BARRON'S

PROFILES OF AMERICAN Colleges

2019

35TH EDITION

Compiled and Edited by
the College Division of
Barron's Educational Series

All inquiries should be addressed to:
Barron's Educational Series, Inc.
250 Wireless Boulevard
Hauppauge, New York 11788
www.barronseduc.com

ISBN: 978-1-4380-1073-1

International Standard Serial No. 1065-5026

PRINTED IN THE UNITED STATES OF AMERICA
9 8 7 6 5 4 3 2 1

CONTENTS

PREFACE

Barron's *Profiles of American Colleges* is the most all-encompassing, easy-to-use guide available. All four-year institutions that offer bachelor's degrees are described if they are fully accredited or are recognized candidates for accreditation. The comprehensive, concise capsule and detailed essay on each school give an easy-to-absorb, complete picture of the colleges that interest the reader. The attractive graphic design provides added readability.

The capsule of each profile lists important information for quick reference: address and phone and fax numbers; enrollment; calendar; fall application deadline; size and salary level of the faculty; percentage of faculty members who hold doctorates; student/faculty ratio; tuition and fees; room-and-board costs; the number of students who applied to the freshman class, were accepted, and enrolled; the median SAT* and/or ACT scores; CEEB Code; and finally, the College Admissions Selector Rating for the school. The information in the essay portion of each profile ranges from available housing and the financial aid climate to admissions requirements and the success of graduates. There are twenty-one categories of information under eight main headings: Student Life, Faculty/Classrooms, Programs of Study, Activities, Services, Requirements, Admissions, and Financial Aid. The Admissions section also gives contact information and Internet addresses.

As a purchaser of the 35th edition of *Profiles of American Colleges*, you are eligible for a free six-month subscription to our *Profiles of American Colleges* on-line edition. The web site will simplify your college search and ease your college application process. To access, go to BarronsPAC.com and register today!

A Word of Thanks

To all the admissions officers, institutional research staff at the colleges, to participating high school advisers, to the students, parents, and other supporters of *Barron's Profiles of American Colleges*, over the last thirty-four editions, we offer our sincere thanks and appreciation.

Our appreciation to the editorial staff, including Bruce Morris, Lena Perfetto; production department, including production director Chris Ciaschini, art director Jeffrey Batzli, and designer Tara O'Hare. Thanks and appreciation to Greg Hammond of Reliable Internet Solutions for database management and technical support.

CONTRIBUTORS

Steven R. Antonoff, Ph.D.
Educational Consultant
Antonoff Associates, Inc.
Denver, Colorado

Barbara J. Aronson
Career Center Coordinator
Miramonte High School
Orinda, California

Marguerite J. Dennis
Former Vice President for Enrollment and International Programs
Suffolk University
Boston, Massachusetts

Benjamin W. Griffith
Former Dean
University of West Georgia
Carrolton, Georgia

Sheldon Halpern
Former Dean
Enrollment Management
Caldwell College
Caldwell, New Jersey

Anthony F. Capraro, III, Ph.D.
President, Teach Inc.
College Counseling
Ocoee, Florida

James Wagner
Center for Academic Support and Advisement Center
Associate Professor of Education
Liberty University

AN EXPLANATION OF THE BOOK

You have been thinking about going to college within the coming years, and have decided that it's time to get serious and take the necessary steps that will lead to your ultimate college decisions, right?

But how do you take these steps? How much will your college education cost? How can you and your parents afford it? What about the entrance exams? What kinds of scores are you going to need to be considered? How do you decide what to major in? Which colleges offer the skills and career preparation that you're going to need? Even if you get past these hurdles, what if you decide which colleges you want to attend, apply to them, and then get turned down? Is there anything you can do to prevent that from happening?

So where do you begin? In addition to hundreds of two-year schools, there are more than 1,650 accredited four-year colleges in the United States, and your options are almost unlimited. Barron's Profiles of American Colleges can help by pointing you in the right direction, and guiding you through the coming months of preparation and decision making.

Within the pages of this directory, you will find articles that will assist you in evaluating your own needs and interests, selecting the colleges you want to apply to, filling out the application, writing the essay, going through the interview process, finding the money, and surviving your freshman year.

The Index of College Majors lists which colleges offer the field that you're interested in. The section also offers advice on deciding your major, career opportunities and the skills you are going to need for the occupation you choose. More than 700 majors are listed, along with the in-state costs and the Admissions Selector Rating in easy-to-read columns.

Advice for international students is included, as well as a list of schools' in-state costs from least to most expensive. The Colleges at a Glance geographic chart provides students quick information about the schools on a state-by-state basis.

The College Admissions Selector Ratings give applicants an idea of the competition they will encounter when applying to a particular school. For your convenience, a key to abbreviations is also included, as well as an explanation of the actual college entries.

The heart of the book, of course, is the detailed descriptions of the colleges, including a special section of religious schools, for those students wishing to pursue a career in the clergy and related fields. The college Profiles are arranged in alphabetical order by state. Each chapter opens with a map that pinpoints the geographic location of the colleges mentioned. Barron's *Profiles of American Colleges* covers the United States; and describes colleges in Puerto Rico, and universities in Canada and abroad (along with advice for international students), for a total of approximately 1650 Profile entries.

This updated and revised edition of *Profiles of American Colleges* will prove to be a valuable resource as you embark on a tremendous learning and growth time of your life—your college education.

KEY TO ABBREVIATIONS

DEGREES

A.A.—Associate of Arts
A.A.S.—Associate of Applied Science
A.B. or **B.A.**—Bachelor of Arts
A.B.J.—Bachelor of Arts in Journalism
A.S.—Associate of Science

B.A.—Bachelor of Arts
B.A.A.—Bachelor of Applied Arts
B.A.A.S. or **B.Applied A.S.**—Bachelor of Applied Arts and Sciences
B.Ac. or **B.Acc.**—Bachelor of Accountancy
B.A.C.—Bachelor of Science in Air Commerce
B.A.C.V.I.—Bachelor of Arts in Computer and Video Imaging
B.A.E. or **B.A.Ed.**—Bachelor of Arts in Education
B.A.G.E.—Bachelor of Arts in General Education
B.Agri.—Bachelor of Agriculture
B.A.G.S.—Bachelor of Arts in General Studies
B.A.J.S.—Bachelor of Arts in Judaic Studies
B.A.M.—Bachelor of Arts in Music
B.Applied Sc.—Bachelor of Applied Science
B.A.R.—Bachelor of Religion
B.Arch.—Bachelor of Architecture
B.Arch.Hist.—Bachelor of Architectural History
B.Arch.Tech.—Bachelor of Architectural Technology
B.Ar.Sc.—Baccalaurium Artium et Scientiae (honors college degree) (Bachelor of Arts & Sciences)
B.Art.Ed.—Bachelor of Art Education
B.A.S.—Bachelor of Applied Science
B.A.S.—Bachelor of Arts and Sciences
B.A.Sec.Ed.—Bachelor of Arts in Secondary Ed.
B.A.S.W.—Bachelor of Arts in Social Work
B.A.T.—Bachelor of Arts in Teaching
B.B. or **B.Bus.**—Bachelor of Business
B.B.A.—Bachelor of Business Administration
B.B.E.—Bachelor of Business Education
B.C. or **B.Com.** or **B.Comm.**—Bachelor of Commerce
B.C.A.—Bachelor of Creative Arts
B.C.E.—Bachelor of Civil Engineering
B.C.E.—Bachelor of Computer Engineering
B.Ch. or **B.Chem.**—Bachelor of Chemistry
B.Ch.E.—Bachelor of Chemical Engineering
B.C.J.—Bachelor of Criminal Justice
B.C.M.—Bachelor of Christian Ministries
B.Church Mus.—Bachelor of Church Music
B.C.S.—Bachelor of College Studies
B.E.—Bachelor of English
B.E. or **B.Ed.**—Bachelor of Education
B.E.—Bachelor of Engineering
B.E.D.—Bachelor of Environmental Design
B.E.E.—Bachelor of Electrical Engineering
B.En. or **B.Eng.**—Bachelor of Engineering
B.E.S. or **B.Eng.Sc.**—Bachelor of Engineering Science
B.E.T.—Bachelor of Engineering Technology
B.F.A.—Bachelor of Fine Arts
B.G.S.—Bachelor of General Studies
B.G.S.—Bachelor of Geological Sciences
B.H.E.—Bachelor of Health Education
B.H.P.E.—Bachelor of Health and Physical Education
B.H.S.—Bachelor of Health Science
B.I.D.—Bachelor of Industrial Design
B.I.M.—Bachelor of Industrial Management
B.Ind.Tech.—Bachelor of Industrial Technology
B.Int.Arch.—Bachelor of Interior Architecture
B.Int.Design—Bachelor of Interior Design
B.I.S.—Bachelor of Industrial Safety
B.I.S.—Bachelor of Interdisciplinary Studies
B.J.—Bachelor of Journalism
B.J.S.—Bachelor of Judaic Studies
B.L.A. or **B.Lib.Arts**—Bachelor of Liberal Arts
B.L.A. or **B.Land.Arch.**—Bachelor in Landscape Architecture
B.L.I.—Bachelor of Literary Interpretation
B.L.S.—Bachelor of Liberal Studies
B.M. or **B.Mus.** or **Mus.Bac.**—Bachelor of Music
B.M.E.—Bachelor of Mechanical Engineering
B.M.E. or **B.M.Ed.** or **B.Mus.Ed.**—Bachelor of Music Education
B.Med.Lab.Sc.—Bachelor of Medical Laboratory Science
B.Min—Bachelor of Ministry
B.M.P. or **B.Mu.**—Bachelor of Music in Performance
B.Mus.A.—Bachelor of Applied Music
B.M.T.—Bachelor of Music Therapy
B.O.T.—Bachelor of Occupational Therapy
B.P.A.—Bachelor of Public Administration
B.P.E.—Bachelor of Physical Education
B.Perf.Arts—Bachelor of Performing Arts
B.Ph.—Bachelor of Philosophy
B.Pharm.—Bachelor of Pharmacy
B.Phys.Hlth.Ed.—Bachelor of Physical Health Education
B.P.S.—Bachelor of Professional Studies
B.P.T.—Bachelor of Physical Therapy
B.R.E.—Bachelor of Religious Education
B.R.T.—Bachelor of Respiratory Therapy
B.S. or **B.Sc.** or **S.B.**—Bachelor of Science
B.S.A. or **B.S.Ag.** or **B.S.Agr.**—Bachelor of Science in Agriculture
B.Sacred Mus.—Bachelor of Sacred Music
B.Sacred Theol.—Bachelor of Sacred Theology
B.S.A.E.—Bachelor of Science in Agricultural Engineering
B.S.A.E. or **B.S.Art Ed.**—Bachelor of Science in Art Education
B.S.Ag.E.—Bachelor of Science in Agricultural Engineering
B.S.A.S.—Bachelor of Science in Administrative Sciences
B.S.A.T.—Bachelor of Science in Athletic Training
B.S.B.—Bachelor of Science (Business)
B.S.B.A. or **B.S.Bus. Adm.**—Bachelor of Science in Business Administration
B.S.Bus.—Bachelor of Science in Business
B.S.Bus.Ed.—Bachelor of Science in Business Education
B.S.C.—Bachelor of Science in Commerce
B.S.C.E. or **B.S.C.I.E.**—Bachelor of Science in Civil Engineering
B.S.C.E.T.—B.S. in Computer Engineering Technology
B.S.Ch. or **B.S.Chem.** or **B.S. in Ch.**—Bachelor of Science in Chemistry
B.S.C.H.—Bachelor of Science in Community Health
B.S.Ch.E.—Bachelor of Science in Chemical Engineering
B.S.C.I.S.—Bachelor of Science in Computer Information Sciences
B.S.C.J.—Bachelor of Science in Criminal Justice
B.S.C.L.S.—Bachelor of Science in Clinical Laboratory Science
B.S.Comp.Eng.—Bachelor of Science in Computer Engineering
B.S.Comp.Sci. or **B.S.C.S.**—Bachelor of Science in Computer Science
B.S.Comp.Soft—Bachelor of Science in Computer Software
B.S.Comp.Tech.—Bachelor of Science in Computer Technology
B.Sc.P.T.—Bachelor of Science in Physical Therapy
B.S.C.S.T.—Bachelor of Science in Computer Science Technology
B.S.D.H.—Bachelor of Science in Dental Hygiene
B.S.Die—Bachelor of Science in Dietetics
B.S.E. or **B.S.Ed.** or **B.S.Educ.**—Bachelor of Science in Education
B.S.E. or **B.S in E.** or **B.S. in Eng.**—Bachelor of Science in Engineering
B.S.E.E.—Bachelor of Science in Electrical Engineering

B.S.E.E.T.—Bachelor of Science in Electrical Engineering Technology
B.S.E.H.—Bachelor of Science in Environmental Health
B.S.Elect.T.—Bachelor of Science in Electronics Technology
B.S.El.Ed. or **B.S. in Elem. Ed.**—Bachelor of Science in Elementary Education
B.S.E.P.H.—Bachelor of Science in Environmental and Public Health
B.S.E.S.—Bachelor of Science in Engineering Science
B.S.E.S.—Bachelor of Science in Environmental Studies
B.S.E.T.—Bachelor of Science in Engineering Technology
B.S.F.—Bachelor of Science in Forestry
B.S.F.R.—Bachelor of Science in Forestry Resources
B.S.F.W.—Bachelor of Science in Fisheries and Wildlife
B.S.G.—Bachelor of Science in Geology
B.S.G.—Bachelor of Science in Gerontology
B.S.G.E.—Bachelor of Science in Geological Engineering
B.S.G.S.—Bachelor of Science in General Studies
B.S.H.C.A.—Bachelor of Science in Health Care Administration
B.S.H.E.—Bachelor of Science in Home Economics
B.S.H.F.—Bachelor of Science in Health Fitness
B.S.H.M.S.—Bachelor of Science in Health Management Systems
B.S.H.S.—Bachelor of Science in Health Sciences
B.S.H.S.—Bachelor of Science in Human Services
B.S.I.A.—Bachelor of Science in Industrial Arts
B.S.I.E.—Bachelor of Science in Industrial Engineering
B.S.I.M.—Bachelor of Science in Industrial Management
B.S. in Biomed.Eng.—Bachelor of Science in Biomedical Engineering
B.S. in C.D.—Bachelor of Science in Communication Disorders
B.S.Ind.Ed.—Bachelor of Science in Industrial Education
B.S.Ind.Tech.—Bachelor of Science in Industrial Technology
B.S. in Sec.Ed.—Bachelor of Science in Secondary Education
B.S.I.S.—Bachelor of Science in Interdisciplinary Studies
B.S.I.T.—Bachelor of Science in Industrial Technology
B.S.J.—Bachelor of Science in Journalism
B.S.L.E.—Bachelor of Science in Law Enforcement
B.S.M.—Bachelor of Science in Management
B.S.M.—Bachelor of Science in Music
B.S.M.E.—Bachelor of Science in Mechanical Engineering
B.S.Med.Tech. or **B.S.M.T.**—Bachelor of Science in Medical Technology
B.S.Met.E.—Bachelor of Science in Metallurgical Engineering
B.S.M.R.A.—Bachelor of Science in Medical Records Administration
B.S.M.T.—Bachelor of Science in Medical Technology
B.S.M.T.—Bachelor of Science in Music Therapy
B.S.Mt.E.—Bachelor of Science in Materials Engineering
B.S.Mus.Ed.—Bachelor of Science in Music Education
B.S.N.—Bachelor of Science in Nursing
B.S.Nuc.T.—Bachelor of Science in Nuclear Technology
B.S.O.A.—Bachelor of Science in Office Administration
B.S.O.E.—Bachelor of Science in Occupational Education
B.S.O.T.—Bachelor of Science in Occupational Therapy
B.S.P. or **B.S.Pharm**—Bachelor of Science in Pharmacy
B.S.P.A.—Bachelor of Science in Public Administration
B.S.Pcs.—Bachelor of Science in Physics
B.S.P.E.—Bachelor of Science in Physical Education
B.S.P.T.—Bachelor of Science in Physical Therapy
B.S.Rad.Tech.—Bachelor of Science in Radiation Technology
B.S.R.C.—Bachelor of Science in Respiratory Care
B.S.R.S.—Bachelor of Science in Radiological Science
B.S.R.T.T.—Bachelor of Science in Radiation Therapy Technology
B.S.S.—Bachelor of Science in Surveying
B.S.S.—Bachelor of Special Studies
B.S.S.A.—Bachelor of Science in Systems Analysis
B.S.Soc. Work or **B.S.S.W.**—Bachelor of Science in Social Work
B.S.Sp.—Bachelor of Science in Speech
B.S.S.T.—Bachelor of Science in Surveying and Topography
B.S.T. or **B.S.Tech.**—Bachelor of Science in Technology
B.S.S.W.E.—Bachelor of Science in Software Engineering
B.S.V.T.E.—Bachelor of Science in Vocational Technical Education
B.S.W.—Bachelor of Social Work
B.T. or **B.Tech.**—Bachelor of Technology
B.Th.—Bachelor of Theology
B.T.S.—Bachelor of Technical Studies
B.U.S.—Bachelor of Urban Studies
B.V.M.—Bachelor of Veterinarian Medicine
B.Voc.Arts or **B.V.A.**—Bachelor of Vocational Arts
B.V.E.D. or **B.Voc.Ed.**—Bachelor of Vocational Education

D.D.S.—Doctor of Dental Surgery

Ed.D.—Doctor of Education
Ed.S.—Education Specialist

J.D.—Doctor of Jurisprudence

LL.B.—Bachelor of Laws

M.A.—Master of Arts
M.A.Ed.—Master of Arts in Education
M.A.T.—Master of Arts in Teaching
M.B.A.—Master of Business Administration
M.D.—Doctor of Medicine
M.F.A.—Master of Fine Arts
M.P.A.—Master of Public Administration
M.S.—Master of Science
Mus.B. or **Mus.Bac.**—Bachelor of Music

Ph.D.—Doctor of Philosophy

R.N.—Registered Nurse

S.B. or **B.S.** or **B.Sc.**—Bachelor of Science

OTHER ABBREVIATIONS

AAAHC—Accreditation Association for Ambulatory Health Care
AABC—Accrediting Association of Bible Colleges
AABI—Aviation Accreditation Board International
AACN—American Association of Colleges of Nursing
AACSB—American Assembly of Collegiate Schools of Business
AACT—American Association of Community Theatre
AACT—Advanced Application Certification Testing
AACTE—American Association of Colleges for Teacher Education
AAFCS—American Association of Family and Consumer Sciences
AAHE—American Association for Health Education
AAHE—American Association for Higher Education
AAHEP—Accreditation of Allied Health Programs
AAHPERD—American Alliance for Health, Physical Education, Recreation, and Dance
AAHPERD—American Association of Health, Physical Education, Recreation, and Dance
AALE—American Academy for Liberal Education
AALS—Association of American Law Schools
AAM—American Academy of Microbiology
AAMA—American Association for Medical Assistants
AAMA—American Alternative Medical Association

AAMC—Association of American Medical Colleges
AAMFT—American Association for Marriage and Family Therapy
AANA—American Association of Nurse Anesthetists
AAPAR—American Association for Physical Activity and Recreation
AATA—American Art Therapy Association, Inc.
AAVLD—American Association of Veterinary Laboratory Diagnosticians
ABA—American Bar Association
ABAI—American Board of Allergy & Immunology
ABE—Association of Building Engineers Association of Building Engineers
ABET—Accreditation Board for Engineering and Technology
ABFSE—American Board of Funeral Service Education
ABHE—Association for Biblical Higher Education
ABHES—Accrediting Bureau of Health Education Schools
ACA—American Chiropractic Association
ACAE—Accreditation Commission for Audiology Education
ACBSP—Accreditation Council for Business Schools and Programs
ACCE—American Council for Construction Education
ACCGC—Accrediting Council for Collegiate Graphic Communications
ACCME—Accreditation Council for Continuing Medical Education
ACCNE—American Catholic Church of New England
ACE HSA—Accrediting Commission on Education for Health Services Administration
ACEI—Association for Cultural Economics International
ACEJ—American Council on Education for Journalism
ACE JMC—American Council on Education in Journalism and Mass Communication
ACF—American Culinary Federation
ACFEF—American Culinary Federation's Education Foundation, Inc. Accrediting Commission
ACGME—Accreditation Council for Graduate Medical Education
ACICS—Accrediting Council for Independent Colleges and Schools
ACNM—American College of Nuclear Medicine
ACNM—American College of Nurse-Midwives
ACOT—American College of Technology
ACOT—Advanced Communications-Computer Officer Training
ACOTE—Accreditation Council for Occupational Therapy Education
ACPE—Association for Clinical Pastoral Education, Inc.
ACPE—Accreditation Council on Pharmaceutical Education
ACPHA—Accreditation Commission for Programs in Hospitality Administration
ACS—American Chemical Society
ACSCU—Accrediting Commission for Senior Colleges and Universities
ACSI—Association of Christian Schools International
ACT—American College Testing Program
ACTFL—American Council on the Teaching of Foreign Languages
ACU—Association of Commonwealth Universities
ADA—American Dietetic Association
ADA—American Dental Association
ADDA—American Design Drafting Association
AEE—Association for Experiential Education
AFIT—Accelerated Flight & Instrument Training
AFSA—Application for Federal Student Aid
AHEA—American Home Economics Association
AHIMA—American Health Information Management Association
AICE—Advanced International Certificate of Education
AIChe—American Institute of Chemical Engineers
ALA—American Library Association
ALIGU—American Language Institute of Georgetown University
AMA—American Medical Association
AMA- CAHEA—American Medical Association Committee on Allied Health Education and Accreditation
AMTA—American Music Therapy Association
AMTA—American Massage Therapy Association
AOA—American Osteopathic Association
AOA—American Optometric Association
AOBFP—American Osteopathic Board of Family Physicians
AOSA—American Optometric Student Association
AOSA—American Overseas Schools Archive
AOTA—American Occupational Therapy Association
AP—Advanced Placement
APA—American Podiatry Association
APA—American Psychological Association
APET—Asset Placement Evaluation Test
APIEL—Advance Placement International English Language Exam
APMA—American Podiatric Medical Association
APTA—American Physical Therapy Association
ARC-PA—Accreditation Review Commission on Education for the Physician Assistant, Inc.
ARC-PA—Accreditation Review Commission on Education for the Physician Assistant, Inc.
ASABE—American Society of Agricultural and Biological Engineers
ASC—Accredited Standards Committee
ASCP—Association of Collegiate Schools of Planning
ASCP—American Society of Concierge Physicians
ASCP—American Society of Cardiovascular Professionals
ASCP—American Society of Clinical Psychopharmacology
ASCP—American Society of Clinical Pathologists
ASHA—American Social Health Association
ASHA—American School Health Association
ASHA—American Speech-Language-Hearing Association
ASLH—American Society for Legal History
ASHA—American School Health Association
ASLA—American Society of Landscape Architects
ASLHA (ASHA)—American Speech-Language-Hearing Association
ASPT—American Society of Plant Taxonomists
ATEP—Athletic Training Education Program
ATMAE—Association of Technology, Management, and Applied Engineering
ATME—Association of Theatre Movement Educators
ATMNE—Association of Teachers of Mathematics in New England
ATS—Association of Theological Schools in the U.S. and Canada
ATSUSC—Association of Theological Schools in the United States and Canada
AUCC—Association of Universities and Colleges of Canada
AUPHA—Association of University Programs of Health Administration
AVMA—American Veterinary Medical Association
AWI—Agency for Workforce Innovation

BENHA—Board of Examiners of Nursing Home Administrators
BEOG—Basic Educational Opportunity Grant (now Pell Grant)

CAA—Council on Aviation Accreditation
CAADE—California Association for Alcohol/Drug Educators

CAAHEP—Commission on Accreditation of Allied Health Education Programs
CAAP—College Achievement Admission Program
CAAT—Center for Alternatives to Animal Testing
CAATE—Commission on Accreditation of Athletic Training Education
CACREP—Council for Accreditation of Counseling and Related Educational Programs
CADE—Commission on Accreditation for Dietetics Education
CAEP Council for the Accreditation of Educator Preparation
CAHEA—See AMA-CAHEA
CAHIIM—Commission on Accreditation for Health Informatics and Information Management Education
CAHME—Commission on Accreditation of Healthcare Management Education
CANAEP—Council on Accreditation of Nurse Anesthesia Educational Programs
CAPTE—Commission on Accreditation in Physical Therapy Education
CARC—Canadian Agri-Food Research Council
CARF—Commission on Accreditation of Rehabilitation Facilities
CAS—Certificate of Advanced Study
CCE—Council on Chiropractic Education
CCIE—California Colleges for International Education
CCNE—Commission on Collegiate Nursing Education
CCTC—California Commission on Teacher Credentialing
CDN—Canadian/Canada
CEA—Canadian Education Association
CEA—Colorado Education Association
CEC—Commission on Education and Communication
CEC—Community Education Council
CED—Council for Education of the Deaf
CEEB—College Entrance Examination Board
CELT—Comprehensive English Language Test
CEPH—Council on Education for Public Health
CHEA—Council for Higher Education Accreditation
CIDA—Council for Interior Design Accreditation
CLAST—College Level Academic Skills Test
CLEP—College-Level Examination Program
CNNE—Commission on Collegiate Nursing Education
CoA—Committee on Accreditation
CoA-NA—Council on Accreditation of Nurse Anesthesia Educational Programs
COA—Commission on Opticianry Accreditation
COAMFTE—Commission on Accreditation for Marriage and Family Therapy Education
CoARC—Committee on Accreditation for Respiratory Care
COAPRT—Council on Accreditation of Parks, Recreation, Tourism, and Related Professions
COC—Certificate of Completion
COCA—Comprehensive Outcomes of Cognitive Assessment
CODA—Commission on Dental Accreditation
COE—Council on Occupational Education
COLA—Commission on Office Laboratory Accreditation
COPRA—Commission on Peer Review and Accreditation
CORE—Central Operation of Resources for Educators
CORE—Council On Rehabilitation Education
CORE—Consortium for Oceanographic Research and Education
CORE—Center for Organ Recovery and Education
CPME—Council on Podiatric Medical Education
CRDA—Candidates Reply Date Agreement
CRE—Council on Rehabilitation Education
CSAB—Computing Science Accreditation Board
CSAC—Consensus Standards Advisory Committee (of NQF)
CSHSE—Council for Standards in Human Service Education
CSLE—Center for the Study of Law and Economics
CSS—College Scholarship Service
CSS/Profile—College Scholarship Service Financial Aid Profile
CSWE—Council on Social Work Education Office of Social Work Accreditation
CVTEA—Committee on Veterinary Technician Education and Activities
CWS—College Work-Study

DECA—Discovering the Educational Consequences of Advanced Technical Education (DECA), a National Science Foundation funded research grant
DECM—Department of Education of the Commonwealth of MA

EAC—Engineering Accreditation Commission
EESL—Examination of English as a Second Language
EHAC—National Environmental Health Science and Protection Accreditation Council
ELPT—English Language Proficiency Test (SAT subject)
ELS/ALA—English Language Services/American Language Academy
EMH—Educable Mentally Handicapped
EOP—Equal Opportunity Program
EPH—Epidemiology and Public Health
EPSB—Education Professional Standards Board
ESL—English as a Second Language
ETS—Educational Testing Service

FAFSA—Free Application for Federal Student Aid
FEF—Foundry Educational Foundation
FET—Full-time equivalent
FFS—Family Financial Statement
FIDER—Foundation for Interior Design Education Research
FISL—Federally Insured Student Loan
FTE—Full-Time Equivalent

GED—General Educational Development (high school equivalency examination)
GPA—Grade Point Average
GPSC—Georgia Professional Student Commission
GPSC—Graduate and Professional Student Council
GRE—Graduate Record Examination
GSLP—Guaranteed Student Loan Program
G-STEP—Georgia State Test for English Proficiency

HEPAC—Higher Education Program Alumni Council
HEOP—Higher Equal Opportunity Program
HLC—Higher Learning Commission
HPER—Health, Physical Education, and Recreation

IACBE—International Assembly for Collegiate Business Education
IAME—International Association for Management Education
IB—International Baccalaureate
IELTS—International English Language Testing System

JRC-AT—Joint Review Committee on Educational Programs in Athletic Training
JRCE—Joint Review Committee on Education
JRCDMS—Joint Review Committee on Education in Diagnostic Medical Sonography
JRCERT—Joint Review Committee on Education in Radiologic Technology
JRCNMT—Joint Review Committee on Educational Programs in Nuclear Medicine Technology

LAAB—Landscape Architectural Accreditation Board
LCME—Liaison Committee on Medical Education

MACTE—Montessori Accreditation Council for Teacher Education
MAPS—Multiple Assessment Program/Services
MBHE—Massachusetts Board of Higher Education
MDOE—Michigan Department of Education
MELAB—Michigan English Language Assessment Battery
MSACS—Middle States Association of Colleges and Schools
MSCHE—Middle States Commission on Higher Education
MUSIC—Multi User System for Interactive Computing

NAAB—National Architectural Accrediting Board
NAACLS—National Accrediting Agency for Clinical Laboratory Sciences
NAALS—National Assessment of Adult Literacy Survey
NACEP—Nurse Aide Competency Evaluation Program
NAEYC—National Association for the Education of Young Children
NAIT—National Association of Industrial Technology
NAMT—National Association for Music Therapy
NAPNES—National Association for Practical Nurse Education and Service
NASAD—National Association of Schools of Art and Design
NASD—National Association of Schools of Dance
NASDTEC—National Association of State Development Teacher Education
NASSM—North American Society for Sport Management
NASM—National Association of Schools of Music
NASO—National Adult School Organization
NASP—National Association of School Psychologists
NASPAA—National Association of Schools of Public Affairs and Administration
NASPE—National Association of Sport and Physical Education
NAST—National Association of Schools of Theatre
NATA—National Athletic Trainers' Association
NCA—North Central Association of Colleges and Schools, Higher Learning Commission
NCAA—National Collegiate Athletic Association
NCACE—National Council for Accreditation of Coaching Education
NCACS—North Central Association of Colleges and Schools
NCA-HLC—North Central Association of Colleges and Schools, The Higher Learning Commission
NCCAA—National Christian College Athletic Association
NCDPI—North Carolina Department of Public Instruction
NCIDQ—National Council for Interior Design Qualification
NCOPE—National Commission on Orthotic and Prosthetic Education
NCTE—National Council of Teachers of English
NCTM—National Council of Teachers of Mathematics
NDEA—National Defense Education Act
NEASC-CIHE—New England Association of Schools and Colleges, Commission on Institutions of Higher Education
NEASC-CTCI—New England Association of Schools and Colleges, Commission on Technical and Career Institutions
NEHA—National Environmental Health Association
NEHSPAC—National Environmental Health Science and Protection Council
NLN—National League for Nursing
NLNAC—National League for Nursing Accrediting Commission, Inc.
NMPED—New Mexico Public Education Department
NMSA—National Middle School Association
NRPA—National Recreation and Park Association
NSTA—National Science Teachers Association
NWCCU—Northwest Commission on Colleges and Universities
NYSED—New York State Education Department

OAKE—Organization of American Kodály Educators
OBN—Ohio Board of Nursing
ODE—Ohio Department of Education
ODPS—Ohio Department of Public Safety

PAB—Planning Accreditation Board
PAIR—PHEAA Aid Information Request
PCS—Parents' Confidential Statement
PDE—Pennsylvania Department of Education
PEP—Proficiency Examination Program
PHEAA—Pennsylvania Higher Education Assistance Agency
PSAT/NMSQT—Preliminary Scholastic Aptitude Test/National Merit Scholarship Qualifying Test

ROTC—Reserve Officers Training Corps
RSE—Regents Scholarship Examination (New York State)

SAAC—Student Aid Application for California
SACU—Service for Admission to College and University (Canada)
SACS—Southern Association of Colleges and Schools, Commission on Colleges
SAF—Society of American Foresters
SAM—Single Application Method
SAR—Student Aid Report
SAT—Scholastic Assessment Testing (*formerly ATP–Admissions Testing Program*)
SATE—Security Awareness Training & Education
SBEC—State Board for Educator Certification (Texas)
SCAT—Scholastic College Aptitude Test
SCS—Students' Confidential Statement
SDBN—South Dakota Board of Nursing
SEOG—Supplementary Educational Opportunity Grant
SOA—Society of Actuaries

TAC—Technology Accreditation Commission
TAP—Tuition Assistance Program (New York State)
TDD/TTY—Telecommunications Device for the Deaf/TeleTYpewriter
TEA—Texas Education Agency
TOEFL—Test of English as a Foreign Language
TRACS—Transnational Association of Christian Colleges and Schools, Accreditation Commission

UAP—Undergraduate Assessment Program
UMC—United Methodist Church
UP—Undergraduate Program (area tests)

VFAF—Virginia Financial Assistance Form

WASC-ACCJC—Western Association of Schools and Colleges, Accrediting Commission for Community and Junior Colleges
WASC-ACSCU—Western Association of Schools and Colleges, Accrediting Commission for Senior Colleges and Universities
WPCT—Washington Pre-College Test

PART I

AN INTRODUCTION TO COLLEGE

You'll soon be on your way to college—but how much thought have you given it so far? Have you started thinking about the career that's in your future?

- Which college will help you make the most of your natural abilities and interests, and get you ready for life?
- Which courses should you take?

This section will help you find answers to these questions. It will also give you advice on:

- how to apply to schools
- how to increase your chances of acceptance
- how to finance your education

And just as important, this introductory section will give you valuable tips on how to get through that critical freshman year.

It's not just about statistics like median SAT scores, the endowment, the number of majors or student-professor ratios; a college should feel right to you, from the structure of the classrooms to the food that's served in the dining halls.

Arielle Shipper, Connecticut College, Class of 2010

You have in your hands a book that will give you answers to your questions about the qualities and features of more than 1650 colleges. But before you start reading the descriptions and getting the answers, you need to know what questions to ask about finding the college that is right for you. Although you need to ask questions about "getting in" i.e., exploring colleges in terms of ease of admission for you, most of your questions should focus on the more significant issue of "fitting in." Fitting in means finding a college where you will be comfortable; where you are compatible with your peers, and where the overall atmosphere encourages your growth as a student and as a person.

This article is designed to help you assess some values and attitudes that will help you determine where you will fit in. It will enable you to ask the right questions. Not all colleges are for everyone; careful thinking about your interests, ideals, and values will lead you to find the college that is right *for you*. Colleges are not "good" or "bad" in a generic sense; they are either good or bad matches for you.

The two assessments that follow will be helpful in thinking about yourself as a future college student; they should help you make the right college choice.

THE COLLEGE PLANNING VALUES ASSESSMENT

Students have different reasons for going to college. Eleven reasons or values are found to be most important to students as they think about college. Knowing about your values is the important first step in identifying the colleges where you will fit in and be happy.

To complete the assessment, read through the list of ten values—A through K. Think about the outcomes you hope college will produce for you. Each student will rank them differently; hence, there are no "right" answers. Whereas several, or even most, of these values may be significant for you in one way or another, the goal is to decide which three are the most important. After you read each of the values, go back and circle the THREE most important ones on the basis of the following question:

What do you want college to do for you?

—— A. To provide me with a place to learn and study.
—— B. To provide me with opportunities to interact with teachers inside and outside the classroom.
—— C. To provide me with lots of fun experiences.
—— D. To prepare me to make a lot of money.
—— E. To provide me with recognition for accomplishments.
—— F. To get politically involved and/or to use much of my college years to help those who are disadvantaged.
—— G. To help me prepare for a career.
—— H. To enable me to be more independent.
—— I. To provide opportunities for me to grow religiously or spiritually.
—— J. To provide me with a variety of new experiences.
—— K. To enable me to receive a degree from a prestigious school.

What do your college planning values say about you?

If ***A*** was among the top three priorities on your list, you will want to explore the academic character of the colleges you are considering. Although all colleges are, by definition, intellectual centers, some put more priority on challenging students and pushing them to their limits. Reading about the academic features of the colleges you are considering will be important. (In the college Profiles, pay attention to the *special* section to learn about these features.) Your high ranking of this value says that you will be able to take advantage of intellectual opportunities at college. You may want to select a college where your SAT scores are similar to or slightly above the ranges of other admitted students—at those colleges you will be able to shine academically. You may desire to take an active part in classroom discussions and will want a college where the student faculty ratio is low.

If ***B*** was among your top three priorities, you feel challenged and stimulated by academics and classroom learning. You will want to find a college where your mind will be stretched. You will want to choose a college where you can explore a range of new academic subjects. A liberal arts and sciences college may give you an enriching breadth of academic offerings. You will want to look for a college where academic clubs are popular and where you have a good chance of knowing professors and sharing ideas with them. Access to faculty is important to you and you will want to look at the student faculty ratio in colleges you consider. Also note the ratio of undergraduate students to graduate students. Primarily undergraduate institutions will be the colleges that may best be able to meet your needs, because you will be the focus of teachers' attention. Teachers at such colleges place their priority on teaching and are not distracted by the needs of graduate students or by pressure to balance teaching and student time with research and writing.

If ***C*** was circled, you derive satisfaction from social opportunities. You will want a college where the academic demands will not diminish your ability to socialize. You likely will want a good balance between the social and academic sides of campus life. You will want to explore the percentage of students who get involved in intramural sports, clubs, or fraternities and sororities. (This information is listed in each college profile.) Look at your college choices on the basis of school spirit and sporting events offered. The profiles list popular campus events—see if they sound exciting to you. Also look at the percentage of students who stay on campus over the weekend. You will also want a college where it is easy to make friends. Both small and larger colleges would be appropriate for you. Although a larger college would expose you to more students and a larger quantity of potential friends, studies show that students at smaller colleges become more involved in activities and build deep friendships more quickly. Look for supportiveness and camaraderie in the student body.

If ***D*** is circled, you will want to consider earning potential, advancement opportunities, and the future market for the careers you consider. You will want to consider this value in your career planning. Remember, however, that there is no sure road to riches! You not only must pick a career direction carefully, but must choose a college where the potential for academic success—good grades—is high. The name of a particular college is less important than good grades or contributions to campus life when securing a good job or being admitted to graduate school. Even if you find that a particular career has tremendous earning potential, those earnings may come to only those who are most successful in the profession. Look at average salaries, but also consider your interests, values, and personality before making your final career choice. Be sure to take advantage of hands-on learning opportunities. Perhaps, for example, there are internships that meet your needs. Also, finding good, career-focused summer jobs can be helpful.

If ***E*** is high on your list, you take pleasure in being known for your success in an area of interest. For instance, you might feel good about being recognized or known in school as a good student, a top athlete, or a leader in a club. No doubt this type of recognition contributes to your confidence. You might look for colleges where you will be able to acquire or continue to receive this recognition. Often, recognition is easier to achieve at smaller colleges where you would not be competing against large numbers of students hoping to achieve the same recognition. You will also want to choose colleges where it is easy to get involved and where the activities offered are appealing to you. You may want to consider the benefits of being a "big fish in a small pond."

If ***F*** is important, that value will no doubt guide your vocational or avocational pursuits. You may find yourself choosing a career in which this value can be fulfilled, or you may seek opportunities on a college campus where you can be of service to others. You will want to choose a college where community service is valued. Look at the *activities* section and note whether community service-related involvements are available. Colleges vary a great deal in terms of political awareness. At some colleges, students are attuned to national and international events, often express feelings about current issues and policies, and in general, show interest in political affairs. Students at other colleges show little or no interest in these matters and find other ways to interact with peers.

If ***G*** was circled, you may know what career you want to pursue or you may be concerned but uncertain about your career decision. If you have tentatively selected a career, you will want to choose a college where you can take courses leading to the attainment of a degree in your chosen field. Explore the *programs of study* section in the profiles to determine whether a college you are considering offers the course work you desire. You will want to make a note of the most popular majors and the strongest majors as they are listed. If you don't yet know what career would suit you, remember, that for most careers, a broad, solid liberal arts foundation is considered good preparation. You will want to look at opportunities for internships and take advantage of the career planning and placement office at your chosen college. Finding a career that will be fulfilling is one of the most important choices you will make in your life. Your selection of a college will be your first step toward achieving your career goal.

If ***H*** is circled, it suggests that personal autonomy is important to you. College is, in general, a time for independence, and students are often anxious to make their own decisions without parental involvement. If you feel you can handle lots of independence, you will want to look for colleges where there is some freedom in choosing courses and where students are given responsibility for their own lives. Colleges vary in terms of these factors. Note particularly the *required* section under *programs of study*, which tells you the courses that must be fulfilled by all students. Be certain that you will not be stifled by too many rules and regulations. You may also want to look for colleges where the personal development of students receives high priority. A priority on independence also suggests that you will be comfortable being away from home and on your own.

If ***I*** is one of your top three choices, you will want to look first at the religious affiliation of each of your college options. There are two ways to consider religious life on college campuses. First is the question of how religion affects the day-to-day life of the college. For example, are biblical references made in class? Are religious convocations mandatory? Second is the question of whether there is a religious heritage at the college. Many hundreds of colleges have historical relationships with a religious denomination, but this tie does not affect the rules or the general life of the students. (For example, the college may have a certain number of religion classes required to graduate, but these classes are typically broad-based and not doctrinal.) You may want a college that has a relationship with your particular religious group. Or you may desire a large number of students who belong to the same denomination as you do. The profiles will also give you the percentage of students who are members of the major religious denominations. As you explore colleges, you will also want to see if the college has a commitment to the values and ideals held by you or your family.

If ***J*** is appealing, you like newness and will likely be stimulated by new experiences and new activities. You are in for a treat at most colleges. New experiences are the "stuff" of which college life is made. You may see college-going as an adventure and will want to pick colleges where you can meet your need for stimulation and excitement. Because you value newness, you should not hesitate to attend college in a different part of the country or to experience an environment or a climate that is quite different from your high school. You will also want to look for evidence of diversity in the student body. As you read the descriptions, look for colleges with lots of new opportunities for growth and for personal expansion.

If ***K*** is appealing, be cautious. Students who are overly concerned about this value might find college planning traumatic, and even painful, because of the admission selectivity of "name brand" colleges. Even though it is perfectly acceptable for students to be attuned to the overall excellence of a college, academic quality and prestige are not the same thing. Some colleges are well-known because of, say, a fine football team or because of academic excellence in a subject like psychology or physics. Although it is appropriate to look for a strong faculty and a highly regarded college, you want a college that will give you the greatest chance of academic success. It is success in college, not just academic reputation or prestige, that will lead to admission into graduate school or a broad selection of jobs.

Now that you've read about your top three values, answer the following question on a separate sheet of paper: In your own words, what do your top three values say about what you are looking for in a college? Then, share that information with your college adviser as he or she assists you in finding colleges that are right for you.

SELF-KNOWLEDGE QUESTIONNAIRE

The following seven items—A–G—will help you in thinking about yourself as a college student and the ease with which you will likely proceed through the college selection process. Read each statement and determine whether it is true or not true of you. After each question, you will see numbers ranging from 1 to 5. Circle 1 if the statement is very true of you. Circle 5 ifthe statement is not true of you. Use 2, 3, or 4 to reflect varying levels of preference. Be realistic and honest.

A. My academic abilities for college (such as reading, writing, and note taking) are good.

Very true of me 1 2 3 4 5 Not true of me

Academic abilities such as reading speed and comprehension, writing, note taking, calculating, speaking, and listening are important for college students. You will be called upon to use such skills in your college classes. If you are confident about your academic skills, you can approach picking a college with the ease of knowing that you will be able to master the academic rigors of college life. If you circled 3, 4, or 5 you will want to work on these skills in your remaining days in high school. You will want to choose colleges where you can work to strengthen these skills. Some colleges provide a learning skills center in which you are able to get help if you are having difficulty writing a paper or understanding the content of a class. If you are less than confident, you might look to colleges where you will not be intimidated by the skills of the other students.

B. My study skills and time management are good.

Very true of me 1 2 3 4 5 Not true of me

Study skills and time management are two of the most important qualities for an efficient and productive college student. Successful college students are average or above in organizing themselves for studying, scheduling, and using study time productively, and differentiating important content of a lecture or a book from supplementary information. In addition, they complete assignments on time and don't get flustered if they have several papers or a couple of tests due on the same day. If you circled 3, 4, or 5, it is important to work on improving these skills during your remaining high school days. You might consider the following:

- Seek help from your parents, a teacher, a counselor, or a learning specialist in becoming more organized.
- Try keeping a calendar. Anticipate each step necessary in preparing for every test and every paper.
- Be responsible for your own appointments.
- Check to see if a study skills course is offered at a local community college or university. Or consider reading a book on study skills.

C. I am motivated to succeed in college.

Very true of me 1 2 3 4 5 Not true of me

Motivation is definitely the most important skill you bring to college. Those students who want to succeed do succeed! Studies show that it is motivation, not your SAT scores, that determines academic success in college. And motivation means knowing not only that you want to go to college, but that you also want to be a student. Some students want to go to college for the fun aspects, but forget that college is primarily an academic experience. So if you circled 1 or 2, great, you're off to a good start. If you circled 3, 4, or 5, it may be an appropriate time to consider your wants and needs in a college. What sort of college would help motivate you? Would a college with a balance between academics and social life be appealing? Would you be more motivated if you were near a large and interesting city? Would nice weather be a distraction rather than an energizer? Is a trade or technical school best for you? Have you considered taking some time off between high school and college? Considering such questions is important, and the time to do that exploration is now.

D. I am a good decision maker.

Very true of me 1 2 3 4 5 Not true of me

Decisions, decisions, decisions. The college selection process is full of decisions! What colleges will I initially consider? To which colleges will I apply for admission? What college will I eventually attend? You will be facing these decisions in the upcoming months. If you circled 1 or 2, you are on your way. If you circled 3, 4, or 5, think about an important decision you made recently. Why didn't it go well? If you can analyze your decision-making weakness in that situation, it may help to avoid any potential pitfalls in your college decision-making. The following suggestions will help you improve your ability to make the right college choice:

- Clearly articulate what you're looking for in a college. Write down those features that will make a college right for you.
- Involve lots of people and resources in your search for a college. Your parents, counselors, and friends can help you.
- List and compare pros and cons of alternative colleges. Every college has both.
- Evaluate each college on the basis of the criteria you set for yourself.

Remember, you're looking for a college where you will get in *and* fit in.

E. I'm a good information gatherer; for example, I am usually able to find books, articles, and so on to help me do a research paper for, say, a history class.

Very true of me 1 2 3 4 5 Not true of me

Finding a college requires you to be a good researcher. There is so much information about colleges to sort through and analyze. If you feel you can do good research, fine, you're on your way. If you circled 3, 4, or 5, the following ideas may be helpful:

- Start with this book and look for colleges that are consistent with what you want. Remember that your primary concern is where you will fit in. Use your college-going values and your responses in this questionnaire to guide your thinking about colleges that will match you.
- Work closely with your college counselor, and seek impressions from students and others with reliable and up-to-date information about colleges of interest. You will make a better decision with credible and extensive input.
- Look for differences in features that are important to you. Is ease of making friends important to you? What about balance between academics and social life? Do you want teachers to know you?

F. I feel I adapt to new situations easily.

Very true of me 1 2 3 4 5 Not true of me

Everyone goes through changes in life. Some move through transition periods with great ease, others find them more difficult. You may have experienced the changes that come after a change of schools (even from middle school to high school), the illness or death of a relative, or the divorce of your parents. If you circled 1 or 2, you are not likely to be intimidated by a college in another part of the country or a college very different from your high school. If you circled 3, 4, or 5, you may want to carefully look at colleges that are a bit closer to home or colleges where the same values, perceptions, and attitudes exist as were true in your high school. Almost everyone has fear and apprehension about leaving for college. But if that fear is significant, you will want to choose a college where you will feel comfortable. Visits to college campuses may be particularly significant in feeling good about potential choices.

G. It is easy for me to meet people and establish friendships.

Very true of me 1 2 3 4 5 Not true of me

Identifying and nurturing friendships is an important skill for college adjustment. If you circled 3, 4, or 5, you will want to look carefully at colleges where there are few cliques, where there is an atmosphere of sharing, and where students report that it is relatively easy to integrate into the campus environment. Your choice of a college is a quest for a good social fit. Your thorough review of the profiles and even visits to college campuses will be helpful in assuring your ability to fit in and be comfortable.

FINAL THOUGHTS

If you took time to carefully consider the issues raised in both the Values Assessment and the Self-Knowledge Questionnaire, you should have gained new insights and perspectives about yourself. You will want to share these results with your parents and with your guidance counselor. Elicit their help in getting more insight as to how they see you as a prospective college student. Finally, two suggestions:

- As you research colleges, consider what you have learned about yourself. You want a college that is a good match with your values and interests.
- Spend time on your college search. It will take many hours of organized planning and investigation. But the time spent will result in a better choice and a greater likelihood that you will spend four productive and exciting years in college.

Good luck. There are lots of colleges out there that want you. Let your knowledge of yourself and your objective analysis of potential college options guide you to college environments where you will be able to shine. Success in college is in your hands. Make the most of the opportunity.

Steven R. Antonoff, Ph.D., Certified Educational Planner
Educational Consultant
Antonoff Associates, Inc.
Denver, Colorado

Location is a key factor in looking at colleges. Those seeking adventures should look toward city schools where there are endless possibilities, and those looking for a quiet atmosphere should look for schools in rural locations.
Bryan Cosca, Boston University College of Engineering, Class of 2014

Start your college search positively. Start with the knowledge that there are many schools out there that want you. Start with the idea that there are many good college choices for every student. Too often these days, articles on college admission make students and their parents apprehensive. You can have choices. You can get financial aid. You can have a happy, successful college career.

When you begin to think about college, you are embarking on a major research project. You have many choices available to you in order to get the best possible education for which you are qualified. This article is intended to help you think of some of the important variables in your college search.

Let us help make the book work for you!

THE CURRENT ADMISSION SCENE

Today there are approximately 1,650 four-year colleges and universities accredited. Most existing institutions have grown larger, and many have expanded their programs, offering master's and doctoral degrees as well as bachelor's.

Total graduate and undergraduate students has also grown, from under 4 million in 1960 to more than 16 million today. Almost 40 percent are part-time students, including many working adults. Part-time enrollments are mostly concentrated in the two-year colleges, which enroll about a third of all students.

What does this all mean to you? There is good news and bad news. The good news is that most of the colleges you will read about in this book are colleges you can get into! In other words, the vast majority of colleges in the U.S. admit more than 70 percent of those who apply. Many hundreds admit all of those who apply. So, on one level, you shouldn't worry that you won't be able to get a college education. The bad news is for the student with extremely high grades who seeks admission to the 50 or so most competitive colleges in the country. These "brand name" colleges have many times more candidates than they admit. Even incredibly qualified students are sometimes denied admission.

The key to good college planning is, as mentioned above, research. Find out about what makes one college different from another. Find out what students say about their experiences. Rely on many sources of information—many people, many books, many web sites, and so on. There are lots of people and materials available to help you. This book is one of them. Let the information be your guide. But also let your instincts and your sense of what's best for you play a part. The higher education opportunities in the U.S. are unlimited. The opportunity to let education help pave the way to achieving your dreams is a worthy goal of your college search.

MAKING A SHORT LIST

You have probably already started a list of colleges you know about from friends or relatives who have attended them, from recommendations by counselors or teachers, or by their academic or social reputations. This list will grow as you read the Profiles, receive college mailings, and attend college fairs. If you are interested in preparing for a very specific career, such as engineering, agriculture, nursing, or architecture, you should add only institutions that offer that program. If you want to study business, teacher education, or the arts and sciences, almost every college can provide a suitable major. Either way, your list will soon include dozens of institutions. Most students apply to between four and seven colleges. To narrow your list, you should keep the following process in mind:

- As you explore, be attuned to the admission requirements. You will want to have colleges on your list that span the admission selectivity continuum—from "reach" colleges (those where your grades, test scores, etc., suggest less chance of admission) to "safety" schools (those where your credentials are a bit better than the average student admitted), eliminating colleges at which you clearly would not qualify for admission.
- You also will want to keep an eye on cost. You want to consider colleges that are generally in line with your family's ability to finance your education. Be very cautious as you do this. Literally millions of dollars are available each year for students. There is both "need-based" aid (aid based on your family's ability to pay) and "merit-based" aid (aid based on such things as grades, test scores, and leadership ability).
- Screen the list according to your preferences, such as size, academic competitiveness, religious focus, and location.
- Make quality judgments, using published information and campus visits, to decide which colleges can give you the best quality and value.

The following sections are organized around the factors most important in researching a college. Discussion of admission competitiveness and cost comes first. After that, a wide range of factors important to consider as you evaluate colleges is examined. These include size, housing, the faculty, academic programs, internships, accreditation, libraries and computer technology, and religious/racial considerations. The final two sections are a discussion of campus visits and, finally, a checklist of 25 important questions to ask about each of the colleges you are exploring.

In the end, you must allow yourself to be a good decision maker. You will have to make some quality judgments. It is not as difficult as you may think. You have to be willing to read the information in this book and the literature that the schools make available, to visit a few campuses, and to ask plenty of questions. Usually you can ask questions of the admissions office by regular mail, e-mail, or in person during a campus visit. Because colleges sincerely are interested in helping you make the right choice, they generally will welcome your questions and answer them politely and honestly. In addition, your high school counselor is a key person who can offer advice and guidance. Finally, there are many resources available, in printed form and on the web, to help you.

SELECTION FACTORS

Admissions Competitiveness

The first question most students ask about a college is, "How hard is it to get in?" It should certainly not be the last question. Admissions competitiveness is not the only, or even the most important, measurement of institutional quality. It makes sense to avoid wasting time, money, and useless disappointment applying to institutions for which you clearly are not qualified. Nevertheless, there are many colleges for which you are qualified, and you can make a good choice from among them. The most prestigious institutions are rarely affected by market conditions. Most of the better known private and public colleges and universities have raised their admission standards in recent years. But there remain hundreds of fine public and private colleges, with good local reputations, that will welcome your application.

Use the College Admissions Selector to compare your qualifications to the admissions competitiveness of the institutions of your list. Make sure you read the descriptions of standards very carefully. Even if you meet the stated qualifications for *Most Competitive* or *Highly Competitive* institutions, you cannot assume that you will be offered admission. These colleges receive applications from many more students than they can enroll and reject far more than they accept. When considering colleges rated *Very Competitive* or *Competitive*, remember that the median test scores identify the middle of the most recent freshman class; half of the admitted students had scores lower than the median, and half were above. Students of average ability are admissible to most of the colleges and universities rated as *Competitive* and to virtually all of those rated as *Less Competitive*.

Cost

The basic cost of the most expensive colleges and universities can exceed $40,000 a year. This is widely publicized and very frightening, especially to your parents. But you don't have to spend that much for a good education. Private colleges charge an average of nearly $30,000 a year for tuition and room and board. Public institutions generally cost an average of $14,000 a year for in-state residents. Because many states have been cutting budgets in recent years, tuition at public institutions is now rising faster than at private ones. If you can commute to school from home, you can save about $6000 to $12,000 in room and board, but should add the cost of transportation. The least expensive option is to attend a local community college for two years, at about $1500 a year, and then transfer to a four-year institution to complete your bachelor's degree. Depending on what you may qualify for in financial aid, and what your family is willing to sacrifice, you may have more choices than you think.

Size

Only one-fifth of American colleges and universities have enrollments of 5000 or more, but they account for more than half the ten million plus students who are pursuing bachelor's degrees. The rest are spread out among more than 1000 smaller schools. There are advantages and disadvantages that go with size.

At a college of 5000 or fewer students, you will get to know the campus quickly. You will not have to compete with many other students when registering for courses or for use of the library or other facilities. You can get to know your professors personally and become familiar with most of your fellow students. On the other hand, the school may not have as many majors and it may have less emphasis on spectator sports. Students at small schools are not able to be as "anonymous" as those at larger schools.

As colleges and universities enroll more students, they offer more courses and activities. Within a large campus community, you can probably find others who share your special interests and form a circle of good friends. But you may also find the facilities more crowded, classes closed out, and competition very stiff for athletic teams or musical groups.

Many of the largest institutions are universities offering medical, law, or other doctoral programs as well as bachelor's and master's degrees. Many colleges that do not offer these programs call themselves universities; and a few universities, Dartmouth among them, continue to call themselves colleges. Don't go by the name, but by the academic program. Universities emphasize research. University faculty need specialized laboratory equipment, computers, library material, and technical assistance for their research. Colleges tend to emphasize teaching.

Because research is very expensive, universities usually charge higher tuition than colleges, even to their undergraduate students. In effect, undergraduates at universities subsidize the high cost of graduate programs. Freshmen and sophomores usually receive some instruction from graduate student assistants and fellows, who are paid to be apprentice faculty members.

Of course, many larger private universities, and many public ones, have fine reputations. They have larger and more up-to-date libraries, laboratories, computers, and other special resources than colleges. They attract students from many states and countries and provide a rich social and cultural environment.

Housing

Deciding whether you will stay in a residence hall or at home is more than a matter of finances or how close to the college you live. You should be aware that students who live on campus, especially during the freshman year, are more likely to pass their courses and graduate than students who commute from home. Campus residents spend more time with faculty members, have more opportunity to use the library and laboratories, and are linked to other students who help one another with their studies. Residence hall life usually helps students mature faster as they participate in social and organizational activities.

If you commute to school, you can get maximum benefits from your college experience by spending time on campus between and after classes. If you need a part-time job, get employment in the college library, offices, or dining halls. Use the library to do homework in an environment that may be less distracting than home. If possible, have some dinners on campus, to make friends with other students and participate in evening social and cultural events. Get involved in campus activities, participating in athletics, working on the newspaper, attending a meeting, or rehearsing a play.

You will have a choice of food plans. Most meal plans include a certain number of meals per week. Other plans allow you to prepay a fixed dollar amount and purchase food by the item rather than by the meal. Choose a meal plan that fits your own eating habits. Most colleges today offer a tremendous variety of food and are accommodating to most diets and preferences.

Many students live off campus after their freshman or sophomore year, either by choice or because the school does not have room for them on campus. Schools try to provide listings of available off-campus rooms and apartments that meet good standards for safety and cleanliness. Many colleges also offer health care and food services to students who live off campus.

It is usually more expensive to live in an apartment than in a residence hall, especially if you plan to prepare your own meals. But that option is appealing to some students, particularly those in their junior or senior years.

The Faculty

The most important resources of any college or university are its professors. Admissions brochures usually point out the strengths of the faculty, but provide little detail. You should direct your questions about the faculty and other academic matters to the specific department or to the office that coordinates academic advising. Recruiting brochures also emphasize faculty research, because the prestige of professors depends largely on the books and articles they have published. Good researchers may or may not make good teachers. Ask how often the best researchers teach undergraduate courses, and whether they instruct small as well as large classes. For example, a Nobel prize chemist may lecture to 500 students at a time but never show up in the laboratories where graduate assistants actually teach individual students.

Also ask about class size, because this determines the amount of individual attention students get from professors. Student/faculty ratios, which usually range from 10 to 20 students per professor, don't really tell you much. Every school offers a mixture of large and small classes. Ask admission officers for the average size of a freshman class. You will want to look for such factors as those that follow:

- Science and technology courses should enroll only 25 to 30 students in each laboratory session, but may combine a number of laboratory classes for large weekly lectures.
- Skill development courses such as speech, foreign language, English composition, and fine and performing arts should have classes of 25 or fewer. Mathematics and computer science require considerable graded homework, and classes should be no larger than 35.
- Most other courses in humanities, social sciences, and professional areas are taught by classroom lectures and discussion. Classes should average 35 to 45 in introductory courses such as general psychology or American government. They should be smaller in advanced or specialized courses, such as Shakespeare or tax accounting.
- Many introductory courses, especially at universities, are taught in lecture classes of 100 or more. This is acceptable, if those courses also include small weekly discussion groups for individual instruction. Sometimes these discussion groups are taught by graduate student assistants rather than regular professors. Although graduate assistants lack teaching experience, they are very often highly capable. You should ask whether the teaching done by graduate assistants is closely supervised by regular faculty members.

Academic Programs

Even colleges and universities that boast fine and well qualified faculties can be short of professors in certain programs. Some schools depend on instruction by part-time faculty members or fill in with available teachers from other specializations. Many international students are enrolled in technical doctoral programs, so you may find yourself being taught mathematics or engineering by a teaching assistant who is not a native English speaker. If you are interested in these subjects, check to see whether full-time faculty members teach the majority of the courses.

Other programs may have sufficient faculty but too few student majors. Majors such as physics and philosophy, for example, often have many students in required introductory courses, but few taking the major. Because of small enrollments, these departments may not be able to offer their advanced and specialized courses on a regular basis.

Academic departments give strength to the program by bringing together faculty members who share a common area of study and make sure their students get the classes they need. Some programs, usually called interdisciplinary, are taught by groups of faculty members from several departments. These programs generally have the word *studies* in their titles; for example, Middle-Eastern Studies, Communication Studies, Women's Studies, or Ethnic Studies. If you are enrolled in one of these programs, be sure to ask about the student advising. (Sometimes, advising suffers if faculty members are primarily loyal to their own department.)

Internships

Internships are available at many colleges. They provide an opportunity to experience work in your major and learn from experienced people in your field. Many students have received job offers after participating in an internship program during the school year or during summer vacation. These internships can make a big difference as you enter the job market.

Accreditation

General standards of academic quality are established by associations of colleges and universities through a process called voluntary accreditation. The criteria include: standards for admission of students; faculty qualifications; content of courses; grading standards; professional success of alumni; adequacy of libraries, laboratories, computers, and other support facilities; administrative systems and policy decision making; and financial support.

Six regional associations (New England, Middle States, Southern, North Central, Northwest, and Western) evaluate and accredit colleges as total institutions. Bible colleges have their own accrediting association. Other organizations evaluate and accredit specific programs, primarily in technical fields, like engineering and architecture; or those that require licensing, such as teaching and health care.

Libraries and Computer Technology

Most people judge libraries by the size of the collection, the bigger the better. Collection size is important, but only in relation to the variety and level of programs offered. A small liberal arts college can support its baccalaureate programs with a collection of 200,000 to 400,000 volumes. A university with many professional schools and doctoral programs may require over 2 million. Many books and journals are available through various methods of information technology, computer storage, and the Internet.

The main stacks should be open to students, with the possible exception of rare books, bound journals, and other special items. Open stacks encourage browsing and save students from waiting on line while a library assistant fetches a few books at a time. Instead, assistants constantly should be picking up unused materials from reading desks or carts and putting them back on the shelves.

Good circulation policies encourage students to check materials out for short periods and to return them promptly. One week or less loans are appropriate for books regularly used in courses, and four week loans should be the maximum for other materials. A recall system should be available to get back borrowed material when it is needed. Journals, reference material, or books placed on reserve for assigned reading should be used within the library while it is open, and circulated overnight only at closing time.

Using a computer is integral to university study. Some institutions require students to have personal computers. Colleges often offer the best price for new computers. You may want to check out the options on campus before you purchase a computer elsewhere. Many residence hall rooms are wired for computers and direct connections are linked to the main campus system. More and more campuses have wireless capability.

Religious/Ethnic Considerations

For some students, the religious life of the campus is important as college choices are reviewed. Religious life can vary from being pervasive to being absent. Most colleges are independent of religious influence. Some are historically affiliated with a religious group, yet religious matters are not part of student life. Other schools exist, in part, to educate students in the doctrine and the practices of their own religious perspective. Information you find on these pages will give you answers to some of your initial questions about religious life at particular schools.

If connecting with and learning from members of your racial/ethnic heritage is important, you will find many colleges and universities from which to choose. Again, this guide provides information about the diversity of the campus and the composition of students who are white, African-American, Hispanic, Asian-American, Latino, and so forth.

GETTING THE MOST FROM YOUR CAMPUS VISIT

It is best not to eliminate any options without at least visiting a few campuses of different types to judge their feeling and style first hand.

To learn everything important about a college, you need more than the standard presentation and tour given to visiting students and parents. Plan your visit for a weekday during the school term. This will let you see how classes are taught and how students live. It also is the best time to meet faculty and staff members. If the college does not schedule group presentations or tours at the time you want, call the office of admissions to arrange for an individual tour and interview. (This is more likely at a small college.) At the same time, ask the admissions office to make appointments with people you want to meet.

To find out about a specific academic program, ask to meet the department chairperson or a professor. If you are interested in athletics, religion, or music, arrange to meet with the coach, the chaplain, or the conductor of the orchestra. Your parents will also want to talk to a financial aid counselor about scholarships, grants, and loans. The office of academic affairs can help with your questions about courses or the faculty. The office of student affairs is in charge of residence halls, health services, and extracurricular activities. Each of these areas has a dean or vice president and a number of assistants, so you should be able to get your questions answered even if you go in without an appointment.

Take advantage of a group presentation and tour if one is scheduled on the day of your visit. Much of what you learn may be familiar, but other students and parents will ask about some of the same things you want to know. Student tour guides are also good sources of information. They love to talk about their own courses, professors, and campus experiences.

Finally, explore the campus on your own. Check the condition of the buildings and the grounds. If they appear well maintained, the college probably has good overall management. If they look run down, the college may have financial problems that also make it scrimp on the book budget or laboratory supplies. Visit a service office, such as the registrar, career planning, or academic advising. Observe whether they treat students courteously and seem genuinely interested in helping them. Look at bulletin boards for signs of campus activities.

And, perhaps most importantly, talk to some of the students who are already enrolled at the college. They will usually speak frankly about weekend activities, whether they find it easy to talk to professors out of class, and how much drinking or drug abuse there is on campus. Most importantly, meeting other students will help you discover how friendly the campus is and whether the college will suit you socially and intellectually.

More than buildings and courses of study, a college is a community of people. Only during a campus visit can you experience the human environment in which you will live and work during four critical years.

25 CRITICAL QUESTIONS

The following questions form a checklist to evaluate each college or university you are considering. Use the profiles, material from the colleges, and your own inquiries and observations to get the answers.

1. Do I have a reasonable chance of being admitted?
2. Can my family manage the costs?
3. Is the overall size of the school right for my personality?
4. Is the location right? (Consider such specifics as region, distance from a major city, distance from home, and weather.)
5. Are class sizes right for my learning style and my need for involvement in class?
6. Will I be comfortable with the setting of the campus?
7. Are the housing and food services suitable?
8. Does the college offer the program I want to study? (Or, often more importantly, does the college offer people and classes that will help me decide what I want to study?)
9. Will the college push me academically, but not shove me?
10. Do the best professors teach undergraduate courses?
11. Can I change majors easily, if I need to?
12. Do students say the majority of classes are taught by fun, stimulating, interesting professors?
13. Is the library collection adequate and accessible?
14. Are computer facilities readily available and are campus networking opportunities up-to-date?
15. Is the connection to the Internet adequate?
16. Are there resources for career development?
17. Do the people in the financial aid, housing, and other service offices seem attentive and genuinely interested in helping students?
18. Are there opportunities for me to use my abilities on campus—for example, a musical or acting.
19. Does the campus seem well maintained and managed?
20. Will the college meet my religious and/or ethnic needs?

And, finally, the five most critical questions:

21. Is there a good chance I will be academically successful there?
22. Will I be happy as a student there?
23. Do I seem compatible with the student population? Do they seem to enjoy what I enjoy?
24. Does the student life seem in sync with my personality and my goals? Is the student life what I'm looking for in a college?
25. Does the college "feel" right for me?

Steven R. Antonoff
Sheldon Halpern
Barbara Aronson

Take your entrance exams seriously. When the opportunity of a lifetime presents itself, you'd better be ready for everything life has to offer, or live with regrets forever.

2Lt Jocelyn Booker, United States Air Force Academy, Class of 2010

COLLEGE ENTRANCE EXAMINATIONS

By providing you with exactly the same information about each of the colleges in which you are interested, the book you are now reading, *Profiles of American Colleges*, will help you narrow down the list of colleges to which you will apply. Of course, your final decision will be influenced by many other factors, many of which are far more important: actual visits to the colleges; virtual visits on the Internet; viewings of videotapes; advice from guidance counselors, parents, teachers, and friends.

In much the same way, by providing college admissions officers with the same information about thousands of applicants, the results of college entrance exams can help them narrow down the list of students they are considering accepting. The results of these exams help admissions officers compare students with widely differing backgrounds. Students from different high schools in different states who earn the same grade in their biology classes, B+ say, have used different textbooks, have performed different labs, have taken different tests, and in general often exhibit great disparity in their level of mastery of the subject; indeed, even within the same school, a grade of B+ from one teacher might not represent the same level of accomplishment as a B+ from another teacher. However, a grade of 650 on the Biology SAT Subject Test, or a 4 on the Biology AP test means the same thing whether it was earned by a student from a rural community in Idaho, an inner-city school in New York, or a private prep school in Massachusetts. Because students all across the country take the same standardized test on the same day, colleges can give greater credence to the results of those tests than they can to the results of final exams from different schools.

KINDS OF COLLEGE ENTRANCE EXAMINATIONS

Although some students who go from high school to two-year community colleges do not take any college entrance tests, most do, and virtually all students who are applying to four-year colleges will take some of the following exams:

- PSAT/NMSQT or the Preliminary SAT/National Merit Scholarship Qualifying Test.
- SAT Reasoning Test.
- SAT Subject Tests.
- Advanced Placement (AP) Examinations.
- The ACT Assessment.

The PSAT/NMSQT

The PSAT/NMSQT measures verbal and mathematical reasoning necessary for success in college. It is a standardized test taken by students in high schools throughout the country in October of their junior year. The test consists of five sections: two 25-minute critical reading sections, two 25-minute math sections, and one 30-minute writing section.

This Preliminary SAT is also the qualifying test for the scholarship competition conducted by the National Merit Scholarship Corporation, an independent, nonprofit organization supported by grants from over 600 corporations, private foundations, colleges, and universities. All students whose scores are in the top 5% of students taking the exam that year receive National Merit Letters of Commendation. In addition, students whose scores are in the top 1% of those taking the exam that year become National Merit Semifinalists. Those who advance to finalist standing by meeting additional requirements compete for one-time National Merit $2000 Scholarships and renewable four-year Merit Scholarships, which may be worth as much as $2000 a year or more for four years.

In addition, this test is used by the National Achievement Scholarship Program for outstanding African-American students. Top-scoring African-American students in each of the regional selection units established for the competition con-tinue in the competition for nonrenewable National Achieve-ment $2000 Scholarships and for four-year Achievement Scholarships sponsored by more than 175 organizations.

Test-Taking Strategies for the PSAT/NMSQT

1. Know what to expect. Each critical reading section has sentence completion questions and reading comprehension questions. A few of the reading questions are based on short passages (often a single paragraph), whereas most are based on longer passages (typically four to seven paragraphs). The first math section has 20 multiple-choice questions; the second math section has 8 quantitative comparison questions and 10 questions for which no choices are provided and whose answers must be entered in a special grid. Calculators may be used on any question in the math sections. The writing skills section, which does *not* have an essay, has three types of multiple-choice questions that test your knowledge of standard written English (grammar and usage).

2. On average, wild guessing has no effect on your score. Educated guessing, on the other hand, can improve your score dramatically. On all multiple-choice questions, try to eliminate as many obviously incorrect answer choices as possible, and then guess from among the choices still remaining.

3. Expect easy questions at the beginning of each set of the same question type. Within each set (except for the reading comprehension questions), the questions progress from easy to difficult. In other words, the first sentence completion questions in a set will be easier than the last sentence completion questions in that set; the first grid-in questions will be easier than the last ones.

4. Take advantage of the easy questions to boost your score. Remember: each question is worth the same number of points. Whether it is easy or difficult, whether it takes you ten seconds or two minutes to answer, you get the same number of points for each question you answer correctly. Your job is to answer as many questions as you can without rushing so fast that you make careless errors. Take enough time to get those easy questions right!

You should be aware that there are eight primary changes coming to the PSAT/SAT. These begin with the PSAT offered in October 2015. The first SAT with the new changes is scheduled for March 2016. These changes affect the class of 2017 and beyond.

For detailed information on these changes, please refer to the SAT web sites below:

www.collegeboard.org/delivering-opportunity/sat/redesign

www.collegeboard.org/delivering-opportunity/sat

The SAT

The SAT is a reasoning test consisting of three parts—critical reading, mathematical reasoning, and writing. It is designed to measure your ability to do college work. Part of the test deals with verbal skills with an emphasis on critical reading, including a double passage with different points of view. The critical reading sections measure the extent of your vocabulary, your ability to interpret and create ideas, and your ability to reason logically and draw conclusions correctly. The mathematics part measures your ability to reason with numbers and mathematical concepts. It tests your ability to handle general number concepts rather than specific achievement in mathematics. Calculators are permitted on each math section.

The writing part consists of a short essay and multiple-choice questions that test your knowledge of standard written English (grammar and usage).

The SAT is given on seven Saturdays during the year—once each in January, March, May, June, October, November, and December. Applicants may request, for religious reasons, to take the test on the Sunday following the regularly scheduled date.

You can register online at *www.collegeboard.org* or by mail by using the registration form available at your school.

In early 2016, students began taking a new version of the SAT—which was based on the old 1,600-point system. An optional essay is scored separately. The sections on reading and writing were replaced with Evidence-based Reading and Writing. There are many schools that are still reporting the old SAT scores. Any new/old scores would be recorded in each individual college profile under the Admissions section.

Test-Taking Strategies for the SAT

1. Pace yourself properly. It is much better to slow down and avoid careless errors than it is to speed up in an effort to answer all the questions. You can earn an above-average score (over 1000) by correctly answering fewer than half of the questions on the test and omitting the rest. Even scores of 1300 can be achieved by omitting more than 20% of the questions.
2. Read carefully. Make sure you are answering the question asked, not a similar one you once encountered. Underline key words (e.g., NOT and EXCEPT) to make sure you do not answer the opposite of the question asked.
3. Learn the directions for each type of question before taking the test. During the test, do not waste even one second reading the directions or looking at the sample questions.
4. Always answer the easy questions first (the ones at the beginning of each section). Do not panic if you can't answer a question. Do not spend too much time on any one question. If you are truly stuck, make an educated guess if possible (see below), and move on. Remember that each question is worth the same one point, and the next few questions may be much eas-ier for you.
5. On average, wild guessing does not affect your score—it is unlikely to help, but it is equally unlikely to hurt you. The choice is yours. However, educated guessing—when you can eliminate one or more of the answer choices—can significantly increase your score! In particular, don't omit critical reading questions if you have read the passage; you can always eliminate some of the choices. Most math questions contain at least one or two choices that are absurd (for example, negative choices when you know that the answer must be positive); eliminate them and guess.

SAT Subject Tests

These tests are one-hour multiple-choice question tests. You may take one, two, or three tests on any one test date. Some colleges do not require SAT Subject Tests. Of those that do, some colleges require specific subject tests, whereas others allow applicants to choose the ones they wish to present with the admission application. Those colleges that do require these tests may use them to determine acceptance or placement in college courses. The tests in foreign language are used not only for placement but also for possible exemption from a foreign language requirement. If the college of your choice does not require these tests but you would like to demonstrate proficiency in a particular field, take the test anyway and have your scores sent. Tests are given in literature, history, mathematics, sciences, and several foreign languages.

Advanced Placement (AP) Examinations

The College Board also conducts Advanced Placement tests, given to high school students who have completed advanced or honors courses and wish to get college credit. Many secondary schools offer college-level courses in calculus, statistics, art, psychology, European history, American history, Latin, Spanish, French, German, biology, chemistry, and physics. As a result of scores obtained on these tests, colleges grant credit or use the results for placement in advanced college courses.

The ACT Assessment

The registration form for the ACT includes a detailed questionnaire that takes about one hour to complete. As a result of the answers to those questions about your high school courses, personal interests, and career plans, plus the scores on your ACT, an ACT Assessment Student Report is produced. This is made available to you, your high school, and to any college or scholarship source that you request. Decisions regarding college acceptance and award of scholarships are the result. This information is kept confidential and is released only according to your written instructions. To obtain an ACT application form, logon to www.actstudent.org, and click on online registration. When you visit the web site you will find answers to other questions you may have as well.

The ACT measures knowledge, understanding, and skills acquired in the educational process. The test is made up of four distinct sections: English, mathematics, reading, and science reasoning.

In addition, you may register to take an optional fifth section: a 30-minute writing test. Some colleges require their applicants to take the writing test, but most do not. Check with the colleges to which you will be applying to know whether you need to take the writing part of the ACT.

On the ACT, you should answer all questions, because your score is based on the number of questions you answer correctly. There is no penalty for wrong answers. For each of the four tests the total number of correct responses yields a raw score. A table is used to convert the raw scores to *scaled scores.* The highest possible scaled score for each test is 36. The average of the four scaled scores yields the *composite score.*

The ACT English Test is a 75-question, 45-minute test that measures punctuation, grammar, usage, and sentence structure. The test consists of five passages, each accompanied by multiple-choice test items.

Test-Taking Strategies for the ACT English Test

1. Pace yourself. You have 45 minutes to complete 75 questions.
2. Read the sentences immediately before and after the one containing an underlined portion.

The ACT Mathematics Test has 60 questions to answer in 60 minutes. The test emphasizes quantitative reasoning rather than memorized formulas. Five content areas are included in the mathematics test. About 14 questions deal with pre-algebra topics, such as operations with whole numbers, decimals, fractions, and integers and about 10 questions deal with elementary algebra. Usually 18 questions are based on intermediate algebra and coordinate geometry. About 14 questions are based on plane geometry and usually four items are based on right triangle trigonometry and basic trigonometric identities.

Test-Taking Strategies for the ACT Mathematics Test

1. Spend an average of one minute on each question, less on the easy questions, more on the difficult ones.
2. Be sure to answer each question even if you have to guess.
3. Make sure your answers are reasonable.

The ACT Reading Test is a 40-question, 35-minute test that measures reading comprehension. Three scores are reported for this test: a total score, a subscore based on the 20 items in the social studies and natural sciences sections, and a subscore on the 20 items in the prose fiction and humanities sections.

Test-Taking Strategies for the ACT Reading Test

1. Read each passage carefully. Underline important ideas in the passage.
2. Pace yourself. You have 40 questions to answer in 35 minutes.
3. Refer to the passage and in particular to your underlined sections when answering the questions.

The ACT Science Reasoning Test presents seven sets of scientific information in three different formats: data representations (graphs, tables, and other schematic forms); research summaries (description of experiments); and conflicting viewpoints. The 40 questions are to be answered in 35 minutes. The content of the test is drawn from biology, chemistry, physics, geology, astronomy, and meteorology. Background knowledge at the level of a high school general science course is all that is needed to answer these questions. The test emphasizes scientific reasoning skills rather than recall of scientific content, skill in mathematics, or reading ability.

Test-Taking Strategies for the ACT Science Reasoning Test

1. Read the scientific material before you begin answering a question. Read tables and text carefully, underlining important ideas.
2. Look for flaws in the experiments and devise ways of improving the experiments.
3. When you are asked to compare viewpoints, make notes in the margin of the printed material summarizing each viewpoint.

Students who take the ACT also receive new readiness scores and indicators, which are designed to show performance and preparedness in areas important for success after high school. The addition of these new scores and indicators provide students, parents, and educators with a more detailed insight to better plan for future success.

For more information on these changes, please refer to the web site, *act.org*

A FINAL WORD

Don't take any examination without preparation, even though you will find descriptions of these tests that say they test skills developed over years of study both in and out of school. Don't walk in cold, even though you believe that you meet all the qualities colleges are looking for.

Although the College Board suggests no special preparation, it does distribute to applicants the booklet, "Taking the SAT Reasoning Test." It also makes available other publications containing former test questions along with advice on how to cope with the questions. Evidently, all candidates need some form of preparation.

The American College Testing Program furnishes the booklet, "Preparing for the ACT Assessment." This gives specific information about the test, test questions, and strategies for taking each of the four parts. It also describes what to expect on the test day and gives practice with typical questions.

Barron's Educational Series publishes books to help you prepare for these tests. They are available at all bookstores and in many libraries. You should be sure to use them before taking any of these tests.

Although no high school student takes all of the college-entrance exams described above, virtually all students planning to attend a four-year college take at least one of them—the SAT or ACT. Prepare conscientiously for each exam that you take and you will provide the colleges to which you are applying with valuable information about your abilities. Good luck!

Ira K. Wolf
President
PowerPrep, Inc.

Don't be afraid to be yourself in every aspect of the applications process. No admissions officer wants to see the proverbial "perfect" application; rather, they're looking for individuals with unique stories, interests and voices that will contribute to the college community.

Arielle Shipper, Connecticut College, Class of 2010

The college admission process—getting in—begins the minute you start making your first choices in course selection and in cocurricular activities in junior high school, middle school, and high school. These initial and ongoing decisions are crucial to your future well-being. They lay the groundwork for the curriculum you will follow throughout your high school career: they are not easily reversed. These are the decisions that will allow you to market yourself to the colleges of your choice.

STUDENTS TAKE NOTE!

There is a myth prevalent among college-bound students throughout the country that the best way to gain entrance to the selective colleges is to be well rounded. This term usually refers to students who have earned good grades in high school (B+ or better) and participated in a wide range of cocurricular activities.

However, most admission officers at the selective colleges prefer applications from candidates they term angular—students who have demonstrated solid academic achievement in and out of school *and* who have developed one or two particularly strong cocurricular skills, interests, and activities. These angular students are very different in character from the well-rounded students who are very good at everything, yet excel at little, if anything.

William Fitzsimmons, Dean of Admission at Harvard, says that Harvard is looking for a well-rounded class, which means Harvard is most interested in admitting angular students—students who have excelled at something. He cautions, though, that "...It is a mistake to denigrate or underestimate that persuasive power of high grades, rank, triple 800s on the SAT, 36 on the ACT, and equally impressive SAT Subject Test scores. The selective colleges take many of these academically high profile applicants. But the numbers game alone often won't get you in! It would be fairly simple for Harvard to enroll an entire freshman class with a superior academic profile and little depth of quality in areas that make up the personality of the class. We just would not do that!"

Dean Fitzsimmons is saying that the majority of the successful applicants to selective colleges must have some major commitment(s) combined with excellent academic qualities. A strong impact results from quality involvements rather than a proliferation of joinings and transient interests. Essentially, the angular applicant is a committed individual, while the well-rounded candidate is merely involved.

STUDENTS AND PARENTS TAKE AN EARLY, ACTIVE ROLE

Students and parents must make time to ensure an early, active role in the college admissions process. Each year, starting in the seventh grade, students and parents should take the time to sit down with the student's guidance counselor and talk meaningfully about the following:

- selection and level of courses, projecting through the senior year of high school;
- cocurricular activities available, such as drama, music, athletics, academic clubs, community activities, student government, and other special interest groups; and
- summer study, work, or recreation.

Why is this important to getting in? As sure as taxes and death, there is going to come a time in your senior year when you, the college-bound student, will be asked to choose colleges, complete the college application, write your college essay(s), and have an interview—either on the college campus, or in your hometown.

You must create the personal marketing, which will take place during the application process in your senior year, long before your senior year starts. By the time you reach that long-awaited dream of being a senior, you and you alone have created the person you must market to the colleges of your choice. You must understand that the person you have created is the only person you have to market. There is no Madison Avenue glitz involved in this marketing process! You don't create a pseudo marketing campaign that shows you jumping off a bridge with a bungee cord tied to your sneakers. Admission counselors can tell the difference between a real marketing effort and a pseudo marketing campaign.

THE APPLICATION FORM

Each college on-line application form differs from college to college, with the exception of those colleges that use the common application. When you start to work, be sure to note all deadlines, follow all directions, be complete, be neat, fill out the geographical data with accurate facts, and type it all (unless you print exceptionally well). Always review the entire application before you start to fill it out, and complete the entire application before you start the next one. Remember the application is *you* to the admissions committee member reading it. Even though "a book should not be judged by its cover," appearances do influence opinions.

It is best to work through a rough draft of the application before you actually work on the application copy to be submitted. Remember to make a copy of all parts of the finished application in the event that your submission gets lost and a replacement must be sent.

You are responsible for giving the Secondary School Report, found in each application, directly to your high school guidance counselor. Your counselor is responsible for sending official copies of grades, rank in class (if any), the school's profile, and a written recommendation regarding you. It also is your responsibility to call or fill out the appropriate forms for either the SAT and/or SAT Subject Tests or the ACT, to send the appropriate test information directly to each college to which you have applied, even if your scores are on your high school transcript. Your college file will not be considered complete, and will not be sent to the admission committee for a decision, without these official scores. Additionally, many colleges want recommendations from one or two teachers. Choose wisely and allow each teacher plenty of time. Request letters from teachers who know you best. If English is your interest, be sure to choose an English teacher. If you are fluent in Spanish and have future interest in Spanish at college, ask the Spanish teacher. Remember, though you have many interests and have participated in many activities—you are developing an admissions package as part of your marketing of yourself. Emphasize your strengths and show how they are integrated into your activities and achievements.

Cocurricular activities usually are athletic or nonathletic. If you have won athletic awards, note them. If you have had the starring role in the spring musical for the last two years, say so. If you are an editor on the school newspaper, specify this. Admissions people view your activities with special interest. They realize how very time consuming these activities can be and how they sometimes bring very few accolades. List these activities in the order of importance to you. If you do not believe that the application allows you the opportunity to show your depth of commitment to one or two cocurricular areas, you may add an addendum. Use the KISS (Keep It Short and Simple) method. This is an addendum, not an essay, letter, or dissertation. Be honest!

Some applications have mini essays. When space is provided, be sure you are concise, clear, and grammatically correct. Here, less is more. Your ability to organize your thoughts and present them concisely is being tested. You will receive your chance to impress each college with your prose in the long essay segment of the application. Some colleges have as many as four long essays, whereas some require none. In addition to the short and long essay questions, some colleges ask the student for a graded paper signed by the teacher.

Some colleges encourage you to support your application with additional materials. If you are given this option, consider what will strengthen your application: musical tapes, art and/or photography portfolios, published writings, an exceptional graded term paper, all the additional opportunities for the college to get to know you better and for you to increase your image as an angular candidate. Such additions help the admissions committee to get a better handle on who you are in relation to other applicants. Be sure your presentation is clear and as professional as possible. These additions are not going to be evaluated by the admissions committee. Your material will be directed to the appropriate department for evaluation and an evaluative note will be sent back to the admissions committee. It is this note that will become part of your admissions package, the same way an athletic coach evaluates potential student/athletes.

Proofread all parts of the application. Be sure you, the student, place your signature where it is required. If you are not sending your application on-line, then place everything, including the registration fee check, in a large manila envelope and give it to your college guidance counselor. After adding the completed Secondary School Report to the application, your guidance counselor will mail it. Your job is now finished and the waiting begins!

E-Mail, On-line Services through the College or the Internet

Applying online directly to the college(s) of your choice and communicating by e-mail has made the college application process less time consuming and easier than ever before. Certainly ecologically correct, by producing as close to a paperless process as possible, this method is still in cyberspace. Be sure you know what you are doing when you use any of these methods. It is seriously suggested that you take the time to call the college shortly after sending this type of application, to ensure that your application is on file. If you have an addendum or two, you may want to speak to an admission clerk to make sure each addendum has reached the office of admission in the format you desired. If it were my application and I chose any of these methods, I'd still send my musical tape, the slides for my art portfolio, and such, by certified or registered mail. Clarity is so important to the professionals who will be evaluating these addenda for your college admission process!

The Common Application

Almost all colleges in the United States have agreed that students may apply to their colleges by completing one common application. Some of the colleges using the common application also have their own application. Students applying to a college that allows an applicant a choice of using either the college's own application or the common application, obviously face a choice. The use of the common application substantially reduces the time spent composing different essay answers and neatly typing separate application forms. If you are one of those who must make a choice between the common application and the application of the college, you should understand that each college using the common application (either as its only application or as an alternative application) has the right to ask for a supplement. If you choose the common application, be very sure to read the pages surrounding the common application carefully. Each college has a paragraph in which they discuss their deadlines, requirements for admission, and specify if they require supplemental information. The supplemental information can range from an additional essay or two, to additional information about your cocurricular activities.

All the colleges participating in the common application have each member of their admission staff sign a statement that they will NOT discriminate in the admissions process among students who submit the common application versus students who submit the college's application. However, there are counselors who believe that when there is a choice, the applicant has a better chance of conveying information by using the college's application; there is a vast difference in format between the two applications, even if the college requires a supplement. Check with your guidance counselor if you are unsure regarding your choice of format. To access the common application online, go to:

www.commonapp.org

College Web Sites

Most colleges today have their own web site. Here you will find a wealth of information. Some colleges have even put their viewbook, course curriculum guide, a campus tour, as well as their application, on their site. Visit each college's web page—the addresses are in the Admissions Contact section of the college Profiles in this book. You'll be a much better informed consumer.

THE INTERVIEW

The interview is a contrived situation that few people enjoy, of which many people misunderstand the value, and about which everyone is apprehensive. However, no information from a college catalog, no friend's friend, no high school guidance counselor's comments, and no parental remembrances from bygone days can surpass the value of your college campus visit and interview. This first hand opportunity to assess your future alma mater will confirm or contradict other impressions and help you make a sound college acceptance.

Many colleges will recommend or request a personal interview. It is best to travel to the campus to meet with a member of the admissions staff if you can; however, if you can't, many colleges will arrange to have one of their representatives, usually an alumnus, interview you in your hometown.

Even though the thought of an interview might give you enough butterflies to lift you to the top of your high school's flagpole, here are some tips that might make it a little easier.

1. **Go prepared.** Read the college's catalog and this book's Profile ahead of time so you won't ask "How many books are in your library?" or "How many students do you have?" Ask intelligent questions that introduce a topic of conversation that you want the interviewer to know about you. The key is to distinguish yourself in a positive way from thousands of other applicants. Forge the final steps in the marketing process you have been building since your first choices in the college admission process back in junior high school. The interview is your chance to enhance those decisions.

2. **Nervousness** is absolutely and entirely normal. The best way to handle it is to admit it, out loud, to the interviewer. Richard Shaw, Dean of Undergraduate Admissions and Financial Aid at Stanford University, sometimes relates this true story to his apprehensive applicants. One extremely agitated young applicant sat opposite him for her interview with her legs crossed, wearing loafers on her feet. She swung her top leg back and forth to some inaudible rhythm. The loafer on her top foot flew off her foot, hit him in the head, ricocheted to the desk lamp and broke it. She looked at him in terror, but when their glances met, they both dissolved in laughter. The moral of the story—the person on the other side of the desk is also a human being and wants to put you at ease. So admit to your anxiety, and don't swing your foot if you're wearing loafers! (And by the way, she was admitted.)
3. **Be yourself.** Nobody's perfect, and everyone knows nobody's perfect, so admit to a flaw or two before the interviewer goes hunting for them. The truly impressive candidate will convey a thorough knowledge of self.
4. **Interview the interviewer.** Don't passively sit there and allow the interviewer to ask all the questions and direct the conversation. Participate in this responsibility by assuming an active role. A thoughtful questioner will accomplish three important tasks in a successful interview:

   demonstrate interest, initiative, and maturity for taking partial responsibility for the content of the conversation;
   guide the conversation to areas where he/she feels most secure and accomplished; and
   obtain answers. Use your genuine feelings to react to the answers you hear. If you are delighted to learn of a certain program or activity, show it. If you are curious, ask more questions. If you are disappointed by something you learn, try to find a path to a positive answer. Then consider yourself lucky that you discovered this particular inadequacy in time.
5. **Parents** do belong in your college decision process as your advisers! Often it is they who spend the megabucks for your next four years. They can provide psychological support and a stabilizing influence for sensible, rational decisions. However, they do NOT belong in your interview session. In essence, the sage senior will find constructive ways to include parents in the decision-making process as catalysts, without letting them take over (as many are apt to do) the interview process. You may want your parents to meet and speak briefly to your interviewer prior to your interview and that is fine, but parents may not accompany you into the interview session! Arrange with your parents to meet somewhere out of the interview building after your interview is over. You do not want the interviewer inviting your parents back to the interview room. As intelligent as parents may be, they do not perceive the answers to questions the same way you do. The worst scenario I can imagine is the interviewer asking your parents some of the same questions that were asked you, and that is highly likely. Parents just answer questions differently than teenagers. At best, the scenario creates a long, long ride home, and when you get home you can't punish your parents by taking the car keys away from them, or grounding them for a week. At worst, the scenario has caused a blight in your admissions file. This is your time! Keep it that way!
6. **Practice makes perfect.** Begin your interviews at colleges that are low on your list of preferred choices, and leave your first-choice colleges until last. If you are shy, you will have a chance to practice vocalizing what your usually silent inner voice tells you. Others will have the opportunity to commit their inevitable first blunders where they won't count as much.
7. **Departing impressions.** There is a remarkable tendency for the student to base final college preferences on the quality of the interview only, or on the personal reaction to the interviewer as the personification of the entire institution. Do not do yourself the disservice of letting it influence an otherwise rational selection, one based on institutional programs, students, services, and environment. After the last good-bye and thank you has been smiled, and you exhale deeply on your way out the door, go ahead and congratulate yourself. If you used the interview properly, you will know whether or not you wish to attend that college and why.
8. **Send a thank-you note** to your interviewer. A short and simple handwritten or typed note will do—and if you forgot to mention something important about yourself at the interview, here's your chance.

WRITING THE COLLEGE ESSAY

Do the colleges read the essays you write on their applications? You bet your diploma they do. Here is your chance to strut your stuff, stand up, be counted, and stylize your way into the hearts of the decision makers.

Write it, edit it, review it. Rewrite it. Try to show why you are unique and how the college will benefit having you in its student body. This is not a routine homework assignment, but a college level essay that will be carefully examined for spelling, grammar, content, and style of a high school senior. As strenuous an effort as it may be, completing the essay gives the admissions committee a chance to know the real you, a three-dimensional human being with passions, preferences, strengths, weaknesses, imagination, energy, and ambition. Your ability to market yourself will help the deans and directors of admission remember your application from among the sea of thousands that flood their offices each year.

First, maximize your strengths—use your essays to say what you want to say. The answer to a specific question on the college's part still provides an opening for you to furnish background information about yourself, your interests, ambitions, and insights. For example, the essay that asks you to name your favorite book and the reason for your selection could be answered with the title of a Dr. Seuss book because you are considering a career as an elementary school teacher. If you are interested in business, read about a famous businessman you admire and then discuss your interest in business.

Whatever the essay questions are, autobiographical or otherwise, select the person or issue that puts you in the position to discuss the subject in which you are the most well versed. In essence, all of your essay responses are autobiographical in the sense that they will illustrate something important about yourself, your values, and the kind of person you are (or hope to become). If personal values are important to you, and they should be, then here is your opportunity to stress their importance.

Because many colleges will ask for more than one essay, make sure that the *sum* of the essays in any one college application covers your best points. Do not repeat your answers, even if the questions sound alike. Cover the most important academic and cocurricular activities (most important meaning the one in which you excelled and/or in which you spent the most quality time).

If you are fortunate to have a cooperative English teacher, you might request a critique of your first draft, but be sure to allow enough time for a careful evaluation and your revision.

Write the essays yourself—no substitutes or stand-ins. College admission professionals can discern mature adult prose from student prose.

PARTING WORDS

You may wish to ask yourself the following questions to help you decide which is your Paradise College. Most of this information is in the individual college Profiles in this book.

1. **Caliber of School Programs** Is the college known for its English department or chemistry department? What are its strengths?
2. **Selectivity of Admissions** Is the college Most Competitive, Highly Competitive, Very Competitive, Competitive, Less Competitive or Noncompetitive? Check the Selector Ratings.
3. **Chances of Admission** Be realistic. What are your chances of getting in? How far can you reach? Listen when you are given advice!
4. **Location of the School** Is the school near home, one hour away, 300 miles away, or across the United States?
5. **Rural, Suburban, Urban Campus** Is the school in the city or in a rural area?
6. **Size of the School** Can you spend four years at a small liberal arts college of 800 undergraduates? Do you need the larger atmosphere of a university? Do not equate size with social life!
7. **State College vs. Private College** Is the college a large state university with most of the student population from the state where it's located? Is it one of the public "Ivies"? Will you be a minority in the state school?
8. **Geographical Diversity** Is the college a regional one attracting students from the same state or region? Or is it a college, regardless of its size, which attracts students from all over the United States, or the world at large?
9. **Cost of College** What is the tuition? What are the living costs? What travel costs are there from home to campus? Are there hidden costs?
10. **Financial Aid** With a great percentage of undergraduates at many private colleges on financial aid of some type, where do you fit? What monies are available for the students at the schools of your choice? Is the college need blind in its admission program?
11. **Living Conditions** Is housing on campus guaranteed for all four years? Are the dorms coed? Are there single-sex dorms? Are alternatives in housing available?
12. **Socialization** Is it a grind school—all work, work, work? Is it fraternity- and sorority-oriented? What are the on-campus facilities for socialization?
13. **Safety on Campus** Are the dorms secure and locked? What's the safety system on the campus?
14. **Core Curriculum—Distribution Credits** Does the college require (for graduation) a specific number of credits in different academic disciplines? For example, does the student have to take six credits in philosophy before graduating? Is a self-designed curriculum possible?
15. **Sophomore Standing** Does the college accept AP credits? Does it offer advanced standing for an AP course, or just a credit toward graduation?
16. **Junior Year Abroad** Are there opportunities to study in Italy, Japan, or Australia, for example, while you are an undergraduate?
17. **Internships** Are there opportunities for hands-on experience while in college? Which departments have formal internship opportunities?
18. **Graduate School After College** What percentage of its graduates go on to graduate school immediately upon graduation, or within five years? What is the record of those who successfully get into the law, medical, or business school of their choice?
19. **Placement After Graduation** Is there an office for job placement after college? Is there an alumni network that helps in job placement?
20. **Weekend College** Do the students remain on campus on weekends, or is it a suitcase college?
21. **Minorities** What percentage of the students are minorities? Reflect on the racial, ethnic, and religious minority roles in the college you are considering. How would you feel being Jewish at a Roman Catholic college for example—or Catholic at a Jewish college?
22. **Sports Facilities** Is there a swimming pool? Are there horse stables? Is there an ice hockey rink on campus?
23. **Library Facilities** How many books are in the library? Is it computerized? Is the campus library tied into a larger network?
24. **Athletic Programs** Is the ice hockey team a varsity sport? Does the lacrosse team play Division I or III? Is basketball strong? Do they have a women's squash team?
25. **Honors Programs** Are honors programs available? What are they? Who is eligible?
26. **Student Body** Are the students politically active? Are they professional in orientation?
27. **Faculty** Are all classes taught by full professors? Or are TAs (teaching assistants) the norm?
28. **Computer Labs** Are computers required of incoming freshmen? What are the facilities on campus? Can you have your own PC in your room?
29. **Campus Visits** If possible, make a visit to the campus. Spend some time talking to students for a feel of the campus.
30. **Special Talents** Recognize your special talents and discover where they fit best. Often, a special talent becomes a scale-tipper in the admissions process.
31. **Special Family Circumstances** Talk with your parents about their expectations. Discuss your needs as well as their thoughts.
32. **Legacy** Does your family have a history at a specific school? Are you interested in continuing the tradition?
33. **Note Well—Final List** Be sure the final list is a realistic one. It should include "reaches," "targets," and "safeties." No matter which one admits you—it must fit!

Finding and applying to the best colleges for you is not supposed to be easy, but it can be fun. Parents, guidance counselors, and teachers are there to help you, so don't struggle alone. Keep your sense of humor and a smile on your face as you go about researching, exploring, and discovering your ideal college.

Last but not least is The Parent Credo: The right college is the one where your child will fit in scholastically and socially. Be realistic in your aspirations and support the child's choice!

Anthony F. Capraro, III, Ph.D.
President, Teach Inc.
College Counseling
Ocoee, Florida

Sometimes getting more aid is a matter of simply applying for it.

Raymond A. Lutzky, Rensselaer Polytechnic Institute, Class of 2002

Postsecondary education is a major American industry. A greater proportion of students pursue postsecondary education in the United States than in any other industrialized country. Annually, more than 13 million students study at over 8000 institutions of higher learning. The diversity of our system of higher education is admired by educators and students throughout the world. There is no reason to believe that this system will change in the future. However, college costs and the resources available to parents and students to meet those costs have changed.

Unfortunately, many high school students and their parents believe either that there is no financial aid available or that they will not qualify for any type of financial assistance from any source. Neither assumption is correct. College costs have increased and will continue to increase. Federal allocations, for some financial aid programs, have decreased. But this decline has been met with generous increases in financial aid from state and school sources.

American students and their parents should realize that they must assume the primary role in planning to meet their future college costs and that the family financial planning process must begin much earlier than has been the case.

COLLEGE COSTS

- Nearly all parents believe college costs are too expensive.
- Currently, the average cost of education, including tuition and fees for one year at a public college would have been about $23,000 and for a private college and university, the cost could have exceeded $45,000.
- While college costs will increase each year, it is important to remember that currently a majority of all college students attend schools with tuition costs below $5,000.

STUDENT FINANCIAL AID

- The total amount of financial aid available from federal, state, and institutional sources to postsecondary students is over $170 billion.
- A majority of all students enrolled in higher education receive some type of financial assistance.
- Federal student aid remains the largest source of funding.
- Not long ago the majority of federal financial assistance was grants. Today, a greater amount of financial aid is from loan money.

TIMETABLE FOR APPLYING FOR FINANCIAL AID

Sophomore Year of High School

Most families wait until a child has been accepted into a college or university to begin planning on how the family will meet those college costs. However, a family's college financial planning should begin much earlier.

Students, as early as the sophomore year of high school, should begin a systematic search for colleges that offer courses of study that are of interest. There are many computer programs that can be helpful in this process. These programs can match a student's interest with colleges fitting the profile. Considering that half of all students who enter college either drop out or transfer to another school, this type of early selection analysis can be invaluable.

After selecting certain schools for further consideration, you should write to the school and request a viewbook, catalog, and financial aid brochure. After receiving this information, you and your family should compare the schools. Your comparison should include academic considerations as well as financial. Don't rule out a school because you think you can't afford it. Remember the financial aid programs at that school may be more generous than at a lower-priced school. If possible, visit the college and speak with both an admission and financial aid counselor. If it is not possible to visit all the schools, call the schools and obtain answers to your questions about admission, financial aid, and placement after graduation.

Junior Year of High School

The comparative analysis of colleges and universities that you began in your sophomore year should continue in your junior year. By the completion of your junior year, you and your parents should have some idea of what it will cost to attend and the financial aid policies of each of the schools you are considering.

Some colleges and universities offer prospective applicants an early estimate of their financial aid award. This estimate is based upon information supplied by the family and can provide assistance in planning a family's budget. Remember that for most families, financial aid from federal, state, and school sources will probably not meet the total cost of attendance.

Families should remember that college costs can be met over the course of the academic year. It is not necessary to have all of the money needed to attend school available at the beginning of the academic year. Student and family savings, as well as student employment throughout the year, can be used to meet college costs.

Senior Year of High School

January

By January of your senior year of high school you should know which colleges and universities you want to receive your financial aid application forms. Be certain that you have completed not only the federal financial aid application form, but also any necessary state or school forms. Read carefully all of the instructions. Application methods and deadline dates may differ from one college to another. Submit an application clean of erasures or notations in the margins, and sign all of the application forms.

February

You will receive a report from the service agency you selected containing information on your family's expected contribution and your eligibility for financial aid. You and your parents should discuss the results of the financial aid application with regard to family contribution, educational costs, and how those costs can be met.

March

Beginning in March, most colleges begin to make financial aid decisions. If your application is complete, your chances of receiving an award letter early are greater than if additional information is required.

The financial aid award letter you receive from your school serves as your official document indicating the amount of financial aid you will receive for the year. You must sign and return a copy of the award letter to your school if you agree to accept their offer of financial aid.

If your family's financial circumstances change and you need additional funding, you should make an appointment to speak with your school's financial aid director or counselor. College financial aid personnel are permitted to exercise professional judgment and make adjustments to a student's financial need. Your letter of appeal should state explicitly how much money you need and why you need it.

TIPS ON APPLYING FOR FINANCIAL AID

1. Families can no longer wait until a child is accepted into college before deciding how they will finance that education. Earlier college financial planning is necessary.
2. Families should assume a much more active role in locating the resources necessary to fund future college costs.
3. Families should assume that college costs will continue to increase.
4. Families should assume that in the future the federal government will not substantially increase financial aid allocations.
5. Families should obtain information on a wide range of colleges including the many excellent low-cost schools.
6. Families should seek information about all of the funding sources available at each school they are considering.
7. Families should seek the advice and expertise of financial experts for college financing strategies. College financial planning should specify the amount of money a family should invest or save each month in order to meet future college bills.
8. Families should investigate all of the legitimate ways of reducing their income and assets before filing for financial aid.
9. Families should know how financial aid is awarded and the financial aid policies and programs of each school they are considering.
10. Families should realize that although the job of financing a college education rests primarily with them, they probably will not be able to save the entire cost of their child's college education. They probably will be eligible to receive some type of financial aid from some source and they will have to borrow a portion of their child's college education costs.
11. Families should be advised that the federal government frequently changes the rules and regulations governing financial aid eligibility. Check with your high school guidance counselor or college financial aid administrator for the latest program qualifications.
12. Part-time employment during the school year and full-time employment during the summer should be a part of every family's financing plan.
13. Families should investigate all colleges and universities that offer three-year graduation options.
14. Not every student can afford to live on campus. Commuting to college is one way to reduce college costs
15. It is important to find out a school's policy on awarding financial aid on the basis of need and merit.
16. Check with the financial aid office on the availability of loan forgiveness programs.
17. Find out if the aid awarded in the first year will be awarded in subsequent years if the family income does not change.
18. Find out the statistics on graduating seniors: how many were employed or accepted to graduate schools at the time of graduation.
19. Plan for the future. What was the average debt of graduating students in each of the schools you applied to?
20. Going to college should be a family decision. All family members should be aware of the financial implications of attendance, not just for the first year, but for all four years.

Marguerite J. Dennis
Former Vice President for Enrollment
and International Programs
Suffolk University
Boston, Massachusetts

Explore the campus and make yourself aware of all it has to offer. Most colleges have what seems like an endless supply of resources for its students. By taking advantage of these resources sooner, rather than later, they will prepare you for the years to come.

Shannon Scott, James Madison University, Class of 2013

COLLEGE: IT'S DIFFERENT

In college you are likely to hear fellow students say, "I don't know what that prof *wants*, and she won't *tell* me." "I wrote about three papers in high school, and now they want one every week." Though these students may be exaggerating a bit, college *is* different, both in the quality and the amount of work expected. Sometimes in high school the basic concepts of a course are reduced to a set of facts on a study sheet, handed to students to be reviewed and learned for a test.

In college, it is the concepts and ideas that are most important. These can only be grasped through a real understanding of the facts as they interrelate and form larger patterns. Writing papers and answering essay questions on tests can demonstrate a genuine understanding of the concepts, and this is why they are so important to college instructors. Learning to deal with ideas in this way can be a long-term asset, developing your independence, intellectual interests, and self-awareness.

Don't be discouraged; you are not alone. Most of your fellow students are having equally difficult times adjusting to a new learning method. Persist, and you will improve, leading to a lifetime habit of critical thinking and problem solving that can benefit you in many important ways.

College is also different outside of classes. Now that you have the freedom to choose how to spend time and what types of relationships to make, you have a bewildering number of possibilities.

In high school, you competed against the entire population, and you did well enough to get accepted into college. But now the population has changed, and you are competing against the very best high school students, many of whom may have better academic profiles than you. Because of this reality, you need to be at your best from day one. Here are some tips to help you.

MAKING A GOOD IMPRESSION

Here you are, plopped down in a strange place, feeling a bit like Dorothy transported to Oz. Your first goal is to make a good impression, showing your best self to those who will be important in your life for the next four years and even longer.

Impressing Faculty Members Favorably

Faculty members come in all ranks, from the graduate assistant, who teaches part-time while pursuing a degree, to a lofty full professor, who teaches primarily graduate students. Though different in rank and seniority, they respond to their students in roughly the same ways. They are, after all, people, with families and relationships much like your own. To have a good working relationship with them, try the following suggestions:

- **Make up your own mind about your instructors.** Listening to other students talk about teachers can be confusing. If you listen long enough, you will hear arguments for and against each of them. Don't allow hearsay to affect your own personal opinion.
- **Get to know your instructors firsthand.** Set up a meeting, during regular office hours. Don't try to settle important issues in the few moments before and after class.
- **Approach a discussion of grades carefully.** If you honestly believe that you have been graded too low, schedule a conference. Do not attack your instructor's integrity or judgment. Instead, say that you had expected your work to result in a better grade and would like to know ways to improve. Be serious about overcoming faults.
- **Don't make excuses.** Instructors have heard them all and can rarely be fooled. Accept responsibility for your mistakes, and learn from them.
- **Pay attention in class.** Conversing and daydreaming can insult your instructor and inhibit the learning process.
- **Arrive ahead of time for class.** You will be more relaxed, and you can use these moments to review notes or talk with classmates. You also demonstrate to your instructor a commitment to the class.
- **Participate in class discussions.** Ask questions and give answers to the instructor's questions. Nothing pleases an instructor more than an intelligent question that proves you are interested and prepared.
- **Learn from criticism.** It is an instructor's job to correct your errors in thinking. Don't take in-class criticism personally.

Impressing Fellow Students Favorably

Relationships with other students can be complex, but there are some basic suggestions that may make life easier in the residence halls and classrooms:

- **Don't get into the habit of bragging.** Frequent references to your wealth, your outstanding friends, your social status, or your family's successes are offensive to others.
- **Don't pry.** When your fellow students share their feelings and problems, listen carefully and avoid any tendency to intrude or ask embarrassing questions.
- **Don't borrow.** Borrowing a book, a basketball, or a few bucks may seem like a small thing to you, but some people who have trouble saying no may resent your request.
- **Divide chores.** Do your part; agree on a fair division of work in a lab project or a household task.
- **Support others.** Respect your friends' study time and the "Do not disturb" signs on their doors. Helping them to reach their goals will help you as well.
- **Allow others to be upset.** Sometimes, turning someone's anger into a joke, minimizing their difficulties, or belittling their frustration is your worst response. Support them by letting them release their emotions.
- **Don't preach.** Share your opinions when asked for, but don't try to reform the world around you.
- **Tell the truth.** Your reputation is your most important asset. When you make an agreement, keep it.

MANAGING YOUR TIME

Everyone, no matter how prominent or how insignificant, has 168 hours a week to spend. In this one asset we are all equal. There are students on every college campus, however, who seem to accomplish all their goals and still find time for play and socializing. There are others who seem to be alternating between frantic dashes and dull idleness, accomplishing very little. To the first group, college is a happy, fulfilling experience; to the latter, it is maddeningly frustrating. The first group has gained control of time, the second is controlled by that elusive and precious commodity.

- **Know where your time goes.** Unfortunately, we cannot store up time as we do money, to be used when the need is greatest. We use it as it comes, and it is amazing how it sometimes comes slowly (as in the last five minutes of a Friday afternoon class) or quickly (as in the last hour before a final exam). The first step in controlling time is to determine exactly how you use it. For a while, at least, you should carefully record how much time you spend in class, going to and from class, studying, sleeping, eating, listening to music, watching television, and running errands. You need to know what happens to your 168 hours. Only then can you make sensible decisions about managing them.
- **Make a weekly schedule.** You can schedule your routine for the week, using the time plan forms available at most college bookstores or by making your own forms.
- **First schedule the inflexible blocks of time.** Your class periods, transportation time, sleeping, and eating will form relatively routine patterns throughout the week. Trying to shave minutes off these important activities is often a mistake.
- **Plan your study time.** It is preferable, though not always possible, to set your study hours at the same time every weekday. Try to make your study time *prime time,* when your body and mind are ready for a peak performance.
- **Plan time for fun.** No one should plan to spend four years of college as a working robot. Fun and recreation are important, but they can be enjoyed in short periods just as well as long. For example, jogging with friends for 30 minutes can clear the mind, tone up the muscles, and give you those all-important social contacts. Parties and group activities can be scheduled for weekends.
- **Be reasonable in your time allotments.** As you progress through your freshman year, you will learn more precisely how much time is required to write a paper or complete a book report. Until then, schedule some extra minutes for these tasks. You are being unfair to yourself by planning one hour for a job that requires two.
- **Allow flexibility.** The unexpected is to be expected. There will be interruptions to your routine and errands that must be run at certain times. Allow for these unforeseen circumstances.

LISTENING AND NOTE-TAKING IN CLASS

Listening

If you're interested in really improving your chances for success in college, you'll want to evaluate your listening skills to see if there are changes that you need to make. You'll also want to become familiar with note-taking strategies that can help you get more out of a lecture or PowerPoint presentation.

There is a difference between hearing and listening. Hearing just means that your ears are doing what they're designed to do; they're picking up sound waves. Listening requires that you pay attention and process information for later retrieval.

Here are some helpful tips for active listening.

1. Check the syllabus so that you'll be ready to discuss the topic for the day. Also, be sure to see if there's an assignment due in class so that you won't be caught off guard.
2. Reading the assignment before going to class really increases the chance of you being able to understand what is being presented. (Reading before class lays the foundation for the material that is given in class.)
3. Regular attendance at class is important, whether a professor requires it or not. Make class attendance a top priority and attend all classes.
4. Prepare mentally to pay attention to gain as much information as you can.
5. Sit in the "T-zone," or what is referred to in the military as "front and center."
6. Watch your posture. Don't slouch, but sit up straight and focus on what is being said or shown.
7. Do your best to stay healthy. Exercise, good nutrition, and adequate rest can all contribute to your being an active listener in class.

Being a more active listener can definitely lead to greater academic success.

Distractions can be a major problem in class, so here are some tips that may help you win the battle over distractions:

1. Don't sit with a friend.
2. Take careful notes. Taking notes helps you stay focused and can help all types of learners gain more information from a lecture.
3. Drinking water during class may help keep you from getting tired.
4. Avoid distractions during class such as the Internet, e-mail, or cell phones.
5. If you find yourself distracted by hunger, eat something before class or bring a "quiet" snack.
6. Plan ahead so that you arrive on time.

Note-taking

Effective note-taking will provide more material that will help you prepare adequately for tests and quizzes.

Tips for Effective Note-taking:

If you plan on handwriting your notes, consider the following:

1. Using a three ring binder with dividers for each subject is an effective way to take notes. Handouts don't get misplaced. They can easily be punched and added to notes taken in class. Notes can be removed and grouped together when studied.
2. Record the information from PowerPoints, drawings, charts, etc. when copies are not provided for the class.
3. Consider talking to professors and having them assess your note-taking in their classes.

The amount of material that you record should reflect the emphasis that was placed on the subject during the lecture.

You may want to take notes on your computer, but there are some things to consider:

1. The use of a computer in class is receiving mixed reviews from professors. Some welcome technology as a learning aid, while others reject it because it is a distraction.
2. If you want to take notes on your computer, you need to ask each professor.
3. Determine what note-taking or word processing software you're going to use. You may be able to use note-taking software, such as Notes PP or Microsoft OneNote. Most note-taking software allows you to easily format and customize your notes. If you choose word processing software, make sure you don't waste

too much time formatting during the lecture. This could lead to missing valuable information given by your professor.

4. Power up your lap top prior to class. If possible, sit by a power outlet. This will ensure that your computer won't go dead during the middle of a lecture. Turn the brightness of your monitor down, so as not to draw attention to yourself. Make sure you have the mute function turned on.
5. Avoid distractions, such as instant messaging, e-mail, and the Internet.
6. Use the keyboard or a computer pen tablet. Keyboards allow you to type data, while you'll be able to draw and write notes with the help of a computer pen tablet. You may choose to stick with the keyboard method if you type faster than you write. For certain classes, such as engineering and science, you may find that the computer pen tablet provides you with greater note-taking flexibility.

You should be aware that some recent research indicates that taking notes on a computer is less effective than on paper, so choose wisely.

Note-taking Systems

There are several styles of taking notes:

Outline. This works best when the professor presents material in a very structured format. It's easy when main points and subpoints are clearly identified during a presentation. Outlining increases retention and memory recall, because you are determining how points relate to one another as you record them.

Block Style. This is very similar to outlines, but without the Roman numerals and letters. Main ideas are written flush with the left margin. Subpoints and bullets are indented to indicate their relationship to the main points.

Paragraphs. This works well when a main theme is presented with ideas and examples supporting it.

Visual (or Concept) Maps. They are made up of lines and circles. They help you to be able to see how each part fits together to form the whole picture. These maps work great for visual learners.

STUDYING EFFECTIVELY

Your most important activity in college is studying. Efficient study skills separate the inept student (who may spend just as many hours studying as an "A" student) from the excellent student, who thinks while studying and who uses common sense strategies to discover the important core of courses. The following suggested game plan for good study has worked in the past; it can work for you.

- **Make a commitment.** It is universally recommended that you spend two hours studying for every hour in class. At the beginning of your college career, be determined to do just that. It doesn't get easy until you make up your mind to do it.
- **Do the tough jobs first.** If certain courses are boring or particularly difficult, study them first. Don't read the interesting, enjoyable materials first, saving the toughies for the last sleepy twinges of your weary brain.
- **Study in short sessions.** Three two-hour sessions, separated from each other by a different activity, are much better than a long six-hour session.
- **Use your bits of time.** Use those minutes when you're waiting for a bus, a return call, laundry to wash, or a friend to arrive. Some of the best students I know carry 3 × 5 cards filled with definitions, formulas, or equations and learn during brief waiting periods. Most chief executives form the habit early of using bits of time wisely.

Digesting a Textbook

1. **Preview chapters.** Before you read a chapter in your textbook, preview it. Quickly examine the introductory paragraphs, headings, tables, illustrations, and other features of the chapter. The purpose is to discover the major topics. Then you can read with increased comprehension because you know where the author is leading.
2. **Underline the important points as you read.** Underlining should never be overdone; it can leave your textbook almost completely marked and less legible to read. Only the major ideas and concepts should be highlighted.
3. **Seven categories of information are commonly found in textbooks.** Be particularly alert when you see the following; get your marking pen ready.
   Definitions of terms.
   Types or *categories* of items.
   Methods of accomplishing certain tasks.
   Sequences of events or stages in a process.
   Reasons or *causes.*
   Results or *effects.*
   Contrasts or *comparisons* between items.
4. **Repeat information you need to learn.** When the object is to learn information, nothing is so effective as reciting the material, either silently or aloud.
5. **Don't read all material the same way.** Decide what you need to learn from the material and read accordingly. You read a work of fiction to learn the characters and the narrative; a poem, to learn an idea, an emotion, or a theme: a work of history, to learn the interrelationships of events. Do not read every sentence with the same speed and concentration; learn when to skim rapidly along. Remember, your study time is limited and the trick is to discriminate between the most important and the least important. No one can learn *everything* equally well.
6. **The five-minute golden secret.** As soon as possible after class is over—preferably at your desk in the classroom—skim through the chapter that has just been covered, marking the points primarily discussed. Copy what was written on the board. Now you know what the professor thinks is important!

TAKING TESTS SKILLFULLY

Try to predict the test questions. At some college libraries, copies of old examinations are made available to students. If you can legally find out your professor's previous test methods do so.

Ask your professor to describe the format of the upcoming test: multiple-choice? true-false? essay questions? problems? Adjust your study to the format described.

Listen for clues in the professor's lecture. Sometimes the questions posed in class have a way of reappearing on tests. If a statement is repeated several times or recurs in a subsequent lecture, note it as important.

As you review for the test, devise questions based on the material, and answer them. If you are part of a study group, have members ask questions of the others.

Common Sense Tactics

Arrive on the scene early; relax by breathing deeply. If the instructor gives instructions while distributing the test, listen very carefully.

- **Scan the whole test first.** Notice the point value for each section and budget your time accordingly.
- **Read the directions carefully** and then reread them. Don't lose points because you misread the directions.

- **Answer the short, easy questions first.** A bit of early success stimulates the mind and builds your confidence.
- **Leave space between answers.** You may think of a brilliant comment to add later.
- **Your first instinct is often the best** in answering true-false and multiple-choice questions. Look for qualifiers such as *never, all, often,* or *seldom* in true-false statements. Usually a qualifier that is absolute (*never, all,* or *none*) will indicate a false statement. Work fast on short-answer questions: they seldom count many points.
- **Open-book tests are no picnic.** Don't think that less study is required for an open-book test. They are often the most difficult of all examinations. If the material is unfamiliar, you won't have time to locate it and learn it during the test period.

Important Essay Strategies

- **Read the question carefully** and find out exactly what is asked for. If you are asked to contrast the French Revolution with the American Revolution and you spend your time describing each, without any contrasting references, your grade will be lowered.
- **Know the definitions of key words** used in essay questions:

  analyze: discuss the component parts.
  compare: examine for similarities.
  criticize: give a judgment or evaluation.
  define: state precise meaning of terms.
  describe: give a detailed picture of qualities and characteristics.
  discuss: give the pros and cons: debate them, and come to a conclusion.
  enumerate: briefly mention a number of ideas, things, or events.
  evaluate: give an opinion, with supporting evidence.
  illustrate: give examples (illustrations) relating to a general statement.
  interpret: usually means to state in other words, to explain, make clear.
  outline: another way of asking for brief listings of principal ideas or characteristics. Normally the sentence or topic outline format is not required.
  prove: give evidence and facts to support the premise stated in the test.
  summarize: give an abbreviated account, with your conclusions.
- **Write a short outline** before you begin your essay. This organizes your thinking, making you less likely to leave out major topics.
- **Get to the point immediately.** Don't get bogged down in a lengthy introduction.
- **Read your essay over** before you hand it in. Words can be left out or misspelled. Remember that essay answers are graded somewhat subjectively, and papers that are correctly and neatly written make a better impression.
- **Learn from your test paper** when it is returned. Students who look at a test grade and discard the paper are throwing away a valuable tool. Analyze your mistakes honestly; look for clues for improvement in the professor's comments.

WRITING A TERM PAPER

Doing convincing library research and writing a term paper with correct footnotes and bibliography is a complicated procedure. Most first-year English composition courses include this process. Good students will work hard to master this skill because they know that research papers are integral parts of undergraduate and graduate courses.

Many students make the mistake of waiting until near the deadline to begin a term paper. At the busy end of the term, with final exams approaching, they embark on the uncertain time span of research and writing. Begin your term paper early, when the library staff is unhurried and ready to help and when you are under less pressure. It will pay dividends.

REGULATING YOUR RELATIONSHIPS

Find your special friends who believe in your definition of success. In a fast-paced environment like college, it is important to spend most of your time with people who share your ideas toward learning, where you can be yourself, without defensiveness. To find your kind of friends, first ask yourself: What is success? Is it a secure position and a comfortable home? A life of serving others? A position of power with a commodious executive suite? A challenging job that allows you to be creative? When you have answered honestly, you will have a set of long-range personal goals, and you can begin looking for kindred souls to walk with you on the road to success.

There will be, of course, some persons around you who are determined not to succeed, who for some reason program their lives for failure. Many college freshmen never receive a college degree; some may start college with no intention of passing courses. Their goal is to spend one hectic term as a party animal. If you intend to succeed at college, spending time among this type will be a considerable handicap. Consider making friends who will be around longer than the first year.

If possible, steer clear of highly emotional relationships during your first year of college. You don't have time for a broken heart, and relationships that begin with a rush often end that way.

MAINTAINING YOUR HEALTH

Poor health can threaten your success in the first year of college as nothing else can. No matter how busy you are, you must not forget your body and its needs: proper food, sufficient sleep, and healthy exercise. Many students, faced with the stress of college life, find themselves overmunching junk foods and gaining weight. Guard against this. Drugs and alcohol threaten the health and the success of many college students.

A FINAL WORD

So there it is. If you have read this far, you probably have a serious interest in succeeding in your first year of college. You probably have also realized that these suggestions, even if they sound a bit preachy, are practical and workable. They are based on many years of observing college students.

Benjamin W. Griffith
Former Dean,
University of West Georgia
Carrollton, Georgia

PART II

COLLEGE FACTS AND FINANCES

Now that you've read through Part I, you'll need specific information on the colleges that best match your needs and aptitudes. Here's where you'll find essential information in a nutshell.

Facts and figures on all schools are listed in chart form to help you make quick and easy comparisons. Thumbnail data include:

- campus environment
- degrees offered
- composition of the student body
- enrollment figures
- test scores of entering freshmen
- fall application deadlines

You'll also see at a glance how much it's going to cost you for tuition, room-and-board, and related expenses. In-state costs are broken down on a state-by-state basis, each range starting with colleges that don't charge tuition and going up the scale to the most expensive schools.

COLLEGES AT A GLANCE

The charts on these pages present some of the basic data that initially concerns many students. All of the four-year accredited schools in the United States are listed here alphabetically by state. The type of college environment (from urban to rural) is given, followed by degrees offered and whether the institution is public or private. Information about whether the student body is coed or primarily men or women, and whether fraternities or sororities are on campus follows. The undergraduate enrollment for the fall of 2017 is given as well as the median test scores for freshmen who took the ACT or the SAT. Finally, the fall admissions deadline is shown. "Open" usually indicates that admission applications will be accepted until a few weeks before classes begin.

NAME OF SCHOOL	TOWN	ENVIRONMENT U-Urban R-Rural SU-Suburban SM-Small Town	DEGREES AWARDED A-Associate B-Bachelor M-Master D-Doctorate	CONTROL Pri-Private, Pub-Public	FRATERNITIES AND SORORITIES F-Fraternities S-Sororities F, S-Both No-Neither	STUDENTS: C-Coed M-Men W-Women PM-Primarily Men PW-Primarily Women	UNDERGRADUATE ENROLLMENT FALL 2017	TEST SCORES: ACT						SAT CRITICAL READING					SAT MATHEMATICS					SAT WRITING					APPLICATION DEADLINE
								Median	Below 21	21-23	24-26	27-28	Above 28	Median	Below 500	500-599	600-700	Above 700	Median	Below 500	500-599	600-700	Above 700	Median	Below 500	500-599	600-700	Above 700	Month / Day
Alabama																													
Alabama A&M University	Normal	SU	A,B,M,D		F,S	C	4,415																						6/15
Alabama State University	Montgomery	SM	B,M,D	Pub	F,S	C	4,727	17		57	37	5		425	62	34	3		420	69	13	4							4/15
Amridge University	Montgomery	U	A,B,M,D	Pri	No	C	322																						Open
Auburn University	Auburn	SM	B,M,D		F,S	C	22,658	27			17	53	30						600	3	42	41	14						2/1
Auburn University at Montgomery	Montgomery	SU	B,M,D		F,S	C	4,273	21			74	24	1																8/1
Birmingham-Southern College	Birmingham	U	B	Pri	F,S	C	1,346	26			29	50	21	550	31	45	21	3	560	20	47	28	5		16	45	28	12	2/1
Concordia College - Alabama	Selma	SM	A,B	Pri	No	C	600																					12	2/1
Faulkner University	Montgomery	U	A,B,M,D	Pri	F,S	C	2,564	21		1	70	28	1	470	67	26	7		490	59	37	4		450	70	26	4		Open
Huntingdon College	Montgomery	SU	B	Pri	F,S	C	1,148	21		10	62	27	1	548	27	48	22	3	543	22	59	19							Open
Jacksonville State University	Jacksonville	SM	B,M,D	Pub	F,S	C	7,561																						Open
Judson College	Marion	SM	A,B	Pri	No	PW	347		60	18	6	8	8		17	16	50	17			50	50			17	33	50		Open
Miles College	Birmingham	U	B	Pri	F,S	C	1,634																						Open
Oakwood University	Huntsville	SU	A,B	Pri	No	C	2,000																						Open
Samford University	Birmingham	SU	B,M,D	Pri	F,S	C	3,341	26			25	55	20						578	11	49	36	4						5/1
Spring Hill College	Mobile	SU	B,M	Pri	F,S	C	1,395	23		5	53	36	6	560	15	58	19	8	560	15	66	19							7/15
Stillman College	Tuscaloosa	SM	B		F,S	C	1,580																						7/15
Talladega College	Talladega	SM	B		F,S	C	740																						Open
The University of Alabama	Tuscaloosa	SU	B,M,D	Pub	F,S	C	26,234																						3/1
Troy University	Troy	R	A,B,M	Pub	F,S	C	14,064																						Open
Tuskegee University	Tuskegee	R	B,M,D	Pri	F,S	C	2,598	21	17	61	15	6	1	500	67	27	4		480	64	26	8							Open
University of Alabama at Birmingham	Birmingham	U	B,M,D	Pub	F,S	C	12,369	25			41	40	19																6/1
University of Alabama in Huntsville	Huntsville	SU	B,M,D	Pub	F,S	C	6,507			1	24	45	30		14	44	34	8		17	35	37	11						8/20
University of Mobile	Mobile	SU	A,B,M	Pri	No	C	1,466	22							67	24	9			64	33	3							8/1
University of Montevallo	Montevallo	SM	B,M	Pub	F,S	C	2,409	23																					8/1
University of North Alabama	Florence	U	B,M	Pub	F,S	C	6,313	23		1	58	35	6	573	9	50	41		527	50	32	13	5						Open
University of South Alabama	Mobile	SU	B,M,D	Pub	F,S	C		23		1	54	36	9	562	19	52	26	4	543	24	55	18	3						7/15
University of West Alabama	Livingston	SM	A,B,M	Pub	F,S	C	1,978	20																					Open
Alaska																													
Alaska Pacific University	Anchorage	SU	A,B,M	Pri	No	C	545																						8/1
University of Alaska Anchorage	Anchorage	U	A,B,M	Pub	No	C		21						510	43	37	18	3	505	43	40	15	2	490	55	34	12	1	8/1
University of Alaska Fairbanks	Fairbanks	SM	A,B,M,D	Pub	F,S	C	3,597	23		13	41	35	11	565	21	43	30	6	580	11	47	33	9	500	42	35	21	2	6/15
University of Alaska Southeast	Juneau	SU	A,B,M	Pub	No	C								500					483					480					8/1
Arizona																													
Arizona State University at the Downtown Phoenix Campus	Phoenix	U	B,M,D	Pub	No		9,238	24		7	42	44	8						570	12	51	32	6						2/1
Arizona State University at the Polytechnic Campus	Mesa	SU	B,M,D	Pub	No	C	3,869	24		2	44	39	15						600	7	42	37	14						Open
Arizona State University at the Tempe Campus	Tempe	U	B,M,D	Pub	F,S	C	42,477	25		3	30	47	20						620	5	35	42	18						Open
Arizona State University at the West Campus	Glendale	U	B,M,D	Pub	No	C	3,264	22		10	53	33	5						550	19	48	31	2						Open
Embry-Riddle Aeronautical University - Prescott Campus	Prescott	R	B,M	Pri	F,S	C	2,377	26		3	27	47	23						620	5	33	46	16						7/1
Grand Canyon University	Phoenix	SU	B,M,D	Pri	No	C	27,680																						8/22
Northern Arizona University	Flagstaff	SM	B,M,D	Pub	F,S	C	26,506	22		9	53	32	6	540	28	47	22	3	530	31	48	19	2	500	42	44	13	1	Open
Prescott College	Prescott	SM	B,M,D	Pri	No	C	356																						8/15
SAGU American Indian College	Phoenix	SM	A,B		No	C	130																						8/14
The University of Arizona	Tucson	U	B,M,D		F,S	C		24		8	37	43	13	540	32	41	23	5	555	27	41	26	6	525	36	42	18	4	11/5
Arkansas																													
Arkansas Baptist College	Little Rock	SM	A,B	Pri	F,S	C	1,193																					4	11/5
Arkansas State University	State University	SM	A,B,M,D	Pub	F,S	C	9,592	24	20	30	26	14	11	420	64	36			500	44	36	20		450	80	20			8/18
Arkansas Tech University	Russellville	SM	A,B,M,D	Pub	F,S	C	11,053	22		18	44	33	5	485	75	25			455	75	25	7							Open
Harding University	Searcy	SM	B,M,D	Pri	No	C	4,419	25		3	36	42	19	550	31	37	25	7	550	25	45	28	2						6/1
Henderson State University	Arkadelphia	SM	A,B,M	Pub	F,S	C	3,052	22		15	50	30	5	460	58	21	18	1	510	48	30	18	1						8/18
Hendrix College	Conway	SU	B,M	Pri	No	C	1,322	28	1	12	18	18	51	603	10	35	34	21	606	7	36	43	14						11/15
John Brown University	Siloam Springs	SM	A,B,M	Pri	No	C	1,670	26		2	23	51	24						585	8	49	35	8						5/1
Lyon College	Batesville	SM	B	Pri	F,S	C	690	25		2	41	37	20						581	7	46	46							8/1
Ouachita Baptist University	Arkadelphia	SM	A,B	Pri	F,S	C	1,494	25		4	40	40	16	584	13	47	30	10	559	28	36	34	2						Open

Philander Smith College	Little Rock	U	B	Pri	F,S	C	732	18	81	9	8	1	1	450	67	29	5		439	62	38			437	76	24			7/15
Southern Arkansas University	Magnolia	SM	A,B,M	Pub	F,S	C	3,036																						Open
University of Arkansas at Fayetteville	Fayetteville	U	B,M,D	Pub	F,S	C	22,548	26			25	53	22						590	5	47	39	9						8/1
University of Arkansas at Little Rock	Little Rock	U	A,B,M,D	Pub	F,S	C	7,720	21	10	55			35	395	95	5			485	5	58	11							Open
University of Arkansas at Monticello	Monticello	SM	A,B,M	Pub	F,S	C	3,363		63	19	13	3	2																Open
University of Arkansas at Pine Bluff	Pine Bluff	SM	A,B,M,D	Pub	F,S	C	2,545																						8/1
University of Central Arkansas	Conway	SM	A,B,M,D	Pub	F,S	C	9,616			3	44	40	13																Open
University of the Ozarks	Clarksville	SM	B	Pri	No	C	660																						4/1
Williams Baptist College	Walnut Ridge	R	A,B	Pri	No	C	465	21		23	55	20	2																Open

California

American Jewish University - College of Arts and Sciences	Los Angeles	SU	B,M	Pri	No	C	110																						5/31
ArtCenter College of Design	Pasadena	SU	B,M	Pri	No	C																							Open
Ashford University	San Diego	SM	A,B,M	Pri	No	C	45,348																						Open
Azusa Pacific University	Azusa	SM	B,M,D	Pri	No	C	5,883	24		4	42	44	10	530	32	45	21	3	540	4	34	21	2						5/1
Biola University	La Mirada	SU	B,M,D	Pri	No	C		24		4	38	49	10	545	31	40	24	6	540	32	40	24	3	510	32	39	24	4	3/1
California Baptist University	Riverside	SU	A,B,M,D	Pri	No	C	6,937	22		16	52	28	4	480	44	43	10	3	480	43	41	14	2	470	54	33	12	1	Open
California College of the Arts	San Francisco	U	B,M	Pri	F,S	C	1,533	24		7	44	40	9	534	36	38	23	3	550	35	25	28	12	526	39	33	24	4	Open
California Institute of Technology	Pasadena	SU	B,M,D	Pri	No	C							100				7	93				2	98			1	10	88	1/3
California Institute of the Arts	Valencia	SU	B,M,D	Pri	No	C	895																						1/5
California Lutheran University	Thousand Oaks	SU	B,M,D	Pri	No	C	2,892	25		1	37	52	9	545	25	51	22	2	553	22	48	27	3	541	26	51	23	1	1/1
California Polytechnic State University	San Luis Obispo	SU	B,M	Pub	F,S	C		31			9	51	40						710		20	49	31						12/1
California State Polytechnic University, Pomona	Pomona	SU	B,M,D	Pub	F,S	C	23,731	23		11	41	37	11	560	21	48	27	3	570	20	44	28	8						11/1
California State University, Maritime Academy	Vallejo	SU	B,M	Pub	No	C	868	24		6	34	49	11	545	25	47	28		580	11	55	31	3	520	39	53	8		11/30
California State University, Bakersfield	Bakersfield	SM	B,M	Pub	F,S	C	7,118	19						450					450										Open
California State University, Chico	Chico	SM	B,M	Pub	F,S	C	12,498	22	1	15	50	33	3	545	24	53	22	2	537	26	55	18	1						11/30
California State University, Dominguez Hills	Carson	SU	B,M	Pub	F,S	C	12,632	17	2	55	36	6	1	420	86	13	1		430	83	15	2		420	87	11	1		11/30
California State University, East Bay	Hayward	SM	B,M,D	Pub	F,S	C	11,853																						12/15
California State University, Fresno	Fresno	U	B,M,D	Pub	F,S	C		19	2	43	42	12	1	445	74	21	4	1	455	71	24	5		450	78	19	3		11/30
California State University, Fullerton	Fullerton	SU	B,M,D	Pub	F,S	C	34,576	22		5	56	34	5	520	40	45	14	1	550	26	47	24	3						11/30
California State University, Long Beach	Long Beach	U	B,M,D	Pub	F,S	C	32,246	23	42	25	20	7	6	514	42	41	15	2	531	35	41	21	3						11/30
California State University, Los Angeles	Los Angeles	SM	B,M,D	Pub	F,S	C	19,574	17	79	12	6	2	1	430	79	17	3	1	440	70	23	6	1	430	80	17	2	1	6/15
California State University, Monterey Bay	Seaside	SU	B,M	Pub	F,S	C		20		28	48	21	3	475					475					465					1/31
California State University, Northridge	Northridge	U	B,M,D	Pub	F,S	C		19						455	79	23	6		460	67	26	7							11/30
California State University, Sacramento	Sacramento	SU	B,M,D	Pub	F,S	C		21		31	50	16	1	490	67	27	6		500	61	31	8							11/30
California State University, San Bernardino	San Bernardino	SU	B,M	Pub	F,S	C	14,732																						Open
California State University, San Marcos	San Marcos	SU	B,M,D	Pub	F,S	C		20						475	61	32	6		485	57	36	7							11/30
California State University, Stanislaus	Turlock	SU	B,M	Pub	F,S	C		19		41	46	11	1	445	74	22	4		450	71	25	4		435	78	18	3		11/30
Chapman University	Orange	SU	B,M,D	Pri	F,S	C	6,410	27			12	61	26	640					630	2	28	52	18						1/15
Claremont McKenna College	Claremont	SU	B,M	Pri	No	C	1,344	32				19	81	710		4	37	60	730		2	29	69						1/5
Cogswell Polytechnical College	San Jose	SU	B,M	Pri	No	C	656			25	38	25	12		34	42	24			31	45	24			48	34	15	3	Open
Concordia University Irvine	Irvine	SU	A,B,M	Pri	No	C	1,738																					3	Open
Dominican University of California	San Rafael	SU	B,M	Pri	No	C	1,625																						Open
Fresno Pacific University	Fresno	SU	A,B,M	Pri	No	C	2,439																						Open
Golden Gate University	San Francisco	U	B,M,D	Pri	No	C	432																						Open
Harvey Mudd College	Claremont	SU	B	Pri	No	C	814	34				6	94	720		4	31	65	770			12	88	720		4	33	63	1/5
Holy Names University	Oakland	U	B,M	Pri	No	C	640																					63	1/5
Hope International University	Fullerton	U	A,B,M	Pri	No	C	914																						Open
Humboldt State University	Arcata	SM	B,M	Pub	F,S	C	6,830	22		19	49	30	2	515	49	38	12	2	500	53	36	9	1	495	58	33	7		11/30
Humphreys College	Stockton	SU	A,B,D	Pri	No	C	620																						Open
La Sierra University	Riverside	SU	B,M,D	Pri	No	C	1,680																						Open
Laguna College of Art and Design	Laguna Beach	SM	B,M	Pri	No	C	583																						Open
Loyola Marymount University	Los Angeles	SU	B,M,D	Pri	F,S	C	6,261	28			5	62	33	600	7	39	40	14	620	5	34	46	15	600	7	37	43	13	1/15
Menlo College	Atherton	SU	B	Pri	No	C	713	20	50	12	25	10	3	470	63	33	3	1	500	46	43	9	2	480	64	30	6	13	1/15
Mills College	Oakland	U	B,M,D	Pri	No	W	808	27		3	26	51	20	550	24	49	17	10	530	29	46	19	7	550	34	31	25	10	1/15
Mount St. Mary's University - Chalon Campus	Los Angeles	U	A,B,M,D	Pri	S	PW	2,288		67	21	10	2	1		70	26	4			72	25	3			65	30	5		2/15
National University	La Jolla	U	A,B,M	Pri	No	C	5,920																						Open
NewSchool of Architecture & Design	San Diego	U	B,M	Pri	No	C	414																						Open
Notre Dame de Namur University	Belmont	SU	B,M,D	Pri	No	C	1,147	20	54	29	12	2	3	470	60	31	8	1	470	63	28	9		480	59	37	4		Open
Occidental College	Los Angeles	U	B,M	Pri	F,S	C		30			2	51	46	645	2	22	56	20	645	1	23	53	24	648	1	21	55	23	1/15
Otis College of Art and Design	Los Angeles	U	B,M	Pri	No	C	1,158	19	46	31	8	8	7	510	46	34	17	3	500	36	38	20	6	480	48	35	15	2	Open
Pacific Union College	Angwin	R	A,B,M	Pri	No	C	1,375																						Open
Pepperdine University	Malibu	SU	B,M,D	Pri	F,S	C		29			10	54	35	600	8	41	40	11	620	7	34	42	17	600	9	34	47	10	1/5
Pitzer College	Claremont	SU	B	Pri	No	C	1,099	30						652		15	60	25	641		24	60	16						1/1
Point Loma Nazarene University	San Diego	SU	B,M,D	Pri	No	C	3,053			1	26	56	16							6	47	41	6						2/15
Pomona College	Claremont	SU	B	Pri	F	C	1,642	32			1	16	82	720		6	31	63	720		6	29	65	730		6	28	67	1/1
Saint Mary's College of California	Moraga	SU	B,M,D	Pri	No	C	3,035	24	13	33	27	14	11	552	23	49	23	5	558	23	46	29	4						2/1
San Diego Christian College	Santee	SU	A,B	Pri	No	C	752																						Open
San Diego State University	San Diego	U	B,M,D	Pub	F,S	C	29,853	25		3	29	54	15	592					593	8	44	41	8						11/30
San Francisco Art Institute	San Francisco	U	B,M	Pri	No	C	338	24						570					520					560					2/18
San Francisco Conservatory of Music	San Francisco	U	B,M	Pri	No	C	171																						12/1

NAME OF SCHOOL	TOWN	ENVIRONMENT U-Urban R-Rural SU-Suburban SM-Small Town	DEGREES AWARDED A-Associate B-Bachelor M-Master D-Doctorate	CONTROL Pri-Private, Pub-Public	FRATERNITIES AND SORORITIES F-Fraternities S-Sororities F, S-Both No-Neither	STUDENTS: C-Coed M-Men W-Women PM-Primarily Men PW-Primarily Women	UNDERGRADUATE ENROLLMENT FALL 2017	TEST SCORES: ACT Median	ACT Below 21	ACT 21-23	ACT 24-26	ACT 27-28	ACT Above 28	SAT CRITICAL READING Median	SAT CR Below 500	SAT CR 500-599	SAT CR 600-700	SAT CR Above 700	SAT MATHEMATICS Median	SAT Math Below 500	SAT Math 500-599	SAT Math 600-700	SAT Math Above 700	SAT WRITING Median	SAT Writing Below 500	SAT Writing 500-599	SAT Writing 600-700	SAT Writing Above 700	APPLICATION DEADLINE Month / Day
San Francisco State University	San Francisco	U	B,M,D	Pub	F,S	C								490	54	35	10	1	505	46	40	13							11/30
San Jose State University	San Jose	U	B,M,D	Pub	F,S	C	26,432	22		12	48	34	5	503	46	40	13	2	522	37	20	38	4	497	52	34	12	2	11/30
Scripps College	Claremont	SU	B	Pri	No	W	1,030																						1/1
Shepherd University	Los Angeles	U	A,B,M,D	Pri	No	C																							8/15
Simpson University	Redding	SU	A,B,M	Pri	No	C	1,019	21	44	26	13	11	4	500	35	41	22	2	500	36	50	14		490	42	43	15		Open
Sonoma State University	Rohnert Park	SU	B,M	Pub	F,S	C	8,606	21		17	55	26	2						522	30	53	16	1						11/30
Stanford University	Stanford	SU	B,M,D	Pri	F,S	C		33	1		1	12	87	730		5	26	68	750		2	22	75	690		5	23	72	1/15
The Master's University	Santa Clarita	SU	B,M,D	Pri	No	C		25		5	43	39	13	560	25	39	28	8	520	40	38	19	3	550	37	34	24	5	11/15
Thomas Aquinas College	Santa Paula	R	B	Pri	No	C	389	28			8	58	34						620	1	36	44	19						Open
University of California at Berkeley	Berkeley	U	B,M,D	Pub	F,S	C		32		1	8	20	71	685	6	14	33	47	730	4	12	25	60	695	5	13	28	54	11/30
University of California at Davis	Davis	SU	B,M,D		F,S	C	28,414			1	18	48	33		20	39	31	10		11	23	36	29		16	33	38	13	11/30
University of California at Irvine	Irvine	SU	B,M,D	Pub	F,S	C	22,216							595	9	49	28	14	613	9	33	40	17	576	17	42	33	8	11/30
University of California at Los Angeles	Los Angeles	U	B,M,D	Pub	F,S	C		29		1	13	29	57	635	9	25	38	27	660	8	20	30	41	645	8	23	36	32	11/30
University of California at Riverside	Riverside	SU	B,M,D	Pub	F,S	C	19,799			2	32	48	19							7	43	35	14						11/30
University of California at Santa Barbara	Santa Barbara	SU	B,M,D	Pub	F,S	C		28			15	45	39	615	7	31	45	17	650	6	22	41	31	625	5	27	46	22	11/30
University of California San Diego	La Jolla	SU	B,M,D	Pub	F,S	C	26,590	31						641					683					642					11/30
University of California, Santa Cruz	Santa Cruz	SM	B,M,D	Pub	F,S	C	16,962	24	23	21	24	12	18	550	27	36	29	8	560	21	34	33	11	550	26	38	30	6	11/30
University of La Verne	La Verne	SU	A,B,M,D	Pri	F,S	C		22		3	58	34	5	520	39	48	12	1	520	37	45	17	1	510	44	44	11	1	2/1
University of Redlands	Redlands	SU	B,M,D	Pri	F,S	C	2,402	25						590					570										1/15
University of San Diego	San Diego	U	B,M,D	Pri	F,S	C	5,711	28			10	55	35						630	2	29	54	15						12/15
University of San Francisco	San Francisco	U	B,M,D	Pri	F,S	C	6,745	25		1	33	52	14	570	18	47	30	5	560	15	45	33	7	560	19	46	30	5	1/15
University of Southern California	Los Angeles	U	B,M,D	Pri	F,S	C	18,794	32			4	21	75	680	2	14	48	36	710	2	10	32	57	700	2	9	38	50	1/15
University of the Pacific	Stockton	SU	B,M,D	Pri	F,S	C		27		1	28	42	28	565	47	38	29	9	600	16	35	32	17	565	26	38	27	10	8/15
Vanguard University of Southern California	Costa Mesa	SU	A,B,M	Pri	No	C	2,041																					10	8/15
Westmont College	Santa Barbara	SU	B	Pri	No	C		26		1	29	45	25	585	18	35	33	14	575	14	44	34	8	580	18	40	33	9	2/15
Whittier College	Whittier	SU	B,M,D	Pri	F,S	C	1,368	22	36	27	23	8	6	526	38	42	17	3	532	36	41	21	2		40	42	16	2	2/1
Woodbury University	Burbank	SU	B,M	Pri	F,S	C			6	13	50	28	3		26	44	25	5		37	38	22	3						Open
Colorado																													
Adams State University	Alamosa	SM	A,B,M	Pub	No	C	2,143	20	62	21	10	5	2	480	53	37	10		500	49	42	9		460	64	30	6		8/1
Colorado Christian University	Lakewood	SU	A,B,M	Pri	No	C	1,475																						8/1
Colorado College	Colorado Springs	U	B,M	Pri	F,S	C	2,101	31			1	31	68						680		7	54	39						1/15
Colorado Mesa University	Grand Junction	SM	A,B,M,D	Pub	F,S	C	9,266	20		22	52	23	3	480	60	28	11	1	490	57	30	12	1						Open
Colorado School of Mines	Golden	SM	B,M,D	Pub	F,S	C	4,383	30						635					680					605					Open
Colorado State University	Fort Collins	SU	B,M,D		F,S	C	23,768			2	34	50	14							8	43	39	9						2/1
Colorado State University-Pueblo	Pueblo	U	B,M	Pub	F,S	C	36,207	21																					8/1
Colorado Technical University	Colorado Springs	SU	A,B,M,D	Pri	No	C	1,200																						Open
Fort Lewis College	Durango	SM	B,M	Pub	No	C		23		9	55	32	4						555	20	54	24	4						8/1
Johnson & Wales University/Denver Campus	Denver	SU	A,B	Pri	S	C																							Open
Metropolitan State University of Denver	Denver	U	B	Pub	No	C		20		25	56	17	2	500	48	36	16		490	52	40	6	2						7/1
Naropa University	Boulder	U	B,M	Pri	No	C	381																						1/15
Regis University	Denver	SU	B,M,D	Pri	No	C	4,070	24		3	43	43	10	580	17	44	39		563	11	50	33	6	535	22	56	17		Open
Rocky Mountain College of Art and Design	Denver	SU	B,M	Pri	No	C	670																						Open
United States Air Force Academy	Colorado Springs	SU	B	Pub	No	C	4,470																						Open
University of Colorado Boulder	Boulder	SU	B,M,D	Pub	F,S	C	26,491	27			16	53	30	620					624	4	33	44	19						1/15
University of Colorado Colorado Springs	Colorado Springs	SU	B,M,D	Pub	F,S	C	10,187	23		7	48	39	6	534	32	42	21	4	536	32	44	20	4						5/1
University of Colorado Denver	Denver	U	B,M,D	Pub	No	C	10,493	23		5	45	41	9	550	35	29	32	3	550	32	45	16	6						7/22
University of Denver	Denver	U	B,M,D	Pri	F,S	C	5,629	28						595	10	37	44	9	610	5	37	46	12	565	19	45	31	4	1/15
University of Northern Colorado	Greeley	SU	B,M,D	Pub	F,S	C		22						525	41	36	19	3	515	38	46	14	2						8/1
Western State Colorado University	Gunnison	R	B,M	Pub	No	C		22		8	54	33	5						516	25	56	19			25	56	19		6/1
Connecticut																													
Albertus Magnus College	New Haven	SU	A,B,M	Pri	No	C	1,605							456	43	41	14	2	448	53	30	15	1	472	48	36	15	1	Open
Central Connecticut State University	New Britain	SU	B,M,D	Pub	F	C	9,538	21		7	62	27	4		46	44	9	1	530	43	44	12	1		49	42	9	1	5/1
Charter Oak State College	New Britain	SU	A,B,M	Pub	No	C	1,533																						Open
Connecticut College	New London	SM	B,M	Pri	No	C		30			1	47	52	655		15	57	30	655		16	56	27	654		19	56	26	1/1
Eastern Connecticut State University	Willimantic	SM	A,B,M	Pub	No	C	5,171	22		5	58	32	6	568	10	58	30	3	540	21	60	18	1	503	44	44	11		5/1
Fairfield University	Fairfield	SU	B,M,D	Pri	No	C	4,032	27			9	72	19	620					620	1	30	60	9						1/15
Goodwin College	East Hartford	SU	A,B	Pri	No	C	3,388																						Open

Mitchell College	New London	SU	A,B	Pri	No	C	858																						Open
Post University	Waterbury	U	A,B		No	C	1,275																						Open
Quinnipiac University	Hamden	SU	B,M,D	Pri	F,S	C	7,102	25		2	30	57	11	590					580	10	49	35	5						2/1
Sacred Heart University	Fairfield	SU	A,B,M,D	Pri	F,S	C	5,428	25			34	61	5	550	34	52	11	3	565	20	66	13	1	552	43	44	12	1	2/1
Southern Connecticut State University	New Haven	U	B,M,D	Pub	F,S	C	7,963	20		21	53	25	1	481	58	33	8	1	470	61	32	6	1	482	57	35	7	1	4/1
Trinity College	Hartford	U	B,M		F,S	C	2,223	28			4	61	35	610	7	30	49	15	650	2	30	51	17	630	5	29	53	13	1/15
United States Coast Guard Academy	New London	SU	B	Pub	No	C	898	28		1	7	60	33	610	5	35	50	10	650	10	17	59	24	605	7	39	45	9	2/1
University of Bridgeport	Bridgeport	U	A,B,M,D	Pri	F,S	C	2,941	20						468	67	27	6		472	70	23	6	1	457	74	23	3		5/15
University of Connecticut	Storrs	R	A,B,M,D	Pub	F,S	C	18,395																						12/1
University of Hartford	West Hartford	SU	A,B,M,D	Pri	F,S	C	5,284	22	38	28	20	6	8	521	46	39	14	1	530	44	37	17	2						Open
University of New Haven	West Haven	SU	A,B,M,D	Pri	F,S	C	4,936	24		6	45	41	8						550	23	51	23	3						Open
University of Saint Joseph	West Hartford	SU	B,M,D	Pri	No	PW	960							549					520	39	48	13							Open
Wesleyan University	Middletown	SU	B,M,D	Pri	F,S	C	2,971	31			4	24	72						690	1	12	42	46						1/1
Western Connecticut State University	Danbury	SU	A,B,M,D	Pub	F,S	C	5,298							490	53	35	11	1	490	50	39	10	1	490	49	38	12	1	5/1
Yale University	New Haven	U	B,M,D	Pri	F,S	C		33						760		3	17	80	755		1	17	82	750		2	17	81	1/1

Delaware

Delaware State University	Dover	SU	B,M	Pub	F,S	C	3,719																						8/20
Goldey-Beacom College	Wilmington	SU	A,B,M	Pri	No	C	625																						8/20
University of Delaware	Newark	SM	A,B,M,D		F,S	C		26		3	26	51	20	595	8	43	35	14	600	7	37	44	12	590	11	46	36	7	1/15
Wesley College	Dover	SM	A,B,M		F,S	C	1,603							410	83	13	3	1	420	81	18	1		410	87	11	2		Open
Wilmington University	New Castle	U	A,B,M,D	Pri	No	C	9,034																						Open

District of Columbia

Gallaudet University	Washington	U	B,M,D	Pri	F,S	C	1,112	17																					Open
Georgetown University	Washington	U	B,M,D	Pri	No	C		32			2	20	78	710		9	31	60	710		7	35	57						1/10
Howard University	Washington	U	B,M,D	Pri	F,S	C	6,883	24		3	43	47	7	563	22	46	28	4	561	24	45	26	5	555	26	46	25	3	2/15
The American University	Washington	SU	B,M,D	Pri	F,S	C	7,903	28			8	57	34	646	1	18	59	22	616	3	35	51	11	608	10	33	40	16	1/15
The Catholic University of America	Washington	U	B,M,D	Pri	F,S	C		26		3	27	50	20	575	17	43	31	8	570	19	45	30	6						2/15
The George Washington University	Washington	U	A,B,M,D	Pri	F,S	C		30						640	5	24	46	25	650	3	18	51	27	650	5	20	49	26	2/15
Trinity Washington University	Washington	U	A,B,M	Pri	No	W	1,391																						7/31
University of the District of Columbia	Washington	SU	A,B,M	Pub	F,S	C	5,110																						Open

Florida

Adventist University of Health Sciences	Orlando	U	A,B,M	Pri	No	C	2,576	19	71	21	4	2	2	455	72	23	5		440	73	24	3							7/1
Barry University	Miami Shores	SU	B,M,D	Pri	F,S	C	5,150							466					459										Open
Beacon College	Leesburg	SM	A,B	Pri	F,S	C	223																						Open
Bethune-Cookman University	Daytona Beach	SM	B,M	Pri	F,S	C	3,527		93	5	1	1			91	8	1			91	8	1			91	8	1		7/30
Carlos Albizu University	Miami	SM	B,M,D	Pri	No	C	431																						Open
Eckerd College	St. Petersburg	SU	B	Pri	No	C	1,844	26		1	31	50	18	590					560	6	48	40	7						4/1
Edward Waters College	Jacksonville	U	B	Pri	F,S	C	1,400																						4/1
Embry-Riddle Aeronautical University - Daytona Beach	Daytona Beach	U	A,B,M,D	Pri	F,S	C	5,447	26		4	31	47	18						600	8	38	40	14						7/1
Embry-Riddle Aeronautical University - Worldwide	Daytona Beach	SU	A,B,M,D	Pri	No	C	11,137																						Open
Flagler College	St. Augustine	SM	B,M	Pri	No	C	2,616	24			47	47	6	540	24	51	21	3	510	42	43	15	1	530	31	52	15	2	3/1
Florida Agricultural and Mechanical University	Tallahassee	U	A,B,M,D	Pub	F,S	C	7,810	23		18	61	19	2	515	61	27	11	2	503	63	28	9		494	68	23	8		5/15
Florida Atlantic University	Boca Raton	SU	A,B,M,D	Pub	F,S	C	24,823	23			59	37	3	525	30	53	15	3	535	27	53	18	2	520	32	54	13	1	5/1
Florida Gulf Coast University	Fort Myers	SU	A,B,M,D	Pub	F,S	C		24		1	51	44	4	540	24	58	16	2	530	30	55	14	1	525	33	55	11	1	5/1
Florida Institute of Technology	Melbourne	SU	B,M,D	Pri	F,S	C	3,629	25			22	56	22	556	20	49	27	4	604	4	44	42	10						Open
Florida International University	Miami	U	B,M,D	Pub	F,S	C	41,038	24		1	29	59	11						584	3	60	34	3						Open
Florida Memorial University	Miami, Gardens	U	B		No	C																							Open
Florida Southern College	Lakeland	SU	B,M,D	Pri	F,S	C	2,386	26			32	57	11						581	11	56	29	3		33	50	15	3	5/1
Florida State University	Tallahassee	SU	A,B,M,D	Pub	F,S	C	32,706	28		1	19	69	11	623	2	44	46	8	618	3	42	48	6	615	3	45	45	6	1/25
Hodges University	Naples	SU	A,B,M	Pri	No	C	1,515																						Open
Jacksonville University	Jacksonville	SU	B,M	Pri	F,S	C	2,410	22						505					505										Open
Johnson & Wales University/North Miami Campus	North Miami	SM	A,B	Pri	F,S	C																							Open
Keiser University	West Palm Beach	SU	A,B,M	Pri	No	C	497								67	28	4	1		42	42	12	4		80	15	4	1	Open
Lynn"University	Boca Raton	SU	A,B,M,D	Pri	F,S	C	2,095	22		13	58	28	1	528	28	57	15		522	30	59	11							Open
New College of Florida	Sarasota	SU	A,B,M	Pub	No	C	861	28			12	53	35						610	1	41	39	19						2/15
Nova Southeastern University	Fort Lauderdale	SU	A,B,M,D	Pri	F,S	C	4,641	25		1	39	40	20	550	26	45	25	4	550	27	39	29	5						8/1
Palm Beach Atlantic University	West Palm Beach	U	B,M,D	Pri	No	C		24	1	8	47	35	9						535	32	45	21	2						Open
Ringling College of Art and Design	Sarasota	U	B	Pri	No	C	1,341																						Open
Rollins College	Winter Park	SU	B,M	Pri	F,S	C	1,948								4	41	45	10		5	43	40	13		8	44	39	10	2/15
Saint Leo University	Saint Leo	R	A,B,M,D	Pri	F,S	C	2,264	22		5	61	32	2	530	27	51	19	3	520	34	49	15	2	470	54	31	15		Open
Southeastern University	Lakeland	SU	A,B,M,D	Pri	No	C	2,448																						Open
St. Thomas University	Miami	SU	B,M	Pri	No	C	1,145	17	83	13	4			440	78	20	2		440	80	18	2		430	79	19	2		Open
Stetson University	DeLand	SM	B,M,D	Pri	F,S	C	3,089	26		1	28	54	18	611					590	7	49	36	8						Open
University of Central Florida	Orlando	SU	A,B,M,D	Pub	F,S	C	55,776	26			22	59	19						617	2	39	48	11						5/1
University of Florida	Gainesville	SU	A,B,M,D	Pub	F,S	C	34,464	29			3	42	55			3	7	5	651		18	52	30			2	8	5	11/1

NAME OF SCHOOL	TOWN	ENVIRONMENT U-Urban R-Rural SU-Suburban SM-Small Town	DEGREES AWARDED A-Associate B-Bachelor M-Master D-Doctorate	CONTROL Pri-Private, Pub-Public	FRATERNITIES AND SORORITIES F-Fraternities S-Sororities F, S-Both No-Neither	STUDENTS: C-Coed M-Men W-Women PM-Primarily Men PW-Primarily Women	UNDERGRADUATE ENROLLMENT FALL 2017	TEST SCORES: ACT Median	ACT Below 21	ACT 21-23	ACT 24-26	ACT 27-28	ACT Above 28	SAT CRITICAL READING Median	SAT CR Below 500	SAT CR 500-599	SAT CR 600-700	SAT CR Above 700	SAT MATHEMATICS Median	SAT Math Below 500	SAT Math 500-599	SAT Math 600-700	SAT Math Above 700	SAT WRITING Median	SAT Writing Below 500	SAT Writing 500-599	SAT Writing 600-700	SAT Writing Above 700	APPLICATION DEADLINE Month / Day
University of Miami	Coral Gables	SU	B,M,D	Pri	F,S	C		30		1	2	39	58	640	4	21	53	22	660	2	18	49	30	635	4	26	53	18	4/1
University of North Florida	Jacksonville	U	A,B,M,D	Pub	F,S	C	13,846	26				80	20	612	3	37	52	8	597	2	48	47	3		13	52	33	2	Open
University of South Florida St. Petersburg	St. Petersburg	U	B,M	Pub	No	C	4,006	23						530					530					510					3/15
University of South Florida/Tampa	Tampa	U	A,B,M,D	Pub	F,S	C		26			17	64	19	575	9	52	33	6	585	9	48	35	7	555	16	56	26	3	3/15
University of Tampa	Tampa	U	B,M	Pri	F,S	C	7,363	24			43	48	8						590	8	59	31	3						Open
University of West Florida	Pensacola	SU	A,B,M,D	Pub	F,S	C	10,332		8	56	32	2	2		44	44	10	1		49	41	9	1		60	34	5	1	6/30
Warner University	Lake Wales	R	A,B,M	Pri	No	C	1,090																						Open
Webber International University	Babson Park	SM	A,B,M	Pri	No	C	655		70	20		1			68	29	3			63	32	4	1						8/1
Georgia																													
Agnes Scott College	Decatur	U	B	Pri	No	W	927	27			19	55	26	610	8	33	41	18	550	13	48	29	9		8	39	44	9	3/15
Albany State University	Albany	U	A,B,M	Pub	F,S	C	3,025																						7/1
Armstrong State University	Savannah	SU	A,B,M,D	Pub	F,S	C	6,397	21		14	64	19	3	28					517	35	56	8	1	27					7/15
Augusta University	Augusta	U	A,B,M,D	Pub	F,S	C	5,224																						7/15
Berry College	Mount Berry	SU	B,M	Pri	No	C	2,073	26			23	60	17	620	4	35	46	16	590	6	50	39	5						1/15
Brenau University - Women's College	Gainesville	SU	B,M	Pri	S	W	867		42	32	16	7	2		39	46	14	1		59	31	10							Open
Brewton-Parker College	Mt. Vernon	R	B	Pri	F,S	C	629	17		69	27	3	1	435	78	20	2		427	77	22	1		453	67	33			Open
Clark Atlanta University	Atlanta	U	B,M,D		F,S	C	3,093	19		25	63	12		450	76	22	2		440	79	19	2							Open
Clayton State University	Morrow	SU	A,B,M	Pub	F,S	C		20						500					458										Open
Columbus State University	Columbus	SU	A,B,M,D	Pub	F,S	C	6,789	20		12	67	19	2	490	50	36	13	1	480	54	36	9	1	470	59	31	9	1	6/30
Covenant College	Lookout Mountain	SU	B,M	Pri	No	C	1,066	27		1	23	47	29						600	10	38	43	10						2/1
Emory University	Atlanta	SU	B,M,D	Pri	F,S	C	6,861	32				17	83						724		4	29	67						1/1
Fort Valley State University	Fort Valley	R	A,B,M		F,S	C	3,421																						6/15
Georgia College & State University	Milledgeville	SM	B,M,D	Pub	F,S	C	6,047	25			35	58	7						579	8	54	34	4						Open
Georgia Institute of Technology	Atlanta	U	B,M,D	Pub	F,S	C		32			2	15	83	710	1	4	39	57	740	1	3	25	71	670	3	19	42	35	1/1
Georgia Southern University	Statesboro	SM	B,M,D	Pub	F,S	C	17,975	23		1	53	40	6						570	2	67	28	3						5/1
Georgia Southwestern State University	Americus	SM	B,M	Pub	F,S	C	2,558	21		10	67	21	2	490	56	36	7		470	63	31	6							7/21
Georgia State University	Atlanta	U	A,B,M,D	Pub	F,S	C	25,455	23		5	51	36	8						524	34	44	20	3						3/1
Kennesaw State University	Kennesaw	SU	B,M,D	Pub	F,S	C	32,166	23		2	53	38	7						570	4	63	29	4						4/1
LaGrange College	LaGrange	SM	B,M	Pri	F,S	C	902	22		1	70	25	4	557	14	60	23	3	538	24	55	16	2						Open
Mercer University	Macon	SU	B,M,D	Pri	F,S	C	2,538	26						580	9	47	35	9	590	7	48	37	8	560	19	46	29	6	4/1
Morehouse College	Atlanta	U	B	Pri	F	M	2,104	20		23	57	17	3						520	35	49	15	1						2/15
Oglethorpe University	Atlanta	SU	B	Pri	F,S	C	1,184	24	12	30	25	14	19	570	8	51	35	6	550	20	52	23	4	550	24	49	24	3	2/15
Paine College	Augusta	U	B	Pri	F,S	C	924		95	2	1	1	1		94	6				92	8				96	4			7/1
Piedmont College	Demorest	SM	B,M,D	Pri	No	C	1,295	21		13	59	25	3	535	29	50	21		511	39	48	12	1						8/1
Reinhardt University	Waleska	SM	A,B		No	C	1,120																						Open
Savannah College of Art and Design	Savannah	U	B,M	Pri	No	C	10,573	24		6	41	41	12	546	28	42	26	4	519	39	42	17	1	524	37	41	19	2	Open
Savannah State University	Savannah	SU	A,B,M	Pub	F,S	C	4,413																						7/15
Shorter University	Rome	SM	A,B,M	Pri	F,S	C	1,555	20		19	55	24	2	470	63	28	8	1	470	59	32	9		470	61	31	8		Open
South University	Savannah	U	A,B,M,D	Pri	No	C																							Open
Spelman College	Atlanta	U	B		S	W	2,318	25																					2/1
The Art Institute of Atlanta	Atlanta	SU	A,B	Pri	No	C	2,720																						Open
Thomas University	Thomasville	SM	A,B,M	Pri	No	C																							Open
Toccoa Falls College	Toccoa Falls	SM	A,B	Pri	No	C	874	20	69	18	9	3	1	505	44	36	20		500	49	41	9	1						8/1
University of Georgia	Athens	SM	B,M,D	Pub	F,S	C	27,951				7	48	45							2	27	51	20						1/15
University of North Georgia	Dahlonega	SM	A,B,M,D	Pub	F,S	C	17,704	23		7	50	39	3	530	33	47	18	2	530	30	47	21	2	500	45	41	12	1	2/15
University of West Georgia	Carrollton	R	B,M,D	Pub	F,S	C	11,155																						6/1
Valdosta State University	Valdosta	SU	A,B	Pub	F,S	C		21						495	51	41	8		480	61	32	6		475	65	30	5		7/1
Wesleyan College	Macon	SU	B,M	Pri	No	W	592	22	36	27	25	7	7																8/1
Hawaii																													
Brigham Young University/Hawaii	Laie	R	B	Pri	No	C		23	26	22	24	16	12																2/15
Chaminade University of Honolulu	Honolulu	U	A,B,M	Pri	No	C	1,183	21		12	68	20		542	27	45	26	2	536	28	55	13	4						Open
Hawaii Pacific University	Honolulu	U	A,B,M	Pri	No	C	6,168	21	47	30	14	5	5	480	57	35	8	1	490	52	38	9	1	470	63	32	5		8/15
University of Hawaii at Hilo	Hilo	SM	B,M,D	Pub	No	C	2,850																						7/1
University of Hawaii at Manoa	Honolulu	SM	B,M,D	Pub	F,S	C		24		4	48	40	8	530	34	44	18	3	550	26	44	25	5	520	42	43	15	2	5/1

Idaho

Boise State University	Boise	U	A,B,M,D	Pub	F,S	C	20,209	23		6	42	36	10	520	39	37	22	2	520	37	48	14	1	500	44	46	9	1	5/15
Idaho State University	Pocatello	U	A,B,M,D	Pub	F,S	C	11,087	22		17	45	31	5	480	58	31	9	1	470	63	26	10	1	460	69	26	5		8/1
Lewis-Clark State College	Lewiston	U	A,B	Pub	No	C	3,495																						Open
Northwest Nazarene University	Nampa	SM	A,B,M,D	Pri	No	C		19		6	42	45	7						555										8/15
The College of Idaho	Caldwell	SM	B,M	Pri	F,S	C	1,039	23		2	53	37	8	510	40	42	16	2	505	41	40	16	3	490	51	35	13	1	7/15
University of Idaho	Moscow	SM	B,M,D	Pub	F,S	C	9,116	23		10	42	39	9						528	38	38	18	6						8/1

Illinois

Augustana College	Rock Island	SU	B	Pri	F,S	C	2,537	26		1	28	55	16						610	9	34	43	14						Open
Aurora University	Aurora	SU	B,M,D	Pri	F,S	C	3,796	21		9	68	21	2						510	39	46	15							Open
Benedictine University	Lisle	SU	A,B,M,D	Pri	No	C	2,940	23	30	27	26	9	8																Open
Blackburn College	Carlinville	R	B	Pri	No	C	596	20		21	57	19	2	440	100				390	100									8/1
Bradley University	Peoria	SU	B,M,D	Pri	F,S	C	4,473	25			37	50	13																Open
Chicago State University	Chicago	U	B,M,D	Pub	F,S	C	4,618																						7/15
Columbia College Chicago	Chicago	U	B,M	Pri	No	C	7,809	23		11	45	37	7																7/15
Concordia University, Chicago	River Forest	SU	B,M,D	Pri	No	C	1,032		36	23	20	9	12																Open
DePaul University	Chicago	U	B,M,D	Pri	F,S	C	16,153	25		2	32	49	17	610	5	37	44	14	590	9	46	39	6						2/1
Dominican University	River Forest	SU	B,M,D	Pri	No	C	2,269	23		6	59	30	5	620	19	47	34		470	25	59	16							Open
Eastern Illinois University	Charleston	SM	B,M	Pub	F,S	C	5,957	21		15	58	23	4																8/15
Elmhurst College	Elmhurst	SU	B,M	Pri	F,S	C	2,856	23		8	49	37	6	460	67	33			520	33	56	11		530	44	45	11		8/15
Eureka College	Eureka	SM	B	Pri	F,S	C	700	23																					8/1
Greenville College	Greenville	SM	B,M	Pri	No	C	1,382	23	32	20	21	13	14	480	56	26	17	1	490	51	36	13		470	60	21	19		8/1
Illinois College	Jacksonville	SM	B	Pri	No	C																							Open
Illinois Institute of Technology	Chicago	U	B,M,D	Pri	F,S	C	3,046	28	11		53		37	580	13	44	32	11	690		8	44	48	580	12	40	41	7	Open
Illinois State University	Normal	U	B,M,D	Pub	F,S	C	18,427	24		1	54	37	4																4/1
Illinois Wesleyan University	Bloomington	SU	B	Pri	F,S	C		27			13	63	24																3/1
Judson University	Elgin	SU	B,M	Pri	No	C	1,195																						Open
Kendall College	Chicago	U	A,B	Pri	No	C	2,545																						Open
Knox College	Galesburg	SM	B	Pri	F,S	C	1,357	26		1	26	48	26						610	5	35	37	23						1/15
Lake Forest College	Lake Forest	SU	B,M	Pri	F,S	C	1,607																						2/15
Lewis University	Romeoville	SU	A,B,M,D	Pri	F,S	C	4,553	23		3	53	38	6	546	37	33	22	8	548	33	33	30	4						Open
Loyola University Chicago	Chicago	U	A,B,M,D	Pri	F,S	C	11,129	27			19	58	23	619					599	7	44	40	10	31					5/1
MacMurray College	Jacksonville	SM	A,B		F,S	C	701	21	50	28	15	4	3																Open
McKendree University	Lebanon	SU	B,M,D	Pri	F,S	C	2,342	24	27	34	27	4	7		56	44				41	54	5			79	15	5		Open
Millikin University	Decatur	SU	B,M,D	Pri	F,S	C	1,971	23		12	49	32	7																Open
Monmouth College	Monmouth	SM	B	Pri	F,S	C	1,198	23		5	55	33	7																Open
National Louis University	Chicago	SU	B,M,D	Pri	No	PW	2,084																						Open
North Central College	Naperville	SU	B,M	Pri	No	C	2,755	24	11	30	31	15	13																Open
North Park University	Chicago	U	B,M,D	Pri	No	C	2,224	22	41	25	16	9	9	530	33	49	17	1	500	40	43	14	3						6/1
Northeastern Illinois University	Chicago	U	B,M	Pub	F,S	C	8,412	19	72	19	7	2	1																8/1
Northern Illinois University	DeKalb	SM	B,M,D	Pub	F,S	C	18,277	22	37	30	21	7	5																8/1
Northwestern University	Evanston	SU	B,M,D	Pri	F,S	C	8,314				1	12	87			4	26	70			2	18	80						1/1
Olivet Nazarene University	Bourbonnais	SU	A,B,M,D	Pri	No	C	3,358	24		3	46	41	10																8/1
Principia College	Elsah	R	B	Pri	No	C	460	24		12	35	43	10	545	22	45	27	6	485	59	22	14	5	535	22	45	27	6	8/1
Quincy University	Quincy	SM	A,B,M	Pri	F,S	C	1,241	21	44	30	15	8	3	450	79	21			460	53	32	10	5						Open
Rockford University	Rockford	SU	B,M	Pri	No	C	869	22	43	26	24	3																	Open
Roosevelt University	Chicago	U	B,M,D		F,S	C	4,300																						Open
Saint Xavier University	Chicago	U	B,M		No	C	3,070																						5/1
School of the Art Institute of Chicago	Chicago	U	B,M		No	C	3,393	25																560					5/1
Southern Illinois University Carbondale	Carbondale	SM	A,B,M,D	Pub	F,S	C		22		7	53	33	7	490	47	26	16		530	32	42	26							5/1
Southern Illinois University Edwardsville	Edwardsville	SU	B,M,D	Pub	F,S	C	11,720	23	31	30	22	9	8																5/1
Trinity Christian College	Palos Heights	SU	B,M	Pri	No	C	1,450	23	35	22	14	13	16	543	32	52	11	5	552	37	47	16							11/1
Trinity College of Nursing and Health Sciences	Rock Island	U	A,B	Pri	No	C																							11/1
Trinity International University	Deerfield	SU	B,M,D	Pri	No	C	1,265																						Open
University of Chicago	Chicago	U	B,M,D	Pri	F,S	C	5,941	34				5	95						775			8	92						1/1
University of Illinois at Chicago	Chicago	U	B,M,D	Pub	F,S	C	17,959	23		4	50	37	8						616	10	32	39	19						1/1
University of Illinois at Urbana-Champaign	Urbana	SM	B,M,D		F,S	C	32,695																						12/1
University of St. Francis	Joliet	SU	B,M,D	Pri	F,S	C	1,362	23		3	61	32	4							7	57	29	7						8/1
VanderCook College of Music	Chicago	U	B,M		F,S	C	90																						8/1
Western Illinois University	Macomb	R	B,M,D	Pub	F,S	C	8,543	21		13	61	21	5																5/15
Wheaton College	Wheaton	SU	B,M,D	Pri	No	C	2,456	29			7	45	48						650	3	20	53	25						1/10

Indiana

Anderson University	Anderson	SU	A,B,M,D	Pri	No	C	1,883	23		15	41	38	6	512	39	37	12	5	519	44	34	20	2						Open
Ball State University	Muncie	SU	A,B,M,D	Pub	F,S	C	17,011	23		2	56	36	6	589	7	58	31	4	572	13	62	23	2						8/10
Bethel College	Mishawaka	SU	A,B,M	Pri	No	C	1,388	23		17	43	36	4						520	35	46	15	4						Open
Butler University	Indianapolis	SU	A,B,M,D	Pri	F,S	C	4,551	27			16	54	30	614	3	38	48	12	609	4	40	48	9			14	6	1	2/1

NAME OF SCHOOL	TOWN	ENVIRONMENT U-Urban R-Rural SU-Suburban SM-Small Town	DEGREES AWARDED A-Associate B-Bachelor M-Master D-Doctorate	CONTROL Pri-Private, Pub-Public	FRATERNITIES AND SORORITIES F-Fraternities S-Sororities F, S-Both No-Neither	STUDENTS: C-Coed M-Men W-Women PM-Primarily Men PW-Primarily Women	UNDERGRADUATE ENROLLMENT FALL 2017	TEST SCORES: ACT Median	ACT Below 21	ACT 21-23	ACT 24-26	ACT 27-28	ACT Above 28	SAT CRITICAL READING Median	SAT CR Below 500	SAT CR 500-599	SAT CR 600-700	SAT CR Above 700	SAT MATHEMATICS Median	SAT Math Below 500	SAT Math 500-599	SAT Math 600-700	SAT Math Above 700	SAT WRITING Median	SAT Writing Below 500	SAT Writing 500-599	SAT Writing 600-700	SAT Writing Above 700	APPLICATION DEADLINE Month / Day
Calumet College of St. Joseph	Whiting	SM	A,B,M		No	C	1,200																						Open
DePauw University	Greencastle	R	B	Pri	F,S	C	2,225	27						580	14	40	35	10	600	8	36	41	14	580	13	42	37	7	3/1
Earlham College	Richmond	SM	B,M	Pri	No	C	1,031	27			17	57	26						630	2	27	45	26						2/15
Franklin College	Franklin	SM	B,M	Pri	F,S	C	1,016	22		18	50	27	5	495	58	32	5	5	505	46	42	10	2	483	58	32	8	2	Open
Goshen College	Goshen	SM	B,M,D	Pri	No	C	800	24		13	37	40	10	558	26	41	28	6	554	29	37	30	4						8/1
Grace College and Seminary	Winona Lake	SM	A,B,M,D	Pri	No	C	1,934	24		6	34	50	10	519	40	41	17	2	512	40	39	19	2						3/1
Hanover College	Hanover	R	B	Pri	F,S	C	1,090	25		3	37	47	13						572	8	50	29	4						3/1
Huntington University	Huntington	SM	A,B,M,D	Pri	No	C	1,001	22		13	54	31	2	490	34	45	20	1	507	36	47	15	2						Open
Indiana Institute of Technology	Fort Wayne	U	A,B,M,D	Pri	F,S	C	5,697	20	53	27	16	2	2	447	69	27	4		468	59	32	8	1	430	81	18	1		8/15
Indiana State University	Terre Haute	U	B,M,D	Pub	F,S	C	11,257	19						460	69	26	5		455	69	26	6		435	80	18	3		8/15
Indiana University Bloomington	Bloomington	SM	A,B,M,D	Pub	F,S	C	39,184	28		1	16	47	36						626	4	33	43	20						2/1
Indiana University East	Richmond	SM	A,B,M	Pub	F,S	C	4,287	21		18	59	21	2						510	40	50	9	1						Open
Indiana University Kokomo	Kokomo	SM	A,B,M	Pub	S	C	3,977	20		28	55	16	1						515	37	52	10	1						Open
Indiana University Northwest	Gary	U	A,B,M	Pub	F,S	C	5,244	20		26	56	15	3						491	53	38	8	1						7/1
Indiana University South Bend	South Bend	SU	A,B,M	Pub	F,S	C	6,653	21		20	53	24	3						510	44	45	10	1						Open
Indiana University Southeast	New Albany	SU	A,B,M	Pub	F,S	C	5,486	20		29	52	17	2						509	36	54	9	1						8/12
Indiana University-Purdue University Fort Wayne	Fort Wayne	SU	A,B,M,D	Pub	F,S	C	11,453			19	50	24	7																8/1
Indiana University-Purdue University Indianapolis	Indianapolis	U	A,B,M,D	Pub	F,S	C	21,748	23		13	43	37	7						545	25	51	20	4						Open
Indiana Wesleyan University	Marion	SM	A,B,M,D	Pri	No	C		24		7	37	45	11	525	36	40	20	4	535	36	424	19	3	515	44	37	17	2	Open
Manchester University	North Manchester	SM	A,B	Pri	No	C	1,217																						Open
Marian University	Indianapolis	SU	A,B,M,D	Pri	No	C	2,147	22		9	52	34	5	518	23	50	25	2	516	20	49	24	3						8/1
Martin University	Indianapolis	U	B,M	Pri	No	C	615																						Open
Oakland City University	Oakland City	SM	A,B,M	Pri	No	C	2,100																						9/8
Purdue University Northwest	Hammond	U	A,B,M,D	Pub	F,S	C	14,385	22		16	53	28	3						479	63	30	6	1						8/1
Purdue University/West Lafayette	West Lafayette	SU	A,B,M,D	Pub	F,S	C	30,043	29	8	16	23	13	41	570	16	44	32	9	680	7	27	37	28	570	16	43	33	7	8/1
Rose-Hulman Institute of Technology	Terre Haute	SU	B,M	Pri	F,S	C	2,202	30			4	44	53	600	6	41	39	13	660	3	25	45	27	570	8	46	32	4	2/1
Saint Mary-of-the-Woods College	St Mary of the Woods	R	A,B,M	Pri	No	PW		20		28	56	16		479	67	22	11		458	69	26	5		447	65	30	5		Open
Saint Mary's College	Notre Dame	SU	B,M,D	Pri	No	W	1,594	25		1	35	52	11	545	25	51	22	3	529	33	47	17	3	543	28	46	24	1	2/15
Taylor University	Upland	R	A,B,M	Pri	No	C	2,133	26		5	28	47	20						570	16	48	31	11						12/1
Trine University	Angola	SM	A,B,M,D	Pri	F,S	C	1,780	23		8	45	38	9	510	42	38	17	3	540	27	40	29	4						8/1
University of Evansville	Evansville	U	A,B,M,D	Pri	F,S	C	2,234	27		2	27	49	22	560	21	46	25	8	570	20	43	31	6	535	29	46	21	4	8/1
University of Indianapolis	Indianapolis	SU	A,B,M,D	Pri	No	C	4,125	23	2	7	55	31	7	505	50	38	11	1	513	44	40	14	1	492	56	35	8	1	Open
University of Notre Dame	Notre Dame	SU	B,M,D	Pri	No	C	8,530	34			1	10	89						770		3	27	70						1/1
University of Saint Francis	Fort Wayne	U	A,B,M,D	Pri	No	C	1,810	21		15	55	26	4						520	31	54	15							Open
University of Southern Indiana	Evansville	SU	A,B,M,D	Pub	F,S	C	7,956	22		12	52	32	4						533	29	54	15	2						8/15
Valparaiso University	Valparaiso	SM	A,B,M,D	Pri	F,S	C	3,299	26		1	28	50	21						582	9	48	36	7						Open
Wabash College	Crawfordsville	SM	B	Pri	F	M	843	25		3	37	45	15	585	10	45	35	7	598	6	44	37	13	557	39	38	21	2	1/15
Iowa																													
Allen College	Waterloo	SU	A,B,M,D	Pri	No	PW	360																						2/1
Briar Cliff University	Sioux City	SU	A,B,M	Pri	No	C	1,079	21	40	28	20	9	3																Open
Buena Vista University	Storm Lake	SM	B,M	Pri	No	C	795	22		13	55	26	6																Open
Central College	Pella	SM	B	Pri	F,S	C	1,248	23		4	47	39	10						530					540					8/15
Clarke University	Dubuque	SM	A,B,M,D	Pri	No	C	868	22		4	56	37	3	507	43	43	14		520	48	33	14	5						Open
Coe College	Cedar Rapids	U	B	Pri	F,S	C	1,409	25		1	37	46	16	580	13	48	23	16	570	16	42	29	13	545	40	25	30	5	Open
Cornell College	Mount Vernon	SM	B	Pri	F,S	C	974	26		2	30	47	22	560	13	50	13	25	610	7	43	34	16	540	38	38	25		3/1
Dordt College	Sioux Center	R	A,B,M		No	C	1,430	25	15	25	36	20	15		47	29	21	3		22	45	30	3		43	40	17		8/1
Drake University	Des Moines	U	B,M,D	Pri	F,S	C	3,267	27			13	58	29		18	33	38	10		10	40	32	18						3/1
Graceland University	Lamoni	SM	B,M,D	Pri	No	C	1,556			18	55	24	3		87	11	2			78	16	5	1						3/1
Grand View University	Des Moines	U	B,M	Pri	No	C	2,094	21	48	27	18	3	5		96	4				80	20				96	4			8/15
Grinnell College	Grinnell	SM	B	Pri	No	C	1,699	32						685		12	44	43	710		1	9	37						1/15
Iowa State University	Ames	U	B,M,D	Pub	F,S	C	30,671																						1/15
Iowa Wesleyan University	Mount Pleasant	SM	B	Pri	F,S	C	523	22		2	75	22	1																Open
Loras College	Dubuque	SM	A,B,M	Pri	F,S	C	1,463	23		3	54	39	4																Open
Luther College	Decorah	SM	B	Pri	F,S	C	2,169	26		3	29	48	20						590	17	35	31	17						Open
Maharishi University of Management	Fairfield	SM	B,M,D	Pri	No	C	220																						Open
Mercy College of Health Sciences	Des Moines	U	A,B	Pri	No	C	771	21		19	56	23	1																6/15
Morningside College	Sioux City	SU	B,M	Pri	F,S	C	1,321	22		7	58	30	5																Open
Mount Mercy University	Cedar Rapids	U	B,M	Pri	No	C	1,543	22		12	55	28	5																8/14
Northwestern College of Iowa	Orange City	SM	B,M	Pri	No	C	1,099	24		3	42	40	15	540	26	50	24		540	23	46	23	8						Open

Simpson College	Indianola	SM	B,M	Pri	F,S	C	1,543	24		2	41	46	11																Open
St. Ambrose University	Davenport	U	B,M,D	Pri	No	C	2,398	23		1	60	34	5																Open
University of Dubuque	Dubuque	SU	A,B,M,D	Pri	F,S	C	1,185																						8/15
University of Iowa	Iowa City	SM	B,M,D	Pub	F,S	C	24,476	26		1	30	50	19						631	5	33	37	24						4/1
University of Northern Iowa	Cedar Falls	SM	B,M,D	Pub	F,S	C	10,104	23		5	53	36	6																8/15
Upper Iowa University	Fayette	R	A,B,M		F,S	C	720																						Open
Wartburg College	Waverly	SM	B	Pri	No	C	1,482	23		5	48	37	10						520	32	37	26	5						5/1
William Penn University	Oskaloosa	R	A,B,M	Pub	F,S	C	1,835																						Open
Kansas																													
Baker University	Baldwin City	R	B	Pri	F,S	C	989	23		4	48	44	4																Open
Benedictine College	Atchison	SM	A,B,M	Pri	No	C	1,993	25																					Open
Bethany College	Lindsborg	SM	B	Pri	F,S	C	483		36	29	24	6	5		74	26				57	38	5							Open
Bethel College	North Newton	SU	B	Pri	No	C	460			2	68	28	2																Open
Emporia State University	Emporia	SM	B,M,D	Pub	F,S	C	3,702	22		13	54	30	4																Open
Fort Hays State University	Hays	SM	A,B,M	Pub	F,S	C	11,299	21																					Open
Friends University	Wichita	U	A,B,M	Pri	No	C	1,192			6	57	30	7																Open
Kansas State University	Manhattan	SU	A,B,M,D		F,S	C	19,859	25		3	37	44	16																Open
Kansas Wesleyan University	Salina	U	A,B,M	Pri	No	C	800																						Open
McPherson College	McPherson	SM	B,M	Pri	No	C	632																						8/1
MidAmerica Nazarene University	Olathe	SU	A,B,M	Pri	No	C	1,309		1	17	48	29	5																8/1
Newman University	Wichita	U	A,B,M	Pri	No	C	2,795	24						509	38	46		8	548	31	38	31		487	46	46		8	Open
Ottawa University	Ottawa	SM	B	Pri	No	C	585																						Open
Pittsburg State University	Pittsburg	SM	A,B,M,D	Pub	F,S	C		22		12	57	28	3																Open
Southwestern College	Winfield	SM	B,M,D	Pri	F	C	522	22	31	29	27	9	4	455	69	25	3	3	486	61	29	7	3	433	75	22	3		8/1
Sterling College	Sterling	R	B	Pri	No	C	642	21	37	31	20	5	7	460	73	23	4		470	65	31	4		460	77	15	8		Open
Tabor College	Hillsboro	SM	A,B,M	Pri	No	C	670	21																					8/1
University of Kansas	Lawrence	SU	B,M,D	Pub	F,S	C	19,262	26		1	30	50	18																Open
University of Saint Mary	Leavenworth	SM	A,B,M,D	Pri	No	C	837	22																					Open
Washburn University	Topeka	U	A,B,M,D	Pub	F,S	C	5,780	22		15	51	32	2																8/1
Wichita State University	Wichita	U	A,B,M,D	Pub	F,S	C		24		8	43	40	9	530	41	33	18	7	538	22	47	15	16						Open
Kentucky																													
Alice Lloyd College	Pippa Passes	R	B	Pri	No	C	612	20	48	35	13	3	1																Open
Asbury University	Wilmore	SM	A,B,M	Pri	No	C	1,532	24	17	27	26	11	19	568	21	41	33	5	558	24	40	32	4						Open
Bellarmine University	Louisville	SU	B,M,D	Pri	F,S	C		25			40	47	11	540	27	49	23	1	530	31	54	15		500	62	24	9	5	8/15
Berea College	Berea	SU	B	Pri	No	C	1,665	24			47	47	6	547	27	50	18	5	554	30	43	23	5	530	34	48	14	5	Open
Brescia University	Owensboro	U	A,B,M	Pri	No	C	801		20	45	17	15	3							53	47								Open
Campbellsville University	Campbellsville	SM	A,B,M,D	Pri	No	C	3,349	21		20	53	24	3							38	51	11							Open
Centre College	Danville	SM	B	Pri	F,S	C	1,430	29			8	47	45						656		33	31	36						1/15
Eastern Kentucky University	Richmond	SM	A,B,M,D	Pub	F,S	C	14,327																						8/1
Georgetown College	Georgetown	SU	B,M	Pri	F,S	C	984	23		4	50	39	7	494	57	29	14		511	43	46	11							8/1
Kentucky Christian University	Grayson	SM	B,M	Pri	No	C	570	19	62	22	10	3	2	450	73	20	7		460	53	40	7							8/1
Kentucky State University	Frankfort	SM	A,B,M		F,S	C	2,300	17																					Open
Kentucky Wesleyan College	Owensboro	SU	B	Pri	F,S	C	678	22	38	29	16	7	10	470	58	36	6		490	55	36	9		460	61	36	3		Open
Lindsey Wilson College	Columbia	SM	A,B,M,D	Pri	No	C	2,144																						Open
Midway University	Midway	R	A,B,M		No	PW	1,169	20	62	21	10	3	4																Open
Morehead State University	Morehead	SM	A,B,M,D	Pub	F,S	C	9,754	20		5	52	38	5							67	22	11							Open
Murray State University	Murray	SM	A,B,M,D	Pub	F,S	C	8,886	24		1	44	43	12	525	31	57	6	6	565	19	56	25							8/17
Northern Kentucky University	Highland Heights	SU	A,B,M,D	Pub	F,S	C	11,651	23						505	47	38	12	4	505	46	36	14	3	480	55	34	7	4	8/18
Spalding University	Louisville	U	A,B,M,D	Pri	F,S	C	1,316	20		20	55	24	1						510	47	24	29							Open
Thomas More College	Crestview Hills	SU	A,B,M	Pri	F,S	C	1,502	22	28	35	24	5	8	480	55	36	9		490	51	31	13	5						8/1
Transylvania University	Lexington	U	B	Pri	F,S	C	966	27			13	55	32	647	4	15	56	26	621	4	33	44	19						2/1
Union College	Barbourville	SM	B,M	Pri	No	C	912	20		22	61	16	1						506										Open
University of Kentucky	Lexington	SU	B,M,D	Pub	F,S	C		26						560	23	42	24	11	565	22	39	27	12	545	28	44	21	7	2/15
University of Louisville	Louisville	U	A,B,M,D	Pub	F,S	C	15,827	25		1	38	42	19	543	39	32	16	13	546	27	46	20	7						Open
University of Pikeville	Pikeville	SM	A,B,M,D	Pri	No	C	1,658	21		22	54	22	2																8/15
University of the Cumberlands	Williamsburg	SM	A,B,M,D	Pri	No	C	3,082	22		8	57	27	8	482	64	33	3		478	64	28	5	3						8/31
Western Kentucky University	Bowling Green	SU	A,B,M,D	Pub	F,S	C	17,459	23		15	42	33	10	510	41	47	10	2	510	37	47	12	4						8/1
Louisiana																													
Centenary College of Louisiana	Shreveport	U	B,M	Pri	F,S	C		25		2	38	46	14	525	43	37	15	5	530	36	41	15	8						8/1
Dillard University	New Orleans	U	B	Pri	F,S	C	1,249																						8/1
Grambling State University	Grambling	SM	A,B,M,D	Pub	F,S	C	3,883			41	54	14			86	14				80	19	1			91	10			7/1
Louisiana College	Pineville	SM	A,B,M	Pri	No	C	1,056	22	38	29	16	9	8																Open
Louisiana State University and A&M College	Baton Rouge	U	B,M,D	Pub	F,S	C	24,923	26	5	27	31	17	21	559	22	51	24	4	577	15	44	35	6						4/15
Louisiana State University in Shreveport	Shreveport	U	B,M,D	Pub	F,S	C	2,819	22	30	32	24	6	5	500	40	60			530	17	83								4/15
Louisiana Tech University	Ruston	SM	A,B,M,D	Pub	F,S	C	10,800	24																					1/15

NAME OF SCHOOL	TOWN	ENVIRONMENT U-Urban R-Rural SU-Suburban SM-Small Town	DEGREES AWARDED A-Associate B-Bachelor M-Master D-Doctorate	CONTROL Pri-Private, Pub-Public	FRATERNITIES AND SORORITIES F-Fraternities S-Sororities F, S-Both No-Neither	STUDENTS: C-Coed M-Men W-Women PM-Primarily Men PW-Primarily Women	UNDERGRADUATE ENROLLMENT FALL 2017	TEST SCORES: ACT Median	ACT Below 21	ACT 21-23	ACT 24-26	ACT 27-28	ACT Above 28	SAT CRITICAL READING Median	SAT CR Below 500	SAT CR 500-599	SAT CR 600-700	SAT CR Above 700	SAT MATHEMATICS Median	SAT Math Below 500	SAT Math 500-599	SAT Math 600-700	SAT Math Above 700	SAT WRITING Median	SAT Writing Below 500	SAT Writing 500-599	SAT Writing 600-700	SAT Writing Above 700	APPLICATION DEADLINE Month / Day
Loyola University New Orleans	New Orleans	SU	B,M,D	Pri	F,S	C	2,483	25		1	35	50	14	607	3	42	45	10	570	17	47	30	6						Open
McNeese State University	Lake Charles	SU	A,B,M	Pub	F,S	C	7,501	20	36	37	17	5	5						490										Open
Nicholls State University	Thibodaux	SM	A,B,M	Pub	F,S	C		22		50	40	10																	Open
Northwestern State University of Louisiana	Natchitoches	SM	A,B,M,D	Pub	F,S	C	8,690	21		10	65	23	2	476	62	30	6	2	476	72	18	8	2	385	90	10			Open
Southeastern Louisiana University	Hammond	SM	A,B,M,D	Pub	F,S	C	13,586	22		4	64	30	2																8/1
Southern University and A&M College	Baton Rouge	U	B,M,D	Pub	F,S	C	6,491	19					1																7/1
Southern University at New Orleans	New Orleans	SU	A,B,M	Pub	No	C	3,165																						7/1
Tulane University	New Orleans	U	A,B,M,D	Pri	F,S	C	8,339	31			2	20	79	710					710	3	3	35	59						1/15
University of Holy Cross	New Orleans	SU	A,B,M,D	Pri	No	C	773																						1/15
University of Louisiana at Lafayette	Lafayette	U	B,M,D	Pub	F,S	C	14,560																						Open
University of Louisiana at Monroe	Monroe	U	A,B,M,D	Pub	F,S	C	7,778	22		6	58	54	5	500	50	34	14	2	570	32	27	27	14						Open
University of New Orleans	New Orleans	U	B,M,D	Pub	F,S	C	8,653	21	37	35	18	6	4	550	35	31	30	4	550	32	34	29	5	540	35	40	22	3	7/25
Xavier University of Louisiana	New Orleans	U	B,M,D	Pri	F,S	C		24						509					494					476					7/1
Maine																													
Bates College	Lewiston	SM	B	Pri	No	C	1,780	30		1	9	36	54	630	5	28	45	22	640	5	27	42	26	630	6	24	47	23	1/1
Bowdoin College	Brunswick	SM	B	Pri	No	C	1,806	32			3	19	78						700	1	8	36	55						1/1
Colby College	Waterville	SM	B	Pri	No	C	1,879	31				25	75	680	1	11	50	38	680	1	11	45	44	680	2	10	50	38	1/1
College of the Atlantic	Bar Harbor	SM	B,M	Pri	No	C	337	28			6	63	31	650	6	24	49	21	550	15	58	27		600	3	42	46	9	2/1
Husson University	Bangor	SU	A,B,M,D	Pri	F,S	C	2,834	22		8	59	31	2	530	34	49	16	1	520	35	49	15	1						8/1
Maine College of Art	Portland	U	B,M	Pri	No	C	370																						Open
Maine Maritime Academy	Castine	SM	A,B,M	Pub	F	C	935																						5/1
Saint Joseph's College of Maine	Standish	R	A,B		No	C	930	21																					8/1
Thomas College	Waterville	R	A,B,M	Pri	F	C	1,339	18	50	40	10			445	70	26	3	1	453	66	27	7		435	77	19	4		Open
Unity College	Unity	SM	A,B,M	Pri	No	C	729																						2/15
University of Maine	Orono	SM	B,M,D		F,S	C	9,323	24		4	38	47	11						571	14	52	28	6						2/1
University of Maine at Augusta	Augusta	SM	A,B	Pub	No	C	4,990																						8/15
University of Maine at Farmington	Farmington	SM	B,M	Pub	No	C	1,782	23		5	35	60							522	34	51	14	1						Open
University of Maine at Fort Kent	Fort Kent	SM	A,B	Pub	F,S	C	1,904	20		38	50	12		450	72	28			440	79	18	3		440	76	24			Open
University of Maine at Machias	Machias	R	A,B	Pub	F,S	C	1,187	22	43	14	29	7	7																8/15
University of Maine at Presque Isle	Presque Isle	R	A,B	Pub	F,S	C		19						455					445					435					Open
University of New England	Biddeford	SM	B,M,D	Pri	No	C	2,374	24		2	45	43	9						556	18	54	24	3						2/15
University of Southern Maine	Gorham	U	A,B,M,D	Pub	F,S	C	7,618	21	45	32	15	3	5	500	47	39	12	2	500	50	40	9	1	490	51	37	11	1	2/15
Maryland																													
Bowie State University	Bowie	SU	B,M,D	Pub	F,S	C	4,711							410	76	20	4		400	84	14	2		390					4/1
Capitol Technology University	Laurel	R	A,B,M	Pri	No	C	300																						Open
Coppin State University	Baltimore	U	B,M	Pub	F,S	C	3,242																						7/15
Frostburg State University	Frostburg	SM	B,M,D	Pub	F,S	C	4,884	20						488	59	33	6	1	492	58	34	8	1	469	66	27	6	1	Open
Goucher College	Baltimore	SU	B,M	Pri	No	C	1,473	25		3	26	51	20	540					500	22	51	23	4						2/1
Hood College	Frederick	SU	B,M,D	Pri	No	C	1,174	20		22	56	22							530	32	42	25	1	510	40	47	13		Open
Johns Hopkins University	Baltimore	SU	B,M,D	Pri	F,S	C	5,365	34				2	98	740		1	16	84	770		1	8	92	760	1	1	15	83	1/3
Loyola University Maryland	Baltimore	U	B,M,D	Pri	No	C		27			9	62	29	595	3	31	58	8	595	4	44	45	7	595					1/15
Maryland Institute College of Art	Baltimore	SM	B,M	Pri	No	C	1,680																						1/15
McDaniel College	Westminster	SU	B,M	Pri	F,S	C	1,559	25			48	35	17	584					565	16	52	27	5						2/1
Morgan State University	Baltimore	SU	B,M,D	Pub	F,S	C	6,119	17	1	54	41	4		440	80	18	2		440	79	17	4		420	84	15	1		11/15
Mount St. Mary's University	Emmitsburg	R	B,M	Pri	No	C	1,729	21		21	48	28	3	500	48	30	17	5	510	46	39	13	2	480	60	29	9	2	Open
Notre Dame of Maryland University	Baltimore	SU	B,M		No	PW	1,620																						Open
Salisbury University	Salisbury	R	B,M,D	Pub	F,S	C	7,861	23		9	49	38	4	596	5	43	48	4	584	6	52	39	3	560					1/15
St. John's College at Annapolis	Annapolis	SM	B,M	Pri	No	C	412	29			13	33	54	688		7	43	50	675	3	25	45	28						1/15
St. Mary's College of Maryland	St. Marys City	R	B,M	Pub	No	C	1,643	25		6	35	39	20						573	13	50	31	6						2/15
Stevenson University	Stevenson	SU	B,M	Pri	S	C		22		13	57	26	4						548	23	54	21	3						Open
Towson University	Towson	SU	B,M,D	Pub	F,S	C		23		3	56	37	4	535	29	53	16	2	535	28	52	18	2	530	30	55	14	1	1/17
United States Naval Academy	Annapolis	SM	B	Pub	No	C	4,487							620	5	37	38	20	643	2	25	41	40				51	23	1/31
University of Maryland University College	Adelphi	U	B,M,D	Pub	No	C	28,119																						Open
University of Maryland/Baltimore County	Baltimore	SU	B,M,D	Pub	F,S	C	11,274	27	2	1	18	55	24	600	8	43	37	12	620	4	33	48	15	580	12	47	33	8	2/1
University of Maryland/College Park	College Park	SU	B,M,D	Pub	F,S	C	28,472				7	35	58		5	22	49	24		4	15	43	38						1/20
University of Maryland/Eastern Shore	Princess Anne	SM	B,M,D	Pub	F,S	C		19		36	58	3	2	440	81	16	2		430	86	13	2		420	88	11			6/30
Washington Adventist University	Takoma Park	SU	A,B,M	Pri	No	C	995	18	56	24	20			451	74	21	4	1	429	76	22	2							8/1

Washington College	Chestertown	SM	B	Pri	F,S	C	1,479							586	10	46	34	10	571	16	45	34	5						2/15
Massachusetts																													
American International College	Springfield	U	A,B,M,D	Pri	F,S	C	1,729	19	60	30	4	4	2	467	67	28	4	1	471	64	26	10	1	461	66	29	5		8/15
Amherst College	Amherst	SM	B	Pri	No	C	1,849	33				11	89	740		1	31	68	740		1	32	67	730		3	27	70	1/1
Anna Maria College	Paxton	SM	B,M	Pri	No	C	1,128	19						509					500					492					3/15
Assumption College	Worcester	SU	B,M	Pri	No	C	1,976	26			31	51	18						579	7	55	34	4						2/15
Atlantic Union College	South Lancaster	SM	A,B,M	Pri	No	C	450																						8/1
Babson College	Babson Park	SU	B,M	Pri	F,S	C	1,800																						1/4
Bard College at Simon's Rock	Great Barrington	SM	A,B	Pri	No	C	362	28			14	57	14	692		4	41	52	656		22	48	30	661		11	26	19	Open
Bay Path University	Longmeadow	SU	A,B,M	Pri	No	W	1,893			19	48	26	7		55	33	11	1		63	32	5			60	34	5	1	Open
Becker College	Worcester	U	A,B	Pri	No	C	1,826	21						490	54	30	14	2	490	51	32	14	3	470	63	27	9	1	Open
Benjamin Franklin Institute of Technology	Boston	U	A,B	Pri	No	C	500																					1	Open
Bentley University	Waltham	SU	B,M,D	Pri	F,S	C	4,222	29			3	60	37						665	1	14	53	32						1/7
Berklee College of Music	Boston	U	B,M	Pri	No	C																							1/15
Boston Architectural College	Boston	U	B,M	Pri	No	C	329																						Open
Boston College	Chestnut Hill	SU	B,M,D	Pri	No	C	9,309	32			2	15	83	670	2	13	50	34	690	1	10	44	44	685	2	12	41	44	1/1
Boston University	Boston	U	B,M,D	Pri	F,S	C	17,944	31			1	32	67						690		8	44	48						1/2
Brandeis University	Waltham	SU	B,M,D	Pri	No	C	3,608	31			1	25	74						680		13	48	39						1/1
Bridgewater State University	Bridgewater	SU	B,M	Pub	F,S	C	8,307	22		15	55	27	3						523	30	57	13	1						2/15
Cambridge College	Boston	U	B,M,D	Pri	No	C	850																						Open
Clark University	Worcester	U	B,M,D	Pri	No	C	2,289	29			6	53	41						630	3	29	48	20						1/15
College of Art and Design at Lesley University	Boston	U	B,M	Pri	No	C	1,267		9	50	13	24	4		27	47	24	2		41	46	12	1		27	50	20	3	2/15
College of the Holy Cross	Worcester	SU	B	Pri	No	C	2,941	30			1	43	56						665		12	58	30						1/15
Curry College	Milton	SU	B,M	Pri	No	C	2,688			19	58	23	2	515					504	41	51	7							4/1
Eastern Nazarene College	Quincy	SU	A,B,M		No	C	640																						9/1
Elms College	Chicopee	SU	A,B,M		No	C	640																						Open
Emerson College	Boston	U	B,M,D	Pri	F,S	C	3,784	28			11	56	33	660		14	60	26	620	1	35	50	14						1/15
Emmanuel College	Boston	U	B,M	Pri	No	C					17	66	17							7	56	34	3						2/15
Endicott College	Beverly	SU	A,B,M,D	Pri	No	C	3,258	23		2	48	48	2	576					567	12	57	28	3						2/15
Fitchburg State University	Fitchburg	SU	B,M	Pub	F,S	C	4,165	21	41	37	11	7	4	490	48	40	11	1	450	40	46	14	1	480	51	39	9	1	3/1
Framingham State University	Framingham	SU	B,M	Pub	No	C	4,337	22		10	65	23	2						517	37	51	11	1						2/15
Franklin W. Olin College of Engineering	Needham	SU	B	Pri	No	C	378	34				2	98						770			9	91						1/1
Gordon College	Wenham	SU	B,M	Pri	No	C	1,657	25		6	30	43	21	596	11	39	38	12	572	19	44	27	10	549	4	6	3	1	8/1
Hampshire College	Amherst	R	B	Pri	No	C																							1/15
Harvard College/Harvard University	Cambridge	U	B,M,D		No	C	6,670	33				7	93	750					750		1	11	88	740					1/1
Hellenic College/Holy Cross Greek Orthodox School of Theology	Brookline	U	B,M	Pri	No	C	91	22	20	60	20			550	30	35	30	5	450	55	35	5	5	460	45	35	20		8/1
Lasell College	Newton	SU	B,M	Pri	No	C	1,778	21		21	55	18	6	500	45	41	9	5	500	43	52	4		480	64	23	14		9/1
Lesley University	Cambridge	U	A,B,M,D	Pri	No	C		24		5	38	51	5	545	26	44	26	3	520	40	44	15	1	540	31	46	22	2	7/15
Massachusetts College of Art and Design	Boston	U	B,M	Pub	No	C	1,772							560	18	47	30	5	540	26	49	22	3	540	23	49	24	3	2/1
Massachusetts College of Liberal Arts	North Adams	R	B,M	Pub	F,S	C	1,444			16	48	24	12							25	44	26	5						Open
Massachusetts Institute of Technology	Cambridge	U	B,M,D	Pri	F,S	C	4,524	34				2	98	750		3	20	77	780			3	97	740		3	23	74	1/1
Massachusetts Maritime Academy	Buzzards Bay	SM	B,M	Pub	No	C	1,677	23		3	50	40	7						560	10	62	24	4						Open
MCPHS University	Boston	U	B,M,D	Pri	F	C	2,883	24	20	28	34	14	4	525	31	55	13	1	570	16	47	34	4	540	26	51	22	1	2/1
Merrimack College	North Andover	SU	B,M	Pri	F,S	C																							2/15
Montserrat College of Art	Beverly	SU	B	Pri	No	C	305																						Open
Mount Holyoke College	South Hadley	SM	B,M	Pri	No	W	2,126	30			2	34	64	670		15	48	37	660	3	16	43	38	670		11	51	38	1/15
Mount Ida College	Newton	SU	A,B	Pri	No	C	1,130																						8/15
New England Conservatory of Music	Boston	U	B,M,D	Pri	No	C	436																						12/1
Newbury College	Brookline	SU	A,B	Pri	No	C	751	21						500					500										Open
Nichols College	Dudley	SU	A,B,M	Pri	No	C	1,269	20		31	45	24		450	67	25	8		470	58	32	10		450	70	26	4		Open
Northeastern University	Boston	U	B,M,D	Pri	F,S	C		33			1	6	92	695	2	8	37	54	725		6	29	64	680	1	12	43	44	1/1
Pine Manor College	Chestnut Hill	SU	A,B,M	Pri	No	C	461																						Open
Regis College	Weston	SU	A,B,M,D	Pri	No	C	1,235	23		24	33	38	5	480	64	32	4		485	56	36	8		470	65	31	4		6/1
Salem State University	Salem	U	B,M	Pub	No	C	7,298																						Open
Simmons College	Boston	U	B,M,D	Pri	No	PW	1,802	27			25	56	19	614		40	40	20	604	5	39	48	8	599		66	33	1	2/1
Smith College	Northampton	SM	B,M,D	Pri	No	W		32			3	20	77	695		7	43	49	695		11	44	45						1/15
Springfield College	Springfield	SU	B,M,D	Pri	No	C	2,200	23		8	42	44	6						560	17	48	32	3						1/15
Stonehill College	Easton	SU	B	Pri	No	C		25		2	34	50	14	550	24	27	24	4	555	21	49	27	2	550	25	48	26	2	1/15
Suffolk University	Boston	U	A,B,M,D	Pri	F,S	C	5,290	24		6	42	47	5						538	24	57	18	1						2/15
The Boston Conservatory at Berklee	Boston	U	B,M	Pri	F,S	C	512	25						549					577										2/15
Tufts University	Medford	SU	B,M,D	Pri	F,S	C	5,508	32			1	10	89	680		4	32	64	710		2	25	73	690	1	2	31	66	1/1
University of Massachusetts Amherst	Amherst	SM	A,B,M,D		F,S	C		28			10	52	38	630					640	1	27	50	22						1/15
University of Massachusetts Boston	Boston	U	B,M,D	Pub	No	C	12,847			3	48	44	5	560	15	53	28	4	560	11	57	28	4						3/1
University of Massachusetts Dartmouth	North Dartmouth	SU	B,M,D	Pub	F,S	C	6,999	22		9	49	32	10						540	25	51	21	3						Open
University of Massachusetts Lowell	Lowell	U	A,B,M,D	Pub	F,S	C	13,639	26		1	22	55	22						618	1	38	49	12						2/1
Wellesley College	Wellesley	SU	B	Pri	No	W	2,226	31			1	23	76	694		8	34	58	703		9	42	49	696		9	34	57	1/15
Wentworth Institute of Technology	Boston	U	A,B,M	Pri	No	C	4,324	24		6	40	40	13						599	5	45	42	8						2/15
Western New England University	Springfield	SU	A,B,M,D	Pri	No	C	2,724	24		1	40	50	9	525	29	60	10	1	550	22	50	26	2						Open
Westfield State University	Westfield	SU	B,M	Pub	No	C	5,610	22		7	54	32	7						530	30	57	13	1						3/1
Wheaton College	Norton	SU	B	Pri	No	C	1,651	26		2	26	46	27	620	6	29	51	14	590	11	44	37	8						1/1

NAME OF SCHOOL	TOWN	ENVIRONMENT U-Urban R-Rural SU-Suburban SM-Small Town	DEGREES AWARDED A-Associate B-Bachelor M-Master D-Doctorate	CONTROL Pri-Private, Pub-Public	FRATERNITIES AND SORORITIES F-Fraternities S-Sororities F, S-Both No-Neither	STUDENTS: C-Coed M-Men W-Women PM-Primarily Men PW-Primarily Women	UNDERGRADUATE ENROLLMENT FALL 2017	TEST SCORES: ACT						SAT CRITICAL READING					SAT MATHEMATICS					SAT WRITING					APPLICATION DEADLINE Month / Day
								Median	Below 21	21-23	24-26	27-28	Above 28	Median	Below 500	500-599	600-700	Above 700	Median	Below 500	500-599	600-700	Above 700	Median	Below 500	500-599	600-700	Above 700	
Wheelock College	Boston	U	B,M	Pri	No	C	726	19		43	47	10		453	70	23	7		455	69	29	2		460	67	27	6		3/1
Williams College	Williamstown	SM	B,M	Pri	No	C	2,099	33				13	87						750		4	24	73						1/1
Worcester Polytechnic Institute	Worcester	SU	B,M,D	Pri	F,S	C	4,432	30			2	37	61						690		6	45	49						2/1
Worcester State University	Worcester	U	B,M	Pub	No	C	5,381	23		5	48	43	3	501	50	39	11	1	509	44	44	11	1						5/1
Michigan																													
Adrian College	Adrian	SM	A,B,M	Pri	F,S	C	1,606	22	38	34	16	6	6	480	55	45			500	41	52	7							Open
Albion College	Albion	SM	B	Pri	F,S	C	1,418	23		4	52	37	7	557					542	24	53	19	4						Open
Alma College	Alma	SM	B	Pri	F,S	C	1,451	24		2	54	37	7	574					556	17	55	26	2						Open
Andrews University	Berrien Springs	R	A,B,M,D	Pri	F,S	C	1,964	23	34	26	21	11	8																Open
Aquinas College - Michigan	Grand Rapids	SU	A,B,M	Pri	No	C	1,654	24		2	45	47	7																Open
Baker College of Flint	Flint	U	A,B		No	C	4,400																						9/20
Calvin College	Grand Rapids	SU	B,M	Pri	No	C	3,807	27			22	47	31						609	4	42	42	12						8/15
Central Michigan University	Mount Pleasant	SM	B,M,D	Pub	F,S	C	22,239	23	29	34	22	9	6																Open
College for Creative Studies	Detroit	U	B	Pri	No	C	3,901	22																					Open
Concordia University, Ann Arbor	Ann Arbor	SU	A,B,M	Pri	No	C	521	22	36	20	27	11	6	575	36	21	21	22	550	28	43	29		560	43	7	29	21	8/15
Cornerstone University	Grand Rapids	SU	A,B,M	Pri	No	C		22						505	26	37	26	11	495	48	21	32		490	42	37	16	5	8/15
Davenport University	Grand Rapids	SU	A,B,M	Pri	No	C	8,882																						Open
Eastern Michigan University	Ypsilanti	SU	B,M,D	Pub	F,S	C	17,780	22		11	54	32	3	483	47	26	14	3	509	41	40	17	2	486	57	33	9	1	8/30
Ferris State University	Big Rapids	SM	A,B,M,D	Pub	F,S	C	12,870	22		15	48	29	8							35	46	16	3						8/1
Grace Bible College	Grand Rapids	SU	A,B,M	Pri	No	C	303	21		20	70	7	3	560	35	66			540	34	66			500	34	33	33		Open
Grand Valley State University	Allendale	SM	B,M,D	Pub	F,S	C	21,231	24	19	31	28	12	10																5/1
Hillsdale College	Hillsdale	SM	B,M,D	Pri	F,S	C	1,486	30			1	33	66	689		7	45	48	661		17	51	32						4/1
Hope College	Holland	U	B	Pri	F,S	C	3,404	26			24	53	22	608	5	37	47	11	602	6	41	43	10						Open
Kalamazoo College	Kalamazoo	SU	B	Pri	No	C	1,443	28		2	13	48	37	610	16	29	33	22	640	9	22	37	31	610	13	28	39	19	1/15
Kettering University	Flint	SU	B,M	Pri	F,S	C		27			15	60	25						650										Open
Lake Superior State University	Sault Sainte Marie	SM	A,B	Pub	F,S	C	2,222	21	1	12	59	20	1	470	67	22	11		500	45	55			480	55	33	11		8/15
Lawrence Technological University	Southfield	SU	A,B,M,D	Pri	F,S	C	2,164	24		10	31	47	12		16	44	36	4	590	12	44	36	8						Open
Madonna University	Livonia	SU	A,B,M,D	Pri	No	C	2,629	22		13	56	28	3						460	55	37	8							Open
Marygrove College	Detroit	U	A,B,M	Pri	F,S	C	788	17																					8/28
Michigan State University	East Lansing	SU	B,M,D		F,S	C	39,090	26		2	24	56	18							6	40	40	13						5/1
Michigan Technological University	Houghton	SM	A,B,M,D	Pub	F,S	C	5,829	27			17	54	29						630	1	31	51	17						Open
Northern Michigan University	Marquette	U	A,B,M,D	Pub	F,S	C	7,082	22																					Open
Northwood University - Michigan	Midland	SU	A,B,M	Pri	F,S	C	1,819		48	27	16	6	3		76	17	3	3		55	34	10			64	29	7		8/1
Oakland University	Rochester	SU	B,M,D	Pub	F,S	C	17,161	22																					3/24
Olivet College	Olivet	SM	B,M	Pri	F,S	C	1,052	19	25	40	15	15	5																Open
Rochester College	Rochester Hills	SU	A,B,M	Pri	F,S	C	908	20	50	20	21	7	2																8/30
Saginaw Valley State University	University Center	SU	B,M,D	Pub	F,S	C	8,397	23		8	50	35	7							26	53	19	2						Open
Siena Heights University	Adrian	SM	A,B,M		F,S	C	2,407																						8/1
Spring Arbor University	Spring Arbor	SM	A,B,M	Pri	No	C	1,555																						8/1
University of Detroit Mercy	Detroit	U	B,M,D	Pri	F,S	C	2,646	25		2	45	45	9	526	39	32	29		543	32	32	29	7	517	50	21	21	7	8/1
University of Michigan/Ann Arbor	Ann Arbor	SU	B,M,D	Pub	F,S	C		31			2	23	74	685	1	10	45	43	720	1	5	29	64	695	2	9	38	51	2/1
University of Michigan/Dearborn	Dearborn	SU	B,M,D	Pub	F,S	C	7,141	26		2	31	50	17						590	13	43	35	9					51	2/1
University of Michigan/Flint	Flint	U	B,M,D	Pub	F,S	C		23		15	41	37	7	534	30	60		10	542	30	40	30		497	60	20	20		8/20
Wayne State University	Detroit	U	B,M,D	Pub	F,S	C	17,280	24		5	40	42	12						557	19	52	23	5						8/1
Western Michigan University	Kalamazoo	U	B,M,D	Pub	F,S	C	17,984	23		10	48	36	6						532	33	47	17	3						Open
Minnesota																													
Augsburg University	Minneapolis	U	B,M	Pri	No	C	3,124	22	38	27	23	8	4	505	50	25	21	4	565	21	33	38	8						8/15
Bemidji State University	Bemidji	SM	A,B,M	Pub	F,S	C	4,744																						Open
Bethel University	St. Paul	SU	A,B,M,D	Pri	No	C		25		4	38	46	12																Open
Carleton College	Northfield	SM	B	Pri	No	C	2,063				3	22	75								7	29	64						1/15
College of Saint Benedict	St. Joseph	SM	B	Pri	No	C	1,958			2	35	47	16																Open
College of St. Scholastica	Duluth	SU	B,M,D	Pri	No	C	2,841	24		5	48	39	7	580					540	58	32	11		540					Open
Concordia College - Moorhead	Moorhead	SU	B,M	Pri	No	C	2,531	25	13	22	29	16	20	570	23	33	35	10	550	33	29	23	15		31	37	23	10	Open
Concordia University Saint Paul	St. Paul	U	A,B,M,D	Pri	No	C	2,567	21		16	54	25	5																8/1
Gustavus Adolphus College	St. Peter	SM	B	Pri	F,S	C	2,455	27	2	13	31	20	34																11/1
Hamline University	St. Paul	U	B,M,D	Pri	F,S	C	2,242	24	20	24	21	11	19	550	36	32	22	10	540	27	51	19	3	540	31	36	31	3	Open
Macalester College	St. Paul	U	B	Pri	No	C	2,146	31			1	30	68						680		11	49	40						1/15

Metropolitan State University	St. Paul	U	B,M,D	Pub	No	C	6,974																						6/15
Minneapolis College of Art and Design	Minneapolis	U	B,M	Pri	No	C	703	23		9	48	33	10	570	14	53	28	6	495	50	31	19		530	25	50	19	6	12/1
Minnesota State University, Mankato	Mankato	R	A,B,M,D	Pub	F,S	C	13,324	23	3	22	54	18	3																8/22
Minnesota State University, Moorhead	Moorhead	SU	A,B,M,D	Pub	F,S	C	7,012																						8/1
North Central University	Minneapolis	U	A,B,M	Pri	No	C	1,366	21																					6/1
Saint John's University	Collegeville	R	B,M	Pri	No	C	1,754				38	46	16																Open
Saint Mary's University of Minnesota	Winona	SM	B,M,D	Pri	F,S	C	1,590	23		10	47	36	8						534	32	40	28							5/1
Southwest Minnesota State University	Marshall	R	A,B,M	Pub	No	C	2,710																						8/1
St. Catherine University	St. Paul	U	A,B,M,D	Pri	No	W	3,559	24	1		48	44	7	560	27	39	17	17	525	27	56	17							Open
St. Cloud State University	St. Cloud	SU	A,B,M,D	Pub	F,S	C	14,525																						Open
St. Olaf College	Northfield	SM	B	Pri	No	C	3,040	29			13	43	44	640	6	24	46	24	640	7	29	33	31						1/15
University of Minnesota/Crookston	Crookston	SM	B	Pub	F,S	C		22		7	64	25	4																8/15
University of Minnesota/Duluth	Duluth	U	B,M,D		F,S	C	8,929	24	15	33	33	11	8	510	40	34	23	3	540	28	46	21	5	530	36	41	21	2	8/1
University of Minnesota/Morris	Morris	SM	B	Pub	No	C	1,771	25		3	36	45	16	570		80	20		610	4	36	20	40	580	40	20	40		3/15
University of Minnesota/Twin Cities	Minneapolis	U	B,M,D	Pub	F,S	C	34,871	29			8	51	40	630	11	25	32	32	680	4	17	44	35	640	14	15	44	27	Open
University of Northwestern - St. Paul	St. Paul	SU	A,B,M	Pri	No	C	1,890																						8/1
University of St. Thomas	St. Paul	U	B,M,D	Pri	No	C	6,111	26			19	62	19	580	20	34	32	14	590	6	40	42	12						Open
Winona State University	Winona	U	A,B,M,D	Pub	F,S	C	7,656	23		3	60	34	3																7/1

Mississippi

Alcorn State University	Lorman	R	A,B,M	Pub	F,S	C	3,010																						Open
Belhaven University	Jackson	U	A,B,M,D	Pri	No	C	2,641	22		3	65	28	4	573	17	45	33	5	552	17	60	21	2						8/12
Blue Mountain College	Blue Mountain	R	B,M	Pri	No	C	544	21		21	59	15	5	555	50		50		480	50	50			495	50	50			Open
Delta State University	Cleveland	SM	B,M,D	Pub	F,S	C	2,659	20		23	59	15	2	510	38	38	13	13	475	63		25	13						8/1
Jackson State University	Jackson	U	B,M,D	Pub	F,S	C	7,492	19		36	51	12																	9/10
Millsaps College	Jackson	U	B,M	Pri	F,S	C	744	26	9	23	27	18	23	540	25	39	28	8	560	17	47	33	3						9/10
Mississippi College	Clinton	SU	B,M,D	Pri	F,S	C	3,000	24						550					520										Open
Mississippi State University	Mississippi State	SM	B,M,D		F,S	C	18,090	25		3	37	41	20																8/1
Mississippi University for Women	Columbus	SM	A,B,M,D	Pub	F,S	C	3,200																						Open
Mississippi Valley State University	Itta Bena	SM	B,M	Pub	F,S	C	2,748	17	91	6	3																		8/10
Rust College	Holly Springs	SM	A,B		F,S	C	1,015																						8/10
Tougaloo College	Tougaloo	SU	A,B	Pri	F,S	C	940																						Open
University of Mississippi	University	SM	B,M,D	Pub	F,S	C	19,213			4	36	40	20		8	44	39	9		13	47	27	13						Open
University of Southern Mississippi	Hattiesburg	SU	B,M,D	Pub	F,S	C	13,658	22	41	24	19	7	9		35	43	18	4		42	40	18							6/30
William Carey University	Hattiesburg	SM	B,M		F,S	C	1,850																						6/30

Missouri

Avila University	Kansas City	SU	B,M	Pri	No	C	1,135																						8/25
Central Methodist University	Fayette	SM	A,B,M	Pri	F,S	C	1,173																						Open
College of the Ozarks	Point Lookout	SM	B	Pri	No	C	1,512	23		1	50	42	6						580	1	58	33							12/31
Columbia College - Missouri	Columbia	U	A,B,M	Pri	No	C	936			5	50	39	6							5	47	37	11						8/12
Cox College	Springfield	U	A,B,M		No	C	600																						8/12
Culver-Stockton College	Canton	SM	B,M	Pri	F,S	C	1,058	21		11	69	18	2		32	62	6			44	46	10							Open
Drury University	Springfield	U	A,B,M	Pri	F,S	C	1,370	26		2	26	57	15																8/22
Evangel University	Springfield	U	A,B,M	Pri	No	C	1,879																						8/22
Fontbonne University	St. Louis	SU	B,M	Pri	No	C	2,085																						8/22
Hannibal-LaGrange University	Hannibal	SM	A,B,M	Pri	No	C	1,711		20	43	27	4	6																8
Harris-Stowe State University	St. Louis	U	B	Pub	No	C	1,464			58	38	3	1																Open
Kansas City Art Institute	Kansas City	U	B	Pri	No	C	660	23		11	40	38	11	590	3	50	38	9	630	28	41	31							5/1
Lincoln University	Jefferson City	SM	A,B,M	Pub	F,S	C	2,618	16	1	57	36	5	1	440					440	77	23								Open
Lindenwood University	St. Charles	SU	B,M,D	Pri	F,S	C	5,905																						Open
Maryville University of Saint Louis	St. Louis	SU	B,M,D	Pri	No	C	2,967	24		6	41	45	8																8/19
Missouri Baptist University	St. Louis	SU	A,B,M,D	Pri	No	C	4,631	22																					Open
Missouri Southern State University	Joplin	SM	A,B,M	Pub	F,S	C	5,732	22		16	55	25	4																9/1
Missouri State University	Springfield	SU	B,M,D	Pub	F,S	C		24		2	48	42	8						565	22	47	29	3						7/20
Missouri University of Science and Technology	Rolla	SM	B,M,D		F,S	C	6,146	28	1	8	26	19	46	590	14	35	36	15	640	5	21	54	21						7/1
Missouri Valley College	Marshall	SM	A,B,M	Pri	F,S	C	1,430																						Open
Missouri Western State University	St. Joseph	SU	A,B,M	Pub	F,S	C	5,250																						Open
Northwest Missouri State University	Maryville	SM	A,B,M	Pub	F,S	C	5,628	22																					Open
Park University	Parkville	SU	A,B,M	Pri	No	C	1,674	21	50	29	9	5	7																Open
Research College of Nursing	Kansas City	U	B,M	Pri	F,S	C	287	23		33	37	17	13																6/30
Rockhurst University	Kansas City	U	B,M,D		F,S	C	2,325																						6/30
Saint Louis University	St. Louis	U	B,M,D	Pri	F,S	C	8,248	28			13	51	36		13	31	44	12		7	32	45	16						12/1
Southeast Missouri State University	Cape Girardeau	SM	A,B,M	Pub	F,S	C	10,693	23		5	55	33	7																7/1
Southwest Baptist University	Bolivar	SM	A,B,M,D	Pri	No	C	3,009																						Open
Stephens College	Columbia	U	B,M	Pri	S	PW	679		29		14	43																	8/1
Truman State University	Kirksville	SM	B,M	Pub	F,S	C	6,039	27			19	52	28						680		37	21	42						3/1
University of Central Missouri	Warrensburg	SM	A,B,M	Pub	F,S	C	9,739	22	40	29	16	6	4																8/19
University of Missouri-Columbia	Columbia	SU	B,M,D	Pub	F,S	C	25,898	26			27	52	19																5/1

NAME OF SCHOOL	TOWN	ENVIRONMENT U-Urban R-Rural SU-Suburban SM-Small Town	DEGREES AWARDED A-Associate B-Bachelor M-Master D-Doctorate	CONTROL Pri-Private, Pub-Public	FRATERNITIES AND SORORITIES F-Fraternities S-Sororities F, S-Both No-Neither	STUDENTS: C-Coed M-Men W-Women PM-Primarily Men PW-Primarily Women	UNDERGRADUATE ENROLLMENT FALL 2017	TEST SCORES: ACT Median	ACT Below 21	ACT 21-23	ACT 24-26	ACT 27-28	ACT Above 28	SAT CRITICAL READING Median	SAT CR Below 500	SAT CR 500-599	SAT CR 600-700	SAT CR Above 700	SAT MATHEMATICS Median	SAT Math Below 500	SAT Math 500-599	SAT Math 600-700	SAT Math Above 700	SAT WRITING Median	SAT Writing Below 500	SAT Writing 500-599	SAT Writing 600-700	SAT Writing Above 700	APPLICATION DEADLINE Month / Day
University of Missouri-Kansas City	Kansas City	U	B,M,D	Pub	F,S	C	11,708	24		5	39	40	16						609	27	37	19	16	578	23	33	30	14	7/1
University of Missouri-St. Louis	St. Louis	U	B,M,D	Pub	F,S	C	13,923	24		3	40	47	10						595		50	50		29	64				8/20
Washington University in St. Louis	St. Louis	SU	A,B,M,D	Pri	F,S	C	7,540	33				6	94						770			10	90						1/2
Webster University	St. Louis	SU	B,M,D	Pri	S	C	2,622	24		7	39	44	10																8/1
Westminster College	Fulton	SM	B	Pri	F,S	C	933	24	17	28	22	17	18																Open
William Jewell College	Liberty	SU	B	Pri	F,S	C	1,030	26	9	22	25	18	26		24	30	39	7		21	34	39	11						8/15
William Woods University	Fulton	SM	A,B,M,D	Pri	F,S	C	973	22		14	49	28	9	490	53	31	16		500	47	27	16							8/15
Montana																													
Carroll College	Helena	SM	A,B,M	Pri	No	C	1,469	25		4	40	43	13																2/1
Montana State University	Bozeman	SM	A,B,M,D	Pub	F,S	C	13,707	25						570	22	39	32	7	565	22	38	33	7	545	32	39	25	4	Open
Montana State University Billings	Billings	U	A,B,M	Pub	No	C		21		18	57	24	1	480	55	31	11	3	500	52	31	14	3						Open
Montana State University-Northern	Havre	SM	A,B,M	Pub	No	C	1,440																						Open
Montana Tech of the University of Montana	Butte	SM	A,B,M	Pub	No	C	2,770	25			33	59	8	560	21	52	25	2	600	10	35	52	3	510	40	54	6		Open
Rocky Mountain College	Billings	SU	A,B,M	Pri	No	C	908	22		10	56	30	4						518	36	51	13							Open
The University of Montana Western	Dillon	SM	A,B	Pub	No	C		20	1	30	55	13	1	485	61	29	8	2	475	67	30	3							Open
University of Great Falls	Great Falls	U	A,B,M	Pri	No	C	577																						9/1
University of Montana	Missoula	U	A,B,M,D	Pub	F,S	C	11,692	23						550	26	44	25	5	542	26	50	20	3	530	35	45	18	2	3/1
Nebraska																													
Bellevue University	Bellevue	SU	B,M	Pri	No	C	3,775																						Open
Chadron State College	Chadron	R	B,M	Pub	No	C	2,375	22																					Open
Clarkson College	Omaha	U	A,B,M	Pri	No	PW	770																						8/16
College of Saint Mary	Omaha	U	A,B,M,D	Pri	No	PW	770	21		7	63	29	1																Open
Concordia University Nebraska	Seward	SM	B,M	Pri	No	C	1,085																						Open
Creighton University	Omaha	U	A,B,M,D	Pri	F,S	C	4,203	27			18	57	25						603	8	35	45	12						2/15
Doane University	Crete	SM	B	Pri	F,S	C	1,047	23		5	53	37	5																Open
Hastings College	Hastings	R	B,M	Pri	F,S	C	1,104	24	37	23	20	10	10																8/1
Midland University	Fremont	U	B,M	Pri	F,S	C	1,200																						Open
Nebraska Methodist College	Omaha	SU	A,B,M,D	Pri	S	C	747		21	45	28	3	3																3/1
Nebraska Wesleyan University	Lincoln	SU	B,M	Pri	F,S	C	1,903	26																					8/15
Peru State College	Peru	R	B,M	Pub	No	C		20		33	41	17	1																Open
Union College	Lincoln	SU	A,B,M	Pri	No	C	813	22																					Open
University of Nebraska - Kearney	Kearney	R	B,M	Pub	F,S	C		22						445	82	12		6	480	53	35	12							Open
University of Nebraska - Lincoln	Lincoln	U	B,M,D	Pub	F,S	C	20,182	25		3	35	43	19	560	25	37	25	13	580	23	33	30	14						5/1
University of Nebraska - Omaha	Omaha	SU	B,M,D	Pub	F,S	C	11,525																						8/1
Wayne State College	Wayne	R	B,M	Pub	F,S	C	2,991	21	45	26	15	8	6																Open
York College	York	SM	A,B,M	Pri	F,S	C	415																						Open
Nevada																													
Sierra Nevada College	Incline Village	R	B		No	C		23		21	42	34	3																8/22
University of Nevada, Las Vegas	Las Vegas	U	B,M,D	Pub	F,S	C	23,336	22						495	49	39	11	1	500	48	37	13	2	475	62	30	7	1	11/1
University of Nevada, Reno	Reno	U	B,M,D	Pub	F,S	C	18,191	24		7	47	39	7	540	29	46	22	3	550	27	44	26	3	520	39	43	16	1	2/1
New Hampshire																													
Colby-Sawyer College	New London	SM	A,B	Pri	No	C	1,375																					1	2/1
Dartmouth College	Hanover	R	B,M,D	Pri	F,S	C	4,310	33						740		3	22	75	760		2	15	83	750		3	21	76	1/1
Franklin Pierce University	Rindge	R	A,B,M,D	Pri	No	C	1,687	21	9	72			19	480	58	36	6		480	54	37	7		470	63	32	5		Open
Granite State College	Concord	SM	A,B,M	Pub	No	C	1,518																						Open
Keene State College	Keene	SM	B,M	Pub	F,S	C	4,068	21		20	51	25	4						513	40	50	10	1						4/1
New England College	Henniker	SM	A,B,M,D	Pri	S	C	1,782								57	28	10	5		59	30	7	4		62	26	8	3	Open
Plymouth State University	Plymouth	SM	B,M	Pub	S	C	4,064	20	59	20	14	4	1	479	62	31	7		484	57	34	8	1		65	30	5		4/1
Rivier University	Nashua	SU	A,B,M		No	C	1,630																						Open
Saint Anselm College	Manchester	SU	B	Pri	No	C	1,930	26			22	64	14						600	2	38	55	5						2/1
Southern New Hampshire University	Manchester	SU	A,B,M,D	Pri	F,S	C	3,027	23		12	51	37																	2/1
Thomas More College of Liberal Arts	Merrimack	SM	B	Pri	No	C	96																						Open
University of New Hampshire	Durham	SM	A,B,M,D	Pub	F,S	C	12,871	25		1	31	54	14	590	7	48	40	5	582	10	49	35	6						2/1

University of New Hampshire - Manchester	Manchester		A,B,M	Pub	No	C	842	21	40	40	40		20	520	41	46	11	2	517	41	44	15		494	50	41	9		2/1

New Jersey

Berkeley College/New Jersey	Woodland Park	SU	A,B	Pri	No	C	3,052																						Open
Bloomfield College	Bloomfield	SU	B,M	Pri	F,S	C	1,947	17		52	38	10		420	85	14	1		430	78	19	3							8/1
Caldwell University	Caldwell	SU	B,M,D	Pri	No	C	1,595	21	46	31	20	3		490	60	30	9	1	480	50	37	12	1	490	52	39	9	1	Open
Centenary College	Hackettstown	SU	A,B,M	Pri	F,S	C	1,993	21	29	43	7	7	14	465	67	25	7	1	463	65	30	5							Open
College of Saint Elizabeth	Morristown	SU	B,M,D	Pri	No	PW	805												444	78	20	2							8/15
Drew University/College of Liberal Arts	Madison	SU	B,M,D	Pri	No	C	1,521	25			33	53	14						590	7	46	37	10		4	38	49	9	2/1
Fairleigh Dickinson University/College at Florham	Madison	SU	B,M	Pri	F,S	C								510	42	42	14	3	520	36	43	18	2	500	48	40	10	3	2/1
Fairleigh Dickinson University/Metropolitan Campus	Teaneck	SU	A,B,M,D	Pri	F,S	C								510	42	46	11		530	30	52	16		500	43	49	8	3	2/1
Felician University	Lodi	SU	A,B,M,D	Pri	F,S	C	1,648	20		31	59	9	2						497										Open
Georgian Court University	Lakewood	SU	B,M	Pri	No	C	1,591	20		30	55	15		517	43	43	13	1	499	49	43	7	1						8/1
Kean University	Union	SU	B,M,D	Pub	F,S	C	11,812	22		7	63	26	4	526	30	57	13	1	520	30	60	10							4/30
Monmouth University	West Long Branch	SU	A,B,M,D	Pri	F,S	C	4,693	23		1	60	36	3						520	35	52	13							3/1
Montclair State University	Montclair	SU	B,M,D	Pub	F,S	C	16,653							541	25	55	19	1	530	27	56	16	1						3/1
New Jersey City University	Jersey City	U	B,M,D	Pub	F,S	C	6,229							440	77	18	3	1	460	65	29								4/1
New Jersey Institute of Technology	Newark	U	B,M,D	Pub	F,S	C		27			20	48	32						659		16	56	28						3/1
Princeton University	Princeton	SM	B,M,D	Pri	No	C		34				8	92	740		3	23	73	755		2	18	81	745		2	22	76	1/1
Ramapo College of New Jersey	Mahwah	SU	B,M	Pub	F,S	C		24		5	50	37	8	615	35	44	20	2	615	26	47	23	4	615	36	46	17	1	3/1
Rider University	Lawrenceville	SU	A,B,M	Pri	F,S	C	4,060	21		12	53	30	5	490	52	36	11	2	500	44	40	14	1	480	53	34	12	1	Open
Rowan University	Glassboro	SU	B,M,D	Pub	F,S	C	13,169							582	28	46	23	3	622	20	43	31	6	565	35	44	19	2	3/1
Rutgers University - Camden	Camden	U	B,M,D	Pub	No	C	5,021												540	22	56	20	2						12/1
Rutgers University - New Brunswick	Piscataway	U	A,B,M,D	Pub	F,S	C	36,168												660	1	20	44	36						12/1
Rutgers University - Newark	Newark	U	A,B,M,D	Pub	No	C	8,170												540	20	57	20	3						12/1
Saint Peter's University	Jersey City	U	A,B,M,D	Pri	No	C	2,317																						Open
Seton Hall University	South Orange	SU	B,M,D	Pri	F,S	C		23	20	33	27	8	13	530	29	49	21	1	540	26	49	24	2	550	24	48	26	2	Open
Stevens Institute of Technology	Hoboken	U	B,M,D	Pri	F,S	C	2,976	31				27	73						712		3	34	63						1/15
Stockton University	Galloway	SU	B,M,D	Pub	F,S	C	6,790																						1/15
The College of New Jersey	Ewing	SU	B,M	Pub	F,S	C		28			11	63	26	590	8	46	36	10	610	4	35	47	14	595	9	43	38	11	2/1
Thomas Edison State University	Trenton	U	A,B,M,D	Pub	No	C	16,506																						Open
Westminster Choir College	Princeton	SU	B,M	Pri	No	C	355																						Open
William Paterson University of New Jersey	Wayne	SU	B,M,D	Pub	F,S	C								517	49	39	9	2	526	42	46	12							6/1

New Mexico

Eastern New Mexico University	Portales	SM	A,B,M	Pub	F,S	C	4,572	21	56	25	15	2	2	470	60	23	9		490	54	33	9	1						8/20
New Mexico Highlands University	Las Vegas	SM	A,B,M	Pub	No	C	2,275	18	48	44	7			425	76	19	5		430	80	15	5		410	81	19			Open
New Mexico Institute of Mining and Technology	Socorro	SM	A,B,M,D	Pub	No	C	1,569	28			26	51	23	630	14		43	43	680	17	17	50	17						8/1
New Mexico State University	Las Cruces	SM	A,B,M,D		F,S	C	12,784	21	49	24	17	6	4	460	60	30	9	1	480	55	34	11		450	65	28	7		Open
St. John's College, Santa Fe	Santa Fe	SU	B,M	Pri	No	C	330	28		14	19	14	52	695		11	37	52	592	15	41	37	7	642	4	22	52	19	2/15
University of New Mexico	Albuquerque	U	A,B,M,D	Pub	F,S	C		22		13	51	30	6	537					530	16	47	29	8	513					6/15
University of the Southwest	Hobbs	SM	B,M	Pri	No	C	425																						Open
Western New Mexico University	Silver City	SM	A,B,M	Pub	F,S	C	660																						8/1

New York

Adelphi University	Garden City	SU	A,B,M,D	Pri	F,S	C		25						550	24	49	23	4	560	19	50	25	6	550	23	50	23	4	Open
Albany College of Pharmacy and Health Sciences	Albany	U	B,M,D	Pri	F,S	C	902	26			27	61	11	590	6	44	47	3	610	1	47	44	8						2/1
Alfred State College	Alfred	R	A,B	Pub	F,S	C	3,735	23						520	67	26	6	1	540	57	33	9	1	490					Open
Alfred University	Alfred	R	B,M,D	Pri	No	C	1,960	24	16	28	30	15	11	530	27	51	19	3	550	20	49	27	4	510	43	40	15	2	8/1
Bard College	Annandale-on-Hudson	R	A,B,M,D	Pri	No	C	1,970							650					620					650					1/1
Barnard College/Columbia University	New York	U	B	Pri	No	W		31			2	26	72	690	1	7	40	51	680	1	13	50	36	705	1	5	37	57	1/1
Berkeley College/New York City Campus	New York	U	A,B	Pri	No	C	2,622																						Open
Berkeley College/White Plains Campus	White Plains	SU	A,B		No	C	640																						Open
Boricua College	New York	U	A,B	Pri	No	C	1,170																						Open
Canisius College	Buffalo	U	B,M	Pri	F,S	C	2,595	25		2	37	50	11	535	33	45	20	2	545	27	45	24	4						3/1
Cazenovia College	Cazenovia	SM	A,B	Pri	No	C				40	40	20								43	52	5							Open
City University of New York/Baruch College	New York	U	B,M	Pub	No	C	14,857								14	43	35	8		3	25	51	22						2/1
City University of New York/Brooklyn College	Brooklyn	U	B,M	Pub	F,S	C	13,099																						2/1
City University of New York/City College	New York	U	B,M,D	Pub	F,S	C													560	32	49	25	7						1/15
City University of New York/Hunter College	New York	U	B,M	Pub	F,S	C	16,638							574	12	54	26	8	598	3	50	37	10						Open
City University of New York/John Jay College of Criminal Justice	New York	U	B,M	Pub	No	C	13,305							460	71	25	4		480	59	34	7							Open
City University of New York/Lehman College	Bronx	U	B,M	Pub	No	C	9,577							474	67	26	5	2	493	51	38	9	2	460	69	24	5	2	8/15
City University of New York/Medgar Evers College	Brooklyn	U	A,B	Pub	No	C	7,081							380	91	8	1		380	92	8			380	93	6	1		Open
City University of New York/Queens College	Queens	U	B,M	Pub	F,S	C	16,326							526	33	55	9	3	547	22	54	21	2	487	44	28	6	1	Open
City University of New York/York College	Jamaica	U	B,M	Pub	No	C	7,245							430	86	13	1		450	74	23	4		425	86	13	1		Open
Clarkson University	Potsdam	SM	B,M,D	Pri	F,S	C	3,268	26			18	58	24	570	17	45	33	5	610	6	34	47	13	540	30	47	20	3	1/15
Colgate University	Hamilton	R	B,M	Pri	F,S	C	2,915	32				15	85						680		15	40	45						1/15
College of Mount Saint Vincent	Riverdale	U	B,M,D	Pri	No	C	1,595	20						500					500										3/1

NAME OF SCHOOL	TOWN	ENVIRONMENT U-Urban R-Rural SU-Suburban SM-Small Town	DEGREES AWARDED A-Associate B-Bachelor M-Master D-Doctorate	CONTROL Pri-Private, Pub-Public	FRATERNITIES AND SORORITIES F-Fraternities S-Sororities F, S-Both No-Neither	STUDENTS: C-Coed M-Men W-Women PM-Primarily Men PW-Primarily Women	UNDERGRADUATE ENROLLMENT FALL 2017	TEST SCORES ACT Median	ACT Below 21	ACT 21-23	ACT 24-26	ACT 27-28	ACT Above 28	SAT CRITICAL READING Median	SAT CR Below 500	SAT CR 500-599	SAT CR 600-700	SAT CR Above 700	SAT MATHEMATICS Median	SAT Math Below 500	SAT Math 500-599	SAT Math 600-700	SAT Math Above 700	SAT WRITING Median	SAT Writing Below 500	SAT Writing 500-599	SAT Writing 600-700	SAT Writing Above 700	APPLICATION DEADLINE Month / Day
College of Staten Island	Staten Island	U	A,B,M,D	Pub	No	C	12,417							500	42	49	7	2	500	46	40	13	1	470	64	30	6		Open
Columbia University/ School of General Studies	New York	U	B	Pri	F,S	C	2,005				4	23	73		1	12	33	54			10	39	51		3	13	27	57	6/1
Columbia University/City of New York	New York	U	B,M,D	Pri	F,S	C	6,084	33				10	90	740		3	21	76	750		2	20	78	750		2	24	74	1/1
Concordia College - New York	Bronxville	SU	A,B,M	Pri	F,S	C	887	18						460					460					448					8/15
Cooper Union for the Advancement of Science and Art	New York	U	B,M	Pri	F	C		32			2	20	78	660	7	15	43	35	710	12	9	16	63	650	8	19	41	32	8/15
Cornell University	Ithaca	R	B,M,D		F,S	C	14,566				1	10	89			3	26	71			4	20	76						1/2
Daemen College	Amherst	SU	B,M,D	Pri	F,S	C	2,045	24						525					539										Open
Dominican College	Orangeburg	SU	A,B,M,D	Pri	No	C	1,677	18	32	58	5	5		451	77	20	2	1	451	75	21	4		448	75	21	3	1	Open
D'Youville College	Buffalo	U	B,M,D	Pri	No	C	1,716	23		4	51	44	2	500	37	50	12	1	520	48	44	7	1	470	60	34	5	1	Open
Eastman School of Music/University of Rochester	Rochester	U	B,M,D	Pri	F,S	C	548																						12/1
Elmira College	Elmira	SU	A,B,M	Pri	No	C	1,101	24			33	59	8						550	19	55	26							Open
Eugene Lang College of Liberal Arts	New York	U	B	Pri	No	C		26						605	11	32	43	15	545	11	42	30	3	595	11	38	42	9	Open
Excelsior College	Albany	SU	A,B,M	Pri	No	C																							Open
Farmingdale State College	Farmingdale	SU	A,B,M	Pub	F,S	C	9,235	21		11	66	22	1						530	26	59	14	1						6/1
Fashion Institute of Technology/State University of New York	New York	U	A,B,M	Pub	No	C	10,710																						1/4
Five Towns College	Dix Hills	SU	A,B,M,D	Pri	No	C	749	21	40	45	15			450	67	26	5	2	430	68	24	7	1	430	75	21	3	1	1/4
Fordham University	Bronx	U	B,M,D	Pri	No	C	9,258	29			4	47	49						662	1	17	49	33					1	1/4
Hamilton College	Clinton	R	B	Pri	F,S	C	1,867	32				11	89	700		10	38	53	690		11	43	47	700	1	9	39	51	1/1
Hartwick College	Oneonta	SM	B	Pri	F,S	C	1,384	24						505	51	34	15		505	41	45	13	1	480	52	39	9		Open
Hilbert College	Hamburg	SU	A,B,M	Pri	No	C	810	21		15	69	16		465	69	27	4		490	53	44	3		440	84	14	2		Open
Hobart and William Smith Colleges	Geneva	SM	B,M	Pri	F,S	C	2,262	28			4	58	38	646	3	17	64	19	639	1	23	60	16						2/1
Hofstra University	Hempstead	SU	B,M,D	Pri	F,S	C	6,899	27			19	61	20	617	2	35	53	10	607	3	42	45	10						2/1
Houghton College	Houghton	R	A,B,M	Pri	No	C		25		6	36	41	17	601	11	37	36	17	580	17	39	33	11						Open
Iona College	New Rochelle	SU	B,M	Pri	F,S	C	3,462	23		6	51	38	6						530	32	47	19	1						2/15
Ithaca College	Ithaca	SM	B,M,D	Pri	F	C	6,221	27		1	14	62	23						600	3	44	44	9						2/1
Keuka College	Keuka Park	R	B,M	Pri	No	C	1,724	21	1	16	54	27	1	529	29	56	14		525	29	59	11	1						Open
Le Moyne College	Syracuse	SU	B,M	Pri	No	C	2,897	25			45	50	5	585	4	55	37	4	590	4	53	39	4						2/1
LIM College	New York	SM	A,B,M	Pri	No	C	1,357	20	58	29	13			483	61	34	5		474	67	28	5							Open
List College/The Jewish Theological Seminary (JTS)	New York	U	B	Pri	No	C	210																						Open
LIU Brooklyn	Brooklyn	U	A,B,M,D	Pri	F,S	C	4,305	23		12	41	38	9						560	23	40	28	9						Open
LIU Post	Brookville	SU	A,B,M,D	Pri	F,S	C	6,290	24											570	12	53	31	4						Open
Manhattan College	Riverdale	U	A,B,M	Pri	F,S	C	3,351	24	16	27	30	12	15	526	38	44	16	2	535	29	40	27	4	528	35	45	19	2	3/1
Manhattan School of Music	New York	U	B,M,D		F,S	C	430																					2	3/1
Manhattanville College	Purchase	SU	B,M,D	Pri	No	C	1,794	24		9	41	40	10	540	26	48	24	2	528	35	49	15	1	504	37	42	15	6	Open
Mannes School of Music	New York	U	B,M	Pri	No	C	210																						12/1
Marist College	Poughkeepsie	SU	B,M	Pri	F,S	C	5,616	27			12	66	22	580	9	47	37	7	600	7	41	46	6	590	9	44	38	9	2/1
Marymount Manhattan College	New York	U	B	Pri	No	C	1,945	25		5	50	40	5	540	20	40	30	10	512	25	35	30	10						Open
Medaille College	Buffalo	U	A,B,M,D	Pri	No	C	1,843	21						480	80	17	2	1	480	72	22	6							Open
Mercy College	Dobbs Ferry	SU	A,B,M,D	Pri	No	C	8,016																						Open
Metropolitan College of New York	New York	U	A,B,M	Pri	No	C	697																						Open
Molloy College	Rockville Centre	SU	A,B,M,D	Pri	No	C	3,336	24	14	34	36	10	6	520	29	58	11	2	530	26	53	19	2	510	39	45	15	1	Open
Monroe College	Bronx		A,B,M	Pri	No	C	5,480																						8/15
Mount Saint Mary College	Newburgh	SU	B,M	Pri	No	C	2,128	22		6	67	25	2	549			7		540	19	64	15	2						8/15
Nazareth College	Rochester	SU	B,M,D	Pri	No	C		25			34	56	10	540	26	49	22	3	545	27	47	25	1	520	40	41	18	2	2/1
New York City College of Technology	Brooklyn	U	A,B	Pub	No	C	17,424							438	78	21	1		437	81	15	4		406	91	8	1		2/1
New York Institute of Technology	Old Westbury	SU	A,B,M,D	Pri	F,S	C	3,610	24		4	42	39	16	538	32	43	22	4	582	21	31	36	13						Open
New York University	New York	U	A,B,M,D	Pri	F,S	C		31			1	32	67	670	1	13	50	36	695	1	12	40	47	680	1	11	45	43	1/1
Niagara University	Niagara University	SU	A,B,M,D	Pri	F,S	C	3,176	23	27	29	26	13	5	510	10	48	11	1	530	32	51	17	1	500	49	40	10	1	8/1
Nyack College	Nyack	SU	A,B,M,D	Pri	No	C	1,540	19		47	36	18		455	70	24	6		445	69	22	8	1						Open
Pace University	New York	U	A,B,M,D	Pri	F,S	C	8,914	25		2	44	46	8	550	21	53	23	3	540	22	53	23	2						2/15
Parsons The New School for Design	New York	U	A,B,M	Pri	No	C	4,260		29	24	32	7	8		32	41	25	2		28	43	26	3		28	49	22	2	Open
Pratt Institute	Brooklyn	U	A,B,M	Pri	F,S	C	3,158	27			13	62	25						620										1/5
Rensselaer Polytechnic Institute	Troy	SU	B,M,D	Pri	F,S	C	5,781	30			4	43	53	678		10	48	42	722		3	28	69						1/15
Roberts Wesleyan College	Rochester	SU	A,B,M	Pri	No	C		23	5	22	48	34	14	525	35	48	12	5	535	30	46	21	2	500	49	35	15	2	8/20
Rochester Institute of Technology	Rochester	SU	A,B,M,D	Pri	F,S	C	14,224	29			7	50	43	632	7	39	42	12	654	2	27	51	20						1/15
Russell Sage College	Troy	U	B,M	Pri	No	W	823	22						500					500										1/15
Sarah Lawrence College	Bronxville	SU	B,M	Pri	No	C	1,330	29		1	4	47	48						632	4	28	47	21						1/15
School of Visual Arts	New York	U	B,M	Pri	No	C	3,335																						2/1
Siena College	Loudonville	SU	B,M	Pri	No	C	3,186	25		4	34	50	13	530	32	44	21	3	550	24	45	26	6	520	39	44	15	2	2/15
Skidmore College	Saratoga Springs	SM	B	Pri	No	C	2,661	29			5	51	45						650	1	24	47	28						1/15
St. Bonaventure University	St. Bonaventure	SM	B,M	Pri	No	C	1,660	24		6	38	44	12						560	22	47	25	6						7/1

St. Francis College	Brooklyn	U	A,B,M	Pri	F,S	C	2,563			18	57	22	3	474	70	27	3		472	67	28	5			73	25	2		Open
St. John Fisher College	Rochester	SU	B,M,D	Pri	No	C	2,786	24		4	37	20	6						573	9	52	36	3						Open
St. John's University	Queens	SU	A,B,M,D	Pri	F,S	C	16,440	26			31	50	19	570	10	54	33	3	570	13	50	29	8						Open
St. Joseph's College, New York/Brooklyn Campus	Brooklyn	U	B,M	Pri	F,S	C	965	20		14	58	28		470	67	28	4	1	470	65	28	6	1	470	66	28	5	1	8/31
St. Joseph's College, New York/Long Island Campus	Patchogue	SU	B,M	Pri	F,S	C	3,075	23		6	48	43	3	520	37	50	12	1	530	32	48	18	2	500	47	44	8	1	Open
St. Lawrence University	Canton	SM	B,M	Pri	F,S	C	2,377	28			9	58	32	660					650	2	20	56	23						2/1
St. Thomas Aquinas College	Sparkill	SU	A,B,M		No	C	2,120																						2/1
State University of New York /College of Agriculture and Tech at Cobleskill	Cobleskill	R	A,B	Pub	No	C	2,446	20	62	22	10	3	3	440					440	71	25	3							Open
State University of New York Albany	Albany	SU	B,M,D	Pub	F,S	C	13,139																						8/1
State University of New York at Binghamton	Binghamton	SU	B,M,D	Pub	F,S	C	13,632	29			3	47	50	640	2	25	53	20	684	1	11	64	24	674	2	21	56	22	Open
State University of New York at Geneseo	Geneseo	SM	B,M	Pub	F,S	C	5,431	26			17	66	17	618					612	6	40	45	9						1/1
State University of New York at New Paltz	New Paltz	SM	B,M	Pub	F,S	C	6,130																						4/1
State University of New York at Oswego	Oswego	SM	B,M	Pub	F,S	C	7,150	24		2	48	46	4						575	7	60	30	3						1/15
State University of New York at Purchase College	Purchase	SU	B,M	Pub	No	C		24		6	40	42	12	555	23	44	26	6	520	4	35	13	2						3/15
State University of New York Polytechnic Institute	Utica	SU	B,M,D	Pub	No	C	2,082			6	53	32	9	570	16	54	27	3	590	12	50	31	7						7/1
State University of New York/Buffalo State	Buffalo	U	B,M	Pub	F,S	C	9,822							440	77	20	3		435	77	20	4		425					7/1
State University of New York/College at Old Westbury	Old Westbury	SU	B,M	Pub	F,S	C	4,158							490	55	39	5	1		40	50	10			64	32	4		Open
State University of New York/Cortland	Cortland	SM	B,M	Pub	F,S	C		24			36	59	5						567	6	66	27	1						Open
State University of New York/Empire State College	Saratoga Springs		A,B,M	Pub	No	C	10,851																						6/1
State University of New York/Fredonia	Fredonia	SM	B,M	Pub	F,S	C	4,386	24		18	43	33	6	550	24	48	24	4	530	31	48	20	1						Open
State University of New York/Maritime College	Throgs Neck	SU	A,B,M	Pub	No	C	1,575	22	35	40	16	4	5	510	42	45	11	2	550	20	52	26	2						1/31
State University of New York/Oneonta	Oneonta	R	B,M	Pub	F,S	C		23		3	43	50	4	565	29	55	15	1	565	25	56	18	1						Open
State University of New York/Plattsburgh	Plattsburgh	SU	B,M	Pub	F,S	C	5,639		19	42	25	10	4	525	33	51	14	2	535	25	53	21	1						8/1
State University of New York/Potsdam	Potsdam	R	B,M	Pub	F,S	C	3,416	26		10	45	37	9	600					590	24	56	19	2						Open
State University of New York/The College of Environmental Science and Forestry	Syracuse	U	A,B,M,D	Pub	F,S	C	1,753	26			15	63	22	622	2	29	57	12	615	2	36	53	9	555					2/1
State University of New York/University at Buffalo	Buffalo	SU	B,M,D	Pub	F,S	C	20,411	22			19	60	21	559	19	50	26	4	603	8	41	40	12						2/1
Stony Brook University/The State University of New York	Stony Brook	SU	B,M,D	Pub	F,S	C	17,026	29			3	51	46						680		10	46	44						1/15
Syracuse University	Syracuse	U	A,B,M,D	Pri	F,S	C	15,218	27		1	13	61	25						633	3	29	47	21						1/1
The College at Brockport - State University of New York	Brockport	SM	B,M	Pub	F,S	C	7,128	22		6	57	32	4		20	57	21	2	540	22	57	20	1						Open
The College of New Rochelle	New Rochelle	SU	B,M	Pri	No	PW	1,025																						8/31
The College of Saint Rose	Albany	U	B,M	Pri	No	C	2,602	23		7	55	31	7	538	25	54	20	1	522	31	55	13	1						2/1
The Juilliard School	New York	U	B,M,D	Pri	No	C	495																						12/1
Touro College	New York	U	A,B,M,D	Pri	No	C								565	3	32	26	18	540	6	26	27	7	535	50	27	18	5	12/1
Union College	Schenectady	SM	B	Pri	F,S	C	2,208								3	25	53	19		2	17	52	29		4	31	48	17	1/15
United States Merchant Marine Academy	Kings Point	SU	B,M	Pub	No	C	987							630	1	40	40	19	638		17	70	13						3/1
United States Military Academy at West Point	West Point	SM	B	Pub	No	C	4,389	25			29	55	16						650		25	46	29						2/28
University of Rochester	Rochester	SU	B,M,D	Pri	F,S	C	6,390																						1/5
Utica College	Utica	SU	B,M,D	Pri	F,S	C	3,550			9	57	32	3		52	39	8	1		42	45	11	1		62	32	5	1	Open
Vassar College	Poughkeepsie	SU	B,M	Pri	No	C	2,424	32				11	89						713	1	2	34	63						1/1
Vaughn College of Aeronautics and Technology	Flushing	U	A,B,M	Pri	No	C	1,799	22	16	67			17	498	54	37	8	1	547	25	48	24	3						Open
Wagner College	Staten Island	SU	B,M	Pri	F,S	C		25		2	39	53	6	575	26	44	25	5	550	23	50	26	1	550	28	40	29	3	2/15
Webb Institute	Glen Cove	SU	B	Pri	No	C	92	34						700					740										8/16
Wells College	Aurora	SM	B	Pri	No	C	572	24			54	41	5	510	49	37	12	2	500	56	35	7	2	480	59	32	9		3/1
Yeshiva University	New York	U	A,B		No	C	2,869	26						619	6	35	39	20	622	5	35	40	20	610	6	37	40	17	12/1

North Carolina

Appalachian State University	Boone	SM	B,M,D	Pub	F,S	C	15,712	26	3	14	47	19	17	572	11	55	30	4	581	6	52	38	4	548	22	55	21	2	2/1
Barton College	Wilson	SU	B,M	Pri	F,S	C		20		18	63	19		540	31	57	12		520	33	52	13	1						Open
Belmont Abbey College	Belmont	SM	B	Pri	F,S	C	1,648	23	27	33	28	4	7	510	54	29	13	3	510	42	39	17	2						8/15
Bennett College	Greensboro	U	B	Pri	S	W	766								90	10	1			92		8							Open
Cabarrus College of Health Sciences	Concord	SU	A,B	Pri	No	C	524																						Open
Campbell University	Buies Creek	R	A,B,M,D	Pri	F,S	C	4,500																						Open
Catawba College	Salisbury	SM	B,M	Pri	No	C	1,297	20	51	25	18	4	2	480	53	36	11	1	500	48	41	10	1						Open
Davidson College	Davidson	SM	B	Pri	F,S	C	1,796	31			1	35	64	670	2	13	46	40	680		12	50	38	670	3	13	44	40	1/2
Duke University	Durham	SU	B,M,D	Pri	F,S	C		33			1	14	85	725	1	5	27	67	750	1	4	18	77	730	2	6	21	71	1/2
East Carolina University	Greenville	U	B,M,D	Pub	F,S	C	21,298	22	18	55	19	6	3	510	49	43	7	1	540	32	55	12	1	490	57	37	6		3/15
Elizabeth City State University	Elizabeth City	SM	B,M	Pub	F,S	C	3,395								89	10	1			83	16	1			92	8			8/1
Elon University	Elon	SU	B,M,D	Pri	F,S	C	6,008	27		1	14	63	23	576					605	4	40	47	9						1/10
Fayetteville State University	Fayetteville	U	B,M,D	Pub	F,S	C	5,287																						1/10
Gardner-Webb University	Boiling Springs	SM	A,B,M,D	Pri	No	C	2,572		36	31	19	8	6		47	39	13	1		45	38	16	1						Open
Greensboro College	Greensboro	U	B,M	Pri	F,S	C	1,066								70	24	5	1		63	26	11							Open
Guilford College	Greensboro	SU	B,M	Pri	No	C	1,809	22		14	48	29	9	508	45	36	14	5	505	41	50	9		484	58	25	17		12/1
High Point University	High Point	SU	B,M,D	Pri	F,S	C	4,546	24		3	46	42	8						573	12	51	32	5						3/15
Johnson & Wales University/Charlotte Campus	Charlotte	U	A,B	Pri	No	C																							Open
Johnson C. Smith University	Charlotte	U	B,M	Pri	F,S	C	1,326	17	2	60	35	2		420	91	6	3		420	87	11	2							Open
Lees-McRae College	Banner Elk	R	B	Pri	No	C	940																						Open
Lenoir-Rhyne University	Hickory	SU	B,M		F,S	C		20		18	47	24	11	485	57	33	9	1	495	50	38	11	1						Open
Livingstone College	Salisbury	SM	A,B	Pri	F,S	C	895	15																					6
Mars Hill University	Mars Hill	R	B		F,S	C	1,250																						Open

NAME OF SCHOOL	TOWN	ENVIRONMENT U-Urban R-Rural SU-Suburban SM-Small Town	DEGREES AWARDED A-Associate B-Bachelor M-Master D-Doctorate	CONTROL Pri-Private, Pub-Public	FRATERNITIES AND SORORITIES F-Fraternities S-Sororities F, S-Both No-Neither	STUDENTS: C-Coed M-Men W-Women PM-Primarily Men PW-Primarily Women	UNDERGRADUATE ENROLLMENT FALL 2017	ACT Median	ACT Below 21	ACT 21-23	ACT 24-26	ACT 27-28	ACT Above 28	SAT CRITICAL READING Median	SAT CRITICAL READING Below 500	SAT CRITICAL READING 500-599	SAT CRITICAL READING 600-700	SAT CRITICAL READING Above 700	SAT MATHEMATICS Median	SAT MATHEMATICS Below 500	SAT MATHEMATICS 500-599	SAT MATHEMATICS 600-700	SAT MATHEMATICS Above 700	SAT WRITING Median	SAT WRITING Below 500	SAT WRITING 500-599	SAT WRITING 600-700	SAT WRITING Above 700	APPLICATION DEADLINE Month / Day
Meredith College	Raleigh	U	B,M	Pri	No	W		22		12	49	35	4	559	19	49	30	2	536	28	52	17	2						2/15
Methodist University	Fayetteville	SU	A,B,M	Pri	F,S	C	2,280	21	50	30	10	6	4	484	59	34	6	1	510	45	40	14	1	466	60	33	6	1	Open
Montreat College	Montreat	SM	A,B,M	Pri	No	C	735							475	20	73	7	1	466	16	76	7	1	445					Open
North Carolina A&T State University	Greensboro	U	B,M,D	Pub	F,S	C		20		28	60	11	1						506	44	48	7	1						6/30
North Carolina Central University	Durham	U	B,M	Pub	F,S	C	5,300																						8/1
North Carolina State University	Raleigh	U	A,B,M,D		F,S	C	23,847	29			4	57	39						662		15	54	31						1/15
North Carolina Wesleyan College	Rocky Mount	SU	B	Pri	F,S	C	1,756																						Open
Pfeiffer University	Misenheimer	R	B,M	Pri	No	C	955	20	55	32	7	5		460	63	31	6		500	49	40	11		450	71	26	2	1	8/25
Queens University of Charlotte	Charlotte	SU	B,M	Pri	F,S	C	1,703	24	22	26	29	13	10	520	41	44	11	3	520	39	43	17	1	510	45	37	15	3	Open
Saint Augustine's University	Raleigh	U	B		F,S	C	1,360																					3	Open
Salem College	Winston-Salem	U	B,M	Pri	No	W	871	24						550					540										Open
Shaw University	Raleigh	U	B,M	Pri	F,S	C	1,713		6	82	11	1																	7/30
St. Andrews University	Laurinburg	SM	B,M	Pri	No	C	460	19					2	460	67	27	4		480	66	29	5							Open
University of Mount Olive	Mount Olive	SM	A,B		No	C	3,116																						Open
University of North Carolina at Asheville	Asheville	U	B,M	Pub	F,S	C	3,806	25		3	37	49	11	580	16	41	34	8	574	10	54	31	5	544	29	47	21	4	2/15
University of North Carolina at Chapel Hill	Chapel Hill	SU	B,M,D	Pub	F,S	C	18,523	30			6	39	55						670	1	14	50	35						1/15
University of North Carolina at Charlotte	Charlotte	SU	B,M,D	Pub	F,S	C		24		1	51	43	5						597	2	50	42	6						6/1
University of North Carolina at Greensboro	Greensboro	U	B,M,D	Pub	F,S	C	16,281	23			61	35	4	566					551	17	65	16	2	28					3/1
University of North Carolina at Pembroke	Pembroke	R	B,M	Pub	F,S	C	5,514	19		30	59	10							451	53	41	5							6/30
University of North Carolina School of the Arts	Winston-Salem	U	B,M	Pub	No	C	781																						3/1
University of North Carolina Wilmington	Wilmington	SU	B,M,D	Pub	F,S	C		24			42	52	6	595	2	49	42	6	600	3	47	47	3	565	12	57	29	1	2/1
Wake Forest University	Winston-Salem	SU	B,M,D	Pri	F,S	C		30			6	33	61						680	3	14	37	47						1/1
Warren Wilson College	Asheville	SU	B,M	Pri	No	C	650	26	8	21	32	17	22	580	15	39	35	11	540	32	46	20	2						1/1
Western Carolina University	Cullowhee	R	B,M,D	Pub	F,S	C	7,979	22	34	38	16	6	6	515	43	43	13	1	526	36	47	16	1	486	60	32	7	1	3/1
William Peace University	Raleigh	U	B	Pri	S	C	791	18	64	10	15	3	8	440	72	23	5		440	73	24	3							Open
Wingate University	Wingate	SM	B,M,D	Pri	F,S	C	2,084	20		22	59	16	3	520	35	49	14	2	510	39	46	14	1						Open
Winston-Salem State University	Winston-Salem	SU	B,M	Pub	F,S	C	5,458												440	78	12	1		420	79	7	1		Open
North Dakota																													
Dickinson State University	Dickinson	R	A,B	Pub	No	C	1,140	20		19	67	14																	8/1
Mayville State University	Mayville	R	A,B	Pub	No	C	1,036	19	68	20	7	3	2																Open
Minot State University	Minot	SM	A,B,M	Pub	No	C	3,298	22		8	51	21	3						520										Open
North Dakota State University	Fargo	U	B,M,D	Pub	F,S	C	12,010	24			45	44	8		26	36	32	6		23	26	36	15		34	38	26	2	Open
The University of Mary	Bismarck	SU	B,M	Pri	No	C	2,060	23	27	33	27	8	5																8/15
University of Jamestown	Jamestown	SM	B,M,D	Pri	No	C	955	22		6	61	28	4	498	55	28	13	2	495	57	28	11	2						Open
University of North Dakota	Grand Forks	U	B,M,D	Pub	F,S	C	11,255	24		3	43	46	8																7/1
Valley City State University	Valley City	SM	B,M	Pub	F,S	C	1,295	21		17	57	19	3																Open
Ohio																													
Art Academy of Cincinnati	Cincinnati	U	A,B,M	Pri	No	C	138	21	43	36	14		7	550	33	50	6	11	460	68	26	6		500	47	47		6	8/1
Ashland University	Ashland	SM	A,B,M,D	Pri	F,S	C	2,785																						Open
Baldwin Wallace University	Berea	SU	B,M	Pri	F,S	C	3,305	24		6	41	46	8						580	14	44	33	8						Open
Bluffton University	Bluffton	SM	B,M	Pri	No	C	865	22		17	57	24	2																8/15
Bowling Green State University	Bowling Green	SM	B,M,D	Pub	F,S	C	14,852	22		5	55	35	5						540	19	51	34	6						7/15
Capital University	Columbus	SU	B,M,D	Pri	F,S	C	2,718	24		3	38	50	9						573	14	53	30	3						7/15
Case Western Reserve University	Cleveland	U	B,M,D	Pri	F,S	C	5,152	32			1	23	76	700	1	14	35	50	750		3	22	75	690	2	14	37	47	1/15
Cedarville University	Cedarville	SM	B,M,D	Pri	No	C	3,388	26			26	55	19	630	4	25	52	19	610	6	40	39	15						Open
Central State University	Wilberforce	R	B,M	Pub	F,S	C	1,335																						Open
Cleveland Institute of Art	Cleveland	U	B	Pri	F,S	C	625	22	1	9	38	46	6	580	17	40	27	16	540	25	46	25	4	590	14	41	29	16	3/1
Cleveland Institute of Music	Cleveland	U	B,M,D	Pri	No	C	243																					16	3/1
Cleveland State University	Cleveland	U	B,M,D	Pub	F,S	C	12,433	22		14	50	32	4	510	45	37	14	3	510	42	41	14	3					16	3/1
Columbus College of Art and Design	Columbus	U	B,M	Pri	No	C	1,333	22	40	23	22	9	6	540	33	37	27	3	570	39	42	18	1	570	49	37	14		8/15
Defiance College	Defiance	SM	A,B,M	Pri	F,S	C	957	22	42	25	22	6	3	470	60	32	8		490	48	48	4		430	72	28			8/15
Denison University	Granville	SU	B	Pri	F,S	C	2,282	29				57	43	644		22	58	20	640		24	52	24						1/15
Franciscan University of Steubenville	Steubenville	SM	A,B,M	Pri	No	C	2,090	25			32	52	16	590	9	42	32	17	560	21	44	28	7	570	18	45	30	7	1/15
Franklin University	Columbus	U	A,B,M		No	C	7,055																						Open
Heidelberg University	Tiffin	SM	B,M	Pri	F,S	C	1,110	22	48	24	16	7	5	420	51	35	12	2	490	52	35	13		400	60	30	9	2	8/1
Hiram College	Hiram	R	B,M	Pri	S	C	1,090	22		19	51	23	7	550	33	37	18	12	530	41	35	20	4						Open
John Carroll University	University Heights	SU	B,M	Pri	F,S	C	3,028	25		1	36	51	12	544	25	53	19	3	549	22	49	28	3	532	31	51	15	3	2/1

Kent State University	Kent	SU	A,B,M,D	Pub	F,S	C	23,607	23		2	57	35	6	530	63	35	2		530	65	32	3		510	54	41	5		Open
Kenyon College	Gambier	R	B	Pri	F,S	C	1,708	30			3	29	68						650	1	14	46	39						1/15
Lake Erie College	Painesville	SM	B,M	Pri	F,S	C	955	20		21	64	14	1	450	73	22	4		470	69	24	7		410	81	17	2		8/7
Lourdes University	Sylvania	SU	A,B,M	Pri	No	C	2,118	20	63	25	10	3		422	79	21			438	80	13	7							Open
Malone University	Canton	SU	B,M	Pri	No	C	1,311	22		9	63	25	3	530	38	42	14	6	528	33	47	14	6						Open
Marietta College	Marietta	SM	A,B,M	Pri	F,S	C	1,487	24	23	27	23	13	15	539	33	40	25	2	555	27	36	34	3	517	40	42	17	1	Open
Miami University	Oxford	SM	A,B,M,D	Pub	F,S	C	16,981	29			5	57	38							1	19	50	30						2/1
Mount St. Joseph University	Cincinnati	SU	A,B,M,D	Pri	No	C	1,795	22	40	29	22	6	3	475	62	30	7	1	468	61	30	9							2/1
Mount Vernon Nazarene University	Mount Vernon	SM	A,B,M	Pri	No	C	1,831	23		8	53	36	3																5/1
Muskingum University	New Concord	SM	B,M	Pri	F,S	C	1,741	22	40	28	19	6	6	491	50	43	5	2	513	45	36	14	5						5/1
Notre Dame College	South Euclid	SU	A,B,M	Pri	No	C	1,363																						Open
Oberlin College	Oberlin	SM	B,M	Pri	No	C	2,895	31			3	33	64	687		6	50	44	680	1	14	45	40	682					1/15
Ohio Dominican University	Columbus	U	A,B,M	Pri	No	C	2,005		33	33	22	7	4		53	28	14	5		35	42	23							Open
Ohio Northern University	Ada	SM	B,D		F,S	C	2,234	26						570					590					555					8/15
Ohio State University at Columbus	Columbus	U	A,B,M,D	Pub	F,S	C	45,831	30		1	6	41	52						680	1	14	44	41						2/1
Ohio State University at Lima	Lima	SU	A,B,M	Pub	No	C	999	23		9	49	39	3						590	22	45	33							Open
Ohio State University at Mansfield	Mansfield	SU	A,B,M	Pub	No	C	1,189	23		10	48	39	3						560	30	30	38	2						Open
Ohio State University at Marion	Marion	R	A,B	Pub	No	C	1,083	22		12	49	37	2						575	12	42	38	8						Open
Ohio State University at Newark	Newark	SU	A,B,M	Pub	No	C	2,448	22		13	50	35	2						550	18	55	26	1						6/1
Ohio University	Athens	SM	A,B,M,D	Pub	F,S	C	23,795	24		1	45	46	8						580	10	52	33	5						6/1
Ohio Wesleyan University	Delaware	SM	B	Pri	F,S	C	1,639	26	11	23	26	19	25	569	20	44	26	10	581	13	41	36	10						3/1
Otterbein University	Westerville	SU	B,M,D	Pri	F,S	C	2,343	23	31	29	24	9	7	530	35	41	22	2	531	33	43	22	2	527	36	39	20	4	8/15
Shawnee State University	Portsmouth	SM	A,B,M	Pub	F,S	C	3,603	22		12	57	28	3																Open
The College of Wooster	Wooster	SU	B	Pri	F,S	C	2,003	27		1	21	52	26	628	19	35	37	9	636	9	42	40	9	32	13	35	39	13	Open
The University of Akron	Akron	U	A,B,M,D	Pub	F,S	C	19,037	22		17	42	33	9	563	21	40	30	9	571	27	34	24	15						8/11
Tiffin University	Tiffin	SM	A,B,M	Pri	F,S	C	2,459	21		27	56	16	1	480	50	37	13		480	53	38	9							Open
Union Institute & University	Cincinnati	SM	B,M,D	Pri	No	C	1,129																						10/1
University of Cincinnati	Cincinnati	U	A,B,M,D	Pub	F,S	C	25,860	25			30	52	18						610	4	36	41	19						3/1
University of Dayton	Dayton	SU	B,M,D	Pri	F,S	C	8,330	27			21	54	25						604	6	42	41	11						2/1
University of Findlay	Findlay	SM	A,B,M,D	Pri	F,S	C	4,004	23	16	31	27	15	11	510	37	45	16	2	530	31	46	21	2	515	36	41	19	4	8/1
University of Mount Union	Alliance	SU	B,M,D	Pri	F,S	C	2,140	23		8	53	34	5																Open
University of Rio Grande & Rio Grande Community College	Rio Grande	R	A,B,M		F,S	C	1,855																						Open
University of Toledo	Toledo	U	A,B,M,D	Pub	F,S	C	16,877	22	41	25	19	8	6																Open
Urbana University	Urbana	SM	A,B,M	Pri	No	C	1,457																						Open
Ursuline College	Pepper Pike	SU	B,M,D	Pri	No	PW	953	20	56	26	15	2	2	456	68	21	11		459	74	21	5		441	74	21	5		Open
Walsh University	North Canton	SM	A,B,M,D	Pri	No	C	2,136	23		8	57	30	5	520					520										Open
Wilberforce University	Wilberforce	R	B,M		F,S	C	800																						Open
Wilmington College	Wilmington	SM	B,M	Pri	F,S	C	1,395	21	20	59	10	10	1	510	61	28	9	1	550	49	35	16							8/1
Wittenberg University	Springfield	SU	B,M	Pri	F,S	C	1,972	25		3	36	47	14						570	20	35	35	10						3/15
Wright State University	Dayton	SU	A,B,M,D	Pub	F,S	C	12,682	22	40	25	18	9	8	520	40	36	21	3	520	40	39	18	3	490	54	33	11	1	Open
Xavier University	Cincinnati	U	A,B,M,D	Pri	No	C	4,563	25		2	34	50	14						570	15	49	31	5						2/1
Youngstown State University	Youngstown	U	A,B,M,D	Pub	F,S	C	11,391	21		16	53	26	5	490	52	30	12	6	500	45	27	17	11	465	61	19	15	5	8/1

Oklahoma

Cameron University	Lawton	SU	A,B,M	Pub	F,S	C	4,446	20	1	31	50	17	1																Open
East Central University	Ada	SM	B,M	Pub	F,S	C	3,455	20		26	53	18	3		95	5			540	30	48	18	4	400					Open
Langston University	Langston	R	A,B,M	Pub	F,S	C	4,020																						Open
Northeastern State University	Tahlequah	SM	B,M,D	Pub	F,S	C	8,659	24																					Open
Northwestern Oklahoma State University	Alva	SM	B,M	Pub	F,S	C	1,809	19	68	22	8	1	1																Open
Oklahoma Baptist University	Shawnee	SM	A,B,M	Pri	F,S	C	1,904	24		6	51	36	8	538	29	47	21	3	520	35	51	11	3						8/1
Oklahoma Christian University	Oklahoma City	SU	B,M	Pri	F,S	C	1,974	24		8	41	38	14	538	18	46	27	9	553	25	41	28	6	499	49	33	14	4	9/1
Oklahoma City University	Oklahoma City	U	B,M,D	Pri	F,S	C	1,804	25		1	31	55	12	560	28	42	23	7	540	29	42	24	3	550	35	46	14	5	Open
Oklahoma Panhandle State University	Goodwell	R	A,B	Pub	F	C	1,387	22	25	35	28	11	1	525	16	67	17		520	33	50	17							Open
Oklahoma State University	Stillwater	SM	B,M,D		F,S	C	20,581	25						540	28	45	23	4	565	21	45	29	6						Open
Oklahoma Wesleyan University	Bartlesville	SU	A,B,M	Pri	No	C	1,059																						Open
Oral Roberts University	Tulsa	U	B,M,D	Pri	No	C	3,057	22		16	54	24	6	503	47	40	10	3	505	49	35	15	1						Open
Southeastern Oklahoma State University	Durant	R	B,M	Pub	F,S	C		21		19	64	16	2																Open
Southern Nazarene University	Bethany	SU	A,B,M	Pri	No	C	1,653	23	36	26	18	8	12																Open
Southwestern Oklahoma State University	Weatherford	SM	A,B,M,D	Pub	F,S	C	4,546	21		20	50	24	6																Open
St. Gregory's University	Shawnee	SU	A,B,M	Pri	F,S	C	770																						Open
University of Central Oklahoma	Edmond	SU	A,B,M	Pub	F,S	C	15,067	21		14	58	25	3																Open
University of Oklahoma	Norman	SU	B,M,D	Pub	F,S	C	21,628	26			27	50	23	630					620	4	33	38	25						2/1
University of Science and Arts of Oklahoma	Chickasha	SM	B	Pub	F,S	C	845	24	18	29	28	16	9																9/1
University of Tulsa	Tulsa	U	B,M,D	Pri	F,S	C	3,406	29		1	13	40	46	640	7	19	42	32	640	9	25	32	34	600	10	29	33	28	Open

Oregon

Art Institute of Portland	Portland	U	A,B		No	C	1,327																						Open
Concordia University	Portland	U	A,B,M,D	Pri	No	C	1,257	20	40	35	16	9	2	500					500										Open
Corban University	Salem	SU	A,B,M,D	Pri	No	C	975																						8/1

NAME OF SCHOOL	TOWN	ENVIRONMENT U-Urban R-Rural SU-Suburban SM-Small Town	DEGREES AWARDED A-Associate B-Bachelor M-Master D-Doctorate	CONTROL Pri-Private, Pub-Public	FRATERNITIES AND SORORITIES F-Fraternities S-Sororities F, S-Both No-Neither	STUDENTS: C-Coed M-Men W-Women PM-Primarily Men PW-Primarily Women	UNDERGRADUATE ENROLLMENT FALL 2017	TEST SCORES: ACT Median	ACT Below 21	ACT 21-23	ACT 24-26	ACT 27-28	ACT Above 28	SAT CRITICAL READING Median	SAT CR Below 500	SAT CR 500-599	SAT CR 600-700	SAT CR Above 700	SAT MATHEMATICS Median	SAT Math Below 500	SAT Math 500-599	SAT Math 600-700	SAT Math Above 700	SAT WRITING Median	SAT Writing Below 500	SAT Writing 500-599	SAT Writing 600-700	SAT Writing Above 700	APPLICATION DEADLINE Month / Day
Eastern Oregon University	La Grande	R	B,M	Pub	No	C		21		25	58	17			61	31	7			65	27	7			77	19	4		9/1
George Fox University	Newberg	SM	B,M,D	Pri	No	C	2,496	23						540	30	42	22	6	545	29	42	22	6	528	38	41	19	3	2/1
Lewis & Clark College	Portland	SU	B,M,D	Pri	No	C	2,134	29		1	11	62	26						636		30	48	22						1/15
Linfield College	McMinnville	SM	B	Pri	F,S	C	1,632	23		7	50	37	7	560					540	18	48	31	3						2/1
Marylhurst University	Marylhurst	SU	B,M	Pri	No	C	817																						Open
Northwest Christian University	Eugene	U	A,B,M	Pri	No	C	705																						Open
Oregon Institute of Technology	Klamath Falls	SM	A,B,M	Pub	F,S	C	3,070																						6/1
Oregon State University	Corvallis	SM	B,M,D		F,S	C	25,327	25		4	35	44	17						592	11	41	36	12						9/1
Pacific Northwest College of Art	Portland	U	B,M	Pri	No	C	446																						8/1
Pacific University	Forest Grove	SM	B,M,D	Pri	F,S	C		24		5	42	46	7	540	28	48	20	3	550	21	52	25	2						2/15
Portland State University	Portland	U	B,M,D	Pub	F,S	C	23,170	22	38	26	20	10	6	520	39	39	19	3	510	42	4	16	1		50	36	13	1	Open
Reed College	Portland	U	B,M	Pri	No	C		31			1	25	74	715		5	36	59	670	1	12	50	37	685	1	8	50	41	1/15
Southern Oregon University	Ashland	SM	B,M	Pub	No	C	5,444	23						525	39	38	19	3	505	47	40	12		490	52	38	9		Open
University of Oregon	Eugene	SU	B,M,D	Pub	F,S	C	20,047	25		5	32	51	12	30					580	13	46	34	7	30					1/15
University of Portland	Portland	U	B,M,D	Pri	No	C	3,741							590	10	43	32	15	600	8	35	47	9						2/1
Warner Pacific College	Portland	U	A,B	Pri	No	C	1,550								65	26	9			64	31	4	1		53	44	3		Open
Western Oregon University	Monmouth	SM	A,B,M	Pub	F,S	C																							Open
Willamette University	Salem	U	B,M,D	Pri	F,S	C		26			14	59	28	624	5	29	50	16	597	8	41	44	7	572					Open

Pennsylvania

NAME OF SCHOOL	TOWN	ENVIRONMENT	DEGREES AWARDED	CONTROL	FRATERNITIES AND SORORITIES	STUDENTS	UNDERGRADUATE ENROLLMENT FALL 2017	ACT Median	ACT Below 21	ACT 21-23	ACT 24-26	ACT 27-28	ACT Above 28	SAT CR Median	SAT CR Below 500	SAT CR 500-599	SAT CR 600-700	SAT CR Above 700	SAT Math Median	SAT Math Below 500	SAT Math 500-599	SAT Math 600-700	SAT Math Above 700	SAT Writing Median	SAT Writing Below 500	SAT Writing 500-599	SAT Writing 600-700	SAT Writing Above 700	APPLICATION DEADLINE Month / Day
Albright College	Reading	SU	B,M	Pri	F,S	C	2,304	22		9	47	38	6	529					525	26	56	17	1						Open
Allegheny College	Meadville	SU	B	Pri	F,S	C	1,920	26		4	25	50	21						605	5	38	51	6						2/15
Alvernia University	Reading	SU	A,B,M,D	Pri	No	C		21		17	57	24	1						520	36	48	15							Open
Arcadia University	Glenside	SU	B,M,D	Pri	No	C	1,957	24		4	36	49	11						564	15	51	29	5						Open
Bloomsburg University of Pennsylvania	Bloomsburg	SM	B,M,D	Pub	F,S	C	8,995	20		15	52	32	1						524	32	53	14	1						Open
Bryn Athyn College	Bryn Athyn	SU	A,B,M	Pri	No	C	267	22		44	12	44							510	42	42	14	2						Open
Bryn Mawr College	Bryn Mawr	SU	B,M,D	Pri	No	W	1,308	30			1	34	65	670	2	19	42	40	665	1	20	45	34	675	2	14	47	37	1/15
Bucknell University	Lewisburg	SM	B,M	Pri	F,S	C	3,571	30			3	42	55						680		14	49	37						1/15
Cabrini University	Radnor	SU	B,M,D	Pri	F,S	C	1,521	20	55	23	16	6		450	70	26	4		440	73	23	4		440	74	24	2		Open
Cairn University	Langhorne	SU	B,M	Pri	No	C	744	20		27	55	15	3	28					520	37	45	16	2	27					Open
California University of Pennsylvania	California	R	A,B,M	Pub	F,S	C		19	1	41	39	18	1	465	68	25	6	1	455	71	22	6	1	435	78	17	4	1	Open
Carlow University	Pittsburgh	U	B,M,D	Pri	No	PW		22						490	50	39	10	1	480	61	31	7							8/1
Carnegie Mellon University	Pittsburgh	U	B,M,D	Pri	F,S	C	6,673	33			1	13	86	700	1	6	41	52	770	1	3	17	79	720		6	32	62	8/1
Cedar Crest College	Allentown	SU	B,M	Pri	No	W	1,387	22						537	64	30	6		516	57	38	5			70	23	7		Open
Chatham University	Pittsburgh	U	B,M,D	Pri	No	C	1,002	24		1	41	48	10						570	9	53	36	2						8/1
Chestnut Hill College	Philadelphia	SU	A,B,M,D	Pri	No	C	1,373	22		6	75	16	3						520	30	59	11							Open
Cheyney University of Pennsylvania	Cheyney	SU	A,B,M	Pub	F,S	C	1,224								94	5	1			94	6				96	3	1		5/30
Clarion University of Pennsylvania	Clarion	SM	A,B,M,D	Pub	F,S	C	4,330	21	1	20	61	14	4						510										Open
Curtis Institute of Music	Philadelphia	U	B		No	C	130																						Open
Delaware Valley University	Doylestown	SU	A,B,M	Pri	F,S	C	2,000	22	38	25	25	13																	Open
DeSales University	Center Valley	SU	B,M,D	Pri	No	C	2,381								44	37	15	5		46	36	15	3		48	34	15	3	8/1
Dickinson College	Carlisle	SU	B	Pri	F,S	C	2,381	30			4	45	51						660	1	17	49	33						1/15
Drexel University	Philadelphia	U	B,M,D	Pri	F,S	C	15,499	28		1	20	52	28	619	2	33	51	13	633	2	35	44	19						1/15
Duquesne University	Pittsburgh	U	B,M,D	Pri	F,S	C	6,099	26			21	59	20						597	2	51	42	5						7/1
East Stroudsburg University	East Stroudsburg	SM	B,M,D	Pub	F,S	C	6,159	23		7	53	29	10	473	57	39	4		475	61	31	7	1	449	77	21	2		7/1
Eastern University	St. Davids	SU	A,B,M,D	Pri	No	C	2,402	22	29	32	18	14	7	524	39	43	14	4	516	46	34	17	3	513	47	32	20	1	Open
Edinboro University	Edinboro	SM	A,B,M	Pub	F,S	C	5,595	20					1	482	63	29	7	1	478	62	30	7	1	462					Open
Elizabethtown College	Elizabethtown	SM	B,M	Pri	No	C	1,737	25		5	36	45	14	590	8	47	38	7	590	14	42	36	8	510					Open
Elizabethtown College School of Continuing and Professional Studies	Elizabethtown	SM	A,B,M	Pri	No	C	346																						Open
Franklin and Marshall College	Lancaster	SU	B	Pri	F,S	C	2,255	30				41	59	655		11	65	24	680		8	54	38						1/15
Gannon University	Erie	U	A,B,M,D	Pri	F,S	C	3,098	23		9	42	40	8	550	22	46	29	3	550	25	46	25	4						Open
Geneva College	Beaver Falls	SM	A,B,M	Pri	No	C	1,458	25		9	34	41	16	530	32	43	21	4	540	36	34	24	6	500	47	34	15	3	Open
Gettysburg College	Gettysburg	SU	B	Pri	F,S	C	2,384	28											673		4	63	33						1/15
Grove City College	Grove City	SM	B	Pri	F,S	C	2,392	27		1	23	49	27	625	3	33	45	19	607	6	40	41	13						1/15
Gwynedd Mercy University	Gwynedd Valley	SU	A,B,M,D	Pri	No	C	2,035	20		34	49	17		490	67	31	2		490	63	30	7		450	69	29	2		1/15
Haverford College	Haverford	SU	B	Pri	No	C	1,268	33				12	88	710		6	34	60	710		7	32	61	710		3	38	59	1/15
Holy Family University	Philadelphia	SU	A,B,M,D	Pri	No	C	2,139							471	71	25	4		476	64	32	4		472					Open
Immaculata University	Immaculata	SU	A,B,M,D	Pri	F,S	C	1,555																						Open
Indiana University of Pennsylvania	Indiana	SM	A,B,M,D	Pub	F,S	C	10,618												500	48	43	8							Open
Jefferson (Philadelphia University + Thomas Jefferson University)	Philadelphia	SU	A,B,M,D	Pri	F,S	C		24		3	45	41	10						555	18	56	24	2						Open

Juniata College	Huntingdon	SM	B,M	Pri	No	C	1,569			3	31	48	19	59	7	44	39	9	590	6	45	41	8						2/15
Keystone College	La Plume	R	A,B	Pri	No	C	1,641	17	86	6			8	445	80	19	1	1	440	79	18	4		445	82	16	1	1	2/15
King's College	Wilkes Barre	U	B,M	Pri	No	C	2,082	24		7	38	47	8	546	26	47	25	2	543	26	49	23	2						Open
Kutztown University of Pennsylvania	Kutztown	SM	B,M,D	Pub	F,S	C	7,718	21		17	57	22	4	490					525	32	55	12	1	464					Open
La Roche College	Pittsburgh	SU	A,B,M,D	Pri	No	C	1,406	21		23	53	20	4						510	42	48	10							Open
La Salle University	Philadelphia	U	A,B,M,D	Pri	F,S	C	3,652	23		13	47	31	9						533	31	50	16	2						4/1
Lafayette College	Easton	SU	B	Pri	F,S	C	2,550	29			4	43	53						678	1	12	46	41						1/15
Lebanon Valley College	Annville	SM	B,M,D	Pri	F,S	C	1,712	26		5	34	47	10						584	7	56	30	7						Open
Lehigh University	Bethlehem	SU	B,M,D	Pri	F,S	C	5,080	31			3	31	66	660		14	57	29	690		9	43	48						1/1
Lincoln University	Lincoln University	R	B,M	Pub	F,S	C	1,624	18		46	50	4							470	60	33	6	1						5/1
Lock Haven University of Pennsylvania	Lock Haven	R	A,B,M	Pub	F,S	C	4,521	20	54	22	12	4	8	471	66	27	6	1	478	61	31	8		456	74	21	4		Open
Lycoming College	Williamsport	U	B	Pri	F,S	C	1,272	23		4	54	39	3						540	25	50	23	1						8/1
Mansfield University of Pennsylvania	Mansfield	R	A,B,M	Pub	F,S	C								480					480	60	32	7	1	450	38	50	12		8/1
Marywood University	Scranton	SU	B,M,D	Pri	S	C	1,931							515	39	49	12		544	24	54	20	2		43	47	10		Open
Mercyhurst University	Erie	SU	A,B,M,D	Pri	No	C	3,840	23	21	46	33			550					530					510					9/1
Messiah College	Mechanicsburg	SM	B,M,D	Pri	No	C	2,788	26		1	31	51	17						595	8	43	37	11						Open
Millersville University of Pennsylvania	Millersville	SM	A,B,M,D	Pub	F,S	C	6,980	22		17	49	28	6						520	31	52	15	2						Open
Misericordia University	Dallas	SU	B,M,D	Pri	No	C	2,195	23		7	45	48		560	17	53	27	3	550	16	59	23	2						Open
Moore College of Art and Design	Philadelphia	U	B	Pri	No	PW	437																						Open
Moravian College	Bethlehem	SU	B,M,D	Pri	F,S	C	1,770	24						554	18	56	23	3	546	21	53	24	2						3/1
Mount Aloysius College	Cresson	SM	A,B,M	Pri	No	C	1,611								49	49	2			45	52	2							8/3
Muhlenberg College	Allentown	SU	A,B	Pri	F,S	C	2,397	28			9	60	31	605	7	39	40	13	613	10	32	52	10	604	13	42	36	8	2/15
Neumann University	Aston	SU	A,B,M,D	Pri	No	C	2,278	18		41	47	12		440	78	19	3		440	79	18	4		440	80	17	1	1	Open
Peirce College	Philadelphia	U	A,B,M	Pri	No	C	1,962																						Open
Penn State Altoona	Altoona	U	A,B,M		F,S	C		22		8	60	31	2	490	55	35	9		515	42	38	16	4						Open
Penn State Erie,The Behrend College	Erie	SU	A,B,M	Pub	F,S	C		24		7	39	48	7	523	39	45	14	2	575	20	40	28	12						Open
Pennsylvania College of Technology	Williamsport	SU	A,B	Pub	F	C	5,457																						7/1
Pennsylvania State University - University Park	University Park	SU	A,B,M,D	Pub	F,S	C	40,891	27			10	61	29						630	3	31	47	19						11/30
Point Park University	Pittsburgh	U	A,B,M	Pri	No	C	3,226		34	22	25	20	6		45	39	14	2		57	34	8	1		52	35	12	2	Open
Robert Morris University	Moon Township	SU	B,M,D	Pri	F,S	C	4,384	24		2	48	39	12						559	18	55	24	4						5/1
Rosemont College	Rosemont	SU	B,M	Pri	No	C	529	23				17	83	460	67	26	5	2	430	74	18	6	2	440	74	21	3	2	8/1
Saint Francis University	Loretto	R	B,M	Pri	F,S	C	1,772																					2	8/1
Saint Joseph's University	Philadelphia	SU	A,B,M,D	Pri	F,S	C	5,377	26			25	59	16	604	3	42	49	6	597	4	47	44	6						2/1
Saint Vincent College	Latrobe	SU	B,M,D	Pri	No	C	1,646	23		7	48	36	9	565	17	50	26	7	554	21	51	24	4						5/1
Seton Hill University	Greensburg	SM	B,M	Pri	No	C	1,606			7	42	41	10		37	42	16	5		36	45	17	2		43	39	15	3	8/15
Shippensburg University of Pennsylvania	Shippensburg	R	B,M,D	Pub	F,S	C	5,912	21		17	59	21	3						530	28	55	16	1						Open
Slippery Rock University of Pennsylvania	Slippery Rock	SM	B,M,D	Pub	F,S	C	7,065																						Open
Susquehanna University	Selinsgrove	SM	B	Pri	F,S	C	2,196			3	31	54	12		8	48	39	5		8	57	31	3						2/1
Swarthmore College	Swarthmore	SU	B	Pri	F,S	C		32				22	78	730		4	33	62	720		3	34	62	720		4	29	67	1/1
Temple University	Philadelphia	U	A,B,M,D	Pub	F,S	C	28,243	24	16	27	28	12	17	558	22	48	25	5	571	17	46	30	7	553	24	46	25	5	2/1
Thiel College	Greenville	R	A,B	Pri	F,S	C	894	21						472					477									5	2/1
University of Pennsylvania	Philadelphia	U	A,B,M,D	Pri	F,S	C	9,712									5	31	64			2	24	74			3	22	75	1/1
University of Pittsburgh	Pittsburgh	SU	B,M,D	Pub	F,S	C	19,123	30	1	1	14	22	62	660	2	28	50	20	670	1	11	53	35		11	35	37	17	Open
University of Pittsburgh at Bradford	Bradford	SM	A,B	Pub	F,S	C	1,476	22		9	61	23	7						530	28	56	13	3	450	63	30	5	2	Open
University of Pittsburgh at Greensburg	Greensburg	SU	B	Pub	No	C		23		11	49	39	1	510	43	44	12	1	508	43	43	13	1	480	53	39	8		Open
University of Pittsburgh at Johnstown	Johnstown	SU	A,B	Pub	F,S	C		23		10	53	35	2	500	48	41	8	1	520	36	45	17	2	470	63	33	4		Open
University of Scranton	Scranton	U	A,B,M,D	Pri	No	C	4,041								15	56	25	4		12	51	31	5						3/1
University of the Arts	Philadelphia	U	B,M	Pri	No	C	2,079	22	48	11	27	7	7																Open
University of the Sciences	Philadelphia	U	B,M,D	Pri	F,S	C	2,438	26			23	58	19	595					610	1	44	45	10						Open
Ursinus College	Collegeville	SU	B	Pri	F,S	C	1,556	27		2	20	50	28						600	5	41	46	8						2/1
Villanova University	Villanova	SU	A,B,M,D	Pri	F,S	C	6,999	31			2	23	75	650	3	19	52	25	670	2	15	47	36	650	4	20	50	25	1/15
Washington & Jefferson College	Washington	SM	B,M	Pri	F,S	C	1,396	26			27	58	15	610					600	5	49	34	12						3/1
Waynesburg University	Waynesburg	SM	B,M,D	Pri	No	C	1,400	22						540					520					520					Open
West Chester University of Pennsylvania	West Chester	SU	B,M,D	Pub	F,S	C	14,398	24		3	47	44	6						573	15	58	25	2						Open
Westminster College	New Wilmington	R	B,M		F,S	C		25		2	42	44	12	555	23	45	28	4	550	24	48	24	4						Open
Widener University	Chester	SU	A,B,M,D	Pri	F,S	C	3,591			7	53	35	5	551	20	58	19	3	551	20	57	20	3						2/15
Wilkes University	Wilkes Barre	U	B,M,D	Pri	No	C	2,421	24		9	38	46	7	564					564	15	53	27	4						Open
Wilson College	Chambersburg	SM	A,B,M	Pri	No	C	607	21		33	33	42		480	59	36	4	1	470	60	30	9		460	70	25	3		8/1
York College of Pennsylvania	York	SU	A,B,M,D	Pri	F,S	C		23		5	57	36	3	520	37	48	13	1	535	30	49	19	1	500	50	39	11		Open

Puerto Rico

American University of Puerto Rico	Bayamon	U	A,B	Pri	No	C	1,211																						Open
Bayamon Central University	Bayamon	U	A,B,M		No	C	2,910																						Open
Caribbean University	Bayamon	U	A,B,M,D	Pri	No	C	2,920																						Open
Conservatory of Music of Puerto Rico	San Juan	U	B	Pub	No	C	255																						Open
Escuela de Artes Plasticas de Puerto Rico	San Juan	U	B	Pub	No	C	515																						Open
Inter-American University of Puerto Rico Ponce	Ponce	U	B		No	C	5,361																						Open
Inter-American University of Puerto Rico-Aguadilla Campus	Aguadilla	SU	A,B,M	Pri	No	C	4,357																						5/1
Inter-American University of Puerto Rico-Arecibo Campus	Arecibo	SU	A,B,M		F,S	C	4,135																						5/1
Inter-American University of Puerto Rico-Barranquitas	Barranquitas	SM	A,B		No	C	1,720																						5/1
Inter-American University of Puerto Rico-Bayamon	Bayamon	U	A,B,M	Pri	No	C	4,942																						5/1

NAME OF SCHOOL	TOWN	ENVIRONMENT U-Urban R-Rural SU-Suburban SM-Small Town	DEGREES AWARDED A-Associate B-Bachelor M-Master D-Doctorate	CONTROL Pri-Private, Pub-Public	FRATERNITIES AND SORORITIES F-Fraternities S-Sororities F,S-Both No-Neither	STUDENTS: C-Coed M-Men W-Women PM-Primarily Men PW-Primarily Women	UNDERGRADUATE ENROLLMENT FALL 2017	TEST SCORES: ACT Median	ACT Below 21	ACT 21-23	ACT 24-26	ACT 27-28	ACT Above 28	SAT CRITICAL READING Median	SAT CR Below 500	SAT CR 500-599	SAT CR 600-700	SAT CR Above 700	SAT MATHEMATICS Median	SAT Math Below 500	SAT Math 500-599	SAT Math 600-700	SAT Math Above 700	SAT WRITING Median	SAT Writing Below 500	SAT Writing 500-599	SAT Writing 600-700	SAT Writing Above 700	APPLICATION DEADLINE Month / Day
Inter-American University of Puerto Rico-Fajardo Campus	Fajardo	U	A,B,M,D	Pri	No	C	2,171																						8/15
Inter-American University of Puerto Rico-Metropolitan Campus	San Juan	U	A,B,M,D	Pri	No	C	7,100																						8/15
Inter-American University of Puerto Rico-San Germán	San Germán	R	A,B,M,D		No	C	5,090																						8/15
Pontifical Catholic University of Puerto Rico	Ponce	U	A,B,M,D	Pri	F,S	C	8,020																						8/15
Universidad Adventista de las Antillas	Mayaguez	SM	A,B,M	Pri	F,S	C	760																						Open
Universidad del Turabo	Gurabo	SU	A,B,M		No																								Open
Universidad Metropolitana	Rio Piedras	U	A,B,M	Pri	No	C																							Open
Universidad Politecnica de Puerto Rico, Hato Rey campus	Hato Rey	U	A,B,M,D	Pri	F	C	3,357																						Open
University of Puerto Rico, at Arecibo	Arecibo	U	A,B	Pub	No	C	4,146																						11/30
University of Puerto Rico, at Bayamon	Bayamon	SU	A,B	Pub	No	C	5,327																						11/30
University of Puerto Rico, at Cayey	Cayey	U	B	Pub	No	C	3,707																						11/30
University of Puerto Rico, at Humacao	Humacao	SU	A,B	Pub	S	C	4,542																						11/14
University of Puerto Rico, at Mayaguez	Mayaguez	U	A,B,M,D	Pub	F,S	C	11,095																						11/14
University of Puerto Rico-Rio Piedras campus	San Juan	U	B,M,D	Pub	F,S	C	17,860																						11/14
University of the Sacred Heart	Santurce	U	A,B,M	Pri	No	C	4,565																						11/14
Rhode Island																													
Brown University	Providence	U	B,M,D	Pri	F,S	C	6,580	33			1	16	83	740		5	24	71	750		4	23	73	740		6	21	73	1/1
Bryant University	Smithfield	SU	B,M	Pri	F,S	C	3,462	26			17	60	23						607	3	43	46	8					73	1/1
Johnson & Wales University/Providence Campus	Providence	SM	A,B,M,D	Pri	F,S	C																							Open
Providence College	Providence	SU	A,B,M	Pri	No	C	4,270	28			8	62	29	620					620	2	34	53	11	610					1/15
Rhode Island College	Providence	SU	B,M,D	Pub	F,S	C		19		43	52	5		460	72	23	5		455	71	25	4		450	74	22	3		3/15
Rhode Island School of Design	Providence	U	B,M	Pri	No	C	2,000				9			623					640					615					2/1
Roger Williams University	Bristol	SU	A,B,M	Pri	No	C		26		1	20	64	15						588	5	54	36	5						2/1
Salve Regina University	Newport	SU	A,B,M,D	Pri	No	C	2,124	25			40	51	5						576	7	57	34	2						2/1
University of Rhode Island	Kingston	SM	B,M,D		F,S	C	14,801	26		1	30	59	10	588					579	9	53	34	4						2/1
South Carolina																													
Allen University	Columbia	SM	A,B	Pri	F,S	C	350																						2/1
Benedict College	Columbia	U	B	Pri	F,S	C	2,641																						Open
Charleston Southern University	Charleston	SU	A,B,M		No	C	2,490																						8/15
Claflin University	Orangeburg	SU	B,M	Pri	F,S	C	1,883	18	77	17	8			436	78	18	4		440	72	19	8	2						Open
Clemson University	Clemson	SM	B,M,D	Pub	F,S	C	18,599	28			9	50	41	611	6	34	47	12	641	3	22	51	24						12/1
Coastal Carolina University	Conway	SU	B,M,D	Pub	F,S	C	9,747	22		5	64	29	2	554					544	17	64	18	1						8/1
Coker College	Hartsville	SM	B,M	Pri	No	C	1,178	19		31	55	12	2	520					500	47	42	10	1						Open
College of Charleston	Charleston	U	B,M	Pub	F,S	C	10,375	25		1	38	50	11						566	11	60	25	4						2/15
Columbia College	Columbia	U	B,M	Pri	No	PW	1,239							500	49	32	16	3	500	50	36	13	1						8/1
Converse College	Spartanburg	U	B,M	Pri	No	W	690	23	32	25	25	13	6	530	29	43	25	3	520	35	50	14	1						9/1
Erskine College	Due West	R	B,M,D	Pri	No	C	553							531	40	36	19	5	543	37	35	23	5						Open
Francis Marion University	Florence	R	B,M	Pub	F,S	C		20						465	66	28	5		455	70	25	5							8/15
Furman University	Greenville	SU	B,M	Pri	F,S	C	2,731	29		1	9	51	39						628	3	29	47	21						1/15
Lander University	Greenwood	SM	B,M	Pub	F,S	C	2,363	21	47	32	15	4	2	470	59	32	8		500	47	38	14	1						Open
Limestone College	Gaffney	SU	A,B,M	Pri	F,S	C	1,246	21			75	19	4	500	60	31	8		510	39	51	9							Open
Morris College	Sumter	SM	B	Pri	F,S	C	754																						4/30
Newberry College	Newberry	SM	B	Pri	F,S	C	795																						Open
North Greenville University	Tigerville	R	B,M,D	Pub	No	C	2,481	24		4	42	45	9	562	15	60	21	4	552	21	54	22	3	528	20	53	21	6	Open
Presbyterian College	Clinton	SM	B,D	Pri	F,S	C	1,063	25		3	33	46	18	550	21	52	21	6	540	20	48	26	6						2/1
South Carolina State University	Orangeburg	SM	B,M,D	Pub	F,S	C		16	1	75	20	3	1	396	90	9	1	1	410	89	10	1							7/31
Southern Wesleyan University	Central	SM	A,B,M	Pri	No	C	1,677	20						490	54	39	7		490	54	33	13		480	56	36	8		Open
The Citadel, The Military College of South Carolina	Charleston	SU	B,M	Pub	No	C		23		5	56	34	5	525	39	40	18	3	530	31	49	19	1						Open
University of South Carolina Aiken	Aiken	SU	B,M	Pub	F,S	C		20		21	59	18	1						505	45	45	10							8/1
University of South Carolina at Columbia	Columbia	U	A,B,M,D	Pub	F,S	C		28			12	62	26	605	4	42	44	10	605	4	37	48	10						12/1
University of South Carolina Upstate	Spartanburg	U	B,M	Pub	F,S	C	5,334	20	59	25	11	4	1	470	65	29	5	1	470	63	31	6		450	73	23	4		Open
Voorhees College	Denmark	SM	B	Pri	F,S	C	415																						Open
Winthrop University	Rock Hill	SM	B,M	Pub	F,S	C	5,091	22		13	51	32	5	556	22	46	27	5	531	28	51	16	2						5/1
Wofford College	Spartanburg	U	B	Pri	F,S	C	1,584	26	3	15	27	23	32	585	12	40	42	6	597	11	35	42	11		21	38	37	4	2/1

South Dakota

Augustana University	Sioux Falls	U	B,M	Pri	No	C	1,665	26		1	32	47	20							10	42	38	10						Open
Black Hills State University	Spearfish	SM	A,B,M	Pub	F,S	C	4,020	21																					Open
Dakota State University	Madison	R	A,B,M,D	Pub	No	C																							Open
Dakota Wesleyan University	Mitchell	R	A,B,M	Pri	No	C	756	22		13	57	28	2	428					487	55	33	22		423	88	22			8/25
Mount Marty College	Yankton	SM	A,B,M	Pri	No	C	1,092		10	50	30	5	5																Open
Northern State University	Aberdeen	U	A,B,M	Pub	No	C	3,001	22	42	26	115	14	3		58	30	8	4		47	38	12	3						9/1
Oglala Lakota College	Kyle	R	A,B,M		No	C																							Open
Presentation College	Aberdeen	SM	A,B	Pri	No	C	630	21																					8/1
Sinte Gleska University	Rosebud	R	A,B,M	Pri	No	C	341																						Open
South Dakota School of Mines and Technology	Rapid City	SU	A,B,M,D	Pub	F,S	C	2,101	26	4	17	35	20	24	560	31	40	22	7	600	12	40	29	19	500	42	40	16	2	Open
South Dakota State University	Brookings	SM	A,B,M,D		F,S	C	11,007			7	49	37	7																Open
University of Sioux Falls	Sioux Falls	SU	A,B,M	Pri	No	C		23		6	54	36	4						550										Open
University of South Dakota	Vermillion	SM	A,B,M,D	Pub	F,S	C	7,633	23	24	31	26	11	8	509	46	34	18	2	527	39	32	25	4						Open

Tennessee

Aquinas College	Nashville	U	A,B,M	Pri	No	C	312	25			48	39	13	560	21	42	16	21	540	26	37	32	5						Open
Austin Peay State University	Clarksville	U	A,B,M	Pub	F,S	C	9,513	22		12	61	24	3																8/8
Belmont University	Nashville	U	B,M,D	Pri	F,S	C	5,983	27			23	56	21	630	2	28	58	12	595	6	47	37	10						8/1
Bethel University	McKenzie	SM	B,M	Pri	F,S	C	2,232		62	24	15	3	2																8/30
Bryan College	Dayton	SM	A,B,M	Pri	No	C	1,011	23		5	52	36	7																Open
Carson-Newman University	Jefferson City	SM	A,B,M	Pri	F,S	C	1,646	23	9	7	49	35	6																8/1
Christian Brothers University	Memphis	U	B,M	Pri	F,S	C	1,351	25	4	42	28	11	15																8/1
Cumberland University	Lebanon	SM	A,B,M	Pri	F,S	C	623	21	44	33	10	11	2		65	30		5		50	50					88	12		Open
East Tennessee State University	Johnson City	SM	A,B,M,D	Pub	F,S	C	9,580																						Open
Fisk University	Nashville	U	B,M	Pri	F,S	C	868	20	60	21	14	3	1																Open
Freed-Hardeman University	Henderson	SM	A,B,M		No	C	1,479	23	30	27	21	10	12																Open
King University	Bristol	SM	A,B,M,D	Pri	No	C	2,467	23		10	42	41	7	519	41	40	17	2	534	25	56	15	4						Open
Lane College	Jackson	SM	B	Pri	F,S	C		15	2	81	15	2																	Open
Lee University	Cleveland	SU	B,M	Pri	F,S	C		24						520	39	38	21	2	480	46	40	11	2						9/1
LeMoyne-Owen College	Memphis	U	A,B	Pri	F,S	C	785																						9/1
Lincoln Memorial University	Harrogate	R	A,B,M	Pri	F,S	C	1,654																						Open
Lipscomb University	Nashville	SU	A,B,M,D	Pri	F,S	C	2,986	26			31	46	23	600	11	36	36	17	580	15	42	33	10						Open
Maryville College	Maryville	SU	B	Pri	No	C	1,176	24	20	26	23	16	15	537	35	34	27	4	535	34	42	23	1	528	35	37	25	3	3/1
Memphis College of Art	Memphis	U	B,M	Pri	No	C	377	22	23	39	23	13	3																8/3
Middle Tennessee State University	Murfreesboro	U	B,M,D	Pub	F,S	C	22,299	22	32	35	20	7	5																7/1
Milligan College	Milligan College	SU	B,M,D	Pri	No	C	885	25		2	32	52	26	568					555	24	53	16	7	29					8/1
Rhodes College	Memphis	U	B,M	Pri	F,S	C	2,031	28		4	22	24	46	630	3	20	53	24	630	2	22	56	20	620					1/15
Sewanee: The University of the South	Sewanee	SM	B,M,D	Pri	F,S	C	1,731	28			5	60	35						632		32	48	20						2/1
Southern Adventist University	Collegedale	SM	A,B,M	Pri	No	C	2,477	22	34	27	21	10	8																Open
Tennessee State University	Nashville	U	A,B,M,D	Pub	F,S	C	7,007	18	77	17	5	1	1																8/1
Tennessee Technological University	Cookeville	SM	B,M,D	Pub	F,S	C		24		3	41	43	13	525	36	40	20	4	550	24	47	26	3						8/1
Tennessee Wesleyan University	Athens	SM	B,M	Pri	F,S	C	1,015	21		14	59	25	1	470	66	33			490	100									8
The University of Memphis	Memphis	U	B,M,D	Pub	F,S	C		22		12	50	31	7	523	42	32	19	6	500	10	38	15	4	500	46	36	15	3	7/1
The University of Tennessee at Chattanooga	Chattanooga	U	B,M,D	Pub	F,S	C	10,084	23		2	52	38	8	577	15	43	37	5	558	15	59	22	4						5/1
The University of Tennessee at Knoxville	Knoxville	U	B,M,D	Pub	F,S	C	21,396	27						575	15	47	29	10	585	14	44	32	10						12/1
The University of Tennessee at Martin	Martin	R	B,M	Pub	F,S	C	6,279	23		1	59	35	5																8/1
Trevecca Nazarene University	Nashville	U	A,B,M,D	Pri	No	C	1,677	23	28	29	22	8	13	530	31	44	15	10	520	37	41	18	4						8/1
Tusculum College	Greeneville	SM	A,B,M	Pri	No	C	1,585	21		19	62	18	1	450	68	29	3		480	56	37	7							Open
Union University	Jackson	SU	A,B,M,D	Pri	F,S	C	2,829	25	16	21	22	12	29	590	13	23	30	23	590	13	35	36	10						8/15
Vanderbilt University	Nashville	U	B,M,D	Pri	F,S	C	6,871				1	8	91							1	5	19	76						1/1

Texas

Abilene Christian University	Abilene	SM	A,B,M,D	Pri	F,S	C	3,758	24		4	46	42	8						558	19	53	25	3						2/15
Angelo State University	San Angelo	U	B,M,D	Pub	F,S	C	8,094																						8/14
Austin College	Sherman	SU	B,M	Pri	F,S	C		26			25	52	23						625	4	34	44	18						3/1
Baylor University	Waco	SM	B,M,D	Pri	F,S	C	14,348	28			6	56	37						637	1	28	51	20						2/1
Concordia University Texas	Austin	U	A,B,M	Pri	No	C	1,030																						8/15
Dallas Baptist University	Dallas	SU	A,B,M,D	Pri	F,S	C	3,223	22		11	63	23	4						577	9	55	33	3						Open
East Texas Baptist University	Marshall	SM	B,M	Pri	F,S	C	1,233	21		15	66	19		490	61	27	11	1	510	41	45	13	1						8/17
Hardin-Simmons University	Abilene	U	B,M,D	Pri	F,S	C	2,030	22	39	25	24	6	6	510	43	35	20	2	520	38	44	17	1	510	43	45	11	1	Open
Houston Baptist University	Houston	U	B,M	Pri	F,S	C	2,447	22	40	30	16	8	6	530	37	38	22	3	540	35	41	22	2	520	39	40	17	4	Open
Howard Payne University	Brownwood	R	A,B	Pri	F,S	C		21		20	56	20	4		62	28	8	2		58	34	8							3/15
Huston-Tillotson University	Austin	U	A,B,M	Pri	F,S	C	972	16	56	35			7	405	88	9	3		415	84	14	1							7/1
Jarvis Christian College	Hawkins	R	A,B	Pri	F,S	C	863	15	7	73	20	1		360	96	3	1		360	93	6	1		350	100				8/1
Lamar University	Beaumont	U	A,B,M,D	Pub	F,S	C	8,430																						8/1
LeTourneau University	Longview	SM	A,B,M	Pri	No	C	2,253			2	41	38	20							9	38	38	15						Open
Lubbock Christian University	Lubbock	SU	A,B,M	Pri	F,S	C	1,471	22		10	50	32	8						527	36	42	19	3						8/15

NAME OF SCHOOL	TOWN	ENVIRONMENT U-Urban R-Rural SU-Suburban SM-Small Town	DEGREES AWARDED A-Associate B-Bachelor M-Master D-Doctorate	CONTROL Pri-Private, Pub-Public	FRATERNITIES AND SORORITIES F-Fraternities S-Sororities F, S-Both No-Neither	STUDENTS: C-Coed M-Men W-Women PM-Primarily Men PW-Primarily Women	UNDERGRADUATE ENROLLMENT FALL 2017	TEST SCORES ACT Median	ACT Below 21	ACT 21-23	ACT 24-26	ACT 27-28	ACT Above 28	SAT CRITICAL READING Median	SAT CR Below 500	SAT CR 500-599	SAT CR 600-700	SAT CR Above 700	SAT MATHEMATICS Median	SAT Math Below 500	SAT Math 500-599	SAT Math 600-700	SAT Math Above 700	SAT WRITING Median	SAT Writing Below 500	SAT Writing 500-599	SAT Writing 600-700	SAT Writing Above 700	APPLICATION DEADLINE Month / Day
McMurry University	Abilene	U	B	Pri	F,S	C	1,509	21		18	62	19	2	457	68	26	5	1	488	59	31	9	1	433	81	16	3		8/15
Midwestern State University	Wichita Falls	U	A,B,M	Pub	F,S	C		21		16	60	23	2	485	59	30	9		490	53	40	7		460	70	25	4		8/1
Our Lady of the Lake University	San Antonio	U	B,M,D		No	C	1,792	19	68	23	6	2																	Open
Paul Quinn College	Dallas	U	B	Pri	F,S	C	193																						Open
Prairie View A&M University	Prairie View	SM	B,M,D	Pub	F,S	C	6,757	17	57	36	4	4		410	85	13	1		420	82	16	2		417					6/1
Rice University	Houston	U	B,M,D	Pri	No	C		34			3	8	89	730	1	4	23	72	760	1	3	14	82	725	2	4	27	68	6/1
Sam Houston State University	Huntsville	SM	B,M,D	Pub	F,S	C	14,995		25	12	5	2	1		46	30	6	1		40	33	9	1						8/1
Schreiner University	Kerrville	R	A,B,M	Pri	F,S	C	1,182			14	59	23	4		53	38	7	2		47	41	11	1		64	31	4	1	8/1
Southern Methodist University	Dallas	U	B,M,D	Pri	F,S	C	6,487	30			1	36	62						690	1	10	42	47						1/15
Southwestern Adventist University	Keene	R	A,B,M	Pri	No	C	875																						8/15
Southwestern University	Georgetown	SU	B	Pri	F,S	C	1,489	26		1	27	51	21						600	4	44	43	9						2/1
St. Edward's University	Austin	U	B,M	Pri	No	C	4,056	25		1	36	52	11						570	9	58	30	3						5/1
St. Mary's University	San Antonio	SU	B,M,D	Pri	F,S	C	2,268	22		3	56	35	6		9	54	34	3	560	13	54	29	4	510	48	39	12	1	Open
Stephen F. Austin State University	Nacogdoches	SM	B,M,D	Pub	F,S	C	11,269	20	52	26	16	4	2	470	62	29	8	1	490	55	35	10	1	460	67	28	5	1	Open
Sul Ross State University	Alpine	R	B,M	Pub	No	C	1,359		2	53	39	5	1		85	13	2			76	21	3			89	11			Open
Tarleton State University	Stephenville	SM	A,B,M,D	Pub	F,S	C	10,750	20		21	57	20	1	470	65	29	6		480	57	35	7		460	71	26	3		8/1
Texas A&M University at College Station	College Station	U	B,M,D		F,S	C	50,747	27		1	18	55	26	617	5	32	50	14	629	4	30	45	21	617	26	43	26	5	12/1
Texas A&M University at Commerce	Commerce	SM	B,M,D	Pub	F,S	C	5,185	21																					8/15
Texas A&M University at Kingsville	Kingsville	SM	B,M,D	Pub	F,S	C		20						470	67	26	6	2	485	56	32	11	1	435	78	19	3		Open
Texas Christian University	Fort Worth	SU	B,M,D	Pri	F,S	C	8,891																						2/15
Texas Lutheran University	Seguin	SM	B,M	Pri	F,S	C	1,283	21		15	58	23	4						530	31	52	14	3						8/1
Texas Southern University	Houston	U	B,M,D	Pub	F,S	C	7,021	17	93	5	2			400	90	9	1		420	86	13	1		400	92	8			8/15
Texas State University	San Marcos	SU	B,M,D	Pub	F,S	C	34,244	23		9	57	31	3						554	13	64	21	2	480	56	36	7	1	3/1
Texas Tech University	Lubbock	U	B,M,D	Pub	F,S	C	29,963	24		1	44	46	9	510					570	7	56	32	5	490					8/1
Texas Wesleyan University	Fort Worth	U	B,M,D	Pri	F,S	C	1,909	23		3	61	30	6	510	37	55	7	1	527	43	50	7		533	66	25	6	3	Open
Texas Woman's University	Denton	U	B,M,D	Pub	F,S	PW	8,668																						7/15
The University of Texas at Austin	Austin	U	B,M,D	Pub	F,S	C	39,955	29		1	11	37	51	620	9	28	40	22	655	6	24	37	34	615	11	30	38	21	12/1
The University of Texas at San Antonio	San Antonio	SU	B,M,D	Pub	F,S	C		23		11	55	32	4	505	45	40	14	2	520	37	46	15	2	480	56	35	7		6/1
Trinity University	San Antonio	U	B,M	Pri	F,S	C	2,294	30			1	44	55						659		16	53	31						2/1
University of Dallas	Irving	U	B,M,D	Pri	No	C		27			18	48	33	590					575	3	46	38	13	570					8/1
University of Houston	Houston	U	B,M,D	Pub	F,S	C	35,871	25		2	34	51	13		20	48	26	6	606	4	46	45	5						6/30
University of Houston-Downtown	Houston	U	B,M	Pub	F,S	C		19	1	32	63	4		440	80	18			465	70	27	3							8/1
University of Mary Hardin-Baylor	Belton	SM	B,M,D	Pri	No	C	3,278			12	51	32	5		17	51	29	3		19	60	20	1						Open
University of North Texas	Denton	SU	B,M,D	Pub	F,S	C	31,171	24		6	46	40	8							11	55	2	7						8/1
University of St. Thomas - Houston	Houston	U	B,M,D	Pri	No	C	1,814	24			51	37	11						575	6	58	29	6						5/1
University of Texas at Arlington	Arlington	U	B,M,D	Pub	F,S	C		23		7	42	42	9	520	32	41	22	4	550	21	43	29	7	500	42	40	16	2	6/1
University of Texas at Dallas	Richardson	SU	B,M,D	Pub	F,S	C	17,351	29			5	47	48	650	2	22	51	25	670	1	16	46	37						7/1
University of Texas at El Paso	El Paso	U	B,M,D	Pub	F,S	C	15,806																						7/31
University of Texas Rio Grande Valley	Edinburg	SM	B,M,D	Pub	F,S	C	24,433	19		31	60	8		449	77	20	4		454	73	24	3		429	86	13	1		8/8
University of the Incarnate Word	San Antonio	U	A,B,M,D	Pri	F,S	C	6,445	20		24	54	20	1	470	61	31	8		480	55	36	7	1	460	69	25	5		Open
Wayland Baptist University	Plainview	SM	A,B,M,D	Pri	F,S	C	3,776	20	2	31	43	21	3						500	47	43	9	1						Open
West Texas A&M University	Canyon	SM	B,M,D	Pub	F,S	C	6,908	21	49	28	15	5	2																Open
Wiley College	Marshall	SM	B		No		741																						9/3
Utah																													
Brigham Young University	Provo	SU	B,M,D	Pri	No	C	30,979	30			6	46	48						650	2	20	52	25						12/15
Southern Utah University	Cedar City	SM	A,B,M	Pub	F,S	C		23		7	46	41	6	515	41	39	16	3	505	49	34	15	3	495	53	36	10		5/1
The University of Utah	Salt Lake City	U	B,M,D	Pub	F,S	C	23,789	25		4	34	42	20						610										4/1
Utah State University	Logan	SM	A,B,M,D	Pub	F,S	C	24,838	24		9	39	38	14	559	26	46	15	13	569	18	42	33	7						Open
Weber State University	Ogden	U	A,B,M	Pub	F,S	C	25,318	21		23	49	23	4																8/28
Westminster College	Salt Lake City	U	B,M	Pri	No	C	2,127	24		1	42	44	12	540	22	45	28	4	540	21	48	24	4						8/15
Vermont																													
Bennington College	Bennington	SM	B,M	Pri	No	C	688	29	5		23	23	50	690		13	46	41	610	2	38	48	13	660	2	21	51	27	1/3
Castleton University	Castleton	R	A,B,M	Pub	No	C	1,985								60	31	8	1		56	34	9	1		64	28	7	1	Open
Champlain College	Burlington	U	A,B,M	Pri	No	C	2,211	26		10	28	41	21						581	12	46	35	7					1	Open

College of St Joseph	Rutland	SM	A,B,M	Pri	No	C	256	17	100					417	25	75			427	100				435	25	75			Open
Goddard College	Plainfield	R	B,M	Pri	No	C	209																						Open
Green Mountain College	Poultney	SM	B,M	Pri	No	C	573																						Open
Johnson State College	Johnson	SM	A,B,M	Pub	No	C	1,540	20						500					500										Open
Lyndon State College	Lyndonville	SM	A,B,M	Pub	No	C	1,430																						Open
Marlboro College	Marlboro	R	B,M	Pri	No	C	192	25		35	29	29	7	670	8	25	17	50	555	17	58	17	8	620	8	17	67	8	1/15
Middlebury College	Middlebury	SM	B,M,D	Pri	No	C	2,532	32			2	18	81						704		6	37	57					8	1/15
Norwich University	Northfield	R	A,B	Pri	No	C	1,903	22	40	28	20	7	5																Open
Saint Michael's College	Colchester	SU	B,M	Pri	No	C	1,997	27						600	5	45	42	9	585	6	53	37	4	580	6	51	39	4	2/1
Southern Vermont College	Bennington	SM	A,B	Pri	No	C	532	19	5	2	1	1		450	78	19	2	1	450	76	24	1			78	19	1		Open
Sterling College	Craftsbury Common	R	B	Pri	No	C	105	22						555					580					590					2/15
University of Vermont	Burlington	SU	B,M,D		F,S	C	11,159	28			11	55	34						623	2	32	53	13						1/15
Vermont Technical College	Randolph Center	R	A,B	Pub	No	C	1,356																						Open

Virginia

Averett University	Danville	SU	A,B	Pri	F,S	C	859	17		32	52	16		480	58	35	6	1	460	71	26	3		430	73	24	3		7/15
Bluefield College	Bluefield	SM	B	Pri	F,S	C	776	21	57	20	13	3	7																8/31
Bridgewater College	Bridgewater	SM	B,M	Pri	No	C	1,882	22		20	504	29	5						524	34	50	14	2						5/1
Christendom College	Front Royal	R	A,B,M		No	C	433	25	3	28	50	12	7	632	5	33	33	29	570	20	46	24	10	616	11	24	43	22	3/1
Christopher Newport University	Newport News	SU	B,M	Pub	F,S	C	4,930	26		1	24	60	15						590	4	47	44	5						2/1
College of William & Mary	Williamsburg	SM	B,M,D	Pub	F,S	C	6,248	31			3	23	74	690	2	14	34	49	670	2	15	46	37	660	4	17	44	34	1/1
Eastern Mennonite University	Harrisonburg	SM	A,B,M	Pri	No	C	1,221	22		6	16	9	4	505	41	26	13	1	503	43	25	11	2						Open
Emory and Henry College	Emory	R	B,M	Pri	F,S	C	1,211								53	34	11	2		43	42	14	1		55	35	9	1	4/15
Ferrum College	Ferrum	R	B	Pri	F,S	C	1,240																						Open
George Mason University	Fairfax	SU	B,M,D	Pub	F,S	C	19,702	25	4	30	37	15	14	560	15	52	28	6	570	12	49	34	5						1/15
Hampden-Sydney College	Hampden-Sydney	R	B	Pri	F	PM	1,027	25						587	14	42	36	9	571	16	47	32	5						3/1
Hampton University	Hampton	SU	A,B,M,D	Pri	F,S	C	3,836	22			68	28	4	535	31	54	14	1	518	33	57	9	1						3/1
Hollins University	Roanoke	SU	B,M	Pri	No	PW		26		3	31	50	16	630					560	8	61	27	4						2/1
James Madison University	Harrisonburg	SM	B,M,D	Pub	F,S	C	18,107							570	13	52	31	4	580	10	47	39	4	565	14	51	31	4	1/15
Liberty University	Lynchburg	SU	A,B,M,D		No	C	6,330																						Open
Longwood University	Farmville	SM	B,M	Pub	F,S	C	4,375	21						500	43	44	10	1	500	44	45	9							3/1
Mary Baldwin University	Staunton	SM	B,M,D	Pri	No	PW	1,310	23		12	49	29	10						522	41	41	13	5						Open
Marymount University	Arlington	SU	B,M,D	Pri	No	C	2,323	22		13	52	25	10						512	45	41	13	1						Open
Norfolk State University	Norfolk	U	A,B,M,D	Pub	F,S	C	5,337	18	81	13	6																		5/31
Old Dominion University	Norfolk	U	B,M,D	Pub	F,S	C	19,793	21		17	49	30	4						530	30	49	19	1						2/1
Radford University	Radford	SM	B,M,D	Pub	F,S	C	8,453	20		25	54	19	2						510	43	49	8							2/1
Randolph College	Lynchburg	SU	B,M	Pri	No	C		22		14	55	23	7						520	38	44	16	2						11/15
Randolph-Macon College	Ashland	SU	B	Pri	F,S	C	1,446	24		2	39	45	13						550	16	55	25	4	500					3/1
Roanoke College	Salem	SU	B	Pri	F,S	C	1,992	24		4	37	49	9						558	16	55	25	4						3/15
Shenandoah University	Winchester	SM	B,M,D	Pri	No	C	2,099	23		6	50	34	10	560	19	48	29	4	542	24	54	20	2						Open
University of Lynchburg	Lynchburg	SU	B,M,D	Pri	F,S	C	2,079	22		13	59	25	3	503	51	35	14		534	30	51	18	2	476	56	32	8	3	Open
The University of Virginia's College at Wise	Wise	SM	B	Pub	F,S	C	1,892	20	58	24	11	4	3																8/15
University of Mary Washington	Fredericksburg	SU	B,M	Pub	No	C	4,515	25	7	24	34	18	17	570	10	42	37	10	560	14	47	34	4	560	12	45	37	6	2/1
University of Richmond	University of Richmond	SU	B,M,D	Pri	F,S	C	3,036	31			2	28	70						680		15	46	39						1/15
University of Virginia	Charlottesville	SU	B,M,D	Pub	F,S	C	16,331	32			4	21	75						690	1	9	38	52						1/1
Virginia Commonwealth University	Richmond	U	B,M,D	Pub	F,S	C	24,212	24		4	42	39	15	590		44		9	560		53	27	5	530	37	41	18	3	1/15
Virginia Military Institute	Lexington	SM	B	Pub	No	C	1,713	26						580	11	47	35	7	580	10	48	39	5	550	24	48	26	1	2/1
Virginia Polytechnic Institute and State University	Blacksburg	R	B,M,D	Pub	F,S	C								590	10	42	40	9	620	5	32	44	18	580	12	44	37	6	1/15
Virginia State University	Petersburg	SU	B,M		F,S	C	3,600																					6	1/15
Virginia Union University	Richmond	U	B,M,D		F,S	C	1,260																					6	1/15
Virginia Wesleyan University	Norfolk	SU	B	Pri	F,S	C		20		27	45	23	4	480	59	31	8	2	475	64	25	9	1	480	70	24	6		Open
Washington and Lee University	Lexington	SM	B,M,D	Pri	F,S	C	1,830	32				12	88	690		5	47	47	690		2	49	48	683		5	55	40	1/1

Washington

Central Washington University	Ellensburg	SM	B,M	Pub	No	C	11,047	21	1	20	52	24	3	530	33	47	18	2	523	34	52	12	2	466	66	28	5	1	4/1
City University of Seattle	Seattle	U	A,B,M,D	Pri	No	C	1,470																						Open
Cornish College of the Arts	Seattle	U	B	Pri	No	C	724																						8/15
Eastern Washington University	Cheney	SM	B,M	Pub	F,S	C		20						480	57	32	9	2	485	55	33	11	1	455	67	27	5		5/15
Gonzaga University	Spokane	U	B,M,D	Pri	No	C	5,160	28			7	59	34						628	1	29	55	15						2/1
Heritage University	Toppenish	R	A,B,M	Pri	No	C	834																						9/1
Northwest University	Kirkland	SU	A,B,M,D	Pri	No	C	1,057																						8/15
Pacific Lutheran University	Tacoma	SU	B,M,D	Pri	No	C	2,783	25		6	30	48	16	560	27	41	26	6	550	25	42	28	5	530	34	46	18	2	Open
Saint Martin's University	Lacey	SU	B,M	Pri	No	C	1,281	21		20	53	21	6						535	32	46	20	2						7/31
Seattle Pacific University	Seattle	U	B,M,D	Pri	No	C	3,202	25		2	29	54	15	560	18	44	32	6	560	21	44	29	6		23				3/1
Seattle University	Seattle	U	B,M,D	Pri	No	C	4,780	27			15	58	27	590	11	43	36	9	590	11	42	39	8	580	14	45	32	10	1/15
The Evergreen State College	Olympia	SM	B,M	Pub	No	C	3,787	23	1	12	37	40	10	545	32	35	27	6	495	49	37	13	1	509	41	43	14	2	2/1
University of Puget Sound	Tacoma	U	B,M,D	Pri	F,S	C	2,476	28		1	13	53	33						625	5	36	42	17						1/15
University of Washington	Seattle	U	B,M,D	Pub	F,S	C		30		2	9	41	49						665	3	19	40	38						11/15
Walla Walla University	College Place	SM	A,B,M	Pri	No	C		24	8	25	40	20	6	530	33	40	20	6	535	37	37	23	3	510	42	40	17	1	Open

NAME OF SCHOOL	TOWN	ENVIRONMENT U-Urban R-Rural SU-Suburban SM-Small Town	DEGREES AWARDED A-Associate B-Bachelor M-Master D-Doctorate	CONTROL Pri-Private, Pub-Public	FRATERNITIES AND SORORITIES F-Fraternities S-Sororities F, S-Both No-Neither	STUDENTS: C-Coed M-Men W-Women PM-Primarily Men PW-Primarily Women	UNDERGRADUATE ENROLLMENT FALL 2017	TEST SCORES: ACT Median	ACT Below 21	ACT 21-23	ACT 24-26	ACT 27-28	ACT Above 28	SAT CRITICAL READING Median	SAT CR Below 500	SAT CR 500-599	SAT CR 600-700	SAT CR Above 700	SAT MATHEMATICS Median	SAT Math Below 500	SAT Math 500-599	SAT Math 600-700	SAT Math Above 700	SAT WRITING Median	SAT Writing Below 500	SAT Writing 500-599	SAT Writing 600-700	SAT Writing Above 700	APPLICATION DEADLINE Month / Day
Washington State University	Pullman	SM	B,M,D		F,S	C	24,904	23		9	44	38	8						560	18	52	26	4						1/31
Western Washington University	Bellingham	SM	B,M	Pub	No	C	14,592	25		3	34	49	14						580	11	51	33	5						1/31
Whitman College	Walla Walla	SM	B	Pri	F,S	C	1,493	30			3	40	57	650	4	19	44	34	650	2	19	53	25	650	1	23	48	28	1/15
Whitworth University	Spokane	SU	B,M	Pri	No	C	2,308	27		6	26	44	23						590	12	41	39	8						3/1
West Virginia																													
Alderson Broaddus University	Philippi	SM	A,B,M	Pri	F,S	C	1,052	21	47	29	19	3	2	470	57	38	5		470	61	32	7		470	69	29	2		8/1
Bethany College	Bethany	R	B,M	Pri	F,S	C	710	19		35	49	16		450	71	24	5	1	470	61	32	6	1	440	81	17	2		8/20
Bluefield State College	Bluefield	SM	A,B	Pub	F,S	C	2,063	18	73	17	8	1	1		55	43	2			57	33	10							Open
Concord University	Athens	SM	A,B,M	Pub	F,S	C	2,142	21						486	58	32	10		482	58	34	7	1		68	23	8	1	Open
Davis & Elkins College	Elkins	SM	A,B	Pri	F	C	805	20		25	55	18	2	463	68	30	2		482	61	36	3							Open
Fairmont State University	Fairmont	SM	A,B,M	Pub	F,S	C		21		18	60	21	1																8/15
Glenville State College	Glenville	R	A,B	Pub	F,S	C	1,891	20	61	24	12	2	1	428	75	20	4	1	438	77	19	4							Open
Marshall University	Huntington	U	A,B,M,D	Pub	F,S	C	9,762			10	55	30	5																Open
Ohio Valley University	Vienna	SU	A,B	Pri	No	C	659	23	75	25	9	3	2																8/15
Salem International University	Salem	R	A,B,M	Pri	F,S	C	568	21	51	29	18	2																	Open
Shepherd University, West Virginia	Shepherdstown	SM	B,M,D	Pub	F,S	C	3,436	21		14	59	25	2	540					520	34	51	15							Open
University of Charleston	Charleston	SM	A,B,M,D	Pri	F,S	C	1,727	22		10	64	24	1	480	61	35	4		490	54	38	8	1						Open
West Liberty University	West Liberty	R	A,B	Pub	F,S	C		21		19	59	20	2																8/1
West Virginia State University	Institute	SU	A,B	Pub	F,S	C		20		28	56	16		462	69	24	7		450	76	19	4							8/10
West Virginia University	Morgantown	SM	B,M,D	Pub	F,S	C	22,350	24		8	48	37	7							23	53	21	2						8/1
West Virginia University Institute of Technology	Montgomery	SM	B	Pub	F,S	C		21		27	51	21																	8/1
West Virginia Wesleyan College	Buckhannon	SM	B,M	Pri	F,S	C	1,327	23	18	19	16	6	4																8/1
Wheeling Jesuit University	Wheeling	SU	B,M,D	Pri	No	C	945	21		15	60	22	3	486	65	26	9		493	50	43	7		440	79	21			Open
Wisconsin																													
Alverno College	Milwaukee	U	A,B,M	Pri	S	W	1,558	19		36	50	13	1																Open
Beloit College	Beloit	SM	B	Pri	F,S	C	1,394	27		2	18	52	28	630	11	34	30	25	620	13	31	43	13						1/15
Cardinal Stritch University	Milwaukee	SU	A,B,M,D		No	C	3,130																						8/1
Carroll University	Waukesha	SU	B,M,D	Pri	F,S	C	3,015	24	17	31	29	13	10																Open
Carthage College	Kenosha	SU	B,M	Pri	F,S	C	2,265																						Open
Concordia University Wisconsin	Mequon	SU	A,B,M,D	Pri	No	C	4,338	22																					8/15
Edgewood College	Madison	SU	B,M,D	Pri	No	C	1,813	23		9	51	36	4																8/14
Lakeland University	Plymouth	R	B,M	Pri	F,S	C	840																						9/1
Lawrence University	Appleton	U	B	Pri	F,S	C		29			13	40	47	624	13	21	40	26	646	5	23	37	35	630	10	25	42	23	1/15
Marian University	Fond du Lac	SM	B,M,D	Pri	S	C	1,553	21		24	53	21	2																Open
Marquette University	Milwaukee	U	B,M,D	Pri	F,S	C	8,334	27			17	58	25						605										12/1
Milwaukee Institute of Art & Design	Milwaukee	U	B	Pri	No	C	628																						12/1
Milwaukee School of Engineering	Milwaukee	U	B,M	Pri	F,S	C	2,712	27			12	62	26						649		24	44	32						Open
Mount Mary University	Milwaukee	U	B,M,D	Pri	No	PW	816	19		31	57	11	1																Open
Northland College	Ashland	SM	B		No	C	739	24																					Open
Ripon College	Ripon	SM	B	Pri	F,S	C	793	23		9	46	36	9	586	12	38	44	6	591	19	49	13	19						8/1
Silver Lake College of the Holy Family	Manitowoc	R	B,M	Pri	No	C	357	17	2	59	28	9	2																Open
St. Norbert College	De Pere	SU	B,M	Pri	F,S	C	2,102	25		1	43	47	9																Open
University of Wisconsin-Eau Claire	Eau Claire	U	A,B,M,D	Pub	F,S	C	9,981	24		2	48	44	6			33		67		33	33	33							Open
University of Wisconsin-Green Bay	Green Bay	SU	A,B,M	Pub	F,S	C	6,758	22		7	57	31	5																Open
University of Wisconsin-La Crosse	La Crosse	SM	A,B,M,D	Pub	F,S	C	9,699	25			39	54	7						615		48	43	9						Open
University of Wisconsin-Madison	Madison	U	B,M,D	Pub	F,S	C	31,710	29			5	52	43						706		8	34	69						2/1
University of Wisconsin-Milwaukee	Milwaukee	U	B,M,D	Pub	F,S	C	21,375	22		8	56	32	4																7/1
University of Wisconsin-Oshkosh	Oshkosh	U	A,B,M	Pub	F,S	C		22		4	63	31	2																7/1
University of Wisconsin-Parkside	Kenosha	SU	A,B,M	Pub	F,S	C	4,300	21		17	60	20	3																8/1
University of Wisconsin-Platteville	Platteville	SM	A,B,M	Pub	F,S	C	7,793	25		6	51	38	5	540	50			50	318		50	50							Open
University of Wisconsin-River Falls	River Falls	SU	B,M	Pub	F,S	C	390																						Open
University of Wisconsin-Stevens Point	Stevens Point	SM	A,B,M,D	Pub	F,S	C	9,118	23	27	37	23	8	5	546	23	55	14	9	536	32	41	23	5	528	46	32	23		Open
University of Wisconsin-Stout	Menomonie	R	B,M,D	Pub	F,S	C	8,194	22		9	59	29	3																Open
University of Wisconsin-Superior	Superior	U	A,B,M	Pub	No	C	2,362			15	64	19	2																8/1

University of Wisconsin-Whitewater	Whitewater	SM	A,B,M,D	Pub	F,S	C	10,584	23																					5/1
Viterbo University	La Crosse	SU	A,B,M	Pri	No	C	2,105	23	24	34	29	8	5																8/15
Wisconsin Lutheran College	Milwaukee	SU	B,M	Pri	No	C	740																						8/15
Wyoming																													
University of Wyoming	Laramie	SM	B,M,D		F,S	C	10,045	24		4	37	47	11	535	34	41	22	3	553	27	37	31	5						8/10

IN-STATE COST RANGES DIRECTORY

The breakdown of in-state tuition, room, and board costs for the 2017-2018 academic year is arranged from least expensive to most expensive. Within each range are lists of schools that don't charge for tuition or room and board, and those that do. Listings that say (no R & B) means complete information was not provided by the school at press time. For any late additions, please refer to the school profile on our website, *barronspac.com.*

Colleges without Tuition, Room, and Board

Berea College, KY
College of the Ozarks, MO
United States Air Force Academy, CO
United States Coast Guard Academy, CT
United States Merchant Marine Academy, NY
United States Military Academy at West Point, NY
United States Naval Academy, MD

Colleges with Room and Board Only

Alice Lloyd College, KY
Curtis Institute of Music, PA
Metropolitan College of New York, NY

$4000-$5999

Colleges with Tuition, Room, and Board

Augusta University, GA (no R & B)
Bluefield State College, WV (no R & B)
City University of New York/Lehman College, NY (no R & B)

$6000-$7999

Colleges with Tuition, Room, and Board

Charter Oak State College, CT (no R & B)
City University of New York/Brooklyn College, NY
City University of New York/John Jay College of Criminal Justice, NY (no R & B)
City University of New York/Medgar Evers College, NY
City University of New York/York College, NY (no R & B)
Indiana University East, IN (no R & B)
Indiana University Kokomo, IN (no R & B)
Indiana University Northwest, IN (no R & B)
Louisiana State University in Shreveport, LA (no R & B)
McNeese State University, LA (no R & B)
Metropolitan State University, MN (no R & B)
Metropolitan State University of Denver, CO (no R & B)
New York City College of Technology, NY (no R & B)
Ohio State University at Lima, OH (no R & B)
Ohio State University at Marion, OH (no R & B)
Oklahoma Panhandle State University, OK
Thomas Edison State University, NJ (no R & B)
University of Houston-Downtown, TX
University of Maine at Augusta, ME (no R & B)
Webb Institute, NY

$8000-$9999

Colleges with Tuition, Room, and Board

Middle Tennessee State University, TN
North Carolina Central University, NC
Northeastern State University, OK
Southern University at New Orleans, LA
State University of New York/Empire State College, NY (no R & B)
The University of Montana Western, MT
Union Institute & University, OH (no R & B)
University of Rio Grande & Rio Grande Community College, OH
Wilmington University, DE (no R & B)

$10,000-$11,999

Colleges with Tuition, Room, and Board

Amridge University, AL (no R & B)
Ashford University, CA
Boricua College, NY (no R & B)
Brigham Young University/Hawaii, HI
Cabarrus College of Health Sciences, NC (no R & B)
Cameron University, OK
Escuela de Artes Plasticas de Puerto Rico, PR (no R & B)
Franklin University, OH (no R & B)
Louisiana Tech University, LA
Montana State University-Northern, MT
New Mexico Highlands University, NM
Pontifical Catholic University of Puerto Rico, PR (no R & B)
Rust College, MS
Southeastern Oklahoma State University, OK
St. Cloud State University, MN
Texas A&M University at Commerce, TX
University of Science and Arts of Oklahoma, OK

$12,000-$13,999

Colleges with Tuition, Room, and Board

Bayamon Central University, PR (no R & B)
Brigham Young University, UT
Caribbean University, PR
Carlos Albizu University, FL (no R & B)
Conservatory of Music of Puerto Rico, PR (no R & B)
Dakota State University, SD
Delta State University, MS
Dickinson State University, ND
East Central University, OK
Eastern New Mexico University, NM
Fort Hays State University, KS
Georgia Southwestern State University, GA
Granite State College, NH
Idaho State University, ID
Midwestern State University, TX
Minot State University, ND
Mississippi State University, MS
Mississippi Valley State University, MS
Missouri Southern State University, MO
Montana State University Billings, MT
NewSchool of Architecture & Design, CA
North Carolina A&T State University, NC
Northeastern Illinois University, IL
Northwestern Oklahoma State University, OK
Pittsburg State University, KS
Sinte Gleska University, SD
Southern Utah University, UT
Southwestern Oklahoma State University, OK
University of Puerto Rico, at Arecibo, PR (no R & B)
University of Arkansas at Monticello, AR
University of Arkansas at Pine Bluff, AR
University of Massachusetts Boston, MA (no R & B)
University of Michigan/Dearborn, MI (no R & B)
University of New Orleans, LA
University of Puerto Rico, at Bayamon, PR (no R & B)
University of Puerto Rico, at Mayaguez, PR
University of Puerto Rico-Rio Piedras campus, PR (no R & B)
University of Southern Mississippi, MS
University of Wisconsin-Superior, WI
University of Wisconsin-Whitewater, WI
Utah State University, UT
Valley City State University, ND
West Texas A&M University, TX
Western Carolina University, NC

$14,000-$15,999

Colleges with Tuition, Room, and Board

Adams State University, CO
Alcorn State University, MS
Angelo State University, TX
Appalachian State University, NC
Armstrong State University, GA
Auburn University at Montgomery, AL
Blue Mountain College, MS
Cambridge College, MA
Chadron State College, NE
Columbus State University, GA
Concord University, WV
Concordia College - Alabama, AL
Coppin State University, MD
Edinboro University, PA
Elizabeth City State University, NC
Emporia State University, KS
Fairmont State University, WV
Florida Agricultural and Mechanical University, FL
Florida Gulf Coast University, FL
Grambling State University, LA
Harris-Stowe State University, MO
Henderson State University, AR
Jackson State University, MS
Jacksonville State University, AL
Kentucky State University, KY
Langston University, OK
Lewis-Clark State College, ID
Lincoln University, MO
Missouri State University, MO
Montana State University, MT
Montana Tech of the University of Montana, MT
New Mexico Institute of Mining and Technology, NM
New Mexico State University, NM
Nicholls State University, LA
Northern State University, SD
Oglala Lakota College, SD
Ohio State University at Mansfield, OH
Peru State College, NE
Purdue University Northwest, IN
South Dakota State University, SD
Sul Ross State University, TX
Tarleton State University, TX
Tennessee State University, TN
Texas Woman's University, TX
The University of Tennessee at Martin, TN
University of Central Arkansas, AR
University of Central Oklahoma, OK
University of Louisiana at Lafayette, LA
University of Louisiana at Monroe, LA
University of Maine at Fort Kent, ME
University of Montana, MT
University of New Hampshire - Manchester, NH (no R & B)
University of North Alabama, AL
University of North Carolina at Asheville, NC
University of North Carolina at Greensboro, NC
University of North Carolina at Pembroke, NC
University of North Florida, FL
University of Puerto Rico, at Humacao, PR (no R & B)
University of South Florida St. Petersburg, FL
University of Texas Rio Grande Valley, TX
University of West Florida, FL
University of Wisconsin-Green Bay, WI
University of Wisconsin-La Crosse, WI
University of Wisconsin-Oshkosh, WI
University of Wisconsin-Parkside, WI
University of Wisconsin-Platteville, WI
University of Wisconsin-River Falls, WI
University of Wisconsin-Stevens Point, WI
University of Wyoming, WY
Valdosta State University, GA
Washburn University, KS
Weber State University, UT

$16,000-$17,999

Colleges with Tuition, Room, and Board

Alabama State University, AL
American University of Puerto Rico, PR (no R & B)
Arkansas State University, AR
Arkansas Tech University, AR
Austin Peay State University, TN
Bemidji State University, MN
Black Hills State University, SD
Boise State University, ID
California State University, Fresno, CA
California State University, Los Angeles, CA
California State University, Northridge, CA
Central Washington University, WA
East Carolina University, NC
Eastern Kentucky University, KY
Eastern Oregon University, OR
Eastern Washington University, WA
Embry-Riddle Aeronautical University - Worldwide, FL
Fayetteville State University, NC
Florida State University, FL
Fort Valley State University, GA
Frostburg State University, MD
Georgia Southern University, GA
Glenville State College, WV
Goddard College, VT
Indiana University South Bend, IN
Indiana University Southeast, IN
Kansas State University, KS
Lane College, TN
LeMoyne-Owen College, TN
Livingstone College, NC
Marylhurst University, OR (no R & B)
Mercy College of Health Sciences, IA (no R & B)
Miles College, AL
Minnesota State University, Mankato, MN
Mississippi University for Women, MS
Missouri Western State University, MO
Morgan State University, MD
Murray State University, KY
National University, CA
New College of Florida, FL
North Dakota State University, ND
Northern Kentucky University, KY
Northwestern State University of Louisiana, LA
Ohio State University at Newark, OH
Oklahoma State University, OK
Peirce College, PA
Savannah State University, GA
Shawnee State University, OH
Shepherd University, West Virginia, WV
Southeast Missouri State University, MO
Southeastern Louisiana University, LA
Southern University and A&M College, LA
Southwest Minnesota State University, MN
State University of New York/College at Old Westbury, NY
State University of New York/Maritime College, NY
Tennessee Technological University, TN
Texas A&M University at Corpus Christi, TX

Texas A&M University at Kingsville, TX
The Evergreen State College, WA
The University of Tennessee at Chattanooga, TN
Tougaloo College, MS
Troy University, AL
Truman State University, MO
Universidad Adventista de las Antillas, PR (no R & B)
Universidad del Turabo, PR (no R & B)
Universidad Metropolitana, PR (no R & B)
University of Alaska Anchorage, AK
University of Alaska Fairbanks, AK
University of Alaska Southeast, AK
University of Central Florida, FL
University of Florida, FL
University of Idaho, ID
University of Maine at Presque Isle, ME
University of Nebraska - Kearney, NE
University of Nebraska - Omaha, NE
University of Nevada, Las Vegas, NV
University of New Mexico, NM
University of North Carolina at Charlotte, NC
University of North Carolina Wilmington, NC
University of North Dakota, ND
University of North Georgia, GA
University of Northern Iowa, IA
University of South Alabama, AL
University of South Dakota, SD
University of South Florida/Tampa, FL
University of Southern Indiana, IN
University of the Sacred Heart, PR
University of West Alabama, AL
University of West Georgia, GA
University of Wisconsin-Eau Claire, WI
West Liberty University, WV
Western Kentucky University, KY
Western New Mexico University, NM
Wichita State University, KS
Wright State University, OH
Youngstown State University, OH

$18,000-$19,999

Colleges with Tuition, Room, and Board

Alabama A&M University, AL
Albany State University, GA
Alfred State College, NY
Allen University, SC
Baker College of Flint, MI
Ball State University, IN
Bloomsburg University of Pennsylvania, PA
Bowie State University, MD
Bowling Green State University, OH
California State University, Chico, CA
California State University, Dominguez Hills, CA
California State University, Long Beach, CA
California State University, Sacramento, CA
California State University, Stanislaus, CA
Central State University, OH
Clayton State University, GA
Colorado Mesa University, CO
Delaware State University, DE
East Stroudsburg University, PA
East Tennessee State University, TN
Eastern Michigan University, MI
Elizabethtown College School of Continuing and Professional Studies, PA (no R & B)
Fashion Institute of Technology/State University of New York, NY
Florida Atlantic University, FL
Francis Marion University, SC
George Mason University, VA
Golden Gate University, CA (no R & B)
Heritage University, WA (no R & B)
Huston-Tillotson University, TX
Indiana University-Purdue University Fort Wayne, IN
Indiana University-Purdue University Indianapolis, IN
Inter-American University of Puerto Rico Ponce, PR (no R & B)
Inter-American University of Puerto Rico-Arecibo Campus, PR (no R & B)
Inter-American University of Puerto Rico-Barranquitas, PR (no R & B)
Inter-American University of Puerto Rico-Bayamon, PR (no R & B)
Inter-American University of Puerto Rico-Fajardo Campus, PR (no R & B)
Iowa State University, IA
James Madison University, VA
Kennesaw State University, GA
Kutztown University of Pennsylvania, PA
Lake Superior State University, MI
Lamar University, TX
Louisiana State University and A&M College, LA
Marshall University, WV
Mayville State University, ND
Missouri University of Science and Technology, MO
Morehead State University, KY
Morris College, SC
Norfolk State University, VA
Northwest Missouri State University, MO
Oregon Institute of Technology, OR
Paine College, GA
Portland State University, OR
Radford University, VA
Rhode Island College, RI
Saginaw Valley State University, MI
SAGU American Indian College, AZ
Sam Houston State University, TX
San Francisco State University, CA
South Dakota School of Mines and Technology, SD
Southern Oregon University, OR
State University of New York/Plattsburgh, NY
Stephen F. Austin State University, TX
Texas Southern University, TX
Texas State University, TX
The University of Memphis, TN
The University of Utah, UT
The University of Virginia's College at Wise, VA
University of Arkansas at Fayetteville, AR
University of Arkansas at Little Rock, AR
University of Central Missouri, MO
University of Hawaii at Hilo, HI
University of Iowa, IA
University of Louisville, KY
University of Maine at Farmington, ME
University of Michigan/Flint, MI
University of Minnesota/Crookston, MN
University of Mississippi, MS
University of Missouri-Kansas City, MO
University of Missouri-St. Louis, MO
University of Mount Olive, NC
University of Nebraska - Lincoln, NE
University of Nevada, Reno, NV
University of Northern Colorado, CO
University of Oklahoma, OK
University of South Carolina Aiken, SC
University of South Carolina Upstate, SC
University of Southern Maine, ME
University of Texas at Arlington, TX
University of Toledo, OH
University of Wisconsin-Stout, WI
Virginia State University, VA
Voorhees College, SC
West Chester University of Pennsylvania, PA
West Virginia State University, WV
West Virginia University, WV
West Virginia University Institute of Technology, WV
Western Oregon University, OR
Western State Colorado University, CO
Western Washington University, WA
Wilberforce University, OH
Wiley College, TX
Winona State University, MN
Winston-Salem State University, NC

$20,000-$21,999

Colleges with Tuition, Room, and Board

Arizona State University at the West Campus, AZ
Arkansas Baptist College, AR
Bellevue University, NE
Boston Architectural College, MA (no R & B)
California State Polytechnic University, Pomona, CA
California State University, East Bay, CA
California State University, Fullerton, CA
California State University, San Bernardino, CA
California State University, San Marcos, CA
California University of Pennsylvania, PA
Castleton University, VT
Central Michigan University, MI
Cheyney University of Pennsylvania, PA
City University of New York/Baruch College, NY
City University of New York/City College, NY
City University of New York/Queens College, NY
Clarion University of Pennsylvania, PA
Coastal Carolina University, SC
Colorado State University-Pueblo, CO
Colorado Technical University, CO
Cox College, MO
Dillard University, LA
Eastern Illinois University, IL
Farmingdale State College, NY
Ferris State University, MI
Fitchburg State University, MA
Florida International University, FL
Fort Lewis College, CO
Framingham State University, MA
Georgia College & State University, GA
Hodges University, FL (no R & B)
Humboldt State University, CA
Indiana University Bloomington, IN
Inter-American University of Puerto Rico-Aguadilla Campus, PR (no R & B)
Inter-American University of Puerto Rico-Metropolitan Campus, PR (no R & B)
Inter-American University of Puerto Rico-San Germán, PR (no R & B)
Jarvis Christian College, TX
Kent State University, OH
Lincoln University, PA
Lock Haven University of Pennsylvania, PA
Louisiana College, LA
Lyndon State College, VT
Martin University, IN
Massachusetts College of Liberal Arts, MA
Massachusetts Maritime Academy, MA
Minnesota State University, Moorhead, MN
New Jersey City University, NJ
Northern Arizona University, AZ
Northern Illinois University, IL
Northern Michigan University, MI
Oakland University, MI
Old Dominion University, VA
Philander Smith College, AR
Purdue University/West Lafayette, IN
Salem International University, WV
Salisbury University, MD
Slippery Rock University of Pennsylvania, PA
South Carolina State University, SC
Southern Arkansas University, AR
Southern Connecticut State University, CT
Southern Illinois University Edwardsville, IL
State University of New York /College of Agriculture and Tech at Cobleskill, NY
State University of New York at Geneseo, NY
State University of New York at New Paltz, NY
State University of New York at Purchase College, NY
State University of New York Polytechnic Institute, NY
State University of New York/Buffalo State, NY
State University of New York/Cortland, NY
State University of New York/Fredonia, NY
State University of New York/Oneonta, NY
State University of New York/Potsdam, NY
Stillman College, AL
Texas A&M University at College Station, TX
Texas Tech University, TX
The Citadel, The Military College of South Carolina, SC
The College at Brockport - State University of New York, NY
The University of Texas at Austin, TX
The University of Texas at San Antonio, TX
Thomas University, GA
Towson University, MD
University of Alabama in Huntsville, AL
University of Colorado Colorado Springs, CO
University of Georgia, GA
University of Holy Cross, LA
University of Houston, TX
University of Kansas, KS
University of Maine, ME
University of Maryland/College Park, MD
University of Maryland/Eastern Shore, MD
University of Minnesota/Duluth, MN
University of Minnesota/Morris, MN
University of Missouri-Columbia, MO
University of Montevallo, AL
University of North Carolina at Chapel Hill, NC
University of North Texas, TX
University of South Carolina at Columbia, SC
University of the District of Columbia, DC
University of Wisconsin-Madison, WI
University of Wisconsin-Milwaukee, WI
Virginia Polytechnic Institute and State University, VA
Western Connecticut State University, CT
Western Illinois University, IL
Western Michigan University, MI
Westfield State University, MA
Worcester State University, MA

$22,000-$23,999

Colleges with Tuition, Room, and Board

Arizona State University at the Polytechnic Campus, AZ
Arizona State University at the Tempe Campus, AZ
Bethune-Cookman University, FL
Bridgewater State University, MA
California Polytechnic State University, CA
California State University, Maritime Academy, CA
California State University, Bakersfield, CA
California State University, Monterey Bay, CA
Calumet College of St. Joseph, IN
Central Connecticut State University, CT
Cleveland State University, OH
Colorado State University, CO
Eastern Connecticut State University, CT
Florida Memorial University, FL
Georgia Institute of Technology, GA
Grand Valley State University, MI
Illinois State University, IL
Indiana State University, IN
Johnson State College, VT
Lee University, TN
Longwood University, VA
Maine Maritime Academy, ME
Monroe College, NY
North Carolina State University, NC
Ohio State University at Columbus, OH
Ohio University, OH
Oregon State University, OR
Park University, MO
Plymouth State University, NH
San Diego State University, CA
San Jose State University, CA
State University of New York Albany, NY
State University of New York at Oswego, NY
State University of New York/The College of Environmental Science and Forestry, NY
State University of New York/University at Buffalo, NY
Stony Brook University/The State University of New York, NY
The University of Akron, OH
The University of Mary, ND
The University of Tennessee at Knoxville, TN
Union College, NE
Universidad Politecnica de Puerto Rico, Hato Rey campus, PR
University of Alabama at Birmingham, AL
University of Cincinnati, OH
University of Colorado Denver, CO
University of Hawaii at Manoa, HI
University of Maine at Machias, ME

University of Mary Washington, VA
University of Maryland/Baltimore County, MD
University of Pittsburgh at Bradford, PA
University of Pittsburgh at Johnstown, PA
University of Texas at Dallas, TX
University of Washington, WA
Virginia Commonwealth University, VA
Washington State University, WA
Wayland Baptist University, TX
Wayne State University, MI
William Carey University, MS
Winthrop University, SC

$24,000-$25,999

Colleges with Tuition, Room, and Board

Arizona State University at the Downtown Phoenix Campus, AZ
Auburn University, AL
Christopher Newport University, VA
City University of Seattle, WA
Claflin University, SC
College of Charleston, SC
College of Staten Island, NY
Davenport University, MI
Gardner-Webb University, NC
Georgia State University, GA
Grace Bible College, MI
Grand Canyon University, AZ
Harding University, AR
Indiana University of Pennsylvania, PA
Johnson C. Smith University, NC
Kean University, NJ
Keene State College, NH
Lindenwood University, MO
Mansfield University of Pennsylvania, PA
Massachusetts College of Art and Design, MA
Michigan State University, MI
Michigan Technological University, MI
Millersville University of Pennsylvania, PA
Mississippi College, MS
Nebraska Methodist College, NE
North Greenville University, SC
Paul Quinn College, TX
Ramapo College of New Jersey, NJ
Rowan University, NJ
Saint Augustine's University, NC
Shaw University, NC
Shippensburg University of Pennsylvania, PA
Southern Illinois University Carbondale, IL
St. Joseph's College, New York/Brooklyn Campus, NY
St. Joseph's College, New York/Long Island Campus, NY
State University of New York at Binghamton, NY
Stockton University, NJ
Talladega College, AL
Temple University, PA
The University of Alabama, AL
The University of Arizona, AZ
University of Illinois at Chicago, IL
University of Kentucky, KY
University of Michigan/Ann Arbor, MI
University of Minnesota/Twin Cities, MN
University of North Carolina School of the Arts, NC
University of Oregon, OR
University of Pittsburgh at Greensburg, PA
University of Sioux Falls, SD
University of the Southwest, NM
Vermont Technical College, VT
Virginia Union University, VA
Wayne State College, NE
William Paterson University of New Jersey, NJ
Williams Baptist College, AR

$26,000-$29,999

Colleges with Tuition, Room, and Board

Alaska Pacific University, AK
Atlantic Union College, MA
Avila University, MO
Belmont Abbey College, NC
Benedict College, SC
Bennett College, NC
Bethel University, TN
Blackburn College, IL
Brescia University, KY
Brewton-Parker College, GA
College of Saint Mary, NE
Colorado School of Mines, CO
Columbia College - Missouri, MO
Concordia University Saint Paul, MN
Converse College, SC
Cumberland University, TN
Edward Waters College, FL
Evangel University, MO
Faulkner University, AL
Flagler College, FL
Freed-Hardeman University, TN
Goodwin College, CT
Greenville College, IL
Grove City College, PA
Hannibal-LaGrange University, MO
Humphreys College, CA
Husson University, ME
Judson College, AL
Kentucky Christian University, KY
Keystone College, PA
Lincoln Memorial University, TN
Lourdes University, OH
Lubbock Christian University, TX
Miami University, OH
Missouri Valley College, MO
Montclair State University, NJ
Mount Aloysius College, PA
Ohio Valley University, WV
Oklahoma Christian University, OK
Penn State Altoona, PA
Penn State Erie,The Behrend College, PA
Pennsylvania College of Technology, PA
Pennsylvania State University - University Park, PA
Prairie View A&M University, TX
Presentation College, SD
Rochester College, MI
Rockhurst University, MO
Rocky Mountain College of Art and Design, CO
Rutgers University - Camden, NJ
Rutgers University - New Brunswick, NJ
Rutgers University - Newark, NJ
Sonoma State University, CA
Southern Adventist University, TN
Southwestern Adventist University, TX
St. Mary's College of Maryland, MD
The College of New Jersey, NJ
Tuskegee University, AL
University of California at Berkeley, CA
University of California at Davis, CA
University of California at Los Angeles, CA
University of California, Santa Cruz, CA
University of Colorado Boulder, CO
University of Connecticut, CT
University of Illinois at Urbana-Champaign, IL
University of Jamestown, ND
University of Maryland University College, MD
University of Massachusetts Amherst, MA
University of Massachusetts Dartmouth, MA
University of Massachusetts Lowell, MA
University of Mobile, AL
University of New Hampshire, NH
University of Pikeville, KY
University of Rhode Island, RI
University of Vermont, VT
University of Virginia, VA
Virginia Military Institute, VA
Warner University, FL
William Penn University, IA
York College of Pennsylvania, PA

$30,000 and over

Colleges with Tuition, Room, and Board

Abilene Christian University, TX
Adelphi University, NY
Adrian College, MI
Adventist University of Health Sciences, FL
Agnes Scott College, GA
Albany College of Pharmacy and Health Sciences, NY
Albert A. List College of Jewish Studies, NY
Albertus Magnus College, CT
Albion College, MI
Albright College, PA
Alderson Broaddus University, WV
Alfred University, NY
Allegheny College, PA
Allen College, IA
Alma College, MI
Alvernia University, PA
Alverno College, WI
American International College, MA
American Jewish University - College of Arts and Sciences, CA
Amherst College, MA
Anderson University, IN
Andrews University, MI
Anna Maria College, MA
Aquinas College, TN
Aquinas College - Michigan, MI
Arcadia University, PA
Art Academy of Cincinnati, OH
Art Institute of Portland, OR
ArtCenter College of Design, CA (no R & B)
Asbury University, KY
Ashland University, OH
Assumption College, MA
Augsburg University, MN
Augustana College, IL
Augustana University, SD
Aurora University, IL
Austin College, TX
Averett University, VA
Azusa Pacific University, CA
Babson College, MA
Baker University, KS
Baldwin Wallace University, OH
Bard College, NY
Bard College at Simon's Rock, MA
Barnard College/Columbia University, NY
Barry University, FL
Barton College, NC
Bates College, ME
Bay Path University, MA
Baylor University, TX
Beacon College, FL
Becker College, MA
Belhaven University, MS
Bellarmine University, KY
Belmont University, TN
Beloit College, WI
Benedictine College, KS
Benedictine University, IL
Benjamin Franklin Institute of Technology, MA
Bennington College, VT
Bentley University, MA
Berkeley College/New Jersey, NJ
Berkeley College/New York City Campus, NY
Berkeley College/White Plains Campus, NY
Berklee College of Music, MA
Berry College, GA
Bethany College, KS
Bethany College, WV
Bethel College, IN
Bethel College, KS
Bethel University, MN
Biola University, CA
Birmingham-Southern College, AL
Bloomfield College, NJ
Bluefield College, VA
Bluffton University, OH
Boston College, MA
Boston University, MA
Bowdoin College, ME
Bradley University, IL
Brandeis University, MA
Brenau University - Women's College, GA (no R & B)
Briar Cliff University, IA
Bridgewater College, VA
Brown University, RI
Bryan College, TN
Bryant University, RI
Bryn Athyn College, PA
Bryn Mawr College, PA
Bucknell University, PA
Buena Vista University, IA
Butler University, IN
Cabrini University, PA
Cairn University, PA
Caldwell University, NJ
California Baptist University, CA
California College of the Arts, CA
California Institute of Technology, CA
California Institute of the Arts, CA
California Lutheran University, CA
Calvin College, MI
Campbell University, NC
Campbellsville University, KY
Canisius College, NY
Capital University, OH
Capitol Technology University, MD
Cardinal Stritch University, WI
Carleton College, MN
Carlow University, PA
Carnegie Mellon University, PA
Carroll College, MT
Carroll University, WI
Carson-Newman University, TN
Carthage College, WI
Case Western Reserve University, OH
Catawba College, NC
Cazenovia College, NY
Cedar Crest College, PA
Cedarville University, OH
Centenary College, NJ
Centenary College of Louisiana, LA
Central College, IA
Central Methodist University, MO
Centre College, KY
Chaminade University of Honolulu, HI
Champlain College, VT
Chapman University, CA
Charleston Southern University, SC
Chatham University, PA
Chestnut Hill College, PA
Chicago State University, IL
Christendom College, VA
Christian Brothers University, TN
City University of New York/Hunter College, NY
Claremont McKenna College, CA
Clark Atlanta University, GA
Clark University, MA
Clarke University, IA
Clarkson College, NE
Clarkson University, NY
Cleveland Institute of Art, OH
Cleveland Institute of Music, OH
Coe College, IA
Cogswell Polytechnical College, CA
Coker College, SC
Colby College, ME
Colby-Sawyer College, NH
Colgate University, NY
College for Creative Studies, MI
College of Art and Design at Lesley University, MA
College of Mount Saint Vincent, NY
College of Saint Benedict, MN
College of Saint Elizabeth, NJ
College of St Joseph, VT
College of St. Scholastica, MN
College of the Atlantic, ME
College of the Holy Cross, MA
College of William & Mary, VA
Colorado Christian University, CO
Colorado College, CO
Columbia College, SC
Columbia College Chicago, IL
Columbia University/ School of General Studies, NY
Columbia University/City of New York, NY
Columbus College of Art and Design, OH
Concordia College - Moorhead, MN
Concordia College - New York, NY
Concordia University, OR
Concordia University Irvine, CA
Concordia University Nebraska, NE
Concordia University Texas, TX
Concordia University Wisconsin, WI
Concordia University, Ann Arbor, MI
Concordia University, Chicago, IL
Connecticut College, CT (no R & B)
Cooper Union for the Advancement of Science and Art, NY
Corban University, OR
Cornell College, IA
Cornell University, NY
Cornerstone University, MI
Cornish College of the Arts, WA
Covenant College, GA
Creighton University, NE
Culver-Stockton College, MO
Curry College, MA
Daemen College, NY
Dakota Wesleyan University, SD
Dallas Baptist University, TX
Dartmouth College, NH
Davidson College, NC
Davis & Elkins College, WV
Defiance College, OH
Delaware Valley University, PA
Denison University, OH
DePaul University, IL
DePauw University, IN
DeSales University, PA
Dickinson College, PA
Doane University, NE
Dominican College, NY
Dominican University, IL
Dominican University of California, CA
Dordt College, IA

Drake University, IA
Drew University/College of Liberal Arts, NJ
Drexel University, PA
Drury University, MO
Duke University, NC
Duquesne University, PA
D'Youville College, NY
Earlham College, IN
East Texas Baptist University, TX
Eastern Mennonite University, VA
Eastern Nazarene College, MA
Eastern University, PA
Eastman School of Music/University of Rochester, NY
Eckerd College, FL
Edgewood College, WI
Elizabethtown College, PA
Elmhurst College, IL
Elmira College, NY
Elms College, MA
Elon University, NC
Embry-Riddle Aeronautical University - Daytona Beach, FL
Embry-Riddle Aeronautical University - Prescott Campus, AZ
Emerson College, MA
Emmanuel College, MA
Emory and Henry College, VA
Emory University, GA
Endicott College, MA
Erskine College, SC
Eugene Lang College of Liberal Arts, NY
Eureka College, IL
Excelsior College, NY
Fairfield University, CT
Fairleigh Dickinson University/College at Florham, NJ
Fairleigh Dickinson University/ Metropolitan Campus, NJ
Felician University, NJ
Ferrum College, VA
Fisk University, TN
Five Towns College, NY
Florida Institute of Technology, FL
Florida Southern College, FL
Fontbonne University, MO
Fordham University, NY
Franciscan University of Steubenville, OH
Franklin and Marshall College, PA
Franklin College, IN
Franklin Pierce University, NH
Franklin W. Olin College of Engineering, MA
Fresno Pacific University, CA
Friends University, KS
Furman University, SC
Gallaudet University, DC
Gannon University, PA
Geneva College, PA
George Fox University, OR
Georgetown College, KY
Georgetown University, DC
Georgian Court University, NJ
Gettysburg College, PA
Goldey-Beacom College, DE
Gonzaga University, WA
Gordon College, MA
Goshen College, IN
Goucher College, MD
Grace College and Seminary, IN
Graceland University, IA
Grand View University, IA
Green Mountain College, VT
Greensboro College, NC
Grinnell College, IA
Guilford College, NC
Gustavus Adolphus College, MN
Gwynedd Mercy University, PA
Hamilton College, NY
Hamline University, MN
Hampden-Sydney College, VA
Hampshire College, MA
Hampton University, VA
Hanover College, IN
Hardin-Simmons University, TX
Hartwick College, NY
Harvard College/Harvard University, MA
Harvey Mudd College, CA
Hastings College, NE
Haverford College, PA
Hawaii Pacific University, HI
Heidelberg University, OH
Hellenic College/Holy Cross Greek Orthodox School of Theology, MA
Hendrix College, AR
High Point University, NC
Hilbert College, NY
Hillsdale College, MI
Hiram College, OH
Hobart and William Smith Colleges, NY
Hofstra University, NY
Hollins University, VA
Holy Family University, PA
Holy Names University, CA
Hood College, MD
Hope College, MI
Hope International University, CA
Houghton College, NY
Houston Baptist University, TX
Howard Payne University, TX
Howard University, DC
Huntingdon College, AL
Huntington University, IN
Illinois College, IL
Illinois Institute of Technology, IL
Illinois Wesleyan University, IL
Immaculata University, PA
Indiana Institute of Technology, IN
Indiana Wesleyan University, IN
Iona College, NY
Iowa Wesleyan University, IA
Ithaca College, NY
Jacksonville University, FL
Jefferson (Philadelphia University + Thomas Jefferson University), PA
John Brown University, AR
John Carroll University, OH
Johns Hopkins University, MD
Johnson & Wales University/Charlotte Campus, NC
Johnson & Wales University/Denver Campus, CO
Johnson & Wales University/North Miami Campus, FL
Johnson & Wales University/Providence Campus, RI
Judson University, IL
Juniata College, PA
Kalamazoo College, MI
Kansas City Art Institute, MO
Kansas Wesleyan University, KS
Keiser University, FL
Kendall College, IL
Kentucky Wesleyan College, KY
Kenyon College, OH
Kettering University, MI
Keuka College, NY
King University, TN
King's College, PA
Knox College, IL
La Roche College, PA
La Salle University, PA
La Sierra University, CA
Lafayette College, PA
LaGrange College, GA
Laguna College of Art and Design, CA
Lake Erie College, OH
Lake Forest College, IL
Lakeland University, WI
Lander University, SC
Lasell College, MA
Lawrence Technological University, MI
Lawrence University, WI
Le Moyne College, NY
Lebanon Valley College, PA
Lees-McRae College, NC
Lehigh University, PA
Lenoir-Rhyne University, NC
Lesley University, MA
LeTourneau University, TX
Lewis & Clark College, OR
Lewis University, IL
Liberty University, VA
LIM College, NY
Limestone College, SC
Lindsey Wilson College, KY
Linfield College, OR
Lipscomb University, TN
LIU Brooklyn, NY
LIU Post, NY
Loras College, IA
Loyola Marymount University, CA
Loyola University Chicago, IL
Loyola University Maryland, MD
Loyola University New Orleans, LA
Luther College, IA
Lycoming College, PA
Lynn University, FL
Lyon College, AR
Macalester College, MN
MacMurray College, IL
Madonna University, MI
Maharishi University of Management, IA
Maine College of Art, ME
Malone University, OH
Manchester University, IN
Manhattan College, NY
Manhattan School of Music, NY
Manhattanville College, NY
Mannes School of Music, NY
Marian University, IN
Marian University, WI
Marietta College, OH
Marist College, NY
Marlboro College, VT
Marquette University, WI
Mars Hill University, NC
Mary Baldwin University, VA
Marygrove College, MI
Maryland Institute College of Art, MD
Marymount Manhattan College, NY
Marymount University, VA
Maryville College, TN
Maryville University of Saint Louis, MO
Marywood University, PA
Massachusetts Institute of Technology, MA
McDaniel College, MD
McKendree University, IL
McMurry University, TX
McPherson College, KS
MCPHS University, MA
Medaille College, NY
Memphis College of Art, TN
Menlo College, CA
Mercer University, GA
Mercy College, NY
Mercyhurst University, PA
Meredith College, NC
Merrimack College, MA
Messiah College, PA
Methodist University, NC
MidAmerica Nazarene University, KS
Middlebury College, VT
Midland University, NE
Midway University, KY
Milligan College, TN
Millikin University, IL
Mills College, CA
Millsaps College, MS
Milwaukee Institute of Art & Design, WI
Milwaukee School of Engineering, WI
Minneapolis College of Art and Design, MN
Misericordia University, PA
Missouri Baptist University, MO
Mitchell College, CT
Molloy College, NY
Monmouth College, IL
Monmouth University, NJ
Montreat College, NC
Montserrat College of Art, MA
Moore College of Art and Design, PA
Moravian College, PA
Morehouse College, GA
Morningside College, IA
Mount Holyoke College, MA
Mount Ida College, MA
Mount Marty College, SD
Mount Mary University, WI
Mount Mercy University, IA
Mount Saint Mary College, NY
Mount St. Joseph University, OH
Mount St. Mary's University, MD
Mount St. Mary's University - Chalon Campus, CA
Mount Vernon Nazarene University, OH
Muhlenberg College, PA
Muskingum University, OH
Naropa University, CO
National Louis University, IL
Nazareth College, NY
Nebraska Wesleyan University, NE
Neumann University, PA
New England College, NH
New England Conservatory of Music, MA
New Jersey Institute of Technology, NJ
New York Institute of Technology, NY
New York University, NY
Newberry College, SC
Newbury College, MA
Newman University, KS
Niagara University, NY
Nichols College, MA
North Carolina Wesleyan College, NC
North Central College, IL
North Central University, MN
North Park University, IL
Northeastern University, MA
Northland College, WI
Northwest Christian University, OR
Northwest Nazarene University, ID
Northwest University, WA
Northwestern College of Iowa, IA
Northwestern University, IL
Northwood University - Michigan, MI
Norwich University, VT
Notre Dame College, OH
Notre Dame de Namur University, CA
Notre Dame of Maryland University, MD
Nova Southeastern University, FL
Nyack College, NY
Oakland City University, IN
Oakwood University, AL
Oberlin College, OH
Occidental College, CA
Oglethorpe University, GA
Ohio Dominican University, OH
Ohio Northern University, OH
Ohio Wesleyan University, OH
Oklahoma Baptist University, OK
Oklahoma City University, OK
Oklahoma Wesleyan University, OK
Olivet College, MI
Olivet Nazarene University, IL
Oral Roberts University, OK
Otis College of Art and Design, CA
Ottawa University, KS
Otterbein University, OH
Ouachita Baptist University, AR
Our Lady of the Lake University, TX
Pace University, NY
Pacific Lutheran University, WA
Pacific Northwest College of Art, OR
Pacific Union College, CA
Pacific University, OR
Palm Beach Atlantic University, FL
Parsons The New School for Design, NY
Pepperdine University, CA
Pfeiffer University, NC
Piedmont College, GA
Pine Manor College, MA
Pitzer College, CA
Point Loma Nazarene University, CA
Point Park University, PA
Pomona College, CA
Post University, CT
Pratt Institute, NY
Presbyterian College, SC
Prescott College, AZ
Princeton University, NJ
Principia College, IL
Providence College, RI
Queens University of Charlotte, NC
Quincy University, IL
Quinnipiac University, CT
Randolph College, VA
Randolph-Macon College, VA
Reed College, OR
Regis College, MA
Regis University, CO
Reinhardt University, GA
Rensselaer Polytechnic Institute, NY
Research College of Nursing, MO
Rhode Island School of Design, RI
Rhodes College, TN
Rice University, TX
Rider University, NJ
Ringling College of Art and Design, FL
Ripon College, WI
Rivier University, NH
Roanoke College, VA
Robert Morris University, PA
Roberts Wesleyan College, NY
Rochester Institute of Technology, NY
Rockford University, IL
Rocky Mountain College, MT
Roger Williams University, RI
Rollins College, FL
Roosevelt University, IL
Rose-Hulman Institute of Technology, IN
Rosemont College, PA
Russell Sage College, NY
Sacred Heart University, CT
Saint Anselm College, NH
Saint Francis University, PA
Saint John's University, MN
Saint Joseph's College of Maine, ME
Saint Joseph's University, PA
Saint Leo University, FL
Saint Louis University, MO
Saint Martin's University, WA
Saint Mary-of-the-Woods College, IN
Saint Mary's College, IN
Saint Mary's College of California, CA
Saint Mary's University of Minnesota, MN
Saint Michael's College, VT
Saint Peter's University, NJ
Saint Vincent College, PA
Saint Xavier University, IL
Salem College, NC
Salem State University, MA
Salve Regina University, RI
Samford University, AL
San Diego Christian College, CA
San Francisco Art Institute, CA
San Francisco Conservatory of Music, CA
Sarah Lawrence College, NY
Savannah College of Art and Design, GA
School of the Art Institute of Chicago, IL

School of Visual Arts, NY
Schreiner University, TX
Scripps College, CA
Seattle Pacific University, WA
Seattle University, WA
Seton Hall University, NJ
Seton Hill University, PA
Sewanee: The University of the South, TN
Shenandoah University, VA
Shorter University, GA
Siena College, NY
Siena Heights University, MI
Sierra Nevada College, NV
Silver Lake College of the Holy Family, WI
Simmons College, MA
Simpson College, IA
Simpson University, CA
Skidmore College, NY
Smith College, MA
South University, GA
Southeastern University, FL
Southern Methodist University, TX
Southern Nazarene University, OK
Southern New Hampshire University, NH
Southern Vermont College, VT
Southern Wesleyan University, SC
Southwest Baptist University, MO
Southwestern College, KS
Southwestern University, TX
Spalding University, KY
Spelman College, GA
Spring Arbor University, MI
Spring Hill College, AL
Springfield College, MA
St. Ambrose University, IA
St. Andrews University, NC
St. Bonaventure University, NY
St. Catherine University, MN
St. Edward's University, TX
St. Francis College, NY
St. Gregory's University, OK
St. John Fisher College, NY
St. John's College, Santa Fe, NM
St. John's College-Annapolis, MD
St. John's University, NY
St. Lawrence University, NY
St. Mary's University , TX
St. Norbert College, WI
St. Olaf College, MN
St. Thomas Aquinas College, NY
St. Thomas University, FL
Stanford University, CA
Stephens College, MO
Sterling College, KS
Sterling College, VT
Stetson University, FL
Stevens Institute of Technology, NJ
Stevenson University, MD
Stonehill College, MA
Suffolk University, MA
Susquehanna University, PA
Swarthmore College, PA
Syracuse University, NY
Tabor College, KS
Taylor University, IN
Tennessee Wesleyan University, TN
Texas Christian University, TX
Texas Lutheran University, TX
Texas Wesleyan University, TX
The American University, DC
The Art Institute of Atlanta, GA
The Boston Conservatory at Berklee, MA
The Catholic University of America, DC
The College of Idaho, ID
The College of New Rochelle, NY
The College of Saint Rose, NY
The College of Wooster, OH
The George Washington University, DC
The Juilliard School, NY
The Master's University, CA
Thiel College, PA
Thomas Aquinas College, CA
Thomas College, ME
Thomas More College, KY
Thomas More College of Liberal Arts, NH
Tiffin University, OH
Toccoa Falls College, GA
Touro College , NY
Transylvania University, KY
Trevecca Nazarene University, TN
Trine University, IN
Trinity Christian College, IL
Trinity College, CT
Trinity College of Nursing and Health Sciences, IL
Trinity International University, IL
Trinity University, TX
Trinity Washington University, DC
Tufts University, MA
Tulane University, LA
Tusculum College, TN
Union College, KY
Union College, NY
Union University, TN
Unity College, ME
University of Bridgeport, CT
University of California at Irvine, CA
University of California at Riverside, CA
University of California at Santa Barbara, CA
University of California San Diego, CA
University of Charleston, WV
University of Chicago, IL
University of Dallas, TX
University of Dayton, OH
University of Delaware, DE
University of Denver, CO
University of Detroit Mercy, MI
University of Dubuque, IA
University of Evansville, IN
University of Findlay, OH
University of Great Falls, MT
University of Hartford, CT
University of Indianapolis, IN
University of La Verne, CA
University of Lynchburg, VA
University of Mary Hardin-Baylor, TX
University of Miami, FL
University of Mount Union, OH
University of New England, ME
University of New Haven, CT
University of Northwestern - St. Paul, MN
University of Notre Dame, IN
University of Pennsylvania, PA
University of Pittsburgh, PA
University of Portland, OR
University of Puget Sound, WA
University of Redlands, CA
University of Richmond, VA
University of Rochester, NY
University of Saint Francis, IN
University of Saint Joseph, CT
University of Saint Mary, KS
University of San Diego, CA
University of San Francisco, CA
University of Scranton, PA
University of Southern California, CA
University of St. Francis, IL
University of St. Thomas, MN
University of St. Thomas - Houston, TX
University of Tampa, FL
University of Texas at El Paso, TX
University of the Arts, PA
University of the Cumberlands, KY
University of the Incarnate Word, TX
University of the Sciences, PA
University of the Ozarks, AR
University of the Pacific, CA
University of Tulsa, OK
Upper Iowa University, IA
Urbana University, OH
Ursinus College, PA
Ursuline College, OH
Utica College, NY
Valparaiso University, IN
Vanderbilt University, TN
VanderCook College of Music, IL
Vanguard University of Southern California, CA
Vassar College, NY
Vaughn College of Aeronautics and Technology, NY
Villanova University, PA
Virginia Wesleyan University, VA
Viterbo University, WI
Wabash College, IN
Wagner College, NY
Wake Forest University, NC
Walla Walla University, WA
Walsh University, OH
Warner Pacific College, OR
Warren Wilson College, NC
Wartburg College, IA
Washington & Jefferson College, PA
Washington Adventist University, MD
Washington and Lee University, VA
Washington College, MD
Washington University in St. Louis, MO
Waynesburg University, PA
Webber International University, FL
Webster University, MO
Wellesley College, MA
Wells College, NY
Wentworth Institute of Technology, MA
Wesley College, DE
Wesleyan College, GA
Wesleyan University, CT
West Virginia Wesleyan College, WV
Western New England University, MA
Westminster Choir College, NJ
Westminster College, MO
Westminster College, PA
Westminster College, UT
Westmont College, CA
Wheaton College, IL
Wheaton College, MA
Wheeling Jesuit University, WV
Wheelock College, MA
Whitman College, WA
Whittier College, CA
Whitworth University, WA
Widener University, PA
Wilkes University, PA
Willamette University, OR
William Jewell College, MO
William Peace University, NC
William Woods University, MO
Williams College, MA
Wilmington College, OH
Wilson College, PA
Wingate University, NC
Wisconsin Lutheran College, WI
Wittenberg University, OH
Wofford College, SC
Woodbury University, CA
Worcester Polytechnic Institute, MA
Xavier University, OH
Xavier University of Louisiana, LA
Yale University, CT
Yeshiva University, NY
York College, NE

PART III

INDEX OF COLLEGE MAJORS

By now, you either have a clear idea about what your college major will be, or you are worrying about it. This section presents an overview of academic majors as well as information about some of the careers for which each major prepares you.

Majors are listed alphabetically in chart form. This lets you compare the various schools that offer the majors that interest you. You'll also be able to compare each school's Selector Rating and in-state costs.

After you've found a representative sampling of the schools that offer majors in the fields you may want to pursue, go on to the college Profiles that make up this book's main section.

What Is a College Major? A major is a field of study in which a student chooses an academic specialty to receive a college degree. A major consists of a concentration of specialized subject matter in a field of study. Most majors occupy about one-quarter to two-thirds of courses in that subject. Most college and university students must complete a required number of courses in their major to earn a Bachelor of Arts (B.A.) or a Bachelor of Science (B.S.) degree. The other twenty-five to fifty percent of courses are occupied by "general education" requirements for graduation, or electives that enhance and broaden a student's academic knowledge. Students' choice of major should be made carefully considering their interests and special talents.

What Is a College Minor? A minor in a field of study usually consists of a number of courses in a field of study other than the major. However, the required units of study are fewer than those required of the major. Many colleges today do not require a formal minor for graduation. The practical reason for a minor is to supplement and strengthen a major. For example, a computer science major may require specified courses in mathematics that, when totaled up, meet the definition of a minor, or perhaps a dual major.

Majors and Careers. Choosing a field of study is one of the most important decisions a student will make in the process of choosing a college major leading to an associate or bachelor's degree. A major with a structured course of study not only provides for intellectual growth, self-improvement, general knowledge, and a search for truth and understanding, but often provides the required technical training to enter and become successful in the world of work. Personal enlightenment is a noble goal, but most students no longer can afford the monetary expenses and the time to pursue courses that do not lead to a major that ties into career goals. Information on majors and careers is presented here to help students to make wise educational and career decisions. Informed educational and career decisions should include interests, academic abilities, and work values.

WHAT ARE SOME DIFFERENT APPROACHES TO CHOOSING A COLLEGE MAJOR?

JOB TRAINING: A student may want to go to college for one main reason: to acquire specific job skills to qualify for direct job entry. Job training course work is usually work-related and technical and it is evident that the skills learned in class can be directly applied to an occupation. For example, students who want to work as engineers in one of the many engineering specialties should pursue a two-year program course work as engineering technicians, or a four- to five-year engineering curriculum to become professional engineers.

Technical preparation: Technical preparation students generally enroll in associate degree programs that provide them with advanced skills through studies and experiences in applied academics, skills, and advanced technology. These students join the workforce after grade 14 or continue their formal preparation by working toward a baccalaureate degree in applied technology. Technical majors can be planned in agriculture, arts and communications, business, engineering and mechanics, health, human service, and natural science.

A general approach: Students may want to pursue a more general major that may not directly tie in to job entry, but will improve their general knowledge and prepare them as generalists with intellectual and problem-solving skills rather than technical training. This kind of major is often referred to as liberal arts, humanities, or general studies. Liberal arts majors can be planned in Social and Behavioral Sciences, The Arts, Communications, Humanities, and Ethnic Studies. A liberal arts major, leading to a baccalaureate degree, may not guarantee direct entry into an occupation associated with the major.

Special talent approach: Students may want to select a major because of a special talent and a strong interest in a certain field of study. Students with a strong interest in writing, drama, music, art, or an academic subject should select a major that helps to further the talent. College life will be more enjoyable if students select majors that will provide personal satisfaction. Designing a career plan that will allow a lifestyle compatible with the special talent will also provide personal satisfaction.

Double major approach: Students often decide to choose two majors in preparation for a career. A double major may be necessary in preparing for occupations in the science field where it is essential to be well-grounded in both the physical and biological sciences.

Independent approach: Students may have highly divergent interests that cut across two or more fields of study. Many colleges allow students to design a major to satisfy their goals. For example, students may have artistic talents and scientific interests. They might combine the two interests and design a scientific illustration major that meets faculty approval.

CONNECTING COLLEGE MAJOR PLANNING AND CAREER PLANNING

All students from the ninth grade through postsecondary school should be following a program of study that will prepare them for specific careers—studies that blend appropriate academics with appropriate skills and knowledge in a particular career area. All students in postsecondary studies should be preparing for life and work after completing their studies. This assertion eliminates a justification for a "general plan" of studies that in theory "leads anywhere," but in fact "leads nowhere." Students should either be in a postsecondary associate, technical, or baccalaureate educational plan that leads to a satisfying career.

The next section presents relevant educational and career information on 14 fields of study from which students may choose a major based on career plans. Each of the 14 fields of study has specific information on majors and careers that students should consider carefully when choosing a college major. Information about employment, growth, and earnings is taken from the Department of Labor figures for 2016, with growth projected to 2026.

1. AGRICULTURAL SCIENCES

Agriculture is a broad and diverse field of study that trains scientists for many rewarding and satisfying careers. These play an important part in maintaining the nation's food supply through ensuring agricultural productivity and the safety of the food supply. Agricultural scientists engage in research, development, and production of farm crops and animals, food sciences, plant sciences, and soil sciences. Others manage marketing or production operations in companies that produce food products or agricultural chemicals, supplies, and machinery. Other agricultural scientists are consultants to business firms, private clients, or governmental agencies.

Interests: Agricultural research, development, and production of farm crops and animals, and development of ways to improve their quantity and quality

Popular majors in this field of study: Agribusiness, Agricultural Education, Agronomy, Animal Science, Entomology, Farm and Ranch Management, Fisheries and Wildlife, Food Sciences, Forestry, Horticultural Science, and Soil Sciences

Employment information/outlook: More than 2,024,179 people worked in related occupations in this field of study in 2016. The 2016–2026 employment growth is expected to be 9%.

The median annual wages of food scientists and technologists were $58,070; soil and plant scientists, $58,740; and animal scientists, $61,680. Incomes of farmers and ranchers vary greatly from year to year, because prices of farm products fluctuate with weather conditions and other factors that influence the quantity and quality of farm output and the demand for those products. In addition to farm business income, farmers often receive government subsidies or other payments that supplement their incomes and reduce some of the risk of farming. Many farmers—primarily operators of small farms—have recently been relying more and more on off-farm sources of income. Full-time, salaried agricultural managers had median weekly earnings of $1,332.80 in 2016. Farm income can vary substantially depending on a number of factors, including the type of crop or livestock being raised, price fluctuations for various agricultural products, and weather conditions that affect yield. In some cases, government subsidies may supplement a farmer's income. For a growing number of farmers and ranchers, particularly those working on farms for residential and lifestyle reasons, crop or livestock production is not their major occupation or source of income.

Agribusiness

Agribusiness majors will learn the business aspect of farms, firms, and industries that supply and service the farmer and other farm-related businesses. They will study merchandising, advertising, finance, marketing, and international trade.

Interests: Taking initiative, leadership, decision making, problem solving, analyzing data, global interdependence, working with people

Skills and abilities: Planning, organizing, making business decisions, leadership, teamwork, creative and critical thinking, working with people, written and verbal skills, adapting to change

Occupations related to this major: Agricultural Crop Farm Managers, Farm Products Purchasing Agents and Buyers, Farm and Ranch Managers, Fish Hatchery Managers, Farmers and Ranchers, Agricultural Statisticians, and Farm and Home Management advisers.

Agricultural Education

Agricultural Education majors will study those basic courses in agriculture that will prepare them to teach agricultural science in high schools, community colleges, or universities. They will also complete general preparation for a service-type career in agriculture, such as extension services. They will learn to supervise youth and adult groups and to direct programs in both agricultural and human resources.

Interests: Working with people, working with plants, working with animals

Skills and abilities: Communication, science (especially natural sciences and chemistry)

Occupations related to this major: Farm and Home Management Advisers, Park Naturalists, Farmers and Ranchers, Agricultural Science Teachers, and 4-H and Agricultural Extension Agents

Agronomy

Agronomy majors will learn about three basic natural elements—crops, soils, and climates—and their interdependence in producing food, feed, fiber, and fuel. Agronomists study theory and practices for improving crop production while conserving natural resources and maintaining environmental quality.

Interests: Nature and the outdoors, environmental quality (soil, water, and air), conservation of natural resources, biological and physical sciences, problem solving, plant growth and experimentation, weather, climate, geologic formations

Skills and qualities: Oral and written communication skills, group dynamics, leadership, organizational (interpersonal) skills, analytic reasoning, creative thinking

Occupations related to this major: Agricultural Climatologists, Agrochemical Technologists, Environmental Technicians, Food and Drug Inspectors, Farm or Ranch Managers, Plant Breeders, Agricultural Technicians, Soil and Water Conservationists, and Greenhouse Managers

Animal Science

Animal Science majors will learn how to manage livestock and poultry. They will study the role of animals in the economy, how animal products influence eating habits and are part of the global food supply, and how animals help serve people's recreation needs. They will carry out investigations and experiments in the areas of breeding, feeding, management, and disease control in farm and domestic animals.

Interests: Working with plants, working with animals, working with people

Skills and abilities: Speaking and writing effectively

Occupations related to this major: Animal Scientists, Soil and Plant Scientists, Park Naturalists, Biologists, Farm and Ranch Managers, and Soil Conservationists

Entomology

Entomology majors will study the biology, ecology, classification, distribution, physiology, economic importance, and management of insects and their relation to plant and animal life. They will learn to identify species of insects and allied forms, such as mites and spiders. They will study methods of controlling and eliminating agricultural, structural, and forest pests by developing new and improved pesticides and cultural and biological methods, including using natural enemies of pests. They will also study insect distribution and habitat, and methods to prevent importation and spread of injurious species.

Interests: Science, techniques of scientific research, the environment, the health and well-being of people

Skills and abilities: Curiosity, rational thinking, objective thinking, performing laboratory tasks carefully

Occupations related to this major: Entomologists, Environmental Scientists, Soil and Plant Scientists, Biologists, Clinical Laboratory Technologists, and Pest Control Workers

Farm and Ranch Management

Farm and Ranch Management majors will learn to guide and assist farmers and ranchers in maximizing the financial returns to their land by managing the day-to-day activities. Duties and responsibilities may vary widely. For example, the owner of a very large livestock farm may employ a farm manager to oversee a single activity, such as feeding livestock. When managing a small crop farm, on the other hand, a farm manager may assume responsibility for all functions, from selecting the crop to participating in planting and harvesting.

Interests: Directing and coordinating worker activities, decision making, problem solving, nature and the outdoors, conservation of natural resources, biological and physical science

Skills and abilities: Speaking, motivating people, creative and critical thinking, oral and written expression and comprehension, organizational skills, leadership

Occupations related to this major: Agricultural Crop Farm Managers, Farm and Ranch Managers, Foresters, Dairy Farm Managers, Poultry Farm Managers, and Farm and Home Management Advisers

Fisheries and Wildlife

Fisheries and Wildlife majors will learn about fish eggs, larvae, fish parasites, and diseases. They will learn to operate fish culture facilities, tag and mark fish, detect problems of water pollution, analyze, identify, collect, control, and preserve populations of fur and game animals.

Interests: Nature and the outdoors, science, research

Skills and abilities: Solving problems, communicating effectively, working with others

Occupations related to this major: Fish Culturists, Fish Hatchery Managers, Environmental Scientists, Zoo Workers, Fisheries and Wildlife Biologists, and Park Naturalists

Food Sciences

Food Science majors will learn to use biological, physical, and social sciences to transform raw materials into safe, nutritious, and economical foods. They will learn to apply scientific and engineering principles in research, development, and food production technology. They will also work to improve methods of processing, preserving, packaging, distributing, and preparing food.

Interests: Biological and physical science, public well-being, teamwork, observing details, solving complex problems

Skills and abilities: Good laboratory technique, oral and written expression and comprehension, mathematical reasoning

Occupations related to this major: Food Scientists, Food Science Technicians, Food Chemists, Food Plant Managers, Food Microbiologists, and Biological and Agricultural Technologists

Forestry

Forestry majors will learn to manage, protect, and develop forest lands and other resources for economic and recreational purposes; plan and supervise the cutting and harvesting of timber; carry out forestation and reforestation activities and manage parks and camps.

Interests: Nature and the outdoors, working with people, planning activities, investigative research, solving problems

Skills and abilities: Communicating effectively, working with quantitative and qualitative problems, presenting ideas to others

Occupations related to this major: Foresters, Soil Conservationists, Environmental Scientists, Biologists, Range Managers, Nursery and Greenhouse Managers, Agricultural Engineers, and Forest and Conservation Technicians

Horticultural Science

Horticultural Science majors will study problems of plant production, processing, and disease resistance. They will also study soil and climate to learn the conditions in which different types of plants thrive. They will be concerned with orchards, garden plants, flowers, ornamental plants, and nursery stock.

Interests: Science, working with plants, business, working with people, solving problems, improving the environment

Skills and abilities: Biological and physical sciences, written and oral communication, organization, creativity, quantitative thinking, computer competency, working with people

Occupations related to this major: Horticulturists, Foresters, Conservation Scientists, Landscape Architects, Plant Scientists, Farmers, and Farm Managers

Soil Sciences

Soil Science majors will study the physical, chemical, and geological characteristics and behaviors of soils. They will learn how to investigate soil both in the field and in the lab, and to classify soils in terms of their capability in producing crops, grasses, and trees. They also will learn how to make land appraisals.

Interests: Nature and the outdoors, conservation of natural resources, the environment, science

Skills and abilities: Quantitative reasoning, keen observation of natural phenomena, oral and written communication, applying scientific knowledge to complex systems

Occupations related to this major: Plant Scientists, Conservation Scientists, Botanists, Biochemists, Park Naturalists, and Farm and Range Managers

2. ARCHITECTURE AND DESIGN

Architects learn to plan, design, and supervise the construction of buildings, houses, factories, skyscrapers, schools, and other structures. They learn to make them attractive, usable, energy efficient, and economical. Architects must qualify for a state license after graduation. Most architects work for architectural firms. Others work directly for builders, real estate developers, or large construction projects, as well as governmental agencies responsible for housing and community planning, such as the Department of Defense, Interior, and Housing and Urban Development. Students interested in the field of architecture will do well in such courses as architectural theory design, computer graphics, computer science, general engineering urban planning, mathematics, physics, and economics.

Interests: Architects have an interest in planning, designing, and supervising the construction of buildings, houses, factories, skyscrapers, schools, and other structures.

Popular majors in this field of study: Architectural Engineering, Architecture, City and Regional Planning, Construction Science, Interior Design, Landscape Architecture, Marine Architecture, and Surveying

Employment information/outlook: More than 2,474,500 people worked in related occupations in this field of study in 2016. The 2016–2026 employment growth is expected to be 7.3%.

Median annual wages of wage-and-salary architects were $73,900 in 2016. Those just starting their internships can expect to earn considerably less. Earnings of partners in established architectural firms may fluctuate because of changing business conditions. Some architects may have difficulty establishing their own practices and may go through a period when their expenses are greater than their incomes, requiring substantial financial resources. Many firms pay tuition and fees toward continuing education requirements for their employees. Median annual wages of urban and regional planners were $65,230 in 2016. Earnings also vary by the worker's education and experience, type of work, complexity of the construction project, and geographic location. Wages of construction workers often are affected when poor weather prevents them from working. Traditionally, winter is the slack period for construction activity, especially in colder parts of the country, but there is a trend toward more year-round construction, even in colder areas. Construction trades are dependent on one another to complete specific parts of a project—especially on large projects—so work delays affecting one trade can delay or stop the work of another trade.

Architectural Engineering

Architectural Engineering majors will learn how different materials interact. They also will learn to calculate loads and stress and study the strength, durability, and safety-factor of materials. They will use artistic, applied physics, and material science skills in the design of buildings.

Interests: Mathematics, physical science, building things, applying mathematics and science to practical use, design, computers

Skills and abilities: Oral and written expression and comprehension, speech clarity, logical thinking, interpersonal skills, teamwork

Occupations related to this major: Architects, Civil Engineers, Marine Architects, Materials Engineers, and Architectural Drafters

Architecture

Architecture majors learn to plan, design, and supervise the construction of buildings, houses, factories, skyscrapers, schools, and other structures. They learn to make them attractive, usable, energy efficient, and economical. They must qualify for a license after graduation. They work in design studios that develop skills and foster creative expression. Architecture students also study the history of the building environment (rooms, buildings, landscapes, cities), the technology required to create it, and related graphic communication.

Interests: The formation of the physical environment; the history of buildings, cities, and landscapes; applied creative expression

Skills and abilities: Communicating by sketching and drafting; solving spatial problems; sensitivity to visual forms, proportions, and colors

Occupations related to this major: Architects, Naval Architects, Landscape Architects, Civil Engineers, Industrial Designers, Interior Designers, and Drafters

City and Regional Planning

City and Regional Planning majors learn to deal with land use and environmental issues created by population movements. They learn how to draw plans for new city environments including streets, sewers, water, and electricity. They also learn to zone areas for residential, commercial, or industrial use. Students commit themselves, through planning, to the future, and to social and environmental improvement.

Interests: Solving problems, working with people, helping groups, communities, and organizations improve people's lives

Skills and abilities: Working with numbers, listening, interpreting and communicating what was observed or heard

Occupations related to this major: Urban and Regional Planners, Architects, Landscape Architects, City Managers, Civil Engineers, and Environmental Engineers

Construction Science

Construction Science majors learn about all areas of construction technology. These areas include contracting, remodeling, cabinet making, building inspection, carpentry, and estimating the costs of building projects.

Interests: Starting and completing projects; leading people and making decisions; risk taking; activities that include practical, hands-on problems and solutions

Skills and abilities: Listening to and understanding information; reading and understanding information; managing one's own time and the time of others; communicating information and ideas in writing

Occupations related to this major: Architects, Property and Real Estate Managers, Real Estate Appraisers, Construction and Building Inspectors, and Industrial Engineers

Interior Design

Interior Design majors learn to arrange the interiors of buildings to fit the functional and aesthetic needs of their owners. They will design everything from lighting and furniture to home decorating accessories. Interior design majors study all aspects of the building environment: scale, proportion, arrangement, light, acoustics, temperature, textures, colors, and materials. They learn how to develop surroundings that are satisfying, creative, and appropriate to human needs.

Interests: Architecture, design (interior, industrial, graphic), building construction, interaction of colors, nature of materials, and textures

Skills and abilities: Design, organization, working with people, drawing, communicating ideas

Occupations related to this major: Interior Designers, Fashion, Furniture, Textile, and Floral Designers, Exhibition Designers, Architects, and Landscape Architects

Landscape Architecture

Landscape Architecture majors learn skills and techniques for planning, designing, and managing the land. They learn about weather, drainage, botany, and construction. They are frequently involved in mapping and consultation. They creatively apply information and principles drawn from both the arts and the sciences to reshape and conserve landscapes.

Interests: Visual arts, ecology, nature, environmental issues

Skills and abilities: Drawing and graphic expression, problem solving, written communication

Occupations related to this major: Landscape Architects, Architects, Surveyors, Civil Engineers, Urban and Regional Planners, Botanists, and Park Naturalists

Marine Architecture

Marine Architecture majors learn to design and oversee construction and repair of marine craft and floating structures, such as ships, barges, tugs, dredges, submarines, torpedoes, floats, and buoys. May confer with marine engineers.

Interests: Design techniques, engineering science and technology, building materials, construction and repair of structures

Skills and abilities: Problem solving, listening and understanding information and ideas, creativity, communicating information and ideas in writing, fluency of ideas

Occupations related to this major: Marine Architects, Aerospace Engineers, Civil Engineers, Materials Engineers, Engineering Technicians, and Drafters

Surveying

Surveying majors learn to make exact measurements and determine property boundaries. They learn to provide data relevant to the shape, contour, gravitation, location, elevation, or dimension of land, or land features on or near the earth's surface, for engineering, mapping, mining, land evaluation, construction, and other purposes.

Interests: Shapes and elevations of geomorphic and topographic features, geography, and methods for describing the features of land, sea, and air masses

Skills and abilities: Communicating effectively in writing; using mathematics to solve problems; understanding written information; using scientific methods to solve problems; motivating, developing, and directing people as they work

Occupations related to this major: Surveyors, Cartographers, Urban Planners, Civil Drafters, Agricultural Engineers, and Landscape Architects

3. THE ARTS

The Arts is a field of study that includes a wider range of subjects than found in other areas of concentration. If students major in one of the arts, they will learn to design products, articles, and materials; they will develop talents as actors; they will study the theory and practice of film production; they will develop talents to draw, paint, or design interpretations of objects, people, and nature, or they will develop talents dealing with the art of sound that express ideas and emotions either by song, dance, or by instrumental musical instruments. This field, in contrast to a liberal arts education, is often thought of as professional training. A major in this field gives information, methods, procedures, and techniques needed in a career. A professional program in this field will offer students good training to make a contribution in the world of art.

Interests: Developing talents to draw, paint, or design interpretations of objects, people, and nature; or developing the art of sound that expresses ideas and emotions either by speech, song, dance, or musical instruments

Popular majors in this field of study: Art Education, Art History, Arts Management, Dance, Dramatic Arts, Film Arts, Fine Arts, Graphic Design, Music Business Management, Music Education, Music Performance, Music Therapy, Photography, Religious Music, and Studio Art

Employment information/outlook: More than 2,570,900 people worked in related occupations in this field of study in 2016. The 2016–2026 employment growth is expected to be 7.0%.

Median annual wages of salaried art directors were $80,880; advertising, public relations and related services, $115,750; salaried craft artists, $44,380; multimedia artists and animators were $61,370; motion picture and video industries, $71,350; advertising and related services, $46,290. The hourly wages of actors were $20.26; hourly wages for performing arts companies were $15.87; and motion picture and video industry occupations came in at $34.31. The median annual wages in 2016 for producers and directors were $71,350; radio and television broadcasting, $37,090; graphic designers, $44,150. Hourly wages of wage-and-salary musicians and singers were $23.50; performing arts companies, $18.33; and religious organizations, $14.69. The median annual wages for salaried music directors and composers were $47,350 in 2016. Self-employed artist wages vary considerably. Most artists, including actors, musicians, and singers, were not available because of the variation in the number of hours they work, and the lack of guaranteed employment. The more successful performers may belong to one of the talent unions, such as SAG/AFTRA, American Guild of Musical Artists, or The American Federation of Musicians, which negotiates minimum contracts.

Art Education

Art Education majors learn to develop their artistic talents and gain the knowledge and skills needed to teach art at various education levels. They will explore the value of art both to the individual and to various cultures throughout history.

Interests: Visual arts, creating art, teaching

Skills and abilities: Working with others, solving problems creatively, manipulating materials creatively, responding to other people's art with sensitivity

Occupations related to this major: Art Teachers, Curriculum Specialists, Art Administrators, Manual Arts Therapists, Craft Demonstrators, Curators, Archivists, and Museum Research Workers

Art History

Art History majors study works of art—how they came about and what they mean. They will examine works of art as they appear now and also consider appearance and function in their original contexts. Through their visual analysis and extensive reading and writing, students explore the traditions of appearance and technique that guided the creation of art in different cultures.

Interests: Visual arts, past civilizations, the connections between different aspects of a civilization, artists, art technique

Skills and abilities: Observing carefully, information gathering, reading critically, written expression and comprehension

Occupations related to this major: High School Teachers, College Teachers, Curators, Archivists, Conservators, Museum Directors, and Museum Technicians

Arts Management

Arts Management majors learn to organize and manage art organizations and facilities. They receive instruction in business and financial management and labor relations, event promotion and management, public relations and arts advocacy, and arts law. They will learn to analyze and address the issues concerning the health of theaters, dance companies, museums, and other arts organizations.

Interests: Visual and performance arts, leadership, working with people

Skills and abilities: Oral and written communication, organizational ability, creative thinking, critical thinking

Occupations related to this major: Theater Managers, Symphony Orchestra Managers, Dance Company Managers, Curators, and Museum Technicians and Conservators

Dance

Dance majors learn to interpret an idea or a story through physical expression or rhythm and/or sound. Dance forms vary from ballet and modern interpretative dance to tap and chorus lines. Dance is a demanding discipline. Students learn to develop their bodies as articulate instruments for dance expression: to understand contributions that dance has made to the arts, and to create their own dances.

Interests: Dance, other arts, the physicality of movement

Skills and abilities: Sense of rhythm and musicality, physical stamina, dynamic strength, speed of limb movement, gross body coordination

Occupations related to this major: Dance Teachers, Actors and Performers, Choreographers, Dance Researchers, and Dance Therapists

Dramatic Arts

Dramatic Arts majors learn how to play a part to entertain, inform, or instruct an audience. They learn to be involved in interpreting plays or scripts, selecting plays or scripts, or planning and supervising performances. They gain breadth of knowledge about past and present culture, art, literature, politics, psychology, and philosophy.

Interests: Self-expression, communication of ideas and feelings, literature and language, art and music, human personality and motivation

Skills and abilities: Speech clarity, memorization, originality, oral and written expression and comprehension, emotional openness

Occupations related to this major: Actors, Directors, Designers, Playwrights, Stage Managers, Talent Directors, and Teachers

Film Arts

Film Arts majors study the theory and practice of film production and the techniques used in this medium of communication. They learn to do creative work, as well as learn the rapidly changing technology. They study cinema history, screenwriting, and the aesthetic and technical aspects of cinema production, including directing, cinematography, and editing. They also examine the economic, technical, social, cultural, and ideological aspects of film as a medium for communication and personal expression.

Interests: Film literature, psychology, theater, music, art history, biography, current events

Skills and abilities: Creativity, ability to express oneself verbally and visually, self-discipline, understanding of human psychology, organization, attention to detail, flexibility, working with people

Occupations related to this major: Directors—Stage, Motion Pictures, Television and Radio, Cinematographers, Technical Directors, Programming and Script Editors, Production Assistants

Fine Arts

Fine Arts majors learn to draw or design their interpretations of objects, people, and nature, using a wide variety of materials from watercolors and oils to stone and metal. They learn to create art to satisfy their own need for self-expression. They learn about the creation of art historically, in contemporary society, and through their own efforts in studio classes. They may display their work in museums, art galleries, corporate collections, and private homes.

Interests: Making things with the hands, other cultures, history, paintings, sculpture, film, self-expression

Skills and abilities: Oral and written expression and comprehension, fluency of ideas, originality, visual color discrimination, manual and finger dexterity

Occupations related to this major: Fine Artists, Graphic Artists, Sculptors, Painters, Illustrators, and Cartoonists and Animators

Graphic Design

Graphic Design majors study the principles of design to learn how to create attractive and effective advertisements, flyers, brochures, logos, magazines, or books. They learn how to create images through the use of silkscreen, computers, and printing presses. Students learn to communicate information visually using words and images. They also study how people perceive and interpret information.

Interests: Visual arts, creativity, critical thinking, working with people

Skills and abilities: Drawing, photography, originality, fluency of ideas, oral expression, visual color discrimination

Occupations related to this major: Graphic Designers, Painters, Illustrators, Cartoonists, Animators, Fashion Designers, and Interior Designers

Music Business Management

Music Business Management majors learn to organize and manage music operations, facilities, and personnel. They receive instruction in business and financial management, personnel management and labor relations, event promotion, and music products merchandising. They study the functional area of business as well as music performance, history, and theory.

Interests: Music, leadership, organizing people, business, solving problems, negotiating

Skills and abilities: Oral expression and comprehension, written expression and comprehension, leadership, organization, creative thinking

Occupations related to this major: Music Facilities Managers, Recording Studio Managers, Artists' Representatives, Orchestra Managers, Music Directors, and Concert Booking Agents

Music Education

Music Education majors learn to become music teachers in public and private schools. They learn the basics of music and the fundamentals of teaching to share music with people of all ages and abilities.

Interests: Listening to music, performing, working with young people, leadership

Skills and abilities: Musical ability, a sense of rhythm and pitch, oral and written expression and comprehension, speech clarity, discriminating listening

Occupations related to this major: Music Teachers, Music Therapists, Choir Directors, Conductors, Composers, Arrangers, and Music Librarians

Music Performance

Music Performance majors learn to develop a high level of performance skill and musical understanding. They reach a high level of technical proficiency and musical sensitivity as music performance majors. They become well-rounded musicians through the study of core music theory and history courses.

Interests: Communicating through music performance, the theoretical and historical aspects of musical structure and style, the relation of music to society

Skills and abilities: Natural aptitude for music, technical skill, strong background in piano

Occupations related to this major: Musicians, Singers, Music Directors, Music Composers, Music Teachers, and Positions with Orchestras and Ensembles

Music Therapy

Music Therapy majors learn to design music experiences and activities to the treatment of individuals and groups in all age categories who have psychological, emotional, physical, social, intellectual, or medical disorders.

Interests: Music, the arts, behavioral and life sciences, helping others

Skills and abilities: Competency in music performance and theory, oral and written expression and comprehension, working with people

Occupations related to this major: Music Therapists, Occupational Therapists, Physical Therapists, Musicians, Singers, and Music Directors

Photography

Photography majors learn the use of camera and film to portray people, places, and events. They become involved in everything from creating motion pictures and video/television to still, portrait, aerial, and commercial photography. They learn both the artistic and technical aspects of photography and a broad understanding of the social, political, and interpersonal aspects of society.

Interests: Expressing oneself in a visual medium, creating images from ideas, helping people see and understand subjects to which they might not otherwise have access

Skills and abilities: Visualization, far vision, fluency of ideas, arm-hand steadiness, control precision, color discrimination

Occupations related to this major: Commercial Photographers, Portrait Photographers, Graphic Designers, Photojournalists, Photo Editors, and Technical and Science Photographers

Religious Music

Religious Music majors develop their skills and interests as musicians and learn to use music in religious celebrations while focusing on the role and history of music in worship. They study the history, theory, composition, and performance of music for religious or sacred purposes.

Interests: Music, music history, the fine arts, the place of music in religious celebrations, matters of faith, working with people

Skills and abilities: Ability to listen carefully, hearing sensitivity, auditory attention, oral expression and comprehension, working with people

Occupations related to this major: Music Directors, Music Teachers, Music Conductors, Organists, Cantors, Musicians, and Singers

Studio Art

Studio Art majors learn to create works of art by exploring a variety of techniques and materials. They learn to focus on learning to master new media, discovering unique solutions to visual problems, exploring fresh ways to create satisfying images, and evaluating what is worth doing.

Interests: Visual arts, manipulating materials, observing visual phenomena in nature and works of art, communicating and experimenting with forms, colors, images, and symbols

Skills and abilities: Working independently, creativity, problem solving, oral and written expression and comprehension

Occupations related to this major: Fine Artists, Commercial Artists, Graphic Designers, Art Teachers, Exhibit Designers, and Set Designers

4. BIOLOGICAL AND LIFE SCIENCES

Biological and Life Sciences majors are concerned with the world of living things—people and microbes, wild and domestic animals, plants and insects, birds and fish. Some biological scientists conduct research. Still others apply biological knowledge to the solution of practical problems, such as the development of new drugs and vaccines or new strains of plants. Biological scientists, who may also be called life scientists, study the structure of living organisms, their life processes, and evolutionary development. They may be classified into groups characterized by the type of organism with which they work or the specific activity they perform. Examples of these groups are botanists who study plants, microbiologists who work with microorganisms, and zoologists who work with animals.

Interests: The world of living things—people and microbes, wild and domestic animals, plants and insects, birds and fish—or the evolutionary development of living organisms.

Popular majors in this field of study: Biochemistry, Biology, Biophysics, Biotechnology, Botany, Marine/Aquatic Biology; Microbiology, Molecular and Cell Biology, Science Education, Wildlife Management, and Zoology

Employment information/outlook: More than 103,100 people worked in related occupations in this field of study in 2016. The 2016–2026 employment growth is expected to be 13%.

Median annual wages of biochemists and biophysicists were $81,480; microbiologists, $66,260. Median annual wages of zoologists and wildlife biologists were $57,710 in 2016.

Biochemistry

Biochemistry majors learn how chemical substances enter into or are created in living things; how drugs, foods, hormones, serums, and other substances can influence organisms. They perform tests to identify, classify, and analyze various chemical reactions. They learn to use the physical and biological sciences to explore the nature of living organisms. They study the structure and behavior of complex molecules and how they interact to form cells, tissues, and entire organisms. They also gain a fundamental grasp of metabolism, energy flow, and the regulation of various life processes.

Interests: Nature, problem solving, investigative research

Skills and abilities: Using information from many areas of science, inductive and deductive reasoning, handling and interpreting data, written expression and comprehension

Occupations related to this major: Microbiologists, Biologists, Toxicologists, Plant Pathologists, Physiologists, Cytologists, and Food Scientists

Biology

Biology majors learn about the structure of living organisms, their life processes and evolutionary development, and the relation between these organisms and their environment. They may specialize in research centering on plants, animals, or human organisms. They study animals, plants, and microorganisms that constitute the living world at the levels of molecule, cell, organism, and population.

Interests: Quality of life, investigative laboratory work, fieldwork

Skills and abilities: Problem solving, deductive and inductive reasoning, information gathering, written expression and comprehension

Occupations related to this major: Biologists, Biochemists, Botanists, Microbiologists, Geneticists, and Zoologists

Biophysics

Biophysics majors learn to apply the laws of physics to biological systems. They study vision, hearing, nerve action, blood flow, and even the behavior of DNA. They also study the effects of radiation and radioactivity on biological systems, and the use of ultrasound scanners to construct images of body interiors. They use biology, physics, chemistry, and mathematics to explore the properties of biological molecules and groups of molecules. They study the inner workings of biological systems with precision to learn how proteins fold, how genes are switched on and off, how organisms respond to light, how cells move, and how the nervous system works.

Interests: Natural history, investigative problem solving

Skills and abilities: Curiosity, deductive and inductive reasoning, written expression and comprehension, information ordering, manual dexterity

Occupations related to this major: Biophysicists, Biologists, Botanists, Geneticists, Microbiologists, and Soil Scientists

Biotechnology

Biotechnology is an interdisciplinary field of study involving the molecular life sciences and engineering fields of study. Students learn techniques for using living matter to develop new products and services in agriculture (plant growth hormones, food additives), health care (vaccines, improved drugs and vitamins), the environment (detoxification of chemicals), and other areas.

Interests: Science, treating and preventing disease, investigative research, and problem solving

Skills and abilities: Creative thinking, oral and written expression and comprehension, deductive and inductive reasoning, problem sensitivity

Occupations related to this major: Biological Technologists, Agricultural Technologists, Environmental Scientists, Food Scientists, Animal Scientists, Botanists, and Microbiologists

Botany

Botany majors focus on all aspects of plant life including taxonomy, genetics, physiology, and plant anatomy. They learn about the economic value of plants in their application to agronomy, forestry, horticulture, and pharmacology. Students study all aspects of plant biology to become familiar with the cellular and molecular functioning of life.

Interests: Nature, investigative problem solving, analytic reasoning

Skills and abilities: Deductive and inductive reasoning, information ordering, written expression and comprehension

Occupations related to this major: Botanists, Agricultural Scientists, Soil Scientists, Ecologists, Microbiologists, Physiologists

Marine/Aquatic Biology

Marine/Aquatic Biology majors learn to research and study marine organisms and their environments. They receive instruction in freshwater and saltwater organisms, physiological and anatomical marine adaptations, ocean and freshwater ecologies, marine microbiology, marine mammalogy, ichthyology, marine botany, and biochemical products of marine life used by humans. They learn about the diversity of life in the ocean, how ocean species relate to each other as food and prey, and how different species depend on and use the physical and chemical structures of the ocean.

Interests: Life in the ocean, how organisms use the sea as a habitat

Skills and abilities: Quantitative thinking, deductive and inductive reasoning, information ordering, written expression and comprehension

Occupations related to this major: Marine Biologists, Aquatic Biologists, Biochemists, Botanists, Agricultural Scientists, and Zoologists

Microbiology

Microbiology majors concentrate on microorganisms, bacteria, yeasts, fungi, protozoa, and one-celled algae. They learn about the application of these organisms in the production of food products, antibiotics, and industrial chemicals. They learn to use the basic knowledge acquired from other biological sciences, chemistry/biochemistry, and physics to study microscopic organisms such as bacteria, yeasts, molds, viruses, rickettsia, and protozoa.

Interests: Biological sciences, health and medicine, ecology, food production, investigative research

Skills and abilities: Working with detail, analytic thinking, deductive and inductive reasoning, information ordering

Occupations related to this major: Microbiologists, Botanists, Medical Scientists, Zoologists, Physiologists, and Geneticists

Molecular and Cell Biology

Molecular and Cell Biology majors study the nature of biological phenomena at the molecular level through the study of DNA proteins and other macromolecules relating to genetic information and cell function. They study what cells are, how they are put together, what makes them work, what makes them differ from each other, how they associate and interact, what goes wrong in disease states, and how they can intervene beneficially in these processes. They study how molecular biology underlies many aspects of genetic engineering, protein engineering, and other new approaches to improving upon nature.

Interests: Organisms and their development, how things work, the molecular basis of plant, animal, and human disease, disease prevention

Skills and abilities: Investigative research, laboratory skills, information gathering, deductive and inductive reasoning, oral and written expression and comprehension

Occupations related to this major: Molecular Biologists, Medical Doctors, Toxicologists, Botanists, Plant Pathologists, and Biologists

Science Education

Science Education majors prepare to teach science in grades 7 through 12. Students typically major in one science and take additional course work in two other sciences. They learn techniques for teaching science.

Interests: Working with young people, helping others, the learning process, solving practical problems, understanding complex processes, learning how things work

Skills and abilities: Oral and written expression and comprehension, speech clarity, fluency of ideas, deductive reasoning, working with numbers

Occupations related to this major: Biological Technicians, Health Specialties Teachers, Elementary School Teachers, Dietitians, Nutritionists, Pharmacists, Psychiatrists, Veterinarians, and Medical and Clinical Laboratory Technologists

Wildlife Management

Wildlife Management majors receive a solid background in basic biology. They study natural resources and wildlife management. They study conservation of animal populations and their habitats, paying special attention to species that are hunted regularly and species that are threatened or endangered. They learn to analyze characteristics of animals to identify and classify them; to conduct experimental studies with live animals in controlled or natural surroundings; to study animals in their natural habitats; and to study characteristics of animals such as origin, interrelationships, classification, life histories and diseases, development, genetics, and distribution.

Interests: Nature, conservation of natural resources, hunting, bird-watching

Skills and abilities: Using scientific rules and methods to solve problems, mathematics, deductive and inductive reasoning, problem sensitivity

Occupations related to this major: Wildlife Biologists, Environmental Scientists, Park Naturalists, and Research Wildlife Biologists

Zoology

Zoology majors study the identification, description, and classification of animals. They study life histories, habits, diseases, life processes, and distribution of animal species within the environment. They study living organisms in the animal kingdom, exploring their form and function, chemistry and structure, growth, reproduction, maintenance, and interactions with each other and their world. They study the transmission of characteristics from one generation to the next (genetics and evolution).

Interests: Natural history, wildlife, the outdoors, bird-watching, how things work, living things, fossils, working with animals

Skills and abilities: Deductive and inductive reasoning, synthesizing information, gathering and analyzing information, working with numbers

Occupations related to this major: Zoologists, Ecologists, Agricultural Scientists, Physiologists, Cytologists, Microbiologists, and Botanists

5. BUSINESS AND MANAGEMENT

Business and Management majors are found in every industry. Business executives, administrators, managers, and support staff are found in every organization. They direct and coordinate operations and activities of an organization. Business majors must be comfortable with numbers and the manipulation of data, enjoy working with a computer, and have good communication skills, both written and oral. Business majors deal with large amounts of information to make production, personnel, financial, and marketing decisions.

Interests: Business managers and support workers have an interest in directing and coordinating operations and activities of a business or organization; an interest in making production, personnel, financial, and market decisions of a business.

Popular majors in this field of study: Accounting, Business Administration, Business Education, Finance, Human Resource Management, Insurance and Risk Management, International Business Management, Labor Relations Management, Management, Management Information Systems, Management Science, Marketing, and Real Estate

Employment information/outlook: More than 10,228,200 people worked in related occupations in this field of study in 2016. The 2016–2026 employment growth is expected to be 13.8%.

Median annual wages of wage and salary accountants and auditors were $63,550. Median annual wages, excluding annual bonuses and stock options, of wage and salary financial managers were $109,740. Annual salary rates for human resources workers vary according to occupation, level of experience, training, location, and firm size. Median annual wages in 2016 were $80,220 for advertising and promotions managers, $134,250 for marketing managers, $129,870 for sales managers, and $108,260 for public relations managers. Median annual wages of salaried property, real estate, and community association managers were $52,610 in 2016.

Accounting

Accounting majors learn to keep track of expenditures, income, profit and loss, prepare financial reports, and calculate taxes. They may specialize in auditing, taxes, or consulting. Many accountants seek Certified Public Accountant (CPA) certification after graduation. Students will learn to apply this knowledge in all areas of business, government, and nonprofit enterprises.

Interests: Working with numbers, competition, economics, computers, mathematics, entrepreneurship, social and political activism, moral and ethical responsibility

Skills and abilities: Mathematical reasoning, written and oral expression and comprehension, working with people, leadership

Occupations related to this major: Accountants, Auditors, Loan Officers, Loan Counselors, Credit Analysts, Tax Preparers, Budget Analysts, and Marketing Managers

Business Administration

Business Administration majors learn about a variety of managerial opportunities in finance, accounting, marketing, information management, operations and production, general management, retailing, and consulting. They learn the fundamental principles, concepts, and applications of accounting, finance, and management.

Interests: Leadership, organizing people, taking initiative, starting and running a business, working with numbers, solving problems, competing, taking risks, working with people

Skills and abilities: Oral and written expression and comprehension, speech clarity, inductive reasoning, creative and critical thinking

Occupations related to this major: Private Sector Executives, Administrative Services Managers, Human Resources Specialists, Production Managers, Labor Relations Specialists, and Financial Analysts

Business Education

Business Education majors learn to teach vocational business programs at various education levels. They develop instructional methods and training techniques including curriculum design principles, learning theory, group and individual teaching techniques, design of individual development plans, and test design principles.

Interests: Teaching young people, helping people develop their academic interests in business, and helping people develop career plans

Skills and abilities: Working with young people, speech clarity, oral and written expression and comprehension, teaching, learning, understanding human behavior

Occupations related to this major: Business Education Teacher, Education Administrators, Training and Development Managers, and Educational Program Directors

Finance

Finance majors study financial and accounting information, economic models, and analytic techniques that can be applied to financing problems. They learn to determine prices of assets such as stocks, bonds, and businesses, and to manage assets to maximize their economic value.

Interests: Business, the stock market, the economy, budgets

Skills and abilities: Logical thinking, organizational skills, oral and written expression and comprehension, problem sensitivity, mathematical reasoning, working with people, solving problems with computers

Occupations related to this major: Financial Managers, Financial Planners, Treasurers, Controllers, Chief Financial Officers, and Loan Officers and Counselors

Human Resource Management

Human Resource Management majors learn to deal with many personnel activities, including hiring competent workers and dismissing workers when necessary, keeping records, classifying jobs, evaluating and properly placing workers, analyzing and assisting in morale and discipline problems, and promoting and rewarding employees. They learn to deal with issues that affect men and women at work.

Interests: Solving problems, working with numbers, working with people of different ages and backgrounds, leadership

Skills and abilities: Logical and critical thinking, speech clarity, oral and written expression and comprehension, analyzing numerical data, teamwork

Occupations related to this major: Human Resource Specialists, Training and Development Managers, Labor Relations Managers, Employee Assistance Specialists, Employee Benefits Managers, and Career Planning and Placement Counselors

Insurance and Risk Management

Insurance and Risk Management majors learn to analyze and solve problems involving loss of personal and corporate assets. They study programs, integrate knowledge from finance, quantitative analysis, and management, and include study of the legal, social, and institutional environment in which losses may occur.

Interests: Working with numbers, solving problems, competing, leadership, taking initiative

Skills and abilities: Oral and written expression and comprehension, fluency of ideas, problem sensitivity, deductive and inductive reasoning, creative and critical thinking

Occupations related to this major: Insurance Adjusters, Insurance Appraisers, Risk Managers, Insurance Brokers, Insurance Sales Representatives, and Insurance Underwriters

International Business Management

International Business Management majors learn to determine and formulate policies, and provide the overall direction of international companies or private and public sector organizations with international business activities. They learn to conduct management guidelines set up by a board of directors or similar governing body. They learn basic business management techniques and practices and how business is conducted in other countries and between different countries.

Interests: Business operations, other cultures, different people and environments

Skills and abilities: Learning languages, organizing and managing people, oral and written expression and comprehension, deductive and inductive reasoning, fluency of ideas

Occupations related to this major: International Business Managers, International Purchasing Agents and Buyers, International Marketing Managers, International Advertising and Promotions Managers, Compliance Officers and Inspectors, and Investment Bankers

Labor Relations Management

Labor Relations Management majors learn to deal with various aspects of employer-employee relations. They learn to deal with wage and salary negotiations, benefits and welfare, affirmative action, grievances, abuses and demands, labor laws, union organization, and collective bargaining. Particular attention is given to government policies, labor unions, and human resources management.

Interests: The employment relationship, human behavior, problem solving

Skills and abilities: Working with people, oral and written expression and comprehension, problem sensitivity, inductive reasoning

Occupations related to this major: Labor Relations Managers, Human Resource Managers, Training and Development Managers, Employee Assistance Specialists, Employee Benefits Managers, and Union Organizers

Management

Management majors study courses designed for the generalist who wants a broad business background. They take courses in business areas, such as accounting, marketing, finance, and business law, and courses that prepare them to function as managers in any organization.

Interests: Working with people, listening, persuading, leading, starting new systems

Skills and abilities: Thinking analytically, problem sensitivity, oral and written expression and comprehension, speech clarity

Occupations related to this major: General and Operations Managers, Marketing Managers, Public Relations Managers, Corporate Communications Specialists, Human Resource Specialists, and Human Resources Recruiters

Management Information Systems

Management Information Systems majors unite studies in computer science and business knowledge. They learn to act as intermediaries between persons with information needs and the computer programmers who provide the solutions to the problems.

Interests: Computer languages, computer programming, problem solving, logic, taking initiative, organizing groups

Skills and abilities: Oral and written expression and comprehension, deductive and inductive reasoning, information ordering, fluency of ideas, creativity

Occupations related to this major: Management Information Systems Managers, Systems Analysts, Computer Support Specialists, Database Administrators, and Computer Programmers

Management Science

Management Science majors learn to plan, organize, direct, and control the functions and processes of a business firm or organization. They learn about management theory, human resources, management and behavior, accounting and other quantitative methods, purchasing and logistics organization and production, marketing and business decision making. They learn to use mathematics, computers, and statistical and economic analysis to solve managerial and business problems.

Interests: Mathematics, solving business and management problems, computer languages, computer programming

Skills and abilities: Quantitative thinking, computer programming, creativity, oral and written expression and comprehension, speech clarity

Occupations related to this major: Employee Training Specialists, Administrative Service Managers, Purchasing Managers, Association Managers, and Property Managers

Marketing

Marketing majors learn to increase sales of products or services by analyzing and compiling data, and researching and influencing the purchasing power of the public through inventory procedures. They study trend forecasting, product development, management, wholesale selling, and operations. They learn how to display and to buy and sell items through showrooms, department stores, and specialty shops. They learn to make decisions about product design and quality, pricing, advertising, selling, and distribution.

Interests: Running a business, economic issues, social issues, working on new products, problem solving, analyzing data, understanding how people buy, use, and sell products and services

Skills and abilities: Oral and written expression and comprehension, speech clarity, originality, fluency of ideas, mathematical reasoning, persuasion

Occupations related to this major: Marketing Managers, Sales Managers, Public Relations Representatives, Advertising and Promotions Managers, Market Research Analysts, and Advertising Account Executives

Real Estate

Real Estate majors learn to show real estate properties to clients, evaluate and list properties for sale, and advise and arrange financing. They study property management and insurance. They act as independent agents, brokers, or appraisers. They gain an understanding of and proficiency in the business and social principles that affect how real property—buildings and land—is developed, operated, and traded.

Interests: Business, people and social conditions, the economy, public affairs

Skills and abilities: Oral and written expression and comprehension, mathematical reasoning, working independently, critical and analytic thinking

Occupations related to this major: Property Managers, Real Estate Sales Agents, Real Estate Financial Analysts, Real Estate Brokers, Loan Processors, and Real Estate Appraisers

6. COMMUNICATIONS

Communications is the giving or exchanging of information. It is a way to share facts, experiences, or emotions with others. A message can be conveyed through a wide variety of means. These can include writing, speaking, drawing, or using face, hand, and body movements. People receive messages through each of the five senses: taste, touch, sight, smell, and hearing. Communications studies involve the understanding of the role of mass communication in society; broadcast satellites, cable television transmitters, computer networks, and other mass media technology provide a global communication system. The field of communications includes training for those occupations necessary for the system to work efficiently.

Interests: The ways and means of exchanging information; an interest in broadcast satellites, television transmitters, computer networks, and other mass media technology.

Popular majors in this field of study: Advertising, Communications, Creative Writing, Journalism, Public Relations, Radio/Television Broadcasting, and Speech

Employment information/outlook: More than 1,531,000 people worked in related occupations in this field of study in 2016. The 2016–2026 employment growth is expected to be 10.8%.

Nonsupervisory workers in advertising and public relations services earned an average of $747 a week—significantly higher than the $608 a week for all nonsupervisory workers in private industry.

Median annual wages for salaried writers and authors were $51,510 in 2016. Median annual wages were $76,790 for those working in advertising, public relations, and related services and $51,510 for those working for newspaper, periodical, book and directory publishers. In 2016, median annual wages for salaried editors were $53,880; those working for newspaper, periodical, book, and directory publishers were $52,000. Freelance writers earn income from their articles, books, and less commonly, television and movie scripts. While most work on an individual project basis for multiple publishers, many support themselves with income derived from other sources. Unless gotten from another job, freelancers generally have to provide for their own health insurance and pension. Weekly earnings of nonsupervisory workers in broadcasting averaged $852 in 2016, higher than the average of $608 for all private industry. Earnings of broadcast personnel typically are highest in large metropolitan areas.

Advertising

Advertising majors learn to plan and prepare advertisements for newspapers, magazines, radio, television, billboards, and brochures. They may specialize in writing copy, layout, or research. They use creative talents to market a product to prospective clients. They learn how advertising campaigns are produced, how advertising is coordinated with marketing, and how advertising strategies develop from research. They learn to write advertising copy for broadcasting and print, and to select media for advertising campaigns.

Interests: Writing, art and design, analysis, knowing something about lots of things, investigative research

Skills and abilities: Oral and written expression and comprehension, originality, fluency of ideas, analytic reasoning, public speaking, art and design

Occupations related to this major: Advertising and Promotions Managers, Advertising Agency Account Executives, Marketing Managers, Sales Managers, Fund-raising Directors, and Advertising Research Specialists

Communications

Communications majors study the role of mass communication in society. They study the nature, function, content, values, and effects of communication on public policy and opinion. They study the nature of language and how it is communicated. They study the history of political and religious oratory; explore the sociology of interpersonal relations, group dynamics, and messages; examine ways of thinking about human symbol systems (semiotics); and examine the ethics of communication.

Interests: Politics, presentations, advertising, television, film, analyzing oral and electronic messages

Skills and abilities: Oral and written expression and comprehension, critical listening, logical analysis, leadership

Occupations related to this major: Communications Managers, Public Relations Specialists, Television Producers and Directors, Press Secretaries, Reporters, and Speech Writers

Creative Writing

Creative Writing majors study the processes and techniques of original composition in various literary forms, such as short stories, novels, biographies, articles, plays, and scripts. They receive instruction in technical and editorial skills, criticism, and the marketing of finished manuscripts.

Interests: Reading, fiction and nonfiction prose, writing, factual information, English language, critical thinking, computers

Skills and abilities: Written and oral expression and comprehension, information ordering, deductive and inductive reasoning, fluency of ideas

Occupations related to this major: Radio and Television Announcers, Broadcast News Analysts, Reporters and Correspondents, Editors, Technical Writers, and Poets and Lyricists

Journalism

Journalism majors learn to write, edit, manage, and produce newspapers and magazines. They learn to interview people, review records, observe events, and conduct journalistic research. They study the liberal arts and sciences to acquire the depth and breadth of knowledge they need to understand the world better and communicate information about it to others. They learn special skills needed by reporters, editors, broadcasters, and photojournalists.

Interests: Human psychology and behavior, reading widely, photography, world events

Skills and abilities: Writing, oral and written expression and comprehension, speech clarity, learning quickly about a wide range of topics

Occupations related to this major: Reporters and Correspondents, Magazine Writers and Editors, Columnists, Critics, Commentators, Creative Writers, Radio and Television Reporters, and Photojournalists

Public Relations

Public Relations majors learn how to manage an organization's or an individual's communication and relationship with others.

They develop skills to build trust between an organization and the public. They learn how to write news articles and press releases, give speeches, and create audiovisual presentations designed to build trust. They learn technical and managerial skills, such as writing and producing printed and visual materials, and study strategic planning and problem solving.

Interests: Solving problems, mediating between opposing groups, writing, public speaking, giving advice

Skills and abilities: Communicating clearly, oral and written expression and comprehension, speech clarity, fluency of ideas, creative and critical thinking

Occupations related to this major: Public Relations Specialists, Publicity Writers, Advertising and Promotions Managers, Corporate Video Producers, Staff Writers and Editors, Special Events Planners, and Reporters and Correspondents

Radio/Television Broadcasting

Radio/Television Broadcasting majors learn about the planning, preparation, and production of radio and television programs. They may specialize in announcing, programming, engineering, or sales. They study the relationship between the mass media and society and develop skills in such specialties as reporting, performance, production, sales, and management

Interests: Writing, speaking, editing words, pictures, or sound; operating a camera; sound recording

Skills and abilities: Interviewing people, oral and written expression and comprehension, speech clarity, persuasion, operating technical equipment

Occupations related to this major: Broadcast News Analysts, Reporters and Correspondents, Radio/Television Announcers, Radio/Television Producers, Station Managers, Radio/Television Writers

Speech

Speech majors learn about the human communication process. They learn the principles and practical application of speech communication, and the skills and techniques essential for effective interpersonal communication. They learn to develop listening skills.

Interests: Public speaking, human behavior

Skills and abilities: Working with people, oral and written expression and comprehension, speech clarity

Occupations related to this major: Speech Teachers, Speech Writers, Public Relations Specialists, Journalists, Writers, Editors, and Radio and Television Reporters

7. COMPUTER AND INFORMATION SCIENCES

Computer and Information Sciences field of study prepares students for a wide variety of occupations in most sectors of the economy. This field of study prepares a wide range of professionals who design computers and the software that runs them. Information technology occupations are comprised of computer-related occupations engaged in either managing, storing, transmitting, or generating the information organizations use to make decisions, as well as installing and repairing computer hardware and software used to perform such tasks. Computer science is distinguished by a high level of theoretical expertise and innovation applied to complex problems, as well as the creation or application of new technology. Computer scientists and technicians can be theorists, researchers, or inventors. They may work at an academic institution on theory, hardware, or language design. Others work in industry to apply theory, develop specialized languages, or design programming tools and knowledge-based systems.

Interests: Designing computers and the software that runs them; managing, storing, transmitting, or generating and repairing computer hardware and software used to perform such tasks

Popular majors in this field of study: Computer Software Engineering, Computer Science, Information Sciences and Systems, Computer Programming, Mathematics, Mathematics Education, and Statistics

Employment information/outlook: More than 1,549,700 people worked in related occupations in this field of study in 2016. The 2016–2026 employment growth is expected to be 16.8%.

Median annual wages of wage-and-salary computer applications software engineers were $85,430; computer systems software engineers, $92,430; mathematicians, $95,150; and statisticians, $72,610.

Computer Software Engineering

Computer Software Engineering majors study applied mathematical and scientific principles to the design, development, and operational evaluation of computer hardware and software systems and related equipment and facilities. They learn to develop, create, and test applications software and/or operating systems level software. They learn to analyze specific problems in computer applications.

Interests: Computers and electronics, computer programming, problem solving, engineering technology, design

Skills and abilities: Using mathematics to solve problems, computer programming, critical thinking, oral and written expression and comprehension, speech clarity, problem sensitivity

Occupations related to this major: Computer Support Specialists, Mathematical Technicians, Computer Science Teachers, and Numerical Tool and Process Control Programmers

Computer Science

Computer Science majors learn to design new computers, computer languages, and related devices, and research new ways to use computers effectively. They become involved in aspects of artificial intelligence, from pattern recognition to problem solving. They learn how computers work and how to program computers to perform tasks and provide services. They study the physical hardware components of computer systems and software procedures for making computers work.

Interests: Mathematics, electronics, investigative research

Skills and abilities: Oral and written expression and comprehension, mathematical reasoning, problem solving, abstract reasoning, working with people

Occupations related to this major: Computer Scientists, Computer Engineers, Computer Science Teachers, Computer Programmers, Software and Hardware Developers

Information Sciences and Systems

Information Sciences and Systems majors receive broad exposure to computer and programming concepts. They learn to bring people and computers together to solve problems in businesses and other organizations. They learn to plan, direct, and coordinate activities in such fields as electronic data processing, information systems, systems analysis, and computer programming.

Interests: Solving problems, working with details, taking initiative, working with numbers, organizing information, working with people

Skills and abilities: Oral and written expression and comprehension, mathematical reasoning, deductive reasoning, critical and logical thinking, working with changing technology

Occupations related to this major: Computer Programmers, Information Systems Designers, Information Systems Analysts, Computer Security Specialists, Database Administrators

Computer Programming

Computer Programming majors learn to write step-by-step instructions in several computer languages and create video games and software packages. They learn how to write software to handle specific jobs. They learn to convert project specifications and statements of problems and procedures to detailed logical flowcharts for coding into computer language. They learn to develop and write computer programs to store, locate, and retrieve specific documents, data, and information. They learn how to maintain software that controls the operations of entire computer systems.

Interests: Mathematics, electronics, using computers, investigative research, problem solving

Skills and abilities: Programming, critical thinking, active listening, oral and written expression and comprehension, mathematical reasoning, fluency of ideas, problem sensitivity

Occupations related to this major: Computer Programmers, Computer and Information Systems Managers, Computer Support Specialists, Computer Systems Analysts, Numerical Tool and Process Control Programmers, and Computer Science Teachers

Mathematics

Mathematics majors learn to solve both theoretical and practical problems that can be explained in mathematical terms. They study all aspects of algebra, geometry, advanced mathematics, and computer languages. They develop the abilities to explore, conjecture, and reason logically as well as the ability to use various mathematical methods effectively to solve problems.

Interests: Problem solving, working with numbers, games requiring analytic reasoning, investigative research

Skills and abilities: Oral and written comprehension, number facility, mathematical reasoning, deductive reasoning, analytic skills

Occupations related to this major: Mathematicians, Statisticians, Mathematics Teachers, and Financial Analysts

Mathematics Education

Mathematics Education majors learn to teach mathematics at the high school or middle school level. They learn techniques to help students develop skills and knowledge in the field of mathematics; they also take professional education courses.

Interests: Problem solving, analytic reasoning, working with young students, working with computers, leadership, organizing people

Skills and abilities: Oral and written expression and comprehension, speech clarity, organizational skills, creativity, using computers

Occupations related to this major: Middle School Teachers, High School Teachers, Insurance Underwriters, Business Training Specialists, and Education Administrators

Statistics

Statistics majors learn the science of dealing with data. They learn to design efficient data collection systems and to analyze and interpret information derived from the data. They learn to use mathematical theory or apply statistical theory and methods to collect, organize, interpret, and summarize numerical data to provide usable information. They may specialize in fields such as biostatistics, agricultural statistics, business statistics, economic statistics, or other fields.

Interests: Mathematics, working with numbers, problem solving, quantitative problems

Skills and abilities: Mathematical reasoning, computer operations, critical thinking, deductive and inductive reasoning, written expression

Occupations related to this major: Statisticians, Actuaries, Mathematicians, Operations Research Analysts, and Cost Estimators

8. EDUCATION

Education is a people-oriented field of study providing teachers, librarians, and school counselors involved in helping others to learn, acquire information, or gain insight into it. There are many levels on which one can teach. These include preschool and day care facilities, elementary schools, secondary schools, colleges and universities, as well as public and private vocational education institutions, dance, music, and art studios, and many other places. Librarianship and counseling are smaller fields than teaching. Archivists and curators are more involved with things than people. They may also help people learn and gain information, but they do not usually work as closely with people as do teachers, librarians, and counselors. All of these professions usually require a bachelor's degree, although some require a master's or doctoral degree.

Interest: Helping others learn, acquire information; teaching, counseling, or librarianship

Popular majors in this field of study: Early Childhood Education, Elementary School Education, Library Science, Middle School Education, Parks and Recreation Management, Physical Education, Secondary School Education, Special Education, Technology Education, and Vocational and Educational Counseling

Employment information/outlook: More than 6,758,700 people worked in related occupations in this field of study in 2016. The 2016–2026 employment growth is expected to be 15%.

Median annual wages of preschool teachers was $27,130; kindergarten, elementary, middle, and secondary school teachers ranged from $53,090 to $57,810 in that same period. In 2012, the majority of all elementary, middle, and secondary school teachers belonged to unions—mainly the American Federation of Teachers and the National Education Association—that bargain with school systems over salaries, hours, and other terms and conditions of employment. Median annual wages in May 2012 of special education teachers who worked primarily in preschools, kindergartens, and elementary schools was $55,060; middle school special education teachers, $87,760; and special education teachers who worked primarily in secondary schools, $51,260. Median annual wages of vocational education teachers in elementary and secondary schools in 2016 were $56,270.

Early Childhood Education

Early Childhood Education majors learn to teach preschool students through art, music, play, poetry, and stories to prepare for learning language, science, numbers, and social studies. They learn to design programs to develop students' mental capacities, learning abilities, and emotional health. They learn a variety of appropriate teaching methods and strategies.

Interests: Childhood development, working with children, communicating with children and their parents

Skills and abilities: Oral expression and comprehension, speech clarity, problem sensitivity, time sharing, creativity, music or artistic ability

Occupations related to this major: Preschool Teachers, Kindergarten Teachers, Elementary School Teachers, Early Childhood Education Program Directors, Child Care Administrators, and Family Service Coordinators

Elementary School Education

Elementary School Education majors learn to teach young students (kindergarten through grade 6) basic academic, social, and manipulative skills. They learn to instill good study and work habits and an appreciation for learning. They learn to prepare lesson plans, tests, records, and reports, and to conduct conferences with parents. They learn a variety of methods for understanding how and why children develop socially and intellectually, and get professional experience that includes research in teaching and learning.

Interests: Communication, creativity, problem solving, flexibility, ability to organize, energy, enthusiasm

Skills and abilities: Oral and written expression and comprehension, speech clarity, problem sensitivity

Occupations related to this major: Elementary School Teachers, Kindergarten Teachers, Middle School Teachers, Secondary School Teachers, Special Education Teachers, and School Counselors

Library Science

Library Science majors learn the science of acquiring and organizing collections of books, pamphlets, manuscripts, clippings, and reports, and assisting readers in their use. They learn how to analyze reader needs, prepare bibliographies, and organize films, tapes, and maps.

Interests: Reading, multimedia communication, working with people, computers

Skills and abilities: Reading comprehension, active listening, oral and written expression and comprehension, speech clarity, fluency of ideas, information ordering

Occupations related to this major: Librarians, Computer and Information Systems Managers, Elementary School Teachers, Secondary School Teachers, and School Administrators

Middle School Education

Middle School Education majors learn to develop a wide array of instructional skills, which include multimedia approaches, classroom management, advisory ability, effective communication, and alternatives to teacher-centered instruction. They learn to build on and extend basic academic skills developed in elementary school students, and introduce them to the world of more abstract thinking and knowledge that they will encounter in high school.

Interests: Helping or providing service to others, communicating with young people, teaching young people, working with ideas

Skills and abilities: Instructing others, active listening, social perceptiveness, oral and written expression and comprehension, speech clarity, problem sensitivity

Occupations related to this major: Middle School Teachers, High School Teachers, Vocational Education Teachers, School Counselors, and Librarians

Parks and Recreation Management

Parks and Recreation Management majors study how individuals and communities pursue leisure and recreation. They explore what recreation is, investigate what motivates people's recreational choices, and develop skills to manage a variety of leisure and recreation enterprises and organizations.

Interests: Working with people; scientific, historic, and natural features of parks, forests, and other attractions

Skills and abilities: Helping others, leadership, solving problems, oral and written expression, speech clarity, problem sensitivity

Occupations related to this major: Community Recreation Planners/Directors, Social Directors, Park Naturalists, Forest Rangers, Amusement and Recreation Establishment Managers, and Camp Directors

Physical Education

Physical Education majors learn to teach and supervise individual and team sports. They learn to demonstrate sports techniques, analyze physical capabilities and needs of students, and administer corrective exercises and physical conditioning. They learn to provide students with activities to maximize physical fitness.

Interests: Physical activity, sports, working with people, health-related issues, biological science

Skills and abilities: Physical stamina, leadership, oral expression, speech clarity, multilimb coordination

Occupations related to this major: Physical Education Teachers, Sports Coaches, Physical Training Instructors, Aerobic Dance Instructors, Athletic Trainers, Fitness Directors, and Athletic Administrators

Secondary School Education

Secondary School Education majors learn to teach one or more high school subjects using various teaching methods. They learn to develop and plan teaching materials and assignments. They learn to construct tests to evaluate learning. They gain depth of knowledge in the subject they intend to teach and develop teaching skills in subject matters such as science, mathematics, social studies, English, music, art, business, physical education, or other subjects.

Interests: Serving others, teaching young people and helping them develop their academic interests and career choices

Skills and abilities: Working with people, teaching, learning, understanding human behavior, oral and written expression and comprehension, speech clarity

Occupations related to this major: Secondary School Teachers, Middle School Teachers, Special Education Teachers, Vocational Education Teachers, and Vocational and Educational School Counselors

Special Education

Special Education majors prepare for a career working with disabled children and adults in a variety of settings. They learn to coordinate the services available to people with disabilities, and provide appropriate educational experiences for people with varying disabilities, including deafness, blindness, aphasia, and mobility impairments.

Interests: Helping others, working with people

Skills and abilities: Accepting differences in people, communicating effectively, teaching, oral and written expression and comprehension, speech clarity, problem sensitivity

Occupations related to this major: Special Education Teachers; Teachers of the Emotionally and Mentally Impaired; Teachers of the Physically, Visually, and Hearing Impaired; Rehabilitation Counselors

Technology Education

Technology Education majors are trained to teach the design, operation, and impact of technological systems to students. They learn technical skills to be used in advanced communication, applied higher mathematics, and science. This major prepares students to teach technical pathway programs found in middle schools, high schools, and colleges. Technical majors can be planned in agriculture, arts, communication, business, engineering, information science, mechanics, and other fields.

Interests: Helping people, design, technological systems, network technology, graphics and multimedia, system designs, programming, teaching

Skills and abilities: Working with people, oral and written expression and comprehension, analyzing and describing technological systems

Occupations related to this major: Agriculture Teachers, Art Teachers, Computer Science Teachers, Business Teachers, Engineering Technology Teachers, and Science Teachers

Vocational and Educational Counseling

Vocational and Educational Counseling majors learn to counsel individuals and provide group educational and vocational guidance services. They learn to promote and enhance student learning through three broad and interrelated areas of student development: academic development, career development, and personal/social development.

Interests: Working with, communicating with, and teaching people; providing service to others

Skills and abilities: Speaking, active listening, oral and written expression and comprehension, problem sensitivity, speech clarity, fluency of ideas

Occupations related to this major: Educational and Vocational School Counselors, Child, Family, and School Social Workers, Health Educators, and Probation Officers

9. ENGINEERING

Engineering field of study involves planning and designing various things. Engineers design machines, processes, systems, and structures. They apply physical laws and mathematical theories and principles to solve practical technical problems. Engineers work in research, development, design, manufacturing and construction, operations, management, technical sales, teaching, and consulting services.

Interests: Designing machines, processes, systems and structures; research, development, design, manufacturing and construction, operations, management, and technical consulting services

Popular majors in this field of study: Aerospace/Aeronautical Engineering, Agricultural Engineering, Chemical Engineering, Civil Engineering, Computer Engineering, Electrical Engineering, Industrial Engineering, Materials Engineering, Mechanical Engineering, and Petroleum Engineering

Employment information/outlook: More than 1,166,700 people worked in related occupations in this field of study in 2016. The 2016–2026 employment growth is expected to be 9.7%.

Earnings for engineers vary significantly by specialty, industry, and education. Variation in median earnings and in the earnings distributions for engineers in a number of specialties is especially significant. Median annual wages of aerospace engineers in 2016 was $103,720; agricultural engineers, $74,000; chemical engineers, $94,350; civil engineers, $79,340; computer engineers, $100,920; electrical engineers, $89,630; industrial engineers, $78,860; materials engineers, $85,150; mechanical engineers, $80,580; and petroleum engineers, $130,280.

Aerospace/Aeronautical Engineering

Aerospace/Aeronautical Engineering majors learn to perform a variety of engineering work in designing, constructing, and testing aircraft, missiles, and spacecraft. They learn to conduct basic and applied research to evaluate adaptability of materials and equipment to aircraft design and manufacture. They learn to make improvements in testing equipment and techniques.

Interests: Model aircraft and rocketry, astronomy, piloting, space exploration, computers, problem solving, working with people

Skills and abilities: Leadership, computer technology, physical science, oral and written expression and comprehension, mathematical reasoning, deductive and inductive reasoning

Occupations related to this major: Aerospace/Aeronautical Engineers, Electronics Engineers, Nuclear Engineers, Ceramic Engineers, Chemical Engineers, and Civil Engineers

Agricultural Engineering

Agricultural Engineering majors learn to apply knowledge of engineering technology and biological science to agricultural problems concerned with power and machinery, electrification, structures, soil and water conservation, and processing of agricultural products.

Interests: Solving problems, improving the quality of life, computers, leadership

Skills and abilities: Problem solving, oral and written expression and comprehension, computer operation, deductive and inductive reasoning, number facility

Occupations related to this major: Soil Conservationists, Landscape Architects, Geoscientists, Foresters, Chemical Engineers, Industrial Engineers, and Mechanical Engineers

Chemical Engineering

Chemical Engineering majors learn to turn chemicals into products through research and development. They learn to devise economical and efficient production processes. They learn to work in a number of fields, such as cosmetics, fertilizers, paints, dyes, pesticides, oil refining, and pollution prevention.

Interests: Science, chemistry, mathematics

Skills and abilities: Applying knowledge of science and mathematics to real-world problems, written expression and comprehension, mathematical reasoning, originality, deductive reasoning

Occupations related to this major: Chemical Engineers, Nuclear Engineers, Civil Engineers, Petroleum Engineers, Agricultural Engineers, and Electrical Engineers

Civil Engineering

Civil Engineering majors learn to solve technical problems involved in providing buildings, bridges, airports, transportation systems, foundations, coastal facilities, environmental control systems, and water supply and purification systems. They become involved in the conception, planning, design, construction, operation, and maintenance of these important public facilities. Studies will include soil mechanics, hydraulics, and structural engineering.

Interests: Mathematics, physical sciences, computers, building things, public service, applying mathematics and science to practical uses

Skills and abilities: Mathematics, physical sciences, logical thinking, interpersonal skills, oral and written expression and comprehension, inductive and deductive reasoning

Occupations related to this major: Civil Engineers, Civil Engineering Technicians, Architectural Engineers, Nuclear Engineers, Electrical Engineers, and Industrial Engineers

Computer Engineering

Computer Engineering majors learn to design and develop computer and computer-related systems. These systems include software systems, hardware systems, and combined hardware/software systems. Students take courses in basic sciences, mathematics, and engineering science and design.

Interests: Mathematics, science, computing, investigative research

Skills and abilities: Mathematics, computer operations, oral and written expression and comprehension, inductive and deductive reasoning

Occupations related to this major: Computer Hardware Engineers, Computer Software Engineers, Electronics Engineers, and Computer Service Technicians

Electrical Engineering

Electrical Engineering majors learn to design, develop, test, or supervise the manufacturing and installation of electrical equipment components or systems for commercial, industrial, military, or scientific use. They learn to design and manufacture a broad array of electrical and electronic devices and systems to meet society's needs.

Interests: Computer languages, computer programming, electronic equipment

Skills and abilities: Mathematics, physical science, oral and written expression and comprehension, deductive reasoning

Occupations related to this major: Electrical Engineers, Electronics Engineers, Mechanical Engineers, Electricians, Nuclear Engineers, and Production Engineers

Industrial Engineering

Industrial Engineering majors learn to plan, design, and implement complex systems for industry that take into account the availability, capabilities, and needs of people, machines, and materials. They learn to plan the layout of factories for efficiency, and engage in time, motion, and incentive studies. They learn about safety studies, cost, and quality control measures, and long-range planning goals.

Interests: Problem solving, leadership

Skills and abilities: Working with people, critical thinking, written and oral expression and comprehension, fluency of ideas, mathematical reasoning

Occupations related to this major: Aerospace Engineers, Materials Engineers, Petroleum Engineers, Industrial Engineers, Mechanical Engineers, and Engineering Technicians

Materials Engineering

Materials Engineering majors learn to evaluate properties of materials used to manufacture products that must meet specialized design and performance criteria. They learn to develop machinery and processes to manufacture materials, such as polymers, plastics, and alloys.

Interests: Nature and the physical sciences, problem solving, computer operations, working with ideas

Skills and abilities: Creative and critical thinking, problem sensitivity, oral and written expression and comprehension, deductive and inductive reasoning

Occupations related to this major: Materials Engineers, Marine Architects, Mechanical Engineers, Electrical Drafters, and Electrical Engineering Technicians

Mechanical Engineering

Mechanical Engineering majors learn to plan and design tools, engines, machines, and other mechanically functioning equipment. They learn to oversee installation, operation, maintenance, and repair of such equipment as centralized heat, gas, water, and steam systems. They learn to create and build machines, devices, and systems that perform useful services.

Interests: Mechanical devices, computers, cars, solving problems, mathematics, physical science

Skills and abilities: Mathematics, critical thinking, complex problem solving, mathematical reasoning, deductive and inductive reasoning, oral and written comprehension

Occupations related to this major: Mechanical Engineers, Marine Architects, Materials Engineers, Petroleum Engineers, Engineering Technicians, and Mechanical Drafters

Petroleum Engineering

Petroleum Engineering majors learn about exploring and drilling for fossil fuel, both on land and under the sea, and how to maximize the recovery of oil and gas through engineering processes. They learn methods of searching for new sources of energy, for example, geothermal energy. They learn to devise methods to improve oil and gas well production and determine the need for new or modified tool designs.

Interests: Solving problems, working with others, using computers, outdoor activities

Skills and abilities: Mathematics, physics, oral and written expression and comprehension, inductive and deductive reasoning, problem sensitivity, fluency of ideas

Occupations related to this major: Petroleum Engineers, Aerospace Engineers, Marine Engineers, Materials Engineers, Mining and Geological Engineers, and Geologists

10. FAMILY AND CONSUMER SCIENCES

Family and Consumer Sciences majors concentrate on issues concerning feeding, clothing, and caring for children, managing resources, and providing housing for individuals and families. Family and Consumer Science majors provide information, gained through research, about families and individuals as consumers and decision makers. These majors provide information about child care, elder care, food, clothing, housing, finance, and other issues of resource management.

Interests: Issues concerning feeding, clothing, and caring for children, managing resources, and providing housing for individuals and families; an interest in families as consumers and decision makers.

Popular majors in this field of study: Day Care Administration, Family and Consumer Education, Fashion Merchandising, Food Science and Nutrition, Hotel and Motel Management, Housing and Human Development, Individual and Family Development, Leisure Studies, Textile Sciences, and Tourism

Employment information/outlook: More than 1,011,500 people worked in related occupations in this field of study in 2016. The 2016–2026 employment growth is expected to be 7.8%.

Pay depends on the educational attainment of the worker and the type of establishment. Although the pay generally is very low, more education usually means higher earnings. Median hourly wages of child care workers were $9.38 in 2016. Hourly earnings of nonsupervisory workers in clothing, accessory, and general merchandise stores in 2016 were well below the average for all workers in private industry. This reality reflects both the high proportion of part-time and less experienced workers in these stores and the fact that even experienced workers receive relatively low pay compared with the pay of experienced workers in many other industries. Median annual wages of dietitians and nutritionists were $55,240 in 2016. For that same period, lodging managers were $46,810; lodging managers in traveler accommodations, $53,780. Salaries of lodging managers vary greatly according to their responsibilities, location, and the segment of the hotel industry in which they work.

Day Care Administration

Day Care Administration majors learn to manage programs that provide education or social services to young children and their families. They gain knowledge of child development and develop skills in teaching young children, in supervising staff, and in business management.

Interests: Leadership, management, supervising people, administering programs, working with children

Skills and abilities: Organizational and managerial skills, program development, oral and written expression and comprehension, speech clarity

Occupations related to this major: Day Care Director, Preschool Director, Head Start Directors, Early Childhood Education Program Directors, and Child Care Workers

Family and Consumer Education

Family and Consumer Education majors learn to use community resources to meet the needs of the individual and the family in the management of time, energy, and money. They learn about parenting skills, communication skills, relationship skills, wellness, foods and nutrition, consumerism, clothing selection, and job skills. They prepare to become family and consumer teachers for preschool through adult education in subjects related to the family. They study various aspects of family life including human development, nutrition, and decision making, in addition to teaching strategies.

Interests: Family life, using current technology, working with people

Skills and abilities: Critical and analytical thinking, oral and written expression and comprehension, speech clarity

Occupations related to this major: Family and Consumer Science Teachers, Consumer Advocates, Education Consultants, Extension Agents, Financial Planners, Housing Administrators

Fashion Merchandising

Fashion Merchandising majors study how to manufacture fashions for consumers and effectively sell those fashions.

Interests: Current trends in apparel, arts, furnishings, travel and leisure, food business trends, fabrics, fashion and fashion designers

Skills and abilities: Motivating people, leadership, organizational ability, originality, fluency of ideas, color discrimination, oral comprehension

Occupations related to this major: Retail Buyers, Manufacturers' Representatives, Product Designer-Pattern Makers, and Fashion Designers

Food Science and Nutrition

Food Science and Nutrition majors study the nature of foods, the causes of their deterioration, and the principles of food processing. They will learn about the selection, preservation, processing, packaging, distribution, and use of safe, nutritious, and wholesome food.

Interests: Social, health, economic, and political issues involved in food production and availability; chemical reactions and what happens to food when it enters the human body; solving problems

Skills and abilities: Organizational abilities, critical thinking, oral and written expression and comprehension, speech clarity, mathematical reasoning

Occupations related to this major: Dietitians, Nutritionists, Nutrition Educators, and Food Scientists and Technicians

Hotel and Motel Management

Hotel Management majors learn the operation of a hotel. They learn the principles of managing lodging facilities efficiently and profitably. They learn about personnel management, services, supplies, business aspects, decision making, accounting, and public relations. They are introduced to the principles of managing these key components of the hospitality industry.

Interests: Working with people, problem solving, attention to detail, leadership

Skills and abilities: Organization ability, creativity, oral and written expression and comprehension, speech clarity, speech recognition

Occupations related to this major: Lodging Managers, Food Service Managers, Retail Store Managers, and Office Managers

Housing and Human Development

Housing and Human Development majors learn to analyze the use of investment in housing and its impact on families, the community, and the larger economy and society.

Interests: Working with people, serving others, real estate, home automation, the family, marketing, management, interior design, environmental design, finance

Skills and abilities: Computer skills, analytical skills, oral and written expression and comprehension, problem sensitivity

Occupations related to this major: Real Estate Managers, Property Managers, Consumer Affairs Specialists, Extension Agents, and Financial/Mortgage Specialists

Individual and Family Development

Individual and Family Development majors study interpersonal relationships and human development from infancy to old age. They study theories of development with an emphasis on techniques to improve quality of life for individuals and families.

Interests: Helping others, family and individual well-being, prevention and elimination of problems facing people in their daily lives

Skills and abilities: Working with people, critical thinking, oral and written expression and comprehension, curiosity about interpersonal and family dynamics, speech clarity

Occupations related to this major: Child Life Specialists, Day Care Teachers, Recreation Activities Directors, Drug and Alcohol Rehabilitation Counselors, and Crisis Center Directors

Leisure Studies

Leisure Studies majors learn to design, manage, and deliver leisure services to a variety of people in diverse settings. They learn about the impact of leisure services upon individual satisfaction and the quality of life.

Interests: Helping people, leadership, organizing individual and group activities

Skills and abilities: Working with people, oral and written expression and comprehension, speech clarity, problem sensitivity, fluency of ideas, memorization

Occupations related to this major: Amusement and Recreation Establishment Managers, Recreation Workers, Tour Guides and Escorts, Social and Community Service Managers, and Meeting and Convention Planners

Textile Sciences

Textile Sciences majors learn how to design fabrics for garments, upholstery, rugs, and other products. They study print, woven, and embroidery styles, and learn how to buy and sell certain fabrics and trims. They learn how to analyze fabric performance in the marketplace.

Interests: Fashion design, garment fashion, art, history of textiles, textile technology, design principles

Skills and abilities: Originality, visualization, visual color discrimination, fluency of ideas, oral expression and comprehension

Occupations related to this major: Textile Designers, Fashion Designers, Quality Control Analysts, Sales Representatives, and Wardrobe Planners

Tourism

Tourism majors study how to manage travel-related enterprises and conventions and tour services. They learn about travel agency management, travel industry operations and procedures, tourism marketing and promotion strategies, and travel industry law.

Interests: Travel, tourism planning, human resource management, travel industry operations, marketing

Skills and abilities: Oral and written expression and comprehension, mathematical reasoning, speech clarity, fluency of ideas

Occupations related to this major: Travel Agents, Travel Guides, Tour Guides and Escorts, Reservation and Transportation Ticket Agents, and Amusement and Recreation Establishment Managers

11. HEALTH SCIENCE

The **Health Science** field of study trains workers in a vast array of occupations. Occupational titles vary, and the training necessary to fill these occupations requires lengthy postgraduate education. Health practitioners diagnose, treat, and prevent illness and disease. While all health practitioners practice the art of healing, they differ in methods of treatment and areas of specialization. Training for this profession is more rigorous than training for most other professional occupations, but practice also offers unusual rewards. Incomes of health practitioners generally are higher than those of other professional workers with similar years of education. Furthermore, most health practitioners derive considerable satisfaction from knowing that their work contributes directly to the well-being of others. Workers in the industry must have the ability and perseverance to complete the years of study required. They should be emotionally stable, able to make decisions in emergencies, and have a strong desire to help the sick and injured. Sincerity and an ability to gain the confidence of patients are important qualities.

Interests: Diagnosing, treating, and preventing illness and disease; an interest in the well-being of others and a desire to help the sick and injured

Popular majors in this field of study: Athletic Training, Clinical Laboratory Science, Dental Hygiene, Health Services Management, Medical Record Administration, Nuclear Medical Technology, Nursing, Occupational Therapy, Pharmacy, and Physical Therapy

Employment information/outlook: More than 2,775,600 people worked in related occupations in this field of study in 2016. The 2016–2026 employment growth is expected to be 27%.

Most athletic trainers work in full-time positions, and typically receive benefits. The salary of an athletic trainer depends on experience and job responsibilities, and varies by job setting. In 2016, median annual wages for athletic trainers were $42,690; medical and clinical laboratory technologists, $47,820; and dental hygienists, $70,210; Earnings vary by geographic location, employment setting, and years of experience. Dental hygienists may be paid on an hourly, daily, salary, or commission basis. Median annual wages of wage and salary medical and health services managers were $88,580; medical records and health information technicians, $34,160. The median annual wage in May 2012 of nuclear medicine technologists was $70,180; registered nurses, $65,470; occupational therapists, $75,400; salary pharmacists, $116,670; physical therapists, $79,860; and speech-language pathologists, $69,870.

Athletic Training

Athletic Training majors learn to prevent, recognize, refer, and treat injuries and illnesses sustained by athletes. They learn about the administration of athletic training programs in public and private schools, colleges, universities, and with professional teams. They study exercise sciences and the medical aspects of sport. Together with clinical experience, this prepares students for national certification in the field.

Interests: Sports, helping others, health and medicine, physical fitness and exercise, anatomy, nutrition, first aid

Skills and abilities: Manual skills, science, problem solving, interpersonal communication, integrity, oral expression, speech clarity, physical strength

Occupations related to this major: Athletic Trainers, Sports Medicine Clinic Administrators, Exercise Physiologists, Physical and Corrective Therapists, and Occupational Therapists

Clinical Laboratory Science

Clinical Laboratory Science majors learn to perform medical tests to determine the presence and cause of disease. They study sophisticated instrumentation used to perform a variety of laboratory procedures. They study blood and other body fluids that aid in the diagnosis of disease and the maintenance of health.

Interests: Solving problems, working with complex machinery, computer science, laboratory work, helping others, medicine, biological science

Skills and abilities: Computer skills, analytic skills, oral and written expression and comprehension, arm-hand steadiness, visual color discrimination

Occupations related to this major: Laboratory Technologists and Technicians, Research Analysts, Coroners, Clinical Scientists, Environmental Health Officers, and Toxicologists

Dental Hygiene

Dental Hygiene majors learn to work under the supervision of a dentist to clean and polish teeth, massage gums, apply fluoride to prevent decay, and provide dental health education. They obtain the knowledge and clinical skills needed to provide preventive oral health care. They learn skills as an assistant to a dentist performing a number of duties.

Interests: Working with people, helping individuals maintain their health, science

Skills and abilities: Critical thinking, oral expression, arm-hand steadiness, manual dexterity, near vision

Occupations related to this major: Dental Hygienists, Dental Assistants, Dentists, and Medical Assistants

Health Services Management

Health Services Management majors prepare for entry-level positions managing a wide variety of health care organizations such as hospitals, nursing homes, insurance companies, and public agencies. They learn to direct the many activities of health care organizations and coordinate administrative duties with medical services. They learn about space needs, staffing, and supplies. They learn to supervise personnel, prepare budgets, and direct the policies of the organization.

Interests: Working with people, taking initiative, solving problems, working with data

Skills and abilities: Oral and written expression and comprehension, speech clarity, organizational skills, interpersonal skills, critical thinking

Occupations related to this major: Medical and Health Services Managers, Public Health Directors, Educational Program Directors, Nursing Directors, Social Welfare Administrators, and Health Insurance Underwriters

Medical Record Administration

Medical Record Administration majors learn to supervise and manage the preparation, storage, and use of medical records and related information systems. They study the legal and technical aspects of medical records, and the design and management of secure data systems. They learn to merge the study of business and medicine. Students prepare to direct medical record departments in varied health care settings by exploring the health care environment, health care organizations, clinical information systems, medical record department operations, and health care reimbursement systems.

Interests: Leadership, working with people, designing and implementing systems, problem solving, working with detail

Skills and abilities: Writing and speaking effectively, working in a changing environment, oral and written expression and comprehension, near vision, mathematical reasoning

Occupations related to this major: Medical Records Administrators and Directors, Quality Assurance Coordinators, Health Care Administrators, Medical Records Educators, and Research Coordinators

Nuclear Medicine Technology

Nuclear Medicine Technology majors learn how to administer radionuclides to patients and to monitor the characteristics and functions of tissues or organs in which they localize. They learn to operate the cameras that detect the radionuclides and maintain patient records. They learn to prepare and administer radioactive drugs to patients, operate radiation detection equipment, and perform the calculations or computer analysis needed to complete the patient's examination.

Interests: Biological sciences, new technologies, helping others, working in a medical setting, working with people

Skills and abilities: Biological and physical science, working with others, oral and written expression and comprehension, problem sensitivity

Occupations related to this major: Nuclear Medicine Technologists, Radiation Therapists, Radiologic Technologists, Electroneurodiagnostic Technologists, and Medical and Clinical Laboratory Technologists

Nursing

Nursing majors learn to administer nursing care to ill or injured persons. They learn to administer medication and treatments prescribed by medical doctors, observe and record symptoms and behaviors of patients, and promote good health. They learn how to rehabilitate, counsel, and educate patients, and how to work as part of a health care team in many settings. They study humanities, natural sciences, and nursing theory to serve individuals, families, groups, and communities.

Interests: Provide intimate helping services to people, ethical care, chemistry, physics, anatomy, biology

Skills and abilities: Clear thinking, oral and written expression and comprehension, problem sensitivity, speech clarity

Occupations related to this major: Registered Nurses, Doctors of Medicine, Nursing Instructors, Physical Therapists, Medical Assistants, Chiropractors, and Podiatrists

Occupational Therapy

Occupational Therapy majors learn to determine the educational, recreational, and vocational activities needed to hasten a patient's recovery from physical, psychological, social, or developmental problems. They learn to instruct patients in the use of artificial limbs or to regain the use of muscles. They learn to help patients function independently so that they may work, play, take care of themselves, and relate to others in a productive and satisfying manner.

Interests: Solving problems, anatomy, working with people, medicine, health, rehabilitation

Skills and abilities: Logical thinking, working with others, oral and written expression and comprehension, deductive reasoning

Occupations related to this major: Occupational Therapists, Respiratory Therapists, Physical Therapists, Speech-Language Pathologists and Audiologists, Recreational Therapists, and Exercise Physiologists

Pharmacy

Pharmacy majors study the science of drugs, including their chemical and physical properties and composition. They learn to understand the effects of drugs, to test those drugs for purity and strength. They learn to provide drug products and drug information in all areas of patient care. They learn to monitor drug therapy to ensure that the treatment is appropriate, safe, therapeutically effective, and cost-effective.

Interests: Chemistry, biology, mathematics, solving problems, helping others

Skills and abilities: Patience, tact, adapting to change, working carefully, oral and written expression and comprehension, information ordering, mathematical reasoning

Occupations related to this major: Pharmacists, Pharmacy Technicians, Physician Assistants, Opticians, Licensed Practical Nurses, and Dietitians and Nutritionists

Physical Therapy

Physical Therapy majors learn to assist and help persons with injuries, muscle, nerve, and joint problems, burns, and bone diseases. They learn to use exercise, massage, and heat and light to assist in healing. They prepare to take state licensure examinations in this field and qualify for service in the prevention of disabilities and the rehabilitation of the disabled. They learn to test, evaluate, and plan a treatment program for patients who are physically incapacitated as the result of accidents or disease, and for healthy individuals who wish to prevent injuries in work or recreational settings.

Interests: Biological and physical sciences, exercise and fitness, people, analytic reasoning

Skills and abilities: Interpersonal communication, problem solving, visual spatial perception, emotional sensitivity, oral and written expression, speech clarity, problem sensitivity, manual dexterity

Occupations related to this major: Physical Therapists, Occupational Therapists, Respiratory Therapists, Manual Arts Therapists, Corrective Therapists, and Speech-Language Pathologists and Audiologists

Speech Pathology/Audiology

Speech Pathology majors learn to treat people with speech, language, voice, hearing, and communication disorders. These disorders may be the result of hearing loss, brain injury or deterioration, cerebral palsy, stroke, cleft palate, mental retardation, or emotional problems. They receive training in the identification and treatment of human communication disorders. They learn about the normal processes of speech and language development, why problems may occur, and what can be done to minimize their impact.

Interests: Working with children, working with adults, identifying and solving behavioral problems, applying technology to human needs

Skills and abilities: Oral and written expression and comprehension, speech clarity, creativity, working cooperatively in groups

Occupations related to this major: Speech-Language Pathologists and Audiologists, Recreation Therapists, Corrective Therapists, Exercise Physiologists, Occupational Therapists, and Respiratory Therapists

12. HUMANITIES

Humanities students explore thought and expression through aesthetic, historical, philosophical, social, political, psychological, and symbolic contexts. Humanities studies serve as a liberal and broad training for professional careers. Students will enjoy courses in English, literature, history, classics, culture studies, history of art and music, philosophy, foreign language, social and natural sciences. Graduates with a bachelor's degree may qualify for management trainee positions in corporations, banks, and federal and state governmental agencies. Many students use humanities as an undergraduate degree for the teaching or law professions. Other students may become writers or communications specialists in humanistic endeavors.

Interests: Exploring thoughts and expressions through aesthetic, historical, philosophical, social, political, psychological and symbolic contests; literature, history, foreign language, social and natural sciences

Popular majors in this field of study: American Literature, Anthropology, Classics, Comparative Literature, English, English Education, Foreign Language, History, Linguistics, Philosophy, Religion, and Sociology

Employment information/outlook: More than 972,100 people worked in related occupations in this field of study in 2016. The 2016–2026 employment growth is expected to be 11%.

Median annual wages for anthropologists and archaeologists were $57,420; historians, $52,480; sociologists, $74,960. Wages of anthropologists and archaeologists, geographers, and historians vary. The same applies to English and Foreign Language specialists and people in the clergy.

American Literature

American Literature majors study the historical development of the culture in which they live. They study the literature and literary development of the United States from the Colonial Era to the present. They learn about the forces—intellectual, economic, geographic, and social—that have shaped their own character. They study periods and genres, authors, literary criticism, and regional and oral traditions.

Interests: Sensitivity to language, the power of ideas, exploring the development of different regional and ethnic traditions that make up American culture

Skills and abilities: Assessing conflicting points of view, oral and written expression and comprehension, speech clarity

Occupations related to this major: English Teachers, Creative Writers, Art, Drama, and Music Teachers, Reporters and Correspondents, and Publicity Writers

Anthropology

Anthropology majors learn to make comparative studies of the distribution, origin, and evolution of man, cultures that man has created, and their social and physical characteristics. Studies include ancient as well as modern man.

Interests: Writing, archeology, sociology, social sciences, investigative research

Skills and abilities: Writing, science, critical thinking, oral and written expression and comprehension, inductive reasoning, fluency of ideas

Occupations related to this major: Anthropologists, Archeologists, Historians, Sociologists, Linguistic Scientists, and Genealogists

Classics

Classics majors immerse themselves in two cultures fundamental to the West—the cultures of ancient Greece and ancient Rome. Students explore the literature, history, art, philosophy, and architecture of those civilizations. Connecting with the past creates a sense of belonging to humanity and participating in human achievement and evokes reflections on the present. Students will explore their poetry, prose, and drama, and consider the relation of literature to other arts and to other fields of study.

Interests: Language, literature, exploring the past, acquiring a broad liberal education

Skills and abilities: Oral and written expression and comprehension, information ordering, skills of analysis and criticism

Occupations related to this major: Classicists, Anthropologists, Art History Teachers, English Teachers, Foreign Language Teachers, and Literature Teachers

Comparative Literature

Comparative Literature majors study the literature of different countries, cultures, and languages. They explore their poetry, prose, and drama, and consider the relation of literature to other arts and to other fields of study.

Interests: Literature, foreign languages, differences between cultures as expressed in their languages and works of art

Skills and abilities: Reading critically, speaking, active listening, oral and written expression and comprehension, speech recognition, information ordering

Occupations related to this major: English Teachers, Foreign Language Teachers, Postsecondary Teachers, Journalists, Lawyers, Reporters and Correspondents, and Writers

English

English majors study the linguistic and literary richness of the English language as well as some of the cultural history of the English-speaking world. They concentrate on specific areas such as creative writing, comparative or American literature, or semantics. They study important works of literature—drama, prose, and poetry—focusing on the point of view, organization, and language of the works. They develop critical and analytical reading skills, and practice language use and composition.

Interests: Reading, talking, writing about literature; music, theater, and film

Skills and abilities: Speaking, writing, oral and written expression and comprehension, speech clarity

Occupations related to this major: English Teachers, Teachers, Journalists, Publishers, Radio and Television Broadcasters, and Social Workers

English Education

English Education majors learn to teach students about English grammar and linguistics. They learn to instruct students in different types of literature such as poetry, short stories, plays, and novels. They learn how to teach students to research and prepare research papers. They learn how to teach public speaking, drama, and English as a second language

Interests: Nature and history of languages, reading, literature, journalism, creative writing, linguistic development of children and teenagers

Skills and abilities: Speaking, working with students, art, guiding discussions

Occupations related to this major: Elementary School Teachers, Secondary School Teachers, Postsecondary School Teachers, Linguistic Scientists, and Speech-Language Pathologists and Audiologists

Foreign Language

Foreign Language majors study foreign languages (French, German, Italian, Japanese, Russian, Spanish, etc.). They study the language, literature, and culture of the country where the language is spoken.

Interests: Literature, history, culture of a language

Skills and abilities: Fluency in speaking and writing, learning languages, oral and written expression and comprehension, speech clarity

Occupations related to this major: Foreign Language Teachers, Translators, Journalists, Foreign Travel Consultants, Diplomats, and Linguists

History

History majors study the social, economic, and political developments of societies. They learn to analyze historical happenings and, as reporters, writers, or teachers, report on their significance. Students expand their knowledge and understanding of the past. Working with written, oral, visual, and art factual evidence they examine the causes, contexts, and chronologies of historical events, thus cultivating a sense of continuity and change in human experiences.

Interests: Curiosity about when, where, and why historical happenings occurred; what it was like to have lived in different times and places

Skills and abilities: Reading carefully, writing clearly, speaking articulately, thinking analytically, oral and written expression and comprehension, expressing ideas with clarity and precision

Occupations related to this major: Historians, Archeologists, Anthropologists, Genealogists, Curators, Archivists, and Teachers

Linguistics

Linguistics majors study the common properties of the world's languages. They study the structure and development of a specific language or language group. They trace the origin and evolution of words through comparative analysis of ancient parent languages and modern language groups. They study word and structural characteristics, such as phonetics and phonology, morphology, syntax, and semantics.

Interests: Language, foreign languages, how people talk and express themselves

Skills and abilities: Learning foreign languages, problem solving, oral and written expression and comprehension, speech recognition

Occupations related to this major: Linguistic Scientists, English as a Second Language Teachers, English Teachers, Foreign Language Teachers, Interpreters, Translators, Public Relations Specialists, and Speech Pathologists

Philosophy

Philosophy majors learn the process of developing a philosophy. They gain insight into how the great minds of the past and present have attempted to answer the most serious questions of the universe. They participate in a tradition of thought as old as civilized life and as new as artificial intelligence and medical ethics. They examine issues of morality, reality, and knowledge. Philosophy is a foundation for teaching, religion, wisdom, and logical thinking.

Interests: Solitary meditation, argument with family and friends, reading, asking the "why" question, seeing the connections between different things

Skills and abilities: Writing, debating, thinking logically, mathematics, oral and written expression and comprehension, speech recognition, information ordering

Occupations related to this major: Philologists, Political Scientists, Anthropologists, Psychologists, Sociologists, and Historians

Religion

Religion majors study and compare the major world religions, as well as many of the lesser-known religions. They study the various branches, sects, and denominations of particular religions. They learn how religion plays an integral part in all societies. They learn to use a range of approaches when examining religion—historical, textual, psychological, philosophical, sociological, and anthropological.

Interests: Different cultures and societies, world religions, human problems and mysteries, such as birth, growth, love, death, grief

Skills and abilities: Reading carefully and critically, foreign languages, oral and written expression and comprehension, problem sensitivity, speech clarity

Occupations related to this major: Clergy, Directors of Religious Activities and Education, Therapists and Counselors, Psychologists, Social Workers, and Teachers

Sociology

Sociology majors study the origin, development, organization, and functions of human society. They trace the origin and growth of human organizations and the behavior and interaction within social groups. They analyze the influence of group activities on individual and group behavior.

Interests: Anthropology, geography, criminology, psychology, investigative research, politics

Skills and abilities: Reading critically, critical thinking, solving problems, oral and written expression and comprehension, deductive reasoning

Occupations related to this major: Sociologists, Anthropologists, Political Scientists, Counseling Psychologists, Historians, and Linguistic Scientists

13. PHYSICAL SCIENCES

Physical Sciences majors in this field of study investigate the structure and composition of the Earth and the universe. Everything in our physical environment, whether naturally occurring or of human design, is composed of chemicals. Chemists search for, and put to practical use, new knowledge about chemicals. Geological scientists play an important role in preserving and cleaning up the environment. Meteorologists forecast the weather. Physicists design and perform experiments with lasers, cyclotrons, telescopes, mass spectrometers, and other equipment. Physical science technicians use the principles and theories of science and mathematics to solve problems in research and development and to help invent and improve products and processes.

Interests: The structure and composition of the Earth and the universe; an interest in our physical environment, whether naturally occurring or of human design

Popular majors in this field of study: Astronomy, Atmospheric Sciences, Chemistry, Environmental Sciences, Geology, Geophysics, and Physics

Employment information/outlook: More than 978,300 people worked in related occupations in this field of study in 2016. The 2016–2026 employment growth is expected to be 10%.

Median wages for physicists and astronomers were $106,360; chemists were $73,060; and environmental scientists, $63,570.

Astronomy

Astronomy majors study the sizes, shapes, motions, and all other physical properties of the sun, moon, stars, and planets. They may use knowledge of astronomy in space exploration and the development of space technology. Students seek to understand the entire universe—its constituent parts, such as the stars and planets, and the physical and mathematical laws that govern them.

Interests: Nature, the night sky, the expanding universe, physical science, astronomical science

Skills and abilities: Mathematics, science, computers, inductive and deductive reasoning, written comprehension

Occupations related to this major: Astronomers, Geophysicists, Physicists, Geologists, Chemists, and Atmospheric and Space Scientists

Atmospheric Sciences

Atmospheric Sciences majors learn to investigate atmospheric phenomena and interpret meteorological data gathered by surface and air stations, satellites, and radar to prepare reports and weather forecasts for public and other uses. They study the basic principles of atmospheric physics and dynamics and are concerned with understanding and forecasting weather.

Interests: Weather, environment, climate, science, mathematics, computer science, geography, serving the public

Skills and abilities: Analytic reasoning, mechanical reasoning, problem solving, oral and written expression and comprehension, speech clarity, inductive reasoning

Occupations related to this major: Atmospheric Scientists, Space Scientists, Climatologists, Geophysicists, Astronomers, and Meteorologists

Chemistry

Chemistry majors study the sciences of physical substances, atoms, molecules, elements, and compounds. They learn to perform chemical tests, develop new chemical products, and monitor the purity of air, food, and drugs. Because it is an experimental science, students learn to design and perform the experiments that allow a better understanding of the physical world.

Interests: Investigative research, problem solving, curiosity about how things work

Skills and abilities: Analytic and mathematical skills, oral and written expression and comprehension, deductive reasoning, mathematical reasoning

Occupations related to this major: Chemists, Chemical Engineers, Chemical Engineering Technicians, Agricultural Scientists, Biological Scientists, and Physicists

Environmental Sciences

Environmental Sciences majors study the biological and physical aspects of the environment. They learn about the conservation and/or improvement of natural resources, such as air, soil, water, land, fish, and wildlife, as well as methods of controlling environmental pollution. They conduct research or perform investigation for the purpose of identifying, abating, or eliminating sources of pollutants or hazards that affect either the environment or the health of the population.

Interests: Investigative research, solving problems, working with ideas

Skills and abilities: Working with others, oral and written expression and comprehension, problem sensitivity, mathematical reasoning, inductive reasoning

Occupations related to this major: Environmental Scientists, Materials Scientists, Geographers, Geologists, Atmospheric Scientists, and Space Scientists

Geology

Geology majors study the Earth's structure, composition, and history. They examine rocks, minerals, and fossils. They record data, prepare maps, conduct surveys, and advise suitability of sites. They develop skills that are useful for basic research and applied problem solving.

Interests: The outdoors, remote places, problem solving, collecting minerals or fossils

Skills and abilities: Reasoning ability, critical thinking, mathematics, oral and written expression and comprehension, number facility, inductive reasoning

Occupations related to this major: Geologists, Physicists, Geophysicists, Materials Scientists, Geological Data Technicians, and Geographers

Geophysics

Geophysics majors study aspects of the earth, including the atmosphere and hydrosphere. They investigate and measure seismic, gravitational, electrical, thermal, and magnetic forces affecting the Earth, and utilize principles of physics, mathematics, and chemistry. They study the Earth and its atmosphere by physical measurements. Students learn to use mathematics and physics, along with electrical engineering, computer science, geology, and other earth sciences to analyze measurements taken at the surface to infer properties and processes deep within the Earth's complex interior.

Interests: The outdoors, travel, taking measurements, computer languages, graphics, computer programming

Skills and abilities: Natural curiosity, mathematics, physical science, computers, oral and written comprehension, mathematical reasoning, deductive reasoning

Occupations related to this major: Geophysicists, Geologists, Astronomers, Physicists, Atmospheric Scientists, Space Scientists, and Chemists

Physics

Physics majors learn to explore and identify the basic principles of the structure and behavior of matter, the generation and transfer of energy, and the interaction of matter and energy. They learn to use these principles in theoretical areas such as the origin of the universe, or in practical areas to develop advanced materials, electronic devices, or medical equipment.

Interests: Investigative research, mathematics, problem solving, improving the quality of life

Skills and abilities: Computational skills, reasoning logically, solving problems, oral and written expression and comprehension, mathematical reasoning

Occupations related to this major: Physicists, Astronomers, Geologists, Atmospheric Scientists, Space Scientists, Geophysicists, and Environmental Scientists

14. SOCIAL AND BEHAVIORAL SCIENCES

Social and Behavioral Sciences majors learn about the social needs of people. Clinical psychologists help the mentally or emotionally disturbed adjust to life through behavior modification programs and other techniques. Social workers address the needs of individuals, families, groups, and communities. Their work may involve everything from helping an elderly person adjust to life in a nursing home, to organizing fund-raising for community social welfare activities. Other social scientists conduct basic and applied research in the social sciences. They use established methods to assemble a body of fact and theory that contributes to human knowledge. Social scientists investigate all aspects of human society—from anthropologists studying the origins of the human race, or historians studying an ancient civilization—to political scientists analyzing the results of presidential elections.

Interests: Social and emotional needs of people; an interest in all aspects of society—from the origins of the human race, or an ancient civilization, to political results of presidential elections

Popular majors in this field of study: Criminal Justice Studies, Economics, Geography, Gerontology, Political Sciences, Psychology, Public Administration, Social Studies Education, and Social Work

Employment information/outlook: More than 4,153,700 people worked in related occupations in this field of study in 2016. The 2016–2026 employment growth is expected to be 19%.

Median annual wages of probation officers and correctional treatment specialists were $38,970; economists, $91,860; salary clinical, counseling, and school psychologists, $69,280; social and human service assistants, $28,850; political scientists, $102,000; sociologists, $74,960; child, family, and school social workers, $44,200. Public administration positions vary by occupation, size of the state or locality, and region of the country.

Criminal Justice Studies

Criminal Justice Studies majors learn about the dimensions and causes of crime and delinquency; the structure of the American criminal justice system; the operation of criminal courts; and the techniques and theories of law enforcement.

Interests: Serving others, court procedures, criminal law, private security, criminal justice

Skills and abilities: Working with others, making decisions, oral and written expression and comprehension, inductive reasoning, speech clarity, problem sensitivity

Occupations related to this major: Criminal Investigators, United States Marshals, Police Detectives, Sheriffs and Deputy Sheriffs, Correction Officers and Jailers, and Child Support and Missing Persons Investigators

Economics

Economics majors learn to plan, design, and conduct research into activities devoted to satisfying human wants. They learn to analyze the relationship between supply and demand. They study the problems of inflation, unemployment, tariffs, taxation, and foreign trade. They learn to analyze such issues as inflation, unemployment, monopoly, and economic growth. They study theory, policy, and trends and explore ways to deal with the economic problems of society and the individual.

Interests: Current issues such as taxes, poverty, health, inflation, the environment, human behavior

Skills and abilities: Solving problems, oral and written expression and comprehension, mathematical reasoning, logical reasoning

Occupations related to this major: Economists, Market Research Analysts, Urban and Regional Planners, Financial Managers, Financial Analysts, and Underwriters

Geography

Geography majors study the activities of people. Students study where people live, why they are located there, and how they earn a living. Students study the physical characteristics of the Earth, such as landforms, vegetation, climate, locale, and mineral and water resources. They study how people relate to and are shaped by their environment. They gain a broad perspective on the world's environments and its peoples while gaining a strong background in the physical and social sciences.

Interests: Analyzing and solving social and environmental problems, doing social and physical scientific research, the relationship between people and their environment

Skills and abilities: Oral and written expression and comprehension, spatial orientation, working individually and in groups, information gathering, working with computers

Occupations related to this major: Geographers, Geophysicists, Geologists, Atmospheric and Space Scientists, Environmental Scientists, and Materials Scientists

Gerontology

Gerontology majors learn about aging and older persons. They study physical, emotional, and intellectual changes in the elderly, cultural aspects of aging, and governmental policies and programs for the aging.

Interests: Helping people, human development, older people, family relations, improving the quality of life

Skills and abilities: Oral and written expression and comprehension, listening, objectivity, deductive reasoning, determining needs and interests, organizing and managing projects

Occupations related to this major: Gerontologists, Geriatric Nurses, Nursing Home Administrators, Social Welfare Administrators, and Occupational and Physical Therapists

Political Sciences

Political Sciences majors study government and the nature of politics. They analyze the operations of different forms of government, and attempt to find theoretical and practical solutions to political problems. Students learn about the origins, historical development, and social functions of government. They study how electoral, legislative, judicial, and administrative structures and processes vary from one country and one age to another; how and why governments change, fall, and engage in wars. They study the behavior of public officials and other citizens involved in politics.

Interests: Public policy issues such as health care and environmental protection; politicians and public figures, justice, good and bad government, law, criminal justice, the legal system

Skills and abilities: Reading critically, thinking analytically, oral and written expression and comprehension, understanding graphic material

Occupations related to this major: Political Scientists, Legislators, Sociologists, Historians, Anthropologists, and Political Science Teachers

Psychology

Psychology majors learn to collect and interpret scientific data relating to human behavior to understand people and explain their actions. They learn to interview patients, give diagnostic tests, and offer therapy to help people make behavioral adjustments. Students study human and animal behavior and explore the processes involved in normal and abnormal thoughts, feelings, and actions. They increase their understanding of behavior while learning psychological facts, methods, principles, and generalizations about individuals and groups.

Interests: Working with people, scientific method, human and animal behavior

Skills and abilities: Critical thinking, oral and written expression and comprehension, inductive reasoning

Occupations related to this major: Developmental Psychologists, Experimental Psychologists, Educational Psychologists, Social Psychologists, Clinical Psychologists, and Counseling Psychologists

Public Administration

Public Administration majors may study in five areas of specialization: personnel, management, public relations, finance, and planning. They learn to establish government policy, and develop laws, rules and regulations. These studies will prepare students to find positions managing public agencies. Students deal with the operations of all forms and levels of government. Students learn about the many skills and challenges associated with implementing public policy in government and in nonprofit organizations.

Interests: Public and community service, organizing people, leadership, working with people from different backgrounds

Skills and abilities: Leadership, organizational ability, problem solving, oral and written expression and comprehension, inductive reasoning

Occupations related to this major: Government Service Executives, City Managers, Management Analysts, Government Affairs Specialists, and Legislators

Social Studies Education

Social Studies Education majors learn to teach courses pertaining to human society and its characteristic elements. They learn to teach subjects such as psychology, economics, history, political science, and sociology. They learn to teach students in middle school and high school courses in history, citizenship, and other social sciences.

Interests: Serving people, working with people, history, social sciences

Skills and abilities: Speaking, organizing working with people, oral and written expression and comprehension, speech clarity

Occupations related to this major: Middle School Teachers, High School Teachers, Postsecondary School Teachers, Historians, Sociologists, and Psychologists

Social Work

Social Work majors study many types of social issues and needs. They learn to aid families with physical, mental, or social problems, such as poverty, unemployment, illness, broken homes, various disabilities, antisocial behavior, and inadequate housing. Students acquire the knowledge and skills to assist individuals, families, groups, and communities in preventing and alleviating the problems of a modern, rapidly changing society. They learn to help others and to modify harmful social conditions, promote social and economic well being, and increase opportunities for all people to live with dignity and freedom.

Interests: Helping those in need, particularly children, the poor, minorities, the aged, the disabled, and women, enabling others to develop unique, positive responses and solutions to their problems

Skills and abilities: Objectivity, ability to listen, analytic ability, oral and written expression and comprehension, problem sensitivity

Occupations related to this major: Social Workers, Medical and Psychiatric Social Workers, Community Organization Social Workers, Residential Counselors, Probation and Correctional Treatment Specialists, and Human Services Workers

LOCATING OCCUPATIONAL INFORMATION RELATED TO YOUR MAJOR

Students may find occupations in a Field of Study in which they have a work interest. They may wish to conduct research to find specific information about an occupation. Good sources for occupational information are public libraries, high school and college career resource centers, One-Stop Career Centers, America's InfoNet (*www.acinet.org*) and O*Net (*www.online.onetcenter.org*), the occupational information Network.

Recommended books for occupations and college entry research:

Occupational Outlook Handbook, 2016–2026 Edition,
U.S. Bureau of Labor Statistics, Postal Square Building
2 Massachusetts Avenue, NE, Washington, DC 20212-0001
www.bls.gov

A Guide to the College Admission Process,
National Association for College Admissions Counseling,
1050 North Highland Street, Suite 400, Arlington, VA 22201
www.nacacnet.org

Federal Student Aid Information Center,
An Office of the U.S. Department of Education,
400 Maryland Avenue, SW, Washington, DC 20202
www.fafsa.ed.gov

CHOOSING A COLLEGE

A student's choice of institution may depend on individual needs and talents. A person's career goals, career plans, and choice of college major are very important criteria in choosing a college. A student's choice may be limited by financial or other considerations. However, if at all possible, students should give high priority to their career plans and choice of a college major when choosing a college that best matches their career plans. Students' choice of their college major may influence their final college choice.

Some majors are rare and specialized. Special attention must be given to those majors that are fairly rare and specialized. Students will be limited in the number of colleges from which to choose. There are more than 1800 four-year colleges in the United States; only 78 offer aerospace engineering; 42 offer landscape architecture; 81 offer astronomy; 24 offer petroleum engineering; 8 offer statistics; 8 offer business statistics; 26 offer oceanography; 59 offer pharmacy; and 115 offer occupational therapy majors. This is a partial listing. A student who chooses a specialized major may find it necessary to travel a distance to find a college offering that major. School career centers and public libraries may carry listings of colleges that offer the major of the student's choice.

The most widely offered baccalaureate-level majors are found in four-year colleges. No college, not even the largest university, offers every major; some offer relatively few. Students will want to attend a college that offers several of the majors they are considering. Students can keep their choice of major open by selecting a university or college that offers a wide range of majors. The most common majors are found in the Art, Business, Computer and Information Science, Education, Engineering, Health, Humanities, and the Social and Behavioral Science fields of study.

MAKING THE FINAL DECISION

Making important decisions and setting long-range goals is never an easy task. Making a decision on what to study in college for four or more years, and how this will fit into students' lifestyles and career goals is very important and very personal. With the soaring costs of education and the increasing complexity of the job market, students cannot afford the luxury of trial and error in preparing for a career that requires college training; entering college without a career or major in mind can add time and expense to the entire journey. Good decision-making calls for awareness of one's needs and the matching of those needs with a wide variety of alternate choices. It is to this end that sufficient information has been explored for making a final decision.

In making a final decision, students must take a broad view of the fourteen Fields of Study. They should look carefully at all career and major options within the fourteen fields. Students should not limit themselves to a career or major that has been recommended to them by family or friends. The final decision should be the student's, along with the responsibility to reach their goals. In the final analysis, students will have to look at themselves. As Plato once said, "Know thyself, and to thine own self be true."

- **Assess work interests.** Identify work-related interests. Discover the type of work activities and occupations that match work interests. Identify and learn about the most relevant broad interest areas. Use interest results to explore the world of work.
- **Assess work values.** Pinpoint what is important in a job. Identify occupations that provide satisfaction based on the similarity among work values, conditions of work, and the characteristics of an occupation.
- **Assess work abilities.** Identify user ability strength, parts of work that the user likes to do, parts of work that the user finds important, and training needs of the user.

The more students know about their interests, work values, abilities, and career goals, the better their decisions will be. In the final analysis, good decision-making by students is based on knowing oneself and being flexible enough to sense whether they are on the right track, and to alter decisions when they are not in their best interest. No matter what major is chosen, students must keep in ming that intellectual flexibility is the skill that enables them to work productively when the knowledge they have mastered is challenged or replaced by new ideas.

We wish all students well in their college studies and in the career path that they have chosen.

Robert Kauk and Francis Ferry

Occupational information was gathered from *O'Net,* U.S. Department of Labor.

INDEX OF COLLEGE MAJORS

This section of *Profiles of American Colleges* will help you quickly determine which schools offer the major in which you are interested, the in-state tuition, room and board costs, and the Selector Rating. The colleges are listed alphabetically and the first column indicates the state where each is located. These data reflect the 2017-2018 academic year. You will be able to compare schools offering those majors that interest you the most and see what their in-state costs and Selector Ratings are, before reading the Profiles in the main section of the book (see page 259 for Selector Rating details). You may also discover some new schools or majors that interset you.

ACCOUNTING

School	ST	$IS	SR
Abilene Christian Univ	TX	43,708	C+
Adams State Univ	CO	15,420	LC
Adelphi Univ	NY	49,792	C
Adrian College	MI	45,550	C
Alabama A&M Univ	AL	18,796	C
Alabama State Univ	AL	16,490	LC
Albany State Univ	GA	19,462	C
Albertus Magnus College	CT	44,016	LC
Albion College	MI	55,260	C
Albright College	PA	57,326	C
Alcorn State Univ	MS	15,884	C
Alderson Broaddus Univ	WV	35,000	LC
Alfred Univ	NY	37,490	C
Alma College	MI	49,410	VC
Alvernia Univ	PA	45,330	C
Alverno College	WI	33,294	LC
American International College	MA	47,020	LC
Anderson Univ	IN	39,450	C
Andrews Univ	MI	41,732	C
Angelo State Univ	TX	15,882	LC
Appalachian State Univ	NC	15,394	VC
Aquinas College - Mich	MI	38,876	VC
Arcadia Univ	PA	55,990	C+
Arizona State Univ at the Tempe Campus	AZ	23,001	VC
Arizona State Univ at the West Campus	AZ	21,513	VC
Arkansas Baptist College	AR	20,280	NC
Arkansas State Univ	AR	16,190	C
Arkansas Tech Univ	AR	16,534	LC
Asbury Univ	KY	36,450	C+
Ashford Univ	CA	10,480	C
Ashland Univ	OH	30,446	C
Assumption College	MA	48,455	VC
Atlantic Union College	MA	27,228	C
Auburn Univ	AL	24,300	VC+
Auburn Univ at Montgomery	AL	15,000	C
Augsburg Univ	MN	45,129	C
Augusta Univ	GA	4,632	C
Augustana College	IL	51,222	VC+
Augustana Univ	SD	39,968	VC
Aurora Univ	IL	34,990	C
Austin Peay State Univ	TN	16,397	C
Averett Univ	VA	43,034	LC
Avila Univ	MO	27,100	C
Azusa Pacific Univ	CA	43,972	C
Baker College of Flint	MI	19,140	NC
Baker Univ	KS	37,190	C
Baldwin Wallace Univ	OH	42,464	VC
Ball State Univ	IN	19,808	C+
Barry Univ	FL	38,730	LC
Bay Path Univ	MA	46,356	C
Bayamon Central Univ	PR	12,490	
Baylor Univ	TX	56,803	HC
Belhaven Univ	MS	32,250	C
Bellarmine Univ	KY	52,532	C
Bellevue Univ	NE	20,300	NC
Belmont Abbey College	NC	28,794	C
Belmont Univ	TN	44,500	VC+
Bemidji State Univ	MN	17,730	C
Benedict College	SC	28,630	NC
Benedictine College	KS	38,850	VC
Benedictine Univ	IL	38,300	C
Bennett College	NC	27,717	NC
Bentley Univ	MA	63,720	MC
Berkeley College/New Jersey	NJ	38,082	LC
Berkeley College/New York City Campus	NY	35,100	LC
Berkeley College/White Plains Campus	NY	35,100	LC
Berry College	GA	47,466	VC
Bethany College	KS	38,637	LC
Bethany College	WV	38,774	LC
Bethel College	IN	36,830	C
Bethel Univ	MN	46,550	C+
Bethune-Cookman Univ	FL	23,322	C
Biola Univ	CA	48,686	C
Birmingham-Southern College	AL	44,478	C+
Black Hills State Univ	SD	16,622	C
Blackburn College	IL	28,526	LC
Bloomfield College	NJ	40,100	LC
Bloomsburg Univ of Pennsylvania	PA	19,930	C
Bluefield State College	WV	5,832	LC
Bluffton Univ	OH	40,950	C+
Boise State Univ	ID	17,368	C
Boston College	MA	68,043	MC
Bowling Green State Univ	OH	19,975	C
Bradley Univ	IL	43,240	VC
Brenau Univ - Women's College	GA	37,876	LC
Brescia Univ	KY	29,890	VC
Brewton-Parker College	GA	26,120	LC
Briar Cliff Univ	IA	36,956	C
Bridgewater State Univ	MA	22,762	C
Brigham Young Univ	UT	13,248	MC
Brigham Young Univ/Hawaii	HI	11,710	C
Bryant Univ	RI	57,204	VC
Bucknell Univ	PA	67,136	MC
Buena Vista Univ	IA	42,344	C
Butler Univ	IN	52,890	VC+
Cabrini Univ	PA	42,591	LC
Cairn Univ	PA	37,572	C
Caldwell Univ	NJ	42,165	LC
Calif Baptist Univ	CA	42,986	C
Calif Lutheran Univ	CA	52,853	C
Calif State Polytechnic Univ, Pomona	CA	21,811	C
Cal State, East Bay	CA	20,748	C
Cal State, Fresno	CA	16,902	LC
Cal State, Fullerton	CA	21,902	C
Cal State, Long Beach	CA	18,850	C
Cal State, Northridge	CA	17,277	LC
Cal State, Sacramento	CA	19,060	C
Cal State, San Bernardino	CA	20,106	C
Calif Univ of Pennsylvania	PA	20,425	LC
Calumet College of St. Joseph	IN	22,735	C
Calvin College	MI	43,090	HC
Cambridge College	MA	14,940	NC
Cameron Univ	OK	11,632	LC
Campbell Univ	NC	37,570	VC
Campbellsville Univ	KY	33,400	C
Canisius College	NY	49,672	C
Capital Univ	OH	44,778	VC
Cardinal Stritch Univ	WI	37,136	C
Caribbean Univ	PR	12,227	
Carlow Univ	PA	39,696	LC
Carroll College	MT	44,304	C
Carroll Univ	WI	38,100	C+
Carson-Newman Univ	TN	35,900	C
Carthage College	WI	48,835	C
Case Western Reserve Univ	OH	62,284	MC
Catawba College	NC	39,820	LC
Cedar Crest College	PA	51,110	C
Cedarville Univ	OH	36,244	VC
Centenary College	NJ	43,890	LC
Central College	IA	44,592	C
Central Conn State Univ	CT	22,041	C
Central Methodist Univ	MO	31,500	VC
Central Mich Univ	MI	20,330	C
Central State Univ	OH	18,564	C
Central Washington Univ	WA	16,803	C
Chaminade Univ of Honolulu	HI	37,614	C
Champlain College	VT	54,724	VC
Chapman Univ	CA	65,504	HC
Chatham Univ	PA	47,883	VC
Chestnut Hill College	PA	47,180	C
Cheyney Univ of Pennsylvania	PA	20,896	LC
Chicago State Univ	IL	41,620	C
Christian Brothers Univ	TN	31,670	VC
Christopher Newport Univ	VA	24,878	VC+
CUNY/Baruch College	NY	21,609	HC
CUNY/Brooklyn College	NY	7,163	C+
CUNY/Hunter College	NY	31,098	VC
CUNY/Lehman College	NY	5,788	LC
CUNY/Medgar Evers College	NY	6,680	NC
CUNY/Queens College	NY	21,507	C
CUNY/York College	NY	6,747	LC
City Univ of Seattle	WA	24,340	NC
Claremont McKenna College	CA	69,900	MC
Clarion Univ of Pennsylvania	PA	21,608	LC
Clark Atlanta Univ	GA	31,019	LC
Clarke Univ	IA	42,950	C
Clayton State Univ	GA	19,735	LC
Clemson Univ	SC		HC
Cleveland State Univ	OH	22,290	C
Coastal Carolina Univ	SC	20,340	C
Coe College	IA	51,570	VC
College of Charleston	SC	24,046	VC
College of St. Benedict	MN	54,480	C
College of St Joseph	VT	32,400	LC
College of St. Scholastica	MN	45,734	C+
College of Staten Island	NY	24,389	LC
College of the Holy Cross	MA	64,320	MC
College of the Ozarks	MO	7,530	VC
College of William & Mary	VA	34,907	MC
Colo Christian Univ	CO	40,885	VC
Colo Mesa Univ	CO	19,707	LC
Colo State Univ	CO	23,033	C
Colo State Univ-Pueblo	CO	21,581	C
Columbia College	SC	36,550	C
Columbus State Univ	GA	14,336	LC
Concord Univ	WV	14,954	LC
Concordia College - Moorhead	MN	46,418	C
Concordia College - New York	NY	39,035	LC
Concordia Univ Nebr	NE	41,900	VC
Concordia Univ St. Paul	MN	29,050	C
Concordia Univ Texas	TX	41,920	C
Concordia Univ Wisc	WI	35,910	C
Concordia Univ, Ann Arbor	MI	38,878	C+
Concordia Univ, Chicago	IL	41,522	C
Converse College	SC	28,290	C
Coppin State Univ	MD	14,071	VC
Corban Univ	OR	41,700	C
Cornerstone Univ	MI	36,550	C
Creighton Univ	NE	49,452	VC
Culver-Stockton College	MO	34,350	C
Cumberland Univ	TN	27,710	C
Curry College	MA	53,331	C
Daemen College	NY	40,336	C
Dakota Wesleyan Univ	SD	33,980	LC
Dallas Baptist Univ	TX	35,220	VC
Davenport Univ	MI	25,896	LC
Davis & Elkins College	WV	38,242	LC
Defiance College	OH	42,240	LC
Delaware State Univ	DE	19,376	LC
Delaware Valley Univ	PA	51,271	C
Delta State Univ	MS	13,176	LC
DePaul Univ	IL	52,807	VC
DeSales Univ	PA	47,520	C
Dickinson State Univ	ND	12,372	LC
Dillard Univ	LA	20,940	VC
Doane Univ	NE	41,340	VC
Dominican College	NY	40,258	LC
Dominican Univ	IL	42,472	C+
Dordt College	IA	37,860	C+
Drake Univ	IA	49,220	HC
Drexel Univ	PA	65,927	HC
Drury Univ	MO	37,555	VC
Duquesne Univ	PA	48,508	VC
D'Youville College	NY	37,678	C
East Carolina Univ	NC	16,539	C
East Central Univ	OK	13,330	C
East Tenn State Univ	TN	18,141	C
Eastern Conn State Univ	CT	23,059	C
Eastern Illinois Univ	IL	21,414	C
Eastern Kentucky Univ	KY	17,742	C
Eastern Mennonite Univ	VA	42,550	C
Eastern Mich Univ	MI	19,761	C
Eastern Nazarene College	MA	41,114	C
Eastern New Mexico Univ	NM	12,874	LC
Eastern Oregon Univ	OR	17,612	C
Eastern Univ	PA	39,540	C
Eastern Washington Univ	WA	17,896	LC
Edgewood College	WI	35,950	C
Edward Waters College	FL	28,089	NC
Elizabeth City State Univ	NC	14,745	C
Elizabethtown College	PA	56,340	VC
Elizabethtown College School of Continuing and Professional Studies	PA	18,900	C
Elmhurst College	IL	46,514	C
Elmira College	NY	53,900	C
Elms College	MA	49,602	VC
Elon Univ	NC	46,142	HC
Emmanuel College	MA	53,472	C+
Emory Univ	GA	63,286	MC
Emporia State Univ	KS	15,029	C
Endicott College	MA	47,054	C+
Eureka College	IL	34,760	C
Evangel Univ	MO	28,898	C
Excelsior College	NY	38,800	SP
Fairfield Univ	CT	61,445	HC
Fairleigh Dickinson Univ/ College at Florham	NJ	54,770	C
Fairleigh Dickinson Univ/ Metropolitan Campus	NJ	52,392	C
Fairmont State Univ	WV	15,726	C
Faulkner Univ	AL	26,410	C
Fayetteville State Univ	NC	17,756	C
Felician Univ	NJ	46,280	LC
Ferris State Univ	MI	21,458	C
Ferrum College	VA	43,970	C
Fitchburg State Univ	MA	21,819	LC
Flagler College	FL	27,620	C
Florida A&M Univ	FL	15,361	C
Florida Atlantic Univ	FL	18,256	C
Florida Gulf Coast Univ	FL	14,738	C
Florida Inst of Technology	FL	53,306	VC
Florida International Univ	FL	20,281	C
Florida Memorial Univ	FL	22,424	LC
Florida Southern College	FL	45,978	VC
Florida State Univ	FL	16,771	HC
Fontbonne Univ	MO	34,606	C
Fordham Univ	NY	68,431	MC
Fort Hays State Univ	KS	12,677	C
Fort Lewis College	CO	20,154	C
Fort Valley State Univ	GA	17,988	VC
Framingham State Univ	MA	21,740	C
Francis Marion Univ	SC	18,144	LC
Franciscan Univ of Steubenville	OH	33,980	VC
Franklin College	IN	40,550	C
Franklin Pierce Univ	NH	46,750	LC
Franklin Univ	OH	11,616	NC
Freed-Hardeman Univ	TN	29,900	C
Fresno Pacific Univ	CA	38,858	C
Friends Univ	KS	38,000	C
Frostburg State Univ	MD	17,280	LC
Furman Univ	SC	61,098	VC+
Gallaudet Univ	DC	30,088	LC
Gannon Univ	PA	42,922	C
Gardner-Webb Univ	NC	24,935	C+
Geneva College	PA	35,450	C
George Fox Univ	OR	42,938	C
George Mason Univ	VA	19,884	C
Georgetown College	KY	41,440	C
Georgetown Univ	DC	68,970	MC
Georgia College & State Univ	GA	21,884	C+
Georgia Southern Univ	GA	16,540	VC
Georgia Southwestern State Univ	GA	13,870	LC
Georgia State Univ	GA	25,250	C
Georgian Court Univ	NJ	43,068	LC
Glenville State College	WV	17,386	LC
Golden Gate Univ	CA	19,510	C
Goldey-Beacom College	DE	36,038	C
Gonzaga Univ	WA	52,880	HC
Goodwin College	CT	28,370	LC
Gordon College	MA	47,740	VC
Goshen College	IN	44,350	C
Grace College and Seminary	IN	31,524	C
Graceland Univ	IA	35,290	C
Grambling State Univ	LA	15,701	C
Grand Canyon Univ	AZ	25,150	VC
Grand Valley State Univ	MI	22,250	C+
Grand View Univ	IA	32,302	C
Greensboro College	NC	39,790	LC
Greenville College	IL	27,012	LC
Grove City College	PA	26,654	VC
Guilford College	NC	45,973	C
Gustavus Adolphus College	MN	53,943	HC
Gwynedd Mercy Univ	PA	43,780	LC
Hamline Univ	MN	50,152	C
Hampton Univ	VA	36,410	C
Hannibal-LaGrange Univ	MO	29,815	C
Harding Univ	AR	25,440	C
Hardin-Simmons Univ	TX	36,025	C
Harris-Stowe State Univ	MO	14,590	NC
Hartwick College	NY	51,270	C
Hastings College	NE	35,380	C+
Hawaii Pacific Univ	HI	33,420	C
Heidelberg Univ	OH	40,400	LC
Henderson State Univ	AR	15,516	C
Hendrix College	AR	54,020	VC
Heritage Univ	WA	19,825	NC
Hilbert College	NY	32,650	LC
Hillsdale College	MI	37,170	MC
Hiram College	OH	44,590	C
Hodges Univ	FL	20,160	LC
Hofstra Univ	NY	58,210	C+
Holy Family Univ	PA	44,672	LC
Hood College	MD	50,540	C
Hope College	MI	42,840	VC
Houghton College	NY	40,558	VC
Houston Baptist Univ	TX	36,450	C
Howard Payne Univ	TX	35,994	C
Howard Univ	DC	37,616	C+
Humphreys College	CA	27,790	C
Huntingdon College	AL	35,900	C
Huntington Univ	IN	33,996	C
Husson Univ	ME	26,508	C
Idaho State Univ	ID	13,619	LC
Illinois College	IL	41,330	VC
Illinois State Univ	IL	23,418	VC
Illinois Wesleyan Univ	IL	56,430	VC+
Immaculata Univ	PA	39,000	C
Indiana Inst of Technology	IN	34,240	LC
Indiana State Univ	IN	23,223	LC
Indiana Univ of Pennsylvania	PA	24,474	C
Indiana Univ-Purdue Univ Fort Wayne	IN	18,675	C
Indiana Wesleyan Univ	IN	33,674	C

ST = STATE **$IS** = IN-STATE COSTS **SR** = SELECTOR RATING

School	ST	$IS	SR
Inter-American Univ of PR Ponce	PR	19,549	
Inter-American Univ of PR-Aguadilla Campus	PR	21,657	
Inter-American Univ of PR-Arecibo Campus	PR	18,245	
Inter-American Univ of PR-Barranquitas	PR	18,336	
Inter-American Univ of PR-Bayamon	PR	18,785	
Inter-American Univ of PR-Fajardo Campus	PR	18,336	
Inter-American Univ of PR-Metropolitan Campus	PR	20,045	
Inter-American Univ of PR-San Germán	PR	20,042	
Iona College	NY	52,514	C
Iowa State Univ	IA	18,176	C
Iowa Wesleyan Univ	IA	41,000	C
Ithaca College	NY	58,158	VC+
Jackson State Univ	MS	15,879	LC
Jacksonville State Univ	AL	14,628	LC
Jacksonville Univ	FL	49,210	C
James Madison Univ	VA	19,084	VC
Jefferson (Philadelphia Univ + Thomas Jefferson Univ)	PA	53,966	C
John Brown Univ	AR	35,184	VC
John Carroll Univ	OH	51,570	C
Johnson & Wales Univ/Charlotte Campus	NC	44,768	C
Johnson & Wales Univ/North Miami Campus	FL	44,768	C
Johnson & Wales Univ/Providence Campus	RI	44,768	C
Judson Univ	IL	39,174	C
Juniata College	PA	58,118	VC
Kansas State Univ	KS	17,780	VC
Kansas Wesleyan Univ	KS	37,930	C
Kean Univ	NJ	25,620	C
Keiser Univ	FL	35,010	LC
Kennesaw State Univ	GA	18,899	VC
Kent State Univ	OH	20,928	C
Kentucky Wesleyan College	KY	34,260	LC
Keuka College	NY	42,398	C
Keystone College	PA	28,680	LC
King's College	PA	48,240	C
Kutztown Univ of Pennsylvania	PA	19,477	C
La Roche College	PA	38,940	C
La Salle Univ	PA	43,476	C
La Sierra Univ	CA	39,690	VC
LaGrange College	GA	41,310	C
Lake Erie College	OH	38,914	LC
Lake Superior State Univ	MI	19,867	C
Lakeland Univ	WI	35,130	C
Lamar Univ	TX	18,014	LC
Langston Univ	OK	15,659	C
Lasell College	MA	49,400	C
Le Moyne College	NY	47,305	VC
Lebanon Valley College	PA	55,510	VC
Lee Univ	TN	22,045	C
Lehigh Univ	PA	63,860	MC
LeMoyne-Owen College	TN	16,980	C
Lenoir-Rhyne Univ	NC	47,500	LC
LeTourneau Univ	TX	39,190	VC
Lewis Univ	IL	41,710	C
Liberty Univ	VA	31,415	C
Limestone College	SC	32,100	C
Lincoln Memorial Univ	TN	28,430	C
Lincoln Univ	MO	14,402	NC
Lincoln Univ	PA	20,878	LC
Lindenwood Univ	MO	25,760	C
Lindsey Wilson College	KY	33,546	C
Linfield College	OR	53,992	C
Lipscomb Univ	TN	42,984	VC
LIU Brooklyn	NY	50,698	C
LIU Post	NY	50,698	C+
Loras College	IA	40,726	C
Louisiana College	LA	21,274	C
Louisiana State Univ and A&M College	LA	18,677	VC
Louisiana State Univ in Shreveport	LA	6,902	C
Louisiana Tech Univ	LA	11,422	VC
Lourdes Univ	OH	29,140	NC
Loyola Marymount Univ	CA	60,202	VC+
Loyola Univ Chicago	IL	57,158	VC
Loyola Univ Maryland	MD	61,710	VC
Loyola Univ New Orleans	LA	52,456	VC
Lubbock Christian Univ	TX	29,727	C
Luther College	IA	49,990	VC
Lycoming College	PA	50,895	C
Lyndon State College	VT	20,714	C
Lyon College	AR	36,120	VC
MacMurray College	IL	35,025	C
Madonna Univ	MI	30,450	LC
Malone Univ	OH	39,200	C
Manchester Univ	IN	41,540	C
Manhattan College	NY	55,652	C
Manhattanville College	NY	52,430	C
Marian Univ	IN	43,206	C
Marian Univ	WI	34,622	C
Marietta College	OH	46,190	C
Marist College	NY	49,860	VC
Marquette Univ	WI	53,090	VC+
Mars Hill Univ	NC	41,104	C
Marshall Univ	WV	18,044	C
Martin Univ	IN	21,010	LC
Marymount Manhattan College	NY	48,350	C
Maryville Univ of St. Louis	MO	38,558	VC
Marywood Univ	PA	47,840	C
Mass College of Liberal Arts	MA	20,659	C
McDaniel College	MD	52,910	VC
McKendree Univ	IL	37,940	C+
McMurry Univ	TX	34,259	LC
McNeese State Univ	LA	7,838	C
Medaille College	NY	41,700	LC
Menlo College	CA	51,380	LC
Mercer Univ	GA	45,348	VC
Mercy College	NY	32,614	C
Mercyhurst Univ	PA	47,420	C
Meredith College	NC	46,634	C
Merrimack College	MA	55,415	C
Messiah College	PA	44,380	VC
Methodist Univ	NC	58,130	C
Metropolitan State Univ	MN	7,859	C
Metropolitan State Univ of Denver	CO	6,928	LC
Miami Univ	OH	27,190	HC+
Mich State Univ	MI	24,542	VC
Mich Tech Univ	MI	25,551	VC+
MidAmerica Nazarene Univ	KS	37,808	C
Middle Tenn State Univ	TN	8,650	C
Midland Univ	NE	39,512	C
Midwestern State Univ	TX	12,111	LC
Miles College	AL	16,530	NC
Millersville Univ of Pennsylvania	PA	25,298	C
Milligan College	TN	39,450	C
Millikin Univ	IL	44,148	C
Millsaps College	MS	50,080	C+
Minn State Univ, Mankato	MN	17,190	C
Minn State Univ, Moorhead	MN	21,393	C
Minot State Univ	ND	13,285	C
Misericordia Univ	PA	45,210	C
Miss College	MS	25,850	C
Miss State Univ	MS	12,028	C+
Miss Univ for Women	MS	17,065	C
Miss Valley State Univ	MS	13,233	LC
Missouri Baptist Univ	MO	35,594	C
Missouri Southern State Univ	MO	13,071	C
Missouri State Univ	MO	15,837	C+
Missouri Valley College	MO	28,150	C
Missouri Western State Univ	MO	17,822	LC
Molloy College	NY	40,440	C
Monmouth College	IL	42,260	C
Monmouth Univ	NJ	50,184	C
Monroe College	NY	23,996	C
Montclair State Univ	NJ	26,912	C
Moravian College	PA	55,488	C
Morehead State Univ	KY	18,386	LC
Morgan State Univ	MD	17,190	LC
Mount Aloysius College	PA	29,976	C
Mount Marty College	SD	36,862	C
Mount Mary Univ	WI	34,650	LC
Mount Mercy Univ	IA	39,748	C
Mount St. Mary College	NY	44,448	C
Mount St. Joseph Univ	OH	33,880	LC
Mount St. Mary's Univ	MD	53,380	C
Mount Vernon Nazarene Univ	OH	35,944	C
Muhlenberg College	PA	56,645	VC
Murray State Univ	KY	17,726	C+
Muskingum Univ	OH	35,966	C
National Univ	CA	17,849	LC
Nazareth College	NY	46,784	C
Nebr Wesleyan Univ	NE	42,026	C+
Neumann Univ	PA	40,678	LC
New England College	NH	50,828	NC
New Jersey City Univ	NJ	21,456	LC
New Mexico Highlands Univ	NM	11,904	LC
New Mexico State Univ	NM	14,050	LC
New York Inst of Technology	NY	49,980	VC
New York Univ	NY	68,139	MC
Newbury College	MA	48,970	C
Newman Univ	KS	37,382	C
Niagara Univ	NY	41,010	C
Nicholls State Univ	LA	14,959	C
Nichols College	MA	46,900	LC
Norfolk State Univ	VA	18,902	LC
N Car A&T State Univ	NC	13,786	C
N Car Central Univ	NC	9,000	C
N Car State Univ	NC	22,434	HC+
N Car Wesleyan College	NC	39,200	C
North Central College	IL	48,712	C+
North Central Univ	MN	30,610	C
N Dak State Univ	ND	16,245	VC
North Greenville Univ	SC	25,930	C
North Park Univ	IL	35,860	C
Northeastern Illinois Univ	IL	12,529	LC
Northeastern State Univ	OK	8,615	VC
Northeastern Univ	MA	65,352	MC
Northern Arizona Univ	AZ	21,003	C
Northern Illinois Univ	IL	20,176	C
Northern Kentucky Univ	KY	16,486	C
Northern Mich Univ	MI	20,853	C
Northern State Univ	SD	15,570	C
Northwest Christian Univ	OR	36,580	C
Northwest Missouri State Univ	MO	18,286	C
Northwest Nazarene Univ	ID	40,250	C
Northwest Univ	WA	38,720	VC
Northwestern College of Iowa	IA	38,400	C
Northwestern Okla State Univ	OK	13,072	LC
Northwestern State Univ of Louisiana	LA	16,534	LC
Northwood Univ - Mich	MI	35,010	LC
Norwich Univ	VT	56,234	C
Notre Dame College	OH	39,150	VC
Notre Dame de Namur Univ	CA	46,526	LC
Notre Dame of Maryland Univ	MD	47,570	VC
Nova Southeastern Univ	FL	38,534	C+
Nyack College	NY	34,450	LC
Oakland City Univ	IN	33,930	NC
Oakland Univ	MI	20,763	C
Oakwood Univ	AL	43,758	C
Oglethorpe Univ	GA	44,200	C
Ohio Dominican Univ	OH	41,340	C+
Ohio Northern Univ	OH	44,050	VC
Ohio State Univ at Columbus	OH	22,843	MC
Ohio Univ	OH	23,394	VC
Ohio Valley Univ	WV	28,800	C
Ohio Wesleyan Univ	OH	49,460	VC
Okla Baptist Univ	OK	33,990	C
Okla Christian Univ	OK	29,260	C
Okla City Univ	OK	40,476	C
Okla Panhandle State Univ	OK	6,152	C
Okla State Univ	OK	17,180	C+
Okla Wesleyan Univ	OK	34,434	C
Old Dominion Univ	VA	21,618	C
Olivet College	MI	37,661	LC
Olivet Nazarene Univ	IL	41,840	VC
Oral Roberts Univ	OK	34,316	C
Oregon State Univ	OR	23,337	VC
Ottawa Univ	KS	39,980	VC
Otterbein Univ	OH	41,630	C
Ouachita Baptist Univ	AR	33,500	VC
Our Lady of the Lake Univ	TX	37,790	LC
Pace Univ	NY	60,136	C
Palm Beach Atlantic Univ	FL	39,250	C
Park Univ	MO	22,134	C
Paul Quinn College	TX	25,350	LC
Peirce College	PA	16,780	NC
Penn State Erie,The Behrend College	PA	26,688	VC
Pennsylvania College of Technology	PA	27,693	NC
Pennsylvania State Univ - Univ Park	PA	29,716	HC
Pepperdine Univ	CA	66,862	VC+
Peru State College	NE	15,602	LC
Pfeiffer Univ	NC	40,532	LC
Pittsburg State Univ	KS	13,880	C
Plymouth State Univ	NH	23,180	LC
Point Loma Nazarene Univ	CA	46,150	C+
Point Park Univ	PA	41,270	C
Pontifical Catholic Univ of PR	PR	10,534	
Portland State Univ	OR	19,443	C
Post Univ	CT	41,150	C
Prairie View A&M Univ	TX	27,273	LC
Providence College	RI	62,870	HC
Purdue Univ Northwest	IN	15,178	C
Purdue Univ/West Lafayette	IN	20,032	MC
Queens Univ of Charlotte	NC	39,543	C
Quincy Univ	IL	38,170	LC
Quinnipiac Univ	CT	60,970	VC
Radford Univ	VA	19,758	C
Ramapo College of New Jersey	NJ	25,760	VC
Randolph-Macon College	VA	51,480	VC
Regis Univ	CO	46,380	C
Rhode Island College	RI	19,000	LC
Rider Univ	NJ	54,050	C
Robert Morris Univ	PA	40,600	C
Roberts Wesleyan College	NY	41,116	C
Rochester College	MI	28,574	LC
Rochester Inst of Technology	NY	52,734	HC+
Rockford Univ	IL	38,570	C
Rocky Mountain College	MT	35,776	C
Roger Williams Univ	RI	48,074	VC
Roosevelt Univ	IL	41,890	VC
Rosemont College	PA	30,980	LC
Rowan Univ	NJ	24,491	VC
Rutgers Univ - Camden	NJ	26,595	C
Rutgers Univ - New Brunswick	NJ	27,090	HC
Rutgers Univ - Newark	NJ	27,351	C
Sacred Heart Univ	CT	54,590	C
Saginaw Valley State Univ	MI	19,284	C
St. Anselm College	NH	56,636	VC
St. Augustine's Univ	NC	25,582	C
St. Francis Univ	PA	46,146	NC
St. John's Univ	MN	53,472	C
St. Joseph's Univ	PA	58,540	VC
St. Leo Univ	FL	32,850	C
St. Louis Univ	MO	49,866	HC
St. Martin's Univ	WA	45,056	C
St. Mary-of-the-Woods College	IN	40,424	LC
St. Mary's College	IN	50,600	C
St. Mary's College of Calif	CA	57,420	C
St. Mary's Univ of Minn	MN	42,440	C
St. Michael's College	VT	53,275	VC+
St. Peter's Univ	NJ	49,192	C
St. Vincent College	PA	46,229	C
St. Xavier Univ	IL	44,440	C
Salem College	NC	40,206	C
Salem State Univ	MA	42,650	LC
Salisbury Univ	MD	21,132	VC
Salve Regina Univ	RI	53,046	VC
Sam Houston State Univ	TX	18,792	C
Samford Univ	AL	40,770	VC
San Diego State Univ	CA	23,156	VC
San Francisco State Univ	CA	18,514	LC
San Jose State Univ	CA	22,630	C
Savannah State Univ	GA	17,036	C
Schreiner Univ	TX	34,626	LC
Seattle Pacific Univ	WA	47,439	C+
Seattle Univ	WA	54,957	VC
Seton Hall Univ	NJ	58,008	C
Seton Hill Univ	PA	46,972	VC
Shaw Univ	NC	24,638	C
Shawnee State Univ	OH	16,998	C
Shepherd Univ, West Virginia	WV	17,382	C
Shippensburg Univ of Pennsylvania	PA	24,096	C
Shorter Univ	GA	31,130	LC
Siena College	NY	48,916	C
Siena Heights Univ	MI	36,322	C
Silver Lake College of the Holy Family	WI	36,290	LC
Simpson College	IA	45,626	VC
Simpson Univ	CA	34,722	C
Slippery Rock Univ of Pennsylvania	PA	20,450	C
S Car State Univ	SC	21,330	LC
Southeast Missouri State Univ	MO	16,148	C
Southeastern Louisiana Univ	LA	16,237	C
Southeastern Okla State Univ	OK	11,875	C
Southeastern Univ	FL	34,910	LC
Southern Adventist Univ	TN	28,250	C
Southern Arkansas Univ	AR	21,532	C
Southern Conn State Univ	CT	21,924	LC
Southern Illinois Univ Carbondale	IL	24,554	C
Southern Illinois Univ Edwardsville	IL	20,188	C
Southern Methodist Univ	TX	69,008	MC
Southern Nazarene Univ	OK	33,684	C
Southern New Hampshire Univ	NH	44,256	C
Southern Oregon Univ	OR	19,117	C
Southern Univ and A&M College	LA	16,074	LC
Southern Univ at New Orleans	LA	8,014	LC
Southwest Baptist Univ	MO	30,890	LC
Southwest Minn State Univ	MN	17,783	C
Southwestern College	KS	31,531	LC
Southwestern Okla State Univ	OK	12,205	C
Spalding Univ	KY	31,938	C
Spring Arbor Univ	MI	37,390	C
Spring Hill College	AL	48,488	C
St. Bonaventure Univ	NY	45,596	C
St. Catherine Univ	MN	45,630	C
St. Cloud State Univ	MN	10,600	C
St. Edward's Univ	TX	56,190	VC
St. Francis College	NY	38,800	LC
St. John Fisher College	NY	45,270	VC
St. John's Univ	NY	57,160	C+
St. Joseph's College, New York/Brooklyn Campus	NY	25,114	LC
St. Joseph's College, New York/Long Island Campus	NY	25,124	C
St. Mary's Univ	TX	39,120	C
St. Norbert College	WI	46,060	VC
St. Thomas Aquinas College	NY	32,450	C
St. Thomas Univ	FL	51,187	LC
SUNY Albany	NY	22,165	C
SUNY at Binghamton	NY	24,100	MC
SUNY at Geneseo	NY	21,622	VC
SUNY at New Paltz	NY	20,840	C
SUNY at Oswego	NY	22,219	VC
SUNY Polytechnic Inst	NY	20,438	VC
SUNY/College at Old Westbury	NY	16,860	C
SUNY/Empire State College	NY	9,145	NC
SUNY/Fredonia	NY	20,818	C
SUNY/Oneonta	NY	20,794	C
SUNY/Plattsburgh	NY	19,314	C
SUNY/Univ at Buffalo	NY	23,122	C
Stephen F. Austin State Univ	TX	18,484	LC
Stephens College	MO	38,042	C
Stetson Univ	FL	57,174	VC+
Stevenson Univ	MD	48,412	C
Stockton Univ	NJ	25,565	C
Stonehill College	MA	55,130	C
Suffolk Univ	MA	52,316	C
Sul Ross State Univ	TX	15,021	LC
Susquehanna Univ	PA	57,560	VC
Syracuse Univ	NY	62,313	HC
Tabor College	KS	35,870	C
Talladega College	AL	25,919	C
Tarleton State Univ	TX	15,248	LC
Taylor Univ	IN	42,130	VC
Temple Univ	PA	24,392	C+
Tenn State Univ	TN	14,423	LC
Tenn Tech Univ	TN	17,929	C
Texas A&M Univ at College Station	TX	20,771	VC+
Texas A&M Univ at Commerce	TX	10,496	C
Texas A&M Univ at Corpus Christi	TX	16,851	LC
Texas A&M Univ at Kingsville	TX	16,580	LC
Texas Christian Univ	TX	57,120	HC
Texas Lutheran Univ	TX	39,770	C
Texas Southern Univ	TX	19,592	LC
Texas State Univ	TX	18,721	C

ST = STATE $IS = IN-STATE COSTS SR = SELECTOR RATING

School	ST	$IS	SR
Texas Tech Univ	TX	20,156	C+
Texas Wesleyan Univ	TX	37,338	C
Texas Woman's Univ	TX	15,302	LC
The Catholic Univ of America	DC	58,376	VC
The College at Brockport - SUNY	NY	21,058	C
The College of Idaho	ID	36,415	C
The College of New Jersey	NJ	28,675	VC+
The College of St. Rose	NY	44,010	C
The George Washington Univ	DC	68,474	HC+
The Master's Univ	CA	43,870	C
The Univ of Akron	OH	22,566	C
The Univ of Alabama	AL	24,320	C+
The Univ of Arizona	AZ	24,086	C
The Univ of Mary	ND	23,180	C
The Univ of Memphis	TN	18,278	C
The Univ of Tenn at Knoxville	TN	22,112	VC
The Univ of Tenn at Martin	TN	15,212	C
The Univ of Texas at Austin	TX	20,206	MC
The Univ of Texas at San Antonio	TX	21,060	C
The Univ of Utah	UT	18,751	VC
The Univ of Virginia's College at Wise	VA	18,192	LC
Thiel College	PA	42,950	LC
Thomas College	ME	73,888	LC
Thomas Edison State Univ	NJ	6,350	NC
Thomas More College	KY	36,720	LC
Tiffin Univ	OH	34,900	LC
Touro College	NY	31,040	C
Towson Univ	MD	21,878	C
Transylvania Univ	KY	47,450	HC+
Trevecca Nazarene Univ	TN	31,186	C
Trine Univ	IN	41,310	C
Trinity Christian College	IL	35,580	C
Trinity International Univ	IL	31,070	VC
Trinity Univ	TX	54,480	MC
Troy Univ	AL	16,171	C
Truman State Univ	MO	16,286	MC
Tulane Univ	LA	67,496	MC
Tuskegee Univ	AL	28,164	C
Union College	KY	32,310	C
Union College	NE	23,270	C
Union Univ	TN	41,160	VC
Universidad del Turabo	PR	17,828	
Universidad Metropolitana	PR	17,828	
Univ of PR, at Arecibo	PR	12,652	
Univ of Alabama at Birmingham	AL	22,092	C
Univ of Alabama in Huntsville	AL	20,028	VC
Univ of Alaska Anchorage	AK	17,914	C
Univ of Alaska Fairbanks	AK	16,874	VC
Univ of Alaska Southeast	AK	17,615	C
Univ of Arkansas at Little Rock	AR	18,211	LC
Univ of Arkansas at Monticello	AR	13,599	LC
Univ of Arkansas at Pine Bluff	AR	13,541	C
Univ of Bridgeport	CT	44,985	LC
Univ of Calif at Santa Barbara	CA	30,627	HC+
Univ of Central Arkansas	AR	15,042	VC
Univ of Central Florida	FL	16,379	VC
Univ of Central Missouri	MO	18,982	C
Univ of Central Okla	OK	15,150	C
Univ of Charleston	WV	35,000	LC
Univ of Cincinnati	OH	22,118	VC
Univ of Colo Boulder	CO	26,048	HC
Univ of Conn	CT	27,394	
Univ of Dayton	OH	54,930	VC
Univ of Delaware	DE	32,214	VC
Univ of Denver	CO	61,129	VC+
Univ of Detroit Mercy	MI	48,816	C
Univ of Dubuque	IA	37,824	C
Univ of Evansville	IN	44,186	C+
Univ of Findlay	OH	43,040	C
Univ of Florida	FL	16,291	HC+
Univ of Georgia	GA	21,878	HC
Univ of Great Falls	MT	38,524	C
Univ of Hartford	CT	49,776	C
Univ of Hawaii at Hilo	HI	18,038	VC
Univ of Hawaii at Manoa	HI	23,261	C
Univ of Holy Cross	LA	21,523	NC
Univ of Houston	TX	21,871	VC
Univ of Houston-Downtown	TX	7,241	LC
Univ of Idaho	ID	16,158	C
Univ of Illinois at Chicago	IL	24,664	VC
Univ of Illinois at Urbana-Champaign	IL	27,006	HC
Univ of Indianapolis	IN	36,480	VC
Univ of Iowa	IA	19,415	HC
Univ of Jamestown	ND	28,508	C
Univ of Kansas	KS	20,884	VC
Univ of Kentucky	KY	24,800	C+
Univ of La Verne	CA	55,600	C
Univ of Louisiana at Lafayette	LA	14,516	C
Univ of Louisiana at Monroe	LA	15,970	C
Univ of Louisville	KY	19,692	C
Univ of Lynchburg	VA	48,370	C
Univ of Maine	ME	21,038	VC
Univ of Maine at Augusta	ME	7,812	C
Univ of Maine at Machias	ME	22,960	C
Univ of Maine at Presque Isle	ME	16,148	LC
Univ of Mary Hardin-Baylor	TX	35,292	C+
Univ of Maryland Univ College	MD	26,146	LC
Univ of Maryland/College Park	MD	21,938	HC
Univ of Maryland/Eastern Shore	MD	21,861	LC
Univ of Mass Amherst	MA	27,669	HC
Univ of Mass Dartmouth	MA	26,507	C
Univ of Miami	FL	63,494	MC
Univ of Mich/Dearborn	MI	12,472	VC
Univ of Mich/Flint	MI	19,062	C
Univ of Minn/Crookston	MN	19,126	C
Univ of Minn/Duluth	MN	20,292	C
Univ of Minn/Twin Cities	MN	24,269	MC
Univ of Miss	MS	18,802	C
Univ of Missouri-Columbia	MO	20,463	VC
Univ of Missouri-Kansas City	MO	19,563	VC
Univ of Missouri-St. Louis	MO	19,810	VC
Univ of Mobile	AL	28,935	C
Univ of Montana	MT	14,105	C
Univ of Montevallo	AL	20,012	C
Univ of Mount Olive	NC	18,426	C
Univ of Mount Union	OH	39,990	C
Univ of Nebr - Kearney	NE	17,014	LC
Univ of Nebr - Lincoln	NE	18,589	VC
Univ of Nebr - Omaha	NE	16,120	C
Univ of Nevada, Las Vegas	NV	17,553	C
Univ of Nevada, Reno	NV	18,010	C
Univ of New Haven	CT	53,680	C
Univ of New Orleans	LA	12,840	C
Univ of North Alabama	AL	15,964	C
Univ of N Car at Asheville	NC	16,251	VC+
Univ of N Car at Charlotte	NC	17,803	VC
Univ of N Car at Greensboro	NC	15,998	C
Univ of N Car at Pembroke	NC	14,737	LC
Univ of N Dak	ND	16,673	C
Univ of North Florida	FL	15,996	VC
Univ of North Georgia	GA	17,316	C
Univ of North Texas	TX	20,082	C
Univ of Northern Iowa	IA	17,480	C
Univ of Northwestern - St. Paul	MN	39,530	C
Univ of Notre Dame	IN	68,801	MC
Univ of Okla	OK	19,651	HC
Univ of Oregon	OR	24,021	VC
Univ of Pennsylvania	PA	63,526	MC
Univ of Pittsburgh	PA	30,030	MC
Univ of Pittsburgh at Bradford	PA	22,958	C
Univ of Pittsburgh at Greensburg	PA	24,140	C
Univ of Pittsburgh at Johnstown	PA	22,092	C
Univ of Portland	OR	52,152	VC
Univ of PR, at Bayamon	PR	13,145	
Univ of PR, at Cayey	PR		
Univ of PR, at Humacao	PR	14,000	
Univ of PR, at Mayaguez	PR	13,995	
Univ of PR-Rio Piedras campus	PR	13,327	
Univ of Redlands	CA	61,934	VC
Univ of Rhode Island	RI	26,066	VC
Univ of Richmond	VA	62,730	MC
Univ of Rio Grande & Rio Grande Community College	OH	8,750	LC
Univ of St. Francis	IN	38,520	C
Univ of St. Joseph	CT	49,069	C
Univ of St. Mary	KS	37,080	NC
Univ of San Diego	CA	60,338	HC
Univ of San Francisco	CA	60,580	C
Univ of Scranton	PA	54,962	VC
Univ of Sioux Falls	SD	25,630	C
Univ of South Alabama	AL	16,880	C
Univ of S Car at Columbia	SC	21,726	VC
Univ of S Car Upstate	SC	19,272	LC
Univ of S Dak	SD	16,109	C
Univ of South Florida St. Petersburg	FL	15,980	C
Univ of South Florida/Tampa	FL	16,110	VC
Univ of Southern Calif	CA	66,631	MC
Univ of Southern Indiana	IN	16,808	C
Univ of Southern Maine	ME	18,320	C
Univ of Southern Miss	MS	13,170	C
Univ of St. Francis	IL	40,828	C
Univ of St. Thomas - Houston	TX	41,510	VC
Univ of Tampa	FL	38,928	VC
Univ of Texas at Arlington	TX	18,876	C
Univ of Texas at Dallas	TX	23,640	HC
Univ of Texas at El Paso	TX	34,452	NC
Univ of Texas Rio Grande Valley	TX	15,573	LC
Univ of the Cumberlands	KY	32,000	LC
Univ of the District of Columbia	DC	21,260	LC
Univ of the Ozarks	AR	31,050	NC
Univ of the Sacred Heart	PR	17,932	
Univ of the Southwest	NM	24,386	C
Univ of Toledo	OH	19,336	C
Univ of Tulsa	OK	52,625	HC
Univ of Washington	WA	23,091	MC
Univ of West Alabama	AL	16,284	LC
Univ of West Florida	FL	15,848	C
Univ of West Georgia	GA	17,510	LC
Univ of Wisc-Eau Claire	WI	16,354	VC
Univ of Wisc-Green Bay	WI	15,184	C
Univ of Wisc-La Crosse	WI	15,425	VC
Univ of Wisc-Madison	WI	21,647	MC
Univ of Wisc-Milwaukee	WI	21,538	C
Univ of Wisc-Oshkosh	WI	15,392	C
Univ of Wisc-Parkside	WI	15,313	C
Univ of Wisc-Platteville	WI	14,148	C
Univ of Wisc-River Falls	WI	14,541	C
Univ of Wisc-Stevens Point	WI	14,043	C
Univ of Wisc-Superior	WI	14,838	C
Univ of Wisc-Whitewater	WI	13,976	C
Univ of Wyoming	WY	15,537	C
Upper Iowa Univ	IA	34,990	NC
Ursuline College	OH	41,076	LC
Utah State Univ	UT	13,235	C
Utica College	NY	31,510	C
Valparaiso Univ	IN	50,160	VC
Vanguard Univ of Southern Calif	CA	42,400	VC
Villanova Univ	PA	64,922	MC
Virginia Commonwealth Univ	VA	23,811	VC
Virginia Polytechnic Inst and State Univ	VA	21,920	VC
Virginia State Univ	VA	19,802	C+
Virginia Union Univ	VA	25,058	C
Viterbo Univ	WI	34,660	C
Voorhees College	SC	19,976	C
Wagner College	NY	57,240	C+
Wake Forest Univ	NC	69,354	MC
Walsh Univ	OH	39,010	C
Warner Univ	FL	28,216	C
Wartburg College	IA	49,478	C
Washburn Univ	KS	15,827	C
Washington & Jefferson College	PA	58,694	VC
Washington Adventist Univ	MD	32,050	LC
Washington and Lee Univ	VA	59,647	MC
Washington State Univ	WA	22,747	C
Washington Univ in St. Louis	MO	67,539	MC
Wayland Baptist Univ	TX	23,460	LC
Wayne State Univ	MI	23,085	C
Waynesburg Univ	PA	33,530	C
Webber International Univ	FL	31,904	C
Weber State Univ	UT	14,112	C
Webster Univ	MO	37,490	C
Wesley College	DE	37,848	LC
Wesleyan College	GA	31,940	C+
West Chester Univ of Pennsylvania	PA	19,171	VC
West Liberty Univ	WV	16,158	C
West Texas A&M Univ	TX	13,478	C
West Virginia State Univ	WV	19,412	LC
West Virginia Univ	WV	18,952	VC
West Virginia Univ Inst of Technology	WV	18,264	C
West Virginia Wesleyan College	WV	39,188	C
Western Carolina Univ	NC	13,965	C
Western Conn State Univ	CT	21,254	LC
Western Illinois Univ	IL	20,897	C
Western Kentucky Univ	KY	16,850	C
Western Mich Univ	MI	21,791	C
Western New England Univ	MA	49,182	C
Western New Mexico Univ	NM	16,914	LC
Western State Colo Univ	CO	19,348	C
Western Washington Univ	WA	18,904	VC
Westminster College	MO	32,820	C
Westminster College	PA	41,722	C
Westminster College	UT	41,078	C
Wheeling Jesuit Univ	WV	37,106	LC
Whitworth Univ	WA	53,682	VC
Wichita State Univ	KS	17,773	C
Widener Univ	PA	58,190	C
Wilberforce Univ	OH	19,900	C
Wilkes Univ	PA	49,166	C
William Jewell College	MO	42,490	C+
William Paterson Univ of New Jersey	NJ	24,022	C
William Penn Univ	IA	26,000	C
William Woods Univ	MO	32,040	C
Wilmington College	OH	35,100	C
Wilmington Univ	DE	8,762	NC
Wilson College	PA	35,620	LC
Wingate Univ	NC	41,900	C
Winona State Univ	MN	18,109	C
Winston-Salem State Univ	NC	18,005	LC
Wisc Lutheran College	WI	36,290	C
Wittenberg Univ	OH	49,863	VC
Wofford College	SC	49,885	VC
Woodbury Univ	CA	49,593	VC
Wright State Univ	OH	16,983	C
Xavier Univ	OH	49,380	VC
Xavier Univ of Louisiana	LA	31,689	C
Yeshiva Univ	NY	52,750	VC
York College	NE	30,260	C
York College of Pennsylvania	PA	29,240	C
Youngstown State Univ	OH	17,487	C

ACTING

School	ST	$IS	SR
Arcadia Univ	PA	55,990	C+
Azusa Pacific Univ	CA	43,972	C
Baldwin Wallace Univ	OH	42,464	VC
Ball State Univ	IN	19,808	C+
Baylor Univ	TX	56,803	HC
Boston Univ	MA	67,352	MC
Carnegie Mellon Univ	PA	67,980	MC
Chapman Univ	CA	65,504	HC
Columbia College Chicago	IL	40,104	C
DePaul Univ	IL	52,807	VC
Elon Univ	NC	46,142	HC

School	ST	$IS	SR
Howard Univ	DC	37,616	C+
Huntington Univ	IN	33,996	C
Lipscomb Univ	TN	42,984	VC
Loyola Univ New Orleans	LA	52,456	VC
Millikin Univ	IL	44,148	C
Oberlin College	OH	68,942	MC
Ohio Univ	OH	23,394	VC
Okla City Univ	OK	40,476	C
Otterbein Univ	OH	41,630	C
Pace Univ	NY	60,136	C
Pennsylvania State Univ - Univ Park	PA	29,716	HC
Shenandoah Univ	VA	42,100	C
St. Edward's Univ	TX	56,190	VC
SUNY/Fredonia	NY	20,818	C
Syracuse Univ	NY	62,313	HC
Texas Christian Univ	TX	57,120	HC
Univ of Conn	CT	27,394	
Univ of Maryland/Baltimore County	MD	23,004	VC
Univ of Minn/Twin Cities	MN	24,269	MC
Univ of N Car at Greensboro	NC	15,998	C
Webster Univ	MO	37,490	C
Western Kentucky Univ	KY	16,850	C

ACTUARIAL MATHEMATICS

School	ST	$IS	SR
Albion College	MI	55,260	C
Asbury Univ	KY	36,450	C+
Bryant Univ	RI	57,204	VC
Cabrini Univ	PA	42,591	LC
Huntington Univ	IN	33,996	C
Lake Superior State Univ	MI	19,867	C
Lycoming College	PA	50,895	C
Millikin Univ	IL	44,148	C
St. Mary's College	IN	50,600	C
Southeastern Univ	FL	34,910	LC
SUNY at Binghamton	NY	24,100	MC
The Univ of Texas at San Antonio	TX	21,060	C
Univ of Conn	CT	27,394	
Univ of Pittsburgh	PA	30,030	MC
West Chester Univ of Pennsylvania	PA	19,171	VC
Wilson College	PA	35,620	LC
Youngstown State Univ	OH	17,487	C

ACTUARIAL SCIENCE

School	ST	$IS	SR
Appalachian State Univ	NC	15,394	VC
Arcadia Univ	PA	55,990	C+
Arizona State Univ at the Tempe Campus	AZ	23,001	VC
Ashland Univ	OH	30,446	C
Assumption College	MA	48,455	VC
Auburn Univ	AL	24,300	VC+
Aurora Univ	IL	34,990	C
Ball State Univ	IN	19,808	C+
Bellarmine Univ	KY	52,532	C
Bentley Univ	MA	63,720	MC
Bethany College	WV	38,774	LC
Bradley Univ	IL	43,240	VC
Brigham Young Univ	UT	13,248	MC
Bryant Univ	RI	57,204	VC
Butler Univ	IN	52,890	VC+
Calif Baptist Univ	CA	42,986	C
Cal State, Fullerton	CA	21,902	C
Calvin College	MI	43,090	HC
Carroll Univ	WI	38,100	C+
Central College	IA	44,592	C
Central Mich Univ	MI	20,330	C
Central Washington Univ	WA	16,803	C
CUNY/Baruch College	NY	21,609	HC
CUNY/Queens College	NY	21,507	C
DePaul Univ	IL	52,807	VC
Dordt College	IA	37,860	C+
Drake Univ	IA	49,220	HC
Eastern Mich Univ	MI	19,761	C
Elizabethtown College	PA	56,340	VC
Elmhurst College	IL	46,514	C
Ferris State Univ	MI	21,458	C
Florida A&M Univ	FL	15,361	C
Florida State Univ	FL	16,771	HC
Georgia State Univ	GA	25,250	C
High Point Univ	NC	47,355	VC
Hofstra Univ	NY	58,210	C+
Huntington Univ	IN	33,996	C
Indiana Univ Northwest	IN	7,207	LC
Indiana Univ South Bend	IN	16,057	C
Indiana Univ-Purdue Univ Fort Wayne	IN	18,675	C
Le Moyne College	NY	47,305	VC
Lebanon Valley College	PA	55,510	VC
Lycoming College	PA	50,895	C
Maryville Univ of St. Louis	MO	38,558	VC
Messiah College	PA	44,380	VC
Mich State Univ	MI	24,542	VC
Millersville Univ of Pennsylvania	PA	25,298	C
Milwaukee School of Engineering	WI	48,531	HC+
Mount Mercy Univ	IA	39,748	C
New York Univ	NY	68,139	MC
North Central College	IL	48,712	C+
N Dak State Univ	ND	16,245	VC
Northwestern College of Iowa	IA	38,400	C
Ohio State Univ at Columbus	OH	22,843	MC
Ohio Univ	OH	23,394	VC
Olivet Nazarene Univ	IL	41,840	VC

School	ST	$IS	SR
Otterbein Univ	OH	41,630	C
Purdue Univ/West Lafayette	IN	20,032	MC
Rider Univ	NJ	54,050	C
Roanoke College	VA	55,952	VC
Robert Morris Univ	PA	40,600	C
Rochester Inst of Technology	NY	52,734	HC+
Roosevelt Univ	IL	41,890	VC
St. Joseph's Univ	PA	58,540	VC
St. Mary's Univ of Minn	MN	42,440	C
Seton Hill Univ	PA	46,972	VC
Siena College	NY	48,916	C
Silver Lake College of the Holy Family	WI	36,290	LC
Simpson College	IA	45,626	VC
Southeast Missouri State Univ	MO	16,148	C
Southern Illinois Univ Edwardsville	IL	20,188	C
St. John's Univ	NY	57,160	C+
SUNY Albany	NY	22,165	C
Temple Univ	PA	24,392	C+
The Univ of Texas at San Antonio	TX	21,060	C
Thiel College	PA	42,950	LC
Univ of Calif at Santa Barbara	CA	30,627	HC+
Univ of Central Missouri	MO	18,982	C
Univ of Central Okla	OK	15,150	C
Univ of Illinois at Urbana-Champaign	IL	27,006	HC
Univ of Indianapolis	IN	36,480	VC
Univ of Iowa	IA	19,415	HC
Univ of Maine at Farmington	ME	18,792	C
Univ of Minn/Duluth	MN	20,292	C
Univ of Nebr - Lincoln	NE	18,589	VC
Univ of Northern Iowa	IA	17,480	C
Univ of Pennsylvania	PA	63,526	MC
Univ of Texas at Dallas	TX	23,640	HC
Univ of Wisc-Madison	WI	21,647	MC
Univ of Wisc-Milwaukee	WI	21,538	C
Valparaiso Univ	IN	50,160	VC
Wartburg College	IA	49,478	C
Western Kentucky Univ	KY	16,850	C
Western New England Univ	MA	49,182	C
Xavier Univ	OH	49,380	VC

ADDICTION STUDIES

School	ST	$IS	SR
Bethany College	KS	38,637	LC
Elizabethtown College School of Continuing and Professional Studies	PA	18,900	C
Goddard College	VT	17,040	VC
Graceland Univ	IA	35,290	C
Grand Canyon Univ	AZ	25,150	VC
Indiana Wesleyan Univ	IN	33,674	C
Kansas Wesleyan Univ	KS	37,930	C
Keene State College	NH	24,604	C
Lewis-Clark State College	ID	14,202	C
Metropolitan State Univ	MN	7,859	C
Minot State Univ	ND	13,285	C
Missouri Valley College	MO	28,150	C
Northwestern State Univ of Louisiana	LA	16,534	LC
Okla City Univ	OK	40,476	C
Rhode Island College	RI	19,000	LC
Southern Univ at New Orleans	LA	8,014	LC
Texas Tech Univ	TX	20,156	C+
The Univ of Mary	ND	23,180	C
Univ of Central Arkansas	AR	15,042	VC
Univ of Central Okla	OK	15,150	C
Univ of Cincinnati	OH	22,118	VC
Univ of Detroit Mercy	MI	48,816	C
Univ of Great Falls	MT	38,524	C
Univ of S Dak	SD	16,109	C
Univ of St. Francis	IL	40,828	C
Viterbo Univ	WI	34,660	C

ADOLESCENT EDUCATION FOR STUDENTS WITH DISABILITIES

School	ST	$IS	SR
Medaille College	NY	41,700	LC

ADVERTISING

School	ST	$IS	SR
Abilene Christian Univ	TX	43,708	C+
Adams State Univ	CO	15,420	LC
American International College	MA	47,020	LC
Appalachian State Univ	NC	15,394	VC
Art Inst of Portland	OR	132,329	SP
ArtCenter College of Design	CA	42,008	SP
Ball State Univ	IN	19,808	C+
Barry Univ	FL	38,730	LC
Bethany College	WV	38,774	LC
Biola Univ	CA	48,686	C
Bradley Univ	IL	43,240	VC
Brigham Young Univ	UT	13,248	MC
Butler Univ	IN	52,890	VC+
Cal State, East Bay	CA	20,748	C
Cal State, Fullerton	CA	21,902	C
Campbell Univ	NC	37,570	VC
Central Mich Univ	MI	20,330	C
Central State Univ	OH	18,564	C
Champlain College	VT	54,724	VC
Chapman Univ	CA	65,504	HC
CUNY/Baruch College	NY	21,609	HC
College for Creative Studies	MI	51,210	SP
College of St. Scholastica	MN	45,734	C+
Colo State Univ	CO	23,033	C
Columbia College Chicago	IL	40,104	C
Columbus College of Art and Design	OH	47,310	SP
Cornerstone Univ	MI	36,550	C
Davenport Univ	MI	25,896	LC
Dordt College	IA	37,860	C+
Drake Univ	IA	49,220	HC
Drury Univ	MO	37,555	VC
Duquesne Univ	PA	48,508	VC
East Central Univ	OK	13,330	C
Eastern Mich Univ	MI	19,761	C
Eastern Nazarene College	MA	41,114	C
Emerson College	MA	61,824	HC+
Fashion Inst of Technology/SUNY	NY	18,521	SP
Florida International Univ	FL	20,281	C
Florida Southern College	FL	45,978	VC
Florida State Univ	FL	16,771	HC
Fontbonne Univ	MO	34,606	C
Gannon Univ	PA	42,922	C
Grand Valley State Univ	MI	22,250	C+
Harding Univ	AR	25,440	C
Hawaii Pacific Univ	HI	33,420	C
Howard Univ	DC	37,616	C+
Iowa State Univ	IA	18,176	C
Johnson & Wales Univ/Providence Campus	RI	44,768	C
Keiser Univ	FL	35,010	LC
Kent State Univ	OH	20,928	C
Lamar Univ	TX	18,014	LC
Loyola Univ Chicago	IL	57,158	VC
Loyola Univ New Orleans	LA	52,456	VC
Marietta College	OH	46,190	C
Marquette Univ	WI	53,090	VC+
Marshall Univ	WV	18,044	C
Marywood Univ	PA	47,840	C
Mercyhurst Univ	PA	47,420	C
Metropolitan State Univ	MN	7,859	C
Mich State Univ	MI	24,542	VC
Midland Univ	NE	39,512	C
Morningside College	IA	39,780	C
Murray State Univ	KY	17,726	C+
New York Inst of Technology	NY	49,980	VC
North Park Univ	IL	35,860	C
Northeastern State Univ	OK	8,615	VC
Northwest Missouri State Univ	MO	18,286	C
Northwood Univ - Mich	MI	35,010	LC
Okla Christian Univ	OK	29,260	C
Okla City Univ	OK	40,476	C
Otis College of Art and Design	CA	54,670	SP
Pace Univ	NY	60,136	C
Parsons The New School for Design	NY	56,610	SP
Pennsylvania State Univ - Univ Park	PA	29,716	HC
Pepperdine Univ	CA	66,862	VC+
Point Park Univ	PA	41,270	C
Portland State Univ	OR	19,443	C
Purdue Univ Northwest	IN	15,178	C
Purdue Univ/West Lafayette	IN	20,032	MC
Quinnipiac Univ	CT	60,970	VC
Rider Univ	NJ	54,050	C
Ringling College of Art and Design	FL	59,160	SP
Rochester Inst of Technology	NY	52,734	HC+
Roosevelt Univ	IL	41,890	VC
Rowan Univ	NJ	24,491	VC
Salem State Univ	MA	42,650	LC
San Diego State Univ	CA	23,156	VC
San Jose State Univ	CA	22,630	C
Savannah College of Art and Design	GA	49,595	SP
School of Visual Arts	NY	47,500	SP
Southeast Missouri State Univ	MO	16,148	C
Southern Methodist Univ	TX	69,008	MC
Southern New Hampshire Univ	NH	44,256	C
Spring Arbor Univ	MI	37,390	C
St. Cloud State Univ	MN	10,600	C
St. John's Univ	NY	57,160	C+
Suffolk Univ	MA	52,316	C
Syracuse Univ	NY	62,313	HC
Temple Univ	PA	24,392	C+
Texas A&M Univ at Commerce	TX	10,496	C
Texas State Univ	TX	18,721	C
Texas Tech Univ	TX	20,156	C+
The Art Inst of Atlanta	GA	34,334	SP
The Univ of Alabama	AL	24,320	C+
The Univ of Tenn at Knoxville	TN	22,112	VC
The Univ of Texas at Austin	TX	20,206	MC
Union Univ	TN	41,160	VC
Univ of Arkansas at Little Rock	AR	18,211	LC
Univ of Central Florida	FL	16,379	VC
Univ of Central Okla	OK	15,150	C
Univ of Colo Boulder	CO	26,048	HC
Univ of Florida	FL	16,291	HC+
Univ of Georgia	GA	21,878	HC
Univ of Idaho	ID	16,158	C
Univ of Illinois at Urbana-Champaign	IL	27,006	HC
Univ of Kentucky	KY	24,800	C+
Univ of Louisiana at Lafayette	LA	14,516	C
Univ of Miami	FL	63,494	MC
Univ of Missouri-Columbia	MO	20,463	VC
Univ of Nebr - Kearney	NE	17,014	LC
Univ of Nebr - Lincoln	NE	18,589	VC
Univ of Okla	OK	19,651	HC
Univ of Oregon	OR	24,021	VC
Univ of San Francisco	CA	60,580	C
Univ of S Car at Columbia	SC	21,726	VC
Univ of Southern Indiana	IN	16,808	C
Univ of Southern Miss	MS	13,170	C
Univ of Tampa	FL	38,928	VC
Univ of the Sacred Heart	PR	17,932	
Washington State Univ	WA	22,747	C
Washington Univ in St. Louis	MO	67,539	MC
Waynesburg Univ	PA	33,530	C
Weber State Univ	UT	14,112	C
Webster Univ	MO	37,490	C
Wesleyan College	GA	31,940	C+
West Liberty Univ	WV	16,158	C
West Virginia Univ	WV	18,952	VC
Western Kentucky Univ	KY	16,850	C
Western Mich Univ	MI	21,791	C
Western New England Univ	MA	49,182	C
Wilmington College	OH	35,100	C
Xavier Univ	OH	49,380	VC
Youngstown State Univ	OH	17,487	C

AERONAUTICAL ENGINEERING

School	ST	$IS	SR
Auburn Univ	AL	24,300	VC+
Calif Polytechnic State Univ	CA	22,547	MC
Clarkson Univ	NY	60,392	VC
Florida Inst of Technology	FL	53,306	VC
Illinois Inst of Technology	IL	56,826	HC+
Iowa State Univ	IA	18,176	C
Mass Inst of Technology	MA	62,662	MC
Missouri Univ of Science and Technology	MO	18,655	HC
N Car State Univ	NC	22,434	HC+
Ohio State Univ at Columbus	OH	22,843	MC
Princeton Univ	NJ	60,090	MC
Purdue Univ/West Lafayette	IN	20,032	MC
Rensselaer Polytechnic Inst	NY	67,265	MC
St. Louis Univ	MO	49,866	HC
San Jose State Univ	CA	22,630	C
Stanford Univ	CA	62,541	MC
Tuskegee Univ	AL	28,164	C
United States Air Force Academy	CO		C
Univ of Calif at Davis	CA	28,468	HC
Univ of Calif at Irvine	CA	33,857	VC
Univ of Calif at Los Angeles	CA	27,438	HC+
Univ of Central Florida	FL	16,379	VC
Univ of Cincinnati	OH	22,118	VC
Univ of Florida	FL	16,291	HC+
Univ of Illinois at Urbana-Champaign	IL	27,006	HC
Univ of Mich/Ann Arbor	MI	25,274	MC
Univ of Southern Calif	CA	66,631	MC
Univ of Washington	WA	23,091	MC
West Virginia Univ	WV	18,952	VC
Wichita State Univ	KS	17,773	C

AERONAUTICAL SCIENCE

School	ST	$IS	SR
Bridgewater State Univ	MA	22,762	C
Embry-Riddle Aeronautical Univ - Daytona Beach	FL	45,822	VC
Embry-Riddle Aeronautical Univ - Prescott Campus	AZ	45,130	VC
Farmingdale State College	NY	20,968	C
Florida Inst of Technology	FL	53,306	VC
Inter-American Univ of PR-Bayamon	PR	18,785	
Kent State Univ	OH	20,928	C
LeTourneau Univ	TX	39,190	VC
Rocky Mountain College	MT	35,776	C
Univ of Maryland/Eastern Shore	MD	21,861	LC
Wilmington Univ	DE	8,762	NC

AERONAUTICAL TECHNOLOGY

School	ST	$IS	SR
Andrews Univ	MI	41,732	C
Arizona State Univ at the Polytechnic Campus	AZ	22,394	VC
Central Washington Univ	WA	16,803	C
Indiana State Univ	IN	23,223	LC
Inter-American Univ of PR-Bayamon	PR	18,785	
Kansas State Univ	KS	17,780	VC
LeTourneau Univ	TX	39,190	VC
Purdue Univ/West Lafayette	IN	20,032	MC
St. Louis Univ	MO	49,866	HC
Tenn State Univ	TN	14,423	LC
Univ of Alaska Anchorage	AK	17,914	C

AEROSPACE ENGINEERING

School	ST	$IS	SR
Arizona State Univ at the Tempe Campus	AZ	23,001	VC
Calif Inst of Technology	CA	64,704	MC
Calif State Polytechnic Univ, Pomona	CA	21,811	C
Cal State, Fullerton	CA	21,902	C
Cal State, Long Beach	CA	18,850	C
Case Western Reserve Univ	OH	62,284	MC
Embry-Riddle Aeronautical Univ - Daytona Beach	FL	45,822	VC
Embry-Riddle Aeronautical Univ - Prescott Campus	AZ	45,130	VC
Georgia Inst of Technology	GA	23,910	MC
Kent State Univ	OH	20,928	C
New Mexico State Univ	NM	14,050	LC
Pennsylvania State Univ - Univ Park	PA	29,716	HC
Rutgers Univ - New Brunswick	NJ	27,090	HC
St. Louis Univ	MO	49,866	HC
San Diego State Univ	CA	23,156	VC
Syracuse Univ	NY	62,313	HC
Texas A&M Univ at College Station	TX	20,771	VC+
The Univ of Arizona	AZ	24,086	C
United States Naval Academy	MD		HC
Univ of Calif San Diego	CA	30,450	MC
Univ of Colo Boulder	CO	26,048	HC
Univ of Kansas	KS	20,884	VC
Univ of Maryland/College Park	MD	21,938	HC
Univ of Minn/Twin Cities	MN	24,269	MC
Univ of Notre Dame	IN	68,801	MC
Univ of Okla	OK	19,651	HC
Western Mich Univ	MI	21,791	C

AEROSPACE STUDIES

School	ST	$IS	SR
Averett Univ	VA	43,034	LC
Mass Inst of Technology	MA	62,662	MC
Miss State Univ	MS	12,028	C+
New Mexico State Univ	NM	14,050	LC
Okla State Univ	OK	17,180	C+
Rochester Inst of Technology	NY	52,734	HC+
St. Louis Univ	MO	49,866	HC
SUNY/Univ at Buffalo	NY	23,122	C
The Univ of Alabama	AL	24,320	C+
The Univ of Tenn at Knoxville	TN	22,112	VC
The Univ of Texas at Austin	TX	20,206	MC
United States Air Force Academy	CO		C
Univ of Alaska Anchorage	AK	17,914	C
Univ of Calif at Los Angeles	CA	27,438	HC+
Univ of Calif San Diego	CA	30,450	MC
Univ of Central Florida	FL	16,379	VC
Univ of Miami	FL	63,494	MC
Univ of Mich/Ann Arbor	MI	25,274	MC
Univ of Southern Calif	CA	66,631	MC
Univ of Virginia	VA	27,367	MC
Virginia Polytechnic Inst and State Univ	VA	21,920	VC
West Virginia Univ	WV	18,952	VC
Western Kentucky Univ	KY	16,850	C

AFRICAN AMERICAN STUDIES

School	ST	$IS	SR
Amherst College	MA	66,186	MC
Arizona State Univ at the Tempe Campus	AZ	23,001	VC
Bard College at Simon's Rock	MA	65,795	MC
Bates College	ME	64,500	HC
Berea College	KY	7,094	C
Brandeis Univ	MA	68,443	MC
Brown Univ	RI	64,566	MC
Cabrini Univ	PA	42,591	LC
Cal State, Fresno	CA	16,902	LC
Cal State, Fullerton	CA	21,902	C
Cal State, Los Angeles	CA	17,186	LC
Cal State, Northridge	CA	17,277	LC
Carleton College	MN	66,414	MC
Chicago State Univ	IL	41,620	C
CUNY/Hunter College	NY	31,098	VC
CUNY/Lehman College	NY	5,788	LC
CUNY/York College	NY	6,747	LC
Claflin Univ	SC	25,592	LC
Coe College	IA	51,570	VC
Colby College	ME	64,060	MC
College of Charleston	SC	24,046	VC
College of Staten Island	NY	24,389	LC
Columbia Univ/ School of General Studies	NY	61,470	MC
Columbia Univ/City of New York	NY	62,958	MC
Dartmouth College	NH	68,109	MC
Denison Univ	OH	62,770	HC+
DePauw Univ	IN	58,688	VC
Duke Univ	NC	68,298	MC
Earlham College	IN	55,670	HC
East Carolina Univ	NC	16,539	C
Eastern Mich Univ	MI	19,761	C
Elon Univ	NC	46,142	HC
Emory Univ	GA	63,286	MC
Fordham Univ	NY	68,431	MC
Georgia State Univ	GA	25,250	C
Guilford College	NC	45,973	C
Hampshire College	MA	65,214	MC
Harvard College/Harvard Univ	MA	65,609	MC
Howard Univ	DC	37,616	C+
Indiana State Univ	IN	23,223	LC
Indiana Univ Bloomington	IN	20,791	HC
Indiana Univ Northwest	IN	7,207	LC
Loyola Marymount Univ	CA	60,202	VC+
Loyola Univ Chicago	IL	57,158	VC
Luther College	IA	49,990	VC
Martin Univ	IN	21,010	LC

ST = STATE $IS = IN-STATE COSTS SR = SELECTOR RATING

School	ST	$IS	SR
Metropolitan State Univ of Denver	CO	6,928	LC
Miami Univ	OH	27,190	HC+
Middlebury College	VT	67,464	MC
Morehouse College	GA	40,835	C
Morgan State Univ	MD	17,190	LC
New York Univ	NY	68,139	MC
Northeastern Univ	MA	65,352	MC
Northwestern Univ	IL	68,725	MC
Oakland Univ	MI	20,763	C
Oberlin College	OH	68,942	MC
Ohio State Univ at Columbus	OH	22,843	MC
Ohio Univ	OH	23,394	VC
Ohio Wesleyan Univ	OH	49,460	VC
Old Dominion Univ	VA	21,618	C
Pennsylvania State Univ - Univ Park	PA	29,716	HC
Pitzer College	CA	68,500	HC+
Purdue Univ/West Lafayette	IN	20,032	MC
Rhode Island College	RI	19,000	LC
Roosevelt Univ	IL	41,890	VC
Rutgers Univ - Camden	NJ	26,595	C
Rutgers Univ - New Brunswick	NJ	27,090	HC
Rutgers Univ - Newark	NJ	27,351	C
St. Augustine's Univ	NC	25,582	C
St. Louis Univ	MO	49,866	HC
St. Peter's Univ	NJ	49,192	C
San Diego State Univ	CA	23,156	VC
Scripps College	CA	69,260	HC
Seton Hall Univ	NJ	58,008	C
Simmons College	MA	54,400	HC
Smith College	MA	66,774	MC
Sonoma State Univ	CA	27,020	C
Southern Methodist Univ	TX	69,008	MC
Stanford Univ	CA	62,541	MC
SUNY Albany	NY	22,165	C
SUNY at Geneseo	NY	21,622	VC
SUNY at New Paltz	NY	20,840	C
SUNY/Cortland	NY	20,910	C
SUNY/Univ at Buffalo	NY	23,122	C
Suffolk Univ	MA	52,316	C
Syracuse Univ	NY	62,313	HC
Temple Univ	PA	24,392	C+
The College at Brockport - SUNY	NY	21,058	C
The College of Wooster	OH	60,000	HC
The Univ of Memphis	TN	18,278	C
Univ of Alabama at Birmingham	AL	22,092	C
Univ of Calif at Berkeley	CA	29,886	MC
Univ of Calif at Irvine	CA	33,857	VC
Univ of Calif at Los Angeles	CA	27,438	HC+
Univ of Calif at Riverside	CA	32,912	C
Univ of Calif at Santa Barbara	CA	30,627	HC+
Univ of Central Arkansas	AR	15,042	VC
Univ of Chicago	IL	70,551	MC
Univ of Cincinnati	OH	22,118	VC
Univ of Georgia	GA	21,878	HC
Univ of Illinois at Chicago	IL	24,664	VC
Univ of Iowa	IA	19,415	HC
Univ of Kansas	KS	20,884	VC
Univ of Maryland/Baltimore County	MD	23,004	VC
Univ of Maryland/College Park	MD	21,938	HC
Univ of Mass Amherst	MA	27,669	HC
Univ of Mass Boston	MA	13,828	C
Univ of Mich/Ann Arbor	MI	25,274	MC
Univ of Mich/Dearborn	MI	12,472	VC
Univ of Minn/Twin Cities	MN	24,269	MC
Univ of Miss	MS	18,802	C
Univ of Nebr - Omaha	NE	16,120	C
Univ of N Car at Chapel Hill	NC	20,561	MC
Univ of N Car at Greensboro	NC	15,998	C
Univ of Northern Colo	CO	19,658	C
Univ of Okla	OK	19,651	HC
Univ of Pennsylvania	PA	63,526	MC
Univ of Rochester	NY	65,032	MC
Univ of S Car at Columbia	SC	21,726	VC
Univ of South Florida/Tampa	FL	16,110	VC
Univ of Southern Calif	CA	66,631	MC
Univ of Virginia	VA	27,367	MC
Univ of Washington	WA	23,091	MC
Univ of Wisc-Madison	WI	21,647	MC
Univ of Wisc-Milwaukee	WI	21,538	C
Vanderbilt Univ	TN	63,248	MC
Virginia Commonwealth Univ	VA	23,811	VC
Washington Univ in St. Louis	MO	67,539	MC
Wellesley College	MA	66,984	MC
Wesleyan Univ	CT	66,940	MC
Western Kentucky Univ	KY	16,850	C
Western Mich Univ	MI	21,791	C
Wheaton College	MA	63,818	VC
William Paterson Univ of New Jersey	NJ	24,022	C
Wofford College	SC	49,885	VC
Wright State Univ	OH	16,983	C
Yale Univ	CT	64,650	MC

AFRICAN LANGUAGES

School	ST	$IS	SR
Cal State, Northridge	CA	17,277	LC
Duke Univ	NC	68,298	MC
Rutgers Univ - New Brunswick	NJ	27,090	HC
Univ of Wisc-Madison	WI	21,647	MC

AFRICAN STUDIES

School	ST	$IS	SR
Agnes Scott College	GA	51,930	VC+
Bard College	NY	65,924	HC
Berea College	KY	7,094	C
Bowling Green State Univ	OH	19,975	C
Brown Univ	RI	64,566	MC
Cal State, Dominguez Hills	CA	19,022	LC
Cal State, Long Beach	CA	18,850	C
Carleton College	MN	66,414	MC
CUNY/Brooklyn College	NY	7,163	C+
CUNY/Queens College	NY	21,507	C
Claflin Univ	SC	25,592	LC
Claremont McKenna College	CA	69,900	MC
Clayton State Univ	GA	19,735	LC
Colgate Univ	NY	67,500	MC
Conn College	CT	65,000	MC
Delaware State Univ	DE	19,376	LC
DePaul Univ	IL	52,807	VC
Dickinson College	PA	66,166	MC
Drew Univ/College of Liberal Arts	NJ	53,608	VC
Duke Univ	NC	68,298	MC
Eastern Mich Univ	MI	19,761	C
Emory Univ	GA	63,286	MC
Florida International Univ	FL	20,281	C
Fordham Univ	NY	68,431	MC
Franklin and Marshall College	PA	67,960	MC
Hamilton College	NY	64,250	MC
Hampshire College	MA	65,214	MC
Hobart and William Smith Colleges	NY	67,050	HC+
Hofstra Univ	NY	58,210	C+
Howard Univ	DC	37,616	C+
Indiana Univ Bloomington	IN	20,791	HC
Kalamazoo College	MI	53,931	HC
Kennesaw State Univ	GA	18,899	VC
Kent State Univ	OH	20,928	C
Lafayette College	PA	68,520	MC
Lehigh Univ	PA	63,860	MC
Linfield College	OR	53,992	C
Loyola Univ Chicago	IL	57,158	VC
Mercer Univ	GA	45,348	VC
New York Univ	NY	68,139	MC
North Park Univ	IL	35,860	C
Old Dominion Univ	VA	21,618	C
Ramapo College of New Jersey	NJ	25,760	VC
Rowan Univ	NJ	24,491	VC
San Francisco State Univ	CA	18,514	LC
Savannah State Univ	GA	17,036	C
Shaw Univ	NC	24,638	C
Smith College	MA	66,774	MC
St. Lawrence Univ	NY	66,646	HC+
SUNY/Oneonta	NY	20,794	C
Tenn State Univ	TN	14,423	LC
The College at Brockport - SUNY	NY	21,058	C
Tulane Univ	LA	67,496	MC
Univ of Calif at Davis	CA	28,468	HC
Univ of Calif at Los Angeles	CA	27,438	HC+
Univ of Calif San Diego	CA	30,450	MC
Univ of Conn	CT	27,394	
Univ of Kansas	KS	20,884	VC
Univ of Mich/Ann Arbor	MI	25,274	MC
Univ of Mich/Dearborn	MI	12,472	VC
Univ of N Car at Greensboro	NC	15,998	C
Univ of Pennsylvania	PA	63,526	MC
Vassar College	NY	68,110	MC
Washington Univ in St. Louis	MO	67,539	MC
Wayne State Univ	MI	23,085	C
Western Mich Univ	MI	21,791	C
Wheaton College	MA	63,818	VC
Yale Univ	CT	64,650	MC

AFRICANA STUDIES

School	ST	$IS	SR
Augustana College	IL	51,222	VC+
Bowdoin College	ME	65,980	MC
Brown Univ	RI	64,566	MC
College of William & Mary	VA	34,907	MC
Cornell Univ	NY	67,591	MC
Davidson College	NC	60,119	MC
Eastern Illinois Univ	IL	21,414	C
Gettysburg College	PA	65,210	MC
Hobart and William Smith Colleges	NY	67,050	HC+
Indiana Univ-Purdue Univ Indianapolis	IN	18,952	C
Johns Hopkins Univ	MD	68,080	MC
Knox College	IL	54,654	VC+
Lincoln Univ	PA	20,878	LC
Mount Holyoke College	MA	56,746	MC
New York Univ	NY	68,139	MC
Oberlin College	OH	68,942	MC
Pomona College	CA	64,957	MC
Sarah Lawrence College	NY	68,866	MC
Southern Illinois Univ Carbondale	IL	24,554	C
SUNY at Binghamton	NY	24,100	MC
Stony Brook Univ/The SUNY	NY	22,703	MC
The Univ of Arizona	AZ	24,086	C
Tufts Univ	MA		MC
Univ of Maryland/Baltimore County	MD	23,004	VC
Univ of Miami	FL	63,494	MC
Univ of New Mexico	NM	16,808	C
Univ of N Car at Charlotte	NC	17,803	VC
Univ of Notre Dame	IN	68,801	MC
Univ of Pittsburgh	PA	30,030	MC
Univ of Rhode Island	RI	26,066	VC
Western Mich Univ	MI	21,791	C

AGRICULTURAL BUSINESS MANAGEMENT

School	ST	$IS	SR
Abilene Christian Univ	TX	43,708	C+
Adams State Univ	CO	15,420	LC
Alabama A&M Univ	AL	18,796	C
Alcorn State Univ	MS	15,884	C
Angelo State Univ	TX	15,882	LC
Appalachian State Univ	NC	15,394	VC
Arkansas State Univ	AR	16,190	C
Arkansas Tech Univ	AR	16,534	LC
Auburn Univ	AL	24,300	VC+
Brigham Young Univ	UT	13,248	MC
Calif Polytechnic State Univ	CA	22,547	MC
Calif State Polytechnic Univ, Pomona	CA	21,811	C
Cal State, Chico	CA	19,790	VC
Cal State, Fresno	CA	16,902	LC
Cal State, Fullerton	CA	21,902	C
College of the Ozarks	MO	7,530	VC
Colo State Univ	CO	23,033	C
Dakota Wesleyan Univ	SD	33,980	LC
Delaware State Univ	DE	19,376	LC
Dickinson State Univ	ND	12,372	LC
Dordt College	IA	37,860	C+
Eastern New Mexico Univ	NM	12,874	LC
Eastern Oregon Univ	OR	17,612	C
Florida Southern College	FL	45,978	VC
Fort Hays State Univ	KS	12,677	C
Hardin-Simmons Univ	TX	36,025	C
Huntington Univ	IN	33,996	C
Illinois State Univ	IL	23,418	VC
Iowa State Univ	IA	18,176	C
Kansas State Univ	KS	17,780	VC
Lincoln Univ	MO	14,402	NC
Louisiana State Univ and A&M College	LA	18,677	VC
Louisiana Tech Univ	LA	11,422	VC
Mich State Univ	MI	24,542	VC
Middle Tenn State Univ	TN	8,650	C
Miss State Univ	MS	12,028	C+
Montana State Univ	MT	15,500	C+
Morningside College	IA	39,780	C
Murray State Univ	KY	17,726	C+
New Mexico State Univ	NM	14,050	LC
Nicholls State Univ	LA	14,959	C
N Car A&T State Univ	NC	13,786	C
N Car State Univ	NC	22,434	HC+
N Dak State Univ	ND	16,245	VC
Northwest Missouri State Univ	MO	18,286	C
Northwestern College of Iowa	IA	38,400	C
Northwestern Okla State Univ	OK	13,072	LC
Ohio State Univ at Columbus	OH	22,843	MC
Okla Panhandle State Univ	OK	6,152	C
Okla State Univ	OK	17,180	C+
Oregon State Univ	OR	23,337	VC
Pennsylvania State Univ - Univ Park	PA	29,716	HC
Prairie View A&M Univ	TX	27,273	LC
Purdue Univ/West Lafayette	IN	20,032	MC
S Car State Univ	SC	21,330	LC
S Dak State Univ	SD	15,874	C
Southeast Missouri State Univ	MO	16,148	C
Southern Arkansas Univ	AR	21,532	C
Southwest Minn State Univ	MN	17,783	C
SUNY /College of Agriculture and Tech at Cobleskill	NY	20,527	LC
Stephen F. Austin State Univ	TX	18,484	LC
Sul Ross State Univ	TX	15,021	LC
Tarleton State Univ	TX	15,248	LC
Texas A&M Univ at College Station	TX	20,771	VC+
Texas A&M Univ at Kingsville	TX	16,580	LC
Texas State Univ	TX	18,721	C
Texas Tech Univ	TX	20,156	C+
The Univ of Arizona	AZ	24,086	C
The Univ of Tenn at Martin	TN	15,212	C
Truman State Univ	MO	16,286	MC
Univ of Arkansas at Fayetteville	AR	19,766	VC
Univ of Calif at Davis	CA	28,468	HC
Univ of Central Missouri	MO	18,982	C
Univ of Delaware	DE	32,214	VC
Univ of Florida	FL	16,291	HC+
Univ of Idaho	ID	16,158	C
Univ of Illinois at Urbana-Champaign	IL	27,006	HC
Univ of Louisiana at Monroe	LA	15,970	C
Univ of Maine at Machias	ME	22,960	C
Univ of Maryland/College Park	MD	21,938	HC
Univ of Minn/Crookston	MN	19,126	C
Univ of Minn/Twin Cities	MN	24,269	MC
Univ of Missouri-Columbia	MO	20,463	VC
Univ of Nebr - Lincoln	NE	18,589	VC
Univ of Wisc-Madison	WI	21,647	MC
Univ of Wisc-Platteville	WI	14,148	C
Univ of Wisc-River Falls	WI	14,541	C
Univ of Wyoming	WY	15,537	C
Urbana Univ	OH	30,820	C
Utah State Univ	UT	13,235	C
Washington State Univ	WA	22,747	C
West Texas A&M Univ	TX	13,478	C
Wilmington College	OH	35,100	C

AGRICULTURAL COMMUNICATIONS

School	ST	$IS	SR
Auburn Univ	AL	24,300	VC+
Calif Polytechnic State Univ	CA	22,547	MC
Cal State, Fresno	CA	16,902	LC
Cal State, Fullerton	CA	21,902	C
Kansas State Univ	KS	17,780	VC
N Dak State Univ	ND	16,245	VC
Okla State Univ	OK	17,180	C+
Purdue Univ/West Lafayette	IN	20,032	MC
S Dak State Univ	SD	15,874	C
Texas A&M Univ at College Station	TX	20,771	VC+
Texas Tech Univ	TX	20,156	C+
Univ of Arkansas at Fayetteville	AR	19,766	VC
Univ of Georgia	GA	21,878	HC
Univ of Idaho	ID	16,158	C
Univ of Illinois at Urbana-Champaign	IL	27,006	HC
Univ of Minn/Twin Cities	MN	24,269	MC
Univ of Nebr - Lincoln	NE	18,589	VC
Univ of Wisc-Madison	WI	21,647	MC
Univ of Wyoming	WY	15,537	C
Washington State Univ	WA	22,747	C

AGRICULTURAL ECONOMICS

School	ST	$IS	SR
Alabama A&M Univ	AL	18,796	C
Alcorn State Univ	MS	15,884	C
Auburn Univ	AL	24,300	VC+
Cal State, Fullerton	CA	21,902	C
Colo State Univ	CO	23,033	C
Eastern Oregon Univ	OR	17,612	C
Fort Valley State Univ	GA	17,988	VC
Kansas State Univ	KS	17,780	VC
Langston Univ	OK	15,659	C
Miss State Univ	MS	12,028	C+
New Mexico State Univ	NM	14,050	LC
N Car A&T State Univ	NC	13,786	C
N Car State Univ	NC	22,434	HC+
N Dak State Univ	ND	16,245	VC
Northwest Missouri State Univ	MO	18,286	C
Ohio State Univ at Columbus	OH	22,843	MC
Okla State Univ	OK	17,180	C+
Prairie View A&M Univ	TX	27,273	LC
Purdue Univ/West Lafayette	IN	20,032	MC
S Dak State Univ	SD	15,874	C
Southern Illinois Univ Carbondale	IL	24,554	C
Southern Univ and A&M College	LA	16,074	LC
Tarleton State Univ	TX	15,248	LC
Tenn Tech Univ	TN	17,929	C
Texas A&M Univ at College Station	TX	20,771	VC+
Texas A&M Univ at Commerce	TX	10,496	C
Texas Tech Univ	TX	20,156	C+
The Univ of Arizona	AZ	24,086	C
The Univ of Tenn at Knoxville	TN	22,112	VC
Tuskegee Univ	AL	28,164	C
Univ of Calif at Davis	CA	28,468	HC
Univ of Conn	CT	27,394	
Univ of Delaware	DE	32,214	VC
Univ of Idaho	ID	16,158	C
Univ of Illinois at Urbana-Champaign	IL	27,006	HC
Univ of Kentucky	KY	24,800	C+
Univ of Maryland/College Park	MD	21,938	HC
Univ of Mass Amherst	MA	27,669	HC
Univ of Missouri-Columbia	MO	20,463	VC
Univ of Nebr - Lincoln	NE	18,589	VC
Univ of Wisc-Madison	WI	21,647	MC
Utah State Univ	UT	13,235	C
Virginia Polytechnic Inst and State Univ	VA	21,920	VC
Washington State Univ	WA	22,747	C
West Texas A&M Univ	TX	13,478	C
West Virginia Univ	WV	18,952	VC

AGRICULTURAL EDUCATION

School	ST	$IS	SR
Alabama A&M Univ	AL	18,796	C
Arkansas Tech Univ	AR	16,534	LC
Calif Polytechnic State Univ	CA	22,547	MC
Cal State, Fresno	CA	16,902	LC
Cal State, Fullerton	CA	21,902	C
Clemson Univ	SC		HC
College of the Ozarks	MO	7,530	VC
Colo State Univ	CO	23,033	C
Delaware State Univ	DE	19,376	LC
Dordt College	IA	37,860	C+
Eastern New Mexico Univ	NM	12,874	LC
Fort Valley State Univ	GA	17,988	VC
Huntington Univ	IN	33,996	C
Iowa State Univ	IA	18,176	C
Kansas State Univ	KS	17,780	VC
Louisiana State Univ and A&M College	LA	18,677	VC

School	ST	$IS	SR
Mich State Univ	MI	24,542	VC
Miss State Univ	MS	12,028	C+
Missouri State Univ	MO	15,837	C+
Montana State Univ	MT	15,500	C+
Morehead State Univ	KY	18,386	LC
Murray State Univ	KY	17,726	C+
New Mexico State Univ	NM	14,050	LC
N Car A&T State Univ	NC	13,786	C
N Car State Univ	NC	22,434	HC+
N Dak State Univ	ND	16,245	VC
Northwest Missouri State Univ	MO	18,286	C
Ohio State Univ at Columbus	OH	22,843	MC
Okla Panhandle State Univ	OK	6,152	C
Okla State Univ	OK	17,180	C+
Pennsylvania State Univ - Univ Park	PA	29,716	HC
Purdue Univ/West Lafayette	IN	20,032	MC
S Dak State Univ	SD	15,874	C
Southern Arkansas Univ	AR	21,532	C
Southern Univ and A&M College	LA	16,074	LC
SUNY at Oswego	NY	22,219	VC
Stephen F. Austin State Univ	TX	18,484	LC
Tarleton State Univ	TX	15,248	LC
Tenn Tech Univ	TN	17,929	C
Texas A&M Univ at College Station	TX	20,771	VC+
Texas A&M Univ at Commerce	TX	10,496	C
Texas A&M Univ at Kingsville	TX	16,580	LC
The Univ of Arizona	AZ	24,086	C
Univ of Arkansas at Fayetteville	AR	19,766	VC
Univ of Arkansas at Pine Bluff	AR	13,541	C
Univ of Central Missouri	MO	18,982	C
Univ of Conn	CT	27,394	
Univ of Florida	FL	16,291	HC+
Univ of Georgia	GA	21,878	HC
Univ of Idaho	ID	16,158	C
Univ of Illinois at Urbana-Champaign	IL	27,006	HC
Univ of Kentucky	KY	24,800	C+
Univ of Louisiana at Lafayette	LA	14,516	C
Univ of Maryland/Eastern Shore	MD	21,861	LC
Univ of Minn/Twin Cities	MN	24,269	MC
Univ of Nebr - Lincoln	NE	18,589	VC
Univ of Wisc-Platteville	WI	14,148	C
Univ of Wisc-River Falls	WI	14,541	C
Univ of Wyoming	WY	15,537	C
Utah State Univ	UT	13,235	C
Virginia Polytechnic Inst and State Univ	VA	21,920	VC
Washington State Univ	WA	22,747	C
West Virginia Univ	WV	18,952	VC
Western Illinois Univ	IL	20,897	C
Western Kentucky Univ	KY	16,850	C
Wilmington College	OH	35,100	C

AGRICULTURAL ENGINEERING

School	ST	$IS	SR
Auburn Univ	AL	24,300	VC+
Cal State, Fullerton	CA	21,902	C
Clemson Univ	SC		HC
Iowa State Univ	IA	18,176	C
Kansas State Univ	KS	17,780	VC
N Car State Univ	NC	22,434	HC+
N Dak State Univ	ND	16,245	VC
Oregon State Univ	OR	23,337	VC
Purdue Univ/West Lafayette	IN	20,032	MC
Rutgers Univ - New Brunswick	NJ	27,090	HC
S Dak State Univ	SD	15,874	C
The Univ of Arizona	AZ	24,086	C
Univ of Calif at Davis	CA	28,468	HC
Univ of Florida	FL	16,291	HC+
Univ of Georgia	GA	21,878	HC
Univ of Illinois at Urbana-Champaign	IL	27,006	HC
Univ of Nebr - Lincoln	NE	18,589	VC
Univ of Wisc-River Falls	WI	14,541	C
Utah State Univ	UT	13,235	C
Virginia Polytechnic Inst and State Univ	VA	21,920	VC
Washington State Univ	WA	22,747	C

AGRICULTURAL ENGINEERING TECHNOLOGY

School	ST	$IS	SR
Fort Valley State Univ	GA	17,988	VC
Kansas State Univ	KS	17,780	VC
Miss State Univ	MS	12,028	C+
Montana State Univ	MT	15,500	C+
Murray State Univ	KY	17,726	C+
N Dak State Univ	ND	16,245	VC
S Dak State Univ	SD	15,874	C
Univ of Central Missouri	MO	18,982	C
Univ of Minn/Crookston	MN	19,126	C
Washington State Univ	WA	22,747	C
Western Kentucky Univ	KY	16,850	C

AGRICULTURAL MECHANICS

School	ST	$IS	SR
Calif Polytechnic State Univ	CA	22,547	MC
Montana State Univ-Northern	MT	11,370	NC
Murray State Univ	KY	17,726	C+
N Dak State Univ	ND	16,245	VC
Northwest Missouri State Univ	MO	18,286	C
SUNY /College of Agriculture and Tech at Cobleskill	NY	20,527	LC
Stephen F. Austin State Univ	TX	18,484	LC
Tarleton State Univ	TX	15,248	LC
Univ of Idaho	ID	16,158	C
Univ of Illinois at Urbana-Champaign	IL	27,006	HC
Univ of Nebr - Lincoln	NE	18,589	VC
Washington State Univ	WA	22,747	C
Western Kentucky Univ	KY	16,850	C

AGRICULTURAL SCIENCES

School	ST	$IS	SR
Angelo State Univ	TX	15,882	LC
Calif Polytechnic State Univ	CA	22,547	MC
Calif State Polytechnic Univ, Pomona	CA	21,811	C
Cal State, Fullerton	CA	21,902	C
College of the Ozarks	MO	7,530	VC
Cornell Univ	NY	67,591	MC
Huntington Univ	IN	33,996	C
Morningside College	IA	39,780	C
Murray State Univ	KY	17,726	C+
Northwest Missouri State Univ	MO	18,286	C
Pennsylvania State Univ - Univ Park	PA	29,716	HC
Texas A&M Univ at College Station	TX	20,771	VC+
Univ of Arkansas at Pine Bluff	AR	13,541	C
Univ of Idaho	ID	16,158	C
Univ of Maine at Machias	ME	22,960	C
Univ of Nevada, Reno	NV	18,010	C
Washington State Univ	WA	22,747	C
West Virginia Univ	WV	18,952	VC

AGRICULTURE

School	ST	$IS	SR
Andrews Univ	MI	41,732	C
Arkansas State Univ	AR	16,190	C
Auburn Univ	AL	24,300	VC+
Austin Peay State Univ	TN	16,397	C
Berea College	KY	7,094	C
Cal State, Chico	CA	19,790	VC
Cal State, Fullerton	CA	21,902	C
Cal State, Stanislaus	CA	18,053	LC
Cameron Univ	OK	11,632	LC
Clemson Univ	SC		HC
College of the Ozarks	MO	7,530	VC
Colo State Univ	CO	23,033	C
Dordt College	IA	37,860	C+
Eastern Kentucky Univ	KY	17,742	C
Eastern New Mexico Univ	NM	12,874	LC
Ferrum College	VA	43,970	C
Florida Southern College	FL	45,978	VC
Fort Hays State Univ	KS	12,677	C
Green Mountain College	VT	45,228	LC
Hampshire College	MA	65,214	MC
Hardin-Simmons Univ	TX	36,025	C
Huntington Univ	IN	33,996	C
Illinois State Univ	IL	23,418	VC
Iowa State Univ	IA	18,176	C
Lincoln Univ	MO	14,402	NC
McNeese State Univ	LA	7,838	C
Mich State Univ	MI	24,542	VC
Miss State Univ	MS	12,028	C+
Missouri State Univ	MO	15,837	C+
Morehead State Univ	KY	18,386	LC
New Mexico State Univ	NM	14,050	LC
N Car State Univ	NC	22,434	HC+
N Dak State Univ	ND	16,245	VC
Northwest Missouri State Univ	MO	18,286	C
Northwestern Okla State Univ	OK	13,072	LC
Oregon State Univ	OR	23,337	VC
Penn State Erie,The Behrend College	PA	26,688	VC
Purdue Univ/West Lafayette	IN	20,032	MC
Rutgers Univ - New Brunswick	NJ	27,090	HC
Sam Houston State Univ	TX	18,792	C
S Dak State Univ	SD	15,874	C
Southern Arkansas Univ	AR	21,532	C
Southern Illinois Univ Carbondale	IL	24,554	C
Southern Univ and A&M College	LA	16,074	LC
Stephen F. Austin State Univ	TX	18,484	LC
Sterling College	VT	41,894	VC
Tarleton State Univ	TX	15,248	LC
Tenn State Univ	TN	14,423	LC
Tenn Tech Univ	TN	17,929	C
Texas A&M Univ at Commerce	TX	10,496	C
Texas State Univ	TX	18,721	C
Texas Tech Univ	TX	20,156	C+
The Univ of Tenn at Knoxville	TN	22,112	VC
The Univ of Tenn at Martin	TN	15,212	C
Truman State Univ	MO	16,286	MC
Unity College	ME	37,670	C
Univ of Arkansas at Monticello	AR	13,599	LC
Univ of Arkansas at Pine Bluff	AR	13,541	C
Univ of Conn	CT	27,394	
Univ of Delaware	DE	32,214	VC
Univ of Hawaii at Hilo	HI	18,038	VC
Univ of Idaho	ID	16,158	C
Univ of Kentucky	KY	24,800	C+
Univ of Maine	ME	21,038	VC
Univ of Maryland/College Park	MD	21,938	HC
Univ of Maryland/Eastern Shore	MD	21,861	LC
Univ of Missouri-Columbia	MO	20,463	VC
Univ of Nebr - Lincoln	NE	18,589	VC
Virginia State Univ	VA	19,802	C+
Washington State Univ	WA	22,747	C
West Texas A&M Univ	TX	13,478	C
West Virginia Univ	WV	18,952	VC
Western Illinois Univ	IL	20,897	C
Western Kentucky Univ	KY	16,850	C
Xavier Univ	OH	49,380	VC

AGRICULTURE INTERNATIONAL

School	ST	$IS	SR
Cal State, Fullerton	CA	21,902	C
Cornell Univ	NY	67,591	MC
Iowa State Univ	IA	18,176	C
Tarleton State Univ	TX	15,248	LC
Univ of Calif at Davis	CA	28,468	HC
Utah State Univ	UT	13,235	C

AGRONOMY

School	ST	$IS	SR
Alabama A&M Univ	AL	18,796	C
Auburn Univ	AL	24,300	VC+
Calif Polytechnic State Univ	CA	22,547	MC
Cal State, Fullerton	CA	21,902	C
College of the Ozarks	MO	7,530	VC
Colo State Univ	CO	23,033	C
Delaware Valley Univ	PA	51,271	C
Iowa State Univ	IA	18,176	C
Kansas State Univ	KS	17,780	VC
Miss State Univ	MS	12,028	C+
Murray State Univ	KY	17,726	C+
New Mexico State Univ	NM	14,050	LC
N Car State Univ	NC	22,434	HC+
Northwest Missouri State Univ	MO	18,286	C
Okla Panhandle State Univ	OK	6,152	C
Oregon State Univ	OR	23,337	VC
Prairie View A&M Univ	TX	27,273	LC
Purdue Univ/West Lafayette	IN	20,032	MC
S Dak State Univ	SD	15,874	C
Tarleton State Univ	TX	15,248	LC
Texas A&M Univ at College Station	TX	20,771	VC+
Truman State Univ	MO	16,286	MC
Univ of Conn	CT	27,394	
Univ of Florida	FL	16,291	HC+
Univ of Illinois at Urbana-Champaign	IL	27,006	HC
Univ of Minn/Crookston	MN	19,126	C
Univ of Nebr - Lincoln	NE	18,589	VC
Univ of Wisc-Madison	WI	21,647	MC
Univ of Wisc-River Falls	WI	14,541	C
Washington State Univ	WA	22,747	C
West Virginia Univ	WV	18,952	VC
Western Kentucky Univ	KY	16,850	C
Wilmington College	OH	35,100	C

AIR TRAFFIC CONTROL

School	ST	$IS	SR
Florida Memorial Univ	FL	22,424	LC
Lynn Univ	FL	49,680	LC
Purdue Univ/West Lafayette	IN	20,032	MC
Thomas Edison State Univ	NJ	6,350	NC
Univ of Alaska Anchorage	AK	17,914	C
Univ of N Dak	ND	16,673	C
Vaughn College of Aeronautics and Technology	NY	37,180	SP

AIR TRAFFIC MANAGEMENT

School	ST	$IS	SR
Arizona State Univ at the Polytechnic Campus	AZ	22,394	VC
Embry-Riddle Aeronautical Univ - Daytona Beach	FL	45,822	VC
Embry-Riddle Aeronautical Univ - Prescott Campus	AZ	45,130	VC

AIRCRAFT MECHANICS

School	ST	$IS	SR
Andrews Univ	MI	41,732	C
Idaho State Univ	ID	13,619	LC
Pennsylvania College of Technology	PA	27,693	NC
Vaughn College of Aeronautics and Technology	NY	37,180	SP

AIRLINE PILOTING AND NAVIGATION

School	ST	$IS	SR
Averett Univ	VA	43,034	LC
Baylor Univ	TX	56,803	HC
Eastern Kentucky Univ	KY	17,742	C
Eastern Mich Univ	MI	19,761	C
Indiana State Univ	IN	23,223	LC
Kansas State Univ	KS	17,780	VC
Louisiana Tech Univ	LA	11,422	VC
Lynn Univ	FL	49,680	LC
Metropolitan State Univ of Denver	CO	6,928	LC
Ohio Univ	OH	23,394	VC
Pacific Union College	CA	36,009	VC
Purdue Univ/West Lafayette	IN	20,032	MC
St. Louis Univ	MO	49,866	HC
Univ of Alaska Anchorage	AK	17,914	C
Univ of Illinois at Urbana-Champaign	IL	27,006	HC
Univ of Minn/Crookston	MN	19,126	C
Vaughn College of Aeronautics and Technology	NY	37,180	SP
Western Mich Univ	MI	21,791	C

ALLIED HEALTH

School	ST	$IS	SR
Adams State Univ	CO	15,420	LC
Albany State Univ	GA	19,462	C
Andrews Univ	MI	41,732	C
Azusa Pacific Univ	CA	43,972	C
Bloomfield College	NJ	40,100	LC
Cedarville Univ	OH	36,244	VC
Clayton State Univ	GA	19,735	LC
College of Mount St. Vincent	NY	45,620	C
College of the Ozarks	MO	7,530	VC
East Tenn State Univ	TN	18,141	C
Eastern Mich Univ	MI	19,761	C
Fairleigh Dickinson Univ/College at Florham	NJ	54,770	C
Fairleigh Dickinson Univ/Metropolitan Campus	NJ	52,392	C
Felician Univ	NJ	46,280	LC
Ferris State Univ	MI	21,458	C
George Fox Univ	OR	42,938	C
Georgian Court Univ	NJ	43,068	LC
Hendrix College	AR	54,020	VC
Howard Univ	DC	37,616	C+
Immaculata Univ	PA	39,000	C
Ithaca College	NY	58,158	VC+
Johnson State College	VT	22,672	C
Keene State College	NH	24,604	C
Lasell College	MA	49,400	C
Mars Hill Univ	NC	41,104	C
Marshall Univ	WV	18,044	C
Mass College of Liberal Arts	MA	20,659	C
MCPHS Univ	MA	45,470	SP
Millersville Univ of Pennsylvania	PA	25,298	C
Milligan College	TN	39,450	C
Millikin Univ	IL	44,148	C
Minn State Univ, Mankato	MN	17,190	C
Mount Aloysius College	PA	29,976	C
National Univ	CA	17,849	LC
Nebr Methodist College	NE	25,314	C
Northwestern State Univ of Louisiana	LA	16,534	LC
Oakland Univ	MI	20,763	C
Oakwood Univ	AL	43,758	C
Okla Baptist Univ	OK	33,990	C
Ramapo College of New Jersey	NJ	25,760	VC
Rochester Inst of Technology	NY	52,734	HC+
Roosevelt Univ	IL	41,890	VC
Rutgers Univ - Camden	NJ	26,595	C
Rutgers Univ - New Brunswick	NJ	27,090	HC
Rutgers Univ - Newark	NJ	27,351	C
St. Louis Univ	MO	49,866	HC
Silver Lake College of the Holy Family	WI	36,290	LC
Tuskegee Univ	AL	28,164	C
Univ of Central Okla	OK	15,150	C
Univ of Conn	CT	27,394	
Univ of Florida	FL	16,291	HC+
Univ of Illinois at Chicago	IL	24,664	VC
Univ of Maine at Machias	ME	22,960	C
Univ of Maryland/Baltimore County	MD	23,004	VC
Univ of St. Francis	IL	40,828	C
Univ of Tampa	FL	38,928	VC
Univ of Texas at El Paso	TX	34,452	NC
Univ of Tulsa	OK	52,625	HC
Washington Univ in St. Louis	MO	67,539	MC
West Texas A&M Univ	TX	13,478	C
Western Kentucky Univ	KY	16,850	C
Youngstown State Univ	OH	17,487	C

AMERICAN INDIAN STUDIES

School	ST	$IS	SR
Arizona State Univ at the Tempe Campus	AZ	23,001	VC
Black Hills State Univ	SD	16,622	C
Brown Univ	RI	64,566	MC
Fort Lewis College	CO	20,154	C
Minn State Univ, Mankato	MN	17,190	C
Northland College	WI	41,103	C+
San Diego State Univ	CA	23,156	VC
Sonoma State Univ	CA	27,020	C
Southern Oregon Univ	OR	19,117	C
The Univ of Arizona	AZ	24,086	C
Univ of Alaska Fairbanks	AK	16,874	VC
Univ of Calif at Los Angeles	CA	27,438	HC+
Univ of Minn/Morris	MN	21,222	VC
Univ of Minn/Twin Cities	MN	24,269	MC

ST = STATE **$IS** = IN-STATE COSTS **SR** = SELECTOR RATING

School	ST	$IS	SR
Univ of N Car at Pembroke	NC	14,737	LC
Univ of N Dak	ND	16,673	C
Univ of Science and Arts of Okla	OK	11,140	VC
Univ of S Dak	SD	16,109	C
Univ of Wisc-Eau Claire	WI	16,354	VC
Univ of Wisc-Green Bay	WI	15,184	C
Univ of Wyoming	WY	15,537	C
West Virginia Univ	WV	18,952	VC

AMERICAN LITERATURE

School	ST	$IS	SR
Bennington College	VT	66,280	MC
Biola Univ	CA	48,686	C
Brown Univ	RI	64,566	MC
Bryant Univ	RI	57,204	VC
Calvin College	MI	43,090	HC
Eastern Mich Univ	MI	19,761	C
Florida State Univ	FL	16,771	HC
Mount Ida College	MA	46,820	C
New York Univ	NY	68,139	MC
Southern Illinois Univ Edwardsville	IL	20,188	C
The American Univ	DC	61,317	HC
Univ of Calif at Los Angeles	CA	27,438	HC+
Univ of Tulsa	OK	52,625	HC
Washington Univ in St. Louis	MO	67,539	MC
Wellesley College	MA	66,984	MC

AMERICAN SIGN LANGUAGE

School	ST	$IS	SR
Augustana Univ	SD	39,968	VC
Bethel College	IN	36,830	C
Biola Univ	CA	48,686	C
Bloomsburg Univ of Pennsylvania	PA	19,930	C
Columbia College Chicago	IL	40,104	C
Framingham State Univ	MA	21,740	C
Gallaudet Univ	DC	30,088	LC
Gardner-Webb Univ	NC	24,935	C+
Goshen College	IN	44,350	C
Indiana Univ-Purdue Univ Indianapolis	IN	18,952	C
Kent State Univ	OH	20,928	C
Keuka College	NY	42,398	C
Lamar Univ	TX	18,014	LC
Maryville College	TN	44,410	C
Mount Aloysius College	PA	29,976	C
North Central Univ	MN	30,610	C
Northeastern Univ	MA	65,352	MC
Rochester Inst of Technology	NY	52,734	HC+
St. Catherine Univ	MN	45,630	C
Univ of Arkansas at Little Rock	AR	18,211	LC
Univ of Houston	TX	21,871	VC
Univ of Louisville	KY	19,692	C
Univ of New Mexico	NM	16,808	C
Univ of N Car at Greensboro	NC	15,998	C
Univ of North Florida	FL	15,996	VC
Univ of Northern Colo	CO	19,658	C
Univ of Rochester	NY	65,032	MC
Western Oregon Univ	OR	19,965	LC
William Woods Univ	MO	32,040	C
Wright State Univ	OH	16,983	C

AMERICAN STUDIES

School	ST	$IS	SR
Albright College	PA	57,326	C
Amherst College	MA	66,186	MC
Ashland Univ	OH	30,446	C
Augustana Univ	SD	39,968	VC
Austin College	TX	51,059	HC
Bard College	NY	65,924	HC
Barnard College/Columbia Univ	NY	68,762	MC
Bates College	ME	64,500	HC
Baylor Univ	TX	56,803	HC
Bennington College	VT	66,280	MC
Boston Univ	MA	67,352	MC
Bowling Green State Univ	OH	19,975	C
Brandeis Univ	MA	68,443	MC
Brigham Young Univ	UT	13,248	MC
Brown Univ	RI	64,566	MC
Bryant Univ	RI	57,204	VC
Cabrini Univ	PA	42,591	LC
Cal State, Fullerton	CA	21,902	C
Cal State, Long Beach	CA	18,850	C
Cal State, San Bernardino	CA	20,106	C
Carleton College	MN	66,414	MC
Christopher Newport Univ	VA	24,878	VC+
CUNY/Brooklyn College	NY	7,163	C+
CUNY/City College	NY	20,204	C
CUNY/Lehman College	NY	5,788	LC
CUNY/Queens College	NY	21,507	C
Claflin Univ	SC	25,592	LC
Claremont McKenna College	CA	69,900	MC
Coe College	IA	51,570	VC
Colby College	ME	64,060	MC
College of Staten Island	NY	24,389	LC
College of William & Mary	VA	34,907	MC
Columbia College - Missouri	MO	28,179	C
Columbia Univ/City of New York	NY	62,958	MC
Conn College	CT	65,000	MC
Cornell Univ	NY	67,591	MC
Creighton Univ	NE	49,452	VC
Cumberland Univ	TN	27,710	C
DePaul Univ	IL	52,807	VC
Dickinson College	PA	66,166	MC
Dominican Univ	IL	42,472	C+
Eckerd College	FL	55,206	VC
Elmhurst College	IL	46,514	C
Elmira College	NY	53,900	C
Elms College	MA	49,602	VC
Elon Univ	NC	46,142	HC
Emmanuel College	MA	53,472	C+
Emory Univ	GA	63,286	MC
Erskine College	SC	45,460	C
Fairfield Univ	CT	61,445	HC
Florida State Univ	FL	16,771	HC
Fordham Univ	NY	68,431	MC
Franklin and Marshall College	PA	67,960	MC
Franklin Pierce Univ	NH	46,750	LC
Georgetown College	KY	41,440	C
Georgetown Univ	DC	68,970	MC
Goucher College	MD	56,110	VC
Hamilton College	NY	64,250	MC
Hampshire College	MA	65,214	MC
Harding Univ	AR	25,440	C
Harvard College/Harvard Univ	MA	65,609	MC
Hendrix College	AR	54,020	VC
Hillsdale College	MI	37,170	MC
Hobart and William Smith Colleges	NY	67,050	HC+
Hofstra Univ	NY	58,210	C+
Illinois College	IL	41,330	VC
Illinois Wesleyan Univ	IL	56,430	VC+
Indiana Univ Bloomington	IN	20,791	HC
Keene State College	NH	24,604	C
Kent State Univ	OH	20,928	C
Kenyon College	OH	65,840	MC
Knox College	IL	54,654	VC+
Lafayette College	PA	68,520	MC
Lake Forest College	IL	50,652	VC
Lebanon Valley College	PA	55,510	VC
Lenoir-Rhyne Univ	NC	47,500	LC
Lindsey Wilson College	KY	33,546	C
Lipscomb Univ	TN	42,984	VC
LIU Post	NY	50,698	C+
Lycoming College	PA	50,895	C
Lynn Univ	FL	49,680	LC
Macalester College	MN	64,136	MC
Manhattanville College	NY	52,430	C
Marist College	NY	49,860	VC
Miami Univ	OH	27,190	HC+
Mich State Univ	MI	24,542	VC
Middlebury College	VT	67,464	MC
Miss College	MS	25,850	C
Montreat College	NC	34,605	LC
Mount Ida College	MA	46,820	C
Mount St. Mary's Univ - Chalon Campus	CA	50,486	VC+
Muhlenberg College	PA	56,645	VC
Muskingum Univ	OH	35,966	C
Nazareth College	NY	46,784	C
New York Univ	NY	68,139	MC
Northwestern Univ	IL	68,725	MC
Oberlin College	OH	68,942	MC
Occidental College	CA	68,660	MC
Oglethorpe Univ	GA	44,200	C
Okla State Univ	OK	17,180	C+
Oregon State Univ	OR	23,337	VC
Pace Univ	NY	60,136	C
Pitzer College	CA	68,500	HC+
Pomona College	CA	64,957	MC
Providence College	RI	62,870	HC
Ramapo College of New Jersey	NJ	25,760	VC
Reed College	OR	65,300	MC
Rider Univ	NJ	54,050	C
Roger Williams Univ	RI	48,074	VC
Roosevelt Univ	IL	41,890	VC
Rowan Univ	NJ	24,491	VC
Rutgers Univ - New Brunswick	NJ	27,090	HC
Rutgers Univ - Newark	NJ	27,351	C
St. Louis Univ	MO	49,866	HC
St. Michael's College	VT	53,275	VC+
St. Peter's Univ	NJ	49,192	C
Salve Regina Univ	RI	53,046	VC
San Francisco State Univ	CA	18,514	LC
Scripps College	CA	69,260	HC
Sewanee: The Univ of the South	TN	58,000	HC+
Siena College	NY	48,916	C
Skidmore College	NY	66,600	MC
Smith College	MA	66,774	MC
Southern Nazarene Univ	OK	33,684	C
St. John Fisher College	NY	45,270	VC
St. Olaf College	MN	56,430	HC
Stanford Univ	CA	62,541	MC
SUNY at Geneseo	NY	21,622	VC
SUNY at Oswego	NY	22,219	VC
SUNY/College at Old Westbury	NY	16,860	C
SUNY/Fredonia	NY	20,818	C
SUNY/Univ at Buffalo	NY	23,122	C
Stetson Univ	FL	57,174	VC+
Stonehill College	MA	55,130	C
Stony Brook Univ/The SUNY	NY	22,703	MC
Suffolk Univ	MA	52,316	C
Temple Univ	PA	24,392	C+
Texas State Univ	TX	18,721	C
The American Univ	DC	61,317	HC
The George Washington Univ	DC	68,474	HC+
The Univ of Alabama	AL	24,320	C+
The Univ of Texas at Austin	TX	20,206	MC
The Univ of Texas at San Antonio	TX	21,060	C
Trinity College	CT	69,020	HC
Tufts Univ	MA		MC
Tulane Univ	LA	67,496	MC
Union College	NY	64,320	MC
Univ of Calif at Berkeley	CA	29,886	MC
Univ of Calif at Davis	CA	28,468	HC
Univ of Calif, Santa Cruz	CA	28,731	C+
Univ of Conn	CT	27,394	
Univ of Florida	FL	16,291	HC+
Univ of Hawaii at Manoa	HI	23,261	C
Univ of Iowa	IA	19,415	HC
Univ of Kansas	KS	20,884	VC
Univ of Mary Washington	VA	23,039	C+
Univ of Maryland/Baltimore County	MD	23,004	VC
Univ of Maryland/College Park	MD	21,938	HC
Univ of Mass Boston	MA	13,828	C
Univ of Mass Lowell	MA	27,296	VC
Univ of Miami	FL	63,494	MC
Univ of Mich/Ann Arbor	MI	25,274	MC
Univ of Mich/Dearborn	MI	12,472	VC
Univ of Minn/Twin Cities	MN	24,269	MC
Univ of New Mexico	NM	16,808	C
Univ of N Car at Chapel Hill	NC	20,561	MC
Univ of Notre Dame	IN	68,801	MC
Univ of Pennsylvania	PA	63,526	MC
Univ of Pittsburgh at Greensburg	PA	24,140	C
Univ of Pittsburgh at Johnstown	PA	22,092	C
Univ of Richmond	VA	62,730	MC
Univ of Rio Grande & Rio Grande Community College	OH	8,750	LC
Univ of Rochester	NY	65,032	MC
Univ of San Francisco	CA	60,580	C
Univ of South Florida/Tampa	FL	16,110	VC
Univ of Southern Calif	CA	66,631	MC
Univ of Texas at Dallas	TX	23,640	HC
Univ of Wisc-Stevens Point	WI	14,043	C
Univ of Wyoming	WY	15,537	C
Upper Iowa Univ	IA	34,990	NC
Ursinus College	PA	62,920	VC
Utah State Univ	UT	13,235	C
Valparaiso Univ	IN	50,160	VC
Vanderbilt Univ	TN	63,248	MC
Vassar College	NY	68,110	MC
Virginia Wesleyan Univ	VA	45,980	LC
Warner Pacific College	OR	31,610	C
Washington College	MD	56,154	VC
Washington State Univ	WA	22,747	C
Washington Univ in St. Louis	MO	67,539	MC
Webster Univ	MO	37,490	C
Wellesley College	MA	66,984	MC
Wesley College	DE	37,848	LC
Wesleyan Univ	CT	66,940	MC
West Chester Univ of Pennsylvania	PA	19,171	VC
Western Conn State Univ	CT	21,254	LC
Western New England Univ	MA	49,182	C
Western Washington Univ	WA	18,904	VC
Wheaton College	MA	63,818	VC
Wheelock College	MA	51,325	LC
Whitworth Univ	WA	53,682	VC
Willamette Univ	OR	62,514	VC+
Williams College	MA	67,700	MC
Yale Univ	CT	64,650	MC

ANATOMY

School	ST	$IS	SR
Andrews Univ	MI	41,732	C
Bryant Univ	RI	57,204	VC
Cal State, Fullerton	CA	21,902	C
Duke Univ	NC	68,298	MC
Howard Univ	DC	37,616	C+
Marshall Univ	WV	18,044	C

ANIMAL SCIENCE

School	ST	$IS	SR
Abilene Christian Univ	TX	43,708	C+
Alabama A&M Univ	AL	18,796	C
Andrews Univ	MI	41,732	C
Angelo State Univ	TX	15,882	LC
Arkansas State Univ	AR	16,190	C
Auburn Univ	AL	24,300	VC+
Becker College	MA	30,100	LC
Berry College	GA	47,466	VC
Bucknell Univ	PA	67,136	MC
Calif Polytechnic State Univ	CA	22,547	MC
Calif State Polytechnic Univ, Pomona	CA	21,811	C
Cal State, Chico	CA	19,790	VC
Cal State, Fresno	CA	16,902	LC
Cal State, Fullerton	CA	21,902	C
Carroll College	MT	44,304	C
Clemson Univ	SC		HC
College of the Ozarks	MO	7,530	VC
Colo State Univ	CO	23,033	C
Cornell Univ	NY	67,591	MC
Delaware Valley Univ	PA	51,271	C
Dordt College	IA	37,860	C+
Eastern New Mexico Univ	NM	12,874	LC
Florida A&M Univ	FL	15,361	C
Fort Valley State Univ	GA	17,988	VC
Hampshire College	MA	65,214	MC
Hardin-Simmons Univ	TX	36,025	C
Indiana Univ Bloomington	IN	20,791	HC
Iowa State Univ	IA	18,176	C
Kansas State Univ	KS	17,780	VC
Langston Univ	OK	15,659	C
Lincoln Univ	MO	14,402	NC
Louisiana State Univ and A&M College	LA	18,677	VC
Louisiana Tech Univ	LA	11,422	VC
Lubbock Christian Univ	TX	29,727	C
Mich State Univ	MI	24,542	VC
Middle Tenn State Univ	TN	8,650	C
Millersville Univ of Pennsylvania	PA	25,298	C
Miss State Univ	MS	12,028	C+
Missouri State Univ	MO	15,837	C+
Montana State Univ	MT	15,500	C+
New Mexico State Univ	NM	14,050	LC
N Car A&T State Univ	NC	13,786	C
N Car State Univ	NC	22,434	HC+
N Dak State Univ	ND	16,245	VC
Northwest Missouri State Univ	MO	18,286	C
Ohio State Univ at Columbus	OH	22,843	MC
Okla Panhandle State Univ	OK	6,152	C
Okla State Univ	OK	17,180	C+
Oregon State Univ	OR	23,337	VC
Pennsylvania State Univ - Univ Park	PA	29,716	HC
Prairie View A&M Univ	TX	27,273	LC
Purdue Univ/West Lafayette	IN	20,032	MC
Rutgers Univ - New Brunswick	NJ	27,090	HC
Sam Houston State Univ	TX	18,792	C
S Dak State Univ	SD	15,874	C
Southeast Missouri State Univ	MO	16,148	C
Southern Illinois Univ Carbondale	IL	24,554	C
SUNY /College of Agriculture and Tech at Cobleskill	NY	20,527	LC
SUNY/The College of Environmental Science and Forestry	NY	23,728	VC
Stephen F. Austin State Univ	TX	18,484	LC
Sul Ross State Univ	TX	15,021	LC
Tarleton State Univ	TX	15,248	LC
Tenn Tech Univ	TN	17,929	C
Texas A&M Univ at College Station	TX	20,771	VC+
Texas A&M Univ at Commerce	TX	10,496	C
Texas A&M Univ at Kingsville	TX	16,580	LC
Texas State Univ	TX	18,721	C
Texas Tech Univ	TX	20,156	C+
The Univ of Arizona	AZ	24,086	C
The Univ of Montana Western	MT	9,426	LC
The Univ of Tenn at Knoxville	TN	22,112	VC
The Univ of Tenn at Martin	TN	15,212	C
Truman State Univ	MO	16,286	MC
Tuskegee Univ	AL	28,164	C
Unity College	ME	37,670	C
Univ of Arkansas at Fayetteville	AR	19,766	VC
Univ of Calif at Davis	CA	28,468	HC
Univ of Conn	CT	27,394	
Univ of Delaware	DE	32,214	VC
Univ of Findlay	OH	43,040	C
Univ of Florida	FL	16,291	HC+
Univ of Georgia	GA	21,878	HC
Univ of Hawaii at Manoa	HI	23,261	C
Univ of Idaho	ID	16,158	C
Univ of Illinois at Urbana-Champaign	IL	27,006	HC
Univ of Kentucky	KY	24,800	C+
Univ of Maine	ME	21,038	VC
Univ of Maryland/College Park	MD	21,938	HC
Univ of Mass Amherst	MA	27,669	HC
Univ of Minn/Crookston	MN	19,126	C
Univ of Minn/Twin Cities	MN	24,269	MC
Univ of Missouri-Columbia	MO	20,463	VC
Univ of Nebr - Lincoln	NE	18,589	VC
Univ of New England	ME	50,110	C
Univ of New Hampshire	NH	29,333	VC
Univ of PR, at Mayaguez	PR	13,995	
Univ of Rhode Island	RI	26,066	VC
Univ of Vermont	VT	29,792	HC
Univ of Wisc-Madison	WI	21,647	MC
Univ of Wisc-Platteville	WI	14,148	C
Univ of Wisc-River Falls	WI	14,541	C
Univ of Wyoming	WY	15,537	C
Utah State Univ	UT	13,235	C
Utica College	NY	31,510	C
Virginia Polytechnic Inst and State Univ	VA	21,920	VC
Washington State Univ	WA	22,747	C
West Texas A&M Univ	TX	13,478	C
West Virginia Univ	WV	18,952	VC
Western Illinois Univ	IL	20,897	C
Wilmington College	OH	35,100	C
Wilson College	PA	35,620	LC

ANIMATION

School	ST	$IS	SR
Art Inst of Portland	OR	132,329	SP

ST = STATE $IS = IN-STATE COSTS   SR = SELECTOR RATING

School	ST	$IS	SR
Ball State Univ	IN	19,808	C+
Bennington College	VT	66,280	MC
Bloomfield College	NJ	40,100	LC
Bradley Univ	IL	43,240	VC
Brigham Young Univ	UT	13,248	MC
Buena Vista Univ	IA	42,344	C
Calif College of the Arts	CA	52,758	SP
Calif Inst of the Arts	CA	61,366	SP
Cleveland Inst of Art	OH	51,455	SP
Cogswell Polytechnical College	CA	31,511	C
College for Creative Studies	MI	51,210	SP
Colo Mesa Univ	CO	19,707	LC
Columbia College Chicago	IL	40,104	C
Columbus College of Art and Design	OH	47,310	SP
Daemen College	NY	40,336	C
DePaul Univ	IL	52,807	VC
Drexel Univ	PA	65,927	HC
Drury Univ	MO	37,555	VC
Eastern Mich Univ	MI	19,761	C
Fairleigh Dickinson Univ/ College at Florham	NJ	54,770	C
Huntington Univ	IN	33,996	C
Kansas City Art Inst	MO	48,200	SP
Laguna College of Art and Design	CA	41,422	SP
Lawrence Tech Univ	MI	41,630	VC
Loyola Marymount Univ	CA	60,202	VC+
Lynn Univ	FL	49,680	LC
Maryland Inst College of Art	MD	58,740	SP
Mass College of Art and Design	MA	24,800	SP
Memphis College of Art	TN	50,880	SP
Minneapolis College of Art and Design	MN	44,218	SP
Missouri Western State Univ	MO	17,822	LC
Montclair State Univ	NJ	26,912	C
Moore College of Art and Design	PA	55,118	SP
Moore College of Art and Design	PA	55,118	SP
New Mexico State Univ	NM	14,050	LC
New York Univ	NY	68,139	MC
NewSchool of Architecture & Design	CA	12,341	SP
Ringling College of Art and Design	FL	59,160	SP
Rochester Inst of Technology	NY	52,734	HC+
Rocky Mountain College of Art and Design	CO	27,052	SP
Savannah College of Art and Design	GA	49,595	SP
School of Visual Arts	NY	47,500	SP
Shepherd Univ	CA		LC
Southern Adventist Univ	TN	28,250	C
SUNY/Fredonia	NY	20,818	C
The Art Inst of Atlanta	GA	34,334	SP
Univ of Denver	CO	61,129	VC+
Univ of Idaho	ID	16,158	C
Univ of Northwestern - St. Paul	MN	39,530	C
Univ of St. Francis	IN	38,520	C
Webster Univ	MO	37,490	C
Woodbury Univ	CA	49,593	VC

ANTHROPOLOGY

School	ST	$IS	SR
Adelphi Univ	NY	49,792	C
Agnes Scott College	GA	51,930	VC+
Albion College	MI	55,260	C
Alma College	MI	49,410	VC
Amherst College	MA	66,186	MC
Andrews Univ	MI	41,732	C
Appalachian State Univ	NC	15,394	VC
Arizona State Univ at the Tempe Campus	AZ	23,001	VC
Ashford Univ	CA	10,480	C
Auburn Univ	AL	24,300	VC+
Augusta Univ	GA	4,632	C
Augustana College	IL	51,222	VC+
Augustana Univ	SD	39,968	VC
Ball State Univ	IN	19,808	C+
Bard College	NY	65,924	HC
Barnard College/Columbia Univ	NY	68,762	MC
Bates College	ME	64,500	HC
Baylor Univ	TX	56,803	HC
Beloit College	WI	55,206	HC
Bennington College	VT	66,280	MC
Berry College	GA	47,466	VC
Biola Univ	CA	48,686	C
Bloomsburg Univ of Pennsylvania	PA	19,930	C
Boise State Univ	ID	17,368	C
Boston Univ	MA	67,352	MC
Bowdoin College	ME	65,980	MC
Brandeis Univ	MA	68,443	MC
Bridgewater State Univ	MA	22,762	C
Brigham Young Univ	UT	13,248	MC
Brown Univ	RI	64,566	MC
Bryn Mawr College	PA	65,220	MC
Bucknell Univ	PA	67,136	MC
Butler Univ	IN	52,890	VC+
Calif Baptist Univ	CA	42,986	C
Calif Polytechnic State Univ	CA	22,547	MC
Calif State Polytechnic Univ, Pomona	CA	21,811	C
Cal State, Bakersfield	CA	22,397	LC
Cal State, Chico	CA	19,790	VC
Cal State, Dominguez Hills	CA	19,022	LC
Cal State, East Bay	CA	20,748	C
Cal State, Fresno	CA	16,902	LC
Cal State, Fullerton	CA	21,902	C
Cal State, Long Beach	CA	18,850	C
Cal State, Los Angeles	CA	17,186	LC
Cal State, Northridge	CA	17,277	LC
Cal State, Sacramento	CA	19,060	C
Cal State, San Bernardino	CA	20,106	C
Cal State, Stanislaus	CA	18,053	LC
Canisius College	NY	49,672	C
Carleton College	MN	66,414	MC
Case Western Reserve Univ	OH	62,284	MC
Central College	IA	44,592	C
Central Conn State Univ	CT	22,041	C
Central Mich Univ	MI	20,330	C
Central Washington Univ	WA	16,803	C
Centre College	KY	50,680	MC
CUNY/Brooklyn College	NY	7,163	C+
CUNY/City College	NY	20,204	C
CUNY/Hunter College	NY	31,098	VC
CUNY/Lehman College	NY	5,788	LC
CUNY/Queens College	NY	21,507	C
CUNY/York College	NY	6,747	LC
Clarion Univ of Pennsylvania	PA	21,608	LC
Cleveland State Univ	OH	22,290	C
Colby College	ME	64,060	MC
Colgate Univ	NY	67,500	MC
College of Charleston	SC	24,046	VC
College of the Holy Cross	MA	64,320	MC
College of William & Mary	VA	34,907	MC
Colo College	CO	64,894	MC
Colo State Univ	CO	23,033	C
Columbia Univ/ School of General Studies	NY	61,470	MC
Columbia Univ/City of New York	NY	62,958	MC
Conn College	CT	65,000	MC
Cornell Univ	NY	67,591	MC
Dartmouth College	NH	68,109	MC
Davidson College	NC	60,119	MC
Denison Univ	OH	62,770	HC+
DePaul Univ	IL	52,807	VC
DePauw Univ	IN	58,688	VC
Dickinson College	PA	66,166	MC
Drew Univ/College of Liberal Arts	NJ	53,608	VC
Drexel Univ	PA	65,927	HC
Duke Univ	NC	68,298	MC
Earlham College	IN	55,670	HC
East Carolina Univ	NC	16,539	C
Eastern Kentucky Univ	KY	17,742	C
Eastern Mich Univ	MI	19,761	C
Eastern New Mexico Univ	NM	12,874	LC
Eastern Oregon Univ	OR	17,612	C
Eastern Washington Univ	WA	17,896	LC
Eckerd College	FL	55,206	VC
Edinboro Univ	PA	15,940	LC
Elon Univ	NC	46,142	HC
Emory Univ	GA	63,286	MC
Eugene Lang College of Liberal Arts	NY	64,940	VC
Florida Atlantic Univ	FL	18,256	C
Florida Gulf Coast Univ	FL	14,738	C
Florida State Univ	FL	16,771	HC
Fordham Univ	NY	68,431	MC
Fort Lewis College	CO	20,154	C
Franciscan Univ of Steubenville	OH	33,980	VC
Franklin and Marshall College	PA	67,960	MC
Franklin Pierce Univ	NH	46,750	LC
Furman Univ	SC	61,098	VC+
George Mason Univ	VA	19,884	C
Georgetown Univ	DC	68,970	MC
Georgia Southern Univ	GA	16,540	VC
Georgia State Univ	GA	25,250	C
Gettysburg College	PA	65,210	MC
Goucher College	MD	56,110	VC
Grand Valley State Univ	MI	22,250	C+
Grinnell College	IA	63,114	MC
Gustavus Adolphus College	MN	53,943	HC
Hamilton College	NY	64,250	MC
Hamline Univ	MN	50,152	C
Hampshire College	MA	65,214	MC
Hanover College	IN	47,750	C+
Hartwick College	NY	51,270	C
Harvard College/Harvard Univ	MA	65,609	MC
Haverford College	PA	66,490	MC
Hawaii Pacific Univ	HI	33,420	C
Heidelberg Univ	OH	40,400	LC
Hendrix College	AR	54,020	VC
High Point Univ	NC	47,355	VC
Hobart and William Smith Colleges	NY	67,050	HC+
Hofstra Univ	NY	58,210	C+
Howard Univ	DC	37,616	C+
Humboldt State Univ	CA	21,708	C
Idaho State Univ	ID	13,619	LC
Illinois State Univ	IL	23,418	VC
Illinois Wesleyan Univ	IL	56,430	VC+
Indiana State Univ	IN	23,223	LC
Indiana Univ Bloomington	IN	20,791	HC
Indiana Univ Northwest	IN	7,207	LC
Indiana Univ of Pennsylvania	PA	24,474	C
Indiana Univ South Bend	IN	16,057	C
Indiana Univ-Purdue Univ Fort Wayne	IN	18,675	C
Indiana Univ-Purdue Univ Indianapolis	IN	18,952	C
Iowa State Univ	IA	18,176	C
Ithaca College	NY	58,158	VC+
James Madison Univ	VA	19,084	VC
Johns Hopkins Univ	MD	68,080	MC
Johnson State College	VT	22,672	C
Judson Univ	IL	39,174	C
Juniata College	PA	58,118	VC
Kalamazoo College	MI	53,931	HC
Kansas State Univ	KS	17,780	VC
Keene State College	NH	24,604	C
Kennesaw State Univ	GA	18,899	VC
Kent State Univ	OH	20,928	C
Kenyon College	OH	65,840	MC
Knox College	IL	54,654	VC+
Kutztown Univ of Pennsylvania	PA	19,477	C
Lafayette College	PA	68,520	MC
Lake Forest College	IL	50,652	VC
Lawrence Univ	WI	56,133	HC+
Le Moyne College	NY	47,305	VC
Lee Univ	TN	22,045	C
Lehigh Univ	PA	63,860	MC
Lewis & Clark College	OR	60,984	MC
Lincoln Univ	PA	20,878	LC
Linfield College	OR	53,992	C
Longwood Univ	VA	22,184	C
Louisiana State Univ and A&M College	LA	18,677	VC
Loyola Univ Chicago	IL	57,158	VC
Luther College	IA	49,990	VC
Lycoming College	PA	50,895	C
Lyon College	AR	36,120	VC
Macalester College	MN	64,136	MC
Marlboro College	VT	50,832	VC+
Marquette Univ	WI	53,090	VC+
Mass Inst of Technology	MA	62,662	MC
Mercer Univ	GA	45,348	VC
Mercyhurst Univ	PA	47,420	C
Metropolitan State Univ of Denver	CO	6,928	LC
Miami Univ	OH	27,190	HC+
Mich State Univ	MI	24,542	VC
Mich Tech Univ	MI	25,551	VC+
Middle Tenn State Univ	TN	8,650	C
Middlebury College	VT	67,464	MC
Millersville Univ of Pennsylvania	PA	25,298	C
Mills College	CA	43,705	C
Millsaps College	MS	50,080	C+
Minn State Univ, Mankato	MN	17,190	C
Minn State Univ, Moorhead	MN	21,393	C
Miss State Univ	MS	12,028	C+
Missouri State Univ	MO	15,837	C+
Missouri Valley College	MO	28,150	C
Monmouth College	IL	42,260	C
Monmouth Univ	NJ	50,184	C
Montana State Univ	MT	15,500	C+
Montclair State Univ	NJ	26,912	C
Mount Holyoke College	MA	56,746	MC
Muhlenberg College	PA	56,645	VC
National Louis Univ	IL	43,000	LC
Nazareth College	NY	46,784	C
New College of Florida	FL	16,180	HC+
New Mexico Highlands Univ	NM	11,904	LC
New Mexico State Univ	NM	14,050	LC
New York Univ	NY	68,139	MC
North Central College	IL	48,712	C+
N Dak State Univ	ND	16,245	VC
North Park Univ	IL	35,860	C
Northeastern Illinois Univ	IL	12,529	LC
Northeastern Univ	MA	65,352	MC
Northern Arizona Univ	AZ	21,003	C
Northern Illinois Univ	IL	20,176	C
Northern Kentucky Univ	KY	16,486	C
Northwestern Univ	IL	68,725	MC
Nova Southeastern Univ	FL	38,534	C+
Oakland Univ	MI	20,763	C
Oberlin College	OH	68,942	MC
Ohio State Univ at Columbus	OH	22,843	MC
Ohio Univ	OH	23,394	VC
Ohio Wesleyan Univ	OH	49,460	VC
Okla Baptist Univ	OK	33,990	C
Olivet College	MI	37,661	LC
Oregon State Univ	OR	23,337	VC
Pacific Lutheran Univ	WA	49,960	C
Pennsylvania State Univ - Univ Park	PA	29,716	HC
Pitzer College	CA	68,500	HC+
Plymouth State Univ	NH	23,180	LC
Pomona College	CA	64,957	MC
Portland State Univ	OR	19,443	C
Prescott College	AZ	38,201	C
Princeton Univ	NJ	60,090	MC
Purdue Univ/West Lafayette	IN	20,032	MC
Radford Univ	VA	19,758	C
Reed College	OR	65,300	MC
Regis Univ	CO	46,380	C
Rhode Island College	RI	19,000	LC
Rhodes College	TN	51,900	HC
Rice Univ	TX	59,458	MC
Ripon College	WI	49,991	VC
Rochester Inst of Technology	NY	52,734	HC+
Rockford Univ	IL	38,570	C
Roger Williams Univ	RI	48,074	VC
Rollins College	FL	58,670	HC
Rutgers Univ - New Brunswick	NJ	27,090	HC
Rutgers Univ - Newark	NJ	27,351	C
St. Louis Univ	MO	49,866	HC
St. Mary's College of Calif	CA	57,420	C
St. Michael's College	VT	53,275	VC+
St. Vincent College	PA	46,229	C
San Diego State Univ	CA	23,156	VC
San Francisco State Univ	CA	18,514	LC
San Jose State Univ	CA	22,630	C
Sarah Lawrence College	NY	68,866	MC
Scripps College	CA	69,260	HC
Seattle Univ	WA	54,957	VC
Seton Hall Univ	NJ	58,008	C
Sewanee: The Univ of the South	TN	58,000	HC+
Skidmore College	NY	66,600	MC
Slippery Rock Univ of Pennsylvania	PA	20,450	C
Smith College	MA	66,774	MC
Sonoma State Univ	CA	27,020	C
Southern Illinois Univ Carbondale	IL	24,554	C
Southern Illinois Univ Edwardsville	IL	20,188	C
Southern Methodist Univ	TX	69,008	MC
Southern Oregon Univ	OR	19,117	C
Southwestern Univ	TX	52,370	VC
Spelman College	GA	41,642	C
St. Cloud State Univ	MN	10,600	C
St. John Fisher College	NY	45,270	VC
St. John's Univ	NY	57,160	C+
St. Lawrence Univ	NY	66,646	HC+
St. Mary's College of Maryland	MD	27,312	VC
Stanford Univ	CA	62,541	MC
SUNY Albany	NY	22,165	C
SUNY at Binghamton	NY	24,100	MC
SUNY at Geneseo	NY	21,622	VC
SUNY at New Paltz	NY	20,840	C
SUNY at Oswego	NY	22,219	VC
SUNY at Purchase College	NY	21,832	C
SUNY/Buffalo State	NY	20,583	LC
SUNY/Cortland	NY	20,910	C
SUNY/Oneonta	NY	20,794	C
SUNY/Plattsburgh	NY	19,314	C
SUNY/Potsdam	NY	21,051	VC
SUNY/Univ at Buffalo	NY	23,122	C
Stockton Univ	NJ	25,565	C
Stony Brook Univ/The SUNY	NY	22,703	MC
Susquehanna Univ	PA	57,560	VC
Swarthmore College	PA	63,550	MC
Syracuse Univ	NY	62,313	HC
Temple Univ	PA	24,392	C+
Texas A&M Univ at College Station	TX	20,771	VC+
Texas A&M Univ at Commerce	TX	10,496	C
Texas A&M Univ at Kingsville	TX	16,580	LC
Texas Christian Univ	TX	57,120	HC
Texas State Univ	TX	18,721	C
Texas Tech Univ	TX	20,156	C+
The American Univ	DC	61,317	HC
The Catholic Univ of America	DC	58,376	VC
The College at Brockport - SUNY	NY	21,058	C
The College of Idaho	ID	36,415	C
The College of Wooster	OH	60,000	HC
The Evergreen State College	WA	16,599	C
The George Washington Univ	DC	68,474	HC+
The Univ of Akron	OH	22,566	C
The Univ of Alabama	AL	24,320	C+
The Univ of Arizona	AZ	24,086	C
The Univ of Memphis	TN	18,278	C
The Univ of Montana	MT	9,426	LC
The Univ of Tenn at Knoxville	TN	22,112	VC
The Univ of Texas at Austin	TX	20,206	MC
The Univ of Texas at San Antonio	TX	21,060	C
The Univ of Utah	UT	18,751	VC
Thomas Edison State Univ	NJ	6,350	NC
Towson Univ	MD	21,878	C
Transylvania Univ	KY	47,450	HC+
Trinity College	CT	69,020	HC
Trinity Univ	TX	54,480	MC
Truman State Univ	MO	16,286	MC
Tufts Univ	MA		MC
Tulane Univ	LA	67,496	MC
Union College	NY	64,320	MC
Univ of Alabama at Birmingham	AL	22,092	C
Univ of Alaska Anchorage	AK	17,914	C
Univ of Alaska Fairbanks	AK	16,874	VC
Univ of Arkansas at Fayetteville	AR	19,766	VC
Univ of Calif at Berkeley	CA	29,886	MC
Univ of Calif at Davis	CA	28,468	HC
Univ of Calif at Irvine	CA	33,857	VC
Univ of Calif at Los Angeles	CA	27,438	HC+
Univ of Calif at Riverside	CA	32,912	C
Univ of Calif at Santa Barbara	CA	30,627	HC+
Univ of Calif San Diego	CA	30,450	MC
Univ of Calif, Santa Cruz	CA	28,731	C+
Univ of Central Arkansas	AR	15,042	VC

ST = STATE **$IS** = IN-STATE COSTS **SR** = SELECTOR RATING

School	ST	$IS	SR
Univ of Central Florida	FL	16,379	VC
Univ of Chicago	IL	70,551	MC
Univ of Cincinnati	OH	22,118	VC
Univ of Colo Boulder	CO	26,048	HC
Univ of Colo Colo Springs	CO	20,300	C
Univ of Colo Denver	CO	22,238	C
Univ of Conn	CT	27,394	
Univ of Delaware	DE	32,214	VC
Univ of Denver	CO	61,129	VC+
Univ of Florida	FL	16,291	HC+
Univ of Georgia	GA	21,878	HC
Univ of Hawaii at Hilo	HI	18,038	VC
Univ of Hawaii at Manoa	HI	23,261	C
Univ of Houston	TX	21,871	VC
Univ of Idaho	ID	16,158	C
Univ of Illinois at Chicago	IL	24,664	VC
Univ of Illinois at Urbana-Champaign	IL	27,006	HC
Univ of Indianapolis	IN	36,480	VC
Univ of Iowa	IA	19,415	HC
Univ of Kansas	KS	20,884	VC
Univ of Kentucky	KY	24,800	C+
Univ of La Verne	CA	55,600	C
Univ of Louisiana at Lafayette	LA	14,516	C
Univ of Louisville	KY	19,692	C
Univ of Maine	ME	21,038	VC
Univ of Maine at Farmington	ME	18,792	C
Univ of Mary Washington	VA	23,039	C+
Univ of Maryland/Baltimore County	MD	23,004	VC
Univ of Maryland/College Park	MD	21,938	HC
Univ of Mass Amherst	MA	27,669	HC
Univ of Mass Boston	MA	13,828	C
Univ of Mass Dartmouth	MA	26,507	C
Univ of Miami	FL	63,494	MC
Univ of Mich/Ann Arbor	MI	25,274	MC
Univ of Mich/Dearborn	MI	12,472	VC
Univ of Mich/Flint	MI	19,062	C
Univ of Minn/Duluth	MN	20,292	C
Univ of Minn/Morris	MN	21,222	VC
Univ of Minn/Twin Cities	MN	24,269	MC
Univ of Miss	MS	18,802	C
Univ of Missouri-Columbia	MO	20,463	VC
Univ of Missouri-St. Louis	MO	19,810	VC
Univ of Montana	MT	14,105	C
Univ of Nebr - Lincoln	NE	18,589	VC
Univ of Nevada, Las Vegas	NV	17,553	C
Univ of Nevada, Reno	NV	18,010	C
Univ of New Hampshire	NH	29,333	VC
Univ of New Mexico	NM	16,808	C
Univ of New Orleans	LA	12,840	C
Univ of N Car at Asheville	NC	16,251	VC+
Univ of N Car at Chapel Hill	NC	20,561	MC
Univ of N Car at Charlotte	NC	17,803	VC
Univ of N Car at Greensboro	NC	15,998	C
Univ of N Car Wilmington	NC	16,784	VC
Univ of N Dak	ND	16,673	C
Univ of North Florida	FL	15,996	VC
Univ of North Texas	TX	20,082	C
Univ of Northern Colo	CO	19,658	C
Univ of Northern Iowa	IA	17,480	C
Univ of Notre Dame	IN	68,801	MC
Univ of Okla	OK	19,651	HC
Univ of Oregon	OR	24,021	VC
Univ of Pennsylvania	PA	63,526	MC
Univ of Pittsburgh	PA	30,030	MC
Univ of Pittsburgh at Greensburg	PA	24,140	C
Univ of PR-Rio Piedras campus	PR	13,327	
Univ of Redlands	CA	61,934	VC
Univ of Rhode Island	RI	26,066	VC
Univ of Richmond	VA	62,730	MC
Univ of Rochester	NY	65,032	MC
Univ of San Diego	CA	60,338	HC
Univ of South Alabama	AL	16,880	C
Univ of S Car at Columbia	SC	21,726	VC
Univ of S Dak	SD	16,109	C
Univ of South Florida St. Petersburg	FL	15,980	C
Univ of South Florida/Tampa	FL	16,110	VC
Univ of Southern Calif	CA	66,631	MC
Univ of Southern Indiana	IN	16,808	C
Univ of Southern Maine	ME	18,320	C
Univ of Southern Miss	MS	13,170	C
Univ of Texas at Arlington	TX	18,876	C
Univ of Texas at El Paso	TX	34,452	NC
Univ of Texas Rio Grande Valley	TX	15,573	LC
Univ of Toledo	OH	19,336	C
Univ of Tulsa	OK	52,625	HC
Univ of Vermont	VT	29,792	HC
Univ of Virginia	VA	27,367	MC
Univ of Washington	WA	23,091	MC
Univ of West Georgia	GA	17,510	LC
Univ of Wisc-Madison	WI	21,647	MC
Univ of Wisc-Milwaukee	WI	21,538	C
Univ of Wisc-Oshkosh	WI	15,392	C
Univ of Wyoming	WY	15,537	C
Ursinus College	PA	62,920	VC
Vanderbilt Univ	TN	63,248	MC
Vanguard Univ of Southern Calif	CA	42,400	VC
Vassar College	NY	68,110	MC
Virginia Commonwealth Univ	VA	23,811	VC
Wagner College	NY	57,240	C+
Wake Forest Univ	NC	69,354	MC
Warren Wilson College	NC	44,220	VC
Washburn Univ	KS	15,827	C
Washington and Lee Univ	VA	59,647	MC
Washington College	MD	56,154	VC
Washington State Univ	WA	22,747	C
Washington Univ in St. Louis	MO	67,539	MC
Wayne State Univ	MI	23,085	C
Weber State Univ	UT	14,112	C
Wellesley College	MA	66,984	MC
Wells College	NY	50,500	C
Wesleyan Univ	CT	66,940	MC
West Chester Univ of Pennsylvania	PA	19,171	VC
West Virginia Univ	WV	18,952	VC
Western Carolina Univ	NC	13,965	C
Western Conn State Univ	CT	21,254	LC
Western Illinois Univ	IL	20,897	C
Western Kentucky Univ	KY	16,850	C
Western Mich Univ	MI	21,791	C
Western Oregon Univ	OR	19,965	LC
Western State Colo Univ	CO	19,348	C
Western Washington Univ	WA	18,904	VC
Westminster College	MO	32,820	C
Wheaton College	IL	44,993	MC
Wheaton College	MA	63,818	VC
Whitman College	WA	59,772	MC
Wichita State Univ	KS	17,773	C
Widener Univ	PA	58,190	C
Willamette Univ	OR	62,514	VC+
William Paterson Univ of New Jersey	NJ	24,022	C
Williams College	MA	67,700	MC
Wright State Univ	OH	16,983	C
Yale Univ	CT	64,650	MC
Youngstown State Univ	OH	17,487	C

APPAREL AND ACCESSORIES MARKETING

School	ST	$IS	SR
Auburn Univ	AL	24,300	VC+
Baylor Univ	TX	56,803	HC
Calif State Polytechnic Univ, Pomona	CA	21,811	C
Cheyney Univ of Pennsylvania	PA	20,896	LC
Colo State Univ	CO	23,033	C
Dominican Univ	IL	42,472	C+
Eastern Mich Univ	MI	19,761	C
Fashion Inst of Technology/SUNY	NY	18,521	SP
Fontbonne Univ	MO	34,606	C
Johnson & Wales Univ/Denver Campus	CO	44,768	C
Kansas State Univ	KS	17,780	VC
Kentucky State Univ	KY	14,484	LC
S Dak State Univ	SD	15,874	C
Stevenson Univ	MD	48,412	C
Univ of Arkansas at Fayetteville	AR	19,766	VC
Univ of Nebr - Lincoln	NE	18,589	VC
Virginia Polytechnic Inst and State Univ	VA	21,920	VC
Western Illinois Univ	IL	20,897	C
Western Mich Univ	MI	21,791	C
Youngstown State Univ	OH	17,487	C

APPAREL DESIGN

School	ST	$IS	SR
Appalachian State Univ	NC	15,394	VC
Art Inst of Portland	OR	132,329	SP
Auburn Univ	AL	24,300	VC+
Baylor Univ	TX	56,803	HC
Bowling Green State Univ	OH	19,975	C
Central Mich Univ	MI	20,330	C
Colo State Univ	CO	23,033	C
Dominican Univ	IL	42,472	C+
Eastern Kentucky Univ	KY	17,742	C
Florida State Univ	FL	16,771	HC
Indiana Univ Bloomington	IN	20,791	HC
Kansas State Univ	KS	17,780	VC
Kennesaw State Univ	GA	18,899	VC
N Dak State Univ	ND	16,245	VC
Oregon State Univ	OR	23,337	VC
Purdue Univ/West Lafayette	IN	20,032	MC
Rhode Island School of Design	RI	59,960	SP
San Francisco State Univ	CA	18,514	LC
Stevenson Univ	MD	48,412	C
Texas Tech Univ	TX	20,156	C+
Univ of Delaware	DE	32,214	VC
Univ of Hawaii at Manoa	HI	23,261	C
Univ of Idaho	ID	16,158	C
Univ of Minn/Twin Cities	MN	24,269	MC
Univ of Nebr - Lincoln	NE	18,589	VC
Univ of N Car at Greensboro	NC	15,998	C
Univ of Wisc-Stout	WI	19,667	C
Western Mich Univ	MI	21,791	C
Western Washington Univ	WA	18,904	VC

APPLIED ART

School	ST	$IS	SR
Centenary College	NJ	43,890	LC
Daemen College	NY	40,336	C
Edinboro Univ	PA	15,940	LC
Goddard College	VT	17,040	VC
Kutztown Univ of Pennsylvania	PA	19,477	C
Lamar Univ	TX	18,014	LC
Marshall Univ	WV	18,044	C
Memphis College of Art	TN	50,880	SP
Oral Roberts Univ	OK	34,316	C
Oregon State Univ	OR	23,337	VC
Point Park Univ	PA	41,270	C
Roberts Wesleyan College	NY	41,116	C
Rochester Inst of Technology	NY	52,734	HC+
Stevenson Univ	MD	48,412	C
Tabor College	KS	35,870	C
Texas State Univ	TX	18,721	C
Texas Tech Univ	TX	20,156	C+
Univ of Arkansas at Little Rock	AR	18,211	LC
Univ of Idaho	ID	16,158	C
Univ of Maine at Presque Isle	ME	16,148	LC
Univ of Maryland/Baltimore County	MD	23,004	VC
Univ of North Texas	TX	20,082	C
West Texas A&M Univ	TX	13,478	C

APPLIED AVIATION

School	ST	$IS	SR
Calif Baptist Univ	CA	42,986	C
Eastern Mich Univ	MI	19,761	C
San Jose State Univ	CA	22,630	C
Univ of Minn/Crookston	MN	19,126	C
Univ of Okla	OK	19,651	HC

APPLIED CLIMATE SCIENCE

School	ST	$IS	SR
Texas Christian Univ	TX	57,120	HC

APPLIED DATA SCIENCE ANALYTICS

School	ST	$IS	SR
Bryant Univ	RI	57,204	VC
Chatham Univ	PA	47,883	VC
Houghton College	NY	40,558	VC
Valparaiso Univ	IN	50,160	VC

APPLIED MATHEMATICS

School	ST	$IS	SR
Andrews Univ	MI	41,732	C
Arizona State Univ at the Polytechnic Campus	AZ	22,394	VC
Arizona State Univ at the Tempe Campus	AZ	23,001	VC
Arizona State Univ at the West Campus	AZ	21,513	VC
Armstrong State Univ	GA	15,615	C
Asbury Univ	KY	36,450	C+
Auburn Univ	AL	24,300	VC+
Augustana College	IL	51,222	VC+
Baldwin Wallace Univ	OH	42,464	VC
Ball State Univ	IN	19,808	C+
Baylor Univ	TX	56,803	HC
Belmont Univ	TN	44,500	VC+
Berea College	KY	7,094	C
Bethany College	WV	38,774	LC
Biola Univ	CA	48,686	C
Brown Univ	RI	64,566	MC
Bryant Univ	RI	57,204	VC
Bucknell Univ	PA	67,136	MC
Calif Inst of Technology	CA	64,704	MC
Cal State, Fullerton	CA	21,902	C
Cal State, Long Beach	CA	18,850	C
Case Western Reserve Univ	OH	62,284	MC
Christopher Newport Univ	VA	24,878	VC+
Clarkson Univ	NY	60,392	VC
Colby College	ME	64,060	MC
Colo State Univ	CO	23,033	C
Columbia Univ/ School of General Studies	NY	61,470	MC
Columbia Univ/City of New York	NY	62,958	MC
DePaul Univ	IL	52,807	VC
East Central Univ	OK	13,330	C
Eastern Mich Univ	MI	19,761	C
Elon Univ	NC	46,142	HC
Endicott College	MA	47,054	C+
Farmingdale State College	NY	20,968	C
Ferris State Univ	MI	21,458	C
Fitchburg State Univ	MA	21,819	LC
Florida Inst of Technology	FL	53,306	VC
Florida State Univ	FL	16,771	HC
Franklin College	IN	40,550	C
Geneva College	PA	35,450	C
Georgia Inst of Technology	GA	23,910	MC
Hampden-Sydney College	VA	57,806	VC
Harvard College/Harvard Univ	MA	65,609	MC
Hawaii Pacific Univ	HI	33,420	C
Hillsdale College	MI	37,170	MC
Hofstra Univ	NY	58,210	C+
Huntingdon College	AL	35,900	C
Illinois Inst of Technology	IL	56,826	HC+
Iona College	NY	52,514	C
Johns Hopkins Univ	MD	68,080	MC
Johnson C. Smith Univ	NC	25,336	LC
Kent State Univ	OH	20,928	C
Kentucky State Univ	KY	14,484	LC
Kettering Univ	MI	47,570	HC
Lasell College	MA	49,400	C
Le Moyne College	NY	47,305	VC
Lipscomb Univ	TN	42,984	VC
LIU Post	NY	50,698	C+
Louisiana College	LA	21,274	C
Loyola Marymount Univ	CA	60,202	VC+
Marist College	NY	49,860	VC
Marshall Univ	WV	18,044	C
Mary Baldwin Univ	VA	40,495	C
Metropolitan State Univ	MN	7,859	C
Millersville Univ of Pennsylvania	PA	25,298	C
Millsaps College	MS	50,080	C+
Missouri Univ of Science and Technology	MO	18,655	HC
Murray State Univ	KY	17,726	C+
New College of Florida	FL	16,180	HC+
New Jersey Inst of Technology	NJ	30,198	HC
New York City College of Technology	NY	7,185	LC
North Central College	IL	48,712	C+
Northwestern Univ	IL	68,725	MC
Oberlin College	OH	68,942	MC
Ohio Univ	OH	23,394	VC
Pacific Union College	CA	36,009	VC
Piedmont College	GA	34,334	C
Purdue Univ/West Lafayette	IN	20,032	MC
Rice Univ	TX	59,458	MC
Robert Morris Univ	PA	40,600	C
Rochester Inst of Technology	NY	52,734	HC+
Rutgers Univ - Newark	NJ	27,351	C
Saginaw Valley State Univ	MI	19,284	C
St. Augustine's Univ	NC	25,582	C
St. Louis Univ	MO	49,866	HC
St. Mary's College	IN	50,600	C
San Diego State Univ	CA	23,156	VC
San Francisco State Univ	CA	18,514	LC
San Jose State Univ	CA	22,630	C
Seattle Univ	WA	54,957	VC
Southern Illinois Univ Edwardsville	IL	20,188	C
SUNY Albany	NY	22,165	C
SUNY at Oswego	NY	22,219	VC
SUNY Polytechnic Inst	NY	20,438	VC
SUNY/Fredonia	NY	20,818	C
Stevenson Univ	MD	48,412	C
Stony Brook Univ/The SUNY	NY	22,703	MC
Syracuse Univ	NY	62,313	HC
Temple Univ	PA	24,392	C+
Texas A&M Univ at College Station	TX	20,771	VC+
Texas State Univ	TX	18,721	C
The American Univ	DC	61,317	HC
The George Washington Univ	DC	68,474	HC+
The Master's Univ	CA	43,870	C
The Univ of Akron	OH	22,566	C
The Univ of Arizona	AZ	24,086	C
The Univ of Montana Western	MT	9,426	LC
The Univ of Tenn at Chattanooga	TN	17,340	C+
The Univ of Utah	UT	18,751	VC
Tufts Univ	MA		MC
Univ of Arkansas at Little Rock	AR	18,211	LC
Univ of Calif at Berkeley	CA	29,886	MC
Univ of Calif at Los Angeles	CA	27,438	HC+
Univ of Calif San Diego	CA	30,450	MC
Univ of Central Arkansas	AR	15,042	VC
Univ of Central Okla	OK	15,150	C
Univ of Chicago	IL	70,551	MC
Univ of Colo Boulder	CO	26,048	HC
Univ of Conn	CT	27,394	
Univ of Houston-Downtown	TX	7,241	LC
Univ of Idaho	ID	16,158	C
Univ of Mass Lowell	MA	27,296	VC
Univ of New England	ME	50,110	C
Univ of New Hampshire	NH	29,333	VC
Univ of New Haven	CT	53,680	C
Univ of N Car at Chapel Hill	NC	20,561	MC
Univ of North Florida	FL	15,996	VC
Univ of Northwestern - St. Paul	MN	39,530	C
Univ of Notre Dame	IN	68,801	MC
Univ of Pittsburgh	PA	30,030	MC
Univ of Pittsburgh at Bradford	PA	22,958	C
Univ of Pittsburgh at Greensburg	PA	24,140	C
Univ of PR-Rio Piedras campus	PR	13,327	
Univ of Rochester	NY	65,032	MC
Univ of S Car Aiken	SC	18,094	C
Univ of Southern Calif	CA	66,631	MC
Univ of St. Thomas - Houston	TX	41,510	VC
Univ of Texas at El Paso	TX	34,452	NC
Univ of the Pacific	CA	57,446	VC
Univ of Tulsa	OK	52,625	HC
Univ of Wisc-Madison	WI	21,647	MC
Univ of Wisc-Milwaukee	WI	21,538	C
Univ of Wisc-Stout	WI	19,667	C
Washington State Univ	WA	22,747	C
Washington Univ in St. Louis	MO	67,539	MC
Weber State Univ	UT	14,112	C
Wentworth Inst of Technology	MA	48,810	VC
Wesleyan College	GA	31,940	C+
West Virginia State Univ	WV	19,412	LC
West Virginia Univ	WV	18,952	VC
Western Mich Univ	MI	21,791	C
Western Washington Univ	WA	18,904	VC
Wheaton College	IL	44,993	MC
Wofford College	SC	49,885	VC

ST = STATE $IS = IN-STATE COSTS SR = SELECTOR RATING

School	ST	$IS	SR
Wright State Univ	OH	16,983	C
Yale Univ	CT	64,650	MC
Youngstown State Univ	OH	17,487	C

APPLIED MUSIC

School	ST	$IS	SR
Baldwin Wallace Univ	OH	42,464	VC
Baylor Univ	TX	56,803	HC
Concordia College - New York	NY	39,035	LC
Cornerstone Univ	MI	36,550	C
Dallas Baptist Univ	TX	35,220	VC
Eastern Mich Univ	MI	19,761	C
Geneva College	PA	35,450	C
Indiana Wesleyan Univ	IN	33,674	C
Inter-American Univ of PR Ponce	PR	19,549	
Inter-American Univ of PR-Fajardo Campus	PR	18,336	
Judson College	AL	27,066	C
Kansas State Univ	KS	17,780	VC
Lenoir-Rhyne Univ	NC	47,500	LC
Mannes School of Music	NY	44,500	SP
Meredith College	NC	46,634	C
Miss College	MS	25,850	C
Nebr Wesleyan Univ	NE	42,026	C+
New England Conservatory of Music	MA	63,170	SP
Newberry College	SC	34,550	C
Ouachita Baptist Univ	AR	33,500	VC
Roberts Wesleyan College	NY	41,116	C
Seton Hall Univ	NJ	58,008	C
The Univ of Texas at Austin	TX	20,206	MC
Trinity Christian College	IL	35,580	C
Univ of Delaware	DE	32,214	VC
Univ of Houston	TX	21,871	VC
Univ of Idaho	ID	16,158	C
Univ of Illinois at Chicago	IL	24,664	VC
Univ of Nevada, Reno	NV	18,010	C
Wartburg College	IA	49,478	C
West Chester Univ of Pennsylvania	PA	19,171	VC
Western Oregon Univ	OR	19,965	LC
Youngstown State Univ	OH	17,487	C

APPLIED NUTRITION

School	ST	$IS	SR
Johnson & Wales Univ/ Denver Campus	CO	44,768	C
Ohio Univ	OH	23,394	VC
Rochester Inst of Technology	NY	52,734	HC+

APPLIED PHYSICS

School	ST	$IS	SR
Arizona State Univ at the Polytechnic Campus	AZ	22,394	VC
Armstrong State Univ	GA	15,615	C
Ball State Univ	IN	19,808	C+
Beloit College	WI	55,206	HC
Berry College	GA	47,466	VC
Bethel Univ	MN	46,550	C+
Bridgewater College	VA	46,260	C
Calif Inst of Technology	CA	64,704	MC
Cal State, Fullerton	CA	21,902	C
Cal State, San Bernardino	CA	20,106	C
Cal State, Stanislaus	CA	18,053	LC
Carroll Univ	WI	38,100	C+
Christopher Newport Univ	VA	24,878	VC+
Columbia Univ/City of New York	NY	62,958	MC
East Carolina Univ	NC	16,539	C
Hofstra Univ	NY	58,210	C+
Houghton College	NY	40,558	VC
Indiana Univ of Pennsylvania	PA	24,474	C
Kettering Univ	MI	47,570	HC
Linfield College	OR	53,992	C
Marietta College	OH	46,190	C
Mich Tech Univ	MI	25,551	VC+
Murray State Univ	KY	17,726	C+
New Jersey Inst of Technology	NJ	30,198	HC
Northeastern Univ	MA	65,352	MC
Ohio Univ	OH	23,394	VC
Pacific Lutheran Univ	WA	49,960	C
Piedmont College	GA	34,334	C
Providence College	RI	62,870	HC
Purdue Univ/West Lafayette	IN	20,032	MC
Rensselaer Polytechnic Inst	NY	67,265	MC
Rutgers Univ - Newark	NJ	27,351	C
Shippensburg Univ of Pennsylvania	PA	24,096	C
SUNY at Geneseo	NY	21,622	VC
Stetson Univ	FL	57,174	VC+
Tufts Univ	MA		MC
Univ of Calif San Diego	CA	30,450	MC
Univ of Iowa	IA	19,415	HC
Univ of Maryland/Baltimore County	MD	23,004	VC
Univ of Minn/Duluth	MN	20,292	C
Univ of Nevada, Las Vegas	NV	17,553	C
Western Washington Univ	WA	18,904	VC
Whitworth Univ	WA	53,682	VC
Xavier Univ	OH	49,380	VC
Yale Univ	CT	64,650	MC

APPLIED PSYCHOLOGY

School	ST	$IS	SR
Belhaven Univ	MS	32,250	C
Belmont Abbey College	NC	28,794	C
Biola Univ	CA	48,686	C
Boston College	MA	68,043	MC
Bryant Univ	RI	57,204	VC
Cedar Crest College	PA	51,110	C
Christian Brothers Univ	TN	31,670	VC
College of St. Mary	NE	27,500	C
Colo State Univ	CO	23,033	C
Coppin State Univ	MD	14,071	VC
Farmingdale State College	NY	20,968	C
Franklin Univ	OH	11,616	NC
Gwynedd Mercy Univ	PA	43,780	LC
Hodges Univ	FL	20,160	LC
Ithaca College	NY	58,158	VC+
Loyola Univ Chicago	IL	57,158	VC
Mayville State Univ	ND	18,371	NC
New York Univ	NY	68,139	MC
Pace Univ	NY	60,136	C
Regis Univ	CO	46,380	C
Russell Sage College	NY	39,370	C
SUNY /College of Agriculture and Tech at Cobleskill	NY	20,527	LC
Univ of Illinois at Chicago	IL	24,664	VC
Univ of Mich/Flint	MI	19,062	C
Univ of North Texas	TX	20,082	C
Univ of Pittsburgh	PA	30,030	MC
Univ of St. Mary	KS	37,080	NC
Wright State Univ	OH	16,983	C

APPLIED SCIENCE

School	ST	$IS	SR
Alcorn State Univ	MS	15,884	C
Arizona State Univ at the Downtown Phoenix Campus	AZ	24,634	VC
Arizona State Univ at the Polytechnic Campus	AZ	22,394	VC
Arizona State Univ at the West Campus	AZ	21,513	VC
Black Hills State Univ	SD	16,622	C
Bluefield State College	WV	5,832	LC
Cambridge College	MA	14,940	NC
Concordia College - Moorhead	MN	46,418	C
Florida Gulf Coast Univ	FL	14,738	C
Georgian Court Univ	NJ	43,068	LC
Indiana Univ Bloomington	IN	20,791	HC
Indiana Univ East	IN	7,207	C
Indiana Univ Kokomo	IN	7,207	C
Indiana Univ Northwest	IN	7,207	LC
Indiana Univ South Bend	IN	16,057	C
Indiana Univ Southeast	IN	16,931	C
Kent State Univ	OH	20,928	C
King Univ	TN	36,976	C
Lamar Univ	TX	18,014	LC
Lehigh Univ	PA	63,860	MC
Madonna Univ	MI	30,450	LC
Messiah College	PA	44,380	VC
Missouri Southern State Univ	MO	13,071	C
Montana State Univ Billings	MT	13,336	LC
Northern Arizona Univ	AZ	21,003	C
Saginaw Valley State Univ	MI	19,284	C
Southwest Minn State Univ	MN	17,783	C
Southwestern Univ	TX	52,370	VC
Tarleton State Univ	TX	15,248	LC
Texas Lutheran Univ	TX	39,770	C
The Univ of Arizona	AZ	24,086	C
Univ of Arkansas at Little Rock	AR	18,211	LC
Univ of Arkansas at Monticello	AR	13,599	LC
Univ of Central Florida	FL	16,379	VC
Univ of Maine at Augusta	ME	7,812	C
Univ of Mich/Flint	MI	19,062	C
Univ of Montana	MT	14,105	C
Univ of Nebr - Lincoln	NE	18,589	VC
Univ of N Car at Chapel Hill	NC	20,561	MC
Univ of Pennsylvania	PA	63,526	MC
Univ of San Francisco	CA	60,580	C
Univ of Wisc-Stout	WI	19,667	C
Wheeling Jesuit Univ	WV	37,106	LC
Winona State Univ	MN	18,109	C

APPLIED SOCIAL SCIENCE

School	ST	$IS	SR
Bryant Univ	RI	57,204	VC
CUNY/Queens College	NY	21,507	C
East Carolina Univ	NC	16,539	C
St. Leo Univ	FL	32,850	C
Univ of New England	ME	50,110	C
Univ of Wisc-Stout	WI	19,667	C

AQUACULTURE & FISHERY TECHNOLOGY

School	ST	$IS	SR
Lake Superior State Univ	MI	19,867	C
Texas State Univ	TX	18,721	C
Univ of New England	ME	50,110	C
Univ of Rhode Island	RI	26,066	VC

ARABIC

School	ST	$IS	SR
Bard College	NY	65,924	HC
Cal State, Fullerton	CA	21,902	C
Colo State Univ	CO	23,033	C
Dartmouth College	NH	68,109	MC
DePaul Univ	IL	52,807	VC
Georgetown Univ	DC	68,970	MC
Mich State Univ	MI	24,542	VC
Middlebury College	VT	67,464	MC
Montclair State Univ	NJ	26,912	C
New York Univ	NY	68,139	MC
Ohio State Univ at Columbus	OH	22,843	MC
SUNY at Binghamton	NY	24,100	MC
The American Univ	DC	61,317	HC
The Univ of Texas at Austin	TX	20,206	MC
Thomas Edison State Univ	NJ	6,350	NC
Tufts Univ	MA		MC
United States Naval Academy	MD		HC
Univ of Calif at Los Angeles	CA	27,438	HC+
Univ of Cincinnati	OH	22,118	VC
Univ of Georgia	GA	21,878	HC
Univ of Maryland/College Park	MD	21,938	HC
Univ of Mich/Ann Arbor	MI	25,274	MC
Univ of Miss	MS	18,802	C
Univ of Notre Dame	IN	68,801	MC
Univ of Okla	OK	19,651	HC
Univ of Richmond	VA	62,730	MC
Washington Univ in St. Louis	MO	67,539	MC
Wellesley College	MA	66,984	MC
Western Kentucky Univ	KY	16,850	C
Western Washington Univ	WA	18,904	VC
Williams College	MA	67,700	MC

ARCHEOLOGY

School	ST	$IS	SR
Biola Univ	CA	48,686	C
Boston Univ	MA	67,352	MC
Bowdoin College	ME	65,980	MC
Brigham Young Univ	UT	13,248	MC
Brown Univ	RI	64,566	MC
Bryn Mawr College	PA	65,220	MC
Cal State, Fullerton	CA	21,902	C
CUNY/Hunter College	NY	31,098	VC
College of Charleston	SC	24,046	VC
Columbia Univ/ School of General Studies	NY	61,470	MC
Columbia Univ/City of New York	NY	62,958	MC
Cornell Univ	NY	67,591	MC
Dickinson College	PA	66,166	MC
Hamilton College	NY	64,250	MC
Haverford College	PA	66,490	MC
Hood College	MD	50,540	C
Johns Hopkins Univ	MD	68,080	MC
Lycoming College	PA	50,895	C
Mass Inst of Technology	MA	62,662	MC
Mercyhurst Univ	PA	47,420	C
Millersville Univ of Pennsylvania	PA	25,298	C
Murray State Univ	KY	17,726	C+
Oberlin College	OH	68,942	MC
Pennsylvania State Univ - Univ Park	PA	29,716	HC
Princeton Univ	NJ	60,090	MC
Randolph-Macon College	VA	51,480	VC
Stanford Univ	CA	62,541	MC
SUNY/Potsdam	NY	21,051	VC
The College of Wooster	OH	60,000	HC
The George Washington Univ	DC	68,474	HC+
The Univ of Texas at Austin	TX	20,206	MC
Tufts Univ	MA		MC
Univ of Cincinnati	OH	22,118	VC
Univ of Evansville	IN	44,186	C+
Univ of Indianapolis	IN	36,480	VC
Univ of Kansas	KS	20,884	VC
Univ of Mich/Ann Arbor	MI	25,274	MC
Univ of Missouri-Columbia	MO	20,463	VC
Univ of N Car at Chapel Hill	NC	20,561	MC
Univ of N Car at Greensboro	NC	15,998	C
Univ of Rochester	NY	65,032	MC
Univ of Tulsa	OK	52,625	HC
Univ of Wisc-La Crosse	WI	15,425	VC
Washington and Lee Univ	VA	59,647	MC
Washington Univ in St. Louis	MO	67,539	MC
Wellesley College	MA	66,984	MC
Wesleyan Univ	CT	66,940	MC
Western Kentucky Univ	KY	16,850	C
Wheaton College	IL	44,993	MC
Yale Univ	CT	64,650	MC

ARCHITECTURAL ENGINEERING

School	ST	$IS	SR
Calif Polytechnic State Univ	CA	22,547	MC
Cal State, Fullerton	CA	21,902	C
Dordt College	IA	37,860	C+
Drexel Univ	PA	65,927	HC
Illinois Inst of Technology	IL	56,826	HC+
Kansas State Univ	KS	17,780	VC
Lawrence Tech Univ	MI	41,630	VC
Milwaukee School of Engineering	WI	48,531	HC+
Missouri Univ of Science and Technology	MO	18,655	HC
N Car A&T State Univ	NC	13,786	C
Northern Kentucky Univ	KY	16,486	C
Okla State Univ	OK	17,180	C+
Olivet Nazarene Univ	IL	41,840	VC
Parsons The New School for Design	NY	56,610	SP
Pennsylvania State Univ - Univ Park	PA	29,716	HC
Princeton Univ	NJ	60,090	MC
Rice Univ	TX	59,458	MC
Stanford Univ	CA	62,541	MC
Tenn State Univ	TN	14,423	LC
The Univ of Texas at Austin	TX	20,206	MC
Univ of Cincinnati	OH	22,118	VC
Univ of Colo Boulder	CO	26,048	HC
Univ of Detroit Mercy	MI	48,816	C
Univ of Hartford	CT	49,776	C
Univ of Illinois at Urbana-Champaign	IL	27,006	HC
Univ of Kansas	KS	20,884	VC
Univ of Miami	FL	63,494	MC
Univ of Nebr - Lincoln	NE	18,589	VC
Univ of Nevada, Las Vegas	NV	17,553	C
Univ of Okla	OK	19,651	HC
Univ of Wyoming	WY	15,537	C
Vermont Technical College	VT	25,370	C
Washington State Univ	WA	22,747	C
Worcester Polytechnic Inst	MA	62,846	MC

ARCHITECTURAL HISTORY

School	ST	$IS	SR
Boston Univ	MA	67,352	MC
Brown Univ	RI	64,566	MC
DePaul Univ	IL	52,807	VC
Miami Univ	OH	27,190	HC+
Middlebury College	VT	67,464	MC
Savannah College of Art and Design	GA	49,595	SP
Univ of Virginia	VA	27,367	MC

ARCHITECTURAL STUDIES

School	ST	$IS	SR
Amherst College	MA	66,186	MC
Arizona State Univ at the Tempe Campus	AZ	23,001	VC
Boston Univ	MA	67,352	MC
Bowling Green State Univ	OH	19,975	C
Brown Univ	RI	64,566	MC
Clayton State Univ	GA	19,735	LC
College of the Holy Cross	MA	64,320	MC
Hobart and William Smith Colleges	NY	67,050	HC+
Ithaca College	NY	58,158	VC+
Kennesaw State Univ	GA	18,899	VC
Kent State Univ	OH	20,928	C
Lawrence Tech Univ	MI	41,630	VC
New York Univ	NY	68,139	MC
Rutgers Univ - New Brunswick	NJ	27,090	HC
The Univ of Utah	UT	18,751	VC
Univ of Arkansas at Fayetteville	AR	19,766	VC
Univ of Illinois at Chicago	IL	24,664	VC
Univ of Kansas	KS	20,884	VC
Univ of Nebr - Lincoln	NE	18,589	VC
Univ of Pittsburgh	PA	30,030	MC
Univ of San Diego	CA	60,338	HC
Washington State Univ	WA	22,747	C

ARCHITECTURAL TECHNOLOGY

School	ST	$IS	SR
Alfred State College	NY	19,895	C
Drury Univ	MO	37,555	VC
Fairmont State Univ	WV	15,726	C
Farmingdale State College	NY	20,968	C
Fitchburg State Univ	MA	21,819	LC
Murray State Univ	KY	17,726	C+
New York City College of Technology	NY	7,185	LC
New York Inst of Technology	NY	49,980	VC
Pennsylvania College of Technology	PA	27,693	NC
Univ of Cincinnati	OH	22,118	VC
Univ of Southern Miss	MS	13,170	C
Washington Univ in St. Louis	MO	67,539	MC

ARCHITECTURE

School	ST	$IS	SR
Alfred State College	NY	19,895	C
Andrews Univ	MI	41,732	C
Appalachian State Univ	NC	15,394	VC
Auburn Univ	AL	24,300	VC+
Ball State Univ	IN	19,808	C+
Barnard College/Columbia Univ	NY	68,762	MC
Bennington College	VT	66,280	MC
Boston Architectural College	MA	20,666	SP
Brown Univ	RI	64,566	MC
Calif Baptist Univ	CA	42,986	C
Calif College of the Arts	CA	52,758	SP
Calif Polytechnic State Univ	CA	22,547	MC
Calif State Polytechnic Univ, Pomona	CA	21,811	C
Cal State, Fullerton	CA	21,902	C
Carnegie Mellon Univ	PA	67,980	MC
CUNY/City College	NY	20,204	C
Columbia Univ/ School of General Studies	NY	61,470	MC
Columbia Univ/City of New York	NY	62,958	MC
Conn College	CT	65,000	MC
Cooper Union for the Advancement of Science and Art	NY	61,370	MC
Cornell Univ	NY	67,591	MC
Drexel Univ	PA	65,927	HC
Drury Univ	MO	37,555	VC
Fairmont State Univ	WV	15,726	C
Florida Atlantic Univ	FL	18,256	C
Florida International Univ	FL	20,281	C
Fordham Univ	NY	68,431	MC
Georgia Inst of Technology	GA	23,910	MC

ST = STATE $IS = IN-STATE COSTS SR = SELECTOR RATING

School	ST	$IS	SR
Hampshire College	MA	65,214	MC
Hampton Univ	VA	36,410	C
Hobart and William Smith Colleges	NY	67,050	HC+
Howard Univ	DC	37,616	C+
Illinois Inst of Technology	IL	56,826	HC+
Iowa State Univ	IA	18,176	C
Jefferson (Philadelphia Univ + Thomas Jefferson Univ)	PA	53,966	C
Judson Univ	IL	39,174	C
Kansas State Univ	KS	17,780	VC
Kean Univ	NJ	25,620	C
Keene State College	NH	24,604	C
Kent State Univ	OH	20,928	C
Lawrence Tech Univ	MI	41,630	VC
Lehigh Univ	PA	63,860	MC
Louisiana State Univ and A&M College	LA	18,677	VC
Louisiana Tech Univ	LA	11,422	VC
Marywood Univ	PA	47,840	C
Mass College of Art and Design	MA	24,800	SP
Mass Inst of Technology	MA	62,662	MC
Miami Univ	OH	27,190	HC+
Miss State Univ	MS	12,028	C+
Mount Holyoke College	MA	56,746	MC
New Jersey Inst of Technology	NJ	30,198	HC
New York Inst of Technology	NY	49,980	VC
NewSchool of Architecture & Design	CA	12,341	SP
N Car State Univ	NC	22,434	HC+
N Dak State Univ	ND	16,245	VC
Northeastern Univ	MA	65,352	MC
Norwich Univ	VT	56,234	C
Ohio State Univ at Columbus	OH	22,843	MC
Okla State Univ	OK	17,180	C+
Otis College of Art and Design	CA	54,670	SP
Pennsylvania State Univ - Univ Park	PA	29,716	HC
Portland State Univ	OR	19,443	C
Prairie View A&M Univ	TX	27,273	LC
Pratt Inst	NY	59,482	VC+
Princeton Univ	NJ	60,090	MC
Rensselaer Polytechnic Inst	NY	67,265	MC
Rhode Island School of Design	RI	59,960	SP
Rice Univ	TX	59,458	MC
Roger Williams Univ	RI	48,074	VC
Sarah Lawrence College	NY	68,866	MC
Savannah College of Art and Design	GA	49,595	SP
Smith College	MA	66,774	MC
S Dak State Univ	SD	15,874	C
Southern Illinois Univ Carbondale	IL	24,554	C
Southern Univ and A&M College	LA	16,074	LC
SUNY/Univ at Buffalo	NY	23,122	C
Syracuse Univ	NY	62,313	HC
Temple Univ	PA	24,392	C+
Texas Tech Univ	TX	20,156	C+
The Catholic Univ of America	DC	58,376	VC
The College of Wooster	OH	60,000	HC
The Univ of Arizona	AZ	24,086	C
The Univ of Memphis	TN	18,278	C
The Univ of Tenn at Knoxville	TN	22,112	VC
The Univ of Texas at Austin	TX	20,206	MC
The Univ of Texas at San Antonio	TX	21,060	C
Tufts Univ	MA		MC
Tulane Univ	LA	67,496	MC
Tuskegee Univ	AL	28,164	C
Univ of Arkansas at Fayetteville	AR	19,766	VC
Univ of Calif at Berkeley	CA	29,886	MC
Univ of Calif at Los Angeles	CA	27,438	HC+
Univ of Central Florida	FL	16,379	VC
Univ of Colo Denver	CO	22,238	C
Univ of Detroit Mercy	MI	48,816	C
Univ of Florida	FL	16,291	HC+
Univ of Houston	TX	21,871	VC
Univ of Idaho	ID	16,158	C
Univ of Illinois at Chicago	IL	24,664	VC
Univ of Illinois at Urbana-Champaign	IL	27,006	HC
Univ of Kansas	KS	20,884	VC
Univ of Maine at Augusta	ME	7,812	C
Univ of Maryland/College Park	MD	21,938	HC
Univ of Mass Amherst	MA	27,669	HC
Univ of Miami	FL	63,494	MC
Univ of Mich/Ann Arbor	MI	25,274	MC
Univ of Minn/Twin Cities	MN	24,269	MC
Univ of Nebr - Lincoln	NE	18,589	VC
Univ of New Mexico	NM	16,808	C
Univ of N Car at Charlotte	NC	17,803	VC
Univ of Notre Dame	IN	68,801	MC
Univ of Okla	OK	19,651	HC
Univ of Oregon	OR	24,021	VC
Univ of Pennsylvania	PA	63,526	MC
Univ of San Francisco	CA	60,580	C
Univ of Southern Calif	CA	66,631	MC
Univ of Texas at Arlington	TX	18,876	C
Univ of the District of Columbia	DC	21,260	LC
Univ of Virginia	VA	27,367	MC
Univ of Wisc-Milwaukee	WI	21,538	C
Virginia Polytechnic Inst and State Univ	VA	21,920	VC
Washington State Univ	WA	22,747	C
Washington Univ in St. Louis	MO	67,539	MC
Wellesley College	MA	66,984	MC
Wentworth Inst of Technology	MA	48,810	VC
Woodbury Univ	CA	49,593	VC
Yale Univ	CT	64,650	MC

AREA STUDIES

School	ST	$IS	SR
Appalachian State Univ	NC	15,394	VC
Bard College	NY	65,924	HC
Baylor Univ	TX	56,803	HC
Calvin College	MI	43,090	HC
CUNY/City College	NY	20,204	C
Colgate Univ	NY	67,500	MC
Columbia Univ/City of New York	NY	62,958	MC
Duke Univ	NC	68,298	MC
Eastern Mich Univ	MI	19,761	C
Gannon Univ	PA	42,922	C
Huntington Univ	IN	33,996	C
Ithaca College	NY	58,158	VC+
Lake Forest College	IL	50,652	VC
Mercer Univ	GA	45,348	VC
New York Univ	NY	68,139	MC
Penn State Erie,The Behrend College	PA	26,688	VC
Prescott College	AZ	38,201	C
St. Ambrose Univ	IA	40,180	C
Stanford Univ	CA	62,541	MC
The American Univ	DC	61,317	HC
The College of Wooster	OH	60,000	HC
Univ of Alaska Fairbanks	AK	16,874	VC
Univ of Miss	MS	18,802	C
Univ of Redlands	CA	61,934	VC
Univ of Vermont	VT	29,792	HC
Univ of Virginia	VA	27,367	MC
Washington Univ in St. Louis	MO	67,539	MC
Webster Univ	MO	37,490	C

ART

School	ST	$IS	SR
Abilene Christian Univ	TX	43,708	C+
Adams State Univ	CO	15,420	LC
Alabama A&M Univ	AL	18,796	C
Alabama State Univ	AL	16,490	LC
Albany State Univ	GA	19,462	C
Albion College	MI	55,260	C
Albright College	PA	57,326	C
Allegheny College	PA	57,620	VC
Alma College	MI	49,410	VC
Alverno College	WI	33,294	LC
Andrews Univ	MI	41,732	C
Angelo State Univ	TX	15,882	LC
Anna Maria College	MA	51,020	C
Appalachian State Univ	NC	15,394	VC
Aquinas College - Mich	MI	38,876	VC
Arcadia Univ	PA	55,990	C+
Arizona State Univ at the Tempe Campus	AZ	23,001	VC
Arkansas State Univ	AR	16,190	C
Arkansas Tech Univ	AR	16,534	LC
Armstrong State Univ	GA	15,615	C
Asbury Univ	KY	36,450	C+
Ashland Univ	OH	30,446	C
Atlantic Union College	MA	27,228	C
Auburn Univ	AL	24,300	VC+
Augsburg Univ	MN	45,129	C
Augusta Univ	GA	4,632	C
Augustana College	IL	51,222	VC+
Augustana Univ	SD	39,968	VC
Aurora Univ	IL	34,990	C
Austin College	TX	51,059	HC
Austin Peay State Univ	TN	16,397	C
Averett Univ	VA	43,034	LC
Avila Univ	MO	27,100	C
Ball State Univ	IN	19,808	C+
Barry Univ	FL	38,730	LC
Baylor Univ	TX	56,803	HC
Belhaven Univ	MS	32,250	C
Beloit College	WI	55,206	HC
Benedictine College	KS	38,850	VC
Bennington College	VT	66,280	MC
Berea College	KY	7,094	C
Berry College	GA	47,466	VC
Bethany College	KS	38,637	LC
Bethel College	KS	35,370	C
Bethel Univ	MN	46,550	C+
Biola Univ	CA	48,686	C
Birmingham-Southern College	AL	44,478	C+
Black Hills State Univ	SD	16,622	C
Blackburn College	IL	28,526	LC
Bluffton Univ	OH	40,950	C+
Boise State Univ	ID	17,368	C
Bowling Green State Univ	OH	19,975	C
Bradley Univ	IL	43,240	VC
Brescia Univ	KY	29,890	VC
Briar Cliff Univ	IA	36,956	C
Bridgewater College	VA	46,260	C
Bridgewater State Univ	MA	22,762	C
Brigham Young Univ	UT	13,248	MC
Brigham Young Univ/Hawaii	HI	11,710	C
Brown Univ	RI	64,566	MC
Bucknell Univ	PA	67,136	MC
Buena Vista Univ	IA	42,344	C
Butler Univ	IN	52,890	VC+
Caldwell Univ	NJ	42,165	LC
Calif College of the Arts	CA	52,758	SP
Calif Lutheran Univ	CA	52,853	C
Cal State, Bakersfield	CA	22,397	LC
Cal State, Chico	CA	19,790	VC
Cal State, Dominguez Hills	CA	19,022	LC
Cal State, East Bay	CA	20,748	C
Cal State, Fresno	CA	16,902	LC
Cal State, Fullerton	CA	21,902	C
Cal State, Long Beach	CA	18,850	C
Cal State, Northridge	CA	17,277	LC
Cal State, San Bernardino	CA	20,106	C
Cal State, Stanislaus	CA	18,053	LC
Calif Univ of Pennsylvania	PA	20,425	LC
Calvin College	MI	43,090	HC
Cameron Univ	OK	11,632	LC
Campbell Univ	NC	37,570	VC
Campbellsville Univ	KY	33,400	C
Capital Univ	OH	44,778	VC
Cardinal Stritch Univ	WI	37,136	C
Carlow Univ	PA	39,696	LC
Carnegie Mellon Univ	PA	67,980	MC
Carroll Univ	WI	38,100	C+
Carthage College	WI	48,835	C
Castleton Univ	VT	20,186	C
Cedar Crest College	PA	51,110	C
Centenary College of Louisiana	LA	49,050	C+
Central College	IA	44,592	C
Central Conn State Univ	CT	22,041	C
Central Mich Univ	MI	20,330	C
Central Washington Univ	WA	16,803	C
Chadron State College	NE	14,819	LC
Chapman Univ	CA	65,504	HC
Chestnut Hill College	PA	47,180	C
Chicago State Univ	IL	41,620	C
CUNY/Brooklyn College	NY	7,163	C+
CUNY/City College	NY	20,204	C
Claflin Univ	SC	25,592	LC
Clarion Univ of Pennsylvania	PA	21,608	LC
Clark Atlanta Univ	GA	31,019	LC
Cleveland State Univ	OH	22,290	C
Coe College	IA	51,570	VC
Coker College	SC	38,196	C
Colby College	ME	64,060	MC
Colby-Sawyer College	NH	50,790	C
College of St. Benedict	MN	54,480	C
College of St. Elizabeth	NJ	45,700	LC
College of St. Mary	NE	27,500	C
College of St. Scholastica	MN	45,734	C+
College of Staten Island	NY	24,389	LC
College of the Ozarks	MO	7,530	VC
College of William & Mary	VA	34,907	MC
Colo Christian Univ	CO	40,885	VC
Colo Mesa Univ	CO	19,707	LC
Colo State Univ	CO	23,033	C
Colo State Univ-Pueblo	CO	21,581	C
Columbia College - Missouri	MO	28,179	C
Columbus State Univ	GA	14,336	LC
Concordia College - Moorhead	MN	46,418	C
Concordia Univ Irvine	CA	44,860	VC
Concordia Univ St. Paul	MN	29,050	C
Concordia Univ Wisc	WI	35,910	C
Concordia Univ, Ann Arbor	MI	38,878	C+
Concordia Univ, Chicago	IL	41,522	C
Conn College	CT	65,000	MC
Covenant College	GA	44,590	HC
Culver-Stockton College	MO	34,350	C
Daemen College	NY	40,336	C
Dakota Wesleyan Univ	SD	33,980	LC
Dallas Baptist Univ	TX	35,220	VC
Davidson College	NC	60,119	MC
Davis & Elkins College	WV	38,242	LC
Defiance College	OH	42,240	LC
Delta State Univ	MS	13,176	LC
DePaul Univ	IL	52,807	VC
Dillard Univ	LA	20,940	VC
Doane Univ	NE	41,340	VC
Dominican Univ of Calif	CA	58,750	C
Dordt College	IA	37,860	C+
Drew Univ/College of Liberal Arts	NJ	53,608	VC
Earlham College	IN	55,670	HC
East Carolina Univ	NC	16,539	C
East Central Univ	OK	13,330	C
East Tenn State Univ	TN	18,141	C
Eastern Illinois Univ	IL	21,414	C
Eastern Kentucky Univ	KY	17,742	C
Eastern Mennonite Univ	VA	42,550	C
Eastern Mich Univ	MI	19,761	C
Eastern New Mexico Univ	NM	12,874	LC
Eastern Oregon Univ	OR	17,612	C
Eastern Washington Univ	WA	17,896	LC
Edgewood College	WI	35,950	C
Edinboro Univ	PA	15,940	LC
Elizabeth City State Univ	NC	14,745	C
Elmhurst College	IL	46,514	C
Elon Univ	NC	46,142	HC
Emory and Henry College	VA	46,320	C
Emory Univ	GA	63,286	MC
Emporia State Univ	KS	15,029	C
Erskine College	SC	45,460	C
Evangel Univ	MO	28,898	C
Felician Univ	NJ	46,280	LC
Ferrum College	VA	43,970	C
Florida Atlantic Univ	FL	18,256	C
Florida Gulf Coast Univ	FL	14,738	C
Florida International Univ	FL	20,281	C
Fontbonne Univ	MO	34,606	C
Fort Hays State Univ	KS	12,677	C
Fort Lewis College	CO	20,154	C
Freed-Hardeman Univ	TN	29,900	C
Friends Univ	KS	38,000	C
Furman Univ	SC	61,098	VC+
Gardner-Webb Univ	NC	24,935	C+
George Fox Univ	OR	42,938	C
Georgetown College	KY	41,440	C
Georgetown Univ	DC	68,970	MC
Georgia College & State Univ	GA	21,884	C+
Georgia Southern Univ	GA	16,540	VC
Georgia Southwestern State Univ	GA	13,870	LC
Georgia State Univ	GA	25,250	C
Goddard College	VT	17,040	VC
Gonzaga Univ	WA	52,880	HC
Gordon College	MA	47,740	VC
Goshen College	IN	44,350	C
Goucher College	MD	56,110	VC
Grace College and Seminary	IN	31,524	C
Grand Valley State Univ	MI	22,250	C+
Green Mountain College	VT	45,228	LC
Greensboro College	NC	39,790	LC
Greenville College	IL	27,012	LC
Guilford College	NC	45,973	C
Hamilton College	NY	64,250	MC
Hamline Univ	MN	50,152	C
Hampton Univ	VA	36,410	C
Hannibal-LaGrange Univ	MO	29,815	C
Hanover College	IN	47,750	C+
Harding Univ	AR	25,440	C
Hardin-Simmons Univ	TX	36,025	C
Hartwick College	NY	51,270	C
Hendrix College	AR	54,020	VC
Heritage Univ	WA	19,825	NC
Hillsdale College	MI	37,170	MC
Hiram College	OH	44,590	C
Holy Family Univ	PA	44,672	LC
Hood College	MD	50,540	C
Hope College	MI	42,840	VC
Houghton College	NY	40,558	VC
Houston Baptist Univ	TX	36,450	C
Howard Payne Univ	TX	35,994	C
Humboldt State Univ	CA	21,708	C
Huntingdon College	AL	35,900	C
Huntington Univ	IN	33,996	C
Idaho State Univ	ID	13,619	LC
Illinois State Univ	IL	23,418	VC
Illinois Wesleyan Univ	IL	56,430	VC+
Indiana Univ of Pennsylvania	PA	24,474	C
Indiana Wesleyan Univ	IN	33,674	C
Ithaca College	NY	58,158	VC+
Jackson State Univ	MS	15,879	LC
James Madison Univ	VA	19,084	VC
Johnson State College	VT	22,672	C
Judson College	AL	27,066	C
Kalamazoo College	MI	53,931	HC
Kansas State Univ	KS	17,780	VC
Keene State College	NH	24,604	C
Kennesaw State Univ	GA	18,899	VC
Kentucky State Univ	KY	14,484	LC
Kentucky Wesleyan College	KY	34,260	LC
Kenyon College	OH	65,840	MC
La Sierra Univ	CA	39,690	VC
Lafayette College	PA	68,520	MC
LaGrange College	GA	41,310	C
Lake Forest College	IL	50,652	VC
Lakeland Univ	WI	35,130	C
Lebanon Valley College	PA	55,510	VC
Lees-McRae College	NC	33,944	NC
Lehigh Univ	PA	63,860	MC
LeMoyne-Owen College	TN	16,980	C
Lindsey Wilson College	KY	33,546	C
Linfield College	OR	53,992	C
Lipscomb Univ	TN	42,984	VC
LIU Post	NY	50,698	C+
Longwood Univ	VA	22,184	C
Lourdes Univ	OH	29,140	NC
Loyola Univ New Orleans	LA	52,456	VC
Luther College	IA	49,990	VC
Lyon College	AR	36,120	VC
Macalester College	MN	64,136	MC
MacMurray College	IL	35,025	C
Malone Univ	OH	39,200	C
Manchester Univ	IN	41,540	C
Marian Univ	WI	34,622	C
Marshall Univ	WV	18,044	C
Marygrove College	MI	30,100	LC
Marylhurst Univ	OR	16,818	NC
Marymount Univ	VA	43,231	C
Maryville College	TN	44,410	C
Mass College of Liberal Arts	MA	20,659	C
McDaniel College	MD	52,910	VC
McKendree Univ	IL	37,940	C+
McMurry Univ	TX	34,259	LC
McNeese State Univ	LA	7,838	C
McPherson College	KS	36,134	C
Mercer Univ	GA	45,348	VC
Meredith College	NC	46,634	C
Methodist Univ	NC	58,130	C
Metropolitan State Univ of Denver	CO	6,928	LC
Miami Univ	OH	27,190	HC+
Millersville Univ of Pennsylvania	PA	25,298	C

ST = STATE **$IS** = IN-STATE COSTS **SR** = SELECTOR RATING

School	ST	$IS	SR
Milligan College	TN	39,450	C
Millikin Univ	IL	44,148	C
Minn State Univ, Mankato	MN	17,190	C
Minot State Univ	ND	13,285	C
Miss College	MS	25,850	C
Miss State Univ	MS	12,028	C+
Miss Valley State Univ	MS	13,233	LC
Missouri Southern State Univ	MO	13,071	C
Missouri State Univ	MO	15,837	C+
Missouri Valley College	MO	28,150	C
Molloy College	NY	40,440	C
Monmouth College	IL	42,260	C
Monmouth Univ	NJ	50,184	C
Montana State Univ	MT	15,500	C+
Montana State Univ Billings	MT	13,336	LC
Moravian College	PA	55,488	C
Morehouse College	GA	40,835	C
Morningside College	IA	39,780	C
Mount Mercy Univ	IA	39,748	C
Mount St. Joseph Univ	OH	33,880	LC
Mount St. Mary's Univ - Chalon Campus	CA	50,486	VC+
Mount Vernon Nazarene Univ	OH	35,944	C
Muhlenberg College	PA	56,645	VC
Muskingum Univ	OH	35,966	C
Nazareth College	NY	46,784	C
Nebr Wesleyan Univ	NE	42,026	C+
Neumann Univ	PA	40,678	LC
New College of Florida	FL	16,180	HC+
New Mexico Highlands Univ	NM	11,904	LC
New Mexico State Univ	NM	14,050	LC
Newberry College	SC	34,550	C
Newman Univ	KS	37,382	C
Nicholls State Univ	LA	14,959	C
N Car Central Univ	NC	9,000	C
North Central College	IL	48,712	C+
N Dak State Univ	ND	16,245	VC
Northeastern Illinois Univ	IL	12,529	LC
Northeastern Univ	MA	65,352	MC
Northern Illinois Univ	IL	20,176	C
Northwest Missouri State Univ	MO	18,286	C
Northwest Nazarene Univ	ID	40,250	C
Northwestern Univ	IL	68,725	MC
Notre Dame College	OH	39,150	VC
Notre Dame de Namur Univ	CA	46,526	LC
Nova Southeastern Univ	FL	38,534	C+
Oberlin College	OH	68,942	MC
Oglethorpe Univ	GA	44,200	C
Ohio Dominican Univ	OH	41,340	C+
Ohio State Univ at Columbus	OH	22,843	MC
Ohio Univ	OH	23,394	VC
Ohio Wesleyan Univ	OH	49,460	VC
Okla Baptist Univ	OK	33,990	C
Okla Christian Univ	OK	29,260	C
Okla City Univ	OK	40,476	C
Okla State Univ	OK	17,180	C+
Olivet Nazarene Univ	IL	41,840	VC
Oregon State Univ	OR	23,337	VC
Ottawa Univ	KS	39,980	VC
Otterbein Univ	OH	41,630	C
Ouachita Baptist Univ	AR	33,500	VC
Our Lady of the Lake Univ	TX	37,790	LC
Pace Univ	NY	60,136	C
Palm Beach Atlantic Univ	FL	39,250	C
Pennsylvania State Univ - Univ Park	PA	29,716	HC
Pepperdine Univ	CA	66,862	VC+
Pfeiffer Univ	NC	40,532	LC
Piedmont College	GA	34,334	C
Pittsburg State Univ	KS	13,880	C
Pitzer College	CA	68,500	HC+
Plymouth State Univ	NH	23,180	LC
Point Loma Nazarene Univ	CA	46,150	C+
Prairie View A&M Univ	TX	27,273	LC
Presbyterian College	SC	47,186	C
Prescott College	AZ	38,201	C
Queens Univ of Charlotte	NC	39,543	C
Radford Univ	VA	19,758	C
Ramapo College of New Jersey	NJ	25,760	VC
Randolph College	VA	53,970	C
Reed College	OR	65,300	MC
Regis Univ	CO	46,380	C
Rhodes College	TN	51,900	HC
Ripon College	WI	49,991	VC
Roanoke College	VA	55,952	VC
Roberts Wesleyan College	NY	41,116	C
Rochester Inst of Technology	NY	52,734	HC+
Rockford Univ	IL	38,570	C
Rocky Mountain College	MT	35,776	C
Rowan Univ	NJ	24,491	VC
Rutgers Univ - Camden	NJ	26,595	C
Rutgers Univ - New Brunswick	NJ	27,090	HC
Rutgers Univ - Newark	NJ	27,351	C
Saginaw Valley State Univ	MI	19,284	C
St. John's Univ	MN	53,472	C
St. Joseph's Univ	PA	58,540	VC
St. Mary-of-the-Woods College	IN	40,424	LC
St. Mary's College	IN	50,600	C
St. Mary's College of Calif	CA	57,420	C
St. Mary's Univ of Minn	MN	42,440	C
St. Vincent College	PA	46,229	C
Salisbury Univ	MD	21,132	VC
Sam Houston State Univ	TX	18,792	C
Samford Univ	AL	40,770	VC
San Diego State Univ	CA	23,156	VC
San Francisco State Univ	CA	18,514	LC
Savannah College of Art and Design	GA	49,595	SP
Schreiner Univ	TX	34,626	LC
Seattle Pacific Univ	WA	47,439	C+
Shepherd Univ, West Virginia	WV	17,382	C
Shippensburg Univ of Pennsylvania	PA	24,096	C
Shorter Univ	GA	31,130	LC
Silver Lake College of the Holy Family	WI	36,290	LC
Simpson College	IA	45,626	VC
Sinte Gleska Univ	SD	13,154	NC
Skidmore College	NY	66,600	MC
Sonoma State Univ	CA	27,020	C
S Dak State Univ	SD	15,874	C
Southeast Missouri State Univ	MO	16,148	C
Southeastern Louisiana Univ	LA	16,237	C
Southeastern Okla State Univ	OK	11,875	C
Southeastern Univ	FL	34,910	LC
Southern Adventist Univ	TN	28,250	C
Southern Arkansas Univ	AR	21,532	C
Southern Illinois Univ Carbondale	IL	24,554	C
Southern Illinois Univ Edwardsville	IL	20,188	C
Southern Oregon Univ	OR	19,117	C
Southwest Baptist Univ	MO	30,890	LC
Southwest Minn State Univ	MN	17,783	C
Southwestern Okla State Univ	OK	12,205	C
Southwestern Univ	TX	52,370	VC
Spelman College	GA	41,642	C
Spring Arbor Univ	MI	37,390	C
St. Catherine Univ	MN	45,630	C
St. Edward's Univ	TX	56,190	VC
St. Lawrence Univ	NY	66,646	HC+
St. Mary's College of Maryland	MD	27,312	VC
St. Norbert College	WI	46,060	VC
Stanford Univ	CA	62,541	MC
SUNY at Binghamton	NY	24,100	MC
SUNY at Oswego	NY	22,219	VC
SUNY/Buffalo State	NY	20,583	LC
SUNY/Cortland	NY	20,910	C
SUNY/Oneonta	NY	20,794	C
SUNY/Plattsburgh	NY	19,314	C
SUNY/Potsdam	NY	21,051	VC
Stephen F. Austin State Univ	TX	18,484	LC
Sterling College	KS	32,830	LC
Stillman College	AL	20,738	C
Swarthmore College	PA	63,550	MC
Syracuse Univ	NY	62,313	HC
Tarleton State Univ	TX	15,248	LC
Taylor Univ	IN	42,130	VC
Temple Univ	PA	24,392	C+
Tenn State Univ	TN	14,423	LC
Texas A&M Univ at Corpus Christi	TX	16,851	LC
Texas Lutheran Univ	TX	39,770	C
Texas Southern Univ	TX	19,592	LC
Texas State Univ	TX	18,721	C
Texas Tech Univ	TX	20,156	C+
Texas Woman's Univ	TX	15,302	LC
The American Univ	DC	61,317	HC
The Catholic Univ of America	DC	58,376	VC
The College of Idaho	ID	36,415	C
The College of New Jersey	NJ	28,675	VC+
The Univ of Akron	OH	22,566	C
The Univ of Arizona	AZ	24,086	C
The Univ of Memphis	TN	18,278	C
The Univ of Montana Western	MT	9,426	LC
The Univ of Tenn at Chattanooga	TN	17,340	C+
The Univ of Tenn at Knoxville	TN	22,112	VC
The Univ of Texas at San Antonio	TX	21,060	C
The Univ of Utah	UT	18,751	VC
The Univ of Virginia's College at Wise	VA	18,192	LC
Thomas Edison State Univ	NJ	6,350	NC
Thomas More College	KY	36,720	LC
Tougaloo College	MS	17,980	NC
Towson Univ	MD	21,878	C
Transylvania Univ	KY	47,450	HC+
Trinity Christian College	IL	35,580	C
Trinity Univ	TX	54,480	MC
Troy Univ	AL	16,171	C
Truman State Univ	MO	16,286	MC
Union Univ	TN	41,160	VC
Unity College	ME	37,670	C
Univ of Alabama at Birmingham	AL	22,092	C
Univ of Alabama in Huntsville	AL	20,028	VC
Univ of Alaska Anchorage	AK	17,914	C
Univ of Alaska Fairbanks	AK	16,874	VC
Univ of Alaska Southeast	AK	17,615	C
Univ of Arkansas at Fayetteville	AR	19,766	VC
Univ of Arkansas at Little Rock	AR	18,211	LC
Univ of Arkansas at Monticello	AR	13,599	LC
Univ of Arkansas at Pine Bluff	AR	13,541	C
Univ of Calif at Berkeley	CA	29,886	MC
Univ of Calif at Los Angeles	CA	27,438	HC+
Univ of Calif at Riverside	CA	32,912	C
Univ of Calif at Santa Barbara	CA	30,627	HC+
Univ of Calif San Diego	CA	30,450	MC
Univ of Calif, Santa Cruz	CA	28,731	C+
Univ of Central Florida	FL	16,379	VC
Univ of Central Okla	OK	15,150	C
Univ of Charleston	WV	35,000	LC
Univ of Conn	CT	27,394	
Univ of Dayton	OH	54,930	VC
Univ of Delaware	DE	32,214	VC
Univ of Denver	CO	61,129	VC+
Univ of Evansville	IN	44,186	C+
Univ of Findlay	OH	43,040	C
Univ of Florida	FL	16,291	HC+
Univ of Georgia	GA	21,878	HC
Univ of Great Falls	MT	38,524	C
Univ of Hawaii at Hilo	HI	18,038	VC
Univ of Hawaii at Manoa	HI	23,261	C
Univ of Houston	TX	21,871	VC
Univ of Idaho	ID	16,158	C
Univ of Indianapolis	IN	36,480	VC
Univ of Iowa	IA	19,415	HC
Univ of Kansas	KS	20,884	VC
Univ of La Verne	CA	55,600	C
Univ of Louisiana at Monroe	LA	15,970	C
Univ of Louisville	KY	19,692	C
Univ of Lynchburg	VA	48,370	C
Univ of Maine at Augusta	ME	7,812	C
Univ of Maine at Farmington	ME	18,792	C
Univ of Maine at Presque Isle	ME	16,148	LC
Univ of Mary Hardin-Baylor	TX	35,292	C+
Univ of Maryland/Baltimore County	MD	23,004	VC
Univ of Mass Boston	MA	13,828	C
Univ of Mass Lowell	MA	27,296	VC
Univ of Miami	FL	63,494	MC
Univ of Mich/Ann Arbor	MI	25,274	MC
Univ of Mich/Flint	MI	19,062	C
Univ of Minn/Duluth	MN	20,292	C
Univ of Minn/Twin Cities	MN	24,269	MC
Univ of Miss	MS	18,802	C
Univ of Missouri-Columbia	MO	20,463	VC
Univ of Mobile	AL	28,935	C
Univ of Montevallo	AL	20,012	C
Univ of Mount Olive	NC	18,426	C
Univ of Mount Union	OH	39,990	C
Univ of Nebr - Lincoln	NE	18,589	VC
Univ of Nebr - Omaha	NE	16,120	C
Univ of Nevada, Reno	NV	18,010	C
Univ of New Haven	CT	53,680	C
Univ of New Mexico	NM	16,808	C
Univ of New Orleans	LA	12,840	C
Univ of North Alabama	AL	15,964	C
Univ of N Car at Asheville	NC	16,251	VC+
Univ of N Car at Charlotte	NC	17,803	VC
Univ of N Car at Greensboro	NC	15,998	C
Univ of N Car at Pembroke	NC	14,737	LC
Univ of North Florida	FL	15,996	VC
Univ of North Georgia	GA	17,316	C
Univ of North Texas	TX	20,082	C
Univ of Northern Colo	CO	19,658	C
Univ of Northwestern - St. Paul	MN	39,530	C
Univ of Okla	OK	19,651	HC
Univ of Oregon	OR	24,021	VC
Univ of Pikeville	KY	27,838	C
Univ of Puget Sound	WA	60,210	HC
Univ of Redlands	CA	61,934	VC
Univ of Rhode Island	RI	26,066	VC
Univ of Rio Grande & Rio Grande Community College	OH	8,750	LC
Univ of St. Mary	KS	37,080	NC
Univ of Science and Arts of Okla	OK	11,140	VC
Univ of S Dak	SD	16,109	C
Univ of Southern Indiana	IN	16,808	C
Univ of Tampa	FL	38,928	VC
Univ of Texas at El Paso	TX	34,452	NC
Univ of Texas Rio Grande Valley	TX	15,573	LC
Univ of the Cumberlands	KY	32,000	LC
Univ of the Incarnate Word	TX	39,162	LC
Univ of the Ozarks	AR	31,050	NC
Univ of the Pacific	CA	57,446	VC
Univ of Tulsa	OK	52,625	HC
Univ of Vermont	VT	29,792	HC
Univ of Virginia	VA	27,367	MC
Univ of West Georgia	GA	17,510	LC
Univ of Wisc-Eau Claire	WI	16,354	VC
Univ of Wisc-Green Bay	WI	15,184	C
Univ of Wisc-La Crosse	WI	15,425	VC
Univ of Wisc-Madison	WI	21,647	MC
Univ of Wisc-Milwaukee	WI	21,538	C
Univ of Wisc-Oshkosh	WI	15,392	C
Univ of Wisc-Parkside	WI	15,313	C
Univ of Wisc-Platteville	WI	14,148	C
Univ of Wisc-River Falls	WI	14,541	C
Univ of Wisc-Stevens Point	WI	14,043	C
Univ of Wisc-Stout	WI	19,667	C
Univ of Wisc-Superior	WI	14,838	C
Univ of Wyoming	WY	15,537	C
Upper Iowa Univ	IA	34,990	NC
Ursinus College	PA	62,920	VC
Ursuline College	OH	41,076	LC
Valley City State Univ	ND	13,267	C
Valparaiso Univ	IN	50,160	VC
Vanderbilt Univ	TN	63,248	MC
Vassar College	NY	68,110	MC
Virginia Polytechnic Inst and State Univ	VA	21,920	VC
Virginia Wesleyan Univ	VA	45,980	LC
Viterbo Univ	WI	34,660	C
Wabash College	IN	52,100	VC
Wake Forest Univ	NC	69,354	MC
Walla Walla Univ	WA	34,845	C
Warren Wilson College	NC	44,220	VC
Wartburg College	IA	49,478	C
Washburn Univ	KS	15,827	C
Washington College	MD	56,154	VC
Washington State Univ	WA	22,747	C
Wayland Baptist Univ	TX	23,460	LC
Wayne State College	NE	25,746	NC
Wayne State Univ	MI	23,085	C
Waynesburg Univ	PA	33,530	C
Weber State Univ	UT	14,112	C
Webster Univ	MO	37,490	C
Wellesley College	MA	66,984	MC
West Chester Univ of Pennsylvania	PA	19,171	VC
West Texas A&M Univ	TX	13,478	C
West Virginia Univ	WV	18,952	VC
Western Carolina Univ	NC	13,965	C
Western Conn State Univ	CT	21,254	LC
Western Illinois Univ	IL	20,897	C
Western Mich Univ	MI	21,791	C
Western Oregon Univ	OR	19,965	LC
Western State Colo Univ	CO	19,348	C
Western Washington Univ	WA	18,904	VC
Westfield State Univ	MA	20,404	C
Westminster College	PA	41,722	C
Westminster College	UT	41,078	C
Westmont College	CA	57,930	VC
Wheaton College	IL	44,993	MC
Wheaton College	MA	63,818	VC
Whitman College	WA	59,772	MC
Whittier College	CA	57,891	C
Whitworth Univ	WA	53,682	VC
Wichita State Univ	KS	17,773	C
Widener Univ	PA	58,190	C
William Carey Univ	MS	23,950	LC
William Jewell College	MO	42,490	C+
William Woods Univ	MO	32,040	C
Williams Baptist College	AR	24,720	C
Williams College	MA	67,700	MC
Wilmington College	OH	35,100	C
Wilson College	PA	35,620	LC
Winston-Salem State Univ	NC	18,005	LC
Winthrop Univ	SC	23,960	C
Wisc Lutheran College	WI	36,290	C
Wittenberg Univ	OH	49,863	VC
Wright State Univ	OH	16,983	C
Xavier Univ	OH	49,380	VC
Yale Univ	CT	64,650	MC
Youngstown State Univ	OH	17,487	C

ART AND DESIGN

School	ST	$IS	SR
Appalachian State Univ	NC	15,394	VC
Barton College	NC	39,854	C
Calif Polytechnic State Univ	CA	22,547	MC
Calvin College	MI	43,090	HC
DePaul Univ	IL	52,807	VC
Doane Univ	NE	41,340	VC
East Stroudsburg Univ	PA	18,578	LC
Frostburg State Univ	MD	17,280	LC
Judson Univ	IL	39,174	C
Missouri Southern State Univ	MO	13,071	C
Mount Ida College	MA	46,820	C
Northern Mich Univ	MI	20,853	C
Point Loma Nazarene Univ	CA	46,150	C+
Regis Univ	CO	46,380	C
Rochester Inst of Technology	NY	52,734	HC+
Seton Hill Univ	PA	46,972	VC
Sterling College	KS	32,830	LC
Stevenson Univ	MD	48,412	C
Taylor Univ	IN	42,130	VC
Tusculum College	TN	31,625	LC
Univ of Dayton	OH	54,930	VC
Univ of Maryland/Baltimore County	MD	23,004	VC
Univ of New England	ME	50,110	C
Univ of Northwestern - St. Paul	MN	39,530	C
Univ of San Diego	CA	60,338	HC
Univ of St. Francis	IL	40,828	C

ART EDUCATION

School	ST	$IS	SR
Adams State Univ	CO	15,420	LC
Adelphi Univ	NY	49,792	C
Alabama A&M Univ	AL	18,796	C
Alabama State Univ	AL	16,490	LC
Alfred Univ	NY	37,490	C
Alverno College	WI	33,294	LC
Andrews Univ	MI	41,732	C
Appalachian State Univ	NC	15,394	VC
Arkansas Tech Univ	AR	16,534	LC
Armstrong State Univ	GA	15,615	C
Asbury Univ	KY	36,450	C+
Ashland Univ	OH	30,446	C
Augustana College	IL	51,222	VC+
Averett Univ	VA	43,034	LC
Azusa Pacific Univ	CA	43,972	C

ST = STATE $IS = IN-STATE COSTS   SR = SELECTOR RATING

School	ST	$IS	SR
Baldwin Wallace Univ	OH	42,464	VC
Baylor Univ	TX	56,803	HC
Belmont Univ	TN	44,500	VC+
Beloit College	WI	55,206	HC
Bemidji State Univ	MN	17,730	C
Berry College	GA	47,466	VC
Bethany College	KS	38,637	LC
Bethany College	WV	38,774	LC
Bethel College	IN	36,830	C
Boise State Univ	ID	17,368	C
Boston Univ	MA	67,352	MC
Bowling Green State Univ	OH	19,975	C
Bradley Univ	IL	43,240	VC
Brenau Univ - Women's College	GA	37,876	LC
Brescia Univ	KY	29,890	VC
Bridgewater State Univ	MA	22,762	C
Brigham Young Univ	UT	13,248	MC
Brigham Young Univ/Hawaii	HI	11,710	C
Buena Vista Univ	IA	42,344	C
Cal State, Chico	CA	19,790	VC
Calvin College	MI	43,090	HC
Capital Univ	OH	44,778	VC
Carlow Univ	PA	39,696	LC
Carroll Univ	WI	38,100	C+
Carson-Newman Univ	TN	35,900	C
Case Western Reserve Univ	OH	62,284	MC
Central Conn State Univ	CT	22,041	C
Central State Univ	OH	18,564	C
Central Washington Univ	WA	16,803	C
Chicago State Univ	IL	41,620	C
CUNY/Brooklyn College	NY	7,163	C+
CUNY/City College	NY	20,204	C
CUNY/Hunter College	NY	31,098	VC
CUNY/Lehman College	NY	5,788	LC
CUNY/Queens College	NY	21,507	C
Claflin Univ	SC	25,592	LC
Clarke Univ	IA	42,950	C
Clayton State Univ	GA	19,735	LC
Coker College	SC	38,196	C
College for Creative Studies	MI	51,210	SP
College of the Ozarks	MO	7,530	VC
Colo State Univ	CO	23,033	C
Columbus State Univ	GA	14,336	LC
Concord Univ	WV	14,954	LC
Concordia College - Moorhead	MN	46,418	C
Concordia College - New York	NY	39,035	LC
Concordia Univ St. Paul	MN	29,050	C
Converse College	SC	28,290	C
Culver-Stockton College	MO	34,350	C
Daemen College	NY	40,336	C
Defiance College	OH	42,240	LC
Delaware State Univ	DE	19,376	LC
DePaul Univ	IL	52,807	VC
Dickinson State Univ	ND	12,372	LC
Dordt College	IA	37,860	C+
East Carolina Univ	NC	16,539	C
East Central Univ	OK	13,330	C
Eastern Kentucky Univ	KY	17,742	C
Eastern Mich Univ	MI	19,761	C
Eastern Washington Univ	WA	17,896	LC
Edgewood College	WI	35,950	C
Edinboro Univ	PA	15,940	LC
Elizabethtown College	PA	56,340	VC
Elmhurst College	IL	46,514	C
Elmira College	NY	53,900	C
Emporia State Univ	KS	15,029	C
Escuela de Artes Plasticas de PR	PR	11,236	
Fairmont State Univ	WV	15,726	C
Ferris State Univ	MI	21,458	C
Fisk Univ	TN	32,066	LC
Flagler College	FL	27,620	C
Florida A&M Univ	FL	15,361	C
Florida International Univ	FL	20,281	C
Florida Southern College	FL	45,978	VC
Florida State Univ	FL	16,771	HC
Fort Hays State Univ	KS	12,677	C
Francis Marion Univ	SC	18,144	LC
Freed-Hardeman Univ	TN	29,900	C
Friends Univ	KS	38,000	C
Georgia State Univ	GA	25,250	C
Goddard College	VT	17,040	VC
Goshen College	IN	44,350	C
Grace College and Seminary	IN	31,524	C
Grand Valley State Univ	MI	22,250	C+
Grand View Univ	IA	32,302	C
Green Mountain College	VT	45,228	LC
Greensboro College	NC	39,790	LC
Gustavus Adolphus College	MN	53,943	HC
Hardin-Simmons Univ	TX	36,025	C
Hastings College	NE	35,380	C+
Henderson State Univ	AR	15,516	C
Heritage Univ	WA	19,825	NC
Hofstra Univ	NY	58,210	C+
Hope College	MI	42,840	VC
Houston Baptist Univ	TX	36,450	C
Howard Univ	DC	37,616	C+
Huntington Univ	IN	33,996	C
Indiana State Univ	IN	23,223	LC
Indiana Univ of Pennsylvania	PA	24,474	C
Indiana Univ South Bend	IN	16,057	C
Indiana Univ-Purdue Univ Fort Wayne	IN	18,675	C
Indiana Univ-Purdue Univ Indianapolis	IN	18,952	C
Indiana Wesleyan Univ	IN	33,674	C

School	ST	$IS	SR
Inter-American Univ of PR-San Germán	PR	20,042	
Ithaca College	NY	58,158	VC+
Jacksonville Univ	FL	49,210	C
Johnson State College	VT	22,672	C
Kansas State Univ	KS	17,780	VC
Kansas Wesleyan Univ	KS	37,930	C
Kennesaw State Univ	GA	18,899	VC
Kent State Univ	OH	20,928	C
Kentucky State Univ	KY	14,484	LC
Kentucky Wesleyan College	KY	34,260	LC
Keystone College	PA	28,680	LC
Kutztown Univ of Pennsylvania	PA	19,477	C
Lamar Univ	TX	18,014	LC
Lincoln Univ	MO	14,402	NC
Lindsey Wilson College	KY	33,546	C
Lipscomb Univ	TN	42,984	VC
LIU Brooklyn	NY	50,698	C
LIU Post	NY	50,698	C+
Longwood Univ	VA	22,184	C
Louisiana College	LA	21,274	C
Louisiana Tech Univ	LA	11,422	VC
Lubbock Christian Univ	TX	29,727	C
Madonna Univ	MI	30,450	LC
Manchester Univ	IN	41,540	C
Marian Univ	WI	34,622	C
Mars Hill Univ	NC	41,104	C
Marymount Univ	VA	43,231	C
Maryville Univ of St. Louis	MO	38,558	VC
Marywood Univ	PA	47,840	C
Mass College of Art and Design	MA	24,800	SP
McKendree Univ	IL	37,940	C+
McMurry Univ	TX	34,259	LC
Mercyhurst Univ	PA	47,420	C
Messiah College	PA	44,380	VC
Methodist Univ	NC	58,130	C
Miami Univ	OH	27,190	HC+
Mich State Univ	MI	24,542	VC
Middle Tenn State Univ	TN	8,650	C
Midland Univ	NE	39,512	C
Millersville Univ of Pennsylvania	PA	25,298	C
Millikin Univ	IL	44,148	C
Minn State Univ, Mankato	MN	17,190	C
Minn State Univ, Moorhead	MN	21,393	C
Miss College	MS	25,850	C
Miss Univ for Women	MS	17,065	C
Missouri Western State Univ	MO	17,822	LC
Monmouth Univ	NJ	50,184	C
Montana State Univ Billings	MT	13,336	LC
Montserrat College of Art	MA	41,500	SP
Moore College of Art and Design	PA	55,118	SP
Moravian College	PA	55,488	C
Morningside College	IA	39,780	C
Mount Mary Univ	WI	34,650	LC
Mount St. Joseph Univ	OH	33,880	LC
Murray State Univ	KY	17,726	C+
Nazareth College	NY	46,784	C
New Jersey City Univ	NJ	21,456	LC
New York Univ	NY	68,139	MC
N Car A&T State Univ	NC	13,786	C
North Central College	IL	48,712	C+
Northeastern State Univ	OK	8,615	VC
Northern Arizona Univ	AZ	21,003	C
Northern Illinois Univ	IL	20,176	C
Northern Mich Univ	MI	20,853	C
Northern State Univ	SD	15,570	C
Northwest Missouri State Univ	MO	18,286	C
Northwest Nazarene Univ	ID	40,250	C
Northwestern College of Iowa	IA	38,400	C
Notre Dame of Maryland Univ	MD	47,570	VC
Oakland City Univ	IN	33,930	NC
Ohio State Univ at Columbus	OH	22,843	MC
Ohio Wesleyan Univ	OH	49,460	VC
Old Dominion Univ	VA	21,618	C
Olivet Nazarene Univ	IL	41,840	VC
Oral Roberts Univ	OK	34,316	C
Ouachita Baptist Univ	AR	33,500	VC
Our Lady of the Lake Univ	TX	37,790	LC
Palm Beach Atlantic Univ	FL	39,250	C
Pennsylvania State Univ - Univ Park	PA	29,716	HC
Peru State College	NE	15,602	LC
Piedmont College	GA	34,334	C
Plymouth State Univ	NH	23,180	LC
Point Loma Nazarene Univ	CA	46,150	C+
Pontifical Catholic Univ of PR	PR	10,534	
Pratt Inst	NY	59,482	VC+
Prescott College	AZ	38,201	C
Purdue Univ/West Lafayette	IN	20,032	MC
Rhode Island College	RI	19,000	LC
Rivier Univ	NH	41,600	VC
Rocky Mountain College	MT	35,776	C
Rocky Mountain College of Art and Design	CO	27,052	SP
Rosemont College	PA	30,980	LC
Rowan Univ	NJ	24,491	VC
Saginaw Valley State Univ	MI	19,284	C
St. Anselm College	NH	56,636	VC
St. Joseph's Univ	PA	58,540	VC
St. Mary-of-the-Woods College	IN	40,424	LC
St. Michael's College	VT	53,275	VC+

School	ST	$IS	SR
St. Vincent College	PA	46,229	C
St. Xavier Univ	IL	44,440	C
Salem State Univ	MA	42,650	LC
School of the Art Inst of Chicago	IL	61,830	SP
Seton Hill Univ	PA	46,972	VC
Shawnee State Univ	OH	16,998	C
Shepherd Univ, West Virginia	WV	17,382	C
Shippensburg Univ of Pennsylvania	PA	24,096	C
Siena Heights Univ	MI	36,322	C
Silver Lake College of the Holy Family	WI	36,290	LC
S Car State Univ	SC	21,330	LC
S Dak State Univ	SD	15,874	C
Southeast Missouri State Univ	MO	16,148	C
Southeastern Okla State Univ	OK	11,875	C
Southern Arkansas Univ	AR	21,532	C
Southern Conn State Univ	CT	21,924	LC
Southern Illinois Univ Edwardsville	IL	20,188	C
Southern Univ and A&M College	LA	16,074	LC
Southern Univ at New Orleans	LA	8,014	LC
Southwest Baptist Univ	MO	30,890	LC
Southwest Minn State Univ	MN	17,783	C
Southwestern Okla State Univ	OK	12,205	C
Spelman College	GA	41,642	C
St. Ambrose Univ	IA	40,180	C
St. Catherine Univ	MN	45,630	C
St. Cloud State Univ	MN	10,600	C
St. Edward's Univ	TX	56,190	VC
St. Thomas Aquinas College	NY	32,450	C
SUNY at New Paltz	NY	20,840	C
SUNY/Buffalo State	NY	20,583	LC
SUNY/Potsdam	NY	21,051	VC
Sul Ross State Univ	TX	15,021	LC
Syracuse Univ	NY	62,313	HC
Tarleton State Univ	TX	15,248	LC
Taylor Univ	IN	42,130	VC
Temple Univ	PA	24,392	C+
Tenn Tech Univ	TN	17,929	C
Texas Christian Univ	TX	57,120	HC
The Catholic Univ of America	DC	58,376	VC
The College of New Jersey	NJ	28,675	VC+
The College of New Rochelle	NY	46,300	LC
The Univ of Akron	OH	22,566	C
The Univ of Arizona	AZ	24,086	C
The Univ of Montana Western	MT	9,426	LC
The Univ of Tenn at Chattanooga	TN	17,340	C+
The Univ of Utah	UT	18,751	VC
Thomas More College	KY	36,720	LC
Tougaloo College	MS	17,980	NC
Towson Univ	MD	21,878	C
Trinity Christian College	IL	35,580	C
Troy Univ	AL	16,171	C
Union College	NE	23,270	C
Univ of Arkansas at Pine Bluff	AR	13,541	C
Univ of Central Arkansas	AR	15,042	VC
Univ of Central Florida	FL	16,379	VC
Univ of Central Missouri	MO	18,982	C
Univ of Central Okla	OK	15,150	C
Univ of Cincinnati	OH	22,118	VC
Univ of Dallas	TX	50,676	VC
Univ of Dayton	OH	54,930	VC
Univ of Evansville	IN	44,186	C+
Univ of Findlay	OH	43,040	C
Univ of Florida	FL	16,291	HC+
Univ of Georgia	GA	21,878	HC
Univ of Idaho	ID	16,158	C
Univ of Illinois at Chicago	IL	24,664	VC
Univ of Illinois at Urbana-Champaign	IL	27,006	HC
Univ of Indianapolis	IN	36,480	VC
Univ of Iowa	IA	19,415	HC
Univ of Kansas	KS	20,884	VC
Univ of Kentucky	KY	24,800	C+
Univ of Louisiana at Lafayette	LA	14,516	C
Univ of Louisville	KY	19,692	C
Univ of Maine	ME	21,038	VC
Univ of Maine at Presque Isle	ME	16,148	LC
Univ of Mary Hardin-Baylor	TX	35,292	C+
Univ of Maryland/Baltimore County	MD	23,004	VC
Univ of Maryland/College Park	MD	21,938	HC
Univ of Maryland/Eastern Shore	MD	21,861	LC
Univ of Mass Dartmouth	MA	26,507	C
Univ of Minn/Duluth	MN	20,292	C
Univ of Missouri-Columbia	MO	20,463	VC
Univ of Montevallo	AL	20,012	C
Univ of Nebr - Kearney	NE	17,014	LC
Univ of New England	ME	50,110	C
Univ of New Mexico	NM	16,808	C
Univ of North Alabama	AL	15,964	C
Univ of N Car at Greensboro	NC	15,998	C
Univ of North Florida	FL	15,996	VC
Univ of North Georgia	GA	17,316	C
Univ of Northern Iowa	IA	17,480	C
Univ of Northwestern - St. Paul	MN	39,530	C

School	ST	$IS	SR
Univ of Rio Grande & Rio Grande Community College	OH	8,750	LC
Univ of St. Francis	IN	38,520	C
Univ of San Francisco	CA	60,580	C
Univ of Sioux Falls	SD	25,630	C
Univ of S Car at Columbia	SC	21,726	VC
Univ of S Car Upstate	SC	19,272	LC
Univ of S Dak	SD	16,109	C
Univ of South Florida/Tampa	FL	16,110	VC
Univ of Southern Miss	MS	13,170	C
Univ of St. Francis	IL	40,828	C
Univ of the Cumberlands	KY	32,000	LC
Univ of the Incarnate Word	TX	39,162	LC
Univ of Toledo	OH	19,336	C
Univ of Vermont	VT	29,792	HC
Univ of West Florida	FL	15,848	C
Univ of Wisc-Green Bay	WI	15,184	C
Univ of Wisc-Madison	WI	21,647	MC
Univ of Wisc-Milwaukee	WI	21,538	C
Univ of Wisc-Oshkosh	WI	15,392	C
Univ of Wisc-Platteville	WI	14,148	C
Univ of Wisc-River Falls	WI	14,541	C
Univ of Wisc-Stout	WI	19,667	C
Univ of Wisc-Superior	WI	14,838	C
Univ of Wisc-Whitewater	WI	13,976	C
Utah State Univ	UT	13,235	C
Valparaiso Univ	IN	50,160	VC
Virginia Commonwealth Univ	VA	23,811	VC
Virginia Union Univ	VA	25,058	C
Virginia Wesleyan Univ	VA	45,980	LC
Viterbo Univ	WI	34,660	C
Wartburg College	IA	49,478	C
Washburn Univ	KS	15,827	C
Washington & Jefferson College	PA	58,694	VC
Washington Univ in St. Louis	MO	67,539	MC
Weber State Univ	UT	14,112	C
Webster Univ	MO	37,490	C
West Liberty Univ	WV	16,158	C
West Texas A&M Univ	TX	13,478	C
West Virginia State Univ	WV	19,412	LC
West Virginia Univ	WV	18,952	VC
West Virginia Wesleyan College	WV	39,188	C
Western Carolina Univ	NC	13,965	C
Western Illinois Univ	IL	20,897	C
Western Kentucky Univ	KY	16,850	C
Western Mich Univ	MI	21,791	C
Western New Mexico Univ	NM	16,914	LC
Western State Colo Univ	CO	19,348	C
Western Washington Univ	WA	18,904	VC
Westmont College	CA	57,930	VC
Wichita State Univ	KS	17,773	C
Winona State Univ	MN	18,109	C
Wright State Univ	OH	16,983	C
Xavier Univ of Louisiana	LA	31,689	C
Youngstown State Univ	OH	17,487	C

ART HISTORY

School	ST	$IS	SR
Amherst College	MA	66,186	MC
Aquinas College - Mich	MI	38,876	VC
Auburn Univ	AL	24,300	VC+
Austin College	TX	51,059	HC
Baylor Univ	TX	56,803	HC
Belmont Univ	TN	44,500	VC+
Beloit College	WI	55,206	HC
Bloomsburg Univ of Pennsylvania	PA	19,930	C
Bowdoin College	ME	65,980	MC
Bowling Green State Univ	OH	19,975	C
Brandeis Univ	MA	68,443	MC
Brown Univ	RI	64,566	MC
Cal State, Fullerton	CA	21,902	C
Cal State, Long Beach	CA	18,850	C
Canisius College	NY	49,672	C
Case Western Reserve Univ	OH	62,284	MC
Chapman Univ	CA	65,504	HC
CUNY/Queens College	NY	21,507	C
Colby College	ME	64,060	MC
College of Charleston	SC	24,046	VC
College of William & Mary	VA	34,907	MC
Columbia College Chicago	IL	40,104	C
Cornell Univ	NY	67,591	MC
Creighton Univ	NE	49,452	VC
DePaul Univ	IL	52,807	VC
Dickinson College	PA	66,166	MC
Dominican Univ	IL	42,472	C+
Dordt College	IA	37,860	C+
Drexel Univ	PA	65,927	HC
Elon Univ	NC	46,142	HC
Fairfield Univ	CT	61,445	HC
Ferris State Univ	MI	21,458	C
Flagler College	FL	27,620	C
Florida International Univ	FL	20,281	C
Fordham Univ	NY	68,431	MC
Franklin College	IN	40,550	C
Furman Univ	SC	61,098	VC+
Georgetown Univ	DC	68,970	MC
Goucher College	MD	56,110	VC
Hamline Univ	MN	50,152	C
Hiram College	OH	44,590	C
Hobart and William Smith Colleges	NY	67,050	HC+
Indiana Univ Bloomington	IN	20,791	HC
Indiana Univ-Purdue Univ Indianapolis	IN	18,952	C

ST = STATE $IS = IN-STATE COSTS SR = SELECTOR RATING

School	ST	$IS	SR
Ithaca College	NY	58,158	VC+
John Carroll Univ	OH	51,570	C
Kennesaw State Univ	GA	18,899	VC
Kenyon College	OH	65,840	MC
Kutztown Univ of Pennsylvania	PA	19,477	C
Loyola Marymount Univ	CA	60,202	VC+
Loyola Univ Chicago	IL	57,158	VC
McDaniel College	MD	52,910	VC
Merrimack College	MA	55,415	C
Mills College	CA	43,705	C
Missouri State Univ	MO	15,837	C+
Moore College of Art and Design	PA	55,118	SP
Mount St. Joseph Univ	OH	33,880	LC
Murray State Univ	KY	17,726	C+
Nazareth College	NY	46,784	C
New York Univ	NY	68,139	MC
Niagara Univ	NY	41,010	C
North Central College	IL	48,712	C+
Northeastern Illinois Univ	IL	12,529	LC
Oberlin College	OH	68,942	MC
Occidental College	CA	68,660	MC
Ohio Univ	OH	23,394	VC
Ohio Wesleyan Univ	OH	49,460	VC
Pace Univ	NY	60,136	C
Pacific Lutheran Univ	WA	49,960	C
Plymouth State Univ	NH	23,180	LC
Point Loma Nazarene Univ	CA	46,150	C+
Providence College	RI	62,870	HC
Regis Univ	CO	46,380	C
St. Louis Univ	MO	49,866	HC
San Diego State Univ	CA	23,156	VC
San Jose State Univ	CA	22,630	C
Sarah Lawrence College	NY	68,866	MC
Seattle Univ	WA	54,957	VC
Seton Hall Univ	NJ	58,008	C
Sewanee: The Univ of the South	TN	58,000	HC+
Southern Oregon Univ	OR	19,117	C
Southwestern Univ	TX	52,370	VC
St. Ambrose Univ	IA	40,180	C
St. Bonaventure Univ	NY	45,596	C
St. Lawrence Univ	NY	66,646	HC+
SUNY at Binghamton	NY	24,100	MC
SUNY/Potsdam	NY	21,051	VC
Stetson Univ	FL	57,174	VC+
Stony Brook Univ/The SUNY	NY	22,703	MC
Syracuse Univ	NY	62,313	HC
Texas Christian Univ	TX	57,120	HC
The Catholic Univ of America	DC	58,376	VC
The Univ of Arizona	AZ	24,086	C
The Univ of Tenn at Knoxville	TN	22,112	VC
The Univ of Utah	UT	18,751	VC
Transylvania Univ	KY	47,450	HC+
Trinity Univ	TX	54,480	MC
Tufts Univ	MA		MC
Univ of Calif at Irvine	CA	33,857	VC
Univ of Calif at Riverside	CA	32,912	C
Univ of Calif San Diego	CA	30,450	MC
Univ of Central Okla	OK	15,150	C
Univ of Cincinnati	OH	22,118	VC
Univ of Colo Boulder	CO	26,048	HC
Univ of Dayton	OH	54,930	VC
Univ of Denver	CO	61,129	VC+
Univ of Evansville	IN	44,186	C+
Univ of Georgia	GA	21,878	HC
Univ of Illinois at Chicago	IL	24,664	VC
Univ of Kansas	KS	20,884	VC
Univ of Louisville	KY	19,692	C
Univ of Maine	ME	21,038	VC
Univ of Maryland/Baltimore County	MD	23,004	VC
Univ of Miami	FL	63,494	MC
Univ of Mich/Dearborn	MI	12,472	VC
Univ of Nebr - Lincoln	NE	18,589	VC
Univ of Nevada, Reno	NV	18,010	C
Univ of New Hampshire	NH	29,333	VC
Univ of New Mexico	NM	16,808	C
Univ of N Car at Greensboro	NC	15,998	C
Univ of N Car Wilmington	NC	16,784	VC
Univ of Northern Iowa	IA	17,480	C
Univ of Notre Dame	IN	68,801	MC
Univ of Okla	OK	19,651	HC
Univ of Rhode Island	RI	26,066	VC
Univ of Richmond	VA	62,730	MC
Univ of St. Francis	IN	38,520	C
Univ of San Diego	CA	60,338	HC
Univ of Tulsa	OK	52,625	HC
Univ of Wisc-Milwaukee	WI	21,538	C
Univ of Wisc-Superior	WI	14,838	C
Ursinus College	PA	62,920	VC
Vanderbilt Univ	TN	63,248	MC
Vassar College	NY	68,110	MC
Wake Forest Univ	NC	69,354	MC
Walsh Univ	OH	39,010	C
Webster Univ	MO	37,490	C
Wellesley College	MA	66,984	MC
Western Kentucky Univ	KY	16,850	C
Western Mich Univ	MI	21,791	C
Wheaton College	MA	63,818	VC
Whitman College	WA	59,772	MC
Wofford College	SC	49,885	VC
Wright State Univ	OH	16,983	C
Yale Univ	CT	64,650	MC
Youngstown State Univ	OH	17,487	C

ART HISTORY AND APPRECIATION

School	ST	$IS	SR
Adams State Univ	CO	15,420	LC
Adelphi Univ	NY	49,792	C
Agnes Scott College	GA	51,930	VC+
Albertus Magnus College	CT	44,016	LC
Albion College	MI	55,260	C
Alfred Univ	NY	37,490	C
Allegheny College	PA	57,620	VC
Aquinas College - Mich	MI	38,876	VC
Arcadia Univ	PA	55,990	C+
Art Academy of Cincinnati	OH	37,790	SP
Augsburg Univ	MN	45,129	C
Augustana College	IL	51,222	VC+
Bard College	NY	65,924	HC
Bard College at Simon's Rock	MA	65,795	MC
Barnard College/Columbia Univ	NY	68,762	MC
Baylor Univ	TX	56,803	HC
Berry College	GA	47,466	VC
Birmingham-Southern College	AL	44,478	C+
Boston College	MA	68,043	MC
Boston Univ	MA	67,352	MC
Bradley Univ	IL	43,240	VC
Bridgewater State Univ	MA	22,762	C
Brigham Young Univ	UT	13,248	MC
Brown Univ	RI	64,566	MC
Bryn Mawr College	PA	65,220	MC
Bucknell Univ	PA	67,136	MC
Calif State Polytechnic Univ, Pomona	CA	21,811	C
Cal State, San Bernardino	CA	20,106	C
Cal State, Stanislaus	CA	18,053	LC
Carleton College	MN	66,414	MC
Carlow Univ	PA	39,696	LC
Centre College	KY	50,680	MC
Chatham Univ	PA	47,883	VC
CUNY/Brooklyn College	NY	7,163	C+
CUNY/York College	NY	6,747	LC
Clark Univ	MA	53,260	HC+
Clarke Univ	IA	42,950	C
Coe College	IA	51,570	VC
Colgate Univ	NY	67,500	MC
College of the Holy Cross	MA	64,320	MC
Colo College	CO	64,894	MC
Colo State Univ	CO	23,033	C
Columbia Univ/ School of General Studies	NY	61,470	MC
Columbia Univ/City of New York	NY	62,958	MC
Columbus State Univ	GA	14,336	LC
Conn College	CT	65,000	MC
Cornell College	IA	49,900	VC
Dartmouth College	NH	68,109	MC
Denison Univ	OH	62,770	HC+
DePauw Univ	IN	58,688	VC
Dominican Univ of Calif	CA	58,750	C
Drake Univ	IA	49,220	HC
Drew Univ/College of Liberal Arts	NJ	53,608	VC
Drury Univ	MO	37,555	VC
Duke Univ	NC	68,298	MC
Duquesne Univ	PA	48,508	VC
East Carolina Univ	NC	16,539	C
Eastern Mich Univ	MI	19,761	C
Eastern Washington Univ	WA	17,896	LC
Edinboro Univ	PA	15,940	LC
Elizabethtown College	PA	56,340	VC
Emory Univ	GA	63,286	MC
Ferris State Univ	MI	21,458	C
Florida International Univ	FL	20,281	C
Florida Southern College	FL	45,978	VC
Florida State Univ	FL	16,771	HC
Framingham State Univ	MA	21,740	C
Franklin and Marshall College	PA	67,960	MC
George Mason Univ	VA	19,884	C
Georgia State Univ	GA	25,250	C
Gettysburg College	PA	65,210	MC
Grand Valley State Univ	MI	22,250	C+
Grinnell College	IA	63,114	MC
Hamilton College	NY	64,250	MC
Hampshire College	MA	65,214	MC
Hanover College	IN	47,750	C+
Hartwick College	NY	51,270	C
Harvard College/Harvard Univ	MA	65,609	MC
Haverford College	PA	66,490	MC
Hofstra Univ	NY	58,210	C+
Hollins Univ	VA	49,635	VC
Hope College	MI	42,840	VC
Howard Univ	DC	37,616	C+
Indiana State Univ	IN	23,223	LC
Ithaca College	NY	58,158	VC+
Jacksonville Univ	FL	49,210	C
James Madison Univ	VA	19,084	VC
John Carroll Univ	OH	51,570	C
Johns Hopkins Univ	MD	68,080	MC
Juniata College	PA	58,118	VC
Kalamazoo College	MI	53,931	HC
Kansas City Art Inst	MO	48,200	SP
Kent State Univ	OH	20,928	C
Knox College	IL	54,654	VC+
Lawrence Univ	WI	56,133	HC+
Lehigh Univ	PA	63,860	MC
Lewis & Clark College	OR	60,984	MC
Lindenwood Univ	MO	25,760	C
LIU Post	NY	50,698	C+
Lourdes Univ	OH	29,140	NC
Lycoming College	PA	50,895	C
Malone Univ	OH	39,200	C
Manhattanville College	NY	52,430	C
Mansfield Univ of Pennsylvania	PA	24,244	LC
Marlboro College	VT	50,832	VC+
Mars Hill Univ	NC	41,104	C
Maryland Inst College of Art	MD	58,740	SP
Maryville College	TN	44,410	C
Mass College of Art and Design	MA	24,800	SP
Messiah College	PA	44,380	VC
Miami Univ	OH	27,190	HC+
Mich State Univ	MI	24,542	VC
Millsaps College	MS	50,080	C+
Monmouth Univ	NJ	50,184	C
Moravian College	PA	55,488	C
Mount Holyoke College	MA	56,746	MC
New College of Florida	FL	16,180	HC+
New England College	NH	50,828	NC
New York Univ	NY	68,139	MC
Northern Illinois Univ	IL	20,176	C
Northwestern Univ	IL	68,725	MC
Notre Dame of Maryland Univ	MD	47,570	VC
Oakland Univ	MI	20,763	C
Oglethorpe Univ	GA	44,200	C
Ohio State Univ at Columbus	OH	22,843	MC
Old Dominion Univ	VA	21,618	C
Pace Univ	NY	60,136	C
Pepperdine Univ	CA	66,862	VC+
Point Loma Nazarene Univ	CA	46,150	C+
Pomona College	CA	64,957	MC
Portland State Univ	OR	19,443	C
Pratt Inst	NY	59,482	VC+
Presbyterian College	SC	47,186	C
Purdue Univ/West Lafayette	IN	20,032	MC
Randolph-Macon College	VA	51,480	VC
Rhode Island College	RI	19,000	LC
Rice Univ	TX	59,458	MC
Ripon College	WI	49,991	VC
Roanoke College	VA	55,952	VC
Rockford Univ	IL	38,570	C
Roger Williams Univ	RI	48,074	VC
Rollins College	FL	58,670	HC
Roosevelt Univ	IL	41,890	VC
Rutgers Univ - Camden	NJ	26,595	C
Rutgers Univ - New Brunswick	NJ	27,090	HC
St. Peter's Univ	NJ	49,192	C
St. Vincent College	PA	46,229	C
Salem College	NC	40,206	C
Salve Regina Univ	RI	53,046	VC
San Francisco Art Inst	CA	60,865	SP
Savannah College of Art and Design	GA	49,595	SP
School of the Art Inst of Chicago	IL	61,830	SP
Scripps College	CA	69,260	HC
Seton Hill Univ	PA	46,972	VC
Siena Heights Univ	MI	36,322	C
Skidmore College	NY	66,600	MC
Smith College	MA	66,774	MC
Southern Conn State Univ	CT	21,924	LC
Southern Illinois Univ Edwardsville	IL	20,188	C
Southern Methodist Univ	TX	69,008	MC
St. Mary's College of Maryland	MD	27,312	VC
St. Olaf College	MN	56,430	HC
Stanford Univ	CA	62,541	MC
SUNY Albany	NY	22,165	C
SUNY at Geneseo	NY	21,622	VC
SUNY at New Paltz	NY	20,840	C
SUNY at Purchase College	NY	21,832	C
SUNY/Buffalo State	NY	20,583	LC
SUNY/Potsdam	NY	21,051	VC
SUNY/Univ at Buffalo	NY	23,122	C
Stephen F. Austin State Univ	TX	18,484	LC
Stonehill College	MA	55,130	C
Suffolk Univ	MA	52,316	C
Susquehanna Univ	PA	57,560	VC
Swarthmore College	PA	63,550	MC
Syracuse Univ	NY	62,313	HC
Temple Univ	PA	24,392	C+
Texas State Univ	TX	18,721	C
The American Univ	DC	61,317	HC
The Catholic Univ of America	DC	58,376	VC
The College of New Jersey	NJ	28,675	VC+
The College of New Rochelle	NY	46,300	LC
The George Washington Univ	DC	68,474	HC+
The Univ of Alabama	AL	24,320	C+
The Univ of Memphis	TN	18,278	C
The Univ of Texas at Austin	TX	20,206	MC
The Univ of Texas at San Antonio	TX	21,060	C
Trinity College	CT	69,020	HC
Troy Univ	AL	16,171	C
Tulane Univ	LA	67,496	MC
Univ of Arkansas at Little Rock	AR	18,211	LC
Univ of Calif at Berkeley	CA	29,886	MC
Univ of Calif at Davis	CA	28,468	HC
Univ of Calif at Los Angeles	CA	27,438	HC+
Univ of Calif at Riverside	CA	32,912	C
Univ of Calif at Santa Barbara	CA	30,627	HC+
Univ of Calif San Diego	CA	30,450	MC
Univ of Calif, Santa Cruz	CA	28,731	C+
Univ of Chicago	IL	70,551	MC
Univ of Conn	CT	27,394	
Univ of Dallas	TX	50,676	VC
Univ of Dayton	OH	54,930	VC
Univ of Delaware	DE	32,214	VC
Univ of Denver	CO	61,129	VC+
Univ of Florida	FL	16,291	HC+
Univ of Hartford	CT	49,776	C
Univ of Illinois at Chicago	IL	24,664	VC
Univ of Illinois at Urbana-Champaign	IL	27,006	HC
Univ of Iowa	IA	19,415	HC
Univ of Kentucky	KY	24,800	C+
Univ of La Verne	CA	55,600	C
Univ of Louisville	KY	19,692	C
Univ of Mary Washington	VA	23,039	C+
Univ of Maryland/Baltimore County	MD	23,004	VC
Univ of Maryland/College Park	MD	21,938	HC
Univ of Mass Amherst	MA	27,669	HC
Univ of Mass Dartmouth	MA	26,507	C
Univ of Mich/Ann Arbor	MI	25,274	MC
Univ of Minn/Duluth	MN	20,292	C
Univ of Minn/Morris	MN	21,222	VC
Univ of Minn/Twin Cities	MN	24,269	MC
Univ of Miss	MS	18,802	C
Univ of Missouri-Columbia	MO	20,463	VC
Univ of Missouri-Kansas City	MO	19,563	VC
Univ of Missouri-St. Louis	MO	19,810	VC
Univ of Nebr - Lincoln	NE	18,589	VC
Univ of Nebr - Omaha	NE	16,120	C
Univ of Nevada, Las Vegas	NV	17,553	C
Univ of New Orleans	LA	12,840	C
Univ of N Car at Chapel Hill	NC	20,561	MC
Univ of N Car at Charlotte	NC	17,803	VC
Univ of North Texas	TX	20,082	C
Univ of Oregon	OR	24,021	VC
Univ of Pennsylvania	PA	63,526	MC
Univ of Rochester	NY	65,032	MC
Univ of St. Joseph	CT	49,069	C
Univ of San Francisco	CA	60,580	C
Univ of S Car at Columbia	SC	21,726	VC
Univ of Southern Calif	CA	66,631	MC
Univ of Texas at Arlington	TX	18,876	C
Univ of Toledo	OH	19,336	C
Univ of Vermont	VT	29,792	HC
Univ of Washington	WA	23,091	MC
Univ of Wisc-Madison	WI	21,647	MC
Univ of Wisc-Milwaukee	WI	21,538	C
Univ of Wisc-Whitewater	WI	13,976	C
Villanova Univ	PA	64,922	MC
Virginia Commonwealth Univ	VA	23,811	VC
Washburn Univ	KS	15,827	C
Washington and Lee Univ	VA	59,647	MC
Washington Univ in St. Louis	MO	67,539	MC
Wayne State Univ	MI	23,085	C
Webster Univ	MO	37,490	C
Wellesley College	MA	66,984	MC
Wesleyan College	GA	31,940	C+
Wesleyan Univ	CT	66,940	MC
Wichita State Univ	KS	17,773	C
Willamette Univ	OR	62,514	VC+
William Paterson Univ of New Jersey	NJ	24,022	C
Williams College	MA	67,700	MC
Winthrop Univ	SC	23,960	C
Wright State Univ	OH	16,983	C
Youngstown State Univ	OH	17,487	C

ART STUDIES

School	ST	$IS	SR
Amherst College	MA	66,186	MC
Belmont Univ	TN	44,500	VC+
Black Hills State Univ	SD	16,622	C
Cairn Univ	PA	37,572	C
Calvin College	MI	43,090	HC
Colgate Univ	NY	67,500	MC
Gallaudet Univ	DC	30,088	LC
Georgian Court Univ	NJ	43,068	LC
John Brown Univ	AR	35,184	VC
Ohio Wesleyan Univ	OH	49,460	VC
St. Joseph's Univ	PA	58,540	VC
Siena College	NY	48,916	C
Syracuse Univ	NY	62,313	HC
Univ of Denver	CO	61,129	VC+
Univ of Hawaii at Hilo	HI	18,038	VC
Univ of Illinois at Chicago	IL	24,664	VC
Univ of Maryland/Baltimore County	MD	23,004	VC
Wellesley College	MA	66,984	MC

ART THERAPY

School	ST	$IS	SR
Albertus Magnus College	CT	44,016	LC
Alverno College	WI	33,294	LC
Andrews Univ	MI	41,732	C
Anna Maria College	MA	51,020	C
Arcadia Univ	PA	55,990	C+
Bethany College	KS	38,637	LC
Buena Vista Univ	IA	42,344	C
Capital Univ	OH	44,778	VC
Carlow Univ	PA	39,696	LC
Cedar Crest College	PA	51,110	C

ST = STATE $IS = IN-STATE COSTS SR = SELECTOR RATING

School	ST	$IS	SR
Converse College	SC	28,290	C
DePaul Univ	IL	52,807	VC
Edgewood College	WI	35,950	C
Emmanuel College	MA	53,472	C+
Endicott College	MA	47,054	C+
Lipscomb Univ	TN	42,984	VC
LIU Post	NY	50,698	C+
Marygrove College	MI	30,100	LC
Marywood Univ	PA	47,840	C
Mercyhurst Univ	PA	47,420	C
Millikin Univ	IL	44,148	C
Missouri Western State Univ	MO	17,822	LC
Mount Mary Univ	WI	34,650	LC
Naropa Univ	CO	43,278	NC
New York Univ	NY	68,139	MC
Prescott College	AZ	38,201	C
Russell Sage College	NY	39,370	C
Seton Hill Univ	PA	46,972	VC
Springfield College	MA	48,775	C
The College of New Rochelle	NY	46,300	LC
The Univ of Montana Western	MT	9,426	LC
Univ of Indianapolis	IN	36,480	VC
Univ of St. Francis	IN	38,520	C
Univ of Wisc-Superior	WI	14,838	C

ARTS ADMINISTRATION

School	ST	$IS	SR
Drury Univ	MO	37,555	VC
Univ of Oregon	OR	24,021	VC

ARTS ADMINISTRATION/ MANAGEMENT

School	ST	$IS	SR
Adrian College	MI	45,550	C
Appalachian State Univ	NC	15,394	VC
Aquinas College - Mich	MI	38,876	VC
Baldwin Wallace Univ	OH	42,464	VC
Belhaven Univ	MS	32,250	C
Bellarmine Univ	KY	52,532	C
Benedictine Univ	IL	38,300	C
Bennett College	NC	27,717	NC
Bethany College	KS	38,637	LC
Brenau Univ - Women's College	GA	37,876	LC
Buena Vista Univ	IA	42,344	C
Butler Univ	IN	52,890	VC+
Chatham Univ	PA	47,883	VC
College of Charleston	SC	24,046	VC
Columbia College Chicago	IL	40,104	C
Concordia College - New York	NY	39,035	LC
Culver-Stockton College	MO	34,350	C
Daemen College	NY	40,336	C
Eastern Mich Univ	MI	19,761	C
Elmhurst College	IL	46,514	C
Elon Univ	NC	46,142	HC
Franklin Pierce Univ	NH	46,750	LC
Indiana Univ Bloomington	IN	20,791	HC
Iona College	NY	52,514	C
Lasell College	MA	49,400	C
LIU Post	NY	50,698	C+
Mary Baldwin Univ	VA	40,495	C
Marywood Univ	PA	47,840	C
Mass College of Liberal Arts	MA	20,659	C
Messiah College	PA	44,380	VC
New York Univ	NY	68,139	MC
Nova Southeastern Univ	FL	38,534	C+
Piedmont College	GA	34,334	C
Point Park Univ	PA	41,270	C
Randolph-Macon College	VA	51,480	VC
Ringling College of Art and Design	FL	59,160	SP
St. Vincent College	PA	46,229	C
Salem College	NC	40,206	C
Seton Hill Univ	PA	46,972	VC
Simmons College	MA	54,400	HC
Spring Hill College	AL	48,488	C
SUNY/Fredonia	NY	20,818	C
The Univ of Montana Western	MT	9,426	LC
Tiffin Univ	OH	34,900	LC
Univ of Findlay	OH	43,040	C
Univ of Kentucky	KY	24,800	C+
Univ of Maryland/Baltimore County	MD	23,004	VC
Univ of N Car at Greensboro	NC	15,998	C
Univ of North Georgia	GA	17,316	C
Univ of San Francisco	CA	60,580	C
Univ of Tulsa	OK	52,625	HC
Univ of Wisc-Green Bay	WI	15,184	C
Univ of Wisc-Stevens Point	WI	14,043	C
Upper Iowa Univ	IA	34,990	NC
Viterbo Univ	WI	34,660	C
Wagner College	NY	57,240	C+
Waynesburg Univ	PA	33,530	C
Westminster College	UT	41,078	C
Wright State Univ	OH	16,983	C

ASIAN STUDIES

School	ST	$IS	SR
Amherst College	MA	66,186	MC
Arizona State Univ at the Tempe Campus	AZ	23,001	VC
Bates College	ME	64,500	HC
Boston Univ	MA	67,352	MC
Bowdoin College	ME	65,980	MC
Cal State, Chico	CA	19,790	VC
Calvin College	MI	43,090	HC
Case Western Reserve Univ	OH	62,284	MC
Colgate Univ	NY	67,500	MC
Cornell Univ	NY	67,591	MC
Elon Univ	NC	46,142	HC
Indiana Univ Bloomington	IN	20,791	HC
Indiana Univ of Pennsylvania	PA	24,474	C
Kennesaw State Univ	GA	18,899	VC
Kenyon College	OH	65,840	MC
Loyola Marymount Univ	CA	60,202	VC+
McDaniel College	MD	52,910	VC
Nazareth College	NY	46,784	C
New York Univ	NY	68,139	MC
Occidental College	CA	68,660	MC
Pace Univ	NY	60,136	C
Pennsylvania State Univ - Univ Park	PA	29,716	HC
St. Joseph's Univ	PA	58,540	VC
Sarah Lawrence College	NY	68,866	MC
Seattle Univ	WA	54,957	VC
St. Lawrence Univ	NY	66,646	HC+
Univ of Colo Boulder	CO	26,048	HC
Univ of Georgia	GA	21,878	HC
Univ of Louisville	KY	19,692	C
Univ of Mass Boston	MA	13,828	C
Univ of Minn/Twin Cities	MN	24,269	MC
Univ of N Car at Greensboro	NC	15,998	C
Univ of Okla	OK	19,651	HC
Univ of San Francisco	CA	60,580	C
Vanderbilt Univ	TN	63,248	MC
Washington State Univ	WA	22,747	C
Wayne State Univ	MI	23,085	C
Western Kentucky Univ	KY	16,850	C

ASIAN/AMERICAN STUDIES

School	ST	$IS	SR
Arizona State Univ at the Tempe Campus	AZ	23,001	VC
Brigham Young Univ	UT	13,248	MC
Brown Univ	RI	64,566	MC
Cal State, Fullerton	CA	21,902	C
Cal State, Northridge	CA	17,277	LC
Columbia Univ/City of New York	NY	62,958	MC
Emory Univ	GA	63,286	MC
Indiana Univ Bloomington	IN	20,791	HC
New York Univ	NY	68,139	MC
Ohio Univ	OH	23,394	VC
Pitzer College	CA	68,500	HC+
Pomona College	CA	64,957	MC
Purdue Univ/West Lafayette	IN	20,032	MC
San Francisco State Univ	CA	18,514	LC
Scripps College	CA	69,260	HC
St. Olaf College	MN	56,430	HC
Stanford Univ	CA	62,541	MC
SUNY at Binghamton	NY	24,100	MC
Stony Brook Univ/The SUNY	NY	22,703	MC
Univ of Calif at Berkeley	CA	29,886	MC
Univ of Calif at Irvine	CA	33,857	VC
Univ of Calif at Los Angeles	CA	27,438	HC+
Univ of Calif at Riverside	CA	32,912	C
Univ of Calif at Santa Barbara	CA	30,627	HC+
Univ of Denver	CO	61,129	VC+
Univ of Northern Colo	CO	19,658	C
Univ of Southern Calif	CA	66,631	MC
Univ of Washington	WA	23,091	MC
Univ of Wisc-Milwaukee	WI	21,538	C
Wellesley College	MA	66,984	MC

ASIAN/ORIENTAL STUDIES

School	ST	$IS	SR
Augustana College	IL	51,222	VC+
Bard College	NY	65,924	HC
Bard College at Simon's Rock	MA	65,795	MC
Baylor Univ	TX	56,803	HC
Belmont Univ	TN	44,500	VC+
Berea College	KY	7,094	C
Birmingham-Southern College	AL	44,478	C+
Bowling Green State Univ	OH	19,975	C
Brigham Young Univ	UT	13,248	MC
Cal State, Long Beach	CA	18,850	C
Calvin College	MI	43,090	HC
Carleton College	MN	66,414	MC
Central Washington Univ	WA	16,803	C
CUNY/City College	NY	20,204	C
Claremont McKenna College	CA	69,900	MC
Clark Univ	MA	53,260	HC+
Coe College	IA	51,570	VC
College of St. Benedict	MN	54,480	C
College of the Holy Cross	MA	64,320	MC
Colo College	CO	64,894	MC
Dartmouth College	NH	68,109	MC
Duke Univ	NC	68,298	MC
Eastern Mich Univ	MI	19,761	C
Emory Univ	GA	63,286	MC
Florida International Univ	FL	20,281	C
Florida State Univ	FL	16,771	HC
Furman Univ	SC	61,098	VC+
Hamilton College	NY	64,250	MC
Hampshire College	MA	65,214	MC
Harvard College/Harvard Univ	MA	65,609	MC
Hobart and William Smith Colleges	NY	67,050	HC+
Indiana Univ Bloomington	IN	20,791	HC
John Carroll Univ	OH	51,570	C
Kean Univ	NJ	25,620	C
Knox College	IL	54,654	VC+
Lafayette College	PA	68,520	MC
Lake Forest College	IL	50,652	VC
Lehigh Univ	PA	63,860	MC
Macalester College	MN	64,136	MC
Manhattanville College	NY	52,430	C
Marietta College	OH	46,190	C
Mount Holyoke College	MA	56,746	MC
New York Univ	NY	68,139	MC
Northeastern Univ	MA	65,352	MC
Old Dominion Univ	VA	21,618	C
Pitzer College	CA	68,500	HC+
Pomona College	CA	64,957	MC
Purdue Univ/West Lafayette	IN	20,032	MC
Randolph-Macon College	VA	51,480	VC
Rice Univ	TX	59,458	MC
Rollins College	FL	58,670	HC
St. John's Univ	MN	53,472	C
San Diego State Univ	CA	23,156	VC
Scripps College	CA	69,260	HC
Seton Hall Univ	NJ	58,008	C
Sewanee: The Univ of the South	TN	58,000	HC+
Skidmore College	NY	66,600	MC
St. John's Univ	NY	57,160	C+
St. Mary's College of Maryland	MD	27,312	VC
SUNY Albany	NY	22,165	C
SUNY at New Paltz	NY	20,840	C
SUNY/Univ at Buffalo	NY	23,122	C
Swarthmore College	PA	63,550	MC
Temple Univ	PA	24,392	C+
Texas State Univ	TX	18,721	C
The Univ of Texas at Austin	TX	20,206	MC
The Univ of Utah	UT	18,751	VC
Tufts Univ	MA		MC
Tulane Univ	LA	67,496	MC
Union College	NY	64,320	MC
Univ of Calif at Berkeley	CA	29,886	MC
Univ of Calif at Los Angeles	CA	27,438	HC+
Univ of Calif at Riverside	CA	32,912	C
Univ of Calif at Santa Barbara	CA	30,627	HC+
Univ of Cincinnati	OH	22,118	VC
Univ of Florida	FL	16,291	HC+
Univ of Hawaii at Manoa	HI	23,261	C
Univ of Iowa	IA	19,415	HC
Univ of Maryland Univ College	MD	26,146	LC
Univ of Mich/Ann Arbor	MI	25,274	MC
Univ of New Mexico	NM	16,808	C
Univ of N Car at Chapel Hill	NC	20,561	MC
Univ of Oregon	OR	24,021	VC
Univ of Pennsylvania	PA	63,526	MC
Univ of Puget Sound	WA	60,210	HC
Univ of Redlands	CA	61,934	VC
Univ of Vermont	VT	29,792	HC
Univ of Washington	WA	23,091	MC
Univ of Wisc-Madison	WI	21,647	MC
Vassar College	NY	68,110	MC
Washington Univ in St. Louis	MO	67,539	MC
Wellesley College	MA	66,984	MC
Whitman College	WA	59,772	MC
Willamette Univ	OR	62,514	VC+
Williams College	MA	67,700	MC

ASTRONOMY

School	ST	$IS	SR
Amherst College	MA	66,186	MC
Ball State Univ	IN	19,808	C+
Barnard College/Columbia Univ	NY	68,762	MC
Benedictine College	KS	38,850	VC
Bennington College	VT	66,280	MC
Boston Univ	MA	67,352	MC
Brigham Young Univ	UT	13,248	MC
Brown Univ	RI	64,566	MC
Bryn Mawr College	PA	65,220	MC
Cal State, Fullerton	CA	21,902	C
Case Western Reserve Univ	OH	62,284	MC
Colby College	ME	64,060	MC
Colgate Univ	NY	67,500	MC
College of Charleston	SC	24,046	VC
Columbia Univ/ School of General Studies	NY	61,470	MC
Columbia Univ/City of New York	NY	62,958	MC
Cornell Univ	NY	67,591	MC
Dartmouth College	NH	68,109	MC
Eastern Mich Univ	MI	19,761	C
Embry-Riddle Aeronautical Univ - Prescott Campus	AZ	45,130	VC
Florida Inst of Technology	FL	53,306	VC
Franklin and Marshall College	PA	67,960	MC
George Mason Univ	VA	19,884	C
Harvard College/Harvard Univ	MA	65,609	MC
Haverford College	PA	66,490	MC
Indiana Univ Bloomington	IN	20,791	HC
Lehigh Univ	PA	63,860	MC
Lycoming College	PA	50,895	C
Mount Holyoke College	MA	56,746	MC
New Mexico State Univ	NM	14,050	LC
Northern Arizona Univ	AZ	21,003	C
Northwestern Univ	IL	68,725	MC
Oberlin College	OH	68,942	MC
Ohio State Univ at Columbus	OH	22,843	MC
Pennsylvania State Univ - Univ Park	PA	29,716	HC
San Diego State Univ	CA	23,156	VC
San Francisco State Univ	CA	18,514	LC
Smith College	MA	66,774	MC
Stony Brook Univ/The SUNY	NY	22,703	MC
Swarthmore College	PA	63,550	MC
The Univ of Arizona	AZ	24,086	C
The Univ of Texas at Austin	TX	20,206	MC
Union College	NY	64,320	MC
Univ of Colo Boulder	CO	26,048	HC
Univ of Delaware	DE	32,214	VC
Univ of Florida	FL	16,291	HC+
Univ of Hawaii at Hilo	HI	18,038	VC
Univ of Illinois at Urbana-Champaign	IL	27,006	HC
Univ of Iowa	IA	19,415	HC
Univ of Kansas	KS	20,884	VC
Univ of Maryland/College Park	MD	21,938	HC
Univ of Mass Amherst	MA	27,669	HC
Univ of Mich/Ann Arbor	MI	25,274	MC
Univ of Nebr - Lincoln	NE	18,589	VC
Univ of Okla	OK	19,651	HC
Univ of Pittsburgh	PA	30,030	HC
Univ of Rochester	NY	65,032	MC
Univ of Southern Calif	CA	66,631	MC
Univ of Virginia	VA	27,367	MC
Univ of Washington	WA	23,091	MC
Univ of Wisc-Madison	WI	21,647	MC
Valparaiso Univ	IN	50,160	VC
Vassar College	NY	68,110	MC
Villanova Univ	PA	64,922	MC
Wayne State Univ	MI	23,085	C
Wellesley College	MA	66,984	MC
Wesleyan Univ	CT	66,940	MC
Western Kentucky Univ	KY	16,850	C
Whitman College	WA	59,772	MC
Williams College	MA	67,700	MC
Wilmington College	OH	35,100	C
Yale Univ	CT	64,650	MC

ASTRONOMY AND PHYSICS

School	ST	$IS	SR
Albion College	MI	55,260	C
Boston Univ	MA	67,352	MC
Brown Univ	RI	64,566	MC
Dartmouth College	NH	68,109	MC
Embry-Riddle Aeronautical Univ - Daytona Beach	FL	45,822	VC
Oberlin College	OH	68,942	MC
Texas Christian Univ	TX	57,120	HC
Univ of Georgia	GA	21,878	HC
Univ of Mass Dartmouth	MA	26,507	C
Univ of Wyoming	WY	15,537	C
Western Kentucky Univ	KY	16,850	C
Wheaton College	MA	63,818	VC
Youngstown State Univ	OH	17,487	C

ASTROPHYSICS

School	ST	$IS	SR
Agnes Scott College	GA	51,930	VC+
Boston Univ	MA	67,352	MC
Brown Univ	RI	64,566	MC
Calif Inst of Technology	CA	64,704	MC
Cal State, Northridge	CA	17,277	LC
Colgate Univ	NY	67,500	MC
College of Charleston	SC	24,046	VC
Columbia Univ/City of New York	NY	62,958	MC
Dartmouth College	NH	68,109	MC
Florida Inst of Technology	FL	53,306	VC
Franklin and Marshall College	PA	67,960	MC
Haverford College	PA	66,490	MC
Indiana Univ Bloomington	IN	20,791	HC
Lehigh Univ	PA	63,860	MC
Lycoming College	PA	50,895	C
Mich State Univ	MI	24,542	VC
Ohio State Univ at Columbus	OH	22,843	MC
Ohio Univ	OH	23,394	VC
Princeton Univ	NJ	60,090	MC
Rutgers Univ - New Brunswick	NJ	27,090	HC
San Francisco State Univ	CA	18,514	LC
Swarthmore College	PA	63,550	MC
Tufts Univ	MA		MC
Univ of Calif at Berkeley	CA	29,886	MC
Univ of Calif at Los Angeles	CA	27,438	HC+
Univ of Cincinnati	OH	22,118	VC
Univ of Mich/Ann Arbor	MI	25,274	MC
Univ of Minn/Twin Cities	MN	24,269	MC
Univ of New Mexico	NM	16,808	C
Univ of Okla	OK	19,651	HC
Villanova Univ	PA	64,922	MC
Wellesley College	MA	66,984	MC
Whitman College	WA	59,772	MC
Williams College	MA	67,700	MC

ATHLETIC TRAINING

School	ST	$IS	SR
Adams State Univ	CO	15,420	LC
Alderson Broaddus Univ	WV	35,000	LC
Alfred Univ	NY	37,490	C
Alvernia Univ	PA	45,330	C
Anderson Univ	IN	39,450	C
Appalachian State Univ	NC	15,394	VC
Aquinas College - Mich	MI	38,876	VC

ST = STATE **$IS** = IN-STATE COSTS **SR** = SELECTOR RATING

School	ST	$IS	SR
Arkansas State Univ	AR	16,190	C
Ashland Univ	OH	30,446	C
Augustana Univ	SD	39,968	VC
Aurora Univ	IL	34,990	C
Averett Univ	VA	43,034	LC
Azusa Pacific Univ	CA	43,972	C
Baldwin Wallace Univ	OH	42,464	VC
Belhaven Univ	MS	32,250	C
Benedictine College	KS	38,850	VC
Bethany College	KS	38,637	LC
Bethel College	KS	35,370	C
Bethel Univ	MN	46,550	C+
Boston Univ	MA	67,352	MC
Bowling Green State Univ	OH	19,975	C
Bridgewater College	VA	46,260	C
Bridgewater State Univ	MA	22,762	C
Buena Vista Univ	IA	42,344	C
Cal State, Fullerton	CA	21,902	C
Calif Univ of Pennsylvania	PA	20,425	LC
Campbell Univ	NC	37,570	VC
Canisius College	NY	49,672	C
Capital Univ	OH	44,778	VC
Carroll Univ	WI	38,100	C+
Castleton Univ	VT	20,186	C
Catawba College	NC	39,820	LC
Cedarville Univ	OH	36,244	VC
Central College	IA	44,592	C
Central Conn State Univ	CT	22,041	C
Central Methodist Univ	MO	31,500	VC
Central Mich Univ	MI	20,330	C
Chapman Univ	CA	65,504	HC
Clarion Univ of Pennsylvania	PA	21,608	LC
Clarke Univ	IA	42,950	C
Coe College	IA	51,570	VC
Colby-Sawyer College	NH	50,790	C
College of Charleston	SC	24,046	VC
College of St. Scholastica	MN	45,734	C+
Colo Mesa Univ	CO	19,707	LC
Concordia Univ Wisc	WI	35,910	C
Culver-Stockton College	MO	34,350	C
Dakota Wesleyan Univ	SD	33,980	LC
Defiance College	OH	42,240	LC
Dominican College	NY	40,258	LC
Dordt College	IA	37,860	C+
Duquesne Univ	PA	48,508	VC
East Carolina Univ	NC	16,539	C
East Central Univ	OK	13,330	C
East Stroudsburg Univ	PA	18,578	LC
East Texas Baptist Univ	TX	34,444	C
Eastern Illinois Univ	IL	21,414	C
Eastern Mich Univ	MI	19,761	C
Eastern Nazarene College	MA	41,114	C
Eastern Univ	PA	39,540	C
Emporia State Univ	KS	15,029	C
Endicott College	MA	47,054	C+
Erskine College	SC	45,460	C
Eureka College	IL	34,760	C
Florida Gulf Coast Univ	FL	14,738	C
Florida Southern College	FL	45,978	VC
Florida State Univ	FL	16,771	HC
Fort Lewis College	CO	20,154	C
Gardner-Webb Univ	NC	24,935	C+
George Fox Univ	OR	42,938	C
George Mason Univ	VA	19,884	C
Georgetown College	KY	41,440	C
Georgia College & State Univ	GA	21,884	C+
Georgia Southern Univ	GA	16,540	VC
Graceland Univ	IA	35,290	C
Grand Canyon Univ	AZ	25,150	VC
Grand Valley State Univ	MI	22,250	C+
Greensboro College	NC	39,790	LC
Hamline Univ	MN	50,152	C
Harding Univ	AR	25,440	C
Hardin-Simmons Univ	TX	36,025	C
Heidelberg Univ	OH	40,400	LC
Hofstra Univ	NY	58,210	C+
Hope College	MI	42,840	VC
Howard Payne Univ	TX	35,994	C
Immaculata Univ	PA	39,000	C
Indiana Univ Bloomington	IN	20,791	HC
Indiana Wesleyan Univ	IN	33,674	C
Ithaca College	NY	58,158	VC+
James Madison Univ	VA	19,084	VC
Johnson State College	VT	22,672	C
Kansas State Univ	KS	17,780	VC
Kean Univ	NJ	25,620	C
Keene State College	NH	24,604	C
Kent State Univ	OH	20,928	C
King Univ	TN	36,976	C
Lake Superior State Univ	MI	19,867	C
Lasell College	MA	49,400	C
Lebanon Valley College	PA	55,510	VC
Lee Univ	TN	22,045	C
Lees-McRae College	NC	33,944	NC
Lenoir-Rhyne Univ	NC	47,500	LC
Lewis Univ	IL	41,710	C
Liberty Univ	VA	31,415	C
Limestone College	SC	32,100	C
Lincoln Memorial Univ	TN	28,430	C
Lindenwood Univ	MO	25,760	C
Linfield College	OR	53,992	C
LIU Brooklyn	NY	50,698	C
Longwood Univ	VA	22,184	C
Loras College	IA	40,726	C
Louisiana State Univ and A&M College	LA	18,677	VC
Lubbock Christian Univ	TX	29,727	C
Luther College	IA	49,990	VC
Marietta College	OH	46,190	C
Marist College	NY	49,860	VC
Marquette Univ	WI	53,090	VC+
Mars Hill Univ	NC	41,104	C
Marshall Univ	WV	18,044	C
Marywood Univ	PA	47,840	C
Mass College of Liberal Arts	MA	20,659	C
McKendree Univ	IL	37,940	C+
McMurry Univ	TX	34,259	LC
McNeese State Univ	LA	7,838	C
Mercyhurst Univ	PA	47,420	C
Merrimack College	MA	55,415	C
Messiah College	PA	44,380	VC
Methodist Univ	NC	58,130	C
Miami Univ	OH	27,190	HC+
MidAmerica Nazarene Univ	KS	37,808	C
Middle Tenn State Univ	TN	8,650	C
Millersville Univ of Pennsylvania	PA	25,298	C
Millikin Univ	IL	44,148	C
Minn State Univ, Moorhead	MN	21,393	C
Missouri State Univ	MO	15,837	C+
Montana State Univ Billings	MT	13,336	LC
Montclair State Univ	NJ	26,912	C
Mount Marty College	SD	36,862	C
Mount St. Joseph Univ	OH	33,880	LC
Murray State Univ	KY	17,726	C+
Nebr Wesleyan Univ	NE	42,026	C+
Neumann Univ	PA	40,678	LC
New Mexico State Univ	NM	14,050	LC
North Central College	IL	48,712	C+
N Dak State Univ	ND	16,245	VC
North Park Univ	IL	35,860	C
Northern Kentucky Univ	KY	16,486	C
Northwestern College of Iowa	IA	38,400	C
Nova Southeastern Univ	FL	38,534	C+
Ohio Northern Univ	OH	44,050	VC
Ohio State Univ at Columbus	OH	22,843	MC
Ohio Univ	OH	23,394	VC
Okla State Univ	OK	17,180	C+
Olivet College	MI	37,661	LC
Olivet Nazarene Univ	IL	41,840	VC
Otterbein Univ	OH	41,630	C
Palm Beach Atlantic Univ	FL	39,250	C
Park Univ	MO	22,134	C
Pennsylvania State Univ - Univ Park	PA	29,716	HC
Piedmont College	GA	34,334	C
Plymouth State Univ	NH	23,180	LC
Point Loma Nazarene Univ	CA	46,150	C+
Purdue Univ/West Lafayette	IN	20,032	MC
Quinnipiac Univ	CT	60,970	VC
Radford Univ	VA	19,758	C
Rowan Univ	NJ	24,491	VC
Sacred Heart Univ	CT	54,590	C
Saginaw Valley State Univ	MI	19,284	C
Salem International Univ	WV	21,090	C
Salisbury Univ	MD	21,132	VC
Samford Univ	AL	40,770	VC
San Diego State Univ	CA	23,156	VC
Shaw Univ	NC	24,638	C
Shawnee State Univ	OH	16,998	C
S Dak State Univ	SD	15,874	C
Southeast Missouri State Univ	MO	16,148	C
Southeastern Louisiana Univ	LA	16,237	C
Southern Nazarene Univ	OK	33,684	C
Southwest Baptist Univ	MO	30,890	LC
Southwestern College	KS	31,531	LC
St. Edward's Univ	TX	56,190	VC
SUNY/Cortland	NY	20,910	C
Sterling College	KS	32,830	LC
Stony Brook Univ/The SUNY	NY	22,703	MC
Tabor College	KS	35,870	C
Temple Univ	PA	24,392	C+
Texas Christian Univ	TX	57,120	HC
Texas Lutheran Univ	TX	39,770	C
Texas State Univ	TX	18,721	C
Texas Wesleyan Univ	TX	37,338	C
The College at Brockport - SUNY	NY	21,058	C
The Univ of Akron	OH	22,566	C
The Univ of Alabama	AL	24,320	C+
The Univ of Mary	ND	23,180	C
The Univ of Montana Western	MT	9,426	LC
The Univ of Utah	UT	18,751	VC
Towson Univ	MD	21,878	C
Trinity International Univ	IL	31,070	VC
Troy Univ	AL	16,171	C
Tusculum College	TN	31,625	LC
Union College	KY	32,310	C
Univ of Central Arkansas	AR	15,042	VC
Univ of Central Florida	FL	16,379	VC
Univ of Central Okla	OK	15,150	C
Univ of Charleston	WV	35,000	LC
Univ of Cincinnati	OH	22,118	VC
Univ of Conn	CT	27,394	
Univ of Delaware	DE	32,214	VC
Univ of Evansville	IN	44,186	C+
Univ of Georgia	GA	21,878	HC
Univ of Illinois at Urbana-Champaign	IL	27,006	HC
Univ of Indianapolis	IN	36,480	VC
Univ of Iowa	IA	19,415	HC
Univ of Kansas	KS	20,884	VC
Univ of La Verne	CA	55,600	C
Univ of Lynchburg	VA	48,370	C
Univ of Maine	ME	21,038	VC
Univ of Maine at Presque Isle	ME	16,148	LC
Univ of Miami	FL	63,494	MC
Univ of Mich/Ann Arbor	MI	25,274	MC
Univ of Minn/Duluth	MN	20,292	C
Univ of Mobile	AL	28,935	C
Univ of Montana	MT	14,105	C
Univ of Nebr - Lincoln	NE	18,589	VC
Univ of New England	ME	50,110	C
Univ of New Hampshire	NH	29,333	VC
Univ of New Mexico	NM	16,808	C
Univ of N Car at Charlotte	NC	17,803	VC
Univ of N Car at Pembroke	NC	14,737	LC
Univ of N Car Wilmington	NC	16,784	VC
Univ of N Dak	ND	16,673	C
Univ of North Florida	FL	15,996	VC
Univ of Northern Colo	CO	19,658	C
Univ of Northern Iowa	IA	17,480	C
Univ of Pittsburgh	PA	30,030	MC
Univ of Pittsburgh at Bradford	PA	22,958	C
Univ of Tampa	FL	38,928	VC
Univ of the Incarnate Word	TX	39,162	LC
Univ of Tulsa	OK	52,625	HC
Univ of Vermont	VT	29,792	HC
Univ of West Alabama	AL	16,284	LC
Univ of Wisc-Eau Claire	WI	16,354	VC
Univ of Wisc-La Crosse	WI	15,425	VC
Univ of Wisc-Madison	WI	21,647	MC
Univ of Wisc-Milwaukee	WI	21,538	C
Univ of Wisc-Stevens Point	WI	14,043	C
Upper Iowa Univ	IA	34,990	NC
Vanguard Univ of Southern Calif	CA	42,400	VC
Virginia State Univ	VA	19,802	C+
Washburn Univ	KS	15,827	C
Washington State Univ	WA	22,747	C
Waynesburg Univ	PA	33,530	C
Weber State Univ	UT	14,112	C
West Chester Univ of Pennsylvania	PA	19,171	VC
West Texas A&M Univ	TX	13,478	C
West Virginia Univ	WV	18,952	VC
Western Illinois Univ	IL	20,897	C
Western Kentucky Univ	KY	16,850	C
Western Mich Univ	MI	21,791	C
Westfield State Univ	MA	20,404	C
Wheeling Jesuit Univ	WV	37,106	LC
Whitworth Univ	WA	53,682	VC
William Woods Univ	MO	32,040	C
Wilmington College	OH	35,100	C
Wingate Univ	NC	41,900	C
Winona State Univ	MN	18,109	C
Winthrop Univ	SC	23,960	C
Wright State Univ	OH	16,983	C

ATMOSPHERIC SCIENCES AND METEOROLOGY

School	ST	$IS	SR
Cal State, Fullerton	CA	21,902	C
CUNY/City College	NY	20,204	C
East Carolina Univ	NC	16,539	C
Florida Inst of Technology	FL	53,306	VC
Florida State Univ	FL	16,771	HC
Howard Univ	DC	37,616	C+
Iowa State Univ	IA	18,176	C
Jackson State Univ	MS	15,879	LC
Lyndon State College	VT	20,714	C
Metropolitan State Univ of Denver	CO	6,928	LC
Millersville Univ of Pennsylvania	PA	25,298	C
N Car State Univ	NC	22,434	HC+
Northern Illinois Univ	IL	20,176	C
Northland College	WI	41,103	C+
Ohio State Univ at Columbus	OH	22,843	MC
Ohio Univ	OH	23,394	VC
Pennsylvania State Univ - Univ Park	PA	29,716	HC
Plymouth State Univ	NH	23,180	LC
Purdue Univ/West Lafayette	IN	20,032	MC
St. Louis Univ	MO	49,866	HC
San Francisco State Univ	CA	18,514	LC
San Jose State Univ	CA	22,630	C
St. Cloud State Univ	MN	10,600	C
SUNY Albany	NY	22,165	C
SUNY at Oswego	NY	22,219	VC
SUNY/Maritime College	NY	16,020	C
SUNY/Oneonta	NY	20,794	C
The College at Brockport - SUNY	NY	21,058	C
The Univ of Arizona	AZ	24,086	C
The Univ of Utah	UT	18,751	VC
United States Air Force Academy	CO		C
Univ of Calif at Davis	CA	28,468	HC
Univ of Calif at Los Angeles	CA	27,438	HC+
Univ of Hawaii at Manoa	HI	23,261	C
Univ of Kansas	KS	20,884	VC
Univ of Louisville	KY	19,692	C
Univ of Maryland/College Park	MD	21,938	HC
Univ of Miami	FL	63,494	MC
Univ of Mich/Ann Arbor	MI	25,274	MC
Univ of Missouri-Columbia	MO	20,463	VC
Univ of Nebr - Lincoln	NE	18,589	VC
Univ of N Car at Asheville	NC	16,251	VC+
Univ of N Car at Charlotte	NC	17,803	VC
Univ of N Dak	ND	16,673	C
Univ of Okla	OK	19,651	HC
Univ of South Alabama	AL	16,880	C
Univ of Washington	WA	23,091	MC
Univ of Wisc-Madison	WI	21,647	MC
Univ of Wisc-Milwaukee	WI	21,538	C
Valparaiso Univ	IN	50,160	VC
Western Conn State Univ	CT	21,254	LC
Western Kentucky Univ	KY	16,850	C

AUDIO TECHNOLOGY

School	ST	$IS	SR
Belmont Univ	TN	44,500	VC+
Brigham Young Univ	UT	13,248	MC
Cogswell Polytechnical College	CA	31,511	C
Columbia College Chicago	IL	40,104	C
Cornerstone Univ	MI	36,550	C
Five Towns College	NY	35,480	LC
Indiana Univ Bloomington	IN	20,791	HC
Ithaca College	NY	58,158	VC+
Lawrence Tech Univ	MI	41,630	VC
Lebanon Valley College	PA	55,510	VC
Mich Tech Univ	MI	25,551	VC+
Ohio Univ	OH	23,394	VC
Purdue Univ/West Lafayette	IN	20,032	MC
Savannah College of Art and Design	GA	49,595	SP
School of the Art Inst of Chicago	IL	61,830	SP
SUNY/Fredonia	NY	20,818	C
Texas State Univ	TX	18,721	C
The American Univ	DC	61,317	HC
Univ of Hartford	CT	49,776	C
Univ of Mich/Ann Arbor	MI	25,274	MC
Univ of New Haven	CT	53,680	C
Univ of Rochester	NY	65,032	MC
Webster Univ	MO	37,490	C
Wichita State Univ	KS	17,773	C

AUTOMOTIVE TECHNOLOGY

School	ST	$IS	SR
Benjamin Franklin Inst of Technology	MA	33,190	SP
Colo State Univ-Pueblo	CO	21,581	C
Farmingdale State College	NY	20,968	C
Ferris State Univ	MI	21,458	C
Idaho State Univ	ID	13,619	LC
Lewis-Clark State College	ID	14,202	C
Minn State Univ, Mankato	MN	17,190	C
Montana State Univ-Northern	MT	11,370	NC
Pennsylvania College of Technology	PA	27,693	NC
Pittsburg State Univ	KS	13,880	C
Southern Illinois Univ Carbondale	IL	24,554	C
The Univ of Akron	OH	22,566	C
Univ of Central Missouri	MO	18,982	C
Walla Walla Univ	WA	34,845	C
Weber State Univ	UT	14,112	C

AVIAN SCIENCES

School	ST	$IS	SR
Bowling Green State Univ	OH	19,975	C
Eastern New Mexico Univ	NM	12,874	LC
Ohio State Univ at Columbus	OH	22,843	MC
Univ of Calif at Davis	CA	28,468	HC
Univ of Georgia	GA	21,878	HC

AVIATION & AEROSPACE TECHNOLOGY

School	ST	$IS	SR
Lewis Univ	IL	41,710	C

AVIATION ADMINISTRATION/MANAGEMENT

School	ST	$IS	SR
Andrews Univ	MI	41,732	C
Auburn Univ	AL	24,300	VC+
Averett Univ	VA	43,034	LC
Baker College of Flint	MI	19,140	NC
Baylor Univ	TX	56,803	HC
Calif Baptist Univ	CA	42,986	C
Central Washington Univ	WA	16,803	C
Delaware State Univ	DE	19,376	LC
Delta State Univ	MS	13,176	LC
Eastern Mich Univ	MI	19,761	C
Farmingdale State College	NY	20,968	C
Florida Inst of Technology	FL	53,306	VC
Florida Memorial Univ	FL	22,424	LC
Geneva College	PA	35,450	C
Henderson State Univ	AR	15,516	C
Inter-American Univ of PR-Bayamon	PR	18,785	
Jacksonville Univ	FL	49,210	C
Lewis Univ	IL	41,710	C
Louisiana Tech Univ	LA	11,422	VC
Lynn Univ	FL	49,680	LC
Marywood Univ	PA	47,840	C
Metropolitan State Univ of Denver	CO	6,928	LC
Minn State Univ, Mankato	MN	17,190	C
Ohio State Univ at Columbus	OH	22,843	MC
Ohio Univ	OH	23,394	VC
Park Univ	MO	22,134	C
Purdue Univ/West Lafayette	IN	20,032	MC
Quincy Univ	IL	38,170	LC
Rocky Mountain College	MT	35,776	C
Salem International Univ	WV	21,090	C
San Diego Christian College	CA	40,914	C
S Dak State Univ	SD	15,874	C

ST = STATE $IS = IN-STATE COSTS SR = SELECTOR RATING

School	ST	$IS	SR
Southeastern Okla State Univ	OK	11,875	C
Southern Illinois Univ Carbondale	IL	24,554	C
Southern Nazarene Univ	OK	33,684	C
St. Cloud State Univ	MN	10,600	C
Texas Southern Univ	TX	19,592	LC
Univ of Alaska Anchorage	AK	17,914	C
Univ of Dubuque	IA	37,824	C
Univ of Illinois at Urbana-Champaign	IL	27,006	HC
Univ of Nebr - Kearney	NE	17,014	LC
Univ of Nebr - Omaha	NE	16,120	C
Univ of North Texas	TX	20,082	C
Univ of the District of Columbia	DC	21,260	LC
Vaughn College of Aeronautics and Technology	NY	37,180	SP
Western Mich Univ	MI	21,791	C
Westminster College	UT	41,078	C
Wilmington Univ	DE	8,762	NC

AVIATION BUSINESS ADMINISTRATION

School	ST	$IS	SR
Embry-Riddle Aeronautical Univ - Daytona Beach	FL	45,822	VC
Embry-Riddle Aeronautical Univ - Prescott Campus	AZ	45,130	VC
Embry-Riddle Aeronautical Univ - Worldwide	FL	17,720	C
Univ of Louisiana at Monroe	LA	15,970	C

AVIATION COMPUTER TECHNOLOGY

School	ST	$IS	SR
Andrews Univ	MI	41,732	C
Florida Inst of Technology	FL	53,306	VC
Florida Memorial Univ	FL	22,424	LC
Inter-American Univ of PR-Bayamon	PR	18,785	
Metropolitan State Univ of Denver	CO	6,928	LC
Purdue Univ/West Lafayette	IN	20,032	MC
Univ of Central Missouri	MO	18,982	C
Walla Walla Univ	WA	34,845	C
Westminster College	UT	41,078	C

AVIATION FLIGHT MANAGEMENT

School	ST	$IS	SR
Lewis Univ	IL	41,710	C

AVIATION FLIGHT TECHNOLOGY

School	ST	$IS	SR
Calif Baptist Univ	CA	42,986	C
Delta State Univ	MS	13,176	LC
Thomas Edison State Univ	NJ	6,350	NC

AVIATION MAINTENANCE MANAGEMENT

School	ST	$IS	SR
Central Washington Univ	WA	16,803	C
Embry-Riddle Aeronautical Univ - Worldwide	FL	17,720	C
Lewis Univ	IL	41,710	C
S Dak State Univ	SD	15,874	C
Univ of N Dak	ND	16,673	C

AVIATION MAINTENANCE TECHNOLOGY

School	ST	$IS	SR
Southern Illinois Univ Carbondale	IL	24,554	C
Thomas Edison State Univ	NJ	6,350	NC
Univ of Alaska Anchorage	AK	17,914	C
Western Mich Univ	MI	21,791	C

BACTERIOLOGY

School	ST	$IS	SR
Univ of Calif at Davis	CA	28,468	HC
Wilmington College	OH	35,100	C

BALLET

School	ST	$IS	SR
Belhaven Univ	MS	32,250	C
Friends Univ	KS	38,000	C
Indiana Univ Bloomington	IN	20,791	HC
Texas Christian Univ	TX	57,120	HC
The Univ of Utah	UT	18,751	VC
Univ of N Car School of the Arts	NC	25,587	SP
Webster Univ	MO	37,490	C

BANKING AND FINANCE

School	ST	$IS	SR
Adams State Univ	CO	15,420	LC
Adelphi Univ	NY	49,792	C
Alabama A&M Univ	AL	18,796	C
Alabama State Univ	AL	16,490	LC
Alfred State College	NY	19,895	C
Anderson Univ	IN	39,450	C
Andrews Univ	MI	41,732	C
Angelo State Univ	TX	15,882	LC
Appalachian State Univ	NC	15,394	VC
Arcadia Univ	PA	55,990	C+
Arkansas State Univ	AR	16,190	C
Ashland Univ	OH	30,446	C
Auburn Univ	AL	24,300	VC+
Augusta Univ	GA	4,632	C
Avila Univ	MO	27,100	C
Baylor Univ	TX	56,803	HC
Bellarmine Univ	KY	52,532	C
Benedictine Univ	IL	38,300	C
Bethel Univ	MN	46,550	C+
Boston College	MA	68,043	MC
Brescia Univ	KY	29,890	VC
Buena Vista Univ	IA	42,344	C
Butler Univ	IN	52,890	VC+
Cal State, Fullerton	CA	21,902	C
Cal State, Long Beach	CA	18,850	C
Cal State, Northridge	CA	17,277	LC
Cal State, Sacramento	CA	19,060	C
Cal State, San Bernardino	CA	20,106	C
Campbell Univ	NC	37,570	VC
Canisius College	NY	49,672	C
Caribbean Univ	PR	12,227	
Central State Univ	OH	18,564	C
Central Washington Univ	WA	16,803	C
Chicago State Univ	IL	41,620	C
CUNY/Brooklyn College	NY	7,163	C+
Clarion Univ of Pennsylvania	PA	21,608	LC
Clemson Univ	SC		HC
Coastal Carolina Univ	SC	20,340	C
College of William & Mary	VA	34,907	MC
Colo State Univ	CO	23,033	C
Columbus State Univ	GA	14,336	LC
Concord Univ	WV	14,954	LC
Concordia Univ St. Paul	MN	29,050	C
Concordia Univ Wisc	WI	35,910	C
Davenport Univ	MI	25,896	LC
Defiance College	OH	42,240	LC
DePaul Univ	IL	52,807	VC
Dominican College	NY	40,258	LC
Dordt College	IA	37,860	C+
Drake Univ	IA	49,220	HC
Duquesne Univ	PA	48,508	VC
East Carolina Univ	NC	16,539	C
East Central Univ	OK	13,330	C
Eastern Kentucky Univ	KY	17,742	C
Eastern Mich Univ	MI	19,761	C
Eastern Washington Univ	WA	17,896	LC
Emory Univ	GA	63,286	MC
Excelsior College	NY	38,800	SP
Fairleigh Dickinson Univ/ College at Florham	NJ	54,770	C
Fayetteville State Univ	NC	17,756	C
Florida A&M Univ	FL	15,361	C
Florida Atlantic Univ	FL	18,256	C
Florida Gulf Coast Univ	FL	14,738	C
Florida International Univ	FL	20,281	C
Florida State Univ	FL	16,771	HC
Fort Hays State Univ	KS	12,677	C
Francis Marion Univ	SC	18,144	LC
Franklin Pierce Univ	NH	46,750	LC
Franklin Univ	OH	11,616	NC
Freed-Hardeman Univ	TN	29,900	C
Friends Univ	KS	38,000	C
Gannon Univ	PA	42,922	C
George Mason Univ	VA	19,884	C
Georgetown College	KY	41,440	C
Georgetown Univ	DC	68,970	MC
Georgia State Univ	GA	25,250	C
Golden Gate Univ	CA	19,510	C
Goldey-Beacom College	DE	36,038	C
Grand Valley State Univ	MI	22,250	C+
Gwynedd Mercy Univ	PA	43,780	LC
Hampton Univ	VA	36,410	C
Harding Univ	AR	25,440	C
Hardin-Simmons Univ	TX	36,025	C
Hawaii Pacific Univ	HI	33,420	C
Hofstra Univ	NY	58,210	C+
Houston Baptist Univ	TX	36,450	C
Howard Univ	DC	37,616	C+
Husson Univ	ME	26,508	C
Idaho State Univ	ID	13,619	LC
Indiana State Univ	IN	23,223	LC
Indiana Univ-Purdue Univ Fort Wayne	IN	18,675	C
Indiana Wesleyan Univ	IN	33,674	C
Inter-American Univ of PR Ponce	PR	19,549	
Inter-American Univ of PR-Bayamon	PR	18,785	
Inter-American Univ of PR-Fajardo Campus	PR	18,336	
Inter-American Univ of PR-Metropolitan Campus	PR	20,045	
Inter-American Univ of PR-San Germán	PR	20,042	
Iowa State Univ	IA	18,176	C
Jacksonville State Univ	AL	14,628	LC
Jacksonville Univ	FL	49,210	C
James Madison Univ	VA	19,084	VC
Jefferson (Philadelphia Univ + Thomas Jefferson Univ)	PA	53,966	C
John Carroll Univ	OH	51,570	C
Juniata College	PA	58,118	VC
Kansas State Univ	KS	17,780	VC
King's College	PA	48,240	C
La Roche College	PA	38,940	C
La Salle Univ	PA	43,476	C
La Sierra Univ	CA	39,690	VC
Lake Superior State Univ	MI	19,867	C
Le Moyne College	NY	47,305	VC
Lindenwood Univ	MO	25,760	C
Linfield College	OR	53,992	C
Louisiana State Univ and A&M College	LA	18,677	VC
Louisiana State Univ in Shreveport	LA	6,902	C
Louisiana Tech Univ	LA	11,422	VC
Loyola Univ New Orleans	LA	52,456	VC
Lubbock Christian Univ	TX	29,727	C
Manchester Univ	IN	41,540	C
Manhattan College	NY	55,652	C
Manhattanville College	NY	52,430	C
Marietta College	OH	46,190	C
Marshall Univ	WV	18,044	C
Marywood Univ	PA	47,840	C
McKendree Univ	IL	37,940	C+
McMurry Univ	TX	34,259	LC
Mercy College	NY	32,614	C
Mercyhurst Univ	PA	47,420	C
Metropolitan State Univ	MN	7,859	C
Metropolitan State Univ of Denver	CO	6,928	LC
Mich State Univ	MI	24,542	VC
Middle Tenn State Univ	TN	8,650	C
Midwestern State Univ	TX	12,111	LC
Minn State Univ, Mankato	MN	17,190	C
Minn State Univ, Moorhead	MN	21,393	C
Minot State Univ	ND	13,285	C
Miss State Univ	MS	12,028	C+
Monmouth Univ	NJ	50,184	C
Morehead State Univ	KY	18,386	LC
Muhlenberg College	PA	56,645	VC
National Univ	CA	17,849	LC
New Mexico Highlands Univ	NM	11,904	LC
New York Univ	NY	68,139	MC
Nicholls State Univ	LA	14,959	C
Norfolk State Univ	VA	18,902	LC
North Park Univ	IL	35,860	C
Northeastern Illinois Univ	IL	12,529	LC
Northeastern State Univ	OK	8,615	VC
Northern Illinois Univ	IL	20,176	C
Northern Mich Univ	MI	20,853	C
Northern State Univ	SD	15,570	C
Northwest Missouri State Univ	MO	18,286	C
Northwood Univ - Mich	MI	35,010	LC
Notre Dame of Maryland Univ	MD	47,570	VC
Oakland Univ	MI	20,763	C
Ohio Dominican Univ	OH	41,340	C+
Ohio State Univ at Columbus	OH	22,843	MC
Ohio Univ	OH	23,394	VC
Okla Baptist Univ	OK	33,990	C
Okla Christian Univ	OK	29,260	C
Okla City Univ	OK	40,476	C
Okla State Univ	OK	17,180	C+
Oral Roberts Univ	OK	34,316	C
Pace Univ	NY	60,136	C
Palm Beach Atlantic Univ	FL	39,250	C
Penn State Erie,The Behrend College	PA	26,688	VC
Pittsburg State Univ	KS	13,880	C
Pontifical Catholic Univ of PR	PR	10,534	
Post Univ	CT	41,150	C
Prairie View A&M Univ	TX	27,273	LC
Purdue Univ/West Lafayette	IN	20,032	MC
Quincy Univ	IL	38,170	LC
Quinnipiac Univ	CT	60,970	VC
Radford Univ	VA	19,758	C
Rhode Island College	RI	19,000	LC
Rider Univ	NJ	54,050	C
Robert Morris Univ	PA	40,600	C
Rochester Inst of Technology	NY	52,734	HC+
Roger Williams Univ	RI	48,074	VC
Roosevelt Univ	IL	41,890	VC
Saginaw Valley State Univ	MI	19,284	C
St. Anselm College	NH	56,636	VC
St. Vincent College	PA	46,229	C
St. Xavier Univ	IL	44,440	C
Salem State Univ	MA	42,650	LC
Sam Houston State Univ	TX	18,792	C
San Francisco State Univ	CA	18,514	LC
San Jose State Univ	CA	22,630	C
Siena College	NY	48,916	C
Southeastern Univ	FL	34,910	LC
Southern Adventist Univ	TN	28,250	C
Southern Conn State Univ	CT	21,924	LC
Southern Illinois Univ Carbondale	IL	24,554	C
Southern Nazarene Univ	OK	33,684	C
Southern Univ and A&M College	LA	16,074	LC
St. Bonaventure Univ	NY	45,596	C
St. Cloud State Univ	MN	10,600	C
St. Edward's Univ	TX	56,190	VC
St. Mary's Univ	TX	39,120	C
St. Thomas Aquinas College	NY	32,450	C
St. Thomas Univ	FL	51,187	LC
SUNY at New Paltz	NY	20,840	C
SUNY/College at Old Westbury	NY	16,860	C
Stephen F. Austin State Univ	TX	18,484	LC
Stetson Univ	FL	57,174	VC+
Stockton Univ	NJ	25,565	C
Stonehill College	MA	55,130	C
Suffolk Univ	MA	52,316	C
Talladega College	AL	25,919	C
Tarleton State Univ	TX	15,248	LC
Taylor Univ	IN	42,130	VC
Temple Univ	PA	24,392	C+
Tenn Tech Univ	TN	17,929	C
Texas A&M Univ at Commerce	TX	10,496	C
Texas A&M Univ at Corpus Christi	TX	16,851	LC
Texas A&M Univ at Kingsville	TX	16,580	LC
Texas Southern Univ	TX	19,592	LC
Texas State Univ	TX	18,721	C
The Catholic Univ of America	DC	58,376	VC
The George Washington Univ	DC	68,474	HC+
The Univ of Akron	OH	22,566	C
The Univ of Memphis	TN	18,278	C
The Univ of Texas at Austin	TX	20,206	MC
Tiffin Univ	OH	34,900	LC
Touro College	NY	31,040	C
Trine Univ	IN	41,310	C
Troy Univ	AL	16,171	C
Tulane Univ	LA	67,496	MC
Tuskegee Univ	AL	28,164	C
Union College	NE	23,270	C
Union Univ	TN	41,160	VC
Univ of PR, at Arecibo	PR	12,652	
Univ of Alabama at Birmingham	AL	22,092	C
Univ of Alabama in Huntsville	AL	20,028	VC
Univ of Alaska Anchorage	AK	17,914	C
Univ of Arkansas at Little Rock	AR	18,211	LC
Univ of Bridgeport	CT	44,985	LC
Univ of Central Arkansas	AR	15,042	VC
Univ of Central Florida	FL	16,379	VC
Univ of Central Okla	OK	15,150	C
Univ of Cincinnati	OH	22,118	VC
Univ of Conn	CT	27,394	
Univ of Dayton	OH	54,930	VC
Univ of Delaware	DE	32,214	VC
Univ of Denver	CO	61,129	VC+
Univ of Findlay	OH	43,040	C
Univ of Florida	FL	16,291	HC+
Univ of Hartford	CT	49,776	C
Univ of Hawaii at Manoa	HI	23,261	C
Univ of Houston-Downtown	TX	7,241	LC
Univ of Illinois at Chicago	IL	24,664	VC
Univ of Illinois at Urbana-Champaign	IL	27,006	HC
Univ of Indianapolis	IN	36,480	VC
Univ of Iowa	IA	19,415	HC
Univ of Kentucky	KY	24,800	C+
Univ of Louisiana at Lafayette	LA	14,516	C
Univ of Louisville	KY	19,692	C
Univ of Mass Amherst	MA	27,669	HC
Univ of Mich/Flint	MI	19,062	C
Univ of Miss	MS	18,802	C
Univ of Missouri-Columbia	MO	20,463	VC
Univ of Montana	MT	14,105	C
Univ of Montevallo	AL	20,012	C
Univ of Nebr - Kearney	NE	17,014	LC
Univ of Nebr - Lincoln	NE	18,589	VC
Univ of Nebr - Omaha	NE	16,120	C
Univ of Nevada, Las Vegas	NV	17,553	C
Univ of New Haven	CT	53,680	C
Univ of New Orleans	LA	12,840	C
Univ of North Alabama	AL	15,964	C
Univ of N Car at Charlotte	NC	17,803	VC
Univ of N Dak	ND	16,673	C
Univ of North Florida	FL	15,996	VC
Univ of North Georgia	GA	17,316	C
Univ of North Texas	TX	20,082	C
Univ of Northern Iowa	IA	17,480	C
Univ of Northwestern - St. Paul	MN	39,530	C
Univ of Pittsburgh at Johnstown	PA	22,092	C
Univ of Portland	OR	52,152	VC
Univ of PR, at Bayamon	PR	13,145	
Univ of PR, at Mayaguez	PR	13,995	
Univ of PR-Rio Piedras campus	PR	13,327	
Univ of Scranton	PA	54,962	VC
Univ of South Alabama	AL	16,880	C
Univ of S Car at Columbia	SC	21,726	VC
Univ of S Dak	SD	16,109	C
Univ of South Florida/Tampa	FL	16,110	VC
Univ of Southern Miss	MS	13,170	C
Univ of St. Francis	IL	40,828	C
Univ of Tampa	FL	38,928	VC
Univ of Texas at Arlington	TX	18,876	C
Univ of Texas at Dallas	TX	23,640	HC
Univ of Texas at El Paso	TX	34,452	NC
Univ of Texas Rio Grande Valley	TX	15,573	LC
Univ of the District of Columbia	DC	21,260	LC
Univ of Toledo	OH	19,336	C
Univ of Tulsa	OK	52,625	HC
Univ of Washington	WA	23,091	MC
Univ of West Florida	FL	15,848	C
Univ of Wisc-Eau Claire	WI	16,354	VC
Univ of Wisc-Madison	WI	21,647	MC
Univ of Wisc-Oshkosh	WI	15,392	C
Univ of Wisc-Whitewater	WI	13,976	C
Upper Iowa Univ	IA	34,990	NC
Utah State Univ	UT	13,235	C
Valparaiso Univ	IN	50,160	VC

ST = STATE $IS = IN-STATE COSTS SR = SELECTOR RATING

School	ST	$IS	SR
Villanova Univ	PA	64,922	MC
Virginia Polytechnic Inst and State Univ	VA	21,920	VC
Virginia Union Univ	VA	25,058	C
Wake Forest Univ	NC	69,354	MC
Warner Univ	FL	28,216	C
Washburn Univ	KS	15,827	C
Washington Univ in St. Louis	MO	67,539	MC
Webber International Univ	FL	31,904	C
Weber State Univ	UT	14,112	C
West Chester Univ of Pennsylvania	PA	19,171	VC
West Liberty Univ	WV	16,158	C
West Texas A&M Univ	TX	13,478	C
West Virginia State Univ	WV	19,412	LC
West Virginia Univ	WV	18,952	VC
Western Carolina Univ	NC	13,965	C
Western Conn State Univ	CT	21,254	LC
Western Kentucky Univ	KY	16,850	C
Westminster College	PA	41,722	C
Westminster College	UT	41,078	C
Wichita State Univ	KS	17,773	C
Wilberforce Univ	OH	19,900	C
William Paterson Univ of New Jersey	NJ	24,022	C
Wilmington Univ	DE	8,762	NC
Winona State Univ	MN	18,109	C
Wofford College	SC	49,885	VC
Wright State Univ	OH	16,983	C
Xavier Univ	OH	49,380	VC
York College of Pennsylvania	PA	29,240	C
Youngstown State Univ	OH	17,487	C

BEHAVIORAL SCIENCE

School	ST	$IS	SR
Alvernia Univ	PA	45,330	C
Andrews Univ	MI	41,732	C
Ashford Univ	CA	10,480	C
Bethel College	IN	36,830	C
Calif Baptist Univ	CA	42,986	C
Cal State, Dominguez Hills	CA	19,022	LC
Cal State, Fullerton	CA	21,902	C
Cal State, Monterey Bay	CA	22,872	LC
Capital Univ	OH	44,778	VC
Chaminade Univ of Honolulu	HI	37,614	C
College of St. Scholastica	MN	45,734	C+
Concordia College - New York	NY	39,035	LC
Concordia Univ Irvine	CA	44,860	VC
Concordia Univ Nebr	NE	41,900	VC
Concordia Univ Texas	TX	41,920	C
Corban Univ	OR	41,700	C
Dakota Wesleyan Univ	SD	33,980	LC
Drury Univ	MO	37,555	VC
Duquesne Univ	PA	48,508	VC
Elizabethtown College School of Continuing and Professional Studies	PA	18,900	C
Erskine College	SC	45,460	C
Fontbonne Univ	MO	34,606	C
George Fox Univ	OR	42,938	C
Grand Valley State Univ	MI	22,250	C+
Johns Hopkins Univ	MD	68,080	MC
Johnson State College	VT	22,672	C
Lakeland Univ	WI	35,130	C
Lehigh Univ	PA	63,860	MC
Mercy College	NY	32,614	C
Metropolitan State Univ of Denver	CO	6,928	LC
Miles College	AL	16,530	NC
Missouri Baptist Univ	MO	35,594	C
Mount Aloysius College	PA	29,976	C
Mount Marty College	SD	36,862	C
Mount Mary Univ	WI	34,650	LC
National Univ	CA	17,849	LC
New York Inst of Technology	NY	49,980	VC
North Central Univ	MN	30,610	C
Northwest Univ	WA	38,720	VC
Nova Southeastern Univ	FL	38,534	C+
Oglethorpe Univ	GA	44,200	C
Okla City Univ	OK	40,476	C
Okla Wesleyan Univ	OK	34,434	C
Our Lady of the Lake Univ	TX	37,790	LC
Palm Beach Atlantic Univ	FL	39,250	C
Point Park Univ	PA	41,270	C
Purdue Univ Northwest	IN	15,178	C
Purdue Univ/West Lafayette	IN	20,032	MC
Rochester College	MI	28,574	LC
St. Louis Univ	MO	49,866	HC
Savannah State Univ	GA	17,036	C
Southern Adventist Univ	TN	28,250	C
Sterling College	KS	32,830	LC
Tabor College	KS	35,870	C
Tenn Wesleyan Univ	TN	32,680	LC
The Univ of Mary	ND	23,180	C
The Univ of Utah	UT	18,751	VC
Trevecca Nazarene Univ	TN	31,186	C
United States Air Force Academy	CO		C
Univ of Calif at Davis	CA	28,468	HC
Univ of Holy Cross	LA	21,523	NC
Univ of Kansas	KS	20,884	VC
Univ of La Verne	CA	55,600	C
Univ of Maine at Fort Kent	ME	15,165	LC
Univ of Maine at Machias	ME	22,960	C
Univ of Mich/Ann Arbor	MI	25,274	MC
Univ of Mich/Dearborn	MI	12,472	VC
Univ of Rio Grande & Rio Grande Community College	OH	8,750	LC
Univ of St. Mary	KS	37,080	NC
Univ of San Diego	CA	60,338	HC
Univ of Wisc-Milwaukee	WI	21,538	C
Villanova Univ	PA	64,922	MC
Western Mich Univ	MI	21,791	C
Western Washington Univ	WA	18,904	VC
Widener Univ	PA	58,190	C
Wilmington Univ	DE	8,762	NC
York College of Pennsylvania	PA	29,240	C

BIBLICAL LANGUAGES

School	ST	$IS	SR
Asbury Univ	KY	36,450	C+
Belmont Univ	TN	44,500	VC+
Concordia Univ Irvine	CA	44,860	VC
Concordia Univ Wisc	WI	35,910	C
Concordia Univ, Ann Arbor	MI	38,878	C+
Faulkner Univ	AL	26,410	C
Harding Univ	AR	25,440	C
Houston Baptist Univ	TX	36,450	C
Lipscomb Univ	TN	42,984	VC
Luther College	IA	49,990	VC
North Central Univ	MN	30,610	C
Okla Baptist Univ	OK	33,990	C
Olivet Nazarene Univ	IL	41,840	VC
Ouachita Baptist Univ	AR	33,500	VC
The Master's Univ	CA	43,870	C
Union Univ	TN	41,160	VC
Walla Walla Univ	WA	34,845	C

BIBLICAL STUDIES

School	ST	$IS	SR
Abilene Christian Univ	TX	43,708	C+
Amridge Univ	AL	10,860	LC
Asbury Univ	KY	36,450	C+
Azusa Pacific Univ	CA	43,972	C
Belhaven Univ	MS	32,250	C
Belmont Univ	TN	44,500	VC+
Bethel College	IN	36,830	C
Bethel Univ	MN	46,550	C+
Biola Univ	CA	48,686	C
Blue Mountain College	MS	15,949	C
Bluffton Univ	OH	40,950	C+
Cairn Univ	PA	37,572	C
Campbellsville Univ	KY	33,400	C
Canisius College	NY	49,672	C
Cedarville Univ	OH	36,244	VC
College of the Ozarks	MO	7,530	VC
Colo Christian Univ	CO	40,885	VC
Corban Univ	OR	41,700	C
Cornerstone Univ	MI	36,550	C
Covenant College	GA	44,590	HC
Dallas Baptist Univ	TX	35,220	VC
East Texas Baptist Univ	TX	34,444	C
Eastern Mennonite Univ	VA	42,550	C
Eastern Univ	PA	39,540	C
Evangel Univ	MO	28,898	C
Faulkner Univ	AL	26,410	C
Freed-Hardeman Univ	TN	29,900	C
Geneva College	PA	35,450	C
George Fox Univ	OR	42,938	C
Gordon College	MA	47,740	VC
Goshen College	IN	44,350	C
Grace Bible College	MI	25,250	C
Grace College and Seminary	IN	31,524	C
Grove City College	PA	26,654	VC
Hannibal-LaGrange Univ	MO	29,815	C
Harding Univ	AR	25,440	C
Hardin-Simmons Univ	TX	36,025	C
Hope International Univ	CA	42,730	C
Houghton College	NY	40,558	VC
Huntington Univ	IN	33,996	C
Indiana Wesleyan Univ	IN	33,674	C
John Brown Univ	AR	35,184	VC
Judson Univ	IL	39,174	C
Kentucky Christian Univ	KY	26,836	LC
King Univ	TN	36,976	C
Lee Univ	TN	22,045	C
LeTourneau Univ	TX	39,190	VC
Lipscomb Univ	TN	42,984	VC
List College/The Jewish Theological Seminary (JTS)	NY	37,870	SP
Lubbock Christian Univ	TX	29,727	C
Malone Univ	OH	39,200	C
Messiah College	PA	44,380	VC
Milligan College	TN	39,450	C
Montreat College	NC	34,605	LC
Mount Vernon Nazarene Univ	OH	35,944	C
North Central Univ	MN	30,610	C
North Park Univ	IL	35,860	C
Northwest Nazarene Univ	ID	40,250	C
Northwest Univ	WA	38,720	VC
Nyack College	NY	34,450	LC
Ohio Valley Univ	WV	28,800	C
Okla Baptist Univ	OK	33,990	C
Okla Christian Univ	OK	29,260	C
Olivet Nazarene Univ	IL	41,840	VC
Oral Roberts Univ	OK	34,316	C
Ouachita Baptist Univ	AR	33,500	VC
Palm Beach Atlantic Univ	FL	39,250	C
Point Loma Nazarene Univ	CA	46,150	C+
Roberts Wesleyan College	NY	41,116	C
Rochester College	MI	28,574	LC
San Diego Christian College	CA	40,914	C
Shepherd Univ	CA		LC
Simpson Univ	CA	34,722	C
Southeastern Univ	FL	34,910	LC
Southwest Baptist Univ	MO	30,890	LC
Spring Arbor Univ	MI	37,390	C
Sterling College	KS	32,830	LC
Tabor College	KS	35,870	C
Taylor Univ	IN	42,130	VC
The Master's Univ	CA	43,870	C
Toccoa Falls College	GA	30,048	C
Trinity Bible College	ND		
Trinity Christian College	IL	35,580	C
Trinity International Univ	IL	31,070	VC
Union Univ	TN	41,160	VC
Univ of Evansville	IN	44,186	C+
Univ of Mary Hardin-Baylor	TX	35,292	C+
Univ of Mich/Ann Arbor	MI	25,274	MC
Univ of Minn/Twin Cities	MN	24,269	MC
Univ of Northwestern - St. Paul	MN	39,530	C
Vanguard Univ of Southern Calif	CA	42,400	VC
Warner Univ	FL	28,216	C
Waynesburg Univ	PA	33,530	C
Wheaton College	IL	44,993	MC
York College	NE	30,260	C

BILINGUAL/BICULTURAL EDUCATION

School	ST	$IS	SR
Boston Univ	MA	67,352	MC
Cal State, Fullerton	CA	21,902	C
Cal State, San Bernardino	CA	20,106	C
Chicago State Univ	IL	41,620	C
CUNY/Brooklyn College	NY	7,163	C+
CUNY/City College	NY	20,204	C
Eastern Mich Univ	MI	19,761	C
Elms College	MA	49,602	VC
Loyola Univ Chicago	IL	57,158	VC
Mount Mary Univ	WI	34,650	LC
New Mexico State Univ	NM	14,050	LC
New York Univ	NY	68,139	MC
Northeastern Illinois Univ	IL	12,529	LC
St. Thomas Aquinas College	NY	32,450	C
SUNY/College at Old Westbury	NY	16,860	C
Univ of Central Okla	OK	15,150	C
Univ of Findlay	OH	43,040	C
Univ of Minn/Twin Cities	MN	24,269	MC
Univ of Texas Rio Grande Valley	TX	15,573	LC
Washington State Univ	WA	22,747	C
Western Illinois Univ	IL	20,897	C

BIOCHEMISTRY

School	ST	$IS	SR
Abilene Christian Univ	TX	43,708	C+
Adams State Univ	CO	15,420	LC
Adelphi Univ	NY	49,792	C
Agnes Scott College	GA	51,930	VC+
Albion College	MI	55,260	C
Albright College	PA	57,326	C
Allegheny College	PA	57,620	VC
Alma College	MI	49,410	VC
Alvernia Univ	PA	45,330	C
American International College	MA	47,020	LC
Amherst College	MA	66,186	MC
Anderson Univ	IN	39,450	C
Andrews Univ	MI	41,732	C
Arizona State Univ at the Tempe Campus	AZ	23,001	VC
Armstrong State Univ	GA	15,615	C
Asbury Univ	KY	36,450	C+
Auburn Univ	AL	24,300	VC+
Augustana College	IL	51,222	VC+
Augustana Univ	SD	39,968	VC
Austin College	TX	51,059	HC
Averett Univ	VA	43,034	LC
Avila Univ	MO	27,100	C
Azusa Pacific Univ	CA	43,972	C
Baker Univ	KS	37,190	C
Barnard College/Columbia Univ	NY	68,762	MC
Bates College	ME	64,500	HC
Bay Path Univ	MA	46,356	C
Baylor Univ	TX	56,803	HC
Bellarmine Univ	KY	52,532	C
Belmont Univ	TN	44,500	VC+
Beloit College	WI	55,206	HC
Benedictine College	KS	38,850	VC
Benedictine Univ	IL	38,300	C
Berry College	GA	47,466	VC
Bethany College	WV	38,774	LC
Bethel College	IN	36,830	C
Bethel Univ	MN	46,550	C+
Biola Univ	CA	48,686	C
Blackburn College	IL	28,526	LC
Bloomfield College	NJ	40,100	LC
Boston College	MA	68,043	MC
Boston Univ	MA	67,352	MC
Bowdoin College	ME	65,980	MC
Bradley Univ	IL	43,240	VC
Brandeis Univ	MA	68,443	MC
Brescia Univ	KY	29,890	VC
Bridgewater College	VA	46,260	C
Brigham Young Univ	UT	13,248	MC
Brown Univ	RI	64,566	MC
Bryant Univ	RI	57,204	VC
Bucknell Univ	PA	67,136	MC
Buena Vista Univ	IA	42,344	C
Butler Univ	IN	52,890	VC+
Calif Baptist Univ	CA	42,986	C
Calif Lutheran Univ	CA	52,853	C
Calif Polytechnic State Univ	CA	22,547	MC
Cal State, Chico	CA	19,790	VC
Cal State, Dominguez Hills	CA	19,022	LC
Cal State, Fullerton	CA	21,902	C
Cal State, Long Beach	CA	18,850	C
Cal State, Los Angeles	CA	17,186	LC
Cal State, Northridge	CA	17,277	LC
Cal State, San Bernardino	CA	20,106	C
Cal State, San Marcos	CA	20,604	LC
Calvin College	MI	43,090	HC
Campbell Univ	NC	37,570	VC
Canisius College	NY	49,672	C
Capital Univ	OH	44,778	VC
Carnegie Mellon Univ	PA	67,980	MC
Carroll College	MT	44,304	C
Carroll Univ	WI	38,100	C+
Case Western Reserve Univ	OH	62,284	MC
Cedar Crest College	PA	51,110	C
Centenary College of Louisiana	LA	49,050	C+
Central College	IA	44,592	C
Central Conn State Univ	CT	22,041	C
Central Mich Univ	MI	20,330	C
Centre College	KY	50,680	MC
Chaminade Univ of Honolulu	HI	37,614	C
Chapman Univ	CA	65,504	HC
Charleston Southern Univ	SC	34,700	C
Chatham Univ	PA	47,883	VC
Chestnut Hill College	PA	47,180	C
Chicago State Univ	IL	41,620	C
Christian Brothers Univ	TN	31,670	VC
Christopher Newport Univ	VA	24,878	VC+
Claflin Univ	SC	25,592	LC
Claremont McKenna College	CA	69,900	MC
Clark Univ	MA	53,260	HC+
Clarke Univ	IA	42,950	C
Clemson Univ	SC		HC
Coastal Carolina Univ	SC	20,340	C
Coe College	IA	51,570	VC
Colby College	ME	64,060	MC
Colgate Univ	NY	67,500	MC
College of Charleston	SC	24,046	VC
College of Mount St. Vincent	NY	45,620	C
College of St. Benedict	MN	54,480	C
College of St. Elizabeth	NJ	45,700	LC
College of St. Scholastica	MN	45,734	C+
College of Staten Island	NY	24,389	LC
Colo College	CO	64,894	MC
Colo State Univ	CO	23,033	C
Colo State Univ-Pueblo	CO	21,581	C
Columbia Univ/City of New York	NY	62,958	MC
Conn College	CT	65,000	MC
Cornell College	IA	49,900	VC
Culver-Stockton College	MO	34,350	C
Curry College	MA	53,331	C
Daemen College	NY	40,336	C
Dakota Wesleyan Univ	SD	33,980	LC
Dartmouth College	NH	68,109	MC
Denison Univ	OH	62,770	HC+
DePaul Univ	IL	52,807	VC
DePauw Univ	IN	58,688	VC
DeSales Univ	PA	47,520	C
Dickinson College	PA	66,166	MC
Doane Univ	NE	41,340	VC
Dominican Univ	IL	42,472	C+
Drew Univ/College of Liberal Arts	NJ	53,608	VC
Drury Univ	MO	37,555	VC
Duquesne Univ	PA	48,508	VC
Earlham College	IN	55,670	HC
East Carolina Univ	NC	16,539	C
East Stroudsburg Univ	PA	18,578	LC
Eastern Conn State Univ	CT	23,059	C
Eastern Mennonite Univ	VA	42,550	C
Eastern Mich Univ	MI	19,761	C
Eastern New Mexico Univ	NM	12,874	LC
Eastern Univ	PA	39,540	C
Eastern Washington Univ	WA	17,896	LC
Eckerd College	FL	55,206	VC
Elizabethtown College	PA	56,340	VC
Elmira College	NY	53,900	C
Elon Univ	NC	46,142	HC
Emmanuel College	MA	53,472	C+
Emporia State Univ	KS	15,029	C
Fairfield Univ	CT	61,445	HC
Fairleigh Dickinson Univ/College at Florham	NJ	54,770	C
Fairleigh Dickinson Univ/Metropolitan Campus	NJ	52,392	C
Faulkner Univ	AL	26,410	C
Ferris State Univ	MI	21,458	C
Florida Inst of Technology	FL	53,306	VC
Florida Southern College	FL	45,978	VC
Florida State Univ	FL	16,771	HC
Fort Lewis College	CO	20,154	C
Framingham State Univ	MA	21,740	C
Franklin and Marshall College	PA	67,960	MC
Freed-Hardeman Univ	TN	29,900	C
Gannon Univ	PA	42,922	C
Georgetown College	KY	41,440	C
Georgetown Univ	DC	68,970	MC

ST = STATE $IS = IN-STATE COSTS SR = SELECTOR RATING

School	ST	$IS	SR
Georgia Inst of Technology	GA	23,910	MC
Georgian Court Univ	NJ	43,068	LC
Gettysburg College	PA	65,210	MC
Gonzaga Univ	WA	52,880	HC
Goshen College	IN	44,350	C
Goucher College	MD	56,110	VC
Grand View Univ	IA	32,302	C
Grinnell College	IA	63,114	MC
Grove City College	PA	26,654	VC
Gustavus Adolphus College	MN	53,943	HC
Hamilton College	NY	64,250	MC
Hamline Univ	MN	50,152	C
Hanover College	IN	47,750	C+
Harding Univ	AR	25,440	C
Hardin-Simmons Univ	TX	36,025	C
Hartwick College	NY	51,270	C
Harvard College/Harvard Univ	MA	65,609	MC
Hawaii Pacific Univ	HI	33,420	C
Heidelberg Univ	OH	40,400	LC
Hendrix College	AR	54,020	VC
High Point Univ	NC	47,355	VC
Hillsdale College	MI	37,170	MC
Hiram College	OH	44,590	C
Hobart and William Smith Colleges	NY	67,050	HC+
Hofstra Univ	NY	58,210	C+
Holy Family Univ	PA	44,672	LC
Hood College	MD	50,540	C
Hope College	MI	42,840	VC
Houghton College	NY	40,558	VC
Howard Univ	DC	37,616	C+
Huntingdon College	AL	35,900	C
Husson Univ	ME	26,508	C
Idaho State Univ	ID	13,619	LC
Illinois College	IL	41,330	VC
Illinois Inst of Technology	IL	56,826	HC+
Illinois State Univ	IL	23,418	VC
Indiana Univ Bloomington	IN	20,791	HC
Indiana Univ East	IN	7,207	C
Indiana Univ Kokomo	IN	7,207	C
Indiana Univ Northwest	IN	7,207	LC
Indiana Univ of Pennsylvania	PA	24,474	C
Indiana Univ South Bend	IN	16,057	C
Indiana Univ-Purdue Univ Fort Wayne	IN	18,675	C
Iona College	NY	52,514	C
Iowa State Univ	IA	18,176	C
Ithaca College	NY	58,158	VC+
Jefferson (Philadelphia Univ + Thomas Jefferson Univ)	PA	53,966	C
John Brown Univ	AR	35,184	VC
John Carroll Univ	OH	51,570	C
Juniata College	PA	58,118	VC
Kalamazoo College	MI	53,931	HC
Kansas State Univ	KS	17,780	VC
Kennesaw State Univ	GA	18,899	VC
Kenyon College	OH	65,840	MC
Kettering Univ	MI	47,570	HC
Keuka College	NY	42,398	C
King Univ	TN	36,976	C
Knox College	IL	54,654	VC+
Kutztown Univ of Pennsylvania	PA	19,477	C
La Roche College	PA	38,940	C
La Salle Univ	PA	43,476	C
La Sierra Univ	CA	39,690	VC
Lafayette College	PA	68,520	MC
LaGrange College	GA	41,310	C
Lake Superior State Univ	MI	19,867	C
Lawrence Tech Univ	MI	41,630	VC
Lawrence Univ	WI	56,133	HC+
Le Moyne College	NY	47,305	VC
Lebanon Valley College	PA	55,510	VC
Lee Univ	TN	22,045	C
Lehigh Univ	PA	63,860	MC
Lewis & Clark College	OR	60,984	MC
Lewis Univ	IL	41,710	C
Lincoln Univ	PA	20,878	LC
Linfield College	OR	53,992	C
Lipscomb Univ	TN	42,984	VC
LIU Brooklyn	NY	50,698	C
Loras College	IA	40,726	C
Louisiana State Univ and A&M College	LA	18,677	VC
Louisiana State Univ in Shreveport	LA	6,902	C
Loyola Marymount Univ	CA	60,202	VC+
Loyola Univ Chicago	IL	57,158	VC
Lubbock Christian Univ	TX	29,727	C
Lycoming College	PA	50,895	C
Madonna Univ	MI	30,450	LC
Malone Univ	OH	39,200	C
Manchester Univ	IN	41,540	C
Manhattan College	NY	55,652	C
Manhattanville College	NY	52,430	C
Marietta College	OH	46,190	C
Marist College	NY	49,860	VC
Marlboro College	VT	50,832	VC+
Marquette Univ	WI	53,090	VC+
Marshall Univ	WV	18,044	C
Marymount Univ	VA	43,231	C
Maryville College	TN	44,410	C
Maryville Univ of St. Louis	MO	38,558	VC
McMurry Univ	TX	34,259	LC
Mercer Univ	GA	45,348	VC
Mercyhurst Univ	PA	47,420	C
Merrimack College	MA	55,415	C
Messiah College	PA	44,380	VC
Miami Univ	OH	27,190	HC+
Mich State Univ	MI	24,542	VC
Mich Tech Univ	MI	25,551	VC+
Middlebury College	VT	67,464	MC
Millersville Univ of Pennsylvania	PA	25,298	C
Millikin Univ	IL	44,148	C
Mills College	CA	43,705	C
Millsaps College	MS	50,080	C+
Minn State Univ, Mankato	MN	17,190	C
Misericordia Univ	PA	45,210	C
Miss College	MS	25,850	C
Miss State Univ	MS	12,028	C+
Missouri Baptist Univ	MO	35,594	C
Missouri Southern State Univ	MO	13,071	C
Missouri Western State Univ	MO	17,822	LC
Monmouth College	IL	42,260	C
Montclair State Univ	NJ	26,912	C
Moravian College	PA	55,488	C
Mount Holyoke College	MA	56,746	MC
Mount St. Joseph Univ	OH	33,880	LC
Mount St. Mary's Univ	MD	53,380	C
Mount St. Mary's Univ - Chalon Campus	CA	50,486	VC+
Muhlenberg College	PA	56,645	VC
Nazareth College	NY	46,784	C
Nebr Wesleyan Univ	NE	42,026	C+
New College of Florida	FL	16,180	HC+
New Mexico State Univ	NM	14,050	LC
New York Univ	NY	68,139	MC
Newman Univ	KS	37,382	C
Niagara Univ	NY	41,010	C
N Car State Univ	NC	22,434	HC+
North Central College	IL	48,712	C+
N Dak State Univ	ND	16,245	VC
Northeastern Univ	MA	65,352	MC
Northern Mich Univ	MI	20,853	C
Northwest Nazarene Univ	ID	40,250	C
Northwestern College of Iowa	IA	38,400	C
Norwich Univ	VT	56,234	C
Notre Dame de Namur Univ	CA	46,526	LC
Oakland Univ	MI	20,763	C
Oakwood Univ	AL	43,758	C
Oberlin College	OH	68,942	MC
Occidental College	CA	68,660	MC
Ohio Northern Univ	OH	44,050	VC
Ohio State Univ at Columbus	OH	22,843	MC
Ohio Univ	OH	23,394	VC
Ohio Valley Univ	WV	28,800	C
Ohio Wesleyan Univ	OH	49,460	VC
Okla Christian Univ	OK	29,260	C
Okla City Univ	OK	40,476	C
Okla State Univ	OK	17,180	C+
Old Dominion Univ	VA	21,618	C
Olivet College	MI	37,661	LC
Oregon State Univ	OR	23,337	VC
Otterbein Univ	OH	41,630	C
Pace Univ	NY	60,136	C
Pennsylvania State Univ - Univ Park	PA	29,716	HC
Pittsburg State Univ	KS	13,880	C
Pitzer College	CA	68,500	HC+
Point Loma Nazarene Univ	CA	46,150	C+
Portland State Univ	OR	19,443	C
Presbyterian College	SC	47,186	C
Providence College	RI	62,870	HC
Purdue Univ/West Lafayette	IN	20,032	MC
Queens Univ of Charlotte	NC	39,543	C
Quinnipiac Univ	CT	60,970	VC
Ramapo College of New Jersey	NJ	25,760	VC
Reed College	OR	65,300	MC
Regis College	MA	51,920	LC
Regis Univ	CO	46,380	C
Rensselaer Polytechnic Inst	NY	67,265	MC
Rhodes College	TN	51,900	HC
Rider Univ	NJ	54,050	C
Ripon College	WI	49,991	VC
Roanoke College	VA	55,952	VC
Roberts Wesleyan College	NY	41,116	C
Rochester Inst of Technology	NY	52,734	HC+
Rockford Univ	IL	38,570	C
Rockhurst Univ	MO	28,990	C
Roger Williams Univ	RI	48,074	VC
Rollins College	FL	58,670	HC
Rose-Hulman Inst of Technology	IN	59,823	MC
Rosemont College	PA	30,980	LC
Rowan Univ	NJ	24,491	VC
Russell Sage College	NY	39,370	C
Rutgers Univ - Camden	NJ	26,595	C
Rutgers Univ - New Brunswick	NJ	27,090	HC
Saginaw Valley State Univ	MI	19,284	C
St. Anselm College	NH	56,636	VC
St. John's Univ	MN	53,472	C
St. Joseph's Univ	PA	58,540	VC
St. Louis Univ	MO	49,866	HC
St. Mary's Univ of Minn	MN	42,440	C
St. Michael's College	VT	53,275	VC+
St. Peter's Univ	NJ	49,192	C
St. Vincent College	PA	46,229	C
Samford Univ	AL	40,770	VC
San Francisco State Univ	CA	18,514	LC
San Jose State Univ	CA	22,630	C
Schreiner Univ	TX	34,626	LC
Seattle Pacific Univ	WA	47,439	C+
Seattle Univ	WA	54,957	VC
Seton Hall Univ	NJ	58,008	C
Seton Hill Univ	PA	46,972	VC
Sewanee: The Univ of the South	TN	58,000	HC+
Siena College	NY	48,916	C
Simmons College	MA	54,400	HC
Simpson College	IA	45,626	VC
Smith College	MA	66,774	MC
Sonoma State Univ	CA	27,020	C
S Dak State Univ	SD	15,874	C
Southern Conn State Univ	CT	21,924	LC
Southern Illinois Univ Edwardsville	IL	20,188	C
Southern Methodist Univ	TX	69,008	MC
Southern Nazarene Univ	OK	33,684	C
Southwestern College	KS	31,531	LC
Southwestern Univ	TX	52,370	VC
Spelman College	GA	41,642	C
Spring Arbor Univ	MI	37,390	C
Spring Hill College	AL	48,488	C
Springfield College	MA	48,775	C
St. Bonaventure Univ	NY	45,596	C
St. Catherine Univ	MN	45,630	C
St. Edward's Univ	TX	56,190	VC
St. Lawrence Univ	NY	66,646	HC+
St. Mary's College of Maryland	MD	27,312	VC
St. Mary's Univ	TX	39,120	C
SUNY Albany	NY	22,165	C
SUNY at Binghamton	NY	24,100	MC
SUNY at Geneseo	NY	21,622	VC
SUNY at Oswego	NY	22,219	VC
SUNY/College at Old Westbury	NY	16,860	C
SUNY/Fredonia	NY	20,818	C
SUNY/Plattsburgh	NY	19,314	C
SUNY/Potsdam	NY	21,051	VC
SUNY/Univ at Buffalo	NY	23,122	C
Stetson Univ	FL	57,174	VC+
Stevens Inst of Technology	NJ	64,954	MC
Stevenson Univ	MD	48,412	C
Stockton Univ	NJ	25,565	C
Stonehill College	MA	55,130	C
Stony Brook Univ/The SUNY	NY	22,703	MC
Suffolk Univ	MA	52,316	C
Susquehanna Univ	PA	57,560	VC
Swarthmore College	PA	63,550	MC
Syracuse Univ	NY	62,313	HC
Tabor College	KS	35,870	C
Taylor Univ	IN	42,130	VC
Temple Univ	PA	24,392	C+
Tenn Tech Univ	TN	17,929	C
Texas A&M Univ at College Station	TX	20,771	VC+
Texas Christian Univ	TX	57,120	HC
Texas Lutheran Univ	TX	39,770	C
Texas State Univ	TX	18,721	C
Texas Tech Univ	TX	20,156	C+
Texas Wesleyan Univ	TX	37,338	C
The American Univ	DC	61,317	HC
The Catholic Univ of America	DC	58,376	VC
The College at Brockport - SUNY	NY	21,058	C
The College of St. Rose	NY	44,010	C
The College of Wooster	OH	60,000	HC
The Univ of Arizona	AZ	24,086	C
The Univ of Texas at Austin	TX	20,206	MC
The Univ of Texas at San Antonio	TX	21,060	C
Transylvania Univ	KY	47,450	HC+
Trinity Christian College	IL	35,580	C
Trinity College	CT	69,020	HC
Trinity Univ	TX	54,480	MC
Trinity Washington Univ	DC	33,826	C+
Tufts Univ	MA		MC
Tulane Univ	LA	67,496	MC
Union College	NY	64,320	MC
Univ of Calif at Davis	CA	28,468	HC
Univ of Calif at Irvine	CA	33,857	VC
Univ of Calif at Los Angeles	CA	27,438	HC+
Univ of Calif at Riverside	CA	32,912	C
Univ of Calif at Santa Barbara	CA	30,627	HC+
Univ of Calif San Diego	CA	30,450	MC
Univ of Calif, Santa Cruz	CA	28,731	C+
Univ of Chicago	IL	70,551	MC
Univ of Cincinnati	OH	22,118	VC
Univ of Colo Boulder	CO	26,048	HC
Univ of Colo Colo Springs	CO	20,300	C
Univ of Dallas	TX	50,676	VC
Univ of Dayton	OH	54,930	VC
Univ of Delaware	DE	32,214	VC
Univ of Denver	CO	61,129	VC+
Univ of Detroit Mercy	MI	48,816	C
Univ of Evansville	IN	44,186	C+
Univ of Georgia	GA	21,878	HC
Univ of Idaho	ID	16,158	C
Univ of Illinois at Chicago	IL	24,664	VC
Univ of Iowa	IA	19,415	HC
Univ of Jamestown	ND	28,508	C
Univ of Kansas	KS	20,884	VC
Univ of Maine	ME	21,038	VC
Univ of Maryland/Baltimore County	MD	23,004	VC
Univ of Maryland/College Park	MD	21,938	HC
Univ of Mass Amherst	MA	27,669	HC
Univ of Mass Boston	MA	13,828	C
Univ of Mass Dartmouth	MA	26,507	C
Univ of Miami	FL	63,494	MC
Univ of Mich/Ann Arbor	MI	25,274	MC
Univ of Mich/Dearborn	MI	12,472	VC
Univ of Minn/Duluth	MN	20,292	C
Univ of Minn/Twin Cities	MN	24,269	MC
Univ of Missouri-Columbia	MO	20,463	VC
Univ of Missouri-St. Louis	MO	19,810	VC
Univ of Montana	MT	14,105	C
Univ of Mount Union	OH	39,990	C
Univ of Nebr - Lincoln	NE	18,589	VC
Univ of Nevada, Reno	NV	18,010	C
Univ of New England	ME	50,110	C
Univ of New Hampshire	NH	29,333	VC
Univ of New Mexico	NM	16,808	C
Univ of N Car at Greensboro	NC	15,998	C
Univ of North Texas	TX	20,082	C
Univ of Northern Iowa	IA	17,480	C
Univ of Northwestern - St. Paul	MN	39,530	C
Univ of Notre Dame	IN	68,801	MC
Univ of Okla	OK	19,651	HC
Univ of Oregon	OR	24,021	VC
Univ of Pennsylvania	PA	63,526	MC
Univ of PR, at Mayaguez	PR	13,995	
Univ of Puget Sound	WA	60,210	HC
Univ of Redlands	CA	61,934	VC
Univ of Richmond	VA	62,730	MC
Univ of Rochester	NY	65,032	MC
Univ of St. Joseph	CT	49,069	C
Univ of San Diego	CA	60,338	HC
Univ of Scranton	PA	54,962	VC
Univ of Southern Indiana	IN	16,808	C
Univ of St. Thomas - Houston	TX	41,510	VC
Univ of Tampa	FL	38,928	VC
Univ of Texas at Arlington	TX	18,876	C
Univ of Texas at Dallas	TX	23,640	HC
Univ of the Pacific	CA	57,446	VC
Univ of the Sciences	PA	40,738	VC
Univ of Tulsa	OK	52,625	HC
Univ of Vermont	VT	29,792	HC
Univ of Washington	WA	23,091	MC
Univ of Wisc-Eau Claire	WI	16,354	VC
Univ of Wisc-La Crosse	WI	15,425	VC
Univ of Wisc-Madison	WI	21,647	MC
Univ of Wisc-Milwaukee	WI	21,538	C
Univ of Wisc-Stevens Point	WI	14,043	C
Ursinus College	PA	62,920	VC
Utah State Univ	UT	13,235	C
Utica College	NY	31,510	C
Valparaiso Univ	IN	50,160	VC
Vanderbilt Univ	TN	63,248	MC
Vanguard Univ of Southern Calif	CA	42,400	VC
Vassar College	NY	68,110	MC
Villanova Univ	PA	64,922	MC
Virginia Polytechnic Inst and State Univ	VA	21,920	VC
Viterbo Univ	WI	34,660	C
Wabash College	IN	52,100	VC
Walla Walla Univ	WA	34,845	C
Walsh Univ	OH	39,010	C
Warren Wilson College	NC	44,220	VC
Wartburg College	IA	49,478	C
Washburn Univ	KS	15,827	C
Washington & Jefferson College	PA	58,694	VC
Washington Adventist Univ	MD	32,050	LC
Washington and Lee Univ	VA	59,647	MC
Washington State Univ	WA	22,747	C
Washington Univ in St. Louis	MO	67,539	MC
Wayne State Univ	MI	23,085	C
Wellesley College	MA	66,984	MC
Wells College	NY	50,500	C
West Chester Univ of Pennsylvania	PA	19,171	VC
West Virginia Wesleyan College	WV	39,188	C
Western Kentucky Univ	KY	16,850	C
Western Mich Univ	MI	21,791	C
Western Washington Univ	WA	18,904	VC
Westminster College	MO	32,820	C
Wheaton College	MA	63,818	VC
Whitman College	WA	59,772	MC
Whittier College	CA	57,891	C
Widener Univ	PA	58,190	C
Wilkes Univ	PA	49,166	C
William Jewell College	MO	42,490	C+
Wilmington College	OH	35,100	C
Wilson College	PA	35,620	LC
Wisc Lutheran College	WI	36,290	C
Wittenberg Univ	OH	49,863	VC
Worcester Polytechnic Inst	MA	62,846	MC
Xavier Univ of Louisiana	LA	31,689	C
Yale Univ	CT	64,650	MC
Youngstown State Univ	OH	17,487	C

BIOENGINEERING

School	ST	$IS	SR
Brown Univ	RI	64,566	MC
Calif Baptist Univ	CA	42,986	C
Calif Inst of Technology	CA	64,704	MC
Colo State Univ	CO	23,033	C
Cornell Univ	NY	67,591	MC
Dordt College	IA	37,860	C+
Endicott College	MA	47,054	C+
Fairfield Univ	CT	61,445	HC
Florida State Univ	FL	16,771	HC
Georgia Inst of Technology	GA	23,910	MC

ST = STATE **$IS** = IN-STATE COSTS **SR** = SELECTOR RATING

School	ST	$IS	SR
Lehigh Univ	PA	63,860	MC
Louisiana State Univ and A&M College	LA	18,677	VC
Loyola Univ Chicago	IL	57,158	VC
Marquette Univ	WI	53,090	VC+
Mass Inst of Technology	MA	62,662	MC
Miami Univ	OH	27,190	HC+
Miss State Univ	MS	12,028	C+
Ohio Univ	OH	23,394	VC
Okla State Univ	OK	17,180	C+
Oral Roberts Univ	OK	34,316	C
Oregon State Univ	OR	23,337	VC
Purdue Univ/West Lafayette	IN	20,032	MC
Rice Univ	TX	59,458	MC
Rutgers Univ - New Brunswick	NJ	27,090	HC
St. Louis Univ	MO	49,866	HC
Stanford Univ	CA	62,541	MC
SUNY at Binghamton	NY	24,100	MC
Syracuse Univ	NY	62,313	HC
Texas A&M Univ at College Station	TX	20,771	VC+
Union College	NY	64,320	MC
Univ of Arkansas at Fayetteville	AR	19,766	VC
Univ of Calif at Berkeley	CA	29,886	MC
Univ of Calif at Davis	CA	28,468	HC
Univ of Calif at Los Angeles	CA	27,438	HC+
Univ of Calif at Riverside	CA	32,912	C
Univ of Calif San Diego	CA	30,450	MC
Univ of Cincinnati	OH	22,118	VC
Univ of Colo Boulder	CO	26,048	HC
Univ of Colo Denver	CO	22,238	C
Univ of Delaware	DE	32,214	VC
Univ of Denver	CO	61,129	VC+
Univ of Georgia	GA	21,878	HC
Univ of Hawaii at Manoa	HI	23,261	C
Univ of Idaho	ID	16,158	C
Univ of Illinois at Chicago	IL	24,664	VC
Univ of Illinois at Urbana-Champaign	IL	27,006	HC
Univ of Louisville	KY	19,692	C
Univ of Maine	ME	21,038	VC
Univ of Maryland/College Park	MD	21,938	HC
Univ of Mass Amherst	MA	27,669	HC
Univ of Mass Dartmouth	MA	26,507	C
Univ of Mich/Dearborn	MI	12,472	VC
Univ of Minn/Twin Cities	MN	24,269	MC
Univ of Nebr - Lincoln	NE	18,589	VC
Univ of New Hampshire	NH	29,333	VC
Univ of Okla	OK	19,651	HC
Univ of Pennsylvania	PA	63,526	MC
Univ of Pittsburgh	PA	30,030	MC
Univ of Toledo	OH	19,336	C
Univ of Wisc-Madison	WI	21,647	MC
Vanderbilt Univ	TN	63,248	MC
Virginia Commonwealth Univ	VA	23,811	VC
Walla Walla Univ	WA	34,845	C
Washington State Univ	WA	22,747	C
Washington Univ in St. Louis	MO	67,539	MC

BIOINFORMATICS

School	ST	$IS	SR
Baylor Univ	TX	56,803	HC
Brigham Young Univ	UT	13,248	MC
Cal State, Fullerton	CA	21,902	C
Canisius College	NY	49,672	C
Claflin Univ	SC	25,592	LC
Gannon Univ	PA	42,922	C
Inter-American Univ of PR-Bayamon	PR	18,785	
King Univ	TN	36,976	C
Loyola Univ Chicago	IL	57,158	VC
MCPHS Univ	MA	45,470	SP
Mich State Univ	MI	24,542	VC
Mich Tech Univ	MI	25,551	VC+
Missouri Southern State Univ	MO	13,071	C
New York City College of Technology	NY	7,185	LC
Niagara Univ	NY	41,010	C
Ramapo College of New Jersey	NJ	25,760	VC
Rochester Inst of Technology	NY	52,734	HC+
Rockhurst Univ	MO	28,990	C
Rowan Univ	NJ	24,491	VC
Rutgers Univ - Camden	NJ	26,595	C
St. Vincent College	PA	46,229	C
St. Bonaventure Univ	NY	45,596	C
St. Edward's Univ	TX	56,190	VC
SUNY/Univ at Buffalo	NY	23,122	C
Stevens Inst of Technology	NJ	64,954	MC
The Univ of Arizona	AZ	24,086	C
Trinity Christian College	IL	35,580	C
Univ of Arkansas at Little Rock	AR	18,211	LC
Univ of Calif at Irvine	CA	33,857	VC
Univ of Calif San Diego	CA	30,450	MC
Univ of Calif, Santa Cruz	CA	28,731	C+
Univ of Denver	CO	61,129	VC+
Univ of Idaho	ID	16,158	C
Univ of Maryland/Baltimore County	MD	23,004	VC
Univ of Missouri-Kansas City	MO	19,563	VC
Univ of Nebr - Omaha	NE	16,120	C
Univ of Northern Iowa	IA	17,480	C
Univ of Pittsburgh	PA	30,030	MC
Univ of St. Thomas - Houston	TX	41,510	VC
Univ of the Sciences	PA	40,738	VC
Virginia Commonwealth Univ	VA	23,811	VC
Walsh Univ	OH	39,010	C
Washington Univ in St. Louis	MO	67,539	MC
Wheaton College	MA	63,818	VC
Whitworth Univ	WA	53,682	VC
Worcester Polytechnic Inst	MA	62,846	MC

BIOLOGICAL SCIENCES

School	ST	$IS	SR
Arizona State Univ at the Tempe Campus	AZ	23,001	VC
Arkansas State Univ	AR	16,190	C
Brown Univ	RI	64,566	MC
Cabrini Univ	PA	42,591	LC
Drury Univ	MO	37,555	VC
Huntington Univ	IN	33,996	C
Kutztown Univ of Pennsylvania	PA	19,477	C
Loyola Univ New Orleans	LA	52,456	VC
Miami Univ	OH	27,190	HC+
Mich State Univ	MI	24,542	VC
Missouri Western State Univ	MO	17,822	LC
North Greenville Univ	SC	25,930	C
Northwestern State Univ of Louisiana	LA	16,534	LC
Nova Southeastern Univ	FL	38,534	C+
Ohio Wesleyan Univ	OH	49,460	VC
Olivet Nazarene Univ	IL	41,840	VC
Southern Vermont College	VT	34,670	LC
The Master's Univ	CA	43,870	C
Univ of Calif San Diego	CA	30,450	MC
Univ of Louisiana at Monroe	LA	15,970	C
Univ of Maine at Machias	ME	22,960	C
Univ of Maryland/Baltimore County	MD	23,004	VC
Univ of Mich/Dearborn	MI	12,472	VC
Univ of New Hampshire - Manchester	NH	14,490	C
Univ of Notre Dame	IN	68,801	MC
Univ of Rhode Island	RI	26,066	VC
Univ of South Florida St. Petersburg	FL	15,980	C
Wellesley College	MA	66,984	MC
West Virginia Wesleyan College	WV	39,188	C

BIOLOGY

School	ST	$IS	SR
Angelo State Univ	TX	15,882	LC
Arizona State Univ at the West Campus	AZ	21,513	VC
Arkansas Tech Univ	AR	16,534	LC
Aurora Univ	IL	34,990	C
Averett Univ	VA	43,034	LC
Azusa Pacific Univ	CA	43,972	C
Black Hills State Univ	SD	16,622	C
Bloomfield College	NJ	40,100	LC
Bowling Green State Univ	OH	19,975	C
Brown Univ	RI	64,566	MC
Cabrini Univ	PA	42,591	LC
Calvin College	MI	43,090	HC
Campbell Univ	NC	37,570	VC
CUNY/Queens College	NY	21,507	C
Clayton State Univ	GA	19,735	LC
Colgate Univ	NY	67,500	MC
College of William & Mary	VA	34,907	MC
Colo State Univ	CO	23,033	C
Creighton Univ	NE	49,452	VC
Dallas Baptist Univ	TX	35,220	VC
Davis & Elkins College	WV	38,242	LC
DePaul Univ	IL	52,807	VC
East Stroudsburg Univ	PA	18,578	LC
East Texas Baptist Univ	TX	34,444	C
Edgewood College	WI	35,950	C
Elon Univ	NC	46,142	HC
Ferris State Univ	MI	21,458	C
Franklin College	IN	40,550	C
Georgian Court Univ	NJ	43,068	LC
Huntington Univ	IN	33,996	C
Indiana Univ Bloomington	IN	20,791	HC
Indiana Univ East	IN	7,207	C
Indiana Univ Kokomo	IN	7,207	C
Indiana Univ Northwest	IN	7,207	LC
Indiana Univ Southeast	IN	16,931	C
Indiana Univ-Purdue Univ Indianapolis	IN	18,952	C
Iowa Wesleyan Univ	IA	41,000	C
Kutztown Univ of Pennsylvania	PA	19,477	C
Lebanon Valley College	PA	55,510	VC
Lewis Univ	IL	41,710	C
Loras College	IA	40,726	C
Louisiana College	LA	21,274	C
Loyola Univ New Orleans	LA	52,456	VC
Lynn Univ	FL	49,680	LC
Medaille College	NY	41,700	LC
MidAmerica Nazarene Univ	KS	37,808	C
Millersville Univ of Pennsylvania	PA	25,298	C
Missouri Southern State Univ	MO	13,071	C
Missouri Western State Univ	MO	17,822	LC
Montreat College	NC	34,605	LC
Mount Vernon Nazarene Univ	OH	35,944	C
New York Inst of Technology	NY	49,980	VC
Niagara Univ	NY	41,010	C
Northwest Missouri State Univ	MO	18,286	C
Northwest Univ	WA	38,720	VC
Northwestern State Univ of Louisiana	LA	16,534	LC
Nova Southeastern Univ	FL	38,534	C+
Nyack College	NY	34,450	LC
Oberlin College	OH	68,942	MC
Ohio Valley Univ	WV	28,800	C
Ohio Wesleyan Univ	OH	49,460	VC
Okla Christian Univ	OK	29,260	C
Okla City Univ	OK	40,476	C
Olivet Nazarene Univ	IL	41,840	VC
Otterbein Univ	OH	41,630	C
Palm Beach Atlantic Univ	FL	39,250	C
Providence College	RI	62,870	HC
Regis Univ	CO	46,380	C
Roberts Wesleyan College	NY	41,116	C
Rochester Inst of Technology	NY	52,734	HC+
Rocky Mountain College	MT	35,776	C
St. Louis Univ	MO	49,866	HC
Seton Hill Univ	PA	46,972	VC
Silver Lake College of the Holy Family	WI	36,290	LC
Southeast Missouri State Univ	MO	16,148	C
Southern Oregon Univ	OR	19,117	C
St. Ambrose Univ	IA	40,180	C
Syracuse Univ	NY	62,313	HC
Taylor Univ	IN	42,130	VC
Tenn Wesleyan Univ	TN	32,680	LC
Texas Christian Univ	TX	57,120	HC
Texas Tech Univ	TX	20,156	C+
Texas Wesleyan Univ	TX	37,338	C
The Master's Univ	CA	43,870	C
Thomas Edison State Univ	NJ	6,350	NC
Tougaloo College	MS	17,980	NC
Trevecca Nazarene Univ	TN	31,186	C
Tufts Univ	MA		MC
Univ of Bridgeport	CT	44,985	LC
Univ of Chicago	IL	70,551	MC
Univ of Dayton	OH	54,930	VC
Univ of Denver	CO	61,129	VC+
Univ of Georgia	GA	21,878	HC
Univ of Hawaii at Hilo	HI	18,038	VC
Univ of Maine at Machias	ME	22,960	C
Univ of Maryland/Baltimore County	MD	23,004	VC
Univ of Miami	FL	63,494	MC
Univ of Minn/Twin Cities	MN	24,269	MC
Univ of Mount Union	OH	39,990	C
Univ of N Car at Greensboro	NC	15,998	C
Univ of Northwestern - St. Paul	MN	39,530	C
Univ of Okla	OK	19,651	HC
Univ of Rhode Island	RI	26,066	VC
Univ of St. Mary	KS	37,080	NC
Univ of Tulsa	OK	52,625	HC
Univ of Wisc-Superior	WI	14,838	C
Univ of Wyoming	WY	15,537	C
Vassar College	NY	68,110	MC
Warren Wilson College	NC	44,220	VC
Wartburg College	IA	49,478	C
Washington State Univ	WA	22,747	C
Wayne State Univ	MI	23,085	C
Wellesley College	MA	66,984	MC
West Virginia Univ	WV	18,952	VC
Western Illinois Univ	IL	20,897	C
Western Kentucky Univ	KY	16,850	C
Wheaton College	MA	63,818	VC
Whitman College	WA	59,772	MC
Wilson College	PA	35,620	LC
Wingate Univ	NC	41,900	C
Worcester Polytechnic Inst	MA	62,846	MC

BIOLOGY AND SOCIETY

School	ST	$IS	SR
Brown Univ	RI	64,566	MC
Cornell Univ	NY	67,591	MC
Univ of Minn/Twin Cities	MN	24,269	MC

BIOLOGY ECOLOGY AND FIELD BIOLOGY

School	ST	$IS	SR
Beloit College	WI	55,206	HC
Bradley Univ	IL	43,240	VC
Brown Univ	RI	64,566	MC
College of the Ozarks	MO	7,530	VC
Colo College	CO	64,894	MC
Franklin College	IN	40,550	C
Iowa Wesleyan Univ	IA	41,000	C
Missouri Western State Univ	MO	17,822	LC
Northland College	WI	41,103	C+
Palm Beach Atlantic Univ	FL	39,250	C
St. Leo Univ	FL	32,850	C
Univ of Maine at Machias	ME	22,960	C
Univ of Maryland/Baltimore County	MD	23,004	VC
Univ of Tulsa	OK	52,625	HC
West Chester Univ of Pennsylvania	PA	19,171	VC

BIOLOGY/ADOLESCENCE EDUCATION

School	ST	$IS	SR
Arkansas State Univ	AR	16,190	C
Augustana College	IL	51,222	VC+
Bethany College	WV	38,774	LC
Biola Univ	CA	48,686	C
Black Hills State Univ	SD	16,622	C
Cabrini Univ	PA	42,591	LC
College of the Ozarks	MO	7,530	VC
Duquesne Univ	PA	48,508	VC
Edgewood College	WI	35,950	C
Elizabethtown College	PA	56,340	VC
Faulkner Univ	AL	26,410	C
Hope College	MI	42,840	VC
Houghton College	NY	40,558	VC
Huntingdon College	AL	35,900	C
Indiana Univ Northwest	IN	7,207	LC
Indiana Univ South Bend	IN	16,057	C
Indiana Univ Southeast	IN	16,931	C
Lipscomb Univ	TN	42,984	VC
LIU Brooklyn	NY	50,698	C
LIU Post	NY	50,698	C+
Marist College	NY	49,860	VC
Messiah College	PA	44,380	VC
Millikin Univ	IL	44,148	C
Missouri Southern State Univ	MO	13,071	C
Murray State Univ	KY	17,726	C+
Nazareth College	NY	46,784	C
Niagara Univ	NY	41,010	C
Northern Kentucky Univ	KY	16,486	C
Old Dominion Univ	VA	21,618	C
Pace Univ	NY	60,136	C
Roberts Wesleyan College	NY	41,116	C
Seattle Univ	WA	54,957	VC
Southern Illinois Univ Carbondale	IL	24,554	C
St. John's Univ	NY	57,160	C+
SUNY at Oswego	NY	22,219	VC
SUNY/Fredonia	NY	20,818	C
SUNY/Plattsburgh	NY	19,314	C
Temple Univ	PA	24,392	C+
Texas Wesleyan Univ	TX	37,338	C
The College of St. Rose	NY	44,010	C
Univ of Mary Hardin-Baylor	TX	35,292	C+

BIOLOGY/BIOLOGICAL SCIENCE

School	ST	$IS	SR
Abilene Christian Univ	TX	43,708	C+
Adams State Univ	CO	15,420	LC
Adelphi Univ	NY	49,792	C
Adrian College	MI	45,550	C
Agnes Scott College	GA	51,930	VC+
Alabama A&M Univ	AL	18,796	C
Alabama State Univ	AL	16,490	LC
Albany State Univ	GA	19,462	C
Albertus Magnus College	CT	44,016	LC
Albion College	MI	55,260	C
Albright College	PA	57,326	C
Alcorn State Univ	MS	15,884	C
Alderson Broaddus Univ	WV	35,000	LC
Alfred Univ	NY	37,490	C
Alice Lloyd College	KY	8,190	LC
Allegheny College	PA	57,620	VC
Allen Univ	SC	19,920	NC
Alma College	MI	49,410	VC
Alvernia Univ	PA	45,330	C
Alverno College	WI	33,294	LC
American International College	MA	47,020	LC
Amherst College	MA	66,186	MC
Anderson Univ	IN	39,450	C
Andrews Univ	MI	41,732	C
Angelo State Univ	TX	15,882	LC
Appalachian State Univ	NC	15,394	VC
Aquinas College - Mich	MI	38,876	VC
Arcadia Univ	PA	55,990	C+
Arkansas Tech Univ	AR	16,534	LC
Armstrong State Univ	GA	15,615	C
Asbury Univ	KY	36,450	C+
Ashford Univ	CA	10,480	C
Ashland Univ	OH	30,446	C
Assumption College	MA	48,455	VC
Atlantic Union College	MA	27,228	C
Auburn Univ	AL	24,300	VC+
Auburn Univ at Montgomery	AL	15,000	C
Augsburg Univ	MN	45,129	C
Augusta Univ	GA	4,632	C
Augustana College	IL	51,222	VC+
Augustana Univ	SD	39,968	VC
Aurora Univ	IL	34,990	C
Austin College	TX	51,059	HC
Austin Peay State Univ	TN	16,397	C
Averett Univ	VA	43,034	LC
Avila Univ	MO	27,100	C
Azusa Pacific Univ	CA	43,972	C
Baker Univ	KS	37,190	C
Baldwin Wallace Univ	OH	42,464	VC
Ball State Univ	IN	19,808	C+
Bard College	NY	65,924	HC
Bard College at Simon's Rock	MA	65,795	MC
Barnard College/Columbia Univ	NY	68,762	MC
Barry Univ	FL	38,730	LC
Barton College	NC	39,854	C
Bates College	ME	64,500	HC
Bay Path Univ	MA	46,356	C
Bayamon Central Univ	PR	12,490	
Baylor Univ	TX	56,803	HC
Becker College	MA	30,100	LC
Belhaven Univ	MS	32,250	C
Bellarmine Univ	KY	52,532	C
Belmont Abbey College	NC	28,794	C
Belmont Univ	TN	44,500	VC+
Beloit College	WI	55,206	HC

ST = STATE $IS = IN-STATE COSTS SR = SELECTOR RATING

School	ST	$IS	SR
Bemidji State Univ	MN	17,730	C
Benedict College	SC	28,630	NC
Benedictine College	KS	38,850	VC
Benedictine Univ	IL	38,300	C
Bennett College	NC	27,717	NC
Bennington College	VT	66,280	MC
Berea College	KY	7,094	C
Berry College	GA	47,466	VC
Bethany College	KS	38,637	LC
Bethany College	WV	38,774	LC
Bethel College	IN	36,830	C
Bethel College	KS	35,370	C
Bethel Univ	MN	46,550	C+
Bethel Univ	TN	27,142	C
Bethune-Cookman Univ	FL	23,322	C
Biola Univ	CA	48,686	C
Birmingham-Southern College	AL	44,478	C+
Black Hills State Univ	SD	16,622	C
Blackburn College	IL	28,526	LC
Bloomfield College	NJ	40,100	LC
Bloomsburg Univ of Pennsylvania	PA	19,930	C
Blue Mountain College	MS	15,949	C
Bluefield College	VA	34,711	C
Bluefield State College	WV	5,832	LC
Bluffton Univ	OH	40,950	C+
Boise State Univ	ID	17,368	C
Boston College	MA	68,043	MC
Boston Univ	MA	67,352	MC
Bowdoin College	ME	65,980	MC
Bowie State Univ	MD	18,610	LC
Bradley Univ	IL	43,240	VC
Brandeis Univ	MA	68,443	MC
Brenau Univ - Women's College	GA	37,876	LC
Brescia Univ	KY	29,890	VC
Brewton-Parker College	GA	26,120	LC
Briar Cliff Univ	IA	36,956	C
Bridgewater College	VA	46,260	C
Bridgewater State Univ	MA	22,762	C
Brigham Young Univ	UT	13,248	MC
Brigham Young Univ/Hawaii	HI	11,710	C
Brown Univ	RI	64,566	MC
Bryan College	TN	32,900	C
Bryant Univ	RI	57,204	VC
Bryn Athyn College	PA	32,664	C
Bryn Mawr College	PA	65,220	MC
Bucknell Univ	PA	67,136	MC
Buena Vista Univ	IA	42,344	C
Butler Univ	IN	52,890	VC+
Cabrini Univ	PA	42,591	LC
Caldwell Univ	NJ	42,165	LC
Calif Baptist Univ	CA	42,986	C
Calif Inst of Technology	CA	64,704	MC
Calif Lutheran Univ	CA	52,853	C
Calif Polytechnic State Univ	CA	22,547	MC
Calif State Polytechnic Univ, Pomona	CA	21,811	C
Cal State, Bakersfield	CA	22,397	LC
Cal State, Chico	CA	19,790	VC
Cal State, Dominguez Hills	CA	19,022	LC
Cal State, East Bay	CA	20,748	C
Cal State, Fresno	CA	16,902	LC
Cal State, Fullerton	CA	21,902	C
Cal State, Long Beach	CA	18,850	C
Cal State, Los Angeles	CA	17,186	LC
Cal State, Monterey Bay	CA	22,872	LC
Cal State, Northridge	CA	17,277	LC
Cal State, Sacramento	CA	19,060	C
Cal State, San Bernardino	CA	20,106	C
Cal State, San Marcos	CA	20,604	LC
Cal State, Stanislaus	CA	18,053	LC
Calif Univ of Pennsylvania	PA	20,425	LC
Calvin College	MI	43,090	HC
Cameron Univ	OK	11,632	LC
Campbell Univ	NC	37,570	VC
Campbellsville Univ	KY	33,400	C
Canisius College	NY	49,672	C
Capital Univ	OH	44,778	VC
Cardinal Stritch Univ	WI	37,136	C
Caribbean Univ	PR	12,227	
Carleton College	MN	66,414	MC
Carlow Univ	PA	39,696	LC
Carnegie Mellon Univ	PA	67,980	MC
Carroll College	MT	44,304	C
Carroll Univ	WI	38,100	C+
Carson-Newman Univ	TN	35,900	C
Carthage College	WI	48,835	C
Case Western Reserve Univ	OH	62,284	MC
Castleton Univ	VT	20,186	C
Catawba College	NC	39,820	LC
Cedar Crest College	PA	51,110	C
Cedarville Univ	OH	36,244	VC
Centenary College	NJ	43,890	LC
Centenary College of Louisiana	LA	49,050	C+
Central College	IA	44,592	C
Central Conn State Univ	CT	22,041	C
Central Methodist Univ	MO	31,500	VC
Central Mich Univ	MI	20,330	C
Central State Univ	OH	18,564	C
Central Washington Univ	WA	16,803	C
Centre College	KY	50,680	MC
Chadron State College	NE	14,819	LC
Chaminade Univ of Honolulu	HI	37,614	C
Chapman Univ	CA	65,504	HC
Charleston Southern Univ	SC	34,700	C
Chatham Univ	PA	47,883	VC
Chestnut Hill College	PA	47,180	C
Cheyney Univ of Pennsylvania	PA	20,896	LC
Chicago State Univ	IL	41,620	C
Christian Brothers Univ	TN	31,670	VC
Christopher Newport Univ	VA	24,878	VC+
CUNY/Brooklyn College	NY	7,163	C+
CUNY/City College	NY	20,204	C
CUNY/Hunter College	NY	31,098	VC
CUNY/Lehman College	NY	5,788	LC
CUNY/Medgar Evers College	NY	6,680	NC
CUNY/York College	NY	6,747	LC
Claflin Univ	SC	25,592	LC
Claremont McKenna College	CA	69,900	MC
Clarion Univ of Pennsylvania	PA	21,608	LC
Clark Atlanta Univ	GA	31,019	LC
Clark Univ	MA	53,260	HC+
Clarke Univ	IA	42,950	C
Clarkson Univ	NY	60,392	VC
Clemson Univ	SC		HC
Cleveland State Univ	OH	22,290	C
Coastal Carolina Univ	SC	20,340	C
Coe College	IA	51,570	VC
Coker College	SC	38,196	C
Colby College	ME	64,060	MC
Colby-Sawyer College	NH	50,790	C
Colgate Univ	NY	67,500	MC
College of Charleston	SC	24,046	VC
College of Mount St. Vincent	NY	45,620	C
College of St. Benedict	MN	54,480	C
College of St. Elizabeth	NJ	45,700	LC
College of St. Mary	NE	27,500	C
College of St. Scholastica	MN	45,734	C+
College of Staten Island	NY	24,389	LC
College of the Holy Cross	MA	64,320	MC
College of the Ozarks	MO	7,530	VC
Colo Christian Univ	CO	40,885	VC
Colo Mesa Univ	CO	19,707	LC
Colo State Univ	CO	23,033	C
Colo State Univ-Pueblo	CO	21,581	C
Columbia College	SC	36,550	C
Columbia College - Missouri	MO	28,179	C
Columbia Univ/ School of General Studies	NY	61,470	MC
Columbia Univ/City of New York	NY	62,958	MC
Columbus State Univ	GA	14,336	LC
Concord Univ	WV	14,954	LC
Concordia College - Moorhead	MN	46,418	C
Concordia College - New York	NY	39,035	LC
Concordia Univ	OR	35,000	C
Concordia Univ Irvine	CA	44,860	VC
Concordia Univ Nebr	NE	41,900	VC
Concordia Univ St. Paul	MN	29,050	C
Concordia Univ Wisc	WI	35,910	C
Concordia Univ, Ann Arbor	MI	38,878	C+
Concordia Univ, Chicago	IL	41,522	C
Conn College	CT	65,000	MC
Converse College	SC	28,290	C
Coppin State Univ	MD	14,071	VC
Cornell College	IA	49,900	VC
Cornell Univ	NY	67,591	MC
Cornerstone Univ	MI	36,550	C
Covenant College	GA	44,590	HC
Culver-Stockton College	MO	34,350	C
Cumberland Univ	TN	27,710	C
Curry College	MA	53,331	C
Daemen College	NY	40,336	C
Dakota State Univ	SD	12,286	C
Dakota Wesleyan Univ	SD	33,980	LC
Dallas Baptist Univ	TX	35,220	VC
Dartmouth College	NH	68,109	MC
Davidson College	NC	60,119	MC
Defiance College	OH	42,240	LC
Delaware State Univ	DE	19,376	LC
Delaware Valley Univ	PA	51,271	C
Delta State Univ	MS	13,176	LC
Denison Univ	OH	62,770	HC+
DePaul Univ	IL	52,807	VC
DePauw Univ	IN	58,688	VC
DeSales Univ	PA	47,520	C
Dickinson College	PA	66,166	MC
Dickinson State Univ	ND	12,372	LC
Dillard Univ	LA	20,940	VC
Doane Univ	NE	41,340	VC
Dominican College	NY	40,258	LC
Dominican Univ	IL	42,472	C+
Dominican Univ of Calif	CA	58,750	C
Dordt College	IA	37,860	C+
Drake Univ	IA	49,220	HC
Drew Univ/College of Liberal Arts	NJ	53,608	VC
Drexel Univ	PA	65,927	HC
Drury Univ	MO	37,555	VC
Duke Univ	NC	68,298	MC
Duquesne Univ	PA	48,508	VC
D'Youville College	NY	37,678	C
Earlham College	IN	55,670	HC
East Carolina Univ	NC	16,539	C
East Central Univ	OK	13,330	C
East Tenn State Univ	TN	18,141	C
East Texas Baptist Univ	TX	34,444	C
Eastern Conn State Univ	CT	23,059	C
Eastern Illinois Univ	IL	21,414	C
Eastern Kentucky Univ	KY	17,742	C
Eastern Mennonite Univ	VA	42,550	C
Eastern Mich Univ	MI	19,761	C
Eastern Nazarene College	MA	41,114	C
Eastern New Mexico Univ	NM	12,874	LC
Eastern Oregon Univ	OR	17,612	C
Eastern Univ	PA	39,540	C
Eastern Washington Univ	WA	17,896	LC
Eckerd College	FL	55,206	VC
Edinboro Univ	PA	15,940	LC
Edward Waters College	FL	28,089	NC
Elizabeth City State Univ	NC	14,745	C
Elizabethtown College	PA	56,340	VC
Elmhurst College	IL	46,514	C
Elmira College	NY	53,900	C
Elms College	MA	49,602	VC
Emmanuel College	MA	53,472	C+
Emory and Henry College	VA	46,320	C
Emory Univ	GA	63,286	MC
Emporia State Univ	KS	15,029	C
Erskine College	SC	45,460	C
Eureka College	IL	34,760	C
Evangel Univ	MO	28,898	C
Excelsior College	NY	38,800	SP
Fairfield Univ	CT	61,445	HC
Fairleigh Dickinson Univ/ College at Florham	NJ	54,770	C
Fairleigh Dickinson Univ/ Metropolitan Campus	NJ	52,392	C
Fairmont State Univ	WV	15,726	C
Farmingdale State College	NY	20,968	C
Faulkner Univ	AL	26,410	C
Fayetteville State Univ	NC	17,756	C
Felician Univ	NJ	46,280	LC
Ferris State Univ	MI	21,458	C
Ferrum College	VA	43,970	C
Fisk Univ	TN	32,066	LC
Fitchburg State Univ	MA	21,819	LC
Florida A&M Univ	FL	15,361	C
Florida Atlantic Univ	FL	18,256	C
Florida Gulf Coast Univ	FL	14,738	C
Florida Inst of Technology	FL	53,306	VC
Florida International Univ	FL	20,281	C
Florida Memorial Univ	FL	22,424	LC
Florida Southern College	FL	45,978	VC
Florida State Univ	FL	16,771	HC
Fontbonne Univ	MO	34,606	C
Fordham Univ	NY	68,431	MC
Fort Hays State Univ	KS	12,677	C
Fort Lewis College	CO	20,154	C
Fort Valley State Univ	GA	17,988	VC
Framingham State Univ	MA	21,740	C
Francis Marion Univ	SC	18,144	LC
Franciscan Univ of Steubenville	OH	33,980	VC
Franklin and Marshall College	PA	67,960	MC
Franklin College	IN	40,550	C
Franklin Pierce Univ	NH	46,750	LC
Freed-Hardeman Univ	TN	29,900	C
Fresno Pacific Univ	CA	38,858	C
Friends Univ	KS	38,000	C
Frostburg State Univ	MD	17,280	LC
Furman Univ	SC	61,098	VC+
Gallaudet Univ	DC	30,088	LC
Gannon Univ	PA	42,922	C
Gardner-Webb Univ	NC	24,935	C+
Geneva College	PA	35,450	C
George Fox Univ	OR	42,938	C
George Mason Univ	VA	19,884	C
Georgetown College	KY	41,440	C
Georgetown Univ	DC	68,970	MC
Georgia College & State Univ	GA	21,884	C+
Georgia Inst of Technology	GA	23,910	MC
Georgia Southern Univ	GA	16,540	VC
Georgia Southwestern State Univ	GA	13,870	LC
Georgia State Univ	GA	25,250	C
Gettysburg College	PA	65,210	MC
Glenville State College	WV	17,386	LC
Gonzaga Univ	WA	52,880	HC
Gordon College	MA	47,740	VC
Goshen College	IN	44,350	C
Goucher College	MD	56,110	VC
Grace College and Seminary	IN	31,524	C
Graceland Univ	IA	35,290	C
Grambling State Univ	LA	15,701	C
Grand Canyon Univ	AZ	25,150	VC
Grand Valley State Univ	MI	22,250	C+
Grand View Univ	IA	32,302	C
Green Mountain College	VT	45,228	LC
Greensboro College	NC	39,790	LC
Greenville College	IL	27,012	LC
Grinnell College	IA	63,114	MC
Grove City College	PA	26,654	VC
Guilford College	NC	45,973	C
Gustavus Adolphus College	MN	53,943	HC
Gwynedd Mercy Univ	PA	43,780	LC
Hamilton College	NY	64,250	MC
Hamline Univ	MN	50,152	C
Hampden-Sydney College	VA	57,806	VC
Hampshire College	MA	65,214	MC
Hampton Univ	VA	36,410	C
Hannibal-LaGrange Univ	MO	29,815	C
Hanover College	IN	47,750	C+
Harding Univ	AR	25,440	C
Hardin-Simmons Univ	TX	36,025	C
Harris-Stowe State Univ	MO	14,590	NC
Hartwick College	NY	51,270	C
Harvard College/Harvard Univ	MA	65,609	MC
Harvey Mudd College	CA	67,155	MC
Hastings College	NE	35,380	C+
Haverford College	PA	66,490	MC
Hawaii Pacific Univ	HI	33,420	C
Heidelberg Univ	OH	40,400	LC
Henderson State Univ	AR	15,516	C
Hendrix College	AR	54,020	VC
High Point Univ	NC	47,355	VC
Hillsdale College	MI	37,170	MC
Hiram College	OH	44,590	C
Hobart and William Smith Colleges	NY	67,050	HC+
Hofstra Univ	NY	58,210	C+
Hollins Univ	VA	49,635	VC
Holy Family Univ	PA	44,672	LC
Holy Names Univ	CA	46,630	LC
Hood College	MD	50,540	C
Hope College	MI	42,840	VC
Houghton College	NY	40,558	VC
Houston Baptist Univ	TX	36,450	C
Howard Payne Univ	TX	35,994	C
Howard Univ	DC	37,616	C+
Humboldt State Univ	CA	21,708	C
Huntingdon College	AL	35,900	C
Huntington Univ	IN	33,996	C
Husson Univ	ME	26,508	C
Huston-Tillotson Univ	TX	18,124	LC
Idaho State Univ	ID	13,619	LC
Illinois College	IL	41,330	VC
Illinois Inst of Technology	IL	56,826	HC+
Illinois State Univ	IL	23,418	VC
Illinois Wesleyan Univ	IL	56,430	VC+
Immaculata Univ	PA	39,000	C
Indiana State Univ	IN	23,223	LC
Indiana Univ Kokomo	IN	7,207	C
Indiana Univ of Pennsylvania	PA	24,474	C
Indiana Univ South Bend	IN	16,057	C
Indiana Univ-Purdue Univ Fort Wayne	IN	18,675	C
Indiana Wesleyan Univ	IN	33,674	C
Inter-American Univ of PR Ponce	PR	19,549	
Inter-American Univ of PR-Aguadilla Campus	PR	21,657	
Inter-American Univ of PR-Arecibo Campus	PR	18,245	
Inter-American Univ of PR-Bayamon	PR	18,785	
Inter-American Univ of PR-Fajardo Campus	PR	18,336	
Inter-American Univ of PR-Metropolitan Campus	PR	20,045	
Inter-American Univ of PR-San Germán	PR	20,042	
Iona College	NY	52,514	C
Iowa State Univ	IA	18,176	C
Iowa Wesleyan Univ	IA	41,000	C
Ithaca College	NY	58,158	VC+
Jackson State Univ	MS	15,879	LC
Jacksonville State Univ	AL	14,628	LC
Jacksonville Univ	FL	49,210	C
James Madison Univ	VA	19,084	VC
Jarvis Christian College	TX	20,160	NC
Jefferson (Philadelphia Univ + Thomas Jefferson Univ)	PA	53,966	C
John Brown Univ	AR	35,184	VC
John Carroll Univ	OH	51,570	C
Johns Hopkins Univ	MD	68,080	MC
Johnson C. Smith Univ	NC	25,336	LC
Johnson State College	VT	22,672	C
Judson College	AL	27,066	C
Judson Univ	IL	39,174	C
Juniata College	PA	58,118	VC
Kalamazoo College	MI	53,931	HC
Kansas State Univ	KS	17,780	VC
Kansas Wesleyan Univ	KS	37,930	C
Kean Univ	NJ	25,620	C
Keene State College	NH	24,604	C
Kennesaw State Univ	GA	18,899	VC
Kent State Univ	OH	20,928	C
Kentucky State Univ	KY	14,484	LC
Kentucky Wesleyan College	KY	34,260	LC
Kenyon College	OH	65,840	MC
Keuka College	NY	42,398	C
Keystone College	PA	28,680	LC
King Univ	TN	36,976	C
King's College	PA	48,240	C
Knox College	IL	54,654	VC+
Kutztown Univ of Pennsylvania	PA	19,477	C
La Roche College	PA	38,940	C
La Salle Univ	PA	43,476	C
La Sierra Univ	CA	39,690	VC
Lafayette College	PA	68,520	MC
LaGrange College	GA	41,310	C
Lake Erie College	OH	38,914	LC
Lake Forest College	IL	50,652	VC
Lake Superior State Univ	MI	19,867	C
Lakeland Univ	WI	35,130	C
Lamar Univ	TX	18,014	LC
Lander Univ	SC	32,200	C
Lane College	TN	17,960	LC
Langston Univ	OK	15,659	C
Lawrence Univ	WI	56,133	HC+
Le Moyne College	NY	47,305	VC
Lebanon Valley College	PA	55,510	VC
Lee Univ	TN	22,045	C
Lees-McRae College	NC	33,944	NC
Lehigh Univ	PA	63,860	MC
LeMoyne-Owen College	TN	16,980	C

ST = STATE $IS = IN-STATE COSTS   SR = SELECTOR RATING

School	ST	$IS	SR
Lenoir-Rhyne Univ	NC	47,500	LC
LeTourneau Univ	TX	39,190	VC
Lewis & Clark College	OR	60,984	MC
Lewis-Clark State College	ID	14,202	C
Liberty Univ	VA	31,415	C
Limestone College	SC	32,100	C
Lincoln Memorial Univ	TN	28,430	C
Lincoln Univ	MO	14,402	NC
Lincoln Univ	PA	20,878	LC
Lindenwood Univ	MO	25,760	C
Lindsey Wilson College	KY	33,546	C
Linfield College	OR	53,992	C
Lipscomb Univ	TN	42,984	VC
LIU Brooklyn	NY	50,698	C
LIU Post	NY	50,698	C+
Livingstone College	NC	17,815	LC
Lock Haven Univ of Pennsylvania	PA	20,544	LC
Longwood Univ	VA	22,184	C
Louisiana State Univ and A&M College	LA	18,677	VC
Louisiana State Univ in Shreveport	LA	6,902	C
Louisiana Tech Univ	LA	11,422	VC
Lourdes Univ	OH	29,140	NC
Loyola Marymount Univ	CA	60,202	VC+
Loyola Univ Chicago	IL	57,158	VC
Loyola Univ Maryland	MD	61,710	VC
Loyola Univ New Orleans	LA	52,456	VC
Lubbock Christian Univ	TX	29,727	C
Luther College	IA	49,990	VC
Lycoming College	PA	50,895	C
Lyon College	AR	36,120	VC
Macalester College	MN	64,136	MC
MacMurray College	IL	35,025	C
Madonna Univ	MI	30,450	LC
Malone Univ	OH	39,200	C
Manchester Univ	IN	41,540	C
Manhattan College	NY	55,652	C
Manhattanville College	NY	52,430	C
Mansfield Univ of Pennsylvania	PA	24,244	LC
Marian Univ	IN	43,206	C
Marian Univ	WI	34,622	C
Marietta College	OH	46,190	C
Marist College	NY	49,860	VC
Marlboro College	VT	50,832	VC+
Marquette Univ	WI	53,090	VC+
Mars Hill Univ	NC	41,104	C
Marshall Univ	WV	18,044	C
Martin Univ	IN	21,010	LC
Mary Baldwin Univ	VA	40,495	C
Marygrove College	MI	30,100	LC
Marymount Manhattan College	NY	48,350	C
Marymount Univ	VA	43,231	C
Maryville College	TN	44,410	C
Maryville Univ of St. Louis	MO	38,558	VC
Marywood Univ	PA	47,840	C
Mass College of Liberal Arts	MA	20,659	C
Mass Inst of Technology	MA	62,662	MC
Mayville State Univ	ND	18,371	NC
McDaniel College	MD	52,910	VC
McKendree Univ	IL	37,940	C+
McMurry Univ	TX	34,259	LC
McNeese State Univ	LA	7,838	C
McPherson College	KS	36,134	C
Mercer Univ	GA	45,348	VC
Mercy College	NY	32,614	C
Mercyhurst Univ	PA	47,420	C
Meredith College	NC	46,634	C
Merrimack College	MA	55,415	C
Messiah College	PA	44,380	VC
Methodist Univ	NC	58,130	C
Metropolitan State Univ	MN	7,859	C
Metropolitan State Univ of Denver	CO	6,928	LC
Mich State Univ	MI	24,542	VC
Mich Tech Univ	MI	25,551	VC+
Middle Tenn State Univ	TN	8,650	C
Middlebury College	VT	67,464	MC
Midland Univ	NE	39,512	C
Midway Univ	KY	33,940	LC
Midwestern State Univ	TX	12,111	LC
Miles College	AL	16,530	NC
Millersville Univ of Pennsylvania	PA	25,298	C
Milligan College	TN	39,450	C
Millikin Univ	IL	44,148	C
Mills College	CA	43,705	C
Millsaps College	MS	50,080	C+
Minn State Univ, Mankato	MN	17,190	C
Minn State Univ, Moorhead	MN	21,393	C
Minot State Univ	ND	13,285	C
Misericordia Univ	PA	45,210	C
Miss College	MS	25,850	C
Miss State Univ	MS	12,028	C+
Miss Univ for Women	MS	17,065	C
Miss Valley State Univ	MS	13,233	LC
Missouri Baptist Univ	MO	35,594	C
Missouri Southern State Univ	MO	13,071	C
Missouri State Univ	MO	15,837	C+
Missouri Univ of Science and Technology	MO	18,655	HC
Missouri Valley College	MO	28,150	C
Missouri Western State Univ	MO	17,822	LC
Molloy College	NY	40,440	C
Monmouth College	IL	42,260	C
Monmouth Univ	NJ	50,184	C
Montana State Univ	MT	15,500	C+
Montana State Univ Billings	MT	13,336	LC
Montana State Univ-Northern	MT	11,370	NC
Montana Tech of the Univ of Montana	MT	15,447	VC
Montclair State Univ	NJ	26,912	C
Moravian College	PA	55,488	C
Morehead State Univ	KY	18,386	LC
Morehouse College	GA	40,835	C
Morgan State Univ	MD	17,190	LC
Morningside College	IA	39,780	C
Morris College	SC	19,195	LC
Mount Aloysius College	PA	29,976	C
Mount Holyoke College	MA	56,746	MC
Mount Marty College	SD	36,862	C
Mount Mary Univ	WI	34,650	LC
Mount Mercy Univ	IA	39,748	C
Mount St. Mary College	NY	44,448	C
Mount St. Joseph Univ	OH	33,880	LC
Mount St. Mary's Univ	MD	53,380	C
Mount St. Mary's Univ - Chalon Campus	CA	50,486	VC+
Muhlenberg College	PA	56,645	VC
Murray State Univ	KY	17,726	C+
Muskingum Univ	OH	35,966	C
National Louis Univ	IL	43,000	LC
Nazareth College	NY	46,784	C
Nebr Wesleyan Univ	NE	42,026	C+
Neumann Univ	PA	40,678	LC
New College of Florida	FL	16,180	HC+
New England College	NH	50,828	NC
New Jersey City Univ	NJ	21,456	LC
New Jersey Inst of Technology	NJ	30,198	HC
New Mexico Highlands Univ	NM	11,904	LC
New Mexico Inst of Mining and Technology	NM	15,385	HC+
New Mexico State Univ	NM	14,050	LC
New York Univ	NY	68,139	MC
Newberry College	SC	34,550	C
Newman Univ	KS	37,382	C
Niagara Univ	NY	41,010	C
Nicholls State Univ	LA	14,959	C
Norfolk State Univ	VA	18,902	LC
N Car A&T State Univ	NC	13,786	C
N Car Central Univ	NC	9,000	C
N Car State Univ	NC	22,434	HC+
N Car Wesleyan College	NC	39,200	C
North Central College	IL	48,712	C+
N Dak State Univ	ND	16,245	VC
North Park Univ	IL	35,860	C
Northeastern Illinois Univ	IL	12,529	LC
Northeastern State Univ	OK	8,615	VC
Northeastern Univ	MA	65,352	MC
Northern Arizona Univ	AZ	21,003	C
Northern Illinois Univ	IL	20,176	C
Northern Kentucky Univ	KY	16,486	C
Northern Mich Univ	MI	20,853	C
Northern State Univ	SD	15,570	C
Northland College	WI	41,103	C+
Northwest Missouri State Univ	MO	18,286	C
Northwest Nazarene Univ	ID	40,250	C
Northwestern College of Iowa	IA	38,400	C
Northwestern Okla State Univ	OK	13,072	LC
Northwestern State Univ of Louisiana	LA	16,534	LC
Northwestern Univ	IL	68,725	MC
Norwich Univ	VT	56,234	C
Notre Dame College	OH	39,150	VC
Notre Dame de Namur Univ	CA	46,526	LC
Notre Dame of Maryland Univ	MD	47,570	VC
Oakland City Univ	IN	33,930	NC
Oakland Univ	MI	20,763	C
Oakwood Univ	AL	43,758	C
Oberlin College	OH	68,942	MC
Occidental College	CA	68,660	MC
Oglethorpe Univ	GA	44,200	C
Ohio Dominican Univ	OH	41,340	C+
Ohio Northern Univ	OH	44,050	VC
Ohio State Univ at Columbus	OH	22,843	MC
Ohio State Univ at Lima	OH	7,553	C
Ohio State Univ at Marion	OH	7,553	VC
Ohio Univ	OH	23,394	VC
Ohio Wesleyan Univ	OH	49,460	VC
Okla Baptist Univ	OK	33,990	C
Okla Christian Univ	OK	29,260	C
Okla Panhandle State Univ	OK	6,152	C
Okla State Univ	OK	17,180	C+
Okla Wesleyan Univ	OK	34,434	C
Old Dominion Univ	VA	21,618	C
Olivet College	MI	37,661	LC
Olivet Nazarene Univ	IL	41,840	VC
Oral Roberts Univ	OK	34,316	C
Oregon State Univ	OR	23,337	VC
Ottawa Univ	KS	39,980	VC
Ouachita Baptist Univ	AR	33,500	VC
Our Lady of the Lake Univ	TX	37,790	LC
Pace Univ	NY	60,136	C
Pacific Lutheran Univ	WA	49,960	C
Pacific Union College	CA	36,009	VC
Pacific Univ	OR	37,617	C
Paine College	GA	19,506	LC
Palm Beach Atlantic Univ	FL	39,250	C
Park Univ	MO	22,134	C
Penn State Altoona	PA	26,686	C
Penn State Erie,The Behrend College	PA	26,688	VC
Pennsylvania State Univ - Univ Park	PA	29,716	HC
Pepperdine Univ	CA	66,862	VC+
Peru State College	NE	15,602	LC
Pfeiffer Univ	NC	40,532	LC
Philander Smith College	AR	20,814	LC
Piedmont College	GA	34,334	C
Pine Manor College	MA	41,660	LC
Pittsburg State Univ	KS	13,880	C
Pitzer College	CA	68,500	HC+
Plymouth State Univ	NH	23,180	LC
Point Loma Nazarene Univ	CA	46,150	C+
Point Park Univ	PA	41,270	C
Pomona College	CA	64,957	MC
Pontifical Catholic Univ of PR	PR	10,534	
Portland State Univ	OR	19,443	C
Prairie View A&M Univ	TX	27,273	LC
Presbyterian College	SC	47,186	C
Prescott College	AZ	38,201	C
Presentation College	SD	28,575	LC
Principia College	IL	40,350	C
Purdue Univ Northwest	IN	15,178	C
Purdue Univ/West Lafayette	IN	20,032	MC
Queens Univ of Charlotte	NC	39,543	C
Quincy Univ	IL	38,170	LC
Quinnipiac Univ	CT	60,970	VC
Radford Univ	VA	19,758	C
Ramapo College of New Jersey	NJ	25,760	VC
Randolph College	VA	53,970	C
Randolph-Macon College	VA	51,480	VC
Reed College	OR	65,300	MC
Regis College	MA	51,920	LC
Regis Univ	CO	46,380	C
Reinhardt Univ	GA	31,344	C
Rensselaer Polytechnic Inst	NY	67,265	MC
Rhode Island College	RI	19,000	LC
Rhodes College	TN	51,900	HC
Rice Univ	TX	59,458	MC
Rider Univ	NJ	54,050	C
Ripon College	WI	49,991	VC
Rivier Univ	NH	41,600	VC
Roanoke College	VA	55,952	VC
Robert Morris Univ	PA	40,600	C
Roberts Wesleyan College	NY	41,116	C
Rochester Inst of Technology	NY	52,734	HC+
Rockford Univ	IL	38,570	C
Rockhurst Univ	MO	28,990	C
Roger Williams Univ	RI	48,074	VC
Rollins College	FL	58,670	HC
Roosevelt Univ	IL	41,890	VC
Rose-Hulman Inst of Technology	IN	59,823	MC
Rosemont College	PA	30,980	LC
Rowan Univ	NJ	24,491	VC
Russell Sage College	NY	39,370	C
Rust College	MS	10,600	C
Rutgers Univ - Camden	NJ	26,595	C
Rutgers Univ - New Brunswick	NJ	27,090	HC
Rutgers Univ - Newark	NJ	27,351	C
Sacred Heart Univ	CT	54,590	C
Saginaw Valley State Univ	MI	19,284	C
St. Anselm College	NH	56,636	VC
St. Augustine's Univ	NC	25,582	C
St. Francis Univ	PA	46,146	NC
St. John's Univ	MN	53,472	C
St. Joseph's College of Maine	ME	47,890	C
St. Joseph's Univ	PA	58,540	VC
St. Leo Univ	FL	32,850	C
St. Louis Univ	MO	49,866	HC
St. Martin's Univ	WA	45,056	C
St. Mary-of-the-Woods College	IN	40,424	LC
St. Mary's College	IN	50,600	C
St. Mary's College of Calif	CA	57,420	C
St. Mary's Univ of Minn	MN	42,440	C
St. Michael's College	VT	53,275	VC+
St. Peter's Univ	NJ	49,192	C
St. Vincent College	PA	46,229	C
St. Xavier Univ	IL	44,440	C
Salem College	NC	40,206	C
Salem International Univ	WV	21,090	C
Salem State Univ	MA	42,650	LC
Salisbury Univ	MD	21,132	VC
Salve Regina Univ	RI	53,046	VC
Sam Houston State Univ	TX	18,792	C
Samford Univ	AL	40,770	VC
San Diego Christian College	CA	40,914	C
San Diego State Univ	CA	23,156	VC
San Francisco State Univ	CA	18,514	LC
San Jose State Univ	CA	22,630	C
Sarah Lawrence College	NY	68,866	MC
Savannah State Univ	GA	17,036	C
Schreiner Univ	TX	34,626	LC
Scripps College	CA	69,260	HC
Seattle Pacific Univ	WA	47,439	C+
Seattle Univ	WA	54,957	VC
Seton Hall Univ	NJ	58,008	C
Seton Hill Univ	PA	46,972	VC
Sewanee: The Univ of the South	TN	58,000	HC+
Shaw Univ	NC	24,638	C
Shawnee State Univ	OH	16,998	C
Shenandoah Univ	VA	42,100	C
Shepherd Univ, West Virginia	WV	17,382	C
Shippensburg Univ of Pennsylvania	PA	24,096	C
Shorter Univ	GA	31,130	LC
Siena College	NY	48,916	C
Siena Heights Univ	MI	36,322	C
Silver Lake College of the Holy Family	WI	36,290	LC
Simmons College	MA	54,400	HC
Simpson College	IA	45,626	VC
Simpson Univ	CA	34,722	C
Skidmore College	NY	66,600	MC
Slippery Rock Univ of Pennsylvania	PA	20,450	C
Smith College	MA	66,774	MC
Sonoma State Univ	CA	27,020	C
S Car State Univ	SC	21,330	LC
S Dak State Univ	SD	15,874	C
Southeastern Louisiana Univ	LA	16,237	C
Southeastern Okla State Univ	OK	11,875	C
Southeastern Univ	FL	34,910	LC
Southern Adventist Univ	TN	28,250	C
Southern Arkansas Univ	AR	21,532	C
Southern Conn State Univ	CT	21,924	LC
Southern Illinois Univ Carbondale	IL	24,554	C
Southern Illinois Univ Edwardsville	IL	20,188	C
Southern Methodist Univ	TX	69,008	MC
Southern Nazarene Univ	OK	33,684	C
Southern Oregon Univ	OR	19,117	C
Southern Univ and A&M College	LA	16,074	LC
Southern Univ at New Orleans	LA	8,014	LC
Southern Wesleyan Univ	SC	33,670	LC
Southwest Baptist Univ	MO	30,890	LC
Southwest Minn State Univ	MN	17,783	C
Southwestern Adventist Univ	TX	28,232	LC
Southwestern College	KS	31,531	LC
Southwestern Okla State Univ	OK	12,205	C
Southwestern Univ	TX	52,370	VC
Spelman College	GA	41,642	C
Spring Arbor Univ	MI	37,390	C
Spring Hill College	AL	48,488	C
Springfield College	MA	48,775	C
St. Andrews Univ	NC	44,634	LC
St. Bonaventure Univ	NY	45,596	C
St. Catherine Univ	MN	45,630	C
St. Cloud State Univ	MN	10,600	C
St. Edward's Univ	TX	56,190	VC
St. Francis College	NY	38,800	LC
St. John Fisher College	NY	45,270	VC
St. John's College at Annapolis	MD	63,348	MC
St. John's Univ	NY	57,160	C+
St. Joseph's College, New York/Brooklyn Campus	NY	25,114	LC
St. Joseph's College, New York/Long Island Campus	NY	25,124	C
St. Lawrence Univ	NY	66,646	HC+
St. Mary's College of Maryland	MD	27,312	VC
St. Mary's Univ	TX	39,120	C
St. Norbert College	WI	46,060	VC
St. Olaf College	MN	56,430	HC
St. Thomas Univ	FL	51,187	LC
Stanford Univ	CA	62,541	MC
SUNY Albany	NY	22,165	C
SUNY at Binghamton	NY	24,100	MC
SUNY at Geneseo	NY	21,622	VC
SUNY at New Paltz	NY	20,840	C
SUNY at Oswego	NY	22,219	VC
SUNY at Purchase College	NY	21,832	C
SUNY Polytechnic Inst	NY	20,438	VC
SUNY/Buffalo State	NY	20,583	LC
SUNY/College at Old Westbury	NY	16,860	C
SUNY/Cortland	NY	20,910	C
SUNY/Fredonia	NY	20,818	C
SUNY/Oneonta	NY	20,794	C
SUNY/Plattsburgh	NY	19,314	C
SUNY/Potsdam	NY	21,051	VC
SUNY/The College of Environmental Science and Forestry	NY	23,728	VC
SUNY/Univ at Buffalo	NY	23,122	C
Stephen F. Austin State Univ	TX	18,484	LC
Stephens College	MO	38,042	C
Sterling College	KS	32,830	LC
Stetson Univ	FL	57,174	VC+
Stevenson Univ	MD	48,412	C
Stillman College	AL	20,738	C
Stockton Univ	NJ	25,565	C
Stonehill College	MA	55,130	C
Stony Brook Univ/The SUNY	NY	22,703	MC
Suffolk Univ	MA	52,316	C
Sul Ross State Univ	TX	15,021	LC
Susquehanna Univ	PA	57,560	VC
Swarthmore College	PA	63,550	MC
Tabor College	KS	35,870	C
Talladega College	AL	25,919	C
Tarleton State Univ	TX	15,248	LC
Taylor Univ	IN	42,130	VC
Temple Univ	PA	24,392	C+
Tenn State Univ	TN	14,423	LC
Tenn Tech Univ	TN	17,929	C
Texas A&M Univ at College Station	TX	20,771	VC+

ST = STATE **$IS** = IN-STATE COSTS **SR** = SELECTOR RATING

School	ST	$IS	SR
Texas A&M Univ at Commerce	TX	10,496	C
Texas A&M Univ at Corpus Christi	TX	16,851	LC
Texas A&M Univ at Kingsville	TX	16,580	LC
Texas Lutheran Univ	TX	39,770	C
Texas Southern Univ	TX	19,592	LC
Texas State Univ	TX	18,721	C
Texas Wesleyan Univ	TX	37,338	C
Texas Woman's Univ	TX	15,302	LC
The American Univ	DC	61,317	HC
The Catholic Univ of America	DC	58,376	VC
The Citadel, The Military College of S Car	SC	20,679	C
The College at Brockport - SUNY	NY	21,058	C
The College of Idaho	ID	36,415	C
The College of New Jersey	NJ	28,675	VC+
The College of New Rochelle	NY	46,300	LC
The College of St. Rose	NY	44,010	C
The College of Wooster	OH	60,000	HC
The Evergreen State College	WA	16,599	C
The George Washington Univ	DC	68,474	HC+
The Master's Univ	CA	43,870	C
The Univ of Akron	OH	22,566	C
The Univ of Alabama	AL	24,320	C+
The Univ of Arizona	AZ	24,086	C
The Univ of Mary	ND	23,180	C
The Univ of Memphis	TN	18,278	C
The Univ of Tenn at Chattanooga	TN	17,340	C+
The Univ of Tenn at Knoxville	TN	22,112	VC
The Univ of Tenn at Martin	TN	15,212	C
The Univ of Texas at Austin	TX	20,206	MC
The Univ of Texas at San Antonio	TX	21,060	C
The Univ of Utah	UT	18,751	VC
The Univ of Virginia's College at Wise	VA	18,192	LC
Thiel College	PA	42,950	LC
Thomas More College	KY	36,720	LC
Thomas Univ	GA	21,420	NC
Toccoa Falls College	GA	30,048	C
Tougaloo College	MS	17,980	NC
Touro College	NY	31,040	C
Towson Univ	MD	21,878	C
Transylvania Univ	KY	47,450	HC+
Trevecca Nazarene Univ	TN	31,186	C
Trine Univ	IN	41,310	C
Trinity Christian College	IL	35,580	C
Trinity College	CT	69,020	HC
Trinity International Univ	IL	31,070	VC
Trinity Univ	TX	54,480	MC
Trinity Washington Univ	DC	33,826	C+
Troy Univ	AL	16,171	C
Truman State Univ	MO	16,286	MC
Tufts Univ	MA		MC
Tusculum College	TN	31,625	LC
Tuskegee Univ	AL	28,164	C
Union College	KY	32,310	C
Union College	NE	23,270	C
Union College	NY	64,320	MC
Union Univ	TN	41,160	VC
United States Air Force Academy	CO		C
Unity College	ME	37,670	C
Universidad Adventista de las Antillas	PR	16,606	
Universidad del Turabo	PR	17,828	
Univ of Alabama at Birmingham	AL	22,092	C
Univ of Alabama in Huntsville	AL	20,028	VC
Univ of Alaska Anchorage	AK	17,914	C
Univ of Alaska Fairbanks	AK	16,874	VC
Univ of Alaska Southeast	AK	17,615	C
Univ of Arkansas at Fayetteville	AR	19,766	VC
Univ of Arkansas at Little Rock	AR	18,211	LC
Univ of Arkansas at Monticello	AR	13,599	LC
Univ of Arkansas at Pine Bluff	AR	13,541	C
Univ of Bridgeport	CT	44,985	LC
Univ of Calif at Berkeley	CA	29,886	MC
Univ of Calif at Davis	CA	28,468	HC
Univ of Calif at Irvine	CA	33,857	VC
Univ of Calif at Los Angeles	CA	27,438	HC+
Univ of Calif at Riverside	CA	32,912	C
Univ of Calif at Santa Barbara	CA	30,627	HC+
Univ of Calif San Diego	CA	30,450	MC
Univ of Calif, Santa Cruz	CA	28,731	C+
Univ of Central Arkansas	AR	15,042	VC
Univ of Central Florida	FL	16,379	VC
Univ of Central Missouri	MO	18,982	C
Univ of Central Okla	OK	15,150	C
Univ of Charleston	WV	35,000	LC
Univ of Chicago	IL	70,551	MC
Univ of Cincinnati	OH	22,118	VC
Univ of Colo Colo Springs	CO	20,300	C
Univ of Colo Denver	CO	22,238	C
Univ of Conn	CT	27,394	
Univ of Dallas	TX	50,676	VC
Univ of Dayton	OH	54,930	VC

School	ST	$IS	SR
Univ of Delaware	DE	32,214	VC
Univ of Denver	CO	61,129	VC+
Univ of Detroit Mercy	MI	48,816	C
Univ of Dubuque	IA	37,824	C
Univ of Evansville	IN	44,186	C+
Univ of Findlay	OH	43,040	C
Univ of Georgia	GA	21,878	HC
Univ of Great Falls	MT	38,524	C
Univ of Hartford	CT	49,776	C
Univ of Hawaii at Hilo	HI	18,038	VC
Univ of Hawaii at Manoa	HI	23,261	C
Univ of Holy Cross	LA	21,523	NC
Univ of Houston	TX	21,871	VC
Univ of Houston-Downtown	TX	7,241	LC
Univ of Idaho	ID	16,158	C
Univ of Illinois at Chicago	IL	24,664	VC
Univ of Illinois at Urbana-Champaign	IL	27,006	HC
Univ of Indianapolis	IN	36,480	VC
Univ of Iowa	IA	19,415	HC
Univ of Jamestown	ND	28,508	C
Univ of Kansas	KS	20,884	VC
Univ of Kentucky	KY	24,800	C+
Univ of La Verne	CA	55,600	C
Univ of Louisville	KY	19,692	C
Univ of Lynchburg	VA	48,370	C
Univ of Maine	ME	21,038	VC
Univ of Maine at Augusta	ME	7,812	C
Univ of Maine at Farmington	ME	18,792	C
Univ of Maine at Fort Kent	ME	15,165	LC
Univ of Maine at Machias	ME	22,960	C
Univ of Maine at Presque Isle	ME	16,148	LC
Univ of Mary Hardin-Baylor	TX	35,292	C+
Univ of Mary Washington	VA	23,039	C+
Univ of Maryland/Baltimore County	MD	23,004	VC
Univ of Maryland/College Park	MD	21,938	HC
Univ of Maryland/Eastern Shore	MD	21,861	LC
Univ of Mass Amherst	MA	27,669	HC
Univ of Mass Boston	MA	13,828	C
Univ of Mass Dartmouth	MA	26,507	C
Univ of Mass Lowell	MA	27,296	VC
Univ of Mich/Ann Arbor	MI	25,274	MC
Univ of Mich/Flint	MI	19,062	C
Univ of Minn/Crookston	MN	19,126	C
Univ of Minn/Duluth	MN	20,292	C
Univ of Minn/Morris	MN	21,222	VC
Univ of Minn/Twin Cities	MN	24,269	MC
Univ of Miss	MS	18,802	C
Univ of Missouri-Columbia	MO	20,463	VC
Univ of Missouri-Kansas City	MO	19,563	VC
Univ of Missouri-St. Louis	MO	19,810	VC
Univ of Mobile	AL	28,935	C
Univ of Montana	MT	14,105	C
Univ of Montevallo	AL	20,012	C
Univ of Mount Olive	NC	18,426	C
Univ of Nebr - Kearney	NE	17,014	LC
Univ of Nebr - Lincoln	NE	18,589	VC
Univ of Nebr - Omaha	NE	16,120	C
Univ of Nevada, Las Vegas	NV	17,553	C
Univ of Nevada, Reno	NV	18,010	C
Univ of New England	ME	50,110	C
Univ of New Hampshire	NH	29,333	VC
Univ of New Haven	CT	53,680	C
Univ of New Mexico	NM	16,808	C
Univ of New Orleans	LA	12,840	C
Univ of North Alabama	AL	15,964	C
Univ of N Car at Asheville	NC	16,251	VC+
Univ of N Car at Chapel Hill	NC	20,561	MC
Univ of N Car at Charlotte	NC	17,803	VC
Univ of N Car at Pembroke	NC	14,737	LC
Univ of N Car Wilmington	NC	16,784	VC
Univ of N Dak	ND	16,673	C
Univ of North Florida	FL	15,996	VC
Univ of North Georgia	GA	17,316	C
Univ of North Texas	TX	20,082	C
Univ of Northern Colo	CO	19,658	C
Univ of Northern Iowa	IA	17,480	C
Univ of Northwestern - St. Paul	MN	39,530	C
Univ of Oregon	OR	24,021	VC
Univ of Pennsylvania	PA	63,526	MC
Univ of Pikeville	KY	27,838	C
Univ of Pittsburgh	PA	30,030	MC
Univ of Pittsburgh at Bradford	PA	22,958	C
Univ of Pittsburgh at Greensburg	PA	24,140	C
Univ of Pittsburgh at Johnstown	PA	22,092	C
Univ of Portland	OR	52,152	VC
Univ of PR, at Cayey	PR		
Univ of PR, at Humacao	PR	14,000	
Univ of PR, at Mayaguez	PR	13,995	
Univ of PR-Rio Piedras campus	PR	13,327	
Univ of Puget Sound	WA	60,210	HC
Univ of Redlands	CA	61,934	VC
Univ of Richmond	VA	62,730	MC
Univ of Rio Grande & Rio Grande Community College	OH	8,750	LC
Univ of Rochester	NY	65,032	MC
Univ of St. Francis	IN	38,520	C
Univ of St. Joseph	CT	49,069	C
Univ of St. Mary	KS	37,080	NC
Univ of San Diego	CA	60,338	HC

School	ST	$IS	SR
Univ of San Francisco	CA	60,580	C
Univ of Science and Arts of Okla	OK	11,140	VC
Univ of Scranton	PA	54,962	VC
Univ of Sioux Falls	SD	25,630	C
Univ of South Alabama	AL	16,880	C
Univ of S Car Aiken	SC	18,094	C
Univ of S Car at Columbia	SC	21,726	VC
Univ of S Car Upstate	SC	19,272	LC
Univ of S Dak	SD	16,109	C
Univ of South Florida St. Petersburg	FL	15,980	C
Univ of South Florida/Tampa	FL	16,110	VC
Univ of Southern Calif	CA	66,631	MC
Univ of Southern Indiana	IN	16,808	C
Univ of Southern Maine	ME	18,320	C
Univ of Southern Miss	MS	13,170	C
Univ of St. Francis	IL	40,828	C
Univ of St. Thomas - Houston	TX	41,510	VC
Univ of Tampa	FL	38,928	VC
Univ of Texas at Arlington	TX	18,876	C
Univ of Texas at Dallas	TX	23,640	HC
Univ of Texas at El Paso	TX	34,452	NC
Univ of Texas Rio Grande Valley	TX	15,573	LC
Univ of the Cumberlands	KY	32,000	LC
Univ of the District of Columbia	DC	21,260	LC
Univ of the Incarnate Word	TX	39,162	LC
Univ of the Ozarks	AR	31,050	NC
Univ of the Pacific	CA	57,446	VC
Univ of the Sacred Heart	PR	17,932	
Univ of the Sciences	PA	40,738	VC
Univ of the Southwest	NM	24,386	C
Univ of Toledo	OH	19,336	C
Univ of Tulsa	OK	52,625	HC
Univ of Vermont	VT	29,792	HC
Univ of Virginia	VA	27,367	MC
Univ of Washington	WA	23,091	MC
Univ of West Alabama	AL	16,284	LC
Univ of West Florida	FL	15,848	C
Univ of West Georgia	GA	17,510	LC
Univ of Wisc-Eau Claire	WI	16,354	VC
Univ of Wisc-Green Bay	WI	15,184	C
Univ of Wisc-La Crosse	WI	15,425	VC
Univ of Wisc-Madison	WI	21,647	MC
Univ of Wisc-Milwaukee	WI	21,538	C
Univ of Wisc-Oshkosh	WI	15,392	C
Univ of Wisc-Parkside	WI	15,313	C
Univ of Wisc-Platteville	WI	14,148	C
Univ of Wisc-River Falls	WI	14,541	C
Univ of Wisc-Stevens Point	WI	14,043	C
Univ of Wisc-Superior	WI	14,838	C
Univ of Wisc-Whitewater	WI	13,976	C
Upper Iowa Univ	IA	34,990	NC
Ursinus College	PA	62,920	VC
Ursuline College	OH	41,076	LC
Utah State Univ	UT	13,235	C
Utica College	NY	31,510	C
Valley City State Univ	ND	13,267	C
Valparaiso Univ	IN	50,160	VC
Vanderbilt Univ	TN	63,248	MC
Vanguard Univ of Southern Calif	CA	42,400	VC
Villanova Univ	PA	64,922	MC
Virginia Commonwealth Univ	VA	23,811	VC
Virginia Military Inst	VA	26,460	VC
Virginia Polytechnic Inst and State Univ	VA	21,920	VC
Virginia State Univ	VA	19,802	C+
Virginia Union Univ	VA	25,058	C
Virginia Wesleyan Univ	VA	45,980	LC
Viterbo Univ	WI	34,660	C
Voorhees College	SC	19,976	C
Wabash College	IN	52,100	VC
Wagner College	NY	57,240	C+
Wake Forest Univ	NC	69,354	MC
Walla Walla Univ	WA	34,845	C
Walsh Univ	OH	39,010	C
Warner Pacific College	OR	31,610	C
Warner Univ	FL	28,216	C
Warren Wilson College	NC	44,220	VC
Washburn Univ	KS	15,827	C
Washington & Jefferson College	PA	58,694	VC
Washington Adventist Univ	MD	32,050	LC
Washington and Lee Univ	VA	59,647	MC
Washington College	MD	56,154	VC
Washington State Univ	WA	22,747	C
Washington Univ in St. Louis	MO	67,539	MC
Wayland Baptist Univ	TX	23,460	LC
Wayne State College	NE	25,746	NC
Wayne State Univ	MI	23,085	C
Waynesburg Univ	PA	33,530	C
Weber State Univ	UT	14,112	C
Webster Univ	MO	37,490	C
Wellesley College	MA	66,984	MC
Wells College	NY	50,500	C
Wesley College	DE	37,848	LC
Wesleyan College	GA	31,940	C+
Wesleyan Univ	CT	66,940	MC
West Chester Univ of Pennsylvania	PA	19,171	VC
West Liberty Univ	WV	16,158	C
West Texas A&M Univ	TX	13,478	C
West Virginia State Univ	WV	19,412	LC
West Virginia Univ	WV	18,952	VC

School	ST	$IS	SR
West Virginia Univ Inst of Technology	WV	18,264	C
West Virginia Wesleyan College	WV	39,188	C
Western Carolina Univ	NC	13,965	C
Western Conn State Univ	CT	21,254	LC
Western Kentucky Univ	KY	16,850	C
Western Mich Univ	MI	21,791	C
Western New England Univ	MA	49,182	C
Western New Mexico Univ	NM	16,914	LC
Western Oregon Univ	OR	19,965	LC
Western State Colo Univ	CO	19,348	C
Western Washington Univ	WA	18,904	VC
Westfield State Univ	MA	20,404	C
Westminster College	MO	32,820	C
Westminster College	PA	41,722	C
Westminster College	UT	41,078	C
Westmont College	CA	57,930	VC
Wheaton College	IL	44,993	MC
Wheeling Jesuit Univ	WV	37,106	LC
Whittier College	CA	57,891	C
Whitworth Univ	WA	53,682	VC
Wichita State Univ	KS	17,773	C
Widener Univ	PA	58,190	C
Wilberforce Univ	OH	19,900	C
Wiley College	TX	19,255	C
Wilkes Univ	PA	49,166	C
Willamette Univ	OR	62,514	VC+
William Carey Univ	MS	23,950	LC
William Jewell College	MO	42,490	C+
William Paterson Univ of New Jersey	NJ	24,022	C
William Peace Univ	NC	39,300	LC
William Penn Univ	IA	26,000	C
William Woods Univ	MO	32,040	C
Williams Baptist College	AR	24,720	C
Williams College	MA	67,700	MC
Wilmington College	OH	35,100	C
Wilson College	PA	35,620	LC
Wingate Univ	NC	41,900	C
Winona State Univ	MN	18,109	C
Winston-Salem State Univ	NC	18,005	LC
Winthrop Univ	SC	23,960	C
Wisc Lutheran College	WI	36,290	C
Wittenberg Univ	OH	49,863	VC
Wofford College	SC	49,885	VC
Worcester State Univ	MA	20,977	C
Wright State Univ	OH	16,983	C
Xavier Univ	OH	49,380	VC
Xavier Univ of Louisiana	LA	31,689	C
Yale Univ	CT	64,650	MC
Yeshiva Univ	NY	52,750	VC
York College	NE	30,260	C
York College of Pennsylvania	PA	29,240	C
Youngstown State Univ	OH	17,487	C

BIOLOGY/GENERAL SCIENCE SECONDARY EDUCATION

School	ST	$IS	SR
Abilene Christian Univ	TX	43,708	C+
Averett Univ	VA	43,034	LC
Coker College	SC	38,196	C
Ferris State Univ	MI	21,458	C
Grove City College	PA	26,654	VC
Gwynedd Mercy Univ	PA	43,780	LC
King Univ	TN	36,976	C
Kutztown Univ of Pennsylvania	PA	19,477	C
Missouri Western State Univ	MO	17,822	LC
Neumann Univ	PA	40,678	LC
St. Ambrose Univ	IA	40,180	C
St. Edward's Univ	TX	56,190	VC
Syracuse Univ	NY	62,313	HC
Tenn Wesleyan Univ	TN	32,680	LC
The Univ of Utah	UT	18,751	VC
Wartburg College	IA	49,478	C
West Chester Univ of Pennsylvania	PA	19,171	VC
Wilson College	PA	35,620	LC
Wingate Univ	NC	41,900	C

BIOLOGY/GENERAL SCIENCE/ ENVIRONMENTAL SCIENCE SECOND EDUCATION

School	ST	$IS	SR
Bay Path Univ	MA	46,356	C
Lynn Univ	FL	49,680	LC
MidAmerica Nazarene Univ	KS	37,808	C
Missouri Western State Univ	MO	17,822	LC
Northern Mich Univ	MI	20,853	C
Wilson College	PA	35,620	LC

BIOMATHEMATICS

School	ST	$IS	SR
Averett Univ	VA	43,034	LC
Brown Univ	RI	64,566	MC
Emmanuel College	MA	53,472	C+
Florida Inst of Technology	FL	53,306	VC
The Univ of Montana Western	MT	9,426	LC
Univ of Scranton	PA	54,962	VC
Washington Univ in St. Louis	MO	67,539	MC

BIOMEDICAL ART

School	ST	$IS	SR
Cleveland Inst of Art	OH	51,455	SP
Rochester Inst of Technology	NY	52,734	HC+

ST = STATE **$IS** = IN-STATE COSTS **SR** = SELECTOR RATING

BIOMEDICAL ELECTRONICS

School	ST	$IS	SR
Thomas Edison State Univ	NJ	6,350	NC

BIOMEDICAL ENGINEERING

School	ST	$IS	SR
Arizona State Univ at the Tempe Campus	AZ	23,001	VC
Boston Univ	MA	67,352	MC
Brown Univ	RI	64,566	MC
Bucknell Univ	PA	67,136	MC
Butler Univ	IN	52,890	VC+
Calif Baptist Univ	CA	42,986	C
Calif Polytechnic State Univ	CA	22,547	MC
Cal State, Fullerton	CA	21,902	C
Case Western Reserve Univ	OH	62,284	MC
CUNY/City College	NY	20,204	C
Colo State Univ	CO	23,033	C
Columbia Univ/City of New York	NY	62,958	MC
Dartmouth College	NH	68,109	MC
Drexel Univ	PA	65,927	HC
Duke Univ	NC	68,298	MC
Duquesne Univ	PA	48,508	VC
Elon Univ	NC	46,142	HC
Florida Inst of Technology	FL	53,306	VC
Florida International Univ	FL	20,281	C
Florida State Univ	FL	16,771	HC
Gannon Univ	PA	42,922	C
Georgia Inst of Technology	GA	23,910	MC
Harding Univ	AR	25,440	C
Hofstra Univ	NY	58,210	C+
Indiana Inst of Technology	IN	34,240	LC
Indiana Univ-Purdue Univ Indianapolis	IN	18,952	C
Jackson State Univ	MS	15,879	LC
Johns Hopkins Univ	MD	68,080	MC
Lawrence Tech Univ	MI	41,630	VC
Louisiana Tech Univ	LA	11,422	VC
Marquette Univ	WI	53,090	VC+
Mass Inst of Technology	MA	62,662	MC
Mich Tech Univ	MI	25,551	VC+
Milwaukee School of Engineering	WI	48,531	HC+
New Jersey Inst of Technology	NJ	30,198	HC
New York Univ	NY	68,139	MC
N Dak State Univ	ND	16,245	VC
Northwestern Univ	IL	68,725	MC
Ohio State Univ at Columbus	OH	22,843	MC
Pennsylvania State Univ - Univ Park	PA	29,716	HC
Purdue Univ/West Lafayette	IN	20,032	MC
Rensselaer Polytechnic Inst	NY	67,265	MC
Rochester Inst of Technology	NY	52,734	HC+
Rose-Hulman Inst of Technology	IN	59,823	MC
Rowan Univ	NJ	24,491	VC
Rutgers Univ - New Brunswick	NJ	27,090	HC
St. Louis Univ	MO	49,866	HC
San Jose State Univ	CA	22,630	C
SUNY at Binghamton	NY	24,100	MC
SUNY/Univ at Buffalo	NY	23,122	C
Stevens Inst of Technology	NJ	64,954	MC
Stony Brook Univ/The SUNY	NY	22,703	MC
Texas A&M Univ at College Station	TX	20,771	VC+
The Catholic Univ of America	DC	58,376	VC
The College of New Jersey	NJ	28,675	VC+
The Univ of Akron	OH	22,566	C
The Univ of Arizona	AZ	24,086	C
The Univ of Memphis	TN	18,278	C
The Univ of Tenn at Knoxville	TN	22,112	VC
The Univ of Texas at Austin	TX	20,206	MC
The Univ of Texas at San Antonio	TX	21,060	C
The Univ of Utah	UT	18,751	VC
Tufts Univ	MA		MC
Tulane Univ	LA	67,496	MC
Tuskegee Univ	AL	28,164	C
Universidad Politecnica de PR, Hato Rey campus	PR	23,514	
Univ of Alabama at Birmingham	AL	22,092	C
Univ of Arkansas at Fayetteville	AR	19,766	VC
Univ of Calif at Irvine	CA	33,857	VC
Univ of Calif at Los Angeles	CA	27,438	HC+
Univ of Central Okla	OK	15,150	C
Univ of Cincinnati	OH	22,118	VC
Univ of Conn	CT	27,394	
Univ of Hartford	CT	49,776	C
Univ of Houston	TX	21,871	VC
Univ of Idaho	ID	16,158	C
Univ of Iowa	IA	19,415	HC
Univ of Mass Lowell	MA	27,296	VC
Univ of Miami	FL	63,494	MC
Univ of Mich/Ann Arbor	MI	25,274	MC
Univ of Minn/Twin Cities	MN	24,269	MC
Univ of Missouri-Columbia	MO	20,463	VC
Univ of Mount Union	OH	39,990	C
Univ of N Car at Chapel Hill	NC	20,561	MC
Univ of Rhode Island	RI	26,066	VC
Univ of Rochester	NY	65,032	MC
Univ of S Car at Columbia	SC	21,726	VC
Univ of Southern Calif	CA	66,631	MC
Univ of Texas at Dallas	TX	23,640	HC
Univ of Virginia	VA	27,367	MC
Univ of Wisc-Madison	WI	21,647	MC
Vanderbilt Univ	TN	63,248	MC
Virginia Commonwealth Univ	VA	23,811	VC
Washington State Univ	WA	22,747	C
Washington Univ in St. Louis	MO	67,539	MC
Wayne State Univ	MI	23,085	C
Wentworth Inst of Technology	MA	48,810	VC
Western New England Univ	MA	49,182	C
Widener Univ	PA	58,190	C
Wright State Univ	OH	16,983	C
Yale Univ	CT	64,650	MC

BIOMEDICAL EQUIPMENT TECHNOLOGY

School	ST	$IS	SR
Alvernia Univ	PA	45,330	C
Andrews Univ	MI	41,732	C
Roberts Wesleyan College	NY	41,116	C

BIOMEDICAL SCIENCE

School	ST	$IS	SR
Adventist Univ of Health Sciences	FL	48,492	SP
Albany College of Pharmacy and Health Sciences	NY	44,421	SP
Andrews Univ	MI	41,732	C
Arcadia Univ	PA	55,990	C+
Auburn Univ	AL	24,300	VC+
Averett Univ	VA	43,034	LC
Bay Path Univ	MA	46,356	C
Boston Univ	MA	67,352	MC
Brown Univ	RI	64,566	MC
Buena Vista Univ	IA	42,344	C
Cal State, Fullerton	CA	21,902	C
Cal State, Northridge	CA	17,277	LC
Central Mich Univ	MI	20,330	C
Christian Brothers Univ	TN	31,670	VC
CUNY/City College	NY	20,204	C
Colo State Univ	CO	23,033	C
Grand Valley State Univ	MI	22,250	C+
Heritage Univ	WA	19,825	NC
Hiram College	OH	44,590	C
Hodges Univ	FL	20,160	LC
Lewis Univ	IL	41,710	C
LIU Post	NY	50,698	C+
Madonna Univ	MI	30,450	LC
Marquette Univ	WI	53,090	VC+
McMurry Univ	TX	34,259	LC
Murray State Univ	KY	17,726	C+
New Mexico Inst of Mining and Technology	NM	15,385	HC+
Northern Arizona Univ	AZ	21,003	C
Ohio State Univ at Columbus	OH	22,843	MC
Okla City Univ	OK	40,476	C
Oral Roberts Univ	OK	34,316	C
Oregon State Univ	OR	23,337	VC
Quinnipiac Univ	CT	60,970	VC
Rochester Inst of Technology	NY	52,734	HC+
St. Leo Univ	FL	32,850	C
St. Louis Univ	MO	49,866	HC
St. Peter's Univ	NJ	49,192	C
Silver Lake College of the Holy Family	WI	36,290	LC
Southeast Missouri State Univ	MO	16,148	C
Southern Oregon Univ	OR	19,117	C
Southwestern Okla State Univ	OK	12,205	C
SUNY/Univ at Buffalo	NY	23,122	C
Susquehanna Univ	PA	57,560	VC
Tarleton State Univ	TX	15,248	LC
Texas A&M Univ at College Station	TX	20,771	VC+
Texas Wesleyan Univ	TX	37,338	C
Tufts Univ	MA		MC
Univ of Alabama at Birmingham	AL	22,092	C
Univ of Calif at Riverside	CA	32,912	C
Univ of Central Florida	FL	16,379	VC
Univ of Illinois at Urbana-Champaign	IL	27,006	HC
Univ of Lynchburg	VA	48,370	C
Univ of New England	ME	50,110	C
Univ of New Hampshire	NH	29,333	VC
Univ of St. Mary	KS	37,080	NC
Univ of South Alabama	AL	16,880	C
Univ of Texas Rio Grande Valley	TX	15,573	LC
Univ of Vermont	VT	29,792	HC
Univ of Wisc-Milwaukee	WI	21,538	C
Washington State Univ	WA	22,747	C
Western Mich Univ	MI	21,791	C
Xavier Univ	OH	49,380	VC

BIOMETRICS AND BIOSTATISTICS

School	ST	$IS	SR
Bryant Univ	RI	57,204	VC
Cal State, Fullerton	CA	21,902	C
Cornell Univ	NY	67,591	MC
La Sierra Univ	CA	39,690	VC
Rutgers Univ - New Brunswick	NJ	27,090	HC
Simmons College	MA	54,400	HC
The Univ of Arizona	AZ	24,086	C
Univ of N Car at Chapel Hill	NC	20,561	MC

BIOPHYSICS

School	ST	$IS	SR
Amherst College	MA	66,186	MC
Andrews Univ	MI	41,732	C
Arizona State Univ at the Tempe Campus	AZ	23,001	VC
Bellarmine Univ	KY	52,532	C
Brandeis Univ	MA	68,443	MC
Brigham Young Univ	UT	13,248	MC
Brown Univ	RI	64,566	MC
Cal State, Fresno	CA	16,902	LC
Cal State, Fullerton	CA	21,902	C
Centenary College of Louisiana	LA	49,050	C+
Claremont McKenna College	CA	69,900	MC
Columbia Univ/City of New York	NY	62,958	MC
Elon Univ	NC	46,142	HC
Harvard College/Harvard Univ	MA	65,609	MC
Illinois Inst of Technology	IL	56,826	HC+
Iowa State Univ	IA	18,176	C
Johns Hopkins Univ	MD	68,080	MC
La Sierra Univ	CA	39,690	VC
Lipscomb Univ	TN	42,984	VC
Loyola Univ Chicago	IL	57,158	VC
Pacific Union College	CA	36,009	VC
Rensselaer Polytechnic Inst	NY	67,265	MC
St. Mary's Univ of Minn	MN	42,440	C
Southern Nazarene Univ	OK	33,684	C
St. Bonaventure Univ	NY	45,596	C
St. Lawrence Univ	NY	66,646	HC+
SUNY at Geneseo	NY	21,622	VC
SUNY/Univ at Buffalo	NY	23,122	C
Syracuse Univ	NY	62,313	HC
Temple Univ	PA	24,392	C+
Tufts Univ	MA		MC
Univ of Calif at Los Angeles	CA	27,438	HC+
Univ of Calif San Diego	CA	30,450	MC
Univ of Conn	CT	27,394	
Univ of Illinois at Chicago	IL	24,664	VC
Univ of Illinois at Urbana-Champaign	IL	27,006	HC
Univ of Mich/Ann Arbor	MI	25,274	MC
Univ of Pennsylvania	PA	63,526	MC
Univ of San Diego	CA	60,338	HC
Univ of San Francisco	CA	60,580	C
Univ of Scranton	PA	54,962	VC
Univ of Southern Calif	CA	66,631	MC
Univ of Southern Indiana	IN	16,808	C
Walla Walla Univ	WA	34,845	C
Washington & Jefferson College	PA	58,694	VC
Washington Univ in St. Louis	MO	67,539	MC
Wayne State Univ	MI	23,085	C
Western Kentucky Univ	KY	16,850	C
Whitman College	WA	59,772	MC
Whitworth Univ	WA	53,682	VC
Xavier Univ	OH	49,380	VC
Yale Univ	CT	64,650	MC

BIOPSYCHOLOGY

School	ST	$IS	SR
Averett Univ	VA	43,034	LC
Barnard College/Columbia Univ	NY	68,762	MC
Birmingham-Southern College	AL	44,478	C+
Grand Valley State Univ	MI	22,250	C+
Immaculata Univ	PA	39,000	C
Jefferson (Philadelphia Univ + Thomas Jefferson Univ)	PA	53,966	C
McKendree Univ	IL	37,940	C+
Messiah College	PA	44,380	VC
Mills College	CA	43,705	C
Monmouth College	IL	42,260	C
Nebr Wesleyan Univ	NE	42,026	C+
Oglethorpe Univ	GA	44,200	C
Pace Univ	NY	60,136	C
Rider Univ	NJ	54,050	C
Simmons College	MA	54,400	HC
Spring Hill College	AL	48,488	C
Tufts Univ	MA		MC
Univ of Calif at Santa Barbara	CA	30,627	HC+
Viterbo Univ	WI	34,660	C
Washington Univ in St. Louis	MO	67,539	MC
Wellesley College	MA	66,984	MC
York College	NE	30,260	C

BIORESOURCE ENGINEERING

School	ST	$IS	SR
Calif Polytechnic State Univ	CA	22,547	MC
Oregon State Univ	OR	23,337	VC

BIOTECHNOLOGY

School	ST	$IS	SR
Alma College	MI	49,410	VC
Arkansas State Univ	AR	16,190	C
Ashland Univ	OH	30,446	C
Bay Path Univ	MA	46,356	C
Brigham Young Univ	UT	13,248	MC
Calif State Polytechnic Univ, Pomona	CA	21,811	C
Cal State, Fullerton	CA	21,902	C
Cal State, San Marcos	CA	20,604	LC
CUNY/York College	NY	6,747	LC
Claflin Univ	SC	25,592	LC
Colo State Univ-Pueblo	CO	21,581	C
East Stroudsburg Univ	PA	18,578	LC
Elizabethtown College	PA	56,340	VC
Endicott College	MA	47,054	C+
Ferris State Univ	MI	21,458	C
Fitchburg State Univ	MA	21,819	LC
Florida Gulf Coast Univ	FL	14,738	C
Grand View Univ	IA	32,302	C
Indiana Univ Bloomington	IN	20,791	HC
Indiana Univ East	IN	7,207	C
Indiana Univ-Purdue Univ Indianapolis	IN	18,952	C
Inter-American Univ of PR-Bayamon	PR	18,785	
Jackson State Univ	MS	15,879	LC
James Madison Univ	VA	19,084	VC
Kennesaw State Univ	GA	18,899	VC
Kent State Univ	OH	20,928	C
Lawrence Tech Univ	MI	41,630	VC
Marshall Univ	WV	18,044	C
Marywood Univ	PA	47,840	C
Mich State Univ	MI	24,542	VC
Millersville Univ of Pennsylvania	PA	25,298	C
Minn State Univ, Mankato	MN	17,190	C
Missouri Baptist Univ	MO	35,594	C
Missouri Western State Univ	MO	17,822	LC
Montana State Univ	MT	15,500	C+
Mount Aloysius College	PA	29,976	C
New York Inst of Technology	NY	49,980	VC
N Dak State Univ	ND	16,245	VC
Ohio Univ	OH	23,394	VC
Pennsylvania State Univ - Univ Park	PA	29,716	HC
Plymouth State Univ	NH	23,180	LC
Point Park Univ	PA	41,270	C
Purdue Univ Northwest	IN	15,178	C
Quinnipiac Univ	CT	60,970	VC
Roberts Wesleyan College	NY	41,116	C
Rochester Inst of Technology	NY	52,734	HC+
Rutgers Univ - Camden	NJ	26,595	C
Rutgers Univ - New Brunswick	NJ	27,090	HC
S Dak State Univ	SD	15,874	C
Southeastern Okla State Univ	OK	11,875	C
Springfield College	MA	48,775	C
SUNY /College of Agriculture and Tech at Cobleskill	NY	20,527	LC
SUNY/The College of Environmental Science and Forestry	NY	23,728	VC
SUNY/Univ at Buffalo	NY	23,122	C
Stevenson Univ	MD	48,412	C
Suffolk Univ	MA	52,316	C
Syracuse Univ	NY	62,313	HC
The Catholic Univ of America	DC	58,376	VC
Tufts Univ	MA		MC
Univ of Calif San Diego	CA	30,450	MC
Univ of Central Florida	FL	16,379	VC
Univ of Delaware	DE	32,214	VC
Univ of Georgia	GA	21,878	HC
Univ of Houston-Downtown	TX	7,241	LC
Univ of Illinois at Urbana-Champaign	IL	27,006	HC
Univ of Kansas	KS	20,884	VC
Univ of Maryland Univ College	MD	26,146	LC
Univ of Missouri-Kansas City	MO	19,563	VC
Univ of Missouri-St. Louis	MO	19,810	VC
Univ of Nebr - Omaha	NE	16,120	C
Univ of Nevada, Reno	NV	18,010	C
Univ of New Hampshire - Manchester	NH	14,490	C
Univ of New Haven	CT	53,680	C
Univ of N Car at Greensboro	NC	15,998	C
Univ of N Car at Pembroke	NC	14,737	LC
Univ of Northern Iowa	IA	17,480	C
Univ of PR, at Mayaguez	PR	13,995	
Univ of Wisc-River Falls	WI	14,541	C
Ursuline College	OH	41,076	LC
Washington State Univ	WA	22,747	C
West Texas A&M Univ	TX	13,478	C
William Paterson Univ of New Jersey	NJ	24,022	C
William Penn Univ	IA	26,000	C
Worcester Polytechnic Inst	MA	62,846	MC
Worcester State Univ	MA	20,977	C

BOTANY

School	ST	$IS	SR
Andrews Univ	MI	41,732	C
Auburn Univ	AL	24,300	VC+
Bennington College	VT	66,280	MC
Brigham Young Univ	UT	13,248	MC
Calif State Polytechnic Univ, Pomona	CA	21,811	C
Cal State, Fullerton	CA	21,902	C
Cal State, Long Beach	CA	18,850	C
Colo State Univ	CO	23,033	C
Conn College	CT	65,000	MC
Delaware State Univ	DE	19,376	LC
Eastern Washington Univ	WA	17,896	LC
Hampshire College	MA	65,214	MC
Humboldt State Univ	CA	21,708	C
Idaho State Univ	ID	13,619	LC
Kent State Univ	OH	20,928	C
Marlboro College	VT	50,832	VC+
Mars Hill Univ	NC	41,104	C

ST = STATE $IS = IN-STATE COSTS SR = SELECTOR RATING

School	ST	$IS	SR
Miami Univ	OH	27,190	HC+
Mich State Univ	MI	24,542	VC
Millersville Univ of Pennsylvania	PA	25,298	C
N Car State Univ	NC	22,434	HC+
N Dak State Univ	ND	16,245	VC
Northern Mich Univ	MI	20,853	C
Northwest Missouri State Univ	MO	18,286	C
Ohio Univ	OH	23,394	VC
Ohio Wesleyan Univ	OH	49,460	VC
Okla State Univ	OK	17,180	C+
Oregon State Univ	OR	23,337	VC
San Francisco State Univ	CA	18,514	LC
San Jose State Univ	CA	22,630	C
Southern Illinois Univ Carbondale	IL	24,554	C
SUNY/The College of Environmental Science and Forestry	NY	23,728	VC
Texas A&M Univ at Commerce	TX	10,496	C
Univ of Calif at Davis	CA	28,468	HC
Univ of Calif at Irvine	CA	33,857	VC
Univ of Florida	FL	16,291	HC+
Univ of Hawaii at Manoa	HI	23,261	C
Univ of Illinois at Urbana-Champaign	IL	27,006	HC
Univ of Kentucky	KY	24,800	C+
Univ of Maine	ME	21,038	VC
Univ of Mich/Ann Arbor	MI	25,274	MC
Univ of Montana	MT	14,105	C
Univ of Okla	OK	19,651	HC
Univ of Vermont	VT	29,792	HC
Univ of Washington	WA	23,091	MC
Univ of Wisc-Madison	WI	21,647	MC
Univ of Wyoming	WY	15,537	C
Washington State Univ	WA	22,747	C
Weber State Univ	UT	14,112	C
Western New Mexico Univ	NM	16,914	LC

BROADCASTING

School	ST	$IS	SR
Alabama State Univ	AL	16,490	LC
Ashland Univ	OH	30,446	C
Baldwin Wallace Univ	OH	42,464	VC
Barry Univ	FL	38,730	LC
Baylor Univ	TX	56,803	HC
Belhaven Univ	MS	32,250	C
Bemidji State Univ	MN	17,730	C
Biola Univ	CA	48,686	C
Bloomfield College	NJ	40,100	LC
Bluffton Univ	OH	40,950	C+
Cal State, Fullerton	CA	21,902	C
Cedarville Univ	OH	36,244	VC
Central Methodist Univ	MO	31,500	VC
Central Mich Univ	MI	20,330	C
Central State Univ	OH	18,564	C
Central Washington Univ	WA	16,803	C
Champlain College	VT	54,724	VC
Chapman Univ	CA	65,504	HC
Chicago State Univ	IL	41,620	C
CUNY/Brooklyn College	NY	7,163	C+
Colo State Univ-Pueblo	CO	21,581	C
Concord Univ	WV	14,954	LC
Dallas Baptist Univ	TX	35,220	VC
Dordt College	IA	37,860	C+
Drake Univ	IA	49,220	HC
Eastern Kentucky Univ	KY	17,742	C
Eastern Nazarene College	MA	41,114	C
Eastern Washington Univ	WA	17,896	LC
Emerson College	MA	61,824	HC+
Evangel Univ	MO	28,898	C
Florida Southern College	FL	45,978	VC
Florida State Univ	FL	16,771	HC
Freed-Hardeman Univ	TN	29,900	C
Geneva College	PA	35,450	C
Gonzaga Univ	WA	52,880	HC
Goshen College	IN	44,350	C
Grand Valley State Univ	MI	22,250	C+
Grand View Univ	IA	32,302	C
Harding Univ	AR	25,440	C
Hardin-Simmons Univ	TX	36,025	C
Hastings College	NE	35,380	C+
Howard Univ	DC	37,616	C+
Huntington Univ	IN	33,996	C
Ithaca College	NY	58,158	VC+
Lewis Univ	IL	41,710	C
Lincoln Memorial Univ	TN	28,430	C
Madonna Univ	MI	30,450	LC
Malone Univ	OH	39,200	C
Manhattan College	NY	55,652	C
Marietta College	OH	46,190	C
Marquette Univ	WI	53,090	VC+
Marshall Univ	WV	18,044	C
Marywood Univ	PA	47,840	C
Mercy College	NY	32,614	C
Mercyhurst Univ	PA	47,420	C
Millersville Univ of Pennsylvania	PA	25,298	C
Minn State Univ, Moorhead	MN	21,393	C
Minot State Univ	ND	13,285	C
Missouri Baptist Univ	MO	35,594	C
North Central College	IL	48,712	C+
North Greenville Univ	SC	25,930	C
Northern Mich Univ	MI	20,853	C
Northwest Missouri State Univ	MO	18,286	C
Northwestern Okla State Univ	OK	13,072	LC
Ohio Northern Univ	OH	44,050	VC
Ohio Univ	OH	23,394	VC
Okla Baptist Univ	OK	33,990	C
Okla Christian Univ	OK	29,260	C
Okla City Univ	OK	40,476	C
Okla State Univ	OK	17,180	C+
Oral Roberts Univ	OK	34,316	C
Otterbein Univ	OH	41,630	C
Point Loma Nazarene Univ	CA	46,150	C+
Point Park Univ	PA	41,270	C
Prairie View A&M Univ	TX	27,273	LC
Purdue Univ Northwest	IN	15,178	C
Purdue Univ/West Lafayette	IN	20,032	MC
Roosevelt Univ	IL	41,890	VC
Rowan Univ	NJ	24,491	VC
San Francisco State Univ	CA	18,514	LC
San Jose State Univ	CA	22,630	C
Savannah College of Art and Design	GA	49,595	SP
Seton Hall Univ	NJ	58,008	C
Shaw Univ	NC	24,638	C
Southeastern Univ	FL	34,910	LC
Southern Adventist Univ	TN	28,250	C
Southern Arkansas Univ	AR	21,532	C
Southern Methodist Univ	TX	69,008	MC
Southwestern Adventist Univ	TX	28,232	LC
Spring Arbor Univ	MI	37,390	C
St. Cloud State Univ	MN	10,600	C
SUNY at Oswego	NY	22,219	VC
SUNY/Buffalo State	NY	20,583	LC
Stephen F. Austin State Univ	TX	18,484	LC
Suffolk Univ	MA	52,316	C
Syracuse Univ	NY	62,313	HC
Temple Univ	PA	24,392	C+
Texas A&M Univ at Commerce	TX	10,496	C
Texas State Univ	TX	18,721	C
The George Washington Univ	DC	68,474	HC+
Troy Univ	AL	16,171	C
Union Univ	TN	41,160	VC
Univ of Central Florida	FL	16,379	VC
Univ of Central Missouri	MO	18,982	C
Univ of Central Okla	OK	15,150	C
Univ of Cincinnati	OH	22,118	VC
Univ of Findlay	OH	43,040	C
Univ of Idaho	ID	16,158	C
Univ of Illinois at Urbana-Champaign	IL	27,006	HC
Univ of Indianapolis	IN	36,480	VC
Univ of La Verne	CA	55,600	C
Univ of Louisiana at Lafayette	LA	14,516	C
Univ of Missouri-Columbia	MO	20,463	VC
Univ of Nebr - Kearney	NE	17,014	LC
Univ of Nebr - Lincoln	NE	18,589	VC
Univ of Nebr - Omaha	NE	16,120	C
Univ of North Texas	TX	20,082	C
Univ of Northwestern - St. Paul	MN	39,530	C
Univ of S Car at Columbia	SC	21,726	VC
Univ of Southern Calif	CA	66,631	MC
Univ of Southern Indiana	IN	16,808	C
Univ of Texas at Arlington	TX	18,876	C
Vanguard Univ of Southern Calif	CA	42,400	VC
Washington State Univ	WA	22,747	C
Waynesburg Univ	PA	33,530	C
West Liberty Univ	WV	16,158	C
West Texas A&M Univ	TX	13,478	C
West Virginia Univ	WV	18,952	VC
Western Illinois Univ	IL	20,897	C
Western Kentucky Univ	KY	16,850	C
Westminster College	PA	41,722	C
Winona State Univ	MN	18,109	C
York College of Pennsylvania	PA	29,240	C
Youngstown State Univ	OH	17,487	C

BUSINESS (DUEL MAJOR)

School	ST	$IS	SR
Bentley Univ	MA	63,720	MC
CUNY/Brooklyn College	NY	7,163	C+
Clayton State Univ	GA	19,735	LC
John Carroll Univ	OH	51,570	C
Loyola Univ New Orleans	LA	52,456	VC
Mercy College	NY	32,614	C
Neumann Univ	PA	40,678	LC
Regis Univ	CO	46,380	C
Southern Oregon Univ	OR	19,117	C
St. Lawrence Univ	NY	66,646	HC+
The Master's Univ	CA	43,870	C
Univ of New Hampshire - Manchester	NH	14,490	C
Univ of Pittsburgh	PA	30,030	MC
Western Kentucky Univ	KY	16,850	C

BUSINESS ADMINISTRATION

School	ST	$IS	SR
Cairn Univ	PA	37,572	C
DePaul Univ	IL	52,807	VC
Drury Univ	MO	37,555	VC
Embry-Riddle Aeronautical Univ - Prescott Campus	AZ	45,130	VC
Georgia Southern Univ	GA	16,540	VC
King Univ	TN	36,976	C
Medaille College	NY	41,700	LC
Missouri Western State Univ	MO	17,822	LC
Regis Univ	CO	46,380	C
Univ of Kansas	KS	20,884	VC
Univ of N Car at Greensboro	NC	15,998	C
Univ of N Car Wilmington	NC	16,784	VC
Univ of Okla	OK	19,651	HC

BUSINESS ADMINISTRATION - INTERNATIONAL

School	ST	$IS	SR
Aquinas College - Mich	MI	38,876	VC
Ball State Univ	IN	19,808	C+
Bloomfield College	NJ	40,100	LC
Cabrini Univ	PA	42,591	LC
Campbell Univ	NC	37,570	VC
CUNY/Queens College	NY	21,507	C
Clayton State Univ	GA	19,735	LC
College of the Ozarks	MO	7,530	VC
Dallas Baptist Univ	TX	35,220	VC
Franklin College	IN	40,550	C
Lake Superior State Univ	MI	19,867	C
Lynn Univ	FL	49,680	LC
Lyon College	AR	36,120	VC
Millersville Univ of Pennsylvania	PA	25,298	C
Missouri Western State Univ	MO	17,822	LC
Monmouth Univ	NJ	50,184	C
Neumann Univ	PA	40,678	LC
Okla Christian Univ	OK	29,260	C
Point Loma Nazarene Univ	CA	46,150	C+
Regis College	MA	51,920	LC
Rochester Inst of Technology	NY	52,734	HC+
Tenn Wesleyan Univ	TN	32,680	LC
The Master's Univ	CA	43,870	C
Trevecca Nazarene Univ	TN	31,186	C
Univ of Nevada, Reno	NV	18,010	C
Univ of Rhode Island	RI	26,066	VC
Univ of South Alabama	AL	16,880	C
Univ of Tulsa	OK	52,625	HC
Wartburg College	IA	49,478	C
West Chester Univ of Pennsylvania	PA	19,171	VC
Western Kentucky Univ	KY	16,850	C

BUSINESS ADMINISTRATION - MANAGEMENT INFORMATION SYSTEMS

School	ST	$IS	SR
Medaille College	NY	41,700	LC
Missouri Western State Univ	MO	17,822	LC

BUSINESS ADMINISTRATION AND MANAGEMENT

School	ST	$IS	SR
Adams State Univ	CO	15,420	LC
Adelphi Univ	NY	49,792	C
Adrian College	MI	45,550	C
Agnes Scott College	GA	51,930	VC+
Alabama A&M Univ	AL	18,796	C
Alabama State Univ	AL	16,490	LC
Alaska Pacific Univ	AK	28,730	VC
Albertus Magnus College	CT	44,016	LC
Albion College	MI	55,260	C
Albright College	PA	57,326	C
Alcorn State Univ	MS	15,884	C
Alderson Broaddus Univ	WV	35,000	LC
Alfred State College	NY	19,895	C
Alfred Univ	NY	37,490	C
Alice Lloyd College	KY	8,190	LC
Allen Univ	SC	19,920	NC
Alma College	MI	49,410	VC
Alvernia Univ	PA	45,330	C
Alverno College	WI	33,294	LC
American International College	MA	47,020	LC
American Jewish Univ - College of A&S	CA	44,234	C
American Univ of PR	PR	16,130	
Amridge Univ	AL	10,860	LC
Anderson Univ	IN	39,450	C
Andrews Univ	MI	41,732	C
Angelo State Univ	TX	15,882	LC
Anna Maria College	MA	51,020	C
Aquinas College	TN	30,800	C+
Aquinas College - Mich	MI	38,876	VC
Arcadia Univ	PA	55,990	C+
Arizona State Univ at the Polytechnic Campus	AZ	22,394	VC
Arizona State Univ at the Tempe Campus	AZ	23,001	VC
Arizona State Univ at the West Campus	AZ	21,513	VC
Arkansas Baptist College	AR	20,280	NC
Arkansas State Univ	AR	16,190	C
Asbury Univ	KY	36,450	C+
Ashford Univ	CA	10,480	C
Ashland Univ	OH	30,446	C
Assumption College	MA	48,455	VC
Atlantic Union College	MA	27,228	C
Auburn Univ	AL	24,300	VC+
Auburn Univ at Montgomery	AL	15,000	C
Augsburg Univ	MN	45,129	C
Augusta Univ	GA	4,632	C
Augustana College	IL	51,222	VC+
Augustana Univ	SD	39,968	VC
Aurora Univ	IL	34,990	C
Austin College	TX	51,059	HC
Austin Peay State Univ	TN	16,397	C
Averett Univ	VA	43,034	LC
Avila Univ	MO	27,100	C
Azusa Pacific Univ	CA	43,972	C
Babson College	MA	63,664	HC
Baker College of Flint	MI	19,140	NC
Baker Univ	KS	37,190	C
Baldwin Wallace Univ	OH	42,464	VC
Ball State Univ	IN	19,808	C+
Barton College	NC	39,854	C
Bay Path Univ	MA	46,356	C
Bayamon Central Univ	PR	12,490	
Baylor Univ	TX	56,803	HC
Becker College	MA	30,100	LC
Belhaven Univ	MS	32,250	C
Bellarmine Univ	KY	52,532	C
Bellevue Univ	NE	20,300	NC
Belmont Abbey College	NC	28,794	C
Belmont Univ	TN	44,500	VC+
Beloit College	WI	55,206	HC
Bemidji State Univ	MN	17,730	C
Benedict College	SC	28,630	NC
Benedictine College	KS	38,850	VC
Benedictine Univ	IL	38,300	C
Bennett College	NC	27,717	NC
Bentley Univ	MA	63,720	MC
Berea College	KY	7,094	C
Berkeley College/New Jersey	NJ	38,082	LC
Berkeley College/New York City Campus	NY	35,100	LC
Berkeley College/White Plains Campus	NY	35,100	LC
Berry College	GA	47,466	VC
Bethany College	KS	38,637	LC
Bethany College	WV	38,774	LC
Bethel College	IN	36,830	C
Bethel College	KS	35,370	C
Bethel Univ	MN	46,550	C+
Bethel Univ	TN	27,142	C
Bethune-Cookman Univ	FL	23,322	C
Biola Univ	CA	48,686	C
Birmingham-Southern College	AL	44,478	C+
Black Hills State Univ	SD	16,622	C
Blackburn College	IL	28,526	LC
Bloomfield College	NJ	40,100	LC
Bloomsburg Univ of Pennsylvania	PA	19,930	C
Blue Mountain College	MS	15,949	C
Bluefield College	VA	34,711	C
Bluefield State College	WV	5,832	LC
Bluffton Univ	OH	40,950	C+
Boise State Univ	ID	17,368	C
Boricua College	NY	10,100	C
Boston College	MA	68,043	MC
Boston Univ	MA	67,352	MC
Bowie State Univ	MD	18,610	LC
Bowling Green State Univ	OH	19,975	C
Bradley Univ	IL	43,240	VC
Brandeis Univ	MA	68,443	MC
Brenau Univ - Women's College	GA	37,876	LC
Brescia Univ	KY	29,890	VC
Brewton-Parker College	GA	26,120	LC
Briar Cliff Univ	IA	36,956	C
Bridgewater College	VA	46,260	C
Brigham Young Univ	UT	13,248	MC
Bryan College	TN	32,900	C
Bryant Univ	RI	57,204	VC
Bucknell Univ	PA	67,136	MC
Buena Vista Univ	IA	42,344	C
Cabrini Univ	PA	42,591	LC
Caldwell Univ	NJ	42,165	LC
Calif Baptist Univ	CA	42,986	C
Calif Inst of Technology	CA	64,704	MC
Calif Lutheran Univ	CA	52,853	C
Calif Polytechnic State Univ	CA	22,547	MC
Calif State Polytechnic Univ, Pomona	CA	21,811	C
Cal State, Maritime Academy	CA	23,156	C+
Cal State, Bakersfield	CA	22,397	LC
Cal State, Chico	CA	19,790	VC
Cal State, Dominguez Hills	CA	19,022	LC
Cal State, East Bay	CA	20,748	C
Cal State, Fresno	CA	16,902	LC
Cal State, Fullerton	CA	21,902	C
Cal State, Long Beach	CA	18,850	C
Cal State, Los Angeles	CA	17,186	LC
Cal State, Monterey Bay	CA	22,872	LC
Cal State, Northridge	CA	17,277	LC
Cal State, Sacramento	CA	19,060	C
Cal State, San Bernardino	CA	20,106	C
Cal State, San Marcos	CA	20,604	LC
Cal State, Stanislaus	CA	18,053	LC
Calif Univ of Pennsylvania	PA	20,425	LC
Calumet College of St. Joseph	IN	22,735	C
Calvin College	MI	43,090	HC
Cameron Univ	OK	11,632	LC
Campbell Univ	NC	37,570	VC
Campbellsville Univ	KY	33,400	C
Canisius College	NY	49,672	C
Capital Univ	OH	44,778	VC
Cardinal Stritch Univ	WI	37,136	C
Caribbean Univ	PR	12,227	
Carlos Albizu Univ	FL	13,036	LC
Carlow Univ	PA	39,696	LC
Carnegie Mellon Univ	PA	67,980	MC
Carroll College	MT	44,304	C
Carroll Univ	WI	38,100	C+
Carson-Newman Univ	TN	35,900	C
Carthage College	WI	48,835	C
Case Western Reserve Univ	OH	62,284	MC
Castleton Univ	VT	20,186	C

ST = STATE **$IS** = IN-STATE COSTS **SR** = SELECTOR RATING

School	ST	$IS	SR
Catawba College	NC	39,820	LC
Cazenovia College	NY	47,866	C
Cedar Crest College	PA	51,110	C
Cedarville Univ	OH	36,244	VC
Centenary College	NJ	43,890	LC
Centenary College of Louisiana	LA	49,050	C+
Central College	IA	44,592	C
Central Conn State Univ	CT	22,041	C
Central Methodist Univ	MO	31,500	VC
Central Mich Univ	MI	20,330	C
Central State Univ	OH	18,564	C
Central Washington Univ	WA	16,803	C
Chadron State College	NE	14,819	LC
Chaminade Univ of Honolulu	HI	37,614	C
Champlain College	VT	54,724	VC
Chapman Univ	CA	65,504	HC
Charleston Southern Univ	SC	34,700	C
Charter Oak State College	CT	7,983	NC
Chatham Univ	PA	47,883	VC
Chestnut Hill College	PA	47,180	C
Cheyney Univ of Pennsylvania	PA	20,896	LC
Chicago State Univ	IL	41,620	C
Christian Brothers Univ	TN	31,670	VC
Christopher Newport Univ	VA	24,878	VC+
CUNY/Brooklyn College	NY	7,163	C+
CUNY/City College	NY	20,204	C
CUNY/Lehman College	NY	5,788	LC
CUNY/Medgar Evers College	NY	6,680	NC
CUNY/York College	NY	6,747	LC
City Univ of Seattle	WA	24,340	NC
Claflin Univ	SC	25,592	LC
Clarion Univ of Pennsylvania	PA	21,608	LC
Clark Atlanta Univ	GA	31,019	LC
Clark Univ	MA	53,260	HC+
Clarke Univ	IA	42,950	C
Clarkson College	NE	32,480	C
Clayton State Univ	GA	19,735	LC
Clemson Univ	SC		HC
Coastal Carolina Univ	SC	20,340	C
Coe College	IA	51,570	VC
Cogswell Polytechnical College	CA	31,511	C
Coker College	SC	38,196	C
Colby-Sawyer College	NH	50,790	C
College of Charleston	SC	24,046	VC
College of Mount St. Vincent	NY	45,620	C
College of St. Elizabeth	NJ	45,700	LC
College of St Joseph	VT	32,400	LC
College of St. Scholastica	MN	45,734	C+
College of Staten Island	NY	24,389	LC
College of the Ozarks	MO	7,530	VC
College of William & Mary	VA	34,907	MC
Colo Christian Univ	CO	40,885	VC
Colo Mesa Univ	CO	19,707	LC
Colo State Univ	CO	23,033	C
Colo State Univ-Pueblo	CO	21,581	C
Colo Technical Univ	CO	21,455	NC
Columbia College	SC	36,550	C
Columbia College - Missouri	MO	28,179	C
Columbus State Univ	GA	14,336	LC
Concord Univ	WV	14,954	LC
Concordia College - Alabama	AL	15,720	NC
Concordia College - Moorhead	MN	46,418	C
Concordia College - New York	NY	39,035	LC
Concordia Univ	OR	35,000	C
Concordia Univ Irvine	CA	44,860	VC
Concordia Univ Nebr	NE	41,900	VC
Concordia Univ St. Paul	MN	29,050	C
Concordia Univ Texas	TX	41,920	C
Concordia Univ Wisc	WI	35,910	C
Concordia Univ, Ann Arbor	MI	38,878	C+
Concordia Univ, Chicago	IL	41,522	C
Converse College	SC	28,290	C
Coppin State Univ	MD	14,071	VC
Corban Univ	OR	41,700	C
Cornerstone Univ	MI	36,550	C
Covenant College	GA	44,590	HC
Culver-Stockton College	MO	34,350	C
Cumberland Univ	TN	27,710	C
Curry College	MA	53,331	C
Daemen College	NY	40,336	C
Dakota State Univ	SD	12,286	C
Dakota Wesleyan Univ	SD	33,980	LC
Dallas Baptist Univ	TX	35,220	VC
Davenport Univ	MI	25,896	LC
Davis & Elkins College	WV	38,242	LC
Defiance College	OH	42,240	LC
Delaware State Univ	DE	19,376	LC
Delaware Valley Univ	PA	51,271	C
Delta State Univ	MS	13,176	LC
DePaul Univ	IL	52,807	VC
DeSales Univ	PA	47,520	C
Dickinson State Univ	ND	12,372	LC
Dillard Univ	LA	20,940	VC
Doane Univ	NE	41,340	VC
Dominican College	NY	40,258	LC
Dominican Univ	IL	42,472	C+
Dominican Univ of Calif	CA	58,750	C
Dordt College	IA	37,860	C+
Drake Univ	IA	49,220	HC
Drew Univ/College of Liberal Arts	NJ	53,608	VC
Drexel Univ	PA	65,927	HC
Duquesne Univ	PA	48,508	VC
D'Youville College	NY	37,678	C
Earlham College	IN	55,670	HC
East Carolina Univ	NC	16,539	C
East Central Univ	OK	13,330	C
East Texas Baptist Univ	TX	34,444	C
Eastern Conn State Univ	CT	23,059	C
Eastern Illinois Univ	IL	21,414	C
Eastern Kentucky Univ	KY	17,742	C
Eastern Mennonite Univ	VA	42,550	C
Eastern Mich Univ	MI	19,761	C
Eastern Nazarene College	MA	41,114	C
Eastern New Mexico Univ	NM	12,874	LC
Eastern Oregon Univ	OR	17,612	C
Eastern Univ	PA	39,540	C
Eastern Washington Univ	WA	17,896	LC
Eckerd College	FL	55,206	VC
Edgewood College	WI	35,950	C
Edinboro Univ	PA	15,940	LC
Edward Waters College	FL	28,089	NC
Elizabeth City State Univ	NC	14,745	C
Elizabethtown College	PA	56,340	VC
Elizabethtown College School of Continuing and Professional Studies	PA	18,900	C
Elmhurst College	IL	46,514	C
Elmira College	NY	53,900	C
Elms College	MA	49,602	VC
Elon Univ	NC	46,142	HC
Emmanuel College	MA	53,472	C+
Emory and Henry College	VA	46,320	C
Emory Univ	GA	63,286	MC
Emporia State Univ	KS	15,029	C
Endicott College	MA	47,054	C+
Erskine College	SC	45,460	C
Eureka College	IL	34,760	C
Excelsior College	NY	38,800	SP
Fairleigh Dickinson Univ/College at Florham	NJ	54,770	C
Fairleigh Dickinson Univ/Metropolitan Campus	NJ	52,392	C
Fairmont State Univ	WV	15,726	C
Farmingdale State College	NY	20,968	C
Faulkner Univ	AL	26,410	C
Fayetteville State Univ	NC	17,756	C
Felician Univ	NJ	46,280	LC
Ferris State Univ	MI	21,458	C
Ferrum College	VA	43,970	C
Fisk Univ	TN	32,066	LC
Fitchburg State Univ	MA	21,819	LC
Five Towns College	NY	35,480	LC
Flagler College	FL	27,620	C
Florida A&M Univ	FL	15,361	C
Florida Atlantic Univ	FL	18,256	C
Florida Inst of Technology	FL	53,306	VC
Florida International Univ	FL	20,281	C
Florida Memorial Univ	FL	22,424	LC
Florida Southern College	FL	45,978	VC
Florida State Univ	FL	16,771	HC
Fontbonne Univ	MO	34,606	C
Fordham Univ	NY	68,431	MC
Fort Hays State Univ	KS	12,677	C
Fort Lewis College	CO	20,154	C
Fort Valley State Univ	GA	17,988	VC
Framingham State Univ	MA	21,740	C
Francis Marion Univ	SC	18,144	LC
Franciscan Univ of Steubenville	OH	33,980	VC
Franklin and Marshall College	PA	67,960	MC
Franklin College	IN	40,550	C
Franklin Pierce Univ	NH	46,750	LC
Franklin Univ	OH	11,616	NC
Freed-Hardeman Univ	TN	29,900	C
Fresno Pacific Univ	CA	38,858	C
Friends Univ	KS	38,000	C
Frostburg State Univ	MD	17,280	LC
Furman Univ	SC	61,098	VC+
Gallaudet Univ	DC	30,088	LC
Gannon Univ	PA	42,922	C
Gardner-Webb Univ	NC	24,935	C+
Geneva College	PA	35,450	C
George Fox Univ	OR	42,938	C
George Mason Univ	VA	19,884	C
Georgetown College	KY	41,440	C
Georgetown Univ	DC	68,970	MC
Georgia College & State Univ	GA	21,884	C+
Georgia Inst of Technology	GA	23,910	MC
Georgia Southwestern State Univ	GA	13,870	LC
Georgia State Univ	GA	25,250	C
Georgian Court Univ	NJ	43,068	LC
Gettysburg College	PA	65,210	MC
Glenville State College	WV	17,386	LC
Goldey-Beacom College	DE	36,038	C
Gonzaga Univ	WA	52,880	HC
Goodwin College	CT	28,370	LC
Gordon College	MA	47,740	VC
Goshen College	IN	44,350	C
Goucher College	MD	56,110	VC
Grace Bible College	MI	25,250	C
Grace College and Seminary	IN	31,524	C
Graceland Univ	IA	35,290	C
Grambling State Univ	LA	15,701	C
Grand Canyon Univ	AZ	25,150	VC
Grand Valley State Univ	MI	22,250	C+
Grand View Univ	IA	32,302	C
Green Mountain College	VT	45,228	LC
Greensboro College	NC	39,790	LC
Greenville College	IL	27,012	LC
Grove City College	PA	26,654	VC
Guilford College	NC	45,973	C
Gustavus Adolphus College	MN	53,943	HC
Gwynedd Mercy Univ	PA	43,780	LC
Hamline Univ	MN	50,152	C
Hampton Univ	VA	36,410	C
Hannibal-LaGrange Univ	MO	29,815	C
Harding Univ	AR	25,440	C
Hardin-Simmons Univ	TX	36,025	C
Harris-Stowe State Univ	MO	14,590	NC
Hartwick College	NY	51,270	C
Hastings College	NE	35,380	C+
Hawaii Pacific Univ	HI	33,420	C
Heidelberg Univ	OH	40,400	LC
Hellenic College/Holy Cross Greek Orthodox School of Theology	MA	39,906	C
Henderson State Univ	AR	15,516	C
Heritage Univ	WA	19,825	NC
High Point Univ	NC	47,355	VC
Hilbert College	NY	32,650	LC
Hodges Univ	FL	20,160	LC
Hollins Univ	VA	49,635	VC
Holy Family Univ	PA	44,672	LC
Holy Names Univ	CA	46,630	LC
Hood College	MD	50,540	C
Hope College	MI	42,840	VC
Hope International Univ	CA	42,730	C
Houghton College	NY	40,558	VC
Houston Baptist Univ	TX	36,450	C
Howard Payne Univ	TX	35,994	C
Howard Univ	DC	37,616	C+
Humboldt State Univ	CA	21,708	C
Humphreys College	CA	27,790	C
Huntingdon College	AL	35,900	C
Huntington Univ	IN	33,996	C
Husson Univ	ME	26,508	C
Huston-Tillotson Univ	TX	18,124	LC
Idaho State Univ	ID	13,619	LC
Illinois College	IL	41,330	VC
Illinois State Univ	IL	23,418	VC
Illinois Wesleyan Univ	IL	56,430	VC+
Immaculata Univ	PA	39,000	C
Indiana Inst of Technology	IN	34,240	LC
Indiana State Univ	IN	23,223	LC
Indiana Univ Bloomington	IN	20,791	HC
Indiana Univ East	IN	7,207	C
Indiana Univ Kokomo	IN	7,207	C
Indiana Univ Northwest	IN	7,207	LC
Indiana Univ South Bend	IN	16,057	C
Indiana Univ Southeast	IN	16,931	C
Indiana Univ-Purdue Univ Fort Wayne	IN	18,675	C
Indiana Univ-Purdue Univ Indianapolis	IN	18,952	C
Indiana Wesleyan Univ	IN	33,674	C
Inter-American Univ of PR Ponce	PR	19,549	
Inter-American Univ of PR-Aguadilla Campus	PR	21,657	
Inter-American Univ of PR-Arecibo Campus	PR	18,245	
Inter-American Univ of PR-Barranquitas	PR	18,336	
Inter-American Univ of PR-Bayamon	PR	18,785	
Inter-American Univ of PR-Fajardo Campus	PR	18,336	
Inter-American Univ of PR-Metropolitan Campus	PR	20,045	
Inter-American Univ of PR-San Germán	PR	20,042	
Iona College	NY	52,514	C
Iowa State Univ	IA	18,176	C
Iowa Wesleyan Univ	IA	41,000	C
Ithaca College	NY	58,158	VC+
Jackson State Univ	MS	15,879	LC
Jacksonville Univ	FL	49,210	C
James Madison Univ	VA	19,084	VC
Jarvis Christian College	TX	20,160	NC
John Brown Univ	AR	35,184	VC
John Carroll Univ	OH	51,570	C
Johnson & Wales Univ/Charlotte Campus	NC	44,768	C
Johnson & Wales Univ/Denver Campus	CO	44,768	C
Johnson & Wales Univ/North Miami Campus	FL	44,768	C
Johnson & Wales Univ/Providence Campus	RI	44,768	C
Johnson C. Smith Univ	NC	25,336	LC
Johnson State College	VT	22,672	C
Judson College	AL	27,066	C
Judson Univ	IL	39,174	C
Juniata College	PA	58,118	VC
Kansas State Univ	KS	17,780	VC
Keiser Univ	FL	35,010	LC
Kendall College	IL	32,610	C
Kent State Univ	OH	20,928	C
Kentucky Christian Univ	KY	26,836	LC
Kentucky State Univ	KY	14,484	LC
Kentucky Wesleyan College	KY	34,260	LC
Keuka College	NY	42,398	C
Keystone College	PA	28,680	LC
King's College	PA	48,240	C
Kutztown Univ of Pennsylvania	PA	19,477	C
La Roche College	PA	38,940	C
La Salle Univ	PA	43,476	C
La Sierra Univ	CA	39,690	VC
LaGrange College	GA	41,310	C
Lake Erie College	OH	38,914	LC
Lake Superior State Univ	MI	19,867	C
Lakeland Univ	WI	35,130	C
Lamar Univ	TX	18,014	LC
Lander Univ	SC	32,200	C
Lane College	TN	17,960	LC
Langston Univ	OK	15,659	C
Lasell College	MA	49,400	C
Lawrence Tech Univ	MI	41,630	VC
Lebanon Valley College	PA	55,510	VC
Lee Univ	TN	22,045	C
Lees-McRae College	NC	33,944	NC
LeMoyne-Owen College	TN	16,980	C
Lenoir-Rhyne Univ	NC	47,500	LC
LeTourneau Univ	TX	39,190	VC
Lewis Univ	IL	41,710	C
Lewis-Clark State College	ID	14,202	C
Liberty Univ	VA	31,415	C
LIM College	NY	45,075	LC
Limestone College	SC	32,100	C
Lincoln Memorial Univ	TN	28,430	C
Lincoln Univ	MO	14,402	NC
Lindenwood Univ	MO	25,760	C
Lindsey Wilson College	KY	33,546	C
Linfield College	OR	53,992	C
Lipscomb Univ	TN	42,984	VC
LIU Brooklyn	NY	50,698	C
LIU Post	NY	50,698	C+
Livingstone College	NC	17,815	LC
Lock Haven Univ of Pennsylvania	PA	20,544	LC
Longwood Univ	VA	22,184	C
Loras College	IA	40,726	C
Louisiana State Univ and A&M College	LA	18,677	VC
Louisiana State Univ in Shreveport	LA	6,902	C
Louisiana Tech Univ	LA	11,422	VC
Lourdes Univ	OH	29,140	NC
Loyola Univ Chicago	IL	57,158	VC
Loyola Univ Maryland	MD	61,710	VC
Loyola Univ New Orleans	LA	52,456	VC
Lubbock Christian Univ	TX	29,727	C
Lycoming College	PA	50,895	C
Lyndon State College	VT	20,714	C
Lynn Univ	FL	49,680	LC
Lyon College	AR	36,120	VC
MacMurray College	IL	35,025	C
Madonna Univ	MI	30,450	LC
Malone Univ	OH	39,200	C
Manchester Univ	IN	41,540	C
Manhattanville College	NY	52,430	C
Mansfield Univ of Pennsylvania	PA	24,244	LC
Marian Univ	IN	43,206	C
Marian Univ	WI	34,622	C
Marietta College	OH	46,190	C
Marist College	NY	49,860	VC
Marquette Univ	WI	53,090	VC+
Mars Hill Univ	NC	41,104	C
Martin Univ	IN	21,010	LC
Mary Baldwin Univ	VA	40,495	C
Marygrove College	MI	30,100	LC
Marylhurst Univ	OR	16,818	NC
Marymount Manhattan College	NY	48,350	C
Marymount Univ	VA	43,231	C
Maryville College	TN	44,410	C
Maryville Univ of St. Louis	MO	38,558	VC
Marywood Univ	PA	47,840	C
Mass College of Liberal Arts	MA	20,659	C
Mayville State Univ	ND	18,371	NC
McDaniel College	MD	52,910	VC
McKendree Univ	IL	37,940	C+
McMurry Univ	TX	34,259	LC
McNeese State Univ	LA	7,838	C
McPherson College	KS	36,134	C
Mercer Univ	GA	45,348	VC
Mercy College	NY	32,614	C
Mercyhurst Univ	PA	47,420	C
Meredith College	NC	46,634	C
Merrimack College	MA	55,415	C
Messiah College	PA	44,380	VC
Methodist Univ	NC	58,130	C
Metropolitan College of New York	NY		VC
Metropolitan State Univ	MN	7,859	C
Mich State Univ	MI	24,542	VC
MidAmerica Nazarene Univ	KS	37,808	C
Middle Tenn State Univ	TN	8,650	C
Midland Univ	NE	39,512	C
Midway Univ	KY	33,940	LC
Midwestern State Univ	TX	12,111	LC
Miles College	AL	16,530	NC
Millersville Univ of Pennsylvania	PA	25,298	C
Milligan College	TN	39,450	C
Millikin Univ	IL	44,148	C
Mills College	CA	43,705	C
Millsaps College	MS	50,080	C+
Milwaukee School of Engineering	WI	48,531	HC+
Minn State Univ, Mankato	MN	17,190	C
Minn State Univ, Moorhead	MN	21,393	C
Misericordia Univ	PA	45,210	C
Miss College	MS	25,850	C
Miss State Univ	MS	12,028	C+
Miss Univ for Women	MS	17,065	C

ST = STATE **$IS** = IN-STATE COSTS **SR** = SELECTOR RATING

School	ST	$IS	SR
Miss Valley State Univ	MS	13,233	LC
Missouri Baptist Univ	MO	35,594	C
Missouri Southern State Univ	MO	13,071	C
Missouri State Univ	MO	15,837	C+
Missouri Univ of Science and Technology	MO	18,655	HC
Missouri Valley College	MO	28,150	C
Missouri Western State Univ	MO	17,822	LC
Mitchell College	CT	45,192	C
Molloy College	NY	40,440	C
Monmouth College	IL	42,260	C
Monmouth Univ	NJ	50,184	C
Monroe College	NY	23,996	C
Montana State Univ	MT	15,500	C+
Montana State Univ Billings	MT	13,336	LC
Montclair State Univ	NJ	26,912	C
Montreat College	NC	34,605	LC
Moravian College	PA	55,488	C
Morehouse College	GA	40,835	C
Morgan State Univ	MD	17,190	LC
Morningside College	IA	39,780	C
Morris College	SC	19,195	LC
Mount Aloysius College	PA	29,976	C
Mount Ida College	MA	46,820	C
Mount Marty College	SD	36,862	C
Mount Mary Univ	WI	34,650	LC
Mount Mercy Univ	IA	39,748	C
Mount St. Mary College	NY	44,448	C
Mount St. Joseph Univ	OH	33,880	LC
Mount St. Mary's Univ	MD	53,380	C
Mount St. Mary's Univ - Chalon Campus	CA	50,486	VC+
Mount Vernon Nazarene Univ	OH	35,944	C
Muhlenberg College	PA	56,645	VC
Murray State Univ	KY	17,726	C+
Muskingum Univ	OH	35,966	C
National Louis Univ	IL	43,000	LC
Nazareth College	NY	46,784	C
Nebr Wesleyan Univ	NE	42,026	C+
New England College	NH	50,828	NC
New Jersey City Univ	NJ	21,456	LC
New Mexico Highlands Univ	NM	11,904	LC
New Mexico Inst of Mining and Technology	NM	15,385	HC+
New Mexico State Univ	NM	14,050	LC
New York Inst of Technology	NY	49,980	VC
New York Univ	NY	68,139	MC
Newberry College	SC	34,550	C
Newbury College	MA	48,970	C
Newman Univ	KS	37,382	C
Niagara Univ	NY	41,010	C
Nicholls State Univ	LA	14,959	C
Nichols College	MA	46,900	LC
N Car A&T State Univ	NC	13,786	C
N Car Central Univ	NC	9,000	C
N Car State Univ	NC	22,434	HC+
N Car Wesleyan College	NC	39,200	C
North Central College	IL	48,712	C+
North Central Univ	MN	30,610	C
N Dak State Univ	ND	16,245	VC
North Park Univ	IL	35,860	C
Northeastern Illinois Univ	IL	12,529	LC
Northeastern State Univ	OK	8,615	VC
Northeastern Univ	MA	65,352	MC
Northern Arizona Univ	AZ	21,003	C
Northern Illinois Univ	IL	20,176	C
Northern Kentucky Univ	KY	16,486	C
Northern Mich Univ	MI	20,853	C
Northern State Univ	SD	15,570	C
Northland College	WI	41,103	C+
Northwest Christian Univ	OR	36,580	C
Northwest Missouri State Univ	MO	18,286	C
Northwest Nazarene Univ	ID	40,250	C
Northwest Univ	WA	38,720	VC
Northwestern College of Iowa	IA	38,400	C
Northwestern Okla State Univ	OK	13,072	LC
Northwestern State Univ of Louisiana	LA	16,534	LC
Northwood Univ - Mich	MI	35,010	LC
Norwich Univ	VT	56,234	C
Notre Dame de Namur Univ	CA	46,526	LC
Notre Dame of Maryland Univ	MD	47,570	VC
Nova Southeastern Univ	FL	38,534	C+
Nyack College	NY	34,450	LC
Oakland City Univ	IN	33,930	NC
Oakland Univ	MI	20,763	C
Oakwood Univ	AL	43,758	C
Oglala Lakota College	SD	15,050	NC
Oglethorpe Univ	GA	44,200	C
Ohio Dominican Univ	OH	41,340	C+
Ohio Northern Univ	OH	44,050	VC
Ohio State Univ at Columbus	OH	22,843	MC
Ohio State Univ at Lima	OH	7,553	C
Ohio State Univ at Mansfield	OH	15,529	C
Ohio State Univ at Marion	OH	7,553	VC
Ohio State Univ at Newark	OH	16,685	C
Ohio Univ	OH	23,394	VC
Ohio Valley Univ	WV	28,800	C
Ohio Wesleyan Univ	OH	49,460	VC
Okla Baptist Univ	OK	33,990	C
Okla Christian Univ	OK	29,260	C
Okla City Univ	OK	40,476	C
Okla Panhandle State Univ	OK	6,152	C
Okla State Univ	OK	17,180	C+
Okla Wesleyan Univ	OK	34,434	C
Old Dominion Univ	VA	21,618	C
Olivet College	MI	37,661	LC
Olivet Nazarene Univ	IL	41,840	VC
Oral Roberts Univ	OK	34,316	C
Oregon State Univ	OR	23,337	VC
Ottawa Univ	KS	39,980	VC
Otterbein Univ	OH	41,630	C
Ouachita Baptist Univ	AR	33,500	VC
Our Lady of the Lake Univ	TX	37,790	LC
Pace Univ	NY	60,136	C
Pacific Lutheran Univ	WA	49,960	C
Pacific Union College	CA	36,009	VC
Pacific Univ	OR	37,617	C
Paine College	GA	19,506	LC
Palm Beach Atlantic Univ	FL	39,250	C
Park Univ	MO	22,134	C
Paul Quinn College	TX	25,350	LC
Peirce College	PA	16,780	NC
Penn State Altoona	PA	26,686	C
Penn State Erie,The Behrend College	PA	26,688	VC
Pennsylvania College of Technology	PA	27,693	NC
Pepperdine Univ	CA	66,862	VC+
Peru State College	NE	15,602	LC
Pfeiffer Univ	NC	40,532	LC
Philander Smith College	AR	20,814	LC
Piedmont College	GA	34,334	C
Pine Manor College	MA	41,660	LC
Pittsburg State Univ	KS	13,880	C
Plymouth State Univ	NH	23,180	LC
Point Loma Nazarene Univ	CA	46,150	C+
Point Park Univ	PA	41,270	C
Pontifical Catholic Univ of PR	PR	10,534	
Portland State Univ	OR	19,443	C
Post Univ	CT	41,150	C
Prairie View A&M Univ	TX	27,273	LC
Presbyterian College	SC	47,186	C
Presentation College	SD	28,575	LC
Principia College	IL	40,350	C
Providence College	RI	62,870	HC
Queens Univ of Charlotte	NC	39,543	C
Quincy Univ	IL	38,170	LC
Quinnipiac Univ	CT	60,970	VC
Radford Univ	VA	19,758	C
Ramapo College of New Jersey	NJ	25,760	VC
Randolph College	VA	53,970	C
Randolph-Macon College	VA	51,480	VC
Regis Univ	CO	46,380	C
Reinhardt Univ	GA	31,344	C
Rhode Island College	RI	19,000	LC
Rhodes College	TN	51,900	HC
Rider Univ	NJ	54,050	C
Ripon College	WI	49,991	VC
Rivier Univ	NH	41,600	VC
Roanoke College	VA	55,952	VC
Robert Morris Univ	PA	40,600	C
Roberts Wesleyan College	NY	41,116	C
Rochester Inst of Technology	NY	52,734	HC+
Rockford Univ	IL	38,570	C
Rockhurst Univ	MO	28,990	C
Rocky Mountain College	MT	35,776	C
Roger Williams Univ	RI	48,074	VC
Roosevelt Univ	IL	41,890	VC
Rosemont College	PA	30,980	LC
Rowan Univ	NJ	24,491	VC
Rust College	MS	10,600	C
Rutgers Univ - Camden	NJ	26,595	C
Rutgers Univ - New Brunswick	NJ	27,090	HC
Rutgers Univ - Newark	NJ	27,351	C
Sacred Heart Univ	CT	54,590	C
Saginaw Valley State Univ	MI	19,284	C
St. Anselm College	NH	56,636	VC
St. Augustine's Univ	NC	25,582	C
St. Joseph's College of Maine	ME	47,890	C
St. Joseph's Univ	PA	58,540	VC
St. Louis Univ	MO	49,866	HC
St. Martin's Univ	WA	45,056	C
St. Mary-of-the-Woods College	IN	40,424	LC
St. Mary's College	IN	50,600	C
St. Mary's College of Calif	CA	57,420	C
St. Mary's Univ of Minn	MN	42,440	C
St. Michael's College	VT	53,275	VC+
St. Peter's Univ	NJ	49,192	C
St. Vincent College	PA	46,229	C
St. Xavier Univ	IL	44,440	C
Salem College	NC	40,206	C
Salem International Univ	WV	21,090	C
Salem State Univ	MA	42,650	LC
Salisbury Univ	MD	21,132	VC
Salve Regina Univ	RI	53,046	VC
Sam Houston State Univ	TX	18,792	C
San Diego Christian College	CA	40,914	C
San Diego State Univ	CA	23,156	VC
San Francisco State Univ	CA	18,514	LC
San Jose State Univ	CA	22,630	C
Savannah State Univ	GA	17,036	C
Schreiner Univ	TX	34,626	LC
Seattle Pacific Univ	WA	47,439	C+
Seattle Univ	WA	54,957	VC
Seton Hall Univ	NJ	58,008	C
Seton Hill Univ	PA	46,972	VC
Shaw Univ	NC	24,638	C
Shenandoah Univ	VA	42,100	C
Shepherd Univ, West Virginia	WV	17,382	C
Shippensburg Univ of Pennsylvania	PA	24,096	C
Shorter Univ	GA	31,130	LC
Siena College	NY	48,916	C
Siena Heights Univ	MI	36,322	C
Sierra Nevada College	NV	45,403	C
Silver Lake College of the Holy Family	WI	36,290	LC
Simmons College	MA	54,400	HC
Simpson College	IA	45,626	VC
Simpson Univ	CA	34,722	C
Skidmore College	NY	66,600	MC
Slippery Rock Univ of Pennsylvania	PA	20,450	C
Sonoma State Univ	CA	27,020	C
S Car State Univ	SC	21,330	LC
South Univ	GA	36,070	LC
Southeast Missouri State Univ	MO	16,148	C
Southeastern Louisiana Univ	LA	16,237	C
Southeastern Okla State Univ	OK	11,875	C
Southeastern Univ	FL	34,910	LC
Southern Adventist Univ	TN	28,250	C
Southern Arkansas Univ	AR	21,532	C
Southern Conn State Univ	CT	21,924	LC
Southern Illinois Univ Carbondale	IL	24,554	C
Southern Illinois Univ Edwardsville	IL	20,188	C
Southern Methodist Univ	TX	69,008	MC
Southern Nazarene Univ	OK	33,684	C
Southern New Hampshire Univ	NH	44,256	C
Southern Oregon Univ	OR	19,117	C
Southern Univ and A&M College	LA	16,074	LC
Southern Univ at New Orleans	LA	8,014	LC
Southern Vermont College	VT	34,670	LC
Southern Wesleyan Univ	SC	33,670	LC
Southwest Baptist Univ	MO	30,890	LC
Southwest Minn State Univ	MN	17,783	C
Southwestern Adventist Univ	TX	28,232	LC
Southwestern College	KS	31,531	LC
Southwestern Okla State Univ	OK	12,205	C
Southwestern Univ	TX	52,370	VC
Spalding Univ	KY	31,938	C
Spring Arbor Univ	MI	37,390	C
Spring Hill College	AL	48,488	C
Springfield College	MA	48,775	C
St. Ambrose Univ	IA	40,180	C
St. Andrews Univ	NC	44,634	LC
St. Catherine Univ	MN	45,630	C
St. Cloud State Univ	MN	10,600	C
St. Edward's Univ	TX	56,190	VC
St. Francis College	NY	38,800	LC
St. John Fisher College	NY	45,270	VC
St. John's Univ	NY	57,160	C+
St. Joseph's College, New York/Brooklyn Campus	NY	25,114	LC
St. Joseph's College, New York/Long Island Campus	NY	25,124	C
St. Mary's Univ	TX	39,120	C
St. Norbert College	WI	46,060	VC
St. Thomas Aquinas College	NY	32,450	C
St. Thomas Univ	FL	51,187	LC
SUNY /College of Agriculture and Tech at Cobleskill	NY	20,527	LC
SUNY Albany	NY	22,165	C
SUNY at Binghamton	NY	24,100	MC
SUNY at Geneseo	NY	21,622	VC
SUNY at New Paltz	NY	20,840	C
SUNY at Oswego	NY	22,219	VC
SUNY Polytechnic Inst	NY	20,438	VC
SUNY/Buffalo State	NY	20,583	LC
SUNY/College at Old Westbury	NY	16,860	C
SUNY/Empire State College	NY	9,145	NC
SUNY/Fredonia	NY	20,818	C
SUNY/Maritime College	NY	16,020	C
SUNY/Plattsburgh	NY	19,314	C
SUNY/Potsdam	NY	21,051	VC
SUNY/Univ at Buffalo	NY	23,122	C
Stephen F. Austin State Univ	TX	18,484	LC
Stephens College	MO	38,042	C
Sterling College	KS	32,830	LC
Stetson Univ	FL	57,174	VC+
Stevens Inst of Technology	NJ	64,954	MC
Stevenson Univ	MD	48,412	C
Stillman College	AL	20,738	C
Stockton Univ	NJ	25,565	C
Stonehill College	MA	55,130	C
Stony Brook Univ/The SUNY	NY	22,703	MC
Sul Ross State Univ	TX	15,021	LC
Susquehanna Univ	PA	57,560	VC
Tabor College	KS	35,870	C
Talladega College	AL	25,919	C
Tarleton State Univ	TX	15,248	LC
Taylor Univ	IN	42,130	VC
Temple Univ	PA	24,392	C+
Tenn State Univ	TN	14,423	LC
Tenn Tech Univ	TN	17,929	C
Tenn Wesleyan Univ	TN	32,680	LC
Texas A&M Univ at College Station	TX	20,771	VC+
Texas A&M Univ at Commerce	TX	10,496	C
Texas A&M Univ at Corpus Christi	TX	16,851	LC
Texas A&M Univ at Kingsville	TX	16,580	LC
Texas Lutheran Univ	TX	39,770	C
Texas Southern Univ	TX	19,592	LC
Texas State Univ	TX	18,721	C
Texas Wesleyan Univ	TX	37,338	C
Texas Woman's Univ	TX	15,302	LC
The American Univ	DC	61,317	HC
The Catholic Univ of America	DC	58,376	VC
The Citadel, The Military College of S Car	SC	20,679	C
The College at Brockport - SUNY	NY	21,058	C
The College of Idaho	ID	36,415	C
The College of New Jersey	NJ	28,675	VC+
The College of New Rochelle	NY	46,300	LC
The College of St. Rose	NY	44,010	C
The George Washington Univ	DC	68,474	HC+
The Master's Univ	CA	43,870	C
The Univ of Akron	OH	22,566	C
The Univ of Arizona	AZ	24,086	C
The Univ of Mary	ND	23,180	C
The Univ of Tenn at Chattanooga	TN	17,340	C+
The Univ of Tenn at Martin	TN	15,212	C
The Univ of Texas at Austin	TX	20,206	MC
The Univ of Texas at San Antonio	TX	21,060	C
The Univ of Utah	UT	18,751	VC
The Univ of Virginia's College at Wise	VA	18,192	LC
Thiel College	PA	42,950	LC
Thomas College	ME	73,888	LC
Thomas Edison State Univ	NJ	6,350	NC
Thomas More College	KY	36,720	LC
Thomas Univ	GA	21,420	NC
Tiffin Univ	OH	34,900	LC
Toccoa Falls College	GA	30,048	C
Touro College	NY	31,040	C
Towson Univ	MD	21,878	C
Transylvania Univ	KY	47,450	HC+
Trevecca Nazarene Univ	TN	31,186	C
Trine Univ	IN	41,310	C
Trinity Christian College	IL	35,580	C
Trinity International Univ	IL	31,070	VC
Trinity Univ	TX	54,480	MC
Trinity Washington Univ	DC	33,826	C+
Troy Univ	AL	16,171	C
Truman State Univ	MO	16,286	MC
Tulane Univ	LA	67,496	MC
Tuskegee Univ	AL	28,164	C
Union College	KY	32,310	C
Union College	NE	23,270	C
Union Inst & Univ	OH	8,912	SP
Union Univ	TN	41,160	VC
Universidad Adventista de las Antillas	PR	16,606	
Universidad del Turabo	PR	17,828	
Universidad Metropolitana	PR	17,828	
Universidad Politecnica de PR, Hato Rey campus	PR	23,514	
Univ of PR, at Arecibo	PR	12,652	
Univ of Alabama in Huntsville	AL	20,028	VC
Univ of Alaska Anchorage	AK	17,914	C
Univ of Alaska Southeast	AK	17,615	C
Univ of Arkansas at Little Rock	AR	18,211	LC
Univ of Arkansas at Monticello	AR	13,599	LC
Univ of Arkansas at Pine Bluff	AR	13,541	C
Univ of Bridgeport	CT	44,985	LC
Univ of Calif at Berkeley	CA	29,886	MC
Univ of Calif at Irvine	CA	33,857	VC
Univ of Calif at Riverside	CA	32,912	C
Univ of Central Arkansas	AR	15,042	VC
Univ of Central Florida	FL	16,379	VC
Univ of Central Missouri	MO	18,982	C
Univ of Central Okla	OK	15,150	C
Univ of Charleston	WV	35,000	LC
Univ of Cincinnati	OH	22,118	VC
Univ of Colo Boulder	CO	26,048	HC
Univ of Colo Colo Springs	CO	20,300	C
Univ of Colo Denver	CO	22,238	C
Univ of Conn	CT	27,394	
Univ of Dallas	TX	50,676	VC
Univ of Dayton	OH	54,930	VC
Univ of Delaware	DE	32,214	VC
Univ of Denver	CO	61,129	VC+
Univ of Detroit Mercy	MI	48,816	C
Univ of Dubuque	IA	37,824	C
Univ of Evansville	IN	44,186	C+
Univ of Findlay	OH	43,040	C
Univ of Florida	FL	16,291	HC+
Univ of Great Falls	MT	38,524	C
Univ of Hartford	CT	49,776	C
Univ of Hawaii at Hilo	HI	18,038	VC
Univ of Hawaii at Manoa	HI	23,261	C
Univ of Holy Cross	LA	21,523	NC
Univ of Houston-Downtown	TX	7,241	LC
Univ of Idaho	ID	16,158	C
Univ of Illinois at Chicago	IL	24,664	VC
Univ of Indianapolis	IN	36,480	VC
Univ of Iowa	IA	19,415	HC
Univ of Jamestown	ND	28,508	C
Univ of Kansas	KS	20,884	VC
Univ of La Verne	CA	55,600	C

ST = STATE **$IS** = IN-STATE COSTS **SR** = SELECTOR RATING

School	ST	$IS	SR
Univ of Louisiana at Lafayette	LA	14,516	C
Univ of Louisiana at Monroe	LA	15,970	C
Univ of Louisville	KY	19,692	C
Univ of Lynchburg	VA	48,370	C
Univ of Maine	ME	21,038	VC
Univ of Maine at Augusta	ME	7,812	C
Univ of Maine at Farmington	ME	18,792	C
Univ of Maine at Fort Kent	ME	15,165	LC
Univ of Maine at Machias	ME	22,960	C
Univ of Maine at Presque Isle	ME	16,148	LC
Univ of Mary Hardin-Baylor	TX	35,292	C+
Univ of Mary Washington	VA	23,039	C+
Univ of Maryland Univ College	MD	26,146	LC
Univ of Maryland/College Park	MD	21,938	HC
Univ of Maryland/Eastern Shore	MD	21,861	LC
Univ of Mass Amherst	MA	27,669	HC
Univ of Mass Dartmouth	MA	26,507	C
Univ of Mass Lowell	MA	27,296	VC
Univ of Mich/Ann Arbor	MI	25,274	MC
Univ of Mich/Flint	MI	19,062	C
Univ of Minn/Crookston	MN	19,126	C
Univ of Minn/Duluth	MN	20,292	C
Univ of Miss	MS	18,802	C
Univ of Missouri-Columbia	MO	20,463	VC
Univ of Missouri-Kansas City	MO	19,563	VC
Univ of Missouri-St. Louis	MO	19,810	VC
Univ of Mobile	AL	28,935	C
Univ of Montana	MT	14,105	C
Univ of Montevallo	AL	20,012	C
Univ of Mount Olive	NC	18,426	C
Univ of Nebr - Kearney	NE	17,014	LC
Univ of Nebr - Lincoln	NE	18,589	VC
Univ of New England	ME	50,110	C
Univ of New Hampshire	NH	29,333	VC
Univ of New Haven	CT	53,680	C
Univ of New Mexico	NM	16,808	C
Univ of New Orleans	LA	12,840	C
Univ of N Car at Asheville	NC	16,251	VC+
Univ of N Car at Chapel Hill	NC	20,561	MC
Univ of N Car at Charlotte	NC	17,803	VC
Univ of N Car at Pembroke	NC	14,737	LC
Univ of North Florida	FL	15,996	VC
Univ of North Georgia	GA	17,316	C
Univ of North Texas	TX	20,082	C
Univ of Northern Colo	CO	19,658	C
Univ of Northwestern - St. Paul	MN	39,530	C
Univ of Oregon	OR	24,021	VC
Univ of Pennsylvania	PA	63,526	MC
Univ of Pikeville	KY	27,838	C
Univ of Pittsburgh at Bradford	PA	22,958	C
Univ of Pittsburgh at Johnstown	PA	22,092	C
Univ of PR, at Bayamon	PR	13,145	
Univ of PR, at Cayey	PR		
Univ of PR, at Humacao	PR	14,000	
Univ of PR, at Mayaguez	PR	13,995	
Univ of PR-Rio Piedras campus	PR	13,327	
Univ of Puget Sound	WA	60,210	HC
Univ of Redlands	CA	61,934	VC
Univ of Rhode Island	RI	26,066	VC
Univ of Richmond	VA	62,730	MC
Univ of Rio Grande & Rio Grande Community College	OH	8,750	LC
Univ of Rochester	NY	65,032	MC
Univ of St. Francis	IN	38,520	C
Univ of St. Mary	KS	37,080	NC
Univ of San Diego	CA	60,338	HC
Univ of San Francisco	CA	60,580	C
Univ of Science and Arts of Okla	OK	11,140	VC
Univ of Scranton	PA	54,962	VC
Univ of Sioux Falls	SD	25,630	C
Univ of South Alabama	AL	16,880	C
Univ of S Car Aiken	SC	18,094	C
Univ of S Car at Columbia	SC	21,726	VC
Univ of S Car Upstate	SC	19,272	LC
Univ of South Florida St. Petersburg	FL	15,980	C
Univ of South Florida/Tampa	FL	16,110	VC
Univ of Southern Calif	CA	66,631	MC
Univ of Southern Indiana	IN	16,808	C
Univ of Southern Maine	ME	18,320	C
Univ of Southern Miss	MS	13,170	C
Univ of St. Francis	IL	40,828	C
Univ of St. Thomas - Houston	TX	41,510	VC
Univ of Tampa	FL	38,928	VC
Univ of Texas at Arlington	TX	18,876	C
Univ of Texas at Dallas	TX	23,640	HC
Univ of Texas Rio Grande Valley	TX	15,573	LC
Univ of the Cumberlands	KY	32,000	LC
Univ of the District of Columbia	DC	21,260	LC
Univ of the Incarnate Word	TX	39,162	LC
Univ of the Ozarks	AR	31,050	NC
Univ of the Pacific	CA	57,446	VC
Univ of the Sacred Heart	PR	17,932	
Univ of the Southwest	NM	24,386	C
Univ of Toledo	OH	19,336	C
Univ of Tulsa	OK	52,625	HC
Univ of Vermont	VT	29,792	HC
Univ of Virginia	VA	27,367	MC
Univ of Washington	WA	23,091	MC
Univ of West Alabama	AL	16,284	LC
Univ of West Florida	FL	15,848	C
Univ of West Georgia	GA	17,510	LC
Univ of Wisc-Eau Claire	WI	16,354	VC
Univ of Wisc-Green Bay	WI	15,184	C
Univ of Wisc-Milwaukee	WI	21,538	C
Univ of Wisc-Oshkosh	WI	15,392	C
Univ of Wisc-Parkside	WI	15,313	C
Univ of Wisc-Platteville	WI	14,148	C
Univ of Wisc-River Falls	WI	14,541	C
Univ of Wisc-Stevens Point	WI	14,043	C
Univ of Wisc-Stout	WI	19,667	C
Univ of Wisc-Superior	WI	14,838	C
Univ of Wisc-Whitewater	WI	13,976	C
Univ of Wyoming	WY	15,537	C
Upper Iowa Univ	IA	34,990	NC
Urbana Univ	OH	30,820	C
Ursuline College	OH	41,076	LC
Utah State Univ	UT	13,235	C
Utica College	NY	31,510	C
Valley City State Univ	ND	13,267	C
Valparaiso Univ	IN	50,160	VC
Vanguard Univ of Southern Calif	CA	42,400	VC
Vaughn College of Aeronautics and Technology	NY	37,180	SP
Villanova Univ	PA	64,922	MC
Virginia Commonwealth Univ	VA	23,811	VC
Virginia State Univ	VA	19,802	C+
Virginia Union Univ	VA	25,058	C
Virginia Wesleyan Univ	VA	45,980	LC
Voorhees College	SC	19,976	C
Wagner College	NY	57,240	C+
Wake Forest Univ	NC	69,354	MC
Walla Walla Univ	WA	34,845	C
Walsh Univ	OH	39,010	C
Warner Pacific College	OR	31,610	C
Warner Univ	FL	28,216	C
Wartburg College	IA	49,478	C
Washburn Univ	KS	15,827	C
Washington & Jefferson College	PA	58,694	VC
Washington Adventist Univ	MD	32,050	LC
Washington and Lee Univ	VA	59,647	MC
Washington College	MD	56,154	VC
Washington State Univ	WA	22,747	C
Washington Univ in St. Louis	MO	67,539	MC
Wayland Baptist Univ	TX	23,460	LC
Wayne State College	NE	25,746	NC
Wayne State Univ	MI	23,085	C
Webber International Univ	FL	31,904	C
Weber State Univ	UT	14,112	C
Webster Univ	MO	37,490	C
Wells College	NY	50,500	C
Wesley College	DE	37,848	LC
Wesleyan College	GA	31,940	C+
West Chester Univ of Pennsylvania	PA	19,171	VC
West Liberty Univ	WV	16,158	C
West Texas A&M Univ	TX	13,478	C
West Virginia State Univ	WV	19,412	LC
West Virginia Univ	WV	18,952	VC
West Virginia Univ Inst of Technology	WV	18,264	C
West Virginia Wesleyan College	WV	39,188	C
Western Conn State Univ	CT	21,254	LC
Western Illinois Univ	IL	20,897	C
Western Kentucky Univ	KY	16,850	C
Western New England Univ	MA	49,182	C
Western New Mexico Univ	NM	16,914	LC
Western Oregon Univ	OR	19,965	LC
Western State Colo Univ	CO	19,348	C
Western Washington Univ	WA	18,904	VC
Westfield State Univ	MA	20,404	C
Westminster College	MO	32,820	C
Westminster College	PA	41,722	C
Westminster College	UT	41,078	C
Wheaton College	MA	63,818	VC
Wheeling Jesuit Univ	WV	37,106	LC
Whittier College	CA	57,891	C
Whitworth Univ	WA	53,682	VC
Wichita State Univ	KS	17,773	C
Widener Univ	PA	58,190	C
Wilberforce Univ	OH	19,900	C
Wiley College	TX	19,255	C
Wilkes Univ	PA	49,166	C
William Carey Univ	MS	23,950	LC
William Jewell College	MO	42,490	C+
William Paterson Univ of New Jersey	NJ	24,022	C
William Peace Univ	NC	39,300	LC
William Penn Univ	IA	26,000	C
William Woods Univ	MO	32,040	C
Williams Baptist College	AR	24,720	C
Wilmington College	OH	35,100	C
Wilmington Univ	DE	8,762	NC
Wilson College	PA	35,620	LC
Winona State Univ	MN	18,109	C
Winston-Salem State Univ	NC	18,005	LC
Winthrop Univ	SC	23,960	C
Wisc Lutheran College	WI	36,290	C
Wittenberg Univ	OH	49,863	VC
Worcester Polytechnic Inst	MA	62,846	MC
Worcester State Univ	MA	20,977	C
Xavier Univ	OH	49,380	VC
Xavier Univ of Louisiana	LA	31,689	C
Yeshiva Univ	NY	52,750	VC
York College	NE	30,260	C
York College of Pennsylvania	PA	29,240	C
Youngstown State Univ	OH	17,487	C

BUSINESS ADMINISTRATION MARKETING

School	ST	$IS	SR
Aquinas College - Mich	MI	38,876	VC
Bay Path Univ	MA	46,356	C
Black Hills State Univ	SD	16,622	C
Bloomfield College	NJ	40,100	LC
Cabrini Univ	PA	42,591	LC
Calif State Polytechnic Univ, Pomona	CA	21,811	C
Campbell Univ	NC	37,570	VC
Clayton State Univ	GA	19,735	LC
Cogswell Polytechnical College	CA	31,511	C
College of the Ozarks	MO	7,530	VC
Corban Univ	OR	41,700	C
East Central Univ	OK	13,330	C
East Texas Baptist Univ	TX	34,444	C
Fort Lewis College	CO	20,154	C
Franklin College	IN	40,550	C
Gwynedd Mercy Univ	PA	43,780	LC
Harris-Stowe State Univ	MO	14,590	NC
Hood College	MD	50,540	C
Huntington Univ	IN	33,996	C
Iowa Wesleyan Univ	IA	41,000	C
King Univ	TN	36,976	C
Kutztown Univ of Pennsylvania	PA	19,477	C
Lake Superior State Univ	MI	19,867	C
Lynn Univ	FL	49,680	LC
Millersville Univ of Pennsylvania	PA	25,298	C
Missouri Western State Univ	MO	17,822	LC
Monmouth Univ	NJ	50,184	C
Niagara Univ	NY	41,010	C
North Central Univ	MN	30,610	C
Okla Christian Univ	OK	29,260	C
Regis Univ	CO	46,380	C
Rochester Inst of Technology	NY	52,734	HC+
Rutgers Univ - New Brunswick	NJ	27,090	HC
San Jose State Univ	CA	22,630	C
St. Ambrose Univ	IA	40,180	C
Taylor Univ	IN	42,130	VC
Tenn Wesleyan Univ	TN	32,680	LC
The Master's Univ	CA	43,870	C
Univ of Alaska Fairbanks	AK	16,874	VC
Univ of Arkansas at Fayetteville	AR	19,766	VC
Univ of Maine	ME	21,038	VC
Univ of Maine at Machias	ME	22,960	C
Univ of Tulsa	OK	52,625	HC
Urbana Univ	OH	30,820	C
Wartburg College	IA	49,478	C
West Chester Univ of Pennsylvania	PA	19,171	VC
West Virginia Univ	WV	18,952	VC
Western Illinois Univ	IL	20,897	C
Western Kentucky Univ	KY	16,850	C

BUSINESS ADMINISTRATION WITH LEGAL STUDIES

School	ST	$IS	SR
East Central Univ	OK	13,330	C
Ferris State Univ	MI	21,458	C
Ithaca College	NY	58,158	VC+
Milligan College	TN	39,450	C
The Master's Univ	CA	43,870	C
Univ of Central Okla	OK	15,150	C

BUSINESS ADMINISTRATION/AVIATION

School	ST	$IS	SR
Drury Univ	MO	37,555	VC
Embry-Riddle Aeronautical Univ - Daytona Beach	FL	45,822	VC
Ferris State Univ	MI	21,458	C
Lynn Univ	FL	49,680	LC

BUSINESS AND TECHNOLOGY

School	ST	$IS	SR
Bentley Univ	MA	63,720	MC
Cal State, Fullerton	CA	21,902	C
Framingham State Univ	MA	21,740	C
Regis Univ	CO	46,380	C
Trinity Univ	TX	54,480	MC
Univ of Miami	FL	63,494	MC

BUSINESS COMMUNICATIONS

School	ST	$IS	SR
Aquinas College - Mich	MI	38,876	VC
Augustana Univ	SD	39,968	VC
Bentley Univ	MA	63,720	MC
Biola Univ	CA	48,686	C
Bryant Univ	RI	57,204	VC
Calvin College	MI	43,090	HC
Canisius College	NY	49,672	C
Carlow Univ	PA	39,696	LC
Chestnut Hill College	PA	47,180	C
Duquesne Univ	PA	48,508	VC
George Fox Univ	OR	42,938	C
Ithaca College	NY	58,158	VC+
Murray State Univ	KY	17,726	C+
Nichols College	MA	46,900	LC
Northwestern State Univ of Louisiana	LA	16,534	LC
Olivet Nazarene Univ	IL	41,840	VC
Point Loma Nazarene Univ	CA	46,150	C+
Rockhurst Univ	MO	28,990	C
St. Leo Univ	FL	32,850	C
Southeast Missouri State Univ	MO	16,148	C
Southwestern College	KS	31,531	LC
Stevenson Univ	MD	48,412	C
The Univ of Akron	OH	22,566	C
The Univ of Mary	ND	23,180	C
Univ of Indianapolis	IN	36,480	VC
Univ of Nebr - Omaha	NE	16,120	C
Walsh Univ	OH	39,010	C
Webber International Univ	FL	31,904	C
Western Kentucky Univ	KY	16,850	C
Westminster College	MO	32,820	C

BUSINESS DATA PROCESSING

School	ST	$IS	SR
Cal State, Fresno	CA	16,902	LC
Eastern Mich Univ	MI	19,761	C
Ferris State Univ	MI	21,458	C
Idaho State Univ	ID	13,619	LC
Mount Vernon Nazarene Univ	OH	35,944	C
Univ of Northwestern - St. Paul	MN	39,530	C

BUSINESS ECONOMICS

School	ST	$IS	SR
Adams State Univ	CO	15,420	LC
Alabama State Univ	AL	16,490	LC
American International College	MA	47,020	LC
Andrews Univ	MI	41,732	C
Aquinas College - Mich	MI	38,876	VC
Arkansas State Univ	AR	16,190	C
Armstrong State Univ	GA	15,615	C
Ashford Univ	CA	10,480	C
Ashland Univ	OH	30,446	C
Auburn Univ	AL	24,300	VC+
Ball State Univ	IN	19,808	C+
Baylor Univ	TX	56,803	HC
Beloit College	WI	55,206	HC
Benedictine Univ	IL	38,300	C
Bentley Univ	MA	63,720	MC
Bethany College	KS	38,637	LC
Bethel College	IN	36,830	C
Biola Univ	CA	48,686	C
Bloomfield College	NJ	40,100	LC
Bloomsburg Univ of Pennsylvania	PA	19,930	C
Boston College	MA	68,043	MC
Bradley Univ	IL	43,240	VC
Brescia Univ	KY	29,890	VC
Brown Univ	RI	64,566	MC
Bryant Univ	RI	57,204	VC
Bryn Athyn College	PA	32,664	C
Buena Vista Univ	IA	42,344	C
Cal State, Fullerton	CA	21,902	C
Cal State, Long Beach	CA	18,850	C
Cal State, San Bernardino	CA	20,106	C
Campbell Univ	NC	37,570	VC
Campbellsville Univ	KY	33,400	C
Canisius College	NY	49,672	C
Carnegie Mellon Univ	PA	67,980	MC
Carroll Univ	WI	38,100	C+
Carson-Newman Univ	TN	35,900	C
Centenary College of Louisiana	LA	49,050	C+
Central Washington Univ	WA	16,803	C
Chatham Univ	PA	47,883	VC
Clarion Univ of Pennsylvania	PA	21,608	LC
Clayton State Univ	GA	19,735	LC
Cleveland State Univ	OH	22,290	C
College of the Ozarks	MO	7,530	VC
Cornell College	IA	49,900	VC
DePaul Univ	IL	52,807	VC
Dominican College	NY	40,258	LC
Dordt College	IA	37,860	C+
Drexel Univ	PA	65,927	HC
Duquesne Univ	PA	48,508	VC
Eastern Mich Univ	MI	19,761	C
Elizabethtown College	PA	56,340	VC
Elmira College	NY	53,900	C
Emory Univ	GA	63,286	MC
Eureka College	IL	34,760	C
Fairleigh Dickinson Univ/ Metropolitan Campus	NJ	52,392	C
Farmingdale State College	NY	20,968	C
Fayetteville State Univ	NC	17,756	C
Florida A&M Univ	FL	15,361	C
Florida Atlantic Univ	FL	18,256	C
Fordham Univ	NY	68,431	MC
Fort Lewis College	CO	20,154	C
Francis Marion Univ	SC	18,144	LC
Friends Univ	KS	38,000	C
Georgetown College	KY	41,440	C
Georgia State Univ	GA	25,250	C
Gonzaga Univ	WA	52,880	HC
Grambling State Univ	LA	15,701	C
Grand Valley State Univ	MI	22,250	C+
Grove City College	PA	26,654	VC
Gustavus Adolphus College	MN	53,943	HC
Hampden-Sydney College	VA	57,806	VC

ST = STATE $IS = IN-STATE COSTS SR = SELECTOR RATING

School	ST	$IS	SR
Hawaii Pacific Univ	HI	33,420	C
Heidelberg Univ	OH	40,400	LC
Hendrix College	AR	54,020	VC
Hofstra Univ	NY	58,210	C+
Humboldt State Univ	CA	21,708	C
Indiana Univ-Purdue Univ Fort Wayne	IN	18,675	C
Inter-American Univ of PR-Bayamon	PR	18,785	
James Madison Univ	VA	19,084	VC
Johnson C. Smith Univ	NC	25,336	LC
Kalamazoo College	MI	53,931	HC
Kansas Wesleyan Univ	KS	37,930	C
Kentucky Wesleyan College	KY	34,260	LC
King Univ	TN	36,976	C
Kutztown Univ of Pennsylvania	PA	19,477	C
Lafayette College	PA	68,520	MC
Lake Forest College	IL	50,652	VC
Lakeland Univ	WI	35,130	C
Lamar Univ	TX	18,014	LC
Lehigh Univ	PA	63,860	MC
Limestone College	SC	32,100	C
Louisiana Tech Univ	LA	11,422	VC
Loyola Univ Chicago	IL	57,158	VC
Manhattan College	NY	55,652	C
Marquette Univ	WI	53,090	VC+
Marshall Univ	WV	18,044	C
Mary Baldwin Univ	VA	40,495	C
Miami Univ	OH	27,190	HC+
Midland Univ	NE	39,512	C
Midwestern State Univ	TX	12,111	LC
Mills College	CA	43,705	C
Missouri Western State Univ	MO	17,822	LC
Monmouth Univ	NJ	50,184	C
Moravian College	PA	55,488	C
Morehead State Univ	KY	18,386	LC
Mount Aloysius College	PA	29,976	C
New Mexico State Univ	NM	14,050	LC
New York Univ	NY	68,139	MC
Niagara Univ	NY	41,010	C
N Car State Univ	NC	22,434	HC+
Northern Arizona Univ	AZ	21,003	C
Northern State Univ	SD	15,570	C
Northwest Missouri State Univ	MO	18,286	C
Northwestern College of Iowa	IA	38,400	C
Northwood Univ - Mich	MI	35,010	LC
Norwich Univ	VT	56,234	C
Notre Dame College	OH	39,150	VC
Oakland Univ	MI	20,763	C
Ohio Northern Univ	OH	44,050	VC
Ohio Univ	OH	23,394	VC
Ohio Wesleyan Univ	OH	49,460	VC
Pace Univ	NY	60,136	C
Park Univ	MO	22,134	C
Penn State Erie,The Behrend College	PA	26,688	VC
Pittsburg State Univ	KS	13,880	C
Pontifical Catholic Univ of PR	PR	10,534	
Presbyterian College	SC	47,186	C
Providence College	RI	62,870	HC
Purdue Univ Northwest	IN	15,178	C
Regis Univ	CO	46,380	C
Rider Univ	NJ	54,050	C
Rockhurst Univ	MO	28,990	C
Sacred Heart Univ	CT	54,590	C
Saginaw Valley State Univ	MI	19,284	C
St. Louis Univ	MO	49,866	HC
Salisbury Univ	MD	21,132	VC
Seattle Univ	WA	54,957	VC
Seton Hall Univ	NJ	58,008	C
Seton Hill Univ	PA	46,972	VC
Skidmore College	NY	66,600	MC
S Car State Univ	SC	21,330	LC
Southeast Missouri State Univ	MO	16,148	C
Southern Conn State Univ	CT	21,924	LC
Southern Illinois Univ Carbondale	IL	24,554	C
Southern Illinois Univ Edwardsville	IL	20,188	C
Southern Univ and A&M College	LA	16,074	LC
St. Ambrose Univ	IA	40,180	C
St. Cloud State Univ	MN	10,600	C
SUNY/Fredonia	NY	20,818	C
SUNY/Oneonta	NY	20,794	C
SUNY/Potsdam	NY	21,051	VC
Stetson Univ	FL	57,174	VC+
Tenn State Univ	TN	14,423	LC
Texas A&M Univ at Kingsville	TX	16,580	LC
Texas State Univ	TX	18,721	C
Texas Wesleyan Univ	TX	37,338	C
The College of Wooster	OH	60,000	HC
The George Washington Univ	DC	68,474	HC+
The Univ of Arizona	AZ	24,086	C
The Univ of Memphis	TN	18,278	C
The Univ of Tenn at Martin	TN	15,212	C
Thomas College	ME	73,888	LC
Troy Univ	AL	16,171	C
Tuskegee Univ	AL	28,164	C
Univ of Arkansas at Fayetteville	AR	19,766	VC
Univ of Calif at Irvine	CA	33,857	VC
Univ of Calif at Los Angeles	CA	27,438	HC+
Univ of Calif at Riverside	CA	32,912	C
Univ of Calif, Santa Cruz	CA	28,731	C+
Univ of Central Arkansas	AR	15,042	VC
Univ of Central Florida	FL	16,379	VC
Univ of Dayton	OH	54,930	VC
Univ of Denver	CO	61,129	VC+
Univ of Findlay	OH	43,040	C
Univ of Idaho	ID	16,158	C
Univ of Illinois at Chicago	IL	24,664	VC
Univ of Indianapolis	IN	36,480	VC
Univ of Iowa	IA	19,415	HC
Univ of Kentucky	KY	24,800	C+
Univ of La Verne	CA	55,600	C
Univ of Louisville	KY	19,692	C
Univ of Maine	ME	21,038	VC
Univ of Maine at Farmington	ME	18,792	C
Univ of Miss	MS	18,802	C
Univ of Missouri-Columbia	MO	20,463	VC
Univ of Nebr - Kearney	NE	17,014	LC
Univ of Nebr - Lincoln	NE	18,589	VC
Univ of North Alabama	AL	15,964	C
Univ of N Car at Charlotte	NC	17,803	VC
Univ of N Dak	ND	16,673	C
Univ of North Florida	FL	15,996	VC
Univ of North Georgia	GA	17,316	C
Univ of Pittsburgh at Johnstown	PA	22,092	C
Univ of PR, at Mayaguez	PR	13,995	
Univ of PR-Rio Piedras campus	PR	13,327	
Univ of Rio Grande & Rio Grande Community College	OH	8,750	LC
Univ of San Diego	CA	60,338	HC
Univ of San Francisco	CA	60,580	C
Univ of Scranton	PA	54,962	VC
Univ of Sioux Falls	SD	25,630	C
Univ of South Alabama	AL	16,880	C
Univ of S Car at Columbia	SC	21,726	VC
Univ of South Florida/Tampa	FL	16,110	VC
Univ of Southern Miss	MS	13,170	C
Univ of Tampa	FL	38,928	VC
Univ of Texas at Arlington	TX	18,876	C
Univ of Texas at El Paso	TX	34,452	NC
Univ of Washington	WA	23,091	MC
Univ of West Florida	FL	15,848	C
Univ of West Georgia	GA	17,510	LC
Univ of Wisc-Whitewater	WI	13,976	C
Univ of Wyoming	WY	15,537	C
Ursinus College	PA	62,920	VC
Utah State Univ	UT	13,235	C
Utica College	NY	31,510	C
Villanova Univ	PA	64,922	MC
Virginia Military Inst	VA	26,460	VC
Virginia Polytechnic Inst and State Univ	VA	21,920	VC
Washburn Univ	KS	15,827	C
Washington State Univ	WA	22,747	C
Washington Univ in St. Louis	MO	67,539	MC
Weber State Univ	UT	14,112	C
West Chester Univ of Pennsylvania	PA	19,171	VC
West Liberty Univ	WV	16,158	C
West Texas A&M Univ	TX	13,478	C
Western Kentucky Univ	KY	16,850	C
Western Mich Univ	MI	21,791	C
Westmont College	CA	57,930	VC
Wheaton College	IL	44,993	MC
Widener Univ	PA	58,190	C
Wilberforce Univ	OH	19,900	C
William Jewell College	MO	42,490	C+
Wilson College	PA	35,620	LC
Winona State Univ	MN	18,109	C
Wofford College	SC	49,885	VC
Wright State Univ	OH	16,983	C
Xavier Univ	OH	49,380	VC
Xavier Univ of Louisiana	LA	31,689	C
Youngstown State Univ	OH	17,487	C

BUSINESS EDUCATION

School	ST	$IS	SR
Adams State Univ	CO	15,420	LC
Alabama State Univ	AL	16,490	LC
Alfred Univ	NY	37,490	C
Appalachian State Univ	NC	15,394	VC
Arkansas State Univ	AR	16,190	C
Arkansas Tech Univ	AR	16,534	LC
Auburn Univ	AL	24,300	VC+
Avila Univ	MO	27,100	C
Baylor Univ	TX	56,803	HC
Bethany College	KS	38,637	LC
Bethel Univ	MN	46,550	C+
Bethune-Cookman Univ	FL	23,322	C
Black Hills State Univ	SD	16,622	C
Bloomsburg Univ of Pennsylvania	PA	19,930	C
Bowling Green State Univ	OH	19,975	C
Brigham Young Univ/Hawaii	HI	11,710	C
Buena Vista Univ	IA	42,344	C
Cal State, Fullerton	CA	21,902	C
Cal State, Northridge	CA	17,277	LC
Cal State, Sacramento	CA	19,060	C
Canisius College	NY	49,672	C
Caribbean Univ	PR	12,227	
Central Washington Univ	WA	16,803	C
Chicago State Univ	IL	41,620	C
CUNY/Lehman College	NY	5,788	LC
Clark Atlanta Univ	GA	31,019	LC
College of the Ozarks	MO	7,530	VC
Concord Univ	WV	14,954	LC
Concordia College - Moorhead	MN	46,418	C
Concordia Univ Nebr	NE	41,900	VC
Dakota State Univ	SD	12,286	C
Delaware State Univ	DE	19,376	LC
Dickinson State Univ	ND	12,372	LC
Dordt College	IA	37,860	C+
East Carolina Univ	NC	16,539	C
East Central Univ	OK	13,330	C
Eastern Kentucky Univ	KY	17,742	C
Eastern Mich Univ	MI	19,761	C
Eastern New Mexico Univ	NM	12,874	LC
Edgewood College	WI	35,950	C
Elizabeth City State Univ	NC	14,745	C
Emporia State Univ	KS	15,029	C
Evangel Univ	MO	28,898	C
Fayetteville State Univ	NC	17,756	C
Ferris State Univ	MI	21,458	C
Florida A&M Univ	FL	15,361	C
Friends Univ	KS	38,000	C
Glenville State College	WV	17,386	LC
Goshen College	IN	44,350	C
Grace College and Seminary	IN	31,524	C
Gustavus Adolphus College	MN	53,943	HC
Gwynedd Mercy Univ	PA	43,780	LC
Hardin-Simmons Univ	TX	36,025	C
Hastings College	NE	35,380	C+
Henderson State Univ	AR	15,516	C
Humboldt State Univ	CA	21,708	C
Illinois State Univ	IL	23,418	VC
Indiana State Univ	IN	23,223	LC
Indiana Univ of Pennsylvania	PA	24,474	C
Jackson State Univ	MS	15,879	LC
Lakeland Univ	WI	35,130	C
Langston Univ	OK	15,659	C
Lee Univ	TN	22,045	C
LeTourneau Univ	TX	39,190	VC
Lincoln Memorial Univ	TN	28,430	C
Lincoln Univ	MO	14,402	NC
Lindenwood Univ	MO	25,760	C
Louisiana College	LA	21,274	C
McKendree Univ	IL	37,940	C+
McMurry Univ	TX	34,259	LC
Mercyhurst Univ	PA	47,420	C
Middle Tenn State Univ	TN	8,650	C
Midland Univ	NE	39,512	C
Minot State Univ	ND	13,285	C
Miss College	MS	25,850	C
Miss State Univ	MS	12,028	C+
Missouri Baptist Univ	MO	35,594	C
Missouri Southern State Univ	MO	13,071	C
Missouri State Univ	MO	15,837	C+
Montana State Univ-Northern	MT	11,370	NC
Morehead State Univ	KY	18,386	LC
Mount Vernon Nazarene Univ	OH	35,944	C
Nazareth College	NY	46,784	C
Niagara Univ	NY	41,010	C
Nicholls State Univ	LA	14,959	C
Norfolk State Univ	VA	18,902	LC
N Car A&T State Univ	NC	13,786	C
Northern Kentucky Univ	KY	16,486	C
Northern Mich Univ	MI	20,853	C
Northern State Univ	SD	15,570	C
Northwest Missouri State Univ	MO	18,286	C
Northwestern College of Iowa	IA	38,400	C
Northwestern Okla State Univ	OK	13,072	LC
Oakland City Univ	IN	33,930	NC
Oakwood Univ	AL	43,758	C
Oglala Lakota College	SD	15,050	NC
Ohio Univ	OH	23,394	VC
Okla Panhandle State Univ	OK	6,152	C
Okla Wesleyan Univ	OK	34,434	C
Oral Roberts Univ	OK	34,316	C
Ouachita Baptist Univ	AR	33,500	VC
Philander Smith College	AR	20,814	LC
Pontifical Catholic Univ of PR	PR	10,534	
Rider Univ	NJ	54,050	C
Robert Morris Univ	PA	40,600	C
Rust College	MS	10,600	C
SAGU American Indian College	AZ	18,142	C
St. Augustine's Univ	NC	25,582	C
St. Vincent College	PA	46,229	C
Salem State Univ	MA	42,650	LC
S Car State Univ	SC	21,330	LC
Southeastern Okla State Univ	OK	11,875	C
Southern Arkansas Univ	AR	21,532	C
Southern New Hampshire Univ	NH	44,256	C
Southern Univ at New Orleans	LA	8,014	LC
Southwestern Adventist Univ	TX	28,232	LC
St. Ambrose Univ	IA	40,180	C
St. Mary's Univ	TX	39,120	C
SUNY at Oswego	NY	22,219	VC
SUNY/Buffalo State	NY	20,583	LC
SUNY/Oneonta	NY	20,794	C
Suffolk Univ	MA	52,316	C
Tarleton State Univ	TX	15,248	LC
Texas A&M Univ at Commerce	TX	10,496	C
The Univ of Montana Western	MT	9,426	LC
Thomas College	ME	73,888	LC
Thomas More College	KY	36,720	LC
Trevecca Nazarene Univ	TN	31,186	C
Union College	NE	23,270	C
Univ of Arkansas at Fayetteville	AR	19,766	VC
Univ of Arkansas at Pine Bluff	AR	13,541	C
Univ of Central Florida	FL	16,379	VC
Univ of Central Missouri	MO	18,982	C
Univ of Cincinnati	OH	22,118	VC
Univ of Kentucky	KY	24,800	C+
Univ of Louisville	KY	19,692	C
Univ of Maine at Machias	ME	22,960	C
Univ of Maryland/Eastern Shore	MD	21,861	LC
Univ of Minn/Twin Cities	MN	24,269	MC
Univ of Nebr - Kearney	NE	17,014	LC
Univ of Nebr - Lincoln	NE	18,589	VC
Univ of North Alabama	AL	15,964	C
Univ of N Car at Greensboro	NC	15,998	C
Univ of N Dak	ND	16,673	C
Univ of Northern Iowa	IA	17,480	C
Univ of Pittsburgh at Bradford	PA	22,958	C
Univ of Rio Grande & Rio Grande Community College	OH	8,750	LC
Univ of South Florida/Tampa	FL	16,110	VC
Univ of Southern Miss	MS	13,170	C
Univ of the Ozarks	AR	31,050	NC
Univ of Toledo	OH	19,336	C
Univ of Wisc-Whitewater	WI	13,976	C
Utah State Univ	UT	13,235	C
Valley City State Univ	ND	13,267	C
Vermont Technical College	VT	25,370	C
Virginia Polytechnic Inst and State Univ	VA	21,920	VC
Virginia State Univ	VA	19,802	C+
Virginia Union Univ	VA	25,058	C
Viterbo Univ	WI	34,660	C
Walla Walla Univ	WA	34,845	C
Warner Univ	FL	28,216	C
Wayland Baptist Univ	TX	23,460	LC
Weber State Univ	UT	14,112	C
West Texas A&M Univ	TX	13,478	C
Western Kentucky Univ	KY	16,850	C
Western Mich Univ	MI	21,791	C
Western New Mexico Univ	NM	16,914	LC
Wiley College	TX	19,255	C
Winona State Univ	MN	18,109	C
Wright State Univ	OH	16,983	C

BUSINESS INFORMATION SYSTEMS

School	ST	$IS	SR
Ashford Univ	CA	10,480	C
Bentley Univ	MA	63,720	MC
Biola Univ	CA	48,686	C
Bloomfield College	NJ	40,100	LC
Bradley Univ	IL	43,240	VC
CUNY/Brooklyn College	NY	7,163	C+
East Central Univ	OK	13,330	C
Eastern Conn State Univ	CT	23,059	C
Faulkner Univ	AL	26,410	C
Illinois State Univ	IL	23,418	VC
Kent State Univ	OH	20,928	C
Lehigh Univ	PA	63,860	MC
Montana Tech of the Univ of Montana	MT	15,447	VC
Northern Kentucky Univ	KY	16,486	C
Okla Baptist Univ	OK	33,990	C
Point Loma Nazarene Univ	CA	46,150	C+
Rochester Inst of Technology	NY	52,734	HC+
San Jose State Univ	CA	22,630	C
Stetson Univ	FL	57,174	VC+
Stevenson Univ	MD	48,412	C
Tenn Wesleyan Univ	TN	32,680	LC
Texas Christian Univ	TX	57,120	HC
The Master's Univ	CA	43,870	C
Univ of Arkansas at Fayetteville	AR	19,766	VC
Univ of Illinois at Chicago	IL	24,664	VC
Univ of Kansas	KS	20,884	VC
Univ of Mary Hardin-Baylor	TX	35,292	C+
Univ of Pittsburgh	PA	30,030	MC

BUSINESS INSTITUTIONS

School	ST	$IS	SR
Univ of Rhode Island	RI	26,066	VC

BUSINESS INTELLIGENCE AND ANALYTICS

School	ST	$IS	SR
Arkansas Tech Univ	AR	16,534	LC
Clarkson Univ	NY	60,392	VC
College of St. Mary	NE	27,500	C
College of William & Mary	VA	34,907	MC
Cornell College	IA	49,900	VC
Creighton Univ	NE	49,452	VC
Drexel Univ	PA	65,927	HC
Hofstra Univ	NY	58,210	C+
Husson Univ	ME	26,508	C
La Salle Univ	PA	43,476	C
Loyola Univ New Orleans	LA	52,456	VC
Marian Univ	IN	43,206	C
Murray State Univ	KY	17,726	C+
Old Dominion Univ	VA	21,618	C
Purdue Univ Northwest	IN	15,178	C

ST = STATE $IS = IN-STATE COSTS SR = SELECTOR RATING

School	ST	$IS	SR
St. Mary's Univ of Minn	MN	42,440	C
Stetson Univ	FL	57,174	VC+
Trinity Univ	TX	54,480	MC
Univ of Conn	CT	27,394	
Univ of Kansas	KS	20,884	VC
Valparaiso Univ	IN	50,160	VC
Western Mich Univ	MI	21,791	C
Xavier Univ	OH	49,380	VC

BUSINESS LAW

School	ST	$IS	SR
Adams State Univ	CO	15,420	LC
Cal State, Fresno	CA	16,902	LC
Hofstra Univ	NY	58,210	C+
Lamar Univ	TX	18,014	LC
New York Univ	NY	68,139	MC
Ohio Univ	OH	23,394	VC
Peirce College	PA	16,780	NC
Roger Williams Univ	RI	48,074	VC
Warner Univ	FL	28,216	C
Washington State Univ	WA	22,747	C
West Virginia Univ	WV	18,952	VC
Western Carolina Univ	NC	13,965	C
Western Mich Univ	MI	21,791	C

BUSINESS LEADERSHIP

School	ST	$IS	SR
Ashford Univ	CA	10,480	C
Louisiana College	LA	21,274	C
Miami Univ	OH	27,190	HC+

BUSINESS MANAGEMENT

School	ST	$IS	SR
Bentley Univ	MA	63,720	MC
Brewton-Parker College	GA	26,120	LC
Clayton State Univ	GA	19,735	LC
College of St. Scholastica	MN	45,734	C+
DePaul Univ	IL	52,807	VC
East Stroudsburg Univ	PA	18,578	LC
Rochester Inst of Technology	NY	52,734	HC+
Thomas Univ	GA	21,420	NC
Univ of Arkansas at Fayetteville	AR	19,766	VC
Wartburg College	IA	49,478	C
Wentworth Inst of Technology	MA	48,810	VC
West Chester Univ of Pennsylvania	PA	19,171	VC

BUSINESS STATISTICS

School	ST	$IS	SR
Baylor Univ	TX	56,803	HC
Cal State, Fullerton	CA	21,902	C
The Univ of Texas at San Antonio	TX	21,060	C
Univ of Denver	CO	61,129	VC+
Univ of PR-Rio Piedras campus	PR	13,327	
Washington State Univ	WA	22,747	C

BUSINESS SYSTEMS ANALYSIS

School	ST	$IS	SR
Baylor Univ	TX	56,803	HC
CUNY/Brooklyn College	NY	7,163	C+
Cornell College	IA	49,900	VC
Eastern Mich Univ	MI	19,761	C
Elizabethtown College	PA	56,340	VC
Husson Univ	ME	26,508	C
Johnson State College	VT	22,672	C
Louisiana Tech Univ	LA	11,422	VC
Montana Tech of the Univ of Montana	MT	15,447	VC
Oregon State Univ	OR	23,337	VC
Rochester Inst of Technology	NY	52,734	HC+
Stevenson Univ	MD	48,412	C
Texas A&M Univ at College Station	TX	20,771	VC+
The Univ of Tenn at Knoxville	TN	22,112	VC
Univ of Findlay	OH	43,040	C

CANADIAN STUDIES

School	ST	$IS	SR
Duke Univ	NC	68,298	MC
St. Lawrence Univ	NY	66,646	HC+
SUNY/Plattsburgh	NY	19,314	C
Univ of Washington	WA	23,091	MC
Western Washington Univ	WA	18,904	VC

CARDIAC SONOGRAPHY

School	ST	$IS	SR
Piedmont College	GA	34,334	C
St. Mary's Univ of Minn	MN	42,440	C
Thomas Edison State Univ	NJ	6,350	NC
Weber State Univ	UT	14,112	C

CAREER, TECHNICAL EDUCATION & TRAINING

School	ST	$IS	SR
Cal State, Fullerton	CA	21,902	C
Temple Univ	PA	24,392	C+
Univ of Arkansas at Fayetteville	AR	19,766	VC
Univ of Idaho	ID	16,158	C
Univ of Wisc-Stout	WI	19,667	C
Wright State Univ	OH	16,983	C

CARIBBEAN STUDIES

School	ST	$IS	SR
CUNY/Brooklyn College	NY	7,163	C+
Emory Univ	GA	63,286	MC
Florida State Univ	FL	16,771	HC
Gettysburg College	PA	65,210	MC
Hofstra Univ	NY	58,210	C+
Pitzer College	CA	68,500	HC+
SUNY Albany	NY	22,165	C
SUNY at Binghamton	NY	24,100	MC
Union College	NY	64,320	MC
Univ of Mich/Ann Arbor	MI	25,274	MC
Univ of N Car at Greensboro	NC	15,998	C

CARTOGRAPHY

School	ST	$IS	SR
East Central Univ	OK	13,330	C
Salem State Univ	MA	42,650	LC
Texas State Univ	TX	18,721	C
Univ of Wisc-Madison	WI	21,647	MC

CELL & MOLECULAR BIOLOGY

School	ST	$IS	SR
Bradley Univ	IL	43,240	VC
Bryant Univ	RI	57,204	VC
Cal State, Fullerton	CA	21,902	C
Christopher Newport Univ	VA	24,878	VC+
Colo State Univ	CO	23,033	C
Fort Lewis College	CO	20,154	C
Indiana Univ of Pennsylvania	PA	24,474	C
King Univ	TN	36,976	C
Kutztown Univ of Pennsylvania	PA	19,477	C
MCPHS Univ	MA	45,470	SP
Texas Tech Univ	TX	20,156	C+
Univ of Georgia	GA	21,878	HC
Univ of Maryland/Baltimore County	MD	23,004	VC
Univ of Rhode Island	RI	26,066	VC
West Chester Univ of Pennsylvania	PA	19,171	VC

CELL BIOLOGY

School	ST	$IS	SR
Adams State Univ	CO	15,420	LC
Auburn Univ	AL	24,300	VC+
Augusta Univ	GA	4,632	C
Beloit College	WI	55,206	HC
Bucknell Univ	PA	67,136	MC
Cal State, Long Beach	CA	18,850	C
Canisius College	NY	49,672	C
Dallas Baptist Univ	TX	35,220	VC
Florida State Univ	FL	16,771	HC
Grand Valley State Univ	MI	22,250	C+
Hope College	MI	42,840	VC
Huntingdon College	AL	35,900	C
John Carroll Univ	OH	51,570	C
Johnson State College	VT	22,672	C
Marshall Univ	WV	18,044	C
Missouri State Univ	MO	15,837	C+
Montana State Univ	MT	15,500	C+
New York Univ	NY	68,139	MC
Ohio Univ	OH	23,394	VC
Okla City Univ	OK	40,476	C
Okla State Univ	OK	17,180	C+
Purdue Univ/West Lafayette	IN	20,032	MC
Rutgers Univ - New Brunswick	NJ	27,090	HC
San Francisco State Univ	CA	18,514	LC
Seattle Univ	WA	54,957	VC
SUNY at Binghamton	NY	24,100	MC
The Univ of Arizona	AZ	24,086	C
The Univ of Montana Western	MT	9,426	LC
Tulane Univ	LA	67,496	MC
Univ of Calif at Irvine	CA	33,857	VC
Univ of Calif at Los Angeles	CA	27,438	HC+
Univ of Calif at Riverside	CA	32,912	C
Univ of Calif at Santa Barbara	CA	30,627	HC+
Univ of Calif, Santa Cruz	CA	28,731	C+
Univ of Georgia	GA	21,878	HC
Univ of Illinois at Urbana-Champaign	IL	27,006	HC
Univ of Mich/Ann Arbor	MI	25,274	MC
Univ of Minn/Duluth	MN	20,292	C
Univ of Puget Sound	WA	60,210	HC
Univ of Rochester	NY	65,032	MC
Washington & Jefferson College	PA	58,694	VC
Washington State Univ	WA	22,747	C
West Chester Univ of Pennsylvania	PA	19,171	VC
Western Washington Univ	WA	18,904	VC

CELTIC STUDIES

School	ST	$IS	SR
Bard College	NY	65,924	HC
Univ of Calif at Berkeley	CA	29,886	MC

CERAMIC ART AND DESIGN

School	ST	$IS	SR
Adams State Univ	CO	15,420	LC
Alfred Univ	NY	37,490	C
Andrews Univ	MI	41,732	C
Aquinas College - Mich	MI	38,876	VC
Arcadia Univ	PA	55,990	C+
Bennington College	VT	66,280	MC
Calif College of the Arts	CA	52,758	SP
Cal State, San Bernardino	CA	20,106	C
Cleveland Inst of Art	OH	51,455	SP
College for Creative Studies	MI	51,210	SP
Columbia College - Missouri	MO	28,179	C
Hofstra Univ	NY	58,210	C+
Howard Univ	DC	37,616	C+
Indiana Wesleyan Univ	IN	33,674	C
Kansas City Art Inst	MO	48,200	SP
Kutztown Univ of Pennsylvania	PA	19,477	C
Marshall Univ	WV	18,044	C
Maryland Inst College of Art	MD	58,740	SP
Marywood Univ	PA	47,840	C
Mass College of Art and Design	MA	24,800	SP
Northland College	WI	41,103	C+
Ohio Northern Univ	OH	44,050	VC
Ohio Univ	OH	23,394	VC
Rhode Island School of Design	RI	59,960	SP
Rochester Inst of Technology	NY	52,734	HC+
School of the Art Inst of Chicago	IL	61,830	SP
Shawnee State Univ	OH	16,998	C
Syracuse Univ	NY	62,313	HC
Temple Univ	PA	24,392	C+
The Catholic Univ of America	DC	58,376	VC
Univ of Dallas	TX	50,676	VC
Univ of Hartford	CT	49,776	C
Univ of Iowa	IA	19,415	HC
Univ of Kansas	KS	20,884	VC
Univ of Mass Dartmouth	MA	26,507	C
Univ of Miami	FL	63,494	MC
Univ of Mich/Ann Arbor	MI	25,274	MC
Univ of Oregon	OR	24,021	VC
Washington Univ in St. Louis	MO	67,539	MC
Webster Univ	MO	37,490	C
Western Washington Univ	WA	18,904	VC

CERAMIC ENGINEERING

School	ST	$IS	SR
Alfred Univ	NY	37,490	C
Clemson Univ	SC		HC
Missouri Univ of Science and Technology	MO	18,655	HC
Univ of Illinois at Urbana-Champaign	IL	27,006	HC
Univ of Washington	WA	23,091	MC

CERAMIC SCIENCE

School	ST	$IS	SR
Maine College of Art	ME	45,940	SP
Rutgers Univ - New Brunswick	NJ	27,090	HC

CHEMICAL BIOTECHNOLOGY

School	ST	$IS	SR
East Stroudsburg Univ	PA	18,578	LC
Missouri Western State Univ	MO	17,822	LC

CHEMICAL ENGINEERING

School	ST	$IS	SR
Arizona State Univ at the Tempe Campus	AZ	23,001	VC
Auburn Univ	AL	24,300	VC+
Brigham Young Univ	UT	13,248	MC
Brown Univ	RI	64,566	MC
Bucknell Univ	PA	67,136	MC
Calif Baptist Univ	CA	42,986	C
Calif Inst of Technology	CA	64,704	MC
Calif State Polytechnic Univ, Pomona	CA	21,811	C
Cal State, Fullerton	CA	21,902	C
Cal State, Long Beach	CA	18,850	C
Calvin College	MI	43,090	HC
Carnegie Mellon Univ	PA	67,980	MC
Case Western Reserve Univ	OH	62,284	MC
Christian Brothers Univ	TN	31,670	VC
CUNY/City College	NY	20,204	C
Clarkson Univ	NY	60,392	VC
Clemson Univ	SC		HC
Cleveland State Univ	OH	22,290	C
Colo School of Mines	CO	29,319	MC
Colo State Univ	CO	23,033	C
Columbia Univ/City of New York	NY	62,958	MC
Cooper Union for the Advancement of Science and Art	NY	61,370	MC
Cornell Univ	NY	67,591	MC
Delaware State Univ	DE	19,376	LC
Dordt College	IA	37,860	C+
Drexel Univ	PA	65,927	HC
Elon Univ	NC	46,142	HC
Florida A&M Univ	FL	15,361	C
Florida Inst of Technology	FL	53,306	VC
Florida State Univ	FL	16,771	HC
Gannon Univ	PA	42,922	C
Geneva College	PA	35,450	C
Georgia Inst of Technology	GA	23,910	MC
Hampton Univ	VA	36,410	C
Howard Univ	DC	37,616	C+
Illinois Inst of Technology	IL	56,826	HC+
Iowa State Univ	IA	18,176	C
Johns Hopkins Univ	MD	68,080	MC
Kansas State Univ	KS	17,780	VC
Lafayette College	PA	68,520	MC
Lamar Univ	TX	18,014	LC
Lehigh Univ	PA	63,860	MC
Louisiana State Univ and A&M College	LA	18,677	VC
Louisiana Tech Univ	LA	11,422	VC
Manhattan College	NY	55,652	C
Mass Inst of Technology	MA	62,662	MC
Miami Univ	OH	27,190	HC+
Mich State Univ	MI	24,542	VC
Mich Tech Univ	MI	25,551	VC+
Miss State Univ	MS	12,028	C+
Missouri Univ of Science and Technology	MO	18,655	HC
Montana State Univ	MT	15,500	C+
New Jersey Inst of Technology	NJ	30,198	HC
New Mexico Inst of Mining and Technology	NM	15,385	HC+
New Mexico State Univ	NM	14,050	LC
New York Univ	NY	68,139	MC
N Car A&T State Univ	NC	13,786	C
N Car State Univ	NC	22,434	HC+
Northeastern Univ	MA	65,352	MC
Northwestern Univ	IL	68,725	MC
Ohio State Univ at Columbus	OH	22,843	MC
Ohio Univ	OH	23,394	VC
Okla State Univ	OK	17,180	C+
Olivet Nazarene Univ	IL	41,840	VC
Oregon State Univ	OR	23,337	VC
Pennsylvania State Univ - Univ Park	PA	29,716	HC
Prairie View A&M Univ	TX	27,273	LC
Princeton Univ	NJ	60,090	MC
Purdue Univ/West Lafayette	IN	20,032	MC
Rensselaer Polytechnic Inst	NY	67,265	MC
Rice Univ	TX	59,458	MC
Rochester Inst of Technology	NY	52,734	HC+
Rose-Hulman Inst of Technology	IN	59,823	MC
Rowan Univ	NJ	24,491	VC
Rutgers Univ - New Brunswick	NJ	27,090	HC
San Jose State Univ	CA	22,630	C
S Dak School of Mines and Technology	SD	18,570	C+
Southwestern College	KS	31,531	LC
Stanford Univ	CA	62,541	MC
SUNY/The College of Environmental Science and Forestry	NY	23,728	VC
SUNY/Univ at Buffalo	NY	23,122	C
Stevens Inst of Technology	NJ	64,954	MC
Stony Brook Univ/The SUNY	NY	22,703	MC
Syracuse Univ	NY	62,313	HC
Tenn Tech Univ	TN	17,929	C
Texas A&M Univ at College Station	TX	20,771	VC+
Texas A&M Univ at Kingsville	TX	16,580	LC
Texas Tech Univ	TX	20,156	C+
The Univ of Akron	OH	22,566	C
The Univ of Alabama	AL	24,320	C+
The Univ of Arizona	AZ	24,086	C
The Univ of Tenn at Chattanooga	TN	17,340	C+
The Univ of Tenn at Knoxville	TN	22,112	VC
The Univ of Texas at Austin	TX	20,206	MC
The Univ of Utah	UT	18,751	VC
Trine Univ	IN	41,310	C
Tufts Univ	MA		MC
Tulane Univ	LA	67,496	MC
Tuskegee Univ	AL	28,164	C
Universidad Politecnica de PR, Hato Rey campus	PR	23,514	
Univ of Alabama in Huntsville	AL	20,028	VC
Univ of Arkansas at Fayetteville	AR	19,766	VC
Univ of Calif at Berkeley	CA	29,886	MC
Univ of Calif at Davis	CA	28,468	HC
Univ of Calif at Irvine	CA	33,857	VC
Univ of Calif at Los Angeles	CA	27,438	HC+
Univ of Calif at Riverside	CA	32,912	C
Univ of Calif at Santa Barbara	CA	30,627	HC+
Univ of Calif San Diego	CA	30,450	MC
Univ of Cincinnati	OH	22,118	VC
Univ of Colo Boulder	CO	26,048	HC
Univ of Conn	CT	27,394	
Univ of Dayton	OH	54,930	VC
Univ of Delaware	DE	32,214	VC
Univ of Florida	FL	16,291	HC+
Univ of Houston	TX	21,871	VC
Univ of Idaho	ID	16,158	C
Univ of Illinois at Chicago	IL	24,664	VC
Univ of Illinois at Urbana-Champaign	IL	27,006	HC
Univ of Iowa	IA	19,415	HC
Univ of Kansas	KS	20,884	VC
Univ of Kentucky	KY	24,800	C+
Univ of Louisiana at Lafayette	LA	14,516	C
Univ of Louisville	KY	19,692	C
Univ of Maine	ME	21,038	VC
Univ of Maryland/Baltimore County	MD	23,004	VC
Univ of Maryland/College Park	MD	21,938	HC
Univ of Mass Amherst	MA	27,669	HC
Univ of Mass Lowell	MA	27,296	VC

ST = STATE $IS = IN-STATE COSTS SR = SELECTOR RATING

School	ST	$IS	SR
Univ of Mich/Ann Arbor	MI	25,274	MC
Univ of Minn/Duluth	MN	20,292	C
Univ of Minn/Twin Cities	MN	24,269	MC
Univ of Miss	MS	18,802	C
Univ of Missouri-Columbia	MO	20,463	VC
Univ of Nebr - Lincoln	NE	18,589	VC
Univ of Nevada, Reno	NV	18,010	C
Univ of New Hampshire	NH	29,333	VC
Univ of New Haven	CT	53,680	C
Univ of New Mexico	NM	16,808	C
Univ of N Dak	ND	16,673	C
Univ of Notre Dame	IN	68,801	MC
Univ of Okla	OK	19,651	HC
Univ of Pennsylvania	PA	63,526	MC
Univ of Pittsburgh	PA	30,030	MC
Univ of PR, at Mayaguez	PR	13,995	
Univ of Rhode Island	RI	26,066	VC
Univ of Rochester	NY	65,032	MC
Univ of South Alabama	AL	16,880	C
Univ of S Car at Columbia	SC	21,726	VC
Univ of South Florida/Tampa	FL	16,110	VC
Univ of Southern Calif	CA	66,631	MC
Univ of Toledo	OH	19,336	C
Univ of Tulsa	OK	52,625	HC
Univ of Virginia	VA	27,367	MC
Univ of Washington	WA	23,091	MC
Univ of Wisc-Madison	WI	21,647	MC
Univ of Wyoming	WY	15,537	C
Vanderbilt Univ	TN	63,248	MC
Villanova Univ	PA	64,922	MC
Virginia Commonwealth Univ	VA	23,811	VC
Virginia Polytechnic Inst and State Univ	VA	21,920	VC
Washington and Lee Univ	VA	59,647	MC
Washington State Univ	WA	22,747	C
Washington Univ in St. Louis	MO	67,539	MC
Wayne State Univ	MI	23,085	C
West Virginia Univ	WV	18,952	VC
West Virginia Univ Inst of Technology	WV	18,264	C
Western Kentucky Univ	KY	16,850	C
Western Mich Univ	MI	21,791	C
Widener Univ	PA	58,190	C
Worcester Polytechnic Inst	MA	62,846	MC
Yale Univ	CT	64,650	MC
Youngstown State Univ	OH	17,487	C

CHEMICAL ENGINEERING TECHNOLOGY

School	ST	$IS	SR
Purdue Univ/West Lafayette	IN	20,032	MC
Univ of PR, at Arecibo	PR	12,652	
Univ of Calif San Diego	CA	30,450	MC
Univ of Hartford	CT	49,776	C

CHEMICAL PHYSICS

School	ST	$IS	SR
Adams State Univ	CO	15,420	LC
Augustana Univ	SD	39,968	VC
Bowdoin College	ME	65,980	MC
Brown Univ	RI	64,566	MC
Cal State, Fullerton	CA	21,902	C
Centre College	KY	50,680	MC
Hamilton College	NY	64,250	MC
Hendrix College	AR	54,020	VC
Maryville College	TN	44,410	C
Mich State Univ	MI	24,542	VC
Reed College	OR	65,300	MC
Saginaw Valley State Univ	MI	19,284	C
San Diego State Univ	CA	23,156	VC
Swarthmore College	PA	63,550	MC
The Catholic Univ of America	DC	58,376	VC

CHEMICAL TECHNOLOGY

School	ST	$IS	SR
Florida State Univ	FL	16,771	HC
Inter-American Univ of PR Ponce	PR	19,549	
Inter-American Univ of PR-Arecibo Campus	PR	18,245	
Inter-American Univ of PR-Bayamon	PR	18,785	
Inter-American Univ of PR-Fajardo Campus	PR	18,336	
Midwestern State Univ	TX	12,111	LC
Univ of Cincinnati	OH	22,118	VC

CHEMISTRY

School	ST	$IS	SR
Abilene Christian Univ	TX	43,708	C+
Adams State Univ	CO	15,420	LC
Adelphi Univ	NY	49,792	C
Adrian College	MI	45,550	C
Agnes Scott College	GA	51,930	VC+
Alabama A&M Univ	AL	18,796	C
Alabama State Univ	AL	16,490	LC
Albany State Univ	GA	19,462	C
Albion College	MI	55,260	C
Albright College	PA	57,326	C
Alcorn State Univ	MS	15,884	C
Alderson Broaddus Univ	WV	35,000	LC
Alfred Univ	NY	37,490	C
Allegheny College	PA	57,620	VC
Alma College	MI	49,410	VC
Alvernia Univ	PA	45,330	C
Alverno College	WI	33,294	LC
American International College	MA	47,020	LC
Amherst College	MA	66,186	MC
Anderson Univ	IN	39,450	C
Andrews Univ	MI	41,732	C
Angelo State Univ	TX	15,882	LC
Appalachian State Univ	NC	15,394	VC
Aquinas College - Mich	MI	38,876	VC
Arcadia Univ	PA	55,990	C+
Arizona State Univ at the Tempe Campus	AZ	23,001	VC
Arkansas State Univ	AR	16,190	C
Arkansas Tech Univ	AR	16,534	LC
Armstrong State Univ	GA	15,615	C
Asbury Univ	KY	36,450	C+
Ashland Univ	OH	30,446	C
Assumption College	MA	48,455	VC
Auburn Univ	AL	24,300	VC+
Auburn Univ at Montgomery	AL	15,000	C
Augsburg Univ	MN	45,129	C
Augusta Univ	GA	4,632	C
Augustana College	IL	51,222	VC+
Augustana Univ	SD	39,968	VC
Austin College	TX	51,059	HC
Austin Peay State Univ	TN	16,397	C
Averett Univ	VA	43,034	LC
Avila Univ	MO	27,100	C
Azusa Pacific Univ	CA	43,972	C
Baker Univ	KS	37,190	C
Baldwin Wallace Univ	OH	42,464	VC
Ball State Univ	IN	19,808	C+
Bard College	NY	65,924	HC
Bard College at Simon's Rock	MA	65,795	MC
Barnard College/Columbia Univ	NY	68,762	MC
Barry Univ	FL	38,730	LC
Barton College	NC	39,854	C
Bates College	ME	64,500	HC
Bayamon Central Univ	PR	12,490	
Baylor Univ	TX	56,803	HC
Belhaven Univ	MS	32,250	C
Bellarmine Univ	KY	52,532	C
Belmont Univ	TN	44,500	VC+
Beloit College	WI	55,206	HC
Bemidji State Univ	MN	17,730	C
Benedict College	SC	28,630	NC
Benedictine College	KS	38,850	VC
Benedictine Univ	IL	38,300	C
Bennett College	NC	27,717	NC
Bennington College	VT	66,280	MC
Berea College	KY	7,094	C
Berry College	GA	47,466	VC
Bethany College	KS	38,637	LC
Bethany College	WV	38,774	LC
Bethel College	IN	36,830	C
Bethel College	KS	35,370	C
Bethel Univ	MN	46,550	C+
Bethel Univ	TN	27,142	C
Bethune-Cookman Univ	FL	23,322	C
Biola Univ	CA	48,686	C
Birmingham-Southern College	AL	44,478	C+
Black Hills State Univ	SD	16,622	C
Blackburn College	IL	28,526	LC
Bloomfield College	NJ	40,100	LC
Bloomsburg Univ of Pennsylvania	PA	19,930	C
Bluefield College	VA	34,711	C
Bluffton Univ	OH	40,950	C+
Boise State Univ	ID	17,368	C
Boston College	MA	68,043	MC
Boston Univ	MA	67,352	MC
Bowdoin College	ME	65,980	MC
Bowling Green State Univ	OH	19,975	C
Bradley Univ	IL	43,240	VC
Brandeis Univ	MA	68,443	MC
Brescia Univ	KY	29,890	VC
Briar Cliff Univ	IA	36,956	C
Bridgewater College	VA	46,260	C
Bridgewater State Univ	MA	22,762	C
Brigham Young Univ	UT	13,248	MC
Brown Univ	RI	64,566	MC
Bryn Mawr College	PA	65,220	MC
Bucknell Univ	PA	67,136	MC
Buena Vista Univ	IA	42,344	C
Butler Univ	IN	52,890	VC+
Cabrini Univ	PA	42,591	LC
Caldwell Univ	NJ	42,165	LC
Calif Baptist Univ	CA	42,986	C
Calif Inst of Technology	CA	64,704	MC
Calif Lutheran Univ	CA	52,853	C
Calif Polytechnic State Univ	CA	22,547	MC
Calif State Polytechnic Univ, Pomona	CA	21,811	C
Cal State, Bakersfield	CA	22,397	LC
Cal State, Chico	CA	19,790	VC
Cal State, Dominguez Hills	CA	19,022	LC
Cal State, East Bay	CA	20,748	C
Cal State, Fresno	CA	16,902	LC
Cal State, Fullerton	CA	21,902	C
Cal State, Long Beach	CA	18,850	C
Cal State, Los Angeles	CA	17,186	LC
Cal State, Northridge	CA	17,277	LC
Cal State, Sacramento	CA	19,060	C
Cal State, San Bernardino	CA	20,106	C
Cal State, San Marcos	CA	20,604	LC
Cal State, Stanislaus	CA	18,053	LC
Calif Univ of Pennsylvania	PA	20,425	LC
Calvin College	MI	43,090	HC
Cameron Univ	OK	11,632	LC
Campbell Univ	NC	37,570	VC
Campbellsville Univ	KY	33,400	C
Canisius College	NY	49,672	C
Capital Univ	OH	44,778	VC
Cardinal Stritch Univ	WI	37,136	C
Carleton College	MN	66,414	MC
Carlow Univ	PA	39,696	LC
Carnegie Mellon Univ	PA	67,980	MC
Carroll College	MT	44,304	C
Carroll Univ	WI	38,100	C+
Carthage College	WI	48,835	C
Case Western Reserve Univ	OH	62,284	MC
Castleton Univ	VT	20,186	C
Catawba College	NC	39,820	LC
Cedar Crest College	PA	51,110	C
Cedarville Univ	OH	36,244	VC
Centenary College of Louisiana	LA	49,050	C+
Central College	IA	44,592	C
Central Conn State Univ	CT	22,041	C
Central Methodist Univ	MO	31,500	VC
Central Mich Univ	MI	20,330	C
Central State Univ	OH	18,564	C
Central Washington Univ	WA	16,803	C
Centre College	KY	50,680	MC
Chadron State College	NE	14,819	LC
Chapman Univ	CA	65,504	HC
Charleston Southern Univ	SC	34,700	C
Chatham Univ	PA	47,883	VC
Chestnut Hill College	PA	47,180	C
Cheyney Univ of Pennsylvania	PA	20,896	LC
Chicago State Univ	IL	41,620	C
Christian Brothers Univ	TN	31,670	VC
Christopher Newport Univ	VA	24,878	VC+
CUNY/Brooklyn College	NY	7,163	C+
CUNY/City College	NY	20,204	C
CUNY/Hunter College	NY	31,098	VC
CUNY/Lehman College	NY	5,788	LC
CUNY/Queens College	NY	21,507	C
CUNY/York College	NY	6,747	LC
Claflin Univ	SC	25,592	LC
Claremont McKenna College	CA	69,900	MC
Clarion Univ of Pennsylvania	PA	21,608	LC
Clark Atlanta Univ	GA	31,019	LC
Clark Univ	MA	53,260	HC+
Clarke Univ	IA	42,950	C
Clarkson Univ	NY	60,392	VC
Clayton State Univ	GA	19,735	LC
Clemson Univ	SC		HC
Cleveland State Univ	OH	22,290	C
Coastal Carolina Univ	SC	20,340	C
Coe College	IA	51,570	VC
Coker College	SC	38,196	C
Colby College	ME	64,060	MC
Colgate Univ	NY	67,500	MC
College of Charleston	SC	24,046	VC
College of Mount St. Vincent	NY	45,620	C
College of St. Benedict	MN	54,480	C
College of St. Elizabeth	NJ	45,700	LC
College of St. Mary	NE	27,500	C
College of St. Scholastica	MN	45,734	C+
College of Staten Island	NY	24,389	LC
College of the Holy Cross	MA	64,320	MC
College of the Ozarks	MO	7,530	VC
College of William & Mary	VA	34,907	MC
Colo College	CO	64,894	MC
Colo Mesa Univ	CO	19,707	LC
Colo School of Mines	CO	29,319	MC
Colo State Univ	CO	23,033	C
Colo State Univ-Pueblo	CO	21,581	C
Columbia College	SC	36,550	C
Columbia College - Missouri	MO	28,179	C
Columbia Univ/ School of General Studies	NY	61,470	MC
Columbia Univ/City of New York	NY	62,958	MC
Columbus State Univ	GA	14,336	LC
Concord Univ	WV	14,954	LC
Concordia College - Moorhead	MN	46,418	C
Concordia Univ	OR	35,000	C
Concordia Univ Irvine	CA	44,860	VC
Concordia Univ Nebr	NE	41,900	VC
Concordia Univ, Ann Arbor	MI	38,878	C+
Concordia Univ, Chicago	IL	41,522	C
Conn College	CT	65,000	MC
Converse College	SC	28,290	C
Coppin State Univ	MD	14,071	VC
Cornell College	IA	49,900	VC
Cornerstone Univ	MI	36,550	C
Covenant College	GA	44,590	HC
Creighton Univ	NE	49,452	VC
Culver-Stockton College	MO	34,350	C
Dartmouth College	NH	68,109	MC
Davidson College	NC	60,119	MC
Davis & Elkins College	WV	38,242	LC
Delaware State Univ	DE	19,376	LC
Delaware Valley Univ	PA	51,271	C
Delta State Univ	MS	13,176	LC
Denison Univ	OH	62,770	HC+
DePaul Univ	IL	52,807	VC
DePauw Univ	IN	58,688	VC
DeSales Univ	PA	47,520	C
Dickinson College	PA	66,166	MC
Dickinson State Univ	ND	12,372	LC
Dillard Univ	LA	20,940	VC
Doane Univ	NE	41,340	VC
Dominican Univ	IL	42,472	C+
Dordt College	IA	37,860	C+
Drake Univ	IA	49,220	HC
Drew Univ/College of Liberal Arts	NJ	53,608	VC
Drexel Univ	PA	65,927	HC
Drury Univ	MO	37,555	VC
Duke Univ	NC	68,298	MC
Duquesne Univ	PA	48,508	VC
Earlham College	IN	55,670	HC
East Carolina Univ	NC	16,539	C
East Central Univ	OK	13,330	C
East Stroudsburg Univ	PA	18,578	LC
East Tenn State Univ	TN	18,141	C
East Texas Baptist Univ	TX	34,444	C
Eastern Illinois Univ	IL	21,414	C
Eastern Kentucky Univ	KY	17,742	C
Eastern Mennonite Univ	VA	42,550	C
Eastern Mich Univ	MI	19,761	C
Eastern Nazarene College	MA	41,114	C
Eastern New Mexico Univ	NM	12,874	LC
Eastern Oregon Univ	OR	17,612	C
Eastern Univ	PA	39,540	C
Eastern Washington Univ	WA	17,896	LC
Eckerd College	FL	55,206	VC
Edgewood College	WI	35,950	C
Edinboro Univ	PA	15,940	LC
Elizabeth City State Univ	NC	14,745	C
Elizabethtown College	PA	56,340	VC
Elmhurst College	IL	46,514	C
Elmira College	NY	53,900	C
Elms College	MA	49,602	VC
Elon Univ	NC	46,142	HC
Emmanuel College	MA	53,472	C+
Emory and Henry College	VA	46,320	C
Emory Univ	GA	63,286	MC
Emporia State Univ	KS	15,029	C
Erskine College	SC	45,460	C
Eureka College	IL	34,760	C
Evangel Univ	MO	28,898	C
Excelsior College	NY	38,800	SP
Fairfield Univ	CT	61,445	HC
Fairleigh Dickinson Univ/ College at Florham	NJ	54,770	C
Fairleigh Dickinson Univ/ Metropolitan Campus	NJ	52,392	C
Fairmont State Univ	WV	15,726	C
Faulkner Univ	AL	26,410	C
Fayetteville State Univ	NC	17,756	C
Ferris State Univ	MI	21,458	C
Ferrum College	VA	43,970	C
Fisk Univ	TN	32,066	LC
Fitchburg State Univ	MA	21,819	LC
Florida A&M Univ	FL	15,361	C
Florida Atlantic Univ	FL	18,256	C
Florida Gulf Coast Univ	FL	14,738	C
Florida Inst of Technology	FL	53,306	VC
Florida International Univ	FL	20,281	C
Florida Memorial Univ	FL	22,424	LC
Florida Southern College	FL	45,978	VC
Florida State Univ	FL	16,771	HC
Fordham Univ	NY	68,431	MC
Fort Hays State Univ	KS	12,677	C
Fort Lewis College	CO	20,154	C
Fort Valley State Univ	GA	17,988	VC
Framingham State Univ	MA	21,740	C
Francis Marion Univ	SC	18,144	LC
Franciscan Univ of Steubenville	OH	33,980	VC
Franklin and Marshall College	PA	67,960	MC
Franklin College	IN	40,550	C
Freed-Hardeman Univ	TN	29,900	C
Fresno Pacific Univ	CA	38,858	C
Friends Univ	KS	38,000	C
Frostburg State Univ	MD	17,280	LC
Furman Univ	SC	61,098	VC+
Gallaudet Univ	DC	30,088	LC
Gannon Univ	PA	42,922	C
Gardner-Webb Univ	NC	24,935	C+
Geneva College	PA	35,450	C
George Fox Univ	OR	42,938	C
George Mason Univ	VA	19,884	C
Georgetown College	KY	41,440	C
Georgetown Univ	DC	68,970	MC
Georgia College & State Univ	GA	21,884	C+
Georgia Inst of Technology	GA	23,910	MC
Georgia Southern Univ	GA	16,540	VC
Georgia Southwestern State Univ	GA	13,870	LC
Georgia State Univ	GA	25,250	C
Georgian Court Univ	NJ	43,068	LC
Gettysburg College	PA	65,210	MC
Glenville State College	WV	17,386	LC
Gonzaga Univ	WA	52,880	HC
Gordon College	MA	47,740	VC
Goshen College	IN	44,350	C
Goucher College	MD	56,110	VC
Graceland Univ	IA	35,290	C
Grambling State Univ	LA	15,701	C
Grand Valley State Univ	MI	22,250	C+
Greensboro College	NC	39,790	LC
Greenville College	IL	27,012	LC
Grinnell College	IA	63,114	MC
Grove City College	PA	26,654	VC
Guilford College	NC	45,973	C
Gustavus Adolphus College	MN	53,943	HC
Hamilton College	NY	64,250	MC
Hamline Univ	MN	50,152	C

ST = STATE $IS = IN-STATE COSTS SR = SELECTOR RATING

School	ST	$IS	SR
Hampden-Sydney College	VA	57,806	VC
Hampshire College	MA	65,214	MC
Hampton Univ	VA	36,410	C
Hanover College	IN	47,750	C+
Harding Univ	AR	25,440	C
Hardin-Simmons Univ	TX	36,025	C
Hartwick College	NY	51,270	C
Harvard College/Harvard Univ	MA	65,609	MC
Harvey Mudd College	CA	67,155	MC
Hastings College	NE	35,380	C+
Haverford College	PA	66,490	MC
Hawaii Pacific Univ	HI	33,420	C
Heidelberg Univ	OH	40,400	LC
Henderson State Univ	AR	15,516	C
Hendrix College	AR	54,020	VC
High Point Univ	NC	47,355	VC
Hillsdale College	MI	37,170	MC
Hiram College	OH	44,590	C
Hobart and William Smith Colleges	NY	67,050	HC+
Hofstra Univ	NY	58,210	C+
Hollins Univ	VA	49,635	VC
Hood College	MD	50,540	C
Hope College	MI	42,840	VC
Houghton College	NY	40,558	VC
Houston Baptist Univ	TX	36,450	C
Howard Payne Univ	TX	35,994	C
Howard Univ	DC	37,616	C+
Humboldt State Univ	CA	21,708	C
Huntingdon College	AL	35,900	C
Huntington Univ	IN	33,996	C
Huston-Tillotson Univ	TX	18,124	LC
Idaho State Univ	ID	13,619	LC
Illinois College	IL	41,330	VC
Illinois Inst of Technology	IL	56,826	HC+
Illinois State Univ	IL	23,418	VC
Illinois Wesleyan Univ	IL	56,430	VC+
Immaculata Univ	PA	39,000	C
Indiana State Univ	IN	23,223	LC
Indiana Univ Bloomington	IN	20,791	HC
Indiana Univ Kokomo	IN	7,207	C
Indiana Univ Northwest	IN	7,207	LC
Indiana Univ of Pennsylvania	PA	24,474	C
Indiana Univ South Bend	IN	16,057	C
Indiana Univ Southeast	IN	16,931	C
Indiana Univ-Purdue Univ Fort Wayne	IN	18,675	C
Indiana Univ-Purdue Univ Indianapolis	IN	18,952	C
Indiana Wesleyan Univ	IN	33,674	C
Inter-American Univ of PR Ponce	PR	19,549	
Inter-American Univ of PR-Arecibo Campus	PR	18,245	
Inter-American Univ of PR-Bayamon	PR	18,785	
Inter-American Univ of PR-Fajardo Campus	PR	18,336	
Inter-American Univ of PR-Metropolitan Campus	PR	20,045	
Inter-American Univ of PR-San Germán	PR	20,042	
Iona College	NY	52,514	C
Iowa State Univ	IA	18,176	C
Iowa Wesleyan Univ	IA	41,000	C
Ithaca College	NY	58,158	VC+
Jackson State Univ	MS	15,879	LC
Jacksonville State Univ	AL	14,628	LC
Jacksonville Univ	FL	49,210	C
James Madison Univ	VA	19,084	VC
Jarvis Christian College	TX	20,160	NC
Jefferson (Philadelphia Univ + Thomas Jefferson Univ)	PA	53,966	C
John Brown Univ	AR	35,184	VC
John Carroll Univ	OH	51,570	C
Johns Hopkins Univ	MD	68,080	MC
Johnson C. Smith Univ	NC	25,336	LC
Judson College	AL	27,066	C
Judson Univ	IL	39,174	C
Juniata College	PA	58,118	VC
Kalamazoo College	MI	53,931	HC
Kansas State Univ	KS	17,780	VC
Kansas Wesleyan Univ	KS	37,930	C
Kean Univ	NJ	25,620	C
Keene State College	NH	24,604	C
Kennesaw State Univ	GA	18,899	VC
Kent State Univ	OH	20,928	C
Kentucky State Univ	KY	14,484	LC
Kentucky Wesleyan College	KY	34,260	LC
Kenyon College	OH	65,840	MC
Kettering Univ	MI	47,570	HC
King Univ	TN	36,976	C
King's College	PA	48,240	C
Knox College	IL	54,654	VC+
Kutztown Univ of Pennsylvania	PA	19,477	C
La Roche College	PA	38,940	C
La Salle Univ	PA	43,476	C
La Sierra Univ	CA	39,690	VC
Lafayette College	PA	68,520	MC
LaGrange College	GA	41,310	C
Lake Erie College	OH	38,914	LC
Lake Forest College	IL	50,652	VC
Lake Superior State Univ	MI	19,867	C
Lakeland Univ	WI	35,130	C
Lamar Univ	TX	18,014	LC
Lander Univ	SC	32,200	C
Lane College	TN	17,960	LC
Langston Univ	OK	15,659	C
Lawrence Tech Univ	MI	41,630	VC
Lawrence Univ	WI	56,133	HC+
Le Moyne College	NY	47,305	VC
Lebanon Valley College	PA	55,510	VC
Lee Univ	TN	22,045	C
Lehigh Univ	PA	63,860	MC
LeMoyne-Owen College	TN	16,980	C
Lenoir-Rhyne Univ	NC	47,500	LC
LeTourneau Univ	TX	39,190	VC
Lewis & Clark College	OR	60,984	MC
Lewis Univ	IL	41,710	C
Lewis-Clark State College	ID	14,202	C
Limestone College	SC	32,100	C
Lincoln Memorial Univ	TN	28,430	C
Lincoln Univ	MO	14,402	NC
Lincoln Univ	PA	20,878	LC
Lindenwood Univ	MO	25,760	C
Linfield College	OR	53,992	C
Lipscomb Univ	TN	42,984	VC
LIU Brooklyn	NY	50,698	C
LIU Post	NY	50,698	C+
Lock Haven Univ of Pennsylvania	PA	20,544	LC
Longwood Univ	VA	22,184	C
Loras College	IA	40,726	C
Louisiana College	LA	21,274	C
Louisiana State Univ and A&M College	LA	18,677	VC
Louisiana State Univ in Shreveport	LA	6,902	C
Louisiana Tech Univ	LA	11,422	VC
Loyola Marymount Univ	CA	60,202	VC+
Loyola Univ Chicago	IL	57,158	VC
Loyola Univ Maryland	MD	61,710	VC
Loyola Univ New Orleans	LA	52,456	VC
Lubbock Christian Univ	TX	29,727	C
Luther College	IA	49,990	VC
Lycoming College	PA	50,895	C
Lyon College	AR	36,120	VC
Macalester College	MN	64,136	MC
MacMurray College	IL	35,025	C
Madonna Univ	MI	30,450	LC
Malone Univ	OH	39,200	C
Manchester Univ	IN	41,540	C
Manhattan College	NY	55,652	C
Manhattanville College	NY	52,430	C
Mansfield Univ of Pennsylvania	PA	24,244	LC
Marian Univ	IN	43,206	C
Marian Univ	WI	34,622	C
Marietta College	OH	46,190	C
Marist College	NY	49,860	VC
Marlboro College	VT	50,832	VC+
Marquette Univ	WI	53,090	VC+
Mars Hill Univ	NC	41,104	C
Marshall Univ	WV	18,044	C
Martin Univ	IN	21,010	LC
Mary Baldwin Univ	VA	40,495	C
Marygrove College	MI	30,100	LC
Maryville College	TN	44,410	C
Maryville Univ of St. Louis	MO	38,558	VC
Mass College of Liberal Arts	MA	20,659	C
Mass Inst of Technology	MA	62,662	MC
Mayville State Univ	ND	18,371	NC
McDaniel College	MD	52,910	VC
McKendree Univ	IL	37,940	C+
McMurry Univ	TX	34,259	LC
McNeese State Univ	LA	7,838	C
McPherson College	KS	36,134	C
MCPHS Univ	MA	45,470	SP
Mercer Univ	GA	45,348	VC
Mercyhurst Univ	PA	47,420	C
Meredith College	NC	46,634	C
Merrimack College	MA	55,415	C
Messiah College	PA	44,380	VC
Methodist Univ	NC	58,130	C
Metropolitan State Univ of Denver	CO	6,928	LC
Miami Univ	OH	27,190	HC+
Mich State Univ	MI	24,542	VC
Mich Tech Univ	MI	25,551	VC+
MidAmerica Nazarene Univ	KS	37,808	C
Middle Tenn State Univ	TN	8,650	C
Middlebury College	VT	67,464	MC
Midland Univ	NE	39,512	C
Midway Univ	KY	33,940	LC
Midwestern State Univ	TX	12,111	LC
Miles College	AL	16,530	NC
Millersville Univ of Pennsylvania	PA	25,298	C
Milligan College	TN	39,450	C
Millikin Univ	IL	44,148	C
Mills College	CA	43,705	C
Millsaps College	MS	50,080	C+
Minn State Univ, Mankato	MN	17,190	C
Minn State Univ, Moorhead	MN	21,393	C
Minot State Univ	ND	13,285	C
Misericordia Univ	PA	45,210	C
Miss College	MS	25,850	C
Miss State Univ	MS	12,028	C+
Miss Univ for Women	MS	17,065	C
Miss Valley State Univ	MS	13,233	LC
Missouri Baptist Univ	MO	35,594	C
Missouri Southern State Univ	MO	13,071	C
Missouri State Univ	MO	15,837	C+
Missouri Univ of Science and Technology	MO	18,655	HC
Missouri Western State Univ	MO	17,822	LC
Monmouth College	IL	42,260	C
Monmouth Univ	NJ	50,184	C
Montana State Univ	MT	15,500	C+
Montana State Univ Billings	MT	13,336	LC
Montana State Univ-Northern	MT	11,370	NC
Montana Tech of the Univ of Montana	MT	15,447	VC
Montclair State Univ	NJ	26,912	C
Moravian College	PA	55,488	C
Morehead State Univ	KY	18,386	LC
Morehouse College	GA	40,835	C
Morgan State Univ	MD	17,190	LC
Morningside College	IA	39,780	C
Mount Holyoke College	MA	56,746	MC
Mount Marty College	SD	36,862	C
Mount Mary Univ	WI	34,650	LC
Mount St. Mary College	NY	44,448	C
Mount St. Joseph Univ	OH	33,880	LC
Mount St. Mary's Univ	MD	53,380	C
Mount St. Mary's Univ - Chalon Campus	CA	50,486	VC+
Mount Vernon Nazarene Univ	OH	35,944	C
Muhlenberg College	PA	56,645	VC
Murray State Univ	KY	17,726	C+
Muskingum Univ	OH	35,966	C
Nazareth College	NY	46,784	C
Nebr Wesleyan Univ	NE	42,026	C+
New College of Florida	FL	16,180	HC+
New Jersey City Univ	NJ	21,456	LC
New Jersey Inst of Technology	NJ	30,198	HC
New Mexico Highlands Univ	NM	11,904	LC
New Mexico Inst of Mining and Technology	NM	15,385	HC+
New Mexico State Univ	NM	14,050	LC
New York Inst of Technology	NY	49,980	VC
New York Univ	NY	68,139	MC
Newberry College	SC	34,550	C
Newman Univ	KS	37,382	C
Niagara Univ	NY	41,010	C
Nicholls State Univ	LA	14,959	C
Norfolk State Univ	VA	18,902	LC
N Car A&T State Univ	NC	13,786	C
N Car Central Univ	NC	9,000	C
N Car State Univ	NC	22,434	HC+
N Car Wesleyan College	NC	39,200	C
North Central College	IL	48,712	C+
N Dak State Univ	ND	16,245	VC
North Park Univ	IL	35,860	C
Northeastern Illinois Univ	IL	12,529	LC
Northeastern State Univ	OK	8,615	VC
Northeastern Univ	MA	65,352	MC
Northern Arizona Univ	AZ	21,003	C
Northern Illinois Univ	IL	20,176	C
Northern Kentucky Univ	KY	16,486	C
Northern Mich Univ	MI	20,853	C
Northern State Univ	SD	15,570	C
Northland College	WI	41,103	C+
Northwest Missouri State Univ	MO	18,286	C
Northwest Nazarene Univ	ID	40,250	C
Northwestern College of Iowa	IA	38,400	C
Northwestern Okla State Univ	OK	13,072	LC
Northwestern Univ	IL	68,725	MC
Norwich Univ	VT	56,234	C
Notre Dame College	OH	39,150	VC
Notre Dame of Maryland Univ	MD	47,570	VC
Nova Southeastern Univ	FL	38,534	C+
Oakland Univ	MI	20,763	C
Oakwood Univ	AL	43,758	C
Oberlin College	OH	68,942	MC
Occidental College	CA	68,660	MC
Oglethorpe Univ	GA	44,200	C
Ohio Dominican Univ	OH	41,340	C+
Ohio Northern Univ	OH	44,050	VC
Ohio State Univ at Columbus	OH	22,843	MC
Ohio Univ	OH	23,394	VC
Ohio Wesleyan Univ	OH	49,460	VC
Okla Baptist Univ	OK	33,990	C
Okla Christian Univ	OK	29,260	C
Okla City Univ	OK	40,476	C
Okla Panhandle State Univ	OK	6,152	C
Okla State Univ	OK	17,180	C+
Okla Wesleyan Univ	OK	34,434	C
Old Dominion Univ	VA	21,618	C
Olivet College	MI	37,661	LC
Olivet Nazarene Univ	IL	41,840	VC
Oral Roberts Univ	OK	34,316	C
Oregon State Univ	OR	23,337	VC
Ottawa Univ	KS	39,980	VC
Otterbein Univ	OH	41,630	C
Ouachita Baptist Univ	AR	33,500	VC
Our Lady of the Lake Univ	TX	37,790	LC
Pace Univ	NY	60,136	C
Pacific Lutheran Univ	WA	49,960	C
Pacific Union College	CA	36,009	VC
Pacific Univ	OR	37,617	C
Paine College	GA	19,506	LC
Palm Beach Atlantic Univ	FL	39,250	C
Park Univ	MO	22,134	C
Penn State Erie,The Behrend College	PA	26,688	VC
Pennsylvania State Univ - Univ Park	PA	29,716	HC
Pepperdine Univ	CA	66,862	VC+
Pfeiffer Univ	NC	40,532	LC
Philander Smith College	AR	20,814	LC
Piedmont College	GA	34,334	C
Pittsburg State Univ	KS	13,880	C
Pitzer College	CA	68,500	HC+
Plymouth State Univ	NH	23,180	LC
Point Loma Nazarene Univ	CA	46,150	C+
Pomona College	CA	64,957	MC
Pontifical Catholic Univ of PR	PR	10,534	
Portland State Univ	OR	19,443	C
Prairie View A&M Univ	TX	27,273	LC
Presbyterian College	SC	47,186	C
Princeton Univ	NJ	60,090	MC
Principia College	IL	40,350	C
Providence College	RI	62,870	HC
Purdue Univ Northwest	IN	15,178	C
Purdue Univ/West Lafayette	IN	20,032	MC
Queens Univ of Charlotte	NC	39,543	C
Quincy Univ	IL	38,170	LC
Quinnipiac Univ	CT	60,970	VC
Radford Univ	VA	19,758	C
Ramapo College of New Jersey	NJ	25,760	VC
Randolph College	VA	53,970	C
Randolph-Macon College	VA	51,480	VC
Reed College	OR	65,300	MC
Regis College	MA	51,920	LC
Regis Univ	CO	46,380	C
Rensselaer Polytechnic Inst	NY	67,265	MC
Rhode Island College	RI	19,000	LC
Rhodes College	TN	51,900	HC
Rice Univ	TX	59,458	MC
Rider Univ	NJ	54,050	C
Ripon College	WI	49,991	VC
Roanoke College	VA	55,952	VC
Roberts Wesleyan College	NY	41,116	C
Rochester Inst of Technology	NY	52,734	HC+
Rockford Univ	IL	38,570	C
Rockhurst Univ	MO	28,990	C
Rocky Mountain College	MT	35,776	C
Roger Williams Univ	RI	48,074	VC
Rollins College	FL	58,670	HC
Roosevelt Univ	IL	41,890	VC
Rose-Hulman Inst of Technology	IN	59,823	MC
Rosemont College	PA	30,980	LC
Rowan Univ	NJ	24,491	VC
Russell Sage College	NY	39,370	C
Rust College	MS	10,600	C
Rutgers Univ - Camden	NJ	26,595	C
Rutgers Univ - New Brunswick	NJ	27,090	HC
Rutgers Univ - Newark	NJ	27,351	C
Sacred Heart Univ	CT	54,590	C
Saginaw Valley State Univ	MI	19,284	C
St. Anselm College	NH	56,636	VC
St. Augustine's Univ	NC	25,582	C
St. Francis Univ	PA	46,146	NC
St. John's Univ	MN	53,472	C
St. Joseph's College of Maine	ME	47,890	C
St. Joseph's Univ	PA	58,540	VC
St. Louis Univ	MO	49,866	HC
St. Martin's Univ	WA	45,056	C
St. Mary's College	IN	50,600	C
St. Mary's College of Calif	CA	57,420	C
St. Mary's Univ of Minn	MN	42,440	C
St. Michael's College	VT	53,275	VC+
St. Peter's Univ	NJ	49,192	C
St. Vincent College	PA	46,229	C
St. Xavier Univ	IL	44,440	C
Salem College	NC	40,206	C
Salem State Univ	MA	42,650	LC
Salisbury Univ	MD	21,132	VC
Salve Regina Univ	RI	53,046	VC
Sam Houston State Univ	TX	18,792	C
Samford Univ	AL	40,770	VC
San Diego State Univ	CA	23,156	VC
San Francisco State Univ	CA	18,514	LC
San Jose State Univ	CA	22,630	C
Sarah Lawrence College	NY	68,866	MC
Savannah State Univ	GA	17,036	C
Schreiner Univ	TX	34,626	LC
Scripps College	CA	69,260	HC
Seattle Pacific Univ	WA	47,439	C+
Seattle Univ	WA	54,957	VC
Seton Hall Univ	NJ	58,008	C
Seton Hill Univ	PA	46,972	VC
Sewanee: The Univ of the South	TN	58,000	HC+
Shaw Univ	NC	24,638	C
Shawnee State Univ	OH	16,998	C
Shenandoah Univ	VA	42,100	C
Shepherd Univ, West Virginia	WV	17,382	C
Shippensburg Univ of Pennsylvania	PA	24,096	C
Shorter Univ	GA	31,130	LC
Siena College	NY	48,916	C
Siena Heights Univ	MI	36,322	C
Silver Lake College of the Holy Family	WI	36,290	LC
Simmons College	MA	54,400	HC
Simpson College	IA	45,626	VC
Skidmore College	NY	66,600	MC
Slippery Rock Univ of Pennsylvania	PA	20,450	C
Smith College	MA	66,774	MC
Sonoma State Univ	CA	27,020	C
S Car State Univ	SC	21,330	LC

ST = STATE **$IS** = IN-STATE COSTS **SR** = SELECTOR RATING

School	ST	$IS	SR
S Dak School of Mines and Technology	SD	18,570	C+
S Dak State Univ	SD	15,874	C
Southeast Missouri State Univ	MO	16,148	C
Southeastern Louisiana Univ	LA	16,237	C
Southeastern Okla State Univ	OK	11,875	C
Southern Adventist Univ	TN	28,250	C
Southern Arkansas Univ	AR	21,532	C
Southern Conn State Univ	CT	21,924	LC
Southern Illinois Univ Carbondale	IL	24,554	C
Southern Illinois Univ Edwardsville	IL	20,188	C
Southern Methodist Univ	TX	69,008	MC
Southern Nazarene Univ	OK	33,684	C
Southern Oregon Univ	OR	19,117	C
Southern Univ and A&M College	LA	16,074	LC
Southern Univ at New Orleans	LA	8,014	LC
Southern Wesleyan Univ	SC	33,670	LC
Southwest Baptist Univ	MO	30,890	LC
Southwest Minn State Univ	MN	17,783	C
Southwestern Adventist Univ	TX	28,232	LC
Southwestern College	KS	31,531	LC
Southwestern Okla State Univ	OK	12,205	C
Southwestern Univ	TX	52,370	VC
Spelman College	GA	41,642	C
Spring Arbor Univ	MI	37,390	C
Spring Hill College	AL	48,488	C
Springfield College	MA	48,775	C
St. Ambrose Univ	IA	40,180	C
St. Bonaventure Univ	NY	45,596	C
St. Catherine Univ	MN	45,630	C
St. Cloud State Univ	MN	10,600	C
St. Edward's Univ	TX	56,190	VC
St. Francis College	NY	38,800	LC
St. John Fisher College	NY	45,270	VC
St. John's College at Annapolis	MD	63,348	MC
St. John's Univ	NY	57,160	C+
St. Joseph's College, New York/Brooklyn Campus	NY	25,114	LC
St. Joseph's College, New York/Long Island Campus	NY	25,124	C
St. Lawrence Univ	NY	66,646	HC+
St. Mary's College of Maryland	MD	27,312	VC
St. Mary's Univ	TX	39,120	C
St. Norbert College	WI	46,060	VC
St. Olaf College	MN	56,430	HC
Stanford Univ	CA	62,541	MC
SUNY Albany	NY	22,165	C
SUNY at Binghamton	NY	24,100	MC
SUNY at Geneseo	NY	21,622	VC
SUNY at New Paltz	NY	20,840	C
SUNY at Oswego	NY	22,219	VC
SUNY at Purchase College	NY	21,832	C
SUNY/Buffalo State	NY	20,583	LC
SUNY/College at Old Westbury	NY	16,860	C
SUNY/Cortland	NY	20,910	C
SUNY/Fredonia	NY	20,818	C
SUNY/Oneonta	NY	20,794	C
SUNY/Plattsburgh	NY	19,314	C
SUNY/Potsdam	NY	21,051	VC
SUNY/The College of Environmental Science and Forestry	NY	23,728	VC
SUNY/Univ at Buffalo	NY	23,122	C
Stephen F. Austin State Univ	TX	18,484	LC
Sterling College	KS	32,830	LC
Stetson Univ	FL	57,174	VC+
Stevens Inst of Technology	NJ	64,954	MC
Stevenson Univ	MD	48,412	C
Stockton Univ	NJ	25,565	C
Stonehill College	MA	55,130	C
Stony Brook Univ/The SUNY	NY	22,703	MC
Suffolk Univ	MA	52,316	C
Susquehanna Univ	PA	57,560	VC
Swarthmore College	PA	63,550	MC
Syracuse Univ	NY	62,313	HC
Tabor College	KS	35,870	C
Talladega College	AL	25,919	C
Tarleton State Univ	TX	15,248	LC
Taylor Univ	IN	42,130	VC
Temple Univ	PA	24,392	C+
Tenn State Univ	TN	14,423	LC
Tenn Tech Univ	TN	17,929	C
Tenn Wesleyan Univ	TN	32,680	LC
Texas A&M Univ at College Station	TX	20,771	VC+
Texas A&M Univ at Commerce	TX	10,496	C
Texas A&M Univ at Corpus Christi	TX	16,851	LC
Texas A&M Univ at Kingsville	TX	16,580	LC
Texas Christian Univ	TX	57,120	HC
Texas Lutheran Univ	TX	39,770	C
Texas Southern Univ	TX	19,592	LC
Texas State Univ	TX	18,721	C
Texas Tech Univ	TX	20,156	C+
Texas Wesleyan Univ	TX	37,338	C
Texas Woman's Univ	TX	15,302	LC
The American Univ	DC	61,317	HC
The Catholic Univ of America	DC	58,376	VC
The Citadel, The Military College of S Car	SC	20,679	C
The College at Brockport - SUNY	NY	21,058	C
The College of Idaho	ID	36,415	C
The College of New Jersey	NJ	28,675	VC+
The College of New Rochelle	NY	46,300	LC
The College of St. Rose	NY	44,010	C
The College of Wooster	OH	60,000	HC
The George Washington Univ	DC	68,474	HC+
The Univ of Akron	OH	22,566	C
The Univ of Alabama	AL	24,320	C+
The Univ of Arizona	AZ	24,086	C
The Univ of Memphis	TN	18,278	C
The Univ of Tenn at Chattanooga	TN	17,340	C+
The Univ of Tenn at Knoxville	TN	22,112	VC
The Univ of Tenn at Martin	TN	15,212	C
The Univ of Texas at Austin	TX	20,206	MC
The Univ of Texas at San Antonio	TX	21,060	C
The Univ of Utah	UT	18,751	VC
The Univ of Virginia's College at Wise	VA	18,192	LC
Thiel College	PA	42,950	LC
Thomas More College	KY	36,720	LC
Tougaloo College	MS	17,980	NC
Touro College	NY	31,040	C
Towson Univ	MD	21,878	C
Transylvania Univ	KY	47,450	HC+
Trevecca Nazarene Univ	TN	31,186	C
Trine Univ	IN	41,310	C
Trinity Christian College	IL	35,580	C
Trinity College	CT	69,020	HC
Trinity International Univ	IL	31,070	VC
Trinity Univ	TX	54,480	MC
Trinity Washington Univ	DC	33,826	C+
Troy Univ	AL	16,171	C
Truman State Univ	MO	16,286	MC
Tufts Univ	MA		MC
Tulane Univ	LA	67,496	MC
Tusculum College	TN	31,625	LC
Tuskegee Univ	AL	28,164	C
Union College	KY	32,310	C
Union College	NE	23,270	C
Union College	NY	64,320	MC
Union Univ	TN	41,160	VC
United States Air Force Academy	CO		C
United States Military Academy at West Point	NY		HC+
United States Naval Academy	MD		HC
Universidad del Turabo	PR	17,828	
Univ of Alabama at Birmingham	AL	22,092	C
Univ of Alabama in Huntsville	AL	20,028	VC
Univ of Alaska Anchorage	AK	17,914	C
Univ of Alaska Fairbanks	AK	16,874	VC
Univ of Arkansas at Fayetteville	AR	19,766	VC
Univ of Arkansas at Little Rock	AR	18,211	LC
Univ of Arkansas at Monticello	AR	13,599	LC
Univ of Arkansas at Pine Bluff	AR	13,541	C
Univ of Calif at Berkeley	CA	29,886	MC
Univ of Calif at Davis	CA	28,468	HC
Univ of Calif at Irvine	CA	33,857	VC
Univ of Calif at Los Angeles	CA	27,438	HC+
Univ of Calif at Riverside	CA	32,912	C
Univ of Calif at Santa Barbara	CA	30,627	HC+
Univ of Calif San Diego	CA	30,450	MC
Univ of Calif, Santa Cruz	CA	28,731	C+
Univ of Central Arkansas	AR	15,042	VC
Univ of Central Florida	FL	16,379	VC
Univ of Central Missouri	MO	18,982	C
Univ of Central Okla	OK	15,150	C
Univ of Charleston	WV	35,000	LC
Univ of Chicago	IL	70,551	MC
Univ of Cincinnati	OH	22,118	VC
Univ of Colo Boulder	CO	26,048	HC
Univ of Colo Colo Springs	CO	20,300	C
Univ of Colo Denver	CO	22,238	C
Univ of Conn	CT	27,394	
Univ of Dallas	TX	50,676	VC
Univ of Dayton	OH	54,930	VC
Univ of Delaware	DE	32,214	VC
Univ of Denver	CO	61,129	VC+
Univ of Detroit Mercy	MI	48,816	C
Univ of Evansville	IN	44,186	C+
Univ of Findlay	OH	43,040	C
Univ of Florida	FL	16,291	HC+
Univ of Georgia	GA	21,878	HC
Univ of Hartford	CT	49,776	C
Univ of Hawaii at Hilo	HI	18,038	VC
Univ of Hawaii at Manoa	HI	23,261	C
Univ of Houston	TX	21,871	VC
Univ of Houston-Downtown	TX	7,241	LC
Univ of Idaho	ID	16,158	C
Univ of Illinois at Chicago	IL	24,664	VC
Univ of Illinois at Urbana-Champaign	IL	27,006	HC
Univ of Indianapolis	IN	36,480	VC
Univ of Iowa	IA	19,415	HC
Univ of Jamestown	ND	28,508	C
Univ of Kansas	KS	20,884	VC
Univ of Kentucky	KY	24,800	C+
Univ of La Verne	CA	55,600	C
Univ of Louisiana at Lafayette	LA	14,516	C
Univ of Louisville	KY	19,692	C
Univ of Lynchburg	VA	48,370	C
Univ of Maine	ME	21,038	VC
Univ of Mary Hardin-Baylor	TX	35,292	C+
Univ of Mary Washington	VA	23,039	C+
Univ of Maryland/Baltimore County	MD	23,004	VC
Univ of Maryland/College Park	MD	21,938	HC
Univ of Maryland/Eastern Shore	MD	21,861	LC
Univ of Mass Amherst	MA	27,669	HC
Univ of Mass Boston	MA	13,828	C
Univ of Mass Dartmouth	MA	26,507	C
Univ of Mass Lowell	MA	27,296	VC
Univ of Miami	FL	63,494	MC
Univ of Mich/Ann Arbor	MI	25,274	MC
Univ of Mich/Dearborn	MI	12,472	VC
Univ of Mich/Flint	MI	19,062	C
Univ of Minn/Duluth	MN	20,292	C
Univ of Minn/Morris	MN	21,222	VC
Univ of Minn/Twin Cities	MN	24,269	MC
Univ of Miss	MS	18,802	C
Univ of Missouri-Columbia	MO	20,463	VC
Univ of Missouri-Kansas City	MO	19,563	VC
Univ of Missouri-St. Louis	MO	19,810	VC
Univ of Montana	MT	14,105	C
Univ of Montevallo	AL	20,012	C
Univ of Mount Union	OH	39,990	C
Univ of Nebr - Kearney	NE	17,014	LC
Univ of Nebr - Lincoln	NE	18,589	VC
Univ of Nebr - Omaha	NE	16,120	C
Univ of Nevada, Las Vegas	NV	17,553	C
Univ of Nevada, Reno	NV	18,010	C
Univ of New England	ME	50,110	C
Univ of New Hampshire	NH	29,333	VC
Univ of New Haven	CT	53,680	C
Univ of New Mexico	NM	16,808	C
Univ of New Orleans	LA	12,840	C
Univ of North Alabama	AL	15,964	C
Univ of N Car at Asheville	NC	16,251	VC+
Univ of N Car at Chapel Hill	NC	20,561	MC
Univ of N Car at Charlotte	NC	17,803	VC
Univ of N Car at Greensboro	NC	15,998	C
Univ of N Car at Pembroke	NC	14,737	LC
Univ of N Car Wilmington	NC	16,784	VC
Univ of N Dak	ND	16,673	C
Univ of North Florida	FL	15,996	VC
Univ of North Georgia	GA	17,316	C
Univ of North Texas	TX	20,082	C
Univ of Northern Colo	CO	19,658	C
Univ of Northern Iowa	IA	17,480	C
Univ of Notre Dame	IN	68,801	MC
Univ of Okla	OK	19,651	HC
Univ of Oregon	OR	24,021	VC
Univ of Pennsylvania	PA	63,526	MC
Univ of Pikeville	KY	27,838	C
Univ of Pittsburgh	PA	30,030	MC
Univ of Pittsburgh at Bradford	PA	22,958	C
Univ of Pittsburgh at Johnstown	PA	22,092	C
Univ of Portland	OR	52,152	VC
Univ of PR, at Cayey	PR		
Univ of PR, at Humacao	PR	14,000	
Univ of PR, at Mayaguez	PR	13,995	
Univ of PR-Rio Piedras campus	PR	13,327	
Univ of Puget Sound	WA	60,210	HC
Univ of Redlands	CA	61,934	VC
Univ of Rhode Island	RI	26,066	VC
Univ of Richmond	VA	62,730	MC
Univ of Rio Grande & Rio Grande Community College	OH	8,750	LC
Univ of Rochester	NY	65,032	MC
Univ of St. Francis	IN	38,520	C
Univ of St. Joseph	CT	49,069	C
Univ of St. Mary	KS	37,080	NC
Univ of San Diego	CA	60,338	HC
Univ of San Francisco	CA	60,580	C
Univ of Science and Arts of Okla	OK	11,140	VC
Univ of Scranton	PA	54,962	VC
Univ of Sioux Falls	SD	25,630	C
Univ of South Alabama	AL	16,880	C
Univ of S Car Aiken	SC	18,094	C
Univ of S Car at Columbia	SC	21,726	VC
Univ of S Car Upstate	SC	19,272	LC
Univ of S Dak	SD	16,109	C
Univ of South Florida/Tampa	FL	16,110	VC
Univ of Southern Calif	CA	66,631	MC
Univ of Southern Indiana	IN	16,808	C
Univ of Southern Maine	ME	18,320	C
Univ of Southern Miss	MS	13,170	C
Univ of St. Thomas - Houston	TX	41,510	VC
Univ of Tampa	FL	38,928	VC
Univ of Texas at Arlington	TX	18,876	C
Univ of Texas at Dallas	TX	23,640	HC
Univ of Texas at El Paso	TX	34,452	NC
Univ of Texas Rio Grande Valley	TX	15,573	LC
Univ of the Cumberlands	KY	32,000	LC
Univ of the District of Columbia	DC	21,260	LC
Univ of the Incarnate Word	TX	39,162	LC
Univ of the Ozarks	AR	31,050	NC
Univ of the Pacific	CA	57,446	VC
Univ of the Sacred Heart	PR	17,932	
Univ of the Sciences	PA	40,738	VC
Univ of Toledo	OH	19,336	C
Univ of Tulsa	OK	52,625	HC
Univ of Vermont	VT	29,792	HC
Univ of Virginia	VA	27,367	MC
Univ of West Alabama	AL	16,284	LC
Univ of West Florida	FL	15,848	C
Univ of West Georgia	GA	17,510	LC
Univ of Wisc-Eau Claire	WI	16,354	VC
Univ of Wisc-Green Bay	WI	15,184	C
Univ of Wisc-La Crosse	WI	15,425	VC
Univ of Wisc-Madison	WI	21,647	MC
Univ of Wisc-Milwaukee	WI	21,538	C
Univ of Wisc-Oshkosh	WI	15,392	C
Univ of Wisc-Parkside	WI	15,313	C
Univ of Wisc-Platteville	WI	14,148	C
Univ of Wisc-River Falls	WI	14,541	C
Univ of Wisc-Stevens Point	WI	14,043	C
Univ of Wisc-Superior	WI	14,838	C
Univ of Wisc-Whitewater	WI	13,976	C
Univ of Wyoming	WY	15,537	C
Upper Iowa Univ	IA	34,990	NC
Ursinus College	PA	62,920	VC
Utah State Univ	UT	13,235	C
Utica College	NY	31,510	C
Valley City State Univ	ND	13,267	C
Valparaiso Univ	IN	50,160	VC
Vanderbilt Univ	TN	63,248	MC
Vanguard Univ of Southern Calif	CA	42,400	VC
Vassar College	NY	68,110	MC
Villanova Univ	PA	64,922	MC
Virginia Commonwealth Univ	VA	23,811	VC
Virginia Military Inst	VA	26,460	VC
Virginia Polytechnic Inst and State Univ	VA	21,920	VC
Virginia State Univ	VA	19,802	C+
Virginia Union Univ	VA	25,058	C
Virginia Wesleyan Univ	VA	45,980	LC
Viterbo Univ	WI	34,660	C
Wabash College	IN	52,100	VC
Wagner College	NY	57,240	C+
Wake Forest Univ	NC	69,354	MC
Walla Walla Univ	WA	34,845	C
Walsh Univ	OH	39,010	C
Warren Wilson College	NC	44,220	VC
Wartburg College	IA	49,478	C
Washburn Univ	KS	15,827	C
Washington & Jefferson College	PA	58,694	VC
Washington Adventist Univ	MD	32,050	LC
Washington and Lee Univ	VA	59,647	MC
Washington College	MD	56,154	VC
Washington State Univ	WA	22,747	C
Washington Univ in St. Louis	MO	67,539	MC
Wayland Baptist Univ	TX	23,460	LC
Wayne State College	NE	25,746	NC
Wayne State Univ	MI	23,085	C
Waynesburg Univ	PA	33,530	C
Weber State Univ	UT	14,112	C
Wellesley College	MA	66,984	MC
Wells College	NY	50,500	C
Wesleyan College	GA	31,940	C+
Wesleyan Univ	CT	66,940	MC
West Chester Univ of Pennsylvania	PA	19,171	VC
West Liberty Univ	WV	16,158	C
West Texas A&M Univ	TX	13,478	C
West Virginia State Univ	WV	19,412	LC
West Virginia Univ	WV	18,952	VC
West Virginia Univ Inst of Technology	WV	18,264	C
West Virginia Wesleyan College	WV	39,188	C
Western Carolina Univ	NC	13,965	C
Western Conn State Univ	CT	21,254	LC
Western Illinois Univ	IL	20,897	C
Western Kentucky Univ	KY	16,850	C
Western Mich Univ	MI	21,791	C
Western New England Univ	MA	49,182	C
Western New Mexico Univ	NM	16,914	LC
Western Oregon Univ	OR	19,965	LC
Western State Colo Univ	CO	19,348	C
Western Washington Univ	WA	18,904	VC
Westfield State Univ	MA	20,404	C
Westminster College	MO	32,820	C
Westminster College	PA	41,722	C
Westminster College	UT	41,078	C
Westmont College	CA	57,930	VC
Wheaton College	IL	44,993	MC
Wheaton College	MA	63,818	VC
Wheeling Jesuit Univ	WV	37,106	LC
Whitman College	WA	59,772	MC
Whittier College	CA	57,891	C
Whitworth Univ	WA	53,682	VC
Wichita State Univ	KS	17,773	C
Widener Univ	PA	58,190	C
Wilberforce Univ	OH	19,900	C
Wiley College	TX	19,255	C
Wilkes Univ	PA	49,166	C
Willamette Univ	OR	62,514	VC+
William Carey Univ	MS	23,950	LC

ST = STATE **$IS** = IN-STATE COSTS **SR** = SELECTOR RATING

School	ST	$IS	SR
William Jewell College	MO	42,490	C+
William Paterson Univ of New Jersey	NJ	24,022	C
Williams College	MA	67,700	MC
Wilmington College	OH	35,100	C
Wilson College	PA	35,620	LC
Wingate Univ	NC	41,900	C
Winona State Univ	MN	18,109	C
Winston-Salem State Univ	NC	18,005	LC
Winthrop Univ	SC	23,960	C
Wisc Lutheran College	WI	36,290	C
Wittenberg Univ	OH	49,863	VC
Wofford College	SC	49,885	VC
Worcester Polytechnic Inst	MA	62,846	MC
Worcester State Univ	MA	20,977	C
Wright State Univ	OH	16,983	C
Xavier Univ	OH	49,380	VC
Xavier Univ of Louisiana	LA	31,689	C
Yale Univ	CT	64,650	MC
Yeshiva Univ	NY	52,750	VC
York College of Pennsylvania	PA	29,240	C
Youngstown State Univ	OH	17,487	C

CHEMISTRY EDUCATION

School	ST	$IS	SR
Arkansas State Univ	AR	16,190	C
Ashland Univ	OH	30,446	C
Bethany College	WV	38,774	LC
Bloomfield College	NJ	40,100	LC
Boston Univ	MA	67,352	MC
Cedarville Univ	OH	36,244	VC
Edgewood College	WI	35,950	C
Ferris State Univ	MI	21,458	C
Hope College	MI	42,840	VC
Indiana Univ of Pennsylvania	PA	24,474	C
Louisiana College	LA	21,274	C
Mayville State Univ	ND	18,371	NC
Missouri Western State Univ	MO	17,822	LC
Monmouth Univ	NJ	50,184	C
Niagara Univ	NY	41,010	C
Oakwood Univ	AL	43,758	C
Olivet Nazarene Univ	IL	41,840	VC
Silver Lake College of the Holy Family	WI	36,290	LC
St. Ambrose Univ	IA	40,180	C
Univ of Conn	CT	27,394	
Weber State Univ	UT	14,112	C
West Chester Univ of Pennsylvania	PA	19,171	VC

CHEMISTRY SECONDARY EDUCATION

School	ST	$IS	SR
Grove City College	PA	26,654	VC
Immaculata Univ	PA	39,000	C
King Univ	TN	36,976	C
Lake Superior State Univ	MI	19,867	C
Millersville Univ of Pennsylvania	PA	25,298	C
Missouri Western State Univ	MO	17,822	LC
Providence College	RI	62,870	HC
Syracuse Univ	NY	62,313	HC
Tenn Wesleyan Univ	TN	32,680	LC
Univ of N Car at Greensboro	NC	15,998	C
Wartburg College	IA	49,478	C
West Chester Univ of Pennsylvania	PA	19,171	VC
Western Mich Univ	MI	21,791	C
Wilson College	PA	35,620	LC

CHEMISTRY/ADOLESCENCE EDUCATION

School	ST	$IS	SR
Arkansas Tech Univ	AR	16,534	LC
Augustana College	IL	51,222	VC+
Bethany College	WV	38,774	LC
Black Hills State Univ	SD	16,622	C
College of the Ozarks	MO	7,530	VC
Duquesne Univ	PA	48,508	VC
Elizabethtown College	PA	56,340	VC
Houghton College	NY	40,558	VC
Huntingdon College	AL	35,900	C
Indiana Univ Bloomington	IN	20,791	HC
Indiana Univ Northwest	IN	7,207	LC
Indiana Univ South Bend	IN	16,057	C
Lipscomb Univ	TN	42,984	VC
LIU Brooklyn	NY	50,698	C
LIU Post	NY	50,698	C+
Marist College	NY	49,860	VC
Messiah College	PA	44,380	VC
Millikin Univ	IL	44,148	C
Minn State Univ, Mankato	MN	17,190	C
Murray State Univ	KY	17,726	C+
Nazareth College	NY	46,784	C
Niagara Univ	NY	41,010	C
Northern Kentucky Univ	KY	16,486	C
Old Dominion Univ	VA	21,618	C
Roberts Wesleyan College	NY	41,116	C
St. Mary's Univ of Minn	MN	42,440	C
Seattle Univ	WA	54,957	VC
SUNY/Fredonia	NY	20,818	C
SUNY/Plattsburgh	NY	19,314	C
Temple Univ	PA	24,392	C+
Trevecca Nazarene Univ	TN	31,186	C
Univ of Mary Hardin-Baylor	TX	35,292	C+
Univ of Nebr - Lincoln	NE	18,589	VC

CHEMISTRY/CHEMICAL BIOLOGY

School	ST	$IS	SR
Bethany College	WV	38,774	LC
Case Western Reserve Univ	OH	62,284	MC
Cornell Univ	NY	67,591	MC
Huntington Univ	IN	33,996	C
Indiana Univ Kokomo	IN	7,207	C
Murray State Univ	KY	17,726	C+
Univ of Okla	OK	19,651	HC
West Chester Univ of Pennsylvania	PA	19,171	VC

CHEMISTRY/FORENSIC CHEMISTRY

School	ST	$IS	SR
Emmanuel College	MA	53,472	C+
Lake Superior State Univ	MI	19,867	C
Missouri Baptist Univ	MO	35,594	C
Missouri Western State Univ	MO	17,822	LC
Okla Baptist Univ	OK	33,990	C
Olivet Nazarene Univ	IL	41,840	VC
Tenn Wesleyan Univ	TN	32,680	LC
Univ of Rhode Island	RI	26,066	VC
Univ of St. Francis	IN	38,520	C
West Chester Univ of Pennsylvania	PA	19,171	VC
Western New England Univ	MA	49,182	C

CHEMISTRY/GENERAL SCIENCE SECOND EDUCATION

School	ST	$IS	SR
Coker College	SC	38,196	C
Grove City College	PA	26,654	VC
Huntingdon College	AL	35,900	C
Missouri Western State Univ	MO	17,822	LC
St. Edward's Univ	TX	56,190	VC
Syracuse Univ	NY	62,313	HC
Tenn Wesleyan Univ	TN	32,680	LC
Wartburg College	IA	49,478	C
West Chester Univ of Pennsylvania	PA	19,171	VC
Wilson College	PA	35,620	LC

CHILD CARE/CHILD AND FAMILY STUDIES

School	ST	$IS	SR
Abilene Christian Univ	TX	43,708	C+
Albright College	PA	57,326	C
Armstrong State Univ	GA	15,615	C
Ashland Univ	OH	30,446	C
Baylor Univ	TX	56,803	HC
Berea College	KY	7,094	C
Cal State, Fresno	CA	16,902	LC
Cal State, Fullerton	CA	21,902	C
Cal State, Long Beach	CA	18,850	C
Cameron Univ	OK	11,632	LC
Chestnut Hill College	PA	47,180	C
CUNY/Brooklyn College	NY	7,163	C+
College of the Ozarks	MO	7,530	VC
Concordia Univ St. Paul	MN	29,050	C
Davis & Elkins College	WV	38,242	LC
East Carolina Univ	NC	16,539	C
East Central Univ	OK	13,330	C
Eastern Kentucky Univ	KY	17,742	C
Eastern Mich Univ	MI	19,761	C
Edgewood College	WI	35,950	C
Eureka College	IL	34,760	C
Florida State Univ	FL	16,771	HC
Fontbonne Univ	MO	34,606	C
Freed-Hardeman Univ	TN	29,900	C
Georgia Southern Univ	GA	16,540	VC
Goodwin College	CT	28,370	LC
Harding Univ	AR	25,440	C
Indiana State Univ	IN	23,223	LC
Indiana Univ of Pennsylvania	PA	24,474	C
Iowa State Univ	IA	18,176	C
Jackson State Univ	MS	15,879	LC
Kansas State Univ	KS	17,780	VC
La Roche College	PA	38,940	C
Limestone College	SC	32,100	C
Louisiana State Univ and A&M College	LA	18,677	VC
Mayville State Univ	ND	18,371	NC
Messiah College	PA	44,380	VC
Metropolitan College of New York	NY		VC
Montclair State Univ	NJ	26,912	C
Mount Aloysius College	PA	29,976	C
New York Univ	NY	68,139	MC
N Car Central Univ	NC	9,000	C
N Dak State Univ	ND	16,245	VC
Northern Illinois Univ	IL	20,176	C
Northwest Missouri State Univ	MO	18,286	C
Ohio Univ	OH	23,394	VC
Okla Baptist Univ	OK	33,990	C
Okla Christian Univ	OK	29,260	C
Okla State Univ	OK	17,180	C+
Park Univ	MO	22,134	C
Plymouth State Univ	NH	23,180	LC
Portland State Univ	OR	19,443	C
San Jose State Univ	CA	22,630	C
Seton Hill Univ	PA	46,972	VC
Silver Lake College of the Holy Family	WI	36,290	LC
St. Bonaventure Univ	NY	45,596	C
SUNY /College of Agriculture and Tech at Cobleskill	NY	20,527	LC
SUNY/Empire State College	NY	9,145	NC
SUNY/Oneonta	NY	20,794	C
SUNY/Plattsburgh	NY	19,314	C
Syracuse Univ	NY	62,313	HC
Tenn Tech Univ	TN	17,929	C
Texas A&M Univ at Kingsville	TX	16,580	LC
Texas State Univ	TX	18,721	C
Texas Tech Univ	TX	20,156	C+
The Univ of Tenn at Knoxville	TN	22,112	VC
The Univ of Tenn at Martin	TN	15,212	C
The Univ of Texas at Austin	TX	20,206	MC
The Univ of Texas at San Antonio	TX	21,060	C
Univ of Alaska Fairbanks	AK	16,874	VC
Univ of Georgia	GA	21,878	HC
Univ of Idaho	ID	16,158	C
Univ of Maine	ME	21,038	VC
Univ of Missouri-Columbia	MO	20,463	VC
Univ of Nebr - Lincoln	NE	18,589	VC
Univ of Nevada, Reno	NV	18,010	C
Univ of New Mexico	NM	16,808	C
Univ of N Car at Chapel Hill	NC	20,561	MC
Univ of N Car at Charlotte	NC	17,803	VC
Univ of N Car at Greensboro	NC	15,998	C
Univ of North Texas	TX	20,082	C
Univ of the Incarnate Word	TX	39,162	LC
Univ of Vermont	VT	29,792	HC
Univ of Wisc-Stout	WI	19,667	C
Utah State Univ	UT	13,235	C
Weber State Univ	UT	14,112	C
West Virginia Univ	WV	18,952	VC
Western Mich Univ	MI	21,791	C
Wheelock College	MA	51,325	LC
Youngstown State Univ	OH	17,487	C

CHILD PSYCHOLOGY/ DEVELOPMENT

School	ST	$IS	SR
Alcorn State Univ	MS	15,884	C
Angelo State Univ	TX	15,882	LC
Appalachian State Univ	NC	15,394	VC
Ashford Univ	CA	10,480	C
Bay Path Univ	MA	46,356	C
Bennington College	VT	66,280	MC
Bethel Univ	TN	27,142	C
Bluffton Univ	OH	40,950	C+
Calif Polytechnic State Univ	CA	22,547	MC
Cal State, Bakersfield	CA	22,397	LC
Cal State, Chico	CA	19,790	VC
Cal State, Dominguez Hills	CA	19,022	LC
Cal State, Fresno	CA	16,902	LC
Cal State, Long Beach	CA	18,850	C
Cal State, Los Angeles	CA	17,186	LC
Cal State, Northridge	CA	17,277	LC
Cal State, San Bernardino	CA	20,106	C
Cal State, Stanislaus	CA	18,053	LC
Central Mich Univ	MI	20,330	C
Colby-Sawyer College	NH	50,790	C
East Tenn State Univ	TN	18,141	C
East Texas Baptist Univ	TX	34,444	C
Eastern Nazarene College	MA	41,114	C
Florida Gulf Coast Univ	FL	14,738	C
Fort Valley State Univ	GA	17,988	VC
Hope International Univ	CA	42,730	C
Howard Univ	DC	37,616	C+
Humboldt State Univ	CA	21,708	C
Iowa State Univ	IA	18,176	C
Kutztown Univ of Pennsylvania	PA	19,477	C
Madonna Univ	MI	30,450	LC
Marygrove College	MI	30,100	LC
Meredith College	NC	46,634	C
Metropolitan State Univ	MN	7,859	C
Mich State Univ	MI	24,542	VC
Mills College	CA	43,705	C
Missouri Baptist Univ	MO	35,594	C
Missouri State Univ	MO	15,837	C+
Mount Ida College	MA	46,820	C
Mount St. Mary's Univ - Chalon Campus	CA	50,486	VC+
Niagara Univ	NY	41,010	C
N Car A&T State Univ	NC	13,786	C
N Car Central Univ	NC	9,000	C
Okla Baptist Univ	OK	33,990	C
Olivet Nazarene Univ	IL	41,840	VC
Point Loma Nazarene Univ	CA	46,150	C+
San Diego State Univ	CA	23,156	VC
Siena Heights Univ	MI	36,322	C
Southern New Hampshire Univ	NH	44,256	C
Spelman College	GA	41,642	C
St. Joseph's College, New York/Long Island Campus	NY	25,124	C
Stephen F. Austin State Univ	TX	18,484	LC
Texas Christian Univ	TX	57,120	HC
Texas Woman's Univ	TX	15,302	LC
The Univ of Akron	OH	22,566	C
Tougaloo College	MS	17,980	NC
Tufts Univ	MA		MC
Univ of Central Okla	OK	15,150	C
Univ of Illinois at Urbana-Champaign	IL	27,006	HC
Univ of La Verne	CA	55,600	C
Univ of Minn/Twin Cities	MN	24,269	MC
Univ of N Car at Charlotte	NC	17,803	VC
Univ of N Car at Greensboro	NC	15,998	C
Univ of St. Joseph	CT	49,069	C
Univ of St. Mary	KS	37,080	NC
Univ of Texas at Dallas	TX	23,640	HC
Univ of Virginia	VA	27,367	MC
Utica College	NY	31,510	C
Vanderbilt Univ	TN	63,248	MC
Wellesley College	MA	66,984	MC
Western Mich Univ	MI	21,791	C
Western Washington Univ	WA	18,904	VC
Whittier College	CA	57,891	C

CHILDHOOD EDUCATION

School	ST	$IS	SR
Bloomfield College	NJ	40,100	LC
Campbell Univ	NC	37,570	VC
Canisius College	NY	49,672	C
CUNY/Brooklyn College	NY	7,163	C+
Clayton State Univ	GA	19,735	LC
Dordt College	IA	37,860	C+
Hofstra Univ	NY	58,210	C+
Houghton College	NY	40,558	VC
Iona College	NY	52,514	C
Kennesaw State Univ	GA	18,899	VC
Kutztown Univ of Pennsylvania	PA	19,477	C
Lynn Univ	FL	49,680	LC
Marshall Univ	WV	18,044	C
Mass College of Liberal Arts	MA	20,659	C
Medaille College	NY	41,700	LC
Missouri Southern State Univ	MO	13,071	C
Missouri Western State Univ	MO	17,822	LC
Mount Aloysius College	PA	29,976	C
New York Univ	NY	68,139	MC
Niagara Univ	NY	41,010	C
Point Park Univ	PA	41,270	C
Silver Lake College of the Holy Family	WI	36,290	LC
St. Ambrose Univ	IA	40,180	C
SUNY at Oswego	NY	22,219	VC
Taylor Univ	IN	42,130	VC
The Univ of Texas at San Antonio	TX	21,060	C
Univ of Arkansas at Fayetteville	AR	19,766	VC
Univ of Georgia	GA	21,878	HC
Univ of Maryland/Baltimore County	MD	23,004	VC
Univ of Nebr - Lincoln	NE	18,589	VC
Univ of N Car at Greensboro	NC	15,998	C
Univ of N Car at Pembroke	NC	14,737	LC
Wellesley College	MA	66,984	MC
West Chester Univ of Pennsylvania	PA	19,171	VC
Western Kentucky Univ	KY	16,850	C
Western Oregon Univ	OR	19,965	LC
Wilson College	PA	35,620	LC
Wright State Univ	OH	16,983	C
Youngstown State Univ	OH	17,487	C

CHINA ASIA-PACIFIC STUDIES

School	ST	$IS	SR
Cornell Univ	NY	67,591	MC
Hofstra Univ	NY	58,210	C+
Trinity Univ	TX	54,480	MC
Wellesley College	MA	66,984	MC

CHINESE

School	ST	$IS	SR
Ball State Univ	IN	19,808	C+
Bard College	NY	65,924	HC
Bates College	ME	64,500	HC
Beloit College	WI	55,206	HC
Bennington College	VT	66,280	MC
Boston Univ	MA	67,352	MC
Brigham Young Univ	UT	13,248	MC
Cal State, Fullerton	CA	21,902	C
Cal State, Long Beach	CA	18,850	C
Calvin College	MI	43,090	HC
Central Washington Univ	WA	16,803	C
CUNY/Hunter College	NY	31,098	VC
CUNY/Queens College	NY	21,507	C
Colgate Univ	NY	67,500	MC
College of the Holy Cross	MA	64,320	MC
College of William & Mary	VA	34,907	MC
Concordia College - Moorhead	MN	46,418	C
Conn College	CT	65,000	MC
Dartmouth College	NH	68,109	MC
Davidson College	NC	60,119	MC
DePaul Univ	IL	52,807	VC
Drew Univ/College of Liberal Arts	NJ	53,608	VC
Emory Univ	GA	63,286	MC
Georgetown Univ	DC	68,970	MC
Grand Valley State Univ	MI	22,250	C+
Grinnell College	IA	63,114	MC
Hamilton College	NY	64,250	MC
Harvard College/Harvard Univ	MA	65,609	MC
Hofstra Univ	NY	58,210	C+
Lawrence Univ	WI	56,133	HC+
Lehigh Univ	PA	63,860	MC
Macalester College	MN	64,136	MC
Mich State Univ	MI	24,542	VC
Middlebury College	VT	67,464	MC
Nazareth College	NY	46,784	C
New College of Florida	FL	16,180	HC+
North Central College	IL	48,712	C+

School	ST	$IS	SR
Oakland Univ	MI	20,763	C
Occidental College	CA	68,660	MC
Ohio State Univ at Columbus	OH	22,843	MC
Pomona College	CA	64,957	MC
Portland State Univ	OR	19,443	C
Reed College	OR	65,300	MC
Rutgers Univ - New Brunswick	NJ	27,090	HC
San Francisco State Univ	CA	18,514	LC
San Jose State Univ	CA	22,630	C
Sarah Lawrence College	NY	68,866	MC
Scripps College	CA	69,260	HC
St. Olaf College	MN	56,430	HC
Stanford Univ	CA	62,541	MC
SUNY Albany	NY	22,165	C
Swarthmore College	PA	63,550	MC
The American Univ	DC	61,317	HC
The George Washington Univ	DC	68,474	HC+
The Univ of Utah	UT	18,751	VC
Thomas Edison State Univ	NJ	6,350	NC
Trinity Univ	TX	54,480	MC
Tufts Univ	MA		MC
United States Naval Academy	MD		HC
Univ of Calif at Berkeley	CA	29,886	MC
Univ of Calif at Davis	CA	28,468	HC
Univ of Calif at Los Angeles	CA	27,438	HC+
Univ of Calif at Riverside	CA	32,912	C
Univ of Calif at Santa Barbara	CA	30,627	HC+
Univ of Calif San Diego	CA	30,450	MC
Univ of Colo Boulder	CO	26,048	HC
Univ of Conn	CT	27,394	
Univ of Hawaii at Manoa	HI	23,261	C
Univ of Houston	TX	21,871	VC
Univ of Iowa	IA	19,415	HC
Univ of Maryland/College Park	MD	21,938	HC
Univ of Mass Amherst	MA	27,669	HC
Univ of Miss	MS	18,802	C
Univ of N Car at Greensboro	NC	15,998	C
Univ of N Dak	ND	16,673	C
Univ of Notre Dame	IN	68,801	MC
Univ of Oregon	OR	24,021	VC
Univ of Pittsburgh	PA	30,030	MC
Univ of Puget Sound	WA	60,210	HC
Univ of Rhode Island	RI	26,066	VC
Univ of Vermont	VT	29,792	HC
Univ of Wisc-Madison	WI	21,647	MC
Vassar College	NY	68,110	MC
Wake Forest Univ	NC	69,354	MC
Washington State Univ	WA	22,747	C
Washington Univ in St. Louis	MO	67,539	MC
Wellesley College	MA	66,984	MC
Western Kentucky Univ	KY	16,850	C
Whittier College	CA	57,891	C
Williams College	MA	67,700	MC
Wofford College	SC	49,885	VC
Yale Univ	CT	64,650	MC

CHINESE STUDIES

School	ST	$IS	SR
Beloit College	WI	55,206	HC
Bryant Univ	RI	57,204	VC
Carnegie Mellon Univ	PA	67,980	MC
Eugene Lang College of Liberal Arts	NY	64,940	VC
Gettysburg College	PA	65,210	MC
Hofstra Univ	NY	58,210	C+
Messiah College	PA	44,380	VC
Morehouse College	GA	40,835	C
Pacific Lutheran Univ	WA	49,960	C
Pennsylvania State Univ - Univ Park	PA	29,716	HC
SUNY at Binghamton	NY	24,100	MC
Swarthmore College	PA	63,550	MC
Trinity Univ	TX	54,480	MC
Univ of Calif at Irvine	CA	33,857	VC
Univ of Georgia	GA	21,878	HC
Univ of Okla	OK	19,651	HC
Univ of Richmond	VA	62,730	MC
Univ of Tulsa	OK	52,625	HC
Washington State Univ	WA	22,747	C
Wellesley College	MA	66,984	MC
Wisc Lutheran College	WI	36,290	C

CHIROPRACTIC

School	ST	$IS	SR
Colo State Univ-Pueblo	CO	21,581	C
Mount Aloysius College	PA	29,976	C
Walla Walla Univ	WA	34,845	C

CHORAL MUSIC

School	ST	$IS	SR
Baylor Univ	TX	56,803	HC
Campbell Univ	NC	37,570	VC
Concordia Univ St. Paul	MN	29,050	C
Dallas Baptist Univ	TX	35,220	VC
Faulkner Univ	AL	26,410	C
Keene State College	NH	24,604	C
Mannes School of Music	NY	44,500	SP
Missouri Southern State Univ	MO	13,071	C
Missouri Western State Univ	MO	17,822	LC
Mount Aloysius College	PA	29,976	C
Ohio Univ	OH	23,394	VC
Toccoa Falls College	GA	30,048	C
Trinity Univ	TX	54,480	MC
Univ of Kansas	KS	20,884	VC
Univ of North Texas	TX	20,082	C
Webster Univ	MO	37,490	C

CHRISTIAN EDUCATION

School	ST	$IS	SR
Asbury Univ	KY	36,450	C+
Bethany College	KS	38,637	LC
Biola Univ	CA	48,686	C
Cedarville Univ	OH	36,244	VC
Columbia College	SC	36,550	C
Concordia Univ Irvine	CA	44,860	VC
Concordia Univ Nebr	NE	41,900	VC
Concordia Univ St. Paul	MN	29,050	C
Corban Univ	OR	41,700	C
Dallas Baptist Univ	TX	35,220	VC
Defiance College	OH	42,240	LC
Erskine College	SC	45,460	C
Hannibal-LaGrange Univ	MO	29,815	C
Harding Univ	AR	25,440	C
Houghton College	NY	40,558	VC
Lenoir-Rhyne Univ	NC	47,500	LC
Malone Univ	OH	39,200	C
Muskingum Univ	OH	35,966	C
Northwest Nazarene Univ	ID	40,250	C
Northwestern College of Iowa	IA	38,400	C
Olivet Nazarene Univ	IL	41,840	VC
Pfeiffer Univ	NC	40,532	LC
Southern Nazarene Univ	OK	33,684	C
Spring Arbor Univ	MI	37,390	C
Taylor Univ	IN	42,130	VC
The Master's Univ	CA	43,870	C
West Virginia Wesleyan College	WV	39,188	C
Westminster College	PA	41,722	C
Wheaton College	IL	44,993	MC

CHRISTIAN STUDIES

School	ST	$IS	SR
Alderson Broaddus Univ	WV	35,000	LC
Belmont Univ	TN	44,500	VC+
Bethel College	IN	36,830	C
Blue Mountain College	MS	15,949	C
Bluefield College	VA	34,711	C
Brewton-Parker College	GA	26,120	LC
Bryan College	TN	32,900	C
Cairn Univ	PA	37,572	C
Calif Baptist Univ	CA	42,986	C
Campbellsville Univ	KY	33,400	C
College of the Ozarks	MO	7,530	VC
Cornerstone Univ	MI	36,550	C
Dallas Baptist Univ	TX	35,220	VC
Eastern Nazarene College	MA	41,114	C
Friends Univ	KS	38,000	C
Grand Canyon Univ	AZ	25,150	VC
Hillsdale College	MI	37,170	MC
Houghton College	NY	40,558	VC
Houston Baptist Univ	TX	36,450	C
Howard Payne Univ	TX	35,994	C
Huntingdon College	AL	35,900	C
Iowa Wesleyan Univ	IA	41,000	C
John Brown Univ	AR	35,184	VC
Mercer Univ	GA	45,348	VC
Miss College	MS	25,850	C
Missouri Baptist Univ	MO	35,594	C
North Greenville Univ	SC	25,930	C
Okla Baptist Univ	OK	33,990	C
Ouachita Baptist Univ	AR	33,500	VC
Point Loma Nazarene Univ	CA	46,150	C+
Roanoke College	VA	55,952	VC
Roberts Wesleyan College	NY	41,116	C
Seattle Pacific Univ	WA	47,439	C+
Shorter Univ	GA	31,130	LC
Sterling College	KS	32,830	LC
Stonehill College	MA	55,130	C
Tabor College	KS	35,870	C
Taylor Univ	IN	42,130	VC
The Master's Univ	CA	43,870	C
Toccoa Falls College	GA	30,048	C
Trinity International Univ	IL	31,070	VC
Union Univ	TN	41,160	VC
Univ of Mary Hardin-Baylor	TX	35,292	C+
Vanguard Univ of Southern Calif	CA	42,400	VC
Wayland Baptist Univ	TX	23,460	LC

CHURCH MUSIC

School	ST	$IS	SR
Averett Univ	VA	43,034	LC
Belmont Univ	TN	44,500	VC+
Blue Mountain College	MS	15,949	C
Campbell Univ	NC	37,570	VC
Concordia Univ St. Paul	MN	29,050	C
Dallas Baptist Univ	TX	35,220	VC
Dordt College	IA	37,860	C+
Furman Univ	SC	61,098	VC+
Hope International Univ	CA	42,730	C
Madonna Univ	MI	30,450	LC
Montreat College	NC	34,605	LC
Mount Vernon Nazarene Univ	OH	35,944	C
Nyack College	NY	34,450	LC
Okla Baptist Univ	OK	33,990	C
Okla City Univ	OK	40,476	C
Ouachita Baptist Univ	AR	33,500	VC
Shenandoah Univ	VA	42,100	C
Southeastern Univ	FL	34,910	LC
Texas Christian Univ	TX	57,120	HC
The Master's Univ	CA	43,870	C
Univ of Mary Hardin-Baylor	TX	35,292	C+
Univ of the Cumberlands	KY	32,000	LC
Wingate Univ	NC	41,900	C

CINEMA AND CULTURAL STUDIES

School	ST	$IS	SR
Missouri Western State Univ	MO	17,822	LC
Univ of Redlands	CA	61,934	VC

CITY/COMMUNITY/REGIONAL PLANNING

School	ST	$IS	SR
Alabama A&M Univ	AL	18,796	C
Ball State Univ	IN	19,808	C+
Brigham Young Univ	UT	13,248	MC
Calif Polytechnic State Univ	CA	22,547	MC
Cal State, Fullerton	CA	21,902	C
East Carolina Univ	NC	16,539	C
Eastern Mich Univ	MI	19,761	C
Indiana Univ of Pennsylvania	PA	24,474	C
Iowa State Univ	IA	18,176	C
Mich State Univ	MI	24,542	VC
New Mexico State Univ	NM	14,050	LC
Ohio State Univ at Columbus	OH	22,843	MC
Plymouth State Univ	NH	23,180	LC
Rutgers Univ - New Brunswick	NJ	27,090	HC
Temple Univ	PA	24,392	C+
Texas State Univ	TX	18,721	C
Univ of Cincinnati	OH	22,118	VC
Univ of Illinois at Urbana-Champaign	IL	27,006	HC
Univ of New Hampshire	NH	29,333	VC
Univ of Virginia	VA	27,367	MC
Univ of Wisc-Green Bay	WI	15,184	C
Western Kentucky Univ	KY	16,850	C
Western Mich Univ	MI	21,791	C
Westfield State Univ	MA	20,404	C

CIVIL AND ENVIRONMENTAL ENGINEERING

School	ST	$IS	SR
Univ of Minn/Twin Cities	MN	24,269	MC
Univ of Nevada, Reno	NV	18,010	C

CIVIL ENGINEERING

School	ST	$IS	SR
Alabama A&M Univ	AL	18,796	C
Angelo State Univ	TX	15,882	LC
Arizona State Univ at the Tempe Campus	AZ	23,001	VC
Auburn Univ	AL	24,300	VC+
Boise State Univ	ID	17,368	C
Bradley Univ	IL	43,240	VC
Brigham Young Univ	UT	13,248	MC
Bucknell Univ	PA	67,136	MC
Calif Baptist Univ	CA	42,986	C
Calif Polytechnic State Univ	CA	22,547	MC
Calif State Polytechnic Univ, Pomona	CA	21,811	C
Cal State, Chico	CA	19,790	VC
Cal State, Fresno	CA	16,902	LC
Cal State, Fullerton	CA	21,902	C
Cal State, Long Beach	CA	18,850	C
Cal State, Los Angeles	CA	17,186	LC
Cal State, Northridge	CA	17,277	LC
Cal State, Sacramento	CA	19,060	C
Calvin College	MI	43,090	HC
Caribbean Univ	PR	12,227	
Carnegie Mellon Univ	PA	67,980	MC
Carroll College	MT	44,304	C
Case Western Reserve Univ	OH	62,284	MC
Central Conn State Univ	CT	22,041	C
Christian Brothers Univ	TN	31,670	VC
CUNY/City College	NY	20,204	C
Clarkson Univ	NY	60,392	VC
Clemson Univ	SC		HC
Cleveland State Univ	OH	22,290	C
Colo Mesa Univ	CO	19,707	LC
Colo State Univ	CO	23,033	C
Columbia Univ/City of New York	NY	62,958	MC
Cooper Union for the Advancement of Science and Art	NY	61,370	MC
Cornell Univ	NY	67,591	MC
Delaware State Univ	DE	19,376	LC
Dordt College	IA	37,860	C+
Drexel Univ	PA	65,927	HC
Duke Univ	NC	68,298	MC
Embry-Riddle Aeronautical Univ - Daytona Beach	FL	45,822	VC
Florida A&M Univ	FL	15,361	C
Florida Atlantic Univ	FL	18,256	C
Florida Gulf Coast Univ	FL	14,738	C
Florida Inst of Technology	FL	53,306	VC
Florida International Univ	FL	20,281	C
Florida State Univ	FL	16,771	HC
George Mason Univ	VA	19,884	C
Georgia Inst of Technology	GA	23,910	MC
Georgia Southern Univ	GA	16,540	VC
Gonzaga Univ	WA	52,880	HC
Hofstra Univ	NY	58,210	C+
Howard Univ	DC	37,616	C+
Idaho State Univ	ID	13,619	LC
Illinois Inst of Technology	IL	56,826	HC+
Indiana Univ-Purdue Univ Fort Wayne	IN	18,675	C
Iowa State Univ	IA	18,176	C
Jackson State Univ	MS	15,879	LC
Johns Hopkins Univ	MD	68,080	MC
Kansas State Univ	KS	17,780	VC
Kennesaw State Univ	GA	18,899	VC
King's College	PA	48,240	C
Lafayette College	PA	68,520	MC
Lamar Univ	TX	18,014	LC
Lawrence Tech Univ	MI	41,630	VC
Lehigh Univ	PA	63,860	MC
Lipscomb Univ	TN	42,984	VC
Louisiana State Univ and A&M College	LA	18,677	VC
Louisiana Tech Univ	LA	11,422	VC
Loyola Marymount Univ	CA	60,202	VC+
Manhattan College	NY	55,652	C
Marquette Univ	WI	53,090	VC+
Marshall Univ	WV	18,044	C
Mass Inst of Technology	MA	62,662	MC
Merrimack College	MA	55,415	C
Mich State Univ	MI	24,542	VC
Mich Tech Univ	MI	25,551	VC+
Milwaukee School of Engineering	WI	48,531	HC+
Minn State Univ, Mankato	MN	17,190	C
Miss State Univ	MS	12,028	C+
Missouri Univ of Science and Technology	MO	18,655	HC
Montana State Univ	MT	15,500	C+
Morgan State Univ	MD	17,190	LC
New Jersey Inst of Technology	NJ	30,198	HC
New Mexico Inst of Mining and Technology	NM	15,385	HC+
New Mexico State Univ	NM	14,050	LC
New York Univ	NY	68,139	MC
N Car A&T State Univ	NC	13,786	C
N Car State Univ	NC	22,434	HC+
N Dak State Univ	ND	16,245	VC
Northeastern Univ	MA	65,352	MC
Northern Arizona Univ	AZ	21,003	C
Northwestern Univ	IL	68,725	MC
Norwich Univ	VT	56,234	C
Ohio Northern Univ	OH	44,050	VC
Ohio State Univ at Columbus	OH	22,843	MC
Ohio Univ	OH	23,394	VC
Okla State Univ	OK	17,180	C+
Old Dominion Univ	VA	21,618	C
Olivet Nazarene Univ	IL	41,840	VC
Oregon Inst of Technology	OR	19,227	C
Oregon State Univ	OR	23,337	VC
Pennsylvania State Univ - Univ Park	PA	29,716	HC
Point Park Univ	PA	41,270	C
Portland State Univ	OR	19,443	C
Prairie View A&M Univ	TX	27,273	LC
Princeton Univ	NJ	60,090	MC
Purdue Univ Northwest	IN	15,178	C
Purdue Univ/West Lafayette	IN	20,032	MC
Quinnipiac Univ	CT	60,970	VC
Rensselaer Polytechnic Inst	NY	67,265	MC
Rice Univ	TX	59,458	MC
Rose-Hulman Inst of Technology	IN	59,823	MC
Rowan Univ	NJ	24,491	VC
Rutgers Univ - New Brunswick	NJ	27,090	HC
St. Louis Univ	MO	49,866	HC
St. Martin's Univ	WA	45,056	C
San Diego State Univ	CA	23,156	VC
San Francisco State Univ	CA	18,514	LC
San Jose State Univ	CA	22,630	C
Savannah State Univ	GA	17,036	C
Seattle Univ	WA	54,957	VC
S Dak School of Mines and Technology	SD	18,570	C+
S Dak State Univ	SD	15,874	C
Southern Illinois Univ Carbondale	IL	24,554	C
Southern Illinois Univ Edwardsville	IL	20,188	C
Southern Methodist Univ	TX	69,008	MC
Southern Univ and A&M College	LA	16,074	LC
Stanford Univ	CA	62,541	MC
SUNY Polytechnic Inst	NY	20,438	VC
SUNY/Univ at Buffalo	NY	23,122	C
Stevens Inst of Technology	NJ	64,954	MC
Stony Brook Univ/The SUNY	NY	22,703	MC
Syracuse Univ	NY	62,313	HC
Tarleton State Univ	TX	15,248	LC
Temple Univ	PA	24,392	C+
Tenn State Univ	TN	14,423	LC
Tenn Tech Univ	TN	17,929	C
Texas A&M Univ at College Station	TX	20,771	VC+
Texas A&M Univ at Kingsville	TX	16,580	LC
Texas Tech Univ	TX	20,156	C+
The Catholic Univ of America	DC	58,376	VC
The Citadel, The Military College of S Car	SC	20,679	C
The College of New Jersey	NJ	28,675	VC+
The George Washington Univ	DC	68,474	HC+
The Univ of Akron	OH	22,566	C
The Univ of Alabama	AL	24,320	C+
The Univ of Arizona	AZ	24,086	C
The Univ of Memphis	TN	18,278	C

ST = STATE **$IS** = IN-STATE COSTS **SR** = SELECTOR RATING

School	ST	$IS	SR
The Univ of Tenn at Chattanooga	TN	17,340	C+
The Univ of Tenn at Knoxville	TN	22,112	VC
The Univ of Texas at Austin	TX	20,206	MC
The Univ of Texas at San Antonio	TX	21,060	C
The Univ of Utah	UT	18,751	VC
Trine Univ	IN	41,310	C
Tufts Univ	MA		MC
United States Air Force Academy	CO		C
United States Coast Guard Academy	CT	942	HC
United States Military Academy at West Point	NY		HC+
Universidad Politecnica de PR, Hato Rey campus	PR	23,514	
Univ of Alabama at Birmingham	AL	22,092	C
Univ of Alabama in Huntsville	AL	20,028	VC
Univ of Alaska Anchorage	AK	17,914	C
Univ of Alaska Fairbanks	AK	16,874	VC
Univ of Arkansas at Fayetteville	AR	19,766	VC
Univ of Calif at Berkeley	CA	29,886	MC
Univ of Calif at Davis	CA	28,468	HC
Univ of Calif at Irvine	CA	33,857	VC
Univ of Calif at Los Angeles	CA	27,438	HC+
Univ of Central Florida	FL	16,379	VC
Univ of Cincinnati	OH	22,118	VC
Univ of Colo Boulder	CO	26,048	HC
Univ of Colo Denver	CO	22,238	C
Univ of Conn	CT	27,394	
Univ of Dayton	OH	54,930	VC
Univ of Delaware	DE	32,214	VC
Univ of Detroit Mercy	MI	48,816	C
Univ of Evansville	IN	44,186	C+
Univ of Florida	FL	16,291	HC+
Univ of Georgia	GA	21,878	HC
Univ of Hartford	CT	49,776	C
Univ of Hawaii at Manoa	HI	23,261	C
Univ of Houston	TX	21,871	VC
Univ of Idaho	ID	16,158	C
Univ of Illinois at Chicago	IL	24,664	VC
Univ of Illinois at Urbana-Champaign	IL	27,006	HC
Univ of Iowa	IA	19,415	HC
Univ of Kansas	KS	20,884	VC
Univ of Kentucky	KY	24,800	C+
Univ of Louisiana at Lafayette	LA	14,516	C
Univ of Louisville	KY	19,692	C
Univ of Maine	ME	21,038	VC
Univ of Maryland/College Park	MD	21,938	HC
Univ of Mass Amherst	MA	27,669	HC
Univ of Mass Dartmouth	MA	26,507	C
Univ of Mass Lowell	MA	27,296	VC
Univ of Miami	FL	63,494	MC
Univ of Mich/Ann Arbor	MI	25,274	MC
Univ of Minn/Duluth	MN	20,292	C
Univ of Minn/Twin Cities	MN	24,269	MC
Univ of Miss	MS	18,802	C
Univ of Missouri-Columbia	MO	20,463	VC
Univ of Missouri-Kansas City	MO	19,563	VC
Univ of Missouri-St. Louis	MO	19,810	VC
Univ of Mount Union	OH	39,990	C
Univ of Nebr - Lincoln	NE	18,589	VC
Univ of Nevada, Las Vegas	NV	17,553	C
Univ of Nevada, Reno	NV	18,010	C
Univ of New Hampshire	NH	29,333	VC
Univ of New Haven	CT	53,680	C
Univ of New Mexico	NM	16,808	C
Univ of New Orleans	LA	12,840	C
Univ of N Car at Charlotte	NC	17,803	VC
Univ of N Dak	ND	16,673	C
Univ of North Florida	FL	15,996	VC
Univ of Northwestern - St. Paul	MN	39,530	C
Univ of Notre Dame	IN	68,801	MC
Univ of Okla	OK	19,651	HC
Univ of Pennsylvania	PA	63,526	MC
Univ of Pittsburgh	PA	30,030	MC
Univ of Portland	OR	52,152	VC
Univ of PR, at Mayaguez	PR	13,995	
Univ of Rhode Island	RI	26,066	VC
Univ of South Alabama	AL	16,880	C
Univ of S Car at Columbia	SC	21,726	VC
Univ of South Florida/Tampa	FL	16,110	VC
Univ of Southern Calif	CA	66,631	MC
Univ of Texas at Arlington	TX	18,876	C
Univ of Texas at El Paso	TX	34,452	NC
Univ of Texas Rio Grande Valley	TX	15,573	LC
Univ of the District of Columbia	DC	21,260	LC
Univ of the Pacific	CA	57,446	VC
Univ of Toledo	OH	19,336	C
Univ of Vermont	VT	29,792	HC
Univ of Virginia	VA	27,367	MC
Univ of Washington	WA	23,091	MC
Univ of Wisc-Madison	WI	21,647	MC
Univ of Wisc-Milwaukee	WI	21,538	C
Univ of Wisc-Platteville	WI	14,148	C
Univ of Wyoming	WY	15,537	C
Utah State Univ	UT	13,235	C
Valparaiso Univ	IN	50,160	VC
Vanderbilt Univ	TN	63,248	MC
Villanova Univ	PA	64,922	MC
Virginia Military Inst	VA	26,460	VC
Virginia Polytechnic Inst and State Univ	VA	21,920	VC
Washington State Univ	WA	22,747	C
Washington Univ in St. Louis	MO	67,539	MC
Wayne State Univ	MI	23,085	C
Wentworth Inst of Technology	MA	48,810	VC
West Virginia Univ	WV	18,952	VC
West Virginia Univ Inst of Technology	WV	18,264	C
Western Kentucky Univ	KY	16,850	C
Western Mich Univ	MI	21,791	C
Western New England Univ	MA	49,182	C
Widener Univ	PA	58,190	C
Worcester Polytechnic Inst	MA	62,846	MC
Youngstown State Univ	OH	17,487	C

CIVIL ENGINEERING TECHNOLOGY

School	ST	$IS	SR
Alabama A&M Univ	AL	18,796	C
Arkansas State Univ	AR	16,190	C
Cal State, Fresno	CA	16,902	LC
Central Conn State Univ	CT	22,041	C
Colo State Univ-Pueblo	CO	21,581	C
Fairleigh Dickinson Univ/ Metropolitan Campus	NJ	52,392	C
Fairmont State Univ	WV	15,726	C
Idaho State Univ	ID	13,619	LC
Lincoln Univ	MO	14,402	NC
Metropolitan State Univ of Denver	CO	6,928	LC
Montana State Univ-Northern	MT	11,370	NC
Murray State Univ	KY	17,726	C+
Old Dominion Univ	VA	21,618	C
Pennsylvania College of Technology	PA	27,693	NC
Point Park Univ	PA	41,270	C
Rochester Inst of Technology	NY	52,734	HC+
St. Louis Univ	MO	49,866	HC
S Car State Univ	SC	21,330	LC
Southern Univ and A&M College	LA	16,074	LC
SUNY Polytechnic Inst	NY	20,438	VC
Texas Southern Univ	TX	19,592	LC
Univ of N Car at Charlotte	NC	17,803	VC
Univ of Pittsburgh at Johnstown	PA	22,092	C
Univ of Southern Indiana	IN	16,808	C
Western Kentucky Univ	KY	16,850	C
Youngstown State Univ	OH	17,487	C

CLASSICAL AND NEAR EASTERN CIVILIZATION

School	ST	$IS	SR
Brown Univ	RI	64,566	MC
Calvin College	MI	43,090	HC
Creighton Univ	NE	49,452	VC
Indiana Univ Bloomington	IN	20,791	HC

CLASSICAL LANGUAGES

School	ST	$IS	SR
Agnes Scott College	GA	51,930	VC+
Asbury Univ	KY	36,450	C+
Austin College	TX	51,059	HC
Ball State Univ	IN	19,808	C+
Bard College	NY	65,924	HC
Beloit College	WI	55,206	HC
Boston Univ	MA	67,352	MC
Brigham Young Univ	UT	13,248	MC
Bryn Mawr College	PA	65,220	MC
Canisius College	NY	49,672	C
Carroll College	MT	44,304	C
Concordia College - Moorhead	MN	46,418	C
Creighton Univ	NE	49,452	VC
Dartmouth College	NH	68,109	MC
DePauw Univ	IN	58,688	VC
Dickinson College	PA	66,166	MC
Duke Univ	NC	68,298	MC
Duquesne Univ	PA	48,508	VC
Eastern Mich Univ	MI	19,761	C
Fordham Univ	NY	68,431	MC
Hollins Univ	VA	49,635	VC
Hope College	MI	42,840	VC
John Carroll Univ	OH	51,570	C
Luther College	IA	49,990	C
Marquette Univ	WI	53,090	VC+
Miami Univ	OH	27,190	HC+
New York Univ	NY	68,139	MC
Pacific Lutheran Univ	WA	49,960	C
Rutgers Univ - New Brunswick	NJ	27,090	HC
St. Louis Univ	MO	49,866	HC
St. Mary's College of Calif	CA	57,420	C
St. Peter's Univ	NJ	49,192	C
Scripps College	CA	69,260	HC
Sewanee: The Univ of the South	TN	58,000	HC+
Southern Illinois Univ Carbondale	IL	24,554	C
St. Bonaventure Univ	NY	45,596	C
Univ of Calif at Berkeley	CA	29,886	MC
Univ of Calif at Riverside	CA	32,912	C
Univ of Calif, Santa Cruz	CA	28,731	C+
Univ of Georgia	GA	21,878	HC
Univ of Kansas	KS	20,884	VC
Univ of Mass Boston	MA	13,828	C
Univ of Mich/Ann Arbor	MI	25,274	MC
Univ of Minn/Twin Cities	MN	24,269	MC
Univ of Nebr - Lincoln	NE	18,589	VC
Univ of N Car at Greensboro	NC	15,998	C
Univ of N Dak	ND	16,673	C
Vanderbilt Univ	TN	63,248	MC
Washington Univ in St. Louis	MO	67,539	MC
Wellesley College	MA	66,984	MC
Wheaton College	IL	44,993	MC
Wright State Univ	OH	16,983	C
Yeshiva Univ	NY	52,750	VC

CLASSICAL STUDIES

School	ST	$IS	SR
Colgate Univ	NY	67,500	MC
Hollins Univ	VA	49,635	VC
Indiana Univ Bloomington	IN	20,791	HC
Univ of Georgia	GA	21,878	HC
Univ of Minn/Twin Cities	MN	24,269	MC
Univ of N Car at Greensboro	NC	15,998	C
Univ of Notre Dame	IN	68,801	MC
Univ of Okla	OK	19,651	HC
Univ of Rhode Island	RI	26,066	VC
Wellesley College	MA	66,984	MC

CLASSICAL/ANCIENT CIVILIZATION

School	ST	$IS	SR
Agnes Scott College	GA	51,930	VC+
Bard College	NY	65,924	HC
Barnard College/Columbia Univ	NY	68,762	MC
Bates College	ME	64,500	HC
Beloit College	WI	55,206	HC
Boston College	MA	68,043	MC
Boston Univ	MA	67,352	MC
Bowdoin College	ME	65,980	MC
Brigham Young Univ	UT	13,248	MC
Brown Univ	RI	64,566	MC
Carleton College	MN	66,414	MC
Centre College	KY	50,680	MC
Christendom College	VA	32,600	VC
Christopher Newport Univ	VA	24,878	VC+
Clark Univ	MA	53,260	HC+
Cleveland State Univ	OH	22,290	C
Colby College	ME	64,060	MC
College of William & Mary	VA	34,907	MC
Columbia Univ/ School of General Studies	NY	61,470	MC
Columbia Univ/City of New York	NY	62,958	MC
Cornell College	IA	49,900	VC
Dartmouth College	NH	68,109	MC
Denison Univ	OH	62,770	HC+
DePauw Univ	IN	58,688	VC
Dickinson College	PA	66,166	MC
Duke Univ	NC	68,298	MC
Duquesne Univ	PA	48,508	VC
Earlham College	IN	55,670	HC
Eckerd College	FL	55,206	VC
Emory Univ	GA	63,286	MC
Florida State Univ	FL	16,771	HC
Fordham Univ	NY	68,431	MC
Gonzaga Univ	WA	52,880	HC
Hawaii Pacific Univ	HI	33,420	C
Howard Univ	DC	37,616	C+
Indiana Univ Bloomington	IN	20,791	HC
Kalamazoo College	MI	53,931	HC
Lehigh Univ	PA	63,860	MC
Loyola Marymount Univ	CA	60,202	VC+
Loyola Univ Chicago	IL	57,158	VC
Loyola Univ Maryland	MD	61,710	VC
Loyola Univ New Orleans	LA	52,456	VC
Mich State Univ	MI	24,542	VC
Mount Holyoke College	MA	56,746	MC
New York Univ	NY	68,139	MC
North Central College	IL	48,712	C+
Ohio Univ	OH	23,394	VC
Rhodes College	TN	51,900	HC
Rice Univ	TX	59,458	MC
Rollins College	FL	58,670	HC
Rutgers Univ - Newark	NJ	27,351	C
St. Peter's Univ	NJ	49,192	C
Scripps College	CA	69,260	HC
Smith College	MA	66,774	MC
St. Olaf College	MN	56,430	HC
SUNY at Binghamton	NY	24,100	MC
Swarthmore College	PA	63,550	MC
Syracuse Univ	NY	62,313	HC
The Univ of Texas at Austin	TX	20,206	MC
Trinity College	CT	69,020	HC
Univ of Arkansas at Fayetteville	AR	19,766	VC
Univ of Calif at Berkeley	CA	29,886	MC
Univ of Calif at Davis	CA	28,468	HC
Univ of Calif at Irvine	CA	33,857	VC
Univ of Calif at Los Angeles	CA	27,438	HC+
Univ of Calif at Riverside	CA	32,912	C
Univ of Chicago	IL	70,551	MC
Univ of Cincinnati	OH	22,118	VC
Univ of Evansville	IN	44,186	C+
Univ of Florida	FL	16,291	HC+
Univ of Illinois at Chicago	IL	24,664	VC
Univ of Iowa	IA	19,415	HC
Univ of Kansas	KS	20,884	VC
Univ of Maryland/Baltimore County	MD	23,004	VC
Univ of Mich/Ann Arbor	MI	25,274	MC
Univ of Miss	MS	18,802	C
Univ of Nebr - Lincoln	NE	18,589	VC
Univ of N Car at Greensboro	NC	15,998	C
Univ of Oregon	OR	24,021	VC
Univ of Richmond	VA	62,730	MC
Univ of Southern Calif	CA	66,631	MC
Univ of Texas at Arlington	TX	18,876	C
Vassar College	NY	68,110	MC
Wellesley College	MA	66,984	MC
Wesleyan Univ	CT	66,940	MC
Wheaton College	MA	63,818	VC
Willamette Univ	OR	62,514	VC+
Yale Univ	CT	64,650	MC

CLASSICS

School	ST	$IS	SR
Alabama A&M Univ	AL	18,796	C
Amherst College	MA	66,186	MC
Augustana College	IL	51,222	VC+
Augustana Univ	SD	39,968	VC
Austin College	TX	51,059	HC
Ball State Univ	IN	19,808	C+
Barnard College/Columbia Univ	NY	68,762	MC
Baylor Univ	TX	56,803	HC
Beloit College	WI	55,206	HC
Boston College	MA	68,043	MC
Boston Univ	MA	67,352	MC
Bowdoin College	ME	65,980	MC
Bowling Green State Univ	OH	19,975	C
Brandeis Univ	MA	68,443	MC
Brigham Young Univ	UT	13,248	MC
Brown Univ	RI	64,566	MC
Bryn Mawr College	PA	65,220	MC
Bucknell Univ	PA	67,136	MC
Cal State, Long Beach	CA	18,850	C
Carleton College	MN	66,414	MC
Case Western Reserve Univ	OH	62,284	MC
CUNY/Brooklyn College	NY	7,163	C+
CUNY/Hunter College	NY	31,098	VC
CUNY/Queens College	NY	21,507	C
Claremont McKenna College	CA	69,900	MC
Colby College	ME	64,060	MC
Colgate Univ	NY	67,500	MC
College of Charleston	SC	24,046	VC
College of St. Benedict	MN	54,480	C
College of the Holy Cross	MA	64,320	MC
Colo College	CO	64,894	MC
Columbia Univ/ School of General Studies	NY	61,470	MC
Columbia Univ/City of New York	NY	62,958	MC
Concordia College - Moorhead	MN	46,418	C
Conn College	CT	65,000	MC
Cornell Univ	NY	67,591	MC
Dartmouth College	NH	68,109	MC
Davidson College	NC	60,119	MC
Drew Univ/College of Liberal Arts	NJ	53,608	VC
Elmira College	NY	53,900	C
Emory Univ	GA	63,286	MC
Florida State Univ	FL	16,771	HC
Fordham Univ	NY	68,431	MC
Franciscan Univ of Steubenville	OH	33,980	VC
Franklin and Marshall College	PA	67,960	MC
Furman Univ	SC	61,098	VC+
Georgetown Univ	DC	68,970	MC
Georgia State Univ	GA	25,250	C
Gettysburg College	PA	65,210	MC
Gonzaga Univ	WA	52,880	HC
Grand Valley State Univ	MI	22,250	C+
Grinnell College	IA	63,114	MC
Gustavus Adolphus College	MN	53,943	HC
Hamilton College	NY	64,250	MC
Hampden-Sydney College	VA	57,806	VC
Hanover College	IN	47,750	C+
Harvard College/Harvard Univ	MA	65,609	MC
Haverford College	PA	66,490	MC
Hellenic College/Holy Cross Greek Orthodox School of Theology	MA	39,906	C
Hillsdale College	MI	37,170	MC
Hobart and William Smith Colleges	NY	67,050	HC+
Hofstra Univ	NY	58,210	C+
Illinois Wesleyan Univ	IL	56,430	VC+
John Carroll Univ	OH	51,570	C
Johns Hopkins Univ	MD	68,080	MC
Kent State Univ	OH	20,928	C
Kenyon College	OH	65,840	MC
Knox College	IL	54,654	VC+
Lawrence Univ	WI	56,133	HC+
Lehigh Univ	PA	63,860	MC
Lewis & Clark College	OR	60,984	MC
Loyola Univ New Orleans	LA	52,456	VC
Macalester College	MN	64,136	MC
Marquette Univ	WI	53,090	VC+
Marshall Univ	WV	18,044	C
Miami Univ	OH	27,190	HC+
Middlebury College	VT	67,464	MC
Millsaps College	MS	50,080	C+
Monmouth College	IL	42,260	C

ST = STATE $IS = IN-STATE COSTS SR = SELECTOR RATING

School	ST	$IS	SR
Montclair State Univ	NJ	26,912	C
Mount Holyoke College	MA	56,746	MC
New College of Florida	FL	16,180	HC+
New York Univ	NY	68,139	MC
Northwestern Univ	IL	68,725	MC
Notre Dame of Maryland Univ	MD	47,570	VC
Oberlin College	OH	68,942	MC
Ohio State Univ at Columbus	OH	22,843	MC
Ohio Univ	OH	23,394	VC
Ohio Wesleyan Univ	OH	49,460	VC
Pacific Lutheran Univ	WA	49,960	C
Pitzer College	CA	68,500	HC+
Pomona College	CA	64,957	MC
Princeton Univ	NJ	60,090	MC
Providence College	RI	62,870	HC
Purdue Univ/West Lafayette	IN	20,032	MC
Randolph College	VA	53,970	C
Randolph-Macon College	VA	51,480	VC
Reed College	OR	65,300	MC
Rice Univ	TX	59,458	MC
Rockford Univ	IL	38,570	C
St. Anselm College	NH	56,636	VC
St. John's Univ	MN	53,472	C
St. Louis Univ	MO	49,866	HC
Samford Univ	AL	40,770	VC
San Diego State Univ	CA	23,156	VC
San Francisco State Univ	CA	18,514	LC
Sarah Lawrence College	NY	68,866	MC
Seattle Pacific Univ	WA	47,439	C+
Seton Hall Univ	NJ	58,008	C
Siena College	NY	48,916	C
Skidmore College	NY	66,600	MC
Smith College	MA	66,774	MC
Southwestern Univ	TX	52,370	VC
St. Catherine Univ	MN	45,630	C
St. Olaf College	MN	56,430	HC
Stanford Univ	CA	62,541	MC
SUNY at Binghamton	NY	24,100	MC
SUNY/Univ at Buffalo	NY	23,122	C
Swarthmore College	PA	63,550	MC
Syracuse Univ	NY	62,313	HC
Temple Univ	PA	24,392	C+
Texas Tech Univ	TX	20,156	C+
The Catholic Univ of America	DC	58,376	VC
The College of New Rochelle	NY	46,300	LC
The George Washington Univ	DC	68,474	HC+
The Univ of Akron	OH	22,566	C
The Univ of Alabama	AL	24,320	C+
The Univ of Arizona	AZ	24,086	C
The Univ of Tenn at Knoxville	TN	22,112	VC
The Univ of Texas at Austin	TX	20,206	MC
The Univ of Texas at San Antonio	TX	21,060	C
The Univ of Utah	UT	18,751	VC
Transylvania Univ	KY	47,450	HC+
Trinity College	CT	69,020	HC
Trinity Univ	TX	54,480	MC
Truman State Univ	MO	16,286	MC
Tufts Univ	MA		MC
Tulane Univ	LA	67,496	MC
Union College	NY	64,320	MC
Univ of Calif at Irvine	CA	33,857	VC
Univ of Calif at Los Angeles	CA	27,438	HC+
Univ of Calif at Santa Barbara	CA	30,627	HC+
Univ of Calif San Diego	CA	30,450	MC
Univ of Chicago	IL	70,551	MC
Univ of Colo Boulder	CO	26,048	HC
Univ of Conn	CT	27,394	
Univ of Dallas	TX	50,676	VC
Univ of Hawaii at Manoa	HI	23,261	C
Univ of Illinois at Urbana-Champaign	IL	27,006	HC
Univ of Iowa	IA	19,415	HC
Univ of Mary Washington	VA	23,039	C+
Univ of Maryland/College Park	MD	21,938	HC
Univ of Mass Amherst	MA	27,669	HC
Univ of Mass Boston	MA	13,828	C
Univ of Miami	FL	63,494	MC
Univ of Mich/Ann Arbor	MI	25,274	MC
Univ of Missouri-Columbia	MO	20,463	VC
Univ of Montana	MT	14,105	C
Univ of Nebr - Lincoln	NE	18,589	VC
Univ of New Hampshire	NH	29,333	VC
Univ of New Mexico	NM	16,808	C
Univ of N Car at Asheville	NC	16,251	VC+
Univ of N Car at Chapel Hill	NC	20,561	MC
Univ of Oregon	OR	24,021	VC
Univ of Pennsylvania	PA	63,526	MC
Univ of Pittsburgh	PA	30,030	MC
Univ of Puget Sound	WA	60,210	HC
Univ of Rochester	NY	65,032	MC
Univ of S Car at Columbia	SC	21,726	VC
Univ of South Florida/Tampa	FL	16,110	VC
Univ of Southern Calif	CA	66,631	MC
Univ of Vermont	VT	29,792	HC
Univ of Virginia	VA	27,367	MC
Univ of Washington	WA	23,091	MC
Univ of Wisc-Madison	WI	21,647	MC
Univ of Wisc-Milwaukee	WI	21,538	C
Valparaiso Univ	IN	50,160	VC
Vanderbilt Univ	TN	63,248	MC
Villanova Univ	PA	64,922	MC
Virginia Wesleyan Univ	VA	45,980	LC
Wabash College	IN	52,100	VC
Wake Forest Univ	NC	69,354	MC
Washington and Lee Univ	VA	59,647	MC
Washington Univ in St. Louis	MO	67,539	MC
Wayne State Univ	MI	23,085	C
Wellesley College	MA	66,984	MC
Wesleyan Univ	CT	66,940	MC
Western Kentucky Univ	KY	16,850	C
Western Washington Univ	WA	18,904	VC
Wheaton College	MA	63,818	VC
Whitman College	WA	59,772	MC
Williams College	MA	67,700	MC
Xavier Univ	OH	49,380	VC
Yale Univ	CT	64,650	MC

CLINICAL LABORATORY SCIENCE

School	ST	$IS	SR
Albany College of Pharmacy and Health Sciences	NY	44,421	SP
Arkansas State Univ	AR	16,190	C
Bloomfield College	NJ	40,100	LC
Eastern Illinois Univ	IL	21,414	C
Eastern Mennonite Univ	VA	42,550	C
Houghton College	NY	40,558	VC
Indiana Univ of Pennsylvania	PA	24,474	C
Indiana Univ South Bend	IN	16,057	C
Indiana Univ Southeast	IN	16,931	C
Indiana Univ-Purdue Univ Indianapolis	IN	18,952	C
Lake Superior State Univ	MI	19,867	C
Lincoln Univ	MO	14,402	NC
Loyola Univ Chicago	IL	57,158	VC
Marian Univ	IN	43,206	C
Monmouth Univ	NJ	50,184	C
Neumann Univ	PA	40,678	LC
St. Louis Univ	MO	49,866	HC
Stony Brook Univ/The SUNY	NY	22,703	MC
Thomas Edison State Univ	NJ	6,350	NC
Univ of Evansville	IN	44,186	C+
Univ of Mass Lowell	MA	27,296	VC
Univ of St. Francis	IN	38,520	C
Univ of S Car Aiken	SC	18,094	C
Univ of Wisc-La Crosse	WI	15,425	VC
Wartburg College	IA	49,478	C
Western Illinois Univ	IL	20,897	C

CLINICAL PSYCHOLOGY

School	ST	$IS	SR
Averett Univ	VA	43,034	LC
Cal State, Fullerton	CA	21,902	C
Eastern Nazarene College	MA	41,114	C
Faulkner Univ	AL	26,410	C
Goddard College	VT	17,040	VC
Kutztown Univ of Pennsylvania	PA	19,477	C
Marywood Univ	PA	47,840	C
St. Leo Univ	FL	32,850	C
Seattle Pacific Univ	WA	47,439	C+
Univ of Louisville	KY	19,692	C
Univ of New Haven	CT	53,680	C
Western Kentucky Univ	KY	16,850	C

CLINICAL SCIENCE

School	ST	$IS	SR
Bellarmine Univ	KY	52,532	C
Benedictine Univ	IL	38,300	C
Bethune-Cookman Univ	FL	23,322	C
Brigham Young Univ	UT	13,248	MC
Cal State, Bakersfield	CA	22,397	LC
Cal State, Dominguez Hills	CA	19,022	LC
Campbell Univ	NC	37,570	VC
Canisius College	NY	49,672	C
Concordia College - Moorhead	MN	46,418	C
DePaul Univ	IL	52,807	VC
Fairleigh Dickinson Univ/College at Florham	NJ	54,770	C
Fairleigh Dickinson Univ/Metropolitan Campus	NJ	52,392	C
Florida Gulf Coast Univ	FL	14,738	C
Georgian Court Univ	NJ	43,068	LC
Grand Valley State Univ	MI	22,250	C+
Gwynedd Mercy Univ	PA	43,780	LC
Howard Univ	DC	37,616	C+
Ithaca College	NY	58,158	VC+
Lake Superior State Univ	MI	19,867	C
LIU Brooklyn	NY	50,698	C
LIU Post	NY	50,698	C+
Marquette Univ	WI	53,090	VC+
Mary Baldwin Univ	VA	40,495	C
Maryville Univ of St. Louis	MO	38,558	VC
McNeese State Univ	LA	7,838	C
Mich State Univ	MI	24,542	VC
Minn State Univ, Mankato	MN	17,190	C
Missouri State Univ	MO	15,837	C+
New Mexico State Univ	NM	14,050	LC
N Dak State Univ	ND	16,245	VC
Northern Illinois Univ	IL	20,176	C
Northern Mich Univ	MI	20,853	C
Purdue Univ/West Lafayette	IN	20,032	MC
Quincy Univ	IL	38,170	LC
Ramapo College of New Jersey	NJ	25,760	VC
Rockhurst Univ	MO	28,990	C
Rutgers Univ - New Brunswick	NJ	27,090	HC
Rutgers Univ - Newark	NJ	27,351	C
St. Louis Univ	MO	49,866	HC
San Francisco State Univ	CA	18,514	LC
S Dak State Univ	SD	15,874	C
St. John's Univ	NY	57,160	C+
Texas A&M Univ at Corpus Christi	TX	16,851	LC
Texas State Univ	TX	18,721	C
The College of Idaho	ID	36,415	C
The George Washington Univ	DC	68,474	HC+
The Univ of Tenn at Knoxville	TN	22,112	VC
Truman State Univ	MO	16,286	MC
Univ of Jamestown	ND	28,508	C
Univ of Mass Dartmouth	MA	26,507	C
Univ of Nevada, Las Vegas	NV	17,553	C
Univ of N Car at Chapel Hill	NC	20,561	MC
Univ of N Car Wilmington	NC	16,784	VC
Univ of N Dak	ND	16,673	C
Univ of St. Mary	KS	37,080	NC
Univ of Texas at El Paso	TX	34,452	NC
Univ of Texas Rio Grande Valley	TX	15,573	LC
Univ of Wisc-Stevens Point	WI	14,043	C
Virginia Commonwealth Univ	VA	23,811	VC
Walsh Univ	OH	39,010	C
Washburn Univ	KS	15,827	C
Wayne State Univ	MI	23,085	C
Weber State Univ	UT	14,112	C
West Liberty Univ	WV	16,158	C
Wright State Univ	OH	16,983	C
Youngstown State Univ	OH	17,487	C

CLOTHING AND TEXTILES MANAGEMENT/PRODUCTION/SERVICES

School	ST	$IS	SR
Cheyney Univ of Pennsylvania	PA	20,896	LC
College of the Ozarks	MO	7,530	VC
East Carolina Univ	NC	16,539	C
Eastern Mich Univ	MI	19,761	C
Florida State Univ	FL	16,771	HC
Johnson & Wales Univ/Charlotte Campus	NC	44,768	C
Johnson & Wales Univ/North Miami Campus	FL	44,768	C
Johnson & Wales Univ/Providence Campus	RI	44,768	C
N Car A&T State Univ	NC	13,786	C
N Car State Univ	NC	22,434	HC+
San Francisco State Univ	CA	18,514	LC
Southern Illinois Univ Carbondale	IL	24,554	C
The Univ of Alabama	AL	24,320	C+
Univ of N Car at Greensboro	NC	15,998	C
Univ of Northern Iowa	IA	17,480	C
Washington State Univ	WA	22,747	C
Western Mich Univ	MI	21,791	C

COASTAL ENVIORNMENTAL STUDIES

School	ST	$IS	SR
Brown Univ	RI	64,566	MC

COGNITIVE SCIENCE

School	ST	$IS	SR
Ashford Univ	CA	10,480	C
Beloit College	WI	55,206	HC
Brown Univ	RI	64,566	MC
Cal State, Stanislaus	CA	18,053	LC
Canisius College	NY	49,672	C
Case Western Reserve Univ	OH	62,284	MC
Central Mich Univ	MI	20,330	C
Dartmouth College	NH	68,109	MC
Fitchburg State Univ	MA	21,819	LC
George Fox Univ	OR	42,938	C
Hampshire College	MA	65,214	MC
Indiana Univ Bloomington	IN	20,791	HC
Johns Hopkins Univ	MD	68,080	MC
Lawrence Univ	WI	56,133	HC+
Lehigh Univ	PA	63,860	MC
Mass Inst of Technology	MA	62,662	MC
Minn State Univ, Mankato	MN	17,190	C
Northwestern Univ	IL	68,725	MC
Occidental College	CA	68,660	MC
Pomona College	CA	64,957	MC
Rice Univ	TX	59,458	MC
Sarah Lawrence College	NY	68,866	MC
Smith College	MA	66,774	MC
SUNY at Oswego	NY	22,219	VC
Tufts Univ	MA		MC
Tulane Univ	LA	67,496	MC
Univ of Calif at Berkeley	CA	29,886	MC
Univ of Calif at Los Angeles	CA	27,438	HC+
Univ of Calif San Diego	CA	30,450	MC
Univ of Conn	CT	27,394	
Univ of Denver	CO	61,129	VC+
Univ of Evansville	IN	44,186	C+
Univ of Georgia	GA	21,878	HC
Univ of Mich/Ann Arbor	MI	25,274	MC
Univ of Pennsylvania	PA	63,526	MC
Univ of Richmond	VA	62,730	MC
Univ of Rochester	NY	65,032	MC
Univ of Texas at Dallas	TX	23,640	HC
Univ of Wisc-Stout	WI	19,667	C
Vanderbilt Univ	TN	63,248	MC
Vassar College	NY	68,110	MC
Villanova Univ	PA	64,922	MC
Wellesley College	MA	66,984	MC
Wright State Univ	OH	16,983	C
Yale Univ	CT	64,650	MC

COLLABORATIVE DESIGN

School	ST	$IS	SR
Ferris State Univ	MI	21,458	C

COLLABORATIVE EDUCATION

School	ST	$IS	SR
Birmingham-Southern College	AL	44,478	C+
Goddard College	VT	17,040	VC
Huntingdon College	AL	35,900	C
Rowan Univ	NJ	24,491	VC
Troy Univ	AL	16,171	C

COLLABORATIVE PIANO

School	ST	$IS	SR
Shenandoah Univ	VA	42,100	C

COMBINED SCIENCE

School	ST	$IS	SR
Calif Baptist Univ	CA	42,986	C
Louisiana College	LA	21,274	C
Texas Christian Univ	TX	57,120	HC
Univ of Montana	MT	14,105	C
Univ of Okla	OK	19,651	HC

COMMERCIAL ART

School	ST	$IS	SR
Ashland Univ	OH	30,446	C
Brenau Univ - Women's College	GA	37,876	LC
Calif Univ of Pennsylvania	PA	20,425	LC
Cazenovia College	NY	47,866	C
Fort Valley State Univ	GA	17,988	VC
Graceland Univ	IA	35,290	C
Millikin Univ	IL	44,148	C
Missouri Western State Univ	MO	17,822	LC
Oral Roberts Univ	OK	34,316	C
Southwest Baptist Univ	MO	30,890	LC
St. Norbert College	WI	46,060	VC
St. Thomas Aquinas College	NY	32,450	C
Univ of Central Missouri	MO	18,982	C
Univ of Indianapolis	IN	36,480	VC
Univ of North Texas	TX	20,082	C
Univ of S Car Upstate	SC	19,272	LC
Washington Univ in St. Louis	MO	67,539	MC

COMMUNICATION ARTS - SPEECH

School	ST	$IS	SR
Black Hills State Univ	SD	16,622	C
Cal State, Fullerton	CA	21,902	C
CUNY/Queens College	NY	21,507	C
College of the Ozarks	MO	7,530	VC
East Central Univ	OK	13,330	C
Kutztown Univ of Pennsylvania	PA	19,477	C
LIU Brooklyn	NY	50,698	C
Millersville Univ of Pennsylvania	PA	25,298	C
Missouri Western State Univ	MO	17,822	LC
San Diego State Univ	CA	23,156	VC
St. Joseph's College, New York/Brooklyn Campus	NY	25,114	LC
St. Joseph's College, New York/Long Island Campus	NY	25,124	C
SUNY/Potsdam	NY	21,051	VC
Univ of Wisc-Platteville	WI	14,148	C
Washington State Univ	WA	22,747	C

COMMUNICATION DESIGN

School	ST	$IS	SR
Cal State, Chico	CA	19,790	VC
Dallas Baptist Univ	TX	35,220	VC
Elon Univ	NC	46,142	HC
Kutztown Univ of Pennsylvania	PA	19,477	C
Lynn Univ	FL	49,680	LC
New York City College of Technology	NY	7,185	LC
Purdue Univ Northwest	IN	15,178	C
Rochester Inst of Technology	NY	52,734	HC+
Stevenson Univ	MD	48,412	C
Syracuse Univ	NY	62,313	HC
Texas State Univ	TX	18,721	C
Western Oregon Univ	OR	19,965	LC

COMMUNICATION INFORMATION DESIGN

School	ST	$IS	SR
Missouri Western State Univ	MO	17,822	LC
SUNY Polytechnic Inst	NY	20,438	VC

COMMUNICATION RHETORIC/COMMUNICATION

School	ST	$IS	SR
Bryant Univ	RI	57,204	VC
Cedarville Univ	OH	36,244	VC
Florida Southern College	FL	45,978	VC
Hobart and William Smith Colleges	NY	67,050	HC+
Huntingdon College	AL	35,900	C
Marshall Univ	WV	18,044	C
Mercer Univ	GA	45,348	VC

ST = STATE **$IS** = IN-STATE COSTS **SR** = SELECTOR RATING

School	ST	$IS	SR
Nazareth College	NY	46,784	C
Nyack College	NY	34,450	LC
Spalding Univ	KY	31,938	C
St. Lawrence Univ	NY	66,646	HC+
Syracuse Univ	NY	62,313	HC
Univ of Nebr - Lincoln	NE	18,589	VC
Univ of N Car Wilmington	NC	16,784	VC
Univ of Pittsburgh	PA	30,030	MC
Univ of Rhode Island	RI	26,066	VC
Univ of Richmond	VA	62,730	MC
Washington & Jefferson College	PA	58,694	VC
Waynesburg Univ	PA	33,530	C
Whitman College	WA	59,772	MC
Wingate Univ	NC	41,900	C
Xavier Univ	OH	49,380	VC

COMMUNICATION SCIENCE

School	ST	$IS	SR
Elmhurst College	IL	46,514	C
Howard Univ	DC	37,616	C+
Idaho State Univ	ID	13,619	LC
Lebanon Valley College	PA	55,510	VC
LIU Brooklyn	NY	50,698	C
Missouri State Univ	MO	15,837	C+
Pennsylvania State Univ - Univ Park	PA	29,716	HC
Univ of Cincinnati	OH	22,118	VC
Univ of Georgia	GA	21,878	HC
Univ of Miss	MS	18,802	C
Univ of Oregon	OR	24,021	VC
Univ of Pittsburgh	PA	30,030	MC
Univ of Wisc-Madison	WI	21,647	MC

COMMUNICATION SCIENCES & DISORDERS

School	ST	$IS	SR
Abilene Christian Univ	TX	43,708	C+
Arkansas State Univ	AR	16,190	C
Armstrong State Univ	GA	15,615	C
Augustana College	IL	51,222	VC+
Baldwin Wallace Univ	OH	42,464	VC
Calif Baptist Univ	CA	42,986	C
Cal State, Chico	CA	19,790	VC
Cal State, Fullerton	CA	21,902	C
Eastern Illinois Univ	IL	21,414	C
Elmhurst College	IL	46,514	C
Fontbonne Univ	MO	34,606	C
Jackson State Univ	MS	15,879	LC
Marywood Univ	PA	47,840	C
Mercy College	NY	32,614	C
Minn State Univ, Mankato	MN	17,190	C
Montclair State Univ	NJ	26,912	C
Mount Vernon Nazarene Univ	OH	35,944	C
Nazareth College	NY	46,784	C
Ohio Univ	OH	23,394	VC
Pace Univ	NY	60,136	C
St. Louis Univ	MO	49,866	HC
St. Mary's College	IN	50,600	C
Samford Univ	AL	40,770	VC
San Jose State Univ	CA	22,630	C
Southeastern Louisiana Univ	LA	16,237	C
Southern Illinois Univ Carbondale	IL	24,554	C
SUNY/Plattsburgh	NY	19,314	C
Syracuse Univ	NY	62,313	HC
Texas State Univ	TX	18,721	C
The College of St. Rose	NY	44,010	C
Univ of Arkansas at Fayetteville	AR	19,766	VC
Univ of Central Arkansas	AR	15,042	VC
Univ of Montana	MT	14,105	C
Univ of Redlands	CA	61,934	VC
Univ of South Alabama	AL	16,880	C
Univ of Tulsa	OK	52,625	HC
Univ of Vermont	VT	29,792	HC
Univ of Wisc-Eau Claire	WI	16,354	VC
Univ of Wisc-Milwaukee	WI	21,538	C
Wayne State Univ	MI	23,085	C
West Chester Univ of Pennsylvania	PA	19,171	VC
Western Illinois Univ	IL	20,897	C
Western Kentucky Univ	KY	16,850	C

COMMUNICATION STUDIES

School	ST	$IS	SR
Albion College	MI	55,260	C
Ashford Univ	CA	10,480	C
Augustana College	IL	51,222	VC+
Averett Univ	VA	43,034	LC
Baldwin Wallace Univ	OH	42,464	VC
Black Hills State Univ	SD	16,622	C
Bloomsburg Univ of Pennsylvania	PA	19,930	C
Calif Baptist Univ	CA	42,986	C
Calif Polytechnic State Univ	CA	22,547	MC
Cal State, Northridge	CA	17,277	LC
Chapman Univ	CA	65,504	HC
Creighton Univ	NE	49,452	VC
DePaul Univ	IL	52,807	VC
Drury Univ	MO	37,555	VC
East Stroudsburg Univ	PA	18,578	LC
Eastern Illinois Univ	IL	21,414	C
Edgewood College	WI	35,950	C
Fordham Univ	NY	68,431	MC
Georgia Southern Univ	GA	16,540	VC
Grove City College	PA	26,654	VC
Illinois State Univ	IL	23,418	VC
Indiana Univ Bloomington	IN	20,791	HC
Indiana Univ East	IN	7,207	C
Indiana Univ South Bend	IN	16,057	C
Indiana Univ-Purdue Univ Indianapolis	IN	18,952	C
Kent State Univ	OH	20,928	C
Kutztown Univ of Pennsylvania	PA	19,477	C
Loras College	IA	40,726	C
Loyola Marymount Univ	CA	60,202	VC+
Lynn Univ	FL	49,680	LC
Madonna Univ	MI	30,450	LC
Mary Baldwin Univ	VA	40,495	C
Millersville Univ of Pennsylvania	PA	25,298	C
Minn State Univ, Mankato	MN	17,190	C
Missouri Western State Univ	MO	17,822	LC
Mount Vernon Nazarene Univ	OH	35,944	C
Niagara Univ	NY	41,010	C
Northwest Univ	WA	38,720	VC
Nova Southeastern Univ	FL	38,534	C+
Okla Baptist Univ	OK	33,990	C
Olivet Nazarene Univ	IL	41,840	VC
Pace Univ	NY	60,136	C
San Jose State Univ	CA	22,630	C
Southeast Missouri State Univ	MO	16,148	C
St. Joseph's College, New York/Brooklyn Campus	NY	25,114	LC
SUNY/Fredonia	NY	20,818	C
Tenn Wesleyan Univ	TN	32,680	LC
Texas Christian Univ	TX	57,120	HC
Texas State Univ	TX	18,721	C
Texas Tech Univ	TX	20,156	C+
The American Univ	DC	61,317	HC
The Master's Univ	CA	43,870	C
Tiffin Univ	OH	34,900	LC
Trevecca Nazarene Univ	TN	31,186	C
Univ of Denver	CO	61,129	VC+
Univ of Georgia	GA	21,878	HC
Univ of Kansas	KS	20,884	VC
Univ of Miami	FL	63,494	MC
Univ of Minn/Twin Cities	MN	24,269	MC
Univ of N Car at Greensboro	NC	15,998	C
Univ of N Car at Pembroke	NC	14,737	LC
Univ of North Georgia	GA	17,316	C
Univ of Northwestern - St. Paul	MN	39,530	C
Univ of Rhode Island	RI	26,066	VC
Univ of San Francisco	CA	60,580	C
Univ of S Dak	SD	16,109	C
Univ of Texas Rio Grande Valley	TX	15,573	LC
Univ of Wisc-La Crosse	WI	15,425	VC
Wartburg College	IA	49,478	C
West Chester Univ of Pennsylvania	PA	19,171	VC
West Virginia Wesleyan College	WV	39,188	C
Western Kentucky Univ	KY	16,850	C
Western Mich Univ	MI	21,791	C
Western Oregon Univ	OR	19,965	LC
Wingate Univ	NC	41,900	C
Winona State Univ	MN	18,109	C

COMMUNICATIONS

School	ST	$IS	SR
Abilene Christian Univ	TX	43,708	C+
Adams State Univ	CO	15,420	LC
Adelphi Univ	NY	49,792	C
Adrian College	MI	45,550	C
Alabama State Univ	AL	16,490	LC
Albertus Magnus College	CT	44,016	LC
Albright College	PA	57,326	C
Alcorn State Univ	MS	15,884	C
Alderson Broaddus Univ	WV	35,000	LC
Alfred Univ	NY	37,490	C
Allegheny College	PA	57,620	VC
Alma College	MI	49,410	VC
Alvernia Univ	PA	45,330	C
Alverno College	WI	33,294	LC
American International College	MA	47,020	LC
Anderson Univ	IN	39,450	C
Andrews Univ	MI	41,732	C
Angelo State Univ	TX	15,882	LC
Appalachian State Univ	NC	15,394	VC
Aquinas College - Mich	MI	38,876	VC
Arcadia Univ	PA	55,990	C+
Arizona State Univ at the Downtown Phoenix Campus	AZ	24,634	VC
Arizona State Univ at the Polytechnic Campus	AZ	22,394	VC
Arizona State Univ at the Tempe Campus	AZ	23,001	VC
Arizona State Univ at the West Campus	AZ	21,513	VC
Arkansas State Univ	AR	16,190	C
Arkansas Tech Univ	AR	16,534	LC
Asbury Univ	KY	36,450	C+
Ashland Univ	OH	30,446	C
Auburn Univ	AL	24,300	VC+
Auburn Univ at Montgomery	AL	15,000	C
Augsburg Univ	MN	45,129	C
Augusta Univ	GA	4,632	C
Augustana Univ	SD	39,968	VC
Aurora Univ	IL	34,990	C
Austin College	TX	51,059	HC
Austin Peay State Univ	TN	16,397	C
Avila Univ	MO	27,100	C
Azusa Pacific Univ	CA	43,972	C
Baker Univ	KS	37,190	C
Barry Univ	FL	38,730	LC
Barton College	NC	39,854	C
Bay Path Univ	MA	46,356	C
Baylor Univ	TX	56,803	HC
Becker College	MA	30,100	LC
Belhaven Univ	MS	32,250	C
Bellarmine Univ	KY	52,532	C
Bellevue Univ	NE	20,300	NC
Belmont Univ	TN	44,500	VC+
Bemidji State Univ	MN	17,730	C
Benedictine Univ	IL	38,300	C
Bennett College	NC	27,717	NC
Berea College	KY	7,094	C
Berry College	GA	47,466	VC
Bethany College	KS	38,637	LC
Bethany College	WV	38,774	LC
Bethel College	IN	36,830	C
Bethel College	KS	35,370	C
Bethel Univ	MN	46,550	C+
Bethune-Cookman Univ	FL	23,322	C
Biola Univ	CA	48,686	C
Black Hills State Univ	SD	16,622	C
Blackburn College	IL	28,526	LC
Bloomfield College	NJ	40,100	LC
Bloomsburg Univ of Pennsylvania	PA	19,930	C
Bluefield College	VA	34,711	C
Bluffton Univ	OH	40,950	C+
Boise State Univ	ID	17,368	C
Boston College	MA	68,043	MC
Boston Univ	MA	67,352	MC
Bowling Green State Univ	OH	19,975	C
Bradley Univ	IL	43,240	VC
Brenau Univ - Women's College	GA	37,876	LC
Brewton-Parker College	GA	26,120	LC
Briar Cliff Univ	IA	36,956	C
Bridgewater College	VA	46,260	C
Brigham Young Univ	UT	13,248	MC
Bryan College	TN	32,900	C
Buena Vista Univ	IA	42,344	C
Butler Univ	IN	52,890	VC+
Cabrini Univ	PA	42,591	LC
Caldwell Univ	NJ	42,165	LC
Calif Baptist Univ	CA	42,986	C
Calif Lutheran Univ	CA	52,853	C
Calif State Polytechnic Univ, Pomona	CA	21,811	C
Cal State, Bakersfield	CA	22,397	LC
Cal State, Chico	CA	19,790	VC
Cal State, Dominguez Hills	CA	19,022	LC
Cal State, East Bay	CA	20,748	C
Cal State, Fresno	CA	16,902	LC
Cal State, Fullerton	CA	21,902	C
Cal State, Long Beach	CA	18,850	C
Cal State, Sacramento	CA	19,060	C
Cal State, San Bernardino	CA	20,106	C
Cal State, San Marcos	CA	20,604	LC
Cal State, Stanislaus	CA	18,053	LC
Calvin College	MI	43,090	HC
Cameron Univ	OK	11,632	LC
Campbell Univ	NC	37,570	VC
Campbellsville Univ	KY	33,400	C
Canisius College	NY	49,672	C
Capital Univ	OH	44,778	VC
Cardinal Stritch Univ	WI	37,136	C
Carlow Univ	PA	39,696	LC
Carnegie Mellon Univ	PA	67,980	MC
Carroll College	MT	44,304	C
Carroll Univ	WI	38,100	C+
Carson-Newman Univ	TN	35,900	C
Castleton Univ	VT	20,186	C
Catawba College	NC	39,820	LC
Cazenovia College	NY	47,866	C
Cedar Crest College	PA	51,110	C
Centenary College	NJ	43,890	LC
Centenary College of Louisiana	LA	49,050	C+
Central College	IA	44,592	C
Central Methodist Univ	MO	31,500	VC
Central Mich Univ	MI	20,330	C
Central Washington Univ	WA	16,803	C
Chaminade Univ of Honolulu	HI	37,614	C
Champlain College	VT	54,724	VC
Chatham Univ	PA	47,883	VC
Chestnut Hill College	PA	47,180	C
Cheyney Univ of Pennsylvania	PA	20,896	LC
Christopher Newport Univ	VA	24,878	VC+
CUNY/Baruch College	NY	21,609	HC
CUNY/Brooklyn College	NY	7,163	C+
CUNY/City College	NY	20,204	C
CUNY/Lehman College	NY	5,788	LC
Claflin Univ	SC	25,592	LC
Clarion Univ of Pennsylvania	PA	21,608	LC
Clark Atlanta Univ	GA	31,019	LC
Clark Univ	MA	53,260	HC+
Clarke Univ	IA	42,950	C
Clarkson Univ	NY	60,392	VC
Clemson Univ	SC		HC
Cleveland State Univ	OH	22,290	C
Coastal Carolina Univ	SC	20,340	C
Coe College	IA	51,570	VC
Coker College	SC	38,196	C
Colby-Sawyer College	NH	50,790	C
College of Charleston	SC	24,046	VC
College of Mount St. Vincent	NY	45,620	C
College of St. Benedict	MN	54,480	C
College of St. Elizabeth	NJ	45,700	LC
College of St. Scholastica	MN	45,734	C+
College of Staten Island	NY	24,389	LC
College of the Ozarks	MO	7,530	VC
Colo Christian Univ	CO	40,885	VC
Colo Mesa Univ	CO	19,707	LC
Colo State Univ	CO	23,033	C
Colo State Univ-Pueblo	CO	21,581	C
Columbia College	SC	36,550	C
Columbia College - Missouri	MO	28,179	C
Columbia College Chicago	IL	40,104	C
Columbus State Univ	GA	14,336	LC
Concord Univ	WV	14,954	LC
Concordia College - Moorhead	MN	46,418	C
Concordia Univ Irvine	CA	44,860	VC
Concordia Univ Nebr	NE	41,900	VC
Concordia Univ St. Paul	MN	29,050	C
Concordia Univ Texas	TX	41,920	C
Concordia Univ Wisc	WI	35,910	C
Concordia Univ, Ann Arbor	MI	38,878	C+
Concordia Univ, Chicago	IL	41,522	C
Corban Univ	OR	41,700	C
Cornell Univ	NY	67,591	MC
Cornerstone Univ	MI	36,550	C
Culver-Stockton College	MO	34,350	C
Curry College	MA	53,331	C
Dakota Wesleyan Univ	SD	33,980	LC
Dallas Baptist Univ	TX	35,220	VC
Defiance College	OH	42,240	LC
Denison Univ	OH	62,770	HC+
DePaul Univ	IL	52,807	VC
DePauw Univ	IN	58,688	VC
DeSales Univ	PA	47,520	C
Dickinson State Univ	ND	12,372	LC
Dillard Univ	LA	20,940	VC
Dominican Univ	IL	42,472	C+
Dominican Univ of Calif	CA	58,750	C
Dordt College	IA	37,860	C+
Drake Univ	IA	49,220	HC
Drew Univ/College of Liberal Arts	NJ	53,608	VC
Drexel Univ	PA	65,927	HC
Duquesne Univ	PA	48,508	VC
East Carolina Univ	NC	16,539	C
East Central Univ	OK	13,330	C
East Tenn State Univ	TN	18,141	C
East Texas Baptist Univ	TX	34,444	C
Eastern Conn State Univ	CT	23,059	C
Eastern Mennonite Univ	VA	42,550	C
Eastern Mich Univ	MI	19,761	C
Eastern Nazarene College	MA	41,114	C
Eastern New Mexico Univ	NM	12,874	LC
Eastern Univ	PA	39,540	C
Eastern Washington Univ	WA	17,896	LC
Eckerd College	FL	55,206	VC
Edinboro Univ	PA	15,940	LC
Edward Waters College	FL	28,089	NC
Elizabethtown College	PA	56,340	VC
Elizabethtown College School of Continuing and Professional Studies	PA	18,900	C
Elmhurst College	IL	46,514	C
Elon Univ	NC	46,142	HC
Embry-Riddle Aeronautical Univ - Daytona Beach	FL	45,822	VC
Embry-Riddle Aeronautical Univ - Worldwide	FL	17,720	C
Emerson College	MA	61,824	HC+
Emmanuel College	MA	53,472	C+
Emory and Henry College	VA	46,320	C
Emporia State Univ	KS	15,029	C
Endicott College	MA	47,054	C+
Eureka College	IL	34,760	C
Evangel Univ	MO	28,898	C
Excelsior College	NY	38,800	SP
Fairfield Univ	CT	61,445	HC
Fairleigh Dickinson Univ/College at Florham	NJ	54,770	C
Fairleigh Dickinson Univ/Metropolitan Campus	NJ	52,392	C
Fairmont State Univ	WV	15,726	C
Felician Univ	NJ	46,280	LC
Ferris State Univ	MI	21,458	C
Fitchburg State Univ	MA	21,819	LC
Five Towns College	NY	35,480	LC
Flagler College	FL	27,620	C
Florida Atlantic Univ	FL	18,256	C
Florida Gulf Coast Univ	FL	14,738	C
Florida Inst of Technology	FL	53,306	VC
Florida Southern College	FL	45,978	VC
Florida State Univ	FL	16,771	HC
Fontbonne Univ	MO	34,606	C
Fort Hays State Univ	KS	12,677	C
Fort Valley State Univ	GA	17,988	VC
Framingham State Univ	MA	21,740	C
Francis Marion Univ	SC	18,144	LC
Franciscan Univ of Steubenville	OH	33,980	VC
Franklin Pierce Univ	NH	46,750	LC
Freed-Hardeman Univ	TN	29,900	C
Friends Univ	KS	38,000	C
Frostburg State Univ	MD	17,280	LC
Furman Univ	SC	61,098	VC+
Gallaudet Univ	DC	30,088	LC

ST = STATE $IS = IN-STATE COSTS SR = SELECTOR RATING

School	ST	$IS	SR
Gannon Univ	PA	42,922	C
Gardner-Webb Univ	NC	24,935	C+
Geneva College	PA	35,450	C
George Fox Univ	OR	42,938	C
George Mason Univ	VA	19,884	C
Georgetown College	KY	41,440	C
Gonzaga Univ	WA	52,880	HC
Gordon College	MA	47,740	VC
Goshen College	IN	44,350	C
Goucher College	MD	56,110	VC
Grace College and Seminary	IN	31,524	C
Graceland Univ	IA	35,290	C
Grambling State Univ	LA	15,701	C
Grand Canyon Univ	AZ	25,150	VC
Grand Valley State Univ	MI	22,250	C+
Grand View Univ	IA	32,302	C
Green Mountain College	VT	45,228	LC
Greenville College	IL	27,012	LC
Gustavus Adolphus College	MN	53,943	HC
Gwynedd Mercy Univ	PA	43,780	LC
Hamline Univ	MN	50,152	C
Hampshire College	MA	65,214	MC
Hampton Univ	VA	36,410	C
Hannibal-LaGrange Univ	MO	29,815	C
Hanover College	IN	47,750	C+
Harding Univ	AR	25,440	C
Hardin-Simmons Univ	TX	36,025	C
Hastings College	NE	35,380	C+
Hawaii Pacific Univ	HI	33,420	C
Heidelberg Univ	OH	40,400	LC
Henderson State Univ	AR	15,516	C
High Point Univ	NC	47,355	VC
Hiram College	OH	44,590	C
Hollins Univ	VA	49,635	VC
Holy Family Univ	PA	44,672	LC
Holy Names Univ	CA	46,630	LC
Hood College	MD	50,540	C
Hope College	MI	42,840	VC
Houghton College	NY	40,558	VC
Houston Baptist Univ	TX	36,450	C
Howard Payne Univ	TX	35,994	C
Howard Univ	DC	37,616	C+
Humboldt State Univ	CA	21,708	C
Huntington Univ	IN	33,996	C
Idaho State Univ	ID	13,619	LC
Illinois College	IL	41,330	VC
Immaculata Univ	PA	39,000	C
Indiana Inst of Technology	IN	34,240	LC
Indiana State Univ	IN	23,223	LC
Indiana Univ Kokomo	IN	7,207	C
Indiana Univ Northwest	IN	7,207	LC
Indiana Univ Southeast	IN	16,931	C
Indiana Univ-Purdue Univ Fort Wayne	IN	18,675	C
Indiana Wesleyan Univ	IN	33,674	C
Iona College	NY	52,514	C
Iowa State Univ	IA	18,176	C
Ithaca College	NY	58,158	VC+
Jackson State Univ	MS	15,879	LC
Jacksonville State Univ	AL	14,628	LC
Jacksonville Univ	FL	49,210	C
James Madison Univ	VA	19,084	VC
John Brown Univ	AR	35,184	VC
John Carroll Univ	OH	51,570	C
Johnson & Wales Univ/ Denver Campus	CO	44,768	C
Johnson C. Smith Univ	NC	25,336	LC
Judson Univ	IL	39,174	C
Juniata College	PA	58,118	VC
Kansas State Univ	KS	17,780	VC
Kansas Wesleyan Univ	KS	37,930	C
Kean Univ	NJ	25,620	C
Keene State College	NH	24,604	C
Kennesaw State Univ	GA	18,899	VC
Kentucky Wesleyan College	KY	34,260	LC
Keuka College	NY	42,398	C
Keystone College	PA	28,680	LC
King Univ	TN	36,976	C
King's College	PA	48,240	C
Kutztown Univ of Pennsylvania	PA	19,477	C
La Roche College	PA	38,940	C
La Salle Univ	PA	43,476	C
La Sierra Univ	CA	39,690	VC
Lake Erie College	OH	38,914	LC
Lake Forest College	IL	50,652	VC
Lake Superior State Univ	MI	19,867	C
Lamar Univ	TX	18,014	LC
Lander Univ	SC	32,200	C
Lane College	TN	17,960	LC
Lasell College	MA	49,400	C
Lawrence Tech Univ	MI	41,630	VC
Le Moyne College	NY	47,305	VC
Lee Univ	TN	22,045	C
Lees-McRae College	NC	33,944	NC
Lenoir-Rhyne Univ	NC	47,500	LC
Lewis & Clark College	OR	60,984	MC
Lewis-Clark State College	ID	14,202	C
Liberty Univ	VA	31,415	C
Limestone College	SC	32,100	C
Lincoln Memorial Univ	TN	28,430	C
Lincoln Univ	PA	20,878	LC
Lindenwood Univ	MO	25,760	C
Lindsey Wilson College	KY	33,546	C
Linfield College	OR	53,992	C
Lipscomb Univ	TN	42,984	VC
Lock Haven Univ of Pennsylvania	PA	20,544	LC
Longwood Univ	VA	22,184	C
Louisiana College	LA	21,274	C
Louisiana State Univ and A&M College	LA	18,677	VC
Louisiana State Univ in Shreveport	LA	6,902	C
Loyola Univ Chicago	IL	57,158	VC
Loyola Univ Maryland	MD	61,710	VC
Loyola Univ New Orleans	LA	52,456	VC
Lubbock Christian Univ	TX	29,727	C
Luther College	IA	49,990	VC
Lyndon State College	VT	20,714	C
Malone Univ	OH	39,200	C
Manchester Univ	IN	41,540	C
Manhattan College	NY	55,652	C
Manhattanville College	NY	52,430	C
Mansfield Univ of Pennsylvania	PA	24,244	LC
Marian Univ	IN	43,206	C
Marian Univ	WI	34,622	C
Marietta College	OH	46,190	C
Marist College	NY	49,860	VC
Marquette Univ	WI	53,090	VC+
Mars Hill Univ	NC	41,104	C
Marshall Univ	WV	18,044	C
Martin Univ	IN	21,010	LC
Marylhurst Univ	OR	16,818	NC
Marymount Manhattan College	NY	48,350	C
Marymount Univ	VA	43,231	C
Maryville Univ of St. Louis	MO	38,558	VC
Marywood Univ	PA	47,840	C
Mass College of Liberal Arts	MA	20,659	C
Mayville State Univ	ND	18,371	NC
McDaniel College	MD	52,910	VC
McNeese State Univ	LA	7,838	C
McPherson College	KS	36,134	C
Medaille College	NY	41,700	LC
Mercer Univ	GA	45,348	VC
Mercy College	NY	32,614	C
Mercyhurst Univ	PA	47,420	C
Meredith College	NC	46,634	C
Merrimack College	MA	55,415	C
Messiah College	PA	44,380	VC
Methodist Univ	NC	58,130	C
Metropolitan State Univ	MN	7,859	C
Metropolitan State Univ of Denver	CO	6,928	LC
Miami Univ	OH	27,190	HC+
Mich State Univ	MI	24,542	VC
Mich Tech Univ	MI	25,551	VC+
MidAmerica Nazarene Univ	KS	37,808	C
Middle Tenn State Univ	TN	8,650	C
Midland Univ	NE	39,512	C
Midwestern State Univ	TX	12,111	LC
Miles College	AL	16,530	NC
Milligan College	TN	39,450	C
Millikin Univ	IL	44,148	C
Millsaps College	MS	50,080	C+
Minn State Univ, Mankato	MN	17,190	C
Minn State Univ, Moorhead	MN	21,393	C
Minot State Univ	ND	13,285	C
Misericordia Univ	PA	45,210	C
Miss College	MS	25,850	C
Miss State Univ	MS	22,028	C+
Miss Univ for Women	MS	17,065	C
Miss Valley State Univ	MS	13,233	LC
Missouri Baptist Univ	MO	35,594	C
Missouri Southern State Univ	MO	13,071	C
Missouri State Univ	MO	15,837	C+
Missouri Valley College	MO	28,150	C
Missouri Western State Univ	MO	17,822	LC
Mitchell College	CT	45,192	C
Molloy College	NY	40,440	C
Monmouth College	IL	42,260	C
Monmouth Univ	NJ	50,184	C
Montana State Univ Billings	MT	13,336	LC
Montana State Univ-Northern	MT	11,370	NC
Montana Tech of the Univ of Montana	MT	15,447	VC
Montreat College	NC	34,605	LC
Morehead State Univ	KY	18,386	LC
Morningside College	IA	39,780	C
Morris College	SC	19,195	LC
Mount Ida College	MA	46,820	C
Mount Mary Univ	WI	34,650	LC
Mount Mercy Univ	IA	39,748	C
Mount St. Joseph Univ	OH	33,880	LC
Mount St. Mary's Univ	MD	53,380	C
Mount Vernon Nazarene Univ	OH	35,944	C
Muhlenberg College	PA	56,645	VC
Muskingum Univ	OH	35,966	C
Nebr Wesleyan Univ	NE	42,026	C+
New England College	NH	50,828	NC
New Jersey Inst of Technology	NJ	30,198	HC
New Mexico Highlands Univ	NM	11,904	LC
New Mexico State Univ	NM	14,050	LC
New York Inst of Technology	NY	49,980	VC
New York Univ	NY	68,139	MC
Newberry College	SC	34,550	C
Newbury College	MA	48,970	C
Newman Univ	KS	37,382	C
Niagara Univ	NY	41,010	C
Nicholls State Univ	LA	14,959	C
Norfolk State Univ	VA	18,902	LC
N Car A&T State Univ	NC	13,786	C
N Car State Univ	NC	22,434	HC+
North Central College	IL	48,712	C+
North Central Univ	MN	30,610	C
N Dak State Univ	ND	16,245	VC
North Park Univ	IL	35,860	C
Northeastern Illinois Univ	IL	12,529	LC
Northeastern State Univ	OK	8,615	VC
Northeastern Univ	MA	65,352	MC
Northern Arizona Univ	AZ	21,003	C
Northern Illinois Univ	IL	20,176	C
Northern Kentucky Univ	KY	16,486	C
Northern Mich Univ	MI	20,853	C
Northwest Christian Univ	OR	36,580	C
Northwest Missouri State Univ	MO	18,286	C
Northwest Nazarene Univ	ID	40,250	C
Northwestern Okla State Univ	OK	13,072	LC
Northwestern State Univ of Louisiana	LA	16,534	LC
Northwestern Univ	IL	68,725	MC
Norwich Univ	VT	56,234	C
Notre Dame College	OH	39,150	VC
Notre Dame de Namur Univ	CA	46,526	LC
Notre Dame of Maryland Univ	MD	47,570	VC
Nyack College	NY	34,450	LC
Oakland Univ	MI	20,763	C
Oakwood Univ	AL	43,758	C
Oglethorpe Univ	GA	44,200	C
Ohio Dominican Univ	OH	41,340	C+
Ohio Northern Univ	OH	44,050	VC
Ohio State Univ at Columbus	OH	22,843	MC
Ohio Univ	OH	23,394	VC
Ohio Wesleyan Univ	OH	49,460	VC
Okla Baptist Univ	OK	33,990	C
Okla Christian Univ	OK	29,260	C
Okla City Univ	OK	40,476	C
Okla Wesleyan Univ	OK	34,434	C
Old Dominion Univ	VA	21,618	C
Olivet College	MI	37,661	LC
Olivet Nazarene Univ	IL	41,840	VC
Oral Roberts Univ	OK	34,316	C
Ottawa Univ	KS	39,980	VC
Otterbein Univ	OH	41,630	C
Ouachita Baptist Univ	AR	33,500	VC
Our Lady of the Lake Univ	TX	37,790	LC
Pace Univ	NY	60,136	C
Pacific Lutheran Univ	WA	49,960	C
Pacific Union College	CA	36,009	VC
Paine College	GA	19,506	LC
Palm Beach Atlantic Univ	FL	39,250	C
Park Univ	MO	22,134	C
Paul Quinn College	TX	25,350	LC
Penn State Altoona	PA	26,686	C
Penn State Erie,The Behrend College	PA	26,688	VC
Pepperdine Univ	CA	66,862	VC+
Pfeiffer Univ	NC	40,532	LC
Piedmont College	GA	34,334	C
Pine Manor College	MA	41,660	LC
Pittsburg State Univ	KS	13,880	C
Plymouth State Univ	NH	23,180	LC
Point Loma Nazarene Univ	CA	46,150	C+
Point Park Univ	PA	41,270	C
Pontifical Catholic Univ of PR	PR	10,534	
Prairie View A&M Univ	TX	27,273	LC
Pratt Inst	NY	59,482	VC+
Presentation College	SD	28,575	LC
Principia College	IL	40,350	C
Purdue Univ Northwest	IN	15,178	C
Purdue Univ/West Lafayette	IN	20,032	MC
Queens Univ of Charlotte	NC	39,543	C
Quincy Univ	IL	38,170	LC
Quinnipiac Univ	CT	60,970	VC
Radford Univ	VA	19,758	C
Ramapo College of New Jersey	NJ	25,760	VC
Randolph College	VA	53,970	C
Randolph-Macon College	VA	51,480	VC
Regis College	MA	51,920	LC
Regis Univ	CO	46,380	C
Reinhardt Univ	GA	31,344	C
Rensselaer Polytechnic Inst	NY	67,265	MC
Rhode Island College	RI	19,000	LC
Rider Univ	NJ	54,050	C
Ripon College	WI	49,991	VC
Rivier Univ	NH	41,600	VC
Roanoke College	VA	55,952	VC
Robert Morris Univ	PA	40,600	C
Roberts Wesleyan College	NY	41,116	C
Rochester College	MI	28,574	LC
Rochester Inst of Technology	NY	52,734	HC+
Rockhurst Univ	MO	28,990	C
Rocky Mountain College	MT	35,776	C
Roger Williams Univ	RI	48,074	VC
Rollins College	FL	58,670	HC
Roosevelt Univ	IL	41,890	VC
Rosemont College	PA	30,980	LC
Rowan Univ	NJ	24,491	VC
Rust College	MS	10,600	C
Sacred Heart Univ	CT	54,590	C
Saginaw Valley State Univ	MI	19,284	C
St. Augustine's Univ	NC	25,582	C
St. Francis Univ	PA	46,146	NC
St. John's Univ	MN	53,472	C
St. Joseph's College of Maine	ME	47,890	C
St. Joseph's Univ	PA	58,540	VC
St. Louis Univ	MO	49,866	HC
St. Martin's Univ	WA	45,056	C
St. Mary's College	IN	50,600	C
St. Mary's College of Calif	CA	57,420	C
St. Peter's Univ	NJ	49,192	C
St. Vincent College	PA	46,229	C
St. Xavier Univ	IL	44,440	C
Salem College	NC	40,206	C
Salem International Univ	WV	21,090	C
Salem State Univ	MA	42,650	LC
Salisbury Univ	MD	21,132	VC
Salve Regina Univ	RI	53,046	VC
Samford Univ	AL	40,770	VC
San Diego Christian College	CA	40,914	C
San Diego State Univ	CA	23,156	VC
San Francisco State Univ	CA	18,514	LC
Savannah College of Art and Design	GA	49,595	SP
Savannah State Univ	GA	17,036	C
Scripps College	CA	69,260	HC
Seattle Pacific Univ	WA	47,439	C+
Seattle Univ	WA	54,957	VC
Seton Hall Univ	NJ	58,008	C
Seton Hill Univ	PA	46,972	VC
Shepherd Univ, West Virginia	WV	17,382	C
Shippensburg Univ of Pennsylvania	PA	24,096	C
Shorter Univ	GA	31,130	LC
Siena Heights Univ	MI	36,322	C
Simmons College	MA	54,400	HC
Simpson College	IA	45,626	VC
Simpson Univ	CA	34,722	C
Slippery Rock Univ of Pennsylvania	PA	20,450	C
Sonoma State Univ	CA	27,020	C
S Dak State Univ	SD	15,874	C
Southeastern Louisiana Univ	LA	16,237	C
Southeastern Okla State Univ	OK	11,875	C
Southeastern Univ	FL	34,910	LC
Southern Adventist Univ	TN	28,250	C
Southern Arkansas Univ	AR	21,532	C
Southern Conn State Univ	CT	21,924	LC
Southern Illinois Univ Edwardsville	IL	20,188	C
Southern Methodist Univ	TX	69,008	MC
Southern Nazarene Univ	OK	33,684	C
Southern New Hampshire Univ	NH	44,256	C
Southern Oregon Univ	OR	19,117	C
Southern Univ and A&M College	LA	16,074	LC
Southern Vermont College	VT	34,670	LC
Southern Wesleyan Univ	SC	33,670	LC
Southwest Baptist Univ	MO	30,890	LC
Southwest Minn State Univ	MN	17,783	C
Southwestern Adventist Univ	TX	28,232	LC
Southwestern College	KS	31,531	LC
Southwestern Okla State Univ	OK	12,205	C
Southwestern Univ	TX	52,370	VC
Spring Arbor Univ	MI	37,390	C
Spring Hill College	AL	48,488	C
St. Bonaventure Univ	NY	45,596	C
St. Catherine Univ	MN	45,630	C
St. Cloud State Univ	MN	10,600	C
St. Edward's Univ	TX	56,190	VC
St. Francis College	NY	38,800	LC
St. John Fisher College	NY	45,270	VC
St. John's Univ	NY	57,160	C+
St. Mary's Univ	TX	39,120	C
St. Norbert College	WI	46,060	VC
St. Thomas Aquinas College	NY	32,450	C
St. Thomas Univ	FL	51,187	LC
Stanford Univ	CA	62,541	MC
SUNY /College of Agriculture and Tech at Cobleskill	NY	20,527	LC
SUNY Albany	NY	22,165	C
SUNY at Geneseo	NY	21,622	VC
SUNY at New Paltz	NY	20,840	C
SUNY at Oswego	NY	22,219	VC
SUNY at Purchase College	NY	21,832	C
SUNY/Buffalo State	NY	20,583	LC
SUNY/College at Old Westbury	NY	16,860	C
SUNY/Cortland	NY	20,910	C
SUNY/Fredonia	NY	20,818	C
SUNY/Oneonta	NY	20,794	C
SUNY/Plattsburgh	NY	19,314	C
SUNY/Potsdam	NY	21,051	VC
SUNY/Univ at Buffalo	NY	23,122	C
Stephen F. Austin State Univ	TX	18,484	LC
Sterling College	KS	32,830	LC
Stetson Univ	FL	57,174	VC+
Stockton Univ	NJ	25,565	C
Stonehill College	MA	55,130	C
Suffolk Univ	MA	52,316	C
Sul Ross State Univ	TX	15,021	LC
Susquehanna Univ	PA	57,560	VC
Tabor College	KS	35,870	C
Tarleton State Univ	TX	15,248	LC
Taylor Univ	IN	42,130	VC
Temple Univ	PA	24,392	C+
Texas A&M Univ at College Station	TX	20,771	VC+
Texas A&M Univ at Corpus Christi	TX	16,851	LC
Texas A&M Univ at Kingsville	TX	16,580	LC
Texas Lutheran Univ	TX	39,770	C
Texas Southern Univ	TX	19,592	LC
Texas State Univ	TX	18,721	C

ST = STATE **$IS** = IN-STATE COSTS **SR** = SELECTOR RATING

School	ST	$IS	SR
Texas Woman's Univ	TX	15,302	LC
The American Univ	DC	61,317	HC
The Catholic Univ of America	DC	58,376	VC
The College at Brockport - SUNY	NY	21,058	C
The College of New Jersey	NJ	28,675	VC+
The College of New Rochelle	NY	46,300	LC
The College of St. Rose	NY	44,010	C
The College of Wooster	OH	60,000	HC
The George Washington Univ	DC	68,474	HC+
The Master's Univ	CA	43,870	C
The Univ of Alabama	AL	24,320	C+
The Univ of Arizona	AZ	24,086	C
The Univ of Mary	ND	23,180	C
The Univ of Memphis	TN	18,278	C
The Univ of Montana Western	MT	9,426	LC
The Univ of Tenn at Chattanooga	TN	17,340	C+
The Univ of Tenn at Knoxville	TN	22,112	VC
The Univ of Tenn at Martin	TN	15,212	C
The Univ of Texas at San Antonio	TX	21,060	C
The Univ of Utah	UT	18,751	VC
The Univ of Virginia's College at Wise	VA	18,192	LC
Thiel College	PA	42,950	LC
Thomas College	ME	73,888	LC
Thomas Edison State Univ	NJ	6,350	NC
Thomas More College	KY	36,720	LC
Tiffin Univ	OH	34,900	LC
Toccoa Falls College	GA	30,048	C
Tougaloo College	MS	17,980	NC
Towson Univ	MD	21,878	C
Trine Univ	IN	41,310	C
Trinity Christian College	IL	35,580	C
Trinity International Univ	IL	31,070	VC
Trinity Univ	TX	54,480	MC
Trinity Washington Univ	DC	33,826	C+
Troy Univ	AL	16,171	C
Truman State Univ	MO	16,286	MC
Tulane Univ	LA	67,496	MC
Union College	KY	32,310	C
Union College	NE	23,270	C
Union Inst & Univ	OH	8,912	SP
Union Univ	TN	41,160	VC
Univ of Alabama at Birmingham	AL	22,092	C
Univ of Alabama in Huntsville	AL	20,028	VC
Univ of Alaska Anchorage	AK	17,914	C
Univ of Alaska Fairbanks	AK	16,874	VC
Univ of Alaska Southeast	AK	17,615	C
Univ of Arkansas at Fayetteville	AR	19,766	VC
Univ of Bridgeport	CT	44,985	LC
Univ of Calif at Berkeley	CA	29,886	MC
Univ of Calif at Davis	CA	28,468	HC
Univ of Calif at Los Angeles	CA	27,438	HC+
Univ of Calif at Santa Barbara	CA	30,627	HC+
Univ of Calif San Diego	CA	30,450	MC
Univ of Central Arkansas	AR	15,042	VC
Univ of Central Florida	FL	16,379	VC
Univ of Central Missouri	MO	18,982	C
Univ of Central Okla	OK	15,150	C
Univ of Charleston	WV	35,000	LC
Univ of Cincinnati	OH	22,118	VC
Univ of Colo Boulder	CO	26,048	HC
Univ of Colo Colo Springs	CO	20,300	C
Univ of Colo Denver	CO	22,238	C
Univ of Conn	CT	27,394	
Univ of Dayton	OH	54,930	VC
Univ of Delaware	DE	32,214	VC
Univ of Detroit Mercy	MI	48,816	C
Univ of Evansville	IN	44,186	C+
Univ of Findlay	OH	43,040	C
Univ of Hartford	CT	49,776	C
Univ of Hawaii at Hilo	HI	18,038	VC
Univ of Hawaii at Manoa	HI	23,261	C
Univ of Houston	TX	21,871	VC
Univ of Houston-Downtown	TX	7,241	LC
Univ of Illinois at Chicago	IL	24,664	VC
Univ of Illinois at Urbana-Champaign	IL	27,006	HC
Univ of Indianapolis	IN	36,480	VC
Univ of Iowa	IA	19,415	HC
Univ of Jamestown	ND	28,508	C
Univ of Kentucky	KY	24,800	C+
Univ of La Verne	CA	55,600	C
Univ of Louisiana at Lafayette	LA	14,516	C
Univ of Louisiana at Monroe	LA	15,970	C
Univ of Louisville	KY	19,692	C
Univ of Lynchburg	VA	48,370	C
Univ of Maine	ME	21,038	VC
Univ of Mary Hardin-Baylor	TX	35,292	C+
Univ of Maryland Univ College	MD	26,146	LC
Univ of Maryland/Baltimore County	MD	23,004	VC
Univ of Maryland/College Park	MD	21,938	HC
Univ of Mass Amherst	MA	27,669	HC
Univ of Mass Boston	MA	13,828	C
Univ of Miami	FL	63,494	MC
Univ of Mich/Ann Arbor	MI	25,274	MC
Univ of Mich/Dearborn	MI	12,472	VC
Univ of Mich/Flint	MI	19,062	C
Univ of Minn/Crookston	MN	19,126	C
Univ of Minn/Duluth	MN	20,292	C
Univ of Minn/Morris	MN	21,222	VC
Univ of Missouri-Columbia	MO	20,463	VC
Univ of Missouri-Kansas City	MO	19,563	VC
Univ of Missouri-St. Louis	MO	19,810	VC
Univ of Mobile	AL	28,935	C
Univ of Montana	MT	14,105	C
Univ of Montevallo	AL	20,012	C
Univ of Mount Olive	NC	18,426	C
Univ of Mount Union	OH	39,990	C
Univ of Nebr - Kearney	NE	17,014	LC
Univ of Nebr - Lincoln	NE	18,589	VC
Univ of Nebr - Omaha	NE	16,120	C
Univ of Nevada, Las Vegas	NV	17,553	C
Univ of Nevada, Reno	NV	18,010	C
Univ of New England	ME	50,110	C
Univ of New Hampshire	NH	29,333	VC
Univ of New Hampshire - Manchester	NH	14,490	C
Univ of New Haven	CT	53,680	C
Univ of New Mexico	NM	16,808	C
Univ of New Orleans	LA	12,840	C
Univ of North Alabama	AL	15,964	C
Univ of N Car at Asheville	NC	16,251	VC+
Univ of N Car at Chapel Hill	NC	20,561	MC
Univ of N Car at Charlotte	NC	17,803	VC
Univ of N Dak	ND	16,673	C
Univ of North Florida	FL	15,996	VC
Univ of North Texas	TX	20,082	C
Univ of Northern Colo	CO	19,658	C
Univ of Northern Iowa	IA	17,480	C
Univ of Northwestern - St. Paul	MN	39,530	C
Univ of Okla	OK	19,651	HC
Univ of Oregon	OR	24,021	VC
Univ of Pennsylvania	PA	63,526	MC
Univ of Pikeville	KY	27,838	C
Univ of Pittsburgh at Bradford	PA	22,958	C
Univ of Pittsburgh at Greensburg	PA	24,140	C
Univ of Pittsburgh at Johnstown	PA	22,092	C
Univ of Portland	OR	52,152	VC
Univ of Puget Sound	WA	60,210	HC
Univ of Rio Grande & Rio Grande Community College	OH	8,750	LC
Univ of St. Francis	IN	38,520	C
Univ of San Diego	CA	60,338	HC
Univ of San Francisco	CA	60,580	C
Univ of Science and Arts of Okla	OK	11,140	VC
Univ of Scranton	PA	54,962	VC
Univ of Sioux Falls	SD	25,630	C
Univ of South Alabama	AL	16,880	C
Univ of S Car Aiken	SC	18,094	C
Univ of S Car at Columbia	SC	21,726	VC
Univ of S Car Upstate	SC	19,272	LC
Univ of South Florida St. Petersburg	FL	15,980	C
Univ of South Florida/Tampa	FL	16,110	VC
Univ of Southern Calif	CA	66,631	MC
Univ of Southern Indiana	IN	16,808	C
Univ of Southern Maine	ME	18,320	C
Univ of Southern Miss	MS	13,170	C
Univ of St. Francis	IL	40,828	C
Univ of St. Thomas - Houston	TX	41,510	VC
Univ of Tampa	FL	38,928	VC
Univ of Texas at Arlington	TX	18,876	C
Univ of Texas at El Paso	TX	34,452	NC
Univ of Texas Rio Grande Valley	TX	15,573	LC
Univ of the Arts	PA	56,579	SP
Univ of the Cumberlands	KY	32,000	LC
Univ of the Incarnate Word	TX	39,162	LC
Univ of the Ozarks	AR	31,050	NC
Univ of the Pacific	CA	57,446	VC
Univ of the Sacred Heart	PR	17,932	
Univ of Toledo	OH	19,336	C
Univ of Tulsa	OK	52,625	HC
Univ of Vermont	VT	29,792	HC
Univ of Washington	WA	23,091	MC
Univ of West Florida	FL	15,848	C
Univ of Wisc-Eau Claire	WI	16,354	VC
Univ of Wisc-Green Bay	WI	15,184	C
Univ of Wisc-Madison	WI	21,647	MC
Univ of Wisc-Milwaukee	WI	21,538	C
Univ of Wisc-Parkside	WI	15,313	C
Univ of Wisc-River Falls	WI	14,541	C
Univ of Wisc-Stevens Point	WI	14,043	C
Univ of Wisc-Stout	WI	19,667	C
Univ of Wisc-Superior	WI	14,838	C
Univ of Wisc-Whitewater	WI	13,976	C
Univ of Wyoming	WY	15,537	C
Upper Iowa Univ	IA	34,990	NC
Urbana Univ	OH	30,820	C
Ursinus College	PA	62,920	VC
Utica College	NY	31,510	C
Valparaiso Univ	IN	50,160	VC
Vanderbilt Univ	TN	63,248	MC
Vanguard Univ of Southern Calif	CA	42,400	VC
Villanova Univ	PA	64,922	MC
Virginia Commonwealth Univ	VA	23,811	VC
Virginia Polytechnic Inst and State Univ	VA	21,920	VC
Virginia Wesleyan Univ	VA	45,980	LC
Viterbo Univ	WI	34,660	C
Voorhees College	SC	19,976	C
Wake Forest Univ	NC	69,354	MC
Walla Walla Univ	WA	34,845	C
Walsh Univ	OH	39,010	C
Warner Univ	FL	28,216	C
Washburn Univ	KS	15,827	C
Washington Adventist Univ	MD	32,050	LC
Washington State Univ	WA	22,747	C
Washington Univ in St. Louis	MO	67,539	MC
Wayland Baptist Univ	TX	23,460	LC
Wayne State College	NE	25,746	NC
Wayne State Univ	MI	23,085	C
Weber State Univ	UT	14,112	C
Webster Univ	MO	37,490	C
Wesleyan College	GA	31,940	C+
West Chester Univ of Pennsylvania	PA	19,171	VC
West Liberty Univ	WV	16,158	C
West Virginia State Univ	WV	19,412	LC
West Virginia Univ	WV	18,952	VC
Western Carolina Univ	NC	13,965	C
Western Conn State Univ	CT	21,254	LC
Western Illinois Univ	IL	20,897	C
Western Kentucky Univ	KY	16,850	C
Western Mich Univ	MI	21,791	C
Western New England Univ	MA	49,182	C
Western State Colo Univ	CO	19,348	C
Western Washington Univ	WA	18,904	VC
Westfield State Univ	MA	20,404	C
Westminster College	PA	41,722	C
Westminster College	UT	41,078	C
Westmont College	CA	57,930	VC
Wheaton College	IL	44,993	MC
Wheeling Jesuit Univ	WV	37,106	LC
Wheelock College	MA	51,325	LC
Whitworth Univ	WA	53,682	VC
Wichita State Univ	KS	17,773	C
Widener Univ	PA	58,190	C
Wilberforce Univ	OH	19,900	C
Wiley College	TX	19,255	C
Wilkes Univ	PA	49,166	C
William Carey Univ	MS	23,950	LC
William Jewell College	MO	42,490	C+
William Paterson Univ of New Jersey	NJ	24,022	C
William Peace Univ	NC	39,300	LC
William Penn Univ	IA	26,000	C
William Woods Univ	MO	32,040	C
Wilmington College	OH	35,100	C
Wilson College	PA	35,620	LC
Winston-Salem State Univ	NC	18,005	LC
Winthrop Univ	SC	23,960	C
Wisc Lutheran College	WI	36,290	C
Wittenberg Univ	OH	49,863	VC
Woodbury Univ	CA	49,593	VC
Worcester State Univ	MA	20,977	C
Wright State Univ	OH	16,983	C
Xavier Univ of Louisiana	LA	31,689	C
Yeshiva Univ	NY	52,750	VC
York College	NE	30,260	C
York College of Pennsylvania	PA	29,240	C
Youngstown State Univ	OH	17,487	C

COMMUNICATIONS TECHNOLOGY

School	ST	$IS	SR
Alverno College	WI	33,294	LC
Calif College of the Arts	CA	52,758	SP
Cal State, Monterey Bay	CA	22,872	LC
Champlain College	VT	54,724	VC
Chestnut Hill College	PA	47,180	C
College of the Ozarks	MO	7,530	VC
Dakota State Univ	SD	12,286	C
Eastern Mich Univ	MI	19,761	C
George Mason Univ	VA	19,884	C
Grand Canyon Univ	AZ	25,150	VC
Indiana Univ of Pennsylvania	PA	24,474	C
Inter-American Univ of PR-Bayamon	PR	18,785	
James Madison Univ	VA	19,084	VC
Lebanon Valley College	PA	55,510	VC
Lubbock Christian Univ	TX	29,727	C
Missouri Western State Univ	MO	17,822	LC
Montana Tech of the Univ of Montana	MT	15,447	VC
Montclair State Univ	NJ	26,912	C
New York Univ	NY	68,139	MC
Northwestern Univ	IL	68,725	MC
Ohio Univ	OH	23,394	VC
Rochester Inst of Technology	NY	52,734	HC+
Salve Regina Univ	RI	53,046	VC
Taylor Univ	IN	42,130	VC
The College of Wooster	OH	60,000	HC
Univ of New Haven	CT	53,680	C
Univ of S Dak	SD	16,109	C
Western Kentucky Univ	KY	16,850	C
Wilmington Univ	DE	8,762	NC

COMMUNICATIVE DISORDERS

School	ST	$IS	SR
Calif Baptist Univ	CA	42,986	C
East Stroudsburg Univ	PA	18,578	LC
Jackson State Univ	MS	15,879	LC
Lebanon Valley College	PA	55,510	VC
San Diego State Univ	CA	23,156	VC
Southeastern Univ	FL	34,910	LC
Univ of Georgia	GA	21,878	HC
Univ of Kansas	KS	20,884	VC
Univ of Northern Iowa	IA	17,480	C
Univ of Rhode Island	RI	26,066	VC
Univ of Texas Rio Grande Valley	TX	15,573	LC
Western Kentucky Univ	KY	16,850	C

COMMUNITY AND BEHAVIORAL HEALTH

School	ST	$IS	SR
Drury Univ	MO	37,555	VC
Keene State College	NH	24,604	C
Missouri Western State Univ	MO	17,822	LC
SUNY Polytechnic Inst	NY	20,438	VC

COMMUNITY HEALTH WORK

School	ST	$IS	SR
Arizona State Univ at the Downtown Phoenix Campus	AZ	24,634	VC
Arizona State Univ at the West Campus	AZ	21,513	VC
Ashford Univ	CA	10,480	C
Bethel Univ	MN	46,550	C+
Bradley Univ	IL	43,240	VC
Brown Univ	RI	64,566	MC
Central Mich Univ	MI	20,330	C
Central Washington Univ	WA	16,803	C
CUNY/York College	NY	6,747	LC
Concordia Univ St. Paul	MN	29,050	C
Delaware State Univ	DE	19,376	LC
Elmira College	NY	53,900	C
Florida Gulf Coast Univ	FL	14,738	C
Florida State Univ	FL	16,771	HC
George Mason Univ	VA	19,884	C
Georgia College & State Univ	GA	21,884	C+
Hofstra Univ	NY	58,210	C+
Howard Univ	DC	37,616	C+
Ithaca College	NY	58,158	VC+
Johnson C. Smith Univ	NC	25,336	LC
Kent State Univ	OH	20,928	C
Liberty Univ	VA	31,415	C
Longwood Univ	VA	22,184	C
Louisiana State Univ in Shreveport	LA	6,902	C
Malone Univ	OH	39,200	C
Mass College of Liberal Arts	MA	20,659	C
Minn State Univ, Mankato	MN	17,190	C
Minn State Univ, Moorhead	MN	21,393	C
Missouri Western State Univ	MO	17,822	LC
Morris College	SC	19,195	LC
Murray State Univ	KY	17,726	C+
New Mexico State Univ	NM	14,050	LC
Northern Illinois Univ	IL	20,176	C
Ohio Univ	OH	23,394	VC
Pine Manor College	MA	41,660	LC
Rhode Island College	RI	19,000	LC
Salisbury Univ	MD	21,132	VC
Slippery Rock Univ of Pennsylvania	PA	20,450	C
Southern Illinois Univ Edwardsville	IL	20,188	C
SUNY/College at Old Westbury	NY	16,860	C
SUNY/Potsdam	NY	21,051	VC
Texas A&M Univ at College Station	TX	20,771	VC+
Tufts Univ	MA		MC
Tulane Univ	LA	67,496	MC
Univ of Calif at Davis	CA	28,468	HC
Univ of Central Okla	OK	15,150	C
Univ of Illinois at Urbana-Champaign	IL	27,006	HC
Univ of Kansas	KS	20,884	VC
Univ of Maine at Farmington	ME	18,792	C
Univ of Maryland/College Park	MD	21,938	HC
Univ of Mass Lowell	MA	27,296	VC
Univ of Nebr - Omaha	NE	16,120	C
Univ of N Car at Greensboro	NC	15,998	C
Univ of Scranton	PA	54,962	VC
Univ of Wisc-La Crosse	WI	15,425	VC
Univ of Wisc-Superior	WI	14,838	C
Western Mich Univ	MI	21,791	C
Whitworth Univ	WA	53,682	VC
William Paterson Univ of New Jersey	NJ	24,022	C
Winona State Univ	MN	18,109	C
Wright State Univ	OH	16,983	C

COMMUNITY PSYCHOLOGY

School	ST	$IS	SR
Mount Aloysius College	PA	29,976	C
Okla Baptist Univ	OK	33,990	C
Univ of Mich/Flint	MI	19,062	C
Univ of New Haven	CT	53,680	C

COMMUNITY SERVICES

School	ST	$IS	SR
Alverno College	WI	33,294	LC
Aquinas College - Mich	MI	38,876	VC
Bemidji State Univ	MN	17,730	C
Bryant Univ	RI	57,204	VC
Cal State, Fullerton	CA	21,902	C
Central Mich Univ	MI	20,330	C

ST = STATE $IS = IN-STATE COSTS SR = SELECTOR RATING

School	ST	$IS	SR
DePaul Univ	IL	52,807	VC
Emory and Henry College	VA	46,320	C
Humphreys College	CA	27,790	C
Martin Univ	IN	21,010	LC
Metropolitan College of New York	NY		VC
Midland Univ	NE	39,512	C
New Mexico State Univ	NM	14,050	LC
Northern State Univ	SD	15,570	C
Ohio State Univ at Columbus	OH	22,843	MC
Ohio Univ	OH	23,394	VC
Portland State Univ	OR	19,443	C
Prescott College	AZ	38,201	C
Providence College	RI	62,870	HC
Queens Univ of Charlotte	NC	39,543	C
Roger Williams Univ	RI	48,074	VC
Southern Arkansas Univ	AR	21,532	C
SUNY/Empire State College	NY	9,145	NC
Univ of Calif, Santa Cruz	CA	28,731	C+
Univ of Mass Boston	MA	13,828	C
Univ of Toledo	OH	19,336	C

COMPARATIVE LITERATURE

School	ST	$IS	SR
Barnard College/Columbia Univ	NY	68,762	MC
Beloit College	WI	55,206	HC
Bennington College	VT	66,280	MC
Brandeis Univ	MA	68,443	MC
Brigham Young Univ	UT	13,248	MC
Brown Univ	RI	64,566	MC
Bryn Mawr College	PA	65,220	MC
Cal State, Fullerton	CA	21,902	C
Cal State, Long Beach	CA	18,850	C
Case Western Reserve Univ	OH	62,284	MC
CUNY/Brooklyn College	NY	7,163	C+
CUNY/City College	NY	20,204	C
CUNY/Hunter College	NY	31,098	VC
CUNY/Lehman College	NY	5,788	LC
CUNY/Queens College	NY	21,507	C
Clark Univ	MA	53,260	HC+
Colo College	CO	64,894	MC
Columbia Univ/ School of General Studies	NY	61,470	MC
Columbia Univ/City of New York	NY	62,958	MC
Cornell Univ	NY	67,591	MC
Dartmouth College	NH	68,109	MC
Eckerd College	FL	55,206	VC
Emory Univ	GA	63,286	MC
Fordham Univ	NY	68,431	MC
Georgetown Univ	DC	68,970	MC
Goddard College	VT	17,040	VC
Hamilton College	NY	64,250	MC
Hampshire College	MA	65,214	MC
Haverford College	PA	66,490	MC
Hillsdale College	MI	37,170	MC
Hobart and William Smith Colleges	NY	67,050	HC+
Hofstra Univ	NY	58,210	C+
Indiana Univ Bloomington	IN	20,791	HC
Lycoming College	PA	50,895	C
Middlebury College	VT	67,464	MC
New York Univ	NY	68,139	MC
Northland College	WI	41,103	C+
Northwestern Univ	IL	68,725	MC
Oberlin College	OH	68,942	MC
Pennsylvania State Univ - Univ Park	PA	29,716	HC
Princeton Univ	NJ	60,090	MC
Purdue Univ/West Lafayette	IN	20,032	MC
Rutgers Univ - New Brunswick	NJ	27,090	HC
San Diego State Univ	CA	23,156	VC
San Francisco State Univ	CA	18,514	LC
Smith College	MA	66,774	MC
Stanford Univ	CA	62,541	MC
SUNY at Binghamton	NY	24,100	MC
SUNY at Geneseo	NY	21,622	VC
Stony Brook Univ/The SUNY	NY	22,703	MC
Swarthmore College	PA	63,550	MC
The College of Wooster	OH	60,000	HC
The Univ of Utah	UT	18,751	VC
Trinity College	CT	69,020	HC
Univ of Calif at Berkeley	CA	29,886	MC
Univ of Calif at Davis	CA	28,468	HC
Univ of Calif at Irvine	CA	33,857	VC
Univ of Calif at Riverside	CA	32,912	C
Univ of Calif at Santa Barbara	CA	30,627	HC+
Univ of Chicago	IL	70,551	MC
Univ of Cincinnati	OH	22,118	VC
Univ of Delaware	DE	32,214	VC
Univ of Georgia	GA	21,878	HC
Univ of Illinois at Urbana-Champaign	IL	27,006	HC
Univ of Iowa	IA	19,415	HC
Univ of La Verne	CA	55,600	C
Univ of Mass Amherst	MA	27,669	HC
Univ of Mich/Ann Arbor	MI	25,274	MC
Univ of Minn/Twin Cities	MN	24,269	MC
Univ of New Mexico	NM	16,808	C
Univ of N Car at Chapel Hill	NC	20,561	MC
Univ of Oregon	OR	24,021	VC
Univ of Pennsylvania	PA	63,526	MC
Univ of PR-Rio Piedras campus	PR	13,327	
Univ of Rochester	NY	65,032	MC
Univ of San Francisco	CA	60,580	C
Univ of S Car at Columbia	SC	21,726	VC
Univ of Southern Calif	CA	66,631	MC
Univ of Virginia	VA	27,367	MC
Univ of Washington	WA	23,091	MC
Univ of Wisc-Madison	WI	21,647	MC
Univ of Wisc-Milwaukee	WI	21,538	C
Washington Univ in St. Louis	MO	67,539	MC
Wellesley College	MA	66,984	MC
Willamette Univ	OR	62,514	VC+
Williams College	MA	67,700	MC

COMPOSITION

School	ST	$IS	SR
Arizona State Univ at the Tempe Campus	AZ	23,001	VC
DePaul Univ	IL	52,807	VC
Georgia Southern Univ	GA	16,540	VC
Mich State Univ	MI	24,542	VC
Oberlin College	OH	68,942	MC
Samford Univ	AL	40,770	VC
Shenandoah Univ	VA	42,100	C
Univ of N Car at Greensboro	NC	15,998	C
Vanderbilt Univ	TN	63,248	MC

COMPUTATIONAL SCIENCES

School	ST	$IS	SR
Arizona State Univ at the Tempe Campus	AZ	23,001	VC
Biola Univ	CA	48,686	C
Brown Univ	RI	64,566	MC
Cal State, Fullerton	CA	21,902	C
Canisius College	NY	49,672	C
Carroll Univ	WI	38,100	C+
Champlain College	VT	54,724	VC
DePaul Univ	IL	52,807	VC
Fairfield Univ	CT	61,445	HC
George Mason Univ	VA	19,884	C
Hood College	MD	50,540	C
Huntington Univ	IN	33,996	C
Indiana Univ Bloomington	IN	20,791	HC
Marquette Univ	WI	53,090	VC+
Mercer Univ	GA	45,348	VC
Mich State Univ	MI	24,542	VC
Mount Aloysius College	PA	29,976	C
New College of Florida	FL	16,180	HC+
New York Univ	NY	68,139	MC
Park Univ	MO	22,134	C
Purdue Univ/West Lafayette	IN	20,032	MC
SUNY/Univ at Buffalo	NY	23,122	C
Stevens Inst of Technology	NJ	64,954	MC
Stockton Univ	NJ	25,565	C
The American Univ	DC	61,317	HC
The College at Brockport - SUNY	NY	21,058	C
Univ of Illinois at Urbana-Champaign	IL	27,006	HC
Univ of Wisc-Superior	WI	14,838	C
Western Kentucky Univ	KY	16,850	C

COMPUTER EDUCATION

School	ST	$IS	SR
Abilene Christian Univ	TX	43,708	C+
Appalachian State Univ	NC	15,394	VC
Arkansas Tech Univ	AR	16,534	LC
Baylor Univ	TX	56,803	HC
Cal State, Fullerton	CA	21,902	C
Clayton State Univ	GA	19,735	LC
Concordia Univ, Chicago	IL	41,522	C
Dakota State Univ	SD	12,286	C
Eastern Mich Univ	MI	19,761	C
Eastern Washington Univ	WA	17,896	LC
Edgewood College	WI	35,950	C
Hardin-Simmons Univ	TX	36,025	C
Indiana Univ-Purdue Univ Fort Wayne	IN	18,675	C
Missouri Southern State Univ	MO	13,071	C
Missouri State Univ	MO	15,837	C+
Northern Mich Univ	MI	20,853	C
The Univ of Montana Western	MT	9,426	LC
Union College	NE	23,270	C
Univ of Illinois at Urbana-Champaign	IL	27,006	HC
Univ of Nebr - Lincoln	NE	18,589	VC

COMPUTER ENGINEERING

School	ST	$IS	SR
Alfred State College	NY	19,895	C
Auburn Univ	AL	24,300	VC+
Baylor Univ	TX	56,803	HC
Bellarmine Univ	KY	52,532	C
Benedict College	SC	28,630	NC
Bethune-Cookman Univ	FL	23,322	C
Boston Univ	MA	67,352	MC
Brigham Young Univ	UT	13,248	MC
Brown Univ	RI	64,566	MC
Bucknell Univ	PA	67,136	MC
Calif Polytechnic State Univ	CA	22,547	MC
Calif State Polytechnic Univ, Pomona	CA	21,811	C
Cal State, Chico	CA	19,790	VC
Cal State, Fresno	CA	16,902	LC
Cal State, Fullerton	CA	21,902	C
Cal State, Long Beach	CA	18,850	C
Cal State, Sacramento	CA	19,060	C
Calvin College	MI	43,090	HC
Capitol Technology Univ	MD	46,280	SP
Carnegie Mellon Univ	PA	67,980	MC
Case Western Reserve Univ	OH	62,284	MC
Cedarville Univ	OH	36,244	VC
Christopher Newport Univ	VA	24,878	VC+
CUNY/City College	NY	20,204	C
Claflin Univ	SC	25,592	LC
Clarkson Univ	NY	60,392	VC
Clemson Univ	SC		HC
Cogswell Polytechnical College	CA	31,511	C
Colo State Univ	CO	23,033	C
Colo Technical Univ	CO	21,455	NC
Columbia Univ/City of New York	NY	62,958	MC
Dordt College	IA	37,860	C+
Drexel Univ	PA	65,927	HC
Drury Univ	MO	37,555	VC
Eastern Mich Univ	MI	19,761	C
Eastern Nazarene College	MA	41,114	C
Elizabethtown College	PA	56,340	VC
Elon Univ	NC	46,142	HC
Embry-Riddle Aeronautical Univ - Daytona Beach	FL	45,822	VC
Embry-Riddle Aeronautical Univ - Prescott Campus	AZ	45,130	VC
Fairfield Univ	CT	61,445	HC
Florida Atlantic Univ	FL	18,256	C
Florida Inst of Technology	FL	53,306	VC
Florida International Univ	FL	20,281	C
Florida State Univ	FL	16,771	HC
Fort Lewis College	CO	20,154	C
Gannon Univ	PA	42,922	C
George Mason Univ	VA	19,884	C
Georgia Inst of Technology	GA	23,910	MC
Gonzaga Univ	WA	52,880	HC
Harding Univ	AR	25,440	C
Hofstra Univ	NY	58,210	C+
Howard Univ	DC	37,616	C+
Illinois Inst of Technology	IL	56,826	HC+
Indiana Inst of Technology	IN	34,240	LC
Indiana Univ-Purdue Univ Fort Wayne	IN	18,675	C
Indiana Univ-Purdue Univ Indianapolis	IN	18,952	C
Iowa State Univ	IA	18,176	C
Jackson State Univ	MS	15,879	LC
Johns Hopkins Univ	MD	68,080	MC
Johnson C. Smith Univ	NC	25,336	LC
Kansas State Univ	KS	17,780	VC
Kennesaw State Univ	GA	18,899	VC
Kettering Univ	MI	47,570	HC
Lake Superior State Univ	MI	19,867	C
Lawrence Tech Univ	MI	41,630	VC
Lehigh Univ	PA	63,860	MC
LeTourneau Univ	TX	39,190	VC
Lewis Univ	IL	41,710	C
Lipscomb Univ	TN	42,984	VC
Louisiana State Univ and A&M College	LA	18,677	VC
Marquette Univ	WI	53,090	VC+
Merrimack College	MA	55,415	C
Miami Univ	OH	27,190	HC+
Mich State Univ	MI	24,542	VC
Mich Tech Univ	MI	25,551	VC+
Milwaukee School of Engineering	WI	48,531	HC+
Minn State Univ, Mankato	MN	17,190	C
Miss State Univ	MS	12,028	C+
Missouri Univ of Science and Technology	MO	18,655	HC
Montana State Univ	MT	15,500	C+
Montana Tech of the Univ of Montana	MT	15,447	VC
New Jersey Inst of Technology	NJ	30,198	HC
New York City College of Technology	NY	7,185	LC
New York Univ	NY	68,139	MC
N Car State Univ	NC	22,434	HC+
N Dak State Univ	ND	16,245	VC
Northeastern Univ	MA	65,352	MC
Northwestern Univ	IL	68,725	MC
Norwich Univ	VT	56,234	C
Nova Southeastern Univ	FL	38,534	C+
Oakland Univ	MI	20,763	C
Ohio Northern Univ	OH	44,050	VC
Ohio State Univ at Columbus	OH	22,843	MC
Ohio Univ	OH	23,394	VC
Okla Christian Univ	OK	29,260	C
Okla State Univ	OK	17,180	C+
Old Dominion Univ	VA	21,618	C
Olivet Nazarene Univ	IL	41,840	VC
Oral Roberts Univ	OK	34,316	C
Oregon State Univ	OR	23,337	VC
Penn State Erie,The Behrend College	PA	26,688	VC
Pennsylvania College of Technology	PA	27,693	NC
Pennsylvania State Univ - Univ Park	PA	29,716	HC
Portland State Univ	OR	19,443	C
Prairie View A&M Univ	TX	27,273	LC
Purdue Univ Northwest	IN	15,178	C
Purdue Univ/West Lafayette	IN	20,032	MC
Rensselaer Polytechnic Inst	NY	67,265	MC
Rochester Inst of Technology	NY	52,734	HC+
Rose-Hulman Inst of Technology	IN	59,823	MC
St. Louis Univ	MO	49,866	HC
San Diego State Univ	CA	23,156	VC
San Francisco State Univ	CA	18,514	LC
San Jose State Univ	CA	22,630	C
Seattle Univ	WA	54,957	VC
Shepherd Univ, West Virginia	WV	17,382	C
Shippensburg Univ of Pennsylvania	PA	24,096	C
S Dak School of Mines and Technology	SD	18,570	C+
Southern Illinois Univ Carbondale	IL	24,554	C
Southern Illinois Univ Edwardsville	IL	20,188	C
Southern Methodist Univ	TX	69,008	MC
St. Mary's Univ	TX	39,120	C
SUNY Albany	NY	22,165	C
SUNY at Binghamton	NY	24,100	MC
SUNY at New Paltz	NY	20,840	C
SUNY/Univ at Buffalo	NY	23,122	C
Stevens Inst of Technology	NJ	64,954	MC
Stony Brook Univ/The SUNY	NY	22,703	MC
Suffolk Univ	MA	52,316	C
Syracuse Univ	NY	62,313	HC
Taylor Univ	IN	42,130	VC
Texas A&M Univ at College Station	TX	20,771	VC+
Texas Tech Univ	TX	20,156	C+
The Catholic Univ of America	DC	58,376	VC
The College of New Jersey	NJ	28,675	VC+
The George Washington Univ	DC	68,474	HC+
The Univ of Akron	OH	22,566	C
The Univ of Memphis	TN	18,278	C
The Univ of Tenn at Knoxville	TN	22,112	VC
The Univ of Texas at San Antonio	TX	21,060	C
The Univ of Utah	UT	18,751	VC
Trine Univ	IN	41,310	C
Tufts Univ	MA		MC
Union College	NY	64,320	MC
United States Air Force Academy	CO		C
United States Naval Academy	MD		HC
Universidad Politecnica de PR, Hato Rey campus	PR	23,514	
Univ of Alabama in Huntsville	AL	20,028	VC
Univ of Alaska Fairbanks	AK	16,874	VC
Univ of Arkansas at Fayetteville	AR	19,766	VC
Univ of Bridgeport	CT	44,985	LC
Univ of Calif at Berkeley	CA	29,886	MC
Univ of Calif at Davis	CA	28,468	HC
Univ of Calif at Irvine	CA	33,857	VC
Univ of Calif at Los Angeles	CA	27,438	HC+
Univ of Calif at Santa Barbara	CA	30,627	HC+
Univ of Calif San Diego	CA	30,450	MC
Univ of Calif, Santa Cruz	CA	28,731	C+
Univ of Central Florida	FL	16,379	VC
Univ of Cincinnati	OH	22,118	VC
Univ of Colo Boulder	CO	26,048	HC
Univ of Colo Colo Springs	CO	20,300	C
Univ of Conn	CT	27,394	
Univ of Dayton	OH	54,930	VC
Univ of Delaware	DE	32,214	VC
Univ of Denver	CO	61,129	VC+
Univ of Evansville	IN	44,186	C+
Univ of Florida	FL	16,291	HC+
Univ of Georgia	GA	21,878	HC
Univ of Hartford	CT	49,776	C
Univ of Houston	TX	21,871	VC
Univ of Idaho	ID	16,158	C
Univ of Illinois at Chicago	IL	24,664	VC
Univ of Illinois at Urbana-Champaign	IL	27,006	HC
Univ of Kansas	KS	20,884	VC
Univ of La Verne	CA	55,600	C
Univ of Louisiana at Lafayette	LA	14,516	C
Univ of Louisville	KY	19,692	C
Univ of Maine	ME	21,038	VC
Univ of Maryland/Baltimore County	MD	23,004	VC
Univ of Maryland/College Park	MD	21,938	HC
Univ of Mass Amherst	MA	27,669	HC
Univ of Mass Dartmouth	MA	26,507	C
Univ of Mass Lowell	MA	27,296	VC
Univ of Miami	FL	63,494	MC
Univ of Mich/Ann Arbor	MI	25,274	MC
Univ of Mich/Dearborn	MI	12,472	VC
Univ of Minn/Duluth	MN	20,292	C
Univ of Minn/Twin Cities	MN	24,269	MC
Univ of Missouri-Columbia	MO	20,463	VC
Univ of Mount Union	OH	39,990	C
Univ of Nebr - Lincoln	NE	18,589	VC
Univ of Nevada, Las Vegas	NV	17,553	C
Univ of New Hampshire	NH	29,333	VC
Univ of New Haven	CT	53,680	C
Univ of New Mexico	NM	16,808	C
Univ of N Car at Charlotte	NC	17,803	VC
Univ of North Texas	TX	20,082	C
Univ of Northwestern - St. Paul	MN	39,530	C
Univ of Notre Dame	IN	68,801	MC
Univ of Okla	OK	19,651	HC
Univ of Pennsylvania	PA	63,526	MC
Univ of Pittsburgh	PA	30,030	MC

ST = STATE **$IS** = IN-STATE COSTS **SR** = SELECTOR RATING

School	ST	$IS	SR
Univ of Pittsburgh at Johnstown	PA	22,092	C
Univ of PR, at Mayaguez	PR	13,995	
Univ of Rhode Island	RI	26,066	VC
Univ of Scranton	PA	54,962	VC
Univ of South Alabama	AL	16,880	C
Univ of S Car at Columbia	SC	21,726	VC
Univ of South Florida/Tampa	FL	16,110	VC
Univ of Southern Calif	CA	66,631	MC
Univ of Texas at Arlington	TX	18,876	C
Univ of Texas at Dallas	TX	23,640	HC
Univ of Texas Rio Grande Valley	TX	15,573	LC
Univ of the Pacific	CA	57,446	VC
Univ of Toledo	OH	19,336	C
Univ of Tulsa	OK	52,625	HC
Univ of Virginia	VA	27,367	MC
Univ of Washington	WA	23,091	MC
Univ of West Florida	FL	15,848	C
Univ of Wisc-Madison	WI	21,647	MC
Univ of Wisc-Milwaukee	WI	21,538	C
Univ of Wisc-Stout	WI	19,667	C
Univ of Wyoming	WY	15,537	C
Valparaiso Univ	IN	50,160	VC
Vanderbilt Univ	TN	63,248	MC
Vermont Technical College	VT	25,370	C
Villanova Univ	PA	64,922	MC
Virginia Commonwealth Univ	VA	23,811	VC
Virginia Polytechnic Inst and State Univ	VA	21,920	VC
Washington State Univ	WA	22,747	C
Washington Univ in St. Louis	MO	67,539	MC
Weber State Univ	UT	14,112	C
Wentworth Inst of Technology	MA	48,810	VC
West Virginia Univ	WV	18,952	VC
Western Mich Univ	MI	21,791	C
Western New England Univ	MA	49,182	C
Wichita State Univ	KS	17,773	C
Wright State Univ	OH	16,983	C
York College of Pennsylvania	PA	29,240	C

COMPUTER ENGINEERING TECHNOLOGY

School	ST	$IS	SR
Calif Baptist Univ	CA	42,986	C
Cal State, Fresno	CA	16,902	LC
Cal State, Long Beach	CA	18,850	C
Central Conn State Univ	CT	22,041	C
Drexel Univ	PA	65,927	HC
Farmingdale State College	NY	20,968	C
Hofstra Univ	NY	58,210	C+
Howard Univ	DC	37,616	C+
Indiana Univ-Purdue Univ Indianapolis	IN	18,952	C
Loyola Univ Chicago	IL	57,158	VC
Minn State Univ, Mankato	MN	17,190	C
Missouri Southern State Univ	MO	13,071	C
Missouri Western State Univ	MO	17,822	LC
New York Univ	NY	68,139	MC
Northern Kentucky Univ	KY	16,486	C
Nova Southeastern Univ	FL	38,534	C+
Rochester Inst of Technology	NY	52,734	HC+
Shawnee State Univ	OH	16,998	C
Univ of Cincinnati	OH	22,118	VC
Univ of Conn	CT	27,394	
Univ of Dayton	OH	54,930	VC
Univ of S Car Upstate	SC	19,272	LC

COMPUTER GAME DESIGN/ DEVELOPMENT

School	ST	$IS	SR
Abilene Christian Univ	TX	43,708	C+
Arkansas Tech Univ	AR	16,534	LC
Becker College	MA	30,100	LC
Bloomfield College	NJ	40,100	LC
Champlain College	VT	54,724	VC
Columbia College Chicago	IL	40,104	C
Dakota State Univ	SD	12,286	C
DePaul Univ	IL	52,807	VC
DeSales Univ	PA	47,520	C
Drexel Univ	PA	65,927	HC
Drury Univ	MO	37,555	VC
Elmhurst College	IL	46,514	C
Indiana Inst of Technology	IN	34,240	LC
Kennesaw State Univ	GA	18,899	VC
Loyola Univ New Orleans	LA	52,456	VC
Lynn Univ	FL	49,680	LC
Marist College	NY	49,860	VC
Marshall Univ	WV	18,044	C
Missouri Western State Univ	MO	17,822	LC
Okla Christian Univ	OK	29,260	C
Rochester Inst of Technology	NY	52,734	HC+
Shawnee State Univ	OH	16,998	C
Shepherd Univ	CA		LC
Univ of Calif, Santa Cruz	CA	28,731	C+
Univ of Colo Colo Springs	CO	20,300	C
Univ of Denver	CO	61,129	VC+
Univ of St. Francis	IN	38,520	C
Univ of Tulsa	OK	52,625	HC

COMPUTER GRAPHIC DESIGN

School	ST	$IS	SR
Lewis Univ	IL	41,710	C
Lynn Univ	FL	49,680	LC
Missouri Western State Univ	MO	17,822	LC
Univ of Northwestern - St. Paul	MN	39,530	C

COMPUTER GRAPHICS

School	ST	$IS	SR
Andrews Univ	MI	41,732	C
Ashford Univ	CA	10,480	C
Bloomfield College	NJ	40,100	LC
Brown Univ	RI	64,566	MC
Cal State, Chico	CA	19,790	VC
Cogswell Polytechnical College	CA	31,511	C
Dakota State Univ	SD	12,286	C
DePaul Univ	IL	52,807	VC
Eastern Mich Univ	MI	19,761	C
Escuela de Artes Plasticas de PR	PR	11,236	
Fashion Inst of Technology/ SUNY	NY	18,521	SP
Indiana Univ-Purdue Univ Fort Wayne	IN	18,675	C
Indiana Univ-Purdue Univ Indianapolis	IN	18,952	C
Indiana Wesleyan Univ	IN	33,674	C
Jacksonville Univ	FL	49,210	C
La Salle Univ	PA	43,476	C
Lawrence Tech Univ	MI	41,630	VC
Millikin Univ	IL	44,148	C
Missouri Western State Univ	MO	17,822	LC
Monmouth Univ	NJ	50,184	C
New York Inst of Technology	NY	49,980	VC
Northwest Nazarene Univ	ID	40,250	C
Pennsylvania College of Technology	PA	27,693	NC
Pratt Inst	NY	59,482	VC+
Purdue Univ Northwest	IN	15,178	C
Purdue Univ/West Lafayette	IN	20,032	MC
Rochester Inst of Technology	NY	52,734	HC+
Savannah College of Art and Design	GA	49,595	SP
School of Visual Arts	NY	47,500	SP
Springfield College	MA	48,775	C
Syracuse Univ	NY	62,313	HC
Taylor Univ	IN	42,130	VC
The Art Inst of Atlanta	GA	34,334	SP
Univ of Dubuque	IA	37,824	C
Univ of Mary Hardin-Baylor	TX	35,292	C+
Univ of Miami	FL	63,494	MC
Univ of Tampa	FL	38,928	VC

COMPUTER INFORMATION SYSTEMS

School	ST	$IS	SR
Anderson Univ	IN	39,450	C
Arizona State Univ at the Tempe Campus	AZ	23,001	VC
Averett Univ	VA	43,034	LC
Bentley Univ	MA	63,720	MC
Bloomfield College	NJ	40,100	LC
Bradley Univ	IL	43,240	VC
Bryant Univ	RI	57,204	VC
Cabrini Univ	PA	42,591	LC
Calif State Polytechnic Univ, Pomona	CA	21,811	C
Cal State, Chico	CA	19,790	VC
Campbell Univ	NC	37,570	VC
Carroll College	MT	44,304	C
Clarke Univ	IA	42,950	C
College of Charleston	SC	24,046	VC
College of St. Scholastica	MN	45,734	C+
College of Staten Island	NY	24,389	LC
Delta State Univ	MS	13,176	LC
Faulkner Univ	AL	26,410	C
Ferris State Univ	MI	21,458	C
Grove City College	PA	26,654	VC
Husson Univ	ME	26,508	C
Indiana Univ Northwest	IN	7,207	LC
Keene State College	NH	24,604	C
Livingstone College	NC	17,815	LC
Loyola Univ New Orleans	LA	52,456	VC
Mayville State Univ	ND	18,371	NC
McKendree Univ	IL	37,940	C+
Mich Tech Univ	MI	25,551	VC+
Milligan College	TN	39,450	C
Missouri Southern State Univ	MO	13,071	C
Missouri Western State Univ	MO	17,822	LC
Molloy College	NY	40,440	C
Murray State Univ	KY	17,726	C+
Neumann Univ	PA	40,678	LC
Niagara Univ	NY	41,010	C
North Central Univ	MN	30,610	C
Northwest Nazarene Univ	ID	40,250	C
Northwestern State Univ of Louisiana	LA	16,534	LC
Nova Southeastern Univ	FL	38,534	C+
Okla Baptist Univ	OK	33,990	C
Regis Univ	CO	46,380	C
Rochester Inst of Technology	NY	52,734	HC+
St. Leo Univ	FL	32,850	C
St. Louis Univ	MO	49,866	HC
Siena Heights Univ	MI	36,322	C
Silver Lake College of the Holy Family	WI	36,290	LC
Southeast Missouri State Univ	MO	16,148	C
Southern Oregon Univ	OR	19,117	C
St. Joseph's College, New York/Brooklyn Campus	NY	25,114	LC
St. Joseph's College, New York/Long Island Campus	NY	25,124	C
St. Thomas Aquinas College	NY	32,450	C
SUNY Polytechnic Inst	NY	20,438	VC
SUNY/Fredonia	NY	20,818	C
Stevenson Univ	MD	48,412	C
Tarleton State Univ	TX	15,248	LC
Tenn Wesleyan Univ	TN	32,680	LC
Texas State Univ	TX	18,721	C
The Master's Univ	CA	43,870	C
Thomas Edison State Univ	NJ	6,350	NC
Univ of Dayton	OH	54,930	VC
Univ of Indianapolis	IN	36,480	VC
Univ of Louisiana at Monroe	LA	15,970	C
Univ of North Alabama	AL	15,964	C
Univ of St. Francis	IN	38,520	C
Univ of San Francisco	CA	60,580	C
Univ of Texas Rio Grande Valley	TX	15,573	LC
Univ of West Alabama	AL	16,284	LC
Wartburg College	IA	49,478	C
Wentworth Inst of Technology	MA	48,810	VC
Western Mich Univ	MI	21,791	C
Western New England Univ	MA	49,182	C

COMPUTER INFORMATION TECHNOLOGY

School	ST	$IS	SR
Berkeley College/New York City Campus	NY	35,100	LC
Biola Univ	CA	48,686	C
Cal State, Fullerton	CA	21,902	C
Campbell Univ	NC	37,570	VC
Champlain College	VT	54,724	VC
CUNY/John Jay College of Criminal Justice	NY	6,359	SP
City Univ of Seattle	WA	24,340	NC
Clayton State Univ	GA	19,735	LC
Ferris State Univ	MI	21,458	C
Georgia Southwestern State Univ	GA	13,870	LC
Indiana Univ-Purdue Univ Indianapolis	IN	18,952	C
Kutztown Univ of Pennsylvania	PA	19,477	C
Limestone College	SC	32,100	C
LIU Brooklyn	NY	50,698	C
LIU Post	NY	50,698	C+
Mills College	CA	43,705	C
Minn State Univ, Mankato	MN	17,190	C
Missouri Western State Univ	MO	17,822	LC
New York Inst of Technology	NY	49,980	VC
Niagara Univ	NY	41,010	C
Northern Arizona Univ	AZ	21,003	C
Northern Kentucky Univ	KY	16,486	C
Ohio Valley Univ	WV	28,800	C
Point Loma Nazarene Univ	CA	46,150	C+
Rochester Inst of Technology	NY	52,734	HC+
St. Louis Univ	MO	49,866	HC
St. Edward's Univ	TX	56,190	VC
St. Joseph's College, New York/Brooklyn Campus	NY	25,114	LC
St. Joseph's College, New York/Long Island Campus	NY	25,124	C
Texas Christian Univ	TX	57,120	HC
Thomas College	ME	73,888	LC
Trevecca Nazarene Univ	TN	31,186	C
Univ of Cincinnati	OH	22,118	VC
Univ of New Hampshire - Manchester	NH	14,490	C
Univ of Texas Rio Grande Valley	TX	15,573	LC
Washington & Jefferson College	PA	58,694	VC

COMPUTER MANAGEMENT

School	ST	$IS	SR
Caldwell Univ	NJ	42,165	LC
Chestnut Hill College	PA	47,180	C
Colo Christian Univ	CO	40,885	VC
Emory and Henry College	VA	46,320	C
Johnson & Wales Univ/ Providence Campus	RI	44,768	C
Lake Superior State Univ	MI	19,867	C
Mayville State Univ	ND	18,371	NC
Metropolitan State Univ of Denver	CO	6,928	LC
New Jersey Inst of Technology	NJ	30,198	HC
Northwest Missouri State Univ	MO	18,286	C
Northwood Univ - Mich	MI	35,010	LC
Peirce College	PA	16,780	NC
Peru State College	NE	15,602	LC
Rochester College	MI	28,574	LC
Southern Adventist Univ	TN	28,250	C
Southern Illinois Univ Edwardsville	IL	20,188	C
Univ of Illinois at Urbana-Champaign	IL	27,006	HC
Univ of Mount Olive	NC	18,426	C
Univ of New Haven	CT	53,680	C
Univ of Northern Iowa	IA	17,480	C
Webster Univ	MO	37,490	C

COMPUTER MATHEMATICS

School	ST	$IS	SR
Bethany College	WV	38,774	LC
Biola Univ	CA	48,686	C
Bowdoin College	ME	65,980	MC
Brown Univ	RI	64,566	MC
Calif Inst of Technology	CA	64,704	MC
Florida Southern College	FL	45,978	VC
Hofstra Univ	NY	58,210	C+
Ithaca College	NY	58,158	VC+
Keene State College	NH	24,604	C
LeTourneau Univ	TX	39,190	VC
Lewis & Clark College	OR	60,984	MC
New York Univ	NY	68,139	MC
Oakwood Univ	AL	43,758	C
Rochester Inst of Technology	NY	52,734	HC+
Salem International Univ	WV	21,090	C
Southern Oregon Univ	OR	19,117	C
Southwestern Univ	TX	52,370	VC
Univ of Illinois at Chicago	IL	24,664	VC
Univ of Illinois at Urbana-Champaign	IL	27,006	HC
Univ of S Car Aiken	SC	18,094	C
Wheaton College	MA	63,818	VC
Whitman College	WA	59,772	MC

COMPUTER NETWORKS & SYSTEMS

School	ST	$IS	SR
Bloomfield College	NJ	40,100	LC
Cal State, Fullerton	CA	21,902	C
Ferris State Univ	MI	21,458	C
Frostburg State Univ	MD	17,280	LC
Keene State College	NH	24,604	C
Lake Superior State Univ	MI	19,867	C
Missouri Western State Univ	MO	17,822	LC
Mount Vernon Nazarene Univ	OH	35,944	C
Regis Univ	CO	46,380	C
Rochester Inst of Technology	NY	52,734	HC+
Silver Lake College of the Holy Family	WI	36,290	LC
St. Ambrose Univ	IA	40,180	C
Taylor Univ	IN	42,130	VC
Univ of Alaska Anchorage	AK	17,914	C
Univ of Georgia	GA	21,878	HC
Weber State Univ	UT	14,112	C
Wentworth Inst of Technology	MA	48,810	VC

COMPUTER PROGRAMMING

School	ST	$IS	SR
Baker College of Flint	MI	19,140	NC
Bloomfield College	NJ	40,100	LC
Calvin College	MI	43,090	HC
Caribbean Univ	PR	12,227	
Carnegie Mellon Univ	PA	67,980	MC
Central Washington Univ	WA	16,803	C
City Univ of Seattle	WA	24,340	NC
Cogswell Polytechnical College	CA	31,511	C
Columbia College Chicago	IL	40,104	C
Concord Univ	WV	14,954	LC
Concordia Univ, Chicago	IL	41,522	C
Curry College	MA	53,331	C
Dakota State Univ	SD	12,286	C
DePaul Univ	IL	52,807	VC
Dickinson State Univ	ND	12,372	LC
Dordt College	IA	37,860	C+
Eastern Kentucky Univ	KY	17,742	C
Eastern Mich Univ	MI	19,761	C
Farmingdale State College	NY	20,968	C
Franklin College	IN	40,550	C
Freed-Hardeman Univ	TN	29,900	C
Gannon Univ	PA	42,922	C
Hannibal-LaGrange Univ	MO	29,815	C
Hawaii Pacific Univ	HI	33,420	C
Idaho State Univ	ID	13,619	LC
Indiana Univ-Purdue Univ Fort Wayne	IN	18,675	C
Ithaca College	NY	58,158	VC+
Lamar Univ	TX	18,014	LC
Le Moyne College	NY	47,305	VC
Limestone College	SC	32,100	C
Mayville State Univ	ND	18,371	NC
Midland Univ	NE	39,512	C
Missouri Western State Univ	MO	17,822	LC
Monmouth College	IL	42,260	C
Montana Tech of the Univ of Montana	MT	15,447	VC
Northeastern Univ	MA	65,352	MC
Northern Mich Univ	MI	20,853	C
Peirce College	PA	16,780	NC
Pennsylvania College of Technology	PA	27,693	NC
Peru State College	NE	15,602	LC
Pontifical Catholic Univ of PR	PR	10,534	
Purdue Univ Northwest	IN	15,178	C
St. Louis Univ	MO	49,866	HC
Salem State Univ	MA	42,650	LC
Southern Oregon Univ	OR	19,117	C
St. Thomas Univ	FL	51,187	LC
Stephen F. Austin State Univ	TX	18,484	LC
Suffolk Univ	MA	52,316	C
Tarleton State Univ	TX	15,248	LC
Universidad del Turabo	PR	17,828	
Univ of Arkansas at Little Rock	AR	18,211	LC
Univ of Illinois at Urbana-Champaign	IL	27,006	HC
Univ of Nebr - Kearney	NE	17,014	LC
Univ of New Haven	CT	53,680	C
Univ of St. Francis	IL	40,828	C

ST = STATE **$IS** = IN-STATE COSTS **SR** = SELECTOR RATING

School	ST	$IS	SR
Univ of Wisc-River Falls	WI	14,541	C
Univ of Wisc-Whitewater	WI	13,976	C
Washington Univ in St. Louis	MO	67,539	MC
Weber State Univ	UT	14,112	C
West Virginia Univ Inst of Technology	WV	18,264	C
Youngstown State Univ	OH	17,487	C

COMPUTER SCIENCE

School	ST	$IS	SR
Abilene Christian Univ	TX	43,708	C+
Adams State Univ	CO	15,420	LC
Adelphi Univ	NY	49,792	C
Agnes Scott College	GA	51,930	VC+
Alabama A&M Univ	AL	18,796	C
Albany State Univ	GA	19,462	C
Albright College	PA	57,326	C
Alcorn State Univ	MS	15,884	C
Alderson Broaddus Univ	WV	35,000	LC
Allegheny College	PA	57,620	VC
Alma College	MI	49,410	VC
American Univ of PR	PR	16,130	
Amherst College	MA	66,186	MC
Anderson Univ	IN	39,450	C
Andrews Univ	MI	41,732	C
Angelo State Univ	TX	15,882	LC
Anna Maria College	MA	51,020	C
Appalachian State Univ	NC	15,394	VC
Arcadia Univ	PA	55,990	C+
Arizona State Univ at the Tempe Campus	AZ	23,001	VC
Arkansas Baptist College	AR	20,280	NC
Arkansas State Univ	AR	16,190	C
Arkansas Tech Univ	AR	16,534	LC
Armstrong State Univ	GA	15,615	C
Ashford Univ	CA	10,480	C
Ashland Univ	OH	30,446	C
Assumption College	MA	48,455	VC
Atlantic Union College	MA	27,228	C
Auburn Univ	AL	24,300	VC+
Auburn Univ at Montgomery	AL	15,000	C
Augsburg Univ	MN	45,129	C
Augusta Univ	GA	4,632	C
Augustana College	IL	51,222	VC+
Augustana Univ	SD	39,968	VC
Aurora Univ	IL	34,990	C
Austin College	TX	51,059	HC
Austin Peay State Univ	TN	16,397	C
Averett Univ	VA	43,034	LC
Avila Univ	MO	27,100	C
Azusa Pacific Univ	CA	43,972	C
Baker Univ	KS	37,190	C
Baldwin Wallace Univ	OH	42,464	VC
Ball State Univ	IN	19,808	C+
Bard College	NY	65,924	HC
Bard College at Simon's Rock	MA	65,795	MC
Barnard College/Columbia Univ	NY	68,762	MC
Barry Univ	FL	38,730	LC
Bayamon Central Univ	PR	12,490	
Baylor Univ	TX	56,803	HC
Belhaven Univ	MS	32,250	C
Bellarmine Univ	KY	52,532	C
Belmont Univ	TN	44,500	VC+
Beloit College	WI	55,206	HC
Bemidji State Univ	MN	17,730	C
Benedict College	SC	28,630	NC
Benedictine College	KS	38,850	VC
Benedictine Univ	IL	38,300	C
Bennett College	NC	27,717	NC
Bennington College	VT	66,280	MC
Berea College	KY	7,094	C
Bethany College	WV	38,774	LC
Bethel Univ	MN	46,550	C+
Bethune-Cookman Univ	FL	23,322	C
Biola Univ	CA	48,686	C
Blackburn College	IL	28,526	LC
Bloomfield College	NJ	40,100	LC
Bloomsburg Univ of Pennsylvania	PA	19,930	C
Bluefield State College	WV	5,832	LC
Bluffton Univ	OH	40,950	C+
Boise State Univ	ID	17,368	C
Boston College	MA	68,043	MC
Boston Univ	MA	67,352	MC
Bowdoin College	ME	65,980	MC
Bowie State Univ	MD	18,610	LC
Bowling Green State Univ	OH	19,975	C
Bradley Univ	IL	43,240	VC
Brandeis Univ	MA	68,443	MC
Brescia Univ	KY	29,890	VC
Briar Cliff Univ	IA	36,956	C
Bridgewater College	VA	46,260	C
Bridgewater State Univ	MA	22,762	C
Brigham Young Univ	UT	13,248	MC
Brigham Young Univ/Hawaii	HI	11,710	C
Brown Univ	RI	64,566	MC
Bryn Mawr College	PA	65,220	MC
Bucknell Univ	PA	67,136	MC
Buena Vista Univ	IA	42,344	C
Butler Univ	IN	52,890	VC+
Cairn Univ	PA	37,572	C
Caldwell Univ	NJ	42,165	LC
Calif Baptist Univ	CA	42,986	C
Calif Inst of Technology	CA	64,704	MC
Calif Lutheran Univ	CA	52,853	C
Calif Polytechnic State Univ	CA	22,547	MC
Calif State Polytechnic Univ, Pomona	CA	21,811	C
Cal State, Bakersfield	CA	22,397	LC
Cal State, Chico	CA	19,790	VC
Cal State, Dominguez Hills	CA	19,022	LC
Cal State, East Bay	CA	20,748	C
Cal State, Fresno	CA	16,902	LC
Cal State, Fullerton	CA	21,902	C
Cal State, Long Beach	CA	18,850	C
Cal State, Los Angeles	CA	17,186	LC
Cal State, Monterey Bay	CA	22,872	LC
Cal State, Northridge	CA	17,277	LC
Cal State, Sacramento	CA	19,060	C
Cal State, San Bernardino	CA	20,106	C
Cal State, San Marcos	CA	20,604	LC
Cal State, Stanislaus	CA	18,053	LC
Calvin College	MI	43,090	HC
Cameron Univ	OK	11,632	LC
Campbell Univ	NC	37,570	VC
Campbellsville Univ	KY	33,400	C
Canisius College	NY	49,672	C
Capital Univ	OH	44,778	VC
Cardinal Stritch Univ	WI	37,136	C
Caribbean Univ	PR	12,227	
Carleton College	MN	66,414	MC
Carnegie Mellon Univ	PA	67,980	MC
Carroll College	MT	44,304	C
Carroll Univ	WI	38,100	C+
Case Western Reserve Univ	OH	62,284	MC
Castleton Univ	VT	20,186	C
Catawba College	NC	39,820	LC
Cedarville Univ	OH	36,244	VC
Central College	IA	44,592	C
Central Conn State Univ	CT	22,041	C
Central Methodist Univ	MO	31,500	VC
Central Mich Univ	MI	20,330	C
Central State Univ	OH	18,564	C
Central Washington Univ	WA	16,803	C
Centre College	KY	50,680	MC
Chaminade Univ of Honolulu	HI	37,614	C
Champlain College	VT	54,724	VC
Chapman Univ	CA	65,504	HC
Charleston Southern Univ	SC	34,700	C
Chestnut Hill College	PA	47,180	C
Cheyney Univ of Pennsylvania	PA	20,896	LC
Chicago State Univ	IL	41,620	C
Christian Brothers Univ	TN	31,670	VC
Christopher Newport Univ	VA	24,878	VC+
CUNY/Brooklyn College	NY	7,163	C+
CUNY/City College	NY	20,204	C
CUNY/Hunter College	NY	31,098	VC
CUNY/Lehman College	NY	5,788	LC
CUNY/Medgar Evers College	NY	6,680	NC
CUNY/Queens College	NY	21,507	C
Claflin Univ	SC	25,592	LC
Clarion Univ of Pennsylvania	PA	21,608	LC
Clark Atlanta Univ	GA	31,019	LC
Clark Univ	MA	53,260	HC+
Clarke Univ	IA	42,950	C
Clarkson Univ	NY	60,392	VC
Clemson Univ	SC		HC
Cleveland State Univ	OH	22,290	C
Coastal Carolina Univ	SC	20,340	C
Coe College	IA	51,570	VC
Coker College	SC	38,196	C
Colby College	ME	64,060	MC
Colgate Univ	NY	67,500	MC
College of Charleston	SC	24,046	VC
College of Mount St. Vincent	NY	45,620	C
College of St. Benedict	MN	54,480	C
College of St. Elizabeth	NJ	45,700	LC
College of Staten Island	NY	24,389	LC
College of the Holy Cross	MA	64,320	MC
College of the Ozarks	MO	7,530	VC
College of William & Mary	VA	34,907	MC
Colo College	CO	64,894	MC
Colo Mesa Univ	CO	19,707	LC
Colo State Univ	CO	23,033	C
Colo Technical Univ	CO	21,455	NC
Columbia College - Missouri	MO	28,179	C
Columbia Univ/ School of General Studies	NY	61,470	MC
Columbia Univ/City of New York	NY	62,958	MC
Columbus State Univ	GA	14,336	LC
Concord Univ	WV	14,954	LC
Concordia Univ Nebr	NE	41,900	VC
Concordia Univ St. Paul	MN	29,050	C
Concordia Univ Texas	TX	41,920	C
Concordia Univ, Ann Arbor	MI	38,878	C+
Concordia Univ, Chicago	IL	41,522	C
Converse College	SC	28,290	C
Coppin State Univ	MD	14,071	VC
Cornell College	IA	49,900	VC
Cornell Univ	NY	67,591	MC
Covenant College	GA	44,590	HC
Dakota State Univ	SD	12,286	C
Dallas Baptist Univ	TX	35,220	VC
Dartmouth College	NH	68,109	MC
Davis & Elkins College	WV	38,242	LC
Delaware State Univ	DE	19,376	LC
Delaware Valley Univ	PA	51,271	C
Denison Univ	OH	62,770	HC+
DePaul Univ	IL	52,807	VC
DePauw Univ	IN	58,688	VC
DeSales Univ	PA	47,520	C
Dickinson College	PA	66,166	MC
Dickinson State Univ	ND	12,372	LC
Dillard Univ	LA	20,940	VC
Doane Univ	NE	41,340	VC
Dominican College	NY	40,258	LC
Dominican Univ	IL	42,472	C+
Dordt College	IA	37,860	C+
Drake Univ	IA	49,220	HC
Drew Univ/College of Liberal Arts	NJ	53,608	VC
Drexel Univ	PA	65,927	HC
Duke Univ	NC	68,298	MC
Duquesne Univ	PA	48,508	VC
Earlham College	IN	55,670	HC
East Carolina Univ	NC	16,539	C
East Central Univ	OK	13,330	C
East Stroudsburg Univ	PA	18,578	LC
East Tenn State Univ	TN	18,141	C
Eastern Conn State Univ	CT	23,059	C
Eastern Illinois Univ	IL	21,414	C
Eastern Kentucky Univ	KY	17,742	C
Eastern Mennonite Univ	VA	42,550	C
Eastern Mich Univ	MI	19,761	C
Eastern Nazarene College	MA	41,114	C
Eastern New Mexico Univ	NM	12,874	LC
Eastern Oregon Univ	OR	17,612	C
Eastern Washington Univ	WA	17,896	LC
Eckerd College	FL	55,206	VC
Edinboro Univ	PA	15,940	LC
Edward Waters College	FL	28,089	NC
Elizabeth City State Univ	NC	14,745	C
Elizabethtown College	PA	56,340	VC
Elmhurst College	IL	46,514	C
Elms College	MA	49,602	VC
Elon Univ	NC	46,142	HC
Embry-Riddle Aeronautical Univ - Daytona Beach	FL	45,822	VC
Emory and Henry College	VA	46,320	C
Emory Univ	GA	63,286	MC
Emporia State Univ	KS	15,029	C
Endicott College	MA	47,054	C+
Eureka College	IL	34,760	C
Evangel Univ	MO	28,898	C
Fairleigh Dickinson Univ/ College at Florham	NJ	54,770	C
Fairleigh Dickinson Univ/ Metropolitan Campus	NJ	52,392	C
Fairmont State Univ	WV	15,726	C
Faulkner Univ	AL	26,410	C
Fayetteville State Univ	NC	17,756	C
Fisk Univ	TN	32,066	LC
Fitchburg State Univ	MA	21,819	LC
Florida A&M Univ	FL	15,361	C
Florida Atlantic Univ	FL	18,256	C
Florida Gulf Coast Univ	FL	14,738	C
Florida Inst of Technology	FL	53,306	VC
Florida International Univ	FL	20,281	C
Florida Memorial Univ	FL	22,424	LC
Florida Southern College	FL	45,978	VC
Florida State Univ	FL	16,771	HC
Fontbonne Univ	MO	34,606	C
Fordham Univ	NY	68,431	MC
Fort Hays State Univ	KS	12,677	C
Fort Valley State Univ	GA	17,988	VC
Framingham State Univ	MA	21,740	C
Francis Marion Univ	SC	18,144	LC
Franciscan Univ of Steubenville	OH	33,980	VC
Franklin College	IN	40,550	C
Franklin Univ	OH	11,616	NC
Freed-Hardeman Univ	TN	29,900	C
Friends Univ	KS	38,000	C
Frostburg State Univ	MD	17,280	LC
Furman Univ	SC	61,098	VC+
Gannon Univ	PA	42,922	C
Gardner-Webb Univ	NC	24,935	C+
Geneva College	PA	35,450	C
George Fox Univ	OR	42,938	C
George Mason Univ	VA	19,884	C
Georgetown Univ	DC	68,970	MC
Georgia College & State Univ	GA	21,884	C+
Georgia Inst of Technology	GA	23,910	MC
Georgia Southern Univ	GA	16,540	VC
Georgia Southwestern State Univ	GA	13,870	LC
Georgia State Univ	GA	25,250	C
Gettysburg College	PA	65,210	MC
Gonzaga Univ	WA	52,880	HC
Gordon College	MA	47,740	VC
Goshen College	IN	44,350	C
Goucher College	MD	56,110	VC
Graceland Univ	IA	35,290	C
Grambling State Univ	LA	15,701	C
Grand Valley State Univ	MI	22,250	C+
Grand View Univ	IA	32,302	C
Greenville College	IL	27,012	LC
Grinnell College	IA	63,114	MC
Grove City College	PA	26,654	VC
Gustavus Adolphus College	MN	53,943	HC
Gwynedd Mercy Univ	PA	43,780	LC
Hamilton College	NY	64,250	MC
Hampden-Sydney College	VA	57,806	VC
Hampshire College	MA	65,214	MC
Hampton Univ	VA	36,410	C
Hanover College	IN	47,750	C+
Harding Univ	AR	25,440	C
Hardin-Simmons Univ	TX	36,025	C
Hartwick College	NY	51,270	C
Harvard College/Harvard Univ	MA	65,609	MC
Harvey Mudd College	CA	67,155	MC
Hastings College	NE	35,380	C+
Haverford College	PA	66,490	MC
Hawaii Pacific Univ	HI	33,420	C
Heidelberg Univ	OH	40,400	LC
Henderson State Univ	AR	15,516	C
Hendrix College	AR	54,020	VC
Heritage Univ	WA	19,825	NC
High Point Univ	NC	47,355	VC
Hiram College	OH	44,590	C
Hobart and William Smith Colleges	NY	67,050	HC+
Hofstra Univ	NY	58,210	C+
Holy Names Univ	CA	46,630	LC
Hood College	MD	50,540	C
Hope College	MI	42,840	VC
Houghton College	NY	40,558	VC
Howard Payne Univ	TX	35,994	C
Howard Univ	DC	37,616	C+
Huntington Univ	IN	33,996	C
Huston-Tillotson Univ	TX	18,124	LC
Idaho State Univ	ID	13,619	LC
Illinois College	IL	41,330	VC
Illinois Inst of Technology	IL	56,826	HC+
Illinois State Univ	IL	23,418	VC
Illinois Wesleyan Univ	IL	56,430	VC+
Indiana Inst of Technology	IN	34,240	LC
Indiana State Univ	IN	23,223	LC
Indiana Univ Bloomington	IN	20,791	HC
Indiana Univ of Pennsylvania	PA	24,474	C
Indiana Univ South Bend	IN	16,057	C
Indiana Univ Southeast	IN	16,931	C
Indiana Univ-Purdue Univ Fort Wayne	IN	18,675	C
Indiana Univ-Purdue Univ Indianapolis	IN	18,952	C
Indiana Wesleyan Univ	IN	33,674	C
Inter-American Univ of PR Ponce	PR	19,549	
Inter-American Univ of PR-Aguadilla Campus	PR	21,657	
Inter-American Univ of PR-Arecibo Campus	PR	18,245	
Inter-American Univ of PR-Bayamon	PR	18,785	
Inter-American Univ of PR-Fajardo Campus	PR	18,336	
Inter-American Univ of PR-Metropolitan Campus	PR	20,045	
Inter-American Univ of PR-San Germán	PR	20,042	
Iona College	NY	52,514	C
Iowa State Univ	IA	18,176	C
Ithaca College	NY	58,158	VC+
Jackson State Univ	MS	15,879	LC
Jacksonville State Univ	AL	14,628	LC
Jacksonville Univ	FL	49,210	C
James Madison Univ	VA	19,084	VC
John Carroll Univ	OH	51,080	C
Johns Hopkins Univ	MD	68,080	MC
Johnson & Wales Univ/ Providence Campus	RI	44,768	C
Johnson C. Smith Univ	NC	25,336	LC
Judson Univ	IL	39,174	C
Juniata College	PA	58,118	VC
Kalamazoo College	MI	53,931	HC
Kansas State Univ	KS	17,780	VC
Kansas Wesleyan Univ	KS	37,930	C
Kean Univ	NJ	25,620	C
Keene State College	NH	24,604	C
Kennesaw State Univ	GA	18,899	VC
Kent State Univ	OH	20,928	C
Kentucky State Univ	KY	14,484	LC
Kentucky Wesleyan College	KY	34,260	LC
Kettering Univ	MI	47,570	HC
King's College	PA	48,240	C
Knox College	IL	54,654	VC+
Kutztown Univ of Pennsylvania	PA	19,477	C
La Roche College	PA	38,940	C
La Salle Univ	PA	43,476	C
La Sierra Univ	CA	39,690	VC
Lafayette College	PA	68,520	MC
LaGrange College	GA	41,310	C
Lake Forest College	IL	50,652	VC
Lake Superior State Univ	MI	19,867	C
Lakeland Univ	WI	35,130	C
Lamar Univ	TX	18,014	LC
Lander Univ	SC	32,200	C
Lane College	TN	17,960	LC
Langston Univ	OK	15,659	C
Lawrence Tech Univ	MI	41,630	VC
Lawrence Univ	WI	56,133	HC+
Le Moyne College	NY	47,305	VC
Lebanon Valley College	PA	55,510	VC
Lehigh Univ	PA	63,860	MC
LeMoyne-Owen College	TN	16,980	C
Lenoir-Rhyne Univ	NC	47,500	LC
LeTourneau Univ	TX	39,190	VC
Lewis & Clark College	OR	60,984	MC
Lewis Univ	IL	41,710	C
Lewis-Clark State College	ID	14,202	C
Liberty Univ	VA	31,415	C
Limestone College	SC	32,100	C
Lincoln Univ	MO	14,402	NC
Lincoln Univ	PA	20,878	LC
Lindenwood Univ	MO	25,760	C
Linfield College	OR	53,992	C
Lipscomb Univ	TN	42,984	VC
LIU Brooklyn	NY	50,698	C
LIU Post	NY	50,698	C+

ST = STATE **$IS** = IN-STATE COSTS **SR** = SELECTOR RATING

School	ST	$IS	SR
Lock Haven Univ of Pennsylvania	PA	20,544	LC
Longwood Univ	VA	22,184	C
Loras College	IA	40,726	C
Louisiana State Univ and A&M College	LA	18,677	VC
Louisiana State Univ in Shreveport	LA	6,902	C
Louisiana Tech Univ	LA	11,422	VC
Loyola Marymount Univ	CA	60,202	VC+
Loyola Univ Chicago	IL	57,158	VC
Loyola Univ Maryland	MD	61,710	VC
Luther College	IA	49,990	VC
Macalester College	MN	64,136	MC
MacMurray College	IL	35,025	C
Madonna Univ	MI	30,450	LC
Maharishi Univ of Management	IA	34,930	VC
Malone Univ	OH	39,200	C
Manchester Univ	IN	41,540	C
Manhattan College	NY	55,652	C
Manhattanville College	NY	52,430	C
Mansfield Univ of Pennsylvania	PA	24,244	LC
Marietta College	OH	46,190	C
Marist College	NY	49,860	VC
Marlboro College	VT	50,832	VC+
Marquette Univ	WI	53,090	VC+
Mars Hill Univ	NC	41,104	C
Marshall Univ	WV	18,044	C
Marygrove College	MI	30,100	LC
Maryville College	TN	44,410	C
Mass College of Liberal Arts	MA	20,659	C
Mass Inst of Technology	MA	62,662	MC
McDaniel College	MD	52,910	VC
McKendree Univ	IL	37,940	C+
McMurry Univ	TX	34,259	LC
McNeese State Univ	LA	7,838	C
Mercer Univ	GA	45,348	VC
Mercy College	NY	32,614	C
Meredith College	NC	46,634	C
Merrimack College	MA	55,415	C
Messiah College	PA	44,380	VC
Methodist Univ	NC	58,130	C
Metropolitan State Univ	MN	7,859	C
Metropolitan State Univ of Denver	CO	6,928	LC
Miami Univ	OH	27,190	HC+
Mich State Univ	MI	24,542	VC
Mich Tech Univ	MI	25,551	VC+
Middle Tenn State Univ	TN	8,650	C
Middlebury College	VT	67,464	MC
Midland Univ	NE	39,512	C
Midwestern State Univ	TX	12,111	LC
Miles College	AL	16,530	NC
Millersville Univ of Pennsylvania	PA	25,298	C
Milligan College	TN	39,450	C
Mills College	CA	43,705	C
Minn State Univ, Moorhead	MN	21,393	C
Minot State Univ	ND	13,285	C
Misericordia Univ	PA	45,210	C
Miss College	MS	25,850	C
Miss State Univ	MS	12,028	C+
Miss Valley State Univ	MS	13,233	LC
Missouri Southern State Univ	MO	13,071	C
Missouri State Univ	MO	15,837	C+
Missouri Univ of Science and Technology	MO	18,655	HC
Missouri Western State Univ	MO	17,822	LC
Molloy College	NY	40,440	C
Monmouth College	IL	42,260	C
Monmouth Univ	NJ	50,184	C
Montana State Univ	MT	15,500	C+
Montana Tech of the Univ of Montana	MT	15,447	VC
Montclair State Univ	NJ	26,912	C
Moravian College	PA	55,488	C
Morehead State Univ	KY	18,386	LC
Morehouse College	GA	40,835	C
Morgan State Univ	MD	17,190	LC
Morningside College	IA	39,780	C
Mount Holyoke College	MA	56,746	MC
Mount Marty College	SD	36,862	C
Mount Mercy Univ	IA	39,748	C
Mount St. Mary's Univ	MD	53,380	C
Mount Vernon Nazarene Univ	OH	35,944	C
Muhlenberg College	PA	56,645	VC
Murray State Univ	KY	17,726	C+
Muskingum Univ	OH	35,966	C
National Univ	CA	17,849	LC
Nebr Wesleyan Univ	NE	42,026	C+
New England College	NH	50,828	NC
New Jersey City Univ	NJ	21,456	LC
New Jersey Inst of Technology	NJ	30,198	HC
New Mexico Highlands Univ	NM	11,904	LC
New Mexico Inst of Mining and Technology	NM	15,385	HC+
New Mexico State Univ	NM	14,050	LC
New York Inst of Technology	NY	49,980	VC
New York Univ	NY	68,139	MC
Newberry College	SC	34,550	C
Newbury College	MA	48,970	C
Niagara Univ	NY	41,010	C
Nicholls State Univ	LA	14,959	C
Norfolk State Univ	VA	18,902	LC
N Car A&T State Univ	NC	13,786	C
N Car Central Univ	NC	9,000	C
N Car State Univ	NC	22,434	HC+
North Central College	IL	48,712	C+
North Central Univ	MN	30,610	C
N Dak State Univ	ND	16,245	VC
Northeastern Illinois Univ	IL	12,529	LC
Northeastern State Univ	OK	8,615	VC
Northeastern Univ	MA	65,352	MC
Northern Arizona Univ	AZ	21,003	C
Northern Illinois Univ	IL	20,176	C
Northern Kentucky Univ	KY	16,486	C
Northern Mich Univ	MI	20,853	C
Northwest Christian Univ	OR	36,580	C
Northwest Missouri State Univ	MO	18,286	C
Northwest Nazarene Univ	ID	40,250	C
Northwestern College of Iowa	IA	38,400	C
Northwestern Okla State Univ	OK	13,072	LC
Northwestern Univ	IL	68,725	MC
Norwich Univ	VT	56,234	C
Notre Dame de Namur Univ	CA	46,526	LC
Notre Dame of Maryland Univ	MD	47,570	VC
Nova Southeastern Univ	FL	38,534	C+
Nyack College	NY	34,450	LC
Oakland Univ	MI	20,763	C
Oakwood Univ	AL	43,758	C
Oberlin College	OH	68,942	MC
Ohio Dominican Univ	OH	41,340	C+
Ohio Northern Univ	OH	44,050	VC
Ohio State Univ at Columbus	OH	22,843	MC
Ohio Univ	OH	23,394	VC
Ohio Wesleyan Univ	OH	49,460	VC
Okla Baptist Univ	OK	33,990	C
Okla Christian Univ	OK	29,260	C
Okla State Univ	OK	17,180	C+
Old Dominion Univ	VA	21,618	C
Olivet College	MI	37,661	LC
Olivet Nazarene Univ	IL	41,840	VC
Oral Roberts Univ	OK	34,316	C
Oregon State Univ	OR	23,337	VC
Otterbein Univ	OH	41,630	C
Ouachita Baptist Univ	AR	33,500	VC
Pace Univ	NY	60,136	C
Pacific Lutheran Univ	WA	49,960	C
Pacific Union College	CA	36,009	VC
Pacific Univ	OR	37,617	C
Palm Beach Atlantic Univ	FL	39,250	C
Park Univ	MO	22,134	C
Penn State Erie,The Behrend College	PA	26,688	VC
Pennsylvania College of Technology	PA	27,693	NC
Pepperdine Univ	CA	66,862	VC+
Peru State College	NE	15,602	LC
Philander Smith College	AR	20,814	LC
Plymouth State Univ	NH	23,180	LC
Point Loma Nazarene Univ	CA	46,150	C+
Point Park Univ	PA	41,270	C
Pomona College	CA	64,957	MC
Portland State Univ	OR	19,443	C
Prairie View A&M Univ	TX	27,273	LC
Princeton Univ	NJ	60,090	MC
Principia College	IL	40,350	C
Providence College	RI	62,870	HC
Purdue Univ Northwest	IN	15,178	C
Purdue Univ/West Lafayette	IN	20,032	MC
Quincy Univ	IL	38,170	LC
Quinnipiac Univ	CT	60,970	VC
Radford Univ	VA	19,758	C
Ramapo College of New Jersey	NJ	25,760	VC
Randolph-Macon College	VA	51,480	VC
Regis Univ	CO	46,380	C
Rensselaer Polytechnic Inst	NY	67,265	MC
Rhode Island College	RI	19,000	LC
Rhodes College	TN	51,900	HC
Rice Univ	TX	59,458	MC
Rivier Univ	NH	41,600	VC
Roanoke College	VA	55,952	VC
Rochester Inst of Technology	NY	52,734	HC+
Rockford Univ	IL	38,570	C
Rockhurst Univ	MO	28,990	C
Rocky Mountain College	MT	35,776	C
Roger Williams Univ	RI	48,074	VC
Rollins College	FL	58,670	HC
Roosevelt Univ	IL	41,890	VC
Rose-Hulman Inst of Technology	IN	59,823	MC
Rowan Univ	NJ	24,491	VC
Rust College	MS	10,600	C
Rutgers Univ - Camden	NJ	26,595	C
Rutgers Univ - New Brunswick	NJ	27,090	HC
Rutgers Univ - Newark	NJ	27,351	C
Sacred Heart Univ	CT	54,590	C
Saginaw Valley State Univ	MI	19,284	C
St. Anselm College	NH	56,636	VC
St. Augustine's Univ	NC	25,582	C
St. Francis Univ	PA	46,146	NC
St. John's Univ	MN	53,472	C
St. Joseph's Univ	PA	58,540	VC
St. Louis Univ	MO	49,866	HC
St. Martin's Univ	WA	45,056	C
St. Mary-of-the-Woods College	IN	40,424	LC
St. Mary's College of Calif	CA	57,420	C
St. Mary's Univ of Minn	MN	42,440	C
St. Michael's College	VT	53,275	VC+
St. Peter's Univ	NJ	49,192	C
St. Vincent College	PA	46,229	C
St. Xavier Univ	IL	44,440	C
Salisbury Univ	MD	21,132	VC
Sam Houston State Univ	TX	18,792	C
Samford Univ	AL	40,770	VC
San Diego State Univ	CA	23,156	VC
San Francisco State Univ	CA	18,514	LC
San Jose State Univ	CA	22,630	C
Sarah Lawrence College	NY	68,866	MC
Savannah State Univ	GA	17,036	C
Scripps College	CA	69,260	HC
Seattle Pacific Univ	WA	47,439	C+
Seattle Univ	WA	54,957	VC
Seton Hall Univ	NJ	58,008	C
Seton Hill Univ	PA	46,972	VC
Sewanee: The Univ of the South	TN	58,000	HC+
Shaw Univ	NC	24,638	C
Shepherd Univ, West Virginia	WV	17,382	C
Shippensburg Univ of Pennsylvania	PA	24,096	C
Siena College	NY	48,916	C
Silver Lake College of the Holy Family	WI	36,290	LC
Simmons College	MA	54,400	HC
Simpson College	IA	45,626	VC
Skidmore College	NY	66,600	MC
Slippery Rock Univ of Pennsylvania	PA	20,450	C
Smith College	MA	66,774	MC
Sonoma State Univ	CA	27,020	C
S Car State Univ	SC	21,330	LC
S Dak School of Mines and Technology	SD	18,570	C+
S Dak State Univ	SD	15,874	C
Southeast Missouri State Univ	MO	16,148	C
Southeastern Louisiana Univ	LA	16,237	C
Southeastern Okla State Univ	OK	11,875	C
Southern Adventist Univ	TN	28,250	C
Southern Arkansas Univ	AR	21,532	C
Southern Conn State Univ	CT	21,924	LC
Southern Illinois Univ Carbondale	IL	24,554	C
Southern Illinois Univ Edwardsville	IL	20,188	C
Southern Methodist Univ	TX	69,008	MC
Southern Nazarene Univ	OK	33,684	C
Southern New Hampshire Univ	NH	44,256	C
Southern Oregon Univ	OR	19,117	C
Southern Univ and A&M College	LA	16,074	LC
Southern Univ at New Orleans	LA	8,014	LC
Southern Wesleyan Univ	SC	33,670	LC
Southwest Baptist Univ	MO	30,890	LC
Southwest Minn State Univ	MN	17,783	C
Southwestern Adventist Univ	TX	28,232	LC
Southwestern College	KS	31,531	LC
Southwestern Okla State Univ	OK	12,205	C
Southwestern Univ	TX	52,370	VC
Spelman College	GA	41,642	C
Spring Arbor Univ	MI	37,390	C
Spring Hill College	AL	48,488	C
St. Ambrose Univ	IA	40,180	C
St. Bonaventure Univ	NY	45,596	C
St. Cloud State Univ	MN	10,600	C
St. Edward's Univ	TX	56,190	VC
St. John Fisher College	NY	45,270	VC
St. John's Univ	NY	57,160	C+
St. Joseph's College, New York/Long Island Campus	NY	25,124	C
St. Lawrence Univ	NY	66,646	HC+
St. Mary's College of Maryland	MD	27,312	VC
St. Mary's Univ	TX	39,120	C
St. Norbert College	WI	46,060	VC
St. Olaf College	MN	56,430	HC
St. Thomas Univ	FL	51,187	LC
Stanford Univ	CA	62,541	MC
SUNY Albany	NY	22,165	C
SUNY at Binghamton	NY	24,100	MC
SUNY at New Paltz	NY	20,840	C
SUNY at Oswego	NY	22,219	VC
SUNY Polytechnic Inst	NY	20,438	VC
SUNY/College at Old Westbury	NY	16,860	C
SUNY/Empire State College	NY	9,145	NC
SUNY/Fredonia	NY	20,818	C
SUNY/Oneonta	NY	20,794	C
SUNY/Plattsburgh	NY	19,314	C
SUNY/Potsdam	NY	21,051	VC
SUNY/Univ at Buffalo	NY	23,122	C
Stephen F. Austin State Univ	TX	18,484	LC
Stetson Univ	FL	57,174	VC+
Stevens Inst of Technology	NJ	64,954	MC
Stillman College	AL	20,738	C
Stockton Univ	NJ	25,565	C
Stonehill College	MA	55,130	C
Stony Brook Univ/The SUNY	NY	22,703	MC
Suffolk Univ	MA	52,316	C
Sul Ross State Univ	TX	15,021	LC
Susquehanna Univ	PA	57,560	VC
Swarthmore College	PA	63,550	MC
Syracuse Univ	NY	62,313	HC
Talladega College	AL	25,919	C
Tarleton State Univ	TX	15,248	LC
Taylor Univ	IN	42,130	VC
Temple Univ	PA	24,392	C+
Tenn State Univ	TN	14,423	LC
Tenn Tech Univ	TN	17,929	C
Texas A&M Univ at College Station	TX	20,771	VC+
Texas A&M Univ at Commerce	TX	10,496	C
Texas A&M Univ at Corpus Christi	TX	16,851	LC
Texas A&M Univ at Kingsville	TX	16,580	LC
Texas Christian Univ	TX	57,120	HC
Texas Lutheran Univ	TX	39,770	C
Texas Southern Univ	TX	19,592	LC
Texas State Univ	TX	18,721	C
Texas Tech Univ	TX	20,156	C+
Texas Wesleyan Univ	TX	37,338	C
Texas Woman's Univ	TX	15,302	LC
The American Univ	DC	61,317	HC
The Catholic Univ of America	DC	58,376	VC
The Citadel, The Military College of S Car	SC	20,679	C
The College at Brockport - SUNY	NY	21,058	C
The College of New Jersey	NJ	28,675	VC+
The College of St. Rose	NY	44,010	C
The College of Wooster	OH	60,000	HC
The George Washington Univ	DC	68,474	HC+
The Univ of Akron	OH	22,566	C
The Univ of Alabama	AL	24,320	C+
The Univ of Arizona	AZ	24,086	C
The Univ of Memphis	TN	18,278	C
The Univ of Tenn at Chattanooga	TN	17,340	C+
The Univ of Tenn at Knoxville	TN	22,112	VC
The Univ of Tenn at Martin	TN	15,212	C
The Univ of Texas at Austin	TX	20,206	MC
The Univ of Texas at San Antonio	TX	21,060	C
The Univ of Utah	UT	18,751	VC
Thiel College	PA	42,950	LC
Thomas College	ME	73,888	LC
Thomas Edison State Univ	NJ	6,350	NC
Thomas More College	KY	36,720	LC
Tougaloo College	MS	17,980	NC
Touro College	NY	31,040	C
Towson Univ	MD	21,878	C
Transylvania Univ	KY	47,450	HC+
Trine Univ	IN	41,310	C
Trinity Christian College	IL	35,580	C
Trinity College	CT	69,020	HC
Trinity Univ	TX	54,480	MC
Troy Univ	AL	16,171	C
Truman State Univ	MO	16,286	MC
Tufts Univ	MA		MC
Tusculum College	TN	31,625	LC
Tuskegee Univ	AL	28,164	C
Union College	NE	23,270	C
Union College	NY	64,320	MC
Union Inst & Univ	OH	8,912	SP
Union Univ	TN	41,160	VC
United States Air Force Academy	CO		C
United States Military Academy at West Point	NY		HC+
United States Naval Academy	MD		HC
Universidad Adventista de las Antillas	PR	16,606	
Universidad Politecnica de PR, Hato Rey campus	PR	23,514	
Univ of PR, at Arecibo	PR	12,652	
Univ of Alabama at Birmingham	AL	22,092	C
Univ of Alabama in Huntsville	AL	20,028	VC
Univ of Alaska Anchorage	AK	17,914	C
Univ of Alaska Fairbanks	AK	16,874	VC
Univ of Arkansas at Fayetteville	AR	19,766	VC
Univ of Arkansas at Little Rock	AR	18,211	LC
Univ of Arkansas at Pine Bluff	AR	13,541	C
Univ of Bridgeport	CT	44,985	LC
Univ of Calif at Berkeley	CA	29,886	MC
Univ of Calif at Davis	CA	28,468	HC
Univ of Calif at Irvine	CA	33,857	VC
Univ of Calif at Los Angeles	CA	27,438	HC+
Univ of Calif at Riverside	CA	32,912	C
Univ of Calif at Santa Barbara	CA	30,627	HC+
Univ of Calif San Diego	CA	30,450	MC
Univ of Calif, Santa Cruz	CA	28,731	C+
Univ of Central Arkansas	AR	15,042	VC
Univ of Central Florida	FL	16,379	VC
Univ of Central Missouri	MO	18,982	C
Univ of Central Okla	OK	15,150	C
Univ of Chicago	IL	70,551	MC
Univ of Cincinnati	OH	22,118	VC
Univ of Colo Boulder	CO	26,048	HC
Univ of Colo Colo Springs	CO	20,300	C
Univ of Colo Denver	CO	22,238	C
Univ of Conn	CT	27,394	
Univ of Dallas	TX	50,676	VC
Univ of Dayton	OH	54,930	VC
Univ of Delaware	DE	32,214	VC

ST = STATE **$IS** = IN-STATE COSTS **SR** = SELECTOR RATING

School	ST	$IS	SR
Univ of Denver	CO	61,129	VC+
Univ of Detroit Mercy	MI	48,816	C
Univ of Dubuque	IA	37,824	C
Univ of Evansville	IN	44,186	C+
Univ of Findlay	OH	43,040	C
Univ of Florida	FL	16,291	HC+
Univ of Georgia	GA	21,878	HC
Univ of Great Falls	MT	38,524	C
Univ of Hartford	CT	49,776	C
Univ of Hawaii at Hilo	HI	18,038	VC
Univ of Hawaii at Manoa	HI	23,261	C
Univ of Houston-Downtown	TX	7,241	LC
Univ of Idaho	ID	16,158	C
Univ of Illinois at Chicago	IL	24,664	VC
Univ of Indianapolis	IN	36,480	VC
Univ of Iowa	IA	19,415	HC
Univ of Jamestown	ND	28,508	C
Univ of Kansas	KS	20,884	VC
Univ of Kentucky	KY	24,800	C+
Univ of La Verne	CA	55,600	C
Univ of Louisiana at Lafayette	LA	14,516	C
Univ of Louisiana at Monroe	LA	15,970	C
Univ of Louisville	KY	19,692	C
Univ of Lynchburg	VA	48,370	C
Univ of Maine	ME	21,038	VC
Univ of Maine at Farmington	ME	18,792	C
Univ of Maine at Fort Kent	ME	15,165	LC
Univ of Mary Hardin-Baylor	TX	35,292	C+
Univ of Mary Washington	VA	23,039	C+
Univ of Maryland Univ College	MD	26,146	LC
Univ of Maryland/Baltimore County	MD	23,004	VC
Univ of Maryland/College Park	MD	21,938	HC
Univ of Maryland/Eastern Shore	MD	21,861	LC
Univ of Mass Amherst	MA	27,669	HC
Univ of Mass Boston	MA	13,828	C
Univ of Mass Dartmouth	MA	26,507	C
Univ of Mass Lowell	MA	27,296	VC
Univ of Miami	FL	63,494	MC
Univ of Mich/Ann Arbor	MI	25,274	MC
Univ of Mich/Dearborn	MI	12,472	VC
Univ of Mich/Flint	MI	19,062	C
Univ of Minn/Duluth	MN	20,292	C
Univ of Minn/Morris	MN	21,222	VC
Univ of Minn/Twin Cities	MN	24,269	MC
Univ of Miss	MS	18,802	C
Univ of Missouri-Columbia	MO	20,463	VC
Univ of Missouri-Kansas City	MO	19,563	VC
Univ of Missouri-St. Louis	MO	19,810	VC
Univ of Montana	MT	14,105	C
Univ of Mount Union	OH	39,990	C
Univ of Nebr - Kearney	NE	17,014	LC
Univ of Nebr - Lincoln	NE	18,589	VC
Univ of Nebr - Omaha	NE	16,120	C
Univ of Nevada, Las Vegas	NV	17,553	C
Univ of Nevada, Reno	NV	18,010	C
Univ of New Hampshire	NH	29,333	VC
Univ of New Hampshire - Manchester	NH	14,490	C
Univ of New Haven	CT	53,680	C
Univ of New Mexico	NM	16,808	C
Univ of New Orleans	LA	12,840	C
Univ of North Alabama	AL	15,964	C
Univ of N Car at Asheville	NC	16,251	VC+
Univ of N Car at Chapel Hill	NC	20,561	MC
Univ of N Car at Charlotte	NC	17,803	VC
Univ of N Car at Greensboro	NC	15,998	C
Univ of N Car at Pembroke	NC	14,737	LC
Univ of N Car Wilmington	NC	16,784	VC
Univ of N Dak	ND	16,673	C
Univ of North Florida	FL	15,996	VC
Univ of North Georgia	GA	17,316	C
Univ of North Texas	TX	20,082	C
Univ of Northern Iowa	IA	17,480	C
Univ of Northwestern - St. Paul	MN	39,530	C
Univ of Notre Dame	IN	68,801	MC
Univ of Oregon	OR	24,021	VC
Univ of Pennsylvania	PA	63,526	MC
Univ of Pikeville	KY	27,838	C
Univ of Pittsburgh	PA	30,030	MC
Univ of Pittsburgh at Johnstown	PA	22,092	C
Univ of Portland	OR	52,152	VC
Univ of PR, at Bayamon	PR	13,145	
Univ of PR, at Mayaguez	PR	13,995	
Univ of PR-Rio Piedras campus	PR	13,327	
Univ of Puget Sound	WA	60,210	HC
Univ of Redlands	CA	61,934	VC
Univ of Rhode Island	RI	26,066	VC
Univ of Richmond	VA	62,730	MC
Univ of Rio Grande & Rio Grande Community College	OH	8,750	LC
Univ of Rochester	NY	65,032	MC
Univ of San Diego	CA	60,338	HC
Univ of San Francisco	CA	60,580	C
Univ of Scranton	PA	54,962	VC
Univ of Sioux Falls	SD	25,630	C
Univ of South Alabama	AL	16,880	C
Univ of S Car at Columbia	SC	21,726	VC
Univ of S Car Upstate	SC	19,272	LC
Univ of S Dak	SD	16,109	C
Univ of Southern Calif	CA	66,631	MC
Univ of Southern Indiana	IN	16,808	C
Univ of Southern Maine	ME	18,320	C
Univ of Southern Miss	MS	13,170	C
Univ of St. Francis	IL	40,828	C
Univ of St. Thomas - Houston	TX	41,510	VC
Univ of Texas at Arlington	TX	18,876	C
Univ of Texas at Dallas	TX	23,640	HC
Univ of Texas at El Paso	TX	34,452	NC
Univ of Texas Rio Grande Valley	TX	15,573	LC
Univ of the District of Columbia	DC	21,260	LC
Univ of the Pacific	CA	57,446	VC
Univ of the Sacred Heart	PR	17,932	
Univ of the Sciences	PA	40,738	VC
Univ of Toledo	OH	19,336	C
Univ of Tulsa	OK	52,625	HC
Univ of Vermont	VT	29,792	HC
Univ of Virginia	VA	27,367	MC
Univ of Washington	WA	23,091	MC
Univ of West Florida	FL	15,848	C
Univ of West Georgia	GA	17,510	LC
Univ of Wisc-Eau Claire	WI	16,354	VC
Univ of Wisc-Green Bay	WI	15,184	C
Univ of Wisc-La Crosse	WI	15,425	VC
Univ of Wisc-Madison	WI	21,647	MC
Univ of Wisc-Milwaukee	WI	21,538	C
Univ of Wisc-Oshkosh	WI	15,392	C
Univ of Wisc-Parkside	WI	15,313	C
Univ of Wisc-Platteville	WI	14,148	C
Univ of Wisc-Superior	WI	14,838	C
Univ of Wyoming	WY	15,537	C
Ursinus College	PA	62,920	VC
Utah State Univ	UT	13,235	C
Utica College	NY	31,510	C
Valparaiso Univ	IN	50,160	VC
Vanderbilt Univ	TN	63,248	MC
Vassar College	NY	68,110	MC
Villanova Univ	PA	64,922	MC
Virginia Commonwealth Univ	VA	23,811	VC
Virginia Military Inst	VA	26,460	VC
Virginia Polytechnic Inst and State Univ	VA	21,920	VC
Virginia Wesleyan Univ	VA	45,980	LC
Voorhees College	SC	19,976	C
Wagner College	NY	57,240	C+
Wake Forest Univ	NC	69,354	MC
Walla Walla Univ	WA	34,845	C
Walsh Univ	OH	39,010	C
Wartburg College	IA	49,478	C
Washburn Univ	KS	15,827	C
Washington Adventist Univ	MD	32,050	LC
Washington and Lee Univ	VA	59,647	MC
Washington College	MD	56,154	VC
Washington State Univ	WA	22,747	C
Washington Univ in St. Louis	MO	67,539	MC
Wayland Baptist Univ	TX	23,460	LC
Wayne State College	NE	25,746	NC
Wayne State Univ	MI	23,085	C
Waynesburg Univ	PA	33,530	C
Weber State Univ	UT	14,112	C
Webster Univ	MO	37,490	C
Wellesley College	MA	66,984	MC
Wells College	NY	50,500	C
Wentworth Inst of Technology	MA	48,810	VC
Wesleyan Univ	CT	66,940	MC
West Chester Univ of Pennsylvania	PA	19,171	VC
West Texas A&M Univ	TX	13,478	C
West Virginia Univ	WV	18,952	VC
West Virginia Univ Inst of Technology	WV	18,264	C
West Virginia Wesleyan College	WV	39,188	C
Western Carolina Univ	NC	13,965	C
Western Conn State Univ	CT	21,254	LC
Western Illinois Univ	IL	20,897	C
Western Kentucky Univ	KY	16,850	C
Western Mich Univ	MI	21,791	C
Western New England Univ	MA	49,182	C
Western New Mexico Univ	NM	16,914	LC
Western Oregon Univ	OR	19,965	LC
Western State Colo Univ	CO	19,348	C
Western Washington Univ	WA	18,904	VC
Westfield State Univ	MA	20,404	C
Westminster College	MO	32,820	C
Westminster College	PA	41,722	C
Westminster College	UT	41,078	C
Westmont College	CA	57,930	VC
Wheaton College	IL	44,993	MC
Wheaton College	MA	63,818	VC
Wheeling Jesuit Univ	WV	37,106	LC
Whitworth Univ	WA	53,682	VC
Wichita State Univ	KS	17,773	C
Widener Univ	PA	58,190	C
Wilberforce Univ	OH	19,900	C
Wiley College	TX	19,255	C
Wilkes Univ	PA	49,166	C
Willamette Univ	OR	62,514	VC+
William Paterson Univ of New Jersey	NJ	24,022	C
William Penn Univ	IA	26,000	C
William Woods Univ	MO	32,040	C
Williams Baptist College	AR	24,720	C
Williams College	MA	67,700	MC
Wilmington College	OH	35,100	C
Winona State Univ	MN	18,109	C
Winston-Salem State Univ	NC	18,005	LC
Winthrop Univ	SC	23,960	C
Wisc Lutheran College	WI	36,290	C
Wittenberg Univ	OH	49,863	VC
Wofford College	SC	49,885	VC
Worcester Polytechnic Inst	MA	62,846	MC
Worcester State Univ	MA	20,977	C
Wright State Univ	OH	16,983	C
Xavier Univ	OH	49,380	VC
Xavier Univ of Louisiana	LA	31,689	C
Yale Univ	CT	64,650	MC
Yeshiva Univ	NY	52,750	VC
York College of Pennsylvania	PA	29,240	C
Youngstown State Univ	OH	17,487	C

COMPUTER SCIENCE & INFORMATICS

School	ST	$IS	SR
Creighton Univ	NE	49,452	VC
Lebanon Valley College	PA	55,510	VC
Luther College	IA	49,990	VC
Rochester Inst of Technology	NY	52,734	HC+

COMPUTER SECURITY

School	ST	$IS	SR
Bradley Univ	IL	43,240	VC
East Stroudsburg Univ	PA	18,578	LC
Rochester Inst of Technology	NY	52,734	HC+
St. Leo Univ	FL	32,850	C
St. Ambrose Univ	IA	40,180	C
Taylor Univ	IN	42,130	VC
Univ of St. Francis	IN	38,520	C
Univ of Tampa	FL	38,928	VC

COMPUTER SECURITY AND INFORMATION ASSURANCE

School	ST	$IS	SR
Baldwin Wallace Univ	OH	42,464	VC
Bloomfield College	NJ	40,100	LC
Champlain College	VT	54,724	VC
Charter Oak State College	CT	7,983	NC
Dakota State Univ	SD	12,286	C
DePaul Univ	IL	52,807	VC
Drexel Univ	PA	65,927	HC
Eastern Mich Univ	MI	19,761	C
Felician Univ	NJ	46,280	LC
Florida Atlantic Univ	FL	18,256	C
Florida International Univ	FL	20,281	C
Fontbonne Univ	MO	34,606	C
Frostburg State Univ	MD	17,280	LC
Guilford College	NC	45,973	C
Hilbert College	NY	32,650	LC
Kennesaw State Univ	GA	18,899	VC
Limestone College	SC	32,100	C
Loyola Univ Chicago	IL	57,158	VC
Marshall Univ	WV	18,044	C
Marymount Univ	VA	43,231	C
Metropolitan State Univ	MN	7,859	C
Minn State Univ, Mankato	MN	17,190	C
Minn State Univ, Moorhead	MN	21,393	C
Mount Aloysius College	PA	29,976	C
Norwich Univ	VT	56,234	C
Pace Univ	NY	60,136	C
Pennsylvania College of Technology	PA	27,693	NC
Rochester Inst of Technology	NY	52,734	HC+
Roger Williams Univ	RI	48,074	VC
St. John's Univ	NY	57,160	C+
SUNY Albany	NY	22,165	C
Stevens Inst of Technology	NJ	64,954	MC
Stevenson Univ	MD	48,412	C
The Univ of Akron	OH	22,566	C
The Univ of Texas at San Antonio	TX	21,060	C
Thomas College	ME	73,888	LC
Univ of Maryland Univ College	MD	26,146	LC
Utica College	NY	31,510	C
Webber International Univ	FL	31,904	C
Weber State Univ	UT	14,112	C

COMPUTER TECHNOLOGY

School	ST	$IS	SR
Alcorn State Univ	MS	15,884	C
Alfred State College	NY	19,895	C
Alverno College	WI	33,294	LC
Andrews Univ	MI	41,732	C
Appalachian State Univ	NC	15,394	VC
Bellarmine Univ	KY	52,532	C
Biola Univ	CA	48,686	C
Bowie State Univ	MD	18,610	LC
Cal State, Dominguez Hills	CA	19,022	LC
Calif Univ of Pennsylvania	PA	20,425	LC
Central Mich Univ	MI	20,330	C
Chestnut Hill College	PA	47,180	C
Colo State Univ	CO	23,033	C
DePaul Univ	IL	52,807	VC
Duquesne Univ	PA	48,508	VC
Eastern Mich Univ	MI	19,761	C
Eastern Washington Univ	WA	17,896	LC
Excelsior College	NY	38,800	SP
Guilford College	NC	45,973	C
Hodges Univ	FL	20,160	LC
Idaho State Univ	ID	13,619	LC
Indiana State Univ	IN	23,223	LC
Inter-American Univ of PR-Bayamon	PR	18,785	
LeTourneau Univ	TX	39,190	VC
Limestone College	SC	32,100	C
Martin Univ	IN	21,010	LC
Methodist Univ	NC	58,130	C
Missouri Western State Univ	MO	17,822	LC
New Jersey Inst of Technology	NJ	30,198	HC
New Mexico State Univ	NM	14,050	LC
Norfolk State Univ	VA	18,902	LC
Oregon Inst of Technology	OR	19,227	C
Peirce College	PA	16,780	NC
Purdue Univ Northwest	IN	15,178	C
Purdue Univ/West Lafayette	IN	20,032	MC
Rochester Inst of Technology	NY	52,734	HC+
Rockhurst Univ	MO	28,990	C
St. Louis Univ	MO	49,866	HC
Shepherd Univ, West Virginia	WV	17,382	C
Southern Wesleyan Univ	SC	33,670	LC
SUNY Polytechnic Inst	NY	20,438	VC
The Univ of Memphis	TN	18,278	C
Tulane Univ	LA	67,496	MC
Union College	KY	32,310	C
Univ of Arkansas at Little Rock	AR	18,211	LC
Univ of Dayton	OH	54,930	VC
Univ of Illinois at Urbana-Champaign	IL	27,006	HC
Univ of Maryland Univ College	MD	26,146	LC
Univ of Minn/Crookston	MN	19,126	C
Univ of Northern Iowa	IA	17,480	C
Univ of Rio Grande & Rio Grande Community College	OH	8,750	LC
Univ of Southern Miss	MS	13,170	C
Univ of St. Francis	IL	40,828	C
Univ of Wisc-Stevens Point	WI	14,043	C
Valparaiso Univ	IN	50,160	VC
Wayne State Univ	MI	23,085	C
Youngstown State Univ	OH	17,487	C

CONDUCTING

School	ST	$IS	SR
Oberlin College	OH	68,942	MC
Okla Baptist Univ	OK	33,990	C

CONGREGATIONAL AND YOUTH MINISTRIES

School	ST	$IS	SR
Eastern Mennonite Univ	VA	42,550	C
Okla Baptist Univ	OK	33,990	C

CONSERVATION AND REGULATION

School	ST	$IS	SR
College of the Ozarks	MO	7,530	VC
Florida Inst of Technology	FL	53,306	VC
Grove City College	PA	26,654	VC
Lipscomb Univ	TN	42,984	VC
Marist College	NY	49,860	VC
Missouri Southern State Univ	MO	13,071	C
Missouri Western State Univ	MO	17,822	LC
Mount Mercy Univ	IA	39,748	C
Muskingum Univ	OH	35,966	C
N Car State Univ	NC	22,434	HC+
Northwest Missouri State Univ	MO	18,286	C
Northwestern Okla State Univ	OK	13,072	LC
Southeastern Okla State Univ	OK	11,875	C
St. Lawrence Univ	NY	66,646	HC+
Texas Tech Univ	TX	20,156	C+
Unity College	ME	37,670	C
Univ of Arkansas at Pine Bluff	AR	13,541	C
Univ of Calif at Berkeley	CA	29,886	MC
Univ of Central Missouri	MO	18,982	C
Univ of Montana	MT	14,105	C
Univ of Wisc-River Falls	WI	14,541	C
Upper Iowa Univ	IA	34,990	NC

CONSTRUCTION

School	ST	$IS	SR
Bradley Univ	IL	43,240	VC
Cal State, Northridge	CA	17,277	LC
Missouri Western State Univ	MO	17,822	LC
Thomas Edison State Univ	NJ	6,350	NC
Univ of Alaska Anchorage	AK	17,914	C

CONSTRUCTION ENGINEERING

School	ST	$IS	SR
Arizona State Univ at the Tempe Campus	AZ	23,001	VC
Calif State Polytechnic Univ, Pomona	CA	21,811	C
Cal State, Fullerton	CA	21,902	C
Colo State Univ	CO	23,033	C
Fairleigh Dickinson Univ/ Metropolitan Campus	NJ	52,392	C
Florida Inst of Technology	FL	53,306	VC
Florida International Univ	FL	20,281	C
Iowa State Univ	IA	18,176	C
Kennesaw State Univ	GA	18,899	VC
Louisiana Tech Univ	LA	11,422	VC
Marquette Univ	WI	53,090	VC+
Montana State Univ	MT	15,500	C+
National Univ	CA	17,849	LC
N Dak State Univ	ND	16,245	VC
Purdue Univ/West Lafayette	IN	20,032	MC

ST = STATE **$IS** = IN-STATE COSTS **SR** = SELECTOR RATING

School	ST	$IS	SR
Rensselaer Polytechnic Inst	NY	67,265	MC
San Diego State Univ	CA	23,156	VC
Texas Tech Univ	TX	20,156	C+
The Catholic Univ of America	DC	58,376	VC
Univ of Arkansas at Little Rock	AR	18,211	LC
Univ of Central Florida	FL	16,379	VC
Univ of Florida	FL	16,291	HC+
Univ of Nebr - Lincoln	NE	18,589	VC
Univ of New Mexico	NM	16,808	C
Univ of North Florida	FL	15,996	VC
Univ of North Texas	TX	20,082	C
Univ of Southern Calif	CA	66,631	MC
Univ of the District of Columbia	DC	21,260	LC
Univ of Washington	WA	23,091	MC
Virginia Polytechnic Inst and State Univ	VA	21,920	VC
Western Mich Univ	MI	21,791	C

CONSTRUCTION MANAGEMENT

School	ST	$IS	SR
Alfred State College	NY	19,895	C
Appalachian State Univ	NC	15,394	VC
Arizona State Univ at the Tempe Campus	AZ	23,001	VC
Auburn Univ	AL	24,300	VC+
Boise State Univ	ID	17,368	C
Bowling Green State Univ	OH	19,975	C
Brigham Young Univ	UT	13,248	MC
Calif Baptist Univ	CA	42,986	C
Calif Polytechnic State Univ	CA	22,547	MC
Cal State, Chico	CA	19,790	VC
Cal State, Fresno	CA	16,902	LC
Cal State, Fullerton	CA	21,902	C
Central Conn State Univ	CT	22,041	C
Central Washington Univ	WA	16,803	C
Clemson Univ	SC		HC
Colo Mesa Univ	CO	19,707	LC
Colo State Univ	CO	23,033	C
Dordt College	IA	37,860	C+
Drexel Univ	PA	65,927	HC
East Carolina Univ	NC	16,539	C
Eastern Mich Univ	MI	19,761	C
Ferris State Univ	MI	21,458	C
Florida Inst of Technology	FL	53,306	VC
Florida International Univ	FL	20,281	C
Georgia Southern Univ	GA	16,540	VC
Illinois State Univ	IL	23,418	VC
John Brown Univ	AR	35,184	VC
Kansas State Univ	KS	17,780	VC
Kennesaw State Univ	GA	18,899	VC
Lawrence Tech Univ	MI	41,630	VC
Louisiana State Univ and A&M College	LA	18,677	VC
Mich State Univ	MI	24,542	VC
Mich Tech Univ	MI	25,551	VC+
Millersville Univ of Pennsylvania	PA	25,298	C
Milwaukee School of Engineering	WI	48,531	HC+
Minn State Univ, Mankato	MN	17,190	C
Minn State Univ, Moorhead	MN	21,393	C
Missouri State Univ	MO	15,837	C+
National Univ	CA	17,849	LC
New York Inst of Technology	NY	49,980	VC
New York Univ	NY	68,139	MC
NewSchool of Architecture & Design	CA	12,341	SP
N Car State Univ	NC	22,434	HC+
N Dak State Univ	ND	16,245	VC
Northern Arizona Univ	AZ	21,003	C
Northern Kentucky Univ	KY	16,486	C
Northern Mich Univ	MI	20,853	C
Ohio State Univ at Columbus	OH	22,843	MC
Okla State Univ	OK	17,180	C+
Oregon State Univ	OR	23,337	VC
Pennsylvania College of Technology	PA	27,693	NC
Pittsburg State Univ	KS	13,880	C
Pratt Inst	NY	59,482	VC+
Purdue Univ/West Lafayette	IN	20,032	MC
Roger Williams Univ	RI	48,074	VC
S Dak State Univ	SD	15,874	C
Southern Illinois Univ Edwardsville	IL	20,188	C
SUNY/The College of Environmental Science and Forestry	NY	23,728	VC
Temple Univ	PA	24,392	C+
Texas State Univ	TX	18,721	C
The Univ of Tenn at Chattanooga	TN	17,340	C+
The Univ of Texas at San Antonio	TX	21,060	C
Tuskegee Univ	AL	28,164	C
Univ of Arkansas at Little Rock	AR	18,211	LC
Univ of Central Missouri	MO	18,982	C
Univ of Cincinnati	OH	22,118	VC
Univ of Denver	CO	61,129	VC+
Univ of Houston	TX	21,871	VC
Univ of Louisiana at Monroe	LA	15,970	C
Univ of Minn/Twin Cities	MN	24,269	MC
Univ of Nebr - Kearney	NE	17,014	LC
Univ of Nebr - Lincoln	NE	18,589	VC
Univ of Nevada, Las Vegas	NV	17,553	C
Univ of New Mexico	NM	16,808	C
Univ of N Car at Charlotte	NC	17,803	VC
Univ of North Florida	FL	15,996	VC
Univ of Northern Iowa	IA	17,480	C
Utica College	NY	31,510	C
Virginia Polytechnic Inst and State Univ	VA	21,920	VC
Washington State Univ	WA	22,747	C
Wayne State Univ	MI	23,085	C
Weber State Univ	UT	14,112	C
Wentworth Inst of Technology	MA	48,810	VC
Western Carolina Univ	NC	13,965	C
Western Illinois Univ	IL	20,897	C
Western Kentucky Univ	KY	16,850	C

CONSTRUCTION MANAGEMENT/COMMERCIAL/INDUSTRIAL

School	ST	$IS	SR
Ferris State Univ	MI	21,458	C
Tarleton State Univ	TX	15,248	LC
Western Kentucky Univ	KY	16,850	C

CONSTRUCTION TECHNOLOGY

School	ST	$IS	SR
Appalachian State Univ	NC	15,394	VC
Black Hills State Univ	SD	16,622	C
Eastern Kentucky Univ	KY	17,742	C
Farmingdale State College	NY	20,968	C
Fitchburg State Univ	MA	21,819	LC
Florida International Univ	FL	20,281	C
Idaho State Univ	ID	13,619	LC
Indiana State Univ	IN	23,223	LC
Missouri Western State Univ	MO	17,822	LC
Montana State Univ-Northern	MT	11,370	NC
Murray State Univ	KY	17,726	C+
New York City College of Technology	NY	7,185	LC
Norfolk State Univ	VA	18,902	LC
Northern Kentucky Univ	KY	16,486	C
Okla State Univ	OK	17,180	C+
Pennsylvania College of Technology	PA	27,693	NC
Pittsburg State Univ	KS	13,880	C
Purdue Univ Northwest	IN	15,178	C
Purdue Univ/West Lafayette	IN	20,032	MC
Texas State Univ	TX	18,721	C
The Univ of Akron	OH	22,566	C
Univ of Arkansas at Little Rock	AR	18,211	LC
Univ of Maine	ME	21,038	VC
Univ of Maryland/Eastern Shore	MD	21,861	LC
Univ of Mass Amherst	MA	27,669	HC
Univ of Okla	OK	19,651	HC
Univ of Southern Miss	MS	13,170	C
Univ of Wisc-Stout	WI	19,667	C

CONSUMER SERVICES

School	ST	$IS	SR
San Francisco State Univ	CA	18,514	LC
S Dak State Univ	SD	15,874	C
Texas Woman's Univ	TX	15,302	LC
The Univ of Utah	UT	18,751	VC
Univ of Georgia	GA	21,878	HC

CORE STUDIES

School	ST	$IS	SR
Shenandoah Univ	VA	42,100	C

CORRECTIONS

School	ST	$IS	SR
Adams State Univ	CO	15,420	LC
Cal State, Fullerton	CA	21,902	C
College of the Ozarks	MO	7,530	VC
Eastern Kentucky Univ	KY	17,742	C
Hardin-Simmons Univ	TX	36,025	C
Jackson State Univ	MS	15,879	LC
Minn State Univ, Mankato	MN	17,190	C
Missouri Western State Univ	MO	17,822	LC
Stephen F. Austin State Univ	TX	18,484	LC
Texas State Univ	TX	18,721	C
Tiffin Univ	OH	34,900	LC
Washburn Univ	KS	15,827	C
Western Oregon Univ	OR	19,965	LC

COUNSELING/PSYCHOLOGY

School	ST	$IS	SR
Adams State Univ	CO	15,420	LC
Anna Maria College	MA	51,020	C
Arizona State Univ at the Polytechnic Campus	AZ	22,394	VC
Averett Univ	VA	43,034	LC
Biola Univ	CA	48,686	C
Blackburn College	IL	28,526	LC
Cal State, Fresno	CA	16,902	LC
Cal State, Fullerton	CA	21,902	C
Campbell Univ	NC	37,570	VC
City Univ of Seattle	WA	24,340	NC
Colo State Univ	CO	23,033	C
Corban Univ	OR	41,700	C
Dallas Baptist Univ	TX	35,220	VC
East Central Univ	OK	13,330	C
East Texas Baptist Univ	TX	34,444	C
Eastern Mich Univ	MI	19,761	C
Eastern New Mexico Univ	NM	12,874	LC
Edinboro Univ	PA	15,940	LC
Emmanuel College	MA	53,472	C+
Faulkner Univ	AL	26,410	C
Florida Gulf Coast Univ	FL	14,738	C
Friends Univ	KS	38,000	C
Geneva College	PA	35,450	C
Goddard College	VT	17,040	VC
Grace College and Seminary	IN	31,524	C
Houghton College	NY	40,558	VC
Howard Univ	DC	37,616	C+
Huntington Univ	IN	33,996	C
Husson Univ	ME	26,508	C
Johnson & Wales Univ/Denver Campus	CO	44,768	C
Kentucky Christian Univ	KY	26,836	LC
Kutztown Univ of Pennsylvania	PA	19,477	C
Martin Univ	IN	21,010	LC
Missouri State Univ	MO	15,837	C+
Mount St. Mary's Univ - Chalon Campus	CA	50,486	VC+
New York Univ	NY	68,139	MC
Newman Univ	KS	37,382	C
Northwest Univ	WA	38,720	VC
Okla Baptist Univ	OK	33,990	C
Pittsburg State Univ	KS	13,880	C
Prescott College	AZ	38,201	C
Rochester College	MI	28,574	LC
Samford Univ	AL	40,770	VC
SUNY/Empire State College	NY	9,145	NC
Tarleton State Univ	TX	15,248	LC
The Univ of Arizona	AZ	24,086	C
Toccoa Falls College	GA	30,048	C
Univ of Great Falls	MT	38,524	C
Univ of Idaho	ID	16,158	C
Univ of Missouri-Columbia	MO	20,463	VC
Univ of New Haven	CT	53,680	C
Univ of North Alabama	AL	15,964	C
Univ of N Car at Pembroke	NC	14,737	LC
Univ of North Florida	FL	15,996	VC
Univ of St. Francis	IL	40,828	C
Washington Adventist Univ	MD	32,050	LC
Wayne State College	NE	25,746	NC
Williams Baptist College	AR	24,720	C
Xavier Univ	OH	49,380	VC

CRAFTS

School	ST	$IS	SR
Indiana Univ-Purdue Univ Fort Wayne	IN	18,675	C
Kent State Univ	OH	20,928	C
Kutztown Univ of Pennsylvania	PA	19,477	C
Malone Univ	OH	39,200	C
Rochester Inst of Technology	NY	52,734	HC+
Univ of Illinois at Urbana-Champaign	IL	27,006	HC
Virginia Commonwealth Univ	VA	23,811	VC

CREATIVE WRITING

School	ST	$IS	SR
Adams State Univ	CO	15,420	LC
Agnes Scott College	GA	51,930	VC+
Albion College	MI	55,260	C
Alderson Broaddus Univ	WV	35,000	LC
Andrews Univ	MI	41,732	C
Arkansas Tech Univ	AR	16,534	LC
Asbury Univ	KY	36,450	C+
Ashland Univ	OH	30,446	C
Augustana College	IL	51,222	VC+
Baldwin Wallace Univ	OH	42,464	VC
Bard College	NY	65,924	HC
Bard College at Simon's Rock	MA	65,795	MC
Baylor Univ	TX	56,803	HC
Belhaven Univ	MS	32,250	C
Beloit College	WI	55,206	HC
Benedictine Univ	IL	38,300	C
Bennington College	VT	66,280	MC
Berry College	GA	47,466	VC
Bethany College	WV	38,774	LC
Blackburn College	IL	28,526	LC
Bloomfield College	NJ	40,100	LC
Bluffton Univ	OH	40,950	C+
Bowling Green State Univ	OH	19,975	C
Brandeis Univ	MA	68,443	MC
Brown Univ	RI	64,566	MC
Bryan College	TN	32,900	C
Calif Baptist Univ	CA	42,986	C
Calif College of the Arts	CA	52,758	SP
Cal State, Fullerton	CA	21,902	C
Cal State, Long Beach	CA	18,850	C
Calvin College	MI	43,090	HC
Canisius College	NY	49,672	C
Capital Univ	OH	44,778	VC
Cardinal Stritch Univ	WI	37,136	C
Carlow Univ	PA	39,696	LC
Carnegie Mellon Univ	PA	67,980	MC
Chapman Univ	CA	65,504	HC
Chatham Univ	PA	47,883	VC
CUNY/Brooklyn College	NY	7,163	C+
CUNY/Hunter College	NY	31,098	VC
Coe College	IA	51,570	VC
Colby College	ME	64,060	MC
Colby-Sawyer College	NH	50,790	C
Colo College	CO	64,894	MC
Colo State Univ	CO	23,033	C
Columbia College Chicago	IL	40,104	C
Concordia Univ St. Paul	MN	29,050	C
Corban Univ	OR	41,700	C
DePaul Univ	IL	52,807	VC
Dominican Univ of Calif	CA	58,750	C
Eastern Mich Univ	MI	19,761	C
Eastern Washington Univ	WA	17,896	LC
Eckerd College	FL	55,206	VC
Elon Univ	NC	46,142	HC
Emerson College	MA	61,824	HC+
Emory and Henry College	VA	46,320	C
Emory Univ	GA	63,286	MC
Fairleigh Dickinson Univ/College at Florham	NJ	54,770	C
Florida Southern College	FL	45,978	VC
Florida State Univ	FL	16,771	HC
Franklin College	IN	40,550	C
Geneva College	PA	35,450	C
George Fox Univ	OR	42,938	C
Georgetown College	KY	41,440	C
Goddard College	VT	17,040	VC
Goshen College	IN	44,350	C
Grand Valley State Univ	MI	22,250	C+
Green Mountain College	VT	45,228	LC
Guilford College	NC	45,973	C
Hamilton College	NY	64,250	MC
Hamline Univ	MN	50,152	C
Hampshire College	MA	65,214	MC
Harvard College/Harvard Univ	MA	65,609	MC
Hiram College	OH	44,590	C
Hofstra Univ	NY	58,210	C+
Hope College	MI	42,840	VC
Huntington Univ	IN	33,996	C
Indiana Wesleyan Univ	IN	33,674	C
Iowa State Univ	IA	18,176	C
Ithaca College	NY	58,158	VC+
Johns Hopkins Univ	MD	68,080	MC
Johnson State College	VT	22,672	C
Kansas City Art Inst	MO	48,200	SP
Knox College	IL	54,654	VC+
La Roche College	PA	38,940	C
Lake Superior State Univ	MI	19,867	C
Lakeland Univ	WI	35,130	C
Le Moyne College	NY	47,305	VC
Lesley Univ	MA	42,800	C
Lindenwood Univ	MO	25,760	C
Linfield College	OR	53,992	C
Loras College	IA	40,726	C
Loyola Univ Maryland	MD	61,710	VC
Loyola Univ New Orleans	LA	52,456	VC
Lubbock Christian Univ	TX	29,727	C
Lycoming College	PA	50,895	C
Malone Univ	OH	39,200	C
Marlboro College	VT	50,832	VC+
Marshall Univ	WV	18,044	C
Maryville College	TN	44,410	C
Mass Inst of Technology	MA	62,662	MC
Mercer Univ	GA	45,348	VC
Methodist Univ	NC	58,130	C
Mills College	CA	43,705	C
Millsaps College	MS	50,080	C+
Missouri Western State Univ	MO	17,822	LC
Murray State Univ	KY	17,726	C+
New England College	NH	50,828	NC
New York Univ	NY	68,139	MC
Northland College	WI	41,103	C+
Oberlin College	OH	68,942	MC
Ohio Northern Univ	OH	44,050	VC
Ohio Univ	OH	23,394	VC
Ohio Wesleyan Univ	OH	49,460	VC
Okla Baptist Univ	OK	33,990	C
Okla Christian Univ	OK	29,260	C
Old Dominion Univ	VA	21,618	C
Pacific Univ	OR	37,617	C
Pepperdine Univ	CA	66,862	VC+
Pfeiffer Univ	NC	40,532	LC
Pratt Inst	NY	59,482	VC+
Presbyterian College	SC	47,186	C
Prescott College	AZ	38,201	C
Providence College	RI	62,870	HC
Purdue Univ/West Lafayette	IN	20,032	MC
Queens Univ of Charlotte	NC	39,543	C
Ringling College of Art and Design	FL	59,160	SP
Roanoke College	VA	55,952	VC
Rocky Mountain College	MT	35,776	C
Roger Williams Univ	RI	48,074	VC
Rosemont College	PA	30,980	LC
Saginaw Valley State Univ	MI	19,284	C
St. Mary-of-the-Woods College	IN	40,424	LC
St. Mary's College	IN	50,600	C
Salem College	NC	40,206	C
San Francisco State Univ	CA	18,514	LC
School of the Art Inst of Chicago	IL	61,830	SP
Seattle Pacific Univ	WA	47,439	C+
Seattle Univ	WA	54,957	VC
Seton Hall Univ	NJ	58,008	C
Seton Hill Univ	PA	46,972	VC
Smith College	MA	66,774	MC
Southeastern Univ	FL	34,910	LC
Southern Methodist Univ	TX	69,008	MC
Southern New Hampshire Univ	NH	44,256	C
Southern Vermont College	VT	34,670	LC
Southwest Minn State Univ	MN	17,783	C
Spalding Univ	KY	31,938	C
St. Andrews Univ	NC	44,634	LC
St. Lawrence Univ	NY	66,646	HC+
SUNY at Binghamton	NY	24,100	MC

ST = STATE $IS = IN-STATE COSTS SR = SELECTOR RATING

School	ST	$IS	SR
SUNY at Oswego	NY	22,219	VC
SUNY at Purchase College	NY	21,832	C
SUNY/Potsdam	NY	21,051	VC
Stephens College	MO	38,042	C
Sterling College	KS	32,830	LC
Suffolk Univ	MA	52,316	C
Tenn Wesleyan Univ	TN	32,680	LC
The American Univ	DC	61,317	HC
The College of Idaho	ID	36,415	C
The Univ of Arizona	AZ	24,086	C
The Univ of Montana Western	MT	9,426	LC
The Univ of Texas at Austin	TX	20,206	MC
Truman State Univ	MO	16,286	MC
Univ of Calif at Irvine	CA	33,857	VC
Univ of Calif at Riverside	CA	32,912	C
Univ of Central Arkansas	AR	15,042	VC
Univ of Central Okla	OK	15,150	C
Univ of Cincinnati	OH	22,118	VC
Univ of Evansville	IN	44,186	C+
Univ of Florida	FL	16,291	HC+
Univ of Idaho	ID	16,158	C
Univ of Maine at Farmington	ME	18,792	C
Univ of Maine at Machias	ME	22,960	C
Univ of Mich/Ann Arbor	MI	25,274	MC
Univ of Missouri-Columbia	MO	20,463	VC
Univ of Nebr - Omaha	NE	16,120	C
Univ of New Haven	CT	53,680	C
Univ of N Car Wilmington	NC	16,784	VC
Univ of Pittsburgh	PA	30,030	MC
Univ of Pittsburgh at Greensburg	PA	24,140	C
Univ of Pittsburgh at Johnstown	PA	22,092	C
Univ of Redlands	CA	61,934	VC
Univ of Southern Calif	CA	66,631	MC
Univ of Tampa	FL	38,928	VC
Univ of Tulsa	OK	52,625	HC
Univ of Wisc-Green Bay	WI	15,184	C
Valparaiso Univ	IN	50,160	VC
Warren Wilson College	NC	44,220	VC
Washington Univ in St. Louis	MO	67,539	MC
Waynesburg Univ	PA	33,530	C
Weber State Univ	UT	14,112	C
Webster Univ	MO	37,490	C
Wellesley College	MA	66,984	MC
Wells College	NY	50,500	C
West Virginia Univ	WV	18,952	VC
Western Mich Univ	MI	21,791	C
Western New England Univ	MA	49,182	C
Western Washington Univ	WA	18,904	VC
Wheaton College	MA	63,818	VC
Wichita State Univ	KS	17,773	C
Widener Univ	PA	58,190	C
Wilson College	PA	35,620	LC
Wofford College	SC	49,885	VC
Wright State Univ	OH	16,983	C
York College of Pennsylvania	PA	29,240	C

CRIMINAL JUSTICE

School	ST	$IS	SR
Abilene Christian Univ	TX	43,708	C+
Adelphi Univ	NY	49,792	C
Adrian College	MI	45,550	C
Alabama State Univ	AL	16,490	LC
Albany State Univ	GA	19,462	C
Albright College	PA	57,326	C
Alcorn State Univ	MS	15,884	C
Alfred State College	NY	19,895	C
Alfred Univ	NY	37,490	C
Alvernia Univ	PA	45,330	C
American International College	MA	47,020	LC
Anderson Univ	IN	39,450	C
Angelo State Univ	TX	15,882	LC
Anna Maria College	MA	51,020	C
Appalachian State Univ	NC	15,394	VC
Arcadia Univ	PA	55,990	C+
Arizona State Univ at the Downtown Phoenix Campus	AZ	24,634	VC
Arizona State Univ at the West Campus	AZ	21,513	VC
Armstrong State Univ	GA	15,615	C
Asbury Univ	KY	36,450	C+
Ashford Univ	CA	10,480	C
Ashland Univ	OH	30,446	C
Auburn Univ at Montgomery	AL	15,000	C
Augusta Univ	GA	4,632	C
Aurora Univ	IL	34,990	C
Austin Peay State Univ	TN	16,397	C
Averett Univ	VA	43,034	LC
Azusa Pacific Univ	CA	43,972	C
Baldwin Wallace Univ	OH	42,464	VC
Ball State Univ	IN	19,808	C+
Barton College	NC	39,854	C
Bay Path Univ	MA	46,356	C
Becker College	MA	30,100	LC
Bellarmine Univ	KY	52,532	C
Bellevue Univ	NE	20,300	NC
Belmont Abbey College	NC	28,794	C
Bemidji State Univ	MN	17,730	C
Benedict College	SC	28,630	NC
Berkeley College/New York City Campus	NY	35,100	LC
Bethany College	KS	38,637	LC
Bethel College	IN	36,830	C
Bethune-Cookman Univ	FL	23,322	C
Blackburn College	IL	28,526	LC
Bloomfield College	NJ	40,100	LC
Bloomsburg Univ of Pennsylvania	PA	19,930	C
Blue Mountain College	MS	15,949	C
Bluefield College	VA	34,711	C
Bluefield State College	WV	5,832	LC
Bluffton Univ	OH	40,950	C+
Boise State Univ	ID	17,368	C
Boston Univ	MA	67,352	MC
Bowie State Univ	MD	18,610	LC
Bowling Green State Univ	OH	19,975	C
Bradley Univ	IL	43,240	VC
Brewton-Parker College	GA	26,120	LC
Briar Cliff Univ	IA	36,956	C
Bridgewater State Univ	MA	22,762	C
Bryan College	TN	32,900	C
Buena Vista Univ	IA	42,344	C
Butler Univ	IN	52,890	VC+
Cairn Univ	PA	37,572	C
Caldwell Univ	NJ	42,165	LC
Calif Baptist Univ	CA	42,986	C
Calif Lutheran Univ	CA	52,853	C
Cal State, Bakersfield	CA	22,397	LC
Cal State, Chico	CA	19,790	VC
Cal State, Dominguez Hills	CA	19,022	LC
Cal State, East Bay	CA	20,748	C
Cal State, Fullerton	CA	21,902	C
Cal State, Long Beach	CA	18,850	C
Cal State, Los Angeles	CA	17,186	LC
Cal State, Sacramento	CA	19,060	C
Cal State, San Bernardino	CA	20,106	C
Cal State, Stanislaus	CA	18,053	LC
Calif Univ of Pennsylvania	PA	20,425	LC
Calumet College of St. Joseph	IN	22,735	C
Cameron Univ	OK	11,632	LC
Campbell Univ	NC	37,570	VC
Campbellsville Univ	KY	33,400	C
Canisius College	NY	49,672	C
Capital Univ	OH	44,778	VC
Caribbean Univ	PR	12,227	
Carroll Univ	WI	38,100	C+
Carthage College	WI	48,835	C
Castleton Univ	VT	20,186	C
Cedar Crest College	PA	51,110	C
Cedarville Univ	OH	36,244	VC
Centenary College	NJ	43,890	LC
Central Methodist Univ	MO	31,500	VC
Central Mich Univ	MI	20,330	C
Central Washington Univ	WA	16,803	C
Chadron State College	NE	14,819	LC
Chaminade Univ of Honolulu	HI	37,614	C
Champlain College	VT	54,724	VC
Charleston Southern Univ	SC	34,700	C
Charter Oak State College	CT	7,983	NC
Chestnut Hill College	PA	47,180	C
Cheyney Univ of Pennsylvania	PA	20,896	LC
Chicago State Univ	IL	41,620	C
CUNY/John Jay College of Criminal Justice	NY	6,359	SP
City Univ of Seattle	WA	24,340	NC
Claflin Univ	SC	25,592	LC
Clarion Univ of Pennsylvania	PA	21,608	LC
Clayton State Univ	GA	19,735	LC
College of St. Elizabeth	NJ	45,700	LC
College of St Joseph	VT	32,400	LC
College of the Ozarks	MO	7,530	VC
Colo Mesa Univ	CO	19,707	LC
Colo Technical Univ	CO	21,455	NC
Columbia College - Missouri	MO	28,179	C
Columbus State Univ	GA	14,336	LC
Concordia Univ St. Paul	MN	29,050	C
Concordia Univ Wisc	WI	35,910	C
Concordia Univ, Ann Arbor	MI	38,878	C+
Coppin State Univ	MD	14,071	VC
Corban Univ	OR	41,700	C
Culver-Stockton College	MO	34,350	C
Cumberland Univ	TN	27,710	C
Curry College	MA	53,331	C
Dakota Wesleyan Univ	SD	33,980	LC
Dallas Baptist Univ	TX	35,220	VC
Defiance College	OH	42,240	LC
Delaware Valley Univ	PA	51,271	C
Delta State Univ	MS	13,176	LC
DeSales Univ	PA	47,520	C
Dominican College	NY	40,258	LC
Dominican Univ	IL	42,472	C+
Dordt College	IA	37,860	C+
Drexel Univ	PA	65,927	HC
Drury Univ	MO	37,555	VC
East Carolina Univ	NC	16,539	C
East Central Univ	OK	13,330	C
East Stroudsburg Univ	PA	18,578	LC
East Tenn State Univ	TN	18,141	C
East Texas Baptist Univ	TX	34,444	C
Eastern Mich Univ	MI	19,761	C
Eastern New Mexico Univ	NM	12,874	LC
Eastern Univ	PA	39,540	C
Eastern Washington Univ	WA	17,896	LC
Edgewood College	WI	35,950	C
Edinboro Univ	PA	15,940	LC
Edward Waters College	FL	28,089	NC
Elizabeth City State Univ	NC	14,745	C
Elizabethtown College	PA	56,340	VC
Elizabethtown College School of Continuing and Professional Studies	PA	18,900	C
Elmhurst College	IL	46,514	C
Elmira College	NY	53,900	C
Elon Univ	NC	46,142	HC
Emporia State Univ	KS	15,029	C
Endicott College	MA	47,054	C+
Evangel Univ	MO	28,898	C
Excelsior College	NY	38,800	SP
Fairleigh Dickinson Univ/Metropolitan Campus	NJ	52,392	C
Fairmont State Univ	WV	15,726	C
Farmingdale State College	NY	20,968	C
Faulkner Univ	AL	26,410	C
Fayetteville State Univ	NC	17,756	C
Felician Univ	NJ	46,280	LC
Ferris State Univ	MI	21,458	C
Ferrum College	VA	43,970	C
Fitchburg State Univ	MA	21,819	LC
Florida A&M Univ	FL	15,361	C
Florida Atlantic Univ	FL	18,256	C
Florida Gulf Coast Univ	FL	14,738	C
Florida International Univ	FL	20,281	C
Florida Memorial Univ	FL	22,424	LC
Fort Hays State Univ	KS	12,677	C
Fort Valley State Univ	GA	17,988	VC
Franklin Pierce Univ	NH	46,750	LC
Freed-Hardeman Univ	TN	29,900	C
Friends Univ	KS	38,000	C
Frostburg State Univ	MD	17,280	LC
Gannon Univ	PA	42,922	C
George Mason Univ	VA	19,884	C
Georgia College & State Univ	GA	21,884	C+
Georgia Southern Univ	GA	16,540	VC
Georgia Southwestern State Univ	GA	13,870	LC
Georgia State Univ	GA	25,250	C
Georgian Court Univ	NJ	43,068	LC
Glenville State College	WV	17,386	LC
Goodwin College	CT	28,370	LC
Grace Bible College	MI	25,250	C
Grace College and Seminary	IN	31,524	C
Graceland Univ	IA	35,290	C
Grambling State Univ	LA	15,701	C
Grand Valley State Univ	MI	22,250	C+
Grand View Univ	IA	32,302	C
Greenville College	IL	27,012	LC
Guilford College	NC	45,973	C
Gwynedd Mercy Univ	PA	43,780	LC
Hamline Univ	MN	50,152	C
Hannibal-LaGrange Univ	MO	29,815	C
Harding Univ	AR	25,440	C
Hardin-Simmons Univ	TX	36,025	C
Harris-Stowe State Univ	MO	14,590	NC
Hawaii Pacific Univ	HI	33,420	C
Heidelberg Univ	OH	40,400	LC
Henderson State Univ	AR	15,516	C
Heritage Univ	WA	19,825	NC
High Point Univ	NC	47,355	VC
Hilbert College	NY	32,650	LC
Hodges Univ	FL	20,160	LC
Holy Family Univ	PA	44,672	LC
Hope International Univ	CA	42,730	C
Howard Univ	DC	37,616	C+
Huntingdon College	AL	35,900	C
Huntington Univ	IN	33,996	C
Husson Univ	ME	26,508	C
Huston-Tillotson Univ	TX	18,124	LC
Illinois State Univ	IL	23,418	VC
Indiana Inst of Technology	IN	34,240	LC
Indiana Univ Bloomington	IN	20,791	HC
Indiana Univ East	IN	7,207	C
Indiana Univ Kokomo	IN	7,207	C
Indiana Univ Northwest	IN	7,207	LC
Indiana Univ South Bend	IN	16,057	C
Indiana Univ Southeast	IN	16,931	C
Indiana Univ-Purdue Univ Fort Wayne	IN	18,675	C
Indiana Univ-Purdue Univ Indianapolis	IN	18,952	C
Indiana Wesleyan Univ	IN	33,674	C
Inter-American Univ of PR Ponce	PR	19,549	
Inter-American Univ of PR-Aguadilla Campus	PR	21,657	
Inter-American Univ of PR-Arecibo Campus	PR	18,245	
Inter-American Univ of PR-Barranquitas	PR	18,336	
Inter-American Univ of PR-Fajardo Campus	PR	18,336	
Inter-American Univ of PR-Metropolitan Campus	PR	20,045	
Iona College	NY	52,514	C
Iowa Wesleyan Univ	IA	41,000	C
Jackson State Univ	MS	15,879	LC
Jacksonville State Univ	AL	14,628	LC
James Madison Univ	VA	19,084	VC
Jarvis Christian College	TX	20,160	NC
John Carroll Univ	OH	51,570	C
Johnson & Wales Univ/Denver Campus	CO	44,768	C
Johnson & Wales Univ/North Miami Campus	FL	44,768	C
Johnson & Wales Univ/Providence Campus	RI	44,768	C
Johnson C. Smith Univ	NC	25,336	LC
Judson College	AL	27,066	C
Kansas Wesleyan Univ	KS	37,930	C
Kean Univ	NJ	25,620	C
Keene State College	NH	24,604	C
Kennesaw State Univ	GA	18,899	VC
Kentucky State Univ	KY	14,484	LC
Kentucky Wesleyan College	KY	34,260	LC
Keuka College	NY	42,398	C
Keystone College	PA	28,680	LC
King Univ	TN	36,976	C
King's College	PA	48,240	C
Kutztown Univ of Pennsylvania	PA	19,477	C
La Roche College	PA	38,940	C
La Salle Univ	PA	43,476	C
Lake Erie College	OH	38,914	LC
Lake Superior State Univ	MI	19,867	C
Lakeland Univ	WI	35,130	C
Lamar Univ	TX	18,014	LC
Lane College	TN	17,960	LC
Langston Univ	OK	15,659	C
Lasell College	MA	49,400	C
Lebanon Valley College	PA	55,510	VC
Lees-McRae College	NC	33,944	NC
LeMoyne-Owen College	TN	16,980	C
Lewis Univ	IL	41,710	C
Lewis-Clark State College	ID	14,202	C
Limestone College	SC	32,100	C
Lincoln Univ	MO	14,402	NC
Lincoln Univ	PA	20,878	LC
Lindenwood Univ	MO	25,760	C
Lindsey Wilson College	KY	33,546	C
LIU Post	NY	50,698	C+
Livingstone College	NC	17,815	LC
Lock Haven Univ of Pennsylvania	PA	20,544	LC
Longwood Univ	VA	22,184	C
Loras College	IA	40,726	C
Louisiana College	LA	21,274	C
Lourdes Univ	OH	29,140	NC
Loyola Univ Chicago	IL	57,158	VC
Loyola Univ New Orleans	LA	52,456	VC
Lubbock Christian Univ	TX	29,727	C
Lycoming College	PA	50,895	C
Lynn Univ	FL	49,680	LC
MacMurray College	IL	35,025	C
Madonna Univ	MI	30,450	LC
Malone Univ	OH	39,200	C
Manhattanville College	NY	52,430	C
Mansfield Univ of Pennsylvania	PA	24,244	LC
Marian Univ	WI	34,622	C
Marist College	NY	49,860	VC
Marshall Univ	WV	18,044	C
Martin Univ	IN	21,010	LC
Mary Baldwin Univ	VA	40,495	C
Marygrove College	MI	30,100	LC
Marymount Univ	VA	43,231	C
Marywood Univ	PA	47,840	C
McKendree Univ	IL	37,940	C+
McNeese State Univ	LA	7,838	C
Medaille College	NY	41,700	LC
Mercer Univ	GA	45,348	VC
Mercy College	NY	32,614	C
Mercyhurst Univ	PA	47,420	C
Merrimack College	MA	55,415	C
Messiah College	PA	44,380	VC
Methodist Univ	NC	58,130	C
Metropolitan State Univ	MN	7,859	C
Metropolitan State Univ of Denver	CO	6,928	LC
Miami Univ	OH	27,190	HC+
Mich State Univ	MI	24,542	VC
MidAmerica Nazarene Univ	KS	37,808	C
Middle Tenn State Univ	TN	8,650	C
Midwestern State Univ	TX	12,111	LC
Miles College	AL	16,530	NC
Minn State Univ, Mankato	MN	17,190	C
Minn State Univ, Moorhead	MN	21,393	C
Minot State Univ	ND	13,285	C
Miss College	MS	25,850	C
Miss Valley State Univ	MS	13,233	LC
Missouri Baptist Univ	MO	35,594	C
Missouri Southern State Univ	MO	13,071	C
Missouri Valley College	MO	28,150	C
Missouri Western State Univ	MO	17,822	LC
Mitchell College	CT	45,192	C
Molloy College	NY	40,440	C
Monmouth Univ	NJ	50,184	C
Monroe College	NY	23,996	C
Montana State Univ Billings	MT	13,336	LC
Montclair State Univ	NJ	26,912	C
Morris College	SC	19,195	LC
Mount Aloysius College	PA	29,976	C
Mount Ida College	MA	46,820	C
Mount Marty College	SD	36,862	C
Mount Mercy Univ	IA	39,748	C
Mount St. Mary's Univ	MD	53,380	C
Mount Vernon Nazarene Univ	OH	35,944	C
Murray State Univ	KY	17,726	C+
Muskingum Univ	OH	35,966	C
National Univ	CA	17,849	LC
Neumann Univ	PA	40,678	LC
New England College	NH	50,828	NC
New Jersey City Univ	NJ	21,456	LC
New Mexico State Univ	NM	14,050	LC
New York Inst of Technology	NY	49,980	VC
Newbury College	MA	48,970	C
Newman Univ	KS	37,382	C
Niagara Univ	NY	41,010	C
Nichols College	MA	46,900	LC
N Car Central Univ	NC	9,000	C
N Car State Univ	NC	22,434	HC+
N Car Wesleyan College	NC	39,200	C

ST = STATE $IS = IN-STATE COSTS SR = SELECTOR RATING

School	ST	$IS	SR
N Dak State Univ	ND	16,245	VC
North Park Univ	IL	35,860	C
Northeastern State Univ	OK	8,615	VC
Northeastern Univ	MA	65,352	MC
Northern Arizona Univ	AZ	21,003	C
Northern Kentucky Univ	KY	16,486	C
Northern Mich Univ	MI	20,853	C
Northern State Univ	SD	15,570	C
Northwest Nazarene Univ	ID	40,250	C
Northwestern College of Iowa	IA	38,400	C
Northwestern Okla State Univ	OK	13,072	LC
Northwestern State Univ of Louisiana	LA	16,534	LC
Norwich Univ	VT	56,234	C
Nova Southeastern Univ	FL	38,534	C+
Nyack College	NY	34,450	LC
Ohio Dominican Univ	OH	41,340	C+
Ohio Northern Univ	OH	44,050	VC
Ohio State Univ at Columbus	OH	22,843	MC
Ohio State Univ at Mansfield	OH	15,529	C
Ohio Univ	OH	23,394	VC
Ohio Valley Univ	WV	28,800	C
Okla Baptist Univ	OK	33,990	C
Okla Christian Univ	OK	29,260	C
Okla Wesleyan Univ	OK	34,434	C
Old Dominion Univ	VA	21,618	C
Olivet College	MI	37,661	LC
Olivet Nazarene Univ	IL	41,840	VC
Pace Univ	NY	60,136	C
Park Univ	MO	22,134	C
Penn State Altoona	PA	26,686	C
Pfeiffer Univ	NC	40,532	LC
Piedmont College	GA	34,334	C
Pittsburg State Univ	KS	13,880	C
Plymouth State Univ	NH	23,180	LC
Point Loma Nazarene Univ	CA	46,150	C+
Point Park Univ	PA	41,270	C
Post Univ	CT	41,150	C
Prairie View A&M Univ	TX	27,273	LC
Purdue Univ Northwest	IN	15,178	C
Purdue Univ/West Lafayette	IN	20,032	MC
Quincy Univ	IL	38,170	LC
Quinnipiac Univ	CT	60,970	VC
Radford Univ	VA	19,758	C
Regis College	MA	51,920	LC
Regis Univ	CO	46,380	C
Rhode Island College	RI	19,000	LC
Roanoke College	VA	55,952	VC
Roberts Wesleyan College	NY	41,116	C
Rochester Inst of Technology	NY	52,734	HC+
Roger Williams Univ	RI	48,074	VC
Rowan Univ	NJ	24,491	VC
Russell Sage College	NY	39,370	C
Rutgers Univ - Camden	NJ	26,595	C
Rutgers Univ - New Brunswick	NJ	27,090	HC
Rutgers Univ - Newark	NJ	27,351	C
Sacred Heart Univ	CT	54,590	C
Saginaw Valley State Univ	MI	19,284	C
St. Anselm College	NH	56,636	VC
St. Augustine's Univ	NC	25,582	C
St. Francis Univ	PA	46,146	NC
St. Joseph's College of Maine	ME	47,890	C
St. Joseph's Univ	PA	58,540	VC
St. Leo Univ	FL	32,850	C
St. Louis Univ	MO	49,866	HC
St. Mary's Univ of Minn	MN	42,440	C
St. Peter's Univ	NJ	49,192	C
St. Xavier Univ	IL	44,440	C
Salem International Univ	WV	21,090	C
Salem State Univ	MA	42,650	LC
Salve Regina Univ	RI	53,046	VC
Sam Houston State Univ	TX	18,792	C
Samford Univ	AL	40,770	VC
San Diego State Univ	CA	23,156	VC
San Francisco State Univ	CA	18,514	LC
San Jose State Univ	CA	22,630	C
Savannah State Univ	GA	17,036	C
Seattle Univ	WA	54,957	VC
Seton Hall Univ	NJ	58,008	C
Seton Hill Univ	PA	46,972	VC
Shaw Univ	NC	24,638	C
Shenandoah Univ	VA	42,100	C
Shippensburg Univ of Pennsylvania	PA	24,096	C
Shorter Univ	GA	31,130	LC
Siena Heights Univ	MI	36,322	C
Simpson College	IA	45,626	VC
Sonoma State Univ	CA	27,020	C
S Car State Univ	SC	21,330	LC
South Univ	GA	36,070	LC
Southeast Missouri State Univ	MO	16,148	C
Southeastern Louisiana Univ	LA	16,237	C
Southeastern Okla State Univ	OK	11,875	C
Southeastern Univ	FL	34,910	LC
Southern Illinois Univ Carbondale	IL	24,554	C
Southern Illinois Univ Edwardsville	IL	20,188	C
Southern Oregon Univ	OR	19,117	C
Southern Univ and A&M College	LA	16,074	LC
Southern Univ at New Orleans	LA	8,014	LC
Southern Vermont College	VT	34,670	LC
Southern Wesleyan Univ	SC	33,670	LC
Southwest Baptist Univ	MO	30,890	LC
Southwestern Okla State Univ	OK	12,205	C

School	ST	$IS	SR
St. Cloud State Univ	MN	10,600	C
St. Edward's Univ	TX	56,190	VC
St. Francis College	NY	38,800	LC
St. John's Univ	NY	57,160	C+
St. Joseph's College, New York/Brooklyn Campus	NY	25,114	LC
St. Joseph's College, New York/Long Island Campus	NY	25,124	C
St. Mary's Univ	TX	39,120	C
St. Thomas Aquinas College	NY	32,450	C
St. Thomas Univ	FL	51,187	LC
SUNY Albany	NY	22,165	C
SUNY at Oswego	NY	22,219	VC
SUNY/Buffalo State	NY	20,583	LC
SUNY/Empire State College	NY	9,145	NC
SUNY/Oneonta	NY	20,794	C
SUNY/Plattsburgh	NY	19,314	C
SUNY/Potsdam	NY	21,051	VC
Stephen F. Austin State Univ	TX	18,484	LC
Sterling College	KS	32,830	LC
Stevenson Univ	MD	48,412	C
Stockton Univ	NJ	25,565	C
Suffolk Univ	MA	52,316	C
Sul Ross State Univ	TX	15,021	LC
Tabor College	KS	35,870	C
Tarleton State Univ	TX	15,248	LC
Temple Univ	PA	24,392	C+
Tenn State Univ	TN	14,423	LC
Tenn Wesleyan Univ	TN	32,680	LC
Texas A&M Univ at Commerce	TX	10,496	C
Texas A&M Univ at Corpus Christi	TX	16,851	LC
Texas Christian Univ	TX	57,120	HC
Texas Southern Univ	TX	19,592	LC
Texas State Univ	TX	18,721	C
Texas Wesleyan Univ	TX	37,338	C
Texas Woman's Univ	TX	15,302	LC
The American Univ	DC	61,317	HC
The Citadel, The Military College of S Car	SC	20,679	C
The College at Brockport - SUNY	NY	21,058	C
The College of New Jersey	NJ	28,675	VC+
The College of St. Rose	NY	44,010	C
The George Washington Univ	DC	68,474	HC+
The Univ of Akron	OH	22,566	C
The Univ of Alabama	AL	24,320	C+
The Univ of Arizona	AZ	24,086	C
The Univ of Mary	ND	23,180	C
The Univ of Memphis	TN	18,278	C
The Univ of Montana Western	MT	9,426	LC
The Univ of Tenn at Chattanooga	TN	17,340	C+
The Univ of Tenn at Martin	TN	15,212	C
The Univ of Texas at San Antonio	TX	21,060	C
The Univ of Virginia's College at Wise	VA	18,192	LC
Thiel College	PA	42,950	LC
Thomas College	ME	73,888	LC
Thomas Edison State Univ	NJ	6,350	NC
Thomas More College	KY	36,720	LC
Thomas Univ	GA	21,420	NC
Tiffin Univ	OH	34,900	LC
Trevecca Nazarene Univ	TN	31,186	C
Trine Univ	IN	41,310	C
Trinity Christian College	IL	35,580	C
Trinity International Univ	IL	31,070	VC
Trinity Washington Univ	DC	33,826	C+
Troy Univ	AL	16,171	C
Truman State Univ	MO	16,286	MC
Tusculum College	TN	31,625	LC
Union College	KY	32,310	C
Union Inst & Univ	OH	8,912	SP
Univ of Alabama at Birmingham	AL	22,092	C
Univ of Arkansas at Fayetteville	AR	19,766	VC
Univ of Arkansas at Little Rock	AR	18,211	LC
Univ of Arkansas at Monticello	AR	13,599	LC
Univ of Arkansas at Pine Bluff	AR	13,541	C
Univ of Bridgeport	CT	44,985	LC
Univ of Central Florida	FL	16,379	VC
Univ of Central Missouri	MO	18,982	C
Univ of Central Okla	OK	15,150	C
Univ of Cincinnati	OH	22,118	VC
Univ of Colo Colo Springs	CO	20,300	C
Univ of Colo Denver	CO	22,238	C
Univ of Dayton	OH	54,930	VC
Univ of Delaware	DE	32,214	VC
Univ of Detroit Mercy	MI	48,816	C
Univ of Evansville	IN	44,186	C+
Univ of Findlay	OH	43,040	C
Univ of Georgia	GA	21,878	HC
Univ of Great Falls	MT	38,524	C
Univ of Hartford	CT	49,776	C
Univ of Hawaii at Hilo	HI	18,038	VC
Univ of Houston-Downtown	TX	7,241	LC
Univ of Illinois at Chicago	IL	24,664	VC
Univ of Indianapolis	IN	36,480	VC
Univ of Jamestown	ND	28,508	C
Univ of Louisiana at Lafayette	LA	14,516	C
Univ of Louisiana at Monroe	LA	15,970	C
Univ of Louisville	KY	19,692	C

School	ST	$IS	SR
Univ of Maine at Fort Kent	ME	15,165	LC
Univ of Maine at Machias	ME	22,960	C
Univ of Maine at Presque Isle	ME	16,148	LC
Univ of Mary Hardin-Baylor	TX	35,292	C+
Univ of Maryland Univ College	MD	26,146	LC
Univ of Maryland/College Park	MD	21,938	HC
Univ of Maryland/Eastern Shore	MD	21,861	LC
Univ of Mass Boston	MA	13,828	C
Univ of Mass Dartmouth	MA	26,507	C
Univ of Mass Lowell	MA	27,296	VC
Univ of Mich/Dearborn	MI	12,472	VC
Univ of Mich/Flint	MI	19,062	C
Univ of Minn/Crookston	MN	19,126	C
Univ of Miss	MS	18,802	C
Univ of Missouri-Kansas City	MO	19,563	VC
Univ of Missouri-St. Louis	MO	19,810	VC
Univ of Mount Olive	NC	18,426	C
Univ of Mount Union	OH	39,990	C
Univ of Nebr - Kearney	NE	17,014	LC
Univ of Nebr - Omaha	NE	16,120	C
Univ of Nevada, Las Vegas	NV	17,553	C
Univ of Nevada, Reno	NV	18,010	C
Univ of New Haven	CT	53,680	C
Univ of North Alabama	AL	15,964	C
Univ of N Car at Charlotte	NC	17,803	VC
Univ of N Car at Pembroke	NC	14,737	LC
Univ of N Dak	ND	16,673	C
Univ of North Florida	FL	15,996	VC
Univ of North Georgia	GA	17,316	C
Univ of North Texas	TX	20,082	C
Univ of Northern Colo	CO	19,658	C
Univ of Northern Iowa	IA	17,480	C
Univ of Northwestern - St. Paul	MN	39,530	C
Univ of Okla	OK	19,651	HC
Univ of Pikeville	KY	27,838	C
Univ of Pittsburgh at Bradford	PA	22,958	C
Univ of Pittsburgh at Johnstown	PA	22,092	C
Univ of Rhode Island	RI	26,066	VC
Univ of St. Francis	IN	38,520	C
Univ of St. Joseph	CT	49,069	C
Univ of Scranton	PA	54,962	VC
Univ of South Alabama	AL	16,880	C
Univ of S Car at Columbia	SC	21,726	VC
Univ of S Car Upstate	SC	19,272	LC
Univ of S Dak	SD	16,109	C
Univ of Southern Indiana	IN	16,808	C
Univ of Southern Miss	MS	13,170	C
Univ of St. Francis	IL	40,828	C
Univ of Texas at Arlington	TX	18,876	C
Univ of Texas at El Paso	TX	34,452	NC
Univ of Texas Rio Grande Valley	TX	15,573	LC
Univ of the Cumberlands	KY	32,000	LC
Univ of the District of Columbia	DC	21,260	LC
Univ of the Sacred Heart	PR	17,932	
Univ of the Southwest	NM	24,386	C
Univ of Toledo	OH	19,336	C
Univ of West Florida	FL	15,848	C
Univ of Wisc-Eau Claire	WI	16,354	VC
Univ of Wisc-Milwaukee	WI	21,538	C
Univ of Wisc-Oshkosh	WI	15,392	C
Univ of Wisc-Parkside	WI	15,313	C
Univ of Wisc-Platteville	WI	14,148	C
Univ of Wisc-Superior	WI	14,838	C
Univ of Wyoming	WY	15,537	C
Urbana Univ	OH	30,820	C
Utica College	NY	31,510	C
Villanova Univ	PA	64,922	MC
Virginia Commonwealth Univ	VA	23,811	VC
Virginia Wesleyan Univ	VA	45,980	LC
Viterbo Univ	WI	34,660	C
Voorhees College	SC	19,976	C
Walsh Univ	OH	39,010	C
Washburn Univ	KS	15,827	C
Washington State Univ	WA	22,747	C
Wayland Baptist Univ	TX	23,460	LC
Wayne State College	NE	25,746	NC
Wayne State Univ	MI	23,085	C
Waynesburg Univ	PA	33,530	C
Weber State Univ	UT	14,112	C
West Chester Univ of Pennsylvania	PA	19,171	VC
West Liberty Univ	WV	16,158	C
West Texas A&M Univ	TX	13,478	C
West Virginia State Univ	WV	19,412	LC
West Virginia Wesleyan College	WV	39,188	C
Western Carolina Univ	NC	13,965	C
Western Conn State Univ	CT	21,254	LC
Western Mich Univ	MI	21,791	C
Western New England Univ	MA	49,182	C
Western Oregon Univ	OR	19,965	LC
Westfield State Univ	MA	20,404	C
Westminster College	PA	41,722	C
Westminster College	UT	41,078	C
Wheeling Jesuit Univ	WV	37,106	LC
Wichita State Univ	KS	17,773	C
Widener Univ	PA	58,190	C
Wilmington College	OH	35,100	C
Wilmington Univ	DE	8,762	NC
Wingate Univ	NC	41,900	C

School	ST	$IS	SR
Winona State Univ	MN	18,109	C
Worcester State Univ	MA	20,977	C
Wright State Univ	OH	16,983	C
Xavier Univ	OH	49,380	VC
York College of Pennsylvania	PA	29,240	C
Youngstown State Univ	OH	17,487	C

CRIMINOLOGY

School	ST	$IS	SR
Adams State Univ	CO	15,420	LC
Alabama A&M Univ	AL	18,796	C
Albertus Magnus College	CT	44,016	LC
Alderson Broaddus Univ	WV	35,000	LC
Arizona State Univ at the Downtown Phoenix Campus	AZ	24,634	VC
Arizona State Univ at the West Campus	AZ	21,513	VC
Arkansas State Univ	AR	16,190	C
Assumption College	MA	48,455	VC
Auburn Univ	AL	24,300	VC+
Barry Univ	FL	38,730	LC
Cabrini Univ	PA	42,591	LC
Cal State, Fresno	CA	16,902	LC
Cal State, Fullerton	CA	21,902	C
Cal State, Long Beach	CA	18,850	C
Cal State, Northridge	CA	17,277	LC
Cal State, San Marcos	CA	20,604	LC
Cazenovia College	NY	47,866	C
Central Conn State Univ	CT	22,041	C
Chatham Univ	PA	47,883	VC
CUNY/John Jay College of Criminal Justice	NY	6,359	SP
Cleveland State Univ	OH	22,290	C
Coker College	SC	38,196	C
College of the Ozarks	MO	7,530	VC
Colo State Univ-Pueblo	CO	21,581	C
Corban Univ	OR	41,700	C
Davis & Elkins College	WV	38,242	LC
DePaul Univ	IL	52,807	VC
Drexel Univ	PA	65,927	HC
Drury Univ	MO	37,555	VC
Eastern Conn State Univ	CT	23,059	C
Emmanuel College	MA	53,472	C+
Faulkner Univ	AL	26,410	C
Flagler College	FL	27,620	C
Florida Gulf Coast Univ	FL	14,738	C
Florida Southern College	FL	45,978	VC
Florida State Univ	FL	16,771	HC
Framingham State Univ	MA	21,740	C
Gonzaga Univ	WA	52,880	HC
Hilbert College	NY	32,650	LC
Hofstra Univ	NY	58,210	C+
Immaculata Univ	PA	39,000	C
Indiana Inst of Technology	IN	34,240	LC
Indiana State Univ	IN	23,223	LC
Indiana Univ of Pennsylvania	PA	24,474	C
Indiana Univ Southeast	IN	16,931	C
John Carroll Univ	OH	51,570	C
Johnson & Wales Univ/ Denver Campus	CO	44,768	C
Kent State Univ	OH	20,928	C
Le Moyne College	NY	47,305	VC
Longwood Univ	VA	22,184	C
Loyola Univ Chicago	IL	57,158	VC
Lycoming College	PA	50,895	C
Marquette Univ	WI	53,090	VC+
Maryville Univ of St. Louis	MO	38,558	VC
Meredith College	NC	46,634	C
Millersville Univ of Pennsylvania	PA	25,298	C
Missouri State Univ	MO	15,837	C+
Mount Aloysius College	PA	29,976	C
Mount St. Mary College	NY	44,448	C
Mount St. Joseph Univ	OH	33,880	LC
Niagara Univ	NY	41,010	C
Northern Arizona Univ	AZ	21,003	C
Northwest Missouri State Univ	MO	18,286	C
Ohio State Univ at Columbus	OH	22,843	MC
Ohio State Univ at Mansfield	OH	15,529	C
Ohio Univ	OH	23,394	VC
Pontifical Catholic Univ of PR	PR	10,534	
Regis Univ	CO	46,380	C
St. Martin's Univ	WA	45,056	C
St. Mary-of-the-Woods College	IN	40,424	LC
Southeastern Univ	FL	34,910	LC
Southern Illinois Univ Carbondale	IL	24,554	C
Southern Oregon Univ	OR	19,117	C
St. Edward's Univ	TX	56,190	VC
St. John Fisher College	NY	45,270	VC
SUNY/College at Old Westbury	NY	16,860	C
Stonehill College	MA	55,130	C
The Univ of Akron	OH	22,566	C
The Univ of Memphis	TN	18,278	C
Universidad del Turabo	PR	17,828	
Univ of Calif at Irvine	CA	33,857	VC
Univ of Central Arkansas	AR	15,042	VC
Univ of Denver	CO	61,129	VC+
Univ of Florida	FL	16,291	HC+
Univ of Illinois at Chicago	IL	24,664	VC
Univ of La Verne	CA	55,600	C
Univ of Lynchburg	VA	48,370	C
Univ of Maryland/College Park	MD	21,938	HC

ST = STATE **$IS** = IN-STATE COSTS **SR** = SELECTOR RATING

School	ST	$IS	SR
Univ of Miami	FL	63,494	MC
Univ of Mich/Dearborn	MI	12,472	VC
Univ of Minn/Duluth	MN	20,292	C
Univ of New Haven	CT	53,680	C
Univ of New Mexico	NM	16,808	C
Univ of N Car at Greensboro	NC	15,998	C
Univ of N Car Wilmington	NC	16,784	VC
Univ of Northern Iowa	IA	17,480	C
Univ of Okla	OK	19,651	HC
Univ of Rhode Island	RI	26,066	VC
Univ of St. Mary	KS	37,080	NC
Univ of South Florida St. Petersburg	FL	15,980	C
Univ of South Florida/Tampa	FL	16,110	VC
Univ of St. Thomas - Houston	TX	41,510	VC
Univ of Tampa	FL	38,928	VC
Univ of Texas at Dallas	TX	23,640	HC
Univ of Texas Rio Grande Valley	TX	15,573	LC
Univ of West Georgia	GA	17,510	LC
Upper Iowa Univ	IA	34,990	NC
Valparaiso Univ	IN	50,160	VC
Virginia Union Univ	VA	25,058	C
Wartburg College	IA	49,478	C
Washington State Univ	WA	22,747	C
Webster Univ	MO	37,490	C
West Virginia Univ	WV	18,952	VC
Western Kentucky Univ	KY	16,850	C
Wilkes Univ	PA	49,166	C
William Penn Univ	IA	26,000	C

CROSSCULTURAL STUDIES

School	ST	$IS	SR
Alfred Univ	NY	37,490	C
Andrews Univ	MI	41,732	C
Bard College at Simon's Rock	MA	65,795	MC
Biola Univ	CA	48,686	C
Bryant Univ	RI	57,204	VC
Chatham Univ	PA	47,883	VC
Columbia College Chicago	IL	40,104	C
Corban Univ	OR	41,700	C
Goddard College	VT	17,040	VC
Hampshire College	MA	65,214	MC
Hope International Univ	CA	42,730	C
Houghton College	NY	40,558	VC
Kentucky Christian Univ	KY	26,836	LC
Lee Univ	TN	22,045	C
Linfield College	OR	53,992	C
Malone Univ	OH	39,200	C
National Louis Univ	IL	43,000	LC
Nyack College	NY	34,450	LC
Okla Baptist Univ	OK	33,990	C
Olivet Nazarene Univ	IL	41,840	VC
Palm Beach Atlantic Univ	FL	39,250	C
Rollins College	FL	58,670	HC
Simpson Univ	CA	34,722	C
Stanford Univ	CA	62,541	MC
Toccoa Falls College	GA	30,048	C
Towson Univ	MD	21,878	C
Univ of Northwestern - St. Paul	MN	39,530	C
Villanova Univ	PA	64,922	MC
Washington State Univ	WA	22,747	C
Western Kentucky Univ	KY	16,850	C
Whitworth Univ	WA	53,682	VC
Wofford College	SC	49,885	VC

CULINARY ARTS

School	ST	$IS	SR
Atlantic Union College	MA	27,228	C
College of the Ozarks	MO	7,530	VC
Drexel Univ	PA	65,927	HC
Idaho State Univ	ID	13,619	LC
Kendall College	IL	32,610	C
Kennesaw State Univ	GA	18,899	VC
Livingstone College	NC	17,815	LC
Miss Univ for Women	MS	17,065	C
Ohio State Univ at Columbus	OH	22,843	MC
Pennsylvania College of Technology	PA	27,693	NC
Southern New Hampshire Univ	NH	44,256	C
SUNY /College of Agriculture and Tech at Cobleskill	NY	20,527	LC
The Art Inst of Atlanta	GA	34,334	SP
Univ of Alaska Anchorage	AK	17,914	C
Univ of Nebr - Lincoln	NE	18,589	VC

CULTURAL ANTHROPOLOGY

School	ST	$IS	SR
Creighton Univ	NE	49,452	VC
Univ of Maryland/Baltimore County	MD	23,004	VC
Webster Univ	MO	37,490	C
Western Kentucky Univ	KY	16,850	C

CULTURAL STUDIES/CRITICAL THEORY & ANALYSIS

School	ST	$IS	SR
Arkansas Tech Univ	AR	16,534	LC
Bard College at Simon's Rock	MA	65,795	MC
Bethany College	WV	38,774	LC
Bryant Univ	RI	57,204	VC
Chatham Univ	PA	47,883	VC
Dallas Baptist Univ	TX	35,220	VC
Goddard College	VT	17,040	VC
MidAmerica Nazarene Univ	KS	37,808	C
Northern Arizona Univ	AZ	21,003	C
Northwest Nazarene Univ	ID	40,250	C
Occidental College	CA	68,660	MC
Univ of Maryland/Baltimore County	MD	23,004	VC

CYBER INTELLIGENCE/ SECURITY STUDIES

School	ST	$IS	SR
Alfred State College	NY	19,895	C
Arkansas Tech Univ	AR	16,534	LC
Armstrong State Univ	GA	15,615	C
Bay Path Univ	MA	46,356	C
Bloomsburg Univ of Pennsylvania	PA	19,930	C
Cal State, Fullerton	CA	21,902	C
Champlain College	VT	54,724	VC
DePaul Univ	IL	52,807	VC
Embry-Riddle Aeronautical Univ - Daytona Beach	FL	45,822	VC
Embry-Riddle Aeronautical Univ - Prescott Campus	AZ	45,130	VC
Excelsior College	NY	38,800	SP
Hilbert College	NY	32,650	LC
Kennesaw State Univ	GA	18,899	VC
Le Moyne College	NY	47,305	VC
Maryville Univ of St. Louis	MO	38,558	VC
Montreat College	NC	34,605	LC
Mount St. Mary's Univ	MD	53,380	C
Newbury College	MA	48,970	C
Northern Mich Univ	MI	20,853	C
Old Dominion Univ	VA	21,618	C
Southeast Missouri State Univ	MO	16,148	C
St. Bonaventure Univ	NY	45,596	C
Thomas Edison State Univ	NJ	6,350	NC
Tiffin Univ	OH	34,900	LC
Trine Univ	IN	41,310	C
Univ of Maine at Fort Kent	ME	15,165	LC
Univ of Maryland/Baltimore County	MD	23,004	VC
Univ of Mich/Dearborn	MI	12,472	VC
Utica College	NY	31,510	C
Western Illinois Univ	IL	20,897	C

CYBER OPERATIONS

School	ST	$IS	SR
United States Naval Academy	MD		HC
Univ of Maryland/Baltimore County	MD	23,004	VC
Univ of New Haven	CT	53,680	C

CYBERNETICS

School	ST	$IS	SR
Cal State, Fullerton	CA	21,902	C
Univ of Maryland/Baltimore County	MD	23,004	VC

CYTOTECHNOLOGY

School	ST	$IS	SR
Barry Univ	FL	38,730	LC
Bloomfield College	NJ	40,100	LC
Cal State, Fullerton	CA	21,902	C
Edgewood College	WI	35,950	C
Indiana Univ-Purdue Univ Indianapolis	IN	18,952	C
Marian Univ	WI	34,622	C
Marshall Univ	WV	18,044	C
Mass College of Liberal Arts	MA	20,659	C
Old Dominion Univ	VA	21,618	C
Rutgers Univ - New Brunswick	NJ	27,090	HC
St. Louis Univ	MO	49,866	HC
St. Mary's Univ of Minn	MN	42,440	C
SUNY/Plattsburgh	NY	19,314	C
The College of St. Rose	NY	44,010	C
Thiel College	PA	42,950	LC
Univ of Conn	CT	27,394	
Univ of Kansas	KS	20,884	VC
Univ of Mass Dartmouth	MA	26,507	C
Univ of Miss	MS	18,802	C
Univ of N Dak	ND	16,673	C
Univ of North Texas	TX	20,082	C
Winona State Univ	MN	18,109	C

DAIRY SCIENCE

School	ST	$IS	SR
Calif Polytechnic State Univ	CA	22,547	MC
Cal State, Fresno	CA	16,902	LC
Delaware Valley Univ	PA	51,271	C
Iowa State Univ	IA	18,176	C
S Dak State Univ	SD	15,874	C
Univ of Florida	FL	16,291	HC+
Univ of Georgia	GA	21,878	HC
Univ of Idaho	ID	16,158	C
Univ of New Hampshire	NH	29,333	VC
Univ of Wisc-Madison	WI	21,647	MC
Univ of Wisc-Platteville	WI	14,148	C
Utah State Univ	UT	13,235	C
Virginia Polytechnic Inst and State Univ	VA	21,920	VC
Western Kentucky Univ	KY	16,850	C

DANCE

School	ST	$IS	SR
Adelphi Univ	NY	49,792	C
Agnes Scott College	GA	51,930	VC+
Alma College	MI	49,410	VC
Amherst College	MA	66,186	MC
Anderson Univ	IN	39,450	C
Appalachian State Univ	NC	15,394	VC
Arizona State Univ at the Tempe Campus	AZ	23,001	VC
Baldwin Wallace Univ	OH	42,464	VC
Ball State Univ	IN	19,808	C+
Bard College	NY	65,924	HC
Bard College at Simon's Rock	MA	65,795	MC
Barnard College/Columbia Univ	NY	68,762	MC
Belhaven Univ	MS	32,250	C
Beloit College	WI	55,206	HC
Bennington College	VT	66,280	MC
Bowling Green State Univ	OH	19,975	C
Brenau Univ - Women's College	GA	37,876	LC
Brigham Young Univ	UT	13,248	MC
Butler Univ	IN	52,890	VC+
Calif Inst of the Arts	CA	61,366	SP
Cal State, Fullerton	CA	21,902	C
Cal State, Long Beach	CA	18,850	C
Cal State, Northridge	CA	17,277	LC
Cal State, San Bernardino	CA	20,106	C
Case Western Reserve Univ	OH	62,284	MC
Cedar Crest College	PA	51,110	C
Centenary College of Louisiana	LA	49,050	C+
Chapman Univ	CA	65,504	HC
CUNY/Hunter College	NY	31,098	VC
CUNY/Lehman College	NY	5,788	LC
Coker College	SC	38,196	C
College of Charleston	SC	24,046	VC
Colo College	CO	64,894	MC
Colo Mesa Univ	CO	19,707	LC
Colo State Univ	CO	23,033	C
Columbia College	SC	36,550	C
Columbia College Chicago	IL	40,104	C
Columbia Univ/ School of General Studies	NY	61,470	MC
Columbia Univ/City of New York	NY	62,958	MC
Conn College	CT	65,000	MC
Cornish College of the Arts	WA	47,750	SP
Davis & Elkins College	WV	38,242	LC
Denison Univ	OH	62,770	HC+
DeSales Univ	PA	47,520	C
Dickinson College	PA	66,166	MC
Dominican Univ of Calif	CA	58,750	C
Drexel Univ	PA	65,927	HC
East Carolina Univ	NC	16,539	C
Eastern Mich Univ	MI	19,761	C
Eastern Univ	PA	39,540	C
Eastern Washington Univ	WA	17,896	LC
Elon Univ	NC	46,142	HC
Emory Univ	GA	63,286	MC
Eugene Lang College of Liberal Arts	NY	64,940	VC
Florida Southern College	FL	45,978	VC
Florida State Univ	FL	16,771	HC
Fordham Univ	NY	68,431	MC
Franklin Pierce Univ	NH	46,750	LC
George Mason Univ	VA	19,884	C
Georgian Court Univ	NJ	43,068	LC
Goucher College	MD	56,110	VC
Grand Valley State Univ	MI	22,250	C+
Gustavus Adolphus College	MN	53,943	HC
Hamilton College	NY	64,250	MC
Hampshire College	MA	65,214	MC
Hobart and William Smith Colleges	NY	67,050	HC+
Hofstra Univ	NY	58,210	C+
Hollins Univ	VA	49,635	VC
Hope College	MI	42,840	VC
Howard Univ	DC	37,616	C+
Indiana Univ Bloomington	IN	20,791	HC
Jacksonville Univ	FL	49,210	C
James Madison Univ	VA	19,084	VC
Keene State College	NH	24,604	C
Kennesaw State Univ	GA	18,899	VC
Kent State Univ	OH	20,928	C
Kenyon College	OH	65,840	MC
La Roche College	PA	38,940	C
Lindenwood Univ	MO	25,760	C
LIU Brooklyn	NY	50,698	C
LIU Post	NY	50,698	C+
Loyola Marymount Univ	CA	60,202	VC+
Loyola Univ Chicago	IL	57,158	VC
Luther College	IA	49,990	VC
Manhattanville College	NY	52,430	C
Marlboro College	VT	50,832	VC+
Marygrove College	MI	30,100	LC
Marymount Manhattan College	NY	48,350	C
Mercyhurst Univ	PA	47,420	C
Meredith College	NC	46,634	C
Messiah College	PA	44,380	VC
Middlebury College	VT	67,464	MC
Mills College	CA	43,705	C
Minn State Univ, Mankato	MN	17,190	C
Montclair State Univ	NJ	26,912	C
Morehouse College	GA	40,835	C
Mount Holyoke College	MA	56,746	MC
Muhlenberg College	PA	56,645	VC
New Mexico State Univ	NM	14,050	LC
New York Univ	NY	68,139	MC
Northeastern Illinois Univ	IL	12,529	LC
Northwestern Univ	IL	68,725	MC
Nova Southeastern Univ	FL	38,534	C+
Oakland Univ	MI	20,763	C
Oberlin College	OH	68,942	MC
Ohio State Univ at Columbus	OH	22,843	MC
Ohio Univ	OH	23,394	VC
Ohio Wesleyan Univ	OH	49,460	VC
Okla City Univ	OK	40,476	C
Old Dominion Univ	VA	21,618	C
Oral Roberts Univ	OK	34,316	C
Otterbein Univ	OH	41,630	C
Pace Univ	NY	60,136	C
Palm Beach Atlantic Univ	FL	39,250	C
Pitzer College	CA	68,500	HC+
Point Park Univ	PA	41,270	C
Pomona College	CA	64,957	MC
Radford Univ	VA	19,758	C
Randolph College	VA	53,970	C
Rhode Island College	RI	19,000	LC
Rider Univ	NJ	54,050	C
Roger Williams Univ	RI	48,074	VC
Rutgers Univ - New Brunswick	NJ	27,090	HC
Salem College	NC	40,206	C
Sam Houston State Univ	TX	18,792	C
San Diego State Univ	CA	23,156	VC
San Francisco State Univ	CA	18,514	LC
San Jose State Univ	CA	22,630	C
Sarah Lawrence College	NY	68,866	MC
Scripps College	CA	69,260	HC
Seton Hill Univ	PA	46,972	VC
Shenandoah Univ	VA	42,100	C
Skidmore College	NY	66,600	MC
Slippery Rock Univ of Pennsylvania	PA	20,450	C
Smith College	MA	66,774	MC
Southeast Missouri State Univ	MO	16,148	C
Southern Illinois Univ Edwardsville	IL	20,188	C
Southern Methodist Univ	TX	69,008	MC
St. Olaf College	MN	56,430	HC
SUNY at Binghamton	NY	24,100	MC
SUNY at Purchase College	NY	21,832	C
SUNY/Fredonia	NY	20,818	C
SUNY/Potsdam	NY	21,051	VC
SUNY/Univ at Buffalo	NY	23,122	C
Stephen F. Austin State Univ	TX	18,484	LC
Stephens College	MO	38,042	C
Stockton Univ	NJ	25,565	C
Swarthmore College	PA	63,550	MC
Temple Univ	PA	24,392	C+
Texas State Univ	TX	18,721	C
Texas Tech Univ	TX	20,156	C+
Texas Woman's Univ	TX	15,302	LC
The Boston Conservatory at Berklee	MA	61,042	SP
The College at Brockport - SUNY	NY	21,058	C
The College of Wooster	OH	60,000	HC
The George Washington Univ	DC	68,474	HC+
The Juilliard School	NY	59,226	SP
The Univ of Akron	OH	22,566	C
The Univ of Alabama	AL	24,320	C+
The Univ of Arizona	AZ	24,086	C
The Univ of Texas at Austin	TX	20,206	MC
Towson Univ	MD	21,878	C
Trinity College	CT	69,020	HC
Tulane Univ	LA	67,496	MC
Univ of Arkansas at Little Rock	AR	18,211	LC
Univ of Calif at Berkeley	CA	29,886	MC
Univ of Calif at Irvine	CA	33,857	VC
Univ of Calif at Riverside	CA	32,912	C
Univ of Calif at Santa Barbara	CA	30,627	HC+
Univ of Calif San Diego	CA	30,450	MC
Univ of Central Okla	OK	15,150	C
Univ of Cincinnati	OH	22,118	VC
Univ of Colo Boulder	CO	26,048	HC
Univ of Florida	FL	16,291	HC+
Univ of Georgia	GA	21,878	HC
Univ of Hartford	CT	49,776	C
Univ of Hawaii at Manoa	HI	23,261	C
Univ of Houston	TX	21,871	VC
Univ of Idaho	ID	16,158	C
Univ of Illinois at Urbana-Champaign	IL	27,006	HC
Univ of Iowa	IA	19,415	HC
Univ of Kansas	KS	20,884	VC
Univ of Louisiana at Lafayette	LA	14,516	C
Univ of Maryland/Baltimore County	MD	23,004	VC
Univ of Maryland/College Park	MD	21,938	HC
Univ of Mass Amherst	MA	27,669	HC
Univ of Mich/Ann Arbor	MI	25,274	MC
Univ of Minn/Twin Cities	MN	24,269	MC
Univ of Missouri-Kansas City	MO	19,563	VC
Univ of Missouri-St. Louis	MO	19,810	VC
Univ of Nebr - Lincoln	NE	18,589	VC
Univ of Nevada, Las Vegas	NV	17,553	C
Univ of New Mexico	NM	16,808	C
Univ of N Car at Charlotte	NC	17,803	VC
Univ of N Car at Greensboro	NC	15,998	C
Univ of N Car School of the Arts	NC	25,587	SP
Univ of North Texas	TX	20,082	C
Univ of Okla	OK	19,651	HC
Univ of Oregon	OR	24,021	VC
Univ of Richmond	VA	62,730	MC
Univ of St. Francis	IN	38,520	C
Univ of S Car at Columbia	SC	21,726	VC

School	ST	$IS	SR
Univ of South Florida/Tampa	FL	16,110	VC
Univ of Southern Miss	MS	13,170	C
Univ of Tampa	FL	38,928	VC
Univ of Texas Rio Grande Valley	TX	15,573	LC
Univ of the Arts	PA	56,579	SP
Univ of Washington	WA	23,091	MC
Univ of Wisc-Madison	WI	21,647	MC
Univ of Wisc-Milwaukee	WI	21,538	C
Univ of Wisc-Stevens Point	WI	14,043	C
Univ of Wyoming	WY	15,537	C
Ursinus College	PA	62,920	VC
Utah State Univ	UT	13,235	C
Virginia Commonwealth Univ	VA	23,811	VC
Washington Univ in St. Louis	MO	67,539	MC
Wayne State Univ	MI	23,085	C
Weber State Univ	UT	14,112	C
Webster Univ	MO	37,490	C
Wells College	NY	50,500	C
Wesleyan Univ	CT	66,940	MC
West Chester Univ of Pennsylvania	PA	19,171	VC
West Texas A&M Univ	TX	13,478	C
West Virginia Univ	WV	18,952	VC
Western Kentucky Univ	KY	16,850	C
Western Mich Univ	MI	21,791	C
Western Oregon Univ	OR	19,965	LC
Western Washington Univ	WA	18,904	VC
Wichita State Univ	KS	17,773	C
Winthrop Univ	SC	23,960	C
Wittenberg Univ	OH	49,863	VC
Wright State Univ	OH	16,983	C
Youngstown State Univ	OH	17,487	C

DANCE EDUCATION

School	ST	$IS	SR
Brenau Univ - Women's College	GA	37,876	LC
Bridgewater State Univ	MA	22,762	C
Brigham Young Univ	UT	13,248	MC
Central Conn State Univ	CT	22,041	C
Columbia College	SC	36,550	C
East Carolina Univ	NC	16,539	C
Grand Canyon Univ	AZ	25,150	VC
Hofstra Univ	NY	58,210	C+
Hope College	MI	42,840	VC
Jacksonville Univ	FL	49,210	C
Keene State College	NH	24,604	C
Marywood Univ	PA	47,840	C
Minn State Univ, Mankato	MN	17,190	C
Montclair State Univ	NJ	26,912	C
New York Univ	NY	68,139	MC
Ohio State Univ at Columbus	OH	22,843	MC
Old Dominion Univ	VA	21,618	C
Point Park Univ	PA	41,270	C
Stephen F. Austin State Univ	TX	18,484	LC
Towson Univ	MD	21,878	C
Univ of Central Okla	OK	15,150	C
Univ of N Car at Greensboro	NC	15,998	C
Univ of Okla	OK	19,651	HC
Univ of the Arts	PA	56,579	SP

DATA ANALYTICS

School	ST	$IS	SR
Assumption College	MA	48,455	VC
Ohio State Univ at Columbus	OH	22,843	MC
Washington State Univ	WA	22,747	C

DATA PROCESSING

School	ST	$IS	SR
Ball State Univ	IN	19,808	C+
Cal State, Fullerton	CA	21,902	C
College of Charleston	SC	24,046	VC
Husson Univ	ME	26,508	C
Northwest Missouri State Univ	MO	18,286	C

DATA SCIENCE

School	ST	$IS	SR
Calvin College	MI	43,090	HC
Univ of Mich/Dearborn	MI	12,472	VC
Univ of Oregon	OR	24,021	VC
Univ of Rhode Island	RI	26,066	VC

DENTAL EDUCATION

School	ST	$IS	SR
Seton Hill Univ	PA	46,972	VC
Thomas Edison State Univ	NJ	6,350	NC
Univ of N Car at Greensboro	NC	15,998	C
Wichita State Univ	KS	17,773	C

DENTAL HYGIENE

School	ST	$IS	SR
Allen College	IA	32,367	LC
Augusta Univ	GA	4,632	C
Clayton State Univ	GA	19,735	LC
Creighton Univ	NE	49,452	VC
East Central Univ	OK	13,330	C
East Tenn State Univ	TN	18,141	C
Eastern Washington Univ	WA	17,896	LC
Farmingdale State College	NY	20,968	C
Ferris State Univ	MI	21,458	C
Goodwin College	CT	28,370	LC
Howard Univ	DC	37,616	C+
Idaho State Univ	ID	13,619	LC
Indiana Univ Northwest	IN	7,207	LC
Indiana Univ South Bend	IN	16,057	C
Indiana Univ-Purdue Univ Indianapolis	IN	18,952	C
Lewis Univ	IL	41,710	C
MCPHS Univ	MA	45,470	SP
Metropolitan State Univ	MN	7,859	C
Midwestern State Univ	TX	12,111	LC
Minn State Univ, Mankato	MN	17,190	C
Missouri Southern State Univ	MO	13,071	C
New York Univ	NY	68,139	MC
Northern Arizona Univ	AZ	21,003	C
Ohio State Univ at Columbus	OH	22,843	MC
Ohio State Univ at Lima	OH	7,553	C
Old Dominion Univ	VA	21,618	C
Oregon Inst of Technology	OR	19,227	C
Pennsylvania College of Technology	PA	27,693	NC
Rhode Island College	RI	19,000	LC
Rutgers Univ - New Brunswick	NJ	27,090	HC
Southern Illinois Univ Carbondale	IL	24,554	C
Tenn State Univ	TN	14,423	LC
Texas A&M Univ at College Station	TX	20,771	VC+
Texas Woman's Univ	TX	15,302	LC
The Univ of Tenn at Knoxville	TN	22,112	VC
Thomas Edison State Univ	NJ	6,350	NC
Univ of Alaska Anchorage	AK	17,914	C
Univ of Bridgeport	CT	44,985	LC
Univ of Detroit Mercy	MI	48,816	C
Univ of Hawaii at Manoa	HI	23,261	C
Univ of Louisiana at Monroe	LA	15,970	C
Univ of Louisville	KY	19,692	C
Univ of Maine at Augusta	ME	7,812	C
Univ of Mich/Ann Arbor	MI	25,274	MC
Univ of Minn/Twin Cities	MN	24,269	MC
Univ of Miss	MS	18,802	C
Univ of Missouri-Kansas City	MO	19,563	VC
Univ of New England	ME	50,110	C
Univ of New Haven	CT	53,680	C
Univ of New Mexico	NM	16,808	C
Univ of N Car at Chapel Hill	NC	20,561	MC
Univ of Pittsburgh	PA	30,030	MC
Univ of S Dak	SD	16,109	C
Univ of Southern Calif	CA	66,631	MC
Univ of Southern Indiana	IN	16,808	C
Univ of Washington	WA	23,091	MC
Univ of Wyoming	WY	15,537	C
Virginia Commonwealth Univ	VA	23,811	VC
Walla Walla Univ	WA	34,845	C
Weber State Univ	UT	14,112	C
West Liberty Univ	WV	16,158	C
West Virginia Univ	WV	18,952	VC
Western Kentucky Univ	KY	16,850	C
Youngstown State Univ	OH	17,487	C

DENTAL LABORATORY TECHNOLOGY

School	ST	$IS	SR
Minot State Univ	ND	13,285	C
Southwest Minn State Univ	MN	17,783	C
Univ of Southern Indiana	IN	16,808	C

DESIGN

School	ST	$IS	SR
Adams State Univ	CO	15,420	LC
Adelphi Univ	NY	49,792	C
Andrews Univ	MI	41,732	C
Arizona State Univ at the Tempe Campus	AZ	23,001	VC
ArtCenter College of Design	CA	42,008	SP
Auburn Univ	AL	24,300	VC+
Becker College	MA	30,100	LC
Belmont Univ	TN	44,500	VC+
Bennington College	VT	66,280	MC
Boston Architectural College	MA	20,666	SP
Bowling Green State Univ	OH	19,975	C
Bryant Univ	RI	57,204	VC
Cal State, Fullerton	CA	21,902	C
Cal State, Long Beach	CA	18,850	C
Carnegie Mellon Univ	PA	67,980	MC
Central Mich Univ	MI	20,330	C
CUNY/Queens College	NY	21,507	C
Clemson Univ	SC		HC
College of Art and Design at Lesley Univ	MA	50,525	SP
Concordia Univ St. Paul	MN	29,050	C
Cornish College of the Arts	WA	47,750	SP
Drexel Univ	PA	65,927	HC
East Carolina Univ	NC	16,539	C
Eastern Mich Univ	MI	19,761	C
Evangel Univ	MO	28,898	C
Fashion Inst of Technology/SUNY	NY	18,521	SP
Grand Valley State Univ	MI	22,250	C+
Harding Univ	AR	25,440	C
Hofstra Univ	NY	58,210	C+
Howard Univ	DC	37,616	C+
Iowa State Univ	IA	18,176	C
Kansas City Art Inst	MO	48,200	SP
Lamar Univ	TX	18,014	LC
Lees-McRae College	NC	33,944	NC
Lehigh Univ	PA	63,860	MC
Loyola Univ New Orleans	LA	52,456	VC
Memphis College of Art	TN	50,880	SP
Minneapolis College of Art and Design	MN	44,218	SP
Missouri State Univ	MO	15,837	C+
National Univ	CA	17,849	LC
New York Univ	NY	68,139	MC
N Car State Univ	NC	22,434	HC+
Northern Mich Univ	MI	20,853	C
Ohio Univ	OH	23,394	VC
Okla Christian Univ	OK	29,260	C
Okla State Univ	OK	17,180	C+
Olivet College	MI	37,661	LC
Otis College of Art and Design	CA	54,670	SP
Parsons The New School for Design	NY	56,610	SP
Radford Univ	VA	19,758	C
Rochester Inst of Technology	NY	52,734	HC+
Rutgers Univ - New Brunswick	NJ	27,090	HC
Saginaw Valley State Univ	MI	19,284	C
Salem College	NC	40,206	C
Salem State Univ	MA	42,650	LC
San Francisco State Univ	CA	18,514	LC
San Jose State Univ	CA	22,630	C
Savannah College of Art and Design	GA	49,595	SP
School of the Art Inst of Chicago	IL	61,830	SP
Southern Illinois Univ Carbondale	IL	24,554	C
SUNY/Buffalo State	NY	20,583	LC
Texas Christian Univ	TX	57,120	HC
The Univ of Texas at Austin	TX	20,206	MC
The Univ of Utah	UT	18,751	VC
Troy Univ	AL	16,171	C
Tusculum College	TN	31,625	LC
Univ of Calif at Davis	CA	28,468	HC
Univ of Central Okla	OK	15,150	C
Univ of Cincinnati	OH	22,118	VC
Univ of Hartford	CT	49,776	C
Univ of Idaho	ID	16,158	C
Univ of Kansas	KS	20,884	VC
Univ of Maryland/Baltimore County	MD	23,004	VC
Univ of Mich/Ann Arbor	MI	25,274	MC
Univ of Missouri-Columbia	MO	20,463	VC
Univ of New Haven	CT	53,680	C
Univ of N Car at Greensboro	NC	15,998	C
Univ of North Texas	TX	20,082	C
Univ of Notre Dame	IN	68,801	MC
Univ of Oregon	OR	24,021	VC
Univ of Pennsylvania	PA	63,526	MC
Univ of San Francisco	CA	60,580	C
Univ of Southern Miss	MS	13,170	C
Univ of Wisc-Green Bay	WI	15,184	C
Washington Univ in St. Louis	MO	67,539	MC
Wayne State Univ	MI	23,085	C
Western Kentucky Univ	KY	16,850	C
Western Washington Univ	WA	18,904	VC
Xavier Univ	OH	49,380	VC
Youngstown State Univ	OH	17,487	C

DESIGN AND ENVIRONMENTAL ANALYSIS

School	ST	$IS	SR
Cornell Univ	NY	67,591	MC
Guilford College	NC	45,973	C

DEVELOPMENT ECONOMICS

School	ST	$IS	SR
Calvin College	MI	43,090	HC
Taylor Univ	IN	42,130	VC

DEVELOPMENTAL PSYCHOLOGY

School	ST	$IS	SR
Boston College	MA	68,043	MC
Brown Univ	RI	64,566	MC
Cal State, Fullerton	CA	21,902	C
Cal State, Stanislaus	CA	18,053	LC
Emmanuel College	MA	53,472	C+
Fitchburg State Univ	MA	21,819	LC
Metropolitan State Univ	MN	7,859	C
New York Univ	NY	68,139	MC
Northwestern State Univ of Louisiana	LA	16,534	LC
St. Leo Univ	FL	32,850	C
Silver Lake College of the Holy Family	WI	36,290	LC
Univ of Detroit Mercy	MI	48,816	C

DEVELOPMENTAL SOCIOLOGY

School	ST	$IS	SR
Cornell Univ	NY	67,591	MC

DIAGNOSTIC MEDICAL SONOGRAPHY

School	ST	$IS	SR
Carroll Univ	WI	38,100	C+
Lewis Univ	IL	41,710	C
LIU Brooklyn	NY	50,698	C
Nova Southeastern Univ	FL	38,534	C+
Thomas Edison State Univ	NJ	6,350	NC
Univ of Charleston	WV	35,000	LC

DIETETICS

School	ST	$IS	SR
Andrews Univ	MI	41,732	C
Arkansas State Univ	AR	16,190	C
Ball State Univ	IN	19,808	C+
Baylor Univ	TX	56,803	HC
Bowling Green State Univ	OH	19,975	C
Brigham Young Univ	UT	13,248	MC
Cal State, Chico	CA	19,790	VC
Cal State, Fullerton	CA	21,902	C
Cal State, Los Angeles	CA	17,186	LC
Case Western Reserve Univ	OH	62,284	MC
Central Mich Univ	MI	20,330	C
CUNY/Lehman College	NY	5,788	LC
College of the Ozarks	MO	7,530	VC
Dominican Univ	IL	42,472	C+
D'Youville College	NY	37,678	C
East Carolina Univ	NC	16,539	C
Eastern Kentucky Univ	KY	17,742	C
Eastern Mich Univ	MI	19,761	C
Florida International Univ	FL	20,281	C
Florida State Univ	FL	16,771	HC
Fontbonne Univ	MO	34,606	C
Harding Univ	AR	25,440	C
Idaho State Univ	ID	13,619	LC
Immaculata Univ	PA	39,000	C
Indiana State Univ	IN	23,223	LC
Iowa State Univ	IA	18,176	C
James Madison Univ	VA	19,084	VC
Kansas State Univ	KS	17,780	VC
Lipscomb Univ	TN	42,984	VC
Louisiana Tech Univ	LA	11,422	VC
Madonna Univ	MI	30,450	LC
Marshall Univ	WV	18,044	C
Marywood Univ	PA	47,840	C
Messiah College	PA	44,380	VC
Mich State Univ	MI	24,542	VC
Minn State Univ, Mankato	MN	17,190	C
Missouri State Univ	MO	15,837	C+
Mount Mary Univ	WI	34,650	LC
Nicholls State Univ	LA	14,959	C
N Dak State Univ	ND	16,245	VC
Northern Illinois Univ	IL	20,176	C
Northwest Missouri State Univ	MO	18,286	C
Oakwood Univ	AL	43,758	C
Ohio State Univ at Columbus	OH	22,843	MC
Olivet Nazarene Univ	IL	41,840	VC
Ouachita Baptist Univ	AR	33,500	VC
Point Loma Nazarene Univ	CA	46,150	C+
Prairie View A&M Univ	TX	27,273	LC
Purdue Univ/West Lafayette	IN	20,032	MC
Rochester Inst of Technology	NY	52,734	HC+
San Francisco State Univ	CA	18,514	LC
Seton Hill Univ	PA	46,972	VC
Simmons College	MA	54,400	HC
Southern Illinois Univ Carbondale	IL	24,554	C
St. Catherine Univ	MN	45,630	C
SUNY/Buffalo State	NY	20,583	LC
SUNY/Oneonta	NY	20,794	C
Stephen F. Austin State Univ	TX	18,484	LC
Tarleton State Univ	TX	15,248	LC
Texas Christian Univ	TX	57,120	HC
Texas Southern Univ	TX	19,592	LC
Texas Woman's Univ	TX	15,302	LC
The Univ of Akron	OH	22,566	C
The Univ of Texas at Austin	TX	20,206	MC
Thomas Edison State Univ	NJ	6,350	NC
Tuskegee Univ	AL	28,164	C
Univ of Calif at Davis	CA	28,468	HC
Univ of Central Arkansas	AR	15,042	VC
Univ of Central Missouri	MO	18,982	C
Univ of Cincinnati	OH	22,118	VC
Univ of Conn	CT	27,394	
Univ of Dayton	OH	54,930	VC
Univ of Delaware	DE	32,214	VC
Univ of Georgia	GA	21,878	HC
Univ of Illinois at Urbana-Champaign	IL	27,006	HC
Univ of Louisiana at Lafayette	LA	14,516	C
Univ of Miss	MS	18,802	C
Univ of Nebr - Lincoln	NE	18,589	VC
Univ of New Haven	CT	53,680	C
Univ of N Dak	ND	16,673	C
Univ of North Florida	FL	15,996	VC
Univ of Northern Colo	CO	19,658	C
Univ of Texas Rio Grande Valley	TX	15,573	LC
Univ of Vermont	VT	29,792	HC
Univ of Wisc-Green Bay	WI	15,184	C
Univ of Wisc-Stevens Point	WI	14,043	C
Univ of Wisc-Stout	WI	19,667	C
Virginia Polytechnic Inst and State Univ	VA	21,920	VC
Viterbo Univ	WI	34,660	C
Wayne State Univ	MI	23,085	C
West Chester Univ of Pennsylvania	PA	19,171	VC
Western Carolina Univ	NC	13,965	C
Western Illinois Univ	IL	20,897	C
Western Mich Univ	MI	21,791	C
Youngstown State Univ	OH	17,487	C

DIGITAL ANIMATION & GAME DESIGN

School	ST	$IS	SR
Bloomfield College	NJ	40,100	LC
Columbia College Chicago	IL	40,104	C
Ferris State Univ	MI	21,458	C
Kennesaw State Univ	GA	18,899	VC
Lynn Univ	FL	49,680	LC
Missouri Western State Univ	MO	17,822	LC
Rochester Inst of Technology	NY	52,734	HC+

ST = STATE $IS = IN-STATE COSTS SR = SELECTOR RATING

DIGITAL ARTS/TECHNOLOGY

School	ST	$IS	SR
Art Academy of Cincinnati	OH	37,790	SP
Baldwin Wallace Univ	OH	42,464	VC
Bennington College	VT	66,280	MC
Bowling Green State Univ	OH	19,975	C
Bryant Univ	RI	57,204	VC
Calif Baptist Univ	CA	42,986	C
Calif College of the Arts	CA	52,758	SP
Cal State, Dominguez Hills	CA	19,022	LC
Calvin College	MI	43,090	HC
Chapman Univ	CA	65,504	HC
Claflin Univ	SC	25,592	LC
Clarkson Univ	NY	60,392	VC
Cogswell Polytechnical College	CA	31,511	C
College for Creative Studies	MI	51,210	SP
Dakota State Univ	SD	12,286	C
Delta State Univ	MS	13,176	LC
DePaul Univ	IL	52,807	VC
Dominican Univ	IL	42,472	C+
Drexel Univ	PA	65,927	HC
Elon Univ	NC	46,142	HC
Ferris State Univ	MI	21,458	C
Grand Canyon Univ	AZ	25,150	VC
Greenville College	IL	27,012	LC
Hamline Univ	MN	50,152	C
Huntingdon College	AL	35,900	C
Illinois State Univ	IL	23,418	VC
Jefferson (Philadelphia Univ + Thomas Jefferson Univ)	PA	53,966	C
John Brown Univ	AR	35,184	VC
Kansas City Art Inst	MO	48,200	SP
King Univ	TN	36,976	C
Lake Erie College	OH	38,914	LC
LIU Post	NY	50,698	C+
Lubbock Christian Univ	TX	29,727	C
Memphis College of Art	TN	50,880	SP
Mercy College	NY	32,614	C
Minneapolis College of Art and Design	MN	44,218	SP
Moore College of Art and Design	PA	55,118	SP
Moore College of Art and Design	PA	55,118	SP
New York Univ	NY	68,139	MC
NewSchool of Architecture & Design	CA	12,341	SP
Northeastern Univ	MA	65,352	MC
Ohio Univ	OH	23,394	VC
Olivet Nazarene Univ	IL	41,840	VC
Otis College of Art and Design	CA	54,670	SP
Parsons The New School for Design	NY	56,610	SP
Point Park Univ	PA	41,270	C
Quinnipiac Univ	CT	60,970	VC
Roberts Wesleyan College	NY	41,116	C
San Francisco Art Inst	CA	60,865	SP
Savannah College of Art and Design	GA	49,595	SP
School of the Art Inst of Chicago	IL	61,830	SP
Seattle Univ	WA	54,957	VC
Southern New Hampshire Univ	NH	44,256	C
Southern Oregon Univ	OR	19,117	C
Southwestern College	KS	31,531	LC
Stetson Univ	FL	57,174	VC+
Stevens Inst of Technology	NJ	64,954	MC
The College of New Jersey	NJ	28,675	VC+
Trinity Christian College	IL	35,580	C
Tulane Univ	LA	67,496	MC
Univ of Central Florida	FL	16,379	VC
Univ of Denver	CO	61,129	VC+
Univ of Idaho	ID	16,158	C
Univ of Illinois at Chicago	IL	24,664	VC
Univ of Maryland Univ College	MD	26,146	LC
Univ of N Car Wilmington	NC	16,784	VC
Univ of Pennsylvania	PA	63,526	MC
Univ of Tampa	FL	38,928	VC
Viterbo Univ	WI	34,660	C
Walla Walla Univ	WA	34,845	C
Washington State Univ	WA	22,747	C
Woodbury Univ	CA	49,593	VC
Youngstown State Univ	OH	17,487	C

DIGITAL COMMUNICATIONS

School	ST	$IS	SR
Albright College	PA	57,326	C
Bennington College	VT	66,280	MC
Bethany College	WV	38,774	LC
Bryant Univ	RI	57,204	VC
Cabrini Univ	PA	42,591	LC
Calvin College	MI	43,090	HC
Canisius College	NY	49,672	C
Columbia College Chicago	IL	40,104	C
Endicott College	MA	47,054	C+
Florida Southern College	FL	45,978	VC
Georgia Inst of Technology	GA	23,910	MC
Georgian Court Univ	NJ	43,068	LC
Henderson State Univ	AR	15,516	C
Hilbert College	NY	32,650	LC
Huntington Univ	IN	33,996	C
Indiana Inst of Technology	IN	34,240	LC
Juniata College	PA	58,118	VC
Kansas City Art Inst	MO	48,200	SP
Kutztown Univ of Pennsylvania	PA	19,477	C
Lebanon Valley College	PA	55,510	VC
LIU Brooklyn	NY	50,698	C
Loyola Univ Chicago	IL	57,158	VC
Lycoming College	PA	50,895	C
Madonna Univ	MI	30,450	LC
Marywood Univ	PA	47,840	C
Mass Inst of Technology	MA	62,662	MC
Milwaukee School of Engineering	WI	48,531	HC+
Muskingum Univ	OH	35,966	C
New York Univ	NY	68,139	MC
Newbury College	MA	48,970	C
Ohio Univ	OH	23,394	VC
Olivet Nazarene Univ	IL	41,840	VC
Oregon State Univ	OR	23,337	VC
Queens Univ of Charlotte	NC	39,543	C
Rutgers Univ - Camden	NJ	26,595	C
Spring Hill College	AL	48,488	C
St. Bonaventure Univ	NY	45,596	C
St. Edward's Univ	TX	56,190	VC
St. John Fisher College	NY	45,270	VC
Trevecca Nazarene Univ	TN	31,186	C
Trinity International Univ	IL	31,070	VC
Univ of Alaska Fairbanks	AK	16,874	VC
Univ of Cincinnati	OH	22,118	VC
Univ of Idaho	ID	16,158	C
Univ of Indianapolis	IN	36,480	VC
Univ of Oregon	OR	24,021	VC
Univ of Rochester	NY	65,032	MC
Valparaiso Univ	IN	50,160	VC
Vanguard Univ of Southern Calif	CA	42,400	VC
Washington State Univ	WA	22,747	C
Webster Univ	MO	37,490	C
William Penn Univ	IA	26,000	C

DIGITAL MEDIA

School	ST	$IS	SR
Alfred State College	NY	19,895	C
Ball State Univ	IN	19,808	C+
Bethany College	WV	38,774	LC
Bloomfield College	NJ	40,100	LC
Buena Vista Univ	IA	42,344	C
Calif Baptist Univ	CA	42,986	C
Cedarville Univ	OH	36,244	VC
Columbia College Chicago	IL	40,104	C
Dakota Wesleyan Univ	SD	33,980	LC
Eastern Conn State Univ	CT	23,059	C
Eastern Mennonite Univ	VA	42,550	C
Ferris State Univ	MI	21,458	C
Florida International Univ	FL	20,281	C
Fordham Univ	NY	68,431	MC
Georgia Inst of Technology	GA	23,910	MC
Huntington Univ	IN	33,996	C
Immaculata Univ	PA	39,000	C
Iowa Wesleyan Univ	IA	41,000	C
King Univ	TN	36,976	C
Loyola Univ New Orleans	LA	52,456	VC
Lynn Univ	FL	49,680	LC
Madonna Univ	MI	30,450	LC
Manhattanville College	NY	52,430	C
Marist College	NY	49,860	VC
Messiah College	PA	44,380	VC
Millikin Univ	IL	44,148	C
Neumann Univ	PA	40,678	LC
Ohio Univ	OH	23,394	VC
Okla Baptist Univ	OK	33,990	C
Rochester Inst of Technology	NY	52,734	HC+
Southeastern Univ	FL	34,910	LC
Southern Oregon Univ	OR	19,117	C
Tarleton State Univ	TX	15,248	LC
Taylor Univ	IN	42,130	VC
Texas State Univ	TX	18,721	C
Texas Tech Univ	TX	20,156	C+
Trinity International Univ	IL	31,070	VC
Univ of Bridgeport	CT	44,985	LC
Univ of Conn	CT	27,394	
Univ of Detroit Mercy	MI	48,816	C
Univ of Indianapolis	IN	36,480	VC
Univ of Northern Iowa	IA	17,480	C
Walsh Univ	OH	39,010	C
Xavier Univ	OH	49,380	VC
Youngstown State Univ	OH	17,487	C

DIGITAL MEDIA SOFTWARE ENGINEERING

School	ST	$IS	SR
Ferris State Univ	MI	21,458	C

DIGITAL MEDIA TECHNOLOGIES

School	ST	$IS	SR
Alfred State College	NY	19,895	C
Central Conn State Univ	CT	22,041	C
Chestnut Hill College	PA	47,180	C
East Stroudsburg Univ	PA	18,578	LC
Fordham Univ	NY	68,431	MC

DISABILITIES STUDIES

School	ST	$IS	SR
Aurora Univ	IL	34,990	C
Indiana Univ of Pennsylvania	PA	24,474	C
West Liberty Univ	WV	16,158	C

DRAFTING AND DESIGN

School	ST	$IS	SR
Pennsylvania College of Technology	PA	27,693	NC

DRAFTING AND DESIGN TECHNOLOGY

School	ST	$IS	SR
Alabama A&M Univ	AL	18,796	C
Baker College of Flint	MI	19,140	NC
Millersville Univ of Pennsylvania	PA	25,298	C
Montana State Univ-Northern	MT	11,370	NC
Norfolk State Univ	VA	18,902	LC
School of the Art Inst of Chicago	IL	61,830	SP
Texas Southern Univ	TX	19,592	LC
Trine Univ	IN	41,310	C
Univ of Central Missouri	MO	18,982	C
Univ of Rio Grande & Rio Grande Community College	OH	8,750	LC
Western Mich Univ	MI	21,791	C

DRAMA EDUCATION

School	ST	$IS	SR
Appalachian State Univ	NC	15,394	VC
Augustana Univ	SD	39,968	VC
Averett Univ	VA	43,034	LC
Baylor Univ	TX	56,803	HC
Bennington College	VT	66,280	MC
Bridgewater State Univ	MA	22,762	C
Brigham Young Univ	UT	13,248	MC
Columbus State Univ	GA	14,336	LC
Culver-Stockton College	MO	34,350	C
East Carolina Univ	NC	16,539	C
East Texas Baptist Univ	TX	34,444	C
Eastern Mich Univ	MI	19,761	C
Fontbonne Univ	MO	34,606	C
Friends Univ	KS	38,000	C
Greensboro College	NC	39,790	LC
Hardin-Simmons Univ	TX	36,025	C
Lees-McRae College	NC	33,944	NC
Lipscomb Univ	TN	42,984	VC
Mars Hill Univ	NC	41,104	C
Minot State Univ	ND	13,285	C
Missouri Western State Univ	MO	17,822	LC
Oral Roberts Univ	OK	34,316	C
Point Park Univ	PA	41,270	C
Saginaw Valley State Univ	MI	19,284	C
St. Louis Univ	MO	49,866	HC
Southwestern College	KS	31,531	LC
The Catholic Univ of America	DC	58,376	VC
The Univ of Montana Western	MT	9,426	LC
Trevecca Nazarene Univ	TN	31,186	C
Univ of Evansville	IN	44,186	C+
Univ of Indianapolis	IN	36,480	VC
Univ of Maryland/College Park	MD	21,938	HC
Univ of Nebr - Lincoln	NE	18,589	VC
Univ of New Mexico	NM	16,808	C
Univ of N Car at Greensboro	NC	15,998	C
West Texas A&M Univ	TX	13,478	C
York College	NE	30,260	C

DRAMATIC ARTS

School	ST	$IS	SR
Abilene Christian Univ	TX	43,708	C+
Adams State Univ	CO	15,420	LC
Adelphi Univ	NY	49,792	C
Adrian College	MI	45,550	C
Agnes Scott College	GA	51,930	VC+
Alabama A&M Univ	AL	18,796	C
Alabama State Univ	AL	16,490	LC
Albany State Univ	GA	19,462	C
Albertus Magnus College	CT	44,016	LC
Albright College	PA	57,326	C
Alfred Univ	NY	37,490	C
Allegheny College	PA	57,620	VC
Anderson Univ	IN	39,450	C
Appalachian State Univ	NC	15,394	VC
Arcadia Univ	PA	55,990	C+
Asbury Univ	KY	36,450	C+
Ashland Univ	OH	30,446	C
Auburn Univ	AL	24,300	VC+
Augsburg Univ	MN	45,129	C
Augustana Univ	SD	39,968	VC
Avila Univ	MO	27,100	C
Bard College	NY	65,924	HC
Bard College at Simon's Rock	MA	65,795	MC
Barnard College/Columbia Univ	NY	68,762	MC
Barry Univ	FL	38,730	LC
Barton College	NC	39,854	C
Baylor Univ	TX	56,803	HC
Belhaven Univ	MS	32,250	C
Beloit College	WI	55,206	HC
Benedictine College	KS	38,850	VC
Bennington College	VT	66,280	MC
Berea College	KY	7,094	C
Bethel College	IN	36,830	C
Bethel Univ	MN	46,550	C+
Bethune-Cookman Univ	FL	23,322	C
Biola Univ	CA	48,686	C
Boise State Univ	ID	17,368	C
Boston College	MA	68,043	MC
Boston Univ	MA	67,352	MC
Brenau Univ - Women's College	GA	37,876	LC
Briar Cliff Univ	IA	36,956	C
Brigham Young Univ	UT	13,248	MC
Bucknell Univ	PA	67,136	MC
Butler Univ	IN	52,890	VC+
Calif Inst of the Arts	CA	61,366	SP
Cal State, Bakersfield	CA	22,397	LC
Cal State, Dominguez Hills	CA	19,022	LC
Cal State, East Bay	CA	20,748	C
Cal State, Fresno	CA	16,902	LC
Cal State, Fullerton	CA	21,902	C
Cal State, Long Beach	CA	18,850	C
Cal State, Los Angeles	CA	17,186	LC
Cal State, Northridge	CA	17,277	LC
Cal State, Sacramento	CA	19,060	C
Cal State, San Bernardino	CA	20,106	C
Cal State, Stanislaus	CA	18,053	LC
Calif Univ of Pennsylvania	PA	20,425	LC
Capital Univ	OH	44,778	VC
Cardinal Stritch Univ	WI	37,136	C
Carnegie Mellon Univ	PA	67,980	MC
Carroll Univ	WI	38,100	C+
Case Western Reserve Univ	OH	62,284	MC
Cedar Crest College	PA	51,110	C
Centenary College	NJ	43,890	LC
Centenary College of Louisiana	LA	49,050	C+
Central College	IA	44,592	C
Central Methodist Univ	MO	31,500	VC
Central Mich Univ	MI	20,330	C
Central Washington Univ	WA	16,803	C
Centre College	KY	50,680	MC
Chadron State College	NE	14,819	LC
Chapman Univ	CA	65,504	HC
Charleston Southern Univ	SC	34,700	C
Cheyney Univ of Pennsylvania	PA	20,896	LC
CUNY/City College	NY	20,204	C
CUNY/Hunter College	NY	31,098	VC
CUNY/York College	NY	6,747	LC
Clarion Univ of Pennsylvania	PA	21,608	LC
Clark Univ	MA	53,260	HC+
Clarke Univ	IA	42,950	C
Cleveland State Univ	OH	22,290	C
Coastal Carolina Univ	SC	20,340	C
Coker College	SC	38,196	C
Colgate Univ	NY	67,500	MC
College of Staten Island	NY	24,389	LC
College of the Ozarks	MO	7,530	VC
Colo College	CO	64,894	MC
Colo State Univ	CO	23,033	C
Columbia College Chicago	IL	40,104	C
Columbia Univ/ School of General Studies	NY	61,470	MC
Columbia Univ/City of New York	NY	62,958	MC
Columbus State Univ	GA	14,336	LC
Concordia College - Moorhead	MN	46,418	C
Concordia Univ Irvine	CA	44,860	VC
Concordia Univ Nebr	NE	41,900	VC
Concordia Univ St. Paul	MN	29,050	C
Concordia Univ, Ann Arbor	MI	38,878	C+
Conn College	CT	65,000	MC
Cornish College of the Arts	WA	47,750	SP
Covenant College	GA	44,590	HC
Culver-Stockton College	MO	34,350	C
Dakota Wesleyan Univ	SD	33,980	LC
Davidson College	NC	60,119	MC
Denison Univ	OH	62,770	HC+
DePaul Univ	IL	52,807	VC
DeSales Univ	PA	47,520	C
Doane Univ	NE	41,340	VC
Dominican Univ	IL	42,472	C+
Dordt College	IA	37,860	C+
Drake Univ	IA	49,220	HC
Duke Univ	NC	68,298	MC
Duquesne Univ	PA	48,508	VC
Earlham College	IN	55,670	HC
East Carolina Univ	NC	16,539	C
East Central Univ	OK	13,330	C
Eastern Kentucky Univ	KY	17,742	C
Eastern Mich Univ	MI	19,761	C
Eastern Nazarene College	MA	41,114	C
Eastern New Mexico Univ	NM	12,874	LC
Eastern Oregon Univ	OR	17,612	C
Eastern Washington Univ	WA	17,896	LC
Eckerd College	FL	55,206	VC
Edinboro Univ	PA	15,940	LC
Elizabethtown College	PA	56,340	VC
Elmira College	NY	53,900	C
Elon Univ	NC	46,142	HC
Emerson College	MA	61,824	HC+
Emory and Henry College	VA	46,320	C
Emory Univ	GA	63,286	MC
Emporia State Univ	KS	15,029	C
Eugene Lang College of Liberal Arts	NY	64,940	VC
Eureka College	IL	34,760	C
Evangel Univ	MO	28,898	C
Fairleigh Dickinson Univ/College at Florham	NJ	54,770	C
Fayetteville State Univ	NC	17,756	C
Ferrum College	VA	43,970	C
Fisk Univ	TN	32,066	LC
Fitchburg State Univ	MA	21,819	LC

School	ST	$IS	SR
Five Towns College	NY	35,480	LC
Flagler College	FL	27,620	C
Florida A&M Univ	FL	15,361	C
Florida Atlantic Univ	FL	18,256	C
Florida International Univ	FL	20,281	C
Florida Southern College	FL	45,978	VC
Florida State Univ	FL	16,771	HC
Fontbonne Univ	MO	34,606	C
Fordham Univ	NY	68,431	MC
Fort Lewis College	CO	20,154	C
Francis Marion Univ	SC	18,144	LC
Franciscan Univ of Steubenville	OH	33,980	VC
Franklin and Marshall College	PA	67,960	MC
Franklin Pierce Univ	NH	46,750	LC
Freed-Hardeman Univ	TN	29,900	C
Furman Univ	SC	61,098	VC+
Gannon Univ	PA	42,922	C
George Fox Univ	OR	42,938	C
George Mason Univ	VA	19,884	C
Georgetown College	KY	41,440	C
Georgia Southwestern State Univ	GA	13,870	LC
Gettysburg College	PA	65,210	MC
Goddard College	VT	17,040	VC
Gonzaga Univ	WA	52,880	HC
Goshen College	IN	44,350	C
Graceland Univ	IA	35,290	C
Grand Valley State Univ	MI	22,250	C+
Greensboro College	NC	39,790	LC
Greenville College	IL	27,012	LC
Gustavus Adolphus College	MN	53,943	HC
Hamilton College	NY	64,250	MC
Hamline Univ	MN	50,152	C
Hampshire College	MA	65,214	MC
Hampton Univ	VA	36,410	C
Hannibal-LaGrange Univ	MO	29,815	C
Hanover College	IN	47,750	C+
Harding Univ	AR	25,440	C
Hardin-Simmons Univ	TX	36,025	C
Hartwick College	NY	51,270	C
Hastings College	NE	35,380	C+
Heidelberg Univ	OH	40,400	LC
Henderson State Univ	AR	15,516	C
Hendrix College	AR	54,020	VC
Hofstra Univ	NY	58,210	C+
Hope College	MI	42,840	VC
Howard Payne Univ	TX	35,994	C
Howard Univ	DC	37,616	C+
Humboldt State Univ	CA	21,708	C
Huntington Univ	IN	33,996	C
Idaho State Univ	ID	13,619	LC
Illinois College	IL	41,330	VC
Illinois State Univ	IL	23,418	VC
Indiana State Univ	IN	23,223	LC
Indiana Univ-Purdue Univ Fort Wayne	IN	18,675	C
Ithaca College	NY	58,158	VC+
Jacksonville State Univ	AL	14,628	LC
Jacksonville Univ	FL	49,210	C
James Madison Univ	VA	19,084	VC
Judson Univ	IL	39,174	C
Juniata College	PA	58,118	VC
Kalamazoo College	MI	53,931	HC
Kansas State Univ	KS	17,780	VC
Kansas Wesleyan Univ	KS	37,930	C
Kenyon College	OH	65,840	MC
King's College	PA	48,240	C
Knox College	IL	54,654	VC+
Kutztown Univ of Pennsylvania	PA	19,477	C
Lakeland Univ	WI	35,130	C
Lamar Univ	TX	18,014	LC
Lander Univ	SC	32,200	C
Langston Univ	OK	15,659	C
Lawrence Univ	WI	56,133	HC+
Le Moyne College	NY	47,305	VC
Lee Univ	TN	22,045	C
Lees-McRae College	NC	33,944	NC
Lenoir-Rhyne Univ	NC	47,500	LC
Lewis & Clark College	OR	60,984	MC
Lindenwood Univ	MO	25,760	C
Linfield College	OR	53,992	C
LIU Post	NY	50,698	C+
Louisiana State Univ and A&M College	LA	18,677	VC
Loyola Univ New Orleans	LA	52,456	VC
Lycoming College	PA	50,895	C
Lynn Univ	FL	49,680	LC
Lyon College	AR	36,120	VC
MacMurray College	IL	35,025	C
Maharishi Univ of Management	IA	34,930	VC
Manhattanville College	NY	52,430	C
Marietta College	OH	46,190	C
Marlboro College	VT	50,832	VC+
Marquette Univ	WI	53,090	VC+
Mars Hill Univ	NC	41,104	C
Marymount Manhattan College	NY	48,350	C
Maryville College	TN	44,410	C
Marywood Univ	PA	47,840	C
McDaniel College	MD	52,910	VC
McKendree Univ	IL	37,940	C+
McMurry Univ	TX	34,259	LC
McPherson College	KS	36,134	C
Mercer Univ	GA	45,348	VC
Meredith College	NC	46,634	C
Messiah College	PA	44,380	VC
Methodist Univ	NC	58,130	C
Metropolitan State Univ	MN	7,859	C
Miami Univ	OH	27,190	HC+
Mich State Univ	MI	24,542	VC
Middlebury College	VT	67,464	MC
Midwestern State Univ	TX	12,111	LC
Millikin Univ	IL	44,148	C
Minn State Univ, Mankato	MN	17,190	C
Minn State Univ, Moorhead	MN	21,393	C
Missouri Valley College	MO	28,150	C
Monmouth College	IL	42,260	C
Montana State Univ Billings	MT	13,336	LC
Montana State Univ-Northern	MT	11,370	NC
Morehead State Univ	KY	18,386	LC
Morehouse College	GA	40,835	C
Morgan State Univ	MD	17,190	LC
Morningside College	IA	39,780	C
Mount Holyoke College	MA	56,746	MC
Mount Vernon Nazarene Univ	OH	35,944	C
Muhlenberg College	PA	56,645	VC
Muskingum Univ	OH	35,966	C
Nebr Wesleyan Univ	NE	42,026	C+
New England College	NH	50,828	NC
New Mexico State Univ	NM	14,050	LC
New York Univ	NY	68,139	MC
Newberry College	SC	34,550	C
Niagara Univ	NY	41,010	C
N Car A&T State Univ	NC	13,786	C
N Car Central Univ	NC	9,000	C
N Car Wesleyan College	NC	39,200	C
N Dak State Univ	ND	16,245	VC
Northeastern Univ	MA	65,352	MC
Northern Illinois Univ	IL	20,176	C
Northern Kentucky Univ	KY	16,486	C
Northwest Missouri State Univ	MO	18,286	C
Northwestern College of Iowa	IA	38,400	C
Northwestern Okla State Univ	OK	13,072	LC
Northwestern State Univ of Louisiana	LA	16,534	LC
Northwestern Univ	IL	68,725	MC
Notre Dame de Namur Univ	CA	46,526	LC
Nova Southeastern Univ	FL	38,534	C+
Oakland Univ	MI	20,763	C
Oberlin College	OH	68,942	MC
Ohio Northern Univ	OH	44,050	VC
Ohio Univ	OH	23,394	VC
Ohio Wesleyan Univ	OH	49,460	VC
Okla Baptist Univ	OK	33,990	C
Okla State Univ	OK	17,180	C+
Olivet Nazarene Univ	IL	41,840	VC
Oral Roberts Univ	OK	34,316	C
Ottawa Univ	KS	39,980	VC
Otterbein Univ	OH	41,630	C
Ouachita Baptist Univ	AR	33,500	VC
Our Lady of the Lake Univ	TX	37,790	LC
Pacific Univ	OR	37,617	C
Park Univ	MO	22,134	C
Pepperdine Univ	CA	66,862	VC+
Piedmont College	GA	34,334	C
Pitzer College	CA	68,500	HC+
Point Park Univ	PA	41,270	C
Portland State Univ	OR	19,443	C
Prairie View A&M Univ	TX	27,273	LC
Presbyterian College	SC	47,186	C
Principia College	IL	40,350	C
Purdue Univ/West Lafayette	IN	20,032	MC
Queens Univ of Charlotte	NC	39,543	C
Quinnipiac Univ	CT	60,970	VC
Ramapo College of New Jersey	NJ	25,760	VC
Randolph College	VA	53,970	C
Randolph-Macon College	VA	51,480	VC
Reed College	OR	65,300	MC
Rhode Island College	RI	19,000	LC
Rider Univ	NJ	54,050	C
Ripon College	WI	49,991	VC
Rockford Univ	IL	38,570	C
Roger Williams Univ	RI	48,074	VC
Rollins College	FL	58,670	HC
Roosevelt Univ	IL	41,890	VC
Rowan Univ	NJ	24,491	VC
Rutgers Univ - Camden	NJ	26,595	C
Rutgers Univ - New Brunswick	NJ	27,090	HC
Rutgers Univ - Newark	NJ	27,351	C
Saginaw Valley State Univ	MI	19,284	C
St. Louis Univ	MO	49,866	HC
St. Michael's College	VT	53,275	VC+
Salem State Univ	MA	42,650	LC
Salve Regina Univ	RI	53,046	VC
Sam Houston State Univ	TX	18,792	C
San Francisco State Univ	CA	18,514	LC
San Jose State Univ	CA	22,630	C
Sarah Lawrence College	NY	68,866	MC
Schreiner Univ	TX	34,626	LC
Scripps College	CA	69,260	HC
Seton Hill Univ	PA	46,972	VC
Shenandoah Univ	VA	42,100	C
Shorter Univ	GA	31,130	LC
Simpson College	IA	45,626	VC
Skidmore College	NY	66,600	MC
Smith College	MA	66,774	MC
S Car State Univ	SC	21,330	LC
S Dak State Univ	SD	15,874	C
Southeastern Okla State Univ	OK	11,875	C
Southern Conn State Univ	CT	21,924	LC
Southern Illinois Univ Carbondale	IL	24,554	C
Southern Illinois Univ Edwardsville	IL	20,188	C
Southern Methodist Univ	TX	69,008	MC
Southern Oregon Univ	OR	19,117	C
Southern Univ and A&M College	LA	16,074	LC
Southwest Minn State Univ	MN	17,783	C
Southwestern College	KS	31,531	LC
Spelman College	GA	41,642	C
St. Bonaventure Univ	NY	45,596	C
St. Catherine Univ	MN	45,630	C
St. Cloud State Univ	MN	10,600	C
St. Lawrence Univ	NY	66,646	HC+
St. Mary's College of Maryland	MD	27,312	VC
Stanford Univ	CA	62,541	MC
SUNY at Binghamton	NY	24,100	MC
SUNY at New Paltz	NY	20,840	C
SUNY at Oswego	NY	22,219	VC
SUNY at Purchase College	NY	21,832	C
SUNY/Buffalo State	NY	20,583	LC
SUNY/Fredonia	NY	20,818	C
SUNY/Oneonta	NY	20,794	C
Stephen F. Austin State Univ	TX	18,484	LC
Stephens College	MO	38,042	C
Sterling College	KS	32,830	LC
Stetson Univ	FL	57,174	VC+
Stevenson Univ	MD	48,412	C
Stockton Univ	NJ	25,565	C
Suffolk Univ	MA	52,316	C
Sul Ross State Univ	TX	15,021	LC
Swarthmore College	PA	63,550	MC
Syracuse Univ	NY	62,313	HC
Tarleton State Univ	TX	15,248	LC
Taylor Univ	IN	42,130	VC
Tenn State Univ	TN	14,423	LC
Texas A&M Univ at Commerce	TX	10,496	C
Texas A&M Univ at Corpus Christi	TX	16,851	LC
Texas A&M Univ at Kingsville	TX	16,580	LC
Texas Lutheran Univ	TX	39,770	C
Texas Southern Univ	TX	19,592	LC
Texas State Univ	TX	18,721	C
Texas Wesleyan Univ	TX	37,338	C
Texas Woman's Univ	TX	15,302	LC
The American Univ	DC	61,317	HC
The Catholic Univ of America	DC	58,376	VC
The College of Wooster	OH	60,000	HC
The George Washington Univ	DC	68,474	HC+
The Juilliard School	NY	59,226	SP
The Univ of Memphis	TN	18,278	C
The Univ of Montana Western	MT	9,426	LC
The Univ of Tenn at Chattanooga	TN	17,340	C+
The Univ of Texas at Austin	TX	20,206	MC
The Univ of Virginia's College at Wise	VA	18,192	LC
Thomas More College	KY	36,720	LC
Transylvania Univ	KY	47,450	HC+
Trevecca Nazarene Univ	TN	31,186	C
Trinity College	CT	69,020	HC
Trinity Univ	TX	54,480	MC
Troy Univ	AL	16,171	C
Truman State Univ	MO	16,286	MC
Tufts Univ	MA		MC
Tulane Univ	LA	67,496	MC
Union College	KY	32,310	C
Union Univ	TN	41,160	VC
Univ of Alabama at Birmingham	AL	22,092	C
Univ of Alaska Anchorage	AK	17,914	C
Univ of Arkansas at Fayetteville	AR	19,766	VC
Univ of Arkansas at Little Rock	AR	18,211	LC
Univ of Calif at Berkeley	CA	29,886	MC
Univ of Calif at Davis	CA	28,468	HC
Univ of Calif at Irvine	CA	33,857	VC
Univ of Calif at Los Angeles	CA	27,438	HC+
Univ of Calif at Riverside	CA	32,912	C
Univ of Calif at Santa Barbara	CA	30,627	HC+
Univ of Calif San Diego	CA	30,450	MC
Univ of Calif, Santa Cruz	CA	28,731	C+
Univ of Central Florida	FL	16,379	VC
Univ of Cincinnati	OH	22,118	VC
Univ of Conn	CT	27,394	
Univ of Dallas	TX	50,676	VC
Univ of Denver	CO	61,129	VC+
Univ of Detroit Mercy	MI	48,816	C
Univ of Evansville	IN	44,186	C+
Univ of Findlay	OH	43,040	C
Univ of Hartford	CT	49,776	C
Univ of Hawaii at Manoa	HI	23,261	C
Univ of Idaho	ID	16,158	C
Univ of Illinois at Chicago	IL	24,664	VC
Univ of Illinois at Urbana-Champaign	IL	27,006	HC
Univ of Indianapolis	IN	36,480	VC
Univ of Iowa	IA	19,415	HC
Univ of Kansas	KS	20,884	VC
Univ of Kentucky	KY	24,800	C+
Univ of La Verne	CA	55,600	C
Univ of Louisiana at Lafayette	LA	14,516	C
Univ of Louisville	KY	19,692	C
Univ of Maine	ME	21,038	VC
Univ of Mary Washington	VA	23,039	C+
Univ of Maryland/Baltimore County	MD	23,004	VC
Univ of Maryland/College Park	MD	21,938	HC
Univ of Mass Amherst	MA	27,669	HC
Univ of Mass Boston	MA	13,828	C
Univ of Mich/Ann Arbor	MI	25,274	MC
Univ of Mich/Flint	MI	19,062	C
Univ of Minn/Duluth	MN	20,292	C
Univ of Minn/Morris	MN	21,222	VC
Univ of Missouri-Columbia	MO	20,463	VC
Univ of Missouri-Kansas City	MO	19,563	VC
Univ of Missouri-St. Louis	MO	19,810	VC
Univ of Montana	MT	14,105	C
Univ of Montevallo	AL	20,012	C
Univ of Nebr - Kearney	NE	17,014	LC
Univ of Nebr - Lincoln	NE	18,589	VC
Univ of Nebr - Omaha	NE	16,120	C
Univ of Nevada, Las Vegas	NV	17,553	C
Univ of Nevada, Reno	NV	18,010	C
Univ of New Orleans	LA	12,840	C
Univ of N Car at Asheville	NC	16,251	VC+
Univ of N Car at Chapel Hill	NC	20,561	MC
Univ of N Car at Greensboro	NC	15,998	C
Univ of N Car at Pembroke	NC	14,737	LC
Univ of N Car School of the Arts	NC	25,587	SP
Univ of North Texas	TX	20,082	C
Univ of Northern Iowa	IA	17,480	C
Univ of Northwestern - St. Paul	MN	39,530	C
Univ of Okla	OK	19,651	HC
Univ of Oregon	OR	24,021	VC
Univ of Pennsylvania	PA	63,526	MC
Univ of Pittsburgh at Johnstown	PA	22,092	C
Univ of Portland	OR	52,152	VC
Univ of PR-Rio Piedras campus	PR	13,327	
Univ of Puget Sound	WA	60,210	HC
Univ of Redlands	CA	61,934	VC
Univ of St. Mary	KS	37,080	NC
Univ of Science and Arts of Okla	OK	11,140	VC
Univ of South Alabama	AL	16,880	C
Univ of S Car at Columbia	SC	21,726	VC
Univ of S Dak	SD	16,109	C
Univ of South Florida/Tampa	FL	16,110	VC
Univ of Southern Calif	CA	66,631	MC
Univ of Southern Maine	ME	18,320	C
Univ of Southern Miss	MS	13,170	C
Univ of St. Thomas - Houston	TX	41,510	VC
Univ of Tampa	FL	38,928	VC
Univ of Texas at Arlington	TX	18,876	C
Univ of Texas at El Paso	TX	34,452	NC
Univ of Texas Rio Grande Valley	TX	15,573	LC
Univ of the Cumberlands	KY	32,000	LC
Univ of the District of Columbia	DC	21,260	LC
Univ of the Incarnate Word	TX	39,162	LC
Univ of the Ozarks	AR	31,050	NC
Univ of the Pacific	CA	57,446	VC
Univ of Toledo	OH	19,336	C
Univ of Vermont	VT	29,792	HC
Univ of Virginia	VA	27,367	MC
Univ of Washington	WA	23,091	MC
Univ of Wisc-Green Bay	WI	15,184	C
Univ of Wisc-Madison	WI	21,647	MC
Univ of Wisc-Milwaukee	WI	21,538	C
Univ of Wisc-Stevens Point	WI	14,043	C
Univ of Wisc-Superior	WI	14,838	C
Univ of Wisc-Whitewater	WI	13,976	C
Ursinus College	PA	62,920	VC
Utah State Univ	UT	13,235	C
Valparaiso Univ	IN	50,160	VC
Vanguard Univ of Southern Calif	CA	42,400	VC
Vassar College	NY	68,110	MC
Virginia Commonwealth Univ	VA	23,811	VC
Virginia Polytechnic Inst and State Univ	VA	21,920	VC
Virginia Wesleyan Univ	VA	45,980	LC
Viterbo Univ	WI	34,660	C
Wabash College	IN	52,100	VC
Wagner College	NY	57,240	C+
Washburn Univ	KS	15,827	C
Washington and Lee Univ	VA	59,647	MC
Washington College	MD	56,154	VC
Washington Univ in St. Louis	MO	67,539	MC
Wayland Baptist Univ	TX	23,460	LC
Wayne State College	NE	25,746	NC
Weber State Univ	UT	14,112	C
Webster Univ	MO	37,490	C
Wellesley College	MA	66,984	MC
Wells College	NY	50,500	C
Wesleyan College	GA	31,940	C+
Wesleyan Univ	CT	66,940	MC
West Chester Univ of Pennsylvania	PA	19,171	VC
West Texas A&M Univ	TX	13,478	C

ST = STATE $IS = IN-STATE COSTS SR = SELECTOR RATING

School	ST	$IS	SR
West Virginia Univ	WV	18,952	VC
West Virginia Wesleyan College	WV	39,188	C
Western Carolina Univ	NC	13,965	C
Western Conn State Univ	CT	21,254	LC
Western Kentucky Univ	KY	16,850	C
Western Oregon Univ	OR	19,965	LC
Western State Colo Univ	CO	19,348	C
Western Washington Univ	WA	18,904	VC
Westminster College	PA	41,722	C
Westminster College	UT	41,078	C
Westmont College	CA	57,930	VC
Whittier College	CA	57,891	C
Whitworth Univ	WA	53,682	VC
Wilkes Univ	PA	49,166	C
Willamette Univ	OR	62,514	VC+
William Carey Univ	MS	23,950	LC
William Jewell College	MO	42,490	C+
William Paterson Univ of New Jersey	NJ	24,022	C
William Woods Univ	MO	32,040	C
Williams College	MA	67,700	MC
Wilmington College	OH	35,100	C
Winona State Univ	MN	18,109	C
Wittenberg Univ	OH	49,863	VC
Wofford College	SC	49,885	VC
Wright State Univ	OH	16,983	C
Yale Univ	CT	64,650	MC
York College of Pennsylvania	PA	29,240	C
Youngstown State Univ	OH	17,487	C

DRAWING

School	ST	$IS	SR
Adams State Univ	CO	15,420	LC
Aquinas College - Mich	MI	38,876	VC
Art Academy of Cincinnati	OH	37,790	SP
Bard College at Simon's Rock	MA	65,795	MC
Bennington College	VT	66,280	MC
Biola Univ	CA	48,686	C
Bradley Univ	IL	43,240	VC
Calif College of the Arts	CA	52,758	SP
Cleveland Inst of Art	OH	51,455	SP
Ferris State Univ	MI	21,458	C
Indiana Univ-Purdue Univ Fort Wayne	IN	18,675	C
Kutztown Univ of Pennsylvania	PA	19,477	C
Laguna College of Art and Design	CA	41,422	SP
Lewis Univ	IL	41,710	C
Lubbock Christian Univ	TX	29,727	C
Maryland Inst College of Art	MD	58,740	SP
Memphis College of Art	TN	50,880	SP
Milwaukee Inst of Art & Design	WI	45,880	SP
Minneapolis College of Art and Design	MN	44,218	SP
Old Dominion Univ	VA	21,618	C
Olivet Nazarene Univ	IL	41,840	VC
Pacific Northwest College of Art	OR	38,494	SP
School of the Art Inst of Chicago	IL	61,830	SP
Shawnee State Univ	OH	16,998	C
SUNY at Binghamton	NY	24,100	MC
SUNY/Fredonia	NY	20,818	C
Univ of Hartford	CT	49,776	C
Univ of Iowa	IA	19,415	HC
Univ of Mich/Ann Arbor	MI	25,274	MC
Univ of N Car at Greensboro	NC	15,998	C
Univ of San Francisco	CA	60,580	C
Washington Univ in St. Louis	MO	67,539	MC

DRAWING WITH PRINTMAKING FOCUS

School	ST	$IS	SR
Univ of Mass Dartmouth	MA	26,507	C

EARLY CHILDHOOD EDUCATION

School	ST	$IS	SR
Alabama A&M Univ	AL	18,796	C
Alabama State Univ	AL	16,490	LC
Albany State Univ	GA	19,462	C
Alfred Univ	NY	37,490	C
Alma College	MI	49,410	VC
American International College	MA	47,020	LC
Angelo State Univ	TX	15,882	LC
Anna Maria College	MA	51,020	C
Aquinas College - Mich	MI	38,876	VC
Arcadia Univ	PA	55,990	C+
Arizona State Univ at the Tempe Campus	AZ	23,001	VC
Arkansas State Univ	AR	16,190	C
Arkansas Tech Univ	AR	16,534	LC
Armstrong State Univ	GA	15,615	C
Ashford Univ	CA	10,480	C
Ashland Univ	OH	30,446	C
Atlantic Union College	MA	27,228	C
Auburn Univ	AL	24,300	VC+
Aurora Univ	IL	34,990	C
Averett Univ	VA	43,034	LC
Baldwin Wallace Univ	OH	42,464	VC
Ball State Univ	IN	19,808	C+
Barry Univ	FL	38,730	LC
Bay Path Univ	MA	46,356	C
Becker College	MA	30,100	LC
Belmont Univ	TN	44,500	VC+
Bemidji State Univ	MN	17,730	C
Benedict College	SC	28,630	NC
Bennington College	VT	66,280	MC
Berry College	GA	47,466	VC
Bethel College	IN	36,830	C
Bethel Univ	MN	46,550	C+
Biola Univ	CA	48,686	C
Black Hills State Univ	SD	16,622	C
Bloomfield College	NJ	40,100	LC
Bloomsburg Univ of Pennsylvania	PA	19,930	C
Bluefield State College	WV	5,832	LC
Bluffton Univ	OH	40,950	C+
Boston College	MA	68,043	MC
Boston Univ	MA	67,352	MC
Bowie State Univ	MD	18,610	LC
Bowling Green State Univ	OH	19,975	C
Bradley Univ	IL	43,240	VC
Brenau Univ - Women's College	GA	37,876	LC
Brescia Univ	KY	29,890	VC
Brewton-Parker College	GA	26,120	LC
Bridgewater State Univ	MA	22,762	C
Brigham Young Univ	UT	13,248	MC
Bucknell Univ	PA	67,136	MC
Cal State, Fullerton	CA	21,902	C
Cal State, Sacramento	CA	19,060	C
Calif Univ of Pennsylvania	PA	20,425	LC
Calvin College	MI	43,090	HC
Cambridge College	MA	14,940	NC
Cameron Univ	OK	11,632	LC
Campbell Univ	NC	37,570	VC
Campbellsville Univ	KY	33,400	C
Canisius College	NY	49,672	C
Cardinal Stritch Univ	WI	37,136	C
Carlow Univ	PA	39,696	LC
Carroll Univ	WI	38,100	C+
Carson-Newman Univ	TN	35,900	C
Cazenovia College	NY	47,866	C
Cedar Crest College	PA	51,110	C
Cedarville Univ	OH	36,244	VC
Central Conn State Univ	CT	22,041	C
Central Methodist Univ	MO	31,500	VC
Central Washington Univ	WA	16,803	C
Chadron State College	NE	14,819	LC
Chaminade Univ of Honolulu	HI	37,614	C
Champlain College	VT	54,724	VC
Charleston Southern Univ	SC	34,700	C
Chatham Univ	PA	47,883	VC
Chestnut Hill College	PA	47,180	C
Cheyney Univ of Pennsylvania	PA	20,896	LC
Chicago State Univ	IL	41,620	C
Christian Brothers Univ	TN	31,670	VC
CUNY/Brooklyn College	NY	7,163	C+
CUNY/City College	NY	20,204	C
CUNY/Hunter College	NY	31,098	VC
CUNY/Lehman College	NY	5,788	LC
CUNY/Queens College	NY	21,507	C
Claflin Univ	SC	25,592	LC
Clarion Univ of Pennsylvania	PA	21,608	LC
Clark Atlanta Univ	GA	31,019	LC
Clemson Univ	SC		HC
Cleveland State Univ	OH	22,290	C
Coastal Carolina Univ	SC	20,340	C
Coker College	SC	38,196	C
College of Charleston	SC	24,046	VC
College of St. Mary	NE	27,500	C
College of the Ozarks	MO	7,530	VC
Colo State Univ	CO	23,033	C
Columbia College	SC	36,550	C
Columbia College Chicago	IL	40,104	C
Columbus State Univ	GA	14,336	LC
Concord Univ	WV	14,954	LC
Concordia College - Alabama	AL	15,720	NC
Concordia College - New York	NY	39,035	LC
Concordia Univ	OR	35,000	C
Concordia Univ Irvine	CA	44,860	VC
Concordia Univ Nebr	NE	41,900	VC
Concordia Univ St. Paul	MN	29,050	C
Concordia Univ Wisc	WI	35,910	C
Concordia Univ, Ann Arbor	MI	38,878	C+
Concordia Univ, Chicago	IL	41,522	C
Converse College	SC	28,290	C
Corban Univ	OR	41,700	C
Curry College	MA	53,331	C
Daemen College	NY	40,336	C
Dallas Baptist Univ	TX	35,220	VC
Defiance College	OH	42,240	LC
Delaware State Univ	DE	19,376	LC
DePaul Univ	IL	52,807	VC
DeSales Univ	PA	47,520	C
Dickinson State Univ	ND	12,372	LC
Dominican Univ	IL	42,472	C+
Dordt College	IA	37,860	C+
Duquesne Univ	PA	48,508	VC
East Carolina Univ	NC	16,539	C
East Central Univ	OK	13,330	C
East Stroudsburg Univ	PA	18,578	LC
East Texas Baptist Univ	TX	34,444	C
Eastern Conn State Univ	CT	23,059	C
Eastern Illinois Univ	IL	21,414	C
Eastern Mennonite Univ	VA	42,550	C
Eastern Mich Univ	MI	19,761	C
Eastern New Mexico Univ	NM	12,874	LC
Eastern Univ	PA	39,540	C
Edgewood College	WI	35,950	C
Edinboro Univ	PA	15,940	LC
Edward Waters College	FL	28,089	NC
Elizabethtown College	PA	56,340	VC
Elmhurst College	IL	46,514	C
Elmira College	NY	53,900	C
Elms College	MA	49,602	VC
Elon Univ	NC	46,142	HC
Erskine College	SC	45,460	C
Evangel Univ	MO	28,898	C
Fairmont State Univ	WV	15,726	C
Faulkner Univ	AL	26,410	C
Fayetteville State Univ	NC	17,756	C
Felician Univ	NJ	46,280	LC
Ferris State Univ	MI	21,458	C
Fitchburg State Univ	MA	21,819	LC
Florida A&M Univ	FL	15,361	C
Florida Gulf Coast Univ	FL	14,738	C
Florida International Univ	FL	20,281	C
Florida State Univ	FL	16,771	HC
Fontbonne Univ	MO	34,606	C
Fort Lewis College	CO	20,154	C
Fort Valley State Univ	GA	17,988	VC
Framingham State Univ	MA	21,740	C
Francis Marion Univ	SC	18,144	LC
Freed-Hardeman Univ	TN	29,900	C
Frostburg State Univ	MD	17,280	LC
Gallaudet Univ	DC	30,088	LC
Gannon Univ	PA	42,922	C
Geneva College	PA	35,450	C
Georgia College & State Univ	GA	21,884	C+
Georgia Southern Univ	GA	16,540	VC
Georgia Southwestern State Univ	GA	13,870	LC
Georgia State Univ	GA	25,250	C
Glenville State College	WV	17,386	LC
Goddard College	VT	17,040	VC
Gordon College	MA	47,740	VC
Goshen College	IN	44,350	C
Grambling State Univ	LA	15,701	C
Greensboro College	NC	39,790	LC
Greenville College	IL	27,012	LC
Grove City College	PA	26,654	VC
Hannibal-LaGrange Univ	MO	29,815	C
Harding Univ	AR	25,440	C
Hardin-Simmons Univ	TX	36,025	C
Harris-Stowe State Univ	MO	14,590	NC
Hendrix College	AR	54,020	VC
Heritage Univ	WA	19,825	NC
Hofstra Univ	NY	58,210	C+
Holy Family Univ	PA	44,672	LC
Hood College	MD	50,540	C
Houghton College	NY	40,558	VC
Houston Baptist Univ	TX	36,450	C
Howard Univ	DC	37,616	C+
Humphreys College	CA	27,790	C
Idaho State Univ	ID	13,619	LC
Illinois State Univ	IL	23,418	VC
Immaculata Univ	PA	39,000	C
Indiana State Univ	IN	23,223	LC
Indiana Univ Bloomington	IN	20,791	HC
Indiana Univ Kokomo	IN	7,207	C
Indiana Univ of Pennsylvania	PA	24,474	C
Indiana Univ-Purdue Univ Fort Wayne	IN	18,675	C
Inter-American Univ of PR Ponce	PR	19,549	
Inter-American Univ of PR-Aguadilla Campus	PR	21,657	
Inter-American Univ of PR-Barranquitas	PR	18,336	
Inter-American Univ of PR-Fajardo Campus	PR	18,336	
Inter-American Univ of PR-Metropolitan Campus	PR	20,045	
Inter-American Univ of PR-San Germán	PR	20,042	
Iona College	NY	52,514	C
Iowa State Univ	IA	18,176	C
Iowa Wesleyan Univ	IA	41,000	C
Jacksonville State Univ	AL	14,628	LC
John Brown Univ	AR	35,184	VC
John Carroll Univ	OH	51,570	C
Judson Univ	IL	39,174	C
Juniata College	PA	58,118	VC
Kansas State Univ	KS	17,780	VC
Kean Univ	NJ	25,620	C
Keene State College	NH	24,604	C
Kendall College	IL	32,610	C
Kennesaw State Univ	GA	18,899	VC
Kent State Univ	OH	20,928	C
Kentucky State Univ	KY	14,484	LC
Keystone College	PA	28,680	LC
King's College	PA	48,240	C
Kutztown Univ of Pennsylvania	PA	19,477	C
LaGrange College	GA	41,310	C
Lake Erie College	OH	38,914	LC
Lake Superior State Univ	MI	19,867	C
Lakeland Univ	WI	35,130	C
Lamar Univ	TX	18,014	LC
Lander Univ	SC	32,200	C
Lasell College	MA	49,400	C
Lebanon Valley College	PA	55,510	VC
LeMoyne-Owen College	TN	16,980	C
Lenoir-Rhyne Univ	NC	47,500	LC
Lesley Univ	MA	42,800	C
Lewis Univ	IL	41,710	C
Lewis-Clark State College	ID	14,202	C
Limestone College	SC	32,100	C
Lincoln Memorial Univ	TN	28,430	C
Lindenwood Univ	MO	25,760	C
Lipscomb Univ	TN	42,984	VC
LIU Brooklyn	NY	50,698	C
LIU Post	NY	50,698	C+
Livingstone College	NC	17,815	LC
Lock Haven Univ of Pennsylvania	PA	20,544	LC
Louisiana State Univ and A&M College	LA	18,677	VC
Louisiana Tech Univ	LA	11,422	VC
Loyola Univ Chicago	IL	57,158	VC
Lubbock Christian Univ	TX	29,727	C
Lyndon State College	VT	20,714	C
Lynn Univ	FL	49,680	LC
Lyon College	AR	36,120	VC
Madonna Univ	MI	30,450	LC
Malone Univ	OH	39,200	C
Manhattan College	NY	55,652	C
Mansfield Univ of Pennsylvania	PA	24,244	LC
Marian Univ	WI	34,622	C
Marietta College	OH	46,190	C
Marshall Univ	WV	18,044	C
Martin Univ	IN	21,010	LC
Marygrove College	MI	30,100	LC
Maryville Univ of St. Louis	MO	38,558	VC
Marywood Univ	PA	47,840	C
Mayville State Univ	ND	18,371	NC
McNeese State Univ	LA	7,838	C
Medaille College	NY	41,700	LC
Mercer Univ	GA	45,348	VC
Mercyhurst Univ	PA	47,420	C
Merrimack College	MA	55,415	C
Messiah College	PA	44,380	VC
Metropolitan College of New York	NY		VC
Metropolitan State Univ	MN	7,859	C
Miami Univ	OH	27,190	HC+
Middle Tenn State Univ	TN	8,650	C
Midland Univ	NE	39,512	C
Miles College	AL	16,530	NC
Millersville Univ of Pennsylvania	PA	25,298	C
Milligan College	TN	39,450	C
Millikin Univ	IL	44,148	C
Minn State Univ, Mankato	MN	17,190	C
Minn State Univ, Moorhead	MN	21,393	C
Misericordia Univ	PA	45,210	C
Miss Valley State Univ	MS	13,233	LC
Missouri Baptist Univ	MO	35,594	C
Missouri Southern State Univ	MO	13,071	C
Missouri State Univ	MO	15,837	C+
Missouri Western State Univ	MO	17,822	LC
Mitchell College	CT	45,192	C
Molloy College	NY	40,440	C
Monmouth Univ	NJ	50,184	C
Montana State Univ Billings	MT	13,336	LC
Moravian College	PA	55,488	C
Morehouse College	GA	40,835	C
Morris College	SC	19,195	LC
Mount Aloysius College	PA	29,976	C
Mount Ida College	MA	46,820	C
Mount Mary Univ	WI	34,650	LC
Mount Mercy Univ	IA	39,748	C
Mount St. Joseph Univ	OH	33,880	LC
Mount Vernon Nazarene Univ	OH	35,944	C
Murray State Univ	KY	17,726	C+
Muskingum Univ	OH	35,966	C
Naropa Univ	CO	43,278	NC
National Louis Univ	IL	43,000	LC
New Jersey City Univ	NJ	21,456	LC
New Mexico Highlands Univ	NM	11,904	LC
New Mexico State Univ	NM	14,050	LC
New York Univ	NY	68,139	MC
Newberry College	SC	34,550	C
Newman Univ	KS	37,382	C
Niagara Univ	NY	41,010	C
Norfolk State Univ	VA	18,902	LC
N Car A&T State Univ	NC	13,786	C
North Park Univ	IL	35,860	C
Northeastern Illinois Univ	IL	12,529	LC
Northeastern State Univ	OK	8,615	VC
Northern Arizona Univ	AZ	21,003	C
Northern Illinois Univ	IL	20,176	C
Northern Kentucky Univ	KY	16,486	C
Northern State Univ	SD	15,570	C
Northwest Missouri State Univ	MO	18,286	C
Northwestern College of Iowa	IA	38,400	C
Northwestern Okla State Univ	OK	13,072	LC
Northwestern State Univ of Louisiana	LA	16,534	LC
Notre Dame College	OH	39,150	VC
Notre Dame of Maryland Univ	MD	47,570	VC
Nova Southeastern Univ	FL	38,534	C+
Nyack College	NY	34,450	LC
Oglala Lakota College	SD	15,050	NC
Ohio Dominican Univ	OH	41,340	C+
Ohio Northern Univ	OH	44,050	VC
Ohio State Univ at Mansfield	OH	15,529	C
Ohio State Univ at Newark	OH	16,685	C
Ohio Univ	OH	23,394	VC
Ohio Wesleyan Univ	OH	49,460	VC
Okla Baptist Univ	OK	33,990	C
Okla Christian Univ	OK	29,260	C

ST = STATE $IS = IN-STATE COSTS   SR = SELECTOR RATING

School	ST	$IS	SR
Okla City Univ	OK	40,476	C
Olivet Nazarene Univ	IL	41,840	VC
Oral Roberts Univ	OK	34,316	C
Otterbein Univ	OH	41,630	C
Ouachita Baptist Univ	AR	33,500	VC
Our Lady of the Lake Univ	TX	37,790	LC
Pacific Union College	CA	36,009	VC
Paine College	GA	19,506	LC
Park Univ	MO	22,134	C
Pennsylvania State Univ - Univ Park	PA	29,716	HC
Philander Smith College	AR	20,814	LC
Piedmont College	GA	34,334	C
Pittsburg State Univ	KS	13,880	C
Point Park Univ	PA	41,270	C
Presbyterian College	SC	47,186	C
Prescott College	AZ	38,201	C
Purdue Univ Northwest	IN	15,178	C
Purdue Univ/West Lafayette	IN	20,032	MC
Rhode Island College	RI	19,000	LC
Rider Univ	NJ	54,050	C
Ripon College	WI	49,991	VC
Rivier Univ	NH	41,600	VC
Roberts Wesleyan College	NY	41,116	C
Roosevelt Univ	IL	41,890	VC
Rowan Univ	NJ	24,491	VC
St. Joseph's Univ	PA	58,540	VC
St. Mary-of-the-Woods College	IN	40,424	LC
St. Vincent College	PA	46,229	C
St. Xavier Univ	IL	44,440	C
Salisbury Univ	MD	21,132	VC
Salve Regina Univ	RI	53,046	VC
Samford Univ	AL	40,770	VC
San Jose State Univ	CA	22,630	C
Schreiner Univ	TX	34,626	LC
Seton Hill Univ	PA	46,972	VC
Shawnee State Univ	OH	16,998	C
Shippensburg Univ of Pennsylvania	PA	24,096	C
Shorter Univ	GA	31,130	LC
Silver Lake College of the Holy Family	WI	36,290	LC
Sinte Gleska Univ	SD	13,154	NC
Slippery Rock Univ of Pennsylvania	PA	20,450	C
Smith College	MA	66,774	MC
S Car State Univ	SC	21,330	LC
S Dak State Univ	SD	15,874	C
Southeast Missouri State Univ	MO	16,148	C
Southeastern Louisiana Univ	LA	16,237	C
Southeastern Okla State Univ	OK	11,875	C
Southeastern Univ	FL	34,910	LC
Southern Conn State Univ	CT	21,924	LC
Southern Illinois Univ Carbondale	IL	24,554	C
Southern Illinois Univ Edwardsville	IL	20,188	C
Southern Nazarene Univ	OK	33,684	C
Southern New Hampshire Univ	NH	44,256	C
Southern Oregon Univ	OR	19,117	C
Southern Univ and A&M College	LA	16,074	LC
Southern Univ at New Orleans	LA	8,014	LC
Southern Wesleyan Univ	SC	33,670	LC
Southwest Baptist Univ	MO	30,890	LC
Southwest Minn State Univ	MN	17,783	C
Southwestern College	KS	31,531	LC
Southwestern Okla State Univ	OK	12,205	C
Spring Hill College	AL	48,488	C
Springfield College	MA	48,775	C
St. Catherine Univ	MN	45,630	C
St. Cloud State Univ	MN	10,600	C
St. Joseph's College, New York/Brooklyn Campus	NY	25,114	LC
SUNY at Geneseo	NY	21,622	VC
SUNY at New Paltz	NY	20,840	C
SUNY/College at Old Westbury	NY	16,860	C
SUNY/Fredonia	NY	20,818	C
SUNY/Potsdam	NY	21,051	VC
Stephens College	MO	38,042	C
Stevenson Univ	MD	48,412	C
Susquehanna Univ	PA	57,560	VC
Syracuse Univ	NY	62,313	HC
Taylor Univ	IN	42,130	VC
Temple Univ	PA	24,392	C+
Tenn State Univ	TN	14,423	LC
Tenn Wesleyan Univ	TN	32,680	LC
Texas A&M Univ at Commerce	TX	10,496	C
Texas Christian Univ	TX	57,120	HC
Texas Tech Univ	TX	20,156	C+
The Catholic Univ of America	DC	58,376	VC
The College of New Jersey	NJ	28,675	VC+
The College of St. Rose	NY	44,010	C
The Univ of Akron	OH	22,566	C
The Univ of Alabama	AL	24,320	C+
The Univ of Arizona	AZ	24,086	C
The Univ of Mary	ND	23,180	C
The Univ of Montana Western	MT	9,426	LC
The Univ of Tenn at Chattanooga	TN	17,340	C+
The Univ of Texas at San Antonio	TX	21,060	C

School	ST	$IS	SR
Thomas College	ME	73,888	LC
Thomas Univ	GA	21,420	NC
Toccoa Falls College	GA	30,048	C
Towson Univ	MD	21,878	C
Trevecca Nazarene Univ	TN	31,186	C
Trinity Washington Univ	DC	33,826	C+
Troy Univ	AL	16,171	C
Tulane Univ	LA	67,496	MC
Tusculum College	TN	31,625	LC
Tuskegee Univ	AL	28,164	C
Univ of Alabama at Birmingham	AL	22,092	C
Univ of Arkansas at Fayetteville	AR	19,766	VC
Univ of Arkansas at Little Rock	AR	18,211	LC
Univ of Arkansas at Monticello	AR	13,599	LC
Univ of Arkansas at Pine Bluff	AR	13,541	C
Univ of Central Arkansas	AR	15,042	VC
Univ of Central Florida	FL	16,379	VC
Univ of Central Missouri	MO	18,982	C
Univ of Central Okla	OK	15,150	C
Univ of Cincinnati	OH	22,118	VC
Univ of Dayton	OH	54,930	VC
Univ of Delaware	DE	32,214	VC
Univ of Georgia	GA	21,878	HC
Univ of Hartford	CT	49,776	C
Univ of Illinois at Chicago	IL	24,664	VC
Univ of Illinois at Urbana-Champaign	IL	27,006	HC
Univ of Kansas	KS	20,884	VC
Univ of Kentucky	KY	24,800	C+
Univ of Louisville	KY	19,692	C
Univ of Maine at Farmington	ME	18,792	C
Univ of Mary Hardin-Baylor	TX	35,292	C+
Univ of Maryland/College Park	MD	21,938	HC
Univ of Mass Boston	MA	13,828	C
Univ of Mich/Dearborn	MI	12,472	VC
Univ of Mich/Flint	MI	19,062	C
Univ of Minn/Crookston	MN	19,126	C
Univ of Minn/Twin Cities	MN	24,269	MC
Univ of Missouri-Columbia	MO	20,463	VC
Univ of Missouri-Kansas City	MO	19,563	VC
Univ of Missouri-St. Louis	MO	19,810	VC
Univ of Mobile	AL	28,935	C
Univ of Mount Union	OH	39,990	C
Univ of Nebr - Kearney	NE	17,014	LC
Univ of Nebr - Lincoln	NE	18,589	VC
Univ of Nevada, Reno	NV	18,010	C
Univ of New Mexico	NM	16,808	C
Univ of New Orleans	LA	12,840	C
Univ of North Alabama	AL	15,964	C
Univ of N Car at Greensboro	NC	15,998	C
Univ of N Car at Pembroke	NC	14,737	LC
Univ of N Car Wilmington	NC	16,784	VC
Univ of N Dak	ND	16,673	C
Univ of North Georgia	GA	17,316	C
Univ of Northern Iowa	IA	17,480	C
Univ of Northwestern - St. Paul	MN	39,530	C
Univ of Okla	OK	19,651	HC
Univ of PR, at Bayamon	PR	13,145	
Univ of Rio Grande & Rio Grande Community College	OH	8,750	LC
Univ of Science and Arts of Okla	OK	11,140	VC
Univ of Scranton	PA	54,962	VC
Univ of Sioux Falls	SD	25,630	C
Univ of South Alabama	AL	16,880	C
Univ of S Car Aiken	SC	18,094	C
Univ of S Car at Columbia	SC	21,726	VC
Univ of S Car Upstate	SC	19,272	LC
Univ of Southern Indiana	IN	16,808	C
Univ of Southern Miss	MS	13,170	C
Univ of Texas Rio Grande Valley	TX	15,573	LC
Univ of the District of Columbia	DC	21,260	LC
Univ of the Ozarks	AR	31,050	NC
Univ of Toledo	OH	19,336	C
Univ of Vermont	VT	29,792	HC
Univ of West Alabama	AL	16,284	LC
Univ of West Florida	FL	15,848	C
Univ of West Georgia	GA	17,510	LC
Univ of Wisc-Parkside	WI	15,313	C
Univ of Wisc-Stevens Point	WI	14,043	C
Univ of Wisc-Stout	WI	19,667	C
Univ of Wisc-Whitewater	WI	13,976	C
Urbana Univ	OH	30,820	C
Ursuline College	OH	41,076	LC
Utah State Univ	UT	13,235	C
Vanderbilt Univ	TN	63,248	MC
Virginia Union Univ	VA	25,058	C
Walsh Univ	OH	39,010	C
Washburn Univ	KS	15,827	C
Washington State Univ	WA	22,747	C
Wayland Baptist Univ	TX	23,460	LC
Waynesburg Univ	PA	33,530	C
Weber State Univ	UT	14,112	C
Webster Univ	MO	37,490	C
Wellesley College	MA	66,984	MC
Wells College	NY	50,500	C
Wesleyan College	GA	31,940	C+
West Chester Univ of Pennsylvania	PA	19,171	VC

School	ST	$IS	SR
West Liberty Univ	WV	16,158	C
West Virginia State Univ	WV	19,412	LC
Western Carolina Univ	NC	13,965	C
Western Kentucky Univ	KY	16,850	C
Western Mich Univ	MI	21,791	C
Western Washington Univ	WA	18,904	VC
Westfield State Univ	MA	20,404	C
Westminster College	UT	41,078	C
Wheaton College	MA	63,818	VC
Wheelock College	MA	51,325	LC
Widener Univ	PA	58,190	C
William Woods Univ	MO	32,040	C
Wilmington College	OH	35,100	C
Wilmington Univ	DE	8,762	NC
Wilson College	PA	35,620	LC
Winona State Univ	MN	18,109	C
Winthrop Univ	SC	23,960	C
Worcester State Univ	MA	20,977	C
Wright State Univ	OH	16,983	C
Xavier Univ	OH	49,380	VC
Youngstown State Univ	OH	17,487	C

EARLY CHILDHOOD STUDIES

School	ST	$IS	SR
Becker College	MA	30,100	LC
Biola Univ	CA	48,686	C
Bluffton Univ	OH	40,950	C+
Boise State Univ	ID	17,368	C
Calif Baptist Univ	CA	42,986	C
Cal State, Fullerton	CA	21,902	C
Central Mich Univ	MI	20,330	C
Ferris State Univ	MI	21,458	C
Goodwin College	CT	28,370	LC
Grace Bible College	MI	25,250	C
Idaho State Univ	ID	13,619	LC
Langston Univ	OK	15,659	C
Mayville State Univ	ND	18,371	NC
Metropolitan State Univ	MN	7,859	C
Mills College	CA	43,705	C
Missouri Southern State Univ	MO	13,071	C
Missouri Western State Univ	MO	17,822	LC
Mount Mary Univ	WI	34,650	LC
National Univ	CA	17,849	LC
New York Univ	NY	68,139	MC
Niagara Univ	NY	41,010	C
Northern Illinois Univ	IL	20,176	C
Ohio State Univ at Columbus	OH	22,843	MC
Plymouth State Univ	NH	23,180	LC
Point Park Univ	PA	41,270	C
Rochester College	MI	28,574	LC
S Dak State Univ	SD	15,874	C
SUNY/Empire State College	NY	9,145	NC
SUNY/Fredonia	NY	20,818	C
SUNY/Potsdam	NY	21,051	VC
Univ of Dayton	OH	54,930	VC
Univ of Maryland/College Park	MD	21,938	HC
Univ of Minn/Duluth	MN	20,292	C
Univ of Missouri-Columbia	MO	20,463	VC
Univ of Nebr - Lincoln	NE	18,589	VC
Univ of N Car at Greensboro	NC	15,998	C
Univ of N Dak	ND	16,673	C
Univ of Texas Rio Grande Valley	TX	15,573	LC
Wayne State College	NE	25,746	NC
Weber State Univ	UT	14,112	C
West Chester Univ of Pennsylvania	PA	19,171	VC
Youngstown State Univ	OH	17,487	C

EARTH & SPACE SCIENCE

School	ST	$IS	SR
Arizona State Univ at the Tempe Campus	AZ	23,001	VC
Brown Univ	RI	64,566	MC
East Stroudsburg Univ	PA	18,578	LC
Indiana Univ Bloomington	IN	20,791	HC
Keene State College	NH	24,604	C
Kutztown Univ of Pennsylvania	PA	19,477	C
Stony Brook Univ/The SUNY	NY	22,703	MC
West Chester Univ of Pennsylvania	PA	19,171	VC

EARTH SCIENCE

School	ST	$IS	SR
Adams State Univ	CO	15,420	LC
Adrian College	MI	45,550	C
Alaska Pacific Univ	AK	28,730	VC
Albion College	MI	55,260	C
Arizona State Univ at the Tempe Campus	AZ	23,001	VC
Baylor Univ	TX	56,803	HC
Bemidji State Univ	MN	17,730	C
Boston Univ	MA	67,352	MC
Bowdoin College	ME	65,980	MC
Bowling Green State Univ	OH	19,975	C
Bridgewater State Univ	MA	22,762	C
Calif Polytechnic State Univ	CA	22,547	MC
Cal State, Fullerton	CA	21,902	C
Cal State, Long Beach	CA	18,850	C
Cal State, Monterey Bay	CA	22,872	LC
Cal State, Northridge	CA	17,277	LC
Calvin College	MI	43,090	HC
Central Conn State Univ	CT	22,041	C
Central Mich Univ	MI	20,330	C
Central Washington Univ	WA	16,803	C
CUNY/Brooklyn College	NY	7,163	C+
CUNY/City College	NY	20,204	C
Colo State Univ	CO	23,033	C
Columbia Univ/City of New York	NY	62,958	MC
Columbus State Univ	GA	14,336	LC
Dartmouth College	NH	68,109	MC
DePauw Univ	IN	58,688	VC
Dickinson College	PA	66,166	MC
Dickinson State Univ	ND	12,372	LC
Eastern Mich Univ	MI	19,761	C
Edinboro Univ	PA	15,940	LC
Emporia State Univ	KS	15,029	C
Fitchburg State Univ	MA	21,819	LC
Frostburg State Univ	MD	17,280	LC
George Mason Univ	VA	19,884	C
Georgia Inst of Technology	GA	23,910	MC
Grand Valley State Univ	MI	22,250	C+
Indiana Univ of Pennsylvania	PA	24,474	C
Indiana Univ-Purdue Univ Fort Wayne	IN	18,675	C
Iowa State Univ	IA	18,176	C
Jackson State Univ	MS	15,879	LC
Johns Hopkins Univ	MD	68,080	MC
Kean Univ	NJ	25,620	C
Kent State Univ	OH	20,928	C
Lehigh Univ	PA	63,860	MC
Lock Haven Univ of Pennsylvania	PA	20,544	LC
Mass Inst of Technology	MA	62,662	MC
Mercer Univ	GA	45,348	VC
Mercyhurst Univ	PA	47,420	C
Miami Univ	OH	27,190	HC+
Mich State Univ	MI	24,542	VC
Millersville Univ of Pennsylvania	PA	25,298	C
Minn State Univ, Mankato	MN	17,190	C
Minn State Univ, Moorhead	MN	21,393	C
Minot State Univ	ND	13,285	C
Montana State Univ	MT	15,500	C+
Morehead State Univ	KY	18,386	LC
Murray State Univ	KY	17,726	C+
Muskingum Univ	OH	35,966	C
National Univ	CA	17,849	LC
New Mexico Inst of Mining and Technology	NM	15,385	HC+
New York Univ	NY	68,139	MC
N Car State Univ	NC	22,434	HC+
N Dak State Univ	ND	16,245	VC
Northeastern Illinois Univ	IL	12,529	LC
Northeastern Univ	MA	65,352	MC
Northern Mich Univ	MI	20,853	C
Northland College	WI	41,103	C+
Northwest Missouri State Univ	MO	18,286	C
Ohio State Univ at Columbus	OH	22,843	MC
Ohio Univ	OH	23,394	VC
Ohio Wesleyan Univ	OH	49,460	VC
Old Dominion Univ	VA	21,618	C
Oregon State Univ	OR	23,337	VC
Otterbein Univ	OH	41,630	C
Point Park Univ	PA	41,270	C
Prescott College	AZ	38,201	C
Purdue Univ/West Lafayette	IN	20,032	MC
Rice Univ	TX	59,458	MC
St. Louis Univ	MO	49,866	HC
Salem State Univ	MA	42,650	LC
Salisbury Univ	MD	21,132	VC
San Francisco State Univ	CA	18,514	LC
Shippensburg Univ of Pennsylvania	PA	24,096	C
Slippery Rock Univ of Pennsylvania	PA	20,450	C
Southern Conn State Univ	CT	21,924	LC
Southern Illinois Univ Edwardsville	IL	20,188	C
St. Cloud State Univ	MN	10,600	C
St. Mary's Univ	TX	39,120	C
Stanford Univ	CA	62,541	MC
SUNY Albany	NY	22,165	C
SUNY at Oswego	NY	22,219	VC
SUNY/Buffalo State	NY	20,583	LC
SUNY/Fredonia	NY	20,818	C
SUNY/Oneonta	NY	20,794	C
Susquehanna Univ	PA	57,560	VC
Syracuse Univ	NY	62,313	HC
Tarleton State Univ	TX	15,248	LC
Texas A&M Univ at Commerce	TX	10,496	C
The College at Brockport - SUNY	NY	21,058	C
The Univ of Memphis	TN	18,278	C
The Univ of Utah	UT	18,751	VC
Towson Univ	MD	21,878	C
Trinity Univ	TX	54,480	MC
Tulane Univ	LA	67,496	MC
Univ of Alabama in Huntsville	AL	20,028	VC
Univ of Alaska Fairbanks	AK	16,874	VC
Univ of Arkansas at Fayetteville	AR	19,766	VC
Univ of Calif at Berkeley	CA	29,886	MC
Univ of Calif at Irvine	CA	33,857	VC
Univ of Calif at Los Angeles	CA	27,438	HC+
Univ of Calif at Santa Barbara	CA	30,627	HC+
Univ of Calif San Diego	CA	30,450	MC
Univ of Calif, Santa Cruz	CA	28,731	C+
Univ of Central Missouri	MO	18,982	C
Univ of Florida	FL	16,291	HC+

ST = STATE $IS = IN-STATE COSTS SR = SELECTOR RATING

School	ST	$IS	SR
Univ of Illinois at Chicago	IL	24,664	VC
Univ of Indianapolis	IN	36,480	VC
Univ of Maine	ME	21,038	VC
Univ of Mass Amherst	MA	27,669	HC
Univ of Mass Boston	MA	13,828	C
Univ of Mass Lowell	MA	27,296	VC
Univ of Mich/Ann Arbor	MI	25,274	MC
Univ of Minn/Twin Cities	MN	24,269	MC
Univ of Nevada, Las Vegas	NV	17,553	C
Univ of New Hampshire	NH	29,333	VC
Univ of New Mexico	NM	16,808	C
Univ of New Orleans	LA	12,840	C
Univ of N Car at Charlotte	NC	17,803	VC
Univ of N Car at Greensboro	NC	15,998	C
Univ of Northern Colo	CO	19,658	C
Univ of Northern Iowa	IA	17,480	C
Univ of Oregon	OR	24,021	VC
Univ of S Dak	SD	16,109	C
Univ of Texas at El Paso	TX	34,452	NC
Univ of Wisc-Green Bay	WI	15,184	C
Univ of Wyoming	WY	15,537	C
Utah State Univ	UT	13,235	C
Vanderbilt Univ	TN	63,248	MC
Vassar College	NY	68,110	MC
Virginia Wesleyan Univ	VA	45,980	LC
Washington State Univ	WA	22,747	C
Washington Univ in St. Louis	MO	67,539	MC
Weber State Univ	UT	14,112	C
Wesleyan Univ	CT	66,940	MC
West Chester Univ of Pennsylvania	PA	19,171	VC
Western Conn State Univ	CT	21,254	LC
Western Mich Univ	MI	21,791	C
Western Oregon Univ	OR	19,965	LC
Western Washington Univ	WA	18,904	VC
Wilkes Univ	PA	49,166	C
Winona State Univ	MN	18,109	C

EARTH SCIENCE / ADOLESCENCE EDUCATION

School	ST	$IS	SR
Augustana College	IL	51,222	VC+
Elizabethtown College	PA	56,340	VC
LIU Post	NY	50,698	C+
Murray State Univ	KY	17,726	C+
Old Dominion Univ	VA	21,618	C
Pace Univ	NY	60,136	C
SUNY at Oswego	NY	22,219	VC
SUNY/Potsdam	NY	21,051	VC
Syracuse Univ	NY	62,313	HC
Temple Univ	PA	24,392	C+
Univ of Nebr - Lincoln	NE	18,589	VC
Univ of New Hampshire	NH	29,333	VC
Weber State Univ	UT	14,112	C
Wichita State Univ	KS	17,773	C
Winona State Univ	MN	18,109	C

EAST ASIAN LANGUAGES AND LITERATURE

School	ST	$IS	SR
Austin College	TX	51,059	HC
Beloit College	WI	55,206	HC
Indiana Univ Bloomington	IN	20,791	HC
Miami Univ	OH	27,190	HC+
Mich State Univ	MI	24,542	VC
Smith College	MA	66,774	MC
Univ of Chicago	IL	70,551	MC
Univ of Florida	FL	16,291	HC+
Univ of Illinois at Urbana-Champaign	IL	27,006	HC
Univ of Kansas	KS	20,884	VC
Univ of Puget Sound	WA	60,210	HC
Univ of Southern Calif	CA	66,631	MC
Washington Univ in St. Louis	MO	67,539	MC
Wellesley College	MA	66,984	MC
Yale Univ	CT	64,650	MC

EAST ASIAN STUDIES

School	ST	$IS	SR
Appalachian State Univ	NC	15,394	VC
Augsburg Univ	MN	45,129	C
Barnard College/Columbia Univ	NY	68,762	MC
Bates College	ME	64,500	HC
Brandeis Univ	MA	68,443	MC
Brown Univ	RI	64,566	MC
Bryn Mawr College	PA	65,220	MC
Bucknell Univ	PA	67,136	MC
Cal State, Fullerton	CA	21,902	C
CUNY/Queens College	NY	21,507	C
Colby College	ME	64,060	MC
Columbia Univ/ School of General Studies	NY	61,470	MC
Columbia Univ/City of New York	NY	62,958	MC
Conn College	CT	65,000	MC
Davidson College	NC	60,119	MC
Denison Univ	OH	62,770	HC+
DePaul Univ	IL	52,807	VC
DePauw Univ	IN	58,688	VC
Dickinson College	PA	66,166	MC
Eckerd College	FL	55,206	VC
Emory and Henry College	VA	46,320	C
Gettysburg College	PA	65,210	MC
Hamline Univ	MN	50,152	C
Haverford College	PA	66,490	MC
Indiana Univ Bloomington	IN	20,791	HC
John Carroll Univ	OH	51,570	C
Johns Hopkins Univ	MD	68,080	MC
Kalamazoo College	MI	53,931	HC
Lawrence Univ	WI	56,133	HC+
Lewis & Clark College	OR	60,984	MC
Middlebury College	VT	67,464	MC
Minn State Univ, Moorhead	MN	21,393	C
Mount Holyoke College	MA	56,746	MC
New York Univ	NY	68,139	MC
North Central College	IL	48,712	C+
Oakland Univ	MI	20,763	C
Oberlin College	OH	68,942	MC
Occidental College	CA	68,660	MC
Ohio Wesleyan Univ	OH	49,460	VC
Princeton Univ	NJ	60,090	MC
Rutgers Univ - New Brunswick	NJ	27,090	HC
Simmons College	MA	54,400	HC
Stanford Univ	CA	62,541	MC
SUNY Albany	NY	22,165	C
SUNY at Binghamton	NY	24,100	MC
The George Washington Univ	DC	68,474	HC+
The Univ of Arizona	AZ	24,086	C
Univ of Calif at Davis	CA	28,468	HC
Univ of Calif at Irvine	CA	33,857	VC
Univ of Calif at Los Angeles	CA	27,438	HC+
Univ of Delaware	DE	32,214	VC
Univ of Illinois at Urbana-Champaign	IL	27,006	HC
Univ of Minn/Twin Cities	MN	24,269	MC
Univ of Rochester	NY	65,032	MC
Univ of Southern Calif	CA	66,631	MC
Ursinus College	PA	62,920	VC
Valparaiso Univ	IN	50,160	VC
Vanderbilt Univ	TN	63,248	MC
Washington and Lee Univ	VA	59,647	MC
Washington Univ in St. Louis	MO	67,539	MC
Wesleyan Univ	CT	66,940	MC
Western Washington Univ	WA	18,904	VC
Wittenberg Univ	OH	49,863	VC
Yale Univ	CT	64,650	MC

EASTERN EUROPEAN STUDIES

School	ST	$IS	SR
Bowdoin College	ME	65,980	MC
Florida State Univ	FL	16,771	HC
Indiana Univ Bloomington	IN	20,791	HC
Oberlin College	OH	68,942	MC
Ohio Univ	OH	23,394	VC
The Univ of Texas at Austin	TX	20,206	MC
Univ of Mich/Ann Arbor	MI	25,274	MC
Washington Univ in St. Louis	MO	67,539	MC
Yale Univ	CT	64,650	MC

ECOGASTRONOMY

School	ST	$IS	SR
Univ of New Hampshire	NH	29,333	VC

ECOLOGY

School	ST	$IS	SR
Adams State Univ	CO	15,420	LC
Angelo State Univ	TX	15,882	LC
Appalachian State Univ	NC	15,394	VC
Augusta Univ	GA	4,632	C
Beloit College	WI	55,206	HC
Bennington College	VT	66,280	MC
Boston Univ	MA	67,352	MC
Brewton-Parker College	GA	26,120	LC
Brown Univ	RI	64,566	MC
Bryant Univ	RI	57,204	VC
Cal State, Fullerton	CA	21,902	C
Cal State, Long Beach	CA	18,850	C
Castleton Univ	VT	20,186	C
Colo State Univ	CO	23,033	C
Defiance College	OH	42,240	LC
Florida Inst of Technology	FL	53,306	VC
Florida State Univ	FL	16,771	HC
Goshen College	IN	44,350	C
Hampshire College	MA	65,214	MC
Idaho State Univ	ID	13,619	LC
Kutztown Univ of Pennsylvania	PA	19,477	C
Le Moyne College	NY	47,305	VC
Marshall Univ	WV	18,044	C
Mich Tech Univ	MI	25,551	VC+
Missouri Southern State Univ	MO	13,071	C
Montana State Univ-Northern	MT	11,370	NC
New Mexico State Univ	NM	14,050	LC
Northern Mich Univ	MI	20,853	C
Northwest Missouri State Univ	MO	18,286	C
Northwestern Univ	IL	68,725	MC
Ohio State Univ at Columbus	OH	22,843	MC
Ohio Univ	OH	23,394	VC
Oregon State Univ	OR	23,337	VC
Prescott College	AZ	38,201	C
Princeton Univ	NJ	60,090	MC
Purdue Univ Northwest	IN	15,178	C
Purdue Univ/West Lafayette	IN	20,032	MC
San Diego State Univ	CA	23,156	VC
San Francisco State Univ	CA	18,514	LC
S Dak State Univ	SD	15,874	C
Southern Illinois Univ Edwardsville	IL	20,188	C
SUNY/Plattsburgh	NY	19,314	C
SUNY/The College of Environmental Science and Forestry	NY	23,728	VC
Sterling College	VT	41,894	VC
Susquehanna Univ	PA	57,560	VC
Texas A&M Univ at College Station	TX	20,771	VC+
The Univ of Arizona	AZ	24,086	C
Trinity Univ	TX	54,480	MC
Tulane Univ	LA	67,496	MC
Unity College	ME	37,670	C
Univ of Calif at Davis	CA	28,468	HC
Univ of Calif at Irvine	CA	33,857	VC
Univ of Calif at Los Angeles	CA	27,438	HC+
Univ of Calif at Santa Barbara	CA	30,627	HC+
Univ of Calif San Diego	CA	30,450	MC
Univ of Calif, Santa Cruz	CA	28,731	C+
Univ of Colo Boulder	CO	26,048	HC
Univ of Conn	CT	27,394	
Univ of Denver	CO	61,129	VC+
Univ of Georgia	GA	21,878	HC
Univ of Mich/Ann Arbor	MI	25,274	MC
Univ of Mich/Flint	MI	19,062	C
Univ of Minn/Twin Cities	MN	24,269	MC
Univ of Montana	MT	14,105	C
Univ of Pittsburgh	PA	30,030	MC
Univ of Rochester	NY	65,032	MC
Univ of Wyoming	WY	15,537	C
Vanderbilt Univ	TN	63,248	MC
Washington Univ in St. Louis	MO	67,539	MC
West Liberty Univ	WV	16,158	C
Western Washington Univ	WA	18,904	VC

ECONOMICS

School	ST	$IS	SR
Adams State Univ	CO	15,420	LC
Adelphi Univ	NY	49,792	C
Adrian College	MI	45,550	C
Agnes Scott College	GA	51,930	VC+
Alabama A&M Univ	AL	18,796	C
Albion College	MI	55,260	C
Albright College	PA	57,326	C
Alcorn State Univ	MS	15,884	C
Allegheny College	PA	57,620	VC
Alma College	MI	49,410	VC
American International College	MA	47,020	LC
Amherst College	MA	66,186	MC
Anderson Univ	IN	39,450	C
Andrews Univ	MI	41,732	C
Appalachian State Univ	NC	15,394	VC
Aquinas College - Mich	MI	38,876	VC
Arizona State Univ at the Tempe Campus	AZ	23,001	VC
Arkansas State Univ	AR	16,190	C
Arkansas Tech Univ	AR	16,534	LC
Armstrong State Univ	GA	15,615	C
Ashland Univ	OH	30,446	C
Assumption College	MA	48,455	VC
Auburn Univ	AL	24,300	VC+
Auburn Univ at Montgomery	AL	15,000	C
Augsburg Univ	MN	45,129	C
Augustana College	IL	51,222	VC+
Augustana Univ	SD	39,968	VC
Austin College	TX	51,059	HC
Baker Univ	KS	37,190	C
Baldwin Wallace Univ	OH	42,464	VC
Ball State Univ	IN	19,808	C+
Bard College	NY	65,924	HC
Barnard College/Columbia Univ	NY	68,762	MC
Barry Univ	FL	38,730	LC
Barton College	NC	39,854	C
Bates College	ME	64,500	HC
Baylor Univ	TX	56,803	HC
Bellarmine Univ	KY	52,532	C
Belmont Univ	TN	44,500	VC+
Beloit College	WI	55,206	HC
Bemidji State Univ	MN	17,730	C
Benedict College	SC	28,630	NC
Benedictine College	KS	38,850	VC
Benedictine Univ	IL	38,300	C
Bentley Univ	MA	63,720	MC
Berea College	KY	7,094	C
Berry College	GA	47,466	VC
Bethany College	WV	38,774	LC
Bethel College	IN	36,830	C
Bethel Univ	MN	46,550	C+
Biola Univ	CA	48,686	C+
Birmingham-Southern College	AL	44,478	C+
Black Hills State Univ	SD	16,622	C
Bloomsburg Univ of Pennsylvania	PA	19,930	C
Bluffton Univ	OH	40,950	C+
Boise State Univ	ID	17,368	C
Boston College	MA	68,043	MC
Boston Univ	MA	67,352	MC
Bowdoin College	ME	65,980	MC
Bowling Green State Univ	OH	19,975	C
Bradley Univ	IL	43,240	VC
Brandeis Univ	MA	68,443	MC
Bridgewater College	VA	46,260	C
Bridgewater State Univ	MA	22,762	C
Brigham Young Univ	UT	13,248	MC
Brown Univ	RI	64,566	MC
Bryant Univ	RI	57,204	VC
Bryn Mawr College	PA	65,220	MC
Bucknell Univ	PA	67,136	MC
Butler Univ	IN	52,890	VC+
Cabrini Univ	PA	42,591	LC
Calif Inst of Technology	CA	64,704	MC
Calif Lutheran Univ	CA	52,853	C
Calif Polytechnic State Univ	CA	22,547	MC
Calif State Polytechnic Univ, Pomona	CA	21,811	C
Cal State, Bakersfield	CA	22,397	LC
Cal State, Chico	CA	19,790	VC
Cal State, East Bay	CA	20,748	C
Cal State, Fresno	CA	16,902	LC
Cal State, Fullerton	CA	21,902	C
Cal State, Long Beach	CA	18,850	C
Cal State, Los Angeles	CA	17,186	LC
Cal State, Northridge	CA	17,277	LC
Cal State, Sacramento	CA	19,060	C
Cal State, San Bernardino	CA	20,106	C
Cal State, San Marcos	CA	20,604	LC
Cal State, Stanislaus	CA	18,053	LC
Calvin College	MI	43,090	HC
Campbell Univ	NC	37,570	VC
Campbellsville Univ	KY	33,400	C
Capital Univ	OH	44,778	VC
Carleton College	MN	66,414	MC
Carnegie Mellon Univ	PA	67,980	MC
Carroll Univ	WI	38,100	C+
Carson-Newman Univ	TN	35,900	C
Carthage College	WI	48,835	C
Case Western Reserve Univ	OH	62,284	MC
Castleton Univ	VT	20,186	C
Catawba College	NC	39,820	LC
Cedarville Univ	OH	36,244	VC
Centenary College of Louisiana	LA	49,050	C+
Central College	IA	44,592	C
Central Conn State Univ	CT	22,041	C
Central Mich Univ	MI	20,330	C
Central State Univ	OH	18,564	C
Central Washington Univ	WA	16,803	C
Centre College	KY	50,680	MC
Chapman Univ	CA	65,504	HC
Charleston Southern Univ	SC	34,700	C
Chatham Univ	PA	47,883	VC
Cheyney Univ of Pennsylvania	PA	20,896	LC
Chicago State Univ	IL	41,620	C
Christopher Newport Univ	VA	24,878	VC+
CUNY/Baruch College	NY	21,609	HC
CUNY/Brooklyn College	NY	7,163	C+
CUNY/City College	NY	20,204	C
CUNY/Hunter College	NY	31,098	VC
CUNY/John Jay College of Criminal Justice	NY	6,359	SP
CUNY/Lehman College	NY	5,788	LC
CUNY/Queens College	NY	21,507	C
CUNY/York College	NY	6,747	LC
Claremont McKenna College	CA	69,900	MC
Clarion Univ of Pennsylvania	PA	21,608	LC
Clark Atlanta Univ	GA	31,019	LC
Clark Univ	MA	53,260	HC+
Clayton State Univ	GA	19,735	LC
Clemson Univ	SC		HC
Cleveland State Univ	OH	22,290	C
Coastal Carolina Univ	SC	20,340	C
Coe College	IA	51,570	VC
Colby College	ME	64,060	MC
Colgate Univ	NY	67,500	MC
College of Charleston	SC	24,046	VC
College of Mount St. Vincent	NY	45,620	C
College of St. Benedict	MN	54,480	C
College of St. Scholastica	MN	45,734	C+
College of Staten Island	NY	24,389	LC
College of the Holy Cross	MA	64,320	MC
College of William & Mary	VA	34,907	MC
Colo College	CO	64,894	MC
Colo School of Mines	CO	29,319	MC
Colo State Univ	CO	23,033	C
Colo State Univ-Pueblo	CO	21,581	C
Columbia Univ/ School of General Studies	NY	61,470	MC
Columbia Univ/City of New York	NY	62,958	MC
Conn College	CT	65,000	MC
Converse College	SC	28,290	C
Cornell College	IA	49,900	VC
Cornell Univ	NY	67,591	MC
Covenant College	GA	44,590	HC
Creighton Univ	NE	49,452	VC
Dallas Baptist Univ	TX	35,220	VC
Dartmouth College	NH	68,109	MC
Davidson College	NC	60,119	MC
Davis & Elkins College	WV	38,242	LC
Delaware State Univ	DE	19,376	LC
Denison Univ	OH	62,770	HC+
DePaul Univ	IL	52,807	VC
DePauw Univ	IN	58,688	VC
Dickinson College	PA	66,166	MC
Dillard Univ	LA	20,940	VC
Doane Univ	NE	41,340	VC
Dominican Univ	IL	42,472	C+
Dordt College	IA	37,860	C+
Drake Univ	IA	49,220	HC
Drew Univ/College of Liberal Arts	NJ	53,608	VC
Drexel Univ	PA	65,927	HC
Drury Univ	MO	37,555	VC
Duke Univ	NC	68,298	MC
Duquesne Univ	PA	48,508	VC
Earlham College	IN	55,670	HC
East Carolina Univ	NC	16,539	C
East Stroudsburg Univ	PA	18,578	LC
East Tenn State Univ	TN	18,141	C

ST = STATE **$IS** = IN-STATE COSTS **SR** = SELECTOR RATING

School	ST	$IS	SR
Eastern Conn State Univ	CT	23,059	C
Eastern Illinois Univ	IL	21,414	C
Eastern Kentucky Univ	KY	17,742	C
Eastern Mennonite Univ	VA	42,550	C
Eastern Mich Univ	MI	19,761	C
Eastern Washington Univ	WA	17,896	LC
Eckerd College	FL	55,206	VC
Edgewood College	WI	35,950	C
Edinboro Univ	PA	15,940	LC
Elizabethtown College	PA	56,340	VC
Elmhurst College	IL	46,514	C
Elon Univ	NC	46,142	HC
Emmanuel College	MA	53,472	C+
Emory and Henry College	VA	46,320	C
Emory Univ	GA	63,286	MC
Emporia State Univ	KS	15,029	C
Eugene Lang College of Liberal Arts	NY	64,940	VC
Excelsior College	NY	38,800	SP
Fairfield Univ	CT	61,445	HC
Fairleigh Dickinson Univ/ College at Florham	NJ	54,770	C
Fairleigh Dickinson Univ/ Metropolitan Campus	NJ	52,392	C
Fayetteville State Univ	NC	17,756	C
Fisk Univ	TN	32,066	LC
Fitchburg State Univ	MA	21,819	LC
Flagler College	FL	27,620	C
Florida A&M Univ	FL	15,361	C
Florida Atlantic Univ	FL	18,256	C
Florida Gulf Coast Univ	FL	14,738	C
Florida International Univ	FL	20,281	C
Florida Southern College	FL	45,978	VC
Florida State Univ	FL	16,771	HC
Fordham Univ	NY	68,431	MC
Fort Hays State Univ	KS	12,677	C
Fort Lewis College	CO	20,154	C
Fort Valley State Univ	GA	17,988	VC
Framingham State Univ	MA	21,740	C
Francis Marion Univ	SC	18,144	LC
Franciscan Univ of Steubenville	OH	33,980	VC
Franklin and Marshall College	PA	67,960	MC
Franklin College	IN	40,550	C
Frostburg State Univ	MD	17,280	LC
Furman Univ	SC	61,098	VC+
Gallaudet Univ	DC	30,088	LC
George Fox Univ	OR	42,938	C
George Mason Univ	VA	19,884	C
Georgetown College	KY	41,440	C
Georgetown Univ	DC	68,970	MC
Georgia College & State Univ	GA	21,884	C+
Georgia Inst of Technology	GA	23,910	MC
Georgia Southern Univ	GA	16,540	VC
Georgia State Univ	GA	25,250	C
Gettysburg College	PA	65,210	MC
Goldey-Beacom College	DE	36,038	C
Gonzaga Univ	WA	52,880	HC
Gordon College	MA	47,740	VC
Goshen College	IN	44,350	C
Goucher College	MD	56,110	VC
Graceland Univ	IA	35,290	C
Grambling State Univ	LA	15,701	C
Grand Valley State Univ	MI	22,250	C+
Grinnell College	IA	63,114	MC
Grove City College	PA	26,654	VC
Guilford College	NC	45,973	C
Gustavus Adolphus College	MN	53,943	HC
Hamilton College	NY	64,250	MC
Hamline Univ	MN	50,152	C
Hampden-Sydney College	VA	57,806	VC
Hampshire College	MA	65,214	MC
Hampton Univ	VA	36,410	C
Hanover College	IN	47,750	C+
Harding Univ	AR	25,440	C
Hardin-Simmons Univ	TX	36,025	C
Hartwick College	NY	51,270	C
Harvard College/Harvard Univ	MA	65,609	MC
Hastings College	NE	35,380	C+
Haverford College	PA	66,490	MC
Hawaii Pacific Univ	HI	33,420	C
Heidelberg Univ	OH	40,400	LC
Hendrix College	AR	54,020	VC
Hillsdale College	MI	37,170	MC
Hiram College	OH	44,590	C
Hobart and William Smith Colleges	NY	67,050	HC+
Hofstra Univ	NY	58,210	C+
Hollins Univ	VA	49,635	VC
Hood College	MD	50,540	C
Hope College	MI	42,840	VC
Houston Baptist Univ	TX	36,450	C
Howard Univ	DC	37,616	C+
Huntington Univ	IN	33,996	C
Idaho State Univ	ID	13,619	LC
Illinois College	IL	41,330	VC
Illinois State Univ	IL	23,418	VC
Illinois Wesleyan Univ	IL	56,430	VC+
Immaculata Univ	PA	39,000	C
Indiana State Univ	IN	23,223	LC
Indiana Univ Bloomington	IN	20,791	HC
Indiana Univ Northwest	IN	7,207	LC
Indiana Univ of Pennsylvania	PA	24,474	C
Indiana Univ South Bend	IN	16,057	C
Indiana Univ Southeast	IN	16,931	C
Indiana Univ-Purdue Univ Fort Wayne	IN	18,675	C
Indiana Univ-Purdue Univ Indianapolis	IN	18,952	C
Indiana Wesleyan Univ	IN	33,674	C
Inter-American Univ of PR-San Germán	PR	20,042	
Iona College	NY	52,514	C
Iowa State Univ	IA	18,176	C
Ithaca College	NY	58,158	VC+
Jackson State Univ	MS	15,879	LC
Jacksonville State Univ	AL	14,628	LC
Jacksonville Univ	FL	49,210	C
James Madison Univ	VA	19,084	VC
John Carroll Univ	OH	51,570	C
Johns Hopkins Univ	MD	68,080	MC
Johnson C. Smith Univ	NC	25,336	LC
Juniata College	PA	58,118	VC
Kalamazoo College	MI	53,931	HC
Kansas State Univ	KS	17,780	VC
Kean Univ	NJ	25,620	C
Keene State College	NH	24,604	C
Kennesaw State Univ	GA	18,899	VC
Kent State Univ	OH	20,928	C
Kenyon College	OH	65,840	MC
King's College	PA	48,240	C
Knox College	IL	54,654	VC+
Kutztown Univ of Pennsylvania	PA	19,477	C
La Salle Univ	PA	43,476	C
Lafayette College	PA	68,520	MC
Lake Forest College	IL	50,652	VC
Lake Superior State Univ	MI	19,867	C
Lakeland Univ	WI	35,130	C
Lamar Univ	TX	18,014	LC
Langston Univ	OK	15,659	C
Lawrence Univ	WI	56,133	HC+
Le Moyne College	NY	47,305	VC
Lebanon Valley College	PA	55,510	VC
Lehigh Univ	PA	63,860	MC
Lenoir-Rhyne Univ	NC	47,500	LC
Lewis & Clark College	OR	60,984	MC
Lewis Univ	IL	41,710	C
Limestone College	SC	32,100	C
Linfield College	OR	53,992	C
Lipscomb Univ	TN	42,984	VC
LIU Brooklyn	NY	50,698	C
LIU Post	NY	50,698	C+
Lock Haven Univ of Pennsylvania	PA	20,544	LC
Longwood Univ	VA	22,184	C
Loras College	IA	40,726	C
Louisiana State Univ and A&M College	LA	18,677	VC
Loyola Marymount Univ	CA	60,202	VC+
Loyola Univ Chicago	IL	57,158	VC
Loyola Univ Maryland	MD	61,710	VC
Loyola Univ New Orleans	LA	52,456	VC
Lubbock Christian Univ	TX	29,727	C
Luther College	IA	49,990	VC
Lycoming College	PA	50,895	C
Lyon College	AR	36,120	VC
Macalester College	MN	64,136	MC
Manchester Univ	IN	41,540	C
Manhattan College	NY	55,652	C
Manhattanville College	NY	52,430	C
Marietta College	OH	46,190	C
Marist College	NY	49,860	VC
Marlboro College	VT	50,832	VC+
Marquette Univ	WI	53,090	VC+
Marshall Univ	WV	18,044	C
Mary Baldwin Univ	VA	40,495	C
Marymount Univ	VA	43,231	C
Maryville College	TN	44,410	C
Mass Inst of Technology	MA	62,662	MC
McDaniel College	MD	52,910	VC
McKendree Univ	IL	37,940	C+
Mercer Univ	GA	45,348	VC
Meredith College	NC	46,634	C
Merrimack College	MA	55,415	C
Messiah College	PA	44,380	VC
Methodist Univ	NC	58,130	C
Metropolitan State Univ	MN	7,859	C
Metropolitan State Univ of Denver	CO	6,928	LC
Miami Univ	OH	27,190	HC+
Mich State Univ	MI	24,542	VC
Mich Tech Univ	MI	25,551	VC+
Middle Tenn State Univ	TN	8,650	C
Middlebury College	VT	67,464	MC
Midland Univ	NE	39,512	C
Midwestern State Univ	TX	12,111	LC
Millersville Univ of Pennsylvania	PA	25,298	C
Mills College	CA	43,705	C
Millsaps College	MS	50,080	C+
Minn State Univ, Mankato	MN	17,190	C
Minn State Univ, Moorhead	MN	21,393	C
Minot State Univ	ND	13,285	C
Miss State Univ	MS	12,028	C+
Missouri Southern State Univ	MO	13,071	C
Missouri State Univ	MO	15,837	C+
Missouri Univ of Science and Technology	MO	18,655	HC
Missouri Valley College	MO	28,150	C
Missouri Western State Univ	MO	17,822	LC
Monmouth College	IL	42,260	C
Montana State Univ	MT	15,500	C+
Montclair State Univ	NJ	26,912	C
Moravian College	PA	55,488	C
Morehouse College	GA	40,835	C
Morgan State Univ	MD	17,190	LC
Mount Holyoke College	MA	56,746	MC
Mount St. Mary's Univ	MD	53,380	C
Muhlenberg College	PA	56,645	VC
Murray State Univ	KY	17,726	C+
Muskingum Univ	OH	35,966	C
Nazareth College	NY	46,784	C
Nebr Wesleyan Univ	NE	42,026	C+
New College of Florida	FL	16,180	HC+
New Jersey City Univ	NJ	21,456	LC
New Mexico State Univ	NM	14,050	LC
New York Univ	NY	68,139	MC
Niagara Univ	NY	41,010	C
Nichols College	MA	46,900	LC
N Car A&T State Univ	NC	13,786	C
N Car State Univ	NC	22,434	HC+
North Central College	IL	48,712	C+
North Central Univ	MN	30,610	C
N Dak State Univ	ND	16,245	VC
North Park Univ	IL	35,860	C
Northeastern Illinois Univ	IL	12,529	LC
Northeastern Univ	MA	65,352	MC
Northern Illinois Univ	IL	20,176	C
Northern Kentucky Univ	KY	16,486	C
Northern Mich Univ	MI	20,853	C
Northern State Univ	SD	15,570	C
Northwest Missouri State Univ	MO	18,286	C
Northwestern College of Iowa	IA	38,400	C
Northwestern Okla State Univ	OK	13,072	LC
Northwestern Univ	IL	68,725	MC
Notre Dame College	OH	39,150	VC
Notre Dame of Maryland Univ	MD	47,570	VC
Oakland Univ	MI	20,763	C
Oberlin College	OH	68,942	MC
Occidental College	CA	68,660	MC
Oglethorpe Univ	GA	44,200	C
Ohio Dominican Univ	OH	41,340	C+
Ohio State Univ at Columbus	OH	22,843	MC
Ohio Univ	OH	23,394	VC
Ohio Wesleyan Univ	OH	49,460	VC
Okla City Univ	OK	40,476	C
Okla State Univ	OK	17,180	C+
Old Dominion Univ	VA	21,618	C
Olivet College	MI	37,661	LC
Olivet Nazarene Univ	IL	41,840	VC
Oregon State Univ	OR	23,337	VC
Otterbein Univ	OH	41,630	C
Pace Univ	NY	60,136	C
Pacific Lutheran Univ	WA	49,960	C
Pacific Univ	OR	37,617	C
Park Univ	MO	22,134	C
Penn State Erie,The Behrend College	PA	26,688	VC
Pennsylvania State Univ - Univ Park	PA	29,716	HC
Pepperdine Univ	CA	66,862	VC+
Pitzer College	CA	68,500	HC+
Plymouth State Univ	NH	23,180	LC
Point Loma Nazarene Univ	CA	46,150	C+
Pomona College	CA	64,957	MC
Portland State Univ	OR	19,443	C
Princeton Univ	NJ	60,090	MC
Principia College	IL	40,350	C
Providence College	RI	62,870	HC
Purdue Univ/West Lafayette	IN	20,032	MC
Quinnipiac Univ	CT	60,970	VC
Radford Univ	VA	19,758	C
Ramapo College of New Jersey	NJ	25,760	VC
Randolph College	VA	53,970	C
Randolph-Macon College	VA	51,480	VC
Reed College	OR	65,300	MC
Regis Univ	CO	46,380	C
Rensselaer Polytechnic Inst	NY	67,265	MC
Rhode Island College	RI	19,000	LC
Rhodes College	TN	51,900	HC
Rice Univ	TX	59,458	MC
Rider Univ	NJ	54,050	C
Ripon College	WI	49,991	VC
Roanoke College	VA	55,952	VC
Robert Morris Univ	PA	40,600	C
Rochester Inst of Technology	NY	52,734	HC+
Rockford Univ	IL	38,570	C
Rockhurst Univ	MO	28,990	C
Roger Williams Univ	RI	48,074	VC
Rollins College	FL	58,670	HC
Roosevelt Univ	IL	41,890	VC
Rose-Hulman Inst of Technology	IN	59,823	MC
Rosemont College	PA	30,980	LC
Rowan Univ	NJ	24,491	VC
Rutgers Univ - Camden	NJ	26,595	C
Rutgers Univ - New Brunswick	NJ	27,090	HC
Rutgers Univ - Newark	NJ	27,351	C
Saginaw Valley State Univ	MI	19,284	C
St. Anselm College	NH	56,636	VC
St. Francis Univ	PA	46,146	NC
St. John's Univ	MN	53,472	C
St. Joseph's Univ	PA	58,540	VC
St. Leo Univ	FL	32,850	C
St. Mary's College	IN	50,600	C
St. Mary's College of Calif	CA	57,420	C
St. Michael's College	VT	53,275	VC+
St. Peter's Univ	NJ	49,192	C
St. Vincent College	PA	46,229	C
Salem College	NC	40,206	C
Salem State Univ	MA	42,650	LC
Salisbury Univ	MD	21,132	VC
Salve Regina Univ	RI	53,046	VC
Sam Houston State Univ	TX	18,792	C
Samford Univ	AL	40,770	VC
San Diego State Univ	CA	23,156	VC
San Francisco State Univ	CA	18,514	LC
San Jose State Univ	CA	22,630	C
Sarah Lawrence College	NY	68,866	MC
Scripps College	CA	69,260	HC
Seattle Pacific Univ	WA	47,439	C+
Seattle Univ	WA	54,957	VC
Seton Hall Univ	NJ	58,008	C
Seton Hill Univ	PA	46,972	VC
Sewanee: The Univ of the South	TN	58,000	HC+
Shenandoah Univ	VA	42,100	C
Shepherd Univ, West Virginia	WV	17,382	C
Shippensburg Univ of Pennsylvania	PA	24,096	C
Shorter Univ	GA	31,130	LC
Siena College	NY	48,916	C
Simmons College	MA	54,400	HC
Simpson College	IA	45,626	VC
Skidmore College	NY	66,600	MC
Slippery Rock Univ of Pennsylvania	PA	20,450	C
Smith College	MA	66,774	MC
Sonoma State Univ	CA	27,020	C
S Dak State Univ	SD	15,874	C
Southeast Missouri State Univ	MO	16,148	C
Southeastern Okla State Univ	OK	11,875	C
Southern Conn State Univ	CT	21,924	LC
Southern Illinois Univ Carbondale	IL	24,554	C
Southern Illinois Univ Edwardsville	IL	20,188	C
Southern Methodist Univ	TX	69,008	MC
Southern Oregon Univ	OR	19,117	C
Southern Univ at New Orleans	LA	8,014	LC
Southwest Baptist Univ	MO	30,890	LC
Southwestern Univ	TX	52,370	VC
Spelman College	GA	41,642	C
Spring Hill College	AL	48,488	C
St. Catherine Univ	MN	45,630	C
St. Cloud State Univ	MN	10,600	C
St. Edward's Univ	TX	56,190	VC
St. Francis College	NY	38,800	LC
St. John Fisher College	NY	45,270	VC
St. John's College at Annapolis	MD	63,348	MC
St. John's Univ	NY	57,160	C+
St. Lawrence Univ	NY	66,646	HC+
St. Mary's College of Maryland	MD	27,312	VC
St. Mary's Univ	TX	39,120	C
St. Norbert College	WI	46,060	VC
St. Olaf College	MN	56,430	HC
Stanford Univ	CA	62,541	MC
SUNY Albany	NY	22,165	C
SUNY at Binghamton	NY	24,100	MC
SUNY at Geneseo	NY	21,622	VC
SUNY at New Paltz	NY	20,840	C
SUNY at Oswego	NY	22,219	VC
SUNY at Purchase College	NY	21,832	C
SUNY/Buffalo State	NY	20,583	LC
SUNY/Cortland	NY	20,910	C
SUNY/Empire State College	NY	9,145	NC
SUNY/Fredonia	NY	20,818	C
SUNY/Oneonta	NY	20,794	C
SUNY/Plattsburgh	NY	19,314	C
SUNY/Potsdam	NY	21,051	VC
SUNY/Univ at Buffalo	NY	23,122	C
Stephen F. Austin State Univ	TX	18,484	LC
Stetson Univ	FL	57,174	VC+
Stockton Univ	NJ	25,565	C
Stonehill College	MA	55,130	C
Stony Brook Univ/The SUNY	NY	22,703	MC
Suffolk Univ	MA	52,316	C
Susquehanna Univ	PA	57,560	VC
Swarthmore College	PA	63,550	MC
Syracuse Univ	NY	62,313	HC
Talladega College	AL	25,919	C
Tarleton State Univ	TX	15,248	LC
Taylor Univ	IN	42,130	VC
Temple Univ	PA	24,392	C+
Tenn Tech Univ	TN	17,929	C
Texas A&M Univ at College Station	TX	20,771	VC+
Texas A&M Univ at Commerce	TX	10,496	C
Texas Christian Univ	TX	57,120	HC
Texas Lutheran Univ	TX	39,770	C
Texas Southern Univ	TX	19,592	LC
Texas State Univ	TX	18,721	C
Texas Tech Univ	TX	20,156	C+
The American Univ	DC	61,317	HC
The Catholic Univ of America	DC	58,376	VC
The College of New Jersey	NJ	28,675	VC+
The College of New Rochelle	NY	46,300	LC
The College of Wooster	OH	60,000	HC
The George Washington Univ	DC	68,474	HC+
The Univ of Akron	OH	22,566	C
The Univ of Alabama	AL	24,320	C+
The Univ of Arizona	AZ	24,086	C
The Univ of Memphis	TN	18,278	C

ST = STATE $IS = IN-STATE COSTS SR = SELECTOR RATING

School	ST	$IS	SR
The Univ of Tenn at Chattanooga	TN	17,340	C+
The Univ of Tenn at Knoxville	TN	22,112	VC
The Univ of Tenn at Martin	TN	15,212	C
The Univ of Texas at Austin	TX	20,206	MC
The Univ of Texas at San Antonio	TX	21,060	C
The Univ of Utah	UT	18,751	VC
The Univ of Virginia's College at Wise	VA	18,192	LC
Thomas Edison State Univ	NJ	6,350	NC
Thomas More College	KY	36,720	LC
Tiffin Univ	OH	34,900	LC
Tougaloo College	MS	17,980	NC
Touro College	NY	31,040	C
Towson Univ	MD	21,878	C
Transylvania Univ	KY	47,450	HC+
Trinity College	CT	69,020	HC
Trinity Univ	TX	54,480	MC
Trinity Washington Univ	DC	33,826	C+
Truman State Univ	MO	16,286	MC
Tufts Univ	MA		MC
Tulane Univ	LA	67,496	MC
Tuskegee Univ	AL	28,164	C
Union College	NY	64,320	MC
Union Univ	TN	41,160	VC
United States Air Force Academy	CO		C
United States Military Academy at West Point	NY		HC+
United States Naval Academy	MD		HC
Universidad del Turabo	PR	17,828	
Univ of Alabama at Birmingham	AL	22,092	C
Univ of Alaska Anchorage	AK	17,914	C
Univ of Arkansas at Fayetteville	AR	19,766	VC
Univ of Arkansas at Little Rock	AR	18,211	LC
Univ of Calif at Berkeley	CA	29,886	MC
Univ of Calif at Davis	CA	28,468	HC
Univ of Calif at Irvine	CA	33,857	VC
Univ of Calif at Los Angeles	CA	27,438	HC+
Univ of Calif at Riverside	CA	32,912	C
Univ of Calif at Santa Barbara	CA	30,627	HC+
Univ of Calif San Diego	CA	30,450	MC
Univ of Calif, Santa Cruz	CA	28,731	C+
Univ of Central Arkansas	AR	15,042	VC
Univ of Central Florida	FL	16,379	VC
Univ of Central Missouri	MO	18,982	C
Univ of Central Okla	OK	15,150	C
Univ of Chicago	IL	70,551	MC
Univ of Cincinnati	OH	22,118	VC
Univ of Colo Boulder	CO	26,048	HC
Univ of Colo Colo Springs	CO	20,300	C
Univ of Colo Denver	CO	22,238	C
Univ of Conn	CT	27,394	
Univ of Dallas	TX	50,676	VC
Univ of Dayton	OH	54,930	VC
Univ of Delaware	DE	32,214	VC
Univ of Denver	CO	61,129	VC+
Univ of Detroit Mercy	MI	48,816	C
Univ of Evansville	IN	44,186	C+
Univ of Findlay	OH	43,040	C
Univ of Florida	FL	16,291	HC+
Univ of Georgia	GA	21,878	HC
Univ of Hartford	CT	49,776	C
Univ of Hawaii at Manoa	HI	23,261	C
Univ of Idaho	ID	16,158	C
Univ of Illinois at Chicago	IL	24,664	VC
Univ of Illinois at Urbana-Champaign	IL	27,006	HC
Univ of Indianapolis	IN	36,480	VC
Univ of Iowa	IA	19,415	HC
Univ of Kansas	KS	20,884	VC
Univ of Kentucky	KY	24,800	C+
Univ of Louisiana at Lafayette	LA	14,516	C
Univ of Lynchburg	VA	48,370	C
Univ of Maine	ME	21,038	VC
Univ of Mary Hardin-Baylor	TX	35,292	C+
Univ of Mary Washington	VA	23,039	C+
Univ of Maryland/Baltimore County	MD	23,004	VC
Univ of Maryland/College Park	MD	21,938	HC
Univ of Mass Amherst	MA	27,669	HC
Univ of Mass Boston	MA	13,828	C
Univ of Mass Dartmouth	MA	26,507	C
Univ of Mass Lowell	MA	27,296	VC
Univ of Miami	FL	63,494	MC
Univ of Mich/Ann Arbor	MI	25,274	MC
Univ of Mich/Dearborn	MI	12,472	VC
Univ of Mich/Flint	MI	19,062	C
Univ of Minn/Duluth	MN	20,292	C
Univ of Minn/Morris	MN	21,222	VC
Univ of Minn/Twin Cities	MN	24,269	MC
Univ of Miss	MS	18,802	C
Univ of Missouri-Columbia	MO	20,463	VC
Univ of Missouri-Kansas City	MO	19,563	VC
Univ of Missouri-St. Louis	MO	19,810	VC
Univ of Montana	MT	14,105	C
Univ of Mount Union	OH	39,990	C
Univ of Nebr - Kearney	NE	17,014	LC
Univ of Nebr - Lincoln	NE	18,589	VC
Univ of Nebr - Omaha	NE	16,120	C
Univ of Nevada, Las Vegas	NV	17,553	C
Univ of Nevada, Reno	NV	18,010	C
Univ of New Hampshire	NH	29,333	VC
Univ of New Haven	CT	53,680	C
Univ of New Mexico	NM	16,808	C
Univ of New Orleans	LA	12,840	C
Univ of N Car at Asheville	NC	16,251	VC+
Univ of N Car at Chapel Hill	NC	20,561	MC
Univ of N Car at Charlotte	NC	17,803	VC
Univ of N Car at Greensboro	NC	15,998	C
Univ of N Car Wilmington	NC	16,784	VC
Univ of N Dak	ND	16,673	C
Univ of North Florida	FL	15,996	VC
Univ of North Texas	TX	20,082	C
Univ of Northern Colo	CO	19,658	C
Univ of Northern Iowa	IA	17,480	C
Univ of Notre Dame	IN	68,801	MC
Univ of Okla	OK	19,651	HC
Univ of Oregon	OR	24,021	VC
Univ of Pennsylvania	PA	63,526	MC
Univ of Pittsburgh	PA	30,030	MC
Univ of Pittsburgh at Bradford	PA	22,958	C
Univ of Pittsburgh at Johnstown	PA	22,092	C
Univ of Portland	OR	52,152	VC
Univ of PR, at Cayey	PR		
Univ of PR, at Mayaguez	PR	13,995	
Univ of PR-Rio Piedras campus	PR	13,327	
Univ of Puget Sound	WA	60,210	HC
Univ of Redlands	CA	61,934	VC
Univ of Rhode Island	RI	26,066	VC
Univ of Richmond	VA	62,730	MC
Univ of Rio Grande & Rio Grande Community College	OH	8,750	LC
Univ of Rochester	NY	65,032	MC
Univ of San Diego	CA	60,338	HC
Univ of San Francisco	CA	60,580	C
Univ of Science and Arts of Okla	OK	11,140	VC
Univ of Scranton	PA	54,962	VC
Univ of S Car at Columbia	SC	21,726	VC
Univ of S Car Upstate	SC	19,272	LC
Univ of S Dak	SD	16,109	C
Univ of South Florida St. Petersburg	FL	15,980	C
Univ of South Florida/Tampa	FL	16,110	VC
Univ of Southern Calif	CA	66,631	MC
Univ of Southern Indiana	IN	16,808	C
Univ of Southern Maine	ME	18,320	C
Univ of Southern Miss	MS	13,170	C
Univ of St. Thomas - Houston	TX	41,510	VC
Univ of Tampa	FL	38,928	VC
Univ of Texas at Arlington	TX	18,876	C
Univ of Texas at Dallas	TX	23,640	HC
Univ of Texas at El Paso	TX	34,452	NC
Univ of Texas Rio Grande Valley	TX	15,573	LC
Univ of the District of Columbia	DC	21,260	LC
Univ of the Ozarks	AR	31,050	NC
Univ of the Pacific	CA	57,446	VC
Univ of Toledo	OH	19,336	C
Univ of Tulsa	OK	52,625	HC
Univ of Vermont	VT	29,792	HC
Univ of Virginia	VA	27,367	MC
Univ of Washington	WA	23,091	MC
Univ of West Georgia	GA	17,510	LC
Univ of Wisc-Eau Claire	WI	16,354	VC
Univ of Wisc-Green Bay	WI	15,184	C
Univ of Wisc-La Crosse	WI	15,425	VC
Univ of Wisc-Madison	WI	21,647	MC
Univ of Wisc-Milwaukee	WI	21,538	C
Univ of Wisc-Oshkosh	WI	15,392	C
Univ of Wisc-Parkside	WI	15,313	C
Univ of Wisc-Platteville	WI	14,148	C
Univ of Wisc-River Falls	WI	14,541	C
Univ of Wisc-Stevens Point	WI	14,043	C
Univ of Wisc-Superior	WI	14,838	C
Univ of Wisc-Whitewater	WI	13,976	C
Univ of Wyoming	WY	15,537	C
Ursinus College	PA	62,920	VC
Utah State Univ	UT	13,235	C
Utica College	NY	31,510	C
Valparaiso Univ	IN	50,160	VC
Vanderbilt Univ	TN	63,248	MC
Vassar College	NY	68,110	MC
Villanova Univ	PA	64,922	MC
Virginia Commonwealth Univ	VA	23,811	VC
Virginia Polytechnic Inst and State Univ	VA	21,920	VC
Virginia State Univ	VA	19,802	C+
Wabash College	IN	52,100	VC
Wake Forest Univ	NC	69,354	MC
Wartburg College	IA	49,478	C
Washburn Univ	KS	15,827	C
Washington & Jefferson College	PA	58,694	VC
Washington and Lee Univ	VA	59,647	MC
Washington College	MD	56,154	VC
Washington State Univ	WA	22,747	C
Washington Univ in St. Louis	MO	67,539	MC
Wayland Baptist Univ	TX	23,460	LC
Wayne State Univ	MI	23,085	C
Weber State Univ	UT	14,112	C
Webster Univ	MO	37,490	C
Wellesley College	MA	66,984	MC
Wells College	NY	50,500	C
Wesleyan College	GA	31,940	C+
Wesleyan Univ	CT	66,940	MC
West Chester Univ of Pennsylvania	PA	19,171	VC
West Liberty Univ	WV	16,158	C
West Texas A&M Univ	TX	13,478	C
West Virginia State Univ	WV	19,412	LC
West Virginia Univ	WV	18,952	VC
West Virginia Wesleyan College	WV	39,188	C
Western Conn State Univ	CT	21,254	LC
Western Illinois Univ	IL	20,897	C
Western Kentucky Univ	KY	16,850	C
Western Mich Univ	MI	21,791	C
Western New England Univ	MA	49,182	C
Western Oregon Univ	OR	19,965	LC
Western State Colo Univ	CO	19,348	C
Western Washington Univ	WA	18,904	VC
Westfield State Univ	MA	20,404	C
Westminster College	MO	32,820	C
Westminster College	PA	41,722	C
Westminster College	UT	41,078	C
Wheaton College	IL	44,993	MC
Wheaton College	MA	63,818	VC
Whitman College	WA	59,772	MC
Whittier College	CA	57,891	C
Whitworth Univ	WA	53,682	VC
Wichita State Univ	KS	17,773	C
Widener Univ	PA	58,190	C
Wilberforce Univ	OH	19,900	C
Willamette Univ	OR	62,514	VC+
William Paterson Univ of New Jersey	NJ	24,022	C
Williams College	MA	67,700	MC
Wilmington College	OH	35,100	C
Wilson College	PA	35,620	LC
Winona State Univ	MN	18,109	C
Winston-Salem State Univ	NC	18,005	LC
Winthrop Univ	SC	23,960	C
Wittenberg Univ	OH	49,863	VC
Wofford College	SC	49,885	VC
Worcester Polytechnic Inst	MA	62,846	MC
Worcester State Univ	MA	20,977	C
Wright State Univ	OH	16,983	C
Xavier Univ	OH	49,380	VC
Yale Univ	CT	64,650	MC
Yeshiva Univ	NY	52,750	VC
York College of Pennsylvania	PA	29,240	C
Youngstown State Univ	OH	17,487	C

ECONOMICS – STATISTICS

School	ST	$IS	SR
Augsburg Univ	MN	45,129	C
Ball State Univ	IN	19,808	C+
Biola Univ	CA	48,686	C
Boise State Univ	ID	17,368	C
Brown Univ	RI	64,566	MC
Bryant Univ	RI	57,204	VC
Southern Methodist Univ	TX	69,008	MC
Univ of Alabama in Huntsville	AL	20,028	VC
Univ of Calif at Irvine	CA	33,857	VC
Univ of Calif San Diego	CA	30,450	MC
Univ of Pittsburgh	PA	30,030	MC
Wichita State Univ	KS	17,773	C

ECONOMICS AND FINANCE

School	ST	$IS	SR
Louisiana College	LA	21,274	C
Shenandoah Univ	VA	42,100	C

EDUCATION

School	ST	$IS	SR
Adams State Univ	CO	15,420	LC
Albertus Magnus College	CT	44,016	LC
American Univ of PR	PR	16,130	
Appalachian State Univ	NC	15,394	VC
Aquinas College - Mich	MI	38,876	VC
Arizona State Univ at the Tempe Campus	AZ	23,001	VC
Arkansas Tech Univ	AR	16,534	LC
Ashford Univ	CA	10,480	C
Assumption College	MA	48,455	VC
Auburn Univ	AL	24,300	VC+
Augsburg Univ	MN	45,129	C
Averett Univ	VA	43,034	LC
Belhaven Univ	MS	32,250	C
Belmont Abbey College	NC	28,794	C
Beloit College	WI	55,206	HC
Bennington College	VT	66,280	MC
Berea College	KY	7,094	C
Bethany College	WV	38,774	LC
Bethel College	IN	36,830	C
Bethel Univ	MN	46,550	C+
Bethune-Cookman Univ	FL	23,322	C
Birmingham-Southern College	AL	44,478	C+
Bloomfield College	NJ	40,100	LC
Boise State Univ	ID	17,368	C
Boston Univ	MA	67,352	MC
Bowdoin College	ME	65,980	MC
Bowling Green State Univ	OH	19,975	C
Bradley Univ	IL	43,240	VC
Brandeis Univ	MA	68,443	MC
Brown Univ	RI	64,566	MC
Bryn Athyn College	PA	32,664	C
Bucknell Univ	PA	67,136	MC
Cabrini Univ	PA	42,591	LC
Cairn Univ	PA	37,572	C
Calif Polytechnic State Univ	CA	22,547	MC
Cal State, Fullerton	CA	21,902	C
Cal State, Monterey Bay	CA	22,872	LC
Calif Univ of Pennsylvania	PA	20,425	LC
Calvin College	MI	43,090	HC
Campbell Univ	NC	37,570	VC
Canisius College	NY	49,672	C
Carroll Univ	WI	38,100	C+
Case Western Reserve Univ	OH	62,284	MC
Castleton Univ	VT	20,186	C
Catawba College	NC	39,820	LC
Cedar Crest College	PA	51,110	C
Central Mich Univ	MI	20,330	C
Chapman Univ	CA	65,504	HC
Chatham Univ	PA	47,883	VC
Clayton State Univ	GA	19,735	LC
Coker College	SC	38,196	C
Colgate Univ	NY	67,500	MC
College of St. Mary	NE	27,500	C
College of St. Scholastica	MN	45,734	C+
Colo College	CO	64,894	MC
Colo Mesa Univ	CO	19,707	LC
Colo State Univ	CO	23,033	C
Columbia College - Missouri	MO	28,179	C
Columbia Univ/City of New York	NY	62,958	MC
Concordia College - New York	NY	39,035	LC
Corban Univ	OR	41,700	C
Cornerstone Univ	MI	36,550	C
Culver-Stockton College	MO	34,350	C
Curry College	MA	53,331	C
Dallas Baptist Univ	TX	35,220	VC
Davis & Elkins College	WV	38,242	LC
Denison Univ	OH	62,770	HC+
DePaul Univ	IL	52,807	VC
Dominican Univ	IL	42,472	C+
Dordt College	IA	37,860	C+
Drexel Univ	PA	65,927	HC
Drury Univ	MO	37,555	VC
Duquesne Univ	PA	48,508	VC
East Texas Baptist Univ	TX	34,444	C
Eastern Mich Univ	MI	19,761	C
Eastern Nazarene College	MA	41,114	C
Eastern Oregon Univ	OR	17,612	C
Elizabethtown College	PA	56,340	VC
Elon Univ	NC	46,142	HC
Endicott College	MA	47,054	C+
Eugene Lang College of Liberal Arts	NY	64,940	VC
Eureka College	IL	34,760	C
Faulkner Univ	AL	26,410	C
Felician Univ	NJ	46,280	LC
Fitchburg State Univ	MA	21,819	LC
Florida International Univ	FL	20,281	C
Fontbonne Univ	MO	34,606	C
Fort Lewis College	CO	20,154	C
Franklin Pierce Univ	NH	46,750	LC
Friends Univ	KS	38,000	C
Furman Univ	SC	61,098	VC+
Gallaudet Univ	DC	30,088	LC
Geneva College	PA	35,450	C
Georgian Court Univ	NJ	43,068	LC
Goddard College	VT	17,040	VC
Goucher College	MD	56,110	VC
Grand Canyon Univ	AZ	25,150	VC
Guilford College	NC	45,973	C
Hamline Univ	MN	50,152	C
Hampshire College	MA	65,214	MC
Hardin-Simmons Univ	TX	36,025	C
Harris-Stowe State Univ	MO	14,590	NC
Henderson State Univ	AR	15,516	C
Heritage Univ	WA	19,825	NC
Hiram College	OH	44,590	C
Hope International Univ	CA	42,730	C
Howard Univ	DC	37,616	C+
Huntington Univ	IN	33,996	C
Huston-Tillotson Univ	TX	18,124	LC
Illinois Wesleyan Univ	IL	56,430	VC+
Ithaca College	NY	58,158	VC+
John Carroll Univ	OH	51,570	C
Johnson State College	VT	22,672	C
Judson Univ	IL	39,174	C
Keene State College	NH	24,604	C
Kent State Univ	OH	20,928	C
LaGrange College	GA	41,310	C
Lake Forest College	IL	50,652	VC
Lasell College	MA	49,400	C
Lebanon Valley College	PA	55,510	VC
Lees-McRae College	NC	33,944	NC
LeMoyne-Owen College	TN	16,980	C
Lewis-Clark State College	ID	14,202	C
Lipscomb Univ	TN	42,984	VC
Louisiana College	LA	21,274	C
Lourdes Univ	OH	29,140	NC
Lycoming College	PA	50,895	C
Macalester College	MN	64,136	MC
Maharishi Univ of Management	IA	34,930	VC
Manhattan College	NY	55,652	C
Manhattanville College	NY	52,430	C
Marian Univ	IN	43,206	C
Marquette Univ	WI	53,090	VC+
Marshall Univ	WV	18,044	C
Martin Univ	IN	21,010	LC
Mass College of Liberal Arts	MA	20,659	C
Mayville State Univ	ND	18,371	NC

ST = STATE $IS = IN-STATE COSTS SR = SELECTOR RATING

School	ST	$IS	SR
McDaniel College	MD	52,910	VC
Mercer Univ	GA	45,348	VC
Merrimack College	MA	55,415	C
Mich State Univ	MI	24,542	VC
Midway Univ	KY	33,940	LC
Miles College	AL	16,530	NC
Millikin Univ	IL	44,148	C
Millsaps College	MS	50,080	C+
Minn State Univ, Mankato	MN	17,190	C
Miss State Univ	MS	12,028	C+
Missouri Western State Univ	MO	17,822	LC
Monmouth Univ	NJ	50,184	C
Montana State Univ Billings	MT	13,336	LC
Morningside College	IA	39,780	C
Mount Aloysius College	PA	29,976	C
Mount St. Mary College	NY	44,448	C
New England College	NH	50,828	NC
New York Univ	NY	68,139	MC
Niagara Univ	NY	41,010	C
N Car State Univ	NC	22,434	HC+
North Central Univ	MN	30,610	C
North Greenville Univ	SC	25,930	C
Northland College	WI	41,103	C+
Northwest Christian Univ	OR	36,580	C
Northwest Univ	WA	38,720	VC
Northwestern Univ	IL	68,725	MC
Nova Southeastern Univ	FL	38,534	C+
Oakwood Univ	AL	43,758	C
Ohio State Univ at Columbus	OH	22,843	MC
Ohio State Univ at Lima	OH	7,553	C
Ohio State Univ at Marion	OH	7,553	VC
Ohio Wesleyan Univ	OH	49,460	VC
Okla Baptist Univ	OK	33,990	C
Okla City Univ	OK	40,476	C
Okla State Univ	OK	17,180	C+
Olivet Nazarene Univ	IL	41,840	VC
Oregon State Univ	OR	23,337	VC
Piedmont College	GA	34,334	C
Pittsburg State Univ	KS	13,880	C
Point Loma Nazarene Univ	CA	46,150	C+
Point Park Univ	PA	41,270	C
Prescott College	AZ	38,201	C
Purdue Univ/West Lafayette	IN	20,032	MC
Quincy Univ	IL	38,170	LC
Radford Univ	VA	19,758	C
Randolph College	VA	53,970	C
Regis Univ	CO	46,380	C
Rocky Mountain College	MT	35,776	C
Roger Williams Univ	RI	48,074	VC
Rosemont College	PA	30,980	LC
Rowan Univ	NJ	24,491	VC
Rutgers Univ - Camden	NJ	26,595	C
St. Anselm College	NH	56,636	VC
St. Louis Univ	MO	49,866	HC
Salem State Univ	MA	42,650	LC
San Diego Christian College	CA	40,914	C
San Jose State Univ	CA	22,630	C
Schreiner Univ	TX	34,626	LC
Seattle Pacific Univ	WA	47,439	C+
Shawnee State Univ	OH	16,998	C
Silver Lake College of the Holy Family	WI	36,290	LC
Simmons College	MA	54,400	HC
Smith College	MA	66,774	MC
S Car State Univ	SC	21,330	LC
S Dak State Univ	SD	15,874	C
Southern Nazarene Univ	OK	33,684	C
Southern New Hampshire Univ	NH	44,256	C
Southern Oregon Univ	OR	19,117	C
Southwestern Univ	TX	52,370	VC
Spalding Univ	KY	31,938	C
St. Bonaventure Univ	NY	45,596	C
St. Francis College	NY	38,800	LC
St. John's Univ	NY	57,160	C+
St. Joseph's College, New York/Long Island Campus	NY	25,124	C
SUNY/Empire State College	NY	9,145	NC
SUNY/Fredonia	NY	20,818	C
SUNY/Potsdam	NY	21,051	VC
Stockton Univ	NJ	25,565	C
Stonehill College	MA	55,130	C
Swarthmore College	PA	63,550	MC
Taylor Univ	IN	42,130	VC
Tenn Wesleyan Univ	TN	32,680	LC
Texas A&M Univ at Corpus Christi	TX	16,851	LC
Texas Lutheran Univ	TX	39,770	C
Texas State Univ	TX	18,721	C
Texas Wesleyan Univ	TX	37,338	C
The Catholic Univ of America	DC	58,376	VC
The College of Idaho	ID	36,415	C
The Univ of Akron	OH	22,566	C
The Univ of Arizona	AZ	24,086	C
The Univ of Montana Western	MT	9,426	LC
The Univ of Tenn at Chattanooga	TN	17,340	C+
The Univ of Tenn at Knoxville	TN	22,112	VC
The Univ of Texas at San Antonio	TX	21,060	C
Towson Univ	MD	21,878	C
Transylvania Univ	KY	47,450	HC+
Trevecca Nazarene Univ	TN	31,186	C
Trinity Christian College	IL	35,580	C
Trinity College	CT	69,020	HC
Trinity Univ	TX	54,480	MC
Trinity Washington Univ	DC	33,826	C+
Tufts Univ	MA		MC
Tusculum College	TN	31,625	LC
Union College	KY	32,310	C
Union Inst & Univ	OH	8,912	SP
Union Univ	TN	41,160	VC
Unity College	ME	37,670	C
Univ of Central Arkansas	AR	15,042	VC
Univ of Colo Colo Springs	CO	20,300	C
Univ of Colo Denver	CO	22,238	C
Univ of Conn	CT	27,394	
Univ of Dallas	TX	50,676	VC
Univ of Dayton	OH	54,930	VC
Univ of Delaware	DE	32,214	VC
Univ of Dubuque	IA	37,824	C
Univ of Idaho	ID	16,158	C
Univ of Illinois at Urbana-Champaign	IL	27,006	HC
Univ of La Verne	CA	55,600	C
Univ of Louisiana at Monroe	LA	15,970	C
Univ of Lynchburg	VA	48,370	C
Univ of Maryland/College Park	MD	21,938	HC
Univ of Mass Amherst	MA	27,669	HC
Univ of Mass Lowell	MA	27,296	VC
Univ of Mich/Dearborn	MI	12,472	VC
Univ of Mich/Flint	MI	19,062	C
Univ of Minn/Morris	MN	21,222	VC
Univ of Missouri-Columbia	MO	20,463	VC
Univ of Missouri-St. Louis	MO	19,810	VC
Univ of Nebr - Lincoln	NE	18,589	VC
Univ of New England	ME	50,110	C
Univ of N Car at Greensboro	NC	15,998	C
Univ of Northern Colo	CO	19,658	C
Univ of Northwestern - St. Paul	MN	39,530	C
Univ of Oregon	OR	24,021	VC
Univ of PR-Rio Piedras campus	PR	13,327	
Univ of Redlands	CA	61,934	VC
Univ of St. Mary	KS	37,080	NC
Univ of South Alabama	AL	16,880	C
Univ of S Dak	SD	16,109	C
Univ of South Florida St. Petersburg	FL	15,980	C
Univ of South Florida/Tampa	FL	16,110	VC
Univ of St. Thomas - Houston	TX	41,510	VC
Univ of the Pacific	CA	57,446	VC
Univ of Tulsa	OK	52,625	HC
Univ of Vermont	VT	29,792	HC
Univ of Wisc-Green Bay	WI	15,184	C
Univ of Wisc-Milwaukee	WI	21,538	C
Univ of Wisc-Platteville	WI	14,148	C
Univ of Wisc-Stevens Point	WI	14,043	C
Ursinus College	PA	62,920	VC
Utica College	NY	31,510	C
Vanderbilt Univ	TN	63,248	MC
Vanguard Univ of Southern Calif	CA	42,400	VC
Wake Forest Univ	NC	69,354	MC
Wartburg College	IA	49,478	C
Washburn Univ	KS	15,827	C
Washington & Jefferson College	PA	58,694	VC
Washington State Univ	WA	22,747	C
Washington Univ in St. Louis	MO	67,539	MC
Weber State Univ	UT	14,112	C
Webster Univ	MO	37,490	C
Western Mich Univ	MI	21,791	C
Western Oregon Univ	OR	19,965	LC
Wheaton College	MA	63,818	VC
William Peace Univ	NC	39,300	LC
Wilmington College	OH	35,100	C
Wittenberg Univ	OH	49,863	VC
Wright State Univ	OH	16,983	C
Xavier Univ	OH	49,380	VC
York College	NE	30,260	C
York College of Pennsylvania	PA	29,240	C
Youngstown State Univ	OH	17,487	C

EDUCATION ADMINISTRATION

School	ST	$IS	SR
Ashford Univ	CA	10,480	C
Ashland Univ	OH	30,446	C
Auburn Univ	AL	24,300	VC+
Cairn Univ	PA	37,572	C
Cal State, Fullerton	CA	21,902	C
Canisius College	NY	49,672	C
Columbia College - Missouri	MO	28,179	C
DePaul Univ	IL	52,807	VC
Georgia Southern Univ	GA	16,540	VC
Howard Univ	DC	37,616	C+
Missouri State Univ	MO	15,837	C+
Nova Southeastern Univ	FL	38,534	C+
Radford Univ	VA	19,758	C
San Jose State Univ	CA	22,630	C
The Univ of Tenn at Martin	TN	15,212	C
Univ of Arkansas at Little Rock	AR	18,211	LC
Univ of Missouri-Columbia	MO	20,463	VC
Univ of N Car at Greensboro	NC	15,998	C
Univ of Texas Rio Grande Valley	TX	15,573	LC
West Virginia Univ	WV	18,952	VC
Western Washington Univ	WA	18,904	VC
Wingate Univ	NC	41,900	C

EDUCATION OF THE DEAF AND HEARING IMPAIRED

School	ST	$IS	SR
Barton College	NC	39,854	C
Boston Univ	MA	67,352	MC
Bowling Green State Univ	OH	19,975	C
Cal State, Fullerton	CA	21,902	C
Cal State, Northridge	CA	17,277	LC
Canisius College	NY	49,672	C
Eastern Kentucky Univ	KY	17,742	C
Eastern Mich Univ	MI	19,761	C
Elmira College	NY	53,900	C
Flagler College	FL	27,620	C
Fontbonne Univ	MO	34,606	C
Ithaca College	NY	58,158	VC+
Kutztown Univ of Pennsylvania	PA	19,477	C
MacMurray College	IL	35,025	C
Marywood Univ	PA	47,840	C
Minot State Univ	ND	13,285	C
Pace Univ	NY	60,136	C
Rochester Inst of Technology	NY	52,734	HC+
San Jose State Univ	CA	22,630	C
Southern Univ at New Orleans	LA	8,014	LC
Stephen F. Austin State Univ	TX	18,484	LC
The College of New Jersey	NJ	28,675	VC+
Towson Univ	MD	21,878	C
Univ of Arkansas at Little Rock	AR	18,211	LC
Univ of Montevallo	AL	20,012	C
Univ of N Car at Greensboro	NC	15,998	C
Univ of Science and Arts of Okla	OK	11,140	VC
Univ of Tulsa	OK	52,625	HC
Western Oregon Univ	OR	19,965	LC

EDUCATION OF THE EMOTIONALLY HANDICAPPED

School	ST	$IS	SR
Bradley Univ	IL	43,240	VC
CUNY/City College	NY	20,204	C
Concordia Univ St. Paul	MN	29,050	C
East Carolina Univ	NC	16,539	C
Eastern Mich Univ	MI	19,761	C
Florida State Univ	FL	16,771	HC
Kutztown Univ of Pennsylvania	PA	19,477	C
Manhattan College	NY	55,652	C
Univ of South Florida/Tampa	FL	16,110	VC
Walsh Univ	OH	39,010	C
Western Mich Univ	MI	21,791	C

EDUCATION OF THE EXCEPTIONAL CHILD

School	ST	$IS	SR
Ashland Univ	OH	30,446	C
Bethel Univ	TN	27,142	C
Bethune-Cookman Univ	FL	23,322	C
Bradley Univ	IL	43,240	VC
Canisius College	NY	49,672	C
Edgewood College	WI	35,950	C
Flagler College	FL	27,620	C
Florida Atlantic Univ	FL	18,256	C
Houghton College	NY	40,558	VC
Jacksonville Univ	FL	49,210	C
Kutztown Univ of Pennsylvania	PA	19,477	C
Marian Univ	IN	43,206	C
Mayville State Univ	ND	18,371	NC
Minot State Univ	ND	13,285	C
Missouri Western State Univ	MO	17,822	LC
Niagara Univ	NY	41,010	C
Northwest Nazarene Univ	ID	40,250	C
Nova Southeastern Univ	FL	38,534	C+
St. Augustine's Univ	NC	25,582	C
Southeast Missouri State Univ	MO	16,148	C
Southeastern Univ	FL	34,910	LC
The Univ of Tenn at Chattanooga	TN	17,340	C+
Univ of Central Arkansas	AR	15,042	VC
Univ of Central Florida	FL	16,379	VC
Univ of Great Falls	MT	38,524	C
Univ of Wisc-Stevens Point	WI	14,043	C
Walsh Univ	OH	39,010	C
Warner Univ	FL	28,216	C
Western Kentucky Univ	KY	16,850	C

EDUCATION OF THE MENTALLY HANDICAPPED

School	ST	$IS	SR
Bradley Univ	IL	43,240	VC
Brescia Univ	KY	29,890	VC
Cal State, Fullerton	CA	21,902	C
CUNY/City College	NY	20,204	C
East Carolina Univ	NC	16,539	C
Eastern Mich Univ	MI	19,761	C
Florida State Univ	FL	16,771	HC
Kutztown Univ of Pennsylvania	PA	19,477	C
Minot State Univ	ND	13,285	C
Northwest Missouri State Univ	MO	18,286	C
Prescott College	AZ	38,201	C
Southeastern Okla State Univ	OK	11,875	C
Univ of Rio Grande & Rio Grande Community College	OH	8,750	LC
Univ of South Florida/Tampa	FL	16,110	VC
Urbana Univ	OH	30,820	C
Walsh Univ	OH	39,010	C
Western Mich Univ	MI	21,791	C

EDUCATION OF THE MULTIPLY HANDICAPPED

School	ST	$IS	SR
Aquinas College - Mich	MI	38,876	VC
Bowling Green State Univ	OH	19,975	C
Eastern Mich Univ	MI	19,761	C
Kutztown Univ of Pennsylvania	PA	19,477	C
Univ of Illinois at Urbana-Champaign	IL	27,006	HC

EDUCATION OF THE PHYSICALLY HANDICAPPED

School	ST	$IS	SR
Aquinas College - Mich	MI	38,876	VC
Bradley Univ	IL	43,240	VC
Cal State, Fullerton	CA	21,902	C
Eastern Mich Univ	MI	19,761	C
Kutztown Univ of Pennsylvania	PA	19,477	C
San Jose State Univ	CA	22,630	C
Walsh Univ	OH	39,010	C

EDUCATION OF THE VISUALLY HANDICAPPED

School	ST	$IS	SR
Cal State, Fullerton	CA	21,902	C
Eastern Mich Univ	MI	19,761	C
Florida State Univ	FL	16,771	HC
Kutztown Univ of Pennsylvania	PA	19,477	C
Stephen F. Austin State Univ	TX	18,484	LC

EDUCATIONAL MEDIA

School	ST	$IS	SR
Drury Univ	MO	37,555	VC
Eastern Mich Univ	MI	19,761	C
Wayne State Univ	MI	23,085	C

EDUCATIONAL STUDIES

School	ST	$IS	SR
Alma College	MI	49,410	VC
Arizona State Univ at the Polytechnic Campus	AZ	22,394	VC
Arizona State Univ at the Tempe Campus	AZ	23,001	VC
Arizona State Univ at the West Campus	AZ	21,513	VC
Ashford Univ	CA	10,480	C
Avila Univ	MO	27,100	C
Bay Path Univ	MA	46,356	C
Blackburn College	IL	28,526	LC
Cabrini Univ	PA	42,591	LC
Cedar Crest College	PA	51,110	C
Dickinson College	PA	66,166	MC
Edgewood College	WI	35,950	C
Gwynedd Mercy Univ	PA	43,780	LC
High Point Univ	NC	47,355	VC
John Brown Univ	AR	35,184	VC
Marian Univ	IN	43,206	C
Neumann Univ	PA	40,678	LC
North Central Univ	MN	30,610	C
St. Martin's Univ	WA	45,056	C
Syracuse Univ	NY	62,313	HC
Tabor College	KS	35,870	C
Texas Christian Univ	TX	57,120	HC
Univ of Arkansas at Fayetteville	AR	19,766	VC
Univ of St. Francis	IN	38,520	C
Univ of South Alabama	AL	16,880	C
Vassar College	NY	68,110	MC
Wheelock College	MA	51,325	LC

ELECTED STUDIES

School	ST	$IS	SR
Lewis Univ	IL	41,710	C

ELECTRICAL AND COMPUTER ENGINEERING

School	ST	$IS	SR
Bowling Green State Univ	OH	19,975	C
Bradley Univ	IL	43,240	VC
Calif Baptist Univ	CA	42,986	C
Calif State Polytechnic Univ, Pomona	CA	21,811	C
Cal State, Fullerton	CA	21,902	C
Christopher Newport Univ	VA	24,878	VC+
Cornell Univ	NY	67,591	MC
Embry-Riddle Aeronautical Univ - Daytona Beach	FL	45,822	VC
Franklin W. Olin College of Engineering	MA	65,580	SP
Grove City College	PA	26,654	VC
New York Inst of Technology	NY	49,980	VC
New York Univ	NY	68,139	MC
Ohio Univ	OH	23,394	VC
Okla Christian Univ	OK	29,260	C
SUNY at Oswego	NY	22,219	VC
Univ of Dayton	OH	54,930	VC

ST = STATE $IS = IN-STATE COSTS SR = SELECTOR RATING

School	ST	$IS	SR
Univ of Denver	CO	61,129	VC+
Univ of Idaho	ID	16,158	C
Univ of Kansas	KS	20,884	VC
Univ of Mass Boston	MA	13,828	C
Univ of New Hampshire - Manchester	NH	14,490	C
Univ of Rhode Island	RI	26,066	VC
Wayne State Univ	MI	23,085	C
Western Mich Univ	MI	21,791	C
Worcester Polytechnic Inst	MA	62,846	MC

ELECTRICAL ENGINEERING

School	ST	$IS	SR
Anderson Univ	IN	39,450	C
Brown Univ	RI	64,566	MC
Cal State, Fullerton	CA	21,902	C
Colo State Univ	CO	23,033	C
Embry-Riddle Aeronautical Univ - Daytona Beach	FL	45,822	VC
Embry-Riddle Aeronautical Univ - Prescott Campus	AZ	45,130	VC
Georgia Southern Univ	GA	16,540	VC
Northern Arizona Univ	AZ	21,003	C
Olivet Nazarene Univ	IL	41,840	VC
Purdue Univ Northwest	IN	15,178	C
Syracuse Univ	NY	62,313	HC
Texas Christian Univ	TX	57,120	HC
Texas Tech Univ	TX	20,156	C+
Univ of Dayton	OH	54,930	VC
Univ of Mich/Dearborn	MI	12,472	VC
Univ of Mount Union	OH	39,990	C
Univ of Northwestern - St. Paul	MN	39,530	C
Univ of Okla	OK	19,651	HC
Washington State Univ	WA	22,747	C

ELECTRICAL TECHNOLOGY

School	ST	$IS	SR
New York City College of Technology	NY	7,185	LC
St. Louis Univ	MO	49,866	HC
Thomas Edison State Univ	NJ	6,350	NC

ELECTRICAL/ELECTRONICS ENGINEERING

School	ST	$IS	SR
Alabama A&M Univ	AL	18,796	C
Andrews Univ	MI	41,732	C
Arizona State Univ at the Tempe Campus	AZ	23,001	VC
Arkansas State Univ	AR	16,190	C
Arkansas Tech Univ	AR	16,534	LC
Auburn Univ	AL	24,300	VC+
Baylor Univ	TX	56,803	HC
Benedict College	SC	28,630	NC
Bloomsburg Univ of Pennsylvania	PA	19,930	C
Boise State Univ	ID	17,368	C
Boston Univ	MA	67,352	MC
Bradley Univ	IL	43,240	VC
Brigham Young Univ	UT	13,248	MC
Bucknell Univ	PA	67,136	MC
Calif Baptist Univ	CA	42,986	C
Calif Inst of Technology	CA	64,704	MC
Calif Polytechnic State Univ	CA	22,547	MC
Calif State Polytechnic Univ, Pomona	CA	21,811	C
Cal State, Chico	CA	19,790	VC
Cal State, Fresno	CA	16,902	LC
Cal State, Fullerton	CA	21,902	C
Cal State, Long Beach	CA	18,850	C
Cal State, Los Angeles	CA	17,186	LC
Cal State, Sacramento	CA	19,060	C
Calvin College	MI	43,090	HC
Capitol Technology Univ	MD	46,280	SP
Carnegie Mellon Univ	PA	67,980	MC
Case Western Reserve Univ	OH	62,284	MC
Cedarville Univ	OH	36,244	VC
Central Mich Univ	MI	20,330	C
Central Washington Univ	WA	16,803	C
Christian Brothers Univ	TN	31,670	VC
CUNY/City College	NY	20,204	C
Clarkson Univ	NY	60,392	VC
Clemson Univ	SC		HC
Cleveland State Univ	OH	22,290	C
Colo State Univ	CO	23,033	C
Colo Technical Univ	CO	21,455	NC
Columbia Univ/City of New York	NY	62,958	MC
Cooper Union for the Advancement of Science and Art	NY	61,370	MC
Delaware State Univ	DE	19,376	LC
Dordt College	IA	37,860	C+
Drexel Univ	PA	65,927	HC
Duke Univ	NC	68,298	MC
Elizabethtown College	PA	56,340	VC
Fairfield Univ	CT	61,445	HC
Fairleigh Dickinson Univ/ Metropolitan Campus	NJ	52,392	C
Florida A&M Univ	FL	15,361	C
Florida Atlantic Univ	FL	18,256	C
Florida Inst of Technology	FL	53,306	VC
Florida International Univ	FL	20,281	C
Florida State Univ	FL	16,771	HC
Gannon Univ	PA	42,922	C
George Mason Univ	VA	19,884	C
Georgia Inst of Technology	GA	23,910	MC
Gonzaga Univ	WA	52,880	HC
Hampton Univ	VA	36,410	C
Harding Univ	AR	25,440	C
Hofstra Univ	NY	58,210	C+
Howard Univ	DC	37,616	C+
Idaho State Univ	ID	13,619	LC
Illinois Inst of Technology	IL	56,826	HC+
Indiana Inst of Technology	IN	34,240	LC
Indiana Univ-Purdue Univ Fort Wayne	IN	18,675	C
Indiana Univ-Purdue Univ Indianapolis	IN	18,952	C
Inter-American Univ of PR-Bayamon	PR	18,785	
Iowa State Univ	IA	18,176	C
Jackson State Univ	MS	15,879	LC
Jacksonville Univ	FL	49,210	C
John Brown Univ	AR	35,184	VC
Johns Hopkins Univ	MD	68,080	MC
Johnson & Wales Univ/North Miami Campus	FL	44,768	C
Johnson & Wales Univ/ Providence Campus	RI	44,768	C
Kansas State Univ	KS	17,780	VC
Kennesaw State Univ	GA	18,899	VC
Kettering Univ	MI	47,570	HC
Lafayette College	PA	68,520	MC
Lake Superior State Univ	MI	19,867	C
Lamar Univ	TX	18,014	LC
Lawrence Tech Univ	MI	41,630	VC
Lehigh Univ	PA	63,860	MC
LeTourneau Univ	TX	39,190	VC
Lipscomb Univ	TN	42,984	VC
Louisiana State Univ and A&M College	LA	18,677	VC
Loyola Marymount Univ	CA	60,202	VC+
Manhattan College	NY	55,652	C
Marquette Univ	WI	53,090	VC+
Mass Inst of Technology	MA	62,662	MC
Merrimack College	MA	55,415	C
Miami Univ	OH	27,190	HC+
Mich State Univ	MI	24,542	VC
Mich Tech Univ	MI	25,551	VC+
Milwaukee School of Engineering	WI	48,531	HC+
Minn State Univ, Mankato	MN	17,190	C
Miss State Univ	MS	12,028	C+
Missouri Univ of Science and Technology	MO	18,655	HC
Montana State Univ	MT	15,500	C+
Morgan State Univ	MD	17,190	LC
New Jersey Inst of Technology	NJ	30,198	HC
New Mexico Inst of Mining and Technology	NM	15,385	HC+
New Mexico State Univ	NM	14,050	LC
New York Univ	NY	68,139	MC
N Car A&T State Univ	NC	13,786	C
N Car State Univ	NC	22,434	HC+
N Dak State Univ	ND	16,245	VC
Northeastern Univ	MA	65,352	MC
Northern Illinois Univ	IL	20,176	C
Northwestern Univ	IL	68,725	MC
Norwich Univ	VT	56,234	C
Oakland Univ	MI	20,763	C
Ohio Northern Univ	OH	44,050	VC
Ohio State Univ at Columbus	OH	22,843	MC
Ohio Univ	OH	23,394	VC
Okla Christian Univ	OK	29,260	C
Okla State Univ	OK	17,180	C+
Old Dominion Univ	VA	21,618	C
Oral Roberts Univ	OK	34,316	C
Oregon State Univ	OR	23,337	VC
Pennsylvania State Univ - Univ Park	PA	29,716	HC
Point Park Univ	PA	41,270	C
Portland State Univ	OR	19,443	C
Prairie View A&M Univ	TX	27,273	LC
Princeton Univ	NJ	60,090	MC
Purdue Univ/West Lafayette	IN	20,032	MC
Rensselaer Polytechnic Inst	NY	67,265	MC
Rice Univ	TX	59,458	MC
Rochester Inst of Technology	NY	52,734	HC+
Rose-Hulman Inst of Technology	IN	59,823	MC
Rutgers Univ - New Brunswick	NJ	27,090	HC
Saginaw Valley State Univ	MI	19,284	C
St. Louis Univ	MO	49,866	HC
San Diego State Univ	CA	23,156	VC
San Francisco State Univ	CA	18,514	LC
San Jose State Univ	CA	22,630	C
Seattle Pacific Univ	WA	47,439	C+
Seattle Univ	WA	54,957	VC
Shippensburg Univ of Pennsylvania	PA	24,096	C
S Dak School of Mines and Technology	SD	18,570	C+
S Dak State Univ	SD	15,874	C
Southern Illinois Univ Carbondale	IL	24,554	C
Southern Illinois Univ Edwardsville	IL	20,188	C
Southern Methodist Univ	TX	69,008	MC
Southern Univ and A&M College	LA	16,074	LC
St. Cloud State Univ	MN	10,600	C
St. Mary's Univ	TX	39,120	C
Stanford Univ	CA	62,541	MC
SUNY at Binghamton	NY	24,100	MC
SUNY at New Paltz	NY	20,840	C
SUNY Polytechnic Inst	NY	20,438	VC
SUNY/Maritime College	NY	16,020	C
SUNY/Univ at Buffalo	NY	23,122	C
Stevens Inst of Technology	NJ	64,954	MC
Stony Brook Univ/The SUNY	NY	22,703	MC
Suffolk Univ	MA	52,316	C
Tarleton State Univ	TX	15,248	LC
Temple Univ	PA	24,392	C+
Tenn State Univ	TN	14,423	LC
Tenn Tech Univ	TN	17,929	C
Texas A&M Univ at College Station	TX	20,771	VC+
Texas A&M Univ at Kingsville	TX	16,580	LC
Texas State Univ	TX	18,721	C
The Catholic Univ of America	DC	58,376	VC
The Citadel, The Military College of S Car	SC	20,679	C
The College of New Jersey	NJ	28,675	VC+
The George Washington Univ	DC	68,474	HC+
The Univ of Akron	OH	22,566	C
The Univ of Alabama	AL	24,320	C+
The Univ of Arizona	AZ	24,086	C
The Univ of Memphis	TN	18,278	C
The Univ of Tenn at Chattanooga	TN	17,340	C+
The Univ of Tenn at Knoxville	TN	22,112	VC
The Univ of Texas at Austin	TX	20,206	MC
The Univ of Texas at San Antonio	TX	21,060	C
The Univ of Utah	UT	18,751	VC
Trine Univ	IN	41,310	C
Tufts Univ	MA		MC
Tuskegee Univ	AL	28,164	C
Union College	NY	64,320	MC
United States Air Force Academy	CO		C
United States Coast Guard Academy	CT	942	HC
United States Military Academy at West Point	NY		HC+
United States Naval Academy	MD		HC
Universidad Politecnica de PR, Hato Rey campus	PR	23,514	
Univ of Alabama at Birmingham	AL	22,092	C
Univ of Alabama in Huntsville	AL	20,028	VC
Univ of Alaska Anchorage	AK	17,914	C
Univ of Alaska Fairbanks	AK	16,874	VC
Univ of Arkansas at Fayetteville	AR	19,766	VC
Univ of Calif at Berkeley	CA	29,886	MC
Univ of Calif at Davis	CA	28,468	HC
Univ of Calif at Irvine	CA	33,857	VC
Univ of Calif at Los Angeles	CA	27,438	HC+
Univ of Calif at Riverside	CA	32,912	C
Univ of Calif at Santa Barbara	CA	30,627	HC+
Univ of Calif San Diego	CA	30,450	MC
Univ of Calif, Santa Cruz	CA	28,731	C+
Univ of Central Florida	FL	16,379	VC
Univ of Central Missouri	MO	18,982	C
Univ of Central Okla	OK	15,150	C
Univ of Cincinnati	OH	22,118	VC
Univ of Colo Boulder	CO	26,048	HC
Univ of Colo Colo Springs	CO	20,300	C
Univ of Colo Denver	CO	22,238	C
Univ of Conn	CT	27,394	
Univ of Dayton	OH	54,930	VC
Univ of Delaware	DE	32,214	VC
Univ of Denver	CO	61,129	VC+
Univ of Detroit Mercy	MI	48,816	C
Univ of Evansville	IN	44,186	C+
Univ of Florida	FL	16,291	HC+
Univ of Georgia	GA	21,878	HC
Univ of Hartford	CT	49,776	C
Univ of Hawaii at Manoa	HI	23,261	C
Univ of Houston	TX	21,871	VC
Univ of Idaho	ID	16,158	C
Univ of Illinois at Chicago	IL	24,664	VC
Univ of Illinois at Urbana-Champaign	IL	27,006	HC
Univ of Indianapolis	IN	36,480	VC
Univ of Iowa	IA	19,415	HC
Univ of Kansas	KS	20,884	VC
Univ of Kentucky	KY	24,800	C+
Univ of Louisiana at Lafayette	LA	14,516	C
Univ of Louisville	KY	19,692	C
Univ of Maine	ME	21,038	VC
Univ of Maryland/College Park	MD	21,938	HC
Univ of Mass Amherst	MA	27,669	HC
Univ of Mass Dartmouth	MA	26,507	C
Univ of Mass Lowell	MA	27,296	VC
Univ of Miami	FL	63,494	MC
Univ of Mich/Ann Arbor	MI	25,274	MC
Univ of Minn/Duluth	MN	20,292	C
Univ of Minn/Twin Cities	MN	24,269	MC
Univ of Miss	MS	18,802	C
Univ of Missouri-Columbia	MO	20,463	VC
Univ of Missouri-Kansas City	MO	19,563	VC
Univ of Missouri-St. Louis	MO	19,810	VC
Univ of Nebr - Lincoln	NE	18,589	VC
Univ of Nevada, Las Vegas	NV	17,553	C
Univ of Nevada, Reno	NV	18,010	C
Univ of New Hampshire	NH	29,333	VC
Univ of New Haven	CT	53,680	C
Univ of New Mexico	NM	16,808	C
Univ of New Orleans	LA	12,840	C
Univ of N Car at Charlotte	NC	17,803	VC
Univ of N Dak	ND	16,673	C
Univ of North Florida	FL	15,996	VC
Univ of North Texas	TX	20,082	C
Univ of Notre Dame	IN	68,801	MC
Univ of Pennsylvania	PA	63,526	MC
Univ of Pittsburgh	PA	30,030	MC
Univ of Portland	OR	52,152	VC
Univ of PR, at Mayaguez	PR	13,995	
Univ of Rochester	NY	65,032	MC
Univ of San Diego	CA	60,338	HC
Univ of Scranton	PA	54,962	VC
Univ of South Alabama	AL	16,880	C
Univ of S Car at Columbia	SC	21,726	VC
Univ of South Florida/Tampa	FL	16,110	VC
Univ of Southern Calif	CA	66,631	MC
Univ of Southern Maine	ME	18,320	C
Univ of Texas at Arlington	TX	18,876	C
Univ of Texas at Dallas	TX	23,640	HC
Univ of Texas at El Paso	TX	34,452	NC
Univ of Texas Rio Grande Valley	TX	15,573	LC
Univ of the District of Columbia	DC	21,260	LC
Univ of the Pacific	CA	57,446	VC
Univ of Toledo	OH	19,336	C
Univ of Tulsa	OK	52,625	HC
Univ of Vermont	VT	29,792	HC
Univ of Virginia	VA	27,367	MC
Univ of Washington	WA	23,091	MC
Univ of West Florida	FL	15,848	C
Univ of Wisc-Madison	WI	21,647	MC
Univ of Wisc-Milwaukee	WI	21,538	C
Univ of Wisc-Platteville	WI	14,148	C
Univ of Wyoming	WY	15,537	C
Utah State Univ	UT	13,235	C
Valparaiso Univ	IN	50,160	VC
Vanderbilt Univ	TN	63,248	MC
Villanova Univ	PA	64,922	MC
Virginia Commonwealth Univ	VA	23,811	VC
Virginia Military Inst	VA	26,460	VC
Virginia Polytechnic Inst and State Univ	VA	21,920	VC
Washington State Univ	WA	22,747	C
Washington Univ in St. Louis	MO	67,539	MC
Wayne State Univ	MI	23,085	C
Weber State Univ	UT	14,112	C
Wentworth Inst of Technology	MA	48,810	VC
West Virginia Univ	WV	18,952	VC
West Virginia Univ Inst of Technology	WV	18,264	C
Western Carolina Univ	NC	13,965	C
Western Kentucky Univ	KY	16,850	C
Western New England Univ	MA	49,182	C
Western Washington Univ	WA	18,904	VC
Wichita State Univ	KS	17,773	C
Widener Univ	PA	58,190	C
Wilkes Univ	PA	49,166	C
Wright State Univ	OH	16,983	C
Yale Univ	CT	64,650	MC
York College of Pennsylvania	PA	29,240	C
Youngstown State Univ	OH	17,487	C

ELECTRICAL/ELECTRONICS ENGINEERING TECHNOLOGY

School	ST	$IS	SR
Alabama A&M Univ	AL	18,796	C
Alfred State College	NY	19,895	C
Appalachian State Univ	NC	15,394	VC
Arizona State Univ at the Polytechnic Campus	AZ	22,394	VC
Baker College of Flint	MI	19,140	NC
Bowling Green State Univ	OH	19,975	C
Brigham Young Univ	UT	13,248	MC
Cal State, Fullerton	CA	21,902	C
Calif Univ of Pennsylvania	PA	20,425	LC
Central Conn State Univ	CT	22,041	C
Cleveland State Univ	OH	22,290	C
Colo State Univ-Pueblo	CO	21,581	C
Colo Technical Univ	CO	21,455	NC
East Carolina Univ	NC	16,539	C
Eastern Mich Univ	MI	19,761	C
Eastern New Mexico Univ	NM	12,874	LC
Excelsior College	NY	38,800	SP
Fairleigh Dickinson Univ/ Metropolitan Campus	NJ	52,392	C
Fairmont State Univ	WV	15,726	C
Farmingdale State College	NY	20,968	C
Ferris State Univ	MI	21,458	C
Fitchburg State Univ	MA	21,819	LC
Fort Valley State Univ	GA	17,988	VC
Indiana State Univ	IN	23,223	LC
Indiana Univ-Purdue Univ Fort Wayne	IN	18,675	C
Indiana Univ-Purdue Univ Indianapolis	IN	18,952	C
Inter-American Univ of PR Ponce	PR	19,549	
Inter-American Univ of PR-Aguadilla Campus	PR	21,657	
Inter-American Univ of PR-Bayamon	PR	18,785	

ST = STATE $IS = IN-STATE COSTS SR = SELECTOR RATING

School	ST	$IS	SR
Inter-American Univ of PR-Fajardo Campus	PR	18,336	
Kansas State Univ	KS	17,780	VC
Kennesaw State Univ	GA	18,899	VC
Louisiana Tech Univ	LA	11,422	VC
Metropolitan State Univ of Denver	CO	6,928	LC
Mich Tech Univ	MI	25,551	VC+
Minn State Univ, Mankato	MN	17,190	C
Missouri Western State Univ	MO	17,822	LC
Montana State Univ-Northern	MT	11,370	NC
Murray State Univ	KY	17,726	C+
New York Inst of Technology	NY	49,980	VC
Norfolk State Univ	VA	18,902	LC
Northern Kentucky Univ	KY	16,486	C
Northern Mich Univ	MI	20,853	C
Northwestern State Univ of Louisiana	LA	16,534	LC
Okla State Univ	OK	17,180	C+
Old Dominion Univ	VA	21,618	C
Oregon Inst of Technology	OR	19,227	C
Pennsylvania College of Technology	PA	27,693	NC
Pittsburg State Univ	KS	13,880	C
Point Park Univ	PA	41,270	C
Purdue Univ Northwest	IN	15,178	C
Purdue Univ/West Lafayette	IN	20,032	MC
Rochester Inst of Technology	NY	52,734	HC+
Roosevelt Univ	IL	41,890	VC
St. Louis Univ	MO	49,866	HC
Savannah State Univ	GA	17,036	C
S Car State Univ	SC	21,330	LC
S Dak State Univ	SD	15,874	C
Southern Illinois Univ Carbondale	IL	24,554	C
SUNY Polytechnic Inst	NY	20,438	VC
SUNY/Buffalo State	NY	20,583	LC
Texas Southern Univ	TX	19,592	LC
The Univ of Akron	OH	22,566	C
The Univ of Memphis	TN	18,278	C
Thomas Edison State Univ	NJ	6,350	NC
Tuskegee Univ	AL	28,164	C
Univ of Arkansas at Little Rock	AR	18,211	LC
Univ of Central Missouri	MO	18,982	C
Univ of Cincinnati	OH	22,118	VC
Univ of Dallas	TX	50,676	VC
Univ of Dayton	OH	54,930	VC
Univ of Hartford	CT	49,776	C
Univ of Maine	ME	21,038	VC
Univ of Mass Lowell	MA	27,296	VC
Univ of N Car at Charlotte	NC	17,803	VC
Univ of North Texas	TX	20,082	C
Univ of Northern Iowa	IA	17,480	C
Univ of Pittsburgh at Johnstown	PA	22,092	C
Univ of PR, at Bayamon	PR	13,145	
Univ of Rio Grande & Rio Grande Community College	OH	8,750	LC
Univ of Southern Indiana	IN	16,808	C
Univ of Southern Miss	MS	13,170	C
Univ of Wisc-Green Bay	WI	15,184	C
Vaughn College of Aeronautics and Technology	NY	37,180	SP
Virginia Commonwealth Univ	VA	23,811	VC
Wayne State Univ	MI	23,085	C
Weber State Univ	UT	14,112	C
West Virginia Univ Inst of Technology	WV	18,264	C
Western Carolina Univ	NC	13,965	C
Western Washington Univ	WA	18,904	VC
Youngstown State Univ	OH	17,487	C

ELECTROMECHANICAL TECHNOLOGY

School	ST	$IS	SR
Idaho State Univ	ID	13,619	LC
Penn State Altoona	PA	26,686	C
Univ of the District of Columbia	DC	21,260	LC
Univ of Toledo	OH	19,336	C
Vermont Technical College	VT	25,370	C
Wayne State Univ	MI	23,085	C
Wentworth Inst of Technology	MA	48,810	VC
Western Kentucky Univ	KY	16,850	C

ELECTRONIC BUSINESS

School	ST	$IS	SR
Cal State, Fullerton	CA	21,902	C
Davenport Univ	MI	25,896	LC
Florida Inst of Technology	FL	53,306	VC
La Sierra Univ	CA	39,690	VC
Limestone College	SC	32,100	C
Old Dominion Univ	VA	21,618	C
San Francisco State Univ	CA	18,514	LC
Southern Univ and A&M College	LA	16,074	LC
Thiel College	PA	42,950	LC
Trevecca Nazarene Univ	TN	31,186	C
Univ of La Verne	CA	55,600	C
Univ of North Texas	TX	20,082	C
Univ of Scranton	PA	54,962	VC
Washington State Univ	WA	22,747	C
Winthrop Univ	SC	23,960	C

ELEMENTARY EDUCATION

School	ST	$IS	SR
Adams State Univ	CO	15,420	LC
Adrian College	MI	45,550	C
Alabama A&M Univ	AL	18,796	C
Alabama State Univ	AL	16,490	LC
Alaska Pacific Univ	AK	28,730	VC
Albright College	PA	57,326	C
Alcorn State Univ	MS	15,884	C
Alderson Broaddus Univ	WV	35,000	LC
Alice Lloyd College	KY	8,190	LC
Alma College	MI	49,410	VC
Alvernia Univ	PA	45,330	C
Alverno College	WI	33,294	LC
American International College	MA	47,020	LC
Anderson Univ	IN	39,450	C
Andrews Univ	MI	41,732	C
Anna Maria College	MA	51,020	C
Appalachian State Univ	NC	15,394	VC
Aquinas College	TN	30,800	C+
Aquinas College - Mich	MI	38,876	VC
Arcadia Univ	PA	55,990	C+
Arizona State Univ at the Polytechnic Campus	AZ	22,394	VC
Arizona State Univ at the Tempe Campus	AZ	23,001	VC
Arizona State Univ at the West Campus	AZ	21,513	VC
Arkansas Baptist College	AR	20,280	NC
Arkansas State Univ	AR	16,190	C
Arkansas Tech Univ	AR	16,534	LC
Asbury Univ	KY	36,450	C+
Ashford Univ	CA	10,480	C
Ashland Univ	OH	30,446	C
Atlantic Union College	MA	27,228	C
Auburn Univ	AL	24,300	VC+
Auburn Univ at Montgomery	AL	15,000	C
Augsburg Univ	MN	45,129	C
Augusta Univ	GA	4,632	C
Augustana College	IL	51,222	VC+
Augustana Univ	SD	39,968	VC
Aurora Univ	IL	34,990	C
Avila Univ	MO	27,100	C
Baker Univ	KS	37,190	C
Ball State Univ	IN	19,808	C+
Barton College	NC	39,854	C
Bay Path Univ	MA	46,356	C
Bayamon Central Univ	PR	12,490	
Baylor Univ	TX	56,803	HC
Becker College	MA	30,100	LC
Belhaven Univ	MS	32,250	C
Bellarmine Univ	KY	52,532	C
Belmont Abbey College	NC	28,794	C
Belmont Univ	TN	44,500	VC+
Bemidji State Univ	MN	17,730	C
Benedict College	SC	28,630	NC
Benedictine College	KS	38,850	VC
Benedictine Univ	IL	38,300	C
Bennett College	NC	27,717	NC
Bennington College	VT	66,280	MC
Berea College	KY	7,094	C
Bethany College	KS	38,637	LC
Bethany College	WV	38,774	LC
Bethel College	IN	36,830	C
Bethel College	KS	35,370	C
Bethel Univ	MN	46,550	C+
Bethune-Cookman Univ	FL	23,322	C
Black Hills State Univ	SD	16,622	C
Blackburn College	IL	28,526	LC
Bloomfield College	NJ	40,100	LC
Blue Mountain College	MS	15,949	C
Bluefield State College	WV	5,832	LC
Boise State Univ	ID	17,368	C
Boricua College	NY	10,100	C
Boston College	MA	68,043	MC
Boston Univ	MA	67,352	MC
Bowie State Univ	MD	18,610	LC
Bowling Green State Univ	OH	19,975	C
Bradley Univ	IL	43,240	VC
Brescia Univ	KY	29,890	VC
Briar Cliff Univ	IA	36,956	C
Bridgewater State Univ	MA	22,762	C
Brigham Young Univ	UT	13,248	MC
Brigham Young Univ/Hawaii	HI	11,710	C
Bryan College	TN	32,900	C
Buena Vista Univ	IA	42,344	C
Butler Univ	IN	52,890	VC+
Cabrini Univ	PA	42,591	LC
Cairn Univ	PA	37,572	C
Caldwell Univ	NJ	42,165	LC
Cal State, Fullerton	CA	21,902	C
Cal State, Long Beach	CA	18,850	C
Calif Univ of Pennsylvania	PA	20,425	LC
Calumet College of St. Joseph	IN	22,735	C
Calvin College	MI	43,090	HC
Cameron Univ	OK	11,632	LC
Campbell Univ	NC	37,570	VC
Campbellsville Univ	KY	33,400	C
Canisius College	NY	49,672	C
Capital Univ	OH	44,778	VC
Cardinal Stritch Univ	WI	37,136	C
Caribbean Univ	PR	12,227	
Carlos Albizu Univ	FL	13,036	LC
Carlow Univ	PA	39,696	LC
Carroll College	MT	44,304	C
Carroll Univ	WI	38,100	C+
Carson-Newman Univ	TN	35,900	C
Carthage College	WI	48,835	C
Catawba College	NC	39,820	LC
Cazenovia College	NY	47,866	C
Centenary College	NJ	43,890	LC
Central College	IA	44,592	C
Central Conn State Univ	CT	22,041	C
Central Methodist Univ	MO	31,500	VC
Central Mich Univ	MI	20,330	C
Central State Univ	OH	18,564	C
Central Washington Univ	WA	16,803	C
Chadron State College	NE	14,819	LC
Chaminade Univ of Honolulu	HI	37,614	C
Champlain College	VT	54,724	VC
Charleston Southern Univ	SC	34,700	C
Chatham Univ	PA	47,883	VC
Chestnut Hill College	PA	47,180	C
Cheyney Univ of Pennsylvania	PA	20,896	LC
Chicago State Univ	IL	41,620	C
CUNY/Brooklyn College	NY	7,163	C+
CUNY/City College	NY	20,204	C
CUNY/Hunter College	NY	31,098	VC
CUNY/Lehman College	NY	5,788	LC
CUNY/Medgar Evers College	NY	6,680	NC
CUNY/Queens College	NY	21,507	C
City Univ of Seattle	WA	24,340	NC
Claflin Univ	SC	25,592	LC
Clarion Univ of Pennsylvania	PA	21,608	LC
Clarke Univ	IA	42,950	C
Clemson Univ	SC		HC
Cleveland State Univ	OH	22,290	C
Coastal Carolina Univ	SC	20,340	C
Coe College	IA	51,570	VC
Coker College	SC	38,196	C
College of Charleston	SC	24,046	VC
College of St. Benedict	MN	54,480	C
College of St. Elizabeth	NJ	45,700	LC
College of St. Mary	NE	27,500	C
College of St Joseph	VT	32,400	LC
College of the Ozarks	MO	7,530	VC
Colo Christian Univ	CO	40,885	VC
Columbia College	SC	36,550	C
Columbia College - Missouri	MO	28,179	C
Concord Univ	WV	14,954	LC
Concordia College - Alabama	AL	15,720	NC
Concordia College - Moorhead	MN	46,418	C
Concordia College - New York	NY	39,035	LC
Concordia Univ	OR	35,000	C
Concordia Univ Nebr	NE	41,900	VC
Concordia Univ St. Paul	MN	29,050	C
Concordia Univ Texas	TX	41,920	C
Concordia Univ Wisc	WI	35,910	C
Concordia Univ, Ann Arbor	MI	38,878	C+
Concordia Univ, Chicago	IL	41,522	C
Converse College	SC	28,290	C
Coppin State Univ	MD	14,071	VC
Corban Univ	OR	41,700	C
Cornell College	IA	49,900	VC
Cornerstone Univ	MI	36,550	C
Covenant College	GA	44,590	HC
Creighton Univ	NE	49,452	VC
Culver-Stockton College	MO	34,350	C
Cumberland Univ	TN	27,710	C
Curry College	MA	53,331	C
Daemen College	NY	40,336	C
Dakota State Univ	SD	12,286	C
Dakota Wesleyan Univ	SD	33,980	LC
Dallas Baptist Univ	TX	35,220	VC
Davis & Elkins College	WV	38,242	LC
Defiance College	OH	42,240	LC
Delaware State Univ	DE	19,376	LC
Delta State Univ	MS	13,176	LC
DePaul Univ	IL	52,807	VC
DePauw Univ	IN	58,688	VC
DeSales Univ	PA	47,520	C
Dickinson State Univ	ND	12,372	LC
Doane Univ	NE	41,340	VC
Dominican College	NY	40,258	LC
Dominican Univ	IL	42,472	C+
Dordt College	IA	37,860	C+
Drake Univ	IA	49,220	HC
Drexel Univ	PA	65,927	HC
Drury Univ	MO	37,555	VC
East Carolina Univ	NC	16,539	C
East Central Univ	OK	13,330	C
East Texas Baptist Univ	TX	34,444	C
Eastern Conn State Univ	CT	23,059	C
Eastern Illinois Univ	IL	21,414	C
Eastern Kentucky Univ	KY	17,742	C
Eastern Mennonite Univ	VA	42,550	C
Eastern Mich Univ	MI	19,761	C
Eastern Nazarene College	MA	41,114	C
Eastern New Mexico Univ	NM	12,874	LC
Eastern Washington Univ	WA	17,896	LC
Edgewood College	WI	35,950	C
Edinboro Univ	PA	15,940	LC
Edward Waters College	FL	28,089	NC
Elizabeth City State Univ	NC	14,745	C
Elizabethtown College	PA	56,340	VC
Elmhurst College	IL	46,514	C
Elms College	MA	49,602	VC
Elon Univ	NC	46,142	HC
Emmanuel College	MA	53,472	C+
Emporia State Univ	KS	15,029	C
Erskine College	SC	45,460	C
Eureka College	IL	34,760	C
Evangel Univ	MO	28,898	C
Fairmont State Univ	WV	15,726	C
Faulkner Univ	AL	26,410	C
Fayetteville State Univ	NC	17,756	C
Felician Univ	NJ	46,280	LC
Ferris State Univ	MI	21,458	C
Fitchburg State Univ	MA	21,819	LC
Five Towns College	NY	35,480	LC
Flagler College	FL	27,620	C
Florida A&M Univ	FL	15,361	C
Florida Atlantic Univ	FL	18,256	C
Florida Gulf Coast Univ	FL	14,738	C
Florida International Univ	FL	20,281	C
Florida Memorial Univ	FL	22,424	LC
Florida Southern College	FL	45,978	VC
Florida State Univ	FL	16,771	HC
Fontbonne Univ	MO	34,606	C
Fort Hays State Univ	KS	12,677	C
Framingham State Univ	MA	21,740	C
Francis Marion Univ	SC	18,144	LC
Franciscan Univ of Steubenville	OH	33,980	VC
Franklin College	IN	40,550	C
Franklin Pierce Univ	NH	46,750	LC
Freed-Hardeman Univ	TN	29,900	C
Friends Univ	KS	38,000	C
Frostburg State Univ	MD	17,280	LC
Furman Univ	SC	61,098	VC+
Gallaudet Univ	DC	30,088	LC
Gannon Univ	PA	42,922	C
Gardner-Webb Univ	NC	24,935	C+
Geneva College	PA	35,450	C
George Fox Univ	OR	42,938	C
Georgetown College	KY	41,440	C
Gettysburg College	PA	65,210	MC
Glenville State College	WV	17,386	LC
Goddard College	VT	17,040	VC
Gordon College	MA	47,740	VC
Goshen College	IN	44,350	C
Grace Bible College	MI	25,250	C
Grace College and Seminary	IN	31,524	C
Graceland Univ	IA	35,290	C
Grambling State Univ	LA	15,701	C
Grand Canyon Univ	AZ	25,150	VC
Grand Valley State Univ	MI	22,250	C+
Grand View Univ	IA	32,302	C
Green Mountain College	VT	45,228	LC
Greensboro College	NC	39,790	LC
Greenville College	IL	27,012	LC
Gustavus Adolphus College	MN	53,943	HC
Gwynedd Mercy Univ	PA	43,780	LC
Hamline Univ	MN	50,152	C
Hannibal-LaGrange Univ	MO	29,815	C
Hanover College	IN	47,750	C+
Harding Univ	AR	25,440	C
Hardin-Simmons Univ	TX	36,025	C
Harris-Stowe State Univ	MO	14,590	NC
Hastings College	NE	35,380	C+
Hawaii Pacific Univ	HI	33,420	C
Heidelberg Univ	OH	40,400	LC
Hellenic College/Holy Cross Greek Orthodox School of Theology	MA	39,906	C
Henderson State Univ	AR	15,516	C
Heritage Univ	WA	19,825	NC
High Point Univ	NC	47,355	VC
Hofstra Univ	NY	58,210	C+
Holy Family Univ	PA	44,672	LC
Hood College	MD	50,540	C
Hope College	MI	42,840	VC
Hope International Univ	CA	42,730	C
Houghton College	NY	40,558	VC
Houston Baptist Univ	TX	36,450	C
Howard Payne Univ	TX	35,994	C
Howard Univ	DC	37,616	C+
Humboldt State Univ	CA	21,708	C
Huntingdon College	AL	35,900	C
Huntington Univ	IN	33,996	C
Husson Univ	ME	26,508	C
Huston-Tillotson Univ	TX	18,124	LC
Idaho State Univ	ID	13,619	LC
Illinois College	IL	41,330	VC
Illinois State Univ	IL	23,418	VC
Immaculata Univ	PA	39,000	C
Indiana Inst of Technology	IN	34,240	LC
Indiana State Univ	IN	23,223	LC
Indiana Univ Bloomington	IN	20,791	HC
Indiana Univ East	IN	7,207	C
Indiana Univ Kokomo	IN	7,207	C
Indiana Univ Northwest	IN	7,207	LC
Indiana Univ South Bend	IN	16,057	C
Indiana Univ Southeast	IN	16,931	C
Indiana Univ-Purdue Univ Fort Wayne	IN	18,675	C
Indiana Univ-Purdue Univ Indianapolis	IN	18,952	C
Indiana Wesleyan Univ	IN	33,674	C
Inter-American Univ of PR Ponce	PR	19,549	
Inter-American Univ of PR-Aguadilla Campus	PR	21,657	
Inter-American Univ of PR-Arecibo Campus	PR	18,245	
Inter-American Univ of PR-Barranquitas	PR	18,336	
Inter-American Univ of PR-Fajardo Campus	PR	18,336	
Inter-American Univ of PR-Metropolitan Campus	PR	20,045	

ST = STATE $IS = IN-STATE COSTS SR = SELECTOR RATING

School	ST	$IS	SR
Inter-American Univ of PR-San Germán	PR	20,042	
Iowa State Univ	IA	18,176	C
Iowa Wesleyan Univ	IA	41,000	C
Jackson State Univ	MS	15,879	LC
Jacksonville State Univ	AL	14,628	LC
Jacksonville Univ	FL	49,210	C
Jarvis Christian College	TX	20,160	NC
John Brown Univ	AR	35,184	VC
Johnson State College	VT	22,672	C
Judson College	AL	27,066	C
Judson Univ	IL	39,174	C
Juniata College	PA	58,118	VC
Kansas State Univ	KS	17,780	VC
Kean Univ	NJ	25,620	C
Keene State College	NH	24,604	C
Kentucky Christian Univ	KY	26,836	LC
Kentucky State Univ	KY	14,484	LC
Kentucky Wesleyan College	KY	34,260	LC
Keuka College	NY	42,398	LC
Keystone College	PA	28,680	LC
King Univ	TN	36,976	C
King's College	PA	48,240	C
Knox College	IL	54,654	VC+
Kutztown Univ of Pennsylvania	PA	19,477	C
La Roche College	PA	38,940	C
La Salle Univ	PA	43,476	C
La Sierra Univ	CA	39,690	VC
Lake Superior State Univ	MI	19,867	C
Lakeland Univ	WI	35,130	C
Lamar Univ	TX	18,014	LC
Lander Univ	SC	32,200	C
Langston Univ	OK	15,659	C
Lasell College	MA	49,400	C
Le Moyne College	NY	47,305	VC
Lebanon Valley College	PA	55,510	VC
Lee Univ	TN	22,045	C
Lees-McRae College	NC	33,944	NC
Lenoir-Rhyne Univ	NC	47,500	LC
Lesley Univ	MA	42,800	C
LeTourneau Univ	TX	39,190	VC
Lewis Univ	IL	41,710	C
Lewis-Clark State College	ID	14,202	C
Liberty Univ	VA	31,415	C
Limestone College	SC	32,100	C
Lincoln Memorial Univ	TN	28,430	C
Lincoln Univ	MO	14,402	NC
Lindenwood Univ	MO	25,760	C
Lindsey Wilson College	KY	33,546	C
Linfield College	OR	53,992	C
Lipscomb Univ	TN	42,984	VC
LIU Brooklyn	NY	50,698	C
LIU Post	NY	50,698	C+
Livingstone College	NC	17,815	LC
Lock Haven Univ of Pennsylvania	PA	20,544	LC
Longwood Univ	VA	22,184	C
Loras College	IA	40,726	C
Louisiana College	LA	21,274	C
Louisiana State Univ and A&M College	LA	18,677	VC
Louisiana State Univ in Shreveport	LA	6,902	C
Louisiana Tech Univ	LA	11,422	VC
Loyola Univ Chicago	IL	57,158	VC
Loyola Univ Maryland	MD	61,710	VC
Luther College	IA	49,990	VC
Lyndon State College	VT	20,714	C
MacMurray College	IL	35,025	C
Manchester Univ	IN	41,540	C
Manhattan College	NY	55,652	C
Mansfield Univ of Pennsylvania	PA	24,244	LC
Marian Univ	IN	43,206	C
Marian Univ	WI	34,622	C
Mars Hill Univ	NC	41,104	C
Marshall Univ	WV	18,044	C
Marymount Manhattan College	NY	48,350	C
Maryville College	TN	44,410	C
Maryville Univ of St. Louis	MO	38,558	VC
Marywood Univ	PA	47,840	C
Mayville State Univ	ND	18,371	NC
McKendree Univ	IL	37,940	C+
McMurry Univ	TX	34,259	LC
McNeese State Univ	LA	7,838	C
McPherson College	KS	36,134	C
Mercer Univ	GA	45,348	VC
Mercy College	NY	32,614	C
Mercyhurst Univ	PA	47,420	C
Merrimack College	MA	55,415	C
Messiah College	PA	44,380	VC
Methodist Univ	NC	58,130	C
Miami Univ	OH	27,190	HC+
MidAmerica Nazarene Univ	KS	37,808	C
Midland Univ	NE	39,512	C
Miles College	AL	16,530	NC
Millersville Univ of Pennsylvania	PA	25,298	C
Millikin Univ	IL	44,148	C
Minn State Univ, Mankato	MN	17,190	C
Minn State Univ, Moorhead	MN	21,393	C
Minot State Univ	ND	13,285	C
Miss College	MS	25,850	C
Miss State Univ	MS	12,028	C+
Miss Univ for Women	MS	17,065	C
Miss Valley State Univ	MS	13,233	LC
Missouri Baptist Univ	MO	35,594	C

School	ST	$IS	SR
Missouri Southern State Univ	MO	13,071	C
Missouri State Univ	MO	15,837	C+
Missouri Valley College	MO	28,150	C
Missouri Western State Univ	MO	17,822	LC
Monmouth College	IL	42,260	C
Monmouth Univ	NJ	50,184	C
Montana State Univ	MT	15,500	C+
Montana State Univ Billings	MT	13,336	LC
Montana State Univ-Northern	MT	11,370	NC
Montreat College	NC	34,605	LC
Moravian College	PA	55,488	C
Morehead State Univ	KY	18,386	LC
Morgan State Univ	MD	17,190	LC
Morningside College	IA	39,780	C
Morris College	SC	19,195	LC
Mount Aloysius College	PA	29,976	C
Mount Marty College	SD	36,862	C
Mount Mercy Univ	IA	39,748	C
Mount St. Joseph Univ	OH	33,880	LC
Mount St. Mary's Univ	MD	53,380	C
Mount St. Mary's Univ - Chalon Campus	CA	50,486	VC+
Murray State Univ	KY	17,726	C+
Muskingum Univ	OH	35,966	C
National Louis Univ	IL	43,000	LC
Nazareth College	NY	46,784	C
Nebr Wesleyan Univ	NE	42,026	C+
New England College	NH	50,828	NC
New Jersey City Univ	NJ	21,456	LC
New Mexico Highlands Univ	NM	11,904	LC
New Mexico State Univ	NM	14,050	LC
New York Univ	NY	68,139	MC
Newberry College	SC	34,550	C
Newman Univ	KS	37,382	C
Niagara Univ	NY	41,010	C
Nicholls State Univ	LA	14,959	C
N Car Central Univ	NC	9,000	C
N Car Wesleyan College	NC	39,200	C
North Central College	IL	48,712	C+
North Central Univ	MN	30,610	C
N Dak State Univ	ND	16,245	VC
North Park Univ	IL	35,860	C
Northeastern Illinois Univ	IL	12,529	LC
Northeastern State Univ	OK	8,615	VC
Northern Arizona Univ	AZ	21,003	C
Northern Illinois Univ	IL	20,176	C
Northern Kentucky Univ	KY	16,486	C
Northern Mich Univ	MI	20,853	C
Northern State Univ	SD	15,570	C
Northland College	WI	41,103	C+
Northwest Christian Univ	OR	36,580	C
Northwest Missouri State Univ	MO	18,286	C
Northwest Nazarene Univ	ID	40,250	C
Northwest Univ	WA	38,720	VC
Northwestern College of Iowa	IA	38,400	C
Northwestern Okla State Univ	OK	13,072	LC
Northwestern State Univ of Louisiana	LA	16,534	LC
Notre Dame College	OH	39,150	VC
Notre Dame of Maryland Univ	MD	47,570	VC
Nova Southeastern Univ	FL	38,534	C+
Nyack College	NY	34,450	LC
Oakland City Univ	IN	33,930	NC
Oakland Univ	MI	20,763	C
Oakwood Univ	AL	43,758	C
Oglala Lakota College	SD	15,050	NC
Ohio State Univ at Mansfield	OH	15,529	C
Ohio State Univ at Marion	OH	7,553	VC
Ohio State Univ at Newark	OH	16,685	C
Ohio Valley Univ	WV	28,800	C
Ohio Wesleyan Univ	OH	49,460	VC
Okla Baptist Univ	OK	33,990	C
Okla Christian Univ	OK	29,260	C
Okla City Univ	OK	40,476	C
Okla State Univ	OK	17,180	C+
Okla Wesleyan Univ	OK	34,434	C
Old Dominion Univ	VA	21,618	C
Olivet College	MI	37,661	LC
Olivet Nazarene Univ	IL	41,840	VC
Oral Roberts Univ	OK	34,316	C
Ottawa Univ	KS	39,980	VC
Otterbein Univ	OH	41,630	C
Ouachita Baptist Univ	AR	33,500	VC
Pace Univ	NY	60,136	C
Pacific Lutheran Univ	WA	49,960	C
Palm Beach Atlantic Univ	FL	39,250	C
Park Univ	MO	22,134	C
Penn State Altoona	PA	26,686	C
Pennsylvania State Univ - Univ Park	PA	29,716	HC
Pepperdine Univ	CA	66,862	VC+
Peru State College	NE	15,602	LC
Pfeiffer Univ	NC	40,532	LC
Pittsburg State Univ	KS	13,880	C
Plymouth State Univ	NH	23,180	LC
Point Park Univ	PA	41,270	C
Pontifical Catholic Univ of PR	PR	10,534	
Presbyterian College	SC	47,186	C
Prescott College	AZ	38,201	C
Principia College	IL	40,350	C
Providence College	RI	62,870	HC
Purdue Univ Northwest	IN	15,178	C
Purdue Univ/West Lafayette	IN	20,032	MC
Queens Univ of Charlotte	NC	39,543	C

School	ST	$IS	SR
Quincy Univ	IL	38,170	LC
Quinnipiac Univ	CT	60,970	VC
Rhode Island College	RI	19,000	LC
Rider Univ	NJ	54,050	C
Ripon College	WI	49,991	VC
Rivier Univ	NH	41,600	VC
Robert Morris Univ	PA	40,600	C
Roberts Wesleyan College	NY	41,116	C
Rockford Univ	IL	38,570	C
Rockhurst Univ	MO	28,990	C
Rocky Mountain College	MT	35,776	C
Roger Williams Univ	RI	48,074	VC
Rollins College	FL	58,670	HC
Roosevelt Univ	IL	41,890	VC
Rowan Univ	NJ	24,491	VC
Russell Sage College	NY	39,370	C
Rust College	MS	10,600	C
Saginaw Valley State Univ	MI	19,284	C
SAGU American Indian College	AZ	18,142	C
St. Augustine's Univ	NC	25,582	C
St. Francis Univ	PA	46,146	NC
St. John's Univ	MN	53,472	C
St. Joseph's College of Maine	ME	47,890	C
St. Joseph's Univ	PA	58,540	VC
St. Leo Univ	FL	32,850	C
St. Louis Univ	MO	49,866	HC
St. Martin's Univ	WA	45,056	C
St. Mary-of-the-Woods College	IN	40,424	LC
St. Mary's College	IN	50,600	C
St. Mary's Univ of Minn	MN	42,440	C
St. Michael's College	VT	53,275	VC+
St. Peter's Univ	NJ	49,192	C
St. Xavier Univ	IL	44,440	C
Salem International Univ	WV	21,090	C
Salisbury Univ	MD	21,132	VC
Salve Regina Univ	RI	53,046	VC
Samford Univ	AL	40,770	VC
San Francisco State Univ	CA	18,514	LC
Schreiner Univ	TX	34,626	LC
Seattle Pacific Univ	WA	47,439	C+
Seton Hall Univ	NJ	58,008	C
Seton Hill Univ	PA	46,972	VC
Shaw Univ	NC	24,638	C
Shawnee State Univ	OH	16,998	C
Shepherd Univ, West Virginia	WV	17,382	C
Shippensburg Univ of Pennsylvania	PA	24,096	C
Siena Heights Univ	MI	36,322	C
Silver Lake College of the Holy Family	WI	36,290	LC
Simmons College	MA	54,400	HC
Simpson College	IA	45,626	VC
Simpson Univ	CA	34,722	C
Sinte Gleska Univ	SD	13,154	NC
Skidmore College	NY	66,600	MC
Slippery Rock Univ of Pennsylvania	PA	20,450	C
Smith College	MA	66,774	MC
S Car State Univ	SC	21,330	LC
Southeast Missouri State Univ	MO	16,148	C
Southeastern Louisiana Univ	LA	16,237	C
Southeastern Okla State Univ	OK	11,875	C
Southeastern Univ	FL	34,910	LC
Southern Adventist Univ	TN	28,250	C
Southern Arkansas Univ	AR	21,532	C
Southern Conn State Univ	CT	21,924	LC
Southern Illinois Univ Carbondale	IL	24,554	C
Southern Illinois Univ Edwardsville	IL	20,188	C
Southern Nazarene Univ	OK	33,684	C
Southern New Hampshire Univ	NH	44,256	C
Southern Oregon Univ	OR	19,117	C
Southern Univ and A&M College	LA	16,074	LC
Southern Univ at New Orleans	LA	8,014	LC
Southern Wesleyan Univ	SC	33,670	LC
Southwest Baptist Univ	MO	30,890	LC
Southwest Minn State Univ	MN	17,783	C
Southwestern Adventist Univ	TX	28,232	LC
Southwestern College	KS	31,531	LC
Southwestern Okla State Univ	OK	12,205	C
Spalding Univ	KY	31,938	C
Spring Hill College	AL	48,488	C
Springfield College	MA	48,775	C
St. Andrews Univ	NC	44,634	LC
St. Bonaventure Univ	NY	45,596	C
St. Catherine Univ	MN	45,630	C
St. Cloud State Univ	MN	10,600	C
St. Francis College	NY	38,800	LC
St. John Fisher College	NY	45,270	VC
St. John's Univ	NY	57,160	C+
St. Joseph's College, New York/Brooklyn Campus	NY	25,114	LC
St. Mary's Univ	TX	39,120	C
St. Norbert College	WI	46,060	VC
St. Thomas Aquinas College	NY	32,450	C
St. Thomas Univ	FL	51,187	LC
SUNY at Geneseo	NY	21,622	VC
SUNY at New Paltz	NY	20,840	C
SUNY at Oswego	NY	22,219	VC
SUNY/Buffalo State	NY	20,583	LC
SUNY/College at Old Westbury	NY	16,860	C
SUNY/Fredonia	NY	20,818	C

School	ST	$IS	SR
SUNY/Oneonta	NY	20,794	C
Stephens College	MO	38,042	C
Sterling College	KS	32,830	LC
Stetson Univ	FL	57,174	VC+
Stevenson Univ	MD	48,412	C
Stillman College	AL	20,738	C
Sul Ross State Univ	TX	15,021	LC
Syracuse Univ	NY	62,313	HC
Tabor College	KS	35,870	C
Taylor Univ	IN	42,130	VC
Temple Univ	PA	24,392	C+
Tenn Wesleyan Univ	TN	32,680	LC
Texas A&M Univ at College Station	TX	20,771	VC+
Texas A&M Univ at Commerce	TX	10,496	C
Texas A&M Univ at Kingsville	TX	16,580	LC
Texas Wesleyan Univ	TX	37,338	C
The American Univ	DC	61,317	HC
The Catholic Univ of America	DC	58,376	VC
The College of Idaho	ID	36,415	C
The College of New Jersey	NJ	28,675	VC+
The Master's Univ	CA	43,870	C
The Univ of Alabama	AL	24,320	C+
The Univ of Arizona	AZ	24,086	C
The Univ of Mary	ND	23,180	C
The Univ of Montana Western	MT	9,426	LC
The Univ of Tenn at Martin	TN	15,212	C
The Univ of Utah	UT	18,751	VC
Thomas College	ME	73,888	LC
Thomas More College	KY	36,720	LC
Tougaloo College	MS	17,980	NC
Touro College	NY	31,040	C
Towson Univ	MD	21,878	C
Transylvania Univ	KY	47,450	HC+
Trine Univ	IN	41,310	C
Trinity Bible College	ND		
Trinity Christian College	IL	35,580	C
Trinity International Univ	IL	31,070	VC
Trinity Washington Univ	DC	33,826	C+
Troy Univ	AL	16,171	C
Tusculum College	TN	31,625	LC
Tuskegee Univ	AL	28,164	C
Union College	KY	32,310	C
Union College	NE	23,270	C
Union Univ	TN	41,160	VC
Universidad Adventista de las Antillas	PR	16,606	
Universidad del Turabo	PR	17,828	
Universidad Metropolitana	PR	17,828	
Univ of PR, at Arecibo	PR	12,652	
Univ of Alabama at Birmingham	AL	22,092	C
Univ of Alabama in Huntsville	AL	20,028	VC
Univ of Alaska Anchorage	AK	17,914	C
Univ of Alaska Fairbanks	AK	16,874	VC
Univ of Alaska Southeast	AK	17,615	C
Univ of Arkansas at Fayetteville	AR	19,766	VC
Univ of Arkansas at Little Rock	AR	18,211	LC
Univ of Central Arkansas	AR	15,042	VC
Univ of Central Florida	FL	16,379	VC
Univ of Central Missouri	MO	18,982	C
Univ of Central Okla	OK	15,150	C
Univ of Charleston	WV	35,000	LC
Univ of Cincinnati	OH	22,118	VC
Univ of Colo Boulder	CO	26,048	HC
Univ of Conn	CT	27,394	
Univ of Dallas	TX	50,676	VC
Univ of Dayton	OH	54,930	VC
Univ of Delaware	DE	32,214	VC
Univ of Detroit Mercy	MI	48,816	C
Univ of Evansville	IN	44,186	C+
Univ of Findlay	OH	43,040	C
Univ of Florida	FL	16,291	HC+
Univ of Great Falls	MT	38,524	C
Univ of Hartford	CT	49,776	C
Univ of Hawaii at Manoa	HI	23,261	C
Univ of Holy Cross	LA	21,523	NC
Univ of Idaho	ID	16,158	C
Univ of Illinois at Chicago	IL	24,664	VC
Univ of Illinois at Urbana-Champaign	IL	27,006	HC
Univ of Indianapolis	IN	36,480	VC
Univ of Iowa	IA	19,415	HC
Univ of Jamestown	ND	28,508	C
Univ of Kansas	KS	20,884	VC
Univ of Kentucky	KY	24,800	C+
Univ of Louisiana at Lafayette	LA	14,516	C
Univ of Louisiana at Monroe	LA	15,970	C
Univ of Louisville	KY	19,692	C
Univ of Lynchburg	VA	48,370	C
Univ of Maine	ME	21,038	VC
Univ of Maine at Farmington	ME	18,792	C
Univ of Maine at Fort Kent	ME	15,165	LC
Univ of Maine at Machias	ME	22,960	C
Univ of Maine at Presque Isle	ME	16,148	LC
Univ of Mary Hardin-Baylor	TX	35,292	C+
Univ of Maryland/College Park	MD	21,938	HC
Univ of Maryland/Eastern Shore	MD	21,861	LC
Univ of Miami	FL	63,494	MC
Univ of Mich/Ann Arbor	MI	25,274	MC

ST = STATE $IS = IN-STATE COSTS SR = SELECTOR RATING

School	ST	$IS	SR
Univ of Mich/Dearborn	MI	12,472	VC
Univ of Mich/Flint	MI	19,062	C
Univ of Minn/Crookston	MN	19,126	C
Univ of Minn/Duluth	MN	20,292	C
Univ of Minn/Morris	MN	21,222	VC
Univ of Minn/Twin Cities	MN	24,269	MC
Univ of Miss	MS	18,802	C
Univ of Missouri-Columbia	MO	20,463	VC
Univ of Missouri-Kansas City	MO	19,563	VC
Univ of Missouri-St. Louis	MO	19,810	VC
Univ of Mobile	AL	28,935	C
Univ of Montana	MT	14,105	C
Univ of Montevallo	AL	20,012	C
Univ of Nebr - Kearney	NE	17,014	LC
Univ of Nebr - Lincoln	NE	18,589	VC
Univ of Nebr - Omaha	NE	16,120	C
Univ of Nevada, Las Vegas	NV	17,553	C
Univ of Nevada, Reno	NV	18,010	C
Univ of New England	ME	50,110	C
Univ of New Mexico	NM	16,808	C
Univ of New Orleans	LA	12,840	C
Univ of North Alabama	AL	15,964	C
Univ of N Car at Chapel Hill	NC	20,561	MC
Univ of N Car at Charlotte	NC	17,803	VC
Univ of N Car at Greensboro	NC	15,998	C
Univ of N Car at Pembroke	NC	14,737	LC
Univ of N Car Wilmington	NC	16,784	VC
Univ of N Dak	ND	16,673	C
Univ of North Florida	FL	15,996	VC
Univ of North Georgia	GA	17,316	C
Univ of Northern Iowa	IA	17,480	C
Univ of Northwestern - St. Paul	MN	39,530	C
Univ of Okla	OK	19,651	HC
Univ of Pennsylvania	PA	63,526	MC
Univ of Pikeville	KY	27,838	C
Univ of Pittsburgh at Bradford	PA	22,958	C
Univ of Pittsburgh at Johnstown	PA	22,092	C
Univ of Portland	OR	52,152	VC
Univ of PR, at Bayamon	PR	13,145	
Univ of PR, at Cayey	PR		
Univ of PR, at Humacao	PR	14,000	
Univ of PR-Rio Piedras campus	PR	13,327	
Univ of Rhode Island	RI	26,066	VC
Univ of Rio Grande & Rio Grande Community College	OH	8,750	LC
Univ of St. Francis	IN	38,520	C
Univ of St. Mary	KS	37,080	NC
Univ of Science and Arts of Okla	OK	11,140	VC
Univ of Scranton	PA	54,962	VC
Univ of Sioux Falls	SD	25,630	C
Univ of South Alabama	AL	16,880	C
Univ of S Car Aiken	SC	18,094	C
Univ of S Car at Columbia	SC	21,726	VC
Univ of S Car Upstate	SC	19,272	LC
Univ of S Dak	SD	16,109	C
Univ of South Florida/Tampa	FL	16,110	VC
Univ of Southern Indiana	IN	16,808	C
Univ of Southern Miss	MS	13,170	C
Univ of St. Francis	IL	40,828	C
Univ of Tampa	FL	38,928	VC
Univ of Texas Rio Grande Valley	TX	15,573	LC
Univ of the Cumberlands	KY	32,000	LC
Univ of the District of Columbia	DC	21,260	LC
Univ of the Incarnate Word	TX	39,162	LC
Univ of the Sacred Heart	PR	17,932	
Univ of the Southwest	NM	24,386	C
Univ of Toledo	OH	19,336	C
Univ of Tulsa	OK	52,625	HC
Univ of Vermont	VT	29,792	HC
Univ of West Alabama	AL	16,284	LC
Univ of West Florida	FL	15,848	C
Univ of Wisc-Eau Claire	WI	16,354	VC
Univ of Wisc-Green Bay	WI	15,184	C
Univ of Wisc-La Crosse	WI	15,425	VC
Univ of Wisc-Madison	WI	21,647	MC
Univ of Wisc-Oshkosh	WI	15,392	C
Univ of Wisc-Parkside	WI	15,313	C
Univ of Wisc-Platteville	WI	14,148	C
Univ of Wisc-River Falls	WI	14,541	C
Univ of Wisc-Stevens Point	WI	14,043	C
Univ of Wisc-Superior	WI	14,838	C
Univ of Wisc-Whitewater	WI	13,976	C
Univ of Wyoming	WY	15,537	C
Upper Iowa Univ	IA	34,990	NC
Urbana Univ	OH	30,820	C
Ursuline College	OH	41,076	LC
Utah State Univ	UT	13,235	C
Valley City State Univ	ND	13,267	C
Valparaiso Univ	IN	50,160	VC
Vanderbilt Univ	TN	63,248	MC
Vanguard Univ of Southern Calif	CA	42,400	VC
Virginia Union Univ	VA	25,058	C
Virginia Wesleyan Univ	VA	45,980	LC
Viterbo Univ	WI	34,660	C
Wagner College	NY	57,240	C+
Walla Walla Univ	WA	34,845	C
Walsh Univ	OH	39,010	C
Warner Univ	FL	28,216	C
Wartburg College	IA	49,478	C
Washburn Univ	KS	15,827	C
Washington Adventist Univ	MD	32,050	LC
Washington State Univ	WA	22,747	C
Washington Univ in St. Louis	MO	67,539	MC
Wayne State College	NE	25,746	NC
Wayne State Univ	MI	23,085	C
Waynesburg Univ	PA	33,530	C
Weber State Univ	UT	14,112	C
Webster Univ	MO	37,490	C
Wellesley College	MA	66,984	MC
Wells College	NY	50,500	C
Wesley College	DE	37,848	LC
West Chester Univ of Pennsylvania	PA	19,171	VC
West Liberty Univ	WV	16,158	C
West Virginia State Univ	WV	19,412	LC
West Virginia Wesleyan College	WV	39,188	C
Western Carolina Univ	NC	13,965	C
Western Conn State Univ	CT	21,254	LC
Western Illinois Univ	IL	20,897	C
Western Kentucky Univ	KY	16,850	C
Western Mich Univ	MI	21,791	C
Western New England Univ	MA	49,182	C
Western New Mexico Univ	NM	16,914	LC
Western State Colo Univ	CO	19,348	C
Western Washington Univ	WA	18,904	VC
Westfield State Univ	MA	20,404	C
Westminster College	MO	32,820	C
Westminster College	PA	41,722	C
Westminster College	UT	41,078	C
Wheaton College	IL	44,993	MC
Wheeling Jesuit Univ	WV	37,106	LC
Wheelock College	MA	51,325	LC
Whitworth Univ	WA	53,682	VC
Wichita State Univ	KS	17,773	C
Widener Univ	PA	58,190	C
Wiley College	TX	19,255	C
Wilkes Univ	PA	49,166	C
William Carey Univ	MS	23,950	LC
William Jewell College	MO	42,490	C+
William Penn Univ	IA	26,000	C
William Woods Univ	MO	32,040	C
Williams Baptist College	AR	24,720	C
Wilmington College	OH	35,100	C
Wilmington Univ	DE	8,762	NC
Wilson College	PA	35,620	LC
Wingate Univ	NC	41,900	C
Winona State Univ	MN	18,109	C
Winston-Salem State Univ	NC	18,005	LC
Winthrop Univ	SC	23,960	C
Wisc Lutheran College	WI	36,290	C
Wittenberg Univ	OH	49,863	VC
Worcester State Univ	MA	20,977	C
Wright State Univ	OH	16,983	C
Xavier Univ of Louisiana	LA	31,689	C
York College	NE	30,260	C
York College of Pennsylvania	PA	29,240	C

EMERGENCY MEDICAL SERVICES

School	ST	$IS	SR
Anna Maria College	MA	51,020	C
Creighton Univ	NE	49,452	VC
Lake Superior State Univ	MI	19,867	C
Univ of South Alabama	AL	16,880	C

EMERGENCY MEDICAL TECHNOLOGIES

School	ST	$IS	SR
Central Washington Univ	WA	16,803	C
Drury Univ	MO	37,555	VC
Idaho State Univ	ID	13,619	LC
Pennsylvania College of Technology	PA	27,693	NC
Springfield College	MA	48,775	C
The George Washington Univ	DC	68,474	HC+
Univ of Maryland/Baltimore County	MD	23,004	VC
Univ of New Mexico	NM	16,808	C
Univ of Pittsburgh	PA	30,030	MC
Western Carolina Univ	NC	13,965	C

EMERGENCY/DISASTER SCIENCE

School	ST	$IS	SR
Arkansas State Univ	AR	16,190	C
Arkansas Tech Univ	AR	16,534	LC
Embry-Riddle Aeronautical Univ - Worldwide	FL	17,720	C
N Dak State Univ	ND	16,245	VC
Northwest Missouri State Univ	MO	18,286	C
St. Louis Univ	MO	49,866	HC
Southeast Missouri State Univ	MO	16,148	C
The Univ of Akron	OH	22,566	C
Univ of Florida	FL	16,291	HC+
Univ of Maryland Univ College	MD	26,146	LC
Univ of North Texas	TX	20,082	C
West Texas A&M Univ	TX	13,478	C
Western Carolina Univ	NC	13,965	C
Western Illinois Univ	IL	20,897	C

ENERGY MANAGEMENT TECHNOLOGY

School	ST	$IS	SR
CUNY/Hunter College	NY	31,098	VC
Drury Univ	MO	37,555	VC
Fitchburg State Univ	MA	21,819	LC
Idaho State Univ	ID	13,619	LC
Illinois State Univ	IL	23,418	VC
Ohio Univ	OH	23,394	VC
Univ of Northern Iowa	IA	17,480	C
Univ of Okla	OK	19,651	HC
Univ of Tulsa	OK	52,625	HC
Univ of Wyoming	WY	15,537	C

ENERGY SCIENCE

School	ST	$IS	SR
Indiana Univ-Purdue Univ Indianapolis	IN	18,952	C
Miami Univ	OH	27,190	HC+
Syracuse Univ	NY	62,313	HC

ENERGY SYSTEMS TECHNOLOGY

School	ST	$IS	SR
Ferris State Univ	MI	21,458	C
Thomas Edison State Univ	NJ	6,350	NC
Univ of Illinois at Chicago	IL	24,664	VC
Univ of Wyoming	WY	15,537	C

ENERGY UTILITY TECHNOLOGY

School	ST	$IS	SR
Thomas Edison State Univ	NJ	6,350	NC

ENGINEERING

School	ST	$IS	SR
Abilene Christian Univ	TX	43,708	C+
Agnes Scott College	GA	51,930	VC+
Alabama State Univ	AL	16,490	LC
Albion College	MI	55,260	C
Andrews Univ	MI	41,732	C
Arcadia Univ	PA	55,990	C+
Arizona State Univ at the Polytechnic Campus	AZ	22,394	VC
Arkansas State Univ	AR	16,190	C
Baldwin Wallace Univ	OH	42,464	VC
Baylor Univ	TX	56,803	HC
Benedictine College	KS	38,850	VC
Biola Univ	CA	48,686	C
Birmingham-Southern College	AL	44,478	C+
Boston Univ	MA	67,352	MC
Brown Univ	RI	64,566	MC
Bucknell Univ	PA	67,136	MC
Butler Univ	IN	52,890	VC+
Calif Baptist Univ	CA	42,986	C
Cal State, East Bay	CA	20,748	C
Cal State, Fullerton	CA	21,902	C
Cal State, Los Angeles	CA	17,186	LC
Cal State, Northridge	CA	17,277	LC
Calvin College	MI	43,090	HC
Carnegie Mellon Univ	PA	67,980	MC
Case Western Reserve Univ	OH	62,284	MC
Central College	IA	44,592	C
Colo School of Mines	CO	29,319	MC
Colo State Univ	CO	23,033	C
Cooper Union for the Advancement of Science and Art	NY	61,370	MC
Cornell College	IA	49,900	VC
Dominican Univ	IL	42,472	C+
Dordt College	IA	37,860	C+
Drexel Univ	PA	65,927	HC
East Carolina Univ	NC	16,539	C
Eastern Illinois Univ	IL	21,414	C
Eastern Washington Univ	WA	17,896	LC
Elizabethtown College	PA	56,340	VC
Elon Univ	NC	46,142	HC
Embry-Riddle Aeronautical Univ - Worldwide	FL	17,720	C
Florida Atlantic Univ	FL	18,256	C
Franklin W. Olin College of Engineering	MA	65,580	SP
Frostburg State Univ	MD	17,280	LC
Geneva College	PA	35,450	C
Georgia Southern Univ	GA	16,540	VC
Grand Valley State Univ	MI	22,250	C+
Harvard College/Harvard Univ	MA	65,609	MC
Harvey Mudd College	CA	67,155	MC
Hope College	MI	42,840	VC
Indiana Inst of Technology	IN	34,240	LC
Indiana Univ-Purdue Univ Fort Wayne	IN	18,675	C
Iowa State Univ	IA	18,176	C
James Madison Univ	VA	19,084	VC
Jefferson (Philadelphia Univ + Thomas Jefferson Univ)	PA	53,966	C
John Brown Univ	AR	35,184	VC
Johns Hopkins Univ	MD	68,080	MC
Johnson C. Smith Univ	NC	25,336	LC
Kalamazoo College	MI	53,931	HC
Lafayette College	PA	68,520	MC
Lake Superior State Univ	MI	19,867	C
Lamar Univ	TX	18,014	LC
Lawrence Tech Univ	MI	41,630	VC
LeTourneau Univ	TX	39,190	VC
Lindenwood Univ	MO	25,760	C
Loyola Univ Maryland	MD	61,710	VC
Lubbock Christian Univ	TX	29,727	C
Maine Maritime Academy	ME	22,536	C
Manchester Univ	IN	41,540	C
Marian Univ	IN	43,206	C
Marquette Univ	WI	53,090	VC+
Marshall Univ	WV	18,044	C
Maryville College	TN	44,410	C
Maryville Univ of St. Louis	MO	38,558	VC
Mass Inst of Technology	MA	62,662	MC
Mass Maritime Academy	MA	20,704	C
McNeese State Univ	LA	7,838	C
Mercer Univ	GA	45,348	VC
Messiah College	PA	44,380	VC
Miami Univ	OH	27,190	HC+
Mich State Univ	MI	24,542	VC
Mich Tech Univ	MI	25,551	VC+
Millersville Univ of Pennsylvania	PA	25,298	C
Milligan College	TN	39,450	C
Milwaukee School of Engineering	WI	48,531	HC+
Montana Tech of the Univ of Montana	MT	15,447	VC
Mount Vernon Nazarene Univ	OH	35,944	C
Muskingum Univ	OH	35,966	C
New Mexico Highlands Univ	NM	11,904	LC
New York Univ	NY	68,139	MC
N Car State Univ	NC	22,434	HC+
Northwest Nazarene Univ	ID	40,250	C
Northwestern Univ	IL	68,725	MC
Olivet Nazarene Univ	IL	41,840	VC
Oral Roberts Univ	OK	34,316	C
Penn State Erie,The Behrend College	PA	26,688	VC
Pepperdine Univ	CA	66,862	VC+
Providence College	RI	62,870	HC
Purdue Univ Northwest	IN	15,178	C
Quinnipiac Univ	CT	60,970	VC
Rensselaer Polytechnic Inst	NY	67,265	MC
Robert Morris Univ	PA	40,600	C
Rochester Inst of Technology	NY	52,734	HC+
Roger Williams Univ	RI	48,074	VC
Rowan Univ	NJ	24,491	VC
St. Anselm College	NH	56,636	VC
St. Louis Univ	MO	49,866	HC
St. Vincent College	PA	46,229	C
San Diego State Univ	CA	23,156	VC
San Jose State Univ	CA	22,630	C
Seattle Pacific Univ	WA	47,439	C+
Seton Hill Univ	PA	46,972	VC
Smith College	MA	66,774	MC
S Dak State Univ	SD	15,874	C
Spelman College	GA	41,642	C
Spring Hill College	AL	48,488	C
St. Mary's Univ	TX	39,120	C
Stanford Univ	CA	62,541	MC
SUNY at Binghamton	NY	24,100	MC
SUNY/Maritime College	NY	16,020	C
Swarthmore College	PA	63,550	MC
Tarleton State Univ	TX	15,248	LC
Temple Univ	PA	24,392	C+
Tenn Tech Univ	TN	17,929	C
The Catholic Univ of America	DC	58,376	VC
The George Washington Univ	DC	68,474	HC+
The Univ of Akron	OH	22,566	C
The Univ of Arizona	AZ	24,086	C
The Univ of Tenn at Chattanooga	TN	17,340	C+
The Univ of Tenn at Martin	TN	15,212	C
The Univ of Texas at San Antonio	TX	21,060	C
The Univ of Utah	UT	18,751	VC
Trinity College	CT	69,020	HC
Tufts Univ	MA		MC
United States Air Force Academy	CO		C
United States Naval Academy	MD		HC
Univ of Calif at Irvine	CA	33,857	VC
Univ of Calif San Diego	CA	30,450	MC
Univ of Central Missouri	MO	18,982	C
Univ of Central Okla	OK	15,150	C
Univ of Cincinnati	OH	22,118	VC
Univ of Delaware	DE	32,214	VC
Univ of Detroit Mercy	MI	48,816	C
Univ of Hartford	CT	49,776	C
Univ of Idaho	ID	16,158	C
Univ of Illinois at Chicago	IL	24,664	VC
Univ of Illinois at Urbana-Champaign	IL	27,006	HC
Univ of Iowa	IA	19,415	HC
Univ of Louisville	KY	19,692	C
Univ of Maryland/College Park	MD	21,938	HC
Univ of Mass Boston	MA	13,828	C
Univ of Mich/Ann Arbor	MI	25,274	MC
Univ of Mich/Dearborn	MI	12,472	VC
Univ of Mich/Flint	MI	19,062	C
Univ of Miss	MS	18,802	C
Univ of Missouri-Columbia	MO	20,463	VC
Univ of New Haven	CT	53,680	C
Univ of N Car at Asheville	NC	16,251	VC+
Univ of Northwestern - St. Paul	MN	39,530	C
Univ of Pittsburgh at Bradford	PA	22,958	C
Univ of Portland	OR	52,152	VC
Univ of PR, at Mayaguez	PR	13,995	
Univ of San Diego	CA	60,338	HC
Univ of South Florida/Tampa	FL	16,110	VC
Univ of Southern Indiana	IN	16,808	C
Univ of Toledo	OH	19,336	C
Univ of Vermont	VT	29,792	HC
Univ of Washington	WA	23,091	MC

ST = STATE $IS = IN-STATE COSTS   SR = SELECTOR RATING

School	ST	$IS	SR
Univ of Wisc-Milwaukee	WI	21,538	C
Utah State Univ	UT	13,235	C
Walla Walla Univ	WA	34,845	C
Washington Univ in St. Louis	MO	67,539	MC
Waynesburg Univ	PA	33,530	C
Wentworth Inst of Technology	MA	48,810	VC
West Virginia Univ	WV	18,952	VC
West Virginia Wesleyan College	WV	39,188	C
Western Illinois Univ	IL	20,897	C
Wheaton College	IL	44,993	MC
Wheeling Jesuit Univ	WV	37,106	LC
Whitworth Univ	WA	53,682	VC
Widener Univ	PA	58,190	C
Yale Univ	CT	64,650	MC
York College of Pennsylvania	PA	29,240	C
Youngstown State Univ	OH	17,487	C

ENGINEERING AND APPLIED SCIENCE

School	ST	$IS	SR
Benedictine Univ	IL	38,300	C
Bethel Univ	MN	46,550	C+
Calif Inst of Technology	CA	64,704	MC
Cal State, Fullerton	CA	21,902	C
College of Staten Island	NY	24,389	LC
Colo State Univ	CO	23,033	C
Fort Lewis College	CO	20,154	C
George Fox Univ	OR	42,938	C
Hofstra Univ	NY	58,210	C+
New Jersey Inst of Technology	NJ	30,198	HC
Pacific Lutheran Univ	WA	49,960	C
Seattle Pacific Univ	WA	47,439	C+
The College of New Jersey	NJ	28,675	VC+
The Univ of Mary	ND	23,180	C
Trinity Univ	TX	54,480	MC
Tufts Univ	MA		MC
United States Air Force Academy	CO		C
Univ of Calif at Berkeley	CA	29,886	MC
Univ of Calif at Riverside	CA	32,912	C
Univ of Florida	FL	16,291	HC+
Univ of Rochester	NY	65,032	MC
Univ of Virginia	VA	27,367	MC
Vanderbilt Univ	TN	63,248	MC
Wilkes Univ	PA	49,166	C
Yale Univ	CT	64,650	MC

ENGINEERING CHEMISTRY

School	ST	$IS	SR
Ithaca College	NY	58,158	VC+
New York Univ	NY	68,139	MC
Oakland Univ	MI	20,763	C
Stony Brook Univ/The SUNY	NY	22,703	MC

ENGINEERING GRAPHICS & DESIGN

School	ST	$IS	SR
Murray State Univ	KY	17,726	C+
Western Mich Univ	MI	21,791	C

ENGINEERING MANAGEMENT

School	ST	$IS	SR
Arizona State Univ at the Tempe Campus	AZ	23,001	VC
Bethel College	IN	36,830	C
Cal State, Fullerton	CA	21,902	C
Christian Brothers Univ	TN	31,670	VC
Clarkson Univ	NY	60,392	VC
Columbia Univ/City of New York	NY	62,958	MC
Gonzaga Univ	WA	52,880	HC
Illinois Inst of Technology	IL	56,826	HC+
Kansas State Univ	KS	17,780	VC
Lake Superior State Univ	MI	19,867	C
Miami Univ	OH	27,190	HC+
Missouri Univ of Science and Technology	MO	18,655	HC
New York Inst of Technology	NY	49,980	VC
N Dak State Univ	ND	16,245	VC
Oral Roberts Univ	OK	34,316	C
Park Univ	MO	22,134	C
Point Park Univ	PA	41,270	C
Purdue Univ/West Lafayette	IN	20,032	MC
St. Louis Univ	MO	49,866	HC
Stevens Inst of Technology	NJ	64,954	MC
Texas A&M Univ at Kingsville	TX	16,580	LC
The Univ of Arizona	AZ	24,086	C
The Univ of Tenn at Chattanooga	TN	17,340	C+
Trine Univ	IN	41,310	C
United States Military Academy at West Point	NY		HC+
Univ of Idaho	ID	16,158	C
Univ of Louisville	KY	19,692	C
Univ of N Car at Asheville	NC	16,251	VC+
Univ of Northwestern - St. Paul	MN	39,530	C
Univ of Texas Rio Grande Valley	TX	15,573	LC
Univ of the Incarnate Word	TX	39,162	LC
Univ of the Pacific	CA	57,446	VC
Univ of Vermont	VT	29,792	HC
Western Mich Univ	MI	21,791	C
Wilkes Univ	PA	49,166	C
York College of Pennsylvania	PA	29,240	C

ENGINEERING MECHANICS

School	ST	$IS	SR
Cal State, Fullerton	CA	21,902	C
Columbia Univ/City of New York	NY	62,958	MC
Johns Hopkins Univ	MD	68,080	MC
Lehigh Univ	PA	63,860	MC
Mich State Univ	MI	24,542	VC
Missouri Univ of Science and Technology	MO	18,655	HC
New York Univ	NY	68,139	MC
Purdue Univ Northwest	IN	15,178	C
United States Air Force Academy	CO		C
Univ of Arkansas at Little Rock	AR	18,211	LC
Univ of Calif at Riverside	CA	32,912	C
Univ of Cincinnati	OH	22,118	VC
Univ of Illinois at Urbana-Champaign	IL	27,006	HC
Univ of Wisc-Madison	WI	21,647	MC
Virginia Polytechnic Inst and State Univ	VA	21,920	VC
Washington Univ in St. Louis	MO	67,539	MC

ENGINEERING PHYSICS

School	ST	$IS	SR
Albion College	MI	55,260	C
Arkansas Tech Univ	AR	16,534	LC
Augustana College	IL	51,222	VC+
Augustana Univ	SD	39,968	VC
Belmont Univ	TN	44,500	VC+
Bethel College	IN	36,830	C
Bradley Univ	IL	43,240	VC
Brown Univ	RI	64,566	MC
Case Western Reserve Univ	OH	62,284	MC
Christian Brothers Univ	TN	31,670	VC
Colo State Univ	CO	23,033	C
Cornell Univ	NY	67,591	MC
Dartmouth College	NH	68,109	MC
Doane Univ	NE	41,340	VC
Eastern Mich Univ	MI	19,761	C
Eastern Nazarene College	MA	41,114	C
Edinboro Univ	PA	15,940	LC
Elon Univ	NC	46,142	HC
Embry-Riddle Aeronautical Univ - Daytona Beach	FL	45,822	VC
Fordham Univ	NY	68,431	MC
Hampden-Sydney College	VA	57,806	VC
Henderson State Univ	AR	15,516	C
Ithaca College	NY	58,158	VC+
Jacksonville Univ	FL	49,210	C
John Carroll Univ	OH	51,570	C
Juniata College	PA	58,118	VC
Kettering Univ	MI	47,570	HC
Kutztown Univ of Pennsylvania	PA	19,477	C
Lehigh Univ	PA	63,860	MC
Linfield College	OR	53,992	C
Loras College	IA	40,726	C
Loyola Marymount Univ	CA	60,202	VC+
Miami Univ	OH	27,190	HC+
Miss College	MS	25,850	C
Morehouse College	GA	40,835	C
Morgan State Univ	MD	17,190	LC
Murray State Univ	KY	17,726	C+
New Mexico State Univ	NM	14,050	LC
New York Univ	NY	68,139	MC
N Car A&T State Univ	NC	13,786	C
Northwest Nazarene Univ	ID	40,250	C
Oakland Univ	MI	20,763	C
Ohio State Univ at Columbus	OH	22,843	MC
Ohio Univ	OH	23,394	VC
Point Loma Nazarene Univ	CA	46,150	C+
Purdue Univ Northwest	IN	15,178	C
Ramapo College of New Jersey	NJ	25,760	VC
Randolph College	VA	53,970	C
Randolph-Macon College	VA	51,480	VC
Rensselaer Polytechnic Inst	NY	67,265	MC
Rose-Hulman Inst of Technology	IN	59,823	MC
St. Louis Univ	MO	49,866	HC
St. Mary's Univ of Minn	MN	42,440	C
Samford Univ	AL	40,770	VC
S Dak State Univ	SD	15,874	C
Southeast Missouri State Univ	MO	16,148	C
Southwestern College	KS	31,531	LC
Southwestern Okla State Univ	OK	12,205	C
St. Bonaventure Univ	NY	45,596	C
Stanford Univ	CA	62,541	MC
SUNY/Univ at Buffalo	NY	23,122	C
Stevens Inst of Technology	NJ	64,954	MC
Tarleton State Univ	TX	15,248	LC
Taylor Univ	IN	42,130	VC
Tufts Univ	MA		MC
Tulane Univ	LA	67,496	MC
United States Military Academy at West Point	NY		HC+
Univ of Calif at Berkeley	CA	29,886	MC
Univ of Calif San Diego	CA	30,450	MC
Univ of Central Okla	OK	15,150	C
Univ of Colo Boulder	CO	26,048	HC
Univ of Conn	CT	27,394	
Univ of Illinois at Chicago	IL	24,664	VC
Univ of Illinois at Urbana-Champaign	IL	27,006	HC
Univ of Kansas	KS	20,884	VC
Univ of Maine	ME	21,038	VC
Univ of Mass Boston	MA	13,828	C
Univ of Mich/Ann Arbor	MI	25,274	MC
Univ of Nebr - Omaha	NE	16,120	C
Univ of Nevada, Reno	NV	18,010	C
Univ of New Hampshire	NH	29,333	VC
Univ of North Texas	TX	20,082	C
Univ of Okla	OK	19,651	HC
Univ of Pittsburgh	PA	30,030	MC
Univ of San Francisco	CA	60,580	C
Univ of Texas Rio Grande Valley	TX	15,573	LC
Univ of the Pacific	CA	57,446	VC
Univ of Tulsa	OK	52,625	HC
Univ of Wisc-Madison	WI	21,647	MC
Univ of Wisc-Platteville	WI	14,148	C
Washington and Lee Univ	VA	59,647	MC
West Chester Univ of Pennsylvania	PA	19,171	VC
West Virginia Wesleyan College	WV	39,188	C
Westmont College	CA	57,930	VC
Whitworth Univ	WA	53,682	VC
Wright State Univ	OH	16,983	C
Xavier Univ	OH	49,380	VC

ENGINEERING SCIENCE

School	ST	$IS	SR
Calif Polytechnic State Univ	CA	22,547	MC
Cal State, Fullerton	CA	21,902	C
Carroll College	MT	44,304	C
Cornell College	IA	49,900	VC
Dartmouth College	NH	68,109	MC
Hanover College	IN	47,750	C+
Lincoln Univ	PA	20,878	LC
Loyola Univ Chicago	IL	57,158	VC
Morehouse College	GA	40,835	C
Pennsylvania State Univ - Univ Park	PA	29,716	HC
Rutgers Univ - New Brunswick	NJ	27,090	HC
Shepherd Univ, West Virginia	WV	17,382	C
Stony Brook Univ/The SUNY	NY	22,703	MC
Univ of Mary Hardin-Baylor	TX	35,292	C+
Univ of Miami	FL	63,494	MC
Univ of Pittsburgh	PA	30,030	MC
Wartburg College	IA	49,478	C

ENGINEERING TECHNOLOGY

School	ST	$IS	SR
Appalachian State Univ	NC	15,394	VC
Austin Peay State Univ	TN	16,397	C
Bluefield State College	WV	5,832	LC
Bowling Green State Univ	OH	19,975	C
Calif State Polytechnic Univ, Pomona	CA	21,811	C
Cal State, Maritime Academy	CA	23,156	C+
Cal State, Fullerton	CA	21,902	C
Cal State, Long Beach	CA	18,850	C
Cal State, Sacramento	CA	19,060	C
Calif Univ of Pennsylvania	PA	20,425	LC
Capitol Technology Univ	MD	46,280	SP
Central Mich Univ	MI	20,330	C
Central Washington Univ	WA	16,803	C
Colo Mesa Univ	CO	19,707	LC
Drexel Univ	PA	65,927	HC
East Tenn State Univ	TN	18,141	C
Eastern Mich Univ	MI	19,761	C
Eastern Washington Univ	WA	17,896	LC
Embry-Riddle Aeronautical Univ - Worldwide	FL	17,720	C
Fairmont State Univ	WV	15,726	C
Ferris State Univ	MI	21,458	C
Florida A&M Univ	FL	15,361	C
Grambling State Univ	LA	15,701	C
Grand Canyon Univ	AZ	25,150	VC
Indiana Univ-Purdue Univ Fort Wayne	IN	18,675	C
Indiana Univ-Purdue Univ Indianapolis	IN	18,952	C
Iowa State Univ	IA	18,176	C
Kansas State Univ	KS	17,780	VC
Kent State Univ	OH	20,928	C
Lake Superior State Univ	MI	19,867	C
Lawrence Tech Univ	MI	41,630	VC
LeTourneau Univ	TX	39,190	VC
Maine Maritime Academy	ME	22,536	C
McNeese State Univ	LA	7,838	C
Middle Tenn State Univ	TN	8,650	C
Midwestern State Univ	TX	12,111	LC
Minn State Univ, Mankato	MN	17,190	C
Missouri Western State Univ	MO	17,822	LC
Montana State Univ-Northern	MT	11,370	NC
New Jersey Inst of Technology	NJ	30,198	HC
New Mexico State Univ	NM	14,050	LC
Northwestern State Univ of Louisiana	LA	16,534	LC
Ohio Univ	OH	23,394	VC
Old Dominion Univ	VA	21,618	C
Oregon Inst of Technology	OR	19,227	C
Penn State Erie,The Behrend College	PA	26,688	VC
Pennsylvania College of Technology	PA	27,693	NC
Point Park Univ	PA	41,270	C
Prairie View A&M Univ	TX	27,273	LC
Purdue Univ Northwest	IN	15,178	C
Rochester Inst of Technology	NY	52,734	HC+
Saginaw Valley State Univ	MI	19,284	C
Shawnee State Univ	OH	16,998	C
S Car State Univ	SC	21,330	LC
S Dak State Univ	SD	15,874	C
Southeast Missouri State Univ	MO	16,148	C
Southeastern Louisiana Univ	LA	16,237	C
Southern Illinois Univ Carbondale	IL	24,554	C
Southern Univ and A&M College	LA	16,074	LC
Southwestern Okla State Univ	OK	12,205	C
St. Cloud State Univ	MN	10,600	C
Temple Univ	PA	24,392	C+
Texas A&M Univ at College Station	TX	20,771	VC+
Texas A&M Univ at Commerce	TX	10,496	C
Texas A&M Univ at Corpus Christi	TX	16,851	LC
Texas Southern Univ	TX	19,592	LC
Texas State Univ	TX	18,721	C
The Univ of Memphis	TN	18,278	C
Univ of Arkansas at Little Rock	AR	18,211	LC
Univ of Central Missouri	MO	18,982	C
Univ of Cincinnati	OH	22,118	VC
Univ of Dayton	OH	54,930	VC
Univ of Delaware	DE	32,214	VC
Univ of Hartford	CT	49,776	C
Univ of Houston-Downtown	TX	7,241	LC
Univ of Maryland/Eastern Shore	MD	21,861	LC
Univ of North Alabama	AL	15,964	C
Univ of N Car at Charlotte	NC	17,803	VC
Univ of North Texas	TX	20,082	C
Univ of S Car Upstate	SC	19,272	LC
Univ of Southern Miss	MS	13,170	C
Univ of Texas Rio Grande Valley	TX	15,573	LC
Univ of Toledo	OH	19,336	C
Univ of Wisc-Green Bay	WI	15,184	C
Univ of Wisc-Stout	WI	19,667	C
Virginia State Univ	VA	19,802	C+
West Texas A&M Univ	TX	13,478	C
West Virginia Univ Inst of Technology	WV	18,264	C
Western Carolina Univ	NC	13,965	C
Western Illinois Univ	IL	20,897	C
Western Washington Univ	WA	18,904	VC

ENGINEERING/MECHANICAL EMP ENERGY SYSTEM FOCUS

School	ST	$IS	SR
Malone Univ	OH	39,200	C
Mass Maritime Academy	MA	20,704	C
Oregon State Univ	OR	23,337	VC
Texas Christian Univ	TX	57,120	HC
Univ of S Car Aiken	SC	18,094	C

ENGLISH

School	ST	$IS	SR
Abilene Christian Univ	TX	43,708	C+
Adams State Univ	CO	15,420	LC
Adelphi Univ	NY	49,792	C
Adrian College	MI	45,550	C
Alabama A&M Univ	AL	18,796	C
Alabama State Univ	AL	16,490	LC
Albany State Univ	GA	19,462	C
Albertus Magnus College	CT	44,016	LC
Albion College	MI	55,260	C
Albright College	PA	57,326	C
Alcorn State Univ	MS	15,884	C
Alfred Univ	NY	37,490	C
Alice Lloyd College	KY	8,190	LC
Allegheny College	PA	57,620	VC
Allen Univ	SC	19,920	NC
Alma College	MI	49,410	VC
Alvernia Univ	PA	45,330	C
Alverno College	WI	33,294	LC
American International College	MA	47,020	LC
Amherst College	MA	66,186	MC
Anderson Univ	IN	39,450	C
Andrews Univ	MI	41,732	C
Angelo State Univ	TX	15,882	LC
Anna Maria College	MA	51,020	C
Appalachian State Univ	NC	15,394	VC
Aquinas College	TN	30,800	C+
Aquinas College - Mich	MI	38,876	VC
Arcadia Univ	PA	55,990	C+
Arizona State Univ at the Polytechnic Campus	AZ	22,394	VC
Arizona State Univ at the Tempe Campus	AZ	23,001	VC
Arizona State Univ at the West Campus	AZ	21,513	VC
Arkansas State Univ	AR	16,190	C
Arkansas Tech Univ	AR	16,534	LC
Armstrong State Univ	GA	15,615	C
Asbury Univ	KY	36,450	C+
Ashford Univ	CA	10,480	C
Ashland Univ	OH	30,446	C
Assumption College	MA	48,455	VC
Atlantic Union College	MA	27,228	C
Auburn Univ	AL	24,300	VC+
Auburn Univ at Montgomery	AL	15,000	C
Augsburg Univ	MN	45,129	C

ST = STATE $IS = IN-STATE COSTS SR = SELECTOR RATING

School	ST	$IS	SR
Augusta Univ	GA	4,632	C
Augustana College	IL	51,222	VC+
Augustana Univ	SD	39,968	VC
Aurora Univ	IL	34,990	C
Austin College	TX	51,059	HC
Austin Peay State Univ	TN	16,397	C
Averett Univ	VA	43,034	LC
Avila Univ	MO	27,100	C
Azusa Pacific Univ	CA	43,972	C
Baker Univ	KS	37,190	C
Baldwin Wallace Univ	OH	42,464	VC
Ball State Univ	IN	19,808	C+
Barnard College/Columbia Univ	NY	68,762	MC
Barry Univ	FL	38,730	LC
Barton College	NC	39,854	C
Bates College	ME	64,500	HC
Baylor Univ	TX	56,803	HC
Belhaven Univ	MS	32,250	C
Bellarmine Univ	KY	52,532	C
Bellevue Univ	NE	20,300	NC
Belmont Abbey College	NC	28,794	C
Belmont Univ	TN	44,500	VC+
Beloit College	WI	55,206	HC
Bemidji State Univ	MN	17,730	C
Benedict College	SC	28,630	NC
Benedictine College	KS	38,850	VC
Bennett College	NC	27,717	NC
Bennington College	VT	66,280	MC
Bentley Univ	MA	63,720	MC
Berea College	KY	7,094	C
Berry College	GA	47,466	VC
Bethany College	KS	38,637	LC
Bethany College	WV	38,774	LC
Bethel College	KS	35,370	C
Bethel Univ	MN	46,550	C+
Bethel Univ	TN	27,142	C
Bethune-Cookman Univ	FL	23,322	C
Biola Univ	CA	48,686	C
Birmingham-Southern College	AL	44,478	C+
Black Hills State Univ	SD	16,622	C
Bloomfield College	NJ	40,100	LC
Bloomsburg Univ of Pennsylvania	PA	19,930	C
Blue Mountain College	MS	15,949	C
Bluefield College	VA	34,711	C
Bluffton Univ	OH	40,950	C+
Boise State Univ	ID	17,368	C
Boston College	MA	68,043	MC
Boston Univ	MA	67,352	MC
Bowdoin College	ME	65,980	MC
Bowie State Univ	MD	18,610	LC
Bowling Green State Univ	OH	19,975	C
Bradley Univ	IL	43,240	VC
Brandeis Univ	MA	68,443	MC
Brenau Univ - Women's College	GA	37,876	LC
Brescia Univ	KY	29,890	VC
Brewton-Parker College	GA	26,120	LC
Briar Cliff Univ	IA	36,956	C
Bridgewater College	VA	46,260	C
Bridgewater State Univ	MA	22,762	C
Brigham Young Univ	UT	13,248	MC
Brigham Young Univ/Hawaii	HI	11,710	C
Brown Univ	RI	64,566	MC
Bryan College	TN	32,900	C
Bryant Univ	RI	57,204	VC
Bryn Athyn College	PA	32,664	C
Bryn Mawr College	PA	65,220	MC
Bucknell Univ	PA	67,136	MC
Buena Vista Univ	IA	42,344	C
Butler Univ	IN	52,890	VC+
Cabrini Univ	PA	42,591	LC
Cairn Univ	PA	37,572	C
Caldwell Univ	NJ	42,165	LC
Calif Baptist Univ	CA	42,986	C
Calif College of the Arts	CA	52,758	SP
Calif Inst of Technology	CA	64,704	MC
Calif Lutheran Univ	CA	52,853	C
Calif Polytechnic State Univ	CA	22,547	MC
Calif State Polytechnic Univ, Pomona	CA	21,811	C
Cal State, Bakersfield	CA	22,397	LC
Cal State, Chico	CA	19,790	VC
Cal State, Dominguez Hills	CA	19,022	LC
Cal State, East Bay	CA	20,748	C
Cal State, Fresno	CA	16,902	LC
Cal State, Fullerton	CA	21,902	C
Cal State, Long Beach	CA	18,850	C
Cal State, Los Angeles	CA	17,186	LC
Cal State, Northridge	CA	17,277	LC
Cal State, Sacramento	CA	19,060	C
Cal State, San Bernardino	CA	20,106	C
Cal State, Stanislaus	CA	18,053	LC
Calif Univ of Pennsylvania	PA	20,425	LC
Calumet College of St. Joseph	IN	22,735	C
Calvin College	MI	43,090	HC
Cameron Univ	OK	11,632	LC
Campbell Univ	NC	37,570	VC
Campbellsville Univ	KY	33,400	C
Canisius College	NY	49,672	C
Capital Univ	OH	44,778	VC
Cardinal Stritch Univ	WI	37,136	C
Carleton College	MN	66,414	MC
Carlow Univ	PA	39,696	LC
Carnegie Mellon Univ	PA	67,980	MC
Carroll College	MT	44,304	C
Carroll Univ	WI	38,100	C+
Carson-Newman Univ	TN	35,900	C
Carthage College	WI	48,835	C
Case Western Reserve Univ	OH	62,284	MC
Castleton Univ	VT	20,186	C
Catawba College	NC	39,820	LC
Cazenovia College	NY	47,866	C
Cedar Crest College	PA	51,110	C
Cedarville Univ	OH	36,244	VC
Centenary College	NJ	43,890	LC
Centenary College of Louisiana	LA	49,050	C+
Central College	IA	44,592	C
Central Conn State Univ	CT	22,041	C
Central Methodist Univ	MO	31,500	VC
Central Mich Univ	MI	20,330	C
Central State Univ	OH	18,564	C
Central Washington Univ	WA	16,803	C
Centre College	KY	50,680	MC
Chadron State College	NE	14,819	LC
Chaminade Univ of Honolulu	HI	37,614	C
Chapman Univ	CA	65,504	HC
Charleston Southern Univ	SC	34,700	C
Chatham Univ	PA	47,883	VC
Cheyney Univ of Pennsylvania	PA	20,896	LC
Chicago State Univ	IL	41,620	C
Christendom College	VA	32,600	VC
Christian Brothers Univ	TN	31,670	VC
Christopher Newport Univ	VA	24,878	VC+
CUNY/Baruch College	NY	21,609	HC
CUNY/Brooklyn College	NY	7,163	C+
CUNY/City College	NY	20,204	C
CUNY/Hunter College	NY	31,098	VC
CUNY/John Jay College of Criminal Justice	NY	6,359	SP
CUNY/Lehman College	NY	5,788	LC
CUNY/Medgar Evers College	NY	6,680	NC
CUNY/Queens College	NY	21,507	C
CUNY/York College	NY	6,747	LC
Claflin Univ	SC	25,592	LC
Clarion Univ of Pennsylvania	PA	21,608	LC
Clark Atlanta Univ	GA	31,019	LC
Clark Univ	MA	53,260	HC+
Clarke Univ	IA	42,950	C
Clemson Univ	SC		HC
Cleveland State Univ	OH	22,290	C
Coastal Carolina Univ	SC	20,340	C
Coe College	IA	51,570	VC
Coker College	SC	38,196	C
Colby College	ME	64,060	MC
Colgate Univ	NY	67,500	MC
College of Charleston	SC	24,046	VC
College of Mount St. Vincent	NY	45,620	C
College of St. Benedict	MN	54,480	C
College of St. Elizabeth	NJ	45,700	LC
College of St. Mary	NE	27,500	C
College of St Joseph	VT	32,400	LC
College of St. Scholastica	MN	45,734	C+
College of Staten Island	NY	24,389	LC
College of the Holy Cross	MA	64,320	MC
College of the Ozarks	MO	7,530	VC
College of William & Mary	VA	34,907	MC
Colo Christian Univ	CO	40,885	VC
Colo College	CO	64,894	MC
Colo Mesa Univ	CO	19,707	LC
Colo State Univ	CO	23,033	C
Colo State Univ-Pueblo	CO	21,581	C
Columbia College	SC	36,550	C
Columbia College - Missouri	MO	28,179	C
Columbia Univ/City of New York	NY	62,958	MC
Columbus State Univ	GA	14,336	LC
Concord Univ	WV	14,954	LC
Concordia College - Moorhead	MN	46,418	C
Concordia College - New York	NY	39,035	LC
Concordia Univ	OR	35,000	C
Concordia Univ Irvine	CA	44,860	VC
Concordia Univ Nebr	NE	41,900	VC
Concordia Univ St. Paul	MN	29,050	C
Concordia Univ Texas	TX	41,920	C
Concordia Univ Wisc	WI	35,910	C
Concordia Univ, Ann Arbor	MI	38,878	C+
Concordia Univ, Chicago	IL	41,522	C
Conn College	CT	65,000	MC
Converse College	SC	28,290	C
Coppin State Univ	MD	14,071	VC
Corban Univ	OR	41,700	C
Cornell College	IA	49,900	VC
Cornell Univ	NY	67,591	MC
Cornerstone Univ	MI	36,550	C
Covenant College	GA	44,590	HC
Creighton Univ	NE	49,452	VC
Culver-Stockton College	MO	34,350	C
Cumberland Univ	TN	27,710	C
Curry College	MA	53,331	C
Daemen College	NY	40,336	C
Dakota State Univ	SD	12,286	C
Dakota Wesleyan Univ	SD	33,980	LC
Dallas Baptist Univ	TX	35,220	VC
Dartmouth College	NH	68,109	MC
Davidson College	NC	60,119	MC
Davis & Elkins College	WV	38,242	LC
Delaware State Univ	DE	19,376	LC
Delaware Valley Univ	PA	51,271	C
Delta State Univ	MS	13,176	LC
Denison Univ	OH	62,770	HC+
DePaul Univ	IL	52,807	VC
DePauw Univ	IN	58,688	VC
DeSales Univ	PA	47,520	C
Dickinson College	PA	66,166	MC
Dickinson State Univ	ND	12,372	LC
Dillard Univ	LA	20,940	VC
Doane Univ	NE	41,340	VC
Dominican College	NY	40,258	LC
Dominican Univ	IL	42,472	C+
Dordt College	IA	37,860	C+
Drake Univ	IA	49,220	HC
Drew Univ/College of Liberal Arts	NJ	53,608	VC
Drexel Univ	PA	65,927	HC
Drury Univ	MO	37,555	VC
Duke Univ	NC	68,298	MC
Duquesne Univ	PA	48,508	VC
D'Youville College	NY	37,678	C
Earlham College	IN	55,670	HC
East Carolina Univ	NC	16,539	C
East Central Univ	OK	13,330	C
East Stroudsburg Univ	PA	18,578	LC
East Tenn State Univ	TN	18,141	C
East Texas Baptist Univ	TX	34,444	C
Eastern Conn State Univ	CT	23,059	C
Eastern Illinois Univ	IL	21,414	C
Eastern Kentucky Univ	KY	17,742	C
Eastern Mennonite Univ	VA	42,550	C
Eastern Mich Univ	MI	19,761	C
Eastern Nazarene College	MA	41,114	C
Eastern New Mexico Univ	NM	12,874	LC
Eastern Oregon Univ	OR	17,612	C
Eastern Univ	PA	39,540	C
Eastern Washington Univ	WA	17,896	LC
Edgewood College	WI	35,950	C
Edinboro Univ	PA	15,940	LC
Edward Waters College	FL	28,089	NC
Elizabeth City State Univ	NC	14,745	C
Elizabethtown College	PA	56,340	VC
Elmhurst College	IL	46,514	C
Elms College	MA	49,602	VC
Elon Univ	NC	46,142	HC
Emmanuel College	MA	53,472	C+
Emory Univ	GA	63,286	MC
Emporia State Univ	KS	15,029	C
Endicott College	MA	47,054	C+
Erskine College	SC	45,460	C
Eureka College	IL	34,760	C
Evangel Univ	MO	28,898	C
Fairfield Univ	CT	61,445	HC
Fairmont State Univ	WV	15,726	C
Faulkner Univ	AL	26,410	C
Fayetteville State Univ	NC	17,756	C
Felician Univ	NJ	46,280	LC
Ferris State Univ	MI	21,458	C
Ferrum College	VA	43,970	C
Fisk Univ	TN	32,066	LC
Fitchburg State Univ	MA	21,819	LC
Flagler College	FL	27,620	C
Florida A&M Univ	FL	15,361	C
Florida Atlantic Univ	FL	18,256	C
Florida Gulf Coast Univ	FL	14,738	C
Florida International Univ	FL	20,281	C
Florida Memorial Univ	FL	22,424	LC
Florida Southern College	FL	45,978	VC
Florida State Univ	FL	16,771	HC
Fontbonne Univ	MO	34,606	C
Fordham Univ	NY	68,431	MC
Fort Hays State Univ	KS	12,677	C
Fort Lewis College	CO	20,154	C
Fort Valley State Univ	GA	17,988	VC
Framingham State Univ	MA	21,740	C
Francis Marion Univ	SC	18,144	LC
Franciscan Univ of Steubenville	OH	33,980	VC
Franklin and Marshall College	PA	67,960	MC
Franklin College	IN	40,550	C
Franklin Pierce Univ	NH	46,750	LC
Freed-Hardeman Univ	TN	29,900	C
Fresno Pacific Univ	CA	38,858	C
Friends Univ	KS	38,000	C
Frostburg State Univ	MD	17,280	LC
Furman Univ	SC	61,098	VC+
Gallaudet Univ	DC	30,088	LC
Gannon Univ	PA	42,922	C
Gardner-Webb Univ	NC	24,935	C+
Geneva College	PA	35,450	C
George Mason Univ	VA	19,884	C
Georgetown College	KY	41,440	C
Georgetown Univ	DC	68,970	MC
Georgia College & State Univ	GA	21,884	C+
Georgia Southern Univ	GA	16,540	VC
Georgia Southwestern State Univ	GA	13,870	LC
Georgia State Univ	GA	25,250	C
Georgian Court Univ	NJ	43,068	LC
Gettysburg College	PA	65,210	MC
Glenville State College	WV	17,386	LC
Goddard College	VT	17,040	VC
Gonzaga Univ	WA	52,880	HC
Gordon College	MA	47,740	VC
Goshen College	IN	44,350	C
Goucher College	MD	56,110	VC
Grace College and Seminary	IN	31,524	C
Graceland Univ	IA	35,290	C
Grambling State Univ	LA	15,701	C
Grand Canyon Univ	AZ	25,150	VC
Grand Valley State Univ	MI	22,250	C+
Grand View Univ	IA	32,302	C
Green Mountain College	VT	45,228	LC
Greensboro College	NC	39,790	LC
Greenville College	IL	27,012	LC
Grinnell College	IA	63,114	MC
Grove City College	PA	26,654	VC
Guilford College	NC	45,973	C
Gustavus Adolphus College	MN	53,943	HC
Gwynedd Mercy Univ	PA	43,780	LC
Hamilton College	NY	64,250	MC
Hamline Univ	MN	50,152	C
Hampden-Sydney College	VA	57,806	VC
Hampton Univ	VA	36,410	C
Hannibal-LaGrange Univ	MO	29,815	C
Hanover College	IN	47,750	C+
Harding Univ	AR	25,440	C
Hardin-Simmons Univ	TX	36,025	C
Hartwick College	NY	51,270	C
Harvard College/Harvard Univ	MA	65,609	MC
Hastings College	NE	35,380	C+
Haverford College	PA	66,490	MC
Hawaii Pacific Univ	HI	33,420	C
Heidelberg Univ	OH	40,400	LC
Henderson State Univ	AR	15,516	C
Hendrix College	AR	54,020	VC
Heritage Univ	WA	19,825	NC
Hilbert College	NY	32,650	LC
Hillsdale College	MI	37,170	MC
Hiram College	OH	44,590	C
Hobart and William Smith Colleges	NY	67,050	HC+
Hofstra Univ	NY	58,210	C+
Hollins Univ	VA	49,635	VC
Holy Family Univ	PA	44,672	LC
Holy Names Univ	CA	46,630	LC
Hood College	MD	50,540	C
Hope College	MI	42,840	VC
Houghton College	NY	40,558	VC
Houston Baptist Univ	TX	36,450	C
Howard Payne Univ	TX	35,994	C
Howard Univ	DC	37,616	C+
Humboldt State Univ	CA	21,708	C
Huntingdon College	AL	35,900	C
Huntington Univ	IN	33,996	C
Husson Univ	ME	26,508	C
Huston-Tillotson Univ	TX	18,124	LC
Idaho State Univ	ID	13,619	LC
Illinois College	IL	41,330	VC
Illinois State Univ	IL	23,418	VC
Illinois Wesleyan Univ	IL	56,430	VC+
Immaculata Univ	PA	39,000	C
Indiana State Univ	IN	23,223	LC
Indiana Univ Bloomington	IN	20,791	HC
Indiana Univ East	IN	7,207	C
Indiana Univ Kokomo	IN	7,207	C
Indiana Univ Northwest	IN	7,207	LC
Indiana Univ of Pennsylvania	PA	24,474	C
Indiana Univ South Bend	IN	16,057	C
Indiana Univ Southeast	IN	16,931	C
Indiana Univ-Purdue Univ Fort Wayne	IN	18,675	C
Indiana Univ-Purdue Univ Indianapolis	IN	18,952	C
Indiana Wesleyan Univ	IN	33,674	C
Inter-American Univ of PR-San Germán	PR	20,042	
Iona College	NY	52,514	C
Iowa State Univ	IA	18,176	C
Ithaca College	NY	58,158	VC+
Jackson State Univ	MS	15,879	LC
Jacksonville State Univ	AL	14,628	LC
Jacksonville Univ	FL	49,210	C
James Madison Univ	VA	19,084	VC
Jarvis Christian College	TX	20,160	NC
John Brown Univ	AR	35,184	VC
John Carroll Univ	OH	51,570	C
Johns Hopkins Univ	MD	68,080	MC
Johnson & Wales Univ/Denver Campus	CO	44,768	C
Johnson C. Smith Univ	NC	25,336	LC
Johnson State College	VT	22,672	C
Judson College	AL	27,066	C
Judson Univ	IL	39,174	C
Juniata College	PA	58,118	VC
Kalamazoo College	MI	53,931	HC
Kansas State Univ	KS	17,780	VC
Kansas Wesleyan Univ	KS	37,930	C
Kean Univ	NJ	25,620	C
Keene State College	NH	24,604	C
Kennesaw State Univ	GA	18,899	VC
Kent State Univ	OH	20,928	C
Kentucky State Univ	KY	14,484	LC
Kentucky Wesleyan College	KY	34,260	LC
Kenyon College	OH	65,840	MC
Keuka College	NY	42,398	C
King Univ	TN	36,976	C
King's College	PA	48,240	C
Kutztown Univ of Pennsylvania	PA	19,477	C
La Roche College	PA	38,940	C
La Salle Univ	PA	43,476	C
La Sierra Univ	CA	39,690	VC
Lafayette College	PA	68,520	MC
LaGrange College	GA	41,310	C
Lake Erie College	OH	38,914	LC
Lake Forest College	IL	50,652	VC
Lakeland Univ	WI	35,130	C
Lamar Univ	TX	18,014	LC
Lander Univ	SC	32,200	C

ST = STATE $IS = IN-STATE COSTS SR = SELECTOR RATING

School	ST	$IS	SR
Lane College	TN	17,960	LC
Langston Univ	OK	15,659	C
Lasell College	MA	49,400	C
Lawrence Tech Univ	MI	41,630	VC
Lawrence Univ	WI	56,133	HC+
Le Moyne College	NY	47,305	VC
Lebanon Valley College	PA	55,510	VC
Lee Univ	TN	22,045	C
Lees-McRae College	NC	33,944	NC
Lehigh Univ	PA	63,860	MC
LeMoyne-Owen College	TN	16,980	C
Lenoir-Rhyne Univ	NC	47,500	LC
LeTourneau Univ	TX	39,190	VC
Lewis & Clark College	OR	60,984	MC
Lewis Univ	IL	41,710	C
Lewis-Clark State College	ID	14,202	C
Liberty Univ	VA	31,415	C
Limestone College	SC	32,100	C
Lincoln Memorial Univ	TN	28,430	C
Lincoln Univ	MO	14,402	NC
Lindenwood Univ	MO	25,760	C
Lindsey Wilson College	KY	33,546	C
Linfield College	OR	53,992	C
Lipscomb Univ	TN	42,984	VC
LIU Brooklyn	NY	50,698	C
LIU Post	NY	50,698	C+
Livingstone College	NC	17,815	LC
Lock Haven Univ of Pennsylvania	PA	20,544	LC
Longwood Univ	VA	22,184	C
Louisiana College	LA	21,274	C
Louisiana State Univ and A&M College	LA	18,677	VC
Louisiana State Univ in Shreveport	LA	6,902	C
Louisiana Tech Univ	LA	11,422	VC
Lourdes Univ	OH	29,140	NC
Loyola Marymount Univ	CA	60,202	VC+
Loyola Univ Chicago	IL	57,158	VC
Loyola Univ Maryland	MD	61,710	VC
Luther College	IA	49,990	VC
Lycoming College	PA	50,895	C
Lyndon State College	VT	20,714	C
Lyon College	AR	36,120	VC
Macalester College	MN	64,136	MC
MacMurray College	IL	35,025	C
Madonna Univ	MI	30,450	LC
Malone Univ	OH	39,200	C
Manchester Univ	IN	41,540	C
Manhattan College	NY	55,652	C
Manhattanville College	NY	52,430	C
Mansfield Univ of Pennsylvania	PA	24,244	LC
Marian Univ	IN	43,206	C
Marian Univ	WI	34,622	C
Marietta College	OH	46,190	C
Marist College	NY	49,860	VC
Marlboro College	VT	50,832	VC+
Marquette Univ	WI	53,090	VC+
Mars Hill Univ	NC	41,104	C
Marshall Univ	WV	18,044	C
Mary Baldwin Univ	VA	40,495	C
Marygrove College	MI	30,100	LC
Marymount Manhattan College	NY	48,350	C
Marymount Univ	VA	43,231	C
Maryville College	TN	44,410	C
Maryville Univ of St. Louis	MO	38,558	VC
Marywood Univ	PA	47,840	C
Mass College of Liberal Arts	MA	20,659	C
Mayville State Univ	ND	18,371	NC
McDaniel College	MD	52,910	VC
McKendree Univ	IL	37,940	C+
McMurry Univ	TX	34,259	LC
McNeese State Univ	LA	7,838	C
McPherson College	KS	36,134	C
Medaille College	NY	41,700	LC
Mercy College	NY	32,614	C
Mercyhurst Univ	PA	47,420	C
Meredith College	NC	46,634	C
Merrimack College	MA	55,415	C
Messiah College	PA	44,380	VC
Methodist Univ	NC	58,130	C
Metropolitan State Univ	MN	7,859	C
Metropolitan State Univ of Denver	CO	6,928	LC
Miami Univ	OH	27,190	HC+
Mich State Univ	MI	24,542	VC
Mich Tech Univ	MI	25,551	VC+
MidAmerica Nazarene Univ	KS	37,808	C
Middle Tenn State Univ	TN	8,650	C
Middlebury College	VT	67,464	MC
Midland Univ	NE	39,512	C
Midway Univ	KY	33,940	LC
Midwestern State Univ	TX	12,111	LC
Miles College	AL	16,530	NC
Millersville Univ of Pennsylvania	PA	25,298	C
Milligan College	TN	39,450	C
Millikin Univ	IL	44,148	C
Mills College	CA	43,705	C
Millsaps College	MS	50,080	C+
Minn State Univ, Mankato	MN	17,190	C
Minn State Univ, Moorhead	MN	21,393	C
Minot State Univ	ND	13,285	C
Misericordia Univ	PA	45,210	C
Miss College	MS	25,850	C
Miss State Univ	MS	12,028	C+
Miss Univ for Women	MS	17,065	C
Miss Valley State Univ	MS	13,233	LC
Missouri Baptist Univ	MO	35,594	C
Missouri Southern State Univ	MO	13,071	C
Missouri State Univ	MO	15,837	C+
Missouri Univ of Science and Technology	MO	18,655	HC
Missouri Valley College	MO	28,150	C
Missouri Western State Univ	MO	17,822	LC
Molloy College	NY	40,440	C
Monmouth College	IL	42,260	C
Monmouth Univ	NJ	50,184	C
Montana State Univ	MT	15,500	C+
Montana State Univ Billings	MT	13,336	LC
Montana State Univ-Northern	MT	11,370	NC
Montclair State Univ	NJ	26,912	C
Montreat College	NC	34,605	LC
Moravian College	PA	55,488	C
Morehead State Univ	KY	18,386	LC
Morehouse College	GA	40,835	C
Morgan State Univ	MD	17,190	LC
Morningside College	IA	39,780	C
Morris College	SC	19,195	LC
Mount Aloysius College	PA	29,976	C
Mount Holyoke College	MA	56,746	MC
Mount Ida College	MA	46,820	C
Mount Marty College	SD	36,862	C
Mount Mary Univ	WI	34,650	LC
Mount Mercy Univ	IA	39,748	C
Mount St. Mary College	NY	44,448	C
Mount St. Joseph Univ	OH	33,880	LC
Mount St. Mary's Univ	MD	53,380	C
Mount St. Mary's Univ - Chalon Campus	CA	50,486	VC+
Mount Vernon Nazarene Univ	OH	35,944	C
Muhlenberg College	PA	56,645	VC
Muskingum Univ	OH	35,966	C
Naropa Univ	CO	43,278	NC
National Louis Univ	IL	43,000	LC
National Univ	CA	17,849	LC
Nazareth College	NY	46,784	C
Nebr Wesleyan Univ	NE	42,026	C+
Neumann Univ	PA	40,678	LC
New College of Florida	FL	16,180	HC+
New Jersey City Univ	NJ	21,456	LC
New Mexico Highlands Univ	NM	11,904	LC
New Mexico State Univ	NM	14,050	LC
New York Inst of Technology	NY	49,980	VC
New York Univ	NY	68,139	MC
Newberry College	SC	34,550	C
Newman Univ	KS	37,382	C
Niagara Univ	NY	41,010	C
Nicholls State Univ	LA	14,959	C
Nichols College	MA	46,900	LC
Norfolk State Univ	VA	18,902	LC
N Car A&T State Univ	NC	13,786	C
N Car Central Univ	NC	9,000	C
N Car State Univ	NC	22,434	HC+
N Car Wesleyan College	NC	39,200	C
North Central College	IL	48,712	C+
North Central Univ	MN	30,610	C
N Dak State Univ	ND	16,245	VC
North Park Univ	IL	35,860	C
Northeastern Illinois Univ	IL	12,529	LC
Northeastern State Univ	OK	8,615	VC
Northeastern Univ	MA	65,352	MC
Northern Arizona Univ	AZ	21,003	C
Northern Illinois Univ	IL	20,176	C
Northern Kentucky Univ	KY	16,486	C
Northern Mich Univ	MI	20,853	C
Northern State Univ	SD	15,570	C
Northland College	WI	41,103	C+
Northwest Missouri State Univ	MO	18,286	C
Northwest Nazarene Univ	ID	40,250	C
Northwest Univ	WA	38,720	VC
Northwestern Okla State Univ	OK	13,072	LC
Northwestern State Univ of Louisiana	LA	16,534	LC
Northwestern Univ	IL	68,725	MC
Norwich Univ	VT	56,234	C
Notre Dame College	OH	39,150	VC
Notre Dame de Namur Univ	CA	46,526	LC
Notre Dame of Maryland Univ	MD	47,570	VC
Nyack College	NY	34,450	LC
Oakland City Univ	IN	33,930	NC
Oakland Univ	MI	20,763	C
Oakwood Univ	AL	43,758	C
Oberlin College	OH	68,942	MC
Occidental College	CA	68,660	MC
Oglethorpe Univ	GA	44,200	C
Ohio Dominican Univ	OH	41,340	C+
Ohio Northern Univ	OH	44,050	VC
Ohio State Univ at Columbus	OH	22,843	MC
Ohio State Univ at Lima	OH	7,553	C
Ohio State Univ at Mansfield	OH	15,529	C
Ohio State Univ at Marion	OH	7,553	VC
Ohio State Univ at Newark	OH	16,685	C
Ohio Univ	OH	23,394	VC
Ohio Valley Univ	WV	28,800	C
Ohio Wesleyan Univ	OH	49,460	VC
Okla Baptist Univ	OK	33,990	C
Okla Christian Univ	OK	29,260	C
Okla City Univ	OK	40,476	C
Okla Panhandle State Univ	OK	6,152	C
Okla State Univ	OK	17,180	C+
Okla Wesleyan Univ	OK	34,434	C
Old Dominion Univ	VA	21,618	C
Olivet College	MI	37,661	LC
Olivet Nazarene Univ	IL	41,840	VC
Oral Roberts Univ	OK	34,316	C
Oregon State Univ	OR	23,337	VC
Ottawa Univ	KS	39,980	VC
Otterbein Univ	OH	41,630	C
Ouachita Baptist Univ	AR	33,500	VC
Our Lady of the Lake Univ	TX	37,790	LC
Pace Univ	NY	60,136	C
Pacific Lutheran Univ	WA	49,960	C
Pacific Union College	CA	36,009	VC
Paine College	GA	19,506	LC
Palm Beach Atlantic Univ	FL	39,250	C
Park Univ	MO	22,134	C
Paul Quinn College	TX	25,350	LC
Penn State Altoona	PA	26,686	C
Penn State Erie,The Behrend College	PA	26,688	VC
Pepperdine Univ	CA	66,862	VC+
Peru State College	NE	15,602	LC
Philander Smith College	AR	20,814	LC
Piedmont College	GA	34,334	C
Pine Manor College	MA	41,660	LC
Pittsburg State Univ	KS	13,880	C
Pitzer College	CA	68,500	HC+
Plymouth State Univ	NH	23,180	LC
Point Park Univ	PA	41,270	C
Pomona College	CA	64,957	MC
Pontifical Catholic Univ of PR	PR	10,534	
Portland State Univ	OR	19,443	C
Post Univ	CT	41,150	C
Prairie View A&M Univ	TX	27,273	LC
Presbyterian College	SC	47,186	C
Princeton Univ	NJ	60,090	MC
Principia College	IL	40,350	C
Providence College	RI	62,870	HC
Purdue Univ Northwest	IN	15,178	C
Purdue Univ/West Lafayette	IN	20,032	MC
Quincy Univ	IL	38,170	LC
Quinnipiac Univ	CT	60,970	VC
Radford Univ	VA	19,758	C
Randolph College	VA	53,970	C
Randolph-Macon College	VA	51,480	VC
Regis College	MA	51,920	LC
Regis Univ	CO	46,380	C
Rhode Island College	RI	19,000	LC
Rhodes College	TN	51,900	HC
Rice Univ	TX	59,458	MC
Rider Univ	NJ	54,050	C
Ripon College	WI	49,991	VC
Rivier Univ	NH	41,600	VC
Robert Morris Univ	PA	40,600	C
Roberts Wesleyan College	NY	41,116	C
Rochester College	MI	28,574	LC
Rockford Univ	IL	38,570	C
Rockhurst Univ	MO	28,990	C
Roger Williams Univ	RI	48,074	VC
Rollins College	FL	58,670	HC
Roosevelt Univ	IL	41,890	VC
Rosemont College	PA	30,980	LC
Rowan Univ	NJ	24,491	VC
Russell Sage College	NY	39,370	C
Rust College	MS	10,600	C
Rutgers Univ - Camden	NJ	26,595	C
Rutgers Univ - Newark	NJ	27,351	C
Sacred Heart Univ	CT	54,590	C
Saginaw Valley State Univ	MI	19,284	C
St. Anselm College	NH	56,636	VC
St. Augustine's Univ	NC	25,582	C
St. Francis Univ	PA	46,146	NC
St. John's Univ	MN	53,472	C
St. Joseph's College of Maine	ME	47,890	C
St. Joseph's Univ	PA	58,540	VC
St. Louis Univ	MO	49,866	HC
St. Martin's Univ	WA	45,056	C
St. Mary-of-the-Woods College	IN	40,424	LC
St. Mary's College of Calif	CA	57,420	C
St. Michael's College	VT	53,275	VC+
St. Peter's Univ	NJ	49,192	C
St. Vincent College	PA	46,229	C
St. Xavier Univ	IL	44,440	C
Salem College	NC	40,206	C
Salem State Univ	MA	42,650	LC
Salisbury Univ	MD	21,132	VC
Salve Regina Univ	RI	53,046	VC
Sam Houston State Univ	TX	18,792	C
Samford Univ	AL	40,770	VC
San Diego Christian College	CA	40,914	C
San Diego State Univ	CA	23,156	VC
San Francisco State Univ	CA	18,514	LC
San Jose State Univ	CA	22,630	C
Sarah Lawrence College	NY	68,866	MC
Savannah State Univ	GA	17,036	C
Schreiner Univ	TX	34,626	LC
Scripps College	CA	69,260	HC
Seattle Pacific Univ	WA	47,439	C+
Seattle Univ	WA	54,957	VC
Seton Hall Univ	NJ	58,008	C
Seton Hill Univ	PA	46,972	VC
Sewanee: The Univ of the South	TN	58,000	HC+
Shaw Univ	NC	24,638	C
Shawnee State Univ	OH	16,998	C
Shenandoah Univ	VA	42,100	C
Shepherd Univ, West Virginia	WV	17,382	C
Shippensburg Univ of Pennsylvania	PA	24,096	C
Shorter Univ	GA	31,130	LC
Siena College	NY	48,916	C
Siena Heights Univ	MI	36,322	C
Silver Lake College of the Holy Family	WI	36,290	LC
Simmons College	MA	54,400	HC
Simpson College	IA	45,626	VC
Simpson Univ	CA	34,722	C
Skidmore College	NY	66,600	MC
Slippery Rock Univ of Pennsylvania	PA	20,450	C
Smith College	MA	66,774	MC
Sonoma State Univ	CA	27,020	C
S Car State Univ	SC	21,330	LC
S Dak State Univ	SD	15,874	C
Southeast Missouri State Univ	MO	16,148	C
Southeastern Louisiana Univ	LA	16,237	C
Southeastern Okla State Univ	OK	11,875	C
Southeastern Univ	FL	34,910	LC
Southern Adventist Univ	TN	28,250	C
Southern Arkansas Univ	AR	21,532	C
Southern Conn State Univ	CT	21,924	LC
Southern Illinois Univ Edwardsville	IL	20,188	C
Southern Methodist Univ	TX	69,008	MC
Southern Nazarene Univ	OK	33,684	C
Southern New Hampshire Univ	NH	44,256	C
Southern Oregon Univ	OR	19,117	C
Southern Univ and A&M College	LA	16,074	LC
Southern Univ at New Orleans	LA	8,014	LC
Southern Vermont College	VT	34,670	LC
Southern Wesleyan Univ	SC	33,670	LC
Southwest Baptist Univ	MO	30,890	LC
Southwestern Adventist Univ	TX	28,232	LC
Southwestern College	KS	31,531	LC
Southwestern Okla State Univ	OK	12,205	C
Southwestern Univ	TX	52,370	VC
Spelman College	GA	41,642	C
Spring Arbor Univ	MI	37,390	C
Spring Hill College	AL	48,488	C
Springfield College	MA	48,775	C
St. Ambrose Univ	IA	40,180	C
St. Bonaventure Univ	NY	45,596	C
St. Catherine Univ	MN	45,630	C
St. Cloud State Univ	MN	10,600	C
St. Francis College	NY	38,800	LC
St. John Fisher College	NY	45,270	VC
St. John's Univ	NY	57,160	C+
St. Joseph's College, New York/Brooklyn Campus	NY	25,114	LC
St. Joseph's College, New York/Long Island Campus	NY	25,124	C
St. Lawrence Univ	NY	66,646	HC+
St. Mary's College of Maryland	MD	27,312	VC
St. Mary's Univ	TX	39,120	C
St. Norbert College	WI	46,060	VC
St. Olaf College	MN	56,430	HC
St. Thomas Aquinas College	NY	32,450	C
St. Thomas Univ	FL	51,187	LC
Stanford Univ	CA	62,541	MC
SUNY Albany	NY	22,165	C
SUNY at Binghamton	NY	24,100	MC
SUNY at Geneseo	NY	21,622	VC
SUNY at New Paltz	NY	20,840	C
SUNY at Oswego	NY	22,219	VC
SUNY/Buffalo State	NY	20,583	LC
SUNY/Cortland	NY	20,910	C
SUNY/Fredonia	NY	20,818	C
SUNY/Oneonta	NY	20,794	C
SUNY/Plattsburgh	NY	19,314	C
SUNY/Potsdam	NY	21,051	VC
SUNY/Univ at Buffalo	NY	23,122	C
Stephen F. Austin State Univ	TX	18,484	LC
Stephens College	MO	38,042	C
Sterling College	KS	32,830	LC
Stetson Univ	FL	57,174	VC+
Stillman College	AL	20,738	C
Stonehill College	MA	55,130	C
Stony Brook Univ/The SUNY	NY	22,703	MC
Suffolk Univ	MA	52,316	C
Sul Ross State Univ	TX	15,021	LC
Susquehanna Univ	PA	57,560	VC
Syracuse Univ	NY	62,313	HC
Tabor College	KS	35,870	C
Talladega College	AL	25,919	C
Tarleton State Univ	TX	15,248	LC
Taylor Univ	IN	42,130	VC
Temple Univ	PA	24,392	C+
Tenn State Univ	TN	14,423	LC
Tenn Tech Univ	TN	17,929	C
Tenn Wesleyan Univ	TN	32,680	LC
Texas A&M Univ at College Station	TX	20,771	VC+
Texas A&M Univ at Commerce	TX	10,496	C
Texas A&M Univ at Corpus Christi	TX	16,851	LC
Texas A&M Univ at Kingsville	TX	16,580	LC
Texas Christian Univ	TX	57,120	HC
Texas Lutheran Univ	TX	39,770	C
Texas Southern Univ	TX	19,592	LC
Texas State Univ	TX	18,721	C

ST = STATE **$IS** = IN-STATE COSTS **SR** = SELECTOR RATING

School	ST	$IS	SR
Texas Tech Univ	TX	20,156	C+
Texas Wesleyan Univ	TX	37,338	C
Texas Woman's Univ	TX	15,302	LC
The Catholic Univ of America	DC	58,376	VC
The Citadel, The Military College of S Car	SC	20,679	C
The College at Brockport - SUNY	NY	21,058	C
The College of New Jersey	NJ	28,675	VC+
The College of New Rochelle	NY	46,300	LC
The College of St. Rose	NY	44,010	C
The College of Wooster	OH	60,000	HC
The George Washington Univ	DC	68,474	HC+
The Master's Univ	CA	43,870	C
The Univ of Akron	OH	22,566	C
The Univ of Alabama	AL	24,320	C+
The Univ of Arizona	AZ	24,086	C
The Univ of Mary	ND	23,180	C
The Univ of Memphis	TN	18,278	C
The Univ of Montana Western	MT	9,426	LC
The Univ of Tenn at Chattanooga	TN	17,340	C+
The Univ of Tenn at Knoxville	TN	22,112	VC
The Univ of Tenn at Martin	TN	15,212	C
The Univ of Texas at Austin	TX	20,206	MC
The Univ of Texas at San Antonio	TX	21,060	C
The Univ of Utah	UT	18,751	VC
The Univ of Virginia's College at Wise	VA	18,192	LC
Thiel College	PA	42,950	LC
Thomas College	ME	73,888	LC
Thomas Edison State Univ	NJ	6,350	NC
Thomas More College	KY	36,720	LC
Tiffin Univ	OH	34,900	LC
Toccoa Falls College	GA	30,048	C
Tougaloo College	MS	17,980	NC
Touro College	NY	31,040	C
Towson Univ	MD	21,878	C
Transylvania Univ	KY	47,450	HC+
Trevecca Nazarene Univ	TN	31,186	C
Trinity Christian College	IL	35,580	C
Trinity College	CT	69,020	HC
Trinity International Univ	IL	31,070	VC
Trinity Univ	TX	54,480	MC
Trinity Washington Univ	DC	33,826	C+
Troy Univ	AL	16,171	C
Truman State Univ	MO	16,286	MC
Tufts Univ	MA		MC
Tulane Univ	LA	67,496	MC
Tusculum College	TN	31,625	LC
Tuskegee Univ	AL	28,164	C
Union College	KY	32,310	C
Union College	NE	23,270	C
Union College	NY	64,320	MC
Union Univ	TN	41,160	VC
United States Air Force Academy	CO		C
United States Military Academy at West Point	NY		HC+
United States Naval Academy	MD		HC
Universidad del Turabo	PR	17,828	
Univ of Alabama at Birmingham	AL	22,092	C
Univ of Alabama in Huntsville	AL	20,028	VC
Univ of Alaska Anchorage	AK	17,914	C
Univ of Alaska Fairbanks	AK	16,874	VC
Univ of Arkansas at Fayetteville	AR	19,766	VC
Univ of Arkansas at Little Rock	AR	18,211	LC
Univ of Arkansas at Monticello	AR	13,599	LC
Univ of Arkansas at Pine Bluff	AR	13,541	C
Univ of Bridgeport	CT	44,985	LC
Univ of Calif at Berkeley	CA	29,886	MC
Univ of Calif at Davis	CA	28,468	HC
Univ of Calif at Irvine	CA	33,857	VC
Univ of Calif at Los Angeles	CA	27,438	HC+
Univ of Calif at Riverside	CA	32,912	C
Univ of Calif at Santa Barbara	CA	30,627	HC+
Univ of Central Arkansas	AR	15,042	VC
Univ of Central Florida	FL	16,379	VC
Univ of Central Missouri	MO	18,982	C
Univ of Central Okla	OK	15,150	C
Univ of Chicago	IL	70,551	MC
Univ of Cincinnati	OH	22,118	VC
Univ of Colo Boulder	CO	26,048	HC
Univ of Colo Colo Springs	CO	20,300	C
Univ of Colo Denver	CO	22,238	C
Univ of Conn	CT	27,394	
Univ of Dallas	TX	50,676	VC
Univ of Dayton	OH	54,930	VC
Univ of Delaware	DE	32,214	VC
Univ of Denver	CO	61,129	VC+
Univ of Detroit Mercy	MI	48,816	C
Univ of Dubuque	IA	37,824	C
Univ of Findlay	OH	43,040	C
Univ of Florida	FL	16,291	HC+
Univ of Georgia	GA	21,878	HC
Univ of Great Falls	MT	38,524	C
Univ of Hartford	CT	49,776	C
Univ of Hawaii at Hilo	HI	18,038	VC
Univ of Hawaii at Manoa	HI	23,261	C
Univ of Holy Cross	LA	21,523	NC
Univ of Houston	TX	21,871	VC
Univ of Houston-Downtown	TX	7,241	LC
Univ of Idaho	ID	16,158	C
Univ of Illinois at Chicago	IL	24,664	VC
Univ of Illinois at Urbana-Champaign	IL	27,006	HC
Univ of Indianapolis	IN	36,480	VC
Univ of Iowa	IA	19,415	HC
Univ of Jamestown	ND	28,508	C
Univ of Kansas	KS	20,884	VC
Univ of Kentucky	KY	24,800	C+
Univ of La Verne	CA	55,600	C
Univ of Louisiana at Lafayette	LA	14,516	C
Univ of Louisiana at Monroe	LA	15,970	C
Univ of Louisville	KY	19,692	C
Univ of Lynchburg	VA	48,370	C
Univ of Maine	ME	21,038	VC
Univ of Maine at Augusta	ME	7,812	C
Univ of Maine at Farmington	ME	18,792	C
Univ of Maine at Fort Kent	ME	15,165	LC
Univ of Maine at Machias	ME	22,960	C
Univ of Maine at Presque Isle	ME	16,148	LC
Univ of Mary Hardin-Baylor	TX	35,292	C+
Univ of Mary Washington	VA	23,039	C+
Univ of Maryland Univ College	MD	26,146	LC
Univ of Maryland/Baltimore County	MD	23,004	VC
Univ of Maryland/College Park	MD	21,938	HC
Univ of Maryland/Eastern Shore	MD	21,861	LC
Univ of Mass Amherst	MA	27,669	HC
Univ of Mass Boston	MA	13,828	C
Univ of Mass Lowell	MA	27,296	VC
Univ of Miami	FL	63,494	MC
Univ of Mich/Ann Arbor	MI	25,274	MC
Univ of Mich/Dearborn	MI	12,472	VC
Univ of Mich/Flint	MI	19,062	C
Univ of Minn/Duluth	MN	20,292	C
Univ of Minn/Morris	MN	21,222	VC
Univ of Minn/Twin Cities	MN	24,269	MC
Univ of Miss	MS	18,802	C
Univ of Missouri-Columbia	MO	20,463	VC
Univ of Missouri-Kansas City	MO	19,563	VC
Univ of Missouri-St. Louis	MO	19,810	VC
Univ of Mobile	AL	28,935	C
Univ of Montana	MT	14,105	C
Univ of Montevallo	AL	20,012	C
Univ of Mount Olive	NC	18,426	C
Univ of Mount Union	OH	39,990	C
Univ of Nebr - Kearney	NE	17,014	LC
Univ of Nebr - Lincoln	NE	18,589	VC
Univ of Nebr - Omaha	NE	16,120	C
Univ of Nevada, Las Vegas	NV	17,553	C
Univ of Nevada, Reno	NV	18,010	C
Univ of New England	ME	50,110	C
Univ of New Hampshire	NH	29,333	VC
Univ of New Hampshire - Manchester	NH	14,490	C
Univ of New Haven	CT	53,680	C
Univ of New Mexico	NM	16,808	C
Univ of New Orleans	LA	12,840	C
Univ of North Alabama	AL	15,964	C
Univ of N Car at Asheville	NC	16,251	VC+
Univ of N Car at Chapel Hill	NC	20,561	MC
Univ of N Car at Charlotte	NC	17,803	VC
Univ of N Car at Greensboro	NC	15,998	C
Univ of N Car at Pembroke	NC	14,737	LC
Univ of N Car Wilmington	NC	16,784	VC
Univ of N Dak	ND	16,673	C
Univ of North Florida	FL	15,996	VC
Univ of North Georgia	GA	17,316	C
Univ of North Texas	TX	20,082	C
Univ of Northern Colo	CO	19,658	C
Univ of Northern Iowa	IA	17,480	C
Univ of Northwestern - St. Paul	MN	39,530	C
Univ of Notre Dame	IN	68,801	MC
Univ of Okla	OK	19,651	HC
Univ of Oregon	OR	24,021	VC
Univ of Pennsylvania	PA	63,526	MC
Univ of Pikeville	KY	27,838	C
Univ of Pittsburgh at Bradford	PA	22,958	C
Univ of Pittsburgh at Johnstown	PA	22,092	C
Univ of Portland	OR	52,152	VC
Univ of PR, at Cayey	PR		
Univ of PR, at Humacao	PR	14,000	
Univ of PR, at Mayaguez	PR	13,995	
Univ of PR-Rio Piedras campus	PR	13,327	
Univ of Puget Sound	WA	60,210	HC
Univ of Redlands	CA	61,934	VC
Univ of Rhode Island	RI	26,066	VC
Univ of Richmond	VA	62,730	MC
Univ of Rio Grande & Rio Grande Community College	OH	8,750	LC
Univ of Rochester	NY	65,032	MC
Univ of St. Francis	IN	38,520	C
Univ of St. Joseph	CT	49,069	C
Univ of St. Mary	KS	37,080	NC
Univ of San Diego	CA	60,338	HC
Univ of San Francisco	CA	60,580	C
Univ of Science and Arts of Okla	OK	11,140	VC
Univ of Scranton	PA	54,962	VC
Univ of Sioux Falls	SD	25,630	C
Univ of South Alabama	AL	16,880	C
Univ of S Car Aiken	SC	18,094	C
Univ of S Car at Columbia	SC	21,726	VC
Univ of S Car Upstate	SC	19,272	LC
Univ of S Dak	SD	16,109	C
Univ of South Florida St. Petersburg	FL	15,980	C
Univ of Southern Calif	CA	66,631	MC
Univ of Southern Indiana	IN	16,808	C
Univ of Southern Maine	ME	18,320	C
Univ of Southern Miss	MS	13,170	C
Univ of St. Francis	IL	40,828	C
Univ of St. Thomas - Houston	TX	41,510	VC
Univ of Tampa	FL	38,928	VC
Univ of Texas at Arlington	TX	18,876	C
Univ of Texas at El Paso	TX	34,452	NC
Univ of Texas Rio Grande Valley	TX	15,573	LC
Univ of the Cumberlands	KY	32,000	LC
Univ of the District of Columbia	DC	21,260	LC
Univ of the Incarnate Word	TX	39,162	LC
Univ of the Ozarks	AR	31,050	NC
Univ of the Pacific	CA	57,446	VC
Univ of the Southwest	NM	24,386	C
Univ of Toledo	OH	19,336	C
Univ of Tulsa	OK	52,625	HC
Univ of Vermont	VT	29,792	HC
Univ of Virginia	VA	27,367	MC
Univ of Washington	WA	23,091	MC
Univ of West Alabama	AL	16,284	LC
Univ of West Florida	FL	15,848	C
Univ of West Georgia	GA	17,510	LC
Univ of Wisc-Eau Claire	WI	16,354	VC
Univ of Wisc-Green Bay	WI	15,184	C
Univ of Wisc-La Crosse	WI	15,425	VC
Univ of Wisc-Madison	WI	21,647	MC
Univ of Wisc-Milwaukee	WI	21,538	C
Univ of Wisc-Oshkosh	WI	15,392	C
Univ of Wisc-Parkside	WI	15,313	C
Univ of Wisc-Platteville	WI	14,148	C
Univ of Wisc-River Falls	WI	14,541	C
Univ of Wisc-Stevens Point	WI	14,043	C
Univ of Wisc-Superior	WI	14,838	C
Univ of Wisc-Whitewater	WI	13,976	C
Univ of Wyoming	WY	15,537	C
Upper Iowa Univ	IA	34,990	NC
Urbana Univ	OH	30,820	C
Ursinus College	PA	62,920	VC
Ursuline College	OH	41,076	LC
Utah State Univ	UT	13,235	C
Utica College	NY	31,510	C
Valley City State Univ	ND	13,267	C
Valparaiso Univ	IN	50,160	VC
Vanderbilt Univ	TN	63,248	MC
Vanguard Univ of Southern Calif	CA	42,400	VC
Vassar College	NY	68,110	MC
Villanova Univ	PA	64,922	MC
Virginia Commonwealth Univ	VA	23,811	VC
Virginia Military Inst	VA	26,460	VC
Virginia Polytechnic Inst and State Univ	VA	21,920	VC
Virginia Union Univ	VA	25,058	C
Virginia Wesleyan Univ	VA	45,980	LC
Viterbo Univ	WI	34,660	C
Voorhees College	SC	19,976	C
Wabash College	IN	52,100	VC
Wagner College	NY	57,240	C+
Wake Forest Univ	NC	69,354	MC
Walla Walla Univ	WA	34,845	C
Walsh Univ	OH	39,010	C
Warner Pacific College	OR	31,610	C
Warner Univ	FL	28,216	C
Warren Wilson College	NC	44,220	VC
Wartburg College	IA	49,478	C
Washburn Univ	KS	15,827	C
Washington & Jefferson College	PA	58,694	VC
Washington Adventist Univ	MD	32,050	LC
Washington and Lee Univ	VA	59,647	MC
Washington College	MD	56,154	VC
Washington State Univ	WA	22,747	C
Washington Univ in St. Louis	MO	67,539	MC
Wayland Baptist Univ	TX	23,460	LC
Wayne State College	NE	25,746	NC
Wayne State Univ	MI	23,085	C
Waynesburg Univ	PA	33,530	C
Weber State Univ	UT	14,112	C
Webster Univ	MO	37,490	C
Wellesley College	MA	66,984	MC
Wells College	NY	50,500	C
Wesley College	DE	37,848	LC
Wesleyan College	GA	31,940	C+
Wesleyan Univ	CT	66,940	MC
West Chester Univ of Pennsylvania	PA	19,171	VC
West Liberty Univ	WV	16,158	C
West Texas A&M Univ	TX	13,478	C
West Virginia State Univ	WV	19,412	LC
West Virginia Univ	WV	18,952	VC
West Virginia Wesleyan College	WV	39,188	C
Western Carolina Univ	NC	13,965	C
Western Conn State Univ	CT	21,254	LC
Western Illinois Univ	IL	20,897	C
Western Kentucky Univ	KY	16,850	C
Western Mich Univ	MI	21,791	C
Western New England Univ	MA	49,182	C
Western New Mexico Univ	NM	16,914	LC
Western Oregon Univ	OR	19,965	LC
Western State Colo Univ	CO	19,348	C
Western Washington Univ	WA	18,904	VC
Westfield State Univ	MA	20,404	C
Westminster College	MO	32,820	C
Westminster College	PA	41,722	C
Westminster College	UT	41,078	C
Westmont College	CA	57,930	VC
Wheaton College	IL	44,993	MC
Wheaton College	MA	63,818	VC
Wheeling Jesuit Univ	WV	37,106	LC
Whitman College	WA	59,772	MC
Whittier College	CA	57,891	C
Whitworth Univ	WA	53,682	VC
Wichita State Univ	KS	17,773	C
Widener Univ	PA	58,190	C
Wiley College	TX	19,255	C
Wilkes Univ	PA	49,166	C
Willamette Univ	OR	62,514	VC+
William Carey Univ	MS	23,950	LC
William Jewell College	MO	42,490	C+
William Paterson Univ of New Jersey	NJ	24,022	C
William Peace Univ	NC	39,300	LC
William Penn Univ	IA	26,000	C
William Woods Univ	MO	32,040	C
Williams Baptist College	AR	24,720	C
Williams College	MA	67,700	MC
Wilmington College	OH	35,100	C
Wilson College	PA	35,620	LC
Wingate Univ	NC	41,900	C
Winona State Univ	MN	18,109	C
Winston-Salem State Univ	NC	18,005	LC
Winthrop Univ	SC	23,960	C
Wisc Lutheran College	WI	36,290	C
Wittenberg Univ	OH	49,863	VC
Wofford College	SC	49,885	VC
Worcester State Univ	MA	20,977	C
Wright State Univ	OH	16,983	C
Xavier Univ	OH	49,380	VC
Xavier Univ of Louisiana	LA	31,689	C
Yale Univ	CT	64,650	MC
Yeshiva Univ	NY	52,750	VC
York College	NE	30,260	C
York College of Pennsylvania	PA	29,240	C
Youngstown State Univ	OH	17,487	C

ENGLISH AND PROFESSIONAL COMMUNICATION

School	ST	$IS	SR
Black Hills State Univ	SD	16,622	C
Bloomfield College	NJ	40,100	LC
Farmingdale State College	NY	20,968	C
Johnson & Wales Univ/Denver Campus	CO	44,768	C
Okla Baptist Univ	OK	33,990	C
Taylor Univ	IN	42,130	VC

ENGLISH AS A SECOND/FOREIGN LANGUAGE

School	ST	$IS	SR
Bloomfield College	NJ	40,100	LC
Doane Univ	NE	41,340	VC
Dordt College	IA	37,860	C+
Holy Names Univ	CA	46,630	LC
Houghton College	NY	40,558	VC
Huntington Univ	IN	33,996	C
Kutztown Univ of Pennsylvania	PA	19,477	C
La Sierra Univ	CA	39,690	VC
Lenoir-Rhyne Univ	NC	47,500	LC
Liberty Univ	VA	31,415	C
Maryville College	TN	44,410	C
Millersville Univ of Pennsylvania	PA	25,298	C
Minn State Univ, Mankato	MN	17,190	C
Olivet Nazarene Univ	IL	41,840	VC
Salem International Univ	WV	21,090	C
Salisbury Univ	MD	21,132	VC
Southern New Hampshire Univ	NH	44,256	C
SUNY at Oswego	NY	22,219	VC
Taylor Univ	IN	42,130	VC
The Univ of Arizona	AZ	24,086	C
Union Univ	TN	41,160	VC
Univ of Central Okla	OK	15,150	C
Univ of Findlay	OH	43,040	C
Univ of Hawaii at Manoa	HI	23,261	C
Univ of Northwestern - St. Paul	MN	39,530	C
Univ of Texas Rio Grande Valley	TX	15,573	LC
Univ of Wisc-Green Bay	WI	15,184	C
Western Kentucky Univ	KY	16,850	C

ENGLISH EDUCATION

School	ST	$IS	SR
Abilene Christian Univ	TX	43,708	C+
Adams State Univ	CO	15,420	LC
Alabama State Univ	AL	16,490	LC
Albion College	MI	55,260	C

School	ST	$IS	SR
Andrews Univ	MI	41,732	C
Appalachian State Univ	NC	15,394	VC
Aquinas College - Mich	MI	38,876	VC
Arkansas State Univ	AR	16,190	C
Armstrong State Univ	GA	15,615	C
Asbury Univ	KY	36,450	C+
Ashford Univ	CA	10,480	C
Ashland Univ	OH	30,446	C
Auburn Univ	AL	24,300	VC+
Augustana College	IL	51,222	VC+
Averett Univ	VA	43,034	LC
Bayamon Central Univ	PR	12,490	
Baylor Univ	TX	56,803	HC
Bennett College	NC	27,717	NC
Bethany College	KS	38,637	LC
Bethany College	WV	38,774	LC
Bethel Univ	MN	46,550	C+
Bethune-Cookman Univ	FL	23,322	C
Black Hills State Univ	SD	16,622	C
Blackburn College	IL	28,526	LC
Bloomfield College	NJ	40,100	LC
Blue Mountain College	MS	15,949	C
Boise State Univ	ID	17,368	C
Boston Univ	MA	67,352	MC
Brigham Young Univ	UT	13,248	MC
Brigham Young Univ/Hawaii	HI	11,710	C
Cal State, Fullerton	CA	21,902	C
Calvin College	MI	43,090	HC
Cameron Univ	OK	11,632	LC
Campbell Univ	NC	37,570	VC
Canisius College	NY	49,672	C
Carthage College	WI	48,835	C
Cedarville Univ	OH	36,244	VC
Central Washington Univ	WA	16,803	C
CUNY/Brooklyn College	NY	7,163	C+
CUNY/City College	NY	20,204	C
Claflin Univ	SC	25,592	LC
Coker College	SC	38,196	C
College of the Ozarks	MO	7,530	VC
Colo State Univ	CO	23,033	C
Concordia Univ St. Paul	MN	29,050	C
Cornerstone Univ	MI	36,550	C
Covenant College	GA	44,590	HC
Daemen College	NY	40,336	C
Dakota State Univ	SD	12,286	C
Dallas Baptist Univ	TX	35,220	VC
Delaware State Univ	DE	19,376	LC
Delta State Univ	MS	13,176	LC
Dordt College	IA	37,860	C+
Duquesne Univ	PA	48,508	VC
East Carolina Univ	NC	16,539	C
East Central Univ	OK	13,330	C
East Texas Baptist Univ	TX	34,444	C
Eastern Mich Univ	MI	19,761	C
Edgewood College	WI	35,950	C
Elizabethtown College	PA	56,340	VC
Emory and Henry College	VA	46,320	C
Faulkner Univ	AL	26,410	C
Ferris State Univ	MI	21,458	C
Flagler College	FL	27,620	C
Florida Atlantic Univ	FL	18,256	C
Florida State Univ	FL	16,771	HC
Fontbonne Univ	MO	34,606	C
Franklin College	IN	40,550	C
Fresno Pacific Univ	CA	38,858	C
Friends Univ	KS	38,000	C
Gannon Univ	PA	42,922	C
Georgetown College	KY	41,440	C
Glenville State College	WV	17,386	LC
Goddard College	VT	17,040	VC
Goshen College	IN	44,350	C
Grace College and Seminary	IN	31,524	C
Grambling State Univ	LA	15,701	C
Green Mountain College	VT	45,228	LC
Greensboro College	NC	39,790	LC
Greenville College	IL	27,012	LC
Hardin-Simmons Univ	TX	36,025	C
Hofstra Univ	NY	58,210	C+
Hood College	MD	50,540	C
Hope College	MI	42,840	VC
Houghton College	NY	40,558	VC
Humboldt State Univ	CA	21,708	C
Huntingdon College	AL	35,900	C
Huntington Univ	IN	33,996	C
Husson Univ	ME	26,508	C
Indiana Univ Northwest	IN	7,207	LC
Indiana Univ of Pennsylvania	PA	24,474	C
Indiana Univ South Bend	IN	16,057	C
Indiana Univ-Purdue Univ Fort Wayne	IN	18,675	C
Indiana Univ-Purdue Univ Indianapolis	IN	18,952	C
Indiana Wesleyan Univ	IN	33,674	C
Ithaca College	NY	58,158	VC+
John Brown Univ	AR	35,184	VC
Johnson State College	VT	22,672	C
Judson College	AL	27,066	C
Juniata College	PA	58,118	VC
Kennesaw State Univ	GA	18,899	VC
Kentucky Christian Univ	KY	26,836	LC
Kutztown Univ of Pennsylvania	PA	19,477	C
Le Moyne College	NY	47,305	VC
Lenoir-Rhyne Univ	NC	47,500	LC
Limestone College	SC	32,100	C
Lincoln Univ	MO	14,402	NC
Lipscomb Univ	TN	42,984	VC
LIU Brooklyn	NY	50,698	C
LIU Post	NY	50,698	C+
Lyndon State College	VT	20,714	C
Marian Univ	WI	34,622	C
Marist College	NY	49,860	VC
Marshall Univ	WV	18,044	C
Marymount Univ	VA	43,231	C
Marywood Univ	PA	47,840	C
Mayville State Univ	ND	18,371	NC
McMurry Univ	TX	34,259	LC
Messiah College	PA	44,380	VC
Miami Univ	OH	27,190	HC+
MidAmerica Nazarene Univ	KS	37,808	C
Millersville Univ of Pennsylvania	PA	25,298	C
Millikin Univ	IL	44,148	C
Minn State Univ, Moorhead	MN	21,393	C
Minot State Univ	ND	13,285	C
Miss Valley State Univ	MS	13,233	LC
Missouri Southern State Univ	MO	13,071	C
Missouri Western State Univ	MO	17,822	LC
Monmouth Univ	NJ	50,184	C
Morningside College	IA	39,780	C
Morris College	SC	19,195	LC
Mount Aloysius College	PA	29,976	C
Mount Mary Univ	WI	34,650	LC
Mount Vernon Nazarene Univ	OH	35,944	C
Murray State Univ	KY	17,726	C+
Nazareth College	NY	46,784	C
Nebr Wesleyan Univ	NE	42,026	C+
New York Univ	NY	68,139	MC
Niagara Univ	NY	41,010	C
N Car A&T State Univ	NC	13,786	C
Northeastern Illinois Univ	IL	12,529	LC
Northern Kentucky Univ	KY	16,486	C
Northwest Missouri State Univ	MO	18,286	C
Northwest Nazarene Univ	ID	40,250	C
Northwestern Okla State Univ	OK	13,072	LC
Nova Southeastern Univ	FL	38,534	C+
Nyack College	NY	34,450	LC
Oakwood Univ	AL	43,758	C
Ohio Valley Univ	WV	28,800	C
Okla Baptist Univ	OK	33,990	C
Okla Christian Univ	OK	29,260	C
Okla Wesleyan Univ	OK	34,434	C
Old Dominion Univ	VA	21,618	C
Olivet Nazarene Univ	IL	41,840	VC
Oral Roberts Univ	OK	34,316	C
Palm Beach Atlantic Univ	FL	39,250	C
Pfeiffer Univ	NC	40,532	LC
Piedmont College	GA	34,334	C
Pittsburg State Univ	KS	13,880	C
Purdue Univ Northwest	IN	15,178	C
Purdue Univ/West Lafayette	IN	20,032	MC
Rider Univ	NJ	54,050	C
Rivier Univ	NH	41,600	VC
Roberts Wesleyan College	NY	41,116	C
Rocky Mountain College	MT	35,776	C
Rust College	MS	10,600	C
Saginaw Valley State Univ	MI	19,284	C
St. Augustine's Univ	NC	25,582	C
St. Louis Univ	MO	49,866	HC
St. Mary's Univ of Minn	MN	42,440	C
Schreiner Univ	TX	34,626	LC
Seton Hill Univ	PA	46,972	VC
Shaw Univ	NC	24,638	C
Shepherd Univ, West Virginia	WV	17,382	C
Shippensburg Univ of Pennsylvania	PA	24,096	C
Shorter Univ	GA	31,130	LC
Simpson Univ	CA	34,722	C
Southeast Missouri State Univ	MO	16,148	C
Southeastern Louisiana Univ	LA	16,237	C
Southern Nazarene Univ	OK	33,684	C
Southern New Hampshire Univ	NH	44,256	C
Southern Oregon Univ	OR	19,117	C
Southern Univ and A&M College	LA	16,074	LC
Southern Univ at New Orleans	LA	8,014	LC
Southern Wesleyan Univ	SC	33,670	LC
Southwestern Okla State Univ	OK	12,205	C
St. Edward's Univ	TX	56,190	VC
St. John Fisher College	NY	45,270	VC
SUNY at New Paltz	NY	20,840	C
SUNY at Oswego	NY	22,219	VC
SUNY/Fredonia	NY	20,818	C
SUNY/Oneonta	NY	20,794	C
SUNY/Plattsburgh	NY	19,314	C
SUNY/Potsdam	NY	21,051	VC
Suffolk Univ	MA	52,316	C
Syracuse Univ	NY	62,313	HC
Taylor Univ	IN	42,130	VC
Texas Southern Univ	TX	19,592	LC
The Catholic Univ of America	DC	58,376	VC
The College of New Jersey	NJ	28,675	VC+
The College of St. Rose	NY	44,010	C
The Univ of Mary	ND	23,180	C
The Univ of Montana Western	MT	9,426	LC
The Univ of Tenn at Chattanooga	TN	17,340	C+
The Univ of Utah	UT	18,751	VC
Tiffin Univ	OH	34,900	LC
Tougaloo College	MS	17,980	NC
Trevecca Nazarene Univ	TN	31,186	C
Trine Univ	IN	41,310	C
Troy Univ	AL	16,171	C
Union College	NE	23,270	C
Universidad del Turabo	PR	17,828	
Univ of Arkansas at Pine Bluff	AR	13,541	C
Univ of Central Florida	FL	16,379	VC
Univ of Central Missouri	MO	18,982	C
Univ of Central Okla	OK	15,150	C
Univ of Charleston	WV	35,000	LC
Univ of Conn	CT	27,394	
Univ of Delaware	DE	32,214	VC
Univ of Evansville	IN	44,186	C+
Univ of Georgia	GA	21,878	HC
Univ of Illinois at Chicago	IL	24,664	VC
Univ of Illinois at Urbana-Champaign	IL	27,006	HC
Univ of Indianapolis	IN	36,480	VC
Univ of Louisiana at Lafayette	LA	14,516	C
Univ of Maine at Machias	ME	22,960	C
Univ of Mary Hardin-Baylor	TX	35,292	C+
Univ of Miss	MS	18,802	C
Univ of Missouri-Columbia	MO	20,463	VC
Univ of Nebr - Lincoln	NE	18,589	VC
Univ of New Hampshire - Manchester	NH	14,490	C
Univ of New Orleans	LA	12,840	C
Univ of N Car at Charlotte	NC	17,803	VC
Univ of North Florida	FL	15,996	VC
Univ of Northwestern - St. Paul	MN	39,530	C
Univ of Pittsburgh at Bradford	PA	22,958	C
Univ of Pittsburgh at Johnstown	PA	22,092	C
Univ of Rio Grande & Rio Grande Community College	OH	8,750	LC
Univ of S Car Upstate	SC	19,272	LC
Univ of South Florida/Tampa	FL	16,110	VC
Univ of Southern Indiana	IN	16,808	C
Univ of the Cumberlands	KY	32,000	LC
Univ of Vermont	VT	29,792	HC
Univ of Wisc-Green Bay	WI	15,184	C
Univ of Wisc-Superior	WI	14,838	C
Urbana Univ	OH	30,820	C
Valparaiso Univ	IN	50,160	VC
Viterbo Univ	WI	34,660	C
Warner Univ	FL	28,216	C
Washington Adventist Univ	MD	32,050	LC
Washington State Univ	WA	22,747	C
Weber State Univ	UT	14,112	C
West Chester Univ of Pennsylvania	PA	19,171	VC
West Texas A&M Univ	TX	13,478	C
Western Carolina Univ	NC	13,965	C
Westmont College	CA	57,930	VC
Whitworth Univ	WA	53,682	VC
Wiley College	TX	19,255	C
Wilmington College	OH	35,100	C
Wilson College	PA	35,620	LC
Wingate Univ	NC	41,900	C
Xavier Univ of Louisiana	LA	31,689	C
York College	NE	30,260	C
York College of Pennsylvania	PA	29,240	C
Youngstown State Univ	OH	17,487	C

ENGLISH LITERATURE

School	ST	$IS	SR
Agnes Scott College	GA	51,930	VC+
Aquinas College - Mich	MI	38,876	VC
Bard College	NY	65,924	HC
Beloit College	WI	55,206	HC
Bennington College	VT	66,280	MC
Bethany College	WV	38,774	LC
Bethel Univ	MN	46,550	C+
Blackburn College	IL	28,526	LC
Boise State Univ	ID	17,368	C
Bowling Green State Univ	OH	19,975	C
Brown Univ	RI	64,566	MC
Cal State, Fullerton	CA	21,902	C
Calvin College	MI	43,090	HC
Carroll College	MT	44,304	C
Chatham Univ	PA	47,883	VC
Chestnut Hill College	PA	47,180	C
CUNY/Hunter College	NY	31,098	VC
Colo State Univ	CO	23,033	C
Columbia Univ/ School of General Studies	NY	61,470	MC
Concordia College - New York	NY	39,035	LC
Cornell College	IA	49,900	VC
DePauw Univ	IN	58,688	VC
Dominican Univ of Calif	CA	58,750	C
Drury Univ	MO	37,555	VC
East Texas Baptist Univ	TX	34,444	C
Eastern Mich Univ	MI	19,761	C
Edinboro Univ	PA	15,940	LC
Elizabethtown College	PA	56,340	VC
Elmira College	NY	53,900	C
Emory and Henry College	VA	46,320	C
Excelsior College	NY	38,800	SP
Fairleigh Dickinson Univ/ Metropolitan Campus	NJ	52,392	C
Fontbonne Univ	MO	34,606	C
Fordham Univ	NY	68,431	MC
Hamilton College	NY	64,250	MC
High Point Univ	NC	47,355	VC
Hofstra Univ	NY	58,210	C+
Hope International Univ	CA	42,730	C
Houghton College	NY	40,558	VC
Huntington Univ	IN	33,996	C
Indiana Univ-Purdue Univ Fort Wayne	IN	18,675	C
Ithaca College	NY	58,158	VC+
Johnson & Wales Univ/ Denver Campus	CO	44,768	C
Keene State College	NH	24,604	C
King Univ	TN	36,976	C
Knox College	IL	54,654	VC+
Loras College	IA	40,726	C
Loyola Univ New Orleans	LA	52,456	VC
Madonna Univ	MI	30,450	LC
Marshall Univ	WV	18,044	C
Marylhurst Univ	OR	16,818	NC
Mass College of Liberal Arts	MA	20,659	C
Mercer Univ	GA	45,348	VC
Millersville Univ of Pennsylvania	PA	25,298	C
Mills College	CA	43,705	C
Missouri Southern State Univ	MO	13,071	C
Missouri Western State Univ	MO	17,822	LC
Murray State Univ	KY	17,726	C+
New York Univ	NY	68,139	MC
North Central College	IL	48,712	C+
North Central Univ	MN	30,610	C
Northeastern Illinois Univ	IL	12,529	LC
Northwest Univ	WA	38,720	VC
Oral Roberts Univ	OK	34,316	C
Otterbein Univ	OH	41,630	C
Pace Univ	NY	60,136	C
Pennsylvania State Univ - Univ Park	PA	29,716	HC
Pfeiffer Univ	NC	40,532	LC
Purdue Univ Northwest	IN	15,178	C
Queens Univ of Charlotte	NC	39,543	C
Reed College	OR	65,300	MC
Rider Univ	NJ	54,050	C
Rutgers Univ - New Brunswick	NJ	27,090	HC
St. Leo Univ	FL	32,850	C
St. Louis Univ	MO	49,866	HC
St. Mary's College	IN	50,600	C
Southern Illinois Univ Carbondale	IL	24,554	C
Southern New Hampshire Univ	NH	44,256	C
St. Edward's Univ	TX	56,190	VC
St. Thomas Aquinas College	NY	32,450	C
SUNY at Binghamton	NY	24,100	MC
SUNY/Plattsburgh	NY	19,314	C
Stevenson Univ	MD	48,412	C
Swarthmore College	PA	63,550	MC
Taylor Univ	IN	42,130	VC
The Catholic Univ of America	DC	58,376	VC
The Univ of Montana Western	MT	9,426	LC
Union Univ	TN	41,160	VC
Univ of Calif San Diego	CA	30,450	MC
Univ of Illinois at Chicago	IL	24,664	VC
Univ of Illinois at Urbana-Champaign	IL	27,006	HC
Univ of Maryland/College Park	MD	21,938	HC
Univ of Mass Dartmouth	MA	26,507	C
Univ of Mich/Ann Arbor	MI	25,274	MC
Univ of Missouri-Columbia	MO	20,463	VC
Univ of North Florida	FL	15,996	VC
Univ of Northwestern - St. Paul	MN	39,530	C
Univ of Pittsburgh	PA	30,030	MC
Univ of Pittsburgh at Greensburg	PA	24,140	C
Univ of Redlands	CA	61,934	VC
Univ of Rochester	NY	65,032	MC
Univ of South Florida/Tampa	FL	16,110	VC
Univ of Southern Calif	CA	66,631	MC
Virginia State Univ	VA	19,802	C+
Warren Wilson College	NC	44,220	VC
Washington Univ in St. Louis	MO	67,539	MC
Wellesley College	MA	66,984	MC
Wesleyan Univ	CT	66,940	MC
West Chester Univ of Pennsylvania	PA	19,171	VC
Winthrop Univ	SC	23,960	C
York College of Pennsylvania	PA	29,240	C
Youngstown State Univ	OH	17,487	C

ENGLISH SECONDARY EDUCATION

School	ST	$IS	SR
Abilene Christian Univ	TX	43,708	C+
Bethel College	IN	36,830	C
Cairn Univ	PA	37,572	C
Calvin College	MI	43,090	HC
Grove City College	PA	26,654	VC
Immaculata Univ	PA	39,000	C
Ithaca College	NY	58,158	VC+
King Univ	TN	36,976	C
Kutztown Univ of Pennsylvania	PA	19,477	C
Louisiana College	LA	21,274	C
Missouri Western State Univ	MO	17,822	LC
Neumann Univ	PA	40,678	LC
North Central Univ	MN	30,610	C
North Greenville Univ	SC	25,930	C
Okla Baptist Univ	OK	33,990	C

ST = STATE **$IS** = IN-STATE COSTS **SR** = SELECTOR RATING

School	ST	$IS	SR
Providence College	RI	62,870	HC
St. Leo Univ	FL	32,850	C
Tenn Wesleyan Univ	TN	32,680	LC
Texas Christian Univ	TX	57,120	HC
Univ of N Car at Greensboro	NC	15,998	C
Univ of Northwestern - St. Paul	MN	39,530	C
Wartburg College	IA	49,478	C
West Chester Univ of Pennsylvania	PA	19,171	VC
Western Kentucky Univ	KY	16,850	C
Western Mich Univ	MI	21,791	C
Wilson College	PA	35,620	LC

ENGLISH WRITING

School	ST	$IS	SR
Aquinas College - Mich	MI	38,876	VC
Augustana College	IL	51,222	VC+
Bethel College	IN	36,830	C
Bloomfield College	NJ	40,100	LC
Boise State Univ	ID	17,368	C
Cabrini Univ	PA	42,591	LC
Calvin College	MI	43,090	HC
Carroll College	MT	44,304	C
Concordia Univ St. Paul	MN	29,050	C
Cornell College	IA	49,900	VC
Cornerstone Univ	MI	36,550	C
Drury Univ	MO	37,555	VC
East Texas Baptist Univ	TX	34,444	C
Elizabethtown College	PA	56,340	VC
Fontbonne Univ	MO	34,606	C
Fordham Univ	NY	68,431	MC
Goddard College	VT	17,040	VC
Goshen College	IN	44,350	C
High Point Univ	NC	47,355	VC
Houghton College	NY	40,558	VC
Ithaca College	NY	58,158	VC+
Johnson & Wales Univ/ Denver Campus	CO	44,768	C
Keene State College	NH	24,604	C
King Univ	TN	36,976	C
Kutztown Univ of Pennsylvania	PA	19,477	C
Limestone College	SC	32,100	C
Macalester College	MN	64,136	MC
Marylhurst Univ	OR	16,818	NC
Mass College of Liberal Arts	MA	20,659	C
Millersville Univ of Pennsylvania	PA	25,298	C
Mills College	CA	43,705	C
Missouri Southern State Univ	MO	13,071	C
Missouri Western State Univ	MO	17,822	LC
North Central College	IL	48,712	C+
North Central Univ	MN	30,610	C
Northwest Univ	WA	38,720	VC
Okla Christian Univ	OK	29,260	C
Purdue Univ Northwest	IN	15,178	C
St. Leo Univ	FL	32,850	C
St. Louis Univ	MO	49,866	HC
St. Mary's College	IN	50,600	C
San Diego State Univ	CA	23,156	VC
Seton Hill Univ	PA	46,972	VC
Southern Oregon Univ	OR	19,117	C
Spring Hill College	AL	48,488	C
St. Edward's Univ	TX	56,190	VC
SUNY at Oswego	NY	22,219	VC
SUNY/Plattsburgh	NY	19,314	C
Taylor Univ	IN	42,130	VC
Univ of Colo Denver	CO	22,238	C
Univ of Idaho	ID	16,158	C
Univ of Mass Dartmouth	MA	26,507	C
Univ of North Alabama	AL	15,964	C
Univ of Northwestern - St. Paul	MN	39,530	C
Valparaiso Univ	IN	50,160	VC
Warren Wilson College	NC	44,220	VC
Wellesley College	MA	66,984	MC
West Chester Univ of Pennsylvania	PA	19,171	VC
Wilson College	PA	35,620	LC

ENTOMOLOGY

School	ST	$IS	SR
Cal State, Fullerton	CA	21,902	C
Colo State Univ	CO	23,033	C
Cornell Univ	NY	67,591	MC
Iowa State Univ	IA	18,176	C
Mich State Univ	MI	24,542	VC
Ohio State Univ at Columbus	OH	22,843	MC
Okla State Univ	OK	17,180	C+
Purdue Univ/West Lafayette	IN	20,032	MC
Rutgers Univ - New Brunswick	NJ	27,090	HC
SUNY/The College of Environmental Science and Forestry	NY	23,728	VC
Texas A&M Univ at College Station	TX	20,771	VC+
The Univ of Arizona	AZ	24,086	C
The Univ of Calif at Davis	CA	28,468	HC
Univ of Calif at Riverside	CA	32,912	C
Univ of Delaware	DE	32,214	VC
Univ of Florida	FL	16,291	HC+
Univ of Georgia	GA	21,878	HC
Univ of Idaho	ID	16,158	C
Univ of Illinois at Urbana-Champaign	IL	27,006	HC
Univ of Nebr - Lincoln	NE	18,589	VC
Univ of Wisc-Madison	WI	21,647	MC

School	ST	$IS	SR
Washington State Univ	WA	22,747	C

ENTREPRENEURIAL STUDIES

School	ST	$IS	SR
American International College	MA	47,020	LC
Ashford Univ	CA	10,480	C
Ashland Univ	OH	30,446	C
Auburn Univ at Montgomery	AL	15,000	C
Baldwin Wallace Univ	OH	42,464	VC
Baylor Univ	TX	56,803	HC
Belmont Univ	TN	44,500	VC+
Black Hills State Univ	SD	16,622	C
Bradley Univ	IL	43,240	VC
Brown Univ	RI	64,566	MC
Bryant Univ	RI	57,204	VC
Calif Baptist Univ	CA	42,986	C
Cal State, Fullerton	CA	21,902	C
Canisius College	NY	49,672	C
Central Mich Univ	MI	20,330	C
Clarkson Univ	NY	60,392	VC
Cogswell Polytechnical College	CA	31,511	C
College of William & Mary	VA	34,907	MC
Dallas Baptist Univ	TX	35,220	VC
Davenport Univ	MI	25,896	LC
Drexel Univ	PA	65,927	HC
Duquesne Univ	PA	48,508	VC
East Central Univ	OK	13,330	C
Eastern Mich Univ	MI	19,761	C
Eastern Univ	PA	39,540	C
Elon Univ	NC	46,142	HC
Endicott College	MA	47,054	C+
Fairleigh Dickinson Univ/ College at Florham	NJ	54,770	C
Fairleigh Dickinson Univ/ Metropolitan Campus	NJ	52,392	C
Florida State Univ	FL	16,771	HC
Gannon Univ	PA	42,922	C
Grand Canyon Univ	AZ	25,150	VC
Grove City College	PA	26,654	VC
Hawaii Pacific Univ	HI	33,420	C
High Point Univ	NC	47,355	VC
Hofstra Univ	NY	58,210	C+
Houston Baptist Univ	TX	36,450	C
Huntington Univ	IN	33,996	C
Jackson State Univ	MS	15,879	LC
John Brown Univ	AR	35,184	VC
John Carroll Univ	OH	51,570	C
Johnson & Wales Univ/ Charlotte Campus	NC	44,768	C
Johnson & Wales Univ/ Denver Campus	CO	44,768	C
Johnson & Wales Univ/North Miami Campus	FL	44,768	C
Johnson & Wales Univ/ Providence Campus	RI	44,768	C
Juniata College	PA	58,118	VC
Kansas State Univ	KS	17,780	VC
Kennesaw State Univ	GA	18,899	VC
Kent State Univ	OH	20,928	C
Lake Erie College	OH	38,914	LC
Lasell College	MA	49,400	C
Lipscomb Univ	TN	42,984	VC
LIU Brooklyn	NY	50,698	C
Loyola Marymount Univ	CA	60,202	VC+
Loyola Univ Chicago	IL	57,158	VC
Marquette Univ	WI	53,090	VC+
Menlo College	CA	51,380	LC
Mercy College	NY	32,614	C
Middle Tenn State Univ	TN	8,650	C
Millikin Univ	IL	44,148	C
Minneapolis College of Art and Design	MN	44,218	SP
Missouri State Univ	MO	15,837	C+
Mount Aloysius College	PA	29,976	C
Murray State Univ	KY	17,726	C+
New York Inst of Technology	NY	49,980	VC
North Central Univ	MN	30,610	C
Northern Kentucky Univ	KY	16,486	C
Northern Mich Univ	MI	20,853	C
Ohio Univ	OH	23,394	VC
Okla State Univ	OK	17,180	C+
Pace Univ	NY	60,136	C
Paul Quinn College	TX	25,350	LC
Peirce College	PA	16,780	NC
Pennsylvania State Univ - Univ Park	PA	29,716	HC
Purdue Univ/West Lafayette	IN	20,032	MC
Quinnipiac Univ	CT	60,970	VC
Rowan Univ	NJ	24,491	VC
St. Joseph's Univ	PA	58,540	VC
St. Louis Univ	MO	49,866	HC
St. Mary's Univ of Minn	MN	42,440	C
Samford Univ	AL	40,770	VC
San Francisco State Univ	CA	18,514	LC
San Jose State Univ	CA	22,630	C
Seton Hill Univ	PA	46,972	VC
Shenandoah Univ	VA	42,100	C
Shippensburg Univ of Pennsylvania	PA	24,096	C
S Dak State Univ	SD	15,874	C
Southeast Missouri State Univ	MO	16,148	C
Southern Adventist Univ	TN	28,250	C
Southern Illinois Univ Edwardsville	IL	20,188	C
Southern Vermont College	VT	34,670	LC
Southwestern Okla State Univ	OK	12,205	C
St. Edward's Univ	TX	56,190	VC
SUNY at Binghamton	NY	24,100	MC
SUNY/Plattsburgh	NY	19,314	C
Stetson Univ	FL	57,174	VC+
Suffolk Univ	MA	52,316	C
Syracuse Univ	NY	62,313	HC
Temple Univ	PA	24,392	C+
Texas Christian Univ	TX	57,120	HC
The Univ of Arizona	AZ	24,086	C
The Univ of Utah	UT	18,751	VC
Thomas Edison State Univ	NJ	6,350	NC
Tulane Univ	LA	67,496	MC
Univ of Alaska Anchorage	AK	17,914	C
Univ of Dayton	OH	54,930	VC
Univ of Hartford	CT	49,776	C
Univ of Illinois at Chicago	IL	24,664	VC
Univ of Illinois at Urbana-Champaign	IL	27,006	HC
Univ of Indianapolis	IN	36,480	VC
Univ of Kansas	KS	20,884	VC
Univ of Louisville	KY	19,692	C
Univ of Maine at Machias	ME	22,960	C
Univ of Maryland/Baltimore County	MD	23,004	VC
Univ of Miami	FL	63,494	MC
Univ of Nebr - Lincoln	NE	18,589	VC
Univ of N Car at Pembroke	NC	14,737	LC
Univ of North Texas	TX	20,082	C
Univ of Pennsylvania	PA	63,526	MC
Univ of Portland	OR	52,152	VC
Univ of San Francisco	CA	60,580	C
Univ of South Florida St. Petersburg	FL	15,980	C
Univ of St. Francis	IL	40,828	C
Univ of Tampa	FL	38,928	VC
Univ of Wisc-Milwaukee	WI	21,538	C
Virginia Polytechnic Inst and State Univ	VA	21,920	VC
Washburn Univ	KS	15,827	C
Washington State Univ	WA	22,747	C
Washington Univ in St. Louis	MO	67,539	MC
Waynesburg Univ	PA	33,530	C
West Virginia Univ	WV	18,952	VC
Western Carolina Univ	NC	13,965	C
Western Kentucky Univ	KY	16,850	C
Western Mich Univ	MI	21,791	C
Western New England Univ	MA	49,182	C
Wichita State Univ	KS	17,773	C
Wilkes Univ	PA	49,166	C
Xavier Univ	OH	49,380	VC
York College of Pennsylvania	PA	29,240	C

ENTREPRENURSHIP

School	ST	$IS	SR
Dakota Wesleyan Univ	SD	33,980	LC
Lynn Univ	FL	49,680	LC
Univ of Minn/Twin Cities	MN	24,269	MC
Univ of N Car at Greensboro	NC	15,998	C
Univ of Okla	OK	19,651	HC

ENVIRONMENTAL BIOLOGY

School	ST	$IS	SR
Alvernia Univ	PA	45,330	C
Aquinas College - Mich	MI	38,876	VC
Belmont Univ	TN	44,500	VC+
Beloit College	WI	55,206	HC
Bennington College	VT	66,280	MC
Blackburn College	IL	28,526	LC
Boston Univ	MA	67,352	MC
Brown Univ	RI	64,566	MC
Calif State Polytechnic Univ, Pomona	CA	21,811	C
Cal State, Fullerton	CA	21,902	C
Cal State, Northridge	CA	17,277	LC
Cedar Crest College	PA	51,110	C
Christopher Newport Univ	VA	24,878	VC+
Colby College	ME	64,060	MC
Colgate Univ	NY	67,500	MC
Columbia Univ/City of New York	NY	62,958	MC
Drury Univ	MO	37,555	VC
Faulkner Univ	AL	26,410	C
Fitchburg State Univ	MA	21,819	LC
Fort Lewis College	CO	20,154	C
Georgetown Univ	DC	68,970	MC
Greenville College	IL	27,012	LC
Hanover College	IN	47,750	C+
Heidelberg Univ	OH	40,400	LC
Houghton College	NY	40,558	VC
Kent State Univ	OH	20,928	C
Kutztown Univ of Pennsylvania	PA	19,477	C
Lock Haven Univ of Pennsylvania	PA	20,544	LC
Mercer Univ	GA	45,348	VC
Mich State Univ	MI	24,542	VC
Millersville Univ of Pennsylvania	PA	25,298	C
Missouri Univ of Science and Technology	MO	18,655	HC
Mount Aloysius College	PA	29,976	C
Norfolk State Univ	VA	18,902	LC
Northland College	WI	41,103	C+
Ohio Univ	OH	23,394	VC
Plymouth State Univ	NH	23,180	LC
St. Mary's Univ of Minn	MN	42,440	C
Salve Regina Univ	RI	53,046	VC
Silver Lake College of the Holy Family	WI	36,290	LC
S Dak State Univ	SD	15,874	C
Southeast Missouri State Univ	MO	16,148	C
Southwestern Okla State Univ	OK	12,205	C
SUNY/The College of Environmental Science and Forestry	NY	23,728	VC
Tulane Univ	LA	67,496	MC
Univ of Calif at Davis	CA	28,468	HC
Univ of Calif San Diego	CA	30,450	MC
Univ of Dayton	OH	54,930	VC
Univ of La Verne	CA	55,600	C
Univ of N Car at Greensboro	NC	15,998	C
Washington Univ in St. Louis	MO	67,539	MC
West Chester Univ of Pennsylvania	PA	19,171	VC
Wilmington College	OH	35,100	C
Wingate Univ	NC	41,900	C

ENVIRONMENTAL CHEMISTRY

School	ST	$IS	SR
Ashland Univ	OH	30,446	C
Kutztown Univ of Pennsylvania	PA	19,477	C
Lake Superior State Univ	MI	19,867	C
Lawrence Tech Univ	MI	41,630	VC
Marshall Univ	WV	18,044	C
Millersville Univ of Pennsylvania	PA	25,298	C
Northland College	WI	41,103	C+
Ohio Univ	OH	23,394	VC
Southeast Missouri State Univ	MO	16,148	C
St. Edward's Univ	TX	56,190	VC
SUNY at Binghamton	NY	24,100	MC
Univ of Calif San Diego	CA	30,450	MC
Univ of Denver	CO	61,129	VC+
Univ of Georgia	GA	21,878	HC

ENVIRONMENTAL DESIGN

School	ST	$IS	SR
Arizona State Univ at the Tempe Campus	AZ	23,001	VC
ArtCenter College of Design	CA	42,008	SP
Ball State Univ	IN	19,808	C+
Brigham Young Univ	UT	13,248	MC
Green Mountain College	VT	45,228	LC
Hampshire College	MA	65,214	MC
Harvard College/Harvard Univ	MA	65,609	MC
Maryland Inst College of Art	MD	58,740	SP
Marywood Univ	PA	47,840	C
Montana State Univ	MT	15,500	C+
N Car State Univ	NC	22,434	HC+
N Dak State Univ	ND	16,245	VC
Olivet Nazarene Univ	IL	41,840	VC
Prescott College	AZ	38,201	C
SUNY at Binghamton	NY	24,100	MC
SUNY/The College of Environmental Science and Forestry	NY	23,728	VC
SUNY/Univ at Buffalo	NY	23,122	C
Stony Brook Univ/The SUNY	NY	22,703	MC
Texas A&M Univ at College Station	TX	20,771	VC+
Univ of Calif at Davis	CA	28,468	HC
Univ of Colo Boulder	CO	26,048	HC
Univ of Houston	TX	21,871	VC
Univ of Mass Amherst	MA	27,669	HC
Univ of New Mexico	NM	16,808	C
Univ of Okla	OK	19,651	HC
Univ of PR-Rio Piedras campus	PR	13,327	

ENVIRONMENTAL EARTH RESOURCES

School	ST	$IS	SR
SUNY at Binghamton	NY	24,100	MC
Univ of Notre Dame	IN	68,801	MC

ENVIRONMENTAL EDUCATION

School	ST	$IS	SR
Cal State, Fullerton	CA	21,902	C
Catawba College	NC	39,820	LC
East Stroudsburg Univ	PA	18,578	LC
Goshen College	IN	44,350	C
Johnson State College	VT	22,672	C
Northland College	WI	41,103	C+
Ohio State Univ at Columbus	OH	22,843	MC
Prescott College	AZ	38,201	C
Seattle Univ	WA	54,957	VC
Southern Oregon Univ	OR	19,117	C
SUNY/The College of Environmental Science and Forestry	NY	23,728	VC
The Univ of Montana Western	MT	9,426	LC
Univ of Nebr - Lincoln	NE	18,589	VC
Univ of Pittsburgh at Bradford	PA	22,958	C
Virginia Polytechnic Inst and State Univ	VA	21,920	VC
West Virginia Univ	WV	18,952	VC

ENVIRONMENTAL ENGINEERING

School	ST	$IS	SR
Alabama A&M Univ	AL	18,796	C
Arizona State Univ at the Tempe Campus	AZ	23,001	VC
Brown Univ	RI	64,566	MC

ST = STATE $IS = IN-STATE COSTS SR = SELECTOR RATING

School	ST	$IS	SR
Bucknell Univ	PA	67,136	MC
Calif Polytechnic State Univ	CA	22,547	MC
Cal State, Fullerton	CA	21,902	C
CUNY/City College	NY	20,204	C
Clarkson Univ	NY	60,392	VC
Colo State Univ	CO	23,033	C
Cornell Univ	NY	67,591	MC
Drexel Univ	PA	65,927	HC
Elon Univ	NC	46,142	HC
Florida Gulf Coast Univ	FL	14,738	C
Florida International Univ	FL	20,281	C
Florida State Univ	FL	16,771	HC
Gannon Univ	PA	42,922	C
Georgia Inst of Technology	GA	23,910	MC
Humboldt State Univ	CA	21,708	C
Indiana Univ of Pennsylvania	PA	24,474	C
Johns Hopkins Univ	MD	68,080	MC
Kennesaw State Univ	GA	18,899	VC
Lehigh Univ	PA	63,860	MC
Louisiana State Univ and A&M College	LA	18,677	VC
Loyola Univ Chicago	IL	57,158	VC
Manhattan College	NY	55,652	C
Marquette Univ	WI	53,090	VC+
Mass Inst of Technology	MA	62,662	MC
Mich Tech Univ	MI	25,551	VC+
Missouri Univ of Science and Technology	MO	18,655	HC
Montana Tech of the Univ of Montana	MT	15,447	VC
New Jersey Inst of Technology	NJ	30,198	HC
New Mexico Inst of Mining and Technology	NM	15,385	HC+
New Mexico State Univ	NM	14,050	LC
N Car State Univ	NC	22,434	HC+
Northern Arizona Univ	AZ	21,003	C
Northwestern Univ	IL	68,725	MC
Ohio State Univ at Columbus	OH	22,843	MC
Ohio Univ	OH	23,394	VC
Oregon State Univ	OR	23,337	VC
Rensselaer Polytechnic Inst	NY	67,265	MC
Rice Univ	TX	59,458	MC
San Diego State Univ	CA	23,156	VC
Seattle Univ	WA	54,957	VC
S Dak School of Mines and Technology	SD	18,570	C+
S Dak State Univ	SD	15,874	C
Southern Methodist Univ	TX	69,008	MC
Stanford Univ	CA	62,541	MC
SUNY/The College of Environmental Science and Forestry	NY	23,728	VC
SUNY/Univ at Buffalo	NY	23,122	C
Stevens Inst of Technology	NJ	64,954	MC
Suffolk Univ	MA	52,316	C
Syracuse Univ	NY	62,313	HC
Tarleton State Univ	TX	15,248	LC
Taylor Univ	IN	42,130	VC
Tenn Tech Univ	TN	17,929	C
Texas Tech Univ	TX	20,156	C+
The Catholic Univ of America	DC	58,376	VC
The Univ of Arizona	AZ	24,086	C
The Univ of Tenn at Chattanooga	TN	17,340	C+
Tufts Univ	MA		MC
United States Air Force Academy	CO		C
United States Military Academy at West Point	NY		HC+
Universidad Politecnica de PR, Hato Rey campus	PR	23,514	
Univ of Calif at Berkeley	CA	29,886	MC
Univ of Calif at Irvine	CA	33,857	VC
Univ of Calif at Riverside	CA	32,912	C
Univ of Calif San Diego	CA	30,450	MC
Univ of Central Florida	FL	16,379	VC
Univ of Colo Boulder	CO	26,048	HC
Univ of Conn	CT	27,394	
Univ of Delaware	DE	32,214	VC
Univ of Florida	FL	16,291	HC+
Univ of Georgia	GA	21,878	HC
Univ of Idaho	ID	16,158	C
Univ of Mass Lowell	MA	27,296	VC
Univ of Miami	FL	63,494	MC
Univ of Mich/Ann Arbor	MI	25,274	MC
Univ of New Hampshire	NH	29,333	VC
Univ of Notre Dame	IN	68,801	MC
Univ of Okla	OK	19,651	HC
Univ of Southern Calif	CA	66,631	MC
Univ of Vermont	VT	29,792	HC
Univ of Wisc-Platteville	WI	14,148	C
Wilkes Univ	PA	49,166	C
Worcester Polytechnic Inst	MA	62,846	MC
Yale Univ	CT	64,650	MC

ENVIRONMENTAL ENGINEERING TECHNOLOGY

School	ST	$IS	SR
Cal State, Fullerton	CA	21,902	C
East Carolina Univ	NC	16,539	C
Indiana Inst of Technology	IN	34,240	LC
Inter-American Univ of PR-Bayamon	PR	18,785	
Lake Superior State Univ	MI	19,867	C
Loyola Univ Chicago	IL	57,158	VC
Mich State Univ	MI	24,542	VC
Murray State Univ	KY	17,726	C+
Rochester Inst of Technology	NY	52,734	HC+
Shawnee State Univ	OH	16,998	C
Texas Southern Univ	TX	19,592	LC
Univ of Calif San Diego	CA	30,450	MC
Univ of Conn	CT	27,394	
Univ of North Alabama	AL	15,964	C
Univ of Wisc-Green Bay	WI	15,184	C

ENVIRONMENTAL GEOLOGY

School	ST	$IS	SR
Allegheny College	PA	57,620	VC
Beloit College	WI	55,206	HC
Brown Univ	RI	64,566	MC
Calvin College	MI	43,090	HC
Case Western Reserve Univ	OH	62,284	MC
Colgate Univ	NY	67,500	MC
Hanover College	IN	47,750	C+
Juniata College	PA	58,118	VC
Kutztown Univ of Pennsylvania	PA	19,477	C
Lake Superior State Univ	MI	19,867	C
Millersville Univ of Pennsylvania	PA	25,298	C
Murray State Univ	KY	17,726	C+
Northland College	WI	41,103	C+
Ohio Univ	OH	23,394	VC
Southern Methodist Univ	TX	69,008	MC
SUNY at Binghamton	NY	24,100	MC
SUNY at New Paltz	NY	20,840	C
SUNY at Oswego	NY	22,219	VC
SUNY/Univ at Buffalo	NY	23,122	C
The Univ of Akron	OH	22,566	C
The Univ of Utah	UT	18,751	VC
Univ of Calif at Irvine	CA	33,857	VC
Univ of Dayton	OH	54,930	VC
Univ of Illinois at Chicago	IL	24,664	VC
Univ of Mich/Ann Arbor	MI	25,274	MC
Univ of Notre Dame	IN	68,801	MC
Univ of Okla	OK	19,651	HC
Univ of Wyoming	WY	15,537	C

ENVIRONMENTAL HEALTH SCIENCE

School	ST	$IS	SR
Benedict College	SC	28,630	NC
Boise State Univ	ID	17,368	C
Cal State, Fullerton	CA	21,902	C
Cal State, Sacramento	CA	19,060	C
Cal State, San Bernardino	CA	20,106	C
CUNY/York College	NY	6,747	LC
Clarkson Univ	NY	60,392	VC
Colo State Univ	CO	23,033	C
Colo State Univ-Pueblo	CO	21,581	C
Delaware State Univ	DE	19,376	LC
East Carolina Univ	NC	16,539	C
East Central Univ	OK	13,330	C
East Tenn State Univ	TN	18,141	C
Eastern Kentucky Univ	KY	17,742	C
Illinois State Univ	IL	23,418	VC
Indiana State Univ	IN	23,223	LC
Indiana Univ Bloomington	IN	20,791	HC
Iowa Wesleyan Univ	IA	41,000	C
Lake Superior State Univ	MI	19,867	C
Miss Valley State Univ	MS	13,233	LC
Missouri Southern State Univ	MO	13,071	C
New Mexico State Univ	NM	14,050	LC
New York Univ	NY	68,139	MC
Ohio Univ	OH	23,394	VC
Old Dominion Univ	VA	21,618	C
Point Park Univ	PA	41,270	C
Purdue Univ Northwest	IN	15,178	C
Purdue Univ/West Lafayette	IN	20,032	MC
Springfield College	MA	48,775	C
Texas Southern Univ	TX	19,592	LC
The Univ of Arizona	AZ	24,086	C
Univ of Arkansas at Little Rock	AR	18,211	LC
Univ of Calif at Davis	CA	28,468	HC
Univ of Georgia	GA	21,878	HC
Univ of Mass Lowell	MA	27,296	VC
Univ of Mich/Flint	MI	19,062	C
Univ of N Car at Chapel Hill	NC	20,561	MC
Univ of Southern Maine	ME	18,320	C
Univ of Washington	WA	23,091	MC
West Chester Univ of Pennsylvania	PA	19,171	VC
Western Carolina Univ	NC	13,965	C
Western Kentucky Univ	KY	16,850	C
Wright State Univ	OH	16,983	C

ENVIRONMENTAL SCIENCE

School	ST	$IS	SR
Abilene Christian Univ	TX	43,708	C+
Adrian College	MI	45,550	C
Alaska Pacific Univ	AK	28,730	VC
Albion College	MI	55,260	C
Albright College	PA	57,326	C
Alderson Broaddus Univ	WV	35,000	LC
Allegheny College	PA	57,620	VC
Alverno College	WI	33,294	LC
Andrews Univ	MI	41,732	C
Anna Maria College	MA	51,020	C
Appalachian State Univ	NC	15,394	VC
Aquinas College - Mich	MI	38,876	VC
Arizona State Univ at the West Campus	AZ	21,513	VC
Arkansas Tech Univ	AR	16,534	LC
Ashland Univ	OH	30,446	C
Assumption College	MA	48,455	VC
Auburn Univ	AL	24,300	VC+
Auburn Univ at Montgomery	AL	15,000	C
Aurora Univ	IL	34,990	C
Ball State Univ	IN	19,808	C+
Barnard College/Columbia Univ	NY	68,762	MC
Barton College	NC	39,854	C
Baylor Univ	TX	56,803	HC
Benedictine Univ	IL	38,300	C
Bennington College	VT	66,280	MC
Berry College	GA	47,466	VC
Bethany College	WV	38,774	LC
Bethel Univ	MN	46,550	C+
Biola Univ	CA	48,686	C
Boston College	MA	68,043	MC
Bowling Green State Univ	OH	19,975	C
Bradley Univ	IL	43,240	VC
Briar Cliff Univ	IA	36,956	C
Bridgewater College	VA	46,260	C
Brown Univ	RI	64,566	MC
Bryant Univ	RI	57,204	VC
Bucknell Univ	PA	67,136	MC
Buena Vista Univ	IA	42,344	C
Cabrini Univ	PA	42,591	LC
Calif Baptist Univ	CA	42,986	C
Calif Polytechnic State Univ	CA	22,547	MC
Cal State, Chico	CA	19,790	VC
Cal State, East Bay	CA	20,748	C
Cal State, Fullerton	CA	21,902	C
Cal State, Long Beach	CA	18,850	C
Calif Univ of Pennsylvania	PA	20,425	LC
Calvin College	MI	43,090	HC
Canisius College	NY	49,672	C
Capital Univ	OH	44,778	VC
Carroll College	MT	44,304	C
Carroll Univ	WI	38,100	C+
Case Western Reserve Univ	OH	62,284	MC
Castleton Univ	VT	20,186	C
Catawba College	NC	39,820	LC
Cedarville Univ	OH	36,244	VC
Centenary College of Louisiana	LA	49,050	C+
Central College	IA	44,592	C
Central Methodist Univ	MO	31,500	VC
Central Mich Univ	MI	20,330	C
Chapman Univ	CA	65,504	HC
Charleston Southern Univ	SC	34,700	C
Chatham Univ	PA	47,883	VC
Chestnut Hill College	PA	47,180	C
CUNY/City College	NY	20,204	C
CUNY/Hunter College	NY	31,098	VC
CUNY/Medgar Evers College	NY	6,680	NC
Claflin Univ	SC	25,592	LC
Claremont McKenna College	CA	69,900	MC
Clarion Univ of Pennsylvania	PA	21,608	LC
Clark Univ	MA	53,260	HC+
Clarke Univ	IA	42,950	C
Clarkson Univ	NY	60,392	VC
Cleveland State Univ	OH	22,290	C
Coe College	IA	51,570	VC
Colby-Sawyer College	NH	50,790	C
Colgate Univ	NY	67,500	MC
Colo College	CO	64,894	MC
Colo Mesa Univ	CO	19,707	LC
Columbia Univ/ School of General Studies	NY	61,470	MC
Columbia Univ/City of New York	NY	62,958	MC
Concordia College - Moorhead	MN	46,418	C
Concordia College - New York	NY	39,035	LC
Concordia Univ	OR	35,000	C
Concordia Univ Texas	TX	41,920	C
Conn College	CT	65,000	MC
Cornell College	IA	49,900	VC
Creighton Univ	NE	49,452	VC
Dallas Baptist Univ	TX	35,220	VC
Davis & Elkins College	WV	38,242	LC
Defiance College	OH	42,240	LC
Delaware Valley Univ	PA	51,271	C
Delta State Univ	MS	13,176	LC
DePaul Univ	IL	52,807	VC
DePauw Univ	IN	58,688	VC
Dickinson College	PA	66,166	MC
Doane Univ	NE	41,340	VC
Dominican Univ	IL	42,472	C+
Dordt College	IA	37,860	C+
Drake Univ	IA	49,220	HC
Drexel Univ	PA	65,927	HC
Duke Univ	NC	68,298	MC
Duquesne Univ	PA	48,508	VC
Earlham College	IN	55,670	HC
Eastern Conn State Univ	CT	23,059	C
Eastern Kentucky Univ	KY	17,742	C
Eastern Mennonite Univ	VA	42,550	C
Eastern Nazarene College	MA	41,114	C
Eastern New Mexico Univ	NM	12,874	LC
Eastern Univ	PA	39,540	C
Edinboro Univ	PA	15,940	LC
Elizabethtown College	PA	56,340	VC
Elmhurst College	IL	46,514	C
Elon Univ	NC	46,142	HC
Emory and Henry College	VA	46,320	C
Endicott College	MA	47,054	C+
Ferrum College	VA	43,970	C
Flagler College	FL	27,620	C
Florida Inst of Technology	FL	53,306	VC
Florida International Univ	FL	20,281	C
Florida State Univ	FL	16,771	HC
Fordham Univ	NY	68,431	MC
Framingham State Univ	MA	21,740	C
Franklin and Marshall College	PA	67,960	MC
Franklin Pierce Univ	NH	46,750	LC
Fresno Pacific Univ	CA	38,858	C
Friends Univ	KS	38,000	C
Frostburg State Univ	MD	17,280	LC
Furman Univ	SC	61,098	VC+
Gannon Univ	PA	42,922	C
Georgetown College	KY	41,440	C
Georgia College & State Univ	GA	21,884	C+
Gettysburg College	PA	65,210	MC
Glenville State College	WV	17,386	LC
Goshen College	IN	44,350	C
Hampshire College	MA	65,214	MC
Hanover College	IN	47,750	C+
Hardin-Simmons Univ	TX	36,025	C
Hartwick College	NY	51,270	C
Harvard College/Harvard Univ	MA	65,609	MC
Hawaii Pacific Univ	HI	33,420	C
Heritage Univ	WA	19,825	NC
Hiram College	OH	44,590	C
Hobart and William Smith Colleges	NY	67,050	HC+
Hollins Univ	VA	49,635	VC
Hood College	MD	50,540	C
Houghton College	NY	40,558	VC
Howard Univ	DC	37,616	C+
Humboldt State Univ	CA	21,708	C
Husson Univ	ME	26,508	C
Idaho State Univ	ID	13,619	LC
Illinois College	IL	41,330	VC
Indiana Univ Bloomington	IN	20,791	HC
Indiana Univ-Purdue Univ Indianapolis	IN	18,952	C
Iowa State Univ	IA	18,176	C
Ithaca College	NY	58,158	VC+
Jacksonville Univ	FL	49,210	C
Jefferson (Philadelphia Univ + Thomas Jefferson Univ)	PA	53,966	C
John Carroll Univ	OH	51,570	C
Johnson State College	VT	22,672	C
Juniata College	PA	58,118	VC
Kalamazoo College	MI	53,931	HC
Kennesaw State Univ	GA	18,899	VC
Keuka College	NY	42,398	C
Keystone College	PA	28,680	LC
Kutztown Univ of Pennsylvania	PA	19,477	C
La Salle Univ	PA	43,476	C
Lake Erie College	OH	38,914	LC
Lake Forest College	IL	50,652	VC
Lake Superior State Univ	MI	19,867	C
Lander Univ	SC	32,200	C
Le Moyne College	NY	47,305	VC
Lebanon Valley College	PA	55,510	VC
Lehigh Univ	PA	63,860	MC
Lewis Univ	IL	41,710	C
Lincoln Memorial Univ	TN	28,430	C
Lincoln Univ	MO	14,402	NC
Lincoln Univ	PA	20,878	LC
Lipscomb Univ	TN	42,984	VC
Louisiana State Univ and A&M College	LA	18,677	VC
Louisiana Tech Univ	LA	11,422	VC
Lourdes Univ	OH	29,140	NC
Loyola Marymount Univ	CA	60,202	VC+
Loyola Univ Chicago	IL	57,158	VC
Loyola Univ New Orleans	LA	52,456	VC
Madonna Univ	MI	30,450	LC
Malone Univ	OH	39,200	C
Marietta College	OH	46,190	C
Marist College	NY	49,860	VC
Marshall Univ	WV	18,044	C
Martin Univ	IN	21,010	LC
Marygrove College	MI	30,100	LC
Maryville Univ of St. Louis	MO	38,558	VC
Marywood Univ	PA	47,840	C
McDaniel College	MD	52,910	VC
Mercyhurst Univ	PA	47,420	C
Merrimack College	MA	55,415	C
Messiah College	PA	44,380	VC
Metropolitan State Univ of Denver	CO	6,928	LC
Miami Univ	OH	27,190	HC+
Mich Tech Univ	MI	25,551	VC+
Middle Tenn State Univ	TN	8,650	C
Midway Univ	KY	33,940	LC
Midwestern State Univ	TX	12,111	LC
Miles College	AL	16,530	NC
Mills College	CA	43,705	C
Minn State Univ, Mankato	MN	17,190	C
Monmouth College	IL	42,260	C
Montana State Univ	MT	15,500	C+
Montana State Univ Billings	MT	13,336	LC
Montana State Univ-Northern	MT	11,370	NC
Montclair State Univ	NJ	26,912	C
Montreat College	NC	34,605	LC
Moravian College	PA	55,488	C
Mount Aloysius College	PA	29,976	C
Mount Marty College	SD	36,862	C
Mount St. Mary's Univ	MD	53,380	C
Muhlenberg College	PA	56,645	VC
Muskingum Univ	OH	35,966	C

ST = STATE **$IS** = IN-STATE COSTS **SR** = SELECTOR RATING

School	ST	$IS	SR
National Univ	CA	17,849	LC
Nazareth College	NY	46,784	C
New England College	NH	50,828	NC
New Jersey Inst of Technology	NJ	30,198	HC
New Mexico Highlands Univ	NM	11,904	LC
New Mexico Inst of Mining and Technology	NM	15,385	HC+
New Mexico State Univ	NM	14,050	LC
N Car Central Univ	NC	9,000	C
N Car State Univ	NC	22,434	HC+
N Car Wesleyan College	NC	39,200	C
North Park Univ	IL	35,860	C
Northeastern Univ	MA	65,352	MC
Northern Arizona Univ	AZ	21,003	C
Northern Kentucky Univ	KY	16,486	C
Northern State Univ	SD	15,570	C
Northland College	WI	41,103	C+
Northwest Univ	WA	38,720	VC
Northwestern Univ	IL	68,725	MC
Norwich Univ	VT	56,234	C
Notre Dame College	OH	39,150	VC
Nova Southeastern Univ	FL	38,534	C+
Oakland Univ	MI	20,763	C
Ohio State Univ at Columbus	OH	22,843	MC
Ohio Wesleyan Univ	OH	49,460	VC
Okla State Univ	OK	17,180	C+
Olivet College	MI	37,661	LC
Olivet Nazarene Univ	IL	41,840	VC
Oregon Inst of Technology	OR	19,227	C
Oregon State Univ	OR	23,337	VC
Otterbein Univ	OH	41,630	C
Pace Univ	NY	60,136	C
Pacific Lutheran Univ	WA	49,960	C
Pfeiffer Univ	NC	40,532	LC
Piedmont College	GA	34,334	C
Pitzer College	CA	68,500	HC+
Point Loma Nazarene Univ	CA	46,150	C+
Point Park Univ	PA	41,270	C
Portland State Univ	OR	19,443	C
Prescott College	AZ	38,201	C
Principia College	IL	40,350	C
Purdue Univ/West Lafayette	IN	20,032	MC
Queens Univ of Charlotte	NC	39,543	C
Ramapo College of New Jersey	NJ	25,760	VC
Randolph College	VA	53,970	C
Regis Univ	CO	46,380	C
Rhodes College	TN	51,900	HC
Rider Univ	NJ	54,050	C
Ripon College	WI	49,991	VC
Robert Morris Univ	PA	40,600	C
Rochester Inst of Technology	NY	52,734	HC+
Rocky Mountain College	MT	35,776	C
Roger Williams Univ	RI	48,074	VC
Rollins College	FL	58,670	HC
Roosevelt Univ	IL	41,890	VC
Rosemont College	PA	30,980	LC
Russell Sage College	NY	39,370	C
Rutgers Univ - New Brunswick	NJ	27,090	HC
Rutgers Univ - Newark	NJ	27,351	C
St. Anselm College	NH	56,636	VC
St. Joseph's College of Maine	ME	47,890	C
St. Joseph's Univ	PA	58,540	VC
St. Louis Univ	MO	49,866	HC
St. Mary's College of Calif	CA	57,420	C
St. Vincent College	PA	46,229	C
Salem International Univ	WV	21,090	C
Sam Houston State Univ	TX	18,792	C
Samford Univ	AL	40,770	VC
San Diego State Univ	CA	23,156	VC
Savannah State Univ	GA	17,036	C
Scripps College	CA	69,260	HC
Seattle Univ	WA	54,957	VC
Shaw Univ	NC	24,638	C
Shenandoah Univ	VA	42,100	C
Shippensburg Univ of Pennsylvania	PA	24,096	C
Siena College	NY	48,916	C
Sierra Nevada College	NV	45,403	C
Simpson College	IA	45,626	VC
Smith College	MA	66,774	MC
Sonoma State Univ	CA	27,020	C
Southeast Missouri State Univ	MO	16,148	C
Southern Methodist Univ	TX	69,008	MC
Southern Oregon Univ	OR	19,117	C
Southwest Minn State Univ	MN	17,783	C
St. Bonaventure Univ	NY	45,596	C
St. Edward's Univ	TX	56,190	VC
St. Mary's Univ	TX	39,120	C
St. Norbert College	WI	46,060	VC
SUNY /College of Agriculture and Tech at Cobleskill	NY	20,527	LC
SUNY at Binghamton	NY	24,100	MC
SUNY at Purchase College	NY	21,832	C
SUNY/Cortland	NY	20,910	C
SUNY/Fredonia	NY	20,818	C
SUNY/Maritime College	NY	16,020	C
SUNY/Oneonta	NY	20,794	C
SUNY/Plattsburgh	NY	19,314	C
SUNY/The College of Environmental Science and Forestry	NY	23,728	VC
Stephen F. Austin State Univ	TX	18,484	LC
Stetson Univ	FL	57,174	VC+
Stevenson Univ	MD	48,412	C
Stockton Univ	NJ	25,565	C
Stony Brook Univ/The SUNY	NY	22,703	MC

School	ST	$IS	SR
Suffolk Univ	MA	52,316	C
Susquehanna Univ	PA	57,560	VC
Tarleton State Univ	TX	15,248	LC
Taylor Univ	IN	42,130	VC
Temple Univ	PA	24,392	C+
Texas A&M Univ at College Station	TX	20,771	VC+
Texas A&M Univ at Corpus Christi	TX	16,851	LC
Texas Christian Univ	TX	57,120	HC
Texas State Univ	TX	18,721	C
The American Univ	DC	61,317	HC
The Catholic Univ of America	DC	58,376	VC
The College at Brockport - SUNY	NY	21,058	C
The George Washington Univ	DC	68,474	HC+
The Univ of Alabama	AL	24,320	C+
The Univ of Arizona	AZ	24,086	C
The Univ of Montana Western	MT	9,426	LC
The Univ of Tenn at Chattanooga	TN	17,340	C+
The Univ of Tenn at Knoxville	TN	22,112	VC
The Univ of Texas at San Antonio	TX	21,060	C
The Univ of Virginia's College at Wise	VA	18,192	LC
Thiel College	PA	42,950	LC
Thomas Edison State Univ	NJ	6,350	NC
Thomas More College	KY	36,720	LC
Towson Univ	MD	21,878	C
Trine Univ	IN	41,310	C
Trinity College	CT	69,020	HC
Troy Univ	AL	16,171	C
Tufts Univ	MA		MC
Tulane Univ	LA	67,496	MC
Tusculum College	TN	31,625	LC
Union College	NY	64,320	MC
United States Military Academy at West Point	NY		HC+
Unity College	ME	37,670	C
Univ of Alaska Southeast	AK	17,615	C
Univ of Arkansas at Fayetteville	AR	19,766	VC
Univ of Calif at Berkeley	CA	29,886	MC
Univ of Calif at Davis	CA	28,468	HC
Univ of Calif at Irvine	CA	33,857	VC
Univ of Calif at Los Angeles	CA	27,438	HC+
Univ of Calif at Riverside	CA	32,912	C
Univ of Calif at Santa Barbara	CA	30,627	HC+
Univ of Calif San Diego	CA	30,450	MC
Univ of Central Arkansas	AR	15,042	VC
Univ of Chicago	IL	70,551	MC
Univ of Colo Boulder	CO	26,048	HC
Univ of Conn	CT	27,394	
Univ of Delaware	DE	32,214	VC
Univ of Denver	CO	61,129	VC+
Univ of Dubuque	IA	37,824	C
Univ of Evansville	IN	44,186	C+
Univ of Findlay	OH	43,040	C
Univ of Georgia	GA	21,878	HC
Univ of Hawaii at Hilo	HI	18,038	VC
Univ of Hawaii at Manoa	HI	23,261	C
Univ of Houston	TX	21,871	VC
Univ of Idaho	ID	16,158	C
Univ of Indianapolis	IN	36,480	VC
Univ of Iowa	IA	19,415	HC
Univ of La Verne	CA	55,600	C
Univ of Lynchburg	VA	48,370	C
Univ of Maine	ME	21,038	VC
Univ of Maine at Farmington	ME	18,792	C
Univ of Maine at Fort Kent	ME	15,165	LC
Univ of Maine at Machias	ME	22,960	C
Univ of Maine at Presque Isle	ME	16,148	LC
Univ of Mary Washington	VA	23,039	C+
Univ of Maryland Univ College	MD	26,146	LC
Univ of Maryland/Baltimore County	MD	23,004	VC
Univ of Maryland/College Park	MD	21,938	HC
Univ of Maryland/Eastern Shore	MD	21,861	LC
Univ of Mass Amherst	MA	27,669	HC
Univ of Mass Boston	MA	13,828	C
Univ of Mass Lowell	MA	27,296	VC
Univ of Miami	FL	63,494	MC
Univ of Mich/Dearborn	MI	12,472	VC
Univ of Minn/Crookston	MN	19,126	C
Univ of Minn/Duluth	MN	20,292	C
Univ of Minn/Morris	MN	21,222	VC
Univ of Missouri-Kansas City	MO	19,563	VC
Univ of Montevallo	AL	20,012	C
Univ of Mount Olive	NC	18,426	C
Univ of Mount Union	OH	39,990	C
Univ of Nebr - Lincoln	NE	18,589	VC
Univ of Nevada, Las Vegas	NV	17,553	C
Univ of Nevada, Reno	NV	18,010	C
Univ of New England	ME	50,110	C
Univ of New Hampshire	NH	29,333	VC
Univ of New Haven	CT	53,680	C
Univ of New Mexico	NM	16,808	C
Univ of New Orleans	LA	12,840	C
Univ of N Car at Asheville	NC	16,251	VC+
Univ of N Car at Chapel Hill	NC	20,561	MC
Univ of N Car at Pembroke	NC	14,737	LC

School	ST	$IS	SR
Univ of N Car Wilmington	NC	16,784	VC
Univ of Northern Iowa	IA	17,480	C
Univ of Northwestern - St. Paul	MN	39,530	C
Univ of Notre Dame	IN	68,801	MC
Univ of Okla	OK	19,651	HC
Univ of Oregon	OR	24,021	VC
Univ of Pittsburgh	PA	30,030	MC
Univ of Portland	OR	52,152	VC
Univ of Redlands	CA	61,934	VC
Univ of Rhode Island	RI	26,066	VC
Univ of Rio Grande & Rio Grande Community College	OH	8,750	LC
Univ of Rochester	NY	65,032	MC
Univ of St. Francis	IN	38,520	C
Univ of San Diego	CA	60,338	HC
Univ of San Francisco	CA	60,580	C
Univ of Scranton	PA	54,962	VC
Univ of S Car at Columbia	SC	21,726	VC
Univ of South Florida St. Petersburg	FL	15,980	C
Univ of South Florida/Tampa	FL	16,110	VC
Univ of Southern Calif	CA	66,631	MC
Univ of Southern Indiana	IN	16,808	C
Univ of Southern Maine	ME	18,320	C
Univ of St. Francis	IL	40,828	C
Univ of St. Thomas - Houston	TX	41,510	VC
Univ of Tampa	FL	38,928	VC
Univ of Texas Rio Grande Valley	TX	15,573	LC
Univ of the District of Columbia	DC	21,260	LC
Univ of the Incarnate Word	TX	39,162	LC
Univ of the Ozarks	AR	31,050	NC
Univ of the Pacific	CA	57,446	VC
Univ of the Sciences	PA	40,738	VC
Univ of Toledo	OH	19,336	C
Univ of Vermont	VT	29,792	HC
Univ of Virginia	VA	27,367	MC
Univ of West Alabama	AL	16,284	LC
Univ of Wisc-Green Bay	WI	15,184	C
Univ of Wisc-Madison	WI	21,647	MC
Univ of Wisc-Milwaukee	WI	21,538	C
Ursinus College	PA	62,920	VC
Utah State Univ	UT	13,235	C
Valparaiso Univ	IN	50,160	VC
Villanova Univ	PA	64,922	MC
Virginia Polytechnic Inst and State Univ	VA	21,920	VC
Walla Walla Univ	WA	34,845	C
Walsh Univ	OH	39,010	C
Wartburg College	IA	49,478	C
Washington & Jefferson College	PA	58,694	VC
Washington and Lee Univ	VA	59,647	MC
Washington College	MD	56,154	VC
Washington State Univ	WA	22,747	C
Washington Univ in St. Louis	MO	67,539	MC
Wayland Baptist Univ	TX	23,460	LC
Wayne State Univ	MI	23,085	C
Waynesburg Univ	PA	33,530	C
Weber State Univ	UT	14,112	C
Wells College	NY	50,500	C
Wesley College	DE	37,848	LC
West Texas A&M Univ	TX	13,478	C
West Virginia Univ	WV	18,952	VC
West Virginia Wesleyan College	WV	39,188	C
Western Conn State Univ	CT	21,254	LC
Western Washington Univ	WA	18,904	VC
Westfield State Univ	MA	20,404	C
Westminster College	MO	32,820	C
Wheaton College	IL	44,993	MC
Wheaton College	MA	63,818	VC
Whitman College	WA	59,772	MC
Whittier College	CA	57,891	C
Widener Univ	PA	58,190	C
Willamette Univ	OR	62,514	VC+
William Paterson Univ of New Jersey	NJ	24,022	C
William Penn Univ	IA	26,000	C
Williams College	MA	67,700	MC
Wilson College	PA	35,620	LC
Winthrop Univ	SC	23,960	C
Wisc Lutheran College	WI	36,290	C
Wittenberg Univ	OH	49,863	VC
Worcester State Univ	MA	20,977	C
Wright State Univ	OH	16,983	C
Xavier Univ	OH	49,380	VC

ENVIRONMENTAL STUDIES

School	ST	$IS	SR
Adelphi Univ	NY	49,792	C
Adrian College	MI	45,550	C
Alaska Pacific Univ	AK	28,730	VC
Albion College	MI	55,260	C
Alfred Univ	NY	37,490	C
Allegheny College	PA	57,620	VC
Alma College	MI	49,410	VC
Amherst College	MA	66,186	MC
Appalachian State Univ	NC	15,394	VC
Aquinas College - Mich	MI	38,876	VC
Arizona State Univ at the Polytechnic Campus	AZ	22,394	VC
Arizona State Univ at the Tempe Campus	AZ	23,001	VC
Ashford Univ	CA	10,480	C
Augsburg Univ	MN	45,129	C
Augustana College	IL	51,222	VC+
Averett Univ	VA	43,034	LC
Bard College	NY	65,924	HC
Bard College at Simon's Rock	MA	65,795	MC
Bates College	ME	64,500	HC
Beloit College	WI	55,206	HC
Bemidji State Univ	MN	17,730	C
Bennington College	VT	66,280	MC
Bentley Univ	MA	63,720	MC
Berea College	KY	7,094	C
Berry College	GA	47,466	VC
Bethel Univ	MN	46,550	C+
Birmingham-Southern College	AL	44,478	C+
Blackburn College	IL	28,526	LC
Boise State Univ	ID	17,368	C
Boston Univ	MA	67,352	MC
Bowdoin College	ME	65,980	MC
Bowling Green State Univ	OH	19,975	C
Brandeis Univ	MA	68,443	MC
Brenau Univ - Women's College	GA	37,876	LC
Brigham Young Univ	UT	13,248	MC
Brown Univ	RI	64,566	MC
Bryant Univ	RI	57,204	VC
Calif Lutheran Univ	CA	52,853	C
Cal State, East Bay	CA	20,748	C
Cal State, Fullerton	CA	21,902	C
Cal State, San Bernardino	CA	20,106	C
Calvin College	MI	43,090	HC
Canisius College	NY	49,672	C
Carleton College	MN	66,414	MC
Catawba College	NC	39,820	LC
Cazenovia College	NY	47,866	C
Central Mich Univ	MI	20,330	C
Centre College	KY	50,680	MC
Chaminade Univ of Honolulu	HI	37,614	C
Champlain College	VT	54,724	VC
Chatham Univ	PA	47,883	VC
Christopher Newport Univ	VA	24,878	VC+
CUNY/Brooklyn College	NY	7,163	C+
CUNY/Queens College	NY	21,507	C
Claremont McKenna College	CA	69,900	MC
Clarke Univ	IA	42,950	C
Coe College	IA	51,570	VC
Colby College	ME	64,060	MC
Colby-Sawyer College	NH	50,790	C
College of St. Benedict	MN	54,480	C
College of the Holy Cross	MA	64,320	MC
Colo State Univ	CO	23,033	C
Columbia College - Missouri	MO	28,179	C
Concordia College - New York	NY	39,035	LC
Daemen College	NY	40,336	C
Dartmouth College	NH	68,109	MC
Davidson College	NC	60,119	MC
Denison Univ	OH	62,770	HC+
DePaul Univ	IL	52,807	VC
Dickinson College	PA	66,166	MC
Doane Univ	NE	41,340	VC
Dominican Univ of Calif	CA	58,750	C
Drew Univ/College of Liberal Arts	NJ	53,608	VC
Drexel Univ	PA	65,927	HC
Drury Univ	MO	37,555	VC
Earlham College	IN	55,670	HC
Eckerd College	FL	55,206	VC
Edgewood College	WI	35,950	C
Elon Univ	NC	46,142	HC
Emory Univ	GA	63,286	MC
Eugene Lang College of Liberal Arts	NY	64,940	VC
Fairfield Univ	CT	61,445	HC
Florida Gulf Coast Univ	FL	14,738	C
Florida Inst of Technology	FL	53,306	VC
Florida Southern College	FL	45,978	VC
Florida State Univ	FL	16,771	HC
Fort Lewis College	CO	20,154	C
Franklin and Marshall College	PA	67,960	MC
George Mason Univ	VA	19,884	C
Goddard College	VT	17,040	VC
Gonzaga Univ	WA	52,880	HC
Goodwin College	CT	28,370	LC
Goshen College	IN	44,350	C
Goucher College	MD	56,110	VC
Green Mountain College	VT	45,228	LC
Guilford College	NC	45,973	C
Gustavus Adolphus College	MN	53,943	HC
Hamilton College	NY	64,250	MC
Hamline Univ	MN	50,152	C
Hawaii Pacific Univ	HI	33,420	C
Hendrix College	AR	54,020	VC
Hofstra Univ	NY	58,210	C+
Hollins Univ	VA	49,635	VC
Illinois Wesleyan Univ	IL	56,430	VC+
Indiana Univ Bloomington	IN	20,791	HC
Iona College	NY	52,514	C
Ithaca College	NY	58,158	VC+
Juniata College	PA	58,118	VC
Keene State College	NH	24,604	C
King's College	PA	48,240	C
Knox College	IL	54,654	VC+
Kutztown Univ of Pennsylvania	PA	19,477	C
Lasell College	MA	49,400	C
Lawrence Univ	WI	56,133	HC+
Lehigh Univ	PA	63,860	MC

ST = STATE $IS = IN-STATE COSTS SR = SELECTOR RATING

School	ST	$IS	SR
Lenoir-Rhyne Univ	NC	47,500	LC
Lewis & Clark College	OR	60,984	MC
Linfield College	OR	53,992	C
Louisiana State Univ and A&M College	LA	18,677	VC
Loyola Univ Chicago	IL	57,158	VC
Loyola Univ New Orleans	LA	52,456	VC
Luther College	IA	49,990	VC
Lynn Univ	FL	49,680	LC
Lyon College	AR	36,120	VC
Macalester College	MN	64,136	MC
Malone Univ	OH	39,200	C
Manchester Univ	IN	41,540	C
Manhattanville College	NY	52,430	C
Marietta College	OH	46,190	C
Marlboro College	VT	50,832	VC+
Maryville College	TN	44,410	C
Mass College of Liberal Arts	MA	20,659	C
McKendree Univ	IL	37,940	C+
Mercer Univ	GA	45,348	VC
Meredith College	NC	46,634	C
Mich State Univ	MI	24,542	VC
Middlebury College	VT	67,464	MC
Millersville Univ of Pennsylvania	PA	25,298	C
Millikin Univ	IL	44,148	C
Mills College	CA	43,705	C
Missouri State Univ	MO	15,837	C+
Mitchell College	CT	45,192	C
Molloy College	NY	40,440	C
Moravian College	PA	55,488	C
Mount Holyoke College	MA	56,746	MC
Naropa Univ	CO	43,278	NC
New College of Florida	FL	16,180	HC+
New York Univ	NY	68,139	MC
Niagara Univ	NY	41,010	C
Northeastern Illinois Univ	IL	12,529	LC
Northeastern Univ	MA	65,352	MC
Northern Arizona Univ	AZ	21,003	C
Northern Mich Univ	MI	20,853	C
Northland College	WI	41,103	C+
Oberlin College	OH	68,942	MC
Ohio Dominican Univ	OH	41,340	C+
Ohio Northern Univ	OH	44,050	VC
Okla City Univ	OK	40,476	C
Pace Univ	NY	60,136	C
Penn State Altoona	PA	26,686	C
Piedmont College	GA	34,334	C
Plymouth State Univ	NH	23,180	LC
Point Park Univ	PA	41,270	C
Pomona College	CA	64,957	MC
Prescott College	AZ	38,201	C
Queens Univ of Charlotte	NC	39,543	C
Ramapo College of New Jersey	NJ	25,760	VC
Randolph College	VA	53,970	C
Randolph-Macon College	VA	51,480	VC
Reed College	OR	65,300	MC
Regis Univ	CO	46,380	C
Rhodes College	TN	51,900	HC
Roanoke College	VA	55,952	VC
Rocky Mountain College	MT	35,776	C
Rowan Univ	NJ	24,491	VC
Rutgers Univ - New Brunswick	NJ	27,090	HC
St. John's Univ	MN	53,472	C
St. Louis Univ	MO	49,866	HC
St. Martin's Univ	WA	45,056	C
St. Mary's College of Calif	CA	57,420	C
St. Michael's College	VT	53,275	VC+
Salem College	NC	40,206	C
Salisbury Univ	MD	21,132	VC
San Diego State Univ	CA	23,156	VC
San Francisco State Univ	CA	18,514	LC
San Jose State Univ	CA	22,630	C
Sarah Lawrence College	NY	68,866	MC
Scripps College	CA	69,260	HC
Seattle Univ	WA	54,957	VC
Seton Hall Univ	NJ	58,008	C
Sewanee: The Univ of the South	TN	58,000	HC+
Shepherd Univ, West Virginia	WV	17,382	C
Siena College	NY	48,916	C
Silver Lake College of the Holy Family	WI	36,290	LC
Simmons College	MA	54,400	HC
Skidmore College	NY	66,600	MC
Southeastern Okla State Univ	OK	11,875	C
Southern Methodist Univ	TX	69,008	MC
Southern Nazarene Univ	OK	33,684	C
Southern New Hampshire Univ	NH	44,256	C
Southern Oregon Univ	OR	19,117	C
Southwestern Univ	TX	52,370	VC
St. Bonaventure Univ	NY	45,596	C
St. John's Univ	NY	57,160	C+
St. Lawrence Univ	NY	66,646	HC+
St. Mary's College of Maryland	MD	27,312	VC
St. Olaf College	MN	56,430	HC
SUNY Albany	NY	22,165	C
SUNY at Binghamton	NY	24,100	MC
SUNY/Fredonia	NY	20,818	C
SUNY/Potsdam	NY	21,051	VC
SUNY/The College of Environmental Science and Forestry	NY	23,728	VC
SUNY/Univ at Buffalo	NY	23,122	C
Stonehill College	MA	55,130	C
Stony Brook Univ/The SUNY	NY	22,703	MC
Suffolk Univ	MA	52,316	C
Taylor Univ	IN	42,130	VC
Temple Univ	PA	24,392	C+
The American Univ	DC	61,317	HC
The College of Idaho	ID	36,415	C
The College of New Rochelle	NY	46,300	LC
The Univ of Arizona	AZ	24,086	C
The Univ of Montana Western	MT	9,426	LC
The Univ of Utah	UT	18,751	VC
Thomas Edison State Univ	NJ	6,350	NC
Trinity Univ	TX	54,480	MC
Union College	NY	64,320	MC
United States Military Academy at West Point	NY		HC+
Unity College	ME	37,670	C
Univ of Calif at Irvine	CA	33,857	VC
Univ of Calif at Los Angeles	CA	27,438	HC+
Univ of Calif San Diego	CA	30,450	MC
Univ of Calif, Santa Cruz	CA	28,731	C+
Univ of Cincinnati	OH	22,118	VC
Univ of Conn	CT	27,394	
Univ of Evansville	IN	44,186	C+
Univ of Illinois at Chicago	IL	24,664	VC
Univ of Kansas	KS	20,884	VC
Univ of Lynchburg	VA	48,370	C
Univ of Maine at Farmington	ME	18,792	C
Univ of Maine at Machias	ME	22,960	C
Univ of Maryland/Baltimore County	MD	23,004	VC
Univ of Mass Lowell	MA	27,296	VC
Univ of Mich/Ann Arbor	MI	25,274	MC
Univ of Mich/Dearborn	MI	12,472	VC
Univ of Minn/Duluth	MN	20,292	C
Univ of Minn/Morris	MN	21,222	VC
Univ of Montana	MT	14,105	C
Univ of Nebr - Lincoln	NE	18,589	VC
Univ of Nebr - Omaha	NE	16,120	C
Univ of New England	ME	50,110	C
Univ of New Hampshire	NH	29,333	VC
Univ of N Car at Chapel Hill	NC	20,561	MC
Univ of N Car at Greensboro	NC	15,998	C
Univ of N Dak	ND	16,673	C
Univ of Okla	OK	19,651	HC
Univ of Oregon	OR	24,021	VC
Univ of Pennsylvania	PA	63,526	MC
Univ of Pittsburgh	PA	30,030	MC
Univ of Pittsburgh at Bradford	PA	22,958	C
Univ of Pittsburgh at Johnstown	PA	22,092	C
Univ of Redlands	CA	61,934	VC
Univ of Rhode Island	RI	26,066	VC
Univ of Richmond	VA	62,730	MC
Univ of Rochester	NY	65,032	MC
Univ of San Diego	CA	60,338	HC
Univ of San Francisco	CA	60,580	C
Univ of Southern Calif	CA	66,631	MC
Univ of St. Thomas - Houston	TX	41,510	VC
Univ of Tulsa	OK	52,625	HC
Univ of Vermont	VT	29,792	HC
Univ of Wisc-Green Bay	WI	15,184	C
Univ of Wisc-Madison	WI	21,647	MC
Univ of Wisc-Parkside	WI	15,313	C
Univ of Wyoming	WY	15,537	C
Vanderbilt Univ	TN	63,248	MC
Vassar College	NY	68,110	MC
Villanova Univ	PA	64,922	MC
Virginia Commonwealth Univ	VA	23,811	VC
Virginia Wesleyan Univ	VA	45,980	LC
Viterbo Univ	WI	34,660	C
Warren Wilson College	NC	44,220	VC
Washington & Jefferson College	PA	58,694	VC
Washington College	MD	56,154	VC
Washington Univ in St. Louis	MO	67,539	MC
Wayland Baptist Univ	TX	23,460	LC
Webster Univ	MO	37,490	C
Wellesley College	MA	66,984	MC
Wesleyan College	GA	31,940	C+
Wesleyan Univ	CT	66,940	MC
West Virginia Wesleyan College	WV	39,188	C
Western Kentucky Univ	KY	16,850	C
Western Mich Univ	MI	21,791	C
Western State Colo Univ	CO	19,348	C
Western Washington Univ	WA	18,904	VC
Westminster College	UT	41,078	C
Wheeling Jesuit Univ	WV	37,106	LC
Wheelock College	MA	51,325	LC
Whitman College	WA	59,772	MC
Wilson College	PA	35,620	LC
Winthrop Univ	SC	23,960	C
Wisc Lutheran College	WI	36,290	C
Wofford College	SC	49,885	VC
Worcester Polytechnic Inst	MA	62,846	MC
Yale Univ	CT	64,650	MC
Youngstown State Univ	OH	17,487	C

EQUESTRIAN STUDIES

School	ST	$IS	SR
Averett Univ	VA	43,034	LC
Cazenovia College	NY	47,866	C
Colo State Univ	CO	23,033	C
Rocky Mountain College	MT	35,776	C

EQUINE SCIENCE

School	ST	$IS	SR
Asbury Univ	KY	36,450	C+
Auburn Univ	AL	24,300	VC+
Averett Univ	VA	43,034	LC
Bethany College	WV	38,774	LC
Centenary College	NJ	43,890	LC
Colo State Univ	CO	23,033	C
Delaware Valley Univ	PA	51,271	C
Houghton College	NY	40,558	VC
Johnson & Wales Univ/Providence Campus	RI	44,768	C
Judson College	AL	27,066	C
Lake Erie College	OH	38,914	LC
Midway Univ	KY	33,940	LC
Mount Ida College	MA	46,820	C
Murray State Univ	KY	17,726	C+
N Dak State Univ	ND	16,245	VC
Okla Panhandle State Univ	OK	6,152	C
Otterbein Univ	OH	41,630	C
Rocky Mountain College	MT	35,776	C
St. Mary-of-the-Woods College	IN	40,424	LC
Salem International Univ	WV	21,090	C
Savannah College of Art and Design	GA	49,595	SP
Stephens College	MO	38,042	C
The Univ of Montana Western	MT	9,426	LC
Truman State Univ	MO	16,286	MC
Univ of Findlay	OH	43,040	C
Univ of Louisville	KY	19,692	C
Univ of Minn/Crookston	MN	19,126	C
William Woods Univ	MO	32,040	C
Wilmington College	OH	35,100	C
Wilson College	PA	35,620	LC

ESKIMO

School	ST	$IS	SR
Univ of Alaska Fairbanks	AK	16,874	VC

ETHICS, POLITICS, AND SOCIAL POLICY

School	ST	$IS	SR
American Jewish Univ - College of A&S	CA	44,234	C
Central Mich Univ	MI	20,330	C
Drake Univ	IA	49,220	HC
Ferris State Univ	MI	21,458	C
Goddard College	VT	17,040	VC
Millikin Univ	IL	44,148	C
Northwestern Univ	IL	68,725	MC
Pine Manor College	MA	41,660	LC
Prescott College	AZ	38,201	C
Smith College	MA	66,774	MC
Syracuse Univ	NY	62,313	HC
Unity College	ME	37,670	C
Univ of Dayton	OH	54,930	VC
Univ of Mass Boston	MA	13,828	C
Univ of N Car at Greensboro	NC	15,998	C
Univ of Northern Colo	CO	19,658	C
Univ of Okla	OK	19,651	HC
Univ of Southern Calif	CA	66,631	MC
Yale Univ	CT	64,650	MC

ETHNIC STUDIES

School	ST	$IS	SR
Albion College	MI	55,260	C
Arizona State Univ at the West Campus	AZ	21,513	VC
Bowling Green State Univ	OH	19,975	C
Brown Univ	RI	64,566	MC
Calif Polytechnic State Univ	CA	22,547	MC
Cal State, East Bay	CA	20,748	C
Cal State, Fullerton	CA	21,902	C
Cal State, San Bernardino	CA	20,106	C
Cal State, Stanislaus	CA	18,053	LC
CUNY/City College	NY	20,204	C
Colo College	CO	64,894	MC
Colo State Univ	CO	23,033	C
Cornell College	IA	49,900	VC
Edgewood College	WI	35,950	C
Kalamazoo College	MI	53,931	HC
Kansas State Univ	KS	17,780	VC
Messiah College	PA	44,380	VC
Metropolitan State Univ	MN	7,859	C
Mills College	CA	43,705	C
Minn State Univ, Mankato	MN	17,190	C
New York Univ	NY	68,139	MC
Oregon State Univ	OR	23,337	VC
Sonoma State Univ	CA	27,020	C
St. Catherine Univ	MN	45,630	C
St. Olaf College	MN	56,430	HC
SUNY at Purchase College	NY	21,832	C
Texas Christian Univ	TX	57,120	HC
Texas State Univ	TX	18,721	C
The Univ of Texas at Austin	TX	20,206	MC
The Univ of Utah	UT	18,751	VC
Univ of Calif at Berkeley	CA	29,886	MC
Univ of Calif at Riverside	CA	32,912	C
Univ of Calif San Diego	CA	30,450	MC
Univ of Colo Boulder	CO	26,048	HC
Univ of Colo Colo Springs	CO	20,300	C
Univ of Colo Denver	CO	22,238	C
Univ of Hawaii at Manoa	HI	23,261	C
Univ of Illinois at Chicago	IL	24,664	VC
Univ of Nebr - Lincoln	NE	18,589	VC
Univ of North Florida	FL	15,996	VC
Univ of Oregon	OR	24,021	VC
Univ of San Diego	CA	60,338	HC
Univ of Vermont	VT	29,792	HC
Univ of Washington	WA	23,091	MC
Univ of Wisc-Milwaukee	WI	21,538	C
Washington State Univ	WA	22,747	C
Washington Univ in St. Louis	MO	67,539	MC
Westfield State Univ	MA	20,404	C
Whitman College	WA	59,772	MC
Wichita State Univ	KS	17,773	C
Yale Univ	CT	64,650	MC

EUROPEAN STUDIES

School	ST	$IS	SR
Amherst College	MA	66,186	MC
Barnard College/Columbia Univ	NY	68,762	MC
Bates College	ME	64,500	HC
Bennington College	VT	66,280	MC
Boston Univ	MA	67,352	MC
Brandeis Univ	MA	68,443	MC
Cal State, Fullerton	CA	21,902	C
Canisius College	NY	49,672	C
Central Mich Univ	MI	20,330	C
Emory and Henry College	VA	46,320	C
Georgetown College	KY	41,440	C
Harvard College/Harvard Univ	MA	65,609	MC
Hillsdale College	MI	37,170	MC
Hobart and William Smith Colleges	NY	67,050	HC+
John Carroll Univ	OH	51,570	C
Lipscomb Univ	TN	42,984	VC
Loyola Marymount Univ	CA	60,202	VC+
Middlebury College	VT	67,464	MC
Millsaps College	MS	50,080	C+
New York Univ	NY	68,139	MC
Northwestern State Univ of Louisiana	LA	16,534	LC
Northwestern Univ	IL	68,725	MC
Ohio Univ	OH	23,394	VC
Pitzer College	CA	68,500	HC+
St. Joseph's Univ	PA	58,540	VC
San Diego State Univ	CA	23,156	VC
Scripps College	CA	69,260	HC
Seattle Pacific Univ	WA	47,439	C+
Smith College	MA	66,774	MC
Stony Brook Univ/The SUNY	NY	22,703	MC
Suffolk Univ	MA	52,316	C
Texas State Univ	TX	18,721	C
The George Washington Univ	DC	68,474	HC+
Univ of Calif at Irvine	CA	33,857	VC
Univ of Calif at Los Angeles	CA	27,438	HC+
Univ of Delaware	DE	32,214	VC
Univ of Kansas	KS	20,884	VC
Univ of Mich/Ann Arbor	MI	25,274	MC
Univ of Minn/Morris	MN	21,222	VC
Univ of New Hampshire	NH	29,333	VC
Univ of New Mexico	NM	16,808	C
Univ of N Car at Chapel Hill	NC	20,561	MC
Univ of Okla	OK	19,651	HC
Univ of S Car at Columbia	SC	21,726	VC
Univ of Vermont	VT	29,792	HC
Vanderbilt Univ	TN	63,248	MC
Washington Univ in St. Louis	MO	67,539	MC
Webster Univ	MO	37,490	C
Westmont College	CA	57,930	VC

EVOLUTIONARY BIOLOGY

School	ST	$IS	SR
Angelo State Univ	TX	15,882	LC
Bennington College	VT	66,280	MC
Cal State, Fullerton	CA	21,902	C
Case Western Reserve Univ	OH	62,284	MC
Florida State Univ	FL	16,771	HC
Marshall Univ	WV	18,044	C
Ohio State Univ at Columbus	OH	22,843	MC
Princeton Univ	NJ	60,090	MC
SUNY at Binghamton	NY	24,100	MC
Tulane Univ	LA	67,496	MC
Univ of Calif at Santa Barbara	CA	30,627	HC+
Univ of Calif, Santa Cruz	CA	28,731	C+
Univ of Colo Boulder	CO	26,048	HC
Univ of Conn	CT	27,394	
Univ of Mich/Ann Arbor	MI	25,274	MC
Yale Univ	CT	64,650	MC

EXERCISE AND MOVEMENT SCIENCE

School	ST	$IS	SR
Cal State, Fullerton	CA	21,902	C
Colo State Univ	CO	23,033	C
Lewis Univ	IL	41,710	C
Okla Christian Univ	OK	29,260	C
Salem College	NC	40,206	C
Univ of Dayton	OH	54,930	VC
Univ of Wisc-Parkside	WI	15,313	C

EXERCISE PHYSIOLOGY

School	ST	$IS	SR
Drury Univ	MO	37,555	VC
Univ of Mass Lowell	MA	27,296	VC

EXERCISE SCIENCE

School	ST	$IS	SR
Adams State Univ	CO	15,420	LC
Adrian College	MI	45,550	C

School	ST	$IS	SR
Albion College	MI	55,260	C
Alma College	MI	49,410	VC
Anderson Univ	IN	39,450	C
Angelo State Univ	TX	15,882	LC
Appalachian State Univ	NC	15,394	VC
Arizona State Univ at the Downtown Phoenix Campus	AZ	24,634	VC
Arkansas State Univ	AR	16,190	C
Asbury Univ	KY	36,450	C+
Augustana Univ	SD	39,968	VC
Aurora Univ	IL	34,990	C
Baker Univ	KS	37,190	C
Baldwin Wallace Univ	OH	42,464	VC
Barton College	NC	39,854	C
Becker College	MA	30,100	LC
Belhaven Univ	MS	32,250	C
Bellarmine Univ	KY	52,532	C
Belmont Univ	TN	44,500	VC+
Berry College	GA	47,466	VC
Bethel College	IN	36,830	C
Bethel Univ	MN	46,550	C+
Black Hills State Univ	SD	16,622	C
Bloomsburg Univ of Pennsylvania	PA	19,930	C
Blue Mountain College	MS	15,949	C
Bluefield College	VA	34,711	C
Bowling Green State Univ	OH	19,975	C
Bridgewater College	VA	46,260	C
Brigham Young Univ	UT	13,248	MC
Bryan College	TN	32,900	C
Buena Vista Univ	IA	42,344	C
Cabrini Univ	PA	42,591	LC
Calif Baptist Univ	CA	42,986	C
Calif Lutheran Univ	CA	52,853	C
Cal State, Fullerton	CA	21,902	C
Cal State, Northridge	CA	17,277	LC
Cal State, San Bernardino	CA	20,106	C
Calvin College	MI	43,090	HC
Campbell Univ	NC	37,570	VC
Campbellsville Univ	KY	33,400	C
Canisius College	NY	49,672	C
Capital Univ	OH	44,778	VC
Carroll Univ	WI	38,100	C+
Castleton Univ	VT	20,186	C
Cedarville Univ	OH	36,244	VC
Central College	IA	44,592	C
Central Conn State Univ	CT	22,041	C
Central Washington Univ	WA	16,803	C
Chatham Univ	PA	47,883	VC
CUNY/York College	NY	6,747	LC
Clayton State Univ	GA	19,735	LC
Cleveland State Univ	OH	22,290	C
Coastal Carolina Univ	SC	20,340	C
Colby-Sawyer College	NH	50,790	C
College of Charleston	SC	24,046	VC
College of St. Scholastica	MN	45,734	C+
Colo Mesa Univ	CO	19,707	LC
Colo State Univ	CO	23,033	C
Colo State Univ-Pueblo	CO	21,581	C
Columbus State Univ	GA	14,336	LC
Concordia College - Moorhead	MN	46,418	C
Concordia Univ Irvine	CA	44,860	VC
Concordia Univ Nebr	NE	41,900	VC
Corban Univ	OR	41,700	C
Cornerstone Univ	MI	36,550	C
Creighton Univ	NE	49,452	VC
Davis & Elkins College	WV	38,242	LC
DePaul Univ	IL	52,807	VC
DeSales Univ	PA	47,520	C
Dordt College	IA	37,860	C+
D'Youville College	NY	37,678	C
East Carolina Univ	NC	16,539	C
East Central Univ	OK	13,330	C
East Stroudsburg Univ	PA	18,578	LC
East Texas Baptist Univ	TX	34,444	C
Eastern Mich Univ	MI	19,761	C
Eastern Univ	PA	39,540	C
Elmhurst College	IL	46,514	C
Elon Univ	NC	46,142	HC
Endicott College	MA	47,054	C+
Fitchburg State Univ	MA	21,819	LC
Florida Gulf Coast Univ	FL	14,738	C
Florida International Univ	FL	20,281	C
Florida Southern College	FL	45,978	VC
Fort Lewis College	CO	20,154	C
Franklin College	IN	40,550	C
Frostburg State Univ	MD	17,280	LC
George Fox Univ	OR	42,938	C
Georgetown College	KY	41,440	C
Georgia College & State Univ	GA	21,884	C+
Georgia Southern Univ	GA	16,540	VC
Georgia Southwestern State Univ	GA	13,870	LC
Georgia State Univ	GA	25,250	C
Gonzaga Univ	WA	52,880	HC
Grand Canyon Univ	AZ	25,150	VC
Grand Valley State Univ	MI	22,250	C+
Greensboro College	NC	39,790	LC
Grove City College	PA	26,654	VC
Guilford College	NC	45,973	C
Hamline Univ	MN	50,152	C
Hannibal-LaGrange Univ	MO	29,815	C
Harding Univ	AR	25,440	C
Hardin-Simmons Univ	TX	36,025	C
Hendrix College	AR	54,020	VC
High Point Univ	NC	47,355	VC
Hillsdale College	MI	37,170	MC
Hiram College	OH	44,590	C
Hofstra Univ	NY	58,210	C+
Hope College	MI	42,840	VC
Howard Payne Univ	TX	35,994	C
Huntingdon College	AL	35,900	C
Huntington Univ	IN	33,996	C
Husson Univ	ME	26,508	C
Illinois College	IL	41,330	VC
Illinois State Univ	IL	23,418	VC
Immaculata Univ	PA	39,000	C
Ithaca College	NY	58,158	VC+
John Carroll Univ	OH	51,570	C
Kansas State Univ	KS	17,780	VC
Keene State College	NH	24,604	C
Kennesaw State Univ	GA	18,899	VC
Kent State Univ	OH	20,928	C
King Univ	TN	36,976	C
King's College	PA	48,240	C
La Roche College	PA	38,940	C
La Sierra Univ	CA	39,690	VC
LaGrange College	GA	41,310	C
Lake Superior State Univ	MI	19,867	C
Lander Univ	SC	32,200	C
Lasell College	MA	49,400	C
Lebanon Valley College	PA	55,510	VC
Lenoir-Rhyne Univ	NC	47,500	LC
Liberty Univ	VA	31,415	C
Linfield College	OR	53,992	C
Lipscomb Univ	TN	42,984	VC
Loras College	IA	40,726	C
Louisiana College	LA	21,274	C
Loyola Univ Chicago	IL	57,158	VC
Malone Univ	OH	39,200	C
Marian Univ	IN	43,206	C
Marquette Univ	WI	53,090	VC+
Marshall Univ	WV	18,044	C
McMurry Univ	TX	34,259	LC
Mercy College	NY	32,614	C
Meredith College	NC	46,634	C
Merrimack College	MA	55,415	C
Mich Tech Univ	MI	25,551	VC+
Milligan College	TN	39,450	C
Minn State Univ, Mankato	MN	17,190	C
Minn State Univ, Moorhead	MN	21,393	C
Missouri Baptist Univ	MO	35,594	C
Missouri State Univ	MO	15,837	C+
Missouri Valley College	MO	28,150	C
Missouri Western State Univ	MO	17,822	LC
Monmouth College	IL	42,260	C
Montana State Univ Billings	MT	13,336	LC
Montreat College	NC	34,605	LC
Mount Vernon Nazarene Univ	OH	35,944	C
Murray State Univ	KY	17,726	C+
Nebr Wesleyan Univ	NE	42,026	C+
Norfolk State Univ	VA	18,902	LC
N Car Wesleyan College	NC	39,200	C
North Central College	IL	48,712	C+
North Park Univ	IL	35,860	C
Northern Arizona Univ	AZ	21,003	C
Northern Kentucky Univ	KY	16,486	C
Northern Mich Univ	MI	20,853	C
Northwest Christian Univ	OR	36,580	C
Northwest Univ	WA	38,720	VC
Northwestern State Univ of Louisiana	LA	16,534	LC
Nova Southeastern Univ	FL	38,534	C+
Ohio Dominican Univ	OH	41,340	C+
Ohio State Univ at Columbus	OH	22,843	MC
Ohio Univ	OH	23,394	VC
Okla City Univ	OK	40,476	C
Old Dominion Univ	VA	21,618	C
Olivet Nazarene Univ	IL	41,840	VC
Palm Beach Atlantic Univ	FL	39,250	C
Pennsylvania College of Technology	PA	27,693	NC
Pfeiffer Univ	NC	40,532	LC
Piedmont College	GA	34,334	C
Point Loma Nazarene Univ	CA	46,150	C+
Purdue Univ/West Lafayette	IN	20,032	MC
Queens Univ of Charlotte	NC	39,543	C
Quincy Univ	IL	38,170	LC
Radford Univ	VA	19,758	C
Rice Univ	TX	59,458	MC
Ripon College	WI	49,991	VC
Roanoke College	VA	55,952	VC
Rochester Inst of Technology	NY	52,734	HC+
Rocky Mountain College	MT	35,776	C
Rutgers Univ - New Brunswick	NJ	27,090	HC
Rutgers Univ - New Brunswick	NJ	27,090	HC
Sacred Heart Univ	CT	54,590	C
Saginaw Valley State Univ	MI	19,284	C
St. Louis Univ	MO	49,866	HC
Samford Univ	AL	40,770	VC
San Diego State Univ	CA	23,156	VC
San Francisco State Univ	CA	18,514	LC
Schreiner Univ	TX	34,626	LC
Seattle Pacific Univ	WA	47,439	C+
Seattle Univ	WA	54,957	VC
Shenandoah Univ	VA	42,100	C
Shippensburg Univ of Pennsylvania	PA	24,096	C
Simmons College	MA	54,400	HC
Simpson College	IA	45,626	VC
Skidmore College	NY	66,600	MC
Smith College	MA	66,774	MC
S Dak State Univ	SD	15,874	C
Southern Illinois Univ Edwardsville	IL	20,188	C
Southern Nazarene Univ	OK	33,684	C
Southwestern Adventist Univ	TX	28,232	LC
Southwestern Okla State Univ	OK	12,205	C
Spring Arbor Univ	MI	37,390	C
St. Catherine Univ	MN	45,630	C
St. Olaf College	MN	56,430	HC
SUNY/Potsdam	NY	21,051	VC
SUNY/Univ at Buffalo	NY	23,122	C
Sterling College	KS	32,830	LC
Taylor Univ	IN	42,130	VC
Texas State Univ	TX	18,721	C
Texas Wesleyan Univ	TX	37,338	C
The College at Brockport - SUNY	NY	21,058	C
The College of Idaho	ID	36,415	C
The College of New Jersey	NJ	28,675	VC+
The Univ of Akron	OH	22,566	C
The Univ of Mary	ND	23,180	C
The Univ of Utah	UT	18,751	VC
Thomas Edison State Univ	NJ	6,350	NC
Tiffin Univ	OH	34,900	LC
Towson Univ	MD	21,878	C
Transylvania Univ	KY	47,450	HC+
Trevecca Nazarene Univ	TN	31,186	C
Trinity Washington Univ	DC	33,826	C+
Truman State Univ	MO	16,286	MC
Union College	KY	32,310	C
Univ of Arkansas at Fayetteville	AR	19,766	VC
Univ of Arkansas at Monticello	AR	13,599	LC
Univ of Central Arkansas	AR	15,042	VC
Univ of Central Florida	FL	16,379	VC
Univ of Central Okla	OK	15,150	C
Univ of Conn	CT	27,394	
Univ of Dayton	OH	54,930	VC
Univ of Evansville	IN	44,186	C+
Univ of Florida	FL	16,291	HC+
Univ of Georgia	GA	21,878	HC
Univ of Hawaii at Manoa	HI	23,261	C
Univ of Idaho	ID	16,158	C
Univ of Illinois at Chicago	IL	24,664	VC
Univ of Illinois at Urbana-Champaign	IL	27,006	HC
Univ of Indianapolis	IN	36,480	VC
Univ of Jamestown	ND	28,508	C
Univ of Kansas	KS	20,884	VC
Univ of Louisiana at Monroe	LA	15,970	C
Univ of Lynchburg	VA	48,370	C
Univ of Maine at Machias	ME	22,960	C
Univ of Mary Hardin-Baylor	TX	35,292	C+
Univ of Mass Amherst	MA	27,669	HC
Univ of Mass Boston	MA	13,828	C
Univ of Miami	FL	63,494	MC
Univ of Mich/Ann Arbor	MI	25,274	MC
Univ of Miss	MS	18,802	C
Univ of Mount Union	OH	39,990	C
Univ of Nebr - Lincoln	NE	18,589	VC
Univ of Nevada, Las Vegas	NV	17,553	C
Univ of New England	ME	50,110	C
Univ of New Mexico	NM	16,808	C
Univ of N Car at Chapel Hill	NC	20,561	MC
Univ of N Car at Charlotte	NC	17,803	VC
Univ of N Car at Pembroke	NC	14,737	LC
Univ of Northern Colo	CO	19,658	C
Univ of Northern Iowa	IA	17,480	C
Univ of Northwestern - St. Paul	MN	39,530	C
Univ of Okla	OK	19,651	HC
Univ of Puget Sound	WA	60,210	HC
Univ of St. Francis	IN	38,520	C
Univ of San Francisco	CA	60,580	C
Univ of Scranton	PA	54,962	VC
Univ of S Car Aiken	SC	18,094	C
Univ of S Car at Columbia	SC	21,726	VC
Univ of S Dak	SD	16,109	C
Univ of Southern Calif	CA	66,631	MC
Univ of Southern Indiana	IN	16,808	C
Univ of Tampa	FL	38,928	VC
Univ of Texas Rio Grande Valley	TX	15,573	LC
Univ of the Cumberlands	KY	32,000	LC
Univ of Tulsa	OK	52,625	HC
Univ of Vermont	VT	29,792	HC
Univ of West Alabama	AL	16,284	LC
Univ of Wisc-Green Bay	WI	15,184	C
Univ of Wisc-La Crosse	WI	15,425	VC
Univ of Wisc-Milwaukee	WI	21,538	C
Univ of Wisc-Superior	WI	14,838	C
Urbana Univ	OH	30,820	C
Ursinus College	PA	62,920	VC
Valparaiso Univ	IN	50,160	VC
Vanguard Univ of Southern Calif	CA	42,400	VC
Wake Forest Univ	NC	69,354	MC
Walsh Univ	OH	39,010	C
Warner Univ	FL	28,216	C
Washington Adventist Univ	MD	32,050	LC
Washington State Univ	WA	22,747	C
Wayne State College	NE	25,746	NC
Wayne State Univ	MI	23,085	C
Waynesburg Univ	PA	33,530	C
Webster Univ	MO	37,490	C
Wesley College	DE	37,848	LC
West Chester Univ of Pennsylvania	PA	19,171	VC
West Texas A&M Univ	TX	13,478	C
West Virginia Wesleyan College	WV	39,188	C
Western Illinois Univ	IL	20,897	C
Western Kentucky Univ	KY	16,850	C
Western Mich Univ	MI	21,791	C
Westmont College	CA	57,930	VC
Willamette Univ	OR	62,514	VC+
Wilson College	PA	35,620	LC
Wingate Univ	NC	41,900	C
Winona State Univ	MN	18,109	C
Winthrop Univ	SC	23,960	C
Wisc Lutheran College	WI	36,290	C
Wittenberg Univ	OH	49,863	VC
Wright State Univ	OH	16,983	C
Youngstown State Univ	OH	17,487	C

EXPERIMENTAL PSYCHOLOGY

School	ST	$IS	SR
Blackburn College	IL	28,526	LC
Rutgers Univ - Camden	NJ	26,595	C
Rutgers Univ - New Brunswick	NJ	27,090	HC
Rutgers Univ - Newark	NJ	27,351	C
St. Leo Univ	FL	32,850	C
Univ of Idaho	ID	16,158	C
Univ of S Car at Columbia	SC	21,726	VC
Univ of Texas Rio Grande Valley	TX	15,573	LC

FACILITIES MANAGEMENT

School	ST	$IS	SR
Colo State Univ	CO	23,033	C
Farmingdale State College	NY	20,968	C
Ferris State Univ	MI	21,458	C

FAMILY AND COMMUNITY SERVICES

School	ST	$IS	SR
Central Washington Univ	WA	16,803	C
East Carolina Univ	NC	16,539	C
John Brown Univ	AR	35,184	VC
Kansas State Univ	KS	17,780	VC
Mich State Univ	MI	24,542	VC
Ohio Univ	OH	23,394	VC
Prairie View A&M Univ	TX	27,273	LC
Purdue Univ/West Lafayette	IN	20,032	MC
Trinity International Univ	IL	31,070	VC
Union Univ	TN	41,160	VC
Univ of Delaware	DE	32,214	VC
Univ of Northern Iowa	IA	17,480	C
Univ of Oregon	OR	24,021	VC
Western Kentucky Univ	KY	16,850	C

FAMILY STUDIES/SOCIAL SERVICE/MARRIAGE FAMILY

School	ST	$IS	SR
College of the Ozarks	MO	7,530	VC
Okla Baptist Univ	OK	33,990	C

FAMILY/CONSUMER RESOURCE MANAGEMENT

School	ST	$IS	SR
Cal State, Northridge	CA	17,277	LC
East Central Univ	OK	13,330	C
Indiana Univ of Pennsylvania	PA	24,474	C
Iowa State Univ	IA	18,176	C
Mich State Univ	MI	24,542	VC
Ohio State Univ at Columbus	OH	22,843	MC
Ohio Univ	OH	23,394	VC
Seattle Pacific Univ	WA	47,439	C+
Seton Hill Univ	PA	46,972	VC
S Dak State Univ	SD	15,874	C
Southeastern Louisiana Univ	LA	16,237	C
Univ of Hawaii at Manoa	HI	23,261	C
Univ of Missouri-Columbia	MO	20,463	VC
Univ of N Car at Greensboro	NC	15,998	C
West Virginia Univ	WV	18,952	VC

FAMILY/CONSUMER STUDIES

School	ST	$IS	SR
Alabama A&M Univ	AL	18,796	C
Alderson Broaddus Univ	WV	35,000	LC
Anderson Univ	IN	39,450	C
Andrews Univ	MI	41,732	C
Appalachian State Univ	NC	15,394	VC
Ashford Univ	CA	10,480	C
Ball State Univ	IN	19,808	C+
Baylor Univ	TX	56,803	HC
Bluffton Univ	OH	40,950	C+
Bowling Green State Univ	OH	19,975	C
Bradley Univ	IL	43,240	VC
Bridgewater College	VA	46,260	C
Brigham Young Univ	UT	13,248	MC
Cal State, Fresno	CA	16,902	LC
Cal State, Long Beach	CA	18,850	C
Cal State, Northridge	CA	17,277	LC
Central Mich Univ	MI	20,330	C
Central Washington Univ	WA	16,803	C
CUNY/Queens College	NY	21,507	C
College of the Ozarks	MO	7,530	VC
Colo State Univ	CO	23,033	C
Concordia Univ, Ann Arbor	MI	38,878	C+
Cornerstone Univ	MI	36,550	C
Delta State Univ	MS	13,176	LC
East Central Univ	OK	13,330	C
Eastern Illinois Univ	IL	21,414	C
Florida State Univ	FL	16,771	HC

ST = STATE $IS = IN-STATE COSTS SR = SELECTOR RATING

School	ST	$IS	SR
Fontbonne Univ	MO	34,606	C
Freed-Hardeman Univ	TN	29,900	C
George Fox Univ	OR	42,938	C
Hampshire College	MA	65,214	MC
Henderson State Univ	AR	15,516	C
Idaho State Univ	ID	13,619	LC
Illinois State Univ	IL	23,418	VC
Iowa State Univ	IA	18,176	C
Kansas State Univ	KS	17,780	VC
Lamar Univ	TX	18,014	LC
Liberty Univ	VA	31,415	C
Lipscomb Univ	TN	42,984	VC
Lubbock Christian Univ	TX	29,727	C
Madonna Univ	MI	30,450	LC
Marywood Univ	PA	47,840	C
Mercyhurst Univ	PA	47,420	C
Meredith College	NC	46,634	C
Messiah College	PA	44,380	VC
Miami Univ	OH	27,190	HC+
Mich State Univ	MI	24,542	VC
Middle Tenn State Univ	TN	8,650	C
Minn State Univ, Mankato	MN	17,190	C
Miss College	MS	25,850	C
Missouri State Univ	MO	15,837	C+
Montclair State Univ	NJ	26,912	C
New Mexico State Univ	NM	14,050	LC
Nicholls State Univ	LA	14,959	C
Northwestern State Univ of Louisiana	LA	16,534	LC
Oakwood Univ	AL	43,758	C
Ohio State Univ at Columbus	OH	22,843	MC
Ohio Univ	OH	23,394	VC
Olivet Nazarene Univ	IL	41,840	VC
Pittsburg State Univ	KS	13,880	C
Purdue Univ/West Lafayette	IN	20,032	MC
San Francisco State Univ	CA	18,514	LC
Seattle Pacific Univ	WA	47,439	C+
Seton Hill Univ	PA	46,972	VC
Shepherd Univ, West Virginia	WV	17,382	C
Silver Lake College of the Holy Family	WI	36,290	LC
S Car State Univ	SC	21,330	LC
S Dak State Univ	SD	15,874	C
Southern Univ and A&M College	LA	16,074	LC
St. Catherine Univ	MN	45,630	C
SUNY at Oswego	NY	22,219	VC
Stephen F. Austin State Univ	TX	18,484	LC
Tarleton State Univ	TX	15,248	LC
Tenn State Univ	TN	14,423	LC
Texas State Univ	TX	18,721	C
Texas Tech Univ	TX	20,156	C+
Texas Woman's Univ	TX	15,302	LC
The Master's Univ	CA	43,870	C
The Univ of Akron	OH	22,566	C
The Univ of Arizona	AZ	24,086	C
The Univ of Utah	UT	18,751	VC
Towson Univ	MD	21,878	C
Univ of Arkansas at Pine Bluff	AR	13,541	C
Univ of Central Arkansas	AR	15,042	VC
Univ of Central Okla	OK	15,150	C
Univ of Georgia	GA	21,878	HC
Univ of Idaho	ID	16,158	C
Univ of Illinois at Urbana-Champaign	IL	27,006	HC
Univ of Maryland/College Park	MD	21,938	HC
Univ of Montevallo	AL	20,012	C
Univ of Nebr - Kearney	NE	17,014	LC
Univ of Nebr - Lincoln	NE	18,589	VC
Univ of New Hampshire	NH	29,333	VC
Univ of New Mexico	NM	16,808	C
Univ of N Car at Greensboro	NC	15,998	C
Univ of PR-Rio Piedras campus	PR	13,327	
Univ of St. Joseph	CT	49,069	C
Univ of Wisc-Madison	WI	21,647	MC
Univ of Wisc-Stevens Point	WI	14,043	C
Univ of Wisc-Stout	WI	19,667	C
Univ of Wyoming	WY	15,537	C
Urbana Univ	OH	30,820	C
Washington State Univ	WA	22,747	C
Wayne State College	NE	25,746	NC
Weber State Univ	UT	14,112	C
Western Kentucky Univ	KY	16,850	C
Western Mich Univ	MI	21,791	C
Youngstown State Univ	OH	17,487	C

FAMILY/JUVENILE JUSTICE

School	ST	$IS	SR
East Central Univ	OK	13,330	C
Georgetown College	KY	41,440	C
Missouri Western State Univ	MO	17,822	LC
The Univ of Akron	OH	22,566	C
Univ of New Haven	CT	53,680	C
William Woods Univ	MO	32,040	C

FASHION DESIGN AND TECHNOLOGY

School	ST	$IS	SR
Baylor Univ	TX	56,803	HC
Bennington College	VT	66,280	MC
Calif College of the Arts	CA	52,758	SP
Cazenovia College	NY	47,866	C
Centenary College	NJ	43,890	LC
Columbia College Chicago	IL	40,104	C
Columbus College of Art and Design	OH	47,310	SP
Dominican Univ	IL	42,472	C+
Drexel Univ	PA	65,927	HC
Fashion Inst of Technology/SUNY	NY	18,521	SP
Florida State Univ	FL	16,771	HC
Framingham State Univ	MA	21,740	C
Howard Univ	DC	37,616	C+
Illinois State Univ	IL	23,418	VC
Iowa State Univ	IA	18,176	C
Jefferson (Philadelphia Univ + Thomas Jefferson Univ)	PA	53,966	C
Kent State Univ	OH	20,928	C
Lasell College	MA	49,400	C
Lindenwood Univ	MO	25,760	C
Marist College	NY	49,860	VC
Marymount Univ	VA	43,231	C
Mass College of Art and Design	MA	24,800	SP
Missouri State Univ	MO	15,837	C+
Montclair State Univ	NJ	26,912	C
Moore College of Art and Design	PA	55,118	SP
Mount Ida College	MA	46,820	C
Mount Mary Univ	WI	34,650	LC
Otis College of Art and Design	CA	54,670	SP
Parsons The New School for Design	NY	56,610	SP
Pratt Inst	NY	59,482	VC+
Purdue Univ/West Lafayette	IN	20,032	MC
Savannah College of Art and Design	GA	49,595	SP
School of the Art Inst of Chicago	IL	61,830	SP
St. Catherine Univ	MN	45,630	C
Stephens College	MO	38,042	C
Stevenson Univ	MD	48,412	C
Syracuse Univ	NY	62,313	HC
Texas Woman's Univ	TX	15,302	LC
Univ of Cincinnati	OH	22,118	VC
Univ of Delaware	DE	32,214	VC
Univ of North Texas	TX	20,082	C
Univ of the Incarnate Word	TX	39,162	LC
Ursuline College	OH	41,076	LC
Virginia Commonwealth Univ	VA	23,811	VC
Washington Univ in St. Louis	MO	67,539	MC
Western Mich Univ	MI	21,791	C
Woodbury Univ	CA	49,593	VC

FASHION MERCHANDISING

School	ST	$IS	SR
Albright College	PA	57,326	C
Ashland Univ	OH	30,446	C
Auburn Univ	AL	24,300	VC+
Baylor Univ	TX	56,803	HC
Berkeley College/New York City Campus	NY	35,100	LC
Brenau Univ - Women's College	GA	37,876	LC
Canisius College	NY	49,672	C
Central Washington Univ	WA	16,803	C
Columbia College Chicago	IL	40,104	C
Delaware State Univ	DE	19,376	LC
Dominican Univ	IL	42,472	C+
Drexel Univ	PA	65,927	HC
East Central Univ	OK	13,330	C
Eastern Mich Univ	MI	19,761	C
Fashion Inst of Technology/SUNY	NY	18,521	SP
Florida State Univ	FL	16,771	HC
Fontbonne Univ	MO	34,606	C
Framingham State Univ	MA	21,740	C
Georgia Southern Univ	GA	16,540	VC
Harding Univ	AR	25,440	C
Howard Univ	DC	37,616	C+
Immaculata Univ	PA	39,000	C
Indiana Inst of Technology	IN	34,240	LC
Indiana Univ of Pennsylvania	PA	24,474	C
Iowa State Univ	IA	18,176	C
Jefferson (Philadelphia Univ + Thomas Jefferson Univ)	PA	53,966	C
Johnson & Wales Univ/Providence Campus	RI	44,768	C
Kent State Univ	OH	20,928	C
Lasell College	MA	49,400	C
LIM College	NY	45,075	LC
Lipscomb Univ	TN	42,984	VC
LIU Post	NY	50,698	C+
Lynn Univ	FL	49,680	LC
Marist College	NY	49,860	VC
Mars Hill Univ	NC	41,104	C
Marymount Univ	VA	43,231	C
Mercyhurst Univ	PA	47,420	C
Meredith College	NC	46,634	C
Missouri State Univ	MO	15,837	C+
Mount Ida College	MA	46,820	C
Mount Mary Univ	WI	34,650	LC
New Mexico State Univ	NM	14,050	LC
Northwood Univ - Mich	MI	35,010	LC
Ohio State Univ at Columbus	OH	22,843	MC
Ohio Univ	OH	23,394	VC
Old Dominion Univ	VA	21,618	C
Olivet Nazarene Univ	IL	41,840	VC
Purdue Univ/West Lafayette	IN	20,032	MC
Savannah College of Art and Design	GA	49,595	SP
Southeast Missouri State Univ	MO	16,148	C
Southern Illinois Univ Carbondale	IL	24,554	C
Southern New Hampshire Univ	NH	44,256	C
St. Catherine Univ	MN	45,630	C
SUNY/Oneonta	NY	20,794	C
Stephen F. Austin State Univ	TX	18,484	LC
Stephens College	MO	38,042	C
Stevenson Univ	MD	48,412	C
Tarleton State Univ	TX	15,248	LC
Texas A&M Univ at Kingsville	TX	16,580	LC
Texas State Univ	TX	18,721	C
Texas Woman's Univ	TX	15,302	LC
The Univ of Akron	OH	22,566	C
Univ of Bridgeport	CT	44,985	LC
Univ of Central Okla	OK	15,150	C
Univ of Georgia	GA	21,878	HC
Univ of Louisiana at Lafayette	LA	14,516	C
Univ of Nebr - Lincoln	NE	18,589	VC
Univ of the Incarnate Word	TX	39,162	LC
Ursuline College	OH	41,076	LC
Utah State Univ	UT	13,235	C
West Virginia Univ	WV	18,952	VC
Western Mich Univ	MI	21,791	C
Western Washington Univ	WA	18,904	VC
Woodbury Univ	CA	49,593	VC
Youngstown State Univ	OH	17,487	C

FASHION STUDIES

School	ST	$IS	SR
Columbia College Chicago	IL	40,104	C
Ferris State Univ	MI	21,458	C
Indiana Univ Bloomington	IN	20,791	HC
Lynn Univ	FL	49,680	LC
Marist College	NY	49,860	VC

FIBER SCIENCE AND APPAREL DESIGN

School	ST	$IS	SR
Cornell Univ	NY	67,591	MC

FIBER/TEXTILES/WEAVING

School	ST	$IS	SR
Adams State Univ	CO	15,420	LC
Colo State Univ	CO	23,033	C
Fashion Inst of Technology/SUNY	NY	18,521	SP
Florida State Univ	FL	16,771	HC
Kansas City Art Inst	MO	48,200	SP
Kutztown Univ of Pennsylvania	PA	19,477	C
Maryland Inst College of Art	MD	58,740	SP
Mass College of Art and Design	MA	24,800	SP
Old Dominion Univ	VA	21,618	C
Savannah College of Art and Design	GA	49,595	SP
School of the Art Inst of Chicago	IL	61,830	SP
Temple Univ	PA	24,392	C+
Univ of Kansas	KS	20,884	VC
Univ of Mass Dartmouth	MA	26,507	C
Univ of Mich/Ann Arbor	MI	25,274	MC
Univ of Oregon	OR	24,021	VC

FILM AND MEDIA STUDIES

School	ST	$IS	SR
Anderson Univ	IN	39,450	C
Ball State Univ	IN	19,808	C+
Birmingham-Southern College	AL	44,478	C+
Boston Univ	MA	67,352	MC
Bryant Univ	RI	57,204	VC
Calvin College	MI	43,090	HC
Central Conn State Univ	CT	22,041	C
CUNY/Queens College	NY	21,507	C
Clayton State Univ	GA	19,735	LC
Columbia College Chicago	IL	40,104	C
Flagler College	FL	27,620	C
Gettysburg College	PA	65,210	MC
Kutztown Univ of Pennsylvania	PA	19,477	C
Louisiana College	LA	21,274	C
Lycoming College	PA	50,895	C
Lynn Univ	FL	49,680	LC
Marist College	NY	49,860	VC
Pennsylvania State Univ - Univ Park	PA	29,716	HC
Tufts Univ	MA		MC
Univ of Georgia	GA	21,878	HC
Univ of Kansas	KS	20,884	VC
Univ of N Car at Greensboro	NC	15,998	C
Wellesley College	MA	66,984	MC
Wells College	NY	50,500	C
Western Kentucky Univ	KY	16,850	C
Wheaton College	MA	63,818	VC
Whitman College	WA	59,772	MC

FILM ARTS

School	ST	$IS	SR
Arizona State Univ at the Tempe Campus	AZ	23,001	VC
ArtCenter College of Design	CA	42,008	SP
Bard College	NY	65,924	HC
Barnard College/Columbia Univ	NY	68,762	MC
Belhaven Univ	MS	32,250	C
Bennington College	VT	66,280	MC
Berklee College of Music	MA	60,930	SP
Biola Univ	CA	48,686	C
Boston College	MA	68,043	MC
Boston Univ	MA	67,352	MC
Bowling Green State Univ	OH	19,975	C
Brandeis Univ	MA	68,443	MC
Calif Baptist Univ	CA	42,986	C
Calif College of the Arts	CA	52,758	SP
Cal State, Long Beach	CA	18,850	C
Cal State, Northridge	CA	17,277	LC
Calvin College	MI	43,090	HC
Champlain College	VT	54,724	VC
Chapman Univ	CA	65,504	HC
CUNY/Brooklyn College	NY	7,163	C+
CUNY/City College	NY	20,204	C
CUNY/Hunter College	NY	31,098	VC
Claremont McKenna College	CA	69,900	MC
Clark Univ	MA	53,260	HC+
Clayton State Univ	GA	19,735	LC
Coe College	IA	51,570	VC
College of Staten Island	NY	24,389	LC
Colo College	CO	64,894	MC
Columbia College Chicago	IL	40,104	C
Columbia Univ/ School of General Studies	NY	61,470	MC
Columbia Univ/City of New York	NY	62,958	MC
Columbus College of Art and Design	OH	47,310	SP
Concordia Univ Irvine	CA	44,860	VC
Conn College	CT	65,000	MC
Cornish College of the Arts	WA	47,750	SP
Dartmouth College	NH	68,109	MC
Denison Univ	OH	62,770	HC+
DeSales Univ	PA	47,520	C
Dominican Univ	IL	42,472	C+
Drexel Univ	PA	65,927	HC
Eastern Mich Univ	MI	19,761	C
Elon Univ	NC	46,142	HC
Emerson College	MA	61,824	HC+
Emory Univ	GA	63,286	MC
Fairleigh Dickinson Univ/College at Florham	NJ	54,770	C
Florida State Univ	FL	16,771	HC
George Fox Univ	OR	42,938	C
George Mason Univ	VA	19,884	C
Georgia State Univ	GA	25,250	C
Grand Valley State Univ	MI	22,250	C+
Hamilton College	NY	64,250	MC
Hampshire College	MA	65,214	MC
Hofstra Univ	NY	58,210	C+
Hollins Univ	VA	49,635	VC
Howard Univ	DC	37,616	C+
Huntington Univ	IN	33,996	C
Ithaca College	NY	58,158	VC+
Kansas City Art Inst	MO	48,200	SP
Keene State College	NH	24,604	C
Kenyon College	OH	65,840	MC
LIU Post	NY	50,698	C+
Mary Baldwin Univ	VA	40,495	C
Mass College of Art and Design	MA	24,800	SP
Memphis College of Art	TN	50,880	SP
Messiah College	PA	44,380	VC
Miami Univ	OH	27,190	HC+
Mich State Univ	MI	24,542	VC
Middlebury College	VT	67,464	MC
Minneapolis College of Art and Design	MN	44,218	SP
Minn State Univ, Moorhead	MN	21,393	C
Missouri Western State Univ	MO	17,822	LC
Montclair State Univ	NJ	26,912	C
Mount Holyoke College	MA	56,746	MC
Mount St. Mary's Univ - Chalon Campus	CA	50,486	VC+
Muhlenberg College	PA	56,645	VC
New Mexico State Univ	NM	14,050	LC
New York Univ	NY	68,139	MC
Northeastern Univ	MA	65,352	MC
Oakland Univ	MI	20,763	C
Oberlin College	OH	68,942	MC
Ohio State Univ at Columbus	OH	22,843	MC
Ohio Univ	OH	23,394	VC
Okla City Univ	OK	40,476	C
Old Dominion Univ	VA	21,618	C
Oral Roberts Univ	OK	34,316	C
Pace Univ	NY	60,136	C
Palm Beach Atlantic Univ	FL	39,250	C
Pepperdine Univ	CA	66,862	VC+
Pitzer College	CA	68,500	HC+
Point Park Univ	PA	41,270	C
Pratt Inst	NY	59,482	VC+
Purdue Univ/West Lafayette	IN	20,032	MC
Rhode Island College	RI	19,000	LC
Rhode Island School of Design	RI	59,960	SP
Ringling College of Art and Design	FL	59,160	SP
Rochester Inst of Technology	NY	52,734	HC+
Rutgers Univ - Newark	NJ	27,351	C
San Francisco Art Inst	CA	60,865	SP
San Francisco State Univ	CA	18,514	LC
San Jose State Univ	CA	22,630	C
Sarah Lawrence College	NY	68,866	MC
Savannah College of Art and Design	GA	49,595	SP

School	ST	$IS	SR
School of the Art Inst of Chicago	IL	61,830	SP
School of Visual Arts	NY	47,500	SP
Seattle Univ	WA	54,957	VC
Smith College	MA	66,774	MC
Southern Adventist Univ	TN	28,250	C
Southern Illinois Univ Carbondale	IL	24,554	C
Southern Methodist Univ	TX	69,008	MC
Spring Arbor Univ	MI	37,390	C
St. Mary's College of Maryland	MD	27,312	VC
Stanford Univ	CA	62,541	MC
SUNY at Binghamton	NY	24,100	MC
SUNY at Oswego	NY	22,219	VC
SUNY at Purchase College	NY	21,832	C
SUNY/Cortland	NY	20,910	C
SUNY/Univ at Buffalo	NY	23,122	C
Stephens College	MO	38,042	C
Stevenson Univ	MD	48,412	C
Suffolk Univ	MA	52,316	C
Swarthmore College	PA	63,550	MC
Syracuse Univ	NY	62,313	HC
Taylor Univ	IN	42,130	VC
Temple Univ	PA	24,392	C+
The American Univ	DC	61,317	HC
The Univ of Arizona	AZ	24,086	C
The Univ of Texas at Austin	TX	20,206	MC
The Univ of Utah	UT	18,751	VC
Tulane Univ	LA	67,496	MC
Univ of Alaska Fairbanks	AK	16,874	VC
Univ of Calif at Berkeley	CA	29,886	MC
Univ of Calif at Irvine	CA	33,857	VC
Univ of Calif at Los Angeles	CA	27,438	HC+
Univ of Calif at Riverside	CA	32,912	C
Univ of Calif at Santa Barbara	CA	30,627	HC+
Univ of Calif, Santa Cruz	CA	28,731	C+
Univ of Central Florida	FL	16,379	VC
Univ of Chicago	IL	70,551	MC
Univ of Colo Boulder	CO	26,048	HC
Univ of Denver	CO	61,129	VC+
Univ of Georgia	GA	21,878	HC
Univ of Hartford	CT	49,776	C
Univ of Illinois at Chicago	IL	24,664	VC
Univ of Illinois at Urbana-Champaign	IL	27,006	HC
Univ of Iowa	IA	19,415	HC
Univ of Maryland/College Park	MD	21,938	HC
Univ of Miami	FL	63,494	MC
Univ of Mich/Ann Arbor	MI	25,274	MC
Univ of Nebr - Lincoln	NE	18,589	VC
Univ of Nevada, Las Vegas	NV	17,553	C
Univ of N Car School of the Arts	NC	25,587	SP
Univ of N Car Wilmington	NC	16,784	VC
Univ of Okla	OK	19,651	HC
Univ of Oregon	OR	24,021	VC
Univ of Pittsburgh	PA	30,030	MC
Univ of Richmond	VA	62,730	MC
Univ of Rochester	NY	65,032	MC
Univ of Southern Calif	CA	66,631	MC
Univ of Tampa	FL	38,928	VC
Univ of the Arts	PA	56,579	SP
Univ of Toledo	OH	19,336	C
Univ of Tulsa	OK	52,625	HC
Univ of Vermont	VT	29,792	HC
Univ of Wisc-Milwaukee	WI	21,538	C
Vassar College	NY	68,110	MC
Virginia Commonwealth Univ	VA	23,811	VC
Washington Univ in St. Louis	MO	67,539	MC
Wayne State Univ	MI	23,085	C
Webster Univ	MO	37,490	C
Wellesley College	MA	66,984	MC
Wesleyan Univ	CT	66,940	MC
Western Kentucky Univ	KY	16,850	C
Wright State Univ	OH	16,983	C
Yale Univ	CT	64,650	MC

FILM, TELEVISION AND DIGITAL MEDIA

School	ST	$IS	SR
Amherst College	MA	66,186	MC
Asbury Univ	KY	36,450	C+
Baldwin Wallace Univ	OH	42,464	VC
Calvin College	MI	43,090	HC
Chapman Univ	CA	65,504	HC
Chatham Univ	PA	47,883	VC
CUNY/Queens College	NY	21,507	C
Clayton State Univ	GA	19,735	LC
Cleveland State Univ	OH	22,290	C
Columbia College Chicago	IL	40,104	C
Dallas Baptist Univ	TX	35,220	VC
DePaul Univ	IL	52,807	VC
Dordt College	IA	37,860	C+
Fairfield Univ	CT	61,445	HC
Five Towns College	NY	35,480	LC
Fordham Univ	NY	68,431	MC
Goshen College	IN	44,350	C
Hobart and William Smith Colleges	NY	67,050	HC+
Kalamazoo College	MI	53,931	HC
Kansas City Art Inst	MO	48,200	SP
Kutztown Univ of Pennsylvania	PA	19,477	C
Loyola Marymount Univ	CA	60,202	VC+
Loyola Univ New Orleans	LA	52,456	VC
Lynn Univ	FL	49,680	LC
McDaniel College	MD	52,910	VC
Mercy College	NY	32,614	C
Messiah College	PA	44,380	VC
Millersville Univ of Pennsylvania	PA	25,298	C
Missouri Western State Univ	MO	17,822	LC
Morehouse College	GA	40,835	C
New York Inst of Technology	NY	49,980	VC
Rochester Inst of Technology	NY	52,734	HC+
Rutgers Univ - New Brunswick	NJ	27,090	HC
Southern Oregon Univ	OR	19,117	C
St. John's Univ	NY	57,160	C+
SUNY/Fredonia	NY	20,818	C
Stevenson Univ	MD	48,412	C
Taylor Univ	IN	42,130	VC
Texas Christian Univ	TX	57,120	HC
The Master's Univ	CA	43,870	C
The Univ of Arizona	AZ	24,086	C
The Univ of Utah	UT	18,751	VC
Univ of Georgia	GA	21,878	HC
Univ of Illinois at Chicago	IL	24,664	VC
Univ of Kansas	KS	20,884	VC
Univ of Mary Hardin-Baylor	TX	35,292	C+
Univ of Nebr - Lincoln	NE	18,589	VC
Univ of New Mexico	NM	16,808	C
Univ of Notre Dame	IN	68,801	MC
Univ of Okla	OK	19,651	HC
Univ of Pikeville	KY	27,838	C
Univ of Rhode Island	RI	26,066	VC
Wartburg College	IA	49,478	C
Wayne State Univ	MI	23,085	C
Western Mich Univ	MI	21,791	C
Woodbury Univ	CA	49,593	VC
Youngstown State Univ	OH	17,487	C

FINANCE

School	ST	$IS	SR
Abilene Christian Univ	TX	43,708	C+
Albion College	MI	55,260	C
Alma College	MI	49,410	VC
Alvernia Univ	PA	45,330	C
Anderson Univ	IN	39,450	C
Aquinas College	TN	30,800	C+
Arizona State Univ at the Tempe Campus	AZ	23,001	VC
Arkansas Tech Univ	AR	16,534	LC
Ashford Univ	CA	10,480	C
Auburn Univ at Montgomery	AL	15,000	C
Aurora Univ	IL	34,990	C
Austin Peay State Univ	TN	16,397	C
Baldwin Wallace Univ	OH	42,464	VC
Ball State Univ	IN	19,808	C+
Belmont Univ	TN	44,500	VC+
Bentley Univ	MA	63,720	MC
Berry College	GA	47,466	VC
Bethany College	KS	38,637	LC
Bethany College	WV	38,774	LC
Bloomfield College	NJ	40,100	LC
Boise State Univ	ID	17,368	C
Bradley Univ	IL	43,240	VC
Bridgewater State Univ	MA	22,762	C
Bryant Univ	RI	57,204	VC
Cabrini Univ	PA	42,591	LC
Cal State, Fullerton	CA	21,902	C
Cal State, Long Beach	CA	18,850	C
Calvin College	MI	43,090	HC
Canisius College	NY	49,672	C
Carroll College	MT	44,304	C
Carroll Univ	WI	38,100	C+
Case Western Reserve Univ	OH	62,284	MC
Cedarville Univ	OH	36,244	VC
Central Conn State Univ	CT	22,041	C
Centre College	KY	50,680	MC
Champlain College	VT	54,724	VC
Christopher Newport Univ	VA	24,878	VC+
CUNY/Queens College	NY	21,507	C
Clarkson Univ	NY	60,392	VC
Clayton State Univ	GA	19,735	LC
Cleveland State Univ	OH	22,290	C
College of Charleston	SC	24,046	VC
College of St. Scholastica	MN	45,734	C+
Concordia Univ, Ann Arbor	MI	38,878	C+
Creighton Univ	NE	49,452	VC
Culver-Stockton College	MO	34,350	C
Dallas Baptist Univ	TX	35,220	VC
Davis & Elkins College	WV	38,242	LC
DePaul Univ	IL	52,807	VC
DeSales Univ	PA	47,520	C
Dominican Univ	IL	42,472	C+
Drury Univ	MO	37,555	VC
Eastern Conn State Univ	CT	23,059	C
Eastern Illinois Univ	IL	21,414	C
Elmhurst College	IL	46,514	C
Elon Univ	NC	46,142	HC
Emmanuel College	MA	53,472	C+
Endicott College	MA	47,054	C+
Fairfield Univ	CT	61,445	HC
Ferris State Univ	MI	21,458	C
Fordham Univ	NY	68,431	MC
Fort Lewis College	CO	20,154	C
Framingham State Univ	MA	21,740	C
Gannon Univ	PA	42,922	C
Georgetown Univ	DC	68,970	MC
Georgia Southern Univ	GA	16,540	VC
Gordon College	MA	47,740	VC
Grove City College	PA	26,654	VC
Hardin-Simmons Univ	TX	36,025	C
Harris-Stowe State Univ	MO	14,590	NC
Hawaii Pacific Univ	HI	33,420	C
Hawaii Pacific Univ	HI	33,420	C
Hawaii Pacific Univ	HI	33,420	C
Hillsdale College	MI	37,170	MC
Holy Family Univ	PA	44,672	LC
Illinois State Univ	IL	23,418	VC
Immaculata Univ	PA	39,000	C
Indiana Univ of Pennsylvania	PA	24,474	C
Iona College	NY	52,514	C
Jackson State Univ	MS	15,879	LC
John Carroll Univ	OH	51,570	C
Kean Univ	NJ	25,620	C
Keiser Univ	FL	35,010	LC
Kennesaw State Univ	GA	18,899	VC
Kent State Univ	OH	20,928	C
Kutztown Univ of Pennsylvania	PA	19,477	C
Lake Erie College	OH	38,914	LC
Lake Forest College	IL	50,652	VC
Lasell College	MA	49,400	C
Le Moyne College	NY	47,305	VC
Lebanon Valley College	PA	55,510	VC
Lehigh Univ	PA	63,860	MC
Lewis Univ	IL	41,710	C
Limestone College	SC	32,100	C
Lincoln Univ	PA	20,878	LC
Lipscomb Univ	TN	42,984	VC
LIU Brooklyn	NY	50,698	C
Loras College	IA	40,726	C
Lourdes Univ	OH	29,140	NC
Loyola Marymount Univ	CA	60,202	VC+
Loyola Univ Chicago	IL	57,158	VC
Lubbock Christian Univ	TX	29,727	C
Malone Univ	OH	39,200	C
Manhattanville College	NY	52,430	C
Marian Univ	IN	43,206	C
Marquette Univ	WI	53,090	VC+
Marshall Univ	WV	18,044	C
Menlo College	CA	51,380	LC
Mercer Univ	GA	45,348	VC
Merrimack College	MA	55,415	C
Messiah College	PA	44,380	VC
Miami Univ	OH	27,190	HC+
Mich State Univ	MI	24,542	VC
Mich Tech Univ	MI	25,551	VC+
Millersville Univ of Pennsylvania	PA	25,298	C
Minn State Univ, Mankato	MN	17,190	C
Missouri Southern State Univ	MO	13,071	C
Missouri State Univ	MO	15,837	C+
Missouri Western State Univ	MO	17,822	LC
Molloy College	NY	40,440	C
Mount Mercy Univ	IA	39,748	C
Mount Vernon Nazarene Univ	OH	35,944	C
Murray State Univ	KY	17,726	C+
Nazareth College	NY	46,784	C
Neumann Univ	PA	40,678	LC
New Mexico State Univ	NM	14,050	LC
New York Inst of Technology	NY	49,980	VC
New York Univ	NY	68,139	MC
Niagara Univ	NY	41,010	C
North Central College	IL	48,712	C+
N Dak State Univ	ND	16,245	VC
Northern Arizona Univ	AZ	21,003	C
Northern Kentucky Univ	KY	16,486	C
Northern Mich Univ	MI	20,853	C
Northwest Missouri State Univ	MO	18,286	C
Nova Southeastern Univ	FL	38,534	C+
Ohio State Univ at Columbus	OH	22,843	MC
Ohio Univ	OH	23,394	VC
Okla Christian Univ	OK	29,260	C
Old Dominion Univ	VA	21,618	C
Olivet Nazarene Univ	IL	41,840	VC
Oregon State Univ	OR	23,337	VC
Our Lady of the Lake Univ	TX	37,790	LC
Pace Univ	NY	60,136	C
Pennsylvania State Univ - Univ Park	PA	29,716	HC
Point Loma Nazarene Univ	CA	46,150	C+
Point Park Univ	PA	41,270	C
Providence College	RI	62,870	HC
Purdue Univ Northwest	IN	15,178	C
Queens Univ of Charlotte	NC	39,543	C
Quinnipiac Univ	CT	60,970	VC
Regis Univ	CO	46,380	C
Rochester Inst of Technology	NY	52,734	HC+
Rutgers Univ - Camden	NJ	26,595	C
Rutgers Univ - New Brunswick	NJ	27,090	HC
Rutgers Univ - Newark	NJ	27,351	C
Saginaw Valley State Univ	MI	19,284	C
St. Joseph's Univ	PA	58,540	VC
St. Louis Univ	MO	49,866	HC
St. Mary's Univ of Minn	MN	42,440	C
Salisbury Univ	MD	21,132	VC
Salve Regina Univ	RI	53,046	VC
Samford Univ	AL	40,770	VC
San Diego State Univ	CA	23,156	VC
San Jose State Univ	CA	22,630	C
Seattle Univ	WA	54,957	VC
Seton Hall Univ	NJ	58,008	C
Shippensburg Univ of Pennsylvania	PA	24,096	C
Simmons College	MA	54,400	HC
Southeast Missouri State Univ	MO	16,148	C
Southeastern Louisiana Univ	LA	16,237	C
Southeastern Univ	FL	34,910	LC
Southern Methodist Univ	TX	69,008	MC
Southern Univ and A&M College	LA	16,074	LC
Southwestern Okla State Univ	OK	12,205	C
St. Ambrose Univ	IA	40,180	C
St. John's Univ	NY	57,160	C+
SUNY at Binghamton	NY	24,100	MC
SUNY at Oswego	NY	22,219	VC
SUNY/Fredonia	NY	20,818	C
SUNY/Plattsburgh	NY	19,314	C
Stephen F. Austin State Univ	TX	18,484	LC
Susquehanna Univ	PA	57,560	VC
Syracuse Univ	NY	62,313	HC
Tarleton State Univ	TX	15,248	LC
Taylor Univ	IN	42,130	VC
Temple Univ	PA	24,392	C+
Tenn Wesleyan Univ	TN	32,680	LC
Texas A&M Univ at College Station	TX	20,771	VC+
Texas Christian Univ	TX	57,120	HC
Texas State Univ	TX	18,721	C
Texas Tech Univ	TX	20,156	C+
The Catholic Univ of America	DC	58,376	VC
The College at Brockport - SUNY	NY	21,058	C
The Univ of Arizona	AZ	24,086	C
The Univ of Tenn at Knoxville	TN	22,112	VC
The Univ of Texas at San Antonio	TX	21,060	C
The Univ of Utah	UT	18,751	VC
Thomas College	ME	73,888	LC
Thomas Edison State Univ	NJ	6,350	NC
Tiffin Univ	OH	34,900	LC
Trinity Univ	TX	54,480	MC
Tulane Univ	LA	67,496	MC
Univ of Arkansas at Fayetteville	AR	19,766	VC
Univ of Central Arkansas	AR	15,042	VC
Univ of Central Okla	OK	15,150	C
Univ of Charleston	WV	35,000	LC
Univ of Cincinnati	OH	22,118	VC
Univ of Colo Boulder	CO	26,048	HC
Univ of Denver	CO	61,129	VC+
Univ of Detroit Mercy	MI	48,816	C
Univ of Evansville	IN	44,186	C+
Univ of Georgia	GA	21,878	HC
Univ of Idaho	ID	16,158	C
Univ of Illinois at Chicago	IL	24,664	VC
Univ of Kansas	KS	20,884	VC
Univ of Louisiana at Monroe	LA	15,970	C
Univ of Maine	ME	21,038	VC
Univ of Mary Hardin-Baylor	TX	35,292	C+
Univ of Maryland/College Park	MD	21,938	HC
Univ of Mass Dartmouth	MA	26,507	C
Univ of Miami	FL	63,494	MC
Univ of Mich/Dearborn	MI	12,472	VC
Univ of Minn/Twin Cities	MN	24,269	MC
Univ of Miss	MS	18,802	C
Univ of Missouri-St. Louis	MO	19,810	VC
Univ of Mount Union	OH	39,990	C
Univ of Nebr - Lincoln	NE	18,589	VC
Univ of Nevada, Reno	NV	18,010	C
Univ of N Car at Charlotte	NC	17,803	VC
Univ of N Car at Greensboro	NC	15,998	C
Univ of North Florida	FL	15,996	VC
Univ of North Georgia	GA	17,316	C
Univ of Northwestern - St. Paul	MN	39,530	C
Univ of Notre Dame	IN	68,801	MC
Univ of Okla	OK	19,651	HC
Univ of Pittsburgh	PA	30,030	MC
Univ of Rhode Island	RI	26,066	VC
Univ of St. Francis	IN	38,520	C
Univ of San Diego	CA	60,338	HC
Univ of San Francisco	CA	60,580	C
Univ of S Dak	SD	16,109	C
Univ of South Florida St. Petersburg	FL	15,980	C
Univ of Southern Indiana	IN	16,808	C
Univ of St. Thomas - Houston	TX	41,510	VC
Univ of Texas Rio Grande Valley	TX	15,573	LC
Univ of West Alabama	AL	16,284	LC
Univ of West Georgia	GA	17,510	LC
Univ of Wisc-Green Bay	WI	15,184	C
Univ of Wisc-La Crosse	WI	15,425	VC
Univ of Wisc-Milwaukee	WI	21,538	C
Univ of Wisc-Superior	WI	14,838	C
Univ of Wyoming	WY	15,537	C
Valparaiso Univ	IN	50,160	VC
Villanova Univ	PA	64,922	MC
Wabash College	IN	52,100	VC
Walla Walla Univ	WA	34,845	C
Walsh Univ	OH	39,010	C
Wartburg College	IA	49,478	C
Washburn Univ	KS	15,827	C
Washington State Univ	WA	22,747	C
Washington Univ in St. Louis	MO	67,539	MC
Wayne State Univ	MI	23,085	C
Waynesburg Univ	PA	33,530	C
Weber State Univ	UT	14,112	C
Webster Univ	MO	37,490	C
West Virginia Univ	WV	18,952	VC
Western Illinois Univ	IL	20,897	C

ST = STATE $IS = IN-STATE COSTS SR = SELECTOR RATING

School	ST	$IS	SR
Western Mich Univ	MI	21,791	C
Western New England Univ	MA	49,182	C
Wichita State Univ	KS	17,773	C
Widener Univ	PA	58,190	C
Wilkes Univ	PA	49,166	C
Wingate Univ	NC	41,900	C
Wittenberg Univ	OH	49,863	VC
Wofford College	SC	49,885	VC

FINANCE (FINANCIAL PLANNING)

School	ST	$IS	SR
Alfred State College	NY	19,895	C
Bryant Univ	RI	57,204	VC
Merrimack College	MA	55,415	C
Murray State Univ	KY	17,726	C+
Olivet Nazarene Univ	IL	41,840	VC
Southern Methodist Univ	TX	69,008	MC
Univ of Georgia	GA	21,878	HC

FINANCE ENTERPRISE SYSTEMS

School	ST	$IS	SR
Univ of Tampa	FL	38,928	VC

FINANCIAL INSTITUTIONS MANAGEMENT

School	ST	$IS	SR
Lynn Univ	FL	49,680	LC
San Jose State Univ	CA	22,630	C
San Jose State Univ	CA	22,630	C
Thomas Edison State Univ	NJ	6,350	NC

FINANCIAL SERVICES

School	ST	$IS	SR
Berkeley College/New York City Campus	NY	35,100	LC
Bethel College	IN	36,830	C
Cal State, Fullerton	CA	21,902	C
Missouri Southern State Univ	MO	13,071	C
Old Dominion Univ	VA	21,618	C
San Diego State Univ	CA	23,156	VC
SUNY /College of Agriculture and Tech at Cobleskill	NY	20,527	LC
Univ of Texas at Arlington	TX	18,876	C

FINE ARTS

School	ST	$IS	SR
Abilene Christian Univ	TX	43,708	C+
Adelphi Univ	NY	49,792	C
Alabama State Univ	AL	16,490	LC
Albany State Univ	GA	19,462	C
Albertus Magnus College	CT	44,016	LC
Alfred Univ	NY	37,490	C
Amherst College	MA	66,186	MC
Anderson Univ	IN	39,450	C
Aquinas College - Mich	MI	38,876	VC
Arcadia Univ	PA	55,990	C+
Arkansas Tech Univ	AR	16,534	LC
Art Academy of Cincinnati	OH	37,790	SP
ArtCenter College of Design	CA	42,008	SP
Ashland Univ	OH	30,446	C
Auburn Univ	AL	24,300	VC+
Auburn Univ at Montgomery	AL	15,000	C
Azusa Pacific Univ	CA	43,972	C
Bellarmine Univ	KY	52,532	C
Bellevue Univ	NE	20,300	NC
Bemidji State Univ	MN	17,730	C
Benedictine Univ	IL	38,300	C
Bennington College	VT	66,280	MC
Bethany College	WV	38,774	LC
Biola Univ	CA	48,686	C
Blue Mountain College	MS	15,949	C
Bluefield College	VA	34,711	C
Boise State Univ	ID	17,368	C
Bowie State Univ	MD	18,610	LC
Bowling Green State Univ	OH	19,975	C
Brenau Univ - Women's College	GA	37,876	LC
Bridgewater State Univ	MA	22,762	C
Brigham Young Univ	UT	13,248	MC
Brigham Young Univ/Hawaii	HI	11,710	C
Bryn Mawr College	PA	65,220	MC
Bucknell Univ	PA	67,136	MC
Caldwell Univ	NJ	42,165	LC
Calif Inst of the Arts	CA	61,366	SP
Cal State, Chico	CA	19,790	VC
Cal State, Fullerton	CA	21,902	C
Cal State, Stanislaus	CA	18,053	LC
Calvin College	MI	43,090	HC
Campbell Univ	NC	37,570	VC
Canisius College	NY	49,672	C
Cardinal Stritch Univ	WI	37,136	C
Carnegie Mellon Univ	PA	67,980	MC
Carson-Newman Univ	TN	35,900	C
Carthage College	WI	48,835	C
Central Washington Univ	WA	16,803	C
Centre College	KY	50,680	MC
Champlain College	VT	54,724	VC
Charleston Southern Univ	SC	34,700	C
Christopher Newport Univ	VA	24,878	VC+
CUNY/City College	NY	20,204	C
CUNY/Hunter College	NY	31,098	VC
CUNY/Lehman College	NY	5,788	LC
Clark Univ	MA	53,260	HC+
Clemson Univ	SC		HC
Coastal Carolina Univ	SC	20,340	C
College for Creative Studies	MI	51,210	SP
College of Art and Design at Lesley Univ	MA	50,525	SP
College of St. Elizabeth	NJ	45,700	LC
Colo State Univ	CO	23,033	C
Columbia College - Missouri	MO	28,179	C
Columbia College Chicago	IL	40,104	C
Columbus College of Art and Design	OH	47,310	SP
Concordia Univ Nebr	NE	41,900	VC
Converse College	SC	28,290	C
Cooper Union for the Advancement of Science and Art	NY	61,370	MC
Cornell Univ	NY	67,591	MC
Cornerstone Univ	MI	36,550	C
Cornish College of the Arts	WA	47,750	SP
Culver-Stockton College	MO	34,350	C
Cumberland Univ	TN	27,710	C
Daemen College	NY	40,336	C
Dallas Baptist Univ	TX	35,220	VC
Denison Univ	OH	62,770	HC+
DePaul Univ	IL	52,807	VC
Dickinson State Univ	ND	12,372	LC
Dominican Univ	IL	42,472	C+
Dordt College	IA	37,860	C+
Drury Univ	MO	37,555	VC
East Stroudsburg Univ	PA	18,578	LC
East Tenn State Univ	TN	18,141	C
Eastern Mich Univ	MI	19,761	C
Edinboro Univ	PA	15,940	LC
Elizabethtown College	PA	56,340	VC
Elmira College	NY	53,900	C
Elms College	MA	49,602	VC
Elon Univ	NC	46,142	HC
Emory Univ	GA	63,286	MC
Eureka College	IL	34,760	C
Fairleigh Dickinson Univ/ College at Florham	NJ	54,770	C
Fairleigh Dickinson Univ/ Metropolitan Campus	NJ	52,392	C
Felician Univ	NJ	46,280	LC
Fisk Univ	TN	32,066	LC
Flagler College	FL	27,620	C
Florida A&M Univ	FL	15,361	C
Florida Atlantic Univ	FL	18,256	C
Florida International Univ	FL	20,281	C
Florida Memorial Univ	FL	22,424	LC
Fontbonne Univ	MO	34,606	C
Fordham Univ	NY	68,431	MC
Fort Hays State Univ	KS	12,677	C
Franklin and Marshall College	PA	67,960	MC
Franklin Pierce Univ	NH	46,750	LC
Freed-Hardeman Univ	TN	29,900	C
Friends Univ	KS	38,000	C
Georgetown Univ	DC	68,970	MC
Georgia Southwestern State Univ	GA	13,870	LC
Georgia State Univ	GA	25,250	C
Goddard College	VT	17,040	VC
Grand Valley State Univ	MI	22,250	C+
Green Mountain College	VT	45,228	LC
Gustavus Adolphus College	MN	53,943	HC
Hamline Univ	MN	50,152	C
Hampshire College	MA	65,214	MC
Harding Univ	AR	25,440	C
Harvard College/Harvard Univ	MA	65,609	MC
Hastings College	NE	35,380	C+
Haverford College	PA	66,490	MC
Hobart and William Smith Colleges	NY	67,050	HC+
Hofstra Univ	NY	58,210	C+
Hope College	MI	42,840	VC
Humboldt State Univ	CA	21,708	C
Huntington Univ	IN	33,996	C
Illinois College	IL	41,330	VC
Indiana State Univ	IN	23,223	LC
Indiana Univ Bloomington	IN	20,791	HC
Indiana Univ East	IN	7,207	C
Indiana Univ Kokomo	IN	7,207	C
Indiana Univ Northwest	IN	7,207	LC
Indiana Univ of Pennsylvania	PA	24,474	C
Indiana Univ South Bend	IN	16,057	C
Indiana Univ Southeast	IN	16,931	C
Indiana Univ-Purdue Univ Fort Wayne	IN	18,675	C
Indiana Univ-Purdue Univ Indianapolis	IN	18,952	C
Inter-American Univ of PR-San Germán	PR	20,042	
Iowa State Univ	IA	18,176	C
Iowa Wesleyan Univ	IA	41,000	C
Ithaca College	NY	58,158	VC+
James Madison Univ	VA	19,084	VC
Johnson State College	VT	22,672	C
Judson Univ	IL	39,174	C
Kansas City Art Inst	MO	48,200	SP
Kean Univ	NJ	25,620	C
Kentucky State Univ	KY	14,484	LC
Kentucky Wesleyan College	KY	34,260	LC
Kutztown Univ of Pennsylvania	PA	19,477	C
La Salle Univ	PA	43,476	C
La Sierra Univ	CA	39,690	VC
Lake Erie College	OH	38,914	LC
Lake Superior State Univ	MI	19,867	C
Lamar Univ	TX	18,014	LC
Lewis & Clark College	OR	60,984	MC
Lincoln Memorial Univ	TN	28,430	C
Lincoln Univ	MO	14,402	NC
LIU Brooklyn	NY	50,698	C
LIU Post	NY	50,698	C+
Lock Haven Univ of Pennsylvania	PA	20,544	LC
Louisiana State Univ in Shreveport	LA	6,902	C
Louisiana Tech Univ	LA	11,422	VC
Loyola Univ Chicago	IL	57,158	VC
Loyola Univ Maryland	MD	61,710	VC
Loyola Univ New Orleans	LA	52,456	VC
Madonna Univ	MI	30,450	LC
Maharishi Univ of Management	IA	34,930	VC
Marist College	NY	49,860	VC
Marlboro College	VT	50,832	VC+
Martin Univ	IN	21,010	LC
Maryland Inst College of Art	MD	58,740	SP
Marylhurst Univ	OR	16,818	NC
Marymount Manhattan College	NY	48,350	C
Mass College of Art and Design	MA	24,800	SP
Mass College of Liberal Arts	MA	20,659	C
McDaniel College	MD	52,910	VC
Memphis College of Art	TN	50,880	SP
Mercy College	NY	32,614	C
Meredith College	NC	46,634	C
Metropolitan State Univ of Denver	CO	6,928	LC
Midland Univ	NE	39,512	C
Midwestern State Univ	TX	12,111	LC
Milligan College	TN	39,450	C
Milwaukee Inst of Art & Design	WI	45,880	SP
Minn State Univ, Moorhead	MN	21,393	C
Miss Univ for Women	MS	17,065	C
Miss Valley State Univ	MS	13,233	LC
Missouri Southern State Univ	MO	13,071	C
Missouri Western State Univ	MO	17,822	LC
Montana State Univ	MT	15,500	C+
Montana State Univ-Northern	MT	11,370	NC
Montserrat College of Art	MA	41,500	SP
Moore College of Art and Design	PA	55,118	SP
Morgan State Univ	MD	17,190	LC
Mount Mary Univ	WI	34,650	LC
Mount St. Joseph Univ	OH	33,880	LC
Mount St. Mary's Univ	MD	53,380	C
National Louis Univ	IL	43,000	LC
Nazareth College	NY	46,784	C
New England College	NH	50,828	NC
New Jersey City Univ	NJ	21,456	LC
New Mexico State Univ	NM	14,050	LC
New York Univ	NY	68,139	MC
Norfolk State Univ	VA	18,902	LC
Northeastern State Univ	OK	8,615	VC
Northern Kentucky Univ	KY	16,486	C
Northern Mich Univ	MI	20,853	C
Northern State Univ	SD	15,570	C
Northland College	WI	41,103	C+
Northwest Missouri State Univ	MO	18,286	C
Northwestern State Univ of Louisiana	LA	16,534	LC
Northwestern Univ	IL	68,725	MC
Notre Dame de Namur Univ	CA	46,526	LC
Nova Southeastern Univ	FL	38,534	C+
Oakland City Univ	IN	33,930	NC
Oberlin College	OH	68,942	MC
Ohio Northern Univ	OH	44,050	VC
Ohio State Univ at Columbus	OH	22,843	MC
Ohio Wesleyan Univ	OH	49,460	VC
Okla Baptist Univ	OK	33,990	C
Okla Panhandle State Univ	OK	6,152	C
Old Dominion Univ	VA	21,618	C
Olivet College	MI	37,661	LC
Our Lady of the Lake Univ	TX	37,790	LC
Pace Univ	NY	60,136	C
Pacific Northwest College of Art	OR	38,494	SP
Pacific Union College	CA	36,009	VC
Park Univ	MO	22,134	C
Parsons The New School for Design	NY	56,610	SP
Piedmont College	GA	34,334	C
Pomona College	CA	64,957	MC
Pontifical Catholic Univ of PR	PR	10,534	
Portland State Univ	OR	19,443	C
Pratt Inst	NY	59,482	VC+
Prescott College	AZ	38,201	C
Principia College	IL	40,350	C
Purdue Univ/West Lafayette	IN	20,032	MC
Radford Univ	VA	19,758	C
Regis Univ	CO	46,380	C
Rider Univ	NJ	54,050	C
Ringling College of Art and Design	FL	59,160	SP
Rochester Inst of Technology	NY	52,734	HC+
Rocky Mountain College of Art and Design	CO	27,052	SP
Rosemont College	PA	30,980	LC
Rowan Univ	NJ	24,491	VC
Saginaw Valley State Univ	MI	19,284	C
St. Anselm College	NH	56,636	VC
St. Augustine's Univ	NC	25,582	C
St. Mary's College	IN	50,600	C
St. Michael's College	VT	53,275	VC+
St. Peter's Univ	NJ	49,192	C
St. Vincent College	PA	46,229	C
Salem State Univ	MA	42,650	LC
Salisbury Univ	MD	21,132	VC
San Jose State Univ	CA	22,630	C
Sarah Lawrence College	NY	68,866	MC
School of Visual Arts	NY	47,500	SP
Seattle Pacific Univ	WA	47,439	C+
Seattle Univ	WA	54,957	VC
Seton Hall Univ	NJ	58,008	C
Seton Hill Univ	PA	46,972	VC
Sewanee: The Univ of the South	TN	58,000	HC+
Siena Heights Univ	MI	36,322	C
Sierra Nevada College	NV	45,403	C
Silver Lake College of the Holy Family	WI	36,290	LC
Slippery Rock Univ of Pennsylvania	PA	20,450	C
Sonoma State Univ	CA	27,020	C
S Car State Univ	SC	21,330	LC
Southeastern Okla State Univ	OK	11,875	C
Southern Adventist Univ	TN	28,250	C
Southern Conn State Univ	CT	21,924	LC
Southern Illinois Univ Carbondale	IL	24,554	C
Southern Oregon Univ	OR	19,117	C
Southern Univ and A&M College	LA	16,074	LC
Southern Univ at New Orleans	LA	8,014	LC
Spelman College	GA	41,642	C
Springfield College	MA	48,775	C
St. Catherine Univ	MN	45,630	C
St. Cloud State Univ	MN	10,600	C
St. John's Univ	NY	57,160	C+
St. Lawrence Univ	NY	66,646	HC+
St. Thomas Aquinas College	NY	32,450	C
Stanford Univ	CA	62,541	MC
SUNY Albany	NY	22,165	C
SUNY/Buffalo State	NY	20,583	LC
SUNY/Fredonia	NY	20,818	C
SUNY/Oneonta	NY	20,794	C
SUNY/Univ at Buffalo	NY	23,122	C
Stockton Univ	NJ	25,565	C
Stonehill College	MA	55,130	C
Suffolk Univ	MA	52,316	C
Sul Ross State Univ	TX	15,021	LC
Syracuse Univ	NY	62,313	HC
Tarleton State Univ	TX	15,248	LC
Taylor Univ	IN	42,130	VC
Tenn Tech Univ	TN	17,929	C
Tenn Wesleyan Univ	TN	32,680	LC
Texas A&M Univ at Commerce	TX	10,496	C
Texas A&M Univ at Kingsville	TX	16,580	LC
Texas Woman's Univ	TX	15,302	LC
The American Univ	DC	61,317	HC
The College of New Jersey	NJ	28,675	VC+
The College of Wooster	OH	60,000	HC
The George Washington Univ	DC	68,474	HC+
The Univ of Arizona	AZ	24,086	C
The Univ of Tenn at Chattanooga	TN	17,340	C+
The Univ of Tenn at Martin	TN	15,212	C
Trinity College	CT	69,020	HC
Truman State Univ	MO	16,286	MC
Tusculum College	TN	31,625	LC
Union College	KY	32,310	C
Union College	NY	64,320	MC
Univ of Alaska Anchorage	AK	17,914	C
Univ of Calif at Davis	CA	28,468	HC
Univ of Central Florida	FL	16,379	VC
Univ of Cincinnati	OH	22,118	VC
Univ of Colo Boulder	CO	26,048	HC
Univ of Colo Denver	CO	22,238	C
Univ of Dayton	OH	54,930	VC
Univ of Delaware	DE	32,214	VC
Univ of Great Falls	MT	38,524	C
Univ of Houston-Downtown	TX	7,241	LC
Univ of Idaho	ID	16,158	C
Univ of Illinois at Chicago	IL	24,664	VC
Univ of Illinois at Urbana-Champaign	IL	27,006	HC
Univ of Iowa	IA	19,415	HC
Univ of Jamestown	ND	28,508	C
Univ of Kansas	KS	20,884	VC
Univ of Louisiana at Lafayette	LA	14,516	C
Univ of Maine at Machias	ME	22,960	C
Univ of Maryland/Baltimore County	MD	23,004	VC
Univ of Miami	FL	63,494	MC
Univ of Montana	MT	14,105	C
Univ of Mount Olive	NC	18,426	C
Univ of Nebr - Kearney	NE	17,014	LC
Univ of Nebr - Lincoln	NE	18,589	VC
Univ of Nebr - Omaha	NE	16,120	C
Univ of Nevada, Las Vegas	NV	17,553	C
Univ of New Hampshire	NH	29,333	VC
Univ of New Haven	CT	53,680	C
Univ of New Orleans	LA	12,840	C
Univ of N Car at Asheville	NC	16,251	VC+
Univ of N Car at Charlotte	NC	17,803	VC
Univ of North Florida	FL	15,996	VC
Univ of North Georgia	GA	17,316	C
Univ of Northern Colo	CO	19,658	C

ST = STATE $IS = IN-STATE COSTS SR = SELECTOR RATING

School	ST	$IS	SR
Univ of Northern Iowa	IA	17,480	C
Univ of Oregon	OR	24,021	VC
Univ of Pennsylvania	PA	63,526	MC
Univ of PR, at Mayaguez	PR	13,995	
Univ of PR-Rio Piedras campus	PR	13,327	
Univ of Rio Grande & Rio Grande Community College	OH	8,750	LC
Univ of San Francisco	CA	60,580	C
Univ of Science and Arts of Okla	OK	11,140	VC
Univ of Sioux Falls	SD	25,630	C
Univ of South Alabama	AL	16,880	C
Univ of S Car Aiken	SC	18,094	C
Univ of S Car at Columbia	SC	21,726	VC
Univ of Southern Calif	CA	66,631	MC
Univ of Southern Maine	ME	18,320	C
Univ of Southern Miss	MS	13,170	C
Univ of the District of Columbia	DC	21,260	LC
Univ of the Southwest	NM	24,386	C
Univ of Toledo	OH	19,336	C
Univ of Wisc-Green Bay	WI	15,184	C
Univ of Wisc-Oshkosh	WI	15,392	C
Univ of Wisc-Parkside	WI	15,313	C
Univ of Wisc-River Falls	WI	14,541	C
Univ of Wisc-Stevens Point	WI	14,043	C
Univ of Wisc-Stout	WI	19,667	C
Univ of Wisc-Superior	WI	14,838	C
Upper Iowa Univ	IA	34,990	NC
Utah State Univ	UT	13,235	C
Wagner College	NY	57,240	C+
Washington College	MD	56,154	VC
Washington State Univ	WA	22,747	C
Washington Univ in St. Louis	MO	67,539	MC
Weber State Univ	UT	14,112	C
West Liberty Univ	WV	16,158	C
West Virginia State Univ	WV	19,412	LC
Western Kentucky Univ	KY	16,850	C
Western New Mexico Univ	NM	16,914	LC
Western State Colo Univ	CO	19,348	C
Western Washington Univ	WA	18,904	VC
Westminster College	PA	41,722	C
Westminster College	UT	41,078	C
Widener Univ	PA	58,190	C
Wilberforce Univ	OH	19,900	C
William Paterson Univ of New Jersey	NJ	24,022	C
William Penn Univ	IA	26,000	C
Williams College	MA	67,700	MC
Wilson College	PA	35,620	LC
Winona State Univ	MN	18,109	C
Winthrop Univ	SC	23,960	C
Wittenberg Univ	OH	49,863	VC
Wright State Univ	OH	16,983	C
Xavier Univ	OH	49,380	VC
Xavier Univ of Louisiana	LA	31,689	C
York College of Pennsylvania	PA	29,240	C

FINE ARTS EDUCATION

School	ST	$IS	SR
Kean Univ	NJ	25,620	C
Missouri Western State Univ	MO	17,822	LC
Old Dominion Univ	VA	21,618	C

FINE/STUDIO ARTS, GENERAL

School	ST	$IS	SR
Cal State, Fullerton	CA	21,902	C
East Central Univ	OK	13,330	C
Georgetown College	KY	41,440	C
Kean Univ	NJ	25,620	C
Kutztown Univ of Pennsylvania	PA	19,477	C
Linfield College	OR	53,992	C
Loyola Univ New Orleans	LA	52,456	VC
Missouri Southern State Univ	MO	13,071	C
Missouri Western State Univ	MO	17,822	LC
Montclair State Univ	NJ	26,912	C
Rochester Inst of Technology	NY	52,734	HC+
St. Louis Univ	MO	49,866	HC
Southern Methodist Univ	TX	69,008	MC
Tenn Wesleyan Univ	TN	32,680	LC
Texas Christian Univ	TX	57,120	HC
Univ of Maine at Machias	ME	22,960	C
Univ of New Haven	CT	53,680	C
Washington State Univ	WA	22,747	C
Wellesley College	MA	66,984	MC

FIRE CONTROL AND SAFETY TECHNOLOGY

School	ST	$IS	SR
Okla State Univ	OK	17,180	C+
Univ of New Haven	CT	53,680	C
Univ of N Car at Charlotte	NC	17,803	VC

FIRE PROTECTION

School	ST	$IS	SR
Cal State, Los Angeles	CA	17,186	LC
Eastern Kentucky Univ	KY	17,742	C
Park Univ	MO	22,134	C
Southern Illinois Univ Carbondale	IL	24,554	C
Univ of New Haven	CT	53,680	C
Western Illinois Univ	IL	20,897	C

FIRE PROTECTION ENGINEERING

School	ST	$IS	SR
Univ of Houston-Downtown	TX	7,241	LC
Univ of Maryland/College Park	MD	21,938	HC
Univ of New Haven	CT	53,680	C

FIRE PROTECTION SCIENCE

School	ST	$IS	SR
Lake Superior State Univ	MI	19,867	C
Southwestern Okla State Univ	OK	12,205	C

FIRE SCIENCE

School	ST	$IS	SR
Anna Maria College	MA	51,020	C
CUNY/John Jay College of Criminal Justice	NY	6,359	SP
Lake Superior State Univ	MI	19,867	C
Madonna Univ	MI	30,450	LC
New England College	NH	50,828	NC
Univ of Idaho	ID	16,158	C
Univ of Maryland Univ College	MD	26,146	LC
Univ of New Haven	CT	53,680	C
Univ of the District of Columbia	DC	21,260	LC

FIRE SERVICES ADMINISTRATION

School	ST	$IS	SR
Bowling Green State Univ	OH	19,975	C
CUNY/John Jay College of Criminal Justice	NY	6,359	SP
Colo State Univ	CO	23,033	C
Columbia College - Missouri	MO	28,179	C
Holy Family Univ	PA	44,672	LC
Idaho State Univ	ID	13,619	LC
Park Univ	MO	22,134	C
SUNY/Empire State College	NY	9,145	NC
Univ of New Haven	CT	53,680	C

FISH AND GAME MANAGEMENT

School	ST	$IS	SR
Delaware State Univ	DE	19,376	LC
Frostburg State Univ	MD	17,280	LC
Kansas State Univ	KS	17,780	VC
Lake Superior State Univ	MI	19,867	C
Northland College	WI	41,103	C+
S Dak State Univ	SD	15,874	C
Stephen F. Austin State Univ	TX	18,484	LC
Tenn Tech Univ	TN	17,929	C
The Univ of Montana Western	MT	9,426	LC
Univ of Idaho	ID	16,158	C
Univ of Maine at Machias	ME	22,960	C
Univ of Nebr - Lincoln	NE	18,589	VC
Univ of Wyoming	WY	15,537	C
West Virginia Univ	WV	18,952	VC

FISHING AND FISHERIES

School	ST	$IS	SR
Arkansas Tech Univ	AR	16,534	LC
Auburn Univ	AL	24,300	VC+
Cal State, Fullerton	CA	21,902	C
Colo State Univ	CO	23,033	C
Humboldt State Univ	CA	21,708	C
Mich State Univ	MI	24,542	VC
Miss State Univ	MS	12,028	C+
N Car State Univ	NC	22,434	HC+
Northern Mich Univ	MI	20,853	C
Ohio State Univ at Columbus	OH	22,843	MC
Oregon State Univ	OR	23,337	VC
Purdue Univ/West Lafayette	IN	20,032	MC
SUNY /College of Agriculture and Tech at Cobleskill	NY	20,527	LC
SUNY/The College of Environmental Science and Forestry	NY	23,728	VC
Univ of Alaska Fairbanks	AK	16,874	VC
Univ of Arkansas at Pine Bluff	AR	13,541	C
Univ of Georgia	GA	21,878	HC
Univ of Idaho	ID	16,158	C
Univ of Maine at Machias	ME	22,960	C
Univ of Minn/Twin Cities	MN	24,269	MC
Univ of Missouri-Columbia	MO	20,463	VC
Univ of N Dak	ND	16,673	C
Univ of Vermont	VT	29,792	HC
Univ of Washington	WA	23,091	MC
Univ of Wisc-Stevens Point	WI	14,043	C
West Virginia Univ	WV	18,952	VC

FITNESS MANAGEMENT

School	ST	$IS	SR
Lasell College	MA	49,400	C
Missouri Baptist Univ	MO	35,594	C
Wartburg College	IA	49,478	C

FOLKLORE AND MYTHOLOGY

School	ST	$IS	SR
Goddard College	VT	17,040	VC
Harvard College/Harvard Univ	MA	65,609	MC
Indiana Univ Bloomington	IN	20,791	HC
Univ of Oregon	OR	24,021	VC
Univ of Pennsylvania	PA	63,526	MC

FOOD PRODUCTION/ MANAGEMENT/SERVICES

School	ST	$IS	SR
Belmont Univ	TN	44,500	VC+
Central Mich Univ	MI	20,330	C
Delaware Valley Univ	PA	51,271	C
Dominican Univ	IL	42,472	C+
Guilford College	NC	45,973	C
Johnson & Wales Univ/ Charlotte Campus	NC	44,768	C
Johnson & Wales Univ/ Denver Campus	CO	44,768	C
Johnson & Wales Univ/North Miami Campus	FL	44,768	C
Johnson & Wales Univ/ Providence Campus	RI	44,768	C
Lipscomb Univ	TN	42,984	VC
Loyola Univ New Orleans	LA	52,456	VC
Metropolitan State Univ	MN	7,859	C
Mich State Univ	MI	24,542	VC
Miss Univ for Women	MS	17,065	C
Mount Marty College	SD	36,862	C
Murray State Univ	KY	17,726	C+
Newbury College	MA	48,970	C
Nicholls State Univ	LA	14,959	C
Ohio State Univ at Columbus	OH	22,843	MC
Purdue Univ Northwest	IN	15,178	C
Purdue Univ/West Lafayette	IN	20,032	MC
Rochester Inst of Technology	NY	52,734	HC+
Seton Hill Univ	PA	46,972	VC
Simmons College	MA	54,400	HC
S Dak State Univ	SD	15,874	C
Texas A&M Univ at Kingsville	TX	16,580	LC
Texas Christian Univ	TX	57,120	HC
Univ of Central Florida	FL	16,379	VC
Univ of Delaware	DE	32,214	VC
Univ of Georgia	GA	21,878	HC
Univ of Illinois at Urbana-Champaign	IL	27,006	HC
Univ of Nebr - Lincoln	NE	18,589	VC
Univ of Nevada, Las Vegas	NV	17,553	C
Univ of Wisc-Stout	WI	19,667	C
Western Mich Univ	MI	21,791	C

FOOD SCIENCE

School	ST	$IS	SR
Alabama A&M Univ	AL	18,796	C
Ashland Univ	OH	30,446	C
Auburn Univ	AL	24,300	VC+
Bluffton Univ	OH	40,950	C+
Brigham Young Univ	UT	13,248	MC
Calif Polytechnic State Univ	CA	22,547	MC
Calif State Polytechnic Univ, Pomona	CA	21,811	C
Cal State, Fresno	CA	16,902	LC
Cal State, Fullerton	CA	21,902	C
Cal State, San Bernardino	CA	20,106	C
Central Washington Univ	WA	16,803	C
Clarke Univ	IA	42,950	C
Clemson Univ	SC		HC
College of the Ozarks	MO	7,530	VC
Colo State Univ	CO	23,033	C
Cornell Univ	NY	67,591	MC
Delaware State Univ	DE	19,376	LC
Delaware Valley Univ	PA	51,271	C
Dominican Univ	IL	42,472	C+
Florida State Univ	FL	16,771	HC
Framingham State Univ	MA	21,740	C
Indiana State Univ	IN	23,223	LC
Iowa State Univ	IA	18,176	C
Kansas State Univ	KS	17,780	VC
Madonna Univ	MI	30,450	LC
Mich State Univ	MI	24,542	VC
Miss State Univ	MS	12,028	C+
N Car State Univ	NC	22,434	HC+
N Dak State Univ	ND	16,245	VC
Northwest Missouri State Univ	MO	18,286	C
Ohio State Univ at Columbus	OH	22,843	MC
Okla State Univ	OK	17,180	C+
Oregon State Univ	OR	23,337	VC
Pennsylvania State Univ - Univ Park	PA	29,716	HC
Purdue Univ/West Lafayette	IN	20,032	MC
Rutgers Univ - New Brunswick	NJ	27,090	HC
San Jose State Univ	CA	22,630	C
Seattle Pacific Univ	WA	47,439	C+
Simmons College	MA	54,400	HC
S Car State Univ	SC	21,330	LC
S Dak State Univ	SD	15,874	C
Syracuse Univ	NY	62,313	HC
Texas A&M Univ at Kingsville	TX	16,580	LC
Texas Tech Univ	TX	20,156	C+
The Univ of Alabama	AL	24,320	C+
The Univ of Tenn at Knoxville	TN	22,112	VC
Tuskegee Univ	AL	28,164	C
Univ of Arkansas at Fayetteville	AR	19,766	VC
Univ of Calif at Davis	CA	28,468	HC
Univ of Delaware	DE	32,214	VC
Univ of Florida	FL	16,291	HC+
Univ of Georgia	GA	21,878	HC
Univ of Hawaii at Manoa	HI	23,261	C
Univ of Idaho	ID	16,158	C
Univ of Illinois at Urbana-Champaign	IL	27,006	HC
Univ of Kentucky	KY	24,800	C+
Univ of Maine	ME	21,038	VC
Univ of Mass Amherst	MA	27,669	HC
Univ of Minn/Twin Cities	MN	24,269	MC
Univ of Missouri-Columbia	MO	20,463	VC
Univ of Nebr - Lincoln	NE	18,589	VC
Univ of the District of Columbia	DC	21,260	LC
Univ of Vermont	VT	29,792	HC
Univ of Washington	WA	23,091	MC
Univ of Wisc-Madison	WI	21,647	MC
Univ of Wisc-River Falls	WI	14,541	C
Utah State Univ	UT	13,235	C
Virginia Polytechnic Inst and State Univ	VA	21,920	VC
Washington State Univ	WA	22,747	C
Youngstown State Univ	OH	17,487	C

FOOD SERVICES TECHNOLOGY

School	ST	$IS	SR
Brigham Young Univ	UT	13,248	MC
Delaware Valley Univ	PA	51,271	C
Inter-American Univ of PR-Bayamon	PR	18,785	
Johnson & Wales Univ/ Charlotte Campus	NC	44,768	C
Johnson & Wales Univ/North Miami Campus	FL	44,768	C
Johnson & Wales Univ/ Providence Campus	RI	44,768	C
Minn State Univ, Mankato	MN	17,190	C
Purdue Univ/West Lafayette	IN	20,032	MC
St. Catherine Univ	MN	45,630	C
Univ of Central Florida	FL	16,379	VC
Univ of Wisc-Stout	WI	19,667	C

FOOD TECHNOLOGY FOR COMPANION ANIMALS

School	ST	$IS	SR
Texas A&M Univ at College Station	TX	20,771	VC+
Univ of Nebr - Lincoln	NE	18,589	VC

FOREIGN LANGUAGE

School	ST	$IS	SR
Arkansas State Univ	AR	16,190	C
Austin Peay State Univ	TN	16,397	C
Bentley Univ	MA	63,720	MC
Bloomsburg Univ of Pennsylvania	PA	19,930	C
Bowling Green State Univ	OH	19,975	C
Colo State Univ	CO	23,033	C
Eastern Illinois Univ	IL	21,414	C
Gannon Univ	PA	42,922	C
Kutztown Univ of Pennsylvania	PA	19,477	C
LIU Post	NY	50,698	C+
Missouri Western State Univ	MO	17,822	LC
New Mexico State Univ	NM	14,050	LC
Niagara Univ	NY	41,010	C
Northwestern State Univ of Louisiana	LA	16,534	LC
Oakwood Univ	AL	43,758	C
Penn State Erie,The Behrend College	PA	26,688	VC
Providence College	RI	62,870	HC
Southern Illinois Univ Carbondale	IL	24,554	C
Southern Oregon Univ	OR	19,117	C
St. Ambrose Univ	IA	40,180	C
St. Joseph's College, New York/Brooklyn Campus	NY	25,114	LC
Thomas Edison State Univ	NJ	6,350	NC
United States Military Academy at West Point	NY		HC+
Univ of Alabama at Birmingham	AL	22,092	C
Univ of Alaska Fairbanks	AK	16,874	VC
Univ of Louisiana at Monroe	LA	15,970	C
Univ of Maryland/College Park	MD	21,938	HC
Washington State Univ	WA	22,747	C
West Virginia Univ	WV	18,952	VC
Western Illinois Univ	IL	20,897	C

FOREIGN LANGUAGE INSTRUCTION

School	ST	$IS	SR
Lewis Univ	IL	41,710	C

FOREIGN LANGUAGES EDUCATION

School	ST	$IS	SR
Abilene Christian Univ	TX	43,708	C+
Adams State Univ	CO	15,420	LC
Alabama State Univ	AL	16,490	LC
American International College	MA	47,020	LC
Anderson Univ	IN	39,450	C
Appalachian State Univ	NC	15,394	VC
Arkansas State Univ	AR	16,190	C
Arkansas Tech Univ	AR	16,534	LC
Asbury Univ	KY	36,450	C+
Ashland Univ	OH	30,446	C
Auburn Univ	AL	24,300	VC+
Augusta Univ	GA	4,632	C

ST = STATE $IS = IN-STATE COSTS SR = SELECTOR RATING

School	ST	$IS	SR
Baylor Univ	TX	56,803	HC
Bemidji State Univ	MN	17,730	C
Bennington College	VT	66,280	MC
Bethel Univ	MN	46,550	C+
Boston Univ	MA	67,352	MC
Bowling Green State Univ	OH	19,975	C
Canisius College	NY	49,672	C
Carson-Newman Univ	TN	35,900	C
Carthage College	WI	48,835	C
Central Mich Univ	MI	20,330	C
Central Washington Univ	WA	16,803	C
CUNY/Brooklyn College	NY	7,163	C+
CUNY/City College	NY	20,204	C
CUNY/Hunter College	NY	31,098	VC
CUNY/Lehman College	NY	5,788	LC
Clarion Univ of Pennsylvania	PA	21,608	LC
College of Charleston	SC	24,046	VC
Colo State Univ	CO	23,033	C
Columbus State Univ	GA	14,336	LC
Concordia College - Moorhead	MN	46,418	C
Converse College	SC	28,290	C
Cornell College	IA	49,900	VC
Daemen College	NY	40,336	C
DePaul Univ	IL	52,807	VC
DePauw Univ	IN	58,688	VC
Dordt College	IA	37,860	C+
Duquesne Univ	PA	48,508	VC
East Carolina Univ	NC	16,539	C
East Tenn State Univ	TN	18,141	C
East Texas Baptist Univ	TX	34,444	C
Eastern Kentucky Univ	KY	17,742	C
Eastern Mich Univ	MI	19,761	C
Eastern Washington Univ	WA	17,896	LC
Edinboro Univ	PA	15,940	LC
Elmira College	NY	53,900	C
Elms College	MA	49,602	VC
Elon Univ	NC	46,142	HC
Emporia State Univ	KS	15,029	C
Erskine College	SC	45,460	C
Eugene Lang College of Liberal Arts	NY	64,940	VC
Evangel Univ	MO	28,898	C
Fairmont State Univ	WV	15,726	C
Florida Atlantic Univ	FL	18,256	C
Florida State Univ	FL	16,771	HC
Friends Univ	KS	38,000	C
Gardner-Webb Univ	NC	24,935	C+
Georgetown College	KY	41,440	C
Georgia Inst of Technology	GA	23,910	MC
Gettysburg College	PA	65,210	MC
Goshen College	IN	44,350	C
Grace College and Seminary	IN	31,524	C
Grand Valley State Univ	MI	22,250	C+
Greensboro College	NC	39,790	LC
Gustavus Adolphus College	MN	53,943	HC
Hamline Univ	MN	50,152	C
Harding Univ	AR	25,440	C
Hardin-Simmons Univ	TX	36,025	C
Hastings College	NE	35,380	C+
Heidelberg Univ	OH	40,400	LC
Hofstra Univ	NY	58,210	C+
Holy Family Univ	PA	44,672	LC
Hood College	MD	50,540	C
Hope College	MI	42,840	VC
Houghton College	NY	40,558	VC
Illinois College	IL	41,330	VC
Immaculata Univ	PA	39,000	C
Indiana State Univ	IN	23,223	LC
Indiana Univ-Purdue Univ Fort Wayne	IN	18,675	C
Ithaca College	NY	58,158	VC+
Juniata College	PA	58,118	VC
King's College	PA	48,240	C
Kutztown Univ of Pennsylvania	PA	19,477	C
La Salle Univ	PA	43,476	C
Lamar Univ	TX	18,014	LC
Le Moyne College	NY	47,305	VC
Lenoir-Rhyne Univ	NC	47,500	LC
Lipscomb Univ	TN	42,984	VC
LIU Post	NY	50,698	C+
Lock Haven Univ of Pennsylvania	PA	20,544	LC
Louisiana Tech Univ	LA	11,422	VC
Manhattan College	NY	55,652	C
Marshall Univ	WV	18,044	C
Marywood Univ	PA	47,840	C
Messiah College	PA	44,380	VC
Miami Univ	OH	27,190	HC+
Millikin Univ	IL	44,148	C
Minn State Univ, Mankato	MN	17,190	C
Minn State Univ, Moorhead	MN	21,393	C
Minot State Univ	ND	13,285	C
Missouri Western State Univ	MO	17,822	LC
Monmouth Univ	NJ	50,184	C
Murray State Univ	KY	17,726	C+
Muskingum Univ	OH	35,966	C
Nazareth College	NY	46,784	C
New York Univ	NY	68,139	MC
Niagara Univ	NY	41,010	C
N Car State Univ	NC	22,434	HC+
Northern State Univ	SD	15,570	C
Northwestern College of Iowa	IA	38,400	C
Notre Dame of Maryland Univ	MD	47,570	VC
Ohio Wesleyan Univ	OH	49,460	VC
Old Dominion Univ	VA	21,618	C
Oral Roberts Univ	OK	34,316	C
Ouachita Baptist Univ	AR	33,500	VC
Pennsylvania State Univ - Univ Park	PA	29,716	HC
Providence College	RI	62,870	HC
Purdue Univ Northwest	IN	15,178	C
Purdue Univ/West Lafayette	IN	20,032	MC
Radford Univ	VA	19,758	C
Rhode Island College	RI	19,000	LC
Rider Univ	NJ	54,050	C
Rockhurst Univ	MO	28,990	C
Rosemont College	PA	30,980	LC
Rowan Univ	NJ	24,491	VC
Saginaw Valley State Univ	MI	19,284	C
St. Michael's College	VT	53,275	VC+
St. Xavier Univ	IL	44,440	C
Seton Hill Univ	PA	46,972	VC
Shippensburg Univ of Pennsylvania	PA	24,096	C
Slippery Rock Univ of Pennsylvania	PA	20,450	C
Southeast Missouri State Univ	MO	16,148	C
Southern Conn State Univ	CT	21,924	LC
Southern Univ at New Orleans	LA	8,014	LC
Southwest Minn State Univ	MN	17,783	C
St. Cloud State Univ	MN	10,600	C
St. Edward's Univ	TX	56,190	VC
St. John Fisher College	NY	45,270	VC
St. Thomas Aquinas College	NY	32,450	C
SUNY at New Paltz	NY	20,840	C
SUNY at Oswego	NY	22,219	VC
SUNY/Buffalo State	NY	20,583	LC
SUNY/College at Old Westbury	NY	16,860	C
SUNY/Cortland	NY	20,910	C
SUNY/Fredonia	NY	20,818	C
SUNY/Oneonta	NY	20,794	C
Taylor Univ	IN	42,130	VC
Texas Southern Univ	TX	19,592	LC
Texas Wesleyan Univ	TX	37,338	C
The American Univ	DC	61,317	HC
Universidad del Turabo	PR	17,828	
Univ of Central Arkansas	AR	15,042	VC
Univ of Central Florida	FL	16,379	VC
Univ of Central Missouri	MO	18,982	C
Univ of Central Okla	OK	15,150	C
Univ of Cincinnati	OH	22,118	VC
Univ of Conn	CT	27,394	
Univ of Delaware	DE	32,214	VC
Univ of Evansville	IN	44,186	C+
Univ of Findlay	OH	43,040	C
Univ of Idaho	ID	16,158	C
Univ of Illinois at Urbana-Champaign	IL	27,006	HC
Univ of Indianapolis	IN	36,480	VC
Univ of Iowa	IA	19,415	HC
Univ of Kentucky	KY	24,800	C+
Univ of Louisiana at Lafayette	LA	14,516	C
Univ of Louisville	KY	19,692	C
Univ of Mary Hardin-Baylor	TX	35,292	C+
Univ of Mich/Flint	MI	19,062	C
Univ of Minn/Duluth	MN	20,292	C
Univ of Nebr - Kearney	NE	17,014	LC
Univ of Nebr - Lincoln	NE	18,589	VC
Univ of New Orleans	LA	12,840	C
Univ of North Alabama	AL	15,964	C
Univ of N Car at Charlotte	NC	17,803	VC
Univ of North Georgia	GA	17,316	C
Univ of Northern Iowa	IA	17,480	C
Univ of PR, at Mayaguez	PR	13,995	
Univ of South Florida/Tampa	FL	16,110	VC
Univ of Southern Miss	MS	13,170	C
Univ of Toledo	OH	19,336	C
Univ of Vermont	VT	29,792	HC
Univ of West Georgia	GA	17,510	LC
Univ of Wisc-Green Bay	WI	15,184	C
Univ of Wisc-River Falls	WI	14,541	C
Univ of Wisc-Whitewater	WI	13,976	C
Utah State Univ	UT	13,235	C
Utica College	NY	31,510	C
Valparaiso Univ	IN	50,160	VC
Virginia Commonwealth Univ	VA	23,811	VC
Virginia Polytechnic Inst and State Univ	VA	21,920	VC
Wartburg College	IA	49,478	C
Washington State Univ	WA	22,747	C
Washington Univ in St. Louis	MO	67,539	MC
Weber State Univ	UT	14,112	C
Webster Univ	MO	37,490	C
West Texas A&M Univ	TX	13,478	C
Western Carolina Univ	NC	13,965	C
Western Illinois Univ	IL	20,897	C
Western Mich Univ	MI	21,791	C
Western State Colo Univ	CO	19,348	C
Western Washington Univ	WA	18,904	VC
Whitworth Univ	WA	53,682	VC
Wilson College	PA	35,620	LC
Winona State Univ	MN	18,109	C
Wittenberg Univ	OH	49,863	VC
Wright State Univ	OH	16,983	C

FORENSIC CRIMINAL INVESTIGATION

School	ST	$IS	SR
Lewis Univ	IL	41,710	C
Missouri Western State Univ	MO	17,822	LC

FORENSIC PSYCHOLOGY

School	ST	$IS	SR
Bay Path Univ	MA	46,356	C
Corban Univ	OR	41,700	C
Faulkner Univ	AL	26,410	C
The College of St. Rose	NY	44,010	C
Tiffin Univ	OH	34,900	LC
Univ of Central Okla	OK	15,150	C

FORENSIC SCIENCE

School	ST	$IS	SR
Alvernia Univ	PA	45,330	C
Arizona State Univ at the West Campus	AZ	21,513	VC
Bay Path Univ	MA	46,356	C
Bethany College	KS	38,637	LC
Bethany College	WV	38,774	LC
Bryant Univ	RI	57,204	VC
Cedar Crest College	PA	51,110	C
Hilbert College	NY	32,650	LC
Indiana Univ-Purdue Univ Indianapolis	IN	18,952	C
King Univ	TN	36,976	C
Madonna Univ	MI	30,450	LC
Missouri Southern State Univ	MO	13,071	C
Missouri Western State Univ	MO	17,822	LC
Murray State Univ	KY	17,726	C+
Northern Mich Univ	MI	20,853	C
Okla Baptist Univ	OK	33,990	C
Okla Christian Univ	OK	29,260	C
Pace Univ	NY	60,136	C
Pennsylvania State Univ - Univ Park	PA	29,716	HC
Piedmont College	GA	34,334	C
Point Park Univ	PA	41,270	C
Purdue Univ Northwest	IN	15,178	C
Roberts Wesleyan College	NY	41,116	C
St. Louis Univ	MO	49,866	HC
San Jose State Univ	CA	22,630	C
Southeast Missouri State Univ	MO	16,148	C
Stevenson Univ	MD	48,412	C
Syracuse Univ	NY	62,313	HC
The College of St. Rose	NY	44,010	C
Tiffin Univ	OH	34,900	LC
Univ of Central Florida	FL	16,379	VC
Univ of Central Okla	OK	15,150	C
Univ of Illinois at Chicago	IL	24,664	VC
Univ of Nebr - Lincoln	NE	18,589	VC
Waynesburg Univ	PA	33,530	C
West Virginia Univ	WV	18,952	VC
Western Illinois Univ	IL	20,897	C

FORENSIC STUDIES

School	ST	$IS	SR
Albany State Univ	GA	19,462	C
Alfred State College	NY	19,895	C
Ashland Univ	OH	30,446	C
Bay Path Univ	MA	46,356	C
Baylor Univ	TX	56,803	HC
Becker College	MA	30,100	LC
Cal State, Fresno	CA	16,902	LC
Carlow Univ	PA	39,696	LC
Cedarville Univ	OH	36,244	VC
Chaminade Univ of Honolulu	HI	37,614	C
Champlain College	VT	54,724	VC
Chatham Univ	PA	47,883	VC
Chestnut Hill College	PA	47,180	C
CUNY/John Jay College of Criminal Justice	NY	6,359	SP
Columbia College - Missouri	MO	28,179	C
Defiance College	OH	42,240	LC
Eastern Kentucky Univ	KY	17,742	C
Eastern New Mexico Univ	NM	12,874	LC
Edinboro Univ	PA	15,940	LC
Embry-Riddle Aeronautical Univ - Prescott Campus	AZ	45,130	VC
Fairmont State Univ	WV	15,726	C
Florida Gulf Coast Univ	FL	14,738	C
Florida Inst of Technology	FL	53,306	VC
Friends Univ	KS	38,000	C
Gannon Univ	PA	42,922	C
Grand Canyon Univ	AZ	25,150	VC
Guilford College	NC	45,973	C
Hamline Univ	MN	50,152	C
Heidelberg Univ	OH	40,400	LC
Hilbert College	NY	32,650	LC
Hofstra Univ	NY	58,210	C+
Husson Univ	ME	26,508	C
Inter-American Univ of PR-Aguadilla Campus	PR	21,657	
Inter-American Univ of PR-Bayamon	PR	18,785	
Keystone College	PA	28,680	LC
Lake Superior State Univ	MI	19,867	C
LIU Post	NY	50,698	C+
Loyola Univ Chicago	IL	57,158	VC
Loyola Univ New Orleans	LA	52,456	VC
Lynn Univ	FL	49,680	LC
Marshall Univ	WV	18,044	C
Marygrove College	MI	30,100	LC
Maryville Univ of St. Louis	MO	38,558	VC
Mercyhurst Univ	PA	47,420	C
Missouri Southern State Univ	MO	13,071	C
Missouri Western State Univ	MO	17,822	LC
Newman Univ	KS	37,382	C
Northern Kentucky Univ	KY	16,486	C
Ohio Univ	OH	23,394	VC
Pace Univ	NY	60,136	C
Russell Sage College	NY	39,370	C
St. Anselm College	NH	56,636	VC
St. Louis Univ	MO	49,866	HC
Seattle Univ	WA	54,957	VC
Seton Hill Univ	PA	46,972	VC
Simpson College	IA	45,626	VC
Southern Illinois Univ Edwardsville	IL	20,188	C
Southern Univ at New Orleans	LA	8,014	LC
Southern Wesleyan Univ	SC	33,670	LC
St. Andrews Univ	NC	44,634	LC
St. Edward's Univ	TX	56,190	VC
Stevenson Univ	MD	48,412	C
Texas A&M Univ at College Station	TX	20,771	VC+
Thomas More College	KY	36,720	LC
Tiffin Univ	OH	34,900	LC
Trine Univ	IN	41,310	C
Univ of Central Florida	FL	16,379	VC
Univ of Central Okla	OK	15,150	C
Univ of Findlay	OH	43,040	C
Univ of Illinois at Chicago	IL	24,664	VC
Univ of Miss	MS	18,802	C
Univ of New Haven	CT	53,680	C
Univ of N Dak	ND	16,673	C
Univ of Scranton	PA	54,962	VC
Univ of Tampa	FL	38,928	VC
Univ of Wisc-Milwaukee	WI	21,538	C
Univ of Wisc-Platteville	WI	14,148	C
Virginia Commonwealth Univ	VA	23,811	VC
Washburn Univ	KS	15,827	C
West Chester Univ of Pennsylvania	PA	19,171	VC
West Virginia Univ	WV	18,952	VC
Western Carolina Univ	NC	13,965	C
Western New England Univ	MA	49,182	C
Youngstown State Univ	OH	17,487	C

FOREST ENGINEERING

School	ST	$IS	SR
Auburn Univ	AL	24,300	VC+
Oregon State Univ	OR	23,337	VC
SUNY/The College of Environmental Science and Forestry	NY	23,728	VC
Univ of Maine	ME	21,038	VC
Univ of Washington	WA	23,091	MC

FORESTRY AND RELATED SCIENCES

School	ST	$IS	SR
Alabama A&M Univ	AL	18,796	C
Albion College	MI	55,260	C
Beloit College	WI	55,206	HC
Calif Polytechnic State Univ	CA	22,547	MC
Cal State, Fullerton	CA	21,902	C
Clemson Univ	SC		HC
Colo State Univ	CO	23,033	C
Davis & Elkins College	WV	38,242	LC
Eastern Oregon Univ	OR	17,612	C
Elizabethtown College	PA	56,340	VC
Glenville State College	WV	17,386	LC
Humboldt State Univ	CA	21,708	C
Iowa State Univ	IA	18,176	C
Louisiana State Univ and A&M College	LA	18,677	VC
Louisiana Tech Univ	LA	11,422	VC
Mich State Univ	MI	24,542	VC
Mich Tech Univ	MI	25,551	VC+
N Car State Univ	NC	22,434	HC+
Northern Arizona Univ	AZ	21,003	C
Northland College	WI	41,103	C+
Northwest Missouri State Univ	MO	18,286	C
Ohio State Univ at Columbus	OH	22,843	MC
Oregon State Univ	OR	23,337	VC
Pennsylvania State Univ - Univ Park	PA	29,716	HC
Prescott College	AZ	38,201	C
Purdue Univ/West Lafayette	IN	20,032	MC
Sewanee: The Univ of the South	TN	58,000	HC+
S Dak State Univ	SD	15,874	C
Southern Illinois Univ Carbondale	IL	24,554	C
Southern Univ and A&M College	LA	16,074	LC
SUNY/The College of Environmental Science and Forestry	NY	23,728	VC
Stephen F. Austin State Univ	TX	18,484	LC
The Univ of Tenn at Knoxville	TN	22,112	VC
Univ of Arkansas at Monticello	AR	13,599	LC
Univ of Calif at Berkeley	CA	29,886	MC
Univ of Florida	FL	16,291	HC+
Univ of Georgia	GA	21,878	HC
Univ of Idaho	ID	16,158	C
Univ of Illinois at Urbana-Champaign	IL	27,006	HC
Univ of Kentucky	KY	24,800	C+
Univ of Maine	ME	21,038	VC
Univ of Maine at Fort Kent	ME	15,165	LC
Univ of Minn/Twin Cities	MN	24,269	MC
Univ of Missouri-Columbia	MO	20,463	VC
Univ of Montana	MT	14,105	C

ST = STATE $IS = IN-STATE COSTS SR = SELECTOR RATING

School	ST	$IS	SR
Univ of New Hampshire	NH	29,333	VC
Univ of Vermont	VT	29,792	HC
Univ of Wisc-Madison	WI	21,647	MC
Univ of Wisc-Stevens Point	WI	14,043	C
Utah State Univ	UT	13,235	C
Virginia Polytechnic Inst and State Univ	VA	21,920	VC
Washington State Univ	WA	22,747	C
West Virginia Univ	WV	18,952	VC
Western New Mexico Univ	NM	16,914	LC
Whitman College	WA	59,772	MC

FORESTRY PRODUCTION AND PROCESSING

School	ST	$IS	SR
Auburn Univ	AL	24,300	VC+
Clemson Univ	SC		HC
Miss State Univ	MS	12,028	C+
Stephen F. Austin State Univ	TX	18,484	LC
Univ of Idaho	ID	16,158	C
Univ of Washington	WA	23,091	MC
Washington State Univ	WA	22,747	C

FRENCH

School	ST	$IS	SR
Adelphi Univ	NY	49,792	C
Adrian College	MI	45,550	C
Agnes Scott College	GA	51,930	VC+
Alabama A&M Univ	AL	18,796	C
Alabama State Univ	AL	16,490	LC
Albany State Univ	GA	19,462	C
Albion College	MI	55,260	C
Albright College	PA	57,326	C
Allegheny College	PA	57,620	VC
Alma College	MI	49,410	VC
Amherst College	MA	66,186	MC
Anderson Univ	IN	39,450	C
Andrews Univ	MI	41,732	C
Appalachian State Univ	NC	15,394	VC
Aquinas College - Mich	MI	38,876	VC
Arizona State Univ at the Tempe Campus	AZ	23,001	VC
Armstrong State Univ	GA	15,615	C
Asbury Univ	KY	36,450	C+
Ashland Univ	OH	30,446	C
Auburn Univ	AL	24,300	VC+
Augsburg Univ	MN	45,129	C
Augustana College	IL	51,222	VC+
Augustana Univ	SD	39,968	VC
Austin College	TX	51,059	HC
Baker Univ	KS	37,190	C
Baldwin Wallace Univ	OH	42,464	VC
Ball State Univ	IN	19,808	C+
Bard College	NY	65,924	HC
Barnard College/Columbia Univ	NY	68,762	MC
Barry Univ	FL	38,730	LC
Baylor Univ	TX	56,803	HC
Belmont Univ	TN	44,500	VC+
Beloit College	WI	55,206	HC
Benedictine College	KS	38,850	VC
Bennington College	VT	66,280	MC
Berea College	KY	7,094	C
Berry College	GA	47,466	VC
Bethel Univ	MN	46,550	C+
Boise State Univ	ID	17,368	C
Boston College	MA	68,043	MC
Boston Univ	MA	67,352	MC
Bowdoin College	ME	65,980	MC
Bowling Green State Univ	OH	19,975	C
Brandeis Univ	MA	68,443	MC
Bridgewater College	VA	46,260	C
Brigham Young Univ	UT	13,248	MC
Bryn Mawr College	PA	65,220	MC
Bucknell Univ	PA	67,136	MC
Butler Univ	IN	52,890	VC+
Cabrini Univ	PA	42,591	LC
Caldwell Univ	NJ	42,165	LC
Calif Lutheran Univ	CA	52,853	C
Cal State, Fresno	CA	16,902	LC
Cal State, Fullerton	CA	21,902	C
Cal State, Long Beach	CA	18,850	C
Cal State, Los Angeles	CA	17,186	LC
Cal State, Northridge	CA	17,277	LC
Cal State, Sacramento	CA	19,060	C
Cal State, San Bernardino	CA	20,106	C
Cal State, Stanislaus	CA	18,053	LC
Calif Univ of Pennsylvania	PA	20,425	LC
Calvin College	MI	43,090	HC
Campbell Univ	NC	37,570	VC
Canisius College	NY	49,672	C
Capital Univ	OH	44,778	VC
Cardinal Stritch Univ	WI	37,136	C
Carleton College	MN	66,414	MC
Carnegie Mellon Univ	PA	67,980	MC
Carroll College	MT	44,304	C
Carson-Newman Univ	TN	35,900	C
Carthage College	WI	48,835	C
Case Western Reserve Univ	OH	62,284	MC
Centenary College of Louisiana	LA	49,050	C+
Central College	IA	44,592	C
Central Conn State Univ	CT	22,041	C
Central Mich Univ	MI	20,330	C
Central Washington Univ	WA	16,803	C
Centre College	KY	50,680	MC
Chapman Univ	CA	65,504	HC
Chestnut Hill College	PA	47,180	C
Christopher Newport Univ	VA	24,878	VC+
CUNY/Brooklyn College	NY	7,163	C+
CUNY/City College	NY	20,204	C
CUNY/Hunter College	NY	31,098	VC
CUNY/Lehman College	NY	5,788	LC
CUNY/Queens College	NY	21,507	C
CUNY/York College	NY	6,747	LC
Claremont McKenna College	CA	69,900	MC
Clark Univ	MA	53,260	HC+
Clemson Univ	SC		HC
Cleveland State Univ	OH	22,290	C
Coe College	IA	51,570	VC
Colgate Univ	NY	67,500	MC
College of Mount St. Vincent	NY	45,620	C
College of St. Benedict	MN	54,480	C
College of the Holy Cross	MA	64,320	MC
College of William & Mary	VA	34,907	MC
Colo State Univ	CO	23,033	C
Columbia College	SC	36,550	C
Columbia Univ/ School of General Studies	NY	61,470	MC
Columbia Univ/City of New York	NY	62,958	MC
Concordia College - Moorhead	MN	46,418	C
Conn College	CT	65,000	MC
Converse College	SC	28,290	C
Cornell College	IA	49,900	VC
Cornell Univ	NY	67,591	MC
Covenant College	GA	44,590	HC
Daemen College	NY	40,336	C
Dartmouth College	NH	68,109	MC
Davidson College	NC	60,119	MC
Delaware State Univ	DE	19,376	LC
Denison Univ	OH	62,770	HC+
DePaul Univ	IL	52,807	VC
DePauw Univ	IN	58,688	VC
Dickinson College	PA	66,166	MC
Doane Univ	NE	41,340	VC
Dominican Univ	IL	42,472	C+
Drew Univ/College of Liberal Arts	NJ	53,608	VC
Drury Univ	MO	37,555	VC
Earlham College	IN	55,670	HC
East Carolina Univ	NC	16,539	C
Eastern Kentucky Univ	KY	17,742	C
Eastern Mich Univ	MI	19,761	C
Eastern Nazarene College	MA	41,114	C
Eastern Washington Univ	WA	17,896	LC
Eckerd College	FL	55,206	VC
Edgewood College	WI	35,950	C
Elizabethtown College	PA	56,340	VC
Elmhurst College	IL	46,514	C
Elon Univ	NC	46,142	HC
Emory Univ	GA	63,286	MC
Fairfield Univ	CT	61,445	HC
Fisk Univ	TN	32,066	LC
Florida Atlantic Univ	FL	18,256	C
Florida International Univ	FL	20,281	C
Florida State Univ	FL	16,771	HC
Fordham Univ	NY	68,431	MC
Fort Hays State Univ	KS	12,677	C
Franciscan Univ of Steubenville	OH	33,980	VC
Franklin and Marshall College	PA	67,960	MC
Franklin College	IN	40,550	C
Furman Univ	SC	61,098	VC+
Gardner-Webb Univ	NC	24,935	C+
George Mason Univ	VA	19,884	C
Georgetown College	KY	41,440	C
Georgetown Univ	DC	68,970	MC
Georgia State Univ	GA	25,250	C
Gettysburg College	PA	65,210	MC
Gonzaga Univ	WA	52,880	HC
Gordon College	MA	47,740	VC
Goucher College	MD	56,110	VC
Grace College and Seminary	IN	31,524	C
Grand Valley State Univ	MI	22,250	C+
Greensboro College	NC	39,790	LC
Grinnell College	IA	63,114	MC
Grove City College	PA	26,654	VC
Guilford College	NC	45,973	C
Gustavus Adolphus College	MN	53,943	HC
Hamilton College	NY	64,250	MC
Hamline Univ	MN	50,152	C
Hampden-Sydney College	VA	57,806	VC
Hanover College	IN	47,750	C+
Harding Univ	AR	25,440	C
Hartwick College	NY	51,270	C
Harvard College/Harvard Univ	MA	65,609	MC
Haverford College	PA	66,490	MC
Hendrix College	AR	54,020	VC
High Point Univ	NC	47,355	VC
Hillsdale College	MI	37,170	MC
Hiram College	OH	44,590	C
Hobart and William Smith Colleges	NY	67,050	HC+
Hofstra Univ	NY	58,210	C+
Hollins Univ	VA	49,635	VC
Hood College	MD	50,540	C
Hope College	MI	42,840	VC
Houston Baptist Univ	TX	36,450	C
Howard Univ	DC	37,616	C+
Humboldt State Univ	CA	21,708	C
Idaho State Univ	ID	13,619	LC
Illinois College	IL	41,330	VC
Illinois State Univ	IL	23,418	VC
Illinois Wesleyan Univ	IL	56,430	VC+
Indiana State Univ	IN	23,223	LC
Indiana Univ Bloomington	IN	20,791	HC
Indiana Univ Northwest	IN	7,207	LC
Indiana Univ South Bend	IN	16,057	C
Indiana Univ Southeast	IN	16,931	C
Indiana Univ-Purdue Univ Fort Wayne	IN	18,675	C
Indiana Univ-Purdue Univ Indianapolis	IN	18,952	C
Iona College	NY	52,514	C
Iowa State Univ	IA	18,176	C
Ithaca College	NY	58,158	VC+
Jacksonville Univ	FL	49,210	C
John Carroll Univ	OH	51,570	C
Johns Hopkins Univ	MD	68,080	MC
Johnson C. Smith Univ	NC	25,336	LC
Juniata College	PA	58,118	VC
Kalamazoo College	MI	53,931	HC
Keene State College	NH	24,604	C
Kenyon College	OH	65,840	MC
King Univ	TN	36,976	C
King's College	PA	48,240	C
Knox College	IL	54,654	VC+
Kutztown Univ of Pennsylvania	PA	19,477	C
Lafayette College	PA	68,520	MC
Lake Forest College	IL	50,652	VC
Lamar Univ	TX	18,014	LC
Lane College	TN	17,960	LC
Lawrence Univ	WI	56,133	HC+
Le Moyne College	NY	47,305	VC
Lebanon Valley College	PA	55,510	VC
Lee Univ	TN	22,045	C
Lehigh Univ	PA	63,860	MC
Lenoir-Rhyne Univ	NC	47,500	LC
Lincoln Univ	PA	20,878	LC
Lindenwood Univ	MO	25,760	C
Linfield College	OR	53,992	C
Lipscomb Univ	TN	42,984	VC
LIU Brooklyn	NY	50,698	C
LIU Post	NY	50,698	C+
Lock Haven Univ of Pennsylvania	PA	20,544	LC
Louisiana College	LA	21,274	C
Louisiana State Univ and A&M College	LA	18,677	VC
Louisiana Tech Univ	LA	11,422	VC
Loyola Marymount Univ	CA	60,202	VC+
Loyola Univ Chicago	IL	57,158	VC
Loyola Univ Maryland	MD	61,710	VC
Loyola Univ New Orleans	LA	52,456	VC
Luther College	IA	49,990	VC
Lycoming College	PA	50,895	C
Macalester College	MN	64,136	MC
Manchester Univ	IN	41,540	C
Manhattan College	NY	55,652	C
Manhattanville College	NY	52,430	C
Marist College	NY	49,860	VC
Marlboro College	VT	50,832	VC+
Marquette Univ	WI	53,090	VC+
Marshall Univ	WV	18,044	C
Marywood Univ	PA	47,840	C
McDaniel College	MD	52,910	VC
Mercer Univ	GA	45,348	VC
Methodist Univ	NC	58,130	C
Miami Univ	OH	27,190	HC+
Mich State Univ	MI	24,542	VC
Middle Tenn State Univ	TN	8,650	C
Middlebury College	VT	67,464	MC
Millersville Univ of Pennsylvania	PA	25,298	C
Mills College	CA	43,705	C
Minn State Univ, Mankato	MN	17,190	C
Minot State Univ	ND	13,285	C
Miss College	MS	25,850	C
Missouri Southern State Univ	MO	13,071	C
Missouri State Univ	MO	15,837	C+
Missouri Western State Univ	MO	17,822	LC
Monmouth College	IL	42,260	C
Montana State Univ-Northern	MT	11,370	NC
Montclair State Univ	NJ	26,912	C
Moravian College	PA	55,488	C
Morehouse College	GA	40,835	C
Mount Holyoke College	MA	56,746	MC
Mount St. Mary's Univ	MD	53,380	C
Mount St. Mary's Univ - Chalon Campus	CA	50,486	VC+
Muhlenberg College	PA	56,645	VC
Murray State Univ	KY	17,726	C+
Muskingum Univ	OH	35,966	C
Nazareth College	NY	46,784	C
Nebr Wesleyan Univ	NE	42,026	C+
New College of Florida	FL	16,180	HC+
New York Univ	NY	68,139	MC
Newberry College	SC	34,550	C
Niagara Univ	NY	41,010	C
Nicholls State Univ	LA	14,959	C
N Car A&T State Univ	NC	13,786	C
N Car Central Univ	NC	9,000	C
N Car State Univ	NC	22,434	HC+
North Central College	IL	48,712	C+
N Dak State Univ	ND	16,245	VC
North Park Univ	IL	35,860	C
Northeastern Illinois Univ	IL	12,529	LC
Northern Illinois Univ	IL	20,176	C
Northern Kentucky Univ	KY	16,486	C
Northern Mich Univ	MI	20,853	C
Northern State Univ	SD	15,570	C
Northwestern Univ	IL	68,725	MC
Oakland Univ	MI	20,763	C
Oakwood Univ	AL	43,758	C
Oberlin College	OH	68,942	MC
Occidental College	CA	68,660	MC
Oglethorpe Univ	GA	44,200	C
Ohio Northern Univ	OH	44,050	VC
Ohio State Univ at Columbus	OH	22,843	MC
Ohio Univ	OH	23,394	VC
Ohio Wesleyan Univ	OH	49,460	VC
Okla City Univ	OK	40,476	C
Okla State Univ	OK	17,180	C+
Old Dominion Univ	VA	21,618	C
Oral Roberts Univ	OK	34,316	C
Oregon State Univ	OR	23,337	VC
Otterbein Univ	OH	41,630	C
Pacific Lutheran Univ	WA	49,960	C
Pacific Union College	CA	36,009	VC
Pennsylvania State Univ - Univ Park	PA	29,716	HC
Pepperdine Univ	CA	66,862	VC+
Pitzer College	CA	68,500	HC+
Plymouth State Univ	NH	23,180	LC
Point Loma Nazarene Univ	CA	46,150	C+
Pomona College	CA	64,957	MC
Portland State Univ	OR	19,443	C
Presbyterian College	SC	47,186	C
Princeton Univ	NJ	60,090	MC
Principia College	IL	40,350	C
Providence College	RI	62,870	HC
Purdue Univ Northwest	IN	15,178	C
Purdue Univ/West Lafayette	IN	20,032	MC
Queens Univ of Charlotte	NC	39,543	C
Randolph College	VA	53,970	C
Randolph-Macon College	VA	51,480	VC
Regis Univ	CO	46,380	C
Rhode Island College	RI	19,000	LC
Rhodes College	TN	51,900	HC
Rider Univ	NJ	54,050	C
Roanoke College	VA	55,952	VC
Rockford Univ	IL	38,570	C
Rockhurst Univ	MO	28,990	C
Rollins College	FL	58,670	HC
Roosevelt Univ	IL	41,890	VC
Rosemont College	PA	30,980	LC
Rutgers Univ - Camden	NJ	26,595	C
Saginaw Valley State Univ	MI	19,284	C
St. Anselm College	NH	56,636	VC
St. Augustine's Univ	NC	25,582	C
St. Francis Univ	PA	46,146	NC
St. John's Univ	MN	53,472	C
St. Joseph's Univ	PA	58,540	VC
St. Louis Univ	MO	49,866	HC
St. Mary's College of Calif	CA	57,420	C
St. Michael's College	VT	53,275	VC+
St. Vincent College	PA	46,229	C
St. Xavier Univ	IL	44,440	C
Salem College	NC	40,206	C
Salisbury Univ	MD	21,132	VC
Salve Regina Univ	RI	53,046	VC
Sam Houston State Univ	TX	18,792	C
Samford Univ	AL	40,770	VC
San Diego State Univ	CA	23,156	VC
San Francisco State Univ	CA	18,514	LC
San Jose State Univ	CA	22,630	C
Sarah Lawrence College	NY	68,866	MC
Seattle Pacific Univ	WA	47,439	C+
Seattle Univ	WA	54,957	VC
Seton Hall Univ	NJ	58,008	C
Sewanee: The Univ of the South	TN	58,000	HC+
Shippensburg Univ of Pennsylvania	PA	24,096	C
Shorter Univ	GA	31,130	LC
Siena College	NY	48,916	C
Simmons College	MA	54,400	HC
Simpson College	IA	45,626	VC
Skidmore College	NY	66,600	MC
Slippery Rock Univ of Pennsylvania	PA	20,450	C
Smith College	MA	66,774	MC
Sonoma State Univ	CA	27,020	C
S Car State Univ	SC	21,330	LC
Southern Conn State Univ	CT	21,924	LC
Southern Illinois Univ Edwardsville	IL	20,188	C
Southern Methodist Univ	TX	69,008	MC
Southern Univ and A&M College	LA	16,074	LC
Southwestern Univ	TX	52,370	VC
Spelman College	GA	41,642	C
St. Catherine Univ	MN	45,630	C
St. Edward's Univ	TX	56,190	VC
St. John Fisher College	NY	45,270	VC
St. John's Univ	NY	57,160	C+
St. Mary's Univ	TX	39,120	C
St. Norbert College	WI	46,060	VC
St. Olaf College	MN	56,430	HC
Stanford Univ	CA	62,541	MC
SUNY at Binghamton	NY	24,100	MC
SUNY at Geneseo	NY	21,622	VC
SUNY at New Paltz	NY	20,840	C
SUNY at Oswego	NY	22,219	VC
SUNY/Buffalo State	NY	20,583	LC
SUNY/Fredonia	NY	20,818	C
SUNY/Oneonta	NY	20,794	C
SUNY/Plattsburgh	NY	19,314	C
SUNY/Potsdam	NY	21,051	VC

ST = STATE **$IS** = IN-STATE COSTS **SR** = SELECTOR RATING

School	ST	$IS	SR
SUNY/Univ at Buffalo	NY	23,122	C
Stephen F. Austin State Univ	TX	18,484	LC
Stetson Univ	FL	57,174	VC+
Stonehill College	MA	55,130	C
Suffolk Univ	MA	52,316	C
Susquehanna Univ	PA	57,560	VC
Swarthmore College	PA	63,550	MC
Temple Univ	PA	24,392	C+
Tenn Tech Univ	TN	17,929	C
Texas A&M Univ at College Station	TX	20,771	VC+
Texas A&M Univ at Commerce	TX	10,496	C
Texas State Univ	TX	18,721	C
Texas Tech Univ	TX	20,156	C+
The American Univ	DC	61,317	HC
The Catholic Univ of America	DC	58,376	VC
The Citadel, The Military College of S Car	SC	20,679	C
The College at Brockport - SUNY	NY	21,058	C
The College of New Rochelle	NY	46,300	LC
The College of Wooster	OH	60,000	HC
The George Washington Univ	DC	68,474	HC+
The Univ of Akron	OH	22,566	C
The Univ of Alabama	AL	24,320	C+
The Univ of Arizona	AZ	24,086	C
The Univ of Tenn at Chattanooga	TN	17,340	C+
The Univ of Tenn at Knoxville	TN	22,112	VC
The Univ of Tenn at Martin	TN	15,212	C
The Univ of Texas at Austin	TX	20,206	MC
The Univ of Utah	UT	18,751	VC
The Univ of Virginia's College at Wise	VA	18,192	LC
Thomas Edison State Univ	NJ	6,350	NC
Towson Univ	MD	21,878	C
Transylvania Univ	KY	47,450	HC+
Trinity College	CT	69,020	HC
Trinity Univ	TX	54,480	MC
Truman State Univ	MO	16,286	MC
Tufts Univ	MA		MC
Tulane Univ	LA	67,496	MC
Union College	NE	23,270	C
Union Univ	TN	41,160	VC
Univ of Arkansas at Fayetteville	AR	19,766	VC
Univ of Arkansas at Little Rock	AR	18,211	LC
Univ of Calif at Berkeley	CA	29,886	MC
Univ of Calif at Davis	CA	28,468	HC
Univ of Calif at Irvine	CA	33,857	VC
Univ of Calif at Los Angeles	CA	27,438	HC+
Univ of Calif at Riverside	CA	32,912	C
Univ of Calif at Santa Barbara	CA	30,627	HC+
Univ of Central Arkansas	AR	15,042	VC
Univ of Central Florida	FL	16,379	VC
Univ of Central Missouri	MO	18,982	C
Univ of Central Okla	OK	15,150	C
Univ of Cincinnati	OH	22,118	VC
Univ of Colo Boulder	CO	26,048	HC
Univ of Colo Denver	CO	22,238	C
Univ of Conn	CT	27,394	
Univ of Dallas	TX	50,676	VC
Univ of Dayton	OH	54,930	VC
Univ of Denver	CO	61,129	VC+
Univ of Evansville	IN	44,186	C+
Univ of Florida	FL	16,291	HC+
Univ of Georgia	GA	21,878	HC
Univ of Hawaii at Manoa	HI	23,261	C
Univ of Houston	TX	21,871	VC
Univ of Idaho	ID	16,158	C
Univ of Illinois at Chicago	IL	24,664	VC
Univ of Illinois at Urbana-Champaign	IL	27,006	HC
Univ of Indianapolis	IN	36,480	VC
Univ of Iowa	IA	19,415	HC
Univ of Jamestown	ND	28,508	C
Univ of Kansas	KS	20,884	VC
Univ of Kentucky	KY	24,800	C+
Univ of La Verne	CA	55,600	C
Univ of Louisiana at Lafayette	LA	14,516	C
Univ of Louisville	KY	19,692	C
Univ of Lynchburg	VA	48,370	C
Univ of Maine	ME	21,038	VC
Univ of Maine at Fort Kent	ME	15,165	LC
Univ of Mary Washington	VA	23,039	C+
Univ of Maryland/Baltimore County	MD	23,004	VC
Univ of Maryland/College Park	MD	21,938	HC
Univ of Mass Boston	MA	13,828	C
Univ of Mass Dartmouth	MA	26,507	C
Univ of Miami	FL	63,494	MC
Univ of Mich/Ann Arbor	MI	25,274	MC
Univ of Mich/Flint	MI	19,062	C
Univ of Minn/Morris	MN	21,222	VC
Univ of Minn/Twin Cities	MN	24,269	MC
Univ of Miss	MS	18,802	C
Univ of Missouri-Columbia	MO	20,463	VC
Univ of Missouri-Kansas City	MO	19,563	VC
Univ of Missouri-St. Louis	MO	19,810	VC
Univ of Montana	MT	14,105	C
Univ of Montevallo	AL	20,012	C
Univ of Mount Union	OH	39,990	C
Univ of Nebr - Kearney	NE	17,014	LC
Univ of Nebr - Lincoln	NE	18,589	VC
Univ of Nebr - Omaha	NE	16,120	C
Univ of Nevada, Las Vegas	NV	17,553	C
Univ of Nevada, Reno	NV	18,010	C
Univ of New Hampshire	NH	29,333	VC
Univ of New Mexico	NM	16,808	C
Univ of New Orleans	LA	12,840	C
Univ of North Alabama	AL	15,964	C
Univ of N Car at Asheville	NC	16,251	VC+
Univ of N Car at Charlotte	NC	17,803	VC
Univ of N Car at Greensboro	NC	15,998	C
Univ of N Car Wilmington	NC	16,784	VC
Univ of N Dak	ND	16,673	C
Univ of North Georgia	GA	17,316	C
Univ of North Texas	TX	20,082	C
Univ of Northern Colo	CO	19,658	C
Univ of Notre Dame	IN	68,801	MC
Univ of Oregon	OR	24,021	VC
Univ of Pennsylvania	PA	63,526	MC
Univ of Pittsburgh	PA	30,030	MC
Univ of PR, at Mayaguez	PR	13,995	
Univ of Puget Sound	WA	60,210	HC
Univ of Redlands	CA	61,934	VC
Univ of Rhode Island	RI	26,066	VC
Univ of Richmond	VA	62,730	MC
Univ of Rochester	NY	65,032	MC
Univ of San Diego	CA	60,338	HC
Univ of San Francisco	CA	60,580	C
Univ of Scranton	PA	54,962	VC
Univ of S Car at Columbia	SC	21,726	VC
Univ of South Florida/Tampa	FL	16,110	VC
Univ of Southern Calif	CA	66,631	MC
Univ of Southern Indiana	IN	16,808	C
Univ of Southern Maine	ME	18,320	C
Univ of St. Thomas - Houston	TX	41,510	VC
Univ of Texas at Arlington	TX	18,876	C
Univ of Texas at El Paso	TX	34,452	NC
Univ of Texas Rio Grande Valley	TX	15,573	LC
Univ of the District of Columbia	DC	21,260	LC
Univ of the Pacific	CA	57,446	VC
Univ of Toledo	OH	19,336	C
Univ of Tulsa	OK	52,625	HC
Univ of Vermont	VT	29,792	HC
Univ of Virginia	VA	27,367	MC
Univ of Washington	WA	23,091	MC
Univ of Wisc-Eau Claire	WI	16,354	VC
Univ of Wisc-Green Bay	WI	15,184	C
Univ of Wisc-La Crosse	WI	15,425	VC
Univ of Wisc-Madison	WI	21,647	MC
Univ of Wisc-Milwaukee	WI	21,538	C
Univ of Wisc-Oshkosh	WI	15,392	C
Univ of Wisc-Stevens Point	WI	14,043	C
Univ of Wisc-Whitewater	WI	13,976	C
Univ of Wyoming	WY	15,537	C
Ursinus College	PA	62,920	VC
Utah State Univ	UT	13,235	C
Valparaiso Univ	IN	50,160	VC
Vanderbilt Univ	TN	63,248	MC
Villanova Univ	PA	64,922	MC
Virginia Polytechnic Inst and State Univ	VA	21,920	VC
Virginia Wesleyan Univ	VA	45,980	LC
Wabash College	IN	52,100	VC
Wake Forest Univ	NC	69,354	MC
Walla Walla Univ	WA	34,845	C
Walsh Univ	OH	39,010	C
Washburn Univ	KS	15,827	C
Washington & Jefferson College	PA	58,694	VC
Washington and Lee Univ	VA	59,647	MC
Washington College	MD	56,154	VC
Washington State Univ	WA	22,747	C
Washington Univ in St. Louis	MO	67,539	MC
Weber State Univ	UT	14,112	C
Webster Univ	MO	37,490	C
Wellesley College	MA	66,984	MC
Wesleyan College	GA	31,940	C+
West Chester Univ of Pennsylvania	PA	19,171	VC
Western Carolina Univ	NC	13,965	C
Western Kentucky Univ	KY	16,850	C
Western Mich Univ	MI	21,791	C
Western Washington Univ	WA	18,904	VC
Westminster College	MO	32,820	C
Westminster College	PA	41,722	C
Westmont College	CA	57,930	VC
Wheaton College	IL	44,993	MC
Wheeling Jesuit Univ	WV	37,106	LC
Whitman College	WA	59,772	MC
Whittier College	CA	57,891	C
Whitworth Univ	WA	53,682	VC
Wichita State Univ	KS	17,773	C
Widener Univ	PA	58,190	C
Willamette Univ	OR	62,514	VC+
William Jewell College	MO	42,490	C+
Williams College	MA	67,700	MC
Wilson College	PA	35,620	LC
Winthrop Univ	SC	23,960	C
Wittenberg Univ	OH	49,863	VC
Wofford College	SC	49,885	VC
Wright State Univ	OH	16,983	C
Xavier Univ	OH	49,380	VC
Xavier Univ of Louisiana	LA	31,689	C
Yale Univ	CT	64,650	MC
Yeshiva Univ	NY	52,750	VC

FRENCH AND FRANCOPHONE STUDIES

School	ST	$IS	SR
Bates College	ME	64,500	HC
Brown Univ	RI	64,566	MC
Cal State, Long Beach	CA	18,850	C
Creighton Univ	NE	49,452	VC
Kent State Univ	OH	20,928	C
Linfield College	OR	53,992	C
Moravian College	PA	55,488	C
Rhode Island College	RI	19,000	LC
Syracuse Univ	NY	62,313	HC
Univ of Illinois at Chicago	IL	24,664	VC
Univ of Mich/Dearborn	MI	12,472	VC
Vassar College	NY	68,110	MC
Wellesley College	MA	66,984	MC

FRENCH LANGUAGE AND LITERATURE

School	ST	$IS	SR
Brown Univ	RI	64,566	MC
Bryant Univ	RI	57,204	VC
Merrimack College	MA	55,415	C
Messiah College	PA	44,380	VC
Rutgers Univ - New Brunswick	NJ	27,090	HC
Southern Illinois Univ Carbondale	IL	24,554	C
Stony Brook Univ/The SUNY	NY	22,703	MC
Texas Christian Univ	TX	57,120	HC
Univ of Okla	OK	19,651	HC

FRENCH STUDIES

School	ST	$IS	SR
Appalachian State Univ	NC	15,394	VC
Aquinas College - Mich	MI	38,876	VC
Bard College	NY	65,924	HC
Bard College at Simon's Rock	MA	65,795	MC
Boston Univ	MA	67,352	MC
Bradley Univ	IL	43,240	VC
Brown Univ	RI	64,566	MC
Cal State, Chico	CA	19,790	VC
Cal State, Fresno	CA	16,902	LC
Cal State, Fullerton	CA	21,902	C
Cal State, Northridge	CA	17,277	LC
Case Western Reserve Univ	OH	62,284	MC
Coe College	IA	51,570	VC
Colby College	ME	64,060	MC
College of Charleston	SC	24,046	VC
Colo College	CO	64,894	MC
Columbia Univ/ School of General Studies	NY	61,470	MC
Dartmouth College	NH	68,109	MC
Duke Univ	NC	68,298	MC
Emory Univ	GA	63,286	MC
Fairleigh Dickinson Univ/ College at Florham	NJ	54,770	C
Fordham Univ	NY	68,431	MC
Lake Erie College	OH	38,914	LC
Lake Superior State Univ	MI	19,867	C
Lebanon Valley College	PA	55,510	VC
Lewis & Clark College	OR	60,984	MC
Mills College	CA	43,705	C
New College of Florida	FL	16,180	HC+
New York Univ	NY	68,139	MC
North Park Univ	IL	35,860	C
Northeastern Illinois Univ	IL	12,529	LC
Ohio State Univ at Columbus	OH	22,843	MC
Otterbein Univ	OH	41,630	C
Purdue Univ/West Lafayette	IN	20,032	MC
Reed College	OR	65,300	MC
Rice Univ	TX	59,458	MC
St. Joseph's Univ	PA	58,540	VC
St. Louis Univ	MO	49,866	HC
Scripps College	CA	69,260	HC
Skidmore College	NY	66,600	MC
Smith College	MA	66,774	MC
S Dak State Univ	SD	15,874	C
St. Lawrence Univ	NY	66,646	HC+
SUNY at Oswego	NY	22,219	VC
SUNY/Plattsburgh	NY	19,314	C
SUNY/Potsdam	NY	21,051	VC
Stony Brook Univ/The SUNY	NY	22,703	MC
The American Univ	DC	61,317	HC
The Catholic Univ of America	DC	58,376	VC
Union College	NY	64,320	MC
Univ of Calif at Los Angeles	CA	27,438	HC+
Univ of Calif San Diego	CA	30,450	MC
Univ of Illinois at Chicago	IL	24,664	VC
Univ of Mass Amherst	MA	27,669	HC
Univ of New Hampshire	NH	29,333	VC
Univ of North Florida	FL	15,996	VC
Univ of Portland	OR	52,152	VC
Univ of S Dak	SD	16,109	C
Univ of Texas Rio Grande Valley	TX	15,573	LC
Univ of Wisc-Green Bay	WI	15,184	C
Wellesley College	MA	66,984	MC
Wesleyan Univ	CT	66,940	MC
West Chester Univ of Pennsylvania	PA	19,171	VC
Wheaton College	MA	63,818	VC

FRENCH STUDIES K-12 EDUCATION

School	ST	$IS	SR
Augustana College	IL	51,222	VC+
Carroll College	MT	44,304	C
Colo State Univ	CO	23,033	C
Edgewood College	WI	35,950	C
Grove City College	PA	26,654	VC
Indiana Univ South Bend	IN	16,057	C
Missouri Western State Univ	MO	17,822	LC
Old Dominion Univ	VA	21,618	C
The Univ of Utah	UT	18,751	VC

FUNERAL HOME SERVICES

School	ST	$IS	SR
Gannon Univ	PA	42,922	C
Mount Ida College	MA	46,820	C
Point Park Univ	PA	41,270	C
Southern Illinois Univ Carbondale	IL	24,554	C
Univ of Central Okla	OK	15,150	C
Wayne State Univ	MI	23,085	C

FURNITURE DESIGN

School	ST	$IS	SR
Calif College of the Arts	CA	52,758	SP
Cal State, Fresno	CA	16,902	LC
Minneapolis College of Art and Design	MN	44,218	SP
N Car State Univ	NC	22,434	HC+
Northern Mich Univ	MI	20,853	C
Rhode Island School of Design	RI	59,960	SP
Rochester Inst of Technology	NY	52,734	HC+
Savannah College of Art and Design	GA	49,595	SP

GAME ART

School	ST	$IS	SR
Champlain College	VT	54,724	VC
Ringling College of Art and Design	FL	59,160	SP
Shepherd Univ	CA		LC
Woodbury Univ	CA	49,593	VC

GAME DESIGN AND DEVELOPMENT

School	ST	$IS	SR
Arkansas Tech Univ	AR	16,534	LC
Bloomfield College	NJ	40,100	LC
Bradley Univ	IL	43,240	VC
Cal State, Fullerton	CA	21,902	C
Champlain College	VT	54,724	VC
Cleveland Inst of Art	OH	51,455	SP
Columbia College Chicago	IL	40,104	C
DePaul Univ	IL	52,807	VC
Hofstra Univ	NY	58,210	C+
Indiana Univ Bloomington	IN	20,791	HC
Lawrence Tech Univ	MI	41,630	VC
LIU Post	NY	50,698	C+
Marist College	NY	49,860	VC
Maryville Univ of St. Louis	MO	38,558	VC
Missouri Western State Univ	MO	17,822	LC
Okla Christian Univ	OK	29,260	C
Rocky Mountain College of Art and Design	CO	27,052	SP
Sarah Lawrence College	NY	68,866	MC
Shepherd Univ	CA		LC
St. Edward's Univ	TX	56,190	VC
SUNY Polytechnic Inst	NY	20,438	VC
Univ of Texas at Dallas	TX	23,640	HC
Univ of Tulsa	OK	52,625	HC
Univ of Wisc-Stout	WI	19,667	C
William Peace Univ	NC	39,300	LC

GAME PROGRAMMING

School	ST	$IS	SR
Bloomfield College	NJ	40,100	LC
Champlain College	VT	54,724	VC
Columbia College Chicago	IL	40,104	C
DePaul Univ	IL	52,807	VC
Kansas City Art Inst	MO	48,200	SP
Loyola Univ New Orleans	LA	52,456	VC
New England College	NH	50,828	NC
Shepherd Univ	CA		LC
Univ of Tulsa	OK	52,625	HC

GENDER STUDIES

School	ST	$IS	SR
Albion College	MI	55,260	C
Bard College	NY	65,924	HC
Bard College at Simon's Rock	MA	65,795	MC
Beloit College	WI	55,206	HC
Bowdoin College	ME	65,980	MC
Brown Univ	RI	64,566	MC
Butler Univ	IN	52,890	VC+
Cabrini Univ	PA	42,591	LC
Calif State Polytechnic Univ, Pomona	CA	21,811	C
Cal State, Chico	CA	19,790	VC
Cal State, Fullerton	CA	21,902	C
CUNY/John Jay College of Criminal Justice	NY	6,359	SP
Coe College	IA	51,570	VC
College of St. Benedict	MN	54,480	C
College of William & Mary	VA	34,907	MC
Colo College	CO	64,894	MC

ST = STATE **$IS** = IN-STATE COSTS **SR** = SELECTOR RATING

School	ST	$IS	SR
Conn College	CT	65,000	MC
Cornell College	IA	49,900	VC
Davidson College	NC	60,119	MC
DePauw Univ	IN	58,688	VC
Dominican Univ	IL	42,472	C+
Eastern Mich Univ	MI	19,761	C
Eugene Lang College of Liberal Arts	NY	64,940	VC
Fort Lewis College	CO	20,154	C
Gettysburg College	PA	65,210	MC
Grinnell College	IA	63,114	MC
Hanover College	IN	47,750	C+
Hollins Univ	VA	49,635	VC
Indiana Univ Bloomington	IN	20,791	HC
John Carroll Univ	OH	51,570	C
Kutztown Univ of Pennsylvania	PA	19,477	C
Lawrence Univ	WI	56,133	HC+
McNeese State Univ	LA	7,838	C
Mercer Univ	GA	45,348	VC
Merrimack College	MA	55,415	C
Missouri Baptist Univ	MO	35,594	C
Montclair State Univ	NJ	26,912	C
Mount Holyoke College	MA	56,746	MC
New College of Florida	FL	16,180	HC+
New York Univ	NY	68,139	MC
Northeastern Illinois Univ	IL	12,529	LC
Northern Mich Univ	MI	20,853	C
Northwestern Univ	IL	68,725	MC
Oberlin College	OH	68,942	MC
Ohio Univ	OH	23,394	VC
Prescott College	AZ	38,201	C
Regis Univ	CO	46,380	C
St. John's Univ	MN	53,472	C
St. Michael's College	VT	53,275	VC+
San Diego State Univ	CA	23,156	VC
Seton Hill Univ	PA	46,972	VC
Skidmore College	NY	66,600	MC
Sonoma State Univ	CA	27,020	C
Southern Oregon Univ	OR	19,117	C
St. Ambrose Univ	IA	40,180	C
SUNY/Plattsburgh	NY	19,314	C
Stonehill College	MA	55,130	C
Swarthmore College	PA	63,550	MC
The American Univ	DC	61,317	HC
The Univ of Arizona	AZ	24,086	C
The Univ of Utah	UT	18,751	VC
Tulane Univ	LA	67,496	MC
Univ of Calif San Diego	CA	30,450	MC
Univ of Chicago	IL	70,551	MC
Univ of Dayton	OH	54,930	VC
Univ of Illinois at Chicago	IL	24,664	VC
Univ of Iowa	IA	19,415	HC
Univ of Kansas	KS	20,884	VC
Univ of Maryland/Baltimore County	MD	23,004	VC
Univ of Mass Amherst	MA	27,669	HC
Univ of Miami	FL	63,494	MC
Univ of Minn/Twin Cities	MN	24,269	MC
Univ of Notre Dame	IN	68,801	MC
Univ of Pennsylvania	PA	63,526	MC
Univ of Rhode Island	RI	26,066	VC
Univ of Vermont	VT	29,792	HC
Univ of Wisc-Green Bay	WI	15,184	C
Univ of Wisc-Madison	WI	21,647	MC
Villanova Univ	PA	64,922	MC
Wellesley College	MA	66,984	MC
Wesleyan Univ	CT	66,940	MC
West Virginia Univ	WV	18,952	VC
West Virginia Wesleyan College	WV	39,188	C
Western Mich Univ	MI	21,791	C
Westminster College	UT	41,078	C
Whitman College	WA	59,772	MC
Widener Univ	PA	58,190	C
Wofford College	SC	49,885	VC
Xavier Univ	OH	49,380	VC

GENERAL ART STUDIO

School	ST	$IS	SR
Lewis Univ	IL	41,710	C
Missouri Western State Univ	MO	17,822	LC
Texas State Univ	TX	18,721	C

GENERAL STUDIES

School	ST	$IS	SR
Anderson Univ	IN	39,450	C
Aquinas College - Mich	MI	38,876	VC
Arizona State Univ at the Downtown Phoenix Campus	AZ	24,634	VC
Arizona State Univ at the Tempe Campus	AZ	23,001	VC
Arkansas State Univ	AR	16,190	C
Austin Peay State Univ	TN	16,397	C
Black Hills State Univ	SD	16,622	C
Columbia College Chicago	IL	40,104	C
Drury Univ	MO	37,555	VC
East Central Univ	OK	13,330	C
East Texas Baptist Univ	TX	34,444	C
Eastern Illinois Univ	IL	21,414	C
Fontbonne Univ	MO	34,606	C
Goodwin College	CT	28,370	LC
Houghton College	NY	40,558	VC
Indiana Univ Bloomington	IN	20,791	HC
Indiana Univ East	IN	7,207	C
Indiana Univ Kokomo	IN	7,207	C
Indiana Univ Northwest	IN	7,207	LC
Indiana Univ of Pennsylvania	PA	24,474	C
Indiana Univ South Bend	IN	16,057	C
Indiana Univ Southeast	IN	16,931	C
Indiana Univ-Purdue Univ Indianapolis	IN	18,952	C
Kent State Univ	OH	20,928	C
King Univ	TN	36,976	C
Kutztown Univ of Pennsylvania	PA	19,477	C
Lake Superior State Univ	MI	19,867	C
Louisiana College	LA	21,274	C
Millersville Univ of Pennsylvania	PA	25,298	C
Minn State Univ, Mankato	MN	17,190	C
Missouri Southern State Univ	MO	13,071	C
Mount St. Joseph Univ	OH	33,880	LC
New York Univ	NY	68,139	MC
Nova Southeastern Univ	FL	38,534	C+
Olivet Nazarene Univ	IL	41,840	VC
Rowan Univ	NJ	24,491	VC
St. Louis Univ	MO	49,866	HC
Southeast Missouri State Univ	MO	16,148	C
Tabor College	KS	35,870	C
Texas Christian Univ	TX	57,120	HC
Texas State Univ	TX	18,721	C
Texas Tech Univ	TX	20,156	C+
The Univ of Arizona	AZ	24,086	C
Univ of Central Okla	OK	15,150	C
Univ of Dayton	OH	54,930	VC
Univ of Idaho	ID	16,158	C
Univ of Maine at Machias	ME	22,960	C
Univ of Mich/Dearborn	MI	12,472	VC
Univ of Nevada, Reno	NV	18,010	C
Univ of Texas Rio Grande Valley	TX	15,573	LC
West Virginia Univ	WV	18,952	VC
Western Illinois Univ	IL	20,897	C
Western Kentucky Univ	KY	16,850	C
Western Mich Univ	MI	21,791	C
Wichita State Univ	KS	17,773	C
Youngstown State Univ	OH	17,487	C

GENETICS

School	ST	$IS	SR
Cal State, Fullerton	CA	21,902	C
Cal State, Northridge	CA	17,277	LC
Cedar Crest College	PA	51,110	C
Dartmouth College	NH	68,109	MC
Florida State Univ	FL	16,771	HC
Howard Univ	DC	37,616	C+
Iowa State Univ	IA	18,176	C
Missouri Western State Univ	MO	17,822	LC
New Mexico State Univ	NM	14,050	LC
Northern Mich Univ	MI	20,853	C
Northwestern College of Iowa	IA	38,400	C
Ohio Wesleyan Univ	OH	49,460	VC
Purdue Univ/West Lafayette	IN	20,032	MC
Rutgers Univ - New Brunswick	NJ	27,090	HC
Southern Illinois Univ Edwardsville	IL	20,188	C
SUNY/Fredonia	NY	20,818	C
Texas A&M Univ at College Station	TX	20,771	VC+
The Univ of Arizona	AZ	24,086	C
Univ of Calif at Davis	CA	28,468	HC
Univ of Calif at Irvine	CA	33,857	VC
Univ of Calif at Riverside	CA	32,912	C
Univ of Conn	CT	27,394	
Univ of Georgia	GA	21,878	HC
Univ of Minn/Twin Cities	MN	24,269	MC
Univ of New Hampshire	NH	29,333	VC
Univ of Vermont	VT	29,792	HC
Univ of Wisc-Madison	WI	21,647	MC
Washington State Univ	WA	22,747	C
West Virginia Univ	WV	18,952	VC
Western Kentucky Univ	KY	16,850	C

GEOCHEMISTRY

School	ST	$IS	SR
Bridgewater State Univ	MA	22,762	C
Brown Univ	RI	64,566	MC
Calif Inst of Technology	CA	64,704	MC
Cal State, Fullerton	CA	21,902	C
Columbia Univ/City of New York	NY	62,958	MC
Grand Valley State Univ	MI	22,250	C+
SUNY at Geneseo	NY	21,622	VC
SUNY at Oswego	NY	22,219	VC
SUNY/Cortland	NY	20,910	C
SUNY/Fredonia	NY	20,818	C
Washington Univ in St. Louis	MO	67,539	MC
Western Mich Univ	MI	21,791	C

GEODETIC SCIENCE

School	ST	$IS	SR
Univ of Arkansas at Monticello	AR	13,599	LC

GEOENVIRONMENTAL STUDIES

School	ST	$IS	SR
Northeastern Illinois Univ	IL	12,529	LC
Shippensburg Univ of Pennsylvania	PA	24,096	C
Univ of Illinois at Chicago	IL	24,664	VC
Univ of N Car at Pembroke	NC	14,737	LC
West Chester Univ of Pennsylvania	PA	19,171	VC

GEOGRAPHY

School	ST	$IS	SR
Adams State Univ	CO	15,420	LC
Appalachian State Univ	NC	15,394	VC
Aquinas College - Mich	MI	38,876	VC
Arizona State Univ at the Tempe Campus	AZ	23,001	VC
Auburn Univ	AL	24,300	VC+
Augustana College	IL	51,222	VC+
Ball State Univ	IN	19,808	C+
Bard College at Simon's Rock	MA	65,795	MC
Bellevue Univ	NE	20,300	NC
Bemidji State Univ	MN	17,730	C
Boston Univ	MA	67,352	MC
Bowling Green State Univ	OH	19,975	C
Bridgewater State Univ	MA	22,762	C
Brigham Young Univ	UT	13,248	MC
Bucknell Univ	PA	67,136	MC
Calif State Polytechnic Univ, Pomona	CA	21,811	C
Cal State, Chico	CA	19,790	VC
Cal State, Dominguez Hills	CA	19,022	LC
Cal State, East Bay	CA	20,748	C
Cal State, Fresno	CA	16,902	LC
Cal State, Fullerton	CA	21,902	C
Cal State, Long Beach	CA	18,850	C
Cal State, Los Angeles	CA	17,186	LC
Cal State, Northridge	CA	17,277	LC
Cal State, Sacramento	CA	19,060	C
Cal State, San Bernardino	CA	20,106	C
Cal State, Stanislaus	CA	18,053	LC
Calif Univ of Pennsylvania	PA	20,425	LC
Calvin College	MI	43,090	HC
Carthage College	WI	48,835	C
Central Conn State Univ	CT	22,041	C
Central Mich Univ	MI	20,330	C
Central Washington Univ	WA	16,803	C
Charleston Southern Univ	SC	34,700	C
Cheyney Univ of Pennsylvania	PA	20,896	LC
Chicago State Univ	IL	41,620	C
CUNY/Hunter College	NY	31,098	VC
CUNY/Lehman College	NY	5,788	LC
Clark Univ	MA	53,260	HC+
Colgate Univ	NY	67,500	MC
College of Staten Island	NY	24,389	LC
Concord Univ	WV	14,954	LC
Concordia Univ Nebr	NE	41,900	VC
Concordia Univ, Chicago	IL	41,522	C
Dartmouth College	NH	68,109	MC
DePaul Univ	IL	52,807	VC
DePauw Univ	IN	58,688	VC
Dickinson State Univ	ND	12,372	LC
East Carolina Univ	NC	16,539	C
East Central Univ	OK	13,330	C
East Tenn State Univ	TN	18,141	C
Eastern Illinois Univ	IL	21,414	C
Eastern Kentucky Univ	KY	17,742	C
Eastern Mich Univ	MI	19,761	C
Eastern Washington Univ	WA	17,896	LC
Edinboro Univ	PA	15,940	LC
Elmhurst College	IL	46,514	C
Elon Univ	NC	46,142	HC
Emory and Henry College	VA	46,320	C
Excelsior College	NY	38,800	SP
Fayetteville State Univ	NC	17,756	C
Fitchburg State Univ	MA	21,819	LC
Florida Atlantic Univ	FL	18,256	C
Florida International Univ	FL	20,281	C
Florida State Univ	FL	16,771	HC
Framingham State Univ	MA	21,740	C
Frostburg State Univ	MD	17,280	LC
George Mason Univ	VA	19,884	C
Georgia College & State Univ	GA	21,884	C+
Georgia Southern Univ	GA	16,540	VC
Georgia State Univ	GA	25,250	C
Grand Valley State Univ	MI	22,250	C+
Gustavus Adolphus College	MN	53,943	HC
Hampshire College	MA	65,214	MC
Hofstra Univ	NY	58,210	C+
Howard Univ	DC	37,616	C+
Humboldt State Univ	CA	21,708	C
Illinois State Univ	IL	23,418	VC
Indiana State Univ	IN	23,223	LC
Indiana Univ Bloomington	IN	20,791	HC
Indiana Univ of Pennsylvania	PA	24,474	C
Indiana Univ-Purdue Univ Indianapolis	IN	18,952	C
Jacksonville State Univ	AL	14,628	LC
Jacksonville Univ	FL	49,210	C
James Madison Univ	VA	19,084	VC
Kansas State Univ	KS	17,780	VC
Keene State College	NH	24,604	C
Kennesaw State Univ	GA	18,899	VC
Kent State Univ	OH	20,928	C
Kutztown Univ of Pennsylvania	PA	19,477	C
LIU Post	NY	50,698	C+
Lock Haven Univ of Pennsylvania	PA	20,544	LC
Louisiana State Univ and A&M College	LA	18,677	VC
Louisiana Tech Univ	LA	11,422	VC
Macalester College	MN	64,136	MC
Marshall Univ	WV	18,044	C
Mayville State Univ	ND	18,371	NC
Miami Univ	OH	27,190	HC+
Mich State Univ	MI	24,542	VC
Middle Tenn State Univ	TN	8,650	C
Middlebury College	VT	67,464	MC
Millersville Univ of Pennsylvania	PA	25,298	C
Minn State Univ, Mankato	MN	17,190	C
Missouri State Univ	MO	15,837	C+
Montclair State Univ	NJ	26,912	C
Mount Holyoke College	MA	56,746	MC
New Jersey City Univ	NJ	21,456	LC
New Mexico State Univ	NM	14,050	LC
N Car Central Univ	NC	9,000	C
Northeastern Illinois Univ	IL	12,529	LC
Northeastern State Univ	OK	8,615	VC
Northern Arizona Univ	AZ	21,003	C
Northern Illinois Univ	IL	20,176	C
Northern Kentucky Univ	KY	16,486	C
Northern Mich Univ	MI	20,853	C
Northwest Missouri State Univ	MO	18,286	C
Northwestern State Univ of Louisiana	LA	16,534	LC
Northwestern Univ	IL	68,725	MC
Ohio State Univ at Columbus	OH	22,843	MC
Ohio Univ	OH	23,394	VC
Ohio Wesleyan Univ	OH	49,460	VC
Okla State Univ	OK	17,180	C+
Old Dominion Univ	VA	21,618	C
Olivet Nazarene Univ	IL	41,840	VC
Park Univ	MO	22,134	C
Pittsburg State Univ	KS	13,880	C
Plymouth State Univ	NH	23,180	LC
Portland State Univ	OR	19,443	C
Prairie View A&M Univ	TX	27,273	LC
Rhode Island College	RI	19,000	LC
Rowan Univ	NJ	24,491	VC
Rutgers Univ - New Brunswick	NJ	27,090	HC
Saginaw Valley State Univ	MI	19,284	C
Salem State Univ	MA	42,650	LC
Salisbury Univ	MD	21,132	VC
Sam Houston State Univ	TX	18,792	C
Samford Univ	AL	40,770	VC
San Diego State Univ	CA	23,156	VC
San Francisco State Univ	CA	18,514	LC
San Jose State Univ	CA	22,630	C
Shippensburg Univ of Pennsylvania	PA	24,096	C
Slippery Rock Univ of Pennsylvania	PA	20,450	C
Sonoma State Univ	CA	27,020	C
S Dak State Univ	SD	15,874	C
Southern Conn State Univ	CT	21,924	LC
Southern Illinois Univ Carbondale	IL	24,554	C
Southern Illinois Univ Edwardsville	IL	20,188	C
Southern Oregon Univ	OR	19,117	C
St. Cloud State Univ	MN	10,600	C
SUNY Albany	NY	22,165	C
SUNY at Binghamton	NY	24,100	MC
SUNY at Geneseo	NY	21,622	VC
SUNY at New Paltz	NY	20,840	C
SUNY/Buffalo State	NY	20,583	LC
SUNY/Cortland	NY	20,910	C
SUNY/Oneonta	NY	20,794	C
SUNY/Plattsburgh	NY	19,314	C
SUNY/Univ at Buffalo	NY	23,122	C
Stephen F. Austin State Univ	TX	18,484	LC
Syracuse Univ	NY	62,313	HC
Taylor Univ	IN	42,130	VC
Temple Univ	PA	24,392	C+
Texas A&M Univ at College Station	TX	20,771	VC+
Texas A&M Univ at Commerce	TX	10,496	C
Texas A&M Univ at Corpus Christi	TX	16,851	LC
Texas A&M Univ at Kingsville	TX	16,580	LC
Texas Christian Univ	TX	57,120	HC
Texas State Univ	TX	18,721	C
Texas Tech Univ	TX	20,156	C+
The Evergreen State College	WA	16,599	C
The George Washington Univ	DC	68,474	HC+
The Univ of Akron	OH	22,566	C
The Univ of Alabama	AL	24,320	C+
The Univ of Arizona	AZ	24,086	C
The Univ of Memphis	TN	18,278	C
The Univ of Tenn at Knoxville	TN	22,112	VC
The Univ of Tenn at Martin	TN	15,212	C
The Univ of Texas at Austin	TX	20,206	MC
The Univ of Texas at San Antonio	TX	21,060	C
The Univ of Utah	UT	18,751	VC
Towson Univ	MD	21,878	C
United States Air Force Academy	CO		C
United States Military Academy at West Point	NY		HC+
Univ of Alaska Fairbanks	AK	16,874	VC
Univ of Arkansas at Fayetteville	AR	19,766	VC
Univ of Calif at Berkeley	CA	29,886	MC
Univ of Calif at Davis	CA	28,468	HC
Univ of Calif at Los Angeles	CA	27,438	HC+
Univ of Calif at Santa Barbara	CA	30,627	HC+
Univ of Central Arkansas	AR	15,042	VC

ST = STATE $IS = IN-STATE COSTS SR = SELECTOR RATING

School	ST	$IS	SR
Univ of Central Missouri	MO	18,982	C
Univ of Central Okla	OK	15,150	C
Univ of Chicago	IL	70,551	MC
Univ of Cincinnati	OH	22,118	VC
Univ of Colo Boulder	CO	26,048	HC
Univ of Colo Colo Springs	CO	20,300	C
Univ of Colo Denver	CO	22,238	C
Univ of Conn	CT	27,394	
Univ of Delaware	DE	32,214	VC
Univ of Denver	CO	61,129	VC+
Univ of Florida	FL	16,291	HC+
Univ of Georgia	GA	21,878	HC
Univ of Hawaii at Hilo	HI	18,038	VC
Univ of Hawaii at Manoa	HI	23,261	C
Univ of Idaho	ID	16,158	C
Univ of Illinois at Urbana-Champaign	IL	27,006	HC
Univ of Iowa	IA	19,415	HC
Univ of Kansas	KS	20,884	VC
Univ of Kentucky	KY	24,800	C+
Univ of Louisville	KY	19,692	C
Univ of Maine at Farmington	ME	18,792	C
Univ of Mary Washington	VA	23,039	C+
Univ of Maryland/Baltimore County	MD	23,004	VC
Univ of Maryland/College Park	MD	21,938	HC
Univ of Mass Amherst	MA	27,669	HC
Univ of Mass Boston	MA	13,828	C
Univ of Miami	FL	63,494	MC
Univ of Mich/Flint	MI	19,062	C
Univ of Minn/Duluth	MN	20,292	C
Univ of Minn/Twin Cities	MN	24,269	MC
Univ of Missouri-Columbia	MO	20,463	VC
Univ of Missouri-Kansas City	MO	19,563	VC
Univ of Montana	MT	14,105	C
Univ of Nebr - Kearney	NE	17,014	LC
Univ of Nebr - Lincoln	NE	18,589	VC
Univ of Nebr - Omaha	NE	16,120	C
Univ of Nevada, Reno	NV	18,010	C
Univ of New Hampshire	NH	29,333	VC
Univ of New Mexico	NM	16,808	C
Univ of New Orleans	LA	12,840	C
Univ of North Alabama	AL	15,964	C
Univ of N Car at Chapel Hill	NC	20,561	MC
Univ of N Car at Charlotte	NC	17,803	VC
Univ of N Car at Greensboro	NC	15,998	C
Univ of N Car Wilmington	NC	16,784	VC
Univ of N Dak	ND	16,673	C
Univ of North Texas	TX	20,082	C
Univ of Northern Colo	CO	19,658	C
Univ of Northern Iowa	IA	17,480	C
Univ of Okla	OK	19,651	HC
Univ of Oregon	OR	24,021	VC
Univ of Pittsburgh at Johnstown	PA	22,092	C
Univ of PR-Rio Piedras campus	PR	13,327	
Univ of Richmond	VA	62,730	MC
Univ of South Alabama	AL	16,880	C
Univ of S Car at Columbia	SC	21,726	VC
Univ of South Florida/Tampa	FL	16,110	VC
Univ of Southern Calif	CA	66,631	MC
Univ of Southern Maine	ME	18,320	C
Univ of Southern Miss	MS	13,170	C
Univ of the District of Columbia	DC	21,260	LC
Univ of Toledo	OH	19,336	C
Univ of Vermont	VT	29,792	HC
Univ of Washington	WA	23,091	MC
Univ of West Georgia	GA	17,510	LC
Univ of Wisc-Eau Claire	WI	16,354	VC
Univ of Wisc-La Crosse	WI	15,425	VC
Univ of Wisc-Madison	WI	21,647	MC
Univ of Wisc-Milwaukee	WI	21,538	C
Univ of Wisc-Oshkosh	WI	15,392	C
Univ of Wisc-Parkside	WI	15,313	C
Univ of Wisc-Platteville	WI	14,148	C
Univ of Wisc-River Falls	WI	14,541	C
Univ of Wisc-Stevens Point	WI	14,043	C
Univ of Wisc-Whitewater	WI	13,976	C
Univ of Wyoming	WY	15,537	C
Utah State Univ	UT	13,235	C
Valparaiso Univ	IN	50,160	VC
Vassar College	NY	68,110	MC
Villanova Univ	PA	64,922	MC
Virginia Polytechnic Inst and State Univ	VA	21,920	VC
Wayne State College	NE	25,746	NC
Weber State Univ	UT	14,112	C
West Chester Univ of Pennsylvania	PA	19,171	VC
West Texas A&M Univ	TX	13,478	C
West Virginia Univ	WV	18,952	VC
Western Carolina Univ	NC	13,965	C
Western Illinois Univ	IL	20,897	C
Western Kentucky Univ	KY	16,850	C
Western Mich Univ	MI	21,791	C
Western Oregon Univ	OR	19,965	LC
Western Washington Univ	WA	18,904	VC
William Paterson Univ of New Jersey	NJ	24,022	C
Worcester State Univ	MA	20,977	C
Wright State Univ	OH	16,983	C
Youngstown State Univ	OH	17,487	C

GEOGRAPHY INFORMATION SCIENCE

School	ST	$IS	SR
Appalachian State Univ	NC	15,394	VC
Arizona State Univ at the Tempe Campus	AZ	23,001	VC
Auburn Univ at Montgomery	AL	15,000	C
Cal State, Fullerton	CA	21,902	C
Elmhurst College	IL	46,514	C
Elon Univ	NC	46,142	HC
Kennesaw State Univ	GA	18,899	VC
Murray State Univ	KY	17,726	C+
Northeastern Illinois Univ	IL	12,529	LC
Ohio State Univ at Columbus	OH	22,843	MC
Ohio Univ	OH	23,394	VC
Old Dominion Univ	VA	21,618	C
Pennsylvania State Univ - Univ Park	PA	29,716	HC
SUNY/Univ at Buffalo	NY	23,122	C
Texas State Univ	TX	18,721	C
Univ of Central Arkansas	AR	15,042	VC
Univ of N Car at Greensboro	NC	15,998	C
Univ of Northern Iowa	IA	17,480	C
Univ of Okla	OK	19,651	HC
Univ of Texas at Dallas	TX	23,640	HC

GEOLOGICAL ENGINEERING

School	ST	$IS	SR
Colo School of Mines	CO	29,319	MC
Mich Tech Univ	MI	25,551	VC+
Missouri Univ of Science and Technology	MO	18,655	HC
Montana Tech of the Univ of Montana	MT	15,447	VC
Olivet Nazarene Univ	IL	41,840	VC
Rutgers Univ - Newark	NJ	27,351	C
S Dak School of Mines and Technology	SD	18,570	C+
Texas A&M Univ at College Station	TX	20,771	VC+
The Univ of Akron	OH	22,566	C
The Univ of Utah	UT	18,751	VC
Univ of Alaska Fairbanks	AK	16,874	VC
Univ of Calif at Los Angeles	CA	27,438	HC+
Univ of Idaho	ID	16,158	C
Univ of Illinois at Urbana-Champaign	IL	27,006	HC
Univ of Mich/Ann Arbor	MI	25,274	MC
Univ of Minn/Twin Cities	MN	24,269	MC
Univ of Miss	MS	18,802	C
Univ of Nevada, Reno	NV	18,010	C
Univ of N Dak	ND	16,673	C
Univ of Rochester	NY	65,032	MC
Univ of Wisc-Madison	WI	21,647	MC

GEOLOGY

School	ST	$IS	SR
Adams State Univ	CO	15,420	LC
Albion College	MI	55,260	C
Alfred Univ	NY	37,490	C
Allegheny College	PA	57,620	VC
Amherst College	MA	66,186	MC
Appalachian State Univ	NC	15,394	VC
Arkansas Tech Univ	AR	16,534	LC
Ashland Univ	OH	30,446	C
Auburn Univ	AL	24,300	VC+
Augustana College	IL	51,222	VC+
Ball State Univ	IN	19,808	C+
Bates College	ME	64,500	HC
Baylor Univ	TX	56,803	HC
Beloit College	WI	55,206	HC
Bemidji State Univ	MN	17,730	C
Boise State Univ	ID	17,368	C
Boston College	MA	68,043	MC
Bowling Green State Univ	OH	19,975	C
Brigham Young Univ	UT	13,248	MC
Brown Univ	RI	64,566	MC
Bryn Mawr College	PA	65,220	MC
Bucknell Univ	PA	67,136	MC
Calif Inst of Technology	CA	64,704	MC
Calif Lutheran Univ	CA	52,853	C
Calif State Polytechnic Univ, Pomona	CA	21,811	C
Cal State, Bakersfield	CA	22,397	LC
Cal State, Chico	CA	19,790	VC
Cal State, Dominguez Hills	CA	19,022	LC
Cal State, East Bay	CA	20,748	C
Cal State, Fresno	CA	16,902	LC
Cal State, Fullerton	CA	21,902	C
Cal State, Long Beach	CA	18,850	C
Cal State, Los Angeles	CA	17,186	LC
Cal State, Northridge	CA	17,277	LC
Cal State, Sacramento	CA	19,060	C
Cal State, San Bernardino	CA	20,106	C
Cal State, Stanislaus	CA	18,053	LC
Calif Univ of Pennsylvania	PA	20,425	LC
Calvin College	MI	43,090	HC
Carleton College	MN	66,414	MC
Case Western Reserve Univ	OH	62,284	MC
Castleton Univ	VT	20,186	C
Cedarville Univ	OH	36,244	VC
Centenary College of Louisiana	LA	49,050	C+
Central Mich Univ	MI	20,330	C
Central Washington Univ	WA	16,803	C
Charleston Southern Univ	SC	34,700	C
CUNY/Brooklyn College	NY	7,163	C+
CUNY/City College	NY	20,204	C
CUNY/Lehman College	NY	5,788	LC
CUNY/Queens College	NY	21,507	C
CUNY/York College	NY	6,747	LC
Clarion Univ of Pennsylvania	PA	21,608	LC
Clemson Univ	SC		HC
Cleveland State Univ	OH	22,290	C
Colby College	ME	64,060	MC
Colgate Univ	NY	67,500	MC
College of Charleston	SC	24,046	VC
College of William & Mary	VA	34,907	MC
Colo College	CO	64,894	MC
Colo Mesa Univ	CO	19,707	LC
Colo State Univ	CO	23,033	C
Columbia Univ/City of New York	NY	62,958	MC
Cornell College	IA	49,900	VC
Denison Univ	OH	62,770	HC+
DePauw Univ	IN	58,688	VC
Duke Univ	NC	68,298	MC
Earlham College	IN	55,670	HC
East Carolina Univ	NC	16,539	C
Eastern Illinois Univ	IL	21,414	C
Eastern Kentucky Univ	KY	17,742	C
Eastern Mich Univ	MI	19,761	C
Eastern New Mexico Univ	NM	12,874	LC
Eastern Washington Univ	WA	17,896	LC
Edinboro Univ	PA	15,940	LC
Elizabeth City State Univ	NC	14,745	C
Excelsior College	NY	38,800	SP
Florida Atlantic Univ	FL	18,256	C
Florida International Univ	FL	20,281	C
Florida State Univ	FL	16,771	HC
Fort Hays State Univ	KS	12,677	C
Fort Lewis College	CO	20,154	C
Franklin and Marshall College	PA	67,960	MC
George Mason Univ	VA	19,884	C
Georgia Southern Univ	GA	16,540	VC
Georgia Southwestern State Univ	GA	13,870	LC
Georgia State Univ	GA	25,250	C
Grand Valley State Univ	MI	22,250	C+
Guilford College	NC	45,973	C
Gustavus Adolphus College	MN	53,943	HC
Hampshire College	MA	65,214	MC
Hanover College	IN	47,750	C+
Hardin-Simmons Univ	TX	36,025	C
Hartwick College	NY	51,270	C
Harvard College/Harvard Univ	MA	65,609	MC
Haverford College	PA	66,490	MC
Hofstra Univ	NY	58,210	C+
Hope College	MI	42,840	VC
Humboldt State Univ	CA	21,708	C
Idaho State Univ	ID	13,619	LC
Illinois State Univ	IL	23,418	VC
Indiana State Univ	IN	23,223	LC
Indiana Univ Northwest	IN	7,207	LC
Indiana Univ of Pennsylvania	PA	24,474	C
Indiana Univ-Purdue Univ Fort Wayne	IN	18,675	C
Indiana Univ-Purdue Univ Indianapolis	IN	18,952	C
Iowa State Univ	IA	18,176	C
James Madison Univ	VA	19,084	VC
Juniata College	PA	58,118	VC
Kansas State Univ	KS	17,780	VC
Kent State Univ	OH	20,928	C
Kutztown Univ of Pennsylvania	PA	19,477	C
Lafayette College	PA	68,520	MC
Lake Superior State Univ	MI	19,867	C
Lamar Univ	TX	18,014	LC
Lawrence Univ	WI	56,133	HC+
LIU Post	NY	50,698	C+
Lock Haven Univ of Pennsylvania	PA	20,544	LC
Louisiana State Univ and A&M College	LA	18,677	VC
Louisiana Tech Univ	LA	11,422	VC
Macalester College	MN	64,136	MC
Marietta College	OH	46,190	C
Marshall Univ	WV	18,044	C
Mercyhurst Univ	PA	47,420	C
Miami Univ	OH	27,190	HC+
Mich State Univ	MI	24,542	VC
Mich Tech Univ	MI	25,551	VC+
Middlebury College	VT	67,464	MC
Midwestern State Univ	TX	12,111	LC
Millersville Univ of Pennsylvania	PA	25,298	C
Millsaps College	MS	50,080	C+
Minot State Univ	ND	13,285	C
Missouri State Univ	MO	15,837	C+
Missouri Univ of Science and Technology	MO	18,655	HC
Moravian College	PA	55,488	C
Morehead State Univ	KY	18,386	LC
Mount Holyoke College	MA	56,746	MC
Muskingum Univ	OH	35,966	C
New Jersey City Univ	NJ	21,456	LC
New Mexico State Univ	NM	14,050	LC
N Car State Univ	NC	22,434	HC+
N Dak State Univ	ND	16,245	VC
Northern Arizona Univ	AZ	21,003	C
Northern Illinois Univ	IL	20,176	C
Northern Kentucky Univ	KY	16,486	C
Northland College	WI	41,103	C+
Northwest Missouri State Univ	MO	18,286	C
Northwestern Univ	IL	68,725	MC
Norwich Univ	VT	56,234	C
Oberlin College	OH	68,942	MC
Occidental College	CA	68,660	MC
Ohio State Univ at Columbus	OH	22,843	MC
Ohio Univ	OH	23,394	VC
Ohio Wesleyan Univ	OH	49,460	VC
Okla State Univ	OK	17,180	C+
Old Dominion Univ	VA	21,618	C
Olivet Nazarene Univ	IL	41,840	VC
Pomona College	CA	64,957	MC
Portland State Univ	OR	19,443	C
Purdue Univ/West Lafayette	IN	20,032	MC
Radford Univ	VA	19,758	C
Rensselaer Polytechnic Inst	NY	67,265	MC
Rice Univ	TX	59,458	MC
Rocky Mountain College	MT	35,776	C
Rutgers Univ - New Brunswick	NJ	27,090	HC
Rutgers Univ - Newark	NJ	27,351	C
St. Louis Univ	MO	49,866	HC
Salem State Univ	MA	42,650	LC
Sam Houston State Univ	TX	18,792	C
San Diego State Univ	CA	23,156	VC
San Francisco State Univ	CA	18,514	LC
San Jose State Univ	CA	22,630	C
Scripps College	CA	69,260	HC
Sewanee: The Univ of the South	TN	58,000	HC+
Shawnee State Univ	OH	16,998	C
Skidmore College	NY	66,600	MC
Slippery Rock Univ of Pennsylvania	PA	20,450	C
Smith College	MA	66,774	MC
Sonoma State Univ	CA	27,020	C
S Dak School of Mines and Technology	SD	18,570	C+
Southern Illinois Univ Carbondale	IL	24,554	C
Southern Methodist Univ	TX	69,008	MC
St. Cloud State Univ	MN	10,600	C
St. Lawrence Univ	NY	66,646	HC+
St. Norbert College	WI	46,060	VC
Stanford Univ	CA	62,541	MC
SUNY at Binghamton	NY	24,100	MC
SUNY at Geneseo	NY	21,622	VC
SUNY at New Paltz	NY	20,840	C
SUNY at Oswego	NY	22,219	VC
SUNY/Buffalo State	NY	20,583	LC
SUNY/Cortland	NY	20,910	C
SUNY/Fredonia	NY	20,818	C
SUNY/Oneonta	NY	20,794	C
SUNY/Plattsburgh	NY	19,314	C
SUNY/Potsdam	NY	21,051	VC
SUNY/Univ at Buffalo	NY	23,122	C
Stephen F. Austin State Univ	TX	18,484	LC
Stockton Univ	NJ	25,565	C
Stony Brook Univ/The SUNY	NY	22,703	MC
Sul Ross State Univ	TX	15,021	LC
Tarleton State Univ	TX	15,248	LC
Temple Univ	PA	24,392	C+
Tenn Tech Univ	TN	17,929	C
Texas A&M Univ at College Station	TX	20,771	VC+
Texas A&M Univ at Commerce	TX	10,496	C
Texas A&M Univ at Corpus Christi	TX	16,851	LC
Texas A&M Univ at Kingsville	TX	16,580	LC
Texas Christian Univ	TX	57,120	HC
The College at Brockport - SUNY	NY	21,058	C
The College of Wooster	OH	60,000	HC
The George Washington Univ	DC	68,474	HC+
The Univ of Akron	OH	22,566	C
The Univ of Alabama	AL	24,320	C+
The Univ of Arizona	AZ	24,086	C
The Univ of Montana Western	MT	9,426	LC
The Univ of Tenn at Chattanooga	TN	17,340	C+
The Univ of Tenn at Knoxville	TN	22,112	VC
The Univ of Tenn at Martin	TN	15,212	C
The Univ of Texas at Austin	TX	20,206	MC
The Univ of Texas at San Antonio	TX	21,060	C
The Univ of Utah	UT	18,751	VC
Towson Univ	MD	21,878	C
Tufts Univ	MA		MC
Tulane Univ	LA	67,496	MC
Union College	NY	64,320	MC
Univ of Arkansas at Fayetteville	AR	19,766	VC
Univ of Arkansas at Little Rock	AR	18,211	LC
Univ of Calif at Davis	CA	28,468	HC
Univ of Calif at Irvine	CA	33,857	VC
Univ of Calif at Los Angeles	CA	27,438	HC+
Univ of Calif at Riverside	CA	32,912	C
Univ of Calif at Santa Barbara	CA	30,627	HC+
Univ of Calif, Santa Cruz	CA	28,731	C+
Univ of Central Missouri	MO	18,982	C
Univ of Cincinnati	OH	22,118	VC
Univ of Colo Boulder	CO	26,048	HC

School	ST	$IS	SR
Univ of Conn	CT	27,394	
Univ of Dayton	OH	54,930	VC
Univ of Delaware	DE	32,214	VC
Univ of Florida	FL	16,291	HC+
Univ of Georgia	GA	21,878	HC
Univ of Hawaii at Hilo	HI	18,038	VC
Univ of Hawaii at Manoa	HI	23,261	C
Univ of Houston	TX	21,871	VC
Univ of Idaho	ID	16,158	C
Univ of Illinois at Urbana-Champaign	IL	27,006	HC
Univ of Iowa	IA	19,415	HC
Univ of Kansas	KS	20,884	VC
Univ of Kentucky	KY	24,800	C+
Univ of Louisiana at Lafayette	LA	14,516	C
Univ of Maine at Farmington	ME	18,792	C
Univ of Maryland/College Park	MD	21,938	HC
Univ of Mass Amherst	MA	27,669	HC
Univ of Miami	FL	63,494	MC
Univ of Mich/Ann Arbor	MI	25,274	MC
Univ of Mich/Dearborn	MI	12,472	VC
Univ of Minn/Duluth	MN	20,292	C
Univ of Minn/Morris	MN	21,222	VC
Univ of Miss	MS	18,802	C
Univ of Missouri-Columbia	MO	20,463	VC
Univ of Missouri-Kansas City	MO	19,563	VC
Univ of Montana	MT	14,105	C
Univ of Mount Union	OH	39,990	C
Univ of Nebr - Lincoln	NE	18,589	VC
Univ of Nebr - Omaha	NE	16,120	C
Univ of Nevada, Las Vegas	NV	17,553	C
Univ of Nevada, Reno	NV	18,010	C
Univ of New Hampshire	NH	29,333	VC
Univ of New Orleans	LA	12,840	C
Univ of North Alabama	AL	15,964	C
Univ of N Car at Chapel Hill	NC	20,561	MC
Univ of N Car at Charlotte	NC	17,803	VC
Univ of N Car Wilmington	NC	16,784	VC
Univ of N Dak	ND	16,673	C
Univ of Northern Colo	CO	19,658	C
Univ of Northern Iowa	IA	17,480	C
Univ of Okla	OK	19,651	HC
Univ of Pennsylvania	PA	63,526	MC
Univ of Pittsburgh	PA	30,030	MC
Univ of Pittsburgh at Johnstown	PA	22,092	C
Univ of PR, at Mayaguez	PR	13,995	
Univ of Puget Sound	WA	60,210	HC
Univ of Rochester	NY	65,032	MC
Univ of South Alabama	AL	16,880	C
Univ of S Car at Columbia	SC	21,726	VC
Univ of South Florida/Tampa	FL	16,110	VC
Univ of Southern Calif	CA	66,631	MC
Univ of Southern Indiana	IN	16,808	C
Univ of Southern Maine	ME	18,320	C
Univ of Southern Miss	MS	13,170	C
Univ of Texas at Arlington	TX	18,876	C
Univ of Texas at El Paso	TX	34,452	NC
Univ of the Pacific	CA	57,446	VC
Univ of Toledo	OH	19,336	C
Univ of Tulsa	OK	52,625	HC
Univ of Vermont	VT	29,792	HC
Univ of Washington	WA	23,091	MC
Univ of West Georgia	GA	17,510	LC
Univ of Wisc-Eau Claire	WI	16,354	VC
Univ of Wisc-Madison	WI	21,647	MC
Univ of Wisc-Milwaukee	WI	21,538	C
Univ of Wisc-Oshkosh	WI	15,392	C
Univ of Wisc-Parkside	WI	15,313	C
Univ of Wisc-River Falls	WI	14,541	C
Univ of Wyoming	WY	15,537	C
Utah State Univ	UT	13,235	C
Valparaiso Univ	IN	50,160	VC
Vassar College	NY	68,110	MC
Virginia Polytechnic Inst and State Univ	VA	21,920	VC
Washington and Lee Univ	VA	59,647	MC
Washington State Univ	WA	22,747	C
Washington Univ in St. Louis	MO	67,539	MC
Wayland Baptist Univ	TX	23,460	LC
Wayne State Univ	MI	23,085	C
Weber State Univ	UT	14,112	C
Wellesley College	MA	66,984	MC
West Chester Univ of Pennsylvania	PA	19,171	VC
West Texas A&M Univ	TX	13,478	C
West Virginia Univ	WV	18,952	VC
Western Carolina Univ	NC	13,965	C
Western Illinois Univ	IL	20,897	C
Western Kentucky Univ	KY	16,850	C
Western Mich Univ	MI	21,791	C
Western State Colo Univ	CO	19,348	C
Western Washington Univ	WA	18,904	VC
Wheaton College	IL	44,993	MC
Whitman College	WA	59,772	MC
Wichita State Univ	KS	17,773	C
Wilkes Univ	PA	49,166	C
Williams College	MA	67,700	MC
Wilmington College	OH	35,100	C
Winona State Univ	MN	18,109	C
Wittenberg Univ	OH	49,863	VC
Wright State Univ	OH	16,983	C
Yale Univ	CT	64,650	MC
Youngstown State Univ	OH	17,487	C

GEOLOGY & GEOLOGY OCEANOGRAPHY

School	ST	$IS	SR
Kutztown Univ of Pennsylvania	PA	19,477	C
Univ of Rhode Island	RI	26,066	VC
Wittenberg Univ	OH	49,863	VC

GEOPHYSICAL ENGINEERING

School	ST	$IS	SR
Colo School of Mines	CO	29,319	MC
Montana Tech of the Univ of Montana	MT	15,447	VC
New Jersey Inst of Technology	NJ	30,198	HC
The Univ of Texas at Austin	TX	20,206	MC
Univ of Mich/Ann Arbor	MI	25,274	MC

GEOPHYSICS AND SEISMOLOGY

School	ST	$IS	SR
Baylor Univ	TX	56,803	HC
Boise State Univ	ID	17,368	C
Boston College	MA	68,043	MC
Boston Univ	MA	67,352	MC
Calif Inst of Technology	CA	64,704	MC
Cal State, Fullerton	CA	21,902	C
Colgate Univ	NY	67,500	MC
Columbia Univ/City of New York	NY	62,958	MC
Harvard College/Harvard Univ	MA	65,609	MC
Mich State Univ	MI	24,542	VC
Mich Tech Univ	MI	25,551	VC+
Missouri Univ of Science and Technology	MO	18,655	HC
Rice Univ	TX	59,458	MC
Southern Methodist Univ	TX	69,008	MC
Stanford Univ	CA	62,541	MC
SUNY at Geneseo	NY	21,622	VC
SUNY/Cortland	NY	20,910	C
Texas A&M Univ at College Station	TX	20,771	VC+
The Univ of Akron	OH	22,566	C
The Univ of Texas at Austin	TX	20,206	MC
The Univ of Utah	UT	18,751	VC
Univ of Calif at Los Angeles	CA	27,438	HC+
Univ of Calif at Riverside	CA	32,912	C
Univ of Calif at Santa Barbara	CA	30,627	HC+
Univ of Hawaii at Manoa	HI	23,261	C
Univ of Nevada, Reno	NV	18,010	C
Univ of New Orleans	LA	12,840	C
Univ of Okla	OK	19,651	HC
Univ of S Car at Columbia	SC	21,726	VC
Univ of Texas at El Paso	TX	34,452	NC
Univ of the Pacific	CA	57,446	VC
Univ of Tulsa	OK	52,625	HC
Univ of Wisc-Madison	WI	21,647	MC
Washington Univ in St. Louis	MO	67,539	MC
Western Mich Univ	MI	21,791	C
Wright State Univ	OH	16,983	C

GEOSCIENCE

School	ST	$IS	SR
Angelo State Univ	TX	15,882	LC
Austin Peay State Univ	TN	16,397	C
Bloomsburg Univ of Pennsylvania	PA	19,930	C
Boise State Univ	ID	17,368	C
Brown Univ	RI	64,566	MC
Cal State, Fullerton	CA	21,902	C
Cedarville Univ	OH	36,244	VC
Colby College	ME	64,060	MC
Columbia Univ/ School of General Studies	NY	61,470	MC
Drexel Univ	PA	65,927	HC
Eckerd College	FL	55,206	VC
Hamilton College	NY	64,250	MC
Hobart and William Smith Colleges	NY	67,050	HC+
Idaho State Univ	ID	13,619	LC
Indiana Univ Bloomington	IN	20,791	HC
Indiana Univ Southeast	IN	16,931	C
Lewis-Clark State College	ID	14,202	C
Mansfield Univ of Pennsylvania	PA	24,244	LC
Mich State Univ	MI	24,542	VC
Minn State Univ, Moorhead	MN	21,393	C
Miss State Univ	MS	12,028	C+
Northern Illinois Univ	IL	20,176	C
Ohio Univ	OH	23,394	VC
Olivet Nazarene Univ	IL	41,840	VC
Pacific Lutheran Univ	WA	49,960	C
Princeton Univ	NJ	60,090	MC
Radford Univ	VA	19,758	C
Rider Univ	NJ	54,050	C
Rutgers Univ - Newark	NJ	27,351	C
S Dak State Univ	SD	15,874	C
Stanford Univ	CA	62,541	MC
SUNY/Fredonia	NY	20,818	C
Tarleton State Univ	TX	15,248	LC
Texas Tech Univ	TX	20,156	C+
The Univ of Arizona	AZ	24,086	C
The Univ of Montana Western	MT	9,426	LC
The Univ of Utah	UT	18,751	VC
Towson Univ	MD	21,878	C
Trinity Univ	TX	54,480	MC
Univ of Alaska Fairbanks	AK	16,874	VC
Univ of Calif at Riverside	CA	32,912	C
Univ of Chicago	IL	70,551	MC
Univ of Conn	CT	27,394	
Univ of Miami	FL	63,494	MC
Univ of Mich/Ann Arbor	MI	25,274	MC
Univ of Montana	MT	14,105	C
Univ of Southern Maine	ME	18,320	C
Univ of Texas at Dallas	TX	23,640	HC
Univ of Tulsa	OK	52,625	HC
Univ of Wisc-Eau Claire	WI	16,354	VC
Univ of Wisc-Green Bay	WI	15,184	C
Univ of Wisc-Stevens Point	WI	14,043	C
Utica College	NY	31,510	C
West Chester Univ of Pennsylvania	PA	19,171	VC
West Virginia Univ	WV	18,952	VC

GERMAN

School	ST	$IS	SR
Adrian College	MI	45,550	C
Agnes Scott College	GA	51,930	VC+
Alabama A&M Univ	AL	18,796	C
Albion College	MI	55,260	C
Allegheny College	PA	57,620	VC
Alma College	MI	49,410	VC
Amherst College	MA	66,186	MC
Aquinas College - Mich	MI	38,876	VC
Arizona State Univ at the Tempe Campus	AZ	23,001	VC
Auburn Univ	AL	24,300	VC+
Augsburg Univ	MN	45,129	C
Augustana College	IL	51,222	VC+
Augustana Univ	SD	39,968	VC
Austin College	TX	51,059	HC
Baker Univ	KS	37,190	C
Baldwin Wallace Univ	OH	42,464	VC
Ball State Univ	IN	19,808	C+
Barnard College/Columbia Univ	NY	68,762	MC
Bates College	ME	64,500	HC
Baylor Univ	TX	56,803	HC
Belmont Univ	TN	44,500	VC+
Beloit College	WI	55,206	HC
Bemidji State Univ	MN	17,730	C
Berea College	KY	7,094	C
Berry College	GA	47,466	VC
Boise State Univ	ID	17,368	C
Bowdoin College	ME	65,980	MC
Bowling Green State Univ	OH	19,975	C
Brandeis Univ	MA	68,443	MC
Brigham Young Univ	UT	13,248	MC
Bryn Mawr College	PA	65,220	MC
Bucknell Univ	PA	67,136	MC
Butler Univ	IN	52,890	VC+
Calif Lutheran Univ	CA	52,853	C
Cal State, Chico	CA	19,790	VC
Cal State, Fresno	CA	16,902	LC
Cal State, Fullerton	CA	21,902	C
Cal State, Long Beach	CA	18,850	C
Cal State, Northridge	CA	17,277	LC
Cal State, Sacramento	CA	19,060	C
Canisius College	NY	49,672	C
Carleton College	MN	66,414	MC
Carnegie Mellon Univ	PA	67,980	MC
Carthage College	WI	48,835	C
Case Western Reserve Univ	OH	62,284	MC
Centenary College of Louisiana	LA	49,050	C+
Central College	IA	44,592	C
Central Conn State Univ	CT	22,041	C
Central Mich Univ	MI	20,330	C
Central Washington Univ	WA	16,803	C
Centre College	KY	50,680	MC
Christopher Newport Univ	VA	24,878	VC+
CUNY/Hunter College	NY	31,098	VC
CUNY/Lehman College	NY	5,788	LC
CUNY/Queens College	NY	21,507	C
Clemson Univ	SC		HC
Coe College	IA	51,570	VC
Colgate Univ	NY	67,500	MC
College of Charleston	SC	24,046	VC
College of St. Benedict	MN	54,480	C
College of the Holy Cross	MA	64,320	MC
College of William & Mary	VA	34,907	MC
Colo State Univ	CO	23,033	C
Columbia Univ/ School of General Studies	NY	61,470	MC
Columbia Univ/City of New York	NY	62,958	MC
Concordia College - Moorhead	MN	46,418	C
Conn College	CT	65,000	MC
Cornell College	IA	49,900	VC
Cornell Univ	NY	67,591	MC
Davidson College	NC	60,119	MC
Denison Univ	OH	62,770	HC+
DePaul Univ	IL	52,807	VC
DePauw Univ	IN	58,688	VC
Dickinson College	PA	66,166	MC
Doane Univ	NE	41,340	VC
Dordt College	IA	37,860	C+
Drew Univ/College of Liberal Arts	NJ	53,608	VC
Earlham College	IN	55,670	HC
East Carolina Univ	NC	16,539	C
Eastern Mich Univ	MI	19,761	C
Eastern Washington Univ	WA	17,896	LC
Elizabethtown College	PA	56,340	VC
Elmhurst College	IL	46,514	C
Fairfield Univ	CT	61,445	HC
Florida Atlantic Univ	FL	18,256	C
Florida State Univ	FL	16,771	HC
Fordham Univ	NY	68,431	MC
Fort Hays State Univ	KS	12,677	C
Franciscan Univ of Steubenville	OH	33,980	VC
Franklin and Marshall College	PA	67,960	MC
Furman Univ	SC	61,098	VC+
Georgetown Univ	DC	68,970	MC
Georgia State Univ	GA	25,250	C
Gettysburg College	PA	65,210	MC
Grace College and Seminary	IN	31,524	C
Graceland Univ	IA	35,290	C
Grand Valley State Univ	MI	22,250	C+
Grinnell College	IA	63,114	MC
Guilford College	NC	45,973	C
Hamline Univ	MN	50,152	C
Hampden-Sydney College	VA	57,806	VC
Hartwick College	NY	51,270	C
Harvard College/Harvard Univ	MA	65,609	MC
Hastings College	NE	35,380	C+
Haverford College	PA	66,490	MC
Heidelberg Univ	OH	40,400	LC
Hendrix College	AR	54,020	VC
Hillsdale College	MI	37,170	MC
Hofstra Univ	NY	58,210	C+
Hood College	MD	50,540	C
Hope College	MI	42,840	VC
Humboldt State Univ	CA	21,708	C
Idaho State Univ	ID	13,619	LC
Illinois College	IL	41,330	VC
Illinois State Univ	IL	23,418	VC
Illinois Wesleyan Univ	IL	56,430	VC+
Indiana State Univ	IN	23,223	LC
Indiana Univ South Bend	IN	16,057	C
Indiana Univ Southeast	IN	16,931	C
Indiana Univ-Purdue Univ Fort Wayne	IN	18,675	C
Indiana Univ-Purdue Univ Indianapolis	IN	18,952	C
Iowa State Univ	IA	18,176	C
Ithaca College	NY	58,158	VC+
John Carroll Univ	OH	51,570	C
Johns Hopkins Univ	MD	68,080	MC
Juniata College	PA	58,118	VC
Kalamazoo College	MI	53,931	HC
Kenyon College	OH	65,840	MC
Knox College	IL	54,654	VC+
Kutztown Univ of Pennsylvania	PA	19,477	C
Lafayette College	PA	68,520	MC
Lakeland Univ	WI	35,130	C
Lawrence Univ	WI	56,133	HC+
Lebanon Valley College	PA	55,510	VC
Lehigh Univ	PA	63,860	MC
Lenoir-Rhyne Univ	NC	47,500	LC
Linfield College	OR	53,992	C
Lipscomb Univ	TN	42,984	VC
Lock Haven Univ of Pennsylvania	PA	20,544	LC
Loyola Univ Maryland	MD	61,710	VC
Luther College	IA	49,990	VC
Lycoming College	PA	50,895	C
Manchester Univ	IN	41,540	C
Marlboro College	VT	50,832	VC+
Marquette Univ	WI	53,090	VC+
Marshall Univ	WV	18,044	C
McDaniel College	MD	52,910	VC
Mercer Univ	GA	45,348	VC
Miami Univ	OH	27,190	HC+
Mich State Univ	MI	24,542	VC
Middle Tenn State Univ	TN	8,650	C
Middlebury College	VT	67,464	MC
Millersville Univ of Pennsylvania	PA	25,298	C
Minn State Univ, Mankato	MN	17,190	C
Minot State Univ	ND	13,285	C
Missouri State Univ	MO	15,837	C+
Montclair State Univ	NJ	26,912	C
Moravian College	PA	55,488	C
Mount St. Mary's Univ	MD	53,380	C
Muhlenberg College	PA	56,645	VC
Murray State Univ	KY	17,726	C+
Muskingum Univ	OH	35,966	C
Nazareth College	NY	46,784	C
Nebr Wesleyan Univ	NE	42,026	C+
New York Univ	NY	68,139	MC
Newberry College	SC	34,550	C
North Central College	IL	48,712	C+
Northern Illinois Univ	IL	20,176	C
Northern Kentucky Univ	KY	16,486	C
Northern State Univ	SD	15,570	C
Northwestern Univ	IL	68,725	MC
Oakland Univ	MI	20,763	C
Oberlin College	OH	68,942	MC
Ohio State Univ at Columbus	OH	22,843	MC
Ohio Univ	OH	23,394	VC
Ohio Wesleyan Univ	OH	49,460	VC
Okla State Univ	OK	17,180	C+
Old Dominion Univ	VA	21,618	C
Oral Roberts Univ	OK	34,316	C
Oregon State Univ	OR	23,337	VC
Pacific Lutheran Univ	WA	49,960	C
Pepperdine Univ	CA	66,862	VC+
Portland State Univ	OR	19,443	C

ST = STATE $IS = IN-STATE COSTS SR = SELECTOR RATING

School	ST	$IS	SR
Princeton Univ	NJ	60,090	MC
Providence College	RI	62,870	HC
Purdue Univ/West Lafayette	IN	20,032	MC
Randolph-Macon College	VA	51,480	HC
Rhodes College	TN	51,900	HC
Rider Univ	NJ	54,050	C
Rockford Univ	IL	38,570	C
Rosemont College	PA	30,980	LC
Rutgers Univ - Camden	NJ	26,595	C
St. John's Univ	MN	53,472	C
St. Joseph's Univ	PA	58,540	VC
Sam Houston State Univ	TX	18,792	C
Samford Univ	AL	40,770	VC
San Diego State Univ	CA	23,156	VC
San Francisco State Univ	CA	18,514	LC
San Jose State Univ	CA	22,630	C
Sarah Lawrence College	NY	68,866	MC
Seattle Pacific Univ	WA	47,439	C+
Sewanee: The Univ of the South	TN	58,000	HC+
Simpson College	IA	45,626	VC
Skidmore College	NY	66,600	MC
Slippery Rock Univ of Pennsylvania	PA	20,450	C
S Dak State Univ	SD	15,874	C
Southeast Missouri State Univ	MO	16,148	C
Southern Conn State Univ	CT	21,924	LC
Southern Illinois Univ Edwardsville	IL	20,188	C
Southern Methodist Univ	TX	69,008	MC
Southwestern Univ	TX	52,370	VC
St. Mary's Univ	TX	39,120	C
St. Norbert College	WI	46,060	VC
St. Olaf College	MN	56,430	HC
SUNY at Binghamton	NY	24,100	MC
SUNY at New Paltz	NY	20,840	C
SUNY at Oswego	NY	22,219	VC
SUNY/Univ at Buffalo	NY	23,122	C
Stetson Univ	FL	57,174	VC+
Susquehanna Univ	PA	57,560	VC
Swarthmore College	PA	63,550	MC
Temple Univ	PA	24,392	C+
Tenn Tech Univ	TN	17,929	C
Texas A&M Univ at College Station	TX	20,771	VC+
Texas A&M Univ at Commerce	TX	10,496	C
Texas State Univ	TX	18,721	C
Texas Tech Univ	TX	20,156	C+
The American Univ	DC	61,317	HC
The Catholic Univ of America	DC	58,376	VC
The Citadel, The Military College of S Car	SC	20,679	C
The College of Wooster	OH	60,000	HC
The George Washington Univ	DC	68,474	HC+
The Univ of Alabama	AL	24,320	C+
The Univ of Tenn at Knoxville	TN	22,112	VC
The Univ of Texas at Austin	TX	20,206	MC
The Univ of Utah	UT	18,751	VC
Thomas Edison State Univ	NJ	6,350	NC
Towson Univ	MD	21,878	C
Trinity College	CT	69,020	HC
Trinity Univ	TX	54,480	MC
Truman State Univ	MO	16,286	MC
Tufts Univ	MA		MC
Tulane Univ	LA	67,496	MC
Union College	NE	23,270	C
Univ of Arkansas at Fayetteville	AR	19,766	VC
Univ of Calif at Berkeley	CA	29,886	MC
Univ of Calif at Davis	CA	28,468	HC
Univ of Calif at Los Angeles	CA	27,438	HC+
Univ of Calif at Riverside	CA	32,912	C
Univ of Calif at Santa Barbara	CA	30,627	HC+
Univ of Central Missouri	MO	18,982	C
Univ of Central Okla	OK	15,150	C
Univ of Chicago	IL	70,551	MC
Univ of Cincinnati	OH	22,118	VC
Univ of Conn	CT	27,394	
Univ of Dallas	TX	50,676	VC
Univ of Dayton	OH	54,930	VC
Univ of Denver	CO	61,129	VC+
Univ of Evansville	IN	44,186	C+
Univ of Florida	FL	16,291	HC+
Univ of Georgia	GA	21,878	HC
Univ of Hawaii at Manoa	HI	23,261	C
Univ of Illinois at Chicago	IL	24,664	VC
Univ of Indianapolis	IN	36,480	VC
Univ of Iowa	IA	19,415	HC
Univ of Jamestown	ND	28,508	C
Univ of Kansas	KS	20,884	VC
Univ of Kentucky	KY	24,800	C+
Univ of La Verne	CA	55,600	C+
Univ of Mary Washington	VA	23,039	C+
Univ of Maryland/Baltimore County	MD	23,004	VC
Univ of Miami	FL	63,494	MC
Univ of Mich/Ann Arbor	MI	25,274	MC
Univ of Minn/Morris	MN	21,222	VC
Univ of Minn/Twin Cities	MN	24,269	MC
Univ of Miss	MS	18,802	C
Univ of Missouri-Columbia	MO	20,463	VC
Univ of Missouri-Kansas City	MO	19,563	VC
Univ of Missouri-St. Louis	MO	19,810	VC
Univ of Montana	MT	14,105	C
Univ of Montevallo	AL	20,012	C
Univ of Mount Union	OH	39,990	C
Univ of Nebr - Kearney	NE	17,014	LC
Univ of Nebr - Lincoln	NE	18,589	VC
Univ of Nebr - Omaha	NE	16,120	C
Univ of Nevada, Las Vegas	NV	17,553	C
Univ of New Hampshire	NH	29,333	VC
Univ of New Mexico	NM	16,808	C
Univ of North Alabama	AL	15,964	C
Univ of N Car at Asheville	NC	16,251	VC+
Univ of N Car at Chapel Hill	NC	20,561	MC
Univ of N Car at Charlotte	NC	17,803	VC
Univ of N Car at Greensboro	NC	15,998	C
Univ of N Car Wilmington	NC	16,784	VC
Univ of N Dak	ND	16,673	C
Univ of North Texas	TX	20,082	C
Univ of Northern Colo	CO	19,658	C
Univ of Notre Dame	IN	68,801	MC
Univ of Okla	OK	19,651	HC
Univ of Oregon	OR	24,021	VC
Univ of Pennsylvania	PA	63,526	MC
Univ of Puget Sound	WA	60,210	HC
Univ of Redlands	CA	61,934	VC
Univ of Rhode Island	RI	26,066	VC
Univ of Rochester	NY	65,032	MC
Univ of Scranton	PA	54,962	VC
Univ of S Car at Columbia	SC	21,726	VC
Univ of S Dak	SD	16,109	C
Univ of South Florida/Tampa	FL	16,110	VC
Univ of Southern Indiana	IN	16,808	C
Univ of Texas at Arlington	TX	18,876	C
Univ of Texas at El Paso	TX	34,452	NC
Univ of the Pacific	CA	57,446	VC
Univ of Toledo	OH	19,336	C
Univ of Tulsa	OK	52,625	HC
Univ of Vermont	VT	29,792	HC
Univ of Virginia	VA	27,367	MC
Univ of Wisc-Eau Claire	WI	16,354	VC
Univ of Wisc-Green Bay	WI	15,184	C
Univ of Wisc-Madison	WI	21,647	MC
Univ of Wisc-Oshkosh	WI	15,392	C
Univ of Wisc-Platteville	WI	14,148	C
Univ of Wisc-Stevens Point	WI	14,043	C
Univ of Wisc-Whitewater	WI	13,976	C
Univ of Wyoming	WY	15,537	C
Ursinus College	PA	62,920	VC
Utah State Univ	UT	13,235	C
Valparaiso Univ	IN	50,160	VC
Vanderbilt Univ	TN	63,248	MC
Virginia Polytechnic Inst and State Univ	VA	21,920	VC
Virginia Wesleyan Univ	VA	45,980	LC
Wabash College	IN	52,100	VC
Wake Forest Univ	NC	69,354	MC
Walla Walla Univ	WA	34,845	C
Wartburg College	IA	49,478	C
Washburn Univ	KS	15,827	C
Washington & Jefferson College	PA	58,694	VC
Washington and Lee Univ	VA	59,647	MC
Washington College	MD	56,154	VC
Washington State Univ	WA	22,747	C
Washington Univ in St. Louis	MO	67,539	MC
Wayne State Univ	MI	23,085	C
Weber State Univ	UT	14,112	C
Webster Univ	MO	37,490	C
Wellesley College	MA	66,984	MC
West Chester Univ of Pennsylvania	PA	19,171	VC
Western Carolina Univ	NC	13,965	C
Western Kentucky Univ	KY	16,850	C
Western Mich Univ	MI	21,791	C
Western Washington Univ	WA	18,904	VC
Westminster College	PA	41,722	C
Wheaton College	IL	44,993	MC
Wheaton College	MA	63,818	VC
Willamette Univ	OR	62,514	VC+
Williams College	MA	67,700	MC
Winthrop Univ	SC	23,960	C
Wisc Lutheran College	WI	36,290	C
Wittenberg Univ	OH	49,863	VC
Wofford College	SC	49,885	VC
Wright State Univ	OH	16,983	C
Xavier Univ	OH	49,380	VC

GERMAN AREA STUDIES

School	ST	$IS	SR
Appalachian State Univ	NC	15,394	VC
Bard College	NY	65,924	HC
Bard College at Simon's Rock	MA	65,795	MC
Boston College	MA	68,043	MC
Brown Univ	RI	64,566	MC
Cal State, Northridge	CA	17,277	LC
Case Western Reserve Univ	OH	62,284	MC
Chestnut Hill College	PA	47,180	C
Coe College	IA	51,570	VC
Columbia Univ/ School of General Studies	NY	61,470	MC
Cornell Univ	NY	67,591	MC
Dartmouth College	NH	68,109	MC
Emory Univ	GA	63,286	MC
Fordham Univ	NY	68,431	MC
Gettysburg College	PA	65,210	MC
Hamilton College	NY	64,250	MC
Ithaca College	NY	58,158	VC+
Kutztown Univ of Pennsylvania	PA	19,477	C
Lake Erie College	OH	38,914	LC
Lewis & Clark College	OR	60,984	MC
Linfield College	OR	53,992	C
Macalester College	MN	64,136	MC
Mount Holyoke College	MA	56,746	MC
Muhlenberg College	PA	56,645	VC
New College of Florida	FL	16,180	HC+
Pomona College	CA	64,957	MC
Rice Univ	TX	59,458	MC
St. Anselm College	NH	56,636	VC
Scripps College	CA	69,260	HC
Stanford Univ	CA	62,541	MC
Suffolk Univ	MA	52,316	C
Swarthmore College	PA	63,550	MC
The American Univ	DC	61,317	HC
The Univ of Arizona	AZ	24,086	C
Tufts Univ	MA		MC
Union College	NY	64,320	MC
Univ of Calif at Irvine	CA	33,857	VC
Univ of Calif, Santa Cruz	CA	28,731	C+
Univ of Illinois at Chicago	IL	24,664	VC
Univ of Minn/Duluth	MN	20,292	C
Univ of Portland	OR	52,152	VC
Wellesley College	MA	66,984	MC
Wesleyan Univ	CT	66,940	MC
Whitman College	WA	59,772	MC
Yale Univ	CT	64,650	MC

GERMAN STUDIES

School	ST	$IS	SR
Brown Univ	RI	64,566	MC
Cal State, Northridge	CA	17,277	LC
Calvin College	MI	43,090	HC
Creighton Univ	NE	49,452	VC
Elon Univ	NC	46,142	HC
Kutztown Univ of Pennsylvania	PA	19,477	C
Moravian College	PA	55,488	C
Ohio Wesleyan Univ	OH	49,460	VC
Syracuse Univ	NY	62,313	HC
The Univ of Arizona	AZ	24,086	C
Trinity Univ	TX	54,480	MC
Univ of Colo Boulder	CO	26,048	HC
Univ of Pittsburgh	PA	30,030	MC
Univ of Richmond	VA	62,730	MC
Univ of Wisc-La Crosse	WI	15,425	VC
Vassar College	NY	68,110	MC
Wartburg College	IA	49,478	C
Wellesley College	MA	66,984	MC
West Chester Univ of Pennsylvania	PA	19,171	VC
Wheaton College	MA	63,818	VC

GERMANIC LANGUAGES AND LITERATURE

School	ST	$IS	SR
Bard College	NY	65,924	HC
Bennington College	VT	66,280	MC
Boston Univ	MA	67,352	MC
Brown Univ	RI	64,566	MC
Colby College	ME	64,060	MC
Colo College	CO	64,894	MC
Columbia Univ/City of New York	NY	62,958	MC
Duke Univ	NC	68,298	MC
Indiana Univ Bloomington	IN	20,791	HC
Ithaca College	NY	58,158	VC+
Johns Hopkins Univ	MD	68,080	MC
Kent State Univ	OH	20,928	C
Messiah College	PA	44,380	VC
New College of Florida	FL	16,180	HC+
New York Univ	NY	68,139	MC
Oberlin College	OH	68,942	MC
Ohio State Univ at Columbus	OH	22,843	MC
Pennsylvania State Univ - Univ Park	PA	29,716	HC
Reed College	OR	65,300	MC
Rutgers Univ - New Brunswick	NJ	27,090	HC
St. Louis Univ	MO	49,866	HC
Scripps College	CA	69,260	HC
Smith College	MA	66,774	MC
Southern Illinois Univ Carbondale	IL	24,554	C
SUNY at Binghamton	NY	24,100	MC
Stony Brook Univ/The SUNY	NY	22,703	MC
Texas Christian Univ	TX	57,120	HC
Transylvania Univ	KY	47,450	HC+
Univ of Calif at Riverside	CA	32,912	C
Univ of Calif at Santa Barbara	CA	30,627	HC+
Univ of Calif San Diego	CA	30,450	MC
Univ of Georgia	GA	21,878	HC
Univ of Illinois at Chicago	IL	24,664	VC
Univ of Illinois at Urbana-Champaign	IL	27,006	HC
Univ of Kansas	KS	20,884	VC
Univ of Maryland/College Park	MD	21,938	HC
Univ of Mass Amherst	MA	27,669	HC
Univ of Mich/Ann Arbor	MI	25,274	MC
Univ of Missouri-St. Louis	MO	19,810	VC
Univ of Pittsburgh	PA	30,030	MC
Univ of Washington	WA	23,091	MC
Univ of Wisc-Green Bay	WI	15,184	C
Univ of Wisc-Milwaukee	WI	21,538	C
Washington and Lee Univ	VA	59,647	MC
Washington Univ in St. Louis	MO	67,539	MC
West Chester Univ of Pennsylvania	PA	19,171	VC
Yale Univ	CT	64,650	MC

GERONTOLOGY

School	ST	$IS	SR
Alfred Univ	NY	37,490	C
Ashford Univ	CA	10,480	C
Barton College	NC	39,854	C
Bethune-Cookman Univ	FL	23,322	C
Bloomfield College	NJ	40,100	LC
Bowling Green State Univ	OH	19,975	C
Cal State, Fresno	CA	16,902	LC
Cal State, Fullerton	CA	21,902	C
Cal State, San Bernardino	CA	20,106	C
Calif Univ of Pennsylvania	PA	20,425	LC
Canisius College	NY	49,672	C
Case Western Reserve Univ	OH	62,284	MC
Central Washington Univ	WA	16,803	C
Chestnut Hill College	PA	47,180	C
CUNY/York College	NY	6,747	LC
Eastern Mich Univ	MI	19,761	C
Gwynedd Mercy Univ	PA	43,780	LC
Ithaca College	NY	58,158	VC+
Langston Univ	OK	15,659	C
Madonna Univ	MI	30,450	LC
Marywood Univ	PA	47,840	C
McKendree Univ	IL	37,940	C+
Metropolitan College of New York	NY		VC
Miami Univ	OH	27,190	HC+
Minn State Univ, Moorhead	MN	21,393	C
Missouri State Univ	MO	15,837	C+
Mount St. Mary's Univ - Chalon Campus	CA	50,486	VC+
Northeastern Illinois Univ	IL	12,529	LC
Pontifical Catholic Univ of PR	PR	10,534	
Quinnipiac Univ	CT	60,970	VC
San Diego State Univ	CA	23,156	VC
Shaw Univ	NC	24,638	C
Southeastern Okla State Univ	OK	11,875	C
Southern Illinois Univ Edwardsville	IL	20,188	C
Springfield College	MA	48,775	C
SUNY/Oneonta	NY	20,794	C
Towson Univ	MD	21,878	C
Univ of Arkansas at Pine Bluff	AR	13,541	C
Univ of Central Arkansas	AR	15,042	VC
Univ of Central Okla	OK	15,150	C
Univ of Maryland Univ College	MD	26,146	LC
Univ of Mass Boston	MA	13,828	C
Univ of N Car at Greensboro	NC	15,998	C
Univ of Northern Colo	CO	19,658	C
Univ of Northern Iowa	IA	17,480	C
Univ of South Florida/Tampa	FL	16,110	VC
Univ of Southern Calif	CA	66,631	MC
Utica College	NY	31,510	C
Weber State Univ	UT	14,112	C
Wichita State Univ	KS	17,773	C
Youngstown State Univ	OH	17,487	C

GLASS

School	ST	$IS	SR
Alfred Univ	NY	37,490	C
Calif College of the Arts	CA	52,758	SP
Cleveland Inst of Art	OH	51,455	SP
College for Creative Studies	MI	51,210	SP
Mass College of Art and Design	MA	24,800	SP
Rhode Island School of Design	RI	59,960	SP
Rochester Inst of Technology	NY	52,734	HC+
Temple Univ	PA	24,392	C+

GLOBAL & PUBLIC HEALTH SCIENCES

School	ST	$IS	SR
Cedar Crest College	PA	51,110	C
Cornell Univ	NY	67,591	MC
Frostburg State Univ	MD	17,280	LC
MCPHS Univ	MA	45,470	SP
Missouri Western State Univ	MO	17,822	LC
Moravian College	PA	55,488	C
Univ of Calif San Diego	CA	30,450	MC

GLOBAL STUDIES

School	ST	$IS	SR
Abilene Christian Univ	TX	43,708	C+
Appalachian State Univ	NC	15,394	VC
Aquinas College - Mich	MI	38,876	VC
Bard College at Simon's Rock	MA	65,795	MC
Bentley Univ	MA	63,720	MC
Bridgewater College	VA	46,260	C
Cal State, Maritime Academy	CA	23,156	C+
Castleton Univ	VT	20,186	C
Colby College	ME	64,060	MC
College of St. Scholastica	MN	45,734	C+
Embry-Riddle Aeronautical Univ - Daytona Beach	FL	45,822	VC
Framingham State Univ	MA	21,740	C
Hofstra Univ	NY	58,210	C+
Hood College	MD	50,540	C
Lehigh Univ	PA	63,860	MC
McKendree Univ	IL	37,940	C+
Millersville Univ of Pennsylvania	PA	25,298	C
Missouri State Univ	MO	15,837	C+
New York Univ	NY	68,139	MC
Ohio Univ	OH	23,394	VC

School	ST	$IS	SR
Okla Baptist Univ	OK	33,990	C
Otterbein Univ	OH	41,630	C
Pacific Lutheran Univ	WA	49,960	C
Providence College	RI	62,870	HC
St. Leo Univ	FL	32,850	C
St. Mary's College	IN	50,600	C
St. Mary's Univ of Minn	MN	42,440	C
Samford Univ	AL	40,770	VC
San Jose State Univ	CA	22,630	C
Shenandoah Univ	VA	42,100	C
Shepherd Univ, West Virginia	WV	17,382	C
Southeast Missouri State Univ	MO	16,148	C
St. Edward's Univ	TX	56,190	VC
SUNY/Univ at Buffalo	NY	23,122	C
Texas Tech Univ	TX	20,156	C+
Tulane Univ	LA	67,496	MC
Univ of Calif at Irvine	CA	33,857	VC
Univ of Central Florida	FL	16,379	VC
Univ of Kansas	KS	20,884	VC
Univ of Minn/Twin Cities	MN	24,269	MC
Univ of New Haven	CT	53,680	C
Univ of Vermont	VT	29,792	HC
Univ of West Georgia	GA	17,510	LC
Valparaiso Univ	IN	50,160	VC
Warren Wilson College	NC	44,220	VC
Washington State Univ	WA	22,747	C
Wayne State Univ	MI	23,085	C
Wilson College	PA	35,620	LC
Winona State Univ	MN	18,109	C

GLOBAL/GENERAL MANAGEMENT

School	ST	$IS	SR
Arizona State Univ at the West Campus	AZ	21,513	VC
Farmingdale State College	NY	20,968	C
Hamline Univ	MN	50,152	C
Thomas Edison State Univ	NJ	6,350	NC
Univ of North Florida	FL	15,996	VC
Univ of Pittsburgh	PA	30,030	MC
Univ of South Florida St. Petersburg	FL	15,980	C

GOLF ENTERPRISE MANAGEMENT

School	ST	$IS	SR
Univ of Nebr - Lincoln	NE	18,589	VC
Univ of Wisc-Stout	WI	19,667	C

GOVERNMENT

School	ST	$IS	SR
Claremont McKenna College	CA	69,900	MC
Cornell Univ	NY	67,591	MC
Dartmouth College	NH	68,109	MC
Emmanuel College	MA	53,472	C+
Gallaudet Univ	DC	30,088	LC
Mills College	CA	43,705	C
Missouri Western State Univ	MO	17,822	LC
The American Univ	DC	61,317	HC
Univ of Texas Rio Grande Valley	TX	15,573	LC
Wartburg College	IA	49,478	C
Wellesley College	MA	66,984	MC
West Chester Univ of Pennsylvania	PA	19,171	VC

GRAPHIC AND PRINTING PRODUCTION

School	ST	$IS	SR
Brenau Univ - Women's College	GA	37,876	LC
New York City College of Technology	NY	7,185	LC
Pittsburg State Univ	KS	13,880	C
Rochester Inst of Technology	NY	52,734	HC+
Univ of Wisc-Stout	WI	19,667	C
Western Mich Univ	MI	21,791	C
Youngstown State Univ	OH	17,487	C

GRAPHIC ARTS TECHNOLOGY

School	ST	$IS	SR
Alfred State College	NY	19,895	C
Andrews Univ	MI	41,732	C
Appalachian State Univ	NC	15,394	VC
Arizona State Univ at the Polytechnic Campus	AZ	22,394	VC
Ball State Univ	IN	19,808	C+
Carroll Univ	WI	38,100	C+
Central State Univ	OH	18,564	C
Clemson Univ	SC		HC
College of the Ozarks	MO	7,530	VC
Colo Mesa Univ	CO	19,707	LC
Colo Technical Univ	CO	21,455	NC
Emmanuel College	MA	53,472	C+
Florida State Univ	FL	16,771	HC
Idaho State Univ	ID	13,619	LC
Minn State Univ, Moorhead	MN	21,393	C
New York Univ	NY	68,139	MC
North Central College	IL	48,712	C+
Pacific Union College	CA	36,009	VC
Pennsylvania College of Technology	PA	27,693	NC
Pittsburg State Univ	KS	13,880	C
Rochester Inst of Technology	NY	52,734	HC+
Univ of Central Missouri	MO	18,982	C
Univ of Jamestown	ND	28,508	C
Univ of Wisc-Stout	WI	19,667	C

GRAPHIC COMMUNICATIONS

School	ST	$IS	SR
Bethany College	WV	38,774	LC
Calif Polytechnic State Univ	CA	22,547	MC
Cal State, Fullerton	CA	21,902	C
Illinois State Univ	IL	23,418	VC
Millersville Univ of Pennsylvania	PA	25,298	C
Walla Walla Univ	WA	34,845	C
Western Illinois Univ	IL	20,897	C

GRAPHIC COMMUNICATIONS MANAGEMENT

School	ST	$IS	SR
Black Hills State Univ	SD	16,622	C
Carroll Univ	WI	38,100	C+
Ferris State Univ	MI	21,458	C
Univ of Wisc-Stout	WI	19,667	C

GRAPHIC DESIGN

School	ST	$IS	SR
Abilene Christian Univ	TX	43,708	C+
Adams State Univ	CO	15,420	LC
Alabama A&M Univ	AL	18,796	C
Anderson Univ	IN	39,450	C
Andrews Univ	MI	41,732	C
Anna Maria College	MA	51,020	C
Appalachian State Univ	NC	15,394	VC
Arcadia Univ	PA	55,990	C+
Arizona State Univ at the Tempe Campus	AZ	23,001	VC
Arkansas State Univ	AR	16,190	C
Art Academy of Cincinnati	OH	37,790	SP
Art Inst of Portland	OR	132,329	SP
ArtCenter College of Design	CA	42,008	SP
Assumption College	MA	48,455	VC
Auburn Univ	AL	24,300	VC+
Augustana College	IL	51,222	VC+
Azusa Pacific Univ	CA	43,972	C
Barton College	NC	39,854	C
Becker College	MA	30,100	LC
Bethel College	IN	36,830	C
Bethel College	KS	35,370	C
Biola Univ	CA	48,686	C
Black Hills State Univ	SD	16,622	C
Blackburn College	IL	28,526	LC
Bloomfield College	NJ	40,100	LC
Boston Univ	MA	67,352	MC
Bowling Green State Univ	OH	19,975	C
Brescia Univ	KY	29,890	VC
Briar Cliff Univ	IA	36,956	C
Brigham Young Univ	UT	13,248	MC
Buena Vista Univ	IA	42,344	C
Cabrini Univ	PA	42,591	LC
Cairn Univ	PA	37,572	C
Calif Baptist Univ	CA	42,986	C
Calif College of the Arts	CA	52,758	SP
Calif State Polytechnic Univ, Pomona	CA	21,811	C
Cal State, Chico	CA	19,790	VC
Cal State, Fresno	CA	16,902	LC
Cal State, Fullerton	CA	21,902	C
Cal State, Los Angeles	CA	17,186	LC
Cal State, San Bernardino	CA	20,106	C
Calif Univ of Pennsylvania	PA	20,425	LC
Calvin College	MI	43,090	HC
Campbell Univ	NC	37,570	VC
Carthage College	WI	48,835	C
Cedarville Univ	OH	36,244	VC
Central Conn State Univ	CT	22,041	C
Central Mich Univ	MI	20,330	C
Champlain College	VT	54,724	VC
Chapman Univ	CA	65,504	HC
CUNY/Queens College	NY	21,507	C
Clarke Univ	IA	42,950	C
Cleveland Inst of Art	OH	51,455	SP
Coastal Carolina Univ	SC	20,340	C
Coker College	SC	38,196	C
Colby-Sawyer College	NH	50,790	C
College for Creative Studies	MI	51,210	SP
Colo State Univ	CO	23,033	C
Columbia College - Missouri	MO	28,179	C
Columbia College Chicago	IL	40,104	C
Columbus College of Art and Design	OH	47,310	SP
Concordia Univ St. Paul	MN	29,050	C
Concordia Univ Wisc	WI	35,910	C
Cooper Union for the Advancement of Science and Art	NY	61,370	MC
Cornerstone Univ	MI	36,550	C
Culver-Stockton College	MO	34,350	C
Curry College	MA	53,331	C
Daemen College	NY	40,336	C
Dallas Baptist Univ	TX	35,220	VC
Defiance College	OH	42,240	LC
DePaul Univ	IL	52,807	VC
Dominican Univ	IL	42,472	C+
Dominican Univ of Calif	CA	58,750	C
Dordt College	IA	37,860	C+
Drake Univ	IA	49,220	HC
Drexel Univ	PA	65,927	HC
Drury Univ	MO	37,555	VC
Eastern Mich Univ	MI	19,761	C
Eastern Washington Univ	WA	17,896	LC
Edgewood College	WI	35,950	C
Edinboro Univ	PA	15,940	LC
Elmhurst College	IL	46,514	C
Endicott College	MA	47,054	C+
Fairmont State Univ	WV	15,726	C
Fashion Inst of Technology/ SUNY	NY	18,521	SP
Felician Univ	NJ	46,280	LC
Ferris State Univ	MI	21,458	C
Fitchburg State Univ	MA	21,819	LC
Flagler College	FL	27,620	C
Florida Atlantic Univ	FL	18,256	C
Florida Southern College	FL	45,978	VC
Fordham Univ	NY	68,431	MC
Franklin Pierce Univ	NH	46,750	LC
Georgia Southern Univ	GA	16,540	VC
Grace College and Seminary	IN	31,524	C
Graceland Univ	IA	35,290	C
Grand View Univ	IA	32,302	C
Harding Univ	AR	25,440	C
Hardin-Simmons Univ	TX	36,025	C
High Point Univ	NC	47,355	VC
Howard Univ	DC	37,616	C+
Huntington Univ	IN	33,996	C
Indiana Univ-Purdue Univ Fort Wayne	IN	18,675	C
Iowa State Univ	IA	18,176	C
Jefferson (Philadelphia Univ + Thomas Jefferson Univ)	PA	53,966	C
John Brown Univ	AR	35,184	VC
Kutztown Univ of Pennsylvania	PA	19,477	C
La Roche College	PA	38,940	C
La Sierra Univ	CA	39,690	VC
Laguna College of Art and Design	CA	41,422	SP
Lasell College	MA	49,400	C
Lenoir-Rhyne Univ	NC	47,500	LC
Limestone College	SC	32,100	C
Lipscomb Univ	TN	42,984	VC
Louisiana College	LA	21,274	C
Loyola Univ New Orleans	LA	52,456	VC
Lubbock Christian Univ	TX	29,727	C
Lyndon State College	VT	20,714	C
Madonna Univ	MI	30,450	LC
Maine College of Art	ME	45,940	SP
Malone Univ	OH	39,200	C
Mansfield Univ of Pennsylvania	PA	24,244	LC
Marietta College	OH	46,190	C
Marshall Univ	WV	18,044	C
Maryland Inst College of Art	MD	58,740	SP
Maryville Univ of St. Louis	MO	38,558	VC
Marywood Univ	PA	47,840	C
Mass College of Art and Design	MA	24,800	SP
Memphis College of Art	TN	50,880	SP
Mercyhurst Univ	PA	47,420	C
Miami Univ	OH	27,190	HC+
Mich State Univ	MI	24,542	VC
MidAmerica Nazarene Univ	KS	37,808	C
Middle Tenn State Univ	TN	8,650	C
Millersville Univ of Pennsylvania	PA	25,298	C
Milwaukee Inst of Art & Design	WI	45,880	SP
Minneapolis College of Art and Design	MN	44,218	SP
Miss College	MS	25,850	C
Missouri Southern State Univ	MO	13,071	C
Missouri Western State Univ	MO	17,822	LC
Monmouth Univ	NJ	50,184	C
Montclair State Univ	NJ	26,912	C
Montserrat College of Art	MA	41,500	SP
Moore College of Art and Design	PA	55,118	SP
Morningside College	IA	39,780	C
Mount Ida College	MA	46,820	C
Mount Mary Univ	WI	34,650	LC
Mount Mercy Univ	IA	39,748	C
Mount St. Joseph Univ	OH	33,880	LC
Mount Vernon Nazarene Univ	OH	35,944	C
New Mexico Highlands Univ	NM	11,904	LC
New York Inst of Technology	NY	49,980	VC
New York Univ	NY	68,139	MC
Newbury College	MA	48,970	C
Norfolk State Univ	VA	18,902	LC
N Car State Univ	NC	22,434	HC+
Northeastern Univ	MA	65,352	MC
Northland College	WI	41,103	C+
Northwest Nazarene Univ	ID	40,250	C
Northwestern College of Iowa	IA	38,400	C
Notre Dame College	OH	39,150	VC
Notre Dame de Namur Univ	CA	46,526	LC
Notre Dame of Maryland Univ	MD	47,570	VC
Ohio Dominican Univ	OH	41,340	C+
Ohio Northern Univ	OH	44,050	VC
Ohio Univ	OH	23,394	VC
Okla Baptist Univ	OK	33,990	C
Old Dominion Univ	VA	21,618	C
Oregon State Univ	OR	23,337	VC
Otis College of Art and Design	CA	54,670	SP
Ouachita Baptist Univ	AR	33,500	VC
Pacific Northwest College of Art	OR	38,494	SP
Pacific Union College	CA	36,009	VC
Palm Beach Atlantic Univ	FL	39,250	C
Park Univ	MO	22,134	C
Parsons The New School for Design	NY	56,610	SP
Pennsylvania College of Technology	PA	27,693	NC
Pennsylvania State Univ - Univ Park	PA	29,716	HC
Plymouth State Univ	NH	23,180	LC
Point Loma Nazarene Univ	CA	46,150	C+
Purdue Univ/West Lafayette	IN	20,032	MC
Queens Univ of Charlotte	NC	39,543	C
Quincy Univ	IL	38,170	LC
Rhode Island School of Design	RI	59,960	SP
Ringling College of Art and Design	FL	59,160	SP
Rivier Univ	NH	41,600	VC
Roberts Wesleyan College	NY	41,116	C
Rochester Inst of Technology	NY	52,734	HC+
Rocky Mountain College of Art and Design	CO	27,052	SP
Roger Williams Univ	RI	48,074	VC
St. Mary's Univ of Minn	MN	42,440	C
St. Peter's Univ	NJ	49,192	C
Sam Houston State Univ	TX	18,792	C
Samford Univ	AL	40,770	VC
San Diego State Univ	CA	23,156	VC
Savannah College of Art and Design	GA	49,595	SP
School of Visual Arts	NY	47,500	SP
Schreiner Univ	TX	34,626	LC
Seton Hall Univ	NJ	58,008	C
Seton Hill Univ	PA	46,972	VC
Siena Heights Univ	MI	36,322	C
Silver Lake College of the Holy Family	WI	36,290	LC
Simpson College	IA	45,626	VC
S Dak State Univ	SD	15,874	C
South Univ	GA	36,070	LC
Southeastern Univ	FL	34,910	LC
Southern Adventist Univ	TN	28,250	C
Southern Nazarene Univ	OK	33,684	C
Southern New Hampshire Univ	NH	44,256	C
Southern Oregon Univ	OR	19,117	C
Southwestern Okla State Univ	OK	12,205	C
Spring Hill College	AL	48,488	C
St. Ambrose Univ	IA	40,180	C
St. Edward's Univ	TX	56,190	VC
St. John's Univ	NY	57,160	C+
St. Norbert College	WI	46,060	VC
SUNY /College of Agriculture and Tech at Cobleskill	NY	20,527	LC
SUNY at New Paltz	NY	20,840	C
SUNY at Oswego	NY	22,219	VC
SUNY/Fredonia	NY	20,818	C
SUNY/Potsdam	NY	21,051	VC
Stephens College	MO	38,042	C
Suffolk Univ	MA	52,316	C
Susquehanna Univ	PA	57,560	VC
Syracuse Univ	NY	62,313	HC
Tabor College	KS	35,870	C
Temple Univ	PA	24,392	C+
Texas Christian Univ	TX	57,120	HC
The American Univ	DC	61,317	HC
The Art Inst of Atlanta	GA	34,334	SP
The College of New Jersey	NJ	28,675	VC+
The College of St. Rose	NY	44,010	C
The Univ of Tenn at Knoxville	TN	22,112	VC
Trinity International Univ	IL	31,070	VC
Union College	NE	23,270	C
Union Univ	TN	41,160	VC
Univ of Arkansas at Fayetteville	AR	19,766	VC
Univ of Bridgeport	CT	44,985	LC
Univ of Central Okla	OK	15,150	C
Univ of Cincinnati	OH	22,118	VC
Univ of Dayton	OH	54,930	VC
Univ of Evansville	IN	44,186	C+
Univ of Findlay	OH	43,040	C
Univ of Florida	FL	16,291	HC+
Univ of Illinois at Chicago	IL	24,664	VC
Univ of Illinois at Urbana-Champaign	IL	27,006	HC
Univ of Iowa	IA	19,415	HC
Univ of Kansas	KS	20,884	VC
Univ of Mass Dartmouth	MA	26,507	C
Univ of Miami	FL	63,494	MC
Univ of Mich/Ann Arbor	MI	25,274	MC
Univ of Minn/Duluth	MN	20,292	C
Univ of Minn/Twin Cities	MN	24,269	MC
Univ of New Haven	CT	53,680	C
Univ of N Dak	ND	16,673	C
Univ of Northern Colo	CO	19,658	C
Univ of Northern Iowa	IA	17,480	C
Univ of Northwestern - St. Paul	MN	39,530	C
Univ of St. Francis	IN	38,520	C
Univ of San Francisco	CA	60,580	C
Univ of S Car Upstate	SC	19,272	LC
Univ of South Florida St. Petersburg	FL	15,980	C
Univ of Tampa	FL	38,928	VC
Univ of the Arts	PA	56,579	SP
Univ of the Pacific	CA	57,446	VC
Univ of Washington	WA	23,091	MC
Univ of Wisc-Parkside	WI	15,313	C
Upper Iowa Univ	IA	34,990	NC
Ursuline College	OH	41,076	LC

ST = STATE $IS = IN-STATE COSTS SR = SELECTOR RATING

School	ST	$IS	SR
Virginia Commonwealth Univ	VA	23,811	VC
Viterbo Univ	WI	34,660	C
Walla Walla Univ	WA	34,845	C
Walsh Univ	OH	39,010	C
Wartburg College	IA	49,478	C
Washington Univ in St. Louis	MO	67,539	MC
Wayland Baptist Univ	TX	23,460	LC
Wayne State College	NE	25,746	NC
Waynesburg Univ	PA	33,530	C
Weber State Univ	UT	14,112	C
Webster Univ	MO	37,490	C
West Liberty Univ	WV	16,158	C
West Texas A&M Univ	TX	13,478	C
Western Mich Univ	MI	21,791	C
Western Oregon Univ	OR	19,965	LC
Wichita State Univ	KS	17,773	C
William Woods Univ	MO	32,040	C
Wilson College	PA	35,620	LC
Winona State Univ	MN	18,109	C
Woodbury Univ	CA	49,593	VC
York College of Pennsylvania	PA	29,240	C
Youngstown State Univ	OH	17,487	C

GRAPHIC DESIGN & MEDIA

School	ST	$IS	SR
Alfred State College	NY	19,895	C
Baldwin Wallace Univ	OH	42,464	VC
Bloomfield College	NJ	40,100	LC
Bluffton Univ	OH	40,950	C+
Champlain College	VT	54,724	VC
Creighton Univ	NE	49,452	VC
Drury Univ	MO	37,555	VC
Lynn Univ	FL	49,680	LC
Marymount Univ	VA	43,231	C
Missouri Western State Univ	MO	17,822	LC
Murray State Univ	KY	17,726	C+
Point Loma Nazarene Univ	CA	46,150	C+
Rochester Inst of Technology	NY	52,734	HC+
Southern Oregon Univ	OR	19,117	C
Trinity International Univ	IL	31,070	VC
Univ of Illinois at Chicago	IL	24,664	VC
Univ of N Car at Greensboro	NC	15,998	C
Western Kentucky Univ	KY	16,850	C
Wilson College	PA	35,620	LC

GREAT PLAINS STUDIES

School	ST	$IS	SR
Univ of Nebr - Lincoln	NE	18,589	VC

GREEK

School	ST	$IS	SR
Ball State Univ	IN	19,808	C+
Barnard College/Columbia Univ	NY	68,762	MC
Brigham Young Univ	UT	13,248	MC
Bryn Mawr College	PA	65,220	MC
Carleton College	MN	66,414	MC
CUNY/Hunter College	NY	31,098	VC
CUNY/Lehman College	NY	5,788	LC
CUNY/Queens College	NY	21,507	C
Colgate Univ	NY	67,500	MC
Columbia Univ/City of New York	NY	62,958	MC
Concordia Univ, Ann Arbor	MI	38,878	C+
DePauw Univ	IN	58,688	VC
Dickinson College	PA	66,166	MC
Emory Univ	GA	63,286	MC
Florida State Univ	FL	16,771	HC
Franklin and Marshall College	PA	67,960	MC
Furman Univ	SC	61,098	VC+
Gettysburg College	PA	65,210	MC
Hampden-Sydney College	VA	57,806	VC
Harvard College/Harvard Univ	MA	65,609	MC
Haverford College	PA	66,490	MC
Hillsdale College	MI	37,170	MC
Hobart and William Smith Colleges	NY	67,050	HC+
John Carroll Univ	OH	51,570	C
Marlboro College	VT	50,832	VC+
Monmouth College	IL	42,260	C
Mount Holyoke College	MA	56,746	MC
New York Univ	NY	68,139	MC
Northeastern Illinois Univ	IL	12,529	LC
Ohio State Univ at Columbus	OH	22,843	MC
Ohio Univ	OH	23,394	VC
Randolph-Macon College	VA	51,480	VC
Samford Univ	AL	40,770	VC
Sarah Lawrence College	NY	68,866	MC
Sewanee: The Univ of the South	TN	58,000	HC+
Smith College	MA	66,774	MC
Southwestern Univ	TX	52,370	VC
St. Olaf College	MN	56,430	HC
Swarthmore College	PA	63,550	MC
The Univ of Tenn at Chattanooga	TN	17,340	C+
The Univ of Texas at Austin	TX	20,206	MC
Trinity Univ	TX	54,480	MC
Tufts Univ	MA		MC
Union Univ	TN	41,160	VC
Univ of Calif at Berkeley	CA	29,886	MC
Univ of Calif at Davis	CA	28,468	HC
Univ of Calif at Los Angeles	CA	27,438	HC+
Univ of Georgia	GA	21,878	HC
Univ of Iowa	IA	19,415	HC
Univ of Mich/Ann Arbor	MI	25,274	MC
Univ of Minn/Twin Cities	MN	24,269	MC
Univ of Notre Dame	IN	68,801	MC
Univ of Oregon	OR	24,021	VC
Univ of Richmond	VA	62,730	MC
Univ of Scranton	PA	54,962	VC
Univ of Vermont	VT	29,792	HC
Wabash College	IN	52,100	VC
Wake Forest Univ	NC	69,354	MC
Wellesley College	MA	66,984	MC
Wheaton College	MA	63,818	VC
Wright State Univ	OH	16,983	C

GREEK (CLASSICAL)

School	ST	$IS	SR
Baylor Univ	TX	56,803	HC
Boston Univ	MA	67,352	MC
Butler Univ	IN	52,890	VC+
Duquesne Univ	PA	48,508	VC
Indiana Univ Bloomington	IN	20,791	HC
Kenyon College	OH	65,840	MC
Knox College	IL	54,654	VC+
Loyola Univ Chicago	IL	57,158	VC
Loyola Univ New Orleans	LA	52,456	VC
New York Univ	NY	68,139	MC
Ohio Univ	OH	23,394	VC
The Catholic Univ of America	DC	58,376	VC
The College of Wooster	OH	60,000	HC
Washington Univ in St. Louis	MO	67,539	MC
Wellesley College	MA	66,984	MC
Whitman College	WA	59,772	MC

GREEK (MODERN)

School	ST	$IS	SR
New York Univ	NY	68,139	MC
Tulane Univ	LA	67,496	MC
Univ of Mich/Ann Arbor	MI	25,274	MC

GUIDANCE EDUCATION

School	ST	$IS	SR
Calif Univ of Pennsylvania	PA	20,425	LC
Eastern Washington Univ	WA	17,896	LC
S Car State Univ	SC	21,330	LC
St. Cloud State Univ	MN	10,600	C
Texas A&M Univ at Commerce	TX	10,496	C
Univ of Central Arkansas	AR	15,042	VC
Univ of Cincinnati	OH	22,118	VC
Univ of Southern Miss	MS	13,170	C
Westminster College	PA	41,722	C

GUITAR

School	ST	$IS	SR
Boston Univ	MA	67,352	MC
Central Washington Univ	WA	16,803	C
Illinois Wesleyan Univ	IL	56,430	VC+
Loyola Univ New Orleans	LA	52,456	VC
Mannes School of Music	NY	44,500	SP
Okla City Univ	OK	40,476	C
Roosevelt Univ	IL	41,890	VC
San Francisco Conservatory of Music	CA	57,310	SP
Stetson Univ	FL	57,174	VC+
The Boston Conservatory at Berklee	MA	61,042	SP
Wright State Univ	OH	16,983	C

HABILITATION OF THE DEAF

School	ST	$IS	SR
Texas Christian Univ	TX	57,120	HC

HAWAIIAN

School	ST	$IS	SR
Univ of Hawaii at Hilo	HI	18,038	VC
Univ of Hawaii at Manoa	HI	23,261	C

HAWAIIAN STUDIES

School	ST	$IS	SR
Brigham Young Univ/Hawaii	HI	11,710	C
Univ of Hawaii at Hilo	HI	18,038	VC
Univ of Hawaii at Manoa	HI	23,261	C

HEALTH

School	ST	$IS	SR
Albertus Magnus College	CT	44,016	LC
Aquinas College - Mich	MI	38,876	VC
Averett Univ	VA	43,034	LC
Bentley Univ	MA	63,720	MC
Cal State, Monterey Bay	CA	22,872	LC
Cal State, Northridge	CA	17,277	LC
Central Mich Univ	MI	20,330	C
Chicago State Univ	IL	41,620	C
Coastal Carolina Univ	SC	20,340	C
College of the Ozarks	MO	7,530	VC
Concordia College - Moorhead	MN	46,418	C
Concordia College - New York	NY	39,035	LC
Concordia Univ Nebr	NE	41,900	VC
Coppin State Univ	MD	14,071	VC
DePauw Univ	IN	58,688	VC
Eastern Illinois Univ	IL	21,414	C
Eastern Oregon Univ	OR	17,612	C
George Fox Univ	OR	42,938	C
Georgetown Univ	DC	68,970	MC
Goddard College	VT	17,040	VC
Graceland Univ	IA	35,290	C
Harding Univ	AR	25,440	C
Hodges Univ	FL	20,160	LC
Husson Univ	ME	26,508	C
Idaho State Univ	ID	13,619	LC
Indiana Wesleyan Univ	IN	33,674	C
Ithaca College	NY	58,158	VC+
Johnson & Wales Univ/Denver Campus	CO	44,768	C
Kentucky Wesleyan College	KY	34,260	LC
Lebanon Valley College	PA	55,510	VC
LeTourneau Univ	TX	39,190	VC
Luther College	IA	49,990	VC
McKendree Univ	IL	37,940	C+
Missouri Southern State Univ	MO	13,071	C
Molloy College	NY	40,440	C
Montana State Univ	MT	15,500	C+
Nebr Wesleyan Univ	NE	42,026	C+
New Mexico Highlands Univ	NM	11,904	LC
New York Inst of Technology	NY	49,980	VC
Northeastern Illinois Univ	IL	12,529	LC
Ohio Northern Univ	OH	44,050	VC
Ohio Valley Univ	WV	28,800	C
Olivet College	MI	37,661	LC
Prairie View A&M Univ	TX	27,273	LC
Regis College	MA	51,920	LC
Rowan Univ	NJ	24,491	VC
Rust College	MS	10,600	C
St. Louis Univ	MO	49,866	HC
Sam Houston State Univ	TX	18,792	C
Southeast Missouri State Univ	MO	16,148	C
Southeastern Louisiana Univ	LA	16,237	C
Southern Oregon Univ	OR	19,117	C
Southwestern Adventist Univ	TX	28,232	LC
SUNY/Buffalo State	NY	20,583	LC
SUNY/College at Old Westbury	NY	16,860	C
Texas A&M Univ at College Station	TX	20,771	VC+
Texas Southern Univ	TX	19,592	LC
The College of Idaho	ID	36,415	C
The Evergreen State College	WA	16,599	C
The Univ of Texas at San Antonio	TX	21,060	C
Union College	KY	32,310	C
Union Inst & Univ	OH	8,912	SP
Univ of Bridgeport	CT	44,985	LC
Univ of Delaware	DE	32,214	VC
Univ of Houston	TX	21,871	VC
Univ of Louisville	KY	19,692	C
Univ of Minn/Crookston	MN	19,126	C
Univ of Missouri-Kansas City	MO	19,563	VC
Univ of Mount Union	OH	39,990	C
Univ of New Mexico	NM	16,808	C
Univ of New Orleans	LA	12,840	C
Univ of North Texas	TX	20,082	C
Univ of Pennsylvania	PA	63,526	MC
Univ of Rochester	NY	65,032	MC
Univ of St. Mary	KS	37,080	NC
Univ of Texas Rio Grande Valley	TX	15,573	LC
Univ of the Cumberlands	KY	32,000	LC
Univ of Wisc-Stout	WI	19,667	C
Univ of Wisc-Superior	WI	14,838	C
Upper Iowa Univ	IA	34,990	NC
Voorhees College	SC	19,976	C
Walla Walla Univ	WA	34,845	C
West Chester Univ of Pennsylvania	PA	19,171	VC
Wichita State Univ	KS	17,773	C

HEALTH ADMINISTRATION AND POLICY

School	ST	$IS	SR
Austin College	TX	51,059	HC
College of St. Elizabeth	NJ	45,700	LC
Creighton Univ	NE	49,452	VC
Eastern Washington Univ	WA	17,896	LC
Johnson & Wales Univ/Denver Campus	CO	44,768	C
Old Dominion Univ	VA	21,618	C
Providence College	RI	62,870	HC
St. Louis Univ	MO	49,866	HC
Salve Regina Univ	RI	53,046	VC
Shawnee State Univ	OH	16,998	C
The Univ of Utah	UT	18,751	VC
Univ of Miami	FL	63,494	MC
Univ of New Hampshire	NH	29,333	VC
Univ of St. Francis	IL	40,828	C
Western Illinois Univ	IL	20,897	C
Xavier Univ	OH	49,380	VC

HEALTH AND EDUCATION SCIENCE

School	ST	$IS	SR
Aquinas College - Mich	MI	38,876	VC
Minot State Univ	ND	13,285	C

HEALTH AND PHYSICAL ACTIVITY

School	ST	$IS	SR
Aquinas College - Mich	MI	38,876	VC
Brewton-Parker College	GA	26,120	LC
Drury Univ	MO	37,555	VC
Hanover College	IN	47,750	C+
Henderson State Univ	AR	15,516	C
Millikin Univ	IL	44,148	C
Texas Christian Univ	TX	57,120	HC
Texas State Univ	TX	18,721	C
Univ of Wisc-Superior	WI	14,838	C
Washington State Univ	WA	22,747	C

HEALTH AND PHYSICAL EDUCATION

School	ST	$IS	SR
Aquinas College - Mich	MI	38,876	VC
Baldwin Wallace Univ	OH	42,464	VC
Bethel College	KS	35,370	C
Bridgewater College	VA	46,260	C
Cairn Univ	PA	37,572	C
Chestnut Hill College	PA	47,180	C
Delta State Univ	MS	13,176	LC
Eastern Mennonite Univ	VA	42,550	C
Georgia Southwestern State Univ	GA	13,870	LC
Louisiana College	LA	21,274	C
Marian Univ	IN	43,206	C
Missouri Western State Univ	MO	17,822	LC
Morehouse College	GA	40,835	C
Murray State Univ	KY	17,726	C+
Oakwood Univ	AL	43,758	C
Okla Baptist Univ	OK	33,990	C
Rocky Mountain College	MT	35,776	C
Southwestern Okla State Univ	OK	12,205	C
Syracuse Univ	NY	62,313	HC
Univ of Arkansas at Pine Bluff	AR	13,541	C
Univ of Great Falls	MT	38,524	C
Univ of Pittsburgh	PA	30,030	MC
West Chester Univ of Pennsylvania	PA	19,171	VC
Wilson College	PA	35,620	LC

HEALTH CARE ADMINISTRATION

School	ST	$IS	SR
Adams State Univ	CO	15,420	LC
Alaska Pacific Univ	AK	28,730	VC
Alfred State College	NY	19,895	C
Alma College	MI	49,410	VC
Alvernia Univ	PA	45,330	C
Appalachian State Univ	NC	15,394	VC
Arcadia Univ	PA	55,990	C+
Arizona State Univ at the Downtown Phoenix Campus	AZ	24,634	VC
Arizona State Univ at the West Campus	AZ	21,513	VC
Ashford Univ	CA	10,480	C
Auburn Univ	AL	24,300	VC+
Baker College of Flint	MI	19,140	NC
Baldwin Wallace Univ	OH	42,464	VC
Barton College	NC	39,854	C
Benedictine Univ	IL	38,300	C
Berkeley College/New Jersey	NJ	38,082	LC
Berkeley College/New York City Campus	NY	35,100	LC
Cabarrus College of Health Sciences	NC	11,948	SP
Calif Baptist Univ	CA	42,986	C
Cal State, Chico	CA	19,790	VC
Cal State, Fullerton	CA	21,902	C
Cal State, Long Beach	CA	18,850	C
Cal State, Northridge	CA	17,277	LC
Cal State, San Bernardino	CA	20,106	C
Calumet College of St. Joseph	IN	22,735	C
Cambridge College	MA	14,940	NC
Campbell Univ	NC	37,570	VC
Carlow Univ	PA	39,696	LC
Carroll Univ	WI	38,100	C+
Central Mich Univ	MI	20,330	C
Charter Oak State College	CT	7,983	NC
Chatham Univ	PA	47,883	VC
Chestnut Hill College	PA	47,180	C
Chicago State Univ	IL	41,620	C
CUNY/Lehman College	NY	5,788	LC
Clayton State Univ	GA	19,735	LC
Coastal Carolina Univ	SC	20,340	C
College of St. Scholastica	MN	45,734	C+
Concordia Univ	OR	35,000	C
Dallas Baptist Univ	TX	35,220	VC
Delta State Univ	MS	13,176	LC
Dominican College	NY	40,258	LC
Duquesne Univ	PA	48,508	VC
D'Youville College	NY	37,678	C
East Carolina Univ	NC	16,539	C
Eastern Kentucky Univ	KY	17,742	C
Eastern Mich Univ	MI	19,761	C
Eastern Washington Univ	WA	17,896	LC
Emporia State Univ	KS	15,029	C
Ferris State Univ	MI	21,458	C
Florida Atlantic Univ	FL	18,256	C
Florida International Univ	FL	20,281	C
Franklin Pierce Univ	NH	46,750	LC
Franklin Univ	OH	11,616	NC
Gardner-Webb Univ	NC	24,935	C+
George Fox Univ	OR	42,938	C
Georgia Southern Univ	GA	16,540	VC
Gwynedd Mercy Univ	PA	43,780	LC
Harding Univ	AR	25,440	C
Harris-Stowe State Univ	MO	14,590	NC
Hastings College	NE	35,380	C+
Hodges Univ	FL	20,160	LC
Howard Univ	DC	37,616	C+
Husson Univ	ME	26,508	C
Idaho State Univ	ID	13,619	LC
Illinois State Univ	IL	23,418	VC
Indiana Univ Bloomington	IN	20,791	HC

School	ST	$IS	SR
Indiana Univ South Bend	IN	16,057	C
Indiana Univ-Purdue Univ Fort Wayne	IN	18,675	C
Indiana Univ-Purdue Univ Indianapolis	IN	18,952	C
Jackson State Univ	MS	15,879	LC
James Madison Univ	VA	19,084	VC
Johnson & Wales Univ/ Denver Campus	CO	44,768	C
King Univ	TN	36,976	C
Langston Univ	OK	15,659	C
Lebanon Valley College	PA	55,510	VC
Lee Univ	TN	22,045	C
Limestone College	SC	32,100	C
LIU Brooklyn	NY	50,698	C
LIU Post	NY	50,698	C+
Lourdes Univ	OH	29,140	NC
Mary Baldwin Univ	VA	40,495	C
Marywood Univ	PA	47,840	C
Mercy College of Health Sciences	IA	17,600	SP
Metropolitan State Univ of Denver	CO	6,928	LC
Midwestern State Univ	TX	12,111	LC
Minn State Univ, Moorhead	MN	21,393	C
Misericordia Univ	PA	45,210	C
Missouri Baptist Univ	MO	35,594	C
Missouri State Univ	MO	15,837	C+
Monroe College	NY	23,996	C
Montana State Univ Billings	MT	13,336	LC
Mount Aloysius College	PA	29,976	C
Mount Marty College	SD	36,862	C
Mount Mercy Univ	IA	39,748	C
Mount St. Mary's Univ - Chalon Campus	CA	50,486	VC+
National Louis Univ	IL	43,000	LC
Nebr Methodist College	NE	25,314	C
New England College	NH	50,828	NC
New York City College of Technology	NY	7,185	LC
New York Univ	NY	68,139	MC
Newbury College	MA	48,970	C
Norfolk State Univ	VA	18,902	LC
Northwest Christian Univ	OR	36,580	C
Ohio Univ	OH	23,394	VC
Okla City Univ	OK	40,476	C
Our Lady of the Lake Univ	TX	37,790	LC
Park Univ	MO	22,134	C
Pennsylvania College of Technology	PA	27,693	NC
Pennsylvania State Univ - Univ Park	PA	29,716	HC
Point Park Univ	PA	41,270	C
Presentation College	SD	28,575	LC
Regis Univ	CO	46,380	C
Rhode Island College	RI	19,000	LC
Robert Morris Univ	PA	40,600	C
Roger Williams Univ	RI	48,074	VC
Rutgers Univ - New Brunswick	NJ	27,090	HC
St. Joseph's Univ	PA	58,540	VC
St. Leo Univ	FL	32,850	C
St. Louis Univ	MO	49,866	HC
St. Mary-of-the-Woods College	IN	40,424	LC
St. Peter's Univ	NJ	49,192	C
Samford Univ	AL	40,770	VC
Shenandoah Univ	VA	42,100	C
Shippensburg Univ of Pennsylvania	PA	24,096	C
Simpson Univ	CA	34,722	C
South Univ	GA	36,070	LC
Southeast Missouri State Univ	MO	16,148	C
Southern Adventist Univ	TN	28,250	C
Southern Illinois Univ Carbondale	IL	24,554	C
Southern Univ at New Orleans	LA	8,014	LC
Southern Vermont College	VT	34,670	LC
Southwestern Okla State Univ	OK	12,205	C
Spring Hill College	AL	48,488	C
Springfield College	MA	48,775	C
St. Catherine Univ	MN	45,630	C
St. Francis College	NY	38,800	LC
St. Joseph's College, New York/Brooklyn Campus	NY	25,114	LC
St. Joseph's College, New York/Long Island Campus	NY	25,124	C
SUNY Polytechnic Inst	NY	20,438	VC
SUNY/Empire State College	NY	9,145	NC
SUNY/Fredonia	NY	20,818	C
Stonehill College	MA	55,130	C
Tenn State Univ	TN	14,423	LC
Texas Southern Univ	TX	19,592	LC
Texas State Univ	TX	18,721	C
Thomas More College	KY	36,720	LC
Tiffin Univ	OH	34,900	LC
Towson Univ	MD	21,878	C
Univ of Central Arkansas	AR	15,042	VC
Univ of Central Florida	FL	16,379	VC
Univ of Conn	CT	27,394	
Univ of Detroit Mercy	MI	48,816	C
Univ of Evansville	IN	44,186	C+
Univ of Findlay	OH	43,040	C
Univ of Illinois at Urbana-Champaign	IL	27,006	HC
Univ of La Verne	CA	55,600	C
Univ of Maine at Fort Kent	ME	15,165	LC
Univ of Miami	FL	63,494	MC
Univ of Mich/Flint	MI	19,062	C
Univ of Minn/Crookston	MN	19,126	C
Univ of Nebr - Omaha	NE	16,120	C
Univ of Nevada, Las Vegas	NV	17,553	C
Univ of N Car at Chapel Hill	NC	20,561	MC
Univ of North Florida	FL	15,996	VC
Univ of Pennsylvania	PA	63,526	MC
Univ of St. Mary	KS	37,080	NC
Univ of Scranton	PA	54,962	VC
Univ of S Dak	SD	16,109	C
Univ of Southern Indiana	IN	16,808	C
Univ of St. Francis	IL	40,828	C
Univ of Virginia	VA	27,367	MC
Univ of Washington	WA	23,091	MC
Univ of Wisc-Eau Claire	WI	16,354	VC
Univ of Wisc-Milwaukee	WI	21,538	C
Upper Iowa Univ	IA	34,990	NC
Ursuline College	OH	41,076	LC
Valparaiso Univ	IN	50,160	VC
Viterbo Univ	WI	34,660	C
Washburn Univ	KS	15,827	C
Washington Adventist Univ	MD	32,050	LC
Washington Univ in St. Louis	MO	67,539	MC
Wayland Baptist Univ	TX	23,460	LC
Weber State Univ	UT	14,112	C
West Virginia Univ Inst of Technology	WV	18,264	C
Western Carolina Univ	NC	13,965	C
Western Kentucky Univ	KY	16,850	C
Wheeling Jesuit Univ	WV	37,106	LC
Wichita State Univ	KS	17,773	C
Wilberforce Univ	OH	19,900	C
Winona State Univ	MN	18,109	C
Xavier Univ	OH	49,380	VC

HEALTH CARE LEADERSHIP

School	ST	$IS	SR
Lewis Univ	IL	41,710	C
Univ of Texas at Dallas	TX	23,640	HC

HEALTH COMMUNICATION

School	ST	$IS	SR
Cal State, Fullerton	CA	21,902	C
Campbell Univ	NC	37,570	VC
Johnson & Wales Univ/ Denver Campus	CO	44,768	C
Juniata College	PA	58,118	VC
N Dak State Univ	ND	16,245	VC
San Diego State Univ	CA	23,156	VC
Southeast Missouri State Univ	MO	16,148	C

HEALTH EDUCATION

School	ST	$IS	SR
Albany State Univ	GA	19,462	C
Anderson Univ	IN	39,450	C
Anna Maria College	MA	51,020	C
Appalachian State Univ	NC	15,394	VC
Aquinas College - Mich	MI	38,876	VC
Arizona State Univ at the Downtown Phoenix Campus	AZ	24,634	VC
Arkansas State Univ	AR	16,190	C
Arkansas Tech Univ	AR	16,534	LC
Armstrong State Univ	GA	15,615	C
Ashford Univ	CA	10,480	C
Ashland Univ	OH	30,446	C
Auburn Univ	AL	24,300	VC+
Augsburg Univ	MN	45,129	C
Augusta Univ	GA	4,632	C
Augustana Univ	SD	39,968	VC
Austin Peay State Univ	TN	16,397	C
Averett Univ	VA	43,034	LC
Ball State Univ	IN	19,808	C+
Baylor Univ	TX	56,803	HC
Bemidji State Univ	MN	17,730	C
Bethany College	KS	38,637	LC
Bethel Univ	MN	46,550	C+
Briar Cliff Univ	IA	36,956	C
Bridgewater State Univ	MA	22,762	C
Calif Baptist Univ	CA	42,986	C
Cal State, Sacramento	CA	19,060	C
Cal State, San Bernardino	CA	20,106	C
Cal State, Stanislaus	CA	18,053	LC
Campbellsville Univ	KY	33,400	C
Carson-Newman Univ	TN	35,900	C
Castleton Univ	VT	20,186	C
Central State Univ	OH	18,564	C
Central Washington Univ	WA	16,803	C
Chadron State College	NE	14,819	LC
CUNY/Hunter College	NY	31,098	VC
CUNY/Lehman College	NY	5,788	LC
Cleveland State Univ	OH	22,290	C
College of Mount St. Vincent	NY	45,620	C
Columbus State Univ	GA	14,336	LC
Concordia College - Moorhead	MN	46,418	C
Concordia Univ, Ann Arbor	MI	38,878	C+
Curry College	MA	53,331	C
Dakota State Univ	SD	12,286	C
Defiance College	OH	42,240	LC
Delaware State Univ	DE	19,376	LC
DePaul Univ	IL	52,807	VC
East Carolina Univ	NC	16,539	C
East Stroudsburg Univ	PA	18,578	LC
Eastern Kentucky Univ	KY	17,742	C
Eastern Mich Univ	MI	19,761	C
Eastern Washington Univ	WA	17,896	LC
Edinboro Univ	PA	15,940	LC
Elon Univ	NC	46,142	HC
Emporia State Univ	KS	15,029	C
Fairmont State Univ	WV	15,726	C
Fayetteville State Univ	NC	17,756	C
Florida State Univ	FL	16,771	HC
Freed-Hardeman Univ	TN	29,900	C
Friends Univ	KS	38,000	C
Gardner-Webb Univ	NC	24,935	C+
Glenville State College	WV	17,386	LC
Goddard College	VT	17,040	VC
Goshen College	IN	44,350	C
Gustavus Adolphus College	MN	53,943	HC
Hofstra Univ	NY	58,210	C+
Houghton College	NY	40,558	VC
Howard Univ	DC	37,616	C+
Idaho State Univ	ID	13,619	LC
Illinois State Univ	IL	23,418	VC
Indiana State Univ	IN	23,223	LC
Indiana Univ of Pennsylvania	PA	24,474	C
Inter-American Univ of PR-San Germán	PR	20,042	
Iowa State Univ	IA	18,176	C
Ithaca College	NY	58,158	VC+
Jackson State Univ	MS	15,879	LC
Jacksonville State Univ	AL	14,628	LC
Johnson C. Smith Univ	NC	25,336	LC
Kennesaw State Univ	GA	18,899	VC
Kent State Univ	OH	20,928	C
Lamar Univ	TX	18,014	LC
Lee Univ	TN	22,045	C
Lenoir-Rhyne Univ	NC	47,500	LC
Lincoln Memorial Univ	TN	28,430	C
Linfield College	OR	53,992	C
Lipscomb Univ	TN	42,984	VC
LIU Post	NY	50,698	C+
Manchester Univ	IN	41,540	C
Manhattan College	NY	55,652	C
Mayville State Univ	ND	18,371	NC
McNeese State Univ	LA	7,838	C
MidAmerica Nazarene Univ	KS	37,808	C
Middle Tenn State Univ	TN	8,650	C
Minn State Univ, Mankato	MN	17,190	C
Minn State Univ, Moorhead	MN	21,393	C
Missouri Baptist Univ	MO	35,594	C
Monmouth Univ	NJ	50,184	C
Montana State Univ Billings	MT	13,336	LC
Montclair State Univ	NJ	26,912	C
Morehead State Univ	KY	18,386	LC
Morgan State Univ	MD	17,190	LC
New Jersey City Univ	NJ	21,456	LC
N Car Central Univ	NC	9,000	C
N Dak State Univ	ND	16,245	VC
Northeastern Illinois Univ	IL	12,529	LC
Northeastern State Univ	OK	8,615	VC
Northern Illinois Univ	IL	20,176	C
Northern Mich Univ	MI	20,853	C
Northern State Univ	SD	15,570	C
Northwestern State Univ of Louisiana	LA	16,534	LC
Ohio Northern Univ	OH	44,050	VC
Ohio Valley Univ	WV	28,800	C
Okla State Univ	OK	17,180	C+
Oral Roberts Univ	OK	34,316	C
Otterbein Univ	OH	41,630	C
Pfeiffer Univ	NC	40,532	LC
Plymouth State Univ	NH	23,180	LC
Portland State Univ	OR	19,443	C
Purdue Univ/West Lafayette	IN	20,032	MC
Rhode Island College	RI	19,000	LC
St. Mary's College of Calif	CA	57,420	C
Sarah Lawrence College	NY	68,866	MC
Shepherd Univ, West Virginia	WV	17,382	C
Slippery Rock Univ of Pennsylvania	PA	20,450	C
S Car State Univ	SC	21,330	LC
S Dak State Univ	SD	15,874	C
Southeastern Louisiana Univ	LA	16,237	C
Southern Arkansas Univ	AR	21,532	C
Southern Conn State Univ	CT	21,924	LC
Southern Illinois Univ Carbondale	IL	24,554	C
Southern Illinois Univ Edwardsville	IL	20,188	C
Southern Methodist Univ	TX	69,008	MC
Southwest Baptist Univ	MO	30,890	LC
Southwest Minn State Univ	MN	17,783	C
Springfield College	MA	48,775	C
St. Cloud State Univ	MN	10,600	C
SUNY/Cortland	NY	20,910	C
Tabor College	KS	35,870	C
Taylor Univ	IN	42,130	VC
Tenn State Univ	TN	14,423	LC
Texas A&M Univ at Commerce	TX	10,496	C
Texas A&M Univ at Kingsville	TX	16,580	LC
Texas State Univ	TX	18,721	C
The American Univ	DC	61,317	HC
The Citadel, The Military College of S Car	SC	20,679	C
The College of New Jersey	NJ	28,675	VC+
The Univ of Montana Western	MT	9,426	LC
The Univ of Utah	UT	18,751	VC
Troy Univ	AL	16,171	C
Tulane Univ	LA	67,496	MC
Univ of Alabama at Birmingham	AL	22,092	C
Univ of Arkansas at Little Rock	AR	18,211	LC
Univ of Arkansas at Monticello	AR	13,599	LC
Univ of Cincinnati	OH	22,118	VC
Univ of Florida	FL	16,291	HC+
Univ of Georgia	GA	21,878	HC
Univ of Illinois at Chicago	IL	24,664	VC
Univ of Iowa	IA	19,415	HC
Univ of Kansas	KS	20,884	VC
Univ of Kentucky	KY	24,800	C+
Univ of Louisiana at Lafayette	LA	14,516	C
Univ of Maine at Farmington	ME	18,792	C
Univ of Maine at Presque Isle	ME	16,148	LC
Univ of Maryland/Eastern Shore	MD	21,861	LC
Univ of Minn/Duluth	MN	20,292	C
Univ of Nebr - Kearney	NE	17,014	LC
Univ of Nevada, Las Vegas	NV	17,553	C
Univ of New Mexico	NM	16,808	C
Univ of N Car at Pembroke	NC	14,737	LC
Univ of North Georgia	GA	17,316	C
Univ of Northern Iowa	IA	17,480	C
Univ of Pittsburgh at Bradford	PA	22,958	C
Univ of Rhode Island	RI	26,066	VC
Univ of Rio Grande & Rio Grande Community College	OH	8,750	LC
Univ of Southern Miss	MS	13,170	C
Univ of the Cumberlands	KY	32,000	LC
Univ of the District of Columbia	DC	21,260	LC
Univ of Toledo	OH	19,336	C
Univ of West Florida	FL	15,848	C
Univ of Wisc-La Crosse	WI	15,425	VC
Univ of Wisc-Stevens Point	WI	14,043	C
Univ of Wisc-Superior	WI	14,838	C
Utah State Univ	UT	13,235	C
Valley City State Univ	ND	13,267	C
Virginia Commonwealth Univ	VA	23,811	VC
Wayne State College	NE	25,746	NC
Wayne State Univ	MI	23,085	C
Weber State Univ	UT	14,112	C
West Chester Univ of Pennsylvania	PA	19,171	VC
West Liberty Univ	WV	16,158	C
Western Mich Univ	MI	21,791	C
Western Oregon Univ	OR	19,965	LC
Western Washington Univ	WA	18,904	VC
William Paterson Univ of New Jersey	NJ	24,022	C
William Penn Univ	IA	26,000	C
Wilmington College	OH	35,100	C
Winona State Univ	MN	18,109	C
Worcester State Univ	MA	20,977	C
Youngstown State Univ	OH	17,487	C

HEALTH INFORMATION MANAGEMENT

School	ST	$IS	SR
Arkansas Tech Univ	AR	16,534	LC
Armstrong State Univ	GA	15,615	C
Ashford Univ	CA	10,480	C
Augusta Univ	GA	4,632	C
Bluffton Univ	OH	40,950	C+
Champlain College	VT	54,724	VC
Charter Oak State College	CT	7,983	NC
College of St. Scholastica	MN	45,734	C+
Coppin State Univ	MD	14,071	VC
Dakota State Univ	SD	12,286	C
Drury Univ	MO	37,555	VC
Duquesne Univ	PA	48,508	VC
Ferris State Univ	MI	21,458	C
Gannon Univ	PA	42,922	C
Georgian Court Univ	NJ	43,068	LC
Idaho State Univ	ID	13,619	LC
Illinois State Univ	IL	23,418	VC
Indiana Inst of Technology	IN	34,240	LC
Indiana Univ Bloomington	IN	20,791	HC
Indiana Univ Northwest	IN	7,207	LC
Indiana Univ Southeast	IN	16,931	C
Indiana Univ-Purdue Univ Indianapolis	IN	18,952	C
John Carroll Univ	OH	51,570	C
Kean Univ	NJ	25,620	C
King Univ	TN	36,976	C
Loyola Univ Chicago	IL	57,158	VC
Marymount Univ	VA	43,231	C
Medaille College	NY	41,700	LC
Mercy College of Health Sciences	IA	17,600	SP
Missouri Western State Univ	MO	17,822	LC
Montana Tech of the Univ of Montana	MT	15,447	VC
Mount St. Joseph Univ	OH	33,880	LC
Murray State Univ	KY	17,726	C+
Ohio State Univ at Columbus	OH	22,843	MC
Regis Univ	CO	46,380	C
St. Louis Univ	MO	49,866	HC
Simmons College	MA	54,400	HC
Southern Illinois Univ Carbondale	IL	24,554	C
Southern Illinois Univ Edwardsville	IL	20,188	C
Southern Univ at New Orleans	LA	8,014	LC
Southwestern Okla State Univ	OK	12,205	C

ST = STATE $IS = IN-STATE COSTS SR = SELECTOR RATING

School	ST	$IS	SR
St. John's Univ	NY	57,160	C+
SUNY Polytechnic Inst	NY	20,438	VC
Temple Univ	PA	24,392	C+
Texas State Univ	TX	18,721	C
The Univ of Tenn at Knoxville	TN	22,112	VC
Thomas Edison State Univ	NJ	6,350	NC
Univ of Central Florida	FL	16,379	VC
Univ of Cincinnati	OH	22,118	VC
Univ of Illinois at Chicago	IL	24,664	VC
Univ of Kansas	KS	20,884	VC
Univ of Maine at Farmington	ME	18,792	C
Univ of Maine at Fort Kent	ME	15,165	LC
Univ of Miss	MS	18,802	C
Univ of Pittsburgh	PA	30,030	MC
Univ of South Alabama	AL	16,186	C
Univ of S Car Upstate	SC	19,272	LC
Univ of Southern Indiana	IN	16,808	C
Univ of Wisc-Green Bay	WI	15,184	C
Univ of Wisc-La Crosse	WI	15,425	VC
Univ of Wisc-Parkside	WI	15,313	C
Weber State Univ	UT	14,112	C
Western Mich Univ	MI	21,791	C
Xavier Univ	OH	49,380	VC

HEALTH PROMOTION

School	ST	$IS	SR
Arkansas State Univ	AR	16,190	C
Ashford Univ	CA	10,480	C
Baldwin Wallace Univ	OH	42,464	VC
Barton College	NC	39,854	C
Cambridge College	MA	14,940	NC
Cedar Crest College	PA	51,110	C
Georgia Southern Univ	GA	16,540	VC
Goddard College	VT	17,040	VC
Johnson & Wales Univ/ Denver Campus	CO	44,768	C
Keene State College	NH	24,604	C
Lubbock Christian Univ	TX	29,727	C
Missouri Southern State Univ	MO	13,071	C
Missouri State Univ	MO	15,837	C+
Nebr Methodist College	NE	25,314	C
North Greenville Univ	SC	25,930	C
Nova Southeastern Univ	FL	38,534	C+
Ohio State Univ at Columbus	OH	22,843	MC
Texas State Univ	TX	18,721	C
The American Univ	DC	61,317	HC
Univ of Georgia	GA	21,878	HC
Univ of Lynchburg	VA	48,370	C
Univ of Montana	MT	14,105	C
Univ of N Car at Asheville	NC	16,251	VC+
Univ of Northern Iowa	IA	17,480	C
Univ of Rhode Island	RI	26,066	VC
Univ of Wisc-Superior	WI	14,838	C
Weber State Univ	UT	14,112	C
Western Conn State Univ	CT	21,254	LC

HEALTH PSYCHOLOGY

School	ST	$IS	SR
Emmanuel College	MA	53,472	C+

HEALTH SCIENCE

School	ST	$IS	SR
Adventist Univ of Health Sciences	FL	48,492	SP
Albany College of Pharmacy and Health Sciences	NY	44,421	SP
Alcorn State Univ	MS	15,884	C
Alderson Broaddus Univ	WV	35,000	LC
Alma College	MI	49,410	VC
Alvernia Univ	PA	45,330	C
Appalachian State Univ	NC	15,394	VC
Arizona State Univ at the Downtown Phoenix Campus	AZ	24,634	VC
Arizona State Univ at the West Campus	AZ	21,513	VC
Armstrong State Univ	GA	15,615	C
Asbury Univ	KY	36,450	C+
Ashford Univ	CA	10,480	C
Assumption College	MA	48,455	VC
Aurora Univ	IL	34,990	C
Ball State Univ	IN	19,808	C+
Baylor Univ	TX	56,803	HC
Benedictine Univ	IL	38,300	C
Bloomsburg Univ of Pennsylvania	PA	19,930	C
Boise State Univ	ID	17,368	C
Boston Univ	MA	67,352	MC
Bowling Green State Univ	OH	19,975	C
Bradley Univ	IL	43,240	VC
Brandeis Univ	MA	68,443	MC
Brewton-Parker College	GA	26,120	LC
Brigham Young Univ	UT	13,248	MC
Butler Univ	IN	52,890	VC+
Calif Baptist Univ	CA	42,986	C
Cal State, Chico	CA	19,790	VC
Cal State, Dominguez Hills	CA	19,022	LC
Cal State, East Bay	CA	20,748	C
Cal State, Fresno	CA	16,902	LC
Cal State, Fullerton	CA	21,902	C
Cal State, Long Beach	CA	18,850	C
Cal State, Los Angeles	CA	17,186	LC
Cal State, Northridge	CA	17,277	LC
Cal State, San Bernardino	CA	20,106	C
Carroll College	MT	44,304	C
Castleton Univ	VT	20,186	C
Cedar Crest College	PA	51,110	C
Chapman Univ	CA	65,504	HC
Chicago State Univ	IL	41,620	C
CUNY/Brooklyn College	NY	7,163	C+
Cleveland State Univ	OH	22,290	C
College of St Joseph	VT	32,400	LC
College of St. Scholastica	MN	45,734	C+
College of William & Mary	VA	34,907	MC
Colo State Univ	CO	23,033	C
Columbus State Univ	GA	14,336	LC
Corban Univ	OR	41,700	C
Culver-Stockton College	MO	34,350	C
Daemen College	NY	40,336	C
DePaul Univ	IL	52,807	VC
Dordt College	IA	37,860	C+
Drexel Univ	PA	65,927	HC
Duquesne Univ	PA	48,508	VC
East Tenn State Univ	TN	18,141	C
East Texas Baptist Univ	TX	34,444	C
Eastern Conn State Univ	CT	23,059	C
Elms College	MA	49,602	VC
Emmanuel College	MA	53,472	C+
Emporia State Univ	KS	15,029	C
Excelsior College	NY	38,800	SP
Ferrum College	VA	43,970	C
Fitchburg State Univ	MA	21,819	LC
Florida Atlantic Univ	FL	18,256	C
Florida Gulf Coast Univ	FL	14,738	C
Franklin Pierce Univ	NH	46,750	LC
Friends Univ	KS	38,000	C
Furman Univ	SC	61,098	VC+
Gannon Univ	PA	42,922	C
George Mason Univ	VA	19,884	C
Gettysburg College	PA	65,210	MC
Goddard College	VT	17,040	VC
Goodwin College	CT	28,370	LC
Grand Canyon Univ	AZ	25,150	VC
Grand Valley State Univ	MI	22,250	C+
Grove City College	PA	26,654	VC
Guilford College	NC	45,973	C
Hampshire College	MA	65,214	MC
Harding Univ	AR	25,440	C
Hardin-Simmons Univ	TX	36,025	C
Henderson State Univ	AR	15,516	C
Hofstra Univ	NY	58,210	C+
Howard Univ	DC	37,616	C+
Idaho State Univ	ID	13,619	LC
Indiana Univ East	IN	7,207	C
Indiana Univ Kokomo	IN	7,207	C
Indiana Univ Northwest	IN	7,207	LC
Indiana Univ South Bend	IN	16,057	C
Indiana Univ-Purdue Univ Indianapolis	IN	18,952	C
Ithaca College	NY	58,158	VC+
James Madison Univ	VA	19,084	VC
Johnson & Wales Univ/ Denver Campus	CO	44,768	C
Johnson State College	VT	22,672	C
Kalamazoo College	MI	53,931	HC
Keene State College	NH	24,604	C
Kent State Univ	OH	20,928	C
La Roche College	PA	38,940	C
La Sierra Univ	CA	39,690	VC
Lasell College	MA	49,400	C
Lee Univ	TN	22,045	C
Lincoln Univ	PA	20,878	LC
LIU Brooklyn	NY	50,698	C
LIU Post	NY	50,698	C+
Lock Haven Univ of Pennsylvania	PA	20,544	LC
Loyola Marymount Univ	CA	60,202	VC+
Madonna Univ	MI	30,450	LC
Marietta College	OH	46,190	C
Marshall Univ	WV	18,044	C
Mary Baldwin Univ	VA	40,495	C
Marymount Univ	VA	43,231	C
Maryville Univ of St. Louis	MO	38,558	VC
Marywood Univ	PA	47,840	C
Mass College of Liberal Arts	MA	20,659	C
MCPHS Univ	MA	45,470	SP
Mercy College	NY	32,614	C
Mercy College of Health Sciences	IA	17,600	SP
Merrimack College	MA	55,415	C
Middle Tenn State Univ	TN	8,650	C
Midwestern State Univ	TX	12,111	LC
Minn State Univ, Mankato	MN	17,190	C
Missouri Baptist Univ	MO	35,594	C
Missouri Southern State Univ	MO	13,071	C
Moravian College	PA	55,488	C
Mount St. Mary's Univ	MD	53,380	C
Nazareth College	NY	46,784	C
New England College	NH	50,828	NC
New York Inst of Technology	NY	49,980	VC
Newman Univ	KS	37,382	C
Nicholls State Univ	LA	14,959	C
Norfolk State Univ	VA	18,902	LC
Northeastern Univ	MA	65,352	MC
Northern Arizona Univ	AZ	21,003	C
Northern Illinois Univ	IL	20,176	C
Northern Kentucky Univ	KY	16,486	C
Oakland Univ	MI	20,763	C
Ohio State Univ at Columbus	OH	22,843	MC
Ohio State Univ at Lima	OH	7,553	C
Old Dominion Univ	VA	21,618	C
Oral Roberts Univ	OK	34,316	C
Oregon Inst of Technology	OR	19,227	C
Pace Univ	NY	60,136	C
Pennsylvania College of Technology	PA	27,693	NC
Point Loma Nazarene Univ	CA	46,150	C+
Purdue Univ Northwest	IN	15,178	C
Purdue Univ/West Lafayette	IN	20,032	MC
Quinnipiac Univ	CT	60,970	VC
Randolph College	VA	53,970	C
Regis Univ	CO	46,380	C
Rutgers Univ - New Brunswick	NJ	27,090	HC
Sacred Heart Univ	CT	54,590	C
Saginaw Valley State Univ	MI	19,284	C
St. Joseph's Univ	PA	58,540	VC
St. Mary's College of Calif	CA	57,420	C
Samford Univ	AL	40,770	VC
San Diego State Univ	CA	23,156	VC
San Francisco State Univ	CA	18,514	LC
San Jose State Univ	CA	22,630	C
South Univ	GA	36,070	LC
Southeast Missouri State Univ	MO	16,148	C
Southern Adventist Univ	TN	28,250	C
Southwestern Okla State Univ	OK	12,205	C
Spalding Univ	KY	31,938	C
St. Bonaventure Univ	NY	45,596	C
St. Francis College	NY	38,800	LC
SUNY/Cortland	NY	20,910	C
Stephen F. Austin State Univ	TX	18,484	LC
Sterling College	KS	32,830	LC
Stetson Univ	FL	57,174	VC+
Stony Brook Univ/The SUNY	NY	22,703	MC
Syracuse Univ	NY	62,313	HC
Taylor Univ	IN	42,130	VC
Tenn Wesleyan Univ	TN	32,680	LC
Texas A&M Univ at Corpus Christi	TX	16,851	LC
Texas Woman's Univ	TX	15,302	LC
The College at Brockport - SUNY	NY	21,058	C
The Univ of Memphis	TN	18,278	C
The Univ of Tenn at Martin	TN	15,212	C
Towson Univ	MD	21,878	C
Truman State Univ	MO	16,286	MC
Universidad Adventista de las Antillas	PR	16,606	
Univ of Alabama at Birmingham	AL	22,092	C
Univ of Arkansas at Little Rock	AR	18,211	LC
Univ of Calif, Santa Cruz	CA	28,731	C+
Univ of Central Arkansas	AR	15,042	VC
Univ of Central Florida	FL	16,379	VC
Univ of Colo Colo Springs	CO	20,300	C
Univ of Delaware	DE	32,214	VC
Univ of Findlay	OH	43,040	C
Univ of Florida	FL	16,291	HC+
Univ of Hartford	CT	49,776	C
Univ of Holy Cross	LA	21,523	NC
Univ of Louisiana at Monroe	LA	15,970	C
Univ of Maryland/Baltimore County	MD	23,004	VC
Univ of Miami	FL	63,494	MC
Univ of Mich/Flint	MI	19,062	C
Univ of Minn/Crookston	MN	19,126	C
Univ of Miss	MS	18,802	C
Univ of Missouri-Kansas City	MO	19,563	VC
Univ of Nebr - Lincoln	NE	18,589	VC
Univ of North Florida	FL	15,996	VC
Univ of Northwestern - St. Paul	MN	39,530	C
Univ of Richmond	VA	62,730	MC
Univ of South Alabama	AL	16,880	C
Univ of S Dak	SD	16,109	C
Univ of South Florida St. Petersburg	FL	15,980	C
Univ of Southern Maine	ME	18,320	C
Univ of Texas at El Paso	TX	34,452	NC
Univ of Texas Rio Grande Valley	TX	15,573	LC
Univ of the Sciences	PA	40,738	VC
Univ of Vermont	VT	29,792	HC
Univ of West Alabama	AL	16,284	LC
Univ of Wisc-Parkside	WI	15,313	C
Univ of Wisc-Stevens Point	WI	14,043	C
Valparaiso Univ	IN	50,160	VC
Washington Univ in St. Louis	MO	67,539	MC
Wayne State Univ	MI	23,085	C
West Chester Univ of Pennsylvania	PA	19,171	VC
Western Conn State Univ	CT	21,254	LC
Western New England Univ	MA	49,182	C
Wheaton College	IL	44,993	MC
Whitworth Univ	WA	53,682	VC
William Paterson Univ of New Jersey	NJ	24,022	C
Yeshiva Univ	NY	52,750	VC

HEALTH SCIENCE BIOLOGY INTERDISCIPLINARY

School	ST	$IS	SR
Chatham Univ	PA	47,883	VC
Univ of Texas at Dallas	TX	23,640	HC

HEALTH SCIENCE EXERCISE SCIENCE INTERDISCIPLINARY

School	ST	$IS	SR
Chatham Univ	PA	47,883	VC

HEALTH SERVICES ADMINISTRATION

School	ST	$IS	SR
Armstrong State Univ	GA	15,615	C
Drexel Univ	PA	65,927	HC
Florida International Univ	FL	20,281	C
Indiana Univ Northwest	IN	7,207	LC
Marian Univ	IN	43,206	C
Univ of Detroit Mercy	MI	48,816	C
Univ of Minn/Twin Cities	MN	24,269	MC
Univ of Rhode Island	RI	26,066	VC
Univ of St. Francis	IN	38,520	C
Univ of San Francisco	CA	60,580	C
Weber State Univ	UT	14,112	C

HEALTH SERVICES TECHNOLOGY

School	ST	$IS	SR
Concordia College - New York	NY	39,035	LC
Indiana Univ-Purdue Univ Indianapolis	IN	18,952	C
John Carroll Univ	OH	51,570	C
Thomas Edison State Univ	NJ	6,350	NC
Univ of Pittsburgh	PA	30,030	MC
Univ of Texas Rio Grande Valley	TX	15,573	LC
Weber State Univ	UT	14,112	C
Wichita State Univ	KS	17,773	C

HEALTHCARE MARKETING

School	ST	$IS	SR
Ferris State Univ	MI	21,458	C
MCPHS Univ	MA	45,470	SP

HEALTHY LIFESTYLE MANAGEMENT

School	ST	$IS	SR
Creighton Univ	NE	49,452	VC

HEAVY EQUIPMENT SERVICE ENGINEERING

School	ST	$IS	SR
Ferris State Univ	MI	21,458	C

HEBREW

School	ST	$IS	SR
Bard College	NY	65,924	HC
CUNY/Hunter College	NY	31,098	VC
CUNY/Lehman College	NY	5,788	LC
CUNY/Queens College	NY	21,507	C
Harvard College/Harvard Univ	MA	65,609	MC
Hofstra Univ	NY	58,210	C+
New York Univ	NY	68,139	MC
Ohio State Univ at Columbus	OH	22,843	MC
SUNY at Binghamton	NY	24,100	MC
The American Univ	DC	61,317	HC
The Univ of Texas at Austin	TX	20,206	MC
The Univ of Utah	UT	18,751	VC
Thomas Edison State Univ	NJ	6,350	NC
Touro College	NY	31,040	C
Univ of Calif at Los Angeles	CA	27,438	HC+
Univ of Cincinnati	OH	22,118	VC
Univ of Illinois at Urbana-Champaign	IL	27,006	HC
Univ of Mich/Ann Arbor	MI	25,274	MC
Univ of Minn/Twin Cities	MN	24,269	MC
Washington Univ in St. Louis	MO	67,539	MC
Wellesley College	MA	66,984	MC
Yeshiva Univ	NY	52,750	VC

HISPANIC AMERICAN STUDIES

School	ST	$IS	SR
Boston College	MA	68,043	MC
Boston Univ	MA	67,352	MC
Brown Univ	RI	64,566	MC
Cal State, Long Beach	CA	18,850	C
Carnegie Mellon Univ	PA	67,980	MC
CUNY/Brooklyn College	NY	7,163	C+
CUNY/Hunter College	NY	31,098	VC
Claremont McKenna College	CA	69,900	MC
College of St. Benedict	MN	54,480	C
Colo College	CO	64,894	MC
Columbia Univ/ School of General Studies	NY	61,470	MC
Columbia Univ/City of New York	NY	62,958	MC
Conn College	CT	65,000	MC
Dartmouth College	NH	68,109	MC
East Carolina Univ	NC	16,539	C
Hamilton College	NY	64,250	MC
Lewis & Clark College	OR	60,984	MC
Loyola Marymount Univ	CA	60,202	VC+
Macalester College	MN	64,136	MC
Mills College	CA	43,705	C
Mount St. Mary College	NY	44,448	C
Northeastern Illinois Univ	IL	12,529	LC
Pacific Lutheran Univ	WA	49,960	C
Pepperdine Univ	CA	66,862	VC+
Pomona College	CA	64,957	MC
Rice Univ	TX	59,458	MC
Rutgers Univ - New Brunswick	NJ	27,090	HC
St. John's Univ	MN	53,472	C
Scripps College	CA	69,260	MC
Stanford Univ	CA	62,541	MC
SUNY Albany	NY	22,165	C
SUNY/Oneonta	NY	20,794	C
The Univ of Tenn at Knoxville	TN	22,112	VC

ST = STATE **$IS** = IN-STATE COSTS **SR** = SELECTOR RATING

School	ST	$IS	SR
Univ of Calif at Berkeley	CA	29,886	MC
Univ of Calif at Irvine	CA	33,857	VC
Univ of Mass Boston	MA	13,828	C
Univ of Mich/Ann Arbor	MI	25,274	MC
Univ of Mich/Dearborn	MI	12,472	VC
Univ of Pennsylvania	PA	63,526	MC
Univ of PR, at Cayey	PR		
Vassar College	NY	68,110	MC
Wabash College	IN	52,100	VC
Wellesley College	MA	66,984	MC
Wesleyan Univ	CT	66,940	MC
Western New Mexico Univ	NM	16,914	LC
Wheaton College	MA	63,818	VC

HISTORIC PRESERVATION

School	ST	$IS	SR
College of Charleston	SC	24,046	VC
Eastern Mich Univ	MI	19,761	C
Roger Williams Univ	RI	48,074	VC
Salve Regina Univ	RI	53,046	VC
Savannah College of Art and Design	GA	49,595	SP
Southeast Missouri State Univ	MO	16,148	C
Univ of Delaware	DE	32,214	VC
Univ of Mary Washington	VA	23,039	C+
Univ of Mich/Ann Arbor	MI	25,274	MC
Ursuline College	OH	41,076	LC

HISTORY

School	ST	$IS	SR
Abilene Christian Univ	TX	43,708	C+
Adams State Univ	CO	15,420	LC
Adelphi Univ	NY	49,792	C
Adrian College	MI	45,550	C
Agnes Scott College	GA	51,930	VC+
Alabama A&M Univ	AL	18,796	C
Alabama State Univ	AL	16,490	LC
Albany State Univ	GA	19,462	C
Albertus Magnus College	CT	44,016	LC
Albion College	MI	55,260	C
Albright College	PA	57,326	C
Alcorn State Univ	MS	15,884	C
Alderson Broaddus Univ	WV	35,000	LC
Alfred Univ	NY	37,490	C
Alice Lloyd College	KY	8,190	LC
Allegheny College	PA	57,620	VC
Allen Univ	SC	19,920	NC
Alma College	MI	49,410	VC
Alvernia Univ	PA	45,330	C
Alverno College	WI	33,294	LC
American International College	MA	47,020	LC
Amherst College	MA	66,186	MC
Anderson Univ	IN	39,450	C
Andrews Univ	MI	41,732	C
Angelo State Univ	TX	15,882	LC
Anna Maria College	MA	51,020	C
Appalachian State Univ	NC	15,394	VC
Aquinas College	TN	30,800	C+
Aquinas College - Mich	MI	38,876	VC
Arcadia Univ	PA	55,990	C+
Arizona State Univ at the Polytechnic Campus	AZ	22,394	VC
Arizona State Univ at the Tempe Campus	AZ	23,001	VC
Arizona State Univ at the West Campus	AZ	21,513	VC
Arkansas State Univ	AR	16,190	C
Arkansas Tech Univ	AR	16,534	LC
Armstrong State Univ	GA	15,615	C
Asbury Univ	KY	36,450	C+
Ashford Univ	CA	10,480	C
Ashland Univ	OH	30,446	C
Assumption College	MA	48,455	VC
Atlantic Union College	MA	27,228	C
Auburn Univ	AL	24,300	VC+
Auburn Univ at Montgomery	AL	15,000	C
Augsburg Univ	MN	45,129	C
Augusta Univ	GA	4,632	C
Augustana College	IL	51,222	VC+
Augustana Univ	SD	39,968	VC
Aurora Univ	IL	34,990	C
Austin College	TX	51,059	HC
Austin Peay State Univ	TN	16,397	C
Averett Univ	VA	43,034	LC
Avila Univ	MO	27,100	C
Azusa Pacific Univ	CA	43,972	C
Baker Univ	KS	37,190	C
Baldwin Wallace Univ	OH	42,464	VC
Ball State Univ	IN	19,808	C+
Bard College	NY	65,924	HC
Bard College at Simon's Rock	MA	65,795	MC
Barnard College/Columbia Univ	NY	68,762	MC
Barry Univ	FL	38,730	LC
Barton College	NC	39,854	C
Bates College	ME	64,500	HC
Baylor Univ	TX	56,803	HC
Belhaven Univ	MS	32,250	C
Bellarmine Univ	KY	52,532	C
Bellevue Univ	NE	20,300	NC
Belmont Abbey College	NC	28,794	C
Belmont Univ	TN	44,500	VC+
Beloit College	WI	55,206	HC
Bemidji State Univ	MN	17,730	C
Benedict College	SC	28,630	NC
Benedictine College	KS	38,850	VC
Benedictine Univ	IL	38,300	C
Bennington College	VT	66,280	MC
Bentley Univ	MA	63,720	MC
Berea College	KY	7,094	C
Berry College	GA	47,466	VC
Bethany College	KS	38,637	LC
Bethany College	WV	38,774	LC
Bethel College	IN	36,830	C
Bethel College	KS	35,370	C
Bethel Univ	MN	46,550	C+
Bethel Univ	TN	27,142	C
Bethune-Cookman Univ	FL	23,322	C
Biola Univ	CA	48,686	C
Birmingham-Southern College	AL	44,478	C+
Black Hills State Univ	SD	16,622	C
Blackburn College	IL	28,526	LC
Bloomfield College	NJ	40,100	LC
Bloomsburg Univ of Pennsylvania	PA	19,930	C
Blue Mountain College	MS	15,949	C
Bluefield College	VA	34,711	C
Bluffton Univ	OH	40,950	C+
Boise State Univ	ID	17,368	C
Boston College	MA	68,043	MC
Boston Univ	MA	67,352	MC
Bowdoin College	ME	65,980	MC
Bowie State Univ	MD	18,610	LC
Bowling Green State Univ	OH	19,975	C
Bradley Univ	IL	43,240	VC
Brandeis Univ	MA	68,443	MC
Brenau Univ - Women's College	GA	37,876	LC
Brescia Univ	KY	29,890	VC
Brewton-Parker College	GA	26,120	LC
Briar Cliff Univ	IA	36,956	C
Bridgewater College	VA	46,260	C
Brigham Young Univ	UT	13,248	MC
Brigham Young Univ/Hawaii	HI	11,710	C
Brown Univ	RI	64,566	MC
Bryan College	TN	32,900	C
Bryant Univ	RI	57,204	VC
Bryn Athyn College	PA	32,664	C
Bryn Mawr College	PA	65,220	MC
Bucknell Univ	PA	67,136	MC
Buena Vista Univ	IA	42,344	C
Butler Univ	IN	52,890	VC+
Cairn Univ	PA	37,572	C
Caldwell Univ	NJ	42,165	LC
Calif Baptist Univ	CA	42,986	C
Calif Inst of Technology	CA	64,704	MC
Calif Lutheran Univ	CA	52,853	C
Calif Polytechnic State Univ	CA	22,547	MC
Calif State Polytechnic Univ, Pomona	CA	21,811	C
Cal State, Bakersfield	CA	22,397	LC
Cal State, Chico	CA	19,790	VC
Cal State, Dominguez Hills	CA	19,022	LC
Cal State, East Bay	CA	20,748	C
Cal State, Fresno	CA	16,902	LC
Cal State, Fullerton	CA	21,902	C
Cal State, Long Beach	CA	18,850	C
Cal State, Los Angeles	CA	17,186	LC
Cal State, Northridge	CA	17,277	LC
Cal State, Sacramento	CA	19,060	C
Cal State, San Bernardino	CA	20,106	C
Cal State, San Marcos	CA	20,604	LC
Cal State, Stanislaus	CA	18,053	LC
Calif Univ of Pennsylvania	PA	20,425	LC
Calvin College	MI	43,090	HC
Cameron Univ	OK	11,632	LC
Campbell Univ	NC	37,570	VC
Campbellsville Univ	KY	33,400	C
Canisius College	NY	49,672	C
Capital Univ	OH	44,778	VC
Cardinal Stritch Univ	WI	37,136	C
Carleton College	MN	66,414	MC
Carlow Univ	PA	39,696	LC
Carnegie Mellon Univ	PA	67,980	MC
Carroll College	MT	44,304	C
Carroll Univ	WI	38,100	C+
Carson-Newman Univ	TN	35,900	C
Carthage College	WI	48,835	C
Case Western Reserve Univ	OH	62,284	MC
Castleton Univ	VT	20,186	C
Catawba College	NC	39,820	LC
Cedar Crest College	PA	51,110	C
Cedarville Univ	OH	36,244	VC
Centenary College	NJ	43,890	LC
Centenary College of Louisiana	LA	49,050	C+
Central College	IA	44,592	C
Central Conn State Univ	CT	22,041	C
Central Methodist Univ	MO	31,500	VC
Central Mich Univ	MI	20,330	C
Central State Univ	OH	18,564	C
Central Washington Univ	WA	16,803	C
Centre College	KY	50,680	MC
Chadron State College	NE	14,819	LC
Chaminade Univ of Honolulu	HI	37,614	C
Chapman Univ	CA	65,504	HC
Charleston Southern Univ	SC	34,700	C
Chatham Univ	PA	47,883	VC
Chestnut Hill College	PA	47,180	C
Chicago State Univ	IL	41,620	C
Christendom College	VA	32,600	VC
Christian Brothers Univ	TN	31,670	VC
Christopher Newport Univ	VA	24,878	VC+
CUNY/Baruch College	NY	21,609	HC
CUNY/Brooklyn College	NY	7,163	C+
CUNY/City College	NY	20,204	C
CUNY/Hunter College	NY	31,098	VC
CUNY/Lehman College	NY	5,788	LC
CUNY/Queens College	NY	21,507	C
CUNY/York College	NY	6,747	LC
Claflin Univ	SC	25,592	LC
Claremont McKenna College	CA	69,900	MC
Clarion Univ of Pennsylvania	PA	21,608	LC
Clark Atlanta Univ	GA	31,019	LC
Clark Univ	MA	53,260	HC+
Clarke Univ	IA	42,950	C
Clarkson Univ	NY	60,392	VC
Clayton State Univ	GA	19,735	LC
Clemson Univ	SC		HC
Cleveland State Univ	OH	22,290	C
Coastal Carolina Univ	SC	20,340	C
Coe College	IA	51,570	VC
Coker College	SC	38,196	C
Colby College	ME	64,060	MC
Colby-Sawyer College	NH	50,790	C
Colgate Univ	NY	67,500	MC
College of Charleston	SC	24,046	VC
College of Mount St. Vincent	NY	45,620	C
College of St. Benedict	MN	54,480	C
College of St. Elizabeth	NJ	45,700	LC
College of St Joseph	VT	32,400	LC
College of St. Scholastica	MN	45,734	C+
College of Staten Island	NY	24,389	LC
College of the Holy Cross	MA	64,320	MC
College of the Ozarks	MO	7,530	VC
College of William & Mary	VA	34,907	MC
Colo Christian Univ	CO	40,885	VC
Colo College	CO	64,894	MC
Colo Mesa Univ	CO	19,707	LC
Colo State Univ	CO	23,033	C
Colo State Univ-Pueblo	CO	21,581	C
Columbia College	SC	36,550	C
Columbia College - Missouri	MO	28,179	C
Columbia Univ/ School of General Studies	NY	61,470	MC
Columbia Univ/City of New York	NY	62,958	MC
Columbus State Univ	GA	14,336	LC
Concord Univ	WV	14,954	LC
Concordia College - Moorhead	MN	46,418	C
Concordia College - New York	NY	39,035	LC
Concordia Univ Irvine	CA	44,860	VC
Concordia Univ Nebr	NE	41,900	VC
Concordia Univ St. Paul	MN	29,050	C
Concordia Univ Texas	TX	41,920	C
Concordia Univ Wisc	WI	35,910	C
Concordia Univ, Ann Arbor	MI	38,878	C+
Concordia Univ, Chicago	IL	41,522	C
Conn College	CT	65,000	MC
Converse College	SC	28,290	C
Coppin State Univ	MD	14,071	VC
Corban Univ	OR	41,700	C
Cornell College	IA	49,900	VC
Cornell Univ	NY	67,591	MC
Cornerstone Univ	MI	36,550	C
Covenant College	GA	44,590	HC
Creighton Univ	NE	49,452	VC
Culver-Stockton College	MO	34,350	C
Cumberland Univ	TN	27,710	C
Curry College	MA	53,331	C
Daemen College	NY	40,336	C
Dakota Wesleyan Univ	SD	33,980	LC
Dallas Baptist Univ	TX	35,220	VC
Dartmouth College	NH	68,109	MC
Davidson College	NC	60,119	MC
Davis & Elkins College	WV	38,242	LC
Defiance College	OH	42,240	LC
Delaware State Univ	DE	19,376	LC
Delta State Univ	MS	13,176	LC
Denison Univ	OH	62,770	HC+
DePaul Univ	IL	52,807	VC
DePauw Univ	IN	58,688	VC
DeSales Univ	PA	47,520	C
Dickinson College	PA	66,166	MC
Dickinson State Univ	ND	12,372	LC
Dillard Univ	LA	20,940	VC
Doane Univ	NE	41,340	VC
Dominican College	NY	40,258	LC
Dominican Univ	IL	42,472	C+
Dominican Univ of Calif	CA	58,750	C
Dordt College	IA	37,860	C+
Drake Univ	IA	49,220	HC
Drew Univ/College of Liberal Arts	NJ	53,608	VC
Drexel Univ	PA	65,927	HC
Drury Univ	MO	37,555	VC
Duke Univ	NC	68,298	MC
Duquesne Univ	PA	48,508	VC
D'Youville College	NY	37,678	C
Earlham College	IN	55,670	HC
East Carolina Univ	NC	16,539	C
East Central Univ	OK	13,330	C
East Stroudsburg Univ	PA	18,578	LC
East Tenn State Univ	TN	18,141	C
East Texas Baptist Univ	TX	34,444	C
Eastern Conn State Univ	CT	23,059	C
Eastern Illinois Univ	IL	21,414	C
Eastern Kentucky Univ	KY	17,742	C
Eastern Mennonite Univ	VA	42,550	C
Eastern Mich Univ	MI	19,761	C
Eastern Nazarene College	MA	41,114	C
Eastern New Mexico Univ	NM	12,874	LC
Eastern Oregon Univ	OR	17,612	C
Eastern Univ	PA	39,540	C
Eastern Washington Univ	WA	17,896	LC
Eckerd College	FL	55,206	VC
Edgewood College	WI	35,950	C
Edinboro Univ	PA	15,940	LC
Edward Waters College	FL	28,089	NC
Elizabeth City State Univ	NC	14,745	C
Elizabethtown College	PA	56,340	VC
Elmhurst College	IL	46,514	C
Elmira College	NY	53,900	C
Elon Univ	NC	46,142	HC
Emmanuel College	MA	53,472	C+
Emory and Henry College	VA	46,320	C
Emory Univ	GA	63,286	MC
Emporia State Univ	KS	15,029	C
Endicott College	MA	47,054	C+
Erskine College	SC	45,460	C
Eugene Lang College of Liberal Arts	NY	64,940	VC
Eureka College	IL	34,760	C
Evangel Univ	MO	28,898	C
Excelsior College	NY	38,800	SP
Fairfield Univ	CT	61,445	HC
Fairleigh Dickinson Univ/ College at Florham	NJ	54,770	C
Fairleigh Dickinson Univ/ Metropolitan Campus	NJ	52,392	C
Fairmont State Univ	WV	15,726	C
Faulkner Univ	AL	26,410	C
Fayetteville State Univ	NC	17,756	C
Felician Univ	NJ	46,280	LC
Ferris State Univ	MI	21,458	C
Ferrum College	VA	43,970	C
Fisk Univ	TN	32,066	LC
Fitchburg State Univ	MA	21,819	LC
Flagler College	FL	27,620	C
Florida A&M Univ	FL	15,361	C
Florida Atlantic Univ	FL	18,256	C
Florida Gulf Coast Univ	FL	14,738	C
Florida International Univ	FL	20,281	C
Florida Southern College	FL	45,978	VC
Florida State Univ	FL	16,771	HC
Fontbonne Univ	MO	34,606	C
Fordham Univ	NY	68,431	MC
Fort Hays State Univ	KS	12,677	C
Fort Lewis College	CO	20,154	C
Framingham State Univ	MA	21,740	C
Francis Marion Univ	SC	18,144	LC
Franciscan Univ of Steubenville	OH	33,980	VC
Franklin and Marshall College	PA	67,960	MC
Franklin College	IN	40,550	C
Franklin Pierce Univ	NH	46,750	LC
Freed-Hardeman Univ	TN	29,900	C
Fresno Pacific Univ	CA	38,858	C
Friends Univ	KS	38,000	C
Frostburg State Univ	MD	17,280	LC
Furman Univ	SC	61,098	VC+
Gallaudet Univ	DC	30,088	LC
Gannon Univ	PA	42,922	C
Gardner-Webb Univ	NC	24,935	C+
Geneva College	PA	35,450	C
George Fox Univ	OR	42,938	C
George Mason Univ	VA	19,884	C
Georgetown College	KY	41,440	C
Georgetown Univ	DC	68,970	MC
Georgia College & State Univ	GA	21,884	C+
Georgia Southern Univ	GA	16,540	VC
Georgia Southwestern State Univ	GA	13,870	LC
Georgia State Univ	GA	25,250	C
Georgian Court Univ	NJ	43,068	LC
Gettysburg College	PA	65,210	MC
Glenville State College	WV	17,386	LC
Goddard College	VT	17,040	VC
Gonzaga Univ	WA	52,880	HC
Gordon College	MA	47,740	VC
Goshen College	IN	44,350	C
Goucher College	MD	56,110	VC
Graceland Univ	IA	35,290	C
Grambling State Univ	LA	15,701	C
Grand Canyon Univ	AZ	25,150	VC
Grand Valley State Univ	MI	22,250	C+
Green Mountain College	VT	45,228	LC
Greensboro College	NC	39,790	LC
Greenville College	IL	27,012	LC
Grinnell College	IA	63,114	MC
Grove City College	PA	26,654	VC
Guilford College	NC	45,973	C
Gustavus Adolphus College	MN	53,943	HC
Gwynedd Mercy Univ	PA	43,780	LC
Hamilton College	NY	64,250	MC
Hamline Univ	MN	50,152	C
Hampden-Sydney College	VA	57,806	VC
Hampshire College	MA	65,214	MC
Hampton Univ	VA	36,410	C
Hannibal-LaGrange Univ	MO	29,815	C
Hanover College	IN	47,750	C+
Harding Univ	AR	25,440	C
Hardin-Simmons Univ	TX	36,025	C
Hartwick College	NY	51,270	C
Harvard College/Harvard Univ	MA	65,609	MC
Hastings College	NE	35,380	C+
Haverford College	PA	66,490	MC
Hawaii Pacific Univ	HI	33,420	C
Heidelberg Univ	OH	40,400	LC

ST = STATE **$IS** = IN-STATE COSTS **SR** = SELECTOR RATING

School	ST	$IS	SR
Hellenic College/Holy Cross Greek Orthodox School of Theology	MA	39,906	C
Henderson State Univ	AR	15,516	C
Hendrix College	AR	54,020	VC
High Point Univ	NC	47,355	VC
Hillsdale College	MI	37,170	MC
Hiram College	OH	44,590	C
Hobart and William Smith Colleges	NY	67,050	HC+
Hofstra Univ	NY	58,210	C+
Hollins Univ	VA	49,635	VC
Holy Family Univ	PA	44,672	LC
Holy Names Univ	CA	46,630	LC
Hood College	MD	50,540	C
Hope College	MI	42,840	VC
Houghton College	NY	40,558	VC
Houston Baptist Univ	TX	36,450	C
Howard Payne Univ	TX	35,994	C
Howard Univ	DC	37,616	C+
Humboldt State Univ	CA	21,708	C
Huntingdon College	AL	35,900	C
Huntington Univ	IN	33,996	C
Huston-Tillotson Univ	TX	18,124	LC
Idaho State Univ	ID	13,619	LC
Illinois College	IL	41,330	VC
Illinois State Univ	IL	23,418	VC
Illinois Wesleyan Univ	IL	56,430	VC+
Immaculata Univ	PA	39,000	C
Indiana State Univ	IN	23,223	LC
Indiana Univ Bloomington	IN	20,791	HC
Indiana Univ East	IN	7,207	C
Indiana Univ Northwest	IN	7,207	LC
Indiana Univ of Pennsylvania	PA	24,474	C
Indiana Univ South Bend	IN	16,057	C
Indiana Univ Southeast	IN	16,931	C
Indiana Univ-Purdue Univ Fort Wayne	IN	18,675	C
Indiana Univ-Purdue Univ Indianapolis	IN	18,952	C
Indiana Wesleyan Univ	IN	33,674	C
Inter-American Univ of PR Ponce	PR	19,549	
Inter-American Univ of PR-Fajardo Campus	PR	18,336	
Inter-American Univ of PR-Metropolitan Campus	PR	20,045	
Inter-American Univ of PR-San Germán	PR	20,042	
Iona College	NY	52,514	C
Iowa State Univ	IA	18,176	C
Ithaca College	NY	58,158	VC+
Jackson State Univ	MS	15,879	LC
Jacksonville State Univ	AL	14,628	LC
Jacksonville Univ	FL	49,210	C
James Madison Univ	VA	19,084	VC
Jarvis Christian College	TX	20,160	NC
John Brown Univ	AR	35,184	VC
John Carroll Univ	OH	51,570	C
Johns Hopkins Univ	MD	68,080	MC
Johnson C. Smith Univ	NC	25,336	LC
Johnson State College	VT	22,672	C
Judson College	AL	27,066	C
Judson Univ	IL	39,174	C
Juniata College	PA	58,118	VC
Kalamazoo College	MI	53,931	HC
Kansas State Univ	KS	17,780	VC
Kansas Wesleyan Univ	KS	37,930	C
Kean Univ	NJ	25,620	C
Keene State College	NH	24,604	C
Kennesaw State Univ	GA	18,899	VC
Kent State Univ	OH	20,928	C
Kentucky Christian Univ	KY	26,836	LC
Kentucky State Univ	KY	14,484	LC
Kentucky Wesleyan College	KY	34,260	LC
Kenyon College	OH	65,840	MC
King Univ	TN	36,976	C
King's College	PA	48,240	C
Knox College	IL	54,654	VC+
Kutztown Univ of Pennsylvania	PA	19,477	C
La Roche College	PA	38,940	C
La Salle Univ	PA	43,476	C
La Sierra Univ	CA	39,690	VC
Lafayette College	PA	68,520	MC
LaGrange College	GA	41,310	C
Lake Erie College	OH	38,914	LC
Lake Forest College	IL	50,652	VC
Lake Superior State Univ	MI	19,867	C
Lakeland Univ	WI	35,130	C
Lamar Univ	TX	18,014	LC
Lander Univ	SC	32,200	C
Lane College	TN	17,960	LC
Langston Univ	OK	15,659	C
Lasell College	MA	49,400	C
Lawrence Univ	WI	56,133	HC+
Le Moyne College	NY	47,305	VC
Lebanon Valley College	PA	55,510	VC
Lee Univ	TN	22,045	C
Lees-McRae College	NC	33,944	NC
Lehigh Univ	PA	63,860	MC
LeMoyne-Owen College	TN	16,980	C
Lenoir-Rhyne Univ	NC	47,500	LC
LeTourneau Univ	TX	39,190	VC
Lewis & Clark College	OR	60,984	MC
Lewis Univ	IL	41,710	C
Lewis-Clark State College	ID	14,202	C
Liberty Univ	VA	31,415	C
Limestone College	SC	32,100	C
Lincoln Memorial Univ	TN	28,430	C
Lincoln Univ	MO	14,402	NC
Lincoln Univ	PA	20,878	LC
Lindenwood Univ	MO	25,760	C
Lindsey Wilson College	KY	33,546	C
Linfield College	OR	53,992	C
Lipscomb Univ	TN	42,984	VC
LIU Brooklyn	NY	50,698	C
LIU Post	NY	50,698	C+
Livingstone College	NC	17,815	LC
Lock Haven Univ of Pennsylvania	PA	20,544	LC
Longwood Univ	VA	22,184	C
Loras College	IA	40,726	C
Louisiana College	LA	21,274	C
Louisiana State Univ and A&M College	LA	18,677	VC
Louisiana State Univ in Shreveport	LA	6,902	C
Louisiana Tech Univ	LA	11,422	VC
Lourdes Univ	OH	29,140	NC
Loyola Marymount Univ	CA	60,202	VC+
Loyola Univ Chicago	IL	57,158	VC
Loyola Univ Maryland	MD	61,710	VC
Loyola Univ New Orleans	LA	52,456	VC
Lubbock Christian Univ	TX	29,727	C
Luther College	IA	49,990	VC
Lycoming College	PA	50,895	C
Lyon College	AR	36,120	VC
Macalester College	MN	64,136	MC
MacMurray College	IL	35,025	C
Madonna Univ	MI	30,450	LC
Malone Univ	OH	39,200	C
Manchester Univ	IN	41,540	C
Manhattan College	NY	55,652	C
Manhattanville College	NY	52,430	C
Mansfield Univ of Pennsylvania	PA	24,244	LC
Marian Univ	IN	43,206	C
Marian Univ	WI	34,622	C
Marietta College	OH	46,190	C
Marist College	NY	49,860	VC
Marlboro College	VT	50,832	VC+
Marquette Univ	WI	53,090	VC+
Mars Hill Univ	NC	41,104	C
Marshall Univ	WV	18,044	C
Martin Univ	IN	21,010	LC
Mary Baldwin Univ	VA	40,495	C
Marygrove College	MI	30,100	LC
Marymount Manhattan College	NY	48,350	C
Marymount Univ	VA	43,231	C
Maryville College	TN	44,410	C
Maryville Univ of St. Louis	MO	38,558	VC
Marywood Univ	PA	47,840	C
Mass College of Liberal Arts	MA	20,659	C
Mass Inst of Technology	MA	62,662	MC
Mayville State Univ	ND	18,371	NC
McDaniel College	MD	52,910	VC
McKendree Univ	IL	37,940	C+
McMurry Univ	TX	34,259	LC
McNeese State Univ	LA	7,838	C
McPherson College	KS	36,134	C
Mercer Univ	GA	45,348	VC
Mercy College	NY	32,614	C
Mercyhurst Univ	PA	47,420	C
Meredith College	NC	46,634	C
Merrimack College	MA	55,415	C
Messiah College	PA	44,380	VC
Methodist Univ	NC	58,130	C
Metropolitan State Univ	MN	7,859	C
Metropolitan State Univ of Denver	CO	6,928	LC
Miami Univ	OH	27,190	HC+
Mich State Univ	MI	24,542	VC
Mich Tech Univ	MI	25,551	VC+
MidAmerica Nazarene Univ	KS	37,808	C
Middle Tenn State Univ	TN	8,650	C
Middlebury College	VT	67,464	MC
Midland Univ	NE	39,512	C
Midwestern State Univ	TX	12,111	LC
Miles College	AL	16,530	NC
Millersville Univ of Pennsylvania	PA	25,298	C
Milligan College	TN	39,450	C
Millikin Univ	IL	44,148	C
Mills College	CA	43,705	C
Millsaps College	MS	50,080	C+
Minn State Univ, Mankato	MN	17,190	C
Minn State Univ, Moorhead	MN	21,393	C
Minot State Univ	ND	13,285	C
Misericordia Univ	PA	45,210	C
Miss College	MS	25,850	C
Miss State Univ	MS	12,028	C+
Miss Univ for Women	MS	17,065	C
Miss Valley State Univ	MS	13,233	LC
Missouri Baptist Univ	MO	35,594	C
Missouri Southern State Univ	MO	13,071	C
Missouri State Univ	MO	15,837	C+
Missouri Univ of Science and Technology	MO	18,655	HC
Missouri Valley College	MO	28,150	C
Missouri Western State Univ	MO	17,822	LC
Molloy College	NY	40,440	C
Monmouth College	IL	42,260	C
Monmouth Univ	NJ	50,184	C
Montana State Univ	MT	15,500	C+
Montana State Univ Billings	MT	13,336	LC
Montana State Univ-Northern	MT	11,370	NC
Montclair State Univ	NJ	26,912	C
Montreat College	NC	34,605	LC
Moravian College	PA	55,488	C
Morehead State Univ	KY	18,386	LC
Morehouse College	GA	40,835	C
Morgan State Univ	MD	17,190	LC
Morningside College	IA	39,780	C
Morris College	SC	19,195	LC
Mount Aloysius College	PA	29,976	C
Mount Holyoke College	MA	56,746	MC
Mount Marty College	SD	36,862	C
Mount Mary Univ	WI	34,650	LC
Mount Mercy Univ	IA	39,748	C
Mount St. Mary College	NY	44,448	C
Mount St. Joseph Univ	OH	33,880	LC
Mount St. Mary's Univ	MD	53,380	C
Mount St. Mary's Univ - Chalon Campus	CA	50,486	VC+
Mount Vernon Nazarene Univ	OH	35,944	C
Muhlenberg College	PA	56,645	VC
Murray State Univ	KY	17,726	C+
Muskingum Univ	OH	35,966	C
National Univ	CA	17,849	LC
Nazareth College	NY	46,784	C
Nebr Wesleyan Univ	NE	42,026	C+
New College of Florida	FL	16,180	HC+
New Jersey City Univ	NJ	21,456	LC
New Jersey Inst of Technology	NJ	30,198	HC
New Mexico Highlands Univ	NM	11,904	LC
New Mexico State Univ	NM	14,050	LC
New York Univ	NY	68,139	MC
Newberry College	SC	34,550	C
Newman Univ	KS	37,382	C
Niagara Univ	NY	41,010	C
Nicholls State Univ	LA	14,959	C
Nichols College	MA	46,900	LC
Norfolk State Univ	VA	18,902	LC
N Car A&T State Univ	NC	13,786	C
N Car Central Univ	NC	9,000	C
N Car State Univ	NC	22,434	HC+
N Car Wesleyan College	NC	39,200	C
North Central College	IL	48,712	C+
N Dak State Univ	ND	16,245	VC
North Park Univ	IL	35,860	C
Northeastern Illinois Univ	IL	12,529	LC
Northeastern State Univ	OK	8,615	VC
Northeastern Univ	MA	65,352	MC
Northern Arizona Univ	AZ	21,003	C
Northern Illinois Univ	IL	20,176	C
Northern Kentucky Univ	KY	16,486	C
Northern Mich Univ	MI	20,853	C
Northern State Univ	SD	15,570	C
Northland College	WI	41,103	C+
Northwest Missouri State Univ	MO	18,286	C
Northwest Nazarene Univ	ID	40,250	C
Northwest Univ	WA	38,720	VC
Northwestern College of Iowa	IA	38,400	C
Northwestern Okla State Univ	OK	13,072	LC
Northwestern State Univ of Louisiana	LA	16,534	LC
Northwestern Univ	IL	68,725	MC
Norwich Univ	VT	56,234	C
Notre Dame College	OH	39,150	VC
Notre Dame de Namur Univ	CA	46,526	LC
Notre Dame of Maryland Univ	MD	47,570	VC
Nyack College	NY	34,450	LC
Oakland Univ	MI	20,763	C
Oakwood Univ	AL	43,758	C
Oberlin College	OH	68,942	MC
Occidental College	CA	68,660	MC
Oglala Lakota College	SD	15,050	NC
Oglethorpe Univ	GA	44,200	C
Ohio Dominican Univ	OH	41,340	C+
Ohio Northern Univ	OH	44,050	VC
Ohio State Univ at Columbus	OH	22,843	MC
Ohio State Univ at Lima	OH	7,553	C
Ohio State Univ at Mansfield	OH	15,529	C
Ohio State Univ at Marion	OH	7,553	VC
Ohio State Univ at Newark	OH	16,685	C
Ohio Univ	OH	23,394	VC
Ohio Valley Univ	WV	28,800	C
Ohio Wesleyan Univ	OH	49,460	VC
Okla Baptist Univ	OK	33,990	C
Okla Christian Univ	OK	29,260	C
Okla City Univ	OK	40,476	C
Okla Panhandle State Univ	OK	6,152	C
Okla State Univ	OK	17,180	C+
Okla Wesleyan Univ	OK	34,434	C
Old Dominion Univ	VA	21,618	C
Olivet College	MI	37,661	LC
Olivet Nazarene Univ	IL	41,840	VC
Oral Roberts Univ	OK	34,316	C
Oregon State Univ	OR	23,337	VC
Ottawa Univ	KS	39,980	VC
Otterbein Univ	OH	41,630	C
Ouachita Baptist Univ	AR	33,500	VC
Our Lady of the Lake Univ	TX	37,790	LC
Pace Univ	NY	60,136	C
Pacific Lutheran Univ	WA	49,960	C
Pacific Union College	CA	36,009	VC
Pacific Univ	OR	37,617	C
Paine College	GA	19,506	LC
Palm Beach Atlantic Univ	FL	39,250	C
Park Univ	MO	22,134	C
Penn State Altoona	PA	26,686	C
Penn State Erie,The Behrend College	PA	26,688	VC
Pepperdine Univ	CA	66,862	VC+
Peru State College	NE	15,602	LC
Pfeiffer Univ	NC	40,532	LC
Piedmont College	GA	34,334	C
Pittsburg State Univ	KS	13,880	C
Pitzer College	CA	68,500	HC+
Plymouth State Univ	NH	23,180	LC
Point Loma Nazarene Univ	CA	46,150	C+
Point Park Univ	PA	41,270	C
Pomona College	CA	64,957	MC
Pontifical Catholic Univ of PR	PR	10,534	
Portland State Univ	OR	19,443	C
Post Univ	CT	41,150	C
Prairie View A&M Univ	TX	27,273	LC
Presbyterian College	SC	47,186	C
Princeton Univ	NJ	60,090	MC
Principia College	IL	40,350	C
Providence College	RI	62,870	HC
Purdue Univ Northwest	IN	15,178	C
Purdue Univ/West Lafayette	IN	20,032	MC
Queens Univ of Charlotte	NC	39,543	C
Quincy Univ	IL	38,170	LC
Quinnipiac Univ	CT	60,970	VC
Radford Univ	VA	19,758	C
Ramapo College of New Jersey	NJ	25,760	VC
Randolph College	VA	53,970	C
Randolph-Macon College	VA	51,480	VC
Reed College	OR	65,300	MC
Regis College	MA	51,920	LC
Regis Univ	CO	46,380	C
Rhode Island College	RI	19,000	LC
Rhodes College	TN	51,900	HC
Rice Univ	TX	59,458	MC
Rider Univ	NJ	54,050	C
Ripon College	WI	49,991	VC
Rivier Univ	NH	41,600	VC
Roanoke College	VA	55,952	VC
Robert Morris Univ	PA	40,600	C
Roberts Wesleyan College	NY	41,116	C
Rochester College	MI	28,574	LC
Rockford Univ	IL	38,570	C
Rockhurst Univ	MO	28,990	C
Rocky Mountain College	MT	35,776	C
Roger Williams Univ	RI	48,074	VC
Rollins College	FL	58,670	HC
Roosevelt Univ	IL	41,890	VC
Rosemont College	PA	30,980	LC
Rowan Univ	NJ	24,491	VC
Russell Sage College	NY	39,370	C
Rutgers Univ - Camden	NJ	26,595	C
Rutgers Univ - New Brunswick	NJ	27,090	HC
Rutgers Univ - Newark	NJ	27,351	C
Sacred Heart Univ	CT	54,590	C
Saginaw Valley State Univ	MI	19,284	C
St. Anselm College	NH	56,636	VC
St. Augustine's Univ	NC	25,582	C
St. Francis Univ	PA	46,146	NC
St. John's Univ	MN	53,472	C
St. Joseph's College of Maine	ME	47,890	C
St. Joseph's Univ	PA	58,540	VC
St. Leo Univ	FL	32,850	C
St. Louis Univ	MO	49,866	HC
St. Martin's Univ	WA	45,056	C
St. Mary's College	IN	50,600	C
St. Mary's College of Calif	CA	57,420	C
St. Mary's Univ of Minn	MN	42,440	C
St. Michael's College	VT	53,275	VC+
St. Peter's Univ	NJ	49,192	C
St. Vincent College	PA	46,229	C
St. Xavier Univ	IL	44,440	C
Salem College	NC	40,206	C
Salem State Univ	MA	42,650	LC
Salisbury Univ	MD	21,132	VC
Salve Regina Univ	RI	53,046	VC
Sam Houston State Univ	TX	18,792	C
Samford Univ	AL	40,770	VC
San Diego Christian College	CA	40,914	C
San Diego State Univ	CA	23,156	VC
San Francisco State Univ	CA	18,514	LC
San Jose State Univ	CA	22,630	C
Sarah Lawrence College	NY	68,866	MC
Savannah State Univ	GA	17,036	C
Schreiner Univ	TX	34,626	LC
Scripps College	CA	69,260	HC
Seattle Pacific Univ	WA	47,439	C+
Seattle Univ	WA	54,957	VC
Seton Hall Univ	NJ	58,008	C
Seton Hill Univ	PA	46,972	VC
Sewanee: The Univ of the South	TN	58,000	HC+
Shawnee State Univ	OH	16,998	C
Shenandoah Univ	VA	42,100	C
Shepherd Univ, West Virginia	WV	17,382	C
Shippensburg Univ of Pennsylvania	PA	24,096	C
Shorter Univ	GA	31,130	LC
Siena College	NY	48,916	C
Siena Heights Univ	MI	36,322	C
Silver Lake College of the Holy Family	WI	36,290	LC
Simmons College	MA	54,400	HC

ST = STATE **$IS** = IN-STATE COSTS **SR** = SELECTOR RATING

School	ST	$IS	SR
Simpson College	IA	45,626	VC
Simpson Univ	CA	34,722	C
Skidmore College	NY	66,600	MC
Slippery Rock Univ of Pennsylvania	PA	20,450	C
Smith College	MA	66,774	MC
Sonoma State Univ	CA	27,020	C
S Car State Univ	SC	21,330	LC
S Dak State Univ	SD	15,874	C
Southeast Missouri State Univ	MO	16,148	C
Southeastern Louisiana Univ	LA	16,237	C
Southeastern Okla State Univ	OK	11,875	C
Southeastern Univ	FL	34,910	LC
Southern Adventist Univ	TN	28,250	C
Southern Arkansas Univ	AR	21,532	C
Southern Conn State Univ	CT	21,924	LC
Southern Illinois Univ Carbondale	IL	24,554	C
Southern Illinois Univ Edwardsville	IL	20,188	C
Southern Methodist Univ	TX	69,008	MC
Southern Nazarene Univ	OK	33,684	C
Southern New Hampshire Univ	NH	44,256	C
Southern Oregon Univ	OR	19,117	C
Southern Univ and A&M College	LA	16,074	LC
Southern Univ at New Orleans	LA	8,014	LC
Southern Vermont College	VT	34,670	LC
Southern Wesleyan Univ	SC	33,670	LC
Southwest Baptist Univ	MO	30,890	LC
Southwest Minn State Univ	MN	17,783	C
Southwestern Adventist Univ	TX	28,232	LC
Southwestern College	KS	31,531	LC
Southwestern Okla State Univ	OK	12,205	C
Southwestern Univ	TX	52,370	VC
Spelman College	GA	41,642	C
Spring Arbor Univ	MI	37,390	C
Spring Hill College	AL	48,488	C
Springfield College	MA	48,775	C
St. Ambrose Univ	IA	40,180	C
St. Bonaventure Univ	NY	45,596	C
St. Catherine Univ	MN	45,630	C
St. Cloud State Univ	MN	10,600	C
St. Edward's Univ	TX	56,190	VC
St. Francis College	NY	38,800	LC
St. John Fisher College	NY	45,270	VC
St. John's College at Annapolis	MD	63,348	MC
St. John's Univ	NY	57,160	C+
St. Joseph's College, New York/Brooklyn Campus	NY	25,114	LC
St. Joseph's College, New York/Long Island Campus	NY	25,124	C
St. Lawrence Univ	NY	66,646	HC+
St. Mary's College of Maryland	MD	27,312	VC
St. Mary's Univ	TX	39,120	C
St. Norbert College	WI	46,060	VC
St. Olaf College	MN	56,430	HC
St. Thomas Aquinas College	NY	32,450	C
St. Thomas Univ	FL	51,187	LC
Stanford Univ	CA	62,541	MC
SUNY Albany	NY	22,165	C
SUNY at Binghamton	NY	24,100	MC
SUNY at Geneseo	NY	21,622	VC
SUNY at New Paltz	NY	20,840	C
SUNY at Oswego	NY	22,219	VC
SUNY at Purchase College	NY	21,832	C
SUNY/Buffalo State	NY	20,583	LC
SUNY/College at Old Westbury	NY	16,860	C
SUNY/Cortland	NY	20,910	C
SUNY/Empire State College	NY	9,145	NC
SUNY/Fredonia	NY	20,818	C
SUNY/Oneonta	NY	20,794	C
SUNY/Plattsburgh	NY	19,314	C
SUNY/Potsdam	NY	21,051	VC
SUNY/Univ at Buffalo	NY	23,122	C
Stephen F. Austin State Univ	TX	18,484	LC
Sterling College	KS	32,830	LC
Stetson Univ	FL	57,174	VC+
Stevens Inst of Technology	NJ	64,954	MC
Stillman College	AL	20,738	C
Stockton Univ	NJ	25,565	C
Stonehill College	MA	55,130	C
Stony Brook Univ/The SUNY	NY	22,703	MC
Suffolk Univ	MA	52,316	C
Sul Ross State Univ	TX	15,021	LC
Susquehanna Univ	PA	57,560	VC
Swarthmore College	PA	63,550	MC
Syracuse Univ	NY	62,313	HC
Tabor College	KS	35,870	C
Talladega College	AL	25,919	C
Tarleton State Univ	TX	15,248	LC
Taylor Univ	IN	42,130	VC
Temple Univ	PA	24,392	C+
Tenn State Univ	TN	14,423	LC
Tenn Tech Univ	TN	17,929	C
Tenn Wesleyan Univ	TN	32,680	LC
Texas A&M Univ at College Station	TX	20,771	VC+
Texas A&M Univ at Commerce	TX	10,496	C
Texas A&M Univ at Corpus Christi	TX	16,851	LC
Texas A&M Univ at Kingsville	TX	16,580	LC
Texas Christian Univ	TX	57,120	HC
Texas Lutheran Univ	TX	39,770	C
Texas Southern Univ	TX	19,592	LC
Texas State Univ	TX	18,721	C
Texas Tech Univ	TX	20,156	C+
Texas Wesleyan Univ	TX	37,338	C
Texas Woman's Univ	TX	15,302	LC
The American Univ	DC	61,317	HC
The Catholic Univ of America	DC	58,376	VC
The Citadel, The Military College of S Car	SC	20,679	C
The College at Brockport - SUNY	NY	21,058	C
The College of Idaho	ID	36,415	C
The College of New Jersey	NJ	28,675	VC+
The College of New Rochelle	NY	46,300	LC
The College of St. Rose	NY	44,010	C
The College of Wooster	OH	60,000	HC
The Evergreen State College	WA	16,599	C
The George Washington Univ	DC	68,474	HC+
The Master's Univ	CA	43,870	C
The Univ of Akron	OH	22,566	C
The Univ of Alabama	AL	24,320	C+
The Univ of Arizona	AZ	24,086	C
The Univ of Memphis	TN	18,278	C
The Univ of Montana	MT	9,426	LC
The Univ of Tenn at Chattanooga	TN	17,340	C+
The Univ of Tenn at Knoxville	TN	22,112	VC
The Univ of Tenn at Martin	TN	15,212	C
The Univ of Texas at Austin	TX	20,206	MC
The Univ of Texas at San Antonio	TX	21,060	C
The Univ of Utah	UT	18,751	VC
The Univ of Virginia's College at Wise	VA	18,192	LC
Thiel College	PA	42,950	LC
Thomas Edison State Univ	NJ	6,350	NC
Thomas More College	KY	36,720	LC
Tiffin Univ	OH	34,900	LC
Toccoa Falls College	GA	30,048	C
Tougaloo College	MS	17,980	NC
Touro College	NY	31,040	C
Towson Univ	MD	21,878	C
Transylvania Univ	KY	47,450	HC+
Trevecca Nazarene Univ	TN	31,186	C
Trinity Christian College	IL	35,580	C
Trinity College	CT	69,020	HC
Trinity International Univ	IL	31,070	VC
Trinity Univ	TX	54,480	MC
Trinity Washington Univ	DC	33,826	C+
Troy Univ	AL	16,171	C
Truman State Univ	MO	16,286	MC
Tufts Univ	MA		MC
Tulane Univ	LA	67,496	MC
Tusculum College	TN	31,625	LC
Tuskegee Univ	AL	28,164	C
Union College	KY	32,310	C
Union College	NE	23,270	C
Union College	NY	64,320	MC
Union Univ	TN	41,160	VC
United States Air Force Academy	CO		C
United States Military Academy at West Point	NY		HC+
United States Naval Academy	MD		HC
Universidad Adventista de las Antillas	PR	16,606	
Universidad del Turabo	PR	17,828	
Univ of Alabama at Birmingham	AL	22,092	C
Univ of Alabama in Huntsville	AL	20,028	VC
Univ of Alaska Anchorage	AK	17,914	C
Univ of Alaska Fairbanks	AK	16,874	VC
Univ of Arkansas at Fayetteville	AR	19,766	VC
Univ of Arkansas at Little Rock	AR	18,211	LC
Univ of Arkansas at Monticello	AR	13,599	LC
Univ of Arkansas at Pine Bluff	AR	13,541	C
Univ of Calif at Berkeley	CA	29,886	MC
Univ of Calif at Davis	CA	28,468	HC
Univ of Calif at Irvine	CA	33,857	VC
Univ of Calif at Los Angeles	CA	27,438	HC+
Univ of Calif at Riverside	CA	32,912	C
Univ of Calif at Santa Barbara	CA	30,627	HC+
Univ of Calif San Diego	CA	30,450	MC
Univ of Calif, Santa Cruz	CA	28,731	C+
Univ of Central Arkansas	AR	15,042	VC
Univ of Central Florida	FL	16,379	VC
Univ of Central Missouri	MO	18,982	C
Univ of Central Okla	OK	15,150	C
Univ of Charleston	WV	35,000	LC
Univ of Chicago	IL	70,551	MC
Univ of Cincinnati	OH	22,118	VC
Univ of Colo Boulder	CO	26,048	HC
Univ of Colo Colo Springs	CO	20,300	C
Univ of Colo Denver	CO	22,238	C
Univ of Conn	CT	27,394	
Univ of Dallas	TX	50,676	VC
Univ of Dayton	OH	54,930	VC
Univ of Delaware	DE	32,214	VC
Univ of Denver	CO	61,129	VC+
Univ of Detroit Mercy	MI	48,816	C
Univ of Evansville	IN	44,186	C+
Univ of Findlay	OH	43,040	C
Univ of Florida	FL	16,291	HC+
Univ of Georgia	GA	21,878	HC
Univ of Great Falls	MT	38,524	C
Univ of Hartford	CT	49,776	C
Univ of Hawaii at Hilo	HI	18,038	VC
Univ of Hawaii at Manoa	HI	23,261	C
Univ of Holy Cross	LA	21,523	NC
Univ of Houston-Downtown	TX	7,241	LC
Univ of Idaho	ID	16,158	C
Univ of Illinois at Chicago	IL	24,664	VC
Univ of Illinois at Urbana-Champaign	IL	27,006	HC
Univ of Indianapolis	IN	36,480	VC
Univ of Iowa	IA	19,415	HC
Univ of Jamestown	ND	28,508	C
Univ of Kansas	KS	20,884	VC
Univ of Kentucky	KY	24,800	C+
Univ of La Verne	CA	55,600	C
Univ of Louisiana at Lafayette	LA	14,516	C
Univ of Louisiana at Monroe	LA	15,970	C
Univ of Louisville	KY	19,692	C
Univ of Lynchburg	VA	48,370	C
Univ of Maine	ME	21,038	VC
Univ of Maine at Farmington	ME	18,792	C
Univ of Mary Hardin-Baylor	TX	35,292	C+
Univ of Mary Washington	VA	23,039	C+
Univ of Maryland Univ College	MD	26,146	LC
Univ of Maryland/Baltimore County	MD	23,004	VC
Univ of Maryland/College Park	MD	21,938	HC
Univ of Maryland/Eastern Shore	MD	21,861	LC
Univ of Mass Amherst	MA	27,669	HC
Univ of Mass Boston	MA	13,828	C
Univ of Mass Dartmouth	MA	26,507	C
Univ of Mass Lowell	MA	27,296	VC
Univ of Miami	FL	63,494	MC
Univ of Mich/Ann Arbor	MI	25,274	MC
Univ of Mich/Dearborn	MI	12,472	VC
Univ of Mich/Flint	MI	19,062	C
Univ of Minn/Duluth	MN	20,292	C
Univ of Minn/Morris	MN	21,222	VC
Univ of Minn/Twin Cities	MN	24,269	MC
Univ of Miss	MS	18,802	C
Univ of Missouri-Columbia	MO	20,463	VC
Univ of Missouri-Kansas City	MO	19,563	VC
Univ of Missouri-St. Louis	MO	19,810	VC
Univ of Mobile	AL	28,935	C
Univ of Montana	MT	14,105	C
Univ of Montevallo	AL	20,012	C
Univ of Mount Olive	NC	18,426	C
Univ of Mount Union	OH	39,990	C
Univ of Nebr - Kearney	NE	17,014	LC
Univ of Nebr - Lincoln	NE	18,589	VC
Univ of Nebr - Omaha	NE	16,120	C
Univ of Nevada, Las Vegas	NV	17,553	C
Univ of Nevada, Reno	NV	18,010	C
Univ of New England	ME	50,110	C
Univ of New Hampshire	NH	29,333	VC
Univ of New Hampshire - Manchester	NH	14,490	C
Univ of New Haven	CT	53,680	C
Univ of New Mexico	NM	16,808	C
Univ of New Orleans	LA	12,840	C
Univ of North Alabama	AL	15,964	C
Univ of N Car at Asheville	NC	16,251	VC+
Univ of N Car at Chapel Hill	NC	20,561	MC
Univ of N Car at Charlotte	NC	17,803	VC
Univ of N Car at Greensboro	NC	15,998	C
Univ of N Car at Pembroke	NC	14,737	LC
Univ of N Car Wilmington	NC	16,784	VC
Univ of N Dak	ND	16,673	C
Univ of North Florida	FL	15,996	VC
Univ of North Georgia	GA	17,316	C
Univ of North Texas	TX	20,082	C
Univ of Northern Colo	CO	19,658	C
Univ of Northern Iowa	IA	17,480	C
Univ of Northwestern - St. Paul	MN	39,530	C
Univ of Notre Dame	IN	68,801	MC
Univ of Okla	OK	19,651	HC
Univ of Oregon	OR	24,021	VC
Univ of Pennsylvania	PA	63,526	MC
Univ of Pikeville	KY	27,838	C
Univ of Pittsburgh	PA	30,030	MC
Univ of Pittsburgh at Bradford	PA	22,958	C
Univ of Pittsburgh at Johnstown	PA	22,092	C
Univ of Portland	OR	52,152	VC
Univ of PR, at Cayey	PR		
Univ of PR, at Mayaguez	PR	13,995	
Univ of PR-Rio Piedras campus	PR	13,327	
Univ of Puget Sound	WA	60,210	HC
Univ of Redlands	CA	61,934	VC
Univ of Rhode Island	RI	26,066	VC
Univ of Richmond	VA	62,730	MC
Univ of Rio Grande & Rio Grande Community College	OH	8,750	LC
Univ of Rochester	NY	65,032	MC
Univ of St. Francis	IN	38,520	C
Univ of St. Joseph	CT	49,069	C
Univ of St. Mary	KS	37,080	NC
Univ of San Diego	CA	60,338	HC
Univ of San Francisco	CA	60,580	C
Univ of Science and Arts of Okla	OK	11,140	VC
Univ of Scranton	PA	54,962	VC
Univ of Sioux Falls	SD	25,630	C
Univ of South Alabama	AL	16,880	C
Univ of S Car Aiken	SC	18,094	C
Univ of S Car at Columbia	SC	21,726	VC
Univ of S Car Upstate	SC	19,272	LC
Univ of S Dak	SD	16,109	C
Univ of South Florida St. Petersburg	FL	15,980	C
Univ of South Florida/Tampa	FL	16,110	VC
Univ of Southern Calif	CA	66,631	MC
Univ of Southern Indiana	IN	16,808	C
Univ of Southern Maine	ME	18,320	C
Univ of Southern Miss	MS	13,170	C
Univ of St. Francis	IL	40,828	C
Univ of St. Thomas - Houston	TX	41,510	VC
Univ of Tampa	FL	38,928	VC
Univ of Texas at Arlington	TX	18,876	C
Univ of Texas at Dallas	TX	23,640	HC
Univ of Texas at El Paso	TX	34,452	NC
Univ of Texas Rio Grande Valley	TX	15,573	LC
Univ of the Cumberlands	KY	32,000	LC
Univ of the District of Columbia	DC	21,260	LC
Univ of the Incarnate Word	TX	39,162	LC
Univ of the Ozarks	AR	31,050	NC
Univ of the Pacific	CA	57,446	VC
Univ of the Southwest	NM	24,386	C
Univ of Toledo	OH	19,336	C
Univ of Tulsa	OK	52,625	HC
Univ of Vermont	VT	29,792	HC
Univ of Virginia	VA	27,367	MC
Univ of Washington	WA	23,091	MC
Univ of West Alabama	AL	16,284	LC
Univ of West Florida	FL	15,848	C
Univ of West Georgia	GA	17,510	LC
Univ of Wisc-Eau Claire	WI	16,354	VC
Univ of Wisc-Green Bay	WI	15,184	C
Univ of Wisc-La Crosse	WI	15,425	VC
Univ of Wisc-Madison	WI	21,647	MC
Univ of Wisc-Milwaukee	WI	21,538	C
Univ of Wisc-Oshkosh	WI	15,392	C
Univ of Wisc-Parkside	WI	15,313	C
Univ of Wisc-Platteville	WI	14,148	C
Univ of Wisc-River Falls	WI	14,541	C
Univ of Wisc-Stevens Point	WI	14,043	C
Univ of Wisc-Superior	WI	14,838	C
Univ of Wisc-Whitewater	WI	13,976	C
Univ of Wyoming	WY	15,537	C
Urbana Univ	OH	30,820	C
Ursinus College	PA	62,920	VC
Ursuline College	OH	41,076	LC
Utah State Univ	UT	13,235	C
Utica College	NY	31,510	C
Valley City State Univ	ND	13,267	C
Valparaiso Univ	IN	50,160	VC
Vanderbilt Univ	TN	63,248	MC
Vanguard Univ of Southern Calif	CA	42,400	VC
Vassar College	NY	68,110	MC
Villanova Univ	PA	64,922	MC
Virginia Commonwealth Univ	VA	23,811	VC
Virginia Military Inst	VA	26,460	VC
Virginia Polytechnic Inst and State Univ	VA	21,920	VC
Virginia State Univ	VA	19,802	C+
Virginia Union Univ	VA	25,058	C
Virginia Wesleyan Univ	VA	45,980	LC
Viterbo Univ	WI	34,660	C
Wabash College	IN	52,100	VC
Wagner College	NY	57,240	C+
Wake Forest Univ	NC	69,354	MC
Walla Walla Univ	WA	34,845	C
Walsh Univ	OH	39,010	C
Warner Pacific College	OR	31,610	C
Warner Univ	FL	28,216	C
Warren Wilson College	NC	44,220	VC
Wartburg College	IA	49,478	C
Washburn Univ	KS	15,827	C
Washington & Jefferson College	PA	58,694	VC
Washington Adventist Univ	MD	32,050	LC
Washington and Lee Univ	VA	59,647	MC
Washington College	MD	56,154	VC
Washington State Univ	WA	22,747	C
Washington Univ in St. Louis	MO	67,539	MC
Wayland Baptist Univ	TX	23,460	LC
Wayne State College	NE	25,746	NC
Wayne State Univ	MI	23,085	C
Waynesburg Univ	PA	33,530	C
Weber State Univ	UT	14,112	C
Webster Univ	MO	37,490	C
Wellesley College	MA	66,984	MC
Wells College	NY	50,500	C
Wesley College	DE	37,848	LC
Wesleyan College	GA	31,940	C+
Wesleyan Univ	CT	66,940	MC
West Chester Univ of Pennsylvania	PA	19,171	VC
West Liberty Univ	WV	16,158	C

ST = STATE **$IS** = IN-STATE COSTS **SR** = SELECTOR RATING

School	ST	$IS	SR
West Texas A&M Univ	TX	13,478	C
West Virginia State Univ	WV	19,412	LC
West Virginia Univ	WV	18,952	VC
West Virginia Univ Inst of Technology	WV	18,264	C
West Virginia Wesleyan College	WV	39,188	C
Western Carolina Univ	NC	13,965	C
Western Conn State Univ	CT	21,254	LC
Western Illinois Univ	IL	20,897	C
Western Kentucky Univ	KY	16,850	C
Western Mich Univ	MI	21,791	C
Western New England Univ	MA	49,182	C
Western New Mexico Univ	NM	16,914	LC
Western Oregon Univ	OR	19,965	LC
Western State Colo Univ	CO	19,348	C
Western Washington Univ	WA	18,904	VC
Westfield State Univ	MA	20,404	C
Westminster College	MO	32,820	C
Westminster College	PA	41,722	C
Westminster College	UT	41,078	C
Westmont College	CA	57,930	VC
Wheaton College	IL	44,993	MC
Wheaton College	MA	63,818	VC
Wheeling Jesuit Univ	WV	37,106	LC
Whitman College	WA	59,772	MC
Whittier College	CA	57,891	C
Whitworth Univ	WA	53,682	VC
Wichita State Univ	KS	17,773	C
Widener Univ	PA	58,190	C
Wiley College	TX	19,255	C
Wilkes Univ	PA	49,166	C
Willamette Univ	OR	62,514	VC+
William Carey Univ	MS	23,950	LC
William Jewell College	MO	42,490	C+
William Paterson Univ of New Jersey	NJ	24,022	C
William Penn Univ	IA	26,000	C
William Woods Univ	MO	32,040	C
Williams Baptist College	AR	24,720	C
Williams College	MA	67,700	MC
Wilmington College	OH	35,100	C
Wilson College	PA	35,620	LC
Wingate Univ	NC	41,900	C
Winona State Univ	MN	18,109	C
Winston-Salem State Univ	NC	18,005	LC
Winthrop Univ	SC	23,960	C
Wisc Lutheran College	WI	36,290	C
Wittenberg Univ	OH	49,863	VC
Wofford College	SC	49,885	VC
Woodbury Univ	CA	49,593	VC
Worcester State Univ	MA	20,977	C
Wright State Univ	OH	16,983	C
Xavier Univ	OH	49,380	VC
Xavier Univ of Louisiana	LA	31,689	C
Yale Univ	CT	64,650	MC
Yeshiva Univ	NY	52,750	VC
York College	NE	30,260	C
York College of Pennsylvania	PA	29,240	C
Youngstown State Univ	OH	17,487	C

HISTORY AND POLITICAL SCIENCE

School	ST	$IS	SR
Averett Univ	VA	43,034	LC
Black Hills State Univ	SD	16,622	C
Bridgewater College	VA	46,260	C
Corban Univ	OR	41,700	C
Drury Univ	MO	37,555	VC
Indiana Univ Kokomo	IN	7,207	C
Mount St. Mary College	NY	44,448	C
North Greenville Univ	SC	25,930	C
Okla Christian Univ	OK	29,260	C
Univ of N Car at Asheville	NC	16,251	VC+
Western Illinois Univ	IL	20,897	C

HISTORY EDUCATION

School	ST	$IS	SR
Augustana College	IL	51,222	VC+
Averett Univ	VA	43,034	LC
Bloomfield College	NJ	40,100	LC
East Texas Baptist Univ	TX	34,444	C
Elon Univ	NC	46,142	HC
Ferris State Univ	MI	21,458	C
Georgetown College	KY	41,440	C
Hope College	MI	42,840	VC
Huntingdon College	AL	35,900	C
Kennesaw State Univ	GA	18,899	VC
King Univ	TN	36,976	C
Marist College	NY	49,860	VC
Missouri Western State Univ	MO	17,822	LC
Mount Ida College	MA	46,820	C
Mount Mary Univ	WI	34,650	LC
Murray State Univ	KY	17,726	C+
Nyack College	NY	34,450	LC
Old Dominion Univ	VA	21,618	C
Olivet Nazarene Univ	IL	41,840	VC
Shorter Univ	GA	31,130	LC
Southwestern Okla State Univ	OK	12,205	C
The Univ of Utah	UT	18,751	VC
Wartburg College	IA	49,478	C
Weber State Univ	UT	14,112	C

HISTORY OF ARCHITECTURE/URBAN DEVELOPMENT

School	ST	$IS	SR
Brown Univ	RI	64,566	MC
DePaul Univ	IL	52,807	VC
Univ of Illinois at Chicago	IL	24,664	VC

HISTORY OF PHILOSOPHY

School	ST	$IS	SR
Colo College	CO	64,894	MC
Univ of Pittsburgh	PA	30,030	MC

HISTORY OF SCIENCE

School	ST	$IS	SR
Calif Inst of Technology	CA	64,704	MC
Case Western Reserve Univ	OH	62,284	MC
Georgia Inst of Technology	GA	23,910	MC
Johns Hopkins Univ	MD	68,080	MC
St. John's College at Annapolis	MD	63,348	MC
Univ of Jamestown	ND	28,508	C
Univ of Okla	OK	19,651	HC
Univ of Pennsylvania	PA	63,526	MC
Univ of Wisc-Madison	WI	21,647	MC
Yale Univ	CT	64,650	MC

HOME ECONOMICS

School	ST	$IS	SR
Ball State Univ	IN	19,808	C+
Cal State, Fresno	CA	16,902	LC
CUNY/Queens College	NY	21,507	C
College of the Ozarks	MO	7,530	VC
Florida State Univ	FL	16,771	HC
Harding Univ	AR	25,440	C
Illinois State Univ	IL	23,418	VC
Indiana State Univ	IN	23,223	LC
Langston Univ	OK	15,659	C
Morgan State Univ	MD	17,190	LC
Oakwood Univ	AL	43,758	C
SUNY/Oneonta	NY	20,794	C
SUNY/Plattsburgh	NY	19,314	C
Tarleton State Univ	TX	15,248	LC
Texas A&M Univ at Kingsville	TX	16,580	LC
The Master's Univ	CA	43,870	C
Univ of Florida	FL	16,291	HC+
Univ of Maryland/Eastern Shore	MD	21,861	LC
Univ of PR-Rio Piedras campus	PR	13,327	
Utah State Univ	UT	13,235	C
Virginia State Univ	VA	19,802	C+

HOME ECONOMICS EDUCATION

School	ST	$IS	SR
Alabama A&M Univ	AL	18,796	C
Ashland Univ	OH	30,446	C
Auburn Univ	AL	24,300	VC+
Ball State Univ	IN	19,808	C+
Baylor Univ	TX	56,803	HC
Bluffton Univ	OH	40,950	C+
Brigham Young Univ	UT	13,248	MC
Cal State, Northridge	CA	17,277	LC
Carson-Newman Univ	TN	35,900	C
Central Washington Univ	WA	16,803	C
Cheyney Univ of Pennsylvania	PA	20,896	LC
Concordia Univ Nebr	NE	41,900	VC
Delaware State Univ	DE	19,376	LC
East Carolina Univ	NC	16,539	C
Eastern Kentucky Univ	KY	17,742	C
Eastern New Mexico Univ	NM	12,874	LC
Florida State Univ	FL	16,771	HC
Fort Valley State Univ	GA	17,988	VC
Indiana State Univ	IN	23,223	LC
Jacksonville State Univ	AL	14,628	LC
Langston Univ	OK	15,659	C
Mercyhurst Univ	PA	47,420	C
Murray State Univ	KY	17,726	C+
New Mexico State Univ	NM	14,050	LC
N Car A&T State Univ	NC	13,786	C
N Dak State Univ	ND	16,245	VC
Oakwood Univ	AL	43,758	C
Pittsburg State Univ	KS	13,880	C
Pontifical Catholic Univ of PR	PR	10,534	
San Francisco State Univ	CA	18,514	LC
Seattle Pacific Univ	WA	47,439	C+
Seton Hill Univ	PA	46,972	VC
Shepherd Univ, West Virginia	WV	17,382	C
S Car State Univ	SC	21,330	LC
S Dak State Univ	SD	15,874	C
St. Catherine Univ	MN	45,630	C
SUNY/Oneonta	NY	20,794	C
Tarleton State Univ	TX	15,248	LC
Tenn Tech Univ	TN	17,929	C
The Univ of Akron	OH	22,566	C
Univ of Arkansas at Pine Bluff	AR	13,541	C
Univ of Louisiana at Lafayette	LA	14,516	C
Univ of Maryland/Eastern Shore	MD	21,861	LC
Univ of Montevallo	AL	20,012	C
Univ of Nebr - Lincoln	NE	18,589	VC
Univ of Southern Miss	MS	13,170	C
Univ of Wisc-Stout	WI	19,667	C
Utah State Univ	UT	13,235	C
Wayne State College	NE	25,746	NC
Western Kentucky Univ	KY	16,850	C

HOME FURNISHINGS AND EQUIPMENT MANAGEMENT/PRODUCTION/SERVICES

School	ST	$IS	SR
Auburn Univ	AL	24,300	VC+
Fashion Inst of Technology/SUNY	NY	18,521	SP
Univ of Georgia	GA	21,878	HC
Univ of North Texas	TX	20,082	C

HOMELAND SECURITY

School	ST	$IS	SR
American Univ of PR	PR	16,130	
Angelo State Univ	TX	15,882	LC
Cal State, Sacramento	CA	19,060	C
Campbell Univ	NC	37,570	VC
Embry-Riddle Aeronautical Univ - Daytona Beach	FL	45,822	VC
Excelsior College	NY	38,800	SP
Goodwin College	CT	28,370	LC
Lake Superior State Univ	MI	19,867	C
Marian Univ	WI	34,622	C
Medaille College	NY	41,700	LC
Mitchell College	CT	45,192	C
Monmouth Univ	NJ	50,184	C
New England College	NH	50,828	NC
St. Leo Univ	FL	32,850	C
Savannah State Univ	GA	17,036	C
SUNY Albany	NY	22,165	C
Tiffin Univ	OH	34,900	LC
Univ of New Hampshire - Manchester	NH	14,490	C
Virginia Commonwealth Univ	VA	23,811	VC
Westminster College	UT	41,078	C

HOMELAND SECURITY/EMERGENCY PREPAREDNESS

School	ST	$IS	SR
Ashford Univ	CA	10,480	C
Auburn Univ at Montgomery	AL	15,000	C
Chestnut Hill College	PA	47,180	C
La Roche College	PA	38,940	C
Mass Maritime Academy	MA	20,704	C
St. Louis Univ	MO	49,866	HC
SUNY Albany	NY	22,165	C
Thomas Edison State Univ	NJ	6,350	NC
Tulane Univ	LA	67,496	MC
Univ of Alaska Fairbanks	AK	16,874	VC

HORTICULTURE

School	ST	$IS	SR
Alabama A&M Univ	AL	18,796	C
Andrews Univ	MI	41,732	C
Auburn Univ	AL	24,300	VC+
Cal State, Fullerton	CA	21,902	C
Clemson Univ	SC		HC
College of the Ozarks	MO	7,530	VC
Colo State Univ	CO	23,033	C
Delaware Valley Univ	PA	51,271	C
Eastern Kentucky Univ	KY	17,742	C
Farmingdale State College	NY	20,968	C
Ferrum College	VA	43,970	C
Florida A&M Univ	FL	15,361	C
Florida Southern College	FL	45,978	VC
Fort Valley State Univ	GA	17,988	VC
Iowa State Univ	IA	18,176	C
Kansas State Univ	KS	17,780	VC
Mich State Univ	MI	24,542	VC
Miss State Univ	MS	12,028	C+
Montana State Univ	MT	15,500	C+
Murray State Univ	KY	17,726	C+
New Mexico State Univ	NM	14,050	LC
N Car State Univ	NC	22,434	HC+
N Dak State Univ	ND	16,245	VC
Northwest Missouri State Univ	MO	18,286	C
Okla State Univ	OK	17,180	C+
Oregon State Univ	OR	23,337	VC
Purdue Univ/West Lafayette	IN	20,032	MC
Sam Houston State Univ	TX	18,792	C
S Dak State Univ	SD	15,874	C
Southeast Missouri State Univ	MO	16,148	C
Southern Illinois Univ Carbondale	IL	24,554	C
Stephen F. Austin State Univ	TX	18,484	LC
Tarleton State Univ	TX	15,248	LC
Temple Univ	PA	24,392	C+
Texas A&M Univ at College Station	TX	20,771	VC+
Truman State Univ	MO	16,286	MC
Tuskegee Univ	AL	28,164	C
Univ of Arkansas at Fayetteville	AR	19,766	VC
Univ of Cincinnati	OH	22,118	VC
Univ of Conn	CT	27,394	
Univ of Florida	FL	16,291	HC+
Univ of Georgia	GA	21,878	HC
Univ of Idaho	ID	16,158	C
Univ of Illinois at Urbana-Champaign	IL	27,006	HC
Univ of Maine	ME	21,038	VC
Univ of Minn/Crookston	MN	19,126	C
Univ of Nebr - Lincoln	NE	18,589	VC
Univ of PR, at Mayaguez	PR	13,995	
Univ of Wisc-Madison	WI	21,647	MC
Univ of Wisc-Platteville	WI	14,148	C
Univ of Wisc-River Falls	WI	14,541	C
Virginia Polytechnic Inst and State Univ	VA	21,920	VC
Washington State Univ	WA	22,747	C
West Virginia Univ	WV	18,952	VC
Western Kentucky Univ	KY	16,850	C

HOSPITAL ADMINISTRATION

School	ST	$IS	SR
Missouri State Univ	MO	15,837	C+
Northwestern State Univ of Louisiana	LA	16,534	LC
San Jose State Univ	CA	22,630	C
Thomas Edison State Univ	NJ	6,350	NC
Univ of Minn/Duluth	MN	20,292	C
Univ of Wisc-Milwaukee	WI	21,538	C

HOSPITALITY MANAGEMENT SERVICES

School	ST	$IS	SR
Appalachian State Univ	NC	15,394	VC
Arkansas Tech Univ	AR	16,534	LC
Ashford Univ	CA	10,480	C
Boston Univ	MA	67,352	MC
Bradley Univ	IL	43,240	VC
Brigham Young Univ/Hawaii	HI	11,710	C
Central Conn State Univ	CT	22,041	C
Central Mich Univ	MI	20,330	C
College of Charleston	SC	24,046	VC
Colo Mesa Univ	CO	19,707	LC
Colo State Univ	CO	23,033	C
Concordia Univ, Ann Arbor	MI	38,878	C+
Cornell Univ	NY	67,591	MC
Dallas Baptist Univ	TX	35,220	VC
Davis & Elkins College	WV	38,242	LC
DePaul Univ	IL	52,807	VC
East Carolina Univ	NC	16,539	C
Eastern Mich Univ	MI	19,761	C
Endicott College	MA	47,054	C+
Ferris State Univ	MI	21,458	C
Florida Atlantic Univ	FL	18,256	C
Florida International Univ	FL	20,281	C
Georgia State Univ	GA	25,250	C
Harris-Stowe State Univ	MO	14,590	NC
Husson Univ	ME	26,508	C
Indiana Univ of Pennsylvania	PA	24,474	C
Indiana Univ-Purdue Univ Fort Wayne	IN	18,675	C
James Madison Univ	VA	19,084	VC
Johnson & Wales Univ/Charlotte Campus	NC	44,768	C
Johnson & Wales Univ/Denver Campus	CO	44,768	C
Johnson & Wales Univ/North Miami Campus	FL	44,768	C
Johnson & Wales Univ/Providence Campus	RI	44,768	C
Johnson State College	VT	22,672	C
Kendall College	IL	32,610	C
Kent State Univ	OH	20,928	C
Lakeland Univ	WI	35,130	C
Lasell College	MA	49,400	C
Livingstone College	NC	17,815	LC
Lynn Univ	FL	49,680	LC
Madonna Univ	MI	30,450	LC
Marywood Univ	PA	47,840	C
Metropolitan State Univ	MN	7,859	C
Metropolitan State Univ of Denver	CO	6,928	LC
Mich State Univ	MI	24,542	VC
Mitchell College	CT	45,192	C
Monroe College	NY	23,996	C
Montclair State Univ	NJ	26,912	C
Morgan State Univ	MD	17,190	LC
Mount Ida College	MA	46,820	C
New York City College of Technology	NY	7,185	LC
New York Inst of Technology	NY	49,980	VC
Newbury College	MA	48,970	C
Norfolk State Univ	VA	18,902	LC
N Dak State Univ	ND	16,245	VC
Northwestern State Univ of Louisiana	LA	16,534	LC
Ohio State Univ at Columbus	OH	22,843	MC
Oregon State Univ	OR	23,337	VC
Pace Univ	NY	60,136	C
Pennsylvania State Univ - Univ Park	PA	29,716	HC
Purdue Univ/West Lafayette	IN	20,032	MC
Robert Morris Univ	PA	40,600	C
Rochester Inst of Technology	NY	52,734	HC+
Rutgers Univ - Camden	NJ	26,595	C
St. Leo Univ	FL	32,850	C
San Diego State Univ	CA	23,156	VC
San Francisco State Univ	CA	18,514	LC
Southeast Missouri State Univ	MO	16,148	C
Southern Illinois Univ Carbondale	IL	24,554	C
Southern New Hampshire Univ	NH	44,256	C
Southern Oregon Univ	OR	19,117	C
St. John's Univ	NY	57,160	C+
St. Joseph's College, New York/Brooklyn Campus	NY	25,114	LC
St. Joseph's College, New York/Long Island Campus	NY	25,124	C
St. Thomas Univ	FL	51,187	LC
SUNY/Buffalo State	NY	20,583	LC
Stephen F. Austin State Univ	TX	18,484	LC

School	ST	$IS	SR
The Univ of Memphis	TN	18,278	C
Thomas Edison State Univ	NJ	6,350	NC
Tougaloo College	MS	17,980	NC
Tuskegee Univ	AL	28,164	C
Univ of Arkansas at Fayetteville	AR	19,766	VC
Univ of Central Florida	FL	16,379	VC
Univ of Denver	CO	61,129	VC+
Univ of Findlay	OH	43,040	C
Univ of Illinois at Urbana-Champaign	IL	27,006	HC
Univ of Mass Amherst	MA	27,669	HC
Univ of Miss	MS	18,802	C
Univ of Nebr - Lincoln	NE	18,589	VC
Univ of New Hampshire	NH	29,333	VC
Univ of New Haven	CT	53,680	C
Univ of North Texas	TX	20,082	C
Univ of Pittsburgh at Bradford	PA	22,958	C
Univ of San Francisco	CA	60,580	C
Univ of South Alabama	AL	16,880	C
Univ of Wisc-Stout	WI	19,667	C
Washington State Univ	WA	22,747	C
Webber International Univ	FL	31,904	C
Western Carolina Univ	NC	13,965	C
Western Illinois Univ	IL	20,897	C
Western Kentucky Univ	KY	16,850	C
Widener Univ	PA	58,190	C
Wilkes Univ	PA	49,166	C
Youngstown State Univ	OH	17,487	C

HOTEL/MOTEL AND RESTAURANT MANAGEMENT

School	ST	$IS	SR
Ashland Univ	OH	30,446	C
Auburn Univ	AL	24,300	VC+
Bethune-Cookman Univ	FL	23,322	C
Boston Univ	MA	67,352	MC
Calif State Polytechnic Univ, Pomona	CA	21,811	C
Cal State, Fullerton	CA	21,902	C
Cheyney Univ of Pennsylvania	PA	20,896	LC
College of the Ozarks	MO	7,530	VC
Colo State Univ	CO	23,033	C
Concord Univ	WV	14,954	LC
Delaware State Univ	DE	19,376	LC
Drexel Univ	PA	65,927	HC
Eastern Mich Univ	MI	19,761	C
Endicott College	MA	47,054	C+
Fairleigh Dickinson Univ/College at Florham	NJ	54,770	C
Fairleigh Dickinson Univ/Metropolitan Campus	NJ	52,392	C
Ferris State Univ	MI	21,458	C
Florida State Univ	FL	16,771	HC
Grambling State Univ	LA	15,701	C
Grand Valley State Univ	MI	22,250	C+
Inter-American Univ of PR-Aguadilla Campus	PR	21,657	
Iowa State Univ	IA	18,176	C
Johnson & Wales Univ/Charlotte Campus	NC	44,768	C
Johnson & Wales Univ/Denver Campus	CO	44,768	C
Johnson & Wales Univ/North Miami Campus	FL	44,768	C
Johnson & Wales Univ/Providence Campus	RI	44,768	C
Kansas State Univ	KS	17,780	VC
Keiser Univ	FL	35,010	LC
Kendall College	IL	32,610	C
Mercyhurst Univ	PA	47,420	C
New Mexico State Univ	NM	14,050	LC
New York Univ	NY	68,139	MC
Newbury College	MA	48,970	C
Niagara Univ	NY	41,010	C
N Car Wesleyan College	NC	39,200	C
N Dak State Univ	ND	16,245	VC
Northern Arizona Univ	AZ	21,003	C
Northwood Univ - Mich	MI	35,010	LC
Ohio Univ	OH	23,394	VC
Okla State Univ	OK	17,180	C+
Purdue Univ Northwest	IN	15,178	C
Rochester Inst of Technology	NY	52,734	HC+
Roosevelt Univ	IL	41,890	VC
San Francisco State Univ	CA	18,514	LC
S Dak State Univ	SD	15,874	C
Southwest Minn State Univ	MN	17,783	C
SUNY/Plattsburgh	NY	19,314	C
Tenn State Univ	TN	14,423	LC
Texas Tech Univ	TX	20,156	C+
The Univ of Tenn at Knoxville	TN	22,112	VC
Tougaloo College	MS	17,980	NC
Univ of Alaska Anchorage	AK	17,914	C
Univ of Central Missouri	MO	18,982	C
Univ of Delaware	DE	32,214	VC
Univ of Houston	TX	21,871	VC
Univ of Kentucky	KY	24,800	C+
Univ of Louisiana at Lafayette	LA	14,516	C
Univ of Maryland/Eastern Shore	MD	21,861	LC
Univ of Missouri-Columbia	MO	20,463	VC
Univ of Nevada, Las Vegas	NV	17,553	C
Univ of New Haven	CT	53,680	C
Univ of New Orleans	LA	12,840	C
Univ of San Francisco	CA	60,580	C
Univ of S Car at Columbia	SC	21,726	VC

School	ST	$IS	SR
Univ of Southern Miss	MS	13,170	C
Univ of Wisc-Stout	WI	19,667	C
Virginia Polytechnic Inst and State Univ	VA	21,920	VC
Virginia State Univ	VA	19,802	C+
Washington State Univ	WA	22,747	C
Wiley College	TX	19,255	C
Youngstown State Univ	OH	17,487	C

HUMAN BIOLOGY

School	ST	$IS	SR
Baker Univ	KS	37,190	C
Brown Univ	RI	64,566	MC
Cal State, Fullerton	CA	21,902	C
King Univ	TN	36,976	C
Mich State Univ	MI	24,542	VC
Missouri Western State Univ	MO	17,822	LC
Ohio Univ	OH	23,394	VC
Univ of Calif San Diego	CA	30,450	MC
Univ of Kansas	KS	20,884	VC
Univ of N Car at Greensboro	NC	15,998	C
Univ of Okla	OK	19,651	HC

HUMAN BIOLOGY, HEALTH, AND SOCIETY

School	ST	$IS	SR
Brown Univ	RI	64,566	MC
Cornell Univ	NY	67,591	MC
Indiana Univ Bloomington	IN	20,791	HC

HUMAN DEVELOPMENT

School	ST	$IS	SR
Alabama A&M Univ	AL	18,796	C
Amridge Univ	AL	10,860	LC
Andrews Univ	MI	41,732	C
Anna Maria College	MA	51,020	C
Arizona State Univ at the Tempe Campus	AZ	23,001	VC
Auburn Univ	AL	24,300	VC+
Boston College	MA	68,043	MC
Bowling Green State Univ	OH	19,975	C
Brigham Young Univ	UT	13,248	MC
Brown Univ	RI	64,566	MC
Cal State, East Bay	CA	20,748	C
Cal State, Long Beach	CA	18,850	C
Cal State, San Bernardino	CA	20,106	C
Cal State, San Marcos	CA	20,604	LC
Colo State Univ	CO	23,033	C
Conn College	CT	65,000	MC
Cornell Univ	NY	67,591	MC
Earlham College	IN	55,670	HC
East Tenn State Univ	TN	18,141	C
Eckerd College	FL	55,206	VC
Goddard College	VT	17,040	VC
Hellenic College/Holy Cross Greek Orthodox School of Theology	MA	39,906	C
Hope International Univ	CA	42,730	C
Howard Univ	DC	37,616	C+
Kalamazoo College	MI	53,931	HC
Kent State Univ	OH	20,928	C
Lee Univ	TN	22,045	C
Marylhurst Univ	OR	16,818	NC
Minn State Univ, Mankato	MN	17,190	C
Mitchell College	CT	45,192	C
Montana State Univ	MT	15,500	C+
National Louis Univ	IL	43,000	LC
N Dak State Univ	ND	16,245	VC
Northwestern Univ	IL	68,725	MC
Nova Southeastern Univ	FL	38,534	C+
Oakwood Univ	AL	43,758	C
Ohio State Univ at Columbus	OH	22,843	MC
Ohio Univ	OH	23,394	VC
Okla State Univ	OK	17,180	C+
Oregon State Univ	OR	23,337	VC
Penn State Altoona	PA	26,686	C
Prescott College	AZ	38,201	C
Radford Univ	VA	19,758	C
Rivier Univ	NH	41,600	VC
San Diego Christian College	CA	40,914	C
Sonoma State Univ	CA	27,020	C
S Dak State Univ	SD	15,874	C
Southern Nazarene Univ	OK	33,684	C
SUNY at Binghamton	NY	24,100	MC
SUNY at Oswego	NY	22,219	VC
SUNY/Empire State College	NY	9,145	NC
SUNY/Plattsburgh	NY	19,314	C
Suffolk Univ	MA	52,316	C
Tarleton State Univ	TX	15,248	LC
The Univ of Alabama	AL	24,320	C+
The Univ of Arizona	AZ	24,086	C
The Univ of Memphis	TN	18,278	C
Univ of Arkansas at Fayetteville	AR	19,766	VC
Univ of Bridgeport	CT	44,985	LC
Univ of Calif at Davis	CA	28,468	HC
Univ of Calif San Diego	CA	30,450	MC
Univ of Chicago	IL	70,551	MC
Univ of Conn	CT	27,394	
Univ of Delaware	DE	32,214	VC
Univ of Illinois at Urbana-Champaign	IL	27,006	HC
Univ of Miami	FL	63,494	MC
Univ of Missouri-Columbia	MO	20,463	VC
Univ of Nebr - Kearney	NE	17,014	LC
Univ of New Mexico	NM	16,808	C
Univ of Pittsburgh at Bradford	PA	22,958	C

School	ST	$IS	SR
Univ of Vermont	VT	29,792	HC
Univ of Wisc-Green Bay	WI	15,184	C
Univ of Wisc-Madison	WI	21,647	MC
Univ of Wisc-Stout	WI	19,667	C
Utah State Univ	UT	13,235	C
Vanderbilt Univ	TN	63,248	MC
Virginia Polytechnic Inst and State Univ	VA	21,920	VC
Warner Pacific College	OR	31,610	C
Washington State Univ	WA	22,747	C

HUMAN DEVELOPMENT & FAMILY STUDIES

School	ST	$IS	SR
Merrimack College	MA	55,415	C
Mich State Univ	MI	24,542	VC
Pennsylvania State Univ - Univ Park	PA	29,716	HC
Purdue Univ Northwest	IN	15,178	C
Samford Univ	AL	40,770	VC
Texas Tech Univ	TX	20,156	C+
Univ of Georgia	GA	21,878	HC
Univ of Minn/Twin Cities	MN	24,269	MC
Univ of New Hampshire	NH	29,333	VC
Univ of N Car at Greensboro	NC	15,998	C
Univ of Rhode Island	RI	26,066	VC
Univ of Vermont	VT	29,792	HC
Washington State Univ	WA	22,747	C
Western Kentucky Univ	KY	16,850	C

HUMAN ECOLOGY

School	ST	$IS	SR
College of the Atlantic	ME	53,289	HC+
Goddard College	VT	17,040	VC
Kansas State Univ	KS	17,780	VC
Ohio State Univ at Columbus	OH	22,843	MC
Tenn Tech Univ	TN	17,929	C
The Univ of Texas at Austin	TX	20,206	MC
Univ of Calif at Davis	CA	28,468	HC
Virginia Wesleyan Univ	VA	45,980	LC

HUMAN EVOLUTIONARY BIOLOGY

School	ST	$IS	SR
Stony Brook Univ/The SUNY	NY	22,703	MC

HUMAN PERFORMANCE

School	ST	$IS	SR
Elon Univ	NC	46,142	HC
Keene State College	NH	24,604	C
Tenn Wesleyan Univ	TN	32,680	LC
Univ of Tampa	FL	38,928	VC

HUMAN RELATIONS

School	ST	$IS	SR
High Point Univ	NC	47,355	VC
Missouri Western State Univ	MO	17,822	LC
Univ of Okla	OK	19,651	HC

HUMAN RESOURCE MANAGEMENT

School	ST	$IS	SR
Bryant Univ	RI	57,204	VC
Cal State, Fullerton	CA	21,902	C
Keene State College	NH	24,604	C
Lewis Univ	IL	41,710	C
Lynn Univ	FL	49,680	LC
Merrimack College	MA	55,415	C
Northwest Missouri State Univ	MO	18,286	C
Rutgers Univ - Camden	NJ	26,595	C
Rutgers Univ - New Brunswick	NJ	27,090	HC
Univ of Mich/Dearborn	MI	12,472	VC
Univ of Mount Union	OH	39,990	C

HUMAN RESOURCES

School	ST	$IS	SR
Adelphi Univ	NY	49,792	C
Alderson Broaddus Univ	WV	35,000	LC
Alvernia Univ	PA	45,330	C
American International College	MA	47,020	LC
Amridge Univ	AL	10,860	LC
Aquinas College - Mich	MI	38,876	VC
Baldwin Wallace Univ	OH	42,464	VC
Ball State Univ	IN	19,808	C+
Baylor Univ	TX	56,803	HC
Black Hills State Univ	SD	16,622	C
Blackburn College	IL	28,526	LC
Bluffton Univ	OH	40,950	C+
Boston College	MA	68,043	MC
Brescia Univ	KY	29,890	VC
Briar Cliff Univ	IA	36,956	C
Cal State, San Bernardino	CA	20,106	C
Calvin College	MI	43,090	HC
Carlow Univ	PA	39,696	LC
Central Mich Univ	MI	20,330	C
Chestnut Hill College	PA	47,180	C
Colo Christian Univ	CO	40,885	VC
Concordia Univ, Ann Arbor	MI	38,878	C+
Davenport Univ	MI	25,896	LC
Defiance College	OH	42,240	LC
DePaul Univ	IL	52,807	VC
DeSales Univ	PA	47,520	C
Dominican College	NY	40,258	LC
Elizabethtown College School of Continuing and Professional Studies	PA	18,900	C
Excelsior College	NY	38,800	SP
Faulkner Univ	AL	26,410	C
Ferris State Univ	MI	21,458	C
Florida Atlantic Univ	FL	18,256	C
Franklin Univ	OH	11,616	NC
Friends Univ	KS	38,000	C
Golden Gate Univ	CA	19,510	C
Goldey-Beacom College	DE	36,038	C
Gwynedd Mercy Univ	PA	43,780	LC
Hawaii Pacific Univ	HI	33,420	C
Holy Names Univ	CA	46,630	LC
Idaho State Univ	ID	13,619	LC
Indiana Univ of Pennsylvania	PA	24,474	C
Inter-American Univ of PR-Aguadilla Campus	PR	21,657	
Inter-American Univ of PR-Bayamon	PR	18,785	
John Carroll Univ	OH	51,570	C
Juniata College	PA	58,118	VC
Kentucky Wesleyan College	KY	34,260	LC
Lake Erie College	OH	38,914	LC
Le Moyne College	NY	47,305	VC
Limestone College	SC	32,100	C
Lindenwood Univ	MO	25,760	C
Louisiana State Univ and A&M College	LA	18,677	VC
Lourdes Univ	OH	29,140	NC
Loyola Univ Chicago	IL	57,158	VC
Marietta College	OH	46,190	C
Marquette Univ	WI	53,090	VC+
Menlo College	CA	51,380	LC
Metropolitan State Univ	MN	7,859	C
Mich State Univ	MI	24,542	VC
Midway Univ	KY	33,940	LC
Mount Aloysius College	PA	29,976	C
Mount Mercy Univ	IA	39,748	C
Neumann Univ	PA	40,678	LC
New York Univ	NY	68,139	MC
Niagara Univ	NY	41,010	C
Nichols College	MA	46,900	LC
North Central College	IL	48,712	C+
Northeastern Illinois Univ	IL	12,529	LC
Northern Kentucky Univ	KY	16,486	C
Notre Dame College	OH	39,150	VC
Oakland Univ	MI	20,763	C
Ohio State Univ at Columbus	OH	22,843	MC
Okla Wesleyan Univ	OK	34,434	C
Our Lady of the Lake Univ	TX	37,790	LC
Pace Univ	NY	60,136	C
Park Univ	MO	22,134	C
Peirce College	PA	16,780	NC
Pennsylvania College of Technology	PA	27,693	NC
Point Park Univ	PA	41,270	C
Purdue Univ Northwest	IN	15,178	C
Purdue Univ/West Lafayette	IN	20,032	MC
Rider Univ	NJ	54,050	C
Rowan Univ	NJ	24,491	VC
St. Joseph's Univ	PA	58,540	VC
St. Mary-of-the-Woods College	IN	40,424	LC
San Jose State Univ	CA	22,630	C
Seton Hill Univ	PA	46,972	VC
Silver Lake College of the Holy Family	WI	36,290	LC
Simpson Univ	CA	34,722	C
Southern Illinois Univ Edwardsville	IL	20,188	C
Spalding Univ	KY	31,938	C
St. Mary's Univ	TX	39,120	C
SUNY at Oswego	NY	22,219	VC
SUNY/Empire State College	NY	9,145	NC
Tarleton State Univ	TX	15,248	LC
Tenn Wesleyan Univ	TN	32,680	LC
Texas A&M Univ at College Station	TX	20,771	VC+
The George Washington Univ	DC	68,474	HC+
The Univ of Tenn at Knoxville	TN	22,112	VC
The Univ of Texas at San Antonio	TX	21,060	C
Thomas College	ME	73,888	LC
Trinity International Univ	IL	31,070	VC
Univ of Arkansas at Fayetteville	AR	19,766	VC
Univ of Central Missouri	MO	18,982	C
Univ of Central Okla	OK	15,150	C
Univ of Findlay	OH	43,040	C
Univ of Florida	FL	16,291	HC+
Univ of Hawaii at Manoa	HI	23,261	C
Univ of Idaho	ID	16,158	C
Univ of Illinois at Urbana-Champaign	IL	27,006	HC
Univ of Lynchburg	VA	48,370	C
Univ of Maryland Univ College	MD	26,146	LC
Univ of Mich/Flint	MI	19,062	C
Univ of Minn/Twin Cities	MN	24,269	MC
Univ of Mount Olive	NC	18,426	C
Univ of Nebr - Lincoln	NE	18,589	VC
Univ of Nevada, Las Vegas	NV	17,553	C
Univ of N Car at Greensboro	NC	15,998	C
Univ of N Dak	ND	16,673	C
Univ of North Texas	TX	20,082	C
Univ of Pennsylvania	PA	63,526	MC
Univ of Pittsburgh	PA	30,030	MC

ST = STATE **$IS** = IN-STATE COSTS **SR** = SELECTOR RATING

School	ST	$IS	SR
Univ of PR, at Humacao	PR	14,000	
Univ of Scranton	PA	54,962	VC
Univ of S Dak	SD	16,109	C
Univ of the Incarnate Word	TX	39,162	LC
Univ of Wisc-Green Bay	WI	15,184	C
Univ of Wisc-Madison	WI	21,647	MC
Univ of Wisc-Milwaukee	WI	21,538	C
Univ of Wisc-Oshkosh	WI	15,392	C
Ursuline College	OH	41,076	LC
Valley City State Univ	ND	13,267	C
Washington State Univ	WA	22,747	C
Washington Univ in St. Louis	MO	67,539	MC
Weber State Univ	UT	14,112	C
Western Washington Univ	WA	18,904	VC
Wichita State Univ	KS	17,773	C
Xavier Univ	OH	49,380	VC
York College	NE	30,260	C
Youngstown State Univ	OH	17,487	C

HUMAN RESOURCES/ ORGANIZATIONAL MGMT

School	ST	$IS	SR
Albertus Magnus College	CT	44,016	LC
Ashford Univ	CA	10,480	C
Bay Path Univ	MA	46,356	C
Black Hills State Univ	SD	16,622	C
Bloomfield College	NJ	40,100	LC
Bradley Univ	IL	43,240	VC
Calif State Polytechnic Univ, Pomona	CA	21,811	C
Dallas Baptist Univ	TX	35,220	VC
Georgia Southwestern State Univ	GA	13,870	LC
Immaculata Univ	PA	39,000	C
Lipscomb Univ	TN	42,984	VC
Mercy College	NY	32,614	C
Mich State Univ	MI	24,542	VC
Missouri Southern State Univ	MO	13,071	C
Murray State Univ	KY	17,726	C+
New York Inst of Technology	NY	49,980	VC
Newbury College	MA	48,970	C
Purdue Univ Northwest	IN	15,178	C
San Diego State Univ	CA	23,156	VC
Silver Lake College of the Holy Family	WI	36,290	LC
Southeast Missouri State Univ	MO	16,148	C
Tarleton State Univ	TX	15,248	LC
Thomas Edison State Univ	NJ	6,350	NC
Univ of Miami	FL	63,494	MC
Univ of San Francisco	CA	60,580	C
Western Illinois Univ	IL	20,897	C
Western Mich Univ	MI	21,791	C
Winona State Univ	MN	18,109	C

HUMAN SERVICES

School	ST	$IS	SR
Alaska Pacific Univ	AK	28,730	VC
Albertus Magnus College	CT	44,016	LC
Alfred State College	NY	19,895	C
Aquinas College - Mich	MI	38,876	VC
Arkansas Baptist College	AR	20,280	NC
Assumption College	MA	48,455	VC
Beacon College	FL	46,862	C
Bethel College	IN	36,830	C
Bethel Univ	TN	27,142	C
Black Hills State Univ	SD	16,622	C
Bloomfield College	NJ	40,100	LC
Boricua College	NY	10,100	C
Cal State, Dominguez Hills	CA	19,022	LC
Cal State, Fullerton	CA	21,902	C
Cal State, Monterey Bay	CA	22,872	LC
Cal State, San Bernardino	CA	20,106	C
Calumet College of St. Joseph	IN	22,735	C
Cambridge College	MA	14,940	NC
Cazenovia College	NY	47,866	C
Chestnut Hill College	PA	47,180	C
College of St Joseph	VT	32,400	LC
Columbia College - Missouri	MO	28,179	C
Drury Univ	MO	37,555	VC
East Central Univ	OK	13,330	C
Eastern New Mexico Univ	NM	12,874	LC
Elizabethtown College School of Continuing and Professional Studies	PA	18,900	C
Elmira College	NY	53,900	C
Elon Univ	NC	46,142	HC
Emmanuel College	MA	53,472	C+
Fitchburg State Univ	MA	21,819	LC
Fontbonne Univ	MO	34,606	C
Friends Univ	KS	38,000	C
Geneva College	PA	35,450	C
Goodwin College	CT	28,370	LC
Grace Bible College	MI	25,250	C
Graceland Univ	IA	35,290	C
Grand View Univ	IA	32,302	C
Gwynedd Mercy Univ	PA	43,780	LC
Hastings College	NE	35,380	C+
Hawaii Pacific Univ	HI	33,420	C
Henderson State Univ	AR	15,516	C
Hilbert College	NY	32,650	LC
Holy Names Univ	CA	46,630	LC
Hope International Univ	CA	42,730	C
Indiana Inst of Technology	IN	34,240	LC
Indiana Univ-Purdue Univ Fort Wayne	IN	18,675	C
Kennesaw State Univ	GA	18,899	VC
Lake Superior State Univ	MI	19,867	C
Lasell College	MA	49,400	C
Le Moyne College	NY	47,305	VC
Lenoir-Rhyne Univ	NC	47,500	LC
Lesley Univ	MA	42,800	C
Lincoln Univ	PA	20,878	LC
Lindenwood Univ	MO	25,760	C
Lindsey Wilson College	KY	33,546	C
Loyola Univ Chicago	IL	57,158	VC
Lyndon State College	VT	20,714	C
Metropolitan College of New York	NY		VC
Metropolitan State Univ	MN	7,859	C
Metropolitan State Univ of Denver	CO	6,928	LC
Millikin Univ	IL	44,148	C
Missouri Baptist Univ	MO	35,594	C
Missouri Valley College	MO	28,150	C
Montana State Univ Billings	MT	13,336	LC
Montreat College	NC	34,605	LC
Mount St. Mary College	NY	44,448	C
Mount St. Mary's Univ	MD	53,380	C
National Louis Univ	IL	43,000	LC
New York City College of Technology	NY	7,185	LC
Newbury College	MA	48,970	C
N Car Central Univ	NC	9,000	C
Northern State Univ	SD	15,570	C
Northwest Christian Univ	OR	36,580	C
Notre Dame de Namur Univ	CA	46,526	LC
Nova Southeastern Univ	FL	38,534	C+
Oglala Lakota College	SD	15,050	NC
Old Dominion Univ	VA	21,618	C
Ottawa Univ	KS	39,980	VC
Park Univ	MO	22,134	C
Pfeiffer Univ	NC	40,532	LC
Queens Univ of Charlotte	NC	39,543	C
Quincy Univ	IL	38,170	LC
St. Mary-of-the-Woods College	IN	40,424	LC
St. Mary's Univ of Minn	MN	42,440	C
Salem International Univ	WV	21,090	C
Seton Hill Univ	PA	46,972	VC
Siena Heights Univ	MI	36,322	C
Sinte Gleska Univ	SD	13,154	NC
S Car State Univ	SC	21,330	LC
Southern Oregon Univ	OR	19,117	C
Southern Wesleyan Univ	SC	33,670	LC
Southwest Baptist Univ	MO	30,890	LC
Springfield College	MA	48,775	C
St. John's Univ	NY	57,160	C+
St. Joseph's College, New York/Brooklyn Campus	NY	25,114	LC
St. Joseph's College, New York/Long Island Campus	NY	25,124	C
St. Thomas Univ	FL	51,187	LC
SUNY/Cortland	NY	20,910	C
Stevenson Univ	MD	48,412	C
Suffolk Univ	MA	52,316	C
Tenn Wesleyan Univ	TN	32,680	LC
Texas Southern Univ	TX	19,592	LC
The George Washington Univ	DC	68,474	HC+
Thomas Edison State Univ	NJ	6,350	NC
Touro College	NY	31,040	C
Trinity International Univ	IL	31,070	VC
Trinity Washington Univ	DC	33,826	C+
Troy Univ	AL	16,171	C
Univ of Alaska Anchorage	AK	17,914	C
Univ of Bridgeport	CT	44,985	LC
Univ of Delaware	DE	32,214	VC
Univ of Maine at Machias	ME	22,960	C
Univ of Mass Boston	MA	13,828	C
Univ of Mount Olive	NC	18,426	C
Univ of New Mexico	NM	16,808	C
Univ of North Georgia	GA	17,316	C
Univ of North Texas	TX	20,082	C
Univ of Northern Colo	CO	19,658	C
Univ of Oregon	OR	24,021	VC
Univ of Scranton	PA	54,962	VC
Univ of Wisc-Oshkosh	WI	15,392	C
Upper Iowa Univ	IA	34,990	NC
Washburn Univ	KS	15,827	C
Wayland Baptist Univ	TX	23,460	LC
Waynesburg Univ	PA	33,530	C
Western New Mexico Univ	NM	16,914	LC
Western Washington Univ	WA	18,904	VC
William Penn Univ	IA	26,000	C
Wingate Univ	NC	41,900	C
Wisc Lutheran College	WI	36,290	C
York College	NE	30,260	C

HUMAN STUDIES

School	ST	$IS	SR
St. Edward's Univ	TX	56,190	VC
Texas Tech Univ	TX	20,156	C+
Univ of Rhode Island	RI	26,066	VC

HUMANITIES

School	ST	$IS	SR
Albertus Magnus College	CT	44,016	LC
Anna Maria College	MA	51,020	C
Belhaven Univ	MS	32,250	C
Bennington College	VT	66,280	MC
Biola Univ	CA	48,686	C
Bloomfield College	NJ	40,100	LC
Bluefield State College	WV	5,832	LC
Brigham Young Univ	UT	13,248	MC
Bucknell Univ	PA	67,136	MC
Cal State, Chico	CA	19,790	VC
Cal State, Fresno	CA	16,902	LC
Cal State, Fullerton	CA	21,902	C
Cal State, Monterey Bay	CA	22,872	LC
Cal State, Northridge	CA	17,277	LC
Cal State, San Bernardino	CA	20,106	C
Chaminade Univ of Honolulu	HI	37,614	C
Charleston Southern Univ	SC	34,700	C
Clarkson Univ	NY	60,392	VC
Colby-Sawyer College	NH	50,790	C
Colgate Univ	NY	67,500	MC
College of St. Benedict	MN	54,480	C
College of St. Mary	NE	27,500	C
College of St. Scholastica	MN	45,734	C+
Concordia College - Moorhead	MN	46,418	C
Concordia Univ	OR	35,000	C
Concordia Univ Irvine	CA	44,860	VC
Concordia Univ Wisc	WI	35,910	C
Concordia Univ, Ann Arbor	MI	38,878	C+
Corban Univ	OR	41,700	C
Cornerstone Univ	MI	36,550	C
Defiance College	OH	42,240	LC
DePaul Univ	IL	52,807	VC
Dominican College	NY	40,258	LC
Dominican Univ of Calif	CA	58,750	C
Duquesne Univ	PA	48,508	VC
Eastern Washington Univ	WA	17,896	LC
Eckerd College	FL	55,206	VC
Edinboro Univ	PA	15,940	LC
Fairleigh Dickinson Univ/ College at Florham	NJ	54,770	C
Fairleigh Dickinson Univ/ Metropolitan Campus	NJ	52,392	C
Faulkner Univ	AL	26,410	C
Felician Univ	NJ	46,280	LC
Florida Inst of Technology	FL	53,306	VC
Florida Southern College	FL	45,978	VC
Florida State Univ	FL	16,771	HC
Fort Lewis College	CO	20,154	C
Georgian Court Univ	NJ	43,068	LC
Hampden-Sydney College	VA	57,806	VC
Hampshire College	MA	65,214	MC
Harding Univ	AR	25,440	C
Harvard College/Harvard Univ	MA	65,609	MC
Hawaii Pacific Univ	HI	33,420	C
Heritage Univ	WA	19,825	NC
Hofstra Univ	NY	58,210	C+
Holy Family Univ	PA	44,672	LC
Holy Names Univ	CA	46,630	LC
Houghton College	NY	40,558	VC
Illinois Inst of Technology	IL	56,826	HC+
Indiana Univ East	IN	7,207	C
Indiana Univ Kokomo	IN	7,207	C
Indiana Univ Southeast	IN	16,931	C
Jacksonville Univ	FL	49,210	C
John Carroll Univ	OH	51,570	C
Johns Hopkins Univ	MD	68,080	MC
Johnson State College	VT	22,672	C
Juniata College	PA	58,118	VC
Kansas State Univ	KS	17,780	VC
Kentucky Christian Univ	KY	26,836	LC
Lasell College	MA	49,400	C
Lawrence Tech Univ	MI	41,630	VC
Lee Univ	TN	22,045	C
Lees-McRae College	NC	33,944	NC
LeMoyne-Owen College	TN	16,980	C
Lesley Univ	MA	42,800	C
LIU Brooklyn	NY	50,698	C
Loyola Marymount Univ	CA	60,202	VC+
Loyola Univ New Orleans	LA	52,456	VC
Lubbock Christian Univ	TX	29,727	C
Marshall Univ	WV	18,044	C
Martin Univ	IN	21,010	LC
Mass Inst of Technology	MA	62,662	MC
Mich State Univ	MI	24,542	VC
Midwestern State Univ	TX	12,111	LC
Miles College	AL	16,530	NC
Milligan College	TN	39,450	C
Minn State Univ, Mankato	MN	17,190	C
Montana State Univ-Northern	MT	11,370	NC
Montclair State Univ	NJ	26,912	C
Mount Aloysius College	PA	29,976	C
New College of Florida	FL	16,180	HC+
New York Univ	NY	68,139	MC
N Dak State Univ	ND	16,245	VC
Northland College	WI	41,103	C+
Northwest Christian Univ	OR	36,580	C
Northwest Missouri State Univ	MO	18,286	C
Northwestern State Univ of Louisiana	LA	16,534	LC
Notre Dame de Namur Univ	CA	46,526	LC
Oberlin College	OH	68,942	MC
Ohio Valley Univ	WV	28,800	C
Okla City Univ	OK	40,476	C
Pacific Univ	OR	37,617	C
Paul Quinn College	TX	25,350	LC
Pepperdine Univ	CA	66,862	VC+
Plymouth State Univ	NH	23,180	LC
Prescott College	AZ	38,201	C
Providence College	RI	62,870	HC
Quincy Univ	IL	38,170	LC
Roberts Wesleyan College	NY	41,116	C
Rockford Univ	IL	38,570	C
Roger Williams Univ	RI	48,074	VC
Rollins College	FL	58,670	HC
Rosemont College	PA	30,980	LC
St. John's Univ	MN	53,472	C
St. Mary-of-the-Woods College	IN	40,424	LC
St. Mary's College	IN	50,600	C
St. Peter's Univ	NJ	49,192	C
San Diego State Univ	CA	23,156	VC
San Francisco State Univ	CA	18,514	LC
Schreiner Univ	TX	34,626	LC
Scripps College	CA	69,260	HC
Seattle Univ	WA	54,957	VC
Shawnee State Univ	OH	16,998	C
Siena Heights Univ	MI	36,322	C
Sierra Nevada College	NV	45,403	C
Southern Methodist Univ	TX	69,008	MC
Spring Hill College	AL	48,488	C
St. Andrews Univ	NC	44,634	LC
St. Norbert College	WI	46,060	VC
SUNY/Buffalo State	NY	20,583	LC
SUNY/College at Old Westbury	NY	16,860	C
SUNY/Maritime College	NY	16,020	C
Suffolk Univ	MA	52,316	C
Taylor Univ	IN	42,130	VC
The George Washington Univ	DC	68,474	HC+
The Univ of Tenn at Chattanooga	TN	17,340	C+
The Univ of Texas at Austin	TX	20,206	MC
The Univ of Texas at San Antonio	TX	21,060	C
Thomas Edison State Univ	NJ	6,350	NC
Thomas More College	KY	36,720	LC
Thomas Univ	GA	21,420	NC
Tougaloo College	MS	17,980	NC
Trinity International Univ	IL	31,070	VC
Tulane Univ	LA	67,496	MC
Union College	NY	64,320	MC
United States Air Force Academy	CO		C
United States Military Academy at West Point	NY		HC+
Universidad del Turabo	PR	17,828	
Universidad Metropolitana	PR	17,828	
Univ of Calif at Irvine	CA	33,857	VC
Univ of Central Florida	FL	16,379	VC
Univ of Central Okla	OK	15,150	C
Univ of Chicago	IL	70,551	MC
Univ of Colo Boulder	CO	26,048	HC
Univ of Houston-Downtown	TX	7,241	LC
Univ of Illinois at Chicago	IL	24,664	VC
Univ of Illinois at Urbana-Champaign	IL	27,006	HC
Univ of Kansas	KS	20,884	VC
Univ of Louisville	KY	19,692	C
Univ of Maryland Univ College	MD	26,146	LC
Univ of Mich/Ann Arbor	MI	25,274	MC
Univ of Mich/Dearborn	MI	12,472	VC
Univ of Mobile	AL	28,935	C
Univ of New Hampshire	NH	29,333	VC
Univ of New Hampshire - Manchester	NH	14,490	C
Univ of Northern Iowa	IA	17,480	C
Univ of Oregon	OR	24,021	VC
Univ of Pittsburgh	PA	30,030	MC
Univ of Pittsburgh at Greensburg	PA	24,140	C
Univ of Pittsburgh at Johnstown	PA	22,092	C
Univ of PR, at Cayey	PR		
Univ of Rio Grande & Rio Grande Community College	OH	8,750	LC
Univ of San Diego	CA	60,338	HC
Univ of Sioux Falls	SD	25,630	C
Univ of South Florida/Tampa	FL	16,110	VC
Univ of the Southwest	NM	24,386	C
Univ of Toledo	OH	19,336	C
Univ of Wisc-Green Bay	WI	15,184	C
Univ of Wyoming	WY	15,537	C
Ursuline College	OH	41,076	LC
Valparaiso Univ	IN	50,160	VC
Villanova Univ	PA	64,922	MC
Virginia Wesleyan Univ	VA	45,980	LC
Walla Walla Univ	WA	34,845	C
Washington College	MD	56,154	VC
Washington State Univ	WA	22,747	C
Washington Univ in St. Louis	MO	67,539	MC
Western New Mexico Univ	NM	16,914	LC
Western Oregon Univ	OR	19,965	LC
Wheelock College	MA	51,325	LC
Widener Univ	PA	58,190	C
Willamette Univ	OR	62,514	VC+
Wofford College	SC	49,885	VC
Worcester Polytechnic Inst	MA	62,846	MC
Wright State Univ	OH	16,983	C
Xavier Univ	OH	49,380	VC
Yale Univ	CT	64,650	MC
York College of Pennsylvania	PA	29,240	C

HUMANITIES AND SOCIAL SCIENCE

School	ST	$IS	SR
Alabama A&M Univ	AL	18,796	C
Bennington College	VT	66,280	MC
Bloomfield College	NJ	40,100	LC
Cal State, Fullerton	CA	21,902	C
Canisius College	NY	49,672	C
CUNY/John Jay College of Criminal Justice	NY	6,359	SP

ST = STATE **$IS** = IN-STATE COSTS **SR** = SELECTOR RATING

School	ST	$IS	SR
Franciscan Univ of Steubenville	OH	33,980	VC
Goddard College	VT	17,040	VC
Lock Haven Univ of Pennsylvania	PA	20,544	LC
Mills College	CA	43,705	C
Mount Aloysius College	PA	29,976	C
New York Univ	NY	68,139	MC
Northwestern State Univ of Louisiana	LA	16,534	LC
Prescott College	AZ	38,201	C
San Francisco State Univ	CA	18,514	LC
Spalding Univ	KY	31,938	C
SUNY/Empire State College	NY	9,145	NC
Sterling College	VT	41,894	VC
Univ of Calif at Riverside	CA	32,912	C
Univ of the Sciences	PA	40,738	VC
Washington State Univ	WA	22,747	C

HYDROGEOLOGY

School	ST	$IS	SR
Eastern Mich Univ	MI	19,761	C
Rensselaer Polytechnic Inst	NY	67,265	MC
Western Mich Univ	MI	21,791	C

HYDROLOGY

School	ST	$IS	SR
The Univ of Arizona	AZ	24,086	C
Univ of Calif at Davis	CA	28,468	HC
Univ of Calif at Santa Barbara	CA	30,627	HC+
Univ of Nevada, Reno	NV	18,010	C

IBERIAN STUDIES

School	ST	$IS	SR
New York Univ	NY	68,139	MC
Southern Methodist Univ	TX	69,008	MC
Stanford Univ	CA	62,541	MC
Univ of PR, at Arecibo	PR	12,652	

IDS CURRICULUM AND INSTRUCTION

School	ST	$IS	SR
Lasell College	MA	49,400	C

ILLUSTRATION

School	ST	$IS	SR
Arcadia Univ	PA	55,990	C+
Art Academy of Cincinnati	OH	37,790	SP
ArtCenter College of Design	CA	42,008	SP
Bennington College	VT	66,280	MC
Brigham Young Univ	UT	13,248	MC
Calif College of the Arts	CA	52,758	SP
Cleveland Inst of Art	OH	51,455	SP
College for Creative Studies	MI	51,210	SP
College of Art and Design at Lesley Univ	MA	50,525	SP
Columbia College Chicago	IL	40,104	C
Columbus College of Art and Design	OH	47,310	SP
Fashion Inst of Technology/ SUNY	NY	18,521	SP
Ferris State Univ	MI	21,458	C
Indiana Wesleyan Univ	IN	33,674	C
John Brown Univ	AR	35,184	VC
Kansas City Art Inst	MO	48,200	SP
Kutztown Univ of Pennsylvania	PA	19,477	C
Laguna College of Art and Design	CA	41,422	SP
Lawrence Tech Univ	MI	41,630	VC
Lewis Univ	IL	41,710	C
Maryland Inst College of Art	MD	58,740	SP
Marywood Univ	PA	47,840	C
Mass College of Art and Design	MA	24,800	SP
Memphis College of Art	TN	50,880	SP
Milwaukee Inst of Art & Design	WI	45,880	SP
Minneapolis College of Art and Design	MN	44,218	SP
Montserrat College of Art	MA	41,500	SP
Moore College of Art and Design	PA	55,118	SP
Ohio Univ	OH	23,394	VC
Olivet College	MI	37,661	LC
Otis College of Art and Design	CA	54,670	SP
Pacific Northwest College of Art	OR	38,494	SP
Parsons The New School for Design	NY	56,610	SP
Rhode Island School of Design	RI	59,960	SP
Ringling College of Art and Design	FL	59,160	SP
Rivier Univ	NH	41,600	VC
Rochester Inst of Technology	NY	52,734	HC+
Rocky Mountain College of Art and Design	CO	27,052	SP
Savannah College of Art and Design	GA	49,595	SP
School of Visual Arts	NY	47,500	SP
St. John's Univ	NY	57,160	C+
SUNY/Fredonia	NY	20,818	C
Syracuse Univ	NY	62,313	HC
The Univ of Montana Western	MT	9,426	LC
Univ of Bridgeport	CT	44,985	LC
Univ of Findlay	OH	43,040	C
Univ of Hartford	CT	49,776	C
Univ of Kansas	KS	20,884	VC
Univ of Mass Dartmouth	MA	26,507	C
Univ of Mich/Ann Arbor	MI	25,274	MC
Univ of Northwestern - St. Paul	MN	39,530	C
Univ of San Francisco	CA	60,580	C
Univ of the Arts	PA	56,579	SP
Washington Univ in St. Louis	MO	67,539	MC
Western Conn State Univ	CT	21,254	LC

IMAGING SCIENCES

School	ST	$IS	SR
Thomas Edison State Univ	NJ	6,350	NC

INDUSTRIAL ADMINISTRATION/ MANAGEMENT

School	ST	$IS	SR
Central Mich Univ	MI	20,330	C
Clarion Univ of Pennsylvania	PA	21,608	LC
Clemson Univ	SC		HC
Colo State Univ-Pueblo	CO	21,581	C
Gardner-Webb Univ	NC	24,935	C+
Grove City College	PA	26,654	VC
Illinois Inst of Technology	IL	56,826	HC+
Inter-American Univ of PR-Bayamon	PR	18,785	
Lawrence Tech Univ	MI	41,630	VC
LeTourneau Univ	TX	39,190	VC
Mercer Univ	GA	45,348	VC
Metropolitan State Univ of Denver	CO	6,928	LC
Okla State Univ	OK	17,180	C+
Oregon Inst of Technology	OR	19,227	C
Purdue Univ/West Lafayette	IN	20,032	MC
Saginaw Valley State Univ	MI	19,284	C
St. Augustine's Univ	NC	25,582	C
San Francisco State Univ	CA	18,514	LC
S Dak State Univ	SD	15,874	C
St. Bonaventure Univ	NY	45,596	C
The Univ of Alabama	AL	24,320	C+
Trine Univ	IN	41,310	C
Universidad Politecnica de PR, Hato Rey campus	PR	23,514	
Univ of Alabama at Birmingham	AL	22,092	C
Univ of Arkansas at Little Rock	AR	18,211	LC
Univ of Cincinnati	OH	22,118	VC
Univ of Illinois at Urbana-Champaign	IL	27,006	HC
Univ of Iowa	IA	19,415	HC
Univ of Minn/Crookston	MN	19,126	C
Univ of Nebr - Kearney	NE	17,014	LC
Univ of N Car at Asheville	NC	16,251	VC+
Univ of N Car at Charlotte	NC	17,803	VC
Univ of Southern Indiana	IN	16,808	C
Univ of Wisc-Stout	WI	19,667	C
Washington State Univ	WA	22,747	C
Wentworth Inst of Technology	MA	48,810	VC
West Virginia Univ Inst of Technology	WV	18,264	C
William Penn Univ	IA	26,000	C

INDUSTRIAL AND LABOR RELATIONS

School	ST	$IS	SR
Cornell Univ	NY	67,591	MC
Eastern Conn State Univ	CT	23,059	C
New York Univ	NY	68,139	MC

INDUSTRIAL AND ORGANIZATIONAL PSYCHOLOGY

School	ST	$IS	SR
Albertus Magnus College	CT	44,016	LC
Arizona State Univ at the Polytechnic Campus	AZ	22,394	VC
Baldwin Wallace Univ	OH	42,464	VC
CUNY/Baruch College	NY	21,609	HC
Coe College	IA	51,570	VC
Fitchburg State Univ	MA	21,819	LC
Goddard College	VT	17,040	VC
Holy Family Univ	PA	44,672	LC
Ithaca College	NY	58,158	VC+
Johnson & Wales Univ/ Denver Campus	CO	44,768	C
Kutztown Univ of Pennsylvania	PA	19,477	C
Marywood Univ	PA	47,840	C
Northwest Missouri State Univ	MO	18,286	C
Ohio State Univ at Columbus	OH	22,843	MC
Oregon Inst of Technology	OR	19,227	C
Texas Wesleyan Univ	TX	37,338	C
Univ of PR, at Arecibo	PR	12,652	
Washington Univ in St. Louis	MO	67,539	MC

INDUSTRIAL ARTS EDUCATION

School	ST	$IS	SR
Alabama A&M Univ	AL	18,796	C
Auburn Univ	AL	24,300	VC+
Ball State Univ	IN	19,808	C+
Bemidji State Univ	MN	17,730	C
Cal State, Los Angeles	CA	17,186	LC
Central Washington Univ	WA	16,803	C
Chicago State Univ	IL	41,620	C
Clemson Univ	SC		HC
Concordia Univ Nebr	NE	41,900	VC
Eastern Kentucky Univ	KY	17,742	C
Eastern Mich Univ	MI	19,761	C
Elizabeth City State Univ	NC	14,745	C
Fitchburg State Univ	MA	21,819	LC
Florida A&M Univ	FL	15,361	C
Humboldt State Univ	CA	21,708	C
Indiana State Univ	IN	23,223	LC
Iowa State Univ	IA	18,176	C
Langston Univ	OK	15,659	C
Montana State Univ-Northern	MT	11,370	NC
Murray State Univ	KY	17,726	C+
N Car A&T State Univ	NC	13,786	C
N Car State Univ	NC	22,434	HC+
Northeastern State Univ	OK	8,615	VC
Northern Kentucky Univ	KY	16,486	C
Northern Mich Univ	MI	20,853	C
San Francisco State Univ	CA	18,514	LC
S Car State Univ	SC	21,330	LC
Southeast Missouri State Univ	MO	16,148	C
St. Cloud State Univ	MN	10,600	C
SUNY/Buffalo State	NY	20,583	LC
Tarleton State Univ	TX	15,248	LC
Texas A&M Univ at Commerce	TX	10,496	C
The Univ of Montana Western	MT	9,426	LC
Univ of Arkansas at Pine Bluff	AR	13,541	C
Univ of Central Missouri	MO	18,982	C
Univ of Cincinnati	OH	22,118	VC
Univ of Louisiana at Lafayette	LA	14,516	C
Univ of Maryland/Eastern Shore	MD	21,861	LC
Univ of Southern Miss	MS	13,170	C
Utah State Univ	UT	13,235	C
Wayne State College	NE	25,746	NC

INDUSTRIAL DESIGN

School	ST	$IS	SR
Appalachian State Univ	NC	15,394	VC
Arizona State Univ at the Tempe Campus	AZ	23,001	VC
ArtCenter College of Design	CA	42,008	SP
Auburn Univ	AL	24,300	VC+
Brigham Young Univ	UT	13,248	MC
Calif College of the Arts	CA	52,758	SP
Cedarville Univ	OH	36,244	VC
Cleveland Inst of Art	OH	51,455	SP
College for Creative Studies	MI	51,210	SP
Columbus College of Art and Design	OH	47,310	SP
Escuela de Artes Plasticas de PR	PR	11,236	
Ferris State Univ	MI	21,458	C
Georgia Inst of Technology	GA	23,910	MC
Jefferson (Philadelphia Univ + Thomas Jefferson Univ)	PA	53,966	C
Kean Univ	NJ	25,620	C
Lawrence Tech Univ	MI	41,630	VC
Mass College of Art and Design	MA	24,800	SP
Metropolitan State Univ of Denver	CO	6,928	LC
Milwaukee Inst of Art & Design	WI	45,880	SP
Montclair State Univ	NJ	26,912	C
NewSchool of Architecture & Design	CA	12,341	SP
N Car State Univ	NC	22,434	HC+
Ohio State Univ at Columbus	OH	22,843	MC
Otis College of Art and Design	CA	54,670	SP
Parsons The New School for Design	NY	56,610	SP
Pratt Inst	NY	59,482	VC+
Purdue Univ/West Lafayette	IN	20,032	MC
Rhode Island School of Design	RI	59,960	SP
Rochester Inst of Technology	NY	52,734	HC+
Savannah College of Art and Design	GA	49,595	SP
Syracuse Univ	NY	62,313	HC
Univ of Bridgeport	CT	44,985	LC
Univ of Houston	TX	21,871	VC
Univ of Illinois at Chicago	IL	24,664	VC
Univ of Illinois at Urbana-Champaign	IL	27,006	HC
Univ of Kansas	KS	20,884	VC
Univ of Mich/Ann Arbor	MI	25,274	MC
Univ of the Arts	PA	56,579	SP
Virginia Polytechnic Inst and State Univ	VA	21,920	VC
Wentworth Inst of Technology	MA	48,810	VC

INDUSTRIAL ENGINEERING

School	ST	$IS	SR
Alabama A&M Univ	AL	18,796	C
Arizona State Univ at the Tempe Campus	AZ	23,001	VC
Auburn Univ	AL	24,300	VC+
Bradley Univ	IL	43,240	VC
Calif Baptist Univ	CA	42,986	C
Calif Polytechnic State Univ	CA	22,547	MC
Calif State Polytechnic Univ, Pomona	CA	21,811	C
Cal State, East Bay	CA	20,748	C
Cal State, Fresno	CA	16,902	LC
Cal State, Fullerton	CA	21,902	C
Clemson Univ	SC		HC
Colo State Univ-Pueblo	CO	21,581	C
Elizabethtown College	PA	56,340	VC
Florida A&M Univ	FL	15,361	C
Florida State Univ	FL	16,771	HC
Francis Marion Univ	SC	18,144	LC
George Mason Univ	VA	19,884	C
Georgia Inst of Technology	GA	23,910	MC
Hofstra Univ	NY	58,210	C+
Indiana Inst of Technology	IN	34,240	LC
Inter-American Univ of PR-Bayamon	PR	18,785	
Jefferson (Philadelphia Univ + Thomas Jefferson Univ)	PA	53,966	C
Kansas State Univ	KS	17,780	VC
Kettering Univ	MI	47,570	HC
Lamar Univ	TX	18,014	LC
Lawrence Tech Univ	MI	41,630	VC
Lehigh Univ	PA	63,860	MC
Louisiana State Univ and A&M College	LA	18,677	VC
Louisiana Tech Univ	LA	11,422	VC
Milwaukee School of Engineering	WI	48,531	HC+
Miss State Univ	MS	12,028	C+
Montana State Univ	MT	15,500	C+
New Jersey Inst of Technology	NJ	30,198	HC
New Mexico State Univ	NM	14,050	LC
N Car A&T State Univ	NC	13,786	C
N Car State Univ	NC	22,434	HC+
N Dak State Univ	ND	16,245	VC
Northeastern Univ	MA	65,352	MC
Northern Illinois Univ	IL	20,176	C
Northwestern State Univ of Louisiana	LA	16,534	LC
Northwestern Univ	IL	68,725	MC
Oakland Univ	MI	20,763	C
Ohio State Univ at Columbus	OH	22,843	MC
Ohio Univ	OH	23,394	VC
Okla State Univ	OK	17,180	C+
Olivet Nazarene Univ	IL	41,840	VC
Oregon State Univ	OR	23,337	VC
Pennsylvania State Univ - Univ Park	PA	29,716	HC
Purdue Univ/West Lafayette	IN	20,032	MC
Quinnipiac Univ	CT	60,970	VC
Rensselaer Polytechnic Inst	NY	67,265	MC
Rochester Inst of Technology	NY	52,734	HC+
St. Augustine's Univ	NC	25,582	C
S Dak School of Mines and Technology	SD	18,570	C+
Southern Illinois Univ Edwardsville	IL	20,188	C
St. Ambrose Univ	IA	40,180	C
St. Mary's Univ	TX	39,120	C
Stanford Univ	CA	62,541	MC
SUNY at Binghamton	NY	24,100	MC
SUNY/Univ at Buffalo	NY	23,122	C
Tenn Tech Univ	TN	17,929	C
Texas State Univ	TX	18,721	C
Texas Tech Univ	TX	20,156	C+
The Univ of Alabama	AL	24,320	C+
The Univ of Arizona	AZ	24,086	C
The Univ of Tenn at Chattanooga	TN	17,340	C+
The Univ of Tenn at Knoxville	TN	22,112	VC
Universidad Politecnica de PR, Hato Rey campus	PR	23,514	
Univ of Alabama in Huntsville	AL	20,028	VC
Univ of Arkansas at Fayetteville	AR	19,766	VC
Univ of Calif at Berkeley	CA	29,886	MC
Univ of Central Florida	FL	16,379	VC
Univ of Houston	TX	21,871	VC
Univ of Illinois at Urbana-Champaign	IL	27,006	HC
Univ of Iowa	IA	19,415	HC
Univ of Louisiana at Lafayette	LA	14,516	C
Univ of Louisville	KY	19,692	C
Univ of Mass Amherst	MA	27,669	HC
Univ of Miami	FL	63,494	MC
Univ of Mich/Ann Arbor	MI	25,274	MC
Univ of Mich/Dearborn	MI	12,472	VC
Univ of Minn/Duluth	MN	20,292	C
Univ of Minn/Twin Cities	MN	24,269	MC
Univ of Missouri-Columbia	MO	20,463	VC
Univ of Okla	OK	19,651	HC
Univ of Pittsburgh	PA	30,030	MC
Univ of PR, at Mayaguez	PR	13,995	
Univ of San Diego	CA	60,338	HC
Univ of South Florida/Tampa	FL	16,110	VC
Univ of Southern Calif	CA	66,631	MC
Univ of Toledo	OH	19,336	C
Univ of Wisc-Madison	WI	21,647	MC
Univ of Wisc-Milwaukee	WI	21,538	C
Univ of Wisc-Platteville	WI	14,148	C
Utah State Univ	UT	13,235	C
Virginia Polytechnic Inst and State Univ	VA	21,920	VC
Wayne State Univ	MI	23,085	C
Western Mich Univ	MI	21,791	C

ST = STATE $IS = IN-STATE COSTS SR = SELECTOR RATING

School	ST	$IS	SR
Western New England Univ	MA	49,182	C
Wichita State Univ	KS	17,773	C
Worcester Polytechnic Inst	MA	62,846	MC
Wright State Univ	OH	16,983	C
Youngstown State Univ	OH	17,487	C

INDUSTRIAL ENGINEERING TECHNOLOGY

School	ST	$IS	SR
Alabama A&M Univ	AL	18,796	C
Appalachian State Univ	NC	15,394	VC
Ball State Univ	IN	19,808	C+
Bemidji State Univ	MN	17,730	C
Berea College	KY	7,094	C
Cal State, Fresno	CA	16,902	LC
Cal State, Los Angeles	CA	17,186	LC
Calif Univ of Pennsylvania	PA	20,425	LC
Caribbean Univ	PR	12,227	
Central Conn State Univ	CT	22,041	C
Central Washington Univ	WA	16,803	C
Chadron State College	NE	14,819	LC
Columbia Univ/City of New York	NY	62,958	MC
East Carolina Univ	NC	16,539	C
Eastern Illinois Univ	IL	21,414	C
Elizabeth City State Univ	NC	14,745	C
Farmingdale State College	NY	20,968	C
Fitchburg State Univ	MA	21,819	LC
Grand Valley State Univ	MI	22,250	C+
Humboldt State Univ	CA	21,708	C
Illinois State Univ	IL	23,418	VC
Indiana State Univ	IN	23,223	LC
Indiana Univ-Purdue Univ Fort Wayne	IN	18,675	C
Iowa State Univ	IA	18,176	C
Jackson State Univ	MS	15,879	LC
Kennesaw State Univ	GA	18,899	VC
Lamar Univ	TX	18,014	LC
Langston Univ	OK	15,659	C
Metropolitan State Univ of Denver	CO	6,928	LC
Middle Tenn State Univ	TN	8,650	C
Millersville Univ of Pennsylvania	PA	25,298	C
Minn State Univ, Moorhead	MN	21,393	C
Miss State Univ	MS	12,028	C+
Miss Valley State Univ	MS	13,233	LC
Morehead State Univ	KY	18,386	LC
Morgan State Univ	MD	17,190	LC
Northern Mich Univ	MI	20,853	C
Northwestern State Univ of Louisiana	LA	16,534	LC
Okla Panhandle State Univ	OK	6,152	C
Prairie View A&M Univ	TX	27,273	LC
Purdue Univ Northwest	IN	15,178	C
Purdue Univ/West Lafayette	IN	20,032	MC
Roger Williams Univ	RI	48,074	VC
San Francisco State Univ	CA	18,514	LC
S Car State Univ	SC	21,330	LC
Southeastern Louisiana Univ	LA	16,237	C
Southern Illinois Univ Carbondale	IL	24,554	C
SUNY/Buffalo State	NY	20,583	LC
Tarleton State Univ	TX	15,248	LC
Tenn Tech Univ	TN	17,929	C
Texas A&M Univ at College Station	TX	20,771	VC+
Texas A&M Univ at Kingsville	TX	16,580	LC
Texas Southern Univ	TX	19,592	LC
Texas State Univ	TX	18,721	C
Univ of Arkansas at Pine Bluff	AR	13,541	C
Univ of Central Missouri	MO	18,982	C
Univ of Cincinnati	OH	22,118	VC
Univ of Dayton	OH	54,930	VC
Univ of Florida	FL	16,291	HC+
Univ of Illinois at Chicago	IL	24,664	VC
Univ of N Dak	ND	16,673	C
Univ of Northern Iowa	IA	17,480	C
Univ of Rio Grande & Rio Grande Community College	OH	8,750	LC
Univ of Southern Maine	ME	18,320	C
Univ of Texas at Arlington	TX	18,876	C
Univ of Texas at El Paso	TX	34,452	NC
Univ of West Alabama	AL	16,284	LC
Univ of Wisc-Platteville	WI	14,148	C
Univ of Wisc-Stout	WI	19,667	C
Utah State Univ	UT	13,235	C
Washington State Univ	WA	22,747	C
West Virginia Univ Inst of Technology	WV	18,264	C
Western Kentucky Univ	KY	16,850	C
Western Washington Univ	WA	18,904	VC
William Penn Univ	IA	26,000	C

INDUSTRIAL HYGIENE

School	ST	$IS	SR
Ohio Univ	OH	23,394	VC
St. Augustine's Univ	NC	25,582	C
South Univ	GA	36,070	LC
Univ of Central Okla	OK	15,150	C
Univ of North Alabama	AL	15,964	C

INDUSTRIAL PSYCHOLOGY/ SAFETY

School	ST	$IS	SR
Embry-Riddle Aeronautical Univ - Prescott Campus	AZ	45,130	VC
Faulkner Univ	AL	26,410	C

INDUSTRIAL TECHNOLOGY

School	ST	$IS	SR
Black Hills State Univ	SD	16,622	C
Calif Polytechnic State Univ	CA	22,547	MC
Cal State, Fullerton	CA	21,902	C
Ferris State Univ	MI	21,458	C
Missouri Southern State Univ	MO	13,071	C
Old Dominion Univ	VA	21,618	C
Southwestern Okla State Univ	OK	12,205	C
Univ of Mass Lowell	MA	27,296	VC
Western Kentucky Univ	KY	16,850	C

INDUSTRIAL/ORGANIZATIONAL PSYCHOLOGY

School	ST	$IS	SR
Cal State, Fullerton	CA	21,902	C
Missouri Western State Univ	MO	17,822	LC
Univ of Detroit Mercy	MI	48,816	C

INDUSTRY & SYSTEMS ENGINEERING

School	ST	$IS	SR
Rutgers Univ - New Brunswick	NJ	27,090	HC
Rutgers Univ - New Brunswick	NJ	27,090	HC
San Jose State Univ	CA	22,630	C
Univ of Rhode Island	RI	26,066	VC

INFORMATICS AND COMPUTER SCIENCE

School	ST	$IS	SR
Arizona State Univ at the Tempe Campus	AZ	23,001	VC
Bloomfield College	NJ	40,100	LC
Faulkner Univ	AL	26,410	C
Indiana Univ Bloomington	IN	20,791	HC
Indiana Univ East	IN	7,207	C
Indiana Univ Kokomo	IN	7,207	C
Indiana Univ Northwest	IN	7,207	LC
Indiana Univ South Bend	IN	16,057	C
Indiana Univ Southeast	IN	16,931	C
Indiana Univ-Purdue Univ Indianapolis	IN	18,952	C
Northern Arizona Univ	AZ	21,003	C
Silver Lake College of the Holy Family	WI	36,290	LC
SUNY/Univ at Buffalo	NY	23,122	C
Widener Univ	PA	58,190	C

INFORMATION & COMMUNICATION TECHNOLOGY

School	ST	$IS	SR
Abilene Christian Univ	TX	43,708	C+
Alfred State College	NY	19,895	C
Aquinas College - Mich	MI	38,876	VC
Arizona State Univ at the Polytechnic Campus	AZ	22,394	VC
Bentley Univ	MA	63,720	MC
Bluffton Univ	OH	40,950	C+
Cal State, Fullerton	CA	21,902	C
Cal State, Northridge	CA	17,277	LC
Coastal Carolina Univ	SC	20,340	C
Dominican Univ	IL	42,472	C+
Goshen College	IN	44,350	C
Husson Univ	ME	26,508	C
Kennesaw State Univ	GA	18,899	VC
Marywood Univ	PA	47,840	C
Univ of Scranton	PA	54,962	VC
Univ of Tampa	FL	38,928	VC
Univ of Wisc-Stout	WI	19,667	C

INFORMATION AND TECHNOLOGY

School	ST	$IS	SR
Cal State, Fullerton	CA	21,902	C
Georgia Southern Univ	GA	16,540	VC
Lasell College	MA	49,400	C
Lasell College	MA	49,400	C

INFORMATION SCIENCE

School	ST	$IS	SR
Alfred State College	NY	19,895	C
Bloomfield College	NJ	40,100	LC
Cairn Univ	PA	37,572	C
Christopher Newport Univ	VA	24,878	VC+
Columbus State Univ	GA	14,336	LC
Cornell Univ	NY	67,591	MC
Niagara Univ	NY	41,010	C
Pennsylvania State Univ - Univ Park	PA	29,716	HC
Rochester Inst of Technology	NY	52,734	HC+
Rutgers Univ - New Brunswick	NJ	27,090	HC
Rutgers Univ - New Brunswick	NJ	27,090	HC
Univ of Colo Boulder	CO	26,048	HC
Univ of Okla	OK	19,651	HC
Univ of South Alabama	AL	16,880	C

INFORMATION SCIENCE, SYSTEMS, AND TECHNOLOGY

School	ST	$IS	SR
Alfred State College	NY	19,895	C
Armstrong State Univ	GA	15,615	C
Cornell Univ	NY	67,591	MC
Shawnee State Univ	OH	16,998	C
Syracuse Univ	NY	62,313	HC
Univ of Mass Lowell	MA	27,296	VC
Univ of N Car at Greensboro	NC	15,998	C
Univ of Wisc-Milwaukee	WI	21,538	C

INFORMATION SCIENCES AND SYSTEMS

School	ST	$IS	SR
Abilene Christian Univ	TX	43,708	C+
Alabama State Univ	AL	16,490	LC
Albany State Univ	GA	19,462	C
Albright College	PA	57,326	C
Alfred State College	NY	19,895	C
Andrews Univ	MI	41,732	C
Aquinas College - Mich	MI	38,876	VC
Arkansas Tech Univ	AR	16,534	LC
Atlantic Union College	MA	27,228	C
Auburn Univ at Montgomery	AL	15,000	C
Augusta Univ	GA	4,632	C
Augustana Univ	SD	39,968	VC
Averett Univ	VA	43,034	LC
Avila Univ	MO	27,100	C
Azusa Pacific Univ	CA	43,972	C
Baylor Univ	TX	56,803	HC
Beacon College	FL	46,862	C
Belhaven Univ	MS	32,250	C
Bellevue Univ	NE	20,300	NC
Bethune-Cookman Univ	FL	23,322	C
Biola Univ	CA	48,686	C
Bloomfield College	NJ	40,100	LC
Boise State Univ	ID	17,368	C
Boston College	MA	68,043	MC
Brewton-Parker College	GA	26,120	LC
Briar Cliff Univ	IA	36,956	C
Brigham Young Univ	UT	13,248	MC
Brigham Young Univ/Hawaii	HI	11,710	C
Cabrini Univ	PA	42,591	LC
Caldwell Univ	NJ	42,165	LC
Calif Lutheran Univ	CA	52,853	C
Cal State, Fullerton	CA	21,902	C
Cal State, Los Angeles	CA	17,186	LC
Cal State, Stanislaus	CA	18,053	LC
Calif Univ of Pennsylvania	PA	20,425	LC
Calumet College of St. Joseph	IN	22,735	C
Calvin College	MI	43,090	HC
Campbell Univ	NC	37,570	VC
Campbellsville Univ	KY	33,400	C
Canisius College	NY	49,672	C
Carlow Univ	PA	39,696	LC
Carnegie Mellon Univ	PA	67,980	MC
Catawba College	NC	39,820	LC
Central Mich Univ	MI	20,330	C
Central Washington Univ	WA	16,803	C
Champlain College	VT	54,724	VC
Chapman Univ	CA	65,504	HC
Chestnut Hill College	PA	47,180	C
Chicago State Univ	IL	41,620	C
CUNY/Baruch College	NY	21,609	HC
CUNY/Brooklyn College	NY	7,163	C+
CUNY/York College	NY	6,747	LC
Clarion Univ of Pennsylvania	PA	21,608	LC
Clarkson Univ	NY	60,392	VC
Clayton State Univ	GA	19,735	LC
Clemson Univ	SC		HC
Cleveland State Univ	OH	22,290	C
Coastal Carolina Univ	SC	20,340	C
College of the Ozarks	MO	7,530	VC
Colo State Univ	CO	23,033	C
Colo State Univ-Pueblo	CO	21,581	C
Colo Technical Univ	CO	21,455	NC
Columbia College	SC	36,550	C
Columbia College - Missouri	MO	28,179	C
Concord Univ	WV	14,954	LC
Concordia Univ St. Paul	MN	29,050	C
Curry College	MA	53,331	C
Dakota State Univ	SD	12,286	C
Davenport Univ	MI	25,896	LC
Defiance College	OH	42,240	LC
DePaul Univ	IL	52,807	VC
Doane Univ	NE	41,340	VC
Dominican College	NY	40,258	LC
Dordt College	IA	37,860	C+
Drake Univ	IA	49,220	HC
Drexel Univ	PA	65,927	HC
D'Youville College	NY	37,678	C
East Carolina Univ	NC	16,539	C
East Tenn State Univ	TN	18,141	C
Eastern Mich Univ	MI	19,761	C
Eastern New Mexico Univ	NM	12,874	LC
Eastern Washington Univ	WA	17,896	LC
Edgewood College	WI	35,950	C
Edinboro Univ	PA	15,940	LC
Elizabethtown College	PA	56,340	VC
Elmhurst College	IL	46,514	C
Elon Univ	NC	46,142	HC
Emporia State Univ	KS	15,029	C
Excelsior College	NY	38,800	SP
Fairfield Univ	CT	61,445	HC
Fairleigh Dickinson Univ/ Metropolitan Campus	NJ	52,392	C
Farmingdale State College	NY	20,968	C
Faulkner Univ	AL	26,410	C
Felician Univ	NJ	46,280	LC
Ferrum College	VA	43,970	C
Florida Atlantic Univ	FL	18,256	C
Florida Inst of Technology	FL	53,306	VC
Florida State Univ	FL	16,771	HC
Fontbonne Univ	MO	34,606	C
Fordham Univ	NY	68,431	MC
Fort Hays State Univ	KS	12,677	C
Fort Valley State Univ	GA	17,988	VC
Francis Marion Univ	SC	18,144	LC
Franciscan Univ of Steubenville	OH	33,980	VC
Freed-Hardeman Univ	TN	29,900	C
Friends Univ	KS	38,000	C
Frostburg State Univ	MD	17,280	LC
Furman Univ	SC	61,098	VC+
Gannon Univ	PA	42,922	C
Gardner-Webb Univ	NC	24,935	C+
George Fox Univ	OR	42,938	C
George Mason Univ	VA	19,884	C
Glenville State College	WV	17,386	LC
Goldey-Beacom College	DE	36,038	C
Goshen College	IN	44,350	C
Graceland Univ	IA	35,290	C
Grambling State Univ	LA	15,701	C
Grand Valley State Univ	MI	22,250	C+
Gwynedd Mercy Univ	PA	43,780	LC
Hampton Univ	VA	36,410	C
Hannibal-LaGrange Univ	MO	29,815	C
Harding Univ	AR	25,440	C
Hartwick College	NY	51,270	C
Haverford College	PA	66,490	MC
Heidelberg Univ	OH	40,400	LC
Henderson State Univ	AR	15,516	C
Hodges Univ	FL	20,160	LC
Hofstra Univ	NY	58,210	C+
Holy Family Univ	PA	44,672	LC
Houston Baptist Univ	TX	36,450	C
Humboldt State Univ	CA	21,708	C
Huntington Univ	IN	33,996	C
Idaho State Univ	ID	13,619	LC
Illinois College	IL	41,330	VC
Illinois Inst of Technology	IL	56,826	HC+
Illinois State Univ	IL	23,418	VC
Immaculata Univ	PA	39,000	C
Indiana Inst of Technology	IN	34,240	LC
Indiana Univ Kokomo	IN	7,207	C
Indiana Univ-Purdue Univ Fort Wayne	IN	18,675	C
Indiana Wesleyan Univ	IN	33,674	C
Inter-American Univ of PR-Aguadilla Campus	PR	21,657	
Iona College	NY	52,514	C
Jacksonville Univ	FL	49,210	C
James Madison Univ	VA	19,084	VC
Johnson & Wales Univ/ Providence Campus	RI	44,768	C
Juniata College	PA	58,118	VC
Kansas State Univ	KS	17,780	VC
Kennesaw State Univ	GA	18,899	VC
Keystone College	PA	28,680	LC
King's College	PA	48,240	C
Kutztown Univ of Pennsylvania	PA	19,477	C
La Salle Univ	PA	43,476	C
La Sierra Univ	CA	39,690	VC
Lamar Univ	TX	18,014	LC
Lawrence Tech Univ	MI	41,630	VC
Le Moyne College	NY	47,305	VC
Lee Univ	TN	22,045	C
Limestone College	SC	32,100	C
Lincoln Memorial Univ	TN	28,430	C
Lincoln Univ	MO	14,402	NC
LIU Brooklyn	NY	50,698	C
LIU Post	NY	50,698	C+
Lock Haven Univ of Pennsylvania	PA	20,544	LC
Louisiana State Univ and A&M College	LA	18,677	VC
Loyola Univ Chicago	IL	57,158	VC
Lubbock Christian Univ	TX	29,727	C
Manhattan College	NY	55,652	C
Mansfield Univ of Pennsylvania	PA	24,244	LC
Marian Univ	WI	34,622	C
Marietta College	OH	46,190	C
Marist College	NY	49,860	VC
Marshall Univ	WV	18,044	C
Marymount Manhattan College	NY	48,350	C
Maryville Univ of St. Louis	MO	38,558	VC
Marywood Univ	PA	47,840	C
McKendree Univ	IL	37,940	C+
Mercer Univ	GA	45,348	VC
Mercy College	NY	32,614	C
Meredith College	NC	46,634	C
Metropolitan State Univ	MN	7,859	C
Metropolitan State Univ of Denver	CO	6,928	LC
Miami Univ	OH	27,190	HC+
Mich State Univ	MI	24,542	VC
Middle Tenn State Univ	TN	8,650	C
Midwestern State Univ	TX	12,111	LC
Milligan College	TN	39,450	C
Millikin Univ	IL	44,148	C

ST = STATE **$IS** = IN-STATE COSTS **SR** = SELECTOR RATING

School	ST	$IS	SR
Minn State Univ, Mankato	MN	17,190	C
Misericordia Univ	PA	45,210	C
Miss State Univ	MS	12,028	C+
Missouri Baptist Univ	MO	35,594	C
Missouri Univ of Science and Technology	MO	18,655	HC
Missouri Valley College	MO	28,150	C
Missouri Western State Univ	MO	17,822	LC
Monroe College	NY	23,996	C
Montana State Univ Billings	MT	13,336	LC
Morgan State Univ	MD	17,190	LC
Mount Aloysius College	PA	29,976	C
Mount St. Mary's Univ	MD	53,380	C
National Louis Univ	IL	43,000	LC
National Univ	CA	17,849	LC
Nebr Wesleyan Univ	NE	42,026	C+
New Jersey Inst of Technology	NJ	30,198	HC
New Mexico Inst of Mining and Technology	NM	15,385	HC+
New Mexico State Univ	NM	14,050	LC
New York City College of Technology	NY	7,185	LC
New York Univ	NY	68,139	MC
Newman Univ	KS	37,382	C
Niagara Univ	NY	41,010	C
Nicholls State Univ	LA	14,959	C
N Car Wesleyan College	NC	39,200	C
Northeastern State Univ	OK	8,615	VC
Northeastern Univ	MA	65,352	MC
Northern Illinois Univ	IL	20,176	C
Northern Kentucky Univ	KY	16,486	C
Northern Mich Univ	MI	20,853	C
Northland College	WI	41,103	C+
Northwest Missouri State Univ	MO	18,286	C
Northwestern State Univ of Louisiana	LA	16,534	LC
Northwestern Univ	IL	68,725	MC
Norwich Univ	VT	56,234	C
Notre Dame College	OH	39,150	VC
Notre Dame de Namur Univ	CA	46,526	LC
Notre Dame of Maryland Univ	MD	47,570	VC
Oakland Univ	MI	20,763	C
Oakwood Univ	AL	43,758	C
Ohio State Univ at Columbus	OH	22,843	MC
Okla Baptist Univ	OK	33,990	C
Okla Christian Univ	OK	29,260	C
Okla Panhandle State Univ	OK	6,152	C
Old Dominion Univ	VA	21,618	C
Olivet Nazarene Univ	IL	41,840	VC
Ottawa Univ	KS	39,980	VC
Our Lady of the Lake Univ	TX	37,790	LC
Pace Univ	NY	60,136	C
Park Univ	MO	22,134	C
Peirce College	PA	16,780	NC
Pennsylvania College of Technology	PA	27,693	NC
Pfeiffer Univ	NC	40,532	LC
Pittsburg State Univ	KS	13,880	C
Plymouth State Univ	NH	23,180	LC
Point Park Univ	PA	41,270	C
Portland State Univ	OR	19,443	C
Purdue Univ Northwest	IN	15,178	C
Purdue Univ/West Lafayette	IN	20,032	MC
Quincy Univ	IL	38,170	LC
Radford Univ	VA	19,758	C
Ramapo College of New Jersey	NJ	25,760	VC
Rhode Island College	RI	19,000	LC
Rider Univ	NJ	54,050	C
Robert Morris Univ	PA	40,600	C
Rochester Inst of Technology	NY	52,734	HC+
Roosevelt Univ	IL	41,890	VC
Rutgers Univ - Newark	NJ	27,351	C
Sacred Heart Univ	CT	54,590	C
Saginaw Valley State Univ	MI	19,284	C
St. Augustine's Univ	NC	25,582	C
St. Joseph's Univ	PA	58,540	VC
St. Leo Univ	FL	32,850	C
St. Michael's College	VT	53,275	VC+
Salem International Univ	WV	21,090	C
Salisbury Univ	MD	21,132	VC
San Diego State Univ	CA	23,156	VC
San Francisco State Univ	CA	18,514	LC
Seattle Pacific Univ	WA	47,439	C+
Shepherd Univ, West Virginia	WV	17,382	C
Siena Heights Univ	MI	36,322	C
Simpson College	IA	45,626	VC
Slippery Rock Univ of Pennsylvania	PA	20,450	C
Southeastern Okla State Univ	OK	11,875	C
Southern Adventist Univ	TN	28,250	C
Southern Illinois Univ Carbondale	IL	24,554	C
Southern New Hampshire Univ	NH	44,256	C
Southwest Baptist Univ	MO	30,890	LC
Southwestern Adventist Univ	TX	28,232	LC
Springfield College	MA	48,775	C
St. Catherine Univ	MN	45,630	C
St. Edward's Univ	TX	56,190	VC
St. Francis College	NY	38,800	LC
SUNY /College of Agriculture and Tech at Cobleskill	NY	20,527	LC
SUNY Albany	NY	22,165	C
SUNY at Binghamton	NY	24,100	MC
SUNY at Oswego	NY	22,219	VC
SUNY/Buffalo State	NY	20,583	LC
SUNY/College at Old Westbury	NY	16,860	C
SUNY/Empire State College	NY	9,145	NC
Stephen F. Austin State Univ	TX	18,484	LC
Stevens Inst of Technology	NJ	64,954	MC
Stevenson Univ	MD	48,412	C
Stockton Univ	NJ	25,565	C
Stony Brook Univ/The SUNY	NY	22,703	MC
Suffolk Univ	MA	52,316	C
Syracuse Univ	NY	62,313	HC
Tarleton State Univ	TX	15,248	LC
Temple Univ	PA	24,392	C+
Texas Lutheran Univ	TX	39,770	C
The George Washington Univ	DC	68,474	HC+
The Master's Univ	CA	43,870	C
The Univ of Arizona	AZ	24,086	C
The Univ of Mary	ND	23,180	C
The Univ of Tenn at Martin	TN	15,212	C
The Univ of Texas at San Antonio	TX	21,060	C
The Univ of Utah	UT	18,751	VC
The Univ of Virginia's College at Wise	VA	18,192	LC
Thomas College	ME	73,888	LC
Tiffin Univ	OH	34,900	LC
Towson Univ	MD	21,878	C
Trevecca Nazarene Univ	TN	31,186	C
Trine Univ	IN	41,310	C
Trinity Christian College	IL	35,580	C
Troy Univ	AL	16,171	C
Tulane Univ	LA	67,496	MC
Tusculum College	TN	31,625	LC
United States Naval Academy	MD		HC
Univ of Alabama at Birmingham	AL	22,092	C
Univ of Alabama in Huntsville	AL	20,028	VC
Univ of Arkansas at Fayetteville	AR	19,766	VC
Univ of Arkansas at Little Rock	AR	18,211	LC
Univ of Arkansas at Monticello	AR	13,599	LC
Univ of Calif at Irvine	CA	33,857	VC
Univ of Calif at Riverside	CA	32,912	C
Univ of Calif San Diego	CA	30,450	MC
Univ of Calif, Santa Cruz	CA	28,731	C+
Univ of Central Arkansas	AR	15,042	VC
Univ of Central Florida	FL	16,379	VC
Univ of Central Missouri	MO	18,982	C
Univ of Cincinnati	OH	22,118	VC
Univ of Delaware	DE	32,214	VC
Univ of Denver	CO	61,129	VC+
Univ of Detroit Mercy	MI	48,816	C
Univ of Florida	FL	16,291	HC+
Univ of Hartford	CT	49,776	C
Univ of Hawaii at Manoa	HI	23,261	C
Univ of Houston-Downtown	TX	7,241	LC
Univ of Idaho	ID	16,158	C
Univ of Illinois at Chicago	IL	24,664	VC
Univ of Iowa	IA	19,415	HC
Univ of Jamestown	ND	28,508	C
Univ of Kansas	KS	20,884	VC
Univ of Louisville	KY	19,692	C
Univ of Maine at Augusta	ME	7,812	C
Univ of Mary Hardin-Baylor	TX	35,292	C+
Univ of Maryland Univ College	MD	26,146	LC
Univ of Maryland/Baltimore County	MD	23,004	VC
Univ of Maryland/College Park	MD	21,938	HC
Univ of Mass Boston	MA	13,828	C
Univ of Mass Lowell	MA	27,296	VC
Univ of Minn/Crookston	MN	19,126	C
Univ of Minn/Duluth	MN	20,292	C
Univ of Missouri-St. Louis	MO	19,810	VC
Univ of Mobile	AL	28,935	C
Univ of Mount Olive	NC	18,426	C
Univ of Nebr - Kearney	NE	17,014	LC
Univ of Nebr - Omaha	NE	16,120	C
Univ of Nevada, Reno	NV	18,010	C
Univ of North Alabama	AL	15,964	C
Univ of N Car at Chapel Hill	NC	20,561	MC
Univ of N Dak	ND	16,673	C
Univ of North Florida	FL	15,996	VC
Univ of North Texas	TX	20,082	C
Univ of Northern Colo	CO	19,658	C
Univ of Northern Iowa	IA	17,480	C
Univ of Pennsylvania	PA	63,526	MC
Univ of Pittsburgh	PA	30,030	MC
Univ of PR, at Bayamon	PR	13,145	
Univ of PR, at Mayaguez	PR	13,995	
Univ of PR-Rio Piedras campus	PR	13,327	
Univ of Redlands	CA	61,934	VC
Univ of St. Mary	KS	37,080	NC
Univ of San Francisco	CA	60,580	C
Univ of Scranton	PA	54,962	VC
Univ of S Car Upstate	SC	19,272	LC
Univ of South Florida St. Petersburg	FL	15,980	C
Univ of Southern Miss	MS	13,170	C
Univ of St. Francis	IL	40,828	C
Univ of Texas at Arlington	TX	18,876	C
Univ of Texas at Dallas	TX	23,640	HC
Univ of Texas Rio Grande Valley	TX	15,573	LC
Univ of the Cumberlands	KY	32,000	LC
Univ of the Incarnate Word	TX	39,162	LC
Univ of the Pacific	CA	57,446	VC
Univ of Toledo	OH	19,336	C
Univ of Tulsa	OK	52,625	HC
Univ of Vermont	VT	29,792	HC
Univ of Washington	WA	23,091	MC
Univ of Wisc-Eau Claire	WI	16,354	VC
Univ of Wisc-Green Bay	WI	15,184	C
Univ of Wisc-La Crosse	WI	15,425	VC
Univ of Wisc-Madison	WI	21,647	MC
Univ of Wisc-Milwaukee	WI	21,538	C
Univ of Wisc-Stevens Point	WI	14,043	C
Utah State Univ	UT	13,235	C
Valley City State Univ	ND	13,267	C
Vermont Technical College	VT	25,370	C
Villanova Univ	PA	64,922	MC
Virginia Commonwealth Univ	VA	23,811	VC
Walla Walla Univ	WA	34,845	C
Warner Univ	FL	28,216	C
Washington Adventist Univ	MD	32,050	LC
Washington Univ in St. Louis	MO	67,539	MC
Wayne State Univ	MI	23,085	C
Waynesburg Univ	PA	33,530	C
Webber International Univ	FL	31,904	C
Weber State Univ	UT	14,112	C
Webster Univ	MO	37,490	C
Wentworth Inst of Technology	MA	48,810	VC
West Liberty Univ	WV	16,158	C
West Texas A&M Univ	TX	13,478	C
Western Illinois Univ	IL	20,897	C
Western New England Univ	MA	49,182	C
Western Oregon Univ	OR	19,965	LC
Westfield State Univ	MA	20,404	C
Westminster College	UT	41,078	C
Widener Univ	PA	58,190	C
Wilberforce Univ	OH	19,900	C
Wilkes Univ	PA	49,166	C
William Woods Univ	MO	32,040	C
Wilmington College	OH	35,100	C
Xavier Univ	OH	49,380	VC
Youngstown State Univ	OH	17,487	C

INFORMATION SECURITY & RISK MANAGEMENT

School	ST	$IS	SR
Ferris State Univ	MI	21,458	C
Lewis Univ	IL	41,710	C
Univ of Okla	OK	19,651	HC

INFORMATION TECHNOLOGY

School	ST	$IS	SR
Arkansas State Univ	AR	16,190	C
Bloomfield College	NJ	40,100	LC
Bryant Univ	RI	57,204	VC
Cabrini Univ	PA	42,591	LC
Calif Baptist Univ	CA	42,986	C
Calvin College	MI	43,090	HC
Cameron Univ	OK	11,632	LC
Campbell Univ	NC	37,570	VC
Carroll Univ	WI	38,100	C+
Cedarville Univ	OH	36,244	VC
Champlain College	VT	54,724	VC
Christopher Newport Univ	VA	24,878	VC+
Dakota State Univ	SD	12,286	C
DePaul Univ	IL	52,807	VC
Elizabethtown College School of Continuing and Professional Studies	PA	18,900	C
Elmhurst College	IL	46,514	C
Faulkner Univ	AL	26,410	C
Gallaudet Univ	DC	30,088	LC
Harris-Stowe State Univ	MO	14,590	NC
Juniata College	PA	58,118	VC
Kean Univ	NJ	25,620	C
King Univ	TN	36,976	C
Kutztown Univ of Pennsylvania	PA	19,477	C
La Roche College	PA	38,940	C
La Salle Univ	PA	43,476	C
Lake Erie College	OH	38,914	LC
Lawrence Tech Univ	MI	41,630	VC
LeMoyne-Owen College	TN	16,980	C
Lincoln Univ	PA	20,878	LC
Marquette Univ	WI	53,090	VC+
Marshall Univ	WV	18,044	C
Marymount Univ	VA	43,231	C
Merrimack College	MA	55,415	C
Missouri State Univ	MO	15,837	C+
Missouri Western State Univ	MO	17,822	LC
Montclair State Univ	NJ	26,912	C
Mount St. Mary College	NY	44,448	C
Mount Vernon Nazarene Univ	OH	35,944	C
Nazareth College	NY	46,784	C
New York Univ	NY	68,139	MC
Nova Southeastern Univ	FL	38,534	C+
Okla Baptist Univ	OK	33,990	C
Olivet Nazarene Univ	IL	41,840	VC
Pace Univ	NY	60,136	C
Regis Univ	CO	46,380	C
Rochester Inst of Technology	NY	52,734	HC+
St. Louis Univ	MO	49,866	HC
San Jose State Univ	CA	22,630	C
Silver Lake College of the Holy Family	WI	36,290	LC
Simmons College	MA	54,400	HC
Southeast Missouri State Univ	MO	16,148	C
Southeastern Louisiana Univ	LA	16,237	C
Southern Illinois Univ Carbondale	IL	24,554	C
St. John's Univ	NY	57,160	C+
SUNY Albany	NY	22,165	C
Stephen F. Austin State Univ	TX	18,484	LC
Tarleton State Univ	TX	15,248	LC
Texas Tech Univ	TX	20,156	C+
The College of St. Rose	NY	44,010	C
The Univ of Arizona	AZ	24,086	C
Thomas Edison State Univ	NJ	6,350	NC
Univ of Central Florida	FL	16,379	VC
Univ of Cincinnati	OH	22,118	VC
Univ of Kansas	KS	20,884	VC
Univ of Mass Boston	MA	13,828	C
Univ of Mass Lowell	MA	27,296	VC
Univ of Minn/Twin Cities	MN	24,269	MC
Univ of Missouri-Kansas City	MO	19,563	VC
Univ of Nebr - Lincoln	NE	18,589	VC
Univ of New Hampshire	NH	29,333	VC
Univ of N Car at Greensboro	NC	15,998	C
Univ of N Car Wilmington	NC	16,784	VC
Univ of Notre Dame	IN	68,801	MC
Univ of South Alabama	AL	16,880	C
Univ of Wisc-Milwaukee	WI	21,538	C
Webster Univ	MO	37,490	C
Youngstown State Univ	OH	17,487	C

INFORMATION TECHNOLOGY MANAGEMENT

School	ST	$IS	SR
Lewis Univ	IL	41,710	C
Northwest Univ	WA	38,720	VC
Univ of Mich/Dearborn	MI	12,472	VC

INSTITUTIONAL MANAGEMENT

School	ST	$IS	SR
Calumet College of St. Joseph	IN	22,735	C
Goshen College	IN	44,350	C
New York City College of Technology	NY	7,185	LC
San Francisco State Univ	CA	18,514	LC
SUNY/Fredonia	NY	20,818	C
Univ of La Verne	CA	55,600	C
Warner Univ	FL	28,216	C

INSTRUCTIONAL DESIGN

School	ST	$IS	SR
Ashford Univ	CA	10,480	C
Univ of South Alabama	AL	16,880	C

INSTRUCTIONAL TECHNOLOGY

School	ST	$IS	SR
Drury Univ	MO	37,555	VC
Georgia Southern Univ	GA	16,540	VC

INSTRUMENTAL MUSIC EDUCATION

School	ST	$IS	SR
Arkansas State Univ	AR	16,190	C
Concordia Univ St. Paul	MN	29,050	C
Keene State College	NH	24,604	C
King Univ	TN	36,976	C
Marian Univ	IN	43,206	C
Missouri Southern State Univ	MO	13,071	C
Missouri Western State Univ	MO	17,822	LC
Murray State Univ	KY	17,726	C+
N Dak State Univ	ND	16,245	VC
Ohio Univ	OH	23,394	VC
Okla Baptist Univ	OK	33,990	C
Okla City Univ	OK	40,476	C
Okla City Univ	OK	40,476	C
Ouachita Baptist Univ	AR	33,500	VC
Weber State Univ	UT	14,112	C
Webster Univ	MO	37,490	C
Western Mich Univ	MI	21,791	C

INSTRUMENTAL PERFORMANCE

School	ST	$IS	SR
Anderson Univ	IN	39,450	C
Baldwin Wallace Univ	OH	42,464	VC
Bowling Green State Univ	OH	19,975	C
Houghton College	NY	40,558	VC
Madonna Univ	MI	30,450	LC
Marian Univ	IN	43,206	C
Missouri Western State Univ	MO	17,822	LC
New York Univ	NY	68,139	MC
Okla Baptist Univ	OK	33,990	C
Okla Christian Univ	OK	29,260	C
Okla City Univ	OK	40,476	C
Ouachita Baptist Univ	AR	33,500	VC
Southeast Missouri State Univ	MO	16,148	C
The Master's Univ	CA	43,870	C
Univ of Miami	FL	63,494	MC
Weber State Univ	UT	14,112	C
Webster Univ	MO	37,490	C
Western Mich Univ	MI	21,791	C
Wingate Univ	NC	41,900	C
Wright State Univ	OH	16,983	C

INSURANCE

School	ST	$IS	SR
Baylor Univ	TX	56,803	HC
Cal State, Sacramento	CA	19,060	C
Ferris State Univ	MI	21,458	C

ST = STATE $IS = IN-STATE COSTS SR = SELECTOR RATING

School	ST	$IS	SR
Idaho State Univ	ID	13,619	LC
Illinois State Univ	IL	23,418	VC
Indiana State Univ	IN	23,223	LC
Inter-American Univ of PR Ponce	PR	19,549	
Inter-American Univ of PR-Fajardo Campus	PR	18,336	
Martin Univ	IN	21,010	LC
Miss State Univ	MS	12,028	C+
Old Dominion Univ	VA	21,618	C
Olivet College	MI	37,661	LC
Roosevelt Univ	IL	41,890	VC
Troy Univ	AL	16,171	C
Univ of Central Okla	OK	15,150	C
Univ of Cincinnati	OH	22,118	VC
Univ of Florida	FL	16,291	HC+
Univ of Hartford	CT	49,776	C
Univ of Illinois at Urbana-Champaign	IL	27,006	HC
Univ of Louisiana at Monroe	LA	15,970	C
Univ of Miss	MS	18,802	C
Univ of North Texas	TX	20,082	C
Univ of S Car at Columbia	SC	21,726	VC
Washington State Univ	WA	22,747	C

INSURANCE AND RISK MANAGEMENT

School	ST	$IS	SR
Appalachian State Univ	NC	15,394	VC
Cal State, Fullerton	CA	21,902	C
Excelsior College	NY	38,800	SP
Florida State Univ	FL	16,771	HC
Gannon Univ	PA	42,922	C
Georgia State Univ	GA	25,250	C
Illinois Wesleyan Univ	IL	56,430	VC+
Mercyhurst Univ	PA	47,420	C
Ohio State Univ at Columbus	OH	22,843	MC
Roosevelt Univ	IL	41,890	VC
St. Joseph's Univ	PA	58,540	VC
Southern Methodist Univ	TX	69,008	MC
St. John's Univ	NY	57,160	C+
SUNY at Oswego	NY	22,219	VC
Univ of Central Arkansas	AR	15,042	VC
Univ of Conn	CT	27,394	
Univ of Georgia	GA	21,878	HC
Univ of Houston-Downtown	TX	7,241	LC
Univ of Nebr - Lincoln	NE	18,589	VC
Univ of Pennsylvania	PA	63,526	MC
Univ of St. Francis	IN	38,520	C
Univ of Wisc-Madison	WI	21,647	MC
Utica College	NY	31,510	C

INTEGRATED ART AND DESIGN

School	ST	$IS	SR
East Stroudsburg Univ	PA	18,578	LC
Univ of Idaho	ID	16,158	C

INTEGRATED MARKETING COMMUNICATIONS

School	ST	$IS	SR
Univ of West Alabama	AL	16,284	LC

INTEGRATIVE HEALTH STUDIES

School	ST	$IS	SR
Averett Univ	VA	43,034	LC
Chatham Univ	PA	47,883	VC

INTEGRATIVE STUDIES

School	ST	$IS	SR
Christopher Newport Univ	VA	24,878	VC+
Ferris State Univ	MI	21,458	C
Kennesaw State Univ	GA	18,899	VC
Murray State Univ	KY	17,726	C+
St. Ambrose Univ	IA	40,180	C
Univ of N Car at Greensboro	NC	15,998	C

INTERACTIVE MEDIA

School	ST	$IS	SR
Lewis Univ	IL	41,710	C
SUNY Polytechnic Inst	NY	20,438	VC
Worcester Polytechnic Inst	MA	62,846	MC

INTERDISCIPLINARY ART

School	ST	$IS	SR
Columbia College Chicago	IL	40,104	C
Tufts Univ	MA		MC
Univ of West Alabama	AL	16,284	LC

INTERDISCIPLINARY STUDIES

School	ST	$IS	SR
Adams State Univ	CO	15,420	LC
Alderson Broaddus Univ	WV	35,000	LC
Alfred Univ	NY	37,490	C
Amherst College	MA	66,186	MC
Andrews Univ	MI	41,732	C
Angelo State Univ	TX	15,882	LC
Appalachian State Univ	NC	15,394	VC
Aquinas College	TN	30,800	C+
Aquinas College - Mich	MI	38,876	VC
Arizona State Univ at the Downtown Phoenix Campus	AZ	24,634	VC
Arizona State Univ at the Polytechnic Campus	AZ	22,394	VC
Arizona State Univ at the Tempe Campus	AZ	23,001	VC
Arizona State Univ at the West Campus	AZ	21,513	VC
Arkansas State Univ	AR	16,190	C
Augustana Univ	SD	39,968	VC
Austin College	TX	51,059	HC
Austin Peay State Univ	TN	16,397	C
Averett Univ	VA	43,034	LC
Baldwin Wallace Univ	OH	42,464	VC
Bard College	NY	65,924	HC
Barton College	NC	39,854	C
Bates College	ME	64,500	HC
Baylor Univ	TX	56,803	HC
Belhaven Univ	MS	32,250	C
Bellarmine Univ	KY	52,532	C
Beloit College	WI	55,206	HC
Bennett College	NC	27,717	NC
Bennington College	VT	66,280	MC
Bentley Univ	MA	63,720	MC
Berry College	GA	47,466	VC
Bethany College	WV	38,774	LC
Bethel College	IN	36,830	C
Birmingham-Southern College	AL	44,478	C+
Blackburn College	IL	28,526	LC
Bloomfield College	NJ	40,100	LC
Bluefield College	VA	34,711	C
Boise State Univ	ID	17,368	C
Boston Univ	MA	67,352	MC
Bowdoin College	ME	65,980	MC
Bowie State Univ	MD	18,610	LC
Bowling Green State Univ	OH	19,975	C
Brandeis Univ	MA	68,443	MC
Brigham Young Univ/Hawaii	HI	11,710	C
Bryn Athyn College	PA	32,664	C
Bucknell Univ	PA	67,136	MC
Buena Vista Univ	IA	42,344	C
Calif Baptist Univ	CA	42,986	C
Calif Inst of Technology	CA	64,704	MC
Calif Lutheran Univ	CA	52,853	C
Calif Polytechnic State Univ	CA	22,547	MC
Cal State, Dominguez Hills	CA	19,022	LC
Cal State, Fullerton	CA	21,902	C
Cal State, Long Beach	CA	18,850	C
Cal State, Los Angeles	CA	17,186	LC
Cal State, Stanislaus	CA	18,053	LC
Calvin College	MI	43,090	HC
Cambridge College	MA	14,940	NC
Cameron Univ	OK	11,632	LC
Centenary College	NJ	43,890	LC
Centenary College of Louisiana	LA	49,050	C+
Central Methodist Univ	MO	31,500	VC
Central Mich Univ	MI	20,330	C
Chatham Univ	PA	47,883	VC
Christopher Newport Univ	VA	24,878	VC+
CUNY/Brooklyn College	NY	7,163	C+
Claremont McKenna College	CA	69,900	MC
Clarkson Univ	NY	60,392	VC
Clayton State Univ	GA	19,735	LC
Coastal Carolina Univ	SC	20,340	C
Coe College	IA	51,570	VC
College of the Ozarks	MO	7,530	VC
College of William & Mary	VA	34,907	MC
Colo College	CO	64,894	MC
Colo State Univ	CO	23,033	C
Columbia College - Missouri	MO	28,179	C
Concordia College - New York	NY	39,035	LC
Coppin State Univ	MD	14,071	VC
Corban Univ	OR	41,700	C
Cornerstone Univ	MI	36,550	C
Covenant College	GA	44,590	HC
Dallas Baptist Univ	TX	35,220	VC
Davidson College	NC	60,119	MC
Davis & Elkins College	WV	38,242	LC
Delta State Univ	MS	13,176	LC
DePauw Univ	IN	58,688	VC
D'Youville College	NY	37,678	C
East Stroudsburg Univ	PA	18,578	LC
East Tenn State Univ	TN	18,141	C
East Texas Baptist Univ	TX	34,444	C
Eastern Mich Univ	MI	19,761	C
Embry-Riddle Aeronautical Univ - Daytona Beach	FL	45,822	VC
Embry-Riddle Aeronautical Univ - Prescott Campus	AZ	45,130	VC
Embry-Riddle Aeronautical Univ - Worldwide	FL	17,720	C
Emerson College	MA	61,824	HC+
Emmanuel College	MA	53,472	C+
Emory and Henry College	VA	46,320	C
Emory Univ	GA	63,286	MC
Eugene Lang College of Liberal Arts	NY	64,940	VC
Fairleigh Dickinson Univ/ Metropolitan Campus	NJ	52,392	C
Farmingdale State College	NY	20,968	C
Fitchburg State Univ	MA	21,819	LC
Florida Atlantic Univ	FL	18,256	C
Florida Inst of Technology	FL	53,306	VC
Fort Lewis College	CO	20,154	C
Framingham State Univ	MA	21,740	C
Franklin and Marshall College	PA	67,960	MC
Franklin Pierce Univ	NH	46,750	LC
Gannon Univ	PA	42,922	C
Geneva College	PA	35,450	C
George Mason Univ	VA	19,884	C
Georgetown College	KY	41,440	C
Georgetown Univ	DC	68,970	MC
Georgia Southern Univ	GA	16,540	VC
Georgia State Univ	GA	25,250	C
Gettysburg College	PA	65,210	MC
Goddard College	VT	17,040	VC
Gonzaga Univ	WA	52,880	HC
Goshen College	IN	44,350	C
Goucher College	MD	56,110	VC
Grace Bible College	MI	25,250	C
Grand Canyon Univ	AZ	25,150	VC
Guilford College	NC	45,973	C
Hamilton College	NY	64,250	MC
Haverford College	PA	66,490	MC
Hendrix College	AR	54,020	VC
Heritage Univ	WA	19,825	NC
Hodges Univ	FL	20,160	LC
Hollins Univ	VA	49,635	VC
Houghton College	NY	40,558	VC
Howard Univ	DC	37,616	C+
Huston-Tillotson Univ	TX	18,124	LC
Illinois State Univ	IL	23,418	VC
Illinois Wesleyan Univ	IL	56,430	VC+
Indiana State Univ	IN	23,223	LC
Indiana Univ-Purdue Univ Indianapolis	IN	18,952	C
Iona College	NY	52,514	C
Ithaca College	NY	58,158	VC+
John Brown Univ	AR	35,184	VC
Johns Hopkins Univ	MD	68,080	MC
Judson College	AL	27,066	C
Kalamazoo College	MI	53,931	HC
King Univ	TN	36,976	C
Lafayette College	PA	68,520	MC
LaGrange College	GA	41,310	C
Lake Erie College	OH	38,914	LC
Lander Univ	SC	32,200	C
Lane College	TN	17,960	LC
Lasell College	MA	49,400	C
Lee Univ	TN	22,045	C
Lehigh Univ	PA	63,860	MC
LeMoyne-Owen College	TN	16,980	C
LeTourneau Univ	TX	39,190	VC
Lewis & Clark College	OR	60,984	MC
Lewis-Clark State College	ID	14,202	C
Liberty Univ	VA	31,415	C
Lipscomb Univ	TN	42,984	VC
LIU Brooklyn	NY	50,698	C
Louisiana College	LA	21,274	C
Louisiana State Univ and A&M College	LA	18,677	VC
Lourdes Univ	OH	29,140	NC
Loyola Marymount Univ	CA	60,202	VC+
Lyndon State College	VT	20,714	C
Madonna Univ	MI	30,450	LC
Manchester Univ	IN	41,540	C
Marian Univ	WI	34,622	C
Marietta College	OH	46,190	C
Marlboro College	VT	50,832	VC+
Marquette Univ	WI	53,090	VC+
Marylhurst Univ	OR	16,818	NC
Mass College of Liberal Arts	MA	20,659	C
Mass Inst of Technology	MA	62,662	MC
McMurry Univ	TX	34,259	LC
Mercy College	NY	32,614	C
Messiah College	PA	44,380	VC
Miami Univ	OH	27,190	HC+
Mich State Univ	MI	24,542	VC
MidAmerica Nazarene Univ	KS	37,808	C
Middle Tenn State Univ	TN	8,650	C
Midwestern State Univ	TX	12,111	LC
Millersville Univ of Pennsylvania	PA	25,298	C
Millikin Univ	IL	44,148	C
Miss State Univ	MS	12,028	C+
Molloy College	NY	40,440	C
Montana State Univ-Northern	MT	11,370	NC
Mount St. Mary College	NY	44,448	C
Mount St. Mary's Univ	MD	53,380	C
Naropa Univ	CO	43,278	NC
National Univ	CA	17,849	LC
New York Inst of Technology	NY	49,980	VC
Newman Univ	KS	37,382	C
Norfolk State Univ	VA	18,902	LC
N Car State Univ	NC	22,434	HC+
North Central Univ	MN	30,610	C
Northeastern Illinois Univ	IL	12,529	LC
Northeastern Univ	MA	65,352	MC
Northern Arizona Univ	AZ	21,003	C
Northwest Christian Univ	OR	36,580	C
Northwest Univ	WA	38,720	VC
Notre Dame of Maryland Univ	MD	47,570	VC
Nyack College	NY	34,450	LC
Ohio Dominican Univ	OH	41,340	C+
Ohio Valley Univ	WV	28,800	C
Okla Baptist Univ	OK	33,990	C
Okla Christian Univ	OK	29,260	C
Old Dominion Univ	VA	21,618	C
Palm Beach Atlantic Univ	FL	39,250	C
Piedmont College	GA	34,334	C
Plymouth State Univ	NH	23,180	LC
Prairie View A&M Univ	TX	27,273	LC
Radford Univ	VA	19,758	C
Rensselaer Polytechnic Inst	NY	67,265	MC
Rhodes College	TN	51,900	HC
Roanoke College	VA	55,952	VC
Roberts Wesleyan College	NY	41,116	C
Rochester College	MI	28,574	LC
Russell Sage College	NY	39,370	C
Rutgers Univ - Camden	NJ	26,595	C
Rutgers Univ - New Brunswick	NJ	27,090	HC
Rutgers Univ - Newark	NJ	27,351	C
Saginaw Valley State Univ	MI	19,284	C
St. Martin's Univ	WA	45,056	C
St. Peter's Univ	NJ	49,192	C
San Diego Christian College	CA	40,914	C
San Diego State Univ	CA	23,156	VC
San Francisco State Univ	CA	18,514	LC
San Jose State Univ	CA	22,630	C
Sarah Lawrence College	NY	68,866	MC
Shawnee State Univ	OH	16,998	C
Shippensburg Univ of Pennsylvania	PA	24,096	C
Simmons College	MA	54,400	HC
Simpson College	IA	45,626	VC
Sonoma State Univ	CA	27,020	C
S Dak School of Mines and Technology	SD	18,570	C+
Southeast Missouri State Univ	MO	16,148	C
Southeastern Univ	FL	34,910	LC
Southern Oregon Univ	OR	19,117	C
Southwest Baptist Univ	MO	30,890	LC
Southwest Minn State Univ	MN	17,783	C
Southwestern College	KS	31,531	LC
Southwestern Okla State Univ	OK	12,205	C
Spring Hill College	AL	48,488	C
St. Andrews Univ	NC	44,634	LC
St. Edward's Univ	TX	56,190	VC
St. John Fisher College	NY	45,270	VC
St. Lawrence Univ	NY	66,646	HC+
St. Olaf College	MN	56,430	HC
SUNY Albany	NY	22,165	C
SUNY at Binghamton	NY	24,100	MC
SUNY Polytechnic Inst	NY	20,438	VC
SUNY/Empire State College	NY	9,145	NC
SUNY/Fredonia	NY	20,818	C
SUNY/Plattsburgh	NY	19,314	C
SUNY/Potsdam	NY	21,051	VC
Stephen F. Austin State Univ	TX	18,484	LC
Sterling College	KS	32,830	LC
Stevenson Univ	MD	48,412	C
Stonehill College	MA	55,130	C
Stony Brook Univ/The SUNY	NY	22,703	MC
Tarleton State Univ	TX	15,248	LC
Taylor Univ	IN	42,130	VC
Tenn State Univ	TN	14,423	LC
Texas Christian Univ	TX	57,120	HC
Texas Southern Univ	TX	19,592	LC
Texas State Univ	TX	18,721	C
Texas Wesleyan Univ	TX	37,338	C
Texas Woman's Univ	TX	15,302	LC
The American Univ	DC	61,317	HC
The College of St. Rose	NY	44,010	C
The College of Wooster	OH	60,000	HC
The George Washington Univ	DC	68,474	HC+
The Univ of Akron	OH	22,566	C
The Univ of Alabama	AL	24,320	C+
The Univ of Arizona	AZ	24,086	C
The Univ of Memphis	TN	18,278	C
The Univ of Tenn at Knoxville	TN	22,112	VC
The Univ of Texas at San Antonio	TX	21,060	C
Thomas Univ	GA	21,420	NC
Touro College	NY	31,040	C
Towson Univ	MD	21,878	C
Trinity College	CT	69,020	HC
Truman State Univ	MO	16,286	MC
Tufts Univ	MA		MC
Union College	NY	64,320	MC
Univ of Alaska Anchorage	AK	17,914	C
Univ of Arkansas at Fayetteville	AR	19,766	VC
Univ of Bridgeport	CT	44,985	LC
Univ of Calif at Berkeley	CA	29,886	MC
Univ of Calif at Irvine	CA	33,857	VC
Univ of Calif at Riverside	CA	32,912	C
Univ of Calif at Santa Barbara	CA	30,627	HC+
Univ of Central Florida	FL	16,379	VC
Univ of Chicago	IL	70,551	MC
Univ of Colo Denver	CO	22,238	C
Univ of Conn	CT	27,394	
Univ of Delaware	DE	32,214	VC
Univ of Denver	CO	61,129	VC+
Univ of Evansville	IN	44,186	C+
Univ of Florida	FL	16,291	HC+
Univ of Georgia	GA	21,878	HC
Univ of Hartford	CT	49,776	C
Univ of Hawaii at Manoa	HI	23,261	C
Univ of Houston	TX	21,871	VC
Univ of Houston-Downtown	TX	7,241	LC
Univ of Idaho	ID	16,158	C
Univ of Maine	ME	21,038	VC
Univ of Maine at Augusta	ME	7,812	C
Univ of Maine at Farmington	ME	18,792	C
Univ of Maine at Machias	ME	22,960	C
Univ of Mary Hardin-Baylor	TX	35,292	C+
Univ of Maryland/Baltimore County	MD	23,004	VC
Univ of Maryland/College Park	MD	21,938	HC
Univ of Mass Amherst	MA	27,669	HC
Univ of Mass Dartmouth	MA	26,507	C
Univ of Miami	FL	63,494	MC
Univ of Mich/Ann Arbor	MI	25,274	MC

ST = STATE **$IS** = IN-STATE COSTS **SR** = SELECTOR RATING

School	ST	$IS	SR
Univ of Mich/Dearborn	MI	12,472	VC
Univ of Minn/Duluth	MN	20,292	C
Univ of Minn/Morris	MN	21,222	VC
Univ of Missouri-St. Louis	MO	19,810	VC
Univ of Nebr - Lincoln	NE	18,589	VC
Univ of Nebr - Omaha	NE	16,120	C
Univ of Nevada, Las Vegas	NV	17,553	C
Univ of New Mexico	NM	16,808	C
Univ of N Car at Chapel Hill	NC	20,561	MC
Univ of N Car at Pembroke	NC	14,737	LC
Univ of N Dak	ND	16,673	C
Univ of North Florida	FL	15,996	VC
Univ of North Texas	TX	20,082	C
Univ of Northern Colo	CO	19,658	C
Univ of Northwestern - St. Paul	MN	39,530	C
Univ of Pikeville	KY	27,838	C
Univ of Pittsburgh	PA	30,030	MC
Univ of Pittsburgh at Bradford	PA	22,958	C
Univ of Portland	OR	52,152	VC
Univ of PR-Rio Piedras campus	PR	13,327	
Univ of Redlands	CA	61,934	VC
Univ of Richmond	VA	62,730	MC
Univ of Rochester	NY	65,032	MC
Univ of St. Mary	KS	37,080	NC
Univ of South Alabama	AL	16,880	C
Univ of S Car Aiken	SC	18,094	C
Univ of S Car at Columbia	SC	21,726	VC
Univ of S Car Upstate	SC	19,272	LC
Univ of Texas at Arlington	TX	18,876	C
Univ of Texas at Dallas	TX	23,640	HC
Univ of Texas at El Paso	TX	34,452	NC
Univ of Texas Rio Grande Valley	TX	15,573	LC
Univ of the Sciences	PA	40,738	VC
Univ of Virginia	VA	27,367	MC
Univ of West Alabama	AL	16,284	LC
Univ of Wisc-Green Bay	WI	15,184	C
Univ of Wisc-Milwaukee	WI	21,538	C
Univ of Wisc-Superior	WI	14,838	C
Univ of Wyoming	WY	15,537	C
Valparaiso Univ	IN	50,160	VC
Vanderbilt Univ	TN	63,248	MC
Villanova Univ	PA	64,922	MC
Virginia Commonwealth Univ	VA	23,811	VC
Virginia Polytechnic Inst and State Univ	VA	21,920	VC
Virginia State Univ	VA	19,802	C+
Virginia Wesleyan Univ	VA	45,980	LC
Warren Wilson College	NC	44,220	VC
Wartburg College	IA	49,478	C
Washburn Univ	KS	15,827	C
Washington & Jefferson College	PA	58,694	VC
Washington and Lee Univ	VA	59,647	MC
Washington College	MD	56,154	VC
Washington State Univ	WA	22,747	C
Washington Univ in St. Louis	MO	67,539	MC
Wayland Baptist Univ	TX	23,460	LC
Wayne State College	NE	25,746	NC
Weber State Univ	UT	14,112	C
Webster Univ	MO	37,490	C
Wesleyan College	GA	31,940	C+
West Liberty Univ	WV	16,158	C
West Texas A&M Univ	TX	13,478	C
West Virginia Univ	WV	18,952	VC
Western Illinois Univ	IL	20,897	C
Western Mich Univ	MI	21,791	C
Western Oregon Univ	OR	19,965	LC
Western Washington Univ	WA	18,904	VC
Wheaton College	IL	44,993	MC
William Woods Univ	MO	32,040	C
Williams College	MA	67,700	MC
Wisc Lutheran College	WI	36,290	C
Woodbury Univ	CA	49,593	VC

INTERIOR ARCHITECTURE

School	ST	$IS	SR
Cal State, Fullerton	CA	21,902	C
Chatham Univ	PA	47,883	VC
Cleveland Inst of Art	OH	51,455	SP
Florida International Univ	FL	20,281	C
Lawrence Tech Univ	MI	41,630	VC
Syracuse Univ	NY	62,313	HC
Univ of N Car at Greensboro	NC	15,998	C
Univ of Oregon	OR	24,021	VC
Univ of San Francisco	CA	60,580	C

INTERIOR DESIGN

School	ST	$IS	SR
Abilene Christian Univ	TX	43,708	C+
Adrian College	MI	45,550	C
Appalachian State Univ	NC	15,394	VC
Arcadia Univ	PA	55,990	C+
Arizona State Univ at the Tempe Campus	AZ	23,001	VC
Art Inst of Portland	OR	132,329	SP
Auburn Univ	AL	24,300	VC+
Baker College of Flint	MI	19,140	NC
Bay Path Univ	MA	46,356	C
Baylor Univ	TX	56,803	HC
Boston Architectural College	MA	20,666	SP
Bowling Green State Univ	OH	19,975	C
Brenau Univ - Women's College	GA	37,876	LC
Calif College of the Arts	CA	52,758	SP
Cal State, Fresno	CA	16,902	LC
Cal State, Fullerton	CA	21,902	C
Cazenovia College	NY	47,866	C
Central Mich Univ	MI	20,330	C
Chaminade Univ of Honolulu	HI	37,614	C
Chatham Univ	PA	47,883	VC
College for Creative Studies	MI	51,210	SP
Colo State Univ	CO	23,033	C
Columbia College Chicago	IL	40,104	C
Columbus College of Art and Design	OH	47,310	SP
Concordia Univ Wisc	WI	35,910	C
Converse College	SC	28,290	C
Drexel Univ	PA	65,927	HC
East Carolina Univ	NC	16,539	C
Eastern Kentucky Univ	KY	17,742	C
Eastern Mich Univ	MI	19,761	C
Endicott College	MA	47,054	C+
Fashion Inst of Technology/SUNY	NY	18,521	SP
Florida International Univ	FL	20,281	C
Florida State Univ	FL	16,771	HC
Georgia Southern Univ	GA	16,540	VC
Harding Univ	AR	25,440	C
High Point Univ	NC	47,355	VC
Howard Univ	DC	37,616	C+
Indiana State Univ	IN	23,223	LC
Indiana Univ Bloomington	IN	20,791	HC
Indiana Univ of Pennsylvania	PA	24,474	C
Indiana Univ-Purdue Univ Fort Wayne	IN	18,675	C
Indiana Univ-Purdue Univ Indianapolis	IN	18,952	C
Indiana Wesleyan Univ	IN	33,674	C
Iowa State Univ	IA	18,176	C
Jefferson (Philadelphia Univ + Thomas Jefferson Univ)	PA	53,966	C
Kansas State Univ	KS	17,780	VC
Kean Univ	NJ	25,620	C
Kent State Univ	OH	20,928	C
La Roche College	PA	38,940	C
Lawrence Tech Univ	MI	41,630	VC
Louisiana State Univ and A&M College	LA	18,677	VC
Marist College	NY	49,860	VC
Marymount Univ	VA	43,231	C
Maryville Univ of St. Louis	MO	38,558	VC
Marywood Univ	PA	47,840	C
Mercyhurst Univ	PA	47,420	C
Meredith College	NC	46,634	C
Miami Univ	OH	27,190	HC+
Mich State Univ	MI	24,542	VC
Middle Tenn State Univ	TN	8,650	C
Milwaukee Inst of Art & Design	WI	45,880	SP
Miss College	MS	25,850	C
Missouri State Univ	MO	15,837	C+
Moore College of Art and Design	PA	55,118	SP
Mount Ida College	MA	46,820	C
Mount Mary Univ	WI	34,650	LC
Murray State Univ	KY	17,726	C+
New York Inst of Technology	NY	49,980	VC
Newbury College	MA	48,970	C
N Dak State Univ	ND	16,245	VC
Northern Arizona Univ	AZ	21,003	C
Ohio State Univ at Columbus	OH	22,843	MC
Ohio Univ	OH	23,394	VC
Okla Christian Univ	OK	29,260	C
Olivet Nazarene Univ	IL	41,840	VC
Oregon State Univ	OR	23,337	VC
Park Univ	MO	22,134	C
Parsons The New School for Design	NY	56,610	SP
Pratt Inst	NY	59,482	VC+
Purdue Univ/West Lafayette	IN	20,032	MC
Queens Univ of Charlotte	NC	39,543	C
Rhode Island School of Design	RI	59,960	SP
Ringling College of Art and Design	FL	59,160	SP
Rochester Inst of Technology	NY	52,734	HC+
Rocky Mountain College of Art and Design	CO	27,052	SP
Samford Univ	AL	40,770	VC
San Diego State Univ	CA	23,156	VC
San Francisco State Univ	CA	18,514	LC
San Jose State Univ	CA	22,630	C
Savannah College of Art and Design	GA	49,595	SP
School of the Art Inst of Chicago	IL	61,830	SP
School of Visual Arts	NY	47,500	SP
Seattle Pacific Univ	WA	47,439	C+
S Dak State Univ	SD	15,874	C
Southeast Missouri State Univ	MO	16,148	C
Southern Illinois Univ Carbondale	IL	24,554	C
Stephen F. Austin State Univ	TX	18,484	LC
Stephens College	MO	38,042	C
Suffolk Univ	MA	52,316	C
Texas A&M Univ at Kingsville	TX	16,580	LC
Texas Christian Univ	TX	57,120	HC
Texas State Univ	TX	18,721	C
Texas Tech Univ	TX	20,156	C+
The Art Inst of Atlanta	GA	34,334	SP
The Univ of Akron	OH	22,566	C
The Univ of Alabama	AL	24,320	C+
The Univ of Tenn at Chattanooga	TN	17,340	C+
The Univ of Tenn at Knoxville	TN	22,112	VC
The Univ of Texas at Austin	TX	20,206	MC
The Univ of Texas at San Antonio	TX	21,060	C
Univ of Arkansas at Fayetteville	AR	19,766	VC
Univ of Bridgeport	CT	44,985	LC
Univ of Central Arkansas	AR	15,042	VC
Univ of Central Missouri	MO	18,982	C
Univ of Central Okla	OK	15,150	C
Univ of Charleston	WV	35,000	LC
Univ of Cincinnati	OH	22,118	VC
Univ of Florida	FL	16,291	HC+
Univ of Idaho	ID	16,158	C
Univ of Kansas	KS	20,884	VC
Univ of Louisiana at Lafayette	LA	14,516	C
Univ of Minn/Twin Cities	MN	24,269	MC
Univ of Nebr - Kearney	NE	17,014	LC
Univ of Nebr - Lincoln	NE	18,589	VC
Univ of Nevada, Las Vegas	NV	17,553	C
Univ of New Haven	CT	53,680	C
Univ of North Alabama	AL	15,964	C
Univ of N Car at Greensboro	NC	15,998	C
Univ of North Texas	TX	20,082	C
Univ of Okla	OK	19,651	HC
Univ of San Francisco	CA	60,580	C
Univ of Texas at Arlington	TX	18,876	C
Univ of the Incarnate Word	TX	39,162	LC
Univ of Wisc-Madison	WI	21,647	MC
Univ of Wisc-Stevens Point	WI	14,043	C
Utah State Univ	UT	13,235	C
Virginia Commonwealth Univ	VA	23,811	VC
Virginia Polytechnic Inst and State Univ	VA	21,920	VC
Washington State Univ	WA	22,747	C
Weber State Univ	UT	14,112	C
Wentworth Inst of Technology	MA	48,810	VC
West Virginia Univ	WV	18,952	VC
Western Carolina Univ	NC	13,965	C
Western Mich Univ	MI	21,791	C
Winthrop Univ	SC	23,960	C
Woodbury Univ	CA	49,593	VC

INTERMEDIA/MULTIMEDIA

School	ST	$IS	SR
Bard College at Simon's Rock	MA	65,795	MC
Beloit College	WI	55,206	HC
Bloomfield College	NJ	40,100	LC
Columbia College Chicago	IL	40,104	C
Goddard College	VT	17,040	VC
Lynn Univ	FL	49,680	LC
Mills College	CA	43,705	C
Univ of Mount Union	OH	39,990	C

INTERNATIONAL BUSINESS

School	ST	$IS	SR
Arkansas State Univ	AR	16,190	C
Ashford Univ	CA	10,480	C
Azusa Pacific Univ	CA	43,972	C
Baldwin Wallace Univ	OH	42,464	VC
Bethany College	WV	38,774	LC
Bloomfield College	NJ	40,100	LC
Bradley Univ	IL	43,240	VC
Bryant Univ	RI	57,204	VC
Cal State, Fullerton	CA	21,902	C
Cal State, Long Beach	CA	18,850	C
Campbell Univ	NC	37,570	VC
Cedarville Univ	OH	36,244	VC
Creighton Univ	NE	49,452	VC
Dallas Baptist Univ	TX	35,220	VC
Drexel Univ	PA	65,927	HC
Grove City College	PA	26,654	VC
Illinois State Univ	IL	23,418	VC
John Brown Univ	AR	35,184	VC
Kutztown Univ of Pennsylvania	PA	19,477	C
La Salle Univ	PA	43,476	C
Lake Superior State Univ	MI	19,867	C
Lebanon Valley College	PA	55,510	VC
Lewis Univ	IL	41,710	C
Lynn Univ	FL	49,680	LC
Messiah College	PA	44,380	VC
Millersville Univ of Pennsylvania	PA	25,298	C
Minn State Univ, Mankato	MN	17,190	C
Missouri Southern State Univ	MO	13,071	C
Murray State Univ	KY	17,726	C+
Niagara Univ	NY	41,010	C
Northwest Missouri State Univ	MO	18,286	C
Ohio Wesleyan Univ	OH	49,460	VC
Okla Baptist Univ	OK	33,990	C
Rochester Inst of Technology	NY	52,734	HC+
St. Louis Univ	MO	49,866	HC
St. Mary's Univ of Minn	MN	42,440	C
Salisbury Univ	MD	21,132	VC
San Jose State Univ	CA	22,630	C
St. Ambrose Univ	IA	40,180	C
Tarleton State Univ	TX	15,248	LC
Taylor Univ	IN	42,130	VC
Texas Tech Univ	TX	20,156	C+
Thomas Edison State Univ	NJ	6,350	NC
Trinity Univ	TX	54,480	MC
Univ of Cincinnati	OH	22,118	VC
Univ of Evansville	IN	44,186	C+
Univ of Georgia	GA	21,878	HC
Univ of Mary Hardin-Baylor	TX	35,292	C+
Univ of N Car at Greensboro	NC	15,998	C
Univ of Northwestern - St. Paul	MN	39,530	C
Univ of Okla	OK	19,651	HC
Univ of Redlands	CA	61,934	VC
Univ of San Francisco	CA	60,580	C
Univ of St. Thomas - Houston	TX	41,510	VC
Univ of Wisc-Eau Claire	WI	16,354	VC
Univ of Wisc-Milwaukee	WI	21,538	C
Washington State Univ	WA	22,747	C
West Chester Univ of Pennsylvania	PA	19,171	VC
West Virginia Wesleyan College	WV	39,188	C
Western New England Univ	MA	49,182	C

INTERNATIONAL BUSINESS INFORMATION SYSTEMS

School	ST	$IS	SR
Concordia College - New York	NY	39,035	LC
Holy Family Univ	PA	44,672	LC
Missouri Southern State Univ	MO	13,071	C
North Greenville Univ	SC	25,930	C
Univ of Texas at Arlington	TX	18,876	C

INTERNATIONAL BUSINESS MANAGEMENT

School	ST	$IS	SR
Adams State Univ	CO	15,420	LC
Adrian College	MI	45,550	C
Alma College	MI	49,410	VC
Alverno College	WI	33,294	LC
American International College	MA	47,020	LC
Angelo State Univ	TX	15,882	LC
Appalachian State Univ	NC	15,394	VC
Aquinas College - Mich	MI	38,876	VC
Arcadia Univ	PA	55,990	C+
Assumption College	MA	48,455	VC
Auburn Univ	AL	24,300	VC+
Augsburg Univ	MN	45,129	C
Augustana College	IL	51,222	VC+
Avila Univ	MO	27,100	C
Barry Univ	FL	38,730	LC
Baylor Univ	TX	56,803	HC
Belmont Univ	TN	44,500	VC+
Benedictine Univ	IL	38,300	C
Berkeley College/New Jersey	NJ	38,082	LC
Berkeley College/New York City Campus	NY	35,100	LC
Berkeley College/White Plains Campus	NY	35,100	LC
Berry College	GA	47,466	VC
Bethune-Cookman Univ	FL	23,322	C
Biola Univ	CA	48,686	C
Bloomfield College	NJ	40,100	LC
Bloomsburg Univ of Pennsylvania	PA	19,930	C
Boise State Univ	ID	17,368	C
Brigham Young Univ/Hawaii	HI	11,710	C
Butler Univ	IN	52,890	VC+
Caldwell Univ	NJ	42,165	LC
Calif State Polytechnic Univ, Pomona	CA	21,811	C
Cal State, Fullerton	CA	21,902	C
Cal State, Long Beach	CA	18,850	C
Cal State, Sacramento	CA	19,060	C
Cal State, San Bernardino	CA	20,106	C
Campbell Univ	NC	37,570	VC
Canisius College	NY	49,672	C
Cardinal Stritch Univ	WI	37,136	C
Catawba College	NC	39,820	LC
Central Mich Univ	MI	20,330	C
Central Washington Univ	WA	16,803	C
Champlain College	VT	54,724	VC
Chatham Univ	PA	47,883	VC
Clarion Univ of Pennsylvania	PA	21,608	LC
College of Charleston	SC	24,046	VC
College of the Ozarks	MO	7,530	VC
Columbia College - Missouri	MO	28,179	C
Concordia College - Moorhead	MN	46,418	C
Cornerstone Univ	MI	36,550	C
Davenport Univ	MI	25,896	LC
Dickinson College	PA	66,166	MC
Dominican College	NY	40,258	LC
Dominican Univ	IL	42,472	C+
Dominican Univ of Calif	CA	58,750	C
Drake Univ	IA	49,220	HC
Drury Univ	MO	37,555	VC
Duquesne Univ	PA	48,508	VC
Eastern Mennonite Univ	VA	42,550	C
Eastern Mich Univ	MI	19,761	C
Eckerd College	FL	55,206	VC
Elizabethtown College	PA	56,340	VC
Elmhurst College	IL	46,514	C
Elms College	MA	49,602	VC
Elon Univ	NC	46,142	HC
Endicott College	MA	47,054	C+
Excelsior College	NY	38,800	SP
Fairfield Univ	CT	61,445	HC
Felician Univ	NJ	46,280	LC
Fitchburg State Univ	MA	21,819	LC

ST = STATE $IS = IN-STATE COSTS SR = SELECTOR RATING

School	ST	$IS	SR
Florida Atlantic Univ	FL	18,256	C
Florida Inst of Technology	FL	53,306	VC
Florida International Univ	FL	20,281	C
Florida State Univ	FL	16,771	HC
Fordham Univ	NY	68,431	MC
Franciscan Univ of Steubenville	OH	33,980	VC
Friends Univ	KS	38,000	C
Gannon Univ	PA	42,922	C
Gardner-Webb Univ	NC	24,935	C+
Georgetown College	KY	41,440	C
Georgetown Univ	DC	68,970	MC
Golden Gate Univ	CA	19,510	C
Goldey-Beacom College	DE	36,038	C
Graceland Univ	IA	35,290	C
Grand Valley State Univ	MI	22,250	C+
Gustavus Adolphus College	MN	53,943	HC
Hamline Univ	MN	50,152	C
Harding Univ	AR	25,440	C
Hawaii Pacific Univ	HI	33,420	C
High Point Univ	NC	47,355	VC
Hilbert College	NY	32,650	LC
Hillsdale College	MI	37,170	MC
Hofstra Univ	NY	58,210	C+
Howard Univ	DC	37,616	C+
Illinois Wesleyan Univ	IL	56,430	VC+
Indiana Univ of Pennsylvania	PA	24,474	C
Iona College	NY	52,514	C
Iowa State Univ	IA	18,176	C
Jacksonville Univ	FL	49,210	C
James Madison Univ	VA	19,084	VC
Jefferson (Philadelphia Univ + Thomas Jefferson Univ)	PA	53,966	C
John Carroll Univ	OH	51,570	C
Johnson & Wales Univ/ Providence Campus	RI	44,768	C
Judson Univ	IL	39,174	C
Juniata College	PA	58,118	VC
Kean Univ	NJ	25,620	C
Keiser Univ	FL	35,010	LC
Kennesaw State Univ	GA	18,899	VC
King's College	PA	48,240	C
Kutztown Univ of Pennsylvania	PA	19,477	C
La Roche College	PA	38,940	C
La Sierra Univ	CA	39,690	VC
Lake Erie College	OH	38,914	LC
Lake Superior State Univ	MI	19,867	C
Lakeland Univ	WI	35,130	C
Lasell College	MA	49,400	C
Lawrence Tech Univ	MI	41,630	VC
Lenoir-Rhyne Univ	NC	47,500	LC
Linfield College	OR	53,992	C
Lipscomb Univ	TN	42,984	VC
Loyola Univ Chicago	IL	57,158	VC
Loyola Univ New Orleans	LA	52,456	VC
Madonna Univ	MI	30,450	LC
Maine Maritime Academy	ME	22,536	C
Manhattan College	NY	55,652	C
Marietta College	OH	46,190	C
Marquette Univ	WI	53,090	VC+
Marshall Univ	WV	18,044	C
Maryville Univ of St. Louis	MO	38,558	VC
Marywood Univ	PA	47,840	C
Mass Maritime Academy	MA	20,704	C
Menlo College	CA	51,380	LC
Mercer Univ	GA	45,348	VC
Merrimack College	MA	55,415	C
Metropolitan State Univ	MN	7,859	C
MidAmerica Nazarene Univ	KS	37,808	C
Millikin Univ	IL	44,148	C
Minn State Univ, Mankato	MN	17,190	C
Minn State Univ, Moorhead	MN	21,393	C
Minot State Univ	ND	13,285	C
Monmouth College	IL	42,260	C
Monmouth Univ	NJ	50,184	C
Moravian College	PA	55,488	C
Mount Vernon Nazarene Univ	OH	35,944	C
Muskingum Univ	OH	35,966	C
Nazareth College	NY	46,784	C
Nebr Wesleyan Univ	NE	42,026	C+
New Mexico State Univ	NM	14,050	LC
New York Inst of Technology	NY	49,980	VC
New York Univ	NY	68,139	MC
Nichols College	MA	46,900	LC
North Central College	IL	48,712	C+
North Park Univ	IL	35,860	C
Northeastern Univ	MA	65,352	MC
Northern State Univ	SD	15,570	C
Northwest Missouri State Univ	MO	18,286	C
Northwest Univ	WA	38,720	VC
Northwood Univ - Mich	MI	35,010	LC
Notre Dame de Namur Univ	CA	46,526	LC
Notre Dame of Maryland Univ	MD	47,570	VC
Ohio Dominican Univ	OH	41,340	C+
Ohio Northern Univ	OH	44,050	VC
Ohio State Univ at Columbus	OH	22,843	MC
Ohio Univ	OH	23,394	VC
Ohio Wesleyan Univ	OH	49,460	VC
Okla Christian Univ	OK	29,260	C
Okla State Univ	OK	17,180	C+
Old Dominion Univ	VA	21,618	C
Olivet College	MI	37,661	LC
Olivet Nazarene Univ	IL	41,840	VC
Oral Roberts Univ	OK	34,316	C
Pace Univ	NY	60,136	C
Palm Beach Atlantic Univ	FL	39,250	C
Pepperdine Univ	CA	66,862	VC+
Pfeiffer Univ	NC	40,532	LC
Pittsburg State Univ	KS	13,880	C
Quinnipiac Univ	CT	60,970	VC
Ramapo College of New Jersey	NJ	25,760	VC
Regis Univ	CO	46,380	C
Rider Univ	NJ	54,050	C
Roberts Wesleyan College	NY	41,116	C
Rochester Inst of Technology	NY	52,734	HC+
Roger Williams Univ	RI	48,074	VC
Rollins College	FL	58,670	HC
Saginaw Valley State Univ	MI	19,284	C
St. Augustine's Univ	NC	25,582	C
St. Joseph's Univ	PA	58,540	VC
St. Peter's Univ	NJ	49,192	C
St. Vincent College	PA	46,229	C
St. Xavier Univ	IL	44,440	C
Salem College	NC	40,206	C
Salve Regina Univ	RI	53,046	VC
San Diego State Univ	CA	23,156	VC
San Francisco State Univ	CA	18,514	LC
San Jose State Univ	CA	22,630	C
Seattle Univ	WA	54,957	VC
Seton Hill Univ	PA	46,972	VC
Simpson College	IA	45,626	VC
Slippery Rock Univ of Pennsylvania	PA	20,450	C
Southeast Missouri State Univ	MO	16,148	C
Southern Adventist Univ	TN	28,250	C
Southern Illinois Univ Edwardsville	IL	20,188	C
Southern New Hampshire Univ	NH	44,256	C
Southwest Baptist Univ	MO	30,890	LC
Spring Hill College	AL	48,488	C
St. Catherine Univ	MN	45,630	C
St. Cloud State Univ	MN	10,600	C
St. Edward's Univ	TX	56,190	VC
St. John's Univ	NY	57,160	C+
St. Mary's Univ	TX	39,120	C
St. Norbert College	WI	46,060	VC
St. Thomas Univ	FL	51,187	LC
SUNY at New Paltz	NY	20,840	C
SUNY/Plattsburgh	NY	19,314	C
Stephen F. Austin State Univ	TX	18,484	LC
Stetson Univ	FL	57,174	VC+
Stonehill College	MA	55,130	C
Suffolk Univ	MA	52,316	C
Taylor Univ	IN	42,130	VC
Temple Univ	PA	24,392	C+
The American Univ	DC	61,317	HC
The College at Brockport - SUNY	NY	21,058	C
The George Washington Univ	DC	68,474	HC+
The Univ of Akron	OH	22,566	C
The Univ of Memphis	TN	18,278	C
Thiel College	PA	42,950	LC
Trinity International Univ	IL	31,070	VC
Truman State Univ	MO	16,286	MC
Union College	KY	32,310	C
Univ of Arkansas at Fayetteville	AR	19,766	VC
Univ of Bridgeport	CT	44,985	LC
Univ of Dayton	OH	54,930	VC
Univ of Denver	CO	61,129	VC+
Univ of Findlay	OH	43,040	C
Univ of Hawaii at Manoa	HI	23,261	C
Univ of Houston-Downtown	TX	7,241	LC
Univ of Indianapolis	IN	36,480	VC
Univ of La Verne	CA	55,600	C
Univ of Maryland/College Park	MD	21,938	HC
Univ of Missouri-St. Louis	MO	19,810	VC
Univ of Montana	MT	14,105	C
Univ of Nebr - Lincoln	NE	18,589	VC
Univ of Nevada, Las Vegas	NV	17,553	C
Univ of N Car at Charlotte	NC	17,803	VC
Univ of N Car at Greensboro	NC	15,998	C
Univ of North Florida	FL	15,996	VC
Univ of Northwestern - St. Paul	MN	39,530	C
Univ of Okla	OK	19,651	HC
Univ of Pittsburgh	PA	30,030	MC
Univ of Portland	OR	52,152	VC
Univ of PR, at Humacao	PR	14,000	
Univ of Rio Grande & Rio Grande Community College	OH	8,750	LC
Univ of San Diego	CA	60,338	HC
Univ of Scranton	PA	54,962	VC
Univ of Southern Calif	CA	66,631	MC
Univ of Southern Miss	MS	13,170	C
Univ of St. Francis	IL	40,828	C
Univ of Tampa	FL	38,928	VC
Univ of Texas at Dallas	TX	23,640	HC
Univ of Texas Rio Grande Valley	TX	15,573	LC
Univ of Tulsa	OK	52,625	HC
Univ of Washington	WA	23,091	MC
Univ of Wisc-La Crosse	WI	15,425	VC
Univ of Wisc-Madison	WI	21,647	MC
Univ of Wisc-Superior	WI	14,838	C
Utah State Univ	UT	13,235	C
Vanguard Univ of Southern Calif	CA	42,400	VC
Villanova Univ	PA	64,922	MC
Walsh Univ	OH	39,010	C
Washburn Univ	KS	15,827	C
Washington & Jefferson College	PA	58,694	VC
Washington State Univ	WA	22,747	C
Washington Univ in St. Louis	MO	67,539	MC
Waynesburg Univ	PA	33,530	C
Wesleyan College	GA	31,940	C+
Western Carolina Univ	NC	13,965	C
Western New Mexico Univ	NM	16,914	LC
Western Washington Univ	WA	18,904	VC
Westminster College	MO	32,820	C
Westminster College	PA	41,722	C
Westminster College	UT	41,078	C
Whitworth Univ	WA	53,682	VC
Wichita State Univ	KS	17,773	C
Widener Univ	PA	58,190	C
William Jewell College	MO	42,490	C+
Xavier Univ	OH	49,380	VC

INTERNATIONAL ECONOMICS

School	ST	$IS	SR
Austin College	TX	51,059	HC
Belmont Univ	TN	44,500	VC+
Beloit College	WI	55,206	HC
Bethany College	WV	38,774	LC
Bryant Univ	RI	57,204	VC
Carthage College	WI	48,835	C
Colo College	CO	64,894	MC
Cornerstone Univ	MI	36,550	C
Elon Univ	NC	46,142	HC
Fitchburg State Univ	MA	21,819	LC
Georgia Inst of Technology	GA	23,910	MC
La Salle Univ	PA	43,476	C
Lafayette College	PA	68,520	MC
Louisiana State Univ and A&M College	LA	18,677	VC
Middlebury College	VT	67,464	MC
Midwestern State Univ	TX	12,111	LC
Pontifical Catholic Univ of PR	PR	10,534	
St. Louis Univ	MO	49,866	HC
Seattle Univ	WA	54,957	VC
Southwestern Adventist Univ	TX	28,232	LC
St. Catherine Univ	MN	45,630	C
St. Lawrence Univ	NY	66,646	HC+
Suffolk Univ	MA	52,316	C
Texas Christian Univ	TX	57,120	HC
Texas Tech Univ	TX	20,156	C+
The Catholic Univ of America	DC	58,376	VC
The College of Idaho	ID	36,415	C
Univ of Bridgeport	CT	44,985	LC
Univ of Calif, Santa Cruz	CA	28,731	C+
Univ of Notre Dame	IN	68,801	MC
Univ of Puget Sound	WA	60,210	HC
Univ of San Francisco	CA	60,580	C
Univ of Vermont	VT	29,792	HC
Univ of West Georgia	GA	17,510	LC
Valparaiso Univ	IN	50,160	VC
Washington Univ in St. Louis	MO	67,539	MC
Weber State Univ	UT	14,112	C
Western Washington Univ	WA	18,904	VC

INTERNATIONAL FINANCE

School	ST	$IS	SR
Bryant Univ	RI	57,204	VC
Bucknell Univ	PA	67,136	MC
Univ of Miami	FL	63,494	MC

INTERNATIONAL MARKETING

School	ST	$IS	SR
Bryant Univ	RI	57,204	VC
Pace Univ	NY	60,136	C
Univ of Miami	FL	63,494	MC

INTERNATIONAL POLITICAL SCIENCE

School	ST	$IS	SR
Carnegie Mellon Univ	PA	67,980	MC
La Salle Univ	PA	43,476	C
New England College	NH	50,828	NC
Reed College	OR	65,300	MC
Univ of Georgia	GA	21,878	HC
Univ of Mount Union	OH	39,990	C
Univ of North Georgia	GA	17,316	C

INTERNATIONAL PUBLIC SERVICE

School	ST	$IS	SR
Baylor Univ	TX	56,803	HC
Union College	NE	23,270	C
Univ of Texas at Dallas	TX	23,640	HC
Valparaiso Univ	IN	50,160	VC

INTERNATIONAL RELATIONS

School	ST	$IS	SR
Agnes Scott College	GA	51,930	VC+
Alverno College	WI	33,294	LC
American International College	MA	47,020	LC
Aquinas College - Mich	MI	38,876	VC
Augsburg Univ	MN	45,129	C
Beloit College	WI	55,206	HC
Bennington College	VT	66,280	MC
Bethany College	WV	38,774	LC
Bethel Univ	MN	46,550	C+
Boston Univ	MA	67,352	MC
Brigham Young Univ	UT	13,248	MC
Brown Univ	RI	64,566	MC
Bryant Univ	RI	57,204	VC
Bucknell Univ	PA	67,136	MC
Cal State, Chico	CA	19,790	VC
Cal State, Fullerton	CA	21,902	C
Cal State, Sacramento	CA	19,060	C
Calvin College	MI	43,090	HC
Canisius College	NY	49,672	C
Capital Univ	OH	44,778	VC
Carleton College	MN	66,414	MC
Carroll College	MT	44,304	C
Centre College	KY	50,680	MC
Chaminade Univ of Honolulu	HI	37,614	C
Chatham Univ	PA	47,883	VC
CUNY/Hunter College	NY	31,098	VC
CUNY/Lehman College	NY	5,788	LC
Claremont McKenna College	CA	69,900	MC
Clark Univ	MA	53,260	HC+
Cleveland State Univ	OH	22,290	C
Colgate Univ	NY	67,500	MC
College of William & Mary	VA	34,907	MC
Conn College	CT	65,000	MC
Cornell College	IA	49,900	VC
Creighton Univ	NE	49,452	VC
Dominican Univ	IL	42,472	C+
Drake Univ	IA	49,220	HC
Drew Univ/College of Liberal Arts	NJ	53,608	VC
Duquesne Univ	PA	48,508	VC
Eastern Mich Univ	MI	19,761	C
Eastern Washington Univ	WA	17,896	LC
Eckerd College	FL	55,206	VC
Edgewood College	WI	35,950	C
Emmanuel College	MA	53,472	C+
Florida International Univ	FL	20,281	C
Florida State Univ	FL	16,771	HC
George Mason Univ	VA	19,884	C
Georgetown Univ	DC	68,970	MC
Georgia Inst of Technology	GA	23,910	MC
Gettysburg College	PA	65,210	MC
Goucher College	MD	56,110	VC
Grand Valley State Univ	MI	22,250	C+
Hamilton College	NY	64,250	MC
Hampden-Sydney College	VA	57,806	VC
Hampshire College	MA	65,214	MC
Hawaii Pacific Univ	HI	33,420	C
Hendrix College	AR	54,020	VC
High Point Univ	NC	47,355	VC
Hobart and William Smith Colleges	NY	67,050	HC+
Illinois College	IL	41,330	VC
Immaculata Univ	PA	39,000	C
Iowa State Univ	IA	18,176	C
Kent State Univ	OH	20,928	C
King Univ	TN	36,976	C
Knox College	IL	54,654	VC+
Lafayette College	PA	68,520	MC
Lake Forest College	IL	50,652	VC
Le Moyne College	NY	47,305	VC
Lehigh Univ	PA	63,860	MC
Lewis & Clark College	OR	60,984	MC
Lewis Univ	IL	41,710	C
Linfield College	OR	53,992	C
Loras College	IA	40,726	C
Loyola Marymount Univ	CA	60,202	VC+
Marquette Univ	WI	53,090	VC+
Marshall Univ	WV	18,044	C
Mary Baldwin Univ	VA	40,495	C
Maryville College	TN	44,410	C
McKendree Univ	IL	37,940	C+
Miami Univ	OH	27,190	HC+
Mich State Univ	MI	24,542	VC
Middle Tenn State Univ	TN	8,650	C
Mills College	CA	43,705	C
Minn State Univ, Mankato	MN	17,190	C
Morningside College	IA	39,780	C
Mount Holyoke College	MA	56,746	MC
Muskingum Univ	OH	35,966	C
New York Univ	NY	68,139	MC
North Park Univ	IL	35,860	C
Northern Arizona Univ	AZ	21,003	C
Northwestern State Univ of Louisiana	LA	16,534	LC
Notre Dame of Maryland Univ	MD	47,570	VC
Nova Southeastern Univ	FL	38,534	C+
Oakland Univ	MI	20,763	C
Occidental College	CA	68,660	MC
Ohio Wesleyan Univ	OH	49,460	VC
Okla Baptist Univ	OK	33,990	C
Oral Roberts Univ	OK	34,316	C
Pitzer College	CA	68,500	HC+
Pomona College	CA	64,957	MC
Princeton Univ	NJ	60,090	MC
Principia College	IL	40,350	C
Regis College	MA	51,920	LC
Roanoke College	VA	55,952	VC
Rockhurst Univ	MO	28,990	C
Roger Williams Univ	RI	48,074	VC
Rollins College	FL	58,670	HC
St. Joseph's Univ	PA	58,540	VC
St. Louis Univ	MO	49,866	HC
St. Michael's College	VT	53,275	VC+
Samford Univ	AL	40,770	VC
San Francisco State Univ	CA	18,514	LC
Seton Hall Univ	NJ	58,008	C
Shaw Univ	NC	24,638	C
Shawnee State Univ	OH	16,998	C
Simmons College	MA	54,400	HC

School	ST	$IS	SR
Simpson College	IA	45,626	VC
Skidmore College	NY	66,600	MC
Smith College	MA	66,774	MC
Southern Methodist Univ	TX	69,008	MC
Southwestern Adventist Univ	TX	28,232	LC
St. Catherine Univ	MN	45,630	C
St. Cloud State Univ	MN	10,600	C
St. Edward's Univ	TX	56,190	VC
St. Mary's Univ	TX	39,120	C
St. Norbert College	WI	46,060	VC
St. Thomas Univ	FL	51,187	LC
Stanford Univ	CA	62,541	MC
SUNY at Geneseo	NY	21,622	VC
SUNY at New Paltz	NY	20,840	C
Suffolk Univ	MA	52,316	C
Syracuse Univ	NY	62,313	HC
Taylor Univ	IN	42,130	VC
Texas State Univ	TX	18,721	C
The College of Wooster	OH	60,000	HC
The George Washington Univ	DC	68,474	HC+
Trinity Univ	TX	54,480	MC
Tufts Univ	MA		MC
Univ of Arkansas at Fayetteville	AR	19,766	VC
Univ of Calif at Davis	CA	28,468	HC
Univ of Colo Boulder	CO	26,048	HC
Univ of Delaware	DE	32,214	VC
Univ of Idaho	ID	16,158	C
Univ of Indianapolis	IN	36,480	VC
Univ of Lynchburg	VA	48,370	C
Univ of Mary Washington	VA	23,039	C+
Univ of Minn/Twin Cities	MN	24,269	MC
Univ of Nevada, Reno	NV	18,010	C
Univ of Northern Colo	CO	19,658	C
Univ of Pennsylvania	PA	63,526	MC
Univ of Redlands	CA	61,934	VC
Univ of Rochester	NY	65,032	MC
Univ of San Diego	CA	60,338	HC
Univ of South Florida/Tampa	FL	16,110	VC
Univ of Southern Calif	CA	66,631	MC
Univ of the Pacific	CA	57,446	VC
Univ of Toledo	OH	19,336	C
Univ of Virginia	VA	27,367	MC
Univ of Washington	WA	23,091	MC
Univ of Wisc-Madison	WI	21,647	MC
Ursinus College	PA	62,920	VC
Utah State Univ	UT	13,235	C
Valparaiso Univ	IN	50,160	VC
Virginia Wesleyan Univ	VA	45,980	LC
Walsh Univ	OH	39,010	C
Wartburg College	IA	49,478	C
Washington Univ in St. Louis	MO	67,539	MC
Webster Univ	MO	37,490	C
Wellesley College	MA	66,984	MC
Wesleyan College	GA	31,940	C+
West Chester Univ of Pennsylvania	PA	19,171	VC
Westminster College	PA	41,722	C
Wheaton College	IL	44,993	MC
Wheaton College	MA	63,818	VC
Widener Univ	PA	58,190	C
William Jewell College	MO	42,490	C+
Wilson College	PA	35,620	LC
Wittenberg Univ	OH	49,863	VC
Wright State Univ	OH	16,983	C

INTERNATIONAL SECURITY/ CONFLECT RESOLUTION MANAGEMENT

School	ST	$IS	SR
Baldwin Wallace Univ	OH	42,464	VC
Cal State, Fullerton	CA	21,902	C
San Diego State Univ	CA	23,156	VC

INTERNATIONAL STUDIES

School	ST	$IS	SR
Adrian College	MI	45,550	C
Albion College	MI	55,260	C
Allegheny College	PA	57,620	VC
Aquinas College - Mich	MI	38,876	VC
Arcadia Univ	PA	55,990	C+
Arkansas Tech Univ	AR	16,534	LC
Ashland Univ	OH	30,446	C
Assumption College	MA	48,455	VC
Auburn Univ at Montgomery	AL	15,000	C
Augustana Univ	SD	39,968	VC
Austin College	TX	51,059	HC
Azusa Pacific Univ	CA	43,972	C
Baker Univ	KS	37,190	C
Baldwin Wallace Univ	OH	42,464	VC
Ball State Univ	IN	19,808	C+
Bard College	NY	65,924	HC
Barnard College/Columbia Univ	NY	68,762	MC
Barry Univ	FL	38,730	LC
Belhaven Univ	MS	32,250	C
Bellarmine Univ	KY	52,532	C
Benedictine Univ	IL	38,300	C
Bennington College	VT	66,280	MC
Berry College	GA	47,466	VC
Bethel College	IN	36,830	C
Bethune-Cookman Univ	FL	23,322	C
Bowling Green State Univ	OH	19,975	C
Bradley Univ	IL	43,240	VC
Brandeis Univ	MA	68,443	MC
Brenau Univ - Women's College	GA	37,876	LC
Brigham Young Univ/Hawaii	HI	11,710	C
Brown Univ	RI	64,566	MC
Bryant Univ	RI	57,204	VC
Bryn Mawr College	PA	65,220	MC
Butler Univ	IN	52,890	VC+
Calif Baptist Univ	CA	42,986	C
Calif Lutheran Univ	CA	52,853	C
Cal State, East Bay	CA	20,748	C
Cal State, Fullerton	CA	21,902	C
Cal State, Long Beach	CA	18,850	C
Cal State, Monterey Bay	CA	22,872	LC
Calvin College	MI	43,090	HC
Case Western Reserve Univ	OH	62,284	MC
Cedarville Univ	OH	36,244	VC
Centenary College	NJ	43,890	LC
Central College	IA	44,592	C
Central Conn State Univ	CT	22,041	C
Chatham Univ	PA	47,883	VC
Chestnut Hill College	PA	47,180	C
CUNY/City College	NY	20,204	C
Clark Univ	MA	53,260	HC+
College of Charleston	SC	24,046	VC
College of Staten Island	NY	24,389	LC
College of the Holy Cross	MA	64,320	MC
Colo State Univ	CO	23,033	C
Concordia College - Moorhead	MN	46,418	C
Concordia College - New York	NY	39,035	LC
Concordia Univ Irvine	CA	44,860	VC
Coppin State Univ	MD	14,071	VC
Culver-Stockton College	MO	34,350	C
Defiance College	OH	42,240	LC
Denison Univ	OH	62,770	HC+
DePaul Univ	IL	52,807	VC
Dickinson College	PA	66,166	MC
Doane Univ	NE	41,340	VC
Dominican Univ of Calif	CA	58,750	C
Drexel Univ	PA	65,927	HC
D'Youville College	NY	37,678	C
Earlham College	IN	55,670	HC
East Texas Baptist Univ	TX	34,444	C
Elmira College	NY	53,900	C
Elms College	MA	49,602	VC
Elon Univ	NC	46,142	HC
Emmanuel College	MA	53,472	C+
Emory and Henry College	VA	46,320	C
Emory Univ	GA	63,286	MC
Endicott College	MA	47,054	C+
Evangel Univ	MO	28,898	C
Fairfield Univ	CT	61,445	HC
Fairleigh Dickinson Univ/ Metropolitan Campus	NJ	52,392	C
Ferrum College	VA	43,970	C
Flagler College	FL	27,620	C
Fordham Univ	NY	68,431	MC
Francis Marion Univ	SC	18,144	LC
Frostburg State Univ	MD	17,280	LC
Gallaudet Univ	DC	30,088	LC
Gannon Univ	PA	42,922	C
George Fox Univ	OR	42,938	C
Georgia Inst of Technology	GA	23,910	MC
Georgia Southern Univ	GA	16,540	VC
Gettysburg College	PA	65,210	MC
Gonzaga Univ	WA	52,880	HC
Graceland Univ	IA	35,290	C
Grand Canyon Univ	AZ	25,150	VC
Greenville College	IL	27,012	LC
Guilford College	NC	45,973	C
Hampshire College	MA	65,214	MC
Hanover College	IN	47,750	C+
Harding Univ	AR	25,440	C
Hawaii Pacific Univ	HI	33,420	C
Heidelberg Univ	OH	40,400	LC
Hollins Univ	VA	49,635	VC
Hood College	MD	50,540	C
Hope College	MI	42,840	VC
Houghton College	NY	40,558	VC
Idaho State Univ	ID	13,619	LC
Illinois Wesleyan Univ	IL	56,430	VC+
Indiana Univ Bloomington	IN	20,791	HC
Indiana Univ East	IN	7,207	C
Indiana Univ of Pennsylvania	PA	24,474	C
Indiana Univ Southeast	IN	16,931	C
Indiana Univ-Purdue Univ Indianapolis	IN	18,952	C
Iona College	NY	52,514	C
Jacksonville Univ	FL	49,210	C
James Madison Univ	VA	19,084	VC
Johns Hopkins Univ	MD	68,080	MC
Juniata College	PA	58,118	VC
Kalamazoo College	MI	53,931	HC
Kennesaw State Univ	GA	18,899	VC
Kenyon College	OH	65,840	MC
Knox College	IL	54,654	VC+
La Roche College	PA	38,940	C
Lawrence Univ	WI	56,133	HC+
Le Moyne College	NY	47,305	VC
Liberty Univ	VA	31,415	C
Lindenwood Univ	MO	25,760	C
Lipscomb Univ	TN	42,984	VC
LIU Post	NY	50,698	C+
Lock Haven Univ of Pennsylvania	PA	20,544	LC
Louisiana State Univ and A&M College	LA	18,677	VC
Loyola Univ Chicago	IL	57,158	VC
Luther College	IA	49,990	VC
Lycoming College	PA	50,895	C
Macalester College	MN	64,136	MC
Malone Univ	OH	39,200	C
Manhattanville College	NY	52,430	C
Marlboro College	VT	50,832	VC+
Mars Hill Univ	NC	41,104	C
Marymount Manhattan College	NY	48,350	C
Maryville Univ of St. Louis	MO	38,558	VC
McKendree Univ	IL	37,940	C+
Meredith College	NC	46,634	C
Methodist Univ	NC	58,130	C
Miami Univ	OH	27,190	HC+
Millersville Univ of Pennsylvania	PA	25,298	C
Minn State Univ, Moorhead	MN	21,393	C
Monmouth College	IL	42,260	C
Morehouse College	GA	40,835	C
Mount Mary Univ	WI	34,650	LC
Mount Mercy Univ	IA	39,748	C
Mount St. Mary's Univ	MD	53,380	C
Muhlenberg College	PA	56,645	VC
Murray State Univ	KY	17,726	C+
National Univ	CA	17,849	LC
Nazareth College	NY	46,784	C
Nebr Wesleyan Univ	NE	42,026	C+
New College of Florida	FL	16,180	HC+
Niagara Univ	NY	41,010	C
N Dak State Univ	ND	16,245	VC
Northern Mich Univ	MI	20,853	C
Northwest Christian Univ	OR	36,580	C
Northwest Nazarene Univ	ID	40,250	C
Northwestern Univ	IL	68,725	MC
Norwich Univ	VT	56,234	C
Oakwood Univ	AL	43,758	C
Oberlin College	OH	68,942	MC
Oglethorpe Univ	GA	44,200	C
Ohio Northern Univ	OH	44,050	VC
Ohio State Univ at Columbus	OH	22,843	MC
Ohio Univ	OH	23,394	VC
Old Dominion Univ	VA	21,618	C
Oral Roberts Univ	OK	34,316	C
Oregon State Univ	OR	23,337	VC
Otterbein Univ	OH	41,630	C
Pepperdine Univ	CA	66,862	VC+
Pittsburg State Univ	KS	13,880	C
Point Loma Nazarene Univ	CA	46,150	C+
Point Park Univ	PA	41,270	C
Portland State Univ	OR	19,443	C
Presbyterian College	SC	47,186	C
Prescott College	AZ	38,201	C
Ramapo College of New Jersey	NJ	25,760	VC
Randolph College	VA	53,970	C
Randolph-Macon College	VA	51,480	VC
Rhodes College	TN	51,900	HC
Ripon College	WI	49,991	VC
Rockford Univ	IL	38,570	C
Roosevelt Univ	IL	41,890	VC
Russell Sage College	NY	39,370	C
Saginaw Valley State Univ	MI	19,284	C
St. Francis Univ	PA	46,146	NC
St. Mary's College	IN	50,600	C
St. Mary's College of Calif	CA	57,420	C
St. Peter's Univ	NJ	49,192	C
Salisbury Univ	MD	21,132	VC
Salve Regina Univ	RI	53,046	VC
San Diego State Univ	CA	23,156	VC
Seattle Univ	WA	54,957	VC
Seton Hill Univ	PA	46,972	VC
Sewanee: The Univ of the South	TN	58,000	HC+
Shaw Univ	NC	24,638	C
Shippensburg Univ of Pennsylvania	PA	24,096	C
Sonoma State Univ	CA	27,020	C
Southern Adventist Univ	TN	28,250	C
Southern Illinois Univ Carbondale	IL	24,554	C
Southern Methodist Univ	TX	69,008	MC
Southern Nazarene Univ	OK	33,684	C
Southern Oregon Univ	OR	19,117	C
Southwestern Univ	TX	52,370	VC
Spring Hill College	AL	48,488	C
St. Ambrose Univ	IA	40,180	C
St. Bonaventure Univ	NY	45,596	C
St. Francis College	NY	38,800	LC
St. John Fisher College	NY	45,270	VC
St. Lawrence Univ	NY	66,646	HC+
St. Mary's Univ	TX	39,120	C
SUNY at Binghamton	NY	24,100	MC
SUNY at Oswego	NY	22,219	VC
SUNY/Cortland	NY	20,910	C
SUNY/Oneonta	NY	20,794	C
Stetson Univ	FL	57,174	VC+
Stonehill College	MA	55,130	C
Susquehanna Univ	PA	57,560	VC
Tabor College	KS	35,870	C
Taylor Univ	IN	42,130	VC
Texas A&M Univ at College Station	TX	20,771	VC+
Texas Lutheran Univ	TX	39,770	C
Texas State Univ	TX	18,721	C
The American Univ	DC	61,317	HC
The College at Brockport - SUNY	NY	21,058	C
The College of New Jersey	NJ	28,675	VC+
The College of New Rochelle	NY	46,300	LC
The Univ of Alabama	AL	24,320	C+
The Univ of Memphis	TN	18,278	C
The Univ of Tenn at Martin	TN	15,212	C
The Univ of Utah	UT	18,751	VC
The Univ of Virginia's College at Wise	VA	18,192	LC
Thomas College	ME	73,888	LC
Thomas Edison State Univ	NJ	6,350	NC
Thomas More College	KY	36,720	LC
Towson Univ	MD	21,878	C
Trinity College	CT	69,020	HC
Trinity Washington Univ	DC	33,826	C+
Union College	NE	23,270	C
United States Air Force Academy	CO		C
United States Military Academy at West Point	NY		HC+
Univ of Alabama at Birmingham	AL	22,092	C
Univ of Arkansas at Little Rock	AR	18,211	LC
Univ of Bridgeport	CT	44,985	LC
Univ of Calif at Irvine	CA	33,857	VC
Univ of Calif at Los Angeles	CA	27,438	HC+
Univ of Calif at Santa Barbara	CA	30,627	HC+
Univ of Calif San Diego	CA	30,450	MC
Univ of Central Florida	FL	16,379	VC
Univ of Chicago	IL	70,551	MC
Univ of Cincinnati	OH	22,118	VC
Univ of Colo Denver	CO	22,238	C
Univ of Dayton	OH	54,930	VC
Univ of Denver	CO	61,129	VC+
Univ of Evansville	IN	44,186	C+
Univ of Findlay	OH	43,040	C
Univ of Hartford	CT	49,776	C
Univ of Idaho	ID	16,158	C
Univ of Illinois at Urbana-Champaign	IL	27,006	HC
Univ of Iowa	IA	19,415	HC
Univ of Kansas	KS	20,884	VC
Univ of La Verne	CA	55,600	C
Univ of Maine	ME	21,038	VC
Univ of Maine at Farmington	ME	18,792	C
Univ of Maine at Presque Isle	ME	16,148	LC
Univ of Miami	FL	63,494	MC
Univ of Mich/Ann Arbor	MI	25,274	MC
Univ of Mich/Dearborn	MI	12,472	VC
Univ of Minn/Duluth	MN	20,292	C
Univ of Miss	MS	18,802	C
Univ of Missouri-Columbia	MO	20,463	VC
Univ of Mount Union	OH	39,990	C
Univ of Nebr - Kearney	NE	17,014	LC
Univ of Nebr - Omaha	NE	16,120	C
Univ of New Hampshire	NH	29,333	VC
Univ of New Mexico	NM	16,808	C
Univ of New Orleans	LA	12,840	C
Univ of N Car at Chapel Hill	NC	20,561	MC
Univ of N Car at Charlotte	NC	17,803	VC
Univ of N Car at Greensboro	NC	15,998	C
Univ of N Car Wilmington	NC	16,784	VC
Univ of N Dak	ND	16,673	C
Univ of North Texas	TX	20,082	C
Univ of Okla	OK	19,651	HC
Univ of Oregon	OR	24,021	VC
Univ of Pennsylvania	PA	63,526	MC
Univ of Pittsburgh	PA	30,030	MC
Univ of Richmond	VA	62,730	MC
Univ of St. Joseph	CT	49,069	C
Univ of St. Mary	KS	37,080	NC
Univ of San Francisco	CA	60,580	C
Univ of Scranton	PA	54,962	VC
Univ of South Alabama	AL	16,880	C
Univ of S Dak	SD	16,109	C
Univ of Southern Indiana	IN	16,808	C
Univ of Southern Miss	MS	13,170	C
Univ of St. Thomas - Houston	TX	41,510	VC
Univ of Tampa	FL	38,928	VC
Univ of the Pacific	CA	57,446	VC
Univ of Wisc-Madison	WI	21,647	MC
Univ of Wisc-Milwaukee	WI	21,538	C
Univ of Wisc-Oshkosh	WI	15,392	C
Univ of Wisc-Parkside	WI	15,313	C
Univ of Wisc-Platteville	WI	14,148	C
Univ of Wisc-Stevens Point	WI	14,043	C
Univ of Wisc-Superior	WI	14,838	C
Univ of Wisc-Whitewater	WI	13,976	C
Univ of Wyoming	WY	15,537	C
Vassar College	NY	68,110	MC
Virginia Commonwealth Univ	VA	23,811	VC
Virginia Military Inst	VA	26,460	VC
Virginia Polytechnic Inst and State Univ	VA	21,920	VC
Washington & Jefferson College	PA	58,694	VC
Washington College	MD	56,154	VC
Washington Univ in St. Louis	MO	67,539	MC
Waynesburg Univ	PA	33,530	C
Wells College	NY	50,500	C
Wesley College	DE	37,848	LC
West Virginia Univ	WV	18,952	VC
West Virginia Wesleyan College	WV	39,188	C
Western Mich Univ	MI	21,791	C
Western New England Univ	MA	49,182	C
Western Oregon Univ	OR	19,965	LC
Western Washington Univ	WA	18,904	VC
Westminster College	MO	32,820	C
Wheeling Jesuit Univ	WV	37,106	LC
Whitman College	WA	59,772	MC

ST = STATE $IS = IN-STATE COSTS SR = SELECTOR RATING

School	ST	$IS	SR
Whittier College	CA	57,891	C
Whitworth Univ	WA	53,682	VC
Wilkes Univ	PA	49,166	C
Willamette Univ	OR	62,514	VC+
William Woods Univ	MO	32,040	C
Wilson College	PA	35,620	LC
Worcester Polytechnic Inst	MA	62,846	MC
Xavier Univ	OH	49,380	VC
Yale Univ	CT	64,650	MC

INTERPRETER FOR THE DEAF

School	ST	$IS	SR
Bethel College	IN	36,830	C
Gallaudet Univ	DC	30,088	LC
Gardner-Webb Univ	NC	24,935	C+
Idaho State Univ	ID	13,619	LC
MacMurray College	IL	35,025	C
Madonna Univ	MI	30,450	LC
Maryville College	TN	44,410	C
Mount Aloysius College	PA	29,976	C
Quincy Univ	IL	38,170	LC
Rochester Inst of Technology	NY	52,734	HC+
St. Catherine Univ	MN	45,630	C
Univ of Arkansas at Little Rock	AR	18,211	LC
Univ of N Car at Greensboro	NC	15,998	C
Virginia Polytechnic Inst and State Univ	VA	21,920	VC
Western Oregon Univ	OR	19,965	LC
William Woods Univ	MO	32,040	C

INVESTMENTS AND SECURITIES

School	ST	$IS	SR
Bryant Univ	RI	57,204	VC
Campbell Univ	NC	37,570	VC
CUNY/Baruch College	NY	21,609	HC
St. Joseph's Univ	PA	58,540	VC
Univ of Nebr - Lincoln	NE	18,589	VC
Univ of N Dak	ND	16,673	C
Univ of North Texas	TX	20,082	C
Westminster College	UT	41,078	C

ISLAMIC STUDIES

School	ST	$IS	SR
Brandeis Univ	MA	68,443	MC
DePaul Univ	IL	52,807	VC
Gettysburg College	PA	65,210	MC
New York Univ	NY	68,139	MC
Ohio State Univ at Columbus	OH	22,843	MC
The Univ of Texas at Austin	TX	20,206	MC
Univ of Calif at Santa Barbara	CA	30,627	HC+
Univ of Mich/Ann Arbor	MI	25,274	MC
Washington Univ in St. Louis	MO	67,539	MC

ITALIAN

School	ST	$IS	SR
Arizona State Univ at the Tempe Campus	AZ	23,001	VC
Bard College	NY	65,924	HC
Barnard College/Columbia Univ	NY	68,762	MC
Bennington College	VT	66,280	MC
Boston College	MA	68,043	MC
Brigham Young Univ	UT	13,248	MC
Brown Univ	RI	64,566	MC
Bryn Mawr College	PA	65,220	MC
Cal State, Fullerton	CA	21,902	C
Central Conn State Univ	CT	22,041	C
CUNY/Brooklyn College	NY	7,163	C+
CUNY/Hunter College	NY	31,098	VC
CUNY/Lehman College	NY	5,788	LC
CUNY/Queens College	NY	21,507	C
College of the Holy Cross	MA	64,320	MC
Columbia Univ/ School of General Studies	NY	61,470	MC
Cornell Univ	NY	67,591	MC
Dartmouth College	NH	68,109	MC
DePaul Univ	IL	52,807	VC
Dominican Univ	IL	42,472	C+
Drew Univ/College of Liberal Arts	NJ	53,608	VC
Emory Univ	GA	63,286	MC
Fairfield Univ	CT	61,445	HC
Florida Atlantic Univ	FL	18,256	C
Florida International Univ	FL	20,281	C
Florida State Univ	FL	16,771	HC
Fordham Univ	NY	68,431	MC
Georgetown Univ	DC	68,970	MC
Harvard College/Harvard Univ	MA	65,609	MC
Haverford College	PA	66,490	MC
Hofstra Univ	NY	58,210	C+
Indiana Univ Bloomington	IN	20,791	HC
Iona College	NY	52,514	C
Johns Hopkins Univ	MD	68,080	MC
LIU Post	NY	50,698	C+
Loyola Univ Chicago	IL	57,158	VC
Marist College	NY	49,860	VC
Marlboro College	VT	50,832	VC+
Middlebury College	VT	67,464	MC
Montclair State Univ	NJ	26,912	C
Mount Holyoke College	MA	56,746	MC
Nazareth College	NY	46,784	C
New York Univ	NY	68,139	MC
Northeastern Illinois Univ	IL	12,529	LC
Northwestern Univ	IL	68,725	MC
Ohio State Univ at Columbus	OH	22,843	MC
Pepperdine Univ	CA	66,862	VC+
Princeton Univ	NJ	60,090	MC
Providence College	RI	62,870	HC
Rutgers Univ - New Brunswick	NJ	27,090	HC
Rutgers Univ - New Brunswick	NJ	27,090	HC
St. Joseph's Univ	PA	58,540	VC
St. Louis Univ	MO	49,866	HC
San Francisco State Univ	CA	18,514	LC
Sarah Lawrence College	NY	68,866	MC
Scripps College	CA	69,260	HC
Seton Hall Univ	NJ	58,008	C
Smith College	MA	66,774	MC
Southern Conn State Univ	CT	21,924	LC
St. John's Univ	NY	57,160	C+
Stanford Univ	CA	62,541	MC
SUNY at Binghamton	NY	24,100	MC
SUNY/Univ at Buffalo	NY	23,122	C
Susquehanna Univ	PA	57,560	VC
Temple Univ	PA	24,392	C+
The American Univ	DC	61,317	HC
The Catholic Univ of America	DC	58,376	VC
The Univ of Arizona	AZ	24,086	C
The Univ of Tenn at Knoxville	TN	22,112	VC
The Univ of Texas at Austin	TX	20,206	MC
Thomas Edison State Univ	NJ	6,350	NC
Trinity College	CT	69,020	HC
Tufts Univ	MA		MC
Tulane Univ	LA	67,496	MC
Univ of Calif at Berkeley	CA	29,886	MC
Univ of Calif at Davis	CA	28,468	HC
Univ of Calif at Los Angeles	CA	27,438	HC+
Univ of Calif San Diego	CA	30,450	MC
Univ of Colo Boulder	CO	26,048	HC
Univ of Delaware	DE	32,214	VC
Univ of Denver	CO	61,129	VC+
Univ of Georgia	GA	21,878	HC
Univ of Illinois at Chicago	IL	24,664	VC
Univ of Illinois at Urbana-Champaign	IL	27,006	HC
Univ of Iowa	IA	19,415	HC
Univ of Kentucky	KY	24,800	C+
Univ of Mass Boston	MA	13,828	C
Univ of Mich/Ann Arbor	MI	25,274	MC
Univ of Minn/Twin Cities	MN	24,269	MC
Univ of Notre Dame	IN	68,801	MC
Univ of Okla	OK	19,651	HC
Univ of Oregon	OR	24,021	VC
Univ of Pittsburgh	PA	30,030	MC
Univ of Rhode Island	RI	26,066	VC
Univ of South Florida/Tampa	FL	16,110	VC
Univ of Southern Calif	CA	66,631	MC
Univ of Virginia	VA	27,367	MC
Univ of Washington	WA	23,091	MC
Univ of Wisc-Madison	WI	21,647	MC
Vassar College	NY	68,110	MC
Villanova Univ	PA	64,922	MC
Washington Univ in St. Louis	MO	67,539	MC
Wellesley College	MA	66,984	MC
Yale Univ	CT	64,650	MC
Youngstown State Univ	OH	17,487	C

ITALIAN STUDIES

School	ST	$IS	SR
Bard College	NY	65,924	HC
Boston Univ	MA	67,352	MC
Brown Univ	RI	64,566	MC
Cal State, Fullerton	CA	21,902	C
College of Staten Island	NY	24,389	LC
Colo College	CO	64,894	MC
Columbia Univ/ School of General Studies	NY	61,470	MC
Columbia Univ/City of New York	NY	62,958	MC
Conn College	CT	65,000	MC
Dartmouth College	NH	68,109	MC
Dickinson College	PA	66,166	MC
Duke Univ	NC	68,298	MC
Elon Univ	NC	46,142	HC
Emory Univ	GA	63,286	MC
Fordham Univ	NY	68,431	MC
Gettysburg College	PA	65,210	MC
Gonzaga Univ	WA	52,880	HC
Ithaca College	NY	58,158	VC+
Lake Erie College	OH	38,914	LC
Merrimack College	MA	55,415	C
Miami Univ	OH	27,190	HC+
New York Univ	NY	68,139	MC
Pennsylvania State Univ - Univ Park	PA	29,716	HC
Purdue Univ/West Lafayette	IN	20,032	MC
Rosemont College	PA	30,980	LC
Scripps College	CA	69,260	HC
Southern Methodist Univ	TX	69,008	MC
Stony Brook Univ/The SUNY	NY	22,703	MC
Syracuse Univ	NY	62,313	HC
Univ of Calif at Los Angeles	CA	27,438	HC+
Univ of Calif at Santa Barbara	CA	30,627	HC+
Univ of Calif San Diego	CA	30,450	MC
Univ of Calif, Santa Cruz	CA	28,731	C+
Univ of Conn	CT	27,394	
Univ of Houston	TX	21,871	VC
Univ of Illinois at Chicago	IL	24,664	VC
Univ of Maryland/College Park	MD	21,938	HC
Univ of Mass Amherst	MA	27,669	HC
Univ of New Hampshire	NH	29,333	VC
Univ of Pennsylvania	PA	63,526	MC
Univ of Richmond	VA	62,730	MC
Univ of San Diego	CA	60,338	HC
Univ of Vermont	VT	29,792	HC
Univ of Wisc-Milwaukee	WI	21,538	C
Vanderbilt Univ	TN	63,248	MC
Wellesley College	MA	66,984	MC
Wesleyan Univ	CT	66,940	MC
Wheaton College	MA	63,818	VC
Youngstown State Univ	OH	17,487	C

JAPANESE

School	ST	$IS	SR
Ball State Univ	IN	19,808	C+
Bard College	NY	65,924	HC
Bates College	ME	64,500	HC
Bennington College	VT	66,280	MC
Brigham Young Univ	UT	13,248	MC
Cal State, Fullerton	CA	21,902	C
Cal State, Long Beach	CA	18,850	C
Cal State, Los Angeles	CA	17,186	LC
Calvin College	MI	43,090	HC
Central Washington Univ	WA	16,803	C
Colgate Univ	NY	67,500	MC
Conn College	CT	65,000	MC
Eastern Mich Univ	MI	19,761	C
Elizabethtown College	PA	56,340	VC
Emory Univ	GA	63,286	MC
Furman Univ	SC	61,098	VC+
Georgetown Univ	DC	68,970	MC
Harvard College/Harvard Univ	MA	65,609	MC
Hofstra Univ	NY	58,210	C+
Lawrence Univ	WI	56,133	HC+
Lehigh Univ	PA	63,860	MC
Linfield College	OR	53,992	C
Macalester College	MN	64,136	MC
Marshall Univ	WV	18,044	C
Middlebury College	VT	67,464	MC
Murray State Univ	KY	17,726	C+
North Central College	IL	48,712	C+
Northern Kentucky Univ	KY	16,486	C
Oakland Univ	MI	20,763	C
Occidental College	CA	68,660	MC
Ohio State Univ at Columbus	OH	22,843	MC
Pacific Univ	OR	37,617	C
Pomona College	CA	64,957	MC
Portland State Univ	OR	19,443	C
Purdue Univ/West Lafayette	IN	20,032	MC
San Diego State Univ	CA	23,156	VC
San Francisco State Univ	CA	18,514	LC
San Jose State Univ	CA	22,630	C
Sarah Lawrence College	NY	68,866	MC
Scripps College	CA	69,260	HC
St. Olaf College	MN	56,430	HC
Stanford Univ	CA	62,541	MC
The American Univ	DC	61,317	HC
The George Washington Univ	DC	68,474	HC+
The Univ of Utah	UT	18,751	VC
Thomas Edison State Univ	NJ	6,350	NC
Tufts Univ	MA		MC
Univ of Calif at Berkeley	CA	29,886	MC
Univ of Calif at Davis	CA	28,468	HC
Univ of Calif at Irvine	CA	33,857	VC
Univ of Calif at Los Angeles	CA	27,438	HC+
Univ of Calif at Riverside	CA	32,912	C
Univ of Calif at Santa Barbara	CA	30,627	HC+
Univ of Calif San Diego	CA	30,450	MC
Univ of Colo Boulder	CO	26,048	HC
Univ of Findlay	OH	43,040	C
Univ of Georgia	GA	21,878	HC
Univ of Hawaii at Hilo	HI	18,038	VC
Univ of Hawaii at Manoa	HI	23,261	C
Univ of Iowa	IA	19,415	HC
Univ of Maryland/College Park	MD	21,938	HC
Univ of Mass Amherst	MA	27,669	HC
Univ of Minn/Twin Cities	MN	24,269	MC
Univ of Missouri-St. Louis	MO	19,810	VC
Univ of Montana	MT	14,105	C
Univ of Mount Union	OH	39,990	C
Univ of Notre Dame	IN	68,801	MC
Univ of Okla	OK	19,651	HC
Univ of Oregon	OR	24,021	VC
Univ of Pittsburgh	PA	30,030	MC
Univ of Puget Sound	WA	60,210	HC
Univ of Rochester	NY	65,032	MC
Univ of the Pacific	CA	57,446	VC
Univ of Vermont	VT	29,792	HC
Univ of Washington	WA	23,091	MC
Univ of Wisc-Madison	WI	21,647	MC
Vassar College	NY	68,110	MC
Wake Forest Univ	NC	69,354	MC
Washington State Univ	WA	22,747	C
Washington Univ in St. Louis	MO	67,539	MC
Wellesley College	MA	66,984	MC
Western Mich Univ	MI	21,791	C
Western Washington Univ	WA	18,904	VC
Williams College	MA	67,700	MC
Yale Univ	CT	64,650	MC

JAPANESE STUDIES

School	ST	$IS	SR
Adrian College	MI	45,550	C
Aquinas College - Mich	MI	38,876	VC
Boston Univ	MA	67,352	MC
Carnegie Mellon Univ	PA	67,980	MC
Case Western Reserve Univ	OH	62,284	MC
DePaul Univ	IL	52,807	VC
Earlham College	IN	55,670	HC
Gettysburg College	PA	65,210	MC
Hofstra Univ	NY	58,210	C+
Hope College	MI	42,840	VC
Linfield College	OR	53,992	C
New York Univ	NY	68,139	MC
Pennsylvania State Univ - Univ Park	PA	29,716	HC
Purdue Univ/West Lafayette	IN	20,032	MC
Salem International Univ	WV	21,090	C
Smith College	MA	66,774	MC
SUNY at Binghamton	NY	24,100	MC
Swarthmore College	PA	63,550	MC
Univ of Alaska Fairbanks	AK	16,874	VC
Univ of Calif San Diego	CA	30,450	MC
Univ of Hawaii at Hilo	HI	18,038	VC
Univ of N Car at Charlotte	NC	17,803	VC
Wellesley College	MA	66,984	MC
Willamette Univ	OR	62,514	VC+
William Jewell College	MO	42,490	C+

JAZZ

School	ST	$IS	SR
Alabama A&M Univ	AL	18,796	C
Aquinas College - Mich	MI	38,876	VC
Bennington College	VT	66,280	MC
Berklee College of Music	MA	60,930	SP
Bowling Green State Univ	OH	19,975	C
Brigham Young Univ	UT	13,248	MC
Butler Univ	IN	52,890	VC+
Cal State, Fresno	CA	16,902	LC
DePaul Univ	IL	52,807	VC
Eastman School of Music/ Univ of Rochester	NY	68,060	SP
Elmhurst College	IL	46,514	C
Five Towns College	NY	35,480	LC
Florida Atlantic Univ	FL	18,256	C
Florida State Univ	FL	16,771	HC
Hofstra Univ	NY	58,210	C+
Howard Univ	DC	37,616	C+
Ithaca College	NY	58,158	VC+
Johnson State College	VT	22,672	C
Limestone College	SC	32,100	C
Loyola Univ New Orleans	LA	52,456	VC
Manhattan School of Music	NY	57,200	SP
Marshall Univ	WV	18,044	C
Mich State Univ	MI	24,542	VC
New England Conservatory of Music	MA	63,170	SP
N Car Central Univ	NC	9,000	C
North Central College	IL	48,712	C+
Northwestern Univ	IL	68,725	MC
Ohio State Univ at Columbus	OH	22,843	MC
Roosevelt Univ	IL	41,890	VC
Rowan Univ	NJ	24,491	VC
San Jose State Univ	CA	22,630	C
Shenandoah Univ	VA	42,100	C
Temple Univ	PA	24,392	C+
Texas State Univ	TX	18,721	C
Tulane Univ	LA	67,496	MC
Univ of Cincinnati	OH	22,118	VC
Univ of Denver	CO	61,129	VC+
Univ of Hartford	CT	49,776	C
Univ of Illinois at Chicago	IL	24,664	VC
Univ of Iowa	IA	19,415	HC
Univ of Maine at Augusta	ME	7,812	C
Univ of Miami	FL	63,494	MC
Univ of Mich/Ann Arbor	MI	25,274	MC
Univ of Minn/Duluth	MN	20,292	C
Univ of N Car at Asheville	NC	16,251	VC+
Univ of N Car at Greensboro	NC	15,998	C
Univ of North Florida	FL	15,996	VC
Univ of North Texas	TX	20,082	C
Univ of Oregon	OR	24,021	VC
Univ of Rochester	NY	65,032	MC
Univ of Southern Calif	CA	66,631	MC
Univ of Washington	WA	23,091	MC
Webster Univ	MO	37,490	C
West Chester Univ of Pennsylvania	PA	19,171	VC
Western Mich Univ	MI	21,791	C
Whitman College	WA	59,772	MC
Youngstown State Univ	OH	17,487	C

JOURNALISM

School	ST	$IS	SR
Abilene Christian Univ	TX	43,708	C+
Adrian College	MI	45,550	C
Alabama A&M Univ	AL	18,796	C
American Jewish Univ - College of A&S	CA	44,234	C
Andrews Univ	MI	41,732	C
Appalachian State Univ	NC	15,394	VC
Aquinas College - Mich	MI	38,876	VC
Arkansas State Univ	AR	16,190	C
Arkansas Tech Univ	AR	16,534	LC
Asbury Univ	KY	36,450	C+
Ashford Univ	CA	10,480	C
Ashland Univ	OH	30,446	C
Auburn Univ	AL	24,300	VC+
Augustana Univ	SD	39,968	VC
Averett Univ	VA	43,034	LC
Azusa Pacific Univ	CA	43,972	C
Ball State Univ	IN	19,808	C+
Bayamon Central Univ	PR	12,490	

ST = STATE **$IS** = IN-STATE COSTS **SR** = SELECTOR RATING

School	ST	$IS	SR
Baylor Univ	TX	56,803	HC
Belmont Univ	TN	44,500	VC+
Bemidji State Univ	MN	17,730	C
Benedict College	SC	28,630	NC
Benedictine College	KS	38,850	VC
Bennington College	VT	66,280	MC
Bethel Univ	MN	46,550	C+
Biola Univ	CA	48,686	C
Bloomfield College	NJ	40,100	LC
Bloomsburg Univ of Pennsylvania	PA	19,930	C
Boston Univ	MA	67,352	MC
Bowling Green State Univ	OH	19,975	C
Bradley Univ	IL	43,240	VC
Briar Cliff Univ	IA	36,956	C
Butler Univ	IN	52,890	VC+
Calif Baptist Univ	CA	42,986	C
Calif Polytechnic State Univ	CA	22,547	MC
Cal State, Chico	CA	19,790	VC
Cal State, Fresno	CA	16,902	LC
Cal State, Fullerton	CA	21,902	C
Cal State, Long Beach	CA	18,850	C
Cal State, Northridge	CA	17,277	LC
Cal State, Sacramento	CA	19,060	C
Cameron Univ	OK	11,632	LC
Campbell Univ	NC	37,570	VC
Canisius College	NY	49,672	C
Carnegie Mellon Univ	PA	67,980	MC
Cedarville Univ	OH	36,244	VC
Central Conn State Univ	CT	22,041	C
Central Mich Univ	MI	20,330	C
Central State Univ	OH	18,564	C
Central Washington Univ	WA	16,803	C
CUNY/Baruch College	NY	21,609	HC
CUNY/Brooklyn College	NY	7,163	C+
College of the Ozarks	MO	7,530	VC
Colo State Univ	CO	23,033	C
Colo State Univ-Pueblo	CO	21,581	C
Columbia College Chicago	IL	40,104	C
Concordia College - Moorhead	MN	46,418	C
Concordia Univ, Ann Arbor	MI	38,878	C+
Corban Univ	OR	41,700	C
Creighton Univ	NE	49,452	VC
Delaware State Univ	DE	19,376	LC
DePaul Univ	IL	52,807	VC
Dickinson State Univ	ND	12,372	LC
Doane Univ	NE	41,340	VC
Dominican Univ	IL	42,472	C+
Dordt College	IA	37,860	C+
Drake Univ	IA	49,220	HC
Drury Univ	MO	37,555	VC
Duquesne Univ	PA	48,508	VC
Eastern Illinois Univ	IL	21,414	C
Eastern Kentucky Univ	KY	17,742	C
Eastern Mich Univ	MI	19,761	C
Eastern Nazarene College	MA	41,114	C
Eastern Washington Univ	WA	17,896	LC
Edinboro Univ	PA	15,940	LC
Elon Univ	NC	46,142	HC
Emerson College	MA	61,824	HC+
Emory and Henry College	VA	46,320	C
Emory Univ	GA	63,286	MC
Evangel Univ	MO	28,898	C
Felician Univ	NJ	46,280	LC
Flagler College	FL	27,620	C
Florida A&M Univ	FL	15,361	C
Florida Atlantic Univ	FL	18,256	C
Florida Southern College	FL	45,978	VC
Fordham Univ	NY	68,431	MC
Franklin College	IN	40,550	C
Freed-Hardeman Univ	TN	29,900	C
Gannon Univ	PA	42,922	C
Georgia College & State Univ	GA	21,884	C+
Georgia State Univ	GA	25,250	C
Gonzaga Univ	WA	52,880	HC
Goshen College	IN	44,350	C
Grace College and Seminary	IN	31,524	C
Grand Valley State Univ	MI	22,250	C+
Grand View Univ	IA	32,302	C
Hampshire College	MA	65,214	MC
Harding Univ	AR	25,440	C
Hawaii Pacific Univ	HI	33,420	C
Hofstra Univ	NY	58,210	C+
Howard Univ	DC	37,616	C+
Humboldt State Univ	CA	21,708	C
Huntington Univ	IN	33,996	C
Illinois State Univ	IL	23,418	VC
Indiana State Univ	IN	23,223	LC
Indiana Univ Bloomington	IN	20,791	HC
Indiana Univ of Pennsylvania	PA	24,474	C
Indiana Univ Southeast	IN	16,931	C
Indiana Univ-Purdue Univ Indianapolis	IN	18,952	C
Iowa State Univ	IA	18,176	C
Ithaca College	NY	58,158	VC+
Johnson State College	VT	22,672	C
Kansas State Univ	KS	17,780	VC
Keene State College	NH	24,604	C
Kent State Univ	OH	20,928	C
Lehigh Univ	PA	63,860	MC
Lenoir-Rhyne Univ	NC	47,500	LC
Lewis Univ	IL	41,710	C
Lincoln Univ	MO	14,402	NC
Linfield College	OR	53,992	C
Lipscomb Univ	TN	42,984	VC
LIU Brooklyn	NY	50,698	C
LIU Post	NY	50,698	C+
Lock Haven Univ of Pennsylvania	PA	20,544	LC
Louisiana State Univ and A&M College	LA	18,677	VC
Louisiana Tech Univ	LA	11,422	VC
Loyola Univ Chicago	IL	57,158	VC
Loyola Univ New Orleans	LA	52,456	VC
Lubbock Christian Univ	TX	29,727	C
Lyndon State College	VT	20,714	C
Lynn Univ	FL	49,680	LC
Madonna Univ	MI	30,450	LC
Manhattan College	NY	55,652	C
Marietta College	OH	46,190	C
Marquette Univ	WI	53,090	VC+
Marshall Univ	WV	18,044	C
Mercer Univ	GA	45,348	VC
Mercy College	NY	32,614	C
Mercyhurst Univ	PA	47,420	C
Messiah College	PA	44,380	VC
Metropolitan State Univ of Denver	CO	6,928	LC
Miami Univ	OH	27,190	HC+
Mich State Univ	MI	24,542	VC
Midland Univ	NE	39,512	C
Millersville Univ of Pennsylvania	PA	25,298	C
Millikin Univ	IL	44,148	C
Minn State Univ, Mankato	MN	17,190	C
Minn State Univ, Moorhead	MN	21,393	C
Missouri Baptist Univ	MO	35,594	C
Missouri State Univ	MO	15,837	C+
Montclair State Univ	NJ	26,912	C
Mount Ida College	MA	46,820	C
Mount Marty College	SD	36,862	C
Mount Mercy Univ	IA	39,748	C
Mount Vernon Nazarene Univ	OH	35,944	C
Murray State Univ	KY	17,726	C+
Muskingum Univ	OH	35,966	C
Neumann Univ	PA	40,678	LC
New Mexico State Univ	NM	14,050	LC
New York Inst of Technology	NY	49,980	VC
New York Univ	NY	68,139	MC
Nicholls State Univ	LA	14,959	C
Norfolk State Univ	VA	18,902	LC
North Central College	IL	48,712	C+
North Central Univ	MN	30,610	C
Northeastern State Univ	OK	8,615	VC
Northeastern Univ	MA	65,352	MC
Northern Arizona Univ	AZ	21,003	C
Northern Illinois Univ	IL	20,176	C
Northern Kentucky Univ	KY	16,486	C
Northwest Missouri State Univ	MO	18,286	C
Northwestern College of Iowa	IA	38,400	C
Northwestern Univ	IL	68,725	MC
Oakland Univ	MI	20,763	C
Ohio Northern Univ	OH	44,050	VC
Ohio State Univ at Columbus	OH	22,843	MC
Ohio Univ	OH	23,394	VC
Ohio Wesleyan Univ	OH	49,460	VC
Okla Baptist Univ	OK	33,990	C
Okla Christian Univ	OK	29,260	C
Okla State Univ	OK	17,180	C+
Old Dominion Univ	VA	21,618	C
Olivet College	MI	37,661	LC
Olivet Nazarene Univ	IL	41,840	VC
Otterbein Univ	OH	41,630	C
Pacific Union College	CA	36,009	VC
Palm Beach Atlantic Univ	FL	39,250	C
Pennsylvania State Univ - Univ Park	PA	29,716	HC
Pepperdine Univ	CA	66,862	VC+
Point Loma Nazarene Univ	CA	46,150	C+
Point Park Univ	PA	41,270	C
Prairie View A&M Univ	TX	27,273	LC
Purdue Univ Northwest	IN	15,178	C
Purdue Univ/West Lafayette	IN	20,032	MC
Quinnipiac Univ	CT	60,970	VC
Rider Univ	NJ	54,050	C
Rochester Inst of Technology	NY	52,734	HC+
Roger Williams Univ	RI	48,074	VC
Roosevelt Univ	IL	41,890	VC
Rowan Univ	NJ	24,491	VC
Rust College	MS	10,600	C
Rutgers Univ - New Brunswick	NJ	27,090	HC
Rutgers Univ - New Brunswick	NJ	27,090	HC
Rutgers Univ - Newark	NJ	27,351	C
St. Mary-of-the-Woods College	IN	40,424	LC
St. Mary's Univ of Minn	MN	42,440	C
St. Michael's College	VT	53,275	VC+
Sam Houston State Univ	TX	18,792	C
Samford Univ	AL	40,770	VC
San Diego State Univ	CA	23,156	VC
San Francisco State Univ	CA	18,514	LC
San Jose State Univ	CA	22,630	C
Seattle Univ	WA	54,957	VC
Seton Hall Univ	NJ	58,008	C
Seton Hill Univ	PA	46,972	VC
Shippensburg Univ of Pennsylvania	PA	24,096	C
Simpson College	IA	45,626	VC
S Dak State Univ	SD	15,874	C
Southeast Missouri State Univ	MO	16,148	C
Southeastern Univ	FL	34,910	LC
Southern Adventist Univ	TN	28,250	C
Southern Arkansas Univ	AR	21,532	C
Southern Conn State Univ	CT	21,924	LC
Southern Illinois Univ Carbondale	IL	24,554	C
Southern Illinois Univ Edwardsville	IL	20,188	C
Southern Methodist Univ	TX	69,008	MC
Southern Nazarene Univ	OK	33,684	C
Southern Univ at New Orleans	LA	8,014	LC
Southwest Baptist Univ	MO	30,890	LC
Southwestern Adventist Univ	TX	28,232	LC
Spring Hill College	AL	48,488	C
St. Bonaventure Univ	NY	45,596	C
St. Cloud State Univ	MN	10,600	C
St. John's Univ	NY	57,160	C+
St. Joseph's College, New York/Brooklyn Campus	NY	25,114	LC
St. Joseph's College, New York/Long Island Campus	NY	25,124	C
SUNY at New Paltz	NY	20,840	C
SUNY at Oswego	NY	22,219	VC
SUNY at Purchase College	NY	21,832	C
SUNY/Buffalo State	NY	20,583	LC
SUNY/Fredonia	NY	20,818	C
SUNY/Plattsburgh	NY	19,314	C
Stephen F. Austin State Univ	TX	18,484	LC
Stony Brook Univ/The SUNY	NY	22,703	MC
Suffolk Univ	MA	52,316	C
Taylor Univ	IN	42,130	VC
Temple Univ	PA	24,392	C+
Tenn Tech Univ	TN	17,929	C
Texas A&M Univ at Commerce	TX	10,496	C
Texas Christian Univ	TX	57,120	HC
Texas State Univ	TX	18,721	C
Texas Tech Univ	TX	20,156	C+
Texas Wesleyan Univ	TX	37,338	C
The American Univ	DC	61,317	HC
The College at Brockport - SUNY	NY	21,058	C
The George Washington Univ	DC	68,474	HC+
The Univ of Alabama	AL	24,320	C+
The Univ of Arizona	AZ	24,086	C
The Univ of Memphis	TN	18,278	C
The Univ of Tenn at Knoxville	TN	22,112	VC
The Univ of Texas at Austin	TX	20,206	MC
Tougaloo College	MS	17,980	NC
Trevecca Nazarene Univ	TN	31,186	C
Troy Univ	AL	16,171	C
Truman State Univ	MO	16,286	MC
Tulane Univ	LA	67,496	MC
Union College	NE	23,270	C
Union Univ	TN	41,160	VC
Univ of Alaska Anchorage	AK	17,914	C
Univ of Alaska Fairbanks	AK	16,874	VC
Univ of Arkansas at Fayetteville	AR	19,766	VC
Univ of Arkansas at Little Rock	AR	18,211	LC
Univ of Arkansas at Pine Bluff	AR	13,541	C
Univ of Bridgeport	CT	44,985	LC
Univ of Calif at Irvine	CA	33,857	VC
Univ of Central Arkansas	AR	15,042	VC
Univ of Central Florida	FL	16,379	VC
Univ of Central Missouri	MO	18,982	C
Univ of Central Okla	OK	15,150	C
Univ of Cincinnati	OH	22,118	VC
Univ of Colo Boulder	CO	26,048	HC
Univ of Conn	CT	27,394	
Univ of Delaware	DE	32,214	VC
Univ of Denver	CO	61,129	VC+
Univ of Florida	FL	16,291	HC+
Univ of Georgia	GA	21,878	HC
Univ of Hawaii at Manoa	HI	23,261	C
Univ of Idaho	ID	16,158	C
Univ of Illinois at Urbana-Champaign	IL	27,006	HC
Univ of Indianapolis	IN	36,480	VC
Univ of Iowa	IA	19,415	HC
Univ of Kansas	KS	20,884	VC
Univ of Kentucky	KY	24,800	C+
Univ of La Verne	CA	55,600	C
Univ of Maine	ME	21,038	VC
Univ of Mary Hardin-Baylor	TX	35,292	C+
Univ of Maryland/College Park	MD	21,938	HC
Univ of Mass Amherst	MA	27,669	HC
Univ of Miami	FL	63,494	MC
Univ of Minn/Twin Cities	MN	24,269	MC
Univ of Miss	MS	18,802	C
Univ of Missouri-Columbia	MO	20,463	VC
Univ of Montana	MT	14,105	C
Univ of Montevallo	AL	20,012	C
Univ of Nebr - Kearney	NE	17,014	LC
Univ of Nebr - Lincoln	NE	18,589	VC
Univ of Nebr - Omaha	NE	16,120	C
Univ of Nevada, Reno	NV	18,010	C
Univ of New Mexico	NM	16,808	C
Univ of North Alabama	AL	15,964	C
Univ of N Car at Chapel Hill	NC	20,561	MC
Univ of North Texas	TX	20,082	C
Univ of Northern Colo	CO	19,658	C
Univ of Northwestern - St. Paul	MN	39,530	C
Univ of Okla	OK	19,651	HC
Univ of Oregon	OR	24,021	VC
Univ of Pittsburgh at Johnstown	PA	22,092	C
Univ of PR-Rio Piedras campus	PR	13,327	
Univ of Rhode Island	RI	26,066	VC
Univ of Richmond	VA	62,730	MC
Univ of S Car at Columbia	SC	21,726	VC
Univ of S Dak	SD	16,109	C
Univ of Southern Calif	CA	66,631	MC
Univ of Southern Indiana	IN	16,808	C
Univ of Southern Miss	MS	13,170	C
Univ of St. Francis	IL	40,828	C
Univ of Tampa	FL	38,928	VC
Univ of Texas at Arlington	TX	18,876	C
Univ of Texas at El Paso	TX	34,452	NC
Univ of Texas Rio Grande Valley	TX	15,573	LC
Univ of the Cumberlands	KY	32,000	LC
Univ of West Georgia	GA	17,510	LC
Univ of Wisc-Eau Claire	WI	16,354	VC
Univ of Wisc-Madison	WI	21,647	MC
Univ of Wisc-Oshkosh	WI	15,392	C
Univ of Wisc-River Falls	WI	14,541	C
Univ of Wisc-Whitewater	WI	13,976	C
Univ of Wyoming	WY	15,537	C
Utah State Univ	UT	13,235	C
Utica College	NY	31,510	C
Virginia Union Univ	VA	25,058	C
Virginia Wesleyan Univ	VA	45,980	LC
Wartburg College	IA	49,478	C
Washington Adventist Univ	MD	32,050	LC
Washington and Lee Univ	VA	59,647	MC
Washington State Univ	WA	22,747	C
Washington Univ in St. Louis	MO	67,539	MC
Wayne State Univ	MI	23,085	C
Weber State Univ	UT	14,112	C
Webster Univ	MO	37,490	C
West Virginia Univ	WV	18,952	VC
Western Illinois Univ	IL	20,897	C
Western Kentucky Univ	KY	16,850	C
Western Mich Univ	MI	21,791	C
Western Washington Univ	WA	18,904	VC
Whitworth Univ	WA	53,682	VC
William Penn Univ	IA	26,000	C
William Woods Univ	MO	32,040	C
Wilmington College	OH	35,100	C
Wingate Univ	NC	41,900	C
Winona State Univ	MN	18,109	C
Youngstown State Univ	OH	17,487	C

JOURNALISM - MAGAZINE JOURNALISM

School	ST	$IS	SR
Ohio Univ	OH	23,394	VC
Syracuse Univ	NY	62,313	HC
Washington State Univ	WA	22,747	C

JOURNALISM - NEWS & INFORMATION

School	ST	$IS	SR
Bloomfield College	NJ	40,100	LC
Calif Baptist Univ	CA	42,986	C
Keene State College	NH	24,604	C
Kennesaw State Univ	GA	18,899	VC
Louisiana College	LA	21,274	C
N Dak State Univ	ND	16,245	VC
Ohio Univ	OH	23,394	VC
Okla Baptist Univ	OK	33,990	C
Syracuse Univ	NY	62,313	HC
Univ of Findlay	OH	43,040	C
Washington State Univ	WA	22,747	C

JOURNALISM - NEWSWRITING / EDIT

School	ST	$IS	SR
Ohio Univ	OH	23,394	VC
Texas Tech Univ	TX	20,156	C+
Washington State Univ	WA	22,747	C

JOURNALISM & TECHNICAL COMMUNICATIONS

School	ST	$IS	SR
Arizona State Univ at the Downtown Phoenix Campus	AZ	24,634	VC
Fairfield Univ	CT	61,445	HC
Ferris State Univ	MI	21,458	C
Louisiana College	LA	21,274	C
Syracuse Univ	NY	62,313	HC

JOURNALISM EDUCATION

School	ST	$IS	SR
Abilene Christian Univ	TX	43,708	C+
Baylor Univ	TX	56,803	HC
Cal State, Northridge	CA	17,277	LC
Carlow Univ	PA	39,696	LC
Grace College and Seminary	IN	31,524	C
Indiana Univ Bloomington	IN	20,791	HC
Stephen F. Austin State Univ	TX	18,484	LC
Univ of Nebr - Lincoln	NE	18,589	VC
Univ of S Dak	SD	16,109	C
Univ of Wisc-Milwaukee	WI	21,538	C
Wartburg College	IA	49,478	C
Webster Univ	MO	37,490	C

ST = STATE $IS = IN-STATE COSTS SR = SELECTOR RATING

JUDAIC STUDIES

School	ST	$IS	SR
American Jewish Univ - College of A&S	CA	44,234	C
Arizona State Univ at the Tempe Campus	AZ	23,001	VC
Bard College	NY	65,924	HC
Bennington College	VT	66,280	MC
Brandeis Univ	MA	68,443	MC
Brown Univ	RI	64,566	MC
CUNY/Brooklyn College	NY	7,163	C+
CUNY/Hunter College	NY	31,098	VC
College of Charleston	SC	24,046	VC
DePaul Univ	IL	52,807	VC
Dickinson College	PA	66,166	MC
Elon Univ	NC	46,142	HC
Emory Univ	GA	63,286	MC
Florida Atlantic Univ	FL	18,256	C
Gettysburg College	PA	65,210	MC
Hampshire College	MA	65,214	MC
Hofstra Univ	NY	58,210	C+
Indiana Univ Bloomington	IN	20,791	HC
List College/The Jewish Theological Seminary (JTS)	NY	37,870	SP
New York Univ	NY	68,139	MC
Northeastern Univ	MA	65,352	MC
Oberlin College	OH	68,942	MC
Ohio State Univ at Columbus	OH	22,843	MC
Pennsylvania State Univ - Univ Park	PA	29,716	HC
Purdue Univ/West Lafayette	IN	20,032	MC
Rutgers Univ - New Brunswick	NJ	27,090	HC
Rutgers Univ - New Brunswick	NJ	27,090	HC
San Francisco State Univ	CA	18,514	LC
Scripps College	CA	69,260	HC
Smith College	MA	66,774	MC
Stanford Univ	CA	62,541	MC
SUNY at Binghamton	NY	24,100	MC
The American Univ	DC	61,317	HC
The George Washington Univ	DC	68,474	HC+
The Univ of Arizona	AZ	24,086	C
The Univ of Texas at Austin	TX	20,206	MC
Touro College	NY	31,040	C
Trinity College	CT	69,020	HC
Tufts Univ	MA		MC
Tulane Univ	LA	67,496	MC
Univ of Calif at Los Angeles	CA	27,438	HC+
Univ of Calif San Diego	CA	30,450	MC
Univ of Chicago	IL	70,551	MC
Univ of Cincinnati	OH	22,118	VC
Univ of Colo Boulder	CO	26,048	HC
Univ of Conn	CT	27,394	
Univ of Denver	CO	61,129	VC+
Univ of Florida	FL	16,291	HC+
Univ of Hartford	CT	49,776	C
Univ of Kansas	KS	20,884	VC
Univ of Maryland/College Park	MD	21,938	HC
Univ of Mass Amherst	MA	27,669	HC
Univ of Miami	FL	63,494	MC
Univ of Mich/Ann Arbor	MI	25,274	MC
Univ of Missouri-Kansas City	MO	19,563	VC
Univ of Oregon	OR	24,021	VC
Univ of Pennsylvania	PA	63,526	MC
Univ of Southern Calif	CA	66,631	MC
Univ of Washington	WA	23,091	MC
Univ of Wisc-Madison	WI	21,647	MC
Univ of Wisc-Milwaukee	WI	21,538	C
Vanderbilt Univ	TN	63,248	MC
Vassar College	NY	68,110	MC
Washington Univ in St. Louis	MO	67,539	MC
Wellesley College	MA	66,984	MC
Yale Univ	CT	64,650	MC

JUSTICE AND SOCIETY

School	ST	$IS	SR
Allegheny College	PA	57,620	VC
Concordia Univ, Ann Arbor	MI	38,878	C+
Creighton Univ	NE	49,452	VC
Elon Univ	NC	46,142	HC
Emmanuel College	MA	53,472	C+
Georgetown College	KY	41,440	C
Goddard College	VT	17,040	VC
Guilford College	NC	45,973	C
Miami Univ	OH	27,190	HC+
Missouri Southern State Univ	MO	13,071	C
Montclair State Univ	NJ	26,912	C
Mount Mary Univ	WI	34,650	LC
Northeastern Illinois Univ	IL	12,529	LC
Univ of Alaska Fairbanks	AK	16,874	VC
Univ of New Hampshire	NH	29,333	VC

KEYBOARD - PIANO CONCENTRATION

School	ST	$IS	SR
Aquinas College - Mich	MI	38,876	VC
Baldwin Wallace Univ	OH	42,464	VC
Cedarville Univ	OH	36,244	VC
Chapman Univ	CA	65,504	HC
Dallas Baptist Univ	TX	35,220	VC
East Central Univ	OK	13,330	C
Murray State Univ	KY	17,726	C+
New England Conservatory of Music	MA	63,170	SP
Ouachita Baptist Univ	AR	33,500	VC
Univ of Cincinnati	OH	22,118	VC
Univ of N Car at Greensboro	NC	15,998	C
West Chester Univ of Pennsylvania	PA	19,171	VC
Western Mich Univ	MI	21,791	C
Youngstown State Univ	OH	17,487	C

KINESIOLOGY

School	ST	$IS	SR
Abilene Christian Univ	TX	43,708	C+
Aquinas College - Mich	MI	38,876	VC
Arizona State Univ at the Downtown Phoenix Campus	AZ	24,634	VC
Auburn Univ at Montgomery	AL	15,000	C
Augusta Univ	GA	4,632	C
Calif Baptist Univ	CA	42,986	C
Calif Polytechnic State Univ	CA	22,547	MC
Cal State, Fullerton	CA	21,902	C
Cal State, Long Beach	CA	18,850	C
Calvin College	MI	43,090	HC
Chapman Univ	CA	65,504	HC
College of William & Mary	VA	34,907	MC
Colo Mesa Univ	CO	19,707	LC
Corban Univ	OR	41,700	C
East Central Univ	OK	13,330	C
East Texas Baptist Univ	TX	34,444	C
Eastern Illinois Univ	IL	21,414	C
Gannon Univ	PA	42,922	C
Georgia Southern Univ	GA	16,540	VC
Gonzaga Univ	WA	52,880	HC
Hanover College	IN	47,750	C+
Indiana Univ Bloomington	IN	20,791	HC
Indiana Univ-Purdue Univ Indianapolis	IN	18,952	C
John Brown Univ	AR	35,184	VC
LIU Brooklyn	NY	50,698	C
MidAmerica Nazarene Univ	KS	37,808	C
New Mexico State Univ	NM	14,050	LC
Nova Southeastern Univ	FL	38,534	C+
Ohio Wesleyan Univ	OH	49,460	VC
Okla Baptist Univ	OK	33,990	C
Oregon State Univ	OR	23,337	VC
Our Lady of the Lake Univ	TX	37,790	LC
Pacific Lutheran Univ	WA	49,960	C
Pennsylvania State Univ - Univ Park	PA	29,716	HC
St. Louis Univ	MO	49,866	HC
San Diego State Univ	CA	23,156	VC
San Jose State Univ	CA	22,630	C
Shenandoah Univ	VA	42,100	C
Southeastern Louisiana Univ	LA	16,237	C
Southeastern Univ	FL	34,910	LC
Southern Illinois Univ Carbondale	IL	24,554	C
St. Ambrose Univ	IA	40,180	C
Tarleton State Univ	TX	15,248	LC
Taylor Univ	IN	42,130	VC
Texas Tech Univ	TX	20,156	C+
The College at Brockport - SUNY	NY	21,058	C
The Master's Univ	CA	43,870	C
United States Military Academy at West Point	NY		HC+
Univ of Alabama at Birmingham	AL	22,092	C
Univ of Central Arkansas	AR	15,042	VC
Univ of Louisiana at Monroe	LA	15,970	C
Univ of Maine	ME	21,038	VC
Univ of Minn/Twin Cities	MN	24,269	MC
Univ of Nevada, Reno	NV	18,010	C
Univ of New Hampshire	NH	29,333	VC
Univ of N Car at Greensboro	NC	15,998	C
Univ of Rhode Island	RI	26,066	VC
Univ of Texas Rio Grande Valley	TX	15,573	LC
Univ of Wisc-Madison	WI	21,647	MC
Univ of Wyoming	WY	15,537	C
Washburn Univ	KS	15,827	C
Wayne State Univ	MI	23,085	C
West Virginia Univ	WV	18,952	VC

KNOWLEDGE MANAGEMENT

School	ST	$IS	SR
Cal State, Fullerton	CA	21,902	C
Syracuse Univ	NY	62,313	HC

KOREAN

School	ST	$IS	SR
Brigham Young Univ	UT	13,248	MC
Northeastern Illinois Univ	IL	12,529	LC
Ohio State Univ at Columbus	OH	22,843	MC
SUNY at Binghamton	NY	24,100	MC
The American Univ	DC	61,317	HC
Thomas Edison State Univ	NJ	6,350	NC
Univ of Calif at Irvine	CA	33,857	VC
Univ of Calif at Los Angeles	CA	27,438	HC+
Univ of Hawaii at Manoa	HI	23,261	C
Wellesley College	MA	66,984	MC

LABOR STUDIES

School	ST	$IS	SR
Cal State, Dominguez Hills	CA	19,022	LC
Cal State, Fullerton	CA	21,902	C
CUNY/Queens College	NY	21,507	C
Cleveland State Univ	OH	22,290	C
Eastern Mich Univ	MI	19,761	C
Hofstra Univ	NY	58,210	C+
Howard Univ	DC	37,616	C+
Indiana Univ Bloomington	IN	20,791	HC
Indiana Univ Northwest	IN	7,207	LC
Indiana Univ South Bend	IN	16,057	C
Indiana Univ-Purdue Univ Fort Wayne	IN	18,675	C
Indiana Univ-Purdue Univ Indianapolis	IN	18,952	C
Manhattan College	NY	55,652	C
Northern Kentucky Univ	KY	16,486	C
Rutgers Univ - New Brunswick	NJ	27,090	HC
Rutgers Univ - New Brunswick	NJ	27,090	HC
San Francisco State Univ	CA	18,514	LC
SUNY/College at Old Westbury	NY	16,860	C
SUNY/Empire State College	NY	9,145	NC
The Univ of Akron	OH	22,566	C
Thomas Edison State Univ	NJ	6,350	NC
Univ of Illinois at Urbana-Champaign	IL	27,006	HC
Univ of Mass Boston	MA	13,828	C
Univ of PR-Rio Piedras campus	PR	13,327	
Wayne State Univ	MI	23,085	C

LAND USE MANAGEMENT AND RECLAMATION

School	ST	$IS	SR
Cal State, Bakersfield	CA	22,397	LC
Eastern Mich Univ	MI	19,761	C
Humboldt State Univ	CA	21,708	C
Metropolitan State Univ of Denver	CO	6,928	LC
Montana State Univ	MT	15,500	C+
Texas State Univ	TX	18,721	C
Unity College	ME	37,670	C
Univ of Louisiana at Lafayette	LA	14,516	C
Univ of Wisc-Platteville	WI	14,148	C
Univ of Wisc-River Falls	WI	14,541	C

LANDSCAPE ARCHITECTURE

School	ST	$IS	SR
Arizona State Univ at the Tempe Campus	AZ	23,001	VC
Calif Polytechnic State Univ	CA	22,547	MC
Cal State, Fullerton	CA	21,902	C
Cornell Univ	NY	67,591	MC
Mich State Univ	MI	24,542	VC
Pennsylvania State Univ - Univ Park	PA	29,716	HC
Rutgers Univ - New Brunswick	NJ	27,090	HC
Rutgers Univ - New Brunswick	NJ	27,090	HC
Texas A&M Univ at College Station	TX	20,771	VC+
Texas Tech Univ	TX	20,156	C+
Univ of Arkansas at Fayetteville	AR	19,766	VC
Univ of Georgia	GA	21,878	HC
Univ of Nebr - Lincoln	NE	18,589	VC
Univ of Rhode Island	RI	26,066	VC

LANDSCAPE ARCHITECTURE/ DESIGN

School	ST	$IS	SR
Andrews Univ	MI	41,732	C
Auburn Univ	AL	24,300	VC+
Ball State Univ	IN	19,808	C+
Boston Architectural College	MA	20,666	SP
Brigham Young Univ	UT	13,248	MC
Calif State Polytechnic Univ, Pomona	CA	21,811	C
CUNY/City College	NY	20,204	C
Clemson Univ	SC		HC
Colo State Univ	CO	23,033	C
Florida International Univ	FL	20,281	C
Florida Southern College	FL	45,978	VC
Iowa State Univ	IA	18,176	C
Jefferson (Philadelphia Univ + Thomas Jefferson Univ)	PA	53,966	C
Kansas State Univ	KS	17,780	VC
Louisiana State Univ and A&M College	LA	18,677	VC
Mich State Univ	MI	24,542	VC
Miss State Univ	MS	12,028	C+
N Car A&T State Univ	NC	13,786	C
N Car State Univ	NC	22,434	HC+
N Dak State Univ	ND	16,245	VC
Northeastern Univ	MA	65,352	MC
Ohio State Univ at Columbus	OH	22,843	MC
Okla State Univ	OK	17,180	C+
Purdue Univ/West Lafayette	IN	20,032	MC
S Dak State Univ	SD	15,874	C
SUNY /College of Agriculture and Tech at Cobleskill	NY	20,527	LC
SUNY/The College of Environmental Science and Forestry	NY	23,728	VC
Temple Univ	PA	24,392	C+
Texas A&M Univ at College Station	TX	20,771	VC+
The Univ of Arizona	AZ	24,086	C
The Univ of Texas at Austin	TX	20,206	MC
Univ of Arkansas at Fayetteville	AR	19,766	VC
Univ of Calif at Berkeley	CA	29,886	MC
Univ of Calif at Davis	CA	28,468	HC
Univ of Conn	CT	27,394	
Univ of Delaware	DE	32,214	VC
Univ of Florida	FL	16,291	HC+
Univ of Idaho	ID	16,158	C
Univ of Illinois at Urbana-Champaign	IL	27,006	HC
Univ of Kentucky	KY	24,800	C+
Univ of Maryland/College Park	MD	21,938	HC
Univ of Mass Amherst	MA	27,669	HC
Univ of Minn/Twin Cities	MN	24,269	MC
Univ of Nebr - Lincoln	NE	18,589	VC
Univ of Nevada, Las Vegas	NV	17,553	C
Univ of Oregon	OR	24,021	VC
Univ of Texas at Arlington	TX	18,876	C
Univ of Washington	WA	23,091	MC
Univ of Wisc-Madison	WI	21,647	MC
Utah State Univ	UT	13,235	C
Virginia Polytechnic Inst and State Univ	VA	21,920	VC
Washington State Univ	WA	22,747	C
West Virginia Univ	WV	18,952	VC

LANGUAGE ARTS

School	ST	$IS	SR
Aquinas College - Mich	MI	38,876	VC
Calvin College	MI	43,090	HC
Catawba College	NC	39,820	LC
Central Mich Univ	MI	20,330	C
Central Washington Univ	WA	16,803	C
College of St. Mary	NE	27,500	C
Concordia Univ, Ann Arbor	MI	38,878	C+
Eastern Mich Univ	MI	19,761	C
Hope College	MI	42,840	VC
Kent State Univ	OH	20,928	C
Lake Erie College	OH	38,914	LC
LeMoyne-Owen College	TN	16,980	C
Madonna Univ	MI	30,450	LC
Malone Univ	OH	39,200	C
Marygrove College	MI	30,100	LC
Miles College	AL	16,530	NC
Missouri Southern State Univ	MO	13,071	C
Mount Vernon Nazarene Univ	OH	35,944	C
Nebr Wesleyan Univ	NE	42,026	C+
Northern Mich Univ	MI	20,853	C
Ohio Northern Univ	OH	44,050	VC
Ohio Univ	OH	23,394	VC
Seattle Pacific Univ	WA	47,439	C+
Shawnee State Univ	OH	16,998	C
Spring Arbor Univ	MI	37,390	C
Univ of Calif, Santa Cruz	CA	28,731	C+
Univ of Mich/Dearborn	MI	12,472	VC
Univ of Nebr - Lincoln	NE	18,589	VC
Univ of N Car at Greensboro	NC	15,998	C
Univ of Okla	OK	19,651	HC
Western Kentucky Univ	KY	16,850	C
Wright State Univ	OH	16,983	C

LANGUAGES

School	ST	$IS	SR
Adelphi Univ	NY	49,792	C
Appalachian State Univ	NC	15,394	VC
Arkansas Tech Univ	AR	16,534	LC
Auburn Univ	AL	24,300	VC+
Augsburg Univ	MN	45,129	C
Austin Peay State Univ	TN	16,397	C
Baylor Univ	TX	56,803	HC
Bellarmine Univ	KY	52,532	C
Bemidji State Univ	MN	17,730	C
Bennington College	VT	66,280	MC
Cal State, Northridge	CA	17,277	LC
Cameron Univ	OK	11,632	LC
Carnegie Mellon Univ	PA	67,980	MC
Carroll Univ	WI	38,100	C+
Carson-Newman Univ	TN	35,900	C
Carthage College	WI	48,835	C
CUNY/Hunter College	NY	31,098	VC
CUNY/Lehman College	NY	5,788	LC
Clark Atlanta Univ	GA	31,019	LC
Clark Univ	MA	53,260	HC+
College of St. Scholastica	MN	45,734	C+
Colo State Univ	CO	23,033	C
Columbia College	SC	36,550	C
Converse College	SC	28,290	C
Denison Univ	OH	62,770	HC+
Dordt College	IA	37,860	C+
Earlham College	IN	55,670	HC
Elmira College	NY	53,900	C
Excelsior College	NY	38,800	SP
Frostburg State Univ	MD	17,280	LC
Geneva College	PA	35,450	C
Gordon College	MA	47,740	VC
Grand Valley State Univ	MI	22,250	C+
Hamilton College	NY	64,250	MC
Hartwick College	NY	51,270	C
Ithaca College	NY	58,158	VC+
Jackson State Univ	MS	15,879	LC
Kent State Univ	OH	20,928	C
Lewis & Clark College	OR	60,984	MC
Louisiana College	LA	21,274	C
Loyola Univ New Orleans	LA	52,456	VC
Marlboro College	VT	50,832	VC+
McNeese State Univ	LA	7,838	C
Mercyhurst Univ	PA	47,420	C
Miss College	MS	25,850	C
Miss State Univ	MS	12,028	C+
New York Univ	NY	68,139	MC
Newberry College	SC	34,550	C

ST = STATE $IS = IN-STATE COSTS SR = SELECTOR RATING

School	ST	$IS	SR
Northeastern Univ	MA	65,352	MC
Occidental College	CA	68,660	MC
Pomona College	CA	64,957	MC
Portland State Univ	OR	19,443	C
Principia College	IL	40,350	C
Regis Univ	CO	46,380	C
Roger Williams Univ	RI	48,074	VC
Roosevelt Univ	IL	41,890	VC
Samford Univ	AL	40,770	VC
San Francisco State Univ	CA	18,514	LC
Scripps College	CA	69,260	HC
Southern Illinois Univ Edwardsville	IL	20,188	C
Southern Methodist Univ	TX	69,008	MC
Southern Oregon Univ	OR	19,117	C
St. Cloud State Univ	MN	10,600	C
St. John's College at Annapolis	MD	63,348	MC
St. Lawrence Univ	NY	66,646	HC+
St. Mary's College of Maryland	MD	27,312	VC
Stockton Univ	NJ	25,565	C
Tenn State Univ	TN	14,423	LC
Texas A&M Univ at Commerce	TX	10,496	C
Texas Tech Univ	TX	20,156	C+
The Evergreen State College	WA	16,599	C
The Univ of Memphis	TN	18,278	C
Univ of Alabama in Huntsville	AL	20,028	VC
Univ of Alaska Anchorage	AK	17,914	C
Univ of Calif at Riverside	CA	32,912	C
Univ of Central Florida	FL	16,379	VC
Univ of Delaware	DE	32,214	VC
Univ of Denver	CO	61,129	VC+
Univ of Hartford	CT	49,776	C
Univ of New Mexico	NM	16,808	C
Univ of N Car at Greensboro	NC	15,998	C
Univ of PR-Rio Piedras campus	PR	13,327	
Univ of South Alabama	AL	16,880	C
Univ of Southern Miss	MS	13,170	C
Univ of Texas at El Paso	TX	34,452	NC
Virginia Commonwealth Univ	VA	23,811	VC
Virginia Wesleyan Univ	VA	45,980	LC
Washington Univ in St. Louis	MO	67,539	MC
Wilson College	PA	35,620	LC
Xavier Univ of Louisiana	LA	31,689	C

LASER ELECTRO-OPTICS TECHNOLOGY

School	ST	$IS	SR
Idaho State Univ	ID	13,619	LC
Oregon Inst of Technology	OR	19,227	C

LATIN

School	ST	$IS	SR
Austin College	TX	51,059	HC
Ball State Univ	IN	19,808	C+
Barnard College/Columbia Univ	NY	68,762	MC
Baylor Univ	TX	56,803	HC
Boston Univ	MA	67,352	MC
Bowling Green State Univ	OH	19,975	C
Brigham Young Univ	UT	13,248	MC
Bryn Mawr College	PA	65,220	MC
Butler Univ	IN	52,890	VC+
Carleton College	MN	66,414	MC
Centenary College of Louisiana	LA	49,050	C+
CUNY/Hunter College	NY	31,098	VC
CUNY/Lehman College	NY	5,788	LC
CUNY/Queens College	NY	21,507	C
Colgate Univ	NY	67,500	MC
Columbia Univ/City of New York	NY	62,958	MC
Concordia College - Moorhead	MN	46,418	C
Denison Univ	OH	62,770	HC+
DePauw Univ	IN	58,688	VC
Dickinson College	PA	66,166	MC
Duquesne Univ	PA	48,508	VC
Emory Univ	GA	63,286	MC
Florida State Univ	FL	16,771	HC
Fordham Univ	NY	68,431	MC
Franklin and Marshall College	PA	67,960	MC
Furman Univ	SC	61,098	VC+
Gettysburg College	PA	65,210	MC
Hampden-Sydney College	VA	57,806	VC
Harvard College/Harvard Univ	MA	65,609	MC
Haverford College	PA	66,490	MC
Hillsdale College	MI	37,170	MC
Hobart and William Smith Colleges	NY	67,050	HC+
Hofstra Univ	NY	58,210	C+
Hope College	MI	42,840	VC
John Carroll Univ	OH	51,570	C
Kenyon College	OH	65,840	MC
Knox College	IL	54,654	VC+
Loyola Univ Chicago	IL	57,158	VC
Loyola Univ Maryland	MD	61,710	VC
Marlboro College	VT	50,832	VC+
Mercer Univ	GA	45,348	VC
Mich State Univ	MI	24,542	VC
Missouri State Univ	MO	15,837	C+
Monmouth College	IL	42,260	C
Montclair State Univ	NJ	26,912	C
Mount Holyoke College	MA	56,746	MC
New York Univ	NY	68,139	MC
Ohio Univ	OH	23,394	VC
Purdue Univ/West Lafayette	IN	20,032	MC
Purdue Univ/West Lafayette	IN	20,032	MC
Randolph-Macon College	VA	51,480	VC
Rockford Univ	IL	38,570	C
St. Joseph's Univ	PA	58,540	VC
Samford Univ	AL	40,770	VC
Sarah Lawrence College	NY	68,866	MC
Seattle Pacific Univ	WA	47,439	C+
Sewanee: The Univ of the South	TN	58,000	HC+
Smith College	MA	66,774	MC
Southwestern Univ	TX	52,370	VC
St. Catherine Univ	MN	45,630	C
St. Olaf College	MN	56,430	HC
SUNY at Binghamton	NY	24,100	MC
Swarthmore College	PA	63,550	MC
The Catholic Univ of America	DC	58,376	VC
The College of Wooster	OH	60,000	HC
The Univ of Tenn at Chattanooga	TN	17,340	C+
The Univ of Texas at Austin	TX	20,206	MC
Trinity Univ	TX	54,480	MC
Tufts Univ	MA		MC
Univ of Calif at Berkeley	CA	29,886	MC
Univ of Calif at Davis	CA	28,468	HC
Univ of Calif at Los Angeles	CA	27,438	HC+
Univ of Georgia	GA	21,878	HC
Univ of Iowa	IA	19,415	HC
Univ of Mich/Ann Arbor	MI	25,274	MC
Univ of Minn/Twin Cities	MN	24,269	MC
Univ of Nebr - Lincoln	NE	18,589	VC
Univ of N Car at Greensboro	NC	15,998	C
Univ of Richmond	VA	62,730	MC
Univ of Scranton	PA	54,962	VC
Univ of Vermont	VT	29,792	HC
Univ of Wisc-Madison	WI	21,647	MC
Wabash College	IN	52,100	VC
Wake Forest Univ	NC	69,354	MC
Washington Univ in St. Louis	MO	67,539	MC
Wellesley College	MA	66,984	MC
Western Mich Univ	MI	21,791	C
Westminster College	PA	41,722	C
Wheaton College	MA	63,818	VC
Whitman College	WA	59,772	MC
Wichita State Univ	KS	17,773	C
Wright State Univ	OH	16,983	C

LATIN AMERICAN STUDIES

School	ST	$IS	SR
Adelphi Univ	NY	49,792	C
Albright College	PA	57,326	C
Appalachian State Univ	NC	15,394	VC
Arizona State Univ at the Tempe Campus	AZ	23,001	VC
Arizona State Univ at the West Campus	AZ	21,513	VC
Assumption College	MA	48,455	VC
Austin College	TX	51,059	HC
Bard College	NY	65,924	HC
Bates College	ME	64,500	HC
Baylor Univ	TX	56,803	HC
Bennington College	VT	66,280	MC
Boston Univ	MA	67,352	MC
Bowdoin College	ME	65,980	MC
Brandeis Univ	MA	68,443	MC
Brigham Young Univ	UT	13,248	MC
Brown Univ	RI	64,566	MC
Bucknell Univ	PA	67,136	MC
Cal State, Chico	CA	19,790	VC
Cal State, East Bay	CA	20,748	C
Cal State, Fresno	CA	16,902	LC
Cal State, Fullerton	CA	21,902	C
Cal State, Los Angeles	CA	17,186	LC
Canisius College	NY	49,672	C
Carleton College	MN	66,414	MC
CUNY/Brooklyn College	NY	7,163	C+
CUNY/City College	NY	20,204	C
CUNY/Hunter College	NY	31,098	VC
CUNY/Queens College	NY	21,507	C
Colby College	ME	64,060	MC
Colgate Univ	NY	67,500	MC
College of Charleston	SC	24,046	VC
College of the Holy Cross	MA	64,320	MC
College of William & Mary	VA	34,907	MC
Columbia Univ/ School of General Studies	NY	61,470	MC
Columbia Univ/City of New York	NY	62,958	MC
Conn College	CT	65,000	MC
Cornell College	IA	49,900	VC
Dartmouth College	NH	68,109	MC
Davidson College	NC	60,119	MC
Denison Univ	OH	62,770	HC+
DePaul Univ	IL	52,807	VC
Dickinson College	PA	66,166	MC
Earlham College	IN	55,670	HC
Eastern Mich Univ	MI	19,761	C
Elon Univ	NC	46,142	HC
Emory Univ	GA	63,286	MC
Flagler College	FL	27,620	C
Florida International Univ	FL	20,281	C
Florida State Univ	FL	16,771	HC
Fordham Univ	NY	68,431	MC
George Mason Univ	VA	19,884	C
Gettysburg College	PA	65,210	MC
Hamline Univ	MN	50,152	C
Hampshire College	MA	65,214	MC
Hobart and William Smith Colleges	NY	67,050	HC+
Hofstra Univ	NY	58,210	C+
Hood College	MD	50,540	C
Johns Hopkins Univ	MD	68,080	MC
Knox College	IL	54,654	VC+
Lake Forest College	IL	50,652	VC
Lehigh Univ	PA	63,860	MC
Linfield College	OR	53,992	C
Lock Haven Univ of Pennsylvania	PA	20,544	LC
Loyola Univ New Orleans	LA	52,456	VC
Macalester College	MN	64,136	MC
Miami Univ	OH	27,190	HC+
Middlebury College	VT	67,464	MC
Millsaps College	MS	50,080	C+
Mount Holyoke College	MA	56,746	MC
New College of Florida	FL	16,180	HC+
New York Univ	NY	68,139	MC
Oakland Univ	MI	20,763	C
Oberlin College	OH	68,942	MC
Occidental College	CA	68,660	MC
Ohio Univ	OH	23,394	VC
Pace Univ	NY	60,136	C
Pennsylvania State Univ - Univ Park	PA	29,716	HC
Pitzer College	CA	68,500	HC+
Pomona College	CA	64,957	MC
Rhode Island College	RI	19,000	LC
Rhodes College	TN	51,900	HC
Rollins College	FL	58,670	HC
Rutgers Univ - New Brunswick	NJ	27,090	HC
Rutgers Univ - New Brunswick	NJ	27,090	HC
St. Louis Univ	MO	49,866	HC
St. Peter's Univ	NJ	49,192	C
Samford Univ	AL	40,770	VC
San Diego State Univ	CA	23,156	VC
Scripps College	CA	69,260	HC
Seattle Pacific Univ	WA	47,439	C+
Seton Hall Univ	NJ	58,008	C
Smith College	MA	66,774	MC
Sonoma State Univ	CA	27,020	C
Southern Methodist Univ	TX	69,008	MC
Southern Nazarene Univ	OK	33,684	C
Southwestern Univ	TX	52,370	VC
St. Mary's Univ	TX	39,120	C
Stanford Univ	CA	62,541	MC
SUNY Albany	NY	22,165	C
SUNY at Binghamton	NY	24,100	MC
SUNY at New Paltz	NY	20,840	C
SUNY/Plattsburgh	NY	19,314	C
Stephen F. Austin State Univ	TX	18,484	LC
Syracuse Univ	NY	62,313	HC
Temple Univ	PA	24,392	C+
Texas Christian Univ	TX	57,120	HC
The American Univ	DC	61,317	HC
The College of Wooster	OH	60,000	HC
The George Washington Univ	DC	68,474	HC+
The Univ of Arizona	AZ	24,086	C
The Univ of Texas at Austin	TX	20,206	MC
The Univ of Utah	UT	18,751	VC
Tufts Univ	MA		MC
Tulane Univ	LA	67,496	MC
Union College	KY	32,310	C
Univ of Calif at Berkeley	CA	29,886	MC
Univ of Calif at Los Angeles	CA	27,438	HC+
Univ of Calif at Riverside	CA	32,912	C
Univ of Calif at Santa Barbara	CA	30,627	HC+
Univ of Calif San Diego	CA	30,450	MC
Univ of Calif, Santa Cruz	CA	28,731	C+
Univ of Central Florida	FL	16,379	VC
Univ of Chicago	IL	70,551	MC
Univ of Cincinnati	OH	22,118	VC
Univ of Conn	CT	27,394	
Univ of Delaware	DE	32,214	VC
Univ of Georgia	GA	21,878	HC
Univ of Idaho	ID	16,158	C
Univ of Illinois at Chicago	IL	24,664	VC
Univ of Illinois at Urbana-Champaign	IL	27,006	HC
Univ of Kansas	KS	20,884	VC
Univ of Kentucky	KY	24,800	C+
Univ of Miami	FL	63,494	MC
Univ of Mich/Ann Arbor	MI	25,274	MC
Univ of Minn/Morris	MN	21,222	VC
Univ of Nebr - Lincoln	NE	18,589	VC
Univ of Nebr - Omaha	NE	16,120	C
Univ of New Mexico	NM	16,808	C
Univ of N Car at Chapel Hill	NC	20,561	MC
Univ of N Car at Charlotte	NC	17,803	VC
Univ of N Car at Greensboro	NC	15,998	C
Univ of Okla	OK	19,651	HC
Univ of Oregon	OR	24,021	VC
Univ of Pennsylvania	PA	63,526	MC
Univ of Redlands	CA	61,934	VC
Univ of Rhode Island	RI	26,066	VC
Univ of Rochester	NY	65,032	MC
Univ of San Francisco	CA	60,580	C
Univ of S Car at Columbia	SC	21,726	VC
Univ of Southern Calif	CA	66,631	MC
Univ of Texas at El Paso	TX	34,452	NC
Univ of Texas Rio Grande Valley	TX	15,573	LC
Univ of Vermont	VT	29,792	HC
Univ of Wisc-Eau Claire	WI	16,354	VC
Univ of Wisc-Madison	WI	21,647	MC
Univ of Wisc-Milwaukee	WI	21,538	C
Vanderbilt Univ	TN	63,248	MC
Vassar College	NY	68,110	MC
Villanova Univ	PA	64,922	MC
Washington Univ in St. Louis	MO	67,539	MC
Wellesley College	MA	66,984	MC
Wesleyan Univ	CT	66,940	MC
Willamette Univ	OR	62,514	VC+
Wofford College	SC	49,885	VC
Yale Univ	CT	64,650	MC

LAW

School	ST	$IS	SR
Amherst College	MA	66,186	MC
Central Mich Univ	MI	20,330	C
CUNY/John Jay College of Criminal Justice	NY	6,359	SP
Dickinson College	PA	66,166	MC
Faulkner Univ	AL	26,410	C
Florida Gulf Coast Univ	FL	14,738	C
Grand Valley State Univ	MI	22,250	C+
Hampshire College	MA	65,214	MC
Hood College	MD	50,540	C
Howard Univ	DC	37,616	C+
Indiana Inst of Technology	IN	34,240	LC
Indiana Univ-Purdue Univ Indianapolis	IN	18,952	C
Lasell College	MA	49,400	C
Minn State Univ, Moorhead	MN	21,393	C
Mount Aloysius College	PA	29,976	C
Mount Ida College	MA	46,820	C
New York Univ	NY	68,139	MC
Oberlin College	OH	68,942	MC
Park Univ	MO	22,134	C
Ramapo College of New Jersey	NJ	25,760	VC
Regis College	MA	51,920	LC
Scripps College	CA	69,260	HC
South Univ	GA	36,070	LC
The College of St. Rose	NY	44,010	C
The Univ of Arizona	AZ	24,086	C
Towson Univ	MD	21,878	C
United States Air Force Academy	CO		C
Univ of Arkansas at Little Rock	AR	18,211	LC
Univ of Calif at Berkeley	CA	29,886	MC
Univ of Calif, Santa Cruz	CA	28,731	C+
Univ of Chicago	IL	70,551	MC
Univ of Hartford	CT	49,776	C
Univ of Mass Amherst	MA	27,669	HC
Univ of Pennsylvania	PA	63,526	MC
Univ of Texas Rio Grande Valley	TX	15,573	LC
Univ of Wisc-Superior	WI	14,838	C
Ursuline College	OH	41,076	LC
Wellesley College	MA	66,984	MC
West Virginia Univ	WV	18,952	VC
Western New England Univ	MA	49,182	C
Wilson College	PA	35,620	LC

LAW ENFORCEMENT AND CORRECTIONS

School	ST	$IS	SR
Adams State Univ	CO	15,420	LC
Amridge Univ	AL	10,860	LC
Ashford Univ	CA	10,480	C
Calumet College of St. Joseph	IN	22,735	C
College of the Ozarks	MO	7,530	VC
Drury Univ	MO	37,555	VC
East Central Univ	OK	13,330	C
Faulkner Univ	AL	26,410	C
Frostburg State Univ	MD	17,280	LC
Idaho State Univ	ID	13,619	LC
Indiana Inst of Technology	IN	34,240	LC
Indiana Wesleyan Univ	IN	33,674	C
Johnson & Wales Univ/ Denver Campus	CO	44,768	C
Lake Superior State Univ	MI	19,867	C
Metropolitan State Univ	MN	7,859	C
Minn State Univ, Mankato	MN	17,190	C
Missouri Southern State Univ	MO	13,071	C
Mount Aloysius College	PA	29,976	C
Point Park Univ	PA	41,270	C
Portland State Univ	OR	19,443	C
Sam Houston State Univ	TX	18,792	C
Southwest Minn State Univ	MN	17,783	C
Southwestern Okla State Univ	OK	12,205	C
Stephen F. Austin State Univ	TX	18,484	LC
Tarleton State Univ	TX	15,248	LC
Texas State Univ	TX	18,721	C
The Univ of Virginia's College at Wise	VA	18,192	LC
Thomas Univ	GA	21,420	NC
Tiffin Univ	OH	34,900	LC
Unity College	ME	37,670	C
Univ of Great Falls	MT	38,524	C
Univ of Illinois at Chicago	IL	24,664	VC
Univ of Maine at Augusta	ME	7,812	C
Univ of New Haven	CT	53,680	C
Univ of San Francisco	CA	60,580	C
Washburn Univ	KS	15,827	C
Weber State Univ	UT	14,112	C
Western Conn State Univ	CT	21,254	LC
Western Illinois Univ	IL	20,897	C

ST = STATE $IS = IN-STATE COSTS SR = SELECTOR RATING

School	ST	$IS	SR
Western New Mexico Univ	NM	16,914	LC
Western Oregon Univ	OR	19,965	LC
Youngstown State Univ	OH	17,487	C

LEADERSHIP

School	ST	$IS	SR
Averett Univ	VA	43,034	LC
Calif Baptist Univ	CA	42,986	C
Creighton Univ	NE	49,452	VC
Elon Univ	NC	46,142	HC
Old Dominion Univ	VA	21,618	C
Olivet Nazarene Univ	IL	41,840	VC
Purdue Univ Northwest	IN	15,178	C
Syracuse Univ	NY	62,313	HC
Univ of Okla	OK	19,651	HC

LEARNER DESIGNED AREA OF STUDY

School	ST	$IS	SR
Bloomfield College	NJ	40,100	LC
Bowling Green State Univ	OH	19,975	C
Goddard College	VT	17,040	VC
King Univ	TN	36,976	C
Thomas Edison State Univ	NJ	6,350	NC
Univ of Illinois at Chicago	IL	24,664	VC
Univ of Mich/Dearborn	MI	12,472	VC
Western Mich Univ	MI	21,791	C

LEGAL STUDIES

School	ST	$IS	SR
Auburn Univ at Montgomery	AL	15,000	C
Bay Path Univ	MA	46,356	C
Berkeley College/New York City Campus	NY	35,100	LC
Blackburn College	IL	28,526	LC
Bradley Univ	IL	43,240	VC
Champlain College	VT	54,724	VC
Culver-Stockton College	MO	34,350	C
Dominican Univ	IL	42,472	C+
Drexel Univ	PA	65,927	HC
East Central Univ	OK	13,330	C
Elizabethtown College	PA	56,340	VC
Faulkner Univ	AL	26,410	C
Gannon Univ	PA	42,922	C
Harding Univ	AR	25,440	C
Hardin-Simmons Univ	TX	36,025	C
Hodges Univ	FL	20,160	LC
Howard Univ	DC	37,616	C+
Illinois State Univ	IL	23,418	VC
Ithaca College	NY	58,158	VC+
Lasell College	MA	49,400	C
Lipscomb Univ	TN	42,984	VC
Manhattanville College	NY	52,430	C
Mercy College	NY	32,614	C
Monmouth Univ	NJ	50,184	C
Montclair State Univ	NJ	26,912	C
Nazareth College	NY	46,784	C
Nova Southeastern Univ	FL	38,534	C+
Paul Quinn College	TX	25,350	LC
Point Park Univ	PA	41,270	C
Roger Williams Univ	RI	48,074	VC
St. Louis Univ	MO	49,866	HC
Shawnee State Univ	OH	16,998	C
St. John Fisher College	NY	45,270	VC
St. John's Univ	NY	57,160	C+
Stephen F. Austin State Univ	TX	18,484	LC
Stevenson Univ	MD	48,412	C
Syracuse Univ	NY	62,313	HC
Temple Univ	PA	24,392	C+
Tenn Wesleyan Univ	TN	32,680	LC
The Univ of Tenn at Chattanooga	TN	17,340	C+
Tulane Univ	LA	67,496	MC
United States Military Academy at West Point	NY		HC+
Univ of Central Florida	FL	16,379	VC
Univ of Central Okla	OK	15,150	C
Univ of Detroit Mercy	MI	48,816	C
Univ of Kansas	KS	20,884	VC
Univ of Miami	FL	63,494	MC
Univ of New Haven	CT	53,680	C
Univ of Pittsburgh	PA	30,030	MC
Univ of Wisc-Madison	WI	21,647	MC
Webster Univ	MO	37,490	C
Wesley College	DE	37,848	LC

LIBERAL ARTS, SCIENCES, GENERAL STUDIES, HUMANITIES

School	ST	$IS	SR
American Univ of PR	PR	16,130	
Aquinas College - Mich	MI	38,876	VC
Azusa Pacific Univ	CA	43,972	C
Bloomfield College	NJ	40,100	LC
Bradley Univ	IL	43,240	VC
Cal State, Fullerton	CA	21,902	C
Elmira College	NY	53,900	C
Excelsior College	NY	38,800	SP
Florida International Univ	FL	20,281	C
Gannon Univ	PA	42,922	C
Johnson & Wales Univ/Denver Campus	CO	44,768	C
LIU Post	NY	50,698	C+
Marlboro College	VT	50,832	VC+
Milligan College	TN	39,450	C
Montana State Univ Billings	MT	13,336	LC
Murray State Univ	KY	17,726	C+
Northern Arizona Univ	AZ	21,003	C
Pennsylvania State Univ - Univ Park	PA	29,716	HC
Regis Univ	CO	46,380	C
St. John's College at Annapolis	MD	63,348	MC
St. Thomas Aquinas College	NY	32,450	C
Taylor Univ	IN	42,130	VC
The Master's Univ	CA	43,870	C
Thomas Edison State Univ	NJ	6,350	NC
Univ of Maine at Machias	ME	22,960	C
Univ of Okla	OK	19,651	HC
Univ of St. Thomas - Houston	TX	41,510	VC
Univ of Wisc-Parkside	WI	15,313	C
Washington College	MD	56,154	VC
Washington State Univ	WA	22,747	C
Wellesley College	MA	66,984	MC
West Chester Univ of Pennsylvania	PA	19,171	VC
Western Illinois Univ	IL	20,897	C
Western New England Univ	MA	49,182	C
Wilson College	PA	35,620	LC

LIBERAL ARTS/ENGINEERING STUDIES

School	ST	$IS	SR
Calif Polytechnic State Univ	CA	22,547	MC
Cal State, Fullerton	CA	21,902	C
Wellesley College	MA	66,984	MC
Worcester Polytechnic Inst	MA	62,846	MC

LIBERAL ARTS/GENERAL STUDIES

School	ST	$IS	SR
Abilene Christian Univ	TX	43,708	C+
Adams State Univ	CO	15,420	LC
Alaska Pacific Univ	AK	28,730	VC
Albertus Magnus College	CT	44,016	LC
Alvernia Univ	PA	45,330	C
American International College	MA	47,020	LC
American Jewish Univ - College of A&S	CA	44,234	C
Amridge Univ	AL	10,860	LC
Angelo State Univ	TX	15,882	LC
Anna Maria College	MA	51,020	C
Aquinas College	TN	30,800	C+
Aquinas College - Mich	MI	38,876	VC
Arcadia Univ	PA	55,990	C+
Arizona State Univ at the Polytechnic Campus	AZ	22,394	VC
Armstrong State Univ	GA	15,615	C
Ashford Univ	CA	10,480	C
Atlantic Union College	MA	27,228	C
Auburn Univ at Montgomery	AL	15,000	C
Aurora Univ	IL	34,990	C
Austin Peay State Univ	TN	16,397	C
Averett Univ	VA	43,034	LC
Azusa Pacific Univ	CA	43,972	C
Ball State Univ	IN	19,808	C+
Barry Univ	FL	38,730	LC
Bay Path Univ	MA	46,356	C
Beacon College	FL	46,862	C
Becker College	MA	30,100	LC
Bellarmine Univ	KY	52,532	C
Belmont Abbey College	NC	28,794	C
Belmont Univ	TN	44,500	VC+
Benedictine College	KS	38,850	VC
Bennington College	VT	66,280	MC
Bentley Univ	MA	63,720	MC
Bethel College	IN	36,830	C
Bethune-Cookman Univ	FL	23,322	C
Biola Univ	CA	48,686	C
Bloomfield College	NJ	40,100	LC
Blue Mountain College	MS	15,949	C
Boricua College	NY	10,100	C
Bowling Green State Univ	OH	19,975	C
Brenau Univ - Women's College	GA	37,876	LC
Brescia Univ	KY	29,890	VC
Brewton-Parker College	GA	26,120	LC
Bridgewater College	VA	46,260	C
Bryan College	TN	32,900	C
Cabrini Univ	PA	42,591	LC
Cairn Univ	PA	37,572	C
Calif Baptist Univ	CA	42,986	C
Calif Lutheran Univ	CA	52,853	C
Calif Polytechnic State Univ	CA	22,547	MC
Calif State Polytechnic Univ, Pomona	CA	21,811	C
Cal State, Bakersfield	CA	22,397	LC
Cal State, Chico	CA	19,790	VC
Cal State, Dominguez Hills	CA	19,022	LC
Cal State, East Bay	CA	20,748	C
Cal State, Fresno	CA	16,902	LC
Cal State, Fullerton	CA	21,902	C
Cal State, Los Angeles	CA	17,186	LC
Cal State, Monterey Bay	CA	22,872	LC
Cal State, Northridge	CA	17,277	LC
Cal State, San Bernardino	CA	20,106	C
Cal State, San Marcos	CA	20,604	LC
Cal State, Stanislaus	CA	18,053	LC
Calif Univ of Pennsylvania	PA	20,425	LC
Calumet College of St. Joseph	IN	22,735	C
Canisius College	NY	49,672	C
Carlow Univ	PA	39,696	LC
Castleton Univ	VT	20,186	C
Cazenovia College	NY	47,866	C
Cedarville Univ	OH	36,244	VC
Centenary College of Louisiana	LA	49,050	C+
Central Washington Univ	WA	16,803	C
Champlain College	VT	54,724	VC
Charter Oak State College	CT	7,983	NC
Chestnut Hill College	PA	47,180	C
Cheyney Univ of Pennsylvania	PA	20,896	LC
Christian Brothers Univ	TN	31,670	VC
CUNY/Medgar Evers College	NY	6,680	NC
CUNY/York College	NY	6,747	LC
City Univ of Seattle	WA	24,340	NC
Clarion Univ of Pennsylvania	PA	21,608	LC
Clarke Univ	IA	42,950	C
Cleveland State Univ	OH	22,290	C
College of Mount St. Vincent	NY	45,620	C
College of St. Mary	NE	27,500	C
College of St Joseph	VT	32,400	LC
Colo Christian Univ	CO	40,885	VC
Colo College	CO	64,894	MC
Colo Mesa Univ	CO	19,707	LC
Colo State Univ	CO	23,033	C
Columbia College - Missouri	MO	28,179	C
Columbus State Univ	GA	14,336	LC
Concordia Univ Irvine	CA	44,860	VC
Concordia Univ Texas	TX	41,920	C
Coppin State Univ	MD	14,071	VC
Cornerstone Univ	MI	36,550	C
Curry College	MA	53,331	C
Dallas Baptist Univ	TX	35,220	VC
DeSales Univ	PA	47,520	C
Dominican Univ of Calif	CA	58,750	C
Duquesne Univ	PA	48,508	VC
East Carolina Univ	NC	16,539	C
East Central Univ	OK	13,330	C
East Tenn State Univ	TN	18,141	C
Eastern Conn State Univ	CT	23,059	C
Eastern Mennonite Univ	VA	42,550	C
Eastern Oregon Univ	OR	17,612	C
Edinboro Univ	PA	15,940	LC
Elmhurst College	IL	46,514	C
Emmanuel College	MA	53,472	C+
Emporia State Univ	KS	15,029	C
Endicott College	MA	47,054	C+
Eureka College	IL	34,760	C
Excelsior College	NY	38,800	SP
Fairfield Univ	CT	61,445	HC
Fairleigh Dickinson Univ/College at Florham	NJ	54,770	C
Fairleigh Dickinson Univ/Metropolitan Campus	NJ	52,392	C
Faulkner Univ	AL	26,410	C
Felician Univ	NJ	46,280	LC
Ferrum College	VA	43,970	C
Flagler College	FL	27,620	C
Florida Atlantic Univ	FL	18,256	C
Florida Gulf Coast Univ	FL	14,738	C
Florida International Univ	FL	20,281	C
Fontbonne Univ	MO	34,606	C
Fort Hays State Univ	KS	12,677	C
Francis Marion Univ	SC	18,144	LC
Friends Univ	KS	38,000	C
Frostburg State Univ	MD	17,280	LC
Gallaudet Univ	DC	30,088	LC
Georgetown College	KY	41,440	C
Georgia College & State Univ	GA	21,884	C+
Glenville State College	WV	17,386	LC
Goddard College	VT	17,040	VC
Graceland Univ	IA	35,290	C
Grand Valley State Univ	MI	22,250	C+
Green Mountain College	VT	45,228	LC
Greenville College	IL	27,012	LC
Hannibal-LaGrange Univ	MO	29,815	C
Harding Univ	AR	25,440	C
Harris-Stowe State Univ	MO	14,590	NC
Haverford College	PA	66,490	MC
Hilbert College	NY	32,650	LC
Hofstra Univ	NY	58,210	C+
Holy Names Univ	CA	46,630	LC
Hope International Univ	CA	42,730	C
Houghton College	NY	40,558	VC
Houston Baptist Univ	TX	36,450	C
Howard Payne Univ	TX	35,994	C
Humboldt State Univ	CA	21,708	C
Idaho State Univ	ID	13,619	LC
Indiana State Univ	IN	23,223	LC
Indiana Univ Bloomington	IN	20,791	HC
Indiana Univ-Purdue Univ Fort Wayne	IN	18,675	C
Indiana Wesleyan Univ	IN	33,674	C
Iona College	NY	52,514	C
Iowa State Univ	IA	18,176	C
Ithaca College	NY	58,158	VC+
James Madison Univ	VA	19,084	VC
John Carroll Univ	OH	51,570	C
Johnson & Wales Univ/Denver Campus	CO	44,768	C
Johnson C. Smith Univ	NC	25,336	LC
Johnson State College	VT	22,672	C
Kentucky Christian Univ	KY	26,836	LC
Kentucky State Univ	KY	14,484	LC
Kutztown Univ of Pennsylvania	PA	19,477	C
La Roche College	PA	38,940	C
La Sierra Univ	CA	39,690	VC
Lewis Univ	IL	41,710	C
Lewis-Clark State College	ID	14,202	C
Liberty Univ	VA	31,415	C
Limestone College	SC	32,100	C
Lincoln Univ	MO	14,402	NC
Lincoln Univ	PA	20,878	LC
Lindenwood Univ	MO	25,760	C
Lindsey Wilson College	KY	33,546	C
Lipscomb Univ	TN	42,984	VC
Lock Haven Univ of Pennsylvania	PA	20,544	LC
Longwood Univ	VA	22,184	C
Louisiana State Univ and A&M College	LA	18,677	VC
Louisiana State Univ in Shreveport	LA	6,902	C
Louisiana Tech Univ	LA	11,422	VC
Loyola Marymount Univ	CA	60,202	VC+
Loyola Univ New Orleans	LA	52,456	VC
Lynn Univ	FL	49,680	LC
MacMurray College	IL	35,025	C
Madonna Univ	MI	30,450	LC
Malone Univ	OH	39,200	C
Mansfield Univ of Pennsylvania	PA	24,244	LC
Marist College	NY	49,860	VC
Mary Baldwin Univ	VA	40,495	C
Marymount Manhattan College	NY	48,350	C
Marymount Univ	VA	43,231	C
Maryville Univ of St. Louis	MO	38,558	VC
Mass College of Liberal Arts	MA	20,659	C
Mayville State Univ	ND	18,371	NC
McNeese State Univ	LA	7,838	C
Medaille College	NY	41,700	LC
Mercy College	NY	32,614	C
Merrimack College	MA	55,415	C
Metropolitan State Univ	MN	7,859	C
Mich Tech Univ	MI	25,551	VC+
Middlebury College	VT	67,464	MC
Midway Univ	KY	33,940	LC
Minot State Univ	ND	13,285	C
Misericordia Univ	PA	45,210	C
Miss State Univ	MS	12,028	C+
Missouri Baptist Univ	MO	35,594	C
Missouri Valley College	MO	28,150	C
Mitchell College	CT	45,192	C
Montana State Univ	MT	15,500	C+
Montana State Univ Billings	MT	13,336	LC
Montana Tech of the Univ of Montana	MT	15,447	VC
Montreat College	NC	34,605	LC
Morehead State Univ	KY	18,386	LC
Morris College	SC	19,195	LC
Mount Aloysius College	PA	29,976	C
Mount Ida College	MA	46,820	C
Mount Mary Univ	WI	34,650	LC
Mount St. Joseph Univ	OH	33,880	LC
Mount St. Mary's Univ - Chalon Campus	CA	50,486	VC+
National Univ	CA	17,849	LC
Neumann Univ	PA	40,678	LC
New Mexico Inst of Mining and Technology	NM	15,385	HC+
Newman Univ	KS	37,382	C
Niagara Univ	NY	41,010	C
Northern Arizona Univ	AZ	21,003	C
Northern Illinois Univ	IL	20,176	C
Northern Kentucky Univ	KY	16,486	C
Northwest Nazarene Univ	ID	40,250	C
Northwest Univ	WA	38,720	VC
Northwestern State Univ of Louisiana	LA	16,534	LC
Norwich Univ	VT	56,234	C
Notre Dame de Namur Univ	CA	46,526	LC
Notre Dame of Maryland Univ	MD	47,570	VC
Oakland Univ	MI	20,763	C
Ohio Dominican Univ	OH	41,340	C+
Okla Christian Univ	OK	29,260	C
Okla City Univ	OK	40,476	C
Okla State Univ	OK	17,180	C+
Okla Wesleyan Univ	OK	34,434	C
Oral Roberts Univ	OK	34,316	C
Oregon State Univ	OR	23,337	VC
Otterbein Univ	OH	41,630	C
Our Lady of the Lake Univ	TX	37,790	LC
Palm Beach Atlantic Univ	FL	39,250	C
Park Univ	MO	22,134	C
Paul Quinn College	TX	25,350	LC
Penn State Altoona	PA	26,686	C
Pepperdine Univ	CA	66,862	VC+
Pittsburg State Univ	KS	13,880	C
Point Park Univ	PA	41,270	C
Pontifical Catholic Univ of PR	PR	10,534	
Portland State Univ	OR	19,443	C
Post Univ	CT	41,150	C
Prescott College	AZ	38,201	C
Providence College	RI	62,870	HC
Purdue Univ Northwest	IN	15,178	C
Purdue Univ/West Lafayette	IN	20,032	MC
Quinnipiac Univ	CT	60,970	VC
Radford Univ	VA	19,758	C
Ramapo College of New Jersey	NJ	25,760	VC
Regis College	MA	51,920	LC
Regis Univ	CO	46,380	C
Reinhardt Univ	GA	31,344	C
Rider Univ	NJ	54,050	C
Rivier Univ	NH	41,600	VC
Roberts Wesleyan College	NY	41,116	C

ST = STATE $IS = IN-STATE COSTS SR = SELECTOR RATING

School	ST	$IS	SR
Roosevelt Univ	IL	41,890	VC
Rosemont College	PA	30,980	LC
Rowan Univ	NJ	24,491	VC
Rutgers Univ - Camden	NJ	26,595	C
Sacred Heart Univ	CT	54,590	C
St. Anselm College	NH	56,636	VC
St. Joseph's Univ	PA	58,540	VC
St. Mary's College of Calif	CA	57,420	C
St. Vincent College	PA	46,229	C
Salem International Univ	WV	21,090	C
Salisbury Univ	MD	21,132	VC
Salve Regina Univ	RI	53,046	VC
Samford Univ	AL	40,770	VC
San Diego Christian College	CA	40,914	C
San Diego State Univ	CA	23,156	VC
San Francisco State Univ	CA	18,514	LC
Sarah Lawrence College	NY	68,866	MC
Schreiner Univ	TX	34,626	LC
Seattle Pacific Univ	WA	47,439	C+
Seattle Univ	WA	54,957	VC
Seton Hall Univ	NJ	58,008	C
Seton Hill Univ	PA	46,972	VC
Shaw Univ	NC	24,638	C
Siena Heights Univ	MI	36,322	C
Simpson Univ	CA	34,722	C
Skidmore College	NY	66,600	MC
Sonoma State Univ	CA	27,020	C
S Dak State Univ	SD	15,874	C
Southeastern Louisiana Univ	LA	16,237	C
Southern Illinois Univ Carbondale	IL	24,554	C
Southern Illinois Univ Edwardsville	IL	20,188	C
Southern Methodist Univ	TX	69,008	MC
Southern New Hampshire Univ	NH	44,256	C
Southern Oregon Univ	OR	19,117	C
Southern Vermont College	VT	34,670	LC
Southwestern College	KS	31,531	LC
Spalding Univ	KY	31,938	C
Spring Hill College	AL	48,488	C
St. Francis College	NY	38,800	LC
St. John's College at Annapolis	MD	63,348	MC
St. John's College, Santa Fe	NM	60,109	HC+
St. John's Univ	NY	57,160	C+
St. Joseph's College, New York/Brooklyn Campus	NY	25,114	LC
St. Joseph's College, New York/Long Island Campus	NY	25,124	C
St. Thomas Univ	FL	51,187	LC
SUNY at New Paltz	NY	20,840	C
SUNY at Purchase College	NY	21,832	C
SUNY Polytechnic Inst	NY	20,438	VC
SUNY/Empire State College	NY	9,145	NC
SUNY/Fredonia	NY	20,818	C
Stephens College	MO	38,042	C
Stockton Univ	NJ	25,565	C
Stony Brook Univ/The SUNY	NY	22,703	MC
Susquehanna Univ	PA	57,560	VC
Syracuse Univ	NY	62,313	HC
Tabor College	KS	35,870	C
Tarleton State Univ	TX	15,248	LC
Taylor Univ	IN	42,130	VC
Texas Southern Univ	TX	19,592	LC
Texas State Univ	TX	18,721	C
Texas Tech Univ	TX	20,156	C+
The Catholic Univ of America	DC	58,376	VC
The College at Brockport - SUNY	NY	21,058	C
The Evergreen State College	WA	16,599	C
The George Washington Univ	DC	68,474	HC+
The Master's Univ	CA	43,870	C
The Univ of Mary	ND	23,180	C
The Univ of Memphis	TN	18,278	C
The Univ of Montana Western	MT	9,426	LC
The Univ of Texas at Austin	TX	20,206	MC
The Univ of Virginia's College at Wise	VA	18,192	LC
Thomas Aquinas College	CA	32,450	HC+
Thomas Edison State Univ	NJ	6,350	NC
Thomas More College	KY	36,720	LC
Thomas More College of Liberal Arts	NH	30,100	C
Thomas Univ	GA	21,420	NC
Touro College	NY	31,040	C
Trinity International Univ	IL	31,070	VC
Tulane Univ	LA	67,496	MC
Union College	NY	64,320	MC
Union Inst & Univ	OH	8,912	SP
Univ of Alaska Anchorage	AK	17,914	C
Univ of Alaska Southeast	AK	17,615	C
Univ of Arkansas at Little Rock	AR	18,211	LC
Univ of Arkansas at Monticello	AR	13,599	LC
Univ of Arkansas at Pine Bluff	AR	13,541	C
Univ of Calif at Riverside	CA	32,912	C
Univ of Central Florida	FL	16,379	VC
Univ of Central Okla	OK	15,150	C
Univ of Charleston	WV	35,000	LC
Univ of Cincinnati	OH	22,118	VC
Univ of Delaware	DE	32,214	VC
Univ of Detroit Mercy	MI	48,816	C
Univ of Evansville	IN	44,186	C+
Univ of Hawaii at Hilo	HI	18,038	VC
Univ of Holy Cross	LA	21,523	NC
Univ of Houston	TX	21,871	VC
Univ of Illinois at Urbana-Champaign	IL	27,006	HC
Univ of Iowa	IA	19,415	HC
Univ of Kansas	KS	20,884	VC
Univ of La Verne	CA	55,600	C
Univ of Louisville	KY	19,692	C
Univ of Lynchburg	VA	48,370	C
Univ of Maine at Augusta	ME	7,812	C
Univ of Maine at Farmington	ME	18,792	C
Univ of Maine at Fort Kent	ME	15,165	LC
Univ of Maine at Machias	ME	22,960	C
Univ of Maine at Presque Isle	ME	16,148	LC
Univ of Mary Washington	VA	23,039	C+
Univ of Maryland Univ College	MD	26,146	LC
Univ of Maryland/Eastern Shore	MD	21,861	LC
Univ of Mass Amherst	MA	27,669	HC
Univ of Mass Dartmouth	MA	26,507	C
Univ of Mass Lowell	MA	27,296	VC
Univ of Miami	FL	63,494	MC
Univ of Mich/Ann Arbor	MI	25,274	MC
Univ of Mich/Dearborn	MI	12,472	VC
Univ of Minn/Morris	MN	21,222	VC
Univ of Miss	MS	18,802	C
Univ of Missouri-Columbia	MO	20,463	VC
Univ of Missouri-Kansas City	MO	19,563	VC
Univ of Missouri-St. Louis	MO	19,810	VC
Univ of Mobile	AL	28,935	C
Univ of Montana	MT	14,105	C
Univ of Mount Olive	NC	18,426	C
Univ of Nebr - Lincoln	NE	18,589	VC
Univ of Nebr - Omaha	NE	16,120	C
Univ of New England	ME	50,110	C
Univ of New Haven	CT	53,680	C
Univ of New Mexico	NM	16,808	C
Univ of North Alabama	AL	15,964	C
Univ of N Car at Asheville	NC	16,251	VC+
Univ of N Car at Charlotte	NC	17,803	VC
Univ of N Car at Greensboro	NC	15,998	C
Univ of North Texas	TX	20,082	C
Univ of Northern Iowa	IA	17,480	C
Univ of Notre Dame	IN	68,801	MC
Univ of Pittsburgh	PA	30,030	MC
Univ of Pittsburgh at Bradford	PA	22,958	C
Univ of PR-Rio Piedras campus	PR	13,327	
Univ of Redlands	CA	61,934	VC
Univ of St. Francis	IN	38,520	C
Univ of St. Mary	KS	37,080	NC
Univ of San Diego	CA	60,338	HC
Univ of San Francisco	CA	60,580	C
Univ of S Car Upstate	SC	19,272	LC
Univ of S Dak	SD	16,109	C
Univ of South Florida/Tampa	FL	16,110	VC
Univ of St. Francis	IL	40,828	C
Univ of St. Thomas - Houston	TX	41,510	VC
Univ of Tampa	FL	38,928	VC
Univ of Texas Rio Grande Valley	TX	15,573	LC
Univ of the Ozarks	AR	31,050	NC
Univ of the Pacific	CA	57,446	VC
Univ of Washington	WA	23,091	MC
Univ of Wisc-Eau Claire	WI	16,354	VC
Univ of Wisc-Green Bay	WI	15,184	C
Univ of Wisc-Milwaukee	WI	21,538	C
Univ of Wisc-Oshkosh	WI	15,392	C
Univ of Wisc-Platteville	WI	14,148	C
Univ of Wisc-Stevens Point	WI	14,043	C
Urbana Univ	OH	30,820	C
Utah State Univ	UT	13,235	C
Utica College	NY	31,510	C
Vanguard Univ of Southern Calif	CA	42,400	VC
Villanova Univ	PA	64,922	MC
Virginia Wesleyan Univ	VA	45,980	LC
Viterbo Univ	WI	34,660	C
Walsh Univ	OH	39,010	C
Warner Pacific College	OR	31,610	C
Washburn Univ	KS	15,827	C
Washington Adventist Univ	MD	32,050	LC
Washington State Univ	WA	22,747	C
Weber State Univ	UT	14,112	C
Wellesley College	MA	66,984	MC
Wesley College	DE	37,848	LC
West Chester Univ of Pennsylvania	PA	19,171	VC
West Texas A&M Univ	TX	13,478	C
West Virginia Univ	WV	18,952	VC
Western Carolina Univ	NC	13,965	C
Western Conn State Univ	CT	21,254	LC
Western Kentucky Univ	KY	16,850	C
Western New England Univ	MA	49,182	C
Western Washington Univ	WA	18,904	VC
Westfield State Univ	MA	20,404	C
Westmont College	CA	57,930	VC
Wheeling Jesuit Univ	WV	37,106	LC
Wichita State Univ	KS	17,773	C
Wilberforce Univ	OH	19,900	C
Wiley College	TX	19,255	C
Wilkes Univ	PA	49,166	C
William Carey Univ	MS	23,950	LC
William Peace Univ	NC	39,300	LC
Wilmington College	OH	35,100	C
Wilson College	PA	35,620	LC
Wingate Univ	NC	41,900	C
Worcester State Univ	MA	20,977	C
Wright State Univ	OH	16,983	C
Xavier Univ	OH	49,380	VC
York College	NE	30,260	C

LIBRARY SCIENCE

School	ST	$IS	SR
Ashford Univ	CA	10,480	C
Cal State, Fullerton	CA	21,902	C
Clarion Univ of Pennsylvania	PA	21,608	LC
Kutztown Univ of Pennsylvania	PA	19,477	C
Northwestern Okla State Univ	OK	13,072	LC
San Jose State Univ	CA	22,630	C
Southern Conn State Univ	CT	21,924	LC
The Univ of Arizona	AZ	24,086	C
Univ of Central Arkansas	AR	15,042	VC
Univ of Maine at Augusta	ME	7,812	C
Univ of Nebr - Omaha	NE	16,120	C
West Virginia Univ	WV	18,952	VC

LIFE SCIENCE

School	ST	$IS	SR
Arkansas Tech Univ	AR	16,534	LC
Atlantic Union College	MA	27,228	C
Baylor Univ	TX	56,803	HC
Biola Univ	CA	48,686	C
Bowling Green State Univ	OH	19,975	C
Hofstra Univ	NY	58,210	C+
Indiana Univ East	IN	7,207	C
Kansas State Univ	KS	17,780	VC
Malone Univ	OH	39,200	C
McMurry Univ	TX	34,259	LC
Minn State Univ, Mankato	MN	17,190	C
Missouri Southern State Univ	MO	13,071	C
Missouri Univ of Science and Technology	MO	18,655	HC
Mount Vernon Nazarene Univ	OH	35,944	C
National Univ	CA	17,849	LC
New York Inst of Technology	NY	49,980	VC
Niagara Univ	NY	41,010	C
Ohio Univ	OH	23,394	VC
Otterbein Univ	OH	41,630	C
Suffolk Univ	MA	52,316	C
United States Military Academy at West Point	NY		HC+
Wayland Baptist Univ	TX	23,460	LC
Wayne State College	NE	25,746	NC
Western Washington Univ	WA	18,904	VC
Wright State Univ	OH	16,983	C
Xavier Univ	OH	49,380	VC

LIFE SCIENCE SECONDARY SCHOOL EDUCATION

School	ST	$IS	SR
Cedarville Univ	OH	36,244	VC
Franklin College	IN	40,550	C
Kent State Univ	OH	20,928	C
Minn State Univ, Mankato	MN	17,190	C
St. Mary's Univ of Minn	MN	42,440	C
Univ of Nebr - Lincoln	NE	18,589	VC

LINGUISTICS

School	ST	$IS	SR
Alabama A&M Univ	AL	18,796	C
Ashford Univ	CA	10,480	C
Bard College at Simon's Rock	MA	65,795	MC
Barnard College/Columbia Univ	NY	68,762	MC
Boston College	MA	68,043	MC
Boston Univ	MA	67,352	MC
Brandeis Univ	MA	68,443	MC
Brigham Young Univ	UT	13,248	MC
Brown Univ	RI	64,566	MC
Bryn Mawr College	PA	65,220	MC
Bucknell Univ	PA	67,136	MC
Cal State, Fresno	CA	16,902	LC
Cal State, Fullerton	CA	21,902	C
Cal State, Monterey Bay	CA	22,872	LC
Cal State, Northridge	CA	17,277	LC
Calvin College	MI	43,090	HC
Carleton College	MN	66,414	MC
Carnegie Mellon Univ	PA	67,980	MC
Cedarville Univ	OH	36,244	VC
Central College	IA	44,592	C
CUNY/Brooklyn College	NY	7,163	C+
CUNY/Lehman College	NY	5,788	LC
CUNY/Queens College	NY	21,507	C
Cleveland State Univ	OH	22,290	C
College of William & Mary	VA	34,907	MC
Columbia Univ/City of New York	NY	62,958	MC
Corban Univ	OR	41,700	C
Cornell Univ	NY	67,591	MC
Dartmouth College	NH	68,109	MC
DePauw Univ	IN	58,688	VC
Duke Univ	NC	68,298	MC
Earlham College	IN	55,670	HC
Eastern Mich Univ	MI	19,761	C
Emory Univ	GA	63,286	MC
Florida Atlantic Univ	FL	18,256	C
Florida State Univ	FL	16,771	HC
Georgetown Univ	DC	68,970	MC
Gordon College	MA	47,740	VC
Hampshire College	MA	65,214	MC
Harvard College/Harvard Univ	MA	65,609	MC
Haverford College	PA	66,490	MC
Hofstra Univ	NY	58,210	C+
Indiana Univ Bloomington	IN	20,791	HC
Iowa State Univ	IA	18,176	C
Lawrence Univ	WI	56,133	HC+
Macalester College	MN	64,136	MC
Marlboro College	VT	50,832	VC+
Mass Inst of Technology	MA	62,662	MC
Miami Univ	OH	27,190	HC+
Mich State Univ	MI	24,542	VC
Millersville Univ of Pennsylvania	PA	25,298	C
Montclair State Univ	NJ	26,912	C
New York Univ	NY	68,139	MC
Northeastern Illinois Univ	IL	12,529	LC
Northeastern Univ	MA	65,352	MC
Northwestern Univ	IL	68,725	MC
Oakland Univ	MI	20,763	C
Ohio State Univ at Columbus	OH	22,843	MC
Ohio Univ	OH	23,394	VC
Old Dominion Univ	VA	21,618	C
Pitzer College	CA	68,500	HC+
Pomona College	CA	64,957	MC
Purdue Univ/West Lafayette	IN	20,032	MC
Reed College	OR	65,300	MC
Rice Univ	TX	59,458	MC
Rutgers Univ - Camden	NJ	26,595	C
Rutgers Univ - New Brunswick	NJ	27,090	HC
Rutgers Univ - New Brunswick	NJ	27,090	HC
San Diego State Univ	CA	23,156	VC
San Jose State Univ	CA	22,630	C
Seattle Pacific Univ	WA	47,439	C+
Southern Illinois Univ Carbondale	IL	24,554	C
Stanford Univ	CA	62,541	MC
SUNY Albany	NY	22,165	C
SUNY at Binghamton	NY	24,100	MC
SUNY at Oswego	NY	22,219	VC
SUNY/Univ at Buffalo	NY	23,122	C
Stony Brook Univ/The SUNY	NY	22,703	MC
Swarthmore College	PA	63,550	MC
Syracuse Univ	NY	62,313	HC
Temple Univ	PA	24,392	C+
The Univ of Arizona	AZ	24,086	C
The Univ of Texas at Austin	TX	20,206	MC
The Univ of Utah	UT	18,751	VC
Truman State Univ	MO	16,286	MC
Tulane Univ	LA	67,496	MC
Univ of Alaska Fairbanks	AK	16,874	VC
Univ of Calif at Berkeley	CA	29,886	MC
Univ of Calif at Davis	CA	28,468	HC
Univ of Calif at Los Angeles	CA	27,438	HC+
Univ of Calif at Riverside	CA	32,912	C
Univ of Calif at Santa Barbara	CA	30,627	HC+
Univ of Calif San Diego	CA	30,450	MC
Univ of Calif, Santa Cruz	CA	28,731	C+
Univ of Chicago	IL	70,551	MC
Univ of Cincinnati	OH	22,118	VC
Univ of Colo Boulder	CO	26,048	HC
Univ of Conn	CT	27,394	
Univ of Florida	FL	16,291	HC+
Univ of Georgia	GA	21,878	HC
Univ of Hawaii at Hilo	HI	18,038	VC
Univ of Hawaii at Manoa	HI	23,261	C
Univ of Illinois at Urbana-Champaign	IL	27,006	HC
Univ of Iowa	IA	19,415	HC
Univ of Kansas	KS	20,884	VC
Univ of Kentucky	KY	24,800	C+
Univ of Louisville	KY	19,692	C
Univ of Maryland/Baltimore County	MD	23,004	VC
Univ of Maryland/College Park	MD	21,938	HC
Univ of Mass Amherst	MA	27,669	HC
Univ of Mich/Ann Arbor	MI	25,274	MC
Univ of Minn/Twin Cities	MN	24,269	MC
Univ of Miss	MS	18,802	C
Univ of Missouri-Columbia	MO	20,463	VC
Univ of Montana	MT	14,105	C
Univ of New Hampshire	NH	29,333	VC
Univ of New Mexico	NM	16,808	C
Univ of N Car at Chapel Hill	NC	20,561	MC
Univ of Okla	OK	19,651	HC
Univ of Oregon	OR	24,021	VC
Univ of Pennsylvania	PA	63,526	MC
Univ of Pittsburgh	PA	30,030	MC
Univ of Rochester	NY	65,032	MC
Univ of Southern Calif	CA	66,631	MC
Univ of Texas at Arlington	TX	18,876	C
Univ of Texas at El Paso	TX	34,452	NC
Univ of Toledo	OH	19,336	C
Univ of Vermont	VT	29,792	HC
Univ of Wisc-Madison	WI	21,647	MC
Univ of Wisc-Milwaukee	WI	21,538	C
Washington State Univ	WA	22,747	C
Washington Univ in St. Louis	MO	67,539	MC
Wayne State Univ	MI	23,085	C
Wellesley College	MA	66,984	MC
Western Washington Univ	WA	18,904	VC
Yale Univ	CT	64,650	MC

ST = STATE $IS = IN-STATE COSTS SR = SELECTOR RATING

LITERATURE

School	ST	$IS	SR
Adrian College	MI	45,550	C
American Jewish Univ - College of A&S	CA	44,234	C
Andrews Univ	MI	41,732	C
Aquinas College - Mich	MI	38,876	VC
Ball State Univ	IN	19,808	C+
Bard College	NY	65,924	HC
Bard College at Simon's Rock	MA	65,795	MC
Baylor Univ	TX	56,803	HC
Beloit College	WI	55,206	HC
Benedictine Univ	IL	38,300	C
Bennington College	VT	66,280	MC
Brigham Young Univ	UT	13,248	MC
Bryant Univ	RI	57,204	VC
Calif College of the Arts	CA	52,758	SP
Cal State, San Marcos	CA	20,604	LC
Calvin College	MI	43,090	HC
Castleton Univ	VT	20,186	C
Claremont McKenna College	CA	69,900	MC
Coe College	IA	51,570	VC
College of the Holy Cross	MA	64,320	MC
Columbia Univ/ School of General Studies	NY	61,470	MC
Concordia College - New York	NY	39,035	LC
Cornerstone Univ	MI	36,550	C
DePauw Univ	IN	58,688	VC
Dordt College	IA	37,860	C+
Duke Univ	NC	68,298	MC
Eastern Mich Univ	MI	19,761	C
Eastern Nazarene College	MA	41,114	C
Eastern Washington Univ	WA	17,896	LC
Eckerd College	FL	55,206	VC
Elon Univ	NC	46,142	HC
Emory and Henry College	VA	46,320	C
Eugene Lang College of Liberal Arts	NY	64,940	VC
Fairleigh Dickinson Univ/ College at Florham	NJ	54,770	C
Faulkner Univ	AL	26,410	C
Fitchburg State Univ	MA	21,819	LC
George Fox Univ	OR	42,938	C
Goddard College	VT	17,040	VC
Gonzaga Univ	WA	52,880	HC
Graceland Univ	IA	35,290	C
Hampshire College	MA	65,214	MC
Harvard College/Harvard Univ	MA	65,609	MC
Hellenic College/Holy Cross Greek Orthodox School of Theology	MA	39,906	C
John Carroll Univ	OH	51,570	C
Keene State College	NH	24,604	C
Kutztown Univ of Pennsylvania	PA	19,477	C
Lake Superior State Univ	MI	19,867	C
Le Moyne College	NY	47,305	VC
Linfield College	OR	53,992	C
Lubbock Christian Univ	TX	29,727	C
Lycoming College	PA	50,895	C
Maharishi Univ of Management	IA	34,930	VC
Marshall Univ	WV	18,044	C
Mass Inst of Technology	MA	62,662	MC
Missouri Southern State Univ	MO	13,071	C
Nazareth College	NY	46,784	C
New College of Florida	FL	16,180	HC+
New York Univ	NY	68,139	MC
North Central Univ	MN	30,610	C
Northwestern College of Iowa	IA	38,400	C
Ohio Northern Univ	OH	44,050	VC
Ohio Univ	OH	23,394	VC
Old Dominion Univ	VA	21,618	C
Oral Roberts Univ	OK	34,316	C
Pacific Univ	OR	37,617	C
Point Loma Nazarene Univ	CA	46,150	C+
Pomona College	CA	64,957	MC
Ramapo College of New Jersey	NJ	25,760	VC
Reed College	OR	65,300	MC
Roanoke College	VA	55,952	VC
Rocky Mountain College	MT	35,776	C
Roosevelt Univ	IL	41,890	VC
St. Mary-of-the-Woods College	IN	40,424	LC
St. Mary's Univ of Minn	MN	42,440	C
San Jose State Univ	CA	22,630	C
Sarah Lawrence College	NY	68,866	MC
Seattle Pacific Univ	WA	47,439	C+
Southwest Minn State Univ	MN	17,783	C
St. John's College at Annapolis	MD	63,348	MC
SUNY at Binghamton	NY	24,100	MC
SUNY at Purchase College	NY	21,832	C
Stevens Inst of Technology	NJ	64,954	MC
Stockton Univ	NJ	25,565	C
Swarthmore College	PA	63,550	MC
Texas Tech Univ	TX	20,156	C+
The American Univ	DC	61,317	HC
The College of Idaho	ID	36,415	C
The George Washington Univ	DC	68,474	HC+
Touro College	NY	31,040	C
Union College	NE	23,270	C
United States Military Academy at West Point	NY		HC+
Univ of Alaska Southeast	AK	17,615	C
Univ of Bridgeport	CT	44,985	LC
Univ of Calif at Santa Barbara	CA	30,627	HC+
Univ of Calif San Diego	CA	30,450	MC
Univ of Calif, Santa Cruz	CA	28,731	C+
Univ of Evansville	IN	44,186	C+
Univ of Mich/Ann Arbor	MI	25,274	MC
Univ of New Haven	CT	53,680	C
Univ of N Car at Asheville	NC	16,251	VC+
Univ of Texas at Dallas	TX	23,640	HC
Washington Univ in St. Louis	MO	67,539	MC
Waynesburg Univ	PA	33,530	C
Wellesley College	MA	66,984	MC
Wells College	NY	50,500	C
West Chester Univ of Pennsylvania	PA	19,171	VC
Western Kentucky Univ	KY	16,850	C
Wilberforce Univ	OH	19,900	C
Wright State Univ	OH	16,983	C
Yale Univ	CT	64,650	MC
Youngstown State Univ	OH	17,487	C

LOGISTICS

School	ST	$IS	SR
Central Mich Univ	MI	20,330	C
Embry-Riddle Aeronautical Univ - Worldwide	FL	17,720	C
Georgia Southern Univ	GA	16,540	VC
Inter-American Univ of PR-Bayamon	PR	18,785	
John Carroll Univ	OH	51,570	C
Missouri Southern State Univ	MO	13,071	C
Missouri State Univ	MO	15,837	C+
Ohio State Univ at Columbus	OH	22,843	MC
Rutgers Univ - New Brunswick	NJ	27,090	HC
Rutgers Univ - New Brunswick	NJ	27,090	HC
The Univ of Memphis	TN	18,278	C
The Univ of Tenn at Knoxville	TN	22,112	VC
Univ of Alaska Anchorage	AK	17,914	C
Univ of Illinois at Urbana-Champaign	IL	27,006	HC
Univ of Maryland/College Park	MD	21,938	HC
Univ of Missouri-St. Louis	MO	19,810	VC
Univ of North Texas	TX	20,082	C
Univ of Pennsylvania	PA	63,526	MC
Univ of St. Francis	IL	40,828	C

LUSO-BRAZILIAN STUDIES

School	ST	$IS	SR
Brown Univ	RI	64,566	MC
New York Univ	NY	68,139	MC
Smith College	MA	66,774	MC

MANAGEMENT

School	ST	$IS	SR
Anderson Univ	IN	39,450	C
Arizona State Univ at the Polytechnic Campus	AZ	22,394	VC
Arizona State Univ at the Tempe Campus	AZ	23,001	VC
Arizona State Univ at the West Campus	AZ	21,513	VC
Arkansas Tech Univ	AR	16,534	LC
Cal State, Fullerton	CA	21,902	C
Cambridge College	MA	14,940	NC
Central Conn State Univ	CT	22,041	C
Chatham Univ	PA	47,883	VC
Christopher Newport Univ	VA	24,878	VC+
Clayton State Univ	GA	19,735	LC
Columbia College Chicago	IL	40,104	C
Cornell College	IA	49,900	VC
Creighton Univ	NE	49,452	VC
Davis & Elkins College	WV	38,242	LC
Drury Univ	MO	37,555	VC
East Central Univ	OK	13,330	C
Elon Univ	NC	46,142	HC
Embry-Riddle Aeronautical Univ - Worldwide	FL	17,720	C
Florida International Univ	FL	20,281	C
Framingham State Univ	MA	21,740	C
Franciscan Univ of Steubenville	OH	33,980	VC
Georgia Southern Univ	GA	16,540	VC
Hiram College	OH	44,590	C
Hofstra Univ	NY	58,210	C+
Indiana Univ Bloomington	IN	20,791	HC
John Brown Univ	AR	35,184	VC
Keene State College	NH	24,604	C
Kent State Univ	OH	20,928	C
Kutztown Univ of Pennsylvania	PA	19,477	C
Lewis Univ	IL	41,710	C
Lincoln Univ	PA	20,878	LC
Loyola Marymount Univ	CA	60,202	VC+
Lubbock Christian Univ	TX	29,727	C
Mich State Univ	MI	24,542	VC
Missouri Baptist Univ	MO	35,594	C
Moravian College	PA	55,488	C
Mount Vernon Nazarene Univ	OH	35,944	C
Nichols College	MA	46,900	LC
Northwest Univ	WA	38,720	VC
Okla Baptist Univ	OK	33,990	C
Providence College	RI	62,870	HC
Purdue Univ Northwest	IN	15,178	C
Regis Univ	CO	46,380	C
Rochester Inst of Technology	NY	52,734	HC+
Samford Univ	AL	40,770	VC
Shawnee State Univ	OH	16,998	C
Southeast Missouri State Univ	MO	16,148	C
Southeastern Louisiana Univ	LA	16,237	C
Southwestern Okla State Univ	OK	12,205	C
St. Ambrose Univ	IA	40,180	C
Syracuse Univ	NY	62,313	HC
Texas State Univ	TX	18,721	C
Texas Tech Univ	TX	20,156	C+
The College of St. Rose	NY	44,010	C
Univ of Conn	CT	27,394	
Univ of Georgia	GA	21,878	HC
Univ of Mass Dartmouth	MA	26,507	C
Univ of Mount Union	OH	39,990	C
Univ of N Car at Greensboro	NC	15,998	C
Univ of North Georgia	GA	17,316	C
Univ of Notre Dame	IN	68,801	MC
Univ of Okla	OK	19,651	HC
Univ of Rhode Island	RI	26,066	VC
Univ of St. Francis	IN	38,520	C
Univ of Tampa	FL	38,928	VC
Univ of Wisc-La Crosse	WI	15,425	VC
Villanova Univ	PA	64,922	MC
Washington State Univ	WA	22,747	C
Wingate Univ	NC	41,900	C
Wittenberg Univ	OH	49,863	VC
Woodbury Univ	CA	49,593	VC

MANAGEMENT & STRATEGIC LEADERSHIP

School	ST	$IS	SR
Bradley Univ	IL	43,240	VC
Carroll Univ	WI	38,100	C+
Iowa Wesleyan Univ	IA	41,000	C
Lehigh Univ	PA	63,860	MC
Ohio Univ	OH	23,394	VC
San Diego State Univ	CA	23,156	VC
Tarleton State Univ	TX	15,248	LC
Univ of Louisiana at Monroe	LA	15,970	C
Western Mich Univ	MI	21,791	C

MANAGEMENT ENGINEERING

School	ST	$IS	SR
Appalachian State Univ	NC	15,394	VC
Claremont McKenna College	CA	69,900	MC
Mich Tech Univ	MI	25,551	VC+
Pitzer College	CA	68,500	HC+
Stanford Univ	CA	62,541	MC
Univ of PR, at Bayamon	PR	13,145	
Western Kentucky Univ	KY	16,850	C
Worcester Polytechnic Inst	MA	62,846	MC

MANAGEMENT INFORMATION SYSTEMS

School	ST	$IS	SR
Adams State Univ	CO	15,420	LC
Adelphi Univ	NY	49,792	C
Albertus Magnus College	CT	44,016	LC
Alverno College	WI	33,294	LC
Amridge Univ	AL	10,860	LC
Andrews Univ	MI	41,732	C
Angelo State Univ	TX	15,882	LC
Aquinas College - Mich	MI	38,876	VC
Ashland Univ	OH	30,446	C
Augsburg Univ	MN	45,129	C
Augusta Univ	GA	4,632	C
Barry Univ	FL	38,730	LC
Baylor Univ	TX	56,803	HC
Benedictine Univ	IL	38,300	C
Biola Univ	CA	48,686	C
Bloomfield College	NJ	40,100	LC
Bowling Green State Univ	OH	19,975	C
Bradley Univ	IL	43,240	VC
Bridgewater College	VA	46,260	C
Brigham Young Univ	UT	13,248	MC
Bryant Univ	RI	57,204	VC
Butler Univ	IN	52,890	VC+
Cal State, Fullerton	CA	21,902	C
Cal State, Long Beach	CA	18,850	C
Cal State, Northridge	CA	17,277	LC
Cal State, Sacramento	CA	19,060	C
Cal State, San Bernardino	CA	20,106	C
Calvin College	MI	43,090	HC
Canisius College	NY	49,672	C
Central Conn State Univ	CT	22,041	C
Central Mich Univ	MI	20,330	C
Chatham Univ	PA	47,883	VC
CUNY/Medgar Evers College	NY	6,680	NC
Cleveland State Univ	OH	22,290	C
Colo Christian Univ	CO	40,885	VC
Colo Mesa Univ	CO	19,707	LC
Colo State Univ	CO	23,033	C
Colo Technical Univ	CO	21,455	NC
Columbus State Univ	GA	14,336	LC
Dallas Baptist Univ	TX	35,220	VC
DePaul Univ	IL	52,807	VC
DeSales Univ	PA	47,520	C
Dordt College	IA	37,860	C+
Drexel Univ	PA	65,927	HC
Duquesne Univ	PA	48,508	VC
East Carolina Univ	NC	16,539	C
Eastern Illinois Univ	IL	21,414	C
Eastern Mich Univ	MI	19,761	C
Embry-Riddle Aeronautical Univ - Worldwide	FL	17,720	C
Eureka College	IL	34,760	C
Excelsior College	NY	38,800	SP
Faulkner Univ	AL	26,410	C
Fayetteville State Univ	NC	17,756	C
Florida Atlantic Univ	FL	18,256	C
Florida Inst of Technology	FL	53,306	VC
Fort Hays State Univ	KS	12,677	C
Friends Univ	KS	38,000	C
George Fox Univ	OR	42,938	C
Georgetown College	KY	41,440	C
Georgia College & State Univ	GA	21,884	C+
Georgia Southern Univ	GA	16,540	VC
Georgia State Univ	GA	25,250	C
Goldey-Beacom College	DE	36,038	C
Grace College and Seminary	IN	31,524	C
Grand View Univ	IA	32,302	C
Greenville College	IL	27,012	LC
Hawaii Pacific Univ	HI	33,420	C
Hawaii Pacific Univ	HI	33,420	C
Hawaii Pacific Univ	HI	33,420	C
Hofstra Univ	NY	58,210	C+
Humphreys College	CA	27,790	C
Idaho State Univ	ID	13,619	LC
Indiana State Univ	IN	23,223	LC
Indiana Univ of Pennsylvania	PA	24,474	C
Inter-American Univ of PR Ponce	PR	19,549	
Inter-American Univ of PR-Aguadilla Campus	PR	21,657	
Inter-American Univ of PR-Bayamon	PR	18,785	
Inter-American Univ of PR-Fajardo Campus	PR	18,336	
Inter-American Univ of PR-Metropolitan Campus	PR	20,045	
Jefferson (Philadelphia Univ + Thomas Jefferson Univ)	PA	53,966	C
John Carroll Univ	OH	51,570	C
Johnson & Wales Univ/ Providence Campus	RI	44,768	C
Kansas State Univ	KS	17,780	VC
La Salle Univ	PA	43,476	C
Le Moyne College	NY	47,305	VC
Lenoir-Rhyne Univ	NC	47,500	LC
LeTourneau Univ	TX	39,190	VC
Lewis Univ	IL	41,710	C
Liberty Univ	VA	31,415	C
Lindenwood Univ	MO	25,760	C
Lipscomb Univ	TN	42,984	VC
Loras College	IA	40,726	C
Loyola Marymount Univ	CA	60,202	VC+
Loyola Univ Chicago	IL	57,158	VC
Lubbock Christian Univ	TX	29,727	C
MacMurray College	IL	35,025	C
Madonna Univ	MI	30,450	LC
Marietta College	OH	46,190	C
Marquette Univ	WI	53,090	VC+
Marshall Univ	WV	18,044	C
McMurry Univ	TX	34,259	LC
Medaille College	NY	41,700	LC
Menlo College	CA	51,380	LC
Mercyhurst Univ	PA	47,420	C
Metropolitan State Univ	MN	7,859	C
Miami Univ	OH	27,190	HC+
Mich Tech Univ	MI	25,551	VC+
Midland Univ	NE	39,512	C
Minot State Univ	ND	13,285	C
Missouri Southern State Univ	MO	13,071	C
Missouri Univ of Science and Technology	MO	18,655	HC
Morehead State Univ	KY	18,386	LC
Morningside College	IA	39,780	C
Mount Aloysius College	PA	29,976	C
Mount Mercy Univ	IA	39,748	C
Mount Vernon Nazarene Univ	OH	35,944	C
New Mexico Highlands Univ	NM	11,904	LC
New Mexico State Univ	NM	14,050	LC
New York Univ	NY	68,139	MC
Newman Univ	KS	37,382	C
N Dak State Univ	ND	16,245	VC
Northeastern Univ	MA	65,352	MC
Northwest Christian Univ	OR	36,580	C
Northwood Univ - Mich	MI	35,010	LC
Oakland Univ	MI	20,763	C
Ohio Dominican Univ	OH	41,340	C+
Ohio State Univ at Columbus	OH	22,843	MC
Ohio Univ	OH	23,394	VC
Okla State Univ	OK	17,180	C+
Old Dominion Univ	VA	21,618	C
Oral Roberts Univ	OK	34,316	C
Oregon Inst of Technology	OR	19,227	C
Ottawa Univ	KS	39,980	VC
Our Lady of the Lake Univ	TX	37,790	LC
Park Univ	MO	22,134	C
Peirce College	PA	16,780	NC
Penn State Erie,The Behrend College	PA	26,688	VC
Pennsylvania College of Technology	PA	27,693	NC
Pennsylvania State Univ - Univ Park	PA	29,716	HC
Rensselaer Polytechnic Inst	NY	67,265	MC
Rivier Univ	NH	41,600	VC
Rochester Inst of Technology	NY	52,734	HC+
Rockford Univ	IL	38,570	C
Rutgers Univ - Newark	NJ	27,351	C
St. Francis Univ	PA	46,146	NC
St. Joseph's Univ	PA	58,540	VC
St. Louis Univ	MO	49,866	HC
St. Mary's College	IN	50,600	C

School	ST	$IS	SR
Savannah State Univ	GA	17,036	C
Schreiner Univ	TX	34,626	LC
Seton Hall Univ	NJ	58,008	C
Seton Hill Univ	PA	46,972	VC
Shippensburg Univ of Pennsylvania	PA	24,096	C
Shorter Univ	GA	31,130	LC
Simmons College	MA	54,400	HC
Simpson College	IA	45,626	VC
Southern Illinois Univ Edwardsville	IL	20,188	C
Southern Nazarene Univ	OK	33,684	C
Spring Arbor Univ	MI	37,390	C
St. Bonaventure Univ	NY	45,596	C
St. Catherine Univ	MN	45,630	C
SUNY at Binghamton	NY	24,100	MC
SUNY/College at Old Westbury	NY	16,860	C
SUNY/Empire State College	NY	9,145	NC
SUNY/Plattsburgh	NY	19,314	C
Stephen F. Austin State Univ	TX	18,484	LC
Temple Univ	PA	24,392	C+
Texas A&M Univ at College Station	TX	20,771	VC+
Texas A&M Univ at Corpus Christi	TX	16,851	LC
Texas Tech Univ	TX	20,156	C+
The Univ of Alabama	AL	24,320	C+
The Univ of Arizona	AZ	24,086	C
The Univ of Mary	ND	23,180	C
The Univ of Memphis	TN	18,278	C
The Univ of Montana Western	MT	9,426	LC
The Univ of Texas at Austin	TX	20,206	MC
The Univ of Utah	UT	18,751	VC
Thiel College	PA	42,950	LC
Thomas College	ME	73,888	LC
Trine Univ	IN	41,310	C
Univ of Alaska Anchorage	AK	17,914	C
Univ of Arkansas at Monticello	AR	13,599	LC
Univ of Bridgeport	CT	44,985	LC
Univ of Central Okla	OK	15,150	C
Univ of Conn	CT	27,394	
Univ of Dayton	OH	54,930	VC
Univ of Delaware	DE	32,214	VC
Univ of Georgia	GA	21,878	HC
Univ of Hartford	CT	49,776	C
Univ of Hawaii at Manoa	HI	23,261	C
Univ of Houston	TX	21,871	VC
Univ of Idaho	ID	16,158	C
Univ of Illinois at Urbana-Champaign	IL	27,006	HC
Univ of Indianapolis	IN	36,480	VC
Univ of Jamestown	ND	28,508	C
Univ of Kansas	KS	20,884	VC
Univ of Maryland Univ College	MD	26,146	LC
Univ of Maryland/College Park	MD	21,938	HC
Univ of Mass Dartmouth	MA	26,507	C
Univ of Mich/Dearborn	MI	12,472	VC
Univ of Minn/Duluth	MN	20,292	C
Univ of Miss	MS	18,802	C
Univ of Missouri-St. Louis	MO	19,810	VC
Univ of Montana	MT	14,105	C
Univ of Nebr - Omaha	NE	16,120	C
Univ of Nevada, Las Vegas	NV	17,553	C
Univ of N Car at Charlotte	NC	17,803	VC
Univ of North Texas	TX	20,082	C
Univ of Northern Iowa	IA	17,480	C
Univ of Northwestern - St. Paul	MN	39,530	C
Univ of Okla	OK	19,651	HC
Univ of Pennsylvania	PA	63,526	MC
Univ of Rhode Island	RI	26,066	VC
Univ of San Francisco	CA	60,580	C
Univ of South Florida/Tampa	FL	16,110	VC
Univ of Southern Indiana	IN	16,808	C
Univ of Tampa	FL	38,928	VC
Univ of Texas at El Paso	TX	34,452	NC
Univ of the Sacred Heart	PR	17,932	
Univ of Tulsa	OK	52,625	HC
Univ of West Georgia	GA	17,510	LC
Univ of Wisc-Milwaukee	WI	21,538	C
Univ of Wisc-Oshkosh	WI	15,392	C
Univ of Wisc-Parkside	WI	15,313	C
Upper Iowa Univ	IA	34,990	NC
Ursuline College	OH	41,076	LC
Utah State Univ	UT	13,235	C
Villanova Univ	PA	64,922	MC
Virginia State Univ	VA	19,802	C+
Viterbo Univ	WI	34,660	C
Washington State Univ	WA	22,747	C
Wayland Baptist Univ	TX	23,460	LC
Wayne State Univ	MI	23,085	C
Weber State Univ	UT	14,112	C
West Virginia Univ	WV	18,952	VC
Western Conn State Univ	CT	21,254	LC
Western Kentucky Univ	KY	16,850	C
Western Mich Univ	MI	21,791	C
Western New Mexico Univ	NM	16,914	LC
Western Washington Univ	WA	18,904	VC
Westminster College	MO	32,820	C
Widener Univ	PA	58,190	C
Winona State Univ	MN	18,109	C
Winston-Salem State Univ	NC	18,005	LC
Worcester Polytechnic Inst	MA	62,846	MC
Wright State Univ	OH	16,983	C
York College of Pennsylvania	PA	29,240	C
Youngstown State Univ	OH	17,487	C

MANAGEMENT SCIENCE

School	ST	$IS	SR
Abilene Christian Univ	TX	43,708	C+
Alabama A&M Univ	AL	18,796	C
Anderson Univ	IN	39,450	C
Avila Univ	MO	27,100	C
Barry Univ	FL	38,730	LC
Belmont Univ	TN	44,500	VC+
Bethany College	WV	38,774	LC
Bethel Univ	TN	27,142	C
Biola Univ	CA	48,686	C
Boston College	MA	68,043	MC
Bridgewater State Univ	MA	22,762	C
Brigham Young Univ	UT	13,248	MC
Bryant Univ	RI	57,204	VC
Caldwell Univ	NJ	42,165	LC
Cal State, Fullerton	CA	21,902	C
Cal State, Monterey Bay	CA	22,872	LC
Cal State, San Bernardino	CA	20,106	C
Calif Univ of Pennsylvania	PA	20,425	LC
Canisius College	NY	49,672	C
Central Mich Univ	MI	20,330	C
Chaminade Univ of Honolulu	HI	37,614	C
Champlain College	VT	54,724	VC
Chicago State Univ	IL	41,620	C
CUNY/Baruch College	NY	21,609	HC
CUNY/Lehman College	NY	5,788	LC
Claflin Univ	SC	25,592	LC
Clemson Univ	SC		HC
Cleveland State Univ	OH	22,290	C
College of St. Benedict	MN	54,480	C
Colo Christian Univ	CO	40,885	VC
Colo Technical Univ	CO	21,455	NC
Concordia Univ Wisc	WI	35,910	C
Coppin State Univ	MD	14,071	VC
Cumberland Univ	TN	27,710	C
Davenport Univ	MI	25,896	LC
Defiance College	OH	42,240	LC
Delta State Univ	MS	13,176	LC
DePaul Univ	IL	52,807	VC
Drake Univ	IA	49,220	HC
Duquesne Univ	PA	48,508	VC
East Tenn State Univ	TN	18,141	C
Eastern Mich Univ	MI	19,761	C
Eastern Washington Univ	WA	17,896	LC
Eckerd College	FL	55,206	VC
Elmhurst College	IL	46,514	C
Evangel Univ	MO	28,898	C
Fairfield Univ	CT	61,445	HC
Faulkner Univ	AL	26,410	C
Fitchburg State Univ	MA	21,819	LC
Florida State Univ	FL	16,771	HC
Franklin Pierce Univ	NH	46,750	LC
Franklin Univ	OH	11,616	NC
Gannon Univ	PA	42,922	C
George Fox Univ	OR	42,938	C
Goodwin College	CT	28,370	LC
Grand Canyon Univ	AZ	25,150	VC
Grand Valley State Univ	MI	22,250	C+
Gwynedd Mercy Univ	PA	43,780	LC
Hardin-Simmons Univ	TX	36,025	C
Hawaii Pacific Univ	HI	33,420	C
Heidelberg Univ	OH	40,400	LC
Idaho State Univ	ID	13,619	LC
Indiana Univ-Purdue Univ Fort Wayne	IN	18,675	C
Indiana Wesleyan Univ	IN	33,674	C
Iona College	NY	52,514	C
Iowa State Univ	IA	18,176	C
Jefferson (Philadelphia Univ + Thomas Jefferson Univ)	PA	53,966	C
Kean Univ	NJ	25,620	C
Kennesaw State Univ	GA	18,899	VC
Langston Univ	OK	15,659	C
Lesley Univ	MA	42,800	C
Limestone College	SC	32,100	C
Loras College	IA	40,726	C
Louisiana State Univ and A&M College	LA	18,677	VC
Louisiana State Univ in Shreveport	LA	6,902	C
Louisiana Tech Univ	LA	11,422	VC
Loyola Univ New Orleans	LA	52,456	VC
Luther College	IA	49,990	VC
Madonna Univ	MI	30,450	LC
Maharishi Univ of Management	IA	34,930	VC
Marian Univ	IN	43,206	C
Marian Univ	WI	34,622	C
Marylhurst Univ	OR	16,818	NC
Mass Inst of Technology	MA	62,662	MC
Metropolitan State Univ of Denver	CO	6,928	LC
Miami Univ	OH	27,190	HC+
Mich Tech Univ	MI	25,551	VC+
Midwestern State Univ	TX	12,111	LC
Millikin Univ	IL	44,148	C
Minn State Univ, Mankato	MN	17,190	C
Minn State Univ, Moorhead	MN	21,393	C
Minot State Univ	ND	13,285	C
Missouri State Univ	MO	15,837	C+
Morehead State Univ	KY	18,386	LC
Mount Aloysius College	PA	29,976	C
Murray State Univ	KY	17,726	C+
National Louis Univ	IL	43,000	LC
National Univ	CA	17,849	LC
New Jersey Inst of Technology	NJ	30,198	HC
New York Univ	NY	68,139	MC
N Dak State Univ	ND	16,245	VC
Northeastern Illinois Univ	IL	12,529	LC
Northern Arizona Univ	AZ	21,003	C
Notre Dame College	OH	39,150	VC
Ohio Northern Univ	OH	44,050	VC
Ohio Univ	OH	23,394	VC
Okla City Univ	OK	40,476	C
Oral Roberts Univ	OK	34,316	C
Oregon State Univ	OR	23,337	VC
Palm Beach Atlantic Univ	FL	39,250	C
Pepperdine Univ	CA	66,862	VC+
Point Park Univ	PA	41,270	C
Portland State Univ	OR	19,443	C
Post Univ	CT	41,150	C
Prescott College	AZ	38,201	C
Quinnipiac Univ	CT	60,970	VC
Rensselaer Polytechnic Inst	NY	67,265	MC
Rice Univ	TX	59,458	MC
Rider Univ	NJ	54,050	C
Rivier Univ	NH	41,600	VC
Rochester Inst of Technology	NY	52,734	HC+
Roger Williams Univ	RI	48,074	VC
Roosevelt Univ	IL	41,890	VC
Rutgers Univ - Camden	NJ	26,595	C
Rutgers Univ - New Brunswick	NJ	27,090	HC
Rutgers Univ - Newark	NJ	27,351	C
St. Francis Univ	PA	46,146	NC
St. John's Univ	MN	53,472	C
St. Leo Univ	FL	32,850	C
Salisbury Univ	MD	21,132	VC
Salve Regina Univ	RI	53,046	VC
San Francisco State Univ	CA	18,514	LC
Southern Illinois Univ Carbondale	IL	24,554	C
Southern Methodist Univ	TX	69,008	MC
Southern Nazarene Univ	OK	33,684	C
Southwestern Adventist Univ	TX	28,232	LC
St. Bonaventure Univ	NY	45,596	C
St. Francis College	NY	38,800	LC
St. John's Univ	NY	57,160	C+
SUNY at Binghamton	NY	24,100	MC
SUNY at Oswego	NY	22,219	VC
SUNY/Cortland	NY	20,910	C
SUNY/Empire State College	NY	9,145	NC
Stephen F. Austin State Univ	TX	18,484	LC
Stockton Univ	NJ	25,565	C
Suffolk Univ	MA	52,316	C
Tarleton State Univ	TX	15,248	LC
Tenn Tech Univ	TN	17,929	C
Texas A&M Univ at College Station	TX	20,771	VC+
Texas A&M Univ at Kingsville	TX	16,580	LC
The Catholic Univ of America	DC	58,376	VC
The Univ of Akron	OH	22,566	C
The Univ of Arizona	AZ	24,086	C
The Univ of Memphis	TN	18,278	C
The Univ of Tenn at Knoxville	TN	22,112	VC
The Univ of Tenn at Martin	TN	15,212	C
The Univ of Texas at Austin	TX	20,206	MC
The Univ of Texas at San Antonio	TX	21,060	C
The Univ of Utah	UT	18,751	VC
Thomas College	ME	73,888	LC
Touro College	NY	31,040	C
Trevecca Nazarene Univ	TN	31,186	C
Trine Univ	IN	41,310	C
Troy Univ	AL	16,171	C
Tulane Univ	LA	67,496	MC
Tusculum College	TN	31,625	LC
Tuskegee Univ	AL	28,164	C
Union College	NE	23,270	C
Union Univ	TN	41,160	VC
United States Air Force Academy	CO		C
United States Coast Guard Academy	CT	942	HC
United States Military Academy at West Point	NY		HC+
Universidad del Turabo	PR	17,828	
Universidad Metropolitana	PR	17,828	
Univ of Arkansas at Little Rock	AR	18,211	LC
Univ of Bridgeport	CT	44,985	LC
Univ of Calif at Berkeley	CA	29,886	MC
Univ of Calif at Riverside	CA	32,912	C
Univ of Calif San Diego	CA	30,450	MC
Univ of Central Florida	FL	16,379	VC
Univ of Central Missouri	MO	18,982	C
Univ of Cincinnati	OH	22,118	VC
Univ of Colo Boulder	CO	26,048	HC
Univ of Delaware	DE	32,214	VC
Univ of Florida	FL	16,291	HC+
Univ of Great Falls	MT	38,524	C
Univ of Hartford	CT	49,776	C
Univ of Hawaii at Manoa	HI	23,261	C
Univ of Illinois at Chicago	IL	24,664	VC
Univ of Illinois at Urbana-Champaign	IL	27,006	HC
Univ of Iowa	IA	19,415	HC
Univ of Louisiana at Lafayette	LA	14,516	C
Univ of Louisville	KY	19,692	C
Univ of Lynchburg	VA	48,370	C
Univ of Maryland Univ College	MD	26,146	LC
Univ of Mass Boston	MA	13,828	C
Univ of Miami	FL	63,494	MC
Univ of Minn/Morris	MN	21,222	VC
Univ of Minn/Twin Cities	MN	24,269	MC
Univ of Miss	MS	18,802	C
Univ of Montevallo	AL	20,012	C
Univ of Nebr - Lincoln	NE	18,589	VC
Univ of Nebr - Omaha	NE	16,120	C
Univ of Nevada, Las Vegas	NV	17,553	C
Univ of Nevada, Reno	NV	18,010	C
Univ of N Car at Chapel Hill	NC	20,561	MC
Univ of North Texas	TX	20,082	C
Univ of Northern Colo	CO	19,658	C
Univ of Northern Iowa	IA	17,480	C
Univ of Pittsburgh at Greensburg	PA	24,140	C
Univ of PR, at Cayey	PR		
Univ of PR-Rio Piedras campus	PR	13,327	
Univ of St. Joseph	CT	49,069	C
Univ of S Car at Columbia	SC	21,726	VC
Univ of S Dak	SD	16,109	C
Univ of South Florida St. Petersburg	FL	15,980	C
Univ of South Florida/Tampa	FL	16,110	VC
Univ of St. Francis	IL	40,828	C
Univ of Texas at Arlington	TX	18,876	C
Univ of Texas at El Paso	TX	34,452	NC
Univ of Texas Rio Grande Valley	TX	15,573	LC
Univ of Tulsa	OK	52,625	HC
Univ of Wisc-Stout	WI	19,667	C
Univ of Wyoming	WY	15,537	C
Upper Iowa Univ	IA	34,990	NC
Valparaiso Univ	IN	50,160	VC
Virginia Polytechnic Inst and State Univ	VA	21,920	VC
Viterbo Univ	WI	34,660	C
Waynesburg Univ	PA	33,530	C
Webber International Univ	FL	31,904	C
Webster Univ	MO	37,490	C
West Liberty Univ	WV	16,158	C
West Texas A&M Univ	TX	13,478	C
Western Carolina Univ	NC	13,965	C
Western Kentucky Univ	KY	16,850	C
Western New England Univ	MA	49,182	C
Western Washington Univ	WA	18,904	VC
Wichita State Univ	KS	17,773	C
Wilberforce Univ	OH	19,900	C
Wilmington College	OH	35,100	C
Wright State Univ	OH	16,983	C
Xavier Univ	OH	49,380	VC

MANUFACTURING ENGINEERING

School	ST	$IS	SR
Arizona State Univ at the Polytechnic Campus	AZ	22,394	VC
Boston Univ	MA	67,352	MC
Bradley Univ	IL	43,240	VC
Brigham Young Univ	UT	13,248	MC
Calif Polytechnic State Univ	CA	22,547	MC
Calif State Polytechnic Univ, Pomona	CA	21,811	C
Cal State, Fullerton	CA	21,902	C
Central State Univ	OH	18,564	C
Eastern Mich Univ	MI	19,761	C
Ferris State Univ	MI	21,458	C
Georgia Southern Univ	GA	16,540	VC
Hofstra Univ	NY	58,210	C+
Kansas State Univ	KS	17,780	VC
Miami Univ	OH	27,190	HC+
Mich State Univ	MI	24,542	VC
Midwestern State Univ	TX	12,111	LC
Minn State Univ, Mankato	MN	17,190	C
Missouri Univ of Science and Technology	MO	18,655	HC
New Jersey Inst of Technology	NJ	30,198	HC
N Dak State Univ	ND	16,245	VC
Northern Kentucky Univ	KY	16,486	C
Northwestern Univ	IL	68,725	MC
Oregon State Univ	OR	23,337	VC
Pennsylvania College of Technology	PA	27,693	NC
Purdue Univ/West Lafayette	IN	20,032	MC
Robert Morris Univ	PA	40,600	C
Rochester Inst of Technology	NY	52,734	HC+
Southern Illinois Univ Edwardsville	IL	20,188	C
St. Cloud State Univ	MN	10,600	C
Tarleton State Univ	TX	15,248	LC
Tenn Tech Univ	TN	17,929	C
Texas State Univ	TX	18,721	C
The Univ of Memphis	TN	18,278	C
Univ of Arkansas at Little Rock	AR	18,211	LC
Univ of Calif at Berkeley	CA	29,886	MC
Univ of Conn	CT	27,394	
Univ of Mich/Dearborn	MI	12,472	VC
Univ of North Texas	TX	20,082	C
Univ of Texas Rio Grande Valley	TX	15,573	LC
Univ of Wisc-Stout	WI	19,667	C
Washington State Univ	WA	22,747	C
Weber State Univ	UT	14,112	C
Western Mich Univ	MI	21,791	C

ST = STATE **$IS** = IN-STATE COSTS **SR** = SELECTOR RATING

School	ST	$IS	SR
Wichita State Univ	KS	17,773	C
Youngstown State Univ	OH	17,487	C

MANUFACTURING TECHNOLOGY

School	ST	$IS	SR
Alabama State Univ	AL	16,490	LC
Alfred State College	NY	19,895	C
Arkansas State Univ	AR	16,190	C
Black Hills State Univ	SD	16,622	C
Bradley Univ	IL	43,240	VC
Brigham Young Univ	UT	13,248	MC
Cal State, Northridge	CA	17,277	LC
Central Conn State Univ	CT	22,041	C
Central Mich Univ	MI	20,330	C
Eastern Kentucky Univ	KY	17,742	C
Eastern Mich Univ	MI	19,761	C
Edinboro Univ	PA	15,940	LC
Farmingdale State College	NY	20,968	C
Fitchburg State Univ	MA	21,819	LC
Idaho State Univ	ID	13,619	LC
Illinois Inst of Technology	IL	56,826	HC+
Indiana State Univ	IN	23,223	LC
Lake Superior State Univ	MI	19,867	C
Millersville Univ of Pennsylvania	PA	25,298	C
Minn State Univ, Mankato	MN	17,190	C
Missouri Southern State Univ	MO	13,071	C
Montana State Univ-Northern	MT	11,370	NC
Murray State Univ	KY	17,726	C+
Nicholls State Univ	LA	14,959	C
Northern Kentucky Univ	KY	16,486	C
Northern Mich Univ	MI	20,853	C
Oregon Inst of Technology	OR	19,227	C
Pittsburg State Univ	KS	13,880	C
Purdue Univ/West Lafayette	IN	20,032	MC
Rochester Inst of Technology	NY	52,734	HC+
S Dak State Univ	SD	15,874	C
Southern Arkansas Univ	AR	21,532	C
Tarleton State Univ	TX	15,248	LC
Texas A&M Univ at College Station	TX	20,771	VC+
Texas State Univ	TX	18,721	C
Univ of Central Missouri	MO	18,982	C
Univ of Dayton	OH	54,930	VC
Univ of Northern Iowa	IA	17,480	C
Univ of Rio Grande & Rio Grande Community College	OH	8,750	LC
Univ of Southern Indiana	IN	16,808	C
Washington State Univ	WA	22,747	C
Wayne State Univ	MI	23,085	C
Weber State Univ	UT	14,112	C
Western Carolina Univ	NC	13,965	C
Western Kentucky Univ	KY	16,850	C
Western Mich Univ	MI	21,791	C
Western Washington Univ	WA	18,904	VC

MARINE AFFAIRS

School	ST	$IS	SR
Univ of Miami	FL	63,494	MC
Univ of New England	ME	50,110	C
Univ of Rhode Island	RI	26,066	VC

MARINE BIOLOGY

School	ST	$IS	SR
Alaska Pacific Univ	AK	28,730	VC
Auburn Univ	AL	24,300	VC+
Barry Univ	FL	38,730	LC
Brown Univ	RI	64,566	MC
Cal State, Fullerton	CA	21,902	C
Cal State, Long Beach	CA	18,850	C
Carroll Univ	WI	38,100	C+
Central Methodist Univ	MO	31,500	VC
College of Charleston	SC	24,046	VC
Eastern Nazarene College	MA	41,114	C
Fairleigh Dickinson Univ/Metropolitan Campus	NJ	52,392	C
Florida Atlantic Univ	FL	18,256	C
Florida Inst of Technology	FL	53,306	VC
Florida International Univ	FL	20,281	C
Florida Southern College	FL	45,978	VC
Florida State Univ	FL	16,771	HC
Hampshire College	MA	65,214	MC
Hawaii Pacific Univ	HI	33,420	C
Hawaii Pacific Univ	HI	33,420	C
Hawaii Pacific Univ	HI	33,420	C
Kutztown Univ of Pennsylvania	PA	19,477	C
Millersville Univ of Pennsylvania	PA	25,298	C
Missouri Southern State Univ	MO	13,071	C
Monmouth Univ	NJ	50,184	C
Montclair State Univ	NJ	26,912	C
Murray State Univ	KY	17,726	C+
New College of Florida	FL	16,180	HC+
Northeastern Univ	MA	65,352	MC
Northwest Missouri State Univ	MO	18,286	C
Nova Southeastern Univ	FL	38,534	C+
Ohio Univ	OH	23,394	VC
Old Dominion Univ	VA	21,618	C
Prescott College	AZ	38,201	C
Roger Williams Univ	RI	48,074	VC
Rollins College	FL	58,670	HC
Rutgers Univ - New Brunswick	NJ	27,090	HC
San Francisco State Univ	CA	18,514	LC
Savannah State Univ	GA	17,036	C
Seattle Univ	WA	54,957	VC
Southeast Missouri State Univ	MO	16,148	C
Southwestern College	KS	31,531	LC
Spring Hill College	AL	48,488	C
Stetson Univ	FL	57,174	VC+
Texas A&M Univ at College Station	TX	20,771	VC+
Texas State Univ	TX	18,721	C
Troy Univ	AL	16,171	C
Unity College	ME	37,670	C
Univ of Alaska Southeast	AK	17,615	C
Univ of Calif at Los Angeles	CA	27,438	HC+
Univ of Calif at Santa Barbara	CA	30,627	HC+
Univ of Calif San Diego	CA	30,450	MC
Univ of Calif, Santa Cruz	CA	28,731	C+
Univ of Hawaii at Manoa	HI	23,261	C
Univ of Maine at Machias	ME	22,960	C
Univ of Mass Dartmouth	MA	26,507	C
Univ of Miami	FL	63,494	MC
Univ of New Hampshire	NH	29,333	VC
Univ of New Haven	CT	53,680	C
Univ of N Car Wilmington	NC	16,784	VC
Univ of Oregon	OR	24,021	VC
Univ of PR, at Humacao	PR	14,000	
Univ of Rhode Island	RI	26,066	VC
Univ of Texas Rio Grande Valley	TX	15,573	LC
Univ of West Alabama	AL	16,284	LC
Univ of West Florida	FL	15,848	C
Waynesburg Univ	PA	33,530	C
Western Washington Univ	WA	18,904	VC
Wisc Lutheran College	WI	36,290	C

MARINE ENGINEERING

School	ST	$IS	SR
Cal State, Maritime Academy	CA	23,156	C+
Maine Maritime Academy	ME	22,536	C
Mass Maritime Academy	MA	20,704	C
SUNY/Maritime College	NY	16,020	C
Texas A&M Univ at College Station	TX	20,771	VC+
United States Merchant Marine Academy	NY		HC
Univ of New Orleans	LA	12,840	C

MARINE ENGINEERING SYSTEMS

School	ST	$IS	SR
Texas A&M Univ at College Station	TX	20,771	VC+
United States Merchant Marine Academy	NY		HC

MARINE ENGINEERING/ SHIPYARD MANAGEMENT

School	ST	$IS	SR
United States Merchant Marine Academy	NY		HC

MARINE SCIENCE

School	ST	$IS	SR
Boston Univ	MA	67,352	MC
Cal State, Fullerton	CA	21,902	C
Coastal Carolina Univ	SC	20,340	C
East Stroudsburg Univ	PA	18,578	LC
Eckerd College	FL	55,276	VC
Florida Gulf Coast Univ	FL	14,738	C
Florida International Univ	FL	20,281	C
Hawaii Pacific Univ	HI	33,420	C
Jacksonville Univ	FL	49,210	C
Kutztown Univ of Pennsylvania	PA	19,477	C
Mass Maritime Academy	MA	20,704	C
Nova Southeastern Univ	FL	38,534	C+
Prescott College	AZ	38,201	C
Rider Univ	NJ	54,050	C
Samford Univ	AL	40,770	VC
San Jose State Univ	CA	22,630	C
SUNY/Maritime College	NY	16,020	C
Stockton Univ	NJ	25,565	C
Stony Brook Univ/The SUNY	NY	22,703	MC
Suffolk Univ	MA	52,316	C
Texas A&M Univ at College Station	TX	20,771	VC+
The Univ of Alabama	AL	24,320	C+
United States Coast Guard Academy	CT	942	HC
Univ of Calif San Diego	CA	30,450	MC
Univ of Conn	CT	27,394	
Univ of Hawaii at Hilo	HI	18,038	VC
Univ of Maine	ME	21,038	VC
Univ of Maine at Machias	ME	22,960	C
Univ of Miami	FL	63,494	MC
Univ of Mobile	AL	28,935	C
Univ of New England	ME	50,110	C
Univ of San Diego	CA	60,338	HC
Univ of S Car at Columbia	SC	21,726	VC
Univ of Tampa	FL	38,928	VC
West Chester Univ of Pennsylvania	PA	19,171	VC
Western Washington Univ	WA	18,904	VC

MARINE TRANSPORTATION

School	ST	$IS	SR
Cal State, Fullerton	CA	21,902	C
Mass Maritime Academy	MA	20,704	C
Texas A&M Univ at College Station	TX	20,771	VC+
United States Merchant Marine Academy	NY		HC

MARINE VERTEBRATE BIOLOGY

School	ST	$IS	SR
Stony Brook Univ/The SUNY	NY	22,703	MC

MARITIME LOGISTICS & SECURITY

School	ST	$IS	SR
United States Merchant Marine Academy	NY		HC

MARITIME SCIENCE

School	ST	$IS	SR
Maine Maritime Academy	ME	22,536	C
SUNY/Maritime College	NY	16,020	C
Texas A&M Univ at College Station	TX	20,771	VC+
Univ of Conn	CT	27,394	

MARKETING

School	ST	$IS	SR
Albertus Magnus College	CT	44,016	LC
Alma College	MI	49,410	VC
Anderson Univ	IN	39,450	C
Arkansas State Univ	AR	16,190	C
Arkansas Tech Univ	AR	16,534	LC
Ashford Univ	CA	10,480	C
Aurora Univ	IL	34,990	C
Austin Peay State Univ	TN	16,397	C
Baldwin Wallace Univ	OH	42,464	VC
Ball State Univ	IN	19,808	C+
Bentley Univ	MA	63,720	MC
Bloomfield College	NJ	40,100	LC
Bowling Green State Univ	OH	19,975	C
Bradley Univ	IL	43,240	VC
Bryan College	TN	32,900	C
Bucknell Univ	PA	67,136	MC
Cabrini Univ	PA	42,591	LC
Champlain College	VT	54,724	VC
Chatham Univ	PA	47,883	VC
Christopher Newport Univ	VA	24,878	VC+
Clayton State Univ	GA	19,735	LC
College of Charleston	SC	24,046	VC
Columbia College Chicago	IL	40,104	C
Creighton Univ	NE	49,452	VC
Dallas Baptist Univ	TX	35,220	VC
Davis & Elkins College	WV	38,242	LC
Defiance College	OH	42,240	LC
East Central Univ	OK	13,330	C
Eastern Illinois Univ	IL	21,414	C
Elon Univ	NC	46,142	HC
Emmanuel College	MA	53,472	C+
Fairfield Univ	CT	61,445	HC
Ferris State Univ	MI	21,458	C
Framingham State Univ	MA	21,740	C
Georgia Southwestern State Univ	GA	13,870	LC
High Point Univ	NC	47,355	VC
Hofstra Univ	NY	58,210	C+
Hood College	MD	50,540	C
Illinois State Univ	IL	23,418	VC
Keene State College	NH	24,604	C
Kent State Univ	OH	20,928	C
Le Moyne College	NY	47,305	VC
Lehigh Univ	PA	63,860	MC
Lewis Univ	IL	41,710	C
Limestone College	SC	32,100	C
LIU Brooklyn	NY	50,698	C
Loras College	IA	40,726	C
Loyola Marymount Univ	CA	60,202	VC+
Lubbock Christian Univ	TX	29,727	C
Madonna Univ	MI	30,450	LC
Manhattanville College	NY	52,430	C
Marian Univ	IN	43,206	C
Mary Baldwin Univ	VA	40,495	C
McNeese State Univ	LA	7,838	C
Mich State Univ	MI	24,542	VC
Mich Tech Univ	MI	25,551	VC+
Minn State Univ, Mankato	MN	17,190	C
Missouri Baptist Univ	MO	35,594	C
Missouri Southern State Univ	MO	13,071	C
Molloy College	NY	40,440	C
Mount Vernon Nazarene Univ	OH	35,944	C
Murray State Univ	KY	17,726	C+
Neumann Univ	PA	40,678	LC
New Mexico State Univ	NM	14,050	LC
North Central Univ	MN	30,610	C
N Dak State Univ	ND	16,245	VC
North Greenville Univ	SC	25,930	C
Northwest Univ	WA	38,720	VC
Nova Southeastern Univ	FL	38,534	C+
Okla Baptist Univ	OK	33,990	C
Okla City Univ	OK	40,476	C
Oregon State Univ	OR	23,337	VC
Point Loma Nazarene Univ	CA	46,150	C+
Providence College	RI	62,870	HC
Regis Univ	CO	46,380	C
Roberts Wesleyan College	NY	41,116	C
Rochester Inst of Technology	NY	52,734	HC+
Rutgers Univ - New Brunswick	NJ	27,090	HC
Rutgers Univ - Newark	NJ	27,351	C
St. Anselm College	NH	56,636	VC
St. Louis Univ	MO	49,866	HC
St. Mary's Univ of Minn	MN	42,440	C
Salisbury Univ	MD	21,132	VC
Samford Univ	AL	40,770	VC
Shawnee State Univ	OH	16,998	C
Southeast Missouri State Univ	MO	16,148	C
Southeastern Louisiana Univ	LA	16,237	C
Southern Oregon Univ	OR	19,117	C
Spalding Univ	KY	31,938	C
St. John's Univ	NY	57,160	C+
Stephen F. Austin State Univ	TX	18,484	LC
Susquehanna Univ	PA	57,560	VC
Syracuse Univ	NY	62,313	HC
Taylor Univ	IN	42,130	VC
Texas Christian Univ	TX	57,120	HC
Texas Tech Univ	TX	20,156	C+
The College of St. Rose	NY	44,010	C
The Univ of Arizona	AZ	24,086	C
Thomas Edison State Univ	NJ	6,350	NC
Tiffin Univ	OH	34,900	LC
Trevecca Nazarene Univ	TN	31,186	C
Univ of Central Okla	OK	15,150	C
Univ of Dayton	OH	54,930	VC
Univ of Evansville	IN	44,186	C+
Univ of Georgia	GA	21,878	HC
Univ of Louisiana at Monroe	LA	15,970	C
Univ of Maryland/College Park	MD	21,938	HC
Univ of Miami	FL	63,494	MC
Univ of Mich/Dearborn	MI	12,472	VC
Univ of Mount Union	OH	39,990	C
Univ of Nevada, Reno	NV	18,010	C
Univ of N Car at Charlotte	NC	17,803	VC
Univ of N Car at Greensboro	NC	15,998	C
Univ of Northwestern - St. Paul	MN	39,530	C
Univ of Notre Dame	IN	68,801	MC
Univ of Okla	OK	19,651	HC
Univ of Rhode Island	RI	26,066	VC
Univ of Rochester	NY	65,032	MC
Univ of St. Francis	IN	38,520	C
Univ of San Francisco	CA	60,580	C
Univ of St. Thomas - Houston	TX	41,510	VC
Univ of West Alabama	AL	16,284	LC
Univ of Wisc-Eau Claire	WI	16,354	VC
Univ of Wisc-La Crosse	WI	15,425	VC
Univ of Wisc-Parkside	WI	15,313	C
Univ of Wyoming	WY	15,537	C
Washington State Univ	WA	22,747	C
West Virginia Univ	WV	18,952	VC
Western Illinois Univ	IL	20,897	C
Western Kentucky Univ	KY	16,850	C
Western New England Univ	MA	49,182	C
Wingate Univ	NC	41,900	C
Winona State Univ	MN	18,109	C
Wittenberg Univ	OH	49,863	VC

MARKETING AND DISTRIBUTION

School	ST	$IS	SR
Alvernia Univ	PA	45,330	C
Aquinas College - Mich	MI	38,876	VC
Becker College	MA	30,100	LC
Caldwell Univ	NJ	42,165	LC
Central Mich Univ	MI	20,330	C
Clayton State Univ	GA	19,735	LC
Florida Gulf Coast Univ	FL	14,738	C
Fort Lewis College	CO	20,154	C
Franklin Univ	OH	11,616	NC
Georgia College & State Univ	GA	21,884	C+
Gwynedd Mercy Univ	PA	43,780	LC
Indiana State Univ	IN	23,223	LC
Inter-American Univ of PR-Arecibo Campus	PR	18,245	
Johnson & Wales Univ/Charlotte Campus	NC	44,768	C
Johnson & Wales Univ/Providence Campus	RI	44,768	C
Lake Erie College	OH	38,914	LC
Limestone College	SC	32,100	C
Malone Univ	OH	39,200	C
Metropolitan State Univ	MN	7,859	C
Nazareth College	NY	46,784	C
New Mexico Highlands Univ	NM	11,904	LC
Northern Kentucky Univ	KY	16,486	C
Ohio State Univ at Columbus	OH	22,843	MC
Salve Regina Univ	RI	53,046	VC
Simmons College	MA	54,400	HC
Southern Illinois Univ Edwardsville	IL	20,188	C
Southwest Baptist Univ	MO	30,890	LC
SUNY/Empire State College	NY	9,145	NC
Tarleton State Univ	TX	15,248	LC
Texas A&M Univ at College Station	TX	20,771	VC+
The Catholic Univ of America	DC	58,376	VC
The Univ of Arizona	AZ	24,086	C
Union College	NE	23,270	C
Univ of Houston	TX	21,871	VC
Univ of Illinois at Urbana-Champaign	IL	27,006	HC
Univ of South Florida St. Petersburg	FL	15,980	C
Univ of West Georgia	GA	17,510	LC
West Virginia Univ	WV	18,952	VC
Western Carolina Univ	NC	13,965	C

School	ST	$IS	SR
Western Kentucky Univ	KY	16,850	C
Wilkes Univ	PA	49,166	C
Wilmington College	OH	35,100	C

MARKETING AND DISTRIBUTION EDUCATION

School	ST	$IS	SR
Central Washington Univ	WA	16,803	C
Dakota State Univ	SD	12,286	C
East Carolina Univ	NC	16,539	C
Eastern Washington Univ	WA	17,896	LC
Fayetteville State Univ	NC	17,756	C
Johnson & Wales Univ/ Providence Campus	RI	44,768	C
Murray State Univ	KY	17,726	C+
N Car State Univ	NC	22,434	HC+
Rider Univ	NJ	54,050	C
The Univ of Tenn at Knoxville	TN	22,112	VC
Univ of Nebr - Lincoln	NE	18,589	VC
Univ of Wisc-Stout	WI	19,667	C
Western Kentucky Univ	KY	16,850	C

MARKETING MANAGEMENT

School	ST	$IS	SR
Adrian College	MI	45,550	C
Alverno College	WI	33,294	LC
Aquinas College	TN	30,800	C+
Aquinas College - Mich	MI	38,876	VC
Assumption College	MA	48,455	VC
Auburn Univ at Montgomery	AL	15,000	C
Averett Univ	VA	43,034	LC
Baker College of Flint	MI	19,140	NC
Benedictine Univ	IL	38,300	C
Berry College	GA	47,466	VC
Bethany College	KS	38,637	LC
Biola Univ	CA	48,686	C
Brigham Young Univ	UT	13,248	MC
Bryant Univ	RI	57,204	VC
Calvin College	MI	43,090	HC
Campbellsville Univ	KY	33,400	C
Canisius College	NY	49,672	C
Carthage College	WI	48,835	C
Case Western Reserve Univ	OH	62,284	MC
Catawba College	NC	39,820	LC
Central Conn State Univ	CT	22,041	C
Central Mich Univ	MI	20,330	C
Champlain College	VT	54,724	VC
Chatham Univ	PA	47,883	VC
CUNY/Baruch College	NY	21,609	HC
College of St. Scholastica	MN	45,734	C+
College of the Ozarks	MO	7,530	VC
College of William & Mary	VA	34,907	MC
Concordia Univ St. Paul	MN	29,050	C
Culver-Stockton College	MO	34,350	C
Cumberland Univ	TN	27,710	C
Davenport Univ	MI	25,896	LC
DePaul Univ	IL	52,807	VC
Dominican Univ	IL	42,472	C+
Dordt College	IA	37,860	C+
Drake Univ	IA	49,220	HC
Drury Univ	MO	37,555	VC
East Carolina Univ	NC	16,539	C
Eastern Mich Univ	MI	19,761	C
Elizabethtown College	PA	56,340	VC
Elon Univ	NC	46,142	HC
Emerson College	MA	61,824	HC+
Endicott College	MA	47,054	C+
Felician Univ	NJ	46,280	LC
Fitchburg State Univ	MA	21,819	LC
Florida Inst of Technology	FL	53,306	VC
Fontbonne Univ	MO	34,606	C
Fordham Univ	NY	68,431	MC
Franciscan Univ of Steubenville	OH	33,980	VC
Georgia Southern Univ	GA	16,540	VC
Goldey-Beacom College	DE	36,038	C
Goshen College	IN	44,350	C
Grove City College	PA	26,654	VC
Hardin-Simmons Univ	TX	36,025	C
Harris-Stowe State Univ	MO	14,590	NC
Hawaii Pacific Univ	HI	33,420	C
Huntington Univ	IN	33,996	C
Immaculata Univ	PA	39,000	C
Indiana Univ of Pennsylvania	PA	24,474	C
Iona College	NY	52,514	C
John Brown Univ	AR	35,184	VC
Johnson & Wales Univ/ Charlotte Campus	NC	44,768	C
Johnson & Wales Univ/North Miami Campus	FL	44,768	C
Johnson & Wales Univ/ Providence Campus	RI	44,768	C
Kean Univ	NJ	25,620	C
Keene State College	NH	24,604	C
Keiser Univ	FL	35,010	LC
Kent State Univ	OH	20,928	C
Kutztown Univ of Pennsylvania	PA	19,477	C
La Roche College	PA	38,940	C
La Sierra Univ	CA	39,690	VC
Lakeland Univ	WI	35,130	C
Le Moyne College	NY	47,305	VC
LeTourneau Univ	TX	39,190	VC
LIM College	NY	45,075	LC
Linfield College	OR	53,992	C
Lipscomb Univ	TN	42,984	VC
Louisiana College	LA	21,274	C
Lourdes Univ	OH	29,140	NC
Maryville Univ of St. Louis	MO	38,558	VC
Menlo College	CA	51,380	LC
Mercer Univ	GA	45,348	VC
Metropolitan State Univ	MN	7,859	C
Mich State Univ	MI	24,542	VC
Missouri Southern State Univ	MO	13,071	C
Monmouth Univ	NJ	50,184	C
Morehead State Univ	KY	18,386	LC
Mount Aloysius College	PA	29,976	C
New York Inst of Technology	NY	49,980	VC
New York Univ	NY	68,139	MC
Newbury College	MA	48,970	C
Northern Arizona Univ	AZ	21,003	C
Northwood Univ - Mich	MI	35,010	LC
Ohio Univ	OH	23,394	VC
Okla Christian Univ	OK	29,260	C
Old Dominion Univ	VA	21,618	C
Olivet College	MI	37,661	LC
Olivet Nazarene Univ	IL	41,840	VC
Our Lady of the Lake Univ	TX	37,790	LC
Palm Beach Atlantic Univ	FL	39,250	C
Park Univ	MO	22,134	C
Peirce College	PA	16,780	NC
Penn State Erie,The Behrend College	PA	26,688	VC
Pennsylvania College of Technology	PA	27,693	NC
Pennsylvania State Univ - Univ Park	PA	29,716	HC
Pepperdine Univ	CA	66,862	VC+
Plymouth State Univ	NH	23,180	LC
Purdue Univ/West Lafayette	IN	20,032	MC
Quinnipiac Univ	CT	60,970	VC
Rhode Island College	RI	19,000	LC
Rochester College	MI	28,574	LC
Rochester Inst of Technology	NY	52,734	HC+
Rutgers Univ - Camden	NJ	26,595	C
Sacred Heart Univ	CT	54,590	C
Saginaw Valley State Univ	MI	19,284	C
St. Joseph's Univ	PA	58,540	VC
St. Leo Univ	FL	32,850	C
St. Louis Univ	MO	49,866	HC
Seattle Univ	WA	54,957	VC
Seton Hall Univ	NJ	58,008	C
Shippensburg Univ of Pennsylvania	PA	24,096	C
Siena College	NY	48,916	C
Simpson College	IA	45,626	VC
Southern New Hampshire Univ	NH	44,256	C
Spring Hill College	AL	48,488	C
St. Edward's Univ	TX	56,190	VC
St. John Fisher College	NY	45,270	VC
St. Joseph's College, New York/Brooklyn Campus	NY	25,114	LC
St. Joseph's College, New York/Long Island Campus	NY	25,124	C
SUNY at Binghamton	NY	24,100	MC
Stephen F. Austin State Univ	TX	18,484	LC
Stevenson Univ	MD	48,412	C
Texas Wesleyan Univ	TX	37,338	C
The College at Brockport - SUNY	NY	21,058	C
The George Washington Univ	DC	68,474	HC+
The Univ of Memphis	TN	18,278	C
The Univ of Texas at Austin	TX	20,206	MC
The Univ of Texas at San Antonio	TX	21,060	C
The Univ of Utah	UT	18,751	VC
Thomas College	ME	73,888	LC
Tiffin Univ	OH	34,900	LC
Troy Univ	AL	16,171	C
Tulane Univ	LA	67,496	MC
Union College	KY	32,310	C
Union Univ	TN	41,160	VC
Univ of Colo Boulder	CO	26,048	HC
Univ of Idaho	ID	16,158	C
Univ of Illinois at Urbana-Champaign	IL	27,006	HC
Univ of Iowa	IA	19,415	HC
Univ of Maryland Univ College	MD	26,146	LC
Univ of Mass Amherst	MA	27,669	HC
Univ of Miami	FL	63,494	MC
Univ of Minn/Crookston	MN	19,126	C
Univ of Missouri-St. Louis	MO	19,810	VC
Univ of Nebr - Lincoln	NE	18,589	VC
Univ of N Dak	ND	16,673	C
Univ of North Florida	FL	15,996	VC
Univ of Northwestern - St. Paul	MN	39,530	C
Univ of PR-Rio Piedras campus	PR	13,327	
Univ of Rio Grande & Rio Grande Community College	OH	8,750	LC
Univ of San Diego	CA	60,338	HC
Univ of S Car Upstate	SC	19,272	LC
Univ of Texas at Dallas	TX	23,640	HC
Univ of the Sciences	PA	40,738	VC
Univ of Wisc-Milwaukee	WI	21,538	C
Ursuline College	OH	41,076	LC
Virginia Polytechnic Inst and State Univ	VA	21,920	VC
Virginia State Univ	VA	19,802	C+
Walsh Univ	OH	39,010	C
Warner Univ	FL	28,216	C
Washington State Univ	WA	22,747	C
Washington Univ in St. Louis	MO	67,539	MC
Webber International Univ	FL	31,904	C
Weber State Univ	UT	14,112	C
Webster Univ	MO	37,490	C
West Chester Univ of Pennsylvania	PA	19,171	VC
Western Conn State Univ	CT	21,254	LC
Whitworth Univ	WA	53,682	VC
Wilmington College	OH	35,100	C
Youngstown State Univ	OH	17,487	C

MARKETING/RETAILING/ MERCHANDISING

School	ST	$IS	SR
Abilene Christian Univ	TX	43,708	C+
Adams State Univ	CO	15,420	LC
Alabama A&M Univ	AL	18,796	C
Alabama State Univ	AL	16,490	LC
Albany State Univ	GA	19,462	C
Alderson Broaddus Univ	WV	35,000	LC
Alfred Univ	NY	37,490	C
American International College	MA	47,020	LC
Anderson Univ	IN	39,450	C
Andrews Univ	MI	41,732	C
Angelo State Univ	TX	15,882	LC
Appalachian State Univ	NC	15,394	VC
Arcadia Univ	PA	55,990	C+
Arizona State Univ at the Tempe Campus	AZ	23,001	VC
Ashland Univ	OH	30,446	C
Auburn Univ	AL	24,300	VC+
Auburn Univ at Montgomery	AL	15,000	C
Augsburg Univ	MN	45,129	C
Augusta Univ	GA	4,632	C
Avila Univ	MO	27,100	C
Azusa Pacific Univ	CA	43,972	C
Barry Univ	FL	38,730	LC
Bay Path Univ	MA	46,356	C
Bayamon Central Univ	PR	12,490	
Baylor Univ	TX	56,803	HC
Belmont Univ	TN	44,500	VC+
Benedictine Univ	IL	38,300	C
Berkeley College/New Jersey	NJ	38,082	LC
Berkeley College/New York City Campus	NY	35,100	LC
Berkeley College/White Plains Campus	NY	35,100	LC
Blackburn College	IL	28,526	LC
Bluffton Univ	OH	40,950	C+
Boise State Univ	ID	17,368	C
Boston College	MA	68,043	MC
Brenau Univ - Women's College	GA	37,876	LC
Buena Vista Univ	IA	42,344	C
Butler Univ	IN	52,890	VC+
Calif Baptist Univ	CA	42,986	C
Cal State, Fullerton	CA	21,902	C
Cal State, Long Beach	CA	18,850	C
Cal State, Northridge	CA	17,277	LC
Cal State, Sacramento	CA	19,060	C
Canisius College	NY	49,672	C
Caribbean Univ	PR	12,227	
Carnegie Mellon Univ	PA	67,980	MC
Cedarville Univ	OH	36,244	VC
Central Mich Univ	MI	20,330	C
Central State Univ	OH	18,564	C
Central Washington Univ	WA	16,803	C
Chestnut Hill College	PA	47,180	C
Chicago State Univ	IL	41,620	C
CUNY/Baruch College	NY	21,609	HC
CUNY/York College	NY	6,747	LC
City Univ of Seattle	WA	24,340	NC
Claflin Univ	SC	25,592	LC
Clarion Univ of Pennsylvania	PA	21,608	LC
Clemson Univ	SC		HC
Cleveland State Univ	OH	22,290	C
Coastal Carolina Univ	SC	20,340	C
Colo State Univ	CO	23,033	C
Columbus State Univ	GA	14,336	LC
Concord Univ	WV	14,954	LC
Concordia Univ Wisc	WI	35,910	C
Cornerstone Univ	MI	36,550	C
Defiance College	OH	42,240	LC
Delaware State Univ	DE	19,376	LC
Delaware Valley Univ	PA	51,271	C
Delta State Univ	MS	13,176	LC
DeSales Univ	PA	47,520	C
Dominican College	NY	40,258	LC
Drexel Univ	PA	65,927	HC
Duquesne Univ	PA	48,508	VC
East Carolina Univ	NC	16,539	C
East Tenn State Univ	TN	18,141	C
Eastern Kentucky Univ	KY	17,742	C
Eastern Mich Univ	MI	19,761	C
Eastern New Mexico Univ	NM	12,874	LC
Eastern Univ	PA	39,540	C
Eastern Washington Univ	WA	17,896	LC
Elizabethtown College School of Continuing and Professional Studies	PA	18,900	C
Elmhurst College	IL	46,514	C
Elms College	MA	49,602	VC
Emory Univ	GA	63,286	MC
Emporia State Univ	KS	15,029	C
Evangel Univ	MO	28,898	C
Excelsior College	NY	38,800	SP
Fairleigh Dickinson Univ/ College at Florham	NJ	54,770	C
Fairleigh Dickinson Univ/ Metropolitan Campus	NJ	52,392	C
Fairmont State Univ	WV	15,726	C
Fashion Inst of Technology/ SUNY	NY	18,521	SP
Florida Atlantic Univ	FL	18,256	C
Florida International Univ	FL	20,281	C
Florida State Univ	FL	16,771	HC
Fontbonne Univ	MO	34,606	C
Fort Hays State Univ	KS	12,677	C
Fort Valley State Univ	GA	17,988	VC
Francis Marion Univ	SC	18,144	LC
Franklin Pierce Univ	NH	46,750	LC
Gannon Univ	PA	42,922	C
George Mason Univ	VA	19,884	C
Georgetown College	KY	41,440	C
Georgetown Univ	DC	68,970	MC
Georgia State Univ	GA	25,250	C
Glenville State College	WV	17,386	LC
Grambling State Univ	LA	15,701	C
Grand Canyon Univ	AZ	25,150	VC
Grand Valley State Univ	MI	22,250	C+
Greenville College	IL	27,012	LC
Hampton Univ	VA	36,410	C
Harding Univ	AR	25,440	C
Hillsdale College	MI	37,170	MC
Holy Family Univ	PA	44,672	LC
Howard Univ	DC	37,616	C+
Husson Univ	ME	26,508	C
Huston-Tillotson Univ	TX	18,124	LC
Idaho State Univ	ID	13,619	LC
Indiana State Univ	IN	23,223	LC
Indiana Univ-Purdue Univ Fort Wayne	IN	18,675	C
Indiana Wesleyan Univ	IN	33,674	C
Inter-American Univ of PR Ponce	PR	19,549	
Inter-American Univ of PR- Aguadilla Campus	PR	21,657	
Inter-American Univ of PR- Bayamon	PR	18,785	
Inter-American Univ of PR- Fajardo Campus	PR	18,336	
Inter-American Univ of PR- Metropolitan Campus	PR	20,045	
Inter-American Univ of PR-San Germán	PR	20,042	
Iowa State Univ	IA	18,176	C
Jackson State Univ	MS	15,879	LC
Jacksonville State Univ	AL	14,628	LC
Jacksonville Univ	FL	49,210	C
James Madison Univ	VA	19,084	VC
Jefferson (Philadelphia Univ + Thomas Jefferson Univ)	PA	53,966	C
John Carroll Univ	OH	51,570	C
Johnson & Wales Univ/ Charlotte Campus	NC	44,768	C
Johnson & Wales Univ/ Denver Campus	CO	44,768	C
Johnson & Wales Univ/North Miami Campus	FL	44,768	C
Johnson & Wales Univ/ Providence Campus	RI	44,768	C
Juniata College	PA	58,118	VC
Kansas State Univ	KS	17,780	VC
Kennesaw State Univ	GA	18,899	VC
Keuka College	NY	42,398	C
King's College	PA	48,240	C
Kutztown Univ of Pennsylvania	PA	19,477	C
La Salle Univ	PA	43,476	C
Lake Superior State Univ	MI	19,867	C
Lamar Univ	TX	18,014	LC
Lasell College	MA	49,400	C
LeTourneau Univ	TX	39,190	VC
Lincoln Univ	MO	14,402	NC
Lindenwood Univ	MO	25,760	C
Lipscomb Univ	TN	42,984	VC
LIU Post	NY	50,698	C+
Louisiana State Univ and A&M College	LA	18,677	VC
Louisiana State Univ in Shreveport	LA	6,902	C
Louisiana Tech Univ	LA	11,422	VC
Loyola Univ Chicago	IL	57,158	VC
Loyola Univ New Orleans	LA	52,456	VC
MacMurray College	IL	35,025	C
Manhattan College	NY	55,652	C
Marian Univ	WI	34,622	C
Marietta College	OH	46,190	C
Marquette Univ	WI	53,090	VC+
Marshall Univ	WV	18,044	C
Martin Univ	IN	21,010	LC
Marywood Univ	PA	47,840	C
McKendree Univ	IL	37,940	C+
McMurry Univ	TX	34,259	LC
Mercyhurst Univ	PA	47,420	C
Merrimack College	MA	55,415	C
Messiah College	PA	44,380	VC
Methodist Univ	NC	58,130	C
Metropolitan State Univ of Denver	CO	6,928	LC
Miami Univ	OH	27,190	HC+
Mich State Univ	MI	24,542	VC
MidAmerica Nazarene Univ	KS	37,808	C
Middle Tenn State Univ	TN	8,650	C
Midland Univ	NE	39,512	C
Midwestern State Univ	TX	12,111	LC
Millikin Univ	IL	44,148	C

ST = STATE $IS = IN-STATE COSTS SR = SELECTOR RATING

School	ST	$IS	SR
Minn State Univ, Moorhead	MN	21,393	C
Minot State Univ	ND	13,285	C
Miss College	MS	25,850	C
Miss State Univ	MS	12,028	C+
Missouri State Univ	MO	15,837	C+
Missouri Western State Univ	MO	17,822	LC
Morgan State Univ	MD	17,190	LC
Mount Ida College	MA	46,820	C
Mount Mary Univ	WI	34,650	LC
Mount Mercy Univ	IA	39,748	C
New Mexico Highlands Univ	NM	11,904	LC
New Mexico State Univ	NM	14,050	LC
New York Univ	NY	68,139	MC
Niagara Univ	NY	41,010	C
Nicholls State Univ	LA	14,959	C
North Central College	IL	48,712	C+
North Park Univ	IL	35,860	C
Northeastern Illinois Univ	IL	12,529	LC
Northeastern State Univ	OK	8,615	VC
Northern Illinois Univ	IL	20,176	C
Northern Mich Univ	MI	20,853	C
Northern State Univ	SD	15,570	C
Northwest Missouri State Univ	MO	18,286	C
Notre Dame College	OH	39,150	VC
Notre Dame de Namur Univ	CA	46,526	LC
Notre Dame of Maryland Univ	MD	47,570	VC
Oakland Univ	MI	20,763	C
Okla Christian Univ	OK	29,260	C
Okla State Univ	OK	17,180	C+
Oral Roberts Univ	OK	34,316	C
Oregon State Univ	OR	23,337	VC
Pace Univ	NY	60,136	C
Parsons The New School for Design	NY	56,610	SP
Peru State College	NE	15,602	LC
Pontifical Catholic Univ of PR	PR	10,534	
Portland State Univ	OR	19,443	C
Post Univ	CT	41,150	C
Prairie View A&M Univ	TX	27,273	LC
Purdue Univ Northwest	IN	15,178	C
Purdue Univ/West Lafayette	IN	20,032	MC
Quincy Univ	IL	38,170	LC
Quinnipiac Univ	CT	60,970	VC
Radford Univ	VA	19,758	C
Regis Univ	CO	46,380	C
Rider Univ	NJ	54,050	C
Robert Morris Univ	PA	40,600	C
Roger Williams Univ	RI	48,074	VC
Roosevelt Univ	IL	41,890	VC
Rowan Univ	NJ	24,491	VC
St. Joseph's Univ	PA	58,540	VC
St. Mary-of-the-Woods College	IN	40,424	LC
St. Peter's Univ	NJ	49,192	C
St. Vincent College	PA	46,229	C
St. Xavier Univ	IL	44,440	C
Salem State Univ	MA	42,650	LC
Sam Houston State Univ	TX	18,792	C
San Diego State Univ	CA	23,156	VC
San Francisco State Univ	CA	18,514	LC
San Jose State Univ	CA	22,630	C
Savannah State Univ	GA	17,036	C
Seton Hill Univ	PA	46,972	VC
Slippery Rock Univ of Pennsylvania	PA	20,450	C
S Car State Univ	SC	21,330	LC
Southeastern Univ	FL	34,910	LC
Southern Adventist Univ	TN	28,250	C
Southern Conn State Univ	CT	21,924	LC
Southern Illinois Univ Carbondale	IL	24,554	C
Southern Methodist Univ	TX	69,008	MC
Southern Nazarene Univ	OK	33,684	C
Southern New Hampshire Univ	NH	44,256	C
Southern Oregon Univ	OR	19,117	C
Southern Univ and A&M College	LA	16,074	LC
Southwest Minn State Univ	MN	17,783	C
Southwestern Okla State Univ	OK	12,205	C
St. Bonaventure Univ	NY	45,596	C
St. Catherine Univ	MN	45,630	C
St. Cloud State Univ	MN	10,600	C
St. Mary's Univ	TX	39,120	C
St. Thomas Aquinas College	NY	32,450	C
St. Thomas Univ	FL	51,187	LC
SUNY at New Paltz	NY	20,840	C
SUNY at Oswego	NY	22,219	VC
SUNY/College at Old Westbury	NY	16,860	C
SUNY/Plattsburgh	NY	19,314	C
Stephen F. Austin State Univ	TX	18,484	LC
Stetson Univ	FL	57,174	VC+
Stonehill College	MA	55,130	C
Suffolk Univ	MA	52,316	C
Tarleton State Univ	TX	15,248	LC
Temple Univ	PA	24,392	C+
Tenn Tech Univ	TN	17,929	C
Texas A&M Univ at Commerce	TX	10,496	C
Texas A&M Univ at Corpus Christi	TX	16,851	LC
Texas A&M Univ at Kingsville	TX	16,580	LC
Texas Southern Univ	TX	19,592	LC
Texas State Univ	TX	18,721	C
Texas Wesleyan Univ	TX	37,338	C
Texas Woman's Univ	TX	15,302	LC
The Univ of Akron	OH	22,566	C
The Univ of Tenn at Martin	TN	15,212	C
The Univ of Utah	UT	18,751	VC
Touro College	NY	31,040	C
Trevecca Nazarene Univ	TN	31,186	C
Trine Univ	IN	41,310	C
Trinity International Univ	IL	31,070	VC
Troy Univ	AL	16,171	C
Tuskegee Univ	AL	28,164	C
Union Univ	TN	41,160	VC
Universidad del Turabo	PR	17,828	
Univ of PR, at Arecibo	PR	12,652	
Univ of Alabama at Birmingham	AL	22,092	C
Univ of Alabama in Huntsville	AL	20,028	VC
Univ of Alaska Anchorage	AK	17,914	C
Univ of Arkansas at Fayetteville	AR	19,766	VC
Univ of Arkansas at Little Rock	AR	18,211	LC
Univ of Bridgeport	CT	44,985	LC
Univ of Central Arkansas	AR	15,042	VC
Univ of Central Florida	FL	16,379	VC
Univ of Central Missouri	MO	18,982	C
Univ of Central Okla	OK	15,150	C
Univ of Cincinnati	OH	22,118	VC
Univ of Conn	CT	27,394	
Univ of Dayton	OH	54,930	VC
Univ of Delaware	DE	32,214	VC
Univ of Denver	CO	61,129	VC+
Univ of Findlay	OH	43,040	C
Univ of Florida	FL	16,291	HC+
Univ of Hartford	CT	49,776	C
Univ of Hawaii at Manoa	HI	23,261	C
Univ of Houston-Downtown	TX	7,241	LC
Univ of Idaho	ID	16,158	C
Univ of Illinois at Chicago	IL	24,664	VC
Univ of Illinois at Urbana-Champaign	IL	27,006	HC
Univ of Indianapolis	IN	36,480	VC
Univ of Kansas	KS	20,884	VC
Univ of Kentucky	KY	24,800	C+
Univ of Louisiana at Lafayette	LA	14,516	C
Univ of Louisville	KY	19,692	C
Univ of Lynchburg	VA	48,370	C
Univ of Maine at Machias	ME	22,960	C
Univ of Mary Hardin-Baylor	TX	35,292	C+
Univ of Mass Dartmouth	MA	26,507	C
Univ of Mich/Flint	MI	19,062	C
Univ of Minn/Twin Cities	MN	24,269	MC
Univ of Miss	MS	18,802	C
Univ of Missouri-Columbia	MO	20,463	VC
Univ of Montana	MT	14,105	C
Univ of Montevallo	AL	20,012	C
Univ of Nebr - Kearney	NE	17,014	LC
Univ of Nebr - Lincoln	NE	18,589	VC
Univ of Nebr - Omaha	NE	16,120	C
Univ of Nevada, Las Vegas	NV	17,553	C
Univ of Nevada, Reno	NV	18,010	C
Univ of New Haven	CT	53,680	C
Univ of New Orleans	LA	12,840	C
Univ of North Alabama	AL	15,964	C
Univ of N Car at Charlotte	NC	17,803	VC
Univ of N Car at Greensboro	NC	15,998	C
Univ of North Georgia	GA	17,316	C
Univ of North Texas	TX	20,082	C
Univ of Northern Colo	CO	19,658	C
Univ of Northern Iowa	IA	17,480	C
Univ of Pennsylvania	PA	63,526	MC
Univ of Pittsburgh	PA	30,030	MC
Univ of Portland	OR	52,152	VC
Univ of PR, at Bayamon	PR	13,145	
Univ of PR, at Mayaguez	PR	13,995	
Univ of Scranton	PA	54,962	VC
Univ of Sioux Falls	SD	25,630	C
Univ of South Alabama	AL	16,880	C
Univ of S Car at Columbia	SC	21,726	VC
Univ of South Florida/Tampa	FL	16,110	VC
Univ of Southern Indiana	IN	16,808	C
Univ of Southern Miss	MS	13,170	C
Univ of St. Francis	IL	40,828	C
Univ of Tampa	FL	38,928	VC
Univ of Texas at Arlington	TX	18,876	C
Univ of Texas at El Paso	TX	34,452	NC
Univ of Texas Rio Grande Valley	TX	15,573	LC
Univ of the District of Columbia	DC	21,260	LC
Univ of the Ozarks	AR	31,050	NC
Univ of the Sacred Heart	PR	17,932	
Univ of Toledo	OH	19,336	C
Univ of Tulsa	OK	52,625	HC
Univ of Washington	WA	23,091	MC
Univ of West Florida	FL	15,848	C
Univ of Wisc-Madison	WI	21,647	MC
Univ of Wisc-Oshkosh	WI	15,392	C
Univ of Wisc-Stout	WI	19,667	C
Univ of Wisc-Whitewater	WI	13,976	C
Upper Iowa Univ	IA	34,990	NC
Utah State Univ	UT	13,235	C
Valparaiso Univ	IN	50,160	VC
Vanguard Univ of Southern Calif	CA	42,400	VC
Villanova Univ	PA	64,922	MC
Virginia Commonwealth Univ	VA	23,811	VC
Viterbo Univ	WI	34,660	C
Washburn Univ	KS	15,827	C
Washington Univ in St. Louis	MO	67,539	MC
Wayne State Univ	MI	23,085	C
Waynesburg Univ	PA	33,530	C
West Liberty Univ	WV	16,158	C
West Texas A&M Univ	TX	13,478	C
West Virginia State Univ	WV	19,412	LC
West Virginia Wesleyan College	WV	39,188	C
Western Mich Univ	MI	21,791	C
Western New Mexico Univ	NM	16,914	LC
Western Washington Univ	WA	18,904	VC
Westminster College	PA	41,722	C
Westminster College	UT	41,078	C
Wichita State Univ	KS	17,773	C
Wilberforce Univ	OH	19,900	C
Woodbury Univ	CA	49,593	VC
Wright State Univ	OH	16,983	C
Xavier Univ	OH	49,380	VC
Yeshiva Univ	NY	52,750	VC
York College of Pennsylvania	PA	29,240	C
Youngstown State Univ	OH	17,487	C

MASS COMMUNICATIONS

School	ST	$IS	SR
Shenandoah Univ	VA	42,100	C

MATERIALS ENGINEERING

School	ST	$IS	SR
Alfred Univ	NY	37,490	C
Auburn Univ	AL	24,300	VC+
Brown Univ	RI	64,566	MC
Calif Polytechnic State Univ	CA	22,547	MC
Cal State, Fullerton	CA	21,902	C
Carnegie Mellon Univ	PA	67,980	MC
Drexel Univ	PA	65,927	HC
Florida State Univ	FL	16,771	HC
Georgia Inst of Technology	GA	23,910	MC
Iowa State Univ	IA	18,176	C
Johns Hopkins Univ	MD	68,080	MC
Mass Inst of Technology	MA	62,662	MC
Mich State Univ	MI	24,542	VC
Mich Tech Univ	MI	25,551	VC+
Missouri Univ of Science and Technology	MO	18,655	HC
New Mexico Inst of Mining and Technology	NM	15,385	HC+
Northwestern Univ	IL	68,725	MC
Ohio State Univ at Columbus	OH	22,843	MC
Ohio Univ	OH	23,394	VC
Rensselaer Polytechnic Inst	NY	67,265	MC
San Jose State Univ	CA	22,630	C
SUNY Albany	NY	22,165	C
The Univ of Arizona	AZ	24,086	C
The Univ of Tenn at Knoxville	TN	22,112	VC
The Univ of Utah	UT	18,751	VC
Univ of Alabama at Birmingham	AL	22,092	C
Univ of Calif at Berkeley	CA	29,886	MC
Univ of Calif at Davis	CA	28,468	HC
Univ of Calif at Irvine	CA	33,857	VC
Univ of Calif at Los Angeles	CA	27,438	HC+
Univ of Calif at Riverside	CA	32,912	C
Univ of Cincinnati	OH	22,118	VC
Univ of Conn	CT	27,394	
Univ of Florida	FL	16,291	HC+
Univ of Idaho	ID	16,158	C
Univ of Illinois at Chicago	IL	24,664	VC
Univ of Illinois at Urbana-Champaign	IL	27,006	HC
Univ of Kentucky	KY	24,800	C+
Univ of Maryland/College Park	MD	21,938	HC
Univ of Mich/Ann Arbor	MI	25,274	MC
Univ of Pennsylvania	PA	63,526	MC
Univ of Pittsburgh	PA	30,030	MC
Univ of Wisc-Madison	WI	21,647	MC
Univ of Wisc-Milwaukee	WI	21,538	C
Virginia Polytechnic Inst and State Univ	VA	21,920	VC
Washington State Univ	WA	22,747	C
Winona State Univ	MN	18,109	C
Wright State Univ	OH	16,983	C

MATERIALS SCIENCE

School	ST	$IS	SR
Arizona State Univ at the Tempe Campus	AZ	23,001	VC
Boise State Univ	ID	17,368	C
Brown Univ	RI	64,566	MC
Calif Inst of Technology	CA	64,704	MC
Case Western Reserve Univ	OH	62,284	MC
Columbia Univ/City of New York	NY	62,958	MC
Duke Univ	NC	68,298	MC
Georgia Inst of Technology	GA	23,910	MC
Illinois Inst of Technology	IL	56,826	HC+
Johns Hopkins Univ	MD	68,080	MC
Mass Inst of Technology	MA	62,662	MC
Missouri State Univ	MO	15,837	C+
N Car State Univ	NC	22,434	HC+
Northwestern Univ	IL	68,725	MC
Ohio State Univ at Columbus	OH	22,843	MC
Pennsylvania State Univ - Univ Park	PA	29,716	HC
Purdue Univ Northwest	IN	15,178	C
Purdue Univ/West Lafayette	IN	20,032	MC
Rochester Inst of Technology	NY	52,734	HC+
Stanford Univ	CA	62,541	MC
SUNY Albany	NY	22,165	C
The Univ of Arizona	AZ	24,086	C
The Univ of Utah	UT	18,751	VC
Univ of Calif at Berkeley	CA	29,886	MC
Univ of Calif at Los Angeles	CA	27,438	HC+
Univ of Denver	CO	61,129	VC+
Univ of Illinois at Urbana-Champaign	IL	27,006	HC
Univ of Mich/Ann Arbor	MI	25,274	MC
Univ of Minn/Twin Cities	MN	24,269	MC
Univ of Pittsburgh	PA	30,030	MC
Univ of the Ozarks	AR	31,050	NC
Univ of Washington	WA	23,091	MC
Univ of Wisc-Eau Claire	WI	16,354	VC
Univ of Wisc-Madison	WI	21,647	MC
Washington State Univ	WA	22,747	C

MATERIALS SCIENCE AND ENGINEERING

School	ST	$IS	SR
Brown Univ	RI	64,566	MC
Cornell Univ	NY	67,591	MC
Drexel Univ	PA	65,927	HC
Georgia Inst of Technology	GA	23,910	MC
Lehigh Univ	PA	63,860	MC
Mich State Univ	MI	24,542	VC
Univ of Idaho	ID	16,158	C
Univ of Wisc-Eau Claire	WI	16,354	VC
Washington State Univ	WA	22,747	C

MATHEMATICAL BUSINESS ECONOMICS

School	ST	$IS	SR
Furman Univ	SC	61,098	VC+
Hofstra Univ	NY	58,210	C+

MATHEMATICAL FINANCE

School	ST	$IS	SR
Hofstra Univ	NY	58,210	C+

MATHEMATICAL PROGRAMMING

School	ST	$IS	SR
Univ of Tampa	FL	38,928	VC

MATHEMATICS

School	ST	$IS	SR
Abilene Christian Univ	TX	43,708	C+
Adams State Univ	CO	15,420	LC
Adelphi Univ	NY	49,792	C
Adrian College	MI	45,550	C
Agnes Scott College	GA	51,930	VC+
Alabama A&M Univ	AL	18,796	C
Alabama State Univ	AL	16,490	LC
Albany State Univ	GA	19,462	C
Albertus Magnus College	CT	44,016	LC
Albion College	MI	55,260	C
Albright College	PA	57,326	C
Alcorn State Univ	MS	15,884	C
Alderson Broaddus Univ	WV	35,000	LC
Alfred Univ	NY	37,490	C
Allegheny College	PA	57,620	VC
Allen Univ	SC	19,920	NC
Alma College	MI	49,410	VC
Alvernia Univ	PA	45,330	C
Alverno College	WI	33,294	LC
American International College	MA	47,020	LC
Amherst College	MA	66,186	MC
Anderson Univ	IN	39,450	C
Andrews Univ	MI	41,732	C
Angelo State Univ	TX	15,882	LC
Appalachian State Univ	NC	15,394	VC
Aquinas College	TN	30,800	C+
Aquinas College - Mich	MI	38,876	VC
Arcadia Univ	PA	55,990	C+
Arizona State Univ at the Tempe Campus	AZ	23,001	VC
Arkansas State Univ	AR	16,190	C
Arkansas Tech Univ	AR	16,534	LC
Armstrong State Univ	GA	15,615	C
Asbury Univ	KY	36,450	C+
Ashland Univ	OH	30,446	C
Assumption College	MA	48,455	VC
Atlantic Union College	MA	27,228	C
Auburn Univ	AL	24,300	VC+
Auburn Univ at Montgomery	AL	15,000	C
Augsburg Univ	MN	45,129	C
Augusta Univ	GA	4,632	C
Augustana College	IL	51,222	VC+
Augustana Univ	SD	39,968	VC
Aurora Univ	IL	34,990	C
Austin College	TX	51,059	HC
Austin Peay State Univ	TN	16,397	C
Averett Univ	VA	43,034	LC
Avila Univ	MO	27,100	C
Azusa Pacific Univ	CA	43,972	C
Baker Univ	KS	37,190	C
Baldwin Wallace Univ	OH	42,464	VC
Ball State Univ	IN	19,808	C+
Bard College	NY	65,924	HC
Bard College at Simon's Rock	MA	65,795	MC
Barnard College/Columbia Univ	NY	68,762	MC
Barry Univ	FL	38,730	LC

School	ST	$IS	SR
Barton College	NC	39,854	C
Bates College	ME	64,500	HC
Baylor Univ	TX	56,803	HC
Belhaven Univ	MS	32,250	C
Bellarmine Univ	KY	52,532	C
Belmont Abbey College	NC	28,794	C
Belmont Univ	TN	44,500	VC+
Beloit College	WI	55,206	HC
Bemidji State Univ	MN	17,730	C
Benedict College	SC	28,630	NC
Benedictine College	KS	38,850	VC
Benedictine Univ	IL	38,300	C
Bennett College	NC	27,717	NC
Bennington College	VT	66,280	MC
Bentley Univ	MA	63,720	MC
Berea College	KY	7,094	C
Berry College	GA	47,466	VC
Bethany College	KS	38,637	LC
Bethany College	WV	38,774	LC
Bethel College	IN	36,830	C
Bethel College	KS	35,370	C
Bethel Univ	MN	46,550	C+
Bethel Univ	TN	27,142	C
Bethune-Cookman Univ	FL	23,322	C
Biola Univ	CA	48,686	C
Birmingham-Southern College	AL	44,478	C+
Black Hills State Univ	SD	16,622	C
Blackburn College	IL	28,526	LC
Bloomfield College	NJ	40,100	LC
Bloomsburg Univ of Pennsylvania	PA	19,930	C
Blue Mountain College	MS	15,949	C
Bluefield College	VA	34,711	C
Bluffton Univ	OH	40,950	C+
Boise State Univ	ID	17,368	C
Boston College	MA	68,043	MC
Boston Univ	MA	67,352	MC
Bowdoin College	ME	65,980	MC
Bowie State Univ	MD	18,610	LC
Bowling Green State Univ	OH	19,975	C
Bradley Univ	IL	43,240	VC
Brandeis Univ	MA	68,443	MC
Brescia Univ	KY	29,890	VC
Briar Cliff Univ	IA	36,956	C
Bridgewater College	VA	46,260	C
Bridgewater State Univ	MA	22,762	C
Brigham Young Univ	UT	13,248	MC
Brigham Young Univ/Hawaii	HI	11,710	C
Brown Univ	RI	64,566	MC
Bryan College	TN	32,900	C
Bryn Mawr College	PA	65,220	MC
Bucknell Univ	PA	67,136	MC
Buena Vista Univ	IA	42,344	C
Butler Univ	IN	52,890	VC+
Cabrini Univ	PA	42,591	LC
Caldwell Univ	NJ	42,165	LC
Calif Baptist Univ	CA	42,986	C
Calif Inst of Technology	CA	64,704	MC
Calif Lutheran Univ	CA	52,853	C
Calif Polytechnic State Univ	CA	22,547	MC
Calif State Polytechnic Univ, Pomona	CA	21,811	C
Cal State, Bakersfield	CA	22,397	LC
Cal State, Chico	CA	19,790	VC
Cal State, Dominguez Hills	CA	19,022	LC
Cal State, East Bay	CA	20,748	C
Cal State, Fresno	CA	16,902	LC
Cal State, Fullerton	CA	21,902	C
Cal State, Long Beach	CA	18,850	C
Cal State, Los Angeles	CA	17,186	LC
Cal State, Monterey Bay	CA	22,872	LC
Cal State, Northridge	CA	17,277	LC
Cal State, Sacramento	CA	19,060	C
Cal State, San Bernardino	CA	20,106	C
Cal State, San Marcos	CA	20,604	LC
Cal State, Stanislaus	CA	18,053	LC
Calif Univ of Pennsylvania	PA	20,425	LC
Calvin College	MI	43,090	HC
Cameron Univ	OK	11,632	LC
Campbell Univ	NC	37,570	VC
Campbellsville Univ	KY	33,400	C
Canisius College	NY	49,672	C
Capital Univ	OH	44,778	VC
Cardinal Stritch Univ	WI	37,136	C
Caribbean Univ	PR	12,227	
Carleton College	MN	66,414	MC
Carlow Univ	PA	39,696	LC
Carnegie Mellon Univ	PA	67,980	MC
Carroll College	MT	44,304	C
Carroll Univ	WI	38,100	C+
Carthage College	WI	48,835	C
Case Western Reserve Univ	OH	62,284	MC
Castleton Univ	VT	20,186	C
Catawba College	NC	39,820	LC
Cedar Crest College	PA	51,110	C
Cedarville Univ	OH	36,244	VC
Centenary College	NJ	43,890	LC
Centenary College of Louisiana	LA	49,050	C+
Central College	IA	44,592	C
Central Conn State Univ	CT	22,041	C
Central Methodist Univ	MO	31,500	VC
Central Mich Univ	MI	20,330	C
Central State Univ	OH	18,564	C
Central Washington Univ	WA	16,803	C
Centre College	KY	50,680	MC
Chadron State College	NE	14,819	LC
Chapman Univ	CA	65,504	HC

School	ST	$IS	SR
Charleston Southern Univ	SC	34,700	C
Chatham Univ	PA	47,883	VC
Chestnut Hill College	PA	47,180	C
Cheyney Univ of Pennsylvania	PA	20,896	LC
Chicago State Univ	IL	41,620	C
Christian Brothers Univ	TN	31,670	VC
Christopher Newport Univ	VA	24,878	VC+
CUNY/Baruch College	NY	21,609	HC
CUNY/Brooklyn College	NY	7,163	C+
CUNY/City College	NY	20,204	C
CUNY/Hunter College	NY	31,098	VC
CUNY/Lehman College	NY	5,788	LC
CUNY/Medgar Evers College	NY	6,680	NC
CUNY/Queens College	NY	21,507	C
CUNY/York College	NY	6,747	LC
Claflin Univ	SC	25,592	LC
Claremont McKenna College	CA	69,900	MC
Clarion Univ of Pennsylvania	PA	21,608	LC
Clark Atlanta Univ	GA	31,019	LC
Clark Univ	MA	53,260	HC+
Clarke Univ	IA	42,950	C
Clarkson Univ	NY	60,392	VC
Clayton State Univ	GA	19,735	LC
Clemson Univ	SC		HC
Cleveland State Univ	OH	22,290	C
Coastal Carolina Univ	SC	20,340	C
Coe College	IA	51,570	VC
Coker College	SC	38,196	C
Colby College	ME	64,060	MC
Colgate Univ	NY	67,500	MC
College of Charleston	SC	24,046	VC
College of Mount St. Vincent	NY	45,620	C
College of St. Benedict	MN	54,480	C
College of St. Elizabeth	NJ	45,700	LC
College of St. Mary	NE	27,500	C
College of St. Scholastica	MN	45,734	C+
College of Staten Island	NY	24,389	LC
College of the Holy Cross	MA	64,320	MC
College of the Ozarks	MO	7,530	VC
College of William & Mary	VA	34,907	MC
Colo College	CO	64,894	MC
Colo Mesa Univ	CO	19,707	LC
Colo School of Mines	CO	29,319	MC
Colo State Univ	CO	23,033	C
Colo State Univ-Pueblo	CO	21,581	C
Columbia College	SC	36,550	C
Columbia College - Missouri	MO	28,179	C
Columbia Univ/ School of General Studies	NY	61,470	MC
Columbia Univ/City of New York	NY	62,958	MC
Columbus State Univ	GA	14,336	LC
Concord Univ	WV	14,954	LC
Concordia College - Moorhead	MN	46,418	C
Concordia College - New York	NY	39,035	LC
Concordia Univ Irvine	CA	44,860	VC
Concordia Univ Nebr	NE	41,900	VC
Concordia Univ St. Paul	MN	29,050	C
Concordia Univ Wisc	WI	35,910	C
Concordia Univ, Ann Arbor	MI	38,878	C+
Concordia Univ, Chicago	IL	41,522	C
Conn College	CT	65,000	MC
Converse College	SC	28,290	C
Coppin State Univ	MD	14,071	VC
Corban Univ	OR	41,700	C
Cornell College	IA	49,900	VC
Cornell Univ	NY	67,591	MC
Covenant College	GA	44,590	HC
Creighton Univ	NE	49,452	VC
Culver-Stockton College	MO	34,350	C
Cumberland Univ	TN	27,710	C
Daemen College	NY	40,336	C
Dakota State Univ	SD	12,286	C
Dakota Wesleyan Univ	SD	33,980	LC
Dallas Baptist Univ	TX	35,220	VC
Dartmouth College	NH	68,109	MC
Davidson College	NC	60,119	MC
Davis & Elkins College	WV	38,242	LC
Defiance College	OH	42,240	LC
Delaware State Univ	DE	19,376	LC
Delta State Univ	MS	13,176	LC
Denison Univ	OH	62,770	HC+
DePaul Univ	IL	52,807	VC
DePauw Univ	IN	58,688	VC
DeSales Univ	PA	47,520	C
Dickinson College	PA	66,166	MC
Dickinson State Univ	ND	12,372	LC
Doane Univ	NE	41,340	VC
Dominican College	NY	40,258	LC
Dominican Univ	IL	42,472	C+
Dordt College	IA	37,860	C+
Drake Univ	IA	49,220	HC
Drew Univ/College of Liberal Arts	NJ	53,608	VC
Drexel Univ	PA	65,927	HC
Drury Univ	MO	37,555	VC
Duke Univ	NC	68,298	MC
Duquesne Univ	PA	48,508	VC
D'Youville College	NY	37,678	C
Earlham College	IN	55,670	HC
East Carolina Univ	NC	16,539	C
East Central Univ	OK	13,330	C
East Stroudsburg Univ	PA	18,578	LC
East Tenn State Univ	TN	18,141	C
East Texas Baptist Univ	TX	34,444	C
Eastern Conn State Univ	CT	23,059	C

School	ST	$IS	SR
Eastern Illinois Univ	IL	21,414	C
Eastern Kentucky Univ	KY	17,742	C
Eastern Mennonite Univ	VA	42,550	C
Eastern Mich Univ	MI	19,761	C
Eastern Nazarene College	MA	41,114	C
Eastern New Mexico Univ	NM	12,874	LC
Eastern Oregon Univ	OR	17,612	C
Eastern Univ	PA	39,540	C
Eastern Washington Univ	WA	17,896	LC
Eckerd College	FL	55,206	VC
Edgewood College	WI	35,950	C
Edinboro Univ	PA	15,940	LC
Edward Waters College	FL	28,089	NC
Elizabeth City State Univ	NC	14,745	C
Elizabethtown College	PA	56,340	VC
Elmhurst College	IL	46,514	C
Elmira College	NY	53,900	C
Elms College	MA	49,602	VC
Elon Univ	NC	46,142	HC
Emmanuel College	MA	53,472	C+
Emory and Henry College	VA	46,320	C
Emory Univ	GA	63,286	MC
Emporia State Univ	KS	15,029	C
Endicott College	MA	47,054	C+
Erskine College	SC	45,460	C
Eureka College	IL	34,760	C
Evangel Univ	MO	28,898	C
Excelsior College	NY	38,800	SP
Fairfield Univ	CT	61,445	HC
Fairleigh Dickinson Univ/ College at Florham	NJ	54,770	C
Fairleigh Dickinson Univ/ Metropolitan Campus	NJ	52,392	C
Fairmont State Univ	WV	15,726	C
Faulkner Univ	AL	26,410	C
Fayetteville State Univ	NC	17,756	C
Felician Univ	NJ	46,280	LC
Ferrum College	VA	43,970	C
Fisk Univ	TN	32,066	LC
Fitchburg State Univ	MA	21,819	LC
Florida A&M Univ	FL	15,361	C
Florida Atlantic Univ	FL	18,256	C
Florida Gulf Coast Univ	FL	14,738	C
Florida Inst of Technology	FL	53,306	VC
Florida International Univ	FL	20,281	C
Florida Memorial Univ	FL	22,424	LC
Florida Southern College	FL	45,978	VC
Florida State Univ	FL	16,771	HC
Fontbonne Univ	MO	34,606	C
Fordham Univ	NY	68,431	MC
Fort Hays State Univ	KS	12,677	C
Fort Lewis College	CO	20,154	C
Fort Valley State Univ	GA	17,988	VC
Framingham State Univ	MA	21,740	C
Francis Marion Univ	SC	18,144	LC
Franciscan Univ of Steubenville	OH	33,980	VC
Franklin and Marshall College	PA	67,960	MC
Franklin College	IN	40,550	C
Franklin Pierce Univ	NH	46,750	LC
Freed-Hardeman Univ	TN	29,900	C
Fresno Pacific Univ	CA	38,858	C
Friends Univ	KS	38,000	C
Frostburg State Univ	MD	17,280	LC
Furman Univ	SC	61,098	VC+
Gallaudet Univ	DC	30,088	LC
Gannon Univ	PA	42,922	C
Gardner-Webb Univ	NC	24,935	C+
George Fox Univ	OR	42,938	C
George Mason Univ	VA	19,884	C
Georgetown College	KY	41,440	C
Georgetown Univ	DC	68,970	MC
Georgia College & State Univ	GA	21,884	C+
Georgia Inst of Technology	GA	23,910	MC
Georgia Southern Univ	GA	16,540	VC
Georgia Southwestern State Univ	GA	13,870	LC
Georgia State Univ	GA	25,250	C
Georgian Court Univ	NJ	43,068	LC
Gettysburg College	PA	65,210	MC
Gonzaga Univ	WA	52,880	HC
Gordon College	MA	47,740	VC
Goshen College	IN	44,350	C
Goucher College	MD	56,110	VC
Grace College and Seminary	IN	31,524	C
Graceland Univ	IA	35,290	C
Grambling State Univ	LA	15,701	C
Grand Valley State Univ	MI	22,250	C+
Grand View Univ	IA	32,302	C
Greensboro College	NC	39,790	LC
Greenville College	IL	27,012	LC
Grinnell College	IA	63,114	MC
Grove City College	PA	26,654	VC
Guilford College	NC	45,973	C
Gustavus Adolphus College	MN	53,943	HC
Gwynedd Mercy Univ	PA	43,780	LC
Hamilton College	NY	64,250	MC
Hamline Univ	MN	50,152	C
Hampden-Sydney College	VA	57,806	VC
Hampshire College	MA	65,214	MC
Hampton Univ	VA	36,410	C
Hannibal-LaGrange Univ	MO	29,815	C
Hanover College	IN	47,750	C+
Harding Univ	AR	25,440	C
Hardin-Simmons Univ	TX	36,025	C
Harris-Stowe State Univ	MO	14,590	NC
Hartwick College	NY	51,270	C

School	ST	$IS	SR
Harvard College/Harvard Univ	MA	65,609	MC
Harvey Mudd College	CA	67,155	MC
Hastings College	NE	35,380	C+
Haverford College	PA	66,490	MC
Hawaii Pacific Univ	HI	33,420	C
Heidelberg Univ	OH	40,400	LC
Henderson State Univ	AR	15,516	C
Hendrix College	AR	54,020	VC
Heritage Univ	WA	19,825	NC
High Point Univ	NC	47,355	VC
Hillsdale College	MI	37,170	MC
Hiram College	OH	44,590	C
Hobart and William Smith Colleges	NY	67,050	HC+
Hofstra Univ	NY	58,210	C+
Hollins Univ	VA	49,635	VC
Holy Family Univ	PA	44,672	LC
Hood College	MD	50,540	C
Hope College	MI	42,840	VC
Houghton College	NY	40,558	VC
Houston Baptist Univ	TX	36,450	C
Howard Payne Univ	TX	35,994	C
Howard Univ	DC	37,616	C+
Humboldt State Univ	CA	21,708	C
Huntingdon College	AL	35,900	C
Huntington Univ	IN	33,996	C
Huston-Tillotson Univ	TX	18,124	LC
Idaho State Univ	ID	13,619	LC
Illinois College	IL	41,330	VC
Illinois State Univ	IL	23,418	VC
Immaculata Univ	PA	39,000	C
Indiana State Univ	IN	23,223	LC
Indiana Univ Bloomington	IN	20,791	HC
Indiana Univ East	IN	7,207	C
Indiana Univ Kokomo	IN	7,207	C
Indiana Univ Northwest	IN	7,207	LC
Indiana Univ of Pennsylvania	PA	24,474	C
Indiana Univ South Bend	IN	16,057	C
Indiana Univ Southeast	IN	16,931	C
Indiana Univ-Purdue Univ Fort Wayne	IN	18,675	C
Indiana Univ-Purdue Univ Indianapolis	IN	18,952	C
Indiana Wesleyan Univ	IN	33,674	C
Inter-American Univ of PR Ponce	PR	19,549	
Inter-American Univ of PR-Bayamon	PR	18,785	
Inter-American Univ of PR-Fajardo Campus	PR	18,336	
Inter-American Univ of PR-Metropolitan Campus	PR	20,045	
Inter-American Univ of PR-San Germán	PR	20,042	
Iona College	NY	52,514	C
Iowa State Univ	IA	18,176	C
Ithaca College	NY	58,158	VC+
Jackson State Univ	MS	15,879	LC
Jacksonville State Univ	AL	14,628	LC
Jacksonville Univ	FL	49,210	C
James Madison Univ	VA	19,084	VC
Jarvis Christian College	TX	20,160	NC
John Brown Univ	AR	35,184	VC
John Carroll Univ	OH	51,570	C
Johns Hopkins Univ	MD	68,080	MC
Johnson C. Smith Univ	NC	25,336	LC
Johnson State College	VT	22,672	C
Judson College	AL	27,066	C
Judson Univ	IL	39,174	C
Juniata College	PA	58,118	VC
Kalamazoo College	MI	53,931	HC
Kansas State Univ	KS	17,780	VC
Kansas Wesleyan Univ	KS	37,930	C
Kean Univ	NJ	25,620	C
Keene State College	NH	24,604	C
Kennesaw State Univ	GA	18,899	VC
Kent State Univ	OH	20,928	C
Kentucky State Univ	KY	14,484	LC
Kenyon College	OH	65,840	MC
Keuka College	NY	42,398	C
King Univ	TN	36,976	C
King's College	PA	48,240	C
Knox College	IL	54,654	VC+
Kutztown Univ of Pennsylvania	PA	19,477	C
La Roche College	PA	38,940	C
La Salle Univ	PA	43,476	C
La Sierra Univ	CA	39,690	VC
Lafayette College	PA	68,520	MC
LaGrange College	GA	41,310	C
Lake Erie College	OH	38,914	LC
Lake Forest College	IL	50,652	VC
Lake Superior State Univ	MI	19,867	C
Lakeland Univ	WI	35,130	C
Lamar Univ	TX	18,014	LC
Lander Univ	SC	32,200	C
Lane College	TN	17,960	LC
Langston Univ	OK	15,659	C
Lawrence Tech Univ	MI	41,630	VC
Lawrence Univ	WI	56,133	HC+
Le Moyne College	NY	47,305	VC
Lebanon Valley College	PA	55,510	VC
Lee Univ	TN	22,045	C
Lees-McRae College	NC	33,944	NC
Lehigh Univ	PA	63,860	MC
LeMoyne-Owen College	TN	16,980	C
Lenoir-Rhyne Univ	NC	47,500	LC
LeTourneau Univ	TX	39,190	VC

ST = STATE $IS = IN-STATE COSTS SR = SELECTOR RATING

School	ST	$IS	SR
Lewis & Clark College	OR	60,984	MC
Lewis Univ	IL	41,710	C
Lewis-Clark State College	ID	14,202	C
Liberty Univ	VA	31,415	C
Limestone College	SC	32,100	C
Lincoln Memorial Univ	TN	28,430	C
Lincoln Univ	MO	14,402	NC
Lincoln Univ	PA	20,878	LC
Lindenwood Univ	MO	25,760	C
Lindsey Wilson College	KY	33,546	C
Linfield College	OR	53,992	C
Lipscomb Univ	TN	42,984	VC
LIU Brooklyn	NY	50,698	C
LIU Post	NY	50,698	C+
Livingstone College	NC	17,815	LC
Lock Haven Univ of Pennsylvania	PA	20,544	LC
Longwood Univ	VA	22,184	C
Loras College	IA	40,726	C
Louisiana College	LA	21,274	C
Louisiana State Univ and A&M College	LA	18,677	VC
Louisiana State Univ in Shreveport	LA	6,902	C
Louisiana Tech Univ	LA	11,422	VC
Loyola Marymount Univ	CA	60,202	VC+
Loyola Univ Chicago	IL	57,158	VC
Loyola Univ Maryland	MD	61,710	VC
Loyola Univ New Orleans	LA	52,456	VC
Lubbock Christian Univ	TX	29,727	C
Luther College	IA	49,990	VC
Lycoming College	PA	50,895	C
Lyndon State College	VT	20,714	C
Lyon College	AR	36,120	VC
Macalester College	MN	64,136	MC
MacMurray College	IL	35,025	C
Madonna Univ	MI	30,450	LC
Maharishi Univ of Management	IA	34,930	VC
Malone Univ	OH	39,200	C
Manchester Univ	IN	41,540	C
Manhattan College	NY	55,652	C
Manhattanville College	NY	52,430	C
Mansfield Univ of Pennsylvania	PA	24,244	LC
Marian Univ	IN	43,206	C
Marian Univ	WI	34,622	C
Marietta College	OH	46,190	C
Marist College	NY	49,860	VC
Marlboro College	VT	50,832	VC+
Marquette Univ	WI	53,090	VC+
Mars Hill Univ	NC	41,104	C
Marshall Univ	WV	18,044	C
Martin Univ	IN	21,010	LC
Mary Baldwin Univ	VA	40,495	C
Marygrove College	MI	30,100	LC
Marymount Univ	VA	43,231	C
Maryville College	TN	44,410	C
Maryville Univ of St. Louis	MO	38,558	VC
Marywood Univ	PA	47,840	C
Mass College of Liberal Arts	MA	20,659	C
Mass Inst of Technology	MA	62,662	MC
Mayville State Univ	ND	18,371	NC
McDaniel College	MD	52,910	VC
McKendree Univ	IL	37,940	C+
McMurry Univ	TX	34,259	LC
McNeese State Univ	LA	7,838	C
McPherson College	KS	36,134	C
Mercer Univ	GA	45,348	VC
Mercy College	NY	32,614	C
Mercyhurst Univ	PA	47,420	C
Meredith College	NC	46,634	C
Merrimack College	MA	55,415	C
Messiah College	PA	44,380	VC
Methodist Univ	NC	58,130	C
Metropolitan State Univ of Denver	CO	6,928	LC
Miami Univ	OH	27,190	HC+
Mich State Univ	MI	24,542	VC
Mich Tech Univ	MI	25,551	VC+
MidAmerica Nazarene Univ	KS	37,808	C
Middle Tenn State Univ	TN	8,650	C
Middlebury College	VT	67,464	MC
Midland Univ	NE	39,512	C
Midway Univ	KY	33,940	LC
Midwestern State Univ	TX	12,111	LC
Miles College	AL	16,530	NC
Millersville Univ of Pennsylvania	PA	25,298	C
Milligan College	TN	39,450	C
Millikin Univ	IL	44,148	C
Mills College	CA	43,705	C
Millsaps College	MS	50,080	C+
Minn State Univ, Mankato	MN	17,190	C
Minn State Univ, Moorhead	MN	21,393	C
Minot State Univ	ND	13,285	C
Misericordia Univ	PA	45,210	C
Miss College	MS	25,850	C
Miss State Univ	MS	12,028	C+
Miss Univ for Women	MS	17,065	C
Miss Valley State Univ	MS	13,233	LC
Missouri Baptist Univ	MO	35,594	C
Missouri Southern State Univ	MO	13,071	C
Missouri State Univ	MO	15,837	C+
Missouri Univ of Science and Technology	MO	18,655	HC
Missouri Valley College	MO	28,150	C
Missouri Western State Univ	MO	17,822	LC
Molloy College	NY	40,440	C
Monmouth College	IL	42,260	C
Monmouth Univ	NJ	50,184	C
Montana State Univ	MT	15,500	C+
Montana State Univ Billings	MT	13,336	LC
Montana Tech of the Univ of Montana	MT	15,447	VC
Montclair State Univ	NJ	26,912	C
Moravian College	PA	55,488	C
Morehead State Univ	KY	18,386	LC
Morehouse College	GA	40,835	C
Morgan State Univ	MD	17,190	LC
Morningside College	IA	39,780	C
Morris College	SC	19,195	LC
Mount Holyoke College	MA	56,746	MC
Mount Marty College	SD	36,862	C
Mount Mary Univ	WI	34,650	LC
Mount Mercy Univ	IA	39,748	C
Mount St. Mary College	NY	44,448	C
Mount St. Joseph Univ	OH	33,880	LC
Mount St. Mary's Univ	MD	53,380	C
Mount St. Mary's Univ - Chalon Campus	CA	50,486	VC+
Mount Vernon Nazarene Univ	OH	35,944	C
Muhlenberg College	PA	56,645	VC
Murray State Univ	KY	17,726	C+
Muskingum Univ	OH	35,966	C
National Louis Univ	IL	43,000	LC
National Univ	CA	17,849	LC
Nazareth College	NY	46,784	C
Nebr Wesleyan Univ	NE	42,026	C+
New College of Florida	FL	16,180	HC+
New Jersey City Univ	NJ	21,456	LC
New Jersey Inst of Technology	NJ	30,198	HC
New Mexico Highlands Univ	NM	11,904	LC
New Mexico Inst of Mining and Technology	NM	15,385	HC+
New Mexico State Univ	NM	14,050	LC
New York Univ	NY	68,139	MC
Newberry College	SC	34,550	C
Newman Univ	KS	37,382	C
Niagara Univ	NY	41,010	C
Nicholls State Univ	LA	14,959	C
Nichols College	MA	46,900	LC
Norfolk State Univ	VA	18,902	LC
N Car A&T State Univ	NC	13,786	C
N Car Central Univ	NC	9,000	C
N Car State Univ	NC	22,434	HC+
N Car Wesleyan College	NC	39,200	C
North Central College	IL	48,712	C+
North Central Univ	MN	30,610	C
N Dak State Univ	ND	16,245	VC
North Greenville Univ	SC	25,930	C
North Park Univ	IL	35,860	C
Northeastern Illinois Univ	IL	12,529	LC
Northeastern State Univ	OK	8,615	VC
Northeastern Univ	MA	65,352	MC
Northern Arizona Univ	AZ	21,003	C
Northern Illinois Univ	IL	20,176	C
Northern Kentucky Univ	KY	16,486	C
Northern Mich Univ	MI	20,853	C
Northern State Univ	SD	15,570	C
Northland College	WI	41,103	C+
Northwest Missouri State Univ	MO	18,286	C
Northwest Nazarene Univ	ID	40,250	C
Northwest Univ	WA	38,720	VC
Northwestern College of Iowa	IA	38,400	C
Northwestern Okla State Univ	OK	13,072	LC
Northwestern State Univ of Louisiana	LA	16,534	LC
Northwestern Univ	IL	68,725	MC
Norwich Univ	VT	56,234	C
Notre Dame College	OH	39,150	VC
Notre Dame of Maryland Univ	MD	47,570	VC
Nova Southeastern Univ	FL	38,534	C+
Nyack College	NY	34,450	LC
Oakland City Univ	IN	33,930	NC
Oakland Univ	MI	20,763	C
Oakwood Univ	AL	43,758	C
Oberlin College	OH	68,942	MC
Occidental College	CA	68,660	MC
Oglala Lakota College	SD	15,050	NC
Oglethorpe Univ	GA	44,200	C
Ohio Dominican Univ	OH	41,340	C+
Ohio Northern Univ	OH	44,050	VC
Ohio State Univ at Columbus	OH	22,843	MC
Ohio Univ	OH	23,394	VC
Ohio Valley Univ	WV	28,800	C
Ohio Wesleyan Univ	OH	49,460	VC
Okla Baptist Univ	OK	33,990	C
Okla Christian Univ	OK	29,260	C
Okla City Univ	OK	40,476	C
Okla Panhandle State Univ	OK	6,152	C
Okla State Univ	OK	17,180	C+
Okla Wesleyan Univ	OK	34,434	C
Old Dominion Univ	VA	21,618	C
Olivet College	MI	37,661	LC
Olivet Nazarene Univ	IL	41,840	VC
Oral Roberts Univ	OK	34,316	C
Oregon State Univ	OR	23,337	VC
Ottawa Univ	KS	39,980	VC
Otterbein Univ	OH	41,630	C
Ouachita Baptist Univ	AR	33,500	VC
Our Lady of the Lake Univ	TX	37,790	LC
Pace Univ	NY	60,136	C
Pacific Lutheran Univ	WA	49,960	C
Pacific Union College	CA	36,009	VC
Pacific Univ	OR	37,617	C
Paine College	GA	19,506	LC
Palm Beach Atlantic Univ	FL	39,250	C
Park Univ	MO	22,134	C
Penn State Altoona	PA	26,686	C
Penn State Erie,The Behrend College	PA	26,688	VC
Pennsylvania State Univ - Univ Park	PA	29,716	HC
Pepperdine Univ	CA	66,862	VC+
Peru State College	NE	15,602	LC
Pfeiffer Univ	NC	40,532	LC
Philander Smith College	AR	20,814	LC
Piedmont College	GA	34,334	C
Pittsburg State Univ	KS	13,880	C
Pitzer College	CA	68,500	HC+
Plymouth State Univ	NH	23,180	LC
Point Loma Nazarene Univ	CA	46,150	C+
Pomona College	CA	64,957	MC
Pontifical Catholic Univ of PR	PR	10,534	
Portland State Univ	OR	19,443	C
Prairie View A&M Univ	TX	27,273	LC
Presbyterian College	SC	47,186	C
Princeton Univ	NJ	60,090	MC
Principia College	IL	40,350	C
Providence College	RI	62,870	HC
Purdue Univ Northwest	IN	15,178	C
Purdue Univ/West Lafayette	IN	20,032	MC
Queens Univ of Charlotte	NC	39,543	C
Quincy Univ	IL	38,170	LC
Quinnipiac Univ	CT	60,970	VC
Radford Univ	VA	19,758	C
Ramapo College of New Jersey	NJ	25,760	VC
Randolph College	VA	53,970	C
Randolph-Macon College	VA	51,480	VC
Reed College	OR	65,300	MC
Regis Univ	CO	46,380	C
Rensselaer Polytechnic Inst	NY	67,265	MC
Rhode Island College	RI	19,000	LC
Rhodes College	TN	51,900	HC
Rice Univ	TX	59,458	MC
Rider Univ	NJ	54,050	C
Ripon College	WI	49,991	VC
Rivier Univ	NH	41,600	VC
Roanoke College	VA	55,952	VC
Roberts Wesleyan College	NY	41,116	C
Rochester Inst of Technology	NY	52,734	HC+
Rockford Univ	IL	38,570	C
Rockhurst Univ	MO	28,990	C
Rocky Mountain College	MT	35,776	C
Roger Williams Univ	RI	48,074	VC
Rollins College	FL	58,670	HC
Roosevelt Univ	IL	41,890	VC
Rose-Hulman Inst of Technology	IN	59,823	MC
Rosemont College	PA	30,980	LC
Rowan Univ	NJ	24,491	VC
Russell Sage College	NY	39,370	C
Rust College	MS	10,600	C
Rutgers Univ - Camden	NJ	26,595	C
Rutgers Univ - New Brunswick	NJ	27,090	HC
Rutgers Univ - Newark	NJ	27,351	C
Sacred Heart Univ	CT	54,590	C
Saginaw Valley State Univ	MI	19,284	C
St. Anselm College	NH	56,636	VC
St. Augustine's Univ	NC	25,582	C
St. Francis Univ	PA	46,146	NC
St. John's Univ	MN	53,472	C
St. Joseph's College of Maine	ME	47,890	C
St. Joseph's Univ	PA	58,540	VC
St. Leo Univ	FL	32,850	C
St. Louis Univ	MO	49,866	HC
St. Martin's Univ	WA	45,056	C
St. Mary-of-the-Woods College	IN	40,424	LC
St. Mary's College	IN	50,600	C
St. Mary's College of Calif	CA	57,420	C
St. Mary's Univ of Minn	MN	42,440	C
St. Michael's College	VT	53,275	VC+
St. Peter's Univ	NJ	49,192	C
St. Vincent College	PA	46,229	C
St. Xavier Univ	IL	44,440	C
Salem College	NC	40,206	C
Salem State Univ	MA	42,650	LC
Salisbury Univ	MD	21,132	VC
Salve Regina Univ	RI	53,046	VC
Sam Houston State Univ	TX	18,792	C
Samford Univ	AL	40,770	VC
San Diego Christian College	CA	40,914	C
San Diego State Univ	CA	23,156	VC
San Francisco State Univ	CA	18,514	LC
San Jose State Univ	CA	22,630	C
Sarah Lawrence College	NY	68,866	MC
Savannah State Univ	GA	17,036	C
Schreiner Univ	TX	34,626	LC
Scripps College	CA	69,260	HC
Seattle Pacific Univ	WA	47,439	C+
Seattle Univ	WA	54,957	VC
Seton Hall Univ	NJ	58,008	C
Seton Hill Univ	PA	46,972	VC
Sewanee: The Univ of the South	TN	58,000	HC+
Shaw Univ	NC	24,638	C
Shawnee State Univ	OH	16,998	C
Shenandoah Univ	VA	42,100	C
Shepherd Univ, West Virginia	WV	17,382	C
Shippensburg Univ of Pennsylvania	PA	24,096	C
Shorter Univ	GA	31,130	LC
Siena College	NY	48,916	C
Siena Heights Univ	MI	36,322	C
Silver Lake College of the Holy Family	WI	36,290	LC
Simmons College	MA	54,400	HC
Simpson College	IA	45,626	VC
Simpson Univ	CA	34,722	C
Skidmore College	NY	66,600	MC
Slippery Rock Univ of Pennsylvania	PA	20,450	C
Smith College	MA	66,774	MC
Sonoma State Univ	CA	27,020	C
S Car State Univ	SC	21,330	LC
S Dak School of Mines and Technology	SD	18,570	C+
S Dak State Univ	SD	15,874	C
Southeast Missouri State Univ	MO	16,148	C
Southeastern Louisiana Univ	LA	16,237	C
Southeastern Okla State Univ	OK	11,875	C
Southeastern Univ	FL	34,910	LC
Southern Adventist Univ	TN	28,250	C
Southern Arkansas Univ	AR	21,532	C
Southern Conn State Univ	CT	21,924	LC
Southern Illinois Univ Carbondale	IL	24,554	C
Southern Illinois Univ Edwardsville	IL	20,188	C
Southern Methodist Univ	TX	69,008	MC
Southern Nazarene Univ	OK	33,684	C
Southern Oregon Univ	OR	19,117	C
Southern Univ and A&M College	LA	16,074	LC
Southern Univ at New Orleans	LA	8,014	LC
Southern Wesleyan Univ	SC	33,670	LC
Southwest Baptist Univ	MO	30,890	LC
Southwest Minn State Univ	MN	17,783	C
Southwestern Adventist Univ	TX	28,232	LC
Southwestern College	KS	31,531	LC
Southwestern Okla State Univ	OK	12,205	C
Southwestern Univ	TX	52,370	VC
Spelman College	GA	41,642	C
Spring Arbor Univ	MI	37,390	C
Spring Hill College	AL	48,488	C
Springfield College	MA	48,775	C
St. Ambrose Univ	IA	40,180	C
St. Bonaventure Univ	NY	45,596	C
St. Catherine Univ	MN	45,630	C
St. Cloud State Univ	MN	10,600	C
St. Edward's Univ	TX	56,190	VC
St. Francis College	NY	38,800	LC
St. John Fisher College	NY	45,270	VC
St. John's College at Annapolis	MD	63,348	MC
St. John's College, Santa Fe	NM	60,109	HC+
St. John's Univ	NY	57,160	C+
St. Joseph's College, New York/Brooklyn Campus	NY	25,114	LC
St. Joseph's College, New York/Long Island Campus	NY	25,124	C
St. Lawrence Univ	NY	66,646	HC+
St. Mary's College of Maryland	MD	27,312	VC
St. Mary's Univ	TX	39,120	C
St. Norbert College	WI	46,060	VC
St. Olaf College	MN	56,430	HC
St. Thomas Aquinas College	NY	32,450	C
Stanford Univ	CA	62,541	MC
SUNY Albany	NY	22,165	C
SUNY at Binghamton	NY	24,100	MC
SUNY at Geneseo	NY	21,622	VC
SUNY at New Paltz	NY	20,840	C
SUNY at Oswego	NY	22,219	VC
SUNY at Purchase College	NY	21,832	C
SUNY/Buffalo State	NY	20,583	LC
SUNY/College at Old Westbury	NY	16,860	C
SUNY/Cortland	NY	20,910	C
SUNY/Empire State College	NY	9,145	NC
SUNY/Fredonia	NY	20,818	C
SUNY/Oneonta	NY	20,794	C
SUNY/Plattsburgh	NY	19,314	C
SUNY/Potsdam	NY	21,051	VC
SUNY/Univ at Buffalo	NY	23,122	C
Stephen F. Austin State Univ	TX	18,484	LC
Sterling College	KS	32,830	LC
Stetson Univ	FL	57,174	VC+
Stevens Inst of Technology	NJ	64,954	MC
Stevenson Univ	MD	48,412	C
Stillman College	AL	20,738	C
Stockton Univ	NJ	25,565	C
Stonehill College	MA	55,130	C
Stony Brook Univ/The SUNY	NY	22,703	MC
Suffolk Univ	MA	52,316	C
Sul Ross State Univ	TX	15,021	LC
Susquehanna Univ	PA	57,560	VC
Swarthmore College	PA	63,550	MC
Syracuse Univ	NY	62,313	HC
Tabor College	KS	35,870	C
Talladega College	AL	25,919	C
Tarleton State Univ	TX	15,248	LC
Taylor Univ	IN	42,130	VC
Temple Univ	PA	24,392	C+
Tenn State Univ	TN	14,423	LC

ST = STATE $IS = IN-STATE COSTS SR = SELECTOR RATING

School	ST	$IS	SR
Tenn Tech Univ	TN	17,929	C
Tenn Wesleyan Univ	TN	32,680	LC
Texas A&M Univ at College Station	TX	20,771	VC+
Texas A&M Univ at Commerce	TX	10,496	C
Texas A&M Univ at Corpus Christi	TX	16,851	LC
Texas A&M Univ at Kingsville	TX	16,580	LC
Texas Christian Univ	TX	57,120	HC
Texas Lutheran Univ	TX	39,770	C
Texas Southern Univ	TX	19,592	LC
Texas State Univ	TX	18,721	C
Texas Tech Univ	TX	20,156	C+
Texas Woman's Univ	TX	15,302	LC
The American Univ	DC	61,317	HC
The Catholic Univ of America	DC	58,376	VC
The Citadel, The Military College of S Car	SC	20,679	C
The College at Brockport - SUNY	NY	21,058	C
The College of Idaho	ID	36,415	C
The College of New Jersey	NJ	28,675	VC+
The College of New Rochelle	NY	46,300	LC
The College of St. Rose	NY	44,010	C
The College of Wooster	OH	60,000	HC
The Evergreen State College	WA	16,599	C
The George Washington Univ	DC	68,474	HC+
The Master's Univ	CA	43,870	C
The Univ of Akron	OH	22,566	C
The Univ of Alabama	AL	24,320	C+
The Univ of Arizona	AZ	24,086	C
The Univ of Mary	ND	23,180	C
The Univ of Memphis	TN	18,278	C
The Univ of Montana Western	MT	9,426	LC
The Univ of Tenn at Chattanooga	TN	17,340	C+
The Univ of Tenn at Knoxville	TN	22,112	VC
The Univ of Tenn at Martin	TN	15,212	C
The Univ of Texas at Austin	TX	20,206	MC
The Univ of Texas at San Antonio	TX	21,060	C
The Univ of Utah	UT	18,751	VC
The Univ of Virginia's College at Wise	VA	18,192	LC
Thiel College	PA	42,950	LC
Thomas Edison State Univ	NJ	6,350	NC
Thomas More College	KY	36,720	LC
Tougaloo College	MS	17,980	NC
Touro College	NY	31,040	C
Towson Univ	MD	21,878	C
Transylvania Univ	KY	47,450	HC+
Trevecca Nazarene Univ	TN	31,186	C
Trine Univ	IN	41,310	C
Trinity Christian College	IL	35,580	C
Trinity College	CT	69,020	HC
Trinity International Univ	IL	31,070	VC
Trinity Univ	TX	54,480	MC
Trinity Washington Univ	DC	33,826	C+
Troy Univ	AL	16,171	C
Truman State Univ	MO	16,286	MC
Tufts Univ	MA		MC
Tulane Univ	LA	67,496	MC
Tusculum College	TN	31,625	LC
Tuskegee Univ	AL	28,164	C
Union College	KY	32,310	C
Union College	NE	23,270	C
Union College	NY	64,320	MC
Union Univ	TN	41,160	VC
United States Air Force Academy	CO		C
United States Military Academy at West Point	NY		HC+
United States Naval Academy	MD		HC
Universidad del Turabo	PR	17,828	
Univ of Alabama at Birmingham	AL	22,092	C
Univ of Alabama in Huntsville	AL	20,028	VC
Univ of Alaska Anchorage	AK	17,914	C
Univ of Alaska Fairbanks	AK	16,874	VC
Univ of Alaska Southeast	AK	17,615	C
Univ of Arkansas at Fayetteville	AR	19,766	VC
Univ of Arkansas at Little Rock	AR	18,211	LC
Univ of Arkansas at Monticello	AR	13,599	LC
Univ of Arkansas at Pine Bluff	AR	13,541	C
Univ of Bridgeport	CT	44,985	LC
Univ of Calif at Berkeley	CA	29,886	MC
Univ of Calif at Davis	CA	28,468	HC
Univ of Calif at Irvine	CA	33,857	VC
Univ of Calif at Los Angeles	CA	27,438	HC+
Univ of Calif at Riverside	CA	32,912	C
Univ of Calif at Santa Barbara	CA	30,627	HC+
Univ of Calif San Diego	CA	30,450	MC
Univ of Calif, Santa Cruz	CA	28,731	C+
Univ of Central Arkansas	AR	15,042	VC
Univ of Central Florida	FL	16,379	VC
Univ of Central Missouri	MO	18,982	C
Univ of Central Okla	OK	15,150	C
Univ of Chicago	IL	70,551	MC
Univ of Cincinnati	OH	22,118	VC
Univ of Colo Boulder	CO	26,048	HC
Univ of Colo Colo Springs	CO	20,300	C
Univ of Colo Denver	CO	22,238	C
Univ of Conn	CT	27,394	
Univ of Dallas	TX	50,676	VC
Univ of Dayton	OH	54,930	VC
Univ of Delaware	DE	32,214	VC
Univ of Denver	CO	61,129	VC+
Univ of Detroit Mercy	MI	48,816	C
Univ of Evansville	IN	44,186	C+
Univ of Findlay	OH	43,040	C
Univ of Florida	FL	16,291	HC+
Univ of Georgia	GA	21,878	HC
Univ of Great Falls	MT	38,524	C
Univ of Hartford	CT	49,776	C
Univ of Hawaii at Hilo	HI	18,038	VC
Univ of Hawaii at Manoa	HI	23,261	C
Univ of Houston	TX	21,871	VC
Univ of Houston-Downtown	TX	7,241	LC
Univ of Idaho	ID	16,158	C
Univ of Illinois at Chicago	IL	24,664	VC
Univ of Illinois at Urbana-Champaign	IL	27,006	HC
Univ of Indianapolis	IN	36,480	VC
Univ of Iowa	IA	19,415	HC
Univ of Jamestown	ND	28,508	C
Univ of Kansas	KS	20,884	VC
Univ of Kentucky	KY	24,800	C+
Univ of La Verne	CA	55,600	C
Univ of Louisiana at Lafayette	LA	14,516	C
Univ of Louisiana at Monroe	LA	15,970	C
Univ of Louisville	KY	19,692	C
Univ of Lynchburg	VA	48,370	C
Univ of Maine	ME	21,038	VC
Univ of Maine at Farmington	ME	18,792	C
Univ of Mary Hardin-Baylor	TX	35,292	C+
Univ of Mary Washington	VA	23,039	C+
Univ of Maryland/Baltimore County	MD	23,004	VC
Univ of Maryland/College Park	MD	21,938	HC
Univ of Maryland/Eastern Shore	MD	21,861	LC
Univ of Mass Amherst	MA	27,669	HC
Univ of Mass Boston	MA	13,828	C
Univ of Mass Dartmouth	MA	26,507	C
Univ of Mass Lowell	MA	27,296	VC
Univ of Miami	FL	63,494	MC
Univ of Mich/Ann Arbor	MI	25,274	MC
Univ of Mich/Dearborn	MI	12,472	VC
Univ of Mich/Flint	MI	19,062	C
Univ of Minn/Duluth	MN	20,292	C
Univ of Minn/Morris	MN	21,222	VC
Univ of Minn/Twin Cities	MN	24,269	MC
Univ of Miss	MS	18,802	C
Univ of Missouri-Columbia	MO	20,463	VC
Univ of Missouri-Kansas City	MO	19,563	VC
Univ of Missouri-St. Louis	MO	19,810	VC
Univ of Mobile	AL	28,935	C
Univ of Montana	MT	14,105	C
Univ of Montevallo	AL	20,012	C
Univ of Mount Olive	NC	18,426	C
Univ of Mount Union	OH	39,990	C
Univ of Nebr - Kearney	NE	17,014	LC
Univ of Nebr - Lincoln	NE	18,589	VC
Univ of Nebr - Omaha	NE	16,120	C
Univ of Nevada, Las Vegas	NV	17,553	C
Univ of Nevada, Reno	NV	18,010	C
Univ of New Hampshire	NH	29,333	VC
Univ of New Haven	CT	53,680	C
Univ of New Mexico	NM	16,808	C
Univ of New Orleans	LA	12,840	C
Univ of North Alabama	AL	15,964	C
Univ of N Car at Asheville	NC	16,251	VC+
Univ of N Car at Chapel Hill	NC	20,561	MC
Univ of N Car at Charlotte	NC	17,803	VC
Univ of N Car at Greensboro	NC	15,998	C
Univ of N Car at Pembroke	NC	14,737	LC
Univ of N Car Wilmington	NC	16,784	VC
Univ of N Dak	ND	16,673	C
Univ of North Florida	FL	15,996	VC
Univ of North Georgia	GA	17,316	C
Univ of North Texas	TX	20,082	C
Univ of Northern Colo	CO	19,658	C
Univ of Northern Iowa	IA	17,480	C
Univ of Northwestern - St. Paul	MN	39,530	C
Univ of Notre Dame	IN	68,801	MC
Univ of Okla	OK	19,651	HC
Univ of Oregon	OR	24,021	VC
Univ of Pennsylvania	PA	63,526	MC
Univ of Pikeville	KY	27,838	C
Univ of Pittsburgh	PA	30,030	MC
Univ of Pittsburgh at Bradford	PA	22,958	C
Univ of Pittsburgh at Johnstown	PA	22,092	C
Univ of Portland	OR	52,152	VC
Univ of PR, at Cayey	PR		
Univ of PR, at Humacao	PR	14,000	
Univ of PR, at Mayaguez	PR	13,995	
Univ of Puget Sound	WA	60,210	HC
Univ of Redlands	CA	61,934	VC
Univ of Rhode Island	RI	26,066	VC
Univ of Richmond	VA	62,730	MC
Univ of Rio Grande & Rio Grande Community College	OH	8,750	LC
Univ of Rochester	NY	65,032	MC
Univ of St. Francis	IN	38,520	C
Univ of St. Joseph	CT	49,069	C
Univ of St. Mary	KS	37,080	NC
Univ of San Diego	CA	60,338	HC
Univ of San Francisco	CA	60,580	C
Univ of Science and Arts of Okla	OK	11,140	VC
Univ of Scranton	PA	54,962	VC
Univ of Sioux Falls	SD	25,630	C
Univ of South Alabama	AL	16,880	C
Univ of S Car at Columbia	SC	21,726	VC
Univ of S Car Upstate	SC	19,272	LC
Univ of S Dak	SD	16,109	C
Univ of South Florida/Tampa	FL	16,110	VC
Univ of Southern Calif	CA	66,631	MC
Univ of Southern Indiana	IN	16,808	C
Univ of Southern Maine	ME	18,320	C
Univ of Southern Miss	MS	13,170	C
Univ of St. Francis	IL	40,828	C
Univ of St. Thomas - Houston	TX	41,510	VC
Univ of Tampa	FL	38,928	VC
Univ of Texas at Arlington	TX	18,876	C
Univ of Texas at Dallas	TX	23,640	HC
Univ of Texas at El Paso	TX	34,452	NC
Univ of Texas Rio Grande Valley	TX	15,573	LC
Univ of the Cumberlands	KY	32,000	LC
Univ of the District of Columbia	DC	21,260	LC
Univ of the Incarnate Word	TX	39,162	LC
Univ of the Ozarks	AR	31,050	NC
Univ of the Pacific	CA	57,446	VC
Univ of the Sacred Heart	PR	17,932	
Univ of the Southwest	NM	24,386	C
Univ of Toledo	OH	19,336	C
Univ of Tulsa	OK	52,625	HC
Univ of Vermont	VT	29,792	HC
Univ of Virginia	VA	27,367	MC
Univ of Washington	WA	23,091	MC
Univ of West Alabama	AL	16,284	LC
Univ of West Florida	FL	15,848	C
Univ of West Georgia	GA	17,510	LC
Univ of Wisc-Eau Claire	WI	16,354	VC
Univ of Wisc-Green Bay	WI	15,184	C
Univ of Wisc-La Crosse	WI	15,425	VC
Univ of Wisc-Madison	WI	21,647	MC
Univ of Wisc-Milwaukee	WI	21,538	C
Univ of Wisc-Oshkosh	WI	15,392	C
Univ of Wisc-Parkside	WI	15,313	C
Univ of Wisc-Platteville	WI	14,148	C
Univ of Wisc-River Falls	WI	14,541	C
Univ of Wisc-Stevens Point	WI	14,043	C
Univ of Wisc-Superior	WI	14,838	C
Univ of Wisc-Whitewater	WI	13,976	C
Univ of Wyoming	WY	15,537	C
Upper Iowa Univ	IA	34,990	NC
Urbana Univ	OH	30,820	C
Ursinus College	PA	62,920	VC
Ursuline College	OH	41,076	LC
Utah State Univ	UT	13,235	C
Utica College	NY	31,510	C
Valley City State Univ	ND	13,267	C
Valparaiso Univ	IN	50,160	VC
Vanderbilt Univ	TN	63,248	MC
Vanguard Univ of Southern Calif	CA	42,400	VC
Vassar College	NY	68,110	MC
Villanova Univ	PA	64,922	MC
Virginia Commonwealth Univ	VA	23,811	VC
Virginia Military Inst	VA	26,460	VC
Virginia Polytechnic Inst and State Univ	VA	21,920	VC
Virginia State Univ	VA	19,802	C+
Virginia Union Univ	VA	25,058	C
Virginia Wesleyan Univ	VA	45,980	LC
Viterbo Univ	WI	34,660	C
Voorhees College	SC	19,976	C
Wabash College	IN	52,100	VC
Wagner College	NY	57,240	C+
Wake Forest Univ	NC	69,354	MC
Walla Walla Univ	WA	34,845	C
Walsh Univ	OH	39,010	C
Warren Wilson College	NC	44,220	VC
Wartburg College	IA	49,478	C
Washburn Univ	KS	15,827	C
Washington & Jefferson College	PA	58,694	VC
Washington Adventist Univ	MD	32,050	LC
Washington and Lee Univ	VA	59,647	MC
Washington College	MD	56,154	VC
Washington State Univ	WA	22,747	C
Washington Univ in St. Louis	MO	67,539	MC
Wayland Baptist Univ	TX	23,460	LC
Wayne State College	NE	25,746	NC
Wayne State Univ	MI	23,085	C
Waynesburg Univ	PA	33,530	C
Weber State Univ	UT	14,112	C
Webster Univ	MO	37,490	C
Wellesley College	MA	66,984	MC
Wells College	NY	50,500	C
Wesley College	DE	37,848	LC
Wesleyan College	GA	31,940	C+
Wesleyan Univ	CT	66,940	MC
West Chester Univ of Pennsylvania	PA	19,171	VC
West Liberty Univ	WV	16,158	C
West Texas A&M Univ	TX	13,478	C
West Virginia State Univ	WV	19,412	LC
West Virginia Univ	WV	18,952	VC
West Virginia Wesleyan College	WV	39,188	C
Western Carolina Univ	NC	13,965	C
Western Conn State Univ	CT	21,254	LC
Western Illinois Univ	IL	20,897	C
Western Kentucky Univ	KY	16,850	C
Western Mich Univ	MI	21,791	C
Western New England Univ	MA	49,182	C
Western New Mexico Univ	NM	16,914	LC
Western Oregon Univ	OR	19,965	LC
Western State Colo Univ	CO	19,348	C
Western Washington Univ	WA	18,904	VC
Westfield State Univ	MA	20,404	C
Westminster College	MO	32,820	C
Westminster College	PA	41,722	C
Westminster College	UT	41,078	C
Westmont College	CA	57,930	VC
Wheaton College	IL	44,993	MC
Wheaton College	MA	63,818	VC
Wheeling Jesuit Univ	WV	37,106	LC
Wheelock College	MA	51,325	LC
Whitman College	WA	59,772	MC
Whittier College	CA	57,891	C
Whitworth Univ	WA	53,682	VC
Wichita State Univ	KS	17,773	C
Widener Univ	PA	58,190	C
Wilberforce Univ	OH	19,900	C
Wiley College	TX	19,255	C
Wilkes Univ	PA	49,166	C
Willamette Univ	OR	62,514	VC+
William Carey Univ	MS	23,950	LC
William Jewell College	MO	42,490	C+
William Paterson Univ of New Jersey	NJ	24,022	C
William Woods Univ	MO	32,040	C
Williams College	MA	67,700	MC
Wilmington College	OH	35,100	C
Wilson College	PA	35,620	LC
Wingate Univ	NC	41,900	C
Winona State Univ	MN	18,109	C
Winston-Salem State Univ	NC	18,005	LC
Winthrop Univ	SC	23,960	C
Wisc Lutheran College	WI	36,290	C
Wittenberg Univ	OH	49,863	VC
Wofford College	SC	49,885	VC
Worcester Polytechnic Inst	MA	62,846	MC
Worcester State Univ	MA	20,977	C
Wright State Univ	OH	16,983	C
Xavier Univ	OH	49,380	VC
Xavier Univ of Louisiana	LA	31,689	C
Yale Univ	CT	64,650	MC
Yeshiva Univ	NY	52,750	VC
York College of Pennsylvania	PA	29,240	C
Youngstown State Univ	OH	17,487	C

MATHEMATICS - ACTUARIAL CONCENTRATION

School	ST	$IS	SR
Bethany College	WV	38,774	LC
East Central Univ	OK	13,330	C
Indiana Univ of Pennsylvania	PA	24,474	C
Kent State Univ	OH	20,928	C
Murray State Univ	KY	17,726	C+
Pacific Lutheran Univ	WA	49,960	C
Rochester Inst of Technology	NY	52,734	HC+
Seattle Univ	WA	54,957	VC
Silver Lake College of the Holy Family	WI	36,290	LC
Texas Christian Univ	TX	57,120	HC
West Chester Univ of Pennsylvania	PA	19,171	VC

MATHEMATICS – ECONOMICS

School	ST	$IS	SR
Baldwin Wallace Univ	OH	42,464	VC
Bethany College	WV	38,774	LC
Bowdoin College	ME	65,980	MC
Brown Univ	RI	64,566	MC
Fordham Univ	NY	68,431	MC
Gettysburg College	PA	65,210	MC
High Point Univ	NC	47,355	VC
Hofstra Univ	NY	58,210	C+
Ithaca College	NY	58,158	VC+
New York Univ	NY	68,139	MC
Reed College	OR	65,300	MC
Southern Oregon Univ	OR	19,117	C
SUNY/Univ at Buffalo	NY	23,122	C
Temple Univ	PA	24,392	C+
Univ of Dayton	OH	54,930	VC
Univ of Pittsburgh	PA	30,030	MC
Wake Forest Univ	NC	69,354	MC
Wayne State Univ	MI	23,085	C
Wheaton College	MA	63,818	VC
Whitman College	WA	59,772	MC
Whitworth Univ	WA	53,682	VC
Yale Univ	CT	64,650	MC

MATHEMATICS – PHILOSOPHY

School	ST	$IS	SR
Boston Univ	MA	67,352	MC
Yale Univ	CT	64,650	MC

MATHEMATICS EDUCATION

School	ST	$IS	SR
Abilene Christian Univ	TX	43,708	C+
Adams State Univ	CO	15,420	LC

ST = STATE $IS = IN-STATE COSTS SR = SELECTOR RATING

School	ST	$IS	SR
Alfred Univ	NY	37,490	C
Andrews Univ	MI	41,732	C
Appalachian State Univ	NC	15,394	VC
Aquinas College - Mich	MI	38,876	VC
Arkansas State Univ	AR	16,190	C
Armstrong State Univ	GA	15,615	C
Asbury Univ	KY	36,450	C+
Auburn Univ	AL	24,300	VC+
Augustana College	IL	51,222	VC+
Averett Univ	VA	43,034	LC
Baker Univ	KS	37,190	C
Baylor Univ	TX	56,803	HC
Bennett College	NC	27,717	NC
Bennington College	VT	66,280	MC
Berry College	GA	47,466	VC
Bethany College	KS	38,637	LC
Bethany College	WV	38,774	LC
Bethel College	IN	36,830	C
Bethel Univ	MN	46,550	C+
Biola Univ	CA	48,686	C
Black Hills State Univ	SD	16,622	C
Blackburn College	IL	28,526	LC
Bloomfield College	NJ	40,100	LC
Bloomsburg Univ of Pennsylvania	PA	19,930	C
Blue Mountain College	MS	15,949	C
Boston Univ	MA	67,352	MC
Bowdoin College	ME	65,980	MC
Bowling Green State Univ	OH	19,975	C
Brigham Young Univ	UT	13,248	MC
Brigham Young Univ/Hawaii	HI	11,710	C
Cairn Univ	PA	37,572	C
Calif Baptist Univ	CA	42,986	C
Cal State, Fullerton	CA	21,902	C
Cal State, Long Beach	CA	18,850	C
Calvin College	MI	43,090	HC
Canisius College	NY	49,672	C
Carthage College	WI	48,835	C
Catawba College	NC	39,820	LC
Cedarville Univ	OH	36,244	VC
Central Washington Univ	WA	16,803	C
CUNY/Brooklyn College	NY	7,163	C+
CUNY/City College	NY	20,204	C
Claflin Univ	SC	25,592	LC
Coker College	SC	38,196	C
College of the Ozarks	MO	7,530	VC
Colo State Univ	CO	23,033	C
Concordia College - Moorhead	MN	46,418	C
Concordia College - New York	NY	39,035	LC
Concordia Univ St. Paul	MN	29,050	C
Corban Univ	OR	41,700	C
Covenant College	GA	44,590	HC
Daemen College	NY	40,336	C
Dakota State Univ	SD	12,286	C
Davis & Elkins College	WV	38,242	LC
Defiance College	OH	42,240	LC
Delaware State Univ	DE	19,376	LC
Delta State Univ	MS	13,176	LC
Dominican College	NY	40,258	LC
Dordt College	IA	37,860	C+
Drake Univ	IA	49,220	HC
Drury Univ	MO	37,555	VC
Duquesne Univ	PA	48,508	VC
East Carolina Univ	NC	16,539	C
East Central Univ	OK	13,330	C
East Texas Baptist Univ	TX	34,444	C
Eastern Mich Univ	MI	19,761	C
Eastern Washington Univ	WA	17,896	LC
Edgewood College	WI	35,950	C
Edinboro Univ	PA	15,940	LC
Elizabethtown College	PA	56,340	VC
Elmhurst College	IL	46,514	C
Elon Univ	NC	46,142	HC
Emory and Henry College	VA	46,320	C
Faulkner Univ	AL	26,410	C
Ferris State Univ	MI	21,458	C
Florida Gulf Coast Univ	FL	14,738	C
Florida Inst of Technology	FL	53,306	VC
Florida State Univ	FL	16,771	HC
Fontbonne Univ	MO	34,606	C
Fort Valley State Univ	GA	17,988	VC
Franklin College	IN	40,550	C
Fresno Pacific Univ	CA	38,858	C
Gannon Univ	PA	42,922	C
Geneva College	PA	35,450	C
Georgetown College	KY	41,440	C
Glenville State College	WV	17,386	LC
Goshen College	IN	44,350	C
Grace College and Seminary	IN	31,524	C
Grambling State Univ	LA	15,701	C
Greensboro College	NC	39,790	LC
Greenville College	IL	27,012	LC
Grove City College	PA	26,654	VC
Gwynedd Mercy Univ	PA	43,780	LC
Hardin-Simmons Univ	TX	36,025	C
Hofstra Univ	NY	58,210	C+
Hood College	MD	50,540	C
Houghton College	NY	40,558	VC
Houston Baptist Univ	TX	36,450	C
Humboldt State Univ	CA	21,708	C
Huntingdon College	AL	35,900	C
Huntington Univ	IN	33,996	C
Immaculata Univ	PA	39,000	C
Indiana Univ Bloomington	IN	20,791	HC
Indiana Univ Northwest	IN	7,207	LC
Indiana Univ South Bend	IN	16,057	C
Indiana Univ Southeast	IN	16,931	C
Indiana Univ-Purdue Univ Fort Wayne	IN	18,675	C
Indiana Wesleyan Univ	IN	33,674	C
Ithaca College	NY	58,158	VC+
Jackson State Univ	MS	15,879	LC
John Brown Univ	AR	35,184	VC
John Carroll Univ	OH	51,570	C
Johnson State College	VT	22,672	C
Judson College	AL	27,066	C
Judson Univ	IL	39,174	C
Juniata College	PA	58,118	VC
Keene State College	NH	24,604	C
Kennesaw State Univ	GA	18,899	VC
Kent State Univ	OH	20,928	C
Kentucky State Univ	KY	14,484	LC
Keystone College	PA	28,680	LC
King Univ	TN	36,976	C
Kutztown Univ of Pennsylvania	PA	19,477	C
Langston Univ	OK	15,659	C
Le Moyne College	NY	47,305	VC
Lee Univ	TN	22,045	C
Limestone College	SC	32,100	C
Lincoln Univ	MO	14,402	NC
Lipscomb Univ	TN	42,984	VC
LIU Brooklyn	NY	50,698	C
LIU Post	NY	50,698	C+
Louisiana College	LA	21,274	C
Loyola Univ Chicago	IL	57,158	VC
Marian Univ	WI	34,622	C
Marist College	NY	49,860	VC
Mars Hill Univ	NC	41,104	C
Marymount Univ	VA	43,231	C
Marywood Univ	PA	47,840	C
Mass College of Liberal Arts	MA	20,659	C
Mayville State Univ	ND	18,371	NC
Mercyhurst Univ	PA	47,420	C
Messiah College	PA	44,380	VC
Miami Univ	OH	27,190	HC+
MidAmerica Nazarene Univ	KS	37,808	C
Miles College	AL	16,530	NC
Millersville Univ of Pennsylvania	PA	25,298	C
Milligan College	TN	39,450	C
Millikin Univ	IL	44,148	C
Minn State Univ, Mankato	MN	17,190	C
Minn State Univ, Moorhead	MN	21,393	C
Minot State Univ	ND	13,285	C
Miss Valley State Univ	MS	13,233	LC
Missouri Southern State Univ	MO	13,071	C
Monmouth Univ	NJ	50,184	C
Montana State Univ Billings	MT	13,336	LC
Morningside College	IA	39,780	C
Morris College	SC	19,195	LC
Mount Mary Univ	WI	34,650	LC
Mount Vernon Nazarene Univ	OH	35,944	C
Murray State Univ	KY	17,726	C+
Nazareth College	NY	46,784	C
New York City College of Technology	NY	7,185	LC
New York Univ	NY	68,139	MC
Niagara Univ	NY	41,010	C
N Car A&T State Univ	NC	13,786	C
N Car State Univ	NC	22,434	HC+
North Greenville Univ	SC	25,930	C
Northern Kentucky Univ	KY	16,486	C
Northwest Missouri State Univ	MO	18,286	C
Northwest Nazarene Univ	ID	40,250	C
Northwestern Okla State Univ	OK	13,072	LC
Northwestern Univ	IL	68,725	MC
Nyack College	NY	34,450	LC
Oakwood Univ	AL	43,758	C
Ohio Univ	OH	23,394	VC
Ohio Valley Univ	WV	28,800	C
Okla Christian Univ	OK	29,260	C
Okla Wesleyan Univ	OK	34,434	C
Old Dominion Univ	VA	21,618	C
Olivet Nazarene Univ	IL	41,840	VC
Oral Roberts Univ	OK	34,316	C
Ouachita Baptist Univ	AR	33,500	VC
Pacific Lutheran Univ	WA	49,960	C
Palm Beach Atlantic Univ	FL	39,250	C
Pepperdine Univ	CA	66,862	VC+
Piedmont College	GA	34,334	C
Pittsburg State Univ	KS	13,880	C
Pontifical Catholic Univ of PR	PR	10,534	
Providence College	RI	62,870	HC
Purdue Univ Northwest	IN	15,178	C
Purdue Univ/West Lafayette	IN	20,032	MC
Radford Univ	VA	19,758	C
Regis College	MA	51,920	LC
Rider Univ	NJ	54,050	C
Rivier Univ	NH	41,600	VC
Roberts Wesleyan College	NY	41,116	C
Rocky Mountain College	MT	35,776	C
Rust College	MS	10,600	C
Saginaw Valley State Univ	MI	19,284	C
St. Augustine's Univ	NC	25,582	C
St. Louis Univ	MO	49,866	HC
St. Mary-of-the-Woods College	IN	40,424	LC
St. Mary's Univ of Minn	MN	42,440	C
Schreiner Univ	TX	34,626	LC
Seattle Pacific Univ	WA	47,439	C+
Seattle Univ	WA	54,957	VC
Seton Hill Univ	PA	46,972	VC
Shaw Univ	NC	24,638	C
Shepherd Univ, West Virginia	WV	17,382	C
Shippensburg Univ of Pennsylvania	PA	24,096	C
Shorter Univ	GA	31,130	LC
Silver Lake College of the Holy Family	WI	36,290	LC
Simpson Univ	CA	34,722	C
Southeast Missouri State Univ	MO	16,148	C
Southeastern Okla State Univ	OK	11,875	C
Southern Illinois Univ Carbondale	IL	24,554	C
Southern Illinois Univ Edwardsville	IL	20,188	C
Southern Nazarene Univ	OK	33,684	C
Southern Univ and A&M College	LA	16,074	LC
Southern Univ at New Orleans	LA	8,014	LC
Southern Wesleyan Univ	SC	33,670	LC
Southwest Baptist Univ	MO	30,890	LC
Southwest Minn State Univ	MN	17,783	C
Southwestern College	KS	31,531	LC
Southwestern Okla State Univ	OK	12,205	C
St. Ambrose Univ	IA	40,180	C
St. Edward's Univ	TX	56,190	VC
St. John Fisher College	NY	45,270	VC
SUNY at New Paltz	NY	20,840	C
SUNY at Oswego	NY	22,219	VC
SUNY/College at Old Westbury	NY	16,860	C
SUNY/Fredonia	NY	20,818	C
SUNY/Oneonta	NY	20,794	C
SUNY/Plattsburgh	NY	19,314	C
SUNY/Potsdam	NY	21,051	VC
Suffolk Univ	MA	52,316	C
Syracuse Univ	NY	62,313	HC
Taylor Univ	IN	42,130	VC
Temple Univ	PA	24,392	C+
Texas Christian Univ	TX	57,120	HC
Texas Southern Univ	TX	19,592	LC
Texas Wesleyan Univ	TX	37,338	C
The Catholic Univ of America	DC	58,376	VC
The College of New Jersey	NJ	28,675	VC+
The College of St. Rose	NY	44,010	C
The Univ of Mary	ND	23,180	C
The Univ of Montana Western	MT	9,426	LC
The Univ of Utah	UT	18,751	VC
Tougaloo College	MS	17,980	NC
Trevecca Nazarene Univ	TN	31,186	C
Trine Univ	IN	41,310	C
Troy Univ	AL	16,171	C
Union College	NE	23,270	C
Universidad del Turabo	PR	17,828	
Univ of Arkansas at Pine Bluff	AR	13,541	C
Univ of Calif at Los Angeles	CA	27,438	HC+
Univ of Calif at Riverside	CA	32,912	C
Univ of Calif San Diego	CA	30,450	MC
Univ of Central Florida	FL	16,379	VC
Univ of Central Missouri	MO	18,982	C
Univ of Central Okla	OK	15,150	C
Univ of Conn	CT	27,394	
Univ of Delaware	DE	32,214	VC
Univ of Evansville	IN	44,186	C+
Univ of Georgia	GA	21,878	HC
Univ of Great Falls	MT	38,524	C
Univ of Idaho	ID	16,158	C
Univ of Illinois at Chicago	IL	24,664	VC
Univ of Illinois at Urbana-Champaign	IL	27,006	HC
Univ of Indianapolis	IN	36,480	VC
Univ of Iowa	IA	19,415	HC
Univ of Kentucky	KY	24,800	C+
Univ of Louisiana at Lafayette	LA	14,516	C
Univ of Mary Hardin-Baylor	TX	35,292	C+
Univ of Maryland/Eastern Shore	MD	21,861	LC
Univ of Mich/Dearborn	MI	12,472	VC
Univ of Minn/Duluth	MN	20,292	C
Univ of Miss	MS	18,802	C
Univ of Missouri-Columbia	MO	20,463	VC
Univ of Nebr - Lincoln	NE	18,589	VC
Univ of New Hampshire	NH	29,333	VC
Univ of New Haven	CT	53,680	C
Univ of New Orleans	LA	12,840	C
Univ of N Car at Charlotte	NC	17,803	VC
Univ of N Car at Greensboro	NC	15,998	C
Univ of North Florida	FL	15,996	VC
Univ of North Georgia	GA	17,316	C
Univ of Northwestern - St. Paul	MN	39,530	C
Univ of Okla	OK	19,651	HC
Univ of Pittsburgh at Bradford	PA	22,958	C
Univ of Pittsburgh at Johnstown	PA	22,092	C
Univ of Rio Grande & Rio Grande Community College	OH	8,750	LC
Univ of S Car Upstate	SC	19,272	LC
Univ of South Florida/Tampa	FL	16,110	VC
Univ of Southern Indiana	IN	16,808	C
Univ of the Cumberlands	KY	32,000	LC
Univ of Vermont	VT	29,792	HC
Univ of Wisc-Green Bay	WI	15,184	C
Univ of Wisc-Superior	WI	14,838	C
Utah State Univ	UT	13,235	C
Valparaiso Univ	IN	50,160	VC
Viterbo Univ	WI	34,660	C
Wartburg College	IA	49,478	C
Washington Adventist Univ	MD	32,050	LC
Washington Univ in St. Louis	MO	67,539	MC
Wayne State Univ	MI	23,085	C
Weber State Univ	UT	14,112	C
Webster Univ	MO	37,490	C
West Chester Univ of Pennsylvania	PA	19,171	VC
West Texas A&M Univ	TX	13,478	C
Western Carolina Univ	NC	13,965	C
Westmont College	CA	57,930	VC
Whitworth Univ	WA	53,682	VC
Widener Univ	PA	58,190	C
Wiley College	TX	19,255	C
Wilmington College	OH	35,100	C
Wilson College	PA	35,620	LC
Wingate Univ	NC	41,900	C
Winona State Univ	MN	18,109	C
Wright State Univ	OH	16,983	C
Xavier Univ of Louisiana	LA	31,689	C
York College of Pennsylvania	PA	29,240	C
Youngstown State Univ	OH	17,487	C

MATHEMATICS/ COMPUTATIONAL

School	ST	$IS	SR
Abilene Christian Univ	TX	43,708	C+
Aquinas College - Mich	MI	38,876	VC
Brown Univ	RI	64,566	MC
Calif Inst of Technology	CA	64,704	MC
Christopher Newport Univ	VA	24,878	VC+
Embry-Riddle Aeronautical Univ - Daytona Beach	FL	45,822	VC
Lawrence Tech Univ	MI	41,630	VC
Loyola Univ Chicago	IL	57,158	VC
Loyola Univ New Orleans	LA	52,456	VC
Missouri Southern State Univ	MO	13,071	C
St. Mary's College	IN	50,600	C
Shepherd Univ, West Virginia	WV	17,382	C
Southwestern Univ	TX	52,370	VC
Stanford Univ	CA	62,541	MC
Temple Univ	PA	24,392	C+
Univ of Conn	CT	27,394	
Univ of Illinois at Chicago	IL	24,664	VC
West Chester Univ of Pennsylvania	PA	19,171	VC

MATHEMATICS/THEORETICAL

School	ST	$IS	SR
Aquinas College - Mich	MI	38,876	VC
Biola Univ	CA	48,686	C
Brown Univ	RI	64,566	MC
Seattle Univ	WA	54,957	VC

MECHANICAL DESIGN TECHNOLOGY

School	ST	$IS	SR
Pennsylvania College of Technology	PA	27,693	NC
Southeast Missouri State Univ	MO	16,148	C
Western Washington Univ	WA	18,904	VC

MECHANICAL ENGINEERING

School	ST	$IS	SR
Alabama A&M Univ	AL	18,796	C
Alfred Univ	NY	37,490	C
Anderson Univ	IN	39,450	C
Arizona State Univ at the Tempe Campus	AZ	23,001	VC
Arkansas State Univ	AR	16,190	C
Arkansas Tech Univ	AR	16,534	LC
Auburn Univ	AL	24,300	VC+
Baylor Univ	TX	56,803	HC
Boise State Univ	ID	17,368	C
Boston Univ	MA	67,352	MC
Bradley Univ	IL	43,240	VC
Brigham Young Univ	UT	13,248	MC
Brown Univ	RI	64,566	MC
Bucknell Univ	PA	67,136	MC
Calif Baptist Univ	CA	42,986	C
Calif Inst of Technology	CA	64,704	MC
Calif Polytechnic State Univ	CA	22,547	MC
Calif State Polytechnic Univ, Pomona	CA	21,811	C
Cal State, Maritime Academy	CA	23,156	C+
Cal State, Chico	CA	19,790	VC
Cal State, Fresno	CA	16,902	LC
Cal State, Fullerton	CA	21,902	C
Cal State, Long Beach	CA	18,850	C
Cal State, Los Angeles	CA	17,186	LC
Cal State, Northridge	CA	17,277	LC
Cal State, Sacramento	CA	19,060	C
Calvin College	MI	43,090	HC
Carnegie Mellon Univ	PA	67,980	MC
Case Western Reserve Univ	OH	62,284	MC
Cedarville Univ	OH	36,244	VC
Central Conn State Univ	CT	22,041	C
Central Mich Univ	MI	20,330	C
Central Washington Univ	WA	16,803	C
Christian Brothers Univ	TN	31,670	VC
CUNY/City College	NY	20,204	C
Clarkson Univ	NY	60,392	VC
Clemson Univ	SC		HC
Cleveland State Univ	OH	22,290	C

ST = STATE **$IS** = IN-STATE COSTS **SR** = SELECTOR RATING

School	ST	$IS	SR
Colo State Univ	CO	23,033	C
Columbia Univ/City of New York	NY	62,958	MC
Cooper Union for the Advancement of Science and Art	NY	61,370	MC
Cornell Univ	NY	67,591	MC
Delaware State Univ	DE	19,376	LC
Dordt College	IA	37,860	C+
Drexel Univ	PA	65,927	HC
Duke Univ	NC	68,298	MC
Elizabethtown College	PA	56,340	VC
Embry-Riddle Aeronautical Univ - Daytona Beach	FL	45,822	VC
Embry-Riddle Aeronautical Univ - Prescott Campus	AZ	45,130	VC
Fairfield Univ	CT	61,445	HC
Florida A&M Univ	FL	15,361	C
Florida Atlantic Univ	FL	18,256	C
Florida Inst of Technology	FL	53,306	VC
Florida International Univ	FL	20,281	C
Florida State Univ	FL	16,771	HC
Franklin W. Olin College of Engineering	MA	65,580	SP
Gannon Univ	PA	42,922	C
Georgia Inst of Technology	GA	23,910	MC
Georgia Southern Univ	GA	16,540	VC
Gonzaga Univ	WA	52,880	HC
Grove City College	PA	26,654	VC
Harding Univ	AR	25,440	C
Hofstra Univ	NY	58,210	C+
Howard Univ	DC	37,616	C+
Idaho State Univ	ID	13,619	LC
Illinois Inst of Technology	IL	56,826	HC+
Indiana Inst of Technology	IN	34,240	LC
Indiana Univ-Purdue Univ Fort Wayne	IN	18,675	C
Indiana Univ-Purdue Univ Indianapolis	IN	18,952	C
Inter-American Univ of PR-Bayamon	PR	18,785	
Iowa State Univ	IA	18,176	C
Jacksonville Univ	FL	49,210	C
Johns Hopkins Univ	MD	68,080	MC
Kansas State Univ	KS	17,780	VC
Kennesaw State Univ	GA	18,899	VC
Kettering Univ	MI	47,570	HC
King's College	PA	48,240	C
Lafayette College	PA	68,520	MC
Lake Superior State Univ	MI	19,867	C
Lamar Univ	TX	18,014	LC
Lawrence Tech Univ	MI	41,630	VC
Lehigh Univ	PA	63,860	MC
LeTourneau Univ	TX	39,190	VC
Lipscomb Univ	TN	42,984	VC
Louisiana State Univ and A&M College	LA	18,677	VC
Louisiana Tech Univ	LA	11,422	VC
Loyola Marymount Univ	CA	60,202	VC+
Manhattan College	NY	55,652	C
Marquette Univ	WI	53,090	VC+
Mass Inst of Technology	MA	62,662	MC
Merrimack College	MA	55,415	C
Miami Univ	OH	27,190	HC+
Mich State Univ	MI	24,542	VC
Mich Tech Univ	MI	25,551	VC+
Milwaukee School of Engineering	WI	48,531	HC+
Minn State Univ, Mankato	MN	17,190	C
Miss State Univ	MS	12,028	C+
Missouri Univ of Science and Technology	MO	18,655	HC
Montana State Univ	MT	15,500	C+
New Jersey Inst of Technology	NJ	30,198	HC
New Mexico Inst of Mining and Technology	NM	15,385	HC+
New Mexico State Univ	NM	14,050	LC
New York Inst of Technology	NY	49,980	VC
New York Univ	NY	68,139	MC
N Car A&T State Univ	NC	13,786	C
N Car State Univ	NC	22,434	HC+
N Dak State Univ	ND	16,245	VC
Northeastern Univ	MA	65,352	MC
Northern Arizona Univ	AZ	21,003	C
Northern Illinois Univ	IL	20,176	C
Northwestern Univ	IL	68,725	MC
Norwich Univ	VT	56,234	C
Oakland Univ	MI	20,763	C
Ohio Northern Univ	OH	44,050	VC
Ohio State Univ at Columbus	OH	22,843	MC
Ohio Univ	OH	23,394	VC
Okla Christian Univ	OK	29,260	C
Okla State Univ	OK	17,180	C+
Old Dominion Univ	VA	21,618	C
Olivet Nazarene Univ	IL	41,840	VC
Oral Roberts Univ	OK	34,316	C
Oregon State Univ	OR	23,337	VC
Pennsylvania College of Technology	PA	27,693	NC
Pennsylvania State Univ - Univ Park	PA	29,716	HC
Point Park Univ	PA	41,270	C
Prairie View A&M Univ	TX	27,273	LC
Princeton Univ	NJ	60,090	MC
Purdue Univ Northwest	IN	15,178	C
Purdue Univ/West Lafayette	IN	20,032	MC
Quinnipiac Univ	CT	60,970	VC
Rensselaer Polytechnic Inst	NY	67,265	MC
Rice Univ	TX	59,458	MC
Rochester Inst of Technology	NY	52,734	HC+
Rose-Hulman Inst of Technology	IN	59,823	MC
Rowan Univ	NJ	24,491	VC
Rutgers Univ - New Brunswick	NJ	27,090	HC
Saginaw Valley State Univ	MI	19,284	C
St. Louis Univ	MO	49,866	HC
St. Martin's Univ	WA	45,056	C
San Diego State Univ	CA	23,156	VC
San Francisco State Univ	CA	18,514	LC
San Jose State Univ	CA	22,630	C
Seattle Univ	WA	54,957	VC
S Dak School of Mines and Technology	SD	18,570	C+
S Dak State Univ	SD	15,874	C
Southern Illinois Univ Carbondale	IL	24,554	C
Southern Illinois Univ Edwardsville	IL	20,188	C
Southern Methodist Univ	TX	69,008	MC
Southern Univ and A&M College	LA	16,074	LC
St. Mary's Univ	TX	39,120	C
Stanford Univ	CA	62,541	MC
SUNY at Binghamton	NY	24,100	MC
SUNY Polytechnic Inst	NY	20,438	VC
SUNY/Univ at Buffalo	NY	23,122	C
Stevens Inst of Technology	NJ	64,954	MC
Stony Brook Univ/The SUNY	NY	22,703	MC
Syracuse Univ	NY	62,313	HC
Temple Univ	PA	24,392	C+
Tenn State Univ	TN	14,423	LC
Tenn Tech Univ	TN	17,929	C
Texas A&M Univ at College Station	TX	20,771	VC+
Texas A&M Univ at Kingsville	TX	16,580	LC
Texas Christian Univ	TX	57,120	HC
Texas Tech Univ	TX	20,156	C+
The Catholic Univ of America	DC	58,376	VC
The College of New Jersey	NJ	28,675	VC+
The George Washington Univ	DC	68,474	HC+
The Univ of Akron	OH	22,566	C
The Univ of Alabama	AL	24,320	C+
The Univ of Arizona	AZ	24,086	C
The Univ of Memphis	TN	18,278	C
The Univ of Tenn at Chattanooga	TN	17,340	C+
The Univ of Tenn at Knoxville	TN	22,112	VC
The Univ of Texas at Austin	TX	20,206	MC
The Univ of Texas at San Antonio	TX	21,060	C
The Univ of Utah	UT	18,751	VC
Trine Univ	IN	41,310	C
Tufts Univ	MA		MC
Tuskegee Univ	AL	28,164	C
Union College	NY	64,320	MC
United States Air Force Academy	CO		C
United States Coast Guard Academy	CT	942	HC
United States Military Academy at West Point	NY		HC+
United States Naval Academy	MD		HC
Universidad Politecnica de PR, Hato Rey campus	PR	23,514	
Univ of Alabama at Birmingham	AL	22,092	C
Univ of Alabama in Huntsville	AL	20,028	VC
Univ of Alaska Fairbanks	AK	16,874	VC
Univ of Arkansas at Fayetteville	AR	19,766	VC
Univ of Calif at Berkeley	CA	29,886	MC
Univ of Calif at Davis	CA	28,468	HC
Univ of Calif at Irvine	CA	33,857	VC
Univ of Calif at Los Angeles	CA	27,438	HC+
Univ of Calif at Riverside	CA	32,912	C
Univ of Calif at Santa Barbara	CA	30,627	HC+
Univ of Calif San Diego	CA	30,450	MC
Univ of Central Florida	FL	16,379	VC
Univ of Cincinnati	OH	22,118	VC
Univ of Colo Boulder	CO	26,048	HC
Univ of Colo Colo Springs	CO	20,300	C
Univ of Colo Denver	CO	22,238	C
Univ of Conn	CT	27,394	
Univ of Dayton	OH	54,930	VC
Univ of Delaware	DE	32,214	VC
Univ of Denver	CO	61,129	VC+
Univ of Detroit Mercy	MI	48,816	C
Univ of Evansville	IN	44,186	C+
Univ of Florida	FL	16,291	HC+
Univ of Georgia	GA	21,878	HC
Univ of Hartford	CT	49,776	C
Univ of Hawaii at Manoa	HI	23,261	C
Univ of Houston	TX	21,871	VC
Univ of Idaho	ID	16,158	C
Univ of Illinois at Chicago	IL	24,664	VC
Univ of Illinois at Urbana-Champaign	IL	27,006	HC
Univ of Indianapolis	IN	36,480	VC
Univ of Iowa	IA	19,415	HC
Univ of Kansas	KS	20,884	VC
Univ of Kentucky	KY	24,800	C+
Univ of Louisiana at Lafayette	LA	14,516	C
Univ of Louisville	KY	19,692	C
Univ of Maine	ME	21,038	VC
Univ of Maryland/Baltimore County	MD	23,004	VC
Univ of Maryland/College Park	MD	21,938	HC
Univ of Mass Amherst	MA	27,669	HC
Univ of Mass Dartmouth	MA	26,507	C
Univ of Mass Lowell	MA	27,296	VC
Univ of Miami	FL	63,494	MC
Univ of Mich/Ann Arbor	MI	25,274	MC
Univ of Mich/Dearborn	MI	12,472	VC
Univ of Minn/Duluth	MN	20,292	C
Univ of Minn/Twin Cities	MN	24,269	MC
Univ of Miss	MS	18,802	C
Univ of Missouri-Columbia	MO	20,463	VC
Univ of Missouri-Kansas City	MO	19,563	VC
Univ of Missouri-St. Louis	MO	19,810	VC
Univ of Mount Union	OH	39,990	C
Univ of Nebr - Lincoln	NE	18,589	VC
Univ of Nevada, Las Vegas	NV	17,553	C
Univ of Nevada, Reno	NV	18,010	C
Univ of New Hampshire	NH	29,333	VC
Univ of New Haven	CT	53,680	C
Univ of New Mexico	NM	16,808	C
Univ of New Orleans	LA	12,840	C
Univ of N Car at Charlotte	NC	17,803	VC
Univ of N Dak	ND	16,673	C
Univ of North Florida	FL	15,996	VC
Univ of North Texas	TX	20,082	C
Univ of Northwestern - St. Paul	MN	39,530	C
Univ of Notre Dame	IN	68,801	MC
Univ of Okla	OK	19,651	HC
Univ of Pittsburgh	PA	30,030	MC
Univ of Portland	OR	52,152	VC
Univ of PR, at Mayaguez	PR	13,995	
Univ of Rhode Island	RI	26,066	VC
Univ of Rochester	NY	65,032	MC
Univ of San Diego	CA	60,338	HC
Univ of South Alabama	AL	16,880	C
Univ of S Car at Columbia	SC	21,726	VC
Univ of South Florida/Tampa	FL	16,110	VC
Univ of Southern Calif	CA	66,631	MC
Univ of Texas at Arlington	TX	18,876	C
Univ of Texas at Dallas	TX	23,640	HC
Univ of Texas at El Paso	TX	34,452	NC
Univ of Texas Rio Grande Valley	TX	15,573	LC
Univ of the District of Columbia	DC	21,260	LC
Univ of the Pacific	CA	57,446	VC
Univ of Toledo	OH	19,336	C
Univ of Tulsa	OK	52,625	HC
Univ of Vermont	VT	29,792	HC
Univ of Virginia	VA	27,367	MC
Univ of Wisc-Madison	WI	21,647	MC
Univ of Wisc-Milwaukee	WI	21,538	C
Univ of Wisc-Platteville	WI	14,148	C
Univ of Wyoming	WY	15,537	C
Utah State Univ	UT	13,235	C
Valparaiso Univ	IN	50,160	VC
Vanderbilt Univ	TN	63,248	MC
Villanova Univ	PA	64,922	MC
Virginia Commonwealth Univ	VA	23,811	VC
Virginia Military Inst	VA	26,460	VC
Virginia Polytechnic Inst and State Univ	VA	21,920	VC
Washington State Univ	WA	22,747	C
Washington Univ in St. Louis	MO	67,539	MC
Wayne State Univ	MI	23,085	C
West Texas A&M Univ	TX	13,478	C
West Virginia Univ	WV	18,952	VC
West Virginia Univ Inst of Technology	WV	18,264	C
Western Illinois Univ	IL	20,897	C
Western Kentucky Univ	KY	16,850	C
Western Mich Univ	MI	21,791	C
Western New England Univ	MA	49,182	C
Wichita State Univ	KS	17,773	C
Widener Univ	PA	58,190	C
Wilkes Univ	PA	49,166	C
Worcester Polytechnic Inst	MA	62,846	MC
Wright State Univ	OH	16,983	C
Yale Univ	CT	64,650	MC
York College of Pennsylvania	PA	29,240	C
Youngstown State Univ	OH	17,487	C

MECHANICAL ENGINEERING TECHNOLOGY

School	ST	$IS	SR
Alabama A&M Univ	AL	18,796	C
Alfred State College	NY	19,895	C
Arizona State Univ at the Polytechnic Campus	AZ	22,394	VC
Cal State, Fullerton	CA	21,902	C
Central Conn State Univ	CT	22,041	C
Central Mich Univ	MI	20,330	C
Cleveland State Univ	OH	22,290	C
Colo State Univ-Pueblo	CO	21,581	C
Eastern Mich Univ	MI	19,761	C
Eastern Washington Univ	WA	17,896	LC
Fairleigh Dickinson Univ/Metropolitan Campus	NJ	52,392	C
Fairmont State Univ	WV	15,726	C
Farmingdale State College	NY	20,968	C
Ferris State Univ	MI	21,458	C
Indiana State Univ	IN	23,223	LC
Indiana Univ-Purdue Univ Fort Wayne	IN	18,675	C
Indiana Univ-Purdue Univ Indianapolis	IN	18,952	C
Kennesaw State Univ	GA	18,899	VC
Metropolitan State Univ of Denver	CO	6,928	LC
Mich Tech Univ	MI	25,551	VC+
Montana State Univ	MT	15,500	C+
New York City College of Technology	NY	7,185	LC
Northern Kentucky Univ	KY	16,486	C
Okla State Univ	OK	17,180	C+
Old Dominion Univ	VA	21,618	C
Oregon Inst of Technology	OR	19,227	C
Penn State Erie,The Behrend College	PA	26,688	VC
Pennsylvania College of Technology	PA	27,693	NC
Pittsburg State Univ	KS	13,880	C
Point Park Univ	PA	41,270	C
Purdue Univ Northwest	IN	15,178	C
Purdue Univ/West Lafayette	IN	20,032	MC
Rochester Inst of Technology	NY	52,734	HC+
S Car State Univ	SC	21,330	LC
Southern Univ and A&M College	LA	16,074	LC
SUNY Polytechnic Inst	NY	20,438	VC
SUNY/Buffalo State	NY	20,583	LC
Tarleton State Univ	TX	15,248	LC
Texas A&M Univ at Corpus Christi	TX	16,851	LC
The Univ of Akron	OH	22,566	C
Univ of Arkansas at Little Rock	AR	18,211	LC
Univ of Cincinnati	OH	22,118	VC
Univ of Dayton	OH	54,930	VC
Univ of Hartford	CT	49,776	C
Univ of Houston	TX	21,871	VC
Univ of Maine	ME	21,038	VC
Univ of Mass Lowell	MA	27,296	VC
Univ of New Hampshire - Manchester	NH	14,490	C
Univ of N Car at Charlotte	NC	17,803	VC
Univ of North Texas	TX	20,082	C
Univ of Pittsburgh at Johnstown	PA	22,092	C
Univ of Southern Indiana	IN	16,808	C
Univ of Southern Miss	MS	13,170	C
Univ of Wisc-Green Bay	WI	15,184	C
Vaughn College of Aeronautics and Technology	NY	37,180	SP
Wayne State Univ	MI	23,085	C
Weber State Univ	UT	14,112	C
Western Washington Univ	WA	18,904	VC
Youngstown State Univ	OH	17,487	C

MECHATRONICS ENGINEERING

School	ST	$IS	SR
Cal State, Chico	CA	19,790	VC
Cal State, Fullerton	CA	21,902	C
Central Conn State Univ	CT	22,041	C
Kennesaw State Univ	GA	18,899	VC
Purdue Univ Northwest	IN	15,178	C
Univ of Denver	CO	61,129	VC+
Vaughn College of Aeronautics and Technology	NY	37,180	SP

MEDIA ARTS

School	ST	$IS	SR
Alverno College	WI	33,294	LC
Anna Maria College	MA	51,020	C
Art Inst of Portland	OR	132,329	SP
Ashland Univ	OH	30,446	C
Baker Univ	KS	37,190	C
Bentley Univ	MA	63,720	MC
Briar Cliff Univ	IA	36,956	C
Brigham Young Univ	UT	13,248	MC
Brown Univ	RI	64,566	MC
Butler Univ	IN	52,890	VC+
Cal State, Fresno	CA	16,902	LC
Cal State, Los Angeles	CA	17,186	LC
Calumet College of St. Joseph	IN	22,735	C
Calvin College	MI	43,090	HC
Canisius College	NY	49,672	C
Carleton College	MN	66,414	MC
Carlow Univ	PA	39,696	LC
Cedar Crest College	PA	51,110	C
Champlain College	VT	54,724	VC
Chatham Univ	PA	47,883	VC
CUNY/Hunter College	NY	31,098	VC
Claremont McKenna College	CA	69,900	MC
College of the Ozarks	MO	7,530	VC
Corban Univ	OR	41,700	C
Cornell Univ	NY	67,591	MC
Cornerstone Univ	MI	36,550	C
Denison Univ	OH	62,770	HC+
DePaul Univ	IL	52,807	VC
DeSales Univ	PA	47,520	C
Drexel Univ	PA	65,927	HC
Eastern Mich Univ	MI	19,761	C
Edinboro Univ	PA	15,940	LC
Elon Univ	NC	46,142	HC
Emerson College	MA	61,824	HC+
Florida Atlantic Univ	FL	18,256	C
Goddard College	VT	17,040	VC
Greenville College	IL	27,012	LC

ST = STATE $IS = IN-STATE COSTS SR = SELECTOR RATING

School	ST	$IS	SR
Hampshire College	MA	65,214	MC
Harding Univ	AR	25,440	C
Hofstra Univ	NY	58,210	C+
Houghton College	NY	40,558	VC
Howard Univ	DC	37,616	C+
Huntington Univ	IN	33,996	C
Illinois State Univ	IL	23,418	VC
Indiana Univ Bloomington	IN	20,791	HC
Indiana Univ Kokomo	IN	7,207	C
Indiana Univ-Purdue Univ Indianapolis	IN	18,952	C
Ithaca College	NY	58,158	VC+
James Madison Univ	VA	19,084	VC
Johns Hopkins Univ	MD	68,080	MC
Judson Univ	IL	39,174	C
Kennesaw State Univ	GA	18,899	VC
Lake Erie College	OH	38,914	LC
Lawrence Tech Univ	MI	41,630	VC
Lindsey Wilson College	KY	33,546	C
LIU Brooklyn	NY	50,698	C
Loyola Univ Chicago	IL	57,158	VC
Lycoming College	PA	50,895	C
Macalester College	MN	64,136	MC
Maine College of Art	ME	45,940	SP
Marquette Univ	WI	53,090	VC+
Maryland Inst College of Art	MD	58,740	SP
Marylhurst Univ	OR	16,818	NC
Mass College of Art and Design	MA	24,800	SP
Mass Inst of Technology	MA	62,662	MC
Mercer Univ	GA	45,348	VC
Mercy College	NY	32,614	C
Miami Univ	OH	27,190	HC+
Montana State Univ	MT	15,500	C+
Mount Ida College	MA	46,820	C
Mount St. Mary College	NY	44,448	C
New Jersey City Univ	NJ	21,456	LC
New York Univ	NY	68,139	MC
NewSchool of Architecture & Design	CA	12,341	SP
Northeastern Illinois Univ	IL	12,529	LC
Ohio Univ	OH	23,394	VC
Olivet Nazarene Univ	IL	41,840	VC
Pepperdine Univ	CA	66,862	VC+
Pitzer College	CA	68,500	HC+
Point Loma Nazarene Univ	CA	46,150	C+
Point Park Univ	PA	41,270	C
Pomona College	CA	64,957	MC
Radford Univ	VA	19,758	C
Rensselaer Polytechnic Inst	NY	67,265	MC
Robert Morris Univ	PA	40,600	C
Rochester Inst of Technology	NY	52,734	HC+
Rocky Mountain College of Art and Design	CO	27,052	SP
Roger Williams Univ	RI	48,074	VC
Rollins College	FL	58,670	HC
Roosevelt Univ	IL	41,890	VC
Sacred Heart Univ	CT	54,590	C
Salve Regina Univ	RI	53,046	VC
San Francisco Art Inst	CA	60,865	SP
Savannah College of Art and Design	GA	49,595	SP
Southern Illinois Univ Edwardsville	IL	20,188	C
Southern Methodist Univ	TX	69,008	MC
Spalding Univ	KY	31,938	C
St. Catherine Univ	MN	45,630	C
SUNY/College at Old Westbury	NY	16,860	C+
SUNY/Fredonia	NY	20,818	C
SUNY/Univ at Buffalo	NY	23,122	C
Sterling College	KS	32,830	LC
Suffolk Univ	MA	52,316	C
Swarthmore College	PA	63,550	MC
Taylor Univ	IN	42,130	VC
Temple Univ	PA	24,392	C+
The Univ of Akron	OH	22,566	C
Thiel College	PA	42,950	LC
Towson Univ	MD	21,878	C
Trinity International Univ	IL	31,070	VC
Tulane Univ	LA	67,496	MC
Univ of Calif at Irvine	CA	33,857	VC
Univ of Chicago	IL	70,551	MC
Univ of Denver	CO	61,129	VC+
Univ of Hartford	CT	49,776	C
Univ of Illinois at Urbana-Champaign	IL	27,006	HC
Univ of Maine	ME	21,038	VC
Univ of Maine at Farmington	ME	18,792	C
Univ of Missouri-St. Louis	MO	19,810	VC
Univ of Montana	MT	14,105	C
Univ of Mount Union	OH	39,990	C
Univ of New Mexico	NM	16,808	C
Univ of Pittsburgh	PA	30,030	MC
Univ of Rochester	NY	65,032	MC
Univ of San Francisco	CA	60,580	C
Univ of S Car at Columbia	SC	21,726	VC
Univ of Texas at Austin	TX	23,640	HC
Univ of the District of Columbia	DC	21,260	LC
Univ of Wisc-Platteville	WI	14,148	C
Vanderbilt Univ	TN	63,248	MC
Vassar College	NY	68,110	MC
Virginia Commonwealth Univ	VA	23,811	VC
Washburn Univ	KS	15,827	C
Wayne State Univ	MI	23,085	C
Weber State Univ	UT	14,112	C
Webster Univ	MO	37,490	C
Wellesley College	MA	66,984	MC
Wesley College	DE	37,848	LC
Western Conn State Univ	CT	21,254	LC
Widener Univ	PA	58,190	C
Wilkes Univ	PA	49,166	C
Wilmington Univ	DE	8,762	NC
Wisc Lutheran College	WI	36,290	C
Xavier Univ	OH	49,380	VC
Youngstown State Univ	OH	17,487	C

MEDIA MANAGEMENT

School	ST	$IS	SR
Columbia College Chicago	IL	40,104	C
Elon Univ	NC	46,142	HC
Minn State Univ, Mankato	MN	17,190	C
Ohio Univ	OH	23,394	VC
Pace Univ	NY	60,136	C
San Diego State Univ	CA	23,156	VC
Texas Tech Univ	TX	20,156	C+
Univ of Miami	FL	63,494	MC
Univ of S Dak	SD	16,109	C

MEDICAL ANTHROPOLOGY

School	ST	$IS	SR
Creighton Univ	NE	49,452	VC
Lycoming College	PA	50,895	C

MEDICAL IMAGING

School	ST	$IS	SR
Georgian Court Univ	NJ	43,068	LC
Indiana Univ Kokomo	IN	7,207	C
Indiana Univ Northwest	IN	7,207	LC
Indiana Univ South Bend	IN	16,057	C
Indiana Univ-Purdue Univ Indianapolis	IN	18,952	C
MCPHS Univ	MA	45,470	SP
Rochester Inst of Technology	NY	52,734	HC+
Thomas Edison State Univ	NJ	6,350	NC

MEDICAL LABORATORY SCIENCE

School	ST	$IS	SR
Allen College	IA	32,367	LC
Armstrong State Univ	GA	15,615	C
Auburn Univ at Montgomery	AL	15,000	C
Augusta Univ	GA	4,632	C
Augustana Univ	SD	39,968	VC
Austin Peay State Univ	TN	16,397	C
Bloomfield College	NJ	40,100	LC
Bradley Univ	IL	43,240	VC
Eastern Mich Univ	MI	19,761	C
Ferris State Univ	MI	21,458	C
Heritage Univ	WA	19,825	NC
Idaho State Univ	ID	13,619	LC
Marquette Univ	WI	53,090	VC+
Mich Tech Univ	MI	25,551	VC+
Minn State Univ, Mankato	MN	17,190	C
Monmouth Univ	NJ	50,184	C
Oakland Univ	MI	20,763	C
Ohio State Univ at Columbus	OH	22,843	MC
Rhode Island College	RI	19,000	LC
Saginaw Valley State Univ	MI	19,284	C
St. Louis Univ	MO	49,866	HC
St. Mary's Univ of Minn	MN	42,440	C
S Dak State Univ	SD	15,874	C
Southeast Missouri State Univ	MO	16,148	C
St. Edward's Univ	TX	56,190	VC
Tarleton State Univ	TX	15,248	LC
The Univ of Utah	UT	18,751	VC
Univ of Iowa	IA	19,415	HC
Univ of Louisiana at Monroe	LA	15,970	C
Univ of Mass Dartmouth	MA	26,507	C
Univ of Miss	MS	18,802	C
Univ of Mount Union	OH	39,990	C
Univ of New England	ME	50,110	C
Univ of N Dak	ND	16,673	C
Univ of Rhode Island	RI	26,066	VC
Univ of Vermont	VT	29,792	HC
Weber State Univ	UT	14,112	C
Western Carolina Univ	NC	13,965	C
York College of Pennsylvania	PA	29,240	C

MEDICAL LABORATORY TECHNOLOGY

School	ST	$IS	SR
Alabama A&M Univ	AL	18,796	C
American International College	MA	47,020	LC
Anderson Univ	IN	39,450	C
Andrews Univ	MI	41,732	C
Angelo State Univ	TX	15,882	LC
Arkansas Tech Univ	AR	16,534	LC
Auburn Univ	AL	24,300	VC+
Avila Univ	MO	27,100	C
Baylor Univ	TX	56,803	HC
Bemidji State Univ	MN	17,730	C
Blackburn College	IL	28,526	LC
Bloomsburg Univ of Pennsylvania	PA	19,930	C
Brescia Univ	KY	29,890	VC
Caldwell Univ	NJ	42,165	LC
Cal State, Northridge	CA	17,277	LC
Cal State, Sacramento	CA	19,060	C
Calif Univ of Pennsylvania	PA	20,425	LC
Campbellsville Univ	KY	33,400	C
Canisius College	NY	49,672	C
Cheyney Univ of Pennsylvania	PA	20,896	LC
CUNY/Hunter College	NY	31,098	VC
CUNY/York College	NY	6,747	LC
Clemson Univ	SC		HC
Coker College	SC	38,196	C
College of St. Mary	NE	27,500	C
Columbia College	SC	36,550	C
Concord Univ	WV	14,954	LC
Concordia Univ Nebr	NE	41,900	VC
Defiance College	OH	42,240	LC
Dordt College	IA	37,860	C+
East Stroudsburg Univ	PA	18,578	LC
Eastern Mennonite Univ	VA	42,550	C
Eastern Mich Univ	MI	19,761	C
Eastern New Mexico Univ	NM	12,874	LC
Eastern Washington Univ	WA	17,896	LC
Edinboro Univ	PA	15,940	LC
Elms College	MA	49,602	VC
Eureka College	IL	34,760	C
Evangel Univ	MO	28,898	C
Fairleigh Dickinson Univ/ College at Florham	NJ	54,770	C
Fairleigh Dickinson Univ/ Metropolitan Campus	NJ	52,392	C
Fayetteville State Univ	NC	17,756	C
Florida Atlantic Univ	FL	18,256	C
Graceland Univ	IA	35,290	C
Grand Valley State Univ	MI	22,250	C+
Gwynedd Mercy Univ	PA	43,780	LC
Holy Family Univ	PA	44,672	LC
Illinois College	IL	41,330	VC
Illinois State Univ	IL	23,418	VC
Indiana State Univ	IN	23,223	LC
Indiana Wesleyan Univ	IN	33,674	C
Inter-American Univ of PR-San Germán	PR	20,042	
Judson Univ	IL	39,174	C
Kent State Univ	OH	20,928	C
Keuka College	NY	42,398	C
King's College	PA	48,240	C
Kutztown Univ of Pennsylvania	PA	19,477	C
Lake Superior State Univ	MI	19,867	C
Lamar Univ	TX	18,014	LC
Langston Univ	OK	15,659	C
Lebanon Valley College	PA	55,510	VC
Lee Univ	TN	22,045	C
Lenoir-Rhyne Univ	NC	47,500	LC
Lincoln Memorial Univ	TN	28,430	C
LIU Post	NY	50,698	C+
Lock Haven Univ of Pennsylvania	PA	20,544	LC
Louisiana Tech Univ	LA	11,422	VC
Malone Univ	OH	39,200	C
Manchester Univ	IN	41,540	C
Marshall Univ	WV	18,044	C
Mayville State Univ	ND	18,371	NC
McKendree Univ	IL	37,940	C+
Mercy College	NY	32,614	C
Mercyhurst Univ	PA	47,420	C
Mich State Univ	MI	24,542	VC
Midwestern State Univ	TX	12,111	LC
Minn State Univ, Moorhead	MN	21,393	C
Misericordia Univ	PA	45,210	C
Missouri Western State Univ	MO	17,822	LC
Monmouth Univ	NJ	50,184	C
Morgan State Univ	MD	17,190	LC
Mount Aloysius College	PA	29,976	C
Mount Mercy Univ	IA	39,748	C
National Louis Univ	IL	43,000	LC
N Car State Univ	NC	22,434	HC+
North Park Univ	IL	35,860	C
Northeastern State Univ	OK	8,615	VC
Northern Mich Univ	MI	20,853	C
Northern State Univ	SD	15,570	C
Northwestern College of Iowa	IA	38,400	C
Northwestern Okla State Univ	OK	13,072	LC
Norwich Univ	VT	56,234	C
Okla Christian Univ	OK	29,260	C
Oral Roberts Univ	OK	34,316	C
Pontifical Catholic Univ of PR	PR	10,534	
Purdue Univ Northwest	IN	15,178	C
Purdue Univ/West Lafayette	IN	20,032	MC
Rutgers Univ - Camden	NJ	26,595	C
Rutgers Univ - Newark	NJ	27,351	C
St. Augustine's Univ	NC	25,582	C
St. Francis Univ	PA	46,146	NC
St. Louis Univ	MO	49,866	HC
St. Peter's Univ	NJ	49,192	C
Salem State Univ	MA	42,650	LC
Salisbury Univ	MD	21,132	VC
Seton Hill Univ	PA	46,972	VC
Shorter Univ	GA	31,130	LC
Slippery Rock Univ of Pennsylvania	PA	20,450	C
Southeastern Okla State Univ	OK	11,875	C
Southern Arkansas Univ	AR	21,532	C
Southern Wesleyan Univ	SC	33,670	LC
Southwestern Okla State Univ	OK	12,205	C
St. Francis College	NY	38,800	LC
St. Thomas Aquinas College	NY	32,450	C
SUNY/Fredonia	NY	20,818	C
SUNY/Plattsburgh	NY	19,314	C
Stevenson Univ	MD	48,412	C
Suffolk Univ	MA	52,316	C
Tarleton State Univ	TX	15,248	LC
Texas A&M Univ at Kingsville	TX	16,580	LC
The Catholic Univ of America	DC	58,376	VC
The George Washington Univ	DC	68,474	HC+
The Univ of Utah	UT	18,751	VC
The Univ of Virginia's College at Wise	VA	18,192	LC
Thiel College	PA	42,950	LC
Thomas More College	KY	36,720	LC
Towson Univ	MD	21,878	C
Union College	NE	23,270	C
Union Univ	TN	41,160	VC
Univ of Alaska Anchorage	AK	17,914	C
Univ of Central Florida	FL	16,379	VC
Univ of Central Missouri	MO	18,982	C
Univ of Cincinnati	OH	22,118	VC
Univ of Conn	CT	27,394	
Univ of Delaware	DE	32,214	VC
Univ of Hawaii at Manoa	HI	23,261	C
Univ of Indianapolis	IN	36,480	VC
Univ of Iowa	IA	19,415	HC
Univ of Kansas	KS	20,884	VC
Univ of Louisville	KY	19,692	C
Univ of Maine	ME	21,038	VC
Univ of Mich/Flint	MI	19,062	C
Univ of Minn/Twin Cities	MN	24,269	MC
Univ of New Mexico	NM	16,808	C
Univ of North Texas	TX	20,082	C
Univ of Pittsburgh at Johnstown	PA	22,092	C
Univ of Scranton	PA	54,962	VC
Univ of Sioux Falls	SD	25,630	C
Univ of Southern Miss	MS	13,170	C
Univ of Texas at El Paso	TX	34,452	NC
Univ of Washington	WA	23,091	MC
Univ of West Florida	FL	15,848	C
Univ of Wisc-Oshkosh	WI	15,392	C
Univ of Wyoming	WY	15,537	C
Utah State Univ	UT	13,235	C
Wartburg College	IA	49,478	C
Wesley College	DE	37,848	LC
Western New Mexico Univ	NM	16,914	LC
Wichita State Univ	KS	17,773	C
William Carey Univ	MS	23,950	LC
William Jewell College	MO	42,490	C+
Winthrop Univ	SC	23,960	C
Wright State Univ	OH	16,983	C

MEDICAL PHYSICS

School	ST	$IS	SR
Belmont Univ	TN	44,500	VC+
Cal State, Fullerton	CA	21,902	C
Oakland Univ	MI	20,763	C
Oregon State Univ	OR	23,337	VC
Presbyterian College	SC	47,186	C
The Univ of Arizona	AZ	24,086	C

MEDICAL RECORDS ADMINISTRATION/SERVICES

School	ST	$IS	SR
Dakota State Univ	SD	12,286	C
Davenport Univ	MI	25,896	LC
East Carolina Univ	NC	16,539	C
Louisiana Tech Univ	LA	11,422	VC
Norfolk State Univ	VA	18,902	LC
Pennsylvania College of Technology	PA	27,693	NC
Rutgers Univ - New Brunswick	NJ	27,090	HC
Rutgers Univ - Newark	NJ	27,351	C
St. Louis Univ	MO	49,866	HC
Southwestern Okla State Univ	OK	12,205	C
St. Catherine Univ	MN	45,630	C
Tenn State Univ	TN	14,423	LC
Texas State Univ	TX	18,721	C
Univ of Alabama at Birmingham	AL	22,092	C
Western Carolina Univ	NC	13,965	C

MEDICAL SCIENCE

School	ST	$IS	SR
Bay Path Univ	MA	46,356	C
Bloomfield College	NJ	40,100	LC
Boston Univ	MA	67,352	MC
Edgewood College	WI	35,950	C
Southern Illinois Univ Edwardsville	IL	20,188	C
The Univ of Arizona	AZ	24,086	C
The Univ of Utah	UT	18,751	VC
Univ of Arkansas at Fayetteville	AR	19,766	VC
Univ of Chicago	IL	70,551	MC
Univ of Colo Denver	CO	22,238	C
Univ of Louisville	KY	19,692	C
Univ of Wisc-Milwaukee	WI	21,538	C

MEDICAL TECHNOLOGY

School	ST	$IS	SR
Armstrong State Univ	GA	15,615	C
Augusta Univ	GA	4,632	C
Averett Univ	VA	43,034	LC
Ball State Univ	IN	19,808	C+
Barry Univ	FL	38,730	LC
Bellarmine Univ	KY	52,532	C
Belmont Univ	TN	44,500	VC+
Bloomfield College	NJ	40,100	LC
Blue Mountain College	MS	15,949	C
Bradley Univ	IL	43,240	VC
Brescia Univ	KY	29,890	VC

School	ST	$IS	SR
Briar Cliff Univ	IA	36,956	C
Clarion Univ of Pennsylvania	PA	21,608	LC
Cleveland State Univ	OH	22,290	C
College of Staten Island	NY	24,389	LC
College of the Ozarks	MO	7,530	VC
Colo State Univ-Pueblo	CO	21,581	C
Drury Univ	MO	37,555	VC
East Carolina Univ	NC	16,539	C
East Central Univ	OK	13,330	C
Farmingdale State College	NY	20,968	C
Gannon Univ	PA	42,922	C
Gardner-Webb Univ	NC	24,935	C+
George Mason Univ	VA	19,884	C
Harding Univ	AR	25,440	C
Hartwick College	NY	51,270	C
Henderson State Univ	AR	15,516	C
Houghton College	NY	40,558	VC
Idaho State Univ	ID	13,619	LC
Indiana Univ-Purdue Univ Fort Wayne	IN	18,675	C
Inter-American Univ of PR Ponce	PR	19,549	
Inter-American Univ of PR-Fajardo Campus	PR	18,336	
Inter-American Univ of PR-Metropolitan Campus	PR	20,045	
Kansas State Univ	KS	17,780	VC
Kean Univ	NJ	25,620	C
Kutztown Univ of Pennsylvania	PA	19,477	C
Lincoln Univ	MO	14,402	NC
Lindenwood Univ	MO	25,760	C
Lipscomb Univ	TN	42,984	VC
Louisiana College	LA	21,274	C
Lubbock Christian Univ	TX	29,727	C
Marist College	NY	49,860	VC
Marywood Univ	PA	47,840	C
Millersville Univ of Pennsylvania	PA	25,298	C
Miss State Univ	MS	12,028	C+
Missouri Southern State Univ	MO	13,071	C
Morehead State Univ	KY	18,386	LC
Morningside College	IA	39,780	C
Mount Aloysius College	PA	29,976	C
Mount Marty College	SD	36,862	C
Norfolk State Univ	VA	18,902	LC
Northern Kentucky Univ	KY	16,486	C
Oakwood Univ	AL	43,758	C
Ohio Northern Univ	OH	44,050	VC
Ohio State Univ at Columbus	OH	22,843	MC
Old Dominion Univ	VA	21,618	C
Pittsburg State Univ	KS	13,880	C
Prairie View A&M Univ	TX	27,273	LC
Roosevelt Univ	IL	41,890	VC
Rutgers Univ - New Brunswick	NJ	27,090	HC
Saginaw Valley State Univ	MI	19,284	C
St. Mary-of-the-Woods College	IN	40,424	LC
Sam Houston State Univ	TX	18,792	C
Seattle Univ	WA	54,957	VC
Southern Adventist Univ	TN	28,250	C
Southern Illinois Univ Edwardsville	IL	20,188	C
Southwest Baptist Univ	MO	30,890	LC
Southwest Minn State Univ	MN	17,783	C
Southwestern Adventist Univ	TX	28,232	LC
St. Joseph's College, New York/Brooklyn Campus	NY	25,114	LC
St. Joseph's College, New York/Long Island Campus	NY	25,124	C
SUNY/Plattsburgh	NY	19,314	C
SUNY/Univ at Buffalo	NY	23,122	C
Tenn State Univ	TN	14,423	LC
Texas Southern Univ	TX	19,592	LC
Texas Woman's Univ	TX	15,302	LC
The Catholic Univ of America	DC	58,376	VC
The College at Brockport - SUNY	NY	21,058	C
The College of St. Rose	NY	44,010	C
The Univ of Tenn at Knoxville	TN	22,112	VC
The Univ of Texas at Austin	TX	20,206	MC
Tusculum College	TN	31,625	LC
Univ of Alabama at Birmingham	AL	22,092	C
Univ of Bridgeport	CT	44,985	LC
Univ of Central Arkansas	AR	15,042	VC
Univ of Hawaii at Manoa	HI	23,261	C
Univ of Mass Boston	MA	13,828	C
Univ of Miss	MS	18,802	C
Univ of Montana	MT	14,105	C
Univ of New Orleans	LA	12,840	C
Univ of N Car at Charlotte	NC	17,803	VC
Univ of Rio Grande & Rio Grande Community College	OH	8,750	LC
Univ of S Dak	SD	16,109	C
Univ of South Florida/Tampa	FL	16,110	VC
Univ of St. Francis	IL	40,828	C
Univ of Texas at Arlington	TX	18,876	C
Univ of the Sacred Heart	PR	17,932	
Univ of the Sciences	PA	40,738	VC
West Chester Univ of Pennsylvania	PA	19,171	VC
West Texas A&M Univ	TX	13,478	C
Western Kentucky Univ	KY	16,850	C
Wilkes Univ	PA	49,166	C
Winston-Salem State Univ	NC	18,005	LC

MEDICINE, HEALTH & SOCIETY

School	ST	$IS	SR
Vanderbilt Univ	TN	63,248	MC

MEDIEVAL STUDIES

School	ST	$IS	SR
Bard College	NY	65,924	HC
Barnard College/Columbia Univ	NY	68,762	MC
Bates College	ME	64,500	HC
Brown Univ	RI	64,566	MC
College of William & Mary	VA	34,907	MC
Columbia Univ/City of New York	NY	62,958	MC
Dickinson College	PA	66,166	MC
Duke Univ	NC	68,298	MC
Emory Univ	GA	63,286	MC
Fordham Univ	NY	68,431	MC
Hanover College	IN	47,750	C+
Lycoming College	PA	50,895	C
Mount Holyoke College	MA	56,746	MC
New College of Florida	FL	16,180	HC+
New York Univ	NY	68,139	MC
Ohio State Univ at Columbus	OH	22,843	MC
Pennsylvania State Univ - Univ Park	PA	29,716	HC
Pomona College	CA	64,957	MC
Purdue Univ/West Lafayette	IN	20,032	MC
Rice Univ	TX	59,458	MC
Rutgers Univ - New Brunswick	NJ	27,090	HC
Sewanee: The Univ of the South	TN	58,000	HC+
Smith College	MA	66,774	MC
Southern Methodist Univ	TX	69,008	MC
St. Olaf College	MN	56,430	HC
SUNY Albany	NY	22,165	C
SUNY at Binghamton	NY	24,100	MC
Swarthmore College	PA	63,550	MC
The Catholic Univ of America	DC	58,376	VC
Tulane Univ	LA	67,496	MC
Univ of Calif at Davis	CA	28,468	HC
Univ of Calif at Santa Barbara	CA	30,627	HC+
Univ of Chicago	IL	70,551	MC
Univ of Mich/Ann Arbor	MI	25,274	MC
Univ of Nebr - Lincoln	NE	18,589	VC
Univ of Notre Dame	IN	68,801	MC
Univ of Oregon	OR	24,021	VC
Vassar College	NY	68,110	MC
Washington and Lee Univ	VA	59,647	MC
Wellesley College	MA	66,984	MC
Wesleyan Univ	CT	66,940	MC

MEETING/SPECIAL EVENT MANAGEMENT

School	ST	$IS	SR
College of the Ozarks	MO	7,530	VC
Florida International Univ	FL	20,281	C
Johnson & Wales Univ/Denver Campus	CO	44,768	C
Lasell College	MA	49,400	C

MENTAL HEALTH/HUMAN SERVICES

School	ST	$IS	SR
Bloomfield College	NJ	40,100	LC
Cal State, Fullerton	CA	21,902	C
Calif Univ of Pennsylvania	PA	20,425	LC
Inter-American Univ of PR-Aguadilla Campus	PR	21,657	
Metropolitan College of New York	NY		VC
Morgan State Univ	MD	17,190	LC
Northern Kentucky Univ	KY	16,486	C
Pennsylvania College of Technology	PA	27,693	NC
Sinte Gleska Univ	SD	13,154	NC
Southern Oregon Univ	OR	19,117	C
Univ of Maine at Augusta	ME	7,812	C
Univ of Maine at Machias	ME	22,960	C
Univ of North Florida	FL	15,996	VC
Univ of the Sciences	PA	40,738	VC

METAL/JEWELRY

School	ST	$IS	SR
Adams State Univ	CO	15,420	LC
Arcadia Univ	PA	55,990	C+
Calif College of the Arts	CA	52,758	SP
Cleveland Inst of Art	OH	51,455	SP
College for Creative Studies	MI	51,210	SP
Colo State Univ	CO	23,033	C
Ferris State Univ	MI	21,458	C
Hofstra Univ	NY	58,210	C+
Maine College of Art	ME	45,940	SP
Mass College of Art and Design	MA	24,800	SP
Memphis College of Art	TN	50,880	SP
Rhode Island School of Design	RI	59,960	SP
Rochester Inst of Technology	NY	52,734	HC+
Savannah College of Art and Design	GA	49,595	SP
SUNY at New Paltz	NY	20,840	C
Syracuse Univ	NY	62,313	HC
Temple Univ	PA	24,392	C+
Univ of Iowa	IA	19,415	HC
Univ of Kansas	KS	20,884	VC
Univ of Mass Dartmouth	MA	26,507	C
Univ of Mich/Ann Arbor	MI	25,274	MC
Univ of Oregon	OR	24,021	VC

METALLURGICAL ENGINEERING

School	ST	$IS	SR
Cal State, Fullerton	CA	21,902	C
Colo School of Mines	CO	29,319	MC
Columbia Univ/City of New York	NY	62,958	MC
Illinois Inst of Technology	IL	56,826	HC+
Missouri Univ of Science and Technology	MO	18,655	HC
Montana Tech of the Univ of Montana	MT	15,447	VC
S Dak School of Mines and Technology	SD	18,570	C+
The Univ of Alabama	AL	24,320	C+
The Univ of Utah	UT	18,751	VC
Univ of Cincinnati	OH	22,118	VC
Univ of Idaho	ID	16,158	C
Univ of Illinois at Urbana-Champaign	IL	27,006	HC
Univ of Nevada, Reno	NV	18,010	C
Univ of Texas at El Paso	TX	34,452	NC

MEXICAN-AMERICAN/CHICANO STUDIES

School	ST	$IS	SR
Cal State, Dominguez Hills	CA	19,022	LC
Cal State, Fresno	CA	16,902	LC
Cal State, Fullerton	CA	21,902	C
Cal State, Los Angeles	CA	17,186	LC
Cal State, Northridge	CA	17,277	LC
Concordia Univ Texas	TX	41,920	C
Metropolitan State Univ of Denver	CO	6,928	LC
Our Lady of the Lake Univ	TX	37,790	LC
Pitzer College	CA	68,500	HC+
Pomona College	CA	64,957	MC
San Diego State Univ	CA	23,156	VC
San Jose State Univ	CA	22,630	C
Scripps College	CA	69,260	HC
Sonoma State Univ	CA	27,020	C
Southern Methodist Univ	TX	69,008	MC
The Univ of Arizona	AZ	24,086	C
The Univ of Texas at San Antonio	TX	21,060	C
Univ of Calif at Davis	CA	28,468	HC
Univ of Calif at Los Angeles	CA	27,438	HC+
Univ of Calif at Riverside	CA	32,912	C
Univ of Calif at Santa Barbara	CA	30,627	HC+
Univ of Mich/Ann Arbor	MI	25,274	MC
Univ of Minn/Twin Cities	MN	24,269	MC
Univ of New Mexico	NM	16,808	C
Univ of Northern Colo	CO	19,658	C
Univ of Texas at El Paso	TX	34,452	NC
Univ of Texas Rio Grande Valley	TX	15,573	LC

MICROBIOLOGY

School	ST	$IS	SR
Albany College of Pharmacy and Health Sciences	NY	44,421	SP
Arizona State Univ at the Tempe Campus	AZ	23,001	VC
Auburn Univ	AL	24,300	VC+
Brigham Young Univ	UT	13,248	MC
Calif Polytechnic State Univ	CA	22,547	MC
Calif State Polytechnic Univ, Pomona	CA	21,811	C
Cal State, Chico	CA	19,790	VC
Cal State, Fullerton	CA	21,902	C
Cal State, Long Beach	CA	18,850	C
Cal State, Los Angeles	CA	17,186	LC
Cal State, Northridge	CA	17,277	LC
Cal State, Sacramento	CA	19,060	C
Clemson Univ	SC		HC
Colo State Univ	CO	23,033	C
Eastern Kentucky Univ	KY	17,742	C
Eastern Washington Univ	WA	17,896	LC
Howard Univ	DC	37,616	C+
Idaho State Univ	ID	13,619	LC
Indiana Univ Bloomington	IN	20,791	HC
Inter-American Univ of PR-Aguadilla Campus	PR	21,657	
Inter-American Univ of PR-Arecibo Campus	PR	18,245	
Iowa State Univ	IA	18,176	C
Kansas State Univ	KS	17,780	VC
Kutztown Univ of Pennsylvania	PA	19,477	C
Louisiana State Univ and A&M College	LA	18,677	VC
Marlboro College	VT	50,832	VC+
Miami Univ	OH	27,190	HC+
Mich State Univ	MI	24,542	VC
Mills College	CA	43,705	C
Miss State Univ	MS	12,028	C+
Miss Univ for Women	MS	17,065	C
Missouri Southern State Univ	MO	13,071	C
Montana State Univ	MT	15,500	C+
New Mexico State Univ	NM	14,050	LC
New York Univ	NY	68,139	MC
N Car State Univ	NC	22,434	HC+
N Dak State Univ	ND	16,245	VC
Northern Arizona Univ	AZ	21,003	C
Northern Mich Univ	MI	20,853	C
Ohio State Univ at Columbus	OH	22,843	MC
Ohio Univ	OH	23,394	VC
Ohio Wesleyan Univ	OH	49,460	VC
Okla State Univ	OK	17,180	C+
Oregon State Univ	OR	23,337	VC
Pennsylvania State Univ - Univ Park	PA	29,716	HC
Purdue Univ Northwest	IN	15,178	C
Purdue Univ/West Lafayette	IN	20,032	MC
Quinnipiac Univ	CT	60,970	VC
Rutgers Univ - New Brunswick	NJ	27,090	HC
San Diego State Univ	CA	23,156	VC
San Francisco State Univ	CA	18,514	LC
San Jose State Univ	CA	22,630	C
S Dak State Univ	SD	15,874	C
Southern Illinois Univ Carbondale	IL	24,554	C
Southwestern Okla State Univ	OK	12,205	C
SUNY/The College of Environmental Science and Forestry	NY	23,728	VC
Texas A&M Univ at College Station	TX	20,771	VC+
Texas State Univ	TX	18,721	C
Texas Tech Univ	TX	20,156	C+
The Univ of Alabama	AL	24,320	C+
The Univ of Arizona	AZ	24,086	C
The Univ of Memphis	TN	18,278	C
The Univ of Texas at Austin	TX	20,206	MC
Univ of PR, at Arecibo	PR	12,652	
Univ of Calif at Berkeley	CA	29,886	MC
Univ of Calif at Davis	CA	28,468	HC
Univ of Calif at Irvine	CA	33,857	VC
Univ of Calif at Los Angeles	CA	27,438	HC+
Univ of Calif at Riverside	CA	32,912	C
Univ of Calif at Santa Barbara	CA	30,627	HC+
Univ of Calif San Diego	CA	30,450	MC
Univ of Florida	FL	16,291	HC+
Univ of Georgia	GA	21,878	HC
Univ of Great Falls	MT	38,524	C
Univ of Hawaii at Manoa	HI	23,261	C
Univ of Houston-Downtown	TX	7,241	LC
Univ of Idaho	ID	16,158	C
Univ of Illinois at Urbana-Champaign	IL	27,006	HC
Univ of Iowa	IA	19,415	HC
Univ of Kansas	KS	20,884	VC
Univ of Maine	ME	21,038	VC
Univ of Maryland/College Park	MD	21,938	HC
Univ of Mass Amherst	MA	27,669	HC
Univ of Miami	FL	63,494	MC
Univ of Mich/Ann Arbor	MI	25,274	MC
Univ of Mich/Dearborn	MI	12,472	VC
Univ of Minn/Twin Cities	MN	24,269	MC
Univ of Missouri-Columbia	MO	20,463	VC
Univ of Montana	MT	14,105	C
Univ of Nebr - Lincoln	NE	18,589	VC
Univ of New Hampshire	NH	29,333	VC
Univ of Northern Iowa	IA	17,480	C
Univ of Okla	OK	19,651	HC
Univ of Pittsburgh	PA	30,030	MC
Univ of PR, at Humacao	PR	14,000	
Univ of PR, at Mayaguez	PR	13,995	
Univ of Rhode Island	RI	26,066	VC
Univ of Rochester	NY	65,032	MC
Univ of South Florida/Tampa	FL	16,110	VC
Univ of Texas at Arlington	TX	18,876	C
Univ of Texas at El Paso	TX	34,452	NC
Univ of the Sciences	PA	40,738	VC
Univ of Vermont	VT	29,792	HC
Univ of Washington	WA	23,091	MC
Univ of Wisc-La Crosse	WI	15,425	VC
Univ of Wisc-Madison	WI	21,647	MC
Univ of Wisc-Milwaukee	WI	21,538	C
Univ of Wisc-Oshkosh	WI	15,392	C
Univ of Wyoming	WY	15,537	C
Utah State Univ	UT	13,235	C
Wagner College	NY	57,240	C+
Washington State Univ	WA	22,747	C
Weber State Univ	UT	14,112	C
West Chester Univ of Pennsylvania	PA	19,171	VC
West Liberty Univ	WV	16,158	C

MIDDLE EASTERN STUDIES

School	ST	$IS	SR
Appalachian State Univ	NC	15,394	VC
Bard College	NY	65,924	HC
Barnard College/Columbia Univ	NY	68,762	MC
Baylor Univ	TX	56,803	HC
Boston Univ	MA	67,352	MC
Brandeis Univ	MA	68,443	MC
Brigham Young Univ	UT	13,248	MC
Brown Univ	RI	64,566	MC
Cal State, Fullerton	CA	21,902	C
CUNY/Queens College	NY	21,507	C
Claremont McKenna College	CA	69,900	MC
Colgate Univ	NY	67,500	MC
Columbia Univ/ School of General Studies	NY	61,470	MC
Columbia Univ/City of New York	NY	62,958	MC

ST = STATE $IS = IN-STATE COSTS SR = SELECTOR RATING

School	ST	$IS	SR
Dartmouth College	NH	68,109	MC
Dickinson College	PA	66,166	MC
Eastern Mich Univ	MI	19,761	C
Elon Univ	NC	46,142	HC
Emory and Henry College	VA	46,320	C
Emory Univ	GA	63,286	MC
Fordham Univ	NY	68,431	MC
Gettysburg College	PA	65,210	MC
Hampshire College	MA	65,214	MC
Harvard College/Harvard Univ	MA	65,609	MC
Hood College	MD	50,540	C
McDaniel College	MD	52,910	VC
Middlebury College	VT	67,464	MC
Mount Holyoke College	MA	56,746	MC
New York Univ	NY	68,139	MC
Pomona College	CA	64,957	MC
Rutgers Univ - New Brunswick	NJ	27,090	HC
Sarah Lawrence College	NY	68,866	MC
Smith College	MA	66,774	MC
Syracuse Univ	NY	62,313	HC
Texas State Univ	TX	18,721	C
The College of Wooster	OH	60,000	HC
The George Washington Univ	DC	68,474	HC+
The Univ of Arizona	AZ	24,086	C
The Univ of Texas at Austin	TX	20,206	MC
The Univ of Utah	UT	18,751	VC
Tufts Univ	MA		MC
Univ of Calif at Berkeley	CA	29,886	MC
Univ of Calif at Los Angeles	CA	27,438	HC+
Univ of Calif at Riverside	CA	32,912	C
Univ of Calif at Santa Barbara	CA	30,627	HC+
Univ of Conn	CT	27,394	
Univ of Mass Amherst	MA	27,669	HC
Univ of Mich/Ann Arbor	MI	25,274	MC
Univ of Minn/Twin Cities	MN	24,269	MC
Univ of Okla	OK	19,651	HC
Univ of Pennsylvania	PA	63,526	MC
Washington Univ in St. Louis	MO	67,539	MC
Wellesley College	MA	66,984	MC
Western Kentucky Univ	KY	16,850	C
Yale Univ	CT	64,650	MC

MIDDLE LEVEL EDUCATION

School	ST	$IS	SR
DePaul Univ	IL	52,807	VC
Gannon Univ	PA	42,922	C
Lewis Univ	IL	41,710	C
Moravian College	PA	55,488	C
Ohio State Univ at Mansfield	OH	15,529	C

MIDDLE SCHOOL EDUCATION

School	ST	$IS	SR
Abilene Christian Univ	TX	43,708	C+
Alabama A&M Univ	AL	18,796	C
Albany State Univ	GA	19,462	C
Alice Lloyd College	KY	8,190	LC
Alvernia Univ	PA	45,330	C
Alverno College	WI	33,294	LC
American International College	MA	47,020	LC
Appalachian State Univ	NC	15,394	VC
Arkansas State Univ	AR	16,190	C
Arkansas Tech Univ	AR	16,534	LC
Armstrong State Univ	GA	15,615	C
Asbury Univ	KY	36,450	C+
Auburn Univ	AL	24,300	VC+
Augusta Univ	GA	4,632	C
Augustana Univ	SD	39,968	VC
Avila Univ	MO	27,100	C
Baldwin Wallace Univ	OH	42,464	VC
Barton College	NC	39,854	C
Bellarmine Univ	KY	52,532	C
Belmont Univ	TN	44,500	VC+
Bemidji State Univ	MN	17,730	C
Bennett College	NC	27,717	NC
Bennington College	VT	66,280	MC
Berry College	GA	47,466	VC
Bethany College	KS	38,637	LC
Bethany College	WV	38,774	LC
Bethel Univ	MN	46,550	C+
Bloomsburg Univ of Pennsylvania	PA	19,930	C
Bluefield College	VA	34,711	C
Bluefield State College	WV	5,832	LC
Bluffton Univ	OH	40,950	C+
Bowling Green State Univ	OH	19,975	C
Bradley Univ	IL	43,240	VC
Brenau Univ - Women's College	GA	37,876	LC
Brewton-Parker College	GA	26,120	LC
Butler Univ	IN	52,890	VC+
Cabrini Univ	PA	42,591	LC
Campbell Univ	NC	37,570	VC
Campbellsville Univ	KY	33,400	C
Canisius College	NY	49,672	C
Capital Univ	OH	44,778	VC
Cardinal Stritch Univ	WI	37,136	C
Caribbean Univ	PR	12,227	
Carlow Univ	PA	39,696	LC
Carson-Newman Univ	TN	35,900	C
Carthage College	WI	48,835	C
Catawba College	NC	39,820	LC
Cedarville Univ	OH	36,244	VC
Central Methodist Univ	MO	31,500	VC
Central Washington Univ	WA	16,803	C
Champlain College	VT	54,724	VC
CUNY/Hunter College	NY	31,098	VC
City Univ of Seattle	WA	24,340	NC
Claflin Univ	SC	25,592	LC
Clark Atlanta Univ	GA	31,019	LC
Clayton State Univ	GA	19,735	LC
Coastal Carolina Univ	SC	20,340	C
College of Charleston	SC	24,046	VC
Columbia College - Missouri	MO	28,179	C
Columbus State Univ	GA	14,336	LC
Concord Univ	WV	14,954	LC
Concordia Univ Nebr	NE	41,900	VC
Concordia Univ St. Paul	MN	29,050	C
Concordia Univ, Chicago	IL	41,522	C
Cornerstone Univ	MI	36,550	C
Cumberland Univ	TN	27,710	C
Dallas Baptist Univ	TX	35,220	VC
Dickinson State Univ	ND	12,372	LC
Dordt College	IA	37,860	C+
Duquesne Univ	PA	48,508	VC
East Carolina Univ	NC	16,539	C
East Stroudsburg Univ	PA	18,578	LC
Eastern Illinois Univ	IL	21,414	C
Eastern Kentucky Univ	KY	17,742	C
Eastern Mich Univ	MI	19,761	C
Eastern Univ	PA	39,540	C
Eastern Washington Univ	WA	17,896	LC
Edinboro Univ	PA	15,940	LC
Elizabeth City State Univ	NC	14,745	C
Elms College	MA	49,602	VC
Elon Univ	NC	46,142	HC
Fairmont State Univ	WV	15,726	C
Fayetteville State Univ	NC	17,756	C
Fitchburg State Univ	MA	21,819	LC
Florida Inst of Technology	FL	53,306	VC
Fontbonne Univ	MO	34,606	C
Fort Valley State Univ	GA	17,988	VC
Francis Marion Univ	SC	18,144	LC
Freed-Hardeman Univ	TN	29,900	C
Frostburg State Univ	MD	17,280	LC
Gannon Univ	PA	42,922	C
Gardner-Webb Univ	NC	24,935	C+
Georgetown College	KY	41,440	C
Georgia College & State Univ	GA	21,884	C+
Georgia Southern Univ	GA	16,540	VC
Georgia Southwestern State Univ	GA	13,870	LC
Glenville State College	WV	17,386	LC
Goddard College	VT	17,040	VC
Gordon College	MA	47,740	VC
Goshen College	IN	44,350	C
Grand Valley State Univ	MI	22,250	C+
Greensboro College	NC	39,790	LC
Grove City College	PA	26,654	VC
Gustavus Adolphus College	MN	53,943	HC
Hardin-Simmons Univ	TX	36,025	C
Harris-Stowe State Univ	MO	14,590	NC
Heidelberg Univ	OH	40,400	LC
Henderson State Univ	AR	15,516	C
High Point Univ	NC	47,355	VC
Humboldt State Univ	CA	21,708	C
Illinois State Univ	IL	23,418	VC
Immaculata Univ	PA	39,000	C
Indiana State Univ	IN	23,223	LC
Indiana Univ-Purdue Univ Fort Wayne	IN	18,675	C
Ithaca College	NY	58,158	VC+
John Carroll Univ	OH	51,570	C
Johnson State College	VT	22,672	C
Kean Univ	NJ	25,620	C
Kennesaw State Univ	GA	18,899	VC
Kent State Univ	OH	20,928	C
Kentucky Christian Univ	KY	26,836	LC
Kentucky Wesleyan College	KY	34,260	LC
King's College	PA	48,240	C
Lake Erie College	OH	38,914	LC
Lee Univ	TN	22,045	C
Lenoir-Rhyne Univ	NC	47,500	LC
Lesley Univ	MA	42,800	C
Lincoln Memorial Univ	TN	28,430	C
Lincoln Univ	MO	14,402	NC
Lipscomb Univ	TN	42,984	VC
LIU Brooklyn	NY	50,698	C
Lubbock Christian Univ	TX	29,727	C
Malone Univ	OH	39,200	C
Manchester Univ	IN	41,540	C
Manhattan College	NY	55,652	C
Marian Univ	WI	34,622	C
Mars Hill Univ	NC	41,104	C
Marshall Univ	WV	18,044	C
Maryville Univ of St. Louis	MO	38,558	VC
Mass College of Liberal Arts	MA	20,659	C
McKendree Univ	IL	37,940	C+
McMurry Univ	TX	34,259	LC
Methodist Univ	NC	58,130	C
Miami Univ	OH	27,190	HC+
Midland Univ	NE	39,512	C
Millersville Univ of Pennsylvania	PA	25,298	C
Minn State Univ, Mankato	MN	17,190	C
Misericordia Univ	PA	45,210	C
Missouri Baptist Univ	MO	35,594	C
Missouri Southern State Univ	MO	13,071	C
Missouri State Univ	MO	15,837	C+
Montana State Univ Billings	MT	13,336	LC
Morehead State Univ	KY	18,386	LC
Mount Aloysius College	PA	29,976	C
Mount Mary Univ	WI	34,650	LC
Mount Mercy Univ	IA	39,748	C
Mount St. Joseph Univ	OH	33,880	LC
Mount Vernon Nazarene Univ	OH	35,944	C
Murray State Univ	KY	17,726	C+
Nazareth College	NY	46,784	C
Nebr Wesleyan Univ	NE	42,026	C+
Niagara Univ	NY	41,010	C
N Car Central Univ	NC	9,000	C
N Car State Univ	NC	22,434	HC+
N Car Wesleyan College	NC	39,200	C
North Central Univ	MN	30,610	C
Northern Kentucky Univ	KY	16,486	C
Northern State Univ	SD	15,570	C
Northland College	WI	41,103	C+
Northwest Missouri State Univ	MO	18,286	C
Northwest Univ	WA	38,720	VC
Northwestern College of Iowa	IA	38,400	C
Notre Dame College	OH	39,150	VC
Nova Southeastern Univ	FL	38,534	C+
Oakland City Univ	IN	33,930	NC
Ohio Dominican Univ	OH	41,340	C+
Ohio Northern Univ	OH	44,050	VC
Ohio State Univ at Columbus	OH	22,843	MC
Ohio Wesleyan Univ	OH	49,460	VC
Okla Christian Univ	OK	29,260	C
Okla Wesleyan Univ	OK	34,434	C
Otterbein Univ	OH	41,630	C
Ouachita Baptist Univ	AR	33,500	VC
Paine College	GA	19,506	LC
Philander Smith College	AR	20,814	LC
Piedmont College	GA	34,334	C
Presbyterian College	SC	47,186	C
Prescott College	AZ	38,201	C
Ripon College	WI	49,991	VC
St. Leo Univ	FL	32,850	C
St. Louis Univ	MO	49,866	HC
St. Vincent College	PA	46,229	C
St. Xavier Univ	IL	44,440	C
Schreiner Univ	TX	34,626	LC
Shippensburg Univ of Pennsylvania	PA	24,096	C
Shorter Univ	GA	31,130	LC
Southeast Missouri State Univ	MO	16,148	C
Southeastern Louisiana Univ	LA	16,237	C
Southeastern Univ	FL	34,910	LC
Southern Arkansas Univ	AR	21,532	C
Southern Univ and A&M College	LA	16,074	LC
Southwest Baptist Univ	MO	30,890	LC
Spalding Univ	KY	31,938	C
Springfield College	MA	48,775	C
St. Francis College	NY	38,800	LC
St. John Fisher College	NY	45,270	VC
SUNY at New Paltz	NY	20,840	C
SUNY/College at Old Westbury	NY	16,860	C
SUNY/Cortland	NY	20,910	C
SUNY/Fredonia	NY	20,818	C
Stevenson Univ	MD	48,412	C
Texas Christian Univ	TX	57,120	HC
The Univ of Akron	OH	22,566	C
The Univ of Arizona	AZ	24,086	C
The Univ of Montana Western	MT	9,426	LC
Thomas More College	KY	36,720	LC
Thomas Univ	GA	21,420	NC
Tiffin Univ	OH	34,900	LC
Toccoa Falls College	GA	30,048	C
Transylvania Univ	KY	47,450	HC+
Tusculum College	TN	31,625	LC
Union College	KY	32,310	C
Union Univ	TN	41,160	VC
Univ of Arkansas at Monticello	AR	13,599	LC
Univ of Arkansas at Pine Bluff	AR	13,541	C
Univ of Central Arkansas	AR	15,042	VC
Univ of Central Missouri	MO	18,982	C
Univ of Cincinnati	OH	22,118	VC
Univ of Dayton	OH	54,930	VC
Univ of Detroit Mercy	MI	48,816	C
Univ of Findlay	OH	43,040	C
Univ of Georgia	GA	21,878	HC
Univ of Great Falls	MT	38,524	C
Univ of Indianapolis	IN	36,480	VC
Univ of Iowa	IA	19,415	HC
Univ of Kansas	KS	20,884	VC
Univ of Kentucky	KY	24,800	C+
Univ of Louisville	KY	19,692	C
Univ of Mary Hardin-Baylor	TX	35,292	C+
Univ of Maryland/College Park	MD	21,938	HC
Univ of Minn/Duluth	MN	20,292	C
Univ of Missouri-Columbia	MO	20,463	VC
Univ of Missouri-Kansas City	MO	19,563	VC
Univ of Mount Olive	NC	18,426	C
Univ of Mount Union	OH	39,990	C
Univ of Nebr - Kearney	NE	17,014	LC
Univ of N Car at Chapel Hill	NC	20,561	MC
Univ of N Car at Charlotte	NC	17,803	VC
Univ of N Car at Greensboro	NC	15,998	C
Univ of N Car Wilmington	NC	16,784	VC
Univ of N Dak	ND	16,673	C
Univ of North Florida	FL	15,996	VC
Univ of North Georgia	GA	17,316	C
Univ of Northern Iowa	IA	17,480	C
Univ of Pikeville	KY	27,838	C
Univ of Sioux Falls	SD	25,630	C
Univ of S Car Aiken	SC	18,094	C
Univ of S Car at Columbia	SC	21,726	VC
Univ of S Car Upstate	SC	19,272	LC
Univ of Southern Miss	MS	13,170	C
Univ of the Cumberlands	KY	32,000	LC
Univ of the Ozarks	AR	31,050	NC
Univ of Vermont	VT	29,792	HC
Univ of West Florida	FL	15,848	C
Univ of Wisc-Green Bay	WI	15,184	C
Univ of Wisc-Platteville	WI	14,148	C
Univ of Wisc-Whitewater	WI	13,976	C
Urbana Univ	OH	30,820	C
Ursuline College	OH	41,076	LC
Wagner College	NY	57,240	C+
Walsh Univ	OH	39,010	C
Washington Univ in St. Louis	MO	67,539	MC
Wayne State College	NE	25,746	NC
Waynesburg Univ	PA	33,530	C
Webster Univ	MO	37,490	C
West Chester Univ of Pennsylvania	PA	19,171	VC
West Liberty Univ	WV	16,158	C
Western Carolina Univ	NC	13,965	C
Western Illinois Univ	IL	20,897	C
Western Kentucky Univ	KY	16,850	C
Western Mich Univ	MI	21,791	C
Westminster College	MO	32,820	C
Wilkes Univ	PA	49,166	C
William Woods Univ	MO	32,040	C
Wilmington College	OH	35,100	C
Wilson College	PA	35,620	LC
Wingate Univ	NC	41,900	C
Winthrop Univ	SC	23,960	C
Wittenberg Univ	OH	49,863	VC
Wright State Univ	OH	16,983	C
Xavier Univ	OH	49,380	VC
Xavier Univ of Louisiana	LA	31,689	C
York College	NE	30,260	C
Youngstown State Univ	OH	17,487	C

MILITARY SCIENCE

School	ST	$IS	SR
Ashford Univ	CA	10,480	C
Campbell Univ	NC	37,570	VC
Columbia College - Missouri	MO	28,179	C
Eastern Mich Univ	MI	19,761	C
Eastern Washington Univ	WA	17,896	LC
Florida Inst of Technology	FL	53,306	VC
Furman Univ	SC	61,098	VC+
Hawaii Pacific Univ	HI	33,420	C
Minn State Univ, Mankato	MN	17,190	C
Norfolk State Univ	VA	18,902	LC
Norwich Univ	VT	56,234	C
Olivet Nazarene Univ	IL	41,840	VC
Rochester Inst of Technology	NY	52,734	HC+
S Car State Univ	SC	21,330	LC
United States Air Force Academy	CO		C
United States Military Academy at West Point	NY		HC+
West Virginia Univ	WV	18,952	VC

MILITARY TECHNOLOGY LEADERSHIP

School	ST	$IS	SR
Thomas Edison State Univ	NJ	6,350	NC

MILLING SCIENCE

School	ST	$IS	SR
Kansas State Univ	KS	17,780	VC

MINING AND MINERAL ENGINEERING

School	ST	$IS	SR
Colo School of Mines	CO	29,319	MC
Columbia Univ/City of New York	NY	62,958	MC
Missouri Univ of Science and Technology	MO	18,655	HC
Montana Tech of the Univ of Montana	MT	15,447	VC
New Mexico Inst of Mining and Technology	NM	15,385	HC+
Pennsylvania State Univ - Univ Park	PA	29,716	HC
S Dak School of Mines and Technology	SD	18,570	C+
Southern Illinois Univ Carbondale	IL	24,554	C
The Univ of Arizona	AZ	24,086	C
The Univ of Utah	UT	18,751	VC
Univ of Alaska Fairbanks	AK	16,874	VC
Univ of Kentucky	KY	24,800	C+
Univ of Nevada, Reno	NV	18,010	C
Univ of Southern Indiana	IN	16,808	C
Virginia Polytechnic Inst and State Univ	VA	21,920	VC
West Virginia Univ	WV	18,952	VC

MINISTRIES

School	ST	$IS	SR
Abilene Christian Univ	TX	43,708	C+
Amridge Univ	AL	10,860	LC
Asbury Univ	KY	36,450	C+
Atlantic Union College	MA	27,228	C
Azusa Pacific Univ	CA	43,972	C
Belmont Univ	TN	44,500	VC+
Bethel College	IN	36,830	C
Biola Univ	CA	48,686	C

School	ST	$IS	SR
Bluffton Univ	OH	40,950	C+
Bryan College	TN	32,900	C
College of the Ozarks	MO	7,530	VC
Concordia Univ Wisc	WI	35,910	C
Corban Univ	OR	41,700	C
Dallas Baptist Univ	TX	35,220	VC
Dominican Univ	IL	42,472	C+
Dordt College	IA	37,860	C+
East Texas Baptist Univ	TX	34,444	C
Eastern Mennonite Univ	VA	42,550	C
Eastern Nazarene College	MA	41,114	C
Faulkner Univ	AL	26,410	C
Freed-Hardeman Univ	TN	29,900	C
Fresno Pacific Univ	CA	38,858	C
Geneva College	PA	35,450	C
George Fox Univ	OR	42,938	C
Greenville College	IL	27,012	LC
Grove City College	PA	26,654	VC
Harding Univ	AR	25,440	C
Hardin-Simmons Univ	TX	36,025	C
Hope International Univ	CA	42,730	C
Houghton College	NY	40,558	VC
Huntington Univ	IN	33,996	C
Indiana Wesleyan Univ	IN	33,674	C
John Brown Univ	AR	35,184	VC
Kentucky Christian Univ	KY	26,836	LC
Lee Univ	TN	22,045	C
Lindenwood Univ	MO	25,760	C
Lindsey Wilson College	KY	33,546	C
Louisiana College	LA	21,274	C
Lubbock Christian Univ	TX	29,727	C
Malone Univ	OH	39,200	C
Messiah College	PA	44,380	VC
MidAmerica Nazarene Univ	KS	37,808	C
Missouri Baptist Univ	MO	35,594	C
Mount Vernon Nazarene Univ	OH	35,944	C
North Central Univ	MN	30,610	C
Northwest Christian Univ	OR	36,580	C
Northwest Nazarene Univ	ID	40,250	C
Northwest Univ	WA	38,720	VC
Notre Dame College	OH	39,150	VC
Oakwood Univ	AL	43,758	C
Okla Christian Univ	OK	29,260	C
Okla Wesleyan Univ	OK	34,434	C
Olivet Nazarene Univ	IL	41,840	VC
Oral Roberts Univ	OK	34,316	C
Ouachita Baptist Univ	AR	33,500	VC
Palm Beach Atlantic Univ	FL	39,250	C
Point Loma Nazarene Univ	CA	46,150	C+
Rochester College	MI	28,574	LC
SAGU American Indian College	AZ	18,142	C
Simpson Univ	CA	34,722	C
Southeastern Univ	FL	34,910	LC
Southwest Baptist Univ	MO	30,890	LC
Tabor College	KS	35,870	C
Taylor Univ	IN	42,130	VC
The Univ of Mary	ND	23,180	C
Toccoa Falls College	GA	30,048	C
Trinity Bible College	ND		
Trinity Christian College	IL	35,580	C
Union College	KY	32,310	C
Union Univ	TN	41,160	VC
Univ of Mary Hardin-Baylor	TX	35,292	C+
Univ of Mount Olive	NC	18,426	C
Univ of Northwestern - St. Paul	MN	39,530	C
Univ of St. Francis	IN	38,520	C
Valparaiso Univ	IN	50,160	VC
Vanguard Univ of Southern Calif	CA	42,400	VC
Warner Pacific College	OR	31,610	C
Waynesburg Univ	PA	33,530	C

MISSIONS

School	ST	$IS	SR
Asbury Univ	KY	36,450	C+
Bethel College	IN	36,830	C
Biola Univ	CA	48,686	C
Bryan College	TN	32,900	C
Cedarville Univ	OH	36,244	VC
Dordt College	IA	37,860	C+
East Texas Baptist Univ	TX	34,444	C
Eastern Univ	PA	39,540	C
Evangel Univ	MO	28,898	C
Faulkner Univ	AL	26,410	C
Fresno Pacific Univ	CA	38,858	C
Grace Bible College	MI	25,250	C
Hannibal-LaGrange Univ	MO	29,815	C
Harding Univ	AR	25,440	C
Hardin-Simmons Univ	TX	36,025	C
Lipscomb Univ	TN	42,984	VC
Louisiana College	LA	21,274	C
Lubbock Christian Univ	TX	29,727	C
Mount Vernon Nazarene Univ	OH	35,944	C
North Central Univ	MN	30,610	C
Northwest Univ	WA	38,720	VC
Okla Christian Univ	OK	29,260	C
Olivet Nazarene Univ	IL	41,840	VC
Simpson Univ	CA	34,722	C
Southern Nazarene Univ	OK	33,684	C
Southwest Baptist Univ	MO	30,890	LC
Spring Arbor Univ	MI	37,390	C
The Master's Univ	CA	43,870	C
Trinity Bible College	ND		
Union Univ	TN	41,160	VC
Univ of the Cumberlands	KY	32,000	LC
Vanguard Univ of Southern Calif	CA	42,400	VC

MODERN DANCE

School	ST	$IS	SR
Texas Christian Univ	TX	57,120	HC
The Univ of Utah	UT	18,751	VC

MODERN JEWISH STUDIES

School	ST	$IS	SR
Cal State, Fullerton	CA	21,902	C
Cal State, Northridge	CA	17,277	LC
CUNY/Queens College	NY	21,507	C
San Diego State Univ	CA	23,156	VC
Syracuse Univ	NY	62,313	HC
Univ of Minn/Twin Cities	MN	24,269	MC

MODERN LANGUAGE

School	ST	$IS	SR
Anna Maria College	MA	51,020	C
Aquinas College - Mich	MI	38,876	VC
Augustana Univ	SD	39,968	VC
Averett Univ	VA	43,034	LC
Beloit College	WI	55,206	HC
Bethune-Cookman Univ	FL	23,322	C
Calif Polytechnic State Univ	CA	22,547	MC
Canisius College	NY	49,672	C
Clemson Univ	SC		HC
College of Mount St. Vincent	NY	45,620	C
Converse College	SC	28,290	C
Duquesne Univ	PA	48,508	VC
Elizabethtown College	PA	56,340	VC
Emory and Henry College	VA	46,320	C
Emporia State Univ	KS	15,029	C
Fort Hays State Univ	KS	12,677	C
Framingham State Univ	MA	21,740	C
Francis Marion Univ	SC	18,144	LC
Georgia Southern Univ	GA	16,540	VC
Graceland Univ	IA	35,290	C
Hobart and William Smith Colleges	NY	67,050	HC+
Ithaca College	NY	58,158	VC+
James Madison Univ	VA	19,084	VC
John Carroll Univ	OH	51,570	C
Kansas State Univ	KS	17,780	VC
Kennesaw State Univ	GA	18,899	VC
Kenyon College	OH	65,840	MC
Knox College	IL	54,654	VC+
Kutztown Univ of Pennsylvania	PA	19,477	C
Lamar Univ	TX	18,014	LC
Longwood Univ	VA	22,184	C
Loyola Marymount Univ	CA	60,202	VC+
Metropolitan State Univ of Denver	CO	6,928	LC
Mills College	CA	43,705	C
Miss College	MS	25,850	C
Monmouth Univ	NJ	50,184	C
Montana State Univ	MT	15,500	C+
Northern Arizona Univ	AZ	21,003	C
Notre Dame of Maryland Univ	MD	47,570	VC
Ohio Univ	OH	23,394	VC
Okla Baptist Univ	OK	33,990	C
Pace Univ	NY	60,136	C
Presbyterian College	SC	47,186	C
Regis Univ	CO	46,380	C
St. Francis Univ	PA	46,146	NC
St. Peter's Univ	NJ	49,192	C
Seton Hall Univ	NJ	58,008	C
St. Lawrence Univ	NY	66,646	HC+
Syracuse Univ	NY	62,313	HC
Texas A&M Univ at College Station	TX	20,771	VC+
The Univ of Texas at San Antonio	TX	21,060	C
Trinity College	CT	69,020	HC
Union College	NY	64,320	MC
Univ of Arkansas at Monticello	AR	13,599	LC
Univ of Idaho	ID	16,158	C
Univ of Louisiana at Monroe	LA	15,970	C
Univ of Maine	ME	21,038	VC
Univ of Maryland/Baltimore County	MD	23,004	VC
Univ of Mass Lowell	MA	27,296	VC
Univ of North Georgia	GA	17,316	C
Univ of Wisc-River Falls	WI	14,541	C
Wayne State College	NE	25,746	NC
Westmont College	CA	57,930	VC
Widener Univ	PA	58,190	C
Winthrop Univ	SC	23,960	C
Wright State Univ	OH	16,983	C
Xavier Univ	OH	49,380	VC

MOLECULAR BIOLOGY

School	ST	$IS	SR
Adams State Univ	CO	15,420	LC
Alverno College	WI	33,294	LC
Andrews Univ	MI	41,732	C
Appalachian State Univ	NC	15,394	VC
Arcadia Univ	PA	55,990	C+
Arizona State Univ at the Tempe Campus	AZ	23,001	VC
Assumption College	MA	48,455	VC
Auburn Univ	AL	24,300	VC+
Bellarmine Univ	KY	52,532	C
Benedictine Univ	IL	38,300	C
Bethel Univ	MN	46,550	C+
Brigham Young Univ	UT	13,248	MC
Brown Univ	RI	64,566	MC
Cal State, Fullerton	CA	21,902	C
Cedarville Univ	OH	36,244	VC
Centre College	KY	50,680	MC
Chestnut Hill College	PA	47,180	C
Claremont McKenna College	CA	69,900	MC
Clarion Univ of Pennsylvania	PA	21,608	LC
Clarkson Univ	NY	60,392	VC
Coe College	IA	51,570	VC
Coker College	SC	38,196	C
Colgate Univ	NY	67,500	MC
Colo College	CO	64,894	MC
Florida Inst of Technology	FL	53,306	VC
Florida Southern College	FL	45,978	VC
Florida State Univ	FL	16,771	HC
Goshen College	IN	44,350	C
Grove City College	PA	26,654	VC
Hampden-Sydney College	VA	57,806	VC
Hardin-Simmons Univ	TX	36,025	C
Houston Baptist Univ	TX	36,450	C
Illinois Inst of Technology	IL	56,826	HC+
Illinois State Univ	IL	23,418	VC
John Carroll Univ	OH	51,570	C
Johns Hopkins Univ	MD	68,080	MC
Kenyon College	OH	65,840	MC
Kutztown Univ of Pennsylvania	PA	19,477	C
Lawrence Tech Univ	MI	41,630	VC
Lehigh Univ	PA	63,860	MC
Lipscomb Univ	TN	42,984	VC
Marquette Univ	WI	53,090	VC+
Marshall Univ	WV	18,044	C
Messiah College	PA	44,380	VC
Middlebury College	VT	67,464	MC
Millikin Univ	IL	44,148	C
Mills College	CA	43,705	C
Milwaukee School of Engineering	WI	48,531	HC+
Missouri Western State Univ	MO	17,822	LC
Montclair State Univ	NJ	26,912	C
Murray State Univ	KY	17,726	C+
Muskingum Univ	OH	35,966	C
Nebr Wesleyan Univ	NE	42,026	C+
New Mexico State Univ	NM	14,050	LC
Northwestern Univ	IL	68,725	MC
Ohio Northern Univ	OH	44,050	VC
Ohio State Univ at Columbus	OH	22,843	MC
Ohio Univ	OH	23,394	VC
Okla State Univ	OK	17,180	C+
Otterbein Univ	OH	41,630	C
Pomona College	CA	64,957	MC
Princeton Univ	NJ	60,090	MC
Purdue Univ/West Lafayette	IN	20,032	MC
Rhodes College	TN	51,900	HC
Rutgers Univ - New Brunswick	NJ	27,090	HC
Salem International Univ	WV	21,090	C
Scripps College	CA	69,260	HC
SUNY Albany	NY	22,165	C
SUNY at Binghamton	NY	24,100	MC
SUNY/The College of Environmental Science and Forestry	NY	23,728	VC
Stetson Univ	FL	57,174	VC+
Texas A&M Univ at College Station	TX	20,771	VC+
The Univ of Arizona	AZ	24,086	C
The Univ of Texas at Austin	TX	20,206	MC
Towson Univ	MD	21,878	C
Tulane Univ	LA	67,496	MC
Univ of Calif at Berkeley	CA	29,886	MC
Univ of Calif at Los Angeles	CA	27,438	HC+
Univ of Calif at Santa Barbara	CA	30,627	HC+
Univ of Calif San Diego	CA	30,450	MC
Univ of Calif, Santa Cruz	CA	28,731	C+
Univ of Colo Boulder	CO	26,048	HC
Univ of Conn	CT	27,394	
Univ of Denver	CO	61,129	VC+
Univ of Great Falls	MT	38,524	C
Univ of Idaho	ID	16,158	C
Univ of Illinois at Urbana-Champaign	IL	27,006	HC
Univ of Kansas	KS	20,884	VC
Univ of Maine	ME	21,038	VC
Univ of Mich/Ann Arbor	MI	25,274	MC
Univ of Minn/Duluth	MN	20,292	C
Univ of New Hampshire	NH	29,333	VC
Univ of Pittsburgh	PA	30,030	MC
Univ of Puget Sound	WA	60,210	HC
Univ of Richmond	VA	62,730	MC
Univ of Rochester	NY	65,032	MC
Univ of Texas at Dallas	TX	23,640	HC
Univ of Vermont	VT	29,792	HC
Univ of Wisc-Madison	WI	21,647	MC
Univ of Wisc-Milwaukee	WI	21,538	C
Univ of Wisc-Parkside	WI	15,313	C
Univ of Wyoming	WY	15,537	C
Vanderbilt Univ	TN	63,248	MC
Washburn Univ	KS	15,827	C
Wells College	NY	50,500	C
Wesleyan Univ	CT	66,940	MC
West Chester Univ of Pennsylvania	PA	19,171	VC
Western Washington Univ	WA	18,904	VC
Westminster College	PA	41,722	C
Whitman College	WA	59,772	MC
Yale Univ	CT	64,650	MC

MOLECULAR DIAGNOSTICS

School	ST	$IS	SR
Ferris State Univ	MI	21,458	C

MOVEMENT SCIENCE

School	ST	$IS	SR
Texas Christian Univ	TX	57,120	HC
Univ of Idaho	ID	16,158	C
Winona State Univ	MN	18,109	C

MULTIDISCIPLINARY STUDIES

School	ST	$IS	SR
Gannon Univ	PA	42,922	C
Stony Brook Univ/The SUNY	NY	22,703	MC
Texas Tech Univ	TX	20,156	C+
Univ of Okla	OK	19,651	HC
Wheaton College	MA	63,818	VC

MULTIMEDIA

School	ST	$IS	SR
Abilene Christian Univ	TX	43,708	C+
Arkansas State Univ	AR	16,190	C
Art Inst of Portland	OR	132,329	SP
Augustana College	IL	51,222	VC+
Belmont Univ	TN	44,500	VC+
Bennington College	VT	66,280	MC
Bethel Univ	MN	46,550	C+
Bloomfield College	NJ	40,100	LC
Calif Lutheran Univ	CA	52,853	C
Champlain College	VT	54,724	VC
CUNY/Brooklyn College	NY	7,163	C+
CUNY/City College	NY	20,204	C
Dakota Wesleyan Univ	SD	33,980	LC
Drury Univ	MO	37,555	VC
Duquesne Univ	PA	48,508	VC
Florida Atlantic Univ	FL	18,256	C
Franklin College	IN	40,550	C
George Fox Univ	OR	42,938	C
Georgia Southern Univ	GA	16,540	VC
Hawaii Pacific Univ	HI	33,420	C
Howard Payne Univ	TX	35,994	C
Keene State College	NH	24,604	C
La Salle Univ	PA	43,476	C
Lyndon State College	VT	20,714	C
McMurry Univ	TX	34,259	LC
Minot State Univ	ND	13,285	C
Missouri Western State Univ	MO	17,822	LC
National Univ	CA	17,849	LC
Northeastern Univ	MA	65,352	MC
Ohio Univ	OH	23,394	VC
Point Loma Nazarene Univ	CA	46,150	C+
Rider Univ	NJ	54,050	C
St. Leo Univ	FL	32,850	C
San Diego State Univ	CA	23,156	VC
Simpson College	IA	45,626	VC
The American Univ	DC	61,317	HC
The Art Inst of Atlanta	GA	34,334	SP
The College of New Jersey	NJ	28,675	VC+
The George Washington Univ	DC	68,474	HC+
Univ of Mary Hardin-Baylor	TX	35,292	C+
Univ of N Car at Asheville	NC	16,251	VC+
Univ of the Arts	PA	56,579	SP
Wartburg College	IA	49,478	C
Washington State Univ	WA	22,747	C
Waynesburg Univ	PA	33,530	C
Western Washington Univ	WA	18,904	VC
Wilmington Univ	DE	8,762	NC

MUSEUM STUDIES

School	ST	$IS	SR
Baylor Univ	TX	56,803	HC
Cal State, Fullerton	CA	21,902	C
Juniata College	PA	58,118	VC
Middlebury College	VT	67,464	MC
Niagara Univ	NY	41,010	C
Rochester Inst of Technology	NY	52,734	HC+
Tusculum College	TN	31,625	LC
Univ of Central Okla	OK	15,150	C
Univ of Illinois at Chicago	IL	24,664	VC
Univ of St. Francis	IN	38,520	C
Walsh Univ	OH	39,010	C

MUSIC

School	ST	$IS	SR
Abilene Christian Univ	TX	43,708	C+
Adams State Univ	CO	15,420	LC
Adelphi Univ	NY	49,792	C
Adrian College	MI	45,550	C
Agnes Scott College	GA	51,930	VC+
Alabama State Univ	AL	16,490	LC
Albany State Univ	GA	19,462	C
Albion College	MI	55,260	C
Alcorn State Univ	MS	15,884	C
Alderson Broaddus Univ	WV	35,000	LC
Allegheny College	PA	57,620	VC
Allen Univ	SC	19,920	NC
Alma College	MI	49,410	VC
Alverno College	WI	33,294	LC
Amherst College	MA	66,186	MC
Andrews Univ	MI	41,732	C
Angelo State Univ	TX	15,882	LC
Anna Maria College	MA	51,020	C
Aquinas College - Mich	MI	38,876	VC
Arizona State Univ at the Tempe Campus	AZ	23,001	VC
Arkansas State Univ	AR	16,190	C
Arkansas Tech Univ	AR	16,534	LC

ST = STATE $IS = IN-STATE COSTS   SR = SELECTOR RATING

School	ST	$IS	SR
Armstrong State Univ	GA	15,615	C
Asbury Univ	KY	36,450	C+
Ashland Univ	OH	30,446	C
Assumption College	MA	48,455	VC
Atlantic Union College	MA	27,228	C
Augsburg Univ	MN	45,129	C
Augusta Univ	GA	4,632	C
Augustana College	IL	51,222	VC+
Augustana Univ	SD	39,968	VC
Aurora Univ	IL	34,990	C
Austin College	TX	51,059	HC
Austin Peay State Univ	TN	16,397	C
Averett Univ	VA	43,034	LC
Avila Univ	MO	27,100	C
Azusa Pacific Univ	CA	43,972	C
Baker Univ	KS	37,190	C
Baldwin Wallace Univ	OH	42,464	VC
Ball State Univ	IN	19,808	C+
Bard College	NY	65,924	HC
Bard College at Simon's Rock	MA	65,795	MC
Barnard College/Columbia Univ	NY	68,762	MC
Bates College	ME	64,500	HC
Baylor Univ	TX	56,803	HC
Belhaven Univ	MS	32,250	C
Bellarmine Univ	KY	52,532	C
Belmont Univ	TN	44,500	VC+
Beloit College	WI	55,206	HC
Bemidji State Univ	MN	17,730	C
Benedict College	SC	28,630	NC
Benedictine College	KS	38,850	VC
Benedictine Univ	IL	38,300	C
Bennett College	NC	27,717	NC
Bennington College	VT	66,280	MC
Berea College	KY	7,094	C
Berklee College of Music	MA	60,930	SP
Berry College	GA	47,466	VC
Bethany College	KS	38,637	LC
Bethany College	WV	38,774	LC
Bethel College	IN	36,830	C
Bethel College	KS	35,370	C
Bethel Univ	MN	46,550	C+
Bethel Univ	TN	27,142	C
Bethune-Cookman Univ	FL	23,322	C
Biola Univ	CA	48,686	C
Birmingham-Southern College	AL	44,478	C+
Black Hills State Univ	SD	16,622	C
Bloomsburg Univ of Pennsylvania	PA	19,930	C
Blue Mountain College	MS	15,949	C
Bluefield College	VA	34,711	C
Bluffton Univ	OH	40,950	C+
Boise State Univ	ID	17,368	C
Boston College	MA	68,043	MC
Boston Univ	MA	67,352	MC
Bowdoin College	ME	65,980	MC
Bowling Green State Univ	OH	19,975	C
Bradley Univ	IL	43,240	VC
Brandeis Univ	MA	68,443	MC
Brewton-Parker College	GA	26,120	LC
Briar Cliff Univ	IA	36,956	C
Bridgewater College	VA	46,260	C
Bridgewater State Univ	MA	22,762	C
Brigham Young Univ	UT	13,248	MC
Brigham Young Univ/Hawaii	HI	11,710	C
Brown Univ	RI	64,566	MC
Bryan College	TN	32,900	C
Bryn Mawr College	PA	65,220	MC
Bucknell Univ	PA	67,136	MC
Buena Vista Univ	IA	42,344	C
Butler Univ	IN	52,890	VC+
Cairn Univ	PA	37,572	C
Caldwell Univ	NJ	42,165	LC
Calif Baptist Univ	CA	42,986	C
Calif Lutheran Univ	CA	52,853	C
Calif Polytechnic State Univ	CA	22,547	MC
Calif State Polytechnic Univ, Pomona	CA	21,811	C
Cal State, Bakersfield	CA	22,397	LC
Cal State, Chico	CA	19,790	VC
Cal State, Dominguez Hills	CA	19,022	LC
Cal State, East Bay	CA	20,748	C
Cal State, Fresno	CA	16,902	LC
Cal State, Fullerton	CA	21,902	C
Cal State, Long Beach	CA	18,850	C
Cal State, Los Angeles	CA	17,186	LC
Cal State, Monterey Bay	CA	22,872	LC
Cal State, Northridge	CA	17,277	LC
Cal State, Sacramento	CA	19,060	C
Cal State, San Bernardino	CA	20,106	C
Cal State, Stanislaus	CA	18,053	LC
Calvin College	MI	43,090	HC
Cameron Univ	OK	11,632	LC
Campbell Univ	NC	37,570	VC
Campbellsville Univ	KY	33,400	C
Canisius College	NY	49,672	C
Capital Univ	OH	44,778	VC
Cardinal Stritch Univ	WI	37,136	C
Carleton College	MN	66,414	MC
Carnegie Mellon Univ	PA	67,980	MC
Carroll Univ	WI	38,100	C+
Carson-Newman Univ	TN	35,900	C
Carthage College	WI	48,835	C
Case Western Reserve Univ	OH	62,284	MC
Castleton Univ	VT	20,186	C
Catawba College	NC	39,820	LC
Cedarville Univ	OH	36,244	VC
Centenary College of Louisiana	LA	49,050	C+
Central College	IA	44,592	C
Central Conn State Univ	CT	22,041	C
Central Methodist Univ	MO	31,500	VC
Central Mich Univ	MI	20,330	C
Central State Univ	OH	18,564	C
Central Washington Univ	WA	16,803	C
Centre College	KY	50,680	MC
Chadron State College	NE	14,819	LC
Chapman Univ	CA	65,504	HC
Charleston Southern Univ	SC	34,700	C
Chatham Univ	PA	47,883	VC
Chestnut Hill College	PA	47,180	C
Cheyney Univ of Pennsylvania	PA	20,896	LC
Chicago State Univ	IL	41,620	C
Christopher Newport Univ	VA	24,878	VC+
CUNY/Baruch College	NY	21,609	HC
CUNY/Brooklyn College	NY	7,163	C+
CUNY/City College	NY	20,204	C
CUNY/Hunter College	NY	31,098	VC
CUNY/Lehman College	NY	5,788	LC
CUNY/Queens College	NY	21,507	C
CUNY/York College	NY	6,747	LC
Claflin Univ	SC	25,592	LC
Clark Atlanta Univ	GA	31,019	LC
Clark Univ	MA	53,260	HC+
Clayton State Univ	GA	19,735	LC
Cleveland State Univ	OH	22,290	C
Coastal Carolina Univ	SC	20,340	C
Coe College	IA	51,570	VC
Coker College	SC	38,196	C
Colby College	ME	64,060	MC
Colgate Univ	NY	67,500	MC
College of Charleston	SC	24,046	VC
College of St. Benedict	MN	54,480	C
College of St. Scholastica	MN	45,734	C+
College of Staten Island	NY	24,389	LC
College of the Holy Cross	MA	64,320	MC
College of the Ozarks	MO	7,530	VC
College of William & Mary	VA	34,907	MC
Colo Christian Univ	CO	40,885	VC
Colo College	CO	64,894	MC
Colo Mesa Univ	CO	19,707	LC
Colo State Univ	CO	23,033	C
Columbia College	SC	36,550	C
Columbia College Chicago	IL	40,104	C
Columbia Univ/ School of General Studies	NY	61,470	MC
Columbia Univ/City of New York	NY	62,958	MC
Columbus State Univ	GA	14,336	LC
Concordia College - Moorhead	MN	46,418	C
Concordia College - New York	NY	39,035	LC
Concordia Univ Irvine	CA	44,860	VC
Concordia Univ Nebr	NE	41,900	VC
Concordia Univ St. Paul	MN	29,050	C
Concordia Univ Texas	TX	41,920	C
Concordia Univ Wisc	WI	35,910	C
Concordia Univ, Ann Arbor	MI	38,878	C+
Concordia Univ, Chicago	IL	41,522	C
Conn College	CT	65,000	MC
Conservatory of Music of PR	PR	13,925	
Converse College	SC	28,290	C
Corban Univ	OR	41,700	C
Cornell College	IA	49,900	VC
Cornell Univ	NY	67,591	MC
Cornerstone Univ	MI	36,550	C
Cornish College of the Arts	WA	47,750	SP
Covenant College	GA	44,590	HC
Creighton Univ	NE	49,452	VC
Culver-Stockton College	MO	34,350	C
Cumberland Univ	TN	27,710	C
Curtis Inst of Music	PA	20,944	SP
Dakota Wesleyan Univ	SD	33,980	LC
Dallas Baptist Univ	TX	35,220	VC
Dartmouth College	NH	68,109	MC
Davidson College	NC	60,119	MC
Delaware State Univ	DE	19,376	LC
Delta State Univ	MS	13,176	LC
Denison Univ	OH	62,770	HC+
DePaul Univ	IL	52,807	VC
DePauw Univ	IN	58,688	VC
Dickinson College	PA	66,166	MC
Dickinson State Univ	ND	12,372	LC
Dillard Univ	LA	20,940	VC
Doane Univ	NE	41,340	VC
Dominican Univ	IL	42,472	C+
Dominican Univ of Calif	CA	58,750	C
Dordt College	IA	37,860	C+
Drake Univ	IA	49,220	HC
Drew Univ/College of Liberal Arts	NJ	53,608	VC
Drury Univ	MO	37,555	VC
Duke Univ	NC	68,298	MC
Earlham College	IN	55,670	HC
East Central Univ	OK	13,330	C
East Tenn State Univ	TN	18,141	C
East Texas Baptist Univ	TX	34,444	C
Eastern Conn State Univ	CT	23,059	C
Eastern Illinois Univ	IL	21,414	C
Eastern Kentucky Univ	KY	17,742	C
Eastern Mennonite Univ	VA	42,550	C
Eastern Mich Univ	MI	19,761	C
Eastern Nazarene College	MA	41,114	C
Eastern New Mexico Univ	NM	12,874	LC
Eastern Oregon Univ	OR	17,612	C
Eastern Univ	PA	39,540	C
Eastern Washington Univ	WA	17,896	LC
Eastman School of Music/ Univ of Rochester	NY	68,060	SP
Eckerd College	FL	55,206	VC
Edgewood College	WI	35,950	C
Edinboro Univ	PA	15,940	LC
Elizabeth City State Univ	NC	14,745	C
Elizabethtown College	PA	56,340	VC
Elmhurst College	IL	46,514	C
Elmira College	NY	53,900	C
Elon Univ	NC	46,142	HC
Emory Univ	GA	63,286	MC
Emporia State Univ	KS	15,029	C
Erskine College	SC	45,460	C
Eugene Lang College of Liberal Arts	NY	64,940	VC
Eureka College	IL	34,760	C
Evangel Univ	MO	28,898	C
Excelsior College	NY	38,800	SP
Fairfield Univ	CT	61,445	HC
Faulkner Univ	AL	26,410	C
Felician Univ	NJ	46,280	LC
Fisk Univ	TN	32,066	LC
Florida A&M Univ	FL	15,361	C
Florida Atlantic Univ	FL	18,256	C
Florida Gulf Coast Univ	FL	14,738	C
Florida International Univ	FL	20,281	C
Florida Memorial Univ	FL	22,424	LC
Florida Southern College	FL	45,978	VC
Florida State Univ	FL	16,771	HC
Fordham Univ	NY	68,431	MC
Fort Hays State Univ	KS	12,677	C
Fort Lewis College	CO	20,154	C
Francis Marion Univ	SC	18,144	LC
Franklin and Marshall College	PA	67,960	MC
Franklin College	IN	40,550	C
Franklin Pierce Univ	NH	46,750	LC
Fresno Pacific Univ	CA	38,858	C
Friends Univ	KS	38,000	C
Frostburg State Univ	MD	17,280	LC
Furman Univ	SC	61,098	VC+
Gardner-Webb Univ	NC	24,935	C+
Geneva College	PA	35,450	C
George Fox Univ	OR	42,938	C
George Mason Univ	VA	19,884	C
Georgetown College	KY	41,440	C
Georgia College & State Univ	GA	21,884	C+
Georgia Southern Univ	GA	16,540	VC
Georgia Southwestern State Univ	GA	13,870	LC
Georgia State Univ	GA	25,250	C
Gettysburg College	PA	65,210	MC
Gonzaga Univ	WA	52,880	HC
Gordon College	MA	47,740	VC
Goshen College	IN	44,350	C
Goucher College	MD	56,110	VC
Grace Bible College	MI	25,250	C
Grace College and Seminary	IN	31,524	C
Graceland Univ	IA	35,290	C
Grambling State Univ	LA	15,701	C
Grand Canyon Univ	AZ	25,150	VC
Grand Valley State Univ	MI	22,250	C+
Grand View Univ	IA	32,302	C
Greensboro College	NC	39,790	LC
Greenville College	IL	27,012	LC
Grinnell College	IA	63,114	MC
Grove City College	PA	26,654	VC
Guilford College	NC	45,973	C
Gustavus Adolphus College	MN	53,943	HC
Hamilton College	NY	64,250	MC
Hamline Univ	MN	50,152	C
Hampshire College	MA	65,214	MC
Hampton Univ	VA	36,410	C
Hannibal-LaGrange Univ	MO	29,815	C
Hanover College	IN	47,750	C+
Harding Univ	AR	25,440	C
Hardin-Simmons Univ	TX	36,025	C
Hartwick College	NY	51,270	C
Harvard College/Harvard Univ	MA	65,609	MC
Hastings College	NE	35,380	C+
Haverford College	PA	66,490	MC
Heidelberg Univ	OH	40,400	LC
Henderson State Univ	AR	15,516	C
Hendrix College	AR	54,020	VC
High Point Univ	NC	47,355	VC
Hillsdale College	MI	37,170	MC
Hiram College	OH	44,590	C
Hobart and William Smith Colleges	NY	67,050	HC+
Hofstra Univ	NY	58,210	C+
Hollins Univ	VA	49,635	VC
Holy Names Univ	CA	46,630	LC
Hood College	MD	50,540	C
Hope College	MI	42,840	VC
Houghton College	NY	40,558	VC
Houston Baptist Univ	TX	36,450	C
Howard Payne Univ	TX	35,994	C
Howard Univ	DC	37,616	C+
Humboldt State Univ	CA	21,708	C
Huntingdon College	AL	35,900	C
Huston-Tillotson Univ	TX	18,124	LC
Idaho State Univ	ID	13,619	LC
Illinois College	IL	41,330	VC
Illinois State Univ	IL	23,418	VC
Illinois Wesleyan Univ	IL	56,430	VC+
Immaculata Univ	PA	39,000	C
Indiana State Univ	IN	23,223	LC
Indiana Univ Bloomington	IN	20,791	HC
Indiana Univ of Pennsylvania	PA	24,474	C
Indiana Univ South Bend	IN	16,057	C
Indiana Univ Southeast	IN	16,931	C
Indiana Univ-Purdue Univ Fort Wayne	IN	18,675	C
Indiana Wesleyan Univ	IN	33,674	C
Inter-American Univ of PR-San Germán	PR	20,042	
Iowa State Univ	IA	18,176	C
Iowa Wesleyan Univ	IA	41,000	C
Ithaca College	NY	58,158	VC+
Jacksonville State Univ	AL	14,628	LC
Jacksonville Univ	FL	49,210	C
James Madison Univ	VA	19,084	VC
John Brown Univ	AR	35,184	VC
Johnson State College	VT	22,672	C
Judson Univ	IL	39,174	C
Kalamazoo College	MI	53,931	HC
Kansas State Univ	KS	17,780	VC
Kansas Wesleyan Univ	KS	37,930	C
Kean Univ	NJ	25,620	C
Keene State College	NH	24,604	C
Kennesaw State Univ	GA	18,899	VC
Kent State Univ	OH	20,928	C
Kentucky Christian Univ	KY	26,836	LC
Kentucky Wesleyan College	KY	34,260	LC
Kenyon College	OH	65,840	MC
King Univ	TN	36,976	C
Knox College	IL	54,654	VC+
Kutztown Univ of Pennsylvania	PA	19,477	C
La Sierra Univ	CA	39,690	VC
Lafayette College	PA	68,520	MC
LaGrange College	GA	41,310	C
Lake Forest College	IL	50,652	VC
Lakeland Univ	WI	35,130	C
Lamar Univ	TX	18,014	LC
Lander Univ	SC	32,200	C
Lane College	TN	17,960	LC
Langston Univ	OK	15,659	C
Lebanon Valley College	PA	55,510	VC
Lee Univ	TN	22,045	C
Lehigh Univ	PA	63,860	MC
LeMoyne-Owen College	TN	16,980	C
Lenoir-Rhyne Univ	NC	47,500	LC
Lewis & Clark College	OR	60,984	MC
Lewis Univ	IL	41,710	C
Liberty Univ	VA	31,415	C
Limestone College	SC	32,100	C
Lincoln Univ	PA	20,878	LC
Lindenwood Univ	MO	25,760	C
Linfield College	OR	53,992	C
Lipscomb Univ	TN	42,984	VC
Livingstone College	NC	17,815	LC
Lock Haven Univ of Pennsylvania	PA	20,544	LC
Longwood Univ	VA	22,184	C
Loras College	IA	40,726	C
Louisiana College	LA	21,274	C
Louisiana State Univ and A&M College	LA	18,677	VC
Louisiana Tech Univ	LA	11,422	VC
Loyola Marymount Univ	CA	60,202	VC+
Loyola Univ Chicago	IL	57,158	VC
Loyola Univ New Orleans	LA	52,456	VC
Lubbock Christian Univ	TX	29,727	C
Luther College	IA	49,990	VC
Lycoming College	PA	50,895	C
Lyon College	AR	36,120	VC
Macalester College	MN	64,136	MC
MacMurray College	IL	35,025	C
Madonna Univ	MI	30,450	LC
Malone Univ	OH	39,200	C
Manchester Univ	IN	41,540	C
Manhattan School of Music	NY	57,200	SP
Manhattanville College	NY	52,430	C
Mannes School of Music	NY	44,500	SP
Mansfield Univ of Pennsylvania	PA	24,244	LC
Marian Univ	IN	43,206	C
Marian Univ	WI	34,622	C
Marietta College	OH	46,190	C
Marlboro College	VT	50,832	VC+
Mars Hill Univ	NC	41,104	C
Marshall Univ	WV	18,044	C
Martin Univ	IN	21,010	LC
Mary Baldwin Univ	VA	40,495	C
Marygrove College	MI	30,100	LC
Marylhurst Univ	OR	16,818	NC
Maryville College	TN	44,410	C
Mass Inst of Technology	MA	62,662	MC
Mayville State Univ	ND	18,371	NC
McDaniel College	MD	52,910	VC
McKendree Univ	IL	37,940	C+
McMurry Univ	TX	34,259	LC
McNeese State Univ	LA	7,838	C
McPherson College	KS	36,134	C
Mercer Univ	GA	45,348	VC
Mercy College	NY	32,614	C
Mercyhurst Univ	PA	47,420	C
Meredith College	NC	46,634	C
Messiah College	PA	44,380	VC
Methodist Univ	NC	58,130	C
Miami Univ	OH	27,190	HC+
Mich State Univ	MI	24,542	VC
MidAmerica Nazarene Univ	KS	37,808	C

School	ST	$IS	SR
Middle Tenn State Univ	TN	8,650	C
Middlebury College	VT	67,464	MC
Midland Univ	NE	39,512	C
Midwestern State Univ	TX	12,111	LC
Millersville Univ of Pennsylvania	PA	25,298	C
Milligan College	TN	39,450	C
Millikin Univ	IL	44,148	C
Mills College	CA	43,705	C
Millsaps College	MS	50,080	C+
Minn State Univ, Mankato	MN	17,190	C
Minn State Univ, Moorhead	MN	21,393	C
Minot State Univ	ND	13,285	C
Miss College	MS	25,850	C
Miss Univ for Women	MS	17,065	C
Missouri Baptist Univ	MO	35,594	C
Missouri Southern State Univ	MO	13,071	C
Missouri State Univ	MO	15,837	C+
Missouri Western State Univ	MO	17,822	LC
Molloy College	NY	40,440	C
Monmouth College	IL	42,260	C
Monmouth Univ	NJ	50,184	C
Montana State Univ	MT	15,500	C+
Montana State Univ Billings	MT	13,336	LC
Montana State Univ-Northern	MT	11,370	NC
Montclair State Univ	NJ	26,912	C
Moravian College	PA	55,488	C
Morehead State Univ	KY	18,386	LC
Morehouse College	GA	40,835	C
Morgan State Univ	MD	17,190	LC
Morningside College	IA	39,780	C
Mount Holyoke College	MA	56,746	MC
Mount Marty College	SD	36,862	C
Mount Mercy Univ	IA	39,748	C
Mount St. Joseph Univ	OH	33,880	LC
Mount St. Mary's Univ - Chalon Campus	CA	50,486	VC+
Mount Vernon Nazarene Univ	OH	35,944	C
Muhlenberg College	PA	56,645	VC
Murray State Univ	KY	17,726	C+
Muskingum Univ	OH	35,966	C
Naropa Univ	CO	43,278	NC
Nazareth College	NY	46,784	C
Nebr Wesleyan Univ	NE	42,026	C+
New College of Florida	FL	16,180	HC+
New England Conservatory of Music	MA	63,170	SP
New Jersey City Univ	NJ	21,456	LC
New Mexico Highlands Univ	NM	11,904	LC
New Mexico State Univ	NM	14,050	LC
New York Univ	NY	68,139	MC
Newberry College	SC	34,550	C
Nicholls State Univ	LA	14,959	C
N Car A&T State Univ	NC	13,786	C
N Car Central Univ	NC	9,000	C
North Central College	IL	48,712	C+
North Central Univ	MN	30,610	C
N Dak State Univ	ND	16,245	VC
North Park Univ	IL	35,860	C
Northeastern Illinois Univ	IL	12,529	LC
Northeastern State Univ	OK	8,615	VC
Northeastern Univ	MA	65,352	MC
Northern Arizona Univ	AZ	21,003	C
Northern Illinois Univ	IL	20,176	C
Northern Kentucky Univ	KY	16,486	C
Northern Mich Univ	MI	20,853	C
Northern State Univ	SD	15,570	C
Northwest Christian Univ	OR	36,580	C
Northwest Missouri State Univ	MO	18,286	C
Northwest Nazarene Univ	ID	40,250	C
Northwest Univ	WA	38,720	VC
Northwestern College of Iowa	IA	38,400	C
Northwestern Okla State Univ	OK	13,072	LC
Northwestern State Univ of Louisiana	LA	16,534	LC
Northwestern Univ	IL	68,725	MC
Notre Dame de Namur Univ	CA	46,526	LC
Notre Dame of Maryland Univ	MD	47,570	VC
Nova Southeastern Univ	FL	38,534	C+
Nyack College	NY	34,450	LC
Oakland City Univ	IN	33,930	NC
Oakland Univ	MI	20,763	C
Oakwood Univ	AL	43,758	C
Oberlin College	OH	68,942	MC
Occidental College	CA	68,660	MC
Ohio Northern Univ	OH	44,050	VC
Ohio State Univ at Columbus	OH	22,843	MC
Ohio Univ	OH	23,394	VC
Ohio Wesleyan Univ	OH	49,460	VC
Okla Baptist Univ	OK	33,990	C
Okla Christian Univ	OK	29,260	C
Okla City Univ	OK	40,476	C
Okla Panhandle State Univ	OK	6,152	C
Okla State Univ	OK	17,180	C+
Okla Wesleyan Univ	OK	34,434	C
Old Dominion Univ	VA	21,618	C
Olivet Nazarene Univ	IL	41,840	VC
Oral Roberts Univ	OK	34,316	C
Oregon State Univ	OR	23,337	VC
Ottawa Univ	KS	39,980	VC
Otterbein Univ	OH	41,630	C
Ouachita Baptist Univ	AR	33,500	VC
Our Lady of the Lake Univ	TX	37,790	LC
Pacific Lutheran Univ	WA	49,960	C
Pacific Union College	CA	36,009	VC
Pacific Univ	OR	37,617	C
Palm Beach Atlantic Univ	FL	39,250	C
Park Univ	MO	22,134	C
Pennsylvania State Univ - Univ Park	PA	29,716	HC
Pepperdine Univ	CA	66,862	VC+
Peru State College	NE	15,602	LC
Philander Smith College	AR	20,814	LC
Piedmont College	GA	34,334	C
Pittsburg State Univ	KS	13,880	C
Pitzer College	CA	68,500	HC+
Plymouth State Univ	NH	23,180	LC
Point Loma Nazarene Univ	CA	46,150	C+
Pomona College	CA	64,957	MC
Portland State Univ	OR	19,443	C
Prairie View A&M Univ	TX	27,273	LC
Presbyterian College	SC	47,186	C
Princeton Univ	NJ	60,090	MC
Principia College	IL	40,350	C
Providence College	RI	62,870	HC
Queens Univ of Charlotte	NC	39,543	C
Quincy Univ	IL	38,170	LC
Radford Univ	VA	19,758	C
Ramapo College of New Jersey	NJ	25,760	VC
Randolph College	VA	53,970	C
Randolph-Macon College	VA	51,480	VC
Reed College	OR	65,300	MC
Regis Univ	CO	46,380	C
Rhode Island College	RI	19,000	LC
Rhodes College	TN	51,900	HC
Rice Univ	TX	59,458	MC
Rider Univ	NJ	54,050	C
Ripon College	WI	49,991	VC
Roanoke College	VA	55,952	VC
Roberts Wesleyan College	NY	41,116	C
Rochester College	MI	28,574	LC
Rockford Univ	IL	38,570	C
Roger Williams Univ	RI	48,074	VC
Rollins College	FL	58,670	HC
Roosevelt Univ	IL	41,890	VC
Rowan Univ	NJ	24,491	VC
Rust College	MS	10,600	C
Rutgers Univ - Camden	NJ	26,595	C
Rutgers Univ - New Brunswick	NJ	27,090	HC
Rutgers Univ - Newark	NJ	27,351	C
Saginaw Valley State Univ	MI	19,284	C
St. Augustine's Univ	NC	25,582	C
St. John's Univ	MN	53,472	C
St. Joseph's Univ	PA	58,540	VC
St. Louis Univ	MO	49,866	HC
St. Martin's Univ	WA	45,056	C
St. Mary-of-the-Woods College	IN	40,424	LC
St. Mary's College	IN	50,600	C
St. Mary's Univ of Minn	MN	42,440	C
St. Michael's College	VT	53,275	VC+
St. Vincent College	PA	46,229	C
St. Xavier Univ	IL	44,440	C
Salem College	NC	40,206	C
Salisbury Univ	MD	21,132	VC
Salve Regina Univ	RI	53,046	VC
Sam Houston State Univ	TX	18,792	C
Samford Univ	AL	40,770	VC
San Diego Christian College	CA	40,914	C
San Diego State Univ	CA	23,156	VC
San Francisco Conservatory of Music	CA	57,310	SP
San Francisco State Univ	CA	18,514	LC
San Jose State Univ	CA	22,630	C
Sarah Lawrence College	NY	68,866	MC
Schreiner Univ	TX	34,626	LC
Scripps College	CA	69,260	HC
Seattle Pacific Univ	WA	47,439	C+
Seattle Univ	WA	54,957	VC
Seton Hall Univ	NJ	58,008	C
Seton Hill Univ	PA	46,972	VC
Sewanee: The Univ of the South	TN	58,000	HC+
Shepherd Univ, West Virginia	WV	17,382	C
Shorter Univ	GA	31,130	LC
Siena Heights Univ	MI	36,322	C
Sierra Nevada College	NV	45,403	C
Silver Lake College of the Holy Family	WI	36,290	LC
Simmons College	MA	54,400	HC
Simpson College	IA	45,626	VC
Simpson Univ	CA	34,722	C
Skidmore College	NY	66,600	MC
Slippery Rock Univ of Pennsylvania	PA	20,450	C
Smith College	MA	66,774	MC
Sonoma State Univ	CA	27,020	C
S Dak State Univ	SD	15,874	C
Southeast Missouri State Univ	MO	16,148	C
Southeastern Louisiana Univ	LA	16,237	C
Southeastern Okla State Univ	OK	11,875	C
Southeastern Univ	FL	34,910	LC
Southern Adventist Univ	TN	28,250	C
Southern Illinois Univ Carbondale	IL	24,554	C
Southern Illinois Univ Edwardsville	IL	20,188	C
Southern Nazarene Univ	OK	33,684	C
Southern Oregon Univ	OR	19,117	C
Southern Univ and A&M College	LA	16,074	LC
Southern Wesleyan Univ	SC	33,670	LC
Southwest Baptist Univ	MO	30,890	LC
Southwest Minn State Univ	MN	17,783	C
Southwestern Adventist Univ	TX	28,232	LC
Southwestern College	KS	31,531	LC
Southwestern Okla State Univ	OK	12,205	C
Spelman College	GA	41,642	C
Spring Arbor Univ	MI	37,390	C
St. Bonaventure Univ	NY	45,596	C
St. Catherine Univ	MN	45,630	C
St. Cloud State Univ	MN	10,600	C
St. John's College at Annapolis	MD	63,348	MC
St. Lawrence Univ	NY	66,646	HC+
St. Mary's College of Maryland	MD	27,312	VC
St. Mary's Univ	TX	39,120	C
St. Norbert College	WI	46,060	VC
St. Olaf College	MN	56,430	HC
Stanford Univ	CA	62,541	MC
SUNY Albany	NY	22,165	C
SUNY at Binghamton	NY	24,100	MC
SUNY at Geneseo	NY	21,622	VC
SUNY at New Paltz	NY	20,840	C
SUNY at Oswego	NY	22,219	VC
SUNY at Purchase College	NY	21,832	C
SUNY/Buffalo State	NY	20,583	LC
SUNY/Fredonia	NY	20,818	C
SUNY/Oneonta	NY	20,794	C
SUNY/Plattsburgh	NY	19,314	C
SUNY/Potsdam	NY	21,051	VC
SUNY/Univ at Buffalo	NY	23,122	C
Stephen F. Austin State Univ	TX	18,484	LC
Sterling College	KS	32,830	LC
Stetson Univ	FL	57,174	VC+
Stillman College	AL	20,738	C
Stockton Univ	NJ	25,565	C
Stonehill College	MA	55,130	C
Stony Brook Univ/The SUNY	NY	22,703	MC
Susquehanna Univ	PA	57,560	VC
Swarthmore College	PA	63,550	MC
Syracuse Univ	NY	62,313	HC
Tabor College	KS	35,870	C
Tarleton State Univ	TX	15,248	LC
Taylor Univ	IN	42,130	VC
Temple Univ	PA	24,392	C+
Tenn State Univ	TN	14,423	LC
Tenn Wesleyan Univ	TN	32,680	LC
Texas A&M Univ at College Station	TX	20,771	VC+
Texas A&M Univ at Commerce	TX	10,496	C
Texas A&M Univ at Corpus Christi	TX	16,851	LC
Texas A&M Univ at Kingsville	TX	16,580	LC
Texas Christian Univ	TX	57,120	HC
Texas Lutheran Univ	TX	39,770	C
Texas Southern Univ	TX	19,592	LC
Texas State Univ	TX	18,721	C
Texas Tech Univ	TX	20,156	C+
Texas Wesleyan Univ	TX	37,338	C
Texas Woman's Univ	TX	15,302	LC
The American Univ	DC	61,317	HC
The Boston Conservatory at Berklee	MA	61,042	SP
The Catholic Univ of America	DC	58,376	VC
The College of Idaho	ID	36,415	C
The College of New Jersey	NJ	28,675	VC+
The College of St. Rose	NY	44,010	C
The College of Wooster	OH	60,000	HC
The George Washington Univ	DC	68,474	HC+
The Juilliard School	NY	59,226	SP
The Master's Univ	CA	43,870	C
The Univ of Akron	OH	22,566	C
The Univ of Alabama	AL	24,320	C+
The Univ of Arizona	AZ	24,086	C
The Univ of Mary	ND	23,180	C
The Univ of Memphis	TN	18,278	C
The Univ of Montana Western	MT	9,426	LC
The Univ of Tenn at Chattanooga	TN	17,340	C+
The Univ of Tenn at Knoxville	TN	22,112	VC
The Univ of Tenn at Martin	TN	15,212	C
The Univ of Texas at Austin	TX	20,206	MC
The Univ of Texas at San Antonio	TX	21,060	C
The Univ of Utah	UT	18,751	VC
Thomas Edison State Univ	NJ	6,350	NC
Toccoa Falls College	GA	30,048	C
Tougaloo College	MS	17,980	NC
Towson Univ	MD	21,878	C
Transylvania Univ	KY	47,450	HC+
Trevecca Nazarene Univ	TN	31,186	C
Trinity Christian College	IL	35,580	C
Trinity College	CT	69,020	HC
Trinity International Univ	IL	31,070	VC
Trinity Univ	TX	54,480	MC
Truman State Univ	MO	16,286	MC
Tufts Univ	MA		MC
Tulane Univ	LA	67,496	MC
Union College	NE	23,270	C
Union Univ	TN	41,160	VC
Universidad Adventista de las Antillas	PR	16,606	
Univ of Alabama at Birmingham	AL	22,092	C
Univ of Alabama in Huntsville	AL	20,028	VC
Univ of Alaska Anchorage	AK	17,914	C
Univ of Alaska Fairbanks	AK	16,874	VC
Univ of Arkansas at Fayetteville	AR	19,766	VC
Univ of Arkansas at Little Rock	AR	18,211	LC
Univ of Arkansas at Monticello	AR	13,599	LC
Univ of Arkansas at Pine Bluff	AR	13,541	C
Univ of Bridgeport	CT	44,985	LC
Univ of Calif at Berkeley	CA	29,886	MC
Univ of Calif at Davis	CA	28,468	HC
Univ of Calif at Irvine	CA	33,857	VC
Univ of Calif at Los Angeles	CA	27,438	HC+
Univ of Calif at Riverside	CA	32,912	C
Univ of Calif at Santa Barbara	CA	30,627	HC+
Univ of Calif San Diego	CA	30,450	MC
Univ of Calif, Santa Cruz	CA	28,731	C+
Univ of Central Arkansas	AR	15,042	VC
Univ of Central Florida	FL	16,379	VC
Univ of Central Missouri	MO	18,982	C
Univ of Central Okla	OK	15,150	C
Univ of Chicago	IL	70,551	MC
Univ of Cincinnati	OH	22,118	VC
Univ of Colo Boulder	CO	26,048	HC
Univ of Colo Denver	CO	22,238	C
Univ of Conn	CT	27,394	
Univ of Dayton	OH	54,930	VC
Univ of Delaware	DE	32,214	VC
Univ of Denver	CO	61,129	VC+
Univ of Evansville	IN	44,186	C+
Univ of Florida	FL	16,291	HC+
Univ of Georgia	GA	21,878	HC
Univ of Hartford	CT	49,776	C
Univ of Hawaii at Hilo	HI	18,038	VC
Univ of Hawaii at Manoa	HI	23,261	C
Univ of Idaho	ID	16,158	C
Univ of Illinois at Chicago	IL	24,664	VC
Univ of Illinois at Urbana-Champaign	IL	27,006	HC
Univ of Indianapolis	IN	36,480	VC
Univ of Iowa	IA	19,415	HC
Univ of Jamestown	ND	28,508	C
Univ of Kansas	KS	20,884	VC
Univ of Kentucky	KY	24,800	C+
Univ of La Verne	CA	55,600	C
Univ of Louisiana at Lafayette	LA	14,516	C
Univ of Louisiana at Monroe	LA	15,970	C
Univ of Louisville	KY	19,692	C
Univ of Lynchburg	VA	48,370	C
Univ of Maine	ME	21,038	VC
Univ of Mary Hardin-Baylor	TX	35,292	C+
Univ of Mary Washington	VA	23,039	C+
Univ of Maryland/Baltimore County	MD	23,004	VC
Univ of Maryland/College Park	MD	21,938	HC
Univ of Mass Amherst	MA	27,669	HC
Univ of Mass Boston	MA	13,828	C
Univ of Mass Dartmouth	MA	26,507	C
Univ of Mass Lowell	MA	27,296	VC
Univ of Miami	FL	63,494	MC
Univ of Mich/Ann Arbor	MI	25,274	MC
Univ of Mich/Flint	MI	19,062	C
Univ of Minn/Duluth	MN	20,292	C
Univ of Minn/Morris	MN	21,222	VC
Univ of Minn/Twin Cities	MN	24,269	MC
Univ of Miss	MS	18,802	C
Univ of Missouri-Columbia	MO	20,463	VC
Univ of Missouri-Kansas City	MO	19,563	VC
Univ of Missouri-St. Louis	MO	19,810	VC
Univ of Mobile	AL	28,935	C
Univ of Montana	MT	14,105	C
Univ of Montevallo	AL	20,012	C
Univ of Mount Olive	NC	18,426	C
Univ of Mount Union	OH	39,990	C
Univ of Nebr - Kearney	NE	17,014	LC
Univ of Nebr - Lincoln	NE	18,589	VC
Univ of Nebr - Omaha	NE	16,120	C
Univ of Nevada, Las Vegas	NV	17,553	C
Univ of Nevada, Reno	NV	18,010	C
Univ of New Hampshire	NH	29,333	VC
Univ of New Haven	CT	53,680	C
Univ of New Mexico	NM	16,808	C
Univ of New Orleans	LA	12,840	C
Univ of North Alabama	AL	15,964	C
Univ of N Car at Asheville	NC	16,251	VC+
Univ of N Car at Chapel Hill	NC	20,561	MC
Univ of N Car at Charlotte	NC	17,803	VC
Univ of N Car at Greensboro	NC	15,998	C
Univ of N Car at Pembroke	NC	14,737	LC
Univ of N Car School of the Arts	NC	25,587	SP
Univ of N Car Wilmington	NC	16,784	VC
Univ of N Dak	ND	16,673	C
Univ of North Florida	FL	15,996	VC
Univ of North Georgia	GA	17,316	C
Univ of North Texas	TX	20,082	C
Univ of Northern Colo	CO	19,658	C
Univ of Northern Iowa	IA	17,480	C
Univ of Northwestern - St. Paul	MN	39,530	C
Univ of Notre Dame	IN	68,801	MC

ST = STATE **$IS** = IN-STATE COSTS **SR** = SELECTOR RATING

School	ST	$IS	SR
Univ of Okla	OK	19,651	HC
Univ of Oregon	OR	24,021	VC
Univ of Pennsylvania	PA	63,526	MC
Univ of Pittsburgh	PA	30,030	MC
Univ of Portland	OR	52,152	VC
Univ of PR-Rio Piedras campus	PR	13,327	
Univ of Puget Sound	WA	60,210	HC
Univ of Redlands	CA	61,934	VC
Univ of Rhode Island	RI	26,066	VC
Univ of Richmond	VA	62,730	MC
Univ of Rio Grande & Rio Grande Community College	OH	8,750	LC
Univ of Rochester	NY	65,032	MC
Univ of St. Mary	KS	37,080	NC
Univ of San Diego	CA	60,338	HC
Univ of Science and Arts of Okla	OK	11,140	VC
Univ of Sioux Falls	SD	25,630	C
Univ of South Alabama	AL	16,880	C
Univ of S Car at Columbia	SC	21,726	VC
Univ of S Dak	SD	16,109	C
Univ of South Florida/Tampa	FL	16,110	VC
Univ of Southern Calif	CA	66,631	MC
Univ of Southern Maine	ME	18,320	C
Univ of Southern Miss	MS	13,170	C
Univ of St. Francis	IL	40,828	C
Univ of St. Thomas - Houston	TX	41,510	VC
Univ of Tampa	FL	38,928	VC
Univ of Texas at Arlington	TX	18,876	C
Univ of Texas at El Paso	TX	34,452	NC
Univ of Texas Rio Grande Valley	TX	15,573	LC
Univ of the Cumberlands	KY	32,000	LC
Univ of the District of Columbia	DC	21,260	LC
Univ of the Incarnate Word	TX	39,162	LC
Univ of the Ozarks	AR	31,050	NC
Univ of the Pacific	CA	57,446	VC
Univ of Toledo	OH	19,336	C
Univ of Tulsa	OK	52,625	HC
Univ of Vermont	VT	29,792	HC
Univ of Virginia	VA	27,367	MC
Univ of West Florida	FL	15,848	C
Univ of Wisc-Eau Claire	WI	16,354	VC
Univ of Wisc-Green Bay	WI	15,184	C
Univ of Wisc-La Crosse	WI	15,425	VC
Univ of Wisc-Madison	WI	21,647	MC
Univ of Wisc-Milwaukee	WI	21,538	C
Univ of Wisc-Oshkosh	WI	15,392	C
Univ of Wisc-Parkside	WI	15,313	C
Univ of Wisc-Platteville	WI	14,148	C
Univ of Wisc-River Falls	WI	14,541	C
Univ of Wisc-Stevens Point	WI	14,043	C
Univ of Wisc-Superior	WI	14,838	C
Univ of Wisc-Whitewater	WI	13,976	C
Univ of Wyoming	WY	15,537	C
Ursinus College	PA	62,920	VC
Utah State Univ	UT	13,235	C
Valley City State Univ	ND	13,267	C
Valparaiso Univ	IN	50,160	VC
Vanguard Univ of Southern Calif	CA	42,400	VC
Vassar College	NY	68,110	MC
Virginia Commonwealth Univ	VA	23,811	VC
Virginia Polytechnic Inst and State Univ	VA	21,920	VC
Virginia Union Univ	VA	25,058	C
Virginia Wesleyan Univ	VA	45,980	LC
Wabash College	IN	52,100	VC
Wagner College	NY	57,240	C+
Wake Forest Univ	NC	69,354	MC
Walla Walla Univ	WA	34,845	C
Walsh Univ	OH	39,010	C
Warner Pacific College	OR	31,610	C
Warren Wilson College	NC	44,220	VC
Wartburg College	IA	49,478	C
Washburn Univ	KS	15,827	C
Washington & Jefferson College	PA	58,694	VC
Washington Adventist Univ	MD	32,050	LC
Washington and Lee Univ	VA	59,647	MC
Washington College	MD	56,154	VC
Washington State Univ	WA	22,747	C
Washington Univ in St. Louis	MO	67,539	MC
Wayland Baptist Univ	TX	23,460	LC
Wayne State College	NE	25,746	NC
Wayne State Univ	MI	23,085	C
Weber State Univ	UT	14,112	C
Webster Univ	MO	37,490	C
Wellesley College	MA	66,984	MC
Wesley College	DE	37,848	LC
Wesleyan College	GA	31,940	C+
Wesleyan Univ	CT	66,940	MC
West Chester Univ of Pennsylvania	PA	19,171	VC
West Liberty Univ	WV	16,158	C
West Texas A&M Univ	TX	13,478	C
West Virginia Univ	WV	18,952	VC
West Virginia Wesleyan College	WV	39,188	C
Western Carolina Univ	NC	13,965	C
Western Conn State Univ	CT	21,254	LC
Western Illinois Univ	IL	20,897	C
Western Kentucky Univ	KY	16,850	C
Western Mich Univ	MI	21,791	C
Western New Mexico Univ	NM	16,914	LC
Western Oregon Univ	OR	19,965	LC
Western State Colo Univ	CO	19,348	C
Western Washington Univ	WA	18,904	VC
Westfield State Univ	MA	20,404	C
Westminster Choir College	NJ	53,730	SP
Westminster College	PA	41,722	C
Westminster College	UT	41,078	C
Westmont College	CA	57,930	VC
Wheaton College	IL	44,993	MC
Wheaton College	MA	63,818	VC
Whitman College	WA	59,772	MC
Whittier College	CA	57,891	C
Whitworth Univ	WA	53,682	VC
Wichita State Univ	KS	17,773	C
Wilberforce Univ	OH	19,900	C
Wiley College	TX	19,255	C
Willamette Univ	OR	62,514	VC+
William Carey Univ	MS	23,950	LC
William Jewell College	MO	42,490	C+
William Paterson Univ of New Jersey	NJ	24,022	C
Williams Baptist College	AR	24,720	C
Williams College	MA	67,700	MC
Wilmington College	OH	35,100	C
Wingate Univ	NC	41,900	C
Winona State Univ	MN	18,109	C
Winthrop Univ	SC	23,960	C
Wisc Lutheran College	WI	36,290	C
Wittenberg Univ	OH	49,863	VC
Wright State Univ	OH	16,983	C
Xavier Univ	OH	49,380	VC
Xavier Univ of Louisiana	LA	31,689	C
Yale Univ	CT	64,650	MC
Yeshiva Univ	NY	52,750	VC
York College of Pennsylvania	PA	29,240	C
Youngstown State Univ	OH	17,487	C

MUSIC BUSINESS MANAGEMENT

School	ST	$IS	SR
Albright College	PA	57,326	C
Anderson Univ	IN	39,450	C
Appalachian State Univ	NC	15,394	VC
Aquinas College - Mich	MI	38,876	VC
Belmont Univ	TN	44,500	VC+
Berklee College of Music	MA	60,930	SP
Berry College	GA	47,466	VC
Bethel Univ	TN	27,142	C
Bradley Univ	IL	43,240	VC
Central Washington Univ	WA	16,803	C
College of the Ozarks	MO	7,530	VC
Columbia College Chicago	IL	40,104	C
Concordia Univ St. Paul	MN	29,050	C
Dallas Baptist Univ	TX	35,220	VC
Delta State Univ	MS	13,176	LC
DePaul Univ	IL	52,807	VC
DePauw Univ	IN	58,688	VC
Dillard Univ	LA	20,940	VC
Drake Univ	IA	49,220	HC
Duquesne Univ	PA	48,508	VC
Elmhurst College	IL	46,514	C
Five Towns College	NY	35,480	LC
Florida Southern College	FL	45,978	VC
Geneva College	PA	35,450	C
Georgia State Univ	GA	25,250	C
Greenville College	IL	27,012	LC
Grove City College	PA	26,654	VC
Hardin-Simmons Univ	TX	36,025	C
Hofstra Univ	NY	58,210	C+
Howard Univ	DC	37,616	C+
Huntington Univ	IN	33,996	C
Johnson C. Smith Univ	NC	25,336	LC
Johnson State College	VT	22,672	C
Kentucky Christian Univ	KY	26,836	LC
Kentucky Wesleyan College	KY	34,260	LC
Lebanon Valley College	PA	55,510	VC
Lee Univ	TN	22,045	C
Lewis Univ	IL	41,710	C
Loyola Univ New Orleans	LA	52,456	VC
Lubbock Christian Univ	TX	29,727	C
Madonna Univ	MI	30,450	LC
Mansfield Univ of Pennsylvania	PA	24,244	LC
Marywood Univ	PA	47,840	C
McKendree Univ	IL	37,940	C+
Messiah College	PA	44,380	VC
Middle Tenn State Univ	TN	8,650	C
Millikin Univ	IL	44,148	C
Minn State Univ, Mankato	MN	17,190	C
Monmouth Univ	NJ	50,184	C
Montreat College	NC	34,605	LC
Murray State Univ	KY	17,726	C+
Nazareth College	NY	46,784	C
New York Univ	NY	68,139	MC
North Central Univ	MN	30,610	C
Northwest Univ	WA	38,720	VC
Northwestern State Univ of Louisiana	LA	16,534	LC
Oakwood Univ	AL	43,758	C
Ohio Northern Univ	OH	44,050	VC
Peru State College	NE	15,602	LC
St. Augustine's Univ	NC	25,582	C
S Car State Univ	SC	21,330	LC
Southern Illinois Univ Edwardsville	IL	20,188	C
Southern Nazarene Univ	OK	33,684	C
Southern Oregon Univ	OR	19,117	C
SUNY/Oneonta	NY	20,794	C
SUNY/Potsdam	NY	21,051	VC
The Univ of Memphis	TN	18,278	C
Tiffin Univ	OH	34,900	LC
Trevecca Nazarene Univ	TN	31,186	C
Univ of Evansville	IN	44,186	C+
Univ of Hartford	CT	49,776	C
Univ of Mass Lowell	MA	27,296	VC
Univ of Miami	FL	63,494	MC
Univ of New Haven	CT	53,680	C
Univ of the Incarnate Word	TX	39,162	LC
Univ of the Pacific	CA	57,446	VC
Wichita State Univ	KS	17,773	C
Winston-Salem State Univ	NC	18,005	LC

MUSIC COMPOSITION

School	ST	$IS	SR
Baldwin Wallace Univ	OH	42,464	VC
Biola Univ	CA	48,686	C
Boston Univ	MA	67,352	MC
Bradley Univ	IL	43,240	VC
Brown Univ	RI	64,566	MC
Cairn Univ	PA	37,572	C
Calif Baptist Univ	CA	42,986	C
Carnegie Mellon Univ	PA	67,980	MC
Cedarville Univ	OH	36,244	VC
Cleveland Inst of Music	OH	63,038	SP
Columbia College Chicago	IL	40,104	C
Furman Univ	SC	61,098	VC+
Indiana Univ Bloomington	IN	20,791	HC
Johns Hopkins Univ	MD	68,080	MC
Keene State College	NH	24,604	C
Lipscomb Univ	TN	42,984	VC
Loyola Univ New Orleans	LA	52,456	VC
Lynn Univ	FL	49,680	LC
Murray State Univ	KY	17,726	C+
New England Conservatory of Music	MA	63,170	SP
New York Univ	NY	68,139	MC
Northern Kentucky Univ	KY	16,486	C
Oberlin College	OH	68,942	MC
Ohio Univ	OH	23,394	VC
Ohio Wesleyan Univ	OH	49,460	VC
Okla City Univ	OK	40,476	C
Ouachita Baptist Univ	AR	33,500	VC
Point Loma Nazarene Univ	CA	46,150	C+
San Francisco Conservatory of Music	CA	57,310	SP
Shepherd Univ	CA		LC
Southern Oregon Univ	OR	19,117	C
Southwestern Univ	TX	52,370	VC
SUNY/Potsdam	NY	21,051	VC
Stetson Univ	FL	57,174	VC+
Syracuse Univ	NY	62,313	HC
Temple Univ	PA	24,392	C+
Texas Christian Univ	TX	57,120	HC
The Master's Univ	CA	43,870	C
Tulane Univ	LA	67,496	MC
Univ of Georgia	GA	21,878	HC
Univ of Kansas	KS	20,884	VC
Univ of Miami	FL	63,494	MC
Univ of Okla	OK	19,651	HC
Univ of West Georgia	GA	17,510	LC
Washington State Univ	WA	22,747	C
Western Mich Univ	MI	21,791	C
Whitman College	WA	59,772	MC
Wichita State Univ	KS	17,773	C
Youngstown State Univ	OH	17,487	C

MUSIC EDUCATION

School	ST	$IS	SR
Abilene Christian Univ	TX	43,708	C+
Adams State Univ	CO	15,420	LC
Alabama A&M Univ	AL	18,796	C
Alabama State Univ	AL	16,490	LC
Albany State Univ	GA	19,462	C
Albion College	MI	55,260	C
Alderson Broaddus Univ	WV	35,000	LC
Anderson Univ	IN	39,450	C
Andrews Univ	MI	41,732	C
Anna Maria College	MA	51,020	C
Appalachian State Univ	NC	15,394	VC
Aquinas College - Mich	MI	38,876	VC
Arcadia Univ	PA	55,990	C+
Arizona State Univ at the Tempe Campus	AZ	23,001	VC
Arkansas Tech Univ	AR	16,534	LC
Armstrong State Univ	GA	15,615	C
Asbury Univ	KY	36,450	C+
Ashland Univ	OH	30,446	C
Atlantic Union College	MA	27,228	C
Auburn Univ	AL	24,300	VC+
Augsburg Univ	MN	45,129	C
Augusta Univ	GA	4,632	C
Augustana College	IL	51,222	VC+
Augustana Univ	SD	39,968	VC
Azusa Pacific Univ	CA	43,972	C
Baker Univ	KS	37,190	C
Baldwin Wallace Univ	OH	42,464	VC
Baylor Univ	TX	56,803	HC
Benedictine College	KS	38,850	VC
Bennett College	NC	27,717	NC
Berklee College of Music	MA	60,930	SP
Berry College	GA	47,466	VC
Bethany College	KS	38,637	LC
Bethel College	IN	36,830	C
Bethel Univ	MN	46,550	C+
Bethel Univ	TN	27,142	C
Bethune-Cookman Univ	FL	23,322	C
Biola Univ	CA	48,686	C
Bloomsburg Univ of Pennsylvania	PA	19,930	C
Blue Mountain College	MS	15,949	C
Bluffton Univ	OH	40,950	C+
Boise State Univ	ID	17,368	C
Boston Univ	MA	67,352	MC
Bowling Green State Univ	OH	19,975	C
Bradley Univ	IL	43,240	VC
Brenau Univ - Women's College	GA	37,876	LC
Bridgewater State Univ	MA	22,762	C
Brigham Young Univ	UT	13,248	MC
Bucknell Univ	PA	67,136	MC
Buena Vista Univ	IA	42,344	C
Butler Univ	IN	52,890	VC+
Cairn Univ	PA	37,572	C
Calif Baptist Univ	CA	42,986	C
Cal State, Fresno	CA	16,902	LC
Cal State, Fullerton	CA	21,902	C
Cal State, San Bernardino	CA	20,106	C
Calvin College	MI	43,090	HC
Cameron Univ	OK	11,632	LC
Campbellsville Univ	KY	33,400	C
Carnegie Mellon Univ	PA	67,980	MC
Carroll Univ	WI	38,100	C+
Carson-Newman Univ	TN	35,900	C
Carthage College	WI	48,835	C
Case Western Reserve Univ	OH	62,284	MC
Castleton Univ	VT	20,186	C
Catawba College	NC	39,820	LC
Cedarville Univ	OH	36,244	VC
Central College	IA	44,592	C
Central Conn State Univ	CT	22,041	C
Central Methodist Univ	MO	31,500	VC
Central Mich Univ	MI	20,330	C
Central State Univ	OH	18,564	C
Central Washington Univ	WA	16,803	C
Chapman Univ	CA	65,504	HC
Charleston Southern Univ	SC	34,700	C
Chestnut Hill College	PA	47,180	C
Chicago State Univ	IL	41,620	C
CUNY/Brooklyn College	NY	7,163	C+
CUNY/Hunter College	NY	31,098	VC
CUNY/Queens College	NY	21,507	C
Claflin Univ	SC	25,592	LC
Clarke Univ	IA	42,950	C
Coe College	IA	51,570	VC
Coker College	SC	38,196	C
College of the Ozarks	MO	7,530	VC
Colo Christian Univ	CO	40,885	VC
Colo Mesa Univ	CO	19,707	LC
Colo State Univ	CO	23,033	C
Colo State Univ-Pueblo	CO	21,581	C
Columbia College	SC	36,550	C
Columbus State Univ	GA	14,336	LC
Concord Univ	WV	14,954	LC
Concordia College - Moorhead	MN	46,418	C
Concordia College - New York	NY	39,035	LC
Concordia Univ Nebr	NE	41,900	VC
Concordia Univ St. Paul	MN	29,050	C
Concordia Univ, Chicago	IL	41,522	C
Conservatory of Music of PR	PR	13,925	
Converse College	SC	28,290	C
Corban Univ	OR	41,700	C
Cornell College	IA	49,900	VC
Cornerstone Univ	MI	36,550	C
Culver-Stockton College	MO	34,350	C
Cumberland Univ	TN	27,710	C
Delaware State Univ	DE	19,376	LC
Delta State Univ	MS	13,176	LC
DePaul Univ	IL	52,807	VC
DePauw Univ	IN	58,688	VC
Dickinson State Univ	ND	12,372	LC
Dordt College	IA	37,860	C+
Drake Univ	IA	49,220	HC
Drury Univ	MO	37,555	VC
Duquesne Univ	PA	48,508	VC
East Carolina Univ	NC	16,539	C
East Central Univ	OK	13,330	C
East Texas Baptist Univ	TX	34,444	C
Eastern Kentucky Univ	KY	17,742	C
Eastern Mich Univ	MI	19,761	C
Eastern Nazarene College	MA	41,114	C
Eastern New Mexico Univ	NM	12,874	LC
Eastern Washington Univ	WA	17,896	LC
Eastman School of Music/ Univ of Rochester	NY	68,060	SP
Edgewood College	WI	35,950	C
Edinboro Univ	PA	15,940	LC
Elizabethtown College	PA	56,340	VC
Elmhurst College	IL	46,514	C
Elon Univ	NC	46,142	HC
Emporia State Univ	KS	15,029	C
Eureka College	IL	34,760	C
Evangel Univ	MO	28,898	C
Fairmont State Univ	WV	15,726	C
Faulkner Univ	AL	26,410	C
Fayetteville State Univ	NC	17,756	C
Fisk Univ	TN	32,066	LC
Five Towns College	NY	35,480	LC
Florida A&M Univ	FL	15,361	C
Florida Gulf Coast Univ	FL	14,738	C
Florida Southern College	FL	45,978	VC
Florida State Univ	FL	16,771	HC
Fort Hays State Univ	KS	12,677	C
Freed-Hardeman Univ	TN	29,900	C
Fresno Pacific Univ	CA	38,858	C

School	ST	$IS	SR
Friends Univ	KS	38,000	C
Furman Univ	SC	61,098	VC+
Gardner-Webb Univ	NC	24,935	C+
Geneva College	PA	35,450	C
George Fox Univ	OR	42,938	C
Georgia College & State Univ	GA	21,884	C+
Georgia Southern Univ	GA	16,540	VC
Gettysburg College	PA	65,210	MC
Glenville State College	WV	17,386	LC
Gonzaga Univ	WA	52,880	HC
Gordon College	MA	47,740	VC
Goshen College	IN	44,350	C
Grace College and Seminary	IN	31,524	C
Graceland Univ	IA	35,290	C
Grand Canyon Univ	AZ	25,150	VC
Grand Valley State Univ	MI	22,250	C+
Grand View Univ	IA	32,302	C
Greensboro College	NC	39,790	LC
Greenville College	IL	27,012	LC
Grove City College	PA	26,654	VC
Gustavus Adolphus College	MN	53,943	HC
Hamline Univ	MN	50,152	C
Harding Univ	AR	25,440	C
Hardin-Simmons Univ	TX	36,025	C
Hartwick College	NY	51,270	C
Hastings College	NE	35,380	C+
Heidelberg Univ	OH	40,400	LC
Henderson State Univ	AR	15,516	C
Hofstra Univ	NY	58,210	C+
Hope College	MI	42,840	VC
Houghton College	NY	40,558	VC
Houston Baptist Univ	TX	36,450	C
Howard Univ	DC	37,616	C+
Humboldt State Univ	CA	21,708	C
Huntingdon College	AL	35,900	C
Huntington Univ	IN	33,996	C
Idaho State Univ	ID	13,619	LC
Illinois State Univ	IL	23,418	VC
Illinois Wesleyan Univ	IL	56,430	VC+
Immaculata Univ	PA	39,000	C
Indiana State Univ	IN	23,223	LC
Indiana Univ Bloomington	IN	20,791	HC
Indiana Univ of Pennsylvania	PA	24,474	C
Indiana Univ South Bend	IN	16,057	C
Indiana Univ-Purdue Univ Fort Wayne	IN	18,675	C
Indiana Wesleyan Univ	IN	33,674	C
Inter-American Univ of PR Ponce	PR	19,549	
Inter-American Univ of PR-Fajardo Campus	PR	18,336	
Inter-American Univ of PR-San Germán	PR	20,042	
Iowa State Univ	IA	18,176	C
Iowa Wesleyan Univ	IA	41,000	C
Ithaca College	NY	58,158	VC+
Jackson State Univ	MS	15,879	LC
Jacksonville State Univ	AL	14,628	LC
Jacksonville Univ	FL	49,210	C
John Brown Univ	AR	35,184	VC
Johns Hopkins Univ	MD	68,080	MC
Johnson State College	VT	22,672	C
Judson College	AL	27,066	C
Judson Univ	IL	39,174	C
Kansas State Univ	KS	17,780	VC
Kansas Wesleyan Univ	KS	37,930	C
Kean Univ	NJ	25,620	C
Keene State College	NH	24,604	C
Kennesaw State Univ	GA	18,899	VC
Kent State Univ	OH	20,928	C
Kentucky Christian Univ	KY	26,836	LC
Kentucky State Univ	KY	14,484	LC
Kentucky Wesleyan College	KY	34,260	LC
King Univ	TN	36,976	C
Kutztown Univ of Pennsylvania	PA	19,477	C
La Sierra Univ	CA	39,690	VC
Lake Forest College	IL	50,652	VC
Lakeland Univ	WI	35,130	C
Lamar Univ	TX	18,014	LC
Lander Univ	SC	32,200	C
Lawrence Univ	WI	56,133	HC+
Lebanon Valley College	PA	55,510	VC
Lee Univ	TN	22,045	C
Lenoir-Rhyne Univ	NC	47,500	LC
Limestone College	SC	32,100	C
Lindenwood Univ	MO	25,760	C
Lindsey Wilson College	KY	33,546	C
Lipscomb Univ	TN	42,984	VC
LIU Brooklyn	NY	50,698	C
LIU Post	NY	50,698	C+
Livingstone College	NC	17,815	LC
Longwood Univ	VA	22,184	C
Loras College	IA	40,726	C
Louisiana College	LA	21,274	C
Louisiana State Univ and A&M College	LA	18,677	VC
Louisiana Tech Univ	LA	11,422	VC
Loyola Univ New Orleans	LA	52,456	VC
Lubbock Christian Univ	TX	29,727	C
MacMurray College	IL	35,025	C
Madonna Univ	MI	30,450	LC
Malone Univ	OH	39,200	C
Mansfield Univ of Pennsylvania	PA	24,244	LC
Marian Univ	WI	34,622	C
Marietta College	OH	46,190	C
Mars Hill Univ	NC	41,104	C
Marshall Univ	WV	18,044	C
Maryville College	TN	44,410	C
Marywood Univ	PA	47,840	C
McKendree Univ	IL	37,940	C+
Mercer Univ	GA	45,348	VC
Mercyhurst Univ	PA	47,420	C
Meredith College	NC	46,634	C
Messiah College	PA	44,380	VC
Methodist Univ	NC	58,130	C
Metropolitan State Univ of Denver	CO	6,928	LC
Miami Univ	OH	27,190	HC+
Mich State Univ	MI	24,542	VC
MidAmerica Nazarene Univ	KS	37,808	C
Midland Univ	NE	39,512	C
Midwestern State Univ	TX	12,111	LC
Millersville Univ of Pennsylvania	PA	25,298	C
Milligan College	TN	39,450	C
Millikin Univ	IL	44,148	C
Minn State Univ, Mankato	MN	17,190	C
Minn State Univ, Moorhead	MN	21,393	C
Minot State Univ	ND	13,285	C
Miss College	MS	25,850	C
Miss State Univ	MS	12,028	C+
Miss Univ for Women	MS	17,065	C
Miss Valley State Univ	MS	13,233	LC
Missouri Baptist Univ	MO	35,594	C
Missouri Western State Univ	MO	17,822	LC
Molloy College	NY	40,440	C
Monmouth Univ	NJ	50,184	C
Montana State Univ	MT	15,500	C+
Montana State Univ Billings	MT	13,336	LC
Moravian College	PA	55,488	C
Morningside College	IA	39,780	C
Mount Vernon Nazarene Univ	OH	35,944	C
Muskingum Univ	OH	35,966	C
Nazareth College	NY	46,784	C
Nebr Wesleyan Univ	NE	42,026	C+
New Jersey City Univ	NJ	21,456	LC
New Mexico State Univ	NM	14,050	LC
New York Univ	NY	68,139	MC
Newberry College	SC	34,550	C
Nicholls State Univ	LA	14,959	C
Norfolk State Univ	VA	18,902	LC
N Car A&T State Univ	NC	13,786	C
North Central College	IL	48,712	C+
North Central Univ	MN	30,610	C
N Dak State Univ	ND	16,245	VC
North Greenville Univ	SC	25,930	C
Northeastern Illinois Univ	IL	12,529	LC
Northeastern State Univ	OK	8,615	VC
Northern Arizona Univ	AZ	21,003	C
Northern Illinois Univ	IL	20,176	C
Northern Kentucky Univ	KY	16,486	C
Northern Mich Univ	MI	20,853	C
Northern State Univ	SD	15,570	C
Northwest Missouri State Univ	MO	18,286	C
Northwest Nazarene Univ	ID	40,250	C
Northwestern College of Iowa	IA	38,400	C
Northwestern Okla State Univ	OK	13,072	LC
Northwestern State Univ of Louisiana	LA	16,534	LC
Northwestern Univ	IL	68,725	MC
Notre Dame of Maryland Univ	MD	47,570	VC
Nyack College	NY	34,450	LC
Oakland City Univ	IN	33,930	NC
Oakland Univ	MI	20,763	C
Oakwood Univ	AL	43,758	C
Oberlin College	OH	68,942	MC
Ohio Northern Univ	OH	44,050	VC
Ohio State Univ at Columbus	OH	22,843	MC
Ohio Univ	OH	23,394	VC
Ohio Wesleyan Univ	OH	49,460	VC
Okla Baptist Univ	OK	33,990	C
Okla Christian Univ	OK	29,260	C
Okla City Univ	OK	40,476	C
Okla State Univ	OK	17,180	C+
Okla Wesleyan Univ	OK	34,434	C
Old Dominion Univ	VA	21,618	C
Olivet Nazarene Univ	IL	41,840	VC
Oral Roberts Univ	OK	34,316	C
Otterbein Univ	OH	41,630	C
Ouachita Baptist Univ	AR	33,500	VC
Pacific Lutheran Univ	WA	49,960	C
Palm Beach Atlantic Univ	FL	39,250	C
Pennsylvania State Univ - Univ Park	PA	29,716	HC
Peru State College	NE	15,602	LC
Piedmont College	GA	34,334	C
Pittsburg State Univ	KS	13,880	C
Plymouth State Univ	NH	23,180	LC
Point Loma Nazarene Univ	CA	46,150	C+
Pontifical Catholic Univ of PR	PR	10,534	
Providence College	RI	62,870	HC
Quincy Univ	IL	38,170	LC
Rhode Island College	RI	19,000	LC
Rider Univ	NJ	54,050	C
Roberts Wesleyan College	NY	41,116	C
Rocky Mountain College	MT	35,776	C
Roosevelt Univ	IL	41,890	VC
Rowan Univ	NJ	24,491	VC
Saginaw Valley State Univ	MI	19,284	C
St. Anselm College	NH	56,636	VC
St. Augustine's Univ	NC	25,582	C
St. Mary's Univ of Minn	MN	42,440	C
St. Xavier Univ	IL	44,440	C
Samford Univ	AL	40,770	VC
San Diego State Univ	CA	23,156	VC
San Jose State Univ	CA	22,630	C
Schreiner Univ	TX	34,626	LC
Seattle Pacific Univ	WA	47,439	C+
Seton Hill Univ	PA	46,972	VC
Shawnee State Univ	OH	16,998	C
Shenandoah Univ	VA	42,100	C
Shepherd Univ, West Virginia	WV	17,382	C
Shorter Univ	GA	31,130	LC
Siena Heights Univ	MI	36,322	C
Silver Lake College of the Holy Family	WI	36,290	LC
Simpson College	IA	45,626	VC
Simpson Univ	CA	34,722	C
Slippery Rock Univ of Pennsylvania	PA	20,450	C
S Car State Univ	SC	21,330	LC
S Dak State Univ	SD	15,874	C
Southeast Missouri State Univ	MO	16,148	C
Southeastern Okla State Univ	OK	11,875	C
Southeastern Univ	FL	34,910	LC
Southern Adventist Univ	TN	28,250	C
Southern Arkansas Univ	AR	21,532	C
Southern Illinois Univ Edwardsville	IL	20,188	C
Southern Methodist Univ	TX	69,008	MC
Southern Nazarene Univ	OK	33,684	C
Southern Univ and A&M College	LA	16,074	LC
Southern Univ at New Orleans	LA	8,014	LC
Southern Wesleyan Univ	SC	33,670	LC
Southwest Baptist Univ	MO	30,890	LC
Southwest Minn State Univ	MN	17,783	C
Southwestern College	KS	31,531	LC
Southwestern Okla State Univ	OK	12,205	C
Spring Arbor Univ	MI	37,390	C
St. Ambrose Univ	IA	40,180	C
St. Catherine Univ	MN	45,630	C
St. Cloud State Univ	MN	10,600	C
St. Norbert College	WI	46,060	VC
St. Olaf College	MN	56,430	HC
SUNY/Fredonia	NY	20,818	C
SUNY/Potsdam	NY	21,051	VC
Sterling College	KS	32,830	LC
Stetson Univ	FL	57,174	VC+
Susquehanna Univ	PA	57,560	VC
Syracuse Univ	NY	62,313	HC
Tabor College	KS	35,870	C
Talladega College	AL	25,919	C
Taylor Univ	IN	42,130	VC
Temple Univ	PA	24,392	C+
Tenn Tech Univ	TN	17,929	C
Tenn Wesleyan Univ	TN	32,680	LC
Texas A&M Univ at Commerce	TX	10,496	C
Texas A&M Univ at Kingsville	TX	16,580	LC
Texas Christian Univ	TX	57,120	HC
The Boston Conservatory at Berklee	MA	61,042	SP
The Catholic Univ of America	DC	58,376	VC
The College of New Jersey	NJ	28,675	VC+
The College of St. Rose	NY	44,010	C
The Master's Univ	CA	43,870	C
The Univ of Akron	OH	22,566	C
The Univ of Alabama	AL	24,320	C+
The Univ of Arizona	AZ	24,086	C
The Univ of Mary	ND	23,180	C
The Univ of Montana Western	MT	9,426	LC
The Univ of Tenn at Chattanooga	TN	17,340	C+
Toccoa Falls College	GA	30,048	C
Tougaloo College	MS	17,980	NC
Towson Univ	MD	21,878	C
Trevecca Nazarene Univ	TN	31,186	C
Trinity Christian College	IL	35,580	C
Trinity International Univ	IL	31,070	VC
Trinity Univ	TX	54,480	MC
Troy Univ	AL	16,171	C
Union College	NE	23,270	C
Union Univ	TN	41,160	VC
Universidad Adventista de las Antillas	PR	16,606	
Univ of Alaska Anchorage	AK	17,914	C
Univ of Alaska Fairbanks	AK	16,874	VC
Univ of Arkansas at Monticello	AR	13,599	LC
Univ of Arkansas at Pine Bluff	AR	13,541	C
Univ of Central Arkansas	AR	15,042	VC
Univ of Central Florida	FL	16,379	VC
Univ of Central Missouri	MO	18,982	C
Univ of Central Okla	OK	15,150	C
Univ of Cincinnati	OH	22,118	VC
Univ of Colo Boulder	CO	26,048	HC
Univ of Conn	CT	27,394	
Univ of Dayton	OH	54,930	VC
Univ of Delaware	DE	32,214	VC
Univ of Evansville	IN	44,186	C+
Univ of Florida	FL	16,291	HC+
Univ of Georgia	GA	21,878	HC
Univ of Hartford	CT	49,776	C
Univ of Idaho	ID	16,158	C
Univ of Illinois at Urbana-Champaign	IL	27,006	HC
Univ of Indianapolis	IN	36,480	VC
Univ of Iowa	IA	19,415	HC
Univ of Kansas	KS	20,884	VC
Univ of Kentucky	KY	24,800	C+
Univ of Louisiana at Lafayette	LA	14,516	C
Univ of Louisville	KY	19,692	C
Univ of Lynchburg	VA	48,370	C
Univ of Maine	ME	21,038	VC
Univ of Mary Hardin-Baylor	TX	35,292	C+
Univ of Maryland/College Park	MD	21,938	HC
Univ of Maryland/Eastern Shore	MD	21,861	LC
Univ of Miami	FL	63,494	MC
Univ of Mich/Ann Arbor	MI	25,274	MC
Univ of Mich/Flint	MI	19,062	C
Univ of Minn/Duluth	MN	20,292	C
Univ of Minn/Twin Cities	MN	24,269	MC
Univ of Missouri-Columbia	MO	20,463	VC
Univ of Missouri-Kansas City	MO	19,563	VC
Univ of Missouri-St. Louis	MO	19,810	VC
Univ of Montana	MT	14,105	C
Univ of Montevallo	AL	20,012	C
Univ of Mount Union	OH	39,990	C
Univ of Nebr - Kearney	NE	17,014	LC
Univ of Nebr - Lincoln	NE	18,589	VC
Univ of Nevada, Reno	NV	18,010	C
Univ of New Mexico	NM	16,808	C
Univ of New Orleans	LA	12,840	C
Univ of North Alabama	AL	15,964	C
Univ of N Car at Greensboro	NC	15,998	C
Univ of N Car Wilmington	NC	16,784	VC
Univ of N Dak	ND	16,673	C
Univ of North Florida	FL	15,996	VC
Univ of North Georgia	GA	17,316	C
Univ of Northern Colo	CO	19,658	C
Univ of Northern Iowa	IA	17,480	C
Univ of Northwestern - St. Paul	MN	39,530	C
Univ of Okla	OK	19,651	HC
Univ of Oregon	OR	24,021	VC
Univ of Puget Sound	WA	60,210	HC
Univ of Redlands	CA	61,934	VC
Univ of Rio Grande & Rio Grande Community College	OH	8,750	LC
Univ of Rochester	NY	65,032	MC
Univ of Sioux Falls	SD	25,630	C
Univ of S Car Aiken	SC	18,094	C
Univ of S Car at Columbia	SC	21,726	VC
Univ of S Dak	SD	16,109	C
Univ of South Florida/Tampa	FL	16,110	VC
Univ of Southern Maine	ME	18,320	C
Univ of Southern Miss	MS	13,170	C
Univ of St. Francis	IL	40,828	C
Univ of St. Thomas - Houston	TX	41,510	VC
Univ of Tampa	FL	38,928	VC
Univ of the Cumberlands	KY	32,000	LC
Univ of the Incarnate Word	TX	39,162	LC
Univ of the Pacific	CA	57,446	VC
Univ of Toledo	OH	19,336	C
Univ of Tulsa	OK	52,625	HC
Univ of Vermont	VT	29,792	HC
Univ of Washington	WA	23,091	MC
Univ of West Florida	FL	15,848	C
Univ of West Georgia	GA	17,510	LC
Univ of Wisc-Green Bay	WI	15,184	C
Univ of Wisc-Madison	WI	21,647	MC
Univ of Wisc-Milwaukee	WI	21,538	C
Univ of Wisc-Oshkosh	WI	15,392	C
Univ of Wisc-Platteville	WI	14,148	C
Univ of Wisc-River Falls	WI	14,541	C
Univ of Wisc-Stevens Point	WI	14,043	C
Univ of Wisc-Superior	WI	14,838	C
Univ of Wisc-Whitewater	WI	13,976	C
Univ of Wyoming	WY	15,537	C
Utah State Univ	UT	13,235	C
Valparaiso Univ	IN	50,160	VC
Vanderbilt Univ	TN	63,248	MC
VanderCook College of Music	IL	31,440	SP
Virginia Union Univ	VA	25,058	C
Viterbo Univ	WI	34,660	C
Walla Walla Univ	WA	34,845	C
Warner Pacific College	OR	31,610	C
Warner Univ	FL	28,216	C
Wartburg College	IA	49,478	C
Washburn Univ	KS	15,827	C
Washington Adventist Univ	MD	32,050	LC
Washington State Univ	WA	22,747	C
Wayland Baptist Univ	TX	23,460	LC
Wayne State College	NE	25,746	NC
Weber State Univ	UT	14,112	C
Webster Univ	MO	37,490	C
West Chester Univ of Pennsylvania	PA	19,171	VC
West Liberty Univ	WV	16,158	C
West Texas A&M Univ	TX	13,478	C
West Virginia Wesleyan College	WV	39,188	C
Western Carolina Univ	NC	13,965	C
Western Conn State Univ	CT	21,254	LC
Western Mich Univ	MI	21,791	C
Western State Colo Univ	CO	19,348	C
Western Washington Univ	WA	18,904	VC
Westminster Choir College	NJ	53,730	SP
Westminster College	PA	41,722	C

ST = STATE $IS = IN-STATE COSTS SR = SELECTOR RATING

School	ST	$IS	SR
Westmont College	CA	57,930	VC
Wheaton College	IL	44,993	MC
Whitworth Univ	WA	53,682	VC
Wichita State Univ	KS	17,773	C
Wiley College	TX	19,255	C
Willamette Univ	OR	62,514	VC+
William Carey Univ	MS	23,950	LC
William Jewell College	MO	42,490	C+
William Paterson Univ of New Jersey	NJ	24,022	C
Wingate Univ	NC	41,900	C
Winona State Univ	MN	18,109	C
Winston-Salem State Univ	NC	18,005	LC
Winthrop Univ	SC	23,960	C
Wittenberg Univ	OH	49,863	VC
Wright State Univ	OH	16,983	C
Xavier Univ	OH	49,380	VC
Xavier Univ of Louisiana	LA	31,689	C
York College	NE	30,260	C
York College of Pennsylvania	PA	29,240	C
Youngstown State Univ	OH	17,487	C

MUSIC HISTORY AND APPRECIATION

School	ST	$IS	SR
Aquinas College - Mich	MI	38,876	VC
Baldwin Wallace Univ	OH	42,464	VC
Baylor Univ	TX	56,803	HC
Boston Univ	MA	67,352	MC
Bowling Green State Univ	OH	19,975	C
Bucknell Univ	PA	67,136	MC
Cal State, San Bernardino	CA	20,106	C
Calvin College	MI	43,090	HC
Central Mich Univ	MI	20,330	C
Florida State Univ	FL	16,771	HC
Hardin-Simmons Univ	TX	36,025	C
Hofstra Univ	NY	58,210	C+
Howard Univ	DC	37,616	C+
Johnson State College	VT	22,672	C
Kutztown Univ of Pennsylvania	PA	19,477	C
McKendree Univ	IL	37,940	C+
Nazareth College	NY	46,784	C
New England Conservatory of Music	MA	63,170	SP
Oberlin College	OH	68,942	MC
Ohio State Univ at Columbus	OH	22,843	MC
Ohio Univ	OH	23,394	VC
Rice Univ	TX	59,458	MC
Roosevelt Univ	IL	41,890	VC
Southern Illinois Univ Edwardsville	IL	20,188	C
Southwestern Univ	TX	52,370	VC
Suffolk Univ	MA	52,316	C
Syracuse Univ	NY	62,313	HC
Temple Univ	PA	24,392	C+
The Catholic Univ of America	DC	58,376	VC
The Univ of Akron	OH	22,566	C
Univ of Calif at Los Angeles	CA	27,438	HC+
Univ of Calif San Diego	CA	30,450	MC
Univ of Cincinnati	OH	22,118	VC
Univ of Hartford	CT	49,776	C
Univ of Idaho	ID	16,158	C
Univ of Illinois at Urbana-Champaign	IL	27,006	HC
Univ of Kansas	KS	20,884	VC
Univ of Mich/Ann Arbor	MI	25,274	MC
Univ of North Texas	TX	20,082	C
Univ of the Pacific	CA	57,446	VC
Univ of Washington	WA	23,091	MC
West Chester Univ of Pennsylvania	PA	19,171	VC
Western Washington Univ	WA	18,904	VC
Whitman College	WA	59,772	MC
Wichita State Univ	KS	17,773	C
Wright State Univ	OH	16,983	C
Youngstown State Univ	OH	17,487	C

MUSIC INDUSTRY

School	ST	$IS	SR
Bradley Univ	IL	43,240	VC
Cal State, Chico	CA	19,790	VC
Delaware State Univ	DE	19,376	LC
Drexel Univ	PA	65,927	HC
Edgewood College	WI	35,950	C
Ferris State Univ	MI	21,458	C
Loyola Univ New Orleans	LA	52,456	VC
Mercy College	NY	32,614	C
Minn State Univ, Mankato	MN	17,190	C
Missouri Southern State Univ	MO	13,071	C
Monmouth Univ	NJ	50,184	C
St. Mary's Univ of Minn	MN	42,440	C
Syracuse Univ	NY	62,313	HC
The College of St. Rose	NY	44,010	C

MUSIC MINISTRY

School	ST	$IS	SR
Cairn Univ	PA	37,572	C
College of the Ozarks	MO	7,530	VC
Hope International Univ	CA	42,730	C
John Brown Univ	AR	35,184	VC
Lipscomb Univ	TN	42,984	VC
Marian Univ	IN	43,206	C
Messiah College	PA	44,380	VC
North Central Univ	MN	30,610	C
Point Loma Nazarene Univ	CA	46,150	C+
Samford Univ	AL	40,770	VC
The Master's Univ	CA	43,870	C
Univ of Northwestern - St. Paul	MN	39,530	C

MUSIC PERFORMANCE

School	ST	$IS	SR
Adams State Univ	CO	15,420	LC
Adrian College	MI	45,550	C
Albion College	MI	55,260	C
Anderson Univ	IN	39,450	C
Andrews Univ	MI	41,732	C
Anna Maria College	MA	51,020	C
Appalachian State Univ	NC	15,394	VC
Aquinas College - Mich	MI	38,876	VC
Arizona State Univ at the Tempe Campus	AZ	23,001	VC
Armstrong State Univ	GA	15,615	C
Augusta Univ	GA	4,632	C
Augustana College	IL	51,222	VC+
Averett Univ	VA	43,034	LC
Baldwin Wallace Univ	OH	42,464	VC
Barry Univ	FL	38,730	LC
Baylor Univ	TX	56,803	HC
Belmont Univ	TN	44,500	VC+
Bennington College	VT	66,280	MC
Berklee College of Music	MA	60,930	SP
Bethel College	IN	36,830	C
Bethel Univ	MN	46,550	C+
Biola Univ	CA	48,686	C
Blackburn College	IL	28,526	LC
Boston Univ	MA	67,352	MC
Bowling Green State Univ	OH	19,975	C
Bradley Univ	IL	43,240	VC
Brenau Univ - Women's College	GA	37,876	LC
Brigham Young Univ	UT	13,248	MC
Bucknell Univ	PA	67,136	MC
Butler Univ	IN	52,890	VC+
Cairn Univ	PA	37,572	C
Calif Baptist Univ	CA	42,986	C
Calif Inst of the Arts	CA	61,366	SP
Calif Lutheran Univ	CA	52,853	C
Cal State, Fresno	CA	16,902	LC
Cal State, Fullerton	CA	21,902	C
Cal State, Los Angeles	CA	17,186	LC
Cal State, San Bernardino	CA	20,106	C
Cal State, Stanislaus	CA	18,053	LC
Calvin College	MI	43,090	HC
Campbellsville Univ	KY	33,400	C
Canisius College	NY	49,672	C
Carnegie Mellon Univ	PA	67,980	MC
Cedarville Univ	OH	36,244	VC
Centenary College of Louisiana	LA	49,050	C+
Central Mich Univ	MI	20,330	C
Chapman Univ	CA	65,504	HC
CUNY/Brooklyn College	NY	7,163	C+
CUNY/Queens College	NY	21,507	C
Clayton State Univ	GA	19,735	LC
Cleveland Inst of Music	OH	63,038	SP
Colo State Univ	CO	23,033	C
Colo State Univ-Pueblo	CO	21,581	C
Columbia College	SC	36,550	C
Columbia College Chicago	IL	40,104	C
Columbus State Univ	GA	14,336	LC
Concordia College - Moorhead	MN	46,418	C
Corban Univ	OR	41,700	C
Cornerstone Univ	MI	36,550	C
Covenant College	GA	44,590	HC
Dallas Baptist Univ	TX	35,220	VC
DePaul Univ	IL	52,807	VC
DePauw Univ	IN	58,688	VC
Dillard Univ	LA	20,940	VC
Dordt College	IA	37,860	C+
Drake Univ	IA	49,220	HC
Duquesne Univ	PA	48,508	VC
East Carolina Univ	NC	16,539	C
East Texas Baptist Univ	TX	34,444	C
Eastern Mich Univ	MI	19,761	C
Eastern Nazarene College	MA	41,114	C
Eastern Washington Univ	WA	17,896	LC
Eastman School of Music/ Univ of Rochester	NY	68,060	SP
Elmhurst College	IL	46,514	C
Elon Univ	NC	46,142	HC
Emory and Henry College	VA	46,320	C
Evangel Univ	MO	28,898	C
Five Towns College	NY	35,480	LC
Florida International Univ	FL	20,281	C
Florida Southern College	FL	45,978	VC
Florida State Univ	FL	16,771	HC
Fort Hays State Univ	KS	12,677	C
Friends Univ	KS	38,000	C
Furman Univ	SC	61,098	VC+
Gettysburg College	PA	65,210	MC
Gordon College	MA	47,740	VC
Grand Canyon Univ	AZ	25,150	VC
Grove City College	PA	26,654	VC
Hamline Univ	MN	50,152	C
Hannibal-LaGrange Univ	MO	29,815	C
Hardin-Simmons Univ	TX	36,025	C
Hofstra Univ	NY	58,210	C+
Hope College	MI	42,840	VC
Houghton College	NY	40,558	VC
Houston Baptist Univ	TX	36,450	C
Huntington Univ	IN	33,996	C
Idaho State Univ	ID	13,619	LC
Illinois State Univ	IL	23,418	VC
Illinois Wesleyan Univ	IL	56,430	VC+
Indiana Univ Bloomington	IN	20,791	HC
Indiana Univ of Pennsylvania	PA	24,474	C
Indiana Univ-Purdue Univ Fort Wayne	IN	18,675	C
Inter-American Univ of PR-Metropolitan Campus	PR	20,045	
Ithaca College	NY	58,158	VC+
Jacksonville Univ	FL	49,210	C
John Brown Univ	AR	35,184	VC
Johnson State College	VT	22,672	C
Kean Univ	NJ	25,620	C
Keene State College	NH	24,604	C
Kennesaw State Univ	GA	18,899	VC
Kentucky Christian Univ	KY	26,836	LC
Kentucky State Univ	KY	14,484	LC
Kutztown Univ of Pennsylvania	PA	19,477	C
La Sierra Univ	CA	39,690	VC
Lawrence Univ	WI	56,133	HC+
Lee Univ	TN	22,045	C
Lenoir-Rhyne Univ	NC	47,500	LC
Lipscomb Univ	TN	42,984	VC
LIU Brooklyn	NY	50,698	C
LIU Post	NY	50,698	C+
Louisiana College	LA	21,274	C
Louisiana Tech Univ	LA	11,422	VC
Loyola Univ New Orleans	LA	52,456	VC
Lynn Univ	FL	49,680	LC
Manhattan School of Music	NY	57,200	SP
Mannes School of Music	NY	44,500	SP
Mansfield Univ of Pennsylvania	PA	24,244	LC
Mars Hill Univ	NC	41,104	C
Marshall Univ	WV	18,044	C
Maryville College	TN	44,410	C
Marywood Univ	PA	47,840	C
McKendree Univ	IL	37,940	C+
Messiah College	PA	44,380	VC
Methodist Univ	NC	58,130	C
Metropolitan State Univ of Denver	CO	6,928	LC
Miami Univ	OH	27,190	HC+
Mich State Univ	MI	24,542	VC
Millikin Univ	IL	44,148	C
Missouri Baptist Univ	MO	35,594	C
Missouri Western State Univ	MO	17,822	LC
Montana State Univ Billings	MT	13,336	LC
Murray State Univ	KY	17,726	C+
Nazareth College	NY	46,784	C
New England Conservatory of Music	MA	63,170	SP
New Mexico State Univ	NM	14,050	LC
New York Univ	NY	68,139	MC
Newberry College	SC	34,550	C
North Central Univ	MN	30,610	C
North Greenville Univ	SC	25,930	C
Northern Arizona Univ	AZ	21,003	C
Northern Kentucky Univ	KY	16,486	C
Northwestern Univ	IL	68,725	MC
Nyack College	NY	34,450	LC
Oakwood Univ	AL	43,758	C
Oberlin College	OH	68,942	MC
Ohio Northern Univ	OH	44,050	VC
Ohio State Univ at Columbus	OH	22,843	MC
Ohio Univ	OH	23,394	VC
Ohio Wesleyan Univ	OH	49,460	VC
Old Dominion Univ	VA	21,618	C
Olivet Nazarene Univ	IL	41,840	VC
Oral Roberts Univ	OK	34,316	C
Otterbein Univ	OH	41,630	C
Pacific Lutheran Univ	WA	49,960	C
Palm Beach Atlantic Univ	FL	39,250	C
Point Loma Nazarene Univ	CA	46,150	C+
Regis Univ	CO	46,380	C
Rhode Island College	RI	19,000	LC
Rice Univ	TX	59,458	MC
Roberts Wesleyan College	NY	41,116	C
Rockford Univ	IL	38,570	C
Rocky Mountain College	MT	35,776	C
Rollins College	FL	58,670	HC
Roosevelt Univ	IL	41,890	VC
Rutgers Univ - New Brunswick	NJ	27,090	HC
St. Mary's Univ of Minn	MN	42,440	C
St. Vincent College	PA	46,229	C
Sam Houston State Univ	TX	18,792	C
Samford Univ	AL	40,770	VC
San Diego State Univ	CA	23,156	VC
San Francisco Conservatory of Music	CA	57,310	SP
Shepherd Univ	CA		LC
Silver Lake College of the Holy Family	WI	36,290	LC
Simpson College	IA	45,626	VC
Southeastern Univ	FL	34,910	LC
Southern Illinois Univ Edwardsville	IL	20,188	C
Southern Methodist Univ	TX	69,008	MC
Southern Nazarene Univ	OK	33,684	C
Southern Oregon Univ	OR	19,117	C
Southwestern College	KS	31,531	LC
Southwestern Univ	TX	52,370	VC
St. Olaf College	MN	56,430	HC
SUNY at Binghamton	NY	24,100	MC
SUNY/Fredonia	NY	20,818	C
SUNY/Potsdam	NY	21,051	VC
SUNY/Univ at Buffalo	NY	23,122	C
Stetson Univ	FL	57,174	VC+
Susquehanna Univ	PA	57,560	VC
Talladega College	AL	25,919	C
Taylor Univ	IN	42,130	VC
Temple Univ	PA	24,392	C+
Texas State Univ	TX	18,721	C
The Boston Conservatory at Berklee	MA	61,042	SP
The Catholic Univ of America	DC	58,376	VC
The College of St. Rose	NY	44,010	C
The George Washington Univ	DC	68,474	HC+
The Univ of Akron	OH	22,566	C
Toccoa Falls College	GA	30,048	C
Tougaloo College	MS	17,980	NC
Trinity Christian College	IL	35,580	C
Trinity Univ	TX	54,480	MC
Truman State Univ	MO	16,286	MC
Union College	NE	23,270	C
Union Univ	TN	41,160	VC
Univ of Alaska Anchorage	AK	17,914	C
Univ of Alaska Fairbanks	AK	16,874	VC
Univ of Calif at Irvine	CA	33,857	VC
Univ of Calif at Santa Barbara	CA	30,627	HC+
Univ of Central Florida	FL	16,379	VC
Univ of Cincinnati	OH	22,118	VC
Univ of Colo Boulder	CO	26,048	HC
Univ of Conn	CT	27,394	
Univ of Dayton	OH	54,930	VC
Univ of Denver	CO	61,129	VC+
Univ of Evansville	IN	44,186	C+
Univ of Georgia	GA	21,878	HC
Univ of Hartford	CT	49,776	C
Univ of Idaho	ID	16,158	C
Univ of Illinois at Chicago	IL	24,664	VC
Univ of Illinois at Urbana-Champaign	IL	27,006	HC
Univ of Indianapolis	IN	36,480	VC
Univ of Kansas	KS	20,884	VC
Univ of Kentucky	KY	24,800	C+
Univ of Maine	ME	21,038	VC
Univ of Mary Hardin-Baylor	TX	35,292	C+
Univ of Maryland/College Park	MD	21,938	HC
Univ of Mass Amherst	MA	27,669	HC
Univ of Mass Lowell	MA	27,296	VC
Univ of Miami	FL	63,494	MC
Univ of Mich/Ann Arbor	MI	25,274	MC
Univ of Minn/Duluth	MN	20,292	C
Univ of Missouri-Kansas City	MO	19,563	VC
Univ of Mobile	AL	28,935	C
Univ of Montana	MT	14,105	C
Univ of Montevallo	AL	20,012	C
Univ of New Haven	CT	53,680	C
Univ of N Car at Chapel Hill	NC	20,561	MC
Univ of N Car at Charlotte	NC	17,803	VC
Univ of N Dak	ND	16,673	C
Univ of North Florida	FL	15,996	VC
Univ of North Texas	TX	20,082	C
Univ of Northern Iowa	IA	17,480	C
Univ of Northwestern - St. Paul	MN	39,530	C
Univ of Okla	OK	19,651	HC
Univ of Oregon	OR	24,021	VC
Univ of Puget Sound	WA	60,210	HC
Univ of Rochester	NY	65,032	MC
Univ of S Car Upstate	SC	19,272	LC
Univ of S Dak	SD	16,109	C
Univ of Southern Calif	CA	66,631	MC
Univ of Southern Maine	ME	18,320	C
Univ of St. Francis	IL	40,828	C
Univ of Tampa	FL	38,928	VC
Univ of the Arts	PA	56,579	SP
Univ of the Pacific	CA	57,446	VC
Univ of Tulsa	OK	52,625	HC
Univ of Washington	WA	23,091	MC
Univ of West Georgia	GA	17,510	LC
Univ of Wisc-Madison	WI	21,647	MC
Univ of Wisc-Superior	WI	14,838	C
Univ of Wyoming	WY	15,537	C
Valparaiso Univ	IN	50,160	VC
Vanderbilt Univ	TN	63,248	MC
Virginia State Univ	VA	19,802	C+
Viterbo Univ	WI	34,660	C
Walla Walla Univ	WA	34,845	C
Wartburg College	IA	49,478	C
Washburn Univ	KS	15,827	C
Washington Adventist Univ	MD	32,050	LC
Washington State Univ	WA	22,747	C
Weber State Univ	UT	14,112	C
Webster Univ	MO	37,490	C
West Chester Univ of Pennsylvania	PA	19,171	VC
Western Conn State Univ	CT	21,254	LC
Western Mich Univ	MI	21,791	C
Westminster College	PA	41,722	C
Whitman College	WA	59,772	MC
Wiley College	TX	19,255	C
Willamette Univ	OR	62,514	VC+
William Carey Univ	MS	23,950	LC
Winona State Univ	MN	18,109	C
Winthrop Univ	SC	23,960	C
Xavier Univ of Louisiana	LA	31,689	C
York College	NE	30,260	C
Youngstown State Univ	OH	17,487	C

ST = STATE **$IS** = IN-STATE COSTS **SR** = SELECTOR RATING

MUSIC PRODUCTION/ RECORDING TECHNOLOGY

School	ST	$IS	SR
Buena Vista Univ	IA	42,344	C
Calif Lutheran Univ	CA	52,853	C
Cleveland Inst of Music	OH	63,038	SP
Edgewood College	WI	35,950	C
Kutztown Univ of Pennsylvania	PA	19,477	C
Loyola Marymount Univ	CA	60,202	VC+
Missouri Western State Univ	MO	17,822	LC
North Central Univ	MN	30,610	C
Old Dominion Univ	VA	21,618	C
Shenandoah Univ	VA	42,100	C
Shepherd Univ	CA		LC
Syracuse Univ	NY	62,313	HC
The Master's Univ	CA	43,870	C
Trinity Christian College	IL	35,580	C
Univ of Denver	CO	61,129	VC+

MUSIC TECHNOLOGY

School	ST	$IS	SR
Bellarmine Univ	KY	52,532	C
Berklee College of Music	MA	60,930	SP
Bethany College	WV	38,774	LC
Bloomfield College	NJ	40,100	LC
Brigham Young Univ	UT	13,248	MC
Cal State, Fullerton	CA	21,902	C
Cal State, San Bernardino	CA	20,106	C
Cogswell Polytechnical College	CA	31,511	C
Columbia College Chicago	IL	40,104	C
Conn College	CT	65,000	MC
Culver-Stockton College	MO	34,350	C
Duquesne Univ	PA	48,508	VC
Elon Univ	NC	46,142	HC
Indiana Univ-Purdue Univ Indianapolis	IN	18,952	C
Keene State College	NH	24,604	C
Malone Univ	OH	39,200	C
Mercy College	NY	32,614	C
Millersville Univ of Pennsylvania	PA	25,298	C
Minn State Univ, Moorhead	MN	21,393	C
Missouri Baptist Univ	MO	35,594	C
Missouri Western State Univ	MO	17,822	LC
New York Univ	NY	68,139	MC
Northeastern Univ	MA	65,352	MC
Northwestern Univ	IL	68,725	MC
Shenandoah Univ	VA	42,100	C
Stetson Univ	FL	57,174	VC+
Stevens Inst of Technology	NJ	64,954	MC
Transylvania Univ	KY	47,450	HC+
Univ of Calif San Diego	CA	30,450	MC
Univ of Hartford	CT	49,776	C
Univ of Miami	FL	63,494	MC
Univ of Mich/Ann Arbor	MI	25,274	MC
Univ of New Haven	CT	53,680	C
Univ of N Car at Asheville	NC	16,251	VC+
Univ of St. Francis	IN	38,520	C
York College of Pennsylvania	PA	29,240	C

MUSIC THEATRE ACCOMPANYING

School	ST	$IS	SR
College of the Ozarks	MO	7,530	VC
Shenandoah Univ	VA	42,100	C

MUSIC THEORY AND COMPOSITION

School	ST	$IS	SR
Adams State Univ	CO	15,420	LC
Aquinas College - Mich	MI	38,876	VC
Baldwin Wallace Univ	OH	42,464	VC
Baylor Univ	TX	56,803	HC
Belmont Univ	TN	44,500	VC+
Bennington College	VT	66,280	MC
Berklee College of Music	MA	60,930	SP
Biola Univ	CA	48,686	C
Boston Univ	MA	67,352	MC
Bowling Green State Univ	OH	19,975	C
Brigham Young Univ	UT	13,248	MC
Bucknell Univ	PA	67,136	MC
Butler Univ	IN	52,890	VC+
Calif Inst of the Arts	CA	61,366	SP
Calvin College	MI	43,090	HC
Central Mich Univ	MI	20,330	C
Central Washington Univ	WA	16,803	C
Chapman Univ	CA	65,504	HC
CUNY/Brooklyn College	NY	7,163	C+
Clayton State Univ	GA	19,735	LC
College of the Ozarks	MO	7,530	VC
Colo State Univ	CO	23,033	C
Colo State Univ-Pueblo	CO	21,581	C
Concordia College - Moorhead	MN	46,418	C
Dallas Baptist Univ	TX	35,220	VC
DePaul Univ	IL	52,807	VC
DePauw Univ	IN	58,688	VC
Dordt College	IA	37,860	C+
East Carolina Univ	NC	16,539	C
Eastman School of Music/ Univ of Rochester	NY	68,060	SP
Elmhurst College	IL	46,514	C
Emory and Henry College	VA	46,320	C
Five Towns College	NY	35,480	LC
Florida State Univ	FL	16,771	HC
Fordham Univ	NY	68,431	MC
Fort Hays State Univ	KS	12,677	C
Furman Univ	SC	61,098	VC+
Hardin-Simmons Univ	TX	36,025	C
Hofstra Univ	NY	58,210	C+
Houghton College	NY	40,558	VC
Houston Baptist Univ	TX	36,450	C
Huntington Univ	IN	33,996	C
Illinois Wesleyan Univ	IL	56,430	VC+
Indiana Univ Bloomington	IN	20,791	HC
Indiana Wesleyan Univ	IN	33,674	C
Ithaca College	NY	58,158	VC+
Jacksonville Univ	FL	49,210	C
Lawrence Univ	WI	56,133	HC+
Lehigh Univ	PA	63,860	MC
Loyola Univ New Orleans	LA	52,456	VC
Manhattan School of Music	NY	57,200	SP
Mannes School of Music	NY	44,500	SP
Marshall Univ	WV	18,044	C
Mich State Univ	MI	24,542	VC
Miss College	MS	25,850	C
Nazareth College	NY	46,784	C
New England Conservatory of Music	MA	63,170	SP
New York Univ	NY	68,139	MC
Newberry College	SC	34,550	C
North Park Univ	IL	35,860	C
Northwestern Univ	IL	68,725	MC
Nyack College	NY	34,450	LC
Oberlin College	OH	68,942	MC
Ohio Northern Univ	OH	44,050	VC
Ohio State Univ at Columbus	OH	22,843	MC
Ohio Univ	OH	23,394	VC
Old Dominion Univ	VA	21,618	C
Olivet Nazarene Univ	IL	41,840	VC
Oral Roberts Univ	OK	34,316	C
Pacific Lutheran Univ	WA	49,960	C
Palm Beach Atlantic Univ	FL	39,250	C
Rice Univ	TX	59,458	MC
Roosevelt Univ	IL	41,890	VC
Sam Houston State Univ	TX	18,792	C
Seton Hill Univ	PA	46,972	VC
Southern Illinois Univ Edwardsville	IL	20,188	C
Southern Methodist Univ	TX	69,008	MC
St. Olaf College	MN	56,430	HC
SUNY/Fredonia	NY	20,818	C
Stetson Univ	FL	57,174	VC+
Taylor Univ	IN	42,130	VC
Temple Univ	PA	24,392	C+
Texas Christian Univ	TX	57,120	HC
The Boston Conservatory at Berklee	MA	61,042	SP
The Catholic Univ of America	DC	58,376	VC
The College of Idaho	ID	36,415	C
The College of Wooster	OH	60,000	HC
The Master's Univ	CA	43,870	C
The Univ of Akron	OH	22,566	C
The Univ of Texas at Austin	TX	20,206	MC
Union Univ	TN	41,160	VC
Univ of Calif at Santa Barbara	CA	30,627	HC+
Univ of Cincinnati	OH	22,118	VC
Univ of Dayton	OH	54,930	VC
Univ of Delaware	DE	32,214	VC
Univ of Georgia	GA	21,878	HC
Univ of Hartford	CT	49,776	C
Univ of Idaho	ID	16,158	C
Univ of Illinois at Urbana-Champaign	IL	27,006	HC
Univ of Kansas	KS	20,884	VC
Univ of Maryland/College Park	MD	21,938	HC
Univ of Mich/Ann Arbor	MI	25,274	MC
Univ of Missouri-Kansas City	MO	19,563	VC
Univ of North Texas	TX	20,082	C
Univ of Northern Iowa	IA	17,480	C
Univ of Northwestern - St. Paul	MN	39,530	C
Univ of Oregon	OR	24,021	VC
Univ of Rochester	NY	65,032	MC
Univ of the Arts	PA	56,579	SP
Univ of the Pacific	CA	57,446	VC
Valparaiso Univ	IN	50,160	VC
Vanderbilt Univ	TN	63,248	MC
Washington State Univ	WA	22,747	C
Washington Univ in St. Louis	MO	67,539	MC
Webster Univ	MO	37,490	C
West Chester Univ of Pennsylvania	PA	19,171	VC
West Texas A&M Univ	TX	13,478	C
Western Mich Univ	MI	21,791	C
Westminster Choir College	NJ	53,730	SP
Westminster College	PA	41,722	C
Whitman College	WA	59,772	MC
Willamette Univ	OR	62,514	VC+
Wright State Univ	OH	16,983	C
Youngstown State Univ	OH	17,487	C

MUSIC THERAPY

School	ST	$IS	SR
Alverno College	WI	33,294	LC
Anna Maria College	MA	51,020	C
Appalachian State Univ	NC	15,394	VC
Arizona State Univ at the Tempe Campus	AZ	23,001	VC
Augsburg Univ	MN	45,129	C
Baldwin Wallace Univ	OH	42,464	VC
Berklee College of Music	MA	60,930	SP
Carroll Univ	WI	38,100	C+
Charleston Southern Univ	SC	34,700	C
Colo State Univ	CO	23,033	C
Drury Univ	MO	37,555	VC
Duquesne Univ	PA	48,508	VC
East Carolina Univ	NC	16,539	C
Eastern Mich Univ	MI	19,761	C
Elizabethtown College	PA	56,340	VC
Florida State Univ	FL	16,771	HC
Georgia College & State Univ	GA	21,884	C+
Howard Univ	DC	37,616	C+
Immaculata Univ	PA	39,000	C
Indiana Univ-Purdue Univ Fort Wayne	IN	18,675	C
Loyola Univ New Orleans	LA	52,456	VC
Lubbock Christian Univ	TX	29,727	C
Marylhurst Univ	OR	16,818	NC
Maryville Univ of St. Louis	MO	38,558	VC
Marywood Univ	PA	47,840	C
Mich State Univ	MI	24,542	VC
Molloy College	NY	40,440	C
Montclair State Univ	NJ	26,912	C
Nazareth College	NY	46,784	C
New York Univ	NY	68,139	MC
Ohio Univ	OH	23,394	VC
Queens Univ of Charlotte	NC	39,543	C
St. Mary-of-the-Woods College	IN	40,424	LC
Sam Houston State Univ	TX	18,792	C
Seton Hill Univ	PA	46,972	VC
Shenandoah Univ	VA	42,100	C
Southern Methodist Univ	TX	69,008	MC
Southwestern Okla State Univ	OK	12,205	C
SUNY at New Paltz	NY	20,840	C
SUNY/Fredonia	NY	20,818	C
Taylor Univ	IN	42,130	VC
Temple Univ	PA	24,392	C+
Texas Woman's Univ	TX	15,302	LC
The Univ of Alabama	AL	24,320	C+
Univ of Dayton	OH	54,930	VC
Univ of Evansville	IN	44,186	C+
Univ of Georgia	GA	21,878	HC
Univ of Iowa	IA	19,415	HC
Univ of Kansas	KS	20,884	VC
Univ of Louisville	KY	19,692	C
Univ of Miami	FL	63,494	MC
Univ of Minn/Twin Cities	MN	24,269	MC
Univ of Missouri-Kansas City	MO	19,563	VC
Univ of N Dak	ND	16,673	C
Univ of the Incarnate Word	TX	39,162	LC
Univ of the Pacific	CA	57,446	VC
Univ of Wisc-Oshkosh	WI	15,392	C
Utah State Univ	UT	13,235	C
Wartburg College	IA	49,478	C
West Texas A&M Univ	TX	13,478	C
Western Mich Univ	MI	21,791	C
William Carey Univ	MS	23,950	LC

MUSICAL THEATER

School	ST	$IS	SR
Adrian College	MI	45,550	C
Aquinas College - Mich	MI	38,876	VC
Arcadia Univ	PA	55,990	C+
Arizona State Univ at the Tempe Campus	AZ	23,001	VC
Ashland Univ	OH	30,446	C
Aurora Univ	IL	34,990	C
Baldwin Wallace Univ	OH	42,464	VC
Belmont Univ	TN	44,500	VC+
Birmingham-Southern College	AL	44,478	C+
Blackburn College	IL	28,526	LC
Brenau Univ - Women's College	GA	37,876	LC
Brigham Young Univ	UT	13,248	MC
Bryan College	TN	32,900	C
Cal State, Chico	CA	19,790	VC
Cal State, Fullerton	CA	21,902	C
Catawba College	NC	39,820	LC
Central Mich Univ	MI	20,330	C
Clarke Univ	IA	42,950	C
Clayton State Univ	GA	19,735	LC
Coastal Carolina Univ	SC	20,340	C
Coker College	SC	38,196	C
College of the Ozarks	MO	7,530	VC
Columbia College Chicago	IL	40,104	C
Cornerstone Univ	MI	36,550	C
Creighton Univ	NE	49,452	VC
Culver-Stockton College	MO	34,350	C
Elon Univ	NC	46,142	HC
Emerson College	MA	61,824	HC+
Faulkner Univ	AL	26,410	C
Florida Southern College	FL	45,978	VC
Florida State Univ	FL	16,771	HC
Friends Univ	KS	38,000	C
Howard Univ	DC	37,616	C+
Illinois Wesleyan Univ	IL	56,430	VC+
Indiana Univ Bloomington	IN	20,791	HC
Ithaca College	NY	58,158	VC+
Kutztown Univ of Pennsylvania	PA	19,477	C
Lees-McRae College	NC	33,944	NC
Limestone College	SC	32,100	C
Lipscomb Univ	TN	42,984	VC
Mars Hill Univ	NC	41,104	C
Marywood Univ	PA	47,840	C
Mercyhurst Univ	PA	47,420	C
Messiah College	PA	44,380	VC
Millikin Univ	IL	44,148	C
Missouri Baptist Univ	MO	35,594	C
Missouri State Univ	MO	15,837	C+
Missouri Western State Univ	MO	17,822	LC
Montclair State Univ	NJ	26,912	C
Nazareth College	NY	46,784	C
Neumann Univ	PA	40,678	LC
Northwestern State Univ of Louisiana	LA	16,534	LC
Olivet Nazarene Univ	IL	41,840	VC
Otterbein Univ	OH	41,630	C
Ouachita Baptist Univ	AR	33,500	VC
Pace Univ	NY	60,136	C
Palm Beach Atlantic Univ	FL	39,250	C
Piedmont College	GA	34,334	C
Providence College	RI	62,870	HC
Roosevelt Univ	IL	41,890	VC
Russell Sage College	NY	39,370	C
Sam Houston State Univ	TX	18,792	C
Samford Univ	AL	40,770	VC
Seton Hill Univ	PA	46,972	VC
Shawnee State Univ	OH	16,998	C
Shenandoah Univ	VA	42,100	C
Shorter Univ	GA	31,130	LC
Southern Illinois Univ Edwardsville	IL	20,188	C
St. Catherine Univ	MN	45,630	C
SUNY at Geneseo	NY	21,622	VC
SUNY at Oswego	NY	22,219	VC
SUNY/Cortland	NY	20,910	C
SUNY/Fredonia	NY	20,818	C
SUNY/Univ at Buffalo	NY	23,122	C
Syracuse Univ	NY	62,313	HC
Taylor Univ	IN	42,130	VC
Texas Christian Univ	TX	57,120	HC
Texas State Univ	TX	18,721	C
The American Univ	DC	61,317	HC
The Boston Conservatory at Berklee	MA	61,042	SP
The Catholic Univ of America	DC	58,376	VC
The Univ of Akron	OH	22,566	C
The Univ of Arizona	AZ	24,086	C
Univ of Alabama at Birmingham	AL	22,092	C
Univ of Calif at Irvine	CA	33,857	VC
Univ of Hartford	CT	49,776	C
Univ of Indianapolis	IN	36,480	VC
Univ of Miami	FL	63,494	MC
Univ of Mich/Ann Arbor	MI	25,274	MC
Univ of N Car at Greensboro	NC	15,998	C
Univ of N Dak	ND	16,673	C
Univ of North Texas	TX	20,082	C
Univ of Northern Colo	CO	19,658	C
Univ of Okla	OK	19,651	HC
Univ of Tampa	FL	38,928	VC
Univ of the Arts	PA	56,579	SP
Univ of Tulsa	OK	52,625	HC
Weber State Univ	UT	14,112	C
Webster Univ	MO	37,490	C
West Chester Univ of Pennsylvania	PA	19,171	VC
West Texas A&M Univ	TX	13,478	C
Western Illinois Univ	IL	20,897	C
Western Mich Univ	MI	21,791	C
Westminster Choir College	NJ	53,730	SP
Wilkes Univ	PA	49,166	C
William Peace Univ	NC	39,300	LC
Wright State Univ	OH	16,983	C
Youngstown State Univ	OH	17,487	C

MUSICAL THEATRE ACCOMPANYING

School	ST	$IS	SR
Shenandoah Univ	VA	42,100	C

MUSICOLOGY/ ETHNOMUSICOLOGY

School	ST	$IS	SR
Brown Univ	RI	64,566	MC
Cal State, San Bernardino	CA	20,106	C
Ohio State Univ at Columbus	OH	22,843	MC
Univ of Calif at Los Angeles	CA	27,438	HC+
Univ of Dayton	OH	54,930	VC
Univ of Kansas	KS	20,884	VC

NANOSCALE ENGINEERING

School	ST	$IS	SR
SUNY Polytechnic Inst	NY	20,438	VC

NANOSCALE SCIENCE

School	ST	$IS	SR
SUNY Polytechnic Inst	NY	20,438	VC

NANOTECHNOLOGY

School	ST	$IS	SR
SUNY Polytechnic Inst	NY	20,438	VC
Univ of Wisc-Platteville	WI	14,148	C

NATIVE AMERICAN STUDIES

School	ST	$IS	SR
Black Hills State Univ	SD	16,622	C
Brown Univ	RI	64,566	MC
Cal State, Fullerton	CA	21,902	C
Colgate Univ	NY	67,500	MC
College of St. Scholastica	MN	45,734	C+
Dartmouth College	NH	68,109	MC
East Central Univ	OK	13,330	C

ST = STATE $IS = IN-STATE COSTS SR = SELECTOR RATING

School	ST	$IS	SR
Heritage Univ	WA	19,825	NC
Humboldt State Univ	CA	21,708	C
Montana State Univ-Northern	MT	11,370	NC
Northern Arizona Univ	AZ	21,003	C
Northland College	WI	41,103	C+
Southern Oregon Univ	OR	19,117	C
Stanford Univ	CA	62,541	MC
Univ of Calif at Berkeley	CA	29,886	MC
Univ of Calif at Davis	CA	28,468	HC
Univ of Calif at Riverside	CA	32,912	C
Univ of Minn/Duluth	MN	20,292	C
Univ of Montana	MT	14,105	C
Univ of New Mexico	NM	16,808	C
Univ of Okla	OK	19,651	HC

NATURAL RESOURCE MANAGEMENT

School	ST	$IS	SR
Alaska Pacific Univ	AK	28,730	VC
Angelo State Univ	TX	15,882	LC
Ball State Univ	IN	19,808	C+
Calif Polytechnic State Univ	CA	22,547	MC
Cal State, Sacramento	CA	19,060	C
Central Mich Univ	MI	20,330	C
Colo State Univ	CO	23,033	C
Delaware State Univ	DE	19,376	LC
DePauw Univ	IN	58,688	VC
Drury Univ	MO	37,555	VC
Glenville State College	WV	17,386	LC
Grand Valley State Univ	MI	22,250	C+
Green Mountain College	VT	45,228	LC
Humboldt State Univ	CA	21,708	C
Johnson State College	VT	22,672	C
Keystone College	PA	28,680	LC
Louisiana State Univ and A&M College	LA	18,677	VC
Lubbock Christian Univ	TX	29,727	C
Marshall Univ	WV	18,044	C
McNeese State Univ	LA	7,838	C
Mich State Univ	MI	24,542	VC
Mich Tech Univ	MI	25,551	VC+
Montana State Univ	MT	15,500	C+
New Mexico Highlands Univ	NM	11,904	LC
New Mexico State Univ	NM	14,050	LC
N Car State Univ	NC	22,434	HC+
N Dak State Univ	ND	16,245	VC
Northland College	WI	41,103	C+
Ohio State Univ at Columbus	OH	22,843	MC
Okla State Univ	OK	17,180	C+
Oregon State Univ	OR	23,337	VC
Purdue Univ/West Lafayette	IN	20,032	MC
Rutgers Univ - New Brunswick	NJ	27,090	HC
San Francisco State Univ	CA	18,514	LC
S Dak State Univ	SD	15,874	C
Southern Oregon Univ	OR	19,117	C
SUNY/The College of Environmental Science and Forestry	NY	23,728	VC
Sul Ross State Univ	TX	15,021	LC
Texas Tech Univ	TX	20,156	C+
The Univ of Arizona	AZ	24,086	C
The Univ of Montana Western	MT	9,426	LC
The Univ of Tenn at Martin	TN	15,212	C
Unity College	ME	37,670	C
Univ of Alaska Fairbanks	AK	16,874	VC
Univ of Conn	CT	27,394	
Univ of Delaware	DE	32,214	VC
Univ of Florida	FL	16,291	HC+
Univ of Hawaii at Manoa	HI	23,261	C
Univ of Idaho	ID	16,158	C
Univ of Illinois at Urbana-Champaign	IL	27,006	HC
Univ of Maryland/College Park	MD	21,938	HC
Univ of Mass Amherst	MA	27,669	HC
Univ of Minn/Crookston	MN	19,126	C
Univ of Nebr - Lincoln	NE	18,589	VC
Univ of Nevada, Reno	NV	18,010	C
Univ of Northern Colo	CO	19,658	C
Univ of PR-Rio Piedras campus	PR	13,327	
Univ of Wisc-Stevens Point	WI	14,043	C
Utah State Univ	UT	13,235	C
Washington State Univ	WA	22,747	C
Washington Univ in St. Louis	MO	67,539	MC
West Virginia Univ	WV	18,952	VC
Western Carolina Univ	NC	13,965	C

NATURAL RESOURCE/ ENVIRONMENTAL ECONOMICS

School	ST	$IS	SR
Arizona State Univ at the Polytechnic Campus	AZ	22,394	VC
Cal State, Fullerton	CA	21,902	C
Drury Univ	MO	37,555	VC
Moravian College	PA	55,488	C
Northland College	WI	41,103	C+
Oregon State Univ	OR	23,337	VC
The Univ of Arizona	AZ	24,086	C
Univ of Georgia	GA	21,878	HC
Univ of Maine at Machias	ME	22,960	C
Univ of Nebr - Lincoln	NE	18,589	VC
Univ of New Hampshire	NH	29,333	VC
Univ of Okla	OK	19,651	HC
Univ of Rhode Island	RI	26,066	VC
Western Kentucky Univ	KY	16,850	C

NATURAL RESOURCES

School	ST	$IS	SR
Austin College	TX	51,059	HC
Colo State Univ	CO	23,033	C
Sewanee: The Univ of the South	TN	58,000	HC+
The Univ of Tenn at Knoxville	TN	22,112	VC
Univ of Idaho	ID	16,158	C
Univ of Maine at Machias	ME	22,960	C
Univ of Vermont	VT	29,792	HC

NATURAL SCIENCES

School	ST	$IS	SR
Alderson Broaddus Univ	WV	35,000	LC
Ashford Univ	CA	10,480	C
Austin College	TX	51,059	HC
Benedictine College	KS	38,850	VC
Bethel College	KS	35,370	C
Biola Univ	CA	48,686	C
Cal State, Chico	CA	19,790	VC
Cal State, Fresno	CA	16,902	LC
Cal State, Fullerton	CA	21,902	C
Cal State, Los Angeles	CA	17,186	LC
Calvin College	MI	43,090	HC
Carthage College	WI	48,835	C
Case Western Reserve Univ	OH	62,284	MC
Castleton Univ	VT	20,186	C
Central College	IA	44,592	C
Charleston Southern Univ	SC	34,700	C
Christian Brothers Univ	TN	31,670	VC
Clarion Univ of Pennsylvania	PA	21,608	LC
Colby-Sawyer College	NH	50,790	C
Colgate Univ	NY	67,500	MC
College of St. Benedict	MN	54,480	C
College of St. Mary	NE	27,500	C
College of St. Scholastica	MN	45,734	C+
Colo State Univ	CO	23,033	C
Concordia Univ Nebr	NE	41,900	VC
Concordia Univ, Chicago	IL	41,522	C
Daemen College	NY	40,336	C
Dallas Baptist Univ	TX	35,220	VC
Doane Univ	NE	41,340	VC
Dominican Univ	IL	42,472	C+
Edgewood College	WI	35,950	C
Edinboro Univ	PA	15,940	LC
Elms College	MA	49,602	VC
Erskine College	SC	45,460	C
Felician Univ	NJ	46,280	LC
Fordham Univ	NY	68,431	MC
Fresno Pacific Univ	CA	38,858	C
Georgian Court Univ	NJ	43,068	LC
Gwynedd Mercy Univ	PA	43,780	LC
Hofstra Univ	NY	58,210	C+
Indiana Univ of Pennsylvania	PA	24,474	C
John Carroll Univ	OH	51,570	C
Johns Hopkins Univ	MD	68,080	MC
Keystone College	PA	28,680	LC
LeMoyne-Owen College	TN	16,980	C
Lesley Univ	MA	42,800	C
Lewis-Clark State College	ID	14,202	C
Lyndon State College	VT	20,714	C
Madonna Univ	MI	30,450	LC
Mercer Univ	GA	45,348	VC
Mich State Univ	MI	24,542	VC
Missouri State Univ	MO	15,837	C+
Missouri Western State Univ	MO	17,822	LC
Muhlenberg College	PA	56,645	VC
New College of Florida	FL	16,180	HC+
Oakwood Univ	AL	43,758	C
Oglala Lakota College	SD	15,050	NC
Okla Baptist Univ	OK	33,990	C
Our Lady of the Lake Univ	TX	37,790	LC
Pacific Union College	CA	36,009	VC
Park Univ	MO	22,134	C
Pepperdine Univ	CA	66,862	VC+
Prescott College	AZ	38,201	C
St. Anselm College	NH	56,636	VC
St. John's Univ	MN	53,472	C
St. Peter's Univ	NJ	49,192	C
San Jose State Univ	CA	22,630	C
Shawnee State Univ	OH	16,998	C
Shorter Univ	GA	31,130	LC
Siena Heights Univ	MI	36,322	C
Southwestern Okla State Univ	OK	12,205	C
Spalding Univ	KY	31,938	C
Spelman College	GA	41,642	C
St. Mary's College of Maryland	MD	27,312	VC
St. Norbert College	WI	46,060	VC
SUNY at Geneseo	NY	21,622	VC
Taylor Univ	IN	42,130	VC
The Evergreen State College	WA	16,599	C
The Master's Univ	CA	43,870	C
The Univ of Akron	OH	22,566	C
The Univ of Arizona	AZ	24,086	C
Thomas Edison State Univ	NJ	6,350	NC
Unity College	ME	37,670	C
Universidad del Turabo	PR	17,828	
Universidad Metropolitana	PR	17,828	
Univ of Alabama at Birmingham	AL	22,092	C
Univ of Alaska Anchorage	AK	17,914	C
Univ of Hawaii at Hilo	HI	18,038	VC
Univ of La Verne	CA	55,600	C
Univ of New Haven	CT	53,680	C
Univ of N Dak	ND	16,673	C
Univ of Pittsburgh	PA	30,030	MC
Univ of Pittsburgh at Greensburg	PA	24,140	C
Univ of PR, at Cayey	PR		
Univ of Puget Sound	WA	60,210	HC
Univ of Science and Arts of Okla	OK	11,140	VC
Univ of Sioux Falls	SD	25,630	C
Univ of Wisc-Stevens Point	WI	14,043	C
Virginia Wesleyan Univ	VA	45,980	LC
Viterbo Univ	WI	34,660	C
Washington and Lee Univ	VA	59,647	MC
Western Oregon Univ	OR	19,965	LC
Worcester State Univ	MA	20,977	C
Xavier Univ	OH	49,380	VC
York College	NE	30,260	C

NATURAL SCIENCES/ MATHEMATICS

School	ST	$IS	SR
Indiana Univ East	IN	7,207	C
Miles College	AL	16,530	NC
Thomas Edison State Univ	NJ	6,350	NC

NAVAL ARCHITECTURE AND MARINE ENGINEERING

School	ST	$IS	SR
SUNY/Maritime College	NY	16,020	C
Stevens Inst of Technology	NJ	64,954	MC
United States Coast Guard Academy	CT	942	HC
United States Naval Academy	MD		HC
Univ of Mich/Ann Arbor	MI	25,274	MC
Univ of New Orleans	LA	12,840	C
Univ of Wisc-Madison	WI	21,647	MC
Webb Inst	NY	61,800	MC

NEAR EASTERN STUDIES

School	ST	$IS	SR
Brandeis Univ	MA	68,443	MC
Brigham Young Univ	UT	13,248	MC
Cornell Univ	NY	67,591	MC
Indiana Univ Bloomington	IN	20,791	HC
Johns Hopkins Univ	MD	68,080	MC
Oberlin College	OH	68,942	MC
Princeton Univ	NJ	60,090	MC
The College of Wooster	OH	60,000	HC
Univ of Calif at Berkeley	CA	29,886	MC
Univ of Calif at Los Angeles	CA	27,438	HC+
Univ of Chicago	IL	70,551	MC
Univ of Mich/Ann Arbor	MI	25,274	MC
Univ of Pennsylvania	PA	63,526	MC
Univ of Washington	WA	23,091	MC
Univ of Wisc-Milwaukee	WI	21,538	C
Washington Univ in St. Louis	MO	67,539	MC
Wayne State Univ	MI	23,085	C
Yale Univ	CT	64,650	MC

NETWORK & COMPUTER SECURITY

School	ST	$IS	SR
DePaul Univ	IL	52,807	VC
Hofstra Univ	NY	58,210	C+
SUNY Polytechnic Inst	NY	20,438	VC

NEUROSCIENCES

School	ST	$IS	SR
Agnes Scott College	GA	51,930	VC+
Alabama A&M Univ	AL	18,796	C
Allegheny College	PA	57,620	VC
Alma College	MI	49,410	VC
Amherst College	MA	66,186	MC
Augustana College	IL	51,222	VC+
Baldwin Wallace Univ	OH	42,464	VC
Bates College	ME	64,500	HC
Bay Path Univ	MA	46,356	C
Baylor Univ	TX	56,803	HC
Belmont Univ	TN	44,500	VC+
Boston Univ	MA	67,352	MC
Bowdoin College	ME	65,980	MC
Bowling Green State Univ	OH	19,975	C
Brandeis Univ	MA	68,443	MC
Brigham Young Univ	UT	13,248	MC
Brown Univ	RI	64,566	MC
Bucknell Univ	PA	67,136	MC
Canisius College	NY	49,672	C
Carnegie Mellon Univ	PA	67,980	MC
Cedar Crest College	PA	51,110	C
Centenary College of Louisiana	LA	49,050	C+
Central Mich Univ	MI	20,330	C
Christopher Newport Univ	VA	24,878	VC+
CUNY/Queens College	NY	21,507	C
Claremont McKenna College	CA	69,900	MC
Coe College	IA	51,570	VC
Colby College	ME	64,060	MC
Colgate Univ	NY	67,500	MC
College of William & Mary	VA	34,907	MC
Colo College	CO	64,894	MC
Colo State Univ	CO	23,033	C
Columbia Univ/City of New York	NY	62,958	MC
Conn College	CT	65,000	MC
Creighton Univ	NE	49,452	VC
Dartmouth College	NH	68,109	MC
Delaware State Univ	DE	19,376	LC
DePaul Univ	IL	52,807	VC
Dickinson College	PA	66,166	MC
Dominican Univ	IL	42,472	C+
Drake Univ	IA	49,220	HC
Drew Univ/College of Liberal Arts	NJ	53,608	VC
Earlham College	IN	55,670	HC
Elon Univ	NC	46,142	HC
Emmanuel College	MA	53,472	C+
Emory Univ	GA	63,286	MC
Fitchburg State Univ	MA	21,819	LC
Fordham Univ	NY	68,431	MC
Franklin and Marshall College	PA	67,960	MC
Furman Univ	SC	61,098	VC+
George Mason Univ	VA	19,884	C
Grove City College	PA	26,654	VC
Hamilton College	NY	64,250	MC
High Point Univ	NC	47,355	VC
Hiram College	OH	44,590	C
Hofstra Univ	NY	58,210	C+
Indiana Univ Bloomington	IN	20,791	HC
Indiana Univ Southeast	IN	16,931	C
Indiana Univ-Purdue Univ Indianapolis	IN	18,952	C
Johns Hopkins Univ	MD	68,080	MC
Kalamazoo College	MI	53,931	HC
Kenyon College	OH	65,840	MC
King Univ	TN	36,976	C
King's College	PA	48,240	C
Knox College	IL	54,654	VC+
Lafayette College	PA	68,520	MC
Lake Forest College	IL	50,652	VC
Lebanon Valley College	PA	55,510	VC
Loras College	IA	40,726	C
Luther College	IA	49,990	VC
Lycoming College	PA	50,895	C
Macalester College	MN	64,136	MC
Mass Inst of Technology	MA	62,662	MC
Miami Univ	OH	27,190	HC+
Mich State Univ	MI	24,542	VC
Middlebury College	VT	67,464	MC
Millsaps College	MS	50,080	C+
Montana State Univ	MT	15,500	C+
Moravian College	PA	55,488	C
Morehead State Univ	KY	18,386	LC
Mount Holyoke College	MA	56,746	MC
Mount St. Joseph Univ	OH	33,880	LC
Muhlenberg College	PA	56,645	VC
Muskingum Univ	OH	35,966	C
New College of Florida	FL	16,180	HC+
New York Univ	NY	68,139	MC
Northeastern Univ	MA	65,352	MC
Northwestern Univ	IL	68,725	MC
Nova Southeastern Univ	FL	38,534	C+
Oberlin College	OH	68,942	MC
Ohio State Univ at Columbus	OH	22,843	MC
Ohio Univ	OH	23,394	VC
Ohio Wesleyan Univ	OH	49,460	VC
Pitzer College	CA	68,500	HC+
Pomona College	CA	64,957	MC
Quinnipiac Univ	CT	60,970	VC
Randolph-Macon College	VA	51,480	VC
Regis Univ	CO	46,380	C
Rhodes College	TN	51,900	HC
St. Louis Univ	MO	49,866	HC
St. Michael's College	VT	53,275	VC+
Scripps College	CA	69,260	HC
Simpson College	IA	45,626	VC
Skidmore College	NY	66,600	MC
Smith College	MA	66,774	MC
St. Lawrence Univ	NY	66,646	HC+
SUNY at Binghamton	NY	24,100	MC
SUNY at Geneseo	NY	21,622	VC
Stonehill College	MA	55,130	C
Swarthmore College	PA	63,550	MC
Syracuse Univ	NY	62,313	HC
Texas Christian Univ	TX	57,120	HC
The American Univ	DC	61,317	HC
The Univ of Arizona	AZ	24,086	C
Thiel College	PA	42,950	LC
Transylvania Univ	KY	47,450	HC+
Trinity College	CT	69,020	HC
Trinity Univ	TX	54,480	MC
Tulane Univ	LA	67,496	MC
Union College	NY	64,320	MC
Univ of Alabama at Birmingham	AL	22,092	C
Univ of Calif at Irvine	CA	33,857	VC
Univ of Calif at Los Angeles	CA	27,438	HC+
Univ of Calif at Riverside	CA	32,912	C
Univ of Calif, Santa Cruz	CA	28,731	C+
Univ of Cincinnati	OH	22,118	VC
Univ of Colo Boulder	CO	26,048	HC
Univ of Evansville	IN	44,186	C+
Univ of Idaho	ID	16,158	C
Univ of Illinois at Chicago	IL	24,664	VC
Univ of Miami	FL	63,494	MC
Univ of Mich/Ann Arbor	MI	25,274	MC
Univ of Minn/Twin Cities	MN	24,269	MC
Univ of Mount Union	OH	39,990	C
Univ of Nevada, Reno	NV	18,010	C
Univ of New England	ME	50,110	C
Univ of New Hampshire	NH	29,333	VC
Univ of Notre Dame	IN	68,801	MC
Univ of Pittsburgh	PA	30,030	MC
Univ of Rochester	NY	65,032	MC
Univ of Scranton	PA	54,962	VC

ST = STATE **$IS** = IN-STATE COSTS **SR** = SELECTOR RATING

School	ST	$IS	SR
Univ of Southern Calif	CA	66,631	MC
Univ of Texas at Dallas	TX	23,640	HC
Univ of Vermont	VT	29,792	HC
Univ of Washington	WA	23,091	MC
Ursinus College	PA	62,920	VC
Utica College	NY	31,510	C
Vanderbilt Univ	TN	63,248	MC
Vassar College	NY	68,110	MC
Wartburg College	IA	49,478	C
Washington & Jefferson College	PA	58,694	VC
Washington and Lee Univ	VA	59,647	MC
Washington State Univ	WA	22,747	C
Washington Univ in St. Louis	MO	67,539	MC
Wellesley College	MA	66,984	MC
Wesleyan Univ	CT	66,940	MC
Western New England Univ	MA	49,182	C
Westminster College	UT	41,078	C
Wheaton College	MA	63,818	VC
Wilkes Univ	PA	49,166	C

NEW MEDIA PRODUCTION

School	ST	$IS	SR
Cedar Crest College	PA	51,110	C
Indiana Univ Kokomo	IN	7,207	C
Indiana Univ South Bend	IN	16,057	C
Kutztown Univ of Pennsylvania	PA	19,477	C
Univ of Okla	OK	19,651	HC
Univ of Tampa	FL	38,928	VC

NONPROFIT/PUBLIC ORGANIZATION MANAGEMENT

School	ST	$IS	SR
Aquinas College - Mich	MI	38,876	VC
Arizona State Univ at the Downtown Phoenix Campus	AZ	24,634	VC
Bryant Univ	RI	57,204	VC
Cal State, Fullerton	CA	21,902	C
Dakota Wesleyan Univ	SD	33,980	LC
Duquesne Univ	PA	48,508	VC
High Point Univ	NC	47,355	VC
Huntington Univ	IN	33,996	C
Juniata College	PA	58,118	VC
Moravian College	PA	55,488	C
Mount Aloysius College	PA	29,976	C
Murray State Univ	KY	17,726	C+
Rockhurst Univ	MO	28,990	C
Salem College	NC	40,206	C
Southern Adventist Univ	TN	28,250	C
Univ of Minn/Twin Cities	MN	24,269	MC
Univ of S Car Upstate	SC	19,272	LC
Univ of Wisc-Madison	WI	21,647	MC
Western Kentucky Univ	KY	16,850	C
Wright State Univ	OH	16,983	C

NORWEGIAN

School	ST	$IS	SR
Pacific Lutheran Univ	WA	49,960	C
St. Olaf College	MN	56,430	HC
Univ of N Dak	ND	16,673	C

NUCLEAR ENGINEERING

School	ST	$IS	SR
Cal State, Fullerton	CA	21,902	C
Excelsior College	NY	38,800	SP
Georgia Inst of Technology	GA	23,910	MC
Idaho State Univ	ID	13,619	LC
Mass Inst of Technology	MA	62,662	MC
Missouri Univ of Science and Technology	MO	18,655	HC
N Car State Univ	NC	22,434	HC+
Oregon State Univ	OR	23,337	VC
Pennsylvania State Univ - Univ Park	PA	29,716	HC
Purdue Univ/West Lafayette	IN	20,032	MC
Rensselaer Polytechnic Inst	NY	67,265	MC
Texas A&M Univ at College Station	TX	20,771	VC+
The Univ of Tenn at Chattanooga	TN	17,340	C+
The Univ of Tenn at Knoxville	TN	22,112	VC
United States Military Academy at West Point	NY		HC+
United States Naval Academy	MD		HC
Univ of Calif at Berkeley	CA	29,886	MC
Univ of Cincinnati	OH	22,118	VC
Univ of Florida	FL	16,291	HC+
Univ of Idaho	ID	16,158	C
Univ of Illinois at Urbana-Champaign	IL	27,006	HC
Univ of Mich/Ann Arbor	MI	25,274	MC
Univ of New Mexico	NM	16,808	C
Univ of Wisc-Madison	WI	21,647	MC

NUCLEAR ENGINEERING TECHNOLOGY

School	ST	$IS	SR
Thomas Edison State Univ	NJ	6,350	NC
Univ of Florida	FL	16,291	HC+
Univ of North Texas	TX	20,082	C

NUCLEAR MEDICAL TECHNOLOGY

School	ST	$IS	SR
Adventist Univ of Health Sciences	FL	48,492	SP
Allen College	IA	32,367	LC
Augusta Univ	GA	4,632	C
Barry Univ	FL	38,730	LC
Benedictine Univ	IL	38,300	C
Cedar Crest College	PA	51,110	C
Edinboro Univ	PA	15,940	LC
Ferris State Univ	MI	21,458	C
Indiana Univ of Pennsylvania	PA	24,474	C
Mount Aloysius College	PA	29,976	C
North Central College	IL	48,712	C+
Old Dominion Univ	VA	21,618	C
Rhode Island College	RI	19,000	LC
Robert Morris Univ	PA	40,600	C
Roosevelt Univ	IL	41,890	VC
Rutgers Univ - New Brunswick	NJ	27,090	HC
St. Louis Univ	MO	49,866	HC
SUNY/Univ at Buffalo	NY	23,122	C
The George Washington Univ	DC	68,474	HC+
Univ of Alabama at Birmingham	AL	22,092	C
Univ of Central Arkansas	AR	15,042	VC
Univ of Cincinnati	OH	22,118	VC
Univ of Findlay	OH	43,040	C
Univ of Iowa	IA	19,415	HC
Univ of Nevada, Las Vegas	NV	17,553	C
Univ of St. Francis	IL	40,828	C
Univ of the Incarnate Word	TX	39,162	LC
Univ of Vermont	VT	29,792	HC
Univ of Wisc-La Crosse	WI	15,425	VC
York College of Pennsylvania	PA	29,240	C

NUCLEAR MEDICINE

School	ST	$IS	SR
Thomas Edison State Univ	NJ	6,350	NC
Weber State Univ	UT	14,112	C

NUCLEAR MEDICINE TECHNOLOGY

School	ST	$IS	SR
Cal State, Fullerton	CA	21,902	C
Indiana Univ-Purdue Univ Indianapolis	IN	18,952	C
Lewis Univ	IL	41,710	C
MCPHS Univ	MA	45,470	SP
Millersville Univ of Pennsylvania	PA	25,298	C
Molloy College	NY	40,440	C
St. Mary's Univ of Minn	MN	42,440	C
Thomas Edison State Univ	NJ	6,350	NC

NUCLEAR TECHNOLOGY

School	ST	$IS	SR
Excelsior College	NY	38,800	SP
Peru State College	NE	15,602	LC

NURSING

School	ST	$IS	SR
Abilene Christian Univ	TX	43,708	C+
Adams State Univ	CO	15,420	LC
Adelphi Univ	NY	49,792	C
Adventist Univ of Health Sciences	FL	48,492	SP
Agnes Scott College	GA	51,930	VC+
Alabama A&M Univ	AL	18,796	C
Albany State Univ	GA	19,462	C
Alcorn State Univ	MS	15,884	C
Alderson Broaddus Univ	WV	35,000	LC
Alfred State College	NY	19,895	C
Allen College	IA	32,367	LC
Alma College	MI	49,410	VC
Alvernia Univ	PA	45,330	C
Alverno College	WI	33,294	LC
American International College	MA	47,020	LC
Anderson Univ	IN	39,450	C
Andrews Univ	MI	41,732	C
Angelo State Univ	TX	15,882	LC
Anna Maria College	MA	51,020	C
Appalachian State Univ	NC	15,394	VC
Aquinas College	TN	30,800	C+
Arizona State Univ at the Downtown Phoenix Campus	AZ	24,634	VC
Arkansas State Univ	AR	16,190	C
Arkansas Tech Univ	AR	16,534	LC
Armstrong State Univ	GA	15,615	C
Ashland Univ	OH	30,446	C
Atlantic Union College	MA	27,228	C
Auburn Univ	AL	24,300	VC+
Auburn Univ at Montgomery	AL	15,000	C
Augusta Univ	GA	4,632	C
Augustana Univ	SD	39,968	VC
Aurora Univ	IL	34,990	C
Austin Peay State Univ	TN	16,397	C
Averett Univ	VA	43,034	LC
Avila Univ	MO	27,100	C
Azusa Pacific Univ	CA	43,972	C
Baker Univ	KS	37,190	C
Baldwin Wallace Univ	OH	42,464	VC
Ball State Univ	IN	19,808	C+
Barry Univ	FL	38,730	LC
Barton College	NC	39,854	C
Bayamon Central Univ	PR	12,490	
Baylor Univ	TX	56,803	HC
Becker College	MA	30,100	LC
Belhaven Univ	MS	32,250	C
Bellarmine Univ	KY	52,532	C
Belmont Univ	TN	44,500	VC+
Bemidji State Univ	MN	17,730	C
Benedictine College	KS	38,850	VC
Benedictine Univ	IL	38,300	C
Berea College	KY	7,094	C
Berry College	GA	47,466	VC
Bethel College	IN	36,830	C
Bethel College	KS	35,370	C
Bethel Univ	MN	46,550	C+
Bethel Univ	TN	27,142	C
Bethune-Cookman Univ	FL	23,322	C
Biola Univ	CA	48,686	C
Birmingham-Southern College	AL	44,478	C+
Bloomfield College	NJ	40,100	LC
Bloomsburg Univ of Pennsylvania	PA	19,930	C
Bluefield State College	WV	5,832	LC
Bluffton Univ	OH	40,950	C+
Boise State Univ	ID	17,368	C
Boston College	MA	68,043	MC
Bowie State Univ	MD	18,610	LC
Bowling Green State Univ	OH	19,975	C
Bradley Univ	IL	43,240	VC
Brenau Univ - Women's College	GA	37,876	LC
Briar Cliff Univ	IA	36,956	C
Brigham Young Univ	UT	13,248	MC
Bryn Athyn College	PA	32,664	C
Cabarrus College of Health Sciences	NC	11,948	SP
Caldwell Univ	NJ	42,165	LC
Calif Baptist Univ	CA	42,986	C
Cal State, Bakersfield	CA	22,397	LC
Cal State, Chico	CA	19,790	VC
Cal State, Dominguez Hills	CA	19,022	LC
Cal State, East Bay	CA	20,748	C
Cal State, Fresno	CA	16,902	LC
Cal State, Fullerton	CA	21,902	C
Cal State, Long Beach	CA	18,850	C
Cal State, Los Angeles	CA	17,186	LC
Cal State, Northridge	CA	17,277	LC
Cal State, Sacramento	CA	19,060	C
Cal State, San Bernardino	CA	20,106	C
Cal State, San Marcos	CA	20,604	LC
Cal State, Stanislaus	CA	18,053	LC
Calif Univ of Pennsylvania	PA	20,425	LC
Calvin College	MI	43,090	HC
Campbell Univ	NC	37,570	VC
Campbellsville Univ	KY	33,400	C
Capital Univ	OH	44,778	VC
Cardinal Stritch Univ	WI	37,136	C
Caribbean Univ	PR	12,227	
Carlow Univ	PA	39,696	LC
Carroll College	MT	44,304	C
Carroll Univ	WI	38,100	C+
Carson-Newman Univ	TN	35,900	C
Carthage College	WI	48,835	C
Case Western Reserve Univ	OH	62,284	MC
Castleton Univ	VT	20,186	C
Cedar Crest College	PA	51,110	C
Cedarville Univ	OH	36,244	VC
Central Conn State Univ	CT	22,041	C
Central Methodist Univ	MO	31,500	VC
Chaminade Univ of Honolulu	HI	37,614	C
Charleston Southern Univ	SC	34,700	C
Chatham Univ	PA	47,883	VC
Chicago State Univ	IL	41,620	C
CUNY/Hunter College	NY	31,098	VC
CUNY/Lehman College	NY	5,788	LC
CUNY/Medgar Evers College	NY	6,680	NC
CUNY/York College	NY	6,747	LC
Clarion Univ of Pennsylvania	PA	21,608	LC
Clarke Univ	IA	42,950	C
Clarkson College	NE	32,480	C
Clayton State Univ	GA	19,735	LC
Clemson Univ	SC		HC
Cleveland State Univ	OH	22,290	C
Coastal Carolina Univ	SC	20,340	C
Coe College	IA	51,570	VC
Colby-Sawyer College	NH	50,790	C
College of Mount St. Vincent	NY	45,620	C
College of St. Benedict	MN	54,480	C
College of St. Elizabeth	NJ	45,700	LC
College of St. Mary	NE	27,500	C
College of St. Scholastica	MN	45,734	C+
College of Staten Island	NY	24,389	LC
College of the Ozarks	MO	7,530	VC
Colo Mesa Univ	CO	19,707	LC
Colo State Univ-Pueblo	CO	21,581	C
Columbia College - Missouri	MO	28,179	C
Columbus State Univ	GA	14,336	LC
Concordia College - Moorhead	MN	46,418	C
Concordia College - New York	NY	39,035	LC
Concordia Univ	OR	35,000	C
Concordia Univ St. Paul	MN	29,050	C
Concordia Univ Wisc	WI	35,910	C
Coppin State Univ	MD	14,071	VC
Cox College	MO	20,335	SP
Creighton Univ	NE	49,452	VC
Culver-Stockton College	MO	34,350	C
Cumberland Univ	TN	27,710	C
Curry College	MA	53,331	C
Daemen College	NY	40,336	C
Dakota Wesleyan Univ	SD	33,980	LC
Davenport Univ	MI	25,896	LC
Davis & Elkins College	WV	38,242	LC
Defiance College	OH	42,240	LC
Delaware State Univ	DE	19,376	LC
Delta State Univ	MS	13,176	LC
DePaul Univ	IL	52,807	VC
DeSales Univ	PA	47,520	C
Dickinson State Univ	ND	12,372	LC
Dillard Univ	LA	20,940	VC
Dominican College	NY	40,258	LC
Dominican Univ	IL	42,472	C+
Dominican Univ of Calif	CA	58,750	C
Dordt College	IA	37,860	C+
Drexel Univ	PA	65,927	HC
Duquesne Univ	PA	48,508	VC
D'Youville College	NY	37,678	C
East Carolina Univ	NC	16,539	C
East Central Univ	OK	13,330	C
East Stroudsburg Univ	PA	18,578	LC
East Tenn State Univ	TN	18,141	C
East Texas Baptist Univ	TX	34,444	C
Eastern Illinois Univ	IL	21,414	C
Eastern Kentucky Univ	KY	17,742	C
Eastern Mennonite Univ	VA	42,550	C
Eastern Mich Univ	MI	19,761	C
Eastern New Mexico Univ	NM	12,874	LC
Eastern Oregon Univ	OR	17,612	C
Eastern Univ	PA	39,540	C
Eastern Washington Univ	WA	17,896	LC
Edgewood College	WI	35,950	C
Edinboro Univ	PA	15,940	LC
Elmhurst College	IL	46,514	C
Elmira College	NY	53,900	C
Elms College	MA	49,602	VC
Emory Univ	GA	63,286	MC
Emporia State Univ	KS	15,029	C
Endicott College	MA	47,054	C+
Excelsior College	NY	38,800	SP
Fairfield Univ	CT	61,445	HC
Fairleigh Dickinson Univ/College at Florham	NJ	54,770	C
Fairleigh Dickinson Univ/Metropolitan Campus	NJ	52,392	C
Fairmont State Univ	WV	15,726	C
Farmingdale State College	NY	20,968	C
Fayetteville State Univ	NC	17,756	C
Felician Univ	NJ	46,280	LC
Ferris State Univ	MI	21,458	C
Fitchburg State Univ	MA	21,819	LC
Florida A&M Univ	FL	15,361	C
Florida Atlantic Univ	FL	18,256	C
Florida Gulf Coast Univ	FL	14,738	C
Florida Southern College	FL	45,978	VC
Florida State Univ	FL	16,771	HC
Fort Hays State Univ	KS	12,677	C
Framingham State Univ	MA	21,740	C
Francis Marion Univ	SC	18,144	LC
Franciscan Univ of Steubenville	OH	33,980	VC
Franklin Pierce Univ	NH	46,750	LC
Frostburg State Univ	MD	17,280	LC
Gannon Univ	PA	42,922	C
Gardner-Webb Univ	NC	24,935	C+
George Fox Univ	OR	42,938	C
George Mason Univ	VA	19,884	C
Georgetown Univ	DC	68,970	MC
Georgia College & State Univ	GA	21,884	C+
Georgia Southwestern State Univ	GA	13,870	LC
Georgia State Univ	GA	25,250	C
Georgian Court Univ	NJ	43,068	LC
Glenville State College	WV	17,386	LC
Gonzaga Univ	WA	52,880	HC
Goodwin College	CT	28,370	LC
Goshen College	IN	44,350	C
Graceland Univ	IA	35,290	C
Grambling State Univ	LA	15,701	C
Grand Canyon Univ	AZ	25,150	VC
Grand Valley State Univ	MI	22,250	C+
Grand View Univ	IA	32,302	C
Gustavus Adolphus College	MN	53,943	HC
Gwynedd Mercy Univ	PA	43,780	LC
Hampton Univ	VA	36,410	C
Hannibal-LaGrange Univ	MO	29,815	C
Harding Univ	AR	25,440	C
Hardin-Simmons Univ	TX	36,025	C
Hartwick College	NY	51,270	C
Hawaii Pacific Univ	HI	33,420	C
Henderson State Univ	AR	15,516	C
Heritage Univ	WA	19,825	NC
Hiram College	OH	44,590	C
Holy Family Univ	PA	44,672	LC
Holy Names Univ	CA	46,630	LC
Hood College	MD	50,540	C
Hope College	MI	42,840	VC
Houston Baptist Univ	TX	36,450	C
Howard Univ	DC	37,616	C+
Humboldt State Univ	CA	21,708	C
Huntington Univ	IN	33,996	C
Husson Univ	ME	26,508	C
Idaho State Univ	ID	13,619	LC
Illinois State Univ	IL	23,418	VC
Illinois Wesleyan Univ	IL	56,430	VC+
Immaculata Univ	PA	39,000	C
Indiana State Univ	IN	23,223	LC

ST = STATE $IS = IN-STATE COSTS SR = SELECTOR RATING

School	ST	$IS	SR
Indiana Univ Bloomington	IN	20,791	HC
Indiana Univ East	IN	7,207	C
Indiana Univ Kokomo	IN	7,207	C
Indiana Univ Northwest	IN	7,207	LC
Indiana Univ of Pennsylvania	PA	24,474	C
Indiana Univ South Bend	IN	16,057	C
Indiana Univ Southeast	IN	16,931	C
Indiana Univ-Purdue Univ Fort Wayne	IN	18,675	C
Indiana Univ-Purdue Univ Indianapolis	IN	18,952	C
Indiana Wesleyan Univ	IN	33,674	C
Inter-American Univ of PR Ponce	PR	19,549	
Inter-American Univ of PR-Aguadilla Campus	PR	21,657	
Inter-American Univ of PR-Arecibo Campus	PR	18,245	
Inter-American Univ of PR-Fajardo Campus	PR	18,336	
Inter-American Univ of PR-Metropolitan Campus	PR	20,045	
Inter-American Univ of PR-San Germán	PR	20,042	
Iowa Wesleyan Univ	IA	41,000	C
Jacksonville State Univ	AL	14,628	LC
Jacksonville Univ	FL	49,210	C
James Madison Univ	VA	19,084	VC
John Brown Univ	AR	35,184	VC
Johnson C. Smith Univ	NC	25,336	LC
Judson College	AL	27,066	C
Judson Univ	IL	39,174	C
Kansas Wesleyan Univ	KS	37,930	C
Kean Univ	NJ	25,620	C
Keene State College	NH	24,604	C
Kennesaw State Univ	GA	18,899	VC
Kent State Univ	OH	20,928	C
Kentucky Christian Univ	KY	26,836	LC
Kentucky State Univ	KY	14,484	LC
Keuka College	NY	42,398	C
King Univ	TN	36,976	C
King's College	PA	48,240	C
Kutztown Univ of Pennsylvania	PA	19,477	C
La Roche College	PA	38,940	C
La Salle Univ	PA	43,476	C
LaGrange College	GA	41,310	C
Lake Superior State Univ	MI	19,867	C
Lamar Univ	TX	18,014	LC
Lander Univ	SC	32,200	C
Langston Univ	OK	15,659	C
Le Moyne College	NY	47,305	VC
Lenoir-Rhyne Univ	NC	47,500	LC
LeTourneau Univ	TX	39,190	VC
Lewis Univ	IL	41,710	C
Lewis-Clark State College	ID	14,202	C
Liberty Univ	VA	31,415	C
Lincoln Memorial Univ	TN	28,430	C
Lincoln Univ	MO	14,402	NC
Lincoln Univ	PA	20,878	LC
Lindsey Wilson College	KY	33,546	C
Linfield College	OR	53,992	C
Lipscomb Univ	TN	42,984	VC
LIU Brooklyn	NY	50,698	C
LIU Post	NY	50,698	C+
Longwood Univ	VA	22,184	C
Louisiana College	LA	21,274	C
Lourdes Univ	OH	29,140	NC
Loyola Univ Chicago	IL	57,158	VC
Loyola Univ New Orleans	LA	52,456	VC
Lubbock Christian Univ	TX	29,727	C
Luther College	IA	49,990	VC
MacMurray College	IL	35,025	C
Madonna Univ	MI	30,450	LC
Malone Univ	OH	39,200	C
Mansfield Univ of Pennsylvania	PA	24,244	LC
Marian Univ	IN	43,206	C
Marian Univ	WI	34,622	C
Marquette Univ	WI	53,090	VC+
Marshall Univ	WV	18,044	C
Mary Baldwin Univ	VA	40,495	C
Marymount Univ	VA	43,231	C
Maryville College	TN	44,410	C
Maryville Univ of St. Louis	MO	38,558	VC
Marywood Univ	PA	47,840	C
Mayville State Univ	ND	18,371	NC
McKendree Univ	IL	37,940	C+
McMurry Univ	TX	34,259	LC
McNeese State Univ	LA	7,838	C
MCPHS Univ	MA	45,470	SP
Mercy College	NY	32,614	C
Mercy College of Health Sciences	IA	17,600	SP
Messiah College	PA	44,380	VC
Methodist Univ	NC	58,130	C
Metropolitan State Univ	MN	7,859	C
Metropolitan State Univ of Denver	CO	6,928	LC
Miami Univ	OH	27,190	HC+
Mich State Univ	MI	24,542	VC
MidAmerica Nazarene Univ	KS	37,808	C
Middle Tenn State Univ	TN	8,650	C
Midland Univ	NE	39,512	C
Midway Univ	KY	33,940	LC
Midwestern State Univ	TX	12,111	LC
Millersville Univ of Pennsylvania	PA	25,298	C
Milligan College	TN	39,450	C
Millikin Univ	IL	44,148	C
Mills College	CA	43,705	C
Milwaukee School of Engineering	WI	48,531	HC+
Minn State Univ, Mankato	MN	17,190	C
Minn State Univ, Moorhead	MN	21,393	C
Minot State Univ	ND	13,285	C
Misericordia Univ	PA	45,210	C
Miss College	MS	25,850	C
Miss Univ for Women	MS	17,065	C
Missouri Baptist Univ	MO	35,594	C
Missouri Southern State Univ	MO	13,071	C
Missouri State Univ	MO	15,837	C+
Missouri Western State Univ	MO	17,822	LC
Molloy College	NY	40,440	C
Monmouth Univ	NJ	50,184	C
Montana State Univ	MT	15,500	C+
Montana State Univ-Northern	MT	11,370	NC
Montana Tech of the Univ of Montana	MT	15,447	VC
Montclair State Univ	NJ	26,912	C
Moravian College	PA	55,488	C
Morehead State Univ	KY	18,386	LC
Morningside College	IA	39,780	C
Mount Aloysius College	PA	29,976	C
Mount Marty College	SD	36,862	C
Mount Mercy Univ	IA	39,748	C
Mount St. Mary College	NY	44,448	C
Mount St. Joseph Univ	OH	33,880	LC
Mount St. Mary's Univ - Chalon Campus	CA	50,486	VC+
Mount Vernon Nazarene Univ	OH	35,944	C
Murray State Univ	KY	17,726	C+
Muskingum Univ	OH	35,966	C
National Univ	CA	17,849	LC
Nazareth College	NY	46,784	C
Nebr Methodist College	NE	25,314	C
Nebr Wesleyan Univ	NE	42,026	C+
Neumann Univ	PA	40,678	LC
New Jersey City Univ	NJ	21,456	LC
New Mexico State Univ	NM	14,050	LC
New York City College of Technology	NY	7,185	LC
New York Inst of Technology	NY	49,980	VC
New York Univ	NY	68,139	MC
Newman Univ	KS	37,382	C
Niagara Univ	NY	41,010	C
Nicholls State Univ	LA	14,959	C
Norfolk State Univ	VA	18,902	LC
N Car A&T State Univ	NC	13,786	C
N Car Central Univ	NC	9,000	C
N Dak State Univ	ND	16,245	VC
North Park Univ	IL	35,860	C
Northeastern State Univ	OK	8,615	VC
Northeastern Univ	MA	65,352	MC
Northern Arizona Univ	AZ	21,003	C
Northern Illinois Univ	IL	20,176	C
Northern Kentucky Univ	KY	16,486	C
Northern Mich Univ	MI	20,853	C
Northwest Nazarene Univ	ID	40,250	C
Northwest Univ	WA	38,720	VC
Northwestern College of Iowa	IA	38,400	C
Northwestern Okla State Univ	OK	13,072	LC
Northwestern State Univ of Louisiana	LA	16,534	LC
Norwich Univ	VT	56,234	C
Notre Dame College	OH	39,150	VC
Notre Dame de Namur Univ	CA	46,526	LC
Notre Dame of Maryland Univ	MD	47,570	VC
Nova Southeastern Univ	FL	38,534	C+
Nyack College	NY	34,450	LC
Oakland Univ	MI	20,763	C
Oakwood Univ	AL	43,758	C
Ohio State Univ at Columbus	OH	22,843	MC
Ohio State Univ at Lima	OH	7,553	C
Ohio State Univ at Mansfield	OH	15,529	C
Ohio State Univ at Marion	OH	7,553	VC
Ohio State Univ at Newark	OH	16,685	C
Ohio Univ	OH	23,394	VC
Okla Baptist Univ	OK	33,990	C
Okla Christian Univ	OK	29,260	C
Okla City Univ	OK	40,476	C
Okla Panhandle State Univ	OK	6,152	C
Old Dominion Univ	VA	21,618	C
Olivet Nazarene Univ	IL	41,840	VC
Oral Roberts Univ	OK	34,316	C
Otterbein Univ	OH	41,630	C
Pace Univ	NY	60,136	C
Pacific Lutheran Univ	WA	49,960	C
Pacific Union College	CA	36,009	VC
Palm Beach Atlantic Univ	FL	39,250	C
Penn State Altoona	PA	26,686	C
Pennsylvania College of Technology	PA	27,693	NC
Pennsylvania State Univ - Univ Park	PA	29,716	HC
Pfeiffer Univ	NC	40,532	LC
Piedmont College	GA	34,334	C
Pittsburg State Univ	KS	13,880	C
Plymouth State Univ	NH	23,180	LC
Point Loma Nazarene Univ	CA	46,150	C+
Pontifical Catholic Univ of PR	PR	10,534	
Prairie View A&M Univ	TX	27,273	LC
Presentation College	SD	28,575	LC
Purdue Univ Northwest	IN	15,178	C
Purdue Univ/West Lafayette	IN	20,032	MC
Queens Univ of Charlotte	NC	39,543	C
Quincy Univ	IL	38,170	LC
Quinnipiac Univ	CT	60,970	VC
Radford Univ	VA	19,758	C
Ramapo College of New Jersey	NJ	25,760	VC
Regis College	MA	51,920	LC
Regis Univ	CO	46,380	C
Research College of Nursing	MO	46,510	SP
Rhode Island College	RI	19,000	LC
Rivier Univ	NH	41,600	VC
Robert Morris Univ	PA	40,600	C
Roberts Wesleyan College	NY	41,116	C
Rockford Univ	IL	38,570	C
Rockhurst Univ	MO	28,990	C
Rowan Univ	NJ	24,491	VC
Russell Sage College	NY	39,370	C
Rutgers Univ - Camden	NJ	26,595	C
Rutgers Univ - New Brunswick	NJ	27,090	HC
Saginaw Valley State Univ	MI	19,284	C
St. Anselm College	NH	56,636	VC
St. Francis Univ	PA	46,146	NC
St. John's Univ	MN	53,472	C
St. Joseph's College of Maine	ME	47,890	C
St. Louis Univ	MO	49,866	HC
St. Martin's Univ	WA	45,056	C
St. Mary-of-the-Woods College	IN	40,424	LC
St. Mary's College	IN	50,600	C
St. Peter's Univ	NJ	49,192	C
St. Xavier Univ	IL	44,440	C
Salem State Univ	MA	42,650	LC
Salisbury Univ	MD	21,132	VC
Salve Regina Univ	RI	53,046	VC
Samford Univ	AL	40,770	VC
San Diego State Univ	CA	23,156	VC
San Francisco State Univ	CA	18,514	LC
San Jose State Univ	CA	22,630	C
Schreiner Univ	TX	34,626	LC
Seattle Pacific Univ	WA	47,439	C+
Seattle Univ	WA	54,957	VC
Seton Hall Univ	NJ	58,008	C
Shawnee State Univ	OH	16,998	C
Shenandoah Univ	VA	42,100	C
Shepherd Univ	CA		LC
Shepherd Univ, West Virginia	WV	17,382	C
Shorter Univ	GA	31,130	LC
Siena College	NY	48,916	C
Silver Lake College of the Holy Family	WI	36,290	LC
Simmons College	MA	54,400	HC
Simpson Univ	CA	34,722	C
Sinte Gleska Univ	SD	13,154	NC
Slippery Rock Univ of Pennsylvania	PA	20,450	C
Sonoma State Univ	CA	27,020	C
S Car State Univ	SC	21,330	LC
S Dak State Univ	SD	15,874	C
South Univ	GA	36,070	LC
Southeast Missouri State Univ	MO	16,148	C
Southeastern Louisiana Univ	LA	16,237	C
Southeastern Univ	FL	34,910	LC
Southern Adventist Univ	TN	28,250	C
Southern Conn State Univ	CT	21,924	LC
Southern Illinois Univ Edwardsville	IL	20,188	C
Southern Nazarene Univ	OK	33,684	C
Southern Oregon Univ	OR	19,117	C
Southern Univ and A&M College	LA	16,074	LC
Southern Vermont College	VT	34,670	LC
Southwest Baptist Univ	MO	30,890	LC
Southwestern Adventist Univ	TX	28,232	LC
Southwestern Okla State Univ	OK	12,205	C
Spalding Univ	KY	31,938	C
Spring Arbor Univ	MI	37,390	C
Spring Hill College	AL	48,488	C
St. Ambrose Univ	IA	40,180	C
St. Catherine Univ	MN	45,630	C
St. Francis College	NY	38,800	LC
St. John Fisher College	NY	45,270	VC
St. Joseph's College, New York/Brooklyn Campus	NY	25,114	LC
St. Joseph's College, New York/Long Island Campus	NY	25,124	C
St. Olaf College	MN	56,430	HC
SUNY at Binghamton	NY	24,100	MC
SUNY at New Paltz	NY	20,840	C
SUNY Polytechnic Inst	NY	20,438	VC
SUNY/Empire State College	NY	9,145	NC
SUNY/Plattsburgh	NY	19,314	C
SUNY/Univ at Buffalo	NY	23,122	C
Stephen F. Austin State Univ	TX	18,484	LC
Stevenson Univ	MD	48,412	C
Stockton Univ	NJ	25,565	C
Stony Brook Univ/The SUNY	NY	22,703	MC
Tabor College	KS	35,870	C
Tarleton State Univ	TX	15,248	LC
Temple Univ	PA	24,392	C+
Tenn State Univ	TN	14,423	LC
Tenn Tech Univ	TN	17,929	C
Tenn Wesleyan Univ	TN	32,680	LC
Texas A&M Univ at College Station	TX	20,771	VC+
Texas A&M Univ at Corpus Christi	TX	16,851	LC
Texas A&M Univ at Kingsville	TX	16,580	LC
Texas Christian Univ	TX	57,120	HC
Texas Lutheran Univ	TX	39,770	C
Texas State Univ	TX	18,721	C
Texas Woman's Univ	TX	15,302	LC
The Catholic Univ of America	DC	58,376	VC
The College at Brockport - SUNY	NY	21,058	C
The College of Idaho	ID	36,415	C
The College of New Jersey	NJ	28,675	VC+
The College of New Rochelle	NY	46,300	LC
The Univ of Akron	OH	22,566	C
The Univ of Alabama	AL	24,320	C+
The Univ of Arizona	AZ	24,086	C
The Univ of Mary	ND	23,180	C
The Univ of Memphis	TN	18,278	C
The Univ of Tenn at Chattanooga	TN	17,340	C+
The Univ of Tenn at Knoxville	TN	22,112	VC
The Univ of Tenn at Martin	TN	15,212	C
The Univ of Texas at Austin	TX	20,206	MC
The Univ of Utah	UT	18,751	VC
The Univ of Virginia's College at Wise	VA	18,192	LC
Thomas Edison State Univ	NJ	6,350	NC
Thomas More College	KY	36,720	LC
Thomas Univ	GA	21,420	NC
Toccoa Falls College	GA	30,048	C
Touro College	NY	31,040	C
Towson Univ	MD	21,878	C
Trevecca Nazarene Univ	TN	31,186	C
Trinity Christian College	IL	35,580	C
Trinity College of Nursing and Health Sciences	IL	53,138	SP
Trinity Washington Univ	DC	33,826	C+
Troy Univ	AL	16,171	C
Truman State Univ	MO	16,286	MC
Tusculum College	TN	31,625	LC
Tuskegee Univ	AL	28,164	C
Union College	KY	32,310	C
Union College	NE	23,270	C
Union Univ	TN	41,160	VC
Universidad Adventista de las Antillas	PR	16,606	
Universidad Metropolitana	PR	17,828	
Univ of PR, at Arecibo	PR	12,652	
Univ of Alabama at Birmingham	AL	22,092	C
Univ of Alabama in Huntsville	AL	20,028	VC
Univ of Alaska Anchorage	AK	17,914	C
Univ of Arkansas at Fayetteville	AR	19,766	VC
Univ of Arkansas at Little Rock	AR	18,211	LC
Univ of Arkansas at Monticello	AR	13,599	LC
Univ of Arkansas at Pine Bluff	AR	13,541	C
Univ of Bridgeport	CT	44,985	LC
Univ of Calif at Irvine	CA	33,857	VC
Univ of Calif at Los Angeles	CA	27,438	HC+
Univ of Central Arkansas	AR	15,042	VC
Univ of Central Florida	FL	16,379	VC
Univ of Central Missouri	MO	18,982	C
Univ of Central Okla	OK	15,150	C
Univ of Charleston	WV	35,000	LC
Univ of Cincinnati	OH	22,118	VC
Univ of Colo Colo Springs	CO	20,300	C
Univ of Colo Denver	CO	22,238	C
Univ of Conn	CT	27,394	
Univ of Dallas	TX	50,676	VC
Univ of Delaware	DE	32,214	VC
Univ of Detroit Mercy	MI	48,816	C
Univ of Dubuque	IA	37,824	C
Univ of Evansville	IN	44,186	C+
Univ of Findlay	OH	43,040	C
Univ of Florida	FL	16,291	HC+
Univ of Hartford	CT	49,776	C
Univ of Hawaii at Hilo	HI	18,038	VC
Univ of Hawaii at Manoa	HI	23,261	C
Univ of Holy Cross	LA	21,523	NC
Univ of Illinois at Chicago	IL	24,664	VC
Univ of Indianapolis	IN	36,480	VC
Univ of Iowa	IA	19,415	HC
Univ of Jamestown	ND	28,508	C
Univ of Kansas	KS	20,884	VC
Univ of Kentucky	KY	24,800	C+
Univ of Louisiana at Lafayette	LA	14,516	C
Univ of Louisiana at Monroe	LA	15,970	C
Univ of Louisville	KY	19,692	C
Univ of Lynchburg	VA	48,370	C
Univ of Maine	ME	21,038	VC
Univ of Maine at Augusta	ME	7,812	C
Univ of Maine at Fort Kent	ME	15,165	LC
Univ of Mary Hardin-Baylor	TX	35,292	C+
Univ of Mass Amherst	MA	27,669	HC
Univ of Mass Boston	MA	13,828	C
Univ of Mass Dartmouth	MA	26,507	C
Univ of Mass Lowell	MA	27,296	VC
Univ of Miami	FL	63,494	MC
Univ of Mich/Ann Arbor	MI	25,274	MC
Univ of Mich/Flint	MI	19,062	C
Univ of Minn/Twin Cities	MN	24,269	MC
Univ of Miss	MS	18,802	C
Univ of Missouri-Columbia	MO	20,463	VC

ST = STATE $IS = IN-STATE COSTS SR = SELECTOR RATING

School	ST	$IS	SR
Univ of Missouri-Kansas City	MO	19,563	VC
Univ of Missouri-St. Louis	MO	19,810	VC
Univ of Mobile	AL	28,935	C
Univ of Mount Union	OH	39,990	C
Univ of Nebr - Kearney	NE	17,014	LC
Univ of Nevada, Las Vegas	NV	17,553	C
Univ of Nevada, Reno	NV	18,010	C
Univ of New England	ME	50,110	C
Univ of New Hampshire	NH	29,333	VC
Univ of New Mexico	NM	16,808	C
Univ of North Alabama	AL	15,964	C
Univ of N Car at Chapel Hill	NC	20,561	MC
Univ of N Car at Charlotte	NC	17,803	VC
Univ of N Car at Greensboro	NC	15,998	C
Univ of N Car at Pembroke	NC	14,737	LC
Univ of N Car Wilmington	NC	16,784	VC
Univ of N Dak	ND	16,673	C
Univ of North Florida	FL	15,996	VC
Univ of North Georgia	GA	17,316	C
Univ of Northern Colo	CO	19,658	C
Univ of Northwestern - St. Paul	MN	39,530	C
Univ of Pennsylvania	PA	63,526	MC
Univ of Pikeville	KY	27,838	C
Univ of Pittsburgh	PA	30,030	MC
Univ of Pittsburgh at Bradford	PA	22,958	C
Univ of Pittsburgh at Johnstown	PA	22,092	C
Univ of Portland	OR	52,152	VC
Univ of PR, at Humacao	PR	14,000	
Univ of PR, at Mayaguez	PR	13,995	
Univ of Rhode Island	RI	26,066	VC
Univ of Rio Grande & Rio Grande Community College	OH	8,750	LC
Univ of Rochester	NY	65,032	MC
Univ of St. Francis	IN	38,520	C
Univ of St. Joseph	CT	49,069	C
Univ of St. Mary	KS	37,080	NC
Univ of San Francisco	CA	60,580	C
Univ of Scranton	PA	54,962	VC
Univ of Sioux Falls	SD	25,630	C
Univ of South Alabama	AL	16,880	C
Univ of S Car Aiken	SC	18,094	C
Univ of S Car at Columbia	SC	21,726	VC
Univ of S Car Upstate	SC	19,272	LC
Univ of S Dak	SD	16,109	C
Univ of South Florida/Tampa	FL	16,110	VC
Univ of Southern Indiana	IN	16,808	C
Univ of Southern Maine	ME	18,320	C
Univ of Southern Miss	MS	13,170	C
Univ of St. Francis	IL	40,828	C
Univ of St. Thomas - Houston	TX	41,510	VC
Univ of Tampa	FL	38,928	VC
Univ of Texas at Arlington	TX	18,876	C
Univ of Texas at El Paso	TX	34,452	NC
Univ of Texas Rio Grande Valley	TX	15,573	LC
Univ of the Cumberlands	KY	32,000	LC
Univ of the District of Columbia	DC	21,260	LC
Univ of the Incarnate Word	TX	39,162	LC
Univ of the Sacred Heart	PR	17,932	
Univ of Toledo	OH	19,336	C
Univ of Tulsa	OK	52,625	HC
Univ of Vermont	VT	29,792	HC
Univ of Virginia	VA	27,367	MC
Univ of Washington	WA	23,091	MC
Univ of West Florida	FL	15,848	C
Univ of West Georgia	GA	17,510	LC
Univ of Wisc-Eau Claire	WI	16,354	VC
Univ of Wisc-Green Bay	WI	15,184	C
Univ of Wisc-Madison	WI	21,647	MC
Univ of Wisc-Milwaukee	WI	21,538	C
Univ of Wisc-Oshkosh	WI	15,392	C
Univ of Wyoming	WY	15,537	C
Urbana Univ	OH	30,820	C
Ursuline College	OH	41,076	LC
Utica College	NY	31,510	C
Valparaiso Univ	IN	50,160	VC
Vanguard Univ of Southern Calif	CA	42,400	VC
Villanova Univ	PA	64,922	MC
Virginia Commonwealth Univ	VA	23,811	VC
Viterbo Univ	WI	34,660	C
Wagner College	NY	57,240	C+
Walla Walla Univ	WA	34,845	C
Walsh Univ	OH	39,010	C
Washburn Univ	KS	15,827	C
Washington Adventist Univ	MD	32,050	LC
Washington State Univ	WA	22,747	C
Wayland Baptist Univ	TX	23,460	LC
Wayne State Univ	MI	23,085	C
Waynesburg Univ	PA	33,530	C
Weber State Univ	UT	14,112	C
Webster Univ	MO	37,490	C
Wesley College	DE	37,848	LC
Wesleyan College	GA	31,940	C+
West Chester Univ of Pennsylvania	PA	19,171	VC
West Liberty Univ	WV	16,158	C
West Texas A&M Univ	TX	13,478	C
West Virginia Univ	WV	18,952	VC
West Virginia Univ Inst of Technology	WV	18,264	C
West Virginia Wesleyan College	WV	39,188	C
Western Carolina Univ	NC	13,965	C
Western Conn State Univ	CT	21,254	LC
Western Illinois Univ	IL	20,897	C
Western Kentucky Univ	KY	16,850	C
Western Mich Univ	MI	21,791	C
Western Washington Univ	WA	18,904	VC
Westfield State Univ	MA	20,404	C
Westminster College	MO	32,820	C
Westminster College	UT	41,078	C
Wheaton College	IL	44,993	MC
Wheeling Jesuit Univ	WV	37,106	LC
Whitworth Univ	WA	53,682	VC
Wichita State Univ	KS	17,773	C
Widener Univ	PA	58,190	C
Wilkes Univ	PA	49,166	C
William Carey Univ	MS	23,950	LC
William Jewell College	MO	42,490	C+
William Paterson Univ of New Jersey	NJ	24,022	C
Wilmington Univ	DE	8,762	NC
Wilson College	PA	35,620	LC
Wingate Univ	NC	41,900	C
Winona State Univ	MN	18,109	C
Winston-Salem State Univ	NC	18,005	LC
Wisc Lutheran College	WI	36,290	C
Worcester State Univ	MA	20,977	C
Wright State Univ	OH	16,983	C
Xavier Univ	OH	49,380	VC
York College of Pennsylvania	PA	29,240	C
Youngstown State Univ	OH	17,487	C

NURSING EDUCATION

School	ST	$IS	SR
Allen College	IA	32,367	LC
Cal State, Northridge	CA	17,277	LC
Georgia Southern Univ	GA	16,540	VC
Indiana Wesleyan Univ	IN	33,674	C
New York Univ	NY	68,139	MC
Seattle Pacific Univ	WA	47,439	C+
Southern Univ and A&M College	LA	16,074	LC
Univ of Alaska Anchorage	AK	17,914	C
Walla Walla Univ	WA	34,845	C
Western Washington Univ	WA	18,904	VC

NURSING HOME ADMINISTRATION

School	ST	$IS	SR
Mount Aloysius College	PA	29,976	C
New York Univ	NY	68,139	MC
Ohio Univ	OH	23,394	VC
Youngstown State Univ	OH	17,487	C

NUTRITION

School	ST	$IS	SR
Abilene Christian Univ	TX	43,708	C+
Alabama A&M Univ	AL	18,796	C
Alcorn State Univ	MS	15,884	C
Andrews Univ	MI	41,732	C
Appalachian State Univ	NC	15,394	VC
Arizona State Univ at the Downtown Phoenix Campus	AZ	24,634	VC
Auburn Univ	AL	24,300	VC+
Baylor Univ	TX	56,803	HC
Benedictine Univ	IL	38,300	C
Boston Univ	MA	67,352	MC
Bowling Green State Univ	OH	19,975	C
Brigham Young Univ	UT	13,248	MC
Calif Polytechnic State Univ	CA	22,547	MC
Case Western Reserve Univ	OH	62,284	MC
Cedar Crest College	PA	51,110	C
CUNY/Hunter College	NY	31,098	VC
College of St. Benedict	MN	54,480	C
College of St. Elizabeth	NJ	45,700	LC
Colo State Univ	CO	23,033	C
Concordia College - Moorhead	MN	46,418	C
Dominican Univ	IL	42,472	C+
Drexel Univ	PA	65,927	HC
East Carolina Univ	NC	16,539	C
Eastern Mich Univ	MI	19,761	C
Florida State Univ	FL	16,771	HC
Fort Valley State Univ	GA	17,988	VC
Framingham State Univ	MA	21,740	C
Gannon Univ	PA	42,922	C
Georgia Southern Univ	GA	16,540	VC
Georgia State Univ	GA	25,250	C
Goddard College	VT	17,040	VC
Hampshire College	MA	65,214	MC
Howard Univ	DC	37,616	C+
Indiana Univ of Pennsylvania	PA	24,474	C
Iowa State Univ	IA	18,176	C
Johnson & Wales Univ/ Denver Campus	CO	44,768	C
Kansas State Univ	KS	17,780	VC
Keene State College	NH	24,604	C
Kent State Univ	OH	20,928	C
La Salle Univ	PA	43,476	C
Langston Univ	OK	15,659	C
LIU Post	NY	50,698	C+
Louisiana State Univ and A&M College	LA	18,677	VC
Madonna Univ	MI	30,450	LC
Marshall Univ	WV	18,044	C
Meredith College	NC	46,634	C
Miami Univ	OH	27,190	HC+
Mich State Univ	MI	24,542	VC
Middle Tenn State Univ	TN	8,650	C
Murray State Univ	KY	17,726	C+
New Mexico State Univ	NM	14,050	LC
New York Univ	NY	68,139	MC
N Car Central Univ	NC	9,000	C
N Dak State Univ	ND	16,245	VC
Northern Illinois Univ	IL	20,176	C
Ohio State Univ at Columbus	OH	22,843	MC
Ohio Univ	OH	23,394	VC
Ohio Wesleyan Univ	OH	49,460	VC
Okla State Univ	OK	17,180	C+
Oregon State Univ	OR	23,337	VC
Pennsylvania State Univ - Univ Park	PA	29,716	HC
Pepperdine Univ	CA	66,862	VC+
Point Loma Nazarene Univ	CA	46,150	C+
Purdue Univ/West Lafayette	IN	20,032	MC
Rochester Inst of Technology	NY	52,734	HC+
Russell Sage College	NY	39,370	C
St. John's Univ	MN	53,472	C
San Diego State Univ	CA	23,156	VC
S Car State Univ	SC	21,330	LC
S Dak State Univ	SD	15,874	C
St. Catherine Univ	MN	45,630	C
SUNY/Plattsburgh	NY	19,314	C
Stephen F. Austin State Univ	TX	18,484	LC
Syracuse Univ	NY	62,313	HC
Texas A&M Univ at College Station	TX	20,771	VC+
Texas Christian Univ	TX	57,120	HC
Texas Southern Univ	TX	19,592	LC
Texas State Univ	TX	18,721	C
Texas Tech Univ	TX	20,156	C+
The Univ of Arizona	AZ	24,086	C
The Univ of Tenn at Knoxville	TN	22,112	VC
The Univ of Tenn at Martin	TN	15,212	C
The Univ of Texas at Austin	TX	20,206	MC
Univ of Arkansas at Fayetteville	AR	19,766	VC
Univ of Bridgeport	CT	44,985	LC
Univ of Calif at Berkeley	CA	29,886	MC
Univ of Calif at Davis	CA	28,468	HC
Univ of Central Okla	OK	15,150	C
Univ of Conn	CT	27,394	
Univ of Delaware	DE	32,214	VC
Univ of Georgia	GA	21,878	HC
Univ of Illinois at Chicago	IL	24,664	VC
Univ of Illinois at Urbana-Champaign	IL	27,006	HC
Univ of Maine	ME	21,038	VC
Univ of Maryland/College Park	MD	21,938	HC
Univ of Mass Amherst	MA	27,669	HC
Univ of Minn/Twin Cities	MN	24,269	MC
Univ of Missouri-Columbia	MO	20,463	VC
Univ of Nebr - Lincoln	NE	18,589	VC
Univ of Nevada, Reno	NV	18,010	C
Univ of New England	ME	50,110	C
Univ of New Hampshire	NH	29,333	VC
Univ of New Haven	CT	53,680	C
Univ of New Mexico	NM	16,808	C
Univ of N Car at Chapel Hill	NC	20,561	MC
Univ of N Car at Greensboro	NC	15,998	C
Univ of North Florida	FL	15,996	VC
Univ of Northern Colo	CO	19,658	C
Univ of Northern Iowa	IA	17,480	C
Univ of PR-Rio Piedras campus	PR	13,327	
Univ of St. Francis	IN	38,520	C
Univ of St. Joseph	CT	49,069	C
Univ of Southern Indiana	IN	16,808	C
Univ of the Incarnate Word	TX	39,162	LC
Univ of Vermont	VT	29,792	HC
Univ of Wisc-Madison	WI	21,647	MC
Univ of Wisc-Milwaukee	WI	21,538	C
Univ of Wisc-Stevens Point	WI	14,043	C
Virginia Polytechnic Inst and State Univ	VA	21,920	VC
Wayne State Univ	MI	23,085	C
West Chester Univ of Pennsylvania	PA	19,171	VC
West Virginia Univ	WV	18,952	VC
West Virginia Wesleyan College	WV	39,188	C
Western Illinois Univ	IL	20,897	C
Winthrop Univ	SC	23,960	C
Youngstown State Univ	OH	17,487	C

NUTRITION AND DIETETICS

School	ST	$IS	SR
Bradley Univ	IL	43,240	VC
Calif State Polytechnic Univ, Pomona	CA	21,811	C
CUNY/Queens College	NY	21,507	C
Indiana Univ of Pennsylvania	PA	24,474	C
Mansfield Univ of Pennsylvania	PA	24,244	LC
Montclair State Univ	NJ	26,912	C
Murray State Univ	KY	17,726	C+
Radford Univ	VA	19,758	C
Rochester Inst of Technology	NY	52,734	HC+
St. Louis Univ	MO	49,866	HC
Samford Univ	AL	40,770	VC
Texas Tech Univ	TX	20,156	C+
Thomas Edison State Univ	NJ	6,350	NC
Univ of Nevada, Reno	NV	18,010	C
Univ of N Car at Greensboro	NC	15,998	C
Univ of Rhode Island	RI	26,066	VC
Wayne State Univ	MI	23,085	C

NUTRITION AND WELLNESS

School	ST	$IS	SR
Gannon Univ	PA	42,922	C
Piedmont College	GA	34,334	C
Rochester Inst of Technology	NY	52,734	HC+
Samford Univ	AL	40,770	VC

NUTRITION EDUCATION

School	ST	$IS	SR
Ohio Univ	OH	23,394	VC
St. Louis Univ	MO	49,866	HC
Univ of Cincinnati	OH	22,118	VC
Univ of Illinois at Chicago	IL	24,664	VC

NUTRITIONAL SCIENCES

School	ST	$IS	SR
Bridgewater College	VA	46,260	C
Calif Baptist Univ	CA	42,986	C
Cal State, Long Beach	CA	18,850	C
CUNY/Queens College	NY	21,507	C
Cornell Univ	NY	67,591	MC
Fontbonne Univ	MO	34,606	C
Madonna Univ	MI	30,450	LC
McNeese State Univ	LA	7,838	C
Merrimack College	MA	55,415	C
Okla Christian Univ	OK	29,260	C
Piedmont College	GA	34,334	C
Rochester Inst of Technology	NY	52,734	HC+
Rutgers Univ - New Brunswick	NJ	27,090	HC
St. Louis Univ	MO	49,866	HC
San Jose State Univ	CA	22,630	C
The Univ of Arizona	AZ	24,086	C
Univ of Arkansas at Fayetteville	AR	19,766	VC
Univ of Georgia	GA	21,878	HC
Univ of Illinois at Chicago	IL	24,664	VC
Univ of Mass Lowell	MA	27,296	VC
Univ of Nevada, Reno	NV	18,010	C
Univ of N Car at Greensboro	NC	15,998	C
Univ of Wisc-Milwaukee	WI	21,538	C

OCCUPATIONAL HYGIENE & SAFETY

School	ST	$IS	SR
Ohio Univ	OH	23,394	VC
Southeastern Louisiana Univ	LA	16,237	C

OCCUPATIONAL SAFETY AND HEALTH

School	ST	$IS	SR
Fairmont State Univ	WV	15,726	C
Grand Valley State Univ	MI	22,250	C+
Howard Payne Univ	TX	35,994	C
Keene State College	NH	24,604	C
Madonna Univ	MI	30,450	LC
Marshall Univ	WV	18,044	C
Millersville Univ of Pennsylvania	PA	25,298	C
Montana Tech of the Univ of Montana	MT	15,447	VC
Murray State Univ	KY	17,726	C+
N Car A&T State Univ	NC	13,786	C
Oakland Univ	MI	20,763	C
Purdue Univ/West Lafayette	IN	20,032	MC
Southeastern Louisiana Univ	LA	16,237	C
Southeastern Okla State Univ	OK	11,875	C
Southwest Baptist Univ	MO	30,890	LC
Univ of Central Missouri	MO	18,982	C
Univ of Findlay	OH	43,040	C
Univ of N Dak	ND	16,673	C
Univ of Wisc-Milwaukee	WI	21,538	C
Western Kentucky Univ	KY	16,850	C

OCCUPATIONAL THERAPY

School	ST	$IS	SR
Allen College	IA	32,367	LC
American International College	MA	47,020	LC
Baker College of Flint	MI	19,140	NC
Barry Univ	FL	38,730	LC
Bethany College	WV	38,774	LC
Brenau Univ - Women's College	GA	37,876	LC
Cal State, Dominguez Hills	CA	19,022	LC
Cal State, Fullerton	CA	21,902	C
Calvin College	MI	43,090	HC
Carroll Univ	WI	38,100	C+
CUNY/York College	NY	6,747	LC
Cleveland State Univ	OH	22,290	C
Colo State Univ-Pueblo	CO	21,581	C
Concordia Univ Wisc	WI	35,910	C
Dominican College	NY	40,258	LC
Dominican Univ of Calif	CA	58,750	C
Duquesne Univ	PA	48,508	VC
East Carolina Univ	NC	16,539	C
Eastern Kentucky Univ	KY	17,742	C
Eastern Mich Univ	MI	19,761	C
Elizabethtown College	PA	56,340	VC
Florida A&M Univ	FL	15,361	C
Florida Gulf Coast Univ	FL	14,738	C
Gannon Univ	PA	42,922	C
Goodwin College	CT	28,370	LC
Gwynedd Mercy Univ	PA	43,780	LC

ST = STATE $IS = IN-STATE COSTS SR = SELECTOR RATING

School	ST	$IS	SR
Howard Univ	DC	37,616	C+
Husson Univ	ME	26,508	C
Ithaca College	NY	58,158	VC+
Keuka College	NY	42,398	C
Lamar Univ	TX	18,014	LC
Lenoir-Rhyne Univ	NC	47,500	LC
LIU Brooklyn	NY	50,698	C
Maryville Univ of St. Louis	MO	38,558	VC
McKendree Univ	IL	37,940	C+
Misericordia Univ	PA	45,210	C
Mount Aloysius College	PA	29,976	C
Mount Mary Univ	WI	34,650	LC
New York Univ	NY	68,139	MC
Ohio State Univ at Columbus	OH	22,843	MC
Pennsylvania College of Technology	PA	27,693	NC
Quinnipiac Univ	CT	60,970	VC
Russell Sage College	NY	39,370	C
Rutgers Univ - New Brunswick	NJ	27,090	HC
St. Francis Univ	PA	46,146	NC
St. Louis Univ	MO	49,866	HC
St. Vincent College	PA	46,229	C
San Jose State Univ	CA	22,630	C
Shawnee State Univ	OH	16,998	C
Spalding Univ	KY	31,938	C
St. Ambrose Univ	IA	40,180	C
St. Catherine Univ	MN	45,630	C
SUNY/Univ at Buffalo	NY	23,122	C
Tenn State Univ	TN	14,423	LC
The Univ of Mary	ND	23,180	C
Touro College	NY	31,040	C
Towson Univ	MD	21,878	C
Tuskegee Univ	AL	28,164	C
Univ of Central Arkansas	AR	15,042	VC
Univ of Findlay	OH	43,040	C
Univ of Florida	FL	16,291	HC+
Univ of Illinois at Chicago	IL	24,664	VC
Univ of Kansas	KS	20,884	VC
Univ of Louisiana at Monroe	LA	15,970	C
Univ of Missouri-Columbia	MO	20,463	VC
Univ of New England	ME	50,110	C
Univ of New Hampshire	NH	29,333	VC
Univ of Scranton	PA	54,962	VC
Univ of Southern Calif	CA	66,631	MC
Univ of Southern Indiana	IN	16,808	C
Univ of the Sciences	PA	40,738	VC
Univ of Wisc-Milwaukee	WI	21,538	C
Utica College	NY	31,510	C
Walla Walla Univ	WA	34,845	C
Wartburg College	IA	49,478	C
West Virginia Univ	WV	18,952	VC
Western Mich Univ	MI	21,791	C
Worcester State Univ	MA	20,977	C

OCEAN ENGINEERING

School	ST	$IS	SR
Cal State, Fullerton	CA	21,902	C
Florida Atlantic Univ	FL	18,256	C
Florida Inst of Technology	FL	53,306	VC
Mass Inst of Technology	MA	62,662	MC
Texas A&M Univ at College Station	TX	20,771	VC+
United States Naval Academy	MD		HC
Univ of New Hampshire	NH	29,333	VC
Univ of Rhode Island	RI	26,066	VC
Univ of Washington	WA	23,091	MC
Virginia Polytechnic Inst and State Univ	VA	21,920	VC

OCEANOGRAPHY

School	ST	$IS	SR
Bowdoin College	ME	65,980	MC
Cal State, Fullerton	CA	21,902	C
Central Mich Univ	MI	20,330	C
Florida Inst of Technology	FL	53,306	VC
Hawaii Pacific Univ	HI	33,420	C
Humboldt State Univ	CA	21,708	C
Maine Maritime Academy	ME	22,536	C
Millersville Univ of Pennsylvania	PA	25,298	C
Old Dominion Univ	VA	21,618	C
Prescott College	AZ	38,201	C
United States Naval Academy	MD		HC
Univ of Mich/Ann Arbor	MI	25,274	MC
Univ of New England	ME	50,110	C
Univ of N Car Wilmington	NC	16,784	VC
Univ of Washington	WA	23,091	MC
Whitman College	WA	59,772	MC

OFFICE SUPERVISION AND MANAGEMENT

School	ST	$IS	SR
Adams State Univ	CO	15,420	LC
Alabama A&M Univ	AL	18,796	C
Albany State Univ	GA	19,462	C
Baker College of Flint	MI	19,140	NC
Campbellsville Univ	KY	33,400	C
Central Conn State Univ	CT	22,041	C
Concord Univ	WV	14,954	LC
Eastern Mich Univ	MI	19,761	C
Fayetteville State Univ	NC	17,756	C
Fort Hays State Univ	KS	12,677	C
Fort Valley State Univ	GA	17,988	VC
Georgia State Univ	GA	25,250	C
Inter-American Univ of PR-Bayamon	PR	18,785	
Johnson & Wales Univ/Providence Campus	RI	44,768	C
Middle Tenn State Univ	TN	8,650	C
Miss Valley State Univ	MS	13,233	LC
Northwestern Okla State Univ	OK	13,072	LC
Rider Univ	NJ	54,050	C
S Car State Univ	SC	21,330	LC
Southwestern Adventist Univ	TX	28,232	LC
Sul Ross State Univ	TX	15,021	LC
Tarleton State Univ	TX	15,248	LC
Universidad Adventista de las Antillas	PR	16,606	
Univ of S Car at Columbia	SC	21,726	VC
Univ of the Cumberlands	KY	32,000	LC
Univ of the District of Columbia	DC	21,260	LC
Univ of Wisc-Whitewater	WI	13,976	C
Valley City State Univ	ND	13,267	C
Washington State Univ	WA	22,747	C
Wiley College	TX	19,255	C

OPERA

School	ST	$IS	SR
New England Conservatory of Music	MA	63,170	SP
The Boston Conservatory at Berklee	MA	61,042	SP

OPERATIONS MANAGEMENT

School	ST	$IS	SR
Ashford Univ	CA	10,480	C
Ball State Univ	IN	19,808	C+
Ferris State Univ	MI	21,458	C
George Mason Univ	VA	19,884	C
Le Moyne College	NY	47,305	VC
Marquette Univ	WI	53,090	VC+
Metropolitan State Univ	MN	7,859	C
Minn State Univ, Moorhead	MN	21,393	C
New York Univ	NY	68,139	MC
Oakland Univ	MI	20,763	C
Ohio State Univ at Columbus	OH	22,843	MC
SUNY at Oswego	NY	22,219	VC
The Univ of Arizona	AZ	24,086	C
The Univ of Utah	UT	18,751	VC
Thomas Edison State Univ	NJ	6,350	NC
Univ of Cincinnati	OH	22,118	VC
Univ of Dayton	OH	54,930	VC
Univ of Delaware	DE	32,214	VC
Univ of Idaho	ID	16,158	C
Univ of Maryland/College Park	MD	21,938	HC
Univ of Mass Amherst	MA	27,669	HC
Univ of Mass Dartmouth	MA	26,507	C
Univ of Missouri-St. Louis	MO	19,810	VC
Univ of N Dak	ND	16,673	C
Univ of North Texas	TX	20,082	C
Univ of Pennsylvania	PA	63,526	MC
Univ of Portland	OR	52,152	VC
Univ of Scranton	PA	54,962	VC
Univ of Wisc-Madison	WI	21,647	MC
Univ of Wisc-Milwaukee	WI	21,538	C
Washington State Univ	WA	22,747	C
Western Washington Univ	WA	18,904	VC

OPERATIONS RESEARCH

School	ST	$IS	SR
Boston College	MA	68,043	MC
Canisius College	NY	49,672	C
CUNY/Baruch College	NY	21,609	HC
Columbia Univ/City of New York	NY	62,958	MC
New York Univ	NY	68,139	MC
Princeton Univ	NJ	60,090	MC
United States Air Force Academy	CO		C
United States Coast Guard Academy	CT	942	HC
United States Military Academy at West Point	NY		HC+
United States Naval Academy	MD		HC
Univ of Calif at Berkeley	CA	29,886	MC
Univ of Illinois at Urbana-Champaign	IL	27,006	HC

OPERATIONS RESEARCH AND ENGINEERING

School	ST	$IS	SR
Cal State, Fullerton	CA	21,902	C
Cornell Univ	NY	67,591	MC

OPTICAL ENGINEERING

School	ST	$IS	SR
Rose-Hulman Inst of Technology	IN	59,823	MC
The Univ of Arizona	AZ	24,086	C
Univ of Alabama in Huntsville	AL	20,028	VC
Univ of Rochester	NY	65,032	MC

OPTICS

School	ST	$IS	SR
Capitol Technology Univ	MD	46,280	SP
Saginaw Valley State Univ	MI	19,284	C
The Univ of Arizona	AZ	24,086	C
Univ of Central Florida	FL	16,379	VC
Univ of Rochester	NY	65,032	MC

OPTOMETRY

School	ST	$IS	SR
Baylor Univ	TX	56,803	HC
Indiana Univ Bloomington	IN	20,791	HC
Oral Roberts Univ	OK	34,316	C
Univ of Calif at Berkeley	CA	29,886	MC
Walla Walla Univ	WA	34,845	C

ORGAN PERFORMANCE

School	ST	$IS	SR
Boston Univ	MA	67,352	MC
Houghton College	NY	40,558	VC
Samford Univ	AL	40,770	VC
Texas Christian Univ	TX	57,120	HC
The Master's Univ	CA	43,870	C
Wright State Univ	OH	16,983	C

ORGANIZATIONAL BEHAVIOR

School	ST	$IS	SR
Assumption College	MA	48,455	VC
Benedictine Univ	IL	38,300	C
Coe College	IA	51,570	VC
College of St. Scholastica	MN	45,734	C+
DePaul Univ	IL	52,807	VC
Franklin Univ	OH	11,616	NC
Hannibal-LaGrange Univ	MO	29,815	C
Huntington Univ	IN	33,996	C
Ithaca College	NY	58,158	VC+
Johnson & Wales Univ/Denver Campus	CO	44,768	C
La Salle Univ	PA	43,476	C
Methodist Univ	NC	58,130	C
National Univ	CA	17,849	LC
New York Univ	NY	68,139	MC
Northwestern Univ	IL	68,725	MC
Oral Roberts Univ	OK	34,316	C
Pitzer College	CA	68,500	HC+
Robert Morris Univ	PA	40,600	C
Rollins College	FL	58,670	HC
St. Louis Univ	MO	49,866	HC
United States Military Academy at West Point	NY		HC+
Univ of Calif at Davis	CA	28,468	HC
Univ of Central Missouri	MO	18,982	C
Univ of Cincinnati	OH	22,118	VC
Univ of Illinois at Urbana-Champaign	IL	27,006	HC
Univ of Mich/Ann Arbor	MI	25,274	MC
Univ of Minn/Crookston	MN	19,126	C
Univ of North Texas	TX	20,082	C
Univ of San Francisco	CA	60,580	C
Univ of Tulsa	OK	52,625	HC

ORGANIZATIONAL COMMUNICATION

School	ST	$IS	SR
DePaul Univ	IL	52,807	VC
Lewis Univ	IL	41,710	C

ORGANIZATIONAL LEADERSHIP AND MANAGEMENT

School	ST	$IS	SR
Adams State Univ	CO	15,420	LC
Alderson Broaddus Univ	WV	35,000	LC
Arizona State Univ at the Polytechnic Campus	AZ	22,394	VC
Ashford Univ	CA	10,480	C
Auburn Univ at Montgomery	AL	15,000	C
Aurora Univ	IL	34,990	C
Baldwin Wallace Univ	OH	42,464	VC
Blackburn College	IL	28,526	LC
Bluffton Univ	OH	40,950	C+
Bradley Univ	IL	43,240	VC
Brown Univ	RI	64,566	MC
Bryant Univ	RI	57,204	VC
Calif Baptist Univ	CA	42,986	C
Cameron Univ	OK	11,632	LC
Carroll Univ	WI	38,100	C+
Chestnut Hill College	PA	47,180	C
Claflin Univ	SC	25,592	LC
College of St Joseph	VT	32,400	LC
Concordia Univ St. Paul	MN	29,050	C
Defiance College	OH	42,240	LC
Drexel Univ	PA	65,927	HC
Drury Univ	MO	37,555	VC
Eastern Illinois Univ	IL	21,414	C
Eastern Univ	PA	39,540	C
Edgewood College	WI	35,950	C
George Fox Univ	OR	42,938	C
Greenville College	IL	27,012	LC
Hilbert College	NY	32,650	LC
Indiana Univ Bloomington	IN	20,791	HC
Indiana Univ-Purdue Univ Fort Wayne	IN	18,675	C
Indiana Univ-Purdue Univ Indianapolis	IN	18,952	C
Keystone College	PA	28,680	LC
Le Moyne College	NY	47,305	VC
Lewis Univ	IL	41,710	C
Loyola Univ Chicago	IL	57,158	VC
Lubbock Christian Univ	TX	29,727	C
Marquette Univ	WI	53,090	VC+
Maryville Univ of St. Louis	MO	38,558	VC
McNeese State Univ	LA	7,838	C
MidAmerica Nazarene Univ	KS	37,808	C
Millikin Univ	IL	44,148	C
Missouri Baptist Univ	MO	35,594	C
Morningside College	IA	39,780	C
Mount Aloysius College	PA	29,976	C
Mount St. Joseph Univ	OH	33,880	LC
National Univ	CA	17,849	LC
Northern Kentucky Univ	KY	16,486	C
Northwestern State Univ of Louisiana	LA	16,534	LC
Nyack College	NY	34,450	LC
Ohio Valley Univ	WV	28,800	C
Palm Beach Atlantic Univ	FL	39,250	C
Point Loma Nazarene Univ	CA	46,150	C+
Point Park Univ	PA	41,270	C
Purdue Univ Northwest	IN	15,178	C
Purdue Univ/West Lafayette	IN	20,032	MC
St. Joseph's Univ	PA	58,540	VC
St. Louis Univ	MO	49,866	HC
Samford Univ	AL	40,770	VC
Seattle Univ	WA	54,957	VC
Simpson Univ	CA	34,722	C
Southeastern Univ	FL	34,910	LC
Southwestern Okla State Univ	OK	12,205	C
Spring Hill College	AL	48,488	C
St. Ambrose Univ	IA	40,180	C
St. Joseph's College, New York/Brooklyn Campus	NY	25,114	LC
St. Joseph's College, New York/Long Island Campus	NY	25,124	C
Stetson Univ	FL	57,174	VC+
Thomas Edison State Univ	NJ	6,350	NC
Tiffin Univ	OH	34,900	LC
Union College	KY	32,310	C
Univ of Charleston	WV	35,000	LC
Univ of Delaware	DE	32,214	VC
Univ of Louisiana at Monroe	LA	15,970	C
Univ of Mary Hardin-Baylor	TX	35,292	C+
Univ of Minn/Duluth	MN	20,292	C
Univ of Nebr - Lincoln	NE	18,589	VC
Univ of North Texas	TX	20,082	C
Univ of St. Francis	IL	40,828	C
Univ of Wyoming	WY	15,537	C
Viterbo Univ	WI	34,660	C
Voorhees College	SC	19,976	C
Washington Adventist Univ	MD	32,050	LC
Wayne State Univ	MI	23,085	C
West Liberty Univ	WV	16,158	C
Wheeling Jesuit Univ	WV	37,106	LC
Wright State Univ	OH	16,983	C

OUTDOOR LEADERSHIP/ EDUCATION

School	ST	$IS	SR
Black Hills State Univ	SD	16,622	C
John Brown Univ	AR	35,184	VC
Messiah College	PA	44,380	VC
Montana State Univ Billings	MT	13,336	LC
Montreat College	NC	34,605	LC
North Greenville Univ	SC	25,930	C
West Liberty Univ	WV	16,158	C

OUTDOOR MINISTRY & ADVENTURE LEADERSHIP

School	ST	$IS	SR
Eastern Mennonite Univ	VA	42,550	C

PACIFIC AREA STUDIES

School	ST	$IS	SR
Brigham Young Univ/Hawaii	HI	11,710	C
Hawaii Pacific Univ	HI	33,420	C
New York Univ	NY	68,139	MC
Univ of Hawaii at Manoa	HI	23,261	C

PACKAGING SCIENCE

School	ST	$IS	SR
Cal State, Fullerton	CA	21,902	C
Mich State Univ	MI	24,542	VC
Univ of Wisc-Stout	WI	19,667	C

PAINTING

School	ST	$IS	SR
Adams State Univ	CO	15,420	LC
Andrews Univ	MI	41,732	C
Aquinas College - Mich	MI	38,876	VC
Art Academy of Cincinnati	OH	37,790	SP
Barton College	NC	39,854	C
Bennington College	VT	66,280	MC
Biola Univ	CA	48,686	C
Boston Univ	MA	67,352	MC
Calif College of the Arts	CA	52,758	SP
Cal State, San Bernardino	CA	20,106	C
Cleveland Inst of Art	OH	51,455	SP
College for Creative Studies	MI	51,210	SP
Columbia College - Missouri	MO	28,179	C
Dominican Univ	IL	42,472	C+
Escuela de Artes Plasticas de PR	PR	11,236	
Ferris State Univ	MI	21,458	C
Harding Univ	AR	25,440	C
Hofstra Univ	NY	58,210	C+
Howard Univ	DC	37,616	C+
Indiana Univ-Purdue Univ Fort Wayne	IN	18,675	C
Indiana Wesleyan Univ	IN	33,674	C
Kansas City Art Inst	MO	48,200	SP
Kutztown Univ of Pennsylvania	PA	19,477	C
Laguna College of Art and Design	CA	41,422	SP
Lewis Univ	IL	41,710	C

ST = STATE $IS = IN-STATE COSTS SR = SELECTOR RATING

School	ST	$IS	SR
Maine College of Art	ME	45,940	SP
Marshall Univ	WV	18,044	C
Maryland Inst College of Art	MD	58,740	SP
Marywood Univ	PA	47,840	C
Mass College of Art and Design	MA	24,800	SP
Memphis College of Art	TN	50,880	SP
Milwaukee Inst of Art & Design	WI	45,880	SP
Minneapolis College of Art and Design	MN	44,218	SP
Montserrat College of Art	MA	41,500	SP
Moore College of Art and Design	PA	55,118	SP
Oberlin College	OH	68,942	MC
Ohio Univ	OH	23,394	VC
Old Dominion Univ	VA	21,618	C
Otis College of Art and Design	CA	54,670	SP
Pacific Northwest College of Art	OR	38,494	SP
Rhode Island School of Design	RI	59,960	SP
San Francisco Art Inst	CA	60,865	SP
Savannah College of Art and Design	GA	49,595	SP
School of the Art Inst of Chicago	IL	61,830	SP
St. Ambrose Univ	IA	40,180	C
SUNY at Binghamton	NY	24,100	MC
SUNY at New Paltz	NY	20,840	C
SUNY/Buffalo State	NY	20,583	LC
SUNY/Fredonia	NY	20,818	C
Syracuse Univ	NY	62,313	HC
Temple Univ	PA	24,392	C+
The Catholic Univ of America	DC	58,376	VC
Univ of Dallas	TX	50,676	VC
Univ of Hartford	CT	49,776	C
Univ of Illinois at Chicago	IL	24,664	VC
Univ of Illinois at Urbana-Champaign	IL	27,006	HC
Univ of Iowa	IA	19,415	HC
Univ of Kansas	KS	20,884	VC
Univ of Mass Dartmouth	MA	26,507	C
Univ of Miami	FL	63,494	MC
Univ of Mich/Ann Arbor	MI	25,274	MC
Univ of Oregon	OR	24,021	VC
Univ of San Francisco	CA	60,580	C
Univ of the Arts	PA	56,579	SP
Univ of Washington	WA	23,091	MC
Virginia Commonwealth Univ	VA	23,811	VC
Washington Univ in St. Louis	MO	67,539	MC
Webster Univ	MO	37,490	C
Western Washington Univ	WA	18,904	VC
Youngstown State Univ	OH	17,487	C

PALEONTOLOGY

School	ST	$IS	SR
Univ of Okla	OK	19,651	HC

PAPER AND PULP SCIENCE

School	ST	$IS	SR
N Car State Univ	NC	22,434	HC+
SUNY/The College of Environmental Science and Forestry	NY	23,728	VC
Univ of Maine	ME	21,038	VC
Univ of Washington	WA	23,091	MC
Univ of Wisc-Stevens Point	WI	14,043	C

PAPER ENGINEERING

School	ST	$IS	SR
SUNY/The College of Environmental Science and Forestry	NY	23,728	VC
Western Mich Univ	MI	21,791	C

PARALEGAL STUDIES

School	ST	$IS	SR
Anna Maria College	MA	51,020	C
Avila Univ	MO	27,100	C
Bay Path Univ	MA	46,356	C
Cal State, San Bernardino	CA	20,106	C
Calumet College of St. Joseph	IN	22,735	C
Central Washington Univ	WA	16,803	C
College of St. Mary	NE	27,500	C
Concordia Univ Wisc	WI	35,910	C
Daemen College	NY	40,336	C
Davenport Univ	MI	25,896	LC
Defiance College	OH	42,240	LC
Drury Univ	MO	37,555	VC
Eastern Kentucky Univ	KY	17,742	C
Eastern Mich Univ	MI	19,761	C
Elms College	MA	49,602	VC
Hamline Univ	MN	50,152	C
Hilbert College	NY	32,650	LC
Hodges Univ	FL	20,160	LC
Humphreys College	CA	27,790	C
Husson Univ	ME	26,508	C
Idaho State Univ	ID	13,619	LC
Johnson & Wales Univ/North Miami Campus	FL	44,768	C
Johnson & Wales Univ/ Providence Campus	RI	44,768	C
Kent State Univ	OH	20,928	C
Kutztown Univ of Pennsylvania	PA	19,477	C
Lake Erie College	OH	38,914	LC
Lewis Univ	IL	41,710	C
Lock Haven Univ of Pennsylvania	PA	20,544	LC
Loyola Univ Chicago	IL	57,158	VC
Madonna Univ	MI	30,450	LC
Maryville Univ of St. Louis	MO	38,558	VC
Mercy College	NY	32,614	C
Minn State Univ, Moorhead	MN	21,393	C
Miss College	MS	25,850	C
Miss Univ for Women	MS	17,065	C
Morehead State Univ	KY	18,386	LC
Mount Aloysius College	PA	29,976	C
Mount St. Joseph Univ	OH	33,880	LC
Nebr Wesleyan Univ	NE	42,026	C+
New York City College of Technology	NY	7,185	LC
Nova Southeastern Univ	FL	38,534	C+
Peirce College	PA	16,780	NC
Pennsylvania College of Technology	PA	27,693	NC
Point Park Univ	PA	41,270	C
Quinnipiac Univ	CT	60,970	VC
Roger Williams Univ	RI	48,074	VC
St. Mary-of-the-Woods College	IN	40,424	LC
Samford Univ	AL	40,770	VC
Shawnee State Univ	OH	16,998	C
Southern Illinois Univ Carbondale	IL	24,554	C
Stephen F. Austin State Univ	TX	18,484	LC
Stevenson Univ	MD	48,412	C
Suffolk Univ	MA	52,316	C
Texas Wesleyan Univ	TX	37,338	C
Tiffin Univ	OH	34,900	LC
Tulane Univ	LA	67,496	MC
Univ of Alaska Anchorage	AK	17,914	C
Univ of Detroit Mercy	MI	48,816	C
Univ of Great Falls	MT	38,524	C
Univ of La Verne	CA	55,600	C
Univ of Louisville	KY	19,692	C
Univ of Maryland Univ College	MD	26,146	LC
Univ of Mass Boston	MA	13,828	C
Univ of Miss	MS	18,802	C
Univ of North Georgia	GA	17,316	C
Washburn Univ	KS	15,827	C
Western Kentucky Univ	KY	16,850	C
William Woods Univ	MO	32,040	C
Winona State Univ	MN	18,109	C

PARKS AND RECREATION MANAGEMENT

School	ST	$IS	SR
Alabama State Univ	AL	16,490	LC
Arizona State Univ at the Downtown Phoenix Campus	AZ	24,634	VC
Arkansas Tech Univ	AR	16,534	LC
Aurora Univ	IL	34,990	C
Belmont Abbey College	NC	28,794	C
Bemidji State Univ	MN	17,730	C
Cal State, Sacramento	CA	19,060	C
Calif Univ of Pennsylvania	PA	20,425	LC
Central Mich Univ	MI	20,330	C
Central Washington Univ	WA	16,803	C
Cheyney Univ of Pennsylvania	PA	20,896	LC
Clemson Univ	SC		HC
Concord Univ	WV	14,954	LC
Davenport Univ	MI	25,896	LC
Delaware State Univ	DE	19,376	LC
East Carolina Univ	NC	16,539	C
Eastern Washington Univ	WA	17,896	LC
Evangel Univ	MO	28,898	C
Florida International Univ	FL	20,281	C
George Mason Univ	VA	19,884	C
Houghton College	NY	40,558	VC
Humboldt State Univ	CA	21,708	C
Huntington Univ	IN	33,996	C
Illinois State Univ	IL	23,418	VC
Indiana Inst of Technology	IN	34,240	LC
Indiana State Univ	IN	23,223	LC
Johnson & Wales Univ/ Charlotte Campus	NC	44,768	C
Johnson & Wales Univ/North Miami Campus	FL	44,768	C
Johnson & Wales Univ/ Providence Campus	RI	44,768	C
Kansas State Univ	KS	17,780	VC
Kent State Univ	OH	20,928	C
Lake Superior State Univ	MI	19,867	C
Marshall Univ	WV	18,044	C
Mich State Univ	MI	24,542	VC
Midland Univ	NE	39,512	C
Minn State Univ, Mankato	MN	17,190	C
Missouri Western State Univ	MO	17,822	LC
N Car State Univ	NC	22,434	HC+
Northern Arizona Univ	AZ	21,003	C
Northern Mich Univ	MI	20,853	C
Northland College	WI	41,103	C+
Ohio Univ	OH	23,394	VC
Old Dominion Univ	VA	21,618	C
Oregon State Univ	OR	23,337	VC
Pennsylvania State Univ - Univ Park	PA	29,716	HC
Prescott College	AZ	38,201	C
Slippery Rock Univ of Pennsylvania	PA	20,450	C
S Dak State Univ	SD	15,874	C
Southwest Baptist Univ	MO	30,890	LC
Southwestern Okla State Univ	OK	12,205	C
Springfield College	MA	48,775	C
St. Thomas Aquinas College	NY	32,450	C
Stephen F. Austin State Univ	TX	18,484	LC
The Univ of Utah	UT	18,751	VC
Unity College	ME	37,670	C
Univ of Arkansas at Pine Bluff	AR	13,541	C
Univ of Idaho	ID	16,158	C
Univ of Illinois at Urbana-Champaign	IL	27,006	HC
Univ of Iowa	IA	19,415	HC
Univ of Maine	ME	21,038	VC
Univ of Maine at Machias	ME	22,960	C
Univ of Miss	MS	18,802	C
Univ of Missouri-Columbia	MO	20,463	VC
Univ of Nebr - Lincoln	NE	18,589	VC
Univ of Southern Miss	MS	13,170	C
Univ of Vermont	VT	29,792	HC
Univ of Wisc-La Crosse	WI	15,425	VC
Utah State Univ	UT	13,235	C
Virginia Polytechnic Inst and State Univ	VA	21,920	VC
Virginia Wesleyan Univ	VA	45,980	LC
West Virginia Univ	WV	18,952	VC
Western Carolina Univ	NC	13,965	C
Western Illinois Univ	IL	20,897	C
Western Washington Univ	WA	18,904	VC
Wingate Univ	NC	41,900	C
York College of Pennsylvania	PA	29,240	C

PASTORAL STUDIES

School	ST	$IS	SR
Andrews Univ	MI	41,732	C
Bethel College	IN	36,830	C
Brescia Univ	KY	29,890	VC
Brewton-Parker College	GA	26,120	LC
Cairn Univ	PA	37,572	C
Concordia Univ Wisc	WI	35,910	C
Corban Univ	OR	41,700	C
East Texas Baptist Univ	TX	34,444	C
Grace Bible College	MI	25,250	C
Greenville College	IL	27,012	LC
Hope International Univ	CA	42,730	C
Houghton College	NY	40,558	VC
Kentucky Christian Univ	KY	26,836	LC
Loyola Univ Chicago	IL	57,158	VC
Madonna Univ	MI	30,450	LC
Marian Univ	IN	43,206	C
Morris College	SC	19,195	LC
Mount Vernon Nazarene Univ	OH	35,944	C
Newman Univ	KS	37,382	C
North Central Univ	MN	30,610	C
Northwest Univ	WA	38,720	VC
Nyack College	NY	34,450	LC
Okla Baptist Univ	OK	33,990	C
Okla Wesleyan Univ	OK	34,434	C
Olivet Nazarene Univ	IL	41,840	VC
St. Mary's Univ of Minn	MN	42,440	C
Simpson Univ	CA	34,722	C
Southeastern Univ	FL	34,910	LC
Southwest Baptist Univ	MO	30,890	LC
St. Ambrose Univ	IA	40,180	C
The Master's Univ	CA	43,870	C
The Univ of Mary	ND	23,180	C
Toccoa Falls College	GA	30,048	C
Trevecca Nazarene Univ	TN	31,186	C
Union College	NE	23,270	C
Union Univ	TN	41,160	VC
Universidad Adventista de las Antillas	PR	16,606	
Univ of Dallas	TX	50,676	VC
Univ of Northwestern - St. Paul	MN	39,530	C
Univ of St. Mary	KS	37,080	NC
Vanguard Univ of Southern Calif	CA	42,400	VC
Warner Univ	FL	28,216	C

PEACE STUDIES

School	ST	$IS	SR
Berea College	KY	7,094	C
Cal State, Dominguez Hills	CA	19,022	LC
Chapman Univ	CA	65,504	HC
Colgate Univ	NY	67,500	MC
College of St. Benedict	MN	54,480	C
College of St. Scholastica	MN	45,734	C+
DePaul Univ	IL	52,807	VC
DePauw Univ	IN	58,688	VC
Earlham College	IN	55,670	HC
Eastern Mennonite Univ	VA	42,550	C
Elon Univ	NC	46,142	HC
Goshen College	IN	44,350	C
Goucher College	MD	56,110	VC
Guilford College	NC	45,973	C
Hamline Univ	MN	50,152	C
Hampshire College	MA	65,214	MC
John Carroll Univ	OH	51,570	C
Juniata College	PA	58,118	VC
Le Moyne College	NY	47,305	VC
Manchester Univ	IN	41,540	C
Manhattan College	NY	55,652	C
Marquette Univ	WI	53,090	VC+
Messiah College	PA	44,380	VC
Naropa Univ	CO	43,278	NC
Nazareth College	NY	46,784	C
Norwich Univ	VT	56,234	C
Ohio Dominican Univ	OH	41,340	C+
Regis Univ	CO	46,380	C
St. John's Univ	MN	53,472	C
Salisbury Univ	MD	21,132	VC
Swarthmore College	PA	63,550	MC
The Univ of Utah	UT	18,751	VC
Tufts Univ	MA		MC
Univ of Calif at Berkeley	CA	29,886	MC
Univ of Hawaii at Manoa	HI	23,261	C
Univ of Mass Lowell	MA	27,296	VC
Univ of N Car at Chapel Hill	NC	20,561	MC
Univ of N Car at Greensboro	NC	15,998	C
Univ of Wisc-Milwaukee	WI	21,538	C
Wartburg College	IA	49,478	C
Wellesley College	MA	66,984	MC
Whitworth Univ	WA	53,682	VC

PERCUSSION

School	ST	$IS	SR
Boston Univ	MA	67,352	MC
Central Washington Univ	WA	16,803	C
Eastern Mich Univ	MI	19,761	C
Indiana Univ-Purdue Univ Fort Wayne	IN	18,675	C
Marshall Univ	WV	18,044	C
New England Conservatory of Music	MA	63,170	SP
Northwestern Univ	IL	68,725	MC
Roosevelt Univ	IL	41,890	VC
San Francisco Conservatory of Music	CA	57,310	SP
Southeastern Univ	FL	34,910	LC
Syracuse Univ	NY	62,313	HC
Texas Christian Univ	TX	57,120	HC
Univ of Iowa	IA	19,415	HC
Univ of Kansas	KS	20,884	VC
Univ of N Car at Greensboro	NC	15,998	C
Wright State Univ	OH	16,983	C
Youngstown State Univ	OH	17,487	C

PERFORMING ARTS

School	ST	$IS	SR
Adelphi Univ	NY	49,792	C
Appalachian State Univ	NC	15,394	VC
Aquinas College - Mich	MI	38,876	VC
Arizona State Univ at the Tempe Campus	AZ	23,001	VC
Baylor Univ	TX	56,803	HC
Bennington College	VT	66,280	MC
Biola Univ	CA	48,686	C
Blackburn College	IL	28,526	LC
Boston Univ	MA	67,352	MC
Bowling Green State Univ	OH	19,975	C
Brigham Young Univ	UT	13,248	MC
Brown Univ	RI	64,566	MC
Butler Univ	IN	52,890	VC+
Calif Baptist Univ	CA	42,986	C
Cal State, Fullerton	CA	21,902	C
Carthage College	WI	48,835	C
CUNY/City College	NY	20,204	C
College of the Ozarks	MO	7,530	VC
Colo State Univ	CO	23,033	C
Columbia College	SC	36,550	C
Columbia College Chicago	IL	40,104	C
Cornell Univ	NY	67,591	MC
DePaul Univ	IL	52,807	VC
DeSales Univ	PA	47,520	C
Dominican Univ	IL	42,472	C+
Eastern Kentucky Univ	KY	17,742	C
Eastern Mich Univ	MI	19,761	C
Elizabethtown College	PA	56,340	VC
Emerson College	MA	61,824	HC+
Ferrum College	VA	43,970	C
Fontbonne Univ	MO	34,606	C
Fordham Univ	NY	68,431	MC
Friends Univ	KS	38,000	C
Georgetown College	KY	41,440	C
Hampshire College	MA	65,214	MC
Huntington Univ	IN	33,996	C
Illinois Wesleyan Univ	IL	56,430	VC+
Ithaca College	NY	58,158	VC+
Johnson C. Smith Univ	NC	25,336	LC
Johnson State College	VT	22,672	C
Kean Univ	NJ	25,620	C
Lees-McRae College	NC	33,944	NC
Lindenwood Univ	MO	25,760	C
Mars Hill Univ	NC	41,104	C
Mary Baldwin Univ	VA	40,495	C
Mass College of Liberal Arts	MA	20,659	C
Millikin Univ	IL	44,148	C
Missouri State Univ	MO	15,837	C+
New England Conservatory of Music	MA	63,170	SP
New York Univ	NY	68,139	MC
N Dak State Univ	ND	16,245	VC
Northwestern Univ	IL	68,725	MC
Oakland Univ	MI	20,763	C
Oberlin College	OH	68,942	MC
Ohio Univ	OH	23,394	VC
Old Dominion Univ	VA	21,618	C
Piedmont College	GA	34,334	C
Plymouth State Univ	NH	23,180	LC
Point Park Univ	PA	41,270	C
Roosevelt Univ	IL	41,890	VC
St. Mary's College of Calif	CA	57,420	C
Savannah College of Art and Design	GA	49,595	SP
Seton Hill Univ	PA	46,972	VC

ST = STATE $IS = IN-STATE COSTS SR = SELECTOR RATING

School	ST	$IS	SR
Shenandoah Univ	VA	42,100	C
Southern Methodist Univ	TX	69,008	MC
Southwest Baptist Univ	MO	30,890	LC
St. Lawrence Univ	NY	66,646	HC+
SUNY at Geneseo	NY	21,622	VC
Suffolk Univ	MA	52,316	C
Tarleton State Univ	TX	15,248	LC
Temple Univ	PA	24,392	C+
Texas A&M Univ at College Station	TX	20,771	VC+
The American Univ	DC	61,317	HC
The Univ of Arizona	AZ	24,086	C
The Univ of Tenn at Martin	TN	15,212	C
Univ of Dayton	OH	54,930	VC
Univ of Florida	FL	16,291	HC+
Univ of Hartford	CT	49,776	C
Univ of Iowa	IA	19,415	HC
Univ of Mary Hardin-Baylor	TX	35,292	C+
Univ of Mich/Ann Arbor	MI	25,274	MC
Univ of Missouri-Kansas City	MO	19,563	VC
Univ of N Car at Greensboro	NC	15,998	C
Univ of N Car School of the Arts	NC	25,587	SP
Univ of North Texas	TX	20,082	C
Univ of San Francisco	CA	60,580	C
Univ of Southern Indiana	IN	16,808	C
Univ of Tampa	FL	38,928	VC
Univ of Texas Rio Grande Valley	TX	15,573	LC
Washington Univ in St. Louis	MO	67,539	MC
West Chester Univ of Pennsylvania	PA	19,171	VC
West Texas A&M Univ	TX	13,478	C
Western Kentucky Univ	KY	16,850	C
Western Mich Univ	MI	21,791	C
Wheelock College	MA	51,325	LC
Youngstown State Univ	OH	17,487	C

PERSONAL FINANCIAL PLANNING

School	ST	$IS	SR
Kansas State Univ	KS	17,780	VC
Old Dominion Univ	VA	21,618	C
Texas Tech Univ	TX	20,156	C+
Univ of Wisc-Madison	WI	21,647	MC
Western Mich Univ	MI	21,791	C

PERSONNEL MANAGEMENT

School	ST	$IS	SR
Auburn Univ	AL	24,300	VC+
Auburn Univ at Montgomery	AL	15,000	C
Baylor Univ	TX	56,803	HC
Bellevue Univ	NE	20,300	NC
Bloomfield College	NJ	40,100	LC
Bryant Univ	RI	57,204	VC
Cal State, Long Beach	CA	18,850	C
CUNY/Baruch College	NY	21,609	HC
Dickinson State Univ	ND	12,372	LC
Eastern Mich Univ	MI	19,761	C
Eastern Washington Univ	WA	17,896	LC
Florida State Univ	FL	16,771	HC
Grand Valley State Univ	MI	22,250	C+
Hawaii Pacific Univ	HI	33,420	C
King's College	PA	48,240	C
Lamar Univ	TX	18,014	LC
Limestone College	SC	32,100	C
Louisiana Tech Univ	LA	11,422	VC
Mich State Univ	MI	24,542	VC
Nicholls State Univ	LA	14,959	C
Northern State Univ	SD	15,570	C
Oakland Univ	MI	20,763	C
Our Lady of the Lake Univ	TX	37,790	LC
Portland State Univ	OR	19,443	C
Roosevelt Univ	IL	41,890	VC
Rowan Univ	NJ	24,491	VC
San Francisco State Univ	CA	18,514	LC
Seton Hill Univ	PA	46,972	VC
Silver Lake College of the Holy Family	WI	36,290	LC
St. Cloud State Univ	MN	10,600	C
Tarleton State Univ	TX	15,248	LC
Troy Univ	AL	16,171	C
Univ of Illinois at Urbana-Champaign	IL	27,006	HC
Univ of Louisiana at Lafayette	LA	14,516	C
Univ of Nebr - Kearney	NE	17,014	LC
Univ of PR-Rio Piedras campus	PR	13,327	
Univ of Southern Miss	MS	13,170	C
Univ of the Sacred Heart	PR	17,932	
Univ of Washington	WA	23,091	MC
Univ of Wisc-Whitewater	WI	13,976	C
Utah State Univ	UT	13,235	C
Weber State Univ	UT	14,112	C
Wilmington Univ	DE	8,762	NC

PETROLEUM SYSTEMS / GEOLOGY

School	ST	$IS	SR
Rocky Mountain College	MT	35,776	C

PETROLEUM/NATURAL GAS ENGINEERING

School	ST	$IS	SR
Colo School of Mines	CO	29,319	MC
Louisiana State Univ and A&M College	LA	18,677	VC
Marietta College	OH	46,190	C
Missouri Univ of Science and Technology	MO	18,655	HC
Montana Tech of the Univ of Montana	MT	15,447	VC
New Mexico Inst of Mining and Technology	NM	15,385	HC+
Nicholls State Univ	LA	14,959	C
Pennsylvania State Univ - Univ Park	PA	29,716	HC
Stanford Univ	CA	62,541	MC
Texas A&M Univ at College Station	TX	20,771	VC+
Texas A&M Univ at Kingsville	TX	16,580	LC
Texas Tech Univ	TX	20,156	C+
The Univ of Texas at Austin	TX	20,206	MC
Univ of Alaska Fairbanks	AK	16,874	VC
Univ of Houston	TX	21,871	VC
Univ of Kansas	KS	20,884	VC
Univ of Louisiana at Lafayette	LA	14,516	C
Univ of N Dak	ND	16,673	C
Univ of Okla	OK	19,651	HC
Univ of Southern Calif	CA	66,631	MC
Univ of Tulsa	OK	52,625	HC
Univ of Wyoming	WY	15,537	C
West Virginia Univ	WV	18,952	VC
West Virginia Wesleyan College	WV	39,188	C

PHARMACEUTICAL CHEMISTRY

School	ST	$IS	SR
Lehigh Univ	PA	63,860	MC
Mich Tech Univ	MI	25,551	VC+
Univ of Dayton	OH	54,930	VC
Univ of Mich/Ann Arbor	MI	25,274	MC
Univ of the Sciences	PA	40,738	VC

PHARMACEUTICAL SCIENCE

School	ST	$IS	SR
Albany College of Pharmacy and Health Sciences	NY	44,421	SP
Belmont Univ	TN	44,500	VC+
Cedarville Univ	OH	36,244	VC
CUNY/York College	NY	6,747	LC
Cleveland State Univ	OH	22,290	C
DeSales Univ	PA	47,520	C
Duquesne Univ	PA	48,508	VC
Howard Univ	DC	37,616	C+
MCPHS Univ	MA	45,470	SP
Northeastern Univ	MA	65,352	MC
Ohio State Univ at Columbus	OH	22,843	MC
Purdue Univ/West Lafayette	IN	20,032	MC
S Dak State Univ	SD	15,874	C
SUNY/Univ at Buffalo	NY	23,122	C
The Univ of Arizona	AZ	24,086	C
Univ of Calif at Irvine	CA	33,857	VC
Univ of Georgia	GA	21,878	HC
Univ of Houston	TX	21,871	VC
Univ of Louisiana at Monroe	LA	15,970	C
Univ of Mich/Ann Arbor	MI	25,274	MC
Univ of Miss	MS	18,802	C
Univ of Pittsburgh	PA	30,030	MC
Univ of Rhode Island	RI	26,066	VC
Univ of the Sciences	PA	40,738	VC
West Chester Univ of Pennsylvania	PA	19,171	VC

PHARMACOLOGY

School	ST	$IS	SR
Arizona State Univ at the West Campus	AZ	21,513	VC
Howard Univ	DC	37,616	C+
MCPHS Univ	MA	45,470	SP
New York Univ	NY	68,139	MC
SUNY/Univ at Buffalo	NY	23,122	C
Stony Brook Univ/The SUNY	NY	22,703	MC
The Univ of Arizona	AZ	24,086	C
Univ of Illinois at Chicago	IL	24,664	VC
Univ of Montana	MT	14,105	C
Univ of the Sciences	PA	40,738	VC
Univ of Wisc-Madison	WI	21,647	MC

PHARMACY

School	ST	$IS	SR
Butler Univ	IN	52,890	VC+
Chapman Univ	CA	65,504	HC
Drake Univ	IA	49,220	HC
Duquesne Univ	PA	48,508	VC
Florida A&M Univ	FL	15,361	C
Howard Univ	DC	37,616	C+
Husson Univ	ME	26,508	C
Johnson C. Smith Univ	NC	25,336	LC
Lamar Univ	TX	18,014	LC
LIU Brooklyn	NY	50,698	C
MCPHS Univ	MA	45,470	SP
N Dak State Univ	ND	16,245	VC
Northeastern Univ	MA	65,352	MC
Ohio Northern Univ	OH	44,050	VC
Presbyterian College	SC	47,186	C
Regis Univ	CO	46,380	C
Roberts Wesleyan College	NY	41,116	C
Rutgers Univ - Camden	NJ	26,595	C
Rutgers Univ - New Brunswick	NJ	27,090	HC
Samford Univ	AL	40,770	VC
Seton Hill Univ	PA	46,972	VC
S Dak State Univ	SD	15,874	C
Southwestern Okla State Univ	OK	12,205	C
St. John's Univ	NY	57,160	C+
SUNY/Univ at Buffalo	NY	23,122	C
The College of Idaho	ID	36,415	C
The Univ of Arizona	AZ	24,086	C
The Univ of Texas at Austin	TX	20,206	MC
The Univ of Calif at Santa Barbara	CA	30,627	HC+
Univ of Conn	CT	27,394	
Univ of Illinois at Chicago	IL	24,664	VC
Univ of Iowa	IA	19,415	HC
Univ of Kansas	KS	20,884	VC
Univ of Louisiana at Monroe	LA	15,970	C
Univ of Mich/Ann Arbor	MI	25,274	MC
Univ of the Sciences	PA	40,738	VC
Univ of Toledo	OH	19,336	C
Walla Walla Univ	WA	34,845	C
Washington Univ in St. Louis	MO	67,539	MC
West Virginia Univ	WV	18,952	VC
Wingate Univ	NC	41,900	C

PHILOSOPHY

School	ST	$IS	SR
Adelphi Univ	NY	49,792	C
Adrian College	MI	45,550	C
Agnes Scott College	GA	51,930	VC+
Albertus Magnus College	CT	44,016	LC
Albion College	MI	55,260	C
Albright College	PA	57,326	C
Alfred Univ	NY	37,490	C
Allegheny College	PA	57,620	VC
Alma College	MI	49,410	VC
Alvernia Univ	PA	45,330	C
Alverno College	WI	33,294	LC
American International College	MA	47,020	LC
Amherst College	MA	66,186	MC
Angelo State Univ	TX	15,882	LC
Appalachian State Univ	NC	15,394	VC
Aquinas College	TN	30,800	C+
Aquinas College - Mich	MI	38,876	VC
Arcadia Univ	PA	55,990	C+
Arizona State Univ at the Tempe Campus	AZ	23,001	VC
Arkansas State Univ	AR	16,190	C
Asbury Univ	KY	36,450	C+
Ashland Univ	OH	30,446	C
Assumption College	MA	48,455	VC
Auburn Univ	AL	24,300	VC+
Augsburg Univ	MN	45,129	C
Augustana College	IL	51,222	VC+
Augustana Univ	SD	39,968	VC
Aurora Univ	IL	34,990	C
Austin College	TX	51,059	HC
Azusa Pacific Univ	CA	43,972	C
Baker Univ	KS	37,190	C
Baldwin Wallace Univ	OH	42,464	VC
Ball State Univ	IN	19,808	C+
Bard College	NY	65,924	HC
Bard College at Simon's Rock	MA	65,795	MC
Barnard College/Columbia Univ	NY	68,762	MC
Barry Univ	FL	38,730	LC
Bates College	ME	64,500	HC
Bayamon Central Univ	PR	12,490	
Baylor Univ	TX	56,803	HC
Belhaven Univ	MS	32,250	C
Bellarmine Univ	KY	52,532	C
Bellevue Univ	NE	20,300	NC
Belmont Abbey College	NC	28,794	C
Belmont Univ	TN	44,500	VC+
Beloit College	WI	55,206	HC
Bemidji State Univ	MN	17,730	C
Benedict College	SC	28,630	NC
Benedictine College	KS	38,850	VC
Benedictine Univ	IL	38,300	C
Bennington College	VT	66,280	MC
Bentley Univ	MA	63,720	MC
Berea College	KY	7,094	C
Berry College	GA	47,466	VC
Bethel College	IN	36,830	C
Bethel Univ	MN	46,550	C+
Biola Univ	CA	48,686	C
Birmingham-Southern College	AL	44,478	C+
Bloomfield College	NJ	40,100	LC
Bloomsburg Univ of Pennsylvania	PA	19,930	C
Boise State Univ	ID	17,368	C
Boston College	MA	68,043	MC
Boston Univ	MA	67,352	MC
Bowdoin College	ME	65,980	MC
Bowling Green State Univ	OH	19,975	C
Bradley Univ	IL	43,240	VC
Brandeis Univ	MA	68,443	MC
Bridgewater State Univ	MA	22,762	C
Brigham Young Univ	UT	13,248	MC
Brown Univ	RI	64,566	MC
Bryn Athyn College	PA	32,664	C
Bryn Mawr College	PA	65,220	MC
Bucknell Univ	PA	67,136	MC
Butler Univ	IN	52,890	VC+
Cabrini Univ	PA	42,591	LC
Calif Baptist Univ	CA	42,986	C
Calif Inst of Technology	CA	64,704	MC
Calif Lutheran Univ	CA	52,853	C
Calif Polytechnic State Univ	CA	22,547	MC
Calif State Polytechnic Univ, Pomona	CA	21,811	C
Cal State, Bakersfield	CA	22,397	LC
Cal State, Chico	CA	19,790	VC
Cal State, Dominguez Hills	CA	19,022	LC
Cal State, East Bay	CA	20,748	C
Cal State, Fresno	CA	16,902	LC
Cal State, Fullerton	CA	21,902	C
Cal State, Long Beach	CA	18,850	C
Cal State, Los Angeles	CA	17,186	LC
Cal State, Northridge	CA	17,277	LC
Cal State, Sacramento	CA	19,060	C
Cal State, San Bernardino	CA	20,106	C
Cal State, Stanislaus	CA	18,053	LC
Calif Univ of Pennsylvania	PA	20,425	LC
Calvin College	MI	43,090	HC
Canisius College	NY	49,672	C
Capital Univ	OH	44,778	VC
Caribbean Univ	PR	12,227	
Carleton College	MN	66,414	MC
Carlow Univ	PA	39,696	LC
Carnegie Mellon Univ	PA	67,980	MC
Carroll College	MT	44,304	C
Carson-Newman Univ	TN	35,900	C
Carthage College	WI	48,835	C
Case Western Reserve Univ	OH	62,284	MC
Castleton Univ	VT	20,186	C
Catawba College	NC	39,820	LC
Centenary College of Louisiana	LA	49,050	C+
Central College	IA	44,592	C
Central Conn State Univ	CT	22,041	C
Central Methodist Univ	MO	31,500	VC
Central Mich Univ	MI	20,330	C
Central Washington Univ	WA	16,803	C
Centre College	KY	50,680	MC
Chapman Univ	CA	65,504	HC
Christendom College	VA	32,600	VC
Christopher Newport Univ	VA	24,878	VC+
CUNY/Baruch College	NY	21,609	HC
CUNY/Brooklyn College	NY	7,163	C+
CUNY/City College	NY	20,204	C
CUNY/Hunter College	NY	31,098	VC
CUNY/John Jay College of Criminal Justice	NY	6,359	SP
CUNY/Lehman College	NY	5,788	LC
CUNY/Queens College	NY	21,507	C
CUNY/York College	NY	6,747	LC
Claremont McKenna College	CA	69,900	MC
Clarion Univ of Pennsylvania	PA	21,608	LC
Clark Atlanta Univ	GA	31,019	LC
Clark Univ	MA	53,260	HC+
Clarke Univ	IA	42,950	C
Clemson Univ	SC		HC
Cleveland State Univ	OH	22,290	C
Coastal Carolina Univ	SC	20,340	C
Coe College	IA	51,570	VC
Colby College	ME	64,060	MC
Colgate Univ	NY	67,500	MC
College of Charleston	SC	24,046	VC
College of Mount St. Vincent	NY	45,620	C
College of St. Benedict	MN	54,480	C
College of St. Scholastica	MN	45,734	C+
College of Staten Island	NY	24,389	LC
College of the Holy Cross	MA	64,320	MC
College of the Ozarks	MO	7,530	VC
College of William & Mary	VA	34,907	MC
Colo College	CO	64,894	MC
Colo State Univ	CO	23,033	C
Columbia College - Missouri	MO	28,179	C
Columbia Univ/ School of General Studies	NY	61,470	MC
Columbia Univ/City of New York	NY	62,958	MC
Concordia College - Moorhead	MN	46,418	C
Concordia Univ, Ann Arbor	MI	38,878	C+
Conn College	CT	65,000	MC
Cornell College	IA	49,900	VC
Cornell Univ	NY	67,591	MC
Cornerstone Univ	MI	36,550	C
Covenant College	GA	44,590	HC
Creighton Univ	NE	49,452	VC
Curry College	MA	53,331	C
Dallas Baptist Univ	TX	35,220	VC
Dartmouth College	NH	68,109	MC
Davidson College	NC	60,119	MC
Denison Univ	OH	62,770	HC+
DePaul Univ	IL	52,807	VC
DePauw Univ	IN	58,688	VC
DeSales Univ	PA	47,520	C
Dickinson College	PA	66,166	MC
Doane Univ	NE	41,340	VC
Dominican Univ	IL	42,472	C+
Dordt College	IA	37,860	C+
Drake Univ	IA	49,220	HC
Drew Univ/College of Liberal Arts	NJ	53,608	VC
Drexel Univ	PA	65,927	HC
Drury Univ	MO	37,555	VC
Duke Univ	NC	68,298	MC
Duquesne Univ	PA	48,508	VC
D'Youville College	NY	37,678	C
Earlham College	IN	55,670	HC
East Carolina Univ	NC	16,539	C
East Stroudsburg Univ	PA	18,578	LC
East Tenn State Univ	TN	18,141	C
Eastern Conn State Univ	CT	23,059	C
Eastern Illinois Univ	IL	21,414	C
Eastern Kentucky Univ	KY	17,742	C
Eastern Mennonite Univ	VA	42,550	C
Eastern Mich Univ	MI	19,761	C
Eastern Univ	PA	39,540	C

ST = STATE **$IS** = IN-STATE COSTS **SR** = SELECTOR RATING

School	ST	$IS	SR
Eastern Washington Univ	WA	17,896	LC
Eckerd College	FL	55,206	VC
Edinboro Univ	PA	15,940	LC
Edward Waters College	FL	28,089	NC
Elizabethtown College	PA	56,340	VC
Elmhurst College	IL	46,514	C
Elon Univ	NC	46,142	HC
Emmanuel College	MA	53,472	C+
Emory and Henry College	VA	46,320	C
Emory Univ	GA	63,286	MC
Erskine College	SC	45,460	C
Eugene Lang College of Liberal Arts	NY	64,940	VC
Eureka College	IL	34,760	C
Excelsior College	NY	38,800	SP
Fairfield Univ	CT	61,445	HC
Fairleigh Dickinson Univ/ College at Florham	NJ	54,770	C
Fairleigh Dickinson Univ/ Metropolitan Campus	NJ	52,392	C
Faulkner Univ	AL	26,410	C
Felician Univ	NJ	46,280	LC
Ferrum College	VA	43,970	C
Fisk Univ	TN	32,066	LC
Florida Atlantic Univ	FL	18,256	C
Florida Gulf Coast Univ	FL	14,738	C
Florida International Univ	FL	20,281	C
Florida Memorial Univ	FL	22,424	LC
Florida Southern College	FL	45,978	VC
Florida State Univ	FL	16,771	HC
Fordham Univ	NY	68,431	MC
Fort Hays State Univ	KS	12,677	C
Fort Lewis College	CO	20,154	C
Franciscan Univ of Steubenville	OH	33,980	VC
Franklin and Marshall College	PA	67,960	MC
Franklin College	IN	40,550	C
Fresno Pacific Univ	CA	38,858	C
Frostburg State Univ	MD	17,280	LC
Furman Univ	SC	61,098	VC+
Gallaudet Univ	DC	30,088	LC
Gannon Univ	PA	42,922	C
Geneva College	PA	35,450	C
George Fox Univ	OR	42,938	C
George Mason Univ	VA	19,884	C
Georgetown College	KY	41,440	C
Georgetown Univ	DC	68,970	MC
Georgia College & State Univ	GA	21,884	C+
Georgia Southern Univ	GA	16,540	VC
Georgia State Univ	GA	25,250	C
Gettysburg College	PA	65,210	MC
Gonzaga Univ	WA	52,880	HC
Gordon College	MA	47,740	VC
Goucher College	MD	56,110	VC
Graceland Univ	IA	35,290	C
Grand Valley State Univ	MI	22,250	C+
Green Mountain College	VT	45,228	LC
Greenville College	IL	27,012	LC
Grinnell College	IA	63,114	MC
Grove City College	PA	26,654	VC
Guilford College	NC	45,973	C
Gustavus Adolphus College	MN	53,943	HC
Hamilton College	NY	64,250	MC
Hamline Univ	MN	50,152	C
Hampden-Sydney College	VA	57,806	VC
Hampshire College	MA	65,214	MC
Hanover College	IN	47,750	C+
Hardin-Simmons Univ	TX	36,025	C
Hartwick College	NY	51,270	C
Harvard College/Harvard Univ	MA	65,609	MC
Hastings College	NE	35,380	C+
Haverford College	PA	66,490	MC
Heidelberg Univ	OH	40,400	LC
Hendrix College	AR	54,020	VC
High Point Univ	NC	47,355	VC
Hillsdale College	MI	37,170	MC
Hiram College	OH	44,590	C
Hobart and William Smith Colleges	NY	67,050	HC+
Hofstra Univ	NY	58,210	C+
Hollins Univ	VA	49,635	VC
Holy Names Univ	CA	46,630	LC
Hood College	MD	50,540	C
Hope College	MI	42,840	VC
Houghton College	NY	40,558	VC
Howard Univ	DC	37,616	C+
Humboldt State Univ	CA	21,708	C
Huntington Univ	IN	33,996	C
Idaho State Univ	ID	13,619	LC
Illinois College	IL	41,330	VC
Illinois State Univ	IL	23,418	VC
Illinois Wesleyan Univ	IL	56,430	VC+
Indiana State Univ	IN	23,223	LC
Indiana Univ Bloomington	IN	20,791	HC
Indiana Univ Northwest	IN	7,207	LC
Indiana Univ of Pennsylvania	PA	24,474	C
Indiana Univ South Bend	IN	16,057	C
Indiana Univ Southeast	IN	16,931	C
Indiana Univ-Purdue Univ Fort Wayne	IN	18,675	C
Indiana Univ-Purdue Univ Indianapolis	IN	18,952	C
Iona College	NY	52,514	C
Iowa State Univ	IA	18,176	C
Ithaca College	NY	58,158	VC+
Jacksonville Univ	FL	49,210	C
James Madison Univ	VA	19,084	VC
John Brown Univ	AR	35,184	VC
John Carroll Univ	OH	51,570	C
Johns Hopkins Univ	MD	68,080	MC
Juniata College	PA	58,118	VC
Kalamazoo College	MI	53,931	HC
Kansas State Univ	KS	17,780	VC
Keene State College	NH	24,604	C
Kennesaw State Univ	GA	18,899	VC
Kent State Univ	OH	20,928	C
Kenyon College	OH	65,840	MC
King Univ	TN	36,976	C
King's College	PA	48,240	C
Knox College	IL	54,654	VC+
Kutztown Univ of Pennsylvania	PA	19,477	C
La Salle Univ	PA	43,476	C
Lafayette College	PA	68,520	MC
Lake Forest College	IL	50,652	VC
Lakeland Univ	WI	35,130	C
Lawrence Univ	WI	56,133	HC+
Le Moyne College	NY	47,305	VC
Lebanon Valley College	PA	55,510	VC
Lehigh Univ	PA	63,860	MC
Lenoir-Rhyne Univ	NC	47,500	LC
Lewis & Clark College	OR	60,984	MC
Lewis Univ	IL	41,710	C
Lincoln Univ	PA	20,878	LC
Linfield College	OR	53,992	C
Lipscomb Univ	TN	42,984	VC
LIU Brooklyn	NY	50,698	C
LIU Post	NY	50,698	C+
Lock Haven Univ of Pennsylvania	PA	20,544	LC
Loras College	IA	40,726	C
Louisiana State Univ and A&M College	LA	18,677	VC
Loyola Marymount Univ	CA	60,202	VC+
Loyola Univ Chicago	IL	57,158	VC
Loyola Univ Maryland	MD	61,710	VC
Loyola Univ New Orleans	LA	52,456	VC
Luther College	IA	49,990	VC
Lycoming College	PA	50,895	C
Macalester College	MN	64,136	MC
MacMurray College	IL	35,025	C
Malone Univ	OH	39,200	C
Manchester Univ	IN	41,540	C
Manhattan College	NY	55,652	C
Manhattanville College	NY	52,430	C
Mansfield Univ of Pennsylvania	PA	24,244	LC
Marian Univ	IN	43,206	C
Marist College	NY	49,860	VC
Marlboro College	VT	50,832	VC+
Marquette Univ	WI	53,090	VC+
Marshall Univ	WV	18,044	C
Marymount Univ	VA	43,231	C
Marywood Univ	PA	47,840	C
Mass College of Liberal Arts	MA	20,659	C
Mass Inst of Technology	MA	62,662	MC
McDaniel College	MD	52,910	VC
McKendree Univ	IL	37,940	C+
McPherson College	KS	36,134	C
Mercer Univ	GA	45,348	VC
Mercyhurst Univ	PA	47,420	C
Merrimack College	MA	55,415	C
Messiah College	PA	44,380	VC
Metropolitan State Univ	MN	7,859	C
Metropolitan State Univ of Denver	CO	6,928	LC
Miami Univ	OH	27,190	HC+
Mich State Univ	MI	24,542	VC
Middle Tenn State Univ	TN	8,650	C
Middlebury College	VT	67,464	MC
Millersville Univ of Pennsylvania	PA	25,298	C
Millikin Univ	IL	44,148	C
Mills College	CA	43,705	C
Millsaps College	MS	50,080	C+
Minn State Univ, Mankato	MN	17,190	C
Minn State Univ, Moorhead	MN	21,393	C
Misericordia Univ	PA	45,210	C
Miss State Univ	MS	12,028	C+
Missouri State Univ	MO	15,837	C+
Missouri Univ of Science and Technology	MO	18,655	HC
Missouri Valley College	MO	28,150	C
Molloy College	NY	40,440	C
Monmouth College	IL	42,260	C
Montana State Univ	MT	15,500	C+
Montclair State Univ	NJ	26,912	C
Moravian College	PA	55,488	C
Morehead State Univ	KY	18,386	LC
Morehouse College	GA	40,835	C
Morgan State Univ	MD	17,190	LC
Morningside College	IA	39,780	C
Mount Holyoke College	MA	56,746	MC
Mount Mary Univ	WI	34,650	LC
Mount Mercy Univ	IA	39,748	C
Mount St. Mary's Univ	MD	53,380	C
Mount St. Mary's Univ - Chalon Campus	CA	50,486	VC+
Mount Vernon Nazarene Univ	OH	35,944	C
Muhlenberg College	PA	56,645	VC
Murray State Univ	KY	17,726	C+
Muskingum Univ	OH	35,966	C
Nazareth College	NY	46,784	C
Nebr Wesleyan Univ	NE	42,026	C+
New College of Florida	FL	16,180	HC+
New England College	NH	50,828	NC
New Jersey City Univ	NJ	21,456	LC
New Mexico State Univ	NM	14,050	LC
New York Univ	NY	68,139	MC
Newberry College	SC	34,550	C
Newman Univ	KS	37,382	C
Niagara Univ	NY	41,010	C
N Car State Univ	NC	22,434	HC+
North Central College	IL	48,712	C+
North Park Univ	IL	35,860	C
Northeastern Illinois Univ	IL	12,529	LC
Northeastern Univ	MA	65,352	MC
Northern Arizona Univ	AZ	21,003	C
Northern Illinois Univ	IL	20,176	C
Northern Kentucky Univ	KY	16,486	C
Northern Mich Univ	MI	20,853	C
Northwest Missouri State Univ	MO	18,286	C
Northwestern College of Iowa	IA	38,400	C
Northwestern Univ	IL	68,725	MC
Notre Dame de Namur Univ	CA	46,526	LC
Nova Southeastern Univ	FL	38,534	C+
Nyack College	NY	34,450	LC
Oakland Univ	MI	20,763	C
Oberlin College	OH	68,942	MC
Occidental College	CA	68,660	MC
Oglethorpe Univ	GA	44,200	C
Ohio Dominican Univ	OH	41,340	C+
Ohio Northern Univ	OH	44,050	VC
Ohio State Univ at Columbus	OH	22,843	MC
Ohio Univ	OH	23,394	VC
Ohio Wesleyan Univ	OH	49,460	VC
Okla Baptist Univ	OK	33,990	C
Okla City Univ	OK	40,476	C
Okla State Univ	OK	17,180	C+
Okla Wesleyan Univ	OK	34,434	C
Old Dominion Univ	VA	21,618	C
Olivet Nazarene Univ	IL	41,840	VC
Oral Roberts Univ	OK	34,316	C
Oregon State Univ	OR	23,337	VC
Otterbein Univ	OH	41,630	C
Ouachita Baptist Univ	AR	33,500	VC
Our Lady of the Lake Univ	TX	37,790	LC
Pacific Lutheran Univ	WA	49,960	C
Pacific Univ	OR	37,617	C
Palm Beach Atlantic Univ	FL	39,250	C
Pennsylvania State Univ - Univ Park	PA	29,716	HC
Pepperdine Univ	CA	66,862	VC+
Piedmont College	GA	34,334	C
Pitzer College	CA	68,500	HC+
Plymouth State Univ	NH	23,180	LC
Point Loma Nazarene Univ	CA	46,150	C+
Pomona College	CA	64,957	MC
Pontifical Catholic Univ of PR	PR	10,534	
Portland State Univ	OR	19,443	C
Princeton Univ	NJ	60,090	MC
Principia College	IL	40,350	C
Providence College	RI	62,870	HC
Purdue Univ Northwest	IN	15,178	C
Purdue Univ/West Lafayette	IN	20,032	MC
Queens Univ of Charlotte	NC	39,543	C
Quinnipiac Univ	CT	60,970	VC
Randolph College	VA	53,970	C
Randolph-Macon College	VA	51,480	VC
Reed College	OR	65,300	MC
Regis Univ	CO	46,380	C
Rensselaer Polytechnic Inst	NY	67,265	MC
Rhode Island College	RI	19,000	LC
Rhodes College	TN	51,900	HC
Rice Univ	TX	59,458	MC
Rider Univ	NJ	54,050	C
Ripon College	WI	49,991	VC
Roanoke College	VA	55,952	VC
Roberts Wesleyan College	NY	41,116	C
Rochester Inst of Technology	NY	52,734	HC+
Rockford Univ	IL	38,570	C
Rockhurst Univ	MO	28,990	C
Roger Williams Univ	RI	48,074	VC
Rollins College	FL	58,670	HC
Roosevelt Univ	IL	41,890	VC
Rosemont College	PA	30,980	LC
Rutgers Univ - Camden	NJ	26,595	C
Rutgers Univ - New Brunswick	NJ	27,090	HC
Rutgers Univ - Newark	NJ	27,351	C
St. Anselm College	NH	56,636	VC
St. Francis Univ	PA	46,146	NC
St. John's Univ	MN	53,472	C
St. Joseph's College of Maine	ME	47,890	C
St. Joseph's Univ	PA	58,540	VC
St. Louis Univ	MO	49,866	HC
St. Mary's College	IN	50,600	C
St. Mary's College of Calif	CA	57,420	C
St. Mary's Univ of Minn	MN	42,440	C
St. Michael's College	VT	53,275	VC+
St. Peter's Univ	NJ	49,192	C
St. Vincent College	PA	46,229	C
St. Xavier Univ	IL	44,440	C
Salem College	NC	40,206	C
Salisbury Univ	MD	21,132	VC
Salve Regina Univ	RI	53,046	VC
Sam Houston State Univ	TX	18,792	C
Samford Univ	AL	40,770	VC
San Diego State Univ	CA	23,156	VC
San Francisco State Univ	CA	18,514	LC
San Jose State Univ	CA	22,630	C
Sarah Lawrence College	NY	68,866	MC
Schreiner Univ	TX	34,626	LC
Scripps College	CA	69,260	HC
Seattle Pacific Univ	WA	47,439	C+
Seattle Univ	WA	54,957	VC
Seton Hall Univ	NJ	58,008	C
Seton Hill Univ	PA	46,972	VC
Sewanee: The Univ of the South	TN	58,000	HC+
Siena College	NY	48,916	C
Siena Heights Univ	MI	36,322	C
Silver Lake College of the Holy Family	WI	36,290	LC
Simmons College	MA	54,400	HC
Simpson College	IA	45,626	VC
Skidmore College	NY	66,600	MC
Slippery Rock Univ of Pennsylvania	PA	20,450	C
Smith College	MA	66,774	MC
Sonoma State Univ	CA	27,020	C
Southeast Missouri State Univ	MO	16,148	C
Southern Conn State Univ	CT	21,924	LC
Southern Illinois Univ Carbondale	IL	24,554	C
Southern Illinois Univ Edwardsville	IL	20,188	C
Southern Methodist Univ	TX	69,008	MC
Southern Nazarene Univ	OK	33,684	C
Southern Oregon Univ	OR	19,117	C
Southwestern Univ	TX	52,370	VC
Spelman College	GA	41,642	C
Spring Arbor Univ	MI	37,390	C
Spring Hill College	AL	48,488	C
St. Ambrose Univ	IA	40,180	C
St. Bonaventure Univ	NY	45,596	C
St. Catherine Univ	MN	45,630	C
St. Cloud State Univ	MN	10,600	C
St. Edward's Univ	TX	56,190	VC
St. Francis College	NY	38,800	LC
St. John Fisher College	NY	45,270	VC
St. John's College at Annapolis	MD	63,348	MC
St. John's College, Santa Fe	NM	60,109	HC+
St. John's Univ	NY	57,160	C+
St. Lawrence Univ	NY	66,646	HC+
St. Mary's College of Maryland	MD	27,312	VC
St. Mary's Univ	TX	39,120	C
St. Norbert College	WI	46,060	VC
St. Olaf College	MN	56,430	HC
St. Thomas Aquinas College	NY	32,450	C
Stanford Univ	CA	62,541	MC
SUNY Albany	NY	22,165	C
SUNY at Binghamton	NY	24,100	MC
SUNY at Geneseo	NY	21,622	VC
SUNY at New Paltz	NY	20,840	C
SUNY at Oswego	NY	22,219	VC
SUNY at Purchase College	NY	21,832	C
SUNY/Buffalo State	NY	20,583	LC
SUNY/College at Old Westbury	NY	16,860	C
SUNY/Cortland	NY	20,910	C
SUNY/Fredonia	NY	20,818	C
SUNY/Oneonta	NY	20,794	C
SUNY/Plattsburgh	NY	19,314	C
SUNY/Potsdam	NY	21,051	VC
SUNY/Univ at Buffalo	NY	23,122	C
Stephen F. Austin State Univ	TX	18,484	LC
Stetson Univ	FL	57,174	VC+
Stevens Inst of Technology	NJ	64,954	MC
Stockton Univ	NJ	25,565	C
Stonehill College	MA	55,130	C
Stony Brook Univ/The SUNY	NY	22,703	MC
Suffolk Univ	MA	52,316	C
Susquehanna Univ	PA	57,560	VC
Swarthmore College	PA	63,550	MC
Syracuse Univ	NY	62,313	HC
Taylor Univ	IN	42,130	VC
Temple Univ	PA	24,392	C+
Texas A&M Univ at College Station	TX	20,771	VC+
Texas Christian Univ	TX	57,120	HC
Texas Lutheran Univ	TX	39,770	C
Texas State Univ	TX	18,721	C
Texas Tech Univ	TX	20,156	C+
The American Univ	DC	61,317	HC
The Catholic Univ of America	DC	58,376	VC
The College at Brockport - SUNY	NY	21,058	C
The College of Idaho	ID	36,415	C
The College of New Jersey	NJ	28,675	VC+
The College of New Rochelle	NY	46,300	LC
The College of Wooster	OH	60,000	HC
The George Washington Univ	DC	68,474	HC+
The Univ of Akron	OH	22,566	C
The Univ of Alabama	AL	24,320	C+
The Univ of Arizona	AZ	24,086	C
The Univ of Memphis	TN	18,278	C
The Univ of Tenn at Chattanooga	TN	17,340	C+
The Univ of Tenn at Knoxville	TN	22,112	VC
The Univ of Tenn at Martin	TN	15,212	C
The Univ of Texas at Austin	TX	20,206	MC
The Univ of Texas at San Antonio	TX	21,060	C
The Univ of Utah	UT	18,751	VC
Thiel College	PA	42,950	LC
Thomas Edison State Univ	NJ	6,350	NC

ST = STATE $IS = IN-STATE COSTS SR = SELECTOR RATING

School	ST	$IS	SR
Thomas More College	KY	36,720	LC
Toccoa Falls College	GA	30,048	C
Touro College	NY	31,040	C
Towson Univ	MD	21,878	C
Transylvania Univ	KY	47,450	HC+
Trinity Christian College	IL	35,580	C
Trinity College	CT	69,020	HC
Trinity International Univ	IL	31,070	VC
Trinity Univ	TX	54,480	MC
Truman State Univ	MO	16,286	MC
Tufts Univ	MA		MC
Tulane Univ	LA	67,496	MC
Union College	NY	64,320	MC
Union Univ	TN	41,160	VC
United States Military Academy at West Point	NY		HC+
Univ of Alabama at Birmingham	AL	22,092	C
Univ of Alabama in Huntsville	AL	20,028	VC
Univ of Alaska Anchorage	AK	17,914	C
Univ of Arkansas at Fayetteville	AR	19,766	VC
Univ of Arkansas at Little Rock	AR	18,211	LC
Univ of Calif at Davis	CA	28,468	HC
Univ of Calif at Irvine	CA	33,857	VC
Univ of Calif at Los Angeles	CA	27,438	HC+
Univ of Calif at Riverside	CA	32,912	C
Univ of Calif at Santa Barbara	CA	30,627	HC+
Univ of Calif San Diego	CA	30,450	MC
Univ of Calif, Santa Cruz	CA	28,731	C+
Univ of Central Arkansas	AR	15,042	VC
Univ of Central Florida	FL	16,379	VC
Univ of Central Okla	OK	15,150	C
Univ of Chicago	IL	70,551	MC
Univ of Cincinnati	OH	22,118	VC
Univ of Colo Boulder	CO	26,048	HC
Univ of Colo Colo Springs	CO	20,300	C
Univ of Colo Denver	CO	22,238	C
Univ of Conn	CT	27,394	
Univ of Dallas	TX	50,676	VC
Univ of Dayton	OH	54,930	VC
Univ of Delaware	DE	32,214	VC
Univ of Denver	CO	61,129	VC+
Univ of Detroit Mercy	MI	48,816	C
Univ of Dubuque	IA	37,824	C
Univ of Evansville	IN	44,186	C+
Univ of Findlay	OH	43,040	C
Univ of Florida	FL	16,291	HC+
Univ of Georgia	GA	21,878	HC
Univ of Hartford	CT	49,776	C
Univ of Hawaii at Hilo	HI	18,038	VC
Univ of Hawaii at Manoa	HI	23,261	C
Univ of Houston	TX	21,871	VC
Univ of Houston-Downtown	TX	7,241	LC
Univ of Idaho	ID	16,158	C
Univ of Illinois at Chicago	IL	24,664	VC
Univ of Illinois at Urbana-Champaign	IL	27,006	HC
Univ of Indianapolis	IN	36,480	VC
Univ of Iowa	IA	19,415	HC
Univ of Kansas	KS	20,884	VC
Univ of Kentucky	KY	24,800	C+
Univ of La Verne	CA	55,600	C
Univ of Louisiana at Lafayette	LA	14,516	C
Univ of Louisville	KY	19,692	C
Univ of Lynchburg	VA	48,370	C
Univ of Maine	ME	21,038	VC
Univ of Mary Washington	VA	23,039	C+
Univ of Maryland/Baltimore County	MD	23,004	VC
Univ of Maryland/College Park	MD	21,938	HC
Univ of Mass Amherst	MA	27,669	HC
Univ of Mass Boston	MA	13,828	C
Univ of Mass Dartmouth	MA	26,507	C
Univ of Mass Lowell	MA	27,296	VC
Univ of Miami	FL	63,494	MC
Univ of Mich/Ann Arbor	MI	25,274	MC
Univ of Mich/Dearborn	MI	12,472	VC
Univ of Mich/Flint	MI	19,062	C
Univ of Minn/Duluth	MN	20,292	C
Univ of Minn/Morris	MN	21,222	VC
Univ of Minn/Twin Cities	MN	24,269	MC
Univ of Miss	MS	18,802	C
Univ of Missouri-Columbia	MO	20,463	VC
Univ of Missouri-Kansas City	MO	19,563	VC
Univ of Missouri-St. Louis	MO	19,810	VC
Univ of Montana	MT	14,105	C
Univ of Mount Union	OH	39,990	C
Univ of Nebr - Lincoln	NE	18,589	VC
Univ of Nebr - Omaha	NE	16,120	C
Univ of Nevada, Las Vegas	NV	17,553	C
Univ of Nevada, Reno	NV	18,010	C
Univ of New Hampshire	NH	29,333	VC
Univ of New Mexico	NM	16,808	C
Univ of New Orleans	LA	12,840	C
Univ of N Car at Asheville	NC	16,251	VC+
Univ of N Car at Chapel Hill	NC	20,561	MC
Univ of N Car at Charlotte	NC	17,803	VC
Univ of N Car at Greensboro	NC	15,998	C
Univ of N Dak	ND	16,673	C
Univ of North Florida	FL	15,996	VC
Univ of North Texas	TX	20,082	C
Univ of Northern Colo	CO	19,658	C
Univ of Northern Iowa	IA	17,480	C
Univ of Northwestern - St. Paul	MN	39,530	C
Univ of Notre Dame	IN	68,801	MC
Univ of Okla	OK	19,651	HC
Univ of Oregon	OR	24,021	VC
Univ of Pennsylvania	PA	63,526	MC
Univ of Pittsburgh	PA	30,030	MC
Univ of Portland	OR	52,152	VC
Univ of PR, at Mayaguez	PR	13,995	
Univ of PR-Rio Piedras campus	PR	13,327	
Univ of Puget Sound	WA	60,210	HC
Univ of Redlands	CA	61,934	VC
Univ of Rhode Island	RI	26,066	VC
Univ of Richmond	VA	62,730	MC
Univ of Rochester	NY	65,032	MC
Univ of St. Francis	IN	38,520	C
Univ of St. Joseph	CT	49,069	C
Univ of San Diego	CA	60,338	HC
Univ of San Francisco	CA	60,580	C
Univ of Scranton	PA	54,962	VC
Univ of Sioux Falls	SD	25,630	C
Univ of South Alabama	AL	16,880	C
Univ of S Car at Columbia	SC	21,726	VC
Univ of S Dak	SD	16,109	C
Univ of South Florida/Tampa	FL	16,110	VC
Univ of Southern Calif	CA	66,631	MC
Univ of Southern Indiana	IN	16,808	C
Univ of Southern Maine	ME	18,320	C
Univ of Southern Miss	MS	13,170	C
Univ of St. Thomas - Houston	TX	41,510	VC
Univ of Tampa	FL	38,928	VC
Univ of Texas at Arlington	TX	18,876	C
Univ of Texas at El Paso	TX	34,452	NC
Univ of Texas Rio Grande Valley	TX	15,573	LC
Univ of the District of Columbia	DC	21,260	LC
Univ of the Incarnate Word	TX	39,162	LC
Univ of the Pacific	CA	57,446	VC
Univ of Toledo	OH	19,336	C
Univ of Tulsa	OK	52,625	HC
Univ of Vermont	VT	29,792	HC
Univ of Virginia	VA	27,367	MC
Univ of Washington	WA	23,091	MC
Univ of West Florida	FL	15,848	C
Univ of West Georgia	GA	17,510	LC
Univ of Wisc-Eau Claire	WI	16,354	VC
Univ of Wisc-Green Bay	WI	15,184	C
Univ of Wisc-La Crosse	WI	15,425	VC
Univ of Wisc-Madison	WI	21,647	MC
Univ of Wisc-Milwaukee	WI	21,538	C
Univ of Wisc-Oshkosh	WI	15,392	C
Univ of Wisc-Parkside	WI	15,313	C
Univ of Wisc-Platteville	WI	14,148	C
Univ of Wisc-Stevens Point	WI	14,043	C
Univ of Wyoming	WY	15,537	C
Ursinus College	PA	62,920	VC
Ursuline College	OH	41,076	LC
Utah State Univ	UT	13,235	C
Utica College	NY	31,510	C
Valparaiso Univ	IN	50,160	VC
Vanderbilt Univ	TN	63,248	MC
Vassar College	NY	68,110	MC
Villanova Univ	PA	64,922	MC
Virginia Commonwealth Univ	VA	23,811	VC
Virginia Polytechnic Inst and State Univ	VA	21,920	VC
Virginia Wesleyan Univ	VA	45,980	LC
Viterbo Univ	WI	34,660	C
Wabash College	IN	52,100	VC
Wagner College	NY	57,240	C+
Wake Forest Univ	NC	69,354	MC
Walsh Univ	OH	39,010	C
Warren Wilson College	NC	44,220	VC
Wartburg College	IA	49,478	C
Washburn Univ	KS	15,827	C
Washington & Jefferson College	PA	58,694	VC
Washington and Lee Univ	VA	59,647	MC
Washington College	MD	56,154	VC
Washington State Univ	WA	22,747	C
Washington Univ in St. Louis	MO	67,539	MC
Wayland Baptist Univ	TX	23,460	LC
Wayne State Univ	MI	23,085	C
Weber State Univ	UT	14,112	C
Webster Univ	MO	37,490	C
Wellesley College	MA	66,984	MC
Wells College	NY	50,500	C
Wesleyan Univ	CT	66,940	MC
West Chester Univ of Pennsylvania	PA	19,171	VC
West Virginia Univ	WV	18,952	VC
West Virginia Wesleyan College	WV	39,188	C
Western Carolina Univ	NC	13,965	C
Western Kentucky Univ	KY	16,850	C
Western Mich Univ	MI	21,791	C
Western New England Univ	MA	49,182	C
Western Oregon Univ	OR	19,965	LC
Western Washington Univ	WA	18,904	VC
Westminster College	MO	32,820	C
Westminster College	PA	41,722	C
Westminster College	UT	41,078	C
Westmont College	CA	57,930	VC
Wheaton College	IL	44,993	MC
Wheaton College	MA	63,818	VC
Wheeling Jesuit Univ	WV	37,106	LC
Whitman College	WA	59,772	MC
Whittier College	CA	57,891	C
Whitworth Univ	WA	53,682	VC
Wichita State Univ	KS	17,773	C
Wiley College	TX	19,255	C
Wilkes Univ	PA	49,166	C
Willamette Univ	OR	62,514	VC+
William Jewell College	MO	42,490	C+
William Paterson Univ of New Jersey	NJ	24,022	C
Williams College	MA	67,700	MC
Wilmington College	OH	35,100	C
Wilson College	PA	35,620	LC
Winthrop Univ	SC	23,960	C
Wisc Lutheran College	WI	36,290	C
Wittenberg Univ	OH	49,863	VC
Wofford College	SC	49,885	VC
Wright State Univ	OH	16,983	C
Xavier Univ	OH	49,380	VC
Xavier Univ of Louisiana	LA	31,689	C
Yale Univ	CT	64,650	MC
Yeshiva Univ	NY	52,750	VC
York College of Pennsylvania	PA	29,240	C
Youngstown State Univ	OH	17,487	C

PHILOSOPHY (AESTHETICS/ MEDIA WRITING)

School	ST	$IS	SR
Murray State Univ	KY	17,726	C+

PHILOSOPHY (HISTORY/ CONTEMPORARY THOUGHT)

School	ST	$IS	SR
Murray State Univ	KY	17,726	C+

PHILOSOPHY (POLITICAL THOUGHT)

School	ST	$IS	SR
Claremont McKenna College	CA	69,900	MC
Murray State Univ	KY	17,726	C+
Syracuse Univ	NY	62,313	HC

PHILOSOPHY AND RELIGION

School	ST	$IS	SR
Arizona State Univ at the West Campus	AZ	21,513	VC
Augustana Univ	SD	39,968	VC
Austin Peay State Univ	TN	16,397	C
Beloit College	WI	55,206	HC
Bethel College	IN	36,830	C
Biola Univ	CA	48,686	C
Boston Univ	MA	67,352	MC
Bridgewater College	VA	46,260	C
Bryan College	TN	32,900	C
Cal State, Fresno	CA	16,902	LC
Cal State, Fullerton	CA	21,902	C
Christian Brothers Univ	TN	31,670	VC
Claflin Univ	SC	25,592	LC
Colgate Univ	NY	67,500	MC
Covenant College	GA	44,590	HC
Dakota Wesleyan Univ	SD	33,980	LC
Davis & Elkins College	WV	38,242	LC
Dordt College	IA	37,860	C+
Drury Univ	MO	37,555	VC
Elmira College	NY	53,900	C
Flagler College	FL	27,620	C
Friends Univ	KS	38,000	C
Hendrix College	AR	54,020	VC
Hillsdale College	MI	37,170	MC
Ithaca College	NY	58,158	VC+
Juniata College	PA	58,118	VC
Kutztown Univ of Pennsylvania	PA	19,477	C
Marymount Manhattan College	NY	48,350	C
Mass College of Liberal Arts	MA	20,659	C
Murray State Univ	KY	17,726	C+
New York Univ	NY	68,139	MC
N Dak State Univ	ND	16,245	VC
Northeastern Univ	MA	65,352	MC
Northwest Nazarene Univ	ID	40,250	C
Nova Southeastern Univ	FL	38,534	C+
Nyack College	NY	34,450	LC
Okla Baptist Univ	OK	33,990	C
Okla City Univ	OK	40,476	C
Ouachita Baptist Univ	AR	33,500	VC
Pace Univ	NY	60,136	C
Paine College	GA	19,506	LC
Philander Smith College	AR	20,814	LC
Presbyterian College	SC	47,186	C
Radford Univ	VA	19,758	C
Rocky Mountain College	MT	35,776	C
Rowan Univ	NJ	24,491	VC
Samford Univ	AL	40,770	VC
Shawnee State Univ	OH	16,998	C
S Dak State Univ	SD	15,874	C
Southwestern College	KS	31,531	LC
Spring Arbor Univ	MI	37,390	C
St. Joseph's College, New York/Brooklyn Campus	NY	25,114	LC
St. Joseph's College, New York/Long Island Campus	NY	25,124	C
Taylor Univ	IN	42,130	VC
Tenn Wesleyan Univ	TN	32,680	LC
The Univ of Texas at San Antonio	TX	21,060	C
Univ of Maine at Farmington	ME	18,792	C
Univ of N Car at Pembroke	NC	14,737	LC
Univ of N Car Wilmington	NC	16,784	VC
Univ of Notre Dame	IN	68,801	MC
Urbana Univ	OH	30,820	C
Virginia Commonwealth Univ	VA	23,811	VC
Washington Adventist Univ	MD	32,050	LC
Wesley College	DE	37,848	LC
West Chester Univ of Pennsylvania	PA	19,171	VC
Wilson College	PA	35,620	LC
Winthrop Univ	SC	23,960	C
Youngstown State Univ	OH	17,487	C

PHILOSOPHY OF LAW

School	ST	$IS	SR
Lewis Univ	IL	41,710	C
Univ of N Car at Greensboro	NC	15,998	C

PHOTOGRAPHY

School	ST	$IS	SR
Adams State Univ	CO	15,420	LC
Andrews Univ	MI	41,732	C
Appalachian State Univ	NC	15,394	VC
Aquinas College - Mich	MI	38,876	VC
Arcadia Univ	PA	55,990	C+
Art Academy of Cincinnati	OH	37,790	SP
ArtCenter College of Design	CA	42,008	SP
Bard College	NY	65,924	HC
Barry Univ	FL	38,730	LC
Bellevue Univ	NE	20,300	NC
Bennington College	VT	66,280	MC
Biola Univ	CA	48,686	C
Brigham Young Univ	UT	13,248	MC
Calif Baptist Univ	CA	42,986	C
Calif College of the Arts	CA	52,758	SP
Calif Inst of the Arts	CA	61,366	SP
Cal State, San Bernardino	CA	20,106	C
Carroll Univ	WI	38,100	C+
Central Mich Univ	MI	20,330	C
Cleveland Inst of Art	OH	51,455	SP
Coker College	SC	38,196	C
College for Creative Studies	MI	51,210	SP
College of Art and Design at Lesley Univ	MA	50,525	SP
Colo State Univ	CO	23,033	C
Columbia College - Missouri	MO	28,179	C
Columbia College Chicago	IL	40,104	C
Columbus College of Art and Design	OH	47,310	SP
Dominican Univ	IL	42,472	C+
Drexel Univ	PA	65,927	HC
Eastern Mennonite Univ	VA	42,550	C
Endicott College	MA	47,054	C+
Ferris State Univ	MI	21,458	C
Fitchburg State Univ	MA	21,819	LC
Goddard College	VT	17,040	VC
Grand Valley State Univ	MI	22,250	C+
Hampshire College	MA	65,214	MC
Hofstra Univ	NY	58,210	C+
Howard Univ	DC	37,616	C+
Indiana Univ-Purdue Univ Fort Wayne	IN	18,675	C
Indiana Wesleyan Univ	IN	33,674	C
Ithaca College	NY	58,158	VC+
John Brown Univ	AR	35,184	VC
Kansas City Art Inst	MO	48,200	SP
Kent State Univ	OH	20,928	C
Kutztown Univ of Pennsylvania	PA	19,477	C
LIU Post	NY	50,698	C+
Maine College of Art	ME	45,940	SP
Marlboro College	VT	50,832	VC+
Marshall Univ	WV	18,044	C
Maryland Inst College of Art	MD	58,740	SP
Marywood Univ	PA	47,840	C
Mass College of Art and Design	MA	24,800	SP
Memphis College of Art	TN	50,880	SP
Milligan College	TN	39,450	C
Milwaukee Inst of Art & Design	WI	45,880	SP
Minneapolis College of Art and Design	MN	44,218	SP
Montserrat College of Art	MA	41,500	SP
Moore College of Art and Design	PA	55,118	SP
Moore College of Art and Design	PA	55,118	SP
Morningside College	IA	39,780	C
New Jersey City Univ	NJ	21,456	LC
New York Univ	NY	68,139	MC
Northern Arizona Univ	AZ	21,003	C
Notre Dame of Maryland Univ	MD	47,570	VC
Oberlin College	OH	68,942	MC
Ohio Univ	OH	23,394	VC
Okla Christian Univ	OK	29,260	C
Okla City Univ	OK	40,476	C
Otis College of Art and Design	CA	54,670	SP
Pacific Northwest College of Art	OR	38,494	SP
Pacific Union College	CA	36,009	VC
Parsons The New School for Design	NY	56,610	SP
Point Park Univ	PA	41,270	C
Pratt Inst	NY	59,482	VC+
Purdue Univ/West Lafayette	IN	20,032	MC

ST = STATE **$IS** = IN-STATE COSTS **SR** = SELECTOR RATING

School	ST	$IS	SR
Rhode Island School of Design	RI	59,960	SP
Ringling College of Art and Design	FL	59,160	SP
Rochester Inst of Technology	NY	52,734	HC+
Rocky Mountain College of Art and Design	CO	27,052	SP
Salem State Univ	MA	42,650	LC
Sam Houston State Univ	TX	18,792	C
San Francisco Art Inst	CA	60,865	SP
Savannah College of Art and Design	GA	49,595	SP
School of the Art Inst of Chicago	IL	61,830	SP
School of Visual Arts	NY	47,500	SP
Seattle Univ	WA	54,957	VC
St. Edward's Univ	TX	56,190	VC
St. John's Univ	NY	57,160	C+
SUNY at New Paltz	NY	20,840	C
SUNY/Buffalo State	NY	20,583	LC
SUNY/Fredonia	NY	20,818	C
Syracuse Univ	NY	62,313	HC
Temple Univ	PA	24,392	C+
Texas A&M Univ at Commerce	TX	10,496	C
Texas State Univ	TX	18,721	C
The Art Inst of Atlanta	GA	34,334	SP
Thomas Edison State Univ	NJ	6,350	NC
Univ of Central Florida	FL	16,379	VC
Univ of Central Missouri	MO	18,982	C
Univ of Central Okla	OK	15,150	C
Univ of Dayton	OH	54,930	VC
Univ of Florida	FL	16,291	HC+
Univ of Hartford	CT	49,776	C
Univ of Illinois at Chicago	IL	24,664	VC
Univ of Illinois at Urbana-Champaign	IL	27,006	HC
Univ of Iowa	IA	19,415	HC
Univ of La Verne	CA	55,600	C
Univ of Mass Dartmouth	MA	26,507	C
Univ of Miami	FL	63,494	MC
Univ of Mich/Ann Arbor	MI	25,274	MC
Univ of N Car at Greensboro	NC	15,998	C
Univ of Oregon	OR	24,021	VC
Univ of San Francisco	CA	60,580	C
Univ of the Arts	PA	56,579	SP
Univ of Washington	WA	23,091	MC
Virginia Commonwealth Univ	VA	23,811	VC
Washington Univ in St. Louis	MO	67,539	MC
Weber State Univ	UT	14,112	C
Webster Univ	MO	37,490	C
Western Washington Univ	WA	18,904	VC
Youngstown State Univ	OH	17,487	C

PHYSICAL CHEMISTRY

School	ST	$IS	SR
Aquinas College - Mich	MI	38,876	VC
Centre College	KY	50,680	MC
Union Univ	TN	41,160	VC
Univ of Calif San Diego	CA	30,450	MC

PHYSICAL EDUCATION

School	ST	$IS	SR
Adams State Univ	CO	15,420	LC
Adelphi Univ	NY	49,792	C
Adrian College	MI	45,550	C
Alabama A&M Univ	AL	18,796	C
Albany State Univ	GA	19,462	C
Alderson Broaddus Univ	WV	35,000	LC
Alice Lloyd College	KY	8,190	LC
Anderson Univ	IN	39,450	C
Appalachian State Univ	NC	15,394	VC
Aquinas College - Mich	MI	38,876	VC
Arkansas State Univ	AR	16,190	C
Arkansas Tech Univ	AR	16,534	LC
Armstrong State Univ	GA	15,615	C
Asbury Univ	KY	36,450	C+
Ashford Univ	CA	10,480	C
Ashland Univ	OH	30,446	C
Auburn Univ	AL	24,300	VC+
Augsburg Univ	MN	45,129	C
Augustana Univ	SD	39,968	VC
Aurora Univ	IL	34,990	C
Averett Univ	VA	43,034	LC
Azusa Pacific Univ	CA	43,972	C
Baker Univ	KS	37,190	C
Baldwin Wallace Univ	OH	42,464	VC
Ball State Univ	IN	19,808	C+
Barry Univ	FL	38,730	LC
Barton College	NC	39,854	C
Baylor Univ	TX	56,803	HC
Bellevue Univ	NE	20,300	NC
Belmont Univ	TN	44,500	VC+
Benedictine College	KS	38,850	VC
Berea College	KY	7,094	C
Bethany College	KS	38,637	LC
Bethany College	WV	38,774	LC
Bethel College	IN	36,830	C
Bethel Univ	MN	46,550	C+
Bethel Univ	TN	27,142	C
Bethune-Cookman Univ	FL	23,322	C
Biola Univ	CA	48,686	C
Black Hills State Univ	SD	16,622	C
Blackburn College	IL	28,526	LC
Blue Mountain College	MS	15,949	C
Bluffton Univ	OH	40,950	C+
Boise State Univ	ID	17,368	C
Boston Univ	MA	67,352	MC
Bowling Green State Univ	OH	19,975	C
Bridgewater State Univ	MA	22,762	C
Bryan College	TN	32,900	C
Cal State, Dominguez Hills	CA	19,022	LC
Cal State, Fullerton	CA	21,902	C
Cal State, Los Angeles	CA	17,186	LC
Cal State, Northridge	CA	17,277	LC
Cal State, Stanislaus	CA	18,053	LC
Calvin College	MI	43,090	HC
Campbellsville Univ	KY	33,400	C
Canisius College	NY	49,672	C
Capital Univ	OH	44,778	VC
Carroll Univ	WI	38,100	C+
Carthage College	WI	48,835	C
Castleton Univ	VT	20,186	C
Catawba College	NC	39,820	LC
Cedarville Univ	OH	36,244	VC
Central Conn State Univ	CT	22,041	C
Central Methodist Univ	MO	31,500	VC
Central Mich Univ	MI	20,330	C
Central State Univ	OH	18,564	C
Central Washington Univ	WA	16,803	C
Charleston Southern Univ	SC	34,700	C
Chicago State Univ	IL	41,620	C
CUNY/Brooklyn College	NY	7,163	C+
CUNY/Queens College	NY	21,507	C
CUNY/York College	NY	6,747	LC
Clark Atlanta Univ	GA	31,019	LC
Cleveland State Univ	OH	22,290	C
Coastal Carolina Univ	SC	20,340	C
Coe College	IA	51,570	VC
Coker College	SC	38,196	C
College of Charleston	SC	24,046	VC
College of Mount St. Vincent	NY	45,620	C
College of the Ozarks	MO	7,530	VC
Concordia College - Moorhead	MN	46,418	C
Concordia Univ Nebr	NE	41,900	VC
Concordia Univ St. Paul	MN	29,050	C
Concordia Univ Wisc	WI	35,910	C
Concordia Univ, Ann Arbor	MI	38,878	C+
Concordia Univ, Chicago	IL	41,522	C
Corban Univ	OR	41,700	C
Cornerstone Univ	MI	36,550	C
Culver-Stockton College	MO	34,350	C
Cumberland Univ	TN	27,710	C
Dakota Wesleyan Univ	SD	33,980	LC
Dallas Baptist Univ	TX	35,220	VC
Davis & Elkins College	WV	38,242	LC
Defiance College	OH	42,240	LC
Delaware State Univ	DE	19,376	LC
Denison Univ	OH	62,770	HC+
DePaul Univ	IL	52,807	VC
Doane Univ	NE	41,340	VC
Dordt College	IA	37,860	C+
East Carolina Univ	NC	16,539	C
East Central Univ	OK	13,330	C
East Tenn State Univ	TN	18,141	C
East Texas Baptist Univ	TX	34,444	C
Eastern Conn State Univ	CT	23,059	C
Eastern Kentucky Univ	KY	17,742	C
Eastern Mennonite Univ	VA	42,550	C
Eastern Mich Univ	MI	19,761	C
Eastern New Mexico Univ	NM	12,874	LC
Eastern Oregon Univ	OR	17,612	C
Eastern Washington Univ	WA	17,896	LC
Edinboro Univ	PA	15,940	LC
Edward Waters College	FL	28,089	NC
Elizabeth City State Univ	NC	14,745	C
Elmhurst College	IL	46,514	C
Elon Univ	NC	46,142	HC
Emory and Henry College	VA	46,320	C
Emporia State Univ	KS	15,029	C
Endicott College	MA	47,054	C+
Erskine College	SC	45,460	C
Eureka College	IL	34,760	C
Evangel Univ	MO	28,898	C
Faulkner Univ	AL	26,410	C
Ferrum College	VA	43,970	C
Florida Atlantic Univ	FL	18,256	C
Florida International Univ	FL	20,281	C
Florida Memorial Univ	FL	22,424	LC
Florida State Univ	FL	16,771	HC
Fort Hays State Univ	KS	12,677	C
Fort Valley State Univ	GA	17,988	VC
Franklin College	IN	40,550	C
Freed-Hardeman Univ	TN	29,900	C
Fresno Pacific Univ	CA	38,858	C
Frostburg State Univ	MD	17,280	LC
Gallaudet Univ	DC	30,088	LC
Gardner-Webb Univ	NC	24,935	C+
George Mason Univ	VA	19,884	C
Georgia Southern Univ	GA	16,540	VC
Georgia State Univ	GA	25,250	C
Glenville State College	WV	17,386	LC
Gonzaga Univ	WA	52,880	HC
Goshen College	IN	44,350	C
Grace College and Seminary	IN	31,524	C
Graceland Univ	IA	35,290	C
Grambling State Univ	LA	15,701	C
Grand Canyon Univ	AZ	25,150	VC
Grand View Univ	IA	32,302	C
Greensboro College	NC	39,790	LC
Greenville College	IL	27,012	LC
Hampton Univ	VA	36,410	C
Hardin-Simmons Univ	TX	36,025	C
Heidelberg Univ	OH	40,400	LC
Henderson State Univ	AR	15,516	C
High Point Univ	NC	47,355	VC
Hillsdale College	MI	37,170	MC
Hofstra Univ	NY	58,210	C+
Houghton College	NY	40,558	VC
Houston Baptist Univ	TX	36,450	C
Howard Univ	DC	37,616	C+
Humboldt State Univ	CA	21,708	C
Huntingdon College	AL	35,900	C
Huntington Univ	IN	33,996	C
Husson Univ	ME	26,508	C
Huston-Tillotson Univ	TX	18,124	LC
Idaho State Univ	ID	13,619	LC
Indiana Inst of Technology	IN	34,240	LC
Indiana State Univ	IN	23,223	LC
Indiana Univ of Pennsylvania	PA	24,474	C
Indiana Wesleyan Univ	IN	33,674	C
Inter-American Univ of PR-Aguadilla Campus	PR	21,657	
Iowa State Univ	IA	18,176	C
Iowa Wesleyan Univ	IA	41,000	C
Ithaca College	NY	58,158	VC+
Jacksonville Univ	FL	49,210	C
John Carroll Univ	OH	51,570	C
Johnson C. Smith Univ	NC	25,336	LC
Johnson State College	VT	22,672	C
Judson Univ	IL	39,174	C
Kalamazoo College	MI	53,931	HC
Kansas Wesleyan Univ	KS	37,930	C
Kean Univ	NJ	25,620	C
Keene State College	NH	24,604	C
Kent State Univ	OH	20,928	C
Kentucky State Univ	KY	14,484	LC
Kentucky Wesleyan College	KY	34,260	LC
King Univ	TN	36,976	C
La Sierra Univ	CA	39,690	VC
Lander Univ	SC	32,200	C
Lane College	TN	17,960	LC
Langston Univ	OK	15,659	C
Lee Univ	TN	22,045	C
LeTourneau Univ	TX	39,190	VC
Liberty Univ	VA	31,415	C
Limestone College	SC	32,100	C
Lincoln Univ	MO	14,402	NC
Lindenwood Univ	MO	25,760	C
Linfield College	OR	53,992	C
Lipscomb Univ	TN	42,984	VC
LIU Brooklyn	NY	50,698	C
LIU Post	NY	50,698	C+
Lock Haven Univ of Pennsylvania	PA	20,544	LC
Longwood Univ	VA	22,184	C
Louisiana Tech Univ	LA	11,422	VC
Lubbock Christian Univ	TX	29,727	C
Luther College	IA	49,990	VC
Lyndon State College	VT	20,714	C
MacMurray College	IL	35,025	C
Madonna Univ	MI	30,450	LC
Manhattan College	NY	55,652	C
Mars Hill Univ	NC	41,104	C
Marshall Univ	WV	18,044	C
Maryville College	TN	44,410	C
Marywood Univ	PA	47,840	C
Mayville State Univ	ND	18,371	NC
McDaniel College	MD	52,910	VC
McKendree Univ	IL	37,940	C+
McMurry Univ	TX	34,259	LC
McPherson College	KS	36,134	C
Messiah College	PA	44,380	VC
Methodist Univ	NC	58,130	C
Metropolitan State Univ of Denver	CO	6,928	LC
Mich State Univ	MI	24,542	VC
MidAmerica Nazarene Univ	KS	37,808	C
Middle Tenn State Univ	TN	8,650	C
Midwestern State Univ	TX	12,111	LC
Millikin Univ	IL	44,148	C
Minn State Univ, Mankato	MN	17,190	C
Minn State Univ, Moorhead	MN	21,393	C
Minot State Univ	ND	13,285	C
Miss State Univ	MS	12,028	C+
Miss Valley State Univ	MS	13,233	LC
Missouri Baptist Univ	MO	35,594	C
Missouri Southern State Univ	MO	13,071	C
Missouri State Univ	MO	15,837	C+
Missouri Valley College	MO	28,150	C
Monmouth College	IL	42,260	C
Monmouth Univ	NJ	50,184	C
Montana State Univ Billings	MT	13,336	LC
Montana State Univ-Northern	MT	11,370	NC
Montclair State Univ	NJ	26,912	C
Morehead State Univ	KY	18,386	LC
Morehouse College	GA	40,835	C
Morgan State Univ	MD	17,190	LC
Mount Marty College	SD	36,862	C
Mount Vernon Nazarene Univ	OH	35,944	C
Muskingum Univ	OH	35,966	C
Nebr Wesleyan Univ	NE	42,026	C+
New England College	NH	50,828	NC
New Mexico State Univ	NM	14,050	LC
Newberry College	SC	34,550	C
N Car A&T State Univ	NC	13,786	C
N Car Central Univ	NC	9,000	C
N Dak State Univ	ND	16,245	VC
Northeastern Illinois Univ	IL	12,529	LC
Northern Illinois Univ	IL	20,176	C
Northern Kentucky Univ	KY	16,486	C
Northern Mich Univ	MI	20,853	C
Northern State Univ	SD	15,570	C
Northwest Missouri State Univ	MO	18,286	C
Northwest Nazarene Univ	ID	40,250	C
Northwest Univ	WA	38,720	VC
Northwestern College of Iowa	IA	38,400	C
Northwestern Okla State Univ	OK	13,072	LC
Norwich Univ	VT	56,234	C
Nova Southeastern Univ	FL	38,534	C+
Oakwood Univ	AL	43,758	C
Ohio Northern Univ	OH	44,050	VC
Ohio State Univ at Columbus	OH	22,843	MC
Ohio Univ	OH	23,394	VC
Ohio Wesleyan Univ	OH	49,460	VC
Okla Baptist Univ	OK	33,990	C
Okla Christian Univ	OK	29,260	C
Okla Panhandle State Univ	OK	6,152	C
Okla State Univ	OK	17,180	C+
Okla Wesleyan Univ	OK	34,434	C
Old Dominion Univ	VA	21,618	C
Olivet College	MI	37,661	LC
Olivet Nazarene Univ	IL	41,840	VC
Oral Roberts Univ	OK	34,316	C
Ottawa Univ	KS	39,980	VC
Otterbein Univ	OH	41,630	C
Pacific Lutheran Univ	WA	49,960	C
Pacific Union College	CA	36,009	VC
Palm Beach Atlantic Univ	FL	39,250	C
Pepperdine Univ	CA	66,862	VC+
Peru State College	NE	15,602	LC
Pfeiffer Univ	NC	40,532	LC
Philander Smith College	AR	20,814	LC
Pittsburg State Univ	KS	13,880	C
Plymouth State Univ	NH	23,180	LC
Pontifical Catholic Univ of PR	PR	10,534	
Prairie View A&M Univ	TX	27,273	LC
Quincy Univ	IL	38,170	LC
Radford Univ	VA	19,758	C
Randolph College	VA	53,970	C
Rhode Island College	RI	19,000	LC
Roanoke College	VA	55,952	VC
Roberts Wesleyan College	NY	41,116	C
Rockford Univ	IL	38,570	C
Saginaw Valley State Univ	MI	19,284	C
St. Augustine's Univ	NC	25,582	C
St. Joseph's College of Maine	ME	47,890	C
St. Mary's College of Calif	CA	57,420	C
Salisbury Univ	MD	21,132	VC
Sam Houston State Univ	TX	18,792	C
San Francisco State Univ	CA	18,514	LC
Schreiner Univ	TX	34,626	LC
Seattle Pacific Univ	WA	47,439	C+
Shaw Univ	NC	24,638	C
Shepherd Univ, West Virginia	WV	17,382	C
Simpson College	IA	45,626	VC
S Car State Univ	SC	21,330	LC
S Dak State Univ	SD	15,874	C
Southeastern Louisiana Univ	LA	16,237	C
Southeastern Okla State Univ	OK	11,875	C
Southern Adventist Univ	TN	28,250	C
Southern Conn State Univ	CT	21,924	LC
Southern Illinois Univ Carbondale	IL	24,554	C
Southern Illinois Univ Edwardsville	IL	20,188	C
Southern Nazarene Univ	OK	33,684	C
Southern Oregon Univ	OR	19,117	C
Southern Univ at New Orleans	LA	8,014	LC
Southern Wesleyan Univ	SC	33,670	LC
Southwest Baptist Univ	MO	30,890	LC
Southwest Minn State Univ	MN	17,783	C
Southwestern Adventist Univ	TX	28,232	LC
Southwestern College	KS	31,531	LC
Springfield College	MA	48,775	C
St. Andrews Univ	NC	44,634	LC
St. Bonaventure Univ	NY	45,596	C
St. Catherine Univ	MN	45,630	C
St. Edward's Univ	TX	56,190	VC
St. Francis College	NY	38,800	LC
SUNY/Cortland	NY	20,910	C
Stillman College	AL	20,738	C
Syracuse Univ	NY	62,313	HC
Tabor College	KS	35,870	C
Tarleton State Univ	TX	15,248	LC
Taylor Univ	IN	42,130	VC
Temple Univ	PA	24,392	C+
Tenn Tech Univ	TN	17,929	C
Tenn Wesleyan Univ	TN	32,680	LC
Texas A&M Univ at College Station	TX	20,771	VC+
Texas A&M Univ at Kingsville	TX	16,580	LC
Texas Christian Univ	TX	57,120	HC
Texas Lutheran Univ	TX	39,770	C
Texas Southern Univ	TX	19,592	LC
Texas State Univ	TX	18,721	C
Texas Wesleyan Univ	TX	37,338	C
The Citadel, The Military College of S Car	SC	20,679	C
The College at Brockport - SUNY	NY	21,058	C
The College of Idaho	ID	36,415	C
The College of New Jersey	NJ	28,675	VC+
The Master's Univ	CA	43,870	C
The Univ of Akron	OH	22,566	C
The Univ of Alabama	AL	24,320	C+
The Univ of Mary	ND	23,180	C

ST = STATE $IS = IN-STATE COSTS SR = SELECTOR RATING

School	ST	$IS	SR
The Univ of Memphis	TN	18,278	C
The Univ of Montana Western	MT	9,426	LC
Tougaloo College	MS	17,980	NC
Towson Univ	MD	21,878	C
Trevecca Nazarene Univ	TN	31,186	C
Trine Univ	IN	41,310	C
Trinity International Univ	IL	31,070	VC
Troy Univ	AL	16,171	C
Truman State Univ	MO	16,286	MC
Tusculum College	TN	31,625	LC
Tuskegee Univ	AL	28,164	C
Union College	KY	32,310	C
Union College	NE	23,270	C
Union Univ	TN	41,160	VC
Universidad del Turabo	PR	17,828	
Univ of PR, at Arecibo	PR	12,652	
Univ of Alaska Anchorage	AK	17,914	C
Univ of Arkansas at Monticello	AR	13,599	LC
Univ of Arkansas at Pine Bluff	AR	13,541	C
Univ of Calif at Davis	CA	28,468	HC
Univ of Central Arkansas	AR	15,042	VC
Univ of Central Missouri	MO	18,982	C
Univ of Central Okla	OK	15,150	C
Univ of Charleston	WV	35,000	LC
Univ of Delaware	DE	32,214	VC
Univ of Dubuque	IA	37,824	C
Univ of Findlay	OH	43,040	C
Univ of Great Falls	MT	38,524	C
Univ of Hawaii at Manoa	HI	23,261	C
Univ of Idaho	ID	16,158	C
Univ of Illinois at Chicago	IL	24,664	VC
Univ of Illinois at Urbana-Champaign	IL	27,006	HC
Univ of Indianapolis	IN	36,480	VC
Univ of Jamestown	ND	28,508	C
Univ of Kentucky	KY	24,800	C+
Univ of Louisville	KY	19,692	C
Univ of Maine	ME	21,038	VC
Univ of Maine at Machias	ME	22,960	C
Univ of Maine at Presque Isle	ME	16,148	LC
Univ of Mary Hardin-Baylor	TX	35,292	C+
Univ of Maryland/College Park	MD	21,938	HC
Univ of Maryland/Eastern Shore	MD	21,861	LC
Univ of Mich/Ann Arbor	MI	25,274	MC
Univ of Minn/Duluth	MN	20,292	C
Univ of Missouri-St. Louis	MO	19,810	VC
Univ of Mobile	AL	28,935	C
Univ of Montevallo	AL	20,012	C
Univ of Mount Union	OH	39,990	C
Univ of Nebr - Kearney	NE	17,014	LC
Univ of Nebr - Omaha	NE	16,120	C
Univ of Nevada, Las Vegas	NV	17,553	C
Univ of New Hampshire	NH	29,333	VC
Univ of New Mexico	NM	16,808	C
Univ of New Orleans	LA	12,840	C
Univ of North Alabama	AL	15,964	C
Univ of N Car Wilmington	NC	16,784	VC
Univ of N Dak	ND	16,673	C
Univ of North Florida	FL	15,996	VC
Univ of North Georgia	GA	17,316	C
Univ of Northern Colo	CO	19,658	C
Univ of Northern Iowa	IA	17,480	C
Univ of Northwestern - St. Paul	MN	39,530	C
Univ of Rio Grande & Rio Grande Community College	OH	8,750	LC
Univ of Science and Arts of Okla	OK	11,140	VC
Univ of South Alabama	AL	16,880	C
Univ of S Car at Columbia	SC	21,726	VC
Univ of S Car Upstate	SC	19,272	LC
Univ of S Dak	SD	16,109	C
Univ of South Florida/Tampa	FL	16,110	VC
Univ of Southern Indiana	IN	16,808	C
Univ of Tampa	FL	38,928	VC
Univ of Texas at Arlington	TX	18,876	C
Univ of the Cumberlands	KY	32,000	LC
Univ of the District of Columbia	DC	21,260	LC
Univ of the Incarnate Word	TX	39,162	LC
Univ of the Ozarks	AR	31,050	NC
Univ of the Pacific	CA	57,446	VC
Univ of the Sacred Heart	PR	17,932	
Univ of Toledo	OH	19,336	C
Univ of Vermont	VT	29,792	HC
Univ of West Alabama	AL	16,284	LC
Univ of West Georgia	GA	17,510	LC
Univ of Wisc-Eau Claire	WI	16,354	VC
Univ of Wisc-La Crosse	WI	15,425	VC
Univ of Wisc-Madison	WI	21,647	MC
Univ of Wisc-Oshkosh	WI	15,392	C
Univ of Wisc-Platteville	WI	14,148	C
Univ of Wisc-River Falls	WI	14,541	C
Univ of Wisc-Stevens Point	WI	14,043	C
Univ of Wisc-Superior	WI	14,838	C
Univ of Wisc-Whitewater	WI	13,976	C
Univ of Wyoming	WY	15,537	C
Upper Iowa Univ	IA	34,990	NC
Utah State Univ	UT	13,235	C
Valley City State Univ	ND	13,267	C
Valparaiso Univ	IN	50,160	VC
Vanguard Univ of Southern Calif	CA	42,400	VC
Virginia State Univ	VA	19,802	C+
Walla Walla Univ	WA	34,845	C
Walsh Univ	OH	39,010	C
Warner Pacific College	OR	31,610	C
Warner Univ	FL	28,216	C
Wartburg College	IA	49,478	C
Washburn Univ	KS	15,827	C
Washington Adventist Univ	MD	32,050	LC
Washington State Univ	WA	22,747	C
Wayland Baptist Univ	TX	23,460	LC
Wayne State Univ	MI	23,085	C
Weber State Univ	UT	14,112	C
Wesley College	DE	37,848	LC
West Chester Univ of Pennsylvania	PA	19,171	VC
West Liberty Univ	WV	16,158	C
West Texas A&M Univ	TX	13,478	C
West Virginia Univ	WV	18,952	VC
West Virginia Wesleyan College	WV	39,188	C
Western Carolina Univ	NC	13,965	C
Western Illinois Univ	IL	20,897	C
Western Kentucky Univ	KY	16,850	C
Western Mich Univ	MI	21,791	C
Western New Mexico Univ	NM	16,914	LC
Western Washington Univ	WA	18,904	VC
Westminster College	MO	32,820	C
Wichita State Univ	KS	17,773	C
Wiley College	TX	19,255	C
William Carey Univ	MS	23,950	LC
William Paterson Univ of New Jersey	NJ	24,022	C
William Penn Univ	IA	26,000	C
William Woods Univ	MO	32,040	C
Williams Baptist College	AR	24,720	C
Wilmington College	OH	35,100	C
Wilson College	PA	35,620	LC
Winona State Univ	MN	18,109	C
Winston-Salem State Univ	NC	18,005	LC
Winthrop Univ	SC	23,960	C
Wright State Univ	OH	16,983	C
Youngstown State Univ	OH	17,487	C

PHYSICAL EDUCATION TEACHER EDUCATION

School	ST	$IS	SR
Averett Univ	VA	43,034	LC
East Stroudsburg Univ	PA	18,578	LC
Frostburg State Univ	MD	17,280	LC
Iowa Wesleyan Univ	IA	41,000	C
Old Dominion Univ	VA	21,618	C
Olivet Nazarene Univ	IL	41,840	VC
Tabor College	KS	35,870	C
Texas Christian Univ	TX	57,120	HC
Univ of Kansas	KS	20,884	VC
Univ of N Car at Greensboro	NC	15,998	C
Washburn Univ	KS	15,827	C
William Woods Univ	MO	32,040	C

PHYSICAL EDUCATION/ EXERCISE SCIENCE

School	ST	$IS	SR
CUNY/Queens College	NY	21,507	C
College of the Ozarks	MO	7,530	VC
Keene State College	NH	24,604	C
Salisbury Univ	MD	21,132	VC
Tabor College	KS	35,870	C
Univ of Mary Hardin-Baylor	TX	35,292	C+
Univ of Montana	MT	14,105	C
Univ of Northwestern - St. Paul	MN	39,530	C
Univ of Southern Miss	MS	13,170	C
Univ of Virginia	VA	27,367	MC
Walla Walla Univ	WA	34,845	C
Western Kentucky Univ	KY	16,850	C

PHYSICAL FITNESS/MOVEMENT

School	ST	$IS	SR
Ashland Univ	OH	30,446	C
Auburn Univ	AL	24,300	VC+
Augustana Univ	SD	39,968	VC
Baylor Univ	TX	56,803	HC
Brigham Young Univ/Hawaii	HI	11,710	C
Buena Vista Univ	IA	42,344	C
Calif State Polytechnic Univ, Pomona	CA	21,811	C
Cal State, East Bay	CA	20,748	C
Cal State, Fresno	CA	16,902	LC
Cal State, Monterey Bay	CA	22,872	LC
Cal State, San Marcos	CA	20,604	LC
Campbell Univ	NC	37,570	VC
Capital Univ	OH	44,778	VC
Colo Mesa Univ	CO	19,707	LC
Concordia Univ Nebr	NE	41,900	VC
Concordia Univ St. Paul	MN	29,050	C
Concordia Univ, Chicago	IL	41,522	C
Dallas Baptist Univ	TX	35,220	VC
Defiance College	OH	42,240	LC
DePauw Univ	IN	58,688	VC
East Carolina Univ	NC	16,539	C
East Texas Baptist Univ	TX	34,444	C
Eastern Nazarene College	MA	41,114	C
Eureka College	IL	34,760	C
Grand Canyon Univ	AZ	25,150	VC
Hope College	MI	42,840	VC
Houston Baptist Univ	TX	36,450	C
Humboldt State Univ	CA	21,708	C
Ithaca College	NY	58,158	VC+
James Madison Univ	VA	19,084	VC
Johnson State College	VT	22,672	C
Kansas State Univ	KS	17,780	VC
Lakeland Univ	WI	35,130	C
Lewis-Clark State College	ID	14,202	C
Limestone College	SC	32,100	C
Louisiana State Univ and A&M College	LA	18,677	VC
Lubbock Christian Univ	TX	29,727	C
Marshall Univ	WV	18,044	C
Marywood Univ	PA	47,840	C
Metropolitan State Univ of Denver	CO	6,928	LC
Miami Univ	OH	27,190	HC+
Minot State Univ	ND	13,285	C
Miss Univ for Women	MS	17,065	C
New England College	NH	50,828	NC
New Mexico Highlands Univ	NM	11,904	LC
New Mexico State Univ	NM	14,050	LC
N Dak State Univ	ND	16,245	VC
Northern Illinois Univ	IL	20,176	C
Northern Mich Univ	MI	20,853	C
Northern State Univ	SD	15,570	C
Northwestern College of Iowa	IA	38,400	C
Notre Dame de Namur Univ	CA	46,526	LC
Oakwood Univ	AL	43,758	C
Occidental College	CA	68,660	MC
Ohio State Univ at Columbus	OH	22,843	MC
Purdue Univ/West Lafayette	IN	20,032	MC
St. Augustine's Univ	NC	25,582	C
Sam Houston State Univ	TX	18,792	C
San Diego Christian College	CA	40,914	C
Seattle Pacific Univ	WA	47,439	C+
Sonoma State Univ	CA	27,020	C
Southern Methodist Univ	TX	69,008	MC
Southern Nazarene Univ	OK	33,684	C
Spring Arbor Univ	MI	37,390	C
Springfield College	MA	48,775	C
St. Edward's Univ	TX	56,190	VC
Stephen F. Austin State Univ	TX	18,484	LC
Sul Ross State Univ	TX	15,021	LC
Tarleton State Univ	TX	15,248	LC
Temple Univ	PA	24,392	C+
Texas Southern Univ	TX	19,592	LC
Texas Woman's Univ	TX	15,302	LC
The George Washington Univ	DC	68,474	HC+
The Univ of Texas at Austin	TX	20,206	MC
Truman State Univ	MO	16,286	MC
Union College	NE	23,270	C
Univ of Central Okla	OK	15,150	C
Univ of Florida	FL	16,291	HC+
Univ of Illinois at Chicago	IL	24,664	VC
Univ of La Verne	CA	55,600	C
Univ of Lynchburg	VA	48,370	C
Univ of Mass Boston	MA	13,828	C
Univ of Mich/Ann Arbor	MI	25,274	MC
Univ of Nevada, Las Vegas	NV	17,553	C
Univ of New Hampshire	NH	29,333	VC
Univ of N Car at Charlotte	NC	17,803	VC
Univ of North Texas	TX	20,082	C
Univ of Northern Colo	CO	19,658	C
Univ of Rio Grande & Rio Grande Community College	OH	8,750	LC
Univ of Texas at El Paso	TX	34,452	NC
Univ of Texas Rio Grande Valley	TX	15,573	LC
Univ of Toledo	OH	19,336	C
Upper Iowa Univ	IA	34,990	NC
Virginia Polytechnic Inst and State Univ	VA	21,920	VC
West Liberty Univ	WV	16,158	C
Western State Colo Univ	CO	19,348	C
Westfield State Univ	MA	20,404	C
Whittier College	CA	57,891	C
Winona State Univ	MN	18,109	C

PHYSICAL SCIENCE SECONDARY SCHOOL EDUCATION

School	ST	$IS	SR
Aquinas College - Mich	MI	38,876	VC
Cedarville Univ	OH	36,244	VC
Dordt College	IA	37,860	C+
Duquesne Univ	PA	48,508	VC
Kent State Univ	OH	20,928	C
Murray State Univ	KY	17,726	C+
St. Louis Univ	MO	49,866	HC
St. Edward's Univ	TX	56,190	VC
Univ of Maine at Machias	ME	22,960	C
Univ of Nebr - Lincoln	NE	18,589	VC
Weber State Univ	UT	14,112	C
Youngstown State Univ	OH	17,487	C

PHYSICAL SCIENCES

School	ST	$IS	SR
Arkansas Tech Univ	AR	16,534	LC
Asbury Univ	KY	36,450	C+
Auburn Univ at Montgomery	AL	15,000	C
Austin College	TX	51,059	HC
Bennington College	VT	66,280	MC
Bethany College	WV	38,774	LC
Bethel College	IN	36,830	C
Biola Univ	CA	48,686	C
Black Hills State Univ	SD	16,622	C
Bluffton Univ	OH	40,950	C+
Brescia Univ	KY	29,890	VC
Cal State, East Bay	CA	20,748	C
Cal State, Fullerton	CA	21,902	C
Cal State, Sacramento	CA	19,060	C
Cal State, Stanislaus	CA	18,053	LC
Calif Univ of Pennsylvania	PA	20,425	LC
Central Conn State Univ	CT	22,041	C
Central Mich Univ	MI	20,330	C
Colgate Univ	NY	67,500	MC
Colo Mesa Univ	CO	19,707	LC
Colo State Univ	CO	23,033	C
Concordia Univ Nebr	NE	41,900	VC
Concordia Univ, Ann Arbor	MI	38,878	C+
Concordia Univ, Chicago	IL	41,522	C
Dakota State Univ	SD	12,286	C
DePaul Univ	IL	52,807	VC
Dordt College	IA	37,860	C+
Emporia State Univ	KS	15,029	C
Eureka College	IL	34,760	C
Fort Hays State Univ	KS	12,677	C
Freed-Hardeman Univ	TN	29,900	C
Georgia Southern Univ	GA	16,540	VC
Harvard College/Harvard Univ	MA	65,609	MC
Indiana Univ Kokomo	IN	7,207	C
Indiana Univ-Purdue Univ Fort Wayne	IN	18,675	C
Kansas State Univ	KS	17,780	VC
Kutztown Univ of Pennsylvania	PA	19,477	C
Le Moyne College	NY	47,305	VC
Mayville State Univ	ND	18,371	NC
Mich State Univ	MI	24,542	VC
Minot State Univ	ND	13,285	C
Miss Univ for Women	MS	17,065	C
Muhlenberg College	PA	56,645	VC
Northwestern State Univ of Louisiana	LA	16,534	LC
Okla Panhandle State Univ	OK	6,152	C
Olivet Nazarene Univ	IL	41,840	VC
Peru State College	NE	15,602	LC
Purdue Univ Northwest	IN	15,178	C
Ripon College	WI	49,991	VC
Rowan Univ	NJ	24,491	VC
St. Michael's College	VT	53,275	VC+
San Diego State Univ	CA	23,156	VC
St. John's Univ	NY	57,160	C+
Trine Univ	IN	41,310	C
Union Univ	TN	41,160	VC
Univ of Arkansas at Monticello	AR	13,599	LC
Univ of Calif at Berkeley	CA	29,886	MC
Univ of Calif at Riverside	CA	32,912	C
Univ of Dayton	OH	54,930	VC
Univ of Great Falls	MT	38,524	C
Univ of Maryland/College Park	MD	21,938	HC
Univ of Mich/Flint	MI	19,062	C
Univ of Pittsburgh at Bradford	PA	22,958	C
Univ of Rio Grande & Rio Grande Community College	OH	8,750	LC
Univ of South Florida/Tampa	FL	16,110	VC
Univ of Southern Calif	CA	66,631	MC
Univ of Texas Rio Grande Valley	TX	15,573	LC
Univ of Wisc-Eau Claire	WI	16,354	VC
Univ of Wisc-Platteville	WI	14,148	C
Washington State Univ	WA	22,747	C
Washington Univ in St. Louis	MO	67,539	MC
Wayland Baptist Univ	TX	23,460	LC
Youngstown State Univ	OH	17,487	C

PHYSICAL THERAPY

School	ST	$IS	SR
American International College	MA	47,020	LC
Biola Univ	CA	48,686	C
Boston Univ	MA	67,352	MC
Cal State, Northridge	CA	17,277	LC
Cal State, Sacramento	CA	19,060	C
Carroll Univ	WI	38,100	C+
Carson-Newman Univ	TN	35,900	C
Chatham Univ	PA	47,883	VC
CUNY/Hunter College	NY	31,098	VC
Clarke Univ	IA	42,950	C
Cleveland State Univ	OH	22,290	C
Coe College	IA	51,570	VC
College of St. Scholastica	MN	45,734	C+
DeSales Univ	PA	47,520	C
Duquesne Univ	PA	48,508	VC
Fairleigh Dickinson Univ/ Metropolitan Campus	NJ	52,392	C
Florida A&M Univ	FL	15,361	C
Gannon Univ	PA	42,922	C
Grand Valley State Univ	MI	22,250	C+
Gustavus Adolphus College	MN	53,943	HC
Howard Univ	DC	37,616	C+
Husson Univ	ME	26,508	C
Ithaca College	NY	58,158	VC+
Lamar Univ	TX	18,014	LC
Langston Univ	OK	15,659	C
Lebanon Valley College	PA	55,510	VC
Maryville Univ of St. Louis	MO	38,558	VC
MCPHS Univ	MA	45,470	SP
Misericordia Univ	PA	45,210	C
Missouri State Univ	MO	15,837	C+
Mount Aloysius College	PA	29,976	C
New York Univ	NY	68,139	MC
North Park Univ	IL	35,860	C
Northeastern Univ	MA	65,352	MC

ST = STATE $IS = IN-STATE COSTS SR = SELECTOR RATING

School	ST	$IS	SR
Notre Dame College	OH	39,150	VC
Ohio State Univ at Columbus	OH	22,843	MC
Okla Baptist Univ	OK	33,990	C
Purdue Univ Northwest	IN	15,178	C
Quinnipiac Univ	CT	60,970	VC
Regis Univ	CO	46,380	C
Russell Sage College	NY	39,370	C
St. Francis Univ	PA	46,146	NC
St. Vincent College	PA	46,229	C
Simmons College	MA	54,400	HC
Stockton Univ	NJ	25,565	C
Tarleton State Univ	TX	15,248	LC
Tenn State Univ	TN	14,423	LC
The Univ of Akron	OH	22,566	C
The Univ of Mary	ND	23,180	C
Touro College	NY	31,040	C
Trine Univ	IN	41,310	C
Trinity International Univ	IL	31,070	VC
Truman State Univ	MO	16,286	MC
Univ of Alaska Anchorage	AK	17,914	C
Univ of Central Arkansas	AR	15,042	VC
Univ of Conn	CT	27,394	
Univ of Florida	FL	16,291	HC+
Univ of Hartford	CT	49,776	C
Univ of Illinois at Chicago	IL	24,664	VC
Univ of Kentucky	KY	24,800	C+
Univ of Maryland/Eastern Shore	MD	21,861	LC
Univ of Mich/Flint	MI	19,062	C
Univ of Missouri-Columbia	MO	20,463	VC
Univ of N Dak	ND	16,673	C
Univ of North Florida	FL	15,996	VC
Univ of the Sciences	PA	40,738	VC
Univ of Toledo	OH	19,336	C
Utica College	NY	31,510	C
Vanguard Univ of Southern Calif	CA	42,400	VC
Virginia Polytechnic Inst and State Univ	VA	21,920	VC
Walla Walla Univ	WA	34,845	C
Walsh Univ	OH	39,010	C
West Virginia Univ	WV	18,952	VC
Wingate Univ	NC	41,900	C
Winston-Salem State Univ	NC	18,005	LC

PHYSICAL THERAPY ASSISTANT

School	ST	$IS	SR
Calif Univ of Pennsylvania	PA	20,425	LC
Idaho State Univ	ID	13,619	LC
Missouri Western State Univ	MO	17,822	LC
Mount Aloysius College	PA	29,976	C
Nebr Methodist College	NE	25,314	C
Walla Walla Univ	WA	34,845	C

PHYSICIAN'S ASSISTANT

School	ST	$IS	SR
Carroll Univ	WI	38,100	C+
CUNY/City College	NY	20,204	C
Colo State Univ-Pueblo	CO	21,581	C
Daemen College	NY	40,336	C
DeSales Univ	PA	47,520	C
Duquesne Univ	PA	48,508	VC
D'Youville College	NY	37,678	C
Gannon Univ	PA	42,922	C
Gardner-Webb Univ	NC	24,935	C+
Grand Valley State Univ	MI	22,250	C+
Howard Univ	DC	37,616	C+
Jefferson (Philadelphia Univ + Thomas Jefferson Univ)	PA	53,966	C
King's College	PA	48,240	C
Marietta College	OH	46,190	C
Mars Hill Univ	NC	41,104	C
Marywood Univ	PA	47,840	C
MCPHS Univ	MA	45,470	SP
Methodist Univ	NC	58,130	C
Missouri State Univ	MO	15,837	C+
Mount Aloysius College	PA	29,976	C
Northern Mich Univ	MI	20,853	C
Pennsylvania College of Technology	PA	27,693	NC
Quinnipiac Univ	CT	60,970	VC
Rochester Inst of Technology	NY	52,734	HC+
St. Francis Univ	PA	46,146	NC
St. Vincent College	PA	46,229	C
Seton Hill Univ	PA	46,972	VC
South Univ	GA	36,070	LC
Southern Illinois Univ Carbondale	IL	24,554	C
St. Ambrose Univ	IA	40,180	C
St. Francis College	NY	38,800	LC
St. John's Univ	NY	57,160	C+
The George Washington Univ	DC	68,474	HC+
Union College	NE	23,270	C
Univ of Findlay	OH	43,040	C
Univ of Kentucky	KY	24,800	C+
Univ of Texas Rio Grande Valley	TX	15,573	LC
Univ of the Sciences	PA	40,738	VC
Wagner College	NY	57,240	C+
Walla Walla Univ	WA	34,845	C
Wichita State Univ	KS	17,773	C
Wingate Univ	NC	41,900	C

PHYSICS

School	ST	$IS	SR
Abilene Christian Univ	TX	43,708	C+
Adams State Univ	CO	15,420	LC
Adelphi Univ	NY	49,792	C
Adrian College	MI	45,550	C
Agnes Scott College	GA	51,930	VC+
Alabama A&M Univ	AL	18,796	C
Alabama State Univ	AL	16,490	LC
Albion College	MI	55,260	C
Albright College	PA	57,326	C
Alfred Univ	NY	37,490	C
Allegheny College	PA	57,620	VC
Alma College	MI	49,410	VC
Amherst College	MA	66,186	MC
Anderson Univ	IN	39,450	C
Andrews Univ	MI	41,732	C
Angelo State Univ	TX	15,882	LC
Appalachian State Univ	NC	15,394	VC
Arizona State Univ at the Tempe Campus	AZ	23,001	VC
Arkansas State Univ	AR	16,190	C
Arkansas Tech Univ	AR	16,534	LC
Ashland Univ	OH	30,446	C
Auburn Univ	AL	24,300	VC+
Augsburg Univ	MN	45,129	C
Augusta Univ	GA	4,632	C
Augustana College	IL	51,222	VC+
Augustana Univ	SD	39,968	VC
Austin College	TX	51,059	HC
Austin Peay State Univ	TN	16,397	C
Azusa Pacific Univ	CA	43,972	C
Baker Univ	KS	37,190	C
Baldwin Wallace Univ	OH	42,464	VC
Ball State Univ	IN	19,808	C+
Bard College	NY	65,924	HC
Bard College at Simon's Rock	MA	65,795	MC
Barnard College/Columbia Univ	NY	68,762	MC
Bates College	ME	64,500	HC
Baylor Univ	TX	56,803	HC
Bellarmine Univ	KY	52,532	C
Belmont Univ	TN	44,500	VC+
Beloit College	WI	55,206	HC
Bemidji State Univ	MN	17,730	C
Benedict College	SC	28,630	NC
Benedictine College	KS	38,850	VC
Benedictine Univ	IL	38,300	C
Bennington College	VT	66,280	MC
Berea College	KY	7,094	C
Berry College	GA	47,466	VC
Bethel Univ	MN	46,550	C+
Biola Univ	CA	48,686	C
Birmingham-Southern College	AL	44,478	C+
Bloomsburg Univ of Pennsylvania	PA	19,930	C
Bluffton Univ	OH	40,950	C+
Boise State Univ	ID	17,368	C
Boston College	MA	68,043	MC
Boston Univ	MA	67,352	MC
Bowdoin College	ME	65,980	MC
Bowling Green State Univ	OH	19,975	C
Bradley Univ	IL	43,240	VC
Brandeis Univ	MA	68,443	MC
Bridgewater College	VA	46,260	C
Bridgewater State Univ	MA	22,762	C
Brigham Young Univ	UT	13,248	MC
Brown Univ	RI	64,566	MC
Bryn Mawr College	PA	65,220	MC
Bucknell Univ	PA	67,136	MC
Buena Vista Univ	IA	42,344	C
Butler Univ	IN	52,890	VC+
Calif Inst of Technology	CA	64,704	MC
Calif Lutheran Univ	CA	52,853	C
Calif Polytechnic State Univ	CA	22,547	MC
Calif State Polytechnic Univ, Pomona	CA	21,811	C
Cal State, Bakersfield	CA	22,397	LC
Cal State, Chico	CA	19,790	VC
Cal State, Dominguez Hills	CA	19,022	LC
Cal State, East Bay	CA	20,748	C
Cal State, Fresno	CA	16,902	LC
Cal State, Fullerton	CA	21,902	C
Cal State, Long Beach	CA	18,850	C
Cal State, Los Angeles	CA	17,186	LC
Cal State, Northridge	CA	17,277	LC
Cal State, Sacramento	CA	19,060	C
Cal State, San Bernardino	CA	20,106	C
Cal State, Stanislaus	CA	18,053	LC
Calif Univ of Pennsylvania	PA	20,425	LC
Calvin College	MI	43,090	HC
Cameron Univ	OK	11,632	LC
Canisius College	NY	49,672	C
Carleton College	MN	66,414	MC
Carnegie Mellon Univ	PA	67,980	MC
Carroll College	MT	44,304	C
Carthage College	WI	48,835	C
Case Western Reserve Univ	OH	62,284	MC
Cedarville Univ	OH	36,244	VC
Centenary College of Louisiana	LA	49,050	C+
Central College	IA	44,592	C
Central Conn State Univ	CT	22,041	C
Central Methodist Univ	MO	31,500	VC
Central Mich Univ	MI	20,330	C
Central Washington Univ	WA	16,803	C
Centre College	KY	50,680	MC
Chadron State College	NE	14,819	LC
Chapman Univ	CA	65,504	HC
Chatham Univ	PA	47,883	VC
Chicago State Univ	IL	41,620	C
Christian Brothers Univ	TN	31,670	VC
CUNY/Brooklyn College	NY	7,163	C+
CUNY/City College	NY	20,204	C
CUNY/Hunter College	NY	31,098	VC
CUNY/Lehman College	NY	5,788	LC
CUNY/Queens College	NY	21,507	C
CUNY/York College	NY	6,747	LC
Claremont McKenna College	CA	69,900	MC
Clarion Univ of Pennsylvania	PA	21,608	LC
Clark Atlanta Univ	GA	31,019	LC
Clark Univ	MA	53,260	HC+
Clarkson Univ	NY	60,392	VC
Clemson Univ	SC		HC
Cleveland State Univ	OH	22,290	C
Coastal Carolina Univ	SC	20,340	C
Coe College	IA	51,570	VC
Colby College	ME	64,060	MC
Colgate Univ	NY	67,500	MC
College of Charleston	SC	24,046	VC
College of Mount St. Vincent	NY	45,620	C
College of St. Benedict	MN	54,480	C
College of Staten Island	NY	24,389	LC
College of the Holy Cross	MA	64,320	MC
College of William & Mary	VA	34,907	MC
Colo College	CO	64,894	MC
Colo Mesa Univ	CO	19,707	LC
Colo School of Mines	CO	29,319	MC
Colo State Univ	CO	23,033	C
Colo State Univ-Pueblo	CO	21,581	C
Columbia Univ/ School of General Studies	NY	61,470	MC
Columbia Univ/City of New York	NY	62,958	MC
Concordia College - Moorhead	MN	46,418	C
Concordia Univ, Ann Arbor	MI	38,878	C+
Conn College	CT	65,000	MC
Cornell College	IA	49,900	VC
Cornell Univ	NY	67,591	MC
Covenant College	GA	44,590	HC
Creighton Univ	NE	49,452	VC
Dartmouth College	NH	68,109	MC
Davidson College	NC	60,119	MC
Delaware State Univ	DE	19,376	LC
Denison Univ	OH	62,770	HC+
DePaul Univ	IL	52,807	VC
DePauw Univ	IN	58,688	VC
Dickinson College	PA	66,166	MC
Dillard Univ	LA	20,940	VC
Doane Univ	NE	41,340	VC
Dordt College	IA	37,860	C+
Drake Univ	IA	49,220	HC
Drew Univ/College of Liberal Arts	NJ	53,608	VC
Drexel Univ	PA	65,927	HC
Drury Univ	MO	37,555	VC
Duke Univ	NC	68,298	MC
Duquesne Univ	PA	48,508	VC
Earlham College	IN	55,670	HC
East Carolina Univ	NC	16,539	C
East Central Univ	OK	13,330	C
East Stroudsburg Univ	PA	18,578	LC
East Tenn State Univ	TN	18,141	C
Eastern Illinois Univ	IL	21,414	C
Eastern Mich Univ	MI	19,761	C
Eastern Nazarene College	MA	41,114	C
Eastern Oregon Univ	OR	17,612	C
Eastern Washington Univ	WA	17,896	LC
Eckerd College	FL	55,206	VC
Edgewood College	WI	35,950	C
Edinboro Univ	PA	15,940	LC
Elizabeth City State Univ	NC	14,745	C
Elizabethtown College	PA	56,340	VC
Elmhurst College	IL	46,514	C
Elon Univ	NC	46,142	HC
Emory and Henry College	VA	46,320	C
Emory Univ	GA	63,286	MC
Emporia State Univ	KS	15,029	C
Erskine College	SC	45,460	C
Excelsior College	NY	38,800	SP
Fairfield Univ	CT	61,445	HC
Fisk Univ	TN	32,066	LC
Florida A&M Univ	FL	15,361	C
Florida Atlantic Univ	FL	18,256	C
Florida Inst of Technology	FL	53,306	VC
Florida International Univ	FL	20,281	C
Florida State Univ	FL	16,771	HC
Fordham Univ	NY	68,431	MC
Fort Hays State Univ	KS	12,677	C
Fort Lewis College	CO	20,154	C
Francis Marion Univ	SC	18,144	LC
Franklin and Marshall College	PA	67,960	MC
Frostburg State Univ	MD	17,280	LC
Furman Univ	SC	61,098	VC+
Geneva College	PA	35,450	C
George Mason Univ	VA	19,884	C
Georgetown College	KY	41,440	C
Georgetown Univ	DC	68,970	MC
Georgia College & State Univ	GA	21,884	C+
Georgia Inst of Technology	GA	23,910	MC
Georgia Southern Univ	GA	16,540	VC
Georgia State Univ	GA	25,250	C
Gettysburg College	PA	65,210	MC
Gonzaga Univ	WA	52,880	HC
Gordon College	MA	47,740	VC
Goshen College	IN	44,350	C
Goucher College	MD	56,110	VC
Grambling State Univ	LA	15,701	C
Grand Valley State Univ	MI	22,250	C+
Greenville College	IL	27,012	LC
Grinnell College	IA	63,114	MC
Grove City College	PA	26,654	VC
Guilford College	NC	45,973	C
Gustavus Adolphus College	MN	53,943	HC
Hamilton College	NY	64,250	MC
Hamline Univ	MN	50,152	C
Hampden-Sydney College	VA	57,806	VC
Hampshire College	MA	65,214	MC
Hampton Univ	VA	36,410	C
Hanover College	IN	47,750	C+
Harding Univ	AR	25,440	C
Hardin-Simmons Univ	TX	36,025	C
Hartwick College	NY	51,270	C
Harvard College/Harvard Univ	MA	65,609	MC
Harvey Mudd College	CA	67,155	MC
Hastings College	NE	35,380	C+
Haverford College	PA	66,490	MC
Heidelberg Univ	OH	40,400	LC
Henderson State Univ	AR	15,516	C
Hendrix College	AR	54,020	VC
High Point Univ	NC	47,355	VC
Hillsdale College	MI	37,170	MC
Hiram College	OH	44,590	C
Hobart and William Smith Colleges	NY	67,050	HC+
Hofstra Univ	NY	58,210	C+
Hope College	MI	42,840	VC
Houghton College	NY	40,558	VC
Houston Baptist Univ	TX	36,450	C
Howard Univ	DC	37,616	C+
Humboldt State Univ	CA	21,708	C
Huntington Univ	IN	33,996	C
Idaho State Univ	ID	13,619	LC
Illinois College	IL	41,330	VC
Illinois Inst of Technology	IL	56,826	HC+
Illinois State Univ	IL	23,418	VC
Illinois Wesleyan Univ	IL	56,430	VC+
Indiana State Univ	IN	23,223	LC
Indiana Univ Bloomington	IN	20,791	HC
Indiana Univ of Pennsylvania	PA	24,474	C
Indiana Univ South Bend	IN	16,057	C
Indiana Univ Southeast	IN	16,931	C
Indiana Univ-Purdue Univ Fort Wayne	IN	18,675	C
Indiana Univ-Purdue Univ Indianapolis	IN	18,952	C
Iona College	NY	52,514	C
Iowa State Univ	IA	18,176	C
Ithaca College	NY	58,158	VC+
Jackson State Univ	MS	15,879	LC
Jacksonville State Univ	AL	14,628	LC
Jacksonville Univ	FL	49,210	C
James Madison Univ	VA	19,084	VC
John Carroll Univ	OH	51,570	C
Johns Hopkins Univ	MD	68,080	MC
Johnson C. Smith Univ	NC	25,336	LC
Juniata College	PA	58,118	VC
Kalamazoo College	MI	53,931	HC
Kansas State Univ	KS	17,780	VC
Kansas Wesleyan Univ	KS	37,930	C
Keene State College	NH	24,604	C
Kennesaw State Univ	GA	18,899	VC
Kent State Univ	OH	20,928	C
Kentucky Wesleyan College	KY	34,260	LC
Kenyon College	OH	65,840	MC
King Univ	TN	36,976	C
King's College	PA	48,240	C
Knox College	IL	54,654	VC+
Kutztown Univ of Pennsylvania	PA	19,477	C
La Sierra Univ	CA	39,690	VC
Lafayette College	PA	68,520	MC
Lake Forest College	IL	50,652	VC
Lamar Univ	TX	18,014	LC
Lane College	TN	17,960	LC
Lawrence Tech Univ	MI	41,630	VC
Lawrence Univ	WI	56,133	HC+
Le Moyne College	NY	47,305	VC
Lebanon Valley College	PA	55,510	VC
Lehigh Univ	PA	63,860	MC
Lenoir-Rhyne Univ	NC	47,500	LC
Lewis & Clark College	OR	60,984	MC
Lewis Univ	IL	41,710	C
Lincoln Univ	MO	14,402	NC
Lincoln Univ	PA	20,878	LC
Linfield College	OR	53,992	C
Lipscomb Univ	TN	42,984	VC
LIU Brooklyn	NY	50,698	C
LIU Post	NY	50,698	C+
Lock Haven Univ of Pennsylvania	PA	20,544	LC
Longwood Univ	VA	22,184	C
Louisiana State Univ and A&M College	LA	18,677	VC
Louisiana State Univ in Shreveport	LA	6,902	C
Louisiana Tech Univ	LA	21,422	VC
Loyola Marymount Univ	CA	60,202	VC+
Loyola Univ Chicago	IL	57,158	VC
Loyola Univ Maryland	MD	61,710	VC
Loyola Univ New Orleans	LA	52,456	VC
Luther College	IA	49,990	VC
Lycoming College	PA	50,895	C
Macalester College	MN	64,136	MC
MacMurray College	IL	35,025	C
Madonna Univ	MI	30,450	LC
Manchester Univ	IN	41,540	C
Manhattan College	NY	55,652	C

ST = STATE $IS = IN-STATE COSTS SR = SELECTOR RATING

School	ST	$IS	SR
Marietta College	OH	46,190	C
Marlboro College	VT	50,832	VC+
Marquette Univ	WI	53,090	VC+
Marshall Univ	WV	18,044	C
Mary Baldwin Univ	VA	40,495	C
Mass College of Liberal Arts	MA	20,659	C
Mass Inst of Technology	MA	62,662	MC
McDaniel College	MD	52,910	VC
McMurry Univ	TX	34,259	LC
Mercer Univ	GA	45,348	VC
Merrimack College	MA	55,415	C
Messiah College	PA	44,380	VC
Metropolitan State Univ of Denver	CO	6,928	LC
Miami Univ	OH	27,190	HC+
Mich State Univ	MI	24,542	VC
Mich Tech Univ	MI	25,551	VC+
MidAmerica Nazarene Univ	KS	37,808	C
Middle Tenn State Univ	TN	8,650	C
Middlebury College	VT	67,464	MC
Millersville Univ of Pennsylvania	PA	25,298	C
Millikin Univ	IL	44,148	C
Millsaps College	MS	50,080	C+
Minn State Univ, Mankato	MN	17,190	C
Minn State Univ, Moorhead	MN	21,393	C
Minot State Univ	ND	13,285	C
Miss College	MS	25,850	C
Miss State Univ	MS	12,028	C+
Missouri Southern State Univ	MO	13,071	C
Missouri Univ of Science and Technology	MO	18,655	HC
Monmouth College	IL	42,260	C
Montana State Univ	MT	15,500	C+
Montclair State Univ	NJ	26,912	C
Moravian College	PA	55,488	C
Morehead State Univ	KY	18,386	LC
Morehouse College	GA	40,835	C
Morgan State Univ	MD	17,190	LC
Morningside College	IA	39,780	C
Mount Holyoke College	MA	56,746	MC
Muhlenberg College	PA	56,645	VC
Murray State Univ	KY	17,726	C+
Muskingum Univ	OH	35,966	C
Nebr Wesleyan Univ	NE	42,026	C+
New College of Florida	FL	16,180	HC+
New Jersey City Univ	NJ	21,456	LC
New Mexico Highlands Univ	NM	11,904	LC
New Mexico Inst of Mining and Technology	NM	15,385	HC+
New Mexico State Univ	NM	14,050	LC
New York Univ	NY	68,139	MC
Norfolk State Univ	VA	18,902	LC
N Car A&T State Univ	NC	13,786	C
N Car Central Univ	NC	9,000	C
N Car State Univ	NC	22,434	HC+
North Central College	IL	48,712	C+
N Dak State Univ	ND	16,245	VC
North Park Univ	IL	35,860	C
Northeastern Illinois Univ	IL	12,529	LC
Northeastern Univ	MA	65,352	MC
Northern Arizona Univ	AZ	21,003	C
Northern Illinois Univ	IL	20,176	C
Northern Kentucky Univ	KY	16,486	C
Northern Mich Univ	MI	20,853	C
Northwest Missouri State Univ	MO	18,286	C
Northwest Nazarene Univ	ID	40,250	C
Northwestern Okla State Univ	OK	13,072	LC
Northwestern Univ	IL	68,725	MC
Norwich Univ	VT	56,234	C
Notre Dame of Maryland Univ	MD	47,570	VC
Oakland Univ	MI	20,763	C
Oberlin College	OH	68,942	MC
Occidental College	CA	68,660	MC
Oglethorpe Univ	GA	44,200	C
Ohio Northern Univ	OH	44,050	VC
Ohio State Univ at Columbus	OH	22,843	MC
Ohio Univ	OH	23,394	VC
Ohio Wesleyan Univ	OH	49,460	VC
Okla Baptist Univ	OK	33,990	C
Okla City Univ	OK	40,476	C
Okla State Univ	OK	17,180	C+
Old Dominion Univ	VA	21,618	C
Oral Roberts Univ	OK	34,316	C
Oregon State Univ	OR	23,337	VC
Otterbein Univ	OH	41,630	C
Ouachita Baptist Univ	AR	33,500	VC
Pace Univ	NY	60,136	C
Pacific Lutheran Univ	WA	49,960	C
Pacific Union College	CA	36,009	VC
Pacific Univ	OR	37,617	C
Penn State Erie,The Behrend College	PA	26,688	VC
Pennsylvania State Univ - Univ Park	PA	29,716	HC
Pepperdine Univ	CA	66,862	VC+
Piedmont College	GA	34,334	C
Pittsburg State Univ	KS	13,880	C
Pitzer College	CA	68,500	HC+
Point Loma Nazarene Univ	CA	46,150	C+
Pomona College	CA	64,957	MC
Pontifical Catholic Univ of PR	PR	10,534	
Portland State Univ	OR	19,443	C
Prairie View A&M Univ	TX	27,273	LC
Presbyterian College	SC	47,186	C
Princeton Univ	NJ	60,090	MC
Principia College	IL	40,350	C
Purdue Univ Northwest	IN	15,178	C
Purdue Univ/West Lafayette	IN	20,032	MC
Radford Univ	VA	19,758	C
Randolph College	VA	53,970	C
Randolph-Macon College	VA	51,480	VC
Reed College	OR	65,300	MC
Regis Univ	CO	46,380	C
Rensselaer Polytechnic Inst	NY	67,265	MC
Rhode Island College	RI	19,000	LC
Rhodes College	TN	51,900	HC
Rice Univ	TX	59,458	MC
Rider Univ	NJ	54,050	C
Ripon College	WI	49,991	VC
Roanoke College	VA	55,952	VC
Roberts Wesleyan College	NY	41,116	C
Rochester Inst of Technology	NY	52,734	HC+
Rockhurst Univ	MO	28,990	C
Rollins College	FL	58,670	HC
Rose-Hulman Inst of Technology	IN	59,823	MC
Rowan Univ	NJ	24,491	VC
Rutgers Univ - Camden	NJ	26,595	C
Rutgers Univ - New Brunswick	NJ	27,090	HC
Rutgers Univ - Newark	NJ	27,351	C
Saginaw Valley State Univ	MI	19,284	C
St. John's Univ	MN	53,472	C
St. Joseph's Univ	PA	58,540	VC
St. Louis Univ	MO	49,866	HC
St. Mary's College	IN	50,600	C
St. Mary's College of Calif	CA	57,420	C
St. Mary's Univ of Minn	MN	42,440	C
St. Michael's College	VT	53,275	VC+
St. Peter's Univ	NJ	49,192	C
St. Vincent College	PA	46,229	C
Salisbury Univ	MD	21,132	VC
Sam Houston State Univ	TX	18,792	C
Samford Univ	AL	40,770	VC
San Diego State Univ	CA	23,156	VC
San Francisco State Univ	CA	18,514	LC
San Jose State Univ	CA	22,630	C
Scripps College	CA	69,260	HC
Seattle Pacific Univ	WA	47,439	C+
Seattle Univ	WA	54,957	VC
Seton Hall Univ	NJ	58,008	C
Seton Hill Univ	PA	46,972	VC
Sewanee: The Univ of the South	TN	58,000	HC+
Shaw Univ	NC	24,638	C
Shawnee State Univ	OH	16,998	C
Shippensburg Univ of Pennsylvania	PA	24,096	C
Siena College	NY	48,916	C
Simmons College	MA	54,400	HC
Simpson College	IA	45,626	VC
Skidmore College	NY	66,600	MC
Slippery Rock Univ of Pennsylvania	PA	20,450	C
Smith College	MA	66,774	MC
Sonoma State Univ	CA	27,020	C
S Car State Univ	SC	21,330	LC
S Dak School of Mines and Technology	SD	18,570	C+
S Dak State Univ	SD	15,874	C
Southeast Missouri State Univ	MO	16,148	C
Southeastern Louisiana Univ	LA	16,237	C
Southeastern Okla State Univ	OK	11,875	C
Southern Adventist Univ	TN	28,250	C
Southern Conn State Univ	CT	21,924	LC
Southern Illinois Univ Carbondale	IL	24,554	C
Southern Illinois Univ Edwardsville	IL	20,188	C
Southern Methodist Univ	TX	69,008	MC
Southern Nazarene Univ	OK	33,684	C
Southern Univ and A&M College	LA	16,074	LC
Southern Univ at New Orleans	LA	8,014	LC
Southwestern Adventist Univ	TX	28,232	LC
Southwestern Univ	TX	52,370	VC
Spelman College	GA	41,642	C
Spring Arbor Univ	MI	37,390	C
St. Bonaventure Univ	NY	45,596	C
St. Cloud State Univ	MN	10,600	C
St. John Fisher College	NY	45,270	VC
St. John's College at Annapolis	MD	63,348	MC
St. John's Univ	NY	57,160	C+
St. Lawrence Univ	NY	66,646	HC+
St. Mary's College of Maryland	MD	27,312	VC
St. Mary's Univ	TX	39,120	C
St. Norbert College	WI	46,060	VC
St. Olaf College	MN	56,430	HC
Stanford Univ	CA	62,541	MC
SUNY Albany	NY	22,165	C
SUNY at Binghamton	NY	24,100	MC
SUNY at Geneseo	NY	21,622	VC
SUNY at New Paltz	NY	20,840	C
SUNY at Oswego	NY	22,219	VC
SUNY/Buffalo State	NY	20,583	LC
SUNY/Cortland	NY	20,910	C
SUNY/Fredonia	NY	20,818	C
SUNY/Oneonta	NY	20,794	C
SUNY/Plattsburgh	NY	19,314	C
SUNY/Potsdam	NY	21,051	VC
SUNY/Univ at Buffalo	NY	23,122	C
Stephen F. Austin State Univ	TX	18,484	LC
Stetson Univ	FL	57,174	VC+
Stevens Inst of Technology	NJ	64,954	MC
Stockton Univ	NJ	25,565	C
Stonehill College	MA	55,130	C
Stony Brook Univ/The SUNY	NY	22,703	MC
Suffolk Univ	MA	52,316	C
Susquehanna Univ	PA	57,560	VC
Swarthmore College	PA	63,550	MC
Syracuse Univ	NY	62,313	HC
Talladega College	AL	25,919	C
Tarleton State Univ	TX	15,248	LC
Taylor Univ	IN	42,130	VC
Temple Univ	PA	24,392	C+
Tenn State Univ	TN	14,423	LC
Tenn Tech Univ	TN	17,929	C
Texas A&M Univ at College Station	TX	20,771	VC+
Texas A&M Univ at Commerce	TX	10,496	C
Texas A&M Univ at Kingsville	TX	16,580	LC
Texas Christian Univ	TX	57,120	HC
Texas Lutheran Univ	TX	39,770	C
Texas State Univ	TX	18,721	C
Texas Tech Univ	TX	20,156	C+
The American Univ	DC	61,317	HC
The Catholic Univ of America	DC	58,376	VC
The Citadel, The Military College of S Car	SC	20,679	C
The College at Brockport - SUNY	NY	21,058	C
The College of New Jersey	NJ	28,675	VC+
The College of Wooster	OH	60,000	HC
The George Washington Univ	DC	68,474	HC+
The Univ of Akron	OH	22,566	C
The Univ of Alabama	AL	24,320	C+
The Univ of Arizona	AZ	24,086	C
The Univ of Memphis	TN	18,278	C
The Univ of Tenn at Chattanooga	TN	17,340	C+
The Univ of Tenn at Knoxville	TN	22,112	VC
The Univ of Texas at Austin	TX	20,206	MC
The Univ of Texas at San Antonio	TX	21,060	C
The Univ of Utah	UT	18,751	VC
Thiel College	PA	42,950	LC
Thomas More College	KY	36,720	LC
Tougaloo College	MS	17,980	NC
Touro College	NY	31,040	C
Towson Univ	MD	21,878	C
Transylvania Univ	KY	47,450	HC+
Trevecca Nazarene Univ	TN	31,186	C
Trinity College	CT	69,020	HC
Trinity Univ	TX	54,480	MC
Truman State Univ	MO	16,286	MC
Tufts Univ	MA		MC
Tulane Univ	LA	67,496	MC
Tuskegee Univ	AL	28,164	C
Union College	NE	23,270	C
Union College	NY	64,320	MC
Union Univ	TN	41,160	VC
United States Air Force Academy	CO		C
United States Military Academy at West Point	NY		HC+
United States Naval Academy	MD		HC
Univ of Alabama at Birmingham	AL	22,092	C
Univ of Alabama in Huntsville	AL	20,028	VC
Univ of Alaska Fairbanks	AK	16,874	VC
Univ of Arkansas at Fayetteville	AR	19,766	VC
Univ of Arkansas at Little Rock	AR	18,211	LC
Univ of Arkansas at Pine Bluff	AR	13,541	C
Univ of Calif at Berkeley	CA	29,886	MC
Univ of Calif at Davis	CA	28,468	HC
Univ of Calif at Irvine	CA	33,857	VC
Univ of Calif at Los Angeles	CA	27,438	HC+
Univ of Calif at Riverside	CA	32,912	C
Univ of Calif at Santa Barbara	CA	30,627	HC+
Univ of Calif San Diego	CA	30,450	MC
Univ of Calif, Santa Cruz	CA	28,731	C+
Univ of Central Arkansas	AR	15,042	VC
Univ of Central Florida	FL	16,379	VC
Univ of Central Missouri	MO	18,982	C
Univ of Chicago	IL	70,551	MC
Univ of Cincinnati	OH	22,118	VC
Univ of Colo Boulder	CO	26,048	HC
Univ of Colo Colo Springs	CO	20,300	C
Univ of Colo Denver	CO	22,238	C
Univ of Conn	CT	27,394	
Univ of Dallas	TX	50,676	VC
Univ of Dayton	OH	54,930	VC
Univ of Delaware	DE	32,214	VC
Univ of Denver	CO	61,129	VC+
Univ of Evansville	IN	44,186	C+
Univ of Florida	FL	16,291	HC+
Univ of Georgia	GA	21,878	HC
Univ of Hartford	CT	49,776	C
Univ of Hawaii at Hilo	HI	18,038	VC
Univ of Hawaii at Manoa	HI	23,261	C
Univ of Houston	TX	21,871	VC
Univ of Idaho	ID	16,158	C
Univ of Illinois at Chicago	IL	24,664	VC
Univ of Illinois at Urbana-Champaign	IL	27,006	HC
Univ of Indianapolis	IN	36,480	VC
Univ of Iowa	IA	19,415	HC
Univ of Kansas	KS	20,884	VC
Univ of Kentucky	KY	24,800	C+
Univ of La Verne	CA	55,600	C
Univ of Louisiana at Lafayette	LA	14,516	C
Univ of Louisville	KY	19,692	C
Univ of Lynchburg	VA	48,370	C
Univ of Maine	ME	21,038	VC
Univ of Mary Washington	VA	23,039	C+
Univ of Maryland/Baltimore County	MD	23,004	VC
Univ of Maryland/College Park	MD	21,938	HC
Univ of Mass Amherst	MA	27,669	HC
Univ of Mass Boston	MA	13,828	C
Univ of Mass Dartmouth	MA	26,507	C
Univ of Mass Lowell	MA	27,296	VC
Univ of Miami	FL	63,494	MC
Univ of Mich/Ann Arbor	MI	25,274	MC
Univ of Mich/Dearborn	MI	12,472	VC
Univ of Mich/Flint	MI	19,062	C
Univ of Minn/Duluth	MN	20,292	C
Univ of Minn/Morris	MN	21,222	VC
Univ of Minn/Twin Cities	MN	24,269	MC
Univ of Miss	MS	18,802	C
Univ of Missouri-Columbia	MO	20,463	VC
Univ of Missouri-Kansas City	MO	19,563	VC
Univ of Missouri-St. Louis	MO	19,810	VC
Univ of Montana	MT	14,105	C
Univ of Mount Union	OH	39,990	C
Univ of Nebr - Kearney	NE	17,014	LC
Univ of Nebr - Lincoln	NE	18,589	VC
Univ of Nebr - Omaha	NE	16,120	C
Univ of Nevada, Las Vegas	NV	17,553	C
Univ of Nevada, Reno	NV	18,010	C
Univ of New Hampshire	NH	29,333	VC
Univ of New Mexico	NM	16,808	C
Univ of New Orleans	LA	12,840	C
Univ of North Alabama	AL	15,964	C
Univ of N Car at Asheville	NC	16,251	VC+
Univ of N Car at Chapel Hill	NC	20,561	MC
Univ of N Car at Charlotte	NC	17,803	VC
Univ of N Car at Greensboro	NC	15,998	C
Univ of N Car at Pembroke	NC	14,737	LC
Univ of N Car Wilmington	NC	16,784	VC
Univ of N Dak	ND	16,673	C
Univ of North Florida	FL	15,996	VC
Univ of North Georgia	GA	17,316	C
Univ of North Texas	TX	20,082	C
Univ of Northern Colo	CO	19,658	C
Univ of Northern Iowa	IA	17,480	C
Univ of Notre Dame	IN	68,801	MC
Univ of Okla	OK	19,651	HC
Univ of Oregon	OR	24,021	VC
Univ of Pennsylvania	PA	63,526	MC
Univ of Pittsburgh	PA	30,030	MC
Univ of Portland	OR	52,152	VC
Univ of PR, at Humacao	PR	14,000	
Univ of PR, at Mayaguez	PR	13,995	
Univ of Puget Sound	WA	60,210	HC
Univ of Redlands	CA	61,934	VC
Univ of Rhode Island	RI	26,066	VC
Univ of Richmond	VA	62,730	MC
Univ of Rochester	NY	65,032	MC
Univ of San Diego	CA	60,338	HC
Univ of San Francisco	CA	60,580	C
Univ of Science and Arts of Okla	OK	11,140	VC
Univ of Scranton	PA	54,962	VC
Univ of South Alabama	AL	16,880	C
Univ of S Car at Columbia	SC	21,726	VC
Univ of S Dak	SD	16,109	C
Univ of South Florida/Tampa	FL	16,110	VC
Univ of Southern Calif	CA	66,631	MC
Univ of Southern Indiana	IN	16,808	C
Univ of Southern Maine	ME	18,320	C
Univ of Southern Miss	MS	13,170	C
Univ of Tampa	FL	38,928	VC
Univ of Texas at Arlington	TX	18,876	C
Univ of Texas at Dallas	TX	23,640	HC
Univ of Texas at El Paso	TX	34,452	NC
Univ of Texas Rio Grande Valley	TX	15,573	LC
Univ of the Cumberlands	KY	32,000	LC
Univ of the District of Columbia	DC	21,260	LC
Univ of the Pacific	CA	57,446	VC
Univ of the Sciences	PA	40,738	VC
Univ of Toledo	OH	19,336	C
Univ of Tulsa	OK	52,625	HC
Univ of Vermont	VT	29,792	HC
Univ of Virginia	VA	27,367	MC
Univ of Washington	WA	23,091	MC
Univ of West Florida	FL	15,848	C
Univ of West Georgia	GA	17,510	LC
Univ of Wisc-Eau Claire	WI	16,354	VC
Univ of Wisc-La Crosse	WI	15,425	VC
Univ of Wisc-Madison	WI	21,647	MC
Univ of Wisc-Milwaukee	WI	21,538	C
Univ of Wisc-Oshkosh	WI	15,392	C
Univ of Wisc-Parkside	WI	15,313	C
Univ of Wisc-Platteville	WI	14,148	C
Univ of Wisc-River Falls	WI	14,541	C

ST = STATE **$IS** = IN-STATE COSTS **SR** = SELECTOR RATING

School	ST	$IS	SR
Univ of Wisc-Stevens Point	WI	14,043	C
Univ of Wisc-Whitewater	WI	13,976	C
Univ of Wyoming	WY	15,537	C
Ursinus College	PA	62,920	VC
Utah State Univ	UT	13,235	C
Utica College	NY	31,510	C
Valparaiso Univ	IN	50,160	VC
Vanderbilt Univ	TN	63,248	MC
Vassar College	NY	68,110	MC
Villanova Univ	PA	64,922	MC
Virginia Commonwealth Univ	VA	23,811	VC
Virginia Military Inst	VA	26,460	VC
Virginia Polytechnic Inst and State Univ	VA	21,920	VC
Virginia State Univ	VA	19,802	C+
Wabash College	IN	52,100	VC
Wagner College	NY	57,240	C+
Wake Forest Univ	NC	69,354	MC
Walla Walla Univ	WA	34,845	C
Wartburg College	IA	49,478	C
Washburn Univ	KS	15,827	C
Washington & Jefferson College	PA	58,694	VC
Washington and Lee Univ	VA	59,647	MC
Washington College	MD	56,154	VC
Washington State Univ	WA	22,747	C
Washington Univ in St. Louis	MO	67,539	MC
Wayne State Univ	MI	23,085	C
Weber State Univ	UT	14,112	C
Wellesley College	MA	66,984	MC
Wells College	NY	50,500	C
Wesleyan Univ	CT	66,940	MC
West Chester Univ of Pennsylvania	PA	19,171	VC
West Texas A&M Univ	TX	13,478	C
West Virginia Univ	WV	18,952	VC
West Virginia Univ Inst of Technology	WV	18,264	C
West Virginia Wesleyan College	WV	39,188	C
Western Illinois Univ	IL	20,897	C
Western Kentucky Univ	KY	16,850	C
Western Mich Univ	MI	21,791	C
Western Washington Univ	WA	18,904	VC
Westminster College	MO	32,820	C
Westminster College	PA	41,722	C
Westminster College	UT	41,078	C
Westmont College	CA	57,930	VC
Wheaton College	IL	44,993	MC
Wheaton College	MA	63,818	VC
Wheeling Jesuit Univ	WV	37,106	LC
Whitman College	WA	59,772	MC
Whittier College	CA	57,891	C
Whitworth Univ	WA	53,682	VC
Wichita State Univ	KS	17,773	C
Widener Univ	PA	58,190	C
Wiley College	TX	19,255	C
Wilkes Univ	PA	49,166	C
Willamette Univ	OR	62,514	VC+
William Jewell College	MO	42,490	C+
Williams College	MA	67,700	MC
Winona State Univ	MN	18,109	C
Wisc Lutheran College	WI	36,290	C
Wittenberg Univ	OH	49,863	VC
Wofford College	SC	49,885	VC
Worcester Polytechnic Inst	MA	62,846	MC
Wright State Univ	OH	16,983	C
Xavier Univ	OH	49,380	VC
Xavier Univ of Louisiana	LA	31,689	C
Yale Univ	CT	64,650	MC
Youngstown State Univ	OH	17,487	C

PHYSICS & PHYSICAL OCEANOGRAPHY

School	ST	$IS	SR
Old Dominion Univ	VA	21,618	C
Univ of Rhode Island	RI	26,066	VC

PHYSICS AND MATHEMATICS

School	ST	$IS	SR
Bethany College	WV	38,774	LC
Bridgewater College	VA	46,260	C
Brown Univ	RI	64,566	MC
Ithaca College	NY	58,158	VC+
Keene State College	NH	24,604	C
Missouri Southern State Univ	MO	13,071	C
St. John's Univ	NY	57,160	C+
Whitman College	WA	59,772	MC

PHYSICS SECONDARY EDUCATION

School	ST	$IS	SR
Arkansas Tech Univ	AR	16,534	LC
Augustana College	IL	51,222	VC+
Cedarville Univ	OH	36,244	VC
Colo State Univ	CO	23,033	C
Grove City College	PA	26,654	VC
Indiana Univ Bloomington	IN	20,791	HC
Indiana Univ of Pennsylvania	PA	24,474	C
Indiana Univ South Bend	IN	16,057	C
Ithaca College	NY	58,158	VC+
Millersville Univ of Pennsylvania	PA	25,298	C
Old Dominion Univ	VA	21,618	C
Providence College	RI	62,870	HC
St. John's Univ	NY	57,160	C+
The Univ of Utah	UT	18,751	VC

School	ST	$IS	SR
Univ of N Car at Greensboro	NC	15,998	C
Western Mich Univ	MI	21,791	C

PHYSICS WITH ASTROPHYSICS OPTION

School	ST	$IS	SR
Brown Univ	RI	64,566	MC
Univ of Nebr - Lincoln	NE	18,589	VC

PHYSICS/COMPUTER

School	ST	$IS	SR
Grove City College	PA	26,654	VC
Univ of Dayton	OH	54,930	VC

PHYSICS/GENERAL SCIENCE SECONDARY EDUCATION

School	ST	$IS	SR
Grove City College	PA	26,654	VC
Messiah College	PA	44,380	VC
Moravian College	PA	55,488	C
Syracuse Univ	NY	62,313	HC
Tenn Wesleyan Univ	TN	32,680	LC
Wartburg College	IA	49,478	C

PHYSIOLOGY

School	ST	$IS	SR
Boston Univ	MA	67,352	MC
Brigham Young Univ	UT	13,248	MC
Cal State, Fullerton	CA	21,902	C
Cal State, Long Beach	CA	18,850	C
Emmanuel College	MA	53,472	C+
Florida State Univ	FL	16,771	HC
Hampshire College	MA	65,214	MC
Howard Univ	DC	37,616	C+
Marquette Univ	WI	53,090	VC+
Mich State Univ	MI	24,542	VC
Missouri Southern State Univ	MO	13,071	C
Northern Mich Univ	MI	20,853	C
Okla Baptist Univ	OK	33,990	C
Okla State Univ	OK	17,180	C+
San Francisco State Univ	CA	18,514	LC
Southern Illinois Univ Carbondale	IL	24,554	C
Texas State Univ	TX	18,721	C
The Evergreen State College	WA	16,599	C
The Univ of Arizona	AZ	24,086	C
The Univ of Montana Western	MT	9,426	LC
Univ of Calif at Davis	CA	28,468	HC
Univ of Calif at Los Angeles	CA	27,438	HC+
Univ of Calif at Santa Barbara	CA	30,627	HC+
Univ of Calif San Diego	CA	30,450	MC
Univ of Colo Boulder	CO	26,048	HC
Univ of Conn	CT	27,394	
Univ of Great Falls	MT	38,524	C
Univ of Illinois at Urbana-Champaign	IL	27,006	HC
Univ of Minn/Twin Cities	MN	24,269	MC
Univ of Oregon	OR	24,021	VC
Univ of Wyoming	WY	15,537	C

PIANO PEDAGOGY

School	ST	$IS	SR
Ithaca College	NY	58,158	VC+
Missouri Western State Univ	MO	17,822	LC
Ohio Univ	OH	23,394	VC
Okla Baptist Univ	OK	33,990	C
Okla City Univ	OK	40,476	C
Samford Univ	AL	40,770	VC
Shorter Univ	GA	31,130	LC
Silver Lake College of the Holy Family	WI	36,290	LC
Texas Christian Univ	TX	57,120	HC
The Master's Univ	CA	43,870	C

PIANO PERFORMANCE

School	ST	$IS	SR
Abilene Christian Univ	TX	43,708	C+
Aquinas College - Mich	MI	38,876	VC
Biola Univ	CA	48,686	C
Boston Univ	MA	67,352	MC
Calif Baptist Univ	CA	42,986	C
Dallas Baptist Univ	TX	35,220	VC
East Texas Baptist Univ	TX	34,444	C
Hope College	MI	42,840	VC
Madonna Univ	MI	30,450	LC
Milligan College	TN	39,450	C
Missouri Southern State Univ	MO	13,071	C
Missouri Western State Univ	MO	17,822	LC
New England Conservatory of Music	MA	63,170	SP
New York Univ	NY	68,139	MC
Okla Baptist Univ	OK	33,990	C
Okla City Univ	OK	40,476	C
Ouachita Baptist Univ	AR	33,500	VC
Point Loma Nazarene Univ	CA	46,150	C+
Roberts Wesleyan College	NY	41,116	C
Samford Univ	AL	40,770	VC
Silver Lake College of the Holy Family	WI	36,290	LC
Southeastern Univ	FL	34,910	LC
Texas Christian Univ	TX	57,120	HC
The Master's Univ	CA	43,870	C
Univ of Central Okla	OK	15,150	C
Univ of N Car at Greensboro	NC	15,998	C
Webster Univ	MO	37,490	C

School	ST	$IS	SR
West Chester Univ of Pennsylvania	PA	19,171	VC
Youngstown State Univ	OH	17,487	C

PIANO/ORGAN

School	ST	$IS	SR
Bennington College	VT	66,280	MC
Calif Baptist Univ	CA	42,986	C
Calvin College	MI	43,090	HC
Central Mich Univ	MI	20,330	C
Central Washington Univ	WA	16,803	C
Columbia College	SC	36,550	C
East Central Univ	OK	13,330	C
East Texas Baptist Univ	TX	34,444	C
Eastern Mich Univ	MI	19,761	C
Florida State Univ	FL	16,771	HC
Hardin-Simmons Univ	TX	36,025	C
Hope College	MI	42,840	VC
Illinois Wesleyan Univ	IL	56,430	VC+
Indiana Univ-Purdue Univ Fort Wayne	IN	18,675	C
Jackson State Univ	MS	15,879	LC
Lenoir-Rhyne Univ	NC	47,500	LC
Louisiana College	LA	21,274	C
Loyola Univ New Orleans	LA	52,456	VC
Manhattan School of Music	NY	57,200	SP
Mannes School of Music	NY	44,500	SP
Marshall Univ	WV	18,044	C
Millikin Univ	IL	44,148	C
Miss College	MS	25,850	C
Missouri Western State Univ	MO	17,822	LC
Northwestern Univ	IL	68,725	MC
Nyack College	NY	34,450	LC
Oberlin College	OH	68,942	MC
Ohio State Univ at Columbus	OH	22,843	MC
Ohio Univ	OH	23,394	VC
Okla City Univ	OK	40,476	C
Ouachita Baptist Univ	AR	33,500	VC
Pacific Lutheran Univ	WA	49,960	C
Palm Beach Atlantic Univ	FL	39,250	C
Rider Univ	NJ	54,050	C
Roosevelt Univ	IL	41,890	VC
Samford Univ	AL	40,770	VC
San Francisco Conservatory of Music	CA	57,310	SP
Shorter Univ	GA	31,130	LC
Southern Methodist Univ	TX	69,008	MC
Stetson Univ	FL	57,174	VC+
Syracuse Univ	NY	62,313	HC
Temple Univ	PA	24,392	C+
The Boston Conservatory at Berklee	MA	61,042	SP
The Catholic Univ of America	DC	58,376	VC
Union Univ	TN	41,160	VC
Univ of Cincinnati	OH	22,118	VC
Univ of Iowa	IA	19,415	HC
Univ of Kansas	KS	20,884	VC
Univ of Northwestern - St. Paul	MN	39,530	C
Univ of Tulsa	OK	52,625	HC
Weber State Univ	UT	14,112	C
Westminster Choir College	NJ	53,730	SP
Youngstown State Univ	OH	17,487	C

PLANETARY AND SPACE SCIENCE

School	ST	$IS	SR
Boston Univ	MA	67,352	MC
Brown Univ	RI	64,566	MC
Calif Inst of Technology	CA	64,704	MC
Florida Inst of Technology	FL	53,306	VC
The Univ of Arizona	AZ	24,086	C
Virginia Polytechnic Inst and State Univ	VA	21,920	VC
Wilmington College	OH	35,100	C

PLANT GENETICS

School	ST	$IS	SR
Brigham Young Univ	UT	13,248	MC
Purdue Univ/West Lafayette	IN	20,032	MC
SUNY/The College of Environmental Science and Forestry	NY	23,728	VC
Univ of Calif at Berkeley	CA	29,886	MC
Univ of Calif at Riverside	CA	32,912	C
Washington State Univ	WA	22,747	C

PLANT PATHOLOGY

School	ST	$IS	SR
Cal State, Fullerton	CA	21,902	C
Iowa State Univ	IA	18,176	C
Mich State Univ	MI	24,542	VC
New Mexico State Univ	NM	14,050	LC
Ohio State Univ at Columbus	OH	22,843	MC
SUNY/The College of Environmental Science and Forestry	NY	23,728	VC
The Univ of Arizona	AZ	24,086	C
Univ of Calif at Riverside	CA	32,912	C
Univ of Delaware	DE	32,214	VC
Univ of Wisc-Madison	WI	21,647	MC
Washington State Univ	WA	22,747	C

PLANT PHYSIOLOGY

School	ST	$IS	SR
Brigham Young Univ	UT	13,248	MC
Ohio State Univ at Columbus	OH	22,843	MC

School	ST	$IS	SR
Purdue Univ/West Lafayette	IN	20,032	MC
SUNY/The College of Environmental Science and Forestry	NY	23,728	VC
Univ of Illinois at Urbana-Champaign	IL	27,006	HC

PLANT PROTECTION (PEST MANAGEMENT)

School	ST	$IS	SR
Colo State Univ	CO	23,033	C
Iowa State Univ	IA	18,176	C
Miss State Univ	MS	12,028	C+
N Dak State Univ	ND	16,245	VC
Purdue Univ/West Lafayette	IN	20,032	MC
Univ of Hawaii at Manoa	HI	23,261	C
Washington State Univ	WA	22,747	C
West Texas A&M Univ	TX	13,478	C

PLANT SCIENCE

School	ST	$IS	SR
Arkansas State Univ	AR	16,190	C
Brigham Young Univ	UT	13,248	MC
Calif State Polytechnic Univ, Pomona	CA	21,811	C
Cal State, Fresno	CA	16,902	LC
Cornell Univ	NY	67,591	MC
Florida State Univ	FL	16,771	HC
Fort Valley State Univ	GA	17,988	VC
Iowa State Univ	IA	18,176	C
Lincoln Univ	MO	14,402	NC
Louisiana State Univ and A&M College	LA	18,677	VC
Middle Tenn State Univ	TN	8,650	C
Missouri State Univ	MO	15,837	C+
Montana State Univ	MT	15,500	C+
N Dak State Univ	ND	16,245	VC
Ohio State Univ at Columbus	OH	22,843	MC
Okla State Univ	OK	17,180	C+
Pennsylvania State Univ - Univ Park	PA	29,716	HC
Purdue Univ/West Lafayette	IN	20,032	MC
Rutgers Univ - New Brunswick	NJ	27,090	HC
S Dak State Univ	SD	15,874	C
Southern Illinois Univ Carbondale	IL	24,554	C
SUNY /College of Agriculture and Tech at Cobleskill	NY	20,527	LC
SUNY/The College of Environmental Science and Forestry	NY	23,728	VC
Tarleton State Univ	TX	15,248	LC
Tenn Tech Univ	TN	17,929	C
Texas A&M Univ at College Station	TX	20,771	VC+
Texas A&M Univ at Kingsville	TX	16,580	LC
Texas Tech Univ	TX	20,156	C+
The Univ of Arizona	AZ	24,086	C
The Univ of Tenn at Knoxville	TN	22,112	VC
The Univ of Tenn at Martin	TN	15,212	C
Univ of Calif at Davis	CA	28,468	HC
Univ of Calif, Santa Cruz	CA	28,731	C+
Univ of Delaware	DE	32,214	VC
Univ of Florida	FL	16,291	HC+
Univ of Hawaii at Manoa	HI	23,261	C
Univ of Idaho	ID	16,158	C
Univ of Maryland/College Park	MD	21,938	HC
Univ of Mass Amherst	MA	27,669	HC
Univ of Minn/Twin Cities	MN	24,269	MC
Univ of Missouri-Columbia	MO	20,463	VC
Univ of Nebr - Lincoln	NE	18,589	VC
Univ of Okla	OK	19,651	HC
Univ of Rhode Island	RI	26,066	VC
Univ of Vermont	VT	29,792	HC
Utah State Univ	UT	13,235	C
Washington State Univ	WA	22,747	C
Washington Univ in St. Louis	MO	67,539	MC
West Texas A&M Univ	TX	13,478	C
West Virginia Univ	WV	18,952	VC

PLASTICS ENGINEERING

School	ST	$IS	SR
Ferris State Univ	MI	21,458	C
Pennsylvania College of Technology	PA	27,693	NC
Univ of Illinois at Urbana-Champaign	IL	27,006	HC
Univ of Mass Lowell	MA	27,296	VC
Univ of Wisc-Stout	WI	19,667	C
Weber State Univ	UT	14,112	C
Western Washington Univ	WA	18,904	VC

PLASTICS TECHNOLOGY

School	ST	$IS	SR
Eastern Mich Univ	MI	19,761	C
Penn State Erie,The Behrend College	PA	26,688	VC
Pittsburg State Univ	KS	13,880	C
Shawnee State Univ	OH	16,998	C
Weber State Univ	UT	14,112	C

PLAYWRITING/SCREENWRITING

School	ST	$IS	SR
Bennington College	VT	66,280	MC
Biola Univ	CA	48,686	C

School	ST	$IS	SR
Chapman Univ	CA	65,504	HC
Columbia College Chicago	IL	40,104	C
DePaul Univ	IL	52,807	VC
Goddard College	VT	17,040	VC
Howard Univ	DC	37,616	C+
Loyola Marymount Univ	CA	60,202	VC+
Metropolitan State Univ	MN	7,859	C
Ohio Univ	OH	23,394	VC
Univ of Southern Calif	CA	66,631	MC
Webster Univ	MO	37,490	C

POLICY ANALYSIS AND MANAGEMENT

School	ST	$IS	SR
Bloomfield College	NJ	40,100	LC
Carnegie Mellon Univ	PA	67,980	MC
Cornell Univ	NY	67,591	MC

POLICY STUDIES

School	ST	$IS	SR
Chatham Univ	PA	47,883	VC
Rutgers Univ - New Brunswick	NJ	27,090	HC

POLISH

School	ST	$IS	SR
Univ of Illinois at Chicago	IL	24,664	VC
Univ of Pittsburgh	PA	30,030	MC
Univ of Wisc-Madison	WI	21,647	MC

POLITICAL SCIENCE/ GOVERNMENT

School	ST	$IS	SR
Abilene Christian Univ	TX	43,708	C+
Adams State Univ	CO	15,420	LC
Adelphi Univ	NY	49,792	C
Adrian College	MI	45,550	C
Agnes Scott College	GA	51,930	VC+
Alabama A&M Univ	AL	18,796	C
Alabama State Univ	AL	16,490	LC
Albany State Univ	GA	19,462	C
Albertus Magnus College	CT	44,016	LC
Albion College	MI	55,260	C
Albright College	PA	57,326	C
Alcorn State Univ	MS	15,884	C
Alderson Broaddus Univ	WV	35,000	LC
Alfred Univ	NY	37,490	C
Allegheny College	PA	57,620	VC
Allen Univ	SC	19,920	NC
Alma College	MI	49,410	VC
Alvernia Univ	PA	45,330	C
Alverno College	WI	33,294	LC
American International College	MA	47,020	LC
American Jewish Univ - College of A&S	CA	44,234	C
Amherst College	MA	66,186	MC
Anderson Univ	IN	39,450	C
Andrews Univ	MI	41,732	C
Angelo State Univ	TX	15,882	LC
Anna Maria College	MA	51,020	C
Appalachian State Univ	NC	15,394	VC
Aquinas College - Mich	MI	38,876	VC
Arcadia Univ	PA	55,990	C+
Arizona State Univ at the Polytechnic Campus	AZ	22,394	VC
Arizona State Univ at the Tempe Campus	AZ	23,001	VC
Arizona State Univ at the West Campus	AZ	21,513	VC
Arkansas State Univ	AR	16,190	C
Arkansas Tech Univ	AR	16,534	LC
Armstrong State Univ	GA	15,615	C
Asbury Univ	KY	36,450	C+
Ashford Univ	CA	10,480	C
Ashland Univ	OH	30,446	C
Assumption College	MA	48,455	VC
Auburn Univ	AL	24,300	VC+
Auburn Univ at Montgomery	AL	15,000	C
Augsburg Univ	MN	45,129	C
Augusta Univ	GA	4,632	C
Augustana College	IL	51,222	VC+
Augustana Univ	SD	39,968	VC
Aurora Univ	IL	34,990	C
Austin College	TX	51,059	HC
Austin Peay State Univ	TN	16,397	C
Averett Univ	VA	43,034	LC
Avila Univ	MO	27,100	C
Azusa Pacific Univ	CA	43,972	C
Baldwin Wallace Univ	OH	42,464	VC
Ball State Univ	IN	19,808	C+
Bard College	NY	65,924	HC
Bard College at Simon's Rock	MA	65,795	MC
Barnard College/Columbia Univ	NY	68,762	MC
Barry Univ	FL	38,730	LC
Barton College	NC	39,854	C
Bates College	ME	64,500	HC
Baylor Univ	TX	56,803	HC
Belhaven Univ	MS	32,250	C
Bellarmine Univ	KY	52,532	C
Bellevue Univ	NE	20,300	NC
Belmont Abbey College	NC	28,794	C
Belmont Univ	TN	44,500	VC+
Beloit College	WI	55,206	HC
Bemidji State Univ	MN	17,730	C
Benedict College	SC	28,630	NC
Benedictine College	KS	38,850	VC
Benedictine Univ	IL	38,300	C
Bennett College	NC	27,717	NC
Bennington College	VT	66,280	MC
Berea College	KY	7,094	C
Berry College	GA	47,466	VC
Bethany College	WV	38,774	LC
Bethel College	IN	36,830	C
Bethel Univ	MN	46,550	C+
Bethune-Cookman Univ	FL	23,322	C
Birmingham-Southern College	AL	44,478	C+
Black Hills State Univ	SD	16,622	C
Blackburn College	IL	28,526	LC
Bloomfield College	NJ	40,100	LC
Bloomsburg Univ of Pennsylvania	PA	19,930	C
Boise State Univ	ID	17,368	C
Boston College	MA	68,043	MC
Boston Univ	MA	67,352	MC
Bowdoin College	ME	65,980	MC
Bowling Green State Univ	OH	19,975	C
Bradley Univ	IL	43,240	VC
Brandeis Univ	MA	68,443	MC
Brenau Univ - Women's College	GA	37,876	LC
Briar Cliff Univ	IA	36,956	C
Bridgewater College	VA	46,260	C
Bridgewater State Univ	MA	22,762	C
Brigham Young Univ	UT	13,248	MC
Brigham Young Univ/Hawaii	HI	11,710	C
Brown Univ	RI	64,566	MC
Bryan College	TN	32,900	C
Bryant Univ	RI	57,204	VC
Bryn Athyn College	PA	32,664	C
Bryn Mawr College	PA	65,220	MC
Bucknell Univ	PA	67,136	MC
Buena Vista Univ	IA	42,344	C
Butler Univ	IN	52,890	VC+
Cabrini Univ	PA	42,591	LC
Caldwell Univ	NJ	42,165	LC
Calif Baptist Univ	CA	42,986	C
Calif Inst of Technology	CA	64,704	MC
Calif Lutheran Univ	CA	52,853	C
Calif Polytechnic State Univ	CA	22,547	MC
Calif State Polytechnic Univ, Pomona	CA	21,811	C
Cal State, Bakersfield	CA	22,397	LC
Cal State, Chico	CA	19,790	VC
Cal State, Dominguez Hills	CA	19,022	LC
Cal State, East Bay	CA	20,748	C
Cal State, Fresno	CA	16,902	LC
Cal State, Fullerton	CA	21,902	C
Cal State, Long Beach	CA	18,850	C
Cal State, Los Angeles	CA	17,186	LC
Cal State, Northridge	CA	17,277	LC
Cal State, San Bernardino	CA	20,106	C
Cal State, San Marcos	CA	20,604	LC
Cal State, Stanislaus	CA	18,053	LC
Calif Univ of Pennsylvania	PA	20,425	LC
Calvin College	MI	43,090	HC
Cameron Univ	OK	11,632	LC
Campbell Univ	NC	37,570	VC
Campbellsville Univ	KY	33,400	C
Capital Univ	OH	44,778	VC
Carleton College	MN	66,414	MC
Carlow Univ	PA	39,696	LC
Carnegie Mellon Univ	PA	67,980	MC
Carroll College	MT	44,304	C
Carroll Univ	WI	38,100	C+
Carthage College	WI	48,835	C
Case Western Reserve Univ	OH	62,284	MC
Castleton Univ	VT	20,186	C
Catawba College	NC	39,820	LC
Cedar Crest College	PA	51,110	C
Cedarville Univ	OH	36,244	VC
Centenary College	NJ	43,890	LC
Centenary College of Louisiana	LA	49,050	C+
Central College	IA	44,592	C
Central Conn State Univ	CT	22,041	C
Central Methodist Univ	MO	31,500	VC
Central State Univ	OH	18,564	C
Central Washington Univ	WA	16,803	C
Centre College	KY	50,680	MC
Chadron State College	NE	14,819	LC
Chapman Univ	CA	65,504	HC
Charleston Southern Univ	SC	34,700	C
Chatham Univ	PA	47,883	VC
Chestnut Hill College	PA	47,180	C
Cheyney Univ of Pennsylvania	PA	20,896	LC
Chicago State Univ	IL	41,620	C
Christendom College	VA	32,600	VC
Christopher Newport Univ	VA	24,878	VC+
CUNY/Baruch College	NY	21,609	HC
CUNY/Brooklyn College	NY	7,163	C+
CUNY/City College	NY	20,204	C
CUNY/Hunter College	NY	31,098	VC
CUNY/John Jay College of Criminal Justice	NY	6,359	SP
CUNY/Lehman College	NY	5,788	LC
CUNY/Queens College	NY	21,507	C
CUNY/York College	NY	6,747	LC
Claflin Univ	SC	25,592	LC
Claremont McKenna College	CA	69,900	MC
Clarion Univ of Pennsylvania	PA	21,608	LC
Clark Atlanta Univ	GA	31,019	LC
Clark Univ	MA	53,260	HC+
Clarkson Univ	NY	60,392	VC
Clemson Univ	SC		HC
Cleveland State Univ	OH	22,290	C
Coastal Carolina Univ	SC	20,340	C
Coe College	IA	51,570	VC
Coker College	SC	38,196	C
Colby College	ME	64,060	MC
Colgate Univ	NY	67,500	MC
College of Charleston	SC	24,046	VC
College of St. Benedict	MN	54,480	C
College of Staten Island	NY	24,389	LC
College of the Holy Cross	MA	64,320	MC
College of William & Mary	VA	34,907	MC
Colo College	CO	64,894	MC
Colo Mesa Univ	CO	19,707	LC
Colo State Univ	CO	23,033	C
Colo State Univ-Pueblo	CO	21,581	C
Columbia College	SC	36,550	C
Columbia College - Missouri	MO	28,179	C
Columbia Univ/ School of General Studies	NY	61,470	MC
Columbia Univ/City of New York	NY	62,958	MC
Columbus State Univ	GA	14,336	LC
Concord Univ	WV	14,954	LC
Concordia College - Moorhead	MN	46,418	C
Concordia Univ Irvine	CA	44,860	VC
Concordia Univ, Chicago	IL	41,522	C
Conn College	CT	65,000	MC
Converse College	SC	28,290	C
Coppin State Univ	MD	14,071	VC
Corban Univ	OR	41,700	C
Cornell College	IA	49,900	VC
Creighton Univ	NE	49,452	VC
Culver-Stockton College	MO	34,350	C
Cumberland Univ	TN	27,710	C
Curry College	MA	53,331	C
Daemen College	NY	40,336	C
Dallas Baptist Univ	TX	35,220	VC
Davidson College	NC	60,119	MC
Davis & Elkins College	WV	38,242	LC
Delaware State Univ	DE	19,376	LC
Delta State Univ	MS	13,176	LC
Denison Univ	OH	62,770	HC+
DePaul Univ	IL	52,807	VC
DePauw Univ	IN	58,688	VC
DeSales Univ	PA	47,520	C
Dickinson College	PA	66,166	MC
Dickinson State Univ	ND	12,372	LC
Dillard Univ	LA	20,940	VC
Doane Univ	NE	41,340	VC
Dominican Univ	IL	42,472	C+
Dominican Univ of Calif	CA	58,750	C
Dordt College	IA	37,860	C+
Drake Univ	IA	49,220	HC
Drew Univ/College of Liberal Arts	NJ	53,608	VC
Drexel Univ	PA	65,927	HC
Drury Univ	MO	37,555	VC
Duke Univ	NC	68,298	MC
Duquesne Univ	PA	48,508	VC
Earlham College	IN	55,670	HC
East Carolina Univ	NC	16,539	C
East Central Univ	OK	13,330	C
East Stroudsburg Univ	PA	18,578	LC
East Tenn State Univ	TN	18,141	C
East Texas Baptist Univ	TX	34,444	C
Eastern Conn State Univ	CT	23,059	C
Eastern Illinois Univ	IL	21,414	C
Eastern Kentucky Univ	KY	17,742	C
Eastern Mich Univ	MI	19,761	C
Eastern New Mexico Univ	NM	12,874	LC
Eastern Univ	PA	39,540	C
Eastern Washington Univ	WA	17,896	LC
Eckerd College	FL	55,206	VC
Edgewood College	WI	35,950	C
Edinboro Univ	PA	15,940	LC
Edward Waters College	FL	28,089	NC
Elizabeth City State Univ	NC	14,745	C
Elizabethtown College	PA	56,340	VC
Elmhurst College	IL	46,514	C
Elmira College	NY	53,900	C
Elon Univ	NC	46,142	HC
Emmanuel College	MA	53,472	C+
Emory and Henry College	VA	46,320	C
Emory Univ	GA	63,286	MC
Emporia State Univ	KS	15,029	C
Endicott College	MA	47,054	C+
Eugene Lang College of Liberal Arts	NY	64,940	VC
Eureka College	IL	34,760	C
Evangel Univ	MO	28,898	C
Excelsior College	NY	38,800	SP
Fairfield Univ	CT	61,445	HC
Fairleigh Dickinson Univ/ College at Florham	NJ	54,770	C
Fairleigh Dickinson Univ/ Metropolitan Campus	NJ	52,392	C
Fairmont State Univ	WV	15,726	C
Fayetteville State Univ	NC	17,756	C
Ferris State Univ	MI	21,458	C
Ferrum College	VA	43,970	C
Fisk Univ	TN	32,066	LC
Fitchburg State Univ	MA	21,819	LC
Flagler College	FL	27,620	C
Florida A&M Univ	FL	15,361	C
Florida Atlantic Univ	FL	18,256	C
Florida Gulf Coast Univ	FL	14,738	C
Florida International Univ	FL	20,281	C
Florida Memorial Univ	FL	22,424	LC
Florida Southern College	FL	45,978	VC
Florida State Univ	FL	16,771	HC
Fordham Univ	NY	68,431	MC
Fort Hays State Univ	KS	12,677	C
Fort Lewis College	CO	20,154	C
Fort Valley State Univ	GA	17,988	VC
Framingham State Univ	MA	21,740	C
Francis Marion Univ	SC	18,144	LC
Franciscan Univ of Steubenville	OH	33,980	VC
Franklin and Marshall College	PA	67,960	MC
Franklin College	IN	40,550	C
Franklin Pierce Univ	NH	46,750	LC
Friends Univ	KS	38,000	C
Frostburg State Univ	MD	17,280	LC
Furman Univ	SC	61,098	VC+
Gannon Univ	PA	42,922	C
Geneva College	PA	35,450	C
George Fox Univ	OR	42,938	C
George Mason Univ	VA	19,884	C
Georgetown College	KY	41,440	C
Georgetown Univ	DC	68,970	MC
Georgia College & State Univ	GA	21,884	C+
Georgia Southern Univ	GA	16,540	VC
Georgia Southwestern State Univ	GA	13,870	LC
Georgia State Univ	GA	25,250	C
Gettysburg College	PA	65,210	MC
Gonzaga Univ	WA	52,880	HC
Gordon College	MA	47,740	VC
Goucher College	MD	56,110	VC
Grambling State Univ	LA	15,701	C
Grand Valley State Univ	MI	22,250	C+
Grand View Univ	IA	32,302	C
Greensboro College	NC	39,790	LC
Grinnell College	IA	63,114	MC
Grove City College	PA	26,654	VC
Guilford College	NC	45,973	C
Gustavus Adolphus College	MN	53,943	HC
Hamilton College	NY	64,250	MC
Hamline Univ	MN	50,152	C
Hampden-Sydney College	VA	57,806	VC
Hampshire College	MA	65,214	MC
Hampton Univ	VA	36,410	C
Hanover College	IN	47,750	C+
Harding Univ	AR	25,440	C
Hardin-Simmons Univ	TX	36,025	C
Harris-Stowe State Univ	MO	14,590	NC
Hartwick College	NY	51,270	C
Harvard College/Harvard Univ	MA	65,609	MC
Hastings College	NE	35,380	C+
Haverford College	PA	66,490	MC
Hawaii Pacific Univ	HI	33,420	C
Heidelberg Univ	OH	40,400	LC
Henderson State Univ	AR	15,516	C
Hendrix College	AR	54,020	VC
High Point Univ	NC	47,355	VC
Hilbert College	NY	32,650	LC
Hillsdale College	MI	37,170	MC
Hiram College	OH	44,590	C
Hobart and William Smith Colleges	NY	67,050	HC+
Hofstra Univ	NY	58,210	C+
Hollins Univ	VA	49,635	VC
Holy Family Univ	PA	44,672	LC
Hood College	MD	50,540	C
Hope College	MI	42,840	VC
Houghton College	NY	40,558	VC
Houston Baptist Univ	TX	36,450	C
Howard Payne Univ	TX	35,994	C
Howard Univ	DC	37,616	C+
Humboldt State Univ	CA	21,708	C
Huntingdon College	AL	35,900	C
Huston-Tillotson Univ	TX	18,124	LC
Idaho State Univ	ID	13,619	LC
Illinois College	IL	41,330	VC
Illinois Inst of Technology	IL	56,826	HC+
Illinois State Univ	IL	23,418	VC
Illinois Wesleyan Univ	IL	56,430	VC+
Immaculata Univ	PA	39,000	C
Indiana State Univ	IN	23,223	LC
Indiana Univ Bloomington	IN	20,791	HC
Indiana Univ East	IN	7,207	C
Indiana Univ Northwest	IN	7,207	LC
Indiana Univ of Pennsylvania	PA	24,474	C
Indiana Univ South Bend	IN	16,057	C
Indiana Univ Southeast	IN	16,931	C
Indiana Univ-Purdue Univ Fort Wayne	IN	18,675	C
Indiana Univ-Purdue Univ Indianapolis	IN	18,952	C
Indiana Wesleyan Univ	IN	33,674	C
Inter-American Univ of PR Ponce	PR	19,549	
Inter-American Univ of PR-Fajardo Campus	PR	18,336	
Inter-American Univ of PR-Metropolitan Campus	PR	20,045	
Inter-American Univ of PR-San Germán	PR	20,042	
Iona College	NY	52,514	C
Iowa State Univ	IA	18,176	C
Ithaca College	NY	58,158	VC+
Jackson State Univ	MS	15,879	LC
Jacksonville State Univ	AL	14,628	LC
Jacksonville Univ	FL	49,210	C

ST = STATE $IS = IN-STATE COSTS SR = SELECTOR RATING

School	ST	$IS	SR
James Madison Univ	VA	19,084	VC
John Brown Univ	AR	35,184	VC
John Carroll Univ	OH	51,570	C
Johns Hopkins Univ	MD	68,080	MC
Johnson C. Smith Univ	NC	25,336	LC
Johnson State College	VT	22,672	C
Judson Univ	IL	39,174	C
Juniata College	PA	58,118	VC
Kalamazoo College	MI	53,931	HC
Kansas State Univ	KS	17,780	VC
Kean Univ	NJ	25,620	C
Keene State College	NH	24,604	C
Kennesaw State Univ	GA	18,899	VC
Kent State Univ	OH	20,928	C
Kentucky State Univ	KY	14,484	LC
Kentucky Wesleyan College	KY	34,260	LC
Kenyon College	OH	65,840	MC
Keuka College	NY	42,398	C
King's College	PA	48,240	C
Knox College	IL	54,654	VC+
Kutztown Univ of Pennsylvania	PA	19,477	C
La Roche College	PA	38,940	C
La Salle Univ	PA	43,476	C
La Sierra Univ	CA	39,690	VC
Lafayette College	PA	68,520	MC
LaGrange College	GA	41,310	C
Lake Erie College	OH	38,914	LC
Lake Forest College	IL	50,652	VC
Lake Superior State Univ	MI	19,867	C
Lamar Univ	TX	18,014	LC
Lander Univ	SC	32,200	C
Lawrence Univ	WI	56,133	HC+
Le Moyne College	NY	47,305	VC
Lebanon Valley College	PA	55,510	VC
Lee Univ	TN	22,045	C
Lehigh Univ	PA	63,860	MC
LeMoyne-Owen College	TN	16,980	C
Lenoir-Rhyne Univ	NC	47,500	LC
Lewis & Clark College	OR	60,984	MC
Lewis Univ	IL	41,710	C
Liberty Univ	VA	31,415	C
Lincoln Univ	MO	14,402	NC
Lincoln Univ	PA	20,878	LC
Lindenwood Univ	MO	25,760	C
Linfield College	OR	53,992	C
Lipscomb Univ	TN	42,984	VC
LIU Brooklyn	NY	50,698	C
LIU Post	NY	50,698	C+
Livingstone College	NC	17,815	LC
Lock Haven Univ of Pennsylvania	PA	20,544	LC
Longwood Univ	VA	22,184	C
Loras College	IA	40,726	C
Louisiana State Univ and A&M College	LA	18,677	VC
Louisiana Tech Univ	LA	11,422	VC
Loyola Marymount Univ	CA	60,202	VC+
Loyola Univ Chicago	IL	57,158	VC
Loyola Univ Maryland	MD	61,710	VC
Loyola Univ New Orleans	LA	52,456	VC
Luther College	IA	49,990	VC
Lycoming College	PA	50,895	C
Lynn Univ	FL	49,680	LC
Lyon College	AR	36,120	VC
Macalester College	MN	64,136	MC
MacMurray College	IL	35,025	C
Malone Univ	OH	39,200	C
Manchester Univ	IN	41,540	C
Manhattan College	NY	55,652	C
Manhattanville College	NY	52,430	C
Mansfield Univ of Pennsylvania	PA	24,244	LC
Marian Univ	IN	43,206	C
Marietta College	OH	46,190	C
Marist College	NY	49,860	VC
Marlboro College	VT	50,832	VC+
Marquette Univ	WI	53,090	VC+
Mars Hill Univ	NC	41,104	C
Marshall Univ	WV	18,044	C
Martin Univ	IN	21,010	LC
Mary Baldwin Univ	VA	40,495	C
Marygrove College	MI	30,100	LC
Marymount Manhattan College	NY	48,350	C
Marymount Univ	VA	43,231	C
Maryville College	TN	44,410	C
Marywood Univ	PA	47,840	C
Mass College of Liberal Arts	MA	20,659	C
Mass Inst of Technology	MA	62,662	MC
McDaniel College	MD	52,910	VC
McKendree Univ	IL	37,940	C+
McMurry Univ	TX	34,259	LC
McNeese State Univ	LA	7,838	C
Mercer Univ	GA	45,348	VC
Mercy College	NY	32,614	C
Mercyhurst Univ	PA	47,420	C
Meredith College	NC	46,634	C
Merrimack College	MA	55,415	C
Messiah College	PA	44,380	VC
Methodist Univ	NC	58,130	C
Metropolitan State Univ of Denver	CO	6,928	LC
Miami Univ	OH	27,190	HC+
Mich State Univ	MI	24,542	VC
Middle Tenn State Univ	TN	8,650	C
Middlebury College	VT	67,464	MC
Midwestern State Univ	TX	12,111	LC
Miles College	AL	16,530	NC
Millersville Univ of Pennsylvania	PA	25,298	C
Millikin Univ	IL	44,148	C
Mills College	CA	43,705	C
Millsaps College	MS	50,080	C+
Minn State Univ, Mankato	MN	17,190	C
Minn State Univ, Moorhead	MN	21,393	C
Miss College	MS	25,850	C
Miss State Univ	MS	12,028	C+
Miss Univ for Women	MS	17,065	C
Miss Valley State Univ	MS	13,233	LC
Missouri Southern State Univ	MO	13,071	C
Missouri State Univ	MO	15,837	C+
Missouri Valley College	MO	28,150	C
Missouri Western State Univ	MO	17,822	LC
Molloy College	NY	40,440	C
Monmouth College	IL	42,260	C
Monmouth Univ	NJ	50,184	C
Montana State Univ	MT	15,500	C+
Montana State Univ Billings	MT	13,336	LC
Montclair State Univ	NJ	26,912	C
Moravian College	PA	55,488	C
Morehead State Univ	KY	18,386	LC
Morehouse College	GA	40,835	C
Morgan State Univ	MD	17,190	LC
Morningside College	IA	39,780	C
Morris College	SC	19,195	LC
Mount Aloysius College	PA	29,976	C
Mount Holyoke College	MA	56,746	MC
Mount Mercy Univ	IA	39,748	C
Mount St. Mary College	NY	44,448	C
Mount St. Mary's Univ	MD	53,380	C
Mount St. Mary's Univ - Chalon Campus	CA	50,486	VC+
Mount Vernon Nazarene Univ	OH	35,944	C
Muhlenberg College	PA	56,645	VC
Murray State Univ	KY	17,726	C+
Muskingum Univ	OH	35,966	C
Nazareth College	NY	46,784	C
Nebr Wesleyan Univ	NE	42,026	C+
Neumann Univ	PA	40,678	LC
New College of Florida	FL	16,180	HC+
New England College	NH	50,828	NC
New Jersey City Univ	NJ	21,456	LC
New Mexico Highlands Univ	NM	11,904	LC
New Mexico State Univ	NM	14,050	LC
New York Inst of Technology	NY	49,980	VC
New York Univ	NY	68,139	MC
Newberry College	SC	34,550	C
Niagara Univ	NY	41,010	C
Nicholls State Univ	LA	14,959	C
Norfolk State Univ	VA	18,902	LC
N Car A&T State Univ	NC	13,786	C
N Car Central Univ	NC	9,000	C
N Car State Univ	NC	22,434	HC+
N Car Wesleyan College	NC	39,200	C
North Central College	IL	48,712	C+
N Dak State Univ	ND	16,245	VC
North Park Univ	IL	35,860	C
Northeastern Illinois Univ	IL	12,529	LC
Northeastern State Univ	OK	8,615	VC
Northeastern Univ	MA	65,352	MC
Northern Arizona Univ	AZ	21,003	C
Northern Illinois Univ	IL	20,176	C
Northern Kentucky Univ	KY	16,486	C
Northern Mich Univ	MI	20,853	C
Northern State Univ	SD	15,570	C
Northwest Missouri State Univ	MO	18,286	C
Northwest Nazarene Univ	ID	40,250	C
Northwest Univ	WA	38,720	VC
Northwestern College of Iowa	IA	38,400	C
Northwestern Okla State Univ	OK	13,072	LC
Northwestern Univ	IL	68,725	MC
Norwich Univ	VT	56,234	C
Notre Dame College	OH	39,150	VC
Notre Dame de Namur Univ	CA	46,526	LC
Notre Dame of Maryland Univ	MD	47,570	VC
Nova Southeastern Univ	FL	38,534	C+
Oakland Univ	MI	20,763	C
Oakwood Univ	AL	43,758	C
Oberlin College	OH	68,942	MC
Occidental College	CA	68,660	MC
Oglethorpe Univ	GA	44,200	C
Ohio Dominican Univ	OH	41,340	C+
Ohio Northern Univ	OH	44,050	VC
Ohio State Univ at Columbus	OH	22,843	MC
Ohio Univ	OH	23,394	VC
Ohio Wesleyan Univ	OH	49,460	VC
Okla Baptist Univ	OK	33,990	C
Okla City Univ	OK	40,476	C
Okla State Univ	OK	17,180	C+
Okla Wesleyan Univ	OK	34,434	C
Old Dominion Univ	VA	21,618	C
Olivet Nazarene Univ	IL	41,840	VC
Oral Roberts Univ	OK	34,316	C
Oregon State Univ	OR	23,337	VC
Ottawa Univ	KS	39,980	VC
Otterbein Univ	OH	41,630	C
Ouachita Baptist Univ	AR	33,500	VC
Our Lady of the Lake Univ	TX	37,790	LC
Pace Univ	NY	60,136	C
Pacific Lutheran Univ	WA	49,960	C
Pacific Univ	OR	37,617	C
Palm Beach Atlantic Univ	FL	39,250	C
Park Univ	MO	22,134	C
Paul Quinn College	TX	25,350	LC
Penn State Erie,The Behrend College	PA	26,688	VC
Pennsylvania State Univ - Univ Park	PA	29,716	HC
Pepperdine Univ	CA	66,862	VC+
Pfeiffer Univ	NC	40,532	LC
Philander Smith College	AR	20,814	LC
Piedmont College	GA	34,334	C
Pittsburg State Univ	KS	13,880	C
Pitzer College	CA	68,500	HC+
Plymouth State Univ	NH	23,180	LC
Point Loma Nazarene Univ	CA	46,150	C+
Point Park Univ	PA	41,270	C
Pomona College	CA	64,957	MC
Pontifical Catholic Univ of PR	PR	10,534	
Portland State Univ	OR	19,443	C
Prairie View A&M Univ	TX	27,273	LC
Presbyterian College	SC	47,186	C
Princeton Univ	NJ	60,090	MC
Principia College	IL	40,350	C
Providence College	RI	62,870	HC
Purdue Univ Northwest	IN	15,178	C
Purdue Univ/West Lafayette	IN	20,032	MC
Queens Univ of Charlotte	NC	39,543	C
Quincy Univ	IL	38,170	LC
Quinnipiac Univ	CT	60,970	VC
Radford Univ	VA	19,758	C
Ramapo College of New Jersey	NJ	25,760	VC
Randolph College	VA	53,970	C
Randolph-Macon College	VA	51,480	VC
Reed College	OR	65,300	MC
Regis College	MA	51,920	LC
Regis Univ	CO	46,380	C
Rhode Island College	RI	19,000	LC
Rhodes College	TN	51,900	HC
Rice Univ	TX	59,458	MC
Rider Univ	NJ	54,050	C
Ripon College	WI	49,991	VC
Rivier Univ	NH	41,600	VC
Roanoke College	VA	55,952	VC
Rochester Inst of Technology	NY	52,734	HC+
Rockford Univ	IL	38,570	C
Rockhurst Univ	MO	28,990	C
Rocky Mountain College	MT	35,776	C
Roger Williams Univ	RI	48,074	VC
Rollins College	FL	58,670	HC
Roosevelt Univ	IL	41,890	VC
Rosemont College	PA	30,980	LC
Rowan Univ	NJ	24,491	VC
Russell Sage College	NY	39,370	C
Rust College	MS	10,600	C
Rutgers Univ - Camden	NJ	26,595	C
Rutgers Univ - New Brunswick	NJ	27,090	HC
Rutgers Univ - Newark	NJ	27,351	C
Saginaw Valley State Univ	MI	19,284	C
St. Anselm College	NH	56,636	VC
St. Augustine's Univ	NC	25,582	C
St. Francis Univ	PA	46,146	NC
St. John's Univ	MN	53,472	C
St. Joseph's Univ	PA	58,540	VC
St. Leo Univ	FL	32,850	C
St. Louis Univ	MO	49,866	HC
St. Martin's Univ	WA	45,056	C
St. Mary's College	IN	50,600	C
St. Mary's College of Calif	CA	57,420	C
St. Mary's Univ of Minn	MN	42,440	C
St. Michael's College	VT	53,275	VC+
St. Peter's Univ	NJ	49,192	C
St. Vincent College	PA	46,229	C
St. Xavier Univ	IL	44,440	C
Salem College	NC	40,206	C
Salisbury Univ	MD	21,132	VC
Salve Regina Univ	RI	53,046	VC
Sam Houston State Univ	TX	18,792	C
Samford Univ	AL	40,770	VC
San Diego State Univ	CA	23,156	VC
San Francisco State Univ	CA	18,514	LC
San Jose State Univ	CA	22,630	C
Sarah Lawrence College	NY	68,866	MC
Savannah State Univ	GA	17,036	C
Schreiner Univ	TX	34,626	LC
Scripps College	CA	69,260	HC
Seattle Pacific Univ	WA	47,439	C+
Seattle Univ	WA	54,957	VC
Seton Hall Univ	NJ	58,008	C
Seton Hill Univ	PA	46,972	VC
Sewanee: The Univ of the South	TN	58,000	HC+
Shaw Univ	NC	24,638	C
Shawnee State Univ	OH	16,998	C
Shenandoah Univ	VA	42,100	C
Shepherd Univ, West Virginia	WV	17,382	C
Shippensburg Univ of Pennsylvania	PA	24,096	C
Siena College	NY	48,916	C
Simmons College	MA	54,400	HC
Simpson College	IA	45,626	VC
Skidmore College	NY	66,600	MC
Slippery Rock Univ of Pennsylvania	PA	20,450	C
Smith College	MA	66,774	MC
Sonoma State Univ	CA	27,020	C
S Car State Univ	SC	21,330	LC
S Dak State Univ	SD	15,874	C
Southeast Missouri State Univ	MO	16,148	C
Southeastern Louisiana Univ	LA	16,237	C
Southeastern Okla State Univ	OK	11,875	C
Southern Arkansas Univ	AR	21,532	C
Southern Conn State Univ	CT	21,924	LC
Southern Illinois Univ Carbondale	IL	24,554	C
Southern Illinois Univ Edwardsville	IL	20,188	C
Southern Methodist Univ	TX	69,008	MC
Southern Nazarene Univ	OK	33,684	C
Southern New Hampshire Univ	NH	44,256	C
Southern Oregon Univ	OR	19,117	C
Southern Univ and A&M College	LA	16,074	LC
Southern Univ at New Orleans	LA	8,014	LC
Southwest Baptist Univ	MO	30,890	LC
Southwest Minn State Univ	MN	17,783	C
Southwestern Okla State Univ	OK	12,205	C
Southwestern Univ	TX	52,370	VC
Spelman College	GA	41,642	C
Spring Hill College	AL	48,488	C
Springfield College	MA	48,775	C
St. Ambrose Univ	IA	40,180	C
St. Bonaventure Univ	NY	45,596	C
St. Catherine Univ	MN	45,630	C
St. Cloud State Univ	MN	10,600	C
St. Edward's Univ	TX	56,190	VC
St. Francis College	NY	38,800	LC
St. John Fisher College	NY	45,270	VC
St. John's College at Annapolis	MD	63,348	MC
St. John's Univ	NY	57,160	C+
St. Joseph's College, New York/Brooklyn Campus	NY	25,114	LC
St. Joseph's College, New York/Long Island Campus	NY	25,124	C
St. Lawrence Univ	NY	66,646	HC+
St. Mary's College of Maryland	MD	27,312	VC
St. Mary's Univ	TX	39,120	C
St. Norbert College	WI	46,060	VC
St. Olaf College	MN	56,430	HC
St. Thomas Univ	FL	51,187	LC
Stanford Univ	CA	62,541	MC
SUNY Albany	NY	22,165	C
SUNY at Binghamton	NY	24,100	MC
SUNY at Geneseo	NY	21,622	VC
SUNY at New Paltz	NY	20,840	C
SUNY at Oswego	NY	22,219	VC
SUNY at Purchase College	NY	21,832	C
SUNY/Buffalo State	NY	20,583	LC
SUNY/College at Old Westbury	NY	16,860	C
SUNY/Cortland	NY	20,910	C
SUNY/Fredonia	NY	20,818	C
SUNY/Oneonta	NY	20,794	C
SUNY/Plattsburgh	NY	19,314	C
SUNY/Potsdam	NY	21,051	VC
SUNY/Univ at Buffalo	NY	23,122	C
Stephen F. Austin State Univ	TX	18,484	LC
Stetson Univ	FL	57,174	VC+
Stockton Univ	NJ	25,565	C
Stonehill College	MA	55,130	C
Stony Brook Univ/The SUNY	NY	22,703	MC
Suffolk Univ	MA	52,316	C
Sul Ross State Univ	TX	15,021	LC
Susquehanna Univ	PA	57,560	VC
Swarthmore College	PA	63,550	MC
Syracuse Univ	NY	62,313	HC
Tarleton State Univ	TX	15,248	LC
Taylor Univ	IN	42,130	VC
Temple Univ	PA	24,392	C+
Tenn State Univ	TN	14,423	LC
Tenn Tech Univ	TN	17,929	C
Texas A&M Univ at College Station	TX	20,771	VC+
Texas A&M Univ at Commerce	TX	10,496	C
Texas A&M Univ at Corpus Christi	TX	16,851	LC
Texas A&M Univ at Kingsville	TX	16,580	LC
Texas Christian Univ	TX	57,120	HC
Texas Lutheran Univ	TX	39,770	C
Texas Southern Univ	TX	19,592	LC
Texas State Univ	TX	18,721	C
Texas Tech Univ	TX	20,156	C+
Texas Wesleyan Univ	TX	37,338	C
Texas Woman's Univ	TX	15,302	LC
The American Univ	DC	61,317	HC
The Catholic Univ of America	DC	58,376	VC
The Citadel, The Military College of S Car	SC	20,679	C
The College at Brockport - SUNY	NY	21,058	C
The College of Idaho	ID	36,415	C
The College of New Jersey	NJ	28,675	VC+
The College of New Rochelle	NY	46,300	LC
The College of St. Rose	NY	44,010	C
The College of Wooster	OH	60,000	HC
The Evergreen State College	WA	16,599	C
The George Washington Univ	DC	68,474	HC+
The Master's Univ	CA	43,870	C
The Univ of Akron	OH	22,566	C
The Univ of Alabama	AL	24,320	C+
The Univ of Arizona	AZ	24,086	C

ST = STATE $IS = IN-STATE COSTS SR = SELECTOR RATING

School	ST	$IS	SR
The Univ of Memphis	TN	18,278	C
The Univ of Montana Western	MT	9,426	LC
The Univ of Tenn at Chattanooga	TN	17,340	C+
The Univ of Tenn at Knoxville	TN	22,112	VC
The Univ of Tenn at Martin	TN	15,212	C
The Univ of Texas at Austin	TX	20,206	MC
The Univ of Texas at San Antonio	TX	21,060	C
The Univ of Utah	UT	18,751	VC
The Univ of Virginia's College at Wise	VA	18,192	LC
Thiel College	PA	42,950	LC
Thomas Edison State Univ	NJ	6,350	NC
Thomas More College	KY	36,720	LC
Tougaloo College	MS	17,980	NC
Touro College	NY	31,040	C
Towson Univ	MD	21,878	C
Transylvania Univ	KY	47,450	HC+
Trevecca Nazarene Univ	TN	31,186	C
Trinity College	CT	69,020	HC
Trinity Univ	TX	54,480	MC
Trinity Washington Univ	DC	33,826	C+
Troy Univ	AL	16,171	C
Truman State Univ	MO	16,286	MC
Tufts Univ	MA		MC
Tulane Univ	LA	67,496	MC
Tusculum College	TN	31,625	LC
Tuskegee Univ	AL	28,164	C
Union College	NY	64,320	MC
Union Univ	TN	41,160	VC
United States Air Force Academy	CO		C
United States Coast Guard Academy	CT	942	HC
United States Military Academy at West Point	NY		HC+
United States Naval Academy	MD		HC
Univ of Alabama at Birmingham	AL	22,092	C
Univ of Alabama in Huntsville	AL	20,028	VC
Univ of Alaska Anchorage	AK	17,914	C
Univ of Alaska Fairbanks	AK	16,874	VC
Univ of Alaska Southeast	AK	17,615	C
Univ of Arkansas at Fayetteville	AR	19,766	VC
Univ of Arkansas at Little Rock	AR	18,211	LC
Univ of Arkansas at Monticello	AR	13,599	LC
Univ of Arkansas at Pine Bluff	AR	13,541	C
Univ of Bridgeport	CT	44,985	LC
Univ of Calif at Berkeley	CA	29,886	MC
Univ of Calif at Davis	CA	28,468	HC
Univ of Calif at Irvine	CA	33,857	VC
Univ of Calif at Los Angeles	CA	27,438	HC+
Univ of Calif at Riverside	CA	32,912	C
Univ of Calif at Santa Barbara	CA	30,627	HC+
Univ of Calif San Diego	CA	30,450	MC
Univ of Calif, Santa Cruz	CA	28,731	C+
Univ of Central Arkansas	AR	15,042	VC
Univ of Central Florida	FL	16,379	VC
Univ of Central Missouri	MO	18,982	C
Univ of Central Okla	OK	15,150	C
Univ of Charleston	WV	35,000	LC
Univ of Chicago	IL	70,551	MC
Univ of Cincinnati	OH	22,118	VC
Univ of Colo Boulder	CO	26,048	HC
Univ of Colo Colo Springs	CO	20,300	C
Univ of Colo Denver	CO	22,238	C
Univ of Conn	CT	27,394	
Univ of Dallas	TX	50,676	VC
Univ of Dayton	OH	54,930	VC
Univ of Delaware	DE	32,214	VC
Univ of Denver	CO	61,129	VC+
Univ of Detroit Mercy	MI	48,816	C
Univ of Evansville	IN	44,186	C+
Univ of Findlay	OH	43,040	C
Univ of Florida	FL	16,291	HC+
Univ of Georgia	GA	21,878	HC
Univ of Great Falls	MT	38,524	C
Univ of Hartford	CT	49,776	C
Univ of Hawaii at Hilo	HI	18,038	VC
Univ of Hawaii at Manoa	HI	23,261	C
Univ of Houston-Downtown	TX	7,241	LC
Univ of Idaho	ID	16,158	C
Univ of Illinois at Chicago	IL	24,664	VC
Univ of Illinois at Urbana-Champaign	IL	27,006	HC
Univ of Indianapolis	IN	36,480	VC
Univ of Iowa	IA	19,415	HC
Univ of Kansas	KS	20,884	VC
Univ of Kentucky	KY	24,800	C+
Univ of La Verne	CA	55,600	C
Univ of Louisiana at Lafayette	LA	14,516	C
Univ of Louisiana at Monroe	LA	15,970	C
Univ of Louisville	KY	19,692	C
Univ of Lynchburg	VA	48,370	C
Univ of Maine	ME	21,038	VC
Univ of Maine at Farmington	ME	18,792	C
Univ of Mary Hardin-Baylor	TX	35,292	C+
Univ of Mary Washington	VA	23,039	C+
Univ of Maryland Univ College	MD	26,146	LC
Univ of Maryland/Baltimore County	MD	23,004	VC
Univ of Maryland/College Park	MD	21,938	HC
Univ of Mass Amherst	MA	27,669	HC
Univ of Mass Boston	MA	13,828	C
Univ of Mass Dartmouth	MA	26,507	C
Univ of Mass Lowell	MA	27,296	VC
Univ of Miami	FL	63,494	MC
Univ of Mich/Ann Arbor	MI	25,274	MC
Univ of Mich/Dearborn	MI	12,472	VC
Univ of Mich/Flint	MI	19,062	C
Univ of Minn/Duluth	MN	20,292	C
Univ of Minn/Morris	MN	21,222	VC
Univ of Minn/Twin Cities	MN	24,269	MC
Univ of Miss	MS	18,802	C
Univ of Missouri-Columbia	MO	20,463	VC
Univ of Missouri-Kansas City	MO	19,563	VC
Univ of Missouri-St. Louis	MO	19,810	VC
Univ of Mobile	AL	28,935	C
Univ of Montana	MT	14,105	C
Univ of Montevallo	AL	20,012	C
Univ of Mount Union	OH	39,990	C
Univ of Nebr - Kearney	NE	17,014	LC
Univ of Nebr - Lincoln	NE	18,589	VC
Univ of Nebr - Omaha	NE	16,120	C
Univ of Nevada, Las Vegas	NV	17,553	C
Univ of Nevada, Reno	NV	18,010	C
Univ of New England	ME	50,110	C
Univ of New Hampshire	NH	29,333	VC
Univ of New Haven	CT	53,680	C
Univ of New Mexico	NM	16,808	C
Univ of New Orleans	LA	12,840	C
Univ of North Alabama	AL	15,964	C
Univ of N Car at Asheville	NC	16,251	VC+
Univ of N Car at Chapel Hill	NC	20,561	MC
Univ of N Car at Charlotte	NC	17,803	VC
Univ of N Car at Greensboro	NC	15,998	C
Univ of N Car at Pembroke	NC	14,737	LC
Univ of N Car Wilmington	NC	16,784	VC
Univ of N Dak	ND	16,673	C
Univ of North Florida	FL	15,996	VC
Univ of North Georgia	GA	17,316	C
Univ of North Texas	TX	20,082	C
Univ of Northern Colo	CO	19,658	C
Univ of Northern Iowa	IA	17,480	C
Univ of Notre Dame	IN	68,801	MC
Univ of Okla	OK	19,651	HC
Univ of Oregon	OR	24,021	VC
Univ of Pennsylvania	PA	63,526	MC
Univ of Pikeville	KY	27,838	C
Univ of Pittsburgh	PA	30,030	MC
Univ of Pittsburgh at Greensburg	PA	24,140	C
Univ of Pittsburgh at Johnstown	PA	22,092	C
Univ of Portland	OR	52,152	VC
Univ of PR, at Mayaguez	PR	13,995	
Univ of PR-Rio Piedras campus	PR	13,327	
Univ of Puget Sound	WA	60,210	HC
Univ of Redlands	CA	61,934	VC
Univ of Rhode Island	RI	26,066	VC
Univ of Richmond	VA	62,730	MC
Univ of Rio Grande & Rio Grande Community College	OH	8,750	LC
Univ of Rochester	NY	65,032	MC
Univ of St. Francis	IN	38,520	C
Univ of St. Mary	KS	37,080	NC
Univ of San Diego	CA	60,338	HC
Univ of San Francisco	CA	60,580	C
Univ of Science and Arts of Okla	OK	11,140	VC
Univ of Scranton	PA	54,962	VC
Univ of Sioux Falls	SD	25,630	C
Univ of South Alabama	AL	16,880	C
Univ of S Car Aiken	SC	18,094	C
Univ of S Car at Columbia	SC	21,726	VC
Univ of S Car Upstate	SC	19,272	LC
Univ of S Dak	SD	16,109	C
Univ of South Florida St. Petersburg	FL	15,980	C
Univ of South Florida/Tampa	FL	16,110	VC
Univ of Southern Calif	CA	66,631	MC
Univ of Southern Indiana	IN	16,808	C
Univ of Southern Maine	ME	18,320	C
Univ of Southern Miss	MS	13,170	C
Univ of St. Francis	IL	40,828	C
Univ of St. Thomas - Houston	TX	41,510	VC
Univ of Tampa	FL	38,928	VC
Univ of Texas at Arlington	TX	18,876	C
Univ of Texas at Dallas	TX	23,640	HC
Univ of Texas at El Paso	TX	34,452	NC
Univ of Texas Rio Grande Valley	TX	15,573	LC
Univ of the Cumberlands	KY	32,000	LC
Univ of the District of Columbia	DC	21,260	LC
Univ of the Incarnate Word	TX	39,162	LC
Univ of the Ozarks	AR	31,050	NC
Univ of the Pacific	CA	57,446	VC
Univ of Toledo	OH	19,336	C
Univ of Tulsa	OK	52,625	HC
Univ of Vermont	VT	29,792	HC
Univ of Virginia	VA	27,367	MC
Univ of Washington	WA	23,091	MC
Univ of West Florida	FL	15,848	C
Univ of West Georgia	GA	17,510	LC
Univ of Wisc-Eau Claire	WI	16,354	VC
Univ of Wisc-Green Bay	WI	15,184	C
Univ of Wisc-La Crosse	WI	15,425	VC
Univ of Wisc-Madison	WI	21,647	MC
Univ of Wisc-Milwaukee	WI	21,538	C
Univ of Wisc-Oshkosh	WI	15,392	C
Univ of Wisc-Parkside	WI	15,313	C
Univ of Wisc-Platteville	WI	14,148	C
Univ of Wisc-River Falls	WI	14,541	C
Univ of Wisc-Stevens Point	WI	14,043	C
Univ of Wisc-Superior	WI	14,838	C
Univ of Wisc-Whitewater	WI	13,976	C
Univ of Wyoming	WY	15,537	C
Ursinus College	PA	62,920	VC
Utah State Univ	UT	13,235	C
Utica College	NY	31,510	C
Valparaiso Univ	IN	50,160	VC
Vanderbilt Univ	TN	63,248	MC
Vanguard Univ of Southern Calif	CA	42,400	VC
Vassar College	NY	68,110	MC
Villanova Univ	PA	64,922	MC
Virginia Commonwealth Univ	VA	23,811	VC
Virginia Polytechnic Inst and State Univ	VA	21,920	VC
Virginia State Univ	VA	19,802	C+
Virginia Union Univ	VA	25,058	C
Virginia Wesleyan Univ	VA	45,980	LC
Wabash College	IN	52,100	VC
Wagner College	NY	57,240	C+
Wake Forest Univ	NC	69,354	MC
Walsh Univ	OH	39,010	C
Warren Wilson College	NC	44,220	VC
Wartburg College	IA	49,478	C
Washburn Univ	KS	15,827	C
Washington & Jefferson College	PA	58,694	VC
Washington Adventist Univ	MD	32,050	LC
Washington and Lee Univ	VA	59,647	MC
Washington College	MD	56,154	VC
Washington State Univ	WA	22,747	C
Washington Univ in St. Louis	MO	67,539	MC
Wayland Baptist Univ	TX	23,460	LC
Wayne State College	NE	25,746	NC
Wayne State Univ	MI	23,085	C
Weber State Univ	UT	14,112	C
Webster Univ	MO	37,490	C
Wellesley College	MA	66,984	MC
Wells College	NY	50,500	C
Wesley College	DE	37,848	LC
Wesleyan College	GA	31,940	C+
Wesleyan Univ	CT	66,940	MC
West Chester Univ of Pennsylvania	PA	19,171	VC
West Liberty Univ	WV	16,158	C
West Texas A&M Univ	TX	13,478	C
West Virginia State Univ	WV	19,412	LC
West Virginia Univ	WV	18,952	VC
West Virginia Wesleyan College	WV	39,188	C
Western Carolina Univ	NC	13,965	C
Western Conn State Univ	CT	21,254	LC
Western Kentucky Univ	KY	16,850	C
Western Mich Univ	MI	21,791	C
Western New England Univ	MA	49,182	C
Western Oregon Univ	OR	19,965	LC
Western State Colo Univ	CO	19,348	C
Western Washington Univ	WA	18,904	VC
Westfield State Univ	MA	20,404	C
Westminster College	MO	32,820	C
Westminster College	PA	41,722	C
Westminster College	UT	41,078	C
Westmont College	CA	57,930	VC
Wheaton College	IL	44,993	MC
Wheaton College	MA	63,818	VC
Wheeling Jesuit Univ	WV	37,106	LC
Wheelock College	MA	51,325	LC
Whitman College	WA	59,772	MC
Whittier College	CA	57,891	C
Whitworth Univ	WA	53,682	VC
Wichita State Univ	KS	17,773	C
Widener Univ	PA	58,190	C
Wilberforce Univ	OH	19,900	C
Wilkes Univ	PA	49,166	C
Willamette Univ	OR	62,514	VC+
William Jewell College	MO	42,490	C+
William Paterson Univ of New Jersey	NJ	24,022	C
William Peace Univ	NC	39,300	LC
William Penn Univ	IA	26,000	C
William Woods Univ	MO	32,040	C
Williams College	MA	67,700	MC
Wilmington College	OH	35,100	C
Wilson College	PA	35,620	LC
Wingate Univ	NC	41,900	C
Winona State Univ	MN	18,109	C
Winston-Salem State Univ	NC	18,005	LC
Winthrop Univ	SC	23,960	C
Wittenberg Univ	OH	49,863	VC
Wofford College	SC	49,885	VC
Woodbury Univ	CA	49,593	VC
Wright State Univ	OH	16,983	C
Xavier Univ	OH	49,380	VC
Xavier Univ of Louisiana	LA	31,689	C
Yale Univ	CT	64,650	MC
Yeshiva Univ	NY	52,750	VC
York College of Pennsylvania	PA	29,240	C
Youngstown State Univ	OH	17,487	C

POLYMER SCIENCE

School	ST	$IS	SR
Cal State, Fullerton	CA	21,902	C
Case Western Reserve Univ	OH	62,284	MC
Eastern Mich Univ	MI	19,761	C
Millersville Univ of Pennsylvania	PA	25,298	C
Murray State Univ	KY	17,726	C+
Pittsburg State Univ	KS	13,880	C
Rochester Inst of Technology	NY	52,734	HC+
SUNY/The College of Environmental Science and Forestry	NY	23,728	VC
Univ of Calif at Davis	CA	28,468	HC
Univ of Southern Miss	MS	13,170	C
Western Washington Univ	WA	18,904	VC

POLYSOMNOGRAPHIC TECHNOLOGY

School	ST	$IS	SR
Stony Brook Univ/The SUNY	NY	22,703	MC

PORTUGUESE

School	ST	$IS	SR
Brigham Young Univ	UT	13,248	MC
Brown Univ	RI	64,566	MC
Dartmouth College	NH	68,109	MC
Florida International Univ	FL	20,281	C
Georgetown Univ	DC	68,970	MC
Harvard College/Harvard Univ	MA	65,609	MC
Indiana Univ Bloomington	IN	20,791	HC
New York Univ	NY	68,139	MC
Ohio State Univ at Columbus	OH	22,843	MC
Princeton Univ	NJ	60,090	MC
Rhode Island College	RI	19,000	LC
Rutgers Univ - New Brunswick	NJ	27,090	HC
Rutgers Univ - Newark	NJ	27,351	C
The Univ of Texas at Austin	TX	20,206	MC
Tulane Univ	LA	67,496	MC
Univ of Calif at Los Angeles	CA	27,438	HC+
Univ of Calif at Santa Barbara	CA	30,627	HC+
Univ of Florida	FL	16,291	HC+
Univ of Illinois at Urbana-Champaign	IL	27,006	HC
Univ of Iowa	IA	19,415	HC
Univ of Mass Amherst	MA	27,669	HC
Univ of Mass Dartmouth	MA	26,507	C
Univ of New Mexico	NM	16,808	C
Univ of Wisc-Madison	WI	21,647	MC
Wellesley College	MA	66,984	MC
Yale Univ	CT	64,650	MC

POULTRY SCIENCE

School	ST	$IS	SR
Auburn Univ	AL	24,300	VC+
Cal State, Fullerton	CA	21,902	C
Miss State Univ	MS	12,028	C+
N Car State Univ	NC	22,434	HC+
Stephen F. Austin State Univ	TX	18,484	LC
Texas A&M Univ at College Station	TX	20,771	VC+
Univ of Arkansas at Fayetteville	AR	19,766	VC
Univ of Georgia	GA	21,878	HC
Univ of Maryland/Eastern Shore	MD	21,861	LC
Univ of Wisc-Madison	WI	21,647	MC
Virginia Polytechnic Inst and State Univ	VA	21,920	VC

PRE K-4 EDUCATION

School	ST	$IS	SR
Alvernia Univ	PA	45,330	C
Cairn Univ	PA	37,572	C
Chatham Univ	PA	47,883	VC
Lynn Univ	FL	49,680	LC

PREALLIED HEALTH

School	ST	$IS	SR
Biola Univ	CA	48,686	C
Ithaca College	NY	58,158	VC+
La Salle Univ	PA	43,476	C
Mount Aloysius College	PA	29,976	C
St. Michael's College	VT	53,275	VC+
The Master's Univ	CA	43,870	C
Univ of Maine at Machias	ME	22,960	C
Xavier Univ	OH	49,380	VC

PRECHIROPRACTIC

School	ST	$IS	SR
College of St. Benedict	MN	54,480	C
Hofstra Univ	NY	58,210	C+
Missouri Western State Univ	MO	17,822	LC

PRECISION PRODUCTION

School	ST	$IS	SR
Calif College of the Arts	CA	52,758	SP

PREDENTISTRY

School	ST	$IS	SR
Albertus Magnus College	CT	44,016	LC
American International College	MA	47,020	LC

ST = STATE **$IS** = IN-STATE COSTS **SR** = SELECTOR RATING

School	ST	$IS	SR
Aquinas College - Mich	MI	38,876	VC
Arcadia Univ	PA	55,990	C+
Ashland Univ	OH	30,446	C
Auburn Univ	AL	24,300	VC+
Baldwin Wallace Univ	OH	42,464	VC
Ball State Univ	IN	19,808	C+
Barry Univ	FL	38,730	LC
Baylor Univ	TX	56,803	HC
Bellarmine Univ	KY	52,532	C
Bemidji State Univ	MN	17,730	C
Biola Univ	CA	48,686	C
Boise State Univ	ID	17,368	C
Boston Univ	MA	67,352	MC
Brigham Young Univ/Hawaii	HI	11,710	C
Cabrini Univ	PA	42,591	LC
Calif Lutheran Univ	CA	52,853	C
Calvin College	MI	43,090	HC
Campbell Univ	NC	37,570	VC
Campbellsville Univ	KY	33,400	C
Canisius College	NY	49,672	C
Capital Univ	OH	44,778	VC
Cardinal Stritch Univ	WI	37,136	C
Carroll College	MT	44,304	C
Chadron State College	NE	14,819	LC
Chicago State Univ	IL	41,620	C
Christopher Newport Univ	VA	24,878	VC+
CUNY/City College	NY	20,204	C
CUNY/Hunter College	NY	31,098	VC
CUNY/Lehman College	NY	5,788	LC
Clark Univ	MA	53,260	HC+
Clayton State Univ	GA	19,735	LC
Clemson Univ	SC		HC
Coe College	IA	51,570	VC
College of St. Benedict	MN	54,480	C
Colo State Univ-Pueblo	CO	21,581	C
Concord Univ	WV	14,954	LC
Concordia Univ Nebr	NE	41,900	VC
Concordia Univ, Ann Arbor	MI	38,878	C+
Converse College	SC	28,290	C
Corban Univ	OR	41,700	C
Cornerstone Univ	MI	36,550	C
Davis & Elkins College	WV	38,242	LC
Dominican Univ	IL	42,472	C+
Dordt College	IA	37,860	C+
Eastern Mennonite Univ	VA	42,550	C
Eastern Washington Univ	WA	17,896	LC
Eckerd College	FL	55,206	VC
Elizabethtown College	PA	56,340	VC
Elmira College	NY	53,900	C
Elms College	MA	49,602	VC
Fairmont State Univ	WV	15,726	C
Faulkner Univ	AL	26,410	C
Ferris State Univ	MI	21,458	C
Florida A&M Univ	FL	15,361	C
Florida Southern College	FL	45,978	VC
Florida State Univ	FL	16,771	HC
Fontbonne Univ	MO	34,606	C
Freed-Hardeman Univ	TN	29,900	C
Gannon Univ	PA	42,922	C
George Fox Univ	OR	42,938	C
Georgetown College	KY	41,440	C
Gettysburg College	PA	65,210	MC
Goshen College	IN	44,350	C
Grace College and Seminary	IN	31,524	C
Graceland Univ	IA	35,290	C
Grand Valley State Univ	MI	22,250	C+
Gustavus Adolphus College	MN	53,943	HC
Hardin-Simmons Univ	TX	36,025	C
Heidelberg Univ	OH	40,400	LC
High Point Univ	NC	47,355	VC
Hofstra Univ	NY	58,210	C+
Houghton College	NY	40,558	VC
Howard Univ	DC	37,616	C+
Humboldt State Univ	CA	21,708	C
Indiana Univ-Purdue Univ Fort Wayne	IN	18,675	C
Iowa Wesleyan Univ	IA	41,000	C
Ithaca College	NY	58,158	VC+
Johnson C. Smith Univ	NC	25,336	LC
Judson Univ	IL	39,174	C
Kent State Univ	OH	20,928	C
Kentucky Wesleyan College	KY	34,260	LC
Keuka College	NY	42,398	C
King's College	PA	48,240	C
Kutztown Univ of Pennsylvania	PA	19,477	C
Lake Superior State Univ	MI	19,867	C
Lamar Univ	TX	18,014	LC
Le Moyne College	NY	47,305	VC
Lehigh Univ	PA	63,860	MC
Lenoir-Rhyne Univ	NC	47,500	LC
Lewis Univ	IL	41,710	C
Lincoln Memorial Univ	TN	28,430	C
Lipscomb Univ	TN	42,984	VC
Loyola Univ New Orleans	LA	52,456	VC
Lubbock Christian Univ	TX	29,727	C
MacMurray College	IL	35,025	C
Madonna Univ	MI	30,450	LC
Manhattan College	NY	55,652	C
Mars Hill Univ	NC	41,104	C
Marshall Univ	WV	18,044	C
Maryville College	TN	44,410	C
MCPHS Univ	MA	45,470	SP
Mercer Univ	GA	45,348	VC
Mercyhurst Univ	PA	47,420	C
Methodist Univ	NC	58,130	C
Mich State Univ	MI	24,542	VC
Mich Tech Univ	MI	25,551	VC+
Midland Univ	NE	39,512	C
Midwestern State Univ	TX	12,111	LC
Millikin Univ	IL	44,148	C
Minn State Univ, Mankato	MN	17,190	C
Minn State Univ, Moorhead	MN	21,393	C
Missouri Southern State Univ	MO	13,071	C
Missouri Western State Univ	MO	17,822	LC
Mount Aloysius College	PA	29,976	C
Mount Mary Univ	WI	34,650	LC
Murray State Univ	KY	17,726	C+
New York Univ	NY	68,139	MC
N Car State Univ	NC	22,434	HC+
North Central College	IL	48,712	C+
North Park Univ	IL	35,860	C
Northern Kentucky Univ	KY	16,486	C
Northern Mich Univ	MI	20,853	C
Northern State Univ	SD	15,570	C
Northwest Missouri State Univ	MO	18,286	C
Northwestern College of Iowa	IA	38,400	C
Notre Dame of Maryland Univ	MD	47,570	VC
Ohio Univ	OH	23,394	VC
Ohio Wesleyan Univ	OH	49,460	VC
Okla Wesleyan Univ	OK	34,434	C
Olivet College	MI	37,661	LC
Olivet Nazarene Univ	IL	41,840	VC
Oral Roberts Univ	OK	34,316	C
Oregon State Univ	OR	23,337	VC
Ouachita Baptist Univ	AR	33,500	VC
Quinnipiac Univ	CT	60,970	VC
Rhode Island College	RI	19,000	LC
Rivier Univ	NH	41,600	VC
Roberts Wesleyan College	NY	41,116	C
Rochester Inst of Technology	NY	52,734	HC+
Roosevelt Univ	IL	41,890	VC
Rosemont College	PA	30,980	LC
Saginaw Valley State Univ	MI	19,284	C
St. Anselm College	NH	56,636	VC
St. John's Univ	MN	53,472	C
St. Mary-of-the-Woods College	IN	40,424	LC
St. Peter's Univ	NJ	49,192	C
St. Vincent College	PA	46,229	C
St. Xavier Univ	IL	44,440	C
Seton Hill Univ	PA	46,972	VC
Simpson College	IA	45,626	VC
Spring Hill College	AL	48,488	C
Springfield College	MA	48,775	C
St. Cloud State Univ	MN	10,600	C
St. Mary's Univ	TX	39,120	C
St. Thomas Univ	FL	51,187	LC
SUNY Albany	NY	22,165	C
SUNY at Oswego	NY	22,219	VC
SUNY/Fredonia	NY	20,818	C
SUNY/Oneonta	NY	20,794	C
SUNY/The College of Environmental Science and Forestry	NY	23,728	VC
Syracuse Univ	NY	62,313	HC
Tarleton State Univ	TX	15,248	LC
Temple Univ	PA	24,392	C+
Texas A&M Univ at Commerce	TX	10,496	C
Texas A&M Univ at Kingsville	TX	16,580	LC
The Catholic Univ of America	DC	58,376	VC
The Master's Univ	CA	43,870	C
The Univ of Tenn at Knoxville	TN	22,112	VC
Thiel College	PA	42,950	LC
Touro College	NY	31,040	C
Trinity Christian College	IL	35,580	C
Truman State Univ	MO	16,286	MC
Union Univ	TN	41,160	VC
Univ of Arkansas at Pine Bluff	AR	13,541	C
Univ of Bridgeport	CT	44,985	LC
Univ of Central Arkansas	AR	15,042	VC
Univ of Central Missouri	MO	18,982	C
Univ of Central Okla	OK	15,150	C
Univ of Cincinnati	OH	22,118	VC
Univ of Dayton	OH	54,930	VC
Univ of Detroit Mercy	MI	48,816	C
Univ of Evansville	IN	44,186	C+
Univ of Great Falls	MT	38,524	C
Univ of Hartford	CT	49,776	C
Univ of Illinois at Chicago	IL	24,664	VC
Univ of Iowa	IA	19,415	HC
Univ of Maine at Machias	ME	22,960	C
Univ of Maryland/College Park	MD	21,938	HC
Univ of Mass Amherst	MA	27,669	HC
Univ of Miami	FL	63,494	MC
Univ of Minn/Twin Cities	MN	24,269	MC
Univ of Nebr - Kearney	NE	17,014	LC
Univ of Nebr - Lincoln	NE	18,589	VC
Univ of New England	ME	50,110	C
Univ of N Car at Greensboro	NC	15,998	C
Univ of North Georgia	GA	17,316	C
Univ of Rio Grande & Rio Grande Community College	OH	8,750	LC
Univ of Southern Miss	MS	13,170	C
Univ of St. Francis	IL	40,828	C
Univ of the Cumberlands	KY	32,000	LC
Univ of West Florida	FL	15,848	C
Univ of Wisc-Eau Claire	WI	16,354	VC
Utah State Univ	UT	13,235	C
Virginia Polytechnic Inst and State Univ	VA	21,920	VC
Walsh Univ	OH	39,010	C
Wartburg College	IA	49,478	C
Washington Adventist Univ	MD	32,050	LC
Washington State Univ	WA	22,747	C
Washington Univ in St. Louis	MO	67,539	MC
Waynesburg Univ	PA	33,530	C
Wellesley College	MA	66,984	MC
West Chester Univ of Pennsylvania	PA	19,171	VC
West Liberty Univ	WV	16,158	C
West Texas A&M Univ	TX	13,478	C
Western Carolina Univ	NC	13,965	C
Western New Mexico Univ	NM	16,914	LC
Western State Colo Univ	CO	19,348	C
Westminster College	PA	41,722	C
Whitworth Univ	WA	53,682	VC
Wilson College	PA	35,620	LC
Wingate Univ	NC	41,900	C
Winona State Univ	MN	18,109	C
Wright State Univ	OH	16,983	C
Youngstown State Univ	OH	17,487	C

PREENGINEERING

School	ST	$IS	SR
Adams State Univ	CO	15,420	LC
Alice Lloyd College	KY	8,190	LC
Aquinas College - Mich	MI	38,876	VC
Asbury Univ	KY	36,450	C+
Baldwin Wallace Univ	OH	42,464	VC
Ball State Univ	IN	19,808	C+
Bard College at Simon's Rock	MA	65,795	MC
Barry Univ	FL	38,730	LC
Bellarmine Univ	KY	52,532	C
Beloit College	WI	55,206	HC
Bethany College	WV	38,774	LC
Bethel College	IN	36,830	C
Calif Baptist Univ	CA	42,986	C
Campbellsville Univ	KY	33,400	C
Canisius College	NY	49,672	C
CUNY/Hunter College	NY	31,098	VC
Clayton State Univ	GA	19,735	LC
Coe College	IA	51,570	VC
College of St. Benedict	MN	54,480	C
College of the Ozarks	MO	7,530	VC
Colo State Univ-Pueblo	CO	21,581	C
Concordia Univ, Ann Arbor	MI	38,878	C+
DePauw Univ	IN	58,688	VC
Eastern Mennonite Univ	VA	42,550	C
Elizabethtown College	PA	56,340	VC
Elmhurst College	IL	46,514	C
Freed-Hardeman Univ	TN	29,900	C
Furman Univ	SC	61,098	VC+
Georgetown College	KY	41,440	C
Goshen College	IN	44,350	C
Harvard College/Harvard Univ	MA	65,609	MC
Heidelberg Univ	OH	40,400	LC
Houghton College	NY	40,558	VC
Johnson C. Smith Univ	NC	25,336	LC
Judson Univ	IL	39,174	C
Kentucky Wesleyan College	KY	34,260	LC
Kutztown Univ of Pennsylvania	PA	19,477	C
Le Moyne College	NY	47,305	VC
Lenoir-Rhyne Univ	NC	47,500	LC
Lewis Univ	IL	41,710	C
Lipscomb Univ	TN	42,984	VC
Louisiana College	LA	21,274	C
Loyola Univ New Orleans	LA	52,456	VC
Lubbock Christian Univ	TX	29,727	C
MacMurray College	IL	35,025	C
Madonna Univ	MI	30,450	LC
Marshall Univ	WV	18,044	C
Maryville College	TN	44,410	C
Midwestern State Univ	TX	12,111	LC
Millikin Univ	IL	44,148	C
Minn State Univ, Mankato	MN	17,190	C
Missouri Western State Univ	MO	17,822	LC
North Central College	IL	48,712	C+
Northwest Missouri State Univ	MO	18,286	C
Notre Dame of Maryland Univ	MD	47,570	VC
Oral Roberts Univ	OK	34,316	C
Peru State College	NE	15,602	LC
Pfeiffer Univ	NC	40,532	LC
Providence College	RI	62,870	HC
Regis Univ	CO	46,380	C
Roberts Wesleyan College	NY	41,116	C
Saginaw Valley State Univ	MI	19,284	C
St. John's Univ	MN	53,472	C
St. Mary's College of Calif	CA	57,420	C
St. Michael's College	VT	53,275	VC+
Scripps College	CA	69,260	HC
Shaw Univ	NC	24,638	C
Simpson College	IA	45,626	VC
Southern Oregon Univ	OR	19,117	C
St. Edward's Univ	TX	56,190	VC
SUNY at Oswego	NY	22,219	VC
Stockton Univ	NJ	25,565	C
Texas A&M Univ at Commerce	TX	10,496	C
The College of Idaho	ID	36,415	C
Thiel College	PA	42,950	LC
Truman State Univ	MO	16,286	MC
Union Univ	TN	41,160	VC
Univ of Arkansas at Pine Bluff	AR	13,541	C
Univ of Central Arkansas	AR	15,042	VC
Univ of N Car at Greensboro	NC	15,998	C
Univ of North Georgia	GA	17,316	C
Univ of Rio Grande & Rio Grande Community College	OH	8,750	LC
Univ of San Diego	CA	60,338	HC
Univ of the Cumberlands	KY	32,000	LC
Wartburg College	IA	49,478	C
Wayland Baptist Univ	TX	23,460	LC
Wellesley College	MA	66,984	MC
West Liberty Univ	WV	16,158	C
West Texas A&M Univ	TX	13,478	C
Western Carolina Univ	NC	13,965	C
Western New England Univ	MA	49,182	C
Western State Colo Univ	CO	19,348	C
Whitman College	WA	59,772	MC
Widener Univ	PA	58,190	C
Wilberforce Univ	OH	19,900	C
Wingate Univ	NC	41,900	C
Winona State Univ	MN	18,109	C
Yeshiva Univ	NY	52,750	VC

PRE-HEALTH BIOLOGICAL STUDIES

School	ST	$IS	SR
Bryant Univ	RI	57,204	VC
Elmhurst College	IL	46,514	C
Ferris State Univ	MI	21,458	C
Florida International Univ	FL	20,281	C
John Carroll Univ	OH	51,570	C
Shippensburg Univ of Pennsylvania	PA	24,096	C
SUNY at Oswego	NY	22,219	VC
Univ of Arkansas at Little Rock	AR	18,211	LC
Urbana Univ	OH	30,820	C
Wilson College	PA	35,620	LC

PRE-HEALTH STUDIES

School	ST	$IS	SR
Aquinas College - Mich	MI	38,876	VC
Asbury Univ	KY	36,450	C+
Augsburg Univ	MN	45,129	C
Averett Univ	VA	43,034	LC
Biola Univ	CA	48,686	C
Bloomfield College	NJ	40,100	LC
Clayton State Univ	GA	19,735	LC
Cornerstone Univ	MI	36,550	C
Dakota Wesleyan Univ	SD	33,980	LC
Elmhurst College	IL	46,514	C
Ferris State Univ	MI	21,458	C
Florida International Univ	FL	20,281	C
Fordham Univ	NY	68,431	MC
Hofstra Univ	NY	58,210	C+
Ithaca College	NY	58,158	VC+
Johnson & Wales Univ/ Denver Campus	CO	44,768	C
Kalamazoo College	MI	53,931	HC
Marshall Univ	WV	18,044	C
Mass College of Liberal Arts	MA	20,659	C
Mayville State Univ	ND	18,371	NC
Milligan College	TN	39,450	C
Murray State Univ	KY	17,726	C+
New York Univ	NY	68,139	MC
Okla City Univ	OK	40,476	C
Point Park Univ	PA	41,270	C
Regis Univ	CO	46,380	C
Siena Heights Univ	MI	36,322	C
SUNY at Binghamton	NY	24,100	MC
SUNY at Oswego	NY	22,219	VC
The Univ of Arizona	AZ	24,086	C
Univ of Illinois at Chicago	IL	24,664	VC
Univ of Miami	FL	63,494	MC
Univ of N Car at Greensboro	NC	15,998	C
Valparaiso Univ	IN	50,160	VC
Wilson College	PA	35,620	LC

PRELAW

School	ST	$IS	SR
Adams State Univ	CO	15,420	LC
Albertus Magnus College	CT	44,016	LC
American International College	MA	47,020	LC
Aquinas College - Mich	MI	38,876	VC
Arcadia Univ	PA	55,990	C+
Ashland Univ	OH	30,446	C
Averett Univ	VA	43,034	LC
Ball State Univ	IN	19,808	C+
Barry Univ	FL	38,730	LC
Beloit College	WI	55,206	HC
Bemidji State Univ	MN	17,730	C
Bennington College	VT	66,280	MC
Biola Univ	CA	48,686	C
Blackburn College	IL	28,526	LC
Bradley Univ	IL	43,240	VC
Bryant Univ	RI	57,204	VC
Calif Lutheran Univ	CA	52,853	C
Calvin College	MI	43,090	HC
Campbell Univ	NC	37,570	VC
Campbellsville Univ	KY	33,400	C
Canisius College	NY	49,672	C
Capital Univ	OH	44,778	VC
Cardinal Stritch Univ	WI	37,136	C
Carroll College	MT	44,304	C
Carroll Univ	WI	38,100	C+

ST = STATE $IS = IN-STATE COSTS SR = SELECTOR RATING

School	ST	$IS	SR
Catawba College	NC	39,820	LC
Cedarville Univ	OH	36,244	VC
Central Washington Univ	WA	16,803	C
Chadron State College	NE	14,819	LC
Chicago State Univ	IL	41,620	C
Christopher Newport Univ	VA	24,878	VC+
CUNY/City College	NY	20,204	C
CUNY/Hunter College	NY	31,098	VC
CUNY/Lehman College	NY	5,788	LC
Clark Univ	MA	53,260	HC+
Clemson Univ	SC		HC
Coe College	IA	51,570	VC
College of St. Benedict	MN	54,480	C
College of the Ozarks	MO	7,530	VC
Colo State Univ-Pueblo	CO	21,581	C
Concord Univ	WV	14,954	LC
Concordia Univ Nebr	NE	41,900	VC
Concordia Univ, Chicago	IL	41,522	C
Converse College	SC	28,290	C
Corban Univ	OR	41,700	C
Dakota Wesleyan Univ	SD	33,980	LC
Davis & Elkins College	WV	38,242	LC
Dominican Univ	IL	42,472	C+
Dordt College	IA	37,860	C+
East Central Univ	OK	13,330	C
Eastern Washington Univ	WA	17,896	LC
Eckerd College	FL	55,206	VC
Edinboro Univ	PA	15,940	LC
Elmira College	NY	53,900	C
Elms College	MA	49,602	VC
Faulkner Univ	AL	26,410	C
Fitchburg State Univ	MA	21,819	LC
Florida Inst of Technology	FL	53,306	VC
Florida International Univ	FL	20,281	C
Florida State Univ	FL	16,771	HC
Fontbonne Univ	MO	34,606	C
Fordham Univ	NY	68,431	MC
Fresno Pacific Univ	CA	38,858	C
George Fox Univ	OR	42,938	C
Georgetown College	KY	41,440	C
Gettysburg College	PA	65,210	MC
Grace College and Seminary	IN	31,524	C
Grand Valley State Univ	MI	22,250	C+
Gustavus Adolphus College	MN	53,943	HC
Hamline Univ	MN	50,152	C
Hardin-Simmons Univ	TX	36,025	C
Heidelberg Univ	OH	40,400	LC
High Point Univ	NC	47,355	VC
Hofstra Univ	NY	58,210	C+
Houghton College	NY	40,558	VC
Humboldt State Univ	CA	21,708	C
Huntington Univ	IN	33,996	C
Illinois College	IL	41,330	VC
Immaculata Univ	PA	39,000	C
Indiana Inst of Technology	IN	34,240	LC
Indiana Univ-Purdue Univ Fort Wayne	IN	18,675	C
Indiana Univ-Purdue Univ Indianapolis	IN	18,952	C
Indiana Wesleyan Univ	IN	33,674	C
Iowa Wesleyan Univ	IA	41,000	C
Ithaca College	NY	58,158	VC+
Johnson C. Smith Univ	NC	25,336	LC
Johnson State College	VT	22,672	C
Judson Univ	IL	39,174	C
Kansas Wesleyan Univ	KS	37,930	C
Kentucky Wesleyan College	KY	34,260	LC
Keuka College	NY	42,398	C
King's College	PA	48,240	C
Lafayette College	PA	68,520	MC
Lake Superior State Univ	MI	19,867	C
Lamar Univ	TX	18,014	LC
Le Moyne College	NY	47,305	VC
Lenoir-Rhyne Univ	NC	47,500	LC
LeTourneau Univ	TX	39,190	VC
Lewis Univ	IL	41,710	C
Limestone College	SC	32,100	C
Lincoln Memorial Univ	TN	28,430	C
Lindenwood Univ	MO	25,760	C
Lipscomb Univ	TN	42,984	VC
Louisiana College	LA	21,274	C
Lubbock Christian Univ	TX	29,727	C
MacMurray College	IL	35,025	C
Madonna Univ	MI	30,450	LC
Manchester Univ	IN	41,540	C
Manhattan College	NY	55,652	C
Marlboro College	VT	50,832	VC+
Mars Hill Univ	NC	41,104	C
Marshall Univ	WV	18,044	C
Maryville College	TN	44,410	C
Marywood Univ	PA	47,840	C
Mayville State Univ	ND	18,371	NC
Mercer Univ	GA	45,348	VC
Mercyhurst Univ	PA	47,420	C
Methodist Univ	NC	58,130	C
Mich State Univ	MI	24,542	VC
Middle Tenn State Univ	TN	8,650	C
Midland Univ	NE	39,512	C
Midwestern State Univ	TX	12,111	LC
Millikin Univ	IL	44,148	C
Mills College	CA	43,705	C
Minn State Univ, Mankato	MN	17,190	C
Minn State Univ, Moorhead	MN	21,393	C
Missouri Univ of Science and Technology	MO	18,655	HC
Missouri Western State Univ	MO	17,822	LC
Monmouth Univ	NJ	50,184	C
Mount Aloysius College	PA	29,976	C
Mount Mary Univ	WI	34,650	LC
Mount Vernon Nazarene Univ	OH	35,944	C
National Univ	CA	17,849	LC
Neumann Univ	PA	40,678	LC
N Car State Univ	NC	22,434	HC+
North Central College	IL	48,712	C+
North Park Univ	IL	35,860	C
Northern Arizona Univ	AZ	21,003	C
Northern Kentucky Univ	KY	16,486	C
Northern Mich Univ	MI	20,853	C
Northern State Univ	SD	15,570	C
Northwest Missouri State Univ	MO	18,286	C
Northwestern College of Iowa	IA	38,400	C
Notre Dame of Maryland Univ	MD	47,570	VC
Oakland City Univ	IN	33,930	NC
Oberlin College	OH	68,942	MC
Ohio Univ	OH	23,394	VC
Ohio Wesleyan Univ	OH	49,460	VC
Okla Baptist Univ	OK	33,990	C
Okla Christian Univ	OK	29,260	C
Okla City Univ	OK	40,476	C
Okla Wesleyan Univ	OK	34,434	C
Olivet College	MI	37,661	LC
Olivet Nazarene Univ	IL	41,840	VC
Oral Roberts Univ	OK	34,316	C
Ouachita Baptist Univ	AR	33,500	VC
Palm Beach Atlantic Univ	FL	39,250	C
Peru State College	NE	15,602	LC
Quinnipiac Univ	CT	60,970	VC
Regis Univ	CO	46,380	C
Rensselaer Polytechnic Inst	NY	67,265	MC
Rhode Island College	RI	19,000	LC
Rider Univ	NJ	54,050	C
Rivier Univ	NH	41,600	VC
Roberts Wesleyan College	NY	41,116	C
Rochester Inst of Technology	NY	52,734	HC+
Roosevelt Univ	IL	41,890	VC
Rosemont College	PA	30,980	LC
Saginaw Valley State Univ	MI	19,284	C
St. Anselm College	NH	56,636	VC
St. Augustine's Univ	NC	25,582	C
St. John's Univ	MN	53,472	C
St. Mary-of-the-Woods College	IN	40,424	LC
St. Michael's College	VT	53,275	VC+
St. Peter's Univ	NJ	49,192	C
St. Vincent College	PA	46,229	C
St. Xavier Univ	IL	44,440	C
Schreiner Univ	TX	34,626	LC
Scripps College	CA	69,260	HC
Seattle Pacific Univ	WA	47,439	C+
Seton Hill Univ	PA	46,972	VC
Shawnee State Univ	OH	16,998	C
Simpson College	IA	45,626	VC
Southern Oregon Univ	OR	19,117	C
Springfield College	MA	48,775	C
St. Ambrose Univ	IA	40,180	C
St. Cloud State Univ	MN	10,600	C
St. Edward's Univ	TX	56,190	VC
St. Mary's Univ	TX	39,120	C
St. Thomas Aquinas College	NY	32,450	C
St. Thomas Univ	FL	51,187	LC
SUNY Albany	NY	22,165	C
SUNY at Oswego	NY	22,219	VC
SUNY/Fredonia	NY	20,818	C
SUNY/Oneonta	NY	20,794	C
SUNY/The College of Environmental Science and Forestry	NY	23,728	VC
Stetson Univ	FL	57,174	VC+
Stillman College	AL	20,738	C
Syracuse Univ	NY	62,313	HC
Tarleton State Univ	TX	15,248	LC
Temple Univ	PA	24,392	C+
Texas A&M Univ at Commerce	TX	10,496	C
Texas A&M Univ at Kingsville	TX	16,580	LC
Texas Wesleyan Univ	TX	37,338	C
The Catholic Univ of America	DC	58,376	VC
The Master's Univ	CA	43,870	C
The Univ of Mary	ND	23,180	C
The Univ of Montana Western	MT	9,426	LC
Thiel College	PA	42,950	LC
Touro College	NY	31,040	C
Trinity Christian College	IL	35,580	C
Truman State Univ	MO	16,286	MC
Union Univ	TN	41,160	VC
Univ of Bridgeport	CT	44,985	LC
Univ of Central Missouri	MO	18,982	C
Univ of Cincinnati	OH	22,118	VC
Univ of Detroit Mercy	MI	48,816	C
Univ of Evansville	IN	44,186	C+
Univ of Findlay	OH	43,040	C
Univ of Great Falls	MT	38,524	C
Univ of Illinois at Urbana-Champaign	IL	27,006	HC
Univ of Iowa	IA	19,415	HC
Univ of Maryland/College Park	MD	21,938	HC
Univ of Miami	FL	63,494	MC
Univ of Minn/Duluth	MN	20,292	C
Univ of Minn/Morris	MN	21,222	VC
Univ of Minn/Twin Cities	MN	24,269	MC
Univ of Nebr - Kearney	NE	17,014	LC
Univ of Nebr - Lincoln	NE	18,589	VC
Univ of N Car at Greensboro	NC	15,998	C
Univ of North Georgia	GA	17,316	C
Univ of Rio Grande & Rio Grande Community College	OH	8,750	LC
Univ of Sioux Falls	SD	25,630	C
Univ of Southern Miss	MS	13,170	C
Univ of the Cumberlands	KY	32,000	LC
Univ of the Incarnate Word	TX	39,162	LC
Univ of Tulsa	OK	52,625	HC
Univ of West Florida	FL	15,848	C
Univ of Wisc-Eau Claire	WI	16,354	VC
Univ of Wisc-River Falls	WI	14,541	C
Univ of Wisc-Whitewater	WI	13,976	C
Urbana Univ	OH	30,820	C
Ursuline College	OH	41,076	LC
Utah State Univ	UT	13,235	C
Valparaiso Univ	IN	50,160	VC
Vassar College	NY	68,110	MC
Virginia Polytechnic Inst and State Univ	VA	21,920	VC
Walsh Univ	OH	39,010	C
Wartburg College	IA	49,478	C
Washington Adventist Univ	MD	32,050	LC
Washington State Univ	WA	22,747	C
Wayland Baptist Univ	TX	23,460	LC
Waynesburg Univ	PA	33,530	C
Webber International Univ	FL	31,904	C
Wellesley College	MA	66,984	MC
West Chester Univ of Pennsylvania	PA	19,171	VC
West Liberty Univ	WV	16,158	C
West Texas A&M Univ	TX	13,478	C
Western Carolina Univ	NC	13,965	C
Western State Colo Univ	CO	19,348	C
Westminster College	PA	41,722	C
Westminster College	UT	41,078	C
Whitman College	WA	59,772	MC
Whitworth Univ	WA	53,682	VC
Wilberforce Univ	OH	19,900	C
William Peace Univ	NC	39,300	LC
Wilmington College	OH	35,100	C
Wilson College	PA	35,620	LC
Wingate Univ	NC	41,900	C
Winona State Univ	MN	18,109	C
Wright State Univ	OH	16,983	C
Youngstown State Univ	OH	17,487	C

PREMEDICINE

School	ST	$IS	SR
Adams State Univ	CO	15,420	LC
Albertus Magnus College	CT	44,016	LC
American International College	MA	47,020	LC
American Jewish Univ - College of A&S	CA	44,234	C
Aquinas College - Mich	MI	38,876	VC
Arcadia Univ	PA	55,990	C+
Ashland Univ	OH	30,446	C
Auburn Univ	AL	24,300	VC+
Augustana College	IL	51,222	VC+
Avila Univ	MO	27,100	C
Baldwin Wallace Univ	OH	42,464	VC
Ball State Univ	IN	19,808	C+
Bard College at Simon's Rock	MA	65,795	MC
Barry Univ	FL	38,730	LC
Bayamon Central Univ	PR	12,490	
Baylor Univ	TX	56,803	HC
Bellarmine Univ	KY	52,532	C
Beloit College	WI	55,206	HC
Bemidji State Univ	MN	17,730	C
Bennington College	VT	66,280	MC
Bethel Univ	TN	27,142	C
Biola Univ	CA	48,686	C
Blackburn College	IL	28,526	LC
Bloomfield College	NJ	40,100	LC
Bluffton Univ	OH	40,950	C+
Boise State Univ	ID	17,368	C
Bradley Univ	IL	43,240	VC
Brigham Young Univ/Hawaii	HI	11,710	C
Cabrini Univ	PA	42,591	LC
Calif Lutheran Univ	CA	52,853	C
Cal State, San Bernardino	CA	20,106	C
Calvin College	MI	43,090	HC
Campbell Univ	NC	37,570	VC
Campbellsville Univ	KY	33,400	C
Canisius College	NY	49,672	C
Capital Univ	OH	44,778	VC
Cardinal Stritch Univ	WI	37,136	C
Carroll College	MT	44,304	C
Chadron State College	NE	14,819	LC
Chicago State Univ	IL	41,620	C
Christopher Newport Univ	VA	24,878	VC+
CUNY/City College	NY	20,204	C
CUNY/Hunter College	NY	31,098	VC
CUNY/Lehman College	NY	5,788	LC
Clark Univ	MA	53,260	HC+
Clemson Univ	SC		HC
Cleveland State Univ	OH	22,290	C
Coe College	IA	51,570	VC
Coker College	SC	38,196	C
College of St. Benedict	MN	54,480	C
College of the Ozarks	MO	7,530	VC
Colo State Univ-Pueblo	CO	21,581	C
Concord Univ	WV	14,954	LC
Concordia Univ	OR	35,000	C
Concordia Univ Nebr	NE	41,900	VC
Concordia Univ, Ann Arbor	MI	38,878	C+
Concordia Univ, Chicago	IL	41,522	C
Converse College	SC	28,290	C
Corban Univ	OR	41,700	C
Cornerstone Univ	MI	36,550	C
Dakota State Univ	SD	12,286	C
Dakota Wesleyan Univ	SD	33,980	LC
Davis & Elkins College	WV	38,242	LC
Dominican Univ	IL	42,472	C+
Dominican Univ of Calif	CA	58,750	C
Dordt College	IA	37,860	C+
Drexel Univ	PA	65,927	HC
Earlham College	IN	55,670	HC
East Central Univ	OK	13,330	C
Eastern Mennonite Univ	VA	42,550	C
Eastern Washington Univ	WA	17,896	LC
Eckerd College	FL	55,206	VC
Edinboro Univ	PA	15,940	LC
Elizabethtown College	PA	56,340	VC
Elmhurst College	IL	46,514	C
Elmira College	NY	53,900	C
Elms College	MA	49,602	VC
Faulkner Univ	AL	26,410	C
Florida A&M Univ	FL	15,361	C
Florida Inst of Technology	FL	53,306	VC
Florida International Univ	FL	20,281	C
Florida Southern College	FL	45,978	VC
Florida State Univ	FL	16,771	HC
Fontbonne Univ	MO	34,606	C
Freed-Hardeman Univ	TN	29,900	C
Fresno Pacific Univ	CA	38,858	C
Friends Univ	KS	38,000	C
Gannon Univ	PA	42,922	C
George Fox Univ	OR	42,938	C
Georgetown College	KY	41,440	C
Gettysburg College	PA	65,210	MC
Goshen College	IN	44,350	C
Grace College and Seminary	IN	31,524	C
Graceland Univ	IA	35,290	C
Grand Valley State Univ	MI	22,250	C+
Gustavus Adolphus College	MN	53,943	HC
Hamline Univ	MN	50,152	C
Hampshire College	MA	65,214	MC
Hardin-Simmons Univ	TX	36,025	C
Hawaii Pacific Univ	HI	33,420	C
Heidelberg Univ	OH	40,400	LC
High Point Univ	NC	47,355	VC
Hofstra Univ	NY	58,210	C+
Houghton College	NY	40,558	VC
Howard Univ	DC	37,616	C+
Humboldt State Univ	CA	21,708	C
Huntington Univ	IN	33,996	C
Immaculata Univ	PA	39,000	C
Indiana Univ-Purdue Univ Fort Wayne	IN	18,675	C
Indiana Univ-Purdue Univ Indianapolis	IN	18,952	C
Indiana Wesleyan Univ	IN	33,674	C
Inter-American Univ of PR-San Germán	PR	20,042	
Iowa Wesleyan Univ	IA	41,000	C
Ithaca College	NY	58,158	VC+
Jackson State Univ	MS	15,879	LC
Jefferson (Philadelphia Univ + Thomas Jefferson Univ)	PA	53,966	C
Johnson C. Smith Univ	NC	25,336	LC
Johnson State College	VT	22,672	C
Judson Univ	IL	39,174	C
Kent State Univ	OH	20,928	C
Kentucky Wesleyan College	KY	34,260	LC
Keuka College	NY	42,398	C
King's College	PA	48,240	C
Kutztown Univ of Pennsylvania	PA	19,477	C
Lake Superior State Univ	MI	19,867	C
Lamar Univ	TX	18,014	LC
Le Moyne College	NY	47,305	VC
Lees-McRae College	NC	33,944	NC
Lehigh Univ	PA	63,860	MC
Lenoir-Rhyne Univ	NC	47,500	LC
LeTourneau Univ	TX	39,190	VC
Lewis Univ	IL	41,710	C
Lincoln Memorial Univ	TN	28,430	C
Lipscomb Univ	TN	42,984	VC
Loyola Univ New Orleans	LA	52,456	VC
Lubbock Christian Univ	TX	29,727	C
MacMurray College	IL	35,025	C
Madonna Univ	MI	30,450	LC
Manhattan College	NY	55,652	C
Marlboro College	VT	50,832	VC+
Marquette Univ	WI	53,090	VC+
Mars Hill Univ	NC	41,104	C
Marshall Univ	WV	18,044	C
Marymount Manhattan College	NY	48,350	C
Marymount Univ	VA	43,231	C
Maryville College	TN	44,410	C
Marywood Univ	PA	47,840	C
Mayville State Univ	ND	18,371	NC
MCPHS Univ	MA	45,470	SP
Mercer Univ	GA	45,348	VC
Mercy College of Health Sciences	IA	17,600	SP
Mercyhurst Univ	PA	47,420	C
Mich Tech Univ	MI	25,551	VC+
Midland Univ	NE	39,512	C
Midwestern State Univ	TX	12,111	LC
Milligan College	TN	39,450	C
Millikin Univ	IL	44,148	C
Minn State Univ, Mankato	MN	17,190	C

ST = STATE **$IS** = IN-STATE COSTS **SR** = SELECTOR RATING

School	ST	$IS	SR
Minn State Univ, Moorhead	MN	21,393	C
Missouri Southern State Univ	MO	13,071	C
Missouri Univ of Science and Technology	MO	18,655	HC
Missouri Western State Univ	MO	17,822	LC
Monmouth Univ	NJ	50,184	C
Mount Aloysius College	PA	29,976	C
Mount Mary Univ	WI	34,650	LC
Mount Vernon Nazarene Univ	OH	35,944	C
Murray State Univ	KY	17,726	C+
Neumann Univ	PA	40,678	LC
New York Univ	NY	68,139	MC
N Car State Univ	NC	22,434	HC+
N Car Wesleyan College	NC	39,200	C
North Central College	IL	48,712	C+
North Park Univ	IL	35,860	C
Northern Kentucky Univ	KY	16,486	C
Northern Mich Univ	MI	20,853	C
Northern State Univ	SD	15,570	C
Northwest Missouri State Univ	MO	18,286	C
Northwestern College of Iowa	IA	38,400	C
Northwestern Univ	IL	68,725	MC
Notre Dame of Maryland Univ	MD	47,570	VC
Oakland City Univ	IN	33,930	NC
Oberlin College	OH	68,942	MC
Ohio Univ	OH	23,394	VC
Ohio Wesleyan Univ	OH	49,460	VC
Okla Baptist Univ	OK	33,990	C
Okla City Univ	OK	40,476	C
Okla Wesleyan Univ	OK	34,434	C
Olivet College	MI	37,661	LC
Olivet Nazarene Univ	IL	41,840	VC
Oral Roberts Univ	OK	34,316	C
Oregon State Univ	OR	23,337	VC
Ouachita Baptist Univ	AR	33,500	VC
Pennsylvania State Univ - Univ Park	PA	29,716	HC
Peru State College	NE	15,602	LC
Pfeiffer Univ	NC	40,532	LC
Pittsburg State Univ	KS	13,880	C
Point Park Univ	PA	41,270	C
Providence College	RI	62,870	HC
Quinnipiac Univ	CT	60,970	VC
Regis Univ	CO	46,380	C
Rensselaer Polytechnic Inst	NY	67,265	MC
Rhode Island College	RI	19,000	LC
Rider Univ	NJ	54,050	C
Rivier Univ	NH	41,600	VC
Roberts Wesleyan College	NY	41,116	C
Rochester Inst of Technology	NY	52,734	HC+
Roosevelt Univ	IL	41,890	VC
Rosemont College	PA	30,980	LC
Saginaw Valley State Univ	MI	19,284	C
St. Anselm College	NH	56,636	VC
St. Augustine's Univ	NC	25,582	C
St. John's Univ	MN	53,472	C
St. Mary-of-the-Woods College	IN	40,424	LC
St. Peter's Univ	NJ	49,192	C
St. Vincent College	PA	46,229	C
St. Xavier Univ	IL	44,440	C
Seton Hill Univ	PA	46,972	VC
Shawnee State Univ	OH	16,998	C
Siena Heights Univ	MI	36,322	C
Simpson College	IA	45,626	VC
Southern Oregon Univ	OR	19,117	C
Spring Hill College	AL	48,488	C
Springfield College	MA	48,775	C
St. Cloud State Univ	MN	10,600	C
St. Edward's Univ	TX	56,190	VC
St. Mary's Univ	TX	39,120	C
St. Thomas Aquinas College	NY	32,450	C
St. Thomas Univ	FL	51,187	LC
SUNY Albany	NY	22,165	C
SUNY at Oswego	NY	22,219	VC
SUNY/Fredonia	NY	20,818	C
SUNY/Oneonta	NY	20,794	C
SUNY/The College of Environmental Science and Forestry	NY	23,728	VC
Stillman College	AL	20,738	C
Syracuse Univ	NY	62,313	HC
Tarleton State Univ	TX	15,248	LC
Taylor Univ	IN	42,130	VC
Temple Univ	PA	24,392	C+
Texas A&M Univ at Commerce	TX	10,496	C
Texas A&M Univ at Kingsville	TX	16,580	LC
The Catholic Univ of America	DC	58,376	VC
The George Washington Univ	DC	68,474	HC+
The Univ of Mary	ND	23,180	C
The Univ of Tenn at Knoxville	TN	22,112	VC
Thiel College	PA	42,950	LC
Touro College	NY	31,040	C
Trine Univ	IN	41,310	C
Trinity Christian College	IL	35,580	C
Trinity International Univ	IL	31,070	VC
Truman State Univ	MO	16,286	MC
Tusculum College	TN	31,625	LC
Union Univ	TN	41,160	VC
Univ of Arkansas at Pine Bluff	AR	13,541	C
Univ of Bridgeport	CT	44,985	LC
Univ of Calif at Irvine	CA	33,857	VC
Univ of Central Arkansas	AR	15,042	VC
Univ of Central Missouri	MO	18,982	C
Univ of Central Okla	OK	15,150	C
Univ of Cincinnati	OH	22,118	VC
Univ of Dayton	OH	54,930	VC
Univ of Detroit Mercy	MI	48,816	C
Univ of Evansville	IN	44,186	C+
Univ of Findlay	OH	43,040	C
Univ of Great Falls	MT	38,524	C
Univ of Hartford	CT	49,776	C
Univ of Illinois at Chicago	IL	24,664	VC
Univ of Iowa	IA	19,415	HC
Univ of Maine at Machias	ME	22,960	C
Univ of Mass Amherst	MA	27,669	HC
Univ of Miami	FL	63,494	MC
Univ of Minn/Morris	MN	21,222	VC
Univ of Minn/Twin Cities	MN	24,269	MC
Univ of Nebr - Kearney	NE	17,014	LC
Univ of Nebr - Lincoln	NE	18,589	VC
Univ of New Orleans	LA	12,840	C
Univ of N Car at Greensboro	NC	15,998	C
Univ of North Georgia	GA	17,316	C
Univ of PR, at Mayaguez	PR	13,995	
Univ of Rio Grande & Rio Grande Community College	OH	8,750	LC
Univ of Sioux Falls	SD	25,630	C
Univ of Southern Miss	MS	13,170	C
Univ of St. Francis	IL	40,828	C
Univ of the Cumberlands	KY	32,000	LC
Univ of Tulsa	OK	52,625	HC
Univ of West Florida	FL	15,848	C
Univ of Wisc-Eau Claire	WI	16,354	VC
Univ of Wisc-Milwaukee	WI	21,538	C
Univ of Wisc-River Falls	WI	14,541	C
Urbana Univ	OH	30,820	C
Ursuline College	OH	41,076	LC
Utah State Univ	UT	13,235	C
Valparaiso Univ	IN	50,160	VC
Vanguard Univ of Southern Calif	CA	42,400	VC
Vassar College	NY	68,110	MC
Virginia Polytechnic Inst and State Univ	VA	21,920	VC
Walsh Univ	OH	39,010	C
Wartburg College	IA	49,478	C
Washington State Univ	WA	22,747	C
Washington Univ in St. Louis	MO	67,539	MC
Wayland Baptist Univ	TX	23,460	LC
Waynesburg Univ	PA	33,530	C
Wellesley College	MA	66,984	MC
West Chester Univ of Pennsylvania	PA	19,171	VC
West Liberty Univ	WV	16,158	C
West Texas A&M Univ	TX	13,478	C
Western Carolina Univ	NC	13,965	C
Western New England Univ	MA	49,182	C
Western New Mexico Univ	NM	16,914	LC
Westminster College	PA	41,722	C
Whitworth Univ	WA	53,682	VC
Wilmington College	OH	35,100	C
Wilson College	PA	35,620	LC
Wingate Univ	NC	41,900	C
Winona State Univ	MN	18,109	C
Wright State Univ	OH	16,983	C
Xavier Univ of Louisiana	LA	31,689	C
Youngstown State Univ	OH	17,487	C

PRE-MINISTERIAL STUDIES

School	ST	$IS	SR
Drury Univ	MO	37,555	VC

PRENURSING

School	ST	$IS	SR
Hofstra Univ	NY	58,210	C+
Regis Univ	CO	46,380	C
Univ of N Car at Greensboro	NC	15,998	C

PRE-OCCUPATIONAL THERAPY

School	ST	$IS	SR
Bay Path Univ	MA	46,356	C
Calvin College	MI	43,090	HC
College of St. Benedict	MN	54,480	C
Dakota Wesleyan Univ	SD	33,980	LC
Eastern Mennonite Univ	VA	42,550	C
High Point Univ	NC	47,355	VC
Immaculata Univ	PA	39,000	C
Indiana Univ-Purdue Univ Indianapolis	IN	18,952	C
Lewis Univ	IL	41,710	C
Louisiana College	LA	21,274	C
MCPHS Univ	MA	45,470	SP
Missouri Southern State Univ	MO	13,071	C
Missouri Western State Univ	MO	17,822	LC
Murray State Univ	KY	17,726	C+
Ohio Wesleyan Univ	OH	49,460	VC
St. John's Univ	MN	53,472	C
Univ of N Car at Greensboro	NC	15,998	C
Walsh Univ	OH	39,010	C
Wartburg College	IA	49,478	C
Wilson College	PA	35,620	LC

PREOPTOMETRY

School	ST	$IS	SR
Adams State Univ	CO	15,420	LC
Arcadia Univ	PA	55,990	C+
Ashland Univ	OH	30,446	C
Auburn Univ	AL	24,300	VC+
Ball State Univ	IN	19,808	C+
Calvin College	MI	43,090	HC
Campbell Univ	NC	37,570	VC
Cardinal Stritch Univ	WI	37,136	C
Carroll College	MT	44,304	C
College of St. Benedict	MN	54,480	C
Colo State Univ-Pueblo	CO	21,581	C
Corban Univ	OR	41,700	C
Dordt College	IA	37,860	C+
East Central Univ	OK	13,330	C
Faulkner Univ	AL	26,410	C
Ferris State Univ	MI	21,458	C
Florida State Univ	FL	16,771	HC
Freed-Hardeman Univ	TN	29,900	C
Gannon Univ	PA	42,922	C
Hofstra Univ	NY	58,210	C+
Houghton College	NY	40,558	VC
Indiana Univ-Purdue Univ Fort Wayne	IN	18,675	C
Iowa Wesleyan Univ	IA	41,000	C
Ithaca College	NY	58,158	VC+
Le Moyne College	NY	47,305	VC
Lehigh Univ	PA	63,860	MC
Lenoir-Rhyne Univ	NC	47,500	LC
Lewis Univ	IL	41,710	C
Lipscomb Univ	TN	42,984	VC
Madonna Univ	MI	30,450	LC
Marshall Univ	WV	18,044	C
MCPHS Univ	MA	45,470	SP
Millersville Univ of Pennsylvania	PA	25,298	C
Millikin Univ	IL	44,148	C
Missouri Southern State Univ	MO	13,071	C
Missouri Western State Univ	MO	17,822	LC
Mount Aloysius College	PA	29,976	C
Murray State Univ	KY	17,726	C+
Northern Kentucky Univ	KY	16,486	C
Olivet Nazarene Univ	IL	41,840	VC
Oregon State Univ	OR	23,337	VC
Pittsburg State Univ	KS	13,880	C
Rhode Island College	RI	19,000	LC
St. John's Univ	MN	53,472	C
Simpson College	IA	45,626	VC
SUNY at Oswego	NY	22,219	VC
SUNY/Fredonia	NY	20,818	C
Trinity Christian College	IL	35,580	C
Univ of Central Arkansas	AR	15,042	VC
Univ of Central Okla	OK	15,150	C
Univ of Evansville	IN	44,186	C+
Univ of Hartford	CT	49,776	C
Univ of Iowa	IA	19,415	HC
Univ of St. Francis	IL	40,828	C
Univ of Wisc-Eau Claire	WI	16,354	VC
Walsh Univ	OH	39,010	C
Wartburg College	IA	49,478	C
Washington State Univ	WA	22,747	C
Wellesley College	MA	66,984	MC
Western Carolina Univ	NC	13,965	C
Western New England Univ	MA	49,182	C
Wilson College	PA	35,620	LC
Winona State Univ	MN	18,109	C
Youngstown State Univ	OH	17,487	C

PREOSTEOPATHY

School	ST	$IS	SR
Colo State Univ-Pueblo	CO	21,581	C
Eastern Mennonite Univ	VA	42,550	C
Hofstra Univ	NY	58,210	C+
Kent State Univ	OH	20,928	C
Lewis Univ	IL	41,710	C
Madonna Univ	MI	30,450	LC
Marshall Univ	WV	18,044	C
Marywood Univ	PA	47,840	C
MCPHS Univ	MA	45,470	SP
Mercyhurst Univ	PA	47,420	C
Mount Aloysius College	PA	29,976	C
Seton Hill Univ	PA	46,972	VC
Wilson College	PA	35,620	LC
Youngstown State Univ	OH	17,487	C

PREPHARMACY

School	ST	$IS	SR
Adams State Univ	CO	15,420	LC
Alabama A&M Univ	AL	18,796	C
Alice Lloyd College	KY	8,190	LC
Baldwin Wallace Univ	OH	42,464	VC
Barry Univ	FL	38,730	LC
Biola Univ	CA	48,686	C
Boise State Univ	ID	17,368	C
Cabrini Univ	PA	42,591	LC
Calvin College	MI	43,090	HC
Campbell Univ	NC	37,570	VC
Campbellsville Univ	KY	33,400	C
Canisius College	NY	49,672	C
Carroll College	MT	44,304	C
Carroll Univ	WI	38,100	C+
Christopher Newport Univ	VA	24,878	VC+
Clemson Univ	SC		HC
College of St. Benedict	MN	54,480	C
College of the Ozarks	MO	7,530	VC
Colo State Univ-Pueblo	CO	21,581	C
Concord Univ	WV	14,954	LC
Corban Univ	OR	41,700	C
Dakota Wesleyan Univ	SD	33,980	LC
Davis & Elkins College	WV	38,242	LC
Dominican Univ	IL	42,472	C+
Dordt College	IA	37,860	C+
East Central Univ	OK	13,330	C
Eastern Mennonite Univ	VA	42,550	C
Florida Southern College	FL	45,978	VC
Florida State Univ	FL	16,771	HC
Freed-Hardeman Univ	TN	29,900	C
Georgetown College	KY	41,440	C
Goshen College	IN	44,350	C
High Point Univ	NC	47,355	VC
Houghton College	NY	40,558	VC
Huntington Univ	IN	33,996	C
Husson Univ	ME	26,508	C
Indiana Univ-Purdue Univ Fort Wayne	IN	18,675	C
Indiana Univ-Purdue Univ Indianapolis	IN	18,952	C
Lake Superior State Univ	MI	19,867	C
Le Moyne College	NY	47,305	VC
Lewis Univ	IL	41,710	C
Lipscomb Univ	TN	42,984	VC
Louisiana College	LA	21,274	C
Lubbock Christian Univ	TX	29,727	C
Madonna Univ	MI	30,450	LC
Mars Hill Univ	NC	41,104	C
Marshall Univ	WV	18,044	C
Mercer Univ	GA	45,348	VC
Mercyhurst Univ	PA	47,420	C
Mich Tech Univ	MI	25,551	VC+
Midwestern State Univ	TX	12,111	LC
Millersville Univ of Pennsylvania	PA	25,298	C
Milligan College	TN	39,450	C
Millikin Univ	IL	44,148	C
Minn State Univ, Mankato	MN	17,190	C
Minn State Univ, Moorhead	MN	21,393	C
Missouri Southern State Univ	MO	13,071	C
Missouri Western State Univ	MO	17,822	LC
Mount Aloysius College	PA	29,976	C
Mount Vernon Nazarene Univ	OH	35,944	C
Murray State Univ	KY	17,726	C+
Neumann Univ	PA	40,678	LC
Northern Kentucky Univ	KY	16,486	C
Northwest Missouri State Univ	MO	18,286	C
Notre Dame of Maryland Univ	MD	47,570	VC
Ohio Univ	OH	23,394	VC
Olivet Nazarene Univ	IL	41,840	VC
Oregon State Univ	OR	23,337	VC
Peru State College	NE	15,602	LC
Pittsburg State Univ	KS	13,880	C
Roberts Wesleyan College	NY	41,116	C
Roosevelt Univ	IL	41,890	VC
St. John's Univ	MN	53,472	C
St. Joseph's College of Maine	ME	47,890	C
St. Michael's College	VT	53,275	VC+
St. Vincent College	PA	46,229	C
St. Xavier Univ	IL	44,440	C
Simpson College	IA	45,626	VC
Southern Oregon Univ	OR	19,117	C
SUNY/The College of Environmental Science and Forestry	NY	23,728	VC
Tarleton State Univ	TX	15,248	LC
Texas A&M Univ at Commerce	TX	10,496	C
Texas A&M Univ at Kingsville	TX	16,580	LC
The Univ of Tenn at Knoxville	TN	22,112	VC
Thiel College	PA	42,950	LC
Truman State Univ	MO	16,286	MC
Union Univ	TN	41,160	VC
Univ of Arkansas at Pine Bluff	AR	13,541	C
Univ of Central Arkansas	AR	15,042	VC
Univ of Cincinnati	OH	22,118	VC
Univ of Evansville	IN	44,186	C+
Univ of Florida	FL	16,291	HC+
Univ of Illinois at Chicago	IL	24,664	VC
Univ of Iowa	IA	19,415	HC
Univ of Miami	FL	63,494	MC
Univ of Minn/Twin Cities	MN	24,269	MC
Univ of Nebr - Lincoln	NE	18,589	VC
Univ of New England	ME	50,110	C
Univ of N Car at Greensboro	NC	15,998	C
Univ of North Georgia	GA	17,316	C
Univ of St. Francis	IL	40,828	C
Univ of the Cumberlands	KY	32,000	LC
Univ of the Pacific	CA	57,446	VC
Univ of Wisc-Eau Claire	WI	16,354	VC
Univ of Wisc-River Falls	WI	14,541	C
Walsh Univ	OH	39,010	C
Wartburg College	IA	49,478	C
Washburn Univ	KS	15,827	C
Washington State Univ	WA	22,747	C
Washington Univ in St. Louis	MO	67,539	MC
West Liberty Univ	WV	16,158	C
West Texas A&M Univ	TX	13,478	C
Western Carolina Univ	NC	13,965	C
Western New England Univ	MA	49,182	C
Western New Mexico Univ	NM	16,914	LC
Wilkes Univ	PA	49,166	C
Wilson College	PA	35,620	LC
Wingate Univ	NC	41,900	C
Winona State Univ	MN	18,109	C
Xavier Univ	OH	49,380	VC

PREPHYSICAL THERAPY

School	ST	$IS	SR
Asbury Univ	KY	36,450	C+
Baldwin Wallace Univ	OH	42,464	VC
Bellarmine Univ	KY	52,532	C
Bethany College	WV	38,774	LC
Biola Univ	CA	48,686	C
Boise State Univ	ID	17,368	C
Calif Baptist Univ	CA	42,986	C
Calvin College	MI	43,090	HC
Carroll College	MT	44,304	C
Christopher Newport Univ	VA	24,878	VC+
Coe College	IA	51,570	VC
College of St. Benedict	MN	54,480	C
Corban Univ	OR	41,700	C
Davis & Elkins College	WV	38,242	LC
Dordt College	IA	37,860	C+
Eastern Mennonite Univ	VA	42,550	C
Elizabethtown College	PA	56,340	VC
Elmhurst College	IL	46,514	C
Faulkner Univ	AL	26,410	C
Ferris State Univ	MI	21,458	C
Florida Southern College	FL	45,978	VC
Fontbonne Univ	MO	34,606	C
Georgetown College	KY	41,440	C
High Point Univ	NC	47,355	VC
Hofstra Univ	NY	58,210	C+
Houghton College	NY	40,558	VC
Huntington Univ	IN	33,996	C
Immaculata Univ	PA	39,000	C
Indiana Univ-Purdue Univ Indianapolis	IN	18,952	C
Iowa Wesleyan Univ	IA	41,000	C
Lewis Univ	IL	41,710	C
Lipscomb Univ	TN	42,984	VC
Louisiana College	LA	21,274	C
Lubbock Christian Univ	TX	29,727	C
Marshall Univ	WV	18,044	C
Marymount Univ	VA	43,231	C
Mich Tech Univ	MI	25,551	VC+
Millikin Univ	IL	44,148	C
Missouri Southern State Univ	MO	13,071	C
Missouri Western State Univ	MO	17,822	LC
Mount Aloysius College	PA	29,976	C
Mount Vernon Nazarene Univ	OH	35,944	C
Murray State Univ	KY	17,726	C+
Northern Kentucky Univ	KY	16,486	C
Ohio Univ	OH	23,394	VC
Olivet Nazarene Univ	IL	41,840	VC
Oregon State Univ	OR	23,337	VC
Pittsburg State Univ	KS	13,880	C
Roberts Wesleyan College	NY	41,116	C
Saginaw Valley State Univ	MI	19,284	C
St. John's Univ	MN	53,472	C
St. Mary's Univ of Minn	MN	42,440	C
Simpson College	IA	45,626	VC
Southern Oregon Univ	OR	19,117	C
St. Edward's Univ	TX	56,190	VC
SUNY at Oswego	NY	22,219	VC
Tenn Wesleyan Univ	TN	32,680	LC
The Master's Univ	CA	43,870	C
Trinity International Univ	IL	31,070	VC
Univ of Dayton	OH	54,930	VC
Univ of Iowa	IA	19,415	HC
Univ of Mary Hardin-Baylor	TX	35,292	C+
Univ of Miami	FL	63,494	MC
Univ of N Car at Greensboro	NC	15,998	C
Univ of St. Francis	IL	40,828	C
Univ of the Cumberlands	KY	32,000	LC
Univ of Wisc-Eau Claire	WI	16,354	VC
Walsh Univ	OH	39,010	C
Wartburg College	IA	49,478	C
Washington State Univ	WA	22,747	C
Waynesburg Univ	PA	33,530	C
West Chester Univ of Pennsylvania	PA	19,171	VC
Western Carolina Univ	NC	13,965	C
Widener Univ	PA	58,190	C
Wilson College	PA	35,620	LC
Wingate Univ	NC	41,900	C
Winona State Univ	MN	18,109	C

PRE-PHYSICIAN ASSISTANT

School	ST	$IS	SR
Cabrini Univ	PA	42,591	LC
Carroll College	MT	44,304	C
College of St. Benedict	MN	54,480	C
Dakota Wesleyan Univ	SD	33,980	LC
East Central Univ	OK	13,330	C
Eastern Mennonite Univ	VA	42,550	C
Hofstra Univ	NY	58,210	C+
Indiana Univ-Purdue Univ Indianapolis	IN	18,952	C
Lewis Univ	IL	41,710	C
Louisiana College	LA	21,274	C
Lubbock Christian Univ	TX	29,727	C
Madonna Univ	MI	30,450	LC
Millikin Univ	IL	44,148	C
Missouri Southern State Univ	MO	13,071	C
Murray State Univ	KY	17,726	C+
St. John's Univ	MN	53,472	C
Thomas Univ	GA	21,420	NC
Univ of Maine at Machias	ME	22,960	C
Univ of New England	ME	50,110	C
Wartburg College	IA	49,478	C
Wellesley College	MA	66,984	MC
Western New England Univ	MA	49,182	C
Wilson College	PA	35,620	LC
Wingate Univ	NC	41,900	C

PREPODIATRY

School	ST	$IS	SR
Bloomfield College	NJ	40,100	LC
Colo State Univ-Pueblo	CO	21,581	C
Gannon Univ	PA	42,922	C
Hofstra Univ	NY	58,210	C+
Le Moyne College	NY	47,305	VC
Lewis Univ	IL	41,710	C
Madonna Univ	MI	30,450	LC
Marshall Univ	WV	18,044	C
MCPHS Univ	MA	45,470	SP
Millersville Univ of Pennsylvania	PA	25,298	C
Mount Aloysius College	PA	29,976	C
Oregon State Univ	OR	23,337	VC
Univ of Iowa	IA	19,415	HC
Wellesley College	MA	66,984	MC
Wilson College	PA	35,620	LC
Winona State Univ	MN	18,109	C

PREVENTIVE/WELLNESS HEALTH CARE

School	ST	$IS	SR
Appalachian State Univ	NC	15,394	VC
Daemen College	NY	40,336	C
Mount Aloysius College	PA	29,976	C
Oakland Univ	MI	20,763	C

PREVETERINARY SCIENCE

School	ST	$IS	SR
Adams State Univ	CO	15,420	LC
Alabama A&M Univ	AL	18,796	C
Albertus Magnus College	CT	44,016	LC
Andrews Univ	MI	41,732	C
Arcadia Univ	PA	55,990	C+
Ashland Univ	OH	30,446	C
Auburn Univ	AL	24,300	VC+
Baldwin Wallace Univ	OH	42,464	VC
Ball State Univ	IN	19,808	C+
Becker College	MA	30,100	LC
Bellarmine Univ	KY	52,532	C
Bethany College	WV	38,774	LC
Boise State Univ	ID	17,368	C
Cal State, Fullerton	CA	21,902	C
Calvin College	MI	43,090	HC
Canisius College	NY	49,672	C
Cardinal Stritch Univ	WI	37,136	C
Carroll College	MT	44,304	C
Christopher Newport Univ	VA	24,878	VC+
Clemson Univ	SC		HC
Coe College	IA	51,570	VC
College of St. Benedict	MN	54,480	C
College of the Ozarks	MO	7,530	VC
Colo State Univ-Pueblo	CO	21,581	C
Corban Univ	OR	41,700	C
Cornerstone Univ	MI	36,550	C
Davis & Elkins College	WV	38,242	LC
Dordt College	IA	37,860	C+
Eastern Washington Univ	WA	17,896	LC
Elmhurst College	IL	46,514	C
Faulkner Univ	AL	26,410	C
Florida State Univ	FL	16,771	HC
Freed-Hardeman Univ	TN	29,900	C
Gannon Univ	PA	42,922	C
George Fox Univ	OR	42,938	C
Goshen College	IN	44,350	C
Graceland Univ	IA	35,290	C
High Point Univ	NC	47,355	VC
Hofstra Univ	NY	58,210	C+
Houghton College	NY	40,558	VC
Indiana Univ-Purdue Univ Fort Wayne	IN	18,675	C
Indiana Univ-Purdue Univ Indianapolis	IN	18,952	C
Iowa Wesleyan Univ	IA	41,000	C
Kansas State Univ	KS	17,780	VC
Kent State Univ	OH	20,928	C
Keuka College	NY	42,398	C
Le Moyne College	NY	47,305	VC
Lees-McRae College	NC	33,944	NC
Lenoir-Rhyne Univ	NC	47,500	LC
LeTourneau Univ	TX	39,190	VC
Lewis Univ	IL	41,710	C
Lipscomb Univ	TN	42,984	VC
Loyola Univ New Orleans	LA	52,456	VC
Lubbock Christian Univ	TX	29,727	C
MacMurray College	IL	35,025	C
Madonna Univ	MI	30,450	LC
Mars Hill Univ	NC	41,104	C
Mercyhurst Univ	PA	47,420	C
Mich State Univ	MI	24,542	VC
Midwestern State Univ	TX	12,111	LC
Millikin Univ	IL	44,148	C
Minn State Univ, Mankato	MN	17,190	C
Minn State Univ, Moorhead	MN	21,393	C
Missouri Southern State Univ	MO	13,071	C
Mount Aloysius College	PA	29,976	C
Mount Mary Univ	WI	34,650	LC
Murray State Univ	KY	17,726	C+
N Car State Univ	NC	22,434	HC+
North Central College	IL	48,712	C+
N Dak State Univ	ND	16,245	VC
Northern Kentucky Univ	KY	16,486	C
Northern Mich Univ	MI	20,853	C
Northwest Missouri State Univ	MO	18,286	C
Ohio Wesleyan Univ	OH	49,460	VC
Olivet College	MI	37,661	LC
Olivet Nazarene Univ	IL	41,840	VC
Peru State College	NE	15,602	LC
Pittsburg State Univ	KS	13,880	C
Rhode Island College	RI	19,000	LC
Rivier Univ	NH	41,600	VC
Roberts Wesleyan College	NY	41,116	C
Rochester Inst of Technology	NY	52,734	HC+
Roosevelt Univ	IL	41,890	VC
St. John's Univ	MN	53,472	C
St. Mary-of-the-Woods College	IN	40,424	LC
St. Vincent College	PA	46,229	C
Seton Hill Univ	PA	46,972	VC
Simpson College	IA	45,626	VC
Spring Hill College	AL	48,488	C
SUNY at Oswego	NY	22,219	VC
Tarleton State Univ	TX	15,248	LC
Texas A&M Univ at Kingsville	TX	16,580	LC
The Catholic Univ of America	DC	58,376	VC
The Univ of Montana Western	MT	9,426	LC
The Univ of Tenn at Knoxville	TN	22,112	VC
Thiel College	PA	42,950	LC
Truman State Univ	MO	16,286	MC
Univ of Central Arkansas	AR	15,042	VC
Univ of Central Missouri	MO	18,982	C
Univ of Evansville	IN	44,186	C+
Univ of Findlay	OH	43,040	C
Univ of Illinois at Urbana-Champaign	IL	27,006	HC
Univ of Iowa	IA	19,415	HC
Univ of Maine at Machias	ME	22,960	C
Univ of Maryland/College Park	MD	21,938	HC
Univ of Mass Amherst	MA	27,669	HC
Univ of Miami	FL	63,494	MC
Univ of Minn/Twin Cities	MN	24,269	MC
Univ of New Orleans	LA	12,840	C
Univ of N Car at Greensboro	NC	15,998	C
Univ of North Georgia	GA	17,316	C
Univ of Rio Grande & Rio Grande Community College	OH	8,750	LC
Univ of St. Francis	IL	40,828	C
Univ of the Cumberlands	KY	32,000	LC
Univ of Wisc-Eau Claire	WI	16,354	VC
Walsh Univ	OH	39,010	C
Washington State Univ	WA	22,747	C
Washington Univ in St. Louis	MO	67,539	MC
Waynesburg Univ	PA	33,530	C
Wellesley College	MA	66,984	MC
West Texas A&M Univ	TX	13,478	C
Western Carolina Univ	NC	13,965	C
Wilmington College	OH	35,100	C
Wilson College	PA	35,620	LC
Wingate Univ	NC	41,900	C
Winona State Univ	MN	18,109	C
Youngstown State Univ	OH	17,487	C

PRINTING MANAGEMENT

School	ST	$IS	SR
Ferris State Univ	MI	21,458	C

PRINTING TECHNOLOGY

School	ST	$IS	SR
Pennsylvania College of Technology	PA	27,693	NC
Rochester Inst of Technology	NY	52,734	HC+

PRINTMAKING

School	ST	$IS	SR
Adams State Univ	CO	15,420	LC
Aquinas College - Mich	MI	38,876	VC
Arcadia Univ	PA	55,990	C+
Art Academy of Cincinnati	OH	37,790	SP
Bennington College	VT	66,280	MC
Biola Univ	CA	48,686	C
Boston Univ	MA	67,352	MC
Calif College of the Arts	CA	52,758	SP
Cal State, San Bernardino	CA	20,106	C
Cleveland Inst of Art	OH	51,455	SP
College for Creative Studies	MI	51,210	SP
Columbia College - Missouri	MO	28,179	C
Drake Univ	IA	49,220	HC
Escuela de Artes Plasticas de PR	PR	11,236	
Houghton College	NY	40,558	VC
Howard Univ	DC	37,616	C+
Indiana Univ-Purdue Univ Fort Wayne	IN	18,675	C
Indiana Wesleyan Univ	IN	33,674	C
Kansas City Art Inst	MO	48,200	SP
Kutztown Univ of Pennsylvania	PA	19,477	C
Maine College of Art	ME	45,940	SP
Maryland Inst College of Art	MD	58,740	SP
Mass College of Art and Design	MA	24,800	SP
Milwaukee Inst of Art & Design	WI	45,880	SP
Minneapolis College of Art and Design	MN	44,218	SP
Montserrat College of Art	MA	41,500	SP
Ohio Univ	OH	23,394	VC
Old Dominion Univ	VA	21,618	C
Pacific Northwest College of Art	OR	38,494	SP
Rhode Island School of Design	RI	59,960	SP
San Francisco Art Inst	CA	60,865	SP
Savannah College of Art and Design	GA	49,595	SP
School of the Art Inst of Chicago	IL	61,830	SP
St. Ambrose Univ	IA	40,180	C
SUNY at Binghamton	NY	24,100	MC
SUNY/Buffalo State	NY	20,583	LC
Syracuse Univ	NY	62,313	HC
Temple Univ	PA	24,392	C+
Texas A&M Univ at Commerce	TX	10,496	C
Texas Christian Univ	TX	57,120	HC
Univ of Dallas	TX	50,676	VC
Univ of Hartford	CT	49,776	C
Univ of Iowa	IA	19,415	HC
Univ of Kansas	KS	20,884	VC
Univ of Maine at Machias	ME	22,960	C
Univ of Miami	FL	63,494	MC
Univ of Mich/Ann Arbor	MI	25,274	MC
Univ of N Car at Greensboro	NC	15,998	C
Univ of Oregon	OR	24,021	VC
Univ of the Arts	PA	56,579	SP
Washington Univ in St. Louis	MO	67,539	MC
Webster Univ	MO	37,490	C
Youngstown State Univ	OH	17,487	C

PRODUCT DESIGN

School	ST	$IS	SR
Keene State College	NH	24,604	C
Stanford Univ	CA	62,541	MC

PRODUCT DESIGN ENGINEERING TECHNOLOGY

School	ST	$IS	SR
Ferris State Univ	MI	21,458	C
Univ of Minn/Twin Cities	MN	24,269	MC
Western Mich Univ	MI	21,791	C

PRODUCTION AND OPERATIONS MANAGEMENT

School	ST	$IS	SR
San Diego State Univ	CA	23,156	VC

PROFESSIONAL GOLF MANAGEMENT

School	ST	$IS	SR
Ferris State Univ	MI	21,458	C
Univ of Central Okla	OK	15,150	C
Univ of Idaho	ID	16,158	C

PROFESSIONAL PROGRAM IN ACCOUNTING

School	ST	$IS	SR
Black Hills State Univ	SD	16,622	C
Bloomfield College	NJ	40,100	LC

PROFESSIONAL STUDIES

School	ST	$IS	SR
Austin Peay State Univ	TN	16,397	C
College of Charleston	SC	24,046	VC
Le Moyne College	NY	47,305	VC
Lewis Univ	IL	41,710	C
Old Dominion Univ	VA	21,618	C
Providence College	RI	62,870	HC
Shippensburg Univ of Pennsylvania	PA	24,096	C
Univ of Okla	OK	19,651	HC

PROFESSIONAL TENNIS MANAGEMENT

School	ST	$IS	SR
Carroll Univ	WI	38,100	C+
Ferris State Univ	MI	21,458	C

PROJECT MANAGEMENT

School	ST	$IS	SR
Ashford Univ	CA	10,480	C
Bryant Univ	RI	57,204	VC
Embry-Riddle Aeronautical Univ - Worldwide	FL	17,720	C
Wingate Univ	NC	41,900	C

PROPERTY MANAGEMENT

School	ST	$IS	SR
New York Univ	NY	68,139	MC
Univ of Wisc-Stout	WI	19,667	C

PSYCHOBIOLOGY

School	ST	$IS	SR
Albright College	PA	57,326	C
Arcadia Univ	PA	55,990	C+
Centre College	KY	50,680	MC
Florida Atlantic Univ	FL	18,256	C
Hamilton College	NY	64,250	MC
Houghton College	NY	40,558	VC
La Sierra Univ	CA	39,690	VC
Lebanon Valley College	PA	55,510	VC
Lindsey Wilson College	KY	33,546	C

School	ST	$IS	SR
Quinnipiac Univ	CT	60,970	VC
Ripon College	WI	49,991	VC
Simmons College	MA	54,400	HC
St. John's College at Annapolis	MD	63,348	MC
SUNY at Binghamton	NY	24,100	MC
Swarthmore College	PA	63,550	MC
Univ of Calif at Los Angeles	CA	27,438	HC+
Utica College	NY	31,510	C
Wellesley College	MA	66,984	MC
Wilson College	PA	35,620	LC

PSYCHOLOGY

School	ST	$IS	SR
Abilene Christian Univ	TX	43,708	C+
Adams State Univ	CO	15,420	LC
Adelphi Univ	NY	49,792	C
Adrian College	MI	45,550	C
Agnes Scott College	GA	51,930	VC+
Alabama A&M Univ	AL	18,796	C
Alabama State Univ	AL	16,490	LC
Alaska Pacific Univ	AK	28,730	VC
Albany State Univ	GA	19,462	C
Albertus Magnus College	CT	44,016	LC
Albion College	MI	55,260	C
Albright College	PA	57,326	C
Alcorn State Univ	MS	15,884	C
Alderson Broaddus Univ	WV	35,000	LC
Alfred Univ	NY	37,490	C
Allegheny College	PA	57,620	VC
Alma College	MI	49,410	VC
Alvernia Univ	PA	45,330	C
Alverno College	WI	33,294	LC
American International College	MA	47,020	LC
American Jewish Univ - College of A&S	CA	44,234	C
Amherst College	MA	66,186	MC
Anderson Univ	IN	39,450	C
Andrews Univ	MI	41,732	C
Angelo State Univ	TX	15,882	LC
Anna Maria College	MA	51,020	C
Appalachian State Univ	NC	15,394	VC
Aquinas College	TN	30,800	C+
Aquinas College - Mich	MI	38,876	VC
Arcadia Univ	PA	55,990	C+
Arizona State Univ at the Polytechnic Campus	AZ	22,394	VC
Arizona State Univ at the Tempe Campus	AZ	23,001	VC
Arizona State Univ at the West Campus	AZ	21,513	VC
Arkansas State Univ	AR	16,190	C
Arkansas Tech Univ	AR	16,534	LC
Armstrong State Univ	GA	15,615	C
Asbury Univ	KY	36,450	C+
Ashford Univ	CA	10,480	C
Ashland Univ	OH	30,446	C
Assumption College	MA	48,455	VC
Atlantic Union College	MA	27,228	C
Auburn Univ	AL	24,300	VC+
Auburn Univ at Montgomery	AL	15,000	C
Augsburg Univ	MN	45,129	C
Augusta Univ	GA	4,632	C
Augustana College	IL	51,222	VC+
Augustana Univ	SD	39,968	VC
Aurora Univ	IL	34,990	C
Austin College	TX	51,059	HC
Austin Peay State Univ	TN	16,397	C
Averett Univ	VA	43,034	LC
Avila Univ	MO	27,100	C
Azusa Pacific Univ	CA	43,972	C
Baker Univ	KS	37,190	C
Baldwin Wallace Univ	OH	42,464	VC
Ball State Univ	IN	19,808	C+
Bard College	NY	65,924	HC
Bard College at Simon's Rock	MA	65,795	MC
Barnard College/Columbia Univ	NY	68,762	MC
Barry Univ	FL	38,730	LC
Barton College	NC	39,854	C
Bates College	ME	64,500	HC
Bay Path Univ	MA	46,356	C
Bayamon Central Univ	PR	12,490	
Baylor Univ	TX	56,803	HC
Becker College	MA	30,100	LC
Belhaven Univ	MS	32,250	C
Bellarmine Univ	KY	52,532	C
Bellevue Univ	NE	20,300	NC
Belmont Abbey College	NC	28,794	C
Belmont Univ	TN	44,500	VC+
Beloit College	WI	55,206	HC
Bemidji State Univ	MN	17,730	C
Benedictine College	KS	38,850	VC
Benedictine Univ	IL	38,300	C
Bennett College	NC	27,717	NC
Bennington College	VT	66,280	MC
Berea College	KY	7,094	C
Berry College	GA	47,466	VC
Bethany College	KS	38,637	LC
Bethany College	WV	38,774	LC
Bethel College	IN	36,830	C
Bethel College	KS	35,370	C
Bethel Univ	MN	46,550	C+
Bethel Univ	TN	27,142	C
Bethune-Cookman Univ	FL	23,322	C
Biola Univ	CA	48,686	C
Birmingham-Southern College	AL	44,478	C+
Black Hills State Univ	SD	16,622	C
Blackburn College	IL	28,526	LC
Bloomfield College	NJ	40,100	LC
Bloomsburg Univ of Pennsylvania	PA	19,930	C
Blue Mountain College	MS	15,949	C
Bluefield College	VA	34,711	C
Bluffton Univ	OH	40,950	C+
Boise State Univ	ID	17,368	C
Boston College	MA	68,043	MC
Boston Univ	MA	67,352	MC
Bowdoin College	ME	65,980	MC
Bowie State Univ	MD	18,610	LC
Bowling Green State Univ	OH	19,975	C
Bradley Univ	IL	43,240	VC
Brandeis Univ	MA	68,443	MC
Brenau Univ - Women's College	GA	37,876	LC
Brescia Univ	KY	29,890	VC
Brewton-Parker College	GA	26,120	LC
Briar Cliff Univ	IA	36,956	C
Bridgewater College	VA	46,260	C
Bridgewater State Univ	MA	22,762	C
Brigham Young Univ	UT	13,248	MC
Brigham Young Univ/Hawaii	HI	11,710	C
Brown Univ	RI	64,566	MC
Bryan College	TN	32,900	C
Bryant Univ	RI	57,204	VC
Bryn Athyn College	PA	32,664	C
Bryn Mawr College	PA	65,220	MC
Bucknell Univ	PA	67,136	MC
Buena Vista Univ	IA	42,344	C
Butler Univ	IN	52,890	VC+
Cabrini Univ	PA	42,591	LC
Cairn Univ	PA	37,572	C
Caldwell Univ	NJ	42,165	LC
Calif Baptist Univ	CA	42,986	C
Calif Lutheran Univ	CA	52,853	C
Calif Polytechnic State Univ	CA	22,547	MC
Calif State Polytechnic Univ, Pomona	CA	21,811	C
Cal State, Bakersfield	CA	22,397	LC
Cal State, Chico	CA	19,790	VC
Cal State, Dominguez Hills	CA	19,022	LC
Cal State, East Bay	CA	20,748	C
Cal State, Fresno	CA	16,902	LC
Cal State, Fullerton	CA	21,902	C
Cal State, Long Beach	CA	18,850	C
Cal State, Los Angeles	CA	17,186	LC
Cal State, Monterey Bay	CA	22,872	LC
Cal State, Northridge	CA	17,277	LC
Cal State, Sacramento	CA	19,060	C
Cal State, San Bernardino	CA	20,106	C
Cal State, San Marcos	CA	20,604	LC
Cal State, Stanislaus	CA	18,053	LC
Calif Univ of Pennsylvania	PA	20,425	LC
Calumet College of St. Joseph	IN	22,735	C
Calvin College	MI	43,090	HC
Cambridge College	MA	14,940	NC
Cameron Univ	OK	11,632	LC
Campbell Univ	NC	37,570	VC
Campbellsville Univ	KY	33,400	C
Canisius College	NY	49,672	C
Capital Univ	OH	44,778	VC
Cardinal Stritch Univ	WI	37,136	C
Carleton College	MN	66,414	MC
Carlos Albizu Univ	FL	13,036	LC
Carlow Univ	PA	39,696	LC
Carnegie Mellon Univ	PA	67,980	MC
Carroll College	MT	44,304	C
Carroll Univ	WI	38,100	C+
Carson-Newman Univ	TN	35,900	C
Carthage College	WI	48,835	C
Case Western Reserve Univ	OH	62,284	MC
Castleton Univ	VT	20,186	C
Catawba College	NC	39,820	LC
Cazenovia College	NY	47,866	C
Cedar Crest College	PA	51,110	C
Cedarville Univ	OH	36,244	VC
Centenary College	NJ	43,890	LC
Centenary College of Louisiana	LA	49,050	C+
Central College	IA	44,592	C
Central Conn State Univ	CT	22,041	C
Central Methodist Univ	MO	31,500	VC
Central Mich Univ	MI	20,330	C
Central State Univ	OH	18,564	C
Central Washington Univ	WA	16,803	C
Centre College	KY	50,680	MC
Chadron State College	NE	14,819	LC
Chaminade Univ of Honolulu	HI	37,614	C
Champlain College	VT	54,724	VC
Chapman Univ	CA	65,504	HC
Charleston Southern Univ	SC	34,700	C
Charter Oak State College	CT	7,983	NC
Chatham Univ	PA	47,883	VC
Chestnut Hill College	PA	47,180	C
Cheyney Univ of Pennsylvania	PA	20,896	LC
Chicago State Univ	IL	41,620	C
Christian Brothers Univ	TN	31,670	VC
Christopher Newport Univ	VA	24,878	VC+
CUNY/Baruch College	NY	21,609	HC
CUNY/Brooklyn College	NY	7,163	C+
CUNY/City College	NY	20,204	C
CUNY/Hunter College	NY	31,098	VC
CUNY/John Jay College of Criminal Justice	NY	6,359	SP
CUNY/Lehman College	NY	5,788	LC
CUNY/Medgar Evers College	NY	6,680	NC
CUNY/Queens College	NY	21,507	C
CUNY/York College	NY	6,747	LC
Claremont McKenna College	CA	69,900	MC
Clarion Univ of Pennsylvania	PA	21,608	LC
Clark Atlanta Univ	GA	31,019	LC
Clark Univ	MA	53,260	HC+
Clarke Univ	IA	42,950	C
Clarkson Univ	NY	60,392	VC
Clayton State Univ	GA	19,735	LC
Clemson Univ	SC		HC
Cleveland State Univ	OH	22,290	C
Coastal Carolina Univ	SC	20,340	C
Coe College	IA	51,570	VC
Coker College	SC	38,196	C
Colby College	ME	64,060	MC
Colby-Sawyer College	NH	50,790	C
Colgate Univ	NY	67,500	MC
College of Charleston	SC	24,046	VC
College of Mount St. Vincent	NY	45,620	C
College of St. Benedict	MN	54,480	C
College of St. Elizabeth	NJ	45,700	LC
College of St. Mary	NE	27,500	C
College of St Joseph	VT	32,400	LC
College of St. Scholastica	MN	45,734	C+
College of Staten Island	NY	24,389	LC
College of the Holy Cross	MA	64,320	MC
College of the Ozarks	MO	7,530	VC
College of William & Mary	VA	34,907	MC
Colo Christian Univ	CO	40,885	VC
Colo College	CO	64,894	MC
Colo Mesa Univ	CO	19,707	LC
Colo State Univ	CO	23,033	C
Colo State Univ-Pueblo	CO	21,581	C
Columbia College	SC	36,550	C
Columbia College - Missouri	MO	28,179	C
Columbia Univ/ School of General Studies	NY	61,470	MC
Columbia Univ/City of New York	NY	62,958	MC
Columbus State Univ	GA	14,336	LC
Concord Univ	WV	14,954	LC
Concordia College - Moorhead	MN	46,418	C
Concordia College - New York	NY	39,035	LC
Concordia Univ	OR	35,000	C
Concordia Univ Irvine	CA	44,860	VC
Concordia Univ Nebr	NE	41,900	VC
Concordia Univ St. Paul	MN	29,050	C
Concordia Univ Wisc	WI	35,910	C
Concordia Univ, Ann Arbor	MI	38,878	C+
Concordia Univ, Chicago	IL	41,522	C
Conn College	CT	65,000	MC
Converse College	SC	28,290	C
Coppin State Univ	MD	14,071	VC
Corban Univ	OR	41,700	C
Cornell College	IA	49,900	VC
Cornell Univ	NY	67,591	MC
Cornerstone Univ	MI	36,550	C
Covenant College	GA	44,590	HC
Creighton Univ	NE	49,452	VC
Culver-Stockton College	MO	34,350	C
Cumberland Univ	TN	27,710	C
Curry College	MA	53,331	C
Daemen College	NY	40,336	C
Dakota Wesleyan Univ	SD	33,980	LC
Dallas Baptist Univ	TX	35,220	VC
Dartmouth College	NH	68,109	MC
Davidson College	NC	60,119	MC
Davis & Elkins College	WV	38,242	LC
Defiance College	OH	42,240	LC
Delaware State Univ	DE	19,376	LC
Delta State Univ	MS	13,176	LC
Denison Univ	OH	62,770	HC+
DePaul Univ	IL	52,807	VC
DePauw Univ	IN	58,688	VC
DeSales Univ	PA	47,520	C
Dickinson College	PA	66,166	MC
Dillard Univ	LA	20,940	VC
Doane Univ	NE	41,340	VC
Dominican College	NY	40,258	LC
Dominican Univ	IL	42,472	C+
Dominican Univ of Calif	CA	58,750	C
Dordt College	IA	37,860	C+
Drake Univ	IA	49,220	HC
Drew Univ/College of Liberal Arts	NJ	53,608	VC
Drexel Univ	PA	65,927	HC
Drury Univ	MO	37,555	VC
Duke Univ	NC	68,298	MC
Duquesne Univ	PA	48,508	VC
D'Youville College	NY	37,678	C
Earlham College	IN	55,670	HC
East Carolina Univ	NC	16,539	C
East Central Univ	OK	13,330	C
East Stroudsburg Univ	PA	18,578	LC
East Tenn State Univ	TN	18,141	C
East Texas Baptist Univ	TX	34,444	C
Eastern Conn State Univ	CT	23,059	C
Eastern Illinois Univ	IL	21,414	C
Eastern Kentucky Univ	KY	17,742	C
Eastern Mennonite Univ	VA	42,550	C
Eastern Mich Univ	MI	19,761	C
Eastern Nazarene College	MA	41,114	C
Eastern New Mexico Univ	NM	12,874	LC
Eastern Oregon Univ	OR	17,612	C
Eastern Univ	PA	39,540	C
Eastern Washington Univ	WA	17,896	LC
Eckerd College	FL	55,206	VC
Edgewood College	WI	35,950	C
Edinboro Univ	PA	15,940	LC
Edward Waters College	FL	28,089	NC
Elizabeth City State Univ	NC	14,745	C
Elizabethtown College	PA	56,340	VC
Elmhurst College	IL	46,514	C
Elmira College	NY	53,900	C
Elms College	MA	49,602	VC
Elon Univ	NC	46,142	HC
Emmanuel College	MA	53,472	C+
Emory and Henry College	VA	46,320	C
Emory Univ	GA	63,286	MC
Emporia State Univ	KS	15,029	C
Endicott College	MA	47,054	C+
Erskine College	SC	45,460	C
Eugene Lang College of Liberal Arts	NY	64,940	VC
Eureka College	IL	34,760	C
Evangel Univ	MO	28,898	C
Excelsior College	NY	38,800	SP
Fairfield Univ	CT	61,445	HC
Fairleigh Dickinson Univ/ College at Florham	NJ	54,770	C
Fairleigh Dickinson Univ/ Metropolitan Campus	NJ	52,392	C
Fairmont State Univ	WV	15,726	C
Fayetteville State Univ	NC	17,756	C
Felician Univ	NJ	46,280	LC
Ferris State Univ	MI	21,458	C
Ferrum College	VA	43,970	C
Fisk Univ	TN	32,066	LC
Fitchburg State Univ	MA	21,819	LC
Flagler College	FL	27,620	C
Florida A&M Univ	FL	15,361	C
Florida Atlantic Univ	FL	18,256	C
Florida Gulf Coast Univ	FL	14,738	C
Florida Inst of Technology	FL	53,306	VC
Florida International Univ	FL	20,281	C
Florida Memorial Univ	FL	22,424	LC
Florida Southern College	FL	45,978	VC
Florida State Univ	FL	16,771	HC
Fontbonne Univ	MO	34,606	C
Fordham Univ	NY	68,431	MC
Fort Hays State Univ	KS	12,677	C
Fort Lewis College	CO	20,154	C
Fort Valley State Univ	GA	17,988	VC
Framingham State Univ	MA	21,740	C
Francis Marion Univ	SC	18,144	LC
Franciscan Univ of Steubenville	OH	33,980	VC
Franklin and Marshall College	PA	67,960	MC
Franklin College	IN	40,550	C
Franklin Pierce Univ	NH	46,750	LC
Freed-Hardeman Univ	TN	29,900	C
Fresno Pacific Univ	CA	38,858	C
Friends Univ	KS	38,000	C
Frostburg State Univ	MD	17,280	LC
Furman Univ	SC	61,098	VC+
Gallaudet Univ	DC	30,088	LC
Gannon Univ	PA	42,922	C
Gardner-Webb Univ	NC	24,935	C+
Geneva College	PA	35,450	C
George Fox Univ	OR	42,938	C
George Mason Univ	VA	19,884	C
Georgetown College	KY	41,440	C
Georgetown Univ	DC	68,970	MC
Georgia College & State Univ	GA	21,884	C+
Georgia Inst of Technology	GA	23,910	MC
Georgia Southwestern State Univ	GA	13,870	LC
Georgia State Univ	GA	25,250	C
Georgian Court Univ	NJ	43,068	LC
Gettysburg College	PA	65,210	MC
Glenville State College	WV	17,386	LC
Goddard College	VT	17,040	VC
Goldey-Beacom College	DE	36,038	C
Gonzaga Univ	WA	52,880	HC
Gordon College	MA	47,740	VC
Goshen College	IN	44,350	C
Goucher College	MD	56,110	VC
Grace College and Seminary	IN	31,524	C
Graceland Univ	IA	35,290	C
Grambling State Univ	LA	15,701	C
Grand Canyon Univ	AZ	25,150	VC
Grand Valley State Univ	MI	22,250	C+
Grand View Univ	IA	32,302	C
Green Mountain College	VT	45,228	LC
Greensboro College	NC	39,790	LC
Greenville College	IL	27,012	LC
Grinnell College	IA	63,114	MC
Grove City College	PA	26,654	VC
Guilford College	NC	45,973	C
Gustavus Adolphus College	MN	53,943	HC
Gwynedd Mercy Univ	PA	43,780	LC
Hamilton College	NY	64,250	MC
Hamline Univ	MN	50,152	C
Hampden-Sydney College	VA	57,806	VC
Hampshire College	MA	65,214	MC
Hampton Univ	VA	36,410	C
Hannibal-LaGrange Univ	MO	29,815	C
Hanover College	IN	47,750	C+
Harding Univ	AR	25,440	C
Hardin-Simmons Univ	TX	36,025	C
Hartwick College	NY	51,270	C
Harvard College/Harvard Univ	MA	65,609	MC
Hastings College	NE	35,380	C+

ST = STATE $IS = IN-STATE COSTS SR = SELECTOR RATING

School	ST	$IS	SR
Haverford College	PA	66,490	MC
Hawaii Pacific Univ	HI	33,420	C
Heidelberg Univ	OH	40,400	LC
Henderson State Univ	AR	15,516	C
Hendrix College	AR	54,020	VC
Heritage Univ	WA	19,825	NC
High Point Univ	NC	47,355	VC
Hilbert College	NY	32,650	LC
Hillsdale College	MI	37,170	MC
Hiram College	OH	44,590	C
Hobart and William Smith Colleges	NY	67,050	HC+
Hofstra Univ	NY	58,210	C+
Hollins Univ	VA	49,635	VC
Holy Family Univ	PA	44,672	LC
Holy Names Univ	CA	46,630	LC
Hood College	MD	50,540	C
Hope College	MI	42,840	VC
Hope International Univ	CA	42,730	C
Houghton College	NY	40,558	VC
Houston Baptist Univ	TX	36,450	C
Howard Payne Univ	TX	35,994	C
Howard Univ	DC	37,616	C+
Humboldt State Univ	CA	21,708	C
Huntingdon College	AL	35,900	C
Huntington Univ	IN	33,996	C
Husson Univ	ME	26,508	C
Huston-Tillotson Univ	TX	18,124	LC
Idaho State Univ	ID	13,619	LC
Illinois College	IL	41,330	VC
Illinois Inst of Technology	IL	56,826	HC+
Illinois State Univ	IL	23,418	VC
Illinois Wesleyan Univ	IL	56,430	VC+
Immaculata Univ	PA	39,000	C
Indiana Inst of Technology	IN	34,240	LC
Indiana State Univ	IN	23,223	LC
Indiana Univ Bloomington	IN	20,791	HC
Indiana Univ East	IN	7,207	C
Indiana Univ Kokomo	IN	7,207	C
Indiana Univ Northwest	IN	7,207	LC
Indiana Univ of Pennsylvania	PA	24,474	C
Indiana Univ South Bend	IN	16,057	C
Indiana Univ Southeast	IN	16,931	C
Indiana Univ-Purdue Univ Fort Wayne	IN	18,675	C
Indiana Univ-Purdue Univ Indianapolis	IN	18,952	C
Indiana Wesleyan Univ	IN	33,674	C
Inter-American Univ of PR Ponce	PR	19,549	
Inter-American Univ of PR-Aguadilla Campus	PR	21,657	
Inter-American Univ of PR-Fajardo Campus	PR	18,336	
Inter-American Univ of PR-Metropolitan Campus	PR	20,045	
Inter-American Univ of PR-San Germán	PR	20,042	
Iona College	NY	52,514	C
Iowa State Univ	IA	18,176	C
Iowa Wesleyan Univ	IA	41,000	C
Ithaca College	NY	58,158	VC+
Jackson State Univ	MS	15,879	LC
Jacksonville State Univ	AL	14,628	LC
Jacksonville Univ	FL	49,210	C
James Madison Univ	VA	19,084	VC
Jefferson (Philadelphia Univ + Thomas Jefferson Univ)	PA	53,966	C
John Brown Univ	AR	35,184	VC
John Carroll Univ	OH	51,570	C
Johns Hopkins Univ	MD	68,080	MC
Johnson & Wales Univ/ Denver Campus	CO	44,768	C
Johnson C. Smith Univ	NC	25,336	LC
Johnson State College	VT	22,672	C
Judson College	AL	27,066	C
Judson Univ	IL	39,174	C
Juniata College	PA	58,118	VC
Kalamazoo College	MI	53,931	HC
Kansas State Univ	KS	17,780	VC
Kansas Wesleyan Univ	KS	37,930	C
Kean Univ	NJ	25,620	C
Keene State College	NH	24,604	C
Kennesaw State Univ	GA	18,899	VC
Kent State Univ	OH	20,928	C
Kentucky State Univ	KY	14,484	LC
Kentucky Wesleyan College	KY	34,260	LC
Kenyon College	OH	65,840	MC
Keuka College	NY	42,398	C
Keystone College	PA	28,680	LC
King Univ	TN	36,976	C
King's College	PA	48,240	C
Knox College	IL	54,654	VC+
Kutztown Univ of Pennsylvania	PA	19,477	C
La Roche College	PA	38,940	C
La Salle Univ	PA	43,476	C
La Sierra Univ	CA	39,690	VC
Lafayette College	PA	68,520	MC
LaGrange College	GA	41,310	C
Lake Erie College	OH	38,914	LC
Lake Forest College	IL	50,652	VC
Lake Superior State Univ	MI	19,867	C
Lakeland Univ	WI	35,130	C
Lamar Univ	TX	18,014	LC
Lander Univ	SC	32,200	C
Langston Univ	OK	15,659	C
Lasell College	MA	49,400	C
Lawrence Tech Univ	MI	41,630	VC
Lawrence Univ	WI	56,133	HC+
Le Moyne College	NY	47,305	VC
Lebanon Valley College	PA	55,510	VC
Lee Univ	TN	22,045	C
Lees-McRae College	NC	33,944	NC
Lehigh Univ	PA	63,860	MC
Lenoir-Rhyne Univ	NC	47,500	LC
Lesley Univ	MA	42,800	C
LeTourneau Univ	TX	39,190	VC
Lewis & Clark College	OR	60,984	MC
Lewis Univ	IL	41,710	C
Lewis-Clark State College	ID	14,202	C
Liberty Univ	VA	31,415	C
Limestone College	SC	32,100	C
Lincoln Memorial Univ	TN	28,430	C
Lincoln Univ	MO	14,402	NC
Lincoln Univ	PA	20,878	LC
Lindenwood Univ	MO	25,760	C
Lindsey Wilson College	KY	33,546	C
Linfield College	OR	53,992	C
Lipscomb Univ	TN	42,984	VC
LIU Brooklyn	NY	50,698	C
LIU Post	NY	50,698	C+
Livingstone College	NC	17,815	LC
Lock Haven Univ of Pennsylvania	PA	20,544	LC
Longwood Univ	VA	22,184	C
Loras College	IA	40,726	C
Louisiana College	LA	21,274	C
Louisiana State Univ and A&M College	LA	18,677	VC
Louisiana State Univ in Shreveport	LA	6,902	C
Louisiana Tech Univ	LA	11,422	VC
Lourdes Univ	OH	29,140	NC
Loyola Marymount Univ	CA	60,202	VC+
Loyola Univ Chicago	IL	57,158	VC
Loyola Univ Maryland	MD	61,710	VC
Loyola Univ New Orleans	LA	52,456	VC
Lubbock Christian Univ	TX	29,727	C
Luther College	IA	49,990	VC
Lycoming College	PA	50,895	C
Lyndon State College	VT	20,714	C
Lynn Univ	FL	49,680	LC
Lyon College	AR	36,120	VC
Macalester College	MN	64,136	MC
MacMurray College	IL	35,025	C
Madonna Univ	MI	30,450	LC
Malone Univ	OH	39,200	C
Manchester Univ	IN	41,540	C
Manhattan College	NY	55,652	C
Manhattanville College	NY	52,430	C
Mansfield Univ of Pennsylvania	PA	24,244	LC
Marian Univ	IN	43,206	C
Marian Univ	WI	34,622	C
Marietta College	OH	46,190	C
Marist College	NY	49,860	VC
Marlboro College	VT	50,832	VC+
Marquette Univ	WI	53,090	VC+
Mars Hill Univ	NC	41,104	C
Marshall Univ	WV	18,044	C
Martin Univ	IN	21,010	LC
Mary Baldwin Univ	VA	40,495	C
Marygrove College	MI	30,100	LC
Marylhurst Univ	OR	16,818	NC
Marymount Manhattan College	NY	48,350	C
Marymount Univ	VA	43,231	C
Maryville College	TN	44,410	C
Maryville Univ of St. Louis	MO	38,558	VC
Marywood Univ	PA	47,840	C
Mass College of Liberal Arts	MA	20,659	C
Mayville State Univ	ND	18,371	NC
McDaniel College	MD	52,910	VC
McKendree Univ	IL	37,940	C+
McMurry Univ	TX	34,259	LC
McNeese State Univ	LA	7,838	C
McPherson College	KS	36,134	C
Medaille College	NY	41,700	LC
Menlo College	CA	51,380	LC
Mercer Univ	GA	45,348	VC
Mercy College	NY	32,614	C
Mercyhurst Univ	PA	47,420	C
Meredith College	NC	46,634	C
Merrimack College	MA	55,415	C
Messiah College	PA	44,380	VC
Methodist Univ	NC	58,130	C
Metropolitan State Univ	MN	7,859	C
Metropolitan State Univ of Denver	CO	6,928	LC
Miami Univ	OH	27,190	HC+
Mich State Univ	MI	24,542	VC
Mich Tech Univ	MI	25,551	VC+
MidAmerica Nazarene Univ	KS	37,808	C
Middle Tenn State Univ	TN	8,650	C
Middlebury College	VT	67,464	MC
Midland Univ	NE	39,512	C
Midway Univ	KY	33,940	LC
Midwestern State Univ	TX	12,111	LC
Millersville Univ of Pennsylvania	PA	25,298	C
Milligan College	TN	39,450	C
Millikin Univ	IL	44,148	C
Mills College	CA	43,705	C
Millsaps College	MS	50,080	C+
Minn State Univ, Mankato	MN	17,190	C
Minn State Univ, Moorhead	MN	21,393	C
Minot State Univ	ND	13,285	C
Misericordia Univ	PA	45,210	C
Miss College	MS	25,850	C
Miss State Univ	MS	12,028	C+
Miss Univ for Women	MS	17,065	C
Missouri Baptist Univ	MO	35,594	C
Missouri Southern State Univ	MO	13,071	C
Missouri Univ of Science and Technology	MO	18,655	HC
Missouri Valley College	MO	28,150	C
Missouri Western State Univ	MO	17,822	LC
Mitchell College	CT	45,192	C
Molloy College	NY	40,440	C
Monmouth College	IL	42,260	C
Monmouth Univ	NJ	50,184	C
Montana State Univ	MT	15,500	C+
Montana State Univ Billings	MT	13,336	LC
Montclair State Univ	NJ	26,912	C
Montreat College	NC	34,605	LC
Moravian College	PA	55,488	C
Morehead State Univ	KY	18,386	LC
Morehouse College	GA	40,835	C
Morgan State Univ	MD	17,190	LC
Morningside College	IA	39,780	C
Mount Aloysius College	PA	29,976	C
Mount Holyoke College	MA	56,746	MC
Mount Mary Univ	WI	34,650	LC
Mount Mercy Univ	IA	39,748	C
Mount St. Mary College	NY	44,448	C
Mount St. Joseph Univ	OH	33,880	LC
Mount St. Mary's Univ	MD	53,380	C
Mount St. Mary's Univ - Chalon Campus	CA	50,486	VC+
Mount Vernon Nazarene Univ	OH	35,944	C
Muhlenberg College	PA	56,645	VC
Murray State Univ	KY	17,726	C+
Muskingum Univ	OH	35,966	C
Naropa Univ	CO	43,278	NC
National Louis Univ	IL	43,000	LC
National Univ	CA	17,849	LC
Nazareth College	NY	46,784	C
Nebr Wesleyan Univ	NE	42,026	C+
Neumann Univ	PA	40,678	LC
New College of Florida	FL	16,180	HC+
New England College	NH	50,828	NC
New Jersey City Univ	NJ	21,456	LC
New Mexico Highlands Univ	NM	11,904	LC
New Mexico Inst of Mining and Technology	NM	15,385	HC+
New Mexico State Univ	NM	14,050	LC
New York Inst of Technology	NY	49,980	VC
New York Univ	NY	68,139	MC
Newberry College	SC	34,550	C
Newbury College	MA	48,970	C
Newman Univ	KS	37,382	C
Niagara Univ	NY	41,010	C
Nicholls State Univ	LA	14,959	C
Nichols College	MA	46,900	LC
Norfolk State Univ	VA	18,902	LC
N Car A&T State Univ	NC	13,786	C
N Car Central Univ	NC	9,000	C
N Car State Univ	NC	22,434	HC+
N Car Wesleyan College	NC	39,200	C
North Central College	IL	48,712	C+
North Central Univ	MN	30,610	C
N Dak State Univ	ND	16,245	VC
North Greenville Univ	SC	25,930	C
North Park Univ	IL	35,860	C
Northeastern Illinois Univ	IL	12,529	LC
Northeastern Univ	MA	65,352	MC
Northern Arizona Univ	AZ	21,003	C
Northern Illinois Univ	IL	20,176	C
Northern Kentucky Univ	KY	16,486	C
Northern Mich Univ	MI	20,853	C
Northern State Univ	SD	15,570	C
Northland College	WI	41,103	C+
Northwest Christian Univ	OR	36,580	C
Northwest Missouri State Univ	MO	18,286	C
Northwest Nazarene Univ	ID	40,250	C
Northwest Univ	WA	38,720	VC
Northwestern College of Iowa	IA	38,400	C
Northwestern Okla State Univ	OK	13,072	LC
Northwestern State Univ of Louisiana	LA	16,534	LC
Northwestern Univ	IL	68,725	MC
Norwich Univ	VT	56,234	C
Notre Dame College	OH	39,150	VC
Notre Dame de Namur Univ	CA	46,526	LC
Notre Dame of Maryland Univ	MD	47,570	VC
Nova Southeastern Univ	FL	38,534	C+
Nyack College	NY	34,450	LC
Oakland Univ	MI	20,763	C
Oakwood Univ	AL	43,758	C
Oberlin College	OH	68,942	MC
Occidental College	CA	68,660	MC
Oglethorpe Univ	GA	44,200	C
Ohio Dominican Univ	OH	41,340	C+
Ohio Northern Univ	OH	44,050	VC
Ohio State Univ at Columbus	OH	22,843	MC
Ohio State Univ at Lima	OH	7,553	C
Ohio State Univ at Mansfield	OH	15,529	C
Ohio State Univ at Marion	OH	7,553	VC
Ohio State Univ at Newark	OH	16,685	C
Ohio Univ	OH	23,394	VC
Ohio Valley Univ	WV	28,800	C
Ohio Wesleyan Univ	OH	49,460	VC
Okla Baptist Univ	OK	33,990	C
Okla Christian Univ	OK	29,260	C
Okla City Univ	OK	40,476	C
Okla Panhandle State Univ	OK	6,152	C
Okla State Univ	OK	17,180	C+
Old Dominion Univ	VA	21,618	C
Olivet College	MI	37,661	LC
Olivet Nazarene Univ	IL	41,840	VC
Oral Roberts Univ	OK	34,316	C
Oregon State Univ	OR	23,337	VC
Ottawa Univ	KS	39,980	VC
Otterbein Univ	OH	41,630	C
Ouachita Baptist Univ	AR	33,500	VC
Our Lady of the Lake Univ	TX	37,790	LC
Pace Univ	NY	60,136	C
Pacific Lutheran Univ	WA	49,960	C
Pacific Union College	CA	36,009	VC
Pacific Univ	OR	37,617	C
Paine College	GA	19,506	LC
Palm Beach Atlantic Univ	FL	39,250	C
Park Univ	MO	22,134	C
Paul Quinn College	TX	25,350	LC
Penn State Erie,The Behrend College	PA	26,688	VC
Pennsylvania State Univ - Univ Park	PA	29,716	HC
Pepperdine Univ	CA	66,862	VC+
Peru State College	NE	15,602	LC
Pfeiffer Univ	NC	40,532	LC
Philander Smith College	AR	20,814	LC
Piedmont College	GA	34,334	C
Pine Manor College	MA	41,660	LC
Pittsburg State Univ	KS	13,880	C
Pitzer College	CA	68,500	HC+
Plymouth State Univ	NH	23,180	LC
Point Loma Nazarene Univ	CA	46,150	C+
Point Park Univ	PA	41,270	C
Pomona College	CA	64,957	MC
Pontifical Catholic Univ of PR	PR	10,534	
Portland State Univ	OR	19,443	C
Post Univ	CT	41,150	C
Prairie View A&M Univ	TX	27,273	LC
Presbyterian College	SC	47,186	C
Prescott College	AZ	38,201	C
Princeton Univ	NJ	60,090	MC
Providence College	RI	62,870	HC
Purdue Univ Northwest	IN	15,178	C
Purdue Univ/West Lafayette	IN	20,032	MC
Queens Univ of Charlotte	NC	39,543	C
Quincy Univ	IL	38,170	LC
Quinnipiac Univ	CT	60,970	VC
Radford Univ	VA	19,758	C
Ramapo College of New Jersey	NJ	25,760	VC
Randolph College	VA	53,970	C
Randolph-Macon College	VA	51,480	VC
Reed College	OR	65,300	MC
Regis College	MA	51,920	LC
Regis Univ	CO	46,380	C
Rensselaer Polytechnic Inst	NY	67,265	MC
Rhode Island College	RI	19,000	LC
Rhodes College	TN	51,900	HC
Rice Univ	TX	59,458	MC
Rider Univ	NJ	54,050	C
Ripon College	WI	49,991	VC
Rivier Univ	NH	41,600	VC
Roanoke College	VA	55,952	VC
Robert Morris Univ	PA	40,600	C
Roberts Wesleyan College	NY	41,116	C
Rochester College	MI	28,574	LC
Rochester Inst of Technology	NY	52,734	HC+
Rockford Univ	IL	38,570	C
Rockhurst Univ	MO	28,990	C
Rocky Mountain College	MT	35,776	C
Roger Williams Univ	RI	48,074	VC
Rollins College	FL	58,670	HC
Roosevelt Univ	IL	41,890	VC
Rosemont College	PA	30,980	LC
Rowan Univ	NJ	24,491	VC
Russell Sage College	NY	39,370	C
Rutgers Univ - Camden	NJ	26,595	C
Rutgers Univ - New Brunswick	NJ	27,090	HC
Rutgers Univ - Newark	NJ	27,351	C
Sacred Heart Univ	CT	54,590	C
Saginaw Valley State Univ	MI	19,284	C
St. Anselm College	NH	56,636	VC
St. Augustine's Univ	NC	25,582	C
St. Francis Univ	PA	46,146	NC
St. John's Univ	MN	53,472	C
St. Joseph's College of Maine	ME	47,890	C
St. Joseph's Univ	PA	58,540	VC
St. Leo Univ	FL	32,850	C
St. Louis Univ	MO	49,866	HC
St. Martin's Univ	WA	45,056	C
St. Mary-of-the-Woods College	IN	40,424	LC
St. Mary's College	IN	50,600	C
St. Mary's College of Calif	CA	57,420	C
St. Mary's Univ of Minn	MN	42,440	C
St. Michael's College	VT	53,275	VC+
St. Peter's Univ	NJ	49,192	C
St. Vincent College	PA	46,229	C
St. Xavier Univ	IL	44,440	C
Salem College	NC	40,206	C
Salem State Univ	MA	42,650	LC
Salisbury Univ	MD	21,132	VC
Salve Regina Univ	RI	53,046	VC

ST = STATE **$IS** = IN-STATE COSTS **SR** = SELECTOR RATING

School	ST	$IS	SR
Sam Houston State Univ	TX	18,792	C
Samford Univ	AL	40,770	VC
San Diego Christian College	CA	40,914	C
San Diego State Univ	CA	23,156	VC
San Francisco State Univ	CA	18,514	LC
San Jose State Univ	CA	22,630	C
Sarah Lawrence College	NY	68,866	MC
Schreiner Univ	TX	34,626	LC
Scripps College	CA	69,260	HC
Seattle Pacific Univ	WA	47,439	C+
Seattle Univ	WA	54,957	VC
Seton Hall Univ	NJ	58,008	C
Seton Hill Univ	PA	46,972	VC
Sewanee: The Univ of the South	TN	58,000	HC+
Shaw Univ	NC	24,638	C
Shawnee State Univ	OH	16,998	C
Shenandoah Univ	VA	42,100	C
Shepherd Univ, West Virginia	WV	17,382	C
Shippensburg Univ of Pennsylvania	PA	24,096	C
Shorter Univ	GA	31,130	LC
Siena College	NY	48,916	C
Siena Heights Univ	MI	36,322	C
Silver Lake College of the Holy Family	WI	36,290	LC
Simmons College	MA	54,400	HC
Simpson College	IA	45,626	VC
Simpson Univ	CA	34,722	C
Skidmore College	NY	66,600	MC
Slippery Rock Univ of Pennsylvania	PA	20,450	C
Smith College	MA	66,774	MC
Sonoma State Univ	CA	27,020	C
S Car State Univ	SC	21,330	LC
S Dak State Univ	SD	15,874	C
Southeast Missouri State Univ	MO	16,148	C
Southeastern Louisiana Univ	LA	16,237	C
Southeastern Okla State Univ	OK	11,875	C
Southeastern Univ	FL	34,910	LC
Southern Adventist Univ	TN	28,250	C
Southern Arkansas Univ	AR	21,532	C
Southern Conn State Univ	CT	21,924	LC
Southern Illinois Univ Carbondale	IL	24,554	C
Southern Illinois Univ Edwardsville	IL	20,188	C
Southern Methodist Univ	TX	69,008	MC
Southern Nazarene Univ	OK	33,684	C
Southern New Hampshire Univ	NH	44,256	C
Southern Oregon Univ	OR	19,117	C
Southern Univ and A&M College	LA	16,074	LC
Southern Univ at New Orleans	LA	8,014	LC
Southern Vermont College	VT	34,670	LC
Southern Wesleyan Univ	SC	33,670	LC
Southwest Baptist Univ	MO	30,890	LC
Southwest Minn State Univ	MN	17,783	C
Southwestern Adventist Univ	TX	28,232	LC
Southwestern College	KS	31,531	LC
Southwestern Okla State Univ	OK	12,205	C
Southwestern Univ	TX	52,370	VC
Spalding Univ	KY	31,938	C
Spelman College	GA	41,642	C
Spring Arbor Univ	MI	37,390	C
Spring Hill College	AL	48,488	C
Springfield College	MA	48,775	C
St. Ambrose Univ	IA	40,180	C
St. Andrews Univ	NC	44,634	LC
St. Bonaventure Univ	NY	45,596	C
St. Catherine Univ	MN	45,630	C
St. Cloud State Univ	MN	10,600	C
St. Edward's Univ	TX	56,190	VC
St. Francis College	NY	38,800	LC
St. John Fisher College	NY	45,270	VC
St. John's Univ	NY	57,160	C+
St. Joseph's College, New York/Brooklyn Campus	NY	25,114	LC
St. Joseph's College, New York/Long Island Campus	NY	25,124	C
St. Lawrence Univ	NY	66,646	HC+
St. Mary's College of Maryland	MD	27,312	VC
St. Mary's Univ	TX	39,120	C
St. Norbert College	WI	46,060	VC
St. Olaf College	MN	56,430	HC
St. Thomas Aquinas College	NY	32,450	C
St. Thomas Univ	FL	51,187	LC
Stanford Univ	CA	62,541	MC
SUNY Albany	NY	22,165	C
SUNY at Binghamton	NY	24,100	MC
SUNY at Geneseo	NY	21,622	VC
SUNY at New Paltz	NY	20,840	C
SUNY at Oswego	NY	22,219	VC
SUNY at Purchase College	NY	21,832	C
SUNY Polytechnic Inst	NY	20,438	VC
SUNY/Buffalo State	NY	20,583	LC
SUNY/College at Old Westbury	NY	16,860	C
SUNY/Cortland	NY	20,910	C
SUNY/Empire State College	NY	9,145	NC
SUNY/Fredonia	NY	20,818	C
SUNY/Oneonta	NY	20,794	C
SUNY/Plattsburgh	NY	19,314	C
SUNY/Potsdam	NY	21,051	VC
SUNY/Univ at Buffalo	NY	23,122	C
Stephen F. Austin State Univ	TX	18,484	LC
Sterling College	KS	32,830	LC
Stetson Univ	FL	57,174	VC+
Stevenson Univ	MD	48,412	C
Stockton Univ	NJ	25,565	C
Stonehill College	MA	55,130	C
Stony Brook Univ/The SUNY	NY	22,703	MC
Suffolk Univ	MA	52,316	C
Sul Ross State Univ	TX	15,021	LC
Susquehanna Univ	PA	57,560	VC
Swarthmore College	PA	63,550	MC
Syracuse Univ	NY	62,313	HC
Tabor College	KS	35,870	C
Talladega College	AL	25,919	C
Tarleton State Univ	TX	15,248	LC
Taylor Univ	IN	42,130	VC
Temple Univ	PA	24,392	C+
Tenn State Univ	TN	14,423	LC
Tenn Tech Univ	TN	17,929	C
Tenn Wesleyan Univ	TN	32,680	LC
Texas A&M Univ at College Station	TX	20,771	VC+
Texas A&M Univ at Commerce	TX	10,496	C
Texas A&M Univ at Corpus Christi	TX	16,851	LC
Texas A&M Univ at Kingsville	TX	16,580	LC
Texas Christian Univ	TX	57,120	HC
Texas Lutheran Univ	TX	39,770	C
Texas Southern Univ	TX	19,592	LC
Texas State Univ	TX	18,721	C
Texas Tech Univ	TX	20,156	C+
Texas Wesleyan Univ	TX	37,338	C
Texas Woman's Univ	TX	15,302	LC
The American Univ	DC	61,317	HC
The Catholic Univ of America	DC	58,376	VC
The Citadel, The Military College of S Car	SC	20,679	C
The College at Brockport - SUNY	NY	21,058	C
The College of Idaho	ID	36,415	C
The College of New Jersey	NJ	28,675	VC+
The College of New Rochelle	NY	46,300	LC
The College of St. Rose	NY	44,010	C
The College of Wooster	OH	60,000	HC
The George Washington Univ	DC	68,474	HC+
The Univ of Akron	OH	22,566	C
The Univ of Alabama	AL	24,320	C+
The Univ of Arizona	AZ	24,086	C
The Univ of Mary	ND	23,180	C
The Univ of Memphis	TN	18,278	C
The Univ of Tenn at Chattanooga	TN	17,340	C+
The Univ of Tenn at Knoxville	TN	22,112	VC
The Univ of Tenn at Martin	TN	15,212	C
The Univ of Texas at Austin	TX	20,206	MC
The Univ of Utah	UT	18,751	VC
The Univ of Virginia's College at Wise	VA	18,192	LC
Thiel College	PA	42,950	LC
Thomas College	ME	73,888	LC
Thomas Edison State Univ	NJ	6,350	NC
Thomas More College	KY	36,720	LC
Thomas Univ	GA	21,420	NC
Tiffin Univ	OH	34,900	LC
Tougaloo College	MS	17,980	NC
Touro College	NY	31,040	C
Towson Univ	MD	21,878	C
Transylvania Univ	KY	47,450	HC+
Trevecca Nazarene Univ	TN	31,186	C
Trine Univ	IN	41,310	C
Trinity Christian College	IL	35,580	C
Trinity College	CT	69,020	HC
Trinity International Univ	IL	31,070	VC
Trinity Univ	TX	54,480	MC
Trinity Washington Univ	DC	33,826	C+
Troy Univ	AL	16,171	C
Truman State Univ	MO	16,286	MC
Tufts Univ	MA		MC
Tulane Univ	LA	67,496	MC
Tusculum College	TN	31,625	LC
Tuskegee Univ	AL	28,164	C
Union College	KY	32,310	C
Union College	NE	23,270	C
Union College	NY	64,320	MC
Union Inst & Univ	OH	8,912	SP
Union Univ	TN	41,160	VC
United States Air Force Academy	CO		C
Universidad del Turabo	PR	17,828	
Universidad Metropolitana	PR	17,828	
Univ of Alabama at Birmingham	AL	22,092	C
Univ of Alabama in Huntsville	AL	20,028	VC
Univ of Alaska Anchorage	AK	17,914	C
Univ of Alaska Fairbanks	AK	16,874	VC
Univ of Arkansas at Fayetteville	AR	19,766	VC
Univ of Arkansas at Little Rock	AR	18,211	LC
Univ of Arkansas at Monticello	AR	13,599	LC
Univ of Arkansas at Pine Bluff	AR	13,541	C
Univ of Bridgeport	CT	44,985	LC
Univ of Calif at Berkeley	CA	29,886	MC
Univ of Calif at Davis	CA	28,468	HC
Univ of Calif at Irvine	CA	33,857	VC
Univ of Calif at Los Angeles	CA	27,438	HC+
Univ of Calif at Riverside	CA	32,912	C
Univ of Calif at Santa Barbara	CA	30,627	HC+
Univ of Calif San Diego	CA	30,450	MC
Univ of Calif, Santa Cruz	CA	28,731	C+
Univ of Central Arkansas	AR	15,042	VC
Univ of Central Florida	FL	16,379	VC
Univ of Central Missouri	MO	18,982	C
Univ of Central Okla	OK	15,150	C
Univ of Charleston	WV	35,000	LC
Univ of Chicago	IL	70,551	MC
Univ of Cincinnati	OH	22,118	VC
Univ of Colo Boulder	CO	26,048	HC
Univ of Colo Colo Springs	CO	20,300	C
Univ of Colo Denver	CO	22,238	C
Univ of Conn	CT	27,394	
Univ of Dallas	TX	50,676	VC
Univ of Dayton	OH	54,930	VC
Univ of Delaware	DE	32,214	VC
Univ of Denver	CO	61,129	VC+
Univ of Detroit Mercy	MI	48,816	C
Univ of Dubuque	IA	37,824	C
Univ of Evansville	IN	44,186	C+
Univ of Findlay	OH	43,040	C
Univ of Florida	FL	16,291	HC+
Univ of Georgia	GA	21,878	HC
Univ of Great Falls	MT	38,524	C
Univ of Hartford	CT	49,776	C
Univ of Hawaii at Hilo	HI	18,038	VC
Univ of Hawaii at Manoa	HI	23,261	C
Univ of Houston-Downtown	TX	7,241	LC
Univ of Idaho	ID	16,158	C
Univ of Illinois at Chicago	IL	24,664	VC
Univ of Illinois at Urbana-Champaign	IL	27,006	HC
Univ of Indianapolis	IN	36,480	VC
Univ of Iowa	IA	19,415	HC
Univ of Jamestown	ND	28,508	C
Univ of Kansas	KS	20,884	VC
Univ of Kentucky	KY	24,800	C+
Univ of La Verne	CA	55,600	C
Univ of Louisiana at Lafayette	LA	14,516	C
Univ of Louisiana at Monroe	LA	15,970	C
Univ of Louisville	KY	19,692	C
Univ of Lynchburg	VA	48,370	C
Univ of Maine	ME	21,038	VC
Univ of Maine at Farmington	ME	18,792	C
Univ of Maine at Machias	ME	22,960	C
Univ of Mary Hardin-Baylor	TX	35,292	C+
Univ of Mary Washington	VA	23,039	C+
Univ of Maryland Univ College	MD	26,146	LC
Univ of Maryland/Baltimore County	MD	23,004	VC
Univ of Maryland/College Park	MD	21,938	HC
Univ of Mass Amherst	MA	27,669	HC
Univ of Mass Boston	MA	13,828	C
Univ of Mass Dartmouth	MA	26,507	C
Univ of Mass Lowell	MA	27,296	VC
Univ of Miami	FL	63,494	MC
Univ of Mich/Ann Arbor	MI	25,274	MC
Univ of Mich/Dearborn	MI	12,472	VC
Univ of Mich/Flint	MI	19,062	C
Univ of Minn/Duluth	MN	20,292	C
Univ of Minn/Morris	MN	21,222	VC
Univ of Minn/Twin Cities	MN	24,269	MC
Univ of Miss	MS	18,802	C
Univ of Missouri-Columbia	MO	20,463	VC
Univ of Missouri-Kansas City	MO	19,563	VC
Univ of Missouri-St. Louis	MO	19,810	VC
Univ of Mobile	AL	28,935	C
Univ of Montana	MT	14,105	C
Univ of Montevallo	AL	20,012	C
Univ of Mount Olive	NC	18,426	C
Univ of Mount Union	OH	39,990	C
Univ of Nebr - Kearney	NE	17,014	LC
Univ of Nebr - Lincoln	NE	18,589	VC
Univ of Nebr - Omaha	NE	16,120	C
Univ of Nevada, Las Vegas	NV	17,553	C
Univ of Nevada, Reno	NV	18,010	C
Univ of New England	ME	50,110	C
Univ of New Hampshire	NH	29,333	VC
Univ of New Hampshire - Manchester	NH	14,490	C
Univ of New Haven	CT	53,680	C
Univ of New Mexico	NM	16,808	C
Univ of New Orleans	LA	12,840	C
Univ of North Alabama	AL	15,964	C
Univ of N Car at Asheville	NC	16,251	VC+
Univ of N Car at Chapel Hill	NC	20,561	MC
Univ of N Car at Charlotte	NC	17,803	VC
Univ of N Car at Greensboro	NC	15,998	C
Univ of N Car at Pembroke	NC	14,737	LC
Univ of N Car Wilmington	NC	16,784	VC
Univ of N Dak	ND	16,673	C
Univ of North Florida	FL	15,996	VC
Univ of North Georgia	GA	17,316	C
Univ of North Texas	TX	20,082	C
Univ of Northern Colo	CO	19,658	C
Univ of Northern Iowa	IA	17,480	C
Univ of Northwestern - St. Paul	MN	39,530	C
Univ of Notre Dame	IN	68,801	MC
Univ of Okla	OK	19,651	HC
Univ of Oregon	OR	24,021	VC
Univ of Pennsylvania	PA	63,526	MC
Univ of Pikeville	KY	27,838	C
Univ of Pittsburgh	PA	30,030	MC
Univ of Pittsburgh at Bradford	PA	22,958	C
Univ of Pittsburgh at Greensburg	PA	24,140	C
Univ of Pittsburgh at Johnstown	PA	22,092	C
Univ of Portland	OR	52,152	VC
Univ of PR, at Cayey	PR		
Univ of PR, at Mayaguez	PR	13,995	
Univ of PR-Rio Piedras campus	PR	13,327	
Univ of Puget Sound	WA	60,210	HC
Univ of Redlands	CA	61,934	VC
Univ of Rhode Island	RI	26,066	VC
Univ of Richmond	VA	62,730	MC
Univ of Rio Grande & Rio Grande Community College	OH	8,750	LC
Univ of Rochester	NY	65,032	MC
Univ of St. Francis	IN	38,520	C
Univ of St. Joseph	CT	49,069	C
Univ of St. Mary	KS	37,080	NC
Univ of San Diego	CA	60,338	HC
Univ of San Francisco	CA	60,580	C
Univ of Science and Arts of Okla	OK	11,140	VC
Univ of Scranton	PA	54,962	VC
Univ of Sioux Falls	SD	25,630	C
Univ of South Alabama	AL	16,880	C
Univ of S Car Aiken	SC	18,094	C
Univ of S Car at Columbia	SC	21,726	VC
Univ of S Car Upstate	SC	19,272	LC
Univ of S Dak	SD	16,109	C
Univ of South Florida St. Petersburg	FL	15,980	C
Univ of South Florida/Tampa	FL	16,110	VC
Univ of Southern Calif	CA	66,631	MC
Univ of Southern Indiana	IN	16,808	C
Univ of Southern Maine	ME	18,320	C
Univ of Southern Miss	MS	13,170	C
Univ of St. Francis	IL	40,828	C
Univ of St. Thomas - Houston	TX	41,510	VC
Univ of Tampa	FL	38,928	VC
Univ of Texas at Arlington	TX	18,876	C
Univ of Texas at Dallas	TX	23,640	HC
Univ of Texas at El Paso	TX	34,452	NC
Univ of Texas Rio Grande Valley	TX	15,573	LC
Univ of the Cumberlands	KY	32,000	LC
Univ of the District of Columbia	DC	21,260	LC
Univ of the Incarnate Word	TX	39,162	LC
Univ of the Ozarks	AR	31,050	NC
Univ of the Pacific	CA	57,446	VC
Univ of the Sacred Heart	PR	17,932	
Univ of the Sciences	PA	40,738	VC
Univ of the Southwest	NM	24,386	C
Univ of Toledo	OH	19,336	C
Univ of Tulsa	OK	52,625	HC
Univ of Vermont	VT	29,792	HC
Univ of Virginia	VA	27,367	MC
Univ of Washington	WA	23,091	MC
Univ of West Alabama	AL	16,284	LC
Univ of West Florida	FL	15,848	C
Univ of West Georgia	GA	17,510	LC
Univ of Wisc-Eau Claire	WI	16,354	VC
Univ of Wisc-Green Bay	WI	15,184	C
Univ of Wisc-La Crosse	WI	15,425	VC
Univ of Wisc-Madison	WI	21,647	MC
Univ of Wisc-Milwaukee	WI	21,538	C
Univ of Wisc-Oshkosh	WI	15,392	C
Univ of Wisc-Parkside	WI	15,313	C
Univ of Wisc-Platteville	WI	14,148	C
Univ of Wisc-River Falls	WI	14,541	C
Univ of Wisc-Stevens Point	WI	14,043	C
Univ of Wisc-Stout	WI	19,667	C
Univ of Wisc-Superior	WI	14,838	C
Univ of Wisc-Whitewater	WI	13,976	C
Univ of Wyoming	WY	15,537	C
Upper Iowa Univ	IA	34,990	NC
Urbana Univ	OH	30,820	C
Ursinus College	PA	62,920	VC
Ursuline College	OH	41,076	LC
Utah State Univ	UT	13,235	C
Utica College	NY	31,510	C
Valparaiso Univ	IN	50,160	VC
Vanderbilt Univ	TN	63,248	MC
Vanguard Univ of Southern Calif	CA	42,400	VC
Vassar College	NY	68,110	MC
Villanova Univ	PA	64,922	MC
Virginia Commonwealth Univ	VA	23,811	VC
Virginia Military Inst	VA	26,460	VC
Virginia Polytechnic Inst and State Univ	VA	21,920	VC
Virginia State Univ	VA	19,802	C+
Virginia Union Univ	VA	25,058	C
Virginia Wesleyan Univ	VA	45,980	LC
Viterbo Univ	WI	34,660	C
Wabash College	IN	52,100	VC
Wagner College	NY	57,240	C+
Wake Forest Univ	NC	69,354	MC
Walla Walla Univ	WA	34,845	C
Walsh Univ	OH	39,010	C

ST = STATE **$IS** = IN-STATE COSTS **SR** = SELECTOR RATING

School	ST	$IS	SR
Warner Univ	FL	28,216	C
Warren Wilson College	NC	44,220	VC
Wartburg College	IA	49,478	C
Washburn Univ	KS	15,827	C
Washington & Jefferson College	PA	58,694	VC
Washington Adventist Univ	MD	32,050	LC
Washington and Lee Univ	VA	59,647	MC
Washington College	MD	56,154	VC
Washington State Univ	WA	22,747	C
Washington Univ in St. Louis	MO	67,539	MC
Wayland Baptist Univ	TX	23,460	LC
Wayne State College	NE	25,746	NC
Wayne State Univ	MI	23,085	C
Waynesburg Univ	PA	33,530	C
Weber State Univ	UT	14,112	C
Webster Univ	MO	37,490	C
Wellesley College	MA	66,984	MC
Wells College	NY	50,500	C
Wesley College	DE	37,848	LC
Wesleyan College	GA	31,940	C+
Wesleyan Univ	CT	66,940	MC
West Chester Univ of Pennsylvania	PA	19,171	VC
West Liberty Univ	WV	16,158	C
West Texas A&M Univ	TX	13,478	C
West Virginia State Univ	WV	19,412	LC
West Virginia Univ	WV	18,952	VC
West Virginia Wesleyan College	WV	39,188	C
Western Carolina Univ	NC	13,965	C
Western Conn State Univ	CT	21,254	LC
Western Illinois Univ	IL	20,897	C
Western Kentucky Univ	KY	16,850	C
Western Mich Univ	MI	21,791	C
Western New England Univ	MA	49,182	C
Western New Mexico Univ	NM	16,914	LC
Western Oregon Univ	OR	19,965	LC
Western State Colo Univ	CO	19,348	C
Western Washington Univ	WA	18,904	VC
Westfield State Univ	MA	20,404	C
Westminster College	MO	32,820	C
Westminster College	PA	41,722	C
Westminster College	UT	41,078	C
Westmont College	CA	57,930	VC
Wheaton College	IL	44,993	MC
Wheaton College	MA	63,818	VC
Wheeling Jesuit Univ	WV	37,106	LC
Wheelock College	MA	51,325	LC
Whitman College	WA	59,772	MC
Whittier College	CA	57,891	C
Whitworth Univ	WA	53,682	VC
Wichita State Univ	KS	17,773	C
Widener Univ	PA	58,190	C
Wilberforce Univ	OH	19,900	C
Wilkes Univ	PA	49,166	C
Willamette Univ	OR	62,514	VC+
William Carey Univ	MS	23,950	LC
William Jewell College	MO	42,490	C+
William Paterson Univ of New Jersey	NJ	24,022	C
William Peace Univ	NC	39,300	LC
William Penn Univ	IA	26,000	C
William Woods Univ	MO	32,040	C
Williams Baptist College	AR	24,720	C
Williams College	MA	67,700	MC
Wilmington College	OH	35,100	C
Wilson College	PA	35,620	LC
Wingate Univ	NC	41,900	C
Winona State Univ	MN	18,109	C
Winston-Salem State Univ	NC	18,005	LC
Winthrop Univ	SC	23,960	C
Wisc Lutheran College	WI	36,290	C
Wittenberg Univ	OH	49,863	VC
Wofford College	SC	49,885	VC
Woodbury Univ	CA	49,593	VC
Worcester Polytechnic Inst	MA	62,846	MC
Worcester State Univ	MA	20,977	C
Wright State Univ	OH	16,983	C
Xavier Univ	OH	49,380	VC
Xavier Univ of Louisiana	LA	31,689	C
Yale Univ	CT	64,650	MC
Yeshiva Univ	NY	52,750	VC
York College	NE	30,260	C
York College of Pennsylvania	PA	29,240	C
Youngstown State Univ	OH	17,487	C

PSYCHOLOGY & PSYCHIATRIC REHABILITATION

School	ST	$IS	SR
Kean Univ	NJ	25,620	C

PSYCHOLOGY EDUCATION

School	ST	$IS	SR
Bethany College	WV	38,774	LC
Bloomfield College	NJ	40,100	LC
Cal State, Fullerton	CA	21,902	C
Drury Univ	MO	37,555	VC
Eastern Mich Univ	MI	19,761	C
Georgia Southern Univ	GA	16,540	VC
Kutztown Univ of Pennsylvania	PA	19,477	C
Lamar Univ	TX	18,014	LC
Mount Holyoke College	MA	56,746	MC
Nazareth College	NY	46,784	C
Pittsburg State Univ	KS	13,880	C
Rocky Mountain College	MT	35,776	C
St. Vincent College	PA	46,229	C

School	ST	$IS	SR
The Univ of Arizona	AZ	24,086	C
Tulane Univ	LA	67,496	MC
Univ of Delaware	DE	32,214	VC
Univ of N Car at Greensboro	NC	15,998	C
Univ of Rio Grande & Rio Grande Community College	OH	8,750	LC
Valparaiso Univ	IN	50,160	VC
Wartburg College	IA	49,478	C
Weber State Univ	UT	14,112	C
York College	NE	30,260	C

PUBLIC ADMINISTRATION

School	ST	$IS	SR
American International College	MA	47,020	LC
Anna Maria College	MA	51,020	C
Aquinas College - Mich	MI	38,876	VC
Ashford Univ	CA	10,480	C
Auburn Univ	AL	24,300	VC+
Auburn Univ at Montgomery	AL	15,000	C
Austin Peay State Univ	TN	16,397	C
Baldwin Wallace Univ	OH	42,464	VC
Baylor Univ	TX	56,803	HC
Bentley Univ	MA	63,720	MC
Blackburn College	IL	28,526	LC
Bloomfield College	NJ	40,100	LC
Brown Univ	RI	64,566	MC
Calif Baptist Univ	CA	42,986	C
Cal State, Bakersfield	CA	22,397	LC
Cal State, Chico	CA	19,790	VC
Cal State, Dominguez Hills	CA	19,022	LC
Cal State, Fresno	CA	16,902	LC
Cal State, Fullerton	CA	21,902	C
Cal State, Sacramento	CA	19,060	C
Cal State, San Bernardino	CA	20,106	C
Calvin College	MI	43,090	HC
Carlow Univ	PA	39,696	LC
Carnegie Mellon Univ	PA	67,980	MC
Catawba College	NC	39,820	LC
Cedarville Univ	OH	36,244	VC
Central State Univ	OH	18,564	C
Central Washington Univ	WA	16,803	C
CUNY/John Jay College of Criminal Justice	NY	6,359	SP
CUNY/Medgar Evers College	NY	6,680	NC
Dakota Wesleyan Univ	SD	33,980	LC
Defiance College	OH	42,240	LC
DePaul Univ	IL	52,807	VC
Doane Univ	NE	41,340	VC
Dordt College	IA	37,860	C+
Drury Univ	MO	37,555	VC
Eastern Mich Univ	MI	19,761	C
Elizabethtown College	PA	56,340	VC
Elizabethtown College School of Continuing and Professional Studies	PA	18,900	C
Elon Univ	NC	46,142	HC
Evangel Univ	MO	28,898	C
Fayetteville State Univ	NC	17,756	C
Flagler College	FL	27,620	C
Florida A&M Univ	FL	15,361	C
Florida Atlantic Univ	FL	18,256	C
Florida International Univ	FL	20,281	C
Florida Memorial Univ	FL	22,424	LC
George Mason Univ	VA	19,884	C
Georgia Southern Univ	GA	16,540	VC
Grambling State Univ	LA	15,701	C
Grand Valley State Univ	MI	22,250	C+
Harding Univ	AR	25,440	C
Hawaii Pacific Univ	HI	33,420	C
Heidelberg Univ	OH	40,400	LC
Henderson State Univ	AR	15,516	C
Howard Univ	DC	37,616	C+
Indiana Univ Kokomo	IN	7,207	C
Indiana Univ-Purdue Univ Fort Wayne	IN	18,675	C
Inter-American Univ of PR Ponce	PR	19,549	
Inter-American Univ of PR-Fajardo Campus	PR	18,336	
Inter-American Univ of PR-San Germán	PR	20,042	
James Madison Univ	VA	19,084	VC
Juniata College	PA	58,118	VC
Kalamazoo College	MI	53,931	HC
Kean Univ	NJ	25,620	C
Kentucky State Univ	KY	14,484	LC
Kutztown Univ of Pennsylvania	PA	19,477	C
Lakeland Univ	WI	35,130	C
Lamar Univ	TX	18,014	LC
LeTourneau Univ	TX	39,190	VC
Lincoln Univ	MO	14,402	NC
Lindenwood Univ	MO	25,760	C
LIU Post	NY	50,698	C+
Louisiana College	LA	21,274	C
Mass College of Liberal Arts	MA	20,659	C
Metropolitan State Univ	MN	7,859	C
Miami Univ	OH	27,190	HC+
Mich State Univ	MI	24,542	VC
Middle Tenn State Univ	TN	8,650	C
Mills College	CA	43,705	C
Millsaps College	MS	50,080	C+
Miss Valley State Univ	MS	13,233	LC
Missouri Valley College	MO	28,150	C
Mount Aloysius College	PA	29,976	C
Murray State Univ	KY	17,726	C+
New York Univ	NY	68,139	MC
Norfolk State Univ	VA	18,902	LC
Northern Arizona Univ	AZ	21,003	C
Northern Kentucky Univ	KY	16,486	C
Northern Mich Univ	MI	20,853	C
Northland College	WI	41,103	C+
Northwest Missouri State Univ	MO	18,286	C
Northwestern State Univ of Louisiana	LA	16,534	LC
Nova Southeastern Univ	FL	38,534	C+
Oakland Univ	MI	20,763	C
Ohio Univ	OH	23,394	VC
Ohio Wesleyan Univ	OH	49,460	VC
Otterbein Univ	OH	41,630	C
Park Univ	MO	22,134	C
Plymouth State Univ	NH	23,180	LC
Point Park Univ	PA	41,270	C
Pontifical Catholic Univ of PR	PR	10,534	
Regis Univ	CO	46,380	C
Rhode Island College	RI	19,000	LC
Roger Williams Univ	RI	48,074	VC
Roosevelt Univ	IL	41,890	VC
Rutgers Univ - Newark	NJ	27,351	C
Saginaw Valley State Univ	MI	19,284	C
St. Francis Univ	PA	46,146	NC
St. Joseph's Univ	PA	58,540	VC
Samford Univ	AL	40,770	VC
San Diego State Univ	CA	23,156	VC
Seattle Univ	WA	54,957	VC
Shaw Univ	NC	24,638	C
Shippensburg Univ of Pennsylvania	PA	24,096	C
Siena Heights Univ	MI	36,322	C
Silver Lake College of the Holy Family	WI	36,290	LC
Slippery Rock Univ of Pennsylvania	PA	20,450	C
Southern Adventist Univ	TN	28,250	C
Southern Univ and A&M College	LA	16,074	LC
Southwest Minn State Univ	MN	17,783	C
St. Cloud State Univ	MN	10,600	C
St. John's Univ	NY	57,160	C+
Stanford Univ	CA	62,541	MC
Stephen F. Austin State Univ	TX	18,484	LC
Stetson Univ	FL	57,174	VC+
Stonehill College	MA	55,130	C
Talladega College	AL	25,919	C
Texas A&M Univ at Kingsville	TX	16,580	LC
Texas State Univ	TX	18,721	C
The Univ of Arizona	AZ	24,086	C
The Univ of Tenn at Knoxville	TN	22,112	VC
The Univ of Tenn at Martin	TN	15,212	C
The Univ of Texas at San Antonio	TX	21,060	C
Thomas Edison State Univ	NJ	6,350	NC
Union Inst & Univ	OH	8,912	SP
Universidad del Turabo	PR	17,828	
Univ of Alaska Southeast	AK	17,615	C
Univ of Arkansas at Little Rock	AR	18,211	LC
Univ of Central Arkansas	AR	15,042	VC
Univ of Central Florida	FL	16,379	VC
Univ of Central Okla	OK	15,150	C
Univ of Idaho	ID	16,158	C
Univ of Illinois at Chicago	IL	24,664	VC
Univ of Kansas	KS	20,884	VC
Univ of La Verne	CA	55,600	C
Univ of Louisville	KY	19,692	C
Univ of Maine at Augusta	ME	7,812	C
Univ of Mich/Flint	MI	19,062	C
Univ of Miss	MS	18,802	C
Univ of Missouri-Columbia	MO	20,463	VC
Univ of Missouri-St. Louis	MO	19,810	VC
Univ of Nebr - Omaha	NE	16,120	C
Univ of Nevada, Las Vegas	NV	17,553	C
Univ of N Dak	ND	16,673	C
Univ of North Florida	FL	15,996	VC
Univ of Northern Iowa	IA	17,480	C
Univ of Okla	OK	19,651	HC
Univ of Oregon	OR	24,021	VC
Univ of Pennsylvania	PA	63,526	MC
Univ of Pittsburgh	PA	30,030	MC
Univ of San Francisco	CA	60,580	C
Univ of Southern Indiana	IN	16,808	C
Univ of Texas at Dallas	TX	23,640	HC
Univ of the District of Columbia	DC	21,260	LC
Univ of Virginia	VA	27,367	MC
Univ of Wisc-Green Bay	WI	15,184	C
Univ of Wisc-La Crosse	WI	15,425	VC
Univ of Wisc-Stevens Point	WI	14,043	C
Univ of Wisc-Superior	WI	14,838	C
Univ of Wisc-Whitewater	WI	13,976	C
Virginia State Univ	VA	19,802	C+
Wagner College	NY	57,240	C+
Washburn Univ	KS	15,827	C
West Texas A&M Univ	TX	13,478	C
West Virginia Univ Inst of Technology	WV	18,264	C
Western New Mexico Univ	NM	16,914	LC
Western Oregon Univ	OR	19,965	LC
Wilkes Univ	PA	49,166	C
Winona State Univ	MN	18,109	C
Winston-Salem State Univ	NC	18,005	LC

PUBLIC AFFAIRS

School	ST	$IS	SR
Albion College	MI	55,260	C
Bloomfield College	NJ	40,100	LC
Chatham Univ	PA	47,883	VC
CUNY/Baruch College	NY	21,609	HC
College of William & Mary	VA	34,907	MC
Columbia College	SC	36,550	C
DePaul Univ	IL	52,807	VC
Dickinson College	PA	66,166	MC
Duke Univ	NC	68,298	MC
Emory and Henry College	VA	46,320	C
Georgia Inst of Technology	GA	23,910	MC
Hamilton College	NY	64,250	MC
Howard Univ	DC	37,616	C+
Indiana Univ Bloomington	IN	20,791	HC
Indiana Univ Northwest	IN	7,207	LC
Indiana Univ-Purdue Univ Fort Wayne	IN	18,675	C
Indiana Univ-Purdue Univ Indianapolis	IN	18,952	C
Meredith College	NC	46,634	C
Mills College	CA	43,705	C
Muskingum Univ	OH	35,966	C
New College of Florida	FL	16,180	HC+
Ohio State Univ at Columbus	OH	22,843	MC
Olivet Nazarene Univ	IL	41,840	VC
Pomona College	CA	64,957	MC
Rice Univ	TX	59,458	MC
Rochester Inst of Technology	NY	52,734	HC+
St. Vincent College	PA	46,229	C
Southern Methodist Univ	TX	69,008	MC
Southern New Hampshire Univ	NH	44,256	C
St. Mary's College of Maryland	MD	27,312	VC
SUNY/Empire State College	NY	9,145	NC
Texas Southern Univ	TX	19,592	LC
Trinity College	CT	69,020	HC
Univ of Chicago	IL	70,551	MC
Univ of Denver	CO	61,129	VC+
Univ of Illinois at Chicago	IL	24,664	VC
Univ of Mich/Ann Arbor	MI	25,274	MC
Univ of Missouri-Columbia	MO	20,463	VC
Univ of N Car at Chapel Hill	NC	20,561	MC
Univ of N Car at Greensboro	NC	15,998	C
Univ of Pittsburgh	PA	30,030	MC
Univ of Texas Rio Grande Valley	TX	15,573	LC
Vanderbilt Univ	TN	63,248	MC
Virginia Polytechnic Inst and State Univ	VA	21,920	VC
Washington & Jefferson College	PA	58,694	VC
Washington and Lee Univ	VA	59,647	MC
Washington State Univ	WA	22,747	C
Wayne State Univ	MI	23,085	C
Western Washington Univ	WA	18,904	VC

PUBLIC HEALTH

School	ST	$IS	SR
Agnes Scott College	GA	51,930	VC+
Albany College of Pharmacy and Health Sciences	NY	44,421	SP
Allegheny College	PA	57,620	VC
Allen College	IA	32,367	LC
Andrews Univ	MI	41,732	C
Arcadia Univ	PA	55,990	C+
Arizona State Univ at the Downtown Phoenix Campus	AZ	24,634	VC
Armstrong State Univ	GA	15,615	C
Augustana College	IL	51,222	VC+
Baker Univ	KS	37,190	C
Baldwin Wallace Univ	OH	42,464	VC
Baylor Univ	TX	56,803	HC
Benedict College	SC	28,630	NC
Bluffton Univ	OH	40,950	C+
Bowling Green State Univ	OH	19,975	C
Brown Univ	RI	64,566	MC
Calif Baptist Univ	CA	42,986	C
Cal State, Fresno	CA	16,902	LC
Cal State, Fullerton	CA	21,902	C
Calvin College	MI	43,090	HC
Carroll College	MT	44,304	C
Carroll Univ	WI	38,100	C+
Cedar Crest College	PA	51,110	C
Central Mich Univ	MI	20,330	C
Central Washington Univ	WA	16,803	C
CUNY/Hunter College	NY	31,098	VC
Colby-Sawyer College	NH	50,790	C
College of Charleston	SC	24,046	VC
Colo State Univ	CO	23,033	C
Curry College	MA	53,331	C
Dillard Univ	LA	20,940	VC
Drexel Univ	PA	65,927	HC
East Carolina Univ	NC	16,539	C
East Stroudsburg Univ	PA	18,578	LC
East Tenn State Univ	TN	18,141	C
Edinboro Univ	PA	15,940	LC
Elon Univ	NC	46,142	HC
Ferris State Univ	MI	21,458	C
Fort Lewis College	CO	20,154	C
Furman Univ	SC	61,098	VC+
Georgia Southern Univ	GA	16,540	VC
Goodwin College	CT	28,370	LC
Guilford College	NC	45,973	C
Hawaii Pacific Univ	HI	33,420	C

School	ST	$IS	SR
Hiram College	OH	44,590	C
Howard Univ	DC	37,616	C+
Indiana State Univ	IN	23,223	LC
Indiana Univ Bloomington	IN	20,791	HC
Indiana Univ of Pennsylvania	PA	24,474	C
Indiana Univ-Purdue Univ Indianapolis	IN	18,952	C
Ithaca College	NY	58,158	VC+
Johns Hopkins Univ	MD	68,080	MC
Kennesaw State Univ	GA	18,899	VC
Kent State Univ	OH	20,928	C
LIU Brooklyn	NY	50,698	C
Malone Univ	OH	39,200	C
Mansfield Univ of Pennsylvania	PA	24,244	LC
Marian Univ	IN	43,206	C
Marshall Univ	WV	18,044	C
MCPHS Univ	MA	45,470	SP
Mercy College of Health Sciences	IA	17,600	SP
Merrimack College	MA	55,415	C
Miami Univ	OH	27,190	HC+
Mills College	CA	43,705	C
Minn State Univ, Mankato	MN	17,190	C
Miss Univ for Women	MS	17,065	C
Montclair State Univ	NJ	26,912	C
Moravian College	PA	55,488	C
New Jersey City Univ	NJ	21,456	LC
New York Univ	NY	68,139	MC
Northeastern Illinois Univ	IL	12,529	LC
Ohio State Univ at Columbus	OH	22,843	MC
Ohio Univ	OH	23,394	VC
Old Dominion Univ	VA	21,618	C
Oregon State Univ	OR	23,337	VC
Regis College	MA	51,920	LC
Roanoke College	VA	55,952	VC
Rutgers Univ - New Brunswick	NJ	27,090	HC
St. Louis Univ	MO	49,866	HC
Samford Univ	AL	40,770	VC
San Diego State Univ	CA	23,156	VC
San Jose State Univ	CA	22,630	C
Shenandoah Univ	VA	42,100	C
Simmons College	MA	54,400	HC
Southern Conn State Univ	CT	21,924	LC
St. Ambrose Univ	IA	40,180	C
St. Cloud State Univ	MN	10,600	C
St. Joseph's College, New York/Long Island Campus	NY	25,124	C
Stetson Univ	FL	57,174	VC+
Stockton Univ	NJ	25,565	C
Syracuse Univ	NY	62,313	HC
Tarleton State Univ	TX	15,248	LC
Taylor Univ	IN	42,130	VC
Temple Univ	PA	24,392	C+
Texas A&M Univ at College Station	TX	20,771	VC+
The American Univ	DC	61,317	HC
The College of St. Rose	NY	44,010	C
The Univ of Arizona	AZ	24,086	C
Truman State Univ	MO	16,286	MC
Tulane Univ	LA	67,496	MC
Univ of Alabama at Birmingham	AL	22,092	C
Univ of Arkansas at Fayetteville	AR	19,766	VC
Univ of Calif at Berkeley	CA	29,886	MC
Univ of Calif at Irvine	CA	33,857	VC
Univ of Colo Denver	CO	22,238	C
Univ of Evansville	IN	44,186	C+
Univ of Illinois at Chicago	IL	24,664	VC
Univ of Illinois at Urbana-Champaign	IL	27,006	HC
Univ of Louisville	KY	19,692	C
Univ of Maryland/College Park	MD	21,938	HC
Univ of Mass Amherst	MA	27,669	HC
Univ of Mass Lowell	MA	27,296	VC
Univ of Miami	FL	63,494	MC
Univ of Mich/Dearborn	MI	12,472	VC
Univ of Missouri-Columbia	MO	20,463	VC
Univ of New England	ME	50,110	C
Univ of N Car at Charlotte	NC	17,803	VC
Univ of N Car at Greensboro	NC	15,998	C
Univ of N Car Wilmington	NC	16,784	VC
Univ of Rochester	NY	65,032	MC
Univ of St. Joseph	CT	49,069	C
Univ of S Car at Columbia	SC	21,726	VC
Univ of Tampa	FL	38,928	VC
Univ of the Cumberlands	KY	32,000	LC
Univ of Wisc-Eau Claire	WI	16,354	VC
Univ of Wisc-La Crosse	WI	15,425	VC
Utah State Univ	UT	13,235	C
Valparaiso Univ	IN	50,160	VC
Walla Walla Univ	WA	34,845	C
Wartburg College	IA	49,478	C
Wayne State Univ	MI	23,085	C
West Chester Univ of Pennsylvania	PA	19,171	VC
Western Illinois Univ	IL	20,897	C
Western Kentucky Univ	KY	16,850	C
Western Mich Univ	MI	21,791	C
Western New Mexico Univ	NM	16,914	LC
Winona State Univ	MN	18,109	C
Worcester State Univ	MA	20,977	C
Youngstown State Univ	OH	17,487	C

PUBLIC HISTORY/ARCHIVES

School	ST	$IS	SR
Arkansas Tech Univ	AR	16,534	LC
Baldwin Wallace Univ	OH	42,464	VC
Cal State, Fullerton	CA	21,902	C
East Carolina Univ	NC	16,539	C
Flagler College	FL	27,620	C
Northern Kentucky Univ	KY	16,486	C
Stevenson Univ	MD	48,412	C
Weber State Univ	UT	14,112	C
Western Mich Univ	MI	21,791	C

PUBLIC POLICY

School	ST	$IS	SR
Bryant Univ	RI	57,204	VC
Cal State, Fullerton	CA	21,902	C
DePaul Univ	IL	52,807	VC
Gettysburg College	PA	65,210	MC
Lewis Univ	IL	41,710	C
Mills College	CA	43,705	C
Ohio State Univ at Columbus	OH	22,843	MC
Univ of Texas at Dallas	TX	23,640	HC

PUBLIC POLICY/PUBLIC SERVICE

School	ST	$IS	SR
Hofstra Univ	NY	58,210	C+
Lynn Univ	FL	49,680	LC
San Diego State Univ	CA	23,156	VC

PUBLIC RELATIONS

School	ST	$IS	SR
Abilene Christian Univ	TX	43,708	C+
Andrews Univ	MI	41,732	C
Appalachian State Univ	NC	15,394	VC
Ashford Univ	CA	10,480	C
Auburn Univ	AL	24,300	VC+
Baldwin Wallace Univ	OH	42,464	VC
Barry Univ	FL	38,730	LC
Belmont Univ	TN	44,500	VC+
Bethany College	WV	38,774	LC
Biola Univ	CA	48,686	C
Bluffton Univ	OH	40,950	C+
Brigham Young Univ	UT	13,248	MC
Butler Univ	IN	52,890	VC+
Calif Baptist Univ	CA	42,986	C
Cal State, Fresno	CA	16,902	LC
Cal State, Fullerton	CA	21,902	C
Capital Univ	OH	44,778	VC
Cardinal Stritch Univ	WI	37,136	C
Carroll College	MT	44,304	C
Central Mich Univ	MI	20,330	C
Central Washington Univ	WA	16,803	C
Champlain College	VT	54,724	VC
Chapman Univ	CA	65,504	HC
Coe College	IA	51,570	VC
College of the Ozarks	MO	7,530	VC
Columbia College Chicago	IL	40,104	C
Dallas Baptist Univ	TX	35,220	VC
DePaul Univ	IL	52,807	VC
Drake Univ	IA	49,220	HC
Drury Univ	MO	37,555	VC
Duquesne Univ	PA	48,508	VC
Eastern Kentucky Univ	KY	17,742	C
Eastern Mich Univ	MI	19,761	C
Emerson College	MA	61,824	HC+
Fairfield Univ	CT	61,445	HC
Ferris State Univ	MI	21,458	C
Flagler College	FL	27,620	C
Florida Southern College	FL	45,978	VC
Florida State Univ	FL	16,771	HC
Franklin College	IN	40,550	C
Freed-Hardeman Univ	TN	29,900	C
Georgia Southern Univ	GA	16,540	VC
Gonzaga Univ	WA	52,880	HC
Goshen College	IN	44,350	C
Greenville College	IL	27,012	LC
Gwynedd Mercy Univ	PA	43,780	LC
Hardin-Simmons Univ	TX	36,025	C
Hawaii Pacific Univ	HI	33,420	C
Heidelberg Univ	OH	40,400	LC
Hofstra Univ	NY	58,210	C+
Howard Univ	DC	37,616	C+
Huntington Univ	IN	33,996	C
Illinois State Univ	IL	23,418	VC
Ithaca College	NY	58,158	VC+
Keene State College	NH	24,604	C
Kennesaw State Univ	GA	18,899	VC
Kent State Univ	OH	20,928	C
Lee Univ	TN	22,045	C
LIU Post	NY	50,698	C+
Loras College	IA	40,726	C
Louisiana College	LA	21,274	C
Malone Univ	OH	39,200	C
Marietta College	OH	46,190	C
Marquette Univ	WI	53,090	VC+
Marshall Univ	WV	18,044	C
McKendree Univ	IL	37,940	C+
Mercyhurst Univ	PA	47,420	C
Messiah College	PA	44,380	VC
Middle Tenn State Univ	TN	8,650	C
Millersville Univ of Pennsylvania	PA	25,298	C
Millikin Univ	IL	44,148	C
Minn State Univ, Moorhead	MN	21,393	C
Missouri Baptist Univ	MO	35,594	C
Missouri Southern State Univ	MO	13,071	C
Missouri Western State Univ	MO	17,822	LC
Montana State Univ Billings	MT	13,336	LC
Montclair State Univ	NJ	26,912	C
Mount St. Mary College	NY	44,448	C
Mount Vernon Nazarene Univ	OH	35,944	C
Murray State Univ	KY	17,726	C+
New York Univ	NY	68,139	MC
N Dak State Univ	ND	16,245	VC
Northern Kentucky Univ	KY	16,486	C
Northern Mich Univ	MI	20,853	C
Northwest Missouri State Univ	MO	18,286	C
Northwestern College of Iowa	IA	38,400	C
Northwestern Okla State Univ	OK	13,072	LC
Notre Dame College	OH	39,150	VC
Ohio Dominican Univ	OH	41,340	C+
Ohio Northern Univ	OH	44,050	VC
Ohio Univ	OH	23,394	VC
Okla Christian Univ	OK	29,260	C
Okla City Univ	OK	40,476	C
Olivet Nazarene Univ	IL	41,840	VC
Otterbein Univ	OH	41,630	C
Pace Univ	NY	60,136	C
Pacific Union College	CA	36,009	VC
Park Univ	MO	22,134	C
Pepperdine Univ	CA	66,862	VC+
Point Park Univ	PA	41,270	C
Pontifical Catholic Univ of PR	PR	10,534	
Purdue Univ Northwest	IN	15,178	C
Purdue Univ/West Lafayette	IN	20,032	MC
Quinnipiac Univ	CT	60,970	VC
Rider Univ	NJ	54,050	C
Rochester Inst of Technology	NY	52,734	HC+
Roosevelt Univ	IL	41,890	VC
Rowan Univ	NJ	24,491	VC
St. Mary's Univ of Minn	MN	42,440	C
San Diego State Univ	CA	23,156	VC
San Jose State Univ	CA	22,630	C
Shorter Univ	GA	31,130	LC
Simpson College	IA	45,626	VC
Southeast Missouri State Univ	MO	16,148	C
Southeastern Univ	FL	34,910	LC
Southern Adventist Univ	TN	28,250	C
Southern Illinois Univ Edwardsville	IL	20,188	C
Southern Methodist Univ	TX	69,008	MC
Spring Hill College	AL	48,488	C
St. John's Univ	NY	57,160	C+
SUNY at Oswego	NY	22,219	VC
SUNY/Fredonia	NY	20,818	C
SUNY/Plattsburgh	NY	19,314	C
Stephens College	MO	38,042	C
Suffolk Univ	MA	52,316	C
Syracuse Univ	NY	62,313	HC
Taylor Univ	IN	42,130	VC
Temple Univ	PA	24,392	C+
Texas State Univ	TX	18,721	C
Texas Tech Univ	TX	20,156	C+
The American Univ	DC	61,317	HC
The George Washington Univ	DC	68,474	HC+
The Univ of Akron	OH	22,566	C
The Univ of Alabama	AL	24,320	C+
The Univ of Tenn at Knoxville	TN	22,112	VC
The Univ of Texas at Austin	TX	20,206	MC
Union College	NE	23,270	C
Union Univ	TN	41,160	VC
Univ of Central Florida	FL	16,379	VC
Univ of Central Missouri	MO	18,982	C
Univ of Central Okla	OK	15,150	C
Univ of Florida	FL	16,291	HC+
Univ of Georgia	GA	21,878	HC
Univ of Idaho	ID	16,158	C
Univ of Indianapolis	IN	36,480	VC
Univ of Louisiana at Lafayette	LA	14,516	C
Univ of Miami	FL	63,494	MC
Univ of Mount Union	OH	39,990	C
Univ of Nebr - Lincoln	NE	18,589	VC
Univ of North Alabama	AL	15,964	C
Univ of Northern Iowa	IA	17,480	C
Univ of Northwestern - St. Paul	MN	39,530	C
Univ of Okla	OK	19,651	HC
Univ of Oregon	OR	24,021	VC
Univ of Pittsburgh at Bradford	PA	22,958	C
Univ of Rhode Island	RI	26,066	VC
Univ of Rio Grande & Rio Grande Community College	OH	8,750	LC
Univ of S Car at Columbia	SC	21,726	VC
Univ of Southern Calif	CA	66,631	MC
Univ of Southern Indiana	IN	16,808	C
Univ of Wisc-Whitewater	WI	13,976	C
Ursuline College	OH	41,076	LC
Utica College	NY	31,510	C
Wartburg College	IA	49,478	C
Washington State Univ	WA	22,747	C
Wayne State Univ	MI	23,085	C
Waynesburg Univ	PA	33,530	C
Weber State Univ	UT	14,112	C
Webster Univ	MO	37,490	C
West Liberty Univ	WV	16,158	C
West Texas A&M Univ	TX	13,478	C
West Virginia Univ	WV	18,952	VC
West Virginia Wesleyan College	WV	39,188	C
Western Kentucky Univ	KY	16,850	C
Western Mich Univ	MI	21,791	C
Western New England Univ	MA	49,182	C
Westminster College	PA	41,722	C
William Penn Univ	IA	26,000	C
Wilmington College	OH	35,100	C
Wingate Univ	NC	41,900	C
Winthrop Univ	SC	23,960	C
Xavier Univ	OH	49,380	VC
York College of Pennsylvania	PA	29,240	C
Youngstown State Univ	OH	17,487	C

PUBLIC RELATIONS/ ADVERTISING

School	ST	$IS	SR
DePaul Univ	IL	52,807	VC
Drury Univ	MO	37,555	VC
Florida International Univ	FL	20,281	C
Lewis Univ	IL	41,710	C
Lynn Univ	FL	49,680	LC
Newbury College	MA	48,970	C

PUBLIC SAFETY

School	ST	$IS	SR
Charter Oak State College	CT	7,983	NC
Univ of West Alabama	AL	16,284	LC
Woodbury Univ	CA	49,593	VC

PUBLISHING

School	ST	$IS	SR
Benedictine Univ	IL	38,300	C
Biola Univ	CA	48,686	C
Emerson College	MA	61,824	HC+
Hofstra Univ	NY	58,210	C+
New York Univ	NY	68,139	MC
Rochester Inst of Technology	NY	52,734	HC+
West Texas A&M Univ	TX	13,478	C

PUERTO RICAN STUDIES

School	ST	$IS	SR
CUNY/Brooklyn College	NY	7,163	C+
Univ of Mich/Ann Arbor	MI	25,274	MC

PURCHASING/INVENTORY MANAGEMENT

School	ST	$IS	SR
Bloomfield College	NJ	40,100	LC
Central Mich Univ	MI	20,330	C
Univ of Illinois at Urbana-Champaign	IL	27,006	HC
Univ of North Texas	TX	20,082	C
Weber State Univ	UT	14,112	C
Xavier Univ	OH	49,380	VC

QUANTITATIVE ECONOMICS

School	ST	$IS	SR
Bryant Univ	RI	57,204	VC
United States Naval Academy	MD		HC

QUANTITATIVE METHODS

School	ST	$IS	SR
Bard College at Simon's Rock	MA	65,795	MC
Bryant Univ	RI	57,204	VC
Bucknell Univ	PA	67,136	MC
Cal State, Fullerton	CA	21,902	C
CUNY/City College	NY	20,204	C
James Madison Univ	VA	19,084	VC
Millersville Univ of Pennsylvania	PA	25,298	C
Pace Univ	NY	60,136	C
Univ of Cincinnati	OH	22,118	VC
Univ of Washington	WA	23,091	MC
Whitworth Univ	WA	53,682	VC

RADIATION PROTECTION

School	ST	$IS	SR
Thomas Edison State Univ	NJ	6,350	NC

RADIATION THERAPY

School	ST	$IS	SR
Augusta Univ	GA	4,632	C
Benedictine Univ	IL	38,300	C
Gwynedd Mercy Univ	PA	43,780	LC
Howard Univ	DC	37,616	C+
Indiana Univ Kokomo	IN	7,207	C
Indiana Univ-Purdue Univ Indianapolis	IN	18,952	C
Lewis Univ	IL	41,710	C
MCPHS Univ	MA	45,470	SP
Mount Aloysius College	PA	29,976	C
North Central College	IL	48,712	C+
St. Louis Univ	MO	49,866	HC
Texas State Univ	TX	18,721	C
Thomas Edison State Univ	NJ	6,350	NC
Univ of Mich/Flint	MI	19,062	C
Univ of St. Francis	IL	40,828	C
Univ of Vermont	VT	29,792	HC
Univ of Wisc-La Crosse	WI	15,425	VC
Wayne State Univ	MI	23,085	C
Weber State Univ	UT	14,112	C

RADIO/TELEVISION TECHNOLOGY

School	ST	$IS	SR
Arkansas State Univ	AR	16,190	C

ST = STATE $IS = IN-STATE COSTS SR = SELECTOR RATING

School	ST	$IS	SR
Biola Univ	CA	48,686	C
Bloomfield College	NJ	40,100	LC
Cal State, Fullerton	CA	21,902	C
CUNY/Brooklyn College	NY	7,163	C+
Columbia College Chicago	IL	40,104	C
DeSales Univ	PA	47,520	C
Emerson College	MA	61,824	HC+
Hardin-Simmons Univ	TX	36,025	C
Hofstra Univ	NY	58,210	C+
LIU Post	NY	50,698	C+
Lyndon State College	VT	20,714	C
Marshall Univ	WV	18,044	C
Mount Ida College	MA	46,820	C
Murray State Univ	KY	17,726	C+
New York Univ	NY	68,139	MC
Northern Kentucky Univ	KY	16,486	C
Northwestern Univ	IL	68,725	MC
Ohio Univ	OH	23,394	VC
Pacific Union College	CA	36,009	VC
Rowan Univ	NJ	24,491	VC
San Diego State Univ	CA	23,156	VC
San Francisco State Univ	CA	18,514	LC
Southern Illinois Univ Carbondale	IL	24,554	C
Southern Illinois Univ Edwardsville	IL	20,188	C
St. Ambrose Univ	IA	40,180	C
St. John's Univ	NY	57,160	C+
Stephen F. Austin State Univ	TX	18,484	LC
Univ of Arkansas at Little Rock	AR	18,211	LC
Univ of Central Florida	FL	16,379	VC
Univ of Cincinnati	OH	22,118	VC
Univ of Montana	MT	14,105	C
Univ of N Car at Greensboro	NC	15,998	C
Univ of North Texas	TX	20,082	C
Univ of Southern Indiana	IN	16,808	C
Univ of Southern Miss	MS	13,170	C
Vanguard Univ of Southern Calif	CA	42,400	VC

RADIO/TV BROADCASTING

School	ST	$IS	SR
Cal State, Fullerton	CA	21,902	C
Florida International Univ	FL	20,281	C
Gannon Univ	PA	42,922	C
Lewis Univ	IL	41,710	C
Northern Arizona Univ	AZ	21,003	C

RADIOGRAPH MEDICAL TECHNOLOGY

School	ST	$IS	SR
Alderson Broaddus Univ	WV	35,000	LC
Clarkson College	NE	32,480	C
Drury Univ	MO	37,555	VC
Henderson State Univ	AR	15,516	C
Howard Univ	DC	37,616	C+
La Roche College	PA	38,940	C
Lewis-Clark State College	ID	14,202	C
Misericordia Univ	PA	45,210	C
Mount Aloysius College	PA	29,976	C
Ohio State Univ at Columbus	OH	22,843	MC
Oregon Inst of Technology	OR	19,227	C
Pennsylvania College of Technology	PA	27,693	NC
St. Louis Univ	MO	49,866	HC
Univ of St. Francis	IL	40,828	C
Weber State Univ	UT	14,112	C

RADIOGRAPHY

School	ST	$IS	SR
Lewis Univ	IL	41,710	C

RADIOLOGIC IMAGING MODALITIES

School	ST	$IS	SR
St. Louis Univ	MO	49,866	HC
Thomas Edison State Univ	NJ	6,350	NC
Weber State Univ	UT	14,112	C

RADIOLOGICAL SCIENCE

School	ST	$IS	SR
Adventist Univ of Health Sciences	FL	48,492	SP
Arkansas State Univ	AR	16,190	C
Armstrong State Univ	GA	15,615	C
Austin Peay State Univ	TN	16,397	C
Cal State, Fullerton	CA	21,902	C
Concordia Univ St. Paul	MN	29,050	C
Friends Univ	KS	38,000	C
Idaho State Univ	ID	13,619	LC
Indiana Univ Northwest	IN	7,207	LC
Manhattan College	NY	55,652	C
Midwestern State Univ	TX	12,111	LC
Missouri State Univ	MO	15,837	C+
Mount Aloysius College	PA	29,976	C
New York City College of Technology	NY	7,185	LC
Northwestern State Univ of Louisiana	LA	16,534	LC
Ohio State Univ at Columbus	OH	22,843	MC
Purdue Univ/West Lafayette	IN	20,032	MC
Quinnipiac Univ	CT	60,970	VC
Regis College	MA	51,920	LC
Southern Vermont College	VT	34,670	LC
St. Francis College	NY	38,800	LC
St. John's Univ	NY	57,160	C+
Suffolk Univ	MA	52,316	C
Texas A&M Univ at College Station	TX	20,771	VC+
The George Washington Univ	DC	68,474	HC+
Univ of Central Arkansas	AR	15,042	VC
Univ of Charleston	WV	35,000	LC
Univ of Iowa	IA	19,415	HC
Univ of Mich/Ann Arbor	MI	25,274	MC
Univ of Miss	MS	18,802	C
Univ of Missouri-Columbia	MO	20,463	VC
Univ of New Mexico	NM	16,808	C
Univ of N Car at Chapel Hill	NC	20,561	MC
Univ of Pittsburgh at Bradford	PA	22,958	C
Univ of South Alabama	AL	16,880	C
Univ of Southern Indiana	IN	16,808	C
Weber State Univ	UT	14,112	C

RADIOLOGICAL TECHNOLOGY

School	ST	$IS	SR
Allen College	IA	32,367	LC
Austin Peay State Univ	TN	16,397	C
Averett Univ	VA	43,034	LC
Avila Univ	MO	27,100	C
Bloomsburg Univ of Pennsylvania	PA	19,930	C
Boise State Univ	ID	17,368	C
Briar Cliff Univ	IA	36,956	C
Cal State, Northridge	CA	17,277	LC
Carroll Univ	WI	38,100	C+
Champlain College	VT	54,724	VC
Clarion Univ of Pennsylvania	PA	21,608	LC
Clarkson College	NE	32,480	C
College of St Joseph	VT	32,400	LC
Colo Mesa Univ	CO	19,707	LC
Concordia College - New York	NY	39,035	LC
Concordia Univ Wisc	WI	35,910	C
Drury Univ	MO	37,555	VC
Fairleigh Dickinson Univ/ College at Florham	NJ	54,770	C
Fairleigh Dickinson Univ/ Metropolitan Campus	NJ	52,392	C
Fort Hays State Univ	KS	12,677	C
Friends Univ	KS	38,000	C
Gwynedd Mercy Univ	PA	43,780	LC
Henderson State Univ	AR	15,516	C
Holy Family Univ	PA	44,672	LC
Howard Univ	DC	37,616	C+
Inter-American Univ of PR-Aguadilla Campus	PR	21,657	
LIU Post	NY	50,698	C+
Mansfield Univ of Pennsylvania	PA	24,244	LC
Marian Univ	WI	34,622	C
McNeese State Univ	LA	7,838	C
MCPHS Univ	MA	45,470	SP
Minot State Univ	ND	13,285	C
Missouri Baptist Univ	MO	35,594	C
Missouri Southern State Univ	MO	13,071	C
Mount Aloysius College	PA	29,976	C
Mount Marty College	SD	36,862	C
Mount Mary Univ	WI	34,650	LC
Nebr Methodist College	NE	25,314	C
N Dak State Univ	ND	16,245	VC
Northern Kentucky Univ	KY	16,486	C
Presentation College	SD	28,575	LC
Purdue Univ/West Lafayette	IN	20,032	MC
Rhode Island College	RI	19,000	LC
Southern Illinois Univ Carbondale	IL	24,554	C
The Univ of Mary	ND	23,180	C
Univ of Hartford	CT	49,776	C
Univ of Jamestown	ND	28,508	C
Univ of Louisiana at Monroe	LA	15,970	C
Univ of Nevada, Las Vegas	NV	17,553	C
Walla Walla Univ	WA	34,845	C
Wayne State Univ	MI	23,085	C
William Carey Univ	MS	23,950	LC
Xavier Univ	OH	49,380	VC

RANCH MANAGEMENT

School	ST	$IS	SR
Univ of Nebr - Lincoln	NE	18,589	VC

RANGE/FARM MANAGEMENT

School	ST	$IS	SR
Colo State Univ	CO	23,033	C
Eastern Oregon Univ	OR	17,612	C
Lake Erie College	OH	38,914	LC
New Mexico State Univ	NM	14,050	LC
N Dak State Univ	ND	16,245	VC
Oregon State Univ	OR	23,337	VC
S Dak State Univ	SD	15,874	C
Tarleton State Univ	TX	15,248	LC
Texas A&M Univ at College Station	TX	20,771	VC+
Texas A&M Univ at Kingsville	TX	16,580	LC
Unity College	ME	37,670	C
Univ of Calif at Davis	CA	28,468	HC
Univ of Idaho	ID	16,158	C
Univ of Illinois at Urbana-Champaign	IL	27,006	HC
Univ of Nebr - Lincoln	NE	18,589	VC
Univ of Wyoming	WY	15,537	C
Utah State Univ	UT	13,235	C
Washington State Univ	WA	22,747	C
Wilmington College	OH	35,100	C

READING EDUCATION

School	ST	$IS	SR
Ball State Univ	IN	19,808	C+
Baylor Univ	TX	56,803	HC
Black Hills State Univ	SD	16,622	C
Cal State, Fullerton	CA	21,902	C
Calif Univ of Pennsylvania	PA	20,425	LC
Carroll College	MT	44,304	C
Dallas Baptist Univ	TX	35,220	VC
Defiance College	OH	42,240	LC
Eastern Mich Univ	MI	19,761	C
Florida State Univ	FL	16,771	HC
Georgia Southern Univ	GA	16,540	VC
Hardin-Simmons Univ	TX	36,025	C
Houston Baptist Univ	TX	36,450	C
Howard Univ	DC	37,616	C+
Missouri Southern State Univ	MO	13,071	C
Muskingum Univ	OH	35,966	C
Silver Lake College of the Holy Family	WI	36,290	LC
S Car State Univ	SC	21,330	LC
Univ of Arkansas at Little Rock	AR	18,211	LC
Univ of Great Falls	MT	38,524	C
Univ of Mich/Dearborn	MI	12,472	VC
Univ of Rio Grande & Rio Grande Community College	OH	8,750	LC
Univ of Texas Rio Grande Valley	TX	15,573	LC
West Texas A&M Univ	TX	13,478	C
West Virginia Univ	WV	18,952	VC
Western Washington Univ	WA	18,904	VC
Wingate Univ	NC	41,900	C

REAL ESTATE

School	ST	$IS	SR
Ashford Univ	CA	10,480	C
Baylor Univ	TX	56,803	HC
Cal State, Fullerton	CA	21,902	C
Cal State, Sacramento	CA	19,060	C
Central Mich Univ	MI	20,330	C
CUNY/Baruch College	NY	21,609	HC
Clarion Univ of Pennsylvania	PA	21,608	LC
Colo State Univ	CO	23,033	C
DePaul Univ	IL	52,807	VC
Florida Atlantic Univ	FL	18,256	C
Florida International Univ	FL	20,281	C
Georgia State Univ	GA	25,250	C
Marquette Univ	WI	53,090	VC+
Marylhurst Univ	OR	16,818	NC
Menlo College	CA	51,380	LC
Miss State Univ	MS	12,028	C+
Monmouth Univ	NJ	50,184	C
Morehead State Univ	KY	18,386	LC
New York Univ	NY	68,139	MC
Ohio State Univ at Columbus	OH	22,843	MC
Old Dominion Univ	VA	21,618	C
Peirce College	PA	16,780	NC
San Diego State Univ	CA	23,156	VC
Southern Methodist Univ	TX	69,008	MC
Syracuse Univ	NY	62,313	HC
Temple Univ	PA	24,392	C+
Texas A&M Univ at Kingsville	TX	16,580	LC
Univ of Central Florida	FL	16,379	VC
Univ of Cincinnati	OH	22,118	VC
Univ of Conn	CT	27,394	
Univ of Denver	CO	61,129	VC+
Univ of Georgia	GA	21,878	HC
Univ of Illinois at Chicago	IL	24,664	VC
Univ of Illinois at Urbana-Champaign	IL	27,006	HC
Univ of Miami	FL	63,494	MC
Univ of Miss	MS	18,802	C
Univ of Missouri-Columbia	MO	20,463	VC
Univ of Nebr - Omaha	NE	16,120	C
Univ of Nevada, Las Vegas	NV	17,553	C
Univ of N Car at Charlotte	NC	17,803	VC
Univ of North Texas	TX	20,082	C
Univ of Northern Iowa	IA	17,480	C
Univ of Pennsylvania	PA	63,526	MC
Univ of San Diego	CA	60,338	HC
Univ of S Car at Columbia	SC	21,726	VC
Univ of Texas at Arlington	TX	18,876	C
Univ of West Georgia	GA	17,510	LC
Univ of Wisc-Madison	WI	21,647	MC
Univ of Wisc-Milwaukee	WI	21,538	C
Villanova Univ	PA	64,922	MC
Washington State Univ	WA	22,747	C

REAL ESTATE FINANCE

School	ST	$IS	SR
Calif State Polytechnic Univ, Pomona	CA	21,811	C
Southern Methodist Univ	TX	69,008	MC
Texas Christian Univ	TX	57,120	HC
Wright State Univ	OH	16,983	C

RECREATION ADMINISTRATION

School	ST	$IS	SR
Cal State, Fullerton	CA	21,902	C
Eastern Illinois Univ	IL	21,414	C
Indiana Univ Bloomington	IN	20,791	HC
Kent State Univ	OH	20,928	C
Okla Baptist Univ	OK	33,990	C
San Diego State Univ	CA	23,156	VC
Southeast Missouri State Univ	MO	16,148	C
Univ of Maine at Machias	ME	22,960	C
Univ of New England	ME	50,110	C
Univ of New Hampshire	NH	29,333	VC

RECREATION AND LEISURE SERVICES

School	ST	$IS	SR
Alcorn State Univ	MS	15,884	C
Aquinas College - Mich	MI	38,876	VC
Asbury Univ	KY	36,450	C+
Aurora Univ	IL	34,990	C
Brigham Young Univ	UT	13,248	MC
Calif Polytechnic State Univ	CA	22,547	MC
Cal State, East Bay	CA	20,748	C
Cal State, Long Beach	CA	18,850	C
Cal State, Northridge	CA	17,277	LC
Catawba College	NC	39,820	LC
Central Washington Univ	WA	16,803	C
Chicago State Univ	IL	41,620	C
Colo State Univ-Pueblo	CO	21,581	C
Cumberland Univ	TN	27,710	C
Davis & Elkins College	WV	38,242	LC
East Central Univ	OK	13,330	C
East Stroudsburg Univ	PA	18,578	LC
Eastern Washington Univ	WA	17,896	LC
Emporia State Univ	KS	15,029	C
Ferrum College	VA	43,970	C
Florida State Univ	FL	16,771	HC
Frostburg State Univ	MD	17,280	LC
Georgia College & State Univ	GA	21,884	C+
Gordon College	MA	47,740	VC
Graceland Univ	IA	35,290	C
Grambling State Univ	LA	15,701	C
Green Mountain College	VT	45,228	LC
Greenville College	IL	27,012	LC
Hannibal-LaGrange Univ	MO	29,815	C
Henderson State Univ	AR	15,516	C
Houghton College	NY	40,558	VC
Indiana Inst of Technology	IN	34,240	LC
Indiana State Univ	IN	23,223	LC
Indiana Univ Bloomington	IN	20,791	HC
Ithaca College	NY	58,158	VC+
James Madison Univ	VA	19,084	VC
Johnson & Wales Univ/North Miami Campus	FL	44,768	C
Johnson & Wales Univ/ Providence Campus	RI	44,768	C
Kutztown Univ of Pennsylvania	PA	19,477	C
Lindsey Wilson College	KY	33,546	C
Lyndon State College	VT	20,714	C
Mars Hill Univ	NC	41,104	C
Maryville College	TN	44,410	C
Metropolitan State Univ of Denver	CO	6,928	LC
MidAmerica Nazarene Univ	KS	37,808	C
Middle Tenn State Univ	TN	8,650	C
Minn State Univ, Mankato	MN	17,190	C
Missouri State Univ	MO	15,837	C+
Morris College	SC	19,195	LC
Murray State Univ	KY	17,726	C+
New England College	NH	50,828	NC
New York Univ	NY	68,139	MC
N Car State Univ	NC	22,434	HC+
N Dak State Univ	ND	16,245	VC
Northwest Missouri State Univ	MO	18,286	C
Northwest Nazarene Univ	ID	40,250	C
Ohio Univ	OH	23,394	VC
Okla State Univ	OK	17,180	C+
Olivet Nazarene Univ	IL	41,840	VC
Oral Roberts Univ	OK	34,316	C
Oregon State Univ	OR	23,337	VC
Ouachita Baptist Univ	AR	33,500	VC
Pittsburg State Univ	KS	13,880	C
Plymouth State Univ	NH	23,180	LC
Radford Univ	VA	19,758	C
Rensselaer Polytechnic Inst	NY	67,265	MC
Shaw Univ	NC	24,638	C
Shepherd Univ, West Virginia	WV	17,382	C
Simpson Univ	CA	34,722	C
Southeastern Okla State Univ	OK	11,875	C
Southern Conn State Univ	CT	21,924	LC
Southern Illinois Univ Carbondale	IL	24,554	C
Southern Wesleyan Univ	SC	33,670	LC
Southwest Baptist Univ	MO	30,890	LC
St. Joseph's College, New York/Brooklyn Campus	NY	25,114	LC
St. Joseph's College, New York/Long Island Campus	NY	25,124	C
St. Thomas Aquinas College	NY	32,450	C
The College at Brockport - SUNY	NY	21,058	C
The Univ of Memphis	TN	18,278	C
The Univ of Tenn at Chattanooga	TN	17,340	C+
The Univ of Utah	UT	18,751	VC
Tougaloo College	MS	17,980	NC
Trine Univ	IN	41,310	C
Unity College	ME	37,670	C
Univ of Central Missouri	MO	18,982	C
Univ of Florida	FL	16,291	HC+
Univ of Georgia	GA	21,878	HC
Univ of Hawaii at Manoa	HI	23,261	C
Univ of Idaho	ID	16,158	C
Univ of Illinois at Urbana-Champaign	IL	27,006	HC
Univ of Iowa	IA	19,415	HC

ST = STATE $IS = IN-STATE COSTS SR = SELECTOR RATING

School	ST	$IS	SR
Univ of Maine at Farmington	ME	18,792	C
Univ of Maine at Machias	ME	22,960	C
Univ of Maine at Presque Isle	ME	16,148	LC
Univ of Minn/Twin Cities	MN	24,269	MC
Univ of Mount Olive	NC	18,426	C
Univ of Nebr - Omaha	NE	16,120	C
Univ of N Car Wilmington	NC	16,784	VC
Univ of North Georgia	GA	17,316	C
Univ of North Texas	TX	20,082	C
Univ of Northern Colo	CO	19,658	C
Univ of Northern Iowa	IA	17,480	C
Univ of South Alabama	AL	16,880	C
Univ of S Dak	SD	16,109	C
Univ of Toledo	OH	19,336	C
Upper Iowa Univ	IA	34,990	NC
Voorhees College	SC	19,976	C
West Virginia Univ	WV	18,952	VC
Western Kentucky Univ	KY	16,850	C
Western Mich Univ	MI	21,791	C
Western State Colo Univ	CO	19,348	C
William Penn Univ	IA	26,000	C
Winona State Univ	MN	18,109	C
York College of Pennsylvania	PA	29,240	C

RECREATION EDUCATION

School	ST	$IS	SR
Alderson Broaddus Univ	WV	35,000	LC
Baylor Univ	TX	56,803	HC
Benedict College	SC	28,630	NC
Campbellsville Univ	KY	33,400	C
Claflin Univ	SC	25,592	LC
College of the Ozarks	MO	7,530	VC
Eastern Washington Univ	WA	17,896	LC
Friends Univ	KS	38,000	C
Georgia Southern Univ	GA	16,540	VC
Indiana Univ Bloomington	IN	20,791	HC
Johnson State College	VT	22,672	C
Lyndon State College	VT	20,714	C
Northeastern Illinois Univ	IL	12,529	LC
Northwest Missouri State Univ	MO	18,286	C
Northwest Nazarene Univ	ID	40,250	C
Ohio Univ	OH	23,394	VC
Oral Roberts Univ	OK	34,316	C
Plymouth State Univ	NH	23,180	LC
Prescott College	AZ	38,201	C
St. Mary's College of Calif	CA	57,420	C
San Francisco State Univ	CA	18,514	LC
San Jose State Univ	CA	22,630	C
Southern Adventist Univ	TN	28,250	C
Southern Oregon Univ	OR	19,117	C
Southern Univ at New Orleans	LA	8,014	LC
SUNY/Cortland	NY	20,910	C
The Univ of Tenn at Knoxville	TN	22,112	VC
Toccoa Falls College	GA	30,048	C
Univ of Arkansas at Fayetteville	AR	19,766	VC
Univ of Conn	CT	27,394	
Univ of Maine at Machias	ME	22,960	C
Univ of Minn/Duluth	MN	20,292	C
Univ of Nevada, Las Vegas	NV	17,553	C
Western Washington Univ	WA	18,904	VC

RECREATION THERAPY

School	ST	$IS	SR
Alderson Broaddus Univ	WV	35,000	LC
Ashland Univ	OH	30,446	C
Cal State, Northridge	CA	17,277	LC
Calvin College	MI	43,090	HC
Catawba College	NC	39,820	LC
Central Mich Univ	MI	20,330	C
East Carolina Univ	NC	16,539	C
Eastern Mich Univ	MI	19,761	C
Eastern Washington Univ	WA	17,896	LC
Grand Valley State Univ	MI	22,250	C+
Hampton Univ	VA	36,410	C
Houghton College	NY	40,558	VC
Huntington Univ	IN	33,996	C
Indiana Inst of Technology	IN	34,240	LC
Ithaca College	NY	58,158	VC+
Lake Superior State Univ	MI	19,867	C
Longwood Univ	VA	22,184	C
Nova Southeastern Univ	FL	38,534	C+
Pittsburg State Univ	KS	13,880	C
Shaw Univ	NC	24,638	C
Southern Univ and A&M College	LA	16,074	LC
Springfield College	MA	48,775	C
Temple Univ	PA	24,392	C+
Unity College	ME	37,670	C
Univ of Iowa	IA	19,415	HC
Univ of N Car at Greensboro	NC	15,998	C
Univ of N Car Wilmington	NC	16,784	VC
Univ of Southern Maine	ME	18,320	C
Univ of Wisc-La Crosse	WI	15,425	VC
Univ of Wisc-Milwaukee	WI	21,538	C
Utica College	NY	31,510	C
West Virginia State Univ	WV	19,412	LC
Western Carolina Univ	NC	13,965	C
Winston-Salem State Univ	NC	18,005	LC

RECREATIONAL FACILITIES MANAGEMENT

School	ST	$IS	SR
Alaska Pacific Univ	AK	28,730	VC
Alderson Broaddus Univ	WV	35,000	LC
Appalachian State Univ	NC	15,394	VC
Aquinas College - Mich	MI	38,876	VC
Ashland Univ	OH	30,446	C
Bluffton Univ	OH	40,950	C+
Cal State, Fresno	CA	16,902	LC
Central Methodist Univ	MO	31,500	VC
Central Mich Univ	MI	20,330	C
Colo State Univ	CO	23,033	C
Dordt College	IA	37,860	C+
East Carolina Univ	NC	16,539	C
Eastern Mennonite Univ	VA	42,550	C
Florida Gulf Coast Univ	FL	14,738	C
Florida International Univ	FL	20,281	C
Florida State Univ	FL	16,771	HC
Glenville State College	WV	17,386	LC
Graceland Univ	IA	35,290	C
Houghton College	NY	40,558	VC
Indiana Wesleyan Univ	IN	33,674	C
Johnson & Wales Univ/ Providence Campus	RI	44,768	C
Johnson State College	VT	22,672	C
Kean Univ	NJ	25,620	C
Millikin Univ	IL	44,148	C
Missouri Valley College	MO	28,150	C
Ohio Univ	OH	23,394	VC
Okla Baptist Univ	OK	33,990	C
San Francisco State Univ	CA	18,514	LC
Sierra Nevada College	NV	45,403	C
SUNY at Oswego	NY	22,219	VC
Texas A&M Univ at College Station	TX	20,771	VC+
Texas State Univ	TX	18,721	C
Trine Univ	IN	41,310	C
Union College	KY	32,310	C
Univ of Iowa	IA	19,415	HC
Univ of Maine at Machias	ME	22,960	C
Univ of Minn/Twin Cities	MN	24,269	MC
Univ of Montana	MT	14,105	C
Univ of Nevada, Las Vegas	NV	17,553	C
Univ of N Car at Greensboro	NC	15,998	C
Univ of St. Francis	IL	40,828	C
Univ of the Sciences	PA	40,738	VC

REHABILITATION THERAPY

School	ST	$IS	SR
Armstrong State Univ	GA	15,615	C
Cal State, Los Angeles	CA	17,186	LC
Central Mich Univ	MI	20,330	C
Clarion Univ of Pennsylvania	PA	21,608	LC
Coppin State Univ	MD	14,071	VC
East Carolina Univ	NC	16,539	C
Emporia State Univ	KS	15,029	C
Florida State Univ	FL	16,771	HC
Ithaca College	NY	58,158	VC+
Maryville Univ of St. Louis	MO	38,558	VC
Montana State Univ Billings	MT	13,336	LC
Pennsylvania State Univ - Univ Park	PA	29,716	HC
Rutgers Univ - New Brunswick	NJ	27,090	HC
Shaw Univ	NC	24,638	C
Southern Illinois Univ Carbondale	IL	24,554	C
Southern Univ and A&M College	LA	16,074	LC
Springfield College	MA	48,775	C
St. Catherine Univ	MN	45,630	C
Stephen F. Austin State Univ	TX	18,484	LC
The Univ of Arizona	AZ	24,086	C
Thomas Univ	GA	21,420	NC
Troy Univ	AL	16,171	C
Univ of Arkansas at Pine Bluff	AR	13,541	C
Univ of Florida	FL	16,291	HC+
Univ of Illinois at Urbana-Champaign	IL	27,006	HC
Univ of Maine at Farmington	ME	18,792	C
Univ of Maryland/Eastern Shore	MD	21,861	LC
Univ of North Texas	TX	20,082	C
Univ of Northern Colo	CO	19,658	C
Univ of Pittsburgh	PA	30,030	MC
Univ of Texas Rio Grande Valley	TX	15,573	LC
Univ of Wisc-Stout	WI	19,667	C
Western Washington Univ	WA	18,904	VC
Wilberforce Univ	OH	19,900	C
Wright State Univ	OH	16,983	C

REHABILITATIVE AND HUMAN SERVICES

School	ST	$IS	SR
East Stroudsburg Univ	PA	18,578	LC
Univ of Idaho	ID	16,158	C

RELIGION

School	ST	$IS	SR
Adrian College	MI	45,550	C
Agnes Scott College	GA	51,930	VC+
Albertus Magnus College	CT	44,016	LC
Albion College	MI	55,260	C
Albright College	PA	57,326	C
Allegheny College	PA	57,620	VC
Alma College	MI	49,410	VC
Alverno College	WI	33,294	LC
Amherst College	MA	66,186	MC
Anderson Univ	IN	39,450	C
Andrews Univ	MI	41,732	C
Anna Maria College	MA	51,020	C
Appalachian State Univ	NC	15,394	VC
Aquinas College - Mich	MI	38,876	VC
Arkansas Baptist College	AR	20,280	NC
Asbury Univ	KY	36,450	C+
Ashland Univ	OH	30,446	C
Atlantic Union College	MA	27,228	C
Augsburg Univ	MN	45,129	C
Augustana College	IL	51,222	VC+
Augustana Univ	SD	39,968	VC
Aurora Univ	IL	34,990	C
Austin College	TX	51,059	HC
Averett Univ	VA	43,034	LC
Azusa Pacific Univ	CA	43,972	C
Baker Univ	KS	37,190	C
Baldwin Wallace Univ	OH	42,464	VC
Ball State Univ	IN	19,808	C+
Bard College	NY	65,924	HC
Barnard College/Columbia Univ	NY	68,762	MC
Barton College	NC	39,854	C
Bayamon Central Univ	PR	12,490	
Baylor Univ	TX	56,803	HC
Belmont Univ	TN	44,500	VC+
Beloit College	WI	55,206	HC
Benedict College	SC	28,630	NC
Benedictine College	KS	38,850	VC
Berea College	KY	7,094	C
Berry College	GA	47,466	VC
Bethany College	WV	38,774	LC
Bethel College	IN	36,830	C
Bethel College	KS	35,370	C
Bethune-Cookman Univ	FL	23,322	C
Birmingham-Southern College	AL	44,478	C+
Bloomfield College	NJ	40,100	LC
Bluefield College	VA	34,711	C
Boston Univ	MA	67,352	MC
Bowdoin College	ME	65,980	MC
Brescia Univ	KY	29,890	VC
Brown Univ	RI	64,566	MC
Bryan College	TN	32,900	C
Bryn Athyn College	PA	32,664	C
Bryn Mawr College	PA	65,220	MC
Bucknell Univ	PA	67,136	MC
Butler Univ	IN	52,890	VC+
Calif Lutheran Univ	CA	52,853	C
Cal State, Bakersfield	CA	22,397	LC
Cal State, Fullerton	CA	21,902	C
Cal State, Long Beach	CA	18,850	C
Calumet College of St. Joseph	IN	22,735	C
Calvin College	MI	43,090	HC
Campbell Univ	NC	37,570	VC
Capital Univ	OH	44,778	VC
Cardinal Stritch Univ	WI	37,136	C
Carleton College	MN	66,414	MC
Carroll College	MT	44,304	C
Carroll Univ	WI	38,100	C+
Carson-Newman Univ	TN	35,900	C
Carthage College	WI	48,835	C
Case Western Reserve Univ	OH	62,284	MC
Catawba College	NC	39,820	LC
Centenary College of Louisiana	LA	49,050	C+
Central College	IA	44,592	C
Central Methodist Univ	MO	31,500	VC
Central Mich Univ	MI	20,330	C
Centre College	KY	50,680	MC
Chaminade Univ of Honolulu	HI	37,614	C
Chapman Univ	CA	65,504	HC
Charleston Southern Univ	SC	34,700	C
CUNY/Brooklyn College	NY	7,163	C+
CUNY/Hunter College	NY	31,098	VC
CUNY/Queens College	NY	21,507	C
Claremont McKenna College	CA	69,900	MC
Clark Atlanta Univ	GA	31,019	LC
Clarke Univ	IA	42,950	C
Cleveland State Univ	OH	22,290	C
Coe College	IA	51,570	VC
Colby College	ME	64,060	MC
Colgate Univ	NY	67,500	MC
College of Mount St. Vincent	NY	45,620	C
College of St. Scholastica	MN	45,734	C+
College of the Holy Cross	MA	64,320	MC
College of the Ozarks	MO	7,530	VC
College of William & Mary	VA	34,907	MC
Colo College	CO	64,894	MC
Columbia College	SC	36,550	C
Columbia Univ/ School of General Studies	NY	61,470	MC
Columbia Univ/City of New York	NY	62,958	MC
Concordia College - Moorhead	MN	46,418	C
Concordia College - New York	NY	39,035	LC
Concordia Univ St. Paul	MN	29,050	C
Concordia Univ Wisc	WI	35,910	C
Concordia Univ, Ann Arbor	MI	38,878	C+
Concordia Univ, Chicago	IL	41,522	C
Conn College	CT	65,000	MC
Converse College	SC	28,290	C
Cornell College	IA	49,900	VC
Cornerstone Univ	MI	36,550	C
Culver-Stockton College	MO	34,350	C
Daemen College	NY	40,336	C
Dallas Baptist Univ	TX	35,220	VC
Dartmouth College	NH	68,109	MC
Davidson College	NC	60,119	MC
Defiance College	OH	42,240	LC
Denison Univ	OH	62,770	HC+
DePaul Univ	IL	52,807	VC
DePauw Univ	IN	58,688	VC
Dickinson College	PA	66,166	MC
Doane Univ	NE	41,340	VC
Dominican Univ	IL	42,472	C+
Dominican Univ of Calif	CA	58,750	C
Dordt College	IA	37,860	C+
Drake Univ	IA	49,220	HC
Drew Univ/College of Liberal Arts	NJ	53,608	VC
Drury Univ	MO	37,555	VC
Duke Univ	NC	68,298	MC
Earlham College	IN	55,670	HC
East Texas Baptist Univ	TX	34,444	C
Eastern Mennonite Univ	VA	42,550	C
Eastern Nazarene College	MA	41,114	C
Eastern New Mexico Univ	NM	12,874	LC
Eckerd College	FL	55,206	VC
Edward Waters College	FL	28,089	NC
Elizabethtown College	PA	56,340	VC
Elizabethtown College School of Continuing and Professional Studies	PA	18,900	C
Elmhurst College	IL	46,514	C
Elms College	MA	49,602	VC
Emmanuel College	MA	53,472	C+
Emory and Henry College	VA	46,320	C
Emory Univ	GA	63,286	MC
Erskine College	SC	45,460	C
Eugene Lang College of Liberal Arts	NY	64,940	VC
Eureka College	IL	34,760	C
Evangel Univ	MO	28,898	C
Felician Univ	NJ	46,280	LC
Ferrum College	VA	43,970	C
Fisk Univ	TN	32,066	LC
Florida International Univ	FL	20,281	C
Florida Memorial Univ	FL	22,424	LC
Florida Southern College	FL	45,978	VC
Florida State Univ	FL	16,771	HC
Fontbonne Univ	MO	34,606	C
Fordham Univ	NY	68,431	MC
Franklin and Marshall College	PA	67,960	MC
Franklin College	IN	40,550	C
Fresno Pacific Univ	CA	38,858	C
Friends Univ	KS	38,000	C
Furman Univ	SC	61,098	VC+
Gardner-Webb Univ	NC	24,935	C+
George Fox Univ	OR	42,938	C
George Mason Univ	VA	19,884	C
Georgetown College	KY	41,440	C
Georgetown Univ	DC	68,970	MC
Gettysburg College	PA	65,210	MC
Goshen College	IN	44,350	C
Goucher College	MD	56,110	VC
Grace College and Seminary	IN	31,524	C
Graceland Univ	IA	35,290	C
Greensboro College	NC	39,790	LC
Greenville College	IL	27,012	LC
Grinnell College	IA	63,114	MC
Guilford College	NC	45,973	C
Gustavus Adolphus College	MN	53,943	HC
Hamilton College	NY	64,250	MC
Hamline Univ	MN	50,152	C
Hampden-Sydney College	VA	57,806	VC
Hampshire College	MA	65,214	MC
Harding Univ	AR	25,440	C
Hartwick College	NY	51,270	C
Harvard College/Harvard Univ	MA	65,609	MC
Hastings College	NE	35,380	C+
Haverford College	PA	66,490	MC
Heidelberg Univ	OH	40,400	LC
Hellenic College/Holy Cross Greek Orthodox School of Theology	MA	39,906	C
Hendrix College	AR	54,020	VC
High Point Univ	NC	47,355	VC
Hillsdale College	MI	37,170	MC
Hiram College	OH	44,590	C
Hobart and William Smith Colleges	NY	67,050	HC+
Hofstra Univ	NY	58,210	C+
Hollins Univ	VA	49,635	VC
Holy Family Univ	PA	44,672	LC
Holy Names Univ	CA	46,630	LC
Hood College	MD	50,540	C
Hope College	MI	42,840	VC
Houghton College	NY	40,558	VC
Howard Univ	DC	37,616	C+
Humboldt State Univ	CA	21,708	C
Huntingdon College	AL	35,900	C
Huntington Univ	IN	33,996	C
Illinois College	IL	41,330	VC
Illinois Wesleyan Univ	IL	56,430	VC+
Indiana Wesleyan Univ	IN	33,674	C
Iona College	NY	52,514	C
Iowa State Univ	IA	18,176	C
Iowa Wesleyan Univ	IA	41,000	C
James Madison Univ	VA	19,084	VC
Jarvis Christian College	TX	20,160	NC
John Carroll Univ	OH	51,570	C
Judson College	AL	27,066	C
Kalamazoo College	MI	53,931	HC
Kansas Wesleyan Univ	KS	37,930	C
La Roche College	PA	38,940	C

ST = STATE $IS = IN-STATE COSTS SR = SELECTOR RATING

School	ST	$IS	SR
La Salle Univ	PA	43,476	C
La Sierra Univ	CA	39,690	VC
Lafayette College	PA	68,520	MC
LaGrange College	GA	41,310	C
Lake Forest College	IL	50,652	VC
Lakeland Univ	WI	35,130	C
Lane College	TN	17,960	LC
Le Moyne College	NY	47,305	VC
Lebanon Valley College	PA	55,510	VC
Lees-McRae College	NC	33,944	NC
Lehigh Univ	PA	63,860	MC
Lenoir-Rhyne Univ	NC	47,500	LC
Lewis & Clark College	OR	60,984	MC
Liberty Univ	VA	31,415	C
Lincoln Univ	PA	20,878	LC
Lindenwood Univ	MO	25,760	C
Linfield College	OR	53,992	C
Loras College	IA	40,726	C
Loyola Univ New Orleans	LA	52,456	VC
Luther College	IA	49,990	VC
Lycoming College	PA	50,895	C
Lyon College	AR	36,120	VC
Macalester College	MN	64,136	MC
MacMurray College	IL	35,025	C
Manchester Univ	IN	41,540	C
Manhattan College	NY	55,652	C
Manhattanville College	NY	52,430	C
Marist College	NY	49,860	VC
Marlboro College	VT	50,832	VC+
Mars Hill Univ	NC	41,104	C
Martin Univ	IN	21,010	LC
Marygrove College	MI	30,100	LC
Marylhurst Univ	OR	16,818	NC
Maryville College	TN	44,410	C
Marywood Univ	PA	47,840	C
McDaniel College	MD	52,910	VC
McKendree Univ	IL	37,940	C+
McMurry Univ	TX	34,259	LC
McPherson College	KS	36,134	C
Mercer Univ	GA	45,348	VC
Mercyhurst Univ	PA	47,420	C
Meredith College	NC	46,634	C
Methodist Univ	NC	58,130	C
Miami Univ	OH	27,190	HC+
Mich State Univ	MI	24,542	VC
Middlebury College	VT	67,464	MC
Midland Univ	NE	39,512	C
Millsaps College	MS	50,080	C+
Missouri State Univ	MO	15,837	C+
Missouri Valley College	MO	28,150	C
Missouri Western State Univ	MO	17,822	LC
Monmouth College	IL	42,260	C
Montreat College	NC	34,605	LC
Moravian College	PA	55,488	C
Morehouse College	GA	40,835	C
Morgan State Univ	MD	17,190	LC
Morningside College	IA	39,780	C
Mount Aloysius College	PA	29,976	C
Mount Holyoke College	MA	56,746	MC
Mount Marty College	SD	36,862	C
Mount Mercy Univ	IA	39,748	C
Mount St. Joseph Univ	OH	33,880	LC
Mount St. Mary's Univ - Chalon Campus	CA	50,486	VC+
Mount Vernon Nazarene Univ	OH	35,944	C
Muhlenberg College	PA	56,645	VC
Muskingum Univ	OH	35,966	C
Naropa Univ	CO	43,278	NC
Nazareth College	NY	46,784	C
Nebr Wesleyan Univ	NE	42,026	C+
New College of Florida	FL	16,180	HC+
New York Univ	NY	68,139	MC
Newberry College	SC	34,550	C
Niagara Univ	NY	41,010	C
N Car State Univ	NC	22,434	HC+
N Car Wesleyan College	NC	39,200	C
North Central College	IL	48,712	C+
North Central Univ	MN	30,610	C
Northeastern Univ	MA	65,352	MC
Northland College	WI	41,103	C+
Northwest Univ	WA	38,720	VC
Northwestern College of Iowa	IA	38,400	C
Northwestern Univ	IL	68,725	MC
Notre Dame de Namur Univ	CA	46,526	LC
Notre Dame of Maryland Univ	MD	47,570	VC
Nyack College	NY	34,450	LC
Oakland City Univ	IN	33,930	NC
Oakwood Univ	AL	43,758	C
Oberlin College	OH	68,942	MC
Occidental College	CA	68,660	MC
Ohio Northern Univ	OH	44,050	VC
Ohio Univ	OH	23,394	VC
Ohio Wesleyan Univ	OH	49,460	VC
Okla Baptist Univ	OK	33,990	C
Okla City Univ	OK	40,476	C
Okla Wesleyan Univ	OK	34,434	C
Olivet Nazarene Univ	IL	41,840	VC
Oral Roberts Univ	OK	34,316	C
Ottawa Univ	KS	39,980	VC
Otterbein Univ	OH	41,630	C
Ouachita Baptist Univ	AR	33,500	VC
Our Lady of the Lake Univ	TX	37,790	LC
Pacific Lutheran Univ	WA	49,960	C
Pacific Union College	CA	36,009	VC
Pepperdine Univ	CA	66,862	VC+
Pfeiffer Univ	NC	40,532	LC
Piedmont College	GA	34,334	C

School	ST	$IS	SR
Pontifical Catholic Univ of PR	PR	10,534	
Presbyterian College	SC	47,186	C
Princeton Univ	NJ	60,090	MC
Principia College	IL	40,350	C
Purdue Univ/West Lafayette	IN	20,032	MC
Queens Univ of Charlotte	NC	39,543	C
Randolph College	VA	53,970	C
Randolph-Macon College	VA	51,480	VC
Reed College	OR	65,300	MC
Regis Univ	CO	46,380	C
Rhodes College	TN	51,900	HC
Rice Univ	TX	59,458	MC
Ripon College	WI	49,991	VC
Roanoke College	VA	55,952	VC
Roberts Wesleyan College	NY	41,116	C
Rollins College	FL	58,670	HC
Rosemont College	PA	30,980	LC
Rutgers Univ - Camden	NJ	26,595	C
St. Francis Univ	PA	46,146	NC
St. Leo Univ	FL	32,850	C
St. Mary's College	IN	50,600	C
St. Mary's College of Calif	CA	57,420	C
St. Michael's College	VT	53,275	VC+
St. Xavier Univ	IL	44,440	C
Salem College	NC	40,206	C
Salve Regina Univ	RI	53,046	VC
Samford Univ	AL	40,770	VC
San Francisco State Univ	CA	18,514	LC
San Jose State Univ	CA	22,630	C
Sarah Lawrence College	NY	68,866	MC
Schreiner Univ	TX	34,626	LC
Scripps College	CA	69,260	HC
Seattle Univ	WA	54,957	VC
Seton Hall Univ	NJ	58,008	C
Seton Hill Univ	PA	46,972	VC
Sewanee: The Univ of the South	TN	58,000	HC+
Shaw Univ	NC	24,638	C
Shenandoah Univ	VA	42,100	C
Shorter Univ	GA	31,130	LC
Siena College	NY	48,916	C
Siena Heights Univ	MI	36,322	C
Silver Lake College of the Holy Family	WI	36,290	LC
Simpson College	IA	45,626	VC
Simpson Univ	CA	34,722	C
Skidmore College	NY	66,600	MC
Smith College	MA	66,774	MC
Southeastern Univ	FL	34,910	LC
Southern Methodist Univ	TX	69,008	MC
Southern Wesleyan Univ	SC	33,670	LC
Southwestern Adventist Univ	TX	28,232	LC
Southwestern Univ	TX	52,370	VC
Spelman College	GA	41,642	C
St. Edward's Univ	TX	56,190	VC
St. Francis College	NY	38,800	LC
St. John Fisher College	NY	45,270	VC
St. Lawrence Univ	NY	66,646	HC+
St. Mary's College of Maryland	MD	27,312	VC
St. Norbert College	WI	46,060	VC
St. Olaf College	MN	56,430	HC
St. Thomas Aquinas College	NY	32,450	C
St. Thomas Univ	FL	51,187	LC
Stanford Univ	CA	62,541	MC
SUNY/College at Old Westbury	NY	16,860	C
Stetson Univ	FL	57,174	VC+
Stillman College	AL	20,738	C
Stonehill College	MA	55,130	C
Susquehanna Univ	PA	57,560	VC
Swarthmore College	PA	63,550	MC
Syracuse Univ	NY	62,313	HC
Tabor College	KS	35,870	C
Temple Univ	PA	24,392	C+
Tenn Wesleyan Univ	TN	32,680	LC
Texas A&M Univ at Commerce	TX	10,496	C
Texas Christian Univ	TX	57,120	HC
Texas Wesleyan Univ	TX	37,338	C
The Catholic Univ of America	DC	58,376	VC
The College of Idaho	ID	36,415	C
The College of New Rochelle	NY	46,300	LC
The College of Wooster	OH	60,000	HC
The George Washington Univ	DC	68,474	HC+
The Univ of Alabama	AL	24,320	C+
The Univ of Tenn at Knoxville	TN	22,112	VC
The Univ of Texas at Austin	TX	20,206	MC
Thiel College	PA	42,950	LC
Thomas Edison State Univ	NJ	6,350	NC
Tougaloo College	MS	17,980	NC
Towson Univ	MD	21,878	C
Transylvania Univ	KY	47,450	HC+
Trevecca Nazarene Univ	TN	31,186	C
Trinity College	CT	69,020	HC
Trinity Univ	TX	54,480	MC
Truman State Univ	MO	16,286	MC
Tufts Univ	MA		MC
Tulane Univ	LA	67,496	MC
Union College	KY	32,310	C
Union College	NE	23,270	C
Union College	NY	64,320	MC
Union Univ	TN	41,160	VC
Universidad Adventista de las Antillas	PR	16,606	
Univ of Bridgeport	CT	44,985	LC

School	ST	$IS	SR
Univ of Calif at Berkeley	CA	29,886	MC
Univ of Calif at Davis	CA	28,468	HC
Univ of Calif at Irvine	CA	33,857	VC
Univ of Calif at Los Angeles	CA	27,438	HC+
Univ of Calif at Riverside	CA	32,912	C
Univ of Calif at Santa Barbara	CA	30,627	HC+
Univ of Calif San Diego	CA	30,450	MC
Univ of Central Arkansas	AR	15,042	VC
Univ of Central Florida	FL	16,379	VC
Univ of Chicago	IL	70,551	MC
Univ of Dayton	OH	54,930	VC
Univ of Denver	CO	61,129	VC+
Univ of Detroit Mercy	MI	48,816	C
Univ of Dubuque	IA	37,824	C
Univ of Findlay	OH	43,040	C
Univ of Florida	FL	16,291	HC+
Univ of Georgia	GA	21,878	HC
Univ of Great Falls	MT	38,524	C
Univ of Hawaii at Manoa	HI	23,261	C
Univ of Illinois at Urbana-Champaign	IL	27,006	HC
Univ of Indianapolis	IN	36,480	VC
Univ of Iowa	IA	19,415	HC
Univ of Jamestown	ND	28,508	C
Univ of Kansas	KS	20,884	VC
Univ of La Verne	CA	55,600	C
Univ of Lynchburg	VA	48,370	C
Univ of Mary Washington	VA	23,039	C+
Univ of Miami	FL	63,494	MC
Univ of Mich/Ann Arbor	MI	25,274	MC
Univ of Miss	MS	18,802	C
Univ of Missouri-Columbia	MO	20,463	VC
Univ of Mobile	AL	28,935	C
Univ of Mount Olive	NC	18,426	C
Univ of Mount Union	OH	39,990	C
Univ of New Mexico	NM	16,808	C
Univ of N Car at Asheville	NC	16,251	VC+
Univ of N Car at Chapel Hill	NC	20,561	MC
Univ of N Dak	ND	16,673	C
Univ of North Florida	FL	15,996	VC
Univ of Northern Iowa	IA	17,480	C
Univ of Oregon	OR	24,021	VC
Univ of Pennsylvania	PA	63,526	MC
Univ of Pikeville	KY	27,838	C
Univ of Pittsburgh	PA	30,030	MC
Univ of Puget Sound	WA	60,210	HC
Univ of Redlands	CA	61,934	VC
Univ of Richmond	VA	62,730	MC
Univ of Rochester	NY	65,032	MC
Univ of St. Joseph	CT	49,069	C
Univ of Sioux Falls	SD	25,630	C
Univ of S Car at Columbia	SC	21,726	VC
Univ of South Florida/Tampa	FL	16,110	VC
Univ of Southern Calif	CA	66,631	MC
Univ of the Cumberlands	KY	32,000	LC
Univ of the Incarnate Word	TX	39,162	LC
Univ of the Ozarks	AR	31,050	NC
Univ of the Pacific	CA	57,446	VC
Univ of Tulsa	OK	52,625	HC
Univ of Vermont	VT	29,792	HC
Univ of Virginia	VA	27,367	MC
Univ of Washington	WA	23,091	MC
Univ of West Florida	FL	15,848	C
Univ of Wisc-Madison	WI	21,647	MC
Univ of Wisc-Milwaukee	WI	21,538	C
Univ of Wisc-Oshkosh	WI	15,392	C
Ursuline College	OH	41,076	LC
Valparaiso Univ	IN	50,160	VC
Vassar College	NY	68,110	MC
Villanova Univ	PA	64,922	MC
Virginia Commonwealth Univ	VA	23,811	VC
Virginia Union Univ	VA	25,058	C
Virginia Wesleyan Univ	VA	45,980	LC
Wabash College	IN	52,100	VC
Wake Forest Univ	NC	69,354	MC
Walla Walla Univ	WA	34,845	C
Wartburg College	IA	49,478	C
Washburn Univ	KS	15,827	C
Washington Adventist Univ	MD	32,050	LC
Washington and Lee Univ	VA	59,647	MC
Washington State Univ	WA	22,747	C
Washington Univ in St. Louis	MO	67,539	MC
Wayland Baptist Univ	TX	23,460	LC
Webster Univ	MO	37,490	C
Wellesley College	MA	66,984	MC
Wesleyan College	GA	31,940	C+
Wesleyan Univ	CT	66,940	MC
West Virginia Wesleyan College	WV	39,188	C
Western Kentucky Univ	KY	16,850	C
Western Mich Univ	MI	21,791	C
Westminster College	MO	32,820	C
Westminster College	PA	41,722	C
Westmont College	CA	57,930	VC
Wheaton College	MA	63,818	VC
Whitman College	WA	59,772	MC
Whittier College	CA	57,891	C
Wiley College	TX	19,255	C
Willamette Univ	OR	62,514	VC+
William Carey Univ	MS	23,950	LC
William Jewell College	MO	42,490	C+
Williams Baptist College	AR	24,720	C
Williams College	MA	67,700	MC
Wilmington College	OH	35,100	C
Wilson College	PA	35,620	LC
Winthrop Univ	SC	23,960	C
Wittenberg Univ	OH	49,863	VC

School	ST	$IS	SR
Wofford College	SC	49,885	VC
Wright State Univ	OH	16,983	C
Yale Univ	CT	64,650	MC
Yeshiva Univ	NY	52,750	VC
Youngstown State Univ	OH	17,487	C

RELIGIOUS EDUCATION

School	ST	$IS	SR
Andrews Univ	MI	41,732	C
Baylor Univ	TX	56,803	HC
Bloomfield College	NJ	40,100	LC
Cal State, Northridge	CA	17,277	LC
Campbellsville Univ	KY	33,400	C
Cedarville Univ	OH	36,244	VC
Concordia Univ St. Paul	MN	29,050	C
Cornerstone Univ	MI	36,550	C
Dallas Baptist Univ	TX	35,220	VC
East Texas Baptist Univ	TX	34,444	C
Edgewood College	WI	35,950	C
Franciscan Univ of Steubenville	OH	33,980	VC
Georgia State Univ	GA	25,250	C
Grace Bible College	MI	25,250	C
Houghton College	NY	40,558	VC
Indiana Wesleyan Univ	IN	33,674	C
Kansas Wesleyan Univ	KS	37,930	C
Lenoir-Rhyne Univ	NC	47,500	LC
Loyola Univ Chicago	IL	57,158	VC
Loyola Univ New Orleans	LA	52,456	VC
Marian Univ	IN	43,206	C
Mercyhurst Univ	PA	47,420	C
Morris College	SC	19,195	LC
Mount Mary Univ	WI	34,650	LC
Mount St. Joseph Univ	OH	33,880	LC
Mount Vernon Nazarene Univ	OH	35,944	C
Muskingum Univ	OH	35,966	C
North Central Univ	MN	30,610	C
Northwest Univ	WA	38,720	VC
Oakwood Univ	AL	43,758	C
Okla Christian Univ	OK	29,260	C
Okla City Univ	OK	40,476	C
Oral Roberts Univ	OK	34,316	C
Pfeiffer Univ	NC	40,532	LC
Presbyterian College	SC	47,186	C
Simpson Univ	CA	34,722	C
Southern Adventist Univ	TN	28,250	C
Southwest Baptist Univ	MO	30,890	LC
Sterling College	KS	32,830	LC
Texas Wesleyan Univ	TX	37,338	C
The Univ of Arizona	AZ	24,086	C
Trinity Bible College	ND		
Union College	NE	23,270	C
Univ of Calif at Riverside	CA	32,912	C
Univ of Dayton	OH	54,930	VC
Univ of Jamestown	ND	28,508	C
Univ of Northwestern - St. Paul	MN	39,530	C
Vanguard Univ of Southern Calif	CA	42,400	VC
Viterbo Univ	WI	34,660	C
Wayland Baptist Univ	TX	23,460	LC
West Virginia Wesleyan College	WV	39,188	C
Williams Baptist College	AR	24,720	C

RELIGIOUS MUSIC

School	ST	$IS	SR
Aquinas College - Mich	MI	38,876	VC
Baylor Univ	TX	56,803	HC
Belhaven Univ	MS	32,250	C
Bethel Univ	MN	46,550	C+
Calvin College	MI	43,090	HC
Campbellsville Univ	KY	33,400	C
Centenary College of Louisiana	LA	49,050	C+
Charleston Southern Univ	SC	34,700	C
College of the Ozarks	MO	7,530	VC
Columbia College	SC	36,550	C
Concordia College - New York	NY	39,035	LC
Concordia Univ St. Paul	MN	29,050	C
Concordia Univ Texas	TX	41,920	C
Concordia Univ Wisc	WI	35,910	C
Concordia Univ, Ann Arbor	MI	38,878	C+
Dallas Baptist Univ	TX	35,220	VC
East Texas Baptist Univ	TX	34,444	C
Eastern Nazarene College	MA	41,114	C
Evangel Univ	MO	28,898	C
Franciscan Univ of Steubenville	OH	33,980	VC
Furman Univ	SC	61,098	VC+
Gardner-Webb Univ	NC	24,935	C+
Grove City College	PA	26,654	VC
Hannibal-LaGrange Univ	MO	29,815	C
Hardin-Simmons Univ	TX	36,025	C
Houghton College	NY	40,558	VC
Houston Baptist Univ	TX	36,450	C
Huntington Univ	IN	33,996	C
Indiana Wesleyan Univ	IN	33,674	C
Johnson C. Smith Univ	NC	25,336	LC
Kentucky Christian Univ	KY	26,836	LC
Lee Univ	TN	22,045	C
Lenoir-Rhyne Univ	NC	47,500	LC
Madonna Univ	MI	30,450	LC
Malone Univ	OH	39,200	C
McKendree Univ	IL	37,940	C+
Milligan College	TN	39,450	C
Miss College	MS	25,850	C

ST = STATE **$IS** = IN-STATE COSTS **SR** = SELECTOR RATING

School	ST	$IS	SR
Missouri Baptist Univ	MO	35,594	C
Mount Vernon Nazarene Univ	OH	35,944	C
North Central Univ	MN	30,610	C
Northwest Univ	WA	38,720	VC
Northwestern College of Iowa	IA	38,400	C
Nyack College	NY	34,450	LC
Okla Wesleyan Univ	OK	34,434	C
Olivet Nazarene Univ	IL	41,840	VC
Oral Roberts Univ	OK	34,316	C
Ouachita Baptist Univ	AR	33,500	VC
Pfeiffer Univ	NC	40,532	LC
Seton Hill Univ	PA	46,972	VC
Shorter Univ	GA	31,130	LC
Southeastern Univ	FL	34,910	LC
Southern Nazarene Univ	OK	33,684	C
Southwest Baptist Univ	MO	30,890	LC
St. Olaf College	MN	56,430	HC
Tenn Wesleyan Univ	TN	32,680	LC
Union Univ	TN	41,160	VC
Univ of Mobile	AL	28,935	C
Univ of the Cumberlands	KY	32,000	LC
Valparaiso Univ	IN	50,160	VC
Warner Pacific College	OR	31,610	C
Warner Univ	FL	28,216	C
Wartburg College	IA	49,478	C
Wayland Baptist Univ	TX	23,460	LC
Westminster College	PA	41,722	C
William Carey Univ	MS	23,950	LC
Williams Baptist College	AR	24,720	C

RELIGIOUS STUDIES

School	ST	$IS	SR
Aquinas College - Mich	MI	38,876	VC
Arizona State Univ at the Tempe Campus	AZ	23,001	VC
Ashland Univ	OH	30,446	C
Avila Univ	MO	27,100	C
Bates College	ME	64,500	HC
Beloit College	WI	55,206	HC
Biola Univ	CA	48,686	C
Bradley Univ	IL	43,240	VC
Brown Univ	RI	64,566	MC
Bryn Athyn College	PA	32,664	C
Cabrini Univ	PA	42,591	LC
Cal State, Chico	CA	19,790	VC
Cal State, Fullerton	CA	21,902	C
Cal State, Long Beach	CA	18,850	C
Cal State, Northridge	CA	17,277	LC
College of Charleston	SC	24,046	VC
College of St. Elizabeth	NJ	45,700	LC
Concordia Univ, Ann Arbor	MI	38,878	C+
Cornell Univ	NY	67,591	MC
Dakota Wesleyan Univ	SD	33,980	LC
Dallas Baptist Univ	TX	35,220	VC
Dordt College	IA	37,860	C+
Edgewood College	WI	35,950	C
Elon Univ	NC	46,142	HC
Fairfield Univ	CT	61,445	HC
Fontbonne Univ	MO	34,606	C
Georgian Court Univ	NJ	43,068	LC
Gettysburg College	PA	65,210	MC
Gonzaga Univ	WA	52,880	HC
Hardin-Simmons Univ	TX	36,025	C
Houghton College	NY	40,558	VC
Indiana Univ Bloomington	IN	20,791	HC
Indiana Univ of Pennsylvania	PA	24,474	C
Indiana Univ-Purdue Univ Indianapolis	IN	18,952	C
Kenyon College	OH	65,840	MC
King Univ	TN	36,976	C
Le Moyne College	NY	47,305	VC
Lebanon Valley College	PA	55,510	VC
Madonna Univ	MI	30,450	LC
Marian Univ	IN	43,206	C
McKendree Univ	IL	37,940	C+
Merrimack College	MA	55,415	C
MidAmerica Nazarene Univ	KS	37,808	C
Montclair State Univ	NJ	26,912	C
New York Univ	NY	68,139	MC
Niagara Univ	NY	41,010	C
Ohio State Univ at Columbus	OH	22,843	MC
Okla Baptist Univ	OK	33,990	C
Old Dominion Univ	VA	21,618	C
Olivet Nazarene Univ	IL	41,840	VC
Oregon State Univ	OR	23,337	VC
Pomona College	CA	64,957	MC
Regis Univ	CO	46,380	C
Rutgers Univ - New Brunswick	NJ	27,090	HC
St. Joseph's Univ	PA	58,540	VC
St. Martin's Univ	WA	45,056	C
San Diego State Univ	CA	23,156	VC
San Jose State Univ	CA	22,630	C
Stony Brook Univ/The SUNY	NY	22,703	MC
Syracuse Univ	NY	62,313	HC
The American Univ	DC	61,317	HC
The Univ of Arizona	AZ	24,086	C
The Univ of Utah	UT	18,751	VC
Univ of Calif San Diego	CA	30,450	MC
Univ of Chicago	IL	70,551	MC
Univ of Colo Boulder	CO	26,048	HC
Univ of Findlay	OH	43,040	C
Univ of Great Falls	MT	38,524	C
Univ of Miami	FL	63,494	MC
Univ of Minn/Twin Cities	MN	24,269	MC
Univ of Nebr - Lincoln	NE	18,589	VC
Univ of N Car at Charlotte	NC	17,803	VC
Univ of N Car at Greensboro	NC	15,998	C
Univ of Okla	OK	19,651	HC
Univ of San Francisco	CA	60,580	C
Univ of Wisc-Eau Claire	WI	16,354	VC
Univ of Wyoming	WY	15,537	C
Ursinus College	PA	62,920	VC
Vanderbilt Univ	TN	63,248	MC
Viterbo Univ	WI	34,660	C
Washington State Univ	WA	22,747	C
Webster Univ	MO	37,490	C
Wingate Univ	NC	41,900	C

RESORT MANAGEMENT

School	ST	$IS	SR
Ferris State Univ	MI	21,458	C
Florida International Univ	FL	20,281	C
Lasell College	MA	49,400	C

RESOURCE ECONOMY & COMMERCE

School	ST	$IS	SR
Texas Tech Univ	TX	20,156	C+

RESPIRATORY CARE

School	ST	$IS	SR
Stony Brook Univ/The SUNY	NY	22,703	MC

RESPIRATORY THERAPY

School	ST	$IS	SR
Armstrong State Univ	GA	15,615	C
Augusta Univ	GA	4,632	C
Ball State Univ	IN	19,808	C+
Bellarmine Univ	KY	52,532	C
Boise State Univ	ID	17,368	C
Dakota State Univ	SD	12,286	C
Ferris State Univ	MI	21,458	C
Gannon Univ	PA	42,922	C
Georgia State Univ	GA	25,250	C
Gwynedd Mercy Univ	PA	43,780	LC
Indiana Univ of Pennsylvania	PA	24,474	C
Indiana Univ-Purdue Univ Indianapolis	IN	18,952	C
LIU Brooklyn	NY	50,698	C
Mansfield Univ of Pennsylvania	PA	24,244	LC
Marshall Univ	WV	18,044	C
Midwestern State Univ	TX	12,111	LC
Millersville Univ of Pennsylvania	PA	25,298	C
Missouri Southern State Univ	MO	13,071	C
Missouri State Univ	MO	15,837	C+
Nebr Methodist College	NE	25,314	C
N Dak State Univ	ND	16,245	VC
Nova Southeastern Univ	FL	38,534	C+
Ohio State Univ at Columbus	OH	22,843	MC
Point Park Univ	PA	41,270	C
Rhode Island College	RI	19,000	LC
Rutgers Univ - New Brunswick	NJ	27,090	HC
Salisbury Univ	MD	21,132	VC
Samford Univ	AL	40,770	VC
Shenandoah Univ	VA	42,100	C
St. Catherine Univ	MN	45,630	C
Stony Brook Univ/The SUNY	NY	22,703	MC
Tenn State Univ	TN	14,423	LC
Texas Southern Univ	TX	19,592	LC
Texas State Univ	TX	18,721	C
The Univ of Akron	OH	22,566	C
The Univ of Mary	ND	23,180	C
Thomas Edison State Univ	NJ	6,350	NC
Univ of Alabama at Birmingham	AL	22,092	C
Univ of Cincinnati	OH	22,118	VC
Univ of Indianapolis	IN	36,480	VC
Univ of Kansas	KS	20,884	VC
Univ of Missouri-Columbia	MO	20,463	VC
Univ of N Car at Charlotte	NC	17,803	VC
Univ of South Alabama	AL	16,880	C
Univ of Southern Indiana	IN	16,808	C
Univ of the Ozarks	AR	31,050	NC
Washington Adventist Univ	MD	32,050	LC
Weber State Univ	UT	14,112	C
West Chester Univ of Pennsylvania	PA	19,171	VC
Wheeling Jesuit Univ	WV	37,106	LC
York College of Pennsylvania	PA	29,240	C
Youngstown State Univ	OH	17,487	C

RETAILING

School	ST	$IS	SR
Bradley Univ	IL	43,240	VC
Central Mich Univ	MI	20,330	C
East Central Univ	OK	13,330	C
Johnson & Wales Univ/Denver Campus	CO	44,768	C
Johnson & Wales Univ/Providence Campus	RI	44,768	C
Marywood Univ	PA	47,840	C
Mount Ida College	MA	46,820	C
Ohio Univ	OH	23,394	VC
Purdue Univ/West Lafayette	IN	20,032	MC
Simmons College	MA	54,400	HC
Southern New Hampshire Univ	NH	44,256	C
Syracuse Univ	NY	62,313	HC
Texas Tech Univ	TX	20,156	C+
The Univ of Arizona	AZ	24,086	C
The Univ of Tenn at Knoxville	TN	22,112	VC
Univ of Arkansas at Fayetteville	AR	19,766	VC
Univ of Minn/Twin Cities	MN	24,269	MC
Univ of N Car at Greensboro	NC	15,998	C
Univ of Pennsylvania	PA	63,526	MC
Univ of S Car at Columbia	SC	21,726	VC
Univ of Wisc-Madison	WI	21,647	MC
Univ of Wisc-Stout	WI	19,667	C
Youngstown State Univ	OH	17,487	C

ROBOTIC & MECHATRONIC SYSTEMS ENGINEERING

School	ST	$IS	SR
Millersville Univ of Pennsylvania	PA	25,298	C
Univ of Detroit Mercy	MI	48,816	C
Worcester Polytechnic Inst	MA	62,846	MC

ROMANCE LANGUAGES AND LITERATURE

School	ST	$IS	SR
Boston College	MA	68,043	MC
Bowdoin College	ME	65,980	MC
Bowling Green State Univ	OH	19,975	C
Bryn Mawr College	PA	65,220	MC
Carleton College	MN	66,414	MC
CUNY/City College	NY	20,204	C
Clark Univ	MA	53,260	HC+
Colo College	CO	64,894	MC
Dartmouth College	NH	68,109	MC
DePauw Univ	IN	58,688	VC
Haverford College	PA	66,490	MC
Johns Hopkins Univ	MD	68,080	MC
Merrimack College	MA	55,415	C
Mount Holyoke College	MA	56,746	MC
New York Univ	NY	68,139	MC
Oberlin College	OH	68,942	MC
Pomona College	CA	64,957	MC
Queens Univ of Charlotte	NC	39,543	C
Rockford Univ	IL	38,570	C
St. Thomas Aquinas College	NY	32,450	C
SUNY Albany	NY	22,165	C
Truman State Univ	MO	16,286	MC
Univ of Chicago	IL	70,551	MC
Univ of Georgia	GA	21,878	HC
Univ of Maryland/College Park	MD	21,938	HC
Univ of Nevada, Las Vegas	NV	17,553	C
Univ of N Car at Chapel Hill	NC	20,561	MC
Univ of Notre Dame	IN	68,801	MC
Univ of Oregon	OR	24,021	VC
Univ of PR-Rio Piedras campus	PR	13,327	
Washington and Lee Univ	VA	59,647	MC
Washington Univ in St. Louis	MO	67,539	MC
Wayne State Univ	MI	23,085	C
Wesleyan Univ	CT	66,940	MC
Wheeling Jesuit Univ	WV	37,106	LC

RURAL ECONOMICS

School	ST	$IS	SR
Univ of Idaho	ID	16,158	C

RURAL SOCIOLOGY

School	ST	$IS	SR
Northland College	WI	41,103	C+
S Dak State Univ	SD	15,874	C
Univ of Missouri-Columbia	MO	20,463	VC
Univ of Wisc-Madison	WI	21,647	MC

RUSSIAN

School	ST	$IS	SR
Amherst College	MA	66,186	MC
Arizona State Univ at the Tempe Campus	AZ	23,001	VC
Bard College	NY	65,924	HC
Barnard College/Columbia Univ	NY	68,762	MC
Bates College	ME	64,500	HC
Baylor Univ	TX	56,803	HC
Beloit College	WI	55,206	HC
Bowdoin College	ME	65,980	MC
Bowling Green State Univ	OH	19,975	C
Brigham Young Univ	UT	13,248	MC
Bryn Mawr College	PA	65,220	MC
Bucknell Univ	PA	67,136	MC
Cal State, Fullerton	CA	21,902	C
Cal State, Northridge	CA	17,277	LC
Carleton College	MN	66,414	MC
Central Washington Univ	WA	16,803	C
CUNY/Brooklyn College	NY	7,163	C+
CUNY/Hunter College	NY	31,098	VC
CUNY/Lehman College	NY	5,788	LC
CUNY/Queens College	NY	21,507	C
Colgate Univ	NY	67,500	MC
College of the Holy Cross	MA	64,320	MC
Columbia Univ/City of New York	NY	62,958	MC
Cornell College	IA	49,900	VC
Dartmouth College	NH	68,109	MC
Dickinson College	PA	66,166	MC
Ferrum College	VA	43,970	C
Florida State Univ	FL	16,771	HC
Georgetown Univ	DC	68,970	MC
Goucher College	MD	56,110	VC
Grinnell College	IA	63,114	MC
Gustavus Adolphus College	MN	53,943	HC
Harvard College/Harvard Univ	MA	65,609	MC
Haverford College	PA	66,490	MC
Hofstra Univ	NY	58,210	C+
Iowa State Univ	IA	18,176	C
Juniata College	PA	58,118	VC
Lawrence Univ	WI	56,133	HC+
Luther College	IA	49,990	VC
Macalester College	MN	64,136	MC
Marlboro College	VT	50,832	VC+
Miami Univ	OH	27,190	HC+
Mich State Univ	MI	24,542	VC
Middlebury College	VT	67,464	MC
New York Univ	NY	68,139	MC
Northern Illinois Univ	IL	20,176	C
Oberlin College	OH	68,942	MC
Ohio State Univ at Columbus	OH	22,843	MC
Ohio Univ	OH	23,394	VC
Pomona College	CA	64,957	MC
Portland State Univ	OR	19,443	C
Purdue Univ/West Lafayette	IN	20,032	MC
Rider Univ	NJ	54,050	C
Rutgers Univ - New Brunswick	NJ	27,090	HC
San Diego State Univ	CA	23,156	VC
Sarah Lawrence College	NY	68,866	MC
Scripps College	CA	69,260	HC
Seattle Pacific Univ	WA	47,439	C+
Sewanee: The Univ of the South	TN	58,000	HC+
Smith College	MA	66,774	MC
St. Olaf College	MN	56,430	HC
Swarthmore College	PA	63,550	MC
Texas A&M Univ at College Station	TX	20,771	VC+
The American Univ	DC	61,317	HC
The George Washington Univ	DC	68,474	HC+
The Univ of Alabama	AL	24,320	C+
The Univ of Arizona	AZ	24,086	C
The Univ of Tenn at Knoxville	TN	22,112	VC
The Univ of Texas at Austin	TX	20,206	MC
The Univ of Utah	UT	18,751	VC
Thomas Edison State Univ	NJ	6,350	NC
Trinity College	CT	69,020	HC
Trinity Univ	TX	54,480	MC
Tufts Univ	MA		MC
Tulane Univ	LA	67,496	MC
Univ of Calif at Davis	CA	28,468	HC
Univ of Calif at Riverside	CA	32,912	C
Univ of Calif San Diego	CA	30,450	MC
Univ of Chicago	IL	70,551	MC
Univ of Denver	CO	61,129	VC+
Univ of Florida	FL	16,291	HC+
Univ of Georgia	GA	21,878	HC
Univ of Hawaii at Manoa	HI	23,261	C
Univ of Illinois at Chicago	IL	24,664	VC
Univ of Iowa	IA	19,415	HC
Univ of Kentucky	KY	24,800	C+
Univ of Maryland/Baltimore County	MD	23,004	VC
Univ of Maryland/College Park	MD	21,938	HC
Univ of Mich/Ann Arbor	MI	25,274	MC
Univ of Minn/Twin Cities	MN	24,269	MC
Univ of Missouri-Columbia	MO	20,463	VC
Univ of Montana	MT	14,105	C
Univ of Nebr - Lincoln	NE	18,589	VC
Univ of New Hampshire	NH	29,333	VC
Univ of New Mexico	NM	16,808	C
Univ of N Car at Greensboro	NC	15,998	C
Univ of Notre Dame	IN	68,801	MC
Univ of Okla	OK	19,651	HC
Univ of Pennsylvania	PA	63,526	MC
Univ of Pittsburgh	PA	30,030	MC
Univ of Rochester	NY	65,032	MC
Univ of S Car at Columbia	SC	21,726	VC
Univ of South Florida/Tampa	FL	16,110	VC
Univ of Southern Calif	CA	66,631	MC
Univ of Texas at Arlington	TX	18,876	C
Univ of Vermont	VT	29,792	HC
Univ of Wisc-Madison	WI	21,647	MC
Univ of Wyoming	WY	15,537	C
Vanderbilt Univ	TN	63,248	MC
Vassar College	NY	68,110	MC
Wake Forest Univ	NC	69,354	MC
Washington State Univ	WA	22,747	C
Wellesley College	MA	66,984	MC
West Chester Univ of Pennsylvania	PA	19,171	VC
Western Washington Univ	WA	18,904	VC
Wheaton College	MA	63,818	VC
Williams College	MA	67,700	MC
Yale Univ	CT	64,650	MC

RUSSIAN AND SLAVIC STUDIES

School	ST	$IS	SR
Augsburg Univ	MN	45,129	C
Bard College	NY	65,924	HC
Baylor Univ	TX	56,803	HC
Boston College	MA	68,043	MC
Brown Univ	RI	64,566	MC
Cal State, Fullerton	CA	21,902	C
Carnegie Mellon Univ	PA	67,980	MC
Colgate Univ	NY	67,500	MC
Colo College	CO	64,894	MC
Columbia Univ/City of New York	NY	62,958	MC
Conn College	CT	65,000	MC

ST = STATE $IS = IN-STATE COSTS SR = SELECTOR RATING

School	ST	$IS	SR
Cornell College	IA	49,900	VC
Dartmouth College	NH	68,109	MC
DePauw Univ	IN	58,688	VC
Eastern Mich Univ	MI	19,761	C
Emory Univ	GA	63,286	MC
Florida State Univ	FL	16,771	HC
George Mason Univ	VA	19,884	C
Grand Valley State Univ	MI	22,250	C+
Hamilton College	NY	64,250	MC
Harvard College/Harvard Univ	MA	65,609	MC
Hobart and William Smith Colleges	NY	67,050	HC+
Lafayette College	PA	68,520	MC
Middlebury College	VT	67,464	MC
Mount Holyoke College	MA	56,746	MC
Muhlenberg College	PA	56,645	VC
New York Univ	NY	68,139	MC
Oakland Univ	MI	20,763	C
Oberlin College	OH	68,942	MC
Pomona College	CA	64,957	MC
Purdue Univ/West Lafayette	IN	20,032	MC
Rhodes College	TN	51,900	HC
Rutgers Univ - New Brunswick	NJ	27,090	HC
San Diego State Univ	CA	23,156	VC
Smith College	MA	66,774	MC
St. Olaf College	MN	56,430	HC
Stetson Univ	FL	57,174	VC+
Syracuse Univ	NY	62,313	HC
Texas Tech Univ	TX	20,156	C+
The American Univ	DC	61,317	HC
The College of Wooster	OH	60,000	HC
The Univ of Texas at Austin	TX	20,206	MC
Tufts Univ	MA		MC
Tulane Univ	LA	67,496	MC
Univ of Calif at Los Angeles	CA	27,438	HC+
Univ of Calif at Riverside	CA	32,912	C
Univ of Calif San Diego	CA	30,450	MC
Univ of Illinois at Chicago	IL	24,664	VC
Univ of Illinois at Urbana-Champaign	IL	27,006	HC
Univ of Iowa	IA	19,415	HC
Univ of Kansas	KS	20,884	VC
Univ of Maryland/College Park	MD	21,938	HC
Univ of Mass Amherst	MA	27,669	HC
Univ of Mich/Ann Arbor	MI	25,274	MC
Univ of Minn/Twin Cities	MN	24,269	MC
Univ of N Car at Chapel Hill	NC	20,561	MC
Univ of N Car at Greensboro	NC	15,998	C
Univ of Richmond	VA	62,730	MC
Univ of Rochester	NY	65,032	MC
Univ of Tulsa	OK	52,625	HC
Univ of Vermont	VT	29,792	HC
Univ of Washington	WA	23,091	MC
Wesleyan Univ	CT	66,940	MC
West Chester Univ of Pennsylvania	PA	19,171	VC
Yale Univ	CT	64,650	MC

RUSSIAN LANGUAGES AND LITERATURE

School	ST	$IS	SR
Boston Univ	MA	67,352	MC
Brandeis Univ	MA	68,443	MC
Brown Univ	RI	64,566	MC
Colby College	ME	64,060	MC
Emory Univ	GA	63,286	MC
Hobart and William Smith Colleges	NY	67,050	HC+
Kent State Univ	OH	20,928	C
New College of Florida	FL	16,180	HC+
Oberlin College	OH	68,942	MC
Okla State Univ	OK	17,180	C+
Pennsylvania State Univ - Univ Park	PA	29,716	HC
Reed College	OR	65,300	MC
St. Louis Univ	MO	49,866	HC
Southern Illinois Univ Carbondale	IL	24,554	C
Stony Brook Univ/The SUNY	NY	22,703	MC
Syracuse Univ	NY	62,313	HC
The College of Wooster	OH	60,000	HC
Univ of Calif at Los Angeles	CA	27,438	HC+
Univ of Calif at Riverside	CA	32,912	C
Univ of Colo Boulder	CO	26,048	HC
Univ of Illinois at Chicago	IL	24,664	VC
Univ of Illinois at Urbana-Champaign	IL	27,006	HC
Univ of Mich/Ann Arbor	MI	25,274	MC
Univ of Oregon	OR	24,021	VC
Univ of Wisc-Milwaukee	WI	21,538	C
Washington and Lee Univ	VA	59,647	MC
Wellesley College	MA	66,984	MC
West Chester Univ of Pennsylvania	PA	19,171	VC
Wheaton College	MA	63,818	VC
Yale Univ	CT	64,650	MC

SAFETY AND SECURITY TECHNOLOGY

School	ST	$IS	SR
Davenport Univ	MI	25,896	LC
Farmingdale State College	NY	20,968	C
Georgetown College	KY	41,440	C
Marshall Univ	WV	18,044	C
St. Louis Univ	MO	49,866	HC
Univ of Wisc-Whitewater	WI	13,976	C

SAFETY MANAGEMENT

School	ST	$IS	SR
Amridge Univ	AL	10,860	LC
CUNY/John Jay College of Criminal Justice	NY	6,359	SP
Concordia Univ, Ann Arbor	MI	38,878	C+
Embry-Riddle Aeronautical Univ - Worldwide	FL	17,720	C
Franklin Univ	OH	11,616	NC
Illinois State Univ	IL	23,418	VC
Indiana State Univ	IN	23,223	LC
Mansfield Univ of Pennsylvania	PA	24,244	LC
Marshall Univ	WV	18,044	C
Pittsburg State Univ	KS	13,880	C
St. Louis Univ	MO	49,866	HC
S Dak State Univ	SD	15,874	C
Univ of Central Missouri	MO	18,982	C
Univ of Houston-Downtown	TX	7,241	LC

SAFETY SCIENCE

School	ST	$IS	SR
Central Washington Univ	WA	16,803	C
Indiana Univ of Pennsylvania	PA	24,474	C
Virginia Commonwealth Univ	VA	23,811	VC

SALES MANAGEMENT & LEADERSHIP

School	ST	$IS	SR
High Point Univ	NC	47,355	VC

SANSKRIT AND INDIAN STUDIES

School	ST	$IS	SR
Bard College	NY	65,924	HC
Brown Univ	RI	64,566	MC
Harvard College/Harvard Univ	MA	65,609	MC
Univ of Iowa	IA	19,415	HC

SCANDINAVIAN LANGUAGES

School	ST	$IS	SR
Augsburg Univ	MN	45,129	C
Augustana College	IL	51,222	VC+
Gustavus Adolphus College	MN	53,943	HC
North Park Univ	IL	35,860	C
The Univ of Texas at Austin	TX	20,206	MC
Univ of Calif at Berkeley	CA	29,886	MC
Univ of Calif at Los Angeles	CA	27,438	HC+
Univ of Minn/Twin Cities	MN	24,269	MC
Univ of Washington	WA	23,091	MC

SCANDINAVIAN STUDIES

School	ST	$IS	SR
Augsburg Univ	MN	45,129	C
Concordia College - Moorhead	MN	46,418	C
Minn State Univ, Mankato	MN	17,190	C
Pacific Lutheran Univ	WA	49,960	C
Univ of Wisc-Madison	WI	21,647	MC
Univ of Wisc-Milwaukee	WI	21,538	C

SCENIC AND LIGHTING DESIGN

School	ST	$IS	SR
Boston Univ	MA	67,352	MC
DePaul Univ	IL	52,807	VC
Webster Univ	MO	37,490	C

SCHOOL PSYCHOLOGY

School	ST	$IS	SR
Adams State Univ	CO	15,420	LC
Cal State, Fullerton	CA	21,902	C
Calif Univ of Pennsylvania	PA	20,425	LC
Eastern Mich Univ	MI	19,761	C
Georgia Southern Univ	GA	16,540	VC
Howard Univ	DC	37,616	C+
New York Univ	NY	68,139	MC
The Univ of Arizona	AZ	24,086	C

SCIENCE

School	ST	$IS	SR
Alfred Univ	NY	37,490	C
Alvernia Univ	PA	45,330	C
Alverno College	WI	33,294	LC
American International College	MA	47,020	LC
Arcadia Univ	PA	55,990	C+
Bennington College	VT	66,280	MC
Black Hills State Univ	SD	16,622	C
Bowling Green State Univ	OH	19,975	C
Buena Vista Univ	IA	42,344	C
Cal State, Fullerton	CA	21,902	C
Cambridge College	MA	14,940	NC
Caribbean Univ	PR	12,227	
Central Mich Univ	MI	20,330	C
Cheyney Univ of Pennsylvania	PA	20,896	LC
Coe College	IA	51,570	VC
Colo Christian Univ	CO	40,885	VC
Concordia Univ, Ann Arbor	MI	38,878	C+
Dallas Baptist Univ	TX	35,220	VC
Drexel Univ	PA	65,927	HC
East Stroudsburg Univ	PA	18,578	LC
Eastern Mich Univ	MI	19,761	C
Eastern Nazarene College	MA	41,114	C
Fairleigh Dickinson Univ/Metropolitan Campus	NJ	52,392	C
Fordham Univ	NY	68,431	MC
Fort Hays State Univ	KS	12,677	C
Gannon Univ	PA	42,922	C
Grace College and Seminary	IN	31,524	C
Graceland Univ	IA	35,290	C
Grand Valley State Univ	MI	22,250	C+
Grinnell College	IA	63,114	MC
Hampshire College	MA	65,214	MC
Hawaii Pacific Univ	HI	33,420	C
Heritage Univ	WA	19,825	NC
Houghton College	NY	40,558	VC
Indiana Wesleyan Univ	IN	33,674	C
Johnson C. Smith Univ	NC	25,336	LC
Keene State College	NH	24,604	C
King's College	PA	48,240	C
La Salle Univ	PA	43,476	C
Le Moyne College	NY	47,305	VC
Lee Univ	TN	22,045	C
LeMoyne-Owen College	TN	16,980	C
Lincoln Univ	PA	20,878	LC
Lyndon State College	VT	20,714	C
Madonna Univ	MI	30,450	LC
Marygrove College	MI	30,100	LC
Marylhurst Univ	OR	16,818	NC
Maryville Univ of St. Louis	MO	38,558	VC
Marywood Univ	PA	47,840	C
Mayville State Univ	ND	18,371	NC
Middle Tenn State Univ	TN	8,650	C
Miss State Univ	MS	12,028	C+
Missouri Southern State Univ	MO	13,071	C
Montana Tech of the Univ of Montana	MT	15,447	VC
Mount Aloysius College	PA	29,976	C
Mount St. Mary College	NY	44,448	C
National Louis Univ	IL	43,000	LC
Northern Kentucky Univ	KY	16,486	C
Northwest Missouri State Univ	MO	18,286	C
Okla City Univ	OK	40,476	C
Okla Wesleyan Univ	OK	34,434	C
Penn State Altoona	PA	26,686	C
Penn State Erie,The Behrend College	PA	26,688	VC
Piedmont College	GA	34,334	C
Pitzer College	CA	68,500	HC+
Pomona College	CA	64,957	MC
Purdue Univ/West Lafayette	IN	20,032	MC
Rochester Inst of Technology	NY	52,734	HC+
Rockford Univ	IL	38,570	C
Samford Univ	AL	40,770	VC
Seattle Univ	WA	54,957	VC
Sierra Nevada College	NV	45,403	C
Southern Nazarene Univ	OK	33,684	C
Southern Oregon Univ	OR	19,117	C
St. John's College, Santa Fe	NM	60,109	HC+
SUNY/Empire State College	NY	9,145	NC
Tiffin Univ	OH	34,900	LC
Trevecca Nazarene Univ	TN	31,186	C
Troy Univ	AL	16,171	C
Tulane Univ	LA	67,496	MC
Union College	NE	23,270	C
Union College	NY	64,320	MC
United States Air Force Academy	CO		C
United States Naval Academy	MD		HC
Univ of Alabama in Huntsville	AL	20,028	VC
Univ of Denver	CO	61,129	VC+
Univ of Findlay	OH	43,040	C
Univ of Great Falls	MT	38,524	C
Univ of Mass Amherst	MA	27,669	HC
Univ of Mich/Flint	MI	19,062	C
Univ of Nebr - Lincoln	NE	18,589	VC
Univ of N Dak	ND	16,673	C
Univ of Northern Iowa	IA	17,480	C
Univ of Notre Dame	IN	68,801	MC
Univ of Oregon	OR	24,021	VC
Univ of Texas at El Paso	TX	34,452	NC
Univ of Wisc-River Falls	WI	14,541	C
Univ of Wisc-Stout	WI	19,667	C
Upper Iowa Univ	IA	34,990	NC
Urbana Univ	OH	30,820	C
Valley City State Univ	ND	13,267	C
Villanova Univ	PA	64,922	MC
Virginia Commonwealth Univ	VA	23,811	VC
Walsh Univ	OH	39,010	C
Washburn Univ	KS	15,827	C
Washington State Univ	WA	22,747	C
Wayland Baptist Univ	TX	23,460	LC
West Virginia Univ	WV	18,952	VC
Western New Mexico Univ	NM	16,914	LC
Westfield State Univ	MA	20,404	C
Widener Univ	PA	58,190	C
Wilberforce Univ	OH	19,900	C
Willamette Univ	OR	62,514	VC+
William Woods Univ	MO	32,040	C

SCIENCE AND MANAGEMENT

School	ST	$IS	SR
Claremont McKenna College	CA	69,900	MC
George Mason Univ	VA	19,884	C
Jefferson (Philadelphia Univ + Thomas Jefferson Univ)	PA	53,966	C
Pitzer College	CA	68,500	HC+
Scripps College	CA	69,260	HC
Univ of St. Francis	IN	38,520	C

SCIENCE AND SOCIETY

School	ST	$IS	SR
Bard College	NY	65,924	HC
Brown Univ	RI	64,566	MC
Butler Univ	IN	52,890	VC+
College of Staten Island	NY	24,389	LC
Northwestern Univ	IL	68,725	MC
Ramapo College of New Jersey	NJ	25,760	VC
Univ of Puget Sound	WA	60,210	HC
Vassar College	NY	68,110	MC
Wesleyan Univ	CT	66,940	MC

SCIENCE AND TECHNOLOGY STUDIES

School	ST	$IS	SR
Cornell Univ	NY	67,591	MC
Georgia Inst of Technology	GA	23,910	MC
Kean Univ	NJ	25,620	C
Missouri Western State Univ	MO	17,822	LC
Montclair State Univ	NJ	26,912	C
Oglala Lakota College	SD	15,050	NC

SCIENCE EDUCATION

School	ST	$IS	SR
Adams State Univ	CO	15,420	LC
Alabama A&M Univ	AL	18,796	C
Albany State Univ	GA	19,462	C
Alfred Univ	NY	37,490	C
Alverno College	WI	33,294	LC
American International College	MA	47,020	LC
Anderson Univ	IN	39,450	C
Andrews Univ	MI	41,732	C
Appalachian State Univ	NC	15,394	VC
Aquinas College - Mich	MI	38,876	VC
Arkansas State Univ	AR	16,190	C
Arkansas Tech Univ	AR	16,534	LC
Asbury Univ	KY	36,450	C+
Ashland Univ	OH	30,446	C
Auburn Univ	AL	24,300	VC+
Baldwin Wallace Univ	OH	42,464	VC
Ball State Univ	IN	19,808	C+
Bayamon Central Univ	PR	12,490	
Baylor Univ	TX	56,803	HC
Bemidji State Univ	MN	17,730	C
Bennett College	NC	27,717	NC
Bethany College	KS	38,637	LC
Bethany College	WV	38,774	LC
Bethel College	IN	36,830	C
Bethel Univ	MN	46,550	C+
Bethune-Cookman Univ	FL	23,322	C
Black Hills State Univ	SD	16,622	C
Blackburn College	IL	28,526	LC
Bloomfield College	NJ	40,100	LC
Blue Mountain College	MS	15,949	C
Boston Univ	MA	67,352	MC
Bowie State Univ	MD	18,610	LC
Bowling Green State Univ	OH	19,975	C
Brigham Young Univ	UT	13,248	MC
Brigham Young Univ/Hawaii	HI	11,710	C
Bryan College	TN	32,900	C
Buena Vista Univ	IA	42,344	C
Cal State, Long Beach	CA	18,850	C
Calvin College	MI	43,090	HC
Canisius College	NY	49,672	C
Caribbean Univ	PR	12,227	
Carroll Univ	WI	38,100	C+
Carson-Newman Univ	TN	35,900	C
Catawba College	NC	39,820	LC
Cedarville Univ	OH	36,244	VC
Central Washington Univ	WA	16,803	C
Chadron State College	NE	14,819	LC
Charleston Southern Univ	SC	34,700	C
CUNY/Brooklyn College	NY	7,163	C+
CUNY/Hunter College	NY	31,098	VC
CUNY/Lehman College	NY	5,788	LC
Colo State Univ	CO	23,033	C
Concord Univ	WV	14,954	LC
Concordia Univ Nebr	NE	41,900	VC
Concordia Univ St. Paul	MN	29,050	C
Concordia Univ, Chicago	IL	41,522	C
Converse College	SC	28,290	C
Corban Univ	OR	41,700	C
Cornerstone Univ	MI	36,550	C
Covenant College	GA	44,590	HC
Daemen College	NY	40,336	C
Dallas Baptist Univ	TX	35,220	VC
Defiance College	OH	42,240	LC
Delaware State Univ	DE	19,376	LC
Dickinson State Univ	ND	12,372	LC
Dominican College	NY	40,258	LC
Dordt College	IA	37,860	C+
East Carolina Univ	NC	16,539	C
East Texas Baptist Univ	TX	34,444	C
Eastern Illinois Univ	IL	21,414	C
Eastern Mich Univ	MI	19,761	C
Eastern Nazarene College	MA	41,114	C
Eastern Washington Univ	WA	17,896	LC
Edinboro Univ	PA	15,940	LC
Elizabethtown College	PA	56,340	VC
Elmira College	NY	53,900	C
Elms College	MA	49,602	VC
Elon Univ	NC	46,142	HC
Eureka College	IL	34,760	C
Evangel Univ	MO	28,898	C

ST = STATE $IS = IN-STATE COSTS   SR = SELECTOR RATING

School	ST	$IS	SR
Fairmont State Univ	WV	15,726	C
Faulkner Univ	AL	26,410	C
Florida A&M Univ	FL	15,361	C
Florida Inst of Technology	FL	53,306	VC
Florida International Univ	FL	20,281	C
Florida State Univ	FL	16,771	HC
Freed-Hardeman Univ	TN	29,900	C
Fresno Pacific Univ	CA	38,858	C
Friends Univ	KS	38,000	C
Gettysburg College	PA	65,210	MC
Glenville State College	WV	17,386	LC
Goshen College	IN	44,350	C
Grace College and Seminary	IN	31,524	C
Grand Valley State Univ	MI	22,250	C+
Greensboro College	NC	39,790	LC
Greenville College	IL	27,012	LC
Gustavus Adolphus College	MN	53,943	HC
Gwynedd Mercy Univ	PA	43,780	LC
Hamline Univ	MN	50,152	C
Hardin-Simmons Univ	TX	36,025	C
Hastings College	NE	35,380	C+
Heidelberg Univ	OH	40,400	LC
Heritage Univ	WA	19,825	NC
Hofstra Univ	NY	58,210	C+
Holy Family Univ	PA	44,672	LC
Hood College	MD	50,540	C
Hope College	MI	42,840	VC
Houghton College	NY	40,558	VC
Humboldt State Univ	CA	21,708	C
Huntington Univ	IN	33,996	C
Husson Univ	ME	26,508	C
Illinois College	IL	41,330	VC
Immaculata Univ	PA	39,000	C
Indiana State Univ	IN	23,223	LC
Indiana Univ South Bend	IN	16,057	C
Indiana Univ-Purdue Univ Fort Wayne	IN	18,675	C
Indiana Wesleyan Univ	IN	33,674	C
Inter-American Univ of PR-San Germán	PR	20,042	
Johnson State College	VT	22,672	C
Judson College	AL	27,066	C
Judson Univ	IL	39,174	C
Juniata College	PA	58,118	VC
Keene State College	NH	24,604	C
Kent State Univ	OH	20,928	C
King's College	PA	48,240	C
Kutztown Univ of Pennsylvania	PA	19,477	C
La Salle Univ	PA	43,476	C
Lamar Univ	TX	18,014	LC
Langston Univ	OK	15,659	C
Le Moyne College	NY	47,305	VC
Lenoir-Rhyne Univ	NC	47,500	LC
LeTourneau Univ	TX	39,190	VC
Lincoln Memorial Univ	TN	28,430	C
Lindenwood Univ	MO	25,760	C
LIU Brooklyn	NY	50,698	C
Livingstone College	NC	17,815	LC
Lock Haven Univ of Pennsylvania	PA	20,544	LC
Loyola Univ Chicago	IL	57,158	VC
Lyndon State College	VT	20,714	C
MacMurray College	IL	35,025	C
Malone Univ	OH	39,200	C
Manhattan College	NY	55,652	C
Marian Univ	WI	34,622	C
Mars Hill Univ	NC	41,104	C
Maryville College	TN	44,410	C
Marywood Univ	PA	47,840	C
Mayville State Univ	ND	18,371	NC
Mercyhurst Univ	PA	47,420	C
Messiah College	PA	44,380	VC
Miami Univ	OH	27,190	HC+
MidAmerica Nazarene Univ	KS	37,808	C
Midland Univ	NE	39,512	C
Miles College	AL	16,530	NC
Millersville Univ of Pennsylvania	PA	25,298	C
Minn State Univ, Mankato	MN	17,190	C
Minn State Univ, Moorhead	MN	21,393	C
Minot State Univ	ND	13,285	C
Miss Valley State Univ	MS	13,233	LC
Missouri Southern State Univ	MO	13,071	C
Missouri State Univ	MO	15,837	C+
Missouri Western State Univ	MO	17,822	LC
Monmouth Univ	NJ	50,184	C
Montana State Univ Billings	MT	13,336	LC
Montana State Univ-Northern	MT	11,370	NC
Morningside College	IA	39,780	C
Morris College	SC	19,195	LC
Mount Aloysius College	PA	29,976	LC
Mount Mary Univ	WI	34,650	LC
Mount Vernon Nazarene Univ	OH	35,944	C
Muskingum Univ	OH	35,966	C
Nebr Wesleyan Univ	NE	42,026	C+
New Mexico Highlands Univ	NM	11,904	LC
New York Univ	NY	68,139	MC
Niagara Univ	NY	41,010	C
N Car State Univ	NC	22,434	HC+
Northeastern State Univ	OK	8,615	VC
Northern Mich Univ	MI	20,853	C
Northern State Univ	SD	15,570	C
Northwest Missouri State Univ	MO	18,286	C
Northwestern College of Iowa	IA	38,400	C

School	ST	$IS	SR
Northwestern Okla State Univ	OK	13,072	LC
Notre Dame of Maryland Univ	MD	47,570	VC
Nova Southeastern Univ	FL	38,534	C+
Oakland City Univ	IN	33,930	NC
Oakwood Univ	AL	43,758	C
Ohio Univ	OH	23,394	VC
Ohio Valley Univ	WV	28,800	C
Ohio Wesleyan Univ	OH	49,460	VC
Okla Baptist Univ	OK	33,990	C
Okla Christian Univ	OK	29,260	C
Okla Wesleyan Univ	OK	34,434	C
Olivet Nazarene Univ	IL	41,840	VC
Oral Roberts Univ	OK	34,316	C
Ouachita Baptist Univ	AR	33,500	VC
Palm Beach Atlantic Univ	FL	39,250	C
Peru State College	NE	15,602	LC
Pfeiffer Univ	NC	40,532	LC
Piedmont College	GA	34,334	C
Plymouth State Univ	NH	23,180	LC
Pontifical Catholic Univ of PR	PR	10,534	
Purdue Univ Northwest	IN	15,178	C
Purdue Univ/West Lafayette	IN	20,032	MC
Rhode Island College	RI	19,000	LC
Rider Univ	NJ	54,050	C
Rocky Mountain College	MT	35,776	C
Rowan Univ	NJ	24,491	VC
Rust College	MS	10,600	C
Saginaw Valley State Univ	MI	19,284	C
St. Augustine's Univ	NC	25,582	C
St. Louis Univ	MO	49,866	HC
St. Mary-of-the-Woods College	IN	40,424	LC
St. Michael's College	VT	53,275	VC+
St. Vincent College	PA	46,229	C
St. Xavier Univ	IL	44,440	C
Salem State Univ	MA	42,650	LC
Schreiner Univ	TX	34,626	LC
Seattle Pacific Univ	WA	47,439	C+
Seton Hill Univ	PA	46,972	VC
Shaw Univ	NC	24,638	C
Shepherd Univ, West Virginia	WV	17,382	C
Siena Heights Univ	MI	36,322	C
Slippery Rock Univ of Pennsylvania	PA	20,450	C
Southeast Missouri State Univ	MO	16,148	C
Southeastern Okla State Univ	OK	11,875	C
Southeastern Univ	FL	34,910	LC
Southern Arkansas Univ	AR	21,532	C
Southern Conn State Univ	CT	21,924	LC
Southern Illinois Univ Edwardsville	IL	20,188	C
Southern Nazarene Univ	OK	33,684	C
Southern Univ at New Orleans	LA	8,014	LC
Southwest Minn State Univ	MN	17,783	C
Southwestern Okla State Univ	OK	12,205	C
Springfield College	MA	48,775	C
St. Cloud State Univ	MN	10,600	C
St. Edward's Univ	TX	56,190	VC
St. John Fisher College	NY	45,270	VC
St. Mary's Univ	TX	39,120	C
St. Thomas Aquinas College	NY	32,450	C
SUNY at New Paltz	NY	20,840	C
SUNY/Buffalo State	NY	20,583	LC
SUNY/College at Old Westbury	NY	16,860	C
SUNY/Fredonia	NY	20,818	C
SUNY/Oneonta	NY	20,794	C
SUNY/Potsdam	NY	21,051	VC
Suffolk Univ	MA	52,316	C
Taylor Univ	IN	42,130	VC
Texas A&M Univ at Commerce	TX	10,496	C
Texas Christian Univ	TX	57,120	HC
The College of New Jersey	NJ	28,675	VC+
The College of St. Rose	NY	44,010	C
The Univ of Arizona	AZ	24,086	C
The Univ of Montana Western	MT	9,426	LC
Toccoa Falls College	GA	30,048	C
Tougaloo College	MS	17,980	NC
Trevecca Nazarene Univ	TN	31,186	C
Trine Univ	IN	41,310	C
Troy Univ	AL	16,171	C
Union College	KY	32,310	C
Universidad del Turabo	PR	17,828	
Univ of Arkansas at Pine Bluff	AR	13,541	C
Univ of Calif San Diego	CA	30,450	MC
Univ of Central Arkansas	AR	15,042	VC
Univ of Central Florida	FL	16,379	VC
Univ of Central Missouri	MO	18,982	C
Univ of Central Okla	OK	15,150	C
Univ of Charleston	WV	35,000	LC
Univ of Cincinnati	OH	22,118	VC
Univ of Conn	CT	27,394	
Univ of Delaware	DE	32,214	VC
Univ of Evansville	IN	44,186	C+
Univ of Georgia	GA	21,878	HC
Univ of Great Falls	MT	38,524	C
Univ of Idaho	ID	16,158	C
Univ of Illinois at Urbana-Champaign	IL	27,006	HC
Univ of Indianapolis	IN	36,480	VC
Univ of Iowa	IA	19,415	HC
Univ of Kentucky	KY	24,800	C+

School	ST	$IS	SR
Univ of Louisiana at Lafayette	LA	14,516	C
Univ of Louisville	KY	19,692	C
Univ of Mary Hardin-Baylor	TX	35,292	C+
Univ of Maryland/Eastern Shore	MD	21,861	LC
Univ of Mich/Dearborn	MI	12,472	VC
Univ of Minn/Duluth	MN	20,292	C
Univ of Miss	MS	18,802	C
Univ of Missouri-Columbia	MO	20,463	VC
Univ of Montana	MT	14,105	C
Univ of Nebr - Kearney	NE	17,014	LC
Univ of Nebr - Lincoln	NE	18,589	VC
Univ of North Alabama	AL	15,964	C
Univ of N Car at Greensboro	NC	15,998	C
Univ of N Car at Pembroke	NC	14,737	LC
Univ of North Florida	FL	15,996	VC
Univ of North Georgia	GA	17,316	C
Univ of Northern Colo	CO	19,658	C
Univ of Northern Iowa	IA	17,480	C
Univ of Notre Dame	IN	68,801	MC
Univ of Okla	OK	19,651	HC
Univ of Pittsburgh at Bradford	PA	22,958	C
Univ of Pittsburgh at Johnstown	PA	22,092	C
Univ of Rio Grande & Rio Grande Community College	OH	8,750	LC
Univ of Sioux Falls	SD	25,630	C
Univ of South Florida/Tampa	FL	16,110	VC
Univ of Southern Indiana	IN	16,808	C
Univ of Southern Miss	MS	13,170	C
Univ of the Cumberlands	KY	32,000	LC
Univ of Toledo	OH	19,336	C
Univ of Vermont	VT	29,792	HC
Univ of Wisc-Eau Claire	WI	16,354	VC
Univ of Wisc-La Crosse	WI	15,425	VC
Univ of Wisc-Oshkosh	WI	15,392	C
Univ of Wisc-Stout	WI	19,667	C
Univ of Wisc-Superior	WI	14,838	C
Univ of Wisc-Whitewater	WI	13,976	C
Utah State Univ	UT	13,235	C
Valparaiso Univ	IN	50,160	VC
Vanguard Univ of Southern Calif	CA	42,400	VC
Virginia Polytechnic Inst and State Univ	VA	21,920	VC
Viterbo Univ	WI	34,660	C
Warner Univ	FL	28,216	C
Wartburg College	IA	49,478	C
Washington State Univ	WA	22,747	C
Washington Univ in St. Louis	MO	67,539	MC
Wayne State College	NE	25,746	NC
Wayne State Univ	MI	23,085	C
Weber State Univ	UT	14,112	C
West Chester Univ of Pennsylvania	PA	19,171	VC
West Liberty Univ	WV	16,158	C
West Texas A&M Univ	TX	13,478	C
Western Carolina Univ	NC	13,965	C
Western New Mexico Univ	NM	16,914	LC
Western State Colo Univ	CO	19,348	C
Western Washington Univ	WA	18,904	VC
Wheelock College	MA	51,325	LC
Whitworth Univ	WA	53,682	VC
Widener Univ	PA	58,190	C
William Penn Univ	IA	26,000	C
Wilmington College	OH	35,100	C
Winona State Univ	MN	18,109	C
Wittenberg Univ	OH	49,863	VC
Wright State Univ	OH	16,983	C
Xavier Univ	OH	49,380	VC
Xavier Univ of Louisiana	LA	31,689	C
York College	NE	30,260	C
York College of Pennsylvania	PA	29,240	C
Youngstown State Univ	OH	17,487	C

SCIENCE OF EARTH SYSTEMS

School	ST	$IS	SR
Cornell Univ	NY	67,591	MC
Univ of Illinois at Chicago	IL	24,664	VC

SCIENCE OF NATURAL AND ENVIRONMENTAL SYSTEMS

School	ST	$IS	SR
Cornell Univ	NY	67,591	MC

SCIENCE TECHNOLOGY

School	ST	$IS	SR
Arizona State Univ at the Polytechnic Campus	AZ	22,394	VC
Colby College	ME	64,060	MC
James Madison Univ	VA	19,084	VC
Lehigh Univ	PA	63,860	MC
Marshall Univ	WV	18,044	C
Mass Inst of Technology	MA	62,662	MC
Missouri Southern State Univ	MO	13,071	C
Missouri Western State Univ	MO	17,822	LC
Pennsylvania State Univ - Univ Park	PA	29,716	HC
Rensselaer Polytechnic Inst	NY	67,265	MC
Scripps College	CA	69,260	HC
Stevens Inst of Technology	NJ	64,954	MC
Univ of Pennsylvania	PA	63,526	MC

SCIENTIFIC/MEDICAL MARKETING

School	ST	$IS	SR
Carlow Univ	PA	39,696	LC
Missouri Western State Univ	MO	17,822	LC

SCULPTURE

School	ST	$IS	SR
Adams State Univ	CO	15,420	LC
Aquinas College - Mich	MI	38,876	VC
Art Academy of Cincinnati	OH	37,790	SP
Bennington College	VT	66,280	MC
Boston Univ	MA	67,352	MC
Calif College of the Arts	CA	52,758	SP
Cal State, San Bernardino	CA	20,106	C
Cleveland Inst of Art	OH	51,455	SP
College for Creative Studies	MI	51,210	SP
Colo State Univ	CO	23,033	C
Escuela de Artes Plasticas de PR	PR	11,236	
Ferris State Univ	MI	21,458	C
Howard Univ	DC	37,616	C+
Indiana Univ-Purdue Univ Fort Wayne	IN	18,675	C
Kansas City Art Inst	MO	48,200	SP
Kutztown Univ of Pennsylvania	PA	19,477	C
Maine College of Art	ME	45,940	SP
Marshall Univ	WV	18,044	C
Maryland Inst College of Art	MD	58,740	SP
Marywood Univ	PA	47,840	C
Mass College of Art and Design	MA	24,800	SP
Milwaukee Inst of Art & Design	WI	45,880	SP
Minneapolis College of Art and Design	MN	44,218	SP
Missouri Western State Univ	MO	17,822	LC
Montserrat College of Art	MA	41,500	SP
Moore College of Art and Design	PA	55,118	SP
Ohio Univ	OH	23,394	VC
Pacific Northwest College of Art	OR	38,494	SP
Rhode Island School of Design	RI	59,960	SP
Rochester Inst of Technology	NY	52,734	HC+
San Francisco Art Inst	CA	60,865	SP
Savannah College of Art and Design	GA	49,595	SP
School of the Art Inst of Chicago	IL	61,830	SP
SUNY Albany	NY	22,165	C
SUNY at Binghamton	NY	24,100	MC
SUNY at New Paltz	NY	20,840	C
SUNY/Buffalo State	NY	20,583	LC
Syracuse Univ	NY	62,313	HC
Temple Univ	PA	24,392	C+
Texas Christian Univ	TX	57,120	HC
Univ of Dallas	TX	50,676	VC
Univ of Hartford	CT	49,776	C
Univ of Illinois at Chicago	IL	24,664	VC
Univ of Illinois at Urbana-Champaign	IL	27,006	HC
Univ of Iowa	IA	19,415	HC
Univ of Kansas	KS	20,884	VC
Univ of Mass Dartmouth	MA	26,507	C
Univ of Miami	FL	63,494	MC
Univ of Mich/Ann Arbor	MI	25,274	MC
Univ of N Car at Greensboro	NC	15,998	C
Univ of Oregon	OR	24,021	VC
Univ of the Arts	PA	56,579	SP
Univ of Washington	WA	23,091	MC
Virginia Commonwealth Univ	VA	23,811	VC
Washington Univ in St. Louis	MO	67,539	MC
Webster Univ	MO	37,490	C
Western Washington Univ	WA	18,904	VC

SECONDARY EDUCATION

School	ST	$IS	SR
Abilene Christian Univ	TX	43,708	C+
Adams State Univ	CO	15,420	LC
Adrian College	MI	45,550	C
Alabama A&M Univ	AL	18,796	C
Alabama State Univ	AL	16,490	LC
Albright College	PA	57,326	C
Alderson Broaddus Univ	WV	35,000	LC
Alfred Univ	NY	37,490	C
Alice Lloyd College	KY	8,190	LC
Alma College	MI	49,410	VC
Alvernia Univ	PA	45,330	C
Alverno College	WI	33,294	LC
American International College	MA	47,020	LC
Andrews Univ	MI	41,732	C
Appalachian State Univ	NC	15,394	VC
Aquinas College	TN	30,800	C+
Aquinas College - Mich	MI	38,876	VC
Arcadia Univ	PA	55,990	C+
Arizona State Univ at the Polytechnic Campus	AZ	22,394	VC
Arizona State Univ at the Tempe Campus	AZ	23,001	VC
Arizona State Univ at the West Campus	AZ	21,513	VC
Armstrong State Univ	GA	15,615	C
Asbury Univ	KY	36,450	C+

ST = STATE $IS = IN-STATE COSTS SR = SELECTOR RATING

School	ST	$IS	SR
Ashland Univ	OH	30,446	C
Auburn Univ	AL	24,300	VC+
Auburn Univ at Montgomery	AL	15,000	C
Augsburg Univ	MN	45,129	C
Augustana College	IL	51,222	VC+
Aurora Univ	IL	34,990	C
Averett Univ	VA	43,034	LC
Baker Univ	KS	37,190	C
Bayamon Central Univ	PR	12,490	
Baylor Univ	TX	56,803	HC
Bemidji State Univ	MN	17,730	C
Benedictine College	KS	38,850	VC
Bennington College	VT	66,280	MC
Bethany College	KS	38,637	LC
Bethany College	WV	38,774	LC
Bethel College	IN	36,830	C
Bethel Univ	MN	46,550	C+
Birmingham-Southern College	AL	44,478	C+
Blackburn College	IL	28,526	LC
Bloomfield College	NJ	40,100	LC
Bloomsburg Univ of Pennsylvania	PA	19,930	C
Bluefield College	VA	34,711	C
Boise State Univ	ID	17,368	C
Boston College	MA	68,043	MC
Bowling Green State Univ	OH	19,975	C
Bradley Univ	IL	43,240	VC
Briar Cliff Univ	IA	36,956	C
Buena Vista Univ	IA	42,344	C
Butler Univ	IN	52,890	VC+
Cabrini Univ	PA	42,591	LC
Cairn Univ	PA	37,572	C
Cal State, Fullerton	CA	21,902	C
Calif Univ of Pennsylvania	PA	20,425	LC
Calumet College of St. Joseph	IN	22,735	C
Calvin College	MI	43,090	HC
Capital Univ	OH	44,778	VC
Cardinal Stritch Univ	WI	37,136	C
Caribbean Univ	PR	12,227	
Carlow Univ	PA	39,696	LC
Carroll College	MT	44,304	C
Carson-Newman Univ	TN	35,900	C
Carthage College	WI	48,835	C
Centenary College	NJ	43,890	LC
Central State Univ	OH	18,564	C
Central Washington Univ	WA	16,803	C
Chadron State College	NE	14,819	LC
Chaminade Univ of Honolulu	HI	37,614	C
Champlain College	VT	54,724	VC
Chicago State Univ	IL	41,620	C
CUNY/Brooklyn College	NY	7,163	C+
CUNY/City College	NY	20,204	C
CUNY/Hunter College	NY	31,098	VC
CUNY/Lehman College	NY	5,788	LC
CUNY/Queens College	NY	21,507	C
Clarion Univ of Pennsylvania	PA	21,608	LC
Clarke Univ	IA	42,950	C
Clemson Univ	SC		HC
Cleveland State Univ	OH	22,290	C
Coe College	IA	51,570	VC
College of Charleston	SC	24,046	VC
College of St Joseph	VT	32,400	LC
College of Staten Island	NY	24,389	LC
College of the Ozarks	MO	7,530	VC
Colo Christian Univ	CO	40,885	VC
Columbia College - Missouri	MO	28,179	C
Columbus State Univ	GA	14,336	LC
Concord Univ	WV	14,954	LC
Concordia College - Moorhead	MN	46,418	C
Concordia Univ	OR	35,000	C
Concordia Univ Nebr	NE	41,900	VC
Concordia Univ St. Paul	MN	29,050	C
Concordia Univ Texas	TX	41,920	C
Concordia Univ Wisc	WI	35,910	C
Concordia Univ, Ann Arbor	MI	38,878	C+
Concordia Univ, Chicago	IL	41,522	C
Converse College	SC	28,290	C
Cornell College	IA	49,900	VC
Cornerstone Univ	MI	36,550	C
Cumberland Univ	TN	27,710	C
Dakota State Univ	SD	12,286	C
Dallas Baptist Univ	TX	35,220	VC
Defiance College	OH	42,240	LC
Delaware Valley Univ	PA	51,271	C
DePaul Univ	IL	52,807	VC
Dickinson State Univ	ND	12,372	LC
Dominican College	NY	40,258	LC
Dominican Univ	IL	42,472	C+
Dordt College	IA	37,860	C+
Drake Univ	IA	49,220	HC
Drury Univ	MO	37,555	VC
East Texas Baptist Univ	TX	34,444	C
Eastern Kentucky Univ	KY	17,742	C
Eastern Mennonite Univ	VA	42,550	C
Eastern Mich Univ	MI	19,761	C
Eastern Washington Univ	WA	17,896	LC
Edinboro Univ	PA	15,940	LC
Elizabethtown College	PA	56,340	VC
Elmhurst College	IL	46,514	C
Elmira College	NY	53,900	C
Elms College	MA	49,602	VC
Elon Univ	NC	46,142	HC
Emmanuel College	MA	53,472	C+
Emporia State Univ	KS	15,029	C
Eureka College	IL	34,760	C
Evangel Univ	MO	28,898	C
Fairmont State Univ	WV	15,726	C
Fayetteville State Univ	NC	17,756	C
Felician Univ	NJ	46,280	LC
Fitchburg State Univ	MA	21,819	LC
Florida Gulf Coast Univ	FL	14,738	C
Florida Memorial Univ	FL	22,424	LC
Florida Southern College	FL	45,978	VC
Fontbonne Univ	MO	34,606	C
Fort Valley State Univ	GA	17,988	VC
Franklin College	IN	40,550	C
Franklin Pierce Univ	NH	46,750	LC
Freed-Hardeman Univ	TN	29,900	C
Friends Univ	KS	38,000	C
Gallaudet Univ	DC	30,088	LC
Gannon Univ	PA	42,922	C
Gardner-Webb Univ	NC	24,935	C+
Georgetown College	KY	41,440	C
Georgia Southern Univ	GA	16,540	VC
Gettysburg College	PA	65,210	MC
Glenville State College	WV	17,386	LC
Goddard College	VT	17,040	VC
Gordon College	MA	47,740	VC
Goshen College	IN	44,350	C
Grace Bible College	MI	25,250	C
Grambling State Univ	LA	15,701	C
Grand Canyon Univ	AZ	25,150	VC
Grand Valley State Univ	MI	22,250	C+
Grand View Univ	IA	32,302	C
Green Mountain College	VT	45,228	LC
Greensboro College	NC	39,790	LC
Gustavus Adolphus College	MN	53,943	HC
Gwynedd Mercy Univ	PA	43,780	LC
Hamline Univ	MN	50,152	C
Hannibal-LaGrange Univ	MO	29,815	C
Harding Univ	AR	25,440	C
Hardin-Simmons Univ	TX	36,025	C
Harris-Stowe State Univ	MO	14,590	NC
Hastings College	NE	35,380	C+
Heidelberg Univ	OH	40,400	LC
Heritage Univ	WA	19,825	NC
Hofstra Univ	NY	58,210	C+
Holy Family Univ	PA	44,672	LC
Hood College	MD	50,540	C
Hope College	MI	42,840	VC
Hope International Univ	CA	42,730	C
Houghton College	NY	40,558	VC
Houston Baptist Univ	TX	36,450	C
Howard Payne Univ	TX	35,994	C
Howard Univ	DC	37,616	C+
Humboldt State Univ	CA	21,708	C
Huntington Univ	IN	33,996	C
Idaho State Univ	ID	13,619	LC
Illinois College	IL	41,330	VC
Immaculata Univ	PA	39,000	C
Indiana State Univ	IN	23,223	LC
Indiana Univ Bloomington	IN	20,791	HC
Indiana Univ East	IN	7,207	C
Indiana Univ Kokomo	IN	7,207	C
Indiana Univ Northwest	IN	7,207	LC
Indiana Univ South Bend	IN	16,057	C
Indiana Univ Southeast	IN	16,931	C
Indiana Univ-Purdue Univ Fort Wayne	IN	18,675	C
Indiana Wesleyan Univ	IN	33,674	C
Inter-American Univ of PR Ponce	PR	19,549	
Inter-American Univ of PR-Aguadilla Campus	PR	21,657	
Inter-American Univ of PR-Arecibo Campus	PR	18,245	
Inter-American Univ of PR-Barranquitas	PR	18,336	
Inter-American Univ of PR-Fajardo Campus	PR	18,336	
Inter-American Univ of PR-Metropolitan Campus	PR	20,045	
Inter-American Univ of PR-San Germán	PR	20,042	
Iowa State Univ	IA	18,176	C
Iowa Wesleyan Univ	IA	41,000	C
Ithaca College	NY	58,158	VC+
Jacksonville State Univ	AL	14,628	LC
Jarvis Christian College	TX	20,160	NC
John Carroll Univ	OH	51,570	C
Johnson State College	VT	22,672	C
Judson Univ	IL	39,174	C
Juniata College	PA	58,118	VC
Kansas State Univ	KS	17,780	VC
Kansas Wesleyan Univ	KS	37,930	C
Kean Univ	NJ	25,620	C
Keene State College	NH	24,604	C
Kentucky State Univ	KY	14,484	LC
Kentucky Wesleyan College	KY	34,260	LC
Keuka College	NY	42,398	C
King's College	PA	48,240	C
Knox College	IL	54,654	VC+
Kutztown Univ of Pennsylvania	PA	19,477	C
La Salle Univ	PA	43,476	C
La Sierra Univ	CA	39,690	VC
Lake Superior State Univ	MI	19,867	C
Lakeland Univ	WI	35,130	C
Lamar Univ	TX	18,014	LC
Lasell College	MA	49,400	C
Le Moyne College	NY	47,305	VC
Lenoir-Rhyne Univ	NC	47,500	LC
LeTourneau Univ	TX	39,190	VC
Lewis Univ	IL	41,710	C
Lewis-Clark State College	ID	14,202	C
Lincoln Memorial Univ	TN	28,430	C
Lincoln Univ	MO	14,402	NC
Lindenwood Univ	MO	25,760	C
Lindsey Wilson College	KY	33,546	C
LIU Brooklyn	NY	50,698	C
Livingstone College	NC	17,815	LC
Lock Haven Univ of Pennsylvania	PA	20,544	LC
Louisiana State Univ in Shreveport	LA	6,902	C
Louisiana Tech Univ	LA	11,422	VC
Loyola Univ Chicago	IL	57,158	VC
Lubbock Christian Univ	TX	29,727	C
MacMurray College	IL	35,025	C
Madonna Univ	MI	30,450	LC
Malone Univ	OH	39,200	C
Manchester Univ	IN	41,540	C
Manhattan College	NY	55,652	C
Mansfield Univ of Pennsylvania	PA	24,244	LC
Marian Univ	IN	43,206	C
Marian Univ	WI	34,622	C
Marquette Univ	WI	53,090	VC+
Marshall Univ	WV	18,044	C
Maryville College	TN	44,410	C
Maryville Univ of St. Louis	MO	38,558	VC
Marywood Univ	PA	47,840	C
Mass College of Liberal Arts	MA	20,659	C
Mayville State Univ	ND	18,371	NC
McMurry Univ	TX	34,259	LC
McPherson College	KS	36,134	C
Mercer Univ	GA	45,348	VC
Mercyhurst Univ	PA	47,420	C
Merrimack College	MA	55,415	C
Messiah College	PA	44,380	VC
Methodist Univ	NC	58,130	C
Miami Univ	OH	27,190	HC+
Mich Tech Univ	MI	25,551	VC+
Midland Univ	NE	39,512	C
Miles College	AL	16,530	NC
Millikin Univ	IL	44,148	C
Minn State Univ, Mankato	MN	17,190	C
Miss State Univ	MS	12,028	C+
Missouri Baptist Univ	MO	35,594	C
Missouri Univ of Science and Technology	MO	18,655	HC
Missouri Western State Univ	MO	17,822	LC
Monmouth College	IL	42,260	C
Monmouth Univ	NJ	50,184	C
Montana State Univ	MT	15,500	C+
Montana State Univ Billings	MT	13,336	LC
Montana State Univ-Northern	MT	11,370	NC
Moravian College	PA	55,488	C
Mount Aloysius College	PA	29,976	C
Mount Marty College	SD	36,862	C
Mount Mercy Univ	IA	39,748	C
Muskingum Univ	OH	35,966	C
New England College	NH	50,828	NC
New Jersey City Univ	NJ	21,456	LC
New Mexico State Univ	NM	14,050	LC
New York Univ	NY	68,139	MC
Newman Univ	KS	37,382	C
Niagara Univ	NY	41,010	C
Nicholls State Univ	LA	14,959	C
N Car State Univ	NC	22,434	HC+
North Central College	IL	48,712	C+
North Central Univ	MN	30,610	C
N Dak State Univ	ND	16,245	VC
North Park Univ	IL	35,860	C
Northeastern Illinois Univ	IL	12,529	LC
Northeastern State Univ	OK	8,615	VC
Northern Arizona Univ	AZ	21,003	C
Northern Kentucky Univ	KY	16,486	C
Northern Mich Univ	MI	20,853	C
Northern State Univ	SD	15,570	C
Northland College	WI	41,103	C+
Northwest Missouri State Univ	MO	18,286	C
Northwest Nazarene Univ	ID	40,250	C
Northwest Univ	WA	38,720	VC
Northwestern College of Iowa	IA	38,400	C
Northwestern Okla State Univ	OK	13,072	LC
Northwestern State Univ of Louisiana	LA	16,534	LC
Northwestern Univ	IL	68,725	MC
Notre Dame College	OH	39,150	VC
Notre Dame of Maryland Univ	MD	47,570	VC
Nova Southeastern Univ	FL	38,534	C+
Nyack College	NY	34,450	LC
Oakland City Univ	IN	33,930	NC
Oglala Lakota College	SD	15,050	NC
Okla Baptist Univ	OK	33,990	C
Okla City Univ	OK	40,476	C
Okla State Univ	OK	17,180	C+
Okla Wesleyan Univ	OK	34,434	C
Old Dominion Univ	VA	21,618	C
Olivet College	MI	37,661	LC
Ouachita Baptist Univ	AR	33,500	VC
Pacific Lutheran Univ	WA	49,960	C
Paine College	GA	19,506	LC
Palm Beach Atlantic Univ	FL	39,250	C
Pennsylvania State Univ - Univ Park	PA	29,716	HC
Pepperdine Univ	CA	66,862	VC+
Peru State College	NE	15,602	LC
Pfeiffer Univ	NC	40,532	LC
Piedmont College	GA	34,334	C
Pittsburg State Univ	KS	13,880	C
Point Park Univ	PA	41,270	C
Pontifical Catholic Univ of PR	PR	10,534	
Prescott College	AZ	38,201	C
Providence College	RI	62,870	HC
Purdue Univ Northwest	IN	15,178	C
Purdue Univ/West Lafayette	IN	20,032	MC
Quinnipiac Univ	CT	60,970	VC
Rhode Island College	RI	19,000	LC
Rider Univ	NJ	54,050	C
Ripon College	WI	49,991	VC
Rivier Univ	NH	41,600	VC
Roberts Wesleyan College	NY	41,116	C
Rockhurst Univ	MO	28,990	C
Roger Williams Univ	RI	48,074	VC
Roosevelt Univ	IL	41,890	VC
Rosemont College	PA	30,980	LC
Rust College	MS	10,600	C
St. Anselm College	NH	56,636	VC
St. Francis Univ	PA	46,146	NC
St. Leo Univ	FL	32,850	C
St. Louis Univ	MO	49,866	HC
St. Mary's Univ of Minn	MN	42,440	C
St. Michael's College	VT	53,275	VC+
St. Peter's Univ	NJ	49,192	C
St. Xavier Univ	IL	44,440	C
Salem International Univ	WV	21,090	C
Salem State Univ	MA	42,650	LC
Salve Regina Univ	RI	53,046	VC
Samford Univ	AL	40,770	VC
Schreiner Univ	TX	34,626	LC
Seattle Pacific Univ	WA	47,439	C+
Seton Hall Univ	NJ	58,008	C
Seton Hill Univ	PA	46,972	VC
Shaw Univ	NC	24,638	C
Shepherd Univ, West Virginia	WV	17,382	C
Shippensburg Univ of Pennsylvania	PA	24,096	C
Silver Lake College of the Holy Family	WI	36,290	LC
Simmons College	MA	54,400	HC
Simpson College	IA	45,626	VC
Simpson Univ	CA	34,722	C
Slippery Rock Univ of Pennsylvania	PA	20,450	C
S Dak State Univ	SD	15,874	C
Southeastern Okla State Univ	OK	11,875	C
Southeastern Univ	FL	34,910	LC
Southern Conn State Univ	CT	21,924	LC
Southern New Hampshire Univ	NH	44,256	C
Southern Univ and A&M College	LA	16,074	LC
Southern Univ at New Orleans	LA	8,014	LC
Southwest Baptist Univ	MO	30,890	LC
Southwestern Adventist Univ	TX	28,232	LC
Southwestern College	KS	31,531	LC
Southwestern College	KS	31,531	LC
Spalding Univ	KY	31,938	C
Spring Hill College	AL	48,488	C
Springfield College	MA	48,775	C
St. Ambrose Univ	IA	40,180	C
St. Catherine Univ	MN	45,630	C
St. Cloud State Univ	MN	10,600	C
St. Francis College	NY	38,800	LC
St. John Fisher College	NY	45,270	VC
St. John's Univ	NY	57,160	C+
St. Joseph's College, New York/Brooklyn Campus	NY	25,114	LC
St. Joseph's College, New York/Long Island Campus	NY	25,124	C
St. Mary's Univ	TX	39,120	C
St. Thomas Aquinas College	NY	32,450	C
St. Thomas Univ	FL	51,187	LC
SUNY at New Paltz	NY	20,840	C
SUNY at Oswego	NY	22,219	VC
SUNY/Buffalo State	NY	20,583	LC
SUNY/College at Old Westbury	NY	16,860	C
SUNY/Cortland	NY	20,910	C
SUNY/Fredonia	NY	20,818	C
SUNY/Oneonta	NY	20,794	C
Tabor College	KS	35,870	C
Taylor Univ	IN	42,130	VC
Temple Univ	PA	24,392	C+
Tenn Tech Univ	TN	17,929	C
Tenn Wesleyan Univ	TN	32,680	LC
Texas A&M Univ at College Station	TX	20,771	VC+
Texas A&M Univ at Commerce	TX	10,496	C
Texas A&M Univ at Kingsville	TX	16,580	LC
The American Univ	DC	61,317	HC
The Catholic Univ of America	DC	58,376	VC
The Citadel, The Military College of S Car	SC	20,679	C
The Master's Univ	CA	43,870	C
The Univ of Alabama	AL	24,320	C+
The Univ of Arizona	AZ	24,086	C
The Univ of Montana Western	MT	9,426	LC
The Univ of Tenn at Chattanooga	TN	17,340	C+
The Univ of Tenn at Martin	TN	15,212	C
Thiel College	PA	42,950	LC

ST = STATE   **$IS** = IN-STATE COSTS   **SR** = SELECTOR RATING

School	ST	$IS	SR
Thomas More College	KY	36,720	LC
Thomas Univ	GA	21,420	NC
Trevecca Nazarene Univ	TN	31,186	C
Trine Univ	IN	41,310	C
Trinity International Univ	IL	31,070	VC
Troy Univ	AL	16,171	C
Tuskegee Univ	AL	28,164	C
Union College	KY	32,310	C
Union College	NE	23,270	C
Union Univ	TN	41,160	VC
Unity College	ME	37,670	C
Universidad Adventista de las Antillas	PR	16,606	
Universidad del Turabo	PR	17,828	
Universidad Metropolitana	PR	17,828	
Univ of Alabama at Birmingham	AL	22,092	C
Univ of Alaska Fairbanks	AK	16,874	VC
Univ of Arkansas at Little Rock	AR	18,211	LC
Univ of Central Arkansas	AR	15,042	VC
Univ of Central Missouri	MO	18,982	C
Univ of Central Okla	OK	15,150	C
Univ of Cincinnati	OH	22,118	VC
Univ of Dayton	OH	54,930	VC
Univ of Delaware	DE	32,214	VC
Univ of Detroit Mercy	MI	48,816	C
Univ of Findlay	OH	43,040	C
Univ of Great Falls	MT	38,524	C
Univ of Hartford	CT	49,776	C
Univ of Hawaii at Manoa	HI	23,261	C
Univ of Holy Cross	LA	21,523	NC
Univ of Idaho	ID	16,158	C
Univ of Illinois at Chicago	IL	24,664	VC
Univ of Illinois at Urbana-Champaign	IL	27,006	HC
Univ of Indianapolis	IN	36,480	VC
Univ of Iowa	IA	19,415	HC
Univ of Kansas	KS	20,884	VC
Univ of Kentucky	KY	24,800	C+
Univ of Louisiana at Lafayette	LA	14,516	C
Univ of Louisiana at Monroe	LA	15,970	C
Univ of Louisville	KY	19,692	C
Univ of Maine	ME	21,038	VC
Univ of Maine at Farmington	ME	18,792	C
Univ of Maine at Fort Kent	ME	15,165	LC
Univ of Maine at Presque Isle	ME	16,148	LC
Univ of Mary Hardin-Baylor	TX	35,292	C+
Univ of Maryland/College Park	MD	21,938	HC
Univ of Maryland/Eastern Shore	MD	21,861	LC
Univ of Mich/Dearborn	MI	12,472	VC
Univ of Mich/Flint	MI	19,062	C
Univ of Minn/Duluth	MN	20,292	C
Univ of Minn/Morris	MN	21,222	VC
Univ of Missouri-Columbia	MO	20,463	VC
Univ of Missouri-Kansas City	MO	19,563	VC
Univ of Missouri-St. Louis	MO	19,810	VC
Univ of Montana	MT	14,105	C
Univ of Mount Olive	NC	18,426	C
Univ of Nebr - Kearney	NE	17,014	LC
Univ of Nebr - Lincoln	NE	18,589	VC
Univ of Nebr - Omaha	NE	16,120	C
Univ of Nevada, Las Vegas	NV	17,553	C
Univ of Nevada, Reno	NV	18,010	C
Univ of New England	ME	50,110	C
Univ of New Mexico	NM	16,808	C
Univ of New Orleans	LA	12,840	C
Univ of North Alabama	AL	15,964	C
Univ of North Florida	FL	15,996	VC
Univ of North Georgia	GA	17,316	C
Univ of Pikeville	KY	27,838	C
Univ of Pittsburgh at Johnstown	PA	22,092	C
Univ of Portland	OR	52,152	VC
Univ of PR, at Cayey	PR		
Univ of PR-Rio Piedras campus	PR	13,327	
Univ of Rhode Island	RI	26,066	VC
Univ of Rio Grande & Rio Grande Community College	OH	8,750	LC
Univ of San Francisco	CA	60,580	C
Univ of Scranton	PA	54,962	VC
Univ of Sioux Falls	SD	25,630	C
Univ of South Alabama	AL	16,880	C
Univ of S Car Aiken	SC	18,094	C
Univ of S Car Upstate	SC	19,272	LC
Univ of S Dak	SD	16,109	C
Univ of Southern Indiana	IN	16,808	C
Univ of Southern Miss	MS	13,170	C
Univ of St. Francis	IL	40,828	C
Univ of Tampa	FL	38,928	VC
Univ of Texas Rio Grande Valley	TX	15,573	LC
Univ of the Incarnate Word	TX	39,162	LC
Univ of the Southwest	NM	24,386	C
Univ of Toledo	OH	19,336	C
Univ of Vermont	VT	29,792	HC
Univ of West Alabama	AL	16,284	LC
Univ of West Florida	FL	15,848	C
Univ of Wisc-Green Bay	WI	15,184	C
Univ of Wisc-La Crosse	WI	15,425	VC
Univ of Wisc-Madison	WI	21,647	MC
Univ of Wisc-Oshkosh	WI	15,392	C
Univ of Wisc-Parkside	WI	15,313	C
Univ of Wisc-Platteville	WI	14,148	C
Univ of Wisc-River Falls	WI	14,541	C
Univ of Wisc-Superior	WI	14,838	C
Univ of Wisc-Whitewater	WI	13,976	C
Univ of Wyoming	WY	15,537	C
Urbana Univ	OH	30,820	C
Ursuline College	OH	41,076	LC
Utah State Univ	UT	13,235	C
Valparaiso Univ	IN	50,160	VC
Vanderbilt Univ	TN	63,248	MC
Vanguard Univ of Southern Calif	CA	42,400	VC
Villanova Univ	PA	64,922	MC
Virginia Polytechnic Inst and State Univ	VA	21,920	VC
Virginia Union Univ	VA	25,058	C
Virginia Wesleyan Univ	VA	45,980	LC
Wagner College	NY	57,240	C+
Walsh Univ	OH	39,010	C
Wartburg College	IA	49,478	C
Washburn Univ	KS	15,827	C
Washington State Univ	WA	22,747	C
Washington Univ in St. Louis	MO	67,539	MC
Wayne State Univ	MI	23,085	C
Weber State Univ	UT	14,112	C
Webster Univ	MO	37,490	C
Wellesley College	MA	66,984	MC
West Chester Univ of Pennsylvania	PA	19,171	VC
West Liberty Univ	WV	16,158	C
West Virginia State Univ	WV	19,412	LC
West Virginia Wesleyan College	WV	39,188	C
Western Carolina Univ	NC	13,965	C
Western Conn State Univ	CT	21,254	LC
Western Mich Univ	MI	21,791	C
Western New England Univ	MA	49,182	C
Western New Mexico Univ	NM	16,914	LC
Western State Colo Univ	CO	19,348	C
Western Washington Univ	WA	18,904	VC
Westminster College	MO	32,820	C
Westminster College	PA	41,722	C
Wheaton College	IL	44,993	MC
Wheaton College	MA	63,818	VC
Whitworth Univ	WA	53,682	VC
Wichita State Univ	KS	17,773	C
Wiley College	TX	19,255	C
William Jewell College	MO	42,490	C+
William Penn Univ	IA	26,000	C
Williams Baptist College	AR	24,720	C
Wilmington College	OH	35,100	C
Wilson College	PA	35,620	LC
Winona State Univ	MN	18,109	C
Winthrop Univ	SC	23,960	C
Wisc Lutheran College	WI	36,290	C
Wittenberg Univ	OH	49,863	VC
Wright State Univ	OH	16,983	C
York College	NE	30,260	C
York College of Pennsylvania	PA	29,240	C
Youngstown State Univ	OH	17,487	C

SECRETARIAL STUDIES/OFFICE MANAGEMENT

School	ST	$IS	SR
Cal State, Fullerton	CA	21,902	C
Caribbean Univ	PR	12,227	
Dordt College	IA	37,860	C+
Inter-American Univ of PR Ponce	PR	19,549	
Inter-American Univ of PR-Aguadilla Campus	PR	21,657	
Inter-American Univ of PR-Barranquitas	PR	18,336	
Inter-American Univ of PR-Bayamon	PR	18,785	
Inter-American Univ of PR-Fajardo Campus	PR	18,336	
Inter-American Univ of PR-Metropolitan Campus	PR	20,045	
Inter-American Univ of PR-San Germán	PR	20,042	
Johnson & Wales Univ/ Providence Campus	RI	44,768	C
Southeastern Okla State Univ	OK	11,875	C
Southern Univ at New Orleans	LA	8,014	LC
Universidad del Turabo	PR	17,828	
Univ of PR, at Arecibo	PR	12,652	
Univ of PR, at Cayey	PR		
Univ of PR, at Humacao	PR	14,000	
Univ of PR-Rio Piedras campus	PR	13,327	
Univ of the Sacred Heart	PR	17,932	

SLAVIC LANGUAGES

School	ST	$IS	SR
Columbia Univ/ School of General Studies	NY	61,470	MC
Duke Univ	NC	68,298	MC
Indiana Univ Bloomington	IN	20,791	HC
New York Univ	NY	68,139	MC
Northwestern Univ	IL	68,725	MC
Princeton Univ	NJ	60,090	MC
Stanford Univ	CA	62,541	MC
The Univ of Texas at Austin	TX	20,206	MC
Univ of Calif at Berkeley	CA	29,886	MC
Univ of Calif at Santa Barbara	CA	30,627	HC+
Univ of Chicago	IL	70,551	MC
Univ of Illinois at Chicago	IL	24,664	VC
Univ of Kansas	KS	20,884	VC
Univ of Pittsburgh	PA	30,030	MC
Univ of Virginia	VA	27,367	MC
Univ of Washington	WA	23,091	MC
Wayne State Univ	MI	23,085	C
Yale Univ	CT	64,650	MC

SMALL BUSINESS MANAGEMENT

School	ST	$IS	SR
Adams State Univ	CO	15,420	LC
Bay Path Univ	MA	46,356	C
Bryant Univ	RI	57,204	VC
Cal State, Chico	CA	19,790	VC
Cal State, Fullerton	CA	21,902	C
Cal State, San Bernardino	CA	20,106	C
Calvin College	MI	43,090	HC
Carroll Univ	WI	38,100	C+
Concord Univ	WV	14,954	LC
Florida Atlantic Univ	FL	18,256	C
Florida State Univ	FL	16,771	HC
Hawaii Pacific Univ	HI	33,420	C
Huntington Univ	IN	33,996	C
Johnson & Wales Univ/ Denver Campus	CO	44,768	C
Johnson & Wales Univ/ Providence Campus	RI	44,768	C
Johnson State College	VT	22,672	C
Mount Aloysius College	PA	29,976	C
Mount Ida College	MA	46,820	C
Northern Arizona Univ	AZ	21,003	C
Rowan Univ	NJ	24,491	VC
Stetson Univ	FL	57,174	VC+
The Univ of Montana Western	MT	9,426	LC
Tusculum College	TN	31,625	LC
Union College	NE	23,270	C
Univ of Maine at Machias	ME	22,960	C
Univ of Mich/Dearborn	MI	12,472	VC
Univ of Montana	MT	14,105	C

SOCIAL FOUNDATIONS

School	ST	$IS	SR
Amridge Univ	AL	10,860	LC
Eastern Mich Univ	MI	19,761	C

SOCIAL MEDIA MARKETING

School	ST	$IS	SR
Kutztown Univ of Pennsylvania	PA	19,477	C
Lewis Univ	IL	41,710	C

SOCIAL PSYCHOLOGY

School	ST	$IS	SR
Bennington College	VT	66,280	MC
Cal State, Fullerton	CA	21,902	C
Clarion Univ of Pennsylvania	PA	21,608	LC
Florida Atlantic Univ	FL	18,256	C
Goddard College	VT	17,040	VC
Northwest Missouri State Univ	MO	18,286	C
Park Univ	MO	22,134	C
Univ of Calif at Irvine	CA	33,857	VC
Univ of Holy Cross	LA	21,523	NC

SOCIAL SCIENCE

School	ST	$IS	SR
Adelphi Univ	NY	49,792	C
Anna Maria College	MA	51,020	C
Aquinas College - Mich	MI	38,876	VC
Arizona State Univ at the West Campus	AZ	21,513	VC
Ashford Univ	CA	10,480	C
Ashland Univ	OH	30,446	C
Austin College	TX	51,059	HC
Azusa Pacific Univ	CA	43,972	C
Ball State Univ	IN	19,808	C+
Bellevue Univ	NE	20,300	NC
Bemidji State Univ	MN	17,730	C
Benedict College	SC	28,630	NC
Benedictine College	KS	38,850	VC
Benedictine Univ	IL	38,300	C
Bennington College	VT	66,280	MC
Bethany College	KS	38,637	LC
Biola Univ	CA	48,686	C
Black Hills State Univ	SD	16,622	C
Bluefield State College	WV	5,832	LC
Bluffton Univ	OH	40,950	C+
Boise State Univ	ID	17,368	C
Bowling Green State Univ	OH	19,975	C
Calif Baptist Univ	CA	42,986	C
Calif Lutheran Univ	CA	52,853	C
Cal State, Chico	CA	19,790	VC
Cal State, Fresno	CA	16,902	LC
Cal State, Fullerton	CA	21,902	C
Cal State, Los Angeles	CA	17,186	LC
Cal State, Monterey Bay	CA	22,872	LC
Cal State, Sacramento	CA	19,060	C
Cal State, San Bernardino	CA	20,106	C
Cal State, San Marcos	CA	20,604	LC
Cal State, Stanislaus	CA	18,053	LC
Calif Univ of Pennsylvania	PA	20,425	LC
Canisius College	NY	49,672	C
Cardinal Stritch Univ	WI	37,136	C
Caribbean Univ	PR	12,227	
Carnegie Mellon Univ	PA	67,980	MC
Carson-Newman Univ	TN	35,900	C
Carthage College	WI	48,835	C
Castleton Univ	VT	20,186	C
Cazenovia College	NY	47,866	C
Central Conn State Univ	CT	22,041	C
Central Mich Univ	MI	20,330	C
Central Washington Univ	WA	16,803	C
Chadron State College	NE	14,819	LC
Charleston Southern Univ	SC	34,700	C
Cheyney Univ of Pennsylvania	PA	20,896	LC
CUNY/Hunter College	NY	31,098	VC
Clarion Univ of Pennsylvania	PA	21,608	LC
Cleveland State Univ	OH	22,290	C
Colgate Univ	NY	67,500	MC
College of St. Mary	NE	27,500	C
College of St. Scholastica	MN	45,734	C+
College of the Ozarks	MO	7,530	VC
Colo Christian Univ	CO	40,885	VC
Colo Mesa Univ	CO	19,707	LC
Colo State Univ-Pueblo	CO	21,581	C
Concord Univ	WV	14,954	LC
Concordia Univ Wisc	WI	35,910	C
Concordia Univ, Ann Arbor	MI	38,878	C+
Concordia Univ, Chicago	IL	41,522	C
Coppin State Univ	MD	14,071	VC
Corban Univ	OR	41,700	C
Covenant College	GA	44,590	HC
Cumberland Univ	TN	27,710	C
Delta State Univ	MS	13,176	LC
DePaul Univ	IL	52,807	VC
Dominican College	NY	40,258	LC
Dominican Univ	IL	42,472	C+
Dordt College	IA	37,860	C+
Eastern Conn State Univ	CT	23,059	C
Eastern Mennonite Univ	VA	42,550	C
Eastern Washington Univ	WA	17,896	LC
Edinboro Univ	PA	15,940	LC
Elizabeth City State Univ	NC	14,745	C
Emporia State Univ	KS	15,029	C
Eureka College	IL	34,760	C
Evangel Univ	MO	28,898	C
Faulkner Univ	AL	26,410	C
Fayetteville State Univ	NC	17,756	C
Felician Univ	NJ	46,280	LC
Florida A&M Univ	FL	15,361	C
Florida Atlantic Univ	FL	18,256	C
Florida State Univ	FL	16,771	HC
Fordham Univ	NY	68,431	MC
Fresno Pacific Univ	CA	38,858	C
Frostburg State Univ	MD	17,280	LC
Gardner-Webb Univ	NC	24,935	C+
George Fox Univ	OR	42,938	C
Georgia Southern Univ	GA	16,540	VC
Goddard College	VT	17,040	VC
Graceland Univ	IA	35,290	C
Grand Valley State Univ	MI	22,250	C+
Gustavus Adolphus College	MN	53,943	HC
Hamline Univ	MN	50,152	C
Harding Univ	AR	25,440	C
Harvard College/Harvard Univ	MA	65,609	MC
Hastings College	NE	35,380	C+
Hawaii Pacific Univ	HI	33,420	C
Heidelberg Univ	OH	40,400	LC
Hofstra Univ	NY	58,210	C+
Hope International Univ	CA	42,730	C
Humboldt State Univ	CA	21,708	C
Illinois State Univ	IL	23,418	VC
Immaculata Univ	PA	39,000	C
Indiana Univ of Pennsylvania	PA	24,474	C
Indiana Univ-Purdue Univ Fort Wayne	IN	18,675	C
James Madison Univ	VA	19,084	VC
Johns Hopkins Univ	MD	68,080	MC
Johnson C. Smith Univ	NC	25,336	LC
Juniata College	PA	58,118	VC
Kansas State Univ	KS	17,780	VC
Keystone College	PA	28,680	LC
Lake Erie College	OH	38,914	LC
Lake Superior State Univ	MI	19,867	C
Lamar Univ	TX	18,014	LC
Langston Univ	OK	15,659	C
LeMoyne-Owen College	TN	16,980	C
Lesley Univ	MA	42,800	C
Lewis-Clark State College	ID	14,202	C
Liberty Univ	VA	31,415	C
Lincoln Memorial Univ	TN	28,430	C
Lindsey Wilson College	KY	33,546	C
LIU Brooklyn	NY	50,698	C
Lock Haven Univ of Pennsylvania	PA	20,544	LC
Loyola Univ New Orleans	LA	52,456	VC
Lyndon State College	VT	20,714	C
Marlboro College	VT	50,832	VC+
Marquette Univ	WI	53,090	VC+
Marygrove College	MI	30,100	LC
Marylhurst Univ	OR	16,818	NC
Maryville College	TN	44,410	C
Marywood Univ	PA	47,840	C
Mayville State Univ	ND	18,371	NC
McKendree Univ	IL	37,940	C+
Mercer Univ	GA	45,348	VC
Metropolitan State Univ	MN	7,859	C
Mich State Univ	MI	24,542	VC
Mich Tech Univ	MI	25,551	VC+
Midland Univ	NE	39,512	C
Minot State Univ	ND	13,285	C
Miss Univ for Women	MS	17,065	C
Missouri Baptist Univ	MO	35,594	C
Montana State Univ-Northern	MT	11,370	NC
Morehead State Univ	KY	18,386	LC

ST = STATE **$IS** = IN-STATE COSTS **SR** = SELECTOR RATING

School	ST	$IS	SR
Mount Marty College	SD	36,862	C
Mount St. Mary College	NY	44,448	C
Mount St. Mary's Univ - Chalon Campus	CA	50,486	VC+
Muskingum Univ	OH	35,966	C
National Louis Univ	IL	43,000	LC
Nazareth College	NY	46,784	C
New College of Florida	FL	16,180	HC+
New York Univ	NY	68,139	MC
Niagara Univ	NY	41,010	C
N Car State Univ	NC	22,434	HC+
North Central College	IL	48,712	C+
N Dak State Univ	ND	16,245	VC
Northeastern State Univ	OK	8,615	VC
Northern Kentucky Univ	KY	16,486	C
Northern State Univ	SD	15,570	C
Northwest Christian Univ	OR	36,580	C
Northwest Missouri State Univ	MO	18,286	C
Northwestern Okla State Univ	OK	13,072	LC
Notre Dame de Namur Univ	CA	46,526	LC
Ohio Wesleyan Univ	OH	49,460	VC
Okla Baptist Univ	OK	33,990	C
Olivet Nazarene Univ	IL	41,840	VC
Oregon State Univ	OR	23,337	VC
Pace Univ	NY	60,136	C
Pepperdine Univ	CA	66,862	VC+
Peru State College	NE	15,602	LC
Piedmont College	GA	34,334	C
Plymouth State Univ	NH	23,180	LC
Point Loma Nazarene Univ	CA	46,150	C+
Pontifical Catholic Univ of PR	PR	10,534	
Providence College	RI	62,870	HC
Quinnipiac Univ	CT	60,970	VC
Radford Univ	VA	19,758	C
Ramapo College of New Jersey	NJ	25,760	VC
Regis Univ	CO	46,380	C
Rhode Island College	RI	19,000	LC
Robert Morris Univ	PA	40,600	C
Rockford Univ	IL	38,570	C
Roger Williams Univ	RI	48,074	VC
Roosevelt Univ	IL	41,890	VC
Rosemont College	PA	30,980	LC
Rutgers Univ - New Brunswick	NJ	27,090	HC
St. John's Univ	MN	53,472	C
St. Mary's Univ of Minn	MN	42,440	C
St. Peter's Univ	NJ	49,192	C
St. Xavier Univ	IL	44,440	C
San Diego State Univ	CA	23,156	VC
San Jose State Univ	CA	22,630	C
Seattle Pacific Univ	WA	47,439	C+
Seton Hall Univ	NJ	58,008	C
Shawnee State Univ	OH	16,998	C
Shorter Univ	GA	31,130	LC
Siena Heights Univ	MI	36,322	C
Silver Lake College of the Holy Family	WI	36,290	LC
Simpson Univ	CA	34,722	C
Skidmore College	NY	66,600	MC
Slippery Rock Univ of Pennsylvania	PA	20,450	C
Southeast Missouri State Univ	MO	16,148	C
Southeastern Okla State Univ	OK	11,875	C
Southern Illinois Univ Carbondale	IL	24,554	C
Southern New Hampshire Univ	NH	44,256	C
Southern Oregon Univ	OR	19,117	C
Southwestern Adventist Univ	TX	28,232	LC
Spalding Univ	KY	31,938	C
Spring Arbor Univ	MI	37,390	C
Spring Hill College	AL	48,488	C
St. Andrews Univ	NC	44,634	LC
St. Cloud State Univ	MN	10,600	C
St. Joseph's College, New York/Brooklyn Campus	NY	25,114	LC
St. Joseph's College, New York/Long Island Campus	NY	25,124	C
St. Thomas Aquinas College	NY	32,450	C
SUNY at New Paltz	NY	20,840	C
SUNY/Univ at Buffalo	NY	23,122	C
Suffolk Univ	MA	52,316	C
Sul Ross State Univ	TX	15,021	LC
Temple Univ	PA	24,392	C+
The Catholic Univ of America	DC	58,376	VC
The Univ of Akron	OH	22,566	C
The Univ of Mary	ND	23,180	C
The Univ of Montana Western	MT	9,426	LC
The Univ of Utah	UT	18,751	VC
The Univ of Virginia's College at Wise	VA	18,192	LC
Thomas Edison State Univ	NJ	6,350	NC
Thomas Univ	GA	21,420	NC
Touro College	NY	31,040	C
Towson Univ	MD	21,878	C
Trine Univ	IN	41,310	C
Trinity International Univ	IL	31,070	VC
Troy Univ	AL	16,171	C
Tulane Univ	LA	67,496	MC
Union College	NE	23,270	C
Union College	NY	64,320	MC
Union Inst & Univ	OH	8,912	SP
United States Air Force Academy	CO		C
Universidad del Turabo	PR	17,828	
Universidad Metropolitana	PR	17,828	
Univ of Alaska Southeast	AK	17,615	C
Univ of Bridgeport	CT	44,985	LC
Univ of Calif at Berkeley	CA	29,886	MC
Univ of Calif at Davis	CA	28,468	HC
Univ of Calif at Irvine	CA	33,857	VC
Univ of Central Florida	FL	16,379	VC
Univ of Chicago	IL	70,551	MC
Univ of Cincinnati	OH	22,118	VC
Univ of Denver	CO	61,129	VC+
Univ of Great Falls	MT	38,524	C
Univ of Holy Cross	LA	21,523	NC
Univ of Houston-Downtown	TX	7,241	LC
Univ of Indianapolis	IN	36,480	VC
Univ of Iowa	IA	19,415	HC
Univ of La Verne	CA	55,600	C
Univ of Maine at Augusta	ME	7,812	C
Univ of Maine at Fort Kent	ME	15,165	LC
Univ of Maryland Univ College	MD	26,146	LC
Univ of Mich/Ann Arbor	MI	25,274	MC
Univ of Mich/Flint	MI	19,062	C
Univ of Minn/Morris	MN	21,222	VC
Univ of Missouri-Columbia	MO	20,463	VC
Univ of Mobile	AL	28,935	C
Univ of Montevallo	AL	20,012	C
Univ of Nebr - Kearney	NE	17,014	LC
Univ of Nevada, Las Vegas	NV	17,553	C
Univ of N Car at Greensboro	NC	15,998	C
Univ of N Dak	ND	16,673	C
Univ of North Georgia	GA	17,316	C
Univ of North Texas	TX	20,082	C
Univ of Northern Colo	CO	19,658	C
Univ of Oregon	OR	24,021	VC
Univ of Pittsburgh	PA	30,030	MC
Univ of Pittsburgh at Bradford	PA	22,958	C
Univ of Pittsburgh at Greensburg	PA	24,140	C
Univ of Pittsburgh at Johnstown	PA	22,092	C
Univ of PR, at Mayaguez	PR	13,995	
Univ of PR-Rio Piedras campus	PR	13,327	
Univ of Sioux Falls	SD	25,630	C
Univ of South Florida St. Petersburg	FL	15,980	C
Univ of South Florida/Tampa	FL	16,110	VC
Univ of Southern Calif	CA	66,631	MC
Univ of Southern Indiana	IN	16,808	C
Univ of Southern Miss	MS	13,170	C
Univ of the Ozarks	AR	31,050	NC
Univ of the Pacific	CA	57,446	VC
Univ of West Florida	FL	15,848	C
Univ of Wisc-Platteville	WI	14,148	C
Univ of Wisc-Stevens Point	WI	14,043	C
Univ of Wyoming	WY	15,537	C
Upper Iowa Univ	IA	34,990	NC
Valley City State Univ	ND	13,267	C
Valparaiso Univ	IN	50,160	VC
Virginia Wesleyan Univ	VA	45,980	LC
Warner Pacific College	OR	31,610	C
Washington State Univ	WA	22,747	C
Washington Univ in St. Louis	MO	67,539	MC
Wayland Baptist Univ	TX	23,460	LC
Wayne State College	NE	25,746	NC
Waynesburg Univ	PA	33,530	C
West Liberty Univ	WV	16,158	C
West Texas A&M Univ	TX	13,478	C
West Virginia Wesleyan College	WV	39,188	C
Western Carolina Univ	NC	13,965	C
Western Conn State Univ	CT	21,254	LC
Western New Mexico Univ	NM	16,914	LC
Western Oregon Univ	OR	19,965	LC
Westminster College	PA	41,722	C
Westminster College	UT	41,078	C
Westmont College	CA	57,930	VC
Wheaton College	IL	44,993	MC
Wilberforce Univ	OH	19,900	C
Wiley College	TX	19,255	C
William Carey Univ	MS	23,950	LC
Williams College	MA	67,700	MC
Wilmington College	OH	35,100	C
Wisc Lutheran College	WI	36,290	C

SOCIAL SCIENCE EDUCATION

School	ST	$IS	SR
Appalachian State Univ	NC	15,394	VC
Aquinas College - Mich	MI	38,876	VC
Arkansas State Univ	AR	16,190	C
Auburn Univ	AL	24,300	VC+
Baylor Univ	TX	56,803	HC
Bethune-Cookman Univ	FL	23,322	C
Black Hills State Univ	SD	16,622	C
Blackburn College	IL	28,526	LC
Blue Mountain College	MS	15,949	C
Boise State Univ	ID	17,368	C
Bowling Green State Univ	OH	19,975	C
Brigham Young Univ	UT	13,248	MC
Brigham Young Univ/Hawaii	HI	11,710	C
Campbellsville Univ	KY	33,400	C
Central Methodist Univ	MO	31,500	VC
Coker College	SC	38,196	C
College of St. Scholastica	MN	45,734	C+
Concordia College - New York	NY	39,035	LC
Delta State Univ	MS	13,176	LC
Dordt College	IA	37,860	C+
Drury Univ	MO	37,555	VC
Eastern Illinois Univ	IL	21,414	C
Eastern Nazarene College	MA	41,114	C
Eastern Washington Univ	WA	17,896	LC
Faulkner Univ	AL	26,410	C
Fayetteville State Univ	NC	17,756	C
Florida Gulf Coast Univ	FL	14,738	C
Florida State Univ	FL	16,771	HC
Fresno Pacific Univ	CA	38,858	C
Friends Univ	KS	38,000	C
Hope International Univ	CA	42,730	C
Humboldt State Univ	CA	21,708	C
Illinois State Univ	IL	23,418	VC
Ithaca College	NY	58,158	VC+
Jackson State Univ	MS	15,879	LC
Knox College	IL	54,654	VC+
Kutztown Univ of Pennsylvania	PA	19,477	C
Lincoln Univ	MO	14,402	NC
Marian Univ	WI	34,622	C
Marywood Univ	PA	47,840	C
Mayville State Univ	ND	18,371	NC
Mercyhurst Univ	PA	47,420	C
Miles College	AL	16,530	NC
Millikin Univ	IL	44,148	C
Miss Valley State Univ	MS	13,233	LC
Missouri Southern State Univ	MO	13,071	C
Missouri Western State Univ	MO	17,822	LC
Montana State Univ Billings	MT	13,336	LC
Montana State Univ-Northern	MT	11,370	NC
Nazareth College	NY	46,784	C
Nebr Wesleyan Univ	NE	42,026	C+
New York Univ	NY	68,139	MC
N Car A&T State Univ	NC	13,786	C
N Dak State Univ	ND	16,245	VC
Oakwood Univ	AL	43,758	C
Oglala Lakota College	SD	15,050	NC
Okla Christian Univ	OK	29,260	C
Olivet Nazarene Univ	IL	41,840	VC
Piedmont College	GA	34,334	C
Rocky Mountain College	MT	35,776	C
Rust College	MS	10,600	C
St. Louis Univ	MO	49,866	HC
St. Mary-of-the-Woods College	IN	40,424	LC
Schreiner Univ	TX	34,626	LC
Seattle Pacific Univ	WA	47,439	C+
Seton Hill Univ	PA	46,972	VC
Shawnee State Univ	OH	16,998	C
Silver Lake College of the Holy Family	WI	36,290	LC
Simpson Univ	CA	34,722	C
S Car State Univ	SC	21,330	LC
Southeastern Louisiana Univ	LA	16,237	C
Southern Illinois Univ Carbondale	IL	24,554	C
Southern Illinois Univ Edwardsville	IL	20,188	C
Southwestern Okla State Univ	OK	12,205	C
SUNY/Oneonta	NY	20,794	C
Stetson Univ	FL	57,174	VC+
Texas Christian Univ	TX	57,120	HC
Texas Wesleyan Univ	TX	37,338	C
The College of New Jersey	NJ	28,675	VC+
The Univ of Mary	ND	23,180	C
The Univ of Montana Western	MT	9,426	LC
The Univ of Utah	UT	18,751	VC
Trine Univ	IN	41,310	C
Troy Univ	AL	16,171	C
Union College	NE	23,270	C
Universidad del Turabo	PR	17,828	
Univ of Arkansas at Pine Bluff	AR	13,541	C
Univ of Central Florida	FL	16,379	VC
Univ of Maryland/Eastern Shore	MD	21,861	LC
Univ of Miss	MS	18,802	C
Univ of Nebr - Lincoln	NE	18,589	VC
Univ of North Alabama	AL	15,964	C
Univ of North Georgia	GA	17,316	C
Univ of Northern Colo	CO	19,658	C
Univ of Northern Iowa	IA	17,480	C
Univ of Pittsburgh at Johnstown	PA	22,092	C
Univ of Rio Grande & Rio Grande Community College	OH	8,750	LC
Univ of Southern Indiana	IN	16,808	C
Univ of Wisc-Oshkosh	WI	15,392	C
Univ of Wisc-Superior	WI	14,838	C
Valparaiso Univ	IN	50,160	VC
Warner Univ	FL	28,216	C
Wartburg College	IA	49,478	C
Washington Univ in St. Louis	MO	67,539	MC
Weber State Univ	UT	14,112	C
West Liberty Univ	WV	16,158	C
Western Carolina Univ	NC	13,965	C
Westmont College	CA	57,930	VC
Wiley College	TX	19,255	C
Wilmington College	OH	35,100	C
Wilson College	PA	35,620	LC
Wright State Univ	OH	16,983	C
York College	NE	30,260	C
Youngstown State Univ	OH	17,487	C

SOCIAL STUDIES

School	ST	$IS	SR
Andrews Univ	MI	41,732	C
Aquinas College - Mich	MI	38,876	VC
Arkansas Tech Univ	AR	16,534	LC
Barton College	NC	39,854	C
Bethel Univ	MN	46,550	C+
Bluefield College	VA	34,711	C
Bluffton Univ	OH	40,950	C+
Brescia Univ	KY	29,890	VC
Caldwell Univ	NJ	42,165	LC
Central Mich Univ	MI	20,330	C
Chaminade Univ of Honolulu	HI	37,614	C
Cleveland State Univ	OH	22,290	C
Concordia Univ, Ann Arbor	MI	38,878	C+
DePaul Univ	IL	52,807	VC
Eastern Mich Univ	MI	19,761	C
Eastern Nazarene College	MA	41,114	C
Eastern New Mexico Univ	NM	12,874	LC
Edgewood College	WI	35,950	C
Erskine College	SC	45,460	C
Ferrum College	VA	43,970	C
Hamline Univ	MN	50,152	C
Harvard College/Harvard Univ	MA	65,609	MC
Indiana Univ Bloomington	IN	20,791	HC
Indiana Wesleyan Univ	IN	33,674	C
Ithaca College	NY	58,158	VC+
Madonna Univ	MI	30,450	LC
Mayville State Univ	ND	18,371	NC
McMurry Univ	TX	34,259	LC
Methodist Univ	NC	58,130	C
Millersville Univ of Pennsylvania	PA	25,298	C
Minn State Univ, Mankato	MN	17,190	C
Miss College	MS	25,850	C
Missouri Southern State Univ	MO	13,071	C
Missouri Western State Univ	MO	17,822	LC
Mount Aloysius College	PA	29,976	C
Mount Mary Univ	WI	34,650	LC
Mount St. Mary's Univ	MD	53,380	C
New York Univ	NY	68,139	MC
Northern Kentucky Univ	KY	16,486	C
Ohio Northern Univ	OH	44,050	VC
Okla Christian Univ	OK	29,260	C
Okla Panhandle State Univ	OK	6,152	C
Okla Wesleyan Univ	OK	34,434	C
Olivet College	MI	37,661	LC
Our Lady of the Lake Univ	TX	37,790	LC
Pacific Union College	CA	36,009	VC
Pfeiffer Univ	NC	40,532	LC
Purdue Univ/West Lafayette	IN	20,032	MC
S Car State Univ	SC	21,330	LC
Southern Wesleyan Univ	SC	33,670	LC
Southwestern Adventist Univ	TX	28,232	LC
Spring Arbor Univ	MI	37,390	C
St. Catherine Univ	MN	45,630	C
St. Francis College	NY	38,800	LC
St. John's Univ	NY	57,160	C+
Tulane Univ	LA	67,496	MC
Univ of Great Falls	MT	38,524	C
Univ of Mich/Dearborn	MI	12,472	VC
Univ of Texas Rio Grande Valley	TX	15,573	LC
Univ of Wisc-Eau Claire	WI	16,354	VC
Univ of Wisc-Madison	WI	21,647	MC
Univ of Wisc-River Falls	WI	14,541	C
Univ of Wisc-Superior	WI	14,838	C
Utica College	NY	31,510	C
Virginia Wesleyan Univ	VA	45,980	LC
Viterbo Univ	WI	34,660	C
Washington State Univ	WA	22,747	C
Wayland Baptist Univ	TX	23,460	LC
Wesleyan Univ	CT	66,940	MC
West Liberty Univ	WV	16,158	C
Western Kentucky Univ	KY	16,850	C
Western Washington Univ	WA	18,904	VC
Youngstown State Univ	OH	17,487	C

SOCIAL STUDIES EDUCATION

School	ST	$IS	SR
Adams State Univ	CO	15,420	LC
Alabama State Univ	AL	16,490	LC
Alfred Univ	NY	37,490	C
Alice Lloyd College	KY	8,190	LC
Anderson Univ	IN	39,450	C
Andrews Univ	MI	41,732	C
Appalachian State Univ	NC	15,394	VC
Aquinas College - Mich	MI	38,876	VC
Asbury Univ	KY	36,450	C+
Augustana Univ	SD	39,968	VC
Averett Univ	VA	43,034	LC
Baylor Univ	TX	56,803	HC
Bethany College	WV	38,774	LC
Bethel College	IN	36,830	C
Bethel Univ	MN	46,550	C+
Biola Univ	CA	48,686	C
Bloomsburg Univ of Pennsylvania	PA	19,930	C
Boston Univ	MA	67,352	MC
Cameron Univ	OK	11,632	LC
Canisius College	NY	49,672	C
Catawba College	NC	39,820	LC
Cedarville Univ	OH	36,244	VC
Central Washington Univ	WA	16,803	C
CUNY/Brooklyn College	NY	7,163	C+

ST = STATE **$IS** = IN-STATE COSTS **SR** = SELECTOR RATING

School	ST	$IS	SR
CUNY/City College	NY	20,204	C
College of the Ozarks	MO	7,530	VC
Colo State Univ	CO	23,033	C
Concordia College - Moorhead	MN	46,418	C
Concordia College - New York	NY	39,035	LC
Concordia Univ St. Paul	MN	29,050	C
Corban Univ	OR	41,700	C
Daemen College	NY	40,336	C
Defiance College	OH	42,240	LC
Duquesne Univ	PA	48,508	VC
East Carolina Univ	NC	16,539	C
East Texas Baptist Univ	TX	34,444	C
Eastern Mich Univ	MI	19,761	C
Edinboro Univ	PA	15,940	LC
Elizabethtown College	PA	56,340	VC
Ferris State Univ	MI	21,458	C
Franklin College	IN	40,550	C
Gannon Univ	PA	42,922	C
Glenville State College	WV	17,386	LC
Grambling State Univ	LA	15,701	C
Green Mountain College	VT	45,228	LC
Greensboro College	NC	39,790	LC
Gwynedd Mercy Univ	PA	43,780	LC
Hardin-Simmons Univ	TX	36,025	C
Hofstra Univ	NY	58,210	C+
Huntington Univ	IN	33,996	C
Indiana State Univ	IN	23,223	LC
Indiana Univ Bloomington	IN	20,791	HC
Indiana Univ Northwest	IN	7,207	LC
Indiana Univ of Pennsylvania	PA	24,474	C
Indiana Univ South Bend	IN	16,057	C
Indiana Univ Southeast	IN	16,931	C
Indiana Univ-Purdue Univ Indianapolis	IN	18,952	C
Indiana Wesleyan Univ	IN	33,674	C
Ithaca College	NY	58,158	VC+
John Brown Univ	AR	35,184	VC
Judson College	AL	27,066	C
Juniata College	PA	58,118	VC
Kentucky Christian Univ	KY	26,836	LC
Kentucky State Univ	KY	14,484	LC
Keystone College	PA	28,680	LC
King Univ	TN	36,976	C
Kutztown Univ of Pennsylvania	PA	19,477	C
La Salle Univ	PA	43,476	C
Le Moyne College	NY	47,305	VC
LIU Brooklyn	NY	50,698	C
LIU Post	NY	50,698	C+
Louisiana College	LA	21,274	C
Malone Univ	OH	39,200	C
Mansfield Univ of Pennsylvania	PA	24,244	LC
Mars Hill Univ	NC	41,104	C
Marshall Univ	WV	18,044	C
Marygrove College	MI	30,100	LC
Messiah College	PA	44,380	VC
MidAmerica Nazarene Univ	KS	37,808	C
Millersville Univ of Pennsylvania	PA	25,298	C
Minn State Univ, Mankato	MN	17,190	C
Minn State Univ, Moorhead	MN	21,393	C
Missouri Southern State Univ	MO	13,071	C
Missouri Valley College	MO	28,150	C
Missouri Western State Univ	MO	17,822	LC
Monmouth Univ	NJ	50,184	C
Montana State Univ Billings	MT	13,336	LC
Morningside College	IA	39,780	C
Morris College	SC	19,195	LC
Mount Aloysius College	PA	29,976	C
Mount Vernon Nazarene Univ	OH	35,944	C
New York Univ	NY	68,139	MC
Niagara Univ	NY	41,010	C
N Car State Univ	NC	22,434	HC+
North Greenville Univ	SC	25,930	C
Ohio Univ	OH	23,394	VC
Okla Baptist Univ	OK	33,990	C
Okla Christian Univ	OK	29,260	C
Okla Wesleyan Univ	OK	34,434	C
Oral Roberts Univ	OK	34,316	C
Ouachita Baptist Univ	AR	33,500	VC
Pfeiffer Univ	NC	40,532	LC
Piedmont College	GA	34,334	C
Pittsburg State Univ	KS	13,880	C
Pontifical Catholic Univ of PR	PR	10,534	
Purdue Univ Northwest	IN	15,178	C
Purdue Univ/West Lafayette	IN	20,032	MC
Rider Univ	NJ	54,050	C
Rivier Univ	NH	41,600	VC
Rocky Mountain College	MT	35,776	C
Saginaw Valley State Univ	MI	19,284	C
St. Augustine's Univ	NC	25,582	C
St. Mary's Univ of Minn	MN	42,440	C
Shaw Univ	NC	24,638	C
Shepherd Univ, West Virginia	WV	17,382	C
Shippensburg Univ of Pennsylvania	PA	24,096	C
Southeast Missouri State Univ	MO	16,148	C
Southeastern Okla State Univ	OK	11,875	C
Southeastern Univ	FL	34,910	LC
Southern Nazarene Univ	OK	33,684	C
Southern New Hampshire Univ	NH	44,256	C
Southern Univ and A&M College	LA	16,074	LC
Southern Univ at New Orleans	LA	8,014	LC
Southwest Baptist Univ	MO	30,890	LC
St. Edward's Univ	TX	56,190	VC
St. John Fisher College	NY	45,270	VC
St. Olaf College	MN	56,430	HC
St. Thomas Univ	FL	51,187	LC
SUNY at New Paltz	NY	20,840	C
SUNY at Oswego	NY	22,219	VC
SUNY/College at Old Westbury	NY	16,860	C
SUNY/Fredonia	NY	20,818	C
SUNY/Potsdam	NY	21,051	VC
Syracuse Univ	NY	62,313	HC
Taylor Univ	IN	42,130	VC
Texas Christian Univ	TX	57,120	HC
Texas Wesleyan Univ	TX	37,338	C
The College of New Jersey	NJ	28,675	VC+
The Univ of Montana Western	MT	9,426	LC
Thomas More College	KY	36,720	LC
Tiffin Univ	OH	34,900	LC
Union College	KY	32,310	C
Univ of Central Missouri	MO	18,982	C
Univ of Central Okla	OK	15,150	C
Univ of Charleston	WV	35,000	LC
Univ of Conn	CT	27,394	
Univ of Evansville	IN	44,186	C+
Univ of Georgia	GA	21,878	HC
Univ of Great Falls	MT	38,524	C
Univ of Indianapolis	IN	36,480	VC
Univ of Kentucky	KY	24,800	C+
Univ of Louisiana at Lafayette	LA	14,516	C
Univ of Maine at Machias	ME	22,960	C
Univ of Mary Hardin-Baylor	TX	35,292	C+
Univ of Mich/Dearborn	MI	12,472	VC
Univ of Minn/Duluth	MN	20,292	C
Univ of Missouri-Columbia	MO	20,463	VC
Univ of N Car at Charlotte	NC	17,803	VC
Univ of North Florida	FL	15,996	VC
Univ of Northwestern - St. Paul	MN	39,530	C
Univ of Okla	OK	19,651	HC
Univ of Pittsburgh at Bradford	PA	22,958	C
Univ of Rio Grande & Rio Grande Community College	OH	8,750	LC
Univ of S Car Upstate	SC	19,272	LC
Univ of South Florida/Tampa	FL	16,110	VC
Univ of the Cumberlands	KY	32,000	LC
Univ of Vermont	VT	29,792	HC
Univ of Wisc-La Crosse	WI	15,425	VC
Univ of Wisc-Whitewater	WI	13,976	C
Valparaiso Univ	IN	50,160	VC
Virginia Wesleyan Univ	VA	45,980	LC
Viterbo Univ	WI	34,660	C
Washington State Univ	WA	22,747	C
Washington Univ in St. Louis	MO	67,539	MC
Wayne State Univ	MI	23,085	C
Webster Univ	MO	37,490	C
West Chester Univ of Pennsylvania	PA	19,171	VC
West Texas A&M Univ	TX	13,478	C
Whitworth Univ	WA	53,682	VC
Wilmington College	OH	35,100	C
Wilson College	PA	35,620	LC
Winona State Univ	MN	18,109	C
Xavier Univ of Louisiana	LA	31,689	C
York College of Pennsylvania	PA	29,240	C
Youngstown State Univ	OH	17,487	C

SOCIAL STUDIES SECONDARY SCHOOL EDUCATION

School	ST	$IS	SR
Aquinas College - Mich	MI	38,876	VC
Biola Univ	CA	48,686	C
Cairn Univ	PA	37,572	C
Concordia Univ St. Paul	MN	29,050	C
East Texas Baptist Univ	TX	34,444	C
Elizabethtown College	PA	56,340	VC
Flagler College	FL	27,620	C
Georgetown College	KY	41,440	C
Grove City College	PA	26,654	VC
Immaculata Univ	PA	39,000	C
Kent State Univ	OH	20,928	C
Kutztown Univ of Pennsylvania	PA	19,477	C
Missouri Southern State Univ	MO	13,071	C
Missouri Western State Univ	MO	17,822	LC
Monmouth Univ	NJ	50,184	C
Murray State Univ	KY	17,726	C+
Neumann Univ	PA	40,678	LC
New York Univ	NY	68,139	MC
Niagara Univ	NY	41,010	C
North Central Univ	MN	30,610	C
Ouachita Baptist Univ	AR	33,500	VC
St. John's Univ	NY	57,160	C+
SUNY/Fredonia	NY	20,818	C
Taylor Univ	IN	42,130	VC
Texas Christian Univ	TX	57,120	HC
The College of St. Rose	NY	44,010	C
Univ of Maine at Machias	ME	22,960	C
Univ of Northwestern - St. Paul	MN	39,530	C
Univ of Wisc-Superior	WI	14,838	C
Wartburg College	IA	49,478	C
Webster Univ	MO	37,490	C
Western Mich Univ	MI	21,791	C
Wilson College	PA	35,620	LC
Youngstown State Univ	OH	17,487	C

SOCIAL WORK

School	ST	$IS	SR
Abilene Christian Univ	TX	43,708	C+
Adams State Univ	CO	15,420	LC
Adelphi Univ	NY	49,792	C
Adrian College	MI	45,550	C
Alabama A&M Univ	AL	18,796	C
Alabama State Univ	AL	16,490	LC
Albany State Univ	GA	19,462	C
Alcorn State Univ	MS	15,884	C
Alvernia Univ	PA	45,330	C
Anderson Univ	IN	39,450	C
Andrews Univ	MI	41,732	C
Angelo State Univ	TX	15,882	LC
Anna Maria College	MA	51,020	C
Appalachian State Univ	NC	15,394	VC
Arizona State Univ at the Downtown Phoenix Campus	AZ	24,634	VC
Arizona State Univ at the West Campus	AZ	21,513	VC
Arkansas State Univ	AR	16,190	C
Asbury Univ	KY	36,450	C+
Ashland Univ	OH	30,446	C
Atlantic Union College	MA	27,228	C
Auburn Univ	AL	24,300	VC+
Augsburg Univ	MN	45,129	C
Augusta Univ	GA	4,632	C
Augustana College	IL	51,222	VC+
Aurora Univ	IL	34,990	C
Austin Peay State Univ	TN	16,397	C
Avila Univ	MO	27,100	C
Azusa Pacific Univ	CA	43,972	C
Ball State Univ	IN	19,808	C+
Barton College	NC	39,854	C
Bayamon Central Univ	PR	12,490	
Baylor Univ	TX	56,803	HC
Belhaven Univ	MS	32,250	C
Belmont Univ	TN	44,500	VC+
Bemidji State Univ	MN	17,730	C
Benedict College	SC	28,630	NC
Bennett College	NC	27,717	NC
Bethany College	WV	38,774	LC
Bethel College	KS	35,370	C
Bethel Univ	MN	46,550	C+
Biola Univ	CA	48,686	C
Bloomfield College	NJ	40,100	LC
Bloomsburg Univ of Pennsylvania	PA	19,930	C
Bluffton Univ	OH	40,950	C+
Boise State Univ	ID	17,368	C
Bowie State Univ	MD	18,610	LC
Bowling Green State Univ	OH	19,975	C
Bradley Univ	IL	43,240	VC
Brescia Univ	KY	29,890	VC
Briar Cliff Univ	IA	36,956	C
Bridgewater State Univ	MA	22,762	C
Brigham Young Univ	UT	13,248	MC
Brigham Young Univ/Hawaii	HI	11,710	C
Buena Vista Univ	IA	42,344	C
Cabrini Univ	PA	42,591	LC
Cairn Univ	PA	37,572	C
Calif Baptist Univ	CA	42,986	C
Cal State, Chico	CA	19,790	VC
Cal State, Fresno	CA	16,902	LC
Cal State, Fullerton	CA	21,902	C
Cal State, Long Beach	CA	18,850	C
Cal State, Los Angeles	CA	17,186	LC
Cal State, Sacramento	CA	19,060	C
Cal State, San Bernardino	CA	20,106	C
Calif Univ of Pennsylvania	PA	20,425	LC
Calvin College	MI	43,090	HC
Campbell Univ	NC	37,570	VC
Campbellsville Univ	KY	33,400	C
Capital Univ	OH	44,778	VC
Caribbean Univ	PR	12,227	
Carlow Univ	PA	39,696	LC
Carthage College	WI	48,835	C
Castleton Univ	VT	20,186	C
Cedar Crest College	PA	51,110	C
Cedarville Univ	OH	36,244	VC
Central Conn State Univ	CT	22,041	C
Central Mich Univ	MI	20,330	C
Central State Univ	OH	18,564	C
Central Washington Univ	WA	16,803	C
Chadron State College	NE	14,819	LC
Champlain College	VT	54,724	VC
Chapman Univ	CA	65,504	HC
Chatham Univ	PA	47,883	VC
Christopher Newport Univ	VA	24,878	VC+
CUNY/Lehman College	NY	5,788	LC
CUNY/York College	NY	6,747	LC
Clark Atlanta Univ	GA	31,019	LC
Clarke Univ	IA	42,950	C
Cleveland State Univ	OH	22,290	C
Coker College	SC	38,196	C
College of St. Elizabeth	NJ	45,700	LC
College of St. Scholastica	MN	45,734	C+
College of Staten Island	NY	24,389	LC
College of the Ozarks	MO	7,530	VC
Colo Mesa Univ	CO	19,707	LC
Colo State Univ	CO	23,033	C
Colo State Univ-Pueblo	CO	21,581	C
Columbia College	SC	36,550	C
Columbia College - Missouri	MO	28,179	C
Concord Univ	WV	14,954	LC
Concordia College - Moorhead	MN	46,418	C
Concordia College - New York	NY	39,035	LC
Concordia Univ	OR	35,000	C
Concordia Univ Wisc	WI	35,910	C
Concordia Univ, Chicago	IL	41,522	C
Coppin State Univ	MD	14,071	VC
Cornerstone Univ	MI	36,550	C
Creighton Univ	NE	49,452	VC
Daemen College	NY	40,336	C
Defiance College	OH	42,240	LC
Delaware State Univ	DE	19,376	LC
Delta State Univ	MS	13,176	LC
Dickinson State Univ	ND	12,372	LC
Dominican College	NY	40,258	LC
Dordt College	IA	37,860	C+
East Carolina Univ	NC	16,539	C
East Central Univ	OK	13,330	C
East Stroudsburg Univ	PA	18,578	LC
East Tenn State Univ	TN	18,141	C
Eastern Conn State Univ	CT	23,059	C
Eastern Kentucky Univ	KY	17,742	C
Eastern Mennonite Univ	VA	42,550	C
Eastern Mich Univ	MI	19,761	C
Eastern Nazarene College	MA	41,114	C
Eastern New Mexico Univ	NM	12,874	LC
Eastern Univ	PA	39,540	C
Eastern Washington Univ	WA	17,896	LC
Edinboro Univ	PA	15,940	LC
Elizabeth City State Univ	NC	14,745	C
Elizabethtown College	PA	56,340	VC
Elms College	MA	49,602	VC
Evangel Univ	MO	28,898	C
Fayetteville State Univ	NC	17,756	C
Ferris State Univ	MI	21,458	C
Ferrum College	VA	43,970	C
Florida A&M Univ	FL	15,361	C
Florida Atlantic Univ	FL	18,256	C
Florida Gulf Coast Univ	FL	14,738	C
Florida International Univ	FL	20,281	C
Florida State Univ	FL	16,771	HC
Fontbonne Univ	MO	34,606	C
Fordham Univ	NY	68,431	MC
Fort Hays State Univ	KS	12,677	C
Fort Valley State Univ	GA	17,988	VC
Franciscan Univ of Steubenville	OH	33,980	VC
Franklin Pierce Univ	NH	46,750	LC
Freed-Hardeman Univ	TN	29,900	C
Fresno Pacific Univ	CA	38,858	C
Frostburg State Univ	MD	17,280	LC
Gallaudet Univ	DC	30,088	LC
Gannon Univ	PA	42,922	C
George Fox Univ	OR	42,938	C
George Mason Univ	VA	19,884	C
Georgia State Univ	GA	25,250	C
Georgian Court Univ	NJ	43,068	LC
Goodwin College	CT	28,370	LC
Gordon College	MA	47,740	VC
Goshen College	IN	44,350	C
Grace College and Seminary	IN	31,524	C
Grambling State Univ	LA	15,701	C
Grand Valley State Univ	MI	22,250	C+
Greenville College	IL	27,012	LC
Grove City College	PA	26,654	VC
Hannibal-LaGrange Univ	MO	29,815	C
Harding Univ	AR	25,440	C
Hardin-Simmons Univ	TX	36,025	C
Hawaii Pacific Univ	HI	33,420	C
Heritage Univ	WA	19,825	NC
Hood College	MD	50,540	C
Hope College	MI	42,840	VC
Howard Payne Univ	TX	35,994	C
Howard Univ	DC	37,616	C+
Humboldt State Univ	CA	21,708	C
Huntington Univ	IN	33,996	C
Idaho State Univ	ID	13,619	LC
Illinois State Univ	IL	23,418	VC
Immaculata Univ	PA	39,000	C
Indiana State Univ	IN	23,223	LC
Indiana Univ Bloomington	IN	20,791	HC
Indiana Univ East	IN	7,207	C
Indiana Univ Northwest	IN	7,207	LC
Indiana Univ South Bend	IN	16,057	C
Indiana Univ-Purdue Univ Indianapolis	IN	18,952	C
Indiana Wesleyan Univ	IN	33,674	C
Inter-American Univ of PR Ponce	PR	19,549	
Inter-American Univ of PR-Aguadilla Campus	PR	21,657	
Inter-American Univ of PR-Arecibo Campus	PR	18,245	
Inter-American Univ of PR-Fajardo Campus	PR	18,336	
Inter-American Univ of PR-Metropolitan Campus	PR	20,045	
Iona College	NY	52,514	C
Jackson State Univ	MS	15,879	LC
Jacksonville State Univ	AL	14,628	LC
James Madison Univ	VA	19,084	VC
Jarvis Christian College	TX	20,160	NC
Johnson C. Smith Univ	NC	25,336	LC
Judson College	AL	27,066	C
Juniata College	PA	58,118	VC
Kansas State Univ	KS	17,780	VC
Kentucky Christian Univ	KY	26,836	LC
Kentucky State Univ	KY	14,484	LC

ST = STATE $IS = IN-STATE COSTS SR = SELECTOR RATING

School	ST	$IS	SR
Keuka College	NY	42,398	C
King Univ	TN	36,976	C
Kutztown Univ of Pennsylvania	PA	19,477	C
La Salle Univ	PA	43,476	C
La Sierra Univ	CA	39,690	VC
Lamar Univ	TX	18,014	LC
LeMoyne-Owen College	TN	16,980	C
Lewis Univ	IL	41,710	C
Lewis-Clark State College	ID	14,202	C
Limestone College	SC	32,100	C
Lincoln Memorial Univ	TN	28,430	C
Lincoln Univ	MO	14,402	NC
Lindenwood Univ	MO	25,760	C
Lipscomb Univ	TN	42,984	VC
LIU Brooklyn	NY	50,698	C
LIU Post	NY	50,698	C+
Livingstone College	NC	17,815	LC
Lock Haven Univ of Pennsylvania	PA	20,544	LC
Longwood Univ	VA	22,184	C
Loras College	IA	40,726	C
Louisiana College	LA	21,274	C
Lourdes Univ	OH	29,140	NC
Loyola Univ Chicago	IL	57,158	VC
Lubbock Christian Univ	TX	29,727	C
Luther College	IA	49,990	VC
MacMurray College	IL	35,025	C
Madonna Univ	MI	30,450	LC
Malone Univ	OH	39,200	C
Manchester Univ	IN	41,540	C
Mansfield Univ of Pennsylvania	PA	24,244	LC
Marian Univ	WI	34,622	C
Marist College	NY	49,860	VC
Mars Hill Univ	NC	41,104	C
Marshall Univ	WV	18,044	C
Mary Baldwin Univ	VA	40,495	C
Marygrove College	MI	30,100	LC
Marywood Univ	PA	47,840	C
McDaniel College	MD	52,910	VC
McKendree Univ	IL	37,940	C+
Mercy College	NY	32,614	C
Mercyhurst Univ	PA	47,420	C
Meredith College	NC	46,634	C
Messiah College	PA	44,380	VC
Methodist Univ	NC	58,130	C
Metropolitan College of New York	NY		VC
Metropolitan State Univ	MN	7,859	C
Metropolitan State Univ of Denver	CO	6,928	LC
Miami Univ	OH	27,190	HC+
Mich State Univ	MI	24,542	VC
Middle Tenn State Univ	TN	8,650	C
Midwestern State Univ	TX	12,111	LC
Miles College	AL	16,530	NC
Millersville Univ of Pennsylvania	PA	25,298	C
Milligan College	TN	39,450	C
Minn State Univ, Mankato	MN	17,190	C
Minn State Univ, Moorhead	MN	21,393	C
Minot State Univ	ND	13,285	C
Misericordia Univ	PA	45,210	C
Miss College	MS	25,850	C
Miss State Univ	MS	12,028	C+
Miss Valley State Univ	MS	13,233	LC
Missouri State Univ	MO	15,837	C+
Missouri Western State Univ	MO	17,822	LC
Molloy College	NY	40,440	C
Monmouth Univ	NJ	50,184	C
Morehead State Univ	KY	18,386	LC
Morgan State Univ	MD	17,190	LC
Mount Mary Univ	WI	34,650	LC
Mount Mercy Univ	IA	39,748	C
Mount St. Joseph Univ	OH	33,880	LC
Mount St. Mary's Univ - Chalon Campus	CA	50,486	VC+
Mount Vernon Nazarene Univ	OH	35,944	C
Murray State Univ	KY	17,726	C+
Nazareth College	NY	46,784	C
Nebr Wesleyan Univ	NE	42,026	C+
Neumann Univ	PA	40,678	LC
New Mexico Highlands Univ	NM	11,904	LC
New Mexico State Univ	NM	14,050	LC
New York Inst of Technology	NY	49,980	VC
New York Univ	NY	68,139	MC
Niagara Univ	NY	41,010	C
N Car A&T State Univ	NC	13,786	C
N Car Central Univ	NC	9,000	C
N Car State Univ	NC	22,434	HC+
North Central Univ	MN	30,610	C
Northeastern Illinois Univ	IL	12,529	LC
Northeastern State Univ	OK	8,615	VC
Northern Arizona Univ	AZ	21,003	C
Northern Kentucky Univ	KY	16,486	C
Northern Mich Univ	MI	20,853	C
Northwest Nazarene Univ	ID	40,250	C
Northwestern College of Iowa	IA	38,400	C
Northwestern Okla State Univ	OK	13,072	LC
Northwestern State Univ of Louisiana	LA	16,534	LC
Nyack College	NY	34,450	LC
Oakland Univ	MI	20,763	C
Oakwood Univ	AL	43,758	C
Oglala Lakota College	SD	15,050	NC
Oglethorpe Univ	GA	44,200	C
Ohio Dominican Univ	OH	41,340	C+
Ohio State Univ at Columbus	OH	22,843	MC
Ohio State Univ at Lima	OH	7,553	C
Ohio State Univ at Mansfield	OH	15,529	C
Ohio State Univ at Marion	OH	7,553	VC
Ohio State Univ at Newark	OH	16,685	C
Ohio Univ	OH	23,394	VC
Okla Baptist Univ	OK	33,990	C
Olivet Nazarene Univ	IL	41,840	VC
Oral Roberts Univ	OK	34,316	C
Our Lady of the Lake Univ	TX	37,790	LC
Pacific Lutheran Univ	WA	49,960	C
Pacific Union College	CA	36,009	VC
Pacific Univ	OR	37,617	C
Park Univ	MO	22,134	C
Philander Smith College	AR	20,814	LC
Pittsburg State Univ	KS	13,880	C
Plymouth State Univ	NH	23,180	LC
Point Loma Nazarene Univ	CA	46,150	C+
Pontifical Catholic Univ of PR	PR	10,534	
Portland State Univ	OR	19,443	C
Prairie View A&M Univ	TX	27,273	LC
Presentation College	SD	28,575	LC
Providence College	RI	62,870	HC
Purdue Univ Northwest	IN	15,178	C
Purdue Univ/West Lafayette	IN	20,032	MC
Quincy Univ	IL	38,170	LC
Radford Univ	VA	19,758	C
Ramapo College of New Jersey	NJ	25,760	VC
Regis College	MA	51,920	LC
Rhode Island College	RI	19,000	LC
Roberts Wesleyan College	NY	41,116	C
Rust College	MS	10,600	C
Rutgers Univ - Camden	NJ	26,595	C
Rutgers Univ - New Brunswick	NJ	27,090	HC
Rutgers Univ - Newark	NJ	27,351	C+
Sacred Heart Univ	CT	54,590	C
Saginaw Valley State Univ	MI	19,284	C
St. Francis Univ	PA	46,146	NC
St. Leo Univ	FL	32,850	C
St. Louis Univ	MO	49,866	HC
St. Martin's Univ	WA	45,056	C
St. Mary's College	IN	50,600	C
Salem State Univ	MA	42,650	LC
Salisbury Univ	MD	21,132	VC
Salve Regina Univ	RI	53,046	VC
San Diego State Univ	CA	23,156	VC
San Francisco State Univ	CA	18,514	LC
San Jose State Univ	CA	22,630	C
Savannah State Univ	GA	17,036	C
Seattle Univ	WA	54,957	VC
Seton Hall Univ	NJ	58,008	C
Seton Hill Univ	PA	46,972	VC
Shaw Univ	NC	24,638	C
Shepherd Univ, West Virginia	WV	17,382	C
Shippensburg Univ of Pennsylvania	PA	24,096	C
Siena College	NY	48,916	C
Siena Heights Univ	MI	36,322	C
Silver Lake College of the Holy Family	WI	36,290	LC
Simmons College	MA	54,400	HC
Skidmore College	NY	66,600	MC
Slippery Rock Univ of Pennsylvania	PA	20,450	C
S Car State Univ	SC	21,330	LC
Southeast Missouri State Univ	MO	16,148	C
Southeastern Louisiana Univ	LA	16,237	C
Southeastern Univ	FL	34,910	LC
Southern Adventist Univ	TN	28,250	C
Southern Conn State Univ	CT	21,924	LC
Southern Illinois Univ Carbondale	IL	24,554	C
Southern Illinois Univ Edwardsville	IL	20,188	C
Southern Univ and A&M College	LA	16,074	LC
Southern Univ at New Orleans	LA	8,014	LC
Southwest Minn State Univ	MN	17,783	C
Southwestern Adventist Univ	TX	28,232	LC
Spalding Univ	KY	31,938	C
Spring Arbor Univ	MI	37,390	C
St. Ambrose Univ	IA	40,180	C
St. Catherine Univ	MN	45,630	C
St. Cloud State Univ	MN	10,600	C
St. Edward's Univ	TX	56,190	VC
St. Olaf College	MN	56,430	HC
SUNY Albany	NY	22,165	C
SUNY/Buffalo State	NY	20,583	LC
SUNY/Fredonia	NY	20,818	C
SUNY/Plattsburgh	NY	19,314	C
Stephen F. Austin State Univ	TX	18,484	LC
Stockton Univ	NJ	25,565	C
Stony Brook Univ/The SUNY	NY	22,703	MC
Syracuse Univ	NY	62,313	HC
Tabor College	KS	35,870	C
Talladega College	AL	25,919	C
Tarleton State Univ	TX	15,248	LC
Taylor Univ	IN	42,130	VC
Temple Univ	PA	24,392	C+
Tenn State Univ	TN	14,423	LC
Tenn Wesleyan Univ	TN	32,680	LC
Texas A&M Univ at Commerce	TX	10,496	C
Texas Christian Univ	TX	57,120	HC
Texas Southern Univ	TX	19,592	LC
Texas State Univ	TX	18,721	C
Texas Tech Univ	TX	20,156	C+
Texas Woman's Univ	TX	15,302	LC
The Catholic Univ of America	DC	58,376	VC
The College at Brockport - SUNY	NY	21,058	C
The College of New Rochelle	NY	46,300	LC
The College of St. Rose	NY	44,010	C
The Univ of Akron	OH	22,566	C
The Univ of Alabama	AL	24,320	C+
The Univ of Mary	ND	23,180	C
The Univ of Memphis	TN	18,278	C
The Univ of Tenn at Chattanooga	TN	17,340	C+
The Univ of Tenn at Knoxville	TN	22,112	VC
The Univ of Tenn at Martin	TN	15,212	C
The Univ of Texas at Austin	TX	20,206	MC
The Univ of Utah	UT	18,751	VC
Thomas Univ	GA	21,420	NC
Trevecca Nazarene Univ	TN	31,186	C
Trinity Christian College	IL	35,580	C
Troy Univ	AL	16,171	C
Tulane Univ	LA	67,496	MC
Tuskegee Univ	AL	28,164	C
Union College	KY	32,310	C
Union College	NE	23,270	C
Union Inst & Univ	OH	8,912	SP
Union Univ	TN	41,160	VC
Univ of Alabama at Birmingham	AL	22,092	C
Univ of Alaska Anchorage	AK	17,914	C
Univ of Alaska Fairbanks	AK	16,874	VC
Univ of Arkansas at Fayetteville	AR	19,766	VC
Univ of Arkansas at Little Rock	AR	18,211	LC
Univ of Arkansas at Monticello	AR	13,599	LC
Univ of Arkansas at Pine Bluff	AR	13,541	C
Univ of Calif at Berkeley	CA	29,886	MC
Univ of Central Florida	FL	16,379	VC
Univ of Central Missouri	MO	18,982	C
Univ of Cincinnati	OH	22,118	VC
Univ of Detroit Mercy	MI	48,816	C
Univ of Findlay	OH	43,040	C
Univ of Georgia	GA	21,878	HC
Univ of Hawaii at Manoa	HI	23,261	C
Univ of Houston-Downtown	TX	7,241	LC
Univ of Indianapolis	IN	36,480	VC
Univ of Iowa	IA	19,415	HC
Univ of Kansas	KS	20,884	VC
Univ of Kentucky	KY	24,800	C+
Univ of Louisiana at Monroe	LA	15,970	C
Univ of Louisville	KY	19,692	C
Univ of Maine	ME	21,038	VC
Univ of Maine at Presque Isle	ME	16,148	LC
Univ of Mary Hardin-Baylor	TX	35,292	C+
Univ of Maryland/Baltimore County	MD	23,004	VC
Univ of Mich/Flint	MI	19,062	C
Univ of Miss	MS	18,802	C
Univ of Missouri-Columbia	MO	20,463	VC
Univ of Missouri-St. Louis	MO	19,810	VC
Univ of Montana	MT	14,105	C
Univ of Montevallo	AL	20,012	C
Univ of Nebr - Kearney	NE	17,014	LC
Univ of Nebr - Omaha	NE	16,120	C
Univ of Nevada, Las Vegas	NV	17,553	C
Univ of Nevada, Reno	NV	18,010	C
Univ of New England	ME	50,110	C
Univ of New Hampshire	NH	29,333	VC
Univ of North Alabama	AL	15,964	C
Univ of N Car at Charlotte	NC	17,803	VC
Univ of N Car at Greensboro	NC	15,998	C
Univ of N Car at Pembroke	NC	14,737	LC
Univ of N Car Wilmington	NC	16,784	VC
Univ of N Dak	ND	16,673	C
Univ of North Texas	TX	20,082	C
Univ of Northern Iowa	IA	17,480	C
Univ of Okla	OK	19,651	HC
Univ of Pikeville	KY	27,838	C
Univ of Pittsburgh	PA	30,030	MC
Univ of Portland	OR	52,152	VC
Univ of PR, at Humacao	PR	14,000	
Univ of PR-Rio Piedras campus	PR	13,327	
Univ of Rio Grande & Rio Grande Community College	OH	8,750	LC
Univ of St. Francis	IN	38,520	C
Univ of St. Joseph	CT	49,069	C
Univ of Sioux Falls	SD	25,630	C
Univ of South Alabama	AL	16,880	C
Univ of S Car at Columbia	SC	21,726	VC
Univ of S Dak	SD	16,109	C
Univ of South Florida/Tampa	FL	16,110	VC
Univ of Southern Indiana	IN	16,808	C
Univ of Southern Maine	ME	18,320	C
Univ of Southern Miss	MS	13,170	C
Univ of St. Francis	IL	40,828	C
Univ of Texas at Arlington	TX	18,876	C
Univ of Texas at El Paso	TX	34,452	NC
Univ of Texas Rio Grande Valley	TX	15,573	LC
Univ of the Cumberlands	KY	32,000	LC
Univ of the District of Columbia	DC	21,260	LC
Univ of the Sacred Heart	PR	17,932	
Univ of Toledo	OH	19,336	C
Univ of Vermont	VT	29,792	HC
Univ of Washington	WA	23,091	MC
Univ of West Florida	FL	15,848	C
Univ of Wisc-Eau Claire	WI	16,354	VC
Univ of Wisc-Green Bay	WI	15,184	C
Univ of Wisc-Madison	WI	21,647	MC
Univ of Wisc-Milwaukee	WI	21,538	C
Univ of Wisc-Oshkosh	WI	15,392	C
Univ of Wisc-River Falls	WI	14,541	C
Univ of Wisc-Stevens Point	WI	14,043	C
Univ of Wisc-Superior	WI	14,838	C
Univ of Wisc-Whitewater	WI	13,976	C
Univ of Wyoming	WY	15,537	C
Ursuline College	OH	41,076	LC
Utah State Univ	UT	13,235	C
Valparaiso Univ	IN	50,160	VC
Virginia Commonwealth Univ	VA	23,811	VC
Virginia State Univ	VA	19,802	C+
Virginia Union Univ	VA	25,058	C
Virginia Wesleyan Univ	VA	45,980	LC
Viterbo Univ	WI	34,660	C
Walla Walla Univ	WA	34,845	C
Warner Univ	FL	28,216	C
Warren Wilson College	NC	44,220	VC
Wartburg College	IA	49,478	C
Washburn Univ	KS	15,827	C
Washington State Univ	WA	22,747	C
Wayne State Univ	MI	23,085	C
Weber State Univ	UT	14,112	C
West Chester Univ of Pennsylvania	PA	19,171	VC
West Texas A&M Univ	TX	13,478	C
West Virginia State Univ	WV	19,412	LC
West Virginia Univ	WV	18,952	VC
Western Carolina Univ	NC	13,965	C
Western Conn State Univ	CT	21,254	LC
Western Illinois Univ	IL	20,897	C
Western Kentucky Univ	KY	16,850	C
Western Mich Univ	MI	21,791	C
Western New England Univ	MA	49,182	C
Western New Mexico Univ	NM	16,914	LC
Westfield State Univ	MA	20,404	C
Wheelock College	MA	51,325	LC
Whittier College	CA	57,891	C
Wichita State Univ	KS	17,773	C
Widener Univ	PA	58,190	C
Wilberforce Univ	OH	19,900	C
William Woods Univ	MO	32,040	C
Wilmington College	OH	35,100	C
Winona State Univ	MN	18,109	C
Winthrop Univ	SC	23,960	C
Wright State Univ	OH	16,983	C
Xavier Univ	OH	49,380	VC
Youngstown State Univ	OH	17,487	C

SOCIOLOGY

School	ST	$IS	SR
Abilene Christian Univ	TX	43,708	C+
Adams State Univ	CO	15,420	LC
Adelphi Univ	NY	49,792	C
Adrian College	MI	45,550	C
Agnes Scott College	GA	51,930	VC+
Alabama A&M Univ	AL	18,796	C
Alabama State Univ	AL	16,490	LC
Albany State Univ	GA	19,462	C
Albertus Magnus College	CT	44,016	LC
Albion College	MI	55,260	C
Albright College	PA	57,326	C
Alcorn State Univ	MS	15,884	C
Alfred Univ	NY	37,490	C
Allen Univ	SC	19,920	NC
Alma College	MI	49,410	VC
Alverno College	WI	33,294	LC
American International College	MA	47,020	LC
Amherst College	MA	66,186	MC
Anderson Univ	IN	39,450	C
Andrews Univ	MI	41,732	C
Angelo State Univ	TX	15,882	LC
Anna Maria College	MA	51,020	C
Appalachian State Univ	NC	15,394	VC
Aquinas College - Mich	MI	38,876	VC
Arcadia Univ	PA	55,990	C+
Arizona State Univ at the Tempe Campus	AZ	23,001	VC
Arizona State Univ at the West Campus	AZ	21,513	VC
Arkansas State Univ	AR	16,190	C
Arkansas Tech Univ	AR	16,534	LC
Asbury Univ	KY	36,450	C+
Ashford Univ	CA	10,480	C
Ashland Univ	OH	30,446	C
Assumption College	MA	48,455	VC
Auburn Univ	AL	24,300	VC+
Auburn Univ at Montgomery	AL	15,000	C
Augsburg Univ	MN	45,129	C
Augusta Univ	GA	4,632	C
Augustana College	IL	51,222	VC+
Augustana Univ	SD	39,968	VC
Aurora Univ	IL	34,990	C
Austin College	TX	51,059	HC
Austin Peay State Univ	TN	16,397	C
Averett Univ	VA	43,034	LC
Avila Univ	MO	27,100	C

ST = STATE **$IS** = IN-STATE COSTS **SR** = SELECTOR RATING

School	ST	$IS	SR
Azusa Pacific Univ	CA	43,972	C
Baker Univ	KS	37,190	C
Baldwin Wallace Univ	OH	42,464	VC
Ball State Univ	IN	19,808	C+
Bard College	NY	65,924	HC
Barnard College/Columbia Univ	NY	68,762	MC
Barry Univ	FL	38,730	LC
Bates College	ME	64,500	HC
Bayamon Central Univ	PR	12,490	
Baylor Univ	TX	56,803	HC
Bellarmine Univ	KY	52,532	C
Bellevue Univ	NE	20,300	NC
Belmont Univ	TN	44,500	VC+
Beloit College	WI	55,206	HC
Bemidji State Univ	MN	17,730	C
Benedict College	SC	28,630	NC
Benedictine College	KS	38,850	VC
Benedictine Univ	IL	38,300	C
Bennington College	VT	66,280	MC
Berea College	KY	7,094	C
Berry College	GA	47,466	VC
Bethel College	IN	36,830	C
Bethel Univ	TN	27,142	C
Bethune-Cookman Univ	FL	23,322	C
Biola Univ	CA	48,686	C
Birmingham-Southern College	AL	44,478	C+
Black Hills State Univ	SD	16,622	C
Bloomfield College	NJ	40,100	LC
Bloomsburg Univ of Pennsylvania	PA	19,930	C
Bluffton Univ	OH	40,950	C+
Boise State Univ	ID	17,368	C
Boston College	MA	68,043	MC
Boston Univ	MA	67,352	MC
Bowdoin College	ME	65,980	MC
Bowie State Univ	MD	18,610	LC
Bowling Green State Univ	OH	19,975	C
Bradley Univ	IL	43,240	VC
Brandeis Univ	MA	68,443	MC
Brewton-Parker College	GA	26,120	LC
Briar Cliff Univ	IA	36,956	C
Bridgewater College	VA	46,260	C
Bridgewater State Univ	MA	22,762	C
Brigham Young Univ	UT	13,248	MC
Brown Univ	RI	64,566	MC
Bryant Univ	RI	57,204	VC
Bryn Mawr College	PA	65,220	MC
Bucknell Univ	PA	67,136	MC
Butler Univ	IN	52,890	VC+
Cabrini Univ	PA	42,591	LC
Caldwell Univ	NJ	42,165	LC
Calif Baptist Univ	CA	42,986	C
Calif Lutheran Univ	CA	52,853	C
Calif Polytechnic State Univ	CA	22,547	MC
Calif State Polytechnic Univ, Pomona	CA	21,811	C
Cal State, Bakersfield	CA	22,397	LC
Cal State, Chico	CA	19,790	VC
Cal State, Dominguez Hills	CA	19,022	LC
Cal State, East Bay	CA	20,748	C
Cal State, Fresno	CA	16,902	LC
Cal State, Fullerton	CA	21,902	C
Cal State, Long Beach	CA	18,850	C
Cal State, Los Angeles	CA	17,186	LC
Cal State, Northridge	CA	17,277	LC
Cal State, Sacramento	CA	19,060	C
Cal State, San Bernardino	CA	20,106	C
Cal State, San Marcos	CA	20,604	LC
Cal State, Stanislaus	CA	18,053	LC
Calvin College	MI	43,090	HC
Cameron Univ	OK	11,632	LC
Campbellsville Univ	KY	33,400	C
Canisius College	NY	49,672	C
Capital Univ	OH	44,778	VC
Cardinal Stritch Univ	WI	37,136	C
Carleton College	MN	66,414	MC
Carlow Univ	PA	39,696	LC
Carroll College	MT	44,304	C
Carroll Univ	WI	38,100	C+
Carson-Newman Univ	TN	35,900	C
Carthage College	WI	48,835	C
Case Western Reserve Univ	OH	62,284	MC
Castleton Univ	VT	20,186	C
Catawba College	NC	39,820	LC
Centenary College	NJ	43,890	LC
Centenary College of Louisiana	LA	49,050	C+
Central College	IA	44,592	C
Central Conn State Univ	CT	22,041	C
Central Methodist Univ	MO	31,500	VC
Central Mich Univ	MI	20,330	C
Central State Univ	OH	18,564	C
Central Washington Univ	WA	16,803	C
Centre College	KY	50,680	MC
Chadron State College	NE	14,819	LC
Chapman Univ	CA	65,504	HC
Charleston Southern Univ	SC	34,700	C
Charter Oak State College	CT	7,983	NC
Chestnut Hill College	PA	47,180	C
Chicago State Univ	IL	41,620	C
Christopher Newport Univ	VA	24,878	VC+
CUNY/Baruch College	NY	21,609	HC
CUNY/Brooklyn College	NY	7,163	C+
CUNY/City College	NY	20,204	C
CUNY/Hunter College	NY	31,098	VC
CUNY/Lehman College	NY	5,788	LC
CUNY/Queens College	NY	21,507	C
CUNY/York College	NY	6,747	LC
Claflin Univ	SC	25,592	LC
Clarion Univ of Pennsylvania	PA	21,608	LC
Clark Atlanta Univ	GA	31,019	LC
Clark Univ	MA	53,260	HC+
Clemson Univ	SC		HC
Cleveland State Univ	OH	22,290	C
Coastal Carolina Univ	SC	20,340	C
Coe College	IA	51,570	VC
Coker College	SC	38,196	C
Colby College	ME	64,060	MC
Colby-Sawyer College	NH	50,790	C
Colgate Univ	NY	67,500	MC
College of Charleston	SC	24,046	VC
College of Mount St. Vincent	NY	45,620	C
College of St. Benedict	MN	54,480	C
College of St. Elizabeth	NJ	45,700	LC
College of Staten Island	NY	24,389	LC
College of the Holy Cross	MA	64,320	MC
College of the Ozarks	MO	7,530	VC
College of William & Mary	VA	34,907	MC
Colo College	CO	64,894	MC
Colo Mesa Univ	CO	19,707	LC
Colo State Univ	CO	23,033	C
Colo State Univ-Pueblo	CO	21,581	C
Columbia College	SC	36,550	C
Columbia College - Missouri	MO	28,179	C
Columbia Univ/ School of General Studies	NY	61,470	MC
Columbia Univ/City of New York	NY	62,958	MC
Columbus State Univ	GA	14,336	LC
Concord Univ	WV	14,954	LC
Concordia College - Moorhead	MN	46,418	C
Concordia College - New York	NY	39,035	LC
Concordia Univ St. Paul	MN	29,050	C
Concordia Univ, Ann Arbor	MI	38,878	C+
Concordia Univ, Chicago	IL	41,522	C
Conn College	CT	65,000	MC
Cornell College	IA	49,900	VC
Cornell Univ	NY	67,591	MC
Covenant College	GA	44,590	HC
Creighton Univ	NE	49,452	VC
Cumberland Univ	TN	27,710	C
Curry College	MA	53,331	C
Dakota Wesleyan Univ	SD	33,980	LC
Dallas Baptist Univ	TX	35,220	VC
Dartmouth College	NH	68,109	MC
Davidson College	NC	60,119	MC
Delaware State Univ	DE	19,376	LC
Denison Univ	OH	62,770	HC+
DePaul Univ	IL	52,807	VC
DePauw Univ	IN	58,688	VC
Dickinson College	PA	66,166	MC
Dickinson State Univ	ND	12,372	LC
Dillard Univ	LA	20,940	VC
Doane Univ	NE	41,340	VC
Dominican Univ	IL	42,472	C+
Dordt College	IA	37,860	C+
Drake Univ	IA	49,220	HC
Drew Univ/College of Liberal Arts	NJ	53,608	VC
Drexel Univ	PA	65,927	HC
Drury Univ	MO	37,555	VC
Duke Univ	NC	68,298	MC
Duquesne Univ	PA	48,508	VC
D'Youville College	NY	37,678	C
Earlham College	IN	55,670	HC
East Carolina Univ	NC	16,539	C
East Central Univ	OK	13,330	C
East Stroudsburg Univ	PA	18,578	LC
East Tenn State Univ	TN	18,141	C
East Texas Baptist Univ	TX	34,444	C
Eastern Conn State Univ	CT	23,059	C
Eastern Illinois Univ	IL	21,414	C
Eastern Kentucky Univ	KY	17,742	C
Eastern Mennonite Univ	VA	42,550	C
Eastern Mich Univ	MI	19,761	C
Eastern Nazarene College	MA	41,114	C
Eastern New Mexico Univ	NM	12,874	LC
Eastern Oregon Univ	OR	17,612	C
Eastern Univ	PA	39,540	C
Eastern Washington Univ	WA	17,896	LC
Eckerd College	FL	55,206	VC
Edgewood College	WI	35,950	C
Edward Waters College	FL	28,089	NC
Elizabeth City State Univ	NC	14,745	C
Elizabethtown College	PA	56,340	VC
Elmhurst College	IL	46,514	C
Elmira College	NY	53,900	C
Elms College	MA	49,602	VC
Elon Univ	NC	46,142	HC
Emmanuel College	MA	53,472	C+
Emory and Henry College	VA	46,320	C
Emory Univ	GA	63,286	MC
Emporia State Univ	KS	15,029	C
Eugene Lang College of Liberal Arts	NY	64,940	VC
Eureka College	IL	34,760	C
Evangel Univ	MO	28,898	C
Excelsior College	NY	38,800	SP
Fairfield Univ	CT	61,445	HC
Fairleigh Dickinson Univ/ College at Florham	NJ	54,770	C
Fairmont State Univ	WV	15,726	C
Fayetteville State Univ	NC	17,756	C
Ferris State Univ	MI	21,458	C
Fisk Univ	TN	32,066	LC
Fitchburg State Univ	MA	21,819	LC
Flagler College	FL	27,620	C
Florida A&M Univ	FL	15,361	C
Florida Atlantic Univ	FL	18,256	C
Florida Gulf Coast Univ	FL	14,738	C
Florida International Univ	FL	20,281	C
Florida Memorial Univ	FL	22,424	LC
Florida State Univ	FL	16,771	HC
Fontbonne Univ	MO	34,606	C
Fordham Univ	NY	68,431	MC
Fort Hays State Univ	KS	12,677	C
Fort Lewis College	CO	20,154	C
Fort Valley State Univ	GA	17,988	VC
Framingham State Univ	MA	21,740	C
Francis Marion Univ	SC	18,144	LC
Franciscan Univ of Steubenville	OH	33,980	VC
Franklin and Marshall College	PA	67,960	MC
Franklin College	IN	40,550	C
Frostburg State Univ	MD	17,280	LC
Furman Univ	SC	61,098	VC+
Gallaudet Univ	DC	30,088	LC
Gardner-Webb Univ	NC	24,935	C+
Geneva College	PA	35,450	C
George Fox Univ	OR	42,938	C
George Mason Univ	VA	19,884	C
Georgetown College	KY	41,440	C
Georgetown Univ	DC	68,970	MC
Georgia College & State Univ	GA	21,884	C+
Georgia Southern Univ	GA	16,540	VC
Georgia Southwestern State Univ	GA	13,870	LC
Georgia State Univ	GA	25,250	C
Gettysburg College	PA	65,210	MC
Gonzaga Univ	WA	52,880	HC
Gordon College	MA	47,740	VC
Goshen College	IN	44,350	C
Goucher College	MD	56,110	VC
Grace College and Seminary	IN	31,524	C
Graceland Univ	IA	35,290	C
Grambling State Univ	LA	15,701	C
Grand Canyon Univ	AZ	25,150	VC
Grand Valley State Univ	MI	22,250	C+
Green Mountain College	VT	45,228	LC
Greensboro College	NC	39,790	LC
Greenville College	IL	27,012	LC
Grinnell College	IA	63,114	MC
Grove City College	PA	26,654	VC
Guilford College	NC	45,973	C
Gustavus Adolphus College	MN	53,943	HC
Hamilton College	NY	64,250	MC
Hamline Univ	MN	50,152	C
Hampshire College	MA	65,214	MC
Hampton Univ	VA	36,410	C
Hannibal-LaGrange Univ	MO	29,815	C
Hanover College	IN	47,750	C+
Hardin-Simmons Univ	TX	36,025	C
Harris-Stowe State Univ	MO	14,590	NC
Hartwick College	NY	51,270	C
Harvard College/Harvard Univ	MA	65,609	MC
Hastings College	NE	35,380	C+
Haverford College	PA	66,490	MC
Hawaii Pacific Univ	HI	33,420	C
Henderson State Univ	AR	15,516	C
Hendrix College	AR	54,020	VC
High Point Univ	NC	47,355	VC
Hillsdale College	MI	37,170	MC
Hiram College	OH	44,590	C
Hobart and William Smith Colleges	NY	67,050	HC+
Hofstra Univ	NY	58,210	C+
Hollins Univ	VA	49,635	VC
Holy Family Univ	PA	44,672	LC
Holy Names Univ	CA	46,630	LC
Hood College	MD	50,540	C
Hope College	MI	42,840	VC
Houghton College	NY	40,558	VC
Houston Baptist Univ	TX	36,450	C
Howard Payne Univ	TX	35,994	C
Howard Univ	DC	37,616	C+
Humboldt State Univ	CA	21,708	C
Huntington Univ	IN	33,996	C
Huston-Tillotson Univ	TX	18,124	LC
Idaho State Univ	ID	13,619	LC
Illinois College	IL	41,330	VC
Illinois State Univ	IL	23,418	VC
Illinois Wesleyan Univ	IL	56,430	VC+
Immaculata Univ	PA	39,000	C
Indiana State Univ	IN	23,223	LC
Indiana Univ Bloomington	IN	20,791	HC
Indiana Univ East	IN	7,207	C
Indiana Univ Kokomo	IN	7,207	C
Indiana Univ Northwest	IN	7,207	LC
Indiana Univ of Pennsylvania	PA	24,474	C
Indiana Univ South Bend	IN	16,057	C
Indiana Univ Southeast	IN	16,931	C
Indiana Univ-Purdue Univ Fort Wayne	IN	18,675	C
Indiana Univ-Purdue Univ Indianapolis	IN	18,952	C
Indiana Wesleyan Univ	IN	33,674	C
Inter-American Univ of PR Ponce	PR	19,549	
Inter-American Univ of PR-Fajardo Campus	PR	18,336	
Inter-American Univ of PR-Metropolitan Campus	PR	20,045	
Inter-American Univ of PR-San Germán	PR	20,042	
Iona College	NY	52,514	C
Iowa State Univ	IA	18,176	C
Iowa Wesleyan Univ	IA	41,000	C
Ithaca College	NY	58,158	VC+
Jackson State Univ	MS	15,879	LC
Jacksonville State Univ	AL	14,628	LC
Jacksonville Univ	FL	49,210	C
James Madison Univ	VA	19,084	VC
Jarvis Christian College	TX	20,160	NC
John Carroll Univ	OH	51,570	C
Johns Hopkins Univ	MD	68,080	MC
Johnson & Wales Univ/ Denver Campus	CO	44,768	C
Johnson C. Smith Univ	NC	25,336	LC
Johnson State College	VT	22,672	C
Judson Univ	IL	39,174	C
Juniata College	PA	58,118	VC
Kalamazoo College	MI	53,931	HC
Kansas State Univ	KS	17,780	VC
Kansas Wesleyan Univ	KS	37,930	C
Kean Univ	NJ	25,620	C
Keene State College	NH	24,604	C
Kennesaw State Univ	GA	18,899	VC
Kent State Univ	OH	20,928	C
Kentucky State Univ	KY	14,484	LC
Kentucky Wesleyan College	KY	34,260	LC
Kenyon College	OH	65,840	MC
Keuka College	NY	42,398	C
King's College	PA	48,240	C
Knox College	IL	54,654	VC+
Kutztown Univ of Pennsylvania	PA	19,477	C
La Roche College	PA	38,940	C
La Salle Univ	PA	43,476	C
La Sierra Univ	CA	39,690	VC
Lafayette College	PA	68,520	MC
LaGrange College	GA	41,310	C
Lake Forest College	IL	50,652	VC
Lake Superior State Univ	MI	19,867	C
Lakeland Univ	WI	35,130	C
Lamar Univ	TX	18,014	LC
Lander Univ	SC	32,200	C
Lane College	TN	17,960	LC
Langston Univ	OK	15,659	C
Lasell College	MA	49,400	C
Le Moyne College	NY	47,305	VC
Lebanon Valley College	PA	55,510	VC
Lee Univ	TN	22,045	C
Lehigh Univ	PA	63,860	MC
LeMoyne-Owen College	TN	16,980	C
Lenoir-Rhyne Univ	NC	47,500	LC
Lewis & Clark College	OR	60,984	MC
Lewis Univ	IL	41,710	C
Lewis-Clark State College	ID	14,202	C
Lincoln Univ	MO	14,402	NC
Lincoln Univ	PA	20,878	LC
Lindenwood Univ	MO	25,760	C
Linfield College	OR	53,992	C
LIU Brooklyn	NY	50,698	C
LIU Post	NY	50,698	C+
Livingstone College	NC	17,815	LC
Lock Haven Univ of Pennsylvania	PA	20,544	LC
Longwood Univ	VA	22,184	C
Loras College	IA	40,726	C
Louisiana State Univ and A&M College	LA	18,677	VC
Louisiana State Univ in Shreveport	LA	6,902	C
Louisiana Tech Univ	LA	11,422	VC
Lourdes Univ	OH	29,140	NC
Loyola Marymount Univ	CA	60,202	VC+
Loyola Univ Chicago	IL	57,158	VC
Loyola Univ Maryland	MD	61,710	VC
Loyola Univ New Orleans	LA	52,456	VC
Luther College	IA	49,990	VC
Lycoming College	PA	50,895	C
Macalester College	MN	64,136	MC
Madonna Univ	MI	30,450	LC
Manchester Univ	IN	41,540	C
Manhattan College	NY	55,652	C
Manhattanville College	NY	52,430	C
Marian Univ	IN	43,206	C
Marlboro College	VT	50,832	VC+
Marquette Univ	WI	53,090	VC+
Mars Hill Univ	NC	41,104	C
Marshall Univ	WV	18,044	C
Martin Univ	IN	21,010	LC
Mary Baldwin Univ	VA	40,495	C
Marymount Manhattan College	NY	48,350	C
Marymount Univ	VA	43,231	C
Maryville College	TN	44,410	C
Maryville Univ of St. Louis	MO	38,558	VC
Mass College of Liberal Arts	MA	20,659	C
Mayville State Univ	ND	18,371	NC
McDaniel College	MD	52,910	VC
McKendree Univ	IL	37,940	C+
McMurry Univ	TX	34,259	LC
McNeese State Univ	LA	7,838	C
McPherson College	KS	36,134	C
Mercer Univ	GA	45,348	VC
Mercy College	NY	32,614	C
Mercyhurst Univ	PA	47,420	C
Meredith College	NC	46,634	C

ST = STATE **$IS** = IN-STATE COSTS **SR** = SELECTOR RATING

School	ST	$IS	SR
Merrimack College	MA	55,415	C
Messiah College	PA	44,380	VC
Methodist Univ	NC	58,130	C
Metropolitan State Univ of Denver	CO	6,928	LC
Miami Univ	OH	27,190	HC+
Mich State Univ	MI	24,542	VC
MidAmerica Nazarene Univ	KS	37,808	C
Middle Tenn State Univ	TN	8,650	C
Middlebury College	VT	67,464	MC
Midland Univ	NE	39,512	C
Midwestern State Univ	TX	12,111	LC
Millersville Univ of Pennsylvania	PA	25,298	C
Milligan College	TN	39,450	C
Millikin Univ	IL	44,148	C
Mills College	CA	43,705	C
Millsaps College	MS	50,080	C+
Minn State Univ, Mankato	MN	17,190	C
Minn State Univ, Moorhead	MN	21,393	C
Minot State Univ	ND	13,285	C
Miss College	MS	25,850	C
Miss State Univ	MS	12,028	C+
Miss Valley State Univ	MS	13,233	LC
Missouri Southern State Univ	MO	13,071	C
Missouri State Univ	MO	15,837	C+
Missouri Valley College	MO	28,150	C
Missouri Western State Univ	MO	17,822	LC
Molloy College	NY	40,440	C
Monmouth College	IL	42,260	C
Monmouth Univ	NJ	50,184	C
Montana State Univ	MT	15,500	C+
Montana State Univ Billings	MT	13,336	LC
Montclair State Univ	NJ	26,912	C
Moravian College	PA	55,488	C
Morehead State Univ	KY	18,386	LC
Morehouse College	GA	40,835	C
Morgan State Univ	MD	17,190	LC
Morris College	SC	19,195	LC
Mount Holyoke College	MA	56,746	MC
Mount Ida College	MA	46,820	C
Mount Mary Univ	WI	34,650	LC
Mount Mercy Univ	IA	39,748	C
Mount St. Mary College	NY	44,448	C
Mount St. Joseph Univ	OH	33,880	LC
Mount St. Mary's Univ	MD	53,380	C
Mount St. Mary's Univ - Chalon Campus	CA	50,486	VC+
Mount Vernon Nazarene Univ	OH	35,944	C
Muhlenberg College	PA	56,645	VC
Murray State Univ	KY	17,726	C+
Muskingum Univ	OH	35,966	C
National Univ	CA	17,849	LC
Nazareth College	NY	46,784	C
Nebr Wesleyan Univ	NE	42,026	C+
New College of Florida	FL	16,180	HC+
New England College	NH	50,828	NC
New Jersey City Univ	NJ	21,456	LC
New Mexico Highlands Univ	NM	11,904	LC
New Mexico State Univ	NM	14,050	LC
New York Inst of Technology	NY	49,980	VC
New York Univ	NY	68,139	MC
Newberry College	SC	34,550	C
Newman Univ	KS	37,382	C
Niagara Univ	NY	41,010	C
Nicholls State Univ	LA	14,959	C
Norfolk State Univ	VA	18,902	LC
N Car A&T State Univ	NC	13,786	C
N Car Central Univ	NC	9,000	C
N Car State Univ	NC	22,434	HC+
N Car Wesleyan College	NC	39,200	C
North Central College	IL	48,712	C+
N Dak State Univ	ND	16,245	VC
North Park Univ	IL	35,860	C
Northeastern Illinois Univ	IL	12,529	LC
Northeastern State Univ	OK	8,615	VC
Northeastern Univ	MA	65,352	MC
Northern Arizona Univ	AZ	21,003	C
Northern Illinois Univ	IL	20,176	C
Northern Kentucky Univ	KY	16,486	C
Northern Mich Univ	MI	20,853	C
Northern State Univ	SD	15,570	C
Northland College	WI	41,103	C+
Northwest Missouri State Univ	MO	18,286	C
Northwestern College of Iowa	IA	38,400	C
Northwestern Okla State Univ	OK	13,072	LC
Northwestern Univ	IL	68,725	MC
Notre Dame de Namur Univ	CA	46,526	LC
Nova Southeastern Univ	FL	38,534	C+
Nyack College	NY	34,450	LC
Oakland Univ	MI	20,763	C
Oberlin College	OH	68,942	MC
Occidental College	CA	68,660	MC
Oglala Lakota College	SD	15,050	NC
Oglethorpe Univ	GA	44,200	C
Ohio Dominican Univ	OH	41,340	C+
Ohio Northern Univ	OH	44,050	VC
Ohio State Univ at Columbus	OH	22,843	MC
Ohio State Univ at Mansfield	OH	15,529	C
Ohio Univ	OH	23,394	VC
Ohio Valley Univ	WV	28,800	C
Ohio Wesleyan Univ	OH	49,460	VC
Okla Baptist Univ	OK	33,990	C
Okla City Univ	OK	40,476	C
Okla State Univ	OK	17,180	C+
Okla Wesleyan Univ	OK	34,434	C
Old Dominion Univ	VA	21,618	C
Olivet College	MI	37,661	LC
Olivet Nazarene Univ	IL	41,840	VC
Oregon State Univ	OR	23,337	VC
Ottawa Univ	KS	39,980	VC
Otterbein Univ	OH	41,630	C
Ouachita Baptist Univ	AR	33,500	VC
Our Lady of the Lake Univ	TX	37,790	LC
Pace Univ	NY	60,136	C
Pacific Lutheran Univ	WA	49,960	C
Pacific Univ	OR	37,617	C
Paine College	GA	19,506	LC
Park Univ	MO	22,134	C
Pennsylvania State Univ - Univ Park	PA	29,716	HC
Pepperdine Univ	CA	66,862	VC+
Peru State College	NE	15,602	LC
Philander Smith College	AR	20,814	LC
Piedmont College	GA	34,334	C
Pittsburg State Univ	KS	13,880	C
Pitzer College	CA	68,500	HC+
Point Loma Nazarene Univ	CA	46,150	C+
Pomona College	CA	64,957	MC
Pontifical Catholic Univ of PR	PR	10,534	
Portland State Univ	OR	19,443	C
Post Univ	CT	41,150	C
Prairie View A&M Univ	TX	27,273	LC
Presbyterian College	SC	47,186	C
Princeton Univ	NJ	60,090	MC
Principia College	IL	40,350	C
Providence College	RI	62,870	HC
Purdue Univ Northwest	IN	15,178	C
Purdue Univ/West Lafayette	IN	20,032	MC
Queens Univ of Charlotte	NC	39,543	C
Quinnipiac Univ	CT	60,970	VC
Radford Univ	VA	19,758	C
Ramapo College of New Jersey	NJ	25,760	VC
Randolph College	VA	53,970	C
Randolph-Macon College	VA	51,480	VC
Reed College	OR	65,300	MC
Regis College	MA	51,920	LC
Regis Univ	CO	46,380	C
Rhode Island College	RI	19,000	LC
Rhodes College	TN	51,900	HC
Rice Univ	TX	59,458	MC
Rider Univ	NJ	54,050	C
Ripon College	WI	49,991	VC
Rivier Univ	NH	41,600	VC
Roanoke College	VA	55,952	VC
Robert Morris Univ	PA	40,600	C
Rochester Inst of Technology	NY	52,734	HC+
Rockford Univ	IL	38,570	C
Rocky Mountain College	MT	35,776	C
Roger Williams Univ	RI	48,074	VC
Rollins College	FL	58,670	HC
Roosevelt Univ	IL	41,890	VC
Rosemont College	PA	30,980	LC
Rowan Univ	NJ	24,491	VC
Russell Sage College	NY	39,370	C
Rust College	MS	10,600	C
Rutgers Univ - Camden	NJ	26,595	C
Rutgers Univ - New Brunswick	NJ	27,090	HC
Rutgers Univ - Newark	NJ	27,351	C
Sacred Heart Univ	CT	54,590	C
Saginaw Valley State Univ	MI	19,284	C
St. Anselm College	NH	56,636	VC
St. Augustine's Univ	NC	25,582	C
St. Francis Univ	PA	46,146	NC
St. Joseph's College of Maine	ME	47,890	C
St. Joseph's Univ	PA	58,540	VC
St. Leo Univ	FL	32,850	C
St. Louis Univ	MO	49,866	HC
St. Martin's Univ	WA	45,056	C
St. Mary's College	IN	50,600	C
St. Mary's College of Calif	CA	57,420	C
St. Mary's Univ of Minn	MN	42,440	C
St. Michael's College	VT	53,275	VC+
St. Peter's Univ	NJ	49,192	C
St. Vincent College	PA	46,229	C
St. Xavier Univ	IL	44,440	C
Salem College	NC	40,206	C
Salem State Univ	MA	42,650	LC
Salisbury Univ	MD	21,132	VC
Salve Regina Univ	RI	53,046	VC
Sam Houston State Univ	TX	18,792	C
Samford Univ	AL	40,770	VC
San Diego State Univ	CA	23,156	VC
San Francisco State Univ	CA	18,514	LC
San Jose State Univ	CA	22,630	C
Sarah Lawrence College	NY	68,866	MC
Savannah State Univ	GA	17,036	C
Scripps College	CA	69,260	HC
Seattle Pacific Univ	WA	47,439	C+
Seattle Univ	WA	54,957	VC
Seton Hall Univ	NJ	58,008	C
Seton Hill Univ	PA	46,972	VC
Shaw Univ	NC	24,638	C
Shawnee State Univ	OH	16,998	C
Shenandoah Univ	VA	42,100	C
Shepherd Univ, West Virginia	WV	17,382	C
Shippensburg Univ of Pennsylvania	PA	24,096	C
Siena College	NY	48,916	C
Simmons College	MA	54,400	HC
Simpson College	IA	45,626	VC
Skidmore College	NY	66,600	MC
Slippery Rock Univ of Pennsylvania	PA	20,450	C
Smith College	MA	66,774	MC
Sonoma State Univ	CA	27,020	C
S Car State Univ	SC	21,330	LC
S Dak State Univ	SD	15,874	C
Southeastern Louisiana Univ	LA	16,237	C
Southeastern Okla State Univ	OK	11,875	C
Southern Arkansas Univ	AR	21,532	C
Southern Conn State Univ	CT	21,924	LC
Southern Illinois Univ Carbondale	IL	24,554	C
Southern Illinois Univ Edwardsville	IL	20,188	C
Southern Methodist Univ	TX	69,008	MC
Southern Nazarene Univ	OK	33,684	C
Southern Oregon Univ	OR	19,117	C
Southern Univ and A&M College	LA	16,074	LC
Southern Univ at New Orleans	LA	8,014	LC
Southwest Baptist Univ	MO	30,890	LC
Southwest Minn State Univ	MN	17,783	C
Southwestern Univ	TX	52,370	VC
Spelman College	GA	41,642	C
Spring Arbor Univ	MI	37,390	C
Spring Hill College	AL	48,488	C
Springfield College	MA	48,775	C
St. Ambrose Univ	IA	40,180	C
St. Bonaventure Univ	NY	45,596	C
St. Catherine Univ	MN	45,630	C
St. Cloud State Univ	MN	10,600	C
St. Edward's Univ	TX	56,190	VC
St. Francis College	NY	38,800	LC
St. John Fisher College	NY	45,270	VC
St. John's Univ	NY	57,160	C+
St. Joseph's College, New York/Brooklyn Campus	NY	25,114	LC
St. Joseph's College, New York/Long Island Campus	NY	25,124	C
St. Lawrence Univ	NY	66,646	HC+
St. Mary's College of Maryland	MD	27,312	VC
St. Mary's Univ	TX	39,120	C
St. Norbert College	WI	46,060	VC
St. Olaf College	MN	56,430	HC
Stanford Univ	CA	62,541	MC
SUNY Albany	NY	22,165	C
SUNY at Binghamton	NY	24,100	MC
SUNY at Geneseo	NY	21,622	VC
SUNY at New Paltz	NY	20,840	C
SUNY at Oswego	NY	22,219	VC
SUNY at Purchase College	NY	21,832	C
SUNY Polytechnic Inst	NY	20,438	VC
SUNY/Buffalo State	NY	20,583	LC
SUNY/College at Old Westbury	NY	16,860	C
SUNY/Cortland	NY	20,910	C
SUNY/Empire State College	NY	9,145	NC
SUNY/Fredonia	NY	20,818	C
SUNY/Oneonta	NY	20,794	C
SUNY/Plattsburgh	NY	19,314	C
SUNY/Potsdam	NY	21,051	VC
SUNY/Univ at Buffalo	NY	23,122	C
Stephen F. Austin State Univ	TX	18,484	LC
Stetson Univ	FL	57,174	VC+
Stonehill College	MA	55,130	C
Stony Brook Univ/The SUNY	NY	22,703	MC
Suffolk Univ	MA	52,316	C
Susquehanna Univ	PA	57,560	VC
Swarthmore College	PA	63,550	MC
Syracuse Univ	NY	62,313	HC
Talladega College	AL	25,919	C
Tarleton State Univ	TX	15,248	LC
Taylor Univ	IN	42,130	VC
Temple Univ	PA	24,392	C+
Tenn State Univ	TN	14,423	LC
Tenn Tech Univ	TN	17,929	C
Tenn Wesleyan Univ	TN	32,680	LC
Texas A&M Univ at College Station	TX	20,771	VC+
Texas A&M Univ at Commerce	TX	10,496	C
Texas A&M Univ at Corpus Christi	TX	16,851	LC
Texas A&M Univ at Kingsville	TX	16,580	LC
Texas Christian Univ	TX	57,120	HC
Texas Lutheran Univ	TX	39,770	C
Texas Southern Univ	TX	19,592	LC
Texas State Univ	TX	18,721	C
Texas Tech Univ	TX	20,156	C+
Texas Wesleyan Univ	TX	37,338	C
Texas Woman's Univ	TX	15,302	LC
The American Univ	DC	61,317	HC
The Catholic Univ of America	DC	58,376	VC
The College at Brockport - SUNY	NY	21,058	C
The College of New Jersey	NJ	28,675	VC+
The College of New Rochelle	NY	46,300	LC
The College of Wooster	OH	60,000	HC
The Evergreen State College	WA	16,599	C
The George Washington Univ	DC	68,474	HC+
The Univ of Akron	OH	22,566	C
The Univ of Arizona	AZ	24,086	C
The Univ of Memphis	TN	18,278	C
The Univ of Montana Western	MT	9,426	LC
The Univ of Tenn at Chattanooga	TN	17,340	C+
The Univ of Tenn at Knoxville	TN	22,112	VC
The Univ of Tenn at Martin	TN	15,212	C
The Univ of Texas at Austin	TX	20,206	MC
The Univ of Texas at San Antonio	TX	21,060	C
The Univ of Utah	UT	18,751	VC
Thiel College	PA	42,950	LC
Thomas Edison State Univ	NJ	6,350	NC
Thomas More College	KY	36,720	LC
Tougaloo College	MS	17,980	NC
Touro College	NY	31,040	C
Towson Univ	MD	21,878	C
Transylvania Univ	KY	47,450	HC+
Trevecca Nazarene Univ	TN	31,186	C
Trinity Christian College	IL	35,580	C
Trinity College	CT	69,020	HC
Trinity Univ	TX	54,480	MC
Trinity Washington Univ	DC	33,826	C+
Troy Univ	AL	16,171	C
Truman State Univ	MO	16,286	MC
Tufts Univ	MA		MC
Tulane Univ	LA	67,496	MC
Tuskegee Univ	AL	28,164	C
Union College	KY	32,310	C
Union College	NY	64,320	MC
Union Univ	TN	41,160	VC
United States Military Academy at West Point	NY		HC+
Universidad del Turabo	PR	17,828	
Universidad Metropolitana	PR	17,828	
Univ of Alabama at Birmingham	AL	22,092	C
Univ of Alabama in Huntsville	AL	20,028	VC
Univ of Alaska Anchorage	AK	17,914	C
Univ of Arkansas at Fayetteville	AR	19,766	VC
Univ of Arkansas at Little Rock	AR	18,211	LC
Univ of Arkansas at Pine Bluff	AR	13,541	C
Univ of Calif at Berkeley	CA	29,886	MC
Univ of Calif at Davis	CA	28,468	HC
Univ of Calif at Irvine	CA	33,857	VC
Univ of Calif at Los Angeles	CA	27,438	HC+
Univ of Calif at Riverside	CA	32,912	C
Univ of Calif at Santa Barbara	CA	30,627	HC+
Univ of Calif San Diego	CA	30,450	MC
Univ of Calif, Santa Cruz	CA	28,731	C+
Univ of Central Arkansas	AR	15,042	VC
Univ of Central Florida	FL	16,379	VC
Univ of Central Missouri	MO	18,982	C
Univ of Central Okla	OK	15,150	C
Univ of Chicago	IL	70,551	MC
Univ of Cincinnati	OH	22,118	VC
Univ of Colo Boulder	CO	26,048	HC
Univ of Colo Colo Springs	CO	20,300	C
Univ of Colo Denver	CO	22,238	C
Univ of Conn	CT	27,394	
Univ of Dayton	OH	54,930	VC
Univ of Delaware	DE	32,214	VC
Univ of Denver	CO	61,129	VC+
Univ of Detroit Mercy	MI	48,816	C
Univ of Dubuque	IA	37,824	C
Univ of Evansville	IN	44,186	C+
Univ of Findlay	OH	43,040	C
Univ of Florida	FL	16,291	HC+
Univ of Georgia	GA	21,878	HC
Univ of Great Falls	MT	38,524	C
Univ of Hartford	CT	49,776	C
Univ of Hawaii at Hilo	HI	18,038	VC
Univ of Hawaii at Manoa	HI	23,261	C
Univ of Houston-Downtown	TX	7,241	LC
Univ of Idaho	ID	16,158	C
Univ of Illinois at Chicago	IL	24,664	VC
Univ of Illinois at Urbana-Champaign	IL	27,006	HC
Univ of Indianapolis	IN	36,480	VC
Univ of Iowa	IA	19,415	HC
Univ of Kansas	KS	20,884	VC
Univ of Kentucky	KY	24,800	C+
Univ of La Verne	CA	55,600	C
Univ of Louisiana at Lafayette	LA	14,516	C
Univ of Louisville	KY	19,692	C
Univ of Lynchburg	VA	48,370	C
Univ of Maine	ME	21,038	VC
Univ of Maine at Farmington	ME	18,792	C
Univ of Mary Hardin-Baylor	TX	35,292	C+
Univ of Mary Washington	VA	23,039	C+
Univ of Maryland/Baltimore County	MD	23,004	VC
Univ of Maryland/College Park	MD	21,938	HC
Univ of Maryland/Eastern Shore	MD	21,861	LC
Univ of Mass Amherst	MA	27,669	HC
Univ of Mass Boston	MA	13,828	C
Univ of Mass Dartmouth	MA	26,507	C
Univ of Mass Lowell	MA	27,296	VC
Univ of Miami	FL	63,494	MC
Univ of Mich/Ann Arbor	MI	25,274	MC
Univ of Mich/Dearborn	MI	12,472	VC
Univ of Mich/Flint	MI	19,062	C
Univ of Minn/Duluth	MN	20,292	C
Univ of Minn/Morris	MN	21,222	VC

ST = STATE **$IS** = IN-STATE COSTS **SR** = SELECTOR RATING

School	ST	$IS	SR
Univ of Minn/Twin Cities	MN	24,269	MC
Univ of Miss	MS	18,802	C
Univ of Missouri-Columbia	MO	20,463	VC
Univ of Missouri-Kansas City	MO	19,563	VC
Univ of Missouri-St. Louis	MO	19,810	VC
Univ of Mobile	AL	28,935	C
Univ of Montana	MT	14,105	C
Univ of Montevallo	AL	20,012	C
Univ of Mount Union	OH	39,990	C
Univ of Nebr - Kearney	NE	17,014	LC
Univ of Nebr - Lincoln	NE	18,589	VC
Univ of Nebr - Omaha	NE	16,120	C
Univ of Nevada, Las Vegas	NV	17,553	C
Univ of Nevada, Reno	NV	18,010	C
Univ of New England	ME	50,110	C
Univ of New Hampshire	NH	29,333	VC
Univ of New Mexico	NM	16,808	C
Univ of New Orleans	LA	12,840	C
Univ of North Alabama	AL	15,964	C
Univ of N Car at Asheville	NC	16,251	VC+
Univ of N Car at Chapel Hill	NC	20,561	MC
Univ of N Car at Charlotte	NC	17,803	VC
Univ of N Car at Greensboro	NC	15,998	C
Univ of N Car at Pembroke	NC	14,737	LC
Univ of N Car Wilmington	NC	16,784	VC
Univ of N Dak	ND	16,673	C
Univ of North Florida	FL	15,996	VC
Univ of North Georgia	GA	17,316	C
Univ of North Texas	TX	20,082	C
Univ of Northern Colo	CO	19,658	C
Univ of Northern Iowa	IA	17,480	C
Univ of Notre Dame	IN	68,801	MC
Univ of Okla	OK	19,651	HC
Univ of Oregon	OR	24,021	VC
Univ of Pennsylvania	PA	63,526	MC
Univ of Pikeville	KY	27,838	C
Univ of Pittsburgh	PA	30,030	MC
Univ of Pittsburgh at Bradford	PA	22,958	C
Univ of Pittsburgh at Johnstown	PA	22,092	C
Univ of Portland	OR	52,152	VC
Univ of PR, at Mayaguez	PR	13,995	
Univ of PR-Rio Piedras campus	PR	13,327	
Univ of Puget Sound	WA	60,210	HC
Univ of Redlands	CA	61,934	VC
Univ of Rhode Island	RI	26,066	VC
Univ of Richmond	VA	62,730	MC
Univ of Rio Grande & Rio Grande Community College	OH	8,750	LC
Univ of St. Francis	IN	38,520	C
Univ of St. Mary	KS	37,080	NC
Univ of San Diego	CA	60,338	HC
Univ of San Francisco	CA	60,580	C
Univ of Science and Arts of Okla	OK	11,140	VC
Univ of Scranton	PA	54,962	VC
Univ of Sioux Falls	SD	25,630	C
Univ of South Alabama	AL	16,880	C
Univ of S Car Aiken	SC	18,094	C
Univ of S Car at Columbia	SC	21,726	VC
Univ of S Car Upstate	SC	19,272	LC
Univ of S Dak	SD	16,109	C
Univ of South Florida/Tampa	FL	16,110	VC
Univ of Southern Calif	CA	66,631	MC
Univ of Southern Indiana	IN	16,808	C
Univ of Southern Maine	ME	18,320	C
Univ of Southern Miss	MS	13,170	C
Univ of Tampa	FL	38,928	VC
Univ of Texas at Arlington	TX	18,876	C
Univ of Texas at Dallas	TX	23,640	HC
Univ of Texas at El Paso	TX	34,452	NC
Univ of Texas Rio Grande Valley	TX	15,573	LC
Univ of the District of Columbia	DC	21,260	LC
Univ of the Incarnate Word	TX	39,162	LC
Univ of the Ozarks	AR	31,050	NC
Univ of the Pacific	CA	57,446	VC
Univ of the Southwest	NM	24,386	C
Univ of Toledo	OH	19,336	C
Univ of Tulsa	OK	52,625	HC
Univ of Vermont	VT	29,792	HC
Univ of Virginia	VA	27,367	MC
Univ of Washington	WA	23,091	MC
Univ of West Alabama	AL	16,284	LC
Univ of West Georgia	GA	17,510	LC
Univ of Wisc-Eau Claire	WI	16,354	VC
Univ of Wisc-La Crosse	WI	15,425	VC
Univ of Wisc-Madison	WI	21,647	MC
Univ of Wisc-Milwaukee	WI	21,538	C
Univ of Wisc-Oshkosh	WI	15,392	C
Univ of Wisc-Parkside	WI	15,313	C
Univ of Wisc-River Falls	WI	14,541	C
Univ of Wisc-Stevens Point	WI	14,043	C
Univ of Wisc-Superior	WI	14,838	C
Univ of Wisc-Whitewater	WI	13,976	C
Univ of Wyoming	WY	15,537	C
Upper Iowa Univ	IA	34,990	NC
Urbana Univ	OH	30,820	C
Ursinus College	PA	62,920	VC
Ursuline College	OH	41,076	LC
Utah State Univ	UT	13,235	C
Utica College	NY	31,510	C
Valparaiso Univ	IN	50,160	VC
Vanderbilt Univ	TN	63,248	MC
Vanguard Univ of Southern Calif	CA	42,400	VC
Vassar College	NY	68,110	MC
Villanova Univ	PA	64,922	MC
Virginia Commonwealth Univ	VA	23,811	VC
Virginia Polytechnic Inst and State Univ	VA	21,920	VC
Virginia State Univ	VA	19,802	C+
Virginia Union Univ	VA	25,058	C
Virginia Wesleyan Univ	VA	45,980	LC
Viterbo Univ	WI	34,660	C
Voorhees College	SC	19,976	C
Wagner College	NY	57,240	C+
Wake Forest Univ	NC	69,354	MC
Walla Walla Univ	WA	34,845	C
Walsh Univ	OH	39,010	C
Warner Pacific College	OR	31,610	C
Warren Wilson College	NC	44,220	VC
Wartburg College	IA	49,478	C
Washburn Univ	KS	15,827	C
Washington & Jefferson College	PA	58,694	VC
Washington and Lee Univ	VA	59,647	MC
Washington College	MD	56,154	VC
Washington State Univ	WA	22,747	C
Wayland Baptist Univ	TX	23,460	LC
Wayne State College	NE	25,746	NC
Wayne State Univ	MI	23,085	C
Waynesburg Univ	PA	33,530	C
Weber State Univ	UT	14,112	C
Webster Univ	MO	37,490	C
Wellesley College	MA	66,984	MC
Wells College	NY	50,500	C
Wesleyan Univ	CT	66,940	MC
West Chester Univ of Pennsylvania	PA	19,171	VC
West Liberty Univ	WV	16,158	C
West Texas A&M Univ	TX	13,478	C
West Virginia State Univ	WV	19,412	LC
West Virginia Univ	WV	18,952	VC
West Virginia Wesleyan College	WV	39,188	C
Western Carolina Univ	NC	13,965	C
Western Conn State Univ	CT	21,254	LC
Western Illinois Univ	IL	20,897	C
Western Kentucky Univ	KY	16,850	C
Western Mich Univ	MI	21,791	C
Western New England Univ	MA	49,182	C
Western New Mexico Univ	NM	16,914	LC
Western Oregon Univ	OR	19,965	LC
Western State Colo Univ	CO	19,348	C
Western Washington Univ	WA	18,904	VC
Westfield State Univ	MA	20,404	C
Westminster College	MO	32,820	C
Westminster College	PA	41,722	C
Westminster College	UT	41,078	C
Westmont College	CA	57,930	VC
Wheaton College	IL	44,993	MC
Wheaton College	MA	63,818	VC
Whitman College	WA	59,772	MC
Whittier College	CA	57,891	C
Whitworth Univ	WA	53,682	VC
Wichita State Univ	KS	17,773	C
Widener Univ	PA	58,190	C
Wilberforce Univ	OH	19,900	C
Wiley College	TX	19,255	C
Wilkes Univ	PA	49,166	C
Willamette Univ	OR	62,514	VC+
William Paterson Univ of New Jersey	NJ	24,022	C
William Penn Univ	IA	26,000	C
Williams College	MA	67,700	MC
Wilmington College	OH	35,100	C
Wilson College	PA	35,620	LC
Wingate Univ	NC	41,900	C
Winona State Univ	MN	18,109	C
Winston-Salem State Univ	NC	18,005	LC
Winthrop Univ	SC	23,960	C
Wittenberg Univ	OH	49,863	VC
Wofford College	SC	49,885	VC
Worcester State Univ	MA	20,977	C
Wright State Univ	OH	16,983	C
Xavier Univ	OH	49,380	VC
Xavier Univ of Louisiana	LA	31,689	C
Yale Univ	CT	64,650	MC
Yeshiva Univ	NY	52,750	VC
York College of Pennsylvania	PA	29,240	C
Youngstown State Univ	OH	17,487	C

SOFTWARE ENGINEERING

School	ST	$IS	SR
Allegheny College	PA	57,620	VC
Arizona State Univ at the Polytechnic Campus	AZ	22,394	VC
Auburn Univ	AL	24,300	VC+
Baldwin Wallace Univ	OH	42,464	VC
Butler Univ	IN	52,890	VC+
Calif Baptist Univ	CA	42,986	C
Calif Polytechnic State Univ	CA	22,547	MC
Cal State, Fullerton	CA	21,902	C
Central Washington Univ	WA	16,803	C
Chapman Univ	CA	65,504	HC
Clarkson Univ	NY	60,392	VC
Drexel Univ	PA	65,927	HC
Drury Univ	MO	37,555	VC
Embry-Riddle Aeronautical Univ - Daytona Beach	FL	45,822	VC
Embry-Riddle Aeronautical Univ - Prescott Campus	AZ	45,130	VC
Fairfield Univ	CT	61,445	HC
Florida Inst of Technology	FL	53,306	VC
Gannon Univ	PA	42,922	C
George Mason Univ	VA	19,884	C
Husson Univ	ME	26,508	C
Indiana Inst of Technology	IN	34,240	LC
Keene State College	NH	24,604	C
Kennesaw State Univ	GA	18,899	VC
Kutztown Univ of Pennsylvania	PA	19,477	C
Lipscomb Univ	TN	42,984	VC
Loyola Univ Chicago	IL	57,158	VC
Miami Univ	OH	27,190	HC+
Mich Tech Univ	MI	25,551	VC+
Milwaukee School of Engineering	WI	48,531	HC+
Monmouth Univ	NJ	50,184	C
National Univ	CA	17,849	LC
Nova Southeastern Univ	FL	38,534	C+
Okla City Univ	OK	40,476	C
Purdue Univ/West Lafayette	IN	20,032	MC
Quinnipiac Univ	CT	60,970	VC
Rochester Inst of Technology	NY	52,734	HC+
Rose-Hulman Inst of Technology	IN	59,823	MC
San Jose State Univ	CA	22,630	C
Shippensburg Univ of Pennsylvania	PA	24,096	C
S Dak State Univ	SD	15,874	C
SUNY at Oswego	NY	22,219	VC
Univ of Calif at Irvine	CA	33,857	VC
Univ of Detroit Mercy	MI	48,816	C
Univ of Mass Dartmouth	MA	26,507	C
Univ of Mich/Dearborn	MI	12,472	VC
Univ of Minn/Crookston	MN	19,126	C
Univ of N Car at Charlotte	NC	17,803	VC
Univ of Texas at Dallas	TX	23,640	HC
Univ of Wisc-Platteville	WI	14,148	C
Vermont Technical College	VT	25,370	C
Washington State Univ	WA	22,747	C

SOFTWARE PRODUCTION & MANAGEMENT

School	ST	$IS	SR
Curry College	MA	53,331	C
Kutztown Univ of Pennsylvania	PA	19,477	C
Univ of Detroit Mercy	MI	48,816	C

SOIL SCIENCE

School	ST	$IS	SR
Alabama A&M Univ	AL	18,796	C
Auburn Univ	AL	24,300	VC+
Calif Polytechnic State Univ	CA	22,547	MC
Cal State, Fullerton	CA	21,902	C
Clemson Univ	SC		HC
Colo State Univ	CO	23,033	C
Eastern Oregon Univ	OR	17,612	C
Lincoln Univ	MO	14,402	NC
Mich State Univ	MI	24,542	VC
New Mexico State Univ	NM	14,050	LC
N Car State Univ	NC	22,434	HC+
N Dak State Univ	ND	16,245	VC
Okla State Univ	OK	17,180	C+
Oregon State Univ	OR	23,337	VC
Purdue Univ/West Lafayette	IN	20,032	MC
Southern Illinois Univ Carbondale	IL	24,554	C
SUNY/The College of Environmental Science and Forestry	NY	23,728	VC
Tenn Tech Univ	TN	17,929	C
Texas A&M Univ at Kingsville	TX	16,580	LC
The Univ of Arizona	AZ	24,086	C
The Univ of Tenn at Knoxville	TN	22,112	VC
Univ of Calif at Davis	CA	28,468	HC
Univ of Calif at Riverside	CA	32,912	C
Univ of Conn	CT	27,394	
Univ of Delaware	DE	32,214	VC
Univ of Florida	FL	16,291	HC+
Univ of Hawaii at Manoa	HI	23,261	C
Univ of Idaho	ID	16,158	C
Univ of Mass Amherst	MA	27,669	HC
Univ of Missouri-Columbia	MO	20,463	VC
Univ of Wisc-Madison	WI	21,647	MC
Univ of Wisc-Platteville	WI	14,148	C
Univ of Wisc-River Falls	WI	14,541	C
Univ of Wisc-Stevens Point	WI	14,043	C
Utah State Univ	UT	13,235	C
Virginia Polytechnic Inst and State Univ	VA	21,920	VC
Washington State Univ	WA	22,747	C
West Texas A&M Univ	TX	13,478	C

SOUTH ASIAN STUDIES

School	ST	$IS	SR
Appalachian State Univ	NC	15,394	VC
Brown Univ	RI	64,566	MC
Cal State, Fullerton	CA	21,902	C
Middlebury College	VT	67,464	MC
Mount Holyoke College	MA	56,746	MC
Oakland Univ	MI	20,763	C
SUNY at Binghamton	NY	24,100	MC
Univ of Calif at Berkeley	CA	29,886	MC
Univ of Calif at Los Angeles	CA	27,438	HC+
Univ of Chicago	IL	70,551	MC
Univ of Minn/Twin Cities	MN	24,269	MC
Univ of Pennsylvania	PA	63,526	MC
Univ of Washington	WA	23,091	MC
Washington Univ in St. Louis	MO	67,539	MC
Yale Univ	CT	64,650	MC

SOUTHWEST AMERICAN STUDIES

School	ST	$IS	SR
Colo College	CO	64,894	MC

SPACE PHYSICS

School	ST	$IS	SR
Embry-Riddle Aeronautical Univ - Daytona Beach	FL	45,822	VC
Embry-Riddle Aeronautical Univ - Prescott Campus	AZ	45,130	VC

SPANISH

School	ST	$IS	SR
Abilene Christian Univ	TX	43,708	C+
Adams State Univ	CO	15,420	LC
Adelphi Univ	NY	49,792	C
Adrian College	MI	45,550	C
Agnes Scott College	GA	51,930	VC+
Alabama State Univ	AL	16,490	LC
Albany State Univ	GA	19,462	C
Albion College	MI	55,260	C
Albright College	PA	57,326	C
Alfred Univ	NY	37,490	C
Allegheny College	PA	57,620	VC
Alma College	MI	49,410	VC
American International College	MA	47,020	LC
Amherst College	MA	66,186	MC
Anderson Univ	IN	39,450	C
Andrews Univ	MI	41,732	C
Angelo State Univ	TX	15,882	LC
Appalachian State Univ	NC	15,394	VC
Aquinas College - Mich	MI	38,876	VC
Arcadia Univ	PA	55,990	C+
Arizona State Univ at the Tempe Campus	AZ	23,001	VC
Arizona State Univ at the West Campus	AZ	21,513	VC
Armstrong State Univ	GA	15,615	C
Asbury Univ	KY	36,450	C+
Ashland Univ	OH	30,446	C
Assumption College	MA	48,455	VC
Auburn Univ	AL	24,300	VC+
Auburn Univ at Montgomery	AL	15,000	C
Augsburg Univ	MN	45,129	C
Augustana College	IL	51,222	VC+
Augustana Univ	SD	39,968	VC
Aurora Univ	IL	34,990	C
Austin College	TX	51,059	HC
Azusa Pacific Univ	CA	43,972	C
Baker Univ	KS	37,190	C
Baldwin Wallace Univ	OH	42,464	VC
Ball State Univ	IN	19,808	C+
Bard College	NY	65,924	HC
Barnard College/Columbia Univ	NY	68,762	MC
Barry Univ	FL	38,730	LC
Bates College	ME	64,500	HC
Bayamon Central Univ	PR	12,490	
Baylor Univ	TX	56,803	HC
Bellarmine Univ	KY	52,532	C
Belmont Univ	TN	44,500	VC+
Beloit College	WI	55,206	HC
Bemidji State Univ	MN	17,730	C
Benedictine College	KS	38,850	VC
Benedictine Univ	IL	38,300	C
Bennington College	VT	66,280	MC
Berea College	KY	7,094	C
Berry College	GA	47,466	VC
Bethany College	WV	38,774	LC
Bethel Univ	MN	46,550	C+
Biola Univ	CA	48,686	C
Birmingham-Southern College	AL	44,478	C+
Black Hills State Univ	SD	16,622	C
Blackburn College	IL	28,526	LC
Bluffton Univ	OH	40,950	C+
Boise State Univ	ID	17,368	C
Boston Univ	MA	67,352	MC
Bowdoin College	ME	65,980	MC
Bowling Green State Univ	OH	19,975	C
Bradley Univ	IL	43,240	VC
Brandeis Univ	MA	68,443	MC
Brescia Univ	KY	29,890	VC
Briar Cliff Univ	IA	36,956	C
Bridgewater College	VA	46,260	C
Bridgewater State Univ	MA	22,762	C
Brigham Young Univ	UT	13,248	MC
Bryn Mawr College	PA	65,220	MC
Bucknell Univ	PA	67,136	MC
Buena Vista Univ	IA	42,344	C
Butler Univ	IN	52,890	VC+
Cabrini Univ	PA	42,591	LC
Caldwell Univ	NJ	42,165	LC
Calif Baptist Univ	CA	42,986	C
Calif Lutheran Univ	CA	52,853	C
Calif State Polytechnic Univ, Pomona	CA	21,811	C
Cal State, Bakersfield	CA	22,397	LC

ST = STATE $IS = IN-STATE COSTS SR = SELECTOR RATING

School	ST	$IS	SR
Cal State, Chico	CA	19,790	VC
Cal State, Dominguez Hills	CA	19,022	LC
Cal State, East Bay	CA	20,748	C
Cal State, Fresno	CA	16,902	LC
Cal State, Fullerton	CA	21,902	C
Cal State, Long Beach	CA	18,850	C
Cal State, Los Angeles	CA	17,186	LC
Cal State, Monterey Bay	CA	22,872	LC
Cal State, Northridge	CA	17,277	LC
Cal State, Sacramento	CA	19,060	C
Cal State, San Bernardino	CA	20,106	C
Cal State, San Marcos	CA	20,604	LC
Cal State, Stanislaus	CA	18,053	LC
Calif Univ of Pennsylvania	PA	20,425	LC
Calvin College	MI	43,090	HC
Campbell Univ	NC	37,570	VC
Canisius College	NY	49,672	C
Capital Univ	OH	44,778	VC
Cardinal Stritch Univ	WI	37,136	C
Carleton College	MN	66,414	MC
Carlow Univ	PA	39,696	LC
Carnegie Mellon Univ	PA	67,980	MC
Carroll College	MT	44,304	C
Carroll Univ	WI	38,100	C+
Carson-Newman Univ	TN	35,900	C
Carthage College	WI	48,835	C
Case Western Reserve Univ	OH	62,284	MC
Castleton Univ	VT	20,186	C
Catawba College	NC	39,820	LC
Cedarville Univ	OH	36,244	VC
Centenary College of Louisiana	LA	49,050	C+
Central College	IA	44,592	C
Central Conn State Univ	CT	22,041	C
Central Methodist Univ	MO	31,500	VC
Central Mich Univ	MI	20,330	C
Central Washington Univ	WA	16,803	C
Centre College	KY	50,680	MC
Chapman Univ	CA	65,504	HC
Charleston Southern Univ	SC	34,700	C
Chatham Univ	PA	47,883	VC
Chestnut Hill College	PA	47,180	C
Chicago State Univ	IL	41,620	C
Christopher Newport Univ	VA	24,878	VC+
CUNY/Baruch College	NY	21,609	HC
CUNY/Brooklyn College	NY	7,163	C+
CUNY/City College	NY	20,204	C
CUNY/Hunter College	NY	31,098	VC
CUNY/Lehman College	NY	5,788	LC
CUNY/Queens College	NY	21,507	C
CUNY/York College	NY	6,747	LC
Claremont McKenna College	CA	69,900	MC
Clarion Univ of Pennsylvania	PA	21,608	LC
Clark Univ	MA	53,260	HC+
Clarke Univ	IA	42,950	C
Clemson Univ	SC		HC
Cleveland State Univ	OH	22,290	C
Coastal Carolina Univ	SC	20,340	C
Coe College	IA	51,570	VC
Coker College	SC	38,196	C
Colby College	ME	64,060	MC
Colgate Univ	NY	67,500	MC
College of Charleston	SC	24,046	VC
College of Mount St. Vincent	NY	45,620	C
College of St. Mary	NE	27,500	C
College of Staten Island	NY	24,389	LC
College of the Holy Cross	MA	64,320	MC
College of the Ozarks	MO	7,530	VC
Colo Mesa Univ	CO	19,707	LC
Colo State Univ	CO	23,033	C
Colo State Univ-Pueblo	CO	21,581	C
Columbia College	SC	36,550	C
Columbia Univ/ School of General Studies	NY	61,470	MC
Columbia Univ/City of New York	NY	62,958	MC
Columbus State Univ	GA	14,336	LC
Concordia College - Moorhead	MN	46,418	C
Concordia Univ Texas	TX	41,920	C
Concordia Univ Wisc	WI	35,910	C
Concordia Univ, Ann Arbor	MI	38,878	C+
Converse College	SC	28,290	C
Cornell College	IA	49,900	VC
Cornell Univ	NY	67,591	MC
Covenant College	GA	44,590	HC
Daemen College	NY	40,336	C
Dartmouth College	NH	68,109	MC
Davidson College	NC	60,119	MC
Delaware State Univ	DE	19,376	LC
Denison Univ	OH	62,770	HC+
DePaul Univ	IL	52,807	VC
DePauw Univ	IN	58,688	VC
DeSales Univ	PA	47,520	C
Dickinson College	PA	66,166	MC
Dickinson State Univ	ND	12,372	LC
Doane Univ	NE	41,340	VC
Dominican College	NY	40,258	LC
Dominican Univ	IL	42,472	C+
Dordt College	IA	37,860	C+
Drew Univ/College of Liberal Arts	NJ	53,608	VC
Drury Univ	MO	37,555	VC
Duke Univ	NC	68,298	MC
Duquesne Univ	PA	48,508	VC
Earlham College	IN	55,670	HC
East Stroudsburg Univ	PA	18,578	LC
East Texas Baptist Univ	TX	34,444	C
Eastern Conn State Univ	CT	23,059	C
Eastern Kentucky Univ	KY	17,742	C
Eastern Mennonite Univ	VA	42,550	C
Eastern Mich Univ	MI	19,761	C
Eastern Nazarene College	MA	41,114	C
Eastern New Mexico Univ	NM	12,874	LC
Eastern Univ	PA	39,540	C
Eastern Washington Univ	WA	17,896	LC
Eckerd College	FL	55,206	VC
Edgewood College	WI	35,950	C
Elizabethtown College	PA	56,340	VC
Elmhurst College	IL	46,514	C
Elms College	MA	49,602	VC
Elon Univ	NC	46,142	HC
Emmanuel College	MA	53,472	C+
Emory Univ	GA	63,286	MC
Evangel Univ	MO	28,898	C
Fairfield Univ	CT	61,445	HC
Fairmont State Univ	WV	15,726	C
Fayetteville State Univ	NC	17,756	C
Ferrum College	VA	43,970	C
Fisk Univ	TN	32,066	LC
Flagler College	FL	27,620	C
Florida Atlantic Univ	FL	18,256	C
Florida Gulf Coast Univ	FL	14,738	C
Florida International Univ	FL	20,281	C
Florida Southern College	FL	45,978	VC
Florida State Univ	FL	16,771	HC
Fordham Univ	NY	68,431	MC
Fort Hays State Univ	KS	12,677	C
Fort Lewis College	CO	20,154	C
Framingham State Univ	MA	21,740	C
Franciscan Univ of Steubenville	OH	33,980	VC
Franklin and Marshall College	PA	67,960	MC
Franklin College	IN	40,550	C
Fresno Pacific Univ	CA	38,858	C
Friends Univ	KS	38,000	C
Furman Univ	SC	61,098	VC+
Gallaudet Univ	DC	30,088	LC
Gardner-Webb Univ	NC	24,935	C+
Geneva College	PA	35,450	C
George Fox Univ	OR	42,938	C
George Mason Univ	VA	19,884	C
Georgetown College	KY	41,440	C
Georgetown Univ	DC	68,970	MC
Georgia Southern Univ	GA	16,540	VC
Georgia State Univ	GA	25,250	C
Georgian Court Univ	NJ	43,068	LC
Gettysburg College	PA	65,210	MC
Gonzaga Univ	WA	52,880	HC
Gordon College	MA	47,740	VC
Goshen College	IN	44,350	C
Goucher College	MD	56,110	VC
Grace College and Seminary	IN	31,524	C
Graceland Univ	IA	35,290	C
Grand Valley State Univ	MI	22,250	C+
Greensboro College	NC	39,790	LC
Greenville College	IL	27,012	LC
Grinnell College	IA	63,114	MC
Grove City College	PA	26,654	VC
Guilford College	NC	45,973	C
Gustavus Adolphus College	MN	53,943	HC
Hamline Univ	MN	50,152	C
Hampden-Sydney College	VA	57,806	VC
Hanover College	IN	47,750	C+
Harding Univ	AR	25,440	C
Hardin-Simmons Univ	TX	36,025	C
Hartwick College	NY	51,270	C
Harvard College/Harvard Univ	MA	65,609	MC
Hastings College	NE	35,380	C+
Haverford College	PA	66,490	MC
Heidelberg Univ	OH	40,400	LC
Henderson State Univ	AR	15,516	C
Hendrix College	AR	54,020	VC
High Point Univ	NC	47,355	VC+
Hillsdale College	MI	37,170	MC
Hiram College	OH	44,590	C
Hofstra Univ	NY	58,210	C+
Hollins Univ	VA	49,635	VC
Hood College	MD	50,540	C
Hope College	MI	42,840	VC
Houghton College	NY	40,558	VC
Houston Baptist Univ	TX	36,450	C
Howard Payne Univ	TX	35,994	C
Howard Univ	DC	37,616	C+
Humboldt State Univ	CA	21,708	C
Idaho State Univ	ID	13,619	LC
Illinois College	IL	41,330	VC
Illinois State Univ	IL	23,418	VC
Immaculata Univ	PA	39,000	C
Indiana State Univ	IN	23,223	LC
Indiana Univ Bloomington	IN	20,791	HC
Indiana Univ East	IN	7,207	C
Indiana Univ Northwest	IN	7,207	LC
Indiana Univ of Pennsylvania	PA	24,474	C
Indiana Univ South Bend	IN	16,057	C
Indiana Univ Southeast	IN	16,931	C
Indiana Univ-Purdue Univ Fort Wayne	IN	18,675	C
Indiana Univ-Purdue Univ Indianapolis	IN	18,952	C
Indiana Wesleyan Univ	IN	33,674	C
Inter-American Univ of PR Ponce	PR	19,549	
Inter-American Univ of PR-Fajardo Campus	PR	18,336	
Inter-American Univ of PR-Metropolitan Campus	PR	20,045	
Inter-American Univ of PR-San Germán	PR	20,042	
Iona College	NY	52,514	C
Iowa State Univ	IA	18,176	C
Ithaca College	NY	58,158	VC+
Jacksonville Univ	FL	49,210	C
John Brown Univ	AR	35,184	VC
John Carroll Univ	OH	51,570	C
Johns Hopkins Univ	MD	68,080	MC
Johnson C. Smith Univ	NC	25,336	LC
Judson College	AL	27,066	C
Juniata College	PA	58,118	VC
Kalamazoo College	MI	53,931	HC
Kansas Wesleyan Univ	KS	37,930	C
Kean Univ	NJ	25,620	C
Keene State College	NH	24,604	C
Kentucky Wesleyan College	KY	34,260	LC
Kenyon College	OH	65,840	MC
King Univ	TN	36,976	C
King's College	PA	48,240	C
Knox College	IL	54,654	VC+
Kutztown Univ of Pennsylvania	PA	19,477	C
La Salle Univ	PA	43,476	C
La Sierra Univ	CA	39,690	VC
Lafayette College	PA	68,520	MC
LaGrange College	GA	41,310	C
Lake Forest College	IL	50,652	VC
Lakeland Univ	WI	35,130	C
Lamar Univ	TX	18,014	LC
Lander Univ	SC	32,200	C
Lawrence Univ	WI	56,133	HC+
Le Moyne College	NY	47,305	VC
Lebanon Valley College	PA	55,510	VC
Lee Univ	TN	22,045	C
Lehigh Univ	PA	63,860	MC
Lenoir-Rhyne Univ	NC	47,500	LC
Liberty Univ	VA	31,415	C
Lincoln Univ	MO	14,402	NC
Lincoln Univ	PA	20,878	LC
Lindenwood Univ	MO	25,760	C
Linfield College	OR	53,992	C
Lipscomb Univ	TN	42,984	VC
LIU Brooklyn	NY	50,698	C
LIU Post	NY	50,698	C+
Lock Haven Univ of Pennsylvania	PA	20,544	LC
Loras College	IA	40,726	C
Louisiana College	LA	21,274	C
Louisiana State Univ and A&M College	LA	18,677	VC
Louisiana Tech Univ	LA	11,422	VC
Loyola Marymount Univ	CA	60,202	VC+
Loyola Univ Chicago	IL	57,158	VC
Loyola Univ Maryland	MD	61,710	VC
Loyola Univ New Orleans	LA	52,456	VC
Luther College	IA	49,990	VC
Lycoming College	PA	50,895	C
Lyon College	AR	36,120	VC
MacMurray College	IL	35,025	C
Madonna Univ	MI	30,450	LC
Manchester Univ	IN	41,540	C
Manhattan College	NY	55,652	C
Manhattanville College	NY	52,430	C
Marian Univ	IN	43,206	C
Marietta College	OH	46,190	C
Marist College	NY	49,860	VC
Marlboro College	VT	50,832	VC+
Marquette Univ	WI	53,090	VC+
Mars Hill Univ	NC	41,104	C
Marshall Univ	WV	18,044	C
Martin Univ	IN	21,010	LC
Maryville College	TN	44,410	C
Marywood Univ	PA	47,840	C
McDaniel College	MD	52,910	VC
McMurry Univ	TX	34,259	LC
McPherson College	KS	36,134	C
Mercer Univ	GA	45,348	VC
Mercy College	NY	32,614	C
Meredith College	NC	46,634	C
Merrimack College	MA	55,415	C
Methodist Univ	NC	58,130	C
Metropolitan State Univ of Denver	CO	6,928	LC
Miami Univ	OH	27,190	HC+
Mich State Univ	MI	24,542	VC
Middle Tenn State Univ	TN	8,650	C
Middlebury College	VT	67,464	MC
Midwestern State Univ	TX	12,111	LC
Millersville Univ of Pennsylvania	PA	25,298	C
Millikin Univ	IL	44,148	C
Mills College	CA	43,705	C
Millsaps College	MS	50,080	C+
Minn State Univ, Mankato	MN	17,190	C
Minn State Univ, Moorhead	MN	21,393	C
Minot State Univ	ND	13,285	C
Miss College	MS	25,850	C
Miss Univ for Women	MS	17,065	C
Missouri State Univ	MO	15,837	C+
Missouri Western State Univ	MO	17,822	LC
Monmouth College	IL	42,260	C
Monmouth Univ	NJ	50,184	C
Montclair State Univ	NJ	26,912	C
Moravian College	PA	55,488	C
Morehouse College	GA	40,835	C
Morningside College	IA	39,780	C
Mount Holyoke College	MA	56,746	MC
Mount Mary Univ	WI	34,650	LC
Mount St. Mary's Univ	MD	53,380	C
Mount St. Mary's Univ - Chalon Campus	CA	50,486	VC+
Mount Vernon Nazarene Univ	OH	35,944	C
Muhlenberg College	PA	56,645	VC
Murray State Univ	KY	17,726	C+
Muskingum Univ	OH	35,966	C
Nazareth College	NY	46,784	C
Nebr Wesleyan Univ	NE	42,026	C+
New College of Florida	FL	16,180	HC+
New Jersey City Univ	NJ	21,456	LC
New Mexico Highlands Univ	NM	11,904	LC
New York Univ	NY	68,139	MC
Newberry College	SC	34,550	C
Niagara Univ	NY	41,010	C
N Car Central Univ	NC	9,000	C
N Car State Univ	NC	22,434	HC+
North Central College	IL	48,712	C+
N Dak State Univ	ND	16,245	VC
North Greenville Univ	SC	25,930	C
North Park Univ	IL	35,860	C
Northeastern Illinois Univ	IL	12,529	LC
Northeastern State Univ	OK	8,615	VC
Northern Arizona Univ	AZ	21,003	C
Northern Illinois Univ	IL	20,176	C
Northern Kentucky Univ	KY	16,486	C
Northern Mich Univ	MI	20,853	C
Northern State Univ	SD	15,570	C
Northwest Missouri State Univ	MO	18,286	C
Northwest Nazarene Univ	ID	40,250	C
Northwestern College of Iowa	IA	38,400	C
Northwestern Univ	IL	68,725	MC
Oakland Univ	MI	20,763	C
Oakwood Univ	AL	43,758	C
Oberlin College	OH	68,942	MC
Occidental College	CA	68,660	MC
Oglethorpe Univ	GA	44,200	C
Ohio Northern Univ	OH	44,050	VC
Ohio State Univ at Columbus	OH	22,843	MC
Ohio Univ	OH	23,394	VC
Ohio Wesleyan Univ	OH	49,460	VC
Okla Baptist Univ	OK	33,990	C
Okla Christian Univ	OK	29,260	C
Okla City Univ	OK	40,476	C
Okla State Univ	OK	17,180	C+
Old Dominion Univ	VA	21,618	C
Olivet Nazarene Univ	IL	41,840	VC
Oral Roberts Univ	OK	34,316	C
Oregon State Univ	OR	23,337	VC
Otterbein Univ	OH	41,630	C
Ouachita Baptist Univ	AR	33,500	VC
Our Lady of the Lake Univ	TX	37,790	LC
Pace Univ	NY	60,136	C
Pacific Lutheran Univ	WA	49,960	C
Pacific Union College	CA	36,009	VC
Pacific Univ	OR	37,617	C
Park Univ	MO	22,134	C
Pepperdine Univ	CA	66,862	VC+
Piedmont College	GA	34,334	C
Pitzer College	CA	68,500	HC+
Plymouth State Univ	NH	23,180	LC
Point Loma Nazarene Univ	CA	46,150	C+
Pomona College	CA	64,957	MC
Pontifical Catholic Univ of PR	PR	10,534	
Portland State Univ	OR	19,443	C
Prairie View A&M Univ	TX	27,273	LC
Presbyterian College	SC	47,186	C
Princeton Univ	NJ	60,090	MC
Principia College	IL	40,350	C
Providence College	RI	62,870	HC
Purdue Univ Northwest	IN	15,178	C
Purdue Univ/West Lafayette	IN	20,032	MC
Queens Univ of Charlotte	NC	39,543	C
Quinnipiac Univ	CT	60,970	VC
Randolph College	VA	53,970	C
Randolph-Macon College	VA	51,480	VC
Regis College	MA	51,920	LC
Regis Univ	CO	46,380	C
Rhode Island College	RI	19,000	LC
Rhodes College	TN	51,900	HC
Rider Univ	NJ	54,050	C
Ripon College	WI	49,991	VC
Roanoke College	VA	55,952	VC
Roberts Wesleyan College	NY	41,116	C
Rockford Univ	IL	38,570	C
Rockhurst Univ	MO	28,990	C
Rollins College	FL	58,670	HC
Roosevelt Univ	IL	41,890	VC
Rosemont College	PA	30,980	LC
Rowan Univ	NJ	24,491	VC
Russell Sage College	NY	39,370	C
Rutgers Univ - Camden	NJ	26,595	C
Rutgers Univ - Newark	NJ	27,351	C
Sacred Heart Univ	CT	54,590	C
Saginaw Valley State Univ	MI	19,284	C
St. Anselm College	NH	56,636	VC
St. Augustine's Univ	NC	25,582	C
St. Francis Univ	PA	46,146	NC
St. Joseph's Univ	PA	58,540	VC
St. Louis Univ	MO	49,866	HC
St. Mary's College	IN	50,600	C
St. Mary's College of Calif	CA	57,420	C
St. Mary's Univ of Minn	MN	42,440	C
St. Michael's College	VT	53,275	VC+

ST = STATE $IS = IN-STATE COSTS SR = SELECTOR RATING

School	ST	$IS	SR
St. Peter's Univ	NJ	49,192	C
St. Vincent College	PA	46,229	C
St. Xavier Univ	IL	44,440	C
Salem College	NC	40,206	C
Salisbury Univ	MD	21,132	VC
Salve Regina Univ	RI	53,046	VC
Sam Houston State Univ	TX	18,792	C
Samford Univ	AL	40,770	VC
San Diego State Univ	CA	23,156	VC
San Francisco State Univ	CA	18,514	LC
San Jose State Univ	CA	22,630	C
Sarah Lawrence College	NY	68,866	MC
Scripps College	CA	69,260	HC
Seattle Pacific Univ	WA	47,439	C+
Seattle Univ	WA	54,957	VC
Seton Hall Univ	NJ	58,008	C
Seton Hill Univ	PA	46,972	VC
Sewanee: The Univ of the South	TN	58,000	HC+
Shenandoah Univ	VA	42,100	C
Shepherd Univ, West Virginia	WV	17,382	C
Shippensburg Univ of Pennsylvania	PA	24,096	C
Shorter Univ	GA	31,130	LC
Siena College	NY	48,916	C
Siena Heights Univ	MI	36,322	C
Simmons College	MA	54,400	HC
Simpson College	IA	45,626	VC
Skidmore College	NY	66,600	MC
Slippery Rock Univ of Pennsylvania	PA	20,450	C
Smith College	MA	66,774	MC
Sonoma State Univ	CA	27,020	C
S Car State Univ	SC	21,330	LC
S Dak State Univ	SD	15,874	C
Southeastern Louisiana Univ	LA	16,237	C
Southern Arkansas Univ	AR	21,532	C
Southern Conn State Univ	CT	21,924	LC
Southern Illinois Univ Edwardsville	IL	20,188	C
Southern Methodist Univ	TX	69,008	MC
Southern Nazarene Univ	OK	33,684	C
Southern Oregon Univ	OR	19,117	C
Southern Univ and A&M College	LA	16,074	LC
Southern Univ at New Orleans	LA	8,014	LC
Southwest Baptist Univ	MO	30,890	LC
Southwest Minn State Univ	MN	17,783	C
Southwestern Univ	TX	52,370	VC
Spelman College	GA	41,642	C
Spring Arbor Univ	MI	37,390	C
St. Ambrose Univ	IA	40,180	C
St. Catherine Univ	MN	45,630	C
St. Edward's Univ	TX	56,190	VC
St. Francis College	NY	38,800	LC
St. John Fisher College	NY	45,270	VC
St. John's Univ	NY	57,160	C+
St. Joseph's College, New York/Brooklyn Campus	NY	25,114	LC
St. Joseph's College, New York/Long Island Campus	NY	25,124	C
St. Mary's Univ	TX	39,120	C
St. Norbert College	WI	46,060	VC
St. Olaf College	MN	56,430	HC
St. Thomas Aquinas College	NY	32,450	C
Stanford Univ	CA	62,541	MC
SUNY Albany	NY	22,165	C
SUNY at Binghamton	NY	24,100	MC
SUNY at Geneseo	NY	21,622	VC
SUNY at New Paltz	NY	20,840	C
SUNY at Oswego	NY	22,219	VC
SUNY/Buffalo State	NY	20,583	LC
SUNY/College at Old Westbury	NY	16,860	C
SUNY/Fredonia	NY	20,818	C
SUNY/Oneonta	NY	20,794	C
SUNY/Plattsburgh	NY	19,314	C
SUNY/Potsdam	NY	21,051	VC
SUNY/Univ at Buffalo	NY	23,122	C
Stephen F. Austin State Univ	TX	18,484	LC
Stetson Univ	FL	57,174	VC+
Stonehill College	MA	55,130	C
Suffolk Univ	MA	52,316	C
Sul Ross State Univ	TX	15,021	LC
Susquehanna Univ	PA	57,560	VC
Swarthmore College	PA	63,550	MC
Tarleton State Univ	TX	15,248	LC
Taylor Univ	IN	42,130	VC
Temple Univ	PA	24,392	C+
Tenn Tech Univ	TN	17,929	C
Texas A&M Univ at College Station	TX	20,771	VC+
Texas A&M Univ at Commerce	TX	10,496	C
Texas A&M Univ at Corpus Christi	TX	16,851	LC
Texas A&M Univ at Kingsville	TX	16,580	LC
Texas Christian Univ	TX	57,120	HC
Texas Lutheran Univ	TX	39,770	C
Texas Southern Univ	TX	19,592	LC
Texas State Univ	TX	18,721	C
Texas Tech Univ	TX	20,156	C+
Texas Wesleyan Univ	TX	37,338	C
The American Univ	DC	61,317	HC
The Catholic Univ of America	DC	58,376	VC
The Citadel, The Military College of S Car	SC	20,679	C
The College at Brockport - SUNY	NY	21,058	C
The College of Idaho	ID	36,415	C
The College of New Jersey	NJ	28,675	VC+
The College of New Rochelle	NY	46,300	LC
The College of Wooster	OH	60,000	HC
The George Washington Univ	DC	68,474	HC+
The Univ of Akron	OH	22,566	C
The Univ of Alabama	AL	24,320	C+
The Univ of Arizona	AZ	24,086	C
The Univ of Tenn at Chattanooga	TN	17,340	C+
The Univ of Tenn at Martin	TN	15,212	C
The Univ of Texas at Austin	TX	20,206	MC
The Univ of Texas at San Antonio	TX	21,060	C
The Univ of Utah	UT	18,751	VC
The Univ of Virginia's College at Wise	VA	18,192	LC
Thomas Edison State Univ	NJ	6,350	NC
Thomas More College	KY	36,720	LC
Towson Univ	MD	21,878	C
Transylvania Univ	KY	47,450	HC+
Trinity Christian College	IL	35,580	C
Trinity College	CT	69,020	HC
Trinity Univ	TX	54,480	MC
Truman State Univ	MO	16,286	MC
Tufts Univ	MA		MC
Tulane Univ	LA	67,496	MC
Union College	NE	23,270	C
Union Univ	TN	41,160	VC
Universidad Adventista de las Antillas	PR	16,606	
Universidad del Turabo	PR	17,828	
Univ of Arkansas at Fayetteville	AR	19,766	VC
Univ of Arkansas at Little Rock	AR	18,211	LC
Univ of Calif at Berkeley	CA	29,886	MC
Univ of Calif at Davis	CA	28,468	HC
Univ of Calif at Irvine	CA	33,857	VC
Univ of Calif at Los Angeles	CA	27,438	HC+
Univ of Calif at Riverside	CA	32,912	C
Univ of Calif at Santa Barbara	CA	30,627	HC+
Univ of Central Arkansas	AR	15,042	VC
Univ of Central Florida	FL	16,379	VC
Univ of Central Missouri	MO	18,982	C
Univ of Central Okla	OK	15,150	C
Univ of Cincinnati	OH	22,118	VC
Univ of Colo Boulder	CO	26,048	HC
Univ of Colo Colo Springs	CO	20,300	C
Univ of Colo Denver	CO	22,238	C
Univ of Conn	CT	27,394	
Univ of Dallas	TX	50,676	VC
Univ of Dayton	OH	54,930	VC
Univ of Denver	CO	61,129	VC+
Univ of Evansville	IN	44,186	C+
Univ of Findlay	OH	43,040	C
Univ of Florida	FL	16,291	HC+
Univ of Georgia	GA	21,878	HC
Univ of Hawaii at Manoa	HI	23,261	C
Univ of Houston	TX	21,871	VC
Univ of Houston-Downtown	TX	7,241	LC
Univ of Idaho	ID	16,158	C
Univ of Illinois at Chicago	IL	24,664	VC
Univ of Illinois at Urbana-Champaign	IL	27,006	HC
Univ of Indianapolis	IN	36,480	VC
Univ of Iowa	IA	19,415	HC
Univ of Jamestown	ND	28,508	C
Univ of Kansas	KS	20,884	VC
Univ of Kentucky	KY	24,800	C+
Univ of La Verne	CA	55,600	C
Univ of Louisiana at Lafayette	LA	14,516	C
Univ of Louisville	KY	19,692	C
Univ of Lynchburg	VA	48,370	C
Univ of Maine	ME	21,038	VC
Univ of Mary Hardin-Baylor	TX	35,292	C+
Univ of Mary Washington	VA	23,039	C+
Univ of Maryland Univ College	MD	26,146	LC
Univ of Maryland/Baltimore County	MD	23,004	VC
Univ of Maryland/College Park	MD	21,938	HC
Univ of Mass Amherst	MA	27,669	HC
Univ of Mass Boston	MA	13,828	C
Univ of Mass Dartmouth	MA	26,507	C
Univ of Miami	FL	63,494	MC
Univ of Mich/Ann Arbor	MI	25,274	MC
Univ of Mich/Flint	MI	19,062	C
Univ of Minn/Duluth	MN	20,292	C
Univ of Minn/Morris	MN	21,222	VC
Univ of Minn/Twin Cities	MN	24,269	MC
Univ of Miss	MS	18,802	C
Univ of Missouri-Columbia	MO	20,463	VC
Univ of Missouri-Kansas City	MO	19,563	VC
Univ of Missouri-St. Louis	MO	19,810	VC
Univ of Montana	MT	14,105	C
Univ of Montevallo	AL	20,012	C
Univ of Mount Union	OH	39,990	C
Univ of Nebr - Kearney	NE	17,014	LC
Univ of Nebr - Lincoln	NE	18,589	VC
Univ of Nebr - Omaha	NE	16,120	C
Univ of Nevada, Las Vegas	NV	17,553	C
Univ of Nevada, Reno	NV	18,010	C
Univ of New Hampshire	NH	29,333	VC
Univ of New Mexico	NM	16,808	C
Univ of New Orleans	LA	12,840	C
Univ of North Alabama	AL	15,964	C
Univ of N Car at Asheville	NC	16,251	VC+
Univ of N Car at Charlotte	NC	17,803	VC
Univ of N Car at Greensboro	NC	15,998	C
Univ of N Car at Pembroke	NC	14,737	LC
Univ of N Car Wilmington	NC	16,784	VC
Univ of N Dak	ND	16,673	C
Univ of North Florida	FL	15,996	VC
Univ of North Georgia	GA	17,316	C
Univ of North Texas	TX	20,082	C
Univ of Northern Colo	CO	19,658	C
Univ of Northern Iowa	IA	17,480	C
Univ of Northwestern - St. Paul	MN	39,530	C
Univ of Notre Dame	IN	68,801	MC
Univ of Okla	OK	19,651	HC
Univ of Oregon	OR	24,021	VC
Univ of Pikeville	KY	27,838	C
Univ of Pittsburgh	PA	30,030	MC
Univ of Portland	OR	52,152	VC
Univ of Puget Sound	WA	60,210	HC
Univ of Redlands	CA	61,934	VC
Univ of Rhode Island	RI	26,066	VC
Univ of Richmond	VA	62,730	MC
Univ of Rochester	NY	65,032	MC
Univ of St. Joseph	CT	49,069	C
Univ of San Diego	CA	60,338	HC
Univ of San Francisco	CA	60,580	C
Univ of Scranton	PA	54,962	VC
Univ of S Car at Columbia	SC	21,726	VC
Univ of S Car Upstate	SC	19,272	LC
Univ of S Dak	SD	16,109	C
Univ of South Florida/Tampa	FL	16,110	VC
Univ of Southern Calif	CA	66,631	MC
Univ of Southern Indiana	IN	16,808	C
Univ of St. Thomas - Houston	TX	41,510	VC
Univ of Tampa	FL	38,928	VC
Univ of Texas at Arlington	TX	18,876	C
Univ of Texas at El Paso	TX	34,452	NC
Univ of Texas Rio Grande Valley	TX	15,573	LC
Univ of the Cumberlands	KY	32,000	LC
Univ of the District of Columbia	DC	21,260	LC
Univ of the Incarnate Word	TX	39,162	LC
Univ of the Pacific	CA	57,446	VC
Univ of Toledo	OH	19,336	C
Univ of Tulsa	OK	52,625	HC
Univ of Vermont	VT	29,792	HC
Univ of Virginia	VA	27,367	MC
Univ of Washington	WA	23,091	MC
Univ of Wisc-Eau Claire	WI	16,354	VC
Univ of Wisc-Green Bay	WI	15,184	C
Univ of Wisc-La Crosse	WI	15,425	VC
Univ of Wisc-Madison	WI	21,647	MC
Univ of Wisc-Oshkosh	WI	15,392	C
Univ of Wisc-Parkside	WI	15,313	C
Univ of Wisc-Platteville	WI	14,148	C
Univ of Wisc-Stevens Point	WI	14,043	C
Univ of Wisc-Whitewater	WI	13,976	C
Univ of Wyoming	WY	15,537	C
Ursinus College	PA	62,920	VC
Utah State Univ	UT	13,235	C
Valley City State Univ	ND	13,267	C
Valparaiso Univ	IN	50,160	VC
Vanderbilt Univ	TN	63,248	MC
Vanguard Univ of Southern Calif	CA	42,400	VC
Villanova Univ	PA	64,922	MC
Virginia Polytechnic Inst and State Univ	VA	21,920	VC
Virginia Wesleyan Univ	VA	45,980	LC
Viterbo Univ	WI	34,660	C
Wabash College	IN	52,100	VC
Wake Forest Univ	NC	69,354	MC
Walla Walla Univ	WA	34,845	C
Walsh Univ	OH	39,010	C
Wartburg College	IA	49,478	C
Washburn Univ	KS	15,827	C
Washington & Jefferson College	PA	58,694	VC
Washington and Lee Univ	VA	59,647	MC
Washington College	MD	56,154	VC
Washington State Univ	WA	22,747	C
Washington Univ in St. Louis	MO	67,539	MC
Wayland Baptist Univ	TX	23,460	LC
Wayne State College	NE	25,746	NC
Weber State Univ	UT	14,112	C
Webster Univ	MO	37,490	C
Wellesley College	MA	66,984	MC
Wells College	NY	50,500	C
Wesleyan College	GA	31,940	C+
West Chester Univ of Pennsylvania	PA	19,171	VC
West Texas A&M Univ	TX	13,478	C
Western Carolina Univ	NC	13,965	C
Western Conn State Univ	CT	21,254	LC
Western Kentucky Univ	KY	16,850	C
Western Mich Univ	MI	21,791	C
Western New Mexico Univ	NM	16,914	LC
Western Oregon Univ	OR	19,965	LC
Western State Colo Univ	CO	19,348	C
Western Washington Univ	WA	18,904	VC
Westfield State Univ	MA	20,404	C
Westminster College	MO	32,820	C
Westminster College	PA	41,722	C
Westmont College	CA	57,930	VC
Wheaton College	IL	44,993	MC
Wheeling Jesuit Univ	WV	37,106	LC
Whitman College	WA	59,772	MC
Whittier College	CA	57,891	C
Whitworth Univ	WA	53,682	VC
Wichita State Univ	KS	17,773	C
Widener Univ	PA	58,190	C
Wiley College	TX	19,255	C
Wilkes Univ	PA	49,166	C
Willamette Univ	OR	62,514	VC+
William Carey Univ	MS	23,950	LC
William Jewell College	MO	42,490	C+
William Paterson Univ of New Jersey	NJ	24,022	C
Williams College	MA	67,700	MC
Wilmington College	OH	35,100	C
Wilson College	PA	35,620	LC
Winona State Univ	MN	18,109	C
Winston-Salem State Univ	NC	18,005	LC
Winthrop Univ	SC	23,960	C
Wisc Lutheran College	WI	36,290	C
Wittenberg Univ	OH	49,863	VC
Wofford College	SC	49,885	VC
Worcester State Univ	MA	20,977	C
Wright State Univ	OH	16,983	C
Xavier Univ	OH	49,380	VC
Xavier Univ of Louisiana	LA	31,689	C
Yale Univ	CT	64,650	MC
York College of Pennsylvania	PA	29,240	C
Youngstown State Univ	OH	17,487	C

SPANISH ADOLESCENSE EDUCATION

School	ST	$IS	SR
Augustana College	IL	51,222	VC+
Bethany College	WV	38,774	LC
Blue Mountain College	MS	15,949	C
Elizabethtown College	PA	56,340	VC
Indiana Univ of Pennsylvania	PA	24,474	C
LIU Post	NY	50,698	C+
Messiah College	PA	44,380	VC
Nazareth College	NY	46,784	C
Niagara Univ	NY	41,010	C
Northern Kentucky Univ	KY	16,486	C
Old Dominion Univ	VA	21,618	C
St. Mary's Univ of Minn	MN	42,440	C
St. John's Univ	NY	57,160	C+
SUNY at Oswego	NY	22,219	VC
SUNY/Plattsburgh	NY	19,314	C
SUNY/Potsdam	NY	21,051	VC
Youngstown State Univ	OH	17,487	C

SPANISH AND HISPANIC STUDIES

School	ST	$IS	SR
Creighton Univ	NE	49,452	VC
Hobart and William Smith Colleges	NY	67,050	HC+
Molloy College	NY	40,440	C
Oberlin College	OH	68,942	MC
Vassar College	NY	68,110	MC

SPANISH EDUCATION K-12

School	ST	$IS	SR
Aquinas College - Mich	MI	38,876	VC
Black Hills State Univ	SD	16,622	C
Carroll College	MT	44,304	C
Cedarville Univ	OH	36,244	VC
CUNY/Queens College	NY	21,507	C
College of the Ozarks	MO	7,530	VC
Colo State Univ	CO	23,033	C
Edgewood College	WI	35,950	C
Grove City College	PA	26,654	VC
Indiana Univ South Bend	IN	16,057	C
Indiana Univ-Purdue Univ Indianapolis	IN	18,952	C
King Univ	TN	36,976	C
Kutztown Univ of Pennsylvania	PA	19,477	C
Louisiana College	LA	21,274	C
Lubbock Christian Univ	TX	29,727	C
Madonna Univ	MI	30,450	LC
Missouri Southern State Univ	MO	13,071	C
Missouri Western State Univ	MO	17,822	LC
Monmouth Univ	NJ	50,184	C
Murray State Univ	KY	17,726	C+
Niagara Univ	NY	41,010	C
St. Ambrose Univ	IA	40,180	C
Syracuse Univ	NY	62,313	HC
Univ of Northwestern - St. Paul	MN	39,530	C
Univ of the Cumberlands	KY	32,000	LC
Wartburg College	IA	49,478	C
Western Mich Univ	MI	21,791	C

SPANISH LANGUAGE AND CULTURE

School	ST	$IS	SR
Lewis Univ	IL	41,710	C

SPANISH LANGUAGE AND LITERATURE

School	ST	$IS	SR
Drury Univ	MO	37,555	VC
Messiah College	PA	44,380	VC

School	ST	$IS	SR
Rutgers Univ - New Brunswick	NJ	27,090	HC
Southern Illinois Univ Carbondale	IL	24,554	C
Stony Brook Univ/The SUNY	NY	22,703	MC
Univ of N Car at Greensboro	NC	15,998	C

SPANISH STUDIES

School	ST	$IS	SR
Ashland Univ	OH	30,446	C
Bard College	NY	65,924	HC
Bard College at Simon's Rock	MA	65,795	MC
Barton College	NC	39,854	C
Bentley Univ	MA	63,720	MC
Blue Mountain College	MS	15,949	C
Bryant Univ	RI	57,204	VC
Cal State, San Bernardino	CA	20,106	C
Cedar Crest College	PA	51,110	C
Coe College	IA	51,570	VC
College of William & Mary	VA	34,907	MC
Dartmouth College	NH	68,109	MC
Fairleigh Dickinson Univ/ College at Florham	NJ	54,770	C
Fairleigh Dickinson Univ/ Metropolitan Campus	NJ	52,392	C
Ferris State Univ	MI	21,458	C
Fordham Univ	NY	68,431	MC
Hobart and William Smith Colleges	NY	67,050	HC+
Holy Names Univ	CA	46,630	LC
Howard Univ	DC	37,616	C+
Kent State Univ	OH	20,928	C
Lake Erie College	OH	38,914	LC
Lebanon Valley College	PA	55,510	VC
Messiah College	PA	44,380	VC
Mills College	CA	43,705	C
Minn State Univ, Moorhead	MN	21,393	C
Montana State Univ Billings	MT	13,336	LC
New College of Florida	FL	16,180	HC+
Northern Mich Univ	MI	20,853	C
Olivet Nazarene Univ	IL	41,840	VC
Pennsylvania State Univ - Univ Park	PA	29,716	HC
Purdue Univ/West Lafayette	IN	20,032	MC
Ramapo College of New Jersey	NJ	25,760	VC
Reed College	OR	65,300	MC
Southern Nazarene Univ	OK	33,684	C
Spring Hill College	AL	48,488	C
St. Lawrence Univ	NY	66,646	HC+
SUNY Albany	NY	22,165	C
Stony Brook Univ/The SUNY	NY	22,703	MC
Syracuse Univ	NY	62,313	HC
Texas A&M Univ at College Station	TX	20,771	VC+
The American Univ	DC	61,317	HC
The Catholic Univ of America	DC	58,376	VC
Union College	NY	64,320	MC
Univ of Calif at Los Angeles	CA	27,438	HC+
Univ of Calif San Diego	CA	30,450	MC
Univ of Illinois at Chicago	IL	24,664	VC
Univ of Wisc-Milwaukee	WI	21,538	C
West Chester Univ of Pennsylvania	PA	19,171	VC
Westminster College	UT	41,078	C
Winthrop Univ	SC	23,960	C
Youngstown State Univ	OH	17,487	C

SPECIAL EDUCATION

School	ST	$IS	SR
Abilene Christian Univ	TX	43,708	C+
Adams State Univ	CO	15,420	LC
Alabama A&M Univ	AL	18,796	C
Alabama State Univ	AL	16,490	LC
Albany State Univ	GA	19,462	C
Albright College	PA	57,326	C
Alcorn State Univ	MS	15,884	C
Alma College	MI	49,410	VC
American International College	MA	47,020	LC
Appalachian State Univ	NC	15,394	VC
Aquinas College - Mich	MI	38,876	VC
Arcadia Univ	PA	55,990	C+
Arizona State Univ at the Polytechnic Campus	AZ	22,394	VC
Arizona State Univ at the Tempe Campus	AZ	23,001	VC
Arizona State Univ at the West Campus	AZ	21,513	VC
Arkansas State Univ	AR	16,190	C
Armstrong State Univ	GA	15,615	C
Auburn Univ	AL	24,300	VC+
Auburn Univ at Montgomery	AL	15,000	C
Augusta Univ	GA	4,632	C
Augustana Univ	SD	39,968	VC
Aurora Univ	IL	34,990	C
Austin Peay State Univ	TN	16,397	C
Avila Univ	MO	27,100	C
Ball State Univ	IN	19,808	C+
Barton College	NC	39,854	C
Baylor Univ	TX	56,803	HC
Bellarmine Univ	KY	52,532	C
Benedictine College	KS	38,850	VC
Benedictine Univ	IL	38,300	C
Bennett College	NC	27,717	NC
Black Hills State Univ	SD	16,622	C
Bloomfield College	NJ	40,100	LC
Bloomsburg Univ of Pennsylvania	PA	19,930	C
Bluffton Univ	OH	40,950	C+
Boise State Univ	ID	17,368	C
Boston College	MA	68,043	MC
Boston Univ	MA	67,352	MC
Bowling Green State Univ	OH	19,975	C
Brenau Univ - Women's College	GA	37,876	LC
Brescia Univ	KY	29,890	VC
Bridgewater State Univ	MA	22,762	C
Brigham Young Univ	UT	13,248	MC
Brigham Young Univ/Hawaii	HI	11,710	C
Buena Vista Univ	IA	42,344	C
Butler Univ	IN	52,890	VC+
Cabrini Univ	PA	42,591	LC
Cal State, Fullerton	CA	21,902	C
Cal State, Long Beach	CA	18,850	C
Calif Univ of Pennsylvania	PA	20,425	LC
Calvin College	MI	43,090	HC
Canisius College	NY	49,672	C
Cardinal Stritch Univ	WI	37,136	C
Caribbean Univ	PR	12,227	
Carlow Univ	PA	39,696	LC
Carroll College	MT	44,304	C
Cedarville Univ	OH	36,244	VC
Central Methodist Univ	MO	31,500	VC
Central State Univ	OH	18,564	C
Central Washington Univ	WA	16,803	C
Cheyney Univ of Pennsylvania	PA	20,896	LC
Christian Brothers Univ	TN	31,670	VC
CUNY/City College	NY	20,204	C
CUNY/Medgar Evers College	NY	6,680	NC
Clarion Univ of Pennsylvania	PA	21,608	LC
Clarke Univ	IA	42,950	C
Clemson Univ	SC		HC
Cleveland State Univ	OH	22,290	C
Coastal Carolina Univ	SC	20,340	C
College of Charleston	SC	24,046	VC
College of Mount St. Vincent	NY	45,620	C
College of St. Mary	NE	27,500	C
Columbia College	SC	36,550	C
Columbus State Univ	GA	14,336	LC
Concord Univ	WV	14,954	LC
Concordia Univ Nebr	NE	41,900	VC
Concordia Univ St. Paul	MN	29,050	C
Coppin State Univ	MD	14,071	VC
Cumberland Univ	TN	27,710	C
Curry College	MA	53,331	C
Dakota Wesleyan Univ	SD	33,980	LC
Delaware State Univ	DE	19,376	LC
DePaul Univ	IL	52,807	VC
Doane Univ	NE	41,340	VC
Dominican College	NY	40,258	LC
Dordt College	IA	37,860	C+
Duquesne Univ	PA	48,508	VC
East Carolina Univ	NC	16,539	C
East Central Univ	OK	13,330	C
East Tenn State Univ	TN	18,141	C
Eastern Illinois Univ	IL	21,414	C
Eastern Kentucky Univ	KY	17,742	C
Eastern Mennonite Univ	VA	42,550	C
Eastern Mich Univ	MI	19,761	C
Eastern New Mexico Univ	NM	12,874	LC
Edgewood College	WI	35,950	C
Edinboro Univ	PA	15,940	LC
Elizabeth City State Univ	NC	14,745	C
Elmhurst College	IL	46,514	C
Elmira College	NY	53,900	C
Elms College	MA	49,602	VC
Elon Univ	NC	46,142	HC
Erskine College	SC	45,460	C
Evangel Univ	MO	28,898	C
Felician Univ	NJ	46,280	LC
Fitchburg State Univ	MA	21,819	LC
Florida Atlantic Univ	FL	18,256	C
Florida Gulf Coast Univ	FL	14,738	C
Florida International Univ	FL	20,281	C
Fontbonne Univ	MO	34,606	C
Freed-Hardeman Univ	TN	29,900	C
Gannon Univ	PA	42,922	C
Georgia College & State Univ	GA	21,884	C+
Georgia Southern Univ	GA	16,540	VC
Georgia Southwestern State Univ	GA	13,870	LC
Glenville State College	WV	17,386	LC
Gonzaga Univ	WA	52,880	HC
Goucher College	MD	56,110	VC
Grace College and Seminary	IN	31,524	C
Grambling State Univ	LA	15,701	C
Grand Valley State Univ	MI	22,250	C+
Greensboro College	NC	39,790	LC
Greenville College	IL	27,012	LC
Grove City College	PA	26,654	VC
Gwynedd Mercy Univ	PA	43,780	LC
Hastings College	NE	35,380	C+
High Point Univ	NC	47,355	VC
Holy Family Univ	PA	44,672	LC
Hood College	MD	50,540	C
Hope College	MI	42,840	VC
Houghton College	NY	40,558	VC
Houston Baptist Univ	TX	36,450	C
Illinois State Univ	IL	23,418	VC
Indiana State Univ	IN	23,223	LC
Indiana Univ Bloomington	IN	20,791	HC
Indiana Univ South Bend	IN	16,057	C
Indiana Univ Southeast	IN	16,931	C
Indiana Wesleyan Univ	IN	33,674	C
Inter-American Univ of PR Ponce	PR	19,549	
Inter-American Univ of PR- Aguadilla Campus	PR	21,657	
Inter-American Univ of PR- Arecibo Campus	PR	18,245	
Inter-American Univ of PR- Fajardo Campus	PR	18,336	
Inter-American Univ of PR- Metropolitan Campus	PR	20,045	
Inter-American Univ of PR-San Germán	PR	20,042	
Jackson State Univ	MS	15,879	LC
Jacksonville State Univ	AL	14,628	LC
Jarvis Christian College	TX	20,160	NC
Juniata College	PA	58,118	VC
Kansas Wesleyan Univ	KS	37,930	C
Kean Univ	NJ	25,620	C
Kent State Univ	OH	20,928	C
King's College	PA	48,240	C
Kutztown Univ of Pennsylvania	PA	19,477	C
La Salle Univ	PA	43,476	C
Lake Erie College	OH	38,914	LC
Lamar Univ	TX	18,014	LC
Lander Univ	SC	32,200	C
Le Moyne College	NY	47,305	VC
Lebanon Valley College	PA	55,510	VC
Lee Univ	TN	22,045	C
LeMoyne-Owen College	TN	16,980	C
Lesley Univ	MA	42,800	C
Lewis Univ	IL	41,710	C
Lincoln Univ	MO	14,402	NC
Lock Haven Univ of Pennsylvania	PA	20,544	LC
Longwood Univ	VA	22,184	C
Louisiana State Univ and A&M College	LA	18,677	VC
Louisiana Tech Univ	LA	11,422	VC
Loyola Univ Chicago	IL	57,158	VC
MacMurray College	IL	35,025	C
Malone Univ	OH	39,200	C
Manhattan College	NY	55,652	C
Marian Univ	IN	43,206	C
Marist College	NY	49,860	VC
Marshall Univ	WV	18,044	C
Marygrove College	MI	30,100	LC
Marymount Univ	VA	43,231	C
Marywood Univ	PA	47,840	C
McKendree Univ	IL	37,940	C+
McPherson College	KS	36,134	C
Mercer Univ	GA	45,348	VC
Mercy College	NY	32,614	C
Mercyhurst Univ	PA	47,420	C
Merrimack College	MA	55,415	C
Methodist Univ	NC	58,130	C
Miami Univ	OH	27,190	HC+
Mich State Univ	MI	24,542	VC
Middle Tenn State Univ	TN	8,650	C
Millersville Univ of Pennsylvania	PA	25,298	C
Milligan College	TN	39,450	C
Minn State Univ, Mankato	MN	17,190	C
Minn State Univ, Moorhead	MN	21,393	C
Miss College	MS	25,850	C
Miss State Univ	MS	12,028	C+
Missouri Baptist Univ	MO	35,594	C
Missouri Southern State Univ	MO	13,071	C
Missouri State Univ	MO	15,837	C+
Missouri Western State Univ	MO	17,822	LC
Monmouth Univ	NJ	50,184	C
Montana State Univ Billings	MT	13,336	LC
Morehead State Univ	KY	18,386	LC
Morningside College	IA	39,780	C
Mount Marty College	SD	36,862	C
Mount St. Joseph Univ	OH	33,880	LC
Mount Vernon Nazarene Univ	OH	35,944	C
Muskingum Univ	OH	35,966	C
Nebr Wesleyan Univ	NE	42,026	C+
New England College	NH	50,828	NC
New Jersey City Univ	NJ	21,456	LC
New Mexico Highlands Univ	NM	11,904	LC
New Mexico State Univ	NM	14,050	LC
New York Univ	NY	68,139	MC
Niagara Univ	NY	41,010	C
Nicholls State Univ	LA	14,959	C
N Car A&T State Univ	NC	13,786	C
Northeastern Illinois Univ	IL	12,529	LC
Northeastern State Univ	OK	8,615	VC
Northern Arizona Univ	AZ	21,003	C
Northern Illinois Univ	IL	20,176	C
Northern Kentucky Univ	KY	16,486	C
Northern State Univ	SD	15,570	C
Northwest Missouri State Univ	MO	18,286	C
Northwest Univ	WA	38,720	VC
Northwestern College of Iowa	IA	38,400	C
Northwestern Okla State Univ	OK	13,072	LC
Notre Dame College	OH	39,150	VC
Notre Dame of Maryland Univ	MD	47,570	VC
Ohio Dominican Univ	OH	41,340	C+
Ohio Univ	OH	23,394	VC
Okla Baptist Univ	OK	33,990	C
Old Dominion Univ	VA	21,618	C
Oral Roberts Univ	OK	34,316	C
Our Lady of the Lake Univ	TX	37,790	LC
Pennsylvania State Univ - Univ Park	PA	29,716	HC
Peru State College	NE	15,602	LC
Pfeiffer Univ	NC	40,532	LC
Piedmont College	GA	34,334	C
Point Park Univ	PA	41,270	C
Pontifical Catholic Univ of PR	PR	10,534	
Prescott College	AZ	38,201	C
Providence College	RI	62,870	HC
Purdue Univ/West Lafayette	IN	20,032	MC
Quincy Univ	IL	38,170	LC
Radford Univ	VA	19,758	C
Rhode Island College	RI	19,000	LC
Roberts Wesleyan College	NY	41,116	C
Rockford Univ	IL	38,570	C
Saginaw Valley State Univ	MI	19,284	C
St. Joseph's Univ	PA	58,540	VC
St. Martin's Univ	WA	45,056	C
St. Mary-of-the-Woods College	IN	40,424	LC
Salve Regina Univ	RI	53,046	VC
Seattle Pacific Univ	WA	47,439	C+
Seton Hall Univ	NJ	58,008	C
Seton Hill Univ	PA	46,972	VC
Shaw Univ	NC	24,638	C
Shawnee State Univ	OH	16,998	C
Shippensburg Univ of Pennsylvania	PA	24,096	C
Siena Heights Univ	MI	36,322	C
Silver Lake College of the Holy Family	WI	36,290	LC
Simmons College	MA	54,400	HC
Slippery Rock Univ of Pennsylvania	PA	20,450	C
S Car State Univ	SC	21,330	LC
Southeastern Louisiana Univ	LA	16,237	C
Southern Conn State Univ	CT	21,924	LC
Southern Illinois Univ Carbondale	IL	24,554	C
Southern Illinois Univ Edwardsville	IL	20,188	C
Southern New Hampshire Univ	NH	44,256	C
Southern Univ and A&M College	LA	16,074	LC
Southern Wesleyan Univ	SC	33,670	LC
Southwestern Okla State Univ	OK	12,205	C
Spring Arbor Univ	MI	37,390	C
St. Ambrose Univ	IA	40,180	C
St. Bonaventure Univ	NY	45,596	C
St. Edward's Univ	TX	56,190	VC
St. John Fisher College	NY	45,270	VC
St. Joseph's College, New York/Brooklyn Campus	NY	25,114	LC
St. Joseph's College, New York/Long Island Campus	NY	25,124	C
St. Thomas Aquinas College	NY	32,450	C
SUNY at Geneseo	NY	21,622	VC
SUNY/Buffalo State	NY	20,583	LC
SUNY/College at Old Westbury	NY	16,860	C
SUNY/Plattsburgh	NY	19,314	C
Stephen F. Austin State Univ	TX	18,484	LC
Tenn State Univ	TN	14,423	LC
Tenn Tech Univ	TN	17,929	C
Tenn Wesleyan Univ	TN	32,680	LC
Texas State Univ	TX	18,721	C
The College of New Jersey	NJ	28,675	VC+
The College of St. Rose	NY	44,010	C
The Univ of Akron	OH	22,566	C
The Univ of Alabama	AL	24,320	C+
The Univ of Arizona	AZ	24,086	C
The Univ of Mary	ND	23,180	C
The Univ of Memphis	TN	18,278	C
The Univ of Montana Western	MT	9,426	LC
The Univ of Tenn at Chattanooga	TN	17,340	C+
The Univ of Tenn at Knoxville	TN	22,112	VC
The Univ of Tenn at Martin	TN	15,212	C
The Univ of Utah	UT	18,751	VC
Thiel College	PA	42,950	LC
Tougaloo College	MS	17,980	NC
Touro College	NY	31,040	C
Towson Univ	MD	21,878	C
Trevecca Nazarene Univ	TN	31,186	C
Trinity Christian College	IL	35,580	C
Troy Univ	AL	16,171	C
Tusculum College	TN	31,625	LC
Tuskegee Univ	AL	28,164	C
Union College	KY	32,310	C
Union Univ	TN	41,160	VC
Universidad del Turabo	PR	17,828	
Univ of Arkansas at Fayetteville	AR	19,766	VC
Univ of Arkansas at Little Rock	AR	18,211	LC
Univ of Arkansas at Pine Bluff	AR	13,541	C
Univ of Central Arkansas	AR	15,042	VC
Univ of Central Missouri	MO	18,982	C
Univ of Central Okla	OK	15,150	C
Univ of Charleston	WV	35,000	LC
Univ of Cincinnati	OH	22,118	VC
Univ of Conn	CT	27,394	
Univ of Dayton	OH	54,930	VC
Univ of Delaware	DE	32,214	VC

ST = STATE $IS = IN-STATE COSTS SR = SELECTOR RATING

School	ST	$IS	SR
Univ of Detroit Mercy	MI	48,816	C
Univ of Evansville	IN	44,186	C+
Univ of Georgia	GA	21,878	HC
Univ of Great Falls	MT	38,524	C
Univ of Hartford	CT	49,776	C
Univ of Idaho	ID	16,158	C
Univ of Kentucky	KY	24,800	C+
Univ of Louisiana at Lafayette	LA	14,516	C
Univ of Louisiana at Monroe	LA	15,970	C
Univ of Maine at Farmington	ME	18,792	C
Univ of Maine at Machias	ME	22,960	C
Univ of Maryland/College Park	MD	21,938	HC
Univ of Mich/Dearborn	MI	12,472	VC
Univ of Minn/Twin Cities	MN	24,269	MC
Univ of Miss	MS	18,802	C
Univ of Missouri-St. Louis	MO	19,810	VC
Univ of Mount Union	OH	39,990	C
Univ of Nebr - Kearney	NE	17,014	LC
Univ of Nebr - Lincoln	NE	18,589	VC
Univ of Nevada, Las Vegas	NV	17,553	C
Univ of Nevada, Reno	NV	18,010	C
Univ of New Mexico	NM	16,808	C
Univ of N Car at Charlotte	NC	17,803	VC
Univ of N Car at Greensboro	NC	15,998	C
Univ of N Car Wilmington	NC	16,784	VC
Univ of North Florida	FL	15,996	VC
Univ of North Georgia	GA	17,316	C
Univ of Northern Colo	CO	19,658	C
Univ of Northern Iowa	IA	17,480	C
Univ of Okla	OK	19,651	HC
Univ of PR, at Cayey	PR		
Univ of PR-Rio Piedras campus	PR	13,327	
Univ of St. Francis	IN	38,520	C
Univ of St. Joseph	CT	49,069	C
Univ of South Alabama	AL	16,880	C
Univ of S Car Aiken	SC	18,094	C
Univ of S Car Upstate	SC	19,272	LC
Univ of S Dak	SD	16,109	C
Univ of South Florida/Tampa	FL	16,110	VC
Univ of Southern Indiana	IN	16,808	C
Univ of St. Francis	IL	40,828	C
Univ of the Cumberlands	KY	32,000	LC
Univ of the Southwest	NM	24,386	C
Univ of Toledo	OH	19,336	C
Univ of Vermont	VT	29,792	HC
Univ of West Alabama	AL	16,284	LC
Univ of West Georgia	GA	17,510	LC
Univ of Wisc-Eau Claire	WI	16,354	VC
Univ of Wisc-Madison	WI	21,647	MC
Univ of Wisc-Milwaukee	WI	21,538	C
Univ of Wisc-Oshkosh	WI	15,392	C
Univ of Wisc-Parkside	WI	15,313	C
Univ of Wisc-Stout	WI	19,667	C
Univ of Wisc-Whitewater	WI	13,976	C
Univ of Wyoming	WY	15,537	C
Ursuline College	OH	41,076	LC
Utah State Univ	UT	13,235	C
Vanderbilt Univ	TN	63,248	MC
Virginia Union Univ	VA	25,058	C
Walla Walla Univ	WA	34,845	C
Walsh Univ	OH	39,010	C
Washington State Univ	WA	22,747	C
Wayne State College	NE	25,746	NC
Wayne State Univ	MI	23,085	C
Waynesburg Univ	PA	33,530	C
Weber State Univ	UT	14,112	C
Webster Univ	MO	37,490	C
West Chester Univ of Pennsylvania	PA	19,171	VC
West Liberty Univ	WV	16,158	C
West Texas A&M Univ	TX	13,478	C
Western Carolina Univ	NC	13,965	C
Western Illinois Univ	IL	20,897	C
Western Mich Univ	MI	21,791	C
Western New Mexico Univ	NM	16,914	LC
Western Washington Univ	WA	18,904	VC
Westfield State Univ	MA	20,404	C
Westminster College	UT	41,078	C
Wheelock College	MA	51,325	LC
Wichita State Univ	KS	17,773	C
Widener Univ	PA	58,190	C
Wiley College	TX	19,255	C
William Paterson Univ of New Jersey	NJ	24,022	C
William Penn Univ	IA	26,000	C
William Woods Univ	MO	32,040	C
Wilson College	PA	35,620	LC
Winona State Univ	MN	18,109	C
Winston-Salem State Univ	NC	18,005	LC
Winthrop Univ	SC	23,960	C
Wittenberg Univ	OH	49,863	VC
Wright State Univ	OH	16,983	C
Xavier Univ	OH	49,380	VC
York College	NE	30,260	C
York College of Pennsylvania	PA	29,240	C
Youngstown State Univ	OH	17,487	C

SPECIAL EDUCATION/EARLY CHILD DUAL PROGRAM

School	ST	$IS	SR
Alvernia Univ	PA	45,330	C
East Stroudsburg Univ	PA	18,578	LC
Millersville Univ of Pennsylvania	PA	25,298	C
Missouri Baptist Univ	MO	35,594	C
Missouri Western State Univ	MO	17,822	LC
Neumann Univ	PA	40,678	LC
Okla Baptist Univ	OK	33,990	C
Syracuse Univ	NY	62,313	HC
West Chester Univ of Pennsylvania	PA	19,171	VC

SPECIFIC LEARNING DISABILITIES

School	ST	$IS	SR
Aquinas College - Mich	MI	38,876	VC
Baldwin Wallace Univ	OH	42,464	VC
Barton College	NC	39,854	C
Florida International Univ	FL	20,281	C
Florida State Univ	FL	16,771	HC
Idaho State Univ	ID	13,619	LC
Murray State Univ	KY	17,726	C+
Northwest Missouri State Univ	MO	18,286	C
Univ of South Florida/Tampa	FL	16,110	VC
Western Mich Univ	MI	21,791	C
Winona State Univ	MN	18,109	C

SPEECH AND THEATRE EDUCATION

School	ST	$IS	SR
College of the Ozarks	MO	7,530	VC
MidAmerica Nazarene Univ	KS	37,808	C
Missouri Baptist Univ	MO	35,594	C
Missouri Southern State Univ	MO	13,071	C
Missouri Western State Univ	MO	17,822	LC
Southwestern College	KS	31,531	LC
Southwestern College	KS	31,531	LC
St. Ambrose Univ	IA	40,180	C

SPEECH CORRECTION

School	ST	$IS	SR
Columbia College	SC	36,550	C
East Texas Baptist Univ	TX	34,444	C
Ithaca College	NY	58,158	VC+
Kutztown Univ of Pennsylvania	PA	19,477	C
New York Univ	NY	68,139	MC
Western Carolina Univ	NC	13,965	C

SPEECH PATHOLOGY/AUDIOLOGY

School	ST	$IS	SR
Adelphi Univ	NY	49,792	C
Alabama A&M Univ	AL	18,796	C
Andrews Univ	MI	41,732	C
Appalachian State Univ	NC	15,394	VC
Arizona State Univ at the Tempe Campus	AZ	23,001	VC
Auburn Univ	AL	24,300	VC+
Auburn Univ at Montgomery	AL	15,000	C
Ball State Univ	IN	19,808	C+
Baylor Univ	TX	56,803	HC
Biola Univ	CA	48,686	C
Bloomsburg Univ of Pennsylvania	PA	19,930	C
Bluffton Univ	OH	40,950	C+
Boston Univ	MA	67,352	MC
Brescia Univ	KY	29,890	VC
Brigham Young Univ	UT	13,248	MC
Butler Univ	IN	52,890	VC+
Cal State, East Bay	CA	20,748	C
Cal State, Fresno	CA	16,902	LC
Cal State, Fullerton	CA	21,902	C
Cal State, Los Angeles	CA	17,186	LC
Cal State, Northridge	CA	17,277	LC
Cal State, Sacramento	CA	19,060	C
Calvin College	MI	43,090	HC
Case Western Reserve Univ	OH	62,284	MC
Central Mich Univ	MI	20,330	C
CUNY/Brooklyn College	NY	7,163	C+
CUNY/Lehman College	NY	5,788	LC
CUNY/Queens College	NY	21,507	C
Clarion Univ of Pennsylvania	PA	21,608	LC
Clemson Univ	SC		HC
Cleveland State Univ	OH	22,290	C
Colo State Univ-Pueblo	CO	21,581	C
Delta State Univ	MS	13,176	LC
Duquesne Univ	PA	48,508	VC
East Carolina Univ	NC	16,539	C
Eastern Mich Univ	MI	19,761	C
Eastern New Mexico Univ	NM	12,874	LC
Eastern Washington Univ	WA	17,896	LC
Edinboro Univ	PA	15,940	LC
Elmhurst College	IL	46,514	C
Elmira College	NY	53,900	C
Elms College	MA	49,602	VC
Emerson College	MA	61,824	HC+
Florida State Univ	FL	16,771	HC
Fontbonne Univ	MO	34,606	C
Fort Hays State Univ	KS	12,677	C
Geneva College	PA	35,450	C
Hampton Univ	VA	36,410	C
Harding Univ	AR	25,440	C
Hardin-Simmons Univ	TX	36,025	C
Hofstra Univ	NY	58,210	C+
Howard Univ	DC	37,616	C+
Idaho State Univ	ID	13,619	LC
Illinois State Univ	IL	23,418	VC
Indiana State Univ	IN	23,223	LC
Indiana Univ Bloomington	IN	20,791	HC
Indiana Univ of Pennsylvania	PA	24,474	C
Indiana Univ-Purdue Univ Fort Wayne	IN	18,675	C
Iona College	NY	52,514	C
Ithaca College	NY	58,158	VC+
James Madison Univ	VA	19,084	VC
Kansas State Univ	KS	17,780	VC
Kean Univ	NJ	25,620	C
Kent State Univ	OH	20,928	C
Kutztown Univ of Pennsylvania	PA	19,477	C
La Salle Univ	PA	43,476	C
Lamar Univ	TX	18,014	LC
LIU Post	NY	50,698	C+
Louisiana State Univ and A&M College	LA	18,677	VC
Louisiana Tech Univ	LA	11,422	VC
Loyola Univ Maryland	MD	61,710	VC
Marquette Univ	WI	53,090	VC+
Marshall Univ	WV	18,044	C
Marymount Manhattan College	NY	48,350	C
Maryville Univ of St. Louis	MO	38,558	VC
Marywood Univ	PA	47,840	C
Mercy College	NY	32,614	C
Miami Univ	OH	27,190	HC+
Mich State Univ	MI	24,542	VC
Minn State Univ, Mankato	MN	17,190	C
Minn State Univ, Moorhead	MN	21,393	C
Minot State Univ	ND	13,285	C
Miss Univ for Women	MS	17,065	C
Missouri State Univ	MO	15,837	C+
Molloy College	NY	40,440	C
Murray State Univ	KY	17,726	C+
Nazareth College	NY	46,784	C
New Mexico State Univ	NM	14,050	LC
New York Univ	NY	68,139	MC
Nicholls State Univ	LA	14,959	C
N Car State Univ	NC	22,434	HC+
Northeastern Univ	MA	65,352	MC
Northern Illinois Univ	IL	20,176	C
Northern Mich Univ	MI	20,853	C
Northern State Univ	SD	15,570	C
Northwestern Univ	IL	68,725	MC
Nova Southeastern Univ	FL	38,534	C+
Ohio State Univ at Columbus	OH	22,843	MC
Okla State Univ	OK	17,180	C+
Old Dominion Univ	VA	21,618	C
Ouachita Baptist Univ	AR	33,500	VC
Our Lady of the Lake Univ	TX	37,790	LC
Purdue Univ/West Lafayette	IN	20,032	MC
Radford Univ	VA	19,758	C
Rockhurst Univ	MO	28,990	C
St. Louis Univ	MO	49,866	HC
St. Mary's College	IN	50,600	C
St. Xavier Univ	IL	44,440	C
San Diego State Univ	CA	23,156	VC
San Francisco State Univ	CA	18,514	LC
San Jose State Univ	CA	22,630	C
Shaw Univ	NC	24,638	C
S Car State Univ	SC	21,330	LC
Southern Illinois Univ Edwardsville	IL	20,188	C
Southern Univ and A&M College	LA	16,074	LC
St. Ambrose Univ	IA	40,180	C
St. Cloud State Univ	MN	10,600	C
St. John's Univ	NY	57,160	C+
SUNY at New Paltz	NY	20,840	C
SUNY/Buffalo State	NY	20,583	LC
SUNY/Cortland	NY	20,910	C
SUNY/Fredonia	NY	20,818	C
SUNY/Univ at Buffalo	NY	23,122	C
Stockton Univ	NJ	25,565	C
Tenn State Univ	TN	14,423	LC
Texas A&M Univ at Kingsville	TX	16,580	LC
Texas Christian Univ	TX	57,120	HC
Texas State Univ	TX	18,721	C
The College of Idaho	ID	36,415	C
The George Washington Univ	DC	68,474	HC+
The Univ of Akron	OH	22,566	C
The Univ of Arizona	AZ	24,086	C
The Univ of Texas at Austin	TX	20,206	MC
The Univ of Utah	UT	18,751	VC
Thiel College	PA	42,950	LC
Towson Univ	MD	21,878	C
Truman State Univ	MO	16,286	MC
Univ of Arkansas at Little Rock	AR	18,211	LC
Univ of Central Arkansas	AR	15,042	VC
Univ of Central Florida	FL	16,379	VC
Univ of Central Missouri	MO	18,982	C
Univ of Central Okla	OK	15,150	C
Univ of Cincinnati	OH	22,118	VC
Univ of Colo Boulder	CO	26,048	HC
Univ of Conn	CT	27,394	
Univ of Florida	FL	16,291	HC+
Univ of Hawaii at Manoa	HI	23,261	C
Univ of Iowa	IA	19,415	HC
Univ of Louisiana at Lafayette	LA	14,516	C
Univ of Louisiana at Monroe	LA	15,970	C
Univ of Maine	ME	21,038	VC
Univ of Maryland/College Park	MD	21,938	HC
Univ of Mass Amherst	MA	27,669	HC
Univ of Minn/Twin Cities	MN	24,269	MC
Univ of Montevallo	AL	20,012	C
Univ of Nebr - Lincoln	NE	18,589	VC
Univ of Nevada, Reno	NV	18,010	C
Univ of New Hampshire	NH	29,333	VC
Univ of New Mexico	NM	16,808	C
Univ of N Car at Greensboro	NC	15,998	C
Univ of North Texas	TX	20,082	C
Univ of Northern Colo	CO	19,658	C
Univ of Northern Iowa	IA	17,480	C
Univ of Oregon	OR	24,021	VC
Univ of Science and Arts of Okla	OK	11,140	VC
Univ of S Dak	SD	16,109	C
Univ of Southern Miss	MS	13,170	C
Univ of Texas at Dallas	TX	23,640	HC
Univ of Texas Rio Grande Valley	TX	15,573	LC
Univ of the District of Columbia	DC	21,260	LC
Univ of the Pacific	CA	57,446	VC
Univ of Toledo	OH	19,336	C
Univ of Tulsa	OK	52,625	HC
Univ of Vermont	VT	29,792	HC
Univ of Virginia	VA	27,367	MC
Univ of Washington	WA	23,091	MC
Univ of West Georgia	GA	17,510	LC
Univ of Wisc-Madison	WI	21,647	MC
Univ of Wisc-Milwaukee	WI	21,538	C
Univ of Wisc-Oshkosh	WI	15,392	C
Univ of Wisc-River Falls	WI	14,541	C
Univ of Wisc-Stevens Point	WI	14,043	C
Univ of Wyoming	WY	15,537	C
Utah State Univ	UT	13,235	C
Washington State Univ	WA	22,747	C
Wayne State Univ	MI	23,085	C
West Chester Univ of Pennsylvania	PA	19,171	VC
West Liberty Univ	WV	16,158	C
West Texas A&M Univ	TX	13,478	C
West Virginia Univ	WV	18,952	VC
Western Kentucky Univ	KY	16,850	C
Western Mich Univ	MI	21,791	C
Western Washington Univ	WA	18,904	VC
Wichita State Univ	KS	17,773	C
Worcester State Univ	MA	20,977	C
Xavier Univ of Louisiana	LA	31,689	C

SPEECH THERAPY

School	ST	$IS	SR
Baylor Univ	TX	56,803	HC
Biola Univ	CA	48,686	C
Cal State, Fresno	CA	16,902	LC
Cleveland State Univ	OH	22,290	C
Ithaca College	NY	58,158	VC+
Misericordia Univ	PA	45,210	C
Northern Mich Univ	MI	20,853	C
Ohio State Univ at Columbus	OH	22,843	MC
Southern Univ and A&M College	LA	16,074	LC
Stephen F. Austin State Univ	TX	18,484	LC
Temple Univ	PA	24,392	C+
Univ of Tulsa	OK	52,625	HC

SPEECH/DEBATE/RHETORIC

School	ST	$IS	SR
Albany State Univ	GA	19,462	C
Arkansas Tech Univ	AR	16,534	LC
Ashland Univ	OH	30,446	C
Auburn Univ	AL	24,300	VC+
Augsburg Univ	MN	45,129	C
Bates College	ME	64,500	HC
Baylor Univ	TX	56,803	HC
Bellarmine Univ	KY	52,532	C
Black Hills State Univ	SD	16,622	C
Bloomsburg Univ of Pennsylvania	PA	19,930	C
Bridgewater State Univ	MA	22,762	C
Butler Univ	IN	52,890	VC+
Cal State, East Bay	CA	20,748	C
Cal State, Fresno	CA	16,902	LC
Cal State, Fullerton	CA	21,902	C
Cal State, Los Angeles	CA	17,186	LC
Cal State, Northridge	CA	17,277	LC
Calif Univ of Pennsylvania	PA	20,425	LC
Canisius College	NY	49,672	C
Capital Univ	OH	44,778	VC
Central Mich Univ	MI	20,330	C
Central Washington Univ	WA	16,803	C
Chadron State College	NE	14,819	LC
Charleston Southern Univ	SC	34,700	C
Chicago State Univ	IL	41,620	C
CUNY/Brooklyn College	NY	7,163	C+
CUNY/Lehman College	NY	5,788	LC
CUNY/York College	NY	6,747	LC
Clark Atlanta Univ	GA	31,019	LC
Concordia Univ Nebr	NE	41,900	VC
Concordia Univ Wisc	WI	35,910	C
Cornerstone Univ	MI	36,550	C
Denison Univ	OH	62,770	HC+
DePaul Univ	IL	52,807	VC
Dickinson State Univ	ND	12,372	LC
Dordt College	IA	37,860	C+
Drake Univ	IA	49,220	HC
Duquesne Univ	PA	48,508	VC
East Carolina Univ	NC	16,539	C
East Central Univ	OK	13,330	C
East Tenn State Univ	TN	18,141	C
East Texas Baptist Univ	TX	34,444	C
Eastern Kentucky Univ	KY	17,742	C
Eastern Mich Univ	MI	19,761	C
Eastern Nazarene College	MA	41,114	C
Eastern Washington Univ	WA	17,896	LC
Emerson College	MA	61,824	HC+
Evangel Univ	MO	28,898	C

ST = STATE $IS = IN-STATE COSTS SR = SELECTOR RATING

School	ST	$IS	SR
Fairmont State Univ	WV	15,726	C
Fayetteville State Univ	NC	17,756	C
Fisk Univ	TN	32,066	LC
Florida State Univ	FL	16,771	HC
Freed-Hardeman Univ	TN	29,900	C
Geneva College	PA	35,450	C
Georgia College & State Univ	GA	21,884	C+
Georgia State Univ	GA	25,250	C
Gonzaga Univ	WA	52,880	HC
Graceland Univ	IA	35,290	C
Greenville College	IL	27,012	LC
Gustavus Adolphus College	MN	53,943	HC
Hannibal-LaGrange Univ	MO	29,815	C
Hardin-Simmons Univ	TX	36,025	C
Hastings College	NE	35,380	C+
Hillsdale College	MI	37,170	MC
Hofstra Univ	NY	58,210	C+
Humboldt State Univ	CA	21,708	C
Illinois College	IL	41,330	VC
Illinois State Univ	IL	23,418	VC
Indiana Univ-Purdue Univ Fort Wayne	IN	18,675	C
Iona College	NY	52,514	C
Iowa State Univ	IA	18,176	C
Jackson State Univ	MS	15,879	LC
James Madison Univ	VA	19,084	VC
Kansas Wesleyan Univ	KS	37,930	C
Kutztown Univ of Pennsylvania	PA	19,477	C
Lamar Univ	TX	18,014	LC
Lander Univ	SC	32,200	C
Langston Univ	OK	15,659	C
Lock Haven Univ of Pennsylvania	PA	20,544	LC
Louisiana Tech Univ	LA	11,422	VC
Marietta College	OH	46,190	C
McKendree Univ	IL	37,940	C+
McPherson College	KS	36,134	C
Metropolitan State Univ of Denver	CO	6,928	LC
Miami Univ	OH	27,190	HC+
Minn State Univ, Mankato	MN	17,190	C
Minn State Univ, Moorhead	MN	21,393	C
Miss Valley State Univ	MS	13,233	LC
Missouri State Univ	MO	15,837	C+
Missouri Valley College	MO	28,150	C
Missouri Western State Univ	MO	17,822	LC
Morgan State Univ	MD	17,190	LC
Muskingum Univ	OH	35,966	C
New York Univ	NY	68,139	MC
N Car A&T State Univ	NC	13,786	C
North Central College	IL	48,712	C+
Northeastern State Univ	OK	8,615	VC
Northern Kentucky Univ	KY	16,486	C
Northern Mich Univ	MI	20,853	C
Northwest Missouri State Univ	MO	18,286	C
Northwestern Okla State Univ	OK	13,072	LC
Ohio Univ	OH	23,394	VC
Okla Baptist Univ	OK	33,990	C
Oral Roberts Univ	OK	34,316	C
Oregon State Univ	OR	23,337	VC
Otterbein Univ	OH	41,630	C
Ouachita Baptist Univ	AR	33,500	VC
Pepperdine Univ	CA	66,862	VC+
Point Loma Nazarene Univ	CA	46,150	C+
Portland State Univ	OR	19,443	C
Prairie View A&M Univ	TX	27,273	LC
Radford Univ	VA	19,758	C
Rowan Univ	NJ	24,491	VC
Rutgers Univ - Camden	NJ	26,595	C
Rutgers Univ - New Brunswick	NJ	27,090	HC
Sam Houston State Univ	TX	18,792	C
San Francisco State Univ	CA	18,514	LC
Shippensburg Univ of Pennsylvania	PA	24,096	C
Southeastern Okla State Univ	OK	11,875	C
Southern Illinois Univ Carbondale	IL	24,554	C
Southern Illinois Univ Edwardsville	IL	20,188	C
Southern Nazarene Univ	OK	33,684	C
Southern Univ at New Orleans	LA	8,014	LC
Southwestern Adventist Univ	TX	28,232	LC
St. Catherine Univ	MN	45,630	C
St. Cloud State Univ	MN	10,600	C
St. John's Univ	NY	57,160	C+
St. Joseph's College, New York/Brooklyn Campus	NY	25,114	LC
St. Joseph's College, New York/Long Island Campus	NY	25,124	C
St. Mary's Univ	TX	39,120	C
SUNY at Binghamton	NY	24,100	MC
SUNY at New Paltz	NY	20,840	C
Stephen F. Austin State Univ	TX	18,484	LC
Suffolk Univ	MA	52,316	C
Tarleton State Univ	TX	15,248	LC
Temple Univ	PA	24,392	C+
Tenn State Univ	TN	14,423	LC
Texas A&M Univ at College Station	TX	20,771	VC+
Texas A&M Univ at Corpus Christi	TX	16,851	LC
The Univ of Texas at Austin	TX	20,206	MC
Touro College	NY	31,040	C
Univ of Alaska Southeast	AK	17,615	C
Univ of Arkansas at Monticello	AR	13,599	LC
Univ of Arkansas at Pine Bluff	AR	13,541	C
Univ of Calif at Berkeley	CA	29,886	MC
Univ of Calif at Davis	CA	28,468	HC
Univ of Central Arkansas	AR	15,042	VC
Univ of Central Missouri	MO	18,982	C
Univ of Cincinnati	OH	22,118	VC
Univ of Dubuque	IA	37,824	C
Univ of Florida	FL	16,291	HC+
Univ of Hawaii at Manoa	HI	23,261	C
Univ of Illinois at Urbana-Champaign	IL	27,006	HC
Univ of Iowa	IA	19,415	HC
Univ of Kansas	KS	20,884	VC
Univ of La Verne	CA	55,600	C
Univ of Mary Hardin-Baylor	TX	35,292	C+
Univ of Mich/Ann Arbor	MI	25,274	MC
Univ of Minn/Morris	MN	21,222	VC
Univ of Minn/Twin Cities	MN	24,269	MC
Univ of Nebr - Kearney	NE	17,014	LC
Univ of Nebr - Lincoln	NE	18,589	VC
Univ of Nebr - Omaha	NE	16,120	C
Univ of Northern Iowa	IA	17,480	C
Univ of Sioux Falls	SD	25,630	C
Univ of S Car at Columbia	SC	21,726	VC
Univ of South Florida/Tampa	FL	16,110	VC
Univ of Southern Miss	MS	13,170	C
Univ of Texas at Arlington	TX	18,876	C
Univ of Texas at El Paso	TX	34,452	NC
Univ of Washington	WA	23,091	MC
Univ of Wisc-Oshkosh	WI	15,392	C
Univ of Wisc-River Falls	WI	14,541	C
Univ of Wisc-Superior	WI	14,838	C
Univ of Wisc-Whitewater	WI	13,976	C
Wabash College	IN	52,100	VC
Walla Walla Univ	WA	34,845	C
Washburn Univ	KS	15,827	C
Wayne State College	NE	25,746	NC
West Texas A&M Univ	TX	13,478	C
West Virginia Univ	WV	18,952	VC
West Virginia Wesleyan College	WV	39,188	C
Western Carolina Univ	NC	13,965	C
Western Oregon Univ	OR	19,965	LC
Whitman College	WA	59,772	MC
Whitworth Univ	WA	53,682	VC
Willamette Univ	OR	62,514	VC+
Wilmington College	OH	35,100	C
Winona State Univ	MN	18,109	C
Yeshiva Univ	NY	52,750	VC

SPORT & LIFESTYLE STUDIES

School	ST	$IS	SR
Ohio State Univ at Columbus	OH	22,843	MC
Ohio Univ	OH	23,394	VC
Univ of Maine at Machias	ME	22,960	C

SPORTS ADMINISTRATION

School	ST	$IS	SR
Baker Univ	KS	37,190	C
Ball State Univ	IN	19,808	C+
Barton College	NC	39,854	C
Berry College	GA	47,466	VC
Bethany College	WV	38,774	LC
Dakota Wesleyan Univ	SD	33,980	LC
East Central Univ	OK	13,330	C
Florida International Univ	FL	20,281	C
Gannon Univ	PA	42,922	C
Lewis-Clark State College	ID	14,202	C
Merrimack College	MA	55,415	C
Ohio Univ	OH	23,394	VC
Samford Univ	AL	40,770	VC
Southern Illinois Univ Carbondale	IL	24,554	C
Southern Methodist Univ	TX	69,008	MC

SPORTS AND WELLNESS STUDIES

School	ST	$IS	SR
Adams State Univ	CO	15,420	LC
Aquinas College - Mich	MI	38,876	VC
Arizona State Univ at the Downtown Phoenix Campus	AZ	24,634	VC
Averett Univ	VA	43,034	LC
College of St. Mary	NE	27,500	C
Corban Univ	OR	41,700	C
Dakota Wesleyan Univ	SD	33,980	LC
Georgian Court Univ	NJ	43,068	LC
Ithaca College	NY	58,158	VC+
Mercy College	NY	32,614	C
Nova Southeastern Univ	FL	38,534	C+
Okla Christian Univ	OK	29,260	C
Southwestern College	KS	31,531	LC
SUNY/Plattsburgh	NY	19,314	C
The Univ of Montana Western	MT	9,426	LC
Univ of Illinois at Chicago	IL	24,664	VC
Univ of Maine at Machias	ME	22,960	C
Univ of Mary Hardin-Baylor	TX	35,292	C+
Westminster College	MO	32,820	C
Winthrop Univ	SC	23,960	C

SPORTS COMMUNICATION

School	ST	$IS	SR
Bethany College	WV	38,774	LC
Bradley Univ	IL	43,240	VC
Bryant Univ	RI	57,204	VC
Ferris State Univ	MI	21,458	C
Millikin Univ	IL	44,148	C
Neumann Univ	PA	40,678	LC
Simpson College	IA	45,626	VC

SPORTS MANAGEMENT

School	ST	$IS	SR
Adams State Univ	CO	15,420	LC
Adrian College	MI	45,550	C
Alfred State College	NY	19,895	C
Alvernia Univ	PA	45,330	C
Anderson Univ	IN	39,450	C
Anna Maria College	MA	51,020	C
Aquinas College - Mich	MI	38,876	VC
Arcadia Univ	PA	55,990	C+
Arkansas State Univ	AR	16,190	C
Asbury Univ	KY	36,450	C+
Ashford Univ	CA	10,480	C
Ashland Univ	OH	30,446	C
Augustana Univ	SD	39,968	VC
Baldwin Wallace Univ	OH	42,464	VC
Ball State Univ	IN	19,808	C+
Barry Univ	FL	38,730	LC
Barton College	NC	39,854	C
Becker College	MA	30,100	LC
Belmont Abbey College	NC	28,794	C
Bethany College	KS	38,637	LC
Bethany College	WV	38,774	LC
Bethel College	IN	36,830	C
Blackburn College	IL	28,526	LC
Bluffton Univ	OH	40,950	C+
Bowling Green State Univ	OH	19,975	C
Buena Vista Univ	IA	42,344	C
Calif Univ of Pennsylvania	PA	20,425	LC
Calvin College	MI	43,090	HC
Cameron Univ	OK	11,632	LC
Campbell Univ	NC	37,570	VC
Campbellsville Univ	KY	33,400	C
Canisius College	NY	49,672	C
Castleton Univ	VT	20,186	C
Catawba College	NC	39,820	LC
Cedarville Univ	OH	36,244	VC
Central Methodist Univ	MO	31,500	VC
Claflin Univ	SC	25,592	LC
Clarke Univ	IA	42,950	C
Coastal Carolina Univ	SC	20,340	C
Colby-Sawyer College	NH	50,790	C
College of St. Elizabeth	NJ	45,700	LC
College of St Joseph	VT	32,400	LC
Colo Mesa Univ	CO	19,707	LC
Columbia College Chicago	IL	40,104	C
Concordia Univ Nebr	NE	41,900	VC
Concordia Univ St. Paul	MN	29,050	C
Coppin State Univ	MD	14,071	VC
Corban Univ	OR	41,700	C
Cornerstone Univ	MI	36,550	C
Culver-Stockton College	MO	34,350	C
Dakota Wesleyan Univ	SD	33,980	LC
Dallas Baptist Univ	TX	35,220	VC
Davis & Elkins College	WV	38,242	LC
Defiance College	OH	42,240	LC
Delaware Valley Univ	PA	51,271	C
DeSales Univ	PA	47,520	C
Dordt College	IA	37,860	C+
Drexel Univ	PA	65,927	HC
Duquesne Univ	PA	48,508	VC
East Stroudsburg Univ	PA	18,578	LC
Eastern Conn State Univ	CT	23,059	C
Edinboro Univ	PA	15,940	LC
Elmhurst College	IL	46,514	C
Elon Univ	NC	46,142	HC
Emmanuel College	MA	53,472	C+
Endicott College	MA	47,054	C+
Erskine College	SC	45,460	C
Farmingdale State College	NY	20,968	C
Faulkner Univ	AL	26,410	C
Ferrum College	VA	43,970	C
Flagler College	FL	27,620	C
Florida Inst of Technology	FL	53,306	VC
Florida International Univ	FL	20,281	C
Florida State Univ	FL	16,771	HC
Fontbonne Univ	MO	34,606	C
Franklin Pierce Univ	NH	46,750	LC
Fresno Pacific Univ	CA	38,858	C
Gannon Univ	PA	42,922	C
Gardner-Webb Univ	NC	24,935	C+
Georgetown College	KY	41,440	C
Georgia Southern Univ	GA	16,540	VC
Glenville State College	WV	17,386	LC
Goldey-Beacom College	DE	36,038	C
Gonzaga Univ	WA	52,880	HC
Grand Canyon Univ	AZ	25,150	VC
Grand View Univ	IA	32,302	C
Guilford College	NC	45,973	C
Gwynedd Mercy Univ	PA	43,780	LC
Hampton Univ	VA	36,410	C
Harding Univ	AR	25,440	C
Heidelberg Univ	OH	40,400	LC
Hilbert College	NY	32,650	LC
Hillsdale College	MI	37,170	MC
Holy Family Univ	PA	44,672	LC
Hope International Univ	CA	42,730	C
Howard Univ	DC	37,616	C+
Huntingdon College	AL	35,900	C
Huntington Univ	IN	33,996	C
Husson Univ	ME	26,508	C
Indiana Inst of Technology	IN	34,240	LC
Indiana State Univ	IN	23,223	LC
Indiana Univ Kokomo	IN	7,207	C
Iowa Wesleyan Univ	IA	41,000	C
Ithaca College	NY	58,158	VC+
Johnson & Wales Univ/ Charlotte Campus	NC	44,768	C
Johnson & Wales Univ/North Miami Campus	FL	44,768	C
Johnson & Wales Univ/ Providence Campus	RI	44,768	C
Johnson C. Smith Univ	NC	25,336	LC
Judson Univ	IL	39,174	C
Keiser Univ	FL	35,010	LC
Kennesaw State Univ	GA	18,899	VC
Kent State Univ	OH	20,928	C
Kentucky Wesleyan College	KY	34,260	LC
Keystone College	PA	28,680	LC
Kutztown Univ of Pennsylvania	PA	19,477	C
Lake Erie College	OH	38,914	LC
Lasell College	MA	49,400	C
Lees-McRae College	NC	33,944	NC
Lenoir-Rhyne Univ	NC	47,500	LC
Lewis Univ	IL	41,710	C
Liberty Univ	VA	31,415	C
Limestone College	SC	32,100	C
Lindenwood Univ	MO	25,760	C
Lipscomb Univ	TN	42,984	VC
LIU Brooklyn	NY	50,698	C
LIU Post	NY	50,698	C+
Livingstone College	NC	17,815	LC
Loras College	IA	40,726	C
Louisiana State Univ and A&M College	LA	18,677	VC
Loyola Univ Chicago	IL	57,158	VC
Lubbock Christian Univ	TX	29,727	C
Lyndon State College	VT	20,714	C
Lynn Univ	FL	49,680	LC
MacMurray College	IL	35,025	C
Madonna Univ	MI	30,450	LC
Malone Univ	OH	39,200	C
Marian Univ	IN	43,206	C
Marian Univ	WI	34,622	C
Marietta College	OH	46,190	C
Marshall Univ	WV	18,044	C
Maryville Univ of St. Louis	MO	38,558	VC
Mayville State Univ	ND	18,371	NC
Medaille College	NY	41,700	LC
Menlo College	CA	51,380	LC
Messiah College	PA	44,380	VC
Methodist Univ	NC	58,130	C
Miami Univ	OH	27,190	HC+
Mich Tech Univ	MI	25,551	VC+
MidAmerica Nazarene Univ	KS	37,808	C
Midway Univ	KY	33,940	LC
Millikin Univ	IL	44,148	C
Minn State Univ, Mankato	MN	17,190	C
Misericordia Univ	PA	45,210	C
Miss Univ for Women	MS	17,065	C
Missouri Baptist Univ	MO	35,594	C
Mitchell College	CT	45,192	C
Mount St. Joseph Univ	OH	33,880	LC
Mount St. Mary's Univ	MD	53,380	C
Mount Vernon Nazarene Univ	OH	35,944	C
Nebr Wesleyan Univ	NE	42,026	C+
Neumann Univ	PA	40,678	LC
New England College	NH	50,828	NC
New York Univ	NY	68,139	MC
Newbury College	MA	48,970	C
Niagara Univ	NY	41,010	C
Nichols College	MA	46,900	LC
North Central College	IL	48,712	C+
North Central Univ	MN	30,610	C
N Dak State Univ	ND	16,245	VC
North Greenville Univ	SC	25,930	C
Northern Kentucky Univ	KY	16,486	C
Northwood Univ - Mich	MI	35,010	LC
Ohio Dominican Univ	OH	41,340	C+
Ohio Northern Univ	OH	44,050	VC
Ohio Univ	OH	23,394	VC
Ohio Valley Univ	WV	28,800	C
Okla Baptist Univ	OK	33,990	C
Old Dominion Univ	VA	21,618	C
Olivet Nazarene Univ	IL	41,840	VC
Ouachita Baptist Univ	AR	33,500	VC
Peru State College	NE	15,602	LC
Pfeiffer Univ	NC	40,532	LC
Point Park Univ	PA	41,270	C
Principia College	IL	40,350	C
Queens Univ of Charlotte	NC	39,543	C
Quincy Univ	IL	38,170	LC
Roanoke College	VA	55,952	VC
Robert Morris Univ	PA	40,600	C
Rochester College	MI	28,574	LC
Rocky Mountain College	MT	35,776	C
Sacred Heart Univ	CT	54,590	C
St. Leo Univ	FL	32,850	C
St. Mary's Univ of Minn	MN	42,440	C
Salem International Univ	WV	21,090	C
Seton Hall Univ	NJ	58,008	C
Seton Hill Univ	PA	46,972	VC
Shawnee State Univ	OH	16,998	C
Shenandoah Univ	VA	42,100	C
Shorter Univ	GA	31,130	LC
Simpson College	IA	45,626	VC
Southeast Missouri State Univ	MO	16,148	C
Southeastern Louisiana Univ	LA	16,237	C

ST = STATE $IS = IN-STATE COSTS SR = SELECTOR RATING

School	ST	$IS	SR
Southeastern Univ	FL	34,910	LC
Southern Nazarene Univ	OK	33,684	C
Southern New Hampshire Univ	NH	44,256	C
Southern Vermont College	VT	34,670	LC
Southern Wesleyan Univ	SC	33,670	LC
Southwest Baptist Univ	MO	30,890	LC
Southwestern College	KS	31,531	LC
Southwestern Okla State Univ	OK	12,205	C
Springfield College	MA	48,775	C
St. Ambrose Univ	IA	40,180	C
St. John Fisher College	NY	45,270	VC
St. John's Univ	NY	57,160	C+
St. Thomas Univ	FL	51,187	LC
SUNY/Cortland	NY	20,910	C
SUNY/Fredonia	NY	20,818	C
Sterling College	KS	32,830	LC
Stetson Univ	FL	57,174	VC+
Syracuse Univ	NY	62,313	HC
Taylor Univ	IN	42,130	VC
Temple Univ	PA	24,392	C+
Tenn Wesleyan Univ	TN	32,680	LC
Texas Tech Univ	TX	20,156	C+
The College at Brockport - SUNY	NY	21,058	C
The Univ of Arizona	AZ	24,086	C
The Univ of Montana Western	MT	9,426	LC
The Univ of Tenn at Knoxville	TN	22,112	VC
Thomas College	ME	73,888	LC
Tiffin Univ	OH	34,900	LC
Towson Univ	MD	21,878	C
Trevecca Nazarene Univ	TN	31,186	C
Trine Univ	IN	41,310	C
Trinity International Univ	IL	31,070	VC
Troy Univ	AL	16,171	C
Tusculum College	TN	31,625	LC
Union College	KY	32,310	C
Union Univ	TN	41,160	VC
Univ of Arkansas at Little Rock	AR	18,211	LC
Univ of Charleston	WV	35,000	LC
Univ of Cincinnati	OH	22,118	VC
Univ of Dayton	OH	54,930	VC
Univ of Delaware	DE	32,214	VC
Univ of Evansville	IN	44,186	C+
Univ of Georgia	GA	21,878	HC
Univ of Indianapolis	IN	36,480	VC
Univ of Kansas	KS	20,884	VC
Univ of Louisville	KY	19,692	C
Univ of Lynchburg	VA	48,370	C
Univ of Maine at Machias	ME	22,960	C
Univ of Mary Hardin-Baylor	TX	35,292	C+
Univ of Mass Amherst	MA	27,669	HC
Univ of Miami	FL	63,494	MC
Univ of Mich/Ann Arbor	MI	25,274	MC
Univ of Minn/Crookston	MN	19,126	C
Univ of Minn/Twin Cities	MN	24,269	MC
Univ of Mount Union	OH	39,990	C
Univ of New England	ME	50,110	C
Univ of New Haven	CT	53,680	C
Univ of North Florida	FL	15,996	VC
Univ of Pittsburgh at Bradford	PA	22,958	C
Univ of St. Mary	KS	37,080	NC
Univ of S Car at Columbia	SC	21,726	VC
Univ of S Dak	SD	16,109	C
Univ of Southern Indiana	IN	16,808	C
Univ of Tampa	FL	38,928	VC
Univ of the Cumberlands	KY	32,000	LC
Univ of the Incarnate Word	TX	39,162	LC
Univ of Tulsa	OK	52,625	HC
Univ of West Alabama	AL	16,284	LC
Univ of West Georgia	GA	17,510	LC
Univ of Wisc-Parkside	WI	15,313	C
Urbana Univ	OH	30,820	C
Valparaiso Univ	IN	50,160	VC
Virginia Commonwealth Univ	VA	23,811	VC
Viterbo Univ	WI	34,660	C
Warner Univ	FL	28,216	C
Washington State Univ	WA	22,747	C
Wayne State College	NE	25,746	NC
Wayne State Univ	MI	23,085	C
Webber International Univ	FL	31,904	C
Wesley College	DE	37,848	LC
West Virginia Univ	WV	18,952	VC
Western Carolina Univ	NC	13,965	C
Western Mich Univ	MI	21,791	C
Western New England Univ	MA	49,182	C
Westminster College	MO	32,820	C
Wichita State Univ	KS	17,773	C
Wilkes Univ	PA	49,166	C
William Penn Univ	IA	26,000	C
Wilmington College	OH	35,100	C
Wilmington Univ	DE	8,762	NC
Wilson College	PA	35,620	LC
Wingate Univ	NC	41,900	C
Winston-Salem State Univ	NC	18,005	LC
Winthrop Univ	SC	23,960	C
Wittenberg Univ	OH	49,863	VC
Xavier Univ	OH	49,380	VC
York College of Pennsylvania	PA	29,240	C

SPORTS MARKETING

School	ST	$IS	SR
Baylor Univ	TX	56,803	HC
Duquesne Univ	PA	48,508	VC
Florida International Univ	FL	20,281	C
Pace Univ	NY	60,136	C
St. Joseph's Univ	PA	58,540	VC
Southeastern Univ	FL	34,910	LC
Southern Nazarene Univ	OK	33,684	C
Thomas More College	KY	36,720	LC
Xavier Univ	OH	49,380	VC

SPORTS MEDIA

School	ST	$IS	SR
Arizona State Univ at the Downtown Phoenix Campus	AZ	24,634	VC
Bethany College	WV	38,774	LC
Ithaca College	NY	58,158	VC+
Louisiana College	LA	21,274	C
Marshall Univ	WV	18,044	C
Newman Univ	KS	37,382	C
Southern Nazarene Univ	OK	33,684	C
Youngstown State Univ	OH	17,487	C

SPORTS MEDICINE

School	ST	$IS	SR
Alcorn State Univ	MS	15,884	C
Aquinas College - Mich	MI	38,876	VC
Avila Univ	MO	27,100	C
Belhaven Univ	MS	32,250	C
Briar Cliff Univ	IA	36,956	C
Campbellsville Univ	KY	33,400	C
Canisius College	NY	49,672	C
Capital Univ	OH	44,778	VC
Central Mich Univ	MI	20,330	C
Concordia Univ Wisc	WI	35,910	C
Eastern Mich Univ	MI	19,761	C
Eastern Nazarene College	MA	41,114	C
Florida State Univ	FL	16,771	HC
Howard Univ	DC	37,616	C+
Ithaca College	NY	58,158	VC+
King's College	PA	48,240	C
Lander Univ	SC	32,200	C
Mercyhurst Univ	PA	47,420	C
Merrimack College	MA	55,415	C
Millersville Univ of Pennsylvania	PA	25,298	C
Norwich Univ	VT	56,234	C
Ohio Univ	OH	23,394	VC
Pepperdine Univ	CA	66,862	VC+
Samford Univ	AL	40,770	VC
Southern Oregon Univ	OR	19,117	C
Towson Univ	MD	21,878	C
Trinity International Univ	IL	31,070	VC
Tusculum College	TN	31,625	LC
Union Univ	TN	41,160	VC
Univ of Kansas	KS	20,884	VC
Univ of Nevada, Las Vegas	NV	17,553	C
Univ of Pittsburgh at Bradford	PA	22,958	C
Univ of Southern Maine	ME	18,320	C
West Chester Univ of Pennsylvania	PA	19,171	VC
Western Carolina Univ	NC	13,965	C

SPORTS PSYCHOLOGY

School	ST	$IS	SR
Arcadia Univ	PA	55,990	C+
Faulkner Univ	AL	26,410	C
Hillsdale College	MI	37,170	MC
Lubbock Christian Univ	TX	29,727	C
Texas Christian Univ	TX	57,120	HC

SPORTS STUDIES

School	ST	$IS	SR
Bethel College	IN	36,830	C
Bryant Univ	RI	57,204	VC
Huntingdon College	AL	35,900	C
Huntington Univ	IN	33,996	C
Ithaca College	NY	58,158	VC+
John Carroll Univ	OH	51,570	C
Lake Erie College	OH	38,914	LC
Manhattanville College	NY	52,430	C
Okla Christian Univ	OK	29,260	C
Okla Wesleyan Univ	OK	34,434	C
Southern Nazarene Univ	OK	33,684	C
St. Andrews Univ	NC	44,634	LC
St. Bonaventure Univ	NY	45,596	C
The Univ of Montana Western	MT	9,426	LC
Trinity Christian College	IL	35,580	C
Univ of Iowa	IA	19,415	HC
Univ of Minn/Morris	MN	21,222	VC
Vanguard Univ of Southern Calif	CA	42,400	VC

STAGE MANAGEMENT

School	ST	$IS	SR
Boston Univ	MA	67,352	MC
Iowa Wesleyan Univ	IA	41,000	C
Ohio Univ	OH	23,394	VC
Pace Univ	NY	60,136	C
Syracuse Univ	NY	62,313	HC
Univ of Conn	CT	27,394	

STATISTICS

School	ST	$IS	SR
Amherst College	MA	66,186	MC
Appalachian State Univ	NC	15,394	VC
Arizona State Univ at the West Campus	AZ	21,513	VC
Barnard College/Columbia Univ	NY	68,762	MC
Biola Univ	CA	48,686	C
Bowling Green State Univ	OH	19,975	C
Bradley Univ	IL	43,240	VC
Brigham Young Univ	UT	13,248	MC
Brown Univ	RI	64,566	MC
Bryant Univ	RI	57,204	VC
Calif Baptist Univ	CA	42,986	C
Calif Polytechnic State Univ	CA	22,547	MC
Cal State, East Bay	CA	20,748	C
Cal State, Fullerton	CA	21,902	C
Cal State, Long Beach	CA	18,850	C
Calvin College	MI	43,090	HC
Carnegie Mellon Univ	PA	67,980	MC
Case Western Reserve Univ	OH	62,284	MC
Central Mich Univ	MI	20,330	C
CUNY/Baruch College	NY	21,609	HC
CUNY/Hunter College	NY	31,098	VC
Colo State Univ	CO	23,033	C
Columbia Univ/ School of General Studies	NY	61,470	MC
Columbia Univ/City of New York	NY	62,958	MC
Cornell Univ	NY	67,591	MC
Eastern Kentucky Univ	KY	17,742	C
Eastern Mich Univ	MI	19,761	C
Elon Univ	NC	46,142	HC
Florida International Univ	FL	20,281	C
Florida State Univ	FL	16,771	HC
Fordham Univ	NY	68,431	MC
Georgia State Univ	GA	25,250	C
Grand Valley State Univ	MI	22,250	C+
Harvard College/Harvard Univ	MA	65,609	MC
Idaho State Univ	ID	13,619	LC
Indiana Univ Bloomington	IN	20,791	HC
Indiana Univ-Purdue Univ Fort Wayne	IN	18,675	C
Iowa State Univ	IA	18,176	C
Jackson State Univ	MS	15,879	LC
James Madison Univ	VA	19,084	VC
Kansas State Univ	KS	17,780	VC
Le Moyne College	NY	47,305	VC
Lehigh Univ	PA	63,860	MC
Loyola Univ Chicago	IL	57,158	VC
Luther College	IA	49,990	VC
Marquette Univ	WI	53,090	VC+
Miami Univ	OH	27,190	HC+
Mich State Univ	MI	24,542	VC
Mich Tech Univ	MI	25,551	VC+
Millersville Univ of Pennsylvania	PA	25,298	C
Missouri Univ of Science and Technology	MO	18,655	HC
Montana Tech of the Univ of Montana	MT	15,447	VC
Mount Holyoke College	MA	56,746	MC
New York Univ	NY	68,139	MC
N Car State Univ	NC	22,434	HC+
N Dak State Univ	ND	16,245	VC
Northern Kentucky Univ	KY	16,486	C
Northwest Missouri State Univ	MO	18,286	C
Northwestern Univ	IL	68,725	MC
Oakland Univ	MI	20,763	C
Ohio Northern Univ	OH	44,050	VC
Ohio Univ	OH	23,394	VC
Okla State Univ	OK	17,180	C+
Pennsylvania State Univ - Univ Park	PA	29,716	HC
Purdue Univ/West Lafayette	IN	20,032	MC
Rice Univ	TX	59,458	MC
Rochester Inst of Technology	NY	52,734	HC+
Roosevelt Univ	IL	41,890	VC
Rutgers Univ - New Brunswick	NJ	27,090	HC
St. Mary's College	IN	50,600	C
San Diego State Univ	CA	23,156	VC
San Francisco State Univ	CA	18,514	LC
San Jose State Univ	CA	22,630	C
Southern Illinois Univ Edwardsville	IL	20,188	C
Southern Methodist Univ	TX	69,008	MC
St. Cloud State Univ	MN	10,600	C
St. John Fisher College	NY	45,270	VC
St. Lawrence Univ	NY	66,646	HC+
SUNY/Oneonta	NY	20,794	C
SUNY/Univ at Buffalo	NY	23,122	C
The American Univ	DC	61,317	HC
The George Washington Univ	DC	68,474	HC+
The Univ of Akron	OH	22,566	C
The Univ of Arizona	AZ	24,086	C
The Univ of Tenn at Knoxville	TN	22,112	VC
The Univ of Texas at San Antonio	TX	21,060	C
Univ of Calif at Berkeley	CA	29,886	MC
Univ of Calif at Davis	CA	28,468	HC
Univ of Calif at Los Angeles	CA	27,438	HC+
Univ of Calif at Riverside	CA	32,912	C
Univ of Calif at Santa Barbara	CA	30,627	HC+
Univ of Central Florida	FL	16,379	VC
Univ of Chicago	IL	70,551	MC
Univ of Conn	CT	27,394	
Univ of Delaware	DE	32,214	VC
Univ of Denver	CO	61,129	VC+
Univ of Florida	FL	16,291	HC+
Univ of Georgia	GA	21,878	HC
Univ of Houston-Downtown	TX	7,241	LC
Univ of Idaho	ID	16,158	C
Univ of Illinois at Chicago	IL	24,664	VC
Univ of Illinois at Urbana-Champaign	IL	27,006	HC
Univ of Iowa	IA	19,415	HC
Univ of Louisiana at Lafayette	LA	14,516	C
Univ of Maryland/Baltimore County	MD	23,004	VC
Univ of Miami	FL	63,494	MC
Univ of Mich/Ann Arbor	MI	25,274	MC
Univ of Minn/Duluth	MN	20,292	C
Univ of Minn/Morris	MN	21,222	VC
Univ of Minn/Twin Cities	MN	24,269	MC
Univ of Missouri-Columbia	MO	20,463	VC
Univ of Nebr - Kearney	NE	17,014	LC
Univ of New Hampshire	NH	29,333	VC
Univ of New Mexico	NM	16,808	C
Univ of N Car at Greensboro	NC	15,998	C
Univ of N Car Wilmington	NC	16,784	VC
Univ of North Florida	FL	15,996	VC
Univ of Northern Colo	CO	19,658	C
Univ of Notre Dame	IN	68,801	MC
Univ of Pennsylvania	PA	63,526	MC
Univ of Pittsburgh	PA	30,030	MC
Univ of Rochester	NY	65,032	MC
Univ of S Car at Columbia	SC	21,726	VC
Univ of Southern Miss	MS	13,170	C
Univ of Texas at El Paso	TX	34,452	NC
Univ of Vermont	VT	29,792	HC
Univ of Washington	WA	23,091	MC
Univ of West Florida	FL	15,848	C
Univ of Wisc-La Crosse	WI	15,425	VC
Univ of Wisc-Madison	WI	21,647	MC
Univ of Wyoming	WY	15,537	C
Utah State Univ	UT	13,235	C
Valparaiso Univ	IN	50,160	VC
Villanova Univ	PA	64,922	MC
Virginia Polytechnic Inst and State Univ	VA	21,920	VC
Washington Univ in St. Louis	MO	67,539	MC
West Chester Univ of Pennsylvania	PA	19,171	VC
Western Mich Univ	MI	21,791	C
Williams College	MA	67,700	MC
Winona State Univ	MN	18,109	C
Wright State Univ	OH	16,983	C
Xavier Univ of Louisiana	LA	31,689	C
Yale Univ	CT	64,650	MC
Youngstown State Univ	OH	17,487	C

STRATEGIC COMMUNICATION

School	ST	$IS	SR
Arkansas State Univ	AR	16,190	C
Butler Univ	IN	52,890	VC+
Calvin College	MI	43,090	HC
Central Conn State Univ	CT	22,041	C
Chapman Univ	CA	65,504	HC
Concordia Univ St. Paul	MN	29,050	C
Elon Univ	NC	46,142	HC
Flagler College	FL	27,620	C
Neumann Univ	PA	40,678	LC
Northern Arizona Univ	AZ	21,003	C
Olivet Nazarene Univ	IL	41,840	VC
Texas Christian Univ	TX	57,120	HC
The American Univ	DC	61,317	HC
Univ of Denver	CO	61,129	VC+
Washington State Univ	WA	22,747	C

STRINGS

School	ST	$IS	SR
Bennington College	VT	66,280	MC
Central Washington Univ	WA	16,803	C
Eastern Mich Univ	MI	19,761	C
Florida State Univ	FL	16,771	HC
Hardin-Simmons Univ	TX	36,025	C
Indiana Univ-Purdue Univ Fort Wayne	IN	18,675	C
Manhattan School of Music	NY	57,200	SP
Mannes School of Music	NY	44,500	SP
Marshall Univ	WV	18,044	C
Missouri Western State Univ	MO	17,822	LC
New England Conservatory of Music	MA	63,170	SP
Northwestern Univ	IL	68,725	MC
Oberlin College	OH	68,942	MC
Roosevelt Univ	IL	41,890	VC
San Francisco Conservatory of Music	CA	57,310	SP
Seattle Univ	WA	54,957	VC
Syracuse Univ	NY	62,313	HC
Texas Christian Univ	TX	57,120	HC
Univ of Iowa	IA	19,415	HC
Univ of Kansas	KS	20,884	VC
Univ of Northwestern - St. Paul	MN	39,530	C
Weber State Univ	UT	14,112	C
Wright State Univ	OH	16,983	C
Youngstown State Univ	OH	17,487	C

STUDIO ART

School	ST	$IS	SR
Adrian College	MI	45,550	C
Agnes Scott College	GA	51,930	VC+
Albertus Magnus College	CT	44,016	LC
Allegheny College	PA	57,620	VC
Angelo State Univ	TX	15,882	LC
Anna Maria College	MA	51,020	C

ST = STATE $IS = IN-STATE COSTS SR = SELECTOR RATING

School	ST	$IS	SR
Appalachian State Univ	NC	15,394	VC
Augsburg Univ	MN	45,129	C
Baker Univ	KS	37,190	C
Baldwin Wallace Univ	OH	42,464	VC
Bard College	NY	65,924	HC
Barton College	NC	39,854	C
Baylor Univ	TX	56,803	HC
Bellarmine Univ	KY	52,532	C
Belmont Univ	TN	44,500	VC+
Beloit College	WI	55,206	HC
Benedict College	SC	28,630	NC
Benedictine Univ	IL	38,300	C
Bennington College	VT	66,280	MC
Berry College	GA	47,466	VC
Bethany College	WV	38,774	LC
Bethel College	IN	36,830	C
Biola Univ	CA	48,686	C
Birmingham-Southern College	AL	44,478	C+
Bloomsburg Univ of Pennsylvania	PA	19,930	C
Boston College	MA	68,043	MC
Bowdoin College	ME	65,980	MC
Brandeis Univ	MA	68,443	MC
Brenau Univ - Women's College	GA	37,876	LC
Brigham Young Univ	UT	13,248	MC
Caldwell Univ	NJ	42,165	LC
Campbell Univ	NC	37,570	VC
Carleton College	MN	66,414	MC
Carthage College	WI	48,835	C
Cazenovia College	NY	47,866	C
Cedarville Univ	OH	36,244	VC
Centenary College of Louisiana	LA	49,050	C+
Central Washington Univ	WA	16,803	C
Christian Brothers Univ	TN	31,670	VC
CUNY/Queens College	NY	21,507	C
CUNY/York College	NY	6,747	LC
Clark Univ	MA	53,260	HC+
Clarke Univ	IA	42,950	C
Coastal Carolina Univ	SC	20,340	C
Colby College	ME	64,060	MC
Colby-Sawyer College	NH	50,790	C
Colgate Univ	NY	67,500	MC
College of Charleston	SC	24,046	VC
College of the Holy Cross	MA	64,320	MC
College of the Ozarks	MO	7,530	VC
Colo College	CO	64,894	MC
Columbia College	SC	36,550	C
Concordia Univ Nebr	NE	41,900	VC
Concordia Univ St. Paul	MN	29,050	C
Cornell College	IA	49,900	VC
Creighton Univ	NE	49,452	VC
Dartmouth College	NH	68,109	MC
Denison Univ	OH	62,770	HC+
DePauw Univ	IN	58,688	VC
Drake Univ	IA	49,220	HC
East Carolina Univ	NC	16,539	C
East Central Univ	OK	13,330	C
Eastern Washington Univ	WA	17,896	LC
Elizabethtown College	PA	56,340	VC
Emmanuel College	MA	53,472	C+
Endicott College	MA	47,054	C+
Fairfield Univ	CT	61,445	HC
Florida Southern College	FL	45,978	VC
Florida State Univ	FL	16,771	HC
Fordham Univ	NY	68,431	MC
Framingham State Univ	MA	21,740	C
Franklin and Marshall College	PA	67,960	MC
Franklin College	IN	40,550	C
Furman Univ	SC	61,098	VC+
Georgia State Univ	GA	25,250	C
Gettysburg College	PA	65,210	MC
Graceland Univ	IA	35,290	C
Grinnell College	IA	63,114	MC
Hamilton College	NY	64,250	MC
Hampden-Sydney College	VA	57,806	VC
Henderson State Univ	AR	15,516	C
High Point Univ	NC	47,355	VC
Hobart and William Smith Colleges	NY	67,050	HC+
Hollins Univ	VA	49,635	VC
Houghton College	NY	40,558	VC
Huntington Univ	IN	33,996	C
Indiana State Univ	IN	23,223	LC
Indiana Univ Bloomington	IN	20,791	HC
Indiana Univ of Pennsylvania	PA	24,474	C
Indiana Wesleyan Univ	IN	33,674	C
Ithaca College	NY	58,158	VC+
Jacksonville Univ	FL	49,210	C
Johnson State College	VT	22,672	C
Juniata College	PA	58,118	VC
Kansas Wesleyan Univ	KS	37,930	C
Kean Univ	NJ	25,620	C
Keene State College	NH	24,604	C
Kentucky State Univ	KY	14,484	LC
Knox College	IL	54,654	VC+
Kutztown Univ of Pennsylvania	PA	19,477	C
Lawrence Univ	WI	56,133	HC+
Lewis & Clark College	OR	60,984	MC
Limestone College	SC	32,100	C
Lindenwood Univ	MO	25,760	C
Linfield College	OR	53,992	C
Lipscomb Univ	TN	42,984	VC
LIU Brooklyn	NY	50,698	C
Louisiana College	LA	21,274	C
Louisiana State Univ and A&M College	LA	18,677	VC
Loyola Marymount Univ	CA	60,202	VC+
Loyola Univ Chicago	IL	57,158	VC
Loyola Univ New Orleans	LA	52,456	VC
Lycoming College	PA	50,895	C
Manhattanville College	NY	52,430	C
Marian Univ	IN	43,206	C
Marietta College	OH	46,190	C
Marist College	NY	49,860	VC
Mary Baldwin Univ	VA	40,495	C
Maryville Univ of St. Louis	MO	38,558	VC
Marywood Univ	PA	47,840	C
Mass College of Art and Design	MA	24,800	SP
Memphis College of Art	TN	50,880	SP
Mercyhurst Univ	PA	47,420	C
Messiah College	PA	44,380	VC
Mich State Univ	MI	24,542	VC
Middle Tenn State Univ	TN	8,650	C
Middlebury College	VT	67,464	MC
Millikin Univ	IL	44,148	C
Mills College	CA	43,705	C
Millsaps College	MS	50,080	C+
Minneapolis College of Art and Design	MN	44,218	SP
Missouri Southern State Univ	MO	13,071	C
Missouri Western State Univ	MO	17,822	LC
Mount Holyoke College	MA	56,746	MC
Murray State Univ	KY	17,726	C+
Nazareth College	NY	46,784	C
Nebr Wesleyan Univ	NE	42,026	C+
New York Univ	NY	68,139	MC
North Central College	IL	48,712	C+
North Greenville Univ	SC	25,930	C
Northeastern Univ	MA	65,352	MC
Northern Arizona Univ	AZ	21,003	C
Northern Illinois Univ	IL	20,176	C
Northern Kentucky Univ	KY	16,486	C
Notre Dame College	OH	39,150	VC
Notre Dame of Maryland Univ	MD	47,570	VC
Oakland Univ	MI	20,763	C
Oberlin College	OH	68,942	MC
Ohio State Univ at Columbus	OH	22,843	MC
Ohio Univ	OH	23,394	VC
Okla City Univ	OK	40,476	C
Old Dominion Univ	VA	21,618	C
Oral Roberts Univ	OK	34,316	C
Pacific Lutheran Univ	WA	49,960	C
Parsons The New School for Design	NY	56,610	SP
Pomona College	CA	64,957	MC
Principia College	IL	40,350	C
Providence College	RI	62,870	HC
Randolph-Macon College	VA	51,480	VC
Rhode Island College	RI	19,000	LC
Ripon College	WI	49,991	VC
Rivier Univ	NH	41,600	VC
Roberts Wesleyan College	NY	41,116	C
Rochester Inst of Technology	NY	52,734	HC+
Rollins College	FL	58,670	HC
St. Louis Univ	MO	49,866	HC
St. Mary's Univ of Minn	MN	42,440	C
St. Vincent College	PA	46,229	C
Salem College	NC	40,206	C
Salve Regina Univ	RI	53,046	VC
San Diego State Univ	CA	23,156	VC
Scripps College	CA	69,260	HC
Seton Hill Univ	PA	46,972	VC
Shawnee State Univ	OH	16,998	C
Siena Heights Univ	MI	36,322	C
Silver Lake College of the Holy Family	WI	36,290	LC
Simpson College	IA	45,626	VC
Smith College	MA	66,774	MC
Southern Conn State Univ	CT	21,924	LC
Southern Illinois Univ Edwardsville	IL	20,188	C
Southern Methodist Univ	TX	69,008	MC
Southern Oregon Univ	OR	19,117	C
Spalding Univ	KY	31,938	C
Spring Hill College	AL	48,488	C
St. Joseph's College, New York/Long Island Campus	NY	25,124	C
St. Lawrence Univ	NY	66,646	HC+
St. Olaf College	MN	56,430	HC
Stanford Univ	CA	62,541	MC
SUNY Albany	NY	22,165	C
SUNY at Binghamton	NY	24,100	MC
SUNY at New Paltz	NY	20,840	C
SUNY/Potsdam	NY	21,051	VC
SUNY/Univ at Buffalo	NY	23,122	C
Stetson Univ	FL	57,174	VC+
Stony Brook Univ/The SUNY	NY	22,703	MC
Susquehanna Univ	PA	57,560	VC
Tabor College	KS	35,870	C
Taylor Univ	IN	42,130	VC
Texas State Univ	TX	18,721	C
The American Univ	DC	61,317	HC
The Catholic Univ of America	DC	58,376	VC
The College at Brockport - SUNY	NY	21,058	C
The College of St. Rose	NY	44,010	C
The Univ of Akron	OH	22,566	C
The Univ of Arizona	AZ	24,086	C
The Univ of Tenn at Knoxville	TN	22,112	VC
The Univ of Texas at Austin	TX	20,206	MC
Transylvania Univ	KY	47,450	HC+
Trinity Christian College	IL	35,580	C
Trinity College	CT	69,020	HC
Troy Univ	AL	16,171	C
Truman State Univ	MO	16,286	MC
Tulane Univ	LA	67,496	MC
Union College	NE	23,270	C
Union College	NY	64,320	MC
Univ of Arkansas at Fayetteville	AR	19,766	VC
Univ of Calif at Davis	CA	28,468	HC
Univ of Calif at Irvine	CA	33,857	VC
Univ of Calif San Diego	CA	30,450	MC
Univ of Central Missouri	MO	18,982	C
Univ of Central Okla	OK	15,150	C
Univ of Colo Boulder	CO	26,048	HC
Univ of Findlay	OH	43,040	C
Univ of Georgia	GA	21,878	HC
Univ of Houston	TX	21,871	VC
Univ of Idaho	ID	16,158	C
Univ of Illinois at Chicago	IL	24,664	VC
Univ of Indianapolis	IN	36,480	VC
Univ of Maine	ME	21,038	VC
Univ of Mary Washington	VA	23,039	C+
Univ of Maryland/College Park	MD	21,938	HC
Univ of Mass Amherst	MA	27,669	HC
Univ of Miami	FL	63,494	MC
Univ of Minn/Duluth	MN	20,292	C
Univ of Minn/Morris	MN	21,222	VC
Univ of Missouri-Kansas City	MO	19,563	VC
Univ of Missouri-St. Louis	MO	19,810	VC
Univ of Montevallo	AL	20,012	C
Univ of Nebr - Lincoln	NE	18,589	VC
Univ of New Hampshire	NH	29,333	VC
Univ of New Mexico	NM	16,808	C
Univ of New Orleans	LA	12,840	C
Univ of N Car at Chapel Hill	NC	20,561	MC
Univ of N Car at Greensboro	NC	15,998	C
Univ of N Car Wilmington	NC	16,784	VC
Univ of North Texas	TX	20,082	C
Univ of Northern Iowa	IA	17,480	C
Univ of Northwestern - St. Paul	MN	39,530	C
Univ of Notre Dame	IN	68,801	MC
Univ of Okla	OK	19,651	HC
Univ of Pittsburgh	PA	30,030	MC
Univ of Redlands	CA	61,934	VC
Univ of Richmond	VA	62,730	MC
Univ of Rochester	NY	65,032	MC
Univ of St. Francis	IN	38,520	C
Univ of S Car at Columbia	SC	21,726	VC
Univ of S Car Upstate	SC	19,272	LC
Univ of Southern Calif	CA	66,631	MC
Univ of St. Thomas - Houston	TX	41,510	VC
Univ of Texas at Arlington	TX	18,876	C
Univ of the Pacific	CA	57,446	VC
Univ of Tulsa	OK	52,625	HC
Univ of Washington	WA	23,091	MC
Univ of West Florida	FL	15,848	C
Univ of Wisc-Stout	WI	19,667	C
Univ of Wisc-Superior	WI	14,838	C
Vassar College	NY	68,110	MC
Viterbo Univ	WI	34,660	C
Wake Forest Univ	NC	69,354	MC
Washington & Jefferson College	PA	58,694	VC
Washington and Lee Univ	VA	59,647	MC
Washington Univ in St. Louis	MO	67,539	MC
Webster Univ	MO	37,490	C
Wellesley College	MA	66,984	MC
Wesleyan College	GA	31,940	C+
Wesleyan Univ	CT	66,940	MC
West Chester Univ of Pennsylvania	PA	19,171	VC
West Texas A&M Univ	TX	13,478	C
Wheaton College	MA	63,818	VC
Wichita State Univ	KS	17,773	C
Willamette Univ	OR	62,514	VC+
William Paterson Univ of New Jersey	NJ	24,022	C
William Woods Univ	MO	32,040	C
Wilson College	PA	35,620	LC
Wofford College	SC	49,885	VC
Wright State Univ	OH	16,983	C
Youngstown State Univ	OH	17,487	C

STUDIO ART CERAMICS

School	ST	$IS	SR
Bard College at Simon's Rock	MA	65,795	MC
College of the Ozarks	MO	7,530	VC
Missouri Western State Univ	MO	17,822	LC
Rochester Inst of Technology	NY	52,734	HC+
Texas Christian Univ	TX	57,120	HC
Univ of N Car at Greensboro	NC	15,998	C

STUDIO ART COMPUTER ART

School	ST	$IS	SR
College of the Ozarks	MO	7,530	VC
Missouri Western State Univ	MO	17,822	LC
Rochester Inst of Technology	NY	52,734	HC+

STUDIO ART FIBERS

School	ST	$IS	SR
College of the Ozarks	MO	7,530	VC

STUDIO ART GRAPHIC DESIGN

School	ST	$IS	SR
Bradley Univ	IL	43,240	VC
Campbell Univ	NC	37,570	VC
College of the Ozarks	MO	7,530	VC
Franklin College	IN	40,550	C
Georgian Court Univ	NJ	43,068	LC
Keene State College	NH	24,604	C
Missouri Western State Univ	MO	17,822	LC
Rochester Inst of Technology	NY	52,734	HC+
Silver Lake College of the Holy Family	WI	36,290	LC
SUNY Albany	NY	22,165	C
Wellesley College	MA	66,984	MC

STUDIO ART PAINTING

School	ST	$IS	SR
Bard College at Simon's Rock	MA	65,795	MC
College of the Ozarks	MO	7,530	VC
Franklin College	IN	40,550	C
Kutztown Univ of Pennsylvania	PA	19,477	C
Missouri Southern State Univ	MO	13,071	C
Missouri Western State Univ	MO	17,822	LC
Oberlin College	OH	68,942	MC
Rochester Inst of Technology	NY	52,734	HC+
SUNY Albany	NY	22,165	C
Texas Christian Univ	TX	57,120	HC
Univ of N Car at Greensboro	NC	15,998	C
Wellesley College	MA	66,984	MC

SUPPLY CHAIN MANAGEMENT

School	ST	$IS	SR
Arizona State Univ at the Tempe Campus	AZ	23,001	VC
Arkansas State Univ	AR	16,190	C
Ashford Univ	CA	10,480	C
Bloomfield College	NJ	40,100	LC
Bloomsburg Univ of Pennsylvania	PA	19,930	C
Boise State Univ	ID	17,368	C
Bradley Univ	IL	43,240	VC
Bryant Univ	RI	57,204	VC
Cal State, Fullerton	CA	21,902	C
Clarkson Univ	NY	60,392	VC
College of Charleston	SC	24,046	VC
Duquesne Univ	PA	48,508	VC
Eastern Mich Univ	MI	19,761	C
Elmhurst College	IL	46,514	C
Florida International Univ	FL	20,281	C
Fontbonne Univ	MO	34,606	C
Gannon Univ	PA	42,922	C
Hofstra Univ	NY	58,210	C+
Howard Univ	DC	37,616	C+
Lehigh Univ	PA	63,860	MC
Lipscomb Univ	TN	42,984	VC
Marquette Univ	WI	53,090	VC+
Miami Univ	OH	27,190	HC+
Mich State Univ	MI	24,542	VC
Missouri Western State Univ	MO	17,822	LC
Murray State Univ	KY	17,726	C+
Old Dominion Univ	VA	21,618	C
Pennsylvania State Univ - Univ Park	PA	29,716	HC
Rutgers Univ - New Brunswick	NJ	27,090	HC
Rutgers Univ - New Brunswick	NJ	27,090	HC
Rutgers Univ - Newark	NJ	27,351	C
Shippensburg Univ of Pennsylvania	PA	24,096	C
Southeastern Louisiana Univ	LA	16,237	C
SUNY at Binghamton	NY	24,100	MC
SUNY/Plattsburgh	NY	19,314	C
Syracuse Univ	NY	62,313	HC
Texas A&M Univ at College Station	TX	20,771	VC+
Texas Christian Univ	TX	57,120	HC
Texas Tech Univ	TX	20,156	C+
Tuskegee Univ	AL	28,164	C
Univ of Houston	TX	21,871	VC
Univ of Houston-Downtown	TX	7,241	LC
Univ of Kansas	KS	20,884	VC
Univ of Maryland/College Park	MD	21,938	HC
Univ of Mich/Dearborn	MI	12,472	VC
Univ of Minn/Twin Cities	MN	24,269	MC
Univ of Nebr - Lincoln	NE	18,589	VC
Univ of N Car at Charlotte	NC	17,803	VC
Univ of N Car at Greensboro	NC	15,998	C
Univ of Northern Iowa	IA	17,480	C
Univ of Okla	OK	19,651	HC
Univ of Pittsburgh	PA	30,030	MC
Univ of Rhode Island	RI	26,066	VC
Univ of Texas at Dallas	TX	23,640	HC
Univ of Wisc-Stout	WI	19,667	C
Wayne State Univ	MI	23,085	C
Weber State Univ	UT	14,112	C
Western Illinois Univ	IL	20,897	C
Western Mich Univ	MI	21,791	C
Wright State Univ	OH	16,983	C
Youngstown State Univ	OH	17,487	C

SURVEY AND MAPPING TECHNOLOGY

School	ST	$IS	SR
Alfred State College	NY	19,895	C
East Tenn State Univ	TN	18,141	C

ST = STATE **$IS** = IN-STATE COSTS **SR** = SELECTOR RATING

School	ST	$IS	SR
Glenville State College	WV	17,386	LC
Kennesaw State Univ	GA	18,899	VC
Metropolitan State Univ of Denver	CO	6,928	LC
Purdue Univ Northwest	IN	15,178	C
SUNY/The College of Environmental Science and Forestry	NY	23,728	VC
The Univ of Akron	OH	22,566	C
Univ of Alaska Anchorage	AK	17,914	C
Univ of Maine at Machias	ME	22,960	C

SURVEYING ENGINEERING

School	ST	$IS	SR
Cal State, Fresno	CA	16,902	LC
Cal State, Fullerton	CA	21,902	C
Ferris State Univ	MI	21,458	C
Metropolitan State Univ of Denver	CO	6,928	LC
Mich Tech Univ	MI	25,551	VC+
New Mexico State Univ	NM	14,050	LC
Oregon Inst of Technology	OR	19,227	C
Purdue Univ/West Lafayette	IN	20,032	MC
Universidad Metropolitana	PR	17,828	
Universidad Politecnica de PR, Hato Rey campus	PR	23,514	
Univ of Arkansas at Little Rock	AR	18,211	LC
Univ of Maine	ME	21,038	VC
Univ of PR, at Mayaguez	PR	13,995	

SUSTAINABILITY

School	ST	$IS	SR
Bryant Univ	RI	57,204	VC
Davis & Elkins College	WV	38,242	LC
Hofstra Univ	NY	58,210	C+
Univ of Conn	CT	27,394	
Univ of New Hampshire	NH	29,333	VC
Univ of N Car at Greensboro	NC	15,998	C

SUSTAINABLE ENERGY

School	ST	$IS	SR
Creighton Univ	NE	49,452	VC

SUSTAINABLE ENERGY SCIENCE

School	ST	$IS	SR
Creighton Univ	NE	49,452	VC
Furman Univ	SC	61,098	VC+
Montclair State Univ	NJ	26,912	C
Shippensburg Univ of Pennsylvania	PA	24,096	C

SUSTAINABLE MANAGEMENT

School	ST	$IS	SR
Ashford Univ	CA	10,480	C
Aurora Univ	IL	34,990	C
Baldwin Wallace Univ	OH	42,464	VC
Bentley Univ	MA	63,720	MC
Catawba College	NC	39,820	LC
Chatham Univ	PA	47,883	VC
College of St. Scholastica	MN	45,734	C+
Goddard College	VT	17,040	VC
Kean Univ	NJ	25,620	C
Lipscomb Univ	TN	42,984	VC
Marylhurst Univ	OR	16,818	NC
Messiah College	PA	44,380	VC
Miami Univ	OH	27,190	HC+
Northland College	WI	41,103	C+
St. Louis Univ	MO	49,866	HC
Taylor Univ	IN	42,130	VC
Univ of Maine at Machias	ME	22,960	C
Univ of Minn/Twin Cities	MN	24,269	MC
Univ of N Car at Greensboro	NC	15,998	C
Univ of Rhode Island	RI	26,066	VC
Univ of Wisc-Green Bay	WI	15,184	C
Univ of Wisc-Stout	WI	19,667	C
Univ of Wisc-Superior	WI	14,838	C
Viterbo Univ	WI	34,660	C
Xavier Univ	OH	49,380	VC

SYSTEMS ANALYSIS

School	ST	$IS	SR
Baldwin Wallace Univ	OH	42,464	VC
Johnson & Wales Univ/ Providence Campus	RI	44,768	C
Rochester Inst of Technology	NY	52,734	HC+
The George Washington Univ	DC	68,474	HC+

SYSTEMS ENGINEERING

School	ST	$IS	SR
Azusa Pacific Univ	CA	43,972	C
Calif Baptist Univ	CA	42,986	C
Calif Inst of Technology	CA	64,704	MC
Cal State, Fullerton	CA	21,902	C
Case Western Reserve Univ	OH	62,284	MC
Embry-Riddle Aeronautical Univ - Daytona Beach	FL	45,822	VC
Embry-Riddle Aeronautical Univ - Worldwide	FL	17,720	C
George Mason Univ	VA	19,884	C
Indiana Univ Bloomington	IN	20,791	HC
Johns Hopkins Univ	MD	68,080	MC
Kennesaw State Univ	GA	18,899	VC
Missouri Univ of Science and Technology	MO	18,655	HC
Point Park Univ	PA	41,270	C
Southern Nazarene Univ	OK	33,684	C
Stanford Univ	CA	62,541	MC
SUNY at Binghamton	NY	24,100	MC
Stevens Inst of Technology	NJ	64,954	MC
Taylor Univ	IN	42,130	VC
The Univ of Arizona	AZ	24,086	C
United States Military Academy at West Point	NY		HC+
United States Naval Academy	MD		HC
Univ of New Haven	CT	53,680	C
Univ of N Car at Charlotte	NC	17,803	VC
Univ of Southern Calif	CA	66,631	MC
Univ of Virginia	VA	27,367	MC
Washington Univ in St. Louis	MO	67,539	MC
West Virginia Univ	WV	18,952	VC
Wright State Univ	OH	16,983	C

SYSTEMS SCIENCE

School	ST	$IS	SR
Case Western Reserve Univ	OH	62,284	MC
Johnson & Wales Univ/ Providence Campus	RI	44,768	C
Stanford Univ	CA	62,541	MC
United States Military Academy at West Point	NY		HC+
Washington Univ in St. Louis	MO	67,539	MC

TEACHING ENGLISH AS A SECOND/FOREIGN LANGUAGE (TESOL/TEFOL)

School	ST	$IS	SR
Andrews Univ	MI	41,732	C
Aquinas College - Mich	MI	38,876	VC
Bethel Univ	MN	46,550	C+
Brigham Young Univ/Hawaii	HI	11,710	C
Cal State, Fullerton	CA	21,902	C
Campbellsville Univ	KY	33,400	C
Canisius College	NY	49,672	C
Caribbean Univ	PR	12,227	
CUNY/Queens College	NY	21,507	C
Elms College	MA	49,602	VC
Goshen College	IN	44,350	C
Hawaii Pacific Univ	HI	33,420	C
Houghton College	NY	40,558	VC
Houston Baptist Univ	TX	36,450	C
Howard Payne Univ	TX	35,994	C
Huntington Univ	IN	33,996	C
Inter-American Univ of PR-Arecibo Campus	PR	18,245	
Inter-American Univ of PR-San Germán	PR	20,042	
Kent State Univ	OH	20,928	C
Le Moyne College	NY	47,305	VC
Mercy College	NY	32,614	C
Missouri Southern State Univ	MO	13,071	C
Murray State Univ	KY	17,726	C+
Niagara Univ	NY	41,010	C
Northeastern Illinois Univ	IL	12,529	LC
Nyack College	NY	34,450	LC
Ohio State Univ at Columbus	OH	22,843	MC
Okla Christian Univ	OK	29,260	C
Olivet Nazarene Univ	IL	41,840	VC
Pontifical Catholic Univ of PR	PR	10,534	
Seattle Pacific Univ	WA	47,439	C+
Simmons College	MA	54,400	HC
SUNY at Oswego	NY	22,219	VC
Taylor Univ	IN	42,130	VC
Texas Wesleyan Univ	TX	37,338	C
The Univ of Arizona	AZ	24,086	C
The Univ of Utah	UT	18,751	VC
Union Univ	TN	41,160	VC
Univ of Idaho	ID	16,158	C
Univ of Louisville	KY	19,692	C
Univ of Nebr - Kearney	NE	17,014	LC
Univ of Northern Iowa	IA	17,480	C
Univ of PR, at Mayaguez	PR	13,995	
Weber State Univ	UT	14,112	C
Western Carolina Univ	NC	13,965	C
Winona State Univ	MN	18,109	C

TECHNICAL & APPLIED STUDIES

School	ST	$IS	SR
Bloomsburg Univ of Pennsylvania	PA	19,930	C
Ohio Univ	OH	23,394	VC

TECHNICAL AND BUSINESS WRITING

School	ST	$IS	SR
Carlow Univ	PA	39,696	LC
Cedarville Univ	OH	36,244	VC
Eastern Mich Univ	MI	19,761	C
Illinois Inst of Technology	IL	56,826	HC+
Indiana Univ-Purdue Univ Fort Wayne	IN	18,675	C
Lawrence Tech Univ	MI	41,630	VC
Madonna Univ	MI	30,450	LC
Metropolitan State Univ	MN	7,859	C
Mich Tech Univ	MI	25,551	VC+
Missouri Univ of Science and Technology	MO	18,655	HC
Mount Mary Univ	WI	34,650	LC
New Jersey Inst of Technology	NJ	30,198	HC
New Mexico Inst of Mining and Technology	NM	15,385	HC+
New York City College of Technology	NY	7,185	LC
New York Univ	NY	68,139	MC
Saginaw Valley State Univ	MI	19,284	C
Taylor Univ	IN	42,130	VC
Tenn Tech Univ	TN	17,929	C
The Univ of Montana Western	MT	9,426	LC
Univ of Arkansas at Little Rock	AR	18,211	LC
Univ of Findlay	OH	43,040	C
Univ of Hartford	CT	49,776	C
Univ of Houston-Downtown	TX	7,241	LC
Univ of Okla	OK	19,651	HC
Univ of Washington	WA	23,091	MC
Valparaiso Univ	IN	50,160	VC
Weber State Univ	UT	14,112	C
Winthrop Univ	SC	23,960	C
Youngstown State Univ	OH	17,487	C

TECHNICAL COMMUNICATION

School	ST	$IS	SR
Arizona State Univ at the Polytechnic Campus	AZ	22,394	VC
Bowling Green State Univ	OH	19,975	C
Carnegie Mellon Univ	PA	67,980	MC
Ferris State Univ	MI	21,458	C
Indiana Univ-Purdue Univ Indianapolis	IN	18,952	C
Kennesaw State Univ	GA	18,899	VC
King Univ	TN	36,976	C
Mercer Univ	GA	45,348	VC
Minn State Univ, Mankato	MN	17,190	C
Missouri Western State Univ	MO	17,822	LC
Texas Tech Univ	TX	20,156	C+
Univ of Minn/Twin Cities	MN	24,269	MC

TECHNICAL EDUCATION

School	ST	$IS	SR
Bowling Green State Univ	OH	19,975	C
Brigham Young Univ	UT	13,248	MC
Central Conn State Univ	CT	22,041	C
Eastern Illinois Univ	IL	21,414	C
Eastern Kentucky Univ	KY	17,742	C
Eastern Mich Univ	MI	19,761	C
Eastern New Mexico Univ	NM	12,874	LC
Elizabeth City State Univ	NC	14,745	C
Ferris State Univ	MI	21,458	C
Fitchburg State Univ	MA	21,819	LC
Fort Hays State Univ	KS	12,677	C
Illinois State Univ	IL	23,418	VC
Millersville Univ of Pennsylvania	PA	25,298	C
Miss State Univ	MS	12,028	C+
Montana State Univ	MT	15,500	C+
Murray State Univ	KY	17,726	C+
New York City College of Technology	NY	7,185	LC
Norfolk State Univ	VA	18,902	LC
N Car State Univ	NC	22,434	HC+
Northern Arizona Univ	AZ	21,003	C
Ohio State Univ at Columbus	OH	22,843	MC
Pittsburg State Univ	KS	13,880	C
Purdue Univ/West Lafayette	IN	20,032	MC
Rhode Island College	RI	19,000	LC
Rochester College	MI	28,574	LC
S Dak State Univ	SD	15,874	C
SUNY at Oswego	NY	22,219	VC
Temple Univ	PA	24,392	C+
Texas State Univ	TX	18,721	C
The College of New Jersey	NJ	28,675	VC+
The Univ of Akron	OH	22,566	C
Thomas Edison State Univ	NJ	6,350	NC
Tuskegee Univ	AL	28,164	C
Univ of Arkansas at Fayetteville	AR	19,766	VC
Univ of Central Florida	FL	16,379	VC
Univ of Idaho	ID	16,158	C
Univ of New Mexico	NM	16,808	C
Univ of Northern Iowa	IA	17,480	C
Univ of Southern Maine	ME	18,320	C
Univ of Wisc-Platteville	WI	14,148	C
Univ of Wisc-Stout	WI	19,667	C
Univ of Wyoming	WY	15,537	C
Valley City State Univ	ND	13,267	C
Western Kentucky Univ	KY	16,850	C
Western Washington Univ	WA	18,904	VC

TECHNICAL OPERATIONS MANAGEMENT

School	ST	$IS	SR
Ohio Univ	OH	23,394	VC

TECHNOLOGICAL MANAGEMENT

School	ST	$IS	SR
Alfred State College	NY	19,895	C
Arizona State Univ at the Polytechnic Campus	AZ	22,394	VC
Arkansas State Univ	AR	16,190	C
Clayton State Univ	GA	19,735	LC
Colo Technical Univ	CO	21,455	NC
Davenport Univ	MI	25,896	LC
Excelsior College	NY	38,800	SP
Franklin Univ	OH	11,616	NC
Golden Gate Univ	CA	19,510	C
Johnson & Wales Univ/ Providence Campus	RI	44,768	C
Lawrence Tech Univ	MI	41,630	VC
New Jersey Inst of Technology	NJ	30,198	HC
Northern Illinois Univ	IL	20,176	C
Ohio Northern Univ	OH	44,050	VC
Okla Panhandle State Univ	OK	6,152	C
Pennsylvania College of Technology	PA	27,693	NC
Pittsburg State Univ	KS	13,880	C
Roger Williams Univ	RI	48,074	VC
Southeast Missouri State Univ	MO	16,148	C
Southern Illinois Univ Carbondale	IL	24,554	C
Southern New Hampshire Univ	NH	44,256	C
Southern Univ at New Orleans	LA	8,014	LC
SUNY /College of Agriculture and Tech at Cobleskill	NY	20,527	LC
SUNY at Oswego	NY	22,219	VC
Stony Brook Univ/The SUNY	NY	22,703	MC
Texas A&M Univ at College Station	TX	20,771	VC+
Texas State Univ	TX	18,721	C
Troy Univ	AL	16,171	C
Univ of Alaska Anchorage	AK	17,914	C
Univ of Findlay	OH	43,040	C
Univ of Idaho	ID	16,158	C
Univ of North Georgia	GA	17,316	C
Washburn Univ	KS	15,827	C
Wayne State College	NE	25,746	NC
Wentworth Inst of Technology	MA	48,810	VC

TECHNOLOGY

School	ST	$IS	SR
Drury Univ	MO	37,555	VC
Univ of West Alabama	AL	16,284	LC

TECHNOLOGY & SCIENCE EDUCATION

School	ST	$IS	SR
Colo State Univ	CO	23,033	C
Excelsior College	NY	38,800	SP
Old Dominion Univ	VA	21,618	C
Univ of Wisc-Stout	WI	19,667	C
Viterbo Univ	WI	34,660	C

TECHNOLOGY AND PUBLIC AFFAIRS

School	ST	$IS	SR
Kent State Univ	OH	20,928	C
New Jersey Inst of Technology	NJ	30,198	HC
Pomona College	CA	64,957	MC
Washington Univ in St. Louis	MO	67,539	MC
Western Kentucky Univ	KY	16,850	C
Western Washington Univ	WA	18,904	VC

TELECOMMUNICATIONS

School	ST	$IS	SR
Alabama A&M Univ	AL	18,796	C
Baylor Univ	TX	56,803	HC
Bowling Green State Univ	OH	19,975	C
Cal State, Fullerton	CA	21,902	C
Cal State, Monterey Bay	CA	22,872	LC
Capitol Technology Univ	MD	46,280	SP
Colo Technical Univ	CO	21,455	NC
Concordia Univ Wisc	WI	35,910	C
Eastern Mich Univ	MI	19,761	C
Fort Hays State Univ	KS	12,677	C
Howard Univ	DC	37,616	C+
Illinois State Univ	IL	23,418	VC
Indiana Univ Bloomington	IN	20,791	HC
Indiana Univ-Purdue Univ Fort Wayne	IN	18,675	C
Ithaca College	NY	58,158	VC+
Kutztown Univ of Pennsylvania	PA	19,477	C
Lee Univ	TN	22,045	C
Mich State Univ	MI	24,542	VC
Morgan State Univ	MD	17,190	LC
New York City College of Technology	NY	7,185	LC
New York Inst of Technology	NY	49,980	VC
Ohio Univ	OH	23,394	VC
Okla Baptist Univ	OK	33,990	C
Pepperdine Univ	CA	66,862	VC+
Rochester Inst of Technology	NY	52,734	HC+
Roosevelt Univ	IL	41,890	VC
St. John's Univ	NY	57,160	C+
Temple Univ	PA	24,392	C+
Texas A&M Univ at College Station	TX	20,771	VC+
The Univ of Alabama	AL	24,320	C+
Univ of PR, at Arecibo	PR	12,652	
Univ of Florida	FL	16,291	HC+
Univ of Idaho	ID	16,158	C
Univ of Kentucky	KY	24,800	C+
Univ of Louisiana at Lafayette	LA	14,516	C
Univ of Nebr - Kearney	NE	17,014	LC
Univ of North Texas	TX	20,082	C
Univ of Northern Colo	CO	19,658	C
Univ of the Sacred Heart	PR	17,932	
Univ of Wisc-Stout	WI	19,667	C
Western Mich Univ	MI	21,791	C
Youngstown State Univ	OH	17,487	C

ST = STATE $IS = IN-STATE COSTS SR = SELECTOR RATING

TELECOMMUNICATIONS ENGINEERING TECHNOLOGY

School	ST	$IS	SR
Farmingdale State College	NY	20,968	C
Jackson State Univ	MS	15,879	LC
Kennesaw State Univ	GA	18,899	VC

TELECOMMUNICATIONS SYSTEMS MANAGEMENT

School	ST	$IS	SR
Cal State, Fullerton	CA	21,902	C
Kent State Univ	OH	20,928	C
Murray State Univ	KY	17,726	C+

TELEVISION & DIGITAL MEDIA PRODUCTION

School	ST	$IS	SR
Bloomfield College	NJ	40,100	LC
Bradley Univ	IL	43,240	VC
Drexel Univ	PA	65,927	HC
Ferris State Univ	MI	21,458	C
Hofstra Univ	NY	58,210	C+
Kent State Univ	OH	20,928	C
Missouri Western State Univ	MO	17,822	LC
Montclair State Univ	NJ	26,912	C
Neumann Univ	PA	40,678	LC
Robert Morris Univ	PA	40,600	C
Syracuse Univ	NY	62,313	HC
Texas Tech Univ	TX	20,156	C+
Wisc Lutheran College	WI	36,290	C

TEXTILE ENGINEERING

School	ST	$IS	SR
Auburn Univ	AL	24,300	VC+
Jefferson (Philadelphia Univ + Thomas Jefferson Univ)	PA	53,966	C
N Car State Univ	NC	22,434	HC+

TEXTILE MARKETING

School	ST	$IS	SR
Univ of Rhode Island	RI	26,066	VC
Wayne State Univ	MI	23,085	C

TEXTILE TECHNOLOGY

School	ST	$IS	SR
Clemson Univ	SC		HC
Fashion Inst of Technology/SUNY	NY	18,521	SP
Jefferson (Philadelphia Univ + Thomas Jefferson Univ)	PA	53,966	C
Mich State Univ	MI	24,542	VC
Univ of Wisc-Madison	WI	21,647	MC

TEXTILE, FASHION MERCHANDISING & DESIGN

School	ST	$IS	SR
East Central Univ	OK	13,330	C
Texas Christian Univ	TX	57,120	HC
Univ of Rhode Island	RI	26,066	VC
Western Mich Univ	MI	21,791	C

TEXTILES AND CLOTHING

School	ST	$IS	SR
Albright College	PA	57,326	C
Auburn Univ	AL	24,300	VC+
Calif College of the Arts	CA	52,758	SP
College for Creative Studies	MI	51,210	SP
Eastern Mich Univ	MI	19,761	C
Fashion Inst of Technology/SUNY	NY	18,521	SP
Framingham State Univ	MA	21,740	C
Howard Univ	DC	37,616	C+
Indiana State Univ	IN	23,223	LC
Iowa State Univ	IA	18,176	C
Kansas State Univ	KS	17,780	VC
Lipscomb Univ	TN	42,984	VC
Louisiana State Univ and A&M College	LA	18,677	VC
Middle Tenn State Univ	TN	8,650	C
Moore College of Art and Design	PA	55,118	SP
New Mexico State Univ	NM	14,050	LC
N Car State Univ	NC	22,434	HC+
N Dak State Univ	ND	16,245	VC
Northern Illinois Univ	IL	20,176	C
Northwest Missouri State Univ	MO	18,286	C
Rhode Island School of Design	RI	59,960	SP
The Univ of Texas at Austin	TX	20,206	MC
Univ of Calif at Davis	CA	28,468	HC
Univ of Central Missouri	MO	18,982	C
Univ of Idaho	ID	16,158	C
Univ of Illinois at Urbana-Champaign	IL	27,006	HC
Univ of Kentucky	KY	24,800	C+
Univ of Missouri-Columbia	MO	20,463	VC
Univ of Nebr - Lincoln	NE	18,589	VC
Univ of Wisc-Madison	WI	21,647	MC
Western Kentucky Univ	KY	16,850	C
Western Mich Univ	MI	21,791	C

THEATER DESIGN

School	ST	$IS	SR
Adelphi Univ	NY	49,792	C
Alabama A&M Univ	AL	18,796	C
Arcadia Univ	PA	55,990	C+
Baldwin Wallace Univ	OH	42,464	VC
Baylor Univ	TX	56,803	HC
Belmont Univ	TN	44,500	VC+
Bennington College	VT	66,280	MC
Biola Univ	CA	48,686	C
Boston Univ	MA	67,352	MC
Calif Inst of the Arts	CA	61,366	SP
Cal State, Fresno	CA	16,902	LC
Cal State, Fullerton	CA	21,902	C
Central Mich Univ	MI	20,330	C
College of the Ozarks	MO	7,530	VC
Colo State Univ	CO	23,033	C
Columbia College Chicago	IL	40,104	C
Cornish College of the Arts	WA	47,750	SP
Davis & Elkins College	WV	38,242	LC
DePaul Univ	IL	52,807	VC
DeSales Univ	PA	47,520	C
Elon Univ	NC	46,142	HC
Emerson College	MA	61,824	HC+
Eugene Lang College of Liberal Arts	NY	64,940	VC
Faulkner Univ	AL	26,410	C
Florida Southern College	FL	45,978	VC
Florida State Univ	FL	16,771	HC
Fordham Univ	NY	68,431	MC
Grand Canyon Univ	AZ	25,150	VC
Hofstra Univ	NY	58,210	C+
Huntington Univ	IN	33,996	C
Illinois Wesleyan Univ	IL	56,430	VC+
Ithaca College	NY	58,158	VC+
Johnson State College	VT	22,672	C
Kean Univ	NJ	25,620	C
Keene State College	NH	24,604	C
Lehigh Univ	PA	63,860	MC
Marshall Univ	WV	18,044	C
Mich Tech Univ	MI	25,551	VC+
Millikin Univ	IL	44,148	C
Missouri Western State Univ	MO	17,822	LC
Niagara Univ	NY	41,010	C
Oberlin College	OH	68,942	MC
Ohio State Univ at Columbus	OH	22,843	MC
Ohio Univ	OH	23,394	VC
Okla City Univ	OK	40,476	C
Pace Univ	NY	60,136	C
Palm Beach Atlantic Univ	FL	39,250	C
Pennsylvania State Univ - Univ Park	PA	29,716	HC
Piedmont College	GA	34,334	C
Roosevelt Univ	IL	41,890	VC
Seton Hill Univ	PA	46,972	VC
Shenandoah Univ	VA	42,100	C
Southern Illinois Univ Edwardsville	IL	20,188	C
SUNY at Binghamton	NY	24,100	MC
SUNY at Geneseo	NY	21,622	VC
SUNY at New Paltz	NY	20,840	C
SUNY at Purchase College	NY	21,832	C
SUNY/Fredonia	NY	20,818	C
Stephens College	MO	38,042	C
Syracuse Univ	NY	62,313	HC
Temple Univ	PA	24,392	C+
Texas Christian Univ	TX	57,120	HC
Texas Wesleyan Univ	TX	37,338	C
Towson Univ	MD	21,878	C
Tulane Univ	LA	67,496	MC
Univ of Central Missouri	MO	18,982	C
Univ of Central Okla	OK	15,150	C
Univ of Cincinnati	OH	22,118	VC
Univ of Conn	CT	27,394	
Univ of Florida	FL	16,291	HC+
Univ of Illinois at Chicago	IL	24,664	VC
Univ of Kansas	KS	20,884	VC
Univ of Maryland/Baltimore County	MD	23,004	VC
Univ of Miami	FL	63,494	MC
Univ of Mich/Ann Arbor	MI	25,274	MC
Univ of Nebr - Lincoln	NE	18,589	VC
Univ of New Mexico	NM	16,808	C
Univ of N Car School of the Arts	NC	25,587	SP
Univ of North Texas	TX	20,082	C
Univ of Southern Calif	CA	66,631	MC
Wagner College	NY	57,240	C+
Washburn Univ	KS	15,827	C
Webster Univ	MO	37,490	C
West Chester Univ of Pennsylvania	PA	19,171	VC
Western Mich Univ	MI	21,791	C
Western Washington Univ	WA	18,904	VC
Wright State Univ	OH	16,983	C

THEATER MANAGEMENT

School	ST	$IS	SR
Aquinas College - Mich	MI	38,876	VC
Baldwin Wallace Univ	OH	42,464	VC
Barry Univ	FL	38,730	LC
Benedictine College	KS	38,850	VC
Bethel Univ	TN	27,142	C
Biola Univ	CA	48,686	C
Boston Univ	MA	67,352	MC
Cal State, Fullerton	CA	21,902	C
Catawba College	NC	39,820	LC
CUNY/Brooklyn College	NY	7,163	C+
Colo Mesa Univ	CO	19,707	LC
DePaul Univ	IL	52,807	VC
DeSales Univ	PA	47,520	C
Emerson College	MA	61,824	HC+
Fitchburg State Univ	MA	21,819	LC
Fontbonne Univ	MO	34,606	C
Grand Canyon Univ	AZ	25,150	VC
Hofstra Univ	NY	58,210	C+
Illinois Wesleyan Univ	IL	56,430	VC+
Ithaca College	NY	58,158	VC+
Johnson State College	VT	22,672	C
Lycoming College	PA	50,895	C
Marywood Univ	PA	47,840	C
Messiah College	PA	44,380	VC
Millikin Univ	IL	44,148	C
New York Univ	NY	68,139	MC
Ohio Univ	OH	23,394	VC
Pace Univ	NY	60,136	C
Roosevelt Univ	IL	41,890	VC
St. Louis Univ	MO	49,866	HC
Seton Hill Univ	PA	46,972	VC
Temple Univ	PA	24,392	C+
The Univ of Akron	OH	22,566	C
Trinity College	CT	69,020	HC
Univ of Delaware	DE	32,214	VC
Univ of Evansville	IN	44,186	C+
Univ of Hartford	CT	49,776	C
Univ of Miami	FL	63,494	MC
Univ of North Texas	TX	20,082	C
Univ of Southern Calif	CA	66,631	MC
Univ of Texas at El Paso	TX	34,452	NC
West Chester Univ of Pennsylvania	PA	19,171	VC
Western Mich Univ	MI	21,791	C
Wright State Univ	OH	16,983	C

THEATRE ACTING

School	ST	$IS	SR
Asbury Univ	KY	36,450	C+
Baldwin Wallace Univ	OH	42,464	VC
Bates College	ME	64,500	HC
Bethany College	WV	38,774	LC
Biola Univ	CA	48,686	C
Cedar Crest College	PA	51,110	C
Colo State Univ	CO	23,033	C
Columbus State Univ	GA	14,336	LC
DeSales Univ	PA	47,520	C
Dordt College	IA	37,860	C+
Eastern Conn State Univ	CT	23,059	C
Elizabethtown College	PA	56,340	VC
Elon Univ	NC	46,142	HC
Eugene Lang College of Liberal Arts	NY	64,940	VC
Fairmont State Univ	WV	15,726	C
Florida Southern College	FL	45,978	VC
Fontbonne Univ	MO	34,606	C
Fordham Univ	NY	68,431	MC
Furman Univ	SC	61,098	VC+
Gonzaga Univ	WA	52,880	HC
Gordon College	MA	47,740	VC
Hiram College	OH	44,590	C
Illinois State Univ	IL	23,418	VC
Keene State College	NH	24,604	C
Lycoming College	PA	50,895	C
Merrimack College	MA	55,415	C
Millersville Univ of Pennsylvania	PA	25,298	C
Missouri Baptist Univ	MO	35,594	C
Missouri Western State Univ	MO	17,822	LC
Montclair State Univ	NJ	26,912	C
Nova Southeastern Univ	FL	38,534	C+
Oberlin College	OH	68,942	MC
Okla City Univ	OK	40,476	C
Pace Univ	NY	60,136	C
Southeast Missouri State Univ	MO	16,148	C
St. Ambrose Univ	IA	40,180	C
SUNY at Oswego	NY	22,219	VC
Texas A&M Univ at College Station	TX	20,771	VC+
The College at Brockport - SUNY	NY	21,058	C
Univ of Central Okla	OK	15,150	C
Univ of Detroit Mercy	MI	48,816	C
Univ of Georgia	GA	21,878	HC
Univ of Illinois at Chicago	IL	24,664	VC
Univ of Miami	FL	63,494	MC
Univ of Tampa	FL	38,928	VC
Univ of Wyoming	WY	15,537	C
Western Mich Univ	MI	21,791	C
Wright State Univ	OH	16,983	C
Youngstown State Univ	OH	17,487	C

THEATRE ARTS

School	ST	$IS	SR
Adams State Univ	CO	15,420	LC
Albion College	MI	55,260	C
Alfred Univ	NY	37,490	C
Alma College	MI	49,410	VC
Alvernia Univ	PA	45,330	C
Angelo State Univ	TX	15,882	LC
Aquinas College - Mich	MI	38,876	VC
Arizona State Univ at the Tempe Campus	AZ	23,001	VC
Arkansas State Univ	AR	16,190	C
Armstrong State Univ	GA	15,615	C
Augustana College	IL	51,222	VC+
Augustana Univ	SD	39,968	VC
Averett Univ	VA	43,034	LC
Azusa Pacific Univ	CA	43,972	C
Bard College	NY	65,924	HC
Belmont Univ	TN	44,500	VC+
Berea College	KY	7,094	C
Berry College	GA	47,466	VC
Bethany College	KS	38,637	LC
Bethel College	IN	36,830	C
Biola Univ	CA	48,686	C
Birmingham-Southern College	AL	44,478	C+
Bloomsburg Univ of Pennsylvania	PA	19,930	C
Boise State Univ	ID	17,368	C
Boston Univ	MA	67,352	MC
Bowdoin College	ME	65,980	MC
Bradley Univ	IL	43,240	VC
Brandeis Univ	MA	68,443	MC
Brown Univ	RI	64,566	MC
Bryan College	TN	32,900	C
Buena Vista Univ	IA	42,344	C
Butler Univ	IN	52,890	VC+
Calif Baptist Univ	CA	42,986	C
Calif Lutheran Univ	CA	52,853	C
Calif Polytechnic State Univ	CA	22,547	MC
Calif State Polytechnic Univ, Pomona	CA	21,811	C
Cal State, Chico	CA	19,790	VC
Cal State, Fresno	CA	16,902	LC
Cal State, Fullerton	CA	21,902	C
Cal State, Long Beach	CA	18,850	C
Cameron Univ	OK	11,632	LC
Campbell Univ	NC	37,570	VC
Campbellsville Univ	KY	33,400	C
Canisius College	NY	49,672	C
Carroll College	MT	44,304	C
Carroll Univ	WI	38,100	C+
Carthage College	WI	48,835	C
Case Western Reserve Univ	OH	62,284	MC
Castleton Univ	VT	20,186	C
Catawba College	NC	39,820	LC
Cedarville Univ	OH	36,244	VC
Central College	IA	44,592	C
Central Conn State Univ	CT	22,041	C
Christopher Newport Univ	VA	24,878	VC+
Coe College	IA	51,570	VC
Colby College	ME	64,060	MC
College of Charleston	SC	24,046	VC
College of St. Benedict	MN	54,480	C
College of the Holy Cross	MA	64,320	MC
College of William & Mary	VA	34,907	MC
Colo Mesa Univ	CO	19,707	LC
Columbia College Chicago	IL	40,104	C
Concordia Univ St. Paul	MN	29,050	C
Creighton Univ	NE	49,452	VC
Dartmouth College	NH	68,109	MC
Davis & Elkins College	WV	38,242	LC
DePaul Univ	IL	52,807	VC
Dickinson College	PA	66,166	MC
Dominican Univ	IL	42,472	C+
Dordt College	IA	37,860	C+
Drew Univ/College of Liberal Arts	NJ	53,608	VC
Drury Univ	MO	37,555	VC
East Central Univ	OK	13,330	C
East Stroudsburg Univ	PA	18,578	LC
East Texas Baptist Univ	TX	34,444	C
Eastern Illinois Univ	IL	21,414	C
Eastern Mennonite Univ	VA	42,550	C
Edgewood College	WI	35,950	C
Elmhurst College	IL	46,514	C
Elmira College	NY	53,900	C
Elon Univ	NC	46,142	HC
Emporia State Univ	KS	15,029	C
Fairfield Univ	CT	61,445	HC
Five Towns College	NY	35,480	LC
Flagler College	FL	27,620	C
Florida Southern College	FL	45,978	VC
Fontbonne Univ	MO	34,606	C
Franklin College	IN	40,550	C
Franklin Pierce Univ	NH	46,750	LC
Frostburg State Univ	MD	17,280	LC
Gallaudet Univ	DC	30,088	LC
Georgia College & State Univ	GA	21,884	C+
Georgia Southern Univ	GA	16,540	VC
Goshen College	IN	44,350	C
Goucher College	MD	56,110	VC
Grand Canyon Univ	AZ	25,150	VC
Grinnell College	IA	63,114	MC
Guilford College	NC	45,973	C
Hamline Univ	MN	50,152	C
Hampden-Sydney College	VA	57,806	VC
Henderson State Univ	AR	15,516	C
High Point Univ	NC	47,355	VC
Hillsdale College	MI	37,170	MC
Hobart and William Smith Colleges	NY	67,050	HC+
Hollins Univ	VA	49,635	VC
Hope College	MI	42,840	VC
Howard Univ	DC	37,616	C+
Huntington Univ	IN	33,996	C
Indiana Univ Bloomington	IN	20,791	HC
Indiana Univ Northwest	IN	7,207	LC
Indiana Univ of Pennsylvania	PA	24,474	C
Indiana Univ South Bend	IN	16,057	C
John Carroll Univ	OH	51,570	C
Kean Univ	NJ	25,620	C
Kennesaw State Univ	GA	18,899	VC
Kent State Univ	OH	20,928	C
King Univ	TN	36,976	C
Knox College	IL	54,654	VC+
LaGrange College	GA	41,310	C
Lake Forest College	IL	50,652	VC
Le Moyne College	NY	47,305	VC
Limestone College	SC	32,100	C
Linfield College	OR	53,992	C

ST = STATE $IS = IN-STATE COSTS SR = SELECTOR RATING

School	ST	$IS	SR
Lipscomb Univ	TN	42,984	VC
LIU Post	NY	50,698	C+
Louisiana College	LA	21,274	C
Loyola Marymount Univ	CA	60,202	VC+
Loyola Univ Chicago	IL	57,158	VC
Lubbock Christian Univ	TX	29,727	C
Luther College	IA	49,990	VC
Macalester College	MN	64,136	MC
Marquette Univ	WI	53,090	VC+
Marshall Univ	WV	18,044	C
Mary Baldwin Univ	VA	40,495	C
Miami Univ	OH	27,190	HC+
Millikin Univ	IL	44,148	C
Missouri Baptist Univ	MO	35,594	C
Missouri Southern State Univ	MO	13,071	C
Missouri State Univ	MO	15,837	C+
Missouri Western State Univ	MO	17,822	LC
Molloy College	NY	40,440	C
Montclair State Univ	NJ	26,912	C
Montreat College	NC	34,605	LC
Murray State Univ	KY	17,726	C+
Nazareth College	NY	46,784	C
New Mexico State Univ	NM	14,050	LC
Niagara Univ	NY	41,010	C
North Central College	IL	48,712	C+
North Central Univ	MN	30,610	C
N Dak State Univ	ND	16,245	VC
North Greenville Univ	SC	25,930	C
Northeastern Illinois Univ	IL	12,529	LC
Northeastern Univ	MA	65,352	MC
Northern Arizona Univ	AZ	21,003	C
Northern Kentucky Univ	KY	16,486	C
Northern Mich Univ	MI	20,853	C
Occidental College	CA	68,660	MC
Ohio State Univ at Columbus	OH	22,843	MC
Ohio State Univ at Lima	OH	7,553	C
Ohio Wesleyan Univ	OH	49,460	VC
Okla City Univ	OK	40,476	C
Old Dominion Univ	VA	21,618	C
Ouachita Baptist Univ	AR	33,500	VC
Pace Univ	NY	60,136	C
Pacific Lutheran Univ	WA	49,960	C
Piedmont College	GA	34,334	C
Plymouth State Univ	NH	23,180	LC
Point Park Univ	PA	41,270	C
Pomona College	CA	64,957	MC
Providence College	RI	62,870	HC
Quinnipiac Univ	CT	60,970	VC
Radford Univ	VA	19,758	C
Rhodes College	TN	51,900	HC
Roanoke College	VA	55,952	VC
Rocky Mountain College	MT	35,776	C
Roger Williams Univ	RI	48,074	VC
Rollins College	FL	58,670	HC
Rowan Univ	NJ	24,491	VC
St. John's Univ	MN	53,472	C
St. Joseph's Univ	PA	58,540	VC
St. Leo Univ	FL	32,850	C
St. Louis Univ	MO	49,866	HC
St. Martin's Univ	WA	45,056	C
St. Mary's Univ of Minn	MN	42,440	C
Salisbury Univ	MD	21,132	VC
Samford Univ	AL	40,770	VC
San Diego State Univ	CA	23,156	VC
San Jose State Univ	CA	22,630	C
Schreiner Univ	TX	34,626	LC
Seattle Univ	WA	54,957	VC
Seton Hall Univ	NJ	58,008	C
Seton Hill Univ	PA	46,972	VC
Sewanee: The Univ of the South	TN	58,000	HC+
Siena Heights Univ	MI	36,322	C
Southern Oregon Univ	OR	19,117	C
Southwestern College	KS	31,531	LC
Spring Hill College	AL	48,488	C
St. Edward's Univ	TX	56,190	VC
St. Norbert College	WI	46,060	VC
St. Olaf College	MN	56,430	HC
SUNY at Binghamton	NY	24,100	MC
SUNY at Oswego	NY	22,219	VC
SUNY/Fredonia	NY	20,818	C
SUNY/Potsdam	NY	21,051	VC
SUNY/Univ at Buffalo	NY	23,122	C
Sterling College	KS	32,830	LC
Stevenson Univ	MD	48,412	C
Stony Brook Univ/The SUNY	NY	22,703	MC
Susquehanna Univ	PA	57,560	VC
Swarthmore College	PA	63,550	MC
Tabor College	KS	35,870	C
Tarleton State Univ	TX	15,248	LC
Taylor Univ	IN	42,130	VC
Texas Christian Univ	TX	57,120	HC
Texas State Univ	TX	18,721	C
Texas Tech Univ	TX	20,156	C+
The College of Idaho	ID	36,415	C
The Univ of Arizona	AZ	24,086	C
The Univ of Tenn at Knoxville	TN	22,112	VC
The Univ of Utah	UT	18,751	VC
Thomas Edison State Univ	NJ	6,350	NC
Transylvania Univ	KY	47,450	HC+
Univ of Alaska Fairbanks	AK	16,874	VC
Univ of Arkansas at Little Rock	AR	18,211	LC
Univ of Calif at Riverside	CA	32,912	C
Univ of Central Florida	FL	16,379	VC
Univ of Central Okla	OK	15,150	C
Univ of Colo Boulder	CO	26,048	HC
Univ of Idaho	ID	16,158	C
Univ of Illinois at Chicago	IL	24,664	VC
Univ of Iowa	IA	19,415	HC
Univ of Kansas	KS	20,884	VC
Univ of Louisville	KY	19,692	C
Univ of Lynchburg	VA	48,370	C
Univ of Maryland/College Park	MD	21,938	HC
Univ of Miami	FL	63,494	MC
Univ of Minn/Twin Cities	MN	24,269	MC
Univ of Miss	MS	18,802	C
Univ of Mount Union	OH	39,990	C
Univ of Nebr - Lincoln	NE	18,589	VC
Univ of New Hampshire	NH	29,333	VC
Univ of New Haven	CT	53,680	C
Univ of N Car at Charlotte	NC	17,803	VC
Univ of N Car Wilmington	NC	16,784	VC
Univ of Northern Iowa	IA	17,480	C
Univ of Oregon	OR	24,021	VC
Univ of Pittsburgh	PA	30,030	MC
Univ of Redlands	CA	61,934	VC
Univ of Rhode Island	RI	26,066	VC
Univ of Richmond	VA	62,730	MC
Univ of Rochester	NY	65,032	MC
Univ of St. Mary	KS	37,080	NC
Univ of San Diego	CA	60,338	HC
Univ of Scranton	PA	54,962	VC
Univ of Southern Indiana	IN	16,808	C
Univ of Tulsa	OK	52,625	HC
Univ of West Georgia	GA	17,510	LC
Univ of Wisc-Eau Claire	WI	16,354	VC
Univ of Wisc-Green Bay	WI	15,184	C
Univ of Wisc-La Crosse	WI	15,425	VC
Univ of Wisc-Madison	WI	21,647	MC
Univ of Wisc-Milwaukee	WI	21,538	C
Univ of Wisc-Parkside	WI	15,313	C
Univ of Wisc-Superior	WI	14,838	C
Valparaiso Univ	IN	50,160	VC
Vanderbilt Univ	TN	63,248	MC
Vanguard Univ of Southern Calif	CA	42,400	VC
Warren Wilson College	NC	44,220	VC
Washington State Univ	WA	22,747	C
Wayne State Univ	MI	23,085	C
Weber State Univ	UT	14,112	C
Wellesley College	MA	66,984	MC
West Chester Univ of Pennsylvania	PA	19,171	VC
West Virginia Wesleyan College	WV	39,188	C
Western Illinois Univ	IL	20,897	C
Western Washington Univ	WA	18,904	VC
Westfield State Univ	MA	20,404	C
Whitman College	WA	59,772	MC
Whitworth Univ	WA	53,682	VC
Wichita State Univ	KS	17,773	C
William Peace Univ	NC	39,300	LC
Winthrop Univ	SC	23,960	C
Wisc Lutheran College	WI	36,290	C
Wofford College	SC	49,885	VC
Xavier Univ	OH	49,380	VC
Youngstown State Univ	OH	17,487	C

THEATRE EDUCATION

School	ST	$IS	SR
Kean Univ	NJ	25,620	C
Missouri Western State Univ	MO	17,822	LC
Old Dominion Univ	VA	21,618	C
Univ of N Car at Greensboro	NC	15,998	C

THEATRE MINISTRY

School	ST	$IS	SR
College of the Ozarks	MO	7,530	VC

THEATRE PRODUCTION

School	ST	$IS	SR
Aquinas College - Mich	MI	38,876	VC
Bethany College	WV	38,774	LC
Boston Univ	MA	67,352	MC
Carthage College	WI	48,835	C
Colo State Univ	CO	23,033	C
DeSales Univ	PA	47,520	C
Elon Univ	NC	46,142	HC
Fontbonne Univ	MO	34,606	C
Fordham Univ	NY	68,431	MC
Keene State College	NH	24,604	C
Lamar Univ	TX	18,014	LC
Millikin Univ	IL	44,148	C
Missouri Western State Univ	MO	17,822	LC
Neumann Univ	PA	40,678	LC
Okla City Univ	OK	40,476	C
Pace Univ	NY	60,136	C
Shenandoah Univ	VA	42,100	C
Southern Oregon Univ	OR	19,117	C
SUNY at Oswego	NY	22,219	VC
SUNY/Fredonia	NY	20,818	C
Stevenson Univ	MD	48,412	C
Texas Christian Univ	TX	57,120	HC
The Univ of Arizona	AZ	24,086	C
Univ of Illinois at Chicago	IL	24,664	VC
West Chester Univ of Pennsylvania	PA	19,171	VC
Youngstown State Univ	OH	17,487	C

THEATRE STUDIES

School	ST	$IS	SR
Amherst College	MA	66,186	MC
Aquinas College - Mich	MI	38,876	VC
Aurora Univ	IL	34,990	C
Baker Univ	KS	37,190	C
Barton College	NC	39,854	C
Baylor Univ	TX	56,803	HC
Bowling Green State Univ	OH	19,975	C
Capital Univ	OH	44,778	VC
Chapman Univ	CA	65,504	HC
Chatham Univ	PA	47,883	VC
Colgate Univ	NY	67,500	MC
College of the Ozarks	MO	7,530	VC
Colo State Univ	CO	23,033	C
Cornell College	IA	49,900	VC
Elon Univ	NC	46,142	HC
Eugene Lang College of Liberal Arts	NY	64,940	VC
Faulkner Univ	AL	26,410	C
Hampden-Sydney College	VA	57,806	VC
Hardin-Simmons Univ	TX	36,025	C
Indiana Univ Bloomington	IN	20,791	HC
John Carroll Univ	OH	51,570	C
Lewis Univ	IL	41,710	C
Lindsey Wilson College	KY	33,546	C
Malone Univ	OH	39,200	C
Marlboro College	VT	50,832	VC+
Mich State Univ	MI	24,542	VC
Mich Tech Univ	MI	25,551	VC+
Mills College	CA	43,705	C
Minn State Univ, Mankato	MN	17,190	C
Missouri Southern State Univ	MO	13,071	C
Missouri Western State Univ	MO	17,822	LC
Montclair State Univ	NJ	26,912	C
Oberlin College	OH	68,942	MC
Shepherd Univ, West Virginia	WV	17,382	C
Southern Oregon Univ	OR	19,117	C
Southwestern Univ	TX	52,370	VC
SUNY/Fredonia	NY	20,818	C
Stephen F. Austin State Univ	TX	18,484	LC
Stevenson Univ	MD	48,412	C
Texas Christian Univ	TX	57,120	HC
Trinity Univ	TX	54,480	MC
Univ of Central Florida	FL	16,379	VC
Univ of Central Okla	OK	15,150	C
Univ of Chicago	IL	70,551	MC
Univ of Dayton	OH	54,930	VC
Univ of Denver	CO	61,129	VC+
Univ of Illinois at Chicago	IL	24,664	VC
Univ of Indianapolis	IN	36,480	VC
Univ of New Mexico	NM	16,808	C
Univ of S Dak	SD	16,109	C
Viterbo Univ	WI	34,660	C
Wake Forest Univ	NC	69,354	MC
Wells College	NY	50,500	C
West Chester Univ of Pennsylvania	PA	19,171	VC
Western Mich Univ	MI	21,791	C
Wright State Univ	OH	16,983	C
Xavier Univ	OH	49,380	VC
Youngstown State Univ	OH	17,487	C

THEATRE/DANCE

School	ST	$IS	SR
Austin Peay State Univ	TN	16,397	C
Keene State College	NH	24,604	C
Macalester College	MN	64,136	MC
Missouri Western State Univ	MO	17,822	LC
Univ of Dayton	OH	54,930	VC
Wheaton College	MA	63,818	VC

THEOLOGICAL STUDIES

School	ST	$IS	SR
Alvernia Univ	PA	45,330	C
Andrews Univ	MI	41,732	C
Aquinas College	TN	30,800	C+
Aquinas College - Mich	MI	38,876	VC
Assumption College	MA	48,455	VC
Atlantic Union College	MA	27,228	C
Avila Univ	MO	27,100	C
Bard College	NY	65,924	HC
Barry Univ	FL	38,730	LC
Bellarmine Univ	KY	52,532	C
Belmont Abbey College	NC	28,794	C
Benedictine Univ	IL	38,300	C
Bethel Univ	MN	46,550	C+
Boston College	MA	68,043	MC
Briar Cliff Univ	IA	36,956	C
Caldwell Univ	NJ	42,165	LC
Calif Lutheran Univ	CA	52,853	C
Calumet College of St. Joseph	IN	22,735	C
Calvin College	MI	43,090	HC
Carlow Univ	PA	39,696	LC
Cedarville Univ	OH	36,244	VC
Christendom College	VA	32,600	VC
College of St. Benedict	MN	54,480	C
College of St. Mary	NE	27,500	C
Colo Christian Univ	CO	40,885	VC
Concordia Univ	OR	35,000	C
Concordia Univ Irvine	CA	44,860	VC
Concordia Univ Nebr	NE	41,900	VC
Concordia Univ St. Paul	MN	29,050	C
Concordia Univ Wisc	WI	35,910	C
Concordia Univ, Chicago	IL	41,522	C
Corban Univ	OR	41,700	C
DeSales Univ	PA	47,520	C
Dominican Univ	IL	42,472	C+
Duquesne Univ	PA	48,508	VC
Eastern Mennonite Univ	VA	42,550	C
Eastern Univ	PA	39,540	C
Elmhurst College	IL	46,514	C
Fordham Univ	NY	68,431	MC
Franciscan Univ of Steubenville	OH	33,980	VC
Gannon Univ	PA	42,922	C
Hanover College	IN	47,750	C+
Hardin-Simmons Univ	TX	36,025	C
Immaculata Univ	PA	39,000	C
John Carroll Univ	OH	51,570	C
Juniata College	PA	58,118	VC
King's College	PA	48,240	C
Lenoir-Rhyne Univ	NC	47,500	LC
Livingstone College	NC	17,815	LC
Lourdes Univ	OH	29,140	NC
Loyola Univ Chicago	IL	57,158	VC
Loyola Univ Maryland	MD	61,710	VC
Malone Univ	OH	39,200	C
Marquette Univ	WI	53,090	VC+
Marymount Univ	VA	43,231	C
Messiah College	PA	44,380	VC
Mount Mary Univ	WI	34,650	LC
Mount St. Mary's Univ	MD	53,380	C
Mount Vernon Nazarene Univ	OH	35,944	C
Newman Univ	KS	37,382	C
North Central Univ	MN	30,610	C
Northwest Univ	WA	38,720	VC
Notre Dame College	OH	39,150	VC
Nyack College	NY	34,450	LC
Ohio Dominican Univ	OH	41,340	C+
Ouachita Baptist Univ	AR	33,500	VC
Pacific Union College	CA	36,009	VC
Pontifical Catholic Univ of PR	PR	10,534	
Providence College	RI	62,870	HC
Quincy Univ	IL	38,170	LC
Rockhurst Univ	MO	28,990	C
St. Anselm College	NH	56,636	VC
St. John's Univ	MN	53,472	C
St. Joseph's College of Maine	ME	47,890	C
St. Joseph's Univ	PA	58,540	VC
St. Louis Univ	MO	49,866	HC
St. Mary-of-the-Woods College	IN	40,424	LC
St. Peter's Univ	NJ	49,192	C
St. Vincent College	PA	46,229	C
Seattle Pacific Univ	WA	47,439	C+
Seattle Univ	WA	54,957	VC
Seton Hall Univ	NJ	58,008	C
Southern Adventist Univ	TN	28,250	C
Southern Nazarene Univ	OK	33,684	C
Southwestern Adventist Univ	TX	28,232	LC
Spring Arbor Univ	MI	37,390	C
Spring Hill College	AL	48,488	C
St. Ambrose Univ	IA	40,180	C
St. Bonaventure Univ	NY	45,596	C
St. Catherine Univ	MN	45,630	C
St. John's College at Annapolis	MD	63,348	MC
St. Mary's Univ	TX	39,120	C
Sterling College	KS	32,830	LC
Texas Lutheran Univ	TX	39,770	C
The Catholic Univ of America	DC	58,376	VC
The Univ of Mary	ND	23,180	C
Thomas More College	KY	36,720	LC
Trinity Christian College	IL	35,580	C
Union College	NE	23,270	C
Universidad Adventista de las Antillas	PR	16,606	
Univ of Chicago	IL	70,551	MC
Univ of Dallas	TX	50,676	VC
Univ of Evansville	IN	44,186	C+
Univ of Great Falls	MT	38,524	C
Univ of Mobile	AL	28,935	C
Univ of Portland	OR	52,152	VC
Univ of St. Mary	KS	37,080	NC
Univ of San Diego	CA	60,338	HC
Univ of San Francisco	CA	60,580	C
Univ of Scranton	PA	54,962	VC
Univ of St. Francis	IL	40,828	C
Univ of St. Thomas - Houston	TX	41,510	VC
Valparaiso Univ	IN	50,160	VC
Vanguard Univ of Southern Calif	CA	42,400	VC
Villanova Univ	PA	64,922	MC
Walla Walla Univ	WA	34,845	C
Walsh Univ	OH	39,010	C
Washington Adventist Univ	MD	32,050	LC
Wheeling Jesuit Univ	WV	37,106	LC
Whitworth Univ	WA	53,682	VC
Wisc Lutheran College	WI	36,290	C
Xavier Univ	OH	49,380	VC
Xavier Univ of Louisiana	LA	31,689	C

THEOLOGY

School	ST	$IS	SR
Aquinas College - Mich	MI	38,876	VC
Azusa Pacific Univ	CA	43,972	C
Calif Baptist Univ	CA	42,986	C
Calvin College	MI	43,090	HC
Carroll College	MT	44,304	C
Creighton Univ	NE	49,452	VC
Lewis Univ	IL	41,710	C
Loyola Marymount Univ	CA	60,202	VC+
Marian Univ	IN	43,206	C
Merrimack College	MA	55,415	C
Molloy College	NY	40,440	C
St. Louis Univ	MO	49,866	HC
St. Mary's Univ of Minn	MN	42,440	C

ST = STATE $IS = IN-STATE COSTS SR = SELECTOR RATING

School	ST	$IS	SR
Silver Lake College of the Holy Family	WI	36,290	LC
St. John's Univ	NY	57,160	C+
The Master's Univ	CA	43,870	C
Univ of Notre Dame	IN	68,801	MC
Univ of St. Francis	IN	38,520	C

THERAPEUTIC RIDING

School	ST	$IS	SR
St. Andrews Univ	NC	44,634	LC
Wilson College	PA	35,620	LC

THIRD WORLD STUDIES

School	ST	$IS	SR
Appalachian State Univ	NC	15,394	VC
Bethel Univ	MN	46,550	C+
Brown Univ	RI	64,566	MC
Pitzer College	CA	68,500	HC+
Univ of Calif San Diego	CA	30,450	MC

TOTAL QUALITY MANAGEMENT (TQM)

School	ST	$IS	SR
Cal State, Dominguez Hills	CA	19,022	LC

TOURISM

School	ST	$IS	SR
Arizona State Univ at the Downtown Phoenix Campus	AZ	24,634	VC
Black Hills State Univ	SD	16,622	C
Bowling Green State Univ	OH	19,975	C
Brigham Young Univ	UT	13,248	MC
Brigham Young Univ/Hawaii	HI	11,710	C
Cal State, Dominguez Hills	CA	19,022	LC
Cal State, Fullerton	CA	21,902	C
Central Washington Univ	WA	16,803	C
Coastal Carolina Univ	SC	20,340	C
Colo State Univ	CO	23,033	C
Eastern Mich Univ	MI	19,761	C
George Mason Univ	VA	19,884	C
Hawaii Pacific Univ	HI	33,420	C
Indiana Univ Kokomo	IN	7,207	C
Indiana Univ-Purdue Univ Indianapolis	IN	18,952	C
James Madison Univ	VA	19,084	VC
Johnson & Wales Univ/ Charlotte Campus	NC	44,768	C
Johnson & Wales Univ/ Denver Campus	CO	44,768	C
Johnson & Wales Univ/North Miami Campus	FL	44,768	C
Johnson & Wales Univ/ Providence Campus	RI	44,768	C
Johnson State College	VT	22,672	C
Kent State Univ	OH	20,928	C
Mich State Univ	MI	24,542	VC
New Mexico State Univ	NM	14,050	LC
Niagara Univ	NY	41,010	C
Northwestern State Univ of Louisiana	LA	16,534	LC
Ohio Univ	OH	23,394	VC
Old Dominion Univ	VA	21,618	C
Oregon State Univ	OR	23,337	VC
Plymouth State Univ	NH	23,180	LC
Purdue Univ/West Lafayette	IN	20,032	MC
Rochester Inst of Technology	NY	52,734	HC+
Seton Hill Univ	PA	46,972	VC
Southern New Hampshire Univ	NH	44,256	C
St. Joseph's College, New York/Brooklyn Campus	NY	25,114	LC
St. Joseph's College, New York/Long Island Campus	NY	25,124	C
St. Thomas Univ	FL	51,187	LC
Temple Univ	PA	24,392	C+
The George Washington Univ	DC	68,474	HC+
The Univ of Montana Western	MT	9,426	LC
Univ of Central Missouri	MO	18,982	C
Univ of Hawaii at Manoa	HI	23,261	C
Univ of Maine at Machias	ME	22,960	C
Univ of Missouri-Columbia	MO	20,463	VC
Univ of New Haven	CT	53,680	C
Univ of New Orleans	LA	12,840	C
Univ of N Car at Greensboro	NC	15,998	C
Univ of the Sacred Heart	PR	17,932	
Virginia Polytechnic Inst and State Univ	VA	21,920	VC
West Liberty Univ	WV	16,158	C
West Virginia Univ	WV	18,952	VC
Western Mich Univ	MI	21,791	C

TOXICOLOGY

School	ST	$IS	SR
Ashland Univ	OH	30,446	C
Bloomfield College	NJ	40,100	LC
Bryant Univ	RI	57,204	VC
Cal State, Fullerton	CA	21,902	C
Colo State Univ	CO	23,033	C
Nazareth College	NY	46,784	C
Pennsylvania State Univ - Univ Park	PA	29,716	HC
St. John's Univ	NY	57,160	C+
Univ of Calif at Davis	CA	28,468	HC
Univ of Louisiana at Monroe	LA	15,970	C
Univ of the Sciences	PA	40,738	VC

TOY DESIGN

School	ST	$IS	SR
Fashion Inst of Technology/ SUNY	NY	18,521	SP
Otis College of Art and Design	CA	54,670	SP

TRADE AND INDUSTRIAL EDUCATION

School	ST	$IS	SR
Alabama A&M Univ	AL	18,796	C
Eastern Mich Univ	MI	19,761	C
Siena Heights Univ	MI	36,322	C
Southern Illinois Univ Carbondale	IL	24,554	C
SUNY at Oswego	NY	22,219	VC
Univ of Nevada, Las Vegas	NV	17,553	C
Univ of Wyoming	WY	15,537	C
Virginia State Univ	VA	19,802	C+

TRADE AND INDUSTRIAL SUPERVISION AND MANAGEMENT

School	ST	$IS	SR
Cal State, Dominguez Hills	CA	19,022	LC
Eastern Mich Univ	MI	19,761	C
Metropolitan State Univ	MN	7,859	C
Miss State Univ	MS	12,028	C+
Washington Univ in St. Louis	MO	67,539	MC

TRANSPORTATION ADMINISTRATION

School	ST	$IS	SR
Lewis Univ	IL	41,710	C

TRANSPORTATION AND TRAVEL MARKETING

School	ST	$IS	SR
Johnson & Wales Univ/ Providence Campus	RI	44,768	C
Keiser Univ	FL	35,010	LC
Northwood Univ - Mich	MI	35,010	LC

TRANSPORTATION ENGINEERING

School	ST	$IS	SR
Calif Polytechnic State Univ	CA	22,547	MC
Lawrence Tech Univ	MI	41,630	VC

TRANSPORTATION MANAGEMENT

School	ST	$IS	SR
Auburn Univ	AL	24,300	VC+
Bryant Univ	RI	57,204	VC
Cal State, Maritime Academy	CA	23,156	C+
Cal State, Fullerton	CA	21,902	C
Florida Memorial Univ	FL	22,424	LC
Iowa State Univ	IA	18,176	C
Niagara Univ	NY	41,010	C
Ohio State Univ at Columbus	OH	22,843	MC
San Jose State Univ	CA	22,630	C
Southern Univ at New Orleans	LA	8,014	LC
SUNY/Maritime College	NY	16,020	C
Univ of Alaska Anchorage	AK	17,914	C
Univ of Arkansas at Fayetteville	AR	19,766	VC
Univ of North Florida	FL	15,996	VC
Univ of Pennsylvania	PA	63,526	MC
Univ of Wisc-Superior	WI	14,838	C

TRANSPORTATION TECHNOLOGY

School	ST	$IS	SR
Maine Maritime Academy	ME	22,536	C
Missouri Southern State Univ	MO	13,071	C

TURFGRASS AND LANDSCAPE MANAGEMENT

School	ST	$IS	SR
New Mexico State Univ	NM	14,050	LC
Pennsylvania State Univ - Univ Park	PA	29,716	HC
Univ of Georgia	GA	21,878	HC
Univ of Nebr - Lincoln	NE	18,589	VC
Washington State Univ	WA	22,747	C

ULTRASOUND TECHNOLOGY

School	ST	$IS	SR
Barry Univ	FL	38,730	LC
MCPHS Univ	MA	45,470	SP
Mount Aloysius College	PA	29,976	C
Newman Univ	KS	37,382	C
Oregon Inst of Technology	OR	19,227	C
Rochester Inst of Technology	NY	52,734	HC+
Rutgers Univ - New Brunswick	NJ	27,090	HC
Seattle Univ	WA	54,957	VC
Washburn Univ	KS	15,827	C

UNIVERSITY STUDIES

School	ST	$IS	SR
East Texas Baptist Univ	TX	34,444	C
Shenandoah Univ	VA	42,100	C
Texas Tech Univ	TX	20,156	C+
Univ of Maine	ME	21,038	VC
Western Mich Univ	MI	21,791	C

UNMANNED AIRCRAFT SYSTEMS

School	ST	$IS	SR
Embry-Riddle Aeronautical Univ - Daytona Beach	FL	45,822	VC
Embry-Riddle Aeronautical Univ - Prescott Campus	AZ	45,130	VC
Lewis Univ	IL	41,710	C

URBAN ADMINISTRATION

School	ST	$IS	SR
Furman Univ	SC	61,098	VC+
New York Inst of Technology	NY	49,980	VC

URBAN AND REGIONAL STUDIES

School	ST	$IS	SR
Arizona State Univ at the Downtown Phoenix Campus	AZ	24,634	VC
Cornell Univ	NY	67,591	MC
Frostburg State Univ	MD	17,280	LC
Ohio Univ	OH	23,394	VC
Salisbury Univ	MD	21,132	VC
Texas A&M Univ at College Station	TX	20,771	VC+
The Univ of Arizona	AZ	24,086	C
Univ of Mich/Dearborn	MI	12,472	VC

URBAN DESIGN

School	ST	$IS	SR
New York Univ	NY	68,139	MC
Parsons The New School for Design	NY	56,610	SP
SUNY Albany	NY	22,165	C
Univ of Virginia	VA	27,367	MC

URBAN ECOLOGY

School	ST	$IS	SR
Harris-Stowe State Univ	MO	14,590	NC
Hofstra Univ	NY	58,210	C+
Seattle Univ	WA	54,957	VC
Xavier Univ	OH	49,380	VC

URBAN PLANNING TECHNOLOGY

School	ST	$IS	SR
Ball State Univ	IN	19,808	C+
Calif State Polytechnic Univ, Pomona	CA	21,811	C
Eastern Mich Univ	MI	19,761	C
Florida Atlantic Univ	FL	18,256	C
Harris-Stowe State Univ	MO	14,590	NC
Mich State Univ	MI	24,542	VC
San Jose State Univ	CA	22,630	C
Texas State Univ	TX	18,721	C
The Univ of Utah	UT	18,751	VC
Univ of Nevada, Las Vegas	NV	17,553	C
Univ of N Car at Greensboro	NC	15,998	C
Univ of Wisc-Milwaukee	WI	21,538	C
West Chester Univ of Pennsylvania	PA	19,171	VC

URBAN STUDIES

School	ST	$IS	SR
Albertus Magnus College	CT	44,016	LC
Arizona State Univ at the Tempe Campus	AZ	23,001	VC
Augsburg Univ	MN	45,129	C
Barnard College/Columbia Univ	NY	68,762	MC
Baylor Univ	TX	56,803	HC
Bellevue Univ	NE	20,300	NC
Boston Univ	MA	67,352	MC
Brown Univ	RI	64,566	MC
Bryn Mawr College	PA	65,220	MC
Calif State Polytechnic Univ, Pomona	CA	21,811	C
Cal State, Fresno	CA	16,902	LC
Cal State, Fullerton	CA	21,902	C
Cal State, Northridge	CA	17,277	LC
Calumet College of St. Joseph	IN	22,735	C
Canisius College	NY	49,672	C
Carnegie Mellon Univ	PA	67,980	MC
CUNY/City College	NY	20,204	C
CUNY/Hunter College	NY	31,098	VC
CUNY/Queens College	NY	21,507	C
Cleveland State Univ	OH	22,290	C
College of Charleston	SC	24,046	VC
College of Mount St. Vincent	NY	45,620	C
Columbia Univ/ School of General Studies	NY	61,470	MC
Columbia Univ/City of New York	NY	62,958	MC
Conn College	CT	65,000	MC
Coppin State Univ	MD	14,071	VC
DePaul Univ	IL	52,807	VC
Dillard Univ	LA	20,940	VC
Eastern Mich Univ	MI	19,761	C
Eastern Washington Univ	WA	17,896	LC
Elmhurst College	IL	46,514	C
Eugene Lang College of Liberal Arts	NY	64,940	VC
Fordham Univ	NY	68,431	MC
Furman Univ	SC	61,098	VC+
Georgia State Univ	GA	25,250	C
Hamline Univ	MN	50,152	C
Hampshire College	MA	65,214	MC
Haverford College	PA	66,490	MC
Howard Univ	DC	37,616	C+
Jackson State Univ	MS	15,879	LC
Langston Univ	OK	15,659	C
LeMoyne-Owen College	TN	16,980	C
Lipscomb Univ	TN	42,984	VC
Loyola Marymount Univ	CA	60,202	VC+
Manhattan College	NY	55,652	C
Mass Inst of Technology	MA	62,662	MC
Metropolitan State Univ of Denver	CO	6,928	LC
Miami Univ	OH	27,190	HC+
Minn State Univ, Mankato	MN	17,190	C
Morehouse College	GA	40,835	C
New College of Florida	FL	16,180	HC+
New York Univ	NY	68,139	MC
Northeastern Illinois Univ	IL	12,529	LC
Northwestern Univ	IL	68,725	MC
Occidental College	CA	68,660	MC
Ohio Univ	OH	23,394	VC
Ohio Wesleyan Univ	OH	49,460	VC
Rhodes College	TN	51,900	HC
Roosevelt Univ	IL	41,890	VC
Rutgers Univ - Camden	NJ	26,595	C
Rutgers Univ - New Brunswick	NJ	27,090	HC
St. Augustine's Univ	NC	25,582	C
St. Louis Univ	MO	49,866	HC
St. Peter's Univ	NJ	49,192	C
San Diego State Univ	CA	23,156	VC
San Francisco State Univ	CA	18,514	LC
Smith College	MA	66,774	MC
Southern Nazarene Univ	OK	33,684	C
St. Cloud State Univ	MN	10,600	C
Stanford Univ	CA	62,541	MC
SUNY/Buffalo State	NY	20,583	LC
The College of Wooster	OH	60,000	HC
The Univ of Texas at Austin	TX	20,206	MC
The Univ of Utah	UT	18,751	VC
Trinity Univ	TX	54,480	MC
Tufts Univ	MA		MC
Univ of Calif at Berkeley	CA	29,886	MC
Univ of Calif at Irvine	CA	33,857	VC
Univ of Calif San Diego	CA	30,450	MC
Univ of Cincinnati	OH	22,118	VC
Univ of Conn	CT	27,394	
Univ of Illinois at Chicago	IL	24,664	VC
Univ of Mich/Flint	MI	19,062	C
Univ of Minn/Duluth	MN	20,292	C
Univ of Minn/Twin Cities	MN	24,269	MC
Univ of Missouri-Kansas City	MO	19,563	VC
Univ of New Orleans	LA	12,840	C
Univ of Northwestern - St. Paul	MN	39,530	C
Univ of Pennsylvania	PA	63,526	MC
Univ of Pittsburgh	PA	30,030	MC
Univ of the District of Columbia	DC	21,260	LC
Univ of the Sacred Heart	PR	17,932	
Univ of Wisc-Green Bay	WI	15,184	C
Univ of Wisc-Milwaukee	WI	21,538	C
Univ of Wisc-Oshkosh	WI	15,392	C
Vassar College	NY	68,110	MC
Virginia Commonwealth Univ	VA	23,811	VC
Virginia Polytechnic Inst and State Univ	VA	21,920	VC
Washington Univ in St. Louis	MO	67,539	MC
Wayne State Univ	MI	23,085	C
Wheaton College	IL	44,993	MC
Worcester State Univ	MA	20,977	C
Wright State Univ	OH	16,983	C

VASCULAR SONOGRAPHY

School	ST	$IS	SR
MCPHS Univ	MA	45,470	SP
Thomas Edison State Univ	NJ	6,350	NC
Weber State Univ	UT	14,112	C

VETERINARY SCIENCE

School	ST	$IS	SR
Becker College	MA	30,100	LC
Colo State Univ	CO	23,033	C
Fort Valley State Univ	GA	17,988	VC
Lincoln Memorial Univ	TN	28,430	C
Mercy College	NY	32,614	C
Mich State Univ	MI	24,542	VC
Mount Ida College	MA	46,820	C
Newberry College	SC	34,550	C
N Dak State Univ	ND	16,245	VC
Pennsylvania State Univ - Univ Park	PA	29,716	HC
The Univ of Arizona	AZ	24,086	C
The Univ of Montana Western	MT	9,426	LC
Tuskegee Univ	AL	28,164	C
Univ of Idaho	ID	16,158	C
Univ of Maine	ME	21,038	VC
Univ of Maryland/College Park	MD	21,938	HC
Univ of Minn/Twin Cities	MN	24,269	MC
Univ of Missouri-Columbia	MO	20,463	VC
Univ of Nebr - Lincoln	NE	18,589	VC
Utah State Univ	UT	13,235	C
Walla Walla Univ	WA	34,845	C
West Virginia Univ	WV	18,952	VC

ST = STATE **$IS** = IN-STATE COSTS **SR** = SELECTOR RATING

School	ST	$IS	SR
Wilson College	PA	35,620	LC

VETERINARY TECHNOLOGY

School	ST	$IS	SR
Medaille College	NY	41,700	LC
Murray State Univ	KY	17,726	C+
Tarleton State Univ	TX	15,248	LC

VICTORIAN STUDIES

School	ST	$IS	SR
Bard College	NY	65,924	HC
Vassar College	NY	68,110	MC

VIDEO

School	ST	$IS	SR
Bennington College	VT	66,280	MC
Bloomfield College	NJ	40,100	LC
Calif Inst of the Arts	CA	61,366	SP
Calvin College	MI	43,090	HC
CUNY/City College	NY	20,204	C
Cornerstone Univ	MI	36,550	C
Drexel Univ	PA	65,927	HC
Fairleigh Dickinson Univ/ College at Florham	NJ	54,770	C
Fitchburg State Univ	MA	21,819	LC
Five Towns College	NY	35,480	LC
George Mason Univ	VA	19,884	C
Hampshire College	MA	65,214	MC
Hofstra Univ	NY	58,210	C+
Ithaca College	NY	58,158	VC+
Madonna Univ	MI	30,450	LC
Maryland Inst College of Art	MD	58,740	SP
Minneapolis College of Art and Design	MN	44,218	SP
Missouri Western State Univ	MO	17,822	LC
New Mexico State Univ	NM	14,050	LC
Ohio Univ	OH	23,394	VC
Point Park Univ	PA	41,270	C
Rochester Inst of Technology	NY	52,734	HC+
School of the Art Inst of Chicago	IL	61,830	SP
School of Visual Arts	NY	47,500	SP
Spring Arbor Univ	MI	37,390	C
SUNY/Fredonia	NY	20,818	C
Stevenson Univ	MD	48,412	C
Syracuse Univ	NY	62,313	HC
The Art Inst of Atlanta	GA	34,334	SP
Univ of Hartford	CT	49,776	C
Univ of Mich/Ann Arbor	MI	25,274	MC
Univ of Northwestern - St. Paul	MN	39,530	C
Univ of Southern Calif	CA	66,631	MC
Webster Univ	MO	37,490	C
Wilmington Univ	DE	8,762	NC

VISUAL AND PERFORMING ARTS

School	ST	$IS	SR
Albion College	MI	55,260	C
Alderson Broaddus Univ	WV	35,000	LC
Andrews Univ	MI	41,732	C
Anna Maria College	MA	51,020	C
Aquinas College - Mich	MI	38,876	VC
Arizona State Univ at the Tempe Campus	AZ	23,001	VC
Armstrong State Univ	GA	15,615	C
Austin College	TX	51,059	HC
Belmont Univ	TN	44,500	VC+
Bennett College	NC	27,717	NC
Bennington College	VT	66,280	MC
Bethel Univ	MN	46,550	C+
Bowling Green State Univ	OH	19,975	C
Brigham Young Univ	UT	13,248	MC
Brown Univ	RI	64,566	MC
Bryn Athyn College	PA	32,664	C
Bucknell Univ	PA	67,136	MC
Calif Baptist Univ	CA	42,986	C
Calif College of the Arts	CA	52,758	SP
Calif Inst of the Arts	CA	61,366	SP
Cal State, Fullerton	CA	21,902	C
Cal State, Monterey Bay	CA	22,872	LC
Cal State, San Marcos	CA	20,604	LC
Central Mich Univ	MI	20,330	C
Central Washington Univ	WA	16,803	C
Chatham Univ	PA	47,883	VC
CUNY/Brooklyn College	NY	7,163	C+
Clark Univ	MA	53,260	HC+
Columbia Univ/ School of General Studies	NY	61,470	MC
Columbia Univ/City of New York	NY	62,958	MC
Columbus State Univ	GA	14,336	LC
Coppin State Univ	MD	14,071	VC
Curry College	MA	53,331	C
Dordt College	IA	37,860	C+
Duke Univ	NC	68,298	MC
East Texas Baptist Univ	TX	34,444	C
Eastern Conn State Univ	CT	23,059	C
Eastern Mich Univ	MI	19,761	C
Eckerd College	FL	55,206	VC
Erskine College	SC	45,460	C
Fayetteville State Univ	NC	17,756	C
Florida Atlantic Univ	FL	18,256	C
Fordham Univ	NY	68,431	MC
Gannon Univ	PA	42,922	C
George Mason Univ	VA	19,884	C
Goddard College	VT	17,040	VC
Grambling State Univ	LA	15,701	C
Grand View Univ	IA	32,302	C
Hampden-Sydney College	VA	57,806	VC
Haverford College	PA	66,490	MC
Heritage Univ	WA	19,825	NC
Hofstra Univ	NY	58,210	C+
Indiana Univ Bloomington	IN	20,791	HC
Inter-American Univ of PR Ponce	PR	19,549	
Inter-American Univ of PR-Bayamon	PR	18,785	
Inter-American Univ of PR-Fajardo Campus	PR	18,336	
Ithaca College	NY	58,158	VC+
Johnson State College	VT	22,672	C
Kean Univ	NJ	25,620	C
Kent State Univ	OH	20,928	C
Keystone College	PA	28,680	LC
Kutztown Univ of Pennsylvania	PA	19,477	C
Lander Univ	SC	32,200	C
Lees-McRae College	NC	33,944	NC
Lesley Univ	MA	42,800	C
Lincoln Univ	PA	20,878	LC
Lipscomb Univ	TN	42,984	VC
LIU Brooklyn	NY	50,698	C
Longwood Univ	VA	22,184	C
Loyola Univ New Orleans	LA	52,456	VC
Mass College of Liberal Arts	MA	20,659	C
Millikin Univ	IL	44,148	C
Missouri Western State Univ	MO	17,822	LC
Naropa Univ	CO	43,278	NC
New England Conservatory of Music	MA	63,170	SP
New Mexico State Univ	NM	14,050	LC
Notre Dame College	OH	39,150	VC
Ohio Univ	OH	23,394	VC
Otterbein Univ	OH	41,630	C
Ouachita Baptist Univ	AR	33,500	VC
Penn State Altoona	PA	26,686	C
Pine Manor College	MA	41,660	LC
Prescott College	AZ	38,201	C
Purdue Univ/West Lafayette	IN	20,032	MC
Ramapo College of New Jersey	NJ	25,760	VC
Regis Univ	CO	46,380	C
Rice Univ	TX	59,458	MC
Roger Williams Univ	RI	48,074	VC
Rutgers Univ - Newark	NJ	27,351	C
St. Augustine's Univ	NC	25,582	C
St. Mary's College	IN	50,600	C
St. Peter's Univ	NJ	49,192	C
St. Vincent College	PA	46,229	C
Sarah Lawrence College	NY	68,866	MC
Savannah State Univ	GA	17,036	C
School of the Art Inst of Chicago	IL	61,830	SP
Schreiner Univ	TX	34,626	LC
Seattle Univ	WA	54,957	VC
Shaw Univ	NC	24,638	C
Siena College	NY	48,916	C
Siena Heights Univ	MI	36,322	C
Sonoma State Univ	CA	27,020	C
S Car State Univ	SC	21,330	LC
Southern Oregon Univ	OR	19,117	C
Spring Arbor Univ	MI	37,390	C
St. Andrews Univ	NC	44,634	LC
St. Bonaventure Univ	NY	45,596	C
St. Lawrence Univ	NY	66,646	HC+
St. Thomas Aquinas College	NY	32,450	C
SUNY at Binghamton	NY	24,100	MC
SUNY at New Paltz	NY	20,840	C
SUNY at Purchase College	NY	21,832	C
SUNY/College at Old Westbury	NY	16,860	C
SUNY/Potsdam	NY	21,051	VC
Susquehanna Univ	PA	57,560	VC
Taylor Univ	IN	42,130	VC
Temple Univ	PA	24,392	C+
The Evergreen State College	WA	16,599	C
The Univ of Montana Western	MT	9,426	LC
The Univ of Texas at Austin	TX	20,206	MC
Univ of Alaska Anchorage	AK	17,914	C
Univ of Arkansas at Little Rock	AR	18,211	LC
Univ of Calif at Riverside	CA	32,912	C
Univ of Calif San Diego	CA	30,450	MC
Univ of Chicago	IL	70,551	MC
Univ of Cincinnati	OH	22,118	VC
Univ of Colo Colo Springs	CO	20,300	C
Univ of Colo Denver	CO	22,238	C
Univ of Conn	CT	27,394	
Univ of Florida	FL	16,291	HC+
Univ of Hartford	CT	49,776	C
Univ of Illinois at Chicago	IL	24,664	VC
Univ of Maine at Farmington	ME	18,792	C
Univ of Maryland/Baltimore County	MD	23,004	VC
Univ of New Haven	CT	53,680	C
Univ of N Dak	ND	16,673	C
Univ of North Texas	TX	20,082	C
Univ of Northern Colo	CO	19,658	C
Univ of Pennsylvania	PA	63,526	MC
Univ of San Diego	CA	60,338	HC
Univ of San Francisco	CA	60,580	C
Univ of Southern Calif	CA	66,631	MC
Univ of St. Francis	IL	40,828	C
Univ of Texas at Dallas	TX	23,640	HC
Univ of the Sacred Heart	PR	17,932	
Univ of Tulsa	OK	52,625	HC
Univ of Wisc-Platteville	WI	14,148	C
Univ of Wisc-Superior	WI	14,838	C
Virginia State Univ	VA	19,802	C+
Wagner College	NY	57,240	C+
Washington Univ in St. Louis	MO	67,539	MC
Weber State Univ	UT	14,112	C
Wells College	NY	50,500	C
West Chester Univ of Pennsylvania	PA	19,171	VC
West Virginia Univ	WV	18,952	VC
Western Kentucky Univ	KY	16,850	C
Western Washington Univ	WA	18,904	VC
Wichita State Univ	KS	17,773	C
Worcester State Univ	MA	20,977	C

VISUAL COMMUNICATION

School	ST	$IS	SR
Iowa Wesleyan Univ	IA	41,000	C
Missouri Western State Univ	MO	17,822	LC
Neumann Univ	PA	40,678	LC
Northern Arizona Univ	AZ	21,003	C
Okla Wesleyan Univ	OK	34,434	C
Purdue Univ Northwest	IN	15,178	C
Rochester Inst of Technology	NY	52,734	HC+
Univ of Okla	OK	19,651	HC

VISUAL DESIGN

School	ST	$IS	SR
Art Academy of Cincinnati	OH	37,790	SP
Calif Inst of the Arts	CA	61,366	SP
Cal State, Fullerton	CA	21,902	C
Cazenovia College	NY	47,866	C
Cedarville Univ	OH	36,244	VC
Eastern New Mexico Univ	NM	12,874	LC
Farmingdale State College	NY	20,968	C
High Point Univ	NC	47,355	VC
Indiana Univ-Purdue Univ Fort Wayne	IN	18,675	C
Kent State Univ	OH	20,928	C
Loyola Univ Chicago	IL	57,158	VC
Lynn Univ	FL	49,680	LC
Missouri Western State Univ	MO	17,822	LC
Nazareth College	NY	46,784	C
Ohio State Univ at Columbus	OH	22,843	MC
Okla Christian Univ	OK	29,260	C
Rochester Inst of Technology	NY	52,734	HC+
San Francisco State Univ	CA	18,514	LC
Stevenson Univ	MD	48,412	C
Truman State Univ	MO	16,286	MC
Univ of Dayton	OH	54,930	VC
Univ of Delaware	DE	32,214	VC
Univ of Mary Hardin-Baylor	TX	35,292	C+
Univ of Mass Dartmouth	MA	26,507	C
Univ of New Haven	CT	53,680	C
Weber State Univ	UT	14,112	C
Western Oregon Univ	OR	19,965	LC
Whitworth Univ	WA	53,682	VC

VISUAL EFFECTS

School	ST	$IS	SR
Bradley Univ	IL	43,240	VC
Missouri Western State Univ	MO	17,822	LC
Otis College of Art and Design	CA	54,670	SP
Ringling College of Art and Design	FL	59,160	SP
Savannah College of Art and Design	GA	49,595	SP
School of Visual Arts	NY	47,500	SP
Shepherd Univ	CA		LC

VITICULTURE AND ENOLOGY

School	ST	$IS	SR
Cornell Univ	NY	67,591	MC
Washington State Univ	WA	22,747	C

VOCAL MUSIC EDUCATION

School	ST	$IS	SR
Aquinas College - Mich	MI	38,876	VC
Calvin College	MI	43,090	HC
Concordia Univ St. Paul	MN	29,050	C
Curtis Inst of Music	PA	20,944	SP
Dordt College	IA	37,860	C+
East Central Univ	OK	13,330	C
Hope College	MI	42,840	VC
Houghton College	NY	40,558	VC
King Univ	TN	36,976	C
Louisiana College	LA	21,274	C
Marian Univ	IN	43,206	C
Missouri Western State Univ	MO	17,822	LC
Murray State Univ	KY	17,726	C+
North Central Univ	MN	30,610	C
Okla Baptist Univ	OK	33,990	C
Silver Lake College of the Holy Family	WI	36,290	LC
St. Ambrose Univ	IA	40,180	C
Wartburg College	IA	49,478	C
Webster Univ	MO	37,490	C
West Chester Univ of Pennsylvania	PA	19,171	VC
Youngstown State Univ	OH	17,487	C

VOCAL PERFORMANCE

School	ST	$IS	SR
Abilene Christian Univ	TX	43,708	C+
Anderson Univ	IN	39,450	C
Aquinas College - Mich	MI	38,876	VC
Arkansas State Univ	AR	16,190	C
Calif Baptist Univ	CA	42,986	C
Dallas Baptist Univ	TX	35,220	VC
East Central Univ	OK	13,330	C
East Texas Baptist Univ	TX	34,444	C
Houghton College	NY	40,558	VC
LIU Post	NY	50,698	C+
Louisiana College	LA	21,274	C
Madonna Univ	MI	30,450	LC
Marian Univ	IN	43,206	C
Missouri Southern State Univ	MO	13,071	C
Missouri Western State Univ	MO	17,822	LC
New England Conservatory of Music	MA	63,170	SP
New York Univ	NY	68,139	MC
Ohio Univ	OH	23,394	VC
Okla Christian Univ	OK	29,260	C
Okla City Univ	OK	40,476	C
Point Loma Nazarene Univ	CA	46,150	C+
Roberts Wesleyan College	NY	41,116	C
Shepherd Univ	CA		LC
Taylor Univ	IN	42,130	VC
Texas Christian Univ	TX	57,120	HC
Univ of Miami	FL	63,494	MC
Univ of N Car at Greensboro	NC	15,998	C
Webster Univ	MO	37,490	C
West Chester Univ of Pennsylvania	PA	19,171	VC
Western Mich Univ	MI	21,791	C
Wingate Univ	NC	41,900	C
Wright State Univ	OH	16,983	C
Youngstown State Univ	OH	17,487	C

VOCATIONAL EDUCATION

School	ST	$IS	SR
Auburn Univ	AL	24,300	VC+
Cal State, Los Angeles	CA	17,186	LC
Cal State, San Bernardino	CA	20,106	C
Chicago State Univ	IL	41,620	C
College of the Ozarks	MO	7,530	VC
Fitchburg State Univ	MA	21,819	LC
Indiana Univ of Pennsylvania	PA	24,474	C
Martin Univ	IN	21,010	LC
New York City College of Technology	NY	7,185	LC
N Car State Univ	NC	22,434	HC+
Okla State Univ	OK	17,180	C+
Pittsburg State Univ	KS	13,880	C
S Dak State Univ	SD	15,874	C
Southern Illinois Univ Carbondale	IL	24,554	C
SUNY at Oswego	NY	22,219	VC
Univ of Illinois at Urbana-Champaign	IL	27,006	HC
Univ of Toledo	OH	19,336	C
Univ of Wisc-Stout	WI	19,667	C
Valley City State Univ	ND	13,267	C
Western Kentucky Univ	KY	16,850	C
Western Mich Univ	MI	21,791	C
Western New Mexico Univ	NM	16,914	LC
Westfield State Univ	MA	20,404	C
Youngstown State Univ	OH	17,487	C

VOICE

School	ST	$IS	SR
Aquinas College - Mich	MI	38,876	VC
Baldwin Wallace Univ	OH	42,464	VC
Bennington College	VT	66,280	MC
Boston Univ	MA	67,352	MC
Bucknell Univ	PA	67,136	MC
Butler Univ	IN	52,890	VC+
Calif Baptist Univ	CA	42,986	C
Calvin College	MI	43,090	HC
Campbellsville Univ	KY	33,400	C
Central Mich Univ	MI	20,330	C
Central Washington Univ	WA	16,803	C
East Central Univ	OK	13,330	C
East Texas Baptist Univ	TX	34,444	C
Eastern Mich Univ	MI	19,761	C
Florida State Univ	FL	16,771	HC
Hardin-Simmons Univ	TX	36,025	C
Houghton College	NY	40,558	VC
Illinois Wesleyan Univ	IL	56,430	VC+
Indiana Univ-Purdue Univ Fort Wayne	IN	18,675	C
Loyola Univ New Orleans	LA	52,456	VC
Manhattan School of Music	NY	57,200	SP
Mannes School of Music	NY	44,500	SP
Marshall Univ	WV	18,044	C
Millikin Univ	IL	44,148	C
Miss College	MS	25,850	C
Missouri Western State Univ	MO	17,822	LC
Mount Aloysius College	PA	29,976	C
New England Conservatory of Music	MA	63,170	SP
New York Univ	NY	68,139	MC
Northwestern Univ	IL	68,725	MC
Nyack College	NY	34,450	LC
Ohio Univ	OH	23,394	VC
Ouachita Baptist Univ	AR	33,500	VC
Pacific Lutheran Univ	WA	49,960	C
Palm Beach Atlantic Univ	FL	39,250	C
Rider Univ	NJ	54,050	C
Roosevelt Univ	IL	41,890	VC
Samford Univ	AL	40,770	VC
San Francisco Conservatory of Music	CA	57,310	SP
Shorter Univ	GA	31,130	LC

ST = STATE $IS = IN-STATE COSTS SR = SELECTOR RATING

School	ST	$IS	SR
Silver Lake College of the Holy Family	WI	36,290	LC
Southeastern Univ	FL	34,910	LC
St. Ambrose Univ	IA	40,180	C
Stetson Univ	FL	57,174	VC+
Syracuse Univ	NY	62,313	HC
The Catholic Univ of America	DC	58,376	VC
The Juilliard School	NY	59,226	SP
Union Univ	TN	41,160	VC
Univ of Cincinnati	OH	22,118	VC
Univ of Illinois at Urbana-Champaign	IL	27,006	HC
Univ of Iowa	IA	19,415	HC
Univ of Kansas	KS	20,884	VC
Univ of Mobile	AL	28,935	C
Univ of Northwestern - St. Paul	MN	39,530	C
Univ of Tulsa	OK	52,625	HC
Valparaiso Univ	IN	50,160	VC
Weber State Univ	UT	14,112	C
Webster Univ	MO	37,490	C
West Chester Univ of Pennsylvania	PA	19,171	VC
Westminster Choir College	NJ	53,730	SP
York College	NE	30,260	C
Youngstown State Univ	OH	17,487	C

WATER AND WASTEWATER TECHNOLOGY

School	ST	$IS	SR
Northland College	WI	41,103	C+
Texas State Univ	TX	18,721	C
Wright State Univ	OH	16,983	C

WATER RESOURCES

School	ST	$IS	SR
Central State Univ	OH	18,564	C
Colo State Univ	CO	23,033	C
Heidelberg Univ	OH	40,400	LC
Northern Mich Univ	MI	20,853	C
Prescott College	AZ	38,201	C
SUNY/Oneonta	NY	20,794	C
Tarleton State Univ	TX	15,248	LC
The College at Brockport - SUNY	NY	21,058	C
Univ of Georgia	GA	21,878	HC
Univ of Idaho	ID	16,158	C
Univ of Nebr - Lincoln	NE	18,589	VC

WEB SERVICES

School	ST	$IS	SR
Bloomfield College	NJ	40,100	LC
Champlain College	VT	54,724	VC
Idaho State Univ	ID	13,619	LC
Indiana Inst of Technology	IN	34,240	LC
Johnson & Wales Univ/ Providence Campus	RI	44,768	C
Keene State College	NH	24,604	C
Limestone College	SC	32,100	C
Lipscomb Univ	TN	42,984	VC
Mercyhurst Univ	PA	47,420	C
Roger Williams Univ	RI	48,074	VC
Southern Adventist Univ	TN	28,250	C
Taylor Univ	IN	42,130	VC
Thiel College	PA	42,950	LC
Univ of Wisc-Milwaukee	WI	21,538	C
Univ of Wisc-Stevens Point	WI	14,043	C

WEB TECHNOLOGY

School	ST	$IS	SR
Belmont Univ	TN	44,500	VC+
Bloomfield College	NJ	40,100	LC
Bradley Univ	IL	43,240	VC
Cogswell Polytechnical College	CA	31,511	C
Davenport Univ	MI	25,896	LC
Drexel Univ	PA	65,927	HC
Edgewood College	WI	35,950	C
Illinois Inst of Technology	IL	56,826	HC+
Keene State College	NH	24,604	C
Limestone College	SC	32,100	C
Mercyhurst Univ	PA	47,420	C
Mount Aloysius College	PA	29,976	C
Pennsylvania College of Technology	PA	27,693	NC
Quinnipiac Univ	CT	60,970	VC
Roger Williams Univ	RI	48,074	VC
Seattle Univ	WA	54,957	VC
Tenn Tech Univ	TN	17,929	C
Tulane Univ	LA	67,496	MC
Univ of St. Francis	IL	40,828	C

WELDING ENGINEERING

School	ST	$IS	SR
Ferris State Univ	MI	21,458	C
Idaho State Univ	ID	13,619	LC
LeTourneau Univ	TX	39,190	VC
Lewis-Clark State College	ID	14,202	C
Ohio State Univ at Columbus	OH	22,843	MC
Pennsylvania College of Technology	PA	27,693	NC
Weber State Univ	UT	14,112	C

WESTERN CIVILIZATION/ CULTURE

School	ST	$IS	SR
St. John's College at Annapolis	MD	63,348	MC
The Univ of Montana Western	MT	9,426	LC

WESTERN EUROPEAN STUDIES

School	ST	$IS	SR
Denison Univ	OH	62,770	HC+
St. John's College at Annapolis	MD	63,348	MC
The College of Wooster	OH	60,000	HC
Univ of Mich/Ann Arbor	MI	25,274	MC
Washington Univ in St. Louis	MO	67,539	MC

WILDLIFE BIOLOGY

School	ST	$IS	SR
Adams State Univ	CO	15,420	LC
Arkansas Tech Univ	AR	16,534	LC
Auburn Univ	AL	24,300	VC+
Colo State Univ	CO	23,033	C
Friends Univ	KS	38,000	C
Humboldt State Univ	CA	21,708	C
Kansas State Univ	KS	17,780	VC
Lees-McRae College	NC	33,944	NC
Missouri Western State Univ	MO	17,822	LC
Murray State Univ	KY	17,726	C+
Ohio Univ	OH	23,394	VC
Oregon State Univ	OR	23,337	VC
Prescott College	AZ	38,201	C
Purdue Univ/West Lafayette	IN	20,032	MC
S Dak State Univ	SD	15,874	C
SUNY/The College of Environmental Science and Forestry	NY	23,728	VC
Tarleton State Univ	TX	15,248	LC
Texas State Univ	TX	18,721	C
The Univ of Montana Western	MT	9,426	LC
The Univ of Tenn at Knoxville	TN	22,112	VC
Unity College	ME	37,670	C
Univ of Calif at Davis	CA	28,468	HC
Univ of Florida	FL	16,291	HC+
Univ of Illinois at Urbana-Champaign	IL	27,006	HC
Univ of Maine at Machias	ME	22,960	C
Univ of Montana	MT	14,105	C
Univ of New Hampshire	NH	29,333	VC
Univ of Vermont	VT	29,792	HC
Univ of Wisc-Madison	WI	21,647	MC
Univ of Wisc-Stevens Point	WI	14,043	C
Univ of Wyoming	WY	15,537	C
Washington State Univ	WA	22,747	C
West Texas A&M Univ	TX	13,478	C

WILDLIFE CONSERVATION BIOLOGY

School	ST	$IS	SR
Lake Superior State Univ	MI	19,867	C
Missouri Western State Univ	MO	17,822	LC
Univ of Alaska Fairbanks	AK	16,874	VC
Univ of Maine at Machias	ME	22,960	C
Univ of Rhode Island	RI	26,066	VC

WILDLIFE MANAGEMENT

School	ST	$IS	SR
Arkansas State Univ	AR	16,190	C
Brigham Young Univ	UT	13,248	MC
Cal State, Fullerton	CA	21,902	C
Colo State Univ	CO	23,033	C
Dakota Wesleyan Univ	SD	33,980	LC
Delaware Valley Univ	PA	51,271	C
Eastern Kentucky Univ	KY	17,742	C
Eastern New Mexico Univ	NM	12,874	LC
Frostburg State Univ	MD	17,280	LC
Kansas State Univ	KS	17,780	VC
Lake Superior State Univ	MI	19,867	C
Lincoln Memorial Univ	TN	28,430	C
Louisiana Tech Univ	LA	11,422	VC
Mich State Univ	MI	24,542	VC
Mich Tech Univ	MI	25,551	VC+
Miss State Univ	MS	12,028	C+
Missouri State Univ	MO	15,837	C+
Missouri Western State Univ	MO	17,822	LC
Northern Mich Univ	MI	20,853	C
Northwest Missouri State Univ	MO	18,286	C
Peru State College	NE	15,602	LC
Prescott College	AZ	38,201	C
SUNY /College of Agriculture and Tech at Cobleskill	NY	20,527	LC
Stephen F. Austin State Univ	TX	18,484	LC
Sul Ross State Univ	TX	15,021	LC
Tarleton State Univ	TX	15,248	LC
Tenn Tech Univ	TN	17,929	C
Texas A&M Univ at Commerce	TX	10,496	C
Unity College	ME	37,670	C
Univ of Arkansas at Monticello	AR	13,599	LC
Univ of Delaware	DE	32,214	VC
Univ of Idaho	ID	16,158	C
Univ of Illinois at Urbana-Champaign	IL	27,006	HC
Univ of Maine	ME	21,038	VC
Univ of Nebr - Lincoln	NE	18,589	VC
Univ of Nevada, Reno	NV	18,010	C
Univ of PR, at Humacao	PR	14,000	
Utah State Univ	UT	13,235	C
Washington State Univ	WA	22,747	C
West Virginia Univ	WV	18,952	VC

WILDLIFE SCIENCE

School	ST	$IS	SR
Embry-Riddle Aeronautical Univ - Prescott Campus	AZ	45,130	VC
Missouri Western State Univ	MO	17,822	LC
New Mexico State Univ	NM	14,050	LC
Texas A&M Univ at College Station	TX	20,771	VC+

WINDS

School	ST	$IS	SR
Eastern Mich Univ	MI	19,761	C
Florida State Univ	FL	16,771	HC
Mannes School of Music	NY	44,500	SP
Miss College	MS	25,850	C
Northwestern Univ	IL	68,725	MC
Oberlin College	OH	68,942	MC
Roosevelt Univ	IL	41,890	VC
San Francisco Conservatory of Music	CA	57,310	SP
Stetson Univ	FL	57,174	VC+
Syracuse Univ	NY	62,313	HC
Texas Christian Univ	TX	57,120	HC
Texas Tech Univ	TX	20,156	C+
Univ of Kansas	KS	20,884	VC
Univ of Mich/Ann Arbor	MI	25,274	MC
Wright State Univ	OH	16,983	C
Youngstown State Univ	OH	17,487	C

WINE AND VITICULTURE

School	ST	$IS	SR
Calif Polytechnic State Univ	CA	22,547	MC

WOMEN & GENDER STUDIES

School	ST	$IS	SR
Allegheny College	PA	57,620	VC
Amherst College	MA	66,186	MC
Aquinas College - Mich	MI	38,876	VC
Arizona State Univ at the Tempe Campus	AZ	23,001	VC
Arizona State Univ at the West Campus	AZ	21,513	VC
Armstrong State Univ	GA	15,615	C
Austin College	TX	51,059	HC
Bates College	ME	64,500	HC
Brown Univ	RI	64,566	MC
Bryant Univ	RI	57,204	VC
Cabrini Univ	PA	42,591	LC
Cal State, Chico	CA	19,790	VC
Cal State, Long Beach	CA	18,850	C
Case Western Reserve Univ	OH	62,284	MC
Castleton Univ	VT	20,186	C
Clarion Univ of Pennsylvania	PA	21,608	LC
College of Staten Island	NY	24,389	LC
Cornell College	IA	49,900	VC
Cornell Univ	NY	67,591	MC
Delaware State Univ	DE	19,376	LC
DePaul Univ	IL	52,807	VC
Duquesne Univ	PA	48,508	VC
Eastern Conn State Univ	CT	23,059	C
Elon Univ	NC	46,142	HC
Gettysburg College	PA	65,210	MC
Goddard College	VT	17,040	VC
Illinois Wesleyan Univ	IL	56,430	VC+
Indiana Univ South Bend	IN	16,057	C
Keene State College	NH	24,604	C
Kenyon College	OH	65,840	MC
Knox College	IL	54,654	VC+
Kutztown Univ of Pennsylvania	PA	19,477	C
Loyola Marymount Univ	CA	60,202	VC+
Mills College	CA	43,705	C
New Jersey City Univ	NJ	21,456	LC
N Dak State Univ	ND	16,245	VC
Northern Arizona Univ	AZ	21,003	C
Northland College	WI	41,103	C+
Oberlin College	OH	68,942	MC
Ohio Univ	OH	23,394	VC
Otterbein Univ	OH	41,630	C
Pace Univ	NY	60,136	C
Pacific Lutheran Univ	WA	49,960	C
St. Mary's College	IN	50,600	C
Sarah Lawrence College	NY	68,866	MC
Seattle Univ	WA	54,957	VC
Seton Hill Univ	PA	46,972	VC
Southern Oregon Univ	OR	19,117	C
St. Ambrose Univ	IA	40,180	C
St. Olaf College	MN	56,430	HC
SUNY Albany	NY	22,165	C
SUNY at Oswego	NY	22,219	VC
Stony Brook Univ/The SUNY	NY	22,703	MC
Syracuse Univ	NY	62,313	HC
Tufts Univ	MA		MC
Univ of Colo Boulder	CO	26,048	HC
Univ of Illinois at Chicago	IL	24,664	VC
Univ of Kansas	KS	20,884	VC
Univ of Maine	ME	21,038	VC
Univ of Maryland/Baltimore County	MD	23,004	VC
Univ of Mass Boston	MA	13,828	C
Univ of Mass Dartmouth	MA	26,507	C
Univ of Mich/Dearborn	MI	12,472	VC
Univ of Nebr - Lincoln	NE	18,589	VC
Univ of N Car at Chapel Hill	NC	20,561	MC
Univ of N Car at Greensboro	NC	15,998	C
Univ of Okla	OK	19,651	HC
Univ of Redlands	CA	61,934	VC
Univ of S Dak	SD	16,109	C
Univ of Tulsa	OK	52,625	HC
Univ of Wyoming	WY	15,537	C
Vanderbilt Univ	TN	63,248	MC
Wayne State Univ	MI	23,085	C
Wellesley College	MA	66,984	MC
Wells College	NY	50,500	C
Wesleyan College	GA	31,940	C+
West Chester Univ of Pennsylvania	PA	19,171	VC
Western Washington Univ	WA	18,904	VC
Wheaton College	MA	63,818	VC
Wichita State Univ	KS	17,773	C
Winona State Univ	MN	18,109	C

WOMEN'S ENTREPRENEURSHIP & INSTITUTIONAL CULTURE

School	ST	$IS	SR
Chatham Univ	PA	47,883	VC

WOMEN'S STUDIES

School	ST	$IS	SR
Agnes Scott College	GA	51,930	VC+
Albion College	MI	55,260	C
Albright College	PA	57,326	C
Alverno College	WI	33,294	LC
Appalachian State Univ	NC	15,394	VC
Aquinas College - Mich	MI	38,876	VC
Arizona State Univ at the West Campus	AZ	21,513	VC
Augsburg Univ	MN	45,129	C
Augustana College	IL	51,222	VC+
Ball State Univ	IN	19,808	C+
Barnard College/Columbia Univ	NY	68,762	MC
Beloit College	WI	55,206	HC
Bennington College	VT	66,280	MC
Berea College	KY	7,094	C
Bloomfield College	NJ	40,100	LC
Bowdoin College	ME	65,980	MC
Bowling Green State Univ	OH	19,975	C
Brandeis Univ	MA	68,443	MC
Brown Univ	RI	64,566	MC
Bucknell Univ	PA	67,136	MC
Cal State, Fresno	CA	16,902	LC
Cal State, Fullerton	CA	21,902	C
Cal State, Long Beach	CA	18,850	C
Cal State, Northridge	CA	17,277	LC
Cal State, San Marcos	CA	20,604	LC
Canisius College	NY	49,672	C
Carleton College	MN	66,414	MC
Central Mich Univ	MI	20,330	C
Chatham Univ	PA	47,883	VC
CUNY/Brooklyn College	NY	7,163	C+
CUNY/Hunter College	NY	31,098	VC
CUNY/Queens College	NY	21,507	C
Clark Univ	MA	53,260	HC+
Cleveland State Univ	OH	22,290	C
Coe College	IA	51,570	VC
Colby College	ME	64,060	MC
Colgate Univ	NY	67,500	MC
College of Charleston	SC	24,046	VC
College of William & Mary	VA	34,907	MC
Colo College	CO	64,894	MC
Colo State Univ	CO	23,033	C
Columbia Univ/ School of General Studies	NY	61,470	MC
Columbia Univ/City of New York	NY	62,958	MC
Dartmouth College	NH	68,109	MC
Denison Univ	OH	62,770	HC+
DePaul Univ	IL	52,807	VC
DePauw Univ	IN	58,688	VC
Dickinson College	PA	66,166	MC
Dominican Univ	IL	42,472	C+
Dominican Univ of Calif	CA	58,750	C
Drew Univ/College of Liberal Arts	NJ	53,608	VC
Duke Univ	NC	68,298	MC
Earlham College	IN	55,670	HC
East Carolina Univ	NC	16,539	C
Eastern Mich Univ	MI	19,761	C
Eckerd College	FL	55,206	VC
Emory Univ	GA	63,286	MC
Florida International Univ	FL	20,281	C
Florida State Univ	FL	16,771	HC
Fordham Univ	NY	68,431	MC
Georgia State Univ	GA	25,250	C
Gettysburg College	PA	65,210	MC
Goucher College	MD	56,110	VC
Guilford College	NC	45,973	C
Gustavus Adolphus College	MN	53,943	HC
Hamilton College	NY	64,250	MC
Hamline Univ	MN	50,152	C
Hampshire College	MA	65,214	MC
Harvard College/Harvard Univ	MA	65,609	MC
Hobart and William Smith Colleges	NY	67,050	HC+
Hofstra Univ	NY	58,210	C+
Hope College	MI	42,840	VC
Howard Univ	DC	37,616	C+

ST = STATE **$IS** = IN-STATE COSTS **SR** = SELECTOR RATING

School	ST	$IS	SR
Indiana Univ-Purdue Univ Fort Wayne	IN	18,675	C
John Carroll Univ	OH	51,570	C
Kansas State Univ	KS	17,780	VC
Kutztown Univ of Pennsylvania	PA	19,477	C
Lehigh Univ	PA	63,860	MC
Loyola Univ Chicago	IL	57,158	VC
Luther College	IA	49,990	VC
Macalester College	MN	64,136	MC
Marshall Univ	WV	18,044	C
Mercer Univ	GA	45,348	VC
Metropolitan State Univ	MN	7,859	C
Miami Univ	OH	27,190	HC+
Mich State Univ	MI	24,542	VC
Middlebury College	VT	67,464	MC
Minn State Univ, Mankato	MN	17,190	C
Minn State Univ, Moorhead	MN	21,393	C
Mount Aloysius College	PA	29,976	C
Nazareth College	NY	46,784	C
Nebr Wesleyan Univ	NE	42,026	C+
New Mexico State Univ	NM	14,050	LC
Northeastern Illinois Univ	IL	12,529	LC
Northern Kentucky Univ	KY	16,486	C
Oakland Univ	MI	20,763	C
Oberlin College	OH	68,942	MC
Ohio State Univ at Columbus	OH	22,843	MC
Ohio Univ	OH	23,394	VC
Ohio Wesleyan Univ	OH	49,460	VC
Old Dominion Univ	VA	21,618	C
Oregon State Univ	OR	23,337	VC
Pennsylvania State Univ - Univ Park	PA	29,716	HC
Pitzer College	CA	68,500	HC+
Pomona College	CA	64,957	MC
Portland State Univ	OR	19,443	C
Prescott College	AZ	38,201	C
Providence College	RI	62,870	HC
Purdue Univ/West Lafayette	IN	20,032	MC
Randolph-Macon College	VA	51,480	VC
Regis Univ	CO	46,380	C
Rhode Island College	RI	19,000	LC
Rice Univ	TX	59,458	MC
Roosevelt Univ	IL	41,890	VC
Rosemont College	PA	30,980	LC
Rutgers Univ - New Brunswick	NJ	27,090	HC
Rutgers Univ - Newark	NJ	27,351	C
St. Louis Univ	MO	49,866	HC
Salem College	NC	40,206	C
San Diego State Univ	CA	23,156	VC
San Francisco State Univ	CA	18,514	LC
Sarah Lawrence College	NY	68,866	MC
Scripps College	CA	69,260	HC
Sewanee: The Univ of the South	TN	58,000	HC+
Simmons College	MA	54,400	HC
Smith College	MA	66,774	MC
Sonoma State Univ	CA	27,020	C
Southwestern Univ	TX	52,370	VC
Spelman College	GA	41,642	C
St. Bonaventure Univ	NY	45,596	C
St. Catherine Univ	MN	45,630	C
Stanford Univ	CA	62,541	MC
SUNY Albany	NY	22,165	C
SUNY at New Paltz	NY	20,840	C
SUNY at Oswego	NY	22,219	VC
SUNY at Purchase College	NY	21,832	C
SUNY/Fredonia	NY	20,818	C
SUNY/Plattsburgh	NY	19,314	C
SUNY/Potsdam	NY	21,051	VC
Suffolk Univ	MA	52,316	C
Temple Univ	PA	24,392	C+
The American Univ	DC	61,317	HC
The College at Brockport - SUNY	NY	21,058	C
The College of New Jersey	NJ	28,675	VC+
The College of New Rochelle	NY	46,300	LC
The College of Wooster	OH	60,000	HC
The Univ of Arizona	AZ	24,086	C
The Univ of Montana Western	MT	9,426	LC
The Univ of Texas at San Antonio	TX	21,060	C
Towson Univ	MD	21,878	C
Trinity College	CT	69,020	HC
Tulane Univ	LA	67,496	MC
Union College	NY	64,320	MC
Univ of Calif at Berkeley	CA	29,886	MC
Univ of Calif at Davis	CA	28,468	HC
Univ of Calif at Irvine	CA	33,857	VC
Univ of Calif at Los Angeles	CA	27,438	HC+
Univ of Calif at Riverside	CA	32,912	C
Univ of Calif at Santa Barbara	CA	30,627	HC+
Univ of Calif, Santa Cruz	CA	28,731	C+
Univ of Cincinnati	OH	22,118	VC
Univ of Colo Colo Springs	CO	20,300	C
Univ of Conn	CT	27,394	
Univ of Dayton	OH	54,930	VC
Univ of Delaware	DE	32,214	VC
Univ of Denver	CO	61,129	VC+
Univ of Georgia	GA	21,878	HC
Univ of Hawaii at Manoa	HI	23,261	C
Univ of Illinois at Urbana-Champaign	IL	27,006	HC
Univ of Iowa	IA	19,415	HC
Univ of Kansas	KS	20,884	VC
Univ of Louisville	KY	19,692	C
Univ of Maryland/Baltimore County	MD	23,004	VC
Univ of Maryland/College Park	MD	21,938	HC
Univ of Mass Amherst	MA	27,669	HC
Univ of Miami	FL	63,494	MC
Univ of Mich/Ann Arbor	MI	25,274	MC
Univ of Minn/Duluth	MN	20,292	C
Univ of Minn/Morris	MN	21,222	VC
Univ of Nebr - Omaha	NE	16,120	C
Univ of Nevada, Las Vegas	NV	17,553	C
Univ of Nevada, Reno	NV	18,010	C
Univ of New Hampshire	NH	29,333	VC
Univ of New Mexico	NM	16,808	C
Univ of N Car at Asheville	NC	16,251	VC+
Univ of Oregon	OR	24,021	VC
Univ of Pennsylvania	PA	63,526	MC
Univ of Pittsburgh	PA	30,030	MC
Univ of Richmond	VA	62,730	MC
Univ of Rochester	NY	65,032	MC
Univ of St. Joseph	CT	49,069	C
Univ of Scranton	PA	54,962	VC
Univ of S Car at Columbia	SC	21,726	VC
Univ of Southern Calif	CA	66,631	MC
Univ of Southern Maine	ME	18,320	C
Univ of Toledo	OH	19,336	C
Univ of Tulsa	OK	52,625	HC
Univ of Washington	WA	23,091	MC
Univ of Wisc-Eau Claire	WI	16,354	VC
Univ of Wisc-Green Bay	WI	15,184	C
Univ of Wisc-La Crosse	WI	15,425	VC
Univ of Wisc-Madison	WI	21,647	MC
Univ of Wisc-Milwaukee	WI	21,538	C
Univ of Wisc-Whitewater	WI	13,976	C
Vassar College	NY	68,110	MC
Virginia Wesleyan Univ	VA	45,980	LC
Washington State Univ	WA	22,747	C
Washington Univ in St. Louis	MO	67,539	MC
Webster Univ	MO	37,490	C
Wellesley College	MA	66,984	MC
West Chester Univ of Pennsylvania	PA	19,171	VC
Western Mich Univ	MI	21,791	C
Western Washington Univ	WA	18,904	VC
Whitworth Univ	WA	53,682	VC
Wichita State Univ	KS	17,773	C
Widener Univ	PA	58,190	C
Willamette Univ	OR	62,514	VC+
Williams College	MA	67,700	MC
Yale Univ	CT	64,650	MC

WOOD SCIENCE

School	ST	$IS	SR
N Car State Univ	NC	22,434	HC+
Pittsburg State Univ	KS	13,880	C
Purdue Univ/West Lafayette	IN	20,032	MC
SUNY/The College of Environmental Science and Forestry	NY	23,728	VC
Univ of Maine	ME	21,038	VC
Univ of Mass Amherst	MA	27,669	HC
West Virginia Univ	WV	18,952	VC

WOODWORKING

School	ST	$IS	SR
Rochester Inst of Technology	NY	52,734	HC+
SUNY at New Paltz	NY	20,840	C
Univ of Rio Grande & Rio Grande Community College	OH	8,750	LC

WORLD CULTURAL STUDIES

School	ST	$IS	SR
Calif Baptist Univ	CA	42,986	C
Georgia College & State Univ	GA	21,884	C+
Univ of Northern Iowa	IA	17,480	C
Univ of Okla	OK	19,651	HC

WORLD LANGUAGE EDUCATION

School	ST	$IS	SR
DePaul Univ	IL	52,807	VC
Indiana Univ Bloomington	IN	20,791	HC
Univ of Georgia	GA	21,878	HC

WRITING

School	ST	$IS	SR
Aquinas College - Mich	MI	38,876	VC
Bay Path Univ	MA	46,356	C
Bloomfield College	NJ	40,100	LC
Cabrini Univ	PA	42,591	LC
Calif College of the Arts	CA	52,758	SP
Calvin College	MI	43,090	HC
Carroll Univ	WI	38,100	C+
Catawba College	NC	39,820	LC
Cedar Crest College	PA	51,110	C
Champlain College	VT	54,724	VC
Coe College	IA	51,570	VC
Columbia College Chicago	IL	40,104	C
Concordia College - New York	NY	39,035	LC
Drury Univ	MO	37,555	VC
Eastern Mennonite Univ	VA	42,550	C
Elon Univ	NC	46,142	HC
Fontbonne Univ	MO	34,606	C
Gettysburg College	PA	65,210	MC
Goshen College	IN	44,350	C
Houghton College	NY	40,558	VC
Johnson State College	VT	22,672	C
Keene State College	NH	24,604	C
Madonna Univ	MI	30,450	LC
Marquette Univ	WI	53,090	VC+
New York Univ	NY	68,139	MC
North Central Univ	MN	30,610	C
Northland College	WI	41,103	C+
Okla Christian Univ	OK	29,260	C
Old Dominion Univ	VA	21,618	C
Point Loma Nazarene Univ	CA	46,150	C+
Sarah Lawrence College	NY	68,866	MC
Savannah College of Art and Design	GA	49,595	SP
Southern Oregon Univ	OR	19,117	C
Taylor Univ	IN	42,130	VC
Texas Christian Univ	TX	57,120	HC
The Univ of Utah	UT	18,751	VC
Univ of Central Florida	FL	16,379	VC
Univ of Maine at Machias	ME	22,960	C
Univ of Mount Union	OH	39,990	C
Univ of Tampa	FL	38,928	VC
Univ of Texas Rio Grande Valley	TX	15,573	LC
Univ of Wisc-Superior	WI	14,838	C
Woodbury Univ	CA	49,593	VC

WRITING & RHETORIC

School	ST	$IS	SR
DePaul Univ	IL	52,807	VC
Johns Hopkins Univ	MD	68,080	MC
Syracuse Univ	NY	62,313	HC
Univ of Rhode Island	RI	26,066	VC
Western Mich Univ	MI	21,791	C

YIDDISH

School	ST	$IS	SR
Thomas Edison State Univ	NJ	6,350	NC

YOUTH MINISTRY

School	ST	$IS	SR
Anderson Univ	IN	39,450	C
Andrews Univ	MI	41,732	C
Asbury Univ	KY	36,450	C+
Augsburg Univ	MN	45,129	C
Azusa Pacific Univ	CA	43,972	C
Benedictine College	KS	38,850	VC
Bethel Univ	MN	46,550	C+
Bluffton Univ	OH	40,950	C+
Cairn Univ	PA	37,572	C
Campbellsville Univ	KY	33,400	C
Cedarville Univ	OH	36,244	VC
Charleston Southern Univ	SC	34,700	C
Colo Christian Univ	CO	40,885	VC
Concordia Univ	OR	35,000	C
Corban Univ	OR	41,700	C
Cornerstone Univ	MI	36,550	C
Dallas Baptist Univ	TX	35,220	VC
Dordt College	IA	37,860	C+
East Texas Baptist Univ	TX	34,444	C
Eastern Univ	PA	39,540	C
Faulkner Univ	AL	26,410	C
Florida Southern College	FL	45,978	VC
Grace Bible College	MI	25,250	C
Grace College and Seminary	IN	31,524	C
Greenville College	IL	27,012	LC
Harding Univ	AR	25,440	C
Hardin-Simmons Univ	TX	36,025	C
Hope International Univ	CA	42,730	C
Huntington Univ	IN	33,996	C
Judson Univ	IL	39,174	C
Kentucky Christian Univ	KY	26,836	LC
King Univ	TN	36,976	C
Lee Univ	TN	22,045	C
Lenoir-Rhyne Univ	NC	47,500	LC
Lipscomb Univ	TN	42,984	VC
Lubbock Christian Univ	TX	29,727	C
MacMurray College	IL	35,025	C
Malone Univ	OH	39,200	C
MidAmerica Nazarene Univ	KS	37,808	C
Milligan College	TN	39,450	C
Mount Vernon Nazarene Univ	OH	35,944	C
North Central Univ	MN	30,610	C
North Greenville Univ	SC	25,930	C
North Park Univ	IL	35,860	C
Northwest Nazarene Univ	ID	40,250	C
Northwest Univ	WA	38,720	VC
Northwestern College of Iowa	IA	38,400	C
Nyack College	NY	34,450	LC
Ohio Northern Univ	OH	44,050	VC
Okla Baptist Univ	OK	33,990	C
Okla Christian Univ	OK	29,260	C
Okla Wesleyan Univ	OK	34,434	C
Olivet Nazarene Univ	IL	41,840	VC
Ouachita Baptist Univ	AR	33,500	VC
Point Loma Nazarene Univ	CA	46,150	C+
Rochester College	MI	28,574	LC
St. Mary's Univ of Minn	MN	42,440	C
Shorter Univ	GA	31,130	LC
Simpson Univ	CA	34,722	C
Southern Nazarene Univ	OK	33,684	C
Spring Arbor Univ	MI	37,390	C
Toccoa Falls College	GA	30,048	C
Trinity International Univ	IL	31,070	VC
Union Univ	TN	41,160	VC
Univ of Northwestern - St. Paul	MN	39,530	C
Vanguard Univ of Southern Calif	CA	42,400	VC
York College	NE	30,260	C

ZOOLOGY

School	ST	$IS	SR
Alabama A&M Univ	AL	18,796	C
Andrews Univ	MI	41,732	C
Auburn Univ	AL	24,300	VC+
Bennington College	VT	66,280	MC
Calif State Polytechnic Univ, Pomona	CA	21,811	C
Cal State, Fullerton	CA	21,902	C
Cal State, Long Beach	CA	18,850	C
Canisius College	NY	49,672	C
Colo State Univ	CO	23,033	C
Delaware Valley Univ	PA	51,271	C
Florida State Univ	FL	16,771	HC
Fort Valley State Univ	GA	17,988	VC
Friends Univ	KS	38,000	C
Humboldt State Univ	CA	21,708	C
Idaho State Univ	ID	13,619	LC
Kent State Univ	OH	20,928	C
Kentucky Wesleyan College	KY	34,260	LC
Malone Univ	OH	39,200	C
Mars Hill Univ	NC	41,104	C
Miami Univ	OH	27,190	HC+
Mich State Univ	MI	24,542	VC
Missouri Western State Univ	MO	17,822	LC
N Car State Univ	NC	22,434	HC+
Northern Mich Univ	MI	20,853	C
Northwest Missouri State Univ	MO	18,286	C
Ohio State Univ at Columbus	OH	22,843	MC
Ohio Univ	OH	23,394	VC
Ohio Wesleyan Univ	OH	49,460	VC
Okla State Univ	OK	17,180	C+
Olivet Nazarene Univ	IL	41,840	VC
Oregon State Univ	OR	23,337	VC
Otterbein Univ	OH	41,630	C
Rutgers Univ - Newark	NJ	27,351	C
San Diego State Univ	CA	23,156	VC
San Francisco State Univ	CA	18,514	LC
San Jose State Univ	CA	22,630	C
Southern Illinois Univ Carbondale	IL	24,554	C
SUNY at Oswego	NY	22,219	VC
Texas A&M Univ at College Station	TX	20,771	VC+
Texas State Univ	TX	18,721	C
Texas Tech Univ	TX	20,156	C+
The Evergreen State College	WA	16,599	C
Univ of Calif at Davis	CA	28,468	HC
Univ of Calif at Santa Barbara	CA	30,627	HC+
Univ of Florida	FL	16,291	HC+
Univ of Hawaii at Manoa	HI	23,261	C
Univ of Kentucky	KY	24,800	C+
Univ of Maine	ME	21,038	VC
Univ of Montana	MT	14,105	C
Univ of New Hampshire	NH	29,333	VC
Univ of Okla	OK	19,651	HC
Univ of Vermont	VT	29,792	HC
Univ of Washington	WA	23,091	MC
Univ of Wisc-Madison	WI	21,647	MC
Univ of Wyoming	WY	15,537	C
Washington State Univ	WA	22,747	C
Weber State Univ	UT	14,112	C
Western New Mexico Univ	NM	16,914	LC

ST = STATE $IS = IN-STATE COSTS SR = SELECTOR RATING

PART IV

A CLOSE LOOK AT THE COLLEGES

This section will help you understand the college Profiles that are at the heart of this directory, so you can get the most out of them.

The College Admissions Selector explains Barron's unique system of comparing every school's degree of admissions competitiveness. Colleges are rated from Most Competitive to Less Competitive, and more.

Explanations of the ratings are followed by an in-depth look at the college capsule and essay.

Next come the Profiles—over 1600 four-year accredited colleges and universities in the United States—followed by encapsulated descriptions of about fifty religious schools. Universities outside the boundaries of this country are profiled here, too, including Canadian, European, and more.

COLLEGE ADMISSIONS SELECTOR

This index groups all the colleges listed in this book according to degree of admissions competitiveness. The *Selector* is not a rating of colleges by academic standards or quality of education; it is rather an attempt to describe, in general terms, the situation a prospective student will meet when applying for admission.

THE CRITERIA USED

The factors used in determining the category for each college were: median entrance examination scores for the 2017–2018 freshman class (the SAT score used was derived by averaging the median criti- cal reading, math, and writing scores; the ACT score used was the median composite score); percentages of 2017–2018 freshmen scoring 500 and above and 600 and above on the critical reading, math, and writing sections of the SAT; percentages of 2017–2018 freshmen scoring 21 and above and 27 and above on the ACT; percentage of 2017–2018 freshmen who ranked in the upper fifth and the upper two-fifths of their high school graduating classes; minimum class rank and grade point average required for admission (if any); and percentage of applicants to the 2017–2018 freshman class who were accepted. The *Selector* cannot and does not take into account all the other factors that each college considers when making admissions decisions. Colleges place varying degrees of emphasis on the factors that comprise each of these categories.

USING THE SELECTOR

To use the *Selector* effectively, the prospective student's records should be compared realistically with the freshmen enrolled by the colleges in each category, as shown by the SAT or ACT scores, the quality of high school record emphasized by the colleges in each category, and the kinds of risks that the applicant wishes to take.

The student should also be aware of what importance a particular school places on various nonacademic factors; when available, this information is presented in the profile of the school. If a student has unusual qualifications that may compensate for exam scores or high school record, the student should examine admissions policies of the colleges in the next higher category than the one that encompasses his or her score and consider those colleges that give major consideration to factors other than exam scores and high school grades. The "safety" college should usually be chosen from the next lower category, where the student can be reasonably sure that his or her scores and high school record will fall above the median scores and records of the freshmen enrolled in the college.

The listing within each category is alphabetical and not in any qualitative order. State-supported institutions have been classified according to the requirements for state residents, but standards for admission of out-of-state students are usually higher. Colleges that are experimenting with the admission of students of higher potential but lower achievement may appear in a less competitive category because of this fact.

A WORD OF CAUTION

The *Selector* is intended primarily for preliminary screening, to eliminate the majority of colleges that are not suitable for a particular student. Be sure to examine the admissions policies spelled out in the *Admissions* section of each profile. And remember that many colleges have to reject *qualified* students; the *Selector* will tell you what your chances are, not which college will accept you.

MOST COMPETITIVE

Even superior students will encounter a great deal of competition for admission to the colleges in this category. In general, these colleges require high school rank in the top 10% to 20% and grade averages of A to B+. Median freshman test scores at these colleges are generally between 655 and 800 on the SAT and 29 and above on the ACT. In addition, many of these colleges admit only a small percentage of those who apply—usually fewer than one third.

Amherst College, MA
Bard College at Simon's Rock, MA
Barnard College/Columbia University, NY
Bennington College, VT
Bentley University, MA
Boston College, MA
Boston University, MA
Bowdoin College, ME
Brandeis University, MA
Brigham Young University, UT
Brown University, RI
Bryn Mawr College, PA
Bucknell University, PA
California Institute of Technology, CA
California Polytechnic State University, CA
Carleton College, MN
Carnegie Mellon University, PA
Case Western Reserve University, OH
Centre College, KY
Claremont McKenna College, CA
Colby College, ME
Colgate University, NY
College of the Holy Cross, MA
College of William & Mary, VA
Colorado College, CO
Colorado School of Mines, CO
Columbia University/ School of General Studies, NY
Columbia University/City of New York, NY
Connecticut College, CT
Cooper Union for the Advancement of Science and Art, NY
Cornell University, NY
Dartmouth College, NH
Davidson College, NC
Dickinson College, PA
Duke University, NC
Emory University, GA
Fordham University, NY
Franklin and Marshall College, PA
Georgetown University, DC
Georgia Institute of Technology, GA
Gettysburg College, PA
Grinnell College, IA
Hamilton College, NY
Hampshire College, MA
Harvard College/Harvard University, MA
Harvey Mudd College, CA
Haverford College, PA
Hillsdale College, MI
Johns Hopkins University, MD
Kenyon College, OH
Lafayette College, PA
Lehigh University, PA
Lewis & Clark College, OR
Macalester College, MN
Massachusetts Institute of Technology, MA
Middlebury College, VT
Mount Holyoke College, MA
New York University, NY
Northeastern University, MA
Northwestern University, IL
Oberlin College, OH
Occidental College, CA
Ohio State University at Columbus, OH
Pomona College, CA
Princeton University, NJ
Purdue University/West Lafayette, IN

Reed College, OR
Rensselaer Polytechnic Institute, NY
Rice University, TX
Rose-Hulman Institute of Technology, IN
Sarah Lawrence College, NY
Skidmore College, NY
Smith College, MA
Southern Methodist University, TX
St. John's College at Annapolis, MD
Stanford University, CA
State University of New York at Binghamton, NY
Stevens Institute of Technology, NJ
Stony Brook University/The State University of New York, NY
Swarthmore College, PA
Trinity University, TX
Truman State University, MO
Tufts University, MA
Tulane University, LA
Union College, NY
University of California at Berkeley, CA
University of California San Diego, CA
University of Chicago, IL
University of Miami, FL
University of Michigan/Ann Arbor, MI
University of Minnesota/Twin Cities, MN
University of North Carolina at Chapel Hill, NC
University of Notre Dame, IN
University of Pennsylvania, PA
University of Pittsburgh, PA
University of Richmond, VA
University of Rochester, NY
University of Southern California, CA
The University of Texas at Austin, TX
University of Texas at Dallas, TX
University of Virginia, VA
University of Washington, WA
University of Wisconsin-Madison, WI
Vanderbilt University, TN
Vassar College, NY
Villanova University, PA
Wake Forest University, NC
Washington and Lee University, VA
Washington University in St. Louis, MO
Webb Institute, NY
Wellesley College, MA
Wesleyan University, CT
Wheaton College, IL
Whitman College, WA
Williams College, MA
Worcester Polytechnic Institute, MA
Yale University, CT

HIGHLY COMPETITIVE

Colleges in this group generally look for students with grade averages of B+ to B and accept most of their students from the top 20% to 35% of the high school class. Median freshman test scores at these colleges generally range from 620 to 654 on the SAT and 27 or 28 on the ACT. These schools generally accept between one third and one half of their applicants.

To provide for finer distinctions within this admissions category, a plus (+) symbol has been placed before some entries. These are colleges with median freshman scores of 645 or more on the SAT or 28 or more on the ACT (depending on which test the college prefers), and colleges that accept fewer than one quarter of their applicants.

The American University, DC
Austin College, TX
Babson College, MA
Bard College, NY
Bates College, ME
Baylor University, TX
Beloit College, WI
Calvin College, MI
Chapman University, CA
City University of New York/Baruch College, NY
+Clark University, MA
Clemson University, SC
+College of the Atlantic, ME
The College of Wooster, OH
Covenant College, GA
+Denison University, OH
Drake University, IA
Drexel University, PA
Earlham College, IN
Elon University, NC
+Emerson College, MA
Fairfield University, CT
Florida State University, FL
+The George Washington University, DC
Gonzaga University, WA
Gustavus Adolphus College, MN
+Hobart and William Smith Colleges, NY
+Illinois Institute of Technology, IL
Indiana University Bloomington, IN
Kalamazoo College, MI
Kettering University, MI
+Lawrence University, WI
+Miami University, OH
+Milwaukee School of Engineering, WI
Missouri University of Science and Technology, MO
+New College of Florida, FL
New Jersey Institute of Technology, NJ
+New Mexico Institute of Mining and Technology, NM
+North Carolina State University, NC
Pennsylvania State University - University Park, PA
+Pitzer College, CA
Providence College, RI
Rhodes College, TN
+Rochester Institute of Technology, NY
Rollins College, FL
Rutgers University - New Brunswick, NJ
Saint Louis University, MO
Scripps College, CA
+Sewanee: The University of the South, TN
Simmons College, MA
+St. John's College, Santa Fe, NM
+St. Lawrence University, NY
St. Olaf College, MN
Syracuse University, NY
Texas Christian University, TX
+Thomas Aquinas College, CA
+Transylvania University, KY
Trinity College, CT
United States Coast Guard Academy, CT
United States Merchant Marine Academy, NY
+United States Military Academy at West Point, NY
United States Naval Academy, MD
University of California at Davis, CA
+University of California at Los Angeles, CA
+University of California at Santa Barbara, CA
University of Colorado Boulder, CO
+University of Florida, FL
University of Georgia, GA
University of Illinois at Urbana-Champaign, IL
University of Iowa, IA
University of Maryland/College Park, MD
University of Massachusetts Amherst, MA
University of Oklahoma, OK
University of Puget Sound, WA
University of San Diego, CA
University of Tulsa, OK
University of Vermont, VT

VERY COMPETITIVE

The colleges in this category generally admit students whose averages are no less than B- and who rank in the top 35% to 50% of their graduating class. They generally report median freshman test scores in the 573 to 619 range on the SAT and from 24 to 26 on the ACT. These schools generally accept between one half and three quarters of their applicants.

The plus (+) has been placed before colleges with median freshman scores of 610 or above on the SAT or 26 or better on the ACT (depending on which test the college prefers), and colleges that accept fewer than one third of their applicants.

+Agnes Scott College, GA
Alaska Pacific University, AK
Allegheny College, PA
Alma College, MI
Appalachian State University, NC
Aquinas College - Michigan, MI
Arizona State University at the Downtown Phoenix Campus, AZ
Arizona State University at the Polytechnic Campus, AZ
Arizona State University at the Tempe Campus, AZ
Arizona State University at the West Campus, AZ
Assumption College, MA
+Auburn University, AL
+Augustana College, IL
Augustana University, SD
Baldwin Wallace University, OH
+Belmont University, TN
Benedictine College, KS
Berry College, GA
Bradley University, IL
Brescia University, KY
Bryant University, RI
+Butler University, IN
California State University, Chico, CA
Campbell University, NC
Capital University, OH
The Catholic University of America, DC
Cedarville University, OH
Central Methodist University, MO
Champlain College, VT
Chatham University, PA
Christendom College, VA
Christian Brothers University, TN
+Christopher Newport University, VA
City University of New York/Hunter College, NY
Clarkson University, NY
Coe College, IA
College of Charleston, SC
+The College of New Jersey, NJ
College of the Ozarks, MO
Colorado Christian University, CO
Concordia University Irvine, CA
Concordia University Nebraska, NE
Coppin State University, MD
Cornell College, IA
Creighton University, NE
Dallas Baptist University, TX
DePaul University, IL
DePauw University, IN
Dillard University, LA
Doane University, NE
Drew University/College of Liberal Arts, NJ
Drury University, MO
Duquesne University, PA
Eckerd College, FL
Elizabethtown College, PA
Elms College, MA
Embry-Riddle Aeronautical University - Daytona Beach, FL
Embry-Riddle Aeronautical University - Prescott Campus, AZ
Eugene Lang College of Liberal Arts, NY
Florida Institute of Technology, FL
Florida Southern College, FL
Fort Valley State University, GA
Franciscan University of Steubenville, OH
+Furman University, SC
Georgia Southern University, GA
Goddard College, VT
Gordon College, MA
Goucher College, MD
Grand Canyon University, AZ
Grove City College, PA
Hampden-Sydney College, VA
Hendrix College, AR
High Point University, NC
Hollins University, VA
Hope College, MI
Houghton College, NY
Illinois College, IL
Illinois State University, IL
+Illinois Wesleyan University, IL
+Ithaca College, NY
James Madison University, VA
John Brown University, AR
Juniata College, PA
Kansas State University, KS
Kennesaw State University, GA
+Knox College, IL
La Sierra University, CA
Lake Forest College, IL
Lawrence Technological University, MI
Le Moyne College, NY
Lebanon Valley College, PA
LeTourneau University, TX
Lipscomb University, TN
Louisiana State University and A&M College, LA
Louisiana Tech University, LA
+Loyola Marymount University, CA
Loyola University Chicago, IL
Loyola University Maryland, MD
Loyola University New Orleans, LA
Luther College, IA
Lyon College, AR
Maharishi University of Management, IA
Marist College, NY
+Marlboro College, VT
+Marquette University, WI
Maryville University of Saint Louis, MO
McDaniel College, MD
Mercer University, GA
Messiah College, PA
Metropolitan College of New York, NY
Michigan State University, MI
+Michigan Technological University, MI
Montana Tech of the University of Montana, MT
+Mount St. Mary's University - Chalon Campus, CA
Muhlenberg College, PA
New York Institute of Technology, NY
North Dakota State University, ND
Northeastern State University, OK
Northwest University, WA
Notre Dame College, OH
Notre Dame of Maryland University, MD
Ohio Northern University, OH
Ohio State University at Marion , OH
Ohio University, OH
Ohio Wesleyan University, OH
Olivet Nazarene University, IL
Oregon State University, OR
Ottawa University, KS
Ouachita Baptist University, AR
Pacific Union College, CA
Penn State Erie,The Behrend College, PA
+Pepperdine University, CA
+Pratt Institute, NY
Quinnipiac University, CT
Ramapo College of New Jersey, NJ
Randolph-Macon College, VA
Ripon College, WI
Rivier University, NH

Roanoke College, VA
Roger Williams University, RI
Roosevelt University, IL
Rowan University, NJ
Saint Anselm College, NH
Saint Joseph's University, PA
+Saint Michael's College, VT
Salisbury University, MD
Salve Regina University, RI
Samford University, AL
San Diego State University, CA
Seattle University, WA
Seton Hill University, PA
Simpson College, IA
Southwestern University, TX
St. Edward's University, TX
St. John Fisher College, NY
St. Mary's College of Maryland, MD
St. Norbert College, WI
State University of New York at Geneseo, NY
State University of New York at Oswego, NY
State University of New York Polytechnic Institute, NY
State University of New York/Potsdam, NY
State University of New York/The College of Environmental Science and Forestry, NY
Sterling College, VT
+Stetson University, FL
Susquehanna University, PA
Taylor University, IN
+Texas A&M University at College Station, TX
Trinity International University, IL
Union University, TN
University of Alabama in Huntsville, AL
University of Alaska Fairbanks, AK
University of Arkansas at Fayetteville, AR
University of California at Irvine, CA
University of Central Arkansas, AR
University of Central Florida, FL
University of Cincinnati, OH
University of Dallas, TX
University of Dayton, OH
University of Delaware, DE
+University of Denver, CO
University of Hawaii at Hilo, HI
University of Houston, TX
University of Illinois at Chicago, IL
University of Indianapolis, IN
University of Kansas, KS
University of Maine, ME
University of Maryland/Baltimore County, MD
University of Massachusetts Lowell, MA
University of Michigan/Dearborn, MI
University of Minnesota/Morris, MN
University of Missouri-Columbia, MO
University of Missouri-Kansas City, MO
University of Missouri-St. Louis, MO
University of Nebraska - Lincoln, NE
University of New Hampshire, NH
+University of North Carolina at Asheville, NC
University of North Carolina at Charlotte, NC
University of North Carolina Wilmington, NC
University of North Florida, FL
University of Oregon, OR
University of Portland, OR
University of Redlands, CA
University of Rhode Island, RI
University of Science and Arts of Oklahoma, OK
University of Scranton, PA
University of South Carolina at Columbia, SC
University of South Florida/Tampa, FL
University of St. Thomas, MN
University of St. Thomas - Houston, TX
University of Tampa, FL
The University of Tennessee at Knoxville, TN
University of the Pacific, CA
University of the Sciences, PA
The University of Utah, UT
University of Wisconsin-Eau Claire, WI
University of Wisconsin-La Crosse, WI
Ursinus College, PA
Valparaiso University, IN
Vanguard University of Southern California, CA
Virginia Commonwealth University, VA
Virginia Military Institute, VA
Virginia Polytechnic Institute and State University, VA
Wabash College, IN
Warren Wilson College, NC
Washington & Jefferson College, PA
Washington College, MD
Wentworth Institute of Technology, MA
West Chester University of Pennsylvania, PA
West Virginia University, WV
Western Washington University, WA
Westmont College, CA
Wheaton College, MA
Whitworth University, WA
+Willamette University, OR
Wittenberg University, OH
Wofford College, SC
Woodbury University, CA
Xavier University, OH
Yeshiva University, NY

COMPETITIVE

This category is a very broad one, covering colleges that generally have median freshman test scores between 500 and 572 on the SAT and between 21 and 23 on the ACT. Some of these colleges require that students have high school averages of B– or better, although others state a minimum of C+ or C. Generally, these colleges prefer students in the top 50% to 65% of the graduating class and accept between 75% and 85% of their applicants.

Colleges with a plus (+) are those with median freshman SAT scores of 563 or more or median freshman ACT scores of 24 or more (depending on which test the colleges prefers), and those that admit fewer than half of their applicants.

+Abilene Christian University, TX
Adelphi University, NY
Adrian College, MI
Alabama A&M University, AL
Albany State University, GA
Albion College, MI
Albright College, PA
Alcorn State University, MS
Alfred State College, NY
Alfred University, NY
Alvernia University, PA
American Jewish University - College of Arts and Sciences, CA
Anderson University, IN
Andrews University, MI
Anna Maria College, MA
+Aquinas College, TN
+Arcadia University, PA
Arkansas State University, AR
Armstrong State University, GA
+Asbury University, KY
Ashford University, CA
Ashland University, OH
Atlantic Union College, MA
Auburn University at Montgomery, AL
Augsburg University, MN
Augusta University, GA
Aurora University, IL
Austin Peay State University, TN
Avila University, MO
Azusa Pacific University, CA
Baker University, KS
+Ball State University, IN
Barton College, NC
Bay Path University, MA
Beacon College, FL
Belhaven University, MS
Bellarmine University, KY
Belmont Abbey College, NC
Bemidji State University, MN
Benedictine University, IL
Berea College, KY
Bethel College, IN
Bethel College, KS
+Bethel University, MN
Bethel University, TN
Bethune-Cookman University, FL
Biola University, CA
+Birmingham-Southern College, AL
Black Hills State University, SD
Bloomsburg University of Pennsylvania, PA
Blue Mountain College, MS
Bluefield College, VA
+Bluffton University, OH
Boise State University, ID
Boricua College, NY
Bowling Green State University, OH
Briar Cliff University, IA
Bridgewater College, VA
Bridgewater State University, MA
Brigham Young University/Hawaii, HI
Bryan College, TN
Bryn Athyn College, PA
Buena Vista University, IA
Cairn University, PA
California Baptist University, CA
California Lutheran University, CA
California State Polytechnic University, Pomona, CA
+California State University, Maritime Academy, CA
California State University, East Bay, CA
California State University, Fullerton, CA
California State University, Long Beach, CA
California State University, Sacramento, CA
California State University, San Bernardino, CA
Calumet College of St. Joseph, IN
Campbellsville University, KY
Canisius College, NY
Cardinal Stritch University, WI
Carroll College, MT
+Carroll University, WI
Carson-Newman University, TN
Carthage College, WI
Castleton University, VT
Cazenovia College, NY
Cedar Crest College, PA
+Centenary College of Louisiana, LA
Central College, IA
Central Connecticut State University, CT
Central Michigan University, MI
Central State University, OH
Central Washington University, WA
Chaminade University of Honolulu, HI
Charleston Southern University, SC
Chestnut Hill College, PA
Chicago State University, IL
The Citadel, The Military College of South Carolina, SC
+City University of New York/Brooklyn College, NY
City University of New York/City College, NY
City University of New York/Queens College, NY
Clarke University, IA
Clarkson College, NE
Cleveland State University, OH
Coastal Carolina University, SC
Cogswell Polytechnical College, CA
Coker College, SC
Colby-Sawyer College, NH
The College at Brockport - State University of New York, NY
The College of Idaho, ID
College of Mount Saint Vincent, NY
College of Saint Benedict, MN
College of Saint Mary, NE
The College of Saint Rose, NY
+College of St. Scholastica, MN
Colorado State University, CO
Colorado State University-Pueblo, CO
Columbia College, SC
Columbia College - Missouri, MO
Columbia College Chicago, IL
Concordia College - Moorhead, MN
Concordia University, OR
Concordia University Saint Paul, MN
Concordia University Texas, TX
Concordia University Wisconsin, WI
+Concordia University, Ann Arbor, MI
Concordia University, Chicago, IL
Converse College, SC
Corban University, OR
Cornerstone University, MI
Culver-Stockton College, MO
Cumberland University, TN
Curry College, MA
Daemen College, NY
Dakota State University, SD
Delaware Valley University, PA
DeSales University, PA
+Dominican University, IL
Dominican University of California, CA
+Dordt College, IA
D'Youville College, NY

East Carolina University, NC
East Central University, OK
East Tennessee State University, TN
East Texas Baptist University, TX
Eastern Connecticut State University, CT
Eastern Illinois University, IL
Eastern Kentucky University, KY
Eastern Mennonite University, VA
Eastern Michigan University, MI
Eastern Nazarene College, MA
Eastern Oregon University, OR
Eastern University, PA
Edgewood College, WI
Elizabeth City State University, NC
Elizabethtown College School of Continuing and Professional Studies, PA
Elmhurst College, IL
Elmira College, NY
Embry-Riddle Aeronautical University - Worldwide, FL
+Emmanuel College, MA
Emory and Henry College, VA
Emporia State University, KS
+Endicott College, MA
Erskine College, SC
Eureka College, IL
Evangel University, MO
The Evergreen State College, WA
Fairleigh Dickinson University/College at Florham, NJ
Fairleigh Dickinson University/Metropolitan Campus, NJ
Fairmont State University, WV
Farmingdale State College, NY
Faulkner University, AL
Fayetteville State University, NC
Ferris State University, MI
Ferrum College, VA
Flagler College, FL
Florida Agricultural and Mechanical University, FL
Florida Atlantic University, FL
Florida Gulf Coast University, FL
Florida International University, FL
Fontbonne University, MO
Fort Hays State University, KS
Fort Lewis College, CO
Framingham State University, MA
Franklin College, IN
Freed-Hardeman University, TN
Fresno Pacific University, CA
Friends University, KS
Gannon University, PA
+Gardner-Webb University, NC
Geneva College, PA
George Fox University, OR
George Mason University, VA
Georgetown College, KY
+Georgia College & State University, GA
Georgia State University, GA
Golden Gate University, CA
Goldey-Beacom College, DE
Goshen College, IN
Grace Bible College, MI
Grace College and Seminary, IN
Graceland University, IA
Grambling State University, LA
+Grand Valley State University, MI
Grand View University, IA
Guilford College, NC
Hamline University, MN
Hampton University, VA
Hannibal-LaGrange University, MO
+Hanover College, IN
Harding University, AR
Hardin-Simmons University, TX
Hartwick College, NY
+Hastings College, NE
Hawaii Pacific University, HI
Hellenic College/Holy Cross Greek Orthodox School of Theology, MA
Henderson State University, AR
Hiram College, OH
+Hofstra University, NY
Hood College, MD
Hope International University, CA
Houston Baptist University, TX
Howard Payne University, TX
+Howard University, DC
Humboldt State University, CA
Humphreys College, CA
Huntingdon College, AL
Huntington University, IN
Husson University, ME
Immaculata University, PA
Indiana University East, IN
Indiana University Kokomo, IN
Indiana University of Pennsylvania, PA
Indiana University South Bend, IN
Indiana University Southeast, IN
Indiana University-Purdue University Fort Wayne, IN
Indiana University-Purdue University Indianapolis, IN
Indiana Wesleyan University, IN
Iona College, NY
Iowa State University, IA
Iowa Wesleyan University, IA
Jacksonville University, FL
Jefferson (Philadelphia University + Thomas Jefferson University), PA
John Carroll University, OH
Johnson & Wales University/Charlotte Campus, NC
Johnson & Wales University/Denver Campus, CO
Johnson & Wales University/North Miami Campus, FL
Johnson & Wales University/Providence Campus, RI
Johnson State College, VT
Judson College, AL
Judson University, IL
Kansas Wesleyan University, KS
Kean University, NJ
Keene State College, NH
Kendall College, IL
Kent State University, OH
Keuka College, NY
King University, TN
King's College, PA
Kutztown University of Pennsylvania, PA
La Roche College, PA
La Salle University, PA
LaGrange College, GA
Lake Superior State University, MI
Lakeland University, WI
Lander University, SC
Langston University, OK
Lasell College, MA
Lee University, TN
LeMoyne-Owen College, TN
Lesley University, MA
Lewis University, IL
Lewis-Clark State College, ID
Liberty University, VA
Limestone College, SC
Lincoln Memorial University, TN
Lindenwood University, MO
Lindsey Wilson College, KY
Linfield College, OR
LIU Brooklyn, NY
+LIU Post, NY
Longwood University, VA
Loras College, IA
Louisiana College, LA
Louisiana State University in Shreveport, LA
Lubbock Christian University, TX
Lycoming College, PA
Lyndon State College, VT
MacMurray College, IL
Maine Maritime Academy, ME
Malone University, OH
Manchester University, IN
Manhattan College, NY
Manhattanville College, NY
Marian University, IN
Marian University, WI
Marietta College, OH
Mars Hill University, NC
Marshall University, WV
Mary Baldwin University, VA
Marymount Manhattan College, NY
Marymount University, VA

Maryville College, TN
Marywood University, PA
Massachusetts College of Liberal Arts, MA
Massachusetts Maritime Academy, MA
The Master's University, CA
+McKendree University, IL
McNeese State University, LA
McPherson College, KS
Mercy College, NY
Mercyhurst University, PA
Meredith College, NC
Merrimack College, MA
Methodist University, NC
Metropolitan State University, MN
MidAmerica Nazarene University, KS
Middle Tennessee State University, TN
Midland University, NE
Millersville University of Pennsylvania, PA
Milligan College, TN
Millikin University, IL
Mills College, CA
+Millsaps College, MS
Minnesota State University, Mankato, MN
Minnesota State University, Moorhead, MN
Minot State University, ND
Misericordia University, PA
Mississippi College, MS
+Mississippi State University, MS
Mississippi University for Women, MS
Missouri Baptist University, MO
Missouri Southern State University, MO
+Missouri State University, MO
Missouri Valley College, MO
Mitchell College, CT
Molloy College, NY
Monmouth College, IL
Monmouth University, NJ
Monroe College, NY
+Montana State University, MT
Montclair State University, NJ
Moravian College, PA
Morehouse College, GA
Morningside College, IA
Mount Aloysius College, PA
Mount Ida College, MA
Mount Marty College, SD
Mount Mercy University, IA
Mount Saint Mary College, NY
Mount St. Mary's University, MD
Mount Vernon Nazarene University, OH
+Murray State University, KY
Muskingum University, OH
Nazareth College, NY
Nebraska Methodist College, NE
+Nebraska Wesleyan University, NE
Newberry College, SC
Newbury College, MA
Newman University, KS
Niagara University, NY
Nicholls State University, LA
North Carolina A&T State University, NC
North Carolina Central University, NC
North Carolina Wesleyan College, NC
+North Central College, IL
North Central University, MN
North Greenville University, SC
North Park University, IL
Northern Arizona University, AZ
Northern Illinois University, IL
Northern Kentucky University, KY
Northern Michigan University, MI
Northern State University, SD
+Northland College, WI
Northwest Christian University, OR
Northwest Missouri State University, MO
Northwest Nazarene University, ID
Northwestern College of Iowa, IA
Norwich University, VT
+Nova Southeastern University, FL
Oakland University, MI
Oakwood University, AL
Oglethorpe University, GA
+Ohio Dominican University, OH
Ohio State University at Lima, OH
Ohio State University at Mansfield, OH
Ohio State University at Newark, OH
Ohio Valley University, WV
Oklahoma Baptist University, OK
Oklahoma Christian University, OK
Oklahoma City University, OK
Oklahoma Panhandle State University, OK
+Oklahoma State University, OK
Oklahoma Wesleyan University, OK
Old Dominion University, VA
Oral Roberts University, OK
Oregon Institute of Technology, OR
Otterbein University, OH
Pace University, NY
Pacific Lutheran University, WA
Pacific University, OR
Palm Beach Atlantic University, FL
Park University, MO
Penn State Altoona, PA
Piedmont College, GA
Pittsburg State University, KS
+Point Loma Nazarene University, CA
Point Park University, PA
Portland State University, OR
Post University, CT
Presbyterian College, SC
Prescott College, AZ
Principia College, IL
Purdue University Northwest, IN
Queens University of Charlotte, NC
Radford University, VA
Randolph College, VA
Regis University, CO
Reinhardt University, GA
Rider University, NJ
Robert Morris University, PA
Roberts Wesleyan College, NY
Rockford University, IL
Rockhurst University, MO
Rocky Mountain College, MT
Russell Sage College, NY
Rust College, MS
Rutgers University - Camden, NJ
Rutgers University - Newark, NJ
Sacred Heart University, CT
Saginaw Valley State University, MI
SAGU American Indian College, AZ
Saint Augustine's University, NC
Saint John's University, MN
Saint Joseph's College of Maine, ME
Saint Leo University, FL
Saint Martin's University, WA
Saint Mary's College, IN
Saint Mary's College of California, CA
Saint Mary's University of Minnesota, MN
Saint Peter's University, NJ
Saint Vincent College, PA
Saint Xavier University, IL
Salem College, NC
Salem International University, WV
Sam Houston State University, TX
San Diego Christian College, CA
San Jose State University, CA
Savannah State University, GA
+Seattle Pacific University, WA
Seton Hall University, NJ
Shaw University, NC
Shawnee State University, OH
Shenandoah University, VA
Shepherd University, West Virginia, WV
Shippensburg University of Pennsylvania, PA
Siena College, NY
Siena Heights University, MI
Sierra Nevada College, NV
Simpson University, CA
Slippery Rock University of Pennsylvania, PA
Sonoma State University, CA
+South Dakota School of Mines and Technology, SD
South Dakota State University, SD
Southeast Missouri State University, MO

Southeastern Louisiana University, LA
Southeastern Oklahoma State University, OK
Southern Adventist University, TN
Southern Arkansas University, AR
Southern Illinois University Carbondale, IL
Southern Illinois University Edwardsville, IL
Southern Nazarene University, OK
Southern New Hampshire University, NH
Southern Oregon University, OR
Southern Utah University, UT
Southwest Minnesota State University, MN
Southwestern Oklahoma State University, OK
Spalding University, KY
Spelman College, GA
Spring Arbor University, MI
Spring Hill College, AL
Springfield College, MA
St. Ambrose University, IA
St. Bonaventure University, NY
St. Catherine University, MN
St. Cloud State University, MN
+St. John's University, NY
St. Joseph's College, New York/Long Island Campus, NY
St. Mary's University, TX
St. Thomas Aquinas College, NY
State University of New York Albany, NY
State University of New York at New Paltz, NY
State University of New York at Purchase College, NY
State University of New York/College at Old Westbury, NY
State University of New York/Cortland, NY
State University of New York/Fredonia, NY
State University of New York/Maritime College, NY
State University of New York/Oneonta, NY
State University of New York/Plattsburgh, NY
State University of New York/University at Buffalo, NY
Stephens College, MO
Stevenson University, MD
Stillman College, AL
Stockton University, NJ
Stonehill College, MA
Suffolk University, MA
Tabor College, KS
Talladega College, AL
+Temple University, PA
Tennessee Technological University, TN
Texas A&M University at Commerce, TX
Texas Lutheran University, TX
Texas State University, TX
+Texas Tech University, TX
Texas Wesleyan University, TX
Thomas More College of Liberal Arts, NH
Toccoa Falls College, GA
Touro College, NY
Towson University, MD
Trevecca Nazarene University, TN
Trine University, IN
Trinity Christian College, IL
+Trinity Washington University, DC
Troy University, AL
Tuskegee University, AL
Union College, KY
Union College, NE
United States Air Force Academy, CO
Unity College, ME
The University of Akron, OH
+The University of Alabama, AL
University of Alabama at Birmingham, AL
University of Alaska Anchorage, AK
University of Alaska Southeast, AK
The University of Arizona, AZ
University of Arkansas at Pine Bluff, AR
University of California at Riverside, CA
+University of California, Santa Cruz, CA
University of Central Missouri, MO
University of Central Oklahoma, OK
University of Colorado Colorado Springs, CO
University of Colorado Denver, CO
University of Detroit Mercy, MI
University of Dubuque, IA
+University of Evansville, IN
University of Findlay, OH
University of Great Falls, MT
University of Hartford, CT
University of Hawaii at Manoa, HI
University of Idaho, ID
University of Jamestown, ND
+University of Kentucky, KY
University of La Verne, CA
University of Louisiana at Lafayette, LA
University of Louisiana at Monroe, LA
University of Louisville, KY
University of Lynchburg, VA
University of Maine at Augusta, ME
University of Maine at Farmington, ME
University of Maine at Machias, ME
The University of Mary, ND
+University of Mary Hardin-Baylor, TX
+University of Mary Washington, VA
University of Massachusetts Boston, MA
University of Massachusetts Dartmouth, MA
The University of Memphis, TN
University of Michigan/Flint, MI
University of Minnesota/Crookston, MN
University of Minnesota/Duluth, MN
University of Mississippi, MS
University of Mobile, AL
University of Montana, MT
University of Montevallo, AL
University of Mount Olive, NC
University of Mount Union, OH
University of Nebraska - Omaha, NE
University of Nevada, Las Vegas, NV
University of Nevada, Reno, NV
University of New England, ME
University of New Hampshire - Manchester, NH
University of New Haven, CT
University of New Mexico, NM
University of New Orleans, LA
University of North Alabama, AL
University of North Carolina at Greensboro, NC
University of North Dakota, ND
University of North Georgia, GA
University of North Texas, TX
University of Northern Colorado, CO
University of Northern Iowa, IA
University of Northwestern - St. Paul, MN
University of Pikeville, KY
University of Pittsburgh at Bradford, PA
University of Pittsburgh at Greensburg, PA
University of Pittsburgh at Johnstown, PA
University of Saint Francis, IN
University of Saint Joseph, CT
University of San Francisco, CA
University of Sioux Falls, SD
University of South Alabama, AL
University of South Carolina Aiken, SC
University of South Dakota, SD
University of South Florida St. Petersburg, FL
University of Southern Indiana, IN
University of Southern Maine, ME
University of Southern Mississippi, MS
University of St. Francis, IL
+The University of Tennessee at Chattanooga, TN
The University of Tennessee at Martin, TN
University of Texas at Arlington, TX
The University of Texas at San Antonio, TX
University of the Southwest, NM
University of Toledo, OH
University of West Florida, FL
University of Wisconsin-Green Bay, WI
University of Wisconsin-Milwaukee, WI
University of Wisconsin-Oshkosh, WI
University of Wisconsin-Parkside, WI
University of Wisconsin-Platteville, WI
University of Wisconsin-River Falls, WI
University of Wisconsin-Stevens Point, WI
University of Wisconsin-Stout, WI
University of Wisconsin-Superior, WI
University of Wisconsin-Whitewater, WI
University of Wyoming, WY
Urbana University, OH
Utah State University, UT
Utica College, NY
Valdosta State University, GA

Valley City State University, ND
Vermont Technical College, VT
+Virginia State University, VA
Virginia Union University, VA
Viterbo University, WI
Voorhees College, SC
+Wagner College, NY
Walla Walla University, WA
Walsh University, OH
Warner Pacific College, OR
Warner University, FL
Wartburg College, IA
Washburn University, KS
Washington State University, WA
Wayne State University, MI
Waynesburg University, PA
Webber International University, FL
Weber State University, UT
Webster University, MO
Wells College, NY
+Wesleyan College, GA
West Liberty University, WV
West Texas A&M University, TX
West Virginia University Institute of Technology, WV
West Virginia Wesleyan College, WV
Western Carolina University, NC
Western Illinois University, IL
Western Kentucky University, KY
Western Michigan University, MI
Western New England University, MA
Western State Colorado University, CO
Westfield State University, MA
Westminster College, MO
Westminster College, PA
Westminster College, UT
Whittier College, CA
Wichita State University, KS
Widener University, PA
Wilberforce University, OH
Wiley College, TX
Wilkes University, PA
+William Jewell College, MO
William Paterson University of New Jersey, NJ
William Penn University, IA
William Woods University, MO
Williams Baptist College, AR
Wilmington College, OH
Wingate University, NC
Winona State University, MN
Winthrop University, SC
Wisconsin Lutheran College, WI
Worcester State University, MA
Wright State University, OH
Xavier University of Louisiana, LA
York College, NE
York College of Pennsylvania, PA
Youngstown State University, OH

LESS COMPETITIVE

Included in this category are colleges with median freshman test scores generally below 500 on the SAT and below 21 on the ACT; some colleges that require entrance examinations but do not report median scores; and colleges that admit students with averages generally below C who rank in the top 65% of the graduating class. These colleges usually admit 85% or more of their applicants. For detailed profiles of these colleges, please go to

Adams State University, CO
Alabama State University, AL
Albertus Magnus College, CT
Alderson Broaddus University, WV
Alice Lloyd College, KY
Allen College, IA
Alverno College, WI
American International College, MA
Amridge University, AL
Angelo State University, TX
Arkansas Tech University, AR
Averett University, VA
Barry University, FL
Becker College, MA
Berkeley College/New Jersey, NJ
Berkeley College/New York City Campus, NY
Berkeley College/White Plains Campus, NY
Bethany College, KS
Bethany College, WV
Blackburn College, IL
Bloomfield College, NJ
Bluefield State College, WV
Bowie State University, MD
Brenau University - Women's College, GA
Brewton-Parker College, GA
Cabrini University, PA
Caldwell University, NJ
California State University, Bakersfield, CA
California State University, Dominguez Hills, CA
California State University, Fresno, CA
California State University, Los Angeles, CA
California State University, Monterey Bay, CA
California State University, Northridge, CA
California State University, San Marcos, CA
California State University, Stanislaus, CA
California University of Pennsylvania, PA
Cameron University, OK
Carlos Albizu University, FL
Carlow University, PA
Catawba College, NC
Centenary College, NJ
Chadron State College, NE
Cheyney University of Pennsylvania, PA
City University of New York/Lehman College, NY
City University of New York/York College, NY
Claflin University, SC
Clarion University of Pennsylvania, PA
Clark Atlanta University, GA
Clayton State University, GA
The College of New Rochelle, NY
College of Saint Elizabeth, NJ
College of St Joseph, VT
College of Staten Island, NY
Colorado Mesa University, CO
Columbus State University, GA
Concord University, WV
Concordia College - New York, NY
Dakota Wesleyan University, SD
Davenport University, MI
Davis & Elkins College, WV
Defiance College, OH
Delaware State University, DE
Delta State University, MS
Dickinson State University, ND
Dominican College, NY
East Stroudsburg University, PA
Eastern New Mexico University, NM
Eastern Washington University, WA
Edinboro University, PA
Felician University, NJ
Fisk University, TN
Fitchburg State University, MA
Five Towns College, NY
Florida Memorial University, FL
Francis Marion University, SC
Franklin Pierce University, NH
Frostburg State University, MD
Gallaudet University, DC
Georgia Southwestern State University, GA
Georgian Court University, NJ
Glenville State College, WV
Goodwin College, CT
Green Mountain College, VT
Greensboro College, NC
Greenville College, IL
Gwynedd Mercy University, PA
Heidelberg University, OH
Hilbert College, NY
Hodges University, FL
Holy Family University, PA
Holy Names University, CA
Huston-Tillotson University, TX
Idaho State University, ID
Indiana Institute of Technology, IN
Indiana State University, IN
Indiana University Northwest, IN
Jackson State University, MS
Jacksonville State University, AL
Johnson C. Smith University, NC
Keiser University, FL
Kentucky Christian University, KY
Kentucky State University, KY
Kentucky Wesleyan College, KY
Keystone College, PA
Lake Erie College, OH
Lamar University, TX
Lane College, TN
Lenoir-Rhyne University, NC
LIM College, NY
Lincoln University, PA
Livingstone College, NC
Lock Haven University of Pennsylvania, PA
Lynn University, FL
Madonna University, MI
Mansfield University of Pennsylvania, PA
Martin University, IN
Marygrove College, MI
McMurry University, TX
Medaille College, NY
Menlo College, CA
Metropolitan State University of Denver, CO
Midway University, KY
Midwestern State University, TX
Mississippi Valley State University, MS
Missouri Western State University, MO
Montana State University Billings, MT
Montreat College, NC
Morehead State University, KY
Morgan State University, MD
Morris College, SC
Mount Mary University, WI
Mount St. Joseph University, OH
National Louis University, IL
National University, CA
Neumann University, PA
New Jersey City University, NJ
New Mexico Highlands University, NM
New Mexico State University, NM
New York City College of Technology, NY
Nichols College, MA
Norfolk State University, VA
Northeastern Illinois University, IL

Northwestern Oklahoma State University, OK
Northwestern State University of Louisiana, LA
Northwood University - Michigan, MI
Notre Dame de Namur University, CA
Nyack College, NY
Olivet College, MI
Our Lady of the Lake University, TX
Paine College, GA
Paul Quinn College, TX
Peru State College, NE
Pfeiffer University, NC
Philander Smith College, AR
Pine Manor College, MA
Plymouth State University, NH
Prairie View A&M University, TX
Presentation College, SD
Quincy University, IL
Regis College, MA
Rhode Island College, RI
Rochester College, MI
Rosemont College, PA
Saint Mary-of-the-Woods College, IN
Salem State University, MA
San Francisco State University, CA
Schreiner University, TX
Shepherd University, CA
Shorter University, GA
Silver Lake College of the Holy Family, WI
South Carolina State University, SC
South University, GA
Southeastern University, FL
Southern Connecticut State University, CT
Southern University and A&M College, LA
Southern University at New Orleans, LA
Southern Vermont College, VT
Southern Wesleyan University, SC
Southwest Baptist University, MO
Southwestern Adventist University, TX
Southwestern College, KS
St. Andrews University, NC
St. Francis College, NY
St. Joseph's College, New York/Brooklyn Campus, NY
St. Thomas University, FL
State University of New York /College of Agriculture and Tech
at Cobleskill, NY
State University of New York/Buffalo State, NY
Stephen F. Austin State University, TX
Sterling College, KS
Sul Ross State University, TX
Tarleton State University, TX
Tennessee State University, TN
Tennessee Wesleyan University, TN
Texas A&M University at Corpus Christi, TX
Texas A&M University at Kingsville, TX
Texas Southern University, TX
Texas Woman's University, TX
Thiel College, PA
Thomas College, ME
Thomas More College, KY
Tiffin University, OH
Tusculum College, TN
University of Arkansas at Little Rock, AR
University of Arkansas at Monticello, AR
University of Bridgeport, CT
University of Charleston, WV
University of Houston-Downtown, TX
University of Maine at Fort Kent, ME
University of Maine at Presque Isle, ME
University of Maryland University College, MD
University of Maryland/Eastern Shore, MD
The University of Montana Western, MT
University of Nebraska - Kearney, NE
University of North Carolina at Pembroke, NC
University of Rio Grande & Rio Grande Community College, OH
University of South Carolina Upstate, SC
University of Texas Rio Grande Valley, TX
University of the Cumberlands, KY
University of the District of Columbia, DC
University of the Incarnate Word, TX
The University of Virginia's College at Wise, VA
University of West Alabama, AL
University of West Georgia, GA
Ursuline College, OH
Virginia Wesleyan University, VA
Washington Adventist University, MD
Wayland Baptist University, TX
Wesley College, DE
West Virginia State University, WV
Western Connecticut State University, CT
Western New Mexico University, NM
Western Oregon University, OR
Wheeling Jesuit University, WV
Wheelock College, MA
William Carey University, MS
William Peace University, NC
Wilson College, PA
Winston-Salem State University, NC

NONCOMPETITIVE

The colleges in this category generally only require evidence of graduation from an accredited high school (although they may also require completion of a certain number of high school units). Some require that entrance examinations be taken for placement purposes only, or only by graduates of unaccredited high schools or only by out-of-state students. In some cases, insufficient capacity may compel a college in this category to limit the number of students that are accepted; generally, however, if a college accepts 98% or more of its applicants, it automatically falls in this category. Colleges are also rated Noncompetitive if they admit all state residents, but have some requirements for nonresidents. For detailed profiles of these colleges, please go to *barronspac.com*

Allen University, SC
Arkansas Baptist College, AR
Baker College of Flint, MI
Bellevue University, NE
Benedict College, SC
Bennett College, NC
Cambridge College, MA
Charter Oak State College, CT
City University of New York/Medgar Evers College, NY
City University of Seattle, WA
Colorado Technical University, CO
Concordia College - Alabama, AL
Edward Waters College, FL
Franklin University, OH
Harris-Stowe State University, MO
Heritage University, WA
Jarvis Christian College, TX
Lees-McRae College, NC
Lincoln University, MO
Lourdes University, OH
Marylhurst University, OR
Mayville State University, ND
Miles College, AL
Montana State University-Northern, MT
Naropa University, CO
New England College, NH
Oakland City University, IN
Oglala Lakota College, SD
Peirce College, PA
Pennsylvania College of Technology, PA
Saint Francis University, PA
Sinte Gleska University, SD
St. Gregory's University, OK
State University of New York/Empire State College, NY
Thomas Edison State University, NJ
Thomas University, GA
Tougaloo College, MS
University of Holy Cross, LA
University of Saint Mary, KS
University of Texas at El Paso, TX
University of the Ozarks, AR
Upper Iowa University, IA
Wayne State College, NE
Wilmington University, DE

SPECIAL

Listed here are colleges whose programs of study are specialized; professional schools of art, music, nursing, and other disciplines. In general, the admissions requirements are not based primarily on academic criteria, but on evidence of talent or special interest in the field. Many other colleges and universities offer special-interest programs *in addition* to regular academic curricula, but such institutions have been given a regular competitive rating based on academic criteria. Schools oriented toward working adults have also been assigned this rating. For detailed profiles of these colleges, please go to *barronspac.com*.

Adventist University of Health Sciences, FL
Albany College of Pharmacy and Health Sciences, NY
Art Academy of Cincinnati, OH
The Art Institute of Atlanta, GA
Art Institute of Portland, OR
ArtCenter College of Design, CA
Benjamin Franklin Institute of Technology, MA
Berklee College of Music, MA
Boston Architectural College, MA
The Boston Conservatory at Berklee, MA
Cabarrus College of Health Sciences, NC
California College of the Arts, CA
California Institute of the Arts, CA
Capitol Technology University, MD
City University of New York/John Jay College of Criminal Justice, NY
Cleveland Institute of Art, OH
Cleveland Institute of Music, OH
College for Creative Studies, MI
College of Art and Design at Lesley University, MA
Columbus College of Art and Design, OH
Cornish College of the Arts, WA
Cox College, MO
Curtis Institute of Music, PA
Eastman School of Music/University of Rochester, NY
Excelsior College, NY
Fashion Institute of Technology/State University of New York, NY
Franklin W. Olin College of Engineering, MA
Granite State College, NH
The Juilliard School, NY
Kansas City Art Institute, MO
Laguna College of Art and Design, CA
List College/The Jewish Theological Seminary (JTS), NY
Maine College of Art, ME
Manhattan School of Music, NY
Mannes School of Music, NY
Maryland Institute College of Art, MD
Massachusetts College of Art and Design, MA
MCPHS University, MA
Memphis College of Art, TN
Mercy College of Health Sciences, IA
Milwaukee Institute of Art & Design, WI
Minneapolis College of Art and Design, MN
Montserrat College of Art, MA
Moore College of Art and Design, PA
New England Conservatory of Music, MA
NewSchool of Architecture & Design, CA
Otis College of Art and Design, CA
Pacific Northwest College of Art, OR
Parsons The New School for Design, NY
Research College of Nursing, MO
Rhode Island School of Design, RI
Ringling College of Art and Design, FL
Rocky Mountain College of Art and Design, CO
San Francisco Art Institute, CA
San Francisco Conservatory of Music, CA
Savannah College of Art and Design, GA
School of the Art Institute of Chicago, IL
School of Visual Arts, NY
Trinity College of Nursing and Health Sciences, IL
Union Institute & University, OH
University of North Carolina School of the Arts, NC
University of the Arts, PA
VanderCook College of Music, IL
Vaughn College of Aeronautics and Technology, NY
Westminster Choir College, NJ

AN EXPLANATION OF THE COLLEGE ENTRIES

THE BASICS

Over 1600 U.S. colleges and universities and Canadian and other foreign universities are described in detail in the Profiles that follow, as well as our web site, www.barronspac.com.

The Choice of Schools

Colleges and universities in this country may achieve recognition from a number of professional organizations, but we have based our choice of U.S. colleges on accreditation from the U.S. regional accrediting associations.

Accreditation amounts to a stamp of approval given to a college. The accreditation process evaluates institutions and programs to determine whether they meet established standards of educational quality. The regional associations listed below supervise an aspect of the accrediting procedure—the study of a detailed report submitted by the institution applying for accreditation, and then an inspection visit by members of the accrediting agency. The six agencies are associated with the Commission on Recognition of Postsecondary Accreditation (CORPA). They include:

Middle States Association of Colleges and Schools
New England Association of Schools and Colleges
North Central Association of Colleges and Schools
Northwest Commission on Colleges and Universities
Southern Association of Colleges and Schools
Western Association of Schools and Colleges

Getting accreditation for the first time can take a school several years. To acknowledge that schools have begun this process, the agencies accord them candidate status. Most candidates eventually are awarded full accreditation.

The U.S. schools included in this book are fully accredited or are candidates for that status. If the latter is the case, it is indicated below the address of the school. Because the U.S. regional accrediting bodies do not officially accredit Canadian colleges and universities, and because there is no equivalent accrediting system in Canada, we have chosen to include only the larger, English-language Canadian schools—those with total full-time undergraduate enrollment of more than 10,000. It should be understood that size in no way relates to quality; there are many excellent Canadian colleges and universities with fewer than 10,000 students.

Four-Year Colleges Only

This book presents Profiles for all accredited four-year colleges that grant bachelor's degrees and admit freshmen with no previous college experience. Most of these colleges also accept transfer students. Profiles of upper-division schools, which offer only the junior or senior year of undergraduate study, are not included, nor are junior or community colleges.

Consistent Entries

Each Profile of a U.S. college is organized in the same way; the only Profiles that vary are those of Canada, schools abroad, and religious schools. The following discussion applies to the U.S. college Profiles, but refers to the other Profiles as well.

Every Profile begins with a capsule and is followed by separate sections covering the campus environment, student life, programs of study, admissions, financial aid, information for international students, computers, graduates, and the admissions contact. These categories are always introduced in the same sequence, so you can find data and compare specific points easily. The following commentary will help you evaluate and interpret the information given for each college.

Data Collection

Barron's *Profiles of American Colleges* was first published in 1964. Since then, it has been revised every year online; comprehensive revisions are undertaken every year for the print edition. Such frequent updating is necessary because so much information about colleges—particularly enrollment figures, costs, programs of study, and admissions standards—changes rapidly.

The facts in the capsule portion of each Profile in this edition were gathered in the fall of 2017 and apply to the 2017–2018 academic year. Figures on tuition and room-and-board costs generally change soon after the book is published. For the most up-to-date information on such items, you should always check with the colleges. Other information—such as the basic nature of the school, its campus, and the educational goals of its students—changes less rapidly. A few new programs of study might be added or new services made available, but the basic educational offerings generally will remain constant.

THE CAPSULE

The capsule of each Profile provides basic information about the college at a glance. An explanation of the standard capsule is shown in the accompanying box.

All toll-free phone numbers are presumed to be out-of-state or both in-state and out-of-state, unless noted.

A former name is given if the name has been changed recently. To use the map code to the right of the college name, turn to the appropriate college-locator map at the beginning of each chapter. Wherever "n/av" is used in the capsule, it means the information was not available. The abbreviation "n/app" means not applicable.

Full-time, Part-time, Graduate

Enrollment figures are the clearest indication of the size of a college, and show whether or not it is coeducational and what the

---

COMPLETE NAME OF SCHOOL — **MAP CODE**
(Former Name, if any)
City, State, Zip Code — **Phone Numbers and E-mail**

Full-time: Full-time undergraduate enrollment
Part-time: Part-time undergraduate enrollment
Graduate: Graduate enrollment
Year: Semesters, quarters, summer sessions
Room & Board: Yearly room-and-board costs
Faculty: Number of full-time faculty; AAUP category of school, salary-level symbol
Ph.D.s: Percentage of faculty holding Ph.D.
Student/Faculty: Full-time student/full-time faculty ratio
Tuition: Yearly tuition and fees (out-of-state if different)
Freshman Class: Number of students who applied, number accepted, number enrolled
SAT: Median Critical Reading, Median Math, Median Writing (abbreviated CR/M/W)
SAT Evidence-Based Reading/Writing
Application Deadline: Fall admission deadline
ACT: Median composite ACT
CEEB Code: 0101
ADMISSIONS SELECTOR RATING

---

male-female ratio is. Graduate enrollment is presented to give a better idea of the size of the entire student body; some schools have far more graduate students enrolled than undergraduates.

Year
Some of the more innovative college calendars include the 4-1-4, 3-2-3, 3-3-1, and 1-3-1-4-3 terms. College administrators sometimes utilize various intersessions or interims—special short terms—for projects, independent study, short courses, or travel programs. The early semester calendar, which allows students to finish spring semesters earlier than those of the traditional semester calendar, gives students a head start on finding summer jobs. A modified semester (4-1-4) system provides a January or winter term, approximately four weeks long, for special projects that usually earn the same credit as one semester-long course. The trimester calendar divides the year into three equal parts; students may attend college during all three but generally take a vacation during any one. The quarter calendar divides the year into four equal parts; students usually attend for three quarters each year. The capsule also indicates schools that offer a summer session.

Application Deadline
Indicated here is the deadline for applications for admission to the fall semester. If there are no specific deadlines, it will say "open." Application deadlines for admission to other semesters are, where available, given in the admissions section of the profile.

CEEB Code
This is a standardized identification number assigned to a college or university by the Educational Testing Service (ETS).

Faculty
The first number given refers to the number of full-time faculty members at the college or university.

The Roman numeral and symbol that follow represent the salary level of faculty at the entire institution as compared with faculty salaries nationally. This information is based on the salary report* published by the American Association of University Professors (AAUP). The Roman numeral refers to the AAUP category to which the particular college or university is assigned. (This allows for comparison of faculty salaries at the same types of schools.) Category I includes "institutions that offer the doctorate degree, and that conferred in the most recent three years an annual average of fifteen or more earned doctorates covering a minimum of three nonrelated disciplines." Category IIA includes "institutions awarding degrees above the baccalaureate, but not included in Category I." Category IIB includes "institutions awarding only the baccalaureate or equivalent degree." Category III includes "institutions with academic ranks, mostly two-year institutions." Category IV includes "institutions without academic ranks." (With the exception of a few liberal arts colleges, this category includes mostly two-year institutions.)

The symbol that follows the Roman numeral indicates into which percentile range the average salary of professors, associate professors, assistant professors, and instructors at the school falls, as compared with other schools in the same AAUP category. The symbols used in this book represent the following:

++$	95th percentile and above
+$	80th–94.9th percentile
av$	60th–79.9th percentile
–$	40th–59.9th percentile
—$	39.9th percentile and below

If the school is not a member of AAUP, nothing will appear.

*Source: Annual Report on the Economic Status of the Profession published in the March-April 2017 issue of *Academe:* Bulletin of the AAUP, American Association of University Professors, 1133 Nineteeneth Street N.W., Suite 200, Washington, DC 20036

Ph.D.s
The figure here indicates the percentage of full-time faculty who have Ph.D.s or the highest terminal degree.

Student/Faculty
Student/faculty ratios may be deceptive because the faculties of many large universities include scholars and scientists who do little or no teaching. Nearly every college has some large lecture classes, usually in required or popular subjects, and many small classes in advanced or specialized fields. Here, the ratio reflects full-time students and full-time faculty, and some colleges utilize the services of a large part-time faculty. Additionally, some institutions factor in an FTE component in determining this ratio. We do not, and thus the Student/Faculty ratio that we report may differ somewhat from what the college reports. In general, a student/faculty ratio of 10 to 1 is very good.

If the faculty and student body are both mostly part-time, the entry will say "n/app."

Tuition
It is important to remember that tuition costs change continually and that in many cases, these changes are substantial. Particularly heavy increases have occurred recently and will continue to occur. On the other hand, some smaller colleges are being encouraged to lower tuitions, in order to make higher education more affordable. Students are therefore urged to contact individual colleges for the most current tuition figures.

The figure given here includes tuition and student fees for the school's standard academic year. If costs differ for state residents and out-of-state residents, the figure for nonresidents is given in parentheses. Where tuition costs are listed per credit hour (p/c), per course (p/course), or per unit (p/unit), student fees are not included. In some university systems, tuition is the same for all schools. However, student fees, and therefore the total tuition figure, may vary from school to school.

Room and Board
It is suggested that students check with individual schools for the most current room-and-board figures because, like tuition figures, they increase continually. The room-and-board figures given here represent the annual cost of a double room and all meals. The word "none" indicates that the college does not charge for room and board; "n/app" indicates that room and board are not provided.

Freshman Class
The numbers apply to the number of students who applied, were accepted, and enrolled in the 2017–2018 freshman class or in a recent class.

SAT, ACT
Whenever available, the median SAT scores—Critical Reading, Math, and Writing--and the median ACT composite score for the 2017–2018 freshmen class are given. If the school has not reported median SAT or ACT scores, the capsule indicates whether the SAT or ACT is required. Note: New SAT scores have been established, but not all schools have adjusted to the new standards. The new procedure is as follows: SAT: Evidence-Based Reading and Writing; SAT: Math. Please refer to our web site in late 2018 for any updates.

Admissions Selector Rating
The College Admissions Selector Rating indicates the degree of competitiveness of admission to the college.

THE GENERAL DESCRIPTION

The Introductory Paragraph
This paragraph indicates, in general, what types of programs the college offers, when it was founded, whether it is public

or private, and its religious affiliation. Baccalaureate program accreditation and information on the size of the school's library collection are also provided.

In evaluating the size of the collection, keep in mind the difference between college and university libraries: A university's graduate and professional schools require many specialized books that would be of no value to an undergraduate. For a university, a ratio of one undergraduate to 500 books generally means an outstanding library, one to 200 an adequate library, one to 100 an inferior library. For a college, a ratio of one to 400 is outstanding, one to 300 superior, one to 200 adequate, one to 50 inferior.

These figures are somewhat arbitrary, because a large university with many professional schools or campuses requires more books than a smaller university. Furthermore, a recently founded college would be expected to have fewer books than an older school, since it has not inherited from the past what might be a great quantity of outdated and useless books. Most libraries can make up for deficiencies through interlibrary loans.

The ratio of students to the number of subscriptions to periodicals is less meaningful, and again, a university requires more periodicals than a college. But for a university, subscription to more than 15,000 periodicals is outstanding, and 6000 is generally more than adequate. For a college, 1500 subscriptions is exceptional, 700 very good, and 400 adequate. Subscription to fewer than 200 periodicals generally implies an inferior library with a very tight budget. Microform items are assuming greater importance within a library's holdings, and this information is included when available. Services of a Learning Resource Center and special facilities, such as a museum, radio or TV station, and Internet access are also described in this paragraph.

This paragraph also provides information on the campus: its size, the type of area in which it is located, and its proximity to a large city.

At most institutions, the existence of classrooms, administrative offices, and dining facilities may be taken for granted, and they generally are not mentioned in the entries unless they have been recently constructed or are considered exceptional.

Student Life

This section, with subdivisions that detail housing, campus activities, sports, facilities for disabled students, services offered to students, and campus safety concentrates on the everyday life of students.

The introductory paragraph, which includes various characteristics of the student body, gives an idea of the mix of attitudes and backgrounds. It includes, where available, percentages of students from out-of-state and from private or public high schools. It also indicates what percentage of the students belong to minority groups and what percentages are Protestant, Catholic, and Jewish. Finally, it tells the average age of all enrolled freshmen and of all undergraduates, and gives data on the freshman dropout rate and the percentage of freshmen who remain to graduate.

Male to Female Ratio. When available, the ratio of male to female students on the college campus is provided for the school.

Housing. Availability of on-campus housing is described here. If you plan to live on campus, note the type, quantity, and capacity of the dormitory accommodations. Some colleges provide dormitory rooms for freshmen, but require upperclass students to make their own arrangements to live in fraternity or sorority houses, off-campus apartments, or rented rooms in private houses. Some small colleges require all students who do not live with parents or other relatives to live on campus. And some colleges have no residence halls.

This paragraph tells whether special housing is available and whether campus housing is single-sex or coed. It gives the percentage of those who live on campus and those who remain on campus on weekends. Finally, it states if alcohol is not permitted on campus and whether students may keep cars on campus.

Faculty/Classrooms. The percentage of male and female faculty is mentioned here if provided by the college, along with the percentage of introductory courses taught by graduate students (if any). The average class size in an introductory lecture, laboratory, and regular class offering may also be indicated.

Programs of Study

Listed here are the bachelor's degrees granted, strongest and most popular majors, and whether associate, master's, and doctoral degrees are awarded. Major areas of study have been included under broader general areas (shown in capital letters in the profiles) for quicker reference; however, the general areas do not necessarily correspond to the academic divisions of the college or university but are more career-oriented.

Activities

Campus organizations play a vital part in students' social lives. This subsection lists types of activities, including student government, special interest or academic clubs, fraternities and sororities, and cultural and popular campus events sponsored at the college.

Sports. Sports are important on campus, so we indicate the extent of the athletic program by giving the number of intercollegiate and intramural sports offered for men and for women. We have also included the athletic and recreation facilities and campus stadium seating capacity.

Graduates. This section gives the number of graduates in the 2016–2017 class, the most popular majors and percentage of graduates earning degrees in those fields, and the percentages of graduates in the 2016 class who enrolled in graduate school or found employment within 6 months of graduation.

Services

Services that may be available to students—free or for a fee—include counseling, tutoring, remedial instruction, and reader service for the blind.

Library/Resources. This section describes the number of publications and media in the library collection of the college. In addition, you will also find computerized library services available to students, as well as any special learning facilities.

Physically Challenged Students. The colleges' own estimates of how accessible their campuses are to the physically disabled are provided. This information should be considered along with the specific kinds of special facilities available. If a Profile does not include a subsection on the disabled, the college did not provide the information.

Special. Special programs are described here. Students at almost every college now have the opportunity to study abroad, either through their college or through other institutions. Internships with businesses, schools, hospitals, and public agencies permit students to gain work experience as they learn. The pass/fail grading option, now quite prevalent, allows students to take courses in unfamiliar areas without threatening their academic average. Many schools offer students the opportunity to earn a combined B.A.-B.S. degree, pursue a general studies (no major) degree, or design their own major. Frequently students may take advantage of a cooperative program offered by two or more universities. Such a program might be referred to, for instance, as a 3-2 engineering program; a student in this program would spend three years at one institution and two at another. The number of national honor societies represented on campus is included. Schools also may conduct honors programs for qualified students, either university-wide or in specific major fields, and these also are listed.

Visiting. Some colleges hold special orientation programs for prospective students to give them a better idea of what the school is like. Many also will provide guides for informal visits, often allowing students to spend a night in the residence halls. You should make arrangements with the college before visiting.

Campus Safety and Security. This section lists the safety and security measures that are in place on the campus. These vary among schools, but may include 24-hour foot and vehicle patrol, self-defense education, security escort services, shuttle buses, informal discussions, pamphlets/posters/films, emergency telephones, and lighted pathways/sidewalks.

Requirements

Wherever possible, information on specific required courses and distribution requirements is supplied, in addition to the number of credits or hours required for graduation. If the college requires students to maintain a certain grade point average (GPA) or pass
comprehensive exams to graduate, that also is given.

This section also specifies the minimum high school class rank and GPA, if any, required by the college for freshman applicants. It indicates what standardized tests (if any) are required, specifically the SAT or ACT, or for Puerto Rican schools, SAT Spanish Subject Test, the CEEB (the Spanish-language version of the SAT). Additional requirements are given such as whether an essay, interview, or audition is necessary, and if AP*/CLEP credit is given. If a college accepts applications on computer disk or on-line, those facts are so noted and described. Other factors used by the school in the admissions decision are also listed.

Procedures. This subsection indicates when you should take entrance exams, the application deadlines for various sessions, the application fee, and when students are notified of the admissions decision. Some schools note that their application deadlines are open; this can mean either that they will consider applications until a class is filled, or that applications are considered right up until registration for the term in which the student wishes to enroll. If a waiting list is an active part of the admissions procedure, the college may indicate the number of applicants placed on that list and the number of wait-listed applicants accepted.

Transfer Students. Nearly every college admits some transfer students. These students may have earned associate degrees at two-year colleges and want to continue their education at a four-year college or wish to attend a different school. One important thing to consider when transferring is how many credits earned at one school will be accepted at another, so entire semesters won't be spent making up lost work. Because most schools require students to spend a specified number of hours in residence to earn a degree, it is best not to wait too long to transfer if you decide to do so.

International Students. This section begins by telling how many of the school's students come from outside the United States. It tells which English proficiency exam, if any, applicants must take. Any necessary college entrance exams, including SAT Subject tests, are listed.

Admissions

The admissions section gives detailed information on standards so you can evaluate your chances for acceptance. Where the SAT or ACT scores of the 2017–2018 freshman class are broken down, you may compare your own scores. Because the role of standardized tests in the admissions process has been subject to criticism, more colleges are considering other factors such as recommendations from high school officials, leadership record, special talents, extracurricular activities, and advanced placement or honors courses completed. A few schools may consider education of parents, ability to pay for college, and relationship to alumni. Some give preference to state residents; others seek a geographically diverse student body.

If a college indicates that it follows an open admissions policy, it is noncompetitive and generally accepts all applicants who meet certain basic requirements, such as graduation from an accredited high school. If a college has rolling admissions, it decides on each application as soon as possible if the applicant's file is complete and does not specify a notification deadline. As a general rule, it is best to submit applications as early as possible.

Some colleges offer special admissions programs for nontraditional applicants. Early admissions programs allow students to begin college either during the summer before their freshman year or during what would have been their last year of high school; in the latter case, a high school diploma is not required. These programs are designed for students who are emotionally and educationally prepared for college at an earlier age than usual.

Deferred admissions plans permit students to spend a year at another activity, such as working or traveling, before beginning college. Students who take advantage of this option can relax during the year off, because they already have been accepted at a college and have a space reserved. During the year off from study, many students become clearer about their educational goals, and they perform better when they do begin study.

Early decision plans allow students to be notified by their first-choice school during the first term of the senior year. This plan may eliminate the anxiety of deciding whether or not to send a deposit to a second-choice college that offers admission before the first-choice college responds.

Admissions Contact. When provided, this is the name or title of the person to whom all correspondence regarding your application should be sent. In addition, internet addresses are included here.

Financial Aid

This paragraph in each Profile describes the availability of financial aid. It includes the percentage of freshmen and continuing students who receive aid, the average freshman award, and average and maximum amounts for various types of need-based and non-need-based financial aid. Aid application deadlines and required forms are also indicated. It also includes the schools required FAFSA Code.

* Advanced Placement and AP are registered trademarks owned by the College Entrance Examination Board. No endorsement of this product is implied or given.

PROFILES OF AMERICAN COLLEGES

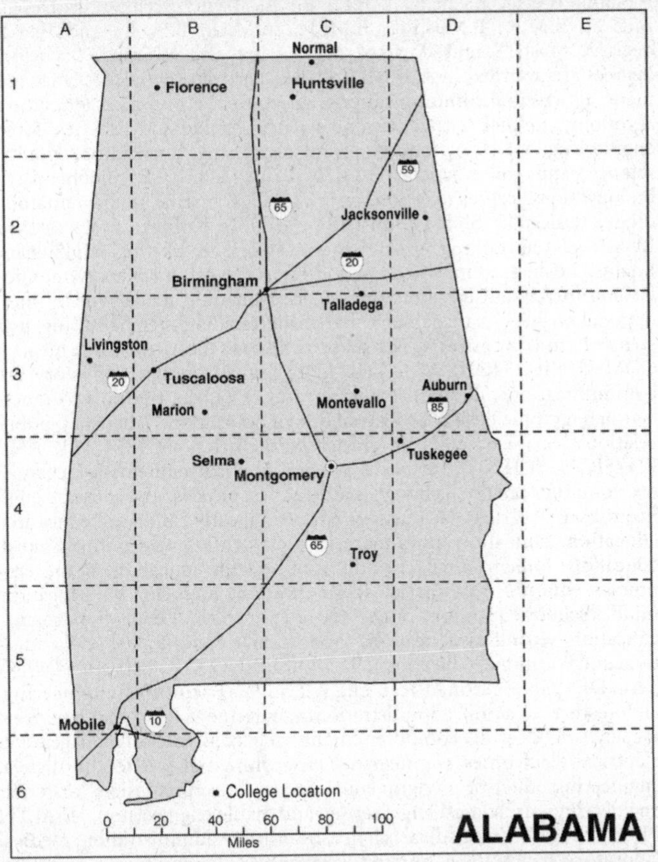

ALABAMA A&M UNIVERSITY
C-1
www.aamu.edu

Normal, AL 35762
(256) 372-5250
(256) 372-5249
Email: admissions@aamu.edu

Full-time: 2015 men, 2015 women
Part-time: 180 men, 205 women
Graduate: 385 men, 810 women
Year: semesters, summer session
Room & Board: $9152
SAT or ACT: required
Application Deadline: June 15

Faculty: n/av
Ph.D.s: 70%
Student/Faculty: 20 to 1
Tuition: $9644 ($17,694)
Freshman Class: n/av
CEEB CODE: 1003
COMPETITIVE

Alabama A&M University, founded in 1875, is a public land-grant institution offering undergraduate and graduate studies. AAMU functions as a teaching, research, and public service institution, including extension. There are 4 undergraduate schools and 1 graduate school. In addition to regional accreditation, AAMU has baccalaureate program accreditation with ABET, ADA, AHEA, CSWE, FIDER, and NCATE. The 2300-acre campus is in a suburban area 90 miles north of Birmingham and 95 miles south of Nashville. Including any residence halls, there are 55 buildings.

STUDENT LIFE: 70% of undergraduates are from Alabama. Others are from 44 states, 11 foreign countries, and Canada. 90% are from public schools. 90% are African American; 6% White; 4% Foreign; 1% Asian American; 1% American Indian/Alaska Native; 1% Hispanic. 98% are Protestant. **Female To Male Ratio:** 1.2:1. The average age of freshmen is 18; all undergraduates, 20. **Housing:** 3100 students can be accommodated in college housing, which includes dorms. On-campus housing is guaranteed for all 4 years. 60% of students live on campus. Alcohol is not permitted. All students may keep cars.

FACULTY/CLASSROOMS: 50% teach undergraduates, 30% do research, and 30% do both. No introductory courses are taught by graduate students. The average class size in an introductory lecture is 90; in a laboratory is 20; and in a regular course is 30.

PROGRAMS OF STUDY: AAMU confers B.A., B.G.S., B.S., B.S.C.E., B.S.E.E., B.S.E.T., and B.S.M.E. degrees. Associate, master's, and doctoral degrees are also awarded. Bachelor's degrees are awarded in AGRICULTURE (agricultural business management, agricultural economics, agronomy, animal science, forestry and related sciences, horticulture, and soil science), BIOLOGICAL SCIENCE (biology/biological science, neurosciences, nutrition, and zoology), BUSINESS (accounting, banking and finance, business administration and management, management science, marketing/retailing/merchandising, and office supervision and management), COMMUNICATIONS AND THE ARTS (art, classics, dramatic arts, English, French, German, graphic design, jazz, journalism, linguistics, telecommunications, and theater design), COMPUTER AND PHYSICAL SCIENCE (chemistry, computer science, mathematics, and physics), EDUCATION (agricultural education, art education, early childhood education, elementary education, home economics education, industrial arts education, middle school education, music education, physical education, science education, secondary education, special education, and trade and industrial education), ENGINEERING AND ENVIRONMENTAL DESIGN (city/community/regional planning, civil engineering, civil engineering technology, drafting and design technology, electrical/electronics engineering, electrical/electronics engineering technology, environmental engineering, industrial engineering, industrial engineering technology, mechanical engineering, and mechanical engineering technology), HEALTH PROFESSIONS (medical laboratory technology, nursing, prepharmacy, preveterinary science, and speech pathology/audiology), SOCIAL SCIENCE (criminology, economics, family/consumer studies, food science, history, human development, humanities and social science, political science/government, psychology, social work, and sociology). Physics, food science, and teacher education are the strongest academically. Business administration, education, and computer science have the largest enrollments.

ACTIVITIES: 7% of men belong to 4 national fraternities; 9% of women belong to 4 national sororities. There are 109 groups on campus, including band, cheerleading, choir, chorus, computers, dance, debate, drama, drill team, ethnic, forensics, honors, international, jazz band, LGBT, marching band, newspaper, orchestra, pep band, political, professional, radio and TV stations, religious, social, student government, symphony, and yearbook. Popular campus events include Magic City Classic, Women's Week, and Men's Week. **Sports:** There are 7 intercollegiate sports for men and 7 for women, and 7 intramural sports for men and 7 for women. Facilities include a gym, Olympic-size pool, bowling alley, an outdoor volley court, suspended 4-lane walking track, racquetball courts, weight room and cardio training area, multi-purpose activity rooms, and aerobic rooms. **Graduates:** The most popular majors were business administration, education, and computer science.

SERVICES: Counseling and information services are available, as is tutoring in most subjects. There is a reader service for the blind. **Library/Resources:** The library contains 253,620 volumes, 48,300 microform items, and 3,010 audio/video tapes/CDs/DVDs, and subscribes to 2,070 periodicals including electronic. Computerized library services include interlibrary loans and database searching. Special learning facilities include an art gallery, radio station, TV station, and the State Black Archives Research Center and Museum. **Physically Challenged Students:** 85% of the campus is accessible. Facilities include wheelchair ramps, elevators, special parking, specially equipped restrooms, and lowered drinking fountains. **Special:** Co-op programs with Georgia Institute of Technology and Tuskegee University, cross-registration with the University of Alabama in Huntsville, Oakwood College, Calhoun Community College, and Athens State College, internships with various government agencies, dual majors, and work-study programs are available. There is a 3-2 engineering degree program with Georgia Institute of Technology. There are 5 national honor societies, a freshman honors program, and 5 departmental honors programs. **Visiting:** There are regularly scheduled orientations for prospective students, consisting of sessions in June, July, and November. Tours are not available during Spring break. The school host an Open House in March. There are guides for informal visits and visitors may stay overnight. To schedule a visit, contact the Office of Admissions. **Campus Safety and Security:** Measures include 24-hour foot and vehicle patrol, self-defense education, and security escort services. There are lighted pathways/sidewalks.

REQUIREMENTS: The SAT or ACT is required, with a satisfactory score on the ACT. Applicants must have 4 years each of English, math, science, social studies, and history. An interview is recommended. The GED is accepted. AP and CLEP credits are accepted. Important factors in the admissions decision are advanced placement or honors courses, leadership record, and recommendations by school officials. All students are required to take at least 52 hours of general studies, including phys ed, music, and art, and to maintain a minimum GPA of 2.0. Students must complete a total of 120 to 126 credit hours, with 30 to 36 in the major. A comprehensive exam is required for some majors. **Procedure:** Freshmen are admitted to all sessions. There are early decision, early admissions, deferred admissions, and rolling admissions plans. Applications should be filed by June 15 for fall entry; December 1 for spring entry; and May 15 for summer entry. The fall 2017 application fee was $30. Applications are accepted online. **Transfer Students:** Transfer students must have a minimum GPA of 2.0 and have earned at least 12 semester credit hours. 30 of 128 credits required for the bachelor's degree must be completed at AAMU. **International Students:** They must take the TOEFL.

Admissions Contact: Venita Clisby King, Director of Admissions. Email: *admissions@aamu.edu* Web: *www.aamu.edu*

FINANCIAL AID: In 2017-2018, 72% of all full-time freshmen received some form of financial aid. 75% of all full-time freshmen received need-based aid. The CCS/Profile, or FAFSA, or FFS, or SFS and the college's own financial statement are required. The FAFSA code is 001002. The priority date for freshman financial aid applications for fall entry is March 1.

ALABAMA STATE UNIVERSITY *(The complete profile is made available exclusively on our website, www.barronspac.com)*

AMRIDGE UNIVERSITY *(The complete profile is made available exclusively on our website, www.barronspac.com)*

AUBURN UNIVERSITY D-3

www.auburn.edu

Auburn, AL 36849 **(334) 844-7577**

Fax: (334) 844-4773
Email: admissions@auburn.edu
Full-time: 10,827 men, 10,935 women
Faculty: I, -$
Part-time: 1473 men, 729 women
Ph.D.s: 88%
Graduate: 3396 men, 2416 women
Student/Faculty: 19 to 1
Year: semesters, summer session
Tuition: $10,968 ($29,640)
Room & Board: $13,332
Freshman Class: 18072 applied, 15168 accepted, 4836 enrolled
SAT EBR-W/M: 610/600 **ACT:** 27
CEEB CODE: 1005
Application Deadline: February 1
VERY COMPETITIVE+

Auburn University, founded in 1856, is a public land-grant institution awarding undergraduate and graduate programs in agriculture, business, education, engineering, forestry, and wildlife sciences, human sciences, liberal arts, nursing and sciences and math, with professional schools of pharmacy, and veterinary medicine, and a graduate school. There are 11 undergraduate schools and 3 graduate schools. In addition to regional accreditation, AU has baccalaureate program accreditation with AACSB, ABET, ACCE, ACEJMC, ACPE, ADA, AHEA, ASLA, CSAB, CSWE, FIDER, NAAB, NASAD, NASM, NCATE, NLN, SAF, AABI, ACEND, ACEN, APA, ASHA, AVMA, CACREP, CCNE, CIDA, COAMFTE, CORE, NASPAA, NAST, and PAB. The 1875-acre campus is in a small town 110 miles southwest of Atlanta, GA., and 54 miles southeast of Montgomery, AL. Including any residence halls, there are 457 buildings.

STUDENT LIFE: 62% of undergraduates are from Alabama. Others are from 51 states, 99 foreign countries, and Canada. 86% are from public schools. 85% are White; 5% African American; 4% Hispanic; 3% two or more races; 2% Asian American; 2% Foreign; 1% American Indian/ Alaska Native; 1% race unknown. **Male To Female Ratio:** 1.1:1. The average age of freshmen is 18; all undergraduates, 20. 9% do not continue beyond their first year; 77% remain to graduate. **Housing:** 4737 students can be accommodated in college housing, which includes married student dorms and on-campus apartments. In addition, there are honors houses, fraternity houses, and living-learning communities. On-campus housing is available on a first-come and first-served basis. 81% of students commute. Alcohol is not permitted. All students may keep cars.

FACULTY/CLASSROOMS: 61% of faculty are male; 39% are female. Graduate students teach 17% of introductory courses.

PROGRAMS OF STUDY: AU confers B.A., B.S., B.A.E., B.Arch., B.B.S.E., B.C.E., B.Che.E., B.E.E., B.F.A., B.Int. Arch., B.Int.Design, B.I.S.E., B.M.E., B.Mus.Ed., B.Mt.Ie., B.M.U., B.Sw.E., and B.W.E. degrees. Master's and doctoral degrees are also awarded. Bachelor's degrees are awarded in AGRICULTURE (agricultural business management, agricultural communications, agricultural economics, agriculture, agronomy, animal science, equine science, fishing and fisheries, forest engineering, forestry production and processing, horticulture, poultry science, and soil science), BIOLOGICAL SCIENCE (biochemistry, biology/biological science, botany, cell biology, marine biology, microbiology, molecular biology, nutrition, wildlife biology, and zoology), BUSINESS (accounting, apparel and accessories marketing, banking and finance, business administration and management, business economics, fashion merchandising, hotel/motel and restaurant management, international business management, marketing/retailing/merchandising, personnel management, and transportation management), COMMUNICATIONS AND THE ARTS (apparel design, art history, art, communications, design, dramatic arts, English, fine arts, French, German, graphic design, industrial design, journalism, languages, public relations, Spanish, and speech/debate/rhetoric), COMPUTER AND PHYSICAL SCIENCE (actuarial science, applied mathematics, chemistry, computer science, geology, mathematics, physics, and software engineering), EDUCATION (business education, early childhood education, education, education administration, elementary education, English education, foreign languages education, health education, home economics education, industrial arts education, mathematics education, middle school education, music education, physical education, science education, secondary education, social science education, special education, and vocational education), ENGINEERING AND ENVIRONMENTAL DESIGN (aeronautical engineering, agricultural engineering, architecture, aviation administration/management, chemical engineering, civil engineering, computer engineering, construction management, electrical/electronics engineering, environmental science, industrial engineering, interior design, landscape architecture/design, materials engineering, mechanical engineering, and textile engineering), HEALTH PROFESSIONS (biomedical science, health care administration, medical laboratory technology, nursing, predentistry, premedicine, preoptometry, preveterinary science, and speech pathology/audiology), SOCIAL SCIENCE (anthropology, criminology, economics, food science, geography, history, home furnishings and equipment management/ production/services, human development, philosophy, physical fitness/ movement, political science/government, psychology, public administration, social work, sociology, and textiles and clothing). Engineering, education, and architecture are the strongest academically. Engineering, business, and liberal arts have the largest enrollments.

ACTIVITIES: 25% of men belong to 34 national fraternities; 44% of women belong to 20 national sororities. There are 490 groups on campus, including art, band, cheerleading, chess, choir, chorale, chorus, computers, dance, drama, drill team, environmental, ethnic, film, honors, international, jazz band, LGBT, literary magazine, marching band, musical theater, newspaper, opera, orchestra, pep band, photography, political, professional, radio and TV, religious, social, social service, student government, symphony, and yearbook. Popular campus events include A Day, Pep Rallies and Tiger Nights. **Sports:** There are 8 intercollegiate sports for men and 11 for women, and 18 intramural sports for men and 18 for women. Facilities include a stadium, coliseum, baseball and softball stadiums, athletics center, tennis center, aquatics center, soccer complex, track, intramural field houses, golf course, equestrian arenas, student activities center with a volleyball arena, racquetball, tennis, basketball courts, fitness/weight room, and an aerobics/cardio theater. **Graduates:** From July 1, 2016 to June 30, 2017, 4396 bachelor's degrees were awarded. The most popular majors were business (22%), engineering (17%), and education (10%). In an average class, 1% graduate in 3 years or less, 49% graduate in 4 years or less, 73% graduate in 5 years or less, and 77% graduate in 6 years or less. Of the 2016 graduating class, 42% were enrolled in graduate school within 6 months of graduation, and 88% were employed.

SERVICES: Counseling and information services are available, as is tutoring in most subjects. There is a reader service for the blind, and remedial writing. Auburn's Academic Support Services provides supplemental instruction and study partners through regularly scheduled peer-review sessions by students selected by the faculty. **Library/Resources:** The library contains 4.6 million volumes, 2.6 million microform items, and 125,322 audio/video tapes/CDs/DVDs, and subscribes to 50,160 periodicals including electronic. Computerized library services include interlibrary loans, database searching, Internet access, and Wi-Fi capability. Special learning facilities include an art gallery, radio station, TV station, a nuclear science center, an arboretum, and electron microscope laboratory, MRI research center and a museum of fine arts. **Physically Challenged Students:** All of the campus is accessible. Facilities include wheelchair ramps, elevators, special parking, specially equipped restrooms, special class scheduling, lowered drinking fountains, special housing, elevators with Braille controls, wheelchair lifts, and asstistive technology lab. **Special:** An Honors College provides enhanced academic opportunities for qualified students, and a University College is available for students with still-developing or wide-ranging academic interests. Opportunities are available for co-op programs, internships, work-study, and dual majors on a program-by-program basis; students should contact their advisers for specific information. 3+2 engineering degrees are offered with numerous other liberal arts colleges or with Auburn's colleges of agriculture, liberal arts, or sciences and mathematics. Other options available to students include study abroad in more than 47 countries, credit by exam, non-degree study, and pass/fail grading on select courses. There are 42 national honor societies, Phi Beta Kappa, a freshman honors program, and 26 departmental honors programs. **Visiting:** There are regularly scheduled orientations for prospective students, including War Eagle Days, held in the fall and spring and offering students and their families an opportunity to meet with representatives from admissions, financial aid, housing, residence life, and various academic departments. There are guides for informal visits and visitors may sit in on classes. To schedule a visit, contact the Office of Enrollment Services and Admissions. **Campus Safety and Security:** Measures include 24-hour foot and vehicle patrol, an emergency notification system, self-defense education, and security escort services. There are shuttle buses, emergency telephones, lighted pathways/sidewalks, and controlled access to dorms/residences.

REQUIREMENTS: The SAT or ACT is required. Favorable consideration for admission will be given to accredited secondary school graduates whose college ability test scores and high school grades give promise of the greatest level of success in college courses. Secondary school students planning to apply for admission are required to complete 4 years of English, 3 years each of social studies and math, and 2 years of science. Applicants of a mature age who are not high school graduates may be considered for admission if their educational attainments are shown through testing to be equivalent to those of high school graduates. Tests include the USAFI General Education Development Test, the American College Test, or other tests recommended by the Admissions Committee. AP credits are accepted. To graduate, students must complete a minimum of 120 credit hours with a cumulative GPA of at least 2.0. All students must complete Auburn's Core Curriculum. These 41-42 credit hours of courses in writing, humanities, social sciences, mathematics, and the natural sciences provide students with a broad foundation for attainment of 11 shared general education competencies. Students must also choose a major curriculum and complete its requirements and those of their college or school. **Procedure:** Freshmen are admitted to all sessions. There are deferred admissions and rolling admissions plans. Applications should be filed by February 1 for fall entry; October 1 for spring entry; and February 1 for summer entry. The fall 2017 application fee was $50. Notification is sent on a rolling basis. Applications are accepted on-line. **Transfer Students:** 1226 transfer students enrolled in 2016-2017. Transfer applicants must provide official transcripts from each college attended. A satisfactory citizenship record, a minimum 2.5 GPA on all college work, and eligibility to re enter the institution last attended are required for transfer admission. All transfer students who have attempted 32 semester hours of college work must have earned a cumulative 2.5 GPA in at least 20 semester hours of standard academic courses, in addition to the overall 2.5 cumulative average. These 20 semester hours must include at least 1 course in English (college-level composition or literature) and 1 in natural science with a lab. 30 of 120 credits required for the bachelor's degree must be completed at Auburn. **International Students:** There are 1124 international students enrolled. They must take the TOEFL with a minimum score of 550 on the paper-based TOEFL (PBT) or 79 on the Internet-based version (iBT). They must also take the SAT or ACT.

ADMISSIONS: 84% of the 2017-2018 applicants were accepted. The SAT scores for the 2017-2018 freshman class were: Math-- 3% below 500, 42% between 500 and 599, 41% between 600 and 699, and 14% between 700 and 800. Evidence-Based Reading/Writing-- 3% below 500, 37% between 500 and 599, 50% between 600 and 699, and 10% between 700 and 800. The ACT scores were 17% between 18 and 23, 53% between 24 and 29, and 30% above 30. 55% of the current freshmen were in the top fifth of their class; 83% were in the top two fifths. **Admissions Contact:** Velda Rooker, Interim, Enrollment Services. Email: *admissions@auburn.edu* Web: *www.auburn.edu*

FINANCIAL AID: In 2017-2018, 73% of all full-time freshmen received some form of financial aid. 36% of all full-time freshmen received need-based aid. The average freshman award was $15,045. Need-based scholarships or need-based grants averaged $8,751; need-based self-help aid (loans and jobs) averaged $3,785; and non-need-based athletic scholarships averaged $37,549. 13% of undergraduate students work part-time. The average financial indebtedness of the 2017 graduate was $29,295. Auburn is a member of CSS. The FAFSA code is 001009. The priority date for freshman financial aid applications for fall entry is February 1.

AUBURN UNIVERSITY AT MONTGOMERY C-4

www.aum.edu

Montgomery, AL 36124	(334) 244-3668
Fax: (334) 244-3795	Email: admissions@aum.edu
Full-time: 1169 men, 2070 women	**Faculty:** 216; IIA, -$
Part-time: 367 men, 707 women	**Ph.D.s:** 82%
Graduate: 193 men, 388 women	**Student/Faculty:** 14 to 1
Year: semesters, summer session	**Tuition:** $8020 ($17,140)
Room & Board: $6980	**Freshman Class:** 2474 applied, 2042 accepted, 673 enrolled
ACT: 21	**CEEB CODE:** 1036
Application Deadline: August 1	**COMPETITIVE**

Auburn University at Montgomery was founded in 1967. The college has 5 academic units: College of Arts and Sciences, College of Business, College of Education, College of Nursing and Health Sciences, and College of Public Policy and Justice. In addition to regional accreditation, AUM has baccalaureate and graduate programs. There are also 4 graduate schools. AUM has baccalaureate program accreditation with AACSB, CAEP, CCNE, NAACLS, and CACREP. The 500-acre campus is in a suburban area 7 miles east of downtown Montgomery. Including any residence halls, there are 53 buildings.

STUDENT LIFE: 92% of undergraduates are from Alabama. Others are from 34 states, and 34 foreign countries. 50% are White; 37% African American; 4% Foreign; 3% Asian American; 3% two or more races; 2% race unknown; 1% American Indian/Alaska Native; 1% Hispanic. **Female To Male Ratio:** 1.8:1. The average age of freshmen is 19; all undergraduates, 23. 33% do not continue beyond their first year; 23% remain to graduate. **Housing:** 1200 students can be accommodated in college housing, which includes gender neutral, coed, married student dorms, on-campus apartments, and special-interest houses. On-campus housing is available on a first-come, first-served basis. 77% of students commute. All students may keep cars.

FACULTY/CLASSROOMS: 54% of faculty are male; 45% are female. All teach undergraduates. No introductory courses are taught by graduate students. The average class size in an introductory lecture is 25 and in a laboratory is 14.

PROGRAMS OF STUDY: AUM confers B.S., B.A., B.F.A., B.I.S., B.S.B.A., and B.S.N. degrees. Master's and doctoral degrees are also awarded. Bachelor's degrees are awarded in BIOLOGICAL SCIENCE (biology/biological science), BUSINESS (accounting, business administration and management, entrepreneurial studies, finance, marketing management, marketing/retailing/merchandising, organizational leadership and management, and personnel management), COMMUNICATIONS AND THE ARTS (communications, English, fine arts, and Spanish), COMPUTER AND PHYSICAL SCIENCE (chemistry, computer science, information sciences and systems, mathematics, and physical sciences), EDUCATION (elementary education, secondary education, and special education), ENGINEERING AND ENVIRONMENTAL DESIGN (environmental science), HEALTH PROFESSIONS (kinesiology, medical laboratory science, nursing, and speech pathology/audiology), SOCIAL SCIENCE (criminal justice, economics, geography information science, history, homeland security/emergency preparedness, international studies, legal studies, liberal arts/general studies, political science/government, psychology, public administration, and sociology). Accounting, management information systems, and psychology are the strongest academically. Nursing, biology, and kinesiology have the largest enrollments.

ACTIVITIES: 2% of men belong to 3 national fraternities; 5% of women

belong to 6 national sororities. There are 52 groups on campus, including art, cheerleading, chorus, computers, dance, drama, environmental, ethnic, honors, international, LGBT, literary magazine, musical theater, newspaper, photography, political, professional, religious, social, social service, and student government. Popular campus events include AUM Fest, Week Of Welcome (WOW), Spring Fest, Mardi Gras, Shriek Week, Dances, and Band Parties. **Sports:** There are 5 intercollegiate sports for men and 6 for women, and 12 intramural sports for men and 12 for women. Facilities include a multipurpose gym-auditorium, an indoor jogging and walking track, baseball and soccer fields, tennis courts, and softball field. A wellness center which provides a climbing wall, 2 workout areas, a swimming pool, walking track, and rooms for exercise classes. **Graduates:** From July 1, 2016 to June 30, 2017, 652 bachelor's degrees were awarded. The most popular majors were business (25%), nursing (20%), and psychology (6%). In an average class, 12% graduate in 4 years or less, 22% graduate in 5 years or less, and 23% graduate in 6 years or less.

SERVICES: Counseling and information services are available, as is tutoring in most subjects. There is a reader service for the blind, and remedial math, reading, and writing, including study skills, Plagiarism Bootcamp, classroom workshops, test prep workshops, and assistive technology services. **Library/Resources:** The library contains 341,612 volumes, 2.4 million microform items, and 2,971 audio/video tapes/CDs/DVDs, and subscribes to 209 periodicals including electronic. Computerized library services include interlibrary loans, database searching, Internet access, and Wi-Fi capability. Special learning facilities include an art gallery, Geographic Information Systems computer and cartography lab technology, Taylor Center, Goodwyn Hall, Sciences Clement Hall, business, education, and developmental math lab. There is also the learning center/instructional support lab, one-on-one appointments in math, business topics, accounting, economics, history, conversational English for ESL students instructional support lab. There are also individual and small group tutoring in math and science. Global Education Office offers educational events to promote learning about world cultures Global Learning Communities Study Abroad Program Enrollment Management: UNIV 1000 first year success course AUM Bridge Program student support program for incoming students lacking full admissions requirements; includes case-managed academic advising and personalized tutoring; opportunity to participate in a residential living and learning Warhawk Warning Program--provides a way for faculty, staff, and administrators to help a student that they perceive as struggling and connect the student with services that may support their future success. AUM Common Reading Program (CRP)--provides students, faculty, staff, and members of the local community with opportunities to interact in meaningful conversations relating to contemporary social and cultural issues via an annual common reading selection. **Physically Challenged Students:** 95% of the campus is accessible. Facilities include wheelchair ramps, elevators, special parking, specially equipped restrooms, special class scheduling, lowered drinking fountains, lowered telephones, and special housing. **Special:** AUM offers study abroad opportunities, co-op program opportunities and internships. Our study abroad programs are located in eight different countries including China, Costa Rica, England (Oxford and Northampton), France, Japan, Mexico, South Korea, and Sri Lanka. AUM also has a cooperative program with Rheem Manufacturing through the Department of Information Systems. Numerous department specific internships are also available. There are 10 national honor societies, a freshman honors program, and 1 departmental honors program. **Visiting:** There are regularly scheduled orientations for prospective students, including meetings with faculty, staff, advising, and registration. There are guides for informal visits and visitors may sit in on classes. To schedule a visit, contact Amanda Brasington at admissions@aum.edu. **Campus Safety and Security:** Measures include 24-hour foot and vehicle patrol, emergency notification system, and security escort services. There are emergency telephones, lighted pathways/sidewalks, controlled access to dorms/residences. There are also personal safety and emergency preparedness seminars.

REQUIREMENTS: High school preparation should include English, math, social studies, science, and foreign language. The GED may be used for admission. Students may submit either the SAT or ACT. A GPA of 2.3 is required. AP and CLEP credits are accepted. To graduate, students must complete a minimum of 120 credit hours with a minimum GPA of 2.0 in the major and overall. All students must fulfill English composition requirements and Core Curriculum requirements. **Procedure:** Freshmen are admitted to all sessions. Entrance exams should be taken in the junior year. There is a rolling admissions plan. Applications should be filed by August 1 for fall entry. Applications are accepted online. **Transfer Students:** 1528 transfer students enrolled in 2016-2017. Applicants for transfer must have a C average and be in good standing at their last school. 30 of 120 credits required for the bachelor's degree must be completed at AUM. **International Students:** There are 154 international students enrolled. They must take the TOEFL with a minimum score of 500 on the paper-based TOEFL (PBT) or 61 on the Internet-based version (iBT), or take the IELTS.

ADMISSIONS: 83% of the 2017-2018 applicants were accepted. The ACT scores were 74% between 18 and 23, 24% between 24 and 29, and 1% above 30. **Admissions Contact:** Shirley Harrington, Director of Admissions. Email: *admissions@aum.edu* Web: *www.aum.edu*

FINANCIAL AID: In 2017-2018, 83% of all full-time freshmen received some form of financial aid. The average freshman award was $10,693. Need-based scholarships or need-based grants averaged $11,715 ($33,252 maximum); and need-based self-help aid (loans and jobs) averaged $8,896 ($34,760 maximum). The average financial indebtedness of the 2017 graduate was $31,485. The FAFSA code is 36124. The priority date for freshman financial aid applications for fall entry is March 1.

BIRMINGHAM-SOUTHERN COLLEGE C-2

www.bsc.edu

Birmingham, AL 35254	**(205) 226-4696** **(800) 523-5793**
Fax: (205) 523-3074	**Email: admission@bsc.edu**
Full-time: 673 men, 664 women	**Faculty:** IIB, av$
Part-time: 3 men, 6 women	**Ph.D.s:** 96%
Graduate: n/av	**Student/Faculty:** 13 to 1
Year: 4-1-4, summer session	**Tuition:** $33,128
Room & Board: $11,350	**Freshman Class:** n/av
SAT CR/M: 550/560 **ACT:** 26	**CEEB CODE:** 1064
Application Deadline: February 1	**COMPETITIVE+**

Birmingham-Southern College, founded in 1856, is a private liberal arts college affiliated with the United Methodist Church. BSC offers 30 undergraduate majors, 23 minors, and 10 special programs. The figures in the above capsule and in this profile are approximate. There is 1 undergraduate school and 1 graduate school. In addition to regional accreditation, BSC has baccalaureate program accreditation with NASM and CAEP. The 192-acre campus is in an urban area 3 miles west of downtown Birmingham. Including any residence halls, there are 50 buildings.

STUDENT LIFE: 54% of undergraduates are from out of state, mostly the South. Students are from 38 states, 21 foreign countries, and Canada. 65% are from public schools. 79% are White; 5% Asian American; 2% Hispanic; 11% African American; 1% American Indian/Alaska Native; 1% two or more races; 1% race unknown. 54% are Protestant; 16% claim no religious affiliation; 13% Catholic. **Male To Female Ratio:** 1.0:1. The average age of freshmen is 18; all undergraduates, 21. 19% do not continue beyond their first year; 71% remain to graduate. **Housing:** 1624 students can be accommodated in college housing, which includes married student dorms and on-campus apartments. In addition, there are honors houses, fraternity houses, and sorority houses. On-campus housing is guaranteed for all 4 years. 90% of students live on campus. All students may keep cars.

FACULTY/CLASSROOMS: 54% of faculty are male; 46% are female. All teach undergraduates. No introductory courses are taught by graduate students. The average class size in an introductory lecture is 16 and in a laboratory is 20.

PROGRAMS OF STUDY: BSC confers B.A., B.F.A., and B.S. degrees. Bachelor's degrees are awarded in AGRICULTURE (environmental studies), BIOLOGICAL SCIENCE (biology/biological science), BUSINESS (accounting and business administration and management), COMMUNICATIONS AND THE ARTS (art, art history and appreciation, English, film and media studies, music, musical theater, Spanish, studio art, and theatre arts), COMPUTER AND PHYSICAL SCIENCE (chemistry, mathematics, and physics), EDUCATION (collaborative education, education, and secondary education), ENGINEERING AND ENVIRONMENTAL DESIGN (engineering), HEALTH PROFESSIONS (nursing), SOCIAL SCIENCE (Asian/Oriental studies, biopsychology, economics, history, interdisciplinary studies, philosophy, political science/government, psychology, religion, and sociology). Biology, business administration, and English have the largest enrollments.

ACTIVITIES: 43% of men belong to 7 national fraternities; 52% of women belong to 7 national sororities. There are 81 groups on campus, including art, band, cheerleading, choir, chorale, chorus, computers, dance, debate, drama, environmental, ethnic, film, honors, international, jazz band, LGBT, literary magazine, marching band, musical theater, newspaper, opera, orchestra, pep band, political, professional, religious, social, social service, student government, symphony, and yearbook. Popular campus events include Halloween on the Hilltop, and E-Fest. **Sports:** There are 10 intercollegiate sports for men and 10 for women, and 10 intramural sports for men and 10 for women. Facilities include a football stadium, urban environmental park, a basketball and volleyball coliseum, baseball field, softball field, racquetball and tennis courts, soccer fields, a weight room, intramural athletic field, indoor pool, game room, indoor jogging track, gyms, a golf simulator, and an aerobics studio. **Graduates:** From July 1, 2016 to June 30, 2017, 220 bachelor's degrees were awarded. The most popular majors were biology, business administration, and English. Of the 2016 graduating class, 42% were enrolled in graduate school within 6 months of graduation, and 52% were employed.

SERVICES: Counseling and information services are available, as is tutoring in most subjects. Through the use of peer tutors and one-on-one assistance, the Academic Resource Center also promotes the Foundation's general education goal of collaborative learning and peer-teaching in most subjects, including specific emphasis on math and writing. **Library/Resources:** The library contains 263,024 volumes, 90,675 microform items, and 38,261 audio/video tapes/CDs/DVDs, and subscribes to 40,000 periodicals including electronic. Computerized library services include interlibrary loans, database searching, Internet access, and Wi-Fi capability. Special learning facilities include an art gallery, planetarium, an environmental center, an outdoor educational center, and two digital classrooms. **Physically Challenged Students:** 90% of the campus is accessible. Facilities include wheelchair ramps, elevators, special parking, specially equipped restrooms, special class scheduling, lowered drinking fountains, lowered telephones, and special housing. **Special:** There is cross-registration with the University of Alabama at Birmingham, Miles College, the University of Montevallo, and Samford University. Student-designed, dual, and interdisciplinary majors, internships, work-study programs, and study abroad are offered. There is a 3-2 nursing program with Vanderbilt University and a 3-2 environmental studies program with Duke University. A 3-2 engineering degree is offered with the University of Alabama at Birmingham, Auburn University, Columbia University, and Washington University. There are 19 national honor societies, Phi Beta Kappa, a freshman honors program, and 5 departmental honors programs. **Visiting:** Visits include a tour of campus and an information session with a member of our staff. From there, you can customize your visit with additional experiences. There are also guides for informal visits, visitors may sit in on classes, and stay overnight. **Campus Safety and Security:** Measures include 24-hour foot and vehicle patrol, emergency notification system, self-defense education, and security escort services. There are shuttle buses, emergency telephones, lighted pathways/sidewalks, and controlled access to dorms/residences.

REQUIREMENTS: The SAT or ACT is required. Your engagement and accomplishments outside the classroom, leadership potential, course preparation, class rank, and more will be taken into consideration by our holistic review process. Applicants should have graduated from an accredited secondary school with 4 courses each in English, math, science, and social studies, and a recommended 2 in foreign language. The GED is also accepted. An essay is required and an interview is recommended. Fine arts majors are advised to submit a portfolio or arrange an interview with the fine arts department. BSC requires applicants to be in the upper 50% of their class. A GPA of 2.3 is required. AP and CLEP credits are accepted. Important factors in the admissions decision are advanced placement or honors courses, leadership record, and recommendations by school officials. All students must complete 32 units, including 2 exploration terms. A GPA of at least 2.0 is required to graduate. **Procedure:** Freshmen are admitted fall, winter, spring, and summer. Entrance exams should be taken in the spring of the junior year or fall of senior year. There are early admissions and deferred admissions plans. Applications should be filed by February 1 for fall entry. The fall 2017 application fee was $50. Notifications are sent March 1. Applications are accepted on-line. **Transfer Students:** 23 transfer students enrolled in 2016-2017. Transfer applicants must have a minimum GPA of 2.0 and leave their former school in good standing. An essay and a school recommendation are required. An interview is recommended. 16 of 32 credits required for the bachelor's degree must be completed at BSC. **International Students:** There are 39 international students enrolled. They must take the TOEFL with a minimum score of 500 on the paper-based TOEFL (PBT) or 61 on the Internet-based version (iBT). The SAT or ACT is required instead of the TOEFL for students whose primary language is English, with minimum English or verbal scores of 21 or 475.

ADMISSIONS: The SAT scores for the 2017-2018 freshman class were: Critical Reading-- 31% below 500, 45% between 500 and 599, 21% between 600 and 699, and 3% between 700 and 800. Math-- 20% below 500, 47% between 500 and 599, 28% between 600 and 699, and 5% between 700 and 800. Writing-- 16% below 500, 45% between 500 and 599, 28% between 600 and 699, and 12% between 700 and 800. The ACT scores were 29% between 18 and 23, 50% between 24 and 29, and 21% above 30. 52% of the current freshmen were in the top fifth of their class; 76% were in the top two fifths. 5 freshmen graduated first in their class. **Admissions Contact:** Sara H. Newhouse, Assoc VP, Admission/Financial Planning. Email: *admission@bsc.edu* Web: *www.bsc.edu*

FINANCIAL AID: In 2017-2018, 100% of all full-time freshmen received some form of financial aid. 30% of all full-time freshmen received need-based aid. The average freshman award was $23,452. The average financial indebtedness of the 2017 graduate was $28,000. The FAFSA code is 001012. The priority date for freshman financial aid applications for fall entry is March 1.

CONCORDIA COLLEGE - ALABAMA *(The complete profile is made available exclusively on our website, www.barronspac.com)*

FAULKNER UNIVERSITY C-4

www.faulkner.edu

Montgomery, AL 36109 (334) 386-7200 (800) 879-9816

Fax: (334) 386-7137 **Email:** admissions@faulkner.edu

Full-time: 745 men, 1026 women	**Faculty:** 98
Part-time: 256 men, 537 women	**Ph.D.s:** 66%
Graduate: 278 men, 420 women	**Student/Faculty:** 18 to 1
Year: semesters, summer session	**Tuition:** $19,280
Room & Board: $7130	**Freshman Class:** 1712 applied, 981 accepted, 297388 enrolled
SAT CR/M/W: required **ACT:** 21	**CEEB CODE:** 1034
Application Deadline: March 15	**COMPETITIVE**

Faulkner University, founded in 1942, is a private, multicampus university affiliated with the Church of Christ, offering undergraduate programs in Bible studies, business, education, and liberal arts and sciences. There are 4 undergraduate schools and 4 graduate schools. In addition to regional accreditation, Faulkner has baccalaureate program accreditation with CAEP and ABA. The 92-acre campus is in an urban area 6.4 miles east of the Alabama State Capital in Montgomery, AL. Including any residence halls, there are 26 buildings.

STUDENT LIFE: 85% of undergraduates are from Alabama. Others are from 26 states, 31 foreign countries, and Canada. 75% are from public schools. 46% are White; 45% African American; 2% Hispanic; 2% Foreign; 2% two or more races; 2% race unknown; 1% American Indian/Alaska Native. 59% are Protestant. **Female To Male Ratio:** 1.6:1. The average age of freshmen is 19; all undergraduates, 28. 40% do not continue beyond their first year; 33% remain to graduate. **Housing:** 652 students can be accommodated in college housing, which includes dorms and on-campus apartments. On-campus housing is available on a first-come and first-served basis. 72% of students commute. Alcohol is not permitted. All students may keep cars.

FACULTY/CLASSROOMS: 61% of faculty are male; 39% are female. 85% teach undergraduates. No introductory courses are taught by graduate students. The average class size in an introductory lecture is 19; in a laboratory is 14; and in a regular course is 13.

PROGRAMS OF STUDY: Faulkner confers B.A. and B.S. degrees. Associate, master's, and doctoral degrees are also awarded. Bachelor's degrees are awarded in BIOLOGICAL SCIENCE (biochemistry, biology/adolescence education, biology/biological science, environmental biology, and forensic psychology), BUSINESS (accounting, business administration and management, business information systems, human resources, management information systems, management science, and sports management), COMMUNICATIONS AND THE ARTS (choral music, English, information technology, literature, music, musical theater, theater design, and theatre studies), COMPUTER AND PHYSICAL SCIENCE (chemistry, computer information systems, computer science, industrial psychology/safety, information sciences and systems, informatics and computer science, and mathematics), EDUCATION (early childhood education, education, elementary education, English education, mathematics education, music education, physical education, science education, and social science education), HEALTH PROFESSIONS (predentistry, premedicine, preoptometry, prephysical therapy, preveterinary science, and sports psychology), SOCIAL SCIENCE (biblical languages, biblical studies, clinical psychology, counseling/psychology, criminal justice, criminology, history, humanities, law, law enforcement and corrections, legal studies, liberal arts/general studies, ministries, missions, philosophy, prelaw, social science, and youth ministry). Criminal justice, biology, and elementary education are the strongest academically. Biology, education, and sports management have the largest enrollments.

ACTIVITIES: 21% of men belong to 5 local fraternities; 34% of women belong to 5 local sororities. There are 26 groups on campus, including band, cheerleading, chorus, drama, honors, jazz band, literary magazine, marching band, musical theater, newspaper, pep band, religious, social, social service, student government, and yearbook. Popular campus events include Annual Bible Lectureship, Jamboree, and Fall Visitation Weekend. **Sports:** There are 5 intercollegiate sports for men and 5 for women, and 6 intramural sports for men and 6 for women. Facilities include a gym, multiplex, weight rooms, walk/run track, exercise room, aerobics room, racquetball courts, game room, baseball and softball fields, and tennis courts. **Graduates:** From July 1, 2016 to June 30, 2017, 452 bachelor's degrees were awarded. The most popular majors were business administration (35%), human resource management (21%), and criminal justice (17%). In an average class, 10% graduate in 4 years or less, 33% graduate in 5 years or less, and 37% graduate in 6 years or less.

SERVICES: Counseling and information services are available, as is tutoring in most subjects. Attempts are made to fulfill all requests for tutoring, sometimes with peers. There is a reader service for the blind, and remedial math, reading, and writing. **Library/Resources:** The library contains 769,046 volumes, 391,849 microform items, and 3,575 audio/video tapes/CDs/DVDs, and subscribes to 1,211 periodicals including electronic. Computerized library services include interlibrary loans, database searching, Internet access, and Wi-Fi capability. **Physically Challenged Students:** All of the campus is accessible. Facilities include wheelchair ramps, elevators, special parking, specially equipped restrooms, special class scheduling, and special housing. **Special:** A second bachelor's degree in a separate major may be completed with a minimum of 24 semester hours earned beyond the first degree. Cross-registration with Auburn University at Montgomery and Huntingdon College, dual majors, credit for life/military/work experience, and nondegree study are offered. Internships in education, psychology, criminal justice, Bible, and sports management are available, as are accelerated degree programs in some majors. There are 8 national honor societies, Phi Beta Kappa, a freshman honors program, and 1 departmental honors program. **Visiting:** There are regularly scheduled orientations for prospective students. We offer three College Bound events (April, June, July) over a two day period that culminate in student registration. The week preceding the fall term is dedicated for an in-depth orientation we call Freshman Experience. There are guides for informal visits, visitors may sit in on classes, and stay overnight. To schedule a visit, contact Robin Byrd at (334) 386-7200. **Campus Safety and Security:** Measures include 24-hour foot and vehicle patrol and security escort services. There are lighted pathways/sidewalks and controlled access to dorms/residences.

REQUIREMENTS: The ACT is required, with a satisfactory score. The SAT is recommended. Candidates must be graduates of an accredited secondary school, or have the GED equivalent, with a minimum of 15 academic units, including 3 in English. A GPA of 2.0 is required. AP and CLEP credits are accepted. Important factors in the admissions decision are leadership record, extracurricular activities record, recommendations by alumni, recommendations by school officials, advanced placement or honors courses, parents or siblings attended your school, and personality/intangible qualities. Students must complete a 52-semester-hour core curriculum, including courses in Bible, history, social science, English composition, literature, speech communication, physical and natural science, math, computer literacy, and phys ed. B.A. students must take 2 semesters of foreign language. At least 120 semester hours with a minimum GPA of 2.0 are required to graduate. **Procedure:** Freshmen are admitted fall, spring, and summer. Entrance exams should be taken during December. There is a rolling admissions plan. Application deadlines are open. The fall 2017 application fee was $25. Applications are accepted on-line. **Transfer Students:** 479 transfer students enrolled in 2016-2017. Applicants must be in good academic standing from another accredited college. 30 of 120 credits required for the bachelor's degree must be completed at Faulkner. **International Students:** There are 49 international students enrolled. They must take the TOEFL with a minimum score of 500 on the paper-based TOEFL (PBT) or 61 on the Internet-based version (iBT). They must also take the SAT or ACT.

ADMISSIONS: 57% of the 2017-2018 applicants were accepted. The SAT scores for the 2017-2018 freshman class were: Critical Reading-- 67% below 500, 26% between 500 and 599, and 7% between 600 and 699. Math-- 59% below 500, 37% between 500 and 599, and 4% between 600 and 699. Writing-- 70% below 500, 26% between 500 and 599, and 4% between 600 and 699. The ACT scores were 1% between 12 and 17, 70% between 18 and 23, 28% between 24 and 29, and 1% above 30. **Admissions Contact:** Neil Scott, Director of Admissions. Email: *admissions@faulkner.edu* Web: *www.faulkner.edu*

FINANCIAL AID: In 2017-2018, 98% of all full-time freshmen received some form of financial aid. 70% of all full-time freshmen received need-based aid. The average freshman award was $9,500. Need-based scholarships or need-based grants averaged $5,100; need-based self-help aid (loans and jobs) averaged $3,722; non-need-based athletic scholarships averaged $5,900; and other non-need-based awards and non-need-based scholarships averaged $9,200. 10% of undergraduate students work part-time. Faulkner is a member of CSS. The state aid form and the college's own financial statement are required. The FAFSA code is 001003. The priority date for freshman financial aid applications for fall entry is February 10.

HUNTINGDON COLLEGE — C-4

www.huntingdon.edu

Montgomery, AL 36106 — (334) 833-4497, (800) 763-0313

Fax: (334) 833-4347 — **Email:** admiss@hawks.huntingdon.edu

Full-time: 463 men, 415 women	**Faculty:** 47; IIB, --$
Part-time: 71 men, 153 women	**Ph.D.s:** 74%
Graduate: n/av	**Student/Faculty:** 19 to 1
Year: semesters, summer session	**Tuition:** $26,400
Room & Board: $9500	**Freshman Class:** 2074 applied, 1161 accepted, 294 enrolled
SAT CR/M: 548/543 **ACT:** 21	**CEEB CODE:** 1303
Application Deadline: rolling	**COMPETITIVE**

Huntingdon College, founded in 1854, and affiliated with the United Methodist Church, is a private institution offering a liberal arts curriculum. Through its Huntingdon plan, the college provides hands-on experience through internships, service, and student-faculty research and exploration of the world through travel/study with faculty and fellow students; each student is also provided with a laptop computer. There is 1 undergraduate school. In addition to regional accreditation, HC has baccalaureate program accreditation with NASM and CAATE. The 71-acre campus is in a suburban area 90 miles south of Birmingham. Including any residence halls, there are 23 buildings.

STUDENT LIFE: 76% of undergraduates are from Alabama. Others are from 22 states, and 4 foreign countries. 82% are from public schools. 64% are White; 6% Hispanic; 5% two or more races; 3% race unknown; 21% African American; 1% American Indian/Alaska Native. 31% are Protestant; 29% Christian, Pentecostal, and Church of Christ, and non-denominational; 17% claim no religious affiliation. **Female To Male Ratio:** 1.1:1. The average age of freshmen is 18; all undergraduates, 23. 35% do not continue beyond their first year; 37% remain to graduate. **Housing:** 629 students can be accommodated in college housing, which includes single sex, and coed dorms. In addition, there are fraternity houses, sorority houses, upperclassmen housing, and special accommodations for students with disabilities. On-campus housing is guaranteed for all 4 years. 68% of students live on campus. Alcohol is not permitted. All students may keep cars.

FACULTY/CLASSROOMS: 55% of faculty are male; 45% are female. All teach undergraduates. No introductory courses are taught by graduate

students. The average class size in an introductory lecture is 27; in a laboratory is 16; and in a regular course is 13.

PROGRAMS OF STUDY: HC confers B.A. and B.S. (B.S. degrees can be earned in the Evening Studies program only) degrees. Bachelor's degrees are awarded in BIOLOGICAL SCIENCE (biochemistry, biology/adolescence education, biology/biological science, and cell biology), BUSINESS (accounting, business administration and management, and sports management), COMMUNICATIONS AND THE ARTS (art, communication rhetoric/communication, English, and music), COMPUTER AND PHYSICAL SCIENCE (applied mathematics, chemistry, chemistry/adolescence education, chemistry/gen science second education, digital arts/technology, and mathematics), EDUCATION (collaborative education, elementary education, English education, history education, mathematics education, music education, physical education, and sports studies), HEALTH PROFESSIONS (exercise science), SOCIAL SCIENCE (Christian studies, criminal justice, history, political science/government, psychology, and religion). Biology and chemistry is the strongest academically. Sport studies, business administration and biology have the largest enrollments.

ACTIVITIES: 18% of men belong to 3 national fraternities; 42% of women belong to 3 national sororities. There are 50 groups on campus, including art, band, cheerleading, choir, chorale, chorus, communications, drama, environmental, ethnic, honors, jazz band, literary magazine, marching band, newspaper, pep band, political, professional, religious, social, social service, student government, and yearbook. Popular campus events include Big Red Weekend, Presidential Convocation, Welcome Back Week, Homecoming Week, Countess of Huntingdon Ball, football games, Service of Lessons and Carols, Stallworth Lecture Series, Miss Huntingdon, CloverJam, Awards Convocation, and Baccalaureate. **Sports:** There are 9 intercollegiate sports for men and 9 for women, and 12 intramural sports for men and 12 for women. Facilities include a multipurpose student center with a gym for basketball. There is also a fitness training facility with fixed and free weight machines, an athletic center for volleyball, sports medicine and athletic training facilities, a football stadium, and weight training and conditioning facilities, outdoor tennis courts, softball, baseball, soccer fields, outdoor basketball court, and a sand volleyball court. **Graduates:** From July 1, 2016 to June 30, 2017, 311 bachelor's degrees were awarded. The most popular majors were business administration/business management (43%), human performance/sport studies (13%), and education (7%).

SERVICES: Counseling and information services are available, as is tutoring in some subjects, such as writing, mathematics, history, English, business and accounting, political science, religion, biology and psychology. **Library/Resources:** The library contains 90,500 volumes, 3,000 microform items, and 4,633 audio/video tapes/CDs/DVDs, and subscribes to 199 periodicals including electronic. Computerized library services include interlibrary loans, database searching, Internet access, and Wi-Fi capability. Special learning facilities include an art gallery, the Bowman Ecological Study Center, Sybil Smith Hall, the Dr. Laurie Jean Weil Center for human performance and Archives for the Alabama-West Florida Conference of the United Methodist Church. **Physically Challenged Students:** 85% of the campus is accessible. Facilities include wheelchair ramps, elevators, special parking, specially equipped restrooms, special class scheduling, lowered drinking fountains, lowered telephones, and special housing. **Special:** Huntingdon currently offers more than 20 majors, the opportunity for travel/study experiences offered as part of regular educational costs, hands-on learning experiences in every program of study, dual majors, internships, and preprofessional advising. Students may participate in the Marine Environmental Sciences Consortium in Dauphin Island, Alabama. Work-study options are also available to qualifying students. There are 17 national honor societies, a freshman honors program, and 12 departmental honors programs. **Visiting:** There are regularly scheduled orientations for prospective students, the Office of Admissions offers personal campus visits during the week (Monday-Friday) and select Saturdays. There are guides for informal visits, visitors may sit in on classes, and stay overnight. To schedule a visit, contact the Office of Admission. **Campus Safety and Security:** Measures include 24-hour foot and vehicle patrol, emergency notification system, self-defense education, and security escort services. There are emergency telephones, lighted pathways/sidewalks, controlled access to dorms/residences, weather alert broadcasts, and parking lot cameras in most lots.

REQUIREMENTS: The SAT or ACT is required. Prospective students must have received a high school diploma or its equivalency. IB and dual enrollment credits are considered for acceptance. AP and CLEP credits are also accepted. Huntingdon's core curriculum includes 39 hours of required courses, including 9 hours of religion/history of the church, 9 hours of writing/communication, and 3 hours each of fine art appreciation, history, literature, mathematics, natural sciences, social science and critical thinking (PACT). Students must maintain a minimum GPA of 2.0 over 120 credits for the bachelor's degree. Major requirements range from 30 to 60+ hours. **Procedure:** Freshmen are admitted fall, spring, and summer. Entrance exams should be taken in the spring of the junior year. There are deferred admissions and rolling admissions plans. Application deadlines are open. Applications are accepted online. **Transfer Students:** 47 transfer students enrolled in 2016-2017. Transfer students must have successfully completed 24 semester hours of non-remedial courses at a regionally accredited college or university and be in good standing at previously attended institutions; otherwise, students must meet the regular freshman admission requirements. Transfer admission to the Evening Studies Program should be referenced in the college catalog (transfer numbers for the ES program are not included in the number shown above). 30 of 120 credits required for the bachelor's degree must be completed at HC. **International Students:** There are 4 international students enrolled. They must take the TOEFL with a minimum score of 500 on the paper-based TOEFL (PBT) or 45 on the Internet-based version (iBT). They must also take the SAT or ACT.

ADMISSIONS: 56% of the 2017-2018 applicants were accepted. The SAT scores for the 2017-2018 freshman class were: Critical Reading-- 27% below 500, 48% between 500 and 599, 22% between 600 and 699, and 3% between 700 and 800. Math-- 22% below 500, 59% between 500 and 599, and 19% between 600 and 699. The ACT scores were 10% between 12 and 17, 62% between 18 and 23, 27% between 24 and 29, and 1% above 30. 22% of the current freshmen were in the top fifth of their class; 53% were in the top two fifths. **Admissions Contact:** Laura Duncan, Vice President for Enrollment Management. Email: *admiss@hawks.huntingdon.edu* Web: *www.huntingdon.edu*

FINANCIAL AID: In 2017-2018, 100% of all full-time freshmen received some form of financial aid. 71% of all full-time freshmen received need-based aid. The average freshman award was $21,949. Need-based scholarships or need-based grants averaged $3,377; need-based self-help aid (loans and jobs) averaged $2,510; and other non-need-based awards and non-need-based scholarships averaged $16,032. 17% of undergraduate students work part-time. The average financial indebtedness of the 2017 graduate was $32,201. The college's own financial statement is required. The FAFSA code is 001019. The priority date for freshman financial aid applications for fall entry is March 1.

JACKSONVILLE STATE UNIVERSITY *(The complete profile is made available exclusively on our website, www.barronspac.com)*

JUDSON COLLEGE — B-3
www.judson.edu

Marion, AL 36756 — **(334) 683-5110**, **(800) 447-9472**

Fax: (334) 683-5282 — **Email: admissions@judson.edu**

Full-time: 261 women	**Faculty:** 31
Part-time: 15 men, 70 women	**Ph.D.s:** 81%
Graduate: n/av	**Student/Faculty:** 9 to 1
Year: semesters, summer session	**Tuition:** $17,088
Room & Board: $9978	**Freshman Class:** 268 applied, 198 accepted, 68 enrolled
SAT or ACT: required	**CEEB CODE:** 1349
Application Deadline: open	**COMPETITIVE**

Judson College, founded in 1838, is a private women's liberal arts college affiliated with the Alabama Baptist Convention. Men are accepted only in the Distance Learning division of the college. The figures in the above capsule and in this profile are approximate. There is 1 undergraduate school. In addition to regional accreditation, Judson has a baccalaureate program accreditation with NASM. The 118-acre campus is in a small town 75 miles southwest of Birmingham. Including any residence halls, there are 18 buildings.

STUDENT LIFE: 82% of undergraduates are from Alabama. Others are from 19 states, and 4 foreign countries. 77% are from public schools. 75% are White; 7% race unknown; 14% African American; 1% Asian

American; 1% Hispanic; 1% Foreign; 1% two or more races. 90% are Protestant. **Female To Male Ratio:** 20.7:1. The average age of freshmen is 18; all undergraduates, 25. 39% do not continue beyond their first year; 37% remain to graduate. **Housing:** 264 students can be accommodated in college housing, which includes dorms. On-campus housing is guaranteed for all 4 years. 57% of students live on campus. Alcohol is not permitted. All students may keep cars.

FACULTY/CLASSROOMS: 53% of faculty are male; 47% are female. All teach undergraduates. No introductory courses are taught by graduate students. The average class size in an introductory lecture is 23; in a laboratory is 12; and in a regular course is 7.

PROGRAMS OF STUDY: Judson confers B.A, B.Min., B.S., and B.S.W. degrees. Associate degrees are also awarded. Bachelor's degrees are awarded in AGRICULTURE (equine science), BIOLOGICAL SCIENCE (biology/biological science), BUSINESS (business administration and management), COMMUNICATIONS AND THE ARTS (applied music, art, English, and Spanish), COMPUTER AND PHYSICAL SCIENCE (chemistry and mathematics), EDUCATION (elementary education, English education, mathematics education, music education, science education, and social studies education), HEALTH PROFESSIONS (nursing), SOCIAL SCIENCE (criminal justice, history, interdisciplinary studies, psychology, religion, and social work). Biology, education, and business are the strongest academically. Biology, nursing, and psychology have the largest enrollments.

ACTIVITIES: There are no fraternities or sororities. There are 26 groups on campus, including art, band, choir, chorale, chorus, computers, departmental clubs, drama, environmental, honors, literary magazine, marching band, musical theater, newspaper, orchestra, photography, political, professional, religious, social, social service, student government, and yearbook. Popular campus events include Hockey Day, Junior-Sophomore Dance, Pageant, Christmas Tea and Vespers, and Rose Sunday. **Sports:** There are 6 intercollegiate sports for women, and 3 intramural sports for women. Facilities include an indoor swimming pool, an equine center with tack rooms, stalls, and a covered riding arena, tennis courts, a wellness center, a gym with an aerobics room and weight training facility, hockey field, softball field, soccer field, and a game room. **Graduates:** From July 1, 2016 to June 30, 2017, 58 bachelor's degrees were awarded. The most popular majors were nursing (34%), biology (12%), and English (9%). In an average class, 3% graduate in 3 years or less, 10% graduate in 4 years or less, 68% graduate in 5 years or less, and 19% graduate in 6 years or less. Of the 2016 graduating class, 9% were enrolled in graduate school within 6 months of graduation, and 47% were employed.

SERVICES: Counseling and information services are available, as is tutoring in most subjects, such as math, English, history, business, and others on request. There is remedial math and writing. **Library/Resources:** The library contains 59,096 volumes, 2,012 microform items, and 1,359 audio/video tapes/CDs/DVDs, and subscribes to 32,679 periodicals including electronic. Computerized library services include interlibrary loans, database searching, Internet access, and Wi-Fi capability. **Physically Challenged Students:** 75% of the campus is accessible. Facilities include wheelchair ramps, elevators, special parking, specially equipped restrooms, lowered drinking fountains, lowered telephones, and special housing. **Special:** Cross-registration with the Marion Military Institute is available for ROTC students. B.A.-B.S. degrees are offered in criminal justice, math, business, biology, psychology, and chemistry. Students study abroad in such places as Salzburg, China, India, Oxford, Uganda, Australia, Latin America, and the Middle East. Dual majors, an equine science program, an accelerated degree program, an interdisciplinary major, work-study programs, and internships are offered. Students may combine their Associate Degree in nursing with biology for a B.S. degree. There are preprofessional programs in health areas, engineering, and law. The Distance Learning program offers credit for prior learning experience and provides individually paced instruction leading to a baccalaureate degree. There are 7 national honor societies, a freshman honors program, and 19 departmental honors programs. **Visiting:** There are regularly scheduled orientations for prospective students, consisting of 3 college Scholarship Days, 1 in September, 1 in November and 1 in February, and a Junior Day in May. Activities include scholarship testing, an equine show, campus tours, faculty meetings, and financial aid planning. There are guides for informal visits, visitors may sit in on classes, and stay overnight. To schedule a visit, contact the Admissions Office. **Campus Safety and Security:** Measures include 24-hour foot and vehicle patrol, emergency notification system, self-defense education, and security escort services. There are emergency telephones, lighted pathways/sidewalks, controlled access to dorms/residences, and card access are for classroom and administrative buildings.

REQUIREMENTS: The SAT or the ACT, with a minimum composite score of 18 is required. SAT applicants should have completed 17 high school credits, including 4 in English. Non-high school graduates must provide the GED equivalent. AP and CLEP credits are accepted. All students are required to complete courses in English, history, multicultural studies, speech, religion, social science, math, science, humanities, computer literacy, health/phys ed, and women's studies. A total of 128 credit hours, with a minimum GPA of 2.0 (2.5 for education majors) is required to graduate. B.A. students must also complete at least 6 hours of foreign languages at the 200-level or above, B.S. students must complete at least 12 hours of math or science electives in addition to the core competency. A passing score is required on the English Language Usage Test and on the senior essay that meets the requirements of the Judson Quality Enhancement Plan. **Procedure:** Freshmen are admitted in the fall, winter, and summer. Entrance exams should be taken in the spring of the junior year. There are early admissions, deferred admissions, and rolling admissions plans. Application deadlines are open. The fall 2017 application fee was $35. Notification is sent on a rolling basis. Applications are accepted on-line. **Transfer Students:** 56 transfer students enrolled in 2016-2017. Transfer students must have a minimum GPA of 2.0 and be eligible to return to the school from which they transfer. 32 of 128 credits required for the bachelor's degree must be completed at Judson. **International Students:** There are 4 international students enrolled. They must take the TOEFL with a minimum score of 500 on the paper-based TOEFL (PBT) or 61 on the Internet-based version (iBT) and the college's own test.

ADMISSIONS: 74% of the 2017-2018 applicants were accepted. 42% of the current freshmen were in the top fifth of their class; 67% were in the top two fifths. **Admissions Contact:** Layne Calhoun, Executive Director of Enrollment Service. Email: *admissions@judson.edu* Web: *www.judson.edu*

FINANCIAL AID: In 2017-2018, 100% of all full-time freshmen received some form of financial aid. 89% of all full-time freshmen received need-based aid. The average freshman award was $10,512. Need-based scholarships or need-based grants averaged $5,812 ($35,222 maximum); need-based self-help aid (loans and jobs) averaged $7,416 ($26,250 maximum); non-need-based athletic scholarships averaged $3,990 ($9,000 maximum); and other non-need-based awards and non-need-based scholarships averaged $8,037 ($35,222 maximum). 31% of undergraduate students work part-time. The average financial indebtedness of the 2017 graduate was $24,374. The FAFSA code is 001023. The priority date for freshman financial aid applications for fall entry is March 1.

MILES COLLEGE *(The complete profile is made available exclusively on our website, www.barronspac.com)*

OAKWOOD UNIVERSITY — C-1

www.oakwood.edu

Huntsville, AL 35896	**(256) 726-7356** **(800) 824-5312**
Fax: (256) 726-7154	**Email: admission@oakwood.edu**
Full-time: 855 men, 857 women	**Faculty:** n/av
Part-time: 143 men, 145 women	**Ph.D.s:** 54%
Graduate: n/av	**Student/Faculty:** n/av
Year: semesters, summer session	**Tuition:** $27,038
Room & Board: $16,720	**Freshman Class:** n/av
SAT or ACT: recommended	**CEEB CODE:** 1586
Application Deadline: open	**COMPETITIVE**

Oakwood University, founded in 1896, is a private, historically black, Seventh-day Adventist institution, that aims to transform students through biblically-based education for service to God and humanity. The figures in the above capsule and in this profile are approximate. There is 1 undergraduate school. In addition to regional accreditation, OU has baccalaureate program accreditation with ACBSP, ADA, CSWE, CAEP, AAADE, CADE, and NLNAC. The 1186-acre campus is in a suburban area 5 miles northwest of Huntsville. Including any residence halls, there are 30 buildings.

STUDENT LIFE: 79% of undergraduates are from out of state, mostly

the South. Students are from 39 states, 22 foreign countries, and Canada. 52% are from public schools. 79% are African American; 12% Foreign. **Female To Male Ratio:** 1.0:1. The average age of freshmen is 19; all undergraduates, 23. 27% do not continue beyond their first year. **Housing:** 1173 students can be accommodated in college housing, which includes single-sex dorms and married student housing. On-campus housing is available on a first-come, first-served basis. Priority is given to out-of-town students. 71% of students live on campus; of those, 98% remain on campus on weekends. Alcohol is not permitted. Upperclassmen may keep cars.

FACULTY/CLASSROOMS: 51% of faculty are male; 49% are female. All teach undergraduates. No introductory courses are taught by graduate students. The average class size in an introductory lecture is 30; in a laboratory is 30; and in a regular course is 40.

PROGRAMS OF STUDY: OU confers B.A., B.S., B.B.A., B.M. and B.S.W. degrees. Associate degrees are also awarded. Bachelor's degrees are awarded in BIOLOGICAL SCIENCE (biochemistry and biology/biological science), BUSINESS (accounting and business administration and management), COMMUNICATIONS AND THE ARTS (communications, English, foreign language, French, music, music business management, music performance, and Spanish), COMPUTER AND PHYSICAL SCIENCE (chemistry, chemistry education, computer mathematics, computer science, information sciences and systems, mathematics, and natural sciences), EDUCATION (business education, education, elementary education, English education, health and physical education, home economics education, mathematics education, music education, physical education, science education, and social science education), HEALTH PROFESSIONS (allied health, medical technology, and nursing), SOCIAL SCIENCE (dietetics, family/consumer studies, history, home economics, human development, international studies, ministries, physical fitness/movement, political science/government, psychology, religion, religious education, and social work). Biochemistry, chemistry, and nursing are the strongest academically. Business and biology have the largest enrollments.

ACTIVITIES: There are no fraternities or sororities. There are 20 groups on campus, including band, choir, chorale, drama, honors, international, newspaper, professional, radio and TV, religious, student government, United Nations children emergency fund social work club, and yearbook. Popular campus events include Convocations, Arts and Lecture Series and Centennial. **Sports:** There are 4 intramural sports for men and 3 for women. Facilities include a gym, skating rink, Olympic-size pool, tennis courts, playing fields, racquetball courts, and a weight room.

SERVICES: Counseling and information services are available, as is tutoring in most subjects. There is remedial math, reading, and writing. Testing, counseling, and developmental guidance services are available through the counseling center. **Library/Resources:** The library contains 125,373 volumes, 2,140 microform items, and 4,816 audio/video tapes/CDs/DVDs, and subscribes to 630 periodicals including electronic. Computerized library services include database searching. Special learning facilities include a radio station, and a Black History Museum. **Physically Challenged Students:** 80% of the campus is accessible. Facilities include wheelchair ramps, elevators, special parking, and specially equipped restrooms. **Special:** Students may cross-register with Alabama A&M, Athens State, or the University of Alabama at Huntsville. The college offers a student missionary abroad program as well as a study abroad program through the Adventist College Consortium. Internships, work-study, dual majors, independent study, life experience credit, and pass/fail options are also available. A second bachelor's degree is offered to students completing at least 160 semester credits. There is 1 national honor society, Phi Beta Kappa, a freshman honors program, and 2 departmental honors programs. **Visiting:** There are guides for informal visits, visitors may sit in on classes, and stay overnight. To schedule a visit, contact the Enrollment Management. **Campus Safety and Security:** Measures include 24-hour foot and vehicle patrol and security escort services. There are lighted pathways/sidewalks.

REQUIREMENTS: The SAT or ACT is recommended. Applicants should be high school graduates with a minimum GPA of 2.0 and at least 11 academic units, distributed as follows: 4 in English, 2 each in math, science, and social studies, and 1 in typing. The GED is accepted. Two character references are required. Students with GPAs between 1.7 and 2.0 may be admitted on probation. Applicants admitted without test scores must take the ACT during freshman orientation. A GPA of 2.0 is required. AP and CLEP credits are accepted. Important factors in the admissions decision are recommendations by school officials, ability to finance college education, and leadership record. To graduate, students must complete 128 semester hours, including 30 in the major and 40 in upper-division courses, with a GPA of 2.0. Regular chapel attendance is required. All students must complete a liberal arts core, and must meet English oral and written proficiency requirements. **Procedure:** Freshmen are admitted to all sessions. Entrance exams should be taken before high school graduation. There are early decision and rolling admissions plans. Application deadlines are open. Application fee is $20. **Transfer Students:** Applicants must submit a college transcript and a statement of honorable dismissal. Grades of C minus or better transfer for credit. 32 of 128 credits required for the bachelor's degree must be completed at OU. **International Students:** They must take the TOEFL and the college's own test. They must also take the SAT or ACT. Students may take the ACT on campus prior to registration.

Admissions Contact: Tracy Moore, Assistant Director of Admissions. E-Mail: *admission@oakwood.edu* Web: *www.oakwood.edu*

FINANCIAL AID: Oakwood is a member of CSS. The college's own financial statement and student and parent federal income tax returns are required. The FAFSA code is 001033. The priority date for freshman financial aid applications for fall entry is March 1.

SAMFORD UNIVERSITY — C-2

www.samford.edu

Birmingham, AL 35229	**(205) 726-2871** **(800) 888-7218**
Fax: (205) 726-2171	**Email: admission@samford.edu**
Full-time: 1103 men, 2163 women	**Faculty:** 230; IIA, av$
Part-time: 41 men, 66 women	**Ph.D.s:** 87%
Graduate: 774 men, 1362 women	**Student/Faculty:** 14 to 1
Year: 4-1-4, summer session	**Tuition:** $30,490
Room & Board: $10,280	**Freshman Class:** 3808 applied, 3168 accepted, 857 enrolled
SAT or ACT: required	**CEEB CODE:** 1302
Application Deadline: May 1	**VERY COMPETITIVE**

Samford University, founded in 1841, is Alabama's top-ranked private university with nationally-ranked academic programs rooted in the university's historic Christian mission. Samford offers 30 undergraduate and graduate degree programs through 10 academic units: arts, arts and sciences, business, divinity, education, health professions, law, nursing, pharmacy and public health. There are 9 undergraduate schools and 10 graduate schools. In addition to regional accreditation, SU has baccalaureate program accreditation with AACSB, ACPE, CSWE, NASM, CAEP CIDA, CCNE, and NAST. The 212-acre campus is in a suburban area 4 miles south of Birmingham, AL. Including any residence halls, there are 82 buildings.

STUDENT LIFE: 68% of undergraduates are from out of state, mostly the South. Students are from 45 states, 29 foreign countries, and Canada. 51% are from public schools. 84% are White; 7% African American; 3% Hispanic; 2% Foreign; 2% two or more races; 1% Asian American; 1% race unknown. 42% are Protestant; 21% claim no religious affiliation. **Female To Male Ratio:** 1.9:1. The average age of freshmen is 18; all undergraduates, 20. 11% do not continue beyond their first year; 72% remain to graduate. **Housing:** 2375 students can be accommodated in college housing, which includes dorms and on-campus apartments. In addition, there are fraternity houses and sorority houses. On-campus housing is guaranteed for all 4 years, and is available on a first-come, first-served basis. 68% of students live on campus. Alcohol is not permitted. All students may keep cars.

FACULTY/CLASSROOMS: 48% of faculty are male; 52% are female. No introductory courses are taught by graduate students. The average class size in an introductory lecture is 23 and in a laboratory is 13.

PROGRAMS OF STUDY: SU confers B.S.B.A., B.S.E., B.S.N., B.A., B.F.A., B.M., B.M.E., and B.S degrees. Master's and doctoral degrees are also awarded. Bachelor's degrees are awarded in BIOLOGICAL SCIENCE (biochemistry, biology/biological science, and marine science), BUSINESS (accounting, entrepreneurial studies, finance, management, marketing, and organizational leadership and management), COMMUNICATIONS AND THE ARTS (art, classics, communications, composition, English, French, German, graphic design, Greek, journalism, languages, Latin, music, music ministry, music performance, musical theater, organ performance, piano/organ, piano pedagogy, piano performance, Spanish, sports administration, theatre arts, and voice), COMPUTER AND PHYSICAL SCIENCE (chemistry, computer science, mathematics, physics, and science), EDUCATION (athletic training, early childhood education, elementary education, global studies, music education, and secondary education), ENGINEERING AND ENVIRONMENTAL DESIGN (engineering physics, environmental science, and interior design), HEALTH PROFESSIONS (exercise science, health care administration, health science, nursing, nutrition and dietetics, nutrition and wellness, pharmacy, public health, respiratory therapy, and sports medicine), SOCIAL SCIENCE (communication sciences & disorders, counseling/psychology, criminal justice, economics, geography, history, human development & family studies, international relations, Latin American studies, liberal arts/general studies, paralegal studies, philosophy, philosophy and religion, political science/government, psychology, public administration, religion, and sociology). Mathematics, biochemistry, English, communication sciences and disorders, early childhood/elem/spec/collaborative, and nutrition and dietetics are the strongest academically. Nursing, journalism and mass communications, and early childhood/elementary/special education have the largest enrollments.

ACTIVITIES: 36% of men belong to 6 national fraternities; 56% of women belong to 9 national sororities. There are 75 groups on campus, including art, band, cheerleading, choir, chorale, chorus, computers, dance, debate, drama, drill team, environmental, ethnic, film, Greek, honors, international, jazz band, literary magazine, marching band, musical theater, newspaper, pep band, photography, political, professional, radio and TV, religious, social, social service, student government, and yearbook. Popular campus events include Homecoming, Family Weekend, Hanging of the Green, Lighting of the Way,Welcome Back Week, Your School/Your City, Samford Arts, Connections, Step Sing, NCAA Division I Athletics, Samford Gives Back, Easter Egg Hunt, and Beeson Ball. **Sports:** There are 8 intercollegiate sports for men and 9 for women, and 10 intramural sports for men and 10 for women. Facilities include a football stadium, basketball courts, track and soccer stadium, baseball field, softball field, tennis pavilion and courts, volleyball court, 4 racquetball courts, a game room with 2 pool tables and 2 ping-pong tables, indoor walking track, dance studio, indoor pool, Alpine Tower is a 50-foot high structure, offering over 30 different climbing routes with varying degrees of difficulty. The Carolina Climbing Wall is a 50-foot high structure with windows that allows social climbing on both sides. **Graduates:** From July 1, 2016 to June 30, 2017, 876 bachelor's degrees were awarded. The most popular majors were health professions and related programs (30%), business and marketing (21%), communications, journalism, and related programs (6%). In an average class, 65% graduate in 4 years or less, 75% graduate in 5 years or less, and 76% graduate in 6 years or less.

SERVICES: Counseling and information services are available, as is tutoring in most subjects. There is a reader service for the blind. There is also skill building for reading, writing, and presentations. **Library/Resources:** The library contains 761,751 volumes, 678,778 microform items, and 13,244 audio/video tapes/CDs/DVDs, and subscribes to 31,549 periodicals including electronic. Computerized library services include interlibrary loans, database searching, Internet access, and Wi-Fi capability. Special learning facilities include an art gallery, planetarium, radio station, Center for Advocacy and Clinical Education, Center for Congregational Resources, Center for Children, law, and ethics, Center for Faith and Health, Center for Healthcare Innovations and Patient Outcomes Research, Center for Law and Civic Education, Center for Science and Religion, EDiscovery Institute and Review Center, Frances Marlin Mann Center for Ethics Leadership, Global Center, Health Care Ethics and Law Institute, Nursing School State of the Art Human Simulation Center, Business School Investment Center, and a Conservatory. **Physically Challenged Students:** All of the campus is accessible. Facilities include wheelchair ramps, elevators, special parking, specially equipped restrooms, special class scheduling, lowered drinking fountains, and lowered telephones. **Special:** The Department of Physics offers a dual-degree engineering program jointly with the following universities: University of Alabama at Birmingham, Auburn University, and Mercer University (Georgia). The five-year program leads to two degrees: a bachelor of science degree from Samford with a major in engineering physics, and a bachelor of engineering degree from the participating university. Students in this five-year program will first pursue a three-year general curriculum at Samford, followed by a two-year general technical curriculum at one of the participating engineering schools. Samford University cooperates with the University of Alabama at Birmingham (UAB), Miles College, University of Montevallo, and Birmingham-Southern College in a student exchange program known as the Birmingham Area Consortium for Higher Education (BACHE). The program is designed to expand the undergraduate educational opportunities for students at these institutions. As part of its commitment to internationalization of the curriculum, Samford University provides a special opportunity for students and faculty to live and study in one of the most cosmopolitan and culturally rich cities of the world—London. Daniel House, Samford's London Study Centre, serves as home and classroom to students and faculty throughout the year in a variety of academic programs. Samford offers opportunities to travel and study in foreign countries for credit. The purpose of these programs is to prepare Samford students for global citizenship in the 21st century. More specifically, Samford seeks to expose students and faculty to the peoples and cultures of other nations; to provide on-site observation of historical, scientific, and cultural phenomena, and to provide opportunities for foreign language study within the cultural context of the target languages. There are 15 national honor societies, a freshman honors program, and 25 departmental honors programs. **Visiting:** There are regularly scheduled orientations for prospective students, campus tours offered 6 days a week. Tours last 90-minutes followed by a 30-minute information session. Special arrangements can be made for overnight stay, class visitation, and/or meeting with Admission and Financial Aid counselors. There are guides for informal visits, visitors may sit in on classes, and stay overnight. To schedule a visit, contact the Office of Admission. **Campus Safety and Security:** Measures include 24-hour foot and vehicle patrol, emergency notification system, and security escort services. There are shuttle buses, emergency telephones, lighted pathways/sidewalks, controlled access to dorms/residences, and restricted access to campus during nighttime hours.

REQUIREMENTS: The SAT or ACT is required. SU seeks to enroll students capable of success in a challenging academic environment. Every applicant is evaluated individually on the basis of academic preparedness and potential, as well as personal fit with the mission and purpose of the university. The Admission Committee considers factors such as the rigor of the high school curriculum, grade point average, standardized test scores, and recommendations. AP and CLEP credits are accepted. The academic requirements for all students are to earn a minimum of 128 successfully completed credits, at least 50% of the credit for the first undergraduate degree from Samford. All undergraduates are required to take the University Core Curriculum at Samford (22 credits). **Procedure:** Freshmen are admitted fall, winter, spring, and summer. Entrance exams should be taken in the junior year. There are deferred admissions and rolling admissions plans. Applications should be filed by May 1 for fall entry. The fall 2017 application fee was $40. Notifications are sent November 1. 206 applicants were on the 2017 waiting list; 70 were admitted. Applications are accepted on-line. **Transfer Students:** 127 transfer students enrolled in 2016-2017. Transfer students generally receive favorable admission review when they present a minimum cumulative 2.50 grade point average on all college-level coursework, provided they have attempted at least 24 credits, or 36 quarter credits, at institutions accredited by one of the regional accrediting agencies. If a student has attempted less than 24 credits of college-level coursework, an official high school transcript and official test scores must also be submitted in order to be considered for admission. 64 of 128 credits required for the bachelor's degree must be completed at SU. **International Students:** There are 57 international students enrolled. They must also take the SAT or ACT.

ADMISSIONS: 83% of the 2017-2018 applicants were accepted. 49% of the current freshmen were in the top fifth of their class; 76% were in the top two fifths. **Admissions Contact:** Jason E. Black, Dean of Admission. Email: *admission@samford.edu* Web: *www.samford.edu*

FINANCIAL AID: In 2017-2018, 98% of all full-time freshmen received some form of financial aid. 49% of all full-time freshmen received need-based aid. The average freshman award was $20,049. Need-based scholarships or need-based grants averaged $4,321 ($39,544 maximum); need-based self-help aid (loans and jobs) averaged $2,904 ($25,000 maximum); non-need-based athletic scholarships averaged $14,165 ($41,000 maximum); and other non-need-based awards and non-need-based scholarships averaged $5,134 ($34,423 maximum). 16% of undergraduate students work part-time. The average financial indebtedness of the 2017 graduate was $29,794. The state aid form is required. The FAFSA code is 001036. The priority date for freshman financial aid applications for fall entry is March 1.

SPRING HILL COLLEGE A-5

www.shc.edu

Mobile, AL 36608
(251) 380-3030
(800) 742-6704
Fax: (251) 460-2186
Email: admit@shc.edu

Full-time: 504 men, 875 women
Part-time: 5 men, 9 women
Graduate: 58 men, 50 women
Year: semesters, summer session
Room & Board: $13,070
SAT CR/M: 560/560 **ACT:** 23
Application Deadline: July 15
Faculty: 86
Ph.D.s: 94%
Student/Faculty: 16 to 1
Tuition: $35,798 ($37,584)
Freshman Class: 8544 applied, 3903 accepted, 395 enrolled
CEEB CODE: 1733
COMPETITIVE

Spring Hill College, founded in 1830, is the oldest Catholic college in the Southeast, as well as the third oldest Jesuit college and fifth oldest Catholic college in the United States. Ranked among the top 20 Southern colleges and universities "America's Best Colleges," its mission is to form students to become responsible leaders in service to others. There are 8 undergraduate schools and 5 graduate schools. In addition to regional accreditation, SHC has baccalaureate program accreditation with CCNE. The 381-acre campus is in a suburban area in Mobile, Alabama. Including any residence halls, there are 34 buildings.

STUDENT LIFE: 58% of undergraduates are from out of state, mostly the South. Students are from 34 states, 23 foreign countries, and Canada. 68% are White; 16% African American; 5% two or more races; 4% Foreign; 3% race unknown; 2% Hispanic; 1% Asian American; 1% American Indian/Alaska Native. 43% are Catholic; 33% Protestant; 21% claim no religious affiliation. **Female To Male Ratio:** 1.6:1. The average age of freshmen is 18; all undergraduates, 20. 22% do not continue beyond their first year; 53% remain to graduate. **Housing:** 1157 students can be accommodated in college housing, which includes dorms and on-campus apartments. In addition, there are special-interest houses. On-campus housing is guaranteed for all 4 years. 71% of students live on campus. All students may keep cars.

FACULTY/CLASSROOMS: 47% of faculty are male; 53% are female. 98% teach undergraduates. No introductory courses are taught by graduate students. The average class size in an introductory lecture is 21; in a laboratory is 14; and in a regular course is 17.

PROGRAMS OF STUDY: SHC confers B.A., B.S., and B.S.N. degrees. Master's degrees are also awarded. Bachelor's degrees are awarded in BIOLOGICAL SCIENCE (biochemistry, biology/biological science, and marine biology), BUSINESS (accounting, business administration and management, international business management, marketing management, and organizational leadership and management), COMMUNICATIONS AND THE ARTS (arts administration/management, communications, digital communications, English, English writing, graphic design, journalism, public relations, studio art, and theatre arts), COMPUTER AND PHYSICAL SCIENCE (chemistry, computer science, and mathematics), EDUCATION (early childhood education, elementary education, and secondary education), ENGINEERING AND ENVIRONMENTAL DESIGN (engineering), HEALTH PROFESSIONS (health care administration, nursing, predentistry, premedicine, and preveterinary science), SOCIAL SCIENCE (biopsychology, economics, history, humanities, interdisciplinary studies, international studies, liberal arts/general studies, philosophy, political science/government, psychology, social science, sociology, Spanish studies, and theological studies). Business, biology, and nursing have the largest enrollments.

ACTIVITIES: 26% of men belong to 4 national fraternities; 28% of women belong to 7 national sororities. There are 49 groups on campus, including art, cheerleading, chorale, communications, computers, dance, drama, environmental, ethnic, film, honors, international, LGBT, literary magazine, newspaper, pep band, photography, political, professional, radio and TV, religious, social, social service, and student government. Popular campus events include Weeks of Welcome, Mardi Gras Ball, Badger Expo, BadgerFest, Christmas on the Hill, Family Weekend, TEDxSpringHillCollege, SGA Tailgate Extravaganza, CPB Crawfish Boil, and International Service Immerson Trips. **Sports:** There are 7 intercollegiate sports for men and 9 for women, and 12 intramural sports for men and 12 for women. Facilities include an 18-hole golf course, basketball courts, outdoor sand volleyball area, baseball, softball, rugby, and soccer fields. A recreation center houses the intercollegiate basketball arena, racquetball courts, weight-training and exercise facilities, an aerobic exercise room, and a running track. **Graduates:** From July 1, 2016 to June 30, 2017, 223 bachelor's degrees were awarded. The most popular majors were business (19%), psychology (13%), and elementary education (6%). In an average class, 44% graduate in 4 years or less, 51% graduate in 5 years or less, and 53% graduate in 6 years or less.

SERVICES: Counseling and information services are available, as is tutoring in some subjects, such as English, theology, math, languages, philosophy, economics, biology, chemistry, psychology, history and accounting. There is remedial math, reading, and writing. **Library/ Resources:** The library contains 205,984 volumes, 351,719 microform items, and 3,620 audio/video tapes/CDs/DVDs, and subscribes to 24,204 periodicals including electronic. Computerized library services include interlibrary loans, database searching, Internet access, and Wi-Fi capability. Special learning facilities include an art gallery, radio station, and a theater. **Physically Challenged Students:** 90% of the campus is accessible. Facilities include wheelchair ramps, elevators, special parking, specially equipped restrooms, special class scheduling, and special housing. **Special:** SHC offers dual degree engineering programs with the University of Alabama-Birmingham, Auburn University, the University of Florida, Marquette University, and Texas A&M University. The college is a member of the Marine Environmental Sciences Consortium and offers marine biology courses at the Dauphin Island Sea Lab. The college offers a study-abroad experience at its Italy Center in Bologna, Italy; other study abroad options are available through the CCSA (Cooperative Center for Study Abroad) consortium and the foreign study programs of other American Jesuit and non-Jesuit colleges and universities. Internships are available in many majors. There are 18 national honor societies and a freshman honors program. **Visiting:** There are regularly scheduled orientations for prospective students, campus tour, faculty appointment, attending a class, interview with an admission counselor. There are guides for informal visits, visitors may sit in on classes, and stay overnight. To schedule a visit, contact the Office of Admissions. **Campus Safety and Security:** Measures include 24-hour foot and vehicle patrol, emergency notification system, self-defense education, and security escort services. There are emergency telephones, lighted pathways/ sidewalks, and controlled access to dorms/residences.

REQUIREMENTS: The SAT is required. The ACT is preferred. Applicants should have completed at least 16 high school units, including 4 in English, 3 each in math, science, and social studies, 2 in foreign languages, and 1 academic elective. The GED equivalent is accepted. AP and CLEP credits are accepted. All students must take core curriculum courses in English composition and literature, history, philosophy, theology, math, science, social science, fine art, and foreign language. Students must also take: one cultural diversity course; at least 3 writing-enriched courses (including one in the major) beyond the required 4 core curriculum English courses; and one LEAP (Learning, Engagement and Awareness, Personal Growth) course. Graduation requirements include completion of a minimum of 128 semester hours with a minimum GPA of 2.0 and 30 to 36 upper-division semester hours in the major with a minimum grade of C/C- (see department policy) in each of the major courses and prerequisites. **Procedure:** Freshmen are admitted fall, spring, and summer. Entrance exams should be taken in spring of the junior year or fall of the senior year. There are deferred admissions and rolling admissions plans. Applications should be filed by July 15 for fall entry; December 1 for spring entry. The fall 2017 application fee was $25. Notification is sent on a rolling basis. Applications are accepted online. **Transfer Students:** 41 transfer students enrolled in 2016-2017. Transfer applicants must have at least 20 semester hours of college credit, a minimum college cumulative GPA of 2.5, good academic standing at the last college or university attended, and satisfactory recommendations. 32 of 128 credits required for the bachelor's degree must be completed at SHC. **International Students:** There are 49 international students enrolled. They must take the TOEFL with a minimum score of 550 on the paper-based TOEFL (PBT) or 80 on the Internet-based version (iBT) or take the MELAB, or the IELTS. Students whose first language is English must take the ACT or SAT.

ADMISSIONS: 46% of the 2017-2018 applicants were accepted. The SAT scores for the 2017-2018 freshman class were: Critical Reading-- 15% below 500, 58% between 500 and 599, 19% between 600 and 699, and 8% between 700 and 800. Math-- 15% below 500, 66% between 500 and 599, and 19% between 600 and 699. The ACT scores were 5% between 12 and 17, 53% between 18 and 23, 36% between 24 and 29, and 6% above 30. 41% of the current freshmen were in the top fifth of their class; 78% were in the top two fifths. 1 freshman graduated first in the class. **Admissions Contact:** Robert Stewart, Vice President for Admissions and Financial Aid. Email: *admit@shc.edu* Web: *www.shc.edu*

FINANCIAL AID: SHC is a member of CSS. The state aid form is required. The FAFSA code is 001041. The priority date for freshman financial aid applications for fall entry is March 1.

STILLMAN COLLEGE B-3

www.stillman.edu

Tuscaloosa, AL 35403	(404) 679-4501 (800) 841-5722
Fax: (205) 366-8817	**Email:** admissions@stillman.edu
Full-time: 700 men, 800 women	**Faculty:** n/av
Part-time: 40 men, 40 women	**Ph.D.s:** 92%
Graduate: n/av	**Student/Faculty:** n/av
Year: semesters, summer session	**Tuition:** $13,682
Room & Board: $7056	**Freshman Class:** n/av
SAT or ACT: required	**CEEB CODE:** 1739
Application Deadline: n/av	**COMPETITIVE**

Stillman College, founded in 1876, is a small, private liberal arts institution affiliated with the Presbyterian Church. The figures in the above capsule and in this profile are approximate. There is 1 undergraduate school. In addition to regional accreditation, SC has baccalaureate program accreditation with NASM, CAEP, NCAA, SIAC, and IACBE. The 105-acre campus is in a small town in Tuscaloosa, Alabama, just 52 miles from Birmingham. Including any residence halls, there are 26 buildings.

STUDENT LIFE: 70% of undergraduates are from Alabama. Others are from 27 states, and 8 foreign countries. 95% are from public schools. 98% are African American. 99% are Protestant. **Female To Male Ratio:** 1.1:1. The average age of freshmen is 19. **Housing:** 750 students can be accommodated in college housing, which includes dorms and off-campus apartments. On-campus housing is available on a first-come and first-served basis. 50% of students commute. Alcohol is not permitted. All students may keep cars.

FACULTY/CLASSROOMS: 40% of faculty are male; 60% are female. All teach undergraduates. No introductory courses are taught by graduate students. The average class size in an introductory lecture is 40; in a laboratory is 40; and in a regular course is 35.

PROGRAMS OF STUDY: SC confers B.A. and B.S. degrees. Bachelor's degrees are awarded in BIOLOGICAL SCIENCE (biology/biological science), BUSINESS (business administration and management), COMMUNICATIONS AND THE ARTS (art, English, and music), COMPUTER AND PHYSICAL SCIENCE (computer science and mathematics), EDUCATION (elementary education and physical education), HEALTH PROFESSIONS (premedicine), SOCIAL SCIENCE (history, prelaw, and religion).

ACTIVITIES: 10% of men belong to 4 national fraternities; 20% of women belong to 4 national sororities. There are 19 groups on campus, including art, band, cheerleading, choir, chorus, dance, debate, drama, honors, international, jazz band, marching band, newspaper, pep band, radio and TV, religious, social, social service, student government, and yearbook. **Sports:** There are 6 intercollegiate sports for men and 6 for women. Facilities include tennis courts, bowling, billiards, swimming pool, a gym, football field, basketball, track, softball, and a weight room.

SERVICES: Counseling and information services are available, as is tutoring in some subjects, such as reading, writing, math, physics, and chemistry. There is remedial math, reading, and writing. **Library/Resources:** The library contains 200,000 volumes, 7,240 microform items, and 3,550 audio/video tapes/CDs/DVDs, and subscribes to 360 periodicals including electronic. Computerized library services include interlibrary loans and database searching. Special learning facilities include an art gallery, radio station, book processing, media area and archives, and the Ashel & Merle Jackson Communications Complex. **Physically Challenged Students:** Facilities include wheelchair ramps, elevators, special parking, and specially equipped restrooms. **Special:** Stillman offers local, national, and international opportunites for cooperative education and internships. Cross-registration is possible with the University of Alabama at Birmingham, with which there also are cooperative degree programs in nursing and allied health. Federal work-study is available on and off campus, and students may earn credit for prior learning experiences. There are 3 national honor societies. **Visiting:** There are regularly scheduled orientations for prospective students. To schedule a visit, contact the Director of Recruitment. **Campus Safety and Security:** Measures include 24-hour foot and vehicle patrol, self-defense education, and security escort services. There are lighted pathways/sidewalks.

REQUIREMENTS: The SAT or ACT is required. Applicants should be high school graduates or have earned the GED. Secondary preparation should include 4 units of English and 1 unit each of math, science, and history. All applicants must have an interview. Music majors must audition. AP and CLEP credits are accepted. To graduate, students must complete a minimum of 124 credit hours, with at least 30 in the major, and maintain a minimum GPA of 2.0 overall and in the major. The 53-credit-hour general education core includes courses in religion, logic, English composition, public speaking, african heritage, African American experience, history, social science, physical and life sciences, math, computer literacy, health, and phys ed. All students must submit a senior thesis and take a senior departmental exam. **Procedure:** Freshmen are admitted to all sessions. There is a rolling admissions plan. Check with the school for current application deadlines. The fall 2017 application fee was $25. **Transfer Students:** Transfer applicants should present at least a C average in previous college work and must plan to spend at least a year in residence. 64 of 124 credits required for the bachelor's degree must be completed at SC. **International Students:** They must take the TOEFL. They must also take the SAT or ACT.

Admissions Contact: Lu Ann Baker, Director of Admissions. Email: *admissions@stillman.edu* Web: *www.stillman.edu*

FINANCIAL AID: The CCS/Profile, FAFSA, and FFS or SFS, and the college's own financial statement are required. The FAFSA code is 001044. The priority date for freshman financial aid applications for fall entry is March 1.

TALLADEGA COLLEGE C-2

www.talladega.edu

Talladega, AL 35160	(256) 761-6416 (800) 633-2440
	Email: admissions@talladega.edu
Full-time: 270 men, 420 women	**Faculty:** n/av
Part-time: 20 men, 30 women	**Ph.D.s:** 60%
Graduate: n/av	**Student/Faculty:** 12 to 1
Year: semesters	**Tuition:** $12,511 ($17,996)
Room & Board: $6704	**Freshman Class:** n/av
SAT or ACT: required	**CEEB CODE:** 1800
Application Deadline: open	**COMPETITIVE**

Talladega College, founded in 1867, is a private liberal arts institution offering emphases on business, sciences, and social work. The figures in above capsule and in this profile are approximate. There is 1 undergraduate school. In addition to regional accreditation, Dega has baccalaureate program accreditation with CSWE. The 50-acre campus is in a small town 55 miles east of Birmingham and 115 miles west of Atlanta. Including any residence halls, there are 41 buildings.

STUDENT LIFE: 60% of undergraduates are from Alabama. Others are from 29 states, and 2 foreign countries. 99% are African American. 90% are Protestant. **Female To Male Ratio:** 1.6:1. The average age of freshmen is 18; all undergraduates, 20. 22% do not continue beyond their first year; 45% remain to graduate. **Housing:** 580 students can be accommodated in college housing, which includes single-sex dorms, on-campus apartments, and honors houses. On-campus housing is guaranteed for all 4 years. 70% of students live on campus; of those, 90% remain on campus on weekends. Alcohol is not permitted. All students may keep cars.

FACULTY/CLASSROOMS: 60% of faculty are male; 40% are female. All teach undergraduates. No introductory courses are taught by graduate students. The average class size in an introductory lecture is 30; in a laboratory is 20; and in a regular course is 18.

PROGRAMS OF STUDY: Dega confers B.A. degrees. Bachelor's degrees are awarded in BIOLOGICAL SCIENCE (biology/biological science), BUSINESS (accounting, banking and finance, and business administration and management), COMMUNICATIONS AND THE ARTS (English and music performance), COMPUTER AND PHYSICAL SCIENCE (chemistry, computer science, mathematics, and physics), EDU-

CATION (music education), SOCIAL SCIENCE (economics, history, psychology, public administration, social work, and sociology). Business, biology, and chemistry are the strongest academically. Biology has the largest enrollment.

ACTIVITIES: 14% of men belong to 4 national fraternities; 40% of women belong to 4 national sororities. There are 23 groups on campus, including art, cheerleading, choir, chorus, computers, dance, drama, honors, jazz band, newspaper, professional, social, student government, and yearbook. Popular campus events include Spring Concert, Carnival and Coronation. **Sports:** There are 4 intercollegiate sports for men and 4 for women, and 8 intramural sports for men and 3 for women. Facilities include a swimming pool, a gym, game rooms, tennis courts, and a baseball field.

SERVICES: Counseling and information services are available, as is tutoring in every subject. There is remedial math, reading, and writing. **Library/Resources:** The library contains 87,960, and 350 audio/video tapes/CDs/DVDs, and subscribes to 330 periodicals including electronic. Computerized library services include interlibrary loans. Special learning facilities include an art gallery, science drop-in center, curriculum and writing labs, and financial computer lab. **Physically Challenged Students:** 50% of the campus is accessible. Facilities include wheelchair ramps, elevators, special parking, and specially equipped restrooms. **Special:** Talladega offers co-op programs with other schools through individual departments, a 3-2 engineering degree with Auburn University, internships involving historic preservation work, work-study plans with Adopt-a-Family and Adult Literacy, and B.A.-B.S. degrees in biology, business administration, chemistry, and computer science. There are dual majors available in law, nursing, engineering, and allied health. There are 4 national honor societies. **Visiting:** There are guides for informal visits, visitors may sit in on classes, and stay overnight. To schedule a visit, contact the Admissions Office. **Campus Safety and Security:** Measures include 24-hour foot and vehicle patrol and security escort services. There are lighted pathways/sidewalks.

REQUIREMENTS: The SAT or ACT is required. Applicants must be graduates of an accredited secondary school with 22 academic units, including 4 in English, 3 in social studies, and 2 each in math, science, health/phys ed, and electives. The GED is considered. An essay and interview are recommended. An audition is required for music majors. A GPA of 2.5 is required. CLEP credits are accepted. Important factors in the admissions decision are advanced placement or honors courses, recommendations by school officials, and recommendations by alumni. To graduate, students must maintain a minimum GPA of 2.5 while taking 124 to 127 total semester hours, including 60 in the major and completion of a core curriculum. Distribution requirements at the freshman level include 8 semester hours in natural sciences, 6 each in communications, social sciences, and humanities, 2 in phys ed, and 1 in freshman orientation; additional hours in these subjects vary by major at the sophomore level. **Procedure:** Freshmen are admitted fall and spring. Entrance exams should be taken in the junior year. There are deferred admissions and rolling admissions plans. Application deadlines are open. The fall 2016 application fee was $10. Applications are accepted on-line. **Transfer Students:** Applicants must have a cumulative GPA of 2.0 in college work. The SAT or ACT is recommended. 60 of 124 credits required for the bachelor's degree must be completed at Dega. **International Students:** The school actively recruits these students. They must take the TOEFL and the college's own test. They must also take the SAT or ACT.

Admissions Contact: Monroe Thornton, Admissions Office. E-Mail: *admissions@talladega.edu* Web: *www.talladega.edu*

FINANCIAL AID: The CCS/Profile, FAFSA, and FFS or SFS, and the college's own financial statement are required. The FAFSA code is 001046. The priority date for freshman financial aid applications for fall entry is March 1.

THE UNIVERSITY OF ALABAMA — B-3

www.ua.edu

Tuscaloosa, AL 35487	**(205) 348-6010** **(800) 933-BAMA**
Fax: (205) 348-9046	**Email: admissions@ua.edu**
Full-time: 11,253 men, 12,692 women	**Faculty:** I, av$
Part-time: 1022 men, 1267 women	**Ph.D.s:** n/av
Graduate: 2244 men, 3169 women	**Student/Faculty:** 19 to 1
Year: semesters, summer session	**Tuition:** $11,270 ($27,750)
Room & Board: $13,050	**Freshman Class:** 22136 applied, 9636 accepted, 5728 enrolled
SAT or ACT: required	**CEEB CODE:** 1830
Application Deadline: March 1	**COMPETITIVE+**

The University of Alabama, is the first public university in Alabama as a senior comprehensive doctoral level institution. The university was established by constitutional provision under statutory mandates and authorizations. It's mission is to advance the intellectual and social condition of the people of the state through quality programs of teaching, research and service. The figures in the above capsule and in this profile are approximate. There are 9 undergraduate schools and 2 graduate schools. In addition to regional accreditation, UA has baccalaureate program accreditation with AACSB, ABET, ACEJMC, ADA, CSWE, FIDER, NASAD, NASM, CAEP, AAFCS, CAAHEP, CCNE, NASD, and NAST. The 1000-acre campus is in a suburban area in Tuscaloosa, 50 miles southwest of Birmingham. Including any residence halls, there are 216 buildings.

STUDENT LIFE: 53% of undergraduates are from out of state, mostly the South. Students are from 50 states, 77 foreign countries, and Canada. 89% are from public schools. 81% are White; 2% Asian American; 2% Hispanic; 12% African American; 1% American Indian/Alaska Native. 56% are Protestant; 32% claim no religious affiliation. **Female To Male Ratio:** 1.2:1. The average age of freshmen is 18; all undergraduates, 21. 14% do not continue beyond their first year; 87% remain to graduate. **Housing:** 5800 students can be accommodated in college housing, which includes married student dorms and on-campus apartments. In addition, there are honors houses, language/international houses, special-interest houses, fraternity houses, and sorority houses. On-campus housing is guaranteed for the freshman year only, and is available on a first-come, first-served basis. 92% of students live on campus. All students may keep cars.

FACULTY/CLASSROOMS: 60% of faculty are male; 40% are female. 71% teach undergraduates, 5% do research, and 4% do both. Graduate students teach 28% of introductory courses. The average class size in an introductory lecture is 52; in a laboratory is 19; and in a regular course is 26.

PROGRAMS OF STUDY: UA, confers B.A., B.S., B.A.Com., B.F.A., B.M., B.S.A.E., B.S.C.B.A., B.S.C.E., B.S.Che.E., B.S.Chem., B.S.C.S., B.S.Ed., B.S.E.E., B.S.Geo., B.S.H.E.S., B.S.I.E., B.S.M.E., B.S.Met., B.S. Micr., B.S.N., and B.S.W. degrees. Master's and doctoral degrees are also awarded. Bachelor's degrees are awarded in BIOLOGICAL SCIENCE (biology/biological science, marine science, and microbiology), BUSINESS (accounting and management information systems), COMMUNICATIONS AND THE ARTS (advertising, art history and appreciation, classics, communications, dance, English, French, German, journalism, music, public relations, Russian, Spanish, and telecommunications), COMPUTER AND PHYSICAL SCIENCE (chemistry, computer science, geology, mathematics, and physics), EDUCATION (athletic training, early childhood education, elementary education, music education, physical education, secondary education, and special education), ENGINEERING AND ENVIRONMENTAL DESIGN (aerospace studies, chemical engineering, civil engineering, electrical/electronics engineering, environmental science, industrial administration/management, industrial engineering, interior design, mechanical engineering, and metallurgical engineering), HEALTH PROFESSIONS (music therapy and nursing), SOCIAL SCIENCE (American studies, anthropology, clothing and textiles management/production/services, criminal justice, economics, food science, geography, history, human development, interdisciplinary studies, international studies, philosophy, political science/government, psychology, religion, and social work). Advertising, accounting, and engineering are the strongest academically. Business, elementary education, and nursing have the largest enrollments.

ACTIVITIES: 28% of men belong to 1 local and 26 national fraternities; 43% of women belong to 1 local and 20 national sororities. There are 391 groups on campus, including leadership and other national honoraries, academic service, art, band, cheerleading, chess, choir, chorale, chorus, computers, dance, debate, drama, drill team, ethnic, film, forensics, honors, international, jazz band, LGBT, literary magazine, marching band, musical theater, newspaper, opera, orchestra, pep band, photography, political, professional, radio and TV, religious, social, social service, student government, symphony, and yearbook. Popular campus events include Honors Week, Get on Board Day, and Family Weekend. **Sports:** There are 9 intercollegiate sports for men and 12 for women, and 17 intramural sports for men and 16 for women. Facilities include football stadium, basketball arena, track and field facility, baseball stadium, softball stadium, indoor football practice facility, tennis courts, an aquatic complex with Olympic-size and standard pools, a weight-lifting facility, soccer field, racquetball, basketball, volleyball courts, and golf course and driving range. **Graduates:** From July 1, 2016 to June 30, 2017, 4463 bachelor's degrees were awarded. The most popular majors were business/marketing (29%), health professions and related programs (10%), and communication/journalism (9%). In an average class, 59% graduate in 3 years or less, 24% graduate in 5 years or less, and 67% graduate in 6 years or less. Of the 2016 graduating class, 87% were enrolled in graduate school within 6 months of graduation.

SERVICES: Counseling and information services are available, as is tutoring in some subjects, such as statistics math, chemistry, physics, computer science, accounting, finance, economics, and foreign languages. There is a reader service for the blind, and remedial math, reading, and writing. Center for teaching and learning, a writing lab, a career center, computer-based self-tutoring a math computer lab. Many departments and colleges offer tutorial services or tutorial referen **Library/Resources:** The library contains 2.5 million volumes, 4.0 million microform items, and 526,856 audio/video tapes/CDs/DVDs, and subscribes to 23,222 periodicals including electronic. Computerized library services include interlibrary loans, database searching, and Internet access. Special learning facilities include an art gallery, natural history museum, radio station, TV station, special collections department, map library, observatory, specialized computer labs, and archeological site. **Physically Challenged Students:** 90% of the campus is accessible. Facilities include wheelchair ramps, elevators, special parking, specially equipped restrooms, special class scheduling, lowered drinking fountains, lowered telephones, special housing, automatic doors, TDD, adaptive technology, and areas of rescue assistance. **Special:** UA offers cross-registration with Stillman College and Shelton State Community College, internships, international study programs, a Washington semester, a 3-week May-June interim term, exchange study within the United States, work-study, co-op programs, accelerated programs, B.A.-B.S. degrees, dual majors, student-designed majors, interdisciplinary majors in the New College arts and sciences program, credit for life experiences, nondegree study, and pass/fail options. There are 27 national honor societies, a chapter of Phi Beta Kappa, a freshman honors program, and 17 departmental honors programs. **Visiting:** There are regularly scheduled orientations for prospective students, consisting of a campus tour followed by meetings with admissions counselors and faculty and staff. Customized visits to suit student and parent needs are possible. University Day (4 times a year) offers tours and information sessions. There are guides for informal visits, visitors may sit in on classes, and stay overnight. To schedule a visit, contact the Office of Undergraduate Admissions. **Campus Safety and Security:** Measures include 24-hour foot and vehicle patrol, self-defense education, and security escort services. There are emergency telephones, lighted pathways/sidewalks, community-oriented police service, UA police bike patrol, educational awareness for personal safety, alcohol awareness, child seat installations, and domestic violence awareness programs.

REQUIREMENTS: The SAT or ACT is required. A minimum GPA of 2.0 is required; admission is based on a sliding scale of test scores and high school GPA. The GED is accepted. High school preparation should include 4 units each of English and social studies, 3 each of math and science, 1 of foreign language, and history and 5 of academic electives. Students with a 3.0 cumulative GPA and a satisfactory ACT or SAT (verbal and math only) score will generally be admitted. AP and CLEP credits are accepted. Important factors in the admissions decision are advanced placement or honors courses, evidence of special talent, and leadership record. To graduate, all students must complete a minimum of 120 semester hours, including at least 27 in the major, with a minimum GPA of 2.0. Core curriculum requirements include 12 hours each of humanities/fine arts and history/social science, 11 of natural science/math, 6 of computer studies or a foreign language, 6 of English composition, and 6 of upper-level courses with a writing component. **Procedure:** Freshmen are admitted in the fall, spring, and summer. Entrance exams should be taken in the spring of the junior year. There are early admissions and rolling admissions plans. Applications should be filed by March 1 for fall entry; December 1 for spring entry; and March 1 for summer entry. The fall 2017 application fee was $40. Notification is sent on a rolling basis. Applications are accepted online. **Transfer Students:** 1463 transfer students enrolled in 2016-2017. Applicants need an overall minimum GPA of 2.0 with at least 24 semester hours earned. Those with fewer than 24 hours must meet freshman standards. 30 of 120 credits required for the bachelor's degree must be completed at UA. **International Students:** They must take the TOEFL, or earn a proficiency certificate from the university's English Language Institute. They must also take the SAT or ACT.

ADMISSIONS: 44% of the 2017-2018 applicants were accepted. **Admissions Contact:** Lorne Kuffel, Director of Undergraduate Admissions. Email: *admissions@ua.edu* Web: *www.ua.edu*

FINANCIAL AID: The FAFSA code is 001051. The priority date for freshman financial aid applications for fall entry is March 1.

TROY UNIVERSITY — C-4

www.troy.edu

Troy, AL 36082 — (334) 670-3179, (800) 551-9716

Fax: (334) 670-3733 — Email: ask@troy.edu

Full-time: 3534 men, 5417 women	**Faculty:** IIA, --$
Part-time: 2175 men, 2438 women	**Ph.D.s:** n/av
Graduate: 1120 men, 3246 women	**Student/Faculty:** n/av
Year: semesters, summer session	**Tuition:** $9646 ($18,256)
Room & Board: $6526	**Freshman Class:** n/av
SAT or ACT: required	**CEEB CODE:** 1738
Application Deadline: open	**COMPETITIVE**

Troy University, founded in 1887, is a public institution composed of a network of campuses throughout Alabama and worldwide. International in scope, Troy University provides a variety of educational programs at the undergraduate and graduate levels for a diverse student body. Academic programs are offered in traditional, nontraditional and emerging electronic formats. Information in this profile applies to the Troy, Phenix City, Dothan, and Montgomery campuses and University College sites. There are 5 undergraduate schools and 5 graduate schools. In addition to regional accreditation, Troy has baccalaureate program accreditation with ACBSP, CSWE, NASM, CAEP, NLN, and CAAHEP. The 768-acre campus is in a rural area 50 miles south of Montgomery. Including any residence halls, there are 111 buildings.

STUDENT LIFE: 59% of undergraduates are from Alabama. Others are from 49 states, 72 foreign countries, and Canada. 53% are White; 31% African American; 4% Hispanic; 4% race unknown; 3% Foreign; 3% two or more races; 1% Asian American; 1% American Indian/Alaska Native. **Female To Male Ratio:** 1.6:1. The average age of freshmen is 22; all undergraduates, 27. 18% do not continue beyond their first year; 34% remain to graduate. **Housing:** 2377 students can be accommodated in college housing, which includes married student dorms, on-campus apartments, and off-campus apartments. In addition, there are honors houses, special-interest houses, fraternity houses, sorority houses, an international house, and substance-free housing. On-campus housing is guaranteed for all 4 years. 66% of students commute. Alcohol is not permitted. All students may keep cars.

FACULTY/CLASSROOMS: All teach undergraduates. No introductory courses are taught by graduate students.

PROGRAMS OF STUDY: Troy confers B.A., B.S., B.A.B.A., B.A.Ed., B.Applied Sc., B.F.A., B.M.Ed., B.S.B.A., B.S.Ed., and B.S.N. degrees. Associate and master's degrees are also awarded. Bachelor's degrees are awarded in BIOLOGICAL SCIENCE (biology/biological science and marine biology), BUSINESS (accounting, banking and finance, business administration and management, business economics, insurance, management science, marketing management, marketing/retailing/merchandising, personnel management, and sports management), COMMUNICATIONS AND THE ARTS (art, art history and appreciation, broadcasting, communications, design, dramatic arts, English, journalism, and studio art), COMPUTER AND PHYSICAL SCIENCE (chemistry, computer science, information sciences and systems, mathematics, and science), EDUCATION (art education, athletic training, collaborative education, early childhood education, elementary education, English education, health education, mathematics education, music education, physical education, science education, secondary education, social science education, and special education), ENGINEERING AND ENVIRONMENTAL DESIGN (environmental science and technological management), HEALTH PROFESSIONS (nursing and rehabilitation therapy), SOCIAL SCIENCE (criminal justice, history, human services, political science/government, psychology, social science, social work, and sociology). Business and education is the strongest academically. Business has the largest enrollment.

ACTIVITIES: 19% of men belong to 13 national fraternities; 18% of women belong to 9 national sororities. There are 197 groups on campus, including art, band, cheerleading, choir, chorale, chorus, computers, dance, debate, drama, drill team, ethnic, film, forensics, honors, international, jazz band, LGBT, literary magazine, marching band, musical theater, newspaper, opera, orchestra, pep band, photography, political, professional, radio and TV, religious, social, social service, student government, and symphony. Popular campus events include ISCO Festival, Spring Picnic and Heritage Week. **Sports:** There are 10 intercollegiate sports for men and 8 for women, and 15 intramural sports for men and 15 for women. Facilities include an auditorium, weight training center, baseball stadium, a 9-hole golf course, football practice fields, basketball, volleyball, an natatorium with an indoor swimming pool, a recreational gym, an outdoor swimming pool and fitness centers, and intramural fields. **Graduates:** From July 1, 2016 to June 30, 2017, 2821 bachelor's degrees were awarded. The most popular majors were psychology (16%), computer information systems (4%), and social sciences (4%).

SERVICES: Counseling and information services are available, as is tutoring in some subjects. There is a reader service for the blind, and remedial math, reading, and writing. Tutors may be provided for students upon request. **Library/Resources:** The library contains 594,716 volumes, 2.1 million microform items, and 19,532 audio/video tapes/CDs/DVDs, and subscribes to 3,263 periodicals including electronic. Computerized library services include interlibrary loans, database searching, Internet access, and Wi-Fi capability. Special learning facilities include an art gallery, planetarium, radio station, TV station, an arboretum, the Davis Theater, and the Rosa L. Parks Library, a museum and children's annex. **Physically Challenged Students:** 95% of the campus is accessible. Facilities include wheelchair ramps, elevators, special parking, specially equipped restrooms, special class scheduling, lowered drinking fountains, and lowered telephones. **Special:** Cross-registration with the Marine Biological Consortium, internships in education, journalism, and nursing, study abroad in 5 countries, work-study programs at the university, and student-designed majors in public relations, advertising, and other fields are offered. Credit for life experience and nondegree study are also offered. There is a dual-degree program with Vyatka State University of Humanities in Kirov, Russia. There are 29 national honor societies, Phi Beta Kappa, a freshman honors program, and 14 departmental honors programs. **Visiting:** There are regularly scheduled orientations for prospective students, including a campus tour, classroom visitation, academic consultation, and interviews. There are guides for informal visits and visitors may sit in on classes. To schedule a visit, contact the Office of Enrollment Services. **Campus Safety and Security:** Measures include 24-hour foot and vehicle patrol, self-defense education, and security escort services. There are lighted pathways/sidewalks.

REQUIREMENTS: The SAT or ACT is required. Applicants must have earned at least 15 Carnegie units, with 11 in academic courses and 3 to 4 in English. An interview is recommended, along with a portfolio or audition for some programs. The GED is accepted. AP and CLEP credits are accepted. Important factors in the admissions decision are evidence of special talent and extracurricular activities record. All students must maintain a minimum GPA of 2.0 while taking 120 to 140 semester credit hours, 54 of which must be in their major field. Distribution requirements include 48 hours of general studies, covering such subjects as English, math, history, science, and fine arts. **Procedure:** Freshmen are admitted fall, spring, and summer. Entrance exams should be taken in the spring of junior year of high school. There is a rolling admissions plan. Application deadlines are open. The fall 2017 application fee was $30. Applications are accepted on-line. **Transfer Students:** Transfer applicants need 20 semester hours attempted at their previous institution, with a GPA of 2.0. **International Students:** They must take the TOEFL with a minimum score of 500 on the paper-based TOEFL (PBT) or 61 on the Internet-based version (iBT), or take the IELTS or the SAT scoring 18.

Admissions Contact: Buddy Starling, Dean of Enrollment Services. Email: *ask@troy.edu* Web: *www.troy.edu*

FINANCIAL AID: The average freshman award was $4,467. Need-based scholarships or need-based grants averaged $4,622 ($5,775 maximum); need-based self-help aid (loans and jobs) averaged $3,628 ($950,000 maximum); non-need-based athletic scholarships averaged $6,204 ($29,444 maximum); and other non-need-based awards and non-need-based scholarships averaged $4,906 ($24,608 maximum). The college's own financial statement is required. The FAFSA code is 001047. The priority date for freshman financial aid applications for fall entry is March 1.

TUSKEGEE UNIVERSITY D-4

www.tuskegee.edu

Tuskegee, AL 36088 (334) 727-8289 (800) 622-6531

Fax: (334) 727 5750 **Email: admissions@tuskegee.edu**

Full-time: 1085 men, 1436 women
Part-time: 38 men, 39 women
Graduate: 161 men, 358 women
Year: semesters, summer session
Room & Board: $9104
SAT CR/M: 500/480 **ACT:** 21
Application Deadline: open

Faculty: 280
Ph.D.s: 70%
Student/Faculty: 12 to 1
Tuition: $19,060
Freshman Class: 5147 applied, 3519 accepted, 650 enrolled
CEEB CODE: 1813
COMPETITIVE

Tuskegee University, founded in 1881, is an independent professional and technical institution offering degree programs in liberal arts and sciences, agriculture, architecture, business, education, engineering, and health professions. There are 7 undergraduate schools and 4 graduate schools. In addition to regional accreditation, TU has baccalaureate program accreditation with ABET, CSWE, NAAB, CAEP, and NLN. The 5200-acre campus is in a rural area 40 miles east of Montgomery, AL and 20 miles west of Auburn, AL. Including any residence halls, there are 160 buildings.

STUDENT LIFE: 67% of undergraduates are from out of state, mostly the South. Students are from 42 states, 31 foreign countries, and Canada. 90% are from public schools. 80% are African American; 2% White; 1% American Indian/Alaska Native; 1% Hispanic; 1% Foreign. **Female To Male Ratio:** 1.4:1. The average age of freshmen is 19; all undergraduates, 22. 22% do not continue beyond their first year; 46% remain to graduate. **Housing:** 2300 students can be accommodated in college housing, which includes married student dorms and on-campus apartments. In addition, there are honors houses. On-campus housing is guaranteed for the freshman year only, and is available on a first-come, and first-served basis. Alcohol is not permitted. All students may keep cars.

FACULTY/CLASSROOMS: 70% of faculty are male; 30% are female. No introductory courses are taught by graduate students.

PROGRAMS OF STUDY: TU confers B.A., B.S., and B.S.N. degrees. Master's and doctoral degrees are also awarded. Bachelor's degrees are awarded in AGRICULTURE (agricultural economics, animal science, and horticulture), BIOLOGICAL SCIENCE (biology/biological science), BUSINESS (accounting, banking and finance, business administration and management, business economics, hospitality management services, management science, marketing/retailing/merchandising, and supply chain management), COMMUNICATIONS AND THE ARTS (English), COMPUTER AND PHYSICAL SCIENCE (chemistry, computer science, mathematics, and physics), EDUCATION (early childhood education, elementary education, physical education, secondary education, special education, and technical education), ENGINEERING AND ENVIRONMENTAL DESIGN (aeronautical engineering, architecture, biomedical engineering, chemical engineering, construction management, electrical/electronics engineering, electrical/electronics engineering technology, and mechanical engineering), HEALTH PROFESSIONS (allied health, nursing, occupational therapy, and veterinary science), SOCIAL SCIENCE (dietetics, economics, food science, history, political science/government, psychology, social work, and sociology). Engineering, nursing, and veterinary science are the strongest academically. Engineering, biology, and veterinary science have the largest enrollments.

ACTIVITIES: 4% of men belong to 6 local and 4 national fraternities; 4% of women belong to 5 local and 4 national sororities. There are 60 groups on campus, including band, cheerleading, choir, chorus, drama, honors, international, jazz band, marching band, newspaper, orchestra, religious, social service, and student government. Popular campus events include Spring Pageant, Campus All-Star Challenge, and Student Leadership Retreat. **Sports:** There are 5 intercollegiate sports for men and 5 for women, and 7 intramural sports for men and 6 for women. Facilities include a stadium, an arena, a student center, tennis courts, a rifle range, playing fields, and an Olympic-size natatorium. **Graduates:** From July 1, 2016 to June 30, 2017, 356 bachelor's degrees were awarded. The most popular majors were engineering (11%), biology (11%), and business (8%). In an average class, 17% graduate in 4 years or less, 28% graduate in 5 years or less, and 43% graduate in 6 years or less.

SERVICES: Counseling and information services are available, as is

tutoring in some subjects. There is a reader service for the blind. **Library/ Resources:** The library contains 380,000 volumes, 2,500 microform items, and 3,000 audio/video tapes/CDs/DVDs, and subscribes to 1,150 periodicals including electronic. Computerized library services include interlibrary loans, database searching, Internet access, and Wi-Fi capability. **Physically Challenged Students:** Facilities include wheelchair ramps, elevators, special parking, specially equipped restrooms, special class scheduling, lowered drinking fountains, and lowered telephones. **Special:** Cooperative programs, internships, work-study programs, dual majors, nondegree study, and a B.A.-B.S. degree are offered. There are 17 national honor societies, a freshman honors program, and 9 departmental honors programs. **Visiting:** There are guides for informal visits, visitors may sit in on classes, and stay overnight. To schedule a visit, contact the Office of Admissions. **Campus Safety and Security:** Measures include 24-hour foot and vehicle patrol and security escort services. There are lighted pathways/sidewalks.

REQUIREMENTS: The SAT or ACT is required. A GPA of 3.0 is recommended. Applicants should be graduates of an accredited secondary school or hold the GED. They should have completed 4 units of English, 3 each of social science and math, and 1 each of physical science and biological science. SAT: Subject tests in mathematics (level I or II) and 1 other subject are recommended. An essay is not required. AP and CLEP credits are accepted. Important factors in the admissions decision are advanced placement or honors courses and geographical diversity. All students must complete a general education curriculum, including courses in history, sociology, philosophy, art, English, humanities, political science, math, natural sciences, and phys ed. A minimum of 124 semester credits with a GPA of 2.0 is required for graduation. **Procedure:** Freshmen are admitted to all sessions. Entrance exams should be taken starting in the junior year. There are early admissions and rolling admissions plans. Application deadlines are open. The fall 2017 application fee was $25. Applications are accepted on-line. **Transfer Students:** 166 transfer students enrolled in 2016-2017. Applicants must be in good standing at all previously attended institutions and have completed 12 or more semester hours with a GPA of 2.5. 44 of 124 credits required for the bachelor's degree must be completed at TU. **International Students:** There are 27 international students enrolled. They must take the TOEFL with a minimum score of 500 on the paper-based TOEFL (PBT) or 62 on the Internet-based version (iBT). They must also take the SAT or ACT.

ADMISSIONS: 68% of the 2017-2018 applicants were accepted. The SAT scores for the 2017-2018 freshman class were: Critical Reading-- 67% below 500, 27% between 500 and 599, and 4% between 600 and 699. Math-- 64% below 500, 26% between 500 and 599, and 8% between 600 and 699. The ACT scores were 17% below 12, 61% between 12 and 17, 15% between 18 and 23, 6% between 24 and 29, and 1% above 30. 60% of the current freshmen were in the top fifth of their class; 80% were in the top two fifths. **Admissions Contact:** Elizabeth Dadzie, Associate VP of Admissions. Email: *admissions@tuskegee.edu* Web: *www.tuskegee.edu*

FINANCIAL AID: In 2017-2018, 87% of all full-time freshmen received some form of financial aid. 71% of all full-time freshmen received need-based aid. 59% of undergraduate students work part-time. TU is a member of CSS. The CSS/Profile, and federal tax returns are required. The FAFSA code is 001050. The priority date for freshman financial aid applications for fall entry is March 1.

UNIVERSITY OF ALABAMA AT BIRMINGHAM — C-2

www.uab.edu

Birmingham, AL 35294	(205) 934-8221 (800) 421-8743
Fax: (205) 975-7114	Email: chooseuab@uab.edu
Full-time: 3933 men, 5744 women	**Faculty:** I, -$
Part-time: 1392 men, 2065 women	**Ph.D.s:** 86%
Graduate: 2783 men, 4985 women	**Student/Faculty:** 18 to 1
Year: semesters, summer session	**Tuition:** $10,410 ($23,790)
Room & Board: $11,882	**Freshman Class:** 7555 applied, 6936 accepted, 2299 enrolled
SAT or ACT: required	**CEEB CODE:** 1856
Application Deadline: June 1	**COMPETITIVE**

University of Alabama at Birmingham, founded in 1969, is a public institution offering degrees in the arts and sciences, business, dentistry, education, engineering, health professions, joint health sciences, medicine, nursing, optometry and public health. There are 9 undergraduate schools and 11 graduate schools. In addition to regional accreditation, University of Alabama at Birmingham has baccalaureate program accreditation with AACSB, ABET, CSWE, NASAD, NASM, CAEP, CCNE, CAHME, and CAAHEP. The 323-acre campus is in an urban area in Birmingham, Alabama. Including any residence halls, there are 246 buildings.

STUDENT LIFE: 86% of undergraduates are from Alabama. Others are from 50 states, 82 foreign countries, and Canada. 92% are from public schools. 60% are White; 21% African American; 6% Asian American; 5% Foreign; 4% two or more races; 3% Hispanic; 1% race unknown. **Female To Male Ratio:** 1.6:1. The average age of freshmen is 18; all undergraduates, 24. 16% do not continue beyond their first year; 53% remain to graduate. **Housing:** 2796 students can be accommodated in college housing, which includes married student dorms and on-campus apartments. On-campus housing is available on a first-come and first-served basis. 77% of students commute. Alcohol is not permitted. All students may keep cars.

FACULTY/CLASSROOMS: 52% of faculty are male; 48% are female. No introductory courses are taught by graduate students.

PROGRAMS OF STUDY: UAB confers B.A., B.S., B.F.A., B.S.B.M.E., B.S.C.E., B.S.E.E., B.S.M.E., B.S.Mt.E., B.S.N., and B.S.S.W. degrees. Master's and doctoral degrees are also awarded. Bachelor's degrees are awarded in BIOLOGICAL SCIENCE (biology/biological science and neurosciences), BUSINESS (accounting, banking and finance, and marketing/retailing/merchandising), COMMUNICATIONS AND THE ARTS (art, communications, dramatic arts, English, foreign language, music, and musical theater), COMPUTER AND PHYSICAL SCIENCE (chemistry, computer science, information sciences and systems, mathematics, natural sciences, and physics), EDUCATION (early childhood education, elementary education, health education, and secondary education), ENGINEERING AND ENVIRONMENTAL DESIGN (biomedical engineering, civil engineering, electrical/electronics engineering, industrial administration/management, materials engineering, and mechanical engineering), HEALTH PROFESSIONS (biomedical science, health science, kinesiology, medical records administration/services, medical technology, nuclear medical technology, nursing, public health, and respiratory therapy), SOCIAL SCIENCE (African American studies, anthropology, criminal justice, economics, history, international studies, philosophy, political science/government, psychology, social work, and sociology). Biology, accounting, and psychology have the largest enrollments.

ACTIVITIES: Groups on campus include band, cheerleading, chess, choir, chorale, chorus, computers, dance, drama, environmental, ethnic, honors, international, jazz band, LGBT, literary magazine, marching band, musical theater, newspaper, opera, orchestra, pep band, political, professional, radio and TV, religious, social, social service, and student government. Popular campus events include Springfest, Homecoming, Camille Armstrong Memorial Scholarship Stepshow, and Talent Search. **Sports:** Facilities include a recreation center with basketball/volleyball courts, racquetball courts (1 of which can be converted to squash and wallyball), aerobics studios, weight and cardio-fitness areas, a KidsZone, an aquatics center with both lap and leisure components, indoor soccer, floor hockey, badminton, indoor track, and a climbing wall. **Graduates:** From July 1, 2016 to June 30, 2017, 2384 bachelor's degrees were awarded. The most popular majors were nursing (14%), psychology (7%), and health care management (6%). In an average class, 40% graduate in 4 years or less, 52% graduate in 5 years or less, and 53% graduate in 6 years or less.

SERVICES: Counseling and information services are available, as is tutoring in some subjects, such as biology, chemistry, physics, psychology, and mathematics. There is a reader service for the blind, and remedial math, reading, and writing. In addition, the college has an academic success center, university writing center, and math learning lab. **Library/ Resources:** The library contains 2.2 million volumes, 1.3 million microform items, and 29,744 audio/video tapes/CDs/DVDs, and subscribes to 39,256 periodicals including electronic. Computerized library services include interlibrary loans, database searching, Internet access, and Wi-Fi capability. Special learning facilities include an art gallery, radio station, TV station, historical library, museum of the health sciences, and performing art center. **Physically Challenged Students:** All of the campus is accessible. Facilities include wheelchair ramps, elevators, special parking, specially equipped restrooms, lowered drinking fountains, lowered telephones, and special housing. **Special:** UAB offers student-designed majors, cross-registration with the Birmingham Area Consortium for Higher Education, internships, study abroad in 32 countries, work-study programs, nondegree study, pass/fail options, and credit by exam and for life experience. Cooperative education programs in the student's area of interest provide full- or part-time work. Additionally, there are several special programs such as the Industrial Scholars Program (provides financial support and industry experience for engineering students), Fifth Year Master of Science program in biology, Mathematics Fast Track Program, and the Early Medical School Acceptance Program. There are 32 national honor societies, a freshman honors program, and 33 departmental honors programs. **Visiting:** There are regularly scheduled orientations for prospective students, including a question-and-answer session, academic advising, sessions for parents, and presentations on student life, financial aid, housing, and student development. There are guides for informal visits and visitors may sit in on classes. To schedule a visit, contact Hilary Murrell at campustour@uab.edu. **Campus Safety and Security:** Measures include 24-hour foot and vehicle patrol, emergency notification system, self-defense education, and security escort services. There are shuttle buses, emergency telephones, and lighted pathways/sidewalks.

REQUIREMENTS: The SAT or ACT is required. Applicants should have completed 17 Carnegie units and a college prep diploma, including 4 units in English, 3 units each in math, science, and social studies, 1 unit in foreign language, and 3 units in electives. The GED is accepted. AP and CLEP credits are accepted. All students must complete a core curriculum that includes courses in math, computers, English, history, science and technology, social sciences, philosophy, fine arts, foreign language or culture, and literature. To receive a bachelor's degree, students must complete 128 semester hours for most programs, with a GPA of at least 2.0. **Procedure:** Freshmen are admitted to all sessions. Entrance exams should be taken during the beginning of the senior year. There are early admissions, deferred admissions, and rolling admissions plans. Applications should be filed by June 1 for fall entry. The fall 2017 application fee was $30. Notification is sent on a rolling basis. Applications are accepted on-line. **Transfer Students:** 1555 transfer students enrolled in 2016-2017. Transfer applicants must have a GPA of 2.0 after completing 24 semester hours (or 36 quarter hours) of college-level work. College transcripts are required of all students. Applicants who have completed fewer than 24 semester hours must meet the requirements of beginning freshmen. **International Students:** There are 268 international students enrolled. They must take the TOEFL with a minimum score of 77 on the Internet-based version (iBT). Students must take the IELTS. They must also take the SAT or ACT, scoring 20.

ADMISSIONS: 92% of the 2017-2018 applicants were accepted. 47% of the current freshmen were in the top fifth of their class; 74% were in the top two fifths. **Admissions Contact:** Sean Kerins, Sr. Institutional Research Analyst. Email: *chooseuab@uab.edu* Web: *www.uab.edu*

FINANCIAL AID: In 2017-2018, 93% of all full-time freshmen received some form of financial aid. 53% of all full-time freshmen received need-based aid. The average freshman award was $13,171. Need-based scholarships or need-based grants averaged $1,998 ($10,920 maximum); need-based self-help aid (loans and jobs) averaged $1,875 ($12,300 maximum); non-need-based athletic scholarships averaged $614 ($42,982 maximum); and other non-need-based awards and non-need-based scholarships averaged $8,030 ($38,901 maximum). 4% of undergraduate students work part-time. The average financial indebtedness of the 2017 graduate was $42,299. The FAFSA code is 001052. The priority date for freshman financial aid applications for fall entry is March 1.

UNIVERSITY OF ALAMA IN HUNTSVILLE C-1

www.uah.edu

Huntsville, AL 35899	(256) 824-2771 (800) UAH-CALL
Fax: (256) 824-4539	Email: uahadmissions@uah.edu
Full-time: 3420 men, 2483 women	Faculty: I, -$
Part-time: 677 men, 510 women	Ph.D.s: 82%
Graduate: 1023 men, 988 women	Student/Faculty: 17 to 1
Year: semesters, summer session	Tuition: $10,280 ($21,480)
Room & Board: $9748	Freshman Class: 4295 applied, 3483 accepted, 1353 enrolled
SAT or ACT: required	CEEB CODE: 1854
Application Deadline: August 20	VERY COMPETITIVE

University of Alabama in Huntsville, founded in 1950 and part of The University of Alabama System, is a public institution specializing in engineering, education, nursing, science, business, the arts, humanities, social sciences, and professional & continuing studies. There are 6 undergraduate schools and 1 graduate school. In addition to regional accreditation, UAH has baccalaureate program accreditation with AACSB, ABET, ACCE, CSAB, NASAD, NASM, CAEP, CCNE, and ACS. The 505-acre campus is in a suburban area 100 miles north of Birmingham and 90 miles south of Nashville. Including any residence halls, there are 59 buildings.

STUDENT LIFE: 86% of undergraduates are from Alabama. Others are from 47 states, 89 foreign countries, and Canada. 72% are White; 10% African American; 5% Foreign; 4% Asian American; 4% Hispanic; 2% two or more races; 1% American Indian/Alaska Native; 1% race unknown. **Male To Female Ratio:** 1.3:1. The average age of freshmen is 18; all undergraduates, 22. 18% do not continue beyond their first year; 49% remain to graduate. **Housing:** 2055 students can be accommodated in college housing, which includes married student dorms and on-campus apartments. In addition, there are honors houses, fraternity houses, sorority houses, athletics teammates, freshman leadership and involvement, engineering, academic success, and discovery. On-campus housing is guaranteed for the freshman year only, and is available on a first-come, and first-served basis. 74% of students commute. Alcohol is not permitted. All students may keep cars.

FACULTY/CLASSROOMS: 55% of faculty are male; 45% are female. No introductory courses are taught by graduate students.

PROGRAMS OF STUDY: UAH confers B.A., B.F.A., B.S., B.S.B.A., B.S.A.E., B.S.Che.E., B.S.C.E., B.S.Cp.E., B.S.E.E., B.S.M.E., B.S.I.S.E., B.S.O.E., and B.S.N. degrees. Master's and doctoral degrees are also awarded. Bachelor's degrees are awarded in BIOLOGICAL SCIENCE (biology/biological science), BUSINESS (accounting, banking and finance, business administration and management, economics – statistics, and marketing/retailing/merchandising), COMMUNICATIONS AND THE ARTS (art, communications, English, languages, and music), COMPUTER AND PHYSICAL SCIENCE (chemistry, computer science, earth science, information sciences and systems, mathematics, physics, and science), EDUCATION (elementary education), ENGINEERING AND ENVIRONMENTAL DESIGN (chemical engineering, civil engineering, computer engineering, electrical/electronics engineering, industrial engineering, mechanical engineering, and optical engineering), HEALTH PROFESSIONS (nursing), SOCIAL SCIENCE (history, philosophy, political science/government, psychology, and sociology). Mechanical engineering, computer science, and aerospace engineering have the largest enrollments.

ACTIVITIES: There are 125 groups on campus, including multicultural club, community service, special interest, academic club, art, band, cheerleading, choir, chorale, chorus, computers, dance, drama, environmental, ethnic, honors, international, jazz band, LGBT, musical theater, newspaper, opera, pep band, political, professional, religious, social, social service, student government, and symphony. Popular campus events include Week of Welcome, Homecoming, Family Weekend, Late Night Breakfast, ChargerCon, The Big Event, Sandella Sounds, and Spring Fling. **Sports:** There are 9 intercollegiate sports for men and 9 for women, and 11 intramural sports for men and 11 for women. Facilities include a gym, swimming pool, racquetball and tennis courts, disc golf course, soccer fields, softball diamonds, a fitness center with cardio equipment, indoor track, weight room, fitness classes, aquatics, sand volleyball, basketball courts, and a sports nutrition center.**Graduates:** From July 1, 2016 to June 30, 2017, 1055 bachelor's degrees were awarded. The most popular majors were nursing (10%), mechanical engineering (10%), and management (9%). In an average class, 25% graduate in 4 years or less, 35% graduate in 5 years or less, and 49% graduate in 6 years or less.

SERVICES: Counseling and information services are available. There are also tutoring services available for most 100-200 level classes, most undergraduate math classes, and undergraduate writing in any discipline. **Library/Resources:** The library contains 289,500 volumes, 571,000 microform items, and 1,489 audio/video tapes/CDs/DVDs, and subscribes to 339 periodicals including electronic. Computerized library services include interlibrary loans, database searching, Internet access, and Wi-Fi capability. Special learning facilities include an art gallery, an optical observatory and a radio telescope, the National Space Science and Technology Center located on our campus, shared between UAHuntsville, NASA and the National Weather Service, and a rooftop greenhouse used for research and laboratory experiences. **Physically Challenged**

Students: 98% of the campus is accessible. Facilities include wheelchair ramps, elevators, special parking, specially equipped restrooms, special class scheduling, lowered drinking fountains, special housing, a swimming pool lift, and sign language interpreters. Special: UAH offers co-op programs in all majors, cross-registration with Alabama Agricultural and Mechanical University, Athens State University, and Calhoun Community College, and internships in business, communications, education, and political science. A 3-2 engineering degree is also available with Oakwood College. Dual majors, B.A.-B.S. degrees in math and biology, study abroad in 28 countries, nondegree study, and a pass/fail option are also offered. Joint Undergraduate Masters Program (JUMP) available in ten majors including atmospheric science, biology, business, chemistry, civil engineering, computer science, earth systems science, electrical and computer engineering, math and physics. There are 15 national honor societies and a freshman honors program. Visiting: There are regularly scheduled orientations for prospective students, including sessions on academics, campus life, financial aid and other important topics are provided as well as time dedicated to advising and class registration. Social activities are available for participants to meet both new and current students. There are guides for informal visits, visitors may sit in on classes, and stay overnight. To schedule a visit, contact Vangie Harris at (800) 824-2773. Campus Safety and Security: Measures include 24-hour foot and vehicle patrol, emergency notification system, self-defense education, and security escort services. There are emergency telephones, lighted pathways/sidewalks, controlled access to dorms/residences, emergency management plan, 911 system, and digitally recorded security cameras.

REQUIREMENTS: The SAT or ACT is required. A sliding scale with the GPA determines the minimum test score needed. The GED is accepted. Students should present a minimum of 20 Carnegie units, including 4 years of English and social studies, and 3 each of math and science. A GPA of 2.0 is required. AP and CLEP credits are accepted. All students must earn a minimum GPA of 2.0 over 120 to 134 credit hours, including 21 to 36 in their major. The core curriculum includes courses in English composition, literature, world history, foreign language and communications, fine arts, math, science and social sciences. Procedure: Freshmen are admitted fall, spring, and summer. Entrance exams should be taken during the junior year. There are early admissions, deferred admissions, and rolling admissions plans. Applications should be filed by August 20 for fall entry; December 15 for spring entry; and May 15 for summer entry. The fall 2017 application fee was $30. Applications are accepted on-line. Transfer Students: 648 transfer students enrolled in 2016-2017. Applicants need a minimum cumulative GPA of 2.0, over at least 24 hours of credit from a regionally accredited college or university. 32 of 128 credits required for the bachelor's degree must be completed at UAH. International Students: There are 179 international students enrolled. They must take the TOEFL with a minimum score of 65 on the Internet-based version (iBT) and the college's own test. They must also take the SAT or ACT.

ADMISSIONS: 81% of the 2017-2018 applicants were accepted. The SAT scores for the 2017-2018 freshman class were: Critical Reading-- 14% below 500, 44% between 500 and 599, 34% between 600 and 699, and 8% between 700 and 800. Math-- 17% below 500, 35% between 500 and 599, 37% between 600 and 699, and 11% between 700 and 800. The ACT scores were 1% between 12 and 17, 24% between 18 and 23, 45% between 24 and 29, and 30% above 30. 58% of the current freshmen were in the top fifth of their class; 82% were in the top two fifths. 24 freshmen graduated first in their class. Admissions Contact: Peggy Masters, Director of Admissions. Email: *uahadmissions@uah.edu* Web: *www.uah.edu*

FINANCIAL AID: The FAFSA code is 001055. The priority date for freshman financial aid applications for fall entry is April 1. The deadline for filing freshman financial aid applications for fall entry is July 31.

UNIVERSITY OF MOBILE A-5

www.umobile.edu

Mobile, AL 36613	**(251) 442-2249** **(800) 946-7267**
Fax: (251) 675-6329	**Email: cwittner@umobile.edu**
Full-time: 473 men, 809 women	**Faculty:** 84
Part-time: 40 men, 144 women	**Ph.D.s:** 62%
Graduate: 25 men, 109 women	**Student/Faculty:** 12 to 1
Year: semesters, summer session	**Tuition:** $19,385
Room & Board: $9550	**Freshman Class:** 1009 applied, 590 accepted, 275 enrolled
ACT: 22	**CEEB CODE:** 1515
Application Deadline: August 1	**COMPETITIVE**

University of Mobile, founded in 1961, is a private liberal arts institution affiliated with the Southern Baptists. There are 7 undergraduate schools and 5 graduate schools. In addition to regional accreditation, UM has baccalaureate program accreditation with ACBSP, NASM, CAATE, CCNE, and ACEN. The 880-acre campus is in a suburban area 10 miles northwest of Mobile. Including any residence halls, there are 60 buildings.

STUDENT LIFE: 74% of undergraduates are from Alabama. Others are from 39 states, 23 foreign countries, and Canada. 63% are White; 5% race unknown; 3% Foreign; 24% African American; 2% American Indian/Alaska Native; 2% two or more races; 1% Hispanic. Female To Male Ratio: 2.0:1. The average age of freshmen is 18; all undergraduates, 24. 23% do not continue beyond their first year; 46% remain to graduate. Housing: 734 students can be accommodated in college housing, which includes dorms and on-campus apartments. On-campus housing is guaranteed for the freshman year only, and is available on a first-come, and first-served basis. 51% of students commute. Alcohol is not permitted. All students may keep cars.

FACULTY/CLASSROOMS: 50% of faculty are male; 50% are female. 98% teach undergraduates. No introductory courses are taught by graduate students. The average class size in an introductory lecture is 16; in a laboratory is 16; and in a regular course is 16.

PROGRAMS OF STUDY: UM confers B.A., B.S., B.B.A., B.M., and B.S.N. degrees. Associate and master's degrees are also awarded. Bachelor's degrees are awarded in BIOLOGICAL SCIENCE (biology/biological science and marine science), BUSINESS (accounting and business administration and management), COMMUNICATIONS AND THE ARTS (art, communications, English, music, music performance, and voice), COMPUTER AND PHYSICAL SCIENCE (information sciences and systems and mathematics), EDUCATION (athletic training, early childhood education, elementary education, and physical education), HEALTH PROFESSIONS (nursing), SOCIAL SCIENCE (history, humanities, liberal arts/general studies, political science/government, psychology, religion, religious music, social science, sociology, and theological studies). Business, education, and nursing are the strongest academically. Business administration, education, and nursing have the largest enrollments.

ACTIVITIES: There are no fraternities or sororities. There are 52 groups on campus, including art, band, cheerleading, choir, chorale, chorus, computers, dance, drama, drum and bugle corps, honors, international, jazz band, musical theater, opera, orchestra, pep band, political, professional, religious, social, social service, student government, and symphony. Popular campus events include College Preview Day, and Christmas Spectacular. Sports: There are 7 intercollegiate sports for men and 8 for women, and 5 intramural sports for men and 5 for women. Facilities include a gym, tennis complex, swimming pool, track, baseball, softball, soccer fields, and a golf driving range with putting greens. Graduates: From July 1, 2016 to June 30, 2017, 272 bachelor's degrees were awarded. The most popular majors were education (22%), nursing (21%), and business (15%). In an average class, 26% graduate in 4 years or less, 14% graduate in 5 years or less, and 42% graduate in 6 years or less. Of the 2016 graduating class, 26% were enrolled in graduate school within 6 months of graduation, and 72% were employed.

SERVICES: Counseling and information services are available, as is tutoring in some subjects, such as writing, English and math. There is remedial math, reading, and writing. There is also additional tutoring provided in other subjects as needed. Library/Resources: The library contains 234,913 volumes, and 1,733 audio/video tapes/CDs/DVDs, and subscribes to 151,268 periodicals including electronic. Computerized library services include interlibrary loans, database searching, Internet access, and Wi-Fi capability. Special learning facilities include an art gallery. Physically Challenged Students: All of the campus is accessible. Facilities include wheelchair ramps, elevators, special parking, specially equipped restrooms, special class scheduling, lowered drinking fountains, and special housing can be arranged as-needed basis. Special: A variety of internships and work-study programs, a five-year B.S./M.B.A. degree, adult programs in business, education, nursing, and leadership/cultural studies, and dual majors are available, as is a 3-2 engineering degree with the University of South Alabama. There are 13 national honor societies, a freshman honors program, and 1 departmental honors program. Visiting: There are regularly scheduled orientations for prospective students, including financial aid seminars, academic seminars, faculty advising, campus tours, and admissions counseling. There are guides for informal visits, visitors may sit in on classes, and stay overnight. To schedule a visit, contact Justin McGehee at (251) 442-2638.

Campus Safety and Security: Measures include 24-hour foot and vehicle patrol and emergency notification system. There are lighted pathways/ sidewalks, controlled access to dorms/residences. A professional campus security service is available 24 hours per day.

REQUIREMENTS: Applicants must have 22 Carnegie units and a minimum composite score of 21 on the ACT. The GED is accepted. The ACT is not required of applicants over age 25. A GPA of 2.8 is required. AP and CLEP credits are accepted. Important factors in the admissions decision are advanced placement or honors courses and leadership record. All students are required to complete 123 credit hours, with at least 30 in their major field, and earn a minimum GPA of 2.0. Distribution requirements include 9 hours in English, 4 hours in lab science, 6 hours in Christian ministries, and 3 hours each in math, history, and public speaking or philosophy. Students select an additional 18 hours of electives from among art, literature, psychology, sociology, political science, philosophy, science, history, economics, music, and Christian ministries. Chapel attendance is also required. **Procedure:** Freshmen are admitted fall, spring, and summer. Entrance exams should be taken in August before the junior year. There are deferred admissions and rolling admissions plans. Applications should be filed by August 1 for fall entry; January 4 for spring entry; and May 1 for summer entry. The fall 2017 application fee was $25. Notification is sent on a rolling basis. Applications are accepted on-line. **Transfer Students:** 113 transfer students enrolled in 2016-2017. Transfer students need to have earned a minimum GPA of 2.0 for previous college work. If fewer than 24 semester hours are accepted, a minimum score of 21 on the ACT and a high school transcript, or GED, are required. 32 of 123 credits required for the bachelor's degree must be completed at UM. **International Students:** There are 64 international students enrolled. They must take the TOEFL with a minimum score of 500 on the paper-based TOEFL (PBT) or 61 on the Internet-based version (iBT). They must also take the SAT or ACT.

ADMISSIONS: 58% of the 2017-2018 applicants were accepted. The SAT scores for the 2017-2018 freshman class were: Critical Reading-- 67% below 500, 24% between 500 and 599, and 9% between 600 and 699. Math-- 64% below 500, 33% between 500 and 599, and 3% between 600 and 699. 50% of the current freshmen were in the top fifth of their class; 84% were in the top two fifths. **Admissions Contact:** Charity Wittner, Director of Enrollment & Admissions. Email: *cwittner@umobile.edu* Web: *www.umobile.edu*

FINANCIAL AID: In 2017-2018, 82% of all full-time freshmen received some form of financial aid. 58% of all full-time freshmen received need-based aid. The average freshman award was $18,602. Need-based scholarships or need-based grants averaged $5,219; need-based self-help aid (loans and jobs) averaged $2,175; non-need-based athletic scholarships averaged $16,508; and other non-need-based awards and non-need-based scholarships averaged $9,377. The average financial indebtedness of the 2017 graduate was $28,250. The state aid form and the college's own financial statement are required. The FAFSA code is 001029. The deadline for filing freshman financial aid applications for fall entry is August 1.

UNIVERSITY OF MONTEVALLO C-3

www.montevallo.edu

Montevallo, AL 35115	(205) 665-6034
Fax: (205) 665-6032	**Email:** admissions@montevallo.edu
Full-time: 685 men, 1416 women	**Faculty:** IIA, --$
Part-time: 79 men, 166 women	**Ph.D.s:** 70%
Graduate: 86 men, 285 women	**Student/Faculty:** 16 to 1
Year: semesters, summer session	**Tuition:** $12,400 ($25,030)
Room & Board: $7612	**Freshman Class:** 2024 applied, 1417 accepted, 505 enrolled
ACT: 23	**CEEB CODE:** 1004
Application Deadline: August 1	**COMPETITIVE**

University of Montevallo, founded in 1896, is a public, liberal arts institution offering courses in business, fine arts, music, teacher preparation and preprofessional training. There are 4 undergraduate schools and 2 graduate schools. In addition to regional accreditation, UM has baccalaureate program accreditation with AACSB, ADA, AHEA, CSWE, NASAD, NASM, SACS, CACREP, and ACS. The 160-acre campus is in a small town 35 miles south of Birmingham. Including any residence halls, there are 40 buildings.

STUDENT LIFE: 91% of undergraduates are from Alabama. Others are from 6 states, 29 foreign countries, and Canada. 70% are White; 5% Hispanic; 3% two or more races; 3% race unknown; 2% Foreign; 16% African American; 1% Asian American. **Female To Male Ratio:** 2.2:1. The average age of freshmen is 18; all undergraduates, 20. 27% do not continue beyond their first year; 45% remain to graduate. **Housing:** 1340 students can be accommodated in college housing, which includes dorms, on-campus apartments, and fraternity houses. On-campus housing is available on a first-come and first-served basis. 52% of students commute. All students may keep cars.

FACULTY/CLASSROOMS: 46% of faculty are male; 54% are female. 99% teach undergraduates. No introductory courses are taught by graduate students. The average class size in an introductory lecture is 24; in a laboratory is 23; and in a regular course is 24.

PROGRAMS OF STUDY: UM confers B.A., B.S., B.B.A., B.F.A., B.M., and B.M.E. degrees. Master's degrees are also awarded. Bachelor's degrees are awarded in BIOLOGICAL SCIENCE (biology/biological science), BUSINESS (accounting, banking and finance, business administration and management, management science, and marketing/retailing/ merchandising), COMMUNICATIONS AND THE ARTS (art, communications, dramatic arts, English, French, German, journalism, music, music performance, Spanish, and studio art), COMPUTER AND PHYSICAL SCIENCE (chemistry and mathematics), EDUCATION (art education, education of the deaf and hearing impaired, elementary education, home economics education, music education, and physical education), ENGINEERING AND ENVIRONMENTAL DESIGN (environmental science), HEALTH PROFESSIONS (speech pathology/ audiology), SOCIAL SCIENCE (family/consumer studies, history, political science/government, psychology, social science, social work, and sociology). Elementary/early childhood education, business and art have the largest enrollments.

ACTIVITIES: 13% of men belong to 7 national fraternities; 19% of women belong to 8 national sororities. There are 93 groups on campus, including art, cheerleading, choir, chorus, computers, dance, debate, drama, environmental, ethnic, forensics, honors, international, jazz band, LGBT, literary magazine, musical theater, newspaper, pep band, photography, political, professional, radio and TV, religious, social, social service, student government, and yearbook. Popular campus events include College Night, and Honors Day. **Sports:** There are 4 intercollegiate sports for men and 7 for women, and 7 intramural sports for men and 4 for women. Facilities include a student activity center with a swimming pool, weight training and cardio-conditioning theater, an arena, athletic fields, tennis courts, sand volleyball facility, golf course and driving range. **Graduates:** From July 1, 2016 to June 30, 2017, 510 bachelor's degrees were awarded. The most popular majors were business/marketing (17%), education (13%), and visual and performing arts (12%). In an average class, 29% graduate in 4 years or less, 46% graduate in 5 years or less, and 49% graduate in 6 years or less.

SERVICES: Counseling and information services are available, as is tutoring in some subjects. There is a reader service for the blind, remedial math, reading, and writing, study skills, and a speech and a hearing center. **Library/Resources:** The library contains 266,236 volumes, 795,344 microform items, and 4,673 audio/video tapes/CDs/DVDs, and subscribes to 27,962 periodicals including electronic. Computerized library services include interlibrary loans, database searching, Internet access, and Wi-Fi capability. Special learning facilities include an art gallery, radio station, TV station, All-Steinway Music Department, Center for Innovative Teaching and Technology, Digital Cafe, distance learning classroom, glass-blowing studio, painting and drawing studios, Ebeneezer Swamp Ecological Preserve, speech and hearing center, an observatory, and a traffic safety center. **Physically Challenged Students:** Facilities include wheelchair ramps, elevators, special parking, specially equipped restrooms, special class scheduling, lowered drinking fountains, and lowered telephones. **Special:** A 3-2 engineering degree is offered with Auburn University, the University of Alabama at Birmingham, and the University of Alabama at Tuscaloosa. Internships are required for some majors. Study abroad, B.A.-B.S. degrees, dual degrees, a Washington semester, and pass/fail options are available. There are 26 national honor societies, a freshman honors program, and 1 departmental honors program. **Visiting:** There are regularly scheduled orientations for prospective students, consisting of a program of orientation, advising, and academic counseling prior to enrollment. There are guides for informal visits, visitors may sit in on classes, and stay overnight. To schedule a visit, contact the Office of Admissions. **Campus Safety and Security:** Measures include 24-hour foot and vehicle patrol, emergency notification system, self-defense education, and security escort services. There are emergency telephones, lighted pathways/sidewalks, controlled access to dorms/residences, and campus lighting and electronic access into residence halls.

REQUIREMENTS: The ACT is preferred. Applicants must present a high school transcript with a minimum GPA of 2.5 and successful completion of a minimum of 16 academic or college-preparatory credits from 9th to 12th grade, including 4 units each of English, social studies, and math, 2 units of science, and 4 units of foreign language or electives. Applicants who have earned a GED should have an official copy of their score report sent in lieu of a high school transcript. AP and CLEP credits are accepted. Important factors in the admissions decision are advanced placement or honors courses, evidence of special talent, and geographical diversity. To graduate, students must complete a minimum of 130 semester hours with an overall 2.0 GPA while meeting core, major, and minor requirements. Core requirements include 12 hours of writing reinforcement courses (usually met with literature and major/minor courses), 7 hours of sciences (2 branches), 6 hours each in foundations in writing, world literature, world civilizations, and institutions and issues courses, 4 hours of health/phys ed, 3 hours each of oral communications, math, computer science, fine arts, and humanities, and 1 additional fine arts or humanity elective. **Procedure:** Freshmen are admitted to all sessions. Entrance exams should be taken in spring of the junior year or fall of the senior year. There are deferred admissions and rolling admissions plans. Applications should be filed by August 1 for fall entry; December 1 for spring entry; and May 1 for summer entry. The fall 2017 application fee was $30. Notification is sent on a rolling basis. Applications are accepted on-line. **Transfer Students:** 157 transfer students enrolled in 2016-2017. A minimum cumulative C average on all college-level study attempted must have been attained. This is a cumulative GPA of 2.0 or better on a 4.0 scale. Applicants must be a student in good standing - neither probation nor suspension can be in effect at the previous or current college of university attended. Transcripts of all previous study attempted must be submitted and evaluated before an application review can be conducted. Collegiate work from post-secondary institutions not accredited nor in candidacy status for accreditation by a regional accrediting association is not transferable to the University of Montevallo. Students who have completed less than 24 semester hours (or 36 quarter hours) of college-level study must also submit a secondary-school transcript and either an ACT or SAT score report and must satisfy all requirements for freshman admission. A maximum of 64 semester hours (or 96 quarter hours) may be transferred for credit from either a community or junior college. 33 of 130 credits required for the bachelor's degree must be completed at UM. **International Students:** There are 58 international students enrolled. They must take the TOEFL with a minimum score of 525 on the paper-based TOEFL (PBT) or 71 on the Internet-based version (iBT). They must also take the SAT or ACT.

ADMISSIONS: 70% of the 2017-2018 applicants were accepted. **Admissions Contact:** Audrey Crawford, Director of Admissions. Email: *admissions@montevallo.edu* Web: *www.montevallo.edu*

FINANCIAL AID: 17% of undergraduate students work part-time. The FAFSA code is 001004. The priority date for freshman financial aid applications for fall entry is August 1.

UNIVERSITY OF NORTH ALABAMA B-1

www.una.edu

Florence, AL 35632	(256) 765-4680
	Email: admissions@una.edu
Full-time: 2079 men, 3071 women	**Faculty:** 253; IIA, --$
Part-time: 450 men, 621 women	**Ph.D.s:** 77%
Graduate: 519 men, 717 women	**Student/Faculty:** 19 to 1
Year: semesters, summer session	**Tuition:** $8480 ($15,128)
Room & Board: $7484	**Freshman Class:** 3163 applied, 2788 accepted, 1098 enrolled
SAT CR/M: 573/527 **ACT:** 23	**CEEB CODE:** 1735
Application Deadline: n/av	**COMPETITIVE**

University of North Alabama was founded as LaGrange College in 1830. It was re-established in 1872 as the first state-supported teachers' college south of the Ohio River. There are 4 undergraduate schools and 1 graduate school. In addition to regional accreditation, UNA has baccalaureate program accreditation with AACSB, ABET, ACBSP, ACEJMC, CSWE, NASAD, NASM, CAEP, ACBSP, ASAC, CAC, CACREP, CAEP, CCNE, CIDA, and NKBA. The 130-acre campus is in an urban area 116 miles north of Birmingham. Including any residence halls, there are 68 buildings.

STUDENT LIFE: 80% of undergraduates are from Alabama. Others are from 46 states, 49 foreign countries, and Canada. 71% are White; 14% African American; 12% Asian American; 3% Hispanic; 3% Foreign; 3% race unknown; 2% two or more races; 1% American Indian/Alaska Native. **Female To Male Ratio:** 1.4:1. The average age of freshmen is 18; all undergraduates, 22. 24% do not continue beyond their first year; 45% remain to graduate. **Housing:** 2139 students can be accommodated in college housing, which includes dorms, on-campus apartments, and off-campus apartments. In addition, there are honors houses, language/international houses, fraternity houses, and sorority houses. On-campus housing is guaranteed for the freshman year only, and is available on a first-come, first-served basis. 75% of students commute. Alcohol is not permitted. All students may keep cars.

FACULTY/CLASSROOMS: 50% of faculty are male; 50% are female. 95% teach undergraduates. No introductory courses are taught by graduate students. The average class size in an introductory lecture is 24; in a laboratory is 22; and in a regular course is 24.

PROGRAMS OF STUDY: UNA confers B.A., B.S., B.S.C.S., B.A.M., B.I.S., B.B.A., B.F.A., B.S.Ed., B.S.M., B.M., B.S.N., and B.S.W. degrees. Master's degrees are also awarded. Bachelor's degrees are awarded in BIOLOGICAL SCIENCE (biology/biological science), BUSINESS (accounting, banking and finance, business economics, and marketing/retailing/merchandising), COMMUNICATIONS AND THE ARTS (art, communications, English, English Writing, French, German, journalism, music, public relations, and Spanish), COMPUTER AND PHYSICAL SCIENCE (chemistry, computer information systems, computer science, geology, information sciences and systems, mathematics, and physics), EDUCATION (art education, business education, early childhood education, elementary education, foreign languages education, music education, physical education, science education, secondary education, and social science education), ENGINEERING AND ENVIRONMENTAL DESIGN (engineering technology, environmental engineering technology, and interior design), HEALTH PROFESSIONS (industrial hygiene and nursing), SOCIAL SCIENCE (counseling/psychology, criminal justice, geography, history, liberal arts/general studies, political science/government, psychology, social work, and sociology). Chemistry, industrial hygiene, secondary education, engineering technology, MBA program, and nursing are the strongest academically. Nursing, elementary education, and biology have the largest enrollments.

ACTIVITIES: 11% of men belong to 2 local and 11 national fraternities; 17% of women belong to 1 local and 9 national sororities. There are 130 groups on campus, including Diversity Student Ambassadors, UNA Nerd Pop Culture, art, band, cheerleading, choir, chorale, chorus, computers, debate, drama, drill team, environmental, ethnic, film, honors, international, jazz band, LGBT, literary magazine, marching band, musical theater, newspaper, opera, orchestra, pep band, photography, political, professional, radio and TV, religious, social, social service, student government, symphony, UNA Video Game Association, and yearbook. Popular campus events include Spring Fling, Miss UNA Pageant, Step Sing, and the George Lindsey Film Festival. **Sports:** There are 6 intercollegiate sports for men and 7 for women, and 7 intramural sports for men and 7 for women. Facilities include a football stadium, a gym, baseball and softball fields, an outdoor track, indoor swimming pool, tennis courts, fitness center, weights and machines, aerobics studio, gaming lounge, an intramural field with multipurpose courts, and track. **Graduates:** From July 1, 2016 to June 30, 2017, 1085 bachelor's degrees were awarded. The most popular majors were nursing (14%), professional management (7%), and elementary Ed K-6 (6%). In an average class, 1% graduate in 3 years or less, 18% graduate in 4 years or less, 38% graduate in 5 years or less, and 46% graduate in 6 years or less.

SERVICES: Counseling and information services are available, as is tutoring in some subjects, such as physics, computer science, writing, math, English, history, biology, chemistry, accounting, finance, economics, qualitative methods, and psychology. There is a reader service for the blind, and remedial math and writing. The academic resource center features computer-assisted tutoring and faculty mentoring. **Library/**

Resources: The library contains 351,273 volumes, 1.1 million microform items, 88,064 audio/video tapes/CDs/DVDs, and subscribes to 32,777 periodicals, including electronic. Computerized library services include interlibrary loans, database searching, Internet access, and Wi-Fi capability. Special learning facilities include an art gallery, a planetarium, a radio station, a learning resource center, and Think Space. **Physically Challenged Students:** 99% of the campus is accessible. Facilities include wheelchair ramps, elevators, special parking, specially equipped restrooms, special class scheduling, lowered drinking fountains, lowered telephones, and special housing. **Special:** University of North Alabama, offers cooperative programs in all majors, internships (Redstone Arsenal, NASA, etc.), accelerated nursing program, study abroads (Tianjin, China, Guatemala, Zimbabwe, France, England, etc.), work-study programs, various B.A.-B.S. degrees, dual majors and a general studies degree, as well as interdisciplinary student designed degrees. Non-degree study is possible. There are 13 national honor societies, Phi Beta Kappa, and a freshman honors program. **Visiting:** There are regularly scheduled orientations for prospective students, including orientation programs conducted each summer prior to the fall semester. There are guides for informal visits. **Campus Safety and Security:** Measures include 24-hour foot and vehicle patrol, an emergency notification system, self-defense education, and security escort services. There are shuttle buses, emergency telephones, lighted pathways/sidewalks, and controlled access to dorms/residences.

REQUIREMENTS: The SAT or ACT is required. Applicants should be graduates of an accredited high school or have earned a GED. 13 High school units required are 4 in English, 3 in social studies, and 2 each in math, and science, and any 2 in foreign languages, history, or computer sciences. A GPA of 2.0 is required. AP and CLEP credits are accepted. Important factors in the admissions decision are advanced placement or honors courses, leadership record, and extracurricular activities record. Students must complete a core curriculum, which includes 12 semester hours in history, social and behavioral sciences, humanities, and fine arts, 11 in natural sciences and math, and 6 in language composition. Total number of hours in majors vary. Passing grades in 1 writing emphasis and 1 computer course also are needed. A minimum of 120 semester hours and a minimum GPA of 2.0 are required to graduate. **Procedure:** Freshmen are admitted fall, spring, and summer. Entrance exams should be taken in the senior year. There are deferred admissions and rolling admissions plans. Application deadlines are open. The fall 2017 application fee was $35. Applications are accepted online. **Transfer Students:** 598 transfer students enrolled in 2016-2017. Applicants should be eligible to return to the school last attended. 30 of 120 credits required for the bachelor's degree must be completed at UNA. **International Students:** There are 147 international students enrolled. They must take the TOEFL with a minimum score of 500 on the paper-based TOEFL (PBT) or 61 on the Internet-based version (iBT). Students may take either the IELTS, TOEIC or PTC.

ADMISSIONS: 88% of the 2017-2018 applicants were accepted. The SAT scores for the 2017-2018 freshman class were: Critical Reading-- 9% below 500, 50% between 500 and 599, and 41% between 600 and 699. Math-- 50% below 500, 32% between 500 and 599, 13% between 600 and 699, and 5% between 700 and 800. The ACT scores were 1% between 12 and 17, 58% between 18 and 23, 35% between 24 and 29, and 6% above 30. **Admissions Contact:** Julie Taylor, Director of Admissions. Email: *admissions@una.edu* Web: *www.una.edu*

FINANCIAL AID: In 2017-2018, 73% of all full-time freshmen received some form of financial aid. 47% of all full-time freshmen received need-based aid. The average freshman award was $5,635. Need-based scholarships or need-based grants averaged $4,914 ($5,816 maximum); need-based self-help aid (loans and jobs) averaged $3,318 ($3,500 maximum); non-need-based athletic scholarships averaged $6,330 ($10,000 maximum); and other non-need-based awards and non-need-based scholarships averaged $5,742. 8% of undergraduate students work part-time. The FAFSA code is 001016. The priority date for freshman financial aid applications for fall entry is June 1.

UNIVERSITY OF SOUTH ALABAMA A-5

www.southalabama.edu

Mobile, AL 36688 **(251) 460-6141** **(800) 872-5247**

Fax: (251) 460-7876 **Email: recruitment@southalabama.edu**

Full-time: 3995 men, 5095 women	**Faculty:** 590; I, --$
Part-time: 784 men, 1114 women	**Ph.D.s:** 76%
Graduate: 1024 men, 3557 women	**Student/Faculty:** 20 to 1
Year: semesters, summer session	**Tuition:** $9390 ($18,780)
Room & Board: $7490	**Freshman Class:** 5855 applied, 4798 accepted, 1843 enrolled
SAT CR/M: 562/543 **ACT:** 23	**CEEB CODE:** 1880
Application Deadline: July 15	**COMPETITIVE**

University of South Alabama, a state-supported institution established in 1963, offers undergraduate and graduate degrees. There are 7 undergraduate schools and 9 graduate schools. In addition to regional accreditation, USA has baccalaureate program accreditation with AACSB, ABET, CSAB, CSWE, NASM, CAEP, JRCERT, CAAHEP, and CCNE. The 1224-acre campus is in a suburban area near the Gulf of Mexico in Mobile, Alabama, and 150 miles east of New Orleans. Including any residence halls, there are 116 buildings.

STUDENT LIFE: 82% of undergraduates are from Alabama. Others are from 50 states, 80 foreign countries, and Canada. 62% are White; 21% African American; 5% Foreign; 3% Asian American; 3% Hispanic; 3% two or more races; 3% race unknown; 1% American Indian/Alaska Native. 15% claim no religious affiliation. **Female To Male Ratio:** 1.7:1. The average age of freshmen is 19; all undergraduates, 22. 22% do not continue beyond their first year; 38% remain to graduate. **Housing:** 3183 students can be accommodated in college housing, which includes dorms, on-campus apartments, and off-campus apartments. In addition, there are special-interest houses, fraternity houses, sorority houses, wellness housing and themed housing. On-campus housing is available on a first-come and first-served basis. 71% of students commute. Alcohol is not permitted. All students may keep cars.

FACULTY/CLASSROOMS: 51% of faculty are male; 49% are female. 73% teach undergraduates. No introductory courses are taught by graduate students.

PROGRAMS OF STUDY: USA confers B.A., B.S., B.F.A., B.M., B.S.B.A., B.S.N., B.P.H.S., B.S.R.S., B.S.I.T., B.S.I.S., B.S.C.S., B.S.C.A., and B.S.W. degrees. Master's and doctoral degrees are also awarded. Bachelor's degrees are awarded in BIOLOGICAL SCIENCE (biology/biological science), BUSINESS (accounting, banking and finance, business administration and management, business administration - international, business economics, hospitality management services, marketing/retailing/merchandising, and recreation and leisure services), COMMUNICATIONS AND THE ARTS (communications, dramatic arts, English, fine arts, information technology, languages, and music), COMPUTER AND PHYSICAL SCIENCE (atmospheric sciences and meteorology, chemistry, computer science, geology, information science, mathematics, and physics), EDUCATION (early childhood education, education, educational studies, elementary education, health information management, physical education, secondary education, and special education), ENGINEERING AND ENVIRONMENTAL DESIGN (chemical engineering, civil engineering, computer engineering, electrical/electronics engineering, instructional design, and mechanical engineering), HEALTH PROFESSIONS (biomedical science, emergency medical services, health science, nursing, radiological science, and respiratory therapy), SOCIAL SCIENCE (anthropology, communication sciences & disorders, criminal justice, geography, history, interdisciplinary studies, international studies, philosophy, political science/government, psychology, social work, and sociology). Health professions, business, and engineering are the strongest academically. Nursing, business administration, and biology have the largest enrollments.

ACTIVITIES: There are 205 groups on campus, including art, band, cheerleading, chess, choir, chorale, chorus, communications, computers, dance, debate, drama, drill team, environmental, ethnic, film, honors, international, jazz band, LGBT, literary magazine, marching band, musical theater, newspaper, opera, orchestra, pep band, political, professional, radio and TV, religious, social, social service, student government, and symphony. Popular campus events include Homecoming, Greek Week, and Winter Jam. **Sports:** There are 8 intercollegiate sports for men and 9 for women, and 9 intramural sports for men and 9 for women. Facilities include an arena, student recreation center, handball courts, fitness rooms, basketball/volleyball courts, indoor track, several intramural fields, and an outdoor swimming pool. **Graduates:** From July 1, 2016 to June 30, 2017, 2066 bachelor's degrees were awarded. The most popular majors were nursing (14%), professional health sciences (6%), and elementary education (6%). In an average class, 19% graduate in 4 years or less, 33% graduate in 5 years or less, and 40% graduate in 6 years or less.

SERVICES: Counseling and information services are available, as is tutoring in some subjects, such as foundational courses. **Library/Resources:** The library contains 431,356 volumes, 1.0 million microform items, and 8,034 audio/video tapes/CDs/DVDs. Computerized library services include interlibrary loans, database searching, Internet access, and Wi-Fi capability. Special learning facilities include an art gallery, radio and TV stations, and an Archaeology Museum. **Physically Challenged Students:** Facilities include wheelchair ramps, elevators, special parking, specially equipped restrooms, lowered drinking fountains, and special housing. **Special:** University of South Alabama, offers co-op programs in most majors, federal work-study, internships, study abroad in many countries, dual majors, an adult degree program, and a personalized studies program. There are 19 national honor societies and a freshman honors program. **Visiting:** There are regularly scheduled orientations for prospective students. Orientation includes a campus tour, class registration, reserving textbooks, team building activities, and obtaining a student ID. There are guides for informal visits. To schedule a visit, contact Scott Henne at recruitment@southalabama.edu. **Campus Safety and Security:** Measures include 24-hour foot and vehicle patrol, emergency notification system, self-defense education, and security escort services. There are shuttle buses, emergency telephones, lighted pathways/sidewalks, and controlled access to dorms/residences.

REQUIREMENTS: Applicants should be high school graduates or have a GED certificate. A minimum ACT score of 19 is required for regular admission. 16 Academic units recommended for admissions are 4 in English, 3 each in math, social studies, and science with those 2 units of lab, and 3 academic electives. A GPA of 2.5 is required. AP and CLEP credits are accepted. General education requirements consist of 12 hours in written composition, 12 hours in humanities and fine arts, at least 12 hours in history and the social and behavioral sciences, and 11 hours in natural science and math. A minimum of 120 semester hours, with a minimum GPA of 2.0, are required for graduation. **Procedure:** Freshmen are admitted to all sessions. Entrance exams should be taken during the junior year or early in the senior year. There are early admissions, deferred admissions, and rolling admissions plans. Applications should be filed by July 15 for fall entry; December 1 for spring entry; and May 1 for summer entry. The fall 2017 application fee was $35. Applications are accepted on-line. **Transfer Students:** 846 transfer students enrolled in 2016-2017. Transfer applicants must have at least a 2.0 GPA on all college work attempted for regular admission. An official transcript from each college or university attended. If the student has earned less than 30 semester or 40 quarter hours, then an official high school transcript is required. If the student graduated from high school less than five years prior to matriculation at USA or is not at least 23 years of age, then ACT or SAT scores are required in addition to the high school transcript. 60 of 120 credits required for the bachelor's degree must be completed at USA. **International Students:** There are 607 international students enrolled. They must take the TOEFL with a minimum score of 61 on the Internet-based version (iBT) and the college's own test. They must also take the SAT or ACT.

ADMISSIONS: 82% of the 2017-2018 applicants were accepted. The SAT scores for the 2017-2018 freshman class were: Critical Reading-- 19% below 500, 52% between 500 and 599, 26% between 600 and 699, and 4% between 700 and 800. Math-- 24% below 500, 55% between 500 and 599, 18% between 600 and 699, and 3% between 700 and 800. The ACT scores were 1% between 12 and 17, 54% between 18 and 23, 36% between 24 and 29, and 9% above 30. **Admissions Contact:** Scott Henne, Director, New Student Recruitment. Email: *recruitment@southalabama.edu* Web: *www.southalabama.edu*

FINANCIAL AID: In 2017-2018, 66% of all full-time freshmen received some form of financial aid. 61% of all full-time freshmen received need-based aid. The average freshman award was $9,894. Need-based scholarships or need-based grants averaged $7,184; need-based self-help aid (loans and jobs) averaged $3,571; non-need-based athletic scholarships averaged $15,708; other non-need-based awards and non-need-based scholarships averaged $3,464; and $4,923 from other forms of aid. The FAFSA code is 001057. The priority date for freshman financial aid applications for fall entry is May 31.

UNIVERSITY OF WEST ALABAMA *(The complete profile is made available exclusively on our website, www.barronspac.com)*

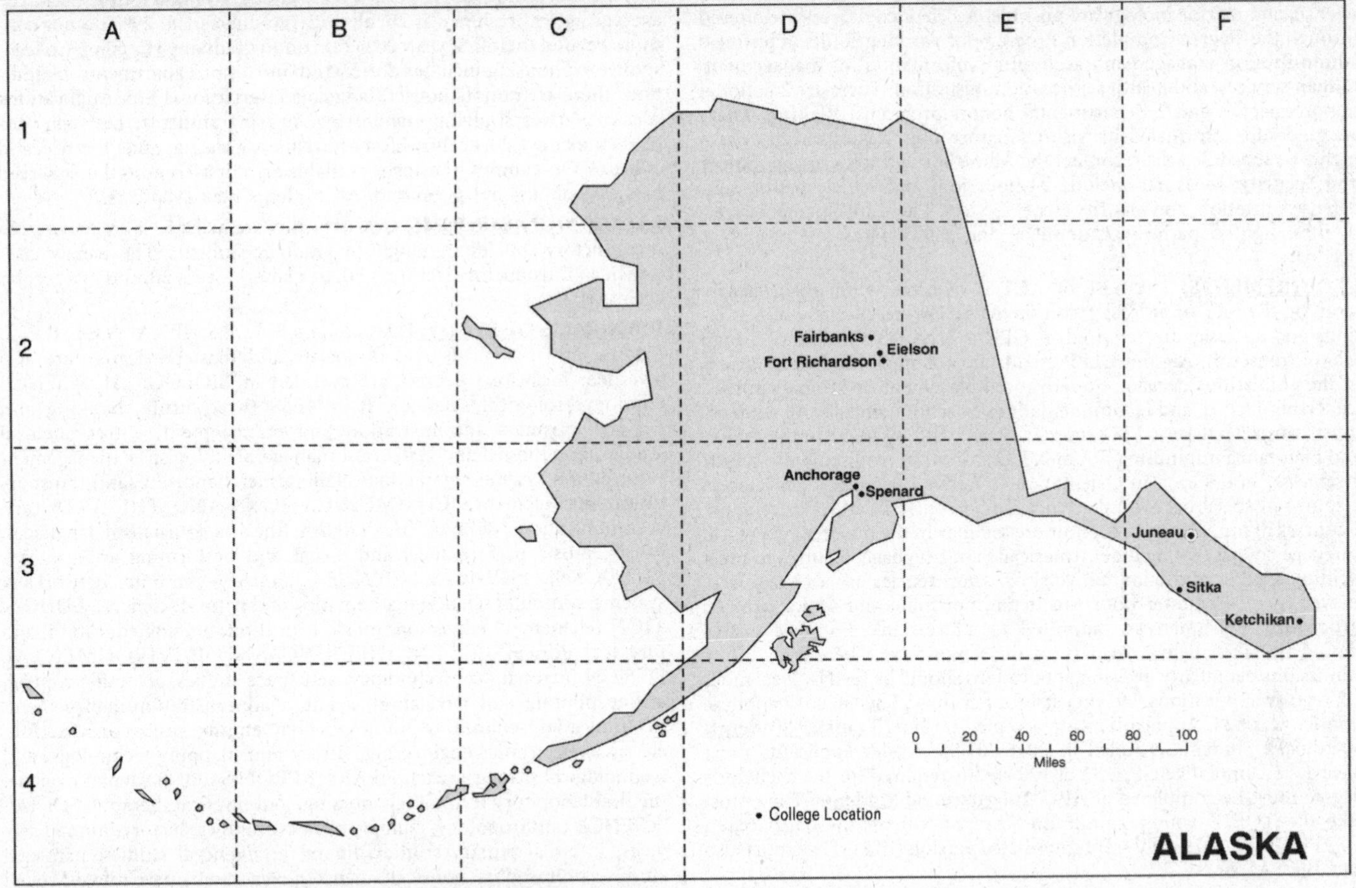

ALASKA PACIFIC UNIVERSITY D-3

www.alaskapacific.edu

Anchorage, AK 99508	**(907) 564-8248** **(800) 252-7528**
Fax: (907) 564-8317	**Email: admissions@alaskapacific.edu**
Full-time: 125 men, 200 women	**Faculty:** n/av
Part-time: 60 men, 160 women	**Ph.D.s:** 60%
Graduate: 85 men, 190 women	**Student/Faculty:** 12 to 1
Year: 4-1-4, summer session	**Tuition:** $20,830
Room & Board: $7900	**Freshman Class:** n/av
SAT or ACT: required	**CEEB CODE:** 4201
Application Deadline: August 1	**VERY COMPETITIVE**

Alaska Pacific University, founded in 1957 and affiliated with the United Methodist Church, is a private institution offering undergraduate, graduate, and adult degree-completion programs. The figures in the above capsule and in this profile are approximate. There are 6 undergraduate schools and 6 graduate schools. In addition to regional accreditation, APU has baccalaureate program accreditation with CAEP. The 170-acre campus is in a suburban area in midtown Anchorage. Including any residence halls, there are 13 buildings.

STUDENT LIFE: 73% of undergraduates are from Alaska. Others are from 37 states, and 2 foreign countries. 68% are White; 5% African American; 5% Hispanic; 3% Asian American; 18% American Indian/Alaska Native; 1% Foreign. **Female To Male Ratio:** 2.0:1. The average age of freshmen is 25; all undergraduates, 30. 25% do not continue beyond their first year; 36% remain to graduate. **Housing:** 170 students can be accommodated in college housing, which includes dorms and on-campus apartments. In addition, there are special-interest houses. On-campus housing is guaranteed for the freshman year only, and is available on a first-come, first-served basis, and is available on a lottery system for upperclassmen. 73% of students commute. Alcohol is not permitted. All students may keep cars.

FACULTY/CLASSROOMS: 42% of faculty are male; 58% are female. 98% teach undergraduates. No introductory courses are taught by graduate students. The average class size in an introductory lecture is 12; in a laboratory is 9; and in a regular course is 10.

PROGRAMS OF STUDY: APU confers B.A. and B.S. degrees. Associate and master's degrees are also awarded. Bachelor's degrees are awarded in AGRICULTURE (environmental studies and natural resource management), BIOLOGICAL SCIENCE (marine biology), BUSINESS (business administration and management and recreational facilities management), COMPUTER AND PHYSICAL SCIENCE (earth science), EDUCATION (elementary education), ENGINEERING AND ENVIRONMENTAL DESIGN (environmental science), HEALTH PROFESSIONS (health care administration), SOCIAL SCIENCE (human services, liberal arts/general studies, and psychology). Environmental science, outdoor studies, and psychology have the largest enrollments.

ACTIVITIES: There are no fraternities or sororities. There are 18 groups on campus, including art, band, chorus, drama, ethnic, international, newspaper, photography, professional, religious, social service, student government, and students in free enterprise. Popular campus events include Earth Day, Spring Honors Convocation, and Fall Academic Convocation. **Sports:** There is no sports program at APU. Facilities include a sports center, indoor swimming pool, cross-country skiing and running trails, climbing wall, soccer fields, boating, a disc golf course, a weight/exercise room, and a trail system. **Graduates:** The most popular majors were business/marketing (19%), health professions and related programs (16%), social sciences, psychology, and engineering (7%).

SERVICES: Counseling and information services are available, as is tutoring in some subjects, such as math, writing, and other subjects as needed. There is remedial math and writing. **Library/Resources:** The library contains 891,103 volumes, 627,916 microform items, and 13,324 audio/video tapes/CDs/DVDs, and subscribes to 3,840 periodicals including electronic. Computerized library services include interlibrary loans and Internet access. Special learning facilities include an art gallery, TV station, the Alaskana collection located in the Consortium Library. **Physically Challenged Students:** 75% of the campus is accessible. Facilities include wheelchair ramps, elevators, special parking, specially equipped restrooms, lowered drinking fountains, and lowered telephones. **Special:** Internships are required, and study abroad, student-designed majors, and B.A.-B.S. degrees in earth sciences, environmental science, and marine biology are possible. Accelerated degrees are offered through the Degree Completion Program for working adults in business administration management, accounting information for management, human services, and health services administration. There are 2 national honor societies and 2 departmental honors programs. **Visiting:** There are guides for informal visits; visitors may sit in on classes and stay overnight. To schedule a visit, contact the Admissions Office. **Campus Safety and Security:** Measures include 24-hour foot and vehicle patrol, self-defense education, and security escort services. There are emergency telephones, lighted pathways/sidewalks, and safety signs are posted as needed.

REQUIREMENTS: The SAT or ACT is required, with a satisfactory score on the SAT or at least 19 on the ACT. Two teacher recommendations and an essay are required. A GED is acceptable in lieu of a high school transcript. AP and CLEP credits are accepted. Important factors in the admissions decision are advanced placement or honors courses, leadership record, and recommendations by school officials. All students must complete at least 128 semester hours, with 39 to 61 in the major, and maintain a minimum GPA of 2.0. Distribution requirements include 4 semester hours each in Orientation to Active Learning, a lab science, a course in social/behavioral science, and a course in ethics or religion, 2 courses in humanities, a sophomore seminar in the major, and a world language course that includes American Sign Language. Courses to meet writing, speech, and quantitative skills competencies are also required, as well as a 3-semester-hour practicum, portfolio, and senior project. **Procedure:** Freshmen are admitted to all sessions. Entrance exams should be taken before January of the senior year. There is a rolling admissions plan. Early decision applications should be filed by December 12; regular applications, by August 1 for fall entry. The fall 2017 application fee was $25. Applications are accepted on-line. **Transfer Students:** 80 transfer students enrolled in 2016-2017. Transfer applicants must have a 2.0 cumulative GPA. 32 of 128 credits required for the bachelor's degree must be completed at APU. **International Students:** They must take the TOEFL with a minimum score of 550 on the paper-based TOEFL (PBT) or 79 on the Internet-based version (iBT). They must also take the SAT or ACT.

ADMISSIONS: 1 freshman graduated first in the class. **Admissions Contact:** Brian McDermott, Assistant Director of Admissions. Email: *admissions@alaskapacific.edu* Web: *www.alaskapacific.edu*

FINANCIAL AID: APU is a member of CSS. The FAFSA code is 001061. The priority date for freshman financial aid applications for fall entry is September 19.

UNIVERSITY OF ALASKA ANCHORAGE D-3

www.uaa.alaska.edu

Anchorage, AK 99508	(907) 786-1480
Fax: (907) 786-4888	**Email:** enroll@uaa.alaska.edu
Full-time: 3215 men, 3622 women	**Faculty:** IIA, av$
Part-time: 2073 men, 3442 women	**Ph.D.s:** 51%
Graduate: 287 men, 556 women	**Student/Faculty:** n/av
Year: semesters, summer session	**Tuition:** $6186
Room & Board: $11,728	**Freshman Class:** 3775 applied, 2665 accepted, 1869 enrolled
SAT CR/M/W: 510/505/490 **ACT:** 21	**CEEB CODE:** 4896
Application Deadline: n/av	**COMPETITIVE**

University of Alaska Anchorage, founded in 1954, is a public institution and a major unit of the University of Alaska statewide system. Its baccalaureate programs are administered through the colleges of arts and sciences, business and public policy, health, education, social welfare, and the school of engineering, and the community and technical college. The figures in the above capsule and in this profile are approximate. There are 5 undergraduate schools and 5 graduate schools. In addition to regional accreditation, UAA has baccalaureate program accreditation with AACSB, ABET, ACEJMC, ADA, CAHEA, CSWE, NASAD, NASDTEC, CAEP, and NLN. The 428-acre campus is in an urban area 3 miles from downtown Anchorage. Including any residence halls, there are 27 buildings.

STUDENT LIFE: 90% of undergraduates are from Alaska. 8% are Asian American; 66% White; 5% Hispanic; 4% African American; 2% Foreign; 11% American Indian/Alaska Native. **Female To Male Ratio:** 1.4:1. The average age of freshmen is 20; all undergraduates, 28. 29% do not continue beyond their first year; 26% remain to graduate. **Housing:** College-sponsored housing includes dorms and on-campus apartments. In addition, there are honors houses, language/international houses, floors for Alaska Natives studying engineering, nursing students, first-year students under age 20, healthy lifestyle, wellness housing, quiet lifestyle, and cultures. On-campus housing is available on a first-come and first-served basis. Alcohol is not permitted. All students may keep cars.

FACULTY/CLASSROOMS: 48% of faculty are male; 52% are female. No introductory courses are taught by graduate students. The average class size in an introductory lecture is 50; in a laboratory is 20; and in a regular course is 35.

PROGRAMS OF STUDY: UAA confers B.A., B.S., B.B.A., B.Ed., B.F.A., B.Mus., and B.S.W. degrees. Associate and master's degrees are also awarded. Bachelor's degrees are awarded in BIOLOGICAL SCIENCE (biology/biological science), BUSINESS (accounting, banking and finance, business administration and management, entrepreneurial studies, hotel/motel and restaurant management, logistics, management information systems, marketing/retailing/merchandising, and transportation management), COMMUNICATIONS AND THE ARTS (art, communications, dramatic arts, English, fine arts, journalism, languages, music, music performance, and visual and performing arts), COMPUTER AND PHYSICAL SCIENCE (chemistry, computer networks & systems, computer science, mathematics, and natural sciences), EDUCATION (elementary education, music education, nursing education, and physical education), ENGINEERING AND ENVIRONMENTAL DESIGN (aeronautical technology, aerospace studies, air traffic control, airline piloting and navigation, aviation administration/management, aviation maintenance technology, civil engineering, construction, electrical/electronics engineering, survey and mapping technology, and technological management), HEALTH PROFESSIONS (dental hygiene, medical laboratory technology, nursing, and physical therapy), SOCIAL SCIENCE (anthropology, culinary arts, economics, history, human services, interdisciplinary studies, liberal arts/general studies, paralegal studies, philosophy, political science/government, psychology, social work, and sociology).

ACTIVITIES: There are no fraternities or sororities. There are 75 groups on campus, including art, cheerleading, chess, choir, chorus, computers, dance, debate, drama, ethnic, film, honors, international, jazz band, LGBT, leadership, literary magazine, newspaper, orchestra, officer training, photography, political, professional, religious, social, social service, student government, and student involvement fairs. Popular campus events include Great Alaska Shoot-Out, Northern Lights Invitational, Student Showcase, Haunted Halloween Fun Night, and Homecoming Shopping Cart Parade. **Sports:** There are 5 intercollegiate sports for men and 6 for women, and 4 intramural sports for men and 4 for women. Facilities include ice hockey, indoor jogging track, a gym, basketball, cross-country, swimming/diving pool, weight room, and racquetball/squash courts, skiing, soccer, volleyball, and water polo. **Graduates:** From July 1, 2016 to June 30, 2017, 1094 bachelor's degrees were awarded. The most popular majors were business/marketing (19%), health professions and related programs (16%), social science, psychology, and engineering (7%). In an average class, 27% graduate in 6 years or less.

SERVICES: Counseling and information services are available, as is tutoring in most subjects. There is a reader service for the blind, and remedial math, reading, and writing. Sign language, interpreters, and note takers are available. **Library/Resources:** The library contains 676,750 volumes, 574,010 microform items, and 7,080 audio/video tapes/CDs/DVDs, and subscribes to 3,480 periodicals including electronic. Computerized library services include interlibrary loans and database searching. Special learning facilities include an art gallery, TV station, a dental clinic, a welding lab, an auto-diesel garage, a theater, photography labs, and a student art museum show case. **Physically Challenged Students:** All of the campus is accessible. Facilities include wheelchair ramps, elevators, special parking, specially equipped restrooms, lowered drinking fountains, lowered telephones, and special housing. **Special:** UAA participates in the National Student Exchange Program and offers study abroad. UAA also offers B.A.-B.S. degrees, student-designed and dual majors, internships, pass/fail options, a 3-2 electrical engineering degree, a general studies degree, nondegree study, and credit for life experience. The Community and Technical College provides educational and vocational courses for career development. There are 2 national honor societies and 3 departmental honors programs. **Visiting:** There are regularly scheduled orientations for prospective students, consisting of registration orientation, application process, campus tours, student appointments, and classes. There are guides for informal visits and visitors may sit in on classes. To schedule a visit, contact the Office of Admissions. **Campus Safety and Security:** Measures include 24-hour foot and vehicle patrol, self-defense education, and security escort services. There are emergency telephones and lighted pathways/sidewalks.

REQUIREMENTS: The SAT or ACT is required. Applicants should be graduates of an accredited secondary school or have a high school or GED certificate. AP and CLEP credits are accepted. General education requirements include 7 credits in natural science, 6 each in written communications, humanities, and social sciences, and 3 each in oral communication, quantitative skills, and fine arts. A total of 120 to 132 credits, with 48 upper-division courses, and a minimum GPA of 2.0 are required to graduate. **Procedure:** Freshmen are admitted to all sessions. Entrance exams should be taken by May of the senior year. There are deferred admissions and rolling admissions plans. Check with the school for current application deadlines. The fall 2017 application fee was $40. Applications are accepted on-line. **Transfer Students:** 794 transfer students enrolled in 2016-2017. Applicants must meet admission requirements and must have a minimum GPA of 2.5 and at least 30 credit hours earned at an accredited post secondary institution. Students may enroll in the fall, spring, and summer. 30 of 120 credits required for the bachelor's degree must be completed at UAA. **International Students:** They must take the TOEFL. They must also take the SAT or ACT.

ADMISSIONS: 71% of the 2017-2018 applicants were accepted. The SAT scores for the 2017-2018 freshman class were: Critical Reading-- 43% below 500, 37% between 500 and 599, 18% between 600 and 699, and 3% between 700 and 800. Math-- 43% below 500, 40% between 500 and 599, 15% between 600 and 699, and 2% between 700 and 800. Writing-- 55% below 500, 34% between 500 and 599, 12% between 600 and 699, and 1% between 700 and 800. **Admissions Contact:** Eric Pedersen, Director of Admission. Email: *enroll@uaa.alaska.edu* Web: *www.uaa.alaska.edu*

FINANCIAL AID: The average freshman award was $8,654. Need-based scholarships or need-based grants averaged $3,476; need-based self-help aid (loans and jobs) averaged $3,470; other non-need-based awards and non-need-based scholarships averaged $3,362; and $3,202 from other forms of aid. The average financial indebtedness of the 2017 graduate was $26,632. UAA is a member of CSS. The college's own financial statement is required. The FAFSA code is 011462. The deadline for filing freshman financial aid applications for fall entry is February 15.

UNIVERSITY OF ALASKA FAIRBANKS D-2

www.uaf.edu

Fairbanks, AK 99775	**(907) 474-7500** **(800) 478-1823**
Fax: (907) 474-7097	**Email: admissions@uaf.edu**
Full-time: 1156 men, 1142 women	**Faculty:** 332; I, -$
Part-time: 458 men, 627 women	**Ph.D.s:** 67%
Graduate: 405 men, 621 women	**Student/Faculty:** 7 to 1
Year: semesters, summer session	**Tuition:** $8144 ($24,149)
Room & Board: $8730	**Freshman Class:** 865 applied, 573 accepted, 380 enrolled
SAT EBR-W/M: 600/580 **ACT:** required	**CEEB CODE:** 4866
Application Deadline: June 15	**VERY COMPETITIVE**

University of Alaska Fairbanks, founded in 1917 is the nation's northernmost Land, Sea, and Space Grant university and international research center. The institution advances and disseminates knowledge through teaching, research, and public service with an emphasis on Alaska and circumpolar regions. There are 8 undergraduate schools and 8 graduate schools. In addition to regional accreditation, UAF has baccalaureate program accreditation with AACSB, ABET, ACEJMC, CSWE, NASM, SAF, ACS, and CAEP. The 2250-acre campus is in a small town 4 miles northwest of Fairbanks. Including any residence halls, there are 68 buildings.

STUDENT LIFE: 80% of undergraduates are from Alaska. Others are from 45 states, 20 foreign countries, and Canada. 55% are White; 16% race unknown; 8% American Indian/Alaska Native; 8% two or more races; 7% Hispanic; 2% African American; 2% Asian American; 2% Foreign. **Female To Male Ratio:** 1.2:1. The average age of freshmen is 18; all undergraduates, 23. 23% do not continue beyond their first year; 38% remain to graduate. **Housing:** 1578 students can be accommodated in college housing, which includes married student dorms and on-campus apartments, first-year experience residence, and Alaska Native cultural housing. On-campus housing is available on a first-come and first-served basis. 61% of students commute. All students may keep cars.

FACULTY/CLASSROOMS: 57% of faculty are male; 43% are female. 60% teach undergraduates, 65% do research, and 41% do both. No introductory courses are taught by graduate students. The average class size in an introductory lecture is 20; in a laboratory is 15; and in a regular course is 18.

PROGRAMS OF STUDY: UAF confers B.A., B.S., B.B.A., B.A.A.S., B.E.M., B.F.A., and B.M. degrees. Associate, master's, and doctoral degrees are also awarded. Bachelor's degrees are awarded in AGRICULTURE (fishing and fisheries and natural resource management), BIOLOGICAL SCIENCE (biology/biological science and wildlife conservation biology), BUSINESS (accounting and business administration marketing), COMMUNICATIONS AND THE ARTS (art, communications, digital communications, English, Eskimo, film arts, foreign language, journalism, linguistics, music, music performance, and theatre arts), COMPUTER AND PHYSICAL SCIENCE (chemistry, computer science, earth science, geoscience, mathematics, and physics), EDUCATION (elementary education, music education, and secondary education), ENGINEERING AND ENVIRONMENTAL DESIGN (civil engineering, computer engineering, electrical/electronics engineering, geological engineering, mechanical engineering, mining and mineral engineering, and petroleum/natural gas engineering), SOCIAL SCIENCE (American Indian studies, anthropology, area studies, child care/child and family studies, geography, history, homeland security/emergency preparedness, Japanese studies, justice and society, political science/government, psychology, and social work). Engineering, fisheries, and biology are the strongest academically. Biological sciences, business administration, and mechanical engineering have the largest enrollments.

ACTIVITIES: There are 175 groups on campus, including art, band, chess, choir, chorus, communications, computers, dance, drama, environmental, ethnic, film, honors, international, jazz band, LGBT, literary magazine, newspaper, orchestra, pep band, photography, political, professional, radio and TV, religious, social, student government, and symphony. Popular campus events include Starvation Gulch, All-Campus Day, and Meltdown. **Sports:** There are 5 intercollegiate sports for men and 6 for women, and 8 intramural sports for men and 8 for women. Facilities include an arena, a gym, skating rink, racquetball courts, weight rooms, basketball courts, an Olympic-size swimming pool, small-bore rifle range, and a lighted 30-mile ski trail. **Graduates:** From July 1, 2016 to June 30, 2017, 581 bachelor's degrees were awarded. The most popular majors were biological sciences (9%), business administration (8%), and mechanical engineering (6%). In an average class, 1% graduate in 3 years or less, 20% graduate in 4 years or less, 34% graduate in 5 years or less, and 38% graduate in 6 years or less.

SERVICES: Counseling and information services are available, as is tutoring in some subjects, such as chemistry, calculus, languages, biology, math, physics, geology and English. There is a reader service for the blind, and remedial math, reading, and writing. **Library/Resources:** The library contains 831,082 volumes, 134,215 microform items, and 99,455 audio/video tapes/CDs/DVDs, and subscribes to 62,484 periodicals including electronic. Computerized library services include interlibrary loans, database searching, Internet access, and Wi-Fi capability. Special learning facilities include an art gallery, natural history museum, radio station, TV station, several research institutes, and labs for study in the physical and natural sciences. **Physically Challenged Students:** 90% of the campus is accessible. Facilities include wheelchair ramps, elevators, special parking, specially equipped restrooms, special class scheduling, lowered drinking fountains, lowered telephones, and special housing. **Special:** The university's Office of eLearning and Distance Education offers satellite education programs to Alaska residents to reach students at remote sites. Study abroad is offered in 42 countries. Internships are offered through the Rural Alaska Honors Institute. Student-designed majors, credit/no credit options, nondegree study, and credit for life, military, and work experience are also available. There are 8 national honor societies and a freshman honors program. **Visiting:** There are regularly scheduled orientations for prospective students, tours generally include academic facilities, dorms, and student recreation center, and may also include meeting with an admissions counselor, professors, advisors, and students, and classroom visits. There are guides for informal visits, visitors may sit in on classes, and stay overnight. To schedule a visit, contact the Office of Admissions. **Campus Safety and Security:** Measures include 24-hour foot and vehicle patrol, emergency notification system, self-defense education, and security escort services. There are shuttle buses, emergency telephones, lighted pathways/sidewalks, controlled access to dorms/residences, 24-hour crisis line, and evening patrols inside dorms.

REQUIREMENTS: The SAT or ACT is required. Applicants should be graduates of an accredited secondary school with 16 academic credits, including 4 in English, and 3 each in math, natural or physical sciences, and social sciences, with a minimum GPA of 2.5 in these courses. Applicants should have an overall high school GPA of at least 3.0 or an overall GPA of at least 2.5 along with an ACT Plus Writing score of at least 18 or SAT total score of at least 955 or a total score of 1290 for the previous version of the SAT. The GED is not accepted. A GPA of 2.5 is required. AP and CLEP credits are accepted. All students must complete core courses in English and oral communication, library skills, humanities, social science, natural science, and math. A minimum of 120 credit hours, with 27 to 30 in the major, and a 2.0 GPA are required for graduation. **Procedure:** Freshmen are admitted to all sessions. Entrance exams should be taken within two years of the start of term. There are early admissions, deferred admissions, and rolling admissions plans. Applications should be filed by June 15 for fall entry; November 1 for spring entry; and May 1 for summer entry. The fall 2017 application fee was $50. Notification is sent on a rolling basis. Applications are accepted online. **Transfer Students:** 225 transfer students enrolled in 2016-2017. A GPA of 2.0 in all previous college work and an honorable dismissal from all schools attended are required. Applicants with fewer than 30 semester hours of transferable credit also must have a high school GPA of 2.0 and ACT or SAT scores. 30 of 120 credits required for the bachelor's degree must be completed at UAF. **International Students:** There are 39 international students enrolled. They must take the TOEFL with a minimum score of 550 on the paper-based TOEFL (PBT) or 79 on the Internet-based version (iBT), or take the IELTS. They must also take the SAT or ACT.

ADMISSIONS: 66% of the 2017-2018 applicants were accepted. The SAT scores for the 2017-2018 freshman class were: Math-- 11% below 500, 47% between 500 and 599, 33% between 600 and 699, and 9% between 700 and 800. Evidence-Based Reading/Writing-- 16% below 500, 33% between 500 and 599, 39% between 600 and 699, and 12% between 700 and 800. 56% of the current freshmen were in the top fifth of their class; 77% were in the top two fifths. 2 freshmen graduated first in their class. **Admissions Contact:** Mary Kreta, Director of Admissions. Email: *admissions@uaf.edu* Web: *www.uaf.edu*

FINANCIAL AID: In 2017-2018, 90% of all full-time freshmen received some form of financial aid. 47% of all full-time freshmen received need-based aid. The average freshman award was $9,715. Need-based scholarships or need-based grants averaged $8,031 ($23,194 maximum); need-based self-help aid (loans and jobs) averaged $5,891 ($8,764 maximum); non-need-based athletic scholarships averaged $15,601 ($40,228 maximum); and other non-need-based awards and non-need-based scholarships averaged $9,187 ($47,032 maximum). 18% of undergraduate students work part-time. The average financial indebtedness of the 2017 graduate was $20,162. The college's own financial statement is required. The FAFSA code is 001063. The deadline for filing freshman financial aid applications for fall entry is February 15.

UNIVERSITY OF ALASKA SOUTHEAST F-3

www.uas.alaska.edu

Juneau, AK 99801	**(907) 465-6457** **(877) 465-4827**
Fax: (907) 465-6365	**Email: admissions@uas.alaska.edu**
Full-time: 213 men, 364 women	**Faculty:** 103; IIA, -$
Part-time: 173 men, 567 women	**Ph.D.s:** 85%
Graduate: 75 men, 238 women	**Student/Faculty:** 8 to 1
Year: semesters, summer session	**Tuition:** $8415 ($22,550)
Room & Board: $9200	**Freshman Class:** 384 applied, 188 accepted, 162 enrolled
SAT or ACT: recommended	**CEEB CODE:** 4897
Application Deadline: August 1	**COMPETITIVE**

University of Alaska Southeast, a multicampus institution founded in 1972, is part of the University of Alaska statewide system, with baccalaureate programs offered in business and public administration, education, and liberal arts and science. There are 4 undergraduate schools and 2 graduate schools. In addition to regional accreditation, UASE has baccalaureate program accreditation with CAEP. The 198-acre campus is in a suburban area 10 miles north of Juneau. Including any residence halls, there are 18 buildings.

STUDENT LIFE: 75% of undergraduates are from Alaska. Others are from 37 states, 12 foreign countries, and Canada. 95% are from public schools. 8% are two or more races; 7% Asian American; 6% Hispanic; 46% White; 23% race unknown; 2% African American; 11% American Indian/Alaska Native. **Female To Male Ratio:** 2.5:1. The average age of freshmen is 19; all undergraduates, 28. **Housing:** 400 students can be accommodated in college housing, which includes married student dorms and on-campus apartments. On-campus housing is available on a first-come and first-served basis. 66% of students commute. All students may keep cars.

FACULTY/CLASSROOMS: 98% teach undergraduates. No introductory courses are taught by graduate students. The average class size in an introductory lecture is 20 and in a laboratory is 12.

PROGRAMS OF STUDY: UASE confers B.A., B.S., B.B.A., B.Ed., and B.L.A. degrees. Associate and master's degrees are also awarded. Bachelor's degrees are awarded in BIOLOGICAL SCIENCE (biology/biological science and marine biology), BUSINESS (accounting and business administration and management), COMMUNICATIONS AND THE ARTS (art, communications, literature, and speech/debate/rhetoric), COMPUTER AND PHYSICAL SCIENCE (mathematics), EDUCATION (elementary education), ENGINEERING AND ENVIRONMENTAL DESIGN (environmental science), SOCIAL SCIENCE (liberal arts/general studies, political science/government, public administration, and social science). Accounting, marine biology, and environmental science are the strongest academically. Liberal arts has the largest enrollment.

ACTIVITIES: There are no fraternities or sororities. There are 16 groups on campus, including choir, dance, drama, ethnic, honors, international, LGBT, literary magazine, music ensembles, newspaper, political, professional, radio station, religious, and student government. Popular campus events include Ski Day, Whale-watching, and Eagle Preserve Field Trips. **Sports:** There are 3 intramural sports for men and 3 for women. Facilities include an activity center, access to a community gym, pool, and health club facilities. **Graduates:** From July 1, 2016 to June 30, 2017, 166 bachelor's degrees were awarded.

SERVICES: Counseling and information services are available, as is tutoring in most subjects. There is a reader service for the blind, and remedial math, reading, and writing. **Library/Resources:** The library contains 250,000 volumes, 250,000 microform items, and 1,850 audio/video tapes/CDs/DVDs, and subscribes to 1,500 periodicals including electronic. Computerized library services include interlibrary loans, database searching, and Internet access. **Physically Challenged Students:** 95% of the campus is accessible. Facilities include wheelchair ramps, elevators, special parking, specially equipped restrooms, lowered drinking fountains, lowered telephones, and special housing. **Special:** UASE offers cross-registration through the National Student Exchange, and internships with federal and state agencies. Study abroad, work-study, dual and student-designed majors, credit/no credit options, and credit for military experience are also available. The School of Career and Continuing Education offers courses and certificate programs in technological skills. **Visiting:** There are regularly scheduled orientations for prospective students. There are guides for informal visits and visitors may sit in on classes. **Campus Safety and Security:** There are shuttle buses, emergency telephones, lighted pathways/sidewalks, and late-night security.

REQUIREMENTS: The SAT or ACT are recommended. Applicants should be graduates of an accredited secondary school or have the GED. A GPA of 2.0 is required. AP and CLEP credits are accepted. All students are required to complete general education courses, including 15 credits in humanities and social science, 10 in math and natural sciences, 6 in written communication skills, and 3 in speech. A total of 120 semester credits, with at least 36 in the major, and a minimum GPA of 2.0 are required in order to graduate. In the liberal arts program, a portfolio is required. **Procedure:** Freshmen are admitted in the fall and spring. There are early admissions, deferred admissions, and rolling admissions plans. Applications should be filed by August 1 for fall entry. The fall 2017 application fee was $35. **Transfer Students:** 180 transfer students enrolled in 2016-2017. A minimum GPA of 2.0 from an accredited institution is required. 30 of 120 credits required for the bachelor's degree must be completed at UASE. **International Students:** They must take the TOEFL. They must also take the SAT or ACT.

ADMISSIONS: 49% of the 2017-2018 applicants were accepted. **Admissions Contact:** Joe G. Nelson J.D., Vice Chancellor of Enrollment/Student Affairs. Email: *admissions@uas.alaska.edu* Web: *www.uas.alaska.edu*

FINANCIAL AID: The average freshman award was $3,205. Need-based scholarships or need-based grants averaged $6,869; need-based self-help aid (loans and jobs) averaged $2,951; other non-need-based awards and non-need-based scholarships averaged $2,518; and $2,904 from other forms of aid. The average financial indebtedness of the 2017 graduate was $25,090. UASE is a member of CSS. The college's own financial statement is required. The FAFSA code is 001065. The priority date for freshman financial aid applications for fall entry is April 15.

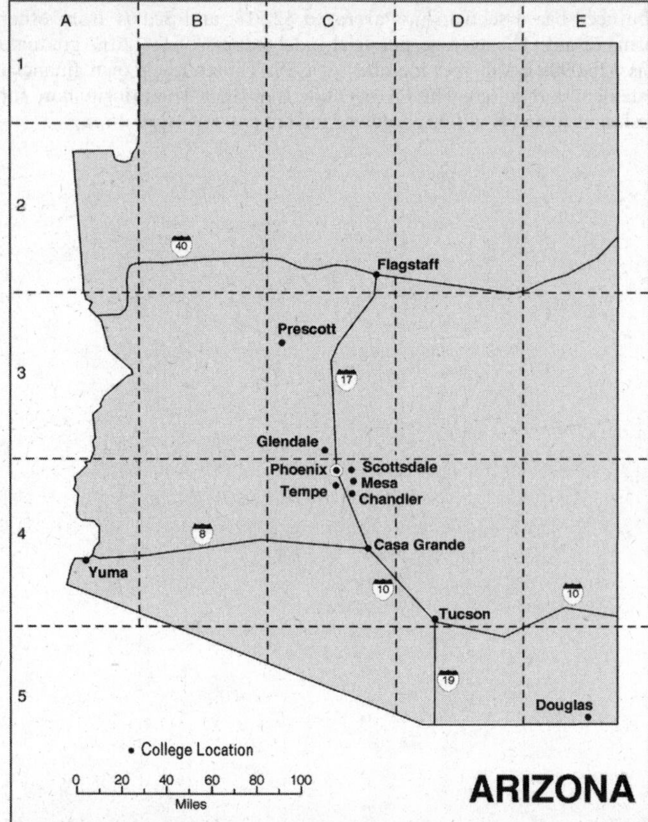

ARIZONA STATE UNIVERSITY AT THE DOWNTOWN PHOENIX CAMPUS C-4

https://campus.asu.edu/downtown-phoenix

Phoenix, AZ 85004 **(480) 965-7788**

Fax: (480) 965-3610	**Email:** admissions@asu.edu
Full-time: 2534 men, 5422 women	**Faculty:** I, --$
Part-time: 355 men, 591 women	**Ph.D.s:** n/av
Graduate: 967 men, 1596 women	**Student/Faculty:** n/av
Year: semesters, summer session	**Tuition:** $10,792 ($27,372)
Room & Board: $13,842	**Freshman Class:** n/av
SAT EBR-W/M: 590/570 **ACT:** 24	**CEEB CODE:** 4007
Application Deadline: February 1	**VERY COMPETITIVE**

Arizona State University's Downtown Phoenix campus, creates strong academic and career connections for students with media, health care, corporate and government organizations. State-of-the-art living and learning facilities offer students a high-quality academic experience woven into the Valley's metropolitan core. U.S. News & World Report recently named ASU the #1 school in the country for innovation for the third year in a row. ASU is a comprehensive public research university, measured not by whom we exclude, but rather by whom we include and how they succeed; advancing research and discovery of public value; and assuming fundamental responsibility for the economic, social, cultural, and overall health of the communities it serves. ASU champions intellectual and cultural diversity. Its research is inspired by real-world application, and blurs the boundaries that traditionally separate academic disciplines. There are 7 undergraduate schools and 6 graduate schools. In addition to regional accreditation, ASU Downtown Phoenix Campus has baccalaureate program accreditation with ACEJMC, CSWE, ACEND, CCNE, COAPRT, and NAACLS. The 18-acre campus is in an urban area in Phoenix, AZ. Including any residence halls, there are 20 buildings.

STUDENT LIFE: 72% of undergraduates are from Arizona. Others are from 36 foreign countries, and Canada. 95% are from public schools. 49% are White; 31% Hispanic; 6% African American; 5% Asian American; 4% two or more races; 2% American Indian/Alaska Native; 2% Foreign; 1% race unknown. **Female To Male Ratio:** 2.0:1. The average age of freshmen is 18; all undergraduates, 22. **Housing:** 1284 students can be accommodated in college housing, which includes dorms and off-campus apartments. In addition, there are special-interest houses, honors are in hall communities, and special interest houses are in groups by major. On-campus housing is guaranteed for the freshman year only, is available on a first-come, first-served basis, and is available on a lottery system for upperclassmen. 83% of students commute. Alcohol is not permitted. All students may keep cars.

FACULTY/CLASSROOMS: No introductory courses are taught by graduate students. The average class size in an introductory lecture is 32; in a laboratory is 20; and in a regular course is 28.

PROGRAMS OF STUDY: ASU Downtown Phoenix Campus confers B.A., B.A.S., B.S., B.S.N., and B.S.W. degrees. Master's and doctoral degrees are also awarded. Bachelor's degrees are awarded in BIOLOGICAL SCIENCE (nutrition), BUSINESS (nonprofit/public organization management and tourism), COMMUNICATIONS AND THE ARTS (communications, journalism & technical communications, and sports media), COMPUTER AND PHYSICAL SCIENCE (applied science), EDUCATION (general studies, health education, and sports and wellness studies), HEALTH PROFESSIONS (community health work, exercise science, health care administration, health science, kinesiology, nursing, and public health), SOCIAL SCIENCE (criminal justice, criminology, interdisciplinary studies, parks and recreation management, social work, and urban and regional studies). Criminology & criminal justice, exercise & wellness, journalism & mass communication have the largest enrollments.

ACTIVITIES: There are no fraternities or sororities. There are 113 groups on campus, including and sports, entrepreneurship, health, technology, art, band, communications, cooking, debate, environmental, ethnic, honors, international, LGBT, musical theater, newspaper, photography, political, professional, radio and TV, religious, social, social service, and student government. Popular campus events include Taylor Fest, Sparky's Carnival, Devils in Disguise, FestDevil, Welcome Back BBQ, Homecoming Dance, Fall Fest, PitchFork Awards, Passport to Phoenix, Spring Bash, Spring Luau, Movies in the Park, and Finals Breakfast. **Sports:** There are 11 intercollegiate sports for men and 15 for women, and 14 intramural sports for men and 14 for women. Facilities include the fitness complex which has weight and fitness areas, with cardiovascular and strength equipment, and multipurpose studios, gymnasium, indoor running track, and a swimming pool. **Graduates:** From July 1, 2016 to June 30, 2017, 2337 bachelor's degrees were awarded. The most popular majors were health professions (21%), parks, recreation, leisure and fitness studies (19%), homeland security, and law enforcement (17%). Of the 2016 graduating class, 16% were enrolled in graduate school within 6 months of graduation, and 85% were employed.

SERVICES: Counseling and information services are available, as is tutoring in most subjects. The University Academic Success Programs offers a range of free academic resources to support students, both in-person and online. Services include: subject area tutoring, writing tutoring, graduate writing tutoring, graduate statistics tutoring, supplemental instruction, and academic mentoring. The Disability Resource Center provides accommodations when needed for tutoring/services, converts print or electronic materials that are not accessible into an accessible format for students who are blind or visually impaired, or who generally have a print related disability. The TRiO student support services provide tutoring on a one-by-one basis. **Library/Resources:** The library contains 4.8 million volumes, 7.8 million microform items, and 180,428 audio/video tapes/CDs/DVDs, and subscribes to 63,322 periodicals including electronic. Computerized library services include interlibrary loans, database searching, Internet access, and Wi-Fi capability. Special learning facilities include a radio station, TV station, writing labs, tutoring, research centers, instructional kitchen, news studio, and news museum. **Physically Challenged Students:** 99% of the campus is accessible. Facilities include wheelchair ramps, elevators, special parking, specially equipped restrooms, special class scheduling, lowered drinking fountains, and special housing. There are flashing alarms for the deaf, modified residence hall rooms and an adaptive exercise program and facility. **Special:** Students on ASU's Downtown Phoenix campus enjoy a variety of academic programs and opportunities to enhance their learning. For example, students in the journalism program produce and broadcast their own televised nightly newscast in an on-campus, state-of-the-art newsroom as part of the Phoenix PBS channel. And nursing students work at the ASU-Mayo Clinic campus, as well as nearby hospitals, gaining practical experience as they help heal patients. Students on the Downtown Phoenix campus can take on an internship in their field of study, as well as have the opportunity to study abroad in 1 of 65 countries, and have the choice such as concurrent degree programs, accelerated degree options, and the selection of 7.5- or 15-week semesters allow students to customize their college experience to exactly what they want it to be. There are 2 national honor societies and a freshman honors program. **Visiting:** There are regularly scheduled orientations for prospective students, and guides for informal visits. To schedule a visit, contact Sean Bryan at visitasu@asu.edu. **Campus Safety and Security:** Measures include 24-hour foot and vehicle patrol, emergency notification system, self-defense education, and security escort services. There are shuttle buses, emergency telephones, lighted pathways/sidewalks, controlled access to dorms/residences, in-room safes, LiveSafe smart phone application; and surveillance cameras in some residence halls.

REQUIREMENTS: The SAT or ACT is recommended. In addition, applicants must successfully complete ASU competency requirement; 4 years each of English (composition/literature based), and math (algebra I, geometry, algebra II and one course requiring algebra II as a prerequisite), 3 years of laboratory science (1 year each from any of the following areas are accepted: biology, chemistry, earth science, integrated sciences, and physics), 2 years each of social science (including one year American history), and second language (same language), and 1 year of fine arts or career and technical education. Applicants must also meet at least one of the following: top 25% in high school graduating class, 3.0 GPA in competency courses (4.0 = A), ACT 22 (24 nonresidents), SAT 1120 (1180 nonresidents). Admission may be granted with one deficiency in no more than two competency areas. Deficiencies cannot be in both math and laboratory science. Students must earn a minimum 2.00 in any subject area. Most competencies may also be met by test scores or college courses. ASU admission decisions begin the first week of Sept. 1. Submission of an ACT or SAT score is highly recommended for merit-based scholarship consideration. Some schools and colleges have higher requirements for admission to their majors. All students who don't meet the above standards will be evaluated through a process called Individual Review. Through this process Admission Services will review all available information about a student's application, carefully considering all aspects of a student's academic background and accomplishments. In some cases, additional information might be requested. ASU welcomes home school students and recognizes the unique academic experiences they contribute to our rich community of scholars. Students may also meet admission requirements by submitting an official GED score of 500 or above for tests taken before Jan. 2014 or a GED score of 170 or above for tests taken after Jan. 2014. A GPA of 3.0 is required. AP and CLEP credits are accepted. To receive a degree from Arizona State University, students must have a minimum cumulative grade point average of 2.00 (though some programs may require a higher GPA) and a minimum total of 120 credit hours, including a minimum of 45 hours of upper-division coursework. The number of hours in the major varies by degree program, and some programs may require more upper-division work. All students must satisfy a minimum of 29 credit hours of approved General Studies coursework in five core areas as well as six credits in literacy (three credit hours) and humanities, art and design/social-behavioral sciences (three credit hours) at the upper division level. **Procedure:** Freshmen are admitted fall and spring. There are deferred admissions and rolling admissions plans. Applications should be filed by February 1 for fall entry; November 1 for spring entry. The fall 2017 application fee was $50. Notification is sent on a rolling basis. Applications are accepted on-line. **Transfer Students:** 895 transfer students enrolled in 2016-2017. Requirements for general admission to Arizona State University: applicant must meet one of the following requirements (1) graduated from high school, (2) earned a GED, (3) completed an associate degree or be in progress toward an associate degree. Transfer students must meet one of the following requirements: less than 24 transferable credit hours - minimum 2.50 cumulative GPA and meet freshman aptitude requirements; 24 or more transferable credit hours - minimum 2.50 cumulative GPA; AGEC from an Arizona community college with a 2.00 or higher cumulative GPA; associate degree from a regionally accredited higher education institution with - 2.00 or higher cumulative GPA (residents) or 2.50 or higher cumulative GPA (nonresidents). "A" = 4.0; ASU accepts transfer college-level courses in which you have earned a "C-" or better. 30 of 120 credits required for the bachelor's degree must be completed at ASU Downtown Phoenix campus. **International Students:** There are 172 international students enrolled. They must take the TOEFL with a minimum score of 500 on the paper-based TOEFL (PBT) or 61 on the Internet-based version (iBT), International English Language Testing Systems (IELTS); Pearson Tesk of English (PTE). They must also take the SAT or ACT.

ADMISSIONS: The SAT scores for the 2017-2018 freshman class were: Math-- 12% below 500, 51% between 500 and 599, 32% between 600 and 699, and 6% between 700 and 800. Evidence-Based Reading/Writing-- 9% below 500, 42% between 500 and 599, 43% between 600 and 699, and 6% between 700 and 800. The ACT scores were 7% between 12 and 17, 42% between 18 and 23, 44% between 24 and 29, and 8% above 30. 62% of the current freshmen were in the top fifth of their class; 88% were in the top two fifths. **Admissions Contact:** Melissa Pizzo, Dean of Admissions and Financial Aid. Email: *admissions@asu.edu* Web: *https:/campus.asu.edu/downtown-phoenix*

FINANCIAL AID: The FAFSA code is 001081. The priority date for freshman financial aid applications for fall entry is January 1.

ARIZONA STATE UNIVERSITY AT THE POLYTECHNIC CAMPUS — C-4

https://campus.asu.edu/polytechnic

Mesa, AZ 85212 — **(480) 965-7788**

Fax: (480) 965-3610	**Email: admissions@asu.edu**
Full-time: 2544 men, 1139 women	**Faculty:** IIA, -$
Part-time: 387 men, 169 women	**Ph.D.s:** n/av
Graduate: 376 men, 194 women	**Student/Faculty:** n/av
Year: semesters, summer session	**Tuition:** $10,301 ($26,038)
Room & Board: $12,093	**Freshman Class:** n/av
SAT EBR-W/M: 590/600 **ACT:** 24	**CEEB CODE:** 4007
Application Deadline: February 1	**VERY COMPETITIVE**

Arizona State University's Polytechnic campus is home to a tight-knit academic community in the fields of interdisciplinary science, engineering and technology, management and business, education, and liberal arts. U.S. News & World Report recently named ASU the #1 school in the country for innovation for the third year in a row. ASU is a comprehensive public research university, measured not by whom we exclude, but rather by whom we include and how they succeed; advancing research and discovery of public value; and assuming fundamental responsibility for the economic, social, cultural and overall health of the communities it serves. ASU champions intellectual and cultural diversity. Its research is inspired by real-world application, and blurs the boundaries that traditionally separate academic disciplines. There are 7 undergraduate schools and 4 graduate schools. In addition to regional accreditation, ASU Polytechnic Campus has baccalaureate program accreditation with ABET, AABI, CAC, and EAC. The 575-acre campus is in a suburban area in Mesa, AZ. Including any residence halls, there are 93 buildings.

STUDENT LIFE: 72% of undergraduates are from Arizona. Others are from 52 foreign countries, and Canada. 94% are from public schools. 53% are White; 21% Hispanic; 8% Foreign; 6% Asian American; 5% African American; 5% two or more races; 1% American Indian/Alaska Native; 1% race unknown. **Male To Female Ratio:** 2.2:1. The average age of freshmen is 18; all undergraduates, 23. **Housing:** 1197 students can be accommodated in college housing, which includes married student dorms. In addition, there are honors houses, special-interest houses, on-campus houses available; honors are in hall communities; special interest houses are residential college model which accomodates students in housing grouped by major. On-campus housing is guaranteed for the freshman year only, is available on a first-come, first-served basis, and is available on a lottery system for upperclassmen. 77% of students commute. Alcohol is not permitted. All students may keep cars.

FACULTY/CLASSROOMS: No introductory courses are taught by graduate students.

PROGRAMS OF STUDY: ASU Polytechnic Campus confers B.A., B.A.E., B.A.S., B.S., and B.S.E degrees. Master's and doctoral degrees are also awarded. Bachelor's degrees are awarded in AGRICULTURE (environmental studies), BUSINESS (business administration and management, environment & natnl resource economics, information & communication technology, management, and organizational leadership and management), COMMUNICATIONS AND THE ARTS (communications, English, and technical communication), COMPUTER AND PHYSICAL SCIENCE (applied mathematics, applied physics, applied science, science technology, and software engineering), EDUCATION (educational studies, elementary education, secondary education, and special education), ENGINEERING AND ENVIRONMENTAL DESIGN (aeronautical technology, air traffic management, electrical/electronics engineering technology, engineering, graphic arts technology, manufacturing engineering, mechanical engineering technology, and technological management), SOCIAL SCIENCE (counseling/psychology, history, industrial and organizational psychology, interdisciplinary studies, liberal arts/general studies, political science/government, and psychology). Engineering, software engineering, and business have the largest enrollments.

ACTIVITIES: There are no fraternities or sororities. There are 81 groups on campus, including art, band, computers, dance, drama, environmental, ethnic, film, honors, international, LGBT, newspaper, photography, professional, religious, social, social service, and student government. Popular campus events include Walter Carter Memorial Fun Run, Blues & BBQ, Devils Royale, Zombie Run, Boo Bash & Polyween, Boat Races, Innovation Showcase, Finals Breakfast, Borderlands, Hunger Banquet, Peace Luncheon, World Food Fest, Gamecon, Club Hub, Spring Involvement Fair. **Sports:** There are 11 intercollegiate sports for men and 15 for women, and 15 intramural sports for men and 15 for women. Facilities include the fitness complex has a recreation space with basketball/badminton/volleyball courts, racquetball courts, tennis courts, sand volleyball courts, multipurpose soccer fields, softball field, cardio and strength equipment, bike co-op and a heated pool. **Graduates:** From July 1, 2016 to June 30, 2017, 806 bachelor's degrees were awarded. The most popular majors were engineering (28%), biological and biomedical sciences (15%), business, and management and marketing (14%). Of the 2016 graduating class, 13% were enrolled in graduate school within 6 months of graduation, and 83% were employed.

SERVICES: Counseling and information services are available, as is tutoring in most subjects. ASU's University Academic Success Programs offers a range of free academic resources to support ASU students, both in-person and online. Services include: subject area tutoring, writing tutoring, graduate writing tutoring, graduate statistics tutoring, Supplemental Instruction (structured study groups), and academic mentoring (a peer mentoring program). ASU's Disability Resource Center (DRC) provides accommodations when needed for tutoring/services that the university provides. The DRC converts print or electronic materials that are not accessible into an accessible format for students who are blind or visually impaired, or who generally have a print related disability which includes learning disabilities. TRiO student support services (extended to those who are accepted into the TRiO program) provide tutoring on a one-by-one basis. **Library/Resources:** The library contains 4.8 million volumes, 7.8 million microform items, and 180,428 audio/video tapes/CDs/DVDs, and subscribes to 63,322 periodicals including electronic. Computerized library services include interlibrary loans, database searching, Internet access, and Wi-Fi capability. **Physically Challenged Students:** 99% of the campus is accessible. Facilities include wheelchair ramps, elevators, special parking, specially equipped restrooms, special class scheduling, lowered drinking fountains, special housing. There are flashing alarms for the deaf, modified residence hall rooms and an adaptive exercise program and facility. **Special:** Students on ASU's Polytechnic campus enjoy a variety of academic programs and opportunities to enhance their learning. For example, students in the aviation and air traffic control programs hone their flying skills in on-campus flight simulators and log flight hours at the adjacent Phoenix-Mesa Gateway Airport. Engineering students work in labs like the ASU Startup Labs, filled with equipment such as 3-D printers, laser cutters, CNC routers and more. Students on the Polytechnic campus can take on an internship in their field of study, as well as have the opportunity to study abroad in one of 55 countries. There are choices such as concurrent degree programs, accelerated degree options, and the selection of 7.5- or 15-week semesters allow students to customize their college experience to exactly what they want it to be. There is 1 national honor society and a freshman honors program. **Visiting:** There are regularly scheduled orientations for prospective students, and guides for informal visits. To schedule a visit, contact Bernadette DiStasi at visitasu@asu.edu. **Campus Safety and Security:** Measures include 24-hour foot and vehicle patrol, emergency notification system, self-defense education, and security escort services. There are shuttle buses, emergency telephones, lighted pathways/sidewalks, controlled access to dorms/residences, in-room safes, LiveSafe smart phone application; and surveillance cameras in some residence halls.

REQUIREMENTS: The SAT or ACT is recommended. Applicants must successfully complete ASU competency requirement; 4 years each of English (composition/literature based), and math (algebra I, geometry, algebra II and one course requiring algebra II as a prerequisite), 3 years of laboratory science (1 year each from any of the following areas are accepted: biology, chemistry, earth science, integrated sciences, and physics), 2 years each of social science (including one year American history), and second language (same language), and 1 year of fine arts or career and technical education. Applicants must also meet at least one of the following: top 25% in high school graduating class, 3.0 GPA in competency courses (4.0 = A), ACT 22 (24 nonresidents), SAT 1120 (1180 nonresidents). Admission may be granted with one deficiency in no more than two competency areas. Deficiencies cannot be in both math and laboratory science. Students must earn a minimum 2.00 in any subject area. Most competencies may also be met by test scores or college courses. ASU admission decisions begin the first week of September 1. Submission of an ACT or SAT score is highly recommended for merit-based scholarship consideration. Some schools and colleges have higher requirements for admission to their majors. All students who don't meet the above standards will be evaluated through a process called Individual Review. Through this process Admission Services will review all available information about a student's application, carefully considering all aspects of a student's academic background and accomplishments. In some cases, additional information might be requested. ASU welcomes home school students and recognizes the unique academic experiences they contribute to our rich community of scholars. Students may also meet admission requirements by submitting an official GED score of 500 or above for tests taken before Jan. 2014 or a GED score of 170 or above for tests taken after Jan. 2014. A GPA of 3.0 is required. AP and CLEP credits are accepted. To receive a degree from Arizona State University, students must have a minimum cumulative grade point average of 2.00 (though some programs may require a higher GPA) and a minimum total of 120 credit hours, including a minimum of 45 hours of upper-division coursework. The number of hours in the major varies by degree program, and some programs may require more upper-division work. All students must satisfy a minimum of 29 credit hours of approved General Studies coursework in five core areas as well as six credits in literacy (three credit hours) and humanities, art and design/social-behavioral sciences (three credit hours) at the upper division level. **Procedure:** Freshmen are admitted fall and spring. There are deferred admissions and rolling admissions plans. Application deadlines are open. The fall 2017 application fee was $50. Notification is sent on a rolling basis. Applications are accepted on-line. **Transfer Students:** 495 transfer students enrolled in 2016-2017. Requirements for general admission to Arizona State University: applicant must meet one of the following requirements (1) graduated from high school, (2) earned a GED, (3) completed an associate degree or be in progress toward an associate degree. Transfer students must meet one of the following requirements: less than 24 transferable credit hours - minimum 2.50 cumulative GPA and meet freshman aptitude requirements; 24 or more transferable credit hours - minimum 2.50 cumulative GPA; AGEC from an Arizona community college with a 2.00 or higher cumulative GPA; associate degree from a regionally accredited higher education institution with - 2.00 or higher cumulative GPA (residents) or 2.50 or higher cumulative GPA (nonresidents). "A" = 4.0; ASU accepts transfer college-level courses in which you have earned a "C-" or better. 30 of 120 credits required for the bachelor's degree must be completed at ASU Polytechnic Campus. **International Students:** There are 331 international students enrolled. They must take the TOEFL with a minimum score of 500 on the paper-based TOEFL (PBT) or 61 on the Internet-based version (iBT), International English Language Testing Systems (IELTS); Pearson Tesk of English (PTE). The SAT or ACT is required for some students.

ADMISSIONS: The SAT scores for the 2017-2018 freshman class were: Math-- 7% below 500, 42% between 500 and 599, 37% between 600 and 699, and 14% between 700 and 800. Evidence-Based Reading/Writing-- 7% below 500, 46% between 500 and 599, 41% between 600 and 699, and 7% between 700 and 800. The ACT scores were 2% between 12 and 17, 44% between 18 and 23, 39% between 24 and 29, and 15% above 30. 43% of the current freshmen were in the top fifth of their class; 76% were in the top two fifths. **Admissions Contact:** Melissa Pizzo, Dean of Admissions and Financial Aid. Email: *admissions@asu.edu* Web: *https:/campus.asu.edu/polytechnic*

FINANCIAL AID: The FAFSA code is 001081. The priority date for freshman financial aid applications for fall entry is January 1.

ARIZONA STATE UNIVERSITY AT THE TEMPE CAMPUS C-4

www.asu.edu

Tempe, AZ 85287 **(480) 965-7788**

Fax: (480) 965-3610
Email: admissions@asu.edu
Full-time: 21,868 men, 16,946 women
Faculty: I, av$
Part-time: 2193 men, 1420 women
Ph.D.s: n/av
Graduate: 5049 men, 3688 women
Student/Faculty: n/av
Year: semesters, summer session
Tuition: $10,792 ($27,372)
Room & Board: $12,209
Freshman Class: n/av
SAT EBR-W/M: 610/620 **ACT:** 25
CEEB CODE: 4007
Application Deadline: February 1
VERY COMPETITIVE

Arizona State University's Tempe campus welcomes students pursuing a wide range of majors including business, liberal arts, engineering and the sciences. Modern classrooms and high-tech laboratories offer a creative and engaging learning environment on this historic college campus. ASU was named the #1 school in the country for innovation for the third year in a row by U.S. News & World Report, and the top public university in the U.S. for international students by the Institute of International Education. ASU is a comprehensive public research university, measured not by whom we exclude, but rather by whom we include and how they succeed; advancing research and discovery of public value; and assuming fundamental responsibility for the economic, social, cultural and overall health of the communities it serves. ASU champions intellectual and cultural diversity. Its research is inspired by real-world application, and blurs the boundaries that traditionally separate academic disciplines. There are 10 undergraduate schools and 9 graduate schools. In addition to regional accreditation, ASU Tempe Campus has baccalaureate program accreditation with AACSB, ABET, ACCE, NAAB, NASAD, NASM, AABI, CAC, CIDA, and LAAB. The 661-acre campus is in an urban area in Tempe, AZ. Including any residence halls, there are 221 buildings.

STUDENT LIFE: 66% of undergraduates are from Arizona. Others are from 116 foreign countries, and Canada. 93% are from public schools. 50% are White; 21% Hispanic; 13% Foreign; 7% Asian American; 4% African American; 4% two or more races; 1% American Indian/Alaska Native; 1% race unknown. **Male To Female Ratio:** 1.3:1. The average age of freshmen is 18; all undergraduates, 21. **Housing:** 11653 students can be accommodated in college housing, which includes dorms, on-campus apartments, and off-campus apartments. In addition, there are honors houses, special-interest houses, fraternity houses, sorority houses, honors are in hall communities; special interest houses are residential college model which accomodates students in housing grouped by major. On-campus housing is guaranteed for the freshman year only, and is available on a first-come, first-served basis, and is available on a lottery system for upperclassmen. 78% of students commute. Alcohol is not permitted. All students may keep cars.

FACULTY/CLASSROOMS: No introductory courses are taught by graduate students. The average class size in an introductory lecture is 37; in a laboratory is 23; and in a regular course is 34.

PROGRAMS OF STUDY: ASU Tempe Campus confers B.A., B.A.E., B.F.A., B.Mus., B.S., B.S.D., B.S.E., B.S.LA., and B.S.P. degrees. Master's and doctoral degrees are also awarded. Bachelor's degrees are awarded in AGRICULTURE (environmental studies), BIOLOGICAL SCIENCE (biochemistry, biological sciences, biophysics, microbiology, and molecular biology), BUSINESS (accounting, business administration and management, finance, management, marketing/retailing/merchandising, and supply chain management), COMMUNICATIONS AND THE ARTS (art, communications, composition, dance, design, English, film arts, French, German, graphic design, industrial design, Italian, music, music performance, musical theater, performing arts, Russian, Spanish, theatre arts, and visual and performing arts), COMPUTER AND PHYSICAL SCIENCE (actuarial science, applied mathematics, chemistry, computer information systems, computer science, earth science, earth & space science, informatics and computer science, mathematics, and physics), EDUCATION (Asian studies, early childhood education, education, educational studies, elementary education, general studies, music education, secondary education, and special education), ENGINEERING AND ENVIRONMENTAL DESIGN (aerospace engineering, biomedical engineering, chemical engineering, civil engineering, computational sciences, construction engineering, construction management, electrical/electronics engineering, engineering management, environmental design, environmental engineering, industrial engineering, interior design, landscape architecture, materials science, and mechanical engineering), HEALTH PROFESSIONS (music therapy and speech pathology/audiology), SOCIAL SCIENCE (African American studies, American Indian studies, anthropology, architectural studies, Asian/American studies, economics, geography, geography information science, history, human development, interdisciplinary studies, Judaic studies, Latin American studies, philosophy, political science/government, psychology, religious studies, sociology, urban studies, and women & gender studies). Business, computer science, and biological science have the largest enrollments.

ACTIVITIES: 10% of men belong to 45 national fraternities; 17% of women belong to 28 national sororities. There are 852 groups on campus, including and sports, health, technology, art, band, cheerleading, chess, choir, chorale, chorus, communications, computers, dance, debate, drama, drill team, entrepreneurship, environmental, ethnic, film, forensics, honors, international, jazz band, LGBT, literary magazine, marching band, musical theater, newspaper, opera, orchestra, pep band, photography, political, professional, radio and TV, religious, social, social service, student government, and symphony. Popular campus events include Devils on Mill, Sorority and Fraternity Recruitment, Passport to ASU, Homecoming, MU After Dark, MU Takeover, Finals Breakfast, Sun Devils UNITE, and Devilpalooza. **Sports:** There are 11 intercollegiate sports for men and 15 for women, and 23 intramural sports for men and 23 for women. Facilities include the fitness complex consists of indoor activity space, outdoor fields, sand volleyball courts and aquatics center, weight and fitness areas with cardiovascular and strength equipment and free weights, multipurpose studios, indoor and outdoor tracks, a multi-activity court gymnasium, softball and baseball stadiums, athletic centers, golf course, aquatic complex, wrestling complex, soccer stadium, gymnastics training facility, track fields, football stadium, basketball arena, and tennis center. **Graduates:** From July 1, 2016 to June 30, 2017, 9366 bachelor's degrees were awarded. The most popular majors were business, management, and marketing (26%), engineering (12%), and social science (9%). Of the 2016 graduating class, 17% were enrolled in graduate school within 6 months of graduation, and 81% were employed.

SERVICES: Counseling and information services are available, as is tutoring in most subjects. ASU's University Academic Success Programs offers a range of free academic resources to support ASU students, both in-person and online. Services include: subject area tutoring, writing tutoring, Supplemental Instruction (structured study groups), and academic mentoring (a peer mentoring program). ASU's Disability Resource Center (DRC) provides accommodations when needed for tutoring/services that the university provides. The DRC converts print or electronic materials that are not accessible into an accessible format for students who are blind or visually impaired, or who generally have a print related disability which includes learning disabilities. TRiO student support services (extended to those who are accepted into the TRiO program) provide tutoring on a one-by-one basis. **Library/Resources:** The library contains 4.8 million volumes, 7.8 million microform items, and 180,428 audio/video tapes/CDs/DVDs, and subscribes to 63,322 periodicals including electronic. Computerized library services include interlibrary loans, database searching, Internet access, and Wi-Fi capability. Special learning facilities include an art gallery, natural history museum, planetarium, radio station, museums, galleries, collections, research labs, digital labs, art, dance and development studios, and research institutes. **Physically Challenged Students:** 99% of the campus is accessible. Facilities include wheelchair ramps, elevators, special parking, specially equipped restrooms, special class scheduling, lowered drinking fountains, special housing. There are flashing alarms for the deaf, modified residence hall rooms and an adaptive exercise program and facility. **Special:** Students on ASU's Tempe campus enjoy a variety of academic programs and opportunities to enhance their learning. For example, Tempe campus is home to the first school entirely dedicated to undergraduate and graduate degrees and research in sustainability. And engineering, design and arts students have access to InnovationSpace, a sustainable product-development program. Students also have opportunities to participate in pioneering research in the Biodesign Institute and other centers, perform in Frank Lloyd Wright-designed ASU Gammage, and to pursue entrepreneurial interests through innovative programs embedded in each college. All students on the Tempe campus can take on an internship in their field of study, as well as have the opportunity to study abroad in one of 65 countries. And choices such as concurrent degree programs, accelerated degree options, and the selection of 7.5- or 15-week semesters allow students to customize their college experience to exactly what they want it to be. There are 26 national honor societies, including Phi Beta Kappa, and a freshman honors program. **Visiting:** There are regularly scheduled orientations for prospective students. There are guides for informal visits. To schedule a visit, contact Lizeth Hill at (480) 727-7013. **Campus Safety and Security:** Measures include 24-hour foot and vehicle patrol, emergency notification system, self-defense education, and security escort services. There are shuttle buses, emergency telephones, lighted pathways/sidewalks, controlled access to dorms/residences, in-room safes, LiveSafe smart phone application; and surveillance cameras in some residence halls.

REQUIREMENTS: The SAT or ACT is recommended. Applicants must successfully complete ASU competency requirement; 4 years each of English (composition/literature based), and math (algebra I, geometry, algebra II and one course requiring algebra II as a prerequisite), 3 years of laboratory science (1 year each from any of the following areas are accepted: biology, chemistry, earth science, integrated sciences, and physics), 2 years each of social science (including one year American history), and second language (same language), and 1 year of fine arts or career and technical education. Applicants must also meet at least one of the following: top 25% in high school graduating class, 3.0 GPA in competency courses (4.0 = A), ACT 22 (24 nonresidents), SAT 1120 (1180 nonresidents). Admission may be granted with one deficiency in no more than two competency areas. Deficiencies cannot be in both math and laboratory science. Students must earn a minimum 2.00 in any subject area. Most competencies may also be met by test scores or college courses. ASU admission decisions begin the first week of Sept. 1. Submission of an ACT or SAT score is highly recommended for merit-based scholarship consideration. Some schools and colleges have higher requirements for admission to their majors. All students who don't meet the above standards will be evaluated through a process called Individual Review. Through this process Admission Services will review all available information about a student's application, carefully considering all aspects of a student's academic background and accomplishments. In some cases, additional information might be requested. ASU welcomes home school students and recognizes the unique academic experiences they contribute to our rich community of scholars. Students may also meet admission requirements by submitting an official GED score of 500 or above for tests taken before Jan. 2014 or a GED score of 170 or above for tests taken after Jan. 2014. A GPA of 3.0 is required. AP and CLEP credits are accepted. To receive a degree from Arizona State University, students must have a minimum cumulative grade point average of 2.00 (though some programs may require a higher GPA) and a minimum total of 120 credit hours, including a minimum of 45 hours of upper-division coursework. The number of hours in the major varies by degree program, and some programs may require more upper-division work. All students must satisfy a minimum of 29 credit hours of approved General Studies coursework in five core areas as well as six credits in literacy (three credit hours) and humanities, art and design/social-behavioral sciences (three credit hours) at the upper division level. **Procedure:** Freshmen are admitted fall and spring. There are deferred admissions and rolling admissions plans. Application deadlines are open. The fall 2017 application fee was $50. Notification is sent on a rolling basis. Applications are accepted on-line. **Transfer Students:** 2897 transfer students enrolled in 2016-2017. Requirements for general admission to Arizona State University: applicant must meet one of the following requirements (1) graduated from high school, (2) earned a GED, (3) completed an associate degree or be in progress toward an associate degree. Transfer students must meet one of the following requirements: less than 24 transferable credit hours - minimum 2.50 cumulative GPA and meet freshman aptitude requirements; 24 or more transferable credit hours - minimum 2.50 cumulative GPA; AGEC from an Arizona community college with a 2.00 or higher cumulative GPA; associate degree from a regionally accredited higher education institution with - 2.00 or higher cumulative GPA (residents) or 2.50 or higher cumulative GPA (nonresidents). "A" = 4.0; ASU accepts transfer college-level courses in which you have earned a "C-" or better. 30 of 120 credits required for the bachelor's degree must be completed at ASU Tempe campus. **International Students:** There are 5110 international students enrolled. They must take the TOEFL with a minimum score of 500 on the paper-based TOEFL (PBT) or 61 on the Internet-based version (iBT), International English Language Testing Systems (IELTS); Pearson Tesk of English (PTE). SAT or ACT is required for the W.P. Carey school of business.

ADMISSIONS: The SAT scores for the 2017-2018 freshman class were: Math-- 5% below 500, 35% between 500 and 599, 42% between 600 and 699, and 18% between 700 and 800. Evidence-Based Reading/Writing-- 6% below 500, 35% between 500 and 599, 44% between 600 and 699, and 14% between 700 and 800. The ACT scores were 3% between 12 and 17, 30% between 18 and 23, 47% between 24 and 29, and 20% above 30. 56% of the current freshmen were in the top fifth of their class; 82% were in the top two fifths. **Admissions Contact:** Melissa Pizzo , Dean of Admissions and Financial Aid. Email: *admissions@asu.edu* Web: *www.asu.edu*

FINANCIAL AID: The FAFSA code is 001081. The priority date for freshman financial aid applications for fall entry is January 1.

ARIZONA STATE UNIVERSITY AT THE WEST CAMPUS — C-4

https://campus.asu.edu/west

Glendale, AZ 85036 — **(480) 965-7788**

Fax: (480) 965-3610	**Email: admissions@asu.edu**
Full-time: 1217 men, 1861 women	**Faculty:** IIA, av$
Part-time: 257 men, 295 women	**Ph.D.s:** n/av
Graduate: 123 men, 310 women	**Student/Faculty:** n/av
Year: semesters, summer session	**Tuition:** $10,301 ($26,038)
Room & Board: $11,212	**Freshman Class:** n/av
SAT EBR-W/M: 580/550 **ACT:** 22	**CEEB CODE:** 4007
Application Deadline: February 1	**VERY COMPETITIVE**

Arizona State University's West campus welcomes students studying business, education, and interdisciplinary arts and sciences. Undergraduate and graduate programs offer the resources of one of the top public research universities in the country within a community-based learning environment. Patterned after the University of Oxford's architecture, this inviting campus creates a close-knit community. Students become master learners, capable of learning anything throughout their lives, on this classic style campus. U.S. News & World Report recently named ASU the #1 school in the country for innovation for the third year in a row. ASU is a comprehensive public research university, measured not by whom we exclude, but rather by whom we include and how they succeed; advancing research and discovery of public value; and assuming fundamental responsibility for the economic, social, cultural and overall health of the communities it serves. ASU champions intellectual and cultural diversity. Its research is inspired by real-world application, and blurs the boundaries that traditionally separate academic disciplines. There are 8 undergraduate schools and 3 graduate schools. In addition to regional accreditation, ASU West Campus has baccalaureate program accreditation with CSWE. The 278-acre campus is in an urban area in Phoenix, AZ. Including any residence halls, there are 26 buildings.

STUDENT LIFE: 83% of undergraduates are from Arizona. Others are from 30 foreign countries, and Canada. 97% are from public schools. 46% are White; 32% Hispanic; 6% Foreign; 5% African American; 5% Asian American; 4% two or more races; 1% American Indian/Alaska Native; 1% race unknown. **Female To Male Ratio:** 1.5:1. The average age of freshmen is 18; all undergraduates, 23. **Housing:** 617 students can be accommodated in college housing, which includes dorms and on-campus apartments. In addition, there are honors houses, special-interest houses, honors are in hall communities. Special interest houses group students by major. On-campus housing is guaranteed for the freshman year only, and is available on a first-come, first-served basis, and is available on a lottery system for upperclassmen. 86% of students commute. Alcohol is not permitted. All students may keep cars.

FACULTY/CLASSROOMS: No introductory courses are taught by graduate students. The average class size in an introductory lecture is 32; in a laboratory is 21; and in a regular course is 28.

PROGRAMS OF STUDY: ASU West Campus confers B.A., B.A.E., B.A.S., B.G.M., B.S., and B.S.W. degrees. Master's and doctoral degrees are also awarded. Bachelor's degrees are awarded in BIOLOGICAL SCIENCE (forensic science), BUSINESS (accounting, business administration and management, global/general management, and management), COMMUNICATIONS AND THE ARTS (communications, English, and Spanish), COMPUTER AND PHYSICAL SCIENCE (applied mathematics, applied science, and statistics), EDUCATION (educational studies, elementary education, secondary education, and special education), ENGINEERING AND ENVIRONMENTAL DESIGN (environmental science), HEALTH PROFESSIONS (biology, community health work, health care administration, health science, and pharmacology), SOCIAL SCIENCE (criminal justice, criminology, ethnic studies, history, interdisciplinary studies, Latin American studies, philosophy and religion, political science/government, psychology, social science, social work, sociology, women & gender studies, and women's studies). Business, psychology, and biology have the largest enrollments.

ACTIVITIES: There are no fraternities or sororities. There are 76 groups on campus, including art, chess, choir, chorale, chorus, communications, computers, dance, debate, drama, environmental, ethnic, film, forensics, honors, international, LGBT, musical theater, newspaper, political, professional, radio and TV, religious, social, social service, and student government. Popular campus events include Solera, Sophomore Serve, Pow Wow, Fiesta Patrias, MLK Mark on West, Spa Night, Rec Ignite, West Fest, Sparky's Carnival & Fun Run, Finals Breakfast, Borderlands Produce Rescue, Dodgeball Tournament, Global Fest, and Pioneer Award Dinner, Gumbo Chall. **Sports:** There are 11 intercollegiate sports for men and 15 for women, and 10 intramural sports for men and 10 for women. Facilities include a free weight fitness area, a two-court gymnasium, a weight machine area, a cardio loft, racquetball courts, basketball courts, indoor running track, and multipurpose studios for group fitness, mind/body classes, and student sport/activity clubs. There is also a wellness space, social gaming area, and a multi-lane pool. Outside of the complex are sand volleyball courts, outdoor basketball courts, softball field, a green quad for campus activities, and a 6-acre multipurpose field, which hosts intramural and sport club programs. **Graduates:** From July 1, 2016 to June 30, 2017, 858 bachelor's degrees were awarded. The most popular majors were business, management, and marketing (21%), psychology (18%), and education (15%). Of the 2016 graduating class, 18% were enrolled in graduate school within 6 months of graduation, and 81% were employed.

SERVICES: Counseling and information services are available, as is tutoring in most subjects. ASU's University Academic Success Programs offers a range of free academic resources to support ASU students, both in-person and online. Services include: subject area tutoring, writing tutoring, graduate writing tutoring, graduate statistics tutoring, Supplemental Instruction (structured study groups), and academic mentoring (a peer mentoring program). ASU's Disability Resource Center (DRC) provides accommodations when needed for tutoring/services that the university provides. The DRC converts print or electronic materials that are not accessible into an accessible format for students who are blind or visually impaired, or who generally have a print related disability which includes learning disabilities. TRiO student support services (extended to those who are accepted into the TRiO program) provides tutoring as well that is 1 on 1. **Library/Resources:** The library contains 4.8 million volumes, 7.8 million microform items, and 180,428 audio/video tapes/CDs/DVDs, and subscribes to 63,322 periodicals including electronic. Computerized library services include interlibrary loans, database searching, Internet access, and Wi-Fi capability. Special learning facilities include an art gallery, radio station, Herberger Young Scholars Academy-school for 7th grade thru 12th grade, art collections, galleries, dance studios, little theatre/black box, Communications Assessment Learning Lab, research labs, digital labs, music labs, cooking labs, performing arts studios, and writing labs. **Physically Challenged Students:** 99% of the campus is accessible. Facilities include wheelchair ramps, elevators, special parking, specially equipped restrooms, special class scheduling, lowered telephones, special housing. There are flashing alarms for the deaf, modified residence hall rooms and an adaptive exercise program and facility. **Special:** Students on ASU's West campus enjoy a variety of academic programs and opportunities to enhance their learning. For example, West campus is home to the first undergraduate degree to be offered by the renowned Thunderbird School of Global Management. And forensic science majors evaluate and process simulated crime scenes. Students on the West campus can take on an internship in their field of study, as well as have the opportunity to study abroad in one of 65 countries. Choices include concurrent degree programs, accelerated degree options, and the selection of 7.5- or 15-week semesters allowing students to customize their college experience to exactly what they want it to be. There are 2 national honor societies and a freshman honors program. **Visiting:** There are regularly scheduled orientations for prospective students. There are guides for informal visits. To schedule a visit, contact Angela Huizar at visitasu@asu.edu. **Campus Safety and Security:** Measures include 24-hour foot and vehicle patrol, emergency notification system, self-defense education, and security escort services. There are shuttle buses, emergency telephones, lighted pathways/sidewalks, controlled access to dorms/residences, in-room safes, LiveSafe smart phone application; and surveillance cameras in some residence halls.

REQUIREMENTS: The SAT or ACT is recommended. Applicants must also successfully complete ASU competency requirement; 4 years each of English (composition/literature based), and math (algebra I, geometry, algebra II and one course requiring algebra II as a prerequisite), 3 years of laboratory science (1 year each from any of the following areas are accepted: biology, chemistry, earth science, integrated sciences, and physics), 2 years each of social science (including one year American history), and second language (same language), and 1 year of fine arts or career and technical education. Applicants must also meet at least one of the following: top 25% in high school graduating class, 3.0 GPA in competency courses (4.0 = A), ACT 22 (24 nonresidents), SAT 1120 (1180 nonresidents). Admission may be granted with one deficiency in no more than two competency areas. Deficiencies cannot be in both math and laboratory science. Students must earn a minimum 2.00 in any subject area. Most competencies may also be met by test scores or college courses. ASU admission decisions begin the first week of Sept. 1. Submission of an ACT or SAT score is highly recommended for merit-based scholarship consideration. Some schools and colleges have higher requirements for admission to their majors. All students who don't meet the above standards will be evaluated through a process called Individual Review. Through this process Admission Services will review all available information about a student's application, carefully considering all aspects of a student's academic background and accomplishments. In some cases, additional information might be requested. ASU welcomes home school students and recognizes the unique academic experiences they contribute to our rich community of scholars. A GPA of 3.0 is required. AP and CLEP credits are accepted. To receive a degree from ASU, students must have a minimum cumulative grade point average of 2.00 (though some programs may require a higher GPA) and a minimum total of 120 credit hours, including a minimum of 45 hours of upper-division coursework. The number of hours in the major varies by degree program, and some programs may require more upper-division work. All students must satisfy a minimum of 29 credit hours of approved General Studies coursework in five core areas as well as six credits in literacy (three credit hours) and humanities, art and design/social-behavioral sciences (three credit hours) at the upper division level. **Procedure:** Freshmen are admitted fall and spring. There are deferred admissions and rolling admissions plans. Application deadlines are open. The fall 2017 application fee was $50. Notification is sent on a rolling basis. Applications are accepted on-line. **Transfer Students:** 603 transfer students enrolled in 2016-2017. Requirements for general admission to Arizona State University: applicant must meet one of the following requirements (1) graduated from high school, (2) earned a GED, (3) completed an associate degree or be in progress toward an associate degree. Transfer students must meet one of the following requirements: less than 24 transferable credit hours - minimum 2.50 cumulative GPA and meet freshman aptitude requirements; 24 or more transferable credit hours - minimum 2.50 cumulative GPA; AGEC from an Arizona community college with a 2.00 or higher cumulative GPA; associate degree from a regionally accredited higher education institution with - 2.00 or higher cumulative GPA (residents) or 2.50 or higher cumulative GPA (nonresidents). "A" = 4.0; ASU accepts transfer college-level courses in which you have earned a "C-" or better. 30 of 120 credits required for the bachelor's degree must be completed at ASU West campus. **International Students:** There are 147 international students enrolled. They must take the TOEFL with a minimum score of 500 on the paper-based TOEFL (PBT) or 61 on the Internet-based version (iBT), International English Language Testing Systems (IELTS); Pearson Tesk of English (PTE). SAT or ACT required for some.

ADMISSIONS: The SAT scores for the 2017-2018 freshman class were: Math-- 19% below 500, 48% between 500 and 599, 31% between 600 and 699, and 2% between 700 and 800. Evidence-Based Reading/Writing-- 14% below 500, 44% between 500 and 599, 37% between 600 and 699, and 5% between 700 and 800. The ACT scores were 10% between 12 and 17, 53% between 18 and 23, 33% between 24 and 29, and 5% above 30. 57% of the current freshmen were in the top fifth of their class; 86% were in the top two fifths. **Admissions Contact:** Melissa Pizzo, Dean of Admissions and Financial Aid. Email: *admissions@asu.edu* Web: *https:/campus.asu.edu/west*

FINANCIAL AID: The FAFSA code is 001081. The priority date for freshman financial aid applications for fall entry is January 1.

EMBRY-RIDDLE AERONAUTICAL UNIVERSITY - PRESCOTT CAMPUS C-3

www.prescott.erau.edu

Prescott, AZ 86301 (928) 777-6600
(800) 888-3728
Email: prescott@erau.edu

Full-time: 1857 men, 614 women
Part-time: 115 men, 20 women
Graduate: 37 men, 20 women
Year: semesters, summer session
Room & Board: $11,394
SAT EBR-W/M: 610/620 **ACT:** 26
Application Deadline: July 1

Faculty: IIB, +$
Ph.D.s: n/av
Student/Faculty: n/av
Tuition: $35,654
Freshman Class: 2168 applied, 1659 accepted, 681 enrolled
CEEB CODE: 4305
VERY COMPETITIVE

Embry-Riddle Aeronautical University-Prescott campus is a private institution offering undergraduate programs in Aviation, Engineering, Business and Security and Intelligence and graduate programs in Safety Science and Security and Intelligence Studies. There are 4 undergraduate schools and 2 graduate schools. In addition to regional accreditation, Prescott Campus has baccalaureate program accreditation with ABET, ACBSP, and AABI. The 539-acre campus is in a rural area 100 miles north of Phoenix. Including any residence halls, there are 71 buildings.

STUDENT LIFE: 77% of undergraduates are from out of state, mostly the West. Students are from 47 states, 38 foreign countries, and Canada. 7% are Foreign; 7% race unknown; 62% White; 6% Asian American; 6% Hispanic; 2% African American; 10% two or more races. **Male To Female Ratio:** 3.1:1. The average age of freshmen is 18; all undergraduates, 21. 13% do not continue beyond their first year. **Housing:** 1200 students can be accommodated in college housing, which includes dorms. In addition, there are language/international houses, students in First Year Experience housing are grouped together by major if possible, and reside with a staff that is specially trained to handle first-year transitional issues. On-campus housing is guaranteed for the freshman year only, is available on a first-come, and first-served basis. 55% of students commute. All students may keep cars.

FACULTY/CLASSROOMS: No introductory courses are taught by graduate students. The average class size in an introductory lecture is 28; in a laboratory is 18; and in a regular course is 28.

PROGRAMS OF STUDY: Prescott Campus confers B.S. degrees. Master's degrees are also awarded. Bachelor's degrees are awarded in AGRICULTURE (wildlife science), BUSINESS (business administration), COMPUTER AND PHYSICAL SCIENCE (astronomy, cyber intelligence/security studies, industrial psychology/safety, space physics, and software engineering), ENGINEERING AND ENVIRONMENTAL DESIGN (aeronautical science, aerospace engineering, air traffic management, aviation business administration, computer engineering, mechanical engineering, and unmanned aircraft systems), HEALTH PROFESSIONS (electrical engineering), SOCIAL SCIENCE (forensic studies and interdisciplinary studies). Aerospace engineering, aeronautical science (flight), and global security & intelligence studies are the strongest academically. Aerospace engineering, aeronautical science (flight), global security & intelligence studies have the largest enrollments.

ACTIVITIES: There are 120 groups on campus, including academic, jet dragster, military, band, choir, computers, dance, debate, drum and bugle corps, environmental, ethnic, forensics, honors, international, jazz band, LGBT, literary magazine, newspaper, orchestra, political, professional, radio and TV, religious, social, social service, and student government. Popular campus events include Hypnotist, Casino Night, OctoberWest, Activity Fair, GreekWeek, Finals Breakfast, Carpe Notcem Events, Smores, and Friday Night Entertainment. **Sports:** There are 6 intercollegiate sports for men and 7 for women. Facilities include athletics and activity centers with weight room and cardio room, aerobics room and exercise classes, gymnasium equipped for basketball, indoor soccer, and an indoor climbing wall, soccer field, track, multipurpose athletic fields, swimming pool complex, courts for racquetball, tennis and sand volleyball. **Graduates:** From July 1, 2016 to June 30, 2017, 436 bachelor's degrees were awarded. The most popular majors were aerospace engineering (27%), aeronautical science (14%), and global security & intelligence studies (14%). In an average class, 3% graduate in 3 years or less, 32% graduate in 4 years or less, 55% graduate in 5 years or less, and 60% graduate in 6 years or less.

SERVICES: Counseling and information services are available, as is tutoring in most subjects. There is remedial math, reading, and writing. **Library/Resources:** The library contains 33,055 volumes, 100,077 microform items, and 3,103 audio/video tapes/CDs/DVDs, and subscribes to 168 periodicals including electronic. Computerized library services include interlibrary loans, database searching, Internet access, and Wi-Fi capability. Special learning facilities include a radio station, Flight Training Center offers a simulator lab and flight operations center; the Academic Complex (AC1) houses design labs, the Weather Center lab and Airway Science Lab; Aerospace Experimentation and Fabrication Building (AXFAB); King Engineering and Technology Center (KEC) houses electrical and computer designs labs; Prescott Observatory Complex; Robertson Aviation Safety Center (RASC) is home to the accident investigation lab; a second building, RASCII, houses the collection of Aviation Safety and Security Archives as well as the Industrial Hygiene and Ergonomics labs. **Physically Challenged Students:** 95% of the campus is accessible. Facilities include wheelchair ramps, special parking, specially equipped restrooms, lowered drinking fountains, lowered telephones, special housing. Pneumatic doors. **Special:** Cooperative and work-study programs, non-degree study, internships in all majors, and study abroad in 22 countries are offered. Flight training may be taken in conjunction with aeronautical science and other degree programs. There is 1 national honor society, a freshman honors program, and 4 departmental honors programs. **Visiting:** There are regularly scheduled orientations for prospective students. Tours are offered 9 am and 1 pm Monday- Friday (Mon-Thurs during summer). There are a variety of options including sitting in on an ERAU class, one-on-one meeting with a professor, and a tour of our Crash Lab. There are guides for informal visits and visitors may sit in on classes. **Campus Safety and Security:** Measures include 24-hour foot and vehicle patrol, emergency notification system, self-defense education, and security escort services. There are emergency telephones, lighted pathways/sidewalks, and controlled access to dorms/residences.

REQUIREMENTS: The SAT or ACT is recommended. AP and CLEP credits are accepted. All students must complete 36 credits of general education requirements, including courses in communication skills, technical report writing, humanities/social sciences, math, physical science, economics, and computer science. A total of 120 to 136 credit hours with a minimum GPA of 2.0 is required to graduate. **Procedure:** Freshmen are admitted fall, spring, and summer. Entrance exams should be taken by the fall of the senior year. There are deferred admissions and rolling admissions plans. Early decision applications should be filed by December 1; regular applications, by July 1 for fall entry; November 1 for spring entry; and April 1 for summer entry. The fall 2017 application fee was $50. Notification is sent on a rolling basis. Applications are accepted online. **Transfer Students:** 147 transfer students enrolled in 2016-2017. A G.P.A. of 2.5 is preferred. 30 of 120 credits required for the bachelor's degree must be completed at the Prescott Campus. **International Students:** There are 152 international students enrolled. They must take the TOEFL with a minimum score of 550 on the paper-based TOEFL (PBT) or 79 on the Internet-based version (iBT). SAT or ACT is strongly recommended.

ADMISSIONS: 77% of the 2017-2018 applicants were accepted. The SAT scores for the 2017-2018 freshman class were: Math-- 5% below 500, 33% between 500 and 599, 46% between 600 and 699, and 16% between 700 and 800. Evidence-Based Reading/Writing-- 7% below 500, 33% between 500 and 599, 48% between 600 and 699, and 12% between 700 and 800. The ACT scores were 3% between 12 and 17, 27% between 18 and 23, 47% between 24 and 29, and 23% above 30. 46% of the current freshmen were in the top fifth of their class; 74% were in the top two fifths. 8 freshmen graduated first in their class. **Admissions Contact:** Prescott Campus Admissions Email: *prescott@erau.edu* Web: *https:/ prescott.erau.edu*

FINANCIAL AID: In 2017-2018, 98% of all full-time freshmen received some form of financial aid. 95% of all full-time freshmen received need-based aid. The average freshman award was $19,131. Need-based scholarships or need-based grants averaged $5,604; need-based self-help aid (loans and jobs) averaged $3,454; and non-need-based athletic scholarships averaged $12,156. 15% of undergraduate students work part-time. The FAFSA code is 001479. The priority date for freshman financial aid applications for fall entry is March 1.

GRAND CANYON UNIVERSITY C-4
www.gcu.edu

Phoenix, AZ 85017	**(855) GCU-LOPE**
	Email: admissions@gcu.edu
Full-time: 1767 men, 3568 women	**Faculty:** 223
Part-time: 4997 men, 17348 women	**Ph.D.s:** 19%
Graduate: 3052 men, 10025 women	**Student/Faculty:** 25 to 1
Year: semesters, summer session	**Tuition:** $16,500
Room & Board: $8650	**Freshman Class:** n/av
SAT or ACT: recommended	**CEEB CODE:** 4331
Application Deadline: August 22	**VERY COMPETITIVE**

Grand Canyon University, founded in 1949, is a small, private, publicly traded nonsectarian liberal arts Christian institution. The figures given in the above capsule and in this profile are approximate. There are 5 undergraduate schools and 5 graduate schools. In addition to regional accreditation, GCU has baccalaureate program accreditation with ACBSP, CAATE, and CCNE. The 179-acre campus is in a suburban area in Phoenix, AZ. Including any residence halls, there are 50 buildings.

STUDENT LIFE: 73% of undergraduates are from out of state, mostly the Southwest. Students are from 50 states, 12 foreign countries, and Canada. 41% are White; 4% Asian American; 25% African American; 10% Hispanic; 1% American Indian/Alaska Native; 1% Foreign. 98% claim no religious affiliation. **Female To Male Ratio:** 3.2:1. The average age of freshmen is 18; all undergraduates, 33. **Housing:** 1600 students can be accommodated in college housing, which includes married student dorms and on-campus apartments. On-campus housing is available on a first-come and first-served basis. 52% of students commute. Alcohol is not permitted. All students may keep cars.

FACULTY/CLASSROOMS: 85% teach undergraduates. No introductory courses are taught by graduate students. The average class size in an introductory lecture is 18; in a laboratory is 14; and in a regular course is 18.

PROGRAMS OF STUDY: GCU confers B.A., B.S., and B.S.N. degrees. Master's and doctoral degrees are also awarded. Bachelor's degrees are awarded in BIOLOGICAL SCIENCE (biology/biological science), BUSINESS (accounting, business administration and management, entrepreneurial studies, management science, marketing/retailing/merchandising, and sports management), COMMUNICATIONS AND THE ARTS (communications, communications technology, English, music, music performance, theatre arts, theater design, and theater management), COMPUTER AND PHYSICAL SCIENCE (digital arts/technology), EDUCATION (athletic training, dance education, education, elementary education, music education, physical education, and secondary education), ENGINEERING AND ENVIRONMENTAL DESIGN (engineering technology), HEALTH PROFESSIONS (exercise science, health science, and nursing), SOCIAL SCIENCE (addiction studies, Christian studies, forensic studies, history, interdisciplinary studies, international studies, physical fitness/movement, psychology, and sociology). Education, business, and nursing are the strongest academically, and have the largest enrollments.

ACTIVITIES: There are no fraternities or sororities. There are 12 groups on campus, including art, band, cheerleading, choir, chorale, chorus, dance, drama, ethnic, film, honors, international, literary magazine, musical theater, newspaper, pep band, photography, political, professional, religious, social, social service, and student government. Popular campus events include Spiritual Emphasis Week, Harvest Festival, and Spring Formal. **Sports:** There are 10 intercollegiate sports for men and 11 for women, and 6 intramural sports for men and 6 for women. Facilities include an arena, intramural fields, baseball stadium, a gymnasium, athlete performance center, soccer/track and field, softball, student recreation center for 2 basketball courts, a student fitness center, aerobics/dance room, cardio/weight facilities, wrestling and basketball intercollegiate training areas. **Graduates:** From July 1, 2016 to June 30, 2017, 2279 bachelor's degrees were awarded. The most popular majors were nursing (17%), curriculum and instruction (5%), and special education (4%).

SERVICES: Counseling and information services are available, as is tutoring in every subject. There is remedial math, reading, and writing. Tutors are also trained in test-taking techniques, study skills, and time management. **Library/Resources:** The library contains 140,456 volumes, 53,459 microform items, and 527 audio/video tapes/CDs/DVDs, and subscribes to 9,502 periodicals including electronic. Computerized library services include interlibrary loans, database searching, Internet access, and Wi-Fi capability. Special learning facilities include an art gallery, a center for Learning and Advancement and a center for Innovation in Research and Teaching. **Physically Challenged Students:** 99% of the campus is accessible. Facilities include wheelchair ramps, elevators, special parking, specially equipped restrooms, lowered drinking fountains, and special housing. **Special:** Internships are offered for most majors through organizatons, corporations, and agencies in the Phoenix area. Study abroad in 5 countries and a Washington semester are possible. There are 3 national honor societies and a freshman honors program. **Visiting:** There are regularly scheduled orientations for prospective students, including student orientation and registration in the summer. There are guides for informal visits, visitors may sit in on classes, and stay overnight. To schedule a visit, contact the Admission Office. **Campus Safety and Security:** Measures include 24-hour foot and vehicle patrol, emergency notification system, self-defense education, and security escort services. There are emergency telephones, lighted pathways/sidewalks, and controlled access to dorms/residences.

REQUIREMENTS: The SAT or ACT is recommended. Applicants need to be graduates of an accredited high school or have a GED. A GPA of 3.0 is required. AP and CLEP credits are accepted. Important factors in the admissions decision are evidence of special talent, extracurricular activities record, and leadership record. All students are required to complete 40 hours of general studies, including 12 hours each in Effective Communication and Critical Thinking, 8 hours in Global Awareness, and 4 hours each in University Foundation and Christian Worldview. A total of 120 semester hours, with a minimum GPA of 2.0, are required to graduate. **Procedure:** Freshmen are admitted to all sessions. Entrance exams should be taken during the junior or senior year of high school. There are early decision and rolling admissions plans. Applications should be filed by August 22 for fall entry. Applications are accepted online. **Transfer Students:** 30 of 120 credits required for the bachelor's degree must be completed at GCU. **International Students:** There are 102 international students enrolled. They must take the TOEFL with a minimum score of 500 on the paper-based TOEFL (PBT) or 61 on the Internet-based version (iBT) and the college's own test.

Admissions Contact: Dr. Antoinette Farmer, Executive Director. Email: *admissions@gcu.edu* Web: *www.gcu.edu*

FINANCIAL AID: 14% of undergraduate students work part-time. The FAFSA code is 001074. The priority date for freshman financial aid applications for fall entry is March 1.

NORTHERN ARIZONA UNIVERSITY C-2
www.nau.edu

Flagstaff, AZ 86011	**(928) 523-5511** **(888) 628-2968**
	Email: admissions@nau.edu
Full-time: 8935 men, 13055 women	**Faculty:** 959; I, --$
Part-time: 1911 men, 3185 women	**Ph.D.s:** 76%
Graduate: 1218 men, 2753 women	**Student/Faculty:** 23 to 1
Year: semesters, summer session	**Tuition:** $11,059 ($24,841)
Room & Board: $9944	**Freshman Class:** 36875 applied, 29812 accepted, 5900 enrolled
SAT CR/M/W: 540/530/500 **ACT:** 22	**CEEB CODE:** 4006
Application Deadline: n/av	**COMPETITIVE**

Northern Arizona University, founded in 1899, is a comprehensive public university. At NAU, we fully prepare students for meaningful life and work through our commitment to learning and teaching in an unparalleled environment. Through our main campus in Flagstaff and our distance-education opportunities throughout Arizona and online, we offer excellence in teaching, research, and public service to the citizens of Arizona and beyond. NAU is a doctoral, higher research institution with undergraduate education at our core and significant research opportunities as well as select master's and doctoral programs. We offer undergraduate and graduate degrees in a full range of disciplines from liberal arts and sciences to professional and career-related fields. Our commitment to high-quality education at all levels is exemplified by small class size and close interaction between students and faculty. There are 6 undergraduate schools and one graduate school. In addition to regional accreditation, NAU has baccalaureate program accreditation with AACSB, ABET, ACBSP, ACCE, ADA, CSWE, NASM, CAEP, NRPA, SAF, ACPHA, CCNE, and CODA. The 683-acre campus is in a small town 140 miles north of Phoenix and 80 miles from the Grand Canyon's South Rim. Including any residence halls, there are 119 buildings.

STUDENT LIFE: 68% of undergraduates are from Arizona. Others are from 50 states, 82 foreign countries, and Canada. 58% are White; 23% Hispanic; 5% two or more races; 4% African American; 4% Foreign; 3% American Indian/Alaska Native; 2% Asian American; 1% race unknown. **Female To Male Ratio:** 1.6:1. The average age of freshmen is 18; all undergraduates, 23. 24% do not continue beyond their first year; 55% remain to graduate. **Housing:** 9854 students can be accommodated in college housing, which includes gender neutral, coed, and married student dorms, on-campus apartments, and off-campus apartments. In addition, there are honors houses, language/international houses, special-interest houses, fraternity houses, and sorority houses. On-campus housing is available on a first-come, first-served basis, and is available on a lottery system for upperclassmen. 65% of students commute. All students may keep cars.

FACULTY/CLASSROOMS: 45% of faculty are male; 55% are female. 89% teach undergraduates. No introductory courses are taught by graduate students. The average class size in an introductory lecture is 35 and in a laboratory is 22.

PROGRAMS OF STUDY: NAU confers B.A., B.A.S., B.A.S.W., B.B.A., B.F.A., B.M.Ed, B.Mus., B.S., B.S.Accy., B.S.B.A., B.S.C.S., B.S.D.H., B.S.E., B.S.Ed, B.S.F., B.S.Jour., B.S.N., B.S.W. and B.U.S. degrees. Master's and doctoral degrees are also awarded. Bachelor's degrees are awarded in AGRICULTURE (environmental studies and forestry and related sciences), BIOLOGICAL SCIENCE (biology/biological science and microbiology), BUSINESS (accounting, business administration and management, business economics, finance, hotel/motel and restaurant management, management science, marketing management, and small business management), COMMUNICATIONS AND THE ARTS (communications, English, journalism, modern language, music, music performance, photography, radio/TV broadcasting, Spanish, strategic communication, studio art, theatre arts, and visual communication), COMPUTER AND PHYSICAL SCIENCE (applied science, astronomy, chemistry, computer information technology, computer science, geology, informatics and computer science, mathematics, and physics), EDUCATION (art education, early childhood education, elementary education, music education, secondary education, special education, and technical education), ENGINEERING AND ENVIRONMENTAL DESIGN (civil engineering, construction management, environmental engineering, environmental science, interior design, and mechanical engineering), HEALTH PROFESSIONS (biomedical science, dental hygiene, electrical engineering, exercise science, health science, and nursing), SOCIAL SCIENCE (anthropology, criminal justice, criminology, cultural studies/critical theory & analysis, geography, history, interdisciplinary studies, international relations, liberal arts/general studies, liberal arts, sciences, general studies, humanities, Native American studies, parks and recreation management, philosophy, political science/ government, prelaw, psychology, public administration, social work, sociology, and women & gender studies). Forestry, physical therapy, engineering and nursing are the strongest academically. Biomedical science, criminology and criminal justice, and nursing have the largest enrollments.

ACTIVITIES: 3% of men belong to 16 national fraternities; 4% of women belong to 15 national sororities. There are 377 groups on campus, including art, band, cheerleading, chess, choir, chorale, chorus, communications, computers, dance, debate, drama, environmental, ethnic, film, forensics, honors, international, jazz band, LGBT, literary magazine, marching band, musical theater, newspaper, opera, orchestra, pep band, photography, political, professional, radio and TV, religious, social, social service, student government, and symphony. Popular campus events include Welcome Week, Family Weekend, Homecoming, Native American Month, International Week and Honors Week. **Sports:** There are 6 intercollegiate sports for men and 9 for women, and 20 intramural sports for men and 20 for women. Facilities include a football field, indoor track and field, outdoor track and field throw facility, 4 basketball courts, a soccer field, 3 volleyball courts, 6 indoor tennis courts, 6 outdoor tennis courts and an indoor Olympic-sized swimming pool with diving facilities. The Health and Learning recreational center include 4 basketball courts, 6 racquetball courts, 2 squash courts, 5 volleyball courts, 3 multipurpose fitness studios, an indoor track, a cardio theater, a climbing wall, a free weight area and challenge course. **Graduates:** From July 1, 2016 to June 30, 2017, 5901 bachelor's degrees were awarded. The most popular majors were nursing (7%), criminology and criminal justice (4%), and elementary education (4%). In an average class, 3% graduate in 3 years or less, 40% graduate in 4 years or less, 53% graduate in 5 years or less, and 55% graduate in 6 years or less.

SERVICES: Counseling and information services are available, as is tutoring in most subjects. There is a reader service for the blind, and remedial math, reading, and writing. **Library/Resources:** The library contains 1.4 million volumes, 587,070 microform items, and 35,327 audio/video tapes/CDs/DVDs, and subscribes to 93,866 periodicals including electronic. Computerized library services include interlibrary loans, database searching, Internet access, and Wi-Fi capability. Special learning facilities include an art gallery, radio station, TV station, an observatory, research centers, and the Centennial Forest. **Physically Challenged Students:** 97% of the campus is accessible. Facilities include wheelchair ramps, elevators, special parking, specially equipped restrooms, special class scheduling, lowered drinking fountains, lowered telephones, and special housing. **Special:** NAU offers co-op programs in business and hotel/restaurant management, cross-registration with many universities through the National Student Exchange, and internships in most majors. Legislative internships are offered through the Arizona State Senate and House of Representatives. Students may study abroad in over 60 countries. Work-study programs are available in numerous fields, including engineering, business, and park services. NAU also offers a Personalized Learning competency based program. There are 18 national honor societies and a freshman honors program. **Visiting:** There are regularly scheduled orientations for prospective students. There are guides for informal visits and visitors may sit in on classes. To schedule a visit, contact the Office of Undergraduate Admissions and Orientation at (928) 523-0922. **Campus Safety and Security:** Measures include 24-hour foot and vehicle patrol, emergency notification system, self-defense education, and security escort services. There are shuttle buses, emergency telephones, lighted pathways/sidewalks, and controlled access to dorms/residences.

REQUIREMENTS: Students will be offered admission if they have a 3.0 or higher core GPA and have no deficiencies in the required college preparatory courses. You will be considered for admission if you have a 2.5 core GPA and have no more than one deficiency in any two areas in the college preparatory courses. If you have a combination of a math and lab science deficiency, you are not admissible. GPA is calculated on a 4.0 scale using only the 16 required core courses. Home schooled students must provide a high school transcript, college transcripts if there is college coursework. AP and CLEP credits are accepted. To receive a bachelor's degree at NAU, you must complete a least 120 units of credit. Within those total units, you must complete: A. All of Northern Arizona University's liberal studies, diversity, junior-level writing, and capstone requirements. B. All requirements for your specific academic plan (s). C. At least 30 units of upper-division courses, which may include transfer work. D. At least 30 units of coursework taken through NAU, of which at least 18 must be upper-division courses (300 level or above). This requirement is not met by credit-by-exam, retro-credits, and transfer coursework. E. A cumulative GPA of at least 2.0 on all work attempted at NAU. **Procedure:** Freshmen are admitted fall, spring, and summer. Entrance exams should be taken the first semester of senior year. There are deferred admissions and rolling admissions plans. Application deadlines are open. The fall 2017 application fee was $25. Applications are accepted on-line. **Transfer Students:** 2694 transfer students enrolled in 2016-2017. Transfer students are high school graduates who have enrolled at a college, university or any other institution since graduating from high school and have earned at least 12 college credits. If you are 22 or older, provide a posted high school degree or equivalent, or demonstrate the completion of a minimum of 12 transferrable college credits. At least six of those credits should be from academic subjects requiring college-level skill in reading, writing and/or analysis. Students applying to NAU's Personalized Learning program must provide official copies of transcripts for all college-level coursework. The Office of Undergraduate Admissions and Orientation will evaluate transcripts to determine the number of transfer credits accepted. Northern Arizona University will accept college-level transfer coursework with grades of C or better or P from an institution that is accredited by one of the following: Northwest Commission on Colleges and Universities, Western Association of Schools and Colleges, Southern Association of Colleges and Schools, The Higher Learning Commission, New England Association of Schools and Colleges, and Middle States Association of Colleges and Schools. You will be offered admission if you have completed AGEC, AGEC-B, AGEC-S, or California IGETC with a cumulative GPA of 2.5;

or you've completed an associate's degree with a cumulative GPA of 2.0. You will be considered for admission if you have no more than two high school deficiencies in the same core subject area or as a combination of math and laboratory science and you have at least 12 transferable credits with a cumulative GPA of 2.0 or above. 30 of 120 credits required for the bachelor's degree must be completed at NAU. **International Students:** There are 1074 international students enrolled. They must take the TOEFL with a minimum score of 525 on the paper-based TOEFL (PBT) or 70 on the Internet-based version (iBT). Students must take any one of these tests the IELTS, ACT, or SAT.

ADMISSIONS: 81% of the 2017-2018 applicants were accepted. The SAT scores for the 2017-2018 freshman class were: Critical Reading-- 28% below 500, 47% between 500 and 599, 22% between 600 and 699, and 3% between 700 and 800. Math-- 31% below 500, 48% between 500 and 599, 19% between 600 and 699, and 2% between 700 and 800. Writing-- 42% below 500, 44% between 500 and 599, 13% between 600 and 699, and 1% between 700 and 800. The ACT scores were 9% between 12 and 17, 53% between 18 and 23, 32% between 24 and 29, and 6% above 30. **Admissions Contact:** Chad Eickhoff, Interim Director of Recruitment. Email: *Chad.Eickhoff@nau.edu* Web: *www.nau.edu*

FINANCIAL AID: 65% of all full-time freshmen received need-based aid. The average freshman award was $13,241. Need-based scholarships or need-based grants averaged $7,547; need-based self-help aid (loans and jobs) averaged $3,577; non-need-based athletic scholarships averaged $18,047; and other non-need-based awards and non-need-based scholarships averaged $6,572. The average financial indebtedness of the 2017 graduate was $22,797. The FAFSA code is 001082. The priority date for freshman financial aid applications for fall entry is November 15.

PRESCOTT COLLEGE C-3
www.prescott.edu

Prescott, AZ 86301	**(928) 350-2100** **(800) 628-6364**
Fax: (928) 776-5242	**Email: admissions@prescott.edu**
Full-time: 130 men, 168 women	**Faculty:** n/av
Part-time: 35 men, 75 women	**Ph.D.s:** 43%
Graduate: 77 men, 245 women	**Student/Faculty:** 9 to 1
Year: semesters, summer session	**Tuition:** $30,501
Room & Board: $7700	**Freshman Class:** 399 applied, 291 accepted, 49 enrolled
SAT CR/M/W: 565/520/534 **ACT:** 23	**CEEB CODE:** 0484
Application Deadline: August 15	**COMPETITIVE**

Prescott College, founded in 1960, is a private liberal arts institution offering a nontraditional undergraduate program complemented with experiential learning focused on sustainability, the environment, and social justice. The curriculum is organized into multidisciplinary courses that allow students to pursue individual areas of competency. Evaluations of a student's work are conducted through a portfolio/contract system and an ongoing series of student self-evaluations. There are 2 undergraduate schools and 2 graduate schools. In addition to regional accreditation, Prescott College has baccalaureate program accreditation with NASDTEC. The 13-acre campus is in a small town 100 miles northwest of Phoenix. Including any residence halls, there are 29 buildings.

STUDENT LIFE: 65% of undergraduates are from out of state, mostly the West. Students are from 43 states, 5 foreign countries, and Canada. 68% are White; 10% race unknown; 9% two or more races; 6% Hispanic; 3% American Indian/Alaska Native; 2% African American; 1% Asian American; 1% Foreign. **Female To Male Ratio:** 2.0:1. The average age of freshmen is 19; all undergraduates, 29. **Housing:** 104 students can be accommodated in college housing, which includes dorms and on-campus apartments, and substance-free housing. On-campus housing is guaranteed for the freshman year only, is available on a first-come, and first-served basis. 70% of students commute. Alcohol is not permitted. All students may keep cars.

FACULTY/CLASSROOMS: 41% of faculty are male; 59% are female. No introductory courses are taught by graduate students. The average class size in an introductory lecture is 12; in a laboratory is 12; and in a regular course is 12.

PROGRAMS OF STUDY: Prescott confers B.A., B.S., and B.F.A degrees. Master's and doctoral degrees are also awarded. Bachelor's degrees are awarded in AGRICULTURE (environmental studies, forestry and related sciences, and wildlife management), BIOLOGICAL SCIENCE (biology/biological science, ecology, marine biology, marine science, and wildlife biology), BUSINESS (management science), COMMUNICATIONS AND THE ARTS (art, creative writing, fine arts, and visual and performing arts), COMPUTER AND PHYSICAL SCIENCE (earth science, natural sciences, and oceanography), EDUCATION (art education, early childhood education, education, education of the mentally handicapped, elementary education, environmental education, middle school education, recreation education, secondary education, and special education), ENGINEERING AND ENVIRONMENTAL DESIGN (environmental design and environmental science), HEALTH PROFESSIONS (art therapy), SOCIAL SCIENCE (anthropology, area studies, community services, counseling/psychology, ethics, politics, and social policy, gender studies, human development, humanities, humanities and social science, international studies, liberal arts/general studies, parks and recreation management, psychology, water resources, and women's studies). Environmental studies and adventure education is the strongest academically. Adventure education, environmental studies and human development have the largest enrollments.

ACTIVITIES: There are no fraternities or sororities. There are 12 groups on campus, including garden club, book club, jugglers and hoopers, meditation club, agriculture, art, dance, drama, environmental, ethnic, international, LGBT, literary magazine, photography, political, social, social service, and student government. Popular campus events include Earth Day, and Southwest Writers Series. **Sports:** There is no sports program at Prescott. There are no sports facilities on campus, but students have access to the local community pool, a weight room, gym at discounted rates and access to city league sports.**Graduates:** From July 1, 2016 to June 30, 2017, 116 bachelor's degrees were awarded. The most popular majors were environmental studies (24%), psychology (23%), and outdoor education (7%).

SERVICES: Counseling and information services are available, as is tutoring in every subject. **Library/Resources:** The library contains 202,000 volumes, 155 microform items, and 2,000 audio/video tapes/CDs/DVDs, and subscribes to 165,000 periodicals including electronic. Computerized library services include interlibrary loans, database searching, Internet access, and Wi-Fi capability. Special learning facilities include an art gallery, an experimental agroecology farm, a field station in Kino Bay, Mexico, a GIS station, a functioning gallery, and an equipment gear warehouse. In the library, there is access to a learning commons for writing and math help. **Physically Challenged Students:** 90% of the campus is accessible. Facilities include wheelchair ramps, elevators, special parking, specially equipped restrooms, and special housing. **Special:** Cross-registration with EcoLeague colleges and the Consortium for Innovative Environments in Learning is possible. Student-coordinated internships, study abroad in almost any country, dual majors, a general studies degree, pass/fail options, and credit for life experience are offered. All majors are student-designed. **Visiting:** There are regularly scheduled orientations for prospective students, including a campus tour, an interview with an admissions counselor, opportunities to sit in classes, faculty interviews, and informational meetings with financial aid and library staff. There are guides for informal visits and visitors may sit in on classes. To schedule a visit, contact the Admissions Office. **Campus Safety and Security:** Measures include emergency notification system and security escort services. There are emergency telephones, lighted pathways/sidewalks, controlled access to dorms/residences, and after hours patrol.

REQUIREMENTS: The SAT is required. The ACT is recommended. A high school diploma is also required, the GED is accepted. The school requires a completed application form, 1 essay, official transcripts, and 1 letter of recommendation. Home-schooled students must submit portfolios and writing samples. GPA of 2.0 is required. AP and CLEP credits are accepted. Important factors in the admissions decision are extracurricular activities record, leadership record, and evidence of special talent. Students must complete an orientation course, fulfill a minimum residency requirement, demonstrate proficiency in college-level writing and math, and meet course and credit requirements. Students design an individual program of studies within 7 multidisciplinary areas: adventure education, arts and letters, cultural and regional studies, education, environmental studies, humanities, and human development. Each student is required to submit a graduation proposal at the end of the junior year to a graduation review committee. **Procedure:** Freshmen are admitted fall and spring. There are early decision, deferred admissions, and rolling admissions plans. Early decision applications should be filed by December 1; regular applications, by August 15 for fall entry; and December 15 for spring entry. Notification of early decision is sent December 15; regular decision, on a rolling basis. 11 early decision candidates were accepted for the 2017-2018 class. Applications are accepted on-line. **Transfer Students:** 39 transfer students enrolled in 2016-2017. Transfer applicants must meet the same requirements as entering freshmen and must also submit official college transcripts and an essay or personal statement. Students who successfully completed 2 years of college work (60 semester hours or 90 quarter credits) need not submit high school transcripts. There is a 1-year residency requirement. 30 of 120 credits required for the bachelor's degree must be completed at Prescott. **International Students:** There are 8 international students enrolled. They must take the TOEFL with a minimum score of 500 on the paper-based TOEFL (PBT) or 61 on the Internet-based version (iBT).

ADMISSIONS: 73% of the 2017-2018 applicants were accepted. The SAT scores for the 2017-2018 freshman class were: Critical Reading-- 29% below 500, 41% between 500 and 599, 18% between 600 and 699, and 12% between 700 and 800. Math-- 44% below 500, 26% between 500 and 599, 24% between 600 and 699, and 6% between 700 and 800. Writing-- 33% below 500, 50% between 500 and 599, 11% between 600 and 699, and 6% between 700 and 800. The ACT scores were 8% below 12, 42% between 12 and 17, % between 18 and 23, 33% between 24 and 29, and 17% above 30. **Admissions Contact:** Paul Burkhardt, Executive VP & Provost. Email: *admissions@prescott.edu* Web: *www.prescott.edu*

FINANCIAL AID: In 2017-2018, 100% of all full-time freshmen received some form of financial aid. 74% of all full-time freshmen received need-based aid. The average freshman award was $25,397. Need-based scholarships or need-based grants averaged $21,355; and need-based self-help aid (loans and jobs) averaged $4,512. The average financial indebtedness of the 2017 graduate was $30,114. The FAFSA code is 013659. The priority date for freshman financial aid applications for fall entry is March 1.

SAGU AMERICAN INDIAN COLLEGE C-4

www.aicag.edu

Phoenix, AZ 85021 (602) 944-3335
(800) 933-3828

Fax: (602) 943-8299 **Email: ALCinfo@sagu.edu**

Full-time: 50 men, 45 women	**Faculty:** n/av
Part-time: 15 men, 20 women	**Ph.D.s:** n/av
Graduate: n/av	**Student/Faculty:** n/av
Year: semesters	**Tuition:** $11,940
Room & Board: $6202	**Freshman Class:** n/av
SAT or ACT: required	**CEEB CODE:** 2597
Application Deadline: August 14	**COMPETITIVE**

SAGU American Indian College (AIC) founded in 1957, is a Christian college and Bible college with a specific mission of preparing American Indians for leadership in churches, education, and the community. AIC serves nearly 25 tribes as well as other ethnicities. AIC is a campus within the Southwestern Assemblies of God University. The figures given in the above capsule and in this profile are approximate. There is 1 undergraduate school. In addition to regional accreditation, AIC has baccalaureate program accreditation with IACBE and SACSCOC. The 10-acre campus is in a small town in north Phoenix, just east of I17 and the Metrocenter area. Including any residence halls, there are 9 buildings.

STUDENT LIFE: 72% of undergraduates are from Arizona. Others are from 10 states, and 1 foreign country. 85% are from public schools. 7% are Hispanic; 67% American Indian/Alaska Native; 4% Asian American; 3% African American; 18% White; 1% Foreign. 100% are Protestant. **Male To Female Ratio:** 1:1. The average age of freshmen is 23; all undergraduates, 26. **Housing:** 80 students can be accommodated in college housing, which includes dorms and off-campus apartments. 52% of students live on campus. Alcohol is not permitted. All students may keep cars.

FACULTY/CLASSROOMS: 65% of faculty are male; 35% are female. All teach undergraduates. No introductory courses are taught by graduate students. The average class size in an introductory lecture is 11; in a laboratory is 6; and in a regular course is 6.

PROGRAMS OF STUDY: AIC confers B.A. degrees. Associate degrees are also awarded. Bachelor's degrees are awarded in EDUCATION (business education and elementary education), SOCIAL SCIENCE (ministries). Christian ministry, elementary education, and business are the strongest academically.

ACTIVITIES: There are no fraternities or sororities. Groups on campus include band, cheerleading, drama, ethnic, religious, student government, and yearbook. Popular campus events include Missions Conventions, and College Days. **Sports:** There is no sports program at AIC. Facilities include a full-size gym and a weight room.

SERVICES: Counseling and information services are available, as is tutoring in most subjects. There is remedial math, reading, and writing. **Library/Resources:** The library contains 21,015 volumes, and 35 audio/video tapes/CDs/DVDs, and subscribes to 102 periodicals including electronic. Computerized library services include Internet access. **Physically Challenged Students:** All of the campus is accessible. Facilities include wheelchair ramps, special parking, specially equipped restrooms, and lowered drinking fountains. **Special:** Internships and dual majors are available. **Visiting:** There are regularly scheduled orientations for prospective students, consisting of College Days in the fall and spring semesters that include class visits, overnight stays in dorms, and meals in the cafeteria for 2 days. To schedule a visit, contact the Admissions Office. **Campus Safety and Security:** There are lighted pathways/sidewalks, night security.

REQUIREMENTS: The SAT or ACT is required. Transcripts from high school and any other secondary schools attended are required along with a pastor's reference form. Applicants are required to take placement tests with satisfactory results. A 2.0 GPA is required and the GED is accepted. AP and CLEP credits are accepted. Important factors in the admissions decision are advanced placement or honors courses, evidence of special talent, and extracurricular activities record. To graduate, all students must maintain a GPA of 2.0 and complete 128 total credits. Students must complete courses in history, science, math, computer, and bible studies. A comprehensive bible exam is required. **Procedure:** Freshmen are admitted to all sessions. Entrance exams should be taken prior to acceptance. There are early decision, early admissions, and deferred admissions plans. Applications should be filed by August 14 for fall entry. **Transfer Students:** Official transcripts from high school and each college attended, plus a pastor's reference form are required. Students must demonstrate proficiency in English, writing, math, and reading. 30 of 128 credits required for the bachelor's degree must be completed at AIC. **International Students:** They must take the TOEFL. They must also take the SAT or ACT.

Admissions Contact: Sandra Gonzales, Director of Student Services. Email: *ALCinfo@sagu.edu* Web: *www.aicag.edu*

FINANCIAL AID: The FAFSA code is 015550. The priority date for freshman financial aid applications for fall entry is March 1.

THE UNIVERSITY OF ARIZONA D-4

www.arizona.edu

Tucson, AZ 85721 (520) 621-3705

Email: admissions@email.arizona.edu

Full-time: 13,998 men, 15,243 women	**Faculty:** 1654; I, av$
Part-time: 2298 men, 2241 women	**Ph.D.s:** 90%
Graduate: 4372 men, 4810 women	**Student/Faculty:** 22 to 1
Year: semesters, summer session	**Tuition:** $12,786 ($35,984)
Room & Board: $11,300	**Freshman Class:** 36166 applied, 28433 accepted, 7753 enrolled
SAT CR/M/W: 540/555/525 **ACT:** 24	**CEEB CODE:** 4832
Application Deadline: November 5	**COMPETITIVE**

The University of Arizona, founded in 1885, is a public land-grant institution controlled by the state of Arizona. Both traditional and online undergraduate programs are offered in agriculture, architecture, arts and sciences, business and public administration, education, engineering and mines, nursing, pharmacy and other health-related professions. There are 43 undergraduate schools and 1 graduate school. In addition to regional accreditation, The University of Arizona has baccalaureate program accreditation with AACSB, ACPE, ADA, NASAD, NASM, and CCNE. The 393-acre campus is in an urban area in Tucson, AZ. Including any residence halls, there are 103 buildings.

STUDENT LIFE: 61% of undergraduates are from Arizona. Others are from 50 states, 138 foreign countries, and Canada. 86% are from public schools. 8% are Foreign; 51% White; 5% Asian American; 4% African American; 4% two or more races; 26% Hispanic. **Female To Male Ratio:** 1.1:1. The average age of freshmen is 18; all undergraduates, 21. 81% do not continue beyond their first year; 61% remain to graduate. **Housing:** 6612 students can be accommodated in college housing, which includes dorms. In addition, there are honors houses, special-interest houses, fraternity houses, sorority houses, women dorms only, apartments for single students, international housing, and theme and wellness housing. On-campus housing is available on a first-come and first-served basis. 73% of students live on campus. Alcohol is not permitted. All students may keep cars.

FACULTY/CLASSROOMS: 61% of faculty are male; 39% are female. 96% teach undergraduates. No introductory courses are taught by graduate students.

PROGRAMS OF STUDY: UA confers B.A., B.A.E., B.Arch., B.A.S., B.E.S., B.F.A., B.G.S., B.Mu., B.S., B.S.Ae.E., B.S.B.A., B.S.Bm.E., B.S.Bs.E., B.S.Ch.E., B.S.Cv.E., B.S.E., B.S.E.C.E., B.S.E.Mg., B.S.H.S., B.S.In.E., B.S.Me.E., B.S.Mn.E., B.S.M.S.E., B.S.N., B.S.O.S.E., B.S.S.B.E., B.S.S.Ed., and B.S.Sy.E. degrees. Master's and doctoral degrees are also awarded. Bachelor's degrees are awarded in AGRICULTURE (agricultural business management, agricultural economics, animal science, environmental studies, natural resource management, plant science, and soil science), BIOLOGICAL SCIENCE (biochemistry, bioinformatics, biology/biological science, biometrics and biostatistics, cell biology, ecology, entomology, genetics, microbiology, molecular biology, neurosciences, nutrition, nutritional sciences, physiology, and plant pathology), BUSINESS (accounting, business administration and management, business economics, entrepreneurial studies, environment & national resource economics, finance, management information systems, management science, marketing, marketing and distribution, operations management, retailing, and sports management), COMMUNICATIONS AND THE ARTS (Africana studies, art history, art, classics, communications, creative writing, dance, English, English as a second/foreign language, film arts, film, television and digital media, fine arts, French, German studies, information technology, Italian, journalism, linguistics, music, musical theater, performing arts, Russian, Spanish, studio art, theatre arts, and theatre production), COMPUTER AND PHYSICAL SCIENCE (applied mathematics, applied science, astronomy, atmospheric sciences and meteorology, chemistry, computer science, geology, geoscience, hydrology, information sciences and systems, mathematics, medical physics, natural sciences, optics, physics, planetary and space science, and statistics), EDUCATION (agricultural education, art education, early childhood education, education, elementary education, general studies, library science, middle school education, music education, psychology education, school psychology, science education, secondary education, special education, and teaching English as a second/foreign language (TESOL/TEFOL), ENGINEERING AND ENVIRONMENTAL DESIGN (aerospace engineering, agricultural engineering, architecture, biomedical engineering, chemical engineering, civil engineering, electrical/electronics engineering, engineering, engineering management, environmental engineering, environmental science, industrial engineering, landscape architecture/design, materials engineering, materials science, mechanical engineering, mining and mineral engineering, optical engineering, and systems engineering), HEALTH PROFESSIONS (environmental health science, medical science, nursing, pharmaceutical science, pharmacology, pharmacy, prehealth studies, public health, rehabilitation therapy, speech pathology/audiology, and veterinary science), SOCIAL SCIENCE (American Indian studies, anthropology, counseling/psychology, criminal justice, East Asian studies, economics, family/consumer studies, gender studies, geography, German area studies, history, human development, interdisciplinary studies, Judaic studies, Latin American studies, law, Mexican-American/Chicano studies, Middle Eastern studies, philosophy, political science/government, psychology, public administration, religious education, religious studies, sociology, urban and regional studies, and women's studies). MIS, entrepreneurship, and engineering are the strongest academically. Psychology, communication, and prephysiology have the largest enrollments.

ACTIVITIES: 12% of men belong to 25 national fraternities; 20% of women belong to 25 national sororities. There are 586 groups on campus, including art, band, cheerleading, chess, choir, chorale, chorus, computers, dance, debate, drama, drill team, environmental, ethnic, honors, international, jazz band, LGBT, literary magazine, marching band, musical theater, newspaper, orchestra, pep band, photography, political, professional, radio and TV, religious, social, student government, and yearbook. Popular campus events include Spring Fling Carnival, Cultural Programs, and Family Weekend. **Sports:** There are 7 intercollegiate sports for men and 10 for women. Facilities include an athletic center, a stadium, arena, recreation facility with a weight room, a waveless swimming pool, gyms, aerobics facilities, treadmills, stair climbers, stationary bicycles, racquetball, squash, handball courts, hiking, backpacking, skiing trails as well as kayaking, caving, and scuba diving. **Graduates:** From July 1, 2016 to June 30, 2017, 7493 bachelor's degrees were awarded. The most popular majors were business/marketing (15%), biological/life sciences (11%), and social sciences (9%). In an average class, 42% graduate in 4 years or less, 14% graduate in 5 years or less, and 4% graduate in 6 years or less.

SERVICES: Counseling and information services are available, as is tutoring in most subjects. There is a reader service for the blind, and remedial math, reading, and writing. **Library/Resources:** The library contains 7.3 million volumes, 5.6 million microform items, and 117,170 audio/video tapes/CDs/DVDs, and subscribes to 79,058 periodicals including electronic. Computerized library services include interlibrary loans, database searching, Internet access, and Wi-Fi capability. Special learning facilities include an art gallery, natural history museum, planetarium, radio station, TV station, the Ansel Adams center for creative photography, and the integrated learning center, and Strategic Alternative Learning Techniques Center. **Physically Challenged Students:** All of the campus is accessible. Facilities include wheelchair ramps, elevators, special parking, specially equipped restrooms, special class scheduling, lowered drinking fountains, lowered telephones, special housing, physical therapy, counseling, interpreters, equipment maintenance and an adaptive athletics program. **Special:** Co-op programs are available in almost all majors. Internships in almost all disciplines. Washington semester for certain internships related to government. Accelerated Masters programs-MBA, MIS, and Entrepreneurship programs. 119 B.A.-B.S. degrees, dual majors, interdisciplinary degrees such as engineering-math and theater arts-education, a 3-2 arts and sciences-business degree, and student designed majors are offered. Study abroad in numerous countries, work-study programs on campus, a general studies degree, and pass/fail options are offered. Non-degree study is possible. There are 33 national honor societies, Phi Beta Kappa, and a freshman honors program. **Visiting:** There are regularly scheduled orientations for prospective students, consisting of an admissions presentation and tour. There are guides for informal visits and visitors may sit in on classes. To schedule a visit, contact the Admissions Office. **Campus Safety and Security:** Measures include 24-hour foot and vehicle patrol, emergency notification system, self-defense education, and security escort services. There are shuttle buses, emergency telephones, lighted pathways/sidewalks, and controlled access to dorms/residences.

REQUIREMENTS: The SAT or ACT is recommended. Applicants should have completed 18 academic high school units such as 4 years each of English and math, 3 in science with lab, 2 units each of foreign language, and social studies, and 1 visual/performing arts. A GED may be considered in place of a high school diploma. Some fine arts programs require auditions prior to admission. A GPA of 2.0 is required. AP and CLEP credits are accepted. Important factors in the admissions decision are evidence of special talent, personality/intangible qualities, and extracurricular activities record. UA offers a research-extensive curriculum and opportunities for all students to engage in real-world experiences designed to enhance classroom learning and meet workforce needs. Engagement experiences include internships, research projects, practicums, work options, study abroad and exchange programs. The UA also offers accelerated master's programs in a variety of disciplines including numerous online degree offerings through UA Online. Dual majors, interdisciplinary degrees, and minors are also available for preparing new generations of college students to address the world's most critical issues. On average, students see a huge ROI from the UA; its graduates are some of the world's most employable, collecting job offers at a 4% higher rate than the national average. **Procedure:** Freshmen are admitted to all sessions. There is a rolling admissions plan. Applications should be filed by November 5 for fall entry. The fall 2017 application fee was $50. Notification is sent on a rolling basis. Applications are accepted on-line. **Transfer Students:** 2175 transfer students enrolled in 2016-2017. Resident transfer applicants must have a minimum GPA of 2.0; and nonresidents must have a minimum GPA of 2.5. Some university divisions have higher requirements. Admission is competitive for out-of-state students. 30 of 120 credits required for the bachelor's degree must be completed at UA. **International Students:** There are 2358 international students enrolled. They must take the TOEFL with a minimum score of 550 on the paper-based TOEFL (PBT) or 70 on the Internet-based version (iBT) and the Comprehensive English Language Test. They must also take the SAT or ACT, scoring 1110.

ADMISSIONS: 79% of the 2017-2018 applicants were accepted. The SAT scores for the 2017-2018 freshman class were: Critical Reading-- 32% below 500, 41% between 500 and 599, 23% between 600 and 699, and 5% between 700 and 800. Math-- 27% below 500, 41% between 500 and 599, 26% between 600 and 699, and 6% between 700 and 800. Writing-- 36% below 500, 42% between 500 and 599, 18% between 600 and 699, and 4% between 700 and 800. The ACT scores were 8% between 12 and 17, 37% between 18 and 23, 43% between 24 and 29, and 13% above 30. 38% of the current freshmen were in the top fifth of their class; 52% were in the top two fifths. **Admissions Contact:** Kasandra Urquidez, Dean of Undergraduate Admissions. Email: *admissions@email.arizona.edu* Web: *www.arizona.edu*

FINANCIAL AID: In 2017-2018, 86% of all full-time freshmen received some form of financial aid. 62% of all full-time freshmen received need-based aid. The average freshman award was $12,542. Need-based scholarships or need-based grants averaged $10,288; need-based self-help aid (loans and jobs) averaged $3,354; non-need-based athletic scholarships averaged $24,494; other non-need-based awards and non-need-based scholarships averaged $7,703; and $3,216 from other forms of aid. The average financial indebtedness of the 2017 graduate was $28,932. The University of Arizona is a member of CSS. The FAFSA code is 001083. The priority date for freshman financial aid applications for fall entry is February 1.

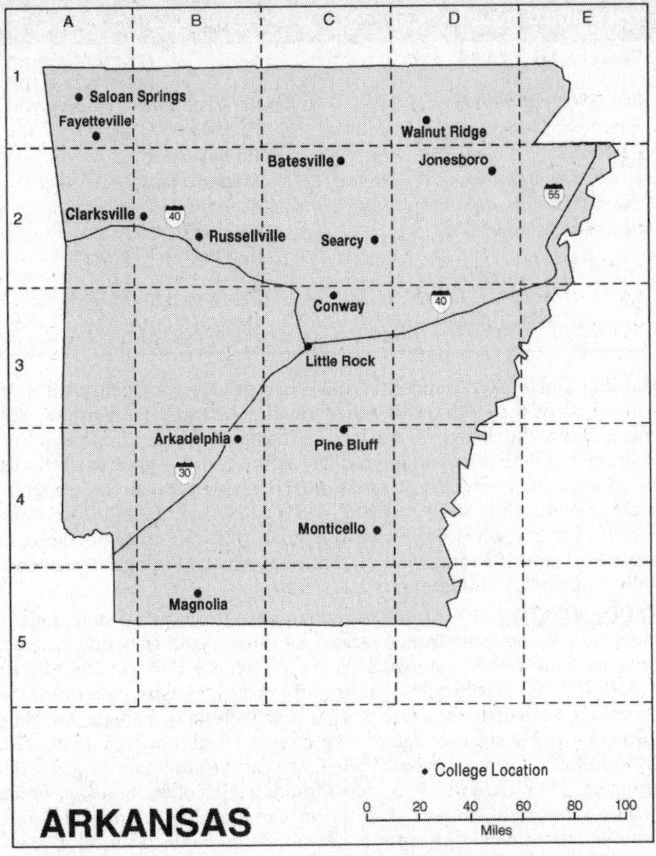

ARKANSAS BAPTIST COLLEGE *(The complete profile is made available exclusively on our website, www.barronspac.com)*

ARKANSAS STATE UNIVERSITY D-2

www.astate.edu

State University, AR 72467 **(870) 972-2782**

Fax: (870) 972-3545
Full-time: 3193 men, 4102 women
Part-time: 919 men, 1378 women
Graduate: 1334 men, 2484 women
Year: semesters, summer session
Room & Board: $8140

Email: admissions@astate.edu
Faculty: 443
Ph.D.s: 85%
Student/Faculty: 17 to 1
Tuition: $8050 ($14,050)
Freshman Class: 5346 applied, 3755 accepted, 1577 enrolled

SAT CR/M/W: 420/500/450 **ACT:** 24
Application Deadline: August 18

CEEB CODE: 6011
COMPETITIVE

Arkansas State University, founded in 1909, and part of the Arkansas State University System, is a state-supported institution offering undergraduate and graduate degrees in agriculture and technology, business, education and behavioral sciences, engineering, fine arts, humanities and social sciences, media and communication, nursing and health professions, sciences and mathematics. There are 6 undergraduate schools and 1 graduate school. In addition to regional accreditation, ASU has baccalaureate program accreditation with AACSB, ABET, ACEJMC, ADA, CSWE, NASAD, NASM, CAEP, NLN, AAM, ACEND, ACS, CAAASLP, CAATE, CACREP, CAEPNET, CALEA, CAPTE, COA, CORE, CSMA, JCERT, JRCDMS, JRCNMT, NAACLS, NACEP, NASP, NASPAA, NAST, and NIBS. The 1376-acre campus is in a small town 70 miles west of Memphis, TN. Including any residence halls, there are 157 buildings.

STUDENT LIFE: 85% of undergraduates are from Arkansas. Others are from 41 states, 50 foreign countries, and Canada. 93% are from public schools. 75% are White; 5% Foreign; 3% Hispanic; 2% two or more races; 13% African American; 1% Asian American; 1% race unknown. **Female To Male Ratio:** 1.5:1. The average age of freshmen is 18; all undergraduates, 23. 24% do not continue beyond their first year; 39% remain to graduate. **Housing:** 3217 students can be accommodated in college housing, which includes married student dorms and on-campus apartments. In addition, there are special-interest houses, fraternity houses, sorority houses, living learning communities (Honors, STEM, ROTC) and first-year residential experience wing. On-campus housing is available on a first-come, first-served basis. 70% of students commute. Alcohol is not permitted. All students may keep cars.

FACULTY/CLASSROOMS: 47% of faculty are male; 53% are female. 90% teach undergraduates, 20% do research, and 20% do both. Graduate students teach 5% of introductory courses. The average class size in an introductory lecture is 30; in a laboratory is 24; and in a regular course is 27.

PROGRAMS OF STUDY: ASU confers B.A., B.G.S., B.S., B.A.S., B.F.A., B.M., B.M.E., B.S.A., B.S.E., B.S.C.E., B.S.E.E., B.S.M.E., B.S.N., B.S.E.N., B.S.R.S., and B.S.W. degrees. Associate, master's, and doctoral degrees are also awarded. Bachelor's degrees are awarded in AGRICULTURE (agricultural business management, agriculture, animal science, plant science, and wildlife management), BIOLOGICAL SCIENCE (biology/adolescence education, biological sciences, and biotechnology), BUSINESS (accounting, banking and finance, business administration and management, business economics, international business, marketing, sports management, and supply chain management), COMMUNICATIONS AND THE ARTS (art, communications, English, foreign language, graphic design, information technology, instrumental music education, journalism, multimedia, music, radio/television technology, strategic communication, theatre arts, and vocal performance), COMPUTER AND PHYSICAL SCIENCE (chemistry, clinical laboratory science, chemistry education, computer science, mathematics, and physics), EDUCATION (athletic training, business education, early childhood education, elementary education, English education, foreign languages education, general studies, health education, mathematics education, middle school education, physical education, science education, social science education, and special education), ENGINEERING AND ENVIRONMENTAL DESIGN (civil engineering technology, electrical/electronics engineering, emergency/disaster science, engineering, manufacturing technology, mechanical engineering, and technological management), HEALTH PROFESSIONS (exercise science, health promotion, nursing, and radiological science), SOCIAL SCIENCE (communication sciences and disorders, criminology, dietetics, economics, history, interdisciplinary studies, philosophy, political science/government, psychology, social work, and sociology). Engineering, nursing, and biological sciences are the strongest academically. Nursing, early childhood education, and interdisciplinary studies have the largest enrollments.

ACTIVITIES: 16% of men belong to 13 national fraternities; 13% of women belong to 7 national sororities. There are 175 groups on campus, including academic clubs, art, cheerleading, choir, computers, dance, debate, drama, drill team, environmental, ethnic, forensics, honors, international, jazz band, LGBT, marching band, musical theater, newspaper, pep band, photography, political, professional, radio and TV, religious, social, social service, student government, symphony, and yearbook. Popular campus events include Welcome Week, Order of the Pack, Homecoming, Residence Life Back to School Luau, Springfest, and Black History Month Celebration. **Sports:** There are 7 intercollegiate sports for men and 9 for women, and 20 intramural sports for men and 20 for women. Facilities include a convocation center for basketball, football, baseball, track, and soccer. **Graduates:** From July 1, 2016 to June 30, 2017, 1766 bachelor's degrees were awarded. The most popular majors were interdisciplinary studies (11%), nursing (8%), and early childhood education (7%). In an average class, 11% graduate in 3 years or less, 28% graduate in 4 years or less, 37% graduate in 5 years or less, and 39% graduate in 6 years or less. Of the 2016 graduating class, 19% were enrolled in graduate school within 6 months of graduation, and 34% were employed.

SERVICES: Counseling and information services are available, as is tutoring in most subjects. There is a reader service for the blind, and remedial math, reading, and writing. Tutoring is provided in virtually all general education subjects. Student Support Services tries to provide as much tutoring as possible for upper level courses when tutors are available for the subject areas. **Library/Resources:** The library contains 838,243 volumes, and 112,847 audio/video tapes/CDs/DVDs, and subscribes to 40,822 periodicals including electronic. Computerized library services include interlibrary loans, database searching, Internet access, and Wi-Fi capability. Special learning facilities include an art gallery, natural history museum, radio station, TV station, Agriculture and Environmental Ecotoxicology Research, the Arkansas Biosciences Institute, the Fowler Center for Performing Arts, distance learning, the Hemingway-Pfeiffer Museum and Educational Center, a geographic information system facility, an electron microscope lab, and the Delta Studies Center. **Physically Challenged Students:** 90% of the campus is accessible. Facilities include wheelchair ramps, elevators, special parking, specially equipped restrooms, special class scheduling, lowered drinking fountains, and lowered telephones. **Special:** An interdisciplinary studies degree, study abroad, and work-study programs are offered. Dual majors and internships are available in many areas. Non-degree study is possible. There are 10 national honor societies and a freshman honors program. **Visiting:** There are regularly scheduled orientations for prospective students, consisting of various sessions held throughout the year. There are guides for informal visits; visitors may sit in on classes and stay overnight. To schedule a visit, contact the Office of Recruitment at (870) 972-2782. **Campus Safety and Security:** Measures include 24-hour foot and vehicle patrol, an emergency notification system, self-defense education, and security escort services. There are shuttle buses, emergency telephones, and lighted pathways/sidewalks.

REQUIREMENTS: SAT, ASSET, or COMPASS scores are required, with ACT scores recommended. Applicants should have completed 14 academic high school units, including 4 each in English and math, 3 each in social studies, and science (must be with labs), and it is recommended to take 2 units in same foreign language. Applicants must have an ACT composite score of 21 and a high school GPA of 2.75 for unconditional admission. A GPA of 2.8 is required. AP and CLEP credits are accepted. All students must complete a 35 hour credit distribution of general education courses. A total of at least 120 credits, with a minimum GPA of 2.0, is required to graduate. **Procedure:** Freshmen are admitted fall, spring, and summer. Entrance exams should be taken before April 1 of the high school senior year. There are early admissions and rolling admissions plans. Applications should be filed by August 18 for fall entry; January 15 for spring entry; and May 27 for summer entry. The fall 2017 application fee was $15. Applications are accepted online. **Transfer Students:** 897 transfer students enrolled in 2016-2017. Transfer applicants should have a minimum GPA of 2.0. Those having completed 12 or fewer credit hours will be admitted on the same basis as freshmen. Official transcripts from every institution attended are required. 32 of 120 credits required for the bachelor's degree must be completed at ASU. **International Students:** There are 441 international students enrolled. They must take the TOEFL with a minimum score of 500 on the paper-based TOEFL (PBT) or 61 on the Internet-based version (iBT).

ADMISSIONS: 70% of the 2017-2018 applicants were accepted. The SAT scores for the 2017-2018 freshman class were: Critical Reading--64% below 500 and 36% between 500 and 599. Math-- 44% below 500, 36% between 500 and 599, and 20% between 600 and 699. Writing--80% below 500 and 20% between 500 and 599. The ACT scores were 20% below 12, 30% between 12 and 17, 26% between 18 and 23, 14% between 24 and 29, and 11% above 30. 43% of the current freshmen were in the top fifth of their class; 66% were in the top two fifths. 49 freshmen graduated first in their class. **Admissions Contact:** Tammy Fowler, Director of Recruitment. Email: *admissions@astate.edu* Web: *www.astate.edu*

FINANCIAL AID: In 2017-2018, 93% of all full-time freshmen received some form of financial aid. 82% of all full-time freshmen received need-based aid. The average freshman award was $13,250. Need-based scholarships or need-based grants averaged $7,800 ($9,000 maximum); need-based self-help aid (loans and jobs) averaged $6,200 ($8,500 maximum); non-need-based athletic scholarships averaged $9,500 ($10,000 maximum); and other non-need-based awards and non-need-based scholarships averaged $6,000 ($12,000 maximum). 9% of undergraduate students work part-time. The average financial indebtedness of the 2017 graduate was $25,000. ASU is a member of CSS. The college's own financial statement is required. The FAFSA code is 001090. The priority date for freshman financial aid applications for fall entry is February 15.

ARKANSAS TECH UNIVERSITY *(The complete profile is made available exclusively on our website, www.barronspac.com)*

HARDING UNIVERSITY — C-2

www.harding.edu

Searcy, AR 72149 — **(501) 279-4407**, **(800) 477-4407**

Fax: (501) 279-4129 — **Email: admissions@harding.edu**

Full-time: 1749 men, 2198 women	**Faculty:** 331; IIA, --$
Part-time: 110 men, 91 women	**Ph.D.s:** 67%
Graduate: 466 men, 890 women	**Student/Faculty:** 16 to 1
Year: semesters, summer session	**Tuition:** $18,440
Room & Board: $6760	**Freshman Class:** 2238 applied, 1617 accepted, 945 enrolled
SAT CR/M: 550/550 **ACT:** required	**CEEB CODE:** 6267
Application Deadline: June 1	**COMPETITIVE**

Harding University, founded in 1924, is a private Christian institution comprised of the Colleges of Allied Health, Arts and Humanities, Sciences, Bible and Religion, Business, Education, Nursing, Honors and Pharmacy. There are 8 undergraduate schools and 5 graduate schools. In addition to regional accreditation, HU has baccalaureate program accreditation with ABET, ACBSP, CSWE, NASM, CAEP, NLN, and CADE. The 350-acre campus is in a small town 50 miles northeast of Little Rock and 105 miles west of Memphis, TN. Including any residence halls, there are 59 buildings.

STUDENT LIFE: 71% of undergraduates are from out of state, mostly the South. Students are from 49 states, 54 foreign countries, and Canada. 65% are from public schools. 82% are White; 6% Foreign; 5% African American; 3% Hispanic; 2% two or more races; 1% Asian American; 1% American Indian/Alaska Native. 93% are Protestant. **Female To Male Ratio:** 1.4:1. The average age of freshmen is 18; all undergraduates, 20. 18% do not continue beyond their first year; 66% remain to graduate. **Housing:** 3245 students can be accommodated in college housing, which includes married student dorms, on-campus apartments, and off-campus apartments. On-campus housing is guaranteed for all 4 years, is available on a first-come, and first-served basis. 72% of students live on campus. Alcohol is not permitted. All students may keep cars.

FACULTY/CLASSROOMS: 66% of faculty are male; 34% are female. 78% teach undergraduates. No introductory courses are taught by graduate students. The average class size in an introductory lecture is 16 and in a laboratory is 14.

PROGRAMS OF STUDY: HU confers B.A., B.S., B.B.A., B.F.A., B.M.E., B.M.N., B.S.N., B.S.W., M.S., M.A.T., M.B.A., M.S.E., M.S.N., M.E.D., E.D.D., and E.D.S. degrees. Master's and doctoral degrees are also awarded. Bachelor's degrees are awarded in BIOLOGICAL SCIENCE (biochemistry and biology/biological science), BUSINESS (accounting, banking and finance, business administration and management, fashion merchandising, international business management, marketing/retailing/merchandising, and sports management), COMMUNICATIONS AND THE ARTS (advertising, art, broadcasting, communications, design, dramatic arts, English, fine arts, French, graphic design, journalism, media arts, music, painting, and Spanish), COMPUTER AND PHYSICAL SCIENCE (chemistry, computer science, information sciences and systems, mathematics, and physics), EDUCATION (athletic training, Christian education, early childhood education, elementary education, foreign languages education, music education, and secondary education), ENGINEERING AND ENVIRONMENTAL DESIGN (biomedical engineering, computer engineering, electrical/electronics engineering, interior design, and mechanical engineering), HEALTH PROFESSIONS (exercise science, health, health care administration, health science, medical technology, nursing, and speech pathology/audiology), SOCIAL SCIENCE (American studies, biblical languages, biblical studies, child care/child and family studies, criminal justice, dietetics, economics, history, home economics, humanities, international studies, legal studies, liberal arts/general studies, ministries, missions, political science/government, psychology, public administration, religion, social science, social work, and youth ministry). Engineering, pharmacy, and physical therapy are the strongest academically. Business, education, and nursing have the largest enrollments.

ACTIVITIES: There are no fraternities or sororities. There are 106 groups on campus, including art, band, cheerleading, choir, chorale, chorus, computers, debate, drama, ethnic, film, honors, international, jazz band, literary magazine, marching band, musical theater, newspaper, orchestra, pep band, photography, political, professional, radio and

TV, religious, social, social service, student government, symphony, and yearbook. Popular campus events include Spring Sing, Homecoming, Bison Days, Family Weekend, and Lectureship. **Sports:** There are 9 intercollegiate sports for men and 9 for women, and 11 intramural sports for men and 9 for women. Facilities include baseball and softball fields, racquetball, handball, tennis courts, a football stadium, indoor and outdoor track, golf practice range, weight rooms, an Olympic-size swimming pool, and gyms. The football and athletic training complex provides a weight room, and rehabilitation area and hydrotherapy area. **Graduates:** From July 1, 2016 to June 30, 2017, 958 bachelor's degrees were awarded. The most popular majors were business/marketing (15%), early childhood licensure (14%), and health professions and related programs (12%). In an average class, 43% graduate in 4 years or less, 61% graduate in 5 years or less, and 64% graduate in 6 years or less. Of the 2016 graduating class, 30% were enrolled in graduate school within 6 months of graduation, and 21% were employed.

SERVICES: Counseling and information services are available, as is tutoring in most subjects. There is a reader service for the blind, and remedial math, reading, and writing. **Library/Resources:** The library contains 367,438 volumes, and subscribes to 174,162 periodicals including electronic. Computerized library services include interlibrary loans, database searching, Internet access, and Wi-Fi capability. Special learning facilities include an art gallery, radio station, and TV station. **Physically Challenged Students:** 95% of the campus is accessible. Facilities include wheelchair ramps, elevators, special parking, specially equipped restrooms, special class scheduling, lowered drinking fountains, lowered telephones, and special housing. **Special:** The Harding campus in Florence, Italy, and Athens, Greece and programs in England, Latin America, France/Switzerland, Australia, and Zambia offer international studies. Internships are given in social work, teaching, nursing, and international missions. Co-op programs in all majors, work-study programs, dual majors, a general studies degree, and non-degree study are available. There are 11 national honor societies and a freshman honors program. **Visiting:** There are regularly scheduled orientations for prospective students. There are guides for informal visits, visitors may sit in on classes, and stay overnight. To schedule a visit, contact the Admissions Office. **Campus Safety and Security:** Measures include 24-hour foot and vehicle patrol, emergency notification system, self-defense education, and security escort services. There are emergency telephones, lighted pathways/sidewalks, and controlled access to dorms/residences.

REQUIREMENTS: The SAT or ACT is required. Applicants should be graduates of an accredited secondary school and have completed 15 high school hours, 4 in English, 3 each in math, social studies, art, history, and music, 2 in science. An interview is highly recommended. AP and CLEP credits are accepted. Important factors in the admissions decision are leadership record, recommendations by school officials, and advanced placement or honors courses. All students must complete 53 hours of general education courses, including religion, English composition, history, speech communications, social sciences, biology, physical science, math, Western literature, music and art appreciation, and phys ed. A total of 128 semester hours, with a minimum GPA of 2.0, is required to graduate. 32 hours must be completed in residence and 45 must be upper-level. **Procedure:** Freshmen are admitted to all sessions. Entrance exams should be taken in the junior year or early in the senior year. There are early admissions, deferred admissions, and rolling admissions plans. Applications should be filed by June 1 for fall entry; November 1 for spring entry. The fall 2017 application fee was $50. Notifications are sent May 1. Applications are accepted online. **Transfer Students:** 129 transfer students enrolled in 2016-2017. Applicants with a minimum GPA of 2.0 and at least 14 semester hours earned are considered for admission. An interview is highly recommended. 32 of 128 credits required for the bachelor's degree must be completed at HU. **International Students:** There are 273 international students enrolled. They must take the TOEFL with a minimum score of 550 on the paper-based TOEFL (PBT) or 79 on the Internet-based version (iBT). They must also take the SAT or ACT.

ADMISSIONS: 72% of the 2017-2018 applicants were accepted. The SAT scores for the 2017-2018 freshman class were: Critical Reading-- 31% below 500, 37% between 500 and 599, 25% between 600 and 699, and 7% between 700 and 800. Math-- 25% below 500, 45% between 500 and 599, 28% between 600 and 699, and 2% between 700 and 800. The ACT scores were 3% between 12 and 17, 36% between 18 and 23, 42% between 24 and 29, and 19% above 30. 38% of the current freshmen were in the top fifth of their class; 56% were in the top two fifths. 39 freshmen graduated first in their class. **Admissions Contact:** Glen Dillard, Assistant Vice President for Enrollment Management. Email: *admissions@harding.edu* Web: *www.harding.edu*

FINANCIAL AID: In 2017-2018, 85% of all full-time freshmen received some form of financial aid. 81% of all full-time freshmen received need-based aid. The average freshman award was $10,283. Need-based scholarships or need-based grants averaged $8,447; and need-based self-help aid (loans and jobs) averaged $8,409. 33% of undergraduate students work part-time. The average financial indebtedness of the 2017 graduate was $26,535. The FAFSA code is 001097. The priority date for freshman financial aid applications for fall entry is February 15.

HENDERSON STATE UNIVERSITY — B-4

www.hsu.edu

Arkadelphia, AR 71999 — **(870) 230-5028**

Fax: (870) 230-5066
Full-time: 1202 men, 1589 women
Part-time: 110 men, 151 women
Graduate: 152 men, 349 women
Year: semesters, summer session
Room & Board: $7400

SAT CR/M: 460/510 **ACT:** 22
Application Deadline: August 18

Email: admissions@hsu.edu
Faculty: 170; IIA, --$
Ph.D.s: 70%
Student/Faculty: 15 to 1
Tuition: $8116 ($14,956)
Freshman Class: 4072 applied, 2692 accepted, 747 enrolled
CEEB CODE: 6272
COMPETITIVE

Henderson State University, was founded in 1890 as Arkadelphia Methodist College and became a state institution in 1929. HSU is known as Arkansas' Public Liberal Arts University. There are 3 undergraduate schools and 1 graduate school. In addition to regional accreditation, HSU has baccalaureate program accreditation with AACSB, ADA, NASM, CCNE, CAATE, CACREP, CAATE, CADE, and CAEP. The 152-acre campus is in a small town in Arkadelphia, a small town in southwest Arkansas, 35 miles from Hot Spring. Including any residence halls, there are 49 buildings.

STUDENT LIFE: 84% of undergraduates are from Arkansas. Others are from 26 states, 26 foreign countries, and Canada. 67% are White; 23% African American; 4% Hispanic; 4% two or more races; 1% Asian American; 1% American Indian/Alaska Native; 1% Foreign; 1% race unknown. **Female To Male Ratio:** 1.4:1. The average age of freshmen is 18; all undergraduates, 22. 40% do not continue beyond their first year; 34% remain to graduate. **Housing:** 2067 students can be accommodated in college housing, which includes dorms and on-campus apartments. In addition, there are honors houses, and international student housing. On-campus housing is available on a first-come, first-served basis. 53% of students live on campus. Alcohol is not permitted. All students may keep cars.

FACULTY/CLASSROOMS: 46% of faculty are male; 54% are female. 95% teach undergraduates. No introductory courses are taught by graduate students. The average class size in an introductory lecture is 50; in a laboratory is 20; and in a regular course is 30.

PROGRAMS OF STUDY: HSU confers A.S, B.A., B.S., B.B.A., B.F.A., B.I.S., B.M., B.S.E., and B.S.N degrees. Associate and master's degrees are also awarded. Bachelor's degrees are awarded in BIOLOGICAL SCIENCE (biology/biological science), BUSINESS (accounting, business administration and management, and recreation and leisure services), COMMUNICATIONS AND THE ARTS (communications, digital communications, dramatic arts, English, music, Spanish, studio art, and theatre arts), COMPUTER AND PHYSICAL SCIENCE (chemistry, computer science, information sciences and systems, mathematics, physics, and radiological technology), EDUCATION (art education, business education, education, elementary education, middle school education, music education, and physical education), ENGINEERING AND ENVIRONMENTAL DESIGN (aviation administration/management and engineering physics), HEALTH PROFESSIONS (health and physical activity, health science, medical technology, nursing, and radiograph medical technology), SOCIAL SCIENCE (criminal justice, family/consumer studies, history, human services, political science/government, psychology, public administration, and sociology). Education, business administration, and biology have the largest enrollments.

ACTIVITIES: There are 90 groups on campus, including art, band, cheerleading, choir, chorale, chorus, dance, debate, drama, ethnic, honors, international, jazz band, LGBT, marching band, musical theater, newspaper, pep band, political, professional, radio and TV, religious, social, social service, student government, and yearbook. Popular campus events include Spring Fling, and Orientation and Family Day. **Sports:** There are 5 intercollegiate sports for men and 7 for women. Facilities include a football stadium, recreation center, auxiliary gym, weight room, swimming pool, tennis courts, women's volleyball, baseball, basketball, golf, softball field, and a track. **Graduates:** From July 1, 2016 to June 30, 2017, 547 bachelor's degrees were awarded. The most popular majors were business administration (12%), Integrated Studies (12%), and accounting (6%). In an average class, 18% graduate in 4 years or less, 29% graduate in 5 years or less, and 33% graduate in 6 years or less.

SERVICES: Counseling and information services are available, as is tutoring in most subjects, such as English, math, history, and sciences. There is a reader service for the blind, and remedial math and reading. We have a writing center to help students with their writing projects. **Library/Resources:** The library contains 237,200 volumes, and 151,230 audio/video tapes/CDs/DVDs. Computerized library services include interlibrary loans, database searching, and Internet access. Special learning facilities include an art gallery, planetarium, radio station, and TV station. **Physically Challenged Students:** 90% of the campus is accessible. Facilities include wheelchair ramps, elevators, special parking, specially equipped restrooms, special class scheduling, lowered drinking fountains, and lowered telephones. **Special:** Henderson offers co-op programs and cross-registration with Ouachita Baptist University, internships in business, psychology, political science, recreation, and education, work-study programs, credit for military experience, nondegree study, and pass/fail options. There is a freshman honors program. **Visiting:** There are regularly scheduled orientations for prospective students, campus tours are given Monday through Friday. There are guides for informal visits and visitors may stay overnight. To schedule a visit, contact the Admissions Office. **Campus Safety and Security:** Measures include 24-hour foot and vehicle patrol and emergency notification system. There are emergency telephones, lighted pathways/sidewalks, controlled access to dorms/residences. The Reddie Rides provide rides to students on campus after hours.

REQUIREMENTS: The SAT is required, with the ACT recommended. Applicants need at least 15 academic credits or Carnegie units consisting of 4 units of English, 3 units each of history, civics, or American government, 2 units each of natural science, math, and foreign language, and a half unit of computer science are recommended. Students with a predicted GPA of 1.5 or below will be admitted conditionally. AP and CLEP credits are accepted. All students must complete a total of 120 credit hours, including 30 in the major, with a minimum GPA of 2.0. Core requirements include 12 semester hours in social science, 11 semester hours in natural science, 9 semester hours in English, 6 semester hours in humanities, 3 semester hours each in non-Western culture, math, and oral communication, and 1 semester hours in phys ed or military science. **Procedure:** Freshmen are admitted fall, spring, and summer. Entrance exams should be taken during the junior year. There is a rolling admissions plan. Applications should be filed by August 18 for fall entry. Applications are accepted on-line. **Transfer Students:** 229 transfer students enrolled in 2016-2017. Applicants with a cumulative GPA below 2.0 will be admitted conditionally. The entire academic record is considered. 30 of 124 credits required for the bachelor's degree must be completed at HSU. **International Students:** There are 35 international students enrolled. They must take the TOEFL with a minimum score of 500 on the paper-based TOEFL (PBT) or 61 on the Internet-based version (iBT) or take the MELAB. They must also take the SAT or ACT, scoring 19.

ADMISSIONS: 66% of the 2017-2018 applicants were accepted. The SAT scores for the 2017-2018 freshman class were: Critical Reading-- 58% below 500, 21% between 500 and 599, 18% between 600 and 699, and 1% between 700 and 800. Math-- 48% below 500, 30% between 500 and 599, 18% between 600 and 699, and 1% between 700 and 800. The ACT scores were 15% between 12 and 17, 50% between 18 and 23, 30% between 24 and 29, and 5% above 30. 27% of the current freshmen were in the top fifth of their class; 52% were in the top two fifths. 3 freshmen graduated first in their class. **Admissions Contact:** Brandie Benton, Director of University Relations/Admissions. Email: *admissions@hsu.edu* Web: *www.hsu.edu*

FINANCIAL AID: The FFS is required. The FAFSA code is 001098. Check with the school for current application deadlines.

HENDRIX COLLEGE — C-3

www.hendrix.edu

Conway, AR 72032	**(501) 450-1362** **(800) 277-9017**
Fax: (501) 450-3843	**Email: adm@hendrix.edu**
Full-time: 621 men, 689 women	**Faculty:** 108; IIB, -$
Part-time: 6 men, 5 women	**Ph.D.s:** 93%
Graduate: 6 men, 1 women	**Student/Faculty:** 11 to 1
Year: semesters	**Tuition:** $42,440
Room & Board: $11,580	**Freshman Class:** 1516 applied, 1412 accepted, 399 enrolled
SAT CR/M: 603/606 **ACT:** 28	**CEEB CODE:** 6273
Application Deadline: November 15	**VERY COMPETITIVE**

Hendrix College, founded in 1876, is a private liberal arts college affiliated with the United Methodist Church. The figures in the above capsule and in this profile are approximate. There is 1 undergraduate school and 1 graduate school. In addition to regional accreditation, HC has baccalaureate program accreditation with NASM, CAEP, ACA, and ASBMB. The 180-acre campus is in a suburban area 25 miles northwest of Little Rock. Including any residence halls, there are 65 buildings.

STUDENT LIFE: 53% of undergraduates are from Arkansas. Others are from 44 states, and 50 foreign countries. 80% are from public schools. 55% are White; 4% African American; 4% Asian American; 4% Foreign; 3% Hispanic; 28% race unknown; 2% two or more races. 42% claim no religious affiliation; 27% Protestant; 11% Catholic. **Female To Male Ratio:** 1.1:1. The average age of freshmen is 18; all undergraduates, 20. 13% do not continue beyond their first year; 85% remain to graduate. **Housing:** 1257 students can be accommodated in college housing, which includes dorms and on-campus apartments. In addition, there are language/international houses, a substance-free house, and an ecology floor. On-campus housing is guaranteed for all 4 years, is available on a first-come, first-served basis, and is available on a lottery system for upperclassmen. 94% of students live on campus. All students may keep cars.

FACULTY/CLASSROOMS: 53% of faculty are male; 47% are female. All teach undergraduates, 75% do research, and do both. No introductory courses are taught by graduate students. The average class size in an introductory lecture is 16; in a laboratory is 18; and in a regular course is 36.

PROGRAMS OF STUDY: HC confers B.A. degrees. Master's degrees are also awarded. Bachelor's degrees are awarded in AGRICULTURE (environmental studies), BIOLOGICAL SCIENCE (biochemistry and biology/biological science), BUSINESS (accounting and business economics), COMMUNICATIONS AND THE ARTS (art, dramatic arts, English, French, German, music, and Spanish), COMPUTER AND PHYSICAL SCIENCE (chemical physics, chemistry, computer science, mathematics, and physics), EDUCATION (early childhood education), HEALTH PROFESSIONS (allied health and exercise science), SOCIAL SCIENCE (American studies, anthropology, economics, history, interdisciplinary studies, international relations, philosophy, philosophy and religion, political science/government, psychology, religion, and sociology). English, and economics & business are the strongest academically. Psychology, English, and biochemistry & molecular biology have the largest enrollments.

ACTIVITIES: There are no fraternities or sororities. There are 70 groups on campus, including art, band, cheerleading, chess, choir, chorale, chorus, dance, debate, drama, environmental, ethnic, film, honors, international, jazz band, LGBT, literary magazine, musical theater, newspaper, orchestra, pep band, photography, political, professional, radio and TV, religious, social, social service, student government, and yearbook. Popular campus events include Campus Kitty, Themed Dance Parties, Shirttails, and Dance Competition. **Sports:** There are 10 intercollegiate sports for men and 11 for women, and 10 intramural sports for men and 10 for women. Facilities include the Wellness and Athletic center includes a competition gym, a fitness center with free weights/weight equipment and cardiovascular machines, an indoor climbing wall, a dance/movement studio, indoor track, indoor 25 meter pool with diving boards, baseball, softball and soccer fields, a multi-purpose turf field, outdoor tennis courts, a stadium, a multi-purpose field house a weight room, an additional multi-purpose turf field, and a tennis bubble with indoor courts. **Graduates:** From July 1, 2016 to June 30, 2017, 281 bachelor's degrees were awarded. The most popular majors were biochemistry, biophysics, and molecular biology (11%), psychology (10%), and English (9%). In an average class, 67% graduate in 4 years or less, 69% graduate in 5 years or less, and 68% graduate in 6 years or less. Of the 2016 graduating class, 32% were enrolled in graduate school within 6 months of graduation.

SERVICES: Counseling and information services are available, as is tutoring in some subjects, such as math, biology, writing, chemistry, foreign languanges, accounting, physics, genetics and zoology. There is a reader service for the blind. **Library/Resources:** The library contains 264,400 volumes, 67,497 microform items, and 4,088 audio/video tapes/CDs/DVDs, and subscribes to 65,518 periodicals including electronic. Computerized library services include interlibrary loans, database searching, Internet access, and Wi-Fi capability. Special learning facilities include an art gallery, radio station, and a writing lab. **Physically Challenged Students:** Facilities include wheelchair ramps, elevators, special parking, specially equipped restrooms, and lowered drinking fountains. **Special:** Internships and work-study may be arranged in all fields. The college offers 3-2 engineering programs with Columbia, Vanderbilt, and Washington Universities. Also available are The Washington Center Program, study abroad, dual majors, and student-designed interdisciplinary studies. Students can pursue minors in all academic departments, as well as African studies, art history, Asian studies, dance, secondary education, gender studies, international business, medical humanities, neuroscience, public health, and applied mathematics. There are 13 national honor societies and a chapter of Phi Beta Kappa. **Visiting:** There are regularly scheduled orientations for prospective students. Student visits include attending a class, visits with current students and faculty, a campus tour, and a luncheon with speakers. Students may also stay overnight in a residence hall. To schedule a visit, contact Jennifer McKenzie at (501) 450-1362. **Campus Safety and Security:** Measures include 24-hour foot and vehicle patrol, emergency notification system, self-defense education, and security escort services. There are emergency telephones, lighted pathways/sidewalks, and controlled access to dorms/residences.

REQUIREMENTS: The SAT or ACT is required. Student must have completed 4 high school units in English, 3 to 4 units each in math and social studies, 2 units in science, and 2 or more in foreign language. The GED is accepted. AP and CLEP credits are accepted. Important factors in the admissions decision are extracurricular activities record, advanced placement or honors courses, and leadership record. The Collegiate Center is the general education program at Hendrix College and it has four distinct parts: First-Year Experience (consists of The Engaged Citizen course that is grouped in faculty dyads and an Explorations seminar that meets weekly), Capacities (consists of a bi-level writing program, foreign language (equivalent to two semesters), a quantitative skills course, and two physical activities), Learning Domains (consists of 7 courses across 7 disciplines) including one course in Expressive Arts, one course in Historical Perspectives, one course in Literary Studies, two courses (one a lab) in Natural Science Inquiry, one course in Social and Behavioral Analysis, and one course in Values, Beliefs and Ethics, The Odyssey Program (consists of 3 reflective, engaged experiences across the six categories of Artistic Creativity, Global Awareness, Professional and Leadership Development, Service to the World, Undergraduate Research, and Special Programs). All majors include a senior capstone experience that varies by major and 32 courses are required for graduation. **Procedure:** Freshmen are admitted fall and spring. Entrance exams should be taken during the junior and senior years. There is an early admissions plan. Applications should be filed by November 15 for fall entry. The fall 2017 application fee was $40. Notification of early decision is sent December 15; regular decision, March 1. Applications are accepted on-line. **Transfer Students:** 15 transfer students enrolled in 2016-2017. Complete the Common Application online for free, or mail a completed Common Application along with $40 nonrefundable application fee. Submit an offical transcript starting in 9th grade, and request your ACT or SAT scores be sent to Hendrix. Have each college or university previously or currently attended send official transcript and a Dean of Student Affairs Recommendation Form. 16 of 32 credits required for the bachelor's degree must be completed at Hendrix. **International Students:** There are 64 international students enrolled. They must take the TOEFL with a minimum score of 550 on the paper-based TOEFL (PBT) or 79 on the Internet-based version (iBT).

ADMISSIONS: 93% of the 2017-2018 applicants were accepted. The SAT scores for the 2017-2018 freshman class were: Critical Reading-- 10% below 500, 35% between 500 and 599, 34% between 600 and 699, and 21% between 700 and 800. Math-- 7% below 500, 36% between 500 and 599, 43% between 600 and 699, and 14% between 700 and 800. The ACT scores were 1% below 12, 12% between 12 and 17, 18% between 18 and 23, 18% between 24 and 29, and 51% above 30. 68% of the current freshmen were in the top fifth of their class; 92% were in the top two fifths. 21 freshmen graduated first in their class. **Admissions Contact:** Karen Foust, Executive Vice President for Enrollment. Email: *adm@hendrix.edu* Web: *www.hendrix.edu*

FINANCIAL AID: In 2017-2018, 100% of all full-time freshmen received some form of financial aid. 74% of all full-time freshmen received need-based aid. The average freshman award was $36,552. Need-based scholarships or need-based grants averaged $32,799 ($52,114 maximum); and need-based self-help aid (loans and jobs) averaged $5,463 ($7,500 maximum). 43% of undergraduate students work part-time. The average financial indebtedness of the 2017 graduate was $30,151. The FAFSA code is 001099. The priority date for freshman financial aid applications for fall entry is March 1.

JOHN BROWN UNIVERSITY — A-1

www.jbu.edu

Siloam Springs, AR 72761 — **(479) 524-7150**

Fax: (479) 524-4196	**Email: jbuinfo@jbu.edu**
Full-time: 609 men, 881 women	**Faculty:** 87; IIA, --$
Part-time: 240 men, 242 women	**Ph.D.s:** 50%
Graduate: 202 men, 439 women	**Student/Faculty:** 14 to 1
Year: semesters, summer session	**Tuition:** $26,144
Room & Board: $9040	**Freshman Class:** 1198 applied, 908 accepted, 327 enrolled
SAT EBR-W/M: 612/585 **ACT:** 26	**CEEB CODE:** 6311
Application Deadline: May 1	**VERY COMPETITIVE**

John Brown University, founded in 1919, is a private, interdenominational Christian university offering more than 40 undergraduate degree programs, 5 online programs, and 11 graduate degree programs. The figures in the above capsule and in this profile are approximate. There are 2 undergraduate schools and 3 graduate schools. In addition to regional accreditation, JBU has baccalaureate program accreditation with ABET, ACBSP, ACCE, and CAEP. The 200-acre campus is in a small town in Siloam Springs, AR, 25 miles west of Rogers, Arkansas and 80 mile east of Tulsa, OK. Including any residence halls, there are 31 buildings.

STUDENT LIFE: 51% of undergraduates are from Arkansas. Others are from 41 states, 50 foreign countries, and Canada. 68% are from public schools. 75% are White; 6% Hispanic; 5% Foreign; 4% two or more races; 4% race unknown; 2% African American; 2% Asian American; 2% American Indian/Alaska Native. **Female To Male Ratio:** 1.5:1. The average age of freshmen is 18; all undergraduates, 22. 17% do not continue beyond their first year; 73% remain to graduate. **Housing:** 1100 students can be accommodated in college housing, which includes married student dorms, on-campus apartments, and off-campus apartments. On-campus housing is guaranteed for all 4 years. 58% of students live on campus. Alcohol is not permitted. All students may keep cars.

FACULTY/CLASSROOMS: 64% of faculty are male; 36% are female. No introductory courses are taught by graduate students.

PROGRAMS OF STUDY: JBU confers B.A., B.S., B.S.N., B.Mus.Ed., B.S.E., and B.S.Eng. degrees. Associate and master's degrees are also awarded. Bachelor's degrees are awarded in BIOLOGICAL SCIENCE (biochemistry and biology/biological science), BUSINESS (accounting, business administration and management, entrepreneurial studies, international business, management, and marketing management), COMMUNICATIONS AND THE ARTS (art studies, communications, English, graphic design, illustration, music, music ministry, music performance, photography, and Spanish), COMPUTER AND PHYSICAL SCIENCE (chemistry, digital arts/technology, and mathematics), EDUCATION (early childhood education, educational studies, elementary education, English education, mathematics education, music education, outdoor leadership/education, and social studies education), ENGINEERING AND ENVIRONMENTAL DESIGN (construction management, electrical/electronics engineering, and engineering), HEALTH PROFESSIONS (kinesiology and nursing), SOCIAL SCIENCE (biblical studies, Christian studies, family and community services, history, interdisciplinary studies, ministries, philosophy, political science/

government, and psychology). Engineering, nursing, and teacher education are the strongest academically. Nursing, engineering, family and human services have the largest enrollments.

ACTIVITIES: There are no fraternities or sororities. Groups on campus include art, cheerleading, choir, chorale, chorus, dance, debate, drama, ethnic, forensics, honors, international, jazz band, literary magazine, musical theater, newspaper, orchestra, pep band, photography, radio and TV, religious, student government, and yearbook. Popular campus events include Fall Breakway, Christmas Candlelight Service, and Toilet Paper Game. **Sports:** There are 6 intercollegiate sports for men and 6 for women, and 10 intramural sports for men and 8 for women. Facilities include a gym, soccer and softball fields, a baseball diamond, training room and a swimming pool. The Lifetime Health Complex includes an indoor track, racquetball courts, a nautilus fitness center, an aerobics room, tennis courts, a rugby pitch and a recreation center. **Graduates:** From July 1, 2016 to June 30, 2017, 424 bachelor's degrees were awarded. The most popular majors were business/marketing (47%), visual and performing arts (12%), and family and consumer sciences (10%). In an average class, 1% graduate in 3 years or less, 59% graduate in 4 years or less, 67% graduate in 5 years or less, and 73% graduate in 6 years or less. Of the 2016 graduating class, 25% were enrolled in graduate school within 6 months of graduation, and 62% were employed.

SERVICES: Counseling and information services are available, as is tutoring in most subjects. There is a reader service for the blind, and remedial math and writing. **Library/Resources:** The library contains 287,410 volumes, 67,763 microform items, and 9,376 audio/video tapes/CDs/DVDs, and subscribes to 41,955 periodicals including electronic. Computerized library services include interlibrary loans, database searching, Internet access, and Wi-Fi capability. Special learning facilities include an art gallery, radio station, TV station, and a wellness assessment laboratory. **Physically Challenged Students:** 95% of the campus is accessible. Facilities include wheelchair ramps, elevators, special parking, specially equipped restrooms, special class scheduling, lowered drinking fountains, lowered telephones, and special housing. **Special:** Internships or field experiences are available in most majors. Study abroad in 15 countries, a Washington semester, work-study, and accelerated degree programs in organizational management and early childhood education are offered. There is a freshman honors program and 12 departmental honors programs. **Visiting:** There are regularly scheduled orientations for prospective students, including campus tours, consultations with faculty and coaches, and examination of financial aid opportunities. There are guides for informal visits, visitors may sit in on classes, and stay overnight. To schedule a visit, contact the Admissions Office. **Campus Safety and Security:** Measures include 24-hour foot and vehicle patrol, emergency notification system, self-defense education, and security escort services. There are lighted pathways/sidewalks and controlled access to dorms/residences.

REQUIREMENTS: Applicants should have completed 14 high school units, including 4 in English, 3 in math, 2 each in science, social studies, and foreign language, and 1 in history. Two references are required: 1 from a high school counselor or teacher, the other from a pastor or church leader. An essay and an interview are recommended. Applicants 21 years of age or older may be admitted without ACT or SAT scores. A GPA of 2.5 is required. AP and CLEP credits are accepted. All students must complete 25 hours of lower-level core courses, 19 to 22 of elective courses in wellness, natural science, mathematics, philosophy, arts, social studies, and global studies, and 8 hours in upper-level core courses. A total of 142 to 145 credit hours (includes hours for minor) with a minimum GPA of 2.25 (2.5 in profession education, teaching, and other state-required courses) is required to graduate. Students must complete an exit assessment before graduation. **Procedure:** Freshmen are admitted in the fall and spring. Entrance exams should be taken during the spring of the junior year or fall of the senior year. There is a rolling admissions plan. Applications should be filed by May 1 for fall entry. The fall 2017 application fee was $25. Notifications are sent November 1. Applications are accepted on-line. **Transfer Students:** 71 transfer students enrolled in 2016-2017. Transfer applicants must have completed at least 12 units of college work, with a minimum 2.5 GPA. 36 of 124 credits required for the bachelor's degree must be completed at JBU. **International Students:** There are 97 international students enrolled. They must take the TOEFL with a minimum score of 80 on the Internet-based version (iBT).

ADMISSIONS: 76% of the 2017-2018 applicants were accepted. The SAT scores for the 2017-2018 freshman class were: Math-- 8% below 500, 49% between 500 and 599, 35% between 600 and 699, and 8% between 700 and 800. Evidence-Based Reading/Writing-- 11% below 500, 25% between 500 and 599, 43% between 600 and 699, and 21% between 700 and 800. The ACT scores were 2% between 12 and 17, 23% between 18 and 23, 51% between 24 and 29, and 24% above 30. 29% of the current freshmen were in the top fifth of their class; 58% were in the top two fifths. **Admissions Contact:** Don Crandall, Vice President for Enrollment. Email: *jbuinfo@jbu.edu* Web: *www.jbu.edu*

FINANCIAL AID: In 2017-2018, 98% of all full-time freshmen received some form of financial aid. 72% of all full-time freshmen received need-based aid. The average freshman award was $20,951. Need-based scholarships or need-based grants averaged $16,845; need-based self-help aid (loans and jobs) averaged $5,560; non-need-based athletic scholarships averaged $14,150; and other non-need-based awards and non-need-based scholarships averaged $15,228. The average financial indebtedness of the 2017 graduate was $24,467. The CSS/Profile and FFS are required. The FAFSA code is 001100. The priority date for freshman financial aid applications for fall entry is March 1.

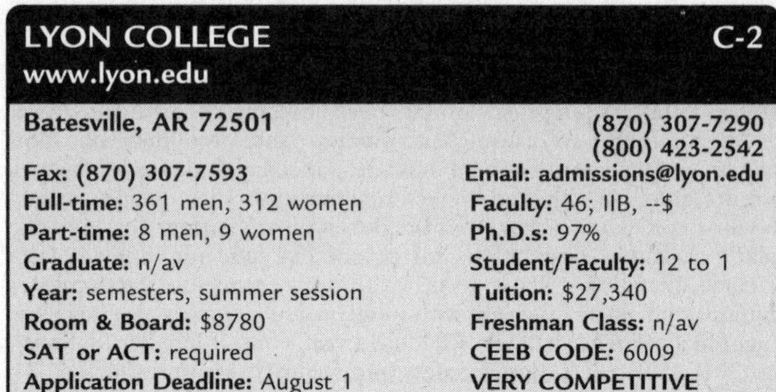

LYON COLLEGE C-2
www.lyon.edu

Batesville, AR 72501	(870) 307-7290 (800) 423-2542
Fax: (870) 307-7593	Email: admissions@lyon.edu
Full-time: 361 men, 312 women	Faculty: 46; IIB, --$
Part-time: 8 men, 9 women	Ph.D.s: 97%
Graduate: n/av	Student/Faculty: 12 to 1
Year: semesters, summer session	Tuition: $27,340
Room & Board: $8780	Freshman Class: n/av
SAT or ACT: required	CEEB CODE: 6009
Application Deadline: August 1	VERY COMPETITIVE

Lyon College, founded in 1872, is a selective, private, residential, liberal arts college affiliated with the Presbyterian Church. There is 1 undergraduate school. In addition to regional accreditation, LC has baccalaureate program accreditation with CAEP. The 136-acre campus is in a small town 90 miles north of Little Rock. Including any residence halls, there are 34 buildings.

STUDENT LIFE: 69% of undergraduates are from Arkansas. Others are from 23 states, and 10 foreign countries. 8% are Hispanic; 8% race unknown; 71% White; 6% African American; 3% American Indian/Alaska Native; 2% Asian American; 1% Foreign. **Male To Female Ratio:** 1.1:1. The average age of freshmen is 18; all undergraduates, 20. 34% do not continue beyond their first year; 50% remain to graduate. **Housing:** 496 students can be accommodated in college housing, which includes married student dorms, on-campus apartments, and off-campus apartments. In addition, there are special-interest houses, and freshman-only housing. On-campus housing is guaranteed for all 4 years. 75% of students live on campus. All students may keep cars.

FACULTY/CLASSROOMS: 66% of faculty are male; 34% are female. All teach undergraduates, and all do research. No introductory courses are taught by graduate students. The average class size in an introductory lecture is 15; in a laboratory is 16; and in a regular course is 15.

PROGRAMS OF STUDY: LC confers B.A. and B.S. degrees. Bachelor's degrees are awarded in AGRICULTURE (environmental studies), BIOLOGICAL SCIENCE (biology/biological science), BUSINESS (accounting, business administration and management, and business administration - international), COMMUNICATIONS AND THE ARTS (art, dramatic arts, English, music, and Spanish), COMPUTER AND PHYSICAL SCIENCE (chemistry and mathematics), EDUCATION (early childhood education), SOCIAL SCIENCE (anthropology, economics, history, political science/government, psychology, and religion). Psychology and biology are the strongest academically. Psychology, biology, and English have the largest enrollments.

ACTIVITIES: 18% of men belong to 3 national fraternities; 26% of women belong to 3 national sororities. There are 51 groups on campus, including art, bagpipe, band, cheerleading, chess, choir, drama, ethnic, film, honors, international, LGBT, literary magazine, marching band, newspaper, orchestra, photography, political, professional, religious, social, social service, student government, and yearbook. Popular campus events include Arkansas Scottish Festival, Service Day, and Baccalaureate Day. **Sports:** There are 6 intercollegiate sports for men and 7 for women, and 14 intramural sports for men and 14 for women. Facilities include a gym, softball, baseball, soccer fields, cross-country trail, indoor swimming pool, tennis courts, indoor baseball practice facility, wrestling facility, indoor football facility, and a weight room. **Graduates:** From July 1, 2016 to June 30, 2017, 109 bachelor's degrees were awarded. The most popular majors were psychology (23%), biology (21%), and English (9%). In an average class, 48% graduate in 4 years or less, 50% graduate in 5 years or less, and 50% graduate in 6 years or less. Of the 2016 graduating class, 50% were enrolled in graduate school within 6 months of graduation, and 44% were employed.

SERVICES: Counseling and information services are available, as is tutoring in every subject, such as foreign language, chemistry, math, english, political science, history, economics, biology, religion & philosophy There is remedial reading and writing. Writing and math labs are available. **Library/Resources:** The library contains 225,191 volumes, 2,928 microform items, and 6,233 audio/video tapes/CDs/DVDs, and subscribes to 43,146 periodicals including electronic. Computerized library services include interlibrary loans, database searching, Internet access, and Wi-Fi capability. Special learning facilities include an art gallery, a writing lab, collaborative learning workstations, a student success center, computer labs. **Physically Challenged Students:** 80% of the campus is accessible. Facilities include wheelchair ramps, elevators, special parking, specially equipped restrooms, and special housing. **Special:** Internships are offered as is cross-registration (for certain courses) with the University of Arkansas Community College at Batesville. A 2-2 engineering program is offered with the University of Missouri in Rolla, and a 3-2 program is offered with the University of Arkansas at Fayetteville. Work-study courses, study abroad in 4 countries, dual majors, student-designed majors, pass/fail options, a Washington semester, and credit for military experience are available. A 3-2 program is available with the University of Minnesota. There are 14 national honor societies and a freshman honors program. **Visiting:** There are regularly scheduled orientations for prospective students, consisting of a campus tour, admission and financial aid orientation, and information sessions with faculty and students. There are guides for informal visits and visitors may sit in on classes. To schedule a visit, contact Dana Bennett at (800) 423-2542. **Campus Safety and Security:** Measures include 24-hour foot and vehicle patrol, emergency notification system, self-defense education, and security escort services. There are lighted pathways/sidewalks and controlled access to dorms/residences.

REQUIREMENTS: The SAT or ACT is required. Applicants should have completed a minimum of 16 high school units, 4 in English, 3 each in science, math, and social sciences, and 2 in foreign language. A letter of recommendation and an admission interview are recommended. AP credits are accepted. All students are required to demonstrate proficiency in English composition, math, and foreign language, meet distribution requirements in social sciences, arts and literature, natural science and math, and religion and philosophy, complete the freshman orientation program, and take 1 semester of phys ed in each of the 4 years. The core curriculum requires 31 to 49 credit hours. A total of 120 credits, with a minimum GPA of 2.0, is required to graduate. **Procedure:** Freshmen are admitted fall and spring. Entrance exams should be taken in spring of the junior year and fall of the senior year. There are deferred admissions and rolling admissions plans. Applications should be filed by August 1 for fall entry; January 1 for spring entry. The fall 2017 application fee was $25. Notification is sent on a rolling basis. Applications are accepted online. **Transfer Students:** 44 transfer students enrolled in 2016-2017. Transfer applicants with 24 or more semester hours must submit a transcript and statement of good standing from each institution attended. Students with fewer than 24 semester hours must submit their final high school transcript and ACT or SAT scores. 30 of 120 credits required for the bachelor's degree must be completed at LC. **International Students:** There are 19 international students enrolled. They must take the TOEFL with a minimum score of 550 on the paper-based TOEFL (PBT) or 79 on the Internet-based version (iBT). Student must take the IELTS. They must also take the SAT or ACT.

ADMISSIONS: The SAT scores for the 2017-2018 freshman class were: Math-- 7% below 500, 46% between 500 and 599, and 46% between 600 and 699. Evidence-Based Reading/Writing-- 16% below 500, 46% between 500 and 599, 30% between 600 and 699, and 7% between 700 and 800. The ACT scores were 2% between 12 and 17, 41% between 18 and 23, 37% between 24 and 29, and 20% above 30. 57% of the current freshmen were in the top fifth of their class; 85% were in the top two fifths. **Admissions Contact:** Michael Kelley, Director of Admissions. Email: *admissions@lyon.edu* Web: *www.lyon.edu*

FINANCIAL AID: In 2017-2018, 100% of all full-time freshmen received some form of financial aid. The average freshman award was $19,512. 16% of undergraduate students work part-time. The FAFSA code is 001088. The priority date for freshman financial aid applications for fall entry is March 1.

OUACHITA BAPTIST UNIVERSITY — B-4

www.obu.edu

Arkadelphia, AR 71998	**(870) 245-5110** **(800) 342-5628**
Fax: (870) 245-5500	**Email: admissions@obu.edu**
Full-time: 671 men, 829 women	**Faculty:** 105; IIB, --$
Part-time: 30 men, 15 women	**Ph.D.s:** 88%
Graduate: n/av	**Student/Faculty:** 14 to 1
Year: semesters, summer session	**Tuition:** $25,870
Room & Board: $7630	**Freshman Class:** 1900 applied, 1230 accepted, 468 enrolled
SAT CR/M: 584/559 **ACT:** 25	**CEEB CODE:** 6549
Application Deadline: open	**VERY COMPETITIVE**

Ouachita Baptist University, founded in 1886, is a private liberal arts institution affiliated with the Arkansas Baptist State Convention. There are 7 undergraduate schools. In addition to regional accreditation, OBU has baccalaureate program accreditation with AACSB, NASM, and CAEP. The 200-acre campus is in a small town 65 miles southwest of Little Rock. Including any residence halls, there are 38 buildings.

STUDENT LIFE: 68% of undergraduates are from Arkansas. Others are from 28 states, and 28 foreign countries. 90% are from public schools. 81% are White; 8% African American; 5% Hispanic; 2% Foreign; 1% Asian American; 1% American Indian/Alaska Native. 81% are Protestant; 15% Unknown denominations. **Female To Male Ratio:** 1.2:1. The average age of freshmen is 18; all undergraduates, 21. 20% do not continue beyond their first year; 64% remain to graduate. **Housing:** 1587 students can be accommodated in college housing, which includes married student dorms, on-campus apartments, and off-campus apartments. On-campus housing is guaranteed for all 4 years. 95% of students live on campus. Alcohol is not permitted. All students may keep cars.

FACULTY/CLASSROOMS: 58% of faculty are male; 42% are female. All teach undergraduates, 50% do research, and 50% do both. No introductory courses are taught by graduate students. The average class size in an introductory lecture is 30; in a laboratory is 12; and in a regular course is 18.

PROGRAMS OF STUDY: OBU confers B.A., B.F.A., B.S., B.M., and B.M.E. degrees. Associate degrees are also awarded. Bachelor's degrees are awarded in BIOLOGICAL SCIENCE (biology/biological science), BUSINESS (accounting, business administration and management, recreation and leisure services, and sports management), COMMUNICATIONS AND THE ARTS (applied music, art, church music, communications, dramatic arts, English, graphic design, instrumental performance, instrumental music education, keyboard - piano concentration, music, music composition, musical theater, piano/organ, piano performance, Spanish, speech/debate/rhetoric, theatre arts, visual and performing arts, and voice), COMPUTER AND PHYSICAL SCIENCE (chemistry, computer science, mathematics, and physics), EDUCATION (art education, business education, early childhood education, elementary education, foreign languages education, mathematics education, middle school education, music education, science education, secondary education, social studies education, and social studies secondary school education), HEALTH PROFESSIONS (predentistry, premedicine, and speech pathology/audiology), SOCIAL SCIENCE (biblical languages, biblical studies, Christian studies, dietetics, history, ministries, philosophy, philosophy and religion, political science/government, prelaw, psychology, religion, religious music, sociology, theological studies, and youth ministry). Biology, business administration, and Christian studies have the largest enrollments.

ACTIVITIES: 20% of men belong to 4 local fraternities; 35% of women belong to 4 local sororities. There are 60 groups on campus, including band, cheerleading, choir, chorale, chorus, computers, drama, drill team, ethnic, film, honors, international, jazz band, literary magazine, marching band, musical theater, newspaper, opera, orchestra, pep band, photography, political, professional, radio and TV, religious, social, social service, student government, and yearbook. Popular campus events include International Student Fair, Tiger Tunes and Tiger Traks. **Sports:**

There are 7 intercollegiate sports for men and 7 for women, and 5 intramural sports for men and 5 for women. Facilities include a football stadium, indoor & outdoor tennis center, indoor complex featuring basketball, a swimming pool, a weight room, racquetball courts, and volleyball courts. **Graduates:** From July 1, 2016 to June 30, 2017, 286 bachelor's degrees were awarded. The most popular majors were business (19%), biology (13%), and visual and performing arts (9%). In an average class, 1% graduate in 3 years or less, 54% graduate in 4 years or less, 63% graduate in 5 years or less, and 64% graduate in 6 years or less. Of the 2016 graduating class, 43% were enrolled in graduate school within 6 months of graduation, and 93% were employed.

SERVICES: Counseling and information services are available, as is tutoring in most subjects. There is a reader service for the blind, and remedial math, reading, and writing. **Library/Resources:** The library contains 854,837 volumes, 325,598 microform items, and 3,612 audio/video tapes/CDs/DVDs, and subscribes to 21,500 periodicals including electronic. Computerized library services include interlibrary loans, database searching, and Wi-Fi capability. Special learning facilities include an art gallery and radio station. **Physically Challenged Students:** 95% of the campus is accessible. Facilities include wheelchair ramps, elevators, special parking, specially equipped restrooms, special class scheduling, and lowered drinking fountains. **Special:** Ouachita offers cross-registration with Henderson State University, a Washington semester for political science majors, internships for business majors and some mass communications and Christian studies majors, B.A.-B.S. degrees, dual majors, pass/fail options, and non-degree study. Study-abroad opportunities are available in Germany, England, France, Italy, Russia, Japan, China, Hong Kong, Australia, Austria, Belize, Scotland, Spain, South Africa, Costa Rica, and Morocco. There are 8 national honor societies and a freshman honors program. **Visiting:** There are regularly scheduled orientations for prospective students, including a campus tour, a question-and-answer session, and meetings with professors and students. There are guides for informal visits, visitors may sit in on classes, and stay overnight. To schedule a visit, contact the Admissions Office. **Campus Safety and Security:** Measures include 24-hour foot and vehicle patrol and emergency notification system. There are emergency telephones, lighted pathways/sidewalks, and controlled access to dorms/residences.

REQUIREMENTS: The SAT or ACT is required. Applicants should have completed 19 high school units, including 4 in English, 3 in social science, and 2 each in natural science, math, and foreign language and 1/2 in computer science are also recommended. A GPA of 2.8 is required. AP and CLEP credits are accepted. All students must fulfill 48 semester hours of general education courses, including 2 semesters of 1 foreign language and 7 chapel credits. A total of 120 semester hours, with a minimum GPA of 2.0, is required for graduation. **Procedure:** Freshmen are admitted fall, spring, and summer. Entrance exams should be taken in the junior year. There are deferred admissions and rolling admissions plans. Application deadlines are open. Applications are accepted on-line. **Transfer Students:** 28 transfer students enrolled in 2016-2017. Applicants must be eligible to return to their previous school. 60 of 120 credits required for the bachelor's degree must be completed at Ouachita. **International Students:** There are 39 international students enrolled. They must take the TOEFL with a minimum score of 550 on the paper-based TOEFL (PBT) or 80 on the Internet-based version (iBT).

ADMISSIONS: 65% of the 2017-2018 applicants were accepted. The SAT scores for the 2017-2018 freshman class were: Critical Reading-- 13% below 500, 47% between 500 and 599, 30% between 600 and 699, and 10% between 700 and 800. Math-- 28% below 500, 36% between 500 and 599, 34% between 600 and 699, and 2% between 700 and 800. The ACT scores were 4% between 12 and 17, 40% between 18 and 23, 40% between 24 and 29, and 16% above 30. 60% of the current freshmen were in the top fifth of their class; 80% were in the top two fifths. 27 freshmen graduated first in their class. **Admissions Contact:** Lori Motl, Director of Admissions Counseling. Email: *admissions@obu.edu* Web: *www.obu.edu*

FINANCIAL AID: In 2017-2018, 98% of all full-time freshmen received some form of financial aid. 69% of all full-time freshmen received need-based aid. The average freshman award was $20,358. Need-based scholarships or need-based grants averaged $14,150; need-based self-help aid (loans and jobs) averaged $4,300; and other non-need-based awards and non-need-based scholarships averaged $2,013. 50% of undergraduate students work part-time. The average financial indebtedness of the 2017 graduate was $27,500. The college's own financial statement is required. The FAFSA code is 001102. The priority date for freshman financial aid applications for fall entry is January 15.

PHILANDER SMITH COLLEGE *(The complete profile is made available exclusively on our website, www.barronspac.com)*

SOUTHERN ARKANSAS UNIVERSITY B-5

www.saumag.edu

Magnolia, AR 71754	**(870) 235-4040** **(800) 332-SAUM**
Fax: (870) 235-4931	**Email: muleriders@saumag.edu**
Full-time: 1298 men, 1536 women	**Faculty:** IIA, --$
Part-time: 77 men, 125 women	**Ph.D.s:** n/av
Graduate: 989 men, 495 women	**Student/Faculty:** n/av
Year: semesters, summer session	**Tuition:** $14,864 ($18,524)
Room & Board: $6668	**Freshman Class:** n/av
ACT: required	**CEEB CODE:** 6661
Application Deadline: August 27	**COMPETITIVE**

Southern Arkansas University, founded in 1909, is a state-supported liberal arts institution. The figures in the above capsule and in this profile are approximate. There are 4 undergraduate schools and 1 graduate school. In addition to regional accreditation, SAU has baccalaureate program accreditation with AACSB, CSWE, NASAD, NASM, and CAEP. The 781-acre campus is in a small town in Magnolia, in Columbia County, Arkansas, situated less than 20 miles north of the Louisiana state line. Including any residence halls, there are 31 buildings.

STUDENT LIFE: 73% of undergraduates are from Arkansas. Others are from 38 states, 40 foreign countries, and Canada. 97% are from public schools. 51% are White; 24% Foreign; 21% African American; 2% Hispanic; 1% Asian American; 1% American Indian/Alaska Native. **Male To Female Ratio:** 1.1:1. The average age of freshmen is 18; all undergraduates, 28. 32% do not continue beyond their first year. **Housing:** 1842 students can be accommodated in college housing, which includes dorms and on-campus apartments. In addition, there are honors houses. On-campus housing is guaranteed for all 4 years. 64% of students commute. Alcohol is not permitted. All students may keep cars.

FACULTY/CLASSROOMS: 56% of faculty are male; 44% are female. 97% teach undergraduates, 10% do research, and 10% do both. No introductory courses are taught by graduate students. The average class size in an introductory lecture is 23; in a laboratory is 18; and in a regular course is 20.

PROGRAMS OF STUDY: SAU confers B.A., B.S., B.A.S., B.B.A., B.M.E., B.S.E., and B.S.W. degrees. Associate and master's degrees are also awarded. Bachelor's degrees are awarded in AGRICULTURE (agricultural business management and agriculture), BIOLOGICAL SCIENCE (biology/biological science), BUSINESS (accounting and business administration and management), COMMUNICATIONS AND THE ARTS (art, broadcasting, communications, English, journalism, and Spanish), COMPUTER AND PHYSICAL SCIENCE (chemistry, computer science, and mathematics), EDUCATION (agricultural education, art education, business education, elementary education, health education, middle school education, music education, and science education), ENGINEERING AND ENVIRONMENTAL DESIGN (manufacturing technology), HEALTH PROFESSIONS (medical laboratory technology), SOCIAL SCIENCE (community services, history, political science/government, psychology, and sociology). Accounting and physical science are the strongest academically. Business administration and health education/kinesiology have the largest enrollment.

ACTIVITIES: 6% of men belong to 7 national fraternities; 5% of women belong to 7 national sororities. There are 80 groups on campus, including art, band, cheerleading, choir, chorale, computers, dance, drama, drill team, ethnic, honors, international, jazz band, literary magazine, marching band, musical theater, newspaper, pep band, photography, political, professional, religious, social, and student government. Popular campus events include Spring Fling, and Celebration of Lights. **Sports:** There are 8 intercollegiate sports for men and 8 for women, and 7 intramural sports for men and 7 for women. Facilities include a stadium, gym, tennis courts, baseball and softball fields, a track, indoor pool, a dance studio, basketball and volleyball courts, and a wellness center.

SERVICES: Counseling and information services are available, as is tutoring in most subjects. There is remedial math, reading, and writing. There is Supplemental instruction in courses for students with high drop/failure rates. **Library/Resources:** The library contains 176,437 volumes, 669,721 microform items, and 12,214 audio/video tapes/CDs/DVDs, and subscribes to 725 periodicals including electronic. Computerized library services include interlibrary loans, database searching, and Internet access. Special learning facilities include an art gallery, biological field station, and a university working farm. **Physically Challenged Students:** 95% of the campus is accessible. Facilities include wheelchair ramps, elevators, special parking, specially equipped restrooms, special class scheduling, lowered drinking fountains, and lowered telephones. **Special:** Work-study programs at SAU, business and Spanish internships, study abroad in Russia and Mexico, and a general studies degree are offered. There is 1 national honor society, a freshman honors program, and 6 departmental honors programs. **Visiting:** There are regularly scheduled orientations for prospective students. There are guides for informal visits, visitors may sit in on classes, and stay overnight. To schedule a visit, contact the Admissions Office. **Campus Safety and Security:** Measures include 24-hour foot and vehicle patrol and security escort services. There are lighted pathways/sidewalks.

REQUIREMENTS: The ACT is required, with a minimum composite of 19. Applicants should have completed 4 high school units in English, 3 each in math and social studies, and 2 each in natural science and foreign language. The GED is accepted. AP and CLEP credits are accepted. All students must complete 43 semester hours of general education courses, including 18 in humanities, 12 in social sciences, 4 each in biological and physical science, 3 in math, and 2 to 3 in physical and health education. A minimum of 124 total semester hours, with a minimum GPA of 2.0, is required to graduate. **Procedure:** Freshmen are admitted to all sessions. Entrance exams should be taken in the fall prior to enrollment. There are deferred admissions and rolling admissions plans. Application deadlines are open. Notification is sent on a rolling basis. Applications are accepted on-line. **Transfer Students:** Applicants must be eligible to return to their previous school and meet GPA requirements. Those with fewer than 24 credit hours must submit ACT or SAT scores and a high school transcript or GED. 30 of 124 credits required for the bachelor's degree must be completed at SAU. **International Students:** They must take the TOEFL. They must also take the ACT.

Admissions Contact: Sarah Jennings, Dean of Enrollment Services. Email: *muleriders@saumag.edu* Web: *www.saumag.edu*

FINANCIAL AID: The FAFSA code is 001107. The priority date for freshman financial aid applications for fall entry is February.

UNIVERSITY OF ARKANSAS AT FAYETTEVILLE — A-1

application.uark.edu

Fayetteville, AR 72701	**(479) 575-5346** **(800) 377-8632**
Fax: (479) 575-7515	**Email: uofa@uark.edu**
Full-time: 9560 men, 10,904 women	**Faculty:** 1151
Part-time: 1245 men, 1335 women	**Ph.D.s:** 79%
Graduate: 2284 men, 2230 women	**Student/Faculty:** 19 to 1
Year: semesters, summer session	**Tuition:** $9062 ($24,308)
Room & Board: $10,704	**Freshman Class:** 21715 applied, 14324 accepted, 5065 enrolled
SAT EBR-W/M: 600/590 **ACT:** 26	**CEEB CODE:** 6866
Application Deadline: August 1	**VERY COMPETITIVE**

University of Arkansas at Fayettville offers high-caliber teaching and hands-on research experiences to undergraduate and graduate students. UA at Fayetteville is the 10th fastest growing public research university in the country. Since its founding, the University of Arkansas has compiled a remarkable record of scientific, technological, intellectual and creative accomplishments. There are 9 undergraduate schools and 2 graduate schools. In addition to regional accreditation, UA at Fayetteville has baccalaureate program accreditation with AACSB, ABET, ACEJMC, ASLA, CSWE, FIDER, NAAB, NASM, CAEP, NAAB, CCNE, and AAFCS. The 718-acre campus is in an urban area in Fayetteville, AR. Including any residence halls, there are 224 buildings.

STUDENT LIFE: 55% of undergraduates are from Arkansas. Others are from 46 states, 83 foreign countries, and Canada. 85% are from public schools. 76% are White; 9% Hispanic; 4% African American; 4% two or more races; 3% Foreign; 2% Asian American; 1% American Indian/Alaska Native; 1% race unknown. **Female To Male Ratio:** 1.1:1. The average age of freshmen is 18; all undergraduates, 21. 18% do not continue beyond their first year; 62% remain to graduate. **Housing:** 5729 students can be accommodated in college housing, which includes single sex, coed dorms and on-campus apartments. In addition, there are honors houses, special-interest houses, fraternity houses, and sorority houses. On-campus housing is guaranteed for the freshman year only, is available on a first-come, and first-served basis. 75% of students commute. All students may keep cars.

FACULTY/CLASSROOMS: 59% of faculty are male; 41% are female. 96% teach undergraduates. Graduate students teach 35% of introductory courses. The average class size in an introductory lecture is 44; in a laboratory is 21; and in a regular course is 36.

PROGRAMS OF STUDY: UA at Fayetteville confers B.A., B.Arch., B.F.A., B.I.D., B.L.A., B.M., B.S., B.S.A., B.S.B.A., B.S.B.E., B.S.B.M.E., B.S.C.E., B.S.ChE., B.S.CmpE., B.S.C.S., B.S.E., B.S.E.E., B.S.H.E.S., B.S.I.B., B.S.I.E., B.S.M.E., B.S.N., and B.S.W. degrees. Master's and doctoral degrees are also awarded. Bachelor's degrees are awarded in AGRICULTURE (agricultural business management, agricultural communications, animal science, horticulture, and poultry science), BIOLOGICAL SCIENCE (biology/biological science, nutrition, and nutritional sciences), BUSINESS (apparel and accessories marketing, business administration marketing, business economics, business information systems, finance, hospitality management services, human resources, international business management, business management, marketing/retailing/merchandising, retailing, and transportation management), COMMUNICATIONS AND THE ARTS (art, communications, dramatic arts, English, French, German, graphic design, journalism, music, Spanish, and studio art), COMPUTER AND PHYSICAL SCIENCE (chemistry, computer science, earth science, geology, information sciences and systems, mathematics, and physics), EDUCATION (agricultural education, business education, childhood education, career, technical education & training, early childhood education, educational studies, elementary education, recreation education, special education, and technical education), ENGINEERING AND ENVIRONMENTAL DESIGN (architecture, bioengineering, biomedical engineering, chemical engineering, civil engineering, computer engineering, electrical/electronics engineering, environmental science, industrial engineering, interior design, landscape architecture, landscape architecture/design, and mechanical engineering), HEALTH PROFESSIONS (exercise science, medical science, nursing, and public health), SOCIAL SCIENCE (anthropology, architectural studies, classical/ancient civilization, communication sciences & disorders, criminal justice, economics, food science, geography, history, human development, interdisciplinary studies, international relations, philosophy, political science/government, psychology, social work, and sociology). Business and architecture is the strongest academically. Business, engineering, and health professions have the largest enrollments.

ACTIVITIES: 21% of men belong to 19 national fraternities; 38% of women belong to 15 national sororities. There are 430 groups on campus, including art, band, cheerleading, chess, choir, chorale, chorus, computers, dance, drama, drill team, environmental, ethnic, film, honors, international, jazz band, LGBT, literary magazine, marching band, musical theater, newspaper, opera, orchestra, pep band, photography, political, professional, radio and TV, religious, social, social service, student government, symphony, and yearbook. Popular campus events include New Student Welcome, ROCK Camp, Welcome Weeks, Campus Blood Drive, MLK Vigil, Black History Month, Student Involvement Awards, Make a Difference Day, Emerging Leaders, Razorbash, Campus Drama Productions, and Distinguished Lecture Series. **Sports:** There are 8 intercollegiate sports for men and 11 for women, and 25 intramural sports for men and 25 for women. Facilities include a football stadium, basketball courts, baseball stadium, volleyball/gymnastics, soccer stadium, cross country course, golf practice facility, indoor swimming and diving pool, outdoor and indoor tennis courts, an indoor practice football field, an indoor running track, outdoor track, and a softball stadium. **Graduates:** From July 1, 2016 to June 30, 2017, 4615 bachelor's degrees were awarded. The most popular majors were business/marketing (23%), engineering (10%), and health professions (8%). In an average class, 42% graduate in 4 years or less, 59% graduate in 5 years or less, and 62% graduate in 6 years or less. Of the 2016 graduating class, 18% were enrolled in graduate school within 6 months of graduation, and 51% were employed.

SERVICES: Counseling and information services are available, as is tutoring in most subjects, such as accounting, anthropology, biology, business law, chemical engineering, chemistry, economics, finance, geosciences, mechanical engineering, mathematics, music, philosophy, political science, psychology, physics, sociology, business,writing, world languages There is a reader service for the blind, and remedial math, reading, and writing. There is a math resource center and a writing center which is a part of CLASS+, and student support services and individual colleges have labs and other facilities. **Library/Resources:** The library contains 2.5 million volumes, 5.6 million microform items, and 42,309 audio/video tapes/CDs/DVDs, and subscribes to 92,699 periodicals including electronic. Computerized library services include interlibrary loans, database searching, Internet access, and Wi-Fi capability. Special learning facilities include an art gallery, radio station, TV station, numerous research centers. **Physically Challenged Students:** All of the campus is accessible. Facilities include wheelchair ramps, elevators, special parking, specially equipped restrooms, special class scheduling, lowered drinking fountains, lowered telephones. **Special:** Co-op programs and internships are available, as well as dual majors and B.A.-B.S. degrees in many majors, and study abroad in 26 countries. 3-3 Program: College of Arts and Sciences/School of Law. 3-3 Program: Dale Bumpers College/School of Law. Law: JD/MBA, JD/MPA (Public Administration). Ag Law: LLM/MS (Ag Econ). Combined Academic - Medical or Dental Degree: Fulbright College of Arts and Sciences. JD/MA in Political Science. MBA/M.P.S. (public service) in conjunction with the Clinton School of Public Service. 5-year BA-MA in Journalism. JD/MSW (Social Work). There are 47 national honor societies, Phi Beta Kappa, a freshman honors program, and 57 departmental honors programs. **Visiting:** There are regularly scheduled orientations for prospective students, including a meeting with an admissions counselor, a walking tour of campus with a student guide, and a residence hall tour. Weekday appointments are encouraged for the best experience, but walk-in visits are also welcome. To schedule a visit, contact Kristen Davidson at visit@uark.edu. **Campus Safety and Security:** Measures include 24-hour foot and vehicle patrol, emergency notification system, self-defense education, and security escort services. There are shuttle buses, emergency telephones, lighted pathways/sidewalks, controlled access to dorms/residences, crime prevention lectures, rape defense program, property engraving, bicycle patrol, and electronic card access in residence halls.

REQUIREMENTS: The SAT or ACT is required. Admissions requirements: 4 years of English and math, 3 years each of social science and natural science. Secondary school record, class rank, essay, recommendations, character, first generation, alumni relations, geographic residence, and volunteer work and work experience considered. A GPA of 3.0 is required. AP and CLEP credits are accepted. Important factors in the admissions decision are leadership record, advanced placement or honors courses, evidence of special talent, personality/intangible qualities, extracurricular activities record, recommendations by alumni, and geographical diversity. To graduate, all students must complete 35 hours of general education courses, including 9 in social sciences, 8 in science, 6 in English, and 3 each in fine arts, math, humanities, and history/government. Students must have a minimum cumulative GPA of 2.0 and no more than 25% of the minimum total of 120 hours may be D or below. **Procedure:** Freshmen are admitted fall, spring, and summer. Entrance exams should be taken during junior year or early during senior year. There are early admissions and rolling admissions plans. Applications should be filed by August 1 for fall entry; December 20 for spring entry; and May 1 for summer entry. The fall 2017 application fee was $40. Notification of early decision is sent December 15; regular decision, on a rolling basis. 490 applicants were on the 2017 waiting list; 167 were admitted. Applications are accepted on-line. **Transfer Students:** 1412 transfer students enrolled in 2016-2017. Applicants must have at least a 2.0 GPA (on a 4-point scale) on all college course work attempted and must be in good standing at the last institution attended. Students with fewer than 24 transferable credit hours must meet admission requirements for entering freshmen, in addition to admission requirements for transfer students. 30 of 120 credits required for the bachelor's degree must be completed at UA at Fayetteville. **International Students:** There are 730 international students enrolled. They must take the TOEFL with a minimum score of 550 on the paper-based TOEFL (PBT) or 79 on the Internet-based version (iBT) and the college's own test, Students must take any one of these tests the IELTS, and PTE-A. They must also take the SAT or ACT.

ADMISSIONS: 66% of the 2017-2018 applicants were accepted. The SAT scores for the 2017-2018 freshman class were: Math-- 5% below 500, 47% between 500 and 599, 39% between 600 and 699, and 9% between 700 and 800. Evidence-Based Reading/Writing-- 4% below 500, 42% between 500 and 599, 45% between 600 and 699, and 9% between 700 and 800. The ACT scores were 25% between 18 and 23, 53% between 24 and 29, and 22% above 30. 46% of the current freshmen were in the top fifth of their class; 75% were in the top two fifths. **Admissions Contact:** Suzanne McCray, Vice Provost of Enrollment. Email: *uofa@uark.edu* Web: *application.uark.edu*

FINANCIAL AID: 12% of undergraduate students work part-time. The SFS is required. The FAFSA code is 001108. The priority date for freshman financial aid applications for fall entry is March 15.

UNIVERSITY OF ARKANSAS AT LITTLE ROCK *(The complete profile is made available exclusively on our website, www.barronspac.com)*

UNIVERSITY OF ARKANSAS AT MONTICELLO *(The complete profile is made available exclusively on our website, www.barronspac.com)*

UNIVERSITY OF ARKANSAS AT PINE BLUFF — C-4

www.uapb.edu

Pine Bluff, AR 71601 — **(870) 575-8492**

Fax: (870) 575-4607	**Email: webadmin@uapb.edu**
Full-time: 1018 men, 1294 women	**Faculty:** n/av
Part-time: 93 men, 140 women	**Ph.D.s:** n/av
Graduate: 55 men, 58 women	**Student/Faculty:** n/av
Year: semesters, summer session	**Tuition:** $6271 ($11,941)
Room & Board: $7270	**Freshman Class:** n/av
SAT: required	**CEEB CODE:** 6004
Application Deadline: August 1	**COMPETITIVE**

University of Arkansas at Pine Bluff, established in 1873, is a historically black land-grant institution providing a liberal arts education as part of the public University of Arkansas system. There are 5 undergraduate schools and 1 graduate school. In addition to regional accreditation, UA at Pine Bluff has baccalaureate program accreditation with ACBSP, AHEA, CSWE, NASAD, NASM, and CAEP. The 318-acre campus is in a small town 40 miles southeast of Little Rock and approximately 142 miles southwest of Memphis. Including any residence halls, there are 49 buildings.

STUDENT LIFE: 61% of undergraduates are from Arkansas. Others are from 38 states, 20 foreign countries, and Canada. 91% are African American; 5% White; 2% Foreign; 1% Hispanic. **Female To Male Ratio:** 1.3:1. The average age of freshmen is 18; all undergraduates, 22. 29% do not continue beyond their first year; 27% remain to graduate. **Housing:** 1495 students can be accommodated in college housing, which includes dorms. Honors clusters are in the dorms. On-campus housing is guaranteed for all 4 years. 65% of students commute. Alcohol is not permitted. All students may keep cars.

FACULTY/CLASSROOMS: 54% of faculty are male; 46% are female. No introductory courses are taught by graduate students. The average class size in a laboratory is 20 and in a regular course is 21.

PROGRAMS OF STUDY: Pine Bluff confers B.A., B.S., B.G.S., and B.S.N. degrees. Associate, master's, and doctoral degrees are also awarded. Bachelor's degrees are awarded in AGRICULTURE (agricultural sciences, agriculture, conservation and regulation, and fishing and fisheries), BIOLOGICAL SCIENCE (biology/biological science), BUSINESS (accounting and business administration and management), COMMUNICATIONS AND THE ARTS (art, English, journalism, music, and speech/debate/rhetoric), COMPUTER AND PHYSICAL SCIENCE (chemistry, computer science, mathematics, and physics), EDUCATION (agricultural education, art education, business education, early childhood education, English education, health and physical education, home economics education, industrial arts education, mathematics education, middle school education, music education, physical education, science education, social science education, and special education), ENGINEERING AND ENVIRONMENTAL DESIGN (industrial engineering technology and preengineering), HEALTH PROFESSIONS (nursing, predentistry, premedicine, prepharmacy, and rehabilitation therapy), SOCIAL SCIENCE (criminal justice, family/consumer studies, gerontology, history, liberal arts/general studies, parks and recreation management, political science/government, psychology, social work, and sociology). STEM disciplines is the strongest academically. Biology, business administration, and criminal justice have the largest enrollments.

ACTIVITIES: There are 104 groups on campus, including art, band,

cheerleading, choir, computers, debate, drama, drill team, honors, jazz band, marching band, newspaper, orchestra, photography, political, professional, radio and TV, religious, social, social service, student government, and yearbook. Popular campus events include Founders Day, Messiah, Spring Emphasis, and Unity Fest. **Sports:** There are 7 intercollegiate sports for men and 8 for women, and 20 intramural sports for men and 19 for women. Facilities include a phys ed complex for flag football, basketball, volleyball, softball, tennis, handball, racquetball, track and field, badminton, swimming pool, and football stadium.

SERVICES: Counseling and information services are available, as is tutoring in most subjects. There is a reader service for the blind, and remedial math, reading, and writing. **Library/Resources:** The library contains 271,547 volumes, 119,205 microform items, and 4,299 audio/video tapes/CDs/DVDs, and subscribes to 1,050 periodicals including electronic. Computerized library services include interlibrary loans and database searching. Special learning facilities include an art gallery, radio station, and TV station. **Physically Challenged Students:** 98% of the campus is accessible. Facilities include wheelchair ramps, elevators, special parking, specially equipped restrooms, special class scheduling, lowered drinking fountains, and lowered telephones. **Special:** The university offers formal co-op education and work-study programs, concurrent registration with members of the University of Arkansas system, internships, B.A.-B.S. degrees, and dual and student-designed majors. Also offered are credit for military experience, nondegree study, individualized programs of study for honors college students, and study abroad. There are 4 national honor societies, a freshman honors program, and 6 departmental honors programs. **Visiting:** There are regularly scheduled orientations for prospective students. There are guides for informal visits, visitors may sit in on classes, and stay overnight. To schedule a visit, contact the Director of Recruitment at (501) 575-8961 or (800) 525-5272. **Campus Safety and Security:** Measures include 24-hour foot and vehicle patrol, self-defense education, and security escort services. There are emergency telephones, lighted pathways/sidewalks. There is a department of public safety and security on campus.

REQUIREMENTS: The SAT is required. The ACT, with a satisfactory score is preferred. Applicants must have earned 22 credits, including 4 units of English and 3 each in social studies, math, and science. The GED is accepted. Students not meeting these requirements may apply for conditional admission. A GPA of 2.0 is required. AP and CLEP credits are accepted. All students must complete at least 120 hours of credit, including 30 hours in their major, while earning an overall 2.0 GPA (2.5 for teacher education majors) and a C or better in all major courses. Distribution requirements include English, math, social and natural science, and phys ed courses. Students must pass a comprehensive exam in their major. **Procedure:** Freshmen are admitted fall, spring, and summer. Entrance exams should be taken during the junior or senior year. There are early admissions, deferred admissions, and rolling admissions plans. Applications should be filed by August 1 for fall entry; January 1 for spring entry. **Transfer Students:** Transfer students must have a minimum GPA of 2.0. Applicants with fewer than 60 semester hours of college credit must submit an application, ACT or SAT I scores, and all college transcripts. 30 of 120 credits required for the bachelor's degree must be completed at UA Pine Buff. **International Students:** They must take the TOEFL with a minimum score of 550 on the paper-based TOEFL (PBT) or 79 on the Internet-based version (iBT). They must also take the SAT or ACT.

Admissions Contact: Philomena Owasoyo, Director of Admissions. Email: *webadmin@uapb.edu* Web: *www.uapb.edu*

FINANCIAL AID: Pine Bluff is a member of CSS. The FAFSA code is 001086. The priority date for freshman financial aid applications for fall entry is January 1.

UNIVERSITY OF CENTRAL ARKANSAS — C-3

www.uca.edu

Conway, AR 72035	(501) 450-3663 (800) 243-8245 Email: helpdesk@uca.edu
Full-time: 3223 men, 4841 women	**Faculty:** IIA, --$
Part-time: 722 men, 756 women	**Ph.D.s:** n/av
Graduate: 472 men, 1336 women	**Student/Faculty:** n/av
Year: semesters, summer session	**Tuition:** $8524 ($15,047)
Room & Board: $6518	**Freshman Class:** 5362 applied, 4823 accepted, 1937 enrolled
SAT or ACT: required	**CEEB CODE:** 6012
Application Deadline: n/av	**VERY COMPETITIVE**

University of Central Arkansas, founded in 1907, offers more than 75 undergraduate and more than 50 graduate certificate and degree programs, including doctoral programs in four disciplines. There are 6 undergraduate schools and 1 graduate school. In addition to regional accreditation, University of Central Arkansas has baccalaureate program accreditation with AACSB, ABET, ADA, APTA, CAHEA, NASAD, NASM, CAEP, and NLN. The 356-acre campus is in a small town 30 miles north of Little Rock. Including any residence halls, there are 124 buildings.

STUDENT LIFE: 88% of undergraduates are from Arkansas. Others are from 43 states, 73 foreign countries, and Canada. 66% are White; 16% African American; 5% Hispanic; 5% Foreign; 4% two or more races; 2% Asian American; 1% American Indian/Alaska Native; 1% race unknown. **Female To Male Ratio:** 1.6:1. The average age of freshmen is 18; all undergraduates, 21. **Housing:** 3867 students can be accommodated in college housing, which includes married student dorms, on-campus apartments, and off-campus apartments. In addition, there are honors houses, sorority houses, and residential colleges. On-campus housing is guaranteed for all 4 years. Alcohol is not permitted. All students may keep cars.

FACULTY/CLASSROOMS: No introductory courses are taught by graduate students.

PROGRAMS OF STUDY: UCA confers B.A., B.S., B.S.E., B.P.S., B.B.A., B.F.A., B.M., and B.S.N. degrees. Associate, master's, and doctoral degrees are also awarded. Bachelor's degrees are awarded in BIOLOGICAL SCIENCE (biology/biological science), BUSINESS (accounting, banking and finance, business administration and management, business economics, finance, insurance and risk management, and marketing/retailing/merchandising), COMMUNICATIONS AND THE ARTS (communications, creative writing, English, French, journalism, music, Spanish, and speech/debate/rhetoric), COMPUTER AND PHYSICAL SCIENCE (applied mathematics, chemistry, computer science, information sciences and systems, mathematics, and physics), EDUCATION (art education, athletic training, early childhood education, education, education of the exceptional child, elementary education, foreign languages education, guidance education, library science, middle school education, music education, physical education, science education, secondary education, and special education), ENGINEERING AND ENVIRONMENTAL DESIGN (environmental science, interior design, and preengineering), HEALTH PROFESSIONS (exercise science, health care administration, health science, kinesiology, medical technology, nuclear medical technology, nursing, occupational therapy, physical therapy, predentistry, premedicine, preoptometry, prepharmacy, preveterinary science, radiological science, and speech pathology/audiology), SOCIAL SCIENCE (addiction studies, African American studies, anthropology, communication sciences & disorders, criminology, dietetics, economics, family/consumer studies, geography, geography information science, gerontology, history, philosophy, political science/government, psychology, public administration, religion, and sociology). Business, health-related sciences, and education are the strongest academically. Health professions & related sciences, business & marketing, and education have the largest enrollments.

ACTIVITIES: There are 230 groups on campus, including art, band, cheerleading, choir, chorale, chorus, computers, dance, debate, drama, environmental, ethnic, film, forensics, honors, international, jazz band, LGBT, literary magazine, marching band, musical theater, newspaper, orchestra, pep band, photography, political, professional, radio and TV, religious, social, social service, student government, symphony, and yearbook. Popular campus events include Bear Facts Day, and Greek God and Miss UCA. **Sports:** There are 7 intercollegiate sports for men and 8 for women, and 14 intramural sports for men and 14 for women. Facilities include a gym, swimming pool, fitness center, racquetball and tennis courts, a track, soccer fields, football field, basketball court, softball fields, and an indoor athletic facility. **Graduates:** From July 1, 2016 to June 30, 2017, 1661 bachelor's degrees were awarded. The most popular majors were health professions and related sciences (22%), business/marketing (18%), and education (9%).

SERVICES: Counseling and information services are available, as is tutoring in most subjects, such as biology, chemistry, physics, algebra, trigonometry, calculus, geometry, sociology, writing, literature, Spanish, accounting, business statistics, French, German, writing and technology. There is a reader service for the blind, and remedial math, reading, and writing. **Library/Resources:** The library contains 446,575 volumes, 618,347 microform items, and 3,173 audio/video tapes/CDs/DVDs, and subscribes to 59,937 periodicals including electronic. Computerized library services include interlibrary loans, database searching, Internet access, and Wi-Fi capability. Special learning facilities include an art gallery, planetarium, radio station, and TV station. **Physically Challenged Students:** Facilities include wheelchair ramps, elevators, special parking, specially equipped restrooms, special class scheduling, lowered drinking fountains, lowered telephones, and special housing. **Special:** Study abroad, work-study programs, a B.S.-B.A. degree, a 3-2 engineering degree with the University of Arkansas at Fayetteville, dual majors, nondegree study, and pass/fail options are available. Co-op programs in business, computer science, and health sciences and internships in education are also possible. There is a freshman honors program. **Visiting:** There are regularly scheduled orientations for prospective students, including tours at 11 a.m. and 2 p.m.; departments and dormitories may be visited. There are also special visitation days that include a campus tour, departmental session, lunch, parents' session, optional residence hall tour, and classroom visit or planetarium show. Visitors may sit in on classes. To schedule a visit, contact the Admissions Office at admissions@uca.edu. **Campus Safety and Security:** Measures include 24-hour foot and vehicle patrol, emergency notification system, self-defense education, and security escort services. There are shuttle buses, emergency telephones, lighted pathways/sidewalks, and controlled access to dorms/residences.

REQUIREMENTS: The SAT or ACT is required. A GPA of 2.8 is required. AP and CLEP credits are accepted. Important factors in the admissions decision are advanced placement or honors courses, evidence of special talent, and recommendations by school officials. To be eligible for graduation with a baccalaureate degree, a student must file a program of study approved by the major and minor advisors that contains at least 120 semester hours of unduplicated credit (at least 40 hours must be upper-division), or more if the curriculum requires it. A grade point average of 2.0 or better is required in each of the major and minor fields and cumulatively. **Procedure:** Freshmen are admitted to all sessions. There is a rolling admissions plan. Application deadlines are open. Applications are accepted on-line. **Transfer Students:** Applicants need, on UCA's scale, a minimum cumulative GPA of 2.0. 15 of 120 credits required for the bachelor's degree must be completed at UCA. **International Students:** There are 520 international students enrolled. They must take the TOEFL.

ADMISSIONS: 90% of the 2017-2018 applicants were accepted. The ACT scores were 3% between 12 and 17, 44% between 18 and 23, 40% between 24 and 29, and 13% above 30. **Admissions Contact:** Amber Hall, Director of Institutional Research. Email: *helpdesk@uca.edu* Web: *www.uca.edu*

FINANCIAL AID: The FAFSA code is 001092. Check with the school for current application deadlines.

UNIVERSITY OF THE OZARKS *(The complete profile is made available exclusively on our website, www.barronspac.com)*

WILLIAMS BAPTIST COLLEGE D-1

www.wbcoll.edu

Walnut Ridge, AR 72476 **(870) 759-4120** **(800) 722-4434**

Fax: (870) 886-3924	**Email:** admissions@wbcoll.edu
Full-time: 262 men, 182 women	**Faculty:** 28
Part-time: 21 men, 28 women	**Ph.D.s:** 61%
Graduate: 1 men, 6 women	**Student/Faculty:** 15 to 1
Year: semesters, summer session	**Tuition:** $17,320
Room & Board: $7400	**Freshman Class:** n/av
SAT or ACT: required	**CEEB CODE:** 6658
Application Deadline: rolling	**COMPETITIVE**

Williams Baptist College, founded in 1941, is a private liberal arts institution providing undergraduate education in business, education, humanities, natural sciences, religion, and social sciences. WBC is affiliated with the Southern Baptist Church and is sponsored by the Arkansas Baptist Convention. There is 1 undergraduate school. The 180-acre campus is in a rural area 100 miles northwest of Memphis, TN and 125 miles north of Little Rock. Including any residence halls, there are 54 buildings.

STUDENT LIFE: 69% of undergraduates are from Arkansas. Others are from 23 states, and 6 foreign countries. 80% are from public schools. 74% are White; 6% Hispanic; 5% Foreign; 2% two or more races; 12% African American; 1% Asian American. 93% are Protestant. **Male To Female Ratio:** 1.3:1. The average age of freshmen is 18; all undergraduates, 20. 30% do not continue beyond their first year; 35% remain to graduate. **Housing:** 473 students can be accommodated in college housing, which includes married student dorms and on-campus apartments. On-campus housing is guaranteed for all 4 years. 74% of students live on campus. Alcohol is not permitted. All students may keep cars.

FACULTY/CLASSROOMS: 61% of faculty are male; 39% are female. All teach undergraduates and all do research. No introductory courses are taught by graduate students. The average class size in an introductory lecture is 16; in a laboratory is 15; and in a regular course is 16.

PROGRAMS OF STUDY: WBC confers B.A., B.S., and B.S.Ed. degrees. Associate degrees are also awarded. Bachelor's degrees are awarded in BIOLOGICAL SCIENCE (biology/biological science), BUSINESS (business administration and management), COMMUNICATIONS AND THE ARTS (art, English, and music), COMPUTER AND PHYSICAL SCIENCE (computer science), EDUCATION (elementary education, physical education, and secondary education), SOCIAL SCIENCE (counseling/psychology, history, psychology, religion, religious education, and religious music). Education, business, and biology have the largest enrollments.

ACTIVITIES: There are no fraternities or sororities. There are 32 groups on campus, including art, cheerleading, choir, chorale, drama, international, literary magazine, professional, religious, social, social service, and student government. Popular campus events include Harvest Fest, Christmas in the Cove, and Spring Fling. **Sports:** There are 3 intercollegiate sports for men and 4 for women, and 4 intramural sports for men and 4 for women. Facilities include a gym, weight room, racquetball and tennis courts, a jogging track, sand volleyball, disc golf, and a student center. **Graduates:** From July 1, 2016 to June 30, 2017, 99 bachelor's degrees were awarded. The most popular majors were psychology (19%), biology (14%), and business/finance (13%). In an average class, 29% graduate in 4 years or less, 37% graduate in 5 years or less, and 40% graduate in 6 years or less.

SERVICES: Counseling and information services are available, as is tutoring in most subjects. There is remedial math. **Library/Resources:** The library contains 101,214 volumes, 119 microform items, and 172 audio/video tapes/CDs/DVDs, and subscribes to 31 periodicals including electronic. Computerized library services include interlibrary loans, database searching, Internet access, and Wi-Fi capability. Special learning facilities include an art gallery, and an education curriculum lab. **Physically Challenged Students:** 90% of the campus is accessible. Facilities include wheelchair ramps, elevators, special parking, specially equipped restrooms, lowered drinking fountains, and special housing. **Special:** WBC offers study abroad in England, Latin America, the Middle East, and Russia, a Washington semester through the American Studies Program, and a general studies major. There are 9 national honor societies and 10 departmental honors programs. **Visiting:** There are regularly scheduled orientations for prospective students, campus tour, visit with professors, and visit with current students. There are guides for informal visits, visitors may sit in on classes, and stay overnight. To schedule a visit, contact Andrew Watson at (800) 722-4434. **Campus Safety and Security:** Measures include 24-hour foot and vehicle patrol and emergency notification system. There are lighted pathways/sidewalks and controlled access to dorms/residences.

REQUIREMENTS: The SAT or ACT is required. First-time freshmen must have a minimum composite score of 20 and 2.6 cumulative high school GPA for unconditional admission. AP and CLEP credits are accepted. To graduate, all students must follow a core curriculum including humanities, social science and religion, natural science and math, and physical activity. Chapel attendance is mandatory. A total of 123 credits, with 36 to 64 hours in the major, and a minimum GPA of 2.0 are required to graduate. **Procedure:** Freshmen are admitted fall and spring. There is a rolling admissions plan. Application deadlines are open. Applications are accepted on-line. **Transfer Students:** 58 transfer students enrolled in 2016-2017. Transfer students must have a GPA of 2.0 for unconditional admission. 32 of 123 credits required for the bachelor's degree must be completed at WBC. **International Students:** There are 19 international students enrolled. They must take the TOEFL with a minimum score of 500 on the paper-based TOEFL (PBT) or 61 on the Internet-based version (iBT). They must also take the SAT or ACT, scoring 20.

ADMISSIONS: 55% of the 2017-2018 applicants were accepted. 25% of the current freshmen were in the top fifth of their class; 44% were in the top two fifths. 3 freshmen graduated first in their class. **Admissions Con-**

tact: Andrew Watson, Director of Admissions. Email: *admissions@wbcoll.edu* Web: *www.wbcoll.edu*

FINANCIAL AID: In 2017-2018, 100% of all full-time freshmen received some form of financial aid. 62% of all full-time freshmen received need-based aid. The average freshman award was $17,643. Need-based scholarships or need-based grants averaged $4,828 ($7,515 maximum); need-based self-help aid (loans and jobs) averaged $3,586 ($6,246 maximum); non-need-based athletic scholarships averaged $8,601 ($19,774 maximum); and other non-need-based awards and non-need-based scholarships averaged $7,280 ($27,702 maximum). 43% of undergraduate students work part-time. The average financial indebtedness of the 2017 graduate was $20,363. The FAFSA code is 001106. The priority date for freshman financial aid applications for fall entry is February 1. The deadline for filing freshman financial aid applications for fall entry is May 1.

AMERICAN JEWISH UNIVERSITY - COLLEGE OF ARTS AND SCIENCES C-5

www.ajula.edu

Los Angeles, CA 90077	**(310) 440-1247** **(877) GO-2-AJULA**
Fax: (310) 471-3657	**Email: admissions@aju.edu**
Full-time: 40 men, 60 women	**Faculty:** n/av
Part-time: 5 men, 5 women	**Ph.D.s:** 100%
Graduate: 65 men, 75 women	**Student/Faculty:** n/av
Year: semesters	**Tuition:** $29,132
Room & Board: $15,102	**Freshman Class:** n/av
SAT or ACT: required	**CEEB CODE:** 4876
Application Deadline: May 31	**COMPETITIVE**

American Jewish University-College of Arts & Sciences, founded in 2007, is distinguished by its core curriculum integrating social justice and ethical leadership. It prepares students for careers and graduate studies in law, business, psychology, education, and other fields. The figures given in the above capsule and in this profile are approximate. There is 1 undergraduate school and 3 graduate schools. In addition to regional accreditation, American Jewish University - College of Arts and Sciences has baccalaureate program accreditation with WASC. The 2700-acre campus is in a suburban area in Los Angeles and Simi Valley. Including any residence halls, there are 9 buildings.

STUDENT LIFE: 71% of undergraduates are from California. Others are from 22 states, and 2 foreign countries. 70% are from public schools. 81% are White; 6% Foreign; 3% African American. 94% are Jewish. **Female To Male Ratio:** 1.3:1. The average age of freshmen is 18; all undergraduates, 23. 5% do not continue beyond their first year; 90% remain to graduate. **Housing:** 192 students can be accommodated in college housing, which includes married student dorms and on-campus apartments. On-campus housing is guaranteed for all 4 years. 70% of students live on campus. All students may keep cars.

FACULTY/CLASSROOMS: 45% of faculty are male; 55% are female. All teach undergraduates, and all do research. No introductory courses are taught by graduate students. The average class size in an introductory lecture is 7 and in a laboratory is 7.

PROGRAMS OF STUDY: AJU College of Arts and Sciences confers B.A. degrees. Master's degrees are also awarded. Bachelor's degrees are awarded in BUSINESS (business administration and management), COMMUNICATIONS AND THE ARTS (journalism and literature), HEALTH PROFESSIONS (premedicine), SOCIAL SCIENCE (ethics, politics, and social policy, Judaic studies, liberal arts/general studies, political science/government, and psychology).

ACTIVITIES: There are no fraternities or sororities. There are 15 groups on campus, including bioethics, Hillel, peer mentoring, psychology, art, choir, dance, drama, Israel action, literary magazine, newspaper, political, radio and TV, religious, social, social service, and student government. Popular campus events include Israel Memorial Day (Yom Hazikaron), and Israel Independence Day (Yom Ha'atzmaut). **Sports:** There is no sports program at AJU. Facilities include a gym, and basketball court, and a soccer field at the Familian campus in Los Angeles and horseback riding, swimming pools, and a ropes course at the Brandeis-Bardin campus in Simi Valley.

SERVICES: Counseling and information services are available, as is tutoring in most subjects. There is remedial math and writing. **Library/ Resources:** The library contains 105,000 volumes, and subscribes to 400 periodicals including electronic. Computerized library services include interlibrary loans, database searching, Internet access, and Wi-Fi capability. Special learning facilities include an art gallery, radio station, and TV station. **Physically Challenged Students:** All of the campus is accessible. Facilities include elevators, special parking, specially equipped restrooms, lowered drinking fountains, and lowered telephones. **Special:** There is a 5-year joint business management program with American Jewish University's Lieber School of Graduate Studies and a 5-year joint master's degree in Jewish education with AJU's Fingerhut School of Education. Student designed and dual majors are available. Internships in all available majors, study abroad, work-study programs, accelerated degree programs, and pass/fail options are offered. Students may apply for independent study projects. There is 1 national honor society. **Visiting:** There are regularly scheduled orientations for prospective students, including meeting with admissions representatives, department chairs, and the Dean of the College of Arts and Sciences, sitting in on classes, sleeping over in the doms, eating meals in the Berg dining hall, meeting current students and touring the campus. There are guides for informal visits, visitors may sit in on classes, and stay overnight. To schedule a visit, contact the Director of Undergraduate Admissions. **Campus Safety and Security:** Measures include 24-hour foot and vehicle patrol, self-defense education, and security escort services. There are emergency telephones and lighted pathways/sidewalks.

REQUIREMENTS: The SAT or ACT is required. Applicants must be graduates of an accredited secondary school or have a GED. A visit and an interview are recommeded for all students. 2 letters of recommendation, an autobiographical essay, and official high school transcripts are required. A GPA of 2.0 is required. AP credits are accepted. Important factors in the admissions decision are extracurricular activities record. All students must complete a core curriculum combining the study of Jewish and Western civilizations, as well as courses in communications and foreign language and 1 in computer science. There are distribution requirements in math, natural and behavioral sciences, English, and fine arts. Other requirements vary according to the major, with at least 32 to 36 upper-division credits needed. A total of 120 semester units, with a minimum GPA of 2.0, is required to graduate. **Procedure:** Freshmen are admitted fall and spring. Entrance exams should be taken no later than November of the year prior to enrollment. There are early decision, deferred admissions, and rolling admissions plans. Applications should be filed by May 31 for fall entry; November 30 for spring entry. The fall 2017 application fee was $35. Notification is sent on a rolling basis. Applications are accepted on-line. **Transfer Students:** 19 transfer students enrolled in 2016-2017. Previous college work should be at the B level to transfer. Students with fewer than 60 college credits should also have a minimum 3.0 high school GPA, at least 1700 on the SAT or 24 on the ACT, recommendations, and an autobiographical essay. The SAT or ACT requirement is waived if the applicant has 60 or more transferable credits. A visit and an interview are recommended. 34 of 120 credits required for the bachelor's degree must be completed at AJU. **International Students:** They must take the TOEFL with a minimum score of 79 on the Internet-based version (iBT). They must also take the SAT or ACT, scoring 1700.

Admissions Contact: Jyllian Siegal, Director of Undergraduate Admissions. Email: *admissions@aju.edu* Web: *www.ajula.edu*

FINANCIAL AID: The college's own financial statement, tax returns, and W2s are required. The deadline for filing freshman financial aid applications for fall entry is March 2.

ARTCENTER COLLEGE OF DESIGN *(The complete profile is made available exclusively on our website, www.barronspac.com)*

ASHFORD UNIVERSITY F-3
www.ashford.edu

San Diego, CA 92123 **(866) 711-1700**

Email: admissions@ashford.edu

Full-time: 13,608 men, 31,716 women	**Faculty:** n/av
Part-time: 8 men, 16 women	**Ph.D.s:** n/av
Graduate: 1505 men, 4384 women	**Student/Faculty:** n/av
Year: varies, summer session	**Tuition:** $10,480
Room & Board: n/app	**Freshman Class:** n/av
SAT or ACT: recommended	**CEEB CODE:** 6418
Application Deadline: n/av	**COMPETITIVE**

Ashford University is a private liberal arts college founded in 1918. There are 4 undergraduate schools and 3 graduate schools. In addition to regional accreditation, AU has baccalaureate program accreditation with IACBE. The 25-acre campus is in a small town 135 miles west of Chicago, IL. Including any residence halls, there are 12 buildings.

STUDENT LIFE: 98% of undergraduates are from out of state, mostly the South. Students are from 50 states, 1 foreign country, and Canada. 47% are White; 35% African American; 3% two or more races; 2% race unknown; 10% Hispanic; 1% Asian American; 1% American Indian/Alaska Native. **Female To Male Ratio:** 2.4:1. The average age of all undergraduates is 35. **Housing:** 573 students can be accommodated in college housing, which includes dorms. On-campus housing is guaranteed for all 4 years. Alcohol is not permitted. All students may keep cars.

FACULTY/CLASSROOMS: No introductory courses are taught by graduate students.

PROGRAMS OF STUDY: AU confers B.A. and B.S. degrees. Associate and master's degrees are also awarded. Bachelor's degrees are awarded in AGRICULTURE (environmental studies), BIOLOGICAL SCIENCE (biology/biological science), BUSINESS (accounting, business administration and management, business economics, business information systems, business leadership, entrepreneurial studies, finance, hospitality management services, human resources/organizational mgmt, international business, marketing, operations management, organizational leadership and management, real estate, sports management, supply chain management, sustainable management, and project management), COMMUNICATIONS AND THE ARTS (communication studies, English, journalism, linguistics, and public relations), COMPUTER AND PHYSICAL SCIENCE (computer science and natural sciences), EDUCATION (early childhood education, education administration, educational studies, elementary education, English education, health education, health information management, library science, and physical education), ENGINEERING AND ENVIRONMENTAL DESIGN (computer graphics, instructional design, and military science), HEALTH PROFESSIONS (community health work, health care administration, health promotion, and health science), SOCIAL SCIENCE (anthropology, behavioral science, child psychology/development, cognitive science, criminal justice, family/consumer studies, gerontology, history, homeland security/emergency preparedness, law enforcement and corrections, liberal arts/general studies, political science/government, psychology, public administration, social science, and sociology). Organizational management, psychology, and early childhood education have the largest enrollments.

ACTIVITIES: There are no fraternities or sororities. Groups on campus include art, band, choir, computers, dance, drama, environmental, ethnic, honors, international, LGBT, literary magazine, musical theater, newspaper, professional, religious, SISEA (Iowa State Education Association), social, social service, and student government. Popular campus events include Family Weekend, Matriculation Ceremony, Earth Day, and Commencement. **Sports:** There are 8 intercollegiate sports for men and 9 for women, and 11 intramural sports for men and 11 for women. Facilities include a gym, an arena with basketball courts, a fitness center, 4-lane perimeter track, artificial turf soccer field, an outdoor all-weather track. . **Graduates:** From July 1, 2016 to June 30, 2017, 11850 bachelor's degrees were awarded. The most popular majors were organizational management (12%), psychology (9%), and early childhood education (9%).

SERVICES: Counseling and information services are available, as is tutoring in every subject. There is also voice-activated computer software, proctoring exams, and prep courses for the GRE and MCAT. **Library/Resources:** The library contains 103,569 volumes, 73,405 microform items, and 2,509 audio/video tapes/CDs/DVDs, and subscribes to 129,376 periodicals including electronic. Computerized library services include interlibrary loans, database searching, Internet access, and Wi-Fi capability. Special learning facilities include an art gallery, a living lab adjacent to the campus. **Physically Challenged Students:** 95% of the campus is accessible. Facilities include wheelchair ramps, elevators, special parking, specially equipped restrooms, lowered drinking fountains, and special housing. **Special:** There are 2 national honor societies, a freshman honors program, and 1 departmental honors program. **Visiting:** There are regularly scheduled orientations for prospective students, including 2-day orientation sessions held prior to the first week of classes for students and parents on campus and an online orientation offered for online students. There are guides for informal visits, visitors may sit in on classes, and stay overnight. To schedule a visit, contact the Admissions Office. **Campus Safety and Security:** Measures include self-defense education and security escort services. There are shuttle buses, emergency telephones, lighted pathways/sidewalks, The campus has 24-hour security through the Clinton police department. On-campus security is available 7 days a week.

REQUIREMENTS: The ACT is recommended. The SAT is accepted. Applicants must be graduates of an accredited secondary school or have earned a GED and must meet 2 of the following requirements: a GPA of 2.0 in college preparatory or regular high school courses, rank in the upper half of the graduating class, and a minimum ACT composite score of 18 or a satisfactory SAT score. AU requires applicants to be in the upper 50% of their class. A GPA of 2.0 is required. AP and CLEP credits are accepted. Students must complete 120 semester hours, including 25 semester hours of general education subject areas, plus 24 hours of general education competencies (communication, critical thinking, mathematical, etc.); 30 hours of upper division coursework, 18-21 of these hours must be in the major (depends on program); minimum GPA of 2.0 although a higher GPA is required for some programs; minimum of 30 credits earned at the University; completion of all major, minor, and specialization course requirements; and a final exam, report, or project is required in every course. **Procedure:** Freshmen are admitted to all sessions. Entrance exams should be taken before enrolling. There are deferred admissions and rolling admissions plans. Check with the school for current application deadlines. Applications are accepted on-line. **Transfer Students:** 5789 transfer students enrolled in 2016-2017. Applicants may apply up to a maximum of 90 semester credit hours 30 of 120 credits required for the bachelor's degree must be completed at AU. **International Students:** They must take the TOEFL with a minimum score of 500 on the paper-based TOEFL (PBT) or 61 on the Internet-based version (iBT).

Admissions Contact: Office of Admissions, Admissions Counselor. Email: *admissions@ashford.edu* Web: *www.ashford.edu*

FINANCIAL AID: The college's own financial statement is required. Check with the school for current application deadlines. Check with the school for current application deadlines.

AZUSA PACIFIC UNIVERSITY D-5
www.apu.edu

Azusa, CA 91702 **(626) 812-3073**
(800) TALK-APU

Fax: (626) 812-3096	**Email: admissions@apu.edu**
Full-time: 1893 men, 3463 women	**Faculty:** 272; I, --$
Part-time: 151 men, 376 women	**Ph.D.s:** 64%
Graduate: 1188 men, 2904 women	**Student/Faculty:** 20 to 1
Year: semesters, summer session	**Tuition:** $34,754
Room & Board: $9218	**Freshman Class:** 6084 applied, 4922 accepted, 1192 enrolled
SAT CR/M: 530/540 **ACT:** 24	**CEEB CODE:** 4596
Application Deadline: May 1	**COMPETITIVE**

Azusa Pacific University, founded in 1899, is a private, interdenominational Christian institution offering undergraduate and graduate programs in the liberal arts and emphasizing spiritual growth. There are 7 undergraduate schools and 8 graduate schools. In addition to regional accreditation, Azusa Pacific University has baccalaureate program accreditation with CSWE, NASAD, NASM, CAEP, NLN, IACBE, ATS, and CAPTE. The 105-acre campus is in a small town 26 miles Notheast of Los Angeles. Including any residence halls, there are 67 buildings.

STUDENT LIFE: Students are from 44 states, 41 foreign countries, and Canada. 9% are Asian American; 8% two or more races; 43% White; 4% African American; 29% Hispanic; 17% race unknown. **Female To Male Ratio:** 2.1:1. The average age of freshmen is 18; all undergraduates, 21. 12% do not continue beyond their first year; 88% remain to graduate. **Housing:** 3101 students can be accommodated in college housing, which includes dorms, on-campus apartments, and off-campus apartments. In addition, there are honors houses and special-interest houses. On-campus housing is available on a first-come, first-served basis, and is available on a lottery system for upperclassmen. 62% of students live on campus. Alcohol is not permitted. All students may keep cars.

FACULTY/CLASSROOMS: 43% of faculty are male; 56% are female. No introductory courses are taught by graduate students.

PROGRAMS OF STUDY: Azusa Pacific University confers B.A., B.S., B.M., B.F.A, B.S.N., and B.S.W. degrees. Master's and doctoral degrees are also awarded. Bachelor's degrees are awarded in BIOLOGICAL SCIENCE (biochemistry and biology/biological science), BUSINESS (accounting, business administration and management, international business, and marketing/retailing/merchandising), COMMUNICATIONS AND THE ARTS (acting, communications, English, fine arts, graphic design, journalism, music, Spanish, and theatre arts), COMPUTER AND PHYSICAL SCIENCE (chemistry, computer science, information sciences and systems, mathematics, and physics), EDUCATION (art education, athletic training, music education, and physical education), ENGINEERING AND ENVIRONMENTAL DESIGN (systems engineering), HEALTH PROFESSIONS (allied health, biology, and nursing), SOCIAL SCIENCE (biblical studies, criminal justice, history, international studies, liberal arts/general studies, liberal arts, sciences, general studies, humanities, ministries, philosophy, political science/government, psychology, religion, social science, social work, sociology, theology, and youth ministry). Nursing, education, and religion are the strongest academically. Business, nursing, and psychology have the largest enrollments.

ACTIVITIES: There are no fraternities or sororities. There are 50 groups on campus, including art, band, cheerleading, choir, chorale, chorus, computers, dance, debate, drama, ethnic, film, honors, international, jazz band, literary magazine, marching band, musical theater, newspaper, opera, orchestra, pep band, photography, political, professional, radio and TV, religious, social, social service, student government, and yearbook. Popular campus events include Missions Week, Mega Weekend-Homecoming, Dinner Rally, and Night of Champions. **Sports:** Facilities include an all-weather track, a football stadium, baseball field, a gym, turf recreation field, sand volleyball courts, indoor/outdoor basketball courts, and a recreation room. **Graduates:** From July 1, 2016 to June 30, 2017, 1783 bachelor's degrees were awarded. The most popular majors were health professions and related programs (23%), business/marketing (21%), and visual and performing arts (9%). In an average class, 8% graduate in 4 years or less, 50% graduate in 5 years or less, and 68% graduate in 6 years or less.

SERVICES: Counseling and information services are available, as is tutoring in most subjects. There is remedial math, reading, and writing. **Library/Resources:** The library contains 386,074 volumes, 703,979 microform items, and subscribes to 93,873 periodicals including electronic. Computerized library services include interlibrary loans, database searching, Internet access, and Wi-Fi capability. Special learning facilities include an art gallery, radio station, and TV station. **Physically Challenged Students:** All of the campus is accessible. Facilities include wheelchair ramps, elevators, special parking, specially equipped restrooms, lowered drinking fountains, lowered telephones, and special housing. **Special:** Internships in ministerial and American studies, study abroad in Japan, Latin America, Taiwan, England, Australia, China, Tanzania, Italy, Israel, France, Lithuania, Spain, Uganda, and South Africa, and a Washington semester are available. In addition, work-study with the university, a B.A.-B.S. degree, dual majors in all programs, and a 3-2 engineering degree are offered. Accelerated degree programs are available in Christian leadership, computer information systems, management information systems, human development, and organizational leadership; there is also a Registered Nurse to Bachelor of Science in Nursing Program. APU awards credit for life experience and allows nondegree study. There are 13 national honor societies and a freshman honors program. **Visiting:** There are regularly scheduled orientations for prospective students, including Seniors Only Day in November, and a brother/sister weekend in February that is open to both juniors and seniors. There are guides for informal visits, visitors may sit in on classes, and stay overnight. To schedule a visit, contact the Admissions Office. **Campus Safety and Security:** Measures include 24-hour foot and vehicle patrol, emergency notification system, self-defense education, and security escort services. There are shuttle buses, emergency telephones, lighted pathways/sidewalks, and controlled access to dorms/residences.

REQUIREMENTS: The SAT or ACT is required, with no minimum score required. An essay is required. A portfolio and an interview are recommended for certain programs. The GED is accepted. A GPA of 3.0 is required. AP and CLEP credits are accepted. Important factors in the admissions decision are personality/intangible qualities, recommendations by school officials, evidence of special talent, and advanced placement or honors courses. All students must take 120 semester units and earn a minimum GPA of 2.0. 18 units of Bible courses, 120 hours of community ministry, and 2 units of health are required. General education requirements include courses in public speaking, fine arts, religion & philosophy, English, algebra, foreign language, phys ed., heritage & institution, identity & relationships, and nature are also required courses. **Procedure:** Freshmen are admitted to all sessions. Entrance exams should be taken prior to enrollment. There are early admissions, deferred admissions, and rolling admissions plans. Early decision applications should be filed by February 15; regular applications, by May 1 for fall entry; and October 15 for spring entry. The fall 2017 application fee was $45. Notification of early decision is sent October 1; regular decision, April 1. Applications are accepted on-line. **Transfer Students:** 534 transfer students enrolled in 2016-2017. Applicants must have a minimum GPA of 2.20 on previous college work. The SAT or ACT is not required if 30 or more semester units have been completed. An associate degree and an interview are recommended. 30 of 120 credits required for the bachelor's degree must be completed at APU. **International Students:** There are 130 international students enrolled. They must take the TOEFL with a minimum score of 587 on the paper-based TOEFL (PBT) or 94 on the Internet-based version (iBT). They must also take the SAT or ACT.

ADMISSIONS: 81% of the 2017-2018 applicants were accepted. The SAT scores for the 2017-2018 freshman class were: Critical Reading--32% below 500, 45% between 500 and 599, 21% between 600 and 699, and 3% between 700 and 800. Math-- 4% below 500, 34% between 500 and 599, 21% between 600 and 699, and 2% between 700 and 800. The ACT scores were 4% between 12 and 17, 42% between 18 and 23, 44% between 24 and 29, and 10% above 30. **Admissions Contact:** Kimberley Wiedefeld, Senior Director Undergraduate Admissions. Email: *admissions@apu.edu* Web: *www.apu.edu*

FINANCIAL AID: In 2017-2018, 93% of all full-time freshmen received some form of financial aid. The average freshman award was $21,492. Need-based scholarships or need-based grants averaged $10,581; need-based self-help aid (loans and jobs) averaged $3,659; non-need-based athletic scholarships averaged $20,225; and other non-need-based awards and non-need-based scholarships averaged $9,432. The average financial indebtedness of the 2017 graduate was $30,516. The college's own financial statement is required. The FAFSA code is 001117. Check with the school for current application deadlines.

BIOLA UNIVERSITY D-5

www.biola.edu

La Mirada, CA 90639	(562) 903-4752
Fax: (562) 903-4709	**Email:** admissions@biola.edu
Full-time: 1425 men, 2522 women	**Faculty:** 274; IIA, av$
Part-time: 56 men, 80 women	**Ph.D.s:** 84%
Graduate: 1246 men, 748 women	**Student/Faculty:** 15 to 1
Year: 4-1-4, summer session	**Tuition:** $38,448
Room & Board: $10,238	**Freshman Class:** 4393 applied, 2849 accepted, 872 enrolled
SAT CR/M/W: 545/540/510 **ACT:** 24	**CEEB CODE:** 4017
Application Deadline: March 1	**COMPETITIVE**

Biola University is a nationally ranked Christian university in the heart of Southern California. Founded in 1908, Biola offers biblically centered education, intentional spiritual development and vocational preparation within a unique learning community where all faculty, staff and students are professing Christians. There are 8 undergraduate schools and 8 graduate schools. In addition to regional accreditation, Biola University has baccalaureate program accreditation with ACBSP, NASAD, NASM, NLN, APA, and ATS. The 95-acre campus is in a suburban area in La Mirada, CA, located on the border of Los Angeles and Orange counties. Including any residence halls, there are 53 buildings.

STUDENT LIFE: 74% of undergraduates are from California. Others are from 40 states, 28 foreign countries, and Canada. 69% are from public schools. 6% are two or more races; 48% White; 3% race unknown; 20% Hispanic; 2% African American; 2% Asian American; 2% Foreign. 99% are Protestant. **Female To Male Ratio:** 1.2:1. The average age of freshmen is 18; all undergraduates, 20. 14% do not continue beyond their first year; 65% remain to graduate. **Housing:** 2307 students can be accommodated in college housing, which includes married student dorms, on-campus apartments, and off-campus apartments. On-campus housing is guaranteed for the freshman year only, is available on a first-come, first-served basis, and is available on a lottery system for upperclassmen. 65% of students live on campus. Alcohol is not permitted. All students may keep cars.

FACULTY/CLASSROOMS: 63% of faculty are male; 37% are female. No introductory courses are taught by graduate students.

PROGRAMS OF STUDY: Biola University confers B.A., B.S., B.F.A., and B.M. degrees. Master's and doctoral degrees are also awarded. Bachelor's degrees are awarded in BIOLOGICAL SCIENCE (biochemistry, biology/adolescence education, biology/biological science, and life science), BUSINESS (accounting, business administration and management, business communications, business economics, business information systems, economics – statistics, international business management, management information systems, management science, and marketing management), COMMUNICATIONS AND THE ARTS (advertising, American literature, American Sign Language, art, broadcasting, communications, dramatic arts, drawing, English, film arts, fine arts, graphic design, journalism, music, music composition, music performance, music theory and composition, painting, performing arts, photography, piano performance, playwriting/screenwriting, printmaking, public relations, publishing, radio/television technology, Spanish, studio art, theatre acting, theatre arts, theater design, and theater management), COMPUTER AND PHYSICAL SCIENCE (applied mathematics, chemistry, computer mathematics, computer information technology, computer science, information sciences and systems, mathematics, mathematics/theoretical, natural sciences, physical sciences, physics, and statistics), EDUCATION (Christian education, early childhood education, mathematics education, music education, physical education, social studies education, and social studies secondary school education), ENGINEERING AND ENVIRONMENTAL DESIGN (computational sciences, computer technology, engineering, and environmental science), HEALTH PROFESSIONS (nursing, physical therapy, preallied health, pre-health studies, predentistry, premedicine, prepharmacy, prephysical therapy, speech pathology/audiology, and speech therapy), SOCIAL SCIENCE (anthropology, applied psychology, archeology, biblical studies, counseling/psychology, crosscultural studies, early childhood studies, economics, history, humanities, liberal arts/general studies, ministries, missions, philosophy, philosophy and religion, prelaw, psychology, religious studies, social science, social work, and sociology). Biblical studies, business administration, and journalism/communication are the strongest academically. Biblical studies, business, and psychology have the largest enrollments.

ACTIVITIES: There are no fraternities or sororities. There are 52 groups on campus, including adventure club, art, band, cheerleading, chess, choir, chorale, debate, drama, environmental, ethnic, film, forensics, honors, international, jazz band, musical theater, newspaper, opera, orchestra, political, professional, radio and TV, religious, social, social service, student government, symphony, and yearbook. Popular campus events include Multicultural Week, Christmas Celebration, Biola Weekend, Missions Conference, and Torrey Conference. **Sports:** There are 12 intercollegiate sports for men and 12 for women, and 10 intramural sports for men and 10 for women. Facilities include a gym/swimming complex, auditorium, athletic fields for soccer, a quarter-mile track, a baseball diamond, tennis, sand volleyball, basketball courts, and a fitness center. **Graduates:** From July 1, 2016 to June 30, 2017, 899 bachelor's degrees were awarded. The most popular majors were business/marketing (15%), communication/journalism (12%), and visual and performing arts (11%). In an average class, 70% graduate in 6 years or less. Of the 2016 graduating class, 50% were employed within 6 months of graduation.

SERVICES: Counseling and information services are available, as is tutoring in most subjects. There is a reader service for the blind, and a writing center is available to all students. **Library/Resources:** The library contains 315,000 volumes, 580,000 microform items, and 9,232 audio/video tapes/CDs/DVDs, and subscribes to 30,000 periodicals including electronic. Computerized library services include interlibrary loans, database searching, Internet access, and Wi-Fi capability. Special learning facilities include an art gallery, radio station, TV station, film studio, a 3-D art facility, an MIDI lab for music composition majors, electronic piano lab, listening lab with music archives, physical science labs, scanning electron microscope, and archeological dig-site. **Physically Challenged Students:** 90% of the campus is accessible. Facilities include wheelchair ramps, elevators, special parking, specially equipped restrooms, special class scheduling, lowered drinking fountains, lowered telephones, and special housing. **Special:** Cross-registration with the Au Sable Institute of Environmental Studies is possible. Biola offers internships, summer travel tours, study abroad in 11 countries, and an American studies program in Washington D.C., sponsored by the Christian College Coalition. Special programs include L.A. Film Studies, a semester in Hollywood working in the film industry; Biola Baja, a 3-week program at Vermillion Sea Field, Baja; a family studies course at Focus on the Family Institute in Colorado Springs; a China studies program at Fudan University in Shanghai, China, and a development theory studies program in Honduras. Also available are on- and off-campus work-study programs, a B.A.- B.S. degree, a 3-2 engineering degree with the University of Southern California, dual majors, and nondegree study. There are several preprofessional programs available, including prelaw, prephysical therapy, and prechiropractic. A 3-1 program with Los Angeles College of Chiropractic is offered. Students can also attend a semester at Martha's Vineyard with the Contemporary Music Center and explore the many areas of the Christian music industry. There are 2 national honor societies, a freshman honors program, and 7 departmental honors programs. **Visiting:** There are regularly scheduled orientations for prospective students, including class visits; orientation with the departments of admissions, financial aid, and student affairs; chapel; a sporting event; and a Disneyland or Knott's Berry Farm visit. There are guides for informal visits, visitors may sit in on classes, and stay overnight. To schedule a visit, contact the Admissions Office. **Campus Safety and Security:** Measures include 24-hour foot and vehicle patrol, emergency notification system, self-defense education, and security escort services. There are shuttle buses, emergency telephones, lighted pathways/sidewalks, controlled access to dorms/residences, bicycle patrol, and the Segway patrol.

REQUIREMENTS: The SAT or ACT is required. Applicants need not be graduates of an accredited secondary school. The GED is accepted. Students should have completed 16 academic credits, including 4 years of English, and foreign language, 3 years of math, and 2 of science with 1 unit of lab, and 1 each of social studies and history. All students must be evangelical Christians who can demonstrate Christian character, leadership ability, and the aptitude for possible success in college. Applicants must submit 1 reference from their pastor or someone on the pastoral staff. A personal essay is required. A GPA of 3.0 is required. AP and CLEP credits are accepted. Important factors in the admissions decision are personality/intangible qualities, advanced placement or honors courses, extracurricular activities record, recommendations by school officials, and leadership record. To graduate, students must pass a writing competency exam, complete 30 units of biblical studies and theology, and fulfill the general education and phys ed requirements. At least 130 semester hours must be completed, with 30 hours in the major and 24 of these in upper-division work. Other requirements vary by major. A minimum 2.0 GPA is required. **Procedure:** Freshmen are admitted to all sessions. There are early decision and rolling admissions plans. Early decision applications should be filed by November 15; regular applications, by March 1 for fall entry; and November 15 for spring entry. The fall 2017 application fee was $45. Notification of early decision is sent January 15; regular decision, April 1. Applications are accepted on-line. **Transfer Students:** 242 transfer students enrolled in 2016-2017. Applicants with fewer than 15 credit hours must submit both college transcripts and SAT scores. All students must provide high school transcripts. A minimum 2.0 GPA and an interview are required. Student may apply in the fall, spring, and summer. 30 of 130 credits required for the bachelor's degree must be completed at Biola. **International Stu-**

dents: There are 180 international students enrolled. They must take the TOEFL with a minimum score of 600 on the paper-based TOEFL (PBT) or 100 on the Internet-based version (iBT). They must also take the SAT or ACT.

ADMISSIONS: 65% of the 2017-2018 applicants were accepted. The SAT scores for the 2017-2018 freshman class were: Critical Reading-- 31% below 500, 40% between 500 and 599, 24% between 600 and 699, and 6% between 700 and 800. Math-- 32% below 500, 40% between 500 and 599, 24% between 600 and 699, and 3% between 700 and 800. Writing-- 32% below 500, 39% between 500 and 599, 24% between 600 and 699, and 4% between 700 and 800. The ACT scores were 4% between 12 and 17, 38% between 18 and 23, 49% between 24 and 29, and 10% above 30. **Admissions Contact:** André Stephens, Senior Director/ Undergraduate Admissions. Email: *admissions@biola.edu* Web: *www.biola.edu*

FINANCIAL AID: In 2017-2018, 69% of all full-time freshmen received some form of financial aid. 55% of all full-time freshmen received need-based aid. The average freshman award was $21,834. Need-based scholarships or need-based grants averaged $16,896; need-based self-help aid (loans and jobs) averaged $6,986; non-need-based athletic scholarships averaged $11,965; other non-need-based awards and non-need-based scholarships averaged $8,961; and $3,293 from other forms of aid. 34% of undergraduate students work part-time. The average financial indebtedness of the 2017 graduate was $48,690. Biola University is a member of CSS. The college's own financial statement is required. California residents should submit the Cal Grant GPA verification form. The FAFSA code is 001122. The priority date for freshman financial aid applications for fall entry is March 1.

CALIFORNIA BAPTIST UNIVERSITY — D-5

www.calbaptist.edu

Riverside, CA 92504	**(951) 343-4212** **(877) 228-8866**
Fax: (951) 343-4525	**Email: admissions@calbaptist.edu**
Full-time: 2408 men, 3961 women	**Faculty:** 352
Part-time: 370 men, 678 women	**Ph.D.s:** 78%
Graduate: 686 men, 1841 women	**Student/Faculty:** 18 to 1
Year: semesters, summer session	**Tuition:** $32,256
Room & Board: $10,730	**Freshman Class:** 4971 applied, 3181 accepted, 1146 enrolled
SAT CR/M/W: required **ACT:** 22	**CEEB CODE:** 4094
Application Deadline: rolling	**COMPETITIVE**

California Baptist University (CBU) is one of the top private Christian colleges and universities in Southern California. CBU offers bachelor's, master's, doctoral and credential programs in Riverside, San Bernardino and online. CBU believes each person has been created for a purpose. CBU strives to help students understand and engage this purpose by providing a Christ-centered educational experience that integrates academics with spiritual and social development opportunities. Graduates are challenged to become individuals whose skills, integrity and sense of purpose glorify God and distinguish them in the workplace and in the world. There are 11 undergraduate schools and 10 graduate schools. In addition to regional accreditation, CBU has baccalaureate program accreditation with ABET, ACBSP, NAAB, NASM, CAATE, CCNE, and CCTC. The 160-acre campus is in a suburban area 60 miles east of Los Angeles. Including any residence halls, there are 172 buildings.

STUDENT LIFE: 91% of undergraduates are from California. Others are from 44 states, 31 foreign countries, and Canada. 90% are from public schools. 39% are White; 36% Hispanic; 7% African American; 6% two or more races; 5% Asian American; 4% race unknown; 2% Foreign; 1% American Indian/Alaska Native. 65% are Protestant; 17% Catholic. **Female To Male Ratio:** 1.9:1. The average age of freshmen is 19; all undergraduates, 23. 24% do not continue beyond their first year; 60% remain to graduate. **Housing:** 3078 students can be accommodated in college housing, which includes single-sex dorms and on-campus apartments. On-campus housing is guaranteed for the freshman year only, is available on a first-come, and first-served basis. 60% of students commute. Alcohol is not permitted. All students may keep cars.

FACULTY/CLASSROOMS: 53% of faculty are male; 47% are female. 95% teach undergraduates, and 88% do both. No introductory courses are taught by graduate students. The average class size in an introductory lecture is 22 and in a laboratory is 15.

PROGRAMS OF STUDY: CBU confers B.A., B.C.S., B.S., B.S.Ch.E., B.S.C.E., B.S.E.C.E., B.S.E., B.S.M.E., B.S.N., B.A.T., B.M., B.C.S., B.S.B.M.E., B.Sw.E., B.S.I.S.E., and B.F.A. degrees. Associate, master's, and doctoral degrees are also awarded. Bachelor's degrees are awarded in BIOLOGICAL SCIENCE (biochemistry, biology/biological science, and nutritional sciences), BUSINESS (accounting, business administration and management, entrepreneurial studies, leadership, marketing/ retailing/merchandising, and organizational leadership and management), COMMUNICATIONS AND THE ARTS (communication studies, communications, creative writing, digital media, English, film arts, graphic design, information technology, journalism, journalism - news & information, music, music composition, music performance, performing arts, photography, piano/organ, piano performance, public relations, Spanish, theatre arts, visual and performing arts, vocal performance, and voice), COMPUTER AND PHYSICAL SCIENCE (actuarial science, chemistry, combined science, computer engineering technology, computer science, digital arts/technology, mathematics, software engineering, and statistics), EDUCATION (health education, mathematics education, and music education), ENGINEERING AND ENVIRONMENTAL DESIGN (applied aviation, architecture, aviation administration/management, aviation flight technology, bioengineering, biomedical engineering, chemical engineering, civil engineering, construction management, electrical and computer engineering, electrical/ electronics engineering, engineering, environmental science, industrial engineering, mechanical engineering, preengineering, and systems engineering), HEALTH PROFESSIONS (communicative disorders, exercise science, health care administration, health science, kinesiology, nursing, prephysical therapy, and public health), SOCIAL SCIENCE (anthropology, behavioral science, Christian studies, communication sciences & disorders, criminal justice, early childhood studies, history, interdisciplinary studies, international studies, liberal arts/general studies, philosophy, political science/government, psychology, public administration, social science, social work, sociology, theology, and world cultural studies). Engineering, nursing, and business administration are the strongest academically. Business administration, nursing/pre-nursing, and psychology have the largest enrollments.

ACTIVITIES: There are no fraternities or sororities. There are 74 groups on campus, including art, band, cheerleading, chess, choir, chorale, chorus, communications, computers, debate, drama, drill team, environmental, ethnic, film, forensics, honors, international, jazz band, literary magazine, musical theater, newspaper, orchestra, pep band, photography, political, professional, religious, social, social service, student government, symphony, and yearbook. Popular campus events include Lancer Cup Soccer Championship, Basketball Midnight Madness, Homecoming Block Party, Fortuna Bowl Flag Football, Yule Festival, Kugel Walk (symbol of Christ's Great Commission), and TWIRP Week-The Woman Is Required to Pay. **Sports:** There are 10 intercollegiate sports for men and 10 for women, and 6 intramural sports for men and 6 for women. Facilities include a gymnasium, recreation center with indoor basketball courts, racquetball courts, climbing wall, and rooftop running track and soccer field, aquatics center with Olympic-size pool, outdoor athletic complex with baseball, softball, and soccer fields, athletic performance center, event center, athletic training clinic, tennis center, and sand volleyball courts. **Graduates:** From July 1, 2016 to June 30, 2017, 1518 bachelor's degrees were awarded. The most popular majors were nursing (11%), business administration (11%), and psychology (8%). In an average class, 4% graduate in 3 years or less, 42% graduate in 4 years or less, 55% graduate in 5 years or less, and 60% graduate in 6 years or less.

SERVICES: Counseling and information services are available, as is tutoring in most subjects. There is remedial math, reading, and writing. **Library/Resources:** The library contains 372,968 volumes, 54,853 microform items, and 32,578 audio/video tapes/CDs/DVDs, and subscribes to 40,749 periodicals including electronic. Computerized library services include interlibrary loans, database searching, Internet access, and Wi-Fi capability. Special learning facilities include an art gallery, music production and recording studios, language lab, digital design and photography studio, architecture studios, theater arts stage production workshop, Bourns engineering laboratories, athletic performance center, recreation and fitness center, and a aquatic center. **Physically Challenged Students:** 95% of the campus is accessible. Facilities include wheelchair ramps, elevators, special parking, specially equipped restrooms, and lowered drinking fountains. **Special:** California Baptist University offers accelerated programs in accounting, business administration, christian ministries, communication studies, computer information technology, criminal justice, early childhood studies, English, graphic design and digital media, kinesiology, liberal studies, marketing, nursing RN to BSN, organizational leadership, psychology, public administration, public health, public relations, and sociology. In addition, CBU offers Study abroad, internships, work-study programs, a Washington semester, double majors, and credit for military/work experience are available. There are 7 national honor societies, a freshman honors program, and 4 departmental honors programs. **Visiting:** There are regularly scheduled orientations for prospective students, consisting of a campus tour, an academic fair, meet the deans/professors, sit in the chapel, and meet current students. There are guides for informal visits, visitors may sit in on classes, and stay overnight. To schedule a visit, contact Taylor Neece at (877) 228-8866. **Campus Safety and Security:** Measures include 24-hour foot and vehicle patrol, emergency notification system, self-defense education, and security escort services. There are shuttle buses, emergency telephones, lighted pathways/sidewalks, and controlled access to dorms/residences.

REQUIREMENTS: The SAT or ACT is required. Applicants should be graduates of an accredited high school or have a GED. Official high school transcripts are required. Standard admission requires a minimum high school GPA of 2.5. and a composite score of 920 on the SAT Critical Reading and Math or 19 on the ACT Composite. Required academic units: 4 years of English, 3 years of mathematics, 2 years each of lab science, foreign language, social studies, and history, 1 year each of fine and performing arts, psychology or sociology, and religion. An essay and two letters of recommendation are required. One of the letters must be an academic reference (from teacher or professor). The second reference is a personal reference and can be completed by a pastor, co-worker or friend. We do not accept recommendations from family or university employees. A GPA of 2.5 is required. AP and CLEP credits are accepted. Important factors in the admissions decision are evidence of special talent, leadership record, and advanced placement or honors courses. Complete at least 124 semester units of credit, at least 39 or which are upper division courses. Complete at least 36 units in residence at CBU, at least 30 or which are upper division courses. Earn a cumulative grade point average of at least 2.0 overall with no grade below C- in the major field of study. Complete all general education requirements*. Complete all course work in a major as selected from the University catalog. Complete a graduation application for planned graduation date. Satisfy all financial obligations, and be in good academic standing at the time of completion. *General education requirements include: competency requirements in English Composition, mathematics, technology coursework, and two semesters of the same foreign language, 3 units in intermediate composition, 4 units in lab science, 9 units in Biblical and Theological Core, 6 units in natural world courses, 6 units in social world courses, 6 units in political world courses, and 6 units in cultural world courses. **Procedure:** Freshmen are admitted fall, spring, and summer. Entrance exams should be taken during the junior year. There are deferred admissions and rolling admissions plans. Application deadlines are open. The fall 2017 application fee was $45. Notification of early decision is sent January 31; regular decision, Nov 9. Applications are accepted on-line. **Transfer Students:** 1107 transfer students enrolled in 2016-2017. Students who have completed 24 or more units from a regionally accredited college or university will be evaluated on the basis of their official college transcripts. Standard admission requires a minimum cumulative GPA of 2.0 for all college work. Only courses with a grade of C- or better may transfer. 36 of 124 credits required for the bachelor's degree must be completed at CBU. **International Students:** There are 145 international students enrolled. They must take the TOEFL with a minimum score of 527 on the paper-based TOEFL (PBT) or 71 on the Internet-based version (iBT). They must also take the SAT or ACT, scoring 430 SAT Reading; 16 ACT Composite.

ADMISSIONS: 64% of the 2017-2018 applicants were accepted. The SAT scores for the 2017-2018 freshman class were: Critical Reading-- 44% below 500, 43% between 500 and 599, 10% between 600 and 699, and 3% between 700 and 800. Math-- 43% below 500, 41% between 500 and 599, 14% between 600 and 699, and 2% between 700 and 800. Writing-- 54% below 500, 33% between 500 and 599, 12% between 600 and 699, and 1% between 700 and 800. Evidence-Based Reading/Writing-- 24% below 500, 50% between 500 and 599, 23% between 600 and 699, and 3% between 700 and 800. The ACT scores were 16% between 12 and 17, 52% between 18 and 23, 28% between 24 and 29, and 4% above 30. **Admissions Contact:** Taylor Neece, Dean of Admissions. Email: *admissions@calbaptist.edu* Web: *www.calbaptist.edu*

FINANCIAL AID: In 2017-2018, 91% of all full-time freshmen received some form of financial aid. 78% of all full-time freshmen received need-based aid. The average freshman award was $33,924. Need-based scholarships or need-based grants averaged $10,386 ($21,666 maximum); need-based self-help aid (loans and jobs) averaged $3,980 ($7,500 maximum); non-need-based athletic scholarships averaged $26,092 ($47,008 maximum); and other non-need-based awards and non-need-based scholarships averaged $17,358 ($34,317 maximum). 15% of undergraduate students work part-time. The average financial indebtedness of the 2017 graduate was $22,798. The FAFSA code is 001125. The priority date for freshman financial aid applications for fall entry is March 2.

CALIFORNIA COLLEGE OF THE ARTS *(The complete profile is made available exclusively on our website, www.barronspac.com)*

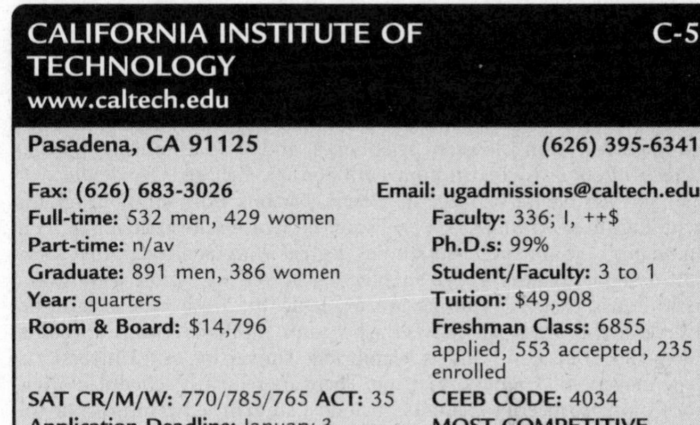

CALIFORNIA INSTITUTE OF TECHNOLOGY C-5

www.caltech.edu

Pasadena, CA 91125	**(626) 395-6341**
Fax: (626) 683-3026	**Email: ugadmissions@caltech.edu**
Full-time: 532 men, 429 women	**Faculty:** 336; I, ++$
Part-time: n/av	**Ph.D.s:** 99%
Graduate: 891 men, 386 women	**Student/Faculty:** 3 to 1
Year: quarters	**Tuition:** $49,908
Room & Board: $14,796	**Freshman Class:** 6855 applied, 553 accepted, 235 enrolled
SAT CR/M/W: 770/785/765 **ACT:** 35	**CEEB CODE:** 4034
Application Deadline: January 3	**MOST COMPETITIVE**

California Institute of Technology, founded in 1891, is a private institution offering programs in engineering, science, and mathematics. There are 6 undergraduate schools and 6 graduate schools. In addition to regional accreditation, CIT has baccalaureate program accreditation with ABET and ACS. The 125-acre campus is in a suburban area 12 miles northeast of Los Angeles. Including any residence halls, there are 123 buildings.

STUDENT LIFE: 66% of undergraduates are from out of state, mostly the South. Students are from 47 states, 23 foreign countries, and Canada. 79% are from public schools. 9% are Foreign; 7% two or more races; 43% Asian American; 28% White; 12% Hispanic; 1% African American. **Male To Female Ratio:** 1.7:1. The average age of freshmen is 18; all undergraduates, 20. 2% do not continue beyond their first year; 89% remain to graduate. **Housing:** 891 students can be accommodated in college housing, which includes both single sex and coed and married student dorms, on-campus apartments, and off-campus apartments, and single family homes. On-campus housing is guaranteed for the freshman year only. Alcohol is not permitted. All students may keep cars.

FACULTY/CLASSROOMS: All teach undergraduates and do research. No introductory courses are taught by graduate students. The average class size in an introductory lecture is 200 and in a regular course is 15.

PROGRAMS OF STUDY: CIT confers B.S. degrees. Master's and doctoral degrees are also awarded. Bachelor's degrees are awarded in BIOLOGICAL SCIENCE (biology/biological science), BUSINESS (business administration and management), COMPUTER AND PHYSICAL SCIENCE (applied mathematics, astrophysics, chemistry, computer mathematics, computer science, geochemistry, geology, geophysics and seismology, mathematics, physics, and planetary and space science), ENGINEERING AND ENVIRONMENTAL DESIGN (chemical engineering, computer engineering, electrical/electronics engineering, engineering and applied science, materials science, and mechanical engineering), HEALTH PROFESSIONS (environmental health science), SOCIAL SCIENCE (economics, history, history of science, philosophy, and political science/government). Engineering, physical science, and computer science have the largest enrollments.

ACTIVITIES: There are no fraternities or sororities. There are 150 groups on campus, including art, band, choir, chorale, chorus, computers, dance, drama, ethnic, honors, international, jazz band, LGBT, literary magazine, musical theater, newspaper, orchestra, pep band, photography, political, professional, religious, social, social service, student government, symphony, and yearbook. Popular campus events include Ditch Day, International Day, and Pre-Frosh Weekend. **Sports:**

There are 9 intercollegiate sports for men and 9 for women, and 9 intramural sports for men and 9 for women. Facilities include 2-25 yd swimming pools, 2-2 full court gymnasia, a 6 lane all-weather track with a natural grass infield, synthetic turf playing space lined for baseball and soccer, 8 tennis courts, 4 racquetball courts, 2 squash courts, 2 strength and conditioning training facilities, and 50 cardio machines. **Graduates:** From July 1, 2016 to June 30, 2017, 249 bachelor's degrees were awarded. The most popular majors were engineering (37%), computer and information sciences (23%), and physical sciences (18%). In an average class, 82% graduate in 4 years or less and 89% graduate in 6 years or less. Of the 2016 graduating class, 55% were enrolled in graduate school within 6 months of graduation.

SERVICES: Counseling and information services are available, as is tutoring in every subject. There is a reader service for the blind. **Library/Resources:** The library contains 624,136 volumes, 10,586 microform items, and 3,033 audio/video tapes/CDs/DVDs, and subscribes to 2,641 periodicals including electronic. Computerized library services include interlibrary loans, database searching, Internet access, and Wi-Fi capability. **Physically Challenged Students:** 98% of the campus is accessible. Facilities include wheelchair ramps, elevators, special parking, specially equipped restrooms, lowered telephones, and special housing. **Special:** Caltech offers cross-registration with Scripps College, Occidental College, and Art Center College of Design, various work-study programs, including those with NASA's Jet Propulsion Laboratory, dual majors in any major, and independent studies degrees with faculty-approved student-designed majors. A 3-2 engineering degree is possible with several institutions. Pass/fail options are available for freshmen. A summer undergraduate research fellowship program is offered. Study abroad at University College in London, Cambridge University, and University of Copenhagen, in Denmark. **Visiting:** There are regularly scheduled orientations for prospective students, include a student-led campus tour followed by an information session. There are guides for informal visits and visitors may sit in on classes. To schedule a visit, contact the Undergadu-ate Admissions Office. **Campus Safety and Security:** Measures include 24-hour foot and vehicle patrol, emergency notification system, self-defense education, and security escort services. There are also emergency telephones, lighted pathways/sidewalks, and controlled access to dorms/residences.

REQUIREMENTS: The SAT or ACT is required. SAT II: Subject tests in math level II and 1 in physics, biology, or chemistry are required. Applicants should have completed 4 years of high school math (including a year of calculus), 3 years of English, 1 year of chemistry, 1 year of physics, and 1 year of U.S. history or government (waived for international students) Important factors in the admissions decision are advanced placement or honors courses, personality/intangible qualities, leadership record, extracurricular activities record, and recommendations by school officials. Caltech's core curriculum consists of the following: 27 units of mathematics: Ma 1 abc: Calculus of One and Several Variables and Linear Algebra. A review of calculus, complex numbers, Taylor polynomials, and infinite series. Comprehensive presentation of linear algebra. Derivatives of vector functions, multiple integrals, line and path integrals, theorems of Green and Stokes. 27 units of physics: Ph 1 abc, classical mechanics and electromagnetism. Newtonian mechanics, electricity and magnetism, special relativity. Emphasis on physical insight and problem solving. 15 units of chemistry, Ch 1 ab, general chemistry. Lectures and recitations dealing with the principles of chemistry. 9 units of biology, a topical course introducing a variety of tools and concepts of modern biology. May be fulfilled with: Bi 1: Principles of Biology or Bi 1 x. The Great Ideas of Biology: An Introduction through Experimentation or Bi 8. Introduction to Molecular Biology: Organization and Expression of Genetic Information. 9 units of freshman menu course include astronomy, geology, energy science, environmental science and engineering, or information science. 12 units of introductory lab courses, freshman chem lab, plus one other lab chosen from offerings in applied physics, biology, chemistry, engineering, or physics. 3 units of scientific writing, students research, write, and revise a 3,000-word paper on a science or engineering topic, which is then published in an online journal established for that purpose. Students work with a faculty mentor on the content of the paper and receive editorial guidance from science writing instructors. 108 units of humanities courses. 2 terms of freshman humanities, 2 terms of introductory social-science, 2 terms of advanced humanities, 2 terms of advanced social-science. The remaining four courses may be chosen from any of the humanities or social-science offerings. 3 writing intensive courses must be taken on grades. 9 units of physical education this requirement may be satisfied entirely or in part by participation in intercollegiate athletics, or successful completion of physical-education class course work. All grades are issued pass/fail. **Procedure:** Freshmen are admitted in the fall. Entrance exams should be taken through December of the senior year. There are early admissions and deferred admissions plans. Applications should be filed by January 3 for fall entry. The fall 2017 application fee was $75. Notifications are sent April 1. 468 applicants were on the 2017 waiting list; 8 were admitted. Applications are accepted on-line. **Transfer Students:** 4 transfer students enrolled in 2016-2017. Transfers, admitted only into sophomore and junior classes, need a minimum GPA of 3.0. Applicants must have completed 1 year (2 years for juniors) of calculus and calculus-based physics, and must take Caltech's entrance exams in math and physics. Chemistry or chemical engineering majors also should have completed 1 year of chemistry and must take an additional entrance exam. 216 of 780 credits required for the bachelor's degree must be completed at Caltech. **International Students:** There are 116 international students enrolled. They must also take the SAT or ACT.

ADMISSIONS: 8% of the 2017-2018 applicants were accepted. The SAT scores for the 2017-2018 freshman class were: Critical Reading-- 8% between 600 and 699 and 92% between 700 and 800. Math-- 1% between 600 and 699 and 99% between 700 and 800. Writing-- 8% between 600 and 699 and 92% between 700 and 800. The ACT scores were 100% above 30. 100% of the current freshmen were in the top fifth of their class; 100% were in the top two fifths. **Admissions Contact:** Jarrid Whitney, Executive Director of Admissions and Financial Aid. Email: *ugadmissions@caltech.edu* Web: *www.caltech.edu*

FINANCIAL AID: In 2017-2018, 100% of all full-time freshmen received some form of financial aid and need-based aid. The average freshman award was $46,283. Need-based scholarships or need-based grants averaged $44,074; need-based self-help aid (loans and jobs) averaged $3,545; other non-need-based awards and non-need-based scholarships averaged $2,702; and $5,000 from other forms of aid. The average financial indebtedness of the 2017 graduate was $70,000. CIT is a member of CSS. The CSS/Profile, the state aid form, the college's own financial statement, noncustodial profile, and business/farm supplement are required. The FAFSA code is 001131. The priority date for freshman financial aid applications for fall entry is March 2.

CALIFORNIA INSTITUTE OF THE ARTS *(The complete profile is made available exclusively on our website, www.barronspac.com)*

CALIFORNIA LUTHERAN UNIVERSITY C-5

www.callutheran.edu

Thousand Oaks, CA 91360 (805) 493-3049
(877) 258-3678

Fax: (805) 493-3645 **Email:** admissions@callutheran.edu

Full-time: 1189 men, 1579 women	**Faculty:** 144; IIA, +$
Part-time: 52 men, 72 women	**Ph.D.s:** 85%
Graduate: 496 men, 785 women	**Student/Faculty:** 14 to 1
Year: semesters, summer session	**Tuition:** $39,793
Room & Board: $13,060	**Freshman Class:** 6013 applied, 3860 accepted, 638 enrolled

SAT CR/M/W: 545/553/541 **ACT:** required
CEEB CODE: 4088

Application Deadline: January 1 **COMPETITIVE**

California Lutheran University is a diverse, scholarly community dedicated to excellence in the liberal arts and sciences and professional studies. Rooted in the Lutheran tradition of Christian faith, the University encourages critical inquiry into matters of both faith and reason. The mission of the University is to educate leaders for a global society who are strong in character and judgment, confident in their identity and vocation, and committed to service and justice. There are 2 undergraduate schools and 4 graduate schools. In addition to regional accreditation, California Lutheran University has baccalaureate program accreditation with WSCUC. The 225-acre campus is in a suburban area 45 miles north of downtown Los Angeles in Ventura County, and 50 miles south of Santa Barbara. Including any residence halls, there are 53 buildings.

STUDENT LIFE: 84% of undergraduates are from California. Others are from 34 states, 45 foreign countries, and Canada. 75% are from public schools. 48% are White; 28% Hispanic; 8% two or more races; 5% Asian American; 4% Foreign; 3% African American; 3% race unknown; 1%

American Indian/Alaska Native. 40% claim no religious affiliation; 22% Catholic; 20% Protestant. **Female To Male Ratio:** 1.4:1. The average age of freshmen is 18; all undergraduates, 22. 15% do not continue beyond their first year; 85% remain to graduate. **Housing:** 1448 students can be accommodated in college housing, which includes dorms, and on-campus apartments. On-campus housing is guaranteed for all 4 years. 52% of students live on campus. Alcohol is not permitted. All students may keep cars.

FACULTY/CLASSROOMS: 51% of faculty are male; 49% are female. 67% teach undergraduates. No introductory courses are taught by graduate students.

PROGRAMS OF STUDY: California Lutheran University confers B.A. and B.S. degrees. Master's and doctoral degrees are also awarded. Bachelor's degrees are awarded in AGRICULTURE (environmental studies), BIOLOGICAL SCIENCE (biochemistry and biology/biological science), BUSINESS (accounting and business administration and management), COMMUNICATIONS AND THE ARTS (art, communications, English, French, German, multimedia, music, music production/recording technology, music performance, Spanish, and theatre arts), COMPUTER AND PHYSICAL SCIENCE (chemistry, computer science, geology, information sciences and systems, mathematics, and physics), HEALTH PROFESSIONS (exercise science, predentistry, and premedicine), SOCIAL SCIENCE (criminal justice, economics, history, interdisciplinary studies, international studies, liberal arts/general studies, philosophy, political science/government, prelaw, psychology, religion, social science, sociology, and theological studies). Biology, accounting, and exercise science are the strongest academically. Business, psychology, and exercise science have the largest enrollments.

ACTIVITIES: There are no fraternities or sororities. There are 80 groups on campus, including Model United Nations, art, band, cheerleading, choir, chorale, chorus, computers, dance, debate, drama, environmental, ethnic, film, forensics, honors, international, jazz band, LGBT, literary magazine, musical theater, newspaper, orchestra, pep band, photography, political, professional, radio and TV, religious, social, social service, Student Alumni, student government, and symphony. Popular campus events include Santa Lucia, Scandinavian Festival, Chinese New Year, World Fair, and Service Day. **Sports:** There are 11 intercollegiate sports for men and 10 for women, and 11 intramural sports for men and 11 for women. Facilities include a sports and fitness center which includes an arena for basketball and volleyball, dance studio, football and soccer fields, a 50-meter pool and diving, cross-country, golf, softball, volleyball, track and field, and water polo. **Graduates:** From July 1, 2016 to June 30, 2017, 817 bachelor's degrees were awarded. The most popular majors were business (22%), communication (15%), and psychology (12%). In an average class, 2% graduate in 3 years or less, 67% graduate in 4 years or less, 73% graduate in 5 years or less, and 73% graduate in 6 years or less. Of the 2016 graduating class, 29% were enrolled in graduate school within 6 months of graduation, and 60% were employed.

SERVICES: Counseling and information services are available, as is tutoring in every subject. The learning resources and writing centers offer help with study and writing skills. There is a reader service for the blind, and remedial math, reading, and writing. A student support services program helps low-income first-generation students adapt to the academic and social life of the campus. We have a coordinator for students with disabilities. **Library/Resources:** The library contains 334,453 volumes, 22,000 microform items, and 2,957 audio/video tapes/CDs/DVDs, and subscribes to 80 periodicals including electronic. Computerized library services include interlibrary loans, database searching, Internet access, and Wi-Fi capability. Special learning facilities include an art gallery, radio station, TV station, a human performance lab, and a SEEd project garden. **Physically Challenged Students:** 95% of the campus is accessible. Facilities include wheelchair ramps, elevators, special parking, specially equipped restrooms, lowered drinking fountains, lowered telephones, and special housing. **Special:** Cal Lutheran offers co-op programs, internships, a Washington semester, and study abroad in over 80 countries. Also available are work-study and student-designed interdisciplinary degree majors, redit for experiential learning, special student status for non degree study, pass/fail options and continuing education. A bachelor's degree for professionals program offers accelerated degrees in accounting, business, computer science, communication, liberal studies, organizational leadership and psychology. There are 9 national honor societies and a freshman honors program. **Visiting:** There are regularly scheduled orientations for prospective students, including an admission and financial aid interview, a tour, visits with faculty or coaches, and lunch. There are guides for informal visits, visitors may sit in on classes, and stay overnight. To schedule a visit, contact the Presidential Host Coordinators at prehost@callutheran.edu. **Campus Safety and Security:** Measures include 24-hour foot and vehicle patrol, emergency notification system, self-defense education, and security escort services. There are emergency telephones, lighted pathways/sidewalks, controlled access to dorms/residences, All residence halls are equipped with security systems.

REQUIREMENTS: The SAT or ACT is required. Applicants must be graduates of an accredited secondary school and have completed a minimum of 4 years of English, 2 years each of math, foreign language, social studies, and lab science. The GED is accepted. An essay is required and an interview is recommended. AP and CLEP credits are accepted. Important factors in the admissions decision are advanced placement or honors courses, recommendations by school officials, and evidence of special talent. To graduate, all students must complete a core curriculum including 16 to 20 units in social science, 8 each in religion, foreign language, and science, 7 in English, 4 to 6 in creative arts, 4 in math, and 1 in phys ed. Students must also fulfill content requirements of a freshman cluster and take one course of each: writing-intensive, speaking intensive, global studies, U.S diversity, and senior level capstone. Also needed are a total of 124 units, 40 of which must be upper division with 32 hours in the major for a B.A. and a minimum of 36 hours for a B.S. The final 30 credits before graduation must be completed at Cal Lutheran. Students must have a minimum 2.0 GPA. **Procedure:** Freshmen are admitted fall and spring. Entrance exams should be taken during spring of junior year, or early fall of senior year. There is an early admissions plan. Early decision applications should be filed by November 1; regular applications, by January 1 for fall entry; and October 1 for spring entry. The fall 2017 application fee was $25. Notification of early decision is sent January 15; regular decision, on a rolling basis. 328 applicants were on the 2017 waiting list; 41 were admitted. Applications are accepted on-line. **Transfer Students:** 270 transfer students enrolled in 2016-2017. Transfers should have at least a 2.75 transferable GPA and 28 transferable units. An application is required. An interview is recommended. Applicants must be in good standing at the previous college and may submit a recommendation from a college professor in lieu of a high school recommendation. 30 of 124 credits required for the bachelor's degree must be completed at Cal Lutheran. **International Students:** There are 97 international students enrolled. They must take the TOEFL with a minimum score of 550 on the paper-based TOEFL (PBT) or 79 on the Internet-based version (iBT). They must also take the SAT or ACT.

ADMISSIONS: 64% of the 2017-2018 applicants were accepted. The SAT scores for the 2017-2018 freshman class were: Critical Reading-- 25% below 500, 51% between 500 and 599, 22% between 600 and 699, and 2% between 700 and 800. Math-- 22% below 500, 48% between 500 and 599, 27% between 600 and 699, and 3% between 700 and 800. Writing-- 26% below 500, 51% between 500 and 599, 23% between 600 and 699, and 1% between 700 and 800. The ACT scores were 1% between 12 and 17, 37% between 18 and 23, 52% between 24 and 29, and 9% above 30. 68% of the current freshmen were in the top fifth of their class; 93% were in the top two fifths. 4 freshmen graduated first in their class. **Admissions Contact:** Michael Elgarico, Director of Undergraduate Admissions. Email: *admissions@callutheran.edu* Web: *www.callutheran.edu*

FINANCIAL AID: In 2017-2018, 97% of all full-time freshmen received some form of financial aid. 75% of all full-time freshmen received need-based aid. The average freshman award was $32,490. Need-based scholarships or need-based grants averaged $29,830 ($57,800 maximum); need-based self-help aid (loans and jobs) averaged $6,900 ($14,500 maximum); and other non-need-based awards and non-need-based scholarships averaged $20,530 ($50,500 maximum). 26% of undergraduate students work part-time. The average financial indebtedness of the 2017 graduate was $20,000. The FAFSA code is 001133. The priority date for freshman financial aid applications for fall entry is March 1.

CALIFORNIA POLYTECHNIC STATE UNIVERSITY B-4
www.calpoly.edu

San Luis Obispo, CA 93407 (805) 756-2311

Fax: (805) 756-5400	**Email:** admissions@calpoly.edu
Full-time: 10,608 men, 9880 women	**Faculty:** 952
Part-time: 488 men, 273 women	**Ph.D.s:** n/av
Graduate: 402 men, 325 women	**Student/Faculty:** 19 to 1
Year: quarters, summer session	**Tuition:** $9432
Room & Board: $13,115	**Freshman Class:** 48588 applied, 16817 accepted, 5241 enrolled
SAT EBR-W/M: 710/690 **ACT:** 31	**CEEB CODE:** 4038
Application Deadline: December 1	**MOST COMPETITIVE**

California Polytechnic State University, founded in 1901, is a public institution that is part of the California State University system. It offers programs in agriculture, architecture and environmental design, business, education, engineering, liberal arts, sciences and math, and pre-professional studies. There are 6 undergraduate schools. In addition to regional accreditation, CPSU has baccalaureate program accreditation with AACSB, ABET, ACCE, ASLA, NAAB, NASAD, NASM, NRPA, SAF, ACEND, CAC, CCTC, COAPRT, ACCGC, AAPAR, ATMAE, EAC, LAAB, and PAB (AICP). The 6000-acre campus is in a suburban area 200 miles north of Los Angeles, and 230 miles south of San Francisco. Including any residence halls, there are 125 buildings.

STUDENT LIFE: 85% of undergraduates are from California. 7% are two or more races; 55% White; 5% race unknown; 2% Foreign; 17% Hispanic; 13% Asian American; 1% African American. **Male To Female Ratio:** 1.1:1. The average age of freshmen is 18; all undergraduates, 20. 7% do not continue beyond their first year. **Housing:** 6323 students can be accommodated in college housing, which includes dorms, on-campus apartments, and off-campus apartments. In addition, there are honors houses, special-interest houses, apartments for single students, international students, theme housing, and gender inclusive housing. On-campus housing is available on a first-come, first-served basis, and is available on a lottery system for upperclassmen. 99% of students live on campus. Alcohol is not permitted. All students may keep cars.

FACULTY/CLASSROOMS: No introductory courses are taught by graduate students.

PROGRAMS OF STUDY: CPSU confers B.A., B.S., B.Arch., B.F.A., and B.L.A. degrees. Master's degrees are also awarded. Bachelor's degrees are awarded in AGRICULTURE (agricultural business management, agricultural communications, agricultural mechanics, agricultural sciences, agronomy, animal science, dairy science, forestry and related sciences, natural resource management, soil science, and wine and viticulture), BIOLOGICAL SCIENCE (biochemistry, biology/biological science, microbiology, and nutrition), BUSINESS (business administration and management and recreation and leisure services), COMMUNICATIONS AND THE ARTS (art and design, communication studies, English, graphic communications, journalism, modern language, music, and theatre arts), COMPUTER AND PHYSICAL SCIENCE (chemistry, computer science, earth science, industrial technology, mathematics, physics, software engineering, and statistics), EDUCATION (agricultural education and education), ENGINEERING AND ENVIRONMENTAL DESIGN (aeronautical engineering, architectural engineering, architecture, biomedical engineering, bioresource engineering, city/community/regional planning, civil engineering, computer engineering, construction management, electrical/electronics engineering, engineering science, environmental engineering, environmental science, industrial engineering, landscape architecture, manufacturing engineering, materials engineering, mechanical engineering, and transportation engineering), HEALTH PROFESSIONS (kinesiology), SOCIAL SCIENCE (anthropology, child psychology/development, economics, ethnic studies, food science, history, interdisciplinary studies, liberal arts/general studies, liberal arts/engineering studies, philosophy, political science/government, psychology, and sociology).

ACTIVITIES: Groups on campus include art, band, cheerleading, chess, choir, chorale, chorus, computers, dance, debate, drama, environmental, ethnic, film, honors, international, jazz band, LGBT, literary magazine, marching band, musical theater, newspaper, opera, orchestra, pep band, photography, political, professional, radio and TV, religious, social, social service, student government, symphony, and various engineering clubs. Popular campus events include Rose Float, Open House, Week of Welcome, and SOAR. **Sports:** There are 10 intercollegiate sports for men and 10 for women, and 7 intramural sports for men and 7 for women. Facilities include outdoor track, outdoor swimming pools, sand volleyball, tennis, basketball and racquetball courts, weight rooms, cardio exercise rooms, martial arts room, synthetic & natural turf playing fields, baseball stadium, softball stadium, and football/soccer stadium. **Graduates:** From July 1, 2016 to June 30, 2017, 4568 bachelor's degrees were awarded. The most popular majors were engineering (26%), business/marketing (15%), and agriculture (11%).

SERVICES: Counseling and information services are available, as is tutoring in most subjects. There is a reader service for the blind. There is also a writing skills lab and test office. Psychological and career services are also available. **Library/Resources:** The library contains 795,216 volumes, 1.8 million microform items, and 3,000 audio/video tapes/CDs/DVDs, and subscribes to 60,000 periodicals including electronic. Computerized library services include interlibrary loans, database searching, Internet access, and Wi-Fi capability. Special learning facilities include an art gallery, radio station, and TV station. **Physically Challenged Students:** 80% of the campus is accessible. Facilities include wheelchair ramps, elevators, special parking, specially equipped restrooms, special class scheduling, lowered drinking fountains, lowered telephones, and special housing. **Special:** Cal Poly offers work-study programs, co-op programs in numerous majors, study abroad, and dual majors. Credit for military experience and pass/fail options are available. There is a freshman honors program. **Visiting:** There are regularly scheduled orientations for prospective students, campus tours are offered Monday through Friday. There are guides for informal visits. To schedule a visit, contact the Admissions Office. **Campus Safety and Security:** Measures include 24-hour foot and vehicle patrol, emergency notification system, self-defense education, and security escort services. There are emergency telephones, lighted pathways/sidewalks, and controlled access to dorms/residences.

REQUIREMENTS: The SAT or ACT is required. Applicants must be graduates of an accredited high school or have a GED. Required are 15 academic credits, (units recommended 21-23) including 4-5 units of English, 3 units of math (4-5 recommended), 2 units each of science with lab (recommended 4 with 2 lab), and foreign language (recommended 4), and 1 unit each of social studies, history, and academic electives. AP and CLEP credits are accepted. Important factors in the admissions decision are leadership record and advanced placement or honors courses. Students must have a minimum 2.0 GPA, 72 quarter units of general education, a minimum of 180 total units, a United States Cultural Pluralism course, completion of the Graduation Writing Requirement, a minimum of 50 units in residence and a senior project are required. **Procedure:** Freshmen are admitted in the fall. Entrance exams should be taken mid-June every year. There are early decision and early admissions plans. Early decision applications should be filed by November 30; regular applications, by December 1 for fall entry. The fall 2017 application fee was $55. Notifications are sent April 1. 1078 early decision candidates were accepted for the 2017-2018 class. 3168 applicants were on the 2017 waiting list; 15 were admitted. Applications are accepted on-line. **Transfer Students:** 878 transfer students enrolled in 2016-2017. Applicants must meet general education and breadth requirements and submit college transcripts with a minimum GPA of 2.0. Students may enroll in the fall. 50 credits required for the bachelor's degree must be completed at CPSU. **International Students:** There are 201 international students enrolled. They must take the TOEFL with a minimum score of 550 on the paper-based TOEFL (PBT) or 80 on the Internet-based version (iBT). Student must take the IELTS.

ADMISSIONS: 35% of the 2017-2018 applicants were accepted. The SAT scores for the 2017-2018 freshman class were: Math-- 20% between 500 and 599, 49% between 600 and 699, and 31% between 700 and 800. Evidence-Based Reading/Writing-- 20% between 500 and 599, 58% between 600 and 699, and 22% between 700 and 800. The ACT scores were: 9% between 18 and 23, 51% between 24 and 29, and 40% above 30. 88% of the current freshmen were in the top fifth of their class; 99% were in the top two fifths. **Admissions Contact:** James Maraviglia, Associate Vice Provost. Email: *admissions@calpoly.edu* Web: *www.calpoly.edu*

FINANCIAL AID: 58% of all full-time freshmen received need-based aid. The average freshman award was $9,996. Need-based scholarships or need-based grants averaged $3,340; need-based self-help aid (loans and jobs) averaged $3,102; non-need-based athletic scholarships averaged $3,847; other non-need-based awards and non-need-based scholarships averaged $2,916; and $3,347 from other forms of aid. The average financial indebtedness of the 2017 graduate was $23,082. The priority date for freshman financial aid applications for fall entry is March 2.

CALIFORNIA STATE POLYTECHNIC UNIVERSITY, POMONA D-5
www.cpp.edu

Pomona, CA 91768 **(909) 869-3427**

Fax: (909) 869-4529
Full-time: 11,509 men, 10,159 women
Part-time: 1578 men, 1073 women
Graduate: 795 men, 780 women
Year: quarters, summer session
Room & Board: $14,514

SAT CR/M: 560/570 **ACT:** 23
Application Deadline: November 1

Email: admissions@cpp.edu
Faculty: 607; IIA, +$
Ph.D.s: 82%
Student/Faculty: 25 to 1
Tuition: $7297 ($19,177)
Freshman Class: 29639 applied, 19225 accepted, 3786 enrolled
CEEB CODE: 4082
COMPETITIVE

California State Polytechnic University, Pomona, an occupationally oriented institution founded in 1938, is part of the state-supported university system. It offers undergraduate and graduate programs in agriculture, liberal arts and sciences, business, engineering, and technical and professional training. There are 8 undergraduate schools and 7 graduate schools. In addition to regional accreditation, CSPU Pomona has baccalaureate program accreditation with AACSB, ABET, ADA, ASLA, CSAB, and NAAB. The 1438-acre campus is in a suburban area 30 miles east of Los Angeles. Including any residence halls, there are 80 buildings.

STUDENT LIFE: 97% of undergraduates are from California. Others are from 31 states, 67 foreign countries, and Canada. 91% are from public schools. 7% are Foreign; 43% Hispanic; 4% two or more races; 4% race unknown; 3% African American; 22% Asian American; 17% White. **Male To Female Ratio:** 1.2:1. The average age of freshmen is 18; all undergraduates, 22. 11% do not continue beyond their first year; 62% remain to graduate. **Housing:** 2400 students can be accommodated in college housing, which includes dorms and on-campus apartments. In addition, there are honors houses, and special-interest houses. On-campus housing is available on a first-come and first-served basis. 90% of students commute. All students may keep cars.

FACULTY/CLASSROOMS: 59% of faculty are male; 41% are female. No introductory courses are taught by graduate students. The average class size in an introductory lecture is 37; in a laboratory is 35; and in a regular course is 35.

PROGRAMS OF STUDY: CSPU Pomona confers B.A., B.S., BArch., and B.F.A. degrees. Master's and doctoral degrees are also awarded. Bachelor's degrees are awarded in AGRICULTURE (agricultural business management, agricultural sciences, animal science, and plant science), BIOLOGICAL SCIENCE (biology/biological science, biotechnology, botany, environmental biology, microbiology, and zoology), BUSINESS (accounting, apparel and accessories marketing, business administration and management, business administration marketing, hotel/motel and restaurant management, human resources/organizational mgmt, international business management, and real estate finance), COMMUNICATIONS AND THE ARTS (art history and appreciation, communications, English, graphic design, music, Spanish, and theatre arts), COMPUTER AND PHYSICAL SCIENCE (chemistry, computer information systems, computer science, geology, mathematics, and physics), ENGINEERING AND ENVIRONMENTAL DESIGN (aerospace engineering, architecture, chemical engineering, civil engineering, computer engineering, construction engineering, electrical and computer engineering, electrical/electronics engineering, engineering technology, industrial engineering, landscape architecture/design, manufacturing engineering, mechanical engineering, and urban planning technology), HEALTH PROFESSIONS (nutrition and dietetics), SOCIAL SCIENCE (anthropology, economics, food science, gender studies, geography, history, liberal arts/general studies, philosophy, physical fitness/movement, political science/government, psychology, sociology, and urban studies). Engineering, architecture, hospitality management, and agriculture are the strongest academically. Mechanical engineering, hospitality management, and biology have the largest enrollments.

ACTIVITIES: 2% of men belong to 7 national fraternities; 1% of women belong to 5 national sororities. There are 306 groups on campus, including Project RISHI, art, band, cheerleading, choir, chorale, chorus, communications, computers, dance, drama, ethnic, film, honors, international, jazz band, LGBT, literary magazine, musical theater, newspaper, opera, orchestra, pep band, photography, political, professional, religious, Rose Float Club, social, social service, student government, and symphony. Popular campus events include BroncoFusion, Hot Dog Caper, Pumpkin Festival, Unity Luncheon, Homecoming, and Commencement. **Sports:** There are 5 intercollegiate sports for men and 5 for women. Facilities include a stadium, tennis and racquetball courts, basketball and volleyball courts, soccer, baseball, softball fields, a track, swimming pool, gymnastics, weight rooms, a horse arena, and dance studios, rock wall, fitness studios, basketball courts, racquetball courts, running track, cardio and strength equipment. **Graduates:** From July 1, 2016 to June 30, 2017, 5193 bachelor's degrees were awarded. The most popular majors were hospitality management (7%), management & human resources (6%), and computer information systems (4%). In an average class, 18% graduate in 4 years or less, 50% graduate in 5 years or less, and 66% graduate in 6 years or less.

SERVICES: Counseling and information services are available, as is tutoring in most subjects. There is a reader service for the blind, and remedial math and writing. **Library/Resources:** The library contains 823,608 volumes, 1.4 million microform items, and 10,557 audio/video tapes/CDs/DVDs, and subscribes to 27,028 periodicals including electronic. Computerized library services include interlibrary loans, database searching, Internet access, and Wi-Fi capability. Special learning facilities include an art gallery, an interactive TV studio, Arabian Horse Center and Equine Research Facility, BioTrek Project (featuring the Rainforest Learning Center, Ethnobotany Gardening Learning Center, Aquatic Biology Learning Center, Mesozoic Garden and Learning Center, and Cal Poly Wildlands), Restaurant at Kellogg Ranch, AGRIscapes Agricultural Outreach Center, and the Lyle Center for Regenerative Studies. **Physically Challenged Students:** 96% of the campus is accessible. Facilities include wheelchair ramps, elevators, special parking, specially equipped restrooms, special class scheduling, lowered drinking fountains, and lowered telephones. There is accessible shuttle transportation, and specialized vans/carts for transport. **Special:** Cross-registration is possible with any California State University school. Internships and co-op programs are available in agriculture, business, environmental design, engineering, science, political science, behavioral science, and phys ed. An international study program in 17 countries, work-study programs, B.A.-B.S. degrees, a liberal studies degree, credit for military experience, an external degree program, and credit/no credit options are offered. Nondegree study is possible. There are 38 national honor societies and a freshman honors program. **Visiting:** There are regularly scheduled orientations for prospective students, consisting of tours of the campus led by current undergraduate students and a 90-minute walking tour. There are guides for informal visits, visitors may sit in on classes, and stay overnight. To schedule a visit, contact Campus Tours at (909) 869-3529. **Campus Safety and Security:** Measures include 24-hour foot and vehicle patrol, emergency notification system, self-defense education, and security escort services. There are shuttle buses, emergency telephones, lighted pathways/sidewalks, controlled access to dorms/residences, vehicle assists, and crime prevention programs.

REQUIREMENTS: The SAT or ACT is recommended. Applicants must be graduates of an accredited secondary school or have a GED equivalent. Secondary school courses must include 4 years of high school English, 3 each of math and electives, 2 of foreign language, and 1 each of science, history, and art. A GPA of 2.0 is required. AP and CLEP credits are accepted. All students must complete general education requirements, including courses in written and oral communications, critical thinking, math, humanities, natural sciences, and social sciences, and must pass a graduation writing test. A total of 180 (B.A.) to 246 (B.S.) quarter units with a minimum GPA of 2.0 is required to graduate. **Procedure:** Freshmen are admitted fall. Entrance exams should be taken during the fall of the senior year. There is a rolling admissions plan. Applications should be filed by November 1 for fall entry; June 1 for winter entry; August 1 for spring entry; and February 1 for summer entry. The fall 2017 application fee was $55. Notification is sent on a rolling basis. Applications are accepted on-line. **Transfer Students:** 3339 transfer students enrolled in 2016-2017. Applicants must have completed 56 semester or 90 quarter units including college preparatory subjects. A 2.0 GPA (2.4 for nonresidents) is required. 50 of 180 credits required for the bachelor's degree must be completed at Cal Poly Pomona. **International Students:** There are 1493 international students enrolled. They must take the TOEFL with a minimum score of 525 on the paper-based TOEFL (PBT) or 70 on the Internet-based version (iBT). They must also take the SAT or ACT.

ADMISSIONS: 65% of the 2017-2018 applicants were accepted. The SAT scores for the 2017-2018 freshman class were: Critical Reading-- 21% below 500, 48% between 500 and 599, 27% between 600 and 699, and 3% between 700 and 800. Math-- 20% below 500, 44% between 500 and 599, 28% between 600 and 699, and 8% between 700 and 800. The ACT scores were 11% between 12 and 17, 41% between 18 and 23, 37% between 24 and 29, and 11% above 30. **Admissions Contact:** Deborah L. Brandon, Executive Director of Admissions. Email: *admissions@cpp.edu* Web: *www.cpp.edu*

FINANCIAL AID: In 2017-2018, 65% of all full-time freshmen received some form of financial aid. 52% of all full-time freshmen received need-based aid. The average freshman award was $10,300. Need-based scholarships or need-based grants averaged $9,973; need-based self-help aid (loans and jobs) averaged $3,461; non-need-based athletic scholarships averaged $1,637; and other non-need-based awards and non-need-based scholarships averaged $1,013. The average financial indebtedness of the 2017 graduate was $21,998. The FAFSA code is 001144. The priority date for freshman financial aid applications for fall entry is March 2.

CALIFORNIA STATE UNIVERSITY, MARITIME ACADEMY B-3

California Maritime Academy
www.csum.edu

Vallejo, CA 94590	**(707) 654-1330** **(800) 561-1945**
Fax: (707) 654-1336	**Email: admission@csum.edu**
Full-time: 824 men, 183 women	**Faculty:** 56; IIB, av$
Part-time: 36 men, 7 women	**Ph.D.s:** n/av
Graduate: 34 men, 6 women	**Student/Faculty:** 19 to 1
Year: semesters, summer session	**Tuition:** $10,834 ($25,882)
Room & Board: $12,322	**Freshman Class:** 968 applied, 769 accepted, 223 enrolled
SAT CR/M/W: 545/580/520 **ACT:** 24	**CEEB CODE:** 4035
Application Deadline: November 30	**COMPETITIVE+**

California State University Maritime Academy, founded in 1929, is a public institution offering undergraduate degrees in marine transportation, business, engineering, and international relations as well as a master's degree in engineering management. All Cal Maritime cadets travel abroad for international experiences or training cruises aboard the 500-foot Training Ship Golden Bear. There are 2 undergraduate schools. In addition to regional accreditation, Cal State Maritime Academy has baccalaureate program accreditation with ABET. The 89-acre campus is in a suburban area on the northern end of San Francisco Bay. Including any residence halls, there are 39 buildings.

STUDENT LIFE: 81% of undergraduates are from California. Others are from 30 states, and 3 foreign countries. 83% are from public schools. 48% are White; 21% Hispanic; 12% two or more races; 9% Asian American; 7% race unknown; 1% African American; 1% American Indian/Alaska Native. **Male To Female Ratio:** 4.6:1. The average age of freshmen is 19; all undergraduates, 22. 25% do not continue beyond their first year; 64% remain to graduate. **Housing:** 727 students can be accommodated in college housing, which includes dorms, and 24-hour quiet residences. On-campus housing is guaranteed for all 4 years. 70% of students live on campus. Alcohol is not permitted. All students may keep cars.

FACULTY/CLASSROOMS: All teach undergraduates. No introductory courses are taught by graduate students. The average class size in an introductory lecture is 27; in a laboratory is 16; and in a regular course is 22.

PROGRAMS OF STUDY: Cal State Maritime Academy confers B.A. and B.S. degrees. Master's degrees are also awarded. Bachelor's degrees are awarded in BUSINESS (business administration and management and transportation management), EDUCATION (global studies), ENGINEERING AND ENVIRONMENTAL DESIGN (engineering technology, marine engineering, and mechanical engineering). Mechanical engineering is the strongest academically. Marine transportation, mechanical engineering, and business administration have the largest enrollments.

ACTIVITIES: There are no fraternities or sororities. There are 26 groups on campus, including American Society of Mechanical Engineers, cycling club, sailing club, Society of Naval Architects and Marine Engineers, sport fishing club, auto shop club, chorale, drill team, environmental, ethnic, honors, international, jazz band, LGBT, newspaper, photography, political, professional, religious, social, social service, and student government. Popular campus events include Movie Nights, Cultural Dinner Nights, and Semiformal Dance. **Sports:** There are 8 intercollegiate sports for men and 6 for women, and 10 intramural sports for men and 8 for women. Facilities include 2 gyms, 2 weight rooms, a 50-meter pool, rugby/soccer field, tennis and basketball courts, spinning, and a yoga room. **Graduates:** From July 1, 2016 to June 30, 2017, 158 bachelor's degrees were awarded. The most popular majors were marine transportation (39%), global studies and maritime affairs (19%), and mechanical engineering (16%). In an average class, 2% graduate in 3 years or less, 51% graduate in 4 years or less, 59% graduate in 5 years or less, and 62% graduate in 6 years or less. Of the 2016 graduating class, 1% were enrolled in graduate school within 6 months of graduation, and 10% were employed.

SERVICES: Counseling and information services are available, as is tutoring in some subjects, such as math, English, engineering, and science. There is remedial math, reading, and writing. **Library/Resources:** The library contains 44,373 volumes, and 1,893 audio/video tapes/CDs/DVDs, and subscribes to 140 periodicals including electronic. Computerized library services include interlibrary loans, database searching, Internet access, and Wi-Fi capabilities. **Physically Challenged Students:** 70% of the campus is accessible. Facilities include wheelchair ramps, special parking, specially equipped restrooms, lowered drinking fountains, and lowered telephones. **Special:** The academy has simulator training and requires a 2-month session aboard the academy's ship for marine transportation and marine engineering majors. Lab time is a major part of each program. Industry internships are available during the summer. Dual majors and co-op programs are available, as is cross-registration with other Cal State institutions. There are B.A.- B.S. degrees in mechanical engineering, business, marine transportation, facilities engineering, global studies, and marine engineering. There are 2 national honor societies and 2 departmental honors programs. **Visiting:** There are regularly scheduled orientations for prospective students. There are guides for informal visits. To schedule a visit, contact the Admissions Office. **Campus Safety and Security:** Measures include 24-hour foot and vehicle patrol, emergency notification system, self-defense education, and security escort services. There are shuttle buses, emergency telephones, lighted pathways/sidewalks, and surveillance cameras.

REQUIREMENTS: The SAT or ACT is required. Secondary school courses must include 4 years of English, 3 each of math and electives, 2 of language, and 1 each of lab science, history, and a visual or performing art. A GPA of 2.0 is required. AP and CLEP credits are accepted. Important factors in the admissions decision are leadership record, advanced placement or honors courses, and evidence of special talent. Graduation requirements for all students include a minimum 2.0 GPA and completion of American government, U.S. and California State history, written communication in the English language, oral communication in the English language, critical thinking, and mathematics or quantitative reasoning with a minimum of 30 upper-division units of coursework. **Procedure:** Freshmen are admitted in the fall. Entrance exams should be taken by December of the senior year. There is a rolling admissions plan. Early decision applications should be filed by November 30. The fall 2017 application fee was $55. Notifications are sent January 1. Applications are accepted on-line. **Transfer Students:** 98 transfer students enrolled in 2016-2017. Applicants must have a 2.0 GPA, provide SAT or ACT scores, and be in good standing at the last institution attended. 30 of 120 credits required for the bachelor's degree must be completed at Cal State Maritime. **International Students:** There are 5 international students enrolled. They must take the TOEFL with a minimum score of 500 on the paper-based TOEFL (PBT) or 61 on the Internet-based version (iBT). They must also take the SAT or ACT.

ADMISSIONS: 79% of the 2017-2018 applicants were accepted. The SAT scores for the 2017-2018 freshman class were: Critical Reading-- 25% below 500, 47% between 500 and 599, and 28% between 600 and 699. Math-- 11% below 500, 55% between 500 and 599, 31% between 600 and 699, and 3% between 700 and 800. Writing-- 39% below 500, 53% between 500 and 599, and 8% between 600 and 699. The ACT scores were 6% between 12 and 17, 34% between 18 and 23, 49% between 24 and 29, and 11% above 30. **Admissions Contact:** Marc McGee, Director of Admissions and Enrollment Services. Email: *admission@csum.edu* Web: *www.csum.edu*

FINANCIAL AID: In 2017-2018, 88% of all full-time freshmen received some form of financial aid. 34% of all full-time freshmen received need-based aid. The average freshman award was $5,932. Need-based scholarships or need-based grants averaged $4,020 ($6,000 maximum); need-based self-help aid (loans and jobs) averaged $2,943 ($4,500 maximum); non-need-based athletic scholarships averaged $842 ($2,500 maximum); other non-need-based awards and non-need-based scholarships averaged $8,251 ($33,716 maximum); and $5,161 from other forms of aid. 40% of undergraduate students work part-time. The average financial indebtedness of the 2017 graduate was $21,818. The FAFSA code is 001134. The priority date for freshman financial aid applications for fall entry is March 2.

CALIFORNIA STATE UNIVERSITY, BAKERSFIELD *(The complete profile is made available exclusively on our website, www.barronspac.com)*

CALIFORNIA STATE UNIVERSITY, CHICO B-2
www.csuchico.edu

Chico, CA 95929	**(530) 898-4428** **(800) 542-4426**
Fax: (530) 898-6456	**Email: info@csuchico.edu**
Full-time: 7120 men, 7928 women	**Faculty:** 507; IIA, av$
Part-time: 735 men, 887 women	**Ph.D.s:** 85%
Graduate: 344 men, 775 women	**Student/Faculty:** 23 to 1
Year: semesters, summer session	**Tuition:** $7078 ($20,834)
Room & Board: $12,712	**Freshman Class:** 22853 applied, 16396 accepted, 2805 enrolled
SAT CR/M: 545/537 **ACT:** 22	**CEEB CODE:** 4048
Application Deadline: November 30	**VERY COMPETITIVE**

California State University, Chico, founded in 1887, is a public institution offering undergraduate programs in behavioral and social sciences, business, communication and education, engineering, computer science and technology, humanities and fine arts, natural sciences, agriculture, and nursing. The university also offers online classes. There are 7 undergraduate schools and 1 graduate school. In addition to regional accreditation, Cal State Chico has baccalaureate program accreditation with AACSB, ABET, ACCE, ACEJMC, ADA, CSAB, CSWE, NASAD, NASM, NRPA, AAAHC, AACN, NASP, COAPRT, ACS, ASHA, ATMAE, AUPHA, and NASPAA. The 130-acre campus is in a small town 90 miles north of Sacramento, and 174 miles northeast of San Francisco. Including any residence halls, there are 66 buildings.

STUDENT LIFE: 96% of undergraduates are from California. Others are from 35 states, 43 foreign countries, and Canada. 93% are from public schools. 42% are White; 32% Hispanic; 8% race unknown; 5% Asian American; 5% two or more races; 3% African American; 3% Foreign; 1% American Indian/Alaska Native. **Female To Male Ratio:** 1.2:1. The average age of freshmen is 19; all undergraduates, 24. 15% do not continue beyond their first year; 85% remain to graduate. **Housing:** 2222 students can be accommodated in college housing, which includes dorms, on-campus apartments, and off-campus apartments. In addition, there are honors houses, language/international houses, special-interest houses, fraternity houses, sorority houses, thematic housing for minorities in engineering and science, math, and business. Theme floors include community service, recreational sports, leadership, adventure outings, and sustainability. On-campus housing is available on a first-come and first-served basis. 99% of students commute. Alcohol is not permitted. All students may keep cars.

FACULTY/CLASSROOMS: 47% of faculty are male; 52% are female. 97% teach undergraduates, and 21% do research. No introductory courses are taught by graduate students. The average class size in an introductory lecture is 30; in a laboratory is 21; and in a regular course is 22.

PROGRAMS OF STUDY: Cal State Chico confers B.A., B.S., and B.F.A. degrees. Master's degrees are also awarded. Bachelor's degrees are awarded in AGRICULTURE (agricultural business management, agriculture, and animal science), BIOLOGICAL SCIENCE (biochemistry, biology/biological science, and microbiology), BUSINESS (business administration and management and small business management), COMMUNICATIONS AND THE ARTS (art, communication design, communications, English, fine arts, German, graphic design, journalism, music, music industry, musical theater, Spanish, and theatre arts), COMPUTER AND PHYSICAL SCIENCE (chemistry, computer information systems, computer science, geology, mathematics, natural sciences, and physics), EDUCATION (art education and Asian studies), ENGINEERING AND ENVIRONMENTAL DESIGN (civil engineering, computer engineering, computer graphics, construction management, electrical/electronics engineering, environmental science, mechanical engineering, and mechatronics engineering), HEALTH PROFESSIONS (health care administration, health science, and nursing), SOCIAL SCIENCE (anthropology, child psychology/development, communication sciences & disorders, criminal justice, dietetics, economics, French studies, gender studies, geography, history, humanities, international relations, Latin American studies, liberal arts/general studies, philosophy, political science/government, psychology, public administration, religious studies, social science, social work, sociology, and women & gender studies). Business administration, health professions, and social sciences are the strongest academically. Business administration, psychology, and liberal studies have the largest enrollments.

ACTIVITIES: 6% of men belong to 2 local and 15 national fraternities; 5% of women belong to 1 local and 13 national sororities. There are 240 groups on campus, including art, band, cheerleading, choir, chorale, chorus, computers, dance, debate, drama, environmental, ethnic, film, forensics, honors, international, jazz band, LGBT, literary magazine, musical theater, newspaper, opera, orchestra, pep band, political, professional, radio and TV, religious, social, social service, student government, symphony, and yearbook. Popular campus events include Cesar Chavez Cats Day (community clean-up), Wildcat Welcome, and Up 'Til Dawn, and St. Jude Hospital Fund-raiser. **Sports:** There are 6 intercollegiate sports for men and 7 for women, and 8 intramural sports for men and 8 for women. Facilities include gyms, athletic training rooms, a dance studio, swimming and diving pools, a par course, putting greens and sand trap, handball/racquetball courts, baseball/softball fields, an all-weather track, a soccer stadium, athletic stadium, a residence hall sports center, a climbing wall, pool, and fitness and weight rooms. **Graduates:** From July 1, 2016 to June 30, 2017, 3771 bachelor's degrees were awarded. The most popular majors were business administration (18%), health professions and related programs (10%), and social sciences (9%). In an average class, 24% graduate in 4 years or less, 53% graduate in 5 years or less, and 59% graduate in 6 years or less.

SERVICES: Counseling and information services are available, as is tutoring in most subjects, such as accounting, anthropology, Arabic, business administration, biology, chemistry, economics, finance, French, German, history, Italian, Japanese, math, management information systems, music, philosophy, physics, political science, and psychology. There is a reader service for the blind, and remedial math and writing. A student learning center offers a tutorial program, study skills development, learning assistance workshops, and writing resources. **Library/Resources:** The library contains 924,281 volumes, 1.2 million microform items, and 23,725 audio/video tapes/CDs/DVDs, and subscribes to 600 periodicals including electronic. Computerized library services include interlibrary loans, database searching, Internet access, and Wi-Fi capability. Special learning facilities include an art gallery, natural history museum, planetarium, radio station, an instructional media center, a university farm, a biological field station, an anthropology museum, a media preparation lab, a computer graphics lab, a recording arts studio, a writing center, and distributed learning technologies, anthropology museum, Gateway science museum, and the Wildcat Recreation Center. **Physically Challenged Students:** 95% of the campus is accessible. Facilities include wheelchair ramps, elevators, special parking, specially equipped restrooms, special class scheduling, lowered drinking fountains, lowered telephones, and special housing. **Special:** The university offers co-op programs and cross-registration as part of the National Student Exchange. In addition, internships, distance learning, teacher certification, study abroad in 38 countries, work-study, student-designed majors, independent study, credit for experience, non-degree study, and pass/fail options are available. Chico State has a nationally recognized sustainability program and an established Institute for Sustainable Development. There are 16 national honor societies, Phi Beta Kappa, a freshman honors program, and 40 departmental honors programs. **Visiting:** There are regularly scheduled orientations for prospective students, consisting of a 1-hour tour given at 11:30 a.m. Monday through Saturday. There are guides for informal visits and visitors may sit in on classes. To schedule a visit, contact the Office of Admissions. **Campus Safety and Security:** Measures include 24-hour foot and vehicle patrol, emergency notification system, self-defense education, and security escort services. There are shuttle buses, emergency telephones, lighted pathways/sidewalks, controlled access to dorms/residences, a freshman safe start program, a victim awareness program, and crime prevention workshops.

REQUIREMENTS: An index combining GPA and SAT and ACT scores is used to determine eligibility for admission. Applicants must be graduates of a secondary school or have a GED and have completed 4 years of English, 3 years of math, 2 years of lab sciences (1 physical and 1 life), 2 years of social science and the same foreign language, and 1 year each of electives, and either visual or performing art. A GPA of 2.0 is required. AP and CLEP credits are accepted. Graduation requirements include: complete a total of 120 to 128 units, 40 units of upper division coursework, a minimum of 12 to 18 units must be in their major, 30 units in residence at Cal State Chico, at least 24 of the 30 units must be upper division (numbered 300 or above), 48 units of prescribed General Education (9 units as a resident at Chico State), minimum of two courses with focus on cultural diversity, demonstrate competent understanding of the Constitution of the United States, U.S. history, mathematics and writing, complete an approved major, and have a GPA of 2.0 or better. General education coursework includes: oral communications, writing, critical thinking, mathematics, 2 laboratory sciences (1 physical science and 1 in the life sciences), US history, US governmental institutions, 4 writing intensive courses, and a GE capstone course. In addition, each student must complete a Pathway, which consists of 18 units of lower division and 9 units of upper division coursework. **Procedure:** Freshmen are admitted fall and spring. Entrance exams should be taken in fall of the senior year. There are deferred admissions and rolling admissions plans. Early decision applications should be filed by October 1; regular applications, by November 30 for fall entry. The fall 2017 application fee was $55. Notifications are sent March 1. Applications are accepted on-line. **Transfer Students:** 1472 transfer students enrolled in 2016-2017. Transfer students who are California residents must have a minimum 2.0 GPA, and nonresidents need 2.4. Students must have made up any missing college preparatory subjects and provide a statement of good standing and transcripts from prior institutions. 30 of 124 credits required for the bachelor's degree must be completed at Cal State Chico. **International Students:** There are 385 international students enrolled. They must take the TOEFL with a minimum score of 500 on the paper-based TOEFL (PBT) or 61 on the Internet-based version (iBT), and take the IELTS.

ADMISSIONS: 72% of the 2017-2018 applicants were accepted. The SAT scores for the 2017-2018 freshman class were: Critical Reading-- 24% below 500, 53% between 500 and 599, 22% between 600 and 699, and 2% between 700 and 800. Math-- 26% below 500, 55% between 500 and 599, 18% between 600 and 699, and 1% between 700 and 800. The ACT scores were 1% below 12, 15% between 12 and 17, 50% between 18 and 23, 33% between 24 and 29, and 3% above 30. **Admissions Contact:** Barbara Fortin, Interim Director of Admissions. Email: *info@csuchico.edu* Web: *www.csuchico.edu*

FINANCIAL AID: The average freshman award was $17,631. Need-based scholarships or need-based grants averaged $10,803; need-based self-help aid (loans and jobs) averaged $3,540; non-need-based athletic scholarships averaged $2,636; and other non-need-based awards and non-need-based scholarships averaged $1,611. The FAFSA code is 001146. The priority date for freshman financial aid applications for fall entry is March 2.

CALIFORNIA STATE UNIVERSITY, DOMINGUEZ HILLS *(The complete profile is made available exclusively on our website, www.barronspac.com)*

CALIFORNIA STATE UNIVERSITY, EAST BAY — B-3

www.csueastbay.edu

Hayward, CA 94542	(510) 885-2310
	Email: admissions@csueastbay.edu
Full-time: 3985 men, 6313 women	**Faculty:** IIA, +$
Part-time: 617 men, 938 women	**Ph.D.s:** n/av
Graduate: 738 men, 1260 women	**Student/Faculty:** n/av
Year: quarters, summer session	**Tuition:** $6564 ($15,492)
Room & Board: $14,184	**Freshman Class:** n/av
SAT or ACT: recommended	**CEEB CODE:** 4011
Application Deadline: December 15	**COMPETITIVE**

California State University, East Bay, founded in 1957, is part of the California State University system. The institution offers degree programs in the arts, sciences, business and economics, and education to a primarily commuter student body. The figures given in the above capsule and in this profile are approximate. There are 4 undergraduate schools and 4 graduate schools. In addition to regional accreditation, Cal State, East Bay has baccalaureate program accreditation with AACSB, NASAD, NASM, CAEP, and NLN. The 342-acre campus is in a small town 20 miles southeast of San Francisco in the Hayward Hills. Including any residence halls, there are 19 buildings.

STUDENT LIFE: 92% of undergraduates are from California. Others are from 31 states, 63 foreign countries, and Canada. 85% are from public schools. 8% are Foreign; 23% Asian American; 23% Hispanic; 21% White; 11% African American; 1% American Indian/Alaska Native. **Female To Male Ratio:** 1.6:1. The average age of all undergraduates is 25. 25% do not continue beyond their first year; 50% remain to graduate. **Housing:** 1300 students can be accommodated in college housing, which includes on-campus apartments. In addition, there are special-interest houses. On-campus housing is available on a first-come and first-served basis. 90% of students commute. All students may keep cars.

FACULTY/CLASSROOMS: 45% of faculty are male; 55% are female. No introductory courses are taught by graduate students.

PROGRAMS OF STUDY: Cal State, East Bay confers B.A. and B.S. degrees. Master's and doctoral degrees are also awarded. Bachelor's degrees are awarded in AGRICULTURE (environmental studies), BIOLOGICAL SCIENCE (biology/biological science), BUSINESS (accounting, business administration and management, and recreation and leisure services), COMMUNICATIONS AND THE ARTS (advertising, art, communications, dramatic arts, English, music, Spanish, and speech/debate/rhetoric), COMPUTER AND PHYSICAL SCIENCE (chemistry, computer science, geology, mathematics, physical sciences, physics, and statistics), ENGINEERING AND ENVIRONMENTAL DESIGN (engineering, environmental science, and industrial engineering), HEALTH PROFESSIONS (health science, nursing, and speech pathology/audiology), SOCIAL SCIENCE (anthropology, criminal justice, economics, ethnic studies, geography, history, human development, international studies, Latin American studies, liberal arts/general studies, philosophy, physical fitness/movement, political science/government, psychology, and sociology).

ACTIVITIES: 1% of men belong to 4 national fraternities; 1% of women belong to 3 national sororities. There are 90 groups on campus, including art, cheerleading, choir, chorale, chorus, computers, dance, drama, environmental, ethnic, film, honors, international, jazz band, LGBT, literary magazine, musical theater, newspaper, opera, orchestra, pep band, photography, political, professional, radio and TV, religious, social, social service, student government, and symphony. Popular campus events include Science Fair, Leadership Conferences, and Al Fresco. **Sports:** There are 5 intercollegiate sports for men and 8 for women. Facilities include tennis and racquetball courts, swimming pools, a track, a soccer field, martial arts facility, dance studio, baseball & softball diamonds, a stadium, and a gym. **Graduates:** From July 1, 2016 to June 30, 2017, 2700 bachelor's degrees were awarded. The most popular majors were business administration (30%), health sciences (7%), and nursing (7%). In an average class, 25% graduate in 4 years or less, 35% graduate in 5 years or less, and 45% graduate in 6 years or less.

SERVICES: Counseling and information services are available, as is tutoring in most subjects. There is a reader service for the blind, and remedial math, reading, and writing. **Library/Resources:** The library contains 912,912 volumes, 873,177 microform items, and 29,768 audio/video tapes/CDs/DVDs, and subscribes to 2,000 periodicals including electronic. Computerized library services include interlibrary loans, database searching, Internet access, and Wi-Fi capability. Special learning facilities include an art gallery, natural history museum, radio station, TV station, a marine biology lab, and geology summer field camp. **Physically Challenged Students:** 95% of the campus is accessible. Facilities include wheelchair ramps, elevators, special parking, specially equipped restrooms, special class scheduling, lowered drinking fountains, lowered telephones, and special housing. The Disabled Student Services Center provides scribe, interpretive, and translation services. **Special:** CSU East Bay offers cross-registration with local community colleges, other CSU campuses, and the University of California, Berkeley. Internships, study abroad in 20 countries, work-study programs, and student-designed majors are also available. The PACE program provides degree opportunities in liberal studies, hospitality and leisure services, and in human development to working adults. There is 1 national honor society, a freshman honors program, and 1 departmental honors program. **Visiting:** There are regularly scheduled orientations for prospective students. There are guides for informal visits and visitors may sit in on classes. To schedule a visit, contact the Welcome Center at admissions@csueastbay.edu. **Campus Safety and Security:** Measures include 24-hour foot and vehicle patrol, self-defense education, and security escort services. There are shuttle buses, emergency telephones, and lighted pathways/sidewalks.

REQUIREMENTS: All students must meet the eligibility index, a combination of the high school GPA and SAT or ACT scores. Applicants must be graduates of an accredited secondary school or have a GED certificate. Secondary school courses must include 4 years of English, 3 of math, 2 each of language other than English, social science, and science with a lab, and 1 elective. A GPA of 2.0 is required. AP and CLEP credits are accepted. In order to graduate, students must fulfill the university writing skills requirement, have a 2.0 minimum GPA, and complete 186 quarter units. **Procedure:** Freshmen are admitted to all sessions. Entrance exams should be taken prior to orientation. There is a rolling admissions plan. Applications should be filed by December 15 for fall entry. The fall 2017 application fee was $55. Notification is sent on a rolling basis. Applications are accepted on-line. **Transfer Students:** Applicants must have a minimum 2.0 GPA (2.45 for nonresidents), be in good standing at the last college attended, and either meet freshman admission requirements or have completed at least 56 transferable semester (84 quarter) units. 45 of 186 credits required for the bachelor's degree must be completed at Cal State East Bay. **International Students:** They must take the TOEFL. They must also take the SAT or ACT.

Admissions Contact: Molly Moya. Email: *admissions@csueastbay.edu*
Web: *www.csueastbay.edu*

FINANCIAL AID: Cal State, East Bay is a member of CSS. The FAFSA code is 001138. Check with the school for current application deadlines.

CALIFORNIA STATE UNIVERSITY, FRESNO *(The complete profile is made available exclusively on our website, www.barronspac.com)*

CALIFORNIA STATE UNIVERSITY, FULLERTON D-5

www.fullerton.edu

Fullerton, CA 92834 (657) 278-2371

Fax: (657) 278-2356	**Email:** admissions@fullerton.edu
Full-time: 12,289 men, 16,173 women	**Faculty:** 1048; I, -$
Part-time: 2981 men, 3477 women	**Ph.D.s:** 84%
Graduate: 2135 men, 3379 women	**Student/Faculty:** 32 to 1
Year: semesters, summer session	**Tuition:** $6560 ($15,488)
Room & Board: $15,342	**Freshman Class:** 44493 applied, 21459 accepted, 4426 enrolled
SAT CR/M: 520/550 **ACT:** 22	**CEEB CODE:** 4589
Application Deadline: November 30	**COMPETITIVE**

California State University, Fullerton, founded in 1957, is part of the California State University system. The school offers programs in the arts, business and economics, communications, engineering and computer science, education, health and human development, humanities and social science, natural science and math. The institution provides a comprehensive teaching credential program. There are 8 undergraduate schools and 8 graduate schools. In addition to regional accreditation, Cal State Fullerton has baccalaureate program accreditation with AACSB, ABET, ACEJMC, NASAD, NASM, CAEP, NLN, ACS, ASHA, CAAHEP, CCNE, CCTE, CSWE, NASD, NASPAA, and NAST. The 240-acre campus is in a suburban area 30 miles southeast of Los Angeles. Including any residence halls, there are 29 buildings.

STUDENT LIFE: 97% of undergraduates are from California. Others are from 38 states, 64 foreign countries, and Canada. 93% are from public schools. 6% are Foreign; 43% Hispanic; 4% two or more races; 4% race unknown; 21% Asian American; 2% African American; 19% White. **Female To Male Ratio:** 1.3:1. The average age of freshmen is 18; all undergraduates, 22. 11% do not continue beyond their first year; 89% remain to graduate. **Housing:** 2000 students can be accommodated in college housing, which includes on-campus apartments and off-campus apartments. In addition, there are fraternity houses and sorority houses. On-campus housing is available on a first-come and first-served basis. 94% of students commute. All students may keep cars.

FACULTY/CLASSROOMS: 51% of faculty are male; 49% are female. 84% teach undergraduates. Graduate students teach 6% of introductory courses. The average class size in an introductory lecture is 38; in a laboratory is 22; and in a regular course is 34.

PROGRAMS OF STUDY: Cal State Fullerton confers B.A., B.S., B.F.A., and B.M. degrees. Master's and doctoral degrees are also awarded. Bachelor's degrees are awarded in BIOLOGICAL SCIENCE (biochemistry and biology/biological science), BUSINESS (accounting, business administration and management, business economics, entrepreneurial studies, finance, international business management, management science, marketing/retailing/merchandising, and tourism), COMMUNICATIONS AND THE ARTS (advertising, art history, art, communications, comparative literature, dance, dramatic arts, English, fine arts, French, Japanese, journalism, linguistics, music, music performance, public relations, radio/television technology, Spanish, speech/debate/rhetoric, theater design, theater management, visual and performing arts, and visual design), COMPUTER AND PHYSICAL SCIENCE (applied mathematics, chemistry, computer science, earth science, geology, information sciences and systems, mathematics, physics, and statistics), EDUCATION (athletic training and music education), ENGINEERING AND ENVIRONMENTAL DESIGN (civil engineering, computer engineering, electrical/electronics engineering, engineering and applied science, and mechanical engineering), HEALTH PROFESSIONS (exercise science, health science, kinesiology, nursing, and speech pathology/audiology), SOCIAL SCIENCE (African American studies, American studies, anthropology, Asian/American studies, child care/child and family studies, criminal justice, economics, ethnic studies, European studies, geography, history, human services, Latin American studies, liberal arts/general studies, Mexican-American/Chicano studies, philosophy, political science/government, psychology, public administration, religion, and women's studies). Business, economics, and teacher credential program are the strongest academically. Business, economics, and humanities have the largest enrollments.

ACTIVITIES: 1% of men belong to 5 local and 13 national fraternities; 2% of women belong to 1 local and 8 national sororities. There are 324 groups on campus, including art, band, cheerleading, choir, chorus, communications, computers, dance, debate, drama, ethnic, film, forensics, honors, international, jazz band, LGBT, literary magazine, musical theater, newspaper, opera, orchestra, pep band, photography, political, professional, radio and TV, religious, social, social service, and student government. Popular campus events include Block Party, Spring Concert, and Snow Day. **Sports:** There are 6 intercollegiate sports for men and 9 for women, and 15 intramural sports for men and 11 for women. Facilities include a gym, a swimming pool, tennis and racquetball courts, baseball/softball, track, and soccer fields, a bowling alley, and a stadium. **Graduates:** From July 1, 2016 to June 30, 2017, 8448 bachelor's degrees were awarded. The most popular majors were business administration (24%), communication/journalism (10%), and psychology (7%). In an average class, 3% graduate in 4 years or less, 42% graduate in 5 years or less, and 81% graduate in 6 years or less.

SERVICES: Counseling and information services are available, as is tutoring in most subjects. There is a reader service for the blind, and remedial math, reading, and writing. **Library/Resources:** The library contains 1.1 million volumes, 1.2 million microform items, and 35,016 audio/video tapes/CDs/DVDs. Computerized library services include interlibrary loans, database searching, Internet access, and Wi-Fi capability. Special learning facilities include an art gallery, radio station, TV station, a wildlife sanctuary, an arboretum, a desert studies center, a demographic research center, and a number of centers for studies in economics and business, the environment, education, oral and public history, and religion in America. **Physically Challenged Students:** All of the campus is accessible. Facilities include wheelchair ramps, elevators, special parking, specially equipped restrooms, lowered drinking fountains, lowered telephones, and automatic doors. **Special:** The university offers distance learning, honors program, freshman program, internships and co-op programs in 45 academic areas, study abroad in 18 countries, and work-study programs both on and off campus. Double majors, and pass/fail options, teacher credential programs, and service learning are also available. There is a freshman honors program. **Visiting:** There are regularly scheduled orientations for prospective students, consisting of daily campus tours and information on academic colleges, student services, student life, and the history of Cal State Fullerton. There are guides for informal visits. To schedule a visit, contact New Student & Parent Programs at (657) 278-2501. **Campus Safety and Security:** Measures include 24-hour foot and vehicle patrol, emergency notification system, self-defense education, and security escort services. There are shuttle buses, emergency telephones, and lighted pathways/sidewalks.

REQUIREMENTS: Applicants must be graduates of an accredited secondary school or have a GED certificate. Secondary school courses must include 4 years of English, 3 years of math, 2 years each of foreign language, science, and history, and 1 of visual or performing arts. Admission is based on the Qualifiable Eligibility Index, a combination of the high school GPA and either the SAT or ACT score. Auditions are required for music majors. A GPA of 2.0 is required. AP and CLEP credits are accepted. Graduation requirements for all students include completion of a minimum of 51 units of general education courses, a 2.0 GPA, and an upper-division writing course designated by the major department. 120 to 135 credit hours must be completed for graduation. **Procedure:** Freshmen are admitted in the fall. Entrance exams should be taken during the senior year of high school. There is a rolling admissions plan. Applications should be filed by November 30 for fall entry. The fall 2017 application fee was $55. Notification is sent on a rolling basis. Applications are accepted on-line. **Transfer Students:** 3755 transfer students enrolled in 2016-2017. Applicants must have a minimum 2.0 GPA. The SAT or ACT is required for students with fewer than 60 transferable units earned. Students with 60 transferable units or more must have 30 units of general education completed with a C or better, including English composition, math, speech, and critical thinking. 30 of 120 credits required for the bachelor's degree must be completed at Cal State Fullerton. **International Students:** There are 1105 international students enrolled. They must take the TOEFL with a minimum score of 500 on the paper-based TOEFL (PBT) or 61 on the Internet-based version (iBT).

ADMISSIONS: 48% of the 2017-2018 applicants were accepted. The SAT scores for the 2017-2018 freshman class were: Critical Reading-- 40% below 500, 45% between 500 and 599, 14% between 600 and 699, and 1% between 700 and 800. Math-- 26% below 500, 47% between 500 and 599, 24% between 600 and 699, and 3% between 700 and 800. The ACT scores were 5% between 12 and 17, 56% between 18 and 23, 34% between 24 and 29, and 5% above 30. 54% of the current freshmen were in the top fifth of their class; 90% were in the top two fifths. 8 freshmen graduated first in their class. **Admissions Contact:** Director of Admissions. Email: *admissions@fullerton.edu* Web: *www.fullerton.edu*

FINANCIAL AID: In 2017-2018, 67% of all full-time freshmen received some form of financial aid. 55% of all full-time freshmen received need-based aid. The average freshman award was $6,717. Need-based scholarships or need-based grants averaged $3,615; need-based self-help aid (loans and jobs) averaged $4,036; non-need-based athletic scholarships averaged $2,538; and other non-need-based awards and non-need-based scholarships averaged $1,287. The priority date for freshman financial aid applications for fall entry is March 2. The deadline for filing freshman financial aid applications for fall entry is June 6.

CALIFORNIA STATE UNIVERSITY, LONG BEACH D-5

www.csulb.edu

Long Beach, CA 90840	(562) 985-8416
Fax: (562) 985-4973	**Email:** eslb@csulb.edu
Full-time: 11,715 men, 15,227 women	**Faculty:** IIA, +$
Part-time: 2333 men, 2971 women	**Ph.D.s:** 72%
Graduate: 2055 men, 3475 women	**Student/Faculty:** 26 to 1
Year: semesters, summer session	**Tuition:** $6452 ($16,124)
Room & Board: $12,398	**Freshman Class:** 60744 applied, 19711 accepted, 4253 enrolled
SAT CR/M: 514/531 **ACT:** 23	**CEEB CODE:** 4389
Application Deadline: November 30	**COMPETITIVE**

California State University, Long Beach, is a diverse, student-centered, globally-engaged public university committed to providing highly-valued undergraduate and graduate educational opportunities through superior teaching, research, creative activity and service for the people of California and the world. CSULB is one of the largest campuses in the CSU system and in the state of California. It is nationally recognized as one of the nations' best values in higher education, offering a high-quality, low-cost education. There are 7 undergraduate schools and 7 graduate schools. In addition to regional accreditation, Cal State Long Beach has baccalaureate program accreditation with AACSB, AALE, ABET, ACEJMC, AHEA, APTA, CAHEA, CSAB, CSWE, FIDER, NASAD, NASM, CAEP, NLN, and NRPA. The 322-acre campus is in an urban area about three miles from the ocean, 25 miles southeast of Los Angeles and a short drive to Orange County. Including any residence halls, there are 95 buildings.

STUDENT LIFE: 95% of undergraduates are from California. Others are from 45 states, 99 foreign countries, and Canada. 46% are from public schools. 7% are Foreign; 5% two or more races; 4% African American; 4% race unknown; 39% Hispanic; 21% Asian American; 19% White. **Female To Male Ratio:** 1.3:1. The average age of freshmen is 18; all undergraduates, 23. 10% do not continue beyond their first year; 90% remain to graduate. **Housing:** 2722 students can be accommodated in college housing, which includes dorms. In addition, there are honors houses, special-interest houses, living-learning communities. On-campus housing is available on a first-come and first-served basis. 92% of students commute. Alcohol is not permitted. All students may keep cars.

FACULTY/CLASSROOMS: 48% of faculty are male; 52% are female. No introductory courses are taught by graduate students.

PROGRAMS OF STUDY: Cal State Long Beach confers B.A., B.S., B.F.A., and B.M. degrees. Master's and doctoral degrees are also awarded. Bachelor's degrees are awarded in BIOLOGICAL SCIENCE (biochemistry, biology/biological science, botany, cell biology, ecology, marine biology, microbiology, nutritional sciences, physiology, and zoology), BUSINESS (accounting, banking and finance, business administration and management, business economics, finance, international business, international business management, management information systems, marketing/retailing/merchandising, personnel management, and recreation and leisure services), COMMUNICATIONS AND THE ARTS (art history, art, Chinese, classics, communications, comparative literature, creative writing, dance, design, dramatic arts, English, film arts, French, French and Francophone studies, German, Japanese, journalism, music, Spanish, and theatre arts), COMPUTER AND PHYSICAL SCIENCE (applied mathematics, chemistry, computer engineering technology, computer science, earth science, geology, mathematics, physics, and statistics), EDUCATION (elementary education, mathematics education, science education, and special education), ENGINEERING AND ENVIRONMENTAL DESIGN (aerospace engineering, chemical engineering, civil engineering, computer engineering, electrical/electronics engineering, engineering technology, environmental science, and mechanical engineering), HEALTH PROFESSIONS (health care administration, health science, kinesiology, and nursing), SOCIAL SCIENCE (African studies, American studies, anthropology, Asian/Oriental studies, child care/child and family studies, child psychology/development, criminal justice, criminology, economics, family/consumer studies, geography, Hispanic American studies, history, human development, interdisciplinary studies, international studies, philosophy, political science/government, psychology, religion, religious studies, social work, sociology, women & gender studies, and women's studies). Art, biological sciences, and music are the strongest academically. Business administration, psychology, and speech communication have the largest enrollments.

ACTIVITIES: 7% of men belong to 24 national fraternities; 6% of women belong to 17 national sororities. There are 395 groups on campus, including art, band, cheerleading, choir, chorale, chorus, communications, computers, dance, debate, drama, drill team, ethnic, film, forensics, honors, international, jazz band, LGBT, literary magazine, musical theater, newspaper, opera, orchestra, pep band, photography, political, professional, radio and TV, religious, social, social service, student government, and symphony. Popular campus events include Homecoming and Smorgasport. **Sports:** There are 7 intercollegiate sports for men and 11 for women, and 14 intramural sports for men and 12 for women. Facilities include basketball or volleyball courts, baseball facilities, softball, women's soccer, a stadium facility that features an all-weather track, and tennis center. The Student Recreation and Wellness Center (SRWC) contains a gym, a multi-activity court gym, an indoor jogging track, weight lifting and cardio equipment, racquetball courts, activity rooms, a custom-made rock climbing wall, and an outdoor pool. **Graduates:** From July 1, 2016 to June 30, 2017, 8679 bachelor's degrees were awarded. The most popular majors were psychology (5%), family

& consumer sciences (5%), and communication (5%). In an average class, 16% graduate in 4 years or less and 68% graduate in 6 years or less.

SERVICES: Counseling and information services are available, as is tutoring in most subjects. There is a reader service for the blind, and remedial math, reading, and writing. **Library/Resources:** The library contains 1.1 million volumes, 1.5 million microform items, and 44,559 audio/video tapes/CDs/DVDs, and subscribes to 68,436 periodicals including electronic. Computerized library services include interlibrary loans, database searching, and Internet access. Special learning facilities include an art gallery, radio station, and TV station. **Physically Challenged Students:** 95% of the campus is accessible. Facilities include wheelchair ramps, elevators, special parking, specially equipped restrooms, special class scheduling, lowered drinking fountains, and lowered telephones. **Special:** There are 23 national honor societies, Phi Beta Kappa, and a freshman honors program. **Visiting:** There are regularly scheduled orientations for prospective students, consisting of a one hour walking tour showcases campus distinctions and facilities, provides a general overview of campus academic programs, student support services and campus life. There are guides for informal visits. To schedule a visit, contact the Office of University Outreach and School Relations at (562) 985-5358. **Campus Safety and Security:** Measures include 24-hour foot and vehicle patrol, emergency notification system, and security escort services. There are shuttle buses, emergency telephones, and lighted pathways/sidewalks.

REQUIREMENTS: The SAT or ACT is required. Applicants must be graduates of an accredited secondary school and have completed 4 years of English, 3 years of math, 2 years each of the same foreign language, lab science, history and social science, 1 year each of visual and performing arts and electives. Students are admitted on the basis of the eligibility index, a formula that combines students' achievement in high school college preparatory courses with the results of the SAT I or ACT. California residents with a minimum 3.0 GPA are automatically admissible. A portfolio is required for art and design students. An audition is required for dance, music and theater students. A GPA of 2.0 is required. AP and CLEP credits are accepted. Graduation requirements for all students include the completion of 40 units of upper-division course work and 30 units in residence at the university. Students must have a minimum 2.0 GPA and a total of 120 to 132 units, depending on the major. Students must also satisfy the Graduation Writing Assessment Requirement. **Procedure:** Freshmen are admitted fall and spring. Entrance exams should be taken during the fall semester of 12th grade. There is a rolling admissions plan. Applications should be filed by November 30 for fall entry; August 31 for spring entry. The fall 2017 application fee was $55. Applications are accepted on-line. **Transfer Students:** 3629 transfer students enrolled in 2016-2017. Upper-division students must have completed a minimum of 56 semester units and have a minimum 2.0 GPA; lower-division students must meet the same requirements as entering freshmen. 30 of 120 credits required for the bachelor's degree must be completed at Cal State Long Beach. **International Students:** There are 1921 international students enrolled. They must take the TOEFL with a minimum score of 500 on the paper-based TOEFL (PBT) or 61 on the Internet-based version (iBT).

ADMISSIONS: 32% of the 2017-2018 applicants were accepted. The SAT scores for the 2017-2018 freshman class were: Critical Reading-- 42% below 500, 41% between 500 and 599, 15% between 600 and 699, and 2% between 700 and 800. Math-- 35% below 500, 41% between 500 and 599, 21% between 600 and 699, and 3% between 700 and 800. The ACT scores were 42% below 12, 25% between 12 and 17, 20% between 18 and 23, 7% between 24 and 29, and 6% above 30. **Admissions Contact:** Donna Green, Interim AVP, and Enrollment Services. Email: *eslb@csulb.edu* Web: *www.csulb.edu*

FINANCIAL AID: Cal State Long Beach is a member of CSS. The deadline for filing freshman financial aid applications for fall entry is March 2.

CALIFORNIA STATE UNIVERSITY, LOS ANGELES *(The complete profile is made available exclusively on our website, www.barronspac.com)*

CALIFORNIA STATE UNIVERSITY, MONTEREY BAY *(The complete profile is made available exclusively on our website, www.barronspac.com)*

CALIFORNIA STATE UNIVERSITY, NORTHRIDGE *(The complete profile is made available exclusively on our website, www.barronspac.com)*

CALIFORNIA STATE UNIVERSITY, SACRAMENTO B-3

www.csus.edu

Sacramento, CA 95819	**(916) 278-7362** **(800) 722-4748**
Fax: (916) 278-5603	**Email: admissions@csus.edu**
Full-time: 10,018 men, 13,100 women	**Faculty:** 662; IIA, av$
Part-time: 2254 men, 2438 women	**Ph.D.s:** 90%
Graduate: 924 men, 1696 women	**Student/Faculty:** 25 to 1
Year: semesters, summer session	**Tuition:** $7204 ($19,084)
Room & Board: $11,856	**Freshman Class:** 23944 applied, 17224 accepted, 3760 enrolled
SAT CR/M: 490/500 **ACT:** 21	**CEEB CODE:** 4671
Application Deadline: November 30	**COMPETITIVE**

California State University, Sacramento, founded in 1947, is dedicated to the life-altering potential of learning that balances a liberal arts education with depth of knowledge in a discipline. We are committed to providing an excellent education to all eligible applicants who aspire to expand their knowledge and prepare themselves for meaningful lives, careers, and service to their community. The figures given in the above capsule and in this profile are approximate. There are 7 undergraduate schools and 7 graduate schools. In addition to regional accreditation, Cal State Sacramento has baccalaureate program accreditation with AACSB, ABET, ACBSP, ACCE, ADA, AHEA, APTA, ASLA, CSWE, FIDER, NASAD, NASM, CAEP, NLN, and NRPA. The 300-acre campus is in a suburban area in Sacramento, California, 90 miles northeast of San Francisco. Including any residence halls, there are 52 buildings.

STUDENT LIFE: 99% of undergraduates are from California. Others are from 37 states, 36 foreign countries, and Canada. 96% are from public schools. 30% are Hispanic; 27% White; 21% Asian American; 6% African American; 6% two or more races; 6% race unknown; 3% Foreign; 1% American Indian/Alaska Native. **Female To Male Ratio:** 1.3:1. The average age of freshmen is 18; all undergraduates, 23. **Housing:** 1100 students can be accommodated in college housing, which includes dorms and off-campus apartments, and theme housing. On-campus housing is available on a first-come and first-served basis. 72% of students commute. All students may keep cars.

FACULTY/CLASSROOMS: 51% of faculty are male; 49% are female. All teach undergraduates, and all do research. No introductory courses are taught by graduate students. The average class size in an introductory lecture is 38; in a laboratory is 19; and in a regular course is 34.

PROGRAMS OF STUDY: Cal State Sacramento confers B.A., B.S., B.M., and B.V.E. degrees. Master's and doctoral degrees are also awarded. Bachelor's degrees are awarded in AGRICULTURE (natural resource management), BIOLOGICAL SCIENCE (biology/biological science and microbiology), BUSINESS (accounting, banking and finance, business administration and management, insurance, international business management, management information systems, marketing/retailing/merchandising, and real estate), COMMUNICATIONS AND THE ARTS (communications, dramatic arts, English, French, German, journalism, music, and Spanish), COMPUTER AND PHYSICAL SCIENCE (chemistry, computer science, geology, mathematics, physical sciences, and physics), EDUCATION (business education, early childhood education, and health education), ENGINEERING AND ENVIRONMENTAL DESIGN (civil engineering, computer engineering, electrical/electronics engineering, engineering technology, and mechanical engineering), HEALTH PROFESSIONS (environmental health science, medical laboratory technology, nursing, physical therapy, and speech pathology/audiology), SOCIAL SCIENCE (anthropology, criminal justice, economics, geography, history, homeland security, international relations, parks and recreation management, philosophy, psychology, public administration, social science, social work, and sociology). Nursing, criminal justice, and business administration. are the strongest academically. Business administration, and communications have the largest enrollments.

ACTIVITIES: 7% of men belong to 3 local and 18 national fraternities; 5% of women belong to 1 local and 20 national sororities. There are 230 groups on campus, including art, band, cheerleading, chess, choir, chorale, chorus, computers, dance, debate, drama, ethnic, film, honors, international, jazz band, LGBT, literary magazine, marching band, musical theater, newspaper, opera, orchestra, pep band, photography, political, professional, radio and TV, religious, social, social service, student government, and symphony. Popular campus events include Greek Week, Festival of New American Music, and River City Days. **Sports:** Facilities include a stadium, gyms, swimming pools, an all-weather outdoor track, tennis courts, baseball, softball, and soccer fields, and an aquatic center, with sailing, wind-surfing, rowing, and canoeing. **Graduates:** From July 1, 2016 to June 30, 2017, 5787 bachelor's degrees were awarded. The most popular majors were social sciences (21%), communication/journalism (8%), psycholgy, homeland security, and parks and recreation (7%).

SERVICES: Counseling and information services are available, as is tutoring in most subjects. There is a reader service for the blind, and remedial math, reading, and writing. **Library/Resources:** The library contains 1.4 million volumes, 2.4 million microform items, and 53,515 audio/video tapes/CDs/DVDs, and subscribes to 2,171 periodicals including electronic. Computerized library services include interlibrary loans, database searching, and Internet access. Special learning facilities include an art gallery, radio station, an aquatic center, an anthropology museum, several art galleries, and a wellness center. **Physically Challenged Students:** 90% of the campus is accessible. Facilities include wheelchair ramps, elevators, special parking, specially equipped restrooms, special class scheduling, lowered drinking fountains, lowered telephones, and special housing. **Special:** The university offers cross-registration with other California State University schools, Co-op programs in many academic programs, internships, a Washington semester, study abroad in 12 countries, and dual and student-designed majors. A joint Ph.D. program in public history is available with the University of California at Santa Barbara. There is a chapter of Phi Beta Kappa and a freshman honors program. **Visiting:** There are regularly scheduled orientations for prospective students. There are guides for informal visits and visitors may sit in on classes. To schedule a visit, contact the University Outreach Services Office. **Campus Safety and Security:** Measures include 24-hour foot and vehicle patrol, self-defense education, and security escort services. There are shuttle buses, emergency telephones, and lighted pathways/sidewalks.

REQUIREMENTS: The SAT or ACT is required of applicants with a high school GPA below 3.0. Applicants should have completed 15 academic high school units 4 years English, 3 years of math, 2 years each of foreign language, history, and lab science, and 1 unit of academic electives and visual/performing arts A GPA of 2.0 is required. AP and CLEP credits are accepted. In order to graduate, students must complete a minimum of 120 semester hours, including 30 to 86 hours in the major, with a minimum 2.0 GPA. Students must complete 51 units in general education requirements and take proficiency exams in writing and a foreign language. Distribution requirements include 15 units in the individual and society; 12 each in arts and humanities and physical universe/life forms, 9 in English language communication, and 3 in understanding personal development. A course in race and ethnicity in American society is required. **Procedure:** Freshmen are admitted fall and spring. Entrance exams should be taken before December of the senior year. There are deferred admissions and rolling admissions plans. Applications should be filed by November 30 for fall entry. The fall 2017 application fee was $55. Notifications are sent October 1. Applications are accepted on-line. **Transfer Students:** 3876 transfer students enrolled in 2016-2017. Applicants must have a 2.0 GPA and 56 transferable semester units, including 30 units of specific general education courses to include oral and written communication, critical thinking, and math. 30 of 120 credits required for the bachelor's degree must be completed at Cal State Sacramento. **International Students:** There are 333 international students enrolled. They must take the TOEFL. They must also take the SAT or ACT.

ADMISSIONS: 72% of the 2017-2018 applicants were accepted. The SAT scores for the 2017-2018 freshman class were: Critical Reading-- 67% below 500, 27% between 500 and 599, and 6% between 600 and 699. Math-- 61% below 500, 31% between 500 and 599, and 8% between 600 and 699. The ACT scores were 31% between 12 and 17, 50% between 18 and 23, 16% between 24 and 29, and 1% above 30. **Admissions Contact:** Emiliano Diaz, Director of University Outreach Services. Email: *admissions@csus.edu* Web: *www.csus.edu*

FINANCIAL AID: In 2017-2018, 62% of all full-time freshmen received some form of financial aid. 60% of all full-time freshmen received need-based aid. The average freshman award was $10,651. Need-based scholarships or need-based grants averaged $8,867; need-based self-help aid (loans and jobs) averaged $3,316; other non-need-based awards and non-need-based scholarships averaged $1,175; and $3,240 from other forms of aid. The average financial indebtedness of the 2017 graduate was $13,187. Cal State Sacramento is a member of CSS. The priority date for freshman financial aid applications for fall entry is March 2.

CALIFORNIA STATE UNIVERSITY, SAN BERNARDINO — D-5

www.csusb.edu

San Bernardino, CA 92407 — **(909) 537-5188**

Fax: (909) 537-7034	**Email:** moreinfo@csusb.edu
Full-time: 4817 men, 8163 women	**Faculty:** IIA, +$
Part-time: 707 men, 1045 women	**Ph.D.s:** n/av
Graduate: 919 men, 1599 women	**Student/Faculty:** n/av
Year: quarters, summer session	**Tuition:** $6885
Room & Board: $13,221	**Freshman Class:** n/av
	CEEB CODE: 4099
Application Deadline: open	**COMPETITIVE**

California State University, San Bernardino, founded in 1965, is a public, comprehensive regional university offering programs in business and public administration, natural sciences, education, arts and letters, and social and behavioral sciences. The figures given in the above capsule and in this profile are approximate. There are 5 undergraduate schools and 19 graduate schools. In addition to regional accreditation, Cal State San Bernardino has baccalaureate program accreditation with AACSB, ABET, ADA, CSAB, CSWE, NASAD, NASM, CAEP, NLN, NAST, CORE, and CCNE. The 430-acre campus is in a suburban area 60 miles east of Los Angeles and 60 miles west of Palm Springs. Including any residence halls, there are 45 buildings.

STUDENT LIFE: 99% of undergraduates are from California. 9% are African American; 7% Asian American; 5% Foreign; 46% Hispanic; 24% White. **Female To Male Ratio:** 1.7:1. The average age of freshmen is 18; all undergraduates, 22. 18% do not continue beyond their first year; 82% remain to graduate. **Housing:** College-sponsored housing includes dorms and on-campus apartments. In addition, there are special-interest houses, and an all-women dorm. On-campus housing is available on a first-come and first-served basis. All students may keep cars.

FACULTY/CLASSROOMS: No introductory courses are taught by graduate students. The average class size in an introductory lecture is 40; in a laboratory is 18; and in a regular course is 24.

PROGRAMS OF STUDY: Cal State San Bernardino confers B.A., B.S., and B.V.E. degrees. Master's degrees are also awarded. Bachelor's degrees are awarded in AGRICULTURE (environmental studies), BIOLOGICAL SCIENCE (biochemistry and biology/biological science), BUSINESS (accounting, banking and finance, business administration and management, business economics, human resources, international business management, management information systems, management science, and small business management), COMMUNICATIONS AND THE ARTS (art, art history and appreciation, ceramic art and design, communications, dance, dramatic arts, English, French, graphic design, music, music history and appreciation, music performance, music technology, musicology/ethnomusicology, painting, photography, printmaking, sculpture, and Spanish), COMPUTER AND PHYSICAL SCIENCE (applied physics, chemistry, computer science, geology, mathematics, and physics), EDUCATION (bilingual/bicultural education, health education, music education, and vocational education), HEALTH PROFESSIONS (environmental health science, exercise science, health care administration, health science, nursing, and premedicine), SOCIAL SCIENCE (American studies, anthropology, child psychology/development, criminal justice, economics, ethnic studies, food science, geography, gerontology, history, human development, human services, humanities, liberal arts/general studies, paralegal studies, philosophy, political science/government, psychology, public administration, social science, social work, sociology, and Spanish studies). Liberal studies, nursing, and psychology have the largest enrollments.

ACTIVITIES: 4% of men belong to 1 local and 8 national fraternities; 3% of women belong to 6 national sororities. There are 80 groups on campus, including art, cheerleading, choir, chorale, chorus, computers, dance, drama, ethnic, honors, international, jazz band, LGBT, musical theater, newspaper, orchestra, political, professional, radio and TV, religious, social, social service, and student government. Popular campus events include Annual Picnic, and California Indian Cultural Awareness

Conference. **Sports:** There are 4 intercollegiate sports for men and 7 for women. Facilities include an arena for basketball and volleyball, baseball, softball, soccer fields, tennis courts, swimming pools for water polo and recreational swimming, and a gym. **Graduates:** From July 1, 2016 to June 30, 2017, 2868 bachelor's degrees were awarded. The most popular majors were psychology (10%), criminal justice (7%), and liberal studies (7%).

SERVICES: Counseling and information services are available, as is tutoring in most subjects. There is a reader service for the blind, and remedial math and writing. **Library/Resources:** Computerized library services include interlibrary loans and database searching. Special learning facilities include an art gallery, radio station, and an observatory. **Physically Challenged Students:** 95% of the campus is accessible. Facilities include wheelchair ramps, elevators, special parking, specially equipped restrooms, lowered drinking fountains, and lowered telephones. **Special:** The university offers cross-registration with other CSU campuses and study abroad in 18 countries. Also available are internships, accelerated study, campus and community work-study programs, B.A.-B.S. degrees, dual and student-designed majors, credit for vocational education and military experience, and nondegree study. There are 3 national honor societies, Phi Beta Kappa, and a freshman honors program. **Visiting:** There are regularly scheduled orientations for prospective students, including sessions on admissions requirements, financial aid information, and campus (student) life information. There are guides for informal visits, visitors may sit in on classes, and stay overnight. To schedule a visit, contact the Outreach Services Office. **Campus Safety and Security:** Measures include 24-hour foot and vehicle patrol, self-defense education, and security escort services. There are emergency telephones, lighted pathways/sidewalks, and Email and web site alerts.

REQUIREMENTS: Applicants must be graduates of an accredited secondary school. Preparatory work should include 4 years of English, 3 of math, and electives, 2 of foreign language, 1 each of U.S. history/government, lab science, and visual and performing arts. Admission is based on an eligibility index that weighs the high school GPA and the SAT or ACT score. Students with GPAs of 3.0 or better (3.6 for nonresidents) are exempt from test score requirements. AP and CLEP credits are accepted. Important factors in the admissions decision are advanced placement or honors courses, recommendations by school officials, and leadership record. To graduate, students must complete 180 to 198 quarter hours, including 60 in upper-division courses and requirements for the major, with a minimum GPA of 2.0. The 82-credit general education program includes courses in basic skills, natural sciences, humanities, social and behavioral sciences, lifelong understanding, upper-division writing, multicultural/gender studies, and electives. Students must also demonstrate an understanding of the U.S. Constitution, American history, and California government. **Procedure:** Freshmen are admitted to all sessions. Entrance exams should be taken prior to applying. There is a rolling admissions plan. Application deadlines are open. The fall 2017 application fee was $55. Notification is sent on a rolling basis. Applications are accepted on-line. **Transfer Students:** 1676 transfer students enrolled in 2016-2017. Applicants must have a minimum college GPA of 2.0 (2.4 for nonresidents) and be in good standing at the previously attended institution. Those with fewer than 56 transferable semester units must submit ACT or SAT scores. 45 of 180 credits required for the bachelor's degree must be completed at Cal State San Berbardino. **International Students:** There are 557 international students enrolled.

Admissions Contact: Olivia Rosas, Director. Email: *moreinfo@csusb.edu* Web: *www.csusb.edu*

FINANCIAL AID: Check with the school for current application deadlines.

CALIFORNIA STATE UNIVERSITY, SAN MARCOS *(The complete profile is made available exclusively on our website, www.barronspac.com)*

CALIFORNIA STATE UNIVERSITY, STANISLAUS *(The complete profile is made available exclusively on our website, www.barronspac.com)*

CHAPMAN UNIVERSITY D-5

www.chapman.edu

Orange, CA 92866 **(714) 997-6711**

Fax: (714) 997-6713
Full-time: 2543 men, 3972 women
Part-time: 243 men, 262 women
Graduate: 969 men, 1403 women
Year: 4-1-4, summer session
Room & Board: $14,910

SAT CR/M: 640/630 **ACT:** 27
Application Deadline: January 15

Email: admit@chapman.edu
Faculty: 377; IIA, ++$
Ph.D.s: 84%
Student/Faculty: 14 to 1
Tuition: $50,594
Freshman Class: 13170 applied, 7539 accepted, 1696 enrolled
CEEB CODE: 4047
HIGHLY COMPETITIVE

Chapman University, founded in 1861, is one of the oldest, and most prestigious private universities in California, known for its blend of liberal arts and professional programs. CU encompasses 7 schools and colleges. The university's mission is to provide personalized education of distinction that leads to inquiring, ethical and productive lives as global citizens. In addition to regional accreditation, CU has baccalaureate program accreditation with AACSB, NASM, CAATE, NASD, and NAST. The 79-acre campus is in a suburban area 35 miles southeast of Los Angeles. Including any residence halls, there are 52 buildings.

STUDENT LIFE: 64% of undergraduates are from California. Others are from 48 states, 57 foreign countries, and Canada. 7% are two or more races; 6% race unknown; 55% White; 4% Foreign; 2% African American; 15% Hispanic; 12% Asian American. 32% are Protestant; 29% claim no religious affiliation; 24% Catholic. **Female To Male Ratio:** 1.5:1. The average age of freshmen is 18; all undergraduates, 20. 9% do not continue beyond their first year; 79% remain to graduate. **Housing:** 1958 students can be accommodated in college housing, which includes married student dorms, on-campus apartments, and off-campus apartments. In addition, there are special-interest houses. On-campus housing is guaranteed for the freshman year only, and is available on a first-come, first-served basis, and is available on a lottery system for upperclassmen. 67% of students commute. All students may keep cars.

FACULTY/CLASSROOMS: 55% of faculty are male; 45% are female. 83% teach undergraduates. Graduate students teach 2% of introductory courses. The average class size in an introductory lecture is 24 and in a laboratory is 21.

PROGRAMS OF STUDY: CU confers B.A., B.S., B.F.A., and B.M. degrees. Master's and doctoral degrees are also awarded. Bachelor's degrees are awarded in BIOLOGICAL SCIENCE (biochemistry and biology/biological science), BUSINESS (accounting and business administration and management), COMMUNICATIONS AND THE ARTS (acting, advertising, art history, art, broadcasting, communication studies, creative writing, dance, dramatic arts, English, film arts, film, television and digital media, French, graphic design, keyboard - piano concentration, music, music performance, music theory and composition, playwriting/screenwriting, public relations, Spanish, strategic communication, and theatre studies), COMPUTER AND PHYSICAL SCIENCE (chemistry, computer science, digital arts/technology, information sciences and systems, mathematics, physics, and software engineering), EDUCATION (athletic training, education, and music education), ENGINEERING AND ENVIRONMENTAL DESIGN (environmental science), HEALTH PROFESSIONS (health science, kinesiology, and pharmacy), SOCIAL SCIENCE (economics, history, peace studies, philosophy, political science/government, psychology, religion, social work, and sociology). Business, film production, computational science, and history are the strongest academically. Business, psychology, and film production have the largest enrollments.

ACTIVITIES: 25% of men belong to 9 national fraternities; 48% of women belong to 8 national sororities. There are 150 groups on campus, including art, band, cheerleading, choir, chorale, chorus, communications, computers, dance, debate, drama, environmental, ethnic, film, forensics, honors, international, jazz band, LGBT, literary magazine, musical theater, newspaper, opera, orchestra, pep band, photography, political, professional, radio and TV, religious, social, social service, student government, symphony, and yearbook. **Sports:** There are 10 intercollegiate sports for men and 11 for women, and 4 intramural sports for men and 4 for women. Facilities include a gym, a weight room, soccer/football field, aquatic center, tennis courts, baseball and softball fields.

Graduates: From July 1, 2016 to June 30, 2017, 1657 bachelor's degrees were awarded. The most popular majors were business administration (20%), strategic and corporate communication (7%), and communication studies (5%). In an average class, 2% graduate in 3 years or less, 69% graduate in 4 years or less, 77% graduate in 5 years or less, and 79% graduate in 6 years or less.

SERVICES: Counseling and information services are available, as is tutoring in most subjects. There is a reader service for the blind, and remedial math, reading, and writing. **Library/Resources:** The library contains 334,330 volumes, 690,324 microform items, 58,921 audio/video tapes/CDs/DVDs, and subscribes to 68,263 periodicals, including electronic. Computerized library services include interlibrary loans, database searching, Internet access, and Wi-Fi capability. Special learning facilities include an art gallery, a radio station, a food science sensory lab, and an economic sciences lab. **Physically Challenged Students:** 75% of the campus is accessible. Facilities include wheelchair ramps, elevators, special parking, specially equipped restrooms, special class scheduling, lowered drinking fountains, lowered telephones, and special housing. **Special:** Internship programs are available. Students are encouraged to study abroad for a semester or spend a semester in Washington, D.C. Dual and student-designed majors are possible. A general studies degree, B.A.-B.S. degrees, nondegree study options, and pass/fail options are also permitted. A 3-2 engineering degree with the University of California, Irvine, is available. There are 13 national honor societies and a freshman honors program. **Visiting:** There are regularly scheduled orientations for prospective students, consisting of fall and spring campus exploration day events. Weekday appointments and campus tours are also available. There are guides for informal visits and visitors may sit in on classes. To schedule a visit, contact the Office of Admissions. **Campus Safety and Security:** Measures include 24-hour foot and vehicle patrol, emergency notification system, self-defense education, and security escort services. There are shuttle buses, emergency telephones, lighted pathways/sidewalks, controlled access to dorms/residences, rape awareness, and victim assistance programs.

REQUIREMENTS: The SAT or ACT is required. The ACT Optional Writing test is also required. Applicants should be graduates of accredited high schools or have earned the GED. Secondary preparation should include 4 years of English, foreign language, math, and social science, and 2 years of science. Prospective art or music majors should show some preparation in those fields. A personal essay is required. An on-campus interview is recommended. Entry to the film school requires portfolio acceptance. Dance performance and theater performance require audition. AP and CLEP credits are accepted. Important factors in the admissions decision are advanced placement or honors courses, evidence of special talent, and leadership record. Students in the baccalaureate program must complete a total of 124 credits with at least a 2.0 GPA. The general education program includes courses in artistic inquiry, natural science inquiry, quantitative inquiry, social inquiry, values and ethical inquiry, and written inquiry. Freshman foundation, global citizenship, and interdisciplinary courses are also required. **Procedure:** Freshmen are admitted in the fall and spring. Entrance exams should be taken by fall of the senior year. There is a early decision plan. Early decision applications should be filed by November 1; regular applications, by January 15 for fall entry; and November 1 for spring entry. The fall 2017 application fee was $70. Notifications are sent March 15. Applications are accepted online. **Transfer Students:** 391 transfer students enrolled in 2016-2017. Transfer applicants should have completed at least 12 credits of transferable college work with a minimum 2.25 GPA. High school records and SAT or ACT scores should be submitted if fewer than 30 transferable credits have been completed. 48 of 120 credits required for the bachelor's degree must be completed at CU. **International Students:** There are 270 international students enrolled. They must take the TOEFL with a minimum score of 550 on the paper-based TOEFL (PBT) or 80 on the Internet-based version (iBT). They must also take the SAT or ACT.

ADMISSIONS: 57% of the 2017-2018 applicants were accepted. The SAT scores for the 2017-2018 freshman class were: Math-- 2% below 500, 28% between 500 and 599, 52% between 600 and 699, and 18% between 700 and 800. Evidence-Based Reading/Writing-- 1% below 500, 22% between 500 and 599, 60% between 600 and 699, and 17% between 700 and 800. The ACT scores were 12% between 18 and 23, 61% between 24 and 29, and 26% above 30. **Admissions Contact:** Marcella Mejia-Martinez, Director of Undergraduate Admission. Email: *admit@chapman.edu* Web: *www.chapman.edu*

FINANCIAL AID: In 2017-2018, 89% of all full-time freshmen received some form of financial aid. 73% of all full-time freshmen received need-based aid. The average freshman award was $38,415. Need-based scholarships or need-based grants averaged $18,018 ($38,250 maximum); need-based self-help aid (loans and jobs) averaged $5,692 ($3,500 maximum); other non-need-based awards and non-need-based scholarships averaged $16,566 ($29,000 maximum); and $23,415 from other forms of aid. The average financial indebtedness of the 2017 graduate was $25,959. CU is a member of CSS. The state aid form is required. The FAFSA code is 001164. The priority date for freshman financial aid applications for fall entry is March 2.

CLAREMONT MCKENNA COLLEGE D-5

www.cmc.edu

Claremont, CA 91711	(909) 621-8088
Fax: (909) 621-8516	**Email:** admission@cmc.edu
Full-time: 697 men, 640 women	**Faculty:** 144
Part-time: 1 women	**Ph.D.s:** 98%
Graduate: 3 men, 4 women	**Student/Faculty:** 8 to 1
Year: semesters	**Tuition:** $52,580
Room & Board: $17,320	**Freshman Class:** 6349 applied, 658 accepted, 352 enrolled
SAT CR/M/W: 710/730 **ACT:** 32	**CEEB CODE:** 4054
Application Deadline: January 1	**MOST COMPETITIVE**

Claremont McKenna College, is one of the nation's top liberal arts colleges, preparing students to make a difference. CMC educates students for thoughtful and productive lives and roles of responsible leadership through its strong, real-world mission. Admission to the college is need-blind and emphasizes the demonstration of leadership accomplishments. The college attracts a student body that is broadly diverse and accomplished beyond the classroom. There is 1 undergraduate school and 1 graduate school. The 69-acre campus is in a suburban area 35 miles east of downtown Los Angeles.

STUDENT LIFE: 61% of undergraduates are from out of state, mostly the West. Students are from 46 states, 43 foreign countries, and Canada. 6% are two or more races; 6% race unknown; 41% White; 4% African American; 17% Foreign; 15% Hispanic; 11% Asian American. **Male To Female Ratio:** 1.1:1. 7% do not continue beyond their first year; 90% remain to graduate. **Housing:** 1212 students can be accommodated in college housing, on-campus housing is guaranteed for the freshman year only and is available on a lottery system for upperclassmen. 97% of students live on campus. Upperclassmen may keep cars.

FACULTY/CLASSROOMS: 64% of faculty are male; 36% are female. No introductory courses are taught by graduate students.

PROGRAMS OF STUDY: CMC confers B.A. degrees. Master's degrees are also awarded. Bachelor's degrees are awarded in AGRICULTURE (environmental studies), BIOLOGICAL SCIENCE (biochemistry, biology/biological science, biophysics, molecular biology, and neurosciences), BUSINESS (accounting and management engineering), COMMUNICATIONS AND THE ARTS (classics, film arts, French, literature, media arts, and Spanish), COMPUTER AND PHYSICAL SCIENCE (chemistry, mathematics, physics, and science and management), ENGINEERING AND ENVIRONMENTAL DESIGN (environmental science), SOCIAL SCIENCE (African studies, American studies, Asian/Oriental studies, economics, government, Hispanic American studies, history, interdisciplinary studies, international relations, Middle Eastern studies, philosophy, philosophy (political thought), political science/government, psychology, and religion).

ACTIVITIES: There are no fraternities or sororities. **Graduates:** From July 1, 2016 to June 30, 2017, 346 bachelor's degrees were awarded. In an average class, 84% graduate in 4 years or less, 89% graduate in 5 years or less, and 90% graduate in 6 years or less.

SERVICES: **Library/Resources:** Computerized library services include interlibrary loans, database searching, Internet access, and Wi-Fi capability. **Special:** There is a chapter of Phi Beta Kappa. **Visiting:** There are regularly scheduled orientations for prospective students. There are guides for informal visits, visitors may sit in on classes, and stay overnight. To schedule a visit, contact the Office of Admission. **Campus Safety and Security:** Measures include security escort services, and emergency telephones.

REQUIREMENTS: The SAT or ACT is required. The ACT Optional

Writing test is also required. AP credits are accepted. All students must complete 32 courses (128 semester hours), including General Education, major and grade-point requirements. **Procedure:** Freshmen are admitted fall. There is an early decision plan. Early decision applications should be filed by November 1; regular applications, by January 1 for fall entry; and November 1 for spring entry. The fall 2017 application fee was $70. Notification of early decision is sent December 15; regular decision, April 1. 207 early decision candidates were accepted for the 2017-2018 class. 404 applicants were on the 2017 waiting list; 1 was admitted. Applications are accepted on-line. **Transfer Students:** 5 transfer students enrolled in 2016-2017. 64 of 128 credits required for the bachelor's degree must be completed at CMC. **International Students:** There are 224 international students enrolled. They must take the TOEFL. They must also take the SAT or ACT.

ADMISSIONS: 10% of the 2017-2018 applicants were accepted. The SAT scores for the 2017-2018 freshman class were: Critical Reading-- 4% between 500 and 599, 37% between 600 and 699, and 60% between 700 and 800. Math-- 2% between 500 and 599, 29% between 600 and 699, and 69% between 700 and 800. The ACT scores were 19% between 24 and 29, and 81% above 30. **Admissions Contact:** Georgette R. DeVeres, AVP and Dean of Admission & Financial Aid. Email: *admission@cmc.edu* Web: *www.cmc.edu*

FINANCIAL AID: In 2017-2018, 47% of all full-time freshmen received some form of financial aid. 46% of all full-time freshmen received need-based aid. The average freshman award was $51,688. Need-based scholarships or need-based grants averaged $49,208; need-based self-help aid (loans and jobs) averaged $4,356; and other non-need-based awards and non-need-based scholarships averaged $20,314. The average financial indebtedness of the 2017 graduate was $21,421. CMC is a member of CSS. The CSS/Profile and the state aid form are required. The FAFSA code is 001170. The priority date for freshman financial aid applications for fall entry is January 1.

COGSWELL POLYTECHNICAL COLLEGE B-3

www.cogswell.edu

San Jose, CA 95134	(408) 498-5103 (800) 264-7955
Fax: (408) 877-7373	**Email:** admissions@cogswell.edu
Full-time: 340 men, 147 women	**Faculty:** 16; IIB, --$
Part-time: 125 men, 44 women	**Ph.D.s:** 25%
Graduate: n/av	**Student/Faculty:** 14 to 1
Year: semesters, summer session	**Tuition:** $19,096
Room & Board: $12,415	**Freshman Class:** 383 applied, 207 accepted, 165 enrolled
SAT or ACT: recommended	**CEEB CODE:** 4057
Application Deadline: n/av	**COMPETITIVE**

Cogswell College provides accredited higher education that empowers students to innovate through the integration of art, engineering and entrepreneurship. There is 1 undergraduate school and 1 graduate school. In addition to regional accreditation, Cogswell Polytechnical College has baccalaureate program accreditation with WASC. The 4-acre campus is in a suburban area 40 miles south of San Francisco in California's Silicon Valley. Including any residence halls, there are 1 buildings.

STUDENT LIFE: 93% of undergraduates are from California. Others are from 14 states, and 6 foreign countries. 65% are from public schools. 36% are White; 21% Asian American; 21% Hispanic; 9% two or more races; 6% race unknown; 5% African American; 1% American Indian/ Alaska Native; 1% Foreign. **Male To Female Ratio:** 2.4:1. The average age of freshmen is 19; all undergraduates, 25. 23% do not continue beyond their first year; 77% remain to graduate. **Housing:** 200 students can be accommodated in college housing, which includes off-campus apartments. Arrangements can be made to accommodate students in private houses or at nearby corporate apartments. Alcohol is not permitted. All students commute. All students may keep cars.

FACULTY/CLASSROOMS: 69% of faculty are male; 31% are female. All teach undergraduates. No introductory courses are taught by graduate students. The average class size in an introductory lecture is 15; in a laboratory is 8; and in a regular course is 20.

PROGRAMS OF STUDY: CPC confers B.A., B.S., B.B.A. degrees. Master's degrees are also awarded. Bachelor's degrees are awarded in BUSINESS (business administration and management, business administration marketing, and entrepreneurial studies), COMMUNICATIONS AND THE ARTS (animation, audio technology, and music technology), COMPUTER AND PHYSICAL SCIENCE (computer programming, digital arts/technology, and web technology), ENGINEERING AND ENVIRONMENTAL DESIGN (computer engineering and computer graphics). Digital art and animation, game design art, game design engineering, and digital audio technology are the strongest academically and have the largest enrollments.

ACTIVITIES: There are no fraternities or sororities. Groups on campus include animation club, audio club, engineering society, game club, art, computers, E-sports, honors, international, literary magazine, newspaper, radio and TV, and student government. Popular campus events include Founders Day, Club Competitions, Cogswell Excelence Awards, Game nights and Friday Concerts. **Sports:** There is no sports program at Cogswell College. Facilities include a game room, student lounge, and access to community athletic facilities. **Graduates:** From July 1, 2016 to June 30, 2017, 64 bachelor's degrees were awarded. The most popular majors were digital art and animation (44%), digital audio technology (23%), and software engineering and digital arts engineering (19%). In an average class, 33% graduate in 3 years or less, 77% graduate in 4 years or less, 97% graduate in 5 years or less, and 100% graduate in 6 years or less.

SERVICES: Counseling and information services are available, as is tutoring in every subject. on campus tutoring is available if needed for any subjects **Library/Resources:** The library contains 103,000 volumes, 250 microform items, and 831 audio/video tapes/CDs/DVDs, and subscribes to 16 periodicals including electronic. Computerized library services include database searching. Special learning facilities include an art gallery, radio station, drawing and sculpture studios, digital arts labs, audio labs, and a recording studio. **Physically Challenged Students:** All of the campus is accessible. Facilities include wheelchair ramps, special parking, specially equipped restrooms, special class scheduling, lowered drinking fountains, and lowered telephones. **Special:** Cogswell offers various internships and work-study programs. Along with on ground programs, the college offers online programs in Game Design Engineering and Game Design Art. There is a freshman honors program. **Visiting:** Visitors may sit in on classes. **Campus Safety and Security:** Measures include emergency notification system. There are emergency telephones, lighted pathways/sidewalks, controlled access to dorms/residences, an emergency evacuation plan with maps in the classrooms.

REQUIREMENTS: The SAT or ACT is recommended. Applicants must be high school graduates or have the GED. Secondary preparation must include 3 years of English, 2 to 3 of math, including algebra, geometry, and trigonometry, and 1 year of science. Cogswell requires a personal essay and recommends a personal interview. A portfolio is required for computer and video imaging programs. AP and CLEP credits are accepted. Important factors in the admissions decision are evidence of special talent and recommendations by school officials. To graduate, students must complete a total of 120 to 126 credits with 18 to 27 in the major and have a 2.0 GPA. 45 credits in general education core courses are required, depending on the major, and include courses in English, math, natural sciences, social sciences, and humanities. **Procedure:** Freshmen are admitted to all sessions. There is a rolling admissions plan. Application deadlines are open. Applications are accepted on-line. **Transfer Students:** Applicants must have completed at least 12 college credits with a 2.2 GPA. An interview is recommended. 40 of 120 credits required for the bachelor's degree must be completed at Cogswell College. **International Students:** There are 7 international students enrolled. They must take the TOEFL with a minimum score of 525 on the paper-based TOEFL (PBT).

ADMISSIONS: 54% of the 2017-2018 applicants were accepted. The SAT scores for the 2017-2018 freshman class were: Critical Reading-- 34% below 500, 42% between 500 and 599, and 24% between 600 and 699. Math-- 31% below 500, 45% between 500 and 599, and 24% between 600 and 699. Writing-- 48% below 500, 34% between 500 and 599, 15% between 600 and 699, and 3% between 700 and 800. The ACT scores were 25% between 12 and 17, 38% between 18 and 23, 25% between 24 and 29, and 12% above 30. **Admissions Contact:** Rick Henson, Director of Admissions. Email: *admissions@cogswell.edu* Web: *www.cogswell.edu*

FINANCIAL AID: In 2017-2018, 77% of all full-time freshmen received some form of financial aid. 75% of all full-time freshmen received need-based aid. 4% of undergraduate students work part-time. The average financial indebtedness of the 2017 graduate was $22,352. Cogswell Polytechnical College is a member of CSS. The college's own financial statement is required. The FAFSA code is 001177. The deadline for filing freshman financial aid applications for fall entry is March 1.

CONCORDIA UNIVERSITY IRVINE D-5

www.cui.edu

Irvine, CA 92612	**(949) 214-3010** **(800) 229-1200**
Fax: (949) 214-3520	**Email: admissions@cui.edu**
Full-time: 618 men, 974 women	**Faculty:** n/av
Part-time: 39 men, 107 women	**Ph.D.s:** n/av
Graduate: 837 men, 944 women	**Student/Faculty:** n/av
Year: semesters, summer session	**Tuition:** $34,100
Room & Board: $10,760	**Freshman Class:** n/av
SAT or ACT: required	**CEEB CODE:** 4069
Application Deadline: n/av	**VERY COMPETITIVE**

Concordia University, founded in 1972, is a private liberal arts college affiliated with the Lutheran Church-Missouri Synod. The figures given in the above capsule and in this profile are approximate. There are 5 undergraduate schools and 4 graduate schools. In addition to regional accreditation, Concordia University Irvine has baccalaureate program accreditation with CAEP, CCNE, IACBE, and CAATE. The 70-acre campus is in a suburban area 40 miles south of Los Angeles. Including any residence halls, there are 26 buildings.

STUDENT LIFE: 89% of undergraduates are from California. Others are from 34 states, 18 foreign countries, and Canada. 66% are White; 6% Foreign; 4% African American; 4% Asian American; 13% Hispanic; 1% American Indian/Alaska Native. 16% are Catholic; 15% Non-denominational. **Female To Male Ratio:** 1.4:1. The average age of freshmen is 18; all undergraduates, 22. 73% remain to graduate. **Housing:** 1077 students can be accommodated in college dorms. On-campus housing is guaranteed for all 4 years. 69% of students live on campus. All students may keep cars.

FACULTY/CLASSROOMS: 63% of faculty are male; 37% are female. No introductory courses are taught by graduate students.

PROGRAMS OF STUDY: CU Irvine confers B.A. degrees. Associate and master's degrees are also awarded. Bachelor's degrees are awarded in BIOLOGICAL SCIENCE (biology/biological science), BUSINESS (business administration and management), COMMUNICATIONS AND THE ARTS (art, communications, dramatic arts, English, film arts, and music), COMPUTER AND PHYSICAL SCIENCE (chemistry and mathematics), EDUCATION (Christian education and early childhood education), HEALTH PROFESSIONS (exercise science), SOCIAL SCIENCE (behavioral science, biblical languages, history, humanities, international studies, liberal arts/general studies, political science/government, psychology, and theological studies). Business administration, education and social science are the strongest academically.

ACTIVITIES: There are no fraternities or sororities. There are 20 groups on campus, including art, choir, chorale, chorus, communications, dance, debate, drama, ethnic, film, forensics, honors, literary magazine, newspaper, political, radio and TV, religious, social, social service, student government, and yearbook. Popular campus events include Closing Banquet, Christmas Dance, and Oktoberfest. **Sports:** There are 9 intercollegiate sports for men and 10 for women, and 7 intramural sports for men and 6 for women. Facilities include a gym, soccer field, baseball/softball diamond, volleyball, tennis, racquetball courts, track field, weight room, and a dance room.

SERVICES: Counseling and information services are available, as is tutoring in some subjects, such as math, chemistry, critical thinking, Spanish, biology and calculus. **Library/Resources:** The library contains 82,600 volumes, 54,550 microform items, and 2,000 audio/video tapes/CDs/DVDs, and subscribes to 10,513 periodicals including electronic. Computerized library services include interlibrary loans, database searching, Internet access, and Wi-Fi capability. Special learning facilities include an art gallery and a radio station. **Physically Challenged Students:** 90% of the campus is accessible. Facilities include wheelchair ramps, elevators, special parking, and specially equipped restrooms. **Special:** Cross-registration is possible with 9 Concordia University institutions nationwide. An accelerated degree program in either applied liberal arts or business administration and leadership. Internships, study abroad, and dual and student-designed majors are available. There are 6 national honor societies, a freshman honors program, and 2 departmental honors programs. **Visiting:** There are regularly scheduled orientations for prospective students. There are guides for informal visits, visitors may sit in on classes, and stay overnight. To schedule a visit, contact the Admission Office. **Campus Safety and Security:** Measures include 24-hour foot and vehicle patrol and security escort services. There are lighted pathways/sidewalks.

REQUIREMENTS: The SAT or ACT is required. Applicants should be high school graduates with 4 years of English, 3 each of math and science, and 2 each of social studies and a foreign language. The GED is accepted. A school reference is also required. A GPA of 2.8 is required. AP and CLEP credits are accepted. All students must complete 49 semester hours of general education requirements, including courses in humanities and fine arts, math and science, social science, religion, and exercise and sport science. A total of 128 credits is required to graduate. A GPA of 2.0 in major and program course work must be maintained. For the CU Accelerate program, 120 semester units are required to graduate. **Procedure:** Freshmen are admitted fall and spring. Entrance exams should be taken by the fall of the senior year. There are deferred admissions and rolling admissions plans. Check with the school for current application deadlines. The fall 2017 application fee was $50. Notifications are sent April 15. Applications are accepted on-line. **Transfer Students:** A GPA of 2.3 is required in a minimum of 24 semester or 36 quarter units completed. An academic reference is required, as are official high school transcripts. 32 of 128 credits required for the bachelor's degree must be completed at Concordia Irvine. **International Students:** They must take the TOEFL, and either the SAT or ACT.

Admissions Contact: Doug Wible, Director of Undergraduate Admissions. Email: *admissions@cui.edu* Web: *www.cui.edu*

FINANCIAL AID: The college's own financial statement is required. The FAFSA code is 013885. The priority date for freshman financial aid applications for fall entry is March 2.

DOMINICAN UNIVERSITY OF CALIFORNIA B-3

www.dominican.edu

San Rafael, CA 94901	**(888) 323-6763** **(888) 323-6763**
Fax: (415) 485-3214	**Email: enroll@dominican.edu**
Full-time: 350 men, 1000 women	**Faculty:** n/av
Part-time: 75 men, 200 women	**Ph.D.s:** 74%
Graduate: 215 men, 500 women	**Student/Faculty:** n/av
Year: semesters, summer session	**Tuition:** $44,690
Room & Board: $14,060	**Freshman Class:** n/av
SAT or ACT: required	**CEEB CODE:** 4284
Application Deadline: open	**COMPETITIVE**

Dominican University of California, founded in 1890, is an independent, international, learner-centered university of Catholic heritage. The figures given in the above capsule and in this profile are approximate. There are 4 undergraduate schools and 4 graduate schools. In addition to regional accreditation, Dominican University of California has baccalaureate program accreditation with AOTA, CCNE, and CCTE. The 80-acre campus is in a suburban area 12 miles north of San Francisco. Including any residence halls, there are 25 buildings.

STUDENT LIFE: 91% of undergraduates are from California. Others are from 31 states, 15 foreign countries, and Canada. 48% are from public schools. 6% are African American; 33% White; 3% Foreign; 25% Asian American; 18% Hispanic; 1% American Indian/Alaska Native. 38% are Catholic. **Female To Male Ratio:** 2.7:1. The average age of freshmen is 18; all undergraduates, 24. 16% do not continue beyond their first year; 34% remain to graduate. **Housing:** 600 students can be accommodated in college housing, which includes dorms. On-campus housing is available on a first-come, first-served basis, and is available on a lottery system for upperclassmen. 55% of students commute. Upperclassmen may keep cars.

FACULTY/CLASSROOMS: 47% of faculty are male; 53% are female. All teach undergraduates, 75% do research, and 75% do both. No introductory courses are taught by graduate students. The average class size in an introductory lecture is 19; in a laboratory is 15; and in a regular course is 15.

PROGRAMS OF STUDY: DU of California confers B.A., B.S., B.F.A., and B.S.N. degrees. Master's degrees are also awarded. Bachelor's degrees are awarded in AGRICULTURE (environmental studies), BIOLOGICAL SCIENCE (biology/biological science), BUSINESS (business administration and management and international business management), COMMUNICATIONS AND THE ARTS (art, art history and appreciation, communications, creative writing, dance, English literature, graphic design, and music), HEALTH PROFESSIONS (nursing, occupational therapy, and premedicine), SOCIAL SCIENCE (history, humanities, international studies, liberal arts/general studies, political science/government, psychology, religion, and women's studies). Nursing, biology, and psychology have the largest enrollments.

ACTIVITIES: There are no fraternities or sororities. There are 27 groups on campus, including art, band, cheerleading, choir, chorale, dance, drama, environmental, ethnic, film, honors, international, jazz band, LGBT, literary magazine, musical theater, newspaper, orchestra, photography, political, professional, radio and TV, religious, social service, and student government. Popular campus events include Shield Day (welcoming the freshman class), Boat Dance, and Penguin Ball. **Sports:** There are 5 intercollegiate sports for men and 7 for women, and 5 intramural sports for men and 5 for women. Facilities include a gym, a fitness center, swimming pool, basketball courts, a multipurpose room for dance and exercise classes, tennis courts, and a soccer field. **Graduates:** From July 1, 2016 to June 30, 2017, 283 bachelor's degrees were awarded. The most popular majors were nursing (27%), psychology (15%), and business (11%). In an average class, 44% graduate in 4 years or less, 46% graduate in 5 years or less, and 51% graduate in 6 years or less.

SERVICES: Counseling and information services are available, as is tutoring in some subjects, such as writing, math, chemistry, economics, time management, study skills, anatomy, physiology, algebra, and physics. There is a reader service for the blind, and remedial math and writing. **Library/Resources:** The library contains 92,536 volumes, 3,500 microform items, and 1,640 audio/video tapes/CDs/DVDs, and subscribes to 597 periodicals including electronic. Computerized library services include interlibrary loans, database searching, Internet access, and Wi-Fi capability. Special learning facilities include an art gallery, radio station, a music library, and art history slide and print collection. **Physically Challenged Students:** 50% of the campus is accessible. Facilities include wheelchair ramps, elevators, special parking, specially equipped restrooms, special class scheduling, and lowered drinking fountains. **Special:** There is a semester interchange program with colleges in Michigan, Florida, or New York. Dominican also offers study abroad, dual majors for students with a 3.0 GPA or better, B.A.-B.S. degrees, student-designed majors, a Washington semester, internships, pass/fail options outside of major and general education courses, and an evening/weekend bachelor's degree program. There are 3 national honor societies, Phi Beta Kappa, a freshman honors program, and 3 departmental honors programs. **Visiting:** There are regularly scheduled orientations for prospective students, including financial aid conferences, lunch on campus, meeting with the prospective academic adviser, and a campus tour. There are guides for informal visits and visitors may sit in on classes. To schedule a visit, contact the Admissions Office. **Campus Safety and Security:** Measures include 24-hour foot and vehicle patrol, emergency notification system, and security escort services. There are emergency telephones, lighted pathways/sidewalks, and controlled access to dorms/residences.

REQUIREMENTS: The SAT or ACT is required. Applicants must be graduates of an accredited high school or have earned the GED. Secondary preparation must include 4 years of English, 2 each of math and a foreign language, and 1 each of lab science and history. An essay and a recommendation are required. An interview and a visit to the campus are highly recommended. Prospective music majors are encouraged to schedule an audition. AP and CLEP credits are accepted. Important factors in the admissions decision are recommendations by school officials, extracurricular activities record, and evidence of special talent. All students must complete 124 credit hours including at least 24 in upper-division work, with a minimum 2.0 GPA. Core requirements include a cultural heritage colloquium of 9 units, 6 units each in religion and first-year interdisciplinary studies, 3 to 4 units each of math and quantitative reasoning, natural science, social science, moral philosophy and ethics, and creative and performing arts, and 1 unit of information and research. Students must pass a computer competency test, and a senior thesis, project, recital, or comprehensive exam is required. **Procedure:** Freshmen are admitted fall and spring. Entrance exams should be taken in the late fall or early spring of the senior year. There are deferred admissions and rolling admissions plans. Application deadlines are open. The fall 2017 application fee was $40. Applications are accepted on-line. **Transfer Students:** 110 transfer students enrolled in 2016-2017. Applicants must have a 2.0 GPA at an accredited college. They must also submit official their high school and college transcripts and a letter of recommendation from a professor, academic dean, or counselor. 30 of 124 credits required for the bachelor's degree must be completed at Dominican. **International Students:** There are 30 international students enrolled. They must take the TOEFL with a minimum score of 550 on the paper-based TOEFL (PBT) or 80 on the Internet-based version (iBT). They must also take the SAT or ACT.

Admissions Contact: Rebecca Finn Kenney, Asst. VP of Undergraduate Admissions. Email: *enroll@dominican.edu* Web: *www.dominican.edu*

FINANCIAL AID: In 2017-2018, 97% of all full-time freshmen received some form of financial aid. 70% of all full-time freshmen received need-based aid. The average freshman award was $34,561. Need-based scholarships or need-based grants averaged $14,006 ($28,922 maximum); need-based self-help aid (loans and jobs) averaged $4,646 ($7,375 maximum); non-need-based athletic scholarships averaged $2,567 ($6,000 maximum); and other non-need-based awards and non-need-based scholarships averaged $7,660 ($15,500 maximum). 17% of undergraduate students work part-time. The average financial indebtedness of the 2017 graduate was $19,092. DU California is a member of CSS. The college's own financial statement is required. The FAFSA code is 001196. Check with the school for current application deadlines.

FRESNO PACIFIC UNIVERSITY C-3

www.fresno.edu

Fresno, CA 93702	**(559) 453-2039** **(800) 660-6089**
Fax: (559) 453-2007	**Email: ugadmis@fresno.edu**
Full-time: 701 men, 1448 women	**Faculty:** IIA, --$
Part-time: 108 men, 182 women	**Ph.D.s:** n/av
Graduate: 320 men, 701 women	**Student/Faculty:** n/av
Year: semesters, summer session	**Tuition:** $30,458
Room & Board: $8400	**Freshman Class:** n/av
SAT or ACT: required	**CEEB CODE:** 4616
Application Deadline: July 31	**COMPETITIVE**

Fresno Pacific University, founded in 1944, and affiliated with the Mennonite Brethren, is a private Christian liberal arts college offering both undergraduate and graduate degrees. The figures in the above capsule and in this profile are approximate. There are 4 undergraduate schools and 5 graduate schools. In addition to regional accreditation, Fresno Pacific University has baccalaureate program accreditation with WASC. The 42-acre campus is in a suburban area 150 miles southeast of San Francisco. Including any residence halls, there are 20 buildings.

STUDENT LIFE: 97% of undergraduates are from California. Others are from 14 states, 12 foreign countries, and Canada. 86% are from public schools. 50% are White; 4% African American; 4% Asian American; 4% Foreign; 29% Hispanic; 1% American Indian/Alaska Native. 79% are Protestant; 15% Catholic. **Female To Male Ratio:** 2.1:1. The average age of freshmen is 20; all undergraduates, 21. 20% do not continue beyond their first year; 62% remain to graduate. **Housing:** 550 students can be accommodated in college housing, which includes dorms, on-campus apartments, and off-campus apartments. In addition, there are special-interest houses. On-campus housing is available on a first-come, first-served basis, and is available on a lottery system for upperclassmen. 51% of students commute. Alcohol is not permitted. All students may keep cars.

FACULTY/CLASSROOMS: 66% of faculty are male; 34% are female. 78% teach undergraduates. No introductory courses are taught by graduate students. The average class size in a laboratory is 14 and in a regular course is 18.

PROGRAMS OF STUDY: Fresno confers B.A. and B.S. degrees. Associate and master's degrees are also awarded. Bachelor's degrees are awarded in BIOLOGICAL SCIENCE (biology/biological science), BUSINESS (accounting, business administration and management, and sports management), COMMUNICATIONS AND THE ARTS (English, music, and Spanish), COMPUTER AND PHYSICAL SCIENCE (chemistry, mathematics, and natural sciences), EDUCATION (English education, mathematics education, music education, physical education, science education, and social science education), ENGINEERING AND ENVI-

RONMENTAL DESIGN (environmental science), HEALTH PROFESSIONS (premedicine), SOCIAL SCIENCE (history, ministries, missions, philosophy, prelaw, psychology, religion, social science, and social work). Business, education, and religion are the strongest academically. Business, education, and psychology have the largest enrollments.

ACTIVITIES: There are no fraternities or sororities. There are 20 groups on campus, including art, cheerleading, choir, chorale, chorus, communications, dance, drama, ethnic, honors, international, jazz band, newspaper, pep band, political, professional, religious, social, social service, and student government. Popular campus events include Carol Sing, Winter Ball, and Junior/Senior Banquet. **Sports:** There are 8 intercollegiate sports for men and 8 for women, and 9 intramural sports for men and 9 for women. Facilities include a gym, soccer fields, swimming pool, track & field facility, weight room, racquetball courts, and tennis courts.

SERVICES: Counseling and information services are available, as is tutoring in every subject. There is a reader service for the blind, and remedial math, reading, and writing. **Library/Resources:** The library contains 197,532 volumes, 315,000 microform items, and 7,840 audio/video tapes/CDs/DVDs, and subscribes to 3,200 periodicals including electronic. Computerized library services include interlibrary loans, database searching, and Internet access. **Physically Challenged Students:** All of the campus is accessible. Facilities include wheelchair ramps, elevators, special parking, specially equipped restrooms, lowered drinking fountains, lowered telephones, and special housing. **Special:** Accelerated degrees and internships are available as is a 1-semester cooperative program with the University of California, Davis. Cross-registration is possible with San Joaquin College of Law and California State University, Fresno. A B.A. in management and organizational development is offered to working adults. Other off-campus learning opportunities include programs in American studies in Washington, D.C., urban studies in Chicago, and study abroad in Israel, Japan, and Costa Rica, and at Brethren Colleges in England, Spain, France, Germany, or China. There are 2 national honor societies, a freshman honors program, and 1 departmental honors program. **Visiting:**There are regularly scheduled orientations for prospective students. There are guides for informal visits, visitors may sit in on classes, and stay overnight. To schedule a visit, contact the Admissions Office. **Campus Safety and Security:** Measures include 24-hour foot and vehicle patrol, self-defense education, and security escort services. There are shuttle buses, emergency telephones, lighted pathways/sidewalks, 24-hour CCTV monitored in real-time closed-circuit security cameras. 16 cameras create a virtual perimeter patrol of the campus with 5 emergency telephones and 8 regular telephones.

REQUIREMENTS: The SAT or ACT is required. Applicants should be graduates of an accredited high school or have the GED. Required secondary preparation includes 4 years of college prep English, 2 years of social studies, algebra 1 and 2, and geometry, and at least 1 year of a lab science. The college recommends that applicants also take courses in art, music, and 2 years of the same foreign language, all with a grade of C or better. An essay is required, and an audition is recommended for prospective music majors. A GPA of 3.1 is required. AP and CLEP credits are accepted. Important factors in the admissions decision are recommendations by school officials, advanced placement or honors courses, and extracurricular activities record. Students must complete 124 semester units, 40 of which are in upper-division courses, with at least a 2.0 GPA. General education requirements include a biblical studies/world civilization series, and 2 courses each in humanities, natural sciences, social sciences, and phys ed and math. Students are required to attend College Hour, a twice-weekly program of lectures, films, and concerts. Students are encouraged to volunteer 2 hours of community service per week. Several majors require internships. **Procedure:** Freshmen are admitted fall and spring. Entrance exams should be taken during the fall of their senior year. There are early admissions and rolling admissions plans. Students must register by July 31 for fall entry. The fall 2017 application fee was $40. Notification is sent on a rolling basis. Applications are accepted on-line. **Transfer Students:** Applicants should have completed at least 24 transferable units of college work with a 2.4 GPA. Those with fewer credits may apply any time but must meet freshman admission requirements. The SAT or ACT scores are recommended. 30 of 124 credits required for the bachelor's degree must be completed at FPU. **International Students:** They must take the TOEFL.

ADMISSIONS: 4 freshmen graduated first in their class. **Admissions Contact:** Krista Brooks, Undergraduate Admissions Director. Email: *ugadmis@fresno.edu* Web: *www.fresno.edu*

FINANCIAL AID: In 2017-2018, 98% of all full-time freshmen received some form of financial aid. The FAFSA code is 001253. Check with the school for current application deadlines.

GOLDEN GATE UNIVERSITY — B-3

www.ggu.edu

San Francisco, CA 94105	**(415) 442-7800** **(800) 448-4968**
Fax: (415) 442-7807	**Email: info@ggu.edu**
Full-time: 90 men, 37 women	**Faculty:** n/av
Part-time: 130 men, 175 women	**Ph.D.s:** n/av
Graduate: 1001 men, 1469 women	**Student/Faculty:** n/av
Year: varies, summer session	**Tuition:** $19,510
Room & Board: n/app	**Freshman Class:** n/av **CEEB CODE:** 4329
Application Deadline: open	**COMPETITIVE**

Golden Gate University, founded in 1901, has been helping adults achieve their professional goals by providing high quality, practice-based undergraduate and graduate educational programs in law, taxation, business and related professions. Many courses are taught by faculty actively working in their field of expertise, providing students with skills that can be applied immediately. Most programs are available fully online or in-person in downtown SF. To learn more, visit www.ggu.edu. There is 1 undergraduate school and 4 graduate schools. In addition to regional accreditation, GGU has baccalaureate program accreditation with WASC. The 1-acre campus is in an urban area in the city's downtown financial district. The school is 1 building.

STUDENT LIFE: 92% of undergraduates are from California. Others are from 41 states, 16 foreign countries, and Canada. 26% are White; 20% Foreign; 18% race unknown; 14% Asian American; 11% Hispanic; 6% African American; 2% two or more races. **Female To Male Ratio:** 1.4:1. The average age of freshmen is 33; all undergraduates, 35. 13% do not continue beyond their first year; 38% remain to graduate. Alcohol is not permitted. All students commute.

FACULTY/CLASSROOMS: All teach undergraduates. No introductory courses are taught by graduate students. The average class size in an introductory lecture is 25; in a laboratory is 15; and in a regular course is 20.

PROGRAMS OF STUDY: GGU confers B.S. and B.B.A. degrees. Master's and doctoral degrees are also awarded. Bachelor's degrees are awarded in BUSINESS (accounting, banking and finance, human resources, and international business management), ENGINEERING AND ENVIRONMENTAL DESIGN (technological management). Accounting, finance, and information systems are the strongest academically. Taxation, law, and arts have the largest enrollments.

ACTIVITIES: There are no fraternities or sororities. There are 5 groups on campus, including ethnic, international, newspaper, professional, and social. A popular campus event is the Commencement Ball. **Sports:** There is no sports program at Golden Gate. **Graduates:** From July 1, 2016 to June 30, 2017, 121 bachelor's degrees were awarded. The most popular majors were MS in taxation (16%), Doctor of jurisprudence (11%), and Bachelor's of arts (9%). In an average class, 56% graduate in 3 years or less, 60% graduate in 4 years or less, 63% graduate in 5 years or less, and 64% graduate in 6 years or less.

SERVICES: Counseling and information services are available, as is tutoring in some subjects. There is remedial math, reading, and writing. **Library/Resources:** The library contains 141,767 volumes, 253,759 microform items, and 160 audio/video tapes/CDs/DVDs, and subscribes to 4,800 periodicals including electronic. Computerized library services include interlibrary loans, database searching, Internet access, and Wi-Fi capability. **Physically Challenged Students:** All of the campus is accessible. Facilities include wheelchair ramps, elevators, special parking, and specially equipped restrooms. **Special:** The university offers cooperative programs, cross-registration with the San Francisco Consortium, internships, an accelerated degree program, dual majors, credit for military experience, nondegree study, and credit/no credit options. Also available are weekend classes and 10-week terms. **Visiting:** Visitors may sit in on classes. To schedule a visit, contact the Student Affairs Office. **Campus Safety and Security:** Measures include security escort services.

REQUIREMENTS: Applicants must be graduates of an accredited secondary school or have a GED. A GPA of 3.0 is required. AP and CLEP credits are accepted. A total of 123 trimester hours, with 21 to 33 in the major, are required to graduate. A minimum GPA of 2.0 is also required. **Procedure:** Freshmen are admitted fall, spring, and summer. There is a rolling admissions plan. Check with the school for current application deadlines. Notification is sent on a rolling basis. Applications are accepted on-line. **Transfer Students:** At least 24 transferable units and a 2.0 overall GPA are required. A minimum of 30 units out of 123, including 21 in the major, must be completed at GGU. **International Students:** They must take the TOEFL.

Admissions Contact: Ayana Richardson, Director. Email: *info@ggu.edu* Web: *www.ggu.edu*

FINANCIAL AID: In 2017-2018, 36% of all full-time freshmen received some form of financial aid. 18% of all full-time freshmen received need-based aid. The average freshman award was $5,718. Need-based scholarships or need-based grants averaged $3,627 ($6,315 maximum); need-based self-help aid (loans and jobs) averaged $5,455 ($6,926 maximum); and other non-need-based awards and non-need-based scholarships averaged $811 ($4,536 maximum). The FAFSA code is 001205. Check with the school for current application deadlines.

HARVEY MUDD COLLEGE D-5
www.hmc.edu

Claremont, CA 91711	(909) 621-8011
Fax: (909) 607-7046	**Email:** admission@hmc.edu
Full-time: 441 men, 403 women	**Faculty:** 93; IIB, ++$
Part-time: n/av	**Ph.D.s:** 100%
Graduate: n/av	**Student/Faculty:** 9 to 1
Year: semesters	**Tuition:** $50,649
Room & Board: $16,506	**Freshman Class:** 4119 applied, 534 accepted, 214 enrolled
SAT CR/M/W: 720/770/720 **ACT:** 34	**CEEB CODE:** 4341
Application Deadline: January 5	**MOST COMPETITIVE**

Harvey Mudd College, founded in 1955, and one of the Claremont Colleges, is a private institution specializing in math, science, and engineering education within a liberal arts tradition. In addition to regional accreditation, Harvey Mudd College has baccalaureate program accreditation with ABET and WASC. The 33-acre campus is in a suburban area 35 miles east of Los Angeles. Including any residence halls, there are 20 buildings.

STUDENT LIFE: 61% of undergraduates are from out of state, mostly the Middle Atlantic. 65% are from public schools. 44% are White; 21% Asian American; 13% Foreign; 10% Hispanic; 6% two or more races; 4% race unknown; 2% African American; 1% American Indian/Alaska Native. **Male To Female Ratio:** 1.1:1. The average age of freshmen is 18; all undergraduates, 19. 3% do not continue beyond their first year; 90% remain to graduate. **Housing:** College-sponsored housing includes married student dorms, on-campus apartments, and off-campus apartments. On-campus housing is guaranteed for the freshman year only and is available on a lottery system for upperclassmen. Upperclassmen may keep cars.

FACULTY/CLASSROOMS: 62% of faculty are male; 38% are female. All teach undergraduates, and all do research. No introductory courses are taught by graduate students. The average class size in an introductory lecture is 65; in a laboratory is 20; and in a regular course is 20.

PROGRAMS OF STUDY: HMC confers B.S. degrees. Bachelor's degrees are awarded in BIOLOGICAL SCIENCE (biology/biological science), COMPUTER AND PHYSICAL SCIENCE (chemistry, computer science, mathematics, and physics), ENGINEERING AND ENVIRONMENTAL DESIGN (engineering). Engineering, computer science, and mathematics have the largest enrollments.

ACTIVITIES: There are no fraternities or sororities. There are 46 groups on campus, including art, band, chess, choir, chorale, chorus, computers, dance, drama, environmental, ethnic, film, international, jazz band, LGBT, literary magazine, musical theater, newspaper, orchestra, photography, political, professional, radio and TV, religious, social, social service, student government, symphony, and yearbook. Popular campus events include 5-Class Competition, Wednesday Nighters, Crib Races, Frosh Soph Games, and Inner Tube Water Polo. **Sports:** There are 10 intercollegiate sports for men and 11 for women, and 9 intramural sports for men and 9 for women. Harvey Mudd, share's an athletic facility with The Clarmont McKenna College and Scripps College, that has 2 gym floors, a weight room, 400-meter track, swimming pool, tennis courts, and sports fields. The HMC campus recreation facility houses a full-size gym floor, an aerobics/dance room, and a fitness room with cardio and weight equipment. **Graduates:** From July 1, 2016 to June 30, 2017, 184 bachelor's degrees were awarded. The most popular majors were computer science (30%), engineering (29%), and joint computer science and mathematics (12%). In an average class, 85% graduate in 4 years or less, 88% graduate in 5 years or less, and 90% graduate in 6 years or less. Of the 2016 graduating class, 27% were enrolled in graduate school within 6 months of graduation, and 64% were employed.

SERVICES: Counseling and information services are available, as is tutoring in most subjects. Additional support is offered on a case-by-case basis in coordination with the Associate Dean of Academic Affairs, the Associate Dean of Student Life, the Academic Excellence Program, and our faculty. **Library/Resources:** The library contains 1.9 million volumes, and subscribes to 87,245 periodicals including electronic. Computerized library services include interlibrary loans, database searching, Internet access, and Wi-Fi capability. Special learning facilities include an art gallery, planetarium, radio station, and TV station. **Physically Challenged Students:** Facilities include wheelchair ramps, elevators, special parking, specially equipped restrooms, special class scheduling, and lowered drinking fountains. **Special:** Students may cross-register at any of the other Claremont Colleges. Industry-sponsored projects (the Clinic Program) are available for all students, and required for Engineering and Computer Science majors. All students may choose to study abroad and an on-campus office supports these students. We offer dual and special majors in Computer Science and Math, Mathematical and Computational Biology, Chemistry and Biology, and student-designed majors are available. A 3-2 engineering degree with Claremont McKenna College or Scripps College is possible. The first semester for freshmen is taken on a pass/fail basis. There are 1 national honor societies and 7 departmental honors programs. **Visiting:** There are regularly scheduled orientations for prospective students, Campus tours and admission interviews are offered Monday through Friday and some Saturday mornings during the fall. Visitors may sit in on classes and stay overnight. To schedule a visit, contact the Office of Admission. **Campus Safety and Security:** Measures include 24-hour foot and vehicle patrol, emergency notification system, self-defense education, and security escort services. There are emergency telephones, lighted pathways/sidewalks, and controlled access to dorms/residences.

REQUIREMENTS: Applicants must have completed 4 years each of English and mathematics (including algebra, demonstrative and analytic geometry, trigonometry, and calculus), 3 years of science (including 1 year each of physics and chemistry), and 1 year of history. The college recommends applicants take 2 years of a foreign language and 2 additional years each of history and social sciences. Students are required to take the SAT or ACT, and SAT subject tests in Math (level 2) and 1 other subject are required. Letters of recommendation are required from the student's counselor, a math or science teacher, and an English, social science, or foreign language teacher. Applicants must submit 2 personal essays and are encouraged to seek an interview. Important factors in the admissions decision are advanced placement or honors courses, personality/intangible qualities, and extracurricular activities record. The required curriculum, as revised by the College in January 2010, is divided into three components: the Common Core, which provides the foundation for advanced study, the program in Humanities, Social Sciences, and the Arts, which completes the liberal arts nature of a Harvey Mudd College education by providing humanistic, social scientific, and aesthetic perspectives; and the Major, which builds depth and technical competence. Unifying all of these is an emphasis on strong oral and written communications, the development of computational skills, and direct experience with a research or design project. In order to be recommended by the faculty for the Bachelor of Science degree, students are required to complete satisfactorily a minimum of 128 credit hours of courses (including approved transfer credits for courses taken at other colleges). **Procedure:** Freshmen are admitted fall. Entrance exams should be taken ED I- Nov test date, ED II- Dec test date, RD- Jan test date. There are early decision and deferred admissions plans. Early decision applications should be filed by November 15; regular applications, by January 5 for fall entry. The fall 2017 application fee was $70. Notification of early decision is sent December 15; regular decision, April 1. 77 early decision candidates were accepted for the 2017-2018 class. 534 applicants were on the 2017 waiting list; 11 were admitted. Applications are accepted on-line. **Transfer Students:** 4 transfer students enrolled in 2016-2017. Applicants must submit high school and college transcripts, course descriptions, and references from a counselor, a college math, science, or engineering teacher, and a college humanities or social science teacher. Test scores for already completed SAT, ACT, and SAT subject tests are highly recommended. Students should aim to complete courses equivalent to the courses in our Common Core. 64 of 128 credits required for the bachelor's degree must be completed at Harvey Mudd College. **International Students:** There are 104 international students enrolled. They must take the TOEFL with a minimum score of 600 on the paper-based TOEFL (PBT) or 100 on the Internet-based version (iBT), or take the IELTS if English has not been their primary language of instruction for the last 5 years. They must also take the SAT or ACT.

ADMISSIONS: 13% of the 2017-2018 applicants were accepted. The SAT scores for the 2017-2018 freshman class were: Critical Reading-- 4% between 500 and 599, 31% between 600 and 699, and 65% between 700 and 800. Math-- 12% between 600 and 699 and 88% between 700 and 800. Writing-- 4% between 500 and 599, 33% between 600 and 699, and 63% between 700 and 800. The ACT scores were 6% between 24 and 29, and 94% above 30. 98% of the current freshmen were in the top fifth of their class; 100% were in the top two fifths. 13 freshmen graduated first in their class. **Admissions Contact:** Peter Osgood, Director of Admission. Email: *admission@hmc.edu* Web: *www.hmc.edu*

FINANCIAL AID: In 2017-2018, 79% of all full-time freshmen received some form of financial aid. 52% of all full-time freshmen received need-based aid. The average freshman award was $39,515. Need-based scholarships or need-based grants averaged $42,553 ($73,143 maximum); need-based self-help aid (loans and jobs) averaged $5,062 ($11,400 maximum); and other non-need-based awards and non-need-based scholarships averaged $8,891 ($55,868 maximum). The average financial indebtedness of the 2017 graduate was $27,483. Harvey Mudd College is a member of CSS. The CSS/Profile and the state aid form are required. The FAFSA code is 001171. The deadline for filing freshman financial aid applications for fall entry is February 1.

HOLY NAMES UNIVERSITY *(The complete profile is made available exclusively on our website, www.barronspac.com)*

HOPE INTERNATIONAL UNIVERSITY D-5

www.hiu.edu

Fullerton, CA 92831	**(714) 879-3901** **(800) 762-1294**
Fax: (714) 524-0231	**Email: undergradadmissions@hiu.edu**
Full-time: 334 men, 394 women	**Faculty:** 43
Part-time: 59 men, 71 women	**Ph.D.s:** 67%
Graduate: 157 men, 263 women	**Student/Faculty:** 14 to 1
Year: 4-1-4, summer session	**Tuition:** $32,800
Room & Board: $9930	**Freshman Class:** n/av
SAT or ACT: required	**CEEB CODE:** 4614
Application Deadline: December 1	**COMPETITIVE**

Hope International University, founded in 1928, is a private liberal arts institution affiliated with the Independent Christian Churches and Churches of Christ. There are 5 undergraduate schools and 4 graduate schools. In addition to regional accreditation, HIU has baccalaureate program accreditation with ABHE. The 15-acre campus is in an urban area 45 miles southeast of Los Angeles. Including any residence halls, there are 9 buildings.

STUDENT LIFE: 69% of undergraduates are from California. Others are from 43 states, 5 foreign countries, and Canada. 44% are White; 26% Hispanic; 11% two or more races; 10% race unknown; 8% African American; 4% Foreign; 3% Asian American; 1% American Indian/Alaska Native. 65% are Protestant; 20% Catholic; 15% claim no religious affiliation. **Female To Male Ratio:** 1.3:1. The average age of freshmen is 18; all undergraduates, 25. 23% do not continue beyond their first year; 38% remain to graduate. **Housing:** 530 students can be accommodated in college housing, which includes dorms and on-campus apartments. On-campus housing is guaranteed for all 4 years, is available on a first-come, and first-served basis. 54% of students commute. Alcohol is not permitted. All students may keep cars.

FACULTY/CLASSROOMS: 53% of faculty are male; 47% are female. All teach undergraduates. No introductory courses are taught by graduate students. The average class size in an introductory lecture is 16; in a laboratory is 7; and in a regular course is 16.

PROGRAMS OF STUDY: HIU confers B.A., B.S., and B.Mus. degrees. Associate and master's degrees are also awarded. Bachelor's degrees are awarded in BUSINESS (business administration and management and sports management), COMMUNICATIONS AND THE ARTS (church music, English literature, and music ministry), EDUCATION (education, elementary education, secondary education, and social science education), SOCIAL SCIENCE (biblical studies, child psychology/development, criminal justice, crosscultural studies, human development, human services, liberal arts/general studies, ministries, pastoral studies, psychology, social science, and youth ministry). Psychology is the strongest academically. Ministry/Biblical studies, psychology, and counseling have the largest enrollments.

ACTIVITIES: There are no fraternities or sororities. There are 17 groups on campus, including cheerleading, choir, chorale, communications, drama, international, jazz band, musical theater, newspaper, religious, social service, yearbook, and student government. Students participate in Model UN at Harvard and Security Council at Yale. and yearbook. Popular campus events include Spring Formal, and Intercultural Awareness Events. **Sports:** There are 8 intercollegiate sports for men and 8 for women, and 4 intramural sports for men and 4 for women. Facilities include a gym with basketball and volleyball courts, a fitness center, recreation room, and an outdoor swimming pool. **Graduates:** From July 1, 2016 to June 30, 2017, 152 bachelor's degrees were awarded. The most popular majors were psychology, social science and human services (54%), ministries and biblical studies (28%), and business (13%). In an average class, 38% graduate in 4 years or less, 44% graduate in 5 years or less, and 47% graduate in 6 years or less.

SERVICES: Counseling and information services are available, as is tutoring in some subjects, such as History, English, mathematics, science, Bible, and financial accounting. There is a reader service for the blind, and remedial math, reading, and writing. **Library/Resources:** The library contains 216,971 volumes, 100 microform items, and 3,049 audio/video tapes/CDs/DVDs, and subscribes to 210 periodicals including electronic. Computerized library services include interlibrary loans, database searching, Internet access, and Wi-Fi capability. **Physically Challenged Students:** 95% of the campus is accessible. Facilities include elevators, special parking, specially equipped restrooms. Priority is given to disabled students for first-floor housing. **Special:** Hope International offers cross-registration with California State University, Fullerton. Internships, study abroad in 7 countries, work-study programs, dual and student-designed majors, non-degree study, pass/fail options, and credit for life, military, and work experience are also offered. Most Leadership and Ethics Curriculum courses are available in the online modality as well. There is 1 national honor society and 1 departmental honors program. **Visiting:** There are guides for informal visits, visitors may sit in on classes, and stay overnight. To schedule a visit, contact Amanda Matthews at ajmatthews@hiu.edu. **Campus Safety and Security:** Measures include 24-hour foot and vehicle patrol, emergency notification system, and security escort services. There are emergency telephones, lighted pathways/sidewalks, and controlled access to dorms/residences.

REQUIREMENTS: The SAT or ACT is required. Applicants must be high school graduates. The GED is accepted. A personal essay and references from a church leader and an academic counselor are required. AP and CLEP credits are accepted. Regular attendance at chapel and participation in Christian service is required. To graduate, students must complete at least 120 credit units with 36 to 51 in the major. A minimum GPA of 2.0 must be maintained. The Leadership and Ethics Core curriculum includes required and elective courses in biblical studies, leadership, written and oral communication, social sciences, humanities, natural sciences, and math. **Procedure:** Freshmen are admitted fall and spring. There are early admissions, deferred admissions, and rolling admissions plans. Application deadlines are open. The fall 2017 application fee was $40. Applications are accepted on-line. **Transfer Students:** 87 transfer students enrolled in 2016-2017. Transfer students must submit copies of college transcripts and SAT or ACT scores if fewer than 30 college units have been completed. A minimum GPA of 2.0 is required. 30 of 120 credits required for the bachelor's degree must be completed at HIU. **International Students:** There are 22 international students enrolled. They must take the TOEFL with a minimum score of 83 on the Internet-based version (iBT).

Admissions Contact: Barbara Moore, Director of Undergraduate Admissions. Email: *undergradadmissions@hiu.edu* Web: *www.hiu.edu*

FINANCIAL AID: The college's own financial statement is required. The FAFSA code is 001252. Check with the school for current application deadlines.

HUMBOLDT STATE UNIVERSITY A-1
www.humboldt.edu

Arcata, CA 95521	**(707) 826-4402** **(866) 850-9556**
Fax: (707) 826-6194	**Email: hsuinfo@humboldt.edu**
Full-time: 3228 men, 4248 women	**Faculty:** 241; IIA, av$
Part-time: 256 men, 210 women	**Ph.D.s:** 41%
Graduate: 218 men, 310 women	**Student/Faculty:** 23 to 1
Year: semesters, summer session	**Tuition:** $8692 ($16,200)
Room & Board: $13,016	**Freshman Class:** 12967 applied, 9895 accepted, 1295 enrolled
SAT CR/M/W: 515/500/495 **ACT:** 22	**CEEB CODE:** 4345
Application Deadline: November 30	**COMPETITIVE**

Humboldt State University, founded in 1913, is a liberal arts institution and is part of the California State University system. Humboldt offers 48 majors, and 11 graduate programs in 3 colleges. The figures given in the above capsule and in this profile are approximate. There are 3 undergraduate schools and 1 graduate school. In addition to regional accreditation, HSU has baccalaureate program accreditation with ABET, CSWE, NASAD, NASM, NLN, SAF, and NAST. The 161-acre campus is in a small town 275 miles north of San Francisco. Including any residence halls, there are 93 buildings.

STUDENT LIFE: 93% of undergraduates are from California. Others are from 50 states, 28 foreign countries, and Canada. 95% are from public schools. 7% are two or more races; 6% race unknown; 43% White; 35% Hispanic; 3% African American; 3% Asian American; 1% Foreign. **Female To Male Ratio:** 1.3:1. The average age of freshmen is 18; all undergraduates, 22. 25% do not continue beyond their first year; 49% remain to graduate. **Housing:** 1400 students can be accommodated in college housing, which includes coed dorms and on-campus apartments, and theme housing. On-campus housing is available on a first-come and first-served basis. 90% of students live on campus. All students may keep cars.

FACULTY/CLASSROOMS: 56% of faculty are male; 44% are female. All teach undergraduates. No introductory courses are taught by graduate students. The average class size in an introductory lecture is 33; in a laboratory is 21; and in a regular course is 24.

PROGRAMS OF STUDY: HSU confers B.A. and B.S. degrees. Master's degrees are also awarded. Bachelor's degrees are awarded in AGRICULTURE (fishing and fisheries, forestry and related sciences, and natural resource management), BIOLOGICAL SCIENCE (biology/biological science, botany, wildlife biology, and zoology), BUSINESS (business administration and management and business economics), COMMUNICATIONS AND THE ARTS (art, communications, dramatic arts, English, fine arts, French, German, journalism, music, Spanish, and speech/debate/rhetoric), COMPUTER AND PHYSICAL SCIENCE (chemistry, geology, information sciences and systems, mathematics, oceanography, and physics), EDUCATION (business education, elementary education, English education, industrial arts education, mathematics education, middle school education, music education, physical education, science education, secondary education, and social science education), ENGINEERING AND ENVIRONMENTAL DESIGN (environmental engineering, environmental science, industrial engineering technology, and land use management and reclamation), HEALTH PROFESSIONS (nursing, predentistry, and premedicine), SOCIAL SCIENCE (anthropology, child psychology/development, geography, history, liberal arts/general studies, Native American studies, parks and recreation management, philosophy, physical fitness/movement, political science/government, prelaw, psychology, religion, social science, social work, and sociology). Environmental resources engineering, natural resources, and performing arts are the strongest academically. Biological sciences has the largest enrollment.

ACTIVITIES: 1% of men belong to 2 national fraternities; 1% of women belong to 4 local sororities. There are 178 groups on campus, including art, band, cheerleading, chorale, chorus, computers, dance, debate, drama, environmental, ethnic, film, honors, international, jazz band, LGBT, literary magazine, marching band, musical theater, newspaper, opera, orchestra, pep band, photography, political, professional, radio and TV, religious, social, social service, student government, and symphony. Popular campus events include Campus Dialogue on Race, International Education week, and International Cultural Festival. **Sports:** There are 5 intercollegiate sports for men and 7 for women, and 4 intramural sports for men and 4 for women. Facilities include a stadium, an all-weather track, a swimming pool, tennis and racquetball courts, playing fields, gyms, a student recreation center with exercise equipment and weight room, and a rock-climbing wall. **Graduates:** From July 1, 2016 to June 30, 2017, 1988 bachelor's degrees were awarded. The most popular majors were natural resurces (15%), biological life sciences (12%), and social sciences (11%).

SERVICES: Counseling and information services are available, as is tutoring in every subject. There is a reader service for the blind, and remedial math, reading, and writing. **Library/Resources:** The library contains 566,531 volumes, 610,992 microform items, and 21,955 audio/video tapes/CDs/DVDs, and subscribes to 1,413 periodicals including electronic. Computerized library services include interlibrary loans, database searching, Internet access, and Wi-Fi capability. Special learning facilities include an art gallery, natural history museum, radio station, observatory, greenhouse, solar hydrogen project, wildlife sanctuaries, the center for Appropriate Technology, child development lab, ceramics lab, jewelry lab, marine lab, marine research vessel, fish hatchery, and wildlife care center. **Physically Challenged Students:** 60% of the campus is accessible. Facilities include wheelchair ramps, elevators, special parking, specially equipped restrooms, special class scheduling, lowered drinking fountains, lowered telephones, wheelchair-accessible transportation, and a study center. **Special:** HSU offers campus work-study programs and co-op programs with a variety of public and private agencies, fisheries, biology, geology, botany, engineering, soil science, hydrology, and range and soil conservation. Internships and study abroad in 25 countries, with semesters in London, China, and Greece, are also offered. Dual majors, student-designed majors, credit for life and military experience, and credit/no credit grading options are also available. **Visiting:** There are regularly scheduled orientations for prospective students, including Preview Day in the spring and mandatory summer orientation for new students, which provides peer and academic counseling, registration, and a variety of social activities. There are guides for informal visits, visitors may sit in on classes, and stay overnight. To schedule a visit, contact the Office of Admissions. **Campus Safety and Security:** Measures include 24-hour foot and vehicle patrol, emergency notification system, self-defense education, and security escort services. There are emergency telephones, lighted pathways/sidewalks, and emergency transportation services.

REQUIREMENTS: The SAT or ACT is recommended. Applicants must be high school graduates with a minimum of 15 academic credits, 4 years in English, 3 in math, 2 in foreign language, and social science with lab, 1 each in U.S. history/government, academic electives, social studies, and visual and performing arts. The GED is accepted. HSU uses an eligibility index that combines GPA and ACT or SAT scores for admission. Requirements are higher for out-of-state applicants. A GPA of 2.0 is required. AP and CLEP credits are accepted. Important factors in the admissions decision are geographical diversity, leadership record, and advanced placement or honors courses. To graduate, students must complete 120 to 132 semester credits, including 48 in general education courses, 24 to 36 in the major, and up to 40 in electives, with a minimum overall GPA of 2.0. Requirements include freshman reading and composition, diversity and common ground course work, and U.S. history course work as required by the California legislature. **Procedure:** Freshmen are admitted fall and spring. Entrance exams should be taken prior to admission. There are early decision and rolling admissions plans. Applications should be filed by November 30 for fall entry. The fall 2017 application fee was $55. Notifications are sent December 15. Applications are accepted on-line. **Transfer Students:** 879 transfer students enrolled in 2016-2017. Applicants must have a minimum college GPA of 2.0 (2.4 for nonresidents). To enter, students need 30 general education units with a grade of C or better, including courses in written and speech communication, critical thinking, and math. Students with fewer than 56 transferable semester units must meet freshman requirements. 30 of 132 credits required for the bachelor's degree must be completed at Humboldt. **International Students:** There are 61 international students enrolled. They must take the TOEFL.

ADMISSIONS: 76% of the 2017-2018 applicants were accepted. The SAT scores for the 2017-2018 freshman class were: Critical Reading-- 49% below 500, 38% between 500 and 599, 12% between 600 and 699, and 2% between 700 and 800. Math-- 53% below 500, 36% between 500 and 599, 9% between 600 and 699, and 1% between 700 and 800. Writing-- 58% below 500, 33% between 500 and 599, and 7% between 600 and 699. The ACT scores were 19% between 12 and 17, 49% between

18 and 23, 30% between 24 and 29, and 2% above 30. **Admissions Contact:** Rebecca Kalal, Assistant Director of Admissions. Email: *hsuinfo@humboldt.edu* Web: *www.humboldt.edu*

FINANCIAL AID: In 2017-2018, 69% of all full-time freshmen received some form of financial aid. 68% of all full-time freshmen received need-based aid. The average freshman award was $13,687. Need-based scholarships or need-based grants averaged $9,186; need-based self-help aid (loans and jobs) averaged $4,511; non-need-based athletic scholarships averaged $2,765; and $5,965 from other forms of aid. The FAFSA code is 001149. The priority date for freshman financial aid applications for fall entry is March 2.

HUMPHREYS COLLEGE B-3
www.humphreys.edu

Stockton, CA 95207	(209) 478-0800
Fax: (209) 478-8721	Email: ugadmission@humphreys.edu
Full-time: 300 men, 320 women	Faculty: n/av
Part-time: n/av	Ph.D.s: n/av
Graduate: n/av	Student/Faculty: n/av
Year: trimesters, summer session	Tuition: $15,323
Room & Board: $12,467	Freshman Class: n/av CEEB CODE: 4346
Application Deadline: open	COMPETITIVE

Humphreys College, founded in 1896, is an independent institution offering undergraduate degrees in business management, accounting, paralegal studies, computer management, law, early childhood education, and liberal arts to a primarily commuter student body. The figures given in the above capsule and in this profile are approximate. There is 1 undergraduate school and 1 graduate school. In addition to regional accreditation, Humphreys College has baccalaureate program accreditation with WASC. The 10-acre campus is in a suburban area 40 miles south of Sacramento. Including any residence halls, there are 9 buildings.

STUDENT LIFE: 97% of undergraduates are from California. Others are from 4 states, and 5 foreign countries. 97% are from public schools. 70% are White; 7% African American; 4% Asian American; 17% Hispanic; 1% American Indian/Alaska Native; 1% Foreign. **Female To Male Ratio:** 1.1:1. The average age of freshmen is 23; all undergraduates, 25. 20% do not continue beyond their first year; 50% remain to graduate. **Housing:** 64 students can be accommodated in college housing, which includes married student on-campus apartments. On-campus housing is available on a first-come and first-served basis. 90% of students commute. Alcohol is not permitted. All students may keep cars.

FACULTY/CLASSROOMS: 51% of faculty are male; 49% are female. All teach undergraduates. No introductory courses are taught by graduate students. The average class size in an introductory lecture is 17.

PROGRAMS OF STUDY: HC confers B.S. degrees. Associate and doctoral degrees are also awarded. Bachelor's degrees are awarded in BUSINESS (accounting, business administration and management, and management information systems), EDUCATION (early childhood education), SOCIAL SCIENCE (community services and paralegal studies). Paralegal studies has the largest enrollment.

ACTIVITIES: There are no fraternities or sororities. There are 4 groups on campus, including professional and student government. Popular campus events include Halloween Party, Christmas Dinner, and a Hot Dog Day Barbecue. **Sports:** There is no sports program at Humphreys. Facilities include a swimming pool, basketball court, tennis court, and sports fields.

SERVICES: Counseling and information services are available, as is tutoring in some subjects. There is also remedial math and writing. **Library/Resources:** The library contains 21,000 volumes, and 1,000 audio/video tapes/CDs/DVDs, and subscribes to 110 periodicals including electronic. Computerized library services include database searching. **Physically Challenged Students:** All of the campus is accessible. Facilities include wheelchair ramps, special parking, specially equipped restrooms, special class scheduling, lowered drinking fountains, and lowered telephones. **Special:** Local internship positions are available for students of paralegal studies and business administration. Dual majors in business studies are possible. **Visiting:** There are regularly scheduled orientations for prospective students, including a campus tour, classroom visits, and meetings with admissions, financial aid, and academic advisers. There are guides for informal visits and visitors may sit in on classes. To schedule a visit, contact the Admissions Office. **Campus Safety and Security:** Measures include 24-hour foot and vehicle patrol and security escort services. There are lighted pathways/sidewalks.

REQUIREMENTS: Applicants must be graduates of an accredited secondary school or have earned a GED. AP and CLEP credits are accepted. To graduate, students must complete a total of 180 quarter units, including 56 in the major and 72 in general education courses, with a minimum GPA of 2.0. **Procedure:** Freshmen are admitted to all sessions. Entrance exams should be taken at any time. There are deferred admissions and rolling admissions plans. Application deadlines are open. The fall 2017 application fee was $35. **Transfer Students:** Applicants must submit official transcripts and have a GPA of at least 2.0. 36 of 180 credits required for the bachelor's degree must be completed at Humphreys. **International Students:** They must take the TOEFL or MELAB.

Admissions Contact: Santa Lopez-Minatre, Director of Admissions. Email: *ugadmission@humphreys.edu* Web: *www.humphreys.edu*

FINANCIAL AID: Humphreys College is a member of CSS. The FAFSA code is 001212. Check with the school for current application deadlines.

LA SIERRA UNIVERSITY D-5
www.lasierra.edu

Riverside, CA 92515	(951) 785-2957 (800) 874-5587
Fax: (951) 785-2447	Email: admissions@lasierra.edu
Full-time: 615 men, 865 women	Faculty: n/av
Part-time: 90 men, 110 women	Ph.D.s: n/av
Graduate: 160 men, 175 women	Student/Faculty: n/av
Year: trimesters, summer session	Tuition: $31,590
Room & Board: $8100	Freshman Class: n/av
SAT or ACT: required	CEEB CODE: 4380
Application Deadline: n/av	VERY COMPETITIVE

La Sierra University, founded originally as La Sierra Academy in 1922, is a Seventh-day Adventist, private university, offering undergraduate and graduate programs in applied and liberal arts and sciences, business and management, religion, and education. The figures in the above capsule and in this profile are approximate. There are 5 undergraduate schools and 4 graduate schools. In addition to regional accreditation, La Sierra University has baccalaureate program accreditation with ABET, CSWE, NASM, CCTC, ATS, and AAA. The 300-acre campus is in a suburban area 40 miles east of Los Angeles. Including any residence halls, there are 48 buildings.

STUDENT LIFE: 29% of undergraduates are from out of state, mostly the Southwest. Students are from 34 states, 58 foreign countries, and Canada. 39% are from public schools. 8% are Foreign; 7% African American; 35% White; 31% Asian American; 19% Hispanic; 1% American Indian/Alaska Native. 90% are Protestant; 12% claim no religious affiliation. **Female To Male Ratio:** 1.3:1. The average age of freshmen is 19; all undergraduates, 22. **Housing:** 850 students can be accommodated in college housing, which includes married student dorms, on-campus apartments, off-campus apartments, and honors houses. On-campus housing is guaranteed for all 4 years, is guaranteed for the freshman year only, is available on a first-come, and first-served basis. 56% of students commute. Alcohol is not permitted. All students may keep cars.

FACULTY/CLASSROOMS: All teach undergraduates, 70% do research, and 70% do both. Graduate students teach 1% of introductory courses. The average class size in an introductory lecture is 30; in a laboratory is 21; and in a regular course is 20.

PROGRAMS OF STUDY: La Sierra confers B.A., B.S., B.F.A., B.Mus., and B.S.W. degrees. Master's and doctoral degrees are also awarded. Bachelor's degrees are awarded in BIOLOGICAL SCIENCE (biochemistry, biology/biological science, biometrics and biostatistics, and biophysics), BUSINESS (accounting, banking and finance, business administration and management, electronic business, international business management, and marketing management), COMMUNICATIONS AND THE ARTS (art, communications, English, English as a second/foreign language, fine arts, graphic design, music, music performance, and Spanish), COMPUTER AND PHYSICAL SCIENCE (chemistry, computer science, information sciences and systems, mathematics, and physics), EDUCATION (elementary education, music education, physical education, and secondary education), HEALTH PROFESSIONS (exercise science and health science), SOCIAL SCIENCE (history, liberal arts/general studies, political science/government, psychobiology, psychology, religion, social work, and sociology). Biology, criminal justice, and business are the strongest academically and has the largest enrollments.

ACTIVITIES: There are no fraternities or sororities. There are 30 groups on campus, including art, band, choir, chorale, chorus, computers, debate, drama, environmental, ethnic, film, honors, international, literary magazine, newspaper, orchestra, photography, professional, religious, social service, student government, symphony, and yearbook. Popular campus events include University Experience, Academic Expo, and Community Service Day. **Sports:** There are 3 intercollegiate sports for men and 3 for women, and 9 intramural sports for men and 9 for women. Facilities include a gym, soccer and flag football fields, running track, swimming pool, and a fitness center. **Graduates:** From July 1, 2016 to June 30, 2017, 208 bachelor's degrees were awarded. The most popular majors were biomedical science (9%), management (7%), and exercise science/scientific basis (5%). In an average class, 35% graduate in 4 years or less and 45% graduate in 6 years or less.

SERVICES: Counseling and information services are available, as is tutoring in most subjects. There is a reader service for the blind, and remedial math, reading, and writing. There is also a learning support center. **Library/Resources:** The library contains 255,694 volumes, 386,372 microform items, and 118,844 audio/video tapes/CDs/DVDs, and subscribes to 792 periodicals including electronic. Computerized library services include interlibrary loans, database searching, Internet access, and Wi-Fi capability. Special learning facilities include an art gallery, natural history museum, an observatory, a Missionary Museum, and a arboretum. **Physically Challenged Students:** 99% of the campus is accessible. Facilities include wheelchair ramps, elevators, special parking, specially equipped restrooms, and special class scheduling. **Special:** Cross-registration with Walla Walla College is necessary for engineering students. Study abroad is available in 3 countries through the Adventist Colleges Abroad Consortium. Liberal studies students work with an adviser to design their own major. There is a freshman honors program. **Visiting:** There are regularly scheduled orientations for prospective students, including a tour and meetings with faculty and administrators. There are guides for informal visits, visitors may sit in on classes, and stay overnight. To schedule a visit, contact the Admissions Office. **Campus Safety and Security:** Measures include 24-hour foot and vehicle patrol, emergency notification system, and security escort services. There are emergency telephones, lighted pathways/sidewalks, and controlled access to dorms/residences.

REQUIREMENTS: The SAT or ACT is required. Prospective students should have a high school diploma or equivalent. Completion of college preparatory work is required, along with a recommendation. A GPA of 2.5 is required. AP and CLEP credits are accepted. Important factors in the admissions decision are recommendations by school officials, leadership record, and evidence of special talent. To graduate, students must complete 190 units, at least 60 of which must be upper-division, with a GPA of 2.0. All students must complete a University Studies curriculum requirements and 3 community service courses. **Procedure:** Freshmen are admitted to all sessions. Entrance exams should be taken during the senior year. There are deferred admissions and rolling admissions plans. Check with the school for current application deadlines. The fall 2017 application fee was $30. **Transfer Students:** Transcripts from all previous colleges are required. 36 of 190 credits required for the bachelor's degree must be completed at La Sierra. **International Students:** There are 283 international students enrolled. They must take the TOEFL with a minimum score of 500 on the paper-based TOEFL (PBT). They must also take the SAT or ACT.

Admissions Contact: Ivy Tejeda, Associate Director of Admissions. Email: *admissions@lasierra.edu* Web: *www.lasierra.edu*

FINANCIAL AID: La Sierra University is a member of CSS. The FAFSA code is 001215. Check with the school for current application deadlines.

LAGUNA COLLEGE OF ART AND DESIGN *(The complete profile is made available exclusively on our website, www.barronspac.com)*

LOYOLA MARYMOUNT UNIVERSITY C-5

www.lmu.edu

Los Angeles, CA 90045 **(310) 338-2750**

Email: admission@lmu.edu

Full-time: 2631 men, 3413 women	**Faculty:** 472
Part-time: 125 men, 92 women	**Ph.D.s:** 96%
Graduate: 1122 men, 1947 women	**Student/Faculty:** 10 to 1
Year: semesters, summer session	**Tuition:** $46,136
Room & Board: $14,066	**Freshman Class:** 13506 applied, 7276 accepted, 1331 enrolled
SAT CR/M/W: 600/620/600 **ACT:** 28	**CEEB CODE:** 4403
Application Deadline: January 15	**VERY COMPETITIVE+**

Loyola Marymount University is one of the largest Catholic universities in the West and one of 28 Jesuit universities in the United States. At LMU the city becomes an extension of the classroom, offering a rich diversity of culture, interests, access and opportunities. That diversity is being put to work at the university's World Policy Institute @LMU, a think-tank idea incubator launched in partnership with the WPI based in New York City. LMU, founded in 1911, is a comprehensive university offering 58 major programs and 53 minor programs for undergraduates; 46 master's degrees; two research level doctoral degrees; one professional practice doctoral degree; and 13 credential programs. Colleges and schools include: Bellarmine College of Liberal Arts, College of Business Administration, College of Communication and Fine Arts, Frank R. Seaver College of Science and Engineering, Loyola Law School, School of Education and School of Film and Television. There are 5 undergraduate schools and 2 graduate schools. The 142-acre campus is in a suburban area 15 miles southwest of downtown Los Angeles.

STUDENT LIFE: 74% of undergraduates are from California. Others are from 75 foreign countries. 52% are from public schools. 8% are two or more races; 6% African American; 44% White; 21% Hispanic; 11% Asian American; 10% Foreign. 38% are Catholic; 17% Christian, Muslim, Buddhist, Armenian Orthodox, Greek Orthodox, Mormon, and Seventh Day Adventist. **Female To Male Ratio:** 1.4:1. The average age of freshmen is 18; all undergraduates, 20. 12% do not continue beyond their first year; 83% remain to graduate. **Housing:** 3210 students can be accommodated in college housing, which includes both single sex and coed dorms and on-campus apartments. On-campus housing is guaranteed for the freshman year only and is available on a lottery system for upperclassmen. All students may keep cars.

FACULTY/CLASSROOMS: 54% of faculty are male; 46% are female. No introductory courses are taught by graduate students.

PROGRAMS OF STUDY: LMU confers B.A., B.S., B.B.A., B.S.A., and B.S.E. degrees. Master's and doctoral degrees are also awarded. Bachelor's degrees are awarded in BIOLOGICAL SCIENCE (biochemistry and biology/biological science), BUSINESS (accounting, entrepreneurial studies, finance, management information systems, management, and marketing), COMMUNICATIONS AND THE ARTS (animation, art history, communication studies, dance, English, film, television and digital media, French, modern language, music, music production/recording technology, playwriting/screenwriting, Spanish, studio art, and theatre arts), COMPUTER AND PHYSICAL SCIENCE (applied mathematics, chemistry, computer science, mathematics, and physics), EDUCATION (Asian studies), ENGINEERING AND ENVIRONMENTAL DESIGN (civil engineering, electrical/electronics engineering, engineering physics, environmental science, and mechanical engineering), HEALTH PROFESSIONS (health science), SOCIAL SCIENCE (African American studies, classical/ancient civilization, economics, European studies, Hispanic American studies, history, humanities, interdisciplinary studies, international relations, liberal arts/general studies, philosophy, political science/government, psychology, sociology, theology, urban studies, and women & gender studies). School of film and television, entreprenuership, and marketing are the strongest academically. Marketing, communication studies, and psychology have the largest enrollments.

ACTIVITIES: 17% of men belong to 10 national fraternities; 33% of women belong to 12 national sororities. There are 193 groups on campus, including choral groups, dance, drama/theater, international student organization, literary magazine, Model UN, music ensembles, opera, radio station, student government, student newspaper, student-run film society, television station, yearbook, and campus ministries.

Popular campus events include Fallapalooza, After Sunset, Greek Life Lip Sync & Stroll Off, Na Kolea's Luau, Charity Ball, Philipino Cultural Night, Fright Night, and Sunken Garden Festival. **Sports:** There are 10 intercollegiate sports for men and 12 for women, and 6 intramural sports for men and 5 for women. Facilities include a recreation and wellness complex, lacrosse, soccer, volleyball, tennis, ski & snowboard, baseball, ice hockey, rugby, basketball, flag football, indoor and outdoor soccer, basketball, billiards, dodgeball, tennis, indoor and sand volleyball, kickball, and table tennis, group fitness classes for yoga, cycling, Zumba and core strength. **Graduates:** From July 1, 2016 to June 30, 2017, 1589 bachelor's degrees were awarded. The most popular majors were marketing (11%), psychology (8%), and communication studies (7%). In an average class, 1% graduate in 3 years or less, 74% graduate in 4 years or less, 82% graduate in 5 years or less, and 83% graduate in 6 years or less. Of the 2016 graduating class, 20% were enrolled in graduate school within 6 months of graduation, and 75% were employed.

SERVICES: Counseling and information services are available, as is tutoring in most subjects. There is a reader service for the blind, and remedial math, reading, and writing. **Library/Resources:** Computerized library services include interlibrary loans, database searching, Internet access, and Wi-Fi capability. Special learning facilities include an art gallery, TV station, fine arts complex with recital hall and recording arts facilities, marine station, a life sciences building with green roof that is a "living laboratory" for research, art gallery, TV production labs, computer graphics lab. **Physically Challenged Students:** 95% of the campus is accessible. Facilities include wheelchair ramps, elevators, special parking, specially equipped restrooms, special class scheduling, lowered drinking fountains, lowered telephones, and special housing. Special test arrangements, adaptive equipment, braille services, interpreters for hearing impaired, note-taking services, talking books, and tape recorders. **Special:** LMU offers accelerated 4+1 masters programs, cross-registration, distance learning, double majors, dual enrollment, English as a Second Language (ESL), a Washington semester exchange student program, honors program, independent study, internships with local firms, a liberal arts/career combination program, student-designed and individualized studies majors, study abroad in over 20 countries, teacher certification, and weekend college. There are 19 national honor societies and a freshman honors program. **Visiting:** There are regularly scheduled orientations for prospective students. There are guides for informal visits and visitors may sit in on classes.

REQUIREMENTS: The ACT is recommended. Prospective students must be graduates of an accredited secondary school and have completed 4 years of English, 3 each of a foreign language, math, and social studies, 2 of science, and 1 of an academic elective. A recommendation from an official of a previous school and essays are required. Either SAT or ACT test scores are required. AP credits are accepted. Regardless of major, all undergraduates must take courses in the following core areas: First year seminar, rhetorical arts, quantitative reasoning, theological inquiry, philosophical inquiry, studies in American diversity, creative experience, historical analysis and perspectives, understanding human behavior, faith and reason, ethics and justice, interdisciplinary connections, and the nature of science, technology and mathematics. A minimum 2.0 GPA is required, as are at least 120 semester hours, with at least 45 semester hours in upper-division courses. At least 30 of the last 36 semester hours of academic work and at least two thirds of the upper-division semester hours of the major must be completed at LMU. **Procedure:** Freshmen are admitted fall and spring. Entrance exams should be taken during the spring of the junior year or fall of senior year. There are early decision, early admissions, deferred admissions, and rolling admissions plans. Early decision applications should be filed by November 1; regular applications, by January 15 for fall entry; and October 15 for spring entry. The fall 2017 application fee was $60. Notification of early decision is sent December 1; regular decision, 2015 applicants were on the 2017 waiting list; 215 were admitted. Applications are accepted on-line. **Transfer Students:** Applicants must have a minimum 3.00 GPA in college work and most recent college work. Students who were not academically eligible for admission as freshmen must have at least 30 semester hours of college work with at least a 3.00 cumulative average. Grades below C (2.0) do not transfer. No minimum credit hours are necessary for students who meet freshman requirements. Standardized test scores (SAT or ACT) are required for those with fewer than 30 transfer hours, and letters of recommendation are recommended for all transfer students. 30 of 120 credits required for the bachelor's degree must be completed at LMU. **International Students:** There are 574 international students enrolled. They must take the TOEFL with a minimum score of 550 on the paper-based TOEFL (PBT) or 80 on the Internet-based version (iBT), or take either the IELTS or PTE test.

ADMISSIONS: 54% of the 2017-2018 applicants were accepted. The SAT scores for the 2017-2018 freshman class were: Critical Reading-- 7% below 500, 39% between 500 and 599, 40% between 600 and 699, and 14% between 700 and 800. Math-- 5% below 500, 34% between 500 and 599, 46% between 600 and 699, and 15% between 700 and 800. Writing-- 7% below 500, 37% between 500 and 599, 43% between 600 and 699, and 13% between 700 and 800. The ACT scores were 5% between 18 and 23, 62% between 24 and 29, and 33% above 30. 62% of the current freshmen were in the top fifth of their class; 95% were in the top two fifths. **Admissions Contact:** Matthew Fissinger, Assistant Vice Provost for Undergraduate. Email: *admission@lmu.edu* Web: *http:/admission.lmu.edu*

FINANCIAL AID: In 2017-2018, 90% of all full-time freshmen received some form of financial aid. 48% of all full-time freshmen received need-based aid. The average financial indebtedness of the 2017 graduate was $30,698. The FAFSA code is 001234. The priority date for freshman financial aid applications for fall entry is February 1.

MENLO COLLEGE *(The complete profile is made available exclusively on our website, www.barronspac.com)*

MILLS COLLEGE — B-3

www.mills.edu

Oakland, CA 94613	**(510) 430-2135** **(800) 87-MILLS**
Fax: (510) 430-3314	**Email: admission@mills.edu**
Full-time: 739 women	**Faculty:** 82; IIA, +$
Part-time: 22 women	**Ph.D.s:** 85%
Graduate: 128 men, 420 women	**Student/Faculty:** 10 to 1
Year: semesters	**Tuition:** $30,257
Room & Board: $13,448	**Freshman Class:** 965 applied, 837 accepted, 174 enrolled
SAT CR/M/W: 550/530/550 **ACT:** required	**CEEB CODE:** 4485
Application Deadline: January 15	**COMPETITIVE**

Mills College offers a challenging liberal arts curriculum that encourages you to think creatively, prepares you to take well-calculated risks, and equips you to put your passions into practice. We are driven by a determination to improve ourselves and the world around us and to work smarter by working together. At Mills, you will be encouraged to stand out, emboldened to think big, and empowered to make a statement. There is 1 undergraduate school and 4 graduate schools. The 135-acre campus is in an urban area in the San Francisco Bay area, 12 miles east of San Francisco and 8 miles from Berkeley. Including any residence halls, there are 64 buildings.

STUDENT LIFE: 81% of undergraduates are from California. Others are from 37 states, and 8 foreign countries. 88% are from public schools. 41% are White; 28% Hispanic; 10% Asian American; 9% African American; 9% two or more races; 1% American Indian/Alaska Native; 1% Foreign; 1% race unknown. 42% are Atheist, and Agnostic; 21% claim no religious affiliation; 15% Protestant; 11% Catholic. **Female To Male Ratio:** 9.2:1. The average age of freshmen is 18; all undergraduates, 22. 21% do not continue beyond their first year; 69% remain to graduate. **Housing:** 794 students can be accommodated in college housing, which includes dorms and on-campus apartments. In addition, there are language/international houses, special-interest houses, and gender-neutral housing. Married-student housing is offered on an equal basis to domestic partners of lesbian and gay students, and a student co-op house is available for juniors and seniors. On-campus housing is guaranteed for all 4 years, is available on a first-come, and first-served basis. 60% of students live on campus. All students may keep cars.

FACULTY/CLASSROOMS: 27% of faculty are male; 73% are female. 97% teach undergraduates and do research. No introductory courses are taught by graduate students. The average class size in an introductory lecture is 25; in a laboratory is 15; and in a regular course is 16.

PROGRAMS OF STUDY: Mills confers B.A. and B.S. degrees. Master's and doctoral degrees are also awarded. Bachelor's degrees are awarded in AGRICULTURE (environmental studies), BIOLOGICAL SCIENCE (biochemistry, biology/biological science, microbiology, and molecular biology), BUSINESS (business administration and management and business economics), COMMUNICATIONS AND THE ARTS (art history, creative writing, dance, English, English literature, English Writing, French, intermedia/multimedia, modern language, music, Spanish, studio art, and theatre studies), COMPUTER AND PHYSICAL SCIENCE (chemistry, computer information technology, computer science, and mathematics), ENGINEERING AND ENVIRONMENTAL DESIGN (environmental science), HEALTH PROFESSIONS (nursing and public health), SOCIAL SCIENCE (anthropology, biopsychology, child psychology/development, early childhood studies, economics, ethnic studies, government, French studies, Hispanic American studies, history, humanities and social science, international relations, philosophy, political science/government, prelaw, psychology, public administration, public affairs, public policy, sociology, Spanish studies, and women & gender studies). Biology, English, computer science, and psychology are the strongest academically. Psychology, English, and sociology have the largest enrollments.

ACTIVITIES: There are no fraternities or sororities. There are 35 groups on campus, including art, cheerleading, choir, chorus, communications, computers, dance, drama, environmental, ethnic, film, honors, international, LGBT, literary magazine, newspaper, photography, political, professional, religious, social, social service, student government, and yearbook. Popular campus events include Black and White Ball, Spring Fling, Heritage Month Celebrations, Alumnae Final Snacks, Midnight Breakfast, and Movie on the Meadow. **Sports:** There are 6 intercollegiate sports for women, and 9 intramural sports for women. Facilities include athletic and recreational facilities include a multi-purpose gymnasium, a fitness center with cardio-fitness and strength training equipment, dance studios, aquatic center and therapy spa, tennis courts, grass soccer field, and on-campus running trail. **Graduates:** From July 1, 2016 to June 30, 2017, 262 bachelor's degrees were awarded. The most popular majors were English (15%), psychology (9%), and biology (9%). In an average class, 5% graduate in 3 years or less, 62% graduate in 4 years or less, 64% graduate in 5 years or less, and 67% graduate in 6 years or less. Of the 2016 graduating class, 10% were enrolled in graduate school within 6 months of graduation, and 79% were employed.

SERVICES: Counseling and information services are available, as is tutoring in every subject. There is a reader service for the blind, and remedial math and writing. **Library/Resources:** The library contains 250,760 volumes, 199 microform items, and 14,831 audio/video tapes/CDs/DVDs, and subscribes to 51,607 periodicals including electronic. Computerized library services include interlibrary loans, database searching, Internet access, and Wi-Fi capability. Special learning facilities include an art gallery, children's school, small book press, electronic/computer music studio, dance and fine arts studios, botanical garden, urban farm, Electronic Collaborative Learning Center, Innovation Lab, Center for Learning, and an Advising and Balance (LAB). **Physically Challenged Students:** All of the campus is accessible. Facilities include wheelchair ramps, elevators, special parking, specially equipped restrooms, special class scheduling, lowered drinking fountains, lowered telephones, and special housing. **Special:** Cross-registration is available for students to attend classes at the University of California at Berkeley, California State University, and California College of the Arts. Mills offers the opportunity to study at other women's colleges in the U.S. Other opportunities include co-op programs, internships, study abroad, and a Washington semester. Students can participate in work-study programs and can declare a dual major, a student-designed major, or an interdisciplinary major such as Public Health and Health Equity. Accelerated degree programs include a 5 year M.B.A., Masters in Public Policy (MPP) or combination MBA/MPP; as well as a B.A./M.A. program in which students graduate in 5 years with a bachelor's degree in psychology and a master's in infant mental health, or in five years, earn a B.A., an M.A. in education, and complete a program qualifying them for a teaching credential. Mills also offers a a 3-2 engineering degree with USC and a prenursing program leading to a bachelor's degree in nursing at Simmons College. Credit by exam, and pass/fail options are also available. There are 5 national honor societies, Phi Beta Kappa, and 1 departmental honors program. **Visiting:** There are regularly scheduled orientations for prospective students, consisting of class visits, campus tours, lunch with faculty, financial aid workshops, and an admissions interview. There are guides for informal visits, visitors may sit in on classes, and stay overnight. **Campus Safety and Security:** Measures include 24-hour foot and vehicle patrol, emergency notification system, self-defense education, and security escort services. There are shuttle buses, emergency telephones, lighted pathways/sidewalks, controlled access to dorms/residences, AED units, vehicle jumps, and a bicycle repair station.

REQUIREMENTS: Students are required to submit a high school transcript, two letters of recommendation, a school report, and a writing sample or personal statement. Official SAT or ACT test scores are optional. Interviews are recommended but not required. GED or High School Proficiency are accepted in lieu of a High School Transcript. We recommend a cumulative GPA of 3.0 or higher and SAT scores above 1500 combined. AP and CLEP credits are accepted. Important factors in the admissions decision are advanced placement or honors courses, personality/intangible qualities, and recommendations by school officials. To graduate, students must fulfill Core Curriculum requirements, earn a total of 120 semester units, with at least 30 in the major, and maintain a minimum GPA of 2.0. Courses are required to fulfill the following core curriculum areas: written and oral communication, information literacy, quantitative literacy, critical analysis, race, gender & power, language other than English, scientific inquiry, international perspectives, community engagement, creativity, innovation, and experimentation. **Procedure:** Freshmen are admitted fall and spring. Entrance exams should be taken at least 1 month prior to application. There are early decision and deferred admissions plans. Early decision applications should be filed by November 15; regular applications, by January 15 for fall entry; and November 1 for spring entry. The fall 2017 application fee was $50. Notification of early decision is sent December 1; regular decision, February 15. 223 early decision candidates were accepted for the 2017-2018 class. Applications are accepted on-line. **Transfer Students:** 122 transfer students enrolled in 2016-2017. A writing sample, two letters of recommendation, a high school transcript, and official transcripts from all colleges attended are required.The recommended minimum GPA to apply to Mills is 3.0. We consider other factors such as writing skills, strength of curriculum, and number of credit hours. 40 of 120 credits required for the bachelor's degree must be completed at Mills. **International Students:** There are 8 international students enrolled. They must take the TOEFL with a minimum score of 550 on the paper-based TOEFL (PBT) or 80 on the Internet-based version (iBT).

ADMISSIONS: 87% of the 2017-2018 applicants were accepted. The SAT scores for the 2017-2018 freshman class were: Critical Reading-- 24% below 500, 49% between 500 and 599, 17% between 600 and 699, and 10% between 700 and 800. Math-- 29% below 500, 46% between 500 and 599, 19% between 600 and 699, and 7% between 700 and 800. Writing-- 34% below 500, 31% between 500 and 599, 25% between 600 and 699, and 10% between 700 and 800. The ACT scores were 3% between 12 and 17, 26% between 18 and 23, 51% between 24 and 29, and 20% above 30. 46% of the current freshmen were in the top fifth of their class; 82% were in the top two fifths. 1 freshman graduated first in the class. **Admissions Contact:** Robynne Lofton, Director of Undergraduate Admission. Email: *admission@mills.edu* Web: *www.mills.edu*

FINANCIAL AID: In 2017-2018, 100% of all full-time freshmen received some form of financial aid. 72% of all full-time freshmen received need-based aid. The average freshman award was $49,405. Need-based scholarships or need-based grants averaged $19,431 ($31,098 maximum); need-based self-help aid (loans and jobs) averaged $9,729 ($14,500 maximum); and other non-need-based awards and non-need-based scholarships averaged $23,124 ($40,500 maximum). 97% of undergraduate students work part-time. The average financial indebtedness of the 2017 graduate was $29,954. The college's own financial statement is required. The FAFSA code is 001238. The priority date for freshman financial aid applications for fall entry is February 1. The deadline for filing freshman financial aid applications for fall entry is February 15.

MOUNT ST. MARY'S UNIVERSITY - CHALON CAMPUS C-5

www.msmu.edu

Los Angeles, CA 90049	**(310) 954-4250** **(800) 999-9893**
Fax: (310) 954-4259	**Email: admissions@msmu.edu**
Full-time: 91 men, 1712 women	**Faculty:** 88
Part-time: 83 men, 402 women	**Ph.D.s:** 61%
Graduate: 126 men, 448 women	**Student/Faculty:** 12 to 1
Year: semesters	**Tuition:** $39,608
Room & Board: $10,878	**Freshman Class:** 1799 applied, 309 accepted, 528 enrolled
SAT or ACT: required	**CEEB CODE:** 4493
Application Deadline: February 15	**VERY COMPETITIVE+**

Mount St. Mary's University-Chalon Campus, founded in 1925, and affiliated with the Catholic Church, is a private, primarily women's institution. The traditional baccalaureate program is offered at the Chalon Campus and associate programs are offered at the Doheny Campus. The figures given in the above capsule and in this profile are approximate. There is 1 undergraduate school and 1 graduate school. In addition to regional accreditation, MSMU-Chalon Campus has baccalaureate program accreditation with NLN, CSC, and UWASC. The 72-acre campus is in an urban area 10 miles west of Los Angeles. Including any residence halls, there are 31 buildings.

STUDENT LIFE: 97% of undergraduates are from California. Others are from 19 states, 5 foreign countries, and Canada. 70% are from public schools. 8% are African American; 7% two or more races; 57% Hispanic; 15% Asian American; 12% White; 1% American Indian/Alaska Native; 1% Foreign. 53% are Catholic; 14% Protestant; 13% claim no religious affiliation. **Female To Male Ratio:** 8.5:1. The average age of freshmen is 18; all undergraduates, 23. 16% do not continue beyond their first year; 84% remain to graduate. **Housing:** 668 students can be accommodated in college housing, which includes dorms. On-campus housing is available on a first-come and first-served basis. 71% of students commute. All students may keep cars.

FACULTY/CLASSROOMS: 27% of faculty are male; 73% are female. 92% teach undergraduates. No introductory courses are taught by graduate students. The average class size in an introductory lecture is 23; in a laboratory is 18; and in a regular course is 23.

PROGRAMS OF STUDY: MSMU-Chalon Campus confers B.A., B.S., and B.S.N. degrees. Associate, master's, and doctoral degrees are also awarded. Bachelor's degrees are awarded in BIOLOGICAL SCIENCE (biochemistry and biology/biological science), BUSINESS (business administration and management), COMMUNICATIONS AND THE ARTS (art, English, film arts, French, music, and Spanish), COMPUTER AND PHYSICAL SCIENCE (chemistry and mathematics), EDUCATION (elementary education), HEALTH PROFESSIONS (health care administration and nursing), SOCIAL SCIENCE (American studies, child psychology/development, counseling/psychology, gerontology, history, liberal arts/general studies, philosophy, political science/government, psychology, religion, social science, social work, and sociology). Nursing, Pre-nursing, psychology, business, biology, sociology, pre-health, and liberal arts is the strongest academically and have the largest enrollments.

ACTIVITIES: There are no fraternities; 1% of women belong to 2 local and 1 national sororities. There are 28 groups on campus, including art, choir, drama, environmental, ethnic, film, honors, international, LGBT, newspaper, political, professional, religious, social, social service, student government, and yearbook. Popular campus events include Leadership Boot Camp, Charity Ball, and Spring Carnival. **Sports:** There are 1 intramural sports for men and 2 for women. Facilities include basketball, tennis, volleyball, a swimming pool, a fitness workout room, and dance studio. **Graduates:** From July 1, 2016 to June 30, 2017, 516 bachelor's degrees were awarded. The most popular majors were nursing (50%), sociology (13%), and business (11%). In an average class, 54% graduate in 4 years or less, 59% graduate in 5 years or less, and 62% graduate in 6 years or less. Of the 2016 graduating class, 26% were enrolled in graduate school within 6 months of graduation, and 31% were employed.

SERVICES: Counseling and information services are available, as is tutoring in most subjects. A peer tutoring program is available. **Library/Resources:** The library contains 140,000 volumes, and 2,520 audio/video tapes/CDs/DVDs, and subscribes to 25,000 periodicals including electronic. Computerized library services include interlibrary loans, database searching, Internet access, and Wi-Fi capability. Special learning facilities include an art gallery, and a film studio. **Physically Challenged Students:** All of the campus is accessible. Facilities include wheelchair ramps, elevators, special parking, specially equipped restrooms, lowered drinking fountains, lowered telephones, and special housing. **Special:** The Mount offers cross-registration with UCLA, the University of Judaism, internships, study abroad in 17 countries, a Washington semester through American University, dual and student-designed majors, work-study programs, and an accelerated degree program in nursing. There are 20 national honor societies, Phi Beta Kappa, and a freshman honors program. **Visiting:** There are regularly scheduled orientations for prospective students, including workshops, student panels, tours, class visits, and faculty presentations. There are guides for informal visits, visitors may sit in on classes, and stay overnight. To schedule a visit, contact the Admissions Office. **Campus Safety and Security:** Measures include 24-hour foot and vehicle patrol, emergency notification system, self-defense education, and security escort services. There are shuttle buses, emergency telephones, lighted pathways/sidewalks, and controlled access to dorms/residences.

REQUIREMENTS: The SAT or ACT is required. Applicants must be graduates of an accredited secondary school or have earned the GED, with 16 academic credits and 16 Carnegie units, including 4 years of English literature and composition, 2 or 3 years each of math, science, and social studies, and 1 or 2 years of history. An essay is required, and an interview is recommended. A GPA of 2.5 is required. AP and CLEP credits are accepted. Important factors in the admissions decision are advanced placement or honors courses, extracurricular activities record, and leadership record. To graduate, students must complete at least 124 semester units with a GPA of 2.0 (C average); a minimum of 45 semester units must be in upper-division work. The total number of hours students must complete in their major varies. All students must satisfy a senior residence requirement and complete a general studies program. Freshmen entering the college with fewer than 24 units must complete Introduction to College Studies. Students must file a graduation application in the Registrar's Office by the end of the term prior to the term of projected completion. **Procedure:** Freshmen are admitted fall and spring. Entrance exams should be taken at the end of the junior year or the beginning of the senior year. There is a rolling admissions plan. Applications should be filed by February 15 for fall entry; November 1 for spring entry. The fall 2017 application fee was $50. Notification is sent on a rolling basis. Applications are accepted on-line. **Transfer Students:** 254 transfer students enrolled in 2016-2017. Transfer students must have a minimum 2.40 GPA with at least 24 completed credit hours. 30 of 124 credits required for the bachelor's degree must be completed at MSMU-Chalon Campus. **International Students:** There are 22 international students enrolled. They must take the TOEFL with a minimum score of 530 on the paper-based TOEFL (PBT) or 75 on the Internet-based version (iBT). They must also take the SAT or ACT.

ADMISSIONS: 17% of the 2017-2018 applicants were accepted. **Admissions Contact:** Yvonne Berumen, Director of Admissions. Email: *admissions@msmu.edu* Web: *www.msmu.edu*

FINANCIAL AID: In 2017-2018, 92% of all full-time freshmen received some form of financial aid. 86% of all full-time freshmen received need-based aid. 45% of undergraduate students work part-time. MSMU-Chalon Campus is a member of CSS. The college's own financial statement is required. The FAFSA code is 001243. The priority date for freshman financial aid applications for fall entry is February 15.

NATIONAL UNIVERSITY *(The complete profile is made available exclusively on our website, www.barronspac.com)*

NEWSCHOOL OF ARCHITECTURE & DESIGN *(The complete profile is made available exclusively on our website, www.barronspac.com)*

NOTRE DAME DE NAMUR UNIVERSITY *(The complete profile is made available exclusively on our website, www.barronspac.com)*

OCCIDENTAL COLLEGE — C-5

www.oxy.edu

Los Angeles, CA 90041 — (323) 259-2700, (800) 825-5262

Fax: (323) 341-4875	**Email:** admission@oxy.edu
Full-time: 883 men, 1186 women	**Faculty:** 172; IIB, ++$
Part-time: 11 men, 8 women	**Ph.D.s:** 95%
Graduate: n/av	**Student/Faculty:** 12 to 1
Year: semesters	**Tuition:** $47,340
Room & Board: $21,320	**Freshman Class:** 5911 applied, 2652 accepted, 518 enrolled
SAT CR/M/W: 645/645/648 **ACT:** 30	**CEEB CODE:** 4581
Application Deadline: January 15	**MOST COMPETITIVE**

Occidental College, founded in 1887, is a private, nonsectarian school of liberal arts and sciences, one of the few top liberal arts colleges in a major city. Even more distinctive is Occidental's ability to sustain its traditional commitment to high achievement while enrolling a diverse student body and faculty. The figures in the above capsule and in this profile are approximate. There is 1 undergraduate school. In addition to regional accreditation, Oxy has baccalaureate program accreditation with WASC. The 120-acre campus is in an urban area in the city of Los Angeles. Including any residence halls, there are 44 buildings.

STUDENT LIFE: 52% of undergraduates are from out of state, mostly the Northwest. Students are from 45 states, 34 foreign countries, and Canada. 58% are from public schools. 6% are Foreign; 51% White; 5% African American; 15% Hispanic; 12% Asian American; 10% two or more races; 1% race unknown. 35% are Protestant; 30% claim no religious affiliation; 19% Catholic; 11% Jewish. **Female To Male Ratio:** 1.3:1. The average age of freshmen is 18; all undergraduates, 20. 7% do not continue beyond their first year; 88% remain to graduate. **Housing:** 1671 students can be accommodated in college housing, which includes dorms. In addition, there are special-interest houses, fraternity houses, multicultural, pets welcome, all-women, theme housing, and gender neutral. On-campus housing is available on a lottery system for upperclassmen. 82% of students live on campus. All students may keep cars.

FACULTY/CLASSROOMS: 50% of faculty are male; 50% are female. All teach undergraduates, and all do research. No introductory courses are taught by graduate students. The average class size in an introductory lecture is 20; in a laboratory is 12; and in a regular course is 15.

PROGRAMS OF STUDY: Oxy confers A.B. degrees. Master's degrees are also awarded. Bachelor's degrees are awarded in BIOLOGICAL SCIENCE (biochemistry and biology/biological science), COMMUNICATIONS AND THE ARTS (art history, Chinese, English, French, Japanese, languages, music, Spanish, and theatre arts), COMPUTER AND PHYSICAL SCIENCE (chemistry, geology, mathematics, and physics), EDUCATION (Asian studies), SOCIAL SCIENCE (American studies, cognitive science, cultural studies/critical theory & analysis, East Asian studies, economics, history, international relations, Latin American studies, philosophy, physical fitness/movement, political science/government, psychology, religion, sociology, and urban studies). Social sciences, biology, and chemistry are the strongest academically. Economics, diplomacy & world affairs, and biology have the largest enrollments.

ACTIVITIES: 10% of men belong to 4 national fraternities; 13% of women belong to 2 local and 2 national sororities. There are 116 groups on campus, including art, cheerleading, choir, chorus, dance, debate, drama, environmental, ethnic, honors, international, LGBT, literary magazine, musical theater, newspaper, orchestra, photography, political, professional, religious, social, social service, student government, student investment fund; entrepreneurs, symphony, and yearbook. Popular campus events include Dance Production, New Play Festival, and Taste of Oxy. **Sports:** There are 10 intercollegiate sports for men and 11 for women, and 6 intramural sports for men and 6 for women. Facilities include football, soccer, baseball, and softball fields, an all-weather track, tennis courts, outdoor pool, outdoor basketball courts, a dance studio, sports medicine center, gym, weight room, and a fitness center. **Graduates:** From July 1, 2016 to June 30, 2017, 504 bachelor's degrees were awarded. The most popular majors were economics (15%), diplomacy and world affairs (8%), and biology (7%). In an average class, 85% graduate in 6 years or less. Of the 2016 graduating class, 22% were enrolled in graduate school within 6 months of graduation, and 64% were employed.

SERVICES: There are peer tutors available in biology, chemistry, geology, kinesiology, mathematics and physics. Peer and faculty advisers are available through the Center for Academic Excellence. **Library/Resources:** The library contains 431,586 volumes, 6,839 microform items, and 12,338 audio/video tapes/CDs/DVDs, and subscribes to 55,322 periodicals including electronic. Computerized library services include interlibrary loans, database searching, Internet access, and Wi-Fi capability. Special learning facilities include an art gallery, student newspaper and yearbook, fully equipped theater, art studio and gallery, ornithology, conchology and geology collections, physics, plasma, paleomagnetic and optic labs, library special collections. **Physically Challenged Students:** 80% of the campus is accessible. Facilities include wheelchair ramps, elevators, special parking, specially equipped restrooms, and lowered drinking fountains. **Special:** Cross-registration is permitted with the California Institute of Technology and the Art Center College of Design. Students may study abroad in 41 countries in Europe, Asia, Africa, and Latin America. Opportunities are provided for internships, a Washington semester, a residential U.N. semester in New York City, dual and student-designed majors, a 3-2 engineering degree with the California Institute of Technology, a 3-3 law program with Columbia, and a 4-2 biotech program with Keck. There are 8 national honor societies, Phi Beta Kappa, and 32 departmental honors programs. **Visiting:** There are regularly scheduled orientations for prospective students, including campus tours Monday through Friday followed by info sessions with an admission officer. There are guides for informal visits, visitors may sit in on classes, and stay overnight. To schedule a visit, contact the Office of Admission at admission@oxy.edu. **Campus Safety and Security:** Measures include 24-hour foot and vehicle patrol, emergency notification system, self-defense education, and security escort services. There are shuttle buses, emergency telephones, lighted pathways/sidewalks, controlled access to dorms/residences, and a whistle alert program.

REQUIREMENTS: The SAT or ACT is required. Applicants should be high school graduates of high academic standing with units recommended 4 years of English, 3 each of math, foreign language and science, and history, 2 of social studies. The GED is accepted. An essay is required and an interview is recommended. A GPA of 3.6 is required. AP credits are accepted. Important factors in the admissions decision are advanced placement or honors courses, personality/intangible qualities, extracurricular activities record, and recommendations by school officials. To graduate, students must complete 32 courses of 4 semester hours each and maintain a minimum GPA of 2.0. In addition, all students must fulfill core course requirements in foreign language, fine arts, writing proficiency, 12 units are required in science and mathematics, foreign language, and cultural studies. To graduate, all students must complete a comprehensive exam; some majors require a thesis. **Procedure:** Freshmen are admitted in the fall. Entrance exams must be taken and the test scores received by February 1. There are early decision and deferred admissions plans. Early decision applications should be filed by November 15; regular applications, by January 15 for fall entry. The fall 2017 application fee was $60. Notification of early decision is sent December 15; regular decision, March 25. 130 early decision candidates were accepted for the 2017-2018 class. 359 applicants were on the 2017 waiting list; 26 were admitted. Applications are accepted on-line. **Transfer Students:** 36 transfer students enrolled in 2016-2017. Students must have at least a B average (3.0 GPA) in all courses submitted for transfer credit. The SAT or ACT is required. All high school and college transcripts, an statement of good standing from prior institution(s), and an interview are recommended. The application deadline is April 1 for fall, and November 1 for spring. 64 of 128 credits required for the bachelor's degree must be completed at Oxy. **International Students:** There are 121 international students enrolled. They must take the TOEFL with a minimum score of 600 on the paper-based TOEFL (PBT). They must also take the SAT or ACT.

ADMISSIONS: 45% of the 2017-2018 applicants were accepted. The SAT scores for the 2017-2018 freshman class were: Critical Reading-- 2% below 500, 22% between 500 and 599, 56% between 600 and 699, and 20% between 700 and 800. Math-- 1% below 500, 23% between 500 and 599, 53% between 600 and 699, and 24% between 700 and 800. Writing-- 1% below 500, 21% between 500 and 599, 55% between 600 and 699, and 23% between 700 and 800. The ACT scores were 2% between 18 and 23, 51% between 24 and 29, and 46% above 30. **Admissions Contact:** M. Teresa Kaldor, PhD., Director of Institutional Research. Email: *admission@oxy.edu* Web: *www.oxy.edu*

FINANCIAL AID: In 2017-2018, 73% of all full-time freshmen received some form of financial aid. 58% of all full-time freshmen received need-based aid. The average freshman award was $43,019. Need-based scholarships or need-based grants averaged $34,600 ($63,194 maximum); need-based self-help aid (loans and jobs) averaged $7,320 ($13,500 maximum); and other non-need-based awards and non-need-based scholarships averaged $11,113 ($49,248 maximum). The average financial indebtedness of the 2017 graduate was $29,940. Oxy is a member of CSS. The CSS/Profile, the state aid form, and non-custodial parent's statement are required. The FAFSA code is 001249. The priority date for freshman financial aid applications for fall entry is January 15.

OTIS COLLEGE OF ART AND DESIGN *(The complete profile is made available exclusively on our website, www.barronspac.com)*

PACIFIC UNION COLLEGE — B-2

www.puc.edu

Angwin, CA 94508	(707) 965-6336 (800) 862-7080
Fax: (707) 965-6432	Email: enroll@puc.edu
Full-time: 500 men, 575 women	**Faculty:** n/av
Part-time: 135 men, 165 women	**Ph.D.s:** n/av
Graduate: no men, 1 women	**Student/Faculty:** n/av
Year: trimesters, summer session	**Tuition:** $28,314
Room & Board: $7695	**Freshman Class:** n/av
SAT or ACT: recommended	**CEEB CODE:** 4600
Application Deadline: open	**VERY COMPETITIVE**

Pacific Union College, founded in 1888, is a private college affiliated with the Seventh-day Adventist Church, offering programs in liberal arts, religion, business, health science, and teacher preparation, among others. The figures in the above capsule and in this profile are approximate. There is 1 undergraduate school and 1 graduate school. In addition to regional accreditation, Pacific Union College has baccalaureate program accreditation with CSWE, NASM, NLN, CCTC, and IACBE. The 1500-acre campus is in a rural area 70 miles north of San Francisco. Including any residence halls, there are 60 buildings.

STUDENT LIFE: 76% of undergraduates are from California. Others are from 42 states, 26 foreign countries, and Canada. 7% are Foreign; 40% White; 4% African American; 29% Asian American; 15% Hispanic; 1% American Indian/Alaska Native. **Female To Male Ratio:** 1.2:1. The average age of freshmen is 19; all undergraduates, 21. 32% do not continue beyond their first year; 40% remain to graduate. **Housing:** 1344 students can be accommodated in college housing, which includes married student dorms. On-campus housing is guaranteed for the freshman year only. 76% of students live on campus. Alcohol is not permitted. All students may keep cars.

FACULTY/CLASSROOMS: 56% of faculty are male; 44% are female. All teach undergraduates. No introductory courses are taught by graduate students. The average class size in an introductory lecture is 19; in a laboratory is 18; and in a regular course is 17.

PROGRAMS OF STUDY: PUC confers B.A., B.S., B.B.A., B.Mus., and B.S.W. degrees. Associate and master's degrees are also awarded. Bachelor's degrees are awarded in BIOLOGICAL SCIENCE (biology/biological science and biophysics), BUSINESS (business administration and management), COMMUNICATIONS AND THE ARTS (communications, English, fine arts, French, graphic design, journalism, music, photography, public relations, radio/television technology, and Spanish), COMPUTER AND PHYSICAL SCIENCE (applied mathematics, chemistry, computer science, mathematics, natural sciences, and physics), EDUCATION (early childhood education and physical education), ENGINEERING AND ENVIRONMENTAL DESIGN (airline piloting and navigation and graphic arts technology), HEALTH PROFESSIONS (nursing), SOCIAL SCIENCE (history, psychology, religion, social studies, social work, and theological studies). Sciences and behavioral science is the strongest academically. Nursing and business administration has the largest enrollment.

ACTIVITIES: There are no fraternities or sororities. There are 50 groups on campus, including campus ministries, academic groups, art, band, chess, choir, chorale, computers, drama, ethnic, film, honors, jazz band, literary magazine, newspaper, orchestra, photography, political, radio and TV, religious, social, student government, symphony, and yearbook. Popular campus events include Picnic and Ski Days, All-College Get-Acquainted Party, Fall and Spring Festivals. **Sports:** There are 3 intercollegiate sports for men and 3 for women, and 6 intramural sports for men and 6 for women. Facilities include a gym, pool, tennis courts, and athletic fields for softball, soccer, volleyball, flag ball, and track and field. **Graduates:** From July 1, 2016 to June 30, 2017, 325 bachelor's degrees were awarded. The most popular majors were nursing (36%), business (19%), and chemistry (5%). In an average class, 12% graduate in 4 years or less, 19% graduate in 5 years or less, and 36% graduate in 6 years or less.

SERVICES: Counseling and information services are available, as is tutoring in most subjects. There is a reader service for the blind, and remedial math and writing. **Library/Resources:** The library contains 148,218 volumes, 125,268 microform items, and 6,623 audio/video tapes/CDs/DVDs, and subscribes to 10,637 periodicals including electronic. Computerized library services include interlibrary loans, database searching, Internet access, and Wi-Fi capability. Special learning facilities include an art gallery, natural history museum, radio station, a video production studio, an observatory and a marine field station. **Physically Challenged Students:** 95% of the campus is accessible. Facilities include wheelchair ramps, elevators, special parking, specially equipped restrooms, and special class scheduling. **Special:** Students may study abroad in Austria, Spain, France, Argentina, and Italy, earn B.A.-B.S. degrees, take dual majors, and pursue a major in interdisciplinary studies. Internships, social work, education, and ministerial field experiences, and accelerated degree programs in business management and early childhood education are also offered. The college offers nondegree study and credit for life, military, and work experience. There are 2 national honor societies and a freshman honors program. **Visiting:** There are regularly scheduled orientations for prospective students. There are guides for informal visits, visitors may sit in on classes, and stay overnight. To schedule a visit, contact the Admissions Office. **Campus Safety and Security:** Measures include 24-hour foot and vehicle patrol, emergency notification system, self-defense education, and security escort services. There are emergency telephones, lighted pathways/sidewalks, and a safety committee.

REQUIREMENTS: The SAT or ACT is recommended. Scores are used only for advising purposes. Candidates for admission should have completed 4 years of English, 2 of math, and 1 each of science and history. A GPA of 2.3 is required. AP and CLEP credits are accepted. Important factors in the admissions decision are recommendations by school officials, leadership record, and advanced placement or honors courses. To graduate, a student must complete a minimum of 192 quarter hours, including 60 in upper-level courses, maintain a minimum GPA of 2.0. Distribution requirements include courses in rhetoric, statistics, historic, philosophy, social science, foreign language, literature, visual and applied arts, music, math, science, and health and fitness. A religion course is required, as is a thesis in some programs. **Procedure:** Freshmen are admitted to all sessions. Entrance exams should be taken in the junior or senior year. There is a rolling admissions plan. Application deadlines are open. The fall 2017 application fee was $30. Applications are accepted on-line. **Transfer Students:** Admission requirements are the same as for nontransfer students. 36 of 192 credits required for the bachelor's degree must be completed at PUC. **International Students:** There are 92 international students enrolled. They must take the TOEFL. They must also take the SAT or ACT.

Admissions Contact: Darren Hagen, Director of Enrollment Services. Email: *enroll@puc.edu* Web: *www.puc.edu*

FINANCIAL AID: In 2017-2018, 100% of all full-time freshmen received some form of financial aid. 95% of all full-time freshmen received need-based aid. 80% of undergraduate students work part-time. The college's own financial statement is required. The FAFSA code is 001258. Check with the school for current application deadlines.

PEPPERDINE UNIVERSITY — C-4
www.pepperdine.edu

Malibu, CA 90263 — **(310) 506-4369**

Fax: (310) 506-4861 — **Email:** admission-seaver@pepperdine.edu

Full-time: 1305 men, 1915 women — **Faculty:** 377; IIA, ++$
Part-time: 149 men, 159 women — **Ph.D.s:** 88%
Graduate: 1735 men, 2549 women — **Student/Faculty:** 14 to 1
Year: semesters, summer session — **Tuition:** $51,992
Room & Board: $14,870 — **Freshman Class:** 11111 applied, 4097 accepted, 743 enrolled
SAT CR/M/W: 600/620/600 **ACT:** required — **CEEB CODE:** 4630
Application Deadline: January 5 — **VERY COMPETITIVE+**

Pepperdine University, founded in 1937, is a private liberal arts university affiliated with the Church of Christ. There are 5 undergraduate schools and 5 graduate schools. In addition to regional accreditation, Pepperdine has baccalaureate program accreditation with AACSB and NCATE. The 830-acre campus is in a suburban area 35 miles northwest of Los Angeles. Including any residence halls, there are 76 buildings.

STUDENT LIFE: 55% of undergraduates are from California. Others are from 50 states, 60 foreign countries, and Canada. 65% are from public schools. 48% are White; 14% Hispanic; 11% Asian American; 11% Foreign; 5% African American; 5% two or more races; 5% race unknown; 1% American Indian/Alaska Native. 16% are Catholic. **Female To Male Ratio:** 1.4:1. The average age of freshmen is 18; all undergraduates, 20. **Housing:** College-sponsored housing includes married student dorms, on-campus apartments, and off-campus apartments. In addition, there are honors houses and special-interest houses. On-campus housing is guaranteed for the freshman year only and is available on a lottery system for upperclassmen. 56% of students live on campus. Alcohol is not permitted. All students may keep cars.

FACULTY/CLASSROOMS: 58% of faculty are male; 42% are female. All teach undergraduates, and all do research. No introductory courses are taught by graduate students. The average class size in an introductory lecture is 18; in a laboratory is 15; and in a regular course is 17.

PROGRAMS OF STUDY: Pepperdine University confers B.A., B.S., and

B.S.M. degrees. Master's and doctoral degrees are also awarded. Bachelor's degrees are awarded in BIOLOGICAL SCIENCE (biology/biological science and nutrition), BUSINESS (accounting, business administration and management, international business management, management science, and marketing management), COMMUNICATIONS AND THE ARTS (advertising, art, art history and appreciation, communications, creative writing, dramatic arts, English, film arts, French, German, Italian, journalism, media arts, music, public relations, Spanish, speech/debate/rhetoric, and telecommunications), COMPUTER AND PHYSICAL SCIENCE (chemistry, computer science, mathematics, natural sciences, and physics), EDUCATION (elementary education, mathematics education, physical education, and secondary education), ENGINEERING AND ENVIRONMENTAL DESIGN (engineering), HEALTH PROFESSIONS (sports medicine), SOCIAL SCIENCE (economics, Hispanic American studies, history, humanities, international studies, liberal arts/general studies, philosophy, political science/government, psychology, religion, social science, and sociology). Natural sciences (premedical), sports medicine, and business administration are the strongest academically. Communication and business has the largest enrollment.

ACTIVITIES: There are 60 groups on campus, including Hawaiian club, women's leadership, art, band, cheerleading, chess, choir, chorale, chorus, computers, dance, debate, drama, environmental, ethnic, film, honors, international, jazz band, literary magazine, medical club, musical theater, newspaper, opera, orchestra, pep band, photography, political, professional, radio and TV, religious, social, social service, student government, symphony, and yearbook. Popular campus events include Waves Weekend, C2F (Culture and Club Fair), Songfest, and REEL Stories Student Film Festival. **Sports:** There are 8 intercollegiate sports for men and 9 for women, and 7 intramural sports for men and 7 for women. Facilities include a field house, pool, weight room, basketball, racquetball, tennis courts, playing fields, an all-weather track, and aerobics room. **Graduates:** From July 1, 2016 to June 30, 2017, 932 bachelor's degrees were awarded. The most popular majors were business/marketing (27%), communication/journalism (19%), and social science (11%).

SERVICES: Counseling and information services are available, as is tutoring in most subjects. **Library/Resources:** The library contains 551,502 volumes, 505,458 microform items, and 15,402 audio/video tapes/CDs/DVDs, and subscribes to 51,798 periodicals including electronic. Computerized library services include interlibrary loans, database searching, and Internet access. Special learning facilities include an art gallery, radio station, TV station, a writing center, and the academic center for excellence. **Physically Challenged Students:** 90% of the campus is accessible. Facilities include wheelchair ramps, elevators, special parking, specially equipped restrooms, special class scheduling, lowered drinking fountains, lowered telephones, and special housing. **Special:** Students may earn 1 to 4 units for an internship, available in most majors, participate in a Washington semester, and study abroad in 8 countries. The school offers a 3-2 engineering degree with Washington University in St. Louis and the University of Southern California. There are dual majors in any discipline, student-designed contract majors, federal work-study programs, nondegree study, and pass/fail options. There are 14 national honor societies and 6 departmental honors programs. **Visiting:** There are regularly scheduled orientations for prospective students, information sessions, campus tours, classroom visits, admission counselor meetings, and meeting faculty member. There are guides for informal visits, visitors may sit in on classes, and stay overnight. To schedule a visit, contact the Housing and Residence Life Office at (310) 506-7586. **Campus Safety and Security:** Measures include 24-hour foot and vehicle patrol, emergency notification system, self-defense education, and security escort services. There are shuttle buses, emergency telephones, lighted pathways/sidewalks, in-room safes, guarded entrances to campus, security cameras, and a campus crimewatch program.

REQUIREMENTS: The SAT or ACT is required. It is strongly recommended that candidates for admission present a college preparatory program that includes 4 years of English, 3 units of math, 2 units each of foreign language and science, speech communication, humanities, and social science. AP and CLEP credits are accepted. Important factors in the admissions decision are advanced placement or honors courses, personality/intangible qualities, extracurricular activities record, recommendations by school officials, and evidence of special talent. To graduate, students must complete 128 units, including 64 units of general education requirements. 2 years of a broad liberal arts core curriculum are needed. Courses are required in English, religion, Western heritage, non-Western heritage, American heritage, behavioral science, foreign language, lab science, math, speech and rhetoric, freshman seminar, and phys ed. Students must take at least 40 upper-division units and complete a 28-unit residency requirement. Pepperdine requires a minimum GPA of 2.0 for graduation. **Procedure:** Freshmen are admitted fall and spring. Entrance exams should be taken in the fall. There is a deferred admissions plan. Applications should be filed by January 5 for fall entry; October 15 for spring entry. The fall 2017 application fee was $65. Notifications are sent April 1. 1082 applicants were on the 2017 waiting list; 18 were admitted. Applications are accepted on-line. **Transfer Students:** 98 transfer students enrolled in 2016-2017. Transfer applicants should have a minimum GPA of 3.0 from an accredited college. SAT or ACT scores are required for applicants who have completed fewer than 30 transferable semester hours at an accredited college. 28 of 128 credits required for the bachelor's degree must be completed at Pepperdine. **International Students:** There are 290 international students enrolled. They must take the TOEFL with a minimum score of 550 on the paper-based TOEFL (PBT) or 80 on the Internet-based version (iBT) and the college's own test. They must also take the SAT.

ADMISSIONS: 37% of the 2017-2018 applicants were accepted. The SAT scores for the 2017-2018 freshman class were: Critical Reading-- 8% below 500, 41% between 500 and 599, 40% between 600 and 699, and 11% between 700 and 800. Math-- 7% below 500, 34% between 500 and 599, 42% between 600 and 699, and 17% between 700 and 800. Writing-- 9% below 500, 34% between 500 and 599, 47% between 600 and 699, and 10% between 700 and 800. The ACT scores were 10% between 18 and 23, 54% between 24 and 29, and 35% above 30. 74% of the current freshmen were in the top fifth of their class; 93% were in the top two fifths. **Admissions Contact:** Michael Truschke, Dean of Admission and Enrollment Management. Email: *admission-seaver@pepperdine.edu* Web: *www.pepperdine.edu*

FINANCIAL AID: In 2017-2018, 76% of all full-time freshmen received some form of financial aid. 53% of all full-time freshmen received need-based aid. The average freshman award was $39,268. Need-based scholarships or need-based grants averaged $35,742; need-based self-help aid (loans and jobs) averaged $4,768; non-need-based athletic scholarships averaged $42,432; other non-need-based awards and non-need-based scholarships averaged $22,552; and $4,474 from other forms of aid. The average financial indebtedness of the 2017 graduate was $23,493. The college's own financial statement, federal income tax form, state scholarship/grant form (California residents), and W-2 wage statements are required. The priority date for freshman financial aid applications for fall entry is February 15.

PITZER COLLEGE — D-5
www.pitzer.edu

Claremont, CA 91711	**(909) 621-8129** **(800) PITZER-1**
Fax: (909) 621-8770	**Email: admission@pitzer.edu**
Full-time: 411 men, 647 women	**Faculty:** 74; IIB, ++$
Part-time: 12 men, 29 women	**Ph.D.s:** 100%
Graduate: n/av	**Student/Faculty:** 12 to 1
Year: semesters, summer session	**Tuition:** $50,430
Room & Board: $16,264	**Freshman Class:** 3743 applied, 903 accepted, 272 enrolled
SAT CR/M: 652/641 **ACT:** 30	**CEEB CODE:** 4619
Application Deadline: January 1	**HIGHLY COMPETITIVE+**

Pitzer College, founded in 1963, is a private liberal arts college that through an interdisciplinary approach emphasizes social justice, intercultural understanding, and environmental sensitivity. Pitzer is one of the Claremont Colleges. The figures in the above capsule and in this profile are approximate. Tuition cost varies by programs chosen. There are 2 undergraduate schools. In addition to regional accreditation, Pitzer College has baccalaureate program accreditation with WASC. The 31-acre campus is in a suburban area 35 miles east of Los Angeles. Including any residence halls, there are 17 buildings.

STUDENT LIFE: 50% of undergraduates are from out of state, mostly the Northwest. Students are from 42 states, 14 foreign countries, and Canada. 8% are Asian American; 6% African American; 46% White; 3% Foreign; 16% Hispanic; 1% American Indian/Alaska Native. **Female To**

Male Ratio: 1.6:1. The average age of freshmen is 18; all undergraduates, 21. 7% do not continue beyond their first year; 80% remain to graduate. **Housing:** 734 students can be accommodated in college housing, which includes dorms and off-campus apartments. In addition, there are special-interest houses, a quiet hall, an involvement tower, food co-op, substance-free, and all-female floors. On-campus housing is guaranteed for the freshman year only. 75% of students live on campus. Upperclassmen may keep cars.

FACULTY/CLASSROOMS: 54% of faculty are male; 46% are female. All teach undergraduates, and all do research. No introductory courses are taught by graduate students. The average class size in an introductory lecture is 20; in a laboratory is 18; and in a regular course is 18.

PROGRAMS OF STUDY: Pitzer confers B.A. degrees. Bachelor's degrees are awarded in BIOLOGICAL SCIENCE (biochemistry, biology/biological science, and neurosciences), BUSINESS (management engineering and organizational behavior), COMMUNICATIONS AND THE ARTS (art, classics, dance, dramatic arts, English, film arts, French, linguistics, media arts, music, and Spanish), COMPUTER AND PHYSICAL SCIENCE (chemistry, mathematics, physics, science, and science and management), ENGINEERING AND ENVIRONMENTAL DESIGN (environmental science), SOCIAL SCIENCE (African American studies, American studies, anthropology, Asian/American studies, Asian/Oriental studies, Caribbean studies, economics, European studies, history, international relations, Latin American studies, Mexican-American/Chicano studies, philosophy, political science/government, psychology, sociology, Third World studies, and women's studies). Social and behavioral sciences are the strongest academically and have the largest enrollments.

ACTIVITIES: There are no fraternities or sororities. There are 50 groups on campus, including art, band, chess, choir, chorale, chorus, computers, dance, debate, drama, environmental, ethnic, film, honors, international, jazz band, LGBT, literary magazine, newspaper, orchestra, photography, political, professional, radio and TV, religious, social, social service, student government, and symphony. Popular campus events include the Kohoutek Festival, Hammock on the Mounds, and Reggae Festival. **Sports:** There are 10 intercollegiate sports for men and 11 for women. Facilities include gyms, swimming pools, tennis courts, numerous playing fields, and volleyball courts. There are also shared intercollegiate sports with Pomona College. The Gold Student Center features a fitness room, lap pool, Frisbee field, basketball and volleyball courts. **Graduates:** From July 1, 2016 to June 30, 2017, 244 bachelor's degrees were awarded. The most popular majors were psychology (17%), political studies, and and sociology (11%). In an average class, 75% graduate in 4 years or less, 80% graduate in 5 years or less, and 85% graduate in 6 years or less. Of the 2016 graduating class, 17% were enrolled in graduate school within 6 months of graduation, and 56% were employed.

SERVICES: Counseling and information services are available, as is tutoring in most subjects. There is tutoring software and programs for the learning disabled. There is a reader service for the blind, and remedial writing. **Library/Resources:** The library contains 250,000 volumes, 1.2 million microform items, and 17,000 audio/video tapes/CDs/DVDs, and subscribes to 35,000 periodicals including electronic. Computerized library services include interlibrary loans, database searching, Internet access, and Wi-Fi capability. Special learning facilities include an art gallery, radio station, a social science lab, an arboretum, and a farm in Costa Rica. **Physically Challenged Students:** 95% of the campus is accessible. Facilities include wheelchair ramps, elevators, special parking, specially equipped restrooms, lowered drinking fountains, lowered telephones, and special housing. **Special:** Students may cross-register at any of the other Claremont Colleges, or study abroad in 60 countries in Africa, Asia, Europe, Latin America, North America, or Oceania. There are co-op programs, work-study, internships, dual majors, student-designed majors, an extensive first-year seminar program, and interdisciplinary study offered in science and technology, and international or intercultural studies. Joint advanced degrees are offered in math, economics, M.I.S., psychology, and public policy, as is a 7-year B.A./D.O. program with the College of Western Health Sciences. There are independent study and limited pass/fail options. There is 1 national honor society and 18 departmental honors programs. **Visiting:** There are regularly scheduled orientations for prospective students. There are guides for informal visits, visitors may sit in on classes, and stay overnight. To schedule a visit, contact the Office of Admissions. **Campus Safety and Security:** Measures include 24-hour foot and vehicle patrol, emergency notification system, self-defense education, and security escort services. There are emergency telephones and lighted pathways/sidewalks.

REQUIREMENTS: Applicants must be graduates of an accredited secondary school or have earned the GED. Secondary school courses must include 4 years of English courses requiring extensive writing, and 3 years each of social and behavioral sciences including history, lab science, foreign language, and math. A personal essay is required and a personal interview is recommended. Students in the top 10% of their class or those with an unweighted GPA in academic subjects of 3.5 are not required to submit ACT or SAT scores. Students without these qualifications must submit either ACT or SAT scores, 2 SAT subject tests, 2 AP test scores of at least 4 (1 in English, 1 in math or science), 2 IB exams (English 1A and Mathematics Methods Standard Level or a higher-level course), or a recent analytical writing sample from a humanities or social science course and a math exam from a course at the algebra II level or higher, both including teacher's comments and grades. AP credits are accepted. Important factors in the admissions decision are advanced placement or honors courses, leadership record, and evidence of special talent. Students must complete a total of 32 courses with a 2.0 GPA. Although requirements vary according to major, most students take introductory or preparatory courses in their first 2 years and courses in or related to their major in the last 2 years. All students must fulfill educational objectives in the following areas: interdisciplinary and intercultural exploration, social responsibility and the ethical implications of knowledge and action, breadth of knowledge, and written expression. More than 10 courses are required in the major. **Procedure:** Freshmen are admitted fall and spring. Entrance exams should be taken by January 1. There are early decision and deferred admissions plans. Early decision applications should be filed by November 1; regular applications, by January 1 for fall entry; and October 15 for spring entry. The fall 2017 application fee was $50. Notifications are sent April 1. Applications are accepted on-line. **Transfer Students:** 21 transfer students enrolled in 2016-2017. No more than 2 years of previous credits may be transferred. 64 of 128 credits required for the bachelor's degree must be completed at Pitzer. **International Students:** There are 36 international students enrolled. They must take the TOEFL with a minimum score of 520 on the paper-based TOEFL (PBT) or 70 on the Internet-based version (iBT).

ADMISSIONS: 24% of the 2017-2018 applicants were accepted. The SAT scores for the 2017-2018 freshman class were: Critical Reading--15% between 500 and 599, 60% between 600 and 699, and 25% between 700 and 800. Math-- 24% between 500 and 599, 60% between 600 and 699, and 16% between 700 and 800. 75% of the current freshmen were in the top fifth of their class; 98% were in the top two fifths. **Admissions Contact:** Angel Perez, Vice President, Admission and Financial Aid. Email: *admission@pitzer.edu* Web: *www.pitzer.edu*

FINANCIAL AID: In 2017-2018, 34% of all full-time freshmen received some form of financial aid. 32% of all full-time freshmen received need-based aid. The average freshman award was $35,509. Need-based scholarships or need-based grants averaged $32,873; need-based self-help aid (loans and jobs) averaged $4,914; and other non-need-based awards and non-need-based scholarships averaged $5,000. Pitzer is a member of CSS. The CSS/Profile and the state aid form are required. The FAFSA code is 001172. The deadline for filing freshman financial aid applications for fall entry is February 1.

POINT LOMA NAZARENE UNIVERSITY D-5

www.pointloma.edu

San Diego, CA 92106 **(619) 849-2541**
(800) 733-7770

Fax: (619) 849-2601 **Email: admissions@pointloma.edu**

Full-time: 955 men, 1666 women	**Faculty:** IIB, ++$
Part-time: 137 men, 392 women	**Ph.D.s:** 85%
Graduate: 391 men, 926 women	**Student/Faculty:** n/av
Year: semesters, summer session	**Tuition:** $35,700
Room & Board: $10,450	**Freshman Class:** 3007 applied, 2294 accepted, 618 enrolled
SAT or ACT: required	**CEEB CODE:** 4605
Application Deadline: February 15	**COMPETITIVE+**

Point Loma Nazarene University, founded in 1902, is a private liberal arts university affiliated with the Church of the Nazarene. There are 6 undergraduate schools and 7 graduate schools. In addition to regional accreditation, PLNU has baccalaureate program accreditation with ACBSP, CSWE, NASM, CAEP, ACEND, CCTC, CAATE, and CCNE.

The 90-acre campus is in a suburban area in San Diego. Including any residence halls, there are 51 buildings.

STUDENT LIFE: 83% of undergraduates are from California. 7% are two or more races; 6% Asian American; 51% White; 3% African American; 3% race unknown; 28% Hispanic; 1% Foreign. **Female To Male Ratio:** 2.0:1. The average age of freshmen is 18; all undergraduates, 22. 11% do not continue beyond their first year; 74% remain to graduate. **Housing:** 1762 students can be accommodated in college housing, which includes dorms, on-campus apartments, and off-campus apartments. On-campus housing is available on a first-come, first-served basis, and is available on a lottery system for upperclassmen. 56% of students live on campus. Alcohol is not permitted. Upperclassmen may keep cars.

FACULTY/CLASSROOMS: 45% of faculty are male; 55% are female. No introductory courses are taught by graduate students.

PROGRAMS OF STUDY: PLNU confers B.A., B.S., B.Mus., B.S.N., B.S.Bus Admin, and B.BusAdmin. degrees. Master's and doctoral degrees are also awarded. Bachelor's degrees are awarded in BIOLOGICAL SCIENCE (biochemistry, biology/biological science, and nutrition), BUSINESS (accounting, business administration and management, business administration-international, business communications, business information systems, finance, marketing, and organizational leadership and management), COMMUNICATIONS AND THE ARTS (art history, art, art and design, art history and appreciation, broadcasting, communications, French, graphic design, graphic design & media, journalism, literature, media arts, multimedia, music, music composition, music ministry, music performance, piano performance, Spanish, speech/debate/rhetoric, vocal performance, and writing), COMPUTER AND PHYSICAL SCIENCE (chemistry, computer information technology, computer science, mathematics, and physics), EDUCATION (art education, athletic training, education, and music education), ENGINEERING AND ENVIRONMENTAL DESIGN (engineering physics and environmental science), HEALTH PROFESSIONS (exercise science, health science, and nursing), SOCIAL SCIENCE (biblical studies, child psychology/development, Christian studies, criminal justice, dietetics, economics, history, international studies, ministries, philosophy, political science/government, psychology, social science, social work, sociology, and youth ministry). Nursing, business administration, and biology are the strongest academically and have the largest enrollments.

ACTIVITIES: There are no fraternities or sororities. Groups on campus include art, band, cheerleading, choir, chorale, chorus, communications, computers, debate, drama, ethnic, film, forensics, honors, international, jazz band, literary magazine, musical theater, newspaper, opera, orchestra, photography, political, professional, radio and TV, religious, social, social service, student government, and yearbook. **Sports:** There are 4 intercollegiate sports for men and 7 for women. Facilities include a gym, baseball and soccer fields, a track, tennis courts, dorm lounges, and table tennis and pool tables. **Graduates:** From July 1, 2016 to June 30, 2017, 761 bachelor's degrees were awarded. In an average class, 67% graduate in 4 years or less, 76% graduate in 5 years or less, and 74% graduate in 6 years or less.

SERVICES: Counseling and information services are available, as is tutoring in most subjects. There is a reader service for the blind, and remedial math, reading, and writing. **Library/Resources:** Computerized library services include interlibrary loans, database searching, and Internet access. Special learning facilities include an art gallery, radio station, TV station, a lab preschool. **Physically Challenged Students:** All of the campus is accessible. Facilities include wheelchair ramps, elevators, special parking, specially equipped restrooms, special class scheduling, lowered drinking fountains, and lowered telephones. **Special:** PLNU offers internships in the church, in state and national governments, in journalism, small business, and in the film industry. Students may study abroad in several world capitals and in more than 40 countries. There are Washington and United Nations semester programs. Various dual or interdepartmental majors are offered, including biology-chemistry, graphic communications, human environmental science-business, and church music-youth ministries. There are pre-professional programs in medicine/dentistry, law, and engineering. A general studies degree in liberal studies is available, as is credit for life, military, and work experience for nursing students. There is a freshman honors program. **Visiting:** There are regularly scheduled orientations for prospective students, including campus tours and appointments with major advisers. There are guides for informal visits, visitors may sit in on classes, and stay overnight. To schedule a visit, contact the Admissions Office. **Campus Safety and Security:** Measures include 24-hour foot and vehicle patrol, emergency notification system, self-defense education, and security escort services. There are shuttle buses, emergency telephones, and lighted pathways/sidewalks.

REQUIREMENTS: The SAT or ACT is required. Candidates for admission should have completed 4 years of English, 3 of math, 2 each of a lab science and the same foreign language, and 1 of history. AP and CLEP credits are accepted. Important factors in the admissions decision are personality/intangible qualities, leadership record, and advanced placement or honors courses. To graduate, students must complete a minimum of 128 semester units. At least 24 upper-division semester units are needed for the major. A minimum GPA of 2.0 is required. Students must complete the general education requirements, though B.S.N. candidates need not take a foreign language. General education requirements include 9 courses in cultural studies, 5 in the sciences, 4 in cognitive studies, and 3 in religious studies. Students must demonstrate proficiency in writing and math. **Procedure:** Freshmen are admitted in the fall. Entrance exams should be taken in the junior year or early in the senior year. Applications should be filed by February 15 for fall entry. The fall 2017 application fee was $55. Notifications are sent April 1. Applications are accepted on-line. **Transfer Students:** 352 transfer students enrolled in 2016-2017. Transfer students must have a minimum cumulative GPA of 2.0 (based on transferable units) to be considered for admission. Applicants with at least 36 transferable units at the time of application need only submit college transcripts (high school transcripts are not required for these applicants). 24 of 128 credits required for the bachelor's degree must be completed at PLNU. **International Students:** There are 23 international students enrolled. They must take the TOEFL with a minimum score of 550 on the paper-based TOEFL (PBT) or 80 on the Internet-based version (iBT).

ADMISSIONS: 76% of the 2017-2018 applicants were accepted. The SAT scores for the 2017-2018 freshman class were: Math-- 6% below 500, 47% between 500 and 599, 41% between 600 and 699, and 6% between 700 and 800. Evidence-Based Reading/Writing-- 4% below 500, 38% between 500 and 599, 51% between 600 and 699, and 7% between 700 and 800. The ACT scores were 1% between 12 and 17, 26% between 18 and 23, 56% between 24 and 29, and 16% above 30. **Admissions Contact:** Shannon Hutchison, Director, Undergrad Admissions. Email: *admissions@pointloma.edu* Web: *www.pointloma.edu*

FINANCIAL AID: The average financial indebtedness of the 2017 graduate was $35,414. PLNU is a member of CSS. The FAFSA code is 001262. The priority date for freshman financial aid applications for fall entry is March 2.

POMONA COLLEGE — D-5

www.pomona.edu

Claremont, CA 91711	(909) 621-8134
Fax: (909) 621-8952	**Email:** admissions@pomona.edu
Full-time: 810 men, 832 women	**Faculty:** 188; IIB, ++$
Part-time: n/av	**Ph.D.s:** 92%
Graduate: n/av	**Student/Faculty:** 8 to 1
Year: semesters	**Tuition:** $49,352
Room & Board: $15,605	**Freshman Class:** 8102 applied, 765 accepted, 411 enrolled
SAT CR/M/W: 720/720/730 **ACT:** 32	**CEEB CODE:** 4607
Application Deadline: January 1	**MOST COMPETITIVE**

Pomona College, founded in 1887, is one of the nation's leading liberal arts colleges and the founding member of The Claremont Colleges, a consortium of 5 undergraduate and 2 graduate schools. In addition to regional accreditation, Pomona College has baccalaureate program accreditation with WASC. The 140-acre campus is in a suburban area 35 miles east of Los Angeles, and 20 miles east of Pasadena. Including any residence halls, there are 63 buildings.

STUDENT LIFE: 74% of undergraduates are from out of state, mostly the Midwest. Students are from 49 states, 63 foreign countries, and Canada. 55% are from public schools. 8% are African American; 7% two or more races; 5% race unknown; 38% White; 15% Hispanic; 14% Asian American; 11% Foreign. **Female To Male Ratio:** 1.0:1. The average age of freshmen is 18; all undergraduates, 20. 3% do not continue beyond their first year; 96% remain to graduate. **Housing:** 1660 students can be accommodated in college housing, which includes dorms and on-campus apartments, and language/international houses. On-campus housing is guaranteed for all 4 years. 98% of students live on campus. Upperclassmen may keep cars.

FACULTY/CLASSROOMS: 54% of faculty are male; 46% are female. All teach undergraduates and do research. No introductory courses are taught by graduate students. The average class size in a regular course is 15.

PROGRAMS OF STUDY: Pomona confers B.A. degrees. Bachelor's degrees are awarded in AGRICULTURE (environmental studies), BIOLOGICAL SCIENCE (biology/biological science, molecular biology, and neurosciences), COMMUNICATIONS AND THE ARTS (Africana studies, art history and appreciation, Chinese, classics, dance, English, fine arts, French, Japanese, languages, linguistics, literature, media arts, music, romance languages and literature, Russian, Spanish, studio art, and theatre arts), COMPUTER AND PHYSICAL SCIENCE (chemistry, computer science, geology, mathematics, physics, and science), ENGINEERING AND ENVIRONMENTAL DESIGN (technology and public affairs), SOCIAL SCIENCE (American studies, anthropology, Asian/American studies, Asian/Oriental studies, cognitive science, economics, German area studies, Hispanic American studies, history, international relations, Latin American studies, medieval studies, Mexican-American/Chicano studies, Middle Eastern studies, philosophy, political science/government, psychology, public affairs, religious studies, Russian and Slavic studies, sociology, and women's studies).

ACTIVITIES: 4% of men belong to 3 local fraternities. There are 200 groups on campus, including the Outdoors Club of the Claremont Colleges, art, band, chess, choir, chorus, dance, debate, drama, environmental, ethnic, film, honors, international, jazz band, LGBT, literary magazine, musical theater, newspaper, orchestra, pep band, photography, political, professional, radio and TV, religious, social, social service, student government, symphony, and yearbook. **Sports:** There are 10 intercollegiate sports for men and 11 for women, and 13 intramural sports for men and 13 for women. Facilities include an all-weather track, swimming pools, weight room, fitness center, dance studio, various playing fields, and courts for tennis, squash, racquetball, basketball, volleyball, and badminton. **Graduates:** From July 1, 2016 to June 30, 2017, 380 bachelor's degrees were awarded. The most popular majors were economics (12%), mathematics (10%), and computer science (8%). In an average class, 92% graduate in 4 years or less, 96% graduate in 5 years or less, and 97% graduate in 6 years or less. Of the 2016 graduating class, 20% were enrolled in graduate school within 6 months of graduation, and 35% were employed.

SERVICES: Counseling and information services are available, as is tutoring in most subjects. There is a reader service for the blind. **Library/Resources:** The library contains 2.0 million volumes, 1.4 million microform items, and 777 audio/video tapes/CDs/DVDs, and subscribes to 6,624 periodicals including electronic. Computerized library services include interlibrary loans, database searching, and Internet access. Special learning facilities include an art gallery, planetarium, radio station, observatory, modern languages and international relations center, and an organic farm. **Physically Challenged Students:** 80% of the campus is accessible. Facilities include wheelchair ramps, elevators, special parking, specially equipped restrooms, special class scheduling, lowered drinking fountains, and lowered telephones. **Special:** Students may cross-register at any of The Claremont Colleges, which are on adjacent campuses and follow the same academic schedule. Study abroad is offered through 49 programs in 31 countries. The Pomona College Internship Program provides students with paid part-time internships in the greater Los Angeles area. Paid internship opportunities are also offered in the summer. The college's Summer Undergraduate Research Program enables students to conduct extended, focused research in close cooperation with a Pomona faculty member. SURP funding includes room and board, a supply budget, and a stipend. Other opportunities include spending a semester in Washington, D.C., a 3-2 engineering program offered with the California Institute of Technology, Washington University in St. Louis, and Dartmouth College, spending one semester at Colby, Smith, Spelman, or Swarthmore colleges, independent study options, and dual and student-designed majors. There is a chapter of Phi Beta Kappa. **Visiting:** There are regularly scheduled orientations for prospective students, including interviews, information sessions, and guided tours. Visitors may sit in on classes and stay overnight. To schedule a visit, contact the Office of Admissions. **Campus Safety and Security:** Measures include 24-hour foot and vehicle patrol, emergency notification system, self-defense education, and security escort services. There are emergency telephones, lighted pathways/sidewalks, and controlled access to dorms/residences.

REQUIREMENTS: The SAT or ACT is required. Although applicants need not be graduates of accredited high schools (some may be admitted after the junior year), most are, or have earned the GED. Secondary preparation must include 4 years of English, 3 years each of math and foreign languages, and 2 years each of lab and social sciences. An interview is strongly recommended. AP credits are accepted. Important factors in the admissions decision are advanced placement or honors courses, recommendations by school officials, and extracurricular activities record. Pomona requires B.A. 32 credits, 30 of which must be completed post-matriculation. Students must satisfy the Breadth of Study requirement (one course in each of five areas), complete a first-year Critical Inquiry seminar, take one P.E. course in the first year, demonstrate proficiency in 3 semesters of the same foreign language, and satisfy the requirements for a major (including a senior exercise). **Procedure:** Freshmen students are admitted in the fall. Entrance exams should be taken before December of the senior year. There is a early decision plan. Early decision applications should be filed by November 1; regular applications, by January 1 for fall entry. The fall 2017 application fee was $70. Notification of early decision is sent December 15; regular decision, April 1. 196 early decision candidates were accepted for the 2017-2018 class. 608 applicants were on the 2017 waiting list; 26 were admitted. Applications are accepted on-line. **Transfer Students:** 13 transfer students enrolled in 2016-2017. Applicants must have completed at least 1 year (24 semester hours) of college-level courses at the time of enrollment. 16 of 32 credits required for the bachelor's degree must be completed at Pomona. **International Students:** There are 180 international students enrolled. They must take the TOEFL with a minimum score of 600 on the paper-based TOEFL (PBT) or 100 on the Internet-based version (iBT). They must also take the SAT or ACT.

ADMISSIONS: 9% of the 2017-2018 applicants were accepted. The SAT scores for the 2017-2018 freshman class were: Critical Reading-- 6% between 500 and 599, 31% between 600 and 699, and 63% between 700 and 800. Math-- 6% between 500 and 599, 29% between 600 and 699, and 65% between 700 and 800. Writing-- 6% between 500 and 599, 28% between 600 and 699, and 67% between 700 and 800. The ACT scores were 1% between 18 and 23, 16% between 24 and 29, and 82% above 30. 97% of the current freshmen were in the top fifth of their class; 100% were in the top two fifths. **Admissions Contact:** Seth Allen, Vice President and Dean of Admissions. Email: *admissions@pomona.edu* Web: *www.pomona.edu*

FINANCIAL AID: In 2017-2018, 57% of all full-time freshmen received some form of financial aid. 57% of all full-time freshmen received need-based aid. The average freshman award was $47,430. Need-based scholarships or need-based grants averaged $45,689; and need-based self-help aid (loans and jobs) averaged $1,741. The average financial indebtedness of the 2017 graduate was $13,381. Pomona is a member of CSS. The CSS/Profile is required. The priority date for freshman financial aid applications for fall entry is February 1. The deadline for filing freshman financial aid applications for fall entry is June 1.

SAINT MARY'S COLLEGE OF CALIFORNIA B-3

www.stmarys-ca.edu

Moraga, CA 94575	**(925) 631-4224** **(800) 800-4SMC**
Fax: (925) 376-7193	**Email: smcadmit@stmarys-ca.edu**
Full-time: 1106 men, 1675 women	**Faculty:** 194
Part-time: 101 men, 153 women	**Ph.D.s:** 95%
Graduate: 396 men, 797 women	**Student/Faculty:** 14 to 1
Year: 4-1-4, summer session	**Tuition:** $42,930
Room & Board: $14,490	**Freshman Class:** 5256 applied, 3448 accepted, 623 enrolled
SAT CR/M: 552/558 **ACT:** required	**CEEB CODE:** 4675
Application Deadline: February 1	**COMPETITIVE**

Saint Mary's College of California, founded in 1863, is a private, independent, liberal arts college affiliated with the Roman Catholic Church. The school offers undergraduate and graduate programs in liberal arts, nursing, economics and business administration, education, and pre-professional studies. There are 4 undergraduate schools and 3 graduate schools. In addition to regional accreditation, Saint Mary's College of California has baccalaureate program accreditation with NLN. The 420-

acre campus is in a suburban area 20 miles east of San Francisco. Including any residence halls, there are 77 buildings.

STUDENT LIFE: 84% of undergraduates are from California. Others are from 40 states, 18 foreign countries, and Canada. 57% are from public schools. 5% are African American; 48% White; 24% Hispanic; 2% Foreign; 11% Asian American; 1% American Indian/Alaska Native. 43% are Catholic; 39% claim no religious affiliation; 13% Protestant. **Female To Male Ratio:** 1.6:1. The average age of freshmen is 19; all undergraduates, 21. 13% do not continue beyond their first year; 87% remain to graduate. **Housing:** 1557 students can be accommodated in college housing, which includes dorms, on-campus apartments, and off-campus apartments. In addition, there are honors houses, special-interest houses, Lasallian and Santiago Living Communities. On-campus housing is guaranteed for the freshman year only and is available on a lottery system for upperclassmen. 62% of students live on campus. All students may keep cars.

FACULTY/CLASSROOMS: 48% of faculty are male; 52% are female. All teach undergraduates, and all do research. No introductory courses are taught by graduate students. The average class size in an introductory lecture is 25; in a laboratory is 16; and in a regular course is 20.

PROGRAMS OF STUDY: Saint Mary's College of California confers B.A. and B.S. degrees. Master's and doctoral degrees are also awarded. Bachelor's degrees are awarded in AGRICULTURE (environmental studies), BIOLOGICAL SCIENCE (biology/biological science), BUSINESS (accounting and business administration and management), COMMUNICATIONS AND THE ARTS (art, classical languages, communications, English, French, performing arts, and Spanish), COMPUTER AND PHYSICAL SCIENCE (chemistry, computer science, mathematics, and physics), EDUCATION (health education, physical education, and recreation education), ENGINEERING AND ENVIRONMENTAL DESIGN (environmental science and preengineering), HEALTH PROFESSIONS (health science), SOCIAL SCIENCE (anthropology, economics, history, international studies, liberal arts/general studies, philosophy, political science/government, psychology, religion, and sociology). Business administration, communications, and psychology have the largest enrollments.

ACTIVITIES: There are no fraternities or sororities. There are 41 groups on campus, including art, cheerleading, choir, chorale, chorus, dance, debate, drama, environmental, ethnic, forensics, honors, international, jazz band, LGBT, literary magazine, musical theater, newspaper, pep band, political, professional, radio and TV, religious, social, social service, and student government. Popular campus events include Cultural Nights, and Coffee House events. **Sports:** There are 7 intercollegiate sports for men and 9 for women, and 7 intramural sports for men and 7 for women. Facilities include a gym, football, baseball and recreational fields, swimming pool, tennis courts, soccer field and rugby pitch, weight room, and workout facility. **Graduates:** From July 1, 2016 to June 30, 2017, 598 bachelor's degrees were awarded. The most popular majors were business administration (19%), communication (12%), and psychology (10%). In an average class, 52% graduate in 4 years or less, 56% graduate in 5 years or less, and 57% graduate in 6 years or less. Of the 2016 graduating class, 14% were enrolled in graduate school within 6 months of graduation, and 64% were employed.

SERVICES: Counseling and information services are available, as is tutoring in most subjects. There is a reader service for the blind, and remedial writing. Tutoring is available in 1-on-1 sessions or group workshops. Readers, note takers, and other services are provided to learning or physically disabled students. **Library/Resources:** The library contains 412,735 volumes, 8,003 microform items, and 9,981 audio/video tapes/CDs/DVDs, and subscribes to 92,291 periodicals including electronic. Computerized library services include interlibrary loans, database searching, Internet access, and Wi-Fi capability. Special learning facilities include an art gallery, radio station, an observatory. **Physically Challenged Students:** 90% of the campus is accessible. Facilities include wheelchair ramps, elevators, special parking, specially equipped restrooms, special class scheduling, lowered drinking fountains, lowered telephones, and special housing. **Special:** The college offers seminars in all fields, dual and student-designed majors, study abroad in 8 countries, a Washington semester, work-study, cross-registration with the Regional Association of East Bay Colleges and Universities, and B.A.-B.S. liberal arts degree. There are 3-2 engineering programs with Washington University, the University of Southern California, and Boston University. There is a freshman honors program and 2 departmental honors programs. **Visiting:** There are regularly scheduled orientations for prospective students, weekdays and weekends (Sept.-May). There are guides for informal visits, visitors may sit in on classes, and stay overnight. **Campus Safety and Security:** Measures include 24-hour foot and vehicle patrol, emergency notification system, and security escort services. There are emergency telephones, lighted pathways/sidewalks, controlled access to dorms/residences, and late night transport/escort service.

REQUIREMENTS: The ACT is required, with the SAT preferred. Candidates should be graduates of an accredited secondary school, with 16 academic units, including 4 units in English and 1 unit each in algebra, advanced algebra, geometry, and U.S. history. It is recommended that the remaining units be made up of foreign language, lab science, and additional academic electives in the student's areas of strength. The GED is accepted. An essay is required. A GPA of 2.0 is required. AP and CLEP credits are accepted. Important factors in the admissions decision are recommendations by school officials, advanced placement or honors courses, and parents or siblings attended your school. To graduate, students must complete 36 course credits, including 17 at the upper-division level, with a GPA of 2.0 overall and in the major. Specific requirements include a 4-course Great Books seminar and 2 courses each in religious studies, humanities, math/science, written English, and social sciences. All students must demonstrate proficiency in a second language. **Procedure:** Freshmen are admitted to all sessions. Entrance exams should be taken by December of the senior year. There are early admissions and deferred admissions plans. Early decision applications should be filed by November 15; regular applications, by February 1 for fall entry; and January 1 for spring entry. The fall 2017 application fee was $55. Notification of early decision is sent December 15; regular decision, March 15. 894 applicants were on the 2017 waiting list; 167 were admitted. Applications are accepted on-line. **Transfer Students:** 199 transfer students enrolled in 2016-2017. Applicants must have a GPA of 2.3 and a minimum of 23 transferable academic semester units. 9 of 36 credits required for the bachelor's degree must be completed at SMC. **International Students:** There are 70 international students enrolled. They must take the TOEFL with a minimum score of 550 on the paper-based TOEFL (PBT) or 79 on the Internet-based version (iBT). Students must take the Comprehensive English Language Test, Nonactive English speakers who submit a minimum score or higher on the TOEFL may be admitted as full-time undergraduates.

ADMISSIONS: 66% of the 2017-2018 applicants were accepted. The SAT scores for the 2017-2018 freshman class were: Critical Reading-- 23% below 500, 49% between 500 and 599, 23% between 600 and 699, and 5% between 700 and 800. Math-- 23% below 500, 46% between 500 and 599, 29% between 600 and 699, and 4% between 700 and 800. The ACT scores were 13% below 12, 33% between 12 and 17, 27% between 18 and 23, 14% between 24 and 29, and 11% above 30. 51% of the current freshmen were in the top fifth of their class; 79% were in the top two fifths. 6 freshmen graduated first in their class. **Admissions Contact:** Michael McKeon, Assistant Vice Provost & Dean of Admissions. Email: *smcadmit@stmarys-ca.edu* Web: *www.stmarys-ca.edu*

FINANCIAL AID: In 2017-2018, 94% of all full-time freshmen received some form of financial aid. 89% of all full-time freshmen received need-based aid. The average freshman award was $31,979. Need-based scholarships or need-based grants averaged $24,082 ($31,200 maximum); need-based self-help aid (loans and jobs) averaged $6,640 ($7,500 maximum); non-need-based athletic scholarships averaged $36,486 ($59,470 maximum); and other non-need-based awards and non-need-based scholarships averaged $14,946 ($39,740 maximum). 60% of undergraduate students work part-time. The average financial indebtedness of the 2017 graduate was $33,000. Saint Mary's is a member of CSS. The priority date for freshman financial aid applications for fall entry is February 15.

SAN DIEGO CHRISTIAN COLLEGE D-5

www.sdcc.edu

Santee, CA 92071	**(619) 588-8700** **(800) 676-2242**
Fax: (619) 590-1739	**Email: admissions@sdcc.edu**
Full-time: 330 men, 335 women	**Faculty:** n/av
Part-time: 40 men, 47 women	**Ph.D.s:** n/av
Graduate: n/av	**Student/Faculty:** n/av
Year: semesters, summer session	**Tuition:** $29,614
Room & Board: $11,300	**Freshman Class:** n/av
SAT or ACT: required	**CEEB CODE:** 4150
Application Deadline: open	**COMPETITIVE**

San Diego Christian College is a small, private institution founded in 1970 by the Scott Memorial Baptist Church of San Diego, offering programs in the liberal arts, business, and education. The figures given in the above capsule and in this profile are approximate. There is 1 undergraduate school. In addition to regional accreditation, SDCC has baccalaureate program accreditation with WASC and ACSI. The 32-acre campus is in a suburban area 15 miles east of San Diego. Including any residence halls, there are 14 buildings.

STUDENT LIFE: 80% of undergraduates are from California. 75% are from public schools. 70% are White; 4% Asian American; 2% Foreign; 10% African American; 10% Hispanic; 1% American Indian/Alaska Native. 100% are Protestant. **Female To Male Ratio:** 1.0:1. The average age of freshmen is 18; all undergraduates, 21. 40% do not continue beyond their first year; 30% remain to graduate. **Housing:** 200 students can be accommodated in college housing, which includes dorms and off-campus apartments. In addition, there are language/international houses. On-campus housing is guaranteed for all 4 years, is available on a first-come, and first-served basis. 50% of students commute. Alcohol is not permitted. All students may keep cars.

FACULTY/CLASSROOMS: 60% of faculty are male; 40% are female. All teach undergraduates. No introductory courses are taught by graduate students. The average class size in an introductory lecture is 40; in a laboratory is 15; and in a regular course is 16.

PROGRAMS OF STUDY: SDCC confers B.A. and B.S. degrees. Associate degrees are also awarded. Bachelor's degrees are awarded in BIOLOGICAL SCIENCE (biology/biological science), BUSINESS (business administration and management), COMMUNICATIONS AND THE ARTS (communications, English, and music), COMPUTER AND PHYSICAL SCIENCE (mathematics), EDUCATION (education), ENGINEERING AND ENVIRONMENTAL DESIGN (aviation administration/management), SOCIAL SCIENCE (biblical studies, history, human development, interdisciplinary studies, liberal arts/general studies, physical fitness/movement, and psychology). Counseling psychology, education, and business are the strongest academically. Business, education, and human development have the largest enrollments.

ACTIVITIES: There are no fraternities or sororities. There are 16 groups on campus, including art, cheerleading, choir, chorale, chorus, computers, drama, honors, international, musical theater, newspaper, pep band, political, religious, social, student government, and yearbook. Popular campus events include Spring, Winter, Valentine's Day Banquets, and the Missions Conference. **Sports:** There are 3 intercollegiate sports for men and 4 for women, and 5 intramural sports for men and 4 for women. Facilities include a swimming pool, gym, outdoor courts for tennis, volleyball, and basketball, soccer and softball fields.

SERVICES: Counseling and information services are available, as is tutoring in some subjects. Tutors are recruited as needed for most general education courses. There is remedial math, reading, and writing. **Library/Resources:** The library contains 69,435 volumes, 80 microform items, and 61,522 audio/video tapes/CDs/DVDs, and subscribes to 30,475 periodicals including electronic. Computerized library services include interlibrary loans, database searching, and Internet access. **Physically Challenged Students:** 90% of the campus is accessible. Facilities include wheelchair ramps, elevators, special parking, and special class scheduling. **Special:** Students attend chapel 3 times each week, participate in an annual Bible conference, and complete a student ministry assignment each semester. Independent study for 1 to 3 credits can be arranged. There are internships in psychology, pastoral studies, and education. **Visiting:** There are regularly scheduled orientations for prospective students, including a campus tour, cafeteria meal, and class and chapel attendance. There are guides for informal visits, visitors may sit in on classes, and stay overnight. To schedule a visit, contact the Admissions Office. **Campus Safety and Security:** Measures include 24-hour foot and vehicle patrol, and emergency notification system. The campus is fenced with lighted pathways/sidewalks.

REQUIREMENTS: The SAT required, the ACT is preferred. Applicants must have a high school diploma or the GED, or have successfully completed the California State High School Proficiency Exam. Secondary preparation should include 4 units of English, 3 each of math, natural science, and social studies, and 2 of a single foreign language. A personal essay is also required. In addition, applicants must meet certain spiritual requirements. A GPA of 2.3 is required. AP and CLEP credits are accepted. Important factors in the admissions decision are recommendations by school officials, leadership record, and extracurricular activities record. The required credits for graduation vary by degree program and major. All students must take 46 to 52 credits in sciences and math, social science, and humanities, 20 credits in personal Christian development and biblical studies, and the balance in major field requirements and electives. A 2.0 GPA is required for graduation. **Procedure:** Freshmen are admitted fall and spring. Entrance exams should be taken during the junior year. There is a rolling admissions plan. Application deadlines are open. The fall 2017 application fee was $25. Notification is sent on a rolling basis. **Transfer Students:** 30 of 124 credits required for the bachelor's degree must be completed at SDCC. **International Students:** They must take the TOEFL and the college's own test. They must also take the SAT or ACT, scoring 900.

Admissions Contact: Christine Roberts, Director of Admissions. Email: *admissions@sdcc.edu* Web: *www.sdcc.edu*

FINANCIAL AID: SDCC is a member of CSS. The college's own financial statement is required. The FAFSA code is 012031. Check with the school for current application deadlines.

SAN DIEGO STATE UNIVERSITY — D-5

www.sdsu.edu

San Diego, CA 92182	**(619) 594-6336** **(855) 594-3983** **Email: admissions@sdsu.edu**
Full-time: 12,318 men, 14,710 women	**Faculty:** 876; I, -$
Part-time: 1506 men, 1631 women	**Ph.D.s:** 88%
Graduate: 1804 men, 2859 women	**Student/Faculty:** n/av
Year: semesters, summer session	**Tuition:** $7190 ($19,340)
Room & Board: $15,966	**Freshman Class:** 60697 applied, 21379 accepted, 5366 enrolled
SAT CR/M: 592/593 **ACT:** 25	**CEEB CODE:** 4682
Application Deadline: November 30	**VERY COMPETITIVE**

San Diego State University, founded in 1897, is a public research university that is part of the California State University system. There are 8 undergraduate schools. In addition to regional accreditation, SDSU has baccalaureate program accreditation with AACSB, ABET, ACEJMC, CAHEA, CSWE, NASAD, NRPA, ACEND, ACGME, ACME, ACS, APA, BRN, CAA, CAATE, CAPTE, CCNE, CEPH, CGS, CIDA, COAMFTE, CORE, CSWE, CTC, NAEYC, NASP, NASPAA, NAST, NCRE, and WAGS. The 283-acre campus is in an urban area 8 miles east of downtown San Diego. Including any residence halls, there are 108 buildings.

STUDENT LIFE: 91% of undergraduates are from California. Others are from 49 states, 114 foreign countries, and Canada. 91% are from public schools. 7% are Foreign; 7% two or more races; 4% African American; 4% race unknown; 33% White; 31% Hispanic; 13% Asian American. **Female To Male Ratio:** 1.2:1. The average age of freshmen is 19; all undergraduates, 22. 11% do not continue beyond their first year. **Housing:** 5187 students can be accommodated in college housing, which includes gender neutral, coed dorms and on-campus apartments. In addition, there are honors houses, language/international houses, special-interest houses, a living/learning center, Aztec engineering residence, substance-free and quiet-study housing, and apartments for single students. On-campus housing is available on a first-come and first-served basis. 86% of students commute. All students may keep cars.

FACULTY/CLASSROOMS: 50% of faculty are male; 50% are female. No introductory courses are taught by graduate students. The average class size in an introductory lecture is 75; in a laboratory is 18; and in a regular course is 54.

PROGRAMS OF STUDY: SDSU confers B.A., B.F.A., B.S., and B.M. degrees. Master's and doctoral degrees are also awarded. Bachelor's degrees are awarded in AGRICULTURE (environmental studies), BIOLOGICAL SCIENCE (biology/biological science, ecology, microbiology, nutrition, and zoology), BUSINESS (accounting, business administration and management, finance, financial services, hospitality management services, human resources/organizational mgmt, international business management, international security/conflict resolution mgmt, management & strategic leadership, marketing/retailing/merchandising, real estate, and production and operations management), COMMUNICATIONS AND THE ARTS (advertising, art history, art, classics, communications, comparative literature, dance, English, English Writing, French, German, graphic design, Japanese, journalism, linguistics, media management, multimedia, music, music performance, public relations, recreation administration, radio/television technology, Russian, Spanish, communication arts - speech, studio art, and theatre arts), COMPUTER AND PHYSICAL SCIENCE (applied mathematics, astronomy, chemical physics, chemistry, computer science, geology, information sciences and systems, mathematics, physical sciences, physics, and statistics), EDUCATION (athletic training and music education), ENGINEERING AND ENVIRONMENTAL DESIGN (aerospace engineering, civil engineering, computer engineering, construction engineering, electrical/electronics engineering, engineering, environmental engineering, environmental science, interior design, and mechanical engineering), HEALTH PROFESSIONS (communicative disorders, exercise science, health communication, health science, kinesiology, nursing, public health, and speech pathology/audiology), SOCIAL SCIENCE (African American studies, American Indian studies, anthropology, Asian/Oriental studies, child psychology/development, criminal justice, economics, European studies, gender studies, geography, gerontology, history, humanities, interdisciplinary studies, international studies, Latin American studies, liberal arts/general studies, Mexican-American/Chicano studies, modern jewish studies, philosophy, political science/government, psychology, public administration, public policy/public service, religious studies, Russian and Slavic studies, social science, social work, sociology, urban studies, and women's studies). Psychology, physical education/kinesiology, and mechanical engineering have the largest enrollments.

ACTIVITIES: 11% of men belong to 23 national fraternities; 13% of women belong to 22 national sororities. There are 310 groups on campus, including art, band, cheerleading, choir, chorale, chorus, dance, debate, drama, drill team, environmental, ethnic, film, honors, international, jazz band, LGBT, literary magazine, marching band, musical theater, newspaper, opera, orchestra, pep band, political, professional, radio and TV, religious, social, social service, student government, and symphony. Popular campus events include Student Involvement Expo, Welcome Week, Aztec Nights, Midnight Breakfast Finals Week, and Explore SDSU. **Sports:** There are 6 intercollegiate sports for men and 13 for women, and 8 intramural sports for men and 8 for women. Facilities include a gym, basketball, racquetball, tennis, volleyball courts, a swimming pool/aquaplex, track, soccer, softball, baseball, football fields, an aquatic center, weight room, bowling and gymnastic equipment, cardio room, and a climbing wall. **Graduates:** From July 1, 2016 to June 30, 2017, 7085 bachelor's degrees were awarded. The most popular majors were psychology (8%), criminal justice administration (5%), and kinesiology (5%). In an average class, 36% graduate in 4 years or less, 67% graduate in 5 years or less, and 75% graduate in 6 years or less.

SERVICES: Counseling and information services are available, as is tutoring in most subjects. There is a reader service for the blind. **Library/Resources:** Computerized library services include interlibrary loans, database searching, Internet access, and Wi-Fi capability. Special learning facilities include an art gallery, planetarium, radio station, TV station, performing arts theatres and recital halls, seismology and weather stations. **Physically Challenged Students:** 99% of the campus is accessible. Facilities include wheelchair ramps, elevators, special parking, specially equipped restrooms, special class scheduling, lowered drinking fountains, lowered telephones, and special housing. **Special:** SDSU has opportunities for cross-registration, distance learning, double major, English as a Second Language (ESL), exchange student program (domestic), external degree program, honors program, independent study, internships, liberal arts/career combination, student-designed major, study abroad, and teacher certification program. There are 26 national honor societies, Phi Beta Kappa, and a freshman honors program. **Visiting:** There are regularly scheduled orientations for prospective students, including tours that can be scheduled with SDSU ambassadors. **Campus Safety and Security:** Measures include 24-hour foot and vehicle patrol, emergency notification system, self-defense education, and security escort services. There are shuttle buses, emergency telephones, lighted pathways/sidewalks, and controlled access to dorms/residences.

REQUIREMENTS: The SAT or ACT is required. Applicants must have a qualifying CSU eligibility index, based on a combination of GPA and standardized test scores. Candidates for admission should have completed 4 years of English, 3 years of math (4 recommended), 2 years each of science and foreign language, and 1 year each of social studies, U.S. history, visual/performing arts, and academic elective. AP and CLEP credits are accepted. To graduate, students must complete a minimum of 120 units, including 49 general education units. The number of units in the major varies by program. A 2.0 or higher GPA must be maintained, depending on the major. Students must demonstrate math and writing competency and fulfill requirements in upper-division writing and in American Institutions. Certain majors require a senior thesis. **Procedure:** Freshmen are admitted fall. Entrance exams should be taken by October of the senior year. Applications should be filed by November 30 for fall entry. The fall 2017 application fee was $55. Notifications are sent in March. 1630 applicants were on the 2017 waiting list; 9 were admitted. Applications are accepted on-line. **Transfer Students:** 3297 transfer students enrolled in 2016-2017. Transfer applicants are required to declare a major and have completed all preparation for the major courses and pre-major requirements if applicable. In addition, all lower division general education (GE) courses must be completed. Must have "C-" grades in four required classes: GE oral communication, GE written communication, GE critical thinking, and GE mathematics (above the level of intermediate algebra). Different application policies apply for applicants in and out of SDSU service area and for applicants in impacted majors. Refer to the Office of Admission website for more information. 30 of 120 credits required for the bachelor's degree must be completed at SDSU. **International Students:** There are 2775 international students enrolled. They must take the TOEFL with a minimum score of 550 on the paper-based TOEFL (PBT) or 80 on the Internet-based version (iBT). Students must take the college's own test, the IELTS, scoring 6.5 or higher, and either the SAT or ACT.

ADMISSIONS: 35% of the 2017-2018 applicants were accepted. The SAT scores for the 2017-2018 freshman class were: Math-- 8% below 500, 44% between 500 and 599, 41% between 600 and 699, and 8% between 700 and 800. Evidence-Based Reading/Writing-- 8% below 500, 43% between 500 and 599, 45% between 600 and 699, and 5% between 700 and 800. The ACT scores were 3% between 12 and 17, 29% between 18 and 23, 54% between 24 and 29, and 15% above 30. 61% of the current freshmen were in the top fifth of their class; 89% were in the top two fifths. **Admissions Contact:** Sabrina Cortell, Director of Admissions. Email: *admissions@sdsu.edu* Web: *www.sdsu.edu*

FINANCIAL AID: In 2017-2018, 61% of all full-time freshmen received some form of financial aid. 50% of all full-time freshmen received need-based aid. The average freshman award was $8,000. Need-based scholarships or need-based grants averaged $9,500; need-based self-help aid (loans and jobs) averaged $3,100; non-need-based athletic scholarships averaged $22,400; and other non-need-based awards and non-need-based scholarships averaged $3,300. The average financial indebtedness of the 2017 graduate was $17,500. SDSU is a member of CSS. The state aid form is required. The FAFSA code is 001151. The priority date for freshman financial aid applications for fall entry is April 1.

SAN FRANCISCO ART INSTITUTE *(The complete profile is made available exclusively on our website, www.barronspac.com)*

SAN FRANCISCO CONSERVATORY OF MUSIC *(The complete profile is made available exclusively on our website, www.barronspac.com)*

SAN FRANCISCO STATE UNIVERSITY *(The complete profile is made available exclusively on our website, www.barronspac.com)*

SAN JOSE STATE UNIVERSITY — B-3

www.sjsu.edu

San Jose, CA 95192 — **(408) 283-7500**

	Email: admissions@sjsu.edu
Full-time: 11,931 men, 11,116 women	**Faculty:** 2001; IIA, +$
Part-time: 2519 men, 2161 women	**Ph.D.s:** n/av
Graduate: 2411 men, 2757 women	**Student/Faculty:** 14 to 1
Year: semesters, summer session	**Tuition:** $7418 ($16,346)
Room & Board: $15,212	**Freshman Class:** 31555 applied, 16862 accepted, 3208 enrolled
SAT CR/M/W: 503/522/497 **ACT:** 22	**CEEB CODE:** 4687
Application Deadline: November 30	**COMPETITIVE**

San Jose State University, founded in 1857 and part of the California State University system, is a public institution offering undergraduate and graduate programs in applied arts and science, social science, and social work to a primarily commuter student body. The figures in the above capsule and in this profile are approximate. There are 8 undergraduate schools and 8 graduate schools. In addition to regional accreditation, San Jose has baccalaureate program accreditation with AACSB,

ABET, ACEJMC, ADA, APTA, CSWE, NASAD, NASM, CAEP, and NRPA. The 154-acre campus is in an urban area in the center of the city of San Jose, CA. Including any residence halls, there are 64 buildings.

STUDENT LIFE: 94% of undergraduates are from California. 128 foreign countries, and Canada. 93% are from public schools. 9% are race unknown; 32% Asian American; 3% African American; 26% Hispanic; 17% White; 12% Foreign. **Male To Female Ratio:** 1.1:1. The average age of freshmen is 19; all undergraduates, 22. 87% do not continue beyond their first year; 65% remain to graduate. **Housing:** 4300 students can be accommodated in college housing, which includes dorms and on-campus apartments. In addition, there are language/international houses, fraternity houses, and sorority houses. On-campus housing is available on a first-come and first-served basis. Alcohol is not permitted. All students may keep cars.

FACULTY/CLASSROOMS: 49% of faculty are male; 51% are female. 97% teach undergraduates. No introductory courses are taught by graduate students. The average class size in an introductory lecture is 32 and in a laboratory is 18.

PROGRAMS OF STUDY: SJSU confers B.A., B.S., B.F.A., and B.Mus. degrees. Master's and doctoral degrees are also awarded. Bachelor's degrees are awarded in AGRICULTURE (environmental studies), BIOLOGICAL SCIENCE (biochemistry, biology/biological science, botany, forensic science, marine science, microbiology, nutritional sciences, and zoology), BUSINESS (accounting, banking and finance, business administration and management, business administration marketing, business information systems, entrepreneurial studies, finance, financial institutions management, financial institutions management, human resources, international business, international business management, marketing/retailing/merchandising, and transportation management), COMMUNICATIONS AND THE ARTS (advertising, art history, broadcasting, Chinese, communication studies, dance, design, dramatic arts, English, film arts, fine arts, French, German, information technology, Japanese, jazz, journalism, linguistics, literature, music, public relations, Spanish, and theatre arts), COMPUTER AND PHYSICAL SCIENCE (applied mathematics, atmospheric sciences and meteorology, chemistry, computer science, geology, mathematics, natural sciences, physics, software engineering, and statistics), EDUCATION (early childhood education, education, education administration, education of the deaf and hearing impaired, education of the physically handicapped, global studies, library science, music education, and recreation education), ENGINEERING AND ENVIRONMENTAL DESIGN (aeronautical engineering, applied aviation, biomedical engineering, chemical engineering, civil engineering, computer engineering, electrical/electronics engineering, engineering, industry & systems engineering, interior design, materials engineering, mechanical engineering, and urban planning technology), HEALTH PROFESSIONS (health science, hospital administration, kinesiology, nursing, occupational therapy, public health, and speech pathology/audiology), SOCIAL SCIENCE (anthropology, child care/child and family studies, communication sciences & disorders, criminal justice, economics, food science, geography, history, interdisciplinary studies, Mexican-American/Chicano studies, philosophy, political science/government, psychology, religion, religious studies, social science, social work, and sociology). Accounting, engineering are the strongest academically. Psychology, accounting, and electrical engineering have the largest enrollments.

ACTIVITIES: There are 394 groups on campus, including cheerleading, choir, chorale, communications, computers, dance, drama, ethnic, film, forensics, international, jazz band, LGBT, literary magazine, marching band, newspaper, opera, orchestra, pep band, professional, radio and TV, religious, student government, and symphony. Popular campus events include International Food Bazaar, Fall Welcome Day, and National Collegiate Alcohol Awareness Week. **Sports:** There are 7 intercollegiate sports for men and 12 for women, and 25 intramural sports for men and 26 for women. Facilities include a gym, pool, track, football field, baseball field, a recreation center with racquetball courts and a bowling alley. **Graduates:** From July 1, 2016 to June 30, 2017, 6186 bachelor's degrees were awarded. The most popular majors were psychology (5%), accounting (4%), and communication studies (4%). In an average class, 13% graduate in 4 years or less, 47% graduate in 5 years or less, and 56% graduate in 6 years or less.

SERVICES: Counseling and information services are available, as is tutoring in most subjects. There is a reader service for the blind, and remedial math, reading, and writing. There are also test accommodations, sign-language interpreters, liaisons to faculty, and note takers. **Library/Resources:** The library contains 920,971 volumes, and 24,527 audio/video tapes/CDs/DVDs, and subscribes to 375,676 periodicals including electronic. Computerized library services include interlibrary loans, database searching, Internet access, and Wi-Fi capability. Special learning facilities include an art gallery and a radio station. **Physically Challenged Students:** All of the campus is accessible. Facilities include wheelchair ramps, elevators, special parking, specially equipped restrooms, special class scheduling, lowered drinking fountains, lowered telephones, special housing, and preadmission assistance. **Special:** San Jose State University offers study abroad programs in Austria, Thailand, South Korea, and Ireland, special majors, university studies, and internships in 12 majors. There are 7 national honor societies, a freshman honors program, and 8 departmental honors programs. **Visiting:** There are regularly scheduled orientations for prospective students, Prospective students are given a 60 minute walking tour around campus with a current student. To schedule a visit, contact the Admission Office. **Campus Safety and Security:** Measures include 24-hour foot and vehicle patrol, emergency notification system, self-defense education, and security escort services. There are shuttle buses, emergency telephones, lighted pathways/sidewalks, controlled access to dorms/residences, and canine patrol.

REQUIREMENTS: The SAT or ACT is required. Scores are used to calculate an eligibility index rating, which determines qualification for admission. Graduation from an accredited secondary school is required; the GED is accepted. Applicants must have completed 4 years of English, 3 each of math and electives, 2 of a foreign language, and 1 each of history, science, and art. A GPA of 2.0 is required. AP and CLEP credits are accepted. Students must complete 39 units of core general education, including 12 units of upper-division courses in residence and 6 units of history and institutions. A minimum of 120 credits, with at least 24 in the major, a minimum GPA of 2.0, and the successful completion of writing, English, and entry-level math tests are required to graduate. **Procedure:** Freshmen are admitted fall. Entrance exams should be taken prior to the fall semester. There are early admissions and rolling admissions plans. Applications should be filed by November 30 for fall entry. The fall 2017 application fee was $55. Notifications are sent November 30. Applications are accepted on-line. **Transfer Students:** 3977 transfer students enrolled in 2016-2017. Applicants must have a minimum GPA of 2.0. The student's rating in the eligibility index is also considered in determining qualification for transfer. 30 of 120 credits required for the bachelor's degree must be completed at SJSU. **International Students:** There are 1616 international students enrolled. They must take the TOEFL with a minimum score of 61 on the Internet-based version (iBT). They must also take the SAT or ACT.

ADMISSIONS: 53% of the 2017-2018 applicants were accepted. The SAT scores for the 2017-2018 freshman class were: Critical Reading-- 46% below 500, 40% between 500 and 599, 13% between 600 and 699, and 2% between 700 and 800. Math-- 37% below 500, 20% between 500 and 599, 38% between 600 and 699, and 4% between 700 and 800. Writing-- 52% below 500, 34% between 500 and 599, 12% between 600 and 699, and 2% between 700 and 800. The ACT scores were 12% between 12 and 17, 48% between 18 and 23, 34% between 24 and 29, and 5% above 30. **Admissions Contact:** Deanna Gonzales, Director of Undergraduate Admission. Email: *admissions@sjsu.edu* Web: *www.sjsu.edu*

FINANCIAL AID: In 2017-2018, 40% of all full-time freshmen received some form of financial aid. 36% of all full-time freshmen received need-based aid. The average freshman award was $17,359. Need-based scholarships or need-based grants averaged $10,649; need-based self-help aid (loans and jobs) averaged $6,781; non-need-based athletic scholarships averaged $12,691; and other non-need-based awards and non-need-based scholarships averaged $813. The average financial indebtedness of the 2017 graduate was $19,797. The state aid form is required. The FAFSA code is 001155. Check with the school for current application deadlines.

SCRIPPS COLLEGE D-5

www.scrippscollege.edu

Claremont, CA 91711	(909) 621-8578 (800) 770-1333
Fax: (909) 607-7508	**Email:** admission@scrippscollege.edu
Full-time: 1056 women	**Faculty:** 94; IIB, ++$
Part-time: 3 women	**Ph.D.s:** 99%
Graduate: 7 men, 11 women	**Student/Faculty:** 10 to 1
Year: semesters	**Tuition:** $52,966
Room & Board: $16,294	**Freshman Class:** 2841 applied, 948 accepted, 327 enrolled
SAT or ACT: required	**CEEB CODE:** 4693
Application Deadline: January 1	**HIGHLY COMPETITIVE**

Scripps College, founded in 1926, is a private liberal arts institution for women. A member of the Claremont Colleges, Scripps emphasizes a challenging core curriculum based on interdisciplinary humanistic studies. There are 5 undergraduate schools. In addition to regional accreditation, Scripps College has baccalaureate program accreditation with WASC. The 33-acre campus is in a suburban area 35 miles east of Los Angeles.

STUDENT LIFE: 53% are White; 5% two or more races; 4% African American; 4% race unknown; 16% Asian American; 13% Hispanic. **Female To Male Ratio:** 152.9:1. **Housing:** College-sponsored housing includes dorms, on-campus apartments, and off-campus apartments, foreign language corridors, and living learning communities. On-campus housing is guaranteed for all 4 years. All students may keep cars.

FACULTY/CLASSROOMS: 38% of faculty are male; 62% are female. All teach and do research. No introductory courses are taught by graduate students. The average class size in a regular course is 15.

PROGRAMS OF STUDY: Scripps confers B.A. and B.S. degrees. Bachelor's degrees are awarded in AGRICULTURE (environmental studies), BIOLOGICAL SCIENCE (biology/biological science, molecular biology, and neurosciences), COMMUNICATIONS AND THE ARTS (art history and appreciation, Chinese, classical languages, communications, dance, dramatic arts, English, Germanic languages and literature, Italian, Japanese, languages, music, Russian, Spanish, and studio art), COMPUTER AND PHYSICAL SCIENCE (chemistry, computer science, geology, mathematics, physics, science and management, and science technology), ENGINEERING AND ENVIRONMENTAL DESIGN (environmental science and preengineering), SOCIAL SCIENCE (African American studies, American studies, anthropology, Asian/American studies, Asian/Oriental studies, classical/ancient civilization, economics, European studies, French studies, German area studies, Hispanic American studies, history, humanities, Italian studies, Judaic studies, Latin American studies, law, Mexican-American/Chicano studies, philosophy, political science/government, prelaw, psychology, religion, sociology, and women's studies). Biology, psychology, and English have the largest enrollments.

ACTIVITIES: There are no fraternities or sororities. There are 35 groups on campus, including art, choir, chorale, chorus, computers, dance, debate, drama, environmental, ethnic, film, honors, international, LGBT, literary magazine, musical theater, newspaper, orchestra, photography, political, professional, religious, social, social service, student government, symphony, and yearbook. Popular campus events include Spring Fling Carnival, Levitt on the Lawn, Weekly Tea, and Scripps Outdoor Adventure Program. **Sports:** There are 11 intercollegiate sports for women, and 6 intramural sports for women. Facilities include a field house with an aerobics studio, cardio machine room, weight room, swimming pool, soccer/lacrosse fields, tennis courts, a climbing wall, an outdoor track, and fields for baseball and softball, and space for fitness and health programs. **Graduates:** From July 1, 2016 to June 30, 2017, 254 bachelor's degrees were awarded. The most popular majors were biology (21%), psychology (7%), and English (6%). In an average class, 83% graduate in 4 years or less, 87% graduate in 5 years or less, and 88% graduate in 6 years or less.

SERVICES: Counseling and information services are available, as is tutoring in every subject. There is a reader service for the blind. **Library/Resources:** Computerized library services include interlibrary loans, database searching, Internet access, and Wi-Fi capability. Special learning facilities include an art gallery, a humanities museum and biological field station. **Physically Challenged Students:** Facilities include wheelchair ramps, elevators, special parking, specially equipped restrooms, special class scheduling, lowered drinking fountains, and special housing. **Special:** Students may cross-register with any of the other Claremont Colleges. Scripps also offers study abroad in 36 countries, a Washington semester, and student-designed, dual, and interdisciplinary majors, including organizational studies and science, technology, and society. Many courses are offered as seminars. There are 4-1 accelerated degree programs in the arts and business administration. A 3-2 engineering program (B.A.-B.S.) is offered with Harvey Mudd College. There are 7 national honor societies and a chapter of Phi Beta Kappa. **Visiting:** There are guides for informal visits, visitors may sit in on classes, and stay overnight. To schedule a visit, contact the Admission Office. **Campus Safety and Security:** Measures include 24-hour foot and vehicle patrol, emergency notification system, self-defense education, and security escort services. There are emergency telephones, lighted pathways/sidewalks, and controlled access to dorms/residences.

REQUIREMENTS: The SAT or ACT is required. Applicants must have completed 4 units each of high school English and math, 3 each of lab science and social studies, and either 3 of a single foreign language or 2 each of 2 languages. SAT Subject Tests and an interview are recommended. An essay and a graded writing assignment from the junior or senior year are required. AP and CLEP credits are accepted. Students must complete a total of 32 courses, or 128 units, with at least a C average. Requirements include a 3-semester humanities core, a first-year writing/critical thinking course, and 1 course each in fine arts, letters, natural science, math, foreign language, social science, gender and women's studies, and race and ethnic studies. A senior thesis or project is also required. **Procedure:** Freshmen are admitted fall and spring. Entrance exams should be taken by December of the senior year. There are early decision, early admissions, and deferred admissions plans. Early decision applications should be filed by November 15; regular applications, by January 1 for fall entry; and November 1 for spring entry. The fall 2017 application fee was $60. Notification of early decision is sent December 15; regular decision, April 1. 239 applicants were on the 2017 waiting list; 1 were admitted. Applications are accepted on-line. **Transfer Students:** 17 transfer students enrolled in 2016-2017. A cumulative college GPA of 3.0 is recommended 16 credits required for the bachelor's degree must be completed at Scripps. **International Students:** They must take the TOEFL with a minimum score of 600 on the paper-based TOEFL (PBT) or 100 on the Internet-based version (iBT). They must also take the SAT or ACT.

ADMISSIONS: 33% of the 2017-2018 applicants were accepted. **Admissions Contact:** Victoria Romero, VP for Enrollment. Email: *admission@scrippscollege.edu* Web: *www.scrippscollege.edu*

FINANCIAL AID: Scripps is a member of CSS. The CSS/Profile and the state aid form are required. The FAFSA code is 001174. The deadline for filing freshman financial aid applications for fall entry is February 1.

SHEPHERD UNIVERSITY *(The complete profile is made available exclusively on our website, www.barronspac.com)*

SIMPSON UNIVERSITY B-2

www.simpsonu.edu

Redding, CA 96003 **(530) 224-5600**

Fax: (530) 226-4861	**Email:** admissions@simpsonu.edu
Full-time: 322 men, 665 women	**Faculty:** 43
Part-time: 12 men, 20 women	**Ph.D.s:** 56%
Graduate: 102 men, 176 women	**Student/Faculty:** 15 to 1
Year: semesters, summer session	**Tuition:** $26,722
Room & Board: $8000	**Freshman Class:** 533 applied, 317 accepted, 158 enrolled
SAT CR/M/W: 500/500/490 **ACT:** 21	**CEEB CODE:** 4698
Application Deadline: open	**COMPETITIVE**

Simpson University, founded in 1921, is a Christian university offering undergraduate, graduate, and teaching credential programs. Simpson University is an official institution of the Christian and Missionary Alliance, and the student population represents more than 25 evangelical denominations. The figures in the above capsule and in this profile are approximate. There is 1 undergraduate school and 3 graduate schools. In addition to regional accreditation, Simpson has baccalaureate program accreditation with WASC. The 92-acre campus is in a suburban area in the northeast city limits of Redding. Including any residence halls, there are 17 buildings.

STUDENT LIFE: 87% of undergraduates are from California. Others are from 27 states, and 7 foreign countries. 59% are from public schools. 9% are Hispanic; 7% Asian American; 60% White; 4% African American; 2% American Indian/Alaska Native; 1% Foreign. 99% are Protestant. **Female To Male Ratio:** 2.0:1. The average age of freshmen is 18; all undergraduates, 25. 35% do not continue beyond their first year; 45% remain to graduate. **Housing:** 590 students can be accommodated in college housing, which includes married student dorms and off-campus apartments. In addition, there are special-interest houses, and the Gatehouse- Missionary Kid housing. On-campus housing is guaranteed for all 4 years. 55% of students commute. Alcohol is not permitted. All students may keep cars.

FACULTY/CLASSROOMS: 52% of faculty are male; 48% are female.

65% teach undergraduates. No introductory courses are taught by graduate students. The average class size in an introductory lecture is 42; in a laboratory is 11; and in a regular course is 11.

PROGRAMS OF STUDY: Simpson confers B.A. and B.S. degrees. Associate and master's degrees are also awarded. Bachelor's degrees are awarded in BIOLOGICAL SCIENCE (biology/biological science), BUSINESS (accounting, business administration and management, human resources, organizational leadership and management, and recreation and leisure services), COMMUNICATIONS AND THE ARTS (communications, English, and music), COMPUTER AND PHYSICAL SCIENCE (mathematics), EDUCATION (elementary education, English education, mathematics education, music education, secondary education, and social science education), HEALTH PROFESSIONS (health care administration and nursing), SOCIAL SCIENCE (biblical studies, crosscultural studies, history, liberal arts/general studies, ministries, missions, pastoral studies, psychology, religion, religious education, social science, and youth ministry). Biology, nursing, and music are the strongest academically. Psychology, business administration, and liberal studies have the largest enrollments.

ACTIVITIES: There are no fraternities or sororities. There are 20 groups on campus, including commuter students association, psychology, band, choir, chorale, computers, drama, ethnic, film, golf, international, jazz band, newspaper, orchestra, photography, professional, religious, social, social service, student government, symphony, and yearbook. Popular campus events include Spring Banquet, Missions Emphasis Week, and Airband. **Sports:** There are 5 intercollegiate sports for men and 6 for women, and 2 intramural sports for men and 1 for women. Facilities include a soccer field, a gym, weight and training rooms, softball field, outdoor volleyball and basketball courts. Students have access to nearby facilities for swimming, boating, mountain climbing, and skiing. **Graduates:** From July 1, 2016 to June 30, 2017, 300 bachelor's degrees were awarded. The most popular majors were liberal arts (18%), psychology (18%), and human resources management (9%). In an average class, 1% graduate in 3 years or less, 32% graduate in 4 years or less, 43% graduate in 5 years or less, and 45% graduate in 6 years or less.

SERVICES: Counseling and information services are available, as is tutoring in every subject. There is remedial math and writing. **Library/Resources:** The library contains 176,640 volumes, 242,910 microform items, and 3,253 audio/video tapes/CDs/DVDs, and subscribes to 24,334 periodicals including electronic. Computerized library services include interlibrary loans, database searching, Internet access, and Wi-Fi capability. **Physically Challenged Students:** 95% of the campus is accessible. Facilities include wheelchair ramps, elevators, special parking, specially equipped restrooms, lowered drinking fountains, lowered telephones, and special housing. **Special:** Off-campus educational programs are offered through the China Studies Program, Contemporary Music Program in Martha's Vineyard, Latin American Studies Program, Los Angeles Film Studies Center, Middle East Studies Program, Oxford Honors Program, and the Russian Studies Program. Students may study abroad in a variety of countries. Internships are available in Christian education, pastoral studies, youth ministries, business, and psychology. Work-study programs in elementary education and with the federal government are also available. There is also a 1-year, nondegree certificate program in Bible and contemporary church music. There are 2 national honor societies and 1 departmental honors program. **Visiting:** There are regularly scheduled orientations for prospective students, Genesis Weekend. There are guides for informal visits, visitors may sit in on classes, and stay overnight. To schedule a visit, contact the Visit Coordinator at (530) 226-4769. **Campus Safety and Security:** Measures include 24-hour foot and vehicle patrol, emergency notification system, and security escort services. There are emergency telephones, lighted pathways/sidewalks, controlled access to dorms/residences, emergency whistle program, local police patrols, and monthly campus safety meetings.

REQUIREMENTS: The SAT or ACT is required. Applicants must be graduates of an accredited high school or have a GED. It is recommended that applicants have completed 4 years of high school English, 3 each of math, science, and social studies/history, and 2 of a foreign language. A GPA of 2.0 is required. AP and CLEP credits are accepted. Important factors in the admissions decision are leadership record, personality/intangible qualities, and recommendations by school officials. Students must complete at least 124 credits, with a minimum of 36 upper-division credits and at least 42 major credits (of which 24 must be upper division). A minimum GPA of 2.0 must be maintained. Foundational studies requirements include 24 credits in biblical studies and theology and 41 credits in human expression, human history and behavior, and global environment. **Procedure:** Freshmen are admitted to all sessions. Entrance exams should be taken during the junior year or in the fall of the senior year. There are deferred admissions and rolling admissions plans. Application deadlines are open. The fall 2017 application fee was $25. Notification is sent on a rolling basis. Applications are accepted on-line. **Transfer Students:** 98 transfer students enrolled in 2016-2017. Transfer applicants with at least 30 semester college credits need not submit SAT or ACT scores. 30 of 124 credits required for the bachelor's degree must be completed at Simpson. **International Students:** There are 7 international students enrolled. They must take the TOEFL with a minimum score of 500 on the paper-based TOEFL (PBT) or 79 on the Internet-based version (iBT). They must also take the SAT or ACT.

ADMISSIONS: 59% of the 2017-2018 applicants were accepted. The SAT scores for the 2017-2018 freshman class were: Critical Reading-- 35% below 500, 41% between 500 and 599, 22% between 600 and 699, and 2% between 700 and 800. Math-- 36% below 500, 50% between 500 and 599, and 14% between 600 and 699. Writing-- 42% below 500, 43% between 500 and 599, and 15% between 600 and 699. The ACT scores were 44% below 12, 26% between 12 and 17, 13% between 18 and 23, 11% between 24 and 29, and 4% above 30. 53% of the current freshmen were in the top fifth of their class; 71% were in the top two fifths. **Admissions Contact:** Kendell Kluttz, Director of Admissions. Email: *admissions@simpsonu.edu* Web: *www.simpsonu.edu*

FINANCIAL AID: In 2017-2018, 100% of all full-time freshmen received some form of financial aid. 91% of all full-time freshmen received need-based aid. The average freshman award was $14,815. Need-based scholarships or need-based grants averaged $15,600 ($25,400 maximum); need-based self-help aid (loans and jobs) averaged $4,300 ($9,000 maximum); non-need-based athletic scholarships averaged $7,227 ($9,000 maximum); and other non-need-based awards and non-need-based scholarships averaged $7,610 ($21,600 maximum). 27% of undergraduate students work part-time. The average financial indebtedness of the 2017 graduate was $17,524. Simpson University is a member of CSS. The college's own financial statement is required. The FAFSA code is 001291. The priority date for freshman financial aid applications for fall entry is October 1.

SONOMA STATE UNIVERSITY — B-3

www.sonoma.edu

Rohnert Park, CA 94928 — (707) 664-2874

Email: student.outreach@sonoma.edu

Full-time: 2902 men, 4955 women	**Faculty:** IIA, av$
Part-time: 321 men, 373 women	**Ph.D.s:** 63%
Graduate: 187 men, 485 women	**Student/Faculty:** 23 to 1
Year: semesters, summer session	**Tuition:** $13,466 ($19,574)
Room & Board: $13,554	**Freshman Class:** 15711 applied, 12888 accepted, 1831 enrolled
SAT EBR-W/M: 539/522 **ACT:** 21	**CEEB CODE:** 4723
Application Deadline: November 30	**COMPETITIVE**

Sonoma State University, founded in 1960, and part of the California State University system, offers undergraduate programs in business and economics, natural sciences, social sciences, and arts and humanities, and graduate programs in education, counseling, public administration, biology and business. There are 6 undergraduate schools and 1 graduate school. In addition to regional accreditation, Sonoma State University has baccalaureate program accreditation with AACSB, NASAD, NASM, CAEP, NLN, ACS, CTC, and NLNAC. The 269-acre campus is in a suburban area 45 miles north of San Francisco.

STUDENT LIFE: 44% are White; 35% Hispanic; 7% two or more races; 6% race unknown; 5% Asian American; 2% African American; 2% Foreign; 1% American Indian/Alaska Native. **Female To Male Ratio:** 1.7:1. The average age of freshmen is 18; all undergraduates, 22. **Housing:** College-sponsored housing includes dorms and on-campus apartments. In addition, there are special-interest houses, women in math/science, housing for learning communities, freshman seminar dorms, wellness housing, substance-free, and intensive-study houses. On-campus housing is available on a first-come and first-served basis. All students may keep cars.

FACULTY/CLASSROOMS: 46% of faculty are male; 54% are female. No introductory courses are taught by graduate students.

PROGRAMS OF STUDY: SSU confers B.A., B.F.A., and B.S. degrees. Master's degrees are also awarded. Bachelor's degrees are awarded in BIOLOGICAL SCIENCE (biochemistry and biology/biological science), BUSINESS (business administration and management), COMMUNICATIONS AND THE ARTS (art, communications, English, fine arts, French, music, Spanish, and visual and performing arts), COMPUTER AND PHYSICAL SCIENCE (chemistry, computer science, geology, mathematics, and physics), ENGINEERING AND ENVIRONMENTAL DESIGN (environmental science), HEALTH PROFESSIONS (nursing), SOCIAL SCIENCE (African American studies, American Indian studies, anthropology, criminal justice, economics, ethnic studies, gender studies, geography, history, human development, interdisciplinary studies, international studies, Latin American studies, liberal arts/general studies, Mexican-American/Chicano studies, philosophy, physical fitness/movement, political science/government, psychology, sociology, and women's studies). Business, psychology, and early childhood studies have the largest enrollments.

ACTIVITIES: Groups on campus include art, cheerleading, chess, choir, chorale, chorus, computers, dance, drama, ethnic, honors, jazz band, LGBT, literary magazine, musical theater, newspaper, opera, orchestra, pep band, political, professional, religious, social, social service, student government, and symphony. Popular campus events include Big Night, Science Night, Parents Day, and Unity Through Diversity Week. **Sports:** There are 5 intercollegiate sports for men and 9 for women. Facilities include a stadium, a gym, a field house, tennis courts, a pool, an auditorium, and various playing fields, a recreation facility includes gymnasiums, a soccer arena, fitness center, climbing wall, outdoor adventure resource and equipment rental area, and exercise studios. **Graduates:** From July 1, 2016 to June 30, 2017, 2461 bachelor's degrees were awarded. The most popular majors were business administration (20%), psychology (9%), and sociology (8%).

SERVICES: Counseling and information services are available, as is tutoring in most subjects. There is a reader service for the blind, and remedial math, reading, and writing. Learning disability assessment is also available. **Library/Resources:** Computerized library services include interlibrary loans, database searching, Internet access, and Wi-Fi capability. Special learning facilities include an art gallery, a performing arts center, an observatory, electron microscope, seismograph, environmental technology center, green music center and natural preserves. **Physically Challenged Students:** All of the campus is accessible. Facilities include wheelchair ramps, elevators, special parking, specially equipped restrooms, special class scheduling, lowered drinking fountains, lowered telephones, a reading machine, phonic listening devices, PC and mainframe access, and interpreters are also available. **Special:** Students may cross-register at Mills College, Oakland, and University of California, Berkeley. Study-abroad programs are available in 17 countries. Community service internships, work-study, nondegree study through Open University, and pass/fail grading options are available. B.A. and B.S. options in biology, chemistry, environmental studies, geology, interdisciplinary studies, math, and physics are offered. The Hutchins School B.A. in liberal studies offers small seminar classes and an interdisciplinary curriculum. Distance learning programs in nursing are available at 3 off-site centers. **Visiting:** There are regularly scheduled orientations for prospective students, consisting of programs in the spring and summer. There are guides for informal visits and visitors may sit in on classes. To schedule a visit, contact the Admissions Development Office. **Campus Safety and Security:** Measures include 24-hour foot and vehicle patrol, emergency notification system, self-defense education, and security escort services. There are emergency telephones and lighted pathways/sidewalks.

REQUIREMENTS: The SAT is required. Applicants should be graduates of accredited high school or have earned the GED. Secondary school preparation should include 4 years of English, 3 year of math, 2 years each of science, foreign language and history, and 1 each of visual/performing arts, academic electives, science with lab. A GPA of 2.0 is required. AP and CLEP credits are accepted. Undergraduate students must complete 120 to 132 units, depending on the degree program, consisting of 48 to 51 units of general education, a concentration of study in a specific major, and electives. General education programs require experience in oral and written communications, critical thinking, natural science and math, arts and humanities, social sciences, and personal integration. All students must take an ethnic studies course and the equivalent of courses in U.S. government, U.S. history, and California government. **Procedure:** Freshmen are admitted fall and spring. There is a rolling admissions plan. Applications should be filed by November 30 for fall entry. The fall 2017 application fee was $55. Applications are accepted on-line. **Transfer Students:** Applicants must have a minimum 2.0 GPA. The maximum number of transferable credits is 70. 30 of 120 credits required for the bachelor's degree must be completed at Sonoma State. **International Students:** There are 188 international students enrolled. They must take the TOEFL with a minimum score of 500 on the paper-based TOEFL (PBT) or 61 on the Internet-based version (iBT). They must also take the SAT or ACT.

ADMISSIONS: 82% of the 2017-2018 applicants were accepted. The SAT scores for the 2017-2018 freshman class were: Math-- 30% below 500, 53% between 500 and 599, 16% between 600 and 699, and 1% between 700 and 800. Evidence-Based Reading/Writing-- 24% below 500, 54% between 500 and 599, 21% between 600 and 699, and 1% between 700 and 800. The ACT scores were 17% between 12 and 17, 55% between 18 and 23, 26% between 24 and 29, and 2% above 30. **Admissions Contact:** Natalie Kalogiannis, Director of Admissions. Email: *student.outreach@sonoma.edu* Web: *www.sonoma.edu*

FINANCIAL AID: The average freshman award was $10,004. Need-based scholarships or need-based grants averaged $10,498; and need-based self-help aid (loans and jobs) averaged $3,145. The FAFSA code is 001156. The priority date for freshman financial aid applications for fall entry is January 31. The deadline for filing freshman financial aid applications for fall entry is rolling.

STANFORD UNIVERSITY — B-3

www.stanford.edu

Stanford, CA 94305 — **(650) 723-2091**

Fax: (650) 723-6050
Email: admission@stanford.edu

Full-time: 3704 men, 3315 women
Part-time: 30 men, 40 women
Graduate: 6687 men, 4693 women
Year: quarters, summer session
Room & Board: $14,107
SAT or ACT: required
Application Deadline: January 3

Faculty: I, ++$
Ph.D.s: 99%
Student/Faculty: 4 to 1
Tuition: $46,302
Freshman Class: 42167 applied, 2145 accepted, 1678 enrolled
CEEB CODE: 4704
MOST COMPETITIVE

Stanford University is a research institution, with seven schools: business, earth sciences, education, engineering, humanities & sciences, law and medicine. Areas of academic excellence cross disciplines, ranging from humanities to social sciences to engineering and the sciences. There are 7 undergraduate schools and 3 graduate schools. In addition to regional accreditation, Stanford has baccalaureate program accreditation with AACSB and ABET. The 8180-acre campus is in an urban area 30 miles south of San Francisco, 20 miles north of San Jose and adjacent to the cities of Palo Alto and Menlo Park. Including any residence halls, there are 700 buildings.

STUDENT LIFE: 53% of undergraduates are from out of state, mostly the South. Students are from 50 states, 90 foreign countries, and Canada. 58% are from public schools. 8% are African American; 8% Foreign; 43% White; 3% race unknown; 23% Asian American; 2% American Indian/Alaska Native; 13% Hispanic. **Male To Female Ratio:** 1.3:1. The average age of freshmen is 18; all undergraduates, 20. 1% do not continue beyond their first year; 95% remain to graduate. **Housing:** 6503 students can be accommodated in college housing, which includes single-sex and coed dorms, on-campus apartments, off-campus apartments, and married student housing. In addition, there are language houses, special-interest houses, fraternity houses, sorority houses, Ethnic theme houses, substance free housing, and academic interest. On-campus housing is guaranteed for all 4 years. 92% of students live on campus; of those, 95% remain on campus on weekends. Upperclassmen may keep cars.

FACULTY/CLASSROOMS: 73% of faculty are male; 27% are female. All teach undergraduates, and do research. No introductory courses are taught by graduate students.

PROGRAMS OF STUDY: Stanford confers A.B., B.S. and B.A.S. degrees. Master's and doctoral degrees are also awarded. Bachelor's degrees are awarded in BIOLOGICAL SCIENCE (biology/biological science), BUSINESS (management engineering and product design), COMMUNICATIONS AND THE ARTS (art, art history and appreciation, Chinese, classics, communications, comparative literature, dramatic arts, English, film arts, fine arts, French, Italian, Japanese, linguistics, music, Slavic languages, Spanish, and studio art), COMPUTER AND PHYSICAL SCIENCE (chemistry, computer science, earth science, geology, geophysics and seismology, geoscience, mathematics, mathematics/computational, and physics), ENGINEERING AND ENVIRONMENTAL DESIGN (aeronautical engineering, architectural engineering, bioengineering, chemical engineering, civil engineering, electrical/electronics engineering, engineering, engineering physics, environmental engineering, industrial engineering, materials science, mechanical engineering, petroleum/natural gas engineering, and systems engineering), SOCIAL SCIENCE (African American studies, American studies, anthropology, archeology, area studies, Asian/American studies, crosscultural studies, East Asian studies, economics, German area studies, Hispanic American studies, history, Iberian studies, international relations, Judaic studies, Latin American studies, Native American studies, philosophy, political science/government, psychology, public administration, religion, sociology, systems science, urban studies, and women's studies). Computer science, human biology, and engineering have the largest enrollments.

ACTIVITIES: 24% of men belong to 16 national fraternities; 28% of women belong to 14 national sororities. There are 625 groups on campus, including art, band, cheerleading, chess, choir, chorale, chorus, computers, dance, debate, drama, environmental, ethnic, film, honors, international, jazz band, LGBT, literary magazine, marching band, musical theater, newspaper, opera, orchestra, pep band, photography, political, professional, radio and TV, religious, social, social service, student government, symphony, and yearbook. Popular campus events include The Big Game, Full Moon on the Quad, Gaities, Fountain Hopping, and Viennese Ball. **Sports:** There are 16 intercollegiate sports for men and 20 for women. Facilities include athletic fields, gyms, swimming pools, volleyball courts, lighted tennis courts, dance studios, climbing wall, weight rooms, golf course, sailing facility, rowing facility, handball, racquetball, squash courts, baseball diamond, football stadium, softball stadium, soccer stadium, field hockey, and lacrosse. **Graduates:** From July 1, 2015 to June 30, 2016, 1723 bachelor's degrees were awarded. The most popular majors were interdisciplinary studies (18%), engineering (16%), and social sciences (15%). 350 companies recruited on campus in 2015-2016. In an average class, 95% graduate in 6 years or less.

SERVICES: Counseling and information services are available, as is tutoring in most subjects. There is a reader service for the blind. Schwab Learning Center offers services for students with learning disabilities and attention-deficit hyperactivity disorder. **Library/Resources:** The 20 libraries contain 9.3 million volumes, 6.0 million microform items, and 2.5 million audio/video tapes/CDs/DVDs, and subscribe to 77,000 periodicals including electronic. Computerized library services include interlibrary loans, database searching, Internet access, and Wi-Fi capability. Special learning facilities include an art gallery, radio station, TV station, 3 art museums, concert hall, biological preserve, linear accelerator, and an observatory. **Physically Challenged Students:** 98% of the campus is accessible. Facilities include wheelchair ramps, elevators, special parking, specially equipped restrooms, special class scheduling, lowered drinking fountains, lowered telephones, special housing. Stanford has a Diversity and Access Office and an Office of Accessible Education to provide help. **Special:** Internships, study abroad, a Washington semester, a New York City program, Marine research center, semester at sea, 12 overseas study programs, dual majors, a B.A.-B.S. degree, research opportunities, honors programs and co-terminal bachelor's and master's programs. Also offered on a pilot basis are joint majors that integrate humanities, and computer science. There is a chapter of Phi Beta Kappa. **Visiting:** There are regularly scheduled orientations for prospective students, including group information sessions and campus tours. There are guides for informal visits, visitors may sit in on classes, and stay overnight. To schedule a visit, contact the Office of Undergraduate Admission at admission@stanford.edu. **Campus Safety and Security:** Measures include 24-hour foot and vehicle patrol, emergency notification system, self-defense education, and security escort services. There are shuttle buses, emergency telephones, lighted pathways/sidewalks, controlled access to dorms/residences, and AlertSU notifies students immediately of safety threats on campus.

REQUIREMENTS: The SAT or ACT Plus Writing is required. SAT Subject Tests are recommended. The university also recommends that applicants have strong preparation in high school English, math, a foreign language, science and social studies. If English is not your native language, we recommend, but do not require, the Test of English as a Foreign Language. Generally speaking, Stanford students have taken the most rigorous classes available to them. Applicants must complete the Common Application, the Stanford University Questions and arrange for recommendations. Candidates choose one topic from the Common Application, as well as complete three Stanford short essays. AP credits are accepted. Important factors in the admissions decision are advanced placement or honors courses, personality/intangible qualities, and recommendations by school officials. To graduate, students must complete 180 units, including requirements for the major, a writing and rhetoric requirement, and 1 year of a foreign language. General education requirements include the one-quarter freshman class Thinking Matters. Also required is Ways of Thinking, Ways of Doing, which includes eleven courses in eight subject areas, including aesthetic and interpretive inquiry, applied quantitative reasoning, creative expression, engaging diversity, ethical reasoning, formal reasoning, scientific method and analysis and social inquiry **Procedure:** Freshmen are admitted in the fall. Entrance exams should be taken by Nov. 1 for early decision; Jan. 15 for regular admission. There are early decision and deferred admissions plans. Early decision applications should be filed by November 1; regular applications, by January 3 for fall entry, along with a $90 fee. Notification of early decision is sent December 15; regular decision, April 1. 748 early decision candidates were accepted for the 2016-2017 class. 958 applicants were on the 2016 waiting list; 7 were admitted. Applications are accepted on-line. **Transfer Students:** 29 transfer students enrolled in 2015-2016. Transfer students must complete 1 full year of academic work prior to enrollment. There is only fall quarter enrollment for transfer students. The application deadline is March 15. 90 of 180 credits required for the bachelor's degree must be completed at Stanford. **International Students:** There are 574 international students enrolled. The school actively recruits these students. They must take the SAT or ACT. SAT Subject tests are recommended.

ADMISSIONS: 5% of the 2016-2017 applicants were accepted. The SAT scores for the 2016-2017 freshman class were: Critical Reading-- 5% between 500 and 599, 26% between 600 and 699, and 69% between 700 and 800. Math-- 3% between 500 and 599, 19% between 600 and 699, and 78% between 700 and 800. Writing-- 4% between 500 and 599, 22% between 600 and 699, and 74% between 700 and 800. The ACT scores were 1% below 12, 11% between 18 and 23, and 88% above 30. 99% of the current freshmen were in the top fifth of their class; 100% were in the top two fifths. **Admissions Contact:** Richard H. Shaw, Dean of Admissions. Email: *admission@stanford.edu* Web: *www.stanford.edu*

FINANCIAL AID: In 2016-2017, 82% of continuing full-time students received some form of financial aid. The average freshman award was $42,514. Need-based scholarships or need-based grants averaged $44,790; need-based self-help aid (loans and jobs) averaged $2,168; and non-need-based athletic scholarships averaged $41,935. The average financial indebtedness of the 2016 graduate was $19,230. Stanford is a member of CSS. The CSS/Profile is required. The FAFSA code is 001305. The priority date for freshman financial aid applications for fall entry is February 15.

THE MASTER'S UNIVERSITY — D-4

www.masters.edu

Santa Clarita, CA 91321 — **(661) 259-3540**, **(800) 568-6248**
Fax: (661) 362-2718 — **Email: admissions@masters.edu**

Full-time: 486 men, 460 women — **Faculty:** 67
Part-time: 139 men, 69 women — **Ph.D.s:** 75%
Graduate: 467 men, 79 women — **Student/Faculty:** 10 to 1
Year: semesters, summer session — **Tuition:** $33,020
Room & Board: $10,850 — **Freshman Class:** 446 applied, 371 accepted, 173 enrolled
SAT CR/M/W: 560/520/550 **ACT:** required — **CEEB CODE:** 4411
Application Deadline: November 15 — **COMPETITIVE**

The Master's University, founded in 1927, is a Christ-centered liberal arts college that exists to advance the kingdom of God by equipping students for moral integrity and lives of service in strategic fields of ministry and vocation. Within this authentic and life-changing community students from around the globe gather to be academically challenged, culturally engaged, and to embrace Biblical fidelity in all things. There is 1 undergraduate school and 1 graduate school. In addition to regional accreditation, The Master's University has baccalaureate program accreditation with ABHES, NASM, WSCUC, ACSI, NASM, WCFA, and AHEAD. The 110-acre campus is in a suburban area 35 miles north of Los Angeles. Including any residence halls, there are 32 buildings.

STUDENT LIFE: 67% of undergraduates are from California. Others are from 40 states, 23 foreign countries, and Canada. 40% are from public schools. 9% are Hispanic; 7% two or more races; 66% White; 6% Asian American; 5% race unknown; 4% Foreign; 3% African American. 100% are Protestant. **Male To Female Ratio:** 1.8:1. The average age of freshmen is 18; all undergraduates, 20. 18% do not continue beyond their first year; 62% remain to graduate. **Housing:** 800 students can be accommodated in college housing, which includes dorms and off-campus apartments. On-campus housing is guaranteed for all 4 years, is available on a first-come, and first-served basis. 75% of students live on campus. Alcohol is not permitted. All students may keep cars.

FACULTY/CLASSROOMS: 73% of faculty are male; 27% are female. All teach undergraduates. No introductory courses are taught by graduate students. The average class size in an introductory lecture is 30; in a laboratory is 11; and in a regular course is 13.

PROGRAMS OF STUDY: The Master's University confers B.A., B.S., and B.Mus. degrees. Master's and doctoral degrees are also awarded. Bachelor's degrees are awarded in BIOLOGICAL SCIENCE (biology/biological science and biological sciences), BUSINESS (accounting, business administration w/legal studies, business administration and management, business (dual major program), business administration - international, business administration marketing, and business information systems), COMMUNICATIONS AND THE ARTS (church music, communication studies, communications, English, film, television and digital media, instrumental performance, music, music composition, music ministry, music production/recording technology, music theory and composition, organ performance, piano pedagogy, and piano performance), COMPUTER AND PHYSICAL SCIENCE (applied mathematics, computer information systems, information sciences and systems, mathematics, and natural sciences), EDUCATION (Christian education, elementary education, music education, physical education, and secondary education), HEALTH PROFESSIONS (biology, kinesiology, preallied health, predentistry, and prephysical therapy), SOCIAL SCIENCE (biblical languages, biblical studies, Christian studies, family/consumer studies, history, home economics, liberal arts/general studies, liberal arts, sciences, general studies, humanities, missions, pastoral studies, political science/government, prelaw, and theology). Biblical studies, business administration, and biological sciences are the strongest academically. Business administration, biblical studies, and communication have the largest enrollments.

ACTIVITIES: There are no fraternities or sororities. There are 15 groups on campus, including Skid Row Evangelism, band, choir, chorale, chorus, drama, ethnic, film, International Justice Mission, jazz band, musical theater, newspaper, opera, orchestra, pep band, photography, political, religious, social, social service, and student government. Popular campus events include Outreach Week, Truth & Life Conference, Disney Week, and Week of Welcome, TMC Blend Coffeehouse, Brother-Sister Dorm Events,. **Sports:** There are 7 intercollegiate sports for men and 6 for women, and 6 intramural sports for men and 6 for women. Facilities include a gymnasium, a field for baseball and soccer, tennis and volleyball courts, batting cages, intramural field, swimming and diving pool, outdoor track and field, and fully-equipped fitness facility. **Graduates:** From July 1, 2016 to June 30, 2017, 267 bachelor's degrees were awarded. The most popular majors were business marketing (22%), theology and religious vocations (16%), and communications/journalism (13%). In an average class, 68% graduate in 6 years or less. Of the 2016 graduating class, 10% were enrolled in graduate school within 6 months of graduation.

SERVICES: Counseling and information services are available, as is tutoring in most subjects. There is remedial math and writing. **Library/Resources:** The library contains 194,000 volumes, 38,500 microform items, and 2,750 audio/video tapes/CDs/DVDs, and subscribes to 35,000 periodicals including electronic. Computerized library services include interlibrary loans, database searching, Internet access, and Wi-Fi capability. **Physically Challenged Students:** 90% of the campus is accessible. Facilities include wheelchair ramps, elevators, special parking, specially equipped restrooms, and lowered drinking fountains. **Special:** Students may cross-register with the Council for Christian Colleges and Universities (CCCU) for additional study abroad programs. Internships are offered with local businesses, churches, radio stations, and newspapers. **Visiting:** There are regularly scheduled orientations for prospective students, class visits, chapel, meetings with faculty, interviews, athletic events, financial aid seminar, and college activities. To schedule a visit, contact the Admissions Office. **Campus Safety and Security:** Measures include 24-hour foot and vehicle patrol, emergency notification system, and security escort services. There are shuttle buses, lighted pathways/sidewalks, and controlled access to dorms/residences.

REQUIREMENTS: The SAT or ACT is required. Applicants must have completed 4 years of English, 3 years of math, and 2 years each of science, and history, and 3 units of electives are recommended. A GPA of 2.8 is required. AP and CLEP credits are accepted. Important factors in the admissions decision are personality/intangible qualities, recommendations by school officials, and leadership record. Students must complete at least 122 semester hours, including a minimum of 61 GE units distributed as follows: 21 in the Scripture Set, 27 in the Worldview Set, and 13 in the Skills Set. Students must complete at least 40 semester hours in upper-division courses and at least 40 in the major and must maintain a minimum GPA of 2.0. **Procedure:** Freshmen are admitted fall and spring. There are early admissions, deferred admissions, and rolling admissions plans. Applications should be filed by November 15 for fall entry. The fall 2017 application fee was $40. Notifications are sent December 1. Applications are accepted on-line. **Transfer Students:** 77 transfer students enrolled in 2016-2017. Applicants must meet freshman requirements. A maximum of 70 units can be transferred from a junior college and 94 units from a 4-year college. Items for admissions also include college transcript (s), and an essay or personal statement. 28 of 122 credits required for the bachelor's degree must be completed at Master's. **International Students:** There are 50 international students enrolled. They must take the TOEFL with a minimum score of 550 on the paper-based TOEFL (PBT) or 80 on the Internet-based version (iBT).

ADMISSIONS: 83% of the 2017-2018 applicants were accepted. The SAT scores for the 2017-2018 freshman class were: Critical Reading-- 25% below 500, 39% between 500 and 599, 28% between 600 and 699, and 8% between 700 and 800. Math-- 40% below 500, 38% between 500 and 599, 19% between 600 and 699, and 3% between 700 and 800. Writing-- 37% below 500, 34% between 500 and 599, 24% between 600 and 699, and 5% between 700 and 800. The ACT scores were 5% between 12 and 17, 43% between 18 and 23, 39% between 24 and 29, and 13% above 30. 43% of the current freshmen were in the top fifth of their class; 67% were in the top two fifths. 2 freshmen graduated first in their class. **Admissions Contact:** Sarah Dyer, Assistant Director of Admissions. Email: *admissions@masters.edu* Web: *www.masters.edu*

FINANCIAL AID: In 2017-2018, 98% of all full-time freshmen received some form of financial aid. 78% of all full-time freshmen received need-based aid. The average freshman award was $23,733. Need-based scholarships or need-based grants averaged $19,981 ($9,084 maximum); need-based self-help aid (loans and jobs) averaged $4,555 ($5,000 maximum); non-need-based athletic scholarships averaged $16,588 ($40,860 maximum); and other non-need-based awards and non-need-based scholarships averaged $9,585 ($14,000 maximum). 21% of undergraduate students work part-time. The average financial indebtedness of the 2017 graduate was $19,233. The Master's is a member of CSS. The college's own financial statement is required. The priority date for freshman financial aid applications for fall entry is January 31.

THOMAS AQUINAS COLLEGE C-4

www.thomasaquinas.edu

Santa Paula, CA 93060 **(800) 634-9797**

Fax: (805) 421-5905 **Email:** admissions@thomasaquinas.edu

Full-time: 176 men, 194 women	**Faculty:** 31
Part-time: n/av	**Ph.D.s:** 87%
Graduate: n/av	**Student/Faculty:** 12 to 1
Year: semesters	**Tuition:** $24,500
Room & Board: $7950	**Freshman Class:** 213 applied, 156 accepted, 102 enrolled
SAT EBR-W/M: 680/620 **ACT:** 28	**CEEB CODE:** 4828
Application Deadline: n/av	**HIGHLY COMPETITIVE+**

Thomas Aquinas College, "great books" replace textbooks, and classroom discussions replace lectures. With truth as their aim, students engage a rigorous, four-year curriculum that spans the major disciplines natural science, mathematics, music, literature, philosophy, and theology in a Catholic community open to members of all faiths. Classes consist of small seminars, where students read and discuss works by the pivotal thinkers of Western civilization, such as Aristotle, St. Thomas Aquinas, Shakespeare, Newton, Einstein, Tocqueville, Tolstoy, and many more. Armed with this broad, integrated education, graduates go on to successful careers in fields ranging from medicine and law to journalism and higher education. College applications are accepted on a rolling basis, and Thomas Aquinas does fill relatively early. There is 1 undergraduate school. The 131-acre campus is in a rural area 70 miles northwest of Los Angeles, and approximately 15 miles east of Ventura. Including any residence halls, there are 20 buildings.

STUDENT LIFE: 58% of undergraduates are from out of state, mostly the Midwest. Students are from 41 states, 7 foreign countries, and Canada. 21% are from public schools. 73% are White; 16% Hispanic; 5% two or more races; 2% Asian American; 2% Foreign; 1% African American; 1% American Indian/Alaska Native; 1% race unknown. 96% are Catholic. **Female To Male Ratio:** 1.1:1. The average age of freshmen is 18; all undergraduates, 20. 8% do not continue beyond their first year; 82% remain to graduate. **Housing:** 398 students can be accommodated in college housing, which includes dorms. On-campus housing is guaranteed for all 4 years. Alcohol is not permitted. All students may keep cars.

FACULTY/CLASSROOMS: 90% of faculty are male; 10% are female. All teach undergraduates. No introductory courses are taught by graduate students. The average class size in a laboratory is 17 and in a regular course is 17.

PROGRAMS OF STUDY: TAC confers B.A. degrees. Bachelor's degrees are awarded in SOCIAL SCIENCE (liberal arts/general studies).

ACTIVITIES: There are no fraternities or sororities. There are 9 groups on campus, including art, choir, chorale, chorus, dance, drama, film, and orchestra. Popular campus events include St. Thomas Aquinas Day, President's Day, St. Patrick's Day, Easter, Open Mic Night, the All-College Picnic, and our Christmas Dance. **Sports:** There are 5 intramural sports for men and 5 for women. Facilities include Tennis, basketball, and volleyball courts; swimming areas; weight-lifting rooms; a soccer field, and a softball field. **Graduates:** From July 1, 2016 to June 30, 2017, 91 bachelor's degrees were awarded. The most popular majors were liberal arts (100%). In an average class, 75% graduate in 4 years or less, 84% graduate in 5 years or less, and 82% graduate in 6 years or less. Of the 2016 graduating class, 10% were enrolled in graduate school within 6 months of graduation, and 100% were employed.

SERVICES: There is remedial writing. The teaching faculty make themselves available to students for tutoring upon request. **Library/Resources:** The library contains 62,852 volumes, and 5,475 audio/video tapes/CDs/DVDs, and subscribes to 78 periodicals including electronic. Computerized library services include database searching and Internet access. **Physically Challenged Students:** All of the campus is accessible. Facilities include wheelchair ramps, elevators, special parking, specially equipped restrooms, special class scheduling, lowered drinking fountains, lowered telephones, and special housing. **Visiting:** There are regularly scheduled orientations for prospective students, The college welcomes prospective students to visit and stay with students in the residence halls for 1-3 days. They are invited to observe classes, dine with the students, and attend lectures, concerts and other special events. There are guides for informal visits, visitors may sit in on classes, and stay overnight. To schedule a visit, contact the Admissions Office.

REQUIREMENTS: The SAT or ACT is required. Candidates for Admission are expected to have completed 4 years of English, 2 years each of natural science, foreign language, and algebra, with 1 year of geometry. Additional work in science, mathematics and language study is recommended. Important factors in the admissions decision are personality/intangible qualities, advanced placement or honors courses, and recommendations by school officials. In order to graduate, students must complete the entire four-year curriculum. All students graduate from TAC with B.A in Liberal Arts; there are no electives, majors, or minors. In each of the four years students take courses in philosophy, theology, math, science, seminar (primarily modern philosophy, history and literature). In their freshman and sophomore years they take an additional course in language, and in their junior year an additional course in music. Seniors must also write and defend a thesis on a topic of their choosing. Students study a total of 146 semester hours and must maintain a minimum GPA of 2.0 to graduate. **Procedure:** Freshmen are admitted in the fall. There is a rolling admissions plan. Application deadlines are open. 28 applicants were on the 2017 waiting list; 14 were admitted. Applications are accepted on-line. **Transfer Students:** The integrated nature of the program requires that all students start as freshmen, and so, regardless of past education, TAC only admits students as freshmen. Approximately 15% of each freshman class has attended college elsewhere prior to enrolling in TAC. 146 of 146 credits required for the bachelor's degree must be completed at TAC. **International Students:** There are 16 international students enrolled. They must take the TOEFL with a minimum score of 570 on the paper-based TOEFL (PBT) or 80 on the Internet-based version (iBT). They must also take the SAT or ACT.

ADMISSIONS: 73% of the 2017-2018 applicants were accepted. The SAT scores for the 2017-2018 freshman class were: Math-- 1% below 500, 36% between 500 and 599, 44% between 600 and 699, and 19% between 700 and 800. Evidence-Based Reading/Writing-- 7% between 500 and 599, 51% between 600 and 699, and 42% between 700 and 800. The ACT scores were 8% between 18 and 23, 58% between 24 and 29, and 34% above 30. 50% of the current freshmen were in the top fifth of their class; 92% were in the top two fifths. **Admissions Contact:** Jonathan P. Daly, Director of Admissions. Email: *admissions@thomasaquinas.edu* Web: *www.thomasaquinas.edu*

FINANCIAL AID: In 2017-2018, 72% of all full-time freshmen received some form of financial aid. 63% of all full-time freshmen received need-based aid. The average freshman award was $18,310. Need-based scholarships or need-based grants averaged $10,597 ($22,334 maximum); need-based self-help aid (loans and jobs) averaged $6,384 ($9,400 maximum); and other non-need-based awards and non-need-based scholarships averaged $21 ($1,000 maximum). 70% of undergraduate students work part-time. The average financial indebtedness of the 2017 graduate was $16,045. The college's own financial statement, and parent and student federal tax returns is required. The FAFSA code is 023580. The priority date for freshman financial aid applications for fall entry is March 2.

UNIVERSITY OF CALIFORNIA AT BERKELEY — B-3

www.berkeley.edu

Berkeley, CA 94720 — **(510) 642-2316**

Email: admissions@berkeley.edu

Full-time: 13,314 men, 14,533 women	**Faculty:** 1606; I, ++$
Part-time: 587 men, 612 women	**Ph.D.s:** 99%
Graduate: 5879 men, 4978 women	**Student/Faculty:** 17 to 1
Year: semesters, summer session	**Tuition:** $14,170 ($42,184)
Room & Board: $15,716	**Freshman Class:** 80374 applied, 13882 accepted, 6057 enrolled
SAT CR/M/W: 685/730/695 **ACT:** 32	**CEEB CODE:** 4833
Application Deadline: November 30	**MOST COMPETITIVE**

University of California at Berkeley, founded in 1868, is a public institution offering a wide variety of programs in the social and physical sciences, liberal arts, and health professional fields. It is the oldest campus of the University of California system. The Berkeley Middle Class Access Plan (MCAP) is a new financial aid program to help middle-class families pay for cost for undergraduate degree programs. MCAP will not cover nonresident tuition. Under the Blue and Gold Opportunity Plan the university will cover tuition and fee cost for low-income California residents. There are 7 undergraduate schools and 14 graduate schools. In addition to regional accreditation, UCB has baccalaureate program accreditation with AACSB, ABET, ADA, ASLA, SAF, and ACS. The 1232-acre campus is in an urban area 10 miles east of San Francisco. Including any residence halls, there are 300 buildings.

STUDENT LIFE: 85% of undergraduates are from California. Others are from 50 states, 80 foreign countries, and Canada. 85% are from public schools. 4% are two or more races; 4% race unknown; 35% Asian American; 26% White; 2% African American; 15% Hispanic; 13% Foreign. **Female To Male Ratio:** 1.0:1. The average age of freshmen is 18; all undergraduates, 21. 4% do not continue beyond their first year; 90% remain to graduate. **Housing:** 8800 students can be accommodated in college housing, which includes married student dorms and off-campus apartments. In addition, there are honors houses, language/international houses, special-interest houses, fraternity houses, sorority houses, substance-free housing, an international house, theme housing, wellness housing, and apartments for student with children, and co-op housing. On-campus housing is guaranteed for the freshman year only and is available on a lottery system for upperclassmen. 97% of students live on campus. All students may keep cars.

FACULTY/CLASSROOMS: 65% of faculty are male; 35% are female. No introductory courses are taught by graduate students.

PROGRAMS OF STUDY: UCB confers A.B. and B.S. degrees. Master's and doctoral degrees are also awarded. Bachelor's degrees are awarded in AGRICULTURE (conservation and regulation and forestry and related sciences), BIOLOGICAL SCIENCE (biology/biological science, microbiology, molecular biology, nutrition, and plant genetics), BUSINESS (business administration and management, management science, and operations research), COMMUNICATIONS AND THE ARTS (art, art history and appreciation, Chinese, classical languages, communications, comparative literature, dance, dramatic arts, English, film arts, French, German, Greek, Italian, Japanese, Latin, linguistics, music, Scandinavian languages, Slavic languages, Spanish, and speech/debate/rhetoric), COMPUTER AND PHYSICAL SCIENCE (applied mathematics, astrophysics, chemistry, computer science, earth science, mathematics, physical sciences, physics, and statistics), ENGINEERING AND ENVIRONMENTAL DESIGN (architecture, bioengineering, chemical engineering, civil engineering, computer engineering, electrical/electronics engineering, engineering and applied science, engineering physics, environmental engineering, environmental science, industrial engineering, landscape architecture/design, manufacturing engineering, materials engineering, materials science, mechanical engineering, and nuclear engineering), HEALTH PROFESSIONS (optometry and public health), SOCIAL SCIENCE (African American studies, American studies, anthropology, Asian/American studies, Asian/Oriental studies, Celtic studies, classical/ancient civilization, cognitive science, economics, ethnic studies, geography, Hispanic American studies, history, interdisciplinary studies, Latin American studies, law, Middle Eastern studies, Native American studies, Near Eastern studies, peace studies, political science/government, psychology, religion, social science, social work, sociology, South Asian studies, urban studies, and women's studies). Electrical engineering & computer science, political science, and economics have the largest enrollments.

ACTIVITIES: There are 400 groups on campus, including art, band, cheerleading, chess, choir, chorale, chorus, computers, dance, debate, drama, ethnic, film, forensics, honors, international, jazz band, LGBT, literary magazine, marching band, model UN, musical theater, newspaper, orchestra, pep band, photography, political, professional, radio and TV, religious, social, social service, student government, symphony, and yearbook. Popular campus events include The Big Game, Cal Performances, and E-Week. **Sports:** Facilities include a football stadium, a track stadium, a basketball pavilion, gyms, martial arts room, swimming pools, weight rooms, squash, racquetball, handball, volleyball, tennis courts, and baseball and softball fields. **Graduates:** From July 1, 2016 to June 30, 2017, 7457 bachelor's degrees were awarded. The most popular majors were social sciences (19%), engineering (12%), and biological/life sciences (11%). In an average class, 3% graduate in 3 years or less, 69% graduate in 4 years or less, 88% graduate in 5 years or less, and 92% graduate in 6 years or less.

SERVICES: Counseling and information services are available, as is tutoring in most subjects. There is a reader service for the blind. **Library/Resources:** The library contains 10.4 million volumes, 6.6 million microform items, and 46,162 audio/video tapes/CDs/DVDs, and subscribes to 82,151 periodicals including electronic. Computerized library services include interlibrary loans and database searching. Special learning facilities include an art gallery, natural history museum, radio station, a botanical garden, an anthropology museum, a hall of science, the University Art Museum and Pacific Film Archive, a seismographic station, an herbaria, The Hall for the Performing Arts, and an observatory. **Physically Challenged Students:** 95% of the campus is accessible. Facilities include wheelchair ramps, elevators, special parking, specially equipped restrooms, special class scheduling, lowered drinking fountains, and lowered telephones. **Special:** Co-op programs, cross-registration with many area schools, internships, work-study programs, and study abroad in 35 countries are available. Interdisciplinary majors are also available, as are pass/fail options, independent study, an independent research and undergraduate research program, and a freshman seminar program, in which 15 to 25 students meet with professors to explore a wide range of majors. There is a 3-2 engineering program with the University of California, Santa Cruz. There is a chapter of Phi Beta Kappa and a freshman honors program. **Visiting:** There are regularly scheduled orientations for prospective students, including 1 1/2 hour student-led walking tours, usually followed by an admissions information presentation; self-guided tours are also available. There are guides for informal visits and visitors may sit in on classes. To schedule a visit, contact the Visitor Services at (510) 642-5215. **Campus Safety and Security:** Measures include 24-hour foot and vehicle patrol, emergency notification system, self-defense education, and security escort services. There are shuttle buses, emergency telephones, lighted pathways/sidewalks, controlled access to dorms/residences, a rape prevention peer education program, an earthquake emergency preparedness program, and safety threats and alerts reports via computer.

REQUIREMENTS: The SAT or ACT is required. Applicants must submit scores from 2 SAT Subject Tests, these are recommended for applicants to chemistry and engineering. High school units required are 4 years of English, 3 of math (4 recommended), 2 each of history/social studies, 2 each of science with lab science (3 recommended), 2 of foreign language (3 recommended), and 1 of college preparatory electives, and or 1 of visual or performing arts. AP credits are accepted. Important factors in the admissions decision are advanced placement or honors courses, evidence of special talent, personality/intangible qualities, and extracurricular activities record. All undergraduate students are required to satisfy the general university requirements of English and writing proficiency and take integrative and comparative courses in American history, institutions, and cultures. Students must complete 120 units with a minimum GPA of 2.0. **Procedure:** Freshmen are admitted in the fall. Entrance exams should be taken no later than December test dates in the senior year. There is a deferred admissions plan. Applications should be filed by November 30 for fall entry. The fall 2017 application fee was $70. Notifications are sent March 31. Applications are accepted on-line. **Transfer Students:** 2574 transfer students enrolled in 2016-2017. Requirements are all college transcripts, and an essay or personal statement. An 2.4 GPA on a scale of 4.0. Students may enroll in the fall-November 30, Notification is April 30, and must reply by June 1. 24 of 120 credits required for the bachelor's degree must be completed at UCB. **International Students:** There are 1073 international students enrolled. They must take the TOEFL with a minimum score of 550 on the paper-based TOEFL (PBT) or 83 on the Internet-based version (iBT). They must also take the SAT or ACT.

ADMISSIONS: 17% of the 2017-2018 applicants were accepted. The SAT scores for the 2017-2018 freshman class were: Critical Reading-- 6% below 500, 14% between 500 and 599, 33% between 600 and 699, and 47% between 700 and 800. Math-- 4% below 500, 12% between 500 and 599, 25% between 600 and 699, and 60% between 700 and 800. Writing-- 5% below 500, 13% between 500 and 599, 28% between 600 and 699, and 54% between 700 and 800. The ACT scores were 1% between 12 and 17, 8% between 18 and 23, 20% between 24 and 29, and 71% above 30. 98% of the current freshmen were in the top fifth of their class; 100% were in the top two fifths. **Admissions Contact:** Walter A. Robinson, Director of Undergraduate Admission. Email: *admissions@berkeley.edu* Web: *www.berkeley.edu*

FINANCIAL AID: In 2017-2018, 88% of all full-time freshmen received some form of financial aid. 89% of all full-time freshmen received need-based aid. The average freshman award was $17,284. Need-based scholarships or need-based grants averaged $15,053; need-based self-help aid (loans and jobs) averaged $7,032; non-need-based athletic scholarships averaged $29,326; other non-need-based awards and non-need-based scholarships averaged $6,686; and $15,053 from other forms of aid. The average financial indebtedness of the 2017 graduate was $28,648. The FAFSA code is 001312. The deadline for filing freshman financial aid applications for fall entry is March 31.

UNIVERSITY OF CALIFORNIA AT DAVIS B-2

www.ucdavis.edu

Davis, CA 95616 **(530) 752-2971**

Fax: (530) 752-1280 **Email:** undergraduateadmissions@ucdavis

Full-time: 11,456 men, 16,510 women
Part-time: 202 men, 216 women
Graduate: 3235 men, 3567 women
Year: quarters, summer session
Room & Board: $14,517

Faculty: I, +$
Ph.D.s: 98%
Student/Faculty: 18 to 1
Tuition: $13,950 ($38,659)
Freshman Class: 64510 applied, 24614 accepted, 5369 enrolled

SAT or ACT: required
Application Deadline: November 30

CEEB CODE: 4834
HIGHLY COMPETITIVE

University of California at Davis, founded in 1908, is a land-grant, comprehensive institution offering programs in arts and science, agricultural and environmental sciences, and engineering. There are 4 undergraduate schools and 5 graduate schools. In addition to regional accreditation, UCD has baccalaureate program accreditation with ABET, ADA, and ASLA. The 5300-acre campus is in a suburban area 15 miles west of Sacramento, and 72 miles northeast of San Francisco. Including any residence halls, there are 1186 buildings.

STUDENT LIFE: 96% of undergraduates are from California. 5% are two or more races; 32% Asian American; 28% White; 2% African American; 2% race unknown; 19% Hispanic; 11% Foreign. **Female To Male Ratio:** 1.4:1. The average age of freshmen is 19; all undergraduates, 21. 8% do not continue beyond their first year; 83% remain to graduate. **Housing:** College-sponsored housing includes married student dorms, on-campus apartments, and off-campus apartments. In addition, there are honors houses, language/international houses, and special-interest houses. On-campus housing is guaranteed for the freshman year only. 75% of students commute. Alcohol is not permitted. No one may keep cars.

FACULTY/CLASSROOMS: 61% of faculty are male; 39% are female. No introductory courses are taught by graduate students.

PROGRAMS OF STUDY: UCD confers B.S., A.B., and B.A.S. degrees. Master's and doctoral degrees are also awarded. Bachelor's degrees are awarded in AGRICULTURE (agricultural business management, agricultural economics, agriculture international, animal science, plant science, range/farm management, and soil science), BIOLOGICAL SCIENCE (avian sciences, bacteriology, biochemistry, biology/biological science, botany, ecology, entomology, environmental biology, genetics, microbiology, nutrition, physiology, toxicology, wildlife biology, and zoology), BUSINESS (organizational behavior), COMMUNICATIONS AND THE ARTS (art history and appreciation, Chinese, communications, comparative literature, design, dramatic arts, English, fine arts, French, German, Greek, Italian, Japanese, Latin, linguistics, music, Russian, Spanish, speech/debate/rhetoric, and studio art), COMPUTER AND PHYSICAL SCIENCE (atmospheric sciences and meteorology, chemistry, computer science, geology, hydrology, mathematics, physics, polymer science, and statistics), EDUCATION (physical education), ENGINEERING AND ENVIRONMENTAL DESIGN (aeronautical engineering, agricultural engineering, bioengineering, chemical engineering, civil engineering, computer engineering, electrical/electronics engineering, environmental design, environmental science, landscape architecture/design, materials engineering, and mechanical engineering), HEALTH PROFESSIONS (community health work and environmental health science), SOCIAL SCIENCE (African studies, American studies, anthropology, behavioral science, classical/ancient civilization, dietetics, East Asian studies, economics, food science, geography, history, human development, human ecology, international relations, medieval studies, Mexican-American/Chicano studies, Native American studies, philosophy, political science/government, psychology, religion, social science, sociology, textiles and clothing, and women's studies). Agricultural, biological, and biotechnical sciences are the strongest academically. Biological science, biochemistry, and psychology have the largest enrollments.

ACTIVITIES: Groups on campus include art, band, cheerleading, chess, choir, chorus, communications, computers, dance, debate, drama, ethnic, film, honors, international, jazz band, LGBT, literary magazine, marching band, musical theater, newspaper, orchestra, pep band, photography, political, professional, radio and TV, religious, social, social service, student government, and symphony. Popular campus events include Picnic Day, Whole Earth Festival, and Asian Pacific Cultural Week. **Sports:** There are 9 intercollegiate sports for men and 14 for women. **Graduates:** From July 1, 2016 to June 30, 2017, 7120 bachelor's degrees were awarded. The most popular majors were psychology (9%), economics (7%), and managerial economics (5%). In an average class, 2% graduate in 3 years or less, 54% graduate in 4 years or less, 79% graduate in 5 years or less, and 83% graduate in 6 years or less.

SERVICES: Counseling and information services are available, as is tutoring in most subjects. There is a reader service for the blind, and remedial math and writing. **Library/Resources:** The library contains 4.5 million volumes, 4.3 million microform items, and 12,977 audio/video tapes/CDs/DVDs, and subscribes to 120,531 periodicals including electronic. Computerized library services include interlibrary loans, database searching, Internet access, and Wi-Fi capability. Special learning facilities include an art gallery, radio station, an experimental farm, a 150-acre arboretum, a raptor center, an equestrian center, a primate research center, and the Crocker Nuclear Laboratory. **Physically Challenged Students:** All of the campus is accessible. Facilities include wheelchair ramps, elevators, special parking, specially equipped restrooms, special class scheduling, lowered drinking fountains, lowered telephones, and lowered automatic teller machines. **Special:** There are credit and noncredit internship programs. Study abroad in more than 32 countries and a Washington semester are offered. Students may participate in college work-study, federal work-study, and California work-study programs. Several A.B.-B.S. degrees are offered. Students may design their own majors, take dual majors, and elect pass/fail options. Interdisciplinary majors are offered in African American and African studies, American studies, Mexican American studies, comparative literature, East Asian studies, exercise science, international relations, linguistics, medieval studies, Native American studies, religious studies, and women's studies. There is a chapter of Phi Beta Kappa and a freshman honors program. **Visiting:** There are regularly scheduled orientations for prospective students, including weekend tours of the campus, weekday tours by appointment, and drop-in counseling with staff and faculty. The campus also offers a 1-day preview for prospective students and their families. There are guides for informal visits, visitors may sit in on classes, and stay overnight. To schedule a visit, contact UC Davis Visitor Services at visit@ucdavis.edu. **Campus Safety and Security:** Measures include 24-hour foot and vehicle patrol, emergency notification system, self-defense education, and security escort services. There are shuttle buses, emergency telephones, lighted pathways/sidewalks, There is also a rape prevention program, crime prevention unit, bike patrol unit, and a K-9 program.

REQUIREMENTS: The SAT or ACT is required. Candidates for admission should have completed 4 units of English, 3 of math, and 2 each of foreign language, history/social science, lab science, and college preparatory electives, for a total of 15 units. Two SAT Subject Tests are required in two different areas. AP credits are accepted. General education requirements vary by college but are based on 3 components: topical breadth, social-cultural diversity, and writing experience. A minimum of 180 quarter units with a minimum GPA of 2.0 are required for graduation, as is proficiency in English composition and American History and Institutions requirement. **Procedure:** Freshmen are admitted fall, winter, and spring. Entrance exams should be taken by December of the senior year. There is a deferred admissions plan. Applications should be filed by November 30 for fall entry. The fall 2017 application fee was $70. Notifications are sent March 15. 2733 applicants were on the 2017 waiting list; 2030 were admitted. Applications are accepted on-line. **Transfer Students:** 2932 transfer students enrolled in 2016-2017. Junior-level transfers have priority. Requirements vary by college, discipline, and major. 35 of 180 credits required for the bachelor's degree must be completed at UCD. **International Students:** They must take the TOEFL with a minimum score of 550 on the paper-based TOEFL (PBT) or 60 on the Internet-based version (iBT). They must also take the SAT or ACT.

ADMISSIONS: 38% of the 2017-2018 applicants were accepted. The SAT scores for the 2017-2018 freshman class were: Critical Reading-- 20% below 500, 39% between 500 and 599, 31% between 600 and 699, and 10% between 700 and 800. Math-- 11% below 500, 23% between 500 and 599, 36% between 600 and 699, and 29% between 700 and 800. Writing-- 16% below 500, 33% between 500 and 599, 38% between 600 and 699, and 13% between 700 and 800. The ACT scores were 1% between 12 and 17, 18% between 18 and 23, 48% between 24 and 29, and 33% above 30. **Admissions Contact:** Walter Robinson, Director, Undergraduate Admissions. Email: *undergraduateadmissions@ucdavis* Web: *www.ucdavis.edu*

FINANCIAL AID: UCD is a member of CSS. The FAFSA code is 001313. The deadline for filing freshman financial aid applications for fall entry is March 2.

UNIVERSITY OF CALIFORNIA AT IRVINE D-5
www.uci.edu

Irvine, CA 92697	**(949) 824-6703**
Fax: (949) 824-2951	**Email: admissions@uci.edu**
Full-time: 13,616 men, 15,235 women	**Faculty:** 1467; I, +$
Part-time: 255 men, 201 women	**Ph.D.s:** 98%
Graduate: 3211 men, 2724 women	**Student/Faculty:** 19 to 1
Year: quarters, summer session	**Tuition:** $15,515 ($43,529)
Room & Board: $14,861	**Freshman Class:** 85102 applied, 31063 accepted, 6545 enrolled
SAT CR/M/W: 595/613/576 **ACT:** required	**CEEB CODE:** 4859
Application Deadline: November 30	**VERY COMPETITIVE**

University of California at Irvine, founded in 1965, is a public research university and part of the University of California System. There are 13 undergraduate schools and 15 graduate schools. In addition to regional accreditation, UCI has baccalaureate program accreditation with AACSB, ABET, ABA, and AAMC. The 1475-acre campus is in a suburban area 40 miles south of Los Angeles. Including any residence halls, there are 494 buildings.

STUDENT LIFE: 79% of undergraduates are from California. Others are from 45 states, 77 foreign countries, and Canada. 75% are from public schools. 4% are two or more races; 36% Asian American; 26% Hispanic; 2% African American; 17% Foreign; 14% White; 1% race unknown. **Female To Male Ratio:** 1.1:1. The average age of freshmen is 18; all undergraduates, 21. 6% do not continue beyond their first year; 94% remain to graduate. **Housing:** 11339 students can be accommodated in college housing, which includes married student dorms and on-campus apartments. In addition, there are honors houses, special-interest houses, fraternity houses, and sorority houses. On-campus housing is available on a first-come, first-served basis, and is available on a lottery system for upperclassmen. 61% of students commute. All students may keep cars.

FACULTY/CLASSROOMS: 64% of faculty are male; 36% are female. All teach undergraduates, and all do research. No introductory courses are taught by graduate students. The average class size in an introductory lecture is 103; in a laboratory is 23; and in a regular course is 39.

PROGRAMS OF STUDY: UCI confers B.A., B.S., B.F.A., and B.Mus. degrees. Master's and doctoral degrees are also awarded. Bachelor's degrees are awarded in AGRICULTURE (environmental studies), BIOLOGICAL SCIENCE (biochemistry, bioinformatics, biology/biological science, botany, cell biology, ecology, genetics, microbiology, and neurosciences), BUSINESS (business administration and management, business economics, and economics – statistics), COMMUNICATIONS AND THE ARTS (art history, classics, comparative literature, creative writing, dance, dramatic arts, English, film arts, French, Japanese, journalism, Korean, media arts, music, music performance, musical theater, Spanish, and studio art), COMPUTER AND PHYSICAL SCIENCE (chemistry, computer science, earth science, environmental geology, geology, information sciences and systems, mathematics, physics, and software engineering), EDUCATION (global studies), ENGINEERING AND ENVIRONMENTAL DESIGN (aeronautical engineering, biomedical engineering, chemical engineering, civil engineering, computer engineering, electrical/electronics engineering, engineering, environmental engineering, environmental science, materials engineering, and mechanical engineering), HEALTH PROFESSIONS (nursing, pharmaceutical science, premedicine, and public health), SOCIAL SCIENCE (African American studies, anthropology, Asian/American studies, Chinese Studies, classical/ancient civilization, criminology, East Asian studies, economics, European studies, German area studies, Hispanic American studies, history, humanities, interdisciplinary studies, international studies, philosophy, political science/government, psychology, religion, social psychology, social science, sociology, urban studies, and women's studies). Biological sciences, computer science, business economics, and psychology have the largest enrollments.

ACTIVITIES: 8% of men belong to 24 national fraternities; 9% of women belong to 25 national sororities. There are 568 groups on campus, including art, band, cheerleading, chess, choir, chorus, communications, computers, dance, debate, drama, environmental, ethnic, film, honors, international, jazz band, LGBT, literary magazine, marching band, musical theater, newspaper, opera, orchestra, pep band, political, professional, radio and TV, religious, social, social service, student government, symphony, and yearbook. Popular campus events include Celebrate UCI, Shocktoberfest, Homecoming, and Welcome Week's All-UCI Dance Battle. **Sports:** There are 42 intercollegiate sports for men and 42 for women. Facilities include a track stadium, an event center, soccer, tennis, baseball, swimming pool, indoor handball/racquetball/squash courts, and an activities hall with areas for badminton, basketball, volleyball, combatives, fencing, and weight training. **Graduates:** From July 1, 2016 to June 30, 2017, 7495 bachelor's degrees were awarded. The most popular majors were social psychology (9%), public health (7%), and biology (7%). In an average class, 5% graduate in 3 years or less, 71% graduate in 4 years or less, 86% graduate in 5 years or less, and 87% graduate in 6 years or less.

SERVICES: Counseling and information services are available, as is tutoring in some subjects. There is a reader service for the blind, and remedial reading and writing. **Library/Resources:** The library contains 3.2 million volumes, 2.2 million microform items, and 123,396 audio/video tapes/CDs/DVDs, and subscribes to 132,134 periodicals including electronic. Computerized library services include interlibrary loans, database searching, and Internet access. Special learning facilities include an art gallery, radio station, a freshwater marsh reserve, an arboretum, a laser institute, and numerous research centers. **Physically Challenged Students:** 96% of the campus is accessible. Facilities include wheelchair ramps, elevators, special parking, specially equipped restrooms, special class scheduling, lowered drinking fountains, lowered telephones, and special housing. **Special:** Students may study abroad in dozens of locations. UCI also offers internships, a Washington semester, semester at sea, work-study programs with the university, B.A.-B.S. degrees, dual majors, and pass/fail options. There are 7 national honor societies, Phi Beta Kappa, and a freshman honors program. **Visiting:** There are regularly scheduled orientations for prospective students. There are guides for informal visits, visitors may sit in on classes, and stay overnight. To schedule a visit, contact the Visitor Center at (949) 824.4636. **Campus Safety and Security:** Measures include 24-hour foot and vehicle patrol, emergency notification system, self-defense education, and security escort services. There are shuttle buses, emergency telephones, and lighted pathways/sidewalks.

REQUIREMENTS: The SAT or ACT is required. Required minimum scores are determined by an eligibility index. Applicants need 15 academic credits, including 4 years of English, 3 in math, and 2 each in foreign language, history/social science, lab science, and electives. An additional year each in foreign language, math, and science is recommended. An essay also is needed. The GED is accepted. AP credits are accepted. To graduate, students must maintain a GPA of at least 2.0, earn 180 quarter units, satisfy all the requirements for their majors, and fulfill requirements in English composition and in American history and institutions. Students must also meet the following General Education requirements: Writing (two lower-division plus one upper-division course), Science and Technology (three courses), Social and Behavioral Sciences (three courses), Arts and Humanities (three courses), Quantitative, Symbolic, and Computational Reasoning (three courses that may also satisfy another GE category), Language Other Than English (one course), Multicultural Studies (one course that may also satisfy another GE category), International/Global Issues (one course that may also satisfy another GE category). **Procedure:** Freshmen are admitted in the fall. Entrance exams should be taken no later than December of the senior year. Applications should be filed by November 30 for fall entry. The fall 2017 application fee was $70. Notifications are sent March 31. Applications are accepted on-line. **Transfer Students:** 2970 transfer students enrolled in 2016-2017. UCI requirements for admission as a transfer applicant vary according to the high school record. Please see catalog for full details. 36 of 180 credits required for the bachelor's degree must be completed at UCI. **International Students:** There are 4906 international students enrolled. They must take the TOEFL with a minimum score of 550 on the paper-based TOEFL (PBT) or 80 on the Internet-based version (iBT). They must also take the SAT or ACT.

ADMISSIONS: 37% of the 2017-2018 applicants were accepted. The SAT scores for the 2017-2018 freshman class were: Critical Reading-- 9% below 500, 49% between 500 and 599, 28% between 600 and 699, and 14% between 700 and 800. Math-- 9% below 500, 33% between 500 and 599, 40% between 600 and 699, and 17% between 700 and 800. Writing-- 17% below 500, 42% between 500 and 599, 33% between 600 and 699, and 8% between 700 and 800. **Admissions Contact:** Brent Yunek, Assistant Vice Chancellor, and Enrollment Services. Email: *admissions@uci.edu* Web: *www.uci.edu*

FINANCIAL AID: UCI is a member of CSS. The FAFSA code is 001314. The priority date for freshman financial aid applications for fall entry is March 2. The deadline for filing freshman financial aid applications for fall entry is May 2.

UNIVERSITY OF CALIFORNIA AT LOS ANGELES — C-5

www.ucla.edu

Los Angeles, CA 90095	(310) 825-3101
Fax: (310) 206-1206	**Email:** ugadm@admissions.ucla.edu
Full-time: 13,069 men, 17,257 women	**Faculty:** I, ++$
Part-time: 287 men, 243 women	**Ph.D.s:** 98%
Graduate: 6888 men, 5787 women	**Student/Faculty:** n/av
Year: quarters, summer session	**Tuition:** $13,409 ($40,091)
Room & Board: $14,029	**Freshman Class:** 97121 applied, 17474 accepted, 6545 enrolled
SAT CR/M/W: 635/660/645 **ACT:** 29	**CEEB CODE:** 4837
Application Deadline: November 30	**HIGHLY COMPETITIVE+**

University of California at Los Angeles (UCLA), founded in 1919, is a public research university offering undergraduate and graduate degrees. Its disciplines include arts and sciences, engineering, applied science, health sciences, law, management, and theater, film, and television. The figures given in the above capsule and in this profile are approximate. There are 5 undergraduate schools and 12 graduate schools. In addition to regional accreditation, UCLA has baccalaureate program accreditation with AACSB, ABET, ADA, CSAB, CSWE, FIDER, NAAB, NLN, CCNE, and NAST. The 419-acre campus is in an urban area in Los Angeles. Including any residence halls, there are 190 buildings.

STUDENT LIFE: 86% of undergraduates are from California. Others are from 46 states, 71 foreign countries, and Canada. 77% are from public schools. 5% are two or more races; 3% African American; 27% White; 27% Asian American; 22% Hispanic; 2% race unknown; 12% Foreign. **Female To Male Ratio:** 1.2:1. The average age of freshmen is 19; all undergraduates, 21. 3% do not continue beyond their first year; 92% remain to graduate. **Housing:** 13300 students can be accommodated in college housing, which includes married student dorms and off-campus apartments. In addition, there are special-interest houses, fraternity houses, sorority houses, and theme and wellness housing. On-campus housing is available on a lottery system for upperclassmen. 64% of students commute. Alcohol is not permitted. Some may keep cars.

FACULTY/CLASSROOMS: 65% of faculty are male; 35% are female. All teach undergraduates, and all do research. No introductory courses are taught by graduate students.

PROGRAMS OF STUDY: UCLA confers B.A. and B.S degrees. Master's and doctoral degrees are also awarded. Bachelor's degrees are awarded in AGRICULTURE (environmental studies), BIOLOGICAL SCIENCE (biochemistry, biology/biological science, biophysics, cell biology, ecology, marine biology, microbiology, molecular biology, neurosciences, and physiology), BUSINESS (business economics), COMMUNICATIONS AND THE ARTS (American literature, Arabic, art, art history and appreciation, Chinese, classics, communications, dramatic arts, English, film arts, French, German, Greek, Hebrew, Italian, Japanese, Korean, Latin, linguistics, music, music history and appreciation, musicology/ethnomusicology, Portuguese, Russian languages and literature, Scandinavian languages, and Spanish), COMPUTER AND PHYSICAL SCIENCE (applied mathematics, astrophysics, atmospheric sciences and meteorology, chemistry, computer science, earth science, geology, geophysics and seismology, mathematics, physics, and statistics), EDUCATION (mathematics education), ENGINEERING AND ENVIRONMENTAL DESIGN (aeronautical engineering, aerospace studies, architecture, bioengineering, biomedical engineering, chemical engineering, civil engineering, computer engineering, electrical/electronics engineering, environmental science, geological engineering, materials engineering, materials science, and mechanical engineering), HEALTH PROFESSIONS (nursing), SOCIAL SCIENCE (African studies, African American studies, American Indian studies, anthropology, Asian/American studies, Asian/Oriental studies, classical/ancient civilization, cognitive science, East Asian studies, economics, European studies, French studies, geography, history, international studies, Italian studies, Judaic studies, Latin American studies, Mexican-American/Chicano studies, Middle Eastern studies, Near Eastern studies, philosophy, political science/government, psychobiology, psychology, religion, Russian and Slavic studies, sociology, South Asian studies, Spanish studies, and women's studies). Economics, psychology, and political science have the largest enrollments.

ACTIVITIES: 11% of men belong to 32 national fraternities; 11% of women belong to 33 national sororities. There are 1000 groups on campus, including art, band, cheerleading, chess, choir, chorale, chorus, computers, dance, debate, drama, environmental, ethnic, film, forensics, honors, international, jazz band, LGBT, literary magazine, marching band, musical theater, newspaper, opera, orchestra, pep band, photography, political, professional, radio and TV, religious, social, social service, student government, symphony, and yearbook. Popular campus events include Career Week, Casino Night, and Welcome Week. **Sports:** There are 10 intercollegiate sports for men and 12 for women, and 21 intramural sports for men and 19 for women. Facilities include a pavilion, stadium, tennis center, and a recreation & sports center. **Graduates:** From July 1, 2016 to June 30, 2017, 8066 bachelor's degrees were awarded. The most popular majors were social sciences (27%), biological life sciences (13%), and psychology (10%). In an average class, 3% graduate in 3 years or less, 70% graduate in 4 years or less, 87% graduate in 5 years or less, and 91% graduate in 6 years or less.

SERVICES: Counseling and information services are available, as is tutoring in most subjects. There is a reader service for the blind. **Library/Resources:** The library contains 9.2 million volumes, 6.2 million microform items, and 5.0 million audio/video tapes/CDs/DVDs, and subscribes to 78,463 periodicals including electronic. Computerized library services include interlibrary loans, database searching, and Internet access. Special learning facilities include a natural history museum, planetarium, radio station, Air Photo Archives, Arts Library, Biomed Library, Young Research Library, Clark Memorial Library, College Library, Cuneiform Digital Library, Darling Biomedical Library, Darling Law Library, Film and Television Archive, Folklore and Mythology Archive, Ethnomusicology Archive, Institute for Social Science Library, Libraries of the Ethnic Studies Centers, Music Library, Rudolph East Asian Library, Rosenfeld Management Library, Science and Engineering Library, UES Gonda Library, University Archives, and the Performing Arts Special Collections. MUSEUMS--Fowler Museum, Hammer Museum of Art and Culture Center, Grunwald Center for Graphic Arts, New Wright Gallery, GARDENS--Mildred E. Mathias Botanical Garden, Franklin D. Murphy Sculpture Garden, Hannah Carter Japanese Garden, ART--Eli and Edythe Broad Art Center, DANCE--Glorya Kaufman Hall, THEATER--Geffen Playhouse, Macgowan Little Theater, Freud Playhouse, Billy Wilder Theater, MUSIC--Royce Hall, Schoenberg Hall, Pauley Pavilion, and the FILM--James Bridges Theater. **Physically Challenged Students:** All of the campus is accessible. Facilities include wheelchair ramps, elevators, special parking, specially equipped restrooms, special class scheduling, lowered drinking fountains, and lowered telephones. **Special:** Opportunities are provided for internships, work-study programs, study abroad in 33 countries, student-designed majors, dual majors, and interdisciplinary majors, including chemistry and materials science, Chicana and Chicano studies, and math and engineering. There is a Washington, D.C., program for 20 to 30 students selected each fall and spring. There are 21 national honor societies, Phi Beta Kappa, a freshman honors program, and 100 departmental honors programs. **Visiting:** There are regularly scheduled orientations for prospective students, including campus tours by current UCLA students, offered weekdays at 10:15 a.m. and 2:15 p.m. Reservations are required. Visitors may sit in on classes. To schedule a visit, contact the Undergraduate Admissions. **Campus Safety and Security:** Measures include 24-hour foot and vehicle patrol, emergency notification system, self-defense education, and security escort services. There are shuttle buses, emergency telephones, lighted pathways/sidewalks, and controlled access to dorms/residences.

REQUIREMENTS: Freshmen applicants applying for admission to Fall Quarter, we will no longer require two SAT subject exams. We will still review these exams if applicants choose to send them to us, and certain SAT subject exams may be recommended for some majors. The SAT Reasoning or ACT with Writing examination are required. 15 required high school units including 4 in English, 3 in math, 2 each in science with lab, foreign language, and history, 1 each in academic electives and visual/performing arts. AP credits are accepted. Important factors in the admissions decision are advanced placement or honors courses, evidence of special talent, personality/intangible qualities, and extracurricular activities record. Students must complete a minimum of 180 quarter units and maintain a minimum GPA of 2.0 in all courses. All students must demonstrate a proficiency in English composition, or take specific courses to achieve this proficiency, and must also meet course requirements in American history and institutions. Other requirements vary by major and college or school. **Procedure:** Freshmen are admitted in the fall. Entrance exams should be taken preferably in the junior year, but no later than December of the senior year. Applications should be filed by November 30 for fall entry. The fall 2017 application fee was $70. Notifications are sent March 31. Applications are accepted on-line. **Transfer Students:** 3346 transfer students enrolled in 2016-2017. Students must have earned 90 quarter units at the previous college and have completed preparatory courses for the selected major. Most students selected present a GPA of 3.0 or better. 68 of 180 credits required for the bachelor's degree must be completed at UCLA. **International Students:** There are 1498 international students enrolled. They must take the TOEFL with a minimum score of 550 on the paper-based TOEFL (PBT) or 83 on the Internet-based version (iBT). Student must take the IELTS, scoring at least 7. They must also take the SAT or ACT.

ADMISSIONS: 18% of the 2017-2018 applicants were accepted. The SAT scores for the 2017-2018 freshman class were: Critical Reading-- 9% below 500, 25% between 500 and 599, 38% between 600 and 699, and 27% between 700 and 800. Math-- 8% below 500, 20% between 500 and 599, 30% between 600 and 699, and 41% between 700 and 800. Writing-- 8% below 500, 23% between 500 and 599, 36% between 600 and

699, and 32% between 700 and 800. The ACT scores were 1% between 12 and 17, 13% between 18 and 23, 29% between 24 and 29, and 57% above 30. **Admissions Contact:** Gary Clark A, Jr., Director of Undergraduate Admissions. Email: *ugadm@admissions.ucla.edu* Web: *www.ucla.edu*

FINANCIAL AID: In 2017-2018, 56% of all full-time freshmen received some form of financial aid. 54% of all full-time freshmen received need-based aid. The average freshman award was $19,561. Need-based scholarships or need-based grants averaged $16,080; need-based self-help aid (loans and jobs) averaged $6,144; non-need-based athletic scholarships averaged $18,580; and other non-need-based awards and non-need-based scholarships averaged $5,493. The average financial indebtedness of the 2017 graduate was $18,203. The college's own financial statement is required. The deadline for filing freshman financial aid applications for fall entry is March 2.

UNIVERSITY OF CALIFORNIA AT RIVERSIDE D-5
www.ucr.edu

Riverside, CA 92521 (951) 827-4531

Fax: (951) 827-6346
Email: admissions@ucr.edu

Full-time: 8958 men, 10,758 women	**Faculty:** 976
Part-time: 205 men, 104 women	**Ph.D.s:** 98%
Graduate: 1792 men, 1417 women	**Student/Faculty:** 22 to 1
Year: quarters, summer session	**Tuition:** $15,912 ($43,926)
Room & Board: $17,000	**Freshman Class:** 43682 applied, 25001 accepted, 4598 enrolled
SAT or ACT: required	**CEEB CODE:** 4839
Application Deadline: November 30	**COMPETITIVE**

University of California at Riverside, founded in 1954, is a public research university with undergraduate and graduate programs in engineering, humanities, arts, social sciences, natural and agricultural sciences, medicine, public policy, health sciences, education and business. The figures given in the above capsule and in this profile are approximate. There are 3 undergraduate schools and 9 graduate schools. In addition to regional accreditation, UCR has baccalaureate program accreditation with AACSB, ABET, and ACS. The 1200-acre campus is in a suburban area 50 miles east of Los Angeles. Including any residence halls, there are 668 buildings.

STUDENT LIFE: 99% of undergraduates are from California. Others are from 35 states, 43 foreign countries, and Canada. 92% are from public schools. 6% are two or more races; 41% Hispanic; 34% Asian American; 3% African American; 11% White; 1% race unknown. **Female To Male Ratio:** 1.1:1. The average age of freshmen is 18; all undergraduates, 20. 11% do not continue beyond their first year; 89% remain to graduate. **Housing:** 6045 students can be accommodated in college housing, which includes gender neutral, coed, married student dorms, and on-campus apartments. In addition, there are honors houses, special-interest houses, and international village. On-campus housing is guaranteed for the freshman year only, is available on a first-come, first-served basis, and is available on a lottery system for upperclassmen. 70% of students commute. All students may keep cars.

FACULTY/CLASSROOMS: 64% of faculty are male; 36% are female. No introductory courses are taught by graduate students.

PROGRAMS OF STUDY: UCR confers B.A. and B.S. degrees. Master's and doctoral degrees are also awarded. Bachelor's degrees are awarded in AGRICULTURE (soil science), BIOLOGICAL SCIENCE (biochemistry, biology/biological science, cell biology, entomology, genetics, microbiology, neurosciences, plant genetics, and plant pathology), BUSINESS (business administration and management, business economics, and management science), COMMUNICATIONS AND THE ARTS (art history, art, art history and appreciation, Chinese, classical languages, comparative literature, creative writing, dance, dramatic arts, English, film arts, French, German, Germanic languages and literature, Japanese, languages, linguistics, music, Russian, Russian languages and literature, Spanish, theatre arts, and visual and performing arts), COMPUTER AND PHYSICAL SCIENCE (chemistry, computer science, geology, geophysics and seismology, geoscience, information sciences and systems, mathematics, physical sciences, physics, and statistics), EDUCATION (mathematics education), ENGINEERING AND ENVIRONMENTAL DESIGN (bioengineering, chemical engineering, electrical/electronics engineering, engineering and applied science, engineering mechanics, environmental engineering, environmental science, materials engineering, and mechanical engineering), HEALTH PROFESSIONS (biomedical science), SOCIAL SCIENCE (African American studies, anthropology, Asian/American studies, Asian/Oriental studies, classical/ancient civilization, economics, ethnic studies, history, humanities and social science, interdisciplinary studies, Latin American studies, liberal arts/general studies, Mexican-American/Chicano studies, Middle Eastern studies, Native American studies, philosophy, political science/government, psychology, religion, religious education, Russian and Slavic studies, sociology, and women's studies). Engineering is the strongest academically. Business administration, biology, and psychology have the largest enrollments.

ACTIVITIES: 4% of men belong to 4 local and 15 national fraternities; 7% of women belong to 4 local and 15 national sororities. There are 446 groups on campus, including art, bagpipe, cheerleading, chorus, computers, dance, drama, ethnic, film, honors, international, jazz band, LGBT, literary magazine, musical theater, newspaper, pep band, photography, political, professional, radio and TV, social, social service, student government, and symphony. Popular campus events include HEAT Festival, Block Party, and Spring Splash. **Sports:** There are 7 intercollegiate sports for men and 8 for women, and 8 intramural sports for men and 9 for women. Facilities include a swimming pool, a student recreation center with a weight room/fitness, indoor multi-use courts, racquetball courts, squash court, fitness studios, tennis courts, a roller hockey rink, challenge ropes course, and a jogging trail. **Graduates:** From July 1, 2016 to June 30, 2017, 4549 bachelor's degrees were awarded. The most popular majors were social sciences (21%), business/marketing (18%), and biological/life sciences (14%). In an average class, 47% graduate in 4 years or less, 69% graduate in 5 years or less, and 73% graduate in 6 years or less. Of the 2016 graduating class, 10% were enrolled in graduate school within 6 months of graduation, and 34% were employed.

SERVICES: Counseling and information services are available, as is tutoring in most subjects, such as individual and group tutoring. There is a reader service for the blind. There are also study skills classes, and preparation sessions for graduate entrance exams, study groups, individual counseling and lab work, and speed-reading classes. **Library/Resources:** The library contains 3.2 million volumes, 2.3 million microform items, and subscribes to 97,678 periodicals including electronic. Computerized library services include interlibrary loans, database searching, Internet access, and Wi-Fi capability. Special learning facilities include an art gallery, radio station, Culver Center for the Arts, museum of photography, College of Engineering-Center for Environmental Research and Technology, air pollution research center, Agricultural Research Institute for Deserts, Citrus Variety Collection, agricultural experiment station, Botanic Gardens, Entomology Museum, George E. Brown Salinity Lab, and Core Instrumentation Facility for Genomics Research. **Physically Challenged Students:** Facilities include wheelchair ramps, elevators, special parking, specially equipped restrooms, special class scheduling, lowered drinking fountains, lowered telephones, special housing, and automatic doors. **Special:** Internships, work-study programs with various agencies and employers on and off campus, study abroad in 35 countries, and a semester in Washington are available. The campus also has a School of Medicine and a School of Public Policy. Student-dual majors, opportunities for undergraduate research, and pass/fail options in elective subjects are possible. Grants are available for research, fieldwork, or other creative activity. Academic internships and co-op programs are offered in all majors. There are 14 national honor societies, Phi Beta Kappa, a freshman honors program, and 13 departmental honors programs. **Visiting:** There are regularly scheduled orientations for prospective students. There are tours available throughout the year on weekdays and some Saturdays. There are guides for informal visits, visitors may sit in on classes, and stay overnight. To schedule a visit, contact Visitor Relations Manager at (951) 827-4531. **Campus Safety and Security:** Measures include 24-hour foot and vehicle patrol, emergency notification system, self-defense education, and security escort services. There are emergency telephones, lighted pathways/sidewalks, off campus point to point shuttle service, and 24/7 University of California police department.

REQUIREMENTS: The SAT or ACT is required. The ACT Optional Writing test is also required. The minimum GPA varies depending on SAT or ACT scores. Candidates for admission should have completed 4 years of English, 3 years of math, and 2 years each of foreign language, history, and science, and 1 each of visual/performing arts and electives. UCR requires applicants to be in the upper 25% of their class. AP credits are accepted. Students must demonstrate proficiency in English and a knowledge of American history and institutions. A total of 180 quarter credit hours with a minimum GPA of 2.0 is required in order to graduate. The number of hours in the major varies. All students must complete a 1-year sequence in English composition, in computers, math, or statistics, and in concepts/issues of ethnicity. There are breadth requirements in humanities, social sciences, and natural sciences/math. For all students; the number of units/courses in each group depends on the student's college and major. A thesis is required for honors program students. **Procedure:** Freshmen are admitted in the fall. Entrance exams should be taken by December of the senior year. Applications should be filed by November 30 for fall entry. The fall 2017 application fee was $70. Notifications are sent February 1. Applications are accepted on-line. **Transfer Students:** 1234 transfer students enrolled in 2016-2017. Transfer students applying to selecting majors must meet major preparation and GPA requirements for that major. 45 of 180 credits required for the bachelor's degree must be completed at UCR. **International Students:** They must take the TOEFL with a minimum score of 550 on the paper-based TOEFL (PBT) or 80 on the Internet-based version (iBT), and take the IELTS. They must also take the SAT or ACT.

ADMISSIONS: 57% of the 2017-2018 applicants were accepted. The SAT scores for the 2017-2018 freshman class were: Math-- 7% below 500, 43% between 500 and 599, 35% between 600 and 699, and 14% between 700 and 800. Evidence-Based Reading/Writing-- 8% below 500, 44% between 500 and 599, 41% between 600 and 699, and 7% between 700 and 800. The ACT scores were 2% between 12 and 17, 32% between 18 and 23, 48% between 24 and 29, and 19% above 30. 100% of the current freshmen were in the top fifth of their class; 100% were in the top two fifths. **Admissions Contact:** Emily Engelschall, Director, Undergraduate Admissions. Email: *admissions@ucr.edu* Web: *www.ucr.edu*

FINANCIAL AID: In 2017-2018, 79% of all full-time freshmen received some form of financial aid. 78% of all full-time freshmen received need-based aid. The average freshman award was $26,448. Need-based scholarships or need-based grants averaged $20,892 ($36,395 maximum); need-based self-help aid (loans and jobs) averaged $4,987 ($45,268 maximum); non-need-based athletic scholarships averaged $23,837 ($60,833 maximum); and other non-need-based awards and non-need-based scholarships averaged $9,123 ($54,931 maximum). The average financial indebtedness of the 2017 graduate was $21,104. The FAFSA code is 001316. The priority date for freshman financial aid applications for fall entry is March 2. The deadline for filing freshman financial aid applications for fall entry is May 1.

UNIVERSITY OF CALIFORNIA AT SANTA BARBARA C-5

www.ucsb.edu

Santa Barbara, CA 93106	(805) 893-2881
Fax: (805) 893-8779	Email: ucinfo@applyucsupport.net
Full-time: 9839 men, 11,359 women	Faculty: 967; I, +$
Part-time: 221 men, 155 women	Ph.D.s: 85%
Graduate: 1565 men, 1207 women	Student/Faculty: 17 to 1
Year: quarters, summer session	Tuition: $14,409 ($42,423)
Room & Board: $16,218	Freshman Class: 77098 applied, 27580 accepted, 4996 enrolled
SAT CR/M/W: 615/650/625 ACT: 28	CEEB CODE: 4835
Application Deadline: November 30	HIGHLY COMPETITIVE+

University of California at Santa Barbara, founded in 1891, is a public liberal arts institution offering programs in creative studies, engineering, and letters and science. There are 3 undergraduate schools and 1 graduate school. In addition to regional accreditation, UCSB has baccalaureate program accreditation with ABET, CSAB, APA, and NASD. The 1055-acre campus is in a suburban area 10 miles north of Santa Barbara. Including any residence halls, there are 399 buildings.

STUDENT LIFE: 95% of undergraduates are from California. Others are from 48 states, 80 foreign countries, and Canada. 86% are from public schools. 34% are White; 26% Hispanic; 21% Asian American; 8% Foreign; 6% two or more races; 2% African American; 1% American Indian/Alaska Native; 1% race unknown. **Female To Male Ratio:** 1.1:1. The average age of freshmen is 18; all undergraduates, 20. 9% do not continue beyond their first year; 91% remain to graduate. **Housing:** 6300 students can be accommodated in college housing, which includes married student dorms, on-campus apartments, and off-campus apartments. In addition, there are special-interest houses, wellness and theme housing, and cooperative housing. On-campus housing is guaranteed for the freshman year only, is available on a first-come, and first-served basis. 94% of students live on campus. All students may keep cars.

FACULTY/CLASSROOMS: All teach undergraduates and do research. No introductory courses are taught by graduate students. The average class size in an introductory lecture is 100; in a laboratory is 17; and in a regular course is 40.

PROGRAMS OF STUDY: UCSB confers B.A., B.F.A., B.M. and B.S. degrees. Master's and doctoral degrees are also awarded. Bachelor's degrees are awarded in BIOLOGICAL SCIENCE (biochemistry, biology/biological science, cell biology, ecology, evolutionary biology, marine biology, microbiology, molecular biology, physiology, and zoology), BUSINESS (accounting), COMMUNICATIONS AND THE ARTS (art, art history and appreciation, Chinese, classics, communications, comparative literature, dance, dramatic arts, English, film arts, French, German, Germanic languages and literature, Japanese, linguistics, literature, music, music performance, music theory and composition, Portuguese, Slavic languages, and Spanish), COMPUTER AND PHYSICAL SCIENCE (actuarial science, chemistry, computer science, earth science, geology, geophysics and seismology, hydrology, mathematics, physics, and statistics), ENGINEERING AND ENVIRONMENTAL DESIGN (chemical engineering, computer engineering, electrical/electronics engineering, environmental science, and mechanical engineering), HEALTH PROFESSIONS (pharmacy), SOCIAL SCIENCE (African American studies, anthropology, Asian/American studies, Asian/Oriental studies, biopsychology, economics, geography, history, interdisciplinary studies, international studies, Islamic studies, Italian studies, Latin American studies, medieval studies, Mexican-American/Chicano studies, Middle Eastern studies, philosophy, political science/government, psychology, religion, sociology, and women's studies). Economics, biological science, and psychology have the largest enrollments.

ACTIVITIES: 6% of men belong to 20 national fraternities; 11% of women belong to 24 national sororities. There are 455 groups on campus, including art, band, cheerleading, chess, choir, chorale, chorus, computers, dance, drama, environmental, ethnic, film, honors, international, jazz band, LGBT, literary magazine, musical theater, newspaper, opera, pep band, photography, political, professional, radio and TV, religious, social, social service, student government, symphony, and yearbook. Popular campus events include Club Day, Activities Fair, and UCEN Cultural Festival, and Exxtravaganza. **Sports:** There are 10 intercollegiate sports for men and 10 for women, and 19 intramural sports for men and 19 for women. Facilities include a gymnastics facility, rock-climbing walls, indoor and outdoor basketball courts, outdoor tennis and sand volleyball courts, swimming pools, a football/soccer stadium, softball diamond, baseball stadium, indoor/outdoor racquetball/squash courts, weight rooms, fitness center, and a synthetic track. **Graduates:** From July 1, 2016 to June 30, 2017, 5722 bachelor's degrees were awarded. The most popular majors were social sciences (26%), interdisciplinary studies (10%), and biological/life sciences (9%). In an average class, 66% graduate in 6 years or less.

SERVICES: Counseling and information services are available, as is tutoring in most subjects. There is a reader service for the blind, and remedial reading and writing. **Library/Resources:** The library contains 3.0 million volumes, 3.8 million microform items, and 5.5 million audio/video tapes/CDs/DVDs, and subscribes to 92,139 periodicals including electronic. Computerized library services include interlibrary loans, database searching, Internet access, and Wi-Fi capability. Special learning facilities include an art gallery, radio station, a language and learning lab, and numerous national and multicampus research institutes. **Physically Challenged Students:** All of the campus is accessible. Facilities include wheelchair ramps, elevators, special parking, specially equipped restrooms, special class scheduling, lowered drinking fountains, and lowered telephones. **Special:** A Washington semester, internships, cross-registration with all University of California campuses, study abroad in 34 countries, work-study programs, dual majors, student-designed majors, the B.A.-B.S. degree, and an accelerated degree program in electrical engineering are offered. There are 3 national honor societies, Phi Beta Kappa, and a freshman honors program. **Visiting:** There are regularly scheduled orientations for prospective students, consisting of a campus film, an information session, and a walking tour of the campus led by a student guide. There are guides for informal visits, visitors may sit in on classes, and stay overnight. To schedule a visit, contact the Office of Relations at (805) 893-2485. **Campus Safety and Security:** Measures include 24-hour foot and vehicle patrol, emergency notification system, self-defense education, and security escort services. There are emergency telephones and lighted pathways/sidewalks.

REQUIREMENTS: The SAT is required. The ACT and ACT Writing Test are recommended. In addition, SAT Subject tests in math and 1 other choice. Candidates for admission must have completed 4 years of English, 3-4 of math, and 2 each of foreign language, history, 2-3 of lab science, and 1 each of academic electives and visual/performing arts A GPA of 3.3 is required. AP credits are accepted. Graduation requirements vary by college. Generally, students will take one third of their distribution in the major subject, one third in general education courses, and one third in elective courses. General subject requirements include courses in English, foreign language, science/math/technology, social sciences, civilization and thought, literature, and the arts. Specific subject requirements include 6 writing-intensive courses and 1 course each in non-Western culture, quantitative relationships, and ethnic studies. To graduate, students must earn at least 180 quarter units, with a minimum GPA of 2.0, and have completed the American History and Institutions requirement. **Procedure:** Freshmen are admitted in the fall. Entrance exams should be taken by December of the senior year. Applications should be filed by November 30 for fall entry. The fall 2017 application fee was $70. Notifications are sent March 15. Applications are accepted on-line. **Transfer Students:** 2045 transfer students enrolled in 2016-2017. High school transcripts, college transcripts, and an essay or personal statement are required for all transfer applicants. Standardized test scores are required of all lower division transfers. An applicant must be in good standing at prior institution but no statement to this request is required. Preference is given to students who have completed 90 quarter (60 a semester) units and who transfer from community colleges. California residents should have a minimum 2.0 GPA in transferable coursework; nonresidents, a 2.8 GPA. Students with fewer than 12 quarter or semester units of transferable coursework must provide standardized test scores. 35 of 180 credits required for the bachelor's degree must be completed at UCSB. **International Students:** There are 552 international students enrolled. They must take the TOEFL with a minimum score of 550 on the paper-based TOEFL (PBT) or 80 on the Internet-based version (iBT). They must also take the SAT or ACT.

ADMISSIONS: 36% of the 2017-2018 applicants were accepted. The SAT scores for the 2017-2018 freshman class were: Critical Reading-- 7% below 500, 31% between 500 and 599, 45% between 600 and 699, and 17% between 700 and 800. Math-- 6% below 500, 22% between 500 and 599, 41% between 600 and 699, and 31% between 700 and 800. Writing-- 5% below 500, 27% between 500 and 599, 46% between 600 and 699, and 22% between 700 and 800. The ACT scores were 15% between 18 and 23, 45% between 24 and 29, and 39% above 30. 100% of the current freshmen were in the top fifth of their class; 100% were in the top two fifths. **Admissions Contact:** Office of Admissions Email: *ucinfo@applyucsupport.net* Web: *www.ucsb.edu*

FINANCIAL AID: In 2017-2018, 62% of all full-time freshmen received some form of financial aid. 58% of all full-time freshmen received need-based aid. The average freshman award was $24,479. Need-based scholarships or need-based grants averaged $20,526; need-based self-help aid (loans and jobs) averaged $6,748; non-need-based athletic scholarships averaged $14,233; other non-need-based awards and non-need-based scholarships averaged $6,450; and $10,012 from other forms of aid. 19% of undergraduate students work part-time. The average financial indebtedness of the 2017 graduate was $27,086. UCSB is a member of CSS. The FAFSA code is 001320. The priority date for freshman financial aid applications for fall entry is March 2. The deadline for filing freshman financial aid applications for fall entry is May 31.

UNIVERSITY OF CALIFORNIA SAN DIEGO D-5

www.ucsd.edu

La Jolla, CA 92093 **(858) 534-3156**

Fax: (858) 534-5629 **Email: admissionsdirector@ucsd.edu**

Full-time: 14,626 men, 13,501 women
Part-time: n/av
Graduate: n/av
Year: quarters, summer session
Room & Board: $13,307

Faculty: I, +$
Ph.D.s: 98%
Student/Faculty: 19 to 1
Tuition: $18,259 ($46,273)
Freshman Class: 88427 applied, 30210 accepted, 5710 enrolled

SAT CR/M/W: 641/683/642 **ACT:** 31
Application Deadline: November 30

CEEB CODE: 4836
MOST COMPETITIVE

University of California San Diego, founded in 1960, is a public institution located just off the California coast in La Jolla. There are 6 undergraduate schools and 5 graduate schools. In addition to regional accreditation, UCSD has baccalaureate program accreditation with ABET. The 2141-acre campus is in a suburban area Just off the California coast in La Jolla, about 12 miles north of downtown San Diego. Including any residence halls, there are 772 buildings.

STUDENT LIFE: 75% of undergraduates are from California. Others are from 50 states, 90 foreign countries, and Canada. 88% are from public schools. 9% are race unknown; 46% Asian American; 20% White; 2% African American; 19% Foreign; 16% Hispanic. **Male To Female Ratio:** 1.1:1. The average age of freshmen is 18; all undergraduates, 21. 5% do not continue beyond their first year; 95% remain to graduate. **Housing:** 11500 students can be accommodated in college housing, which includes married student dorms and on-campus apartments. In addition, there are language/international houses, special-interest houses, and identity housing. On-campus housing is available on a lottery system for upperclassmen. 57% of students commute. Upperclassmen may keep cars.

FACULTY/CLASSROOMS: 68% of faculty are male; 32% are female. No introductory courses are taught by graduate students. The average class size in an introductory lecture is 350 and in a laboratory is 40.

PROGRAMS OF STUDY: UCSD confers B.A. and B.S. degrees. Master's and doctoral degrees are also awarded. Bachelor's degrees are awarded in AGRICULTURE (environmental studies), BIOLOGICAL SCIENCE (biochemistry, bioinformatics, biology/biological science, biological sciences, biophysics, biotechnology, ecology, environmental biology, marine biology, marine science, microbiology, molecular biology, and physiology), BUSINESS (economics – statistics and management science), COMMUNICATIONS AND THE ARTS (art history, art, art history and appreciation, Chinese, classics, communications, dance, dramatic arts, English literature, Germanic languages and literature, Italian, Japanese, linguistics, literature, music, music history and appreciation, music technology, Russian, studio art, and visual and performing arts), COMPUTER AND PHYSICAL SCIENCE (applied mathematics, applied physics, chemistry, computer science, earth science, environmental chemistry, information sciences and systems, mathematics, physical chemistry, and physics), EDUCATION (mathematics education and science education), ENGINEERING AND ENVIRONMENTAL DESIGN (aerospace engineering, aerospace studies, bioengineering, chemical engineering, chemical engineering technology, computer engineering, electrical/electronics engineering, engineering, engineering physics, environmental engineering, environmental engineering technology, environmental science, and mechanical engineering), HEALTH PROFESSIONS (global & public health sciences and human biology), SOCIAL SCIENCE (African studies, anthropology, cognitive science, economics, ethnic studies, French studies, gender studies, history, human development, international studies, Italian studies, Japanese studies, Judaic studies, Latin American studies, philosophy, political science/government, psychology, religion, religious studies, Russian and Slavic studies, sociology, Spanish studies, Third World studies, and urban studies). Sciences, engineering, and the arts are the strongest academically. Biology, economics, and psychology have the largest enrollments.

ACTIVITIES: 12% of men belong to 23 national fraternities; 12% of women belong to 20 national sororities. There are 600 groups on campus, including an enterprise club, academic, art, band, cheerleading, chess, choir, chorale, chorus, communications, computers, dance, debate, drama, environmental, ethnic, film, honors, international, jazz band, LGBT, literary magazine, musical theater, newspaper, opera, orchestra, pep band, photography, political, professional, radio and TV, religious, social, social service, student government, symphony, and yearbook. Popular campus events include Sun God Festival, Founders Day Celebration. **Sports:** There are 12 intercollegiate sports for men and 11 for women, and 11 intramural sports for men and 11 for women. Facilities include an all-weather track, soccer and softball fields, an athletic training facility, swimming pools, a weight room, tennis courts, playing fields, and a golf driving range, a recreation complex features an arena, handball/racquetball courts, squash courts, a weight-training facility, a climbing wall, basketball, volleyball, and badminton courts. **Graduates:** From July 1, 2016 to June 30, 2017, 8058 bachelor's degrees were awarded. The most popular majors were social sciences, engineering technology, and biology.

SERVICES: Counseling and information services are available, as is tutoring in most subjects. There is a reader service for the blind. Office of Academic Support and Instructional Services (OASIS) and a writing lab. **Library/Resources:** The library contains 7.0 million volumes, 2.9 million microform items, and 87,625 audio/video tapes/CDs/DVDs, and subscribes to 42,000 periodicals including electronic. Computerized library services include interlibrary loans, database searching, Internet access, and Wi-Fi capability. Special learning facilities include an art gallery, radio station, TV station, an aquarium-museum, a supercomputer center, a theater, and myriad labs. **Physically Challenged Students:** Facilities include wheelchair ramps, elevators, special parking, specially equipped restrooms, special class scheduling, lowered drinking fountains, and lowered telephones. There is also available special accommodations, and administrative support services. **Special:** Internships in many fields, work-study, study abroad in more than 30 countries, and a Washington semester are offered. B.A.-B.S. degrees, an accelerated degree, dual majors, student-designed majors, and exchange programs with Xavier College, Spelman College, and Morehouse College are available. Nondegree study, credit for military experience, and pass/fail options are possible. There is a chapter of Phi Beta Kappa and a freshman honors program. **Visiting:** There are regularly scheduled orientations for prospective students, Triton Tour includes: 30-minute Admission Information Session, conducted by an Admissions Officer and a 90-minute walking tour led by current students. There are guides for informal visits and visitors may sit in on classes. To schedule a visit, contact Campus Tours at (858) 822-1455. **Campus Safety and Security:** Measures include 24-hour foot and vehicle patrol, emergency notification system, self-defense education, and security escort services. There are shuttle buses, emergency telephones, lighted pathways/sidewalks, an student safety awareness program, peer educators, and on-campus police department.

REQUIREMENTS: The SAT or ACT and ACT Writing Test are recommended. In addition, students must submit scores from either: ACT plus Writing OR SAT Reasoning Test with critical reading, math and writing; scores must be from same sitting. Recommended for engineering, biological or physical sciences majors: 2 SAT Subject Tests closely related to your major. Tests must be taken by December of senior year. A GPA of 3.0 is required. AP credits are accepted. Important factors in the admissions decision are advanced placement or honors courses, leadership record, and extracurricular activities record. Graduation requirements vary by undergraduate college but students must complete 180 to 184 total quarter units or 45 to 46 courses, with a minimum of 60 credit hours or 12 to 22 courses in the major. Students must maintain a minimum GPA of 2.0. **Procedure:** Freshmen are admitted fall. Entrance exams should be taken by December of the senior year. Applications should be filed by November 30 for fall entry. The fall 2017 application fee was $105. Notifications are sent March 30. applicants were on the 2017 waiting list; were admitted. Applications are accepted on-line. **Transfer Students:** 2933 transfer students enrolled in 2016-2017. Complete a minimum of 60 UC-transferable semester (90 quarter) units. Complete the UC-transferable college courses below with a C grade or better in each course. Each course must be 3 semester (4-5 quarter) units. 2 English composition, 1 mathematical concepts and quantitative reasoning, 4 courses from at least 2 of the following: arts and humanities, physical and biological sciences,and social and behavioral sciences. UCSD requires a competitive GPA in UC-transferable courses and good academic standing. 36 of 180 credits required for the bachelor's degree must be completed at UC San Diego. **International Students:** They must take the TOEFL with a minimum score of 550 on the paper-based TOEFL (PBT) or 80 on the Internet-based version (iBT). They must also take the SAT or ACT.

ADMISSIONS: 34% of the 2017-2018 applicants were accepted. **Admissions Contact:** Adele Brumfield, Associate Vice Chancellor of Enrollment. Email: *admissionsdirector@ucsd.edu* Web: *www.ucsd.edu*

FINANCIAL AID: 55% of all full-time freshmen received need-based aid. 70% of undergraduate students work part-time. UCSD is a member of CSS. The state aid form is required. The FAFSA code is 001317. The deadline for filing freshman financial aid applications for fall entry is March 2.

UNIVERSITY OF CALIFORNIA, SANTA CRUZ — B-3

www.ucsc.edu

Santa Cruz, CA 95064 — **(831) 459-4008**

Fax: (831) 459-4452	**Email: admissions@ucsc.edu**
Full-time: 8045 men, 8466 women	**Faculty:** I, +$
Part-time: 145 men, 165 women	**Ph.D.s:** 98%
Graduate: 1019 men, 764 women	**Student/Faculty:** 18 to 1
Year: trimesters, summer session	**Tuition:** $13,515 ($40,197)
Room & Board: $15,216	**Freshman Class:** 38640 applied, 20039 accepted, 3303 enrolled
SAT CR/M/W: 550/560/550 **ACT:** 24	**CEEB CODE:** 4860
Application Deadline: November 30	**COMPETITIVE+**

University of California, Santa Cruz is a public university, founded in 1965. UCSC began as a showcase for progressive, cross-disciplinary undergraduate education, innovative teaching methods and contemporary architecture. Since then, it has evolved into a modern research university with a wide variety of undergraduate and graduate programs, while retaining its reputation for strong undergraduate support and political activism. The residential college system, consisting of 10 small colleges, combines the student support of a small college with the resources of a major university. The figures given in the above capsule and in this profile are approximate. There is 1 graduate school. In addition to regional accreditation, University of California, Santa Cruz has baccalaureate program accreditation with ABET. The 2000-acre campus is located at the top of the Monterey Bay on the Central California coast, approximately 75 miles south of San Francisco and 30 miles south of San Jose. Including any residence halls, there are 559 buildings.

STUDENT LIFE: 96% of undergraduates are from California. Others are from 48 states, 65 foreign countries, and Canada. 8% are two or more races; 5% Foreign; 32% White; 30% Hispanic; 22% Asian American; 2% African American; 2% race unknown. **Female To Male Ratio:** 1.0:1. The average age of freshmen is 19; all undergraduates, 23. 9% do not continue beyond their first year; 77% remain to graduate. **Housing:** 8415 students can be accommodated in college housing, which includes married student dorms, on-campus apartments, and off-campus apartments. In addition, there are language/international houses, special-interest houses, multicultural residence halls, and family student housing. On-campus housing is guaranteed for the freshman year only and is available on a lottery system for upperclassmen. 53% of students live on campus. Alcohol is not permitted. Upperclassmen may keep cars.

FACULTY/CLASSROOMS: 58% of faculty are male; 42% are female. All teach undergraduates, and all do research. Graduate students teach 1% of introductory courses.

PROGRAMS OF STUDY: UCSC confers B.A., B.S., and B.M. degrees. Master's and doctoral degrees are also awarded. Bachelor's degrees are awarded in AGRICULTURE (environmental studies and plant science), BIOLOGICAL SCIENCE (biochemistry, bioinformatics, biology/biological science, cell biology, ecology, evolutionary biology, marine biology, molecular biology, and neurosciences), BUSINESS (business economics and international economics), COMMUNICATIONS AND THE ARTS (art, art history and appreciation, classical languages, dramatic arts, film arts, language arts, linguistics, literature, and music), COMPUTER AND PHYSICAL SCIENCE (chemistry, computer game design/development, computer science, earth science, geology, information sciences and systems, mathematics, and physics), ENGINEERING AND ENVIRONMENTAL DESIGN (computer engineering and electrical/electronics engineering), HEALTH PROFESSIONS (health science), SOCIAL SCIENCE (American studies, anthropology, community services, economics, German area studies, history, Italian studies, Latin American studies, law, philosophy, political science/government, psychology, sociology, and women's studies). Psychology, business management economics, and biology have the largest enrollments.

ACTIVITIES: There are 160 groups on campus, including art, band, cheerleading, chess, choir, chorale, chorus, computers, dance, debate, drama, environmental, ethnic, film, honors, international, jazz band, LGBT, literary magazine, musical theater, newspaper, opera, orchestra, photography, political, professional, radio and TV, religious, social, social service, student government, and symphony. Popular campus events include Multicultural Festival, and Martin Luther King Convocation. **Sports:** There are 7 intercollegiate sports for men and 8 for women, and 6 intramural sports for men and 6 for women. Facilities include a pool, playing fields, a weight room, an all-weather jogging track, fully equipped gyms, a fitness course, racquetball, tennis, and basketball courts, and a fitness center. **Graduates:** From July 1, 2016 to June 30, 2017, 3958 bachelor's degrees were awarded. The most popular majors were biological and life sciences (16%), social sciences (15%), and psychology (13%). In an average class, 4% graduate in 3 years or less, 55% graduate in 4 years or less, 70% graduate in 5 years or less, and 74% graduate in 6 years or less.

SERVICES: Counseling and information services are available, as is tutoring in most subjects. There is a reader service for the blind. A learning center helps SAA/EOP students with math and writing skills. There is also a program to help any student who is having trouble with certain courses. **Library/Resources:** The library contains 2.4 million volumes, and 523,053 audio/video tapes/CDs/DVDs. Computerized library services include interlibrary loans, database searching, Internet access, and Wi-Fi capability. Special learning facilities include an art gallery, natural history museum, radio station, TV station, Agroecology Program The Farm, Arboretum, Long Marine Lab, Seymour Marine Discovery Center, Lick Observatory on Mt. Hamilton, Silicon Valley Center, Digital Arts Research Center, and Genome Bioinformatics Project. **Physically Challenged Students:** Facilities include wheelchair ramps, elevators, special parking, specially equipped restrooms, special class scheduling, lowered drinking fountains, and lowered telephones. There is also a wheelchair lift-equipped transportation. **Special:** Cross-registration is possible with other Universities of California campuses, such as Hampshire College, University of New Hampshire, and University of New Mexico. UCSC also offers work-study, a Washington semester, internships in many arenas, study abroad in 34 countries, student-designed majors, dual majors, and a B.A.-B.S. degree in earth sciences, chemistry, and computer science. There is a chapter of Phi Beta Kappa and a freshman honors program. **Visiting:** There are regularly scheduled orientations for prospective students. There are guides for informal visits and visitors may sit in on classes. To schedule a visit, contact the Office of Admissions at (831) 459-4008. **Campus Safety and Security:** Measures include 24-hour foot and vehicle patrol, emergency notification system, self-defense education, and security escort services. There are shuttle buses, emergency telephones, lighted pathways/sidewalks, a rape prevention program, seminars for residential staff, and guards at each entrance.

REQUIREMENTS: The SAT or ACT is required. The ACT Optional Writing test is also required. Applicants must be graduates of an accredited secondary school or have a GED certificate. They should have completed 15 academic credits, including 4 years of English, 3 of math, and 2 each of foreign language, history, lab science, visual or performing arts, and college preparatory electives. Auditions are required for music majors, and portfolios are required for art majors. All students must submit a personal statement. Nonresidents must meet additional requirements. A GPA of 2.8 is required. AP credits are accepted. Important factors in the admissions decision are advanced placement or honors courses, evidence of special talent, and extracurricular activities record. To graduate, all students must complete 36 full-credit courses (180 quarter units) with a minimum GPA of 2.0. Courses are required in arts, English, history, writing-intensive, U.S. ethnic minorities/non-Western society, humanities, math, sciences, and social sciences. They must satisfy university requirements in U.S. history and institutions and in English composition, the residence requirement, the core course, and a comprehensive exam or equivalent body of work, or a senior thesis. Particular college requirements and those of an approved major vary. All students must also satisfy each of the UCSC general education requirements with a course graded C or better. **Procedure:** Freshmen are admitted fall and winter. Entrance exams should be taken by December of the senior year. Applications should be filed by November 30 for fall entry. The fall 2017 application fee was $70. Notifications are sent March 31. Applications are accepted on-line. **Transfer Students:** 1005 transfer students enrolled in 2016-2017. Applicants should have completed 84 quarter credits, with a GPA of 2.4 required for California residents and 2.8 for nonresidents, and all subject areas must be completed. No senior transfers are accepted. 35 of 180 credits required for the bachelor's degree must be completed at UCSC. **International Students:** There are 806 international students enrolled. They must take the TOEFL with a minimum score of 550 on the paper-based TOEFL (PBT) or 83 on the Internet-based version (iBT). They must also take the SAT or ACT.

ADMISSIONS: 52% of the 2017-2018 applicants were accepted. The SAT scores for the 2017-2018 freshman class were: Critical Reading-- 27% below 500, 36% between 500 and 599, 29% between 600 and 699, and 8% between 700 and 800. Math-- 21% below 500, 34% between 500 and 599, 33% between 600 and 699, and 11% between 700 and 800. Writing-- 26% below 500, 38% between 500 and 599, 30% between 600 and 699, and 6% between 700 and 800. The ACT scores were 23% below 12, 21% between 12 and 17, 24% between 18 and 23, 12% between 24 and 29, and 18% above 30. 100% of the current freshmen were in the top fifth of their class; 100% were in the top two fifths. **Admissions Contact:** Michael Mc Cawley, Director of Admissions. Email: *admissions@ucsc.edu* Web: *www.ucsc.edu*

FINANCIAL AID: The FAFSA code is 001321. The priority date for freshman financial aid applications for fall entry is January 1. The deadline for filing freshman financial aid applications for fall entry is March 2.

UNIVERSITY OF LA VERNE — D-5

www.laverne.edu

La Verne, CA 91750	**(909) 392-2800** **(800) 876-4858**
Fax: (909) 392-2714	**Email: admission@laverne.edu**
Full-time: 1130 men, 1643 women	**Faculty:** 245
Part-time: 41 men, 45 women	**Ph.D.s:** 81%
Graduate: 692 men, 1326 women	**Student/Faculty:** 13 to 1
Year: 4-1-4, summer session	**Tuition:** $39,900
Room & Board: $15,700	**Freshman Class:** 8179 applied, 3859 accepted, 724 enrolled
SAT CR/M/W: 520/520/510 **ACT:** 22	**CEEB CODE:** 4381
Application Deadline: February 1	**COMPETITIVE**

University of La Verne, founded in 1891, has been dedicated to the belief that a quality, values-based education enriches the human condition by engendering service, scholarly accomplishment, and professionalism. Though decades of growth have changed its appearance and reach, La Verne has retained its sense of purpose, seeking to provide students with individual attention to spark personal growth through intellectual challenge and development. The figures given in the above capsule and in this profile are approximate. There are 3 undergraduate schools and 4 graduate schools. In addition to regional accreditation, ULV has baccalaureate program accreditation with CAEP, CCTC, and CAATE. The 38-acre campus is in a suburban area on the eastern edge of Los Angeles County, some 30 miles from downtown Los Angeles. Including any residence halls, there are 35 buildings.

STUDENT LIFE: 96% of undergraduates are from California. Others are from 19 states, and 10 foreign countries. 7% are Asian American; 51% Hispanic; 5% African American; 5% Foreign; 4% two or more races; 26% White; 2% race unknown. **Female To Male Ratio:** 1.6:1. The average age of freshmen is 18; all undergraduates, 20. 13% do not continue beyond their first year; 59% remain to graduate. **Housing:** 837 students can be accommodated in college housing, which includes dorms, special-interest houses, international housing, and theme housing. On-campus housing is available on a first-come, first-served basis, and is available on a lottery system for upperclassmen. 69% of students commute. Alcohol is not permitted. All students may keep cars.

FACULTY/CLASSROOMS: 50% of faculty are male; 50% are female. No introductory courses are taught by graduate students. The average class size in an introductory lecture is 17 and in a regular course is 17.

PROGRAMS OF STUDY: ULV confers B.A. and B.S. degrees. Associate, master's, and doctoral degrees are also awarded. Bachelor's degrees are awarded in BIOLOGICAL SCIENCE (biology/biological science and environmental biology), BUSINESS (accounting, business administration and management, business economics, electronic business, institutional management, and international business management), COMMUNICATIONS AND THE ARTS (art, art history and appreciation, broadcasting, communications, comparative literature, dramatic arts, English, French, German, journalism, music, photography, Spanish, and speech/debate/rhetoric), COMPUTER AND PHYSICAL SCIENCE (chemistry, computer science, mathematics, natural sciences, and physics), EDUCATION (athletic training and education), ENGINEERING AND ENVIRONMENTAL DESIGN (computer engineering and environmental science), HEALTH PROFESSIONS (health care administration), SOCIAL SCIENCE (anthropology, behavioral science, child psychology/development, criminology, history, international studies, liberal arts/general studies, paralegal studies, philosophy, physical fitness/movement, political science/government, psychology, public administration, religion, social science, and sociology). Business administration, natural science, and education are the strongest academically. Business administration, organizational management, and liberal studies have the largest enrollments.

ACTIVITIES: 8% of men belong to 1 local and 2 national fraternities; 12% of women belong to 2 local and 3 national sororities. There are 66 groups on campus, including art, band, choir, chorale, chorus, communications, computers, dance, debate, drama, environmental, ethnic, forensics, honors, international, jazz band, LGBT, literary magazine, musical theater, newspaper, pep band, photography, political, professional, radio and TV, religious, social, social service, and student government. Popular campus events include Homecoming, Club Day, and Greek Week. **Sports:** There are 11 intercollegiate sports for men and 9 for women. Facilities include a football field, soccer field, track, and indoor gym with weight and fitness centers. **Graduates:** From July 1, 2016 to June 30, 2017, 549 bachelor's degrees were awarded. The most popular majors were business/marketing (21%), social sciences (16%), and psychology (14%). In an average class, 64% graduate in 6 years or less.

SERVICES: Counseling and information services are available, as is tutoring in most subjects. There is a reader service for the blind, and remedial math and writing. Students may use the Learning Enhancement Center or schedule tutoring free of charge. **Library/Resources:** The library contains 181,576 volumes, 1,068 microform items, and 1,640 audio/video tapes/CDs/DVDs, and subscribes to 37,287 periodicals including electronic. Computerized library services include interlibrary loans, database searching, Internet access, and Wi-Fi capability. Special learning facilities include an art gallery, natural history museum, radio station, TV station, a theater, an archeology lab, and a nuclear magnetic resonance (NMR) facility. **Physically Challenged Students:** Facilities include wheelchair ramps, elevators, special parking, specially equipped restrooms, lowered drinking fountains, and lowered telephones. **Special:** La Verne offers study abroad programs, work-study programs, student-designed majors, exchange student programs (domestic) distance learning and double major, liberal arts/career combination, and accelerated programs for adults. There are 9 national honor societies and a freshman honors program. **Visiting:** There are regularly scheduled orientations for prospective students, Student visits include campus tours, faculty and student panels, and meals. There are guides for informal visits, visitors may sit in on classes, and stay overnight. To schedule a visit, contact the Admissions Office. **Campus Safety and Security:** Measures include 24-hour foot and vehicle patrol, emergency notification system, and security escort services. There are shuttle buses, emergency telephones, lighted pathways/sidewalks, and controlled access to dorms/residences.

REQUIREMENTS: The ACT Optional Writing test is required. The SAT or ACT is recommended. Applicants must be graduates of an accredited secondary school. To apply for admission to the University, the following documents must be submitted to the Office of Admission: Application for Admission and Application Fee (using the La Verne Application for Admission or the Common Application), personal statement, High School transcripts, SAT I or ACT Test Scores, letter of recommendation. AP and CLEP credits are accepted. Important factors in the admissions decision are leadership record, advanced placement or honors courses, personality/intangible qualities, extracurricular activities record, geographical diversity, and recommendations by school officials. 128 semester hours, 44 must be taken at La Verne. At least 16 semester hours of the last 32 must be taken at ULV. The La Verne Experience integrates curricular, co-curricular, and community engagement activities for traditional undergraduates and spans throughout their four years at La Verne. **Procedure:** Freshmen are admitted in the fall and spring. Entrance exams should be taken during the junior or senior year. There are deferred admissions and rolling admissions plans. Applications should be filed by February 1 for fall entry; December 1 for spring entry. The fall 2017 application fee was $50. Notifications are sent December 1. Applications are accepted on-line. **Transfer Students:** 175 transfer students enrolled in 2016-2017. Transfer requirements include: 28 college semester units completed upon enrollment at La Verne, 2.7 GPA, College-level English and college-level math (typically college algebra or statistics or pre-calculus and higher). Students may enroll in the fall, April 1, and spring, December 1. 44 of 128 credits required for the bachelor's degree must be completed at ULV. **International Students:** There are 123 international students enrolled. They must take the TOEFL with a minimum score of 550 on the paper-based TOEFL (PBT) or 80 on the Internet-based version (iBT). Students must also take the Comprehensive English Language Test, the college's own test, SAT critical reading with a score of 550, and a minimum score of 6.5 on IELTS.

ADMISSIONS: 47% of the 2017-2018 applicants were accepted. The SAT scores for the 2017-2018 freshman class were: Critical Reading-- 39% below 500, 48% between 500 and 599, 12% between 600 and 699, and 1% between 700 and 800. Math-- 37% below 500, 45% between 500 and 599, 17% between 600 and 699, and 1% between 700 and 800. Writing-- 44% below 500, 44% between 500 and 599, 11% between 600 and 699, and 1% between 700 and 800. The ACT scores were 3% between 12 and 17, 58% between 18 and 23, 34% between 24 and 29, and 5% above 30. 54% of the current freshmen were in the top fifth of their class; 86% were in the top two fifths. 3 freshmen graduated first in their class. **Admissions Contact:** Ana Liza V. Zell, Associate Dean of Undergraduate Admissions. Email: *admission@laverne.edu* Web: *www.laverne.edu*

FINANCIAL AID: In 2017-2018, 86% of all full-time freshmen received some form of financial aid. 82% of all full-time freshmen received need-based aid. The average freshman award was $34,418. Need-based scholarships or need-based grants averaged $11,116; need-based self-help aid (loans and jobs) averaged $3,904; non-need-based athletic scholarships averaged $20,998; and $3,749 from other forms of aid. The average financial indebtedness of the 2017 graduate was $30,844. The state aid form, and the Cal Grant Application if available are required. The FAFSA code is 001216. The priority date for freshman financial aid applications for fall entry is March 2.

UNIVERSITY OF REDLANDS E-5

www.redlands.edu

Redlands, CA 92373	**909-748-8074** **800-455-5064**
Fax: 909-335-4089	**Email: admissions@redlands.edu**
Full-time: 1005 men, 1380 women	**Faculty:** 308; IIA, +$
Part-time: 12 men, 5 women	**Ph.D.s:** 89%
Graduate: 37 men, 61 women	**Student/Faculty:** 13 to 1
Year: other	**Tuition:** $48,072
Room & Board: $13,862	**Freshman Class:** n/av
SAT CR/M: 590/570 **ACT:** 25	**CEEB CODE:** 4848
Application Deadline: January 15	**VERY COMPETITIVE**

Since its founding in 1907, the University of Redlands emphasizes academic rigor, curricular diversity and innovative teaching. A Redlands education goes beyond training to embrace reflective understanding of our world; it proceeds from information to insight, from knowledge to meaning. The University blends liberal arts and professional programs, applied and theoretical study, traditional majors and self-designed contracts for graduation. There are 2 undergraduate schools and 5 graduate schools. In addition to regional accreditation, University of Redlands has baccalaureate program accreditation with ASLA, NASM, and WASC. The 160-acre campus is in a suburban area 20 miles north of Riverside and 60 miles east of Los Angeles. Including any residence halls, there are 86 buildings.

STUDENT LIFE: 70% of undergraduates are from California. Others are from 45 states, 43 foreign countries, and Canada. 51% are White; 25% Hispanic; 6% Asian American; 6% race unknown; 5% two or more races; 3% African American; 3% Foreign; 1% American Indian/Alaska Native. **Female To Male Ratio:** 1.4:1. The average age of freshmen is 18; all undergraduates, 20. 13% do not continue beyond their first year; 87% remain to graduate. **Housing:** 1621 students can be accommodated in college housing, which includes gender neutral and both single sex and coed dorms, on-campus apartments, and off-campus apartments. In addition, there are honors houses, language/international houses, special-interest houses, fraternity houses, and sorority houses. On-campus housing is guaranteed for all 4 years. 89% of students live on campus. All students may keep cars.

FACULTY/CLASSROOMS: 49% of faculty are male; 51% are female. All teach undergraduates. No introductory courses are taught by graduate students. The average class size in an introductory lecture is 20; in a laboratory is 10; and in a regular course is 12.

PROGRAMS OF STUDY: University of Redlands confers B.A., B.S. and B.Mus. degrees. Master's and doctoral degrees are also awarded. Bachelor's degrees are awarded in AGRICULTURE (environmental studies), BIOLOGICAL SCIENCE (biochemistry and biology/biological science), BUSINESS (accounting, business administration and management, and international business), COMMUNICATIONS AND THE ARTS (art, creative writing, dramatic arts, English, English literature, French, German, music, Spanish, studio art, theatre arts, and cinema and cultural studies), COMPUTER AND PHYSICAL SCIENCE (chemistry, computer science, information sciences and systems, mathematics, and physics), EDUCATION (education and music education), ENGINEERING AND ENVIRONMENTAL DESIGN (environmental science), SOCIAL SCIENCE (anthropology, area studies, Asian/Oriental studies, communication sciences & disorders, economics, history, interdisciplinary studies, international relations, Latin American studies, liberal arts/general studies, philosophy, political science/government, psychology, religion, sociology, and women & gender studies). Business, psychology, creative writing, interdisciplinary studies, environmental studies, and biology are the strongest academically. Business, psychology, interdisciplinary studies, and biology have the largest enrollments.

ACTIVITIES: 11% of men belong to 6 local and 1 national fraternities; 16% of women belong to 7 local sororities. There are 120 groups on campus, including and intramurals., big buddies club, art, band, cheerleading, chess, choir, chorale, chorus, communications, computers, dance, debate, drama, environmental, ethnic, film, honors, international, jazz band, LGBT, literary magazine, musical theater, newspaper, opera, orchestra, outdoor programs, pep band, photography, political, professional, radio and TV, religious, social, social service, student government, symphony, and yearbook. Popular campus events include Convocation Lecture Speaker Series, Multicultural Festival, Film Festival, Feast of Lights, Rah Rah Redlands, May Fest, and Fall Fest. **Sports:** There are 10 intercollegiate sports for men and 11 for women, and 6 intramural sports for men and 6 for women. Facilities include a fitness center, an aquatic center, a football stadium, tennis courts, and baseball, softball, soccer, and lacrosse fields.

SERVICES: Counseling and information services are available, as is tutoring in every subject. There is a reader service for the blind. **Library/Resources:** The library contains 421,219 volumes, 317,465 microform items, and 6,091 audio/video tapes/CDs/DVDs, and subscribes to 12,800 periodicals including electronic. Computerized library services include interlibrary loans, database searching, Internet access, and Wi-Fi capability. Special learning facilities include an art gallery, radio station, a language lab, a computer center, and a geographic information systems lab. **Physically Challenged Students:** 25% of the campus is accessible. Facilities include wheelchair ramps, elevators, special parking, specially equipped restrooms, special class scheduling, lowered drinking fountains, and lowered telephones. **Special:** Cross-registration with sister colleges, various internships, and study abroad in 50 countries are offered. A Salzburg semester, various work-study programs, B.A.-B.S. degrees, a liberal studies degree, dual majors, and accelerated degree programs are available. Students may pursue nondegree study, and take advantage of pass/fail option. At the Johnston Center for Integrative Studies, students design their own majors and courses of study. There are 4 national honor societies, Phi Beta Kappa, a freshman honors program, and 27 departmental honors programs. **Visiting:** There are regularly scheduled orientations for prospective students, including campus tours at 10 a.m., 1 p.m., and 4 p.m., on weekdays and 10 a.m. and 1 p.m. on Saturdays during the school year, interviews with counselors, department heads, and coaches, and sitting in on classes. There are guides for informal visits, and stay overnight. To schedule a visit, contact Office of Admission at admissions@redlands.edu. **Campus Safety and Security:** Measures include 24-hour foot and vehicle patrol, emergency notification system, self-defense education, and security escort services. There are shuttle buses, emergency telephones, lighted pathways/sidewalks, controlled access to dorms/residences, and safety whistles.

REQUIREMENTS: The SAT or ACT is required. Applicants should complete at least 16 credits in academic areas, including 4 years of English, 3 years of math, up to and including Algebra II, and 2 to 3 years of foreign language, sciences, and social studies. AP credits are accepted. Important factors in the admissions decision are advanced placement or honors courses, leadership record, and personality/intangible qualities. Requirements for graduation vary according to the degree and major. Students must complete at least 128 units with at least 32 in residence and maintain a minimum GPA of 2.0. A comprehensive exam is required for some programs. A liberal arts core curriculum, first-year seminar and community service are required. **Procedure:** Freshmen are admitted fall and spring. Entrance exams should be taken prior to application. There are early decision, early admissions, deferred admissions, and rolling admissions plans. Early decision applications should be filed by November 15; regular applications, by January 15 for fall entry. The fall 2017 application fee was $50. Applications are accepted on-line. **Transfer Students:** The SAT or the ACT may be required of transfer applicants, depending on how many units are accepted. 32 of 128 credits required for the bachelor's degree must be completed at Redlands. **International Students:** They must take the TOEFL with a minimum score of 550 on the paper-based TOEFL (PBT) or 81 on the Internet-based version (iBT), IELTS. They must also take the SAT or ACT.

Admissions Contact: Belinda Sandoval Zazueta, Director of Undergraduate Admissions. Email: *admissions@redlands.edu* Web: *www.redlands.edu*

FINANCIAL AID: The college's own financial statement, and the GPA verification form for California residents are required. The FAFSA code is 001322. The priority date for freshman financial aid applications for fall entry is November 15. The deadline for filing freshman financial aid applications for fall entry is March 2.

UNIVERSITY OF SAN DIEGO — D-5

www.sandiego.edu

San Diego, CA 92110 — **(619) 260-4506**, **(800) 248-4873**

Fax: (619) 260-6836	**Email:** admissions@sandiego.edu
Full-time: 2537 men, 3068 women	**Faculty:** 349; I, +$
Part-time: 96 men, 73 women	**Ph.D.s:** 95%
Graduate: 1209 men, 1922 women	**Student/Faculty:** 14 to 1
Year: 4-1-4, summer session	**Tuition:** $47,708
Room & Board: $12,630	**Freshman Class:** 14739 applied, 7339 accepted, 1210 enrolled
SAT EBR-W/M: 633/630 **ACT:** 28	**CEEB CODE:** 4849
Application Deadline: December 15	**HIGHLY COMPETITIVE**

University of San Diego, founded in 1949, is a private, Catholic liberal arts university. There are 3 undergraduate schools and 8 graduate schools. In addition to regional accreditation, USD has baccalaureate program accreditation with AACSB, ABET, and CAEP. The 180-acre campus is in an urban area 5 miles north of downtown San Diego. Including any residence halls, there are 85 buildings.

STUDENT LIFE: 62% of undergraduates are from California. Others are from 50 states, 75 foreign countries, and Canada. 55% are from public schools. 51% are White; 20% Hispanic; 9% Foreign; 7% Asian American; 6% two or more races; 4% African American; 2% race unknown; 1% American Indian/Alaska Native. 41% are Catholic; 31% claim no religious affiliation; 21% Protestant. **Female To Male Ratio:** 1.3:1. The average age of freshmen is 18; all undergraduates, 20. 10% do not continue beyond their first year; 82% remain to graduate. **Housing:** 2675 students can be accommodated in college housing, which includes both single sex and coed dorms and on-campus apartments. In addition, there are special-interest houses. On-campus housing is available on a first-come, first-served basis, and is available on a lottery system for upperclassmen. 54% of students commute. All students may keep cars.

FACULTY/CLASSROOMS: 51% of faculty are male; 49% are female. No introductory courses are taught by graduate students. The average class size in a laboratory is 18 and in a regular course is 22.

PROGRAMS OF STUDY: USD confers B.A., B.A./B.S., B.Acc. and B.B.A. degrees. Master's and doctoral degrees are also awarded. Bachelor's degrees are awarded in AGRICULTURE (environmental studies), BIOLOGICAL SCIENCE (biochemistry, biology/biological science, biophysics, and marine science), BUSINESS (accounting, business administration and management, business economics, finance, international business management, marketing management, and real estate), COMMUNICATIONS AND THE ARTS (art history, art and design, communications, English, French, music, Spanish, theatre arts, and visual and performing arts), COMPUTER AND PHYSICAL SCIENCE (chemistry, computer science, mathematics, and physics), ENGINEERING AND ENVIRONMENTAL DESIGN (electrical/electronics engineering, engineering, environmental science, industrial engineering, mechanical engineering, and preengineering), SOCIAL SCIENCE (anthropology, architectural studies, behavioral science, economics, ethnic studies, history, humanities, international relations, Italian studies, liberal arts/

general studies, philosophy, political science/government, psychology, sociology, and theological studies). Business administration, finance and accountancy have the largest enrollments.

ACTIVITIES: 23% of men belong to 9 national fraternities; 31% of women belong to 9 national sororities. There are 177 groups on campus, including environmental, LGBT, multicultural, political, service and outreach/diversity clubs, academic, cheerleading, choir, chorale, dance, debate, drama, environmental, ethnic, film, honors, international, LGBT, musical theater, newspaper, opera, pep band, political, professional, radio and TV, religious, social, social service, and student government. Popular campus events include Involvement Fair, International Student Organization Expo, Multicultural Night, Big Blue Bash/ Homecoming Concert, Greek Week, Open Mic Nights, Walk a Mile in Her Shoes, Life Week, and Changemaker Fest. **Sports:** There are 8 intercollegiate sports for men and 9 for women, and 10 intramural sports for men and 10 for women. Facilities include a sports center, a stadium for football and soccer, tennis courts, swimming pools, baseball facility, and an aquatic center. **Graduates:** From July 1, 2016 to June 30, 2017, 1396 bachelor's degrees were awarded. The most popular majors were finance (12%), business administration (10%), and marketing (8%). In an average class, 69% graduate in 4 years or less, 81% graduate in 5 years or less, and 82% graduate in 6 years or less. Of the 2016 graduating class, 15% were enrolled in graduate school within 6 months of graduation, and 98% were employed.

SERVICES: Counseling and information services are available, as is tutoring in most subjects. **Library/Resources:** Computerized library services include interlibrary loans, database searching, Internet access, and Wi-Fi capability. Special learning facilities include an art gallery, radio station, TV station, a media center, child development center, and a greenhouse. **Physically Challenged Students:** 85% of the campus is accessible. Facilities include wheelchair ramps, elevators, special parking, specially equipped restrooms, and lowered drinking fountains. **Special:** A B.A.-B.S. degree is offered in electrical, industrial and mechanical engineering. Internships in all disciplines, study abroad in over 30 countries and work-study programs on campus are available. Undergraduate research is a focus and available in many disciplines. The Washington Center Academic Seminar takes place each January in Washington, DC. The Department of Political Science and International Relations offers an intersession course (PS434) which enables students to earn 3 units for attending the seminar. There are 22 national honor societies, Phi Beta Kappa, and a freshman honors program. **Visiting:** There are regularly scheduled orientations for prospective students, tours and information sessions offered by the Admissions Office Monday through Friday 10 a.m. and 1:30 p.m., and most Saturdays from November through April at 11:00 a.m. There are guides for informal visits, visitors may sit in on classes, and stay overnight. To schedule a visit, contact the Undergraduate Admissions Office at (800) 248-4873. **Campus Safety and Security:** Measures include 24-hour foot and vehicle patrol, emergency notification system, self-defense education, and security escort services. There are shuttle buses, emergency telephones, lighted pathways/sidewalks, and controlled access to dorms/residences.

REQUIREMENTS: The SAT is required. Applicants should present a well-balanced secondary school program of college preparatory courses in English, foreign language, math, laboratory science, history, and social science. Both the content of the academic program as well as the quality of performance is considered. In addition, SAT/ACT results are used to broaden understanding of the applicant's potential. Participation in extracurricular activities at the school and in the community or church is taken into consideration in the admission decision. AP and CLEP credits are accepted. Important factors in the admissions decision are advanced placement or honors courses, parents or siblings attended your school, and personality/intangible qualities. All students must take 124 credit hours, including 36 to 72 in their major, while maintaining a minimum GPA of 2.0. The new Core curriculum includes basic competencies in writing, mathematical reasoning and a second language. Students will receive a foundation in theological and religious inquiry, philosophical inquiry and ethical inquiry. They will explore through scientific and technological inquiry, historical inquiry, social and behavioral inquiry, literary inquiry, and artistic inquiry. They will enhance their skills through studies in diversity, inclusion, and social justice as well as advanced writing, oral communication, and quantitative reasoning. They will be required to complete a culmination project or learning experience integrating these ideas. **Procedure:** Freshmen are admitted fall, spring, and summer. Applications should be filed by December 15 for fall entry; October 1 for spring entry. The fall 2017 application fee was $55. 1913 applicants were on the 2017 waiting list; 896 were admitted. Applications are accepted on-line. **Transfer Students:** 419 transfer students enrolled in 2016-2017. Transfer students must have a minimum GPA of 3.0 and have earned 24 credit hours. 30 of 124 credits required for the bachelor's degree must be completed at USD. **International Students:** There are 532 international students enrolled. They must take the TOEFL with a minimum score of 550 on the paper-based TOEFL (PBT) or 80 on the Internet-based version (iBT). They must also take the SAT or ACT.

ADMISSIONS: 50% of the 2017-2018 applicants were accepted. The SAT scores for the 2017-2018 freshman class were: Math-- 2% below 500, 29% between 500 and 599, 54% between 600 and 699, and 15% between 700 and 800. Evidence-Based Reading/Writing-- 1% below 500, 25% between 500 and 599, 60% between 600 and 699, and 14% between 700 and 800. The ACT scores were 10% between 18 and 23, 55% between 24 and 29, and 35% above 30. 67% of the current freshmen were in the top fifth of their class; 91% were in the top two fifths. **Admissions Contact:** Minh-Ha Hoang, Director of Admissions. Email: *admissions@sandiego.edu* Web: *www.sandiego.edu*

FINANCIAL AID: In 2017-2018, 84% of all full-time freshmen received some form of financial aid. 52% of all full-time freshmen received need-based aid. The average freshman award was $33,801. Need-based scholarships or need-based grants averaged $27,519; need-based self-help aid (loans and jobs) averaged $6,874; non-need-based athletic scholarships averaged $41,970; and other non-need-based awards and non-need-based scholarships averaged $14,503. 25% of undergraduate students work part-time. The average financial indebtedness of the 2017 graduate was $30,854. The FAFSA code is 010395. The priority date for freshman financial aid applications for fall entry is March 2.

UNIVERSITY OF SAN FRANCISCO B-3

www.usfca.edu

San Francisco, CA 94117 **(415) 422-6563**

Fax: (415) 422-2217
Email: admissions@usfca.edu
Full-time: 2460 men, 4126 women
Part-time: 116 men, 145 women
Graduate: 1449 men, 2784 women
Year: semesters, summer session
Room & Board: $14,330
Faculty: 346; I, +$
Ph.D.s: 95%
Student/Faculty: 14 to 1
Tuition: $46,250
Freshman Class: 15441 applied, 10907 accepted, 1587 enrolled
SAT or ACT: required
CEEB CODE: 4850
Application Deadline: January 15
COMPETITIVE

University of San Francisco, founded in 1855, is a private Roman Catholic institution run by the Jesuit Fathers and offering degree programs in the arts and sciences, business, education, nursing, and law. There are 3 undergraduate schools and 5 graduate schools. In addition to regional accreditation, USF has baccalaureate program accreditation with AACSB, CSAB, NLN, NASPAA, CCNE, and ABA. The 55-acre campus is in an urban area in the heart of San Francisco. Including any residence halls, there are 21 buildings.

STUDENT LIFE: 66% of undergraduates are from California. Others are from 49 states, 84 foreign countries, and Canada. 60% are from public schools. 26% are White; 22% Asian American; 21% Hispanic; 17% Foreign; 7% two or more races; 4% African American; 2% race unknown; 1% American Indian/Alaska Native. 35% are Buddhist, Hindu, Muslim, and Unknown; 30% Catholic; 24% claim no religious affiliation. **Female To Male Ratio:** 1.8:1. The average age of freshmen is 18; all undergraduates, 21. 15% do not continue beyond their first year; 76% remain to graduate. **Housing:** 2600 students can be accommodated in college housing, which includes dorms, on-campus apartments, and off-campus apartments. In addition, there are special-interest houses, multicultural floor, an academic interest floor, a freshman experiences floor, and a quiet floor. On-campus housing is guaranteed for the freshman year only. 63% of students commute. Alcohol is not permitted. All students may keep cars.

FACULTY/CLASSROOMS: 48% of faculty are male; 52% are female. 69% teach undergraduates. No introductory courses are taught by graduate students. The average class size in an introductory lecture is 22; in a laboratory is 14; and in a regular course is 27.

PROGRAMS OF STUDY: USF confers B.B.A., B.A., B.S., B.Arch.,

B.F.A., B.P.A., B.S.B.A., B.H.S. and B.S.N. degrees. Master's and doctoral degrees are also awarded. Bachelor's degrees are awarded in AGRICULTURE (environmental studies), BIOLOGICAL SCIENCE (biology/biological science and biophysics), BUSINESS (accounting, business administration and management, business economics, entrepreneurial studies, finance, hospitality management services, hotel/motel and restaurant management, human resources/organizational mgmt, international business, international economics, management information systems, marketing, and organizational behavior), COMMUNICATIONS AND THE ARTS (advertising, art history and appreciation, arts administration/management, communication studies, communications, comparative literature, design, drawing, English, fine arts, French, graphic design, illustration, media arts, painting, performing arts, photography, Spanish, and visual and performing arts), COMPUTER AND PHYSICAL SCIENCE (applied science, chemistry, computer information systems, computer science, information sciences and systems, mathematics, and physics), EDUCATION (art education, Asian studies, and secondary education), ENGINEERING AND ENVIRONMENTAL DESIGN (architecture, engineering physics, environmental science, interior architecture, and interior design), HEALTH PROFESSIONS (exercise science, health services administration, and nursing), SOCIAL SCIENCE (American studies, economics, history, international studies, Latin American studies, law enforcement and corrections, liberal arts/general studies, philosophy, political science/government, psychology, public administration, religious studies, sociology, and theological studies). Nursing, Sciences, Business are the strongest academically. Business, nursing, and psychology have the largest enrollments.

ACTIVITIES: 1% of men belong to 4 national fraternities; 1% of women belong to 5 national sororities. There are 117 groups on campus, including art, band, cheerleading, choir, chorale, chorus, communications, computers, dance, drama, environmental, ethnic, film, honors, international, jazz band, LGBT, literary magazine, marching band, musical theater, newspaper, orchestra, pep band, political, professional, radio and TV, religious, social, social service, student government, and yearbook. Popular campus events include Founders Day, and International Week. **Sports:** There are 7 intercollegiate sports for men and 8 for women, and 6 intramural sports for men and 6 for women. Facilities include a soccer stadium, a recreation center, swimming pool, multipurpose gym, weight room, dance and aerobics room, a martial arts room, and racquetball/handball courts, and a baseball field. **Graduates:** From July 1, 2016 to June 30, 2017, 1699 bachelor's degrees were awarded. The most popular majors were nursing (9%), finance (9%), and psychology (7%). In an average class, 3% graduate in 3 years or less, 62% graduate in 4 years or less, 71% graduate in 5 years or less, and 72% graduate in 6 years or less.

SERVICES: Counseling and information services are available, as is tutoring in every subject. There is a reader service for the blind. There is a full-time counselor for learning-disabled students, as well as a learning and writing center for students in need of academic assistance. **Library/Resources:** The library contains 1,000,000 volumes, 900,000 microform items, and 6,000 audio/video tapes/CDs/DVDs, and subscribes to 2,500 periodicals including electronic. Computerized library services include interlibrary loans, database searching, Internet access, and Wi-Fi capability. Special learning facilities include an art gallery, radio station, TV station, a rare book room, the Institute for Chinese-Western Cultural History, and the Center for Pacific Rim Studies. School of Nursing and Health Professions Learning Resource Center and Simulation Center for emulation of an acute care facility to practice hands on clinical nursing skills. Kudlick High-Tech Interactive Classroom for lectures, labs and individual student work equipped with 30 high end computers, two plasma screens, electronic white board, a camera capable of projecting physical objects onto a screen and individual presentation screens and workstations for students. **Physically Challenged Students:** 95% of the campus is accessible. Facilities include wheelchair ramps, elevators, special parking, specially equipped restrooms, and lowered drinking fountains. **Special:** Cross-registration with the San Francisco Consortium, internships with local business, social services, and research opportunities are available. Study abroad in Europe and Japan, work-study programs on and off campus and with social service agencies, a B.A.-B.S. degree in exercise and sports science, dual majors in liberal arts and education, 3-2 engineering degrees with the University of Southern California, student-designed majors, nondegree study, and limited pass/fail options are also available. The College of Professional Studies is a degree completion program for working adults. There are 13 national honor societies and a freshman honors program. **Visiting:** There are regularly scheduled orientations for prospective students, including a tour of campus, academic buildings, library, residence halls, recreation centers, and a group information session hosted by an admissions staff member. There are guides for informal visits, visitors may sit in on classes, and stay overnight. To schedule a visit, contact the Office of Admissions. **Campus Safety and Security:** Measures include 24-hour foot and vehicle patrol, emergency notification system, self-defense education, and security escort services. There are shuttle buses, emergency telephones, lighted pathways/sidewalks, and controlled access to dorms/residences.

REQUIREMENTS: The SAT or ACT is required. Applicants are required to have 20 academic units, based on 6 years of academic electives, 4 of English, 3 each of math and social studies, and 2 each of foreign language and lab science. An essay is required. The GED is accepted. A GPA of 3.0 is required. AP and CLEP credits are accepted. Important factors in the admissions decision are extracurricular activities record, evidence of special talent, and leadership record. All students must maintain a GPA of at least 2.0 and take 128 credit hours, including 58 in upper-division courses. 36 to 58 hours are required in the major. The current general education requirements include 9 units each of basic skills and history/social science, 6 each of philosophy, religious studies, cultural perspectives, natural science, and literature and fine arts, and 3 of ethics. **Procedure:** Freshmen are admitted fall and spring. Entrance exams should be taken during the first half of the senior year. There are early decision, early admissions, deferred admissions, and rolling admissions plans. Early decision applications should be filed by November 15; regular applications, by January 15 for fall entry. The fall 2017 application fee was $65. Notification of early decision is sent January 1; regular decision, on a rolling basis. 198 applicants were on the 2017 waiting list. Applications are accepted on-line. **Transfer Students:** 462 transfer students enrolled in 2016-2017. Applicants need a GPA of 3.0 or higher to be competitive for admission. 45 of 128 credits required for the bachelor's degree must be completed at USF. **International Students:** There are 1200 international students enrolled. They must take the TOEFL with a minimum score of 550 on the paper-based TOEFL (PBT) or 80 on the Internet-based version (iBT).

ADMISSIONS: 71% of the 2017-2018 applicants were accepted.; 3% were in the top two fifths. 5 freshmen graduated first in their class. **Admissions Contact:** April Crabtree, Director, Undergraduate Admissions. Email: *admissions@usfca.edu* Web: *www.usfca.edu*

FINANCIAL AID: In 2017-2018, 85% of all full-time freshmen received some form of financial aid. 62% of all full-time freshmen received need-based aid. The average freshman award was $35,575. Need-based scholarships or need-based grants averaged $21,677 ($51,484 maximum); need-based self-help aid (loans and jobs) averaged $13,047 ($68,084 maximum); non-need-based athletic scholarships averaged $43,498 ($63,214 maximum); and other non-need-based awards and non-need-based scholarships averaged $16,075 ($66,040 maximum). 47% of undergraduate students work part-time. The average financial indebtedness of the 2017 graduate was $47,322. The CSS/Profile is required. The FAFSA code is 001325. The deadline for filing freshman financial aid applications for fall entry is February 15.

UNIVERSITY OF SOUTHERN CALIFORNIA C-5

www.usc.edu

Los Angeles, CA 90089 (213) 740-1111

Fax: (213) 740-6364	**Email:** admdean@usc.edu
Full-time: 8758 men, 9437 women	**Faculty:** 1785; I, +$
Part-time: 318 men, 281 women	**Ph.D.s:** 90%
Graduate: 11545 men, 13532 women	**Student/Faculty:** 9 to 1
Year: semesters, summer session	**Tuition:** $52,283
Room & Board: $14,348	**Freshman Class:** 54280 applied, 9022 accepted, 3068 enrolled
SAT CR/M/W: 680/710/700 **ACT:** 32	**CEEB CODE:** 4852
Application Deadline: January 15	**MOST COMPETITIVE**

University of Southern California, founded in 1880, is a private institution offering undergraduate and graduate programs in liberal arts, fine arts, education, business, law, dentistry, engineering, communications, and health professions. There are 13 undergraduate schools and 18 graduate schools. In addition to regional accreditation, University of Southern California has baccalaureate program accreditation with AACSB,

ABET, ACEJMC, ACPE, ADA, APTA, CSWE, NAAB, NASM, CAEP, NLN, ACS, AOTA, ACPOTE, CODA, and CAPTE. The 226-acre campus is in an urban area 3 miles south of the Los Angeles Civic Center. Including any residence halls, there are 275 buildings.

STUDENT LIFE: 55% of undergraduates are from California. Others are from 50 states, 126 foreign countries, and Canada. 6% are African American; 33% White; 3% two or more races; 3% race unknown; 24% Foreign; 18% Asian American; 13% Hispanic. **Female To Male Ratio:** 1.1:1. The average age of freshmen is 18; all undergraduates, 20. 4% do not continue beyond their first year; 96% remain to graduate. **Housing:** 6500 students can be accommodated in college housing, which includes married student dorms, on-campus apartments, and off-campus apartments. In addition, there are honors houses, special-interest houses, fraternity houses, sorority houses, multicultural floors, substance-free housing, and international housing. On-campus housing is guaranteed for the freshman year only, is available on a first-come, first-served basis, and is available on a lottery system for upperclassmen. All students may keep cars.

FACULTY/CLASSROOMS: 61% of faculty are male; 39% are female. 90% teach undergraduates. No introductory courses are taught by graduate students.

PROGRAMS OF STUDY: USC confers B.A., B.S., B.Arch., B.F.A., B.Land.Arch. and B.M. degrees. Master's and doctoral degrees are also awarded. Bachelor's degrees are awarded in AGRICULTURE (environmental studies), BIOLOGICAL SCIENCE (biology/biological science, biophysics, and neurosciences), BUSINESS (accounting, business administration and management, and international business management), COMMUNICATIONS AND THE ARTS (art history and appreciation, broadcasting, classics, communications, comparative literature, creative writing, dramatic arts, East Asian languages and literature, English, English literature, film arts, fine arts, French, Italian, jazz, journalism, linguistics, music, music performance, playwriting/screenwriting, public relations, Russian, Spanish, studio art, theater design, theater management, video, and visual and performing arts), COMPUTER AND PHYSICAL SCIENCE (applied mathematics, astronomy, chemistry, computer science, geology, mathematics, physical sciences, and physics), ENGINEERING AND ENVIRONMENTAL DESIGN (aeronautical engineering, aerospace studies, architecture, biomedical engineering, chemical engineering, civil engineering, computer engineering, construction engineering, electrical/electronics engineering, environmental engineering, environmental science, industrial engineering, mechanical engineering, petroleum/natural gas engineering, and systems engineering), HEALTH PROFESSIONS (dental hygiene, exercise science, and occupational therapy), SOCIAL SCIENCE (African American studies, American studies, anthropology, Asian/American studies, classical/ancient civilization, East Asian studies, economics, ethics, politics, and social policy, geography, gerontology, history, international relations, Judaic studies, Latin American studies, philosophy, political science/government, psychology, religion, social science, sociology, and women's studies). Business, communications, and biological sciences have the largest enrollments.

ACTIVITIES: 4% of men belong to 2 local and 35 national fraternities; 4% of women belong to 3 local and 22 national sororities. There are 858 groups on campus, including art, band, cheerleading, chess, choir, chorale, chorus, computers, dance, debate, drama, drill team, environmental, ethnic, film, forensics, honors, international, jazz band, LGBT, literary magazine, marching band, musical theater, newspaper, opera, orchestra, pep band, photography, political, professional, radio and TV, religious, social, social service, student government, symphony, and yearbook. Popular campus events include Springfest, International Food and Cultural Fair, and Spectrum Concert Series. **Sports:** There are 9 intercollegiate sports for men and 13 for women, and 30 intramural sports for men and 23 for women. Facilities include a student athletic center, a track, gym, swimming pools, tennis, and baseball stadiums. **Graduates:** The most popular majors were business (25%), engineering (10%), and communication (9%). In an average class, 3% graduate in 3 years or less, 77% graduate in 4 years or less, 90% graduate in 5 years or less, and 92% graduate in 6 years or less.

SERVICES: Counseling and information services are available, as is tutoring in every subject. There is a reader service for the blind. Accommodations are made for students with disabilities. **Library/Resources:** The library contains 4.8 million volumes, 6.6 million microform items, and 84,953 audio/video tapes/CDs/DVDs. Computerized library services include interlibrary loans, database searching, Internet access, and Wi-Fi capability. Special learning facilities include an art gallery, natural history museum, radio station, TV station, state-of-the-art cinema/film-making facilities, labs, wind tunnel, and a marine science center. **Physically Challenged Students:** 97% of the campus is accessible. Facilities include wheelchair ramps, elevators, special parking, specially equipped restrooms, special class scheduling, and special housing. There are also a shuttle service for students with temporary disabilities. **Special:** Cross-registration is permitted with Hebrew Union College and Howard University. Internships in various majors, a Washington semester, work-study programs, study abroad in 29 countries, dual majors, a general studies degree, student-designed majors, a 3-2 engineering degree, and pass/fail options are available. Students are encouraged to pursue interdisciplinary study linking core art and science disciplines to professional programs. There are 39 national honor societies, Phi Beta Kappa, and a freshman honors program. **Visiting:** There are regularly scheduled orientations for prospective students. There are guides for informal visits, visitors may sit in on classes, and stay overnight. To schedule a visit, contact the Admission Office. **Campus Safety and Security:** Measures include 24-hour foot and vehicle patrol, emergency notification system, self-defense education, and security escort services. There are shuttle buses, emergency telephones, and lighted pathways/sidewalks. The safety department responds to calls for service on and off campus.

REQUIREMENTS: The SAT or ACT is required. The ACT Optional Writing test is also required. In addition, 3 SAT Subject Tests are recommended. Graduation from an accredited secondary school is required. Applicants must have completed at least 16 academic units combined in English, humanities, math, natural sciences, social sciences, and foreign languages, and academic electives in computer science, and with some exceptions, theater, fine arts, journalism, music or speech. AP credits are accepted. Important factors in the admissions decision are advanced placement or honors courses, recommendations by school officials, and evidence of special talent. All students must satisfy requirements in foreign language, freshman writing, general education, and take 1 multicultural course. Graduation requirements include a minimum of 128 credit hours and a minimum GPA of 2.0. **Procedure:** Freshmen are admitted fall and spring. Entrance exams should be taken by November of the senior year for scholarship applicants; by December for all others. Applications should be filed by January 15 for fall entry. The fall 2017 application fee was $80. Notifications are sent April 1. Applications are accepted on-line. **Transfer Students:** 1505 transfer students enrolled in 2016-2017. Transfer applicants must submit 30 units of transferable work with a strong GPA in a rigorous selection of courses. SAT or ACT scores are considered if 30 units have not been completed. 64 of 128 credits required for the bachelor's degree must be completed at USC. **International Students:** There are 2669 international students enrolled. They must take the TOEFL, Undergraduate students who score 500 or better on the verbal portion of the SAT are exempted from providing TOEFL scores. Upon arrival students with low TOEFL scores are required to take our local English proficiency examination. They must also take the SAT or ACT.

ADMISSIONS: 17% of the 2017-2018 applicants were accepted. The SAT scores for the 2017-2018 freshman class were: Critical Reading-- 2% below 500, 14% between 500 and 599, 48% between 600 and 699, and 36% between 700 and 800. Math-- 2% below 500, 10% between 500 and 599, 32% between 600 and 699, and 57% between 700 and 800. Writing-- 2% below 500, 9% between 500 and 599, 38% between 600 and 699, and 50% between 700 and 800. The ACT scores were 4% between 18 and 23, 21% between 24 and 29, and 75% above 30. **Admissions Contact:** Timothy Brunold, Dean of Admission. Email: *admdean@usc.edu* Web: *www.usc.edu*

FINANCIAL AID: USC is a member of CSS. The CSS/Profile, and parent and student federal income tax forms are required. The FAFSA code is 001328. The priority date for freshman financial aid applications for fall entry is December 1.

UNIVERSITY OF THE PACIFIC — B-3

www.pacific.edu

Stockton, CA 95211	(209) 946-2211 (800) 959-2867
Fax: (209) 946-2413	**Email:** admission@pacific.edu
Full-time: 1567 men, 1809 women	**Faculty:** 443; IIA, +$
Part-time: 53 men, 45 women	**Ph.D.s:** 91%
Graduate: 1076 men, 1566 women	**Student/Faculty:** 12 to 1
Year: semesters, summer session	**Tuition:** $44,588
Room & Board: $12,858	**Freshman Class:** 8870 applied, 5853 accepted, 726 enrolled
SAT CR/M/W: 565/600/565 **ACT:** 27	**CEEB CODE:** 4065
Application Deadline: August 15	**VERY COMPETITIVE**

University of the Pacific, founded in 1851, is a private institution that offers undergraduate and graduate programs in the arts and sciences, and professional programs in pharmacy, law, and dentistry. There are 8 undergraduate schools and 1 graduate school. In addition to regional accreditation, University of the Pacific has baccalaureate program accreditation with AACSB, ABET, NASAD, NASM, CAEP, ACS, and CAAHEP. The 175-acre campus is in a suburban area 80 miles east of San Francisco, and 40 miles south of Sacramento. Including any residence halls, there are 68 buildings.

STUDENT LIFE: 93% of undergraduates are from California. 37% are Asian American; 25% White; 19% Hispanic; 6% Foreign; 5% two or more races; 4% race unknown; 3% African American; 1% American Indian/Alaska Native. **Female To Male Ratio:** 1.3:1. The average age of freshmen is 18; all undergraduates, 20. 13% do not continue beyond their first year; 82% remain to graduate. **Housing:** 2208 students can be accommodated in college housing, which includes married student dorms and on-campus apartments. In addition, there are honors houses, special-interest houses, fraternity houses, sorority houses, intercultural, wellness, pharmacy, honors, and learning involvement theme houses. On-campus housing is guaranteed for the freshman year only, is available on a first-come, first-served basis, and is available on a lottery system for upperclassmen. 76% of students live on campus. Alcohol is not permitted. All students may keep cars.

FACULTY/CLASSROOMS: All teach undergraduates. No introductory courses are taught by graduate students. The average class size in a regular course is 19.

PROGRAMS OF STUDY: University of the Pacific confers B.A., B.S., B.F.A., B.M., B.S.B.A., B.S.B.E., B.S.C.E., B.S.E.E., B.S.E.M., B.S.E.P. and B.S.M.E. degrees. Master's and doctoral degrees are also awarded. Bachelor's degrees are awarded in BIOLOGICAL SCIENCE (biochemistry and biology/biological science), BUSINESS (business administration and management), COMMUNICATIONS AND THE ARTS (art, communications, dramatic arts, English, French, German, graphic design, Japanese, music, music business management, music history and appreciation, music performance, music theory and composition, Spanish, and studio art), COMPUTER AND PHYSICAL SCIENCE (applied mathematics, chemistry, computer science, geology, geophysics and seismology, information sciences and systems, mathematics, and physics), EDUCATION (education, music education, and physical education), ENGINEERING AND ENVIRONMENTAL DESIGN (civil engineering, computer engineering, electrical/electronics engineering, engineering management, engineering physics, environmental science, and mechanical engineering), HEALTH PROFESSIONS (music therapy, prepharmacy, and speech pathology/audiology), SOCIAL SCIENCE (economics, history, international relations, international studies, liberal arts/general studies, philosophy, political science/government, psychology, religion, social science, and sociology). Natural sciences, and the health professions are the strongest academically. Arts and sciences, pharmacy, and business have the largest enrollments.

ACTIVITIES: 15% of men belong to 1 local and 7 national fraternities; 22% of women belong to 1 local and 6 national sororities. There are 100 groups on campus, including the resident hall association, intramurals, residential learning, band, cheerleading, choir, chorale, chorus, club sports, computers, dance, debate, drama, ethnic, forensics, honors, international, jazz band, LGBT, literary magazine, musical theater, newspaper, opera, orchestra, pep band, photography, political, professional, radio and TV, religious, social, social service, student government, symphony, and yearbook. Popular campus events include Alumni Weekend, Pacific Boardwalk Carnival, and Cultural Diversity Week. **Sports:** There are 7 intercollegiate sports for men and 9 for women, and 30 intramural sports for men and 30 for women. Facilities include a sports arena, swimming pool, tennis courts, softball field, and a fitness center. **Graduates:** From July 1, 2016 to June 30, 2017, 823 bachelor's degrees were awarded. The most popular majors were business/marketing (16%), biological/life sciences and engineering (13%), and interdisciplinary studies (8%).

SERVICES: Counseling and information services are available, as is tutoring in every subject. There is a reader service for the blind, and remedial math, reading, and writing. **Library/Resources:** The library contains 381,686 volumes, 691,985 microform items, and 12,732 audio/video tapes/CDs/DVDs, and subscribes to 12,732 periodicals including electronic. Computerized library services include interlibrary loans, database searching, and Internet access. Special learning facilities include an art gallery, radio station, and the Brubeck Institute. **Physically Challenged Students:** 90% of the campus is accessible. Facilities include wheelchair ramps, elevators, special parking, specially equipped restrooms, special class scheduling, lowered drinking fountains, and lowered telephones. **Special:** The engineering school requires and guarantees a co-op program for specialized training in the field. Internships for credit or pay in all majors, more than 230 study-abroad programs in more than 80 countries, a Washington semester, and more than 20 work-study programs also are available. Student-designed majors, B.A./B.S. degrees, dual majors in most disciplines, and pass/fail options are possible. There are 18 national honor societies, a freshman honors program, and 42 departmental honors programs. **Visiting:** There are regularly scheduled orientations for prospective students, a tour and schedule appointments with faculty, admissions, financial aid personnel, and class visits, visitors may sit in on classes, and stay overnight. To schedule a visit, contact the Admissions Office. **Campus Safety and Security:** Measures include 24-hour foot and vehicle patrol and security escort services. There are emergency telephones and lighted pathways/sidewalks.

REQUIREMENTS: The SAT or ACT is required. Applicants must have 16 academic credits, 4 years English, (3 recommended) 3 of math (4 recommended), 2 each in same foreign language, and social studies, 2 lab science (3 recommended), 1 unit each of U.S history or government, fine or performing arts, and academic electives, and science majors are also recommended. An essay is required and an interview is recommended. In addition, music students must audition. The GED is accepted. Students must also have one year of math and science for science and health related majors. A GPA of 2.5 is required. AP and CLEP credits are accepted. Important factors in the admissions decision are advanced placement or honors courses, leadership record, parents or siblings attended your school, and extracurricular activities record. Students must complete at least 124 credit hours to graduate. The required general education program consists of 3 "mentor seminars" and 6 to 9 other courses chosen from categories such as the Individual and Society, the Human Heritage, and the Natural World and Formal Systems of Thought. **Procedure:** Freshmen are admitted fall and spring. Entrance exams should be taken in the spring of the junior year or fall of the senior year. There are early decision, early admissions, deferred admissions, and rolling admissions plans. Applications should be filed by August 15 for fall entry. The fall 2017 application fee was $35. Notifications are sent November 15. 143 applicants were on the 2017 waiting list; 14 were admitted. Applications are accepted on-line. **Transfer Students:** 162 transfer students enrolled in 2016-2017. Applicants should have a minimum GPA of 3.0 and at least 16 credit hours. The SAT or ACT and high school transcripts are required if fewer than 30 units of college work have been completed. 32 of 124 credits required for the bachelor's degree must be completed at Pacific. **International Students:** There are 125 international students enrolled. They must take the TOEFL. The SAT or ACT is required if the student has attended a U.S. high school.

ADMISSIONS: 66% of the 2017-2018 applicants were accepted. The SAT scores for the 2017-2018 freshman class were: Critical Reading-- 47% below 500, 38% between 500 and 599, 29% between 600 and 699, and 9% between 700 and 800. Math-- 16% below 500, 35% between 500 and 599, 32% between 600 and 699, and 17% between 700 and 800. Writing-- 26% below 500, 38% between 500 and 599, 27% between 600 and 699, and 10% between 700 and 800. The ACT scores were 1% between 12 and 17, 28% between 18 and 23, 42% between 24 and 29, and 28% above 30. **Admissions Contact:** Margaret Adkins, Director of Admissions. Email: *admission@pacific.edu* Web: *www.pacific.edu*

FINANCIAL AID: The average freshman award was $32,756. Need-based scholarships or need-based grants averaged $27,538; need-based self-help aid (loans and jobs) averaged $7,009; non-need-based athletic scholarships averaged $42,678; other non-need-based awards and non-need-based scholarships averaged $6,074; and $12,591 from other forms of aid. The average financial indebtedness of the 2017 graduate was $34,023. University of the Pacific is a member of CSS. The FAFSA code is 001329. The priority date for freshman financial aid applications for fall entry is February 15.

VANGUARD UNIVERSITY OF SOUTHERN CALIFORNIA D-5
www.vanguard.edu

Costa Mesa, CA 92626	(714) 966-5421 (800) 722-6279
Fax: (714) 966-5471	**Email:** admissions@vanguard.edu
Full-time: 511 men, 948 women	**Faculty:** 97
Part-time: 17 men, 10 women	**Ph.D.s:** 81%
Graduate: 80 men, 231 women	**Student/Faculty:** 13 to 1
Year: semesters, summer session	**Tuition:** $32,430
Room & Board: $9970	**Freshman Class:** 1418 applied, 917 accepted, 408 enrolled
SAT or ACT: required	**CEEB CODE:** 4701
Application Deadline: n/av	**VERY COMPETITIVE**

Vanguard University of Southern California, founded in 1920, is a private Christian comprehensive university of liberal arts and professional studies affiliated with the Assemblies of God. The figures given in the above capsule and in this profile are approximate. There is 1 undergraduate school and 4 graduate schools. In addition to regional accreditation, VUSC has baccalaureate program accreditation with WASC. The 38-acre campus is in a suburban area 40 miles southeast of Los Angeles, and 5 miles north of Newport Beach. Including any residence halls, there are 25 buildings.

STUDENT LIFE: 95% of undergraduates are from California. Others are from 29 states, 8 foreign countries, and Canada. 75% are from public schools. 43% are White; 37% Hispanic; 6% African American; 5% race unknown; 4% Asian American; 4% two or more races; 1% American Indian/Alaska Native. 74% are Protestant; 22% Unknown denominations. **Female To Male Ratio:** 2.0:1. The average age of freshmen is 19; all undergraduates, 24. 28% do not continue beyond their first year; 71% remain to graduate. **Housing:** 1074 students can be accommodated in college housing, which includes married student dorms, on-campus apartments, and off-campus apartments. On-campus housing is available on a first-come, first-served basis, and is available on a lottery system for upperclassmen. 68% of students live on campus. Alcohol is not permitted. All students may keep cars.

FACULTY/CLASSROOMS: 47% of faculty are male; 52% are female. 57% teach undergraduates. No introductory courses are taught by graduate students. The average class size in an introductory lecture is 40; in a laboratory is 12; and in a regular course is 19.

PROGRAMS OF STUDY: VUSC confers B.A. and B.S. degrees. Associate and master's degrees are also awarded. Bachelor's degrees are awarded in BIOLOGICAL SCIENCE (biochemistry and biology/biological science), BUSINESS (accounting, business administration and management, international business management, and marketing/retailing/merchandising), COMMUNICATIONS AND THE ARTS (broadcasting, communications, digital communications, dramatic arts, English, music, radio/television technology, Spanish, and theatre arts), COMPUTER AND PHYSICAL SCIENCE (chemistry and mathematics), EDUCATION (athletic training, education, elementary education, physical education, science education, secondary education, and sports studies), HEALTH PROFESSIONS (exercise science, nursing, physical therapy, and premedicine), SOCIAL SCIENCE (anthropology, biblical studies, Christian studies, history, liberal arts/general studies, ministries, missions, pastoral studies, political science/government, psychology, religious education, sociology, theological studies, and youth ministry). Religion, social sciences, natural sciences, and kinesiology are the strongest academically. Business, psychology, and communication have the largest enrollments.

ACTIVITIES: There are no fraternities or sororities. There are 35 groups on campus, including art, band, cheerleading, choir, chorale, chorus, communications, computers, dance, drama, environmental, ethnic, film, international, jazz band, literary magazine, musical theater, newspaper, opera, orchestra, photography, political, professional, radio and TV, religious, social, social service, student government, symphony, and yearbook. Popular campus events include Harvest Party, International Missions Week, Residence Rallies, and Christmas Party. **Sports:** There are 7 intercollegiate sports for men and 8 for women, and 4 intramural sports for men and 4 for women. Facilities include a gym, baseball, softball, soccer, a weight room, and contracted off-campus tennis courts and track course. **Graduates:** From July 1, 2016 to June 30, 2017, 545 bachelor's degrees were awarded. The most popular majors were psychology (20%), business administration (17%), and communications (11%). In an average class, 54% graduate in 4 years or less, 60% graduate in 5 years or less, and 61% graduate in 6 years or less.

SERVICES: Counseling and information services are available, as is tutoring in most subjects. There is also time management, organization skill, a writing center, and learning strategy. **Library/Resources:** The library contains 175,877 volumes, 20,795 microform items, and 7,962 audio/video tapes/CDs/DVDs, and subscribes to 10,000 periodicals including electronic. Computerized library services include interlibrary loans, database searching, and Internet access. Special learning facilities include a radio station. **Physically Challenged Students:** 95% of the campus is accessible. Facilities include wheelchair ramps, elevators, special parking, specially equipped restrooms, special class scheduling, lowered drinking fountains, and special housing. **Special:** Study abroad in cooperation with Assemblies of God programs and programs in the CCCU with placement in over 100 countries, a general studies degree, work-study, accelerated degree programs in business, psychology, and religion, and pass/fail options are available. 3 summer sessions are offered. There are 9 national honor societies and 6 departmental honors programs. **Visiting:** There are regularly scheduled orientations for prospective students, A typical campus visit includes a tour, and an appointment with an Admissions Counselor . There are guides for informal visits, visitors may sit in on classes, and stay overnight. To schedule a visit, contact Kyla Whittenberg at (714) 966-5496. **Campus Safety and Security:** Measures include 24-hour foot and vehicle patrol, emergency notification system, self-defense education, and security escort services. There are emergency telephones, lighted pathways/sidewalks, controlled access to dorms/residences, in-room safes and locks, and vehicle locks.

REQUIREMENTS: The SAT or ACT is required. High school courses should include 4 years of English, 3 years of social studies, and 2 years of math and science. Applicants are required to write an application essay and submit 2 references; 1 academic and 1 from a pastor/minister. A GPA of 2.8 is required. AP and CLEP credits are accepted. Important factors in the admissions decision are leadership record, advanced placement or honors courses, and evidence of special talent. Students must complete a minimum of 124 credits, with 40 to 70 in the major. General education requirements include 16 credits in religion, 15 in humanities and fine arts, 12 in social science, 7 in natural sciences and math, and 2 in phys ed. **Procedure:** Freshmen are admitted fall and spring. Entrance exams should be taken in the junior year. There are deferred admissions and rolling admissions plans. Early decision applications should be filed by December 1; regular applications, by March 2 for spring entry; and August 1 for summer entry. The fall 2017 application fee was $45. Notification of early decision is sent January 15; regular decision, November 1. Applications are accepted online. **Transfer Students:** 97 transfer students enrolled in 2016-2017. Transfer applicants must submit college transcripts and have a minimum college GPA of 2.5. 24 of 124 credits required for the bachelor's degree must be completed at VUSC. **International Students:** They must take the TOEFL with a minimum score of 550 on the paper-based TOEFL (PBT) or 80 on the Internet-based version (iBT). They must also take the SAT or ACT.

ADMISSIONS: 65% of the 2017-2018 applicants were accepted. 5 freshmen graduated first in their class. **Admissions Contact:** Katy Neric, Director of Admissions Operations and Communications. Email: *admissions@vanguard.edu* Web: *www.vanguard.edu*

FINANCIAL AID: In 2017-2018, 92% of all full-time freshmen received some form of financial aid. The FAFSA code is 001293. Check with the school for current application deadlines.

WESTMONT COLLEGE C-5
www.westmont.edu

Santa Barbara, CA 93108	(805) 565-6005 (800) 777-9011
Fax: (805) 565-6234	**Email:** admissions@westmont.edu
Full-time: 497 men, 775 women	**Faculty:** 94; IIB, ++$
Part-time: 1 men, 2 women	**Ph.D.s:** 90%
Graduate: n/av	**Student/Faculty:** 11 to 1
Year: semesters, summer session	**Tuition:** $44,044
Room & Board: $13,886	**Freshman Class:** 2001 applied, 1656 accepted, 363 enrolled
SAT CR/M/W: 585/575/580 **ACT:** 26	**CEEB CODE:** 4950
Application Deadline: February 15	**VERY COMPETITIVE**

Westmont College, founded in 1937, is a private, nondenominational Christian institution offering undergraduate liberal arts degrees. There is 1 undergraduate school. In addition to regional accreditation, WC has baccalaureate program accreditation with WASC. The 111-acre campus is in a suburban area 90 miles north of Los Angeles. Including any residence halls, there are 30 buildings.

STUDENT LIFE: 69% of undergraduates are from California. Others are from 41 states, 8 foreign countries, and Canada. 70% are from public schools. 61% are White; 16% Hispanic; 8% Asian American; 6% two or more races; 3% Foreign; 3% race unknown; 1% African American; 1% American Indian/Alaska Native. 95% are Protestant. **Female To Male Ratio:** 1.6:1. The average age of freshmen is 18; all undergraduates, 20. 13% do not continue beyond their first year; 70% remain to graduate. **Housing:** 1113 students can be accommodated in college housing, which includes dorms, and apartments for single students. On-campus housing is guaranteed for all 4 years. Alcohol is not permitted. Upperclassmen may keep cars.

FACULTY/CLASSROOMS: All teach undergraduates and do research. No introductory courses are taught by graduate students. The average class size in an introductory lecture is 30; in a laboratory is 15; and in a regular course is 20.

PROGRAMS OF STUDY: WC confers B.A. and B.S. degrees. Bachelor's degrees are awarded in BIOLOGICAL SCIENCE (biology/biological science), BUSINESS (business economics), COMMUNICATIONS AND THE ARTS (art, communications, dramatic arts, English, French, modern language, music, and Spanish), COMPUTER AND PHYSICAL SCIENCE (chemistry, computer science, mathematics, and physics), EDUCATION (art education, English education, mathematics education, music education, and social science education), ENGINEERING AND ENVIRONMENTAL DESIGN (engineering physics), HEALTH PROFESSIONS (exercise science), SOCIAL SCIENCE (European studies, history, liberal arts/general studies, philosophy, political science/government, psychology, religion, social science, and sociology). Biology, communication studies, and economics/business have the largest enrollments.

ACTIVITIES: There are no fraternities or sororities. There are 50 groups on campus, including art, band, chess, choir, chorale, chorus, computers, dance, debate, drama, ethnic, film, honors, international, jazz band, literary magazine, musical theater, newspaper, opera, orchestra, pep band, photography, political, professional, radio and TV, religious, social, social service, student government, symphony, and yearbook. Popular campus events include Spring Sing Musical/Talent Show, Multicultural Fellowship Week, and Theatrical and Musical Productions. **Sports:** There are 6 intercollegiate sports for men and 6 for women, and 10 intramural sports for men and 10 for women. Facilities include a gym, soccer/baseball field, swimming pool, fitness room, dance studio, a track, volleyball, tennis, basketball, and racquetball courts. **Graduates:** From July 1, 2016 to June 30, 2017, 307 bachelor's degrees were awarded. The most popular majors were parks and recreation (16%), business/marketing (14%), and biological/life sciences (11%). In an average class, 73% graduate in 4 years or less. Of the 2016 graduating class, 48% were enrolled in graduate school within 6 months of graduation, and 85% were employed.

SERVICES: Counseling and information services are available, as is tutoring in every subject. There is a reader service for the blind, and remedial math, and writers' corner supervised by tutors. **Library/Resources:** The library contains 162,274 volumes, 20,687 microform items, and 7,926 audio/video tapes/CDs/DVDs, and subscribes to 3,211 periodicals including electronic. Computerized library services include interlibrary loans, database searching, and Internet access. Special learning facilities include an art gallery, radio station, an observatory, a science center with a premedical center, and a physiology lab. **Physically Challenged Students:** 60% of the campus is accessible. Facilities include wheelchair ramps, elevators, special parking, specially equipped restrooms, special class scheduling, lowered drinking fountains, lowered telephones, and special housing. **Special:** Westmont offers cross-registration with 12 Christian colleges in the Christian College Consortium, internships in local businesses and social agencies, study abroad in 11 countries, and semesters in Washington, D.C., San Francisco, and Los Angeles. B.A.-B.S. degrees, student-designed majors, work-study programs, a 3-2 engineering program with several California universities, the University of Washington, and Boston University, and pass/fail options are also available. There are preprofessional programs in sports medicine, dentistry, engineering, law, medicine, ministry/missions, optometry, pharmacology, physical therapy, teaching, and veterinary medicine. There are 8 national honor societies, a freshman honors program, and 9 departmental honors programs. **Visiting:** There are regularly scheduled orientations for prospective students, consisting of meeting faculty and administrators and attending classes, academic seminars, student/parent panels, academic open houses, admission and financial aid sessions, student led small groups, campus tours, and various cultural events. There are guides for informal visits, visitors may sit in on classes, and stay overnight. To schedule a visit, contact Admissions/Campus Visit Coordinator. **Campus Safety and Security:** Measures include 24-hour foot and vehicle patrol, self-defense education, and security escort services. There are shuttle buses, emergency telephones, and lighted pathways/sidewalks.

REQUIREMENTS: The SAT or ACT and the ACT Optional Writing test are required. Applicants need 16 academic credits, including 4 years of high school English, 3 of math, 2 each of a foreign language, social science, and physical science, and 1 each of history and biological science. Interviews are recommended. Essays are required. The GED is accepted. AP and CLEP credits are accepted. Important factors in the admissions decision are advanced placement or honors courses, leadership record, and extracurricular activities record. Of the 124 semester units required for graduation, the college's general education requirements include 20 semester units of Common Context courses and 32 semester units of Common Inquiries courses. In addition, students must complete Common Skills courses and courses relating to Competent and Compassionate Action. Courses in religions studies and phys ed are required, as are courses in the history of Western civilization and English composition. Math proficiency is also required. There are distribution requirements in social sciences, humanities, and natural sciences. The total number of hours in the major varies from 36 to 66. A GPA of 2.0 must be maintained. **Procedure:** Freshmen are admitted fall and spring. Entrance exams should be taken during the spring of the junior year or the beginning of the senior year. Applications should be filed by February 15 for fall entry. The fall 2017 application fee was $50. 23 applicants were on the 2017 waiting list; 9 were admitted. Applications are accepted online. **Transfer Students:** 58 transfer students enrolled in 2016-2017. Transfer students from 2-year colleges should have a minimum GPA of 2.8 and students from 4-year colleges or universities, a 2.5. The college will not accept more than 64 transferable units from a community college; there is no maximum number of transferable units from a 4-year college. High school transcripts and test scores are required if the student has fewer than 24 transferable units. 32 of 124 credits required for the bachelor's degree must be completed at WC. **International Students:** There are 9 international students enrolled. They must take the TOEFL with a minimum score of 560 on the paper-based TOEFL (PBT) or 83 on the Internet-based version (iBT). They must also take the SAT or ACT.

ADMISSIONS: 83% of the 2017-2018 applicants were accepted. The SAT scores for the 2017-2018 freshman class were: Critical Reading-- 18% below 500, 35% between 500 and 599, 33% between 600 and 699, and 14% between 700 and 800. Math-- 14% below 500, 44% between 500 and 599, 34% between 600 and 699, and 8% between 700 and 800. Writing-- 18% below 500, 40% between 500 and 599, 33% between 600 and 699, and 9% between 700 and 800. The ACT scores were 1% between 12 and 17, 29% between 18 and 23, 45% between 24 and 29, and 25% above 30. **Admissions Contact:** Silvio E. Vazquez, Dean of Admissions. Email: *admissions@westmont.edu* Web: *www.westmont.edu*

FINANCIAL AID: In 2017-2018, 83% of all full-time freshmen received some form of financial aid. 83% of all full-time freshmen received need-based aid. The average freshman award was $35,569. Need-based scholarships or need-based grants averaged $28,676; need-based self-help aid (loans and jobs) averaged $5,370; non-need-based athletic scholarships averaged $11,059; other non-need-based awards and non-need-based scholarships averaged $3,891; and $17,726 from other forms of aid. 54% of undergraduate students work part-time. The average financial indebtedness of the 2017 graduate was $41,108. The FAFSA code is 001341. The priority date for freshman financial aid applications for fall entry is March 1.

WHITTIER COLLEGE D-5

www.whittier.edu

Whittier, CA 90608 **(562) 907-4238**

Fax: (562) 907-4870
Email: admissions@whittier.edu
Full-time: 634 men, 720 women
Faculty: 92; IIB, ++$
Part-time: 7 men, 7 women
Ph.D.s: 100%
Graduate: 258 men, 286 women
Student/Faculty: 15 to 1
Year: 4-1-4, summer session
Tuition: $46,604
Room & Board: $11,287
Freshman Class: 1970 applied, 1639 accepted, 358 enrolled
SAT CR/M: 526/532 **ACT:** 22
CEEB CODE: 4952
Application Deadline: February 1
COMPETITIVE

Whittier College, founded in 1887 by the Society of Friends and chartered by the state of California in 1901, is an independent, secular, and liberal arts institution. There is 1 undergraduate school and 2 graduate schools. In addition to regional accreditation, WC has baccalaureate program accreditation with CSWE. The 75-acre campus is in a suburban area 18 miles southeast of Los Angeles, in the foothills of the San Gabriel Mountains. Including any residence halls, there are 51 buildings.

STUDENT LIFE: 71% of undergraduates are from California. Others are from 25 states, 16 foreign countries, and Canada. 8% are Asian American; 6% African American; 40% White; 29% Hispanic; 2% Foreign; 1% American Indian/Alaska Native. **Female To Male Ratio:** 1.1:1. The average age of freshmen is 18; all undergraduates, 20. 26% do not continue beyond their first year; 54% remain to graduate. **Housing:** 840 students can be accommodated in college housing, dorms, and special-interest houses. On-campus housing is guaranteed for all 4 years. 61% of students live on campus. All students may keep cars.

FACULTY/CLASSROOMS: 47% of faculty are male; 53% are female. All teach undergraduates and do research. No introductory courses are taught by graduate students. The average class size in an introductory lecture is 20; in a laboratory is 24; and in a regular course is 22.

PROGRAMS OF STUDY: WC confers B.A. degrees. Master's and doctoral degrees are also awarded. Bachelor's degrees are awarded in BIOLOGICAL SCIENCE (biochemistry and biology/biological science), BUSINESS (business administration and management), COMMUNICATIONS AND THE ARTS (art, Chinese, dramatic arts, English, French, music, and Spanish), COMPUTER AND PHYSICAL SCIENCE (chemistry, mathematics, and physics), ENGINEERING AND ENVIRONMENTAL DESIGN (environmental science), SOCIAL SCIENCE (child psychology/development, economics, history, international studies, philosophy, physical fitness/movement, political science/government, psychology, religion, social work, and sociology). Business administration, political science, and English have the largest enrollments.

ACTIVITIES: 13% of men belong to 4 local fraternities; 21% of women belong to 6 local sororities. There are 90 groups on campus, including art, band, cheerleading, choir, chorale, chorus, computers, dance, drama, ethnic, film, honors, international, jazz band, LGBT, literary magazine, musical theater, newspaper, photography, political, professional, radio and TV, religious, social, social service, and student government. Popular campus events include Helping Hands Day, Tardeada-Latino Cultural Celebration, and MLK Jr. Oratorical Contest. **Sports:** There are 11 intercollegiate sports for men and 10 for women, and 5 intramural sports for men and 5 for women. Facilities include a stadium, gym, playing fields, athletics center, aquatics center, fitness center, and tennis courts. **Graduates:** From July 1, 2016 to June 30, 2017, 259 bachelor's degrees were awarded. The most popular majors were business (12%), political science (10%), and English (10%). In an average class, 49% graduate in 4 years or less, 62% graduate in 5 years or less, and 64% graduate in 6 years or less. Of the 2016 graduating class, 37% were enrolled in graduate school within 6 months of graduation, and 57% were employed.

SERVICES: Counseling and information services are available, as is tutoring in every subject. **Library/Resources:** The library contains 127,410 volumes, 6,877 microform items, and 1,793 audio/video tapes/CDs/DVDs, and subscribes to 26,365 periodicals including electronic. Computerized library services include interlibrary loans, database searching, Internet access, and Wi-Fi capability. Special learning facilities include an art gallery, radio station, a performing arts center, and writing center. **Physically Challenged Students:** 75% of the campus is accessible. Facilities include wheelchair ramps, elevators, special parking, specially equipped restrooms, special class scheduling, lowered drinking fountains, lowered telephones, and special housing. **Special:** Internships are possible fall, spring, and summer. Study abroad is offered in 30 countries. The Whittier Scholars Program offers self-designed interdisciplinary curricula, and dual majors are possible in all majors. Nondegree study and pass/fail options are available. Whittier offers a 3-2 engineering program with the Universities of Southern California and Minnesota, and a 3-3 law degree with Whittier Law School. There are 17 national honor societies and 16 departmental honors programs. **Visiting:** There are regularly scheduled orientations for prospective students, consisting of an interview with an admission officer and a campus tour. Customized visits can be arranged to include faculty, coaches, extracurricular activities, class visits, and residence hall tours. There are guides for informal visits, visitors may sit in on classes, and stay overnight. To schedule a visit, contact the Office of Admissions. **Campus Safety and Security:** Measures include 24-hour foot and vehicle patrol, emergency notification system, self-defense education, and security escort services. There are emergency telephones and lighted pathways/sidewalks.

REQUIREMENTS: The SAT or ACT is required. The SAT I is preferred. The college recommends that applicants have 4 years of high school English, 3 years each of history, math, and science, and 2 years of a foreign language. An essay is required. An interview is recommended. A GPA of 2.5 is required. AP credits are accepted. Important factors in the admissions decision are advanced placement or honors courses, recommendations by school officials, and leadership record. All students must take a total of 120 credits, including at least 30 in the major field, with a minimum GPA of 2.0. Distribution requirements include 4 courses in 4 distinct areas of communication, 4 courses in culture from 4 distinct areas, and a pair of courses in science and society. **Procedure:** Freshmen are admitted in the fall and spring. Entrance exams should be taken during the junior year or fall of the senior year. There are early admissions, deferred admissions, and rolling admissions plans. Early decision applications should be filed by December 1; regular applications, by February 1 for fall entry. The fall 2017 application fee was $50. Notification of early decision is sent December 29; regular decision, March 1. Applications are accepted online. **Transfer Students:** 95 transfer students enrolled in 2016-2017. Transfer applicants are considered on a case-by-case basis, but a minimum GPA of 2.5 is recommended in academic course work. The SAT or the ACT is required for students with fewer than 30 academic units. The GED is accepted for transfer applicants with at least 30 academic units. 30 of 120 credits required for the bachelor's degree must be completed at Whittier. **International Students:** There are 32 international students enrolled. They must take the TOEFL and either the SAT or ACT.

ADMISSIONS: 83% of the 2017-2018 applicants were accepted. The SAT scores for the 2017-2018 freshman class were: Critical Reading-- 38% below 500, 42% between 500 and 599, 17% between 600 and 699, and 3% between 700 and 800. Math-- 36% below 500, 41% between 500 and 599, 21% between 600 and 699, and 2% between 700 and 800. Writing-- 40% below 500, 42% between 500 and 599, 16% between 600 and 699, and 2% between 700 and 800. The ACT scores were 36% below 12, 27% between 12 and 17, 23% between 18 and 23, 8% between 24 and 29, and 6% above 30. 54% of the current freshmen were in the top fifth of their class; 75% were in the top two fifths. 16 freshmen graduated first in their class. **Admissions Contact:** Lisa Meyer, Vice President of Enrollment. Email: *admissions@whittier.edu* Web: *www.whittier.edu*

FINANCIAL AID: In 2017-2018, 83% of all full-time freshmen received some form of financial aid. 67% of all full-time freshmen received need-based aid. The average freshman award was $31,970. 64% of undergraduate students work part-time. The average financial indebtedness of the 2017 graduate was $30,970. WC is a member of CSS. The college's own financial statement is required. The FAFSA code is 001342. The deadline for filing freshman financial aid applications for fall entry is February 15.

WOODBURY UNIVERSITY C-5

www.woodbury.edu

Burbank, CA 91504 **(818) 252-5221** **(800) 784-9663**

Fax: (818) 767-7520
Email: info@woodbury.edu
Full-time: 458 men, 455 women
Faculty: n/av
Part-time: 40 men, 57 women
Ph.D.s: 71%
Graduate: 59 men, 75 women
Student/Faculty: n/av
Year: semesters, summer session
Tuition: $38,460
Room & Board: $11,133
Freshman Class: 1327 applied, 818 accepted, 116 enrolled
SAT: recommended
CEEB CODE: 4955
Application Deadline: March 1
VERY COMPETITIVE

Woodbury University, founded in 1884, is a private institution that emphasizes business and professional design education. There are 4 undergraduate schools and 3 graduate schools. In addition to regional accreditation, WU has baccalaureate program accreditation with AACSB, ACBSP, NAAB, NASAD, and CIDA. The 22-acre campus is in a suburban area 17 miles north of Los Angeles. Including any residence halls, there are 22 buildings.

STUDENT LIFE: 85% of undergraduates are from California. 9% are Asian American; 32% White; 31% Hispanic; 3% African American; 3% two or more races; 20% Foreign; 1% race unknown. **Female To Male Ratio:** 1.1:1. The average age of freshmen is 18; all undergraduates, 23. 28% do not continue beyond their first year; 52% remain to graduate. **Housing:** 227 students can be accommodated in college housing, which includes dorms and off-campus apartments, and nonsmoking suites. On-campus housing is available on a first-come and first-served basis. Alcohol is not permitted. All students may keep cars.

FACULTY/CLASSROOMS: 59% of faculty are male; 41% are female. No introductory courses are taught by graduate students. The average class size in an introductory lecture is 25; in a laboratory is 15; and in a regular course is 15.

PROGRAMS OF STUDY: WC confers B.A., B.S., B.Arch., B.B.A., and B.F.A. degrees. Master's degrees are also awarded. Bachelor's degrees are awarded in BUSINESS (accounting, fashion merchandising, management, and marketing/retailing/merchandising), COMMUNICATIONS AND THE ARTS (animation, communications, film, television and digital media, game art, graphic design, and writing), COMPUTER AND PHYSICAL SCIENCE (digital arts/technology), ENGINEERING AND ENVIRONMENTAL DESIGN (architecture and interior design), SOCIAL SCIENCE (fashion design and technology, history, interdisciplinary studies, political science/government, psychology, and public safety).

ACTIVITIES: Groups on campus include a fashion club, drama, ethnic, film, international, newspaper, professional, religious, social, social service, and student government. **Sports:** There is no sports program at Woodbury. Facilities include basketball and volleyball courts, weight training and aerobics rooms, an outdoor swimming pool, quarter-mile track, and a field for soccer and other sports. **Graduates:** From July 1, 2016 to June 30, 2017, 314 bachelor's degrees were awarded. In an average class, 26% graduate in 4 years or less, 43% graduate in 5 years or less, and 52% graduate in 6 years or less.

SERVICES: Counseling and information services are available, as is tutoring in some subjects, such as accounting, physics, structures, economics, and math. There is remedial math, reading, and writing. Books on tape are available for the blind. **Library/Resources:** Computerized library services include interlibrary loans, database searching, and Internet access. Special learning facilities include an art gallery, an architecture gallery, art/design gallery, and a fashion center. **Physically Challenged Students:** 95% of the campus is accessible. Facilities include wheelchair ramps, elevators, special parking, specially equipped restrooms, special class scheduling, and special housing. **Special:** Internships or verified work experience is required for all majors with the exception of organizational leadership. Concurrent registration with area institutions, work-study programs, study abroad in France, Spain, China, Korea, England, and Germany, dual majors, and pass/fail options are also offered. In addition there is limited pass/fail options; mostly in internships and some software workshop courses. **Visiting:** There are regularly scheduled orientations for prospective students, consisting of meeting with admissions counselors, the president, faculty members, students, financial aid counselors, and student services staff. There are guides for informal visits. To schedule a visit, contact the Admissions Office. **Campus Safety and Security:** Measures include 24-hour foot and vehicle patrol, self-defense education, and security escort services. There are emergency telephones, and lighted pathways/sidewalks.

REQUIREMENTS: The SAT is recommended. Required: an application form along with a $75 nonrefundable application fee and official high school transcripts. Optional: college entrance exams, letters of recommendation, and/or personal essay. Priority deadline for Spring Semester is November 1st and Fall Semester is March 1st. A GPA of 2.0 is required. AP and CLEP credits are accepted. Important factors in the admissions decision are advanced placement or honors courses, evidence of special talent, and recommendations by school officials. To graduate with a B.S., students must complete 120 semester units, including 61 to 66 in the major, with a B.A. 120 including 45 to 54 in the major, with a B.F.A., 128 including 68 in the major, with a B.Arch., 160 semester units, including 98 in the major. All students must maintain a minimum GPA of 2.0 and take freshman composition, information literacy, and public speaking courses. Course work in behavioral and social sciences, fine arts, humanities, environmental studies and natural sciences, and math are also part of the curriculum. **Procedure:** Freshmen are admitted in the fall, spring, and summer. Entrance exams should be taken prior to application. There are deferred admissions and rolling admissions plans. Application deadlines are open. The fall 2017 application fee was $75. Notification is sent on a rolling basis. Applications are accepted online. **Transfer Students:** 145 transfer students enrolled in 2016-2017. Applicants are required to have maintained a minimum GPA of 2.5 and to take the SAT or ACT if they have completed fewer than 30 semester units. 45 credits required for the bachelor's degree must be completed at WC. **International Students:** They must take the TOEFL with a minimum score of 61 on the Internet-based version (iBT). They must also take the SAT or ACT.

ADMISSIONS: 62% of the 2017-2018 applicants were accepted. The SAT scores for the 2017-2018 freshman class were: Critical Reading-- 26% below 500, 44% between 500 and 599, 25% between 600 and 699, and 5% between 700 and 800. Math-- 37% below 500, 38% between 500 and 599, 22% between 600 and 699, and 3% between 700 and 800. The ACT scores were 6% below 12, 13% between 12 and 17, 50% between 18 and 23, 28% between 24 and 29, and 3% above 30. **Admissions Contact:** Sabrina Taylor, Associate Vice President of Admissions. Email: *info@woodbury.edu* Web: *www.woodbury.edu*

FINANCIAL AID: Woodbury is a member of CSS. The college's own financial statement is required. The FAFSA code is 001343. The priority date for freshman financial aid applications for fall entry is October 1.

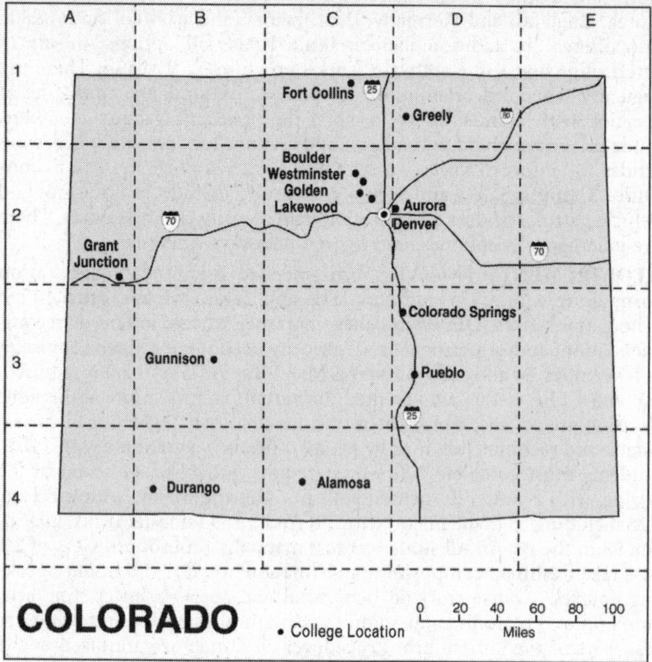

ADAMS STATE UNIVERSITY *(The complete profile is made available exclusively on our website, www.barronspac.com)*

COLORADO CHRISTIAN UNIVERSITY C-2

www.ccu.edu

Lakewood, CO 80226 **(303) 963-3207**
(800) 44-FAITH

Fax: (303) 963-3401	**Email: ccuadmissions@ccu.edu**
Full-time: 425 men, 700 women	**Faculty:** n/av
Part-time: 175 men, 175 women	**Ph.D.s:** 85%
Graduate: 55 men, 80 women	**Student/Faculty:** n/av
Year: semesters, summer session	**Tuition:** $30,370
Room & Board: $10,516	**Freshman Class:** n/av
SAT or ACT: required	**CEEB CODE:** 4659
Application Deadline: August 1	**VERY COMPETITIVE**

Colorado Christian University, founded in 1914, is a private, Christian interdenominational institution offering undergraduate and graduate programs in the arts and sciences, biblical studies, music, and education. The figures in the above capsule and in this profile are approximate. There are 4 undergraduate schools and 3 graduate schools. In addition to regional accreditation, CCU has baccalaureate program accreditation with NCA. The 29-acre campus is in a suburban area 10 miles west of Denver. Including any residence halls, there are 21 buildings.

STUDENT LIFE: 55% of undergraduates are from Colorado. Others are from 50 states, 16 foreign countries, and Canada. 81% are White; 7% African American; 6% Hispanic; 1% Asian American; 1% American Indian/Alaska Native; 1% Foreign. 99% are Protestant. **Female To Male Ratio:** 1.5:1. The average age of freshmen is 19; all undergraduates, 20. 33% do not continue beyond their first year. **Housing:** 732 students can be accommodated in college housing, which includes married student dorms, on-campus apartments, and off-campus apartments. In addition, there are special-interest houses. On-campus housing is guaranteed for the freshman year only, is available on a first-come, first-served basis, and is available on a lottery system for upperclassmen. 65% of students live on campus. Alcohol is not permitted. All students may keep cars.

FACULTY/CLASSROOMS: 65% of faculty are male; 35% are female. No introductory courses are taught by graduate students. The average class size in an introductory lecture is 25; in a laboratory is 18; and in a regular course is 30.

PROGRAMS OF STUDY: CCU confers B.A., B.S. and B.M. degrees. Associate and master's degrees are also awarded. Bachelor's degrees are awarded in BIOLOGICAL SCIENCE (biology/biological science), BUSINESS (accounting, business administration and management, human resources, management information systems, and management science), COMMUNICATIONS AND THE ARTS (art, communications, English, and music), COMPUTER AND PHYSICAL SCIENCE (computer management and science), EDUCATION (elementary education, music education, and secondary education), SOCIAL SCIENCE (biblical studies, history, liberal arts/general studies, psychology, social science, theological studies, and youth ministry). Science, biology, and education are the strongest academically. Human resources management, computer/information technology, and liberal arts have the largest enrollments.

ACTIVITIES: There are no fraternities or sororities. There are 21 groups on campus, including band, cheerleading, choir, chorus, computers, drama, honors, international, jazz band, literary magazine, musical theater, newspaper, orchestra, photography, professional, religious, social, social service, student government, symphony, and yearbook. Popular campus events include Preview Days, Spring Retreat, and New Student Retreat. **Sports:** There are 5 intercollegiate sports for men and 5 for women, and 6 intramural sports for men and 6 for women. Facilities include a gym, soccer and practice fields.

SERVICES: Counseling and information services are available, as is tutoring in every subject. There is remedial math, reading, and writing. **Library/Resources:** The library contains 53,532 volumes, 281,234 microform items, and 3,917 audio/video tapes/CDs/DVDs, and subscribes to 415 periodicals including electronic. Computerized library services include interlibrary loans, database searching, and Internet access. Special learning facilities include an art gallery. **Physically Challenged Students:** 85% of the campus is accessible. Facilities include wheelchair ramps, special parking, specially equipped restrooms, special class scheduling, lowered drinking fountains, lowered telephones, and special housing. **Special:** The school offers an ROTC program in cooperation with CU Boulder, cross-registration with the Focus on the Family Institute, internships, study abroad in 7 countries, a Washington semester, and work-study programs. Accelerated degree programs are available in Christian leadership, organizational management, and management of information systems. Dual and student-designed majors, nondegree study, pass/fail options, and credit for life, military, and work experience are also available. There are 2 national honor societies, a freshman honors program, and 1 departmental honors program. **Visiting:** There are regularly scheduled orientations for prospective students. There are guides for informal visits, visitors may sit in on classes, and stay overnight. To schedule a visit, contact the Office of Admissions. **Campus Safety and Security:** Measures include 24-hour foot and vehicle patrol and security escort services. There are emergency telephones and lighted pathways/sidewalks.

REQUIREMENTS: The SAT or ACT is required. In addition, applicants must be graduates of an accredited secondary school, and completed 4 years of English, 3 years of math, 2-3 years of science, and 2 years of a foreign language. The GED is accepted. Two essay are required. If you don't meet the admission requirements, your application file will be reviewed by a committee. A campus visit is recommended. A GPA of 2.8 is required. AP and CLEP credits are accepted. To graduate, students must complete at least 128 semester hours, including the 48-hour general education requirement and courses specified for the major, a minimum cumulative GPA of 2.0, with 2.5 in the major. The university requires 4 semesters of Christian service and regular chapel attendance. All students must complete 12 credits in biblical studies. **Procedure:** Freshmen are admitted to all sessions. There are deferred admissions and rolling admissions plans. Applications should be filed by August 1 for fall entry. The fall 2017 application fee was $40. Applications are accepted on-line. **Transfer Students:** Applicants for transfer should have completed 12 college credits with a minimum GPA of 2.0. 30 of 128 credits required for the bachelor's degree must be completed at CCU. **International Students:** They must take the TOEFL and the college's own test. They must also take the SAT or ACT.

Admissions Contact: Simeon Turner, Assoc. Director of Admissions. Email: *ccuadmissions@ccu.edu* Web: *www.ccu.edu*

FINANCIAL AID: In 2017-2018, 90% of all full-time freshmen received some form of financial aid. 90% of all full-time freshmen received need-based aid. The FAFSA code is 009401. The priority date for freshman financial aid applications for fall entry is October 1.

COLORADO COLLEGE D-3
www.coloradocollege.edu

Colorado Springs, CO 80903 (719) 389-6344 (800) 542-7214
Fax: (719) 389-6816 Email: admission@coloradocollege.edu

Full-time: 971 men, 1120 women	**Faculty:** 190; IIB, ++$
Part-time: 8 men, 8 women	**Ph.D.s:** 99%
Graduate: 3 men, 8 women	**Student/Faculty:** 10 to 1
Year: other, summer session	**Tuition:** $52,818
Room & Board: $12,076	**Freshman Class:** 8223 applied, 1244 accepted, 544 enrolled
SAT or ACT: required	**CEEB CODE:** 4072
Application Deadline: January 15	**MOST COMPETITIVE**

Colorado College, founded in 1874, is an independent liberal arts and sciences institution. The academic year is based on the "Block Plan," under which students take one course during each of the eight three-and-a-half week long blocks of study. There is also a two-block Summer Session. There is 1 undergraduate school and 1 graduate school. In addition to regional accreditation, CC has baccalaureate program accreditation with NCA. The 90-acre campus is in an urban area in Colorado Springs, 70 miles south of Denver. Including any residence halls, there are 107 buildings.

STUDENT LIFE: 83% of undergraduates are from out of state, mostly the Northeast. Students are from 49 states, 56 foreign countries, and Canada. 9% are Foreign; 9% two or more races; 8% Hispanic; 66% White; 4% Asian American; 2% African American; 1% race unknown. **Female To Male Ratio:** 1.2:1. The average age of freshmen is 18; all undergraduates, 20. 6% do not continue beyond their first year; 88% remain to graduate. **Housing:** 1649 students can be accommodated in college housing, which includes single-sex and coed dorms, on-campus apartments, and off-campus apartments. In addition, there are language/international houses, fraternity houses, substance-free, smoke-free, diversity, community arts, and sustainable living houses. On-campus housing is guaranteed for all 4 years. 78% of students live on campus. Upperclassmen may keep cars.

FACULTY/CLASSROOMS: 52% of faculty are male; 48% are female. All teach undergraduates. No introductory courses are taught by graduate students. The average class size in a regular course is 15.

PROGRAMS OF STUDY: CC confers B.A. degrees. Master's degrees are also awarded. Bachelor's degrees are awarded in BIOLOGICAL SCIENCE (biology ecology and field biology, biochemistry, molecular biology, and neurosciences), BUSINESS (international economics), COMMUNICATIONS AND THE ARTS (art history and appreciation, classics, comparative literature, creative writing, dance, dramatic arts, English, film arts, Germanic languages and literature, music, romance languages and literature, and studio art), COMPUTER AND PHYSICAL SCIENCE (chemistry, computer science, geology, mathematics, and physics), EDUCATION (education), ENGINEERING AND ENVIRONMENTAL DESIGN (environmental science), SOCIAL SCIENCE (anthropology, Asian/Oriental studies, economics, ethnic studies, French studies, gender studies, Hispanic American studies, history, history of philosophy, interdisciplinary studies, Italian studies, liberal arts/general studies, philosophy, political science/government, psychology, religion, Russian and Slavic studies, sociology, Southwest American studies, and women's studies). Economics, sociology, and political science have the largest enrollments.

ACTIVITIES: There are 143 groups on campus, including and health awareness, science, art, band, chess, choir, chorale, chorus, communications, computers, dance, debate, drama, environmental, ethnic, film, forensics, honors, international, jazz band, LGBT, literary magazine, musical theater, newspaper, orchestra, other major clubs are outdoor, photography, political, professional, religious, social, social service, student government, symphony, and yearbook. Popular campus events include Afternoon and Evening Blues, Rock, Folk, Jazz, World Music Concerts, Annual Arts and Crafts Sale, Winter Ball and Homecoming. **Sports:** There are 8 intercollegiate sports for men and 8 for women, and 14 intramural sports for men and 12 for women. Facilities include a sports center with two gyms, weight & exercise rooms, squash, tennis, racquetball courts, a pool, ice rink, and playing fields. **Graduates:** From July 1, 2016 to June 30, 2017, 566 bachelor's degrees were awarded. The most popular majors were economics (8%), sociology (6%), and political science (6%). In an average class, 1% graduate in 3 years or less, 82% graduate in 4 years or less, 88% graduate in 5 years or less, and 88% graduate in 6 years or less.

SERVICES: There are a variety of services and resources to help students succeed. **Library/Resources:** The library contains 543,881 volumes, 132,510 microform items, and 76,543 audio/video tapes/CDs/DVDs, and subscribes to 77,278 periodicals including electronic. Computerized library services include interlibrary loans, database searching, Internet access, and Wi-Fi capability. Special learning facilities include an art gallery, an electronic music studio, music library, telescope dome, multimedia computer lab, the Colorado College Press, an herbarium, Fourier transform nuclear magnetic resonance spectrometer, a scanning electronic microscope and transmission electronic microscope, an environmental service van equipped for field research, petrographic microscopes, an X-ray diffractometer, sedimentology lab, metabolic equipment, hydrostatic weighing equipment, and a cadaver study in sports science. **Physically Challenged Students:** Staff members work closely with students who have documented disabilities requiring accommodation to ensure equal access to the college's programs, activities, and services. **Special:** CC offers study abroad in many countries, a Washington semester, student-designed majors, 3-3 law program opportunity with Columbia University School of Law, and 3-2 engineering degrees with Columbia University, Rensselaer Polytechnic Institute, University of Southern California, and Washington University. There are 12 national honor societies and a chapter of Phi Beta Kappa. **Visiting:** There are regularly scheduled orientations for prospective students, a class visit, an information session with an admissions director, and a student-led tour. There are guides for informal visits, visitors may sit in on classes, and stay overnight. To schedule a visit, contact Admission Office. **Campus Safety and Security:** Measures include 24-hour foot and vehicle patrol, emergency notification system, self-defense education, and security escort services. There are emergency telephones, lighted pathways/sidewalks, controlled access to dorms/residences, whistle stop program, and fire safety inspections.

REQUIREMENTS: Applicants should have completed at least 16 (18 to 20 recommended) high school academic credits. The GED is accepted. An essay is required. Colorado College has adopted a flexible testing policy which allows applicants an expanded set of choices for meeting standardized test requirements. We require that applicants submit either the SAT Reasoning Test or ACT test, or elect a third option including three exams of the applicant's choice chosen from a list of acceptable exams (ACT, SAT, AP, IB, TOEFL) of the applicant's choice, which must include one quantitative test, one verbal/writing test, and a third test of your choice. AP credits are accepted. Important factors in the admissions decision are advanced placement or honors courses, extracurricular activities record, and evidence of special talent. To graduate, students must complete 32 units with a cumulative GPA of 2.0. No major may require more than 14 units in any one department and no more than 16 overall (including prerequisites). Students must take and pass at least one full unit in each academic division. They must complete a Critical Perspectives requirement, consisting of "West in Time" units (one two-block course, two units); a "Global Cultures" unit (one unit); a "Social Inequality" unit (one unit); Scientific Investigation of the Natural World (two units, including at least one lab or field course); Quantitative Reasoning (one unit). Courses may meet more than one designation (for example, a course may be designated both "West in Time" and "Global Cultures") but students must choose one designation or the other, except in the case of "Quantitative Reasoning," which may be fulfilled along with any of the other Critical Perspectives requirements. Basic competency in a foreign language is also required, as is two units of a First-Year Experience course. **Procedure:** Freshmen are admitted fall and spring. Entrance exams must be received by January 15 for fall entry. There are early decision, early admissions, and deferred admissions plans. Early decision applications should be filed by November 10; regular applications, by January 15 for fall entry. The fall 2017 application fee was $60. Notification of early decision is sent December 15; regular decision, April 1. 301 early decision candidates were accepted for the 2017-2018 class. 212 applicants were on the 2017 waiting list; 16 were admitted. Applications are accepted on-line. **Transfer Students:** 25 transfer students enrolled in 2016-2017. Requirements needed are the Common Application and Writing Supplement to the Common Application, $60 application fee or fee waiver request, Transfer College Report (from College Registrar), Final high school transcript, Official transcript (s) for all colleges/universities attended, Standardized test scores (may be waived if not required for entry to current college/university), Two college instructor academic evaluations. 64 of 128 credits required for the bachelor's degree must be completed at CC. **International Students:** There are 177 international students enrolled. Applicants must submit either the SAT Reasoning, ACT test, or three exams of the applicant's choice selected from a list.

ADMISSIONS: 15% of the 2017-2018 applicants were accepted. 89% of the current freshmen were in the top fifth of their class; 98% were in the top two fifths. **Admissions Contact:** Carlos Jiminez, Director of Admissions/Outreach & Recuitment. Email: *admission@coloradocollege .edu* Web: *www.coloradocollege.edu*

FINANCIAL AID: In 2017-2018, 50% of all full-time freshmen received some form of financial aid. 33% of all full-time freshmen received need-based aid. The average freshman award was $41,970. Need-based scholarships or need-based grants averaged $48,492 ($68,522 maximum); need-based self-help aid (loans and jobs) averaged $3,341 ($5,600 maximum); non-need-based athletic scholarships averaged $48,288 ($68,616 maximum); and other non-need-based awards and non-need-based scholarships averaged $15,638 ($66,124 maximum). 50% of undergraduate students work part-time. The average financial indebtedness of the 2017 graduate was $25,470. CC is a member of CSS. The CSS/Profile, noncustodial parents' form, parent and student tax return are required. The FAFSA code is 001347. The priority date for freshman financial aid applications for fall entry is November 10.

COLORADO MESA UNIVERSITY *(The complete profile is made available exclusively on our website, www.barronspac.com)*

COLORADO SCHOOL OF MINES C-2

www.mines.edu

Golden, CO 80401	(303) 273-3220 (888) 446-9489
Fax: (303) 273-3509	Email: admit@mines.edu
Full-time: 3080 men, 1129 women	Faculty: I, av$
Part-time: 136 men, 38 women	Ph.D.s: 90%
Graduate: 936 men, 354 women	Student/Faculty: n/av
Year: semesters, summer session	Tuition: $17,842 ($36,148)
Room & Board: $11,477	Freshman Class: 12340 applied, 4501 accepted, 999 enrolled
SAT CR/M/W: 635/680/605 ACT: 30	CEEB CODE: 4073
Application Deadline: n/av	MOST COMPETITIVE

Colorado School of Mines, founded in 1874, is a public institution offering programs in math, science, economics, and engineering. The figures in the above capsule and in this profile are approximate. There is 1 undergraduate school. In addition to regional accreditation, CSM has baccalaureate program accreditation with ABET. The 373-acre campus is in a small town 20 miles west of Denver. Including any residence halls, there are 40 buildings.

STUDENT LIFE: 76% of undergraduates are from Colorado. Others are from 44 states, 52 foreign countries, and Canada. 90% are from public schools. 79% are White; 7% Hispanic; 7% Foreign; 5% Asian American; 2% African American; 1% American Indian/Alaska Native. 52% are Protestant; 21% Catholic; 20% claim no religious affiliation. **Male To Female Ratio:** 2.7:1. The average age of freshmen is 18; all undergraduates, 20. 14% do not continue beyond their first year; 67% remain to graduate. **Housing:** 855 students can be accommodated in college housing, which includes married student dorms and on-campus apartments. In addition, there are fraternity houses and sorority houses. On-campus housing is guaranteed for the freshman year only, is available on a first-come, and first-served basis. 10% of students commute. All students may keep cars.

FACULTY/CLASSROOMS: 80% of faculty are male; 20% are female. 93% teach undergraduates, 50% do research, and 50% do both. No introductory courses are taught by graduate students. The average class size in an introductory lecture is 100; in a laboratory is 22; and in a regular course is 29.

PROGRAMS OF STUDY: CSM confers B.S. degrees. Master's and doctoral degrees are also awarded. Bachelor's degrees are awarded in COMPUTER AND PHYSICAL SCIENCE (chemistry, mathematics, and physics), ENGINEERING AND ENVIRONMENTAL DESIGN (chemical engineering, engineering, geological engineering, geophysical engineering, metallurgical engineering, mining and mineral engineering, and petroleum/natural gas engineering), SOCIAL SCIENCE (economics). Chemical engineering, geological engineering, and petroleum engineering are the strongest academically. General engineering, chemical engineering, and engineering physics have the largest enrollments.

ACTIVITIES: 19% of men belong to 7 national fraternities; 19% of women belong to 3 national sororities. There are 95 groups on campus, including band, cheerleading, choir, chorus, computers, drama, ethnic, honors, international, jazz band, literary magazine, marching band, musical theater, newspaper, pep band, political, professional, radio station, religious, social, social service, student government, symphony, and yearbook. Popular campus events include International Day, and Parents Day. **Sports:** There are 9 intercollegiate sports for men and 7 for women, and 20 intramural sports for men and 20 for women. Facilities include a stadium, a recreation center, gym, numerous intramural fields, tennis courts, and a field house. **Graduates:** From July 1, 2016 to June 30, 2017, 889 bachelor's degrees were awarded. The most popular majors were general engineering (34%), petroleum engineering (12%), and chemical engineering (11%). In an average class, 1% graduate in 3 years or less, 40% graduate in 4 years or less, 66% graduate in 5 years or less, and 69% graduate in 6 years or less.

SERVICES: Counseling and information services are available, as is tutoring in most subjects. There is a reader service for the blind, and remedial math and writing. **Library/Resources:** The library contains 356,000 volumes, 236,000 microform items, and subscribes to 2,700 periodicals including electronic. Computerized library services include interlibrary loans, database searching, and Internet access. **Physically Challenged Students:** All of the campus is accessible. Facilities include wheelchair ramps, elevators, special parking, specially equipped restrooms, special class scheduling, lowered drinking fountains, lowered telephones, and special housing. **Special:** Co-op programs, internships in the McBride honors program in humanities, accelerated degree programs in all majors, dual majors, study abroad in 20 countries, and non-degree study are offered. There is 1 national honor society, a freshman honors program, and 3 departmental honors programs. **Visiting:** There are regularly scheduled orientations for prospective students, including a half day-long visitation program twice each fall where students may visit departments and talk with faculty. Sessions in admissions and financial aid also are given. There are guides for informal visits and visitors may sit in on classes. To schedule a visit, contact the Admissions Office. **Campus Safety and Security:** Measures include 24-hour foot and vehicle patrol, emergency notification system, and self-defense education. There are emergency telephones and lighted pathways/sidewalks.

REQUIREMENTS: The SAT or ACT is required. Applicants must be graduates of an accredited secondary school. The GED is accepted. Students should have completed 17 high school academic credits, including 4 units each of English and math, 3 units of science (of these units including lab- 3), 1 unit of foreign language, 3 units of social studies, and 2 units of academic electives. AP credits are accepted. Important factors in the admissions decision are advanced placement or honors courses, leadership record, evidence of special talent, personality/intangible qualities, extracurricular activities record, recommendations by alumni, geographical diversity, and recommendations by school officials. Students must complete 138 to 148 credit hours, with 35 to 40 hours in the major and a GPA of 2.0. Required courses include humanities, calculus, physics, computer science, chemistry, and phys ed. **Procedure:** Freshmen are admitted to all sessions. Entrance exams should be taken by late in the junior year or early in the senior year. There are deferred admissions and rolling admissions plans. Check with the school for current application deadlines. The fall 2017 application fee was $45. Applications are accepted on-line. **Transfer Students:** 159 transfer students enrolled in 2016-2017. Transfer applicants must have a minimum GPA of 2.75 30 of 138 credits required for the bachelor's degree must be completed at Mines. **International Students:** There are 204 international students enrolled. They must take the TOEFL with a minimum score of 550 on the paper-based TOEFL (PBT) or 79 on the Internet-based version (iBT) and the Comprehensive English Language Test.

ADMISSIONS: 36% of the 2017-2018 applicants were accepted. 75 freshmen graduated first in their class. **Admissions Contact:** Bruce Goetz, Director of Admissions. Email: *admit@mines.edu* Web: *www. mines.edu*

FINANCIAL AID: In 2017-2018, 85% of all full-time freshmen received some form of financial aid. The average freshman award was $12,181. Need-based scholarships or need-based grants averaged $4,835; need-based self-help aid (loans and jobs) averaged $5,263; non-need-based athletic scholarships averaged $7,129; other non-need-based awards and non-need-based scholarships averaged $4,764; and $7,666 from other forms of aid. The average financial indebtedness of the 2017 graduate was $23,667. CSM is a member of CSS. The FAFSA code is 001348. Check with the school for current application deadlines.

COLORADO STATE UNIVERSITY C-1

www.colostate.edu

Fort Collins, CO 80523 (970) 491-6909

Fax: (970) 491-7799 Email: admissions@colostate.edu

Full-time: 10,732 men, 11,237 women	**Faculty:** 1318; I, av$
Part-time: 1730 men, 2204 women	**Ph.D.s:** 89%
Graduate: 3446 men, 3888 women	**Student/Faculty:** 18 to 1
Year: semesters, summer session	**Tuition:** $11,519 ($29,027)
Room & Board: $11,514	**Freshman Class:** 23137 applied, 19116 accepted, 5124 enrolled
SAT or ACT: required	**CEEB CODE:** 4075
Application Deadline: February 1	**COMPETITIVE**

Colorado State University, founded in 1870 and part of the Colorado State University system, is a public, land-grant institution offering 76 undergraduate degrees in 55 departments. There are 8 undergraduate schools and 1 graduate school. In addition to regional accreditation, CSU has baccalaureate program accreditation with AACSB, ABET, ACCE, ACEJMC, CSWE, NASAD, NASM, SAF, CAEP, SRM, CIDA, ACEND, CACREP, NAEYC, ACOTE, AVMA, AAVLD, CDHE, COAMFTE, CAEP, AFE, ACS, APA, and LAAB. The 4773-acre campus is in a suburban area about 65 miles north of Denver. Including any residence halls, there are 705 buildings.

STUDENT LIFE: 73% of undergraduates are from Colorado. Others are from 50 states, 116 foreign countries, and Canada. 70% are White; 6% Foreign; 4% two or more races; 3% Asian American; 2% African American; 2% race unknown; 12% Hispanic. **Female To Male Ratio:** 1.1:1. The average age of freshmen is 18; all undergraduates, 21. 16% do not continue beyond their first year; 68% remain to graduate. **Housing:** 8050 students can be accommodated in college housing, which includes coed and married student dorms, on-campus apartments, and off-campus apartments. In addition, there are honors houses, language/international houses, special-interest houses, honors floors, and more than 10 different residential learning communities. On-campus housing is guaranteed for the freshman year only, is available on a first-come, and first-served basis. 74% of students commute. All students may keep cars.

FACULTY/CLASSROOMS: 54% of faculty are male; 46% are female. 61% teach undergraduates, 58% do research, and 33% do both. Graduate students teach 12% of introductory courses. The average class size in an introductory lecture is 58; in a laboratory is 23; and in a regular course is 38.

PROGRAMS OF STUDY: CSU confers B.A., B.S., B.F.A., B.S.W, and B.M. degrees. Master's and doctoral degrees are also awarded. Bachelor's degrees are awarded in AGRICULTURE (agricultural business management, agricultural economics, agriculture, agronomy, animal science, environmental studies, equestrian studies, equine science, fishing and fisheries, forestry and related sciences, horticulture, natural resources, natural resource management, plant protection (pest management), range/farm management, soil science, and wildlife management), BIOLOGICAL SCIENCE (biochemistry, biology/biological science, botany, cell & molecular biology, ecology, entomology, microbiology, neurosciences, nutrition, toxicology, wildlife biology, and zoology), BUSINESS (accounting, apparel and accessories marketing, banking and finance, business administration and management, facilities management, hospitality management services, hotel/motel and restaurant management, management information systems, marketing/retailing/merchandising, real estate, recreational facilities management, and tourism), COMMUNICATIONS AND THE ARTS (advertising, apparel design, Arabic, art, art history and appreciation, communications, creative writing, dance, dramatic arts, English, English literature, fiber/textiles/weaving, fine arts, foreign language, French, German, graphic design, journalism, languages, metal/jewelry, music, music performance, music theory and composition, performing arts, photography, sculpture, Spanish, theatre acting, theater design, theatre production, and theatre studies), COMPUTER AND PHYSICAL SCIENCE (applied mathematics, chemistry, computer science, earth science, geology, information sciences and systems, mathematics, natural sciences, physical sciences, physics secondary education, physics, and statistics), EDUCATION (agricultural education, art education, early childhood education, education, English education, foreign languages education, French studies K-12 education, mathematics education, music education, science education, social studies education, Spanish education K-12, and technology & science education), ENGINEERING AND ENVIRONMENTAL DESIGN (bioengineering, biomedical engineering, chemical engineering, civil engineering, computer engineering, computer technology, construction engineering, construction management, electrical/electronics engineering, engineering, engineering and applied science, engineering physics, environmental engineering, interior design, landscape architecture/design, and mechanical engineering), HEALTH PROFESSIONS (biology, biomedical science, electrical engineering, environmental health science, exercise science, exercise and movement science, health science, music therapy, public health, and veterinary science), SOCIAL SCIENCE (anthropology, applied psychology, counseling/psychology, economics, ethnic studies, family/consumer studies, fire services administration, food science, history, human development, interdisciplinary studies, international studies, liberal arts/general studies, philosophy, political science/government, psychology, social work, sociology, water resources, and women's studies). Veterinary medicine, atmospheric sciences, and engineering are the strongest academically. Biological science, psychology, and mechanical engineering have the largest enrollments.

ACTIVITIES: 2% of men belong to 27 national fraternities; 4% of women belong to 19 national sororities. There are 453 groups on campus, including art, band, cheerleading, chess, choir, chorale, chorus, computers, dance, drama, drill team, environmental, ethnic, film, honors, international, jazz band, LGBT, literary magazine, marching band, musical theater, newspaper, opera, orchestra, pep band, photography, political, professional, radio and TV, religious, social, social service, student government, and symphony. Popular campus events include Homecoming, Ag Day, President's Annual Address and Picnic. **Sports:** There are 5 intercollegiate sports for men and 9 for women, and 35 intramural sports for men and 35 for women. Facilities include on-campus stadium, an arena, indoor and outdoor tracks, tennis complex, intramural fields, indoor swimming pools, a comprehensive student recreation center featuring free weights, fitness equipment, climbing wall and sports courts, and a ropes course. **Graduates:** From July 1, 2016 to June 30, 2017, 5332 bachelor's degrees were awarded. The most popular majors were business/marketing (14%), biological/life sciences (11%), and social sciences (9%). In an average class, 2% graduate in 3 years or less, 44% graduate in 4 years or less, 64% graduate in 5 years or less, and 67% graduate in 6 years or less. Of the 2016 graduating class, 21% were enrolled in graduate school within 6 months of graduation, and 64% were employed.

SERVICES: Counseling and information services are available, as is tutoring in most subjects. There is a reader service for the blind. Interpreters and note takers are available and pre-college algebra hybrid courses. **Library/Resources:** The library contains 2.4 million volumes, and 142,264 audio/video tapes/CDs/DVDs, and subscribes to 124,969 periodicals including electronic. Computerized library services include interlibrary loans, database searching, Internet access, and Wi-Fi capability. Special learning facilities include an art gallery, radio station, TV station, Colorado State University boasts many unique state-of-the-art learning facilities including a concert hall, a Thrust theatre, a music hall, engineering research center, equine center, veterinary teaching hospital, environmental learning center, and a plant environmental research center. These are just a few of the cutting-edge learning facilities that serve the many disciplines at CSU. **Physically Challenged Students:** 99% of the campus is accessible. Facilities include wheelchair ramps, elevators, special parking, specially equipped restrooms, special class scheduling, lowered drinking fountains, lowered telephones, and special housing. **Special:** Colorado State offers a co-op program in Engineering, study abroad, a semester at sea, work-study programs, internships, B.A.-B.S. degrees, dual majors, and pass/fail options are available. Teaching certification students receive a bachelor's degree in their chosen subject and also complete a certification sequence through the School of Education. There are 41 national honor societies, Phi Beta Kappa, a freshman honors program, and 55 departmental honors programs. **Visiting:** There are regularly scheduled orientations for prospective students. Regularly scheduled visit days provide specialized information for particular groups including high school seniors and juniors, transfer students, special interests and others. A daily information session and campus tour are presented each weekday. There are guides for informal visits, visitors may sit in on classes, and stay overnight. To schedule a visit, contact the Office of Admissions. **Campus Safety and Security:** Measures include 24-hour foot and vehicle patrol, emergency notification system, self-defense education, and security escort services. There are shuttle buses, emergency telephones, lighted pathways/sidewalks, controlled access to dorms/residences, and lectures by campus police on a variety of safety issues, a crime victim support unit, safe walk escort, and a bike patrol.

REQUIREMENTS: The SAT or ACT is required. Graduation from secondary school is required. The GED is accepted. Priority consideration is given to applicants who have earned a minimum 3.25 GPA with no D/F grades and who will have successfully satisfied our academic course work standards before enrolling at CSU. Applicants with a GPA below 3.25, occasional D/F grades, and/or fewer than the 18 recommended high school units are encouraged to apply, since many factors are considered in the holistic review process. The 18 recommended high school credits are to include 4 English, 4 math, 3 science (at least 2 must include a lab), 2 social studies, 1 history, 2 foreign language (must be the same language), and 2 academic electives. An essay (minimum 250 words) and 1 recommendation are required. AP and CLEP credits are accepted. In order to graduate, students must complete a minimum of 120 credit hours (more for some programs), 42 of which must be upper division. The minimum GPA required for graduation is 2.0. Students must complete the All-University Core and all curricular requirements as described in the current catalog. A minimum of 30 upper-division semester credits must be completed in residence at CSU. "In residence" courses include any authorized Colorado State University course recorded as CSU credit on the CSU transcript. **Procedure:** Freshmen are admitted fall, spring, and summer. Entrance exams should be taken during the junior year or early fall of the senior year. There are deferred admissions and rolling admissions plans. Applications should be filed by February 1 for fall entry; November 1 for spring entry. The fall 2017 application fee was $50. Notification is sent on a rolling basis. Applications are accepted on-line. **Transfer Students:** 1688 transfer students enrolled in 2016-2017. Strong candidates for transfer admission have earned a minimum 2.5 cumulative GPA in 30 or more college-level academic semester credits and have satisfied the transfer admissions requirement in mathematics. Students holding an Associate Degree from an accredited Colorado institution are guaranteed admission provided that it is the last institution attended and that a cumulative 2.0 GPA has been achieved from all institutions attended. Specific majors may require additional course work and a higher GPA. 30 of 120 credits required for the bachelor's degree must be completed at Colorado State. **International Students:** There are 946 international students enrolled. They must take the TOEFL with a minimum score of 550 on the paper-based TOEFL (PBT) or 79 on the Internet-based version (iBT). Scores from other English language proficiency exams may be considered in lieu of the TOEFL. They must also take the SAT or ACT.

ADMISSIONS: 83% of the 2017-2018 applicants were accepted. The SAT scores for the 2017-2018 freshman class were: Math-- 8% below 500, 43% between 500 and 599, 39% between 600 and 699, and 9% between 700 and 800. Evidence-Based Reading/Writing-- 7% below 500, 36% between 500 and 599, 47% between 600 and 699, and 10% between 700 and 800. The ACT scores were 2% between 12 and 17, 34% between 18 and 23, 50% between 24 and 29, and 14% above 30. 38% of the current freshmen were in the top fifth of their class; 70% were in the top two fifths. 65 freshmen graduated first in their class. **Admissions Contact:** Director of Admissions Email: *admissions@colostate.edu* Web: *www.colostate.edu*

FINANCIAL AID: In 2017-2018, 64% of all full-time freshmen received some form of financial aid. 45% of all full-time freshmen received need-based aid. The average freshman award was $11,572. Need-based scholarships or need-based grants averaged $8,904; need-based self-help aid (loans and jobs) averaged $5,533; non-need-based athletic scholarships averaged $26,673; other non-need-based awards and non-need-based scholarships averaged $5,215; and $5,156 from other forms of aid. 80% of undergraduate students work part-time. The average financial indebtedness of the 2017 graduate was $13,138. The FAFSA code is 001350. The priority date for freshman financial aid applications for fall entry is March 1.

COLORADO STATE UNIVERSITY-PUEBLO D-3

www.csupueblo.edu

Pueblo, CO 81001 (719) 549-2462
(719) 549-2100

Fax: (719) 549-2419 **Email: chrissy.holiday@csupueblo.edu**

Full-time: 1774 men, 1968 women	**Faculty:** n/av
Part-time: 540 men, 925 women	**Ph.D.s:** 70%
Graduate: 374 men, 1508 women	**Student/Faculty:** n/av
Year: semesters, summer session	**Tuition:** $10,941 ($26,872)
Room & Board: $10,640	**Freshman Class:** n/av
SAT: required **ACT:** 21	**CEEB CODE:** 4611
Application Deadline: August 1	**COMPETITIVE**

Colorado State University-Pueblo, founded in 1933, is part of the Colorado State University System. The public institution offers undergraduate programs in humanities and social sciences, fine arts, business administration, nursing, the natural sciences, technology, engineering, and education. There are 4 undergraduate schools and 1 graduate school. In addition to regional accreditation, CSU-Pueblo has baccalaureate program accreditation with AACSB, ABET, CSWE, NASM, NLN, CAEP, ACS, and CAATE. The 275-acre campus is in an urban area 100 miles south of Denver, 50 miles south of Colorado Springs, 100 miles north of New Mexico. Including any residence halls, there are 23 buildings.

STUDENT LIFE: 87% of undergraduates are from Colorado. Others are from 41 states, 40 foreign countries, and Canada. 51% are White; 30% Hispanic; 7% African American; 3% Foreign; 3% two or more races; 3% race unknown; 2% Asian American; 1% American Indian/Alaska Native. **Female To Male Ratio:** 1.6:1. The average age of freshmen is 19; all undergraduates, 26. 39% do not continue beyond their first year; 27% remain to graduate. **Housing:** 652 students can be accommodated in college housing, which includes dorms and on-campus apartments. On-campus housing is guaranteed for the freshman year only, is available on a first-come, and first-served basis. 81% of students commute. Alcohol is not permitted. All students may keep cars.

FACULTY/CLASSROOMS: 57% of faculty are male; 43% are female. 99% teach undergraduates, 10% do research, and 4% do both. No introductory courses are taught by graduate students. The average class size in an introductory lecture is 70; in a laboratory is 24; and in a regular course is 22.

PROGRAMS OF STUDY: CSU-Pueblo confers B.A., B.S., B.S.B.A., B.F.A., B.S.C.E.T., B.S.I.En., B.S.N. and B.S.W. degrees. Master's degrees are also awarded. Bachelor's degrees are awarded in BIOLOGICAL SCIENCE (biochemistry, biology/biological science, and biotechnology), BUSINESS (accounting, business administration and management, and recreation and leisure services), COMMUNICATIONS AND THE ARTS (art, broadcasting, communications, English, journalism, music performance, music theory and composition, and Spanish), COMPUTER AND PHYSICAL SCIENCE (chemistry, information sciences and systems, mathematics, and physics), EDUCATION (music education), ENGINEERING AND ENVIRONMENTAL DESIGN (automotive technology, civil engineering technology, electrical/electronics engineering technology, industrial administration/management, industrial engineering, mechanical engineering technology, and preengineering), HEALTH PROFESSIONS (chiropractic, environmental health science, exercise science, medical technology, nursing, occupational therapy, physician's assistant, predentistry, premedicine, preoptometry, preosteopathy, prepharmacy, prepodiatry, preveterinary science, and speech pathology/audiology), SOCIAL SCIENCE (criminology, economics, history, political science/government, prelaw, psychology, social science, social work, and sociology). Business, engineering, and nursing are the strongest academically. Business, nursing, and biology have the largest enrollments.

ACTIVITIES: 1% of men belong to 2 national fraternities; 1% of women belong to 1 local sorority. There are 68 groups on campus, including art, cheerleading, choir, chorale, computers, drama, ethnic, forensics, honors, international, jazz band, LGBT, literary magazine, marching band, newspaper, pep band, political, professional, radio and TV, religious, social, social service, student government, and symphony. Popular campus events include Distinguished Lecture Series and Departmental Lecture Series, Pueblo Symphony, Career Fair, and Homecoming. **Sports:** There are 7 intercollegiate sports for men and 8 for women, and 7 intramural sports for men and 7 for women. Facilities include an arena with an indoor swimming pool, a weight room, rock-climbing wall, racquetball, basketball, and volleyball courts, a sports complex with tennis courts, baseball, softball, football and soccer fields, bike trails, and a rope course. **Graduates:** From July 1, 2016 to June 30, 2017, 889 bachelor's degrees were awarded. In an average class, 18% graduate in 4 years or less, 28% graduate in 5 years or less, and 33% graduate in 6 years or less.

SERVICES: Counseling and information services are available, as is tutoring in most subjects. **Library/Resources:** The library contains 350,000 volumes, 10,000 microform items, and 16,862 audio/video tapes/CDs/DVDs, and subscribes to 1,327 periodicals including electronic. Computerized library services include interlibrary loans and database searching. Special learning facilities include an art gallery, radio station, TV station, observatory at nature center. **Physically Challenged Students:** All of the campus is accessible. Facilities include wheelchair ramps, elevators, special parking, specially equipped restrooms, special class scheduling, lowered drinking fountains, and lowered telephones. **Special:** CSU-Pueblo offers co-op programs, internships, study abroad in 8 countries, and on-campus work-study programs. Also available are 5-year combined B.S.B.A./M.B.A. degrees, a 3-2 engineering degree with Colorado State University, dual majors, nondegree study, and preprofessional programs in forestry, physical therapy, and wildlife management. CSU-Pueblo is a member of the National Student Exchange. There are 10 national honor societies, a freshman honors program, and 10 departmental honors programs. **Visiting:** There are regularly scheduled orientations for prospective students, including a tour, lunch, and mini-sessions on financial aid, athletics, scholarships, and student services. There are guides for informal visits and visitors may sit in on classes. To schedule a visit, contact Tiffany Kingrey at tiffany.kingrey@colostate-pueblo.edu. **Campus Safety and Security:** Measures include 24-hour foot and vehicle patrol, self-defense education, and security escort services. There are emergency telephones and lighted pathways/sidewalks.

REQUIREMENTS: The SAT or ACT is required. Applicants must be graduates of an accredited secondary school or have a GED certificate with a minimum score of 45. CSU-Pueblo computes a CCHE admission index, comprised of the high school GPA and SAT or ACT scores. Students scoring below the minimum will still be considered by an admissions committee. Academic preparation should consist of 4 years of English, 3 of math including algebra and geometry, 2 of natural science including physical science, 3 years of social studies including American government, and 1 year of a foreign language. A GPA of 2.0 is required. AP and CLEP credits are accepted. Important factors in the admissions decision are advanced placement or honors courses, leadership record, and recommendations by school officials. To graduate, all students must complete at least 120 semester hours, including 40 in upper-division courses and 30 to 48 in the major, with a minimum GPA of 2.0. General education requirements include a 14-credit skills component of courses in communication, computer literacy, and quantitative skills, as well as a 19-credit knowledge component of courses in humanities, social sciences, and science and technology. Other requirements vary with the major. **Procedure:** Freshmen are admitted to all sessions. Entrance exams should be taken during spring of the junior year or fall of the senior year. There is a rolling admissions plan. Applications should be filed by August 1 for fall entry. The fall 2017 application fee was $25. Notification is sent on a rolling basis. **Transfer Students:** A minimum GPA of 2.0 and official transcripts of previous college work are required. Applicants with fewer than 30 credit hours must submit ACT or SAT scores and high school transcripts. 30 of 120 credits required for the bachelor's degree must be completed at CSU-Pueblo. **International Students:** They must take the TOEFL or MELAB.

Admissions Contact: Christin Holliday, Director of Admissions. Email: *chrissy.holiday@csupueblo.edu* Web: *www.csupueblo.edu*

FINANCIAL AID: 54% of all full-time freshmen received need-based aid. The average freshman award was $8,637. Need-based scholarships or need-based grants averaged $6,610; need-based self-help aid (loans and jobs) averaged $3,336; non-need-based athletic scholarships averaged $3,688; and other non-need-based awards and non-need-based scholarships averaged $3,483. The FAFSA code is 001365. Check with the school for current application deadlines.

COLORADO TECHNICAL UNIVERSITY *(The complete profile is made available exclusively on our website, www.barronspac.com)*

FORT LEWIS COLLEGE — B-4

www.fortlewis.edu

Durango, CO 81301 — **(970) 247-7180**

Fax: (970) 247-7179
Email: admission@fortlewis.edu
Full-time: 1389 men, 1509 women
Faculty: 161; IIB, av$
Part-time: 157 men, 132 women
Ph.D.s: 96%
Graduate: 10 men, 22 women
Student/Faculty: 16 to 1
Year: varies, summer session
Tuition: $10,498 ($20,650)
Room & Board: $9658
Freshman Class: 4473 applied, 3722 accepted, 706 enrolled
SAT EBR-W/M: 560/555 **ACT:** 23
CEEB CODE: 4310
Application Deadline: August 1
COMPETITIVE

Fort Lewis College, founded in 1911, is a public institution with undergraduate programs in arts and sciences, business and education. There are 3 undergraduate schools and 1 graduate school. In addition to regional accreditation, Fort Lewis has baccalaureate program accreditation with AACSB, ABET, NASM, and CAEP. The 362-acre campus is in a small town in Durango Colorado, the southwestern corner of Colorado, about 330 miles southwest of Denver. Including any residence halls, there are 59 buildings.

STUDENT LIFE: 55% of undergraduates are from out of state, mostly the Southwest. Students are from 48 states, 17 foreign countries, and Canada. 48% are White; 26% American Indian/Alaska Native; 11% Hispanic; 9% two or more races; 3% race unknown; 1% African American; 1% Asian American; 1% Foreign. **Female To Male Ratio:** 1.1:1. The average age of freshmen is 18; all undergraduates, 21. 41% do not continue beyond their first year; 45% remain to graduate. **Housing:** 1528 students can be accommodated in college housing, which includes coed and married student dorms and on-campus apartments. In addition, there are special-interest houses, living learning community, and theme housing. On-campus housing is guaranteed for the freshman year only, is available on a first-come, and first-served basis. 91% of students live on campus. Alcohol is not permitted. All students may keep cars.

FACULTY/CLASSROOMS: 43% of faculty are male; 57% are female. All teach undergraduates, and 52% do both. No introductory courses are taught by graduate students. The average class size in an introductory lecture is 21; in a laboratory is 20; and in a regular course is 21.

PROGRAMS OF STUDY: Fort Lewis confers B.A. and B.S. degrees. Master's degrees are also awarded. Bachelor's degrees are awarded in AGRICULTURE (environmental studies), BIOLOGICAL SCIENCE (biochemistry, biology/biological science, cell & molecular biology, and environmental biology), BUSINESS (accounting, business administration and management, business administration marketing, business economics, finance, and marketing and distribution), COMMUNICATIONS AND THE ARTS (art, dramatic arts, English, music, and Spanish), COMPUTER AND PHYSICAL SCIENCE (chemistry, geology, mathematics, and physics), EDUCATION (athletic training, early childhood education, and education), ENGINEERING AND ENVIRONMENTAL DESIGN (computer engineering and engineering and applied science), HEALTH PROFESSIONS (exercise science and public health), SOCIAL SCIENCE (American Indian studies, anthropology, economics, gender studies, history, humanities, interdisciplinary studies, philosophy, political science/government, psychology, and sociology). Business, exercise science, and psychology have the largest enrollments.

ACTIVITIES: There are no fraternities or sororities. There are 70 groups on campus, including art, band, cheerleading, choir, chorale, chorus, computers, dance, drama, environmental, ethnic, honors, jazz band, LGBT, literary magazine, newspaper, pep band, political, professional, radio station, religious, social, social service, and student government. Popular campus events include Fiesta on the Mesa, Fall Blaze, Homecoming, and Hozhoni Days. **Sports:** There are 5 intercollegiate sports for men and 8 for women, and 13 intramural sports for men and 13 for women. Facilities include a field house, an outdoor sports complex, indoor swimming pool, student life center, which includes a gym, racquetball court, aerobic/dance studio, track, climbing wall, and cardio/weight area. **Graduates:** From July 1, 2016 to June 30, 2017, 728 bachelor's degrees were awarded. The most popular majors were business/marketing (20%), social sciences (12%), and parks and recreation (10%). In an average class, 21% graduate in 4 years or less and 40% graduate in 6 years or less. Of the 2016 graduating class, 16% were enrolled in graduate school within 6 months of graduation.

SERVICES: Counseling and information services are available, as is tutoring in most subjects. There is a reader service for the blind, and remedial math, reading, and writing. **Library/Resources:** The library contains 381,520 volumes, 392 microform items, and 179,671 audio/video tapes/CDs/DVDs, and subscribes to 62,280 periodicals including electronic. Computerized library services include interlibrary loans, database searching, Internet access, and Wi-Fi capability. Special learning facilities include an art gallery, a center for Southwest studies. **Physically Challenged Students:** All of the campus is accessible. Facilities include wheelchair ramps, elevators, special parking, specially equipped restrooms, special class scheduling, lowered drinking fountains, lowered telephones, special housing, and workstations modified for individual needs. **Special:** The college offers cooperative programs in most majors, numerous internships, a Washington semester for political science majors, study abroad in 32 countries, student-designed majors, a general studies degree, nondegree study, pass/fail option, and B.A.-B.S. degrees. There are 3-2 engineering degrees with 4 universities and a preforestry degree with Colorado State and Northern Arizona Universities. There are 5 national honor societies and a freshman honors program. **Visiting:** There are regularly scheduled orientations for prospective students. There are guides for informal visits, visitors may sit in on classes, and stay overnight. To schedule a visit, contact the Office of Admission. **Campus Safety and Security:** Measures include 24-hour foot and vehicle patrol, emergency notification system, self-defense education, and security escort services. There are shuttle buses, emergency telephones, lighted pathways/sidewalks, and controlled access to dorms/residences.

REQUIREMENTS: The SAT or ACT is required. Applicants must be graduates of an accredited secondary school or have a GED certificate. An interview is recommended. 17 academic units are required: 4 units each in English, and math, 3 units in science, of those, 2 must be lab, and academic electives, 2 each in social studies, and 1 each in foreign language, and history. A GPA of 2.0 is required. AP and CLEP credits are accepted. Important factors in the admissions decision are leadership record, advanced placement or honors courses, parents or siblings attended your school, evidence of special talent, personality/intangible qualities, recommendations by alumni, and recommendations by school officials. To graduate, students must complete 120 semester hours with 30 to 40 hours in the major, 50 credits outside the major, and a minimum GPA of 2.0 overall and in the major. A total of 32 to 44 hours in general distribution courses is required. **Procedure:** Freshmen are admitted to all sessions. Entrance exams should be taken in spring of the junior year. There are deferred admissions and rolling admissions plans. Applications should be filed by August 1 for fall entry. The fall 2017 application fee was $40. Notifications are sent September 15. Applications are accepted on-line. **Transfer Students:** 296 transfer students enrolled in 2016-2017. Applicants for transfer should have completed a minimum of 12 credit hours and have a GPA of 2.40. Courses completed with a grade of C- or better may transfer. An interview is recommended. Student may enroll in the fall, spring, and summer. 30 of 120 credits required for the bachelor's degree must be completed at Fort Lewis. **International Students:** There are 30 international students enrolled. They must take the TOEFL with a minimum score of 500 on the paper-based TOEFL (PBT) or 61 on the Internet-based version (iBT).

ADMISSIONS: 83% of the 2017-2018 applicants were accepted. The SAT scores for the 2017-2018 freshman class were: Math-- 20% below 500, 54% between 500 and 599, 24% between 600 and 699, and 4% between 700 and 800. Evidence-Based Reading/Writing-- 22% below 500, 49% between 500 and 599, 26% between 600 and 699, and 3% between 700 and 800. The ACT scores were 9% between 12 and 17, 55% between 18 and 23, 32% between 24 and 29, and 4% above 30. 21% of the current freshmen were in the top fifth of their class; 73% were in the top two fifths. 4 freshmen graduated first in their class. **Admissions Contact:** Carol Smith, Interim Director of Admissions. Email: *admission@fortlewis.edu* Web: *www.fortlewis.edu*

FINANCIAL AID: In 2017-2018, 88% of all full-time freshmen received some form of financial aid. 90% of all full-time freshmen received need-based aid. The average freshman award was $15,593. Need-based scholarships or need-based grants averaged $4,951; need-based self-help aid (loans and jobs) averaged $3,676; non-need-based athletic scholarships averaged $6,657; other non-need-based awards and non-need-based scholarships averaged $4,687; and $3,367 from other forms of aid. The average financial indebtedness of the 2017 graduate was $16,525. Fort Lewis is a member of CSS. The FAFSA code is 001353. The priority date for freshman financial aid applications for fall entry is November 15.

JOHNSON & WALES UNIVERSITY/ DENVER CAMPUS — C-2

www.jwu.edu/denver

Denver, CO 80220 — (303) 256-9300, (877) 598-3368

Fax: (303) 256-9333 — Email: den@admissions.jwu.edu

Full-time: 496 men, 731 women	**Faculty:** 48
Part-time: 56 men, 73 women	**Ph.D.s:** n/av
Graduate: 13 men, 19 women	**Student/Faculty:** 17 to 1
Year: quarters, summer session	**Tuition:** $30,746
Room & Board: $11,961	**Freshman Class:** 2319 applied, 1883 accepted, 339 enrolled
	CEEB CODE: 3567
Application Deadline: n/av	**COMPETITIVE**

Johnson & Wales University/Denver Campus, founded in 2000, offers degree programs in its college of business, college of culinary arts, hospitality college, and school of education. The figures given in the above capsule and in this profile are approximate. There are 5 undergraduate schools and 1 graduate school. In addition to regional accreditation, JWU has baccalaureate program accreditation with NEASC. The 26-acre campus is in a suburban area in Park Hill. Including any residence halls, there are 19 buildings.

STUDENT LIFE: 63% of undergraduates are from out of state, mostly the West. Students are from 50 states, 11 foreign countries, and Canada. 48% are White; 4% African American; 3% Asian American; 2% Foreign; 11% Hispanic; 1% American Indian/Alaska Native. **Female To Male Ratio:** 1.5:1. The average age of freshmen is 18; all undergraduates, 22. 67% remain to graduate. **Housing:** College-sponsored housing includes coed dorms, and on-campus apartments, and wellness housing. On-campus housing is available on a lottery system for upperclassmen. 53% of students commute. Alcohol is not permitted. All students may keep cars.

FACULTY/CLASSROOMS: No introductory courses are taught by graduate students.

PROGRAMS OF STUDY: JWU confers B.S. degrees. Associate degrees are also awarded. Bachelor's degrees are awarded in BIOLOGICAL SCIENCE (nutrition), BUSINESS (apparel and accessories marketing, business administration and management, entrepreneurial studies, hospitality management services, hotel/motel and restaurant management, marketing/retailing/merchandising, meeting / special event mgmt, organizational behavior, retailing, small business management, and tourism), COMMUNICATIONS AND THE ARTS (applied communication, communications, English, English literature, English Writing, and English and Professional Communication), HEALTH PROFESSIONS (applied nutrition, health, health administration and policy, health communication, health care administration, health promotion, health science, and pre-health studies), SOCIAL SCIENCE (counseling/psychology, criminal justice, criminology, food production/management/services, industrial and organizational psychology, law enforcement and corrections, liberal arts/general studies, liberal arts, sciences, general studies, humanities, psychology, and sociology). Culinary, sports entertainment event management, and food service management have the largest enrollments.

ACTIVITIES: There are no fraternities; 1% of women belong to 1 national sorority. There are 26 groups on campus, including leadership academy, campus activities board, cheerleading, dance, drama, international, LGBT, literary magazine, musical theater, newspaper, professional, social, student government, and yearbook. Popular campus events include Winter Week, Love Fest, and Spring Fling. **Sports:** There are 5 intercollegiate sports for men and 6 for women, and 5 intramural sports for men and 6 for women. Facilities include a gym, weight room, cardio room, a sand volleyball pit, and an outdoor basketball court. **Graduates:** From July 1, 2015 to June 30, 2016, 238 bachelor's degrees were awarded. The most popular majors were family and consumer sciences (35%), business/marketing (29%), and personal and culinary services (17%). 120 companies recruited on campus in 2015-2016. In an average class, 53% graduate in 6 years or less.

SERVICES: Counseling and information services are available, as is tutoring in every subject. **Library/Resources:** The library contains 29,000 volumes, and 1,200 audio/video tapes/CDs/DVDs, and subscribes to 215 periodicals including electronic. Computerized library services include interlibrary loans, database searching, Internet access, and Wi-Fi capability. **Physically Challenged Students:** All of the campus is accessible. Facilities include wheelchair ramps, elevators, special parking, specially equipped restrooms, special class scheduling, lowered drinking fountains, and lowered telephones. **Special:** The university offers co-op programs, accelerated degree programs, dual majors, study abroad, and worldwide work-study opportunities in business, hospitality, technology, and culinary arts. Most majors require 11-week internships. There are a freshman honors program. **Visiting:** There are guides for informal visits, visitors may sit in on classes, and stay overnight. To schedule a visit, contact the Admissions Office. **Campus Safety and Security:** Measures include 24-hour foot and vehicle patrol, emergency notification system, self-defense education, and security escort services. There are emergency telephones, lighted pathways/sidewalks, and controlled access to dorms/residences.

REQUIREMENTS: Although SAT and ACT scores are required only for students applying for honors admissions, students who have taken these tests are encouraged to submit their scores. High school diploma is required, and the GED is accepted. Requirements are 4 years of English, 3 years each of mathematics, and science, and 2 years of social studies. A GPA of 2.0 is required. AP and CLEP credits are accepted. Important factors in the admissions decision are advanced placement or honors courses, extracurricular activities record, parents or siblings attended your school, and recommendations by school officials. To graduate, students must complete 180 quarter credit hours, including at least 36 in the major, with a minimum GPA of 2.0. Required classes include English, math, history, psychology, sociology, economics, science, and professional development. **Procedure:** Freshmen are admitted to all sessions. There are early admissions, deferred admissions, and rolling admissions plans. Application deadlines are open. Applications are accepted on-line. **Transfer Students:** 96 transfer students enrolled in 2015-2016. Applicants are required to submit official high school and college transcripts and must have earned a minimum college GPA of 2.0. Student may enroll in the fall, winter, spring and summer. 45 of 180 credits required for the bachelor's degree must be completed at JWU. **International Students:** There are 18 international students enrolled. The school actively recruits these students. They must take the TOEFL with a minimum score of 550 on the paper-based TOEFL (PBT) or 80 on the Internet-based version (iBT) and the Comprehensive English Language Test.

ADMISSIONS: 81% of the 2016-2017 applicants were accepted. **Admissions Contact:** Michael Rusk, Assistant Director of Admissions. Email: *den@admissions.jwu.edu* Web: *www.jwu.edu/denver*

FINANCIAL AID: In 2016-2017, 95% of all full-time freshmen received some form of financial aid. The average freshman award was $25,367. Need-based scholarships or need-based grants averaged $9,346; need-based self-help aid (loans and jobs) averaged $4,393; other non-need-based awards and non-need-based scholarships averaged $3,390; and $11,224 from other forms of aid. JWU is a member of CSS. The FAFSA code is 003404. The priority date for freshman financial aid applications for fall entry is March 1.

METROPOLITAN STATE UNIVERSITY OF DENVER *(The complete profile is made available exclusively on our website, www.barronspac.com)*

NAROPA UNIVERSITY *(The complete profile is made available exclusively on our website, www.barronspac.com)*

REGIS UNIVERSITY — C-2

www.regis.edu

Denver, CO 80221 — **(303) 458-4300** **(800) 388-2366**

Fax: (303) 964-5534 — **Email: ruadmissions@regis.edu**

Full-time: 821 men, 1506 women	**Faculty:** n/av
Part-time: 680 men, 865 women	**Ph.D.s:** n/av
Graduate: 1539 men, 2718 women	**Student/Faculty:** n/av
Year: varies, summer session	**Tuition:** $35,610
Room & Board: $10,770	**Freshman Class:** 6761 applied, 3827 accepted, 553 enrolled
SAT or ACT: required	**CEEB CODE:** 4656
Application Deadline: August 1	**COMPETITIVE**

Regis University was founded in 1877 by a group of exiled Italian Jesuits. Regis University is the only Jesuit Catholic university in the Rocky Mountain West, and one of 28 Jesuit colleges and universities in the United States. Inspired by St. Ignatius Loyola, the mission of Regis University is to educate men and women of all ages to make a positive impact in a rapidly-changing global society. We encourage our students to seek truth, live purposeful lives, and continually examine and attempt to answer the question: "How ought we to live?". There are 5 undergraduate schools and 5 graduate schools. In addition to regional accreditation, Regis University has baccalaureate program accreditation with ABET, ACPE, CACREP, CAPTE, GAC, CAHIIM, COAMFTE, CCNE, and CPT. The 100-acre campus is in a suburban area in Northwest Denver. Including any residence halls, there are 17 buildings.

STUDENT LIFE: 61% of undergraduates are from Colorado. Others are from 49 states, 20 foreign countries, and Canada. 7% are race unknown; 54% White; 5% Asian American; 4% African American; 4% Foreign; 4% two or more races; 21% Hispanic. 71% are Agnostic, Baptist, Buddhist, Episcopal, Greek Orthodox, Hindu, Islamic, Latter-Day Saints, Lutheran, Methodist, Presbyterian, Unknown denomination; 31% Catholic. **Female To Male Ratio:** 1.7:1. The average age of freshmen is 18; all undergraduates, 28. **Housing:** College-sponsored housing includes dorms and on-campus apartments. In addition, there are honors houses and special-interest houses. On-campus housing is guaranteed for all 4 years. All students may keep cars.

FACULTY/CLASSROOMS: No introductory courses are taught by graduate students.

PROGRAMS OF STUDY: Regis confers B.A., B.S., B.S.N., B.A.S., B.A.S.C. degrees. Master's and doctoral degrees are also awarded. Bachelor's degrees are awarded in AGRICULTURE (environmental studies), BIOLOGICAL SCIENCE (biochemistry, biology/biological science, and neurosciences), BUSINESS (accounting, business administration and management, business economics, business and technology, finance, international business management, and marketing/retailing/merchandising), COMMUNICATIONS AND THE ARTS (art history, communications, English, French, information technology, music, music performance, Spanish, and visual and performing arts), COMPUTER AND PHYSICAL SCIENCE (chemistry, computer networks & systems, computer science, mathematics, and physics), EDUCATION (education and health information management), ENGINEERING AND ENVIRONMENTAL DESIGN (environmental science and preengineering), HEALTH PROFESSIONS (biology, health care administration, health science, nursing, pharmacy, physical therapy, and premedicine), SOCIAL SCIENCE (applied psychology, criminology, economics, history, liberal arts/general studies, peace studies, philosophy, political science/government, prelaw, psychology, public administration, religion, sociology, and women's studies). Nursing is the strongest academically. Nursing, business, and computer science have the largest enrollments.

ACTIVITIES: There are no fraternities or sororities. There are 26 groups on campus, including art, cheerleading, chess, choir, chorus, dance, debate, environmental, ethnic, forensics, honors, international, jazz band, Leadership Club , LGBT, literary magazine, musical theater, newspaper, orchestra, photography, political, professional, radio and TV, religious, social, social service, student government, and yearbook. Popular campus events include Mistletoe Madness, Ranger Week, Hall Olympics, Snow Week, Best of Colorado, Senior Life Last Call, Thursday Thrills, and Twelve Programs. **Sports:** There are 5 intercollegiate sports for men and 7 for women, and 8 intramural sports for men and 8 for women. Facilities include a field-house, baseball field, soccer/lacrosse pitch, fitness center, and indoor golf facility. **Graduates:** From July 1, 2016 to June 30, 2017, 1331 bachelor's degrees were awarded. The most popular majors were nursing (29%), business administration (10%), and accounting (7%). In an average class, 49% graduate in 4 years or less, 62% graduate in 5 years or less, and 64% graduate in 6 years or less.

SERVICES: Counseling and information services are available, as is tutoring in every subject. There is a reader service for the blind. **Library/Resources:** The library contains 393,000 volumes, 118,000 microform items, and 13,000 audio/video tapes/CDs/DVDs. Computerized library services include interlibrary loans, database searching, Internet access, and Wi-Fi capability. Special learning facilities include an art gallery, radio station, nursing labs, physical therapy labs, a cadaver lab, music labs, classrooms in residence halls, and an arboretum. **Physically Challenged Students:** 80% of the campus is accessible. Facilities include wheelchair ramps, elevators, special parking, specially equipped restrooms, special class scheduling, lowered drinking fountains, and lowered telephones. **Special:** Cross-registration is possible with Denver University and Metropolitan State. Internships, study abroad, and work-study programs with Regis are available. The college offers B.A.-B.S. degrees, dual majors, student-designed majors, a 3-2 engineering degree with Washington University, and pass/fail options. An accelerated degree program in nursing is also offered. There are 7 national honor societies and a freshman honors program. **Visiting:** There are guides for informal visits, visitors may sit in on classes, and stay overnight. To schedule a visit, contact the Admissions Office. **Campus Safety and Security:** Measures include 24-hour foot and vehicle patrol, emergency notification system, self-defense education, and security escort services. There are shuttle buses, emergency telephones, lighted pathways/sidewalks, and controlled access to dorms/residences.

REQUIREMENTS: The SAT or ACT is required. Applicants should be graduates of an accredited secondary school. The GED is accepted. A recommendation from the high school counselor and an essay are required. An interview is recommended. AP and CLEP credits are accepted. Important factors in the admissions decision are advanced placement or honors courses, leadership record, and recommendations by school officials. Students must complete 128 credit hours with a minimum GPA of 2.0. Required courses include 58 credit hours in the core curriculum, of which 12 are seminars, 7 to 8 are math and natural science, 6 are in literature/humanities, social science, religious studies, and philosophy, and 3 each are in economics, communication arts, and fine arts. **Procedure:** Freshmen are admitted fall and spring. Entrance exams should be taken in the fall. There are deferred admissions and rolling admissions plans. Application deadlines are open. The fall 2017 application fee was $40. Notification is sent on a rolling basis. Applications are accepted online. **Transfer Students:** 65 transfer students enrolled in 2016-2017. Applicants must have a GPA of 2.5. All previous college work is considered. The university reviews each applicant individually. 30 of 128 credits required for the bachelor's degree must be completed at Regis. **International Students:** There are 48 international students enrolled. They must take the TOEFL with a minimum score of 550 on the paper-based TOEFL (PBT) or 82 on the Internet-based version (iBT). Students must take the MELAB or the ELS.

ADMISSIONS: 57% of the 2017-2018 applicants were accepted. The SAT scores for the 2017-2018 freshman class were: Critical Reading-- 25% below 500, 47% between 500 and 599, 24% between 600 and 699, and 4% between 700 and 800. Math-- 37% below 500, 43% between 500 and 599, 18% between 600 and 699, and 2% between 700 and 800. Writing-- 38% below 500, 43% between 500 and 599, and 19% between 600 and 699. The ACT scores were 6% between 12 and 17, 35% between 18 and 23, 29% between 24 and 29, and 28% above 30. 47% of the current freshmen were in the top fifth of their class; 77% were in the top two fifths. 30 freshmen graduated first in their class. **Admissions Contact:** Regis University, Director of Admissions. Email: *ruadmissions@regis.edu* Web: *www.regis.edu*

FINANCIAL AID: In 2017-2018, 99% of all full-time freshmen received some form of financial aid. The average freshman award was $28,628. The college's own financial statement is required. The FAFSA code is 001363. The priority date for freshman financial aid applications for fall entry is April 15.

ROCKY MOUNTAIN COLLEGE OF ART AND DESIGN *(The complete profile is made available exclusively on our website, www.barronspac.com)*

UNITED STATES AIR FORCE ACADEMY D-3
www.usafa.af.mil

Colorado Springs, CO 80840 **(719) 333-2520** **(800) 443-9266**

Fax: (719) 333-3012	**Email:** alo_webmail@usafa.edu
Full-time: 3635 men, 835 women	**Faculty:** n/av
Part-time: n/av	**Ph.D.s:** 49%
Graduate: n/av	**Student/Faculty:** n/av
Year: semesters, summer session	**Tuition:** see profile
Room & Board: see profile	**Freshman Class:** n/av
SAT or ACT: required	**CEEB CODE:** 4830
Application Deadline: n/av	**COMPETITIVE**

The United States Air Force Academy, founded in 1954, is a public institution. Graduates receive the B.S. degree and a second lieutenant's commission in the regular Air Force. All graduates are obligated to serve at least 5 years of active duty military service. Tuition, room and board, medical, and dental expenses are paid by the U.S. government. Each cadet receives a monthly salary from which they can pay for uniforms, supplies, and personal expenses. Entering freshmen are required to deposit $2,500 to defray the initial costs of uniforms and personal expenses incurred upon entry. Students who are unable to submit the full deposit will receive a reduced monthly cash allotment until prescribed levels are reached. There is one undergraduate school. In addition to regional accreditation, United States Air Force Academy has baccalaureate program accreditation with ABET and CSAB. The 18000-acre campus is in a suburban area 70 miles south of downtown Denver and 8 miles north of downtown Colorado Springs. Including any residence halls, there are 13 buildings.

STUDENT LIFE: 95% of undergraduates are from out of state, mostly the South. Students are from 30 foreign countries. 8% are Asian American; 77% White; 7% Hispanic; 5% African American; 2% American Indian/Alaska Native; 1% Foreign. 58% are Protestant; 30% Catholic. **Male To Female Ratio:** 4.4:1. The average age of freshmen is 18; all undergraduates, 20. 15% do not continue beyond their first year; 85% remain to graduate. **Housing:** 4550 students can be accommodated in college housing, which includes dorms. On-campus housing is guaranteed for all 4 years. Alcohol is not permitted. Upperclassmen may keep cars.

FACULTY/CLASSROOMS: 85% of faculty are male; 15% are female. All teach undergraduates, and 10% do research. No introductory courses are taught by graduate students. The average class size in an introductory lecture is 17; in a laboratory is 17; and in a regular course is 17.

PROGRAMS OF STUDY: US Air Force Academy confers B.S. degrees. Bachelor's degrees are awarded in BIOLOGICAL SCIENCE (biology/biological science), BUSINESS (management science and operations research), COMMUNICATIONS AND THE ARTS (English), COMPUTER AND PHYSICAL SCIENCE (atmospheric sciences and meteorology, chemistry, computer science, mathematics, physics, and science), ENGINEERING AND ENVIRONMENTAL DESIGN (aeronautical engineering, aerospace studies, civil engineering, computer engineering, electrical/electronics engineering, engineering, engineering and applied science, engineering mechanics, environmental engineering, mechanical engineering, and military science), SOCIAL SCIENCE (behavioral science, economics, geography, history, humanities, international studies, law, political science/government, psychology, and social science). Engineering, and basic sciences are the strongest academically. Engineering, management, and social sciences have the largest enrollments.

ACTIVITIES: There are no fraternities or sororities. There are 87 groups on campus, including band, chamber music, cheerleading, chess, choir, chorale, chorus, computers, drama, drill team, drum and bugle corps, ethnic, film, forensics, honors, marching band, musical theater, pep band, photography, professional, radio and TV, religious, social, social service, and student government. Popular campus events include Acceptance Parade, and Christmas events. **Sports:** There are 17 intercollegiate sports for men and 10 for women, and 14 intramural sports for men and 13 for women. Facilities include a stadium, a cadet gym, field house, athletic facilities and recreational areas, basketball gyms, indoor tennis courts, an Olympic-size swimming pool, squash and racquetball/handball courts, weight-training rooms, and golf courses. **Graduates:** From July 1, 2016 to June 30, 2017, 986 bachelor's degrees were awarded. The most popular majors were social sciences (36%), engineering (35%), and basic sciences (15%). In an average class, 71% graduate in 4 years or less and 77% graduate in 5 years or less. Of the 2016 graduating class, 3% were enrolled in graduate school within 6 months of graduation, and 97% were employed.

SERVICES: Counseling and information services are available, as is tutoring in every subject. There is remedial math, reading, and writing. **Library/Resources:** The library contains 551,476 volumes, 729,880 microform items, and 3,643 audio/video tapes/CDs/DVDs, and subscribes to 36,252 periodicals including electronic. Computerized library services include interlibrary loans, database searching, Internet access, and Wi-Fi capability. Special learning facilities include an art gallery, planetarium, radio station, TV station, a field engineering and readiness lab, and an aeronautics lab/aeronautical research center. **Physically Challenged Students:** All of the campus is accessible. Facilities include wheelchair ramps, elevators, special parking, specially equipped restrooms, and lowered drinking fountains. **Special:** All cadets receive orientation flights in Air Force aircraft and take aviation science courses. A semester exchange program is available with the French Air Force Academy and U.S. Army, Naval, and Coast Guard academies. Freshman classes start in June, and basic cadet training must be completed before academics begin in August. Work-study programs are available, and dual majors are possible in all areas. There is an interdisciplinary space operations major. There are 2 national honor societies and a freshman honors program. **Visiting:** There are regularly scheduled orientations for prospective students, consisting of a 2-day orientation held in March and April. Students are given briefings by the superintendent, the commandant of cadets, the dean of cadets, and the director of athletics. Students stay overnight in the dormitories and shadow their escort cadets the second day, attending classes, training, and meals. There is also a daily tour. There are guides for informal visits. To schedule a visit, contact the Director of Admissions. **Campus Safety and Security:** Measures include 24-hour foot and vehicle patrol, self-defense education, and security escort services. There are emergency telephones and lighted pathways/ sidewalks.

REQUIREMENTS: The SAT or ACT is required. Candidates must be U.S. citizens between 17 and 22 years of age, unmarried and with no dependents, and nominated from a legal source. Students should have completed 4 years each of English, math, and lab sciences and 2 years each of social sciences and foreign languages. A computer course is recommended. A personal interview is required, as is an essay and a drug and alcohol abuse certificate. A GPA of 2.0 is required. AP credits are accepted. Important factors in the admissions decision are advanced placement or honors courses, leadership record, and personality/ intangible qualities. Cadets must complete the requirements for the core curriculum and for an academic major. They must be proficient in phys ed and military training and demonstrate an aptitude for commissioned service and leadership. A total of 145 to 161 semester hours is required, with a minimum GPA of 2.0, to graduate. The required curriculum includes 9 hours of military arts and sciences, 6 hours of phys ed, and 1 hour of aviation. **Procedure:** Freshmen are admitted in the summer. Entrance exams should be taken in the spring of the junior year. Check with the school for current application deadlines. Applications are accepted on-line. **Transfer Students:** All students must enter as freshmen and attend 4 years. 145 of 145 credits required for the bachelor's degree must be completed at US Air Force Academy. **International Students:** There are 52 international students enrolled. They must also take the SAT or ACT.

ADMISSIONS: 45 freshmen graduated first in their class. **Admissions Contact:** Maj. Andrew L Mattson, Associate Director, Admissions/ Selections. Email: *alo_webmail@usafa.edu* Web: *www.usafa.af.mil*

FINANCIAL AID: Check with the school for current application deadlines.

UNIVERSITY OF COLORADO BOULDER C-2

www.colorado.edu

Boulder, CO 80309 **(303) 492-6301**

Fax: (303) 492-7115 **Email:** admissions@colorado.edu

Full-time: 14,899 men, 11,955 women	**Faculty:** 1560; I, av$
Part-time: 1105 men, 708 women	**Ph.D.s:** n/av
Graduate: 3370 men, 2521 women	**Student/Faculty:** 17 to 1
Year: semesters, summer session	**Tuition:** $12,086 ($36,220)
Room & Board: $13,998	**Freshman Class:** 36150 applied, 28862 accepted, 6570 enrolled
SAT CR/M: 620/624 **ACT:** 27	**CEEB CODE:** 4841
Application Deadline: January 15	**HIGHLY COMPETITIVE**

University of Colorado Boulder, established in 1876, is a public institution offering undergraduate and graduate programs in arts and sciences, business, engineering, environmental design, music, education, journalism and mass communication, and law. There are 6 undergraduate schools and 3 graduate schools. In addition to regional accreditation, UC Boulder has baccalaureate program accreditation with AACSB, ABET, ACEJMC, NASM, and CAEP. The 600-acre campus is in a suburban area 30 miles northwest of Denver. Including any residence halls, there are 200 buildings.

STUDENT LIFE: 58% of undergraduates are from Colorado. Others are from 50 states, 82 foreign countries, and Canada. 88% are from public schools. 7% are Foreign; 68% White; 6% Asian American; 5% two or more races; 2% African American; 12% Hispanic; 1% race unknown. **Male To Female Ratio:** 1.3:1. The average age of freshmen is 18; all undergraduates, 20. 12% do not continue beyond their first year; 69% remain to graduate. **Housing:** 8072 students can be accommodated in college housing, which includes coed and married student dorms and on-campus apartments. In addition, there are honors houses, special-interest houses, theme housing, and residential academic programs in specific dorms. On-campus housing is guaranteed for the freshman year only, is available on a first-come, and first-served basis. 72% of students commute. All students may keep cars.

FACULTY/CLASSROOMS: 71% of faculty are male; 67% are female. 88% teach undergraduates and all do research. Graduate students teach 8% of introductory courses. The average class size in an introductory lecture is 40; in a laboratory is 21; and in a regular course is 24.

PROGRAMS OF STUDY: UC-Boulder confers B.A., B.Envd., B.F.A., B.A.Mus., B.Mus., B.Mus.Ed., B.S., and I.B.A. degrees. Master's and doctoral degrees are also awarded. Bachelor's degrees are awarded in BIOLOGICAL SCIENCE (biochemistry, ecology, evolutionary biology, molecular biology, neurosciences, and physiology), BUSINESS (accounting, business administration and management, finance, management science, and marketing management), COMMUNICATIONS AND THE ARTS (advertising, art history, Chinese, classics, communications, dance, English, film arts, fine arts, French, German studies, Italian, Japanese, journalism, linguistics, music, music performance, Russian languages and literature, Spanish, studio art, and theatre arts), COMPUTER AND PHYSICAL SCIENCE (applied mathematics, astronomy, chemistry, computer science, geology, information science, mathematics, and physics), EDUCATION (Asian studies, elementary education, and music education), ENGINEERING AND ENVIRONMENTAL DESIGN (aerospace engineering, architectural engineering, bioengineering, chemical engineering, civil engineering, computer engineering, electrical/ electronics engineering, engineering physics, environmental design, environmental engineering, environmental science, and mechanical engineering), HEALTH PROFESSIONS (speech pathology/audiology), SOCIAL SCIENCE (anthropology, economics, ethnic studies, geography, history, humanities, international relations, Judaic studies, philosophy, political science/government, psychology, religious studies, sociology, and women & gender studies). Psychology, integrative physiology, and finance have the largest enrollments.

ACTIVITIES: 12% of men belong to 23 national fraternities; 21% of women belong to 14 national sororities. There are 475 groups on campus, including art, band, cheerleading, chess, choir, chorale, chorus, communications, computers, dance, debate, drama, drill team, environmental, ethnic, film, honors, international, jazz band, LGBT, literary magazine, marching band, musical theater, newspaper, opera, orchestra, pep band, photography, political, professional, radio and TV, religious, social, social service, student government, and symphony. Popular campus events include Conference on World Affairs, Colorado Shakespeare Festival, Holiday Festival, Football Games, International Festival, and Global Jam. **Sports:** There are 6 intercollegiate sports for men and 9 for women, and 13 intramural sports for men and 13 for women. Facilities include a stadium, an events center, 4 outdoor basketball courts, and 5 outdoor recreational fields to accommodate rugby, ultimate frisbee, and soccer. The student recreation center facilities include an 8-lane swimming pool and diving pool, 2 large general purpose gyms, 3 indoor basketball courts, a 1/10th-mile indoor running track, courts for handball, racquetball, and squash, an aerobics studio, extensive weight training and cardio space, a wellness suite, private area for health screenings, 5 fitness studios including mind & body, indoor cycling, and functional training, an ice rink, 3 outdoor tennis courts, outdoor pool, and a climbing wall. **Graduates:** From July 1, 2016 to June 30, 2017, 5512 bachelor's degrees were awarded. The most popular majors were psychology (8%), integrative physiology (6%), and comunication (6%). In an average class, 47% graduate in 4 years or less, 66% graduate in 5 years or less, and 70% graduate in 6 years or less. Of the 2016 graduating class, 20% were enrolled in graduate school within 6 months of graduation, and 74% were employed.

SERVICES: Counseling and information services are available, as is tutoring in most subjects. The Disability Services Academic Skills Kit (ASK) service assists students in improving study habits, organizing their workload, and developing strategies to prepare for exams. **Library/ Resources:** The library contains 6.9 million volumes, 120,757 microform items, and subscribes to 584,830 periodicals including electronic. Computerized library services include interlibrary loans, database searching, Internet access, and Wi-Fi capability. Special learning facilities include an art gallery, natural history museum, planetarium, radio station, interactive foreign language video center, mountain research station, integrated teaching and learning lab in engineering, and multidisciplinary information technology center. **Physically Challenged Students:** 87% of the campus is accessible. Facilities include wheelchair ramps, elevators, special parking, specially equipped restrooms, special class scheduling, lowered drinking fountains, lowered telephones, and special housing. **Special:** Twelve residential academic programs for freshmen and sophomores offer a small liberal arts college atmosphere while taking advantage of the resources of a major university. Student-designed and dual majors, internships (including the CU in D.C Program), 5-year B.A.-M.A. degrees, and cooperative programs in engineering and computer science are available. Study abroad in 65 countries, work-study programs in federal labs, and cross-registration with other University of Colorado campuses are also offered. There are 31 national honor societies, Phi Beta Kappa, a freshman honors program, and 78 departmental honors programs. **Visiting:** There are regularly scheduled orientations for prospective students, combined information sessions and campus tours include a one-hour information session hosted by a CU Boulder admissions representative, followed by a student-led, 90-minute walking tour of campus. CU-Boulder also offers all-day-visit programs. There are guides for informal visits and visitors may sit in on classes. To schedule a visit, contact the Admissions Office. **Campus Safety and Security:** Measures include 24-hour foot and vehicle patrol, emergency notification system, self-defense education, and security escort services. There are shuttle buses, emergency telephones, lighted pathways/sidewalks, controlled access to dorms/residences. The campus police are academy-trained and commissioned officers of the Boulder police force.

REQUIREMENTS: Applicants must send an official score report for either the SAT or the ACT and either an official high school transcript or an official copy of certificate of high school equivalency and official GED scores. They are expected to have completed 17 credits of high school work as identified by the CU Boulder Minimum Academic Preparation Standards. High school diploma is required and GED is accepted. Required application materials include 2 short-answer essay questions and one academic letter of recommendation. Interviews are not used in the decision-making process. Auditions are required for consideration to the College of Music. Portfolios are discouraged. A GPA of 2.0 is required. AP and CLEP credits are accepted. Undergraduate degree and graduation requirements (e.g., number of credits overall and in the major, minimum GPA, core curriculum requirements) vary by degree program (e.g., B.A., B.F.A) and by undergraduate college and program. **Procedure:** Freshmen are admitted fall, spring, and summer. Entrance exams should be taken before December for summer or fall admission. There are early admissions and deferred admissions plans. Applications should be filed by January 15 for fall entry; October 1 for spring entry; and January 15 for summer entry. The fall 2017 application fee was $50. Notifications are sent April 1. 173 applicants were on the 2017 waiting list; 173 were admitted. Applications are accepted on-line. **Transfer Students:** 1133 transfer students enrolled in 2016-2017. Transfer applicants must submit official high school and college transcripts. Students who have completed fewer than 24 semester hours of transferable college work must also submit SAT or ACT results. Required application materials include 2 short-answer essay questions and one academic letter of recommendation. College of Music applicants must also complete a College of Music application after their admission application has been submitted, provide a letter of reference, and schedule an audition. 45 of 120 credits required for the bachelor's degree must be completed at UC Boulder. **International Students:** There are 1912 international students enrolled.

ADMISSIONS: 80% of the 2017-2018 applicants were accepted. The SAT scores for the 2017-2018 freshman class were: Math-- 4% below 500, 33% between 500 and 599, 44% between 600 and 699, and 19% between 700 and 800. Evidence-Based Reading/Writing-- 4% below 500, 31% between 500 and 599, 52% between 600 and 699, and 14% between 700 and 800. The ACT scores were 16% between 18 and 23, 53% between 24 and 29, and 30% above 30. 51% of the current freshmen were in the top fifth of their class; 80% were in the top two fifths. 137 freshmen graduated first in their class. **Admissions Contact:** Colleen Newman, Director of Undergraduate Admissions. Email: *admissions@colorado.edu* Web: *www.colorado.edu*

FINANCIAL AID: In 2017-2018, 82% of all full-time freshmen received some form of financial aid. 81% of all full-time freshmen received need-based aid. The average freshman award was $16,237. Need-based scholarships or need-based grants averaged $11,465; need-based self-help aid (loans and jobs) averaged $5,563; non-need-based athletic scholarships averaged $27,447; other non-need-based awards and non-need-based scholarships averaged $8,893; and $2,125 from other forms of aid. 17% of undergraduate students work part-time. The average financial indebtedness of the 2017 graduate was $41,373. The FAFSA code is 001370. The priority date for freshman financial aid applications for fall entry is February 15. The deadline for filing freshman financial aid applications for fall entry is rolling.

UNIVERSITY OF COLORADO COLORADO SPRINGS D-3

www.uccs.edu

Colorado Springs, CO 80918 **(719) 255-3640**

Email: admrec@uccs.edu

Full-time: 3910 men, 4010 women
Part-time: 973 men, 1294 women
Graduate: 818 men, 990 women
Year: semesters, summer session
Room & Board: $9800

SAT CR/M/W: 531/533/502 **ACT:** 23
Application Deadline: May 1

Faculty: 406
Ph.D.s: 67%
Student/Faculty: 19 to 1
Tuition: $9863 ($23,273)
Freshman Class: 12158 applied, 8970 accepted, 2056 enrolled
CEEB CODE: 4874
COMPETITIVE

University of Colorado Colorado Springs is a public institution offering 45 baccalaureate, 22 master's, and 5 doctorate programs in a broad range of disciplines including engineering, education, nursing & health sciences, business, public affairs, and arts & sciences. There are 6 undergraduate schools and 6 graduate schools. In addition to regional accreditation, UCCS has baccalaureate program accreditation with AACSB, ABET, ADA, CAEP, NLN, ACS, APA, Council for the Accreditation of Educator Preparat, and NASPAA. The 548-acre campus is in a suburban area in the heart of Colorado Springs, CO. Including any residence halls, there are 58 buildings.

STUDENT LIFE: 88% of undergraduates are from Colorado. Others are from 50 states, 71 foreign countries, and Canada. 65% are White; 17% Hispanic; 7% two or more races; 4% African American; 3% Asian American; 2% race unknown; 1% American Indian/Alaska Native; 1% Foreign. **Female To Male Ratio:** 1.1:1. The average age of freshmen is 19; all undergraduates, 23. 33% do not continue beyond their first year; 47% remain to graduate. **Housing:** 1684 students can be accommodated in college housing, which includes single-sex and coed dorms and on-campus apartments. In addition, there are honors houses, theme floors, and special interest housing. On-campus housing is available on a first-come and first-served basis. All students may keep cars.

FACULTY/CLASSROOMS: 46% of faculty are male; 54% are female. All teach undergraduates. No introductory courses are taught by graduate students. The average class size in an introductory lecture is 29; in a laboratory is 18; and in a regular course is 27.

PROGRAMS OF STUDY: UCCS confers B.A., B.S. and B.I. degrees. Master's and doctoral degrees are also awarded. Bachelor's degrees are awarded in BIOLOGICAL SCIENCE (biochemistry and biology/biological science), BUSINESS (business administration and management), COMMUNICATIONS AND THE ARTS (communications, English, Spanish, and visual and performing arts), COMPUTER AND PHYSICAL SCIENCE (chemistry, computer game design/development, computer science, mathematics, and physics), EDUCATION (education), ENGINEERING AND ENVIRONMENTAL DESIGN (computer engineering, electrical/electronics engineering, and mechanical engineering), HEALTH PROFESSIONS (health science and nursing), SOCIAL SCIENCE (anthropology, criminal justice, economics, ethnic studies, geography, history, philosophy, political science/government, psychology, sociology, and women's studies). Engineering, and nursing are the strongest academically. Business, nursing, and biology have the largest enrollments.

ACTIVITIES: 1% of men belong to 2 national fraternities; 2% of women belong to 2 national sororities. There are 207 groups on campus, including cheerleading, communications, computers, dance, drama, environmental, ethnic, film, honors, international, LGBT, literary magazine, musical theater, newspaper, pep band, political, professional, radio and TV, religious, social, and student government. Popular campus events include Clyde's Kickoff, DisOrientation Week, Homecoming Week,

Annual Leadership Conference, Roar Daze, Annual Concerts, and Annual Significant Speaker Events. **Sports:** There are 6 intercollegiate sports for men and 8 for women, and 19 intramural sports for men and 19 for women. Facilities include an aquatic center, a fitness center, gymnasium, indoor track, bouldering wall, multipurpose studio, locker rooms, track and field, basketball, cross-country, soccer, golf, softball, and outdoor trails. There is also an recreation and wellness center. **Graduates:** From July 1, 2015 to June 30, 2016, 1531 bachelor's degrees were awarded. The most popular majors were business (16%), nursing (10%), and communication (10%). In an average class, 23% graduate in 4 years or less, 40% graduate in 5 years or less, and 44% graduate in 6 years or less.

SERVICES: Counseling and information services are available, as is tutoring in most subjects. The Office of First Year Experience and the five centers for Academic Excellence (communication, language, science, math, and writing), are also available for students. There is a reader service for the blind, and remedial math, reading, and writing. **Library/Resources:** The library contains 407,599 volumes, 451,929 microform items, and 8,910 audio/video tapes/CDs/DVDs, and subscribes to 3,079 periodicals including electronic. Computerized library services include interlibrary loans, database searching, Internet access, and Wi-Fi capability. Special learning facilities include an art gallery, radio station, TV station, communication center, languages & social sciences center, mathematics center, science center, and the writing center. **Physically Challenged Students:** Facilities include wheelchair ramps, elevators, special parking, specially equipped restrooms, special class scheduling, lowered drinking fountains, lowered telephones, and special housing. **Special:** UCCS offers a distributed studies option that allows students to design their course of study. Additionally, we offer 7 undergraduate online completion programs in health care sciences, nursing, business, sociology, philosophy, criminal justice, and communication. There are 9 national honor societies, Phi Beta Kappa, a freshman honors program, and 8 departmental honors programs. **Visiting:** There are regularly scheduled orientations for prospective students. There are guides for informal visits and visitors may sit in on classes. To schedule a visit, contact Chris Beiswanger at go@uccs.edu. **Campus Safety and Security:** Measures include 24-hour foot and vehicle patrol, emergency notification system, self-defense education, and security escort services. There are shuttle buses, emergency telephones, lighted pathways/sidewalks, and controlled access to dorms/residences. UCCS employs highly-trained officers within the Department of Public Safety. While having the authority via Colorado Revised Statutes and the CU Board of Regents to enforce campus, municipal, county, and state laws, the Department also provides numerous classes and training for personal and public safety on campus.

REQUIREMENTS: AP and CLEP credits are accepted. To earn a baccalaureate degree, students must complete at least 120 credit hours (with at least 30 hours earned in the major) and a minimum GPA of 2.0. Additional requirements vary by academic program. **Procedure:** Freshmen are admitted to all sessions. There are deferred admissions and rolling admissions plans. Applications should be filed by May 1 for fall entry; December 1 for spring entry, along with a $50 fee. Applications are accepted on-line. **Transfer Students:** 1499 transfer students enrolled in 2015-2016. GPA of 2.0 and 13 or more transferable credit hours 30 of 120 credits required for the bachelor's degree must be completed at UCCS. **International Students:** There are 112 international students enrolled. The school actively recruits these students. They must take the TOEFL with a minimum score of 550 on the paper-based TOEFL (PBT) or 85 on the Internet-based version (iBT). They must also take the SAT or ACT.

ADMISSIONS: 23% of the current freshmen were in the top fifth of their class; 46% were in the top two fifths. 11 freshmen graduated first in their class. **Admissions Contact:** Chris Beiswanger, Director of Admissions. Email: *cbeiswan@uccs.edu* Web: *www.uccs.edu*

FINANCIAL AID: The FAFSA code is 004509. The priority date for freshman financial aid applications for fall entry is March 1.

UNIVERSITY OF COLORADO DENVER C-2

www.ucdenver.edu

Denver, CO 80204	**303-315-2601**
Fax: (303) 556-4838	**Email: admissions@cudenver.edu**
Full-time: 3831 men, 4108 women	**Faculty:** 3520; I, av$
Part-time: 1353 men, 1489 women	**Ph.D.s:** 72%
Graduate: 1811 men, 2383 women	**Student/Faculty:** 16 to 1
Year: semesters, summer session	**Tuition:** $10,658 ($31,448)
Room & Board: $11,580	**Freshman Class:** 8615 applied, 5808 accepted, 1372 enrolled
SAT CR/M: 550/550 **ACT:** 23	**CEEB CODE:** 4875
Application Deadline: July 22	**COMPETITIVE**

University of Colorado Denver is a public institution that was established in 1912. The University has two campuses. The downtown Denver campus is a commuter school with programs in the liberal arts and sciences, business, engineering and applied sciences, music, architecture and planning, and education. The Anschutz Medical Campus is a commuter school with programs in medicine, nursing, pharmacy, and dentistry. The downtown campus has housing associated with the University, but which is not owned nor operated by the University. The on-campus cost listed herein represents the cost of said university associated housing. There are 7 undergraduate schools and 8 graduate schools. In addition to regional accreditation, UC-Denver has baccalaureate program accreditation with AACSB, ABET, NAAB, NASM, CAEP, ACS, and CACREP. The 151-acre campus is in an urban area in downtown Denver.

STUDENT LIFE: 86% of undergraduates are from Colorado. Others are from 49 states, 68 foreign countries, and Canada. 6% are two or more races; 5% African American; 5% Foreign; 49% White; 22% Hispanic; 2% race unknown; 10% Asian American. **Female To Male Ratio:** 1.1:1. The average age of freshmen is 18; all undergraduates, 23. 29% do not continue beyond their first year; 48% remain to graduate. **Housing:** On-campus housing is guaranteed for the freshman year only. Alcohol is not permitted. All students may keep cars.

FACULTY/CLASSROOMS: 48% of faculty are male; 52% are female. No introductory courses are taught by graduate students. The average class size in an introductory lecture is 27; in a laboratory is 20; and in a regular course is 27.

PROGRAMS OF STUDY: UC-Denver confers B.A., B.S., and B.F.A degrees. Master's and doctoral degrees are also awarded. Bachelor's degrees are awarded in BIOLOGICAL SCIENCE (biology/biological science), BUSINESS (business administration and management), COMMUNICATIONS AND THE ARTS (communications, English, English Writing, fine arts, French, music, Spanish, and visual and performing arts), COMPUTER AND PHYSICAL SCIENCE (chemistry, computer science, mathematics, and physics), EDUCATION (education), ENGINEERING AND ENVIRONMENTAL DESIGN (architecture, bioengineering, civil engineering, electrical/electronics engineering, and mechanical engineering), HEALTH PROFESSIONS (medical science, nursing, and public health), SOCIAL SCIENCE (anthropology, criminal justice, economics, ethnic studies, geography, history, interdisciplinary studies, international studies, philosophy, political science/government, psychology, and sociology). Biology, psychology, and music have the largest enrollments.

ACTIVITIES: There are no fraternities or sororities. There are 228 groups on campus, including art, cheerleading, chorale, computers, dance, drama, environmental, ethnic, film, honors, international, jazz band, LGBT, men's hockey club, musical theater, newspaper, political, professional, radio and TV, religious, social, social service, and student government. Popular campus events include Fall Festival. **Sports:** There are 10 intramural sports for men and 12 for women. Facilities include a diving well, weight room, squash, racquetball/handball, tennis courts, a basketball half-court, dance studio, 3 gym arenas, a fitness center and a green room, a 400-meter track, a field for football, rugby, lacrosse, softball fields, a baseball field, a soccer field, sand volleyball court, ice hockey for men, utlimate frisbee, and Taekwondo. **Graduates:** From July 1, 2016 to June 30, 2017, 2128 bachelor's degrees were awarded. The most popular majors were biology (10%), psychology (9%), and communication (7%). In an average class, 22% graduate in 4 years or less and 48% graduate in 6 years or less.

SERVICES: Counseling and information services are available, as is

tutoring in most subjects. There is a reader service for the blind. There are ESL classes and study skills courses. **Library/Resources:** The library contains 1.5 million volumes, 38,106 microform items, and 14,651 audio/video tapes/CDs/DVDs, and subscribes to 188,468 periodicals including electronic. Computerized library services include interlibrary loans, database searching, Internet access, and Wi-Fi capability. Special learning facilities include an art gallery, radio station, and a writing center. **Physically Challenged Students:** All of the campus is accessible. Facilities include wheelchair ramps, elevators, special parking, specially equipped restrooms, special class scheduling, lowered drinking fountains, lowered telephones, transit system, and an adaptive computer lab. **Special:** Students can cross-register with Metropolitan State College, Community College of Denver, and Red Rocks Community College. Concurrent enrollment with any University of Colorado campus is possible. Cooperative programs, 1-semester internships, study abroad in 12 countries, work-study programs, an accelerated degree program in liberal arts and arts and media, and B.A.-B.S. degrees are available. The university offers dual majors, a general studies degree, non-degree study, and pass/fail options. There are small individualized classes, peer advocates, and workshops. There is also an international college in Beijing, China. There are 10 national honor societies and a freshman honors program. **Visiting:** There are regularly scheduled orientations for prospective students. Student visits include a mini-lecture, campus tour, and financial aid and academic advising. There are guides for informal visits and visitors may sit in on classes. To schedule a visit, contact the Office of Admissions. **Campus Safety and Security:** Measures include 24-hour foot and vehicle patrol, emergency notification system, self-defense education, and security escort services. There are shuttle buses, emergency telephones, lighted pathways/sidewalks, and crime prevention programs.

REQUIREMENTS: Preference for admission is given to applicants who rank in the top 30% of their high school graduating class and present a composite score of 21 or higher on the ACT, or a combined score of 950 or higher on the SAT. 18 Academic units are required: 4 each in English, and math, 3 each in science, with those 2 must be lab, and social studies, and 1 each in foreign language and history, and 2 in academic electives. AP and CLEP credits are accepted. Important factors in the admissions decision are advanced placement or honors courses, evidence of special talent, and extracurricular activities record. To graduate, students must complete 120 credit hours with a minimum GPA of 2.0. All students must complete the core curriculum courses in addition to the requirements for the major. **Procedure:** Freshmen are admitted fall, spring, and summer. Entrance exams should be taken in the junior or senior year of high school. There are deferred admissions and rolling admissions plans. Applications should be filed by July 22 for fall entry; December 1 for spring entry; and May 3 for summer entry. The fall 2017 application fee was $50. Notification is sent on a rolling basis. Applications are accepted on-line. **Transfer Students:** 1421 transfer students enrolled in 2016-2017. Students transferring less than 30 approved college credits are required to submit standardized test scores and high school GPA and rank. Students transferring 30 approved credits or more from an accredited college only need to submit their current college transcript and proof of good-standing. Students may enroll in the fall, spring and summer. 60 of 120 credits required for the bachelor's degree must be completed at CU Denver. **International Students:** There are 1051 international students enrolled. They must take the TOEFL with a minimum score of 537 on the paper-based TOEFL (PBT) or 75 on the Internet-based version (iBT). They must also take the SAT or ACT.

ADMISSIONS: 67% of the 2017-2018 applicants were accepted. The SAT scores for the 2017-2018 freshman class were: Critical Reading-- 35% below 500, 29% between 500 and 599, 32% between 600 and 699, and 3% between 700 and 800. Math-- 32% below 500, 45% between 500 and 599, 16% between 600 and 699, and 6% between 700 and 800. The ACT scores were 5% between 12 and 17, 45% between 18 and 23, 41% between 24 and 29, and 9% above 30. 50% of the current freshmen were in the top fifth of their class; 80% were in the top two fifths. **Admissions Contact:** Catherine Wilson, Director of Undergraduate Admissions. Email: *admissions@cudenver.edu* Web: *www.ucdenver.edu*

FINANCIAL AID: In 2017-2018, 60% of all full-time freshmen received some form of financial aid. 48% of all full-time freshmen received need-based aid. The average freshman award was $10,904. Need-based scholarships or need-based grants averaged $7,726; need-based self-help aid (loans and jobs) averaged $4,982; other non-need-based awards and non-need-based scholarships averaged $2,348; and $1,883 from other forms of aid. The average financial indebtedness of the 2017 graduate was $19,378. The college's own financial statement, and tax returns are required. The FAFSA code is 004508. The priority date for freshman financial aid applications for fall entry is April 1.

UNIVERSITY OF DENVER — C-2

www.du.edu

Denver, CO 80208 — (303) 871-2036

Fax: (303) 871-3301	**Email:** admission@du.edu
Full-time: 2496 men, 2801 women	**Faculty:** I, av$
Part-time: 118 men, 214 women	**Ph.D.s:** 90%
Graduate: 2473 men, 3519 women	**Student/Faculty:** 11 to 1
Year: quarters, summer session	**Tuition:** $48,780
Room & Board: $12,349	**Freshman Class:** 13670 applied, 10456 accepted, 1424 enrolled
SAT CR/M/W: 595/610/565 **ACT:** 28	**CEEB CODE:** 4852
Application Deadline: January 15	**VERY COMPETITIVE+**

University of Denver, established in 1864, is a private institution offering degrees in arts and sciences, fine arts, music, business, engineering, and education. The figures given in the above capsule and in this profile are approximate. There are 8 undergraduate schools and 10 graduate schools. In addition to regional accreditation, UD has baccalaureate program accreditation with AACSB, ABET, NASAD, NASM, and ACS. The 125-acre campus is in an urban area 8 miles south of downtown Denver. Including any residence halls, there are 74 buildings.

STUDENT LIFE: 59% of undergraduates are from out of state, mostly the Midwest. Students are from 50 states, 47 foreign countries, and Canada. 68% are White; 4% Asian American; 3% African American. **Female To Male Ratio:** 1.3:1. The average age of freshmen is 18; all undergraduates, 21. 14% do not continue beyond their first year; 85% remain to graduate. **Housing:** College-sponsored housing includes married student dorms, on-campus apartments, and off-campus apartments. In addition, there are honors houses, special-interest houses, fraternity houses, sorority houses, five living and learning communities, and a pioneer leadership program floor. On-campus housing is guaranteed for the freshman year only and is available on a lottery system for upperclassmen. 53% of students commute. All students may keep cars.

FACULTY/CLASSROOMS: 50% of faculty are male; 50% are female. 71% teach undergraduates, 70% do research, and 53% do both. Graduate students teach 5% of introductory courses. The average class size in an introductory lecture is 23; in a laboratory is 18; and in a regular course is 19.

PROGRAMS OF STUDY: UD confers B.A., B.S., B.B.A., B.F.A., B.M., B.S.ACC., B.S.B.A., B.S.CH., B.S.CPE., B.S.EE. and B.S.ME. degrees. Master's and doctoral degrees are also awarded. Bachelor's degrees are awarded in BIOLOGICAL SCIENCE (biochemistry, bioinformatics, biology/biological science, ecology, and molecular biology), BUSINESS (accounting, banking and finance, business administration and management, business economics, business statistics, finance, hospitality management services, international business management, marketing/retailing/merchandising, and real estate), COMMUNICATIONS AND THE ARTS (animation, art history, art, art history and appreciation, art studies, communication studies, dramatic arts, English, film arts, French, German, Italian, jazz, journalism, languages, media arts, music, music production/recording technology, music performance, Russian, Spanish, strategic communication, and theatre studies), COMPUTER AND PHYSICAL SCIENCE (chemistry, computer game design/development, computer science, digital arts/technology, environmental chemistry, information sciences and systems, mathematics, physics, science, and statistics), ENGINEERING AND ENVIRONMENTAL DESIGN (bioengineering, computer engineering, construction management, electrical and computer engineering, electrical/electronics engineering, environmental science, materials science, mechanical engineering, and mechatronics engineering), HEALTH PROFESSIONS (biology), SOCIAL SCIENCE (anthropology, Asian/American studies, cognitive science, criminology, economics, geography, history, interdisciplinary studies, international studies, Judaic studies, philosophy, political science/government, psychology, public affairs, religion, social science, sociology, and women's studies). Information technology studies, real estate and construction management, and accounting are the strongest academically. Management, biology, and general business have the largest enrollments.

ACTIVITIES: 24% of men belong to 9 national fraternities; 32% of women belong to 5 national sororities. There are 160 groups on campus, including art, band, cheerleading, chess, choir, chorale, chorus, communications, computers, dance, debate, drama, drum and bugle corps, environmental, ethnic, film, forensics, honors, international, jazz band, LGBT, literary magazine, musical theater, newspaper, opera, orchestra, pep band, photography, political, professional, radio and TV, religious, social, social service, student government, and symphony. Popular campus events include Winter Carnival, May Days, and Festival of Nations Celebration. **Sports:** There are 8 intercollegiate sports for men and 9 for women. Facilities include a sports and wellness center housing 2 ice arenas, a gym, a multipurpose field house, an Olympic-size swimming pool, a fitness center, racquetball courts, studios for yoga, dance, cycling, and karate, a 25-foot climbing wall, a health clinic, a soccer field, a lacrosse stadium, and a tennis pavilion. **Graduates:** From July 1, 2016 to June 30, 2017, 1239 bachelor's degrees were awarded. The most popular majors were business/marketing (28%), social sciences (18%), and visual and performing arts (10%). In an average class, 2% graduate in 3 years or less, 66% graduate in 4 years or less, 76% graduate in 5 years or less, and 78% graduate in 6 years or less.

SERVICES: Counseling and information services are available, as is tutoring in most subjects. There is a reader service for the blind. **Library/Resources:** The library contains 2.3 million volumes, 1.1 million microform items, and 24,425 audio/video tapes/CDs/DVDs, and subscribes to 282,209 periodicals including electronic. Computerized library services include interlibrary loans, database searching, Internet access, and Wi-Fi capability. Special learning facilities include an art gallery, radio station, a high-altitude lab, an observatory, and an elementary and early learning center. **Physically Challenged Students:** 85% of the campus is accessible. Facilities include wheelchair ramps, elevators, special parking, specially equipped restrooms, special class scheduling, lowered drinking fountains, lowered telephones, and special housing. **Special:** DU offers co-op programs, study abroad through more than 59 programs, internships across the country and internationally, a Washington quarter, work-study programs, accelerated degree programs, and dual majors. Non-degree study and pass/fail options are also available. There are 19 national honor societies, Phi Beta Kappa, and a freshman honors program. **Visiting:** There are regularly scheduled orientations for prospective students, including tours and information sessions throughout the year, and 2 day-long open houses in the fall. Visitors may sit in on classes and stay overnight. To schedule a visit, contact the Office of Undergraduate Admission. **Campus Safety and Security:** Measures include 24-hour foot and vehicle patrol, emergency notification system, self-defense education, and security escort services. There are shuttle buses, emergency telephones, lighted pathways/sidewalks, controlled access to dorms/residences, and in-room safes.

REQUIREMENTS: The SAT or ACT is required. Applicants must be graduates of an accredited secondary school. The GED is accepted. DU recommends that applicants have 4 years in English, 3 to 4 each in math, social studies, 3 to 4 in science. of those, 2 must be lab, 2 to 4 in foreign language. An essay and a counselor recommendation are required, and a Hyde interview is strongly encouraged. AP and CLEP credits are accepted. Important factors in the admissions decision are leadership record, advanced placement or honors courses, personality/intangible qualities, extracurricular activities record, recommendations by school officials, parents or siblings attended your school, evidence of special talent, recommendations by alumni, and geographical diversity. For graduation, students must complete 183 to 194 quarter hours, including 40 to 135 in the major, with a minimum GPA of 2.0. They must fulfill foundational requirements in the freshman and sophomore years, and with junior standing take core courses in communities and environments, self and identities, and change and continuity, and must complete a writing-intensive course. Distribution requirements include 12 quarter hours each of English, natural sciences, arts and humanities, and social sciences, 8 of math and computer science, and 4 of oral communication. **Procedure:** Freshmen are admitted to all sessions. Entrance exams should be taken by January of the senior year. There are early admissions and deferred admissions plans. Early decision applications should be filed by November 1; regular applications, by January 15 for fall entry; December 1 for winter entry; February 15 for spring entry; and May 1 for summer entry. The fall 2017 application fee was $60. Notification of early decision is sent January 15; regular decision, March 15. 1659 applicants were on the 2017 waiting list; 108 were admitted. Applications are accepted on-line. **Transfer Students:** 194 transfer students enrolled in 2016-2017. Applicants must submit an official transcript from all colleges attended. Those students with fewer than 30 semester hours of college credit must submit a high school transcript and test scores. A minimum GPA of 2.0 is required, but a GPA of 3.0 is recommended. 45 of 138 credits required for the bachelor's degree must be completed at DU. **International Students:** There are 475 international students enrolled. They must take the TOEFL with a minimum score of 550 on the paper-based TOEFL (PBT) or 80 on the Internet-based version (iBT). Students must also take the IELTS, Intensive English Language Program, and either the SAT or ACT.

ADMISSIONS: 76% of the 2017-2018 applicants were accepted. The SAT scores for the 2017-2018 freshman class were: Critical Reading-- 10% below 500, 37% between 500 and 599, 44% between 600 and 699, and 9% between 700 and 800. Math-- 5% below 500, 37% between 500 and 599, 46% between 600 and 699, and 12% between 700 and 800. Writing-- 19% below 500, 45% between 500 and 599, 31% between 600 and 699, and 4% between 700 and 800. 70% of the current freshmen were in the top fifth of their class; 92% were in the top two fifths. 22 freshmen graduated first in their class. **Admissions Contact:** Hannah Stone, Director of Admissions. Email: *admission@du.edu* Web: *www.du.edu*

FINANCIAL AID: In 2017-2018, 86% of all full-time freshmen received some form of financial aid. The average freshman award was $34,455. Need-based scholarships or need-based grants averaged $28,597; need-based self-help aid (loans and jobs) averaged $5,018; non-need-based athletic scholarships averaged $36,371; other non-need-based awards and non-need-based scholarships averaged $4,181; and $14,724 from other forms of aid. The average financial indebtedness of the 2017 graduate was $29,050. University of Denver is a member of CSS. The CSS/Profile is required. The FAFSA code is 001371. The priority date for freshman financial aid applications for fall entry is February 15. The deadline for filing freshman financial aid applications for fall entry is May 1.

UNIVERSITY OF NORTHERN COLORADO D-1

www.unco.edu

Greeley, CO 80634	(970) 351-2881 (888) 700-4UNC
Fax: (970) 351-2984	Email: admissions@unco.edu
Full-time: 3016 men, 5226 women	Faculty: 490; I, --$
Part-time: 251 men, 602 women	Ph.D.s: n/av
Graduate: 655 men, 1903 women	Student/Faculty: 18 to 1
Year: semesters, summer session	Tuition: $8888 ($20,473)
Room & Board: $10,770	Freshman Class: 6784 applied, 6124 accepted, 2166 enrolled
SAT CR/M: 525/515 ACT: 22	CEEB CODE: 4074
Application Deadline: August 1	COMPETITIVE

University of Northern Colorado, founded in 1890, is a state-supported public institution offering undergraduate and graduate programs in liberal arts and sciences, business, education, health and human sciences, and performing and visual arts. There are 6 undergraduate schools and 1 graduate school. In addition to regional accreditation, University of Northern Colorado has baccalaureate program accreditation with AACSB, ADA, NASM, CAEP, and NLN. The 260-acre campus is in a suburban area 50 miles north of Denver. Including any residence halls, there are 86 buildings.

STUDENT LIFE: 97% of undergraduates are from Colorado. Others are from 50 states, 23 foreign countries, and Canada. 58% are White; 4% African American; 4% two or more races; 2% Asian American; 2% American Indian/Alaska Native; 19% Hispanic; 10% race unknown. **Female To Male Ratio:** 2.0:1. The average age of freshmen is 18; all undergraduates, 21. **Housing:** 3176 students can be accommodated in college housing, which includes married student dorms, on-campus apartments, and off-campus apartments. In addition, there are special-interest houses, fraternity houses, sorority houses, and wellness housing. On-campus housing is guaranteed for the freshman year only, is available on a first-come, first-served basis, and is available on a lottery system for upperclassmen. 90% of students live on campus. All students may keep cars.

FACULTY/CLASSROOMS: All teach undergraduates and all do research. Graduate students teach 17% of introductory courses. The average class size in an introductory lecture is 46; in a laboratory is 27; and in a regular course is 28.

PROGRAMS OF STUDY: UNC confers B.A., B.M., B.M.E. and B.S. degrees. Master's and doctoral degrees are also awarded. Bachelor's degrees are awarded in AGRICULTURE (natural resource management), BIOLOGICAL SCIENCE (biology/biological science and nutrition), BUSINESS (business administration and management, management science, marketing/retailing/merchandising, and recreation and leisure services), COMMUNICATIONS AND THE ARTS (American Sign Language, art, communications, English, fine arts, French, German, graphic design, journalism, music, musical theater, Spanish, telecommunications, and visual and performing arts), COMPUTER AND PHYSICAL SCIENCE (chemistry, earth science, geology, information sciences and systems, mathematics, physics, and statistics), EDUCATION (athletic training, education, music education, physical education, science education, social science education, and special education), HEALTH PROFESSIONS (exercise science, nursing, rehabilitation therapy, and speech pathology/audiology), SOCIAL SCIENCE (African American studies, anthropology, Asian/American studies, criminal justice, dietetics, economics, ethics, politics, and social policy, geography, gerontology, history, human services, interdisciplinary studies, international relations, Mexican-American/Chicano studies, philosophy, physical fitness/movement, political science/government, psychology, social science, and sociology). Business, music, and nursing are the strongest academically. Business, interdisciplinary studies, and sport & exercise science have the largest enrollments.

ACTIVITIES: 6% of men belong to 11 national fraternities; 6% of women belong to 9 national sororities. There are 138 groups on campus, including art, band, cheerleading, chess, choir, chorale, chorus, computers, dance, drama, drill team, ethnic, film, honors, international, jazz band, LGBT, literary magazine, marching band, musical theater, newspaper, opera, orchestra, pep band, photography, political, professional, radio and TV, religious, social, social service, student government, and symphony. Popular campus events include Hawaiian Luau, Academic Excellence Week, and International Dinner. **Sports:** There are 8 intercollegiate sports for men and 9 for women, and 16 intramural sports for men and 16 for women. Facilities include 50-foot rock climbing wall, full high ropes course and bouldering cave, a fitness center, treadmills, spin cycles, ellipticals, strength equipment and free weights, a gymnasium, hockey rink, Olympic-size swimming pool with a diving well, a field house, complete with indoor track, basketball, volleyball, indoor lacrosse courts, racquetball courts, squash courts, dance studio, physical therapy/training room, courts for tennis and basketball, a quarter-mile track, a field for softball and a modern turf field for soccer, lacrosse and intramural competition. **Graduates:** From July 1, 2016 to June 30, 2017, 1901 bachelor's degrees were awarded. The most popular majors were health professions and related programs (15%), interdisciplinary studies (13%), and business/marketing (11%). In an average class, 87% graduate in 4 years or less, 92% graduate in 5 years or less, and 94% graduate in 6 years or less.

SERVICES: Counseling and information services are available, as is tutoring in most subjects. There is a reader service for the blind, and remedial math, reading, and writing. **Library/Resources:** The library contains 1.1 million volumes, 2.1 million microform items, and 36,009 audio/video tapes/CDs/DVDs, and subscribes to 40,304 periodicals including electronic. Computerized library services include interlibrary loans, database searching, Internet access, and Wi-Fi capability. Special learning facilities include an art gallery and radio station. **Physically Challenged Students:** All of the campus is accessible. Facilities include wheelchair ramps, elevators, special parking, specially equipped restrooms, special class scheduling, lowered drinking fountains, lowered telephones, and special housing. Academic support services such as note taking, transportation, interpreters, adaptive computer instruction, and library assistance. **Special:** UNC offers internships and co-op programs in many majors and study abroad in England, Australia, Spain, France, and Germany or through the International Student Exchange Program. Dual majors, student-designed majors, credit by exam, and pass/fail options are also available. There are 7 national honor societies and a freshman honors program. **Visiting:** There are regularly scheduled orientations for prospective students, including academic advising, registration, tours, and special activities. There are guides for informal visits and visitors may sit in on classes. To schedule a visit, contact the UNC Visitors Center at visitors.center@unco.edu. **Campus Safety and Security:** Measures include 24-hour foot and vehicle patrol, emergency notification system, and security escort services. There are shuttle buses, emergency telephones, and lighted pathways/sidewalks.

REQUIREMENTS: The SAT or ACT is required. Admission standards are set by the Colorado Commission on Higher Education, but each applicant is evaluated on an individual basis. In general, an ACT score of 22, or an SAT composite score of 1000, and a cumulative GPA of 2.9 are required. Graduation from an accredited high school is required. 17 academic units are recommended 4 each in English, and math, 3 units in science with 2 lab, 2 each in social studies and academic electives, and 1 in history. AP and CLEP credits are accepted. Important factors in the admissions decision are leadership record, recommendations by school officials, evidence of special talent, advanced placement or honors courses, parents or siblings attended your school, personality/intangible qualities, extracurricular activities record, and geographical diversity. Students must earn a minimum of 120 semester hours (some majors require additional hours) with a minimum GPA of 2.0. All students must complete 40 semester hours in required general education courses and meet all degree requirements in the major. **Procedure:** Freshmen are admitted fall, spring, and summer. Entrance exams should be taken as early as possible. There are deferred admissions and rolling admissions plans. Applications should be filed by August 1 for fall entry; December 20 for spring entry; and May 1 for summer entry. The fall 2017 application fee was $45. Applications are accepted on-line. **Transfer Students:** 807 transfer students enrolled in 2016-2017. Transfer students who have completed 12 or fewer hours of college must meet the same criteria for admission as entering freshmen. Transfers with 13 or more semester hours must have a minimum 2.4 GPA. 30 of 120 credits required for the bachelor's degree must be completed at UNC. **International Students:** There are 130 international students enrolled. They must take the TOEFL with a minimum score of 520 on the paper-based TOEFL (PBT) or 70 on the Internet-based version (iBT) or take the MELAB. They must also take the SAT or ACT.

ADMISSIONS: 90% of the 2017-2018 applicants were accepted. The SAT scores for the 2017-2018 freshman class were: Critical Reading--41% below 500, 36% between 500 and 599, 19% between 600 and 699, and 3% between 700 and 800. Math-- 38% below 500, 46% between 500 and 599, 14% between 600 and 699, and 2% between 700 and 800. 29 freshmen graduated first in their class. **Admissions Contact:** Sean Broghammer, Director of Admissions. Email: *admissions@unco.edu* Web: *www.unco.edu*

FINANCIAL AID: In 2017-2018, 56% of all full-time freshmen received some form of financial aid. 36% of all full-time freshmen received need-based aid. The average freshman award was $11,863. Need-based scholarships or need-based grants averaged $9,347; need-based self-help aid (loans and jobs) averaged $3,416; non-need-based athletic scholarships averaged $14,947; other non-need-based awards and non-need-based scholarships averaged $3,215; and $6,381 from other forms of aid. The average financial indebtedness of the 2017 graduate was $22,832. The FAFSA code is 001349. The priority date for freshman financial aid applications for fall entry is March 1.

WESTERN STATE COLORADO UNIVERSITY — B-3

www.western.edu

Gunnison, CO 81231 — **(970) 943-2119**, **(800) 876-5309**

Fax: (970) 943-2212 — **Email: admissions@western.edu**

Full-time: 1076 men, 758 women
Part-time: 293 men, 298 women
Graduate: 133 men, 244 women
Year: semesters, summer session
Room & Board: $9546
SAT or ACT: required
Application Deadline: June 1
Faculty: 102
Ph.D.s: 83%
Student/Faculty: 19 to 1
Tuition: $9802 ($21,274)
Freshman Class: n/av
CEEB CODE: 4946
COMPETITIVE

Western State Colorado University, founded in 1901, is a public institution offering undergraduate programs in liberal arts and sciences, business, recreation, and education. There are 8 undergraduate schools and 1 graduate school. In addition to regional accreditation, Western State has baccalaureate program accreditation with NASM. The 228-acre campus is in a rural area 210 miles southwest of Denver. Including any residence halls, there are 31 buildings.

STUDENT LIFE: 70% of undergraduates are from Colorado. Others are from 50 states, 8 foreign countries, and Canada. 85% are from public schools. 8% are race unknown; 71% White; 4% two or more races; 3%

African American; 11% Hispanic; 1% Asian American; 1% American Indian/Alaska Native. **Male To Female Ratio:** 1.2:1. The average age of freshmen is 18; all undergraduates, 21. 36% do not continue beyond their first year; 64% remain to graduate. **Housing:** 1234 students can be accommodated in college housing, which includes married student dorms and on-campus apartments. In addition, there are special-interest houses, theme floors on art, science, and outdoor pursuits. On-campus housing is guaranteed for the freshman year only, is available on a first-come, and first-served basis. 62% of students commute. All students may keep cars.

FACULTY/CLASSROOMS: 55% of faculty are male; 45% are female. 97% do both. No introductory courses are taught by graduate students. The average class size in an introductory lecture is 22; in a laboratory is 15; and in a regular course is 19.

PROGRAMS OF STUDY: Western State confers B.A., B.S., and B.F.A. degrees. Master's degrees are also awarded. Bachelor's degrees are awarded in AGRICULTURE (environmental studies), BIOLOGICAL SCIENCE (biology/biological science), BUSINESS (accounting, business administration and management, and recreation and leisure services), COMMUNICATIONS AND THE ARTS (art, communications, dramatic arts, English, fine arts, music, and Spanish), COMPUTER AND PHYSICAL SCIENCE (chemistry, computer science, geology, and mathematics), EDUCATION (art education, elementary education, foreign languages education, music education, science education, and secondary education), ENGINEERING AND ENVIRONMENTAL DESIGN (pre-engineering), HEALTH PROFESSIONS (predentistry), SOCIAL SCIENCE (anthropology, economics, history, physical fitness/movement, political science/government, prelaw, psychology, and sociology). Business, biological sciences, and communications are the strongest academically. Business, exercise & sports science, and recreation & outdoor education have the largest enrollments.

ACTIVITIES: There are no fraternities or sororities. There are 60 groups on campus, including adventure race team, alpine ski, wilderness pursuits, English performance poetry, mountain bike/road cycling, art, band, cheerleading, choir, chorale, chorus, clubs for nordic, dance, drama, environmental, ethnic, honors, international, jazz band, LGBT, literary magazine, marching band, musical theater, newspaper, opera, orchestra, pep band, photography, political, professional, radio and TV, religious, social, social service, student government, and symphony. Popular campus events include Family Weekend, Spring Carnival, and Winter Fest. **Sports:** There are 15 intercollegiate sports for men and 14 for women, and 9 intramural sports for men and 9 for women. Facilities include a fitness center, gyms, a football stadium, an all-weather track, a number of playing fields, a weight room, an indoor swimming pool, a game/pool area, tennis and volleyball courts, men's and women's rugby and soccer, baseball, hockey, and climbing. **Graduates:** From July 1, 2016 to June 30, 2017, 386 bachelor's degrees were awarded. The most popular majors were business (24%), exercise, sports science (15%), and biology (10%). In an average class, 1% graduate in 3 years or less, 21% graduate in 4 years or less, 37% graduate in 5 years or less, and 41% graduate in 6 years or less.

SERVICES: Counseling and information services are available, as is tutoring in most subjects. There is a reader service for the blind, and remedial math and writing. **Library/Resources:** The library contains 252,757 volumes, 105,363 microform items, and 10,268 audio/video tapes/CDs/DVDs, and subscribes to 211 periodicals including electronic. Computerized library services include interlibrary loans and database searching. Special learning facilities include an art gallery, radio station, TV station, a greenhouse, Western mountain archeological site, and media production studio. **Physically Challenged Students:** 90% of the campus is accessible. Facilities include wheelchair ramps, elevators, special parking, specially equipped restrooms, special class scheduling, lowered drinking fountains, lowered telephones, and special housing. There are also screen reader programs available on all student lab computers, ADA compliant rooms in residence halls, and an audio device that increases telephone volume. **Special:** The Department of Business and Accounting offers a co-op program. Study abroad, internships, work-study programs, an accelerated degree program in teacher education, dual and student-designed majors, and credit for military and work experience are available. There are 9 national honor societies and a freshman honors program. **Visiting:** There are regularly scheduled orientations for prospective students, consisting of campus tours, and meetings with faculty, coaches, and admissions counselors are available. There are guides for informal visits and visitors may sit in on classes. To schedule a visit, contact the Admissions Office. **Campus Safety and Security:** Measures include 24-hour foot and vehicle patrol and security escort services. There are emergency telephones, lighted pathways/sidewalks, and special event van shuttle service.

REQUIREMENTS: The SAT or ACT is required. An essay is required and an interview is recommended. Applicants must be graduates of an accredited secondary school. Western recommends that in high school students complete 4 units of English, 4 units of math, 3 units of laboratory science, 3 units of social science, and at least 1 unit of foreign language. A GPA of 2.5 is required. AP and CLEP credits are accepted. Important factors in the admissions decision are advanced placement or honors courses, leadership record, and extracurricular activities record. To be eligible to graduate, students must complete 120 credit hours and attain a minimum GPA of 2.0. Students must complete 35 core curriculum credits, 26 of which must be fulfilled through liberal arts credits in human relationships, natural sciences, and creative arts, as well as completing competencies in written expression, oral communication, and math. **Procedure:** Freshmen are admitted to all sessions. Entrance exams should be taken during spring of junior year or fall of senior year. There are deferred admissions and rolling admissions plans. Applications should be filed by June 1 for fall entry; November 1 for spring entry. The fall 2017 application fee was $30. Notification is sent on a rolling basis. Applications are accepted on-line. **Transfer Students:** 153 transfer students enrolled in 2016-2017. Transfer applicants must have a minimum GPA of 2.0, and may be asked to submit SAT or ACT test scores. 30 of 120 credits required for the bachelor's degree must be completed at Western. **International Students:** There are 9 international students enrolled. They must take the TOEFL with a minimum score of 550 on the paper-based TOEFL (PBT) or 96 on the Internet-based version (iBT).

ADMISSIONS: The SAT scores for the 2017-2018 freshman class were: Math-- 25% below 500, 56% between 500 and 599, and 19% between 600 and 699. Writing-- 25% below 500, 56% between 500 and 599, and 19% between 600 and 699. The ACT scores were 8% between 12 and 17, 54% between 18 and 23, 33% between 24 and 29, and 5% above 30. **Admissions Contact:** Admissions Officer. Email: *admissions@western.edu* Web: *www.western.edu*

FINANCIAL AID: In 2017-2018, 93% of all full-time freshmen received some form of financial aid. 60% of all full-time freshmen received need-based aid. The average freshman award was $11,049. Need-based scholarships or need-based grants averaged $9,266; need-based self-help aid (loans and jobs) averaged $3,169; non-need-based athletic scholarships averaged $6,638; and other non-need-based awards and non-need-based scholarships averaged $4,480. 30% of undergraduate students work part-time. The average financial indebtedness of the 2017 graduate was $26,950. The FAFSA code is 001372. The priority date for freshman financial aid applications for fall entry is March 1.

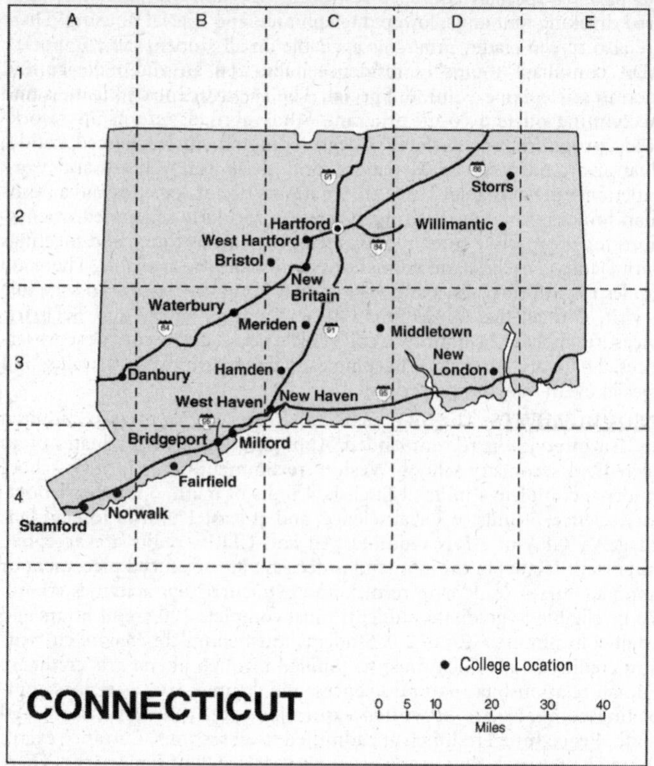

ALBERTUS MAGNUS COLLEGE *(The complete profile is made available exclusively on our website, www.barronspac.com)*

CENTRAL CONNECTICUT STATE UNIVERSITY C-2

www.ccsu.edu

New Britain, CT 06050 **(860) 832-2278**
(888) 733-2278

Fax: (860) 832-2522
Email: admissions@ccsu.edu

Full-time: 3984 men, 3621 women
Part-time: 1092 men, 857 women
Graduate: 840 men, 1486 women
Year: semesters, summer session
Room & Board: $11,816
SAT EBR-W/M: 540/530 **ACT:** 21
Application Deadline: May 1

Faculty: 398; IIA, +$
Ph.D.s: 84%
Student/Faculty: 19 to 1
Tuition: $10,225 ($22,914)
Freshman Class: 7733 applied, 5232 accepted, 1421 enrolled
CEEB CODE: 3898
COMPETITIVE

Central Connecticut State University is a regional, comprehensive master's level public university dedicated to learning in the liberal arts and sciences and to education for the professions. CCSU comprises 5 schools: the Carol A. Ammon School of Arts & Sciences, Business, Education & Professional Studies, Engineering, Science & Technology, and Graduate Studies. CCSU offers over 130 undergraduate and graduate programs through the master's and sixth-year levels, and the Ed.D. in Educational Leadership. In addition to regional accreditation, CCSU has baccalaureate program accreditation with AACSB, ABET, ACCE, CSWE, NASM, ACEI, ATMAE, CAATE. The 314-acre campus is in a suburban area in the northern edge of New Britain, 15 minutes from the state capital of Hartford and about 2 hours from New York City and Boston. Including any residence halls, there are 70 buildings.

STUDENT LIFE: 96% of undergraduates are from Connecticut. Others are from 37 states, 27 foreign countries, and Canada. 61% are White; 4% Asian American; 3% two or more races; 3% race unknown; 2% Foreign; 14% Hispanic; 13% African American. **Female To Male Ratio:** 1.0:1. The average age of freshmen is 18; all undergraduates, 23. 24% do not continue beyond their first year; 52% remain to graduate. **Housing:** 2279 students can be accommodated in college housing, and dorms. On-campus housing is guaranteed for all 4 years, is available on a first-come, first-served basis. 76% of students commute. All students may keep cars.

FACULTY/CLASSROOMS: 54% of faculty are male; 46% are female. 90% teach undergraduates. No introductory courses are taught by graduate students.

PROGRAMS OF STUDY: CCSU confers B.A., B.S., B.F.A., and B.S.N. degrees. Master's and doctoral degrees are also awarded. Bachelor's degrees are awarded in BIOLOGICAL SCIENCE (biochemistry and biology/biological science), BUSINESS (accounting, business administration and management, finance, hospitality management services, management information systems, management, marketing management, and office supervision and management), COMMUNICATIONS AND THE ARTS (art, digital media technologies, English, French, German, graphic design, Italian, journalism, film and media studies, music, Spanish, strategic communication, and theatre arts), COMPUTER AND PHYSICAL SCIENCE (chemistry, computer engineering technology, computer science, earth science, mathematics, physical sciences, and physics), EDUCATION (art education, athletic training, dance education, early childhood education, elementary education, music education, physical education, and technical education), ENGINEERING AND ENVIRONMENTAL DESIGN (civil engineering, civil engineering technology, construction management, electrical/electronics engineering technology, industrial engineering technology, manufacturing technology, mechanical engineering, mechanical engineering technology, and mechatronics engineering), HEALTH PROFESSIONS (exercise science and nursing), SOCIAL SCIENCE (anthropology, criminology, economics, geography, history, international studies, philosophy, political science/government, psychology, social science, social work, and sociology). Psychological science, criminology, and accounting have the largest enrollments.

ACTIVITIES: 1% of men belong to 3 national fraternities. There are no sororities. There are 130 groups on campus, including art, band, cheerleading, choir, chorale, chorus, computers, dance, drama, ethnic, honors, international, jazz band, LGBT, literary magazine, marching band, newspaper, orchestra, pep band, photography, political, professional, radio and TV, religious, social, social service, student government, and symphony. Popular campus events include Welcome week, Spring Concert, Intramural sports, GARBA (South Asian Student Association event), and Lavender Graduation. **Sports:** There are 7 intercollegiate sports for men and 7 for women. Facilities include a gym, football stadium, natatorium, weight training rooms, softball, baseball, and soccer fields. **Graduates:** From July 1, 2016 to June 30, 2017, 1958 bachelor's degrees were awarded. The most popular majors were business/marketing/management (26%), social sciences (13%), and psychology (8%). In an average class, 24% graduate in 4 years or less, 45% graduate in 5 years or less, and 52% graduate in 6 years or less.

SERVICES: Counseling and information services are available, as is tutoring in some subjects. There is a reader service for the blind, and remedial math, reading, and writing. **Library/Resources:** The library contains 595,180 volumes, 86,029 microform items, and 11,897 audio/video tapes/CDs/DVDs, and subscribes to 4,655 periodicals including electronic. Computerized library services include interlibrary loans, database searching, Internet access, and Wi-Fi capability. Special learning facilities include an art gallery, planetarium, radio station, TV station, The Elihu Burritt Collection, Connecticut Polish American Archive, GLBTQ archives, William A. O'Neill Oral History Project, Veterans History Project, and the John Woodcock Lemon Law Archives. **Physically Challenged Students:** 90% of the campus is accessible. Facilities include wheelchair ramps, elevators, special parking, specially equipped restrooms, special class scheduling, lowered drinking fountains, lowered telephones, and personal care attendants as roommates for physically disabled students. **Special:** The university offers co-op programs and cross-registration with several other Connecticut educational institutions, study abroad in more than 45 countries, internships in most departments, work-study programs, dual majors, and student-designed majors. There are 7 national honor societies, a freshman honors program, and 1 departmental honors program. **Visiting:** There are regularly scheduled orientations for prospective students, including a fall open house in October and daily and select Saturday visits throughout the fall and spring. There are guides for informal visits and visitors may sit in on classes. To schedule a visit, contact the Admissions Office. **Campus Safety and Security:** Measures include 24-hour foot and vehicle patrol, emergency notification system, self-defense education, and security escort services. There are shuttle buses, emergency telephones, lighted pathways/sidewalks, and controlled access to dorms/residences.

REQUIREMENTS: The SAT and the ACT Optional Writing test are required. Applicants must be graduates of an accredited secondary school or have earned a GED. An interview is recommended. CCSU also recommends that applicants have 14 academic credits: 4 in English, 3 each in math and foreign language, 2 each in science and social sciences, and 1 in U.S. history. AP and CLEP credits are accepted. Important factors in the admissions decision are extracurricular activities record, recommendations by school officials, and advanced placement or honors courses. Requirements depend on the major. To graduate all students need a minimum 2.0 GPA, and must complete at least 120 credit hours depending on the major. General education requirements total 44 to 46 credits in arts and humanities, sciences, math, communications, and fitness/wellness studies. Students must also demonstrate foreign language proficiency, complete 6 credits in courses with a global context, and satisfy a First-Year Experience requirement. **Procedure:** Freshmen are admitted fall and spring. Entrance exams should be taken in May of the junior year or November of the senior year. There are deferred admissions and rolling admissions plans. Applications should be filed by May 1 for fall entry; December 1 for spring entry. The fall 2017 application fee was $50. Notifications are sent April 1. 35 applicants were on the 2017 waiting list; 25 were admitted. Applications are accepted online. **Transfer Students:** 1039 transfer students enrolled in 2016-2017. Applicants must have a minimum of 12 transferable credits and a GPA of 2.0, and must submit official transcripts from previous schools attended. 30 of 120 credits required for the bachelor's degree must be completed at CCSU. **International Students:** There are 67 international students enrolled. They must take the TOEFL with a minimum score of 500 on the paper-based TOEFL (PBT).

ADMISSIONS: 68% of the 2017-2018 applicants were accepted. The SAT scores for the 2017-2018 freshman class were: Critical Reading-- 46% below 500, 44% between 500 and 599, 9% between 600 and 699, and 1% between 700 and 800. Math-- 43% below 500, 44% between 500 and 599, 12% between 600 and 699, and 1% between 700 and 800. Writing-- 49% below 500, 42% between 500 and 599, 9% between 600 and 699, and 1% between 700 and 800. The ACT scores were 7% between 12 and 17, 62% between 18 and 23, 27% between 24 and 29, and 4% above 30. 4% of the current freshmen were in the top fifth of their class; 22% were in the top two fifths. **Admissions Contact:** Larry Hall, Director of Recruitment and Admissions. Email: *admissions@ccsu.edu* Web: *www.ccsu.edu*

FINANCIAL AID: In 2017-2018, 86% of all full-time freshmen received some form of financial aid. 72% of all full-time freshmen received need-based aid. The average freshman award was $9,344. Need-based scholarships or need-based grants averaged $5,983 ($10,120 maximum); need-based self-help aid (loans and jobs) averaged $3,618 ($6,000 maximum); non-need-based athletic scholarships averaged $10,400 ($24,000 maximum); and other non-need-based awards and non-need-based scholarships averaged $2,000 ($5,000 maximum). 80% of undergraduate students work part-time. The average financial indebtedness of the 2017 graduate was $28,016. CCSU is a member of CSS. The FAFSA code is 001378. The priority date for freshman financial aid applications for fall entry is March 1.

CHARTER OAK STATE COLLEGE *(The complete profile is made available exclusively on our website, www.barronspac.com)*

CONNECTICUT COLLEGE — D-3

www.conncoll.edu

New London, CT 06320 — **(860) 439-2200**

Fax: (860) 439-4301	**Email:** info@conncoll.edu
Full-time: 694 men, 1158 women	**Faculty:** 180; IIB, ++$
Part-time: 1 men, 1 women	**Ph.D.s:** 91%
Graduate: 1 men, 3 women	**Student/Faculty:** 9 to 1
Year: semesters	**Tuition:** $65,000
Room & Board: n/av	**Freshman Class:** 5182 applied, 2071 accepted, 482 enrolled
SAT or ACT: required	**CEEB CODE:** 3284
Application Deadline: January 1	**MOST COMPETITIVE**

Connecticut College, is a highly selective residential liberal arts college known for interdisciplinary studies, international programs, funded internships, strong student-faculty relationships, and service learning. Institutional values include commitment to diversity, academic excellence, shared governance, and sustainability. The approximate figures given in the above capsule and in this profile covers tuition, fee's, room and board depending upon programs chosen for the academic school year. The college operates under a student-adjudicated honor code, has no Greek system, and is a member of the New England Small College Athletic Conference. There are 2 undergraduate schools and 1 graduate school. The 750-acre campus is in a small town midway between Boston and New York City, just off Interstate 95. Including any residence halls, there are 103 buildings.

STUDENT LIFE: 82% of undergraduates are from out of state, mostly the Northeast. Students are from 42 states, 46 foreign countries, and Canada. 50% are from public schools. 8% are Hispanic; 74% White; 4% African American; 4% Foreign; 3% Asian American. 27% are Protestant; 26% Catholic; 17% claim no religious affiliation; 14% Jewish. **Female To Male Ratio:** 1.7:1. The average age of freshmen is 19; all undergraduates, 20. 8% do not continue beyond their first year; 85% remain to graduate. **Housing:** 1790 students can be accommodated in college housing, which includes dorms and on-campus apartments. In addition, there are language/international houses, special-interest houses, quiet housing, theme housing, wellness housing, substance-free housing and gender-neutral housing. On-campus housing is guaranteed for all 4 years and is available on a lottery system for upperclassmen. 99% of students live on campus. Upperclassmen may keep cars.

FACULTY/CLASSROOMS: 49% of faculty are male; 51% are female. All teach undergraduates and do research. No introductory courses are taught by graduate students. The average class size in an introductory lecture is 25; in a laboratory is 13; and in a regular course is 19.

PROGRAMS OF STUDY: CC confers B.A. degrees. Master's degrees are also awarded. Bachelor's degrees are awarded in BIOLOGICAL SCIENCE (biochemistry, biology/biological science, botany, and neurosciences), COMMUNICATIONS AND THE ARTS (art, art history and appreciation, Chinese, classics, dance, dramatic arts, English, film arts, French, German, Japanese, music, and music technology), COMPUTER AND PHYSICAL SCIENCE (chemistry, mathematics, and physics), ENGINEERING AND ENVIRONMENTAL DESIGN (architecture and environmental science), SOCIAL SCIENCE (African studies, American studies, anthropology, East Asian studies, economics, gender studies, Hispanic American studies, history, human development, international relations, Italian studies, Latin American studies, philosophy, political science/government, psychology, religion, Russian and Slavic studies, sociology, and urban studies). Economics, English, and government have the largest enrollments.

ACTIVITIES: There are no fraternities or sororities. There are 55 groups on campus, including a capella group, art, band, choir, chorus, communications, computers, dance, drama, environmental, ethnic, film, international, jazz band, LGBT, literary magazine, newspaper, orchestra, photography, political, professional, radio and TV, religious, social, social service, student government, and symphony. Popular campus events include Eclipse Weekend, Harvestfest, and Floralia. **Sports:** There are 12 intercollegiate sports for men and 14 for women, and 12 intramural sports for men and 10 for women. The athletics complex includes a field house, an arena, fitness/wellness center, lighted artificial-turf field, eight-lane all-weather track, tennis courts, and playing fields. **Graduates:** From July 1, 2016 to June 30, 2017, 444 bachelor's degrees were awarded. The most popular majors were social sciences (32%), biological/life science (16%), and viual and performing arts (10%). In an average class, 83% graduate in 6 years or less. Of the 2016 graduating class, 25% were enrolled in graduate school within 6 months of graduation, and 75% were employed.

SERVICES: Counseling and information services are available, as is tutoring in some subjects, such as math, writing, and biological sciences. **Library/Resources:** Computerized library services include interlibrary loans, database searching, Internet access, and Wi-Fi capability. Special learning facilities include an art gallery, radio station, 750-acre arboretum, greenhouse, ion accelerator, refracting telescope and observatory, scanning and transmission electron microscopes, nuclear magnetic resonance spectrometer, tunable diode laser spectroscopy laboratory, center for electronic and digital sound, neuroscience and animal behavior laboratories, clinical and social psychology research observation suites. **Physically Challenged Students:** Facilities include wheelchair ramps, elevators, special parking, specially equipped restrooms, special class scheduling, lowered drinking fountains, lowered telephones, and special housing. Case-by-case accommodations are made for housing. **Special:** Cross-registration with 12 area colleges, internships in government, human services, and other fields, a Washington semester at American University, dual majors, student-designed majors, a 3-2 engineering degree with Washington University in St. Louis and Boston University, non-degree study, and satisfactory/unsatisfactory options are available. About half of the junior class studies abroad. Students may supplement their majors by earning certificates from one of our four interdisciplinary centers (focused on international studies, arts and technology, community action and public policy, or the environment. Students can also earn a certificate in museum studies or earn Connecticut teacher certification. There are 5 national honor societies and a chapter of Phi Beta Kappa. **Visiting:** There are regularly scheduled orientations for prospective students. Student visits include an introduction to the college, student perspectives, academic programs, a luncheon for parents and students, tours, and stay over night. To schedule a visit, contact the Office of Admission. **Campus Safety and Security:** Measures include 24-hour foot and vehicle patrol, emergency notification system, and security escort services. There are shuttle buses, emergency telephones, lighted pathways/sidewalks, controlled access to dorms/residences, and a campus-wide emergency communications system.

REQUIREMENTS: The submission of standardized test scores is optional. Students whose primary language is not English are required to submit the TOEFL or its equivalent. In addition, applicants must be graduates of an accredited secondary school. An essay is required and an interview is recommended. AP credits are accepted. Important factors in the admissions decision are personality/intangible qualities, evidence of special talent, extracurricular activities record, and recommendations by school officials. To graduate, students must complete at least 128 credit hours with a minimum GPA of 2.0. The number of courses required for our majors varies somewhat. Our General Education distribution requirements cover 7 courses from 7 academic areas, plus a foreign language and 2 writing-intensive courses. **Procedure:** Freshmen are admitted fall and spring. Entrance exams should be taken by January of the senior year. There are early decision and deferred admissions plans. Early decision applications should be filed by November 15; regular applications, by January 1 for fall entry; and December 1 for spring entry. The fall 2017 application fee was $60. Notification of early decision is sent December 15; regular decision, February 15. 268 early decision candidates were accepted for the 2017-2018 class. 637 applicants were on the 2017 waiting list; 61 were admitted. Applications are accepted on-line. **Transfer Students:** 24 transfer students enrolled in 2016-2017. Applicants must have a minimum college GPA of 3.0 and be in good standing at the previous school attended. SAT or ACT scores are required and an interview is recommended. Students may enroll in the fall and spring. 64 of 128 credits required for the bachelor's degree must be completed at Connecticut College. **International Students:** There are 90 international students enrolled. They must take the TOEFL with a minimum score of 600 on the paper-based TOEFL (PBT) or 100 on the Internet-based version (iBT). Student must also take any one of these tests: APIEL, IELTS, MELAB, or ELPT.

ADMISSIONS: 40% of the 2017-2018 applicants were accepted. **Admissions Contact:** Benjamin Brown, Assistant Director of Admissions. Email: *info@conncoll.edu* Web: *www.conncoll.edu*

FINANCIAL AID: In 2017-2018, 48% of all full-time freshmen received some form of financial aid. 48% of all full-time freshmen received need-based aid. The average freshman award was $40,019. Need-based scholarships or need-based grants averaged $37,224; need-based self-help aid (loans and jobs) averaged $4,759; and other non-need-based awards and non-need-based scholarships averaged $3,314. CC is a member of CSS. The CSS/Profile, parent and student tax forms, and noncustodial parent's statement (s) are required. The FAFSA code is 001379. The priority date for freshman financial aid applications for fall entry is February 1.

EASTERN CONNECTICUT STATE UNIVERSITY D-2

www.easternct.edu

Willimantic, CT 06226 **(860) 465-4398**

Email: admissions@easternct.edu

Full-time: 1903 men, 2389 women
Part-time: 372 men, 507 women
Graduate: 62 men, 129 women
Year: semesters, summer session
Room & Board: $12,559

Faculty: 199
Ph.D.s: 95%
Student/Faculty: 22 to 1
Tuition: $10,500 ($23,361)
Freshman Class: 5822 applied, 3678 accepted, 925 enrolled

SAT CR/M/W: 568/540/503 **ACT:** 22
Application Deadline: May 1

CEEB CODE: 3966
COMPETITIVE

Eastern Connecticut State University, founded in 1889, is the state's public liberal arts university. There are 3 undergraduate schools and 1 graduate school. In addition to regional accreditation, ECSU has baccalaureate program accreditation with CSWE, CAEP, and NAEYC. The 182-acre campus is in a small town 29 miles east of Hartford and 90 miles southwest of Boston. Including any residence halls, there are 45 buildings.

STUDENT LIFE: 95% of undergraduates are from Connecticut. Others are from 29 states, 74 foreign countries, and Canada. 95% are from public schools. 67% are White; 11% Hispanic; 8% African American; 8% race unknown; 3% Asian American; 3% two or more races; 1% Foreign. **Female To Male Ratio:** 1.3:1. The average age of freshmen is 18; all undergraduates, 22. 24% do not continue beyond their first year; 54% remain to graduate. **Housing:** 2650 students can be accommodated in college housing, which includes dorms and on-campus apartments. In addition, there are honors houses and special-interest houses. 52% of students live on campus. Alcohol is not permitted. Upperclassmen may keep cars.

FACULTY/CLASSROOMS: 54% of faculty are male; 46% are female. All teach undergraduates. No introductory courses are taught by graduate students. The average class size in an introductory lecture is 26; in a laboratory is 17; and in a regular course is 23.

PROGRAMS OF STUDY: ECSU confers B.A., B.S. and B.G.S. degrees. Associate and master's degrees are also awarded. Bachelor's degrees are awarded in BIOLOGICAL SCIENCE (biochemistry and biology/biological science), BUSINESS (accounting, business administration and management, business information systems, finance, industrial and labor relations, and sports management), COMMUNICATIONS AND THE ARTS (communications, digital media, English, music, Spanish, theatre acting, and visual and performing arts), COMPUTER AND PHYSICAL SCIENCE (computer science and mathematics), EDUCATION (early childhood education, elementary education, and physical education), ENGINEERING AND ENVIRONMENTAL DESIGN (environmental science), HEALTH PROFESSIONS (health science), SOCIAL SCIENCE (criminology, economics, history, liberal arts/general studies, philosophy, political science/government, psychology, social science, social work, sociology, and women & gender studies). Business administration, psychology, and social sciences have the largest enrollments.

ACTIVITIES: There are no fraternities or sororities. There are 95 groups on campus, including art, cheerleading, chorale, computers, dance, drama, environmental, ethnic, film, honors, international, jazz band, LGBT, literary magazine, musical theater, newspaper, photography, political, professional, radio and TV, religious, social, social service, student government, and yearbook. Popular campus events include Jazzin' it Up at Eastern, Day of Giving, University Hour, and Shackathon. **Sports:** There are 5 intercollegiate sports for men and 8 for women, and 15 intramural sports for men and 15 for women. Facilities include a student center, ice hockey, fencing, football, a fitness center, rugby, field house, 6-lane swimming pool, soccer field, baseball complex, softball stadium, 400 meter 8-lane track, field hockey field, tennis, basketball, racquetball, squash courts, weight room, yoga, martial arts, and trails in an arboretum. **Graduates:** From July 1, 2016 to June 30, 2017, 1102 bachelor's degrees were awarded. The most popular majors were business administration (11%), psychology (10%), and general studies (10%). In an average class, 1% graduate in 3 years or less, 47% graduate in 4 years or less, 51% graduate in 5 years or less, and 54% graduate in 6 years or less.

SERVICES: Counseling and information services are available, as is

tutoring in every subject. **Library/Resources:** The library contains 2.0 million volumes, 965,946 microform items, 7,910 audio/video tapes/CDs/DVDs, and subscribes to 55,085 periodicals including electronic. Computerized library services include interlibrary loans, database searching, Internet access, and Wi-Fi capability. Special learning facilities include an art gallery, planetarium, radio station, TV station, an arboretum, child and family development resource center, and the Church Farm Center for the Arts and Sciences. **Physically Challenged Students:** Facilities include wheelchair ramps, elevators, special parking, specially equipped restrooms, special class scheduling, and lowered drinking fountains. **Special:** The University Honors Program promotes undergraduate scholarship by providing academically talented students with opportunities to participate in specially designed courses that prepare them to conduct independent research and/or scholarly activity under the oversight of a faculty mentor. The Individualized Major Plan is a student's self-designed interdisciplinary plan of study, which consists of courses from two or more disciplines and results in a B.A. or B.S. degree. The self-designed plan of study allows the student to take courses in areas that naturally complement each other in today's workplace and to develop a strong educational base in at least one subject to facilitate entrance into a graduate program. There are 9 national honor societies and a freshman honors program. **Visiting:** There are regularly scheduled orientations for prospective students, including small group discussions, a tour of the campus, and a personal interview. There are guides for informal visits and visitors may sit in on classes. To schedule a visit, contact the Office of Admissions. **Campus Safety and Security:** Measures include 24-hour foot and vehicle patrol, emergency notification system, and security escort services. There are shuttle buses, emergency telephones, lighted pathways/sidewalks, and controlled access to dorms/residences.

REQUIREMENTS: Applicants must be graduates of an accredited secondary school or have a GED. They should have completed 15 high school academic credits, including 4 years each of English, and math, and 2 each of foreign language, social studies, and science (including 1 of lab science). While interviews are not generally required of students applying for admission, the Admission staff may request an interview with certain applicants to obtain additional information or clarify information. AP and CLEP credits are accepted. Important factors in the admissions decision are advanced placement or honors courses, personality/intangible qualities, and extracurricular activities record. To graduate, students must complete 120 credit hours, including the requirements of an academic major, with a GPA of 2.0. Liberal Arts Core Curriculum requirements include 26 credits in Methods and Concepts, 15 in Synthesis and Application, and 3 credits in Independent Inquiry. **Procedure:** Freshmen are admitted fall and spring. Entrance exams should be taken in November or December of the senior year. There are deferred admissions and rolling admissions plans. Applications should be filed by May 1 for fall entry. The fall 2017 application fee was $50. Notification is sent on a rolling basis. Applications are accepted on-line. **Transfer Students:** 652 transfer students enrolled in 2016-2017. Official college and high school transcripts are required. 30 of 120 credits required for the bachelor's degree must be completed at ECSU. **International Students:** There are 43 international students enrolled. They must take the TOEFL. They must also take the SAT or ACT.

ADMISSIONS: 63% of the 2017-2018 applicants were accepted. The SAT scores for the 2017-2018 freshman class were: Critical Reading-- 10% below 500, 58% between 500 and 599, 30% between 600 and 699, and 3% between 700 and 800. Math-- 21% below 500, 60% between 500 and 599, 18% between 600 and 699, and 1% between 700 and 800. Writing-- 44% below 500, 44% between 500 and 599, and 11% between 600 and 699. The ACT scores were 5% between 12 and 17, 58% between 18 and 23, 32% between 24 and 29, and 6% above 30. 31% of the current freshmen were in the top fifth of their class; 63% were in the top two fifths. 2 freshmen graduated first in their class. **Admissions Contact:** Christopher Dorsey, Director of Admissions. Email: *admissions@easternct.edu* Web: *www.easternct.edu*

FINANCIAL AID: ECSU is a member of CSS. The FAFSA code is 001425. The deadline for filing freshman financial aid applications for fall entry is March 15.

FAIRFIELD UNIVERSITY — B-4

www.fairfield.edu

Fairfield, CT 06824	(203) 254-4000
Fax: (203) 254-4199	Email: admis@fairfield.edu
Full-time: 1541 men, 2338 women	**Faculty:** 243; IIA, +$
Part-time: 95 men, 139 women	**Ph.D.s:** 92%
Graduate: 328 men, 751 women	**Student/Faculty:** 16 to 1
Year: semesters, summer session	**Tuition:** $47,165
Room & Board: $14,280	**Freshman Class:** 11218 applied, 6794 accepted, 994 enrolled
SAT CR/M: 620/620 **ACT:** 27	**CEEB CODE:** 3390
Application Deadline: January 15	**HIGHLY COMPETITIVE**

Fairfield University is the modern Catholic institution, its education has become more integrated in focus, more global in outlook, and more intentional in its structure than ever before. In the Jesuit tradition, we are committed to creating a student-focused, holistic, and diverse educational environment intended to educate the whole person mind, body, and spirit. We cultivate in both our undergraduate and graduate students a sense of community and strong ethical and spiritual values to guide them on their paths into the future. Our graduates build vital, meaningful lives, they think critically and independently, they know how to lead and how to work together. We can sum up a Fairfield education in two words: cura personalis. That's Latin (and Jesuit) for "care for the whole person." There are 4 undergraduate schools and 5 graduate schools. In addition to regional accreditation, Fairfield University has baccalaureate program accreditation with AACSB, ABET, CAEP, NLN, ACS, CCNE, and IACS. The 200-acre campus is in a suburban area 60 miles northeast of New York City and 1 mile from Long Island Sound. Including any residence halls, there are 65 buildings.

STUDENT LIFE: 72% of undergraduates are from out of state, mostly the Northeast. Students are from 35 states, 49 foreign countries, and Canada. 60% are from public schools. 8% are Hispanic; 78% White; 5% race unknown; 3% Foreign; 2% African American; 2% Asian American; 2% two or more races. 66% are Catholic; 24% claim no religious affiliation. **Female To Male Ratio:** 1.6:1. The average age of freshmen is 18; all undergraduates, 20. 10% do not continue beyond their first year; 90% remain to graduate. **Housing:** 2944 students can be accommodated in college housing, which includes gender neutral dorms and on-campus apartments. In addition, there are special-interest houses, leadership through service, honors housing, women in science, technology, engineering and mathematics (WiSTEM), man to man, sisters inspiring sisters and healthy living (substance free) for our first-year students. For our sophomores we have 3 residential colleges: Creative Life, Service for Justice, and Ignatian. For juniors and seniors: Build-A-House. On-campus housing is guaranteed for all 4 years and is available on a lottery system for upperclassmen. 70% of students live on campus. Upperclassmen may keep cars.

FACULTY/CLASSROOMS: 48% of faculty are male; 52% are female. 84% teach undergraduates. No introductory courses are taught by graduate students. The average class size in an introductory lecture is 19 and in a laboratory is 14.

PROGRAMS OF STUDY: Fairfield confers B.A., B.S. and B.S.N. degrees. Master's and doctoral degrees are also awarded. Bachelor's degrees are awarded in AGRICULTURE (environmental studies), BIOLOGICAL SCIENCE (biochemistry and biology/biological science), BUSINESS (accounting, finance, international business management, management science, and marketing), COMMUNICATIONS AND THE ARTS (art history, communications, English, film, television and digital media, French, German, Italian, journalism & technical communications, music, public relations, Spanish, studio art, and theatre arts), COMPUTER AND PHYSICAL SCIENCE (chemistry, information sciences and systems, mathematics, physics, and software engineering), ENGINEERING AND ENVIRONMENTAL DESIGN (bioengineering, computational sciences, computer engineering, electrical/electronics engineering, and mechanical engineering), HEALTH PROFESSIONS (nursing), SOCIAL SCIENCE (American studies, economics, history, international studies, liberal arts/general studies, philosophy, political science/government, psychology, religious studies, and sociology). Finance, marketing and nursing are the strongest academically, and have the largest enrollments.

ACTIVITIES: There are no fraternities or sororities. There are 95 groups

on campus, including art, band, cheerleading, chess, choir, chorale, chorus, communications, computers, dance, debate, drama, environmental, equestrian and sailing clubs, ethnic, film, honors, international, jazz band, LGBT, literary magazine, musical theater, newspaper, orchestra, pep band, photography, political, professional, radio and TV, religious, social, social service, student government, and yearbook. Popular campus events include Presidential Ball, Dogwoods Dance, Midnight Breakfast, Senior Week, FUSA Concert, Relay for Life, Wit 'n Grit, Glee Club Pops Concert, Clam Jam, Noche Client, Remixx Showcase, Late Night @ Barone, South Side Café, BINGO, La Gala, and Flavors of Asia. **Sports:** There are 9 intercollegiate sports for men and 11 for women, and 25 intramural sports for men and 18 for women. The recreation complex houses multi-use exercise/fitness rooms, an eight lane 25 meter pool and racquetball court, strength and conditioning, free weight training stations, a fieldhouse, which features multipurpose regulation basketball courts, an elevated indoor track, and cardio equipment. **Graduates:** From July 1, 2016 to June 30, 2017, 930 bachelor's degrees were awarded. The most popular majors were nursing (14%), finance (13%), and accounting (11%). In an average class, 80% graduate in 4 years or less, 80% graduate in 5 years or less, and 81% graduate in 6 years or less. Of the 2016 graduating class, 21% were enrolled in graduate school within 6 months of graduation, and 74% were employed.

SERVICES: Counseling and information services are available, as is tutoring in some subjects such as chemistry, biology, engineering, finance, physics, psychology, and nursing. There are also modern languages courses in French, Italian, Japanese and Spanish. There is a reader service for the blind, and additional tutoring is offered in accounting and economics, writing and math. **Library/Resources:** The library contains 1.3 million volumes, 945,373 microform items, 165,139 audio/video tapes/CDs/DVDs, and subscribes to 59,376 periodicals including electronic. Computerized library services include interlibrary loans, database searching, Internet access, and Wi-Fi capability. Special learning facilities include an art gallery, radio station, TV station, a media center, 750-seat concert hall/theater, a rehearsal and improvisation theater, a black box 150 seat theater, language learning lab, business education simulation training (BEST) classroom, SIM/simulated hospital environment and human patient simulators, an art gallery and art museum, model interactive high technology classrooms, and resource center for core science. **Physically Challenged Students:** 95% of the campus is accessible. Facilities include wheelchair ramps, elevators, special parking, specially equipped restrooms, special class scheduling, lowered drinking fountains, special housing, accommodations for assistance service animals, and a library computer station for physically challenged and learning disabled students. **Special:** Fairfield administers its own study abroad centers in London, Madrid, Managua, Florence, Aix-en-Provence, Brisbane and Galway. In addition, Fairfield students may choose from a list of over 60 different study abroad programs in five continents and engage in research, internships and service learning at most of these sites. Fairfield has available to students a federal work-study program, B.A.-B.S. degrees in economics, international studies, and psychology, individually-designed majors, and dual majors in all subjects. The university offers 5th year graduate degree programs in education, psychology, business and engineering. Fairfield offers a four year honors program by special admission, to all undergraduates regardless of the school in which they enrolled. A bachelor of arts/sciences in liberal studies is offered for part time students through the college of arts and sciences. Internships, both credit and noncredit, are offered at area corporations, publications, banks, and other organizations nationally and internationally. Interdisciplinary minors include humanitarian action, women's studies, entrepreneurship, marine science, black studies, environmental studies, jazz, classical performance, Italian studies, Russian and Eastern European studies, Catholic studies and Judaic studies, applied ethics, Asian studies, Irish studies, Latin American and Caribbean studies, and peace and justice. There are 21 national honor societies, Phi Beta Kappa, and a freshman honors program. **Visiting:** There are regularly scheduled orientations for prospective students, seasonal information sessions and tours offered weekdays and some weekends. Individualized class visits are available. There are guides for informal visits and visitors may sit in on classes. To schedule a visit, contact the Office of Undergraduate Admission. **Campus Safety and Security:** Measures include 24-hour foot and vehicle patrol, emergency notification system, self-defense education, and security escort services. There are shuttle buses, emergency telephones, lighted pathways/sidewalks, controlled access to dorms/residences, EMT public safety officers, bike patrol, closed circuit television system, crime prevention seminars, and the LiveSafe mobile safety application.

REQUIREMENTS: Fairfield has test optional admission. There is no additional information required if students choose not to submit test scores. There is no required grade point average, although most admitted students have a B+ average or better in a solid college preparatory program, which should include advanced and/or honors classes. Students should have completed 15 academic credits, including 4 credits of English, 3 to 4 credits each of history, math, and lab science, and 2 to 4 credits of a foreign language. AP and CLEP credits are accepted. Important factors in the admissions decision are advanced placement or honors courses, extracurricular activities record, and recommendations by school officials. To graduate, students must complete a minimum of 120 credits and complete at least 38 three or four credit courses with a minimum GPA of 2.0 both overall and in the major. 60 of the 120 credits are in general education core requirements. Distribution requirements include 15 credits in philosophy, religious studies, and ethics, 15 credits in English and fine arts, 12 credits in math and natural sciences, 12 credits in history and social sciences, and 6 credits in foreign languages. Students are also required to take courses in US and world diversity. **Procedure:** Freshmen are admitted in the fall. Entrance exams should be taken in the spring of the junior year or fall of the senior year. There are early decision, early admissions, and deferred admissions plans. Early decision applications should be filed by November 15; regular applications, by January 15 for fall entry. The fall 2017 application fee was $60. Notification of early decision is sent December 15; regular decision, April 1. 148 early decision candidates were accepted for the 2017-2018 class. 1118 applicants were on the 2017 waiting list; 56 were admitted. Applications are accepted on-line. **Transfer Students:** 52 transfer students enrolled in 2016-2017. The following are needed to complete the transfer application: common application for transfer students, application fee, personal statement/essay addressing why you are seeking transfer, official high school transcript, official college transcript from all universities attended (whether or not credit was earned), Mid-term grade progress report, Dean of Students Certification Form from all colleges attended, and course catalog descriptions of all classes taken. Additionally required are SAT or ACT results, if you choose to submit them. Refer to our Standardized Test Optional Policy for more details. 60 of 120 credits required for the bachelor's degree must be completed at Fairfield. **International Students:** There are 125 international students enrolled. They must take the TOEFL with a minimum score of 550 on the paper-based TOEFL (PBT) or 80 on the Internet-based version (iBT). Student must also take the IELTS.

ADMISSIONS: 61% of the 2017-2018 applicants were accepted. The SAT scores for the 2017-2018 freshman class were: Math-- 1% below 500, 30% between 500 and 599, 60% between 600 and 699, and 9% between 700 and 800. Evidence-Based Reading/Writing-- 1% below 500, 28% between 500 and 599, 61% between 600 and 699, and 10% between 700 and 800. The ACT scores were 9% between 18 and 23, 72% between 24 and 29, and 19% above 30. 71% of the current freshmen were in the top fifth of their class; 95% were in the top two fifths. **Admissions Contact:** Karen Pellegrino, Vice President for Enrollment Management. Email: *admis@fairfield.edu* Web: *www.fairfield.edu*

FINANCIAL AID: In 2017-2018, 91% of all full-time freshmen received some form of financial aid. 56% of all full-time freshmen received need-based aid. The average freshman award was $24,320. Need-based scholarships or need-based grants averaged $23,375 ($61,445 maximum); need-based self-help aid (loans and jobs) averaged $4,611 ($7,800 maximum); non-need-based athletic scholarships averaged $24,394 ($64,170 maximum); and other non-need-based awards and non-need-based scholarships averaged $10,961 ($46,490 maximum). 92% of undergraduate students work part-time. The average financial indebtedness of the 2017 graduate was $25,609. Fairfield is a member of CSS. The CSS/Profile is required. The FAFSA code is 001385. The priority date for freshman financial aid applications for fall entry is January 15.

GOODWIN COLLEGE *(The complete profile is made available exclusively on our website, www.barronspac.com)*

MITCHELL COLLEGE D-3

www.mitchell.edu

New London, CT 06320	(800) 443-2811
Fax: (860) 444-1209	**Email:** admissions@mitchell.edu
Full-time: 395 men, 336 women	**Faculty:** 35
Part-time: 59 men, 68 women	**Ph.D.s:** 74%
Graduate: n/av	**Student/Faculty:** 14 to 1
Year: semesters, summer session	**Tuition:** $32,442
Room & Board: $12,750	**Freshman Class:** n/av **CEEB CODE:** 3582
Application Deadline: rolling	**COMPETITIVE**

Mitchell College, founded in 1938, is a private institution offering associate and bachelor degree programs in the liberal arts and professional areas. The figures given in the above capsule and in this profile are approximate. There is 1 undergraduate school. In addition to regional accreditation, MC has baccalaureate program accreditation with NEASCE-CIHE. The 68-acre campus is in a suburban area on the shore of the Thames River where it meets Long Island Sound. Including any residence halls, there are 26 buildings.

STUDENT LIFE: 54% of undergraduates are from Connecticut. Others are from 26 states, and 5 foreign countries. 50% are from public schools. 66% are White; 2% Asian American; 12% Hispanic; 10% African American; 1% American Indian/Alaska Native; 1% Foreign. 61% claim no religious affiliation; 18% Catholic; 12% Protestant. **Male To Female Ratio:** 1.1:1. The average age of freshmen is 19; all undergraduates, 20. 43% do not continue beyond their first year; 47% remain to graduate. **Housing:** 598 students can be accommodated in college housing, which includes dorms and on-campus apartments. On-campus housing is guaranteed for all 4 years. 80% of students live on campus. All students may keep cars.

FACULTY/CLASSROOMS: 49% of faculty are male; 51% are female. All teach undergraduates. No introductory courses are taught by graduate students. The average class size in an introductory lecture is 14; in a laboratory is 10; and in a regular course is 14.

PROGRAMS OF STUDY: MC confers B.A. and B.S. degrees. Associate degrees are also awarded. Bachelor's degrees are awarded in AGRICULTURE (environmental studies), BUSINESS (business administration and management, hospitality management services, and sports management), COMMUNICATIONS AND THE ARTS (communications), EDUCATION (early childhood education), SOCIAL SCIENCE (criminal justice, homeland security, human development, liberal arts/general studies, and psychology). Early childhood education is the strongest academically. Business administration, criminal justice, and sport & fitness management have the largest enrollments.

ACTIVITIES: There are no fraternities or sororities. There are 35 groups on campus, including academic club, art, cheerleading, choir, chorus, computers, dance, drama, ethnic, honors, international, LGBT, professional, radio and TV, religious, social, social service, and student government. **Sports:** There are 8 intercollegiate sports for men and 7 for women, and 4 intramural sports for men and 4 for women. Facilities include a basketball court, fitness center, trails, tennis courts, and athletic fields for all varsity teams. **Graduates:** From July 1, 2016 to June 30, 2017, 190 bachelor's degrees were awarded. The most popular majors were liberal and pressional studies (23%), business administration (22%), and criminal justice (18%).

SERVICES: Counseling and information services are available, as is tutoring in most subjects. There is a reader service for the blind. **Library/Resources:** The library contains 94,542 volumes, and 1,658 audio/video tapes/CDs/DVDs, and subscribes to 90 periodicals including electronic. Computerized library services include interlibrary loans, database searching, Internet access, and Wi-Fi capability. Special learning facilities include a radio station. **Physically Challenged Students:** 50% of the campus is accessible. Facilities include wheelchair ramps, elevators, special parking, specially equipped restrooms, and special class scheduling. **Special:** Internships are available through Academic Department Chairs. Liberal & Professional studies offers an Individualized (student-designed) option. Work study jobs are available. Bachelor degrees (BA or BS) offered. There are 8 national honor societies, Phi Beta Kappa, and 1 departmental honors program. **Visiting:** There are regularly scheduled orientations for prospective students, includes a student-guided tour and an interview with an admissions counselor. There are guides for informal visits and visitors may sit in on classes. To schedule a visit, contact the Visit Coordinator, Admissions Office. **Campus Safety and Security:** Measures include 24-hour foot and vehicle patrol, emergency notification system, and security escort services. There are shuttle buses, emergency telephones, lighted pathways/sidewalks, and controlled access to dorms/residences.

REQUIREMENTS: The GED is accepted. A recommendation and a personal statement are required. A personal interview is recommended but not required. A GPA of 2.0 is required. AP and CLEP credits are accepted. Important factors in the admissions decision are personality/intangible qualities, recommendations by school officials, and extracurricular activities record. To graduate: bachelor-degree-seeking students must complete 120 credits (associate-degree-seeking 60 credits) with a minimum GPA of 2.0 (2.67 for early childhood education). Required general education curriculum. Several majors contain a cumulating experience (a capstone, senior project, or internship). **Procedure:** Freshmen are admitted fall and spring. Entrance exams should be taken during summer orientation. There are early decision, deferred admissions, and rolling admissions plans. Early decision applications should be filed by November 15. The fall 2017 application fee was $30. Notification of early decision is sent December 15; regular decision, on a rolling basis. Applications are accepted on-line. **Transfer Students:** 74 transfer students enrolled in 2016-2017. In addition to fulfilling regular application requirements, transfer applicants must submit official college transcripts from all colleges/universities attended. 30 of 120 credits required for the bachelor's degree must be completed at MC. **International Students:** There are 7 international students enrolled. They must take the TOEFL with a minimum score of 500 on the paper-based TOEFL (PBT), or take the APIEL.

Admissions Contact: Gregg Gorneault, Director of Admissions. Email: *admissions@mitchell.edu* Web: *www.mitchell.edu*

FINANCIAL AID: In 2017-2018, 83% of all full-time freshmen received some form of financial aid. 83% of all full-time freshmen received need-based aid. The average freshman award was $20,235. Need-based scholarships or need-based grants averaged $16,739; need-based self-help aid (loans and jobs) averaged $7,281; and other non-need-based awards and non-need-based scholarships averaged $7,636. The FAFSA code is 001393. The priority date for freshman financial aid applications for fall entry is April 1.

POST UNIVERSITY — B-3
www.post.edu

Waterbury, CT 06723	(203) 596-4520 (800) 345-2562
Fax: (203) 756-5810	**Email:** admissions@post.edu
Full-time: 325 men, 400 women	**Faculty:** n/av
Part-time: 200 men, 350 women	**Ph.D.s:** 61%
Graduate: n/av	**Student/Faculty:** n/av
Year: semesters, summer session	**Tuition:** $29,550
Room & Board: $11,600	**Freshman Class:** n/av
SAT or ACT: required	**CEEB CODE:** 3698
Application Deadline: open	**COMPETITIVE**

Post University, founded in 1890, is a private institution offering liberal arts and business programs. The figures given in the above capsule and in this profile are approximate. There are 2 undergraduate schools. In addition to regional accreditation, Post has baccalaureate program accreditation with NEASC. The 70-acre campus is in an urban area 1 mile west of Waterbury. Including any residence halls, there are 13 buildings.

STUDENT LIFE: 83% of undergraduates are from Connecticut. Others are from 12 states, 20 foreign countries, and Canada. 75% are from public schools. 8% are Hispanic; 63% White; 5% Foreign; 2% Asian American; 17% African American. **Female To Male Ratio:** 1.4:1. The average age of freshmen is 19; all undergraduates, 26. 23% do not continue beyond their first year; 39% remain to graduate. **Housing:** 424 students can be accommodated in college housing, which includes dorms and off-campus apartments. On-campus housing is guaranteed for all 4 years. 58% of students live on campus. All students may keep cars.

FACULTY/CLASSROOMS: 57% of faculty are male; 43% are female. All teach undergraduates. No introductory courses are taught by graduate students. The average class size in an introductory lecture is 20; in a laboratory is 15; and in a regular course is 35.

PROGRAMS OF STUDY: Post confers B.A. and B.S. degrees. Associate degrees are also awarded. Bachelor's degrees are awarded in BUSINESS (accounting, banking and finance, business administration and management, management science, and marketing/retailing/merchandising), COMMUNICATIONS AND THE ARTS (English), SOCIAL SCIENCE (criminal justice, history, liberal arts/general studies, psychology, and sociology). Biology is the strongest academically. Management, and general studies have the largest enrollments.

ACTIVITIES: There are no fraternities or sororities. There are 30 groups on campus, including cheerleading, chorale, chorus, computers, drama, ethnic, honors, international, LGBT, literary magazine, musical theater, social, social service, student government, and yearbook. Popular campus events include Dances, Concerts, and International Food Festivals. **Sports:** There are 5 intercollegiate sports for men and 5 for women, and 4 intramural sports for men and 4 for women. Facilities include a soccer field, a fitness center, weight room, racquetball court, a swimming pool, and tennis courts.

SERVICES: Counseling and information services are available, as is tutoring in most subjects. There is a reader service for the blind, and remedial math, reading, and writing. **Library/Resources:** The library contains 85,000 volumes, 75,158 microform items, 1,027 audio/video tapes/CDs/DVDs, and subscribes to 427 periodicals including electronic. Computerized library services include interlibrary loans and database searching. **Physically Challenged Students:** 70% of the campus is accessible. Facilities include wheelchair ramps, elevators, special parking, specially equipped restrooms, and special class scheduling. **Special:** Co-op programs in all majors, cross-registration with Naugatuck Valley Community College, study abroad in England, the Netherlands, and Japan. There are also internships with area businesses, general studies degrees, accelerated degree programs, B.A.-B.S. degrees, and credit for life experience are available. There are 2 national honor societies and 1 departmental honors program. **Visiting:** There are regularly scheduled orientations for prospective students, including tours, interviews with admissions counselors, and meetings with faculty and students. There are guides for informal visits, visitors may sit in on classes, and stay overnight. To schedule a visit, contact the Admissions Office. **Campus Safety and Security:** Measures include 24-hour foot and vehicle patrol, self-defense education, and security escort services. There are shuttle buses and lighted pathways/sidewalks.

REQUIREMENTS: The SAT or ACT is required. Applicants must be graduates of an accredited secondary school, with 4 years of English and at least 16 total academic credits. The GED is accepted. A GPA of 2.0 is required. AP and CLEP credits are accepted. Important factors in the admissions decision are personality/intangible qualities, extracurricular activities record, and recommendations by school officials. To graduate, all students must maintain a minimum GPA of 2.0, earn a total of 120 credits, including at least 33 in the major, and take a computer course. **Procedure:** Freshmen are admitted to all sessions. There are early admissions, deferred admissions, and rolling admissions plans. Check with the school for current application deadlines. The fall 2017 application fee was $40. Notification is sent on a rolling basis. Applications are accepted on-line. **Transfer Students:** Applicants must have a minimum college GPA of 2.0, submit an official college transcript, and have an interview. The SAT is recommended. 30 of 120 credits required for the bachelor's degree must be completed at TPU. **International Students:** There are 48 international students enrolled. They must take the TOEFL with a minimum score of 500 on the paper-based TOEFL (PBT) or 79 on the Internet-based version (iBT).

Admissions Contact: Aline Rossiter, Dean of Admissions. Email: *admissions@post.edu* Web: *www.post.edu*

FINANCIAL AID: In 2017-2018, 100% of all full-time freshmen received some form of financial aid. The college's own financial statement, parent and student federal tax returns are required. The FAFSA code is 001401. Check with the school for current application deadlines.

QUINNIPIAC UNIVERSITY C-3

www.qu.edu

Hamden, CT 06518	**(203) 582-8600** **(800) 462-1944**
Fax: (203) 582-8906	**Email: admissions@qu.edu**
Full-time: 2721 men, 4238 women	**Faculty:** 360; IIA, ++$
Part-time: 128 men, 218 women	**Ph.D.s:** 89%
Graduate: 986 men, 1818 women	**Student/Faculty:** 16 to 1
Year: semesters, summer session	**Tuition:** $46,780
Room & Board: $14,190	**Freshman Class:** 22048 applied, 16304 accepted, 1966 enrolled
SAT CR/M: 590/580 **ACT:** 25	**CEEB CODE:** 3712
Application Deadline: February 1	**VERY COMPETITIVE**

Quinnipiac University, founded in 1929, is a private institution offering over 58 undergraduate majors and 22 graduate programs through the schools of health sciences, nursing, business, engineering, communications, education, the college of arts and sciences, the school of law and the Frank H. Netter MD School of Medicine. There are 6 undergraduate schools and 9 graduate schools. In addition to regional accreditation, Quinnipiac has baccalaureate program accreditation with AACSB, ABET, APTA, CAHEA, NLN, ABA, ACOTE, ARC-PA, NAACLS, CAATE, CAPTE, CCNE, and COA. The 600-acre campus is in a suburban area in Hamden and North Haven CT, just 8 miles north of New Haven, CT. 80 miles Northeast of NYC. Including any residence halls, there are 80 buildings.

STUDENT LIFE: 75% of undergraduates are from out of state, mostly the Middle Atlantic. Students are from 42 states, 30 foreign countries, and Canada. 76% are from public schools. 8% are Hispanic; 73% White; 6% race unknown; 5% African American; 4% Asian American; 2% Foreign; 2% two or more races. 51% are Catholic; 26% Protestant. **Female To Male Ratio:** 1.6:1. The average age of freshmen is 19; all undergraduates, 21. 14% do not continue beyond their first year; 75% remain to graduate. **Housing:** 5020 students can be accommodated in college housing, which includes dorms, on-campus apartments, and off-campus apartments. In addition, there are honors houses, special-interest houses, wellness housing, nursing cohort, advanced (3+1 BS/MBA) business and advanced (3+1 BA/MA) communications cohort housing. On-campus housing is guaranteed for all 4 years. 75% of students live on campus. Upperclassmen may keep cars.

FACULTY/CLASSROOMS: 43% of faculty are male; 57% are female. 95% teach undergraduates, 40% do research, and 40% do both. No introductory courses are taught by graduate students. The average class size in an introductory lecture is 24; in a laboratory is 18; and in a regular course is 24.

PROGRAMS OF STUDY: Quinnipiac confers B.A., B.S. and B.F.A. degrees. Master's and doctoral degrees are also awarded. Bachelor's degrees are awarded in BIOLOGICAL SCIENCE (biochemistry, biology/biological science, biotechnology, microbiology, and neurosciences), BUSINESS (accounting, banking and finance, business administration and management, entrepreneurial studies, finance, international business management, management science, marketing management, and marketing/retailing/merchandising), COMMUNICATIONS AND THE ARTS (advertising, communications, dramatic arts, English, journalism, public relations, Spanish, and theatre arts), COMPUTER AND PHYSICAL SCIENCE (chemistry, computer science, digital arts/technology, mathematics, software engineering, and web technology), EDUCATION (athletic training, elementary education, and secondary education), ENGINEERING AND ENVIRONMENTAL DESIGN (civil engineering, engineering, industrial engineering, and mechanical engineering), HEALTH PROFESSIONS (biomedical science, health science, nursing, occupational therapy, physical therapy, physician's assistant, predentistry, premedicine, and radiological science), SOCIAL SCIENCE (criminal justice, economics, gerontology, history, liberal arts/general studies, paralegal studies, philosophy, political science/government, prelaw, psychobiology, psychology, social science, and sociology). Physician assistant, physical therapy, and nursing are the strongest academically. Nursing, physical therapy, and management have the largest enrollments.

ACTIVITIES: 20% of men belong to 9 national fraternities; 30% of women belong to 10 national sororities. There are 142 groups on campus, including cheerleading, chorale, chorus, communications, dance, drama, environmental, ethnic, film, honors, international, jazz band, LGBT, literary magazine, newspaper, pep band, political, professional, radio and TV, religious, social, social service, student government, and yearbook. Popular campus events include The BIG Event, Parents Weekend, Relay for Life, Holiday Party, and Fall and Spring Concerts. **Sports:** There are 7 intercollegiate sports for men and 14 for women, and 6 intramural sports for men and 6 for women. Facilities include a sports center with arenas, ice hockey and basketball, playing fields, a recreation center with weight training, indoor tennis, basketball, volleyball, aerobics, a suspended indoor track, a weight room, spinning room, exercise and yoga. **Graduates:** From July 1, 2016 to June 30, 2017, 1654 bachelor's degrees were awarded. The most popular majors were health professions (36%), business (23%), and communications (11%). In an average class, 4% graduate in 3 years or less, 68% graduate in 4 years or less, 74% graduate in 5 years or less, and 75% graduate in 6 years or less. Of the 2016 graduating class, 43% were enrolled in graduate school within 6 months of graduation, and 54% were employed.

SERVICES: Counseling and information services are available, as is tutoring in most subjects, such as all freshman-level courses and others by request. Special workshops on work study skills, library resources, and time management are also available. **Library/Resources:** The library contains 311,000 volumes, 592,900 microform items, and 6,000 audio/

video tapes/CDs/DVDs, and subscribes to 44,700 periodicals including electronic. Computerized library services include interlibrary loans, database searching, Internet access, and Wi-Fi capability. Special learning facilities include an art gallery, radio station, TV station, exhibits on the Irish famine, part of Quinnipiac's Ireland's Great Hunger Museum, and the Albert Schweitzer Institute. **Physically Challenged Students:** All of the campus is accessible. Facilities include wheelchair ramps, elevators, special parking, specially equipped restrooms, special class scheduling, and lowered drinking fountains. **Special:** Internships or clinical placements are available in all majors. Students can choose to study abroad in more than 25 countries such as Australia, Italy, Ireland, Spain, France and England. A 6 or 7-year freshman entry-level doctorate (BS/DPT) in physical therapy and a 5 1/2 year freshman entry-level master's (BS/MOT) in occupational therapy are offered, as well as a 6-year BS in Health Sciences/MHS in a physician assistant master's program. For those interested in teaching elementary or secondary education, a 5-year BA in an academic major plus a master of arts in teaching (MAT) which includes student teaching. An innovative BS/MBA is offered to academically talented Business students in a 4 year (3+1) format to complete both degrees in 4 years. A similar program is offered for talented Communications students to complete their BA/MA in 4 years. In addition, a 3+3 BA or BS/JD degree with the School of Law invites academically talented students who wish to complete both degrees in 6 rather than 7 years. There are 11 national honor societies, a freshman honors program, and 20 departmental honors programs. **Visiting:** There are regularly scheduled orientations for prospective students that include interviews, group information sessions, and student-guided tours. During open houses, there is an opportunity to speak with faculty and various offices and student life groups. There are guides for informal visits and visitors may sit in on classes. To schedule a visit, contact The Admissions Office. **Campus Safety and Security:** Measures include 24-hour foot and vehicle patrol, emergency notification system, self-defense education, and security escort services. There are shuttle buses, emergency telephones, lighted pathways/sidewalks, controlled access to dorms/residences, perimeter security staffed by public safety officers at all entrances, and vehicle and occupant check-in identification.

REQUIREMENTS: A minimum composite score of 1140 on the SAT or 23 composite on the ACT is recommended. All students must have completed 16 academic credits, including 4 in English, 3 in math, 2 each in science and social studies, and 5 in electives. The GED is accepted. An interview is recommended, an essay, and at least one letter of recommendation are required. For majors in the health sciences, 4 years each of math and science are required. Physics is highly recommended for those applying to the physical therapy and physician assistant programs. Test Optional Policy: Test scores (either SAT or ACT) are required for all students applying to the school of health sciences and nursing. All other majors do not require test scores to be submitted for an admissions decision but test scores will be considered if submitted. Quinnipiac requires applicants to be in the upper 60% of their class. A GPA of 2.9 is required. AP and CLEP credits are accepted. Important factors in the admissions decision are advanced placement or honors courses, extracurricular activities record, and personality/intangible qualities. All students must complete the University Curriculum including the first year seminar, English, math, fine arts, social sciences, humanities and sciences, plus the specific course standards and requirements of a student's chosen major and a University Curriculum Capstone course or experience. To graduate, students must maintain a GPA of 2.0 over 120 total semester hours. **Procedure:** Freshmen are admitted fall and spring. Entrance exams should be taken in the junior year and early in the senior year. There are early decision, deferred admissions, and rolling admissions plans. Early decision applications should be filed by November 1; regular applications, by February 1 for fall entry; and December 15 for spring entry. The fall 2017 application fee was $65. Notification of early decision is sent November 30; regular decision, December 15. 248 early decision candidates were accepted for the 2017-2018 class. 1699 applicants were on the 2017 waiting list; 42 were admitted. Applications are accepted on-line. **Transfer Students:** 196 transfer students enrolled in 2016-2017. Transfer students must have a minimum college GPA of 2.5 (some programs require a minimum of 3.0) and must submit SAT scores and high school or college transcripts if they have not received an associate degree prior to enrollment. An interview is recommended. 45 of 120 credits required for the bachelor's degree must be completed at Quinnipiac. **International Students:** There are 136 international students enrolled. They must take the TOEFL with a minimum score of 550 on the paper-based TOEFL (PBT) or 80 on the Internet-based version (iBT). Students must take the IELTS. They must also take the SAT or ACT only if the language of instruction is in English.

ADMISSIONS: 74% of the 2017-2018 applicants were accepted. The SAT scores for the 2017-2018 freshman class were: Math-- 10% below 500, 49% between 500 and 599, 35% between 600 and 699, and 5% between 700 and 800. Evidence-Based Reading/Writing-- 9% below 500, 45% between 500 and 599, 42% between 600 and 699, and 4% between 700 and 800. The ACT scores were 2% between 12 and 17, 30% between 18 and 23, 57% between 24 and 29, and 11% above 30. 51% of the current freshmen were in the top fifth of their class; 84% were in the top two fifths. 19 freshmen graduated first in their class. **Admissions Contact:** Joan Issac Mohr, Vice President of Admissions and Financial Aid. Email: *admissions@qu.edu* Web: *www.qu.edu*

FINANCIAL AID: In 2017-2018, 96% of all full-time freshmen received some form of financial aid. 70% of all full-time freshmen received need-based aid. The average freshman award was $27,621. Need-based scholarships or need-based grants averaged $28,944 ($55,780 maximum); need-based self-help aid (loans and jobs) averaged $4,395 ($11,000 maximum); non-need-based athletic scholarships averaged $31,908 ($57,734 maximum); and other non-need-based awards and non-need-based scholarships averaged $16,331 ($38,000 maximum). 28% of undergraduate students work part-time. The average financial indebtedness of the 2017 graduate was $48,894. The FAFSA code is 001402. The priority date for freshman financial aid applications for fall entry is March 1. The deadline for filing freshman financial aid applications for fall entry is April 1.

SACRED HEART UNIVERSITY — B-4

www.sacredheart.edu

Fairfield, CT 06825 — **(203) 371-7880**

Fax: (203) 365-7607
Email: enroll@sacredheart.edu
Full-time: 1844 men, 3138 women
Faculty: 228
Part-time: 178 men, 443 women
Ph.D.s: 80%
Graduate: 797 men, 2143 women
Student/Faculty: 22 to 1
Year: semesters, summer session
Tuition: $39,820
Room & Board: $14,770
Freshman Class: 9992 applied, 6023 accepted, 1387 enrolled
SAT or ACT: required
CEEB CODE: 3780
Application Deadline: rolling
COMPETITIVE

One of the fastest-growing Catholic institutions in the country, Sacred Heart University offers more than 70 undergraduate, graduate and doctoral programs in business, communications, engineering, sciences, performing and visual arts, education, technology, health professions, and nursing. There are 7 undergraduate schools and 7 graduate schools. In addition to regional accreditation, SHU has baccalaureate program accreditation with AACSB, APTA, CAEP, NLN, AOTA, and CAATE. The 350-acre campus is in a suburban area 90 minutes from Manhattan and 150 minutes from Boston.

STUDENT LIFE: 64% of undergraduates are from out of state, mostly the Northeast. Students are from 50 states, 26 foreign countries, and Canada. 75% are from public schools. 73% are White; 10% Hispanic; 10% Foreign; 6% race unknown; 5% African American; 4% American Indian/Alaska Native; 3% two or more races; 2% Asian American. 61% are Catholic; 23% claim no religious affiliation; 13% Protestant. **Female To Male Ratio:** 2.0:1. The average age of freshmen is 18; all undergraduates, 21. 16% do not continue beyond their first year; 72% remain to graduate. **Housing:** 2926 students can be accommodated in college housing, which includes dorms, on-campus apartments, and off-campus apartments. In addition, there are special-interest houses, living and learning communities with themes such as honors, business, wellness, community service and gaming and technology. On-campus housing is guaranteed for all 4 years, is available on a first-come, first-served basis, and is available on a lottery system for upperclassmen. 51% of students live on campus. Upperclassmen may keep cars.

FACULTY/CLASSROOMS: 47% of faculty are male; 53% are female. 70% teach undergraduates. No introductory courses are taught by graduate students. The average class size in an introductory lecture is 25; in a laboratory is 16; and in a regular course is 22.

PROGRAMS OF STUDY: SHU confers B.A. and B.S. degrees. Associate, master's, and doctoral degrees are also awarded. Bachelor's degrees are awarded in BIOLOGICAL SCIENCE (biology/biological science), BUSI-

NESS (accounting, business administration and management, business economics, marketing management, and sports management), COMMUNICATIONS AND THE ARTS (communications, English, media arts, and Spanish), COMPUTER AND PHYSICAL SCIENCE (chemistry, computer science, information sciences and systems, and mathematics), EDUCATION (athletic training), HEALTH PROFESSIONS (exercise science and health science), SOCIAL SCIENCE (criminal justice, history, liberal arts/general studies, psychology, social work, and sociology). Physical therapy, nursing, and business management are the strongest academically. Nursing, marketing, and psychology have the largest enrollments.

ACTIVITIES: 15% of men belong to 1 local and 5 national fraternities; 36% of women belong to 8 national sororities. There are 162 groups on campus, including art, bagpipe, band, cheerleading, chess, choir, chorale, chorus, communications, computers, dance, debate, drama, drill team, environmental, ethnic, film, Habitat for Humanity, honors, international, jazz band, LGBT, literary magazine, marching band, musical theater, newspaper, orchestra, pep band, photography, political, professional, radio and TV, religious, social, social service, student government, and yearbook. Popular campus events include Spring Concert, Family Weekend, Siblings Weekend, Homecoming, Pack the Pitt, SHU Hoops Madness, President's Gala, and Just SHU it. **Sports:** There are 33 intercollegiate sports for men and 35 for women, and 9 intramural sports for men and 6 for women. Facilities include a health and recreation center for basketball, weight training/fitness, aerobics, fencing, a varsity wrestling room, softball stadium, a spin turf athletic field, eight-lane outdoor running track, and tennis courts. **Graduates:** From July 1, 2016 to June 30, 2017, 1134 bachelor's degrees were awarded. The most popular majors were health professions (33%), business/marketing (26%), and psychology (10%). In an average class, 1% graduate in 3 years or less, 67% graduate in 4 years or less, 72% graduate in 5 years or less, and 72% graduate in 6 years or less. Of the 2016 graduating class, 26% were enrolled in graduate school within 6 months of graduation, and 25% were employed.

SERVICES: Counseling and information services are available, as is tutoring in every subject. There is a reader service for the blind, and remedial math, reading, and writing. **Library/Resources:** The library contains 89,498 volumes, 7,394 microform items, and 1,075 audio/video tapes/CDs/DVDs, and subscribes to 4,083 periodicals including electronic. Computerized library services include interlibrary loans, database searching, Internet access, and Wi-Fi capability. Special learning facilities include an art gallery, center for performing arts, Martire Business and Communications Center featuring an active trading floor with 30 work stations, 13 Bloomberg terminals, wallboard ticker tapes and real time data from NASDAQ and NYSE, screening venues, smart classrooms with multi-media technology, interactive labs, a motion capture lab, and two large television studios, video and film production, center for healthcare education containing an audiology suite, motion analysis and human performance labs, driving simulator, pediatrics clinic, medical gym, an immersive acute care simulation lab with video and data capture capability, a simulated outpatient suite, high-fidelity manikins, home-care suite, cadaver lab, computing facilities with a gaming lab, a closed LAN laboratory, 3D printing lab and the motion lab, fashion design studio, and art studios. The learning center provides academic support including those with disabilities. **Physically Challenged Students:** Facilities include wheelchair ramps, elevators, special parking, specially equipped restrooms, special class scheduling, lowered drinking fountains, and lowered telephones. Special housing rooms are equipped with special audible alarms for students with hearing disabilities and other special accommodations can be made through the departments of Residential Life. **Special:** SHU offers paid and unpaid internships at local, regional and national organizations, including Fortune 500 and 1000 companies, hospitals, media outlets, social service agencies, and schools. Study abroad opportunities exist worldwide and year-round including the SHU campuses in Dingle, Ireland and Luxembourg. The 3+2 dual degree engineering program offers a SHU undergraduate degree in mathematics, computer science or chemistry and a bachelor's degree in a variety of engineering disciplines at Rensselaer Polytechnic Institute and Columbia University. The 3+3 Bachelor's – J.D. program with Seton Hall University Law School is available to students in a variety of majors in the College of Arts and Sciences. There are 2 national honor societies, a freshman honors program, and 1 departmental honors program. **Visiting:** There are regularly scheduled orientations for prospective students, including tours, information sessions and interviews are available Monday through Friday and select Saturdays and Sundays. Open House programs during the academic year and summer. There are guides for informal visits, visitors may sit in on classes, and stay overnight. To schedule a visit, contact Robert Gilmore at (203) 365-7880. **Campus Safety and Security:** Measures include 24-hour foot and vehicle patrol, emergency notification system, self-defense education, and security escort services. There are shuttle buses, emergency telephones, lighted pathways/sidewalks, and controlled access to dorms/residences. The SHUSafe safety app allows students to make medical information instantly available, link to emergency services, pinpoint their location for emergency personnel and set up safety checks. The SHU Safety Week includes programs on self-defense, social media safety, and bystander intervention, personal safety escort program, silent witness program and blue light call boxes. All campus residence halls have sprinklers and alarms and are designated nonsmoking.

REQUIREMENTS: Students must submit a completed application, an essay and one letter of recommendation. An interview is required for early decision candidates and recommended for all other candidates. Required are 4 years of English and 3 years of math, science, history, and language with 4 years preferred. AP and CLEP credits are accepted. Important factors in the admissions decision are advanced placement or honors courses, recommendations by school officials, and leadership record. At the undergraduate level, Sacred Heart University offers two baccalaureate degrees: Bachelor of Arts or Bachelor of Science depending upon the nature of the discipline of the major. The University also offers Associate in Arts and Associate in Science degrees. A central component of undergraduate study is the University's Core Curriculum, the Human Journey, which embodies the University's commitment to academic excellence, social responsibility, and ethical awareness. All candidates for the baccalaureate degree must complete at least 120 credits, with a minimum of 30 credits taken at Sacred Heart University. A minimum cumulative GPA 2.0 is required. **Procedure:** Freshmen are admitted fall and spring. Entrance exams should be taken in May of the junior year through November of the senior year. There are early decision, early admissions, deferred admissions, and rolling admissions plans. Early decision applications should be filed by December 1. The fall 2017 application fee was $50. Notification of early decision is sent December 15; regular decision, April 1. 171 early decision candidates were accepted for the 2017-2018 class. Applications are accepted on-line. **Transfer Students:** 123 transfer students enrolled in 2016-2017. A minimum college GPA of 2.5 is required. 30 of 120 credits required for the bachelor's degree must be completed at SHU. **International Students:** There are 70 international students enrolled. They must take the TOEFL with a minimum score of 550 on the paper-based TOEFL (PBT) or 80 on the Internet-based version (iBT). SHU offers a Test-Optional Admissions Policy.

ADMISSIONS: 60% of the 2017-2018 applicants were accepted. 23% of the current freshmen were in the top fifth of their class; 55% were in the top two fifths. **Admissions Contact:** Kevin O'Sullivan, Executive Director Admissions. Email: *enroll@sacredheart.edu* Web: *www.sacredheart.edu*

FINANCIAL AID: In 2017-2018, 73% of all full-time freshmen received some form of financial aid and need-based aid. The average freshman award was $20,600. Need-based scholarships or need-based grants averaged $16,566; need-based self-help aid (loans and jobs) averaged $5,111; non-need-based athletic scholarships averaged $17,533; other non-need-based awards and non-need-based scholarships averaged $13,114; and $4,167 from other forms of aid. 36% of undergraduate students work part-time. The average financial indebtedness of the 2017 graduate was $24,058. SHU is a member of CSS. The CSS/Profile is required. The FAFSA code is 001403. The priority date for freshman financial aid applications for fall entry is March 1.

SOUTHERN CONNECTICUT STATE UNIVERSITY *(The complete profile is made available exclusively on our website, www.barronspac.com)*

TRINITY COLLEGE — C-2

www.trincoll.edu

Hartford, CT 06106 — **(860) 297-2180**

Fax: (860) 297-2287 — **Email:** admissions.office@trincoll.edu

Full-time: 1115 men, 984 women	**Faculty:** 193
Part-time: 67 men, 57 women	**Ph.D.s:** 93%
Graduate: 49 men, 59 women	**Student/Faculty:** 10 to 1
Year: 4-1-4	**Tuition:** $54,820
Room & Board: $14,200	**Freshman Class:** 7570 applied, 2530 accepted, 559 enrolled
SAT CR/M/W: 610/650/630 **ACT:** 28	**CEEB CODE:** 3899
Application Deadline: January 15	**HIGHLY COMPETITIVE**

Trinity College, founded in 1823, is an independent, nonsectarian liberal arts college. Figures given in the above capsule and in this profile are approximate. There is 1 undergraduate school and 1 graduate school. In addition to regional accreditation, Trinity has baccalaureate program accreditation with ABET. The 100-acre campus is in an urban area southwest of downtown Hartford. Including any residence halls, there are 78 buildings.

STUDENT LIFE: 84% of undergraduates are from out of state, mostly the Northeast. Students are from 44 states, 63 foreign countries, and Canada. 43% are from public schools. 7% are Hispanic; 65% White; 6% African American; 5% race unknown; 4% Asian American; 3% two or more races; 10% Foreign. 30% claim no religious affiliation; 28% Protestant; 27% Catholic. **Male To Female Ratio:** 1.1:1. The average age of freshmen is 18; all undergraduates, 20. 12% do not continue beyond their first year; 86% remain to graduate. **Housing:** 2000 students can be accommodated in college housing, which includes dorms, on-campus apartments, off-campus apartments, and special-interest houses. On-campus housing is guaranteed for all 4 years. 90% of students live on campus. Upperclassmen may keep cars.

FACULTY/CLASSROOMS: 52% of faculty are male; 48% are female. All teach undergraduates and all do research. No introductory courses are taught by graduate students. The average class size in an introductory lecture is 20; in a laboratory is 16; and in a regular course is 13.

PROGRAMS OF STUDY: Trinity confers B.A. and B.S. degrees. Master's degrees are also awarded. Bachelor's degrees are awarded in BIOLOGICAL SCIENCE (biochemistry, biology/biological science, and neurosciences), COMMUNICATIONS AND THE ARTS (art history and appreciation, classics, comparative literature, dance, dramatic arts, English, fine arts, French, German, Italian, modern language, music, Russian, Spanish, studio art, and theater management), COMPUTER AND PHYSICAL SCIENCE (chemistry, computer science, mathematics, and physics), EDUCATION (education), ENGINEERING AND ENVIRONMENTAL DESIGN (engineering and environmental science), SOCIAL SCIENCE (American studies, anthropology, classical/ancient civilization, economics, history, interdisciplinary studies, international studies, Judaic studies, philosophy, political science/government, psychology, public affairs, religion, sociology, and women's studies). Political science, economics, and psychology have the largest enrollments.

ACTIVITIES: 20% of men belong to 7 national fraternities; 16% of women belong to 1 local and 2 national sororities. There are 120 groups on campus, including art, bagpipe, band, cheerleading, chess, choir, chorale, chorus, dance, debate, drama, ethnic, film, honors, international, jazz band, LGBT, literary magazine, musical theater, newspaper, pep band, photography, political, professional, radio and TV, religious, social, social service, student government, and yearbook. Popular campus events include Human Rights Lecture Series, Black History Month, and Latino Heritage Week. **Sports:** There are 15 intercollegiate sports for men and 13 for women, and 14 intramural sports for men and 14 for women. Facilities include a pool, outdoor and indoor tracks, playing fields, a weight room, a fitness center, tennis, squash, and basketball courts. **Graduates:** From July 1, 2016 to June 30, 2017, 523 bachelor's degrees were awarded. The most popular majors were political science (13%), economics (13%), and psychology (7%). In an average class, 1% graduate in 3 years or less, 77% graduate in 4 years or less, 84% graduate in 5 years or less, and 86% graduate in 6 years or less.

SERVICES: Counseling and information services are available, as is tutoring in every subject. There is a reader service for the blind. The writing center offers instruction in all forms of writing, and the math center provides individual tutoring on topics related to math and other courses involving quantitative reasoning. **Library/Resources:** The library contains 992,817 volumes, 399,394 microform items, 225,477 audio/video tapes/CDs/DVDs, and subscribes to 2,438 periodicals including electronic. Computerized library services include interlibrary loans, database searching, Internet access, and Wi-Fi capability. Special learning facilities include an art gallery, radio station, and TV station. **Physically Challenged Students:** 60% of the campus is accessible. Facilities include wheelchair ramps, elevators, special parking, specially equipped restrooms, special class scheduling, lowered drinking fountains, and lowered telephones. **Special:** Trinity offers special freshman programs for exceptional students, including interdisciplinary programs in the sciences and the humanities. There is an intensive study program under which students can devote a semester to 1 subject. Cross-registration through such programs as the Hartford Consortium and the Twelve-College Exchange Program, hundreds of internships (some with Connecticut Public Radio and TV on campus), study abroad virtually worldwide, including Rome, South Africa, Trinidad, Russia, and Nepal, a Washington semester, dual majors in all disciplines, student-designed majors, nondegree study, and pass/fail options also are offered. A 5-year advanced degree in electrical or mechanical engineering with Rensselaer Polytechnic Institute is available. There are 4 national honor societies and a chapter of Phi Beta Kappa. **Visiting:** There are regularly scheduled orientations for prospective students. There are guides for informal visits, visitors may sit in on classes, and stay overnight. To schedule a visit, contact the Admissions Office. **Campus Safety and Security:** Measures include 24-hour foot and vehicle patrol, emergency notification system, self-defense education, and security escort services. There are shuttle buses, emergency telephones, lighted pathways/sidewalks, and controlled access to dorms/residences.

REQUIREMENTS: Trinity strongly emphasizes individual character and personal qualities in admission. Consequently, an interview and essay are recommended. The college requires 4 years of English, 2 years each in foreign language and algebra, and 1 year each in geometry, history, and lab science. AP credits are accepted. Important factors in the admissions decision are advanced placement or honors courses, extracurricular activities record, and evidence of special talent. All students must complete 36 course credits, including 10 to 15 in the major and 1 from each of 5 distribution areas: arts, humanities, natural sciences, numerical and symbolic reasoning, and social sciences. Students must maintain at least a C average overall. **Procedure:** Freshmen are admitted in the fall. Entrance exams should be taken in the fall of the senior year. There are early decision and deferred admissions plans. Early decision applications should be filed by November 15; regular applications, by January 15 for fall entry; and December 15 for spring entry. The fall 2017 application fee was $60. Notifications are sent April 1. 300 early decision candidates were accepted for the 2017-2018 class. 574 applicants were on the 2017 waiting list; 83 were admitted. Applications are accepted on-line. **Transfer Students:** 17 transfer students enrolled in 2016-2017. Transfer applicants must take the SAT or ACT. A minimum college GPA of 3.0 is recommended. 18 of 36 credits required for the bachelor's degree must be completed at Trinity. **International Students:** There are 214 international students enrolled. Students must take the TOEFL.

ADMISSIONS: 33% of the 2017-2018 applicants were accepted. The SAT scores for the 2017-2018 freshman class were: Critical Reading-- 7% below 500, 30% between 500 and 599, 49% between 600 and 699, and 15% between 700 and 800. Math-- 2% below 500, 30% between 500 and 599, 51% between 600 and 699, and 17% between 700 and 800. Writing-- 5% below 500, 29% between 500 and 599, 53% between 600 and 699, and 13% between 700 and 800. The ACT scores were 4% between 18 and 23, 61% between 24 and 29, and 35% above 30. **Admissions Contact:** Angel Perez, Dean of Admissions/Financial Aid. Email: *admissions.office@trincoll.edu* Web: *www.trincoll.edu*

FINANCIAL AID: In 2017-2018, 48% of all full-time freshmen received some form of financial aid. 46% of all full-time freshmen received need-based aid. The average freshman award was $45,859. Need-based scholarships or need-based grants averaged $42,969 ($67,658 maximum); need-based self-help aid (loans and jobs) averaged $5,508 ($11,000 maximum); and other non-need-based awards and non-need-based scholarships averaged $26,799 ($65,650 maximum). 29% of undergraduate students work part-time. The average financial indebtedness of the 2017 graduate was $12,447. Trinity is a member of CSS. The CSS/Profile is required. The FAFSA code is 001414. The priority date for freshman financial aid applications for fall entry is November 15.

UNITED STATES COAST GUARD ACADEMY — D-3

www.cga.edu

New London, CT 06320	(860) 444-8500 (800) 883-8724
Fax: (860) 701-6700	Email: uscga.admissions@uscga.edu
Full-time: 585 men, 313 women	**Faculty:** 147
Part-time: n/av	**Ph.D.s:** 36%
Graduate: n/av	**Student/Faculty:** 6 to 1
Year: semesters, summer session	**Tuition:** $942 (see profile)
Room & Board: see profile	**Freshman Class:** 1948 applied, 388 accepted, 267 enrolled
SAT CR/M/W: 610/650/605 **ACT:** 28	**CEEB CODE:** 5807
Application Deadline: February 1	**HIGHLY COMPETITIVE**

The U.S. Coast Guard Academy, founded in 1876, is an Armed Forces Service Academy for men and women. Appointments are made solely on the basis of an annual nationwide competition. The federal government provides a yearly allowance of $12,192 to help cover cadet expenses. The figure given in the above capsule is for required fees only. There is 1 undergraduate school. In addition to regional accreditation, USCGA has baccalaureate program accreditation with AACSB and ABET. The 103-acre campus is in a suburban area next to New London, 2 hours south of Boston, and 2 hours north of New York City. Including any residence halls, there are 28 buildings.

STUDENT LIFE: 94% of undergraduates are from out of state, mostly the Northeast. Students are from 50 states, and 13 foreign countries. 76% are from public schools. 8% are two or more races; 7% Asian American; 67% White; 4% African American; 10% Hispanic. **Male To Female Ratio:** 1.9:1. The average age of freshmen is 18; all undergraduates, 20. 2% do not continue beyond their first year; 87% remain to graduate. **Housing:** College-sponsored housing includes dorms. On-campus housing is guaranteed for all 4 years. Alcohol is not permitted. Upperclassmen may keep cars.

FACULTY/CLASSROOMS: 70% of faculty are male; 30% are female. All teach undergraduates, 50% do research, and 50% do both. No introductory courses are taught by graduate students. The average class size in an introductory lecture is 25; in a laboratory is 14; and in a regular course is 18.

PROGRAMS OF STUDY: USCGA confers B.S. degrees. Bachelor's degrees are awarded in BIOLOGICAL SCIENCE (marine science), BUSINESS (management science and operations research), ENGINEERING AND ENVIRONMENTAL DESIGN (civil engineering, electrical/electronics engineering, mechanical engineering, and naval architecture and marine engineering), SOCIAL SCIENCE (political science/government). Engineering, marine science, and government have the largest enrollments.

ACTIVITIES: There are no fraternities or sororities. There are 51 groups on campus, including art, band, cheerleading, choir, chorale, chorus, computers, dance, debate, drama, drill team, drum and bugle corps, environmental, ethnic, honors, international, jazz band, LGBT, marching band, musical theater, newspaper, pep band, political, professional, religious, social, social service, student government, and yearbook. Popular campus events include Parents' weekend, Coast Guard Day, Homecoming, Graduation, Cultural History and Heritage Eventsand Sporting Events. **Sports:** There are 15 intercollegiate sports for men and 13 for women, and 22 intramural sports for men and 22 for women. Facilities include a field house with basketball courts, a 6-lane swimming pool, racquetball courts, and facilities for track meets, tennis matches, baseball and softball games, an additional athletic facility with wrestling and weight rooms, basketball courts, gymnastics areas, swimming pool, a stadium, practice and playing fields, outdoor tennis courts, and rowing and seamanship-sailing centers. **Graduates:** From July 1, 2016 to June 30, 2017, 219 bachelor's degrees were awarded. The most popular majors were management (20%), government (19%), and marine & environmental sciences (17%). In an average class, 78% graduate in 4 years or less, 77% graduate in 5 years or less, and 86% graduate in 6 years or less. Of the 2016 graduating class, 100% were employed within 6 months of graduation.

SERVICES: Counseling and information services are available, as is tutoring in every subject. There is remedial math, reading, and writing. **Library/Resources:** The library contains 247,000 volumes, 410,000 microform items, 2,400 audio/video tapes/CDs/DVDs, and subscribes to 74,000 periodicals including electronic. Computerized library services include interlibrary loans, database searching, Internet access, and Wi-Fi capability. **Physically Challenged Students:** 24% of the campus is accessible. Facilities include wheelchair ramps, elevators, special parking, and specially equipped restrooms. **Special:** Cross-registration with Connecticut College, summer cruises to foreign ports, 6-week internships with various government agencies and some engineering and science organizations, and a 1-semester exchange program with the 3 other military academies are available. All U.S. citizen graduates are commissioned in the U.S. Coast Guard (Foreign Nationals are not commissioned in the U.S. Coast Guard). There are 2 national honor societies, a freshman honors program, and 3 departmental honors programs. **Visiting:** There are regularly scheduled orientations for prospective students, including an admissions briefing, and tour of the academy every Monday, Wednesday, and Friday. To schedule a visit, contact the Admissions Receptionist at www.uscga.edu. **Campus Safety and Security:** Measures include 24-hour foot and vehicle patrol, emergency notification system, self-defense education, and security escort services. There are lighted pathways/sidewalks and controlled access to dorms/residences.

REQUIREMENTS: The SAT or ACT is required. The ACT Optional Writing test is also required. Applicants must have reached the age of 17 not the age of 23 by July 1 of the year of admission, must be citizens of the United States, and be single at the time of appointment and remain single while attending the academy. Required secondary school courses include 4 years each of English and math. International non US Citizens must apply through their consulate. These requirements for the degree of Bachelor of Science and a commission as an Ensign in the United States Coast Guard are as follows: a. Pass or validate every course in the core curriculum, b. Pass at least 37 courses of 3.0 credits or greater, c. Attain an average of at least a 2.0 in all required "upper-division" courses in the major, as specified in the official catalog of courses. For repeated courses, all grades earned are included in the average. Satisfy the academic requirements for one of the majors as specified in the official catalog of courses. Attain a cumulative GPA of at least a 2.0. Be in residence at the Academy for at least four academic years. Successfully complete all required portions of the physical education program, including meeting minimum swimming and physical fitness standards. Meet all military performance standards, demonstrating all aspects of personal and professional development necessary to serve as ensigns in the United States Coast Guard, unless a commission will not be offered due to a medical disqualification. International cadets must meet the same standards of personal and professional development as all other graduates, notwithstanding that they are not entitled to appointment in the U.S. Coast Guard. **Procedure:** Freshmen are admitted in the all. There are early admissions, deferred admissions, and rolling admissions plans. Applications should be filed by February 1 for fall entry. Notification is sent on a rolling basis. 148 applicants were on the 2017 waiting list; 36 were admitted. Applications are accepted on-line. **Transfer Students:** All transfer students must meet the same standards as incoming freshmen and must begin as freshmen no matter how many semesters or years of college they have completed. 126 credits are required for the bachelor's degree, and must be completed at USCGA. **International Students:** There are 22 international students enrolled. They must take the TOEFL with a minimum score of 560 on the paper-based TOEFL (PBT). They must also take the SAT or ACT.

ADMISSIONS: 20% of the 2017-2018 applicants were accepted. The SAT scores for the 2017-2018 freshman class were: Critical Reading-- 5% below 500, 35% between 500 and 599, 50% between 600 and 699, and 10% between 700 and 800. Math-- 10% below 500, 17% between 500 and 599, 59% between 600 and 699, and 24% between 700 and 800. Writing-- 7% below 500, 39% between 500 and 599, 45% between 600 and 699, and 9% between 700 and 800. The ACT scores were 1% between 12 and 17, 7% between 18 and 23, 60% between 24 and 29, and 33% above 30. 72% of the current freshmen were in the top fifth of their class; 92% were in the top two fifths. 9 freshmen graduated first in their class. **Admissions Contact:** Captain McKenna, Director of Admissions. Email: *uscga.admissions@uscga.edu* Web: *www.cga.edu*

FINANCIAL AID: Check with the school for current application deadlines.

UNIVERSITY OF BRIDGEPORT *(The complete profile is made available exclusively on our website, www.barronspac.com)*

UNIVERSITY OF CONNECTICUT *(The complete profile is made available exclusively on our website, www.barronspac.com)*

UNIVERSITY OF HARTFORD — C-2

www.hartford.edu

West Hartford, CT 06117	(860) 243-4296 (800) 947-4303
Fax: (860) 768-4961	**Email:** admission@hartford.edu
Full-time: 2281 men, 2222 women	**Faculty:** 347; IIA, av$
Part-time: 315 men, 466 women	**Ph.D.s:** 86%
Graduate: 651 men, 959 women	**Student/Faculty:** 12 to 1
Year: semesters, summer session	**Tuition:** $37,790
Room & Board: $11,986	**Freshman Class:** 14683 applied, 9086 accepted, 1289 enrolled
SAT CR/M: 521/530 **ACT:** 22	**CEEB CODE:** 3436
Application Deadline: open	**COMPETITIVE**

University of Hartford, founded in 1877, is an independent, nonsectarian institution offering extensive undergraduate and graduate programs ranging from liberal arts to business. The figures given in the above capsule and in this profile are approximate. There are 7 undergraduate schools and 6 graduate schools. In addition to regional accreditation, UH has baccalaureate program accreditation with AACSB, ABET, APTA, CAHEA, NASAD, NASM, CEAP, and NLN. The 320-acre campus is in a suburban area 4 miles northwest of Hartford. Including any residence halls, there are 32 buildings.

STUDENT LIFE: 58% of undergraduates are from out of state, mostly the Northeast. Students are from 45 states, 37 foreign countries, and Canada. 80% are from public schools. 7% are Hispanic; 7% Foreign; 61% White; 3% Asian American; 14% African American. 91% claim no religious affiliation. **Female To Male Ratio:** 1.1:1. The average age of freshmen is 18; all undergraduates, 22. 27% do not continue beyond their first year; 57% remain to graduate. **Housing:** 3530 students can be accommodated in college housing, which includes dorms and on-campus apartments. In addition, there are honors houses, special-interest houses, housing for the arts, and the international housing. On-campus housing is guaranteed for all 4 years. 61% of students live on campus. All students may keep cars.

FACULTY/CLASSROOMS: 61% of faculty are male; 39% are female. All teach undergraduates, and 97% do research. No introductory courses are taught by graduate students. The average class size in an introductory lecture is 43; in a laboratory is 21; and in a regular course is 24.

PROGRAMS OF STUDY: UH confers B.A., B.F.A., B.Mus., B.S., B.S.A.E.T., B.S.B.A., B.S.C.E., B.S.Comp.E., B.S.Ed., B.S.E.E. and B.S.M.E. degrees. Associate, master's, and doctoral degrees are also awarded. Bachelor's degrees are awarded in BIOLOGICAL SCIENCE (biology/biological science), BUSINESS (accounting, banking and finance, business administration and management, entrepreneurial studies, insurance, management information systems, management science, and marketing/retailing/merchandising), COMMUNICATIONS AND THE ARTS (art history and appreciation, audio technology, ceramic art and design, communications, dance, design, dramatic arts, drawing, English, film arts, illustration, jazz, languages, media arts, music, music business management, music history and appreciation, music performance, music technology, music theory and composition, musical theater, painting, performing arts, photography, printmaking, sculpture, technical and business writing, theater management, video, and visual and performing arts), COMPUTER AND PHYSICAL SCIENCE (chemistry, computer science, information sciences and systems, mathematics, physics, and radiological technology), EDUCATION (early childhood education, elementary education, music education, secondary education, and special education), ENGINEERING AND ENVIRONMENTAL DESIGN (architectural engineering, biomedical engineering, chemical engineering technology, civil engineering, computer engineering, electrical/electronics engineering, electrical/electronics engineering technology, engineering, engineering technology, mechanical engineering, and mechanical engineering technology), HEALTH PROFESSIONS (health science, nursing, physical therapy, predentistry, premedicine, and preoptometry), SOCIAL SCIENCE (criminal justice, economics, history, interdisciplinary studies, international studies, Judaic studies, law, philosophy, political science/government, psychology, and sociology). Physical therapy, radiologic technology, and acoustical engineering are the strongest academically. Communication, architectural engineering technology, and psychology have the largest enrollments.

ACTIVITIES: 17% of men belong to 7 national fraternities; 21% of women belong to 7 national sororities. There are 100 groups on campus, including art, band, cheerleading, choir, chorale, chorus, communications, computers, drama, ethnic, film, honors, international, jazz band, LGBT, literary magazine, musical theater, newspaper, opera, orchestra, pep band, political, professional, radio and TV, religious, social, social service, student government, and symphony. Popular campus events include Spring Fling, and Hawktober Weekend. **Sports:** There are 7 intercollegiate sports for men and 8 for women, and 15 intramural sports for men and 15 for women. Facilities include playing fields, a 25-meter outdoor pool, tennis courts, golf practice cages, a fitness trail, and a sports center with multipurpose court, an 8-lane swimming pool, a weight room, racquetball courts, and squash court. **Graduates:** From July 1, 2016 to June 30, 2017, 955 bachelor's degrees were awarded. The most popular majors were communications (7%), psychology (4%), and architectural engineering tech. (4%). In an average class, 53% graduate in 4 years or less, 58% graduate in 5 years or less, and 59% graduate in 6 years or less. Of the 2016 graduating class, 35% were enrolled in graduate school within 6 months of graduation, and 75% were employed.

SERVICES: Counseling and information services are available, as is tutoring in most subjects. There is a reader service for the blind, and remedial math, reading, and writing. The health education office offers peer counseling and workshops on health-related topics. Professional counseling is also available. **Library/Resources:** The library contains 590,724 volumes, 383,386 microform items, 5,921 audio/video tapes/CDs/DVDs, and subscribes to 49,600 periodicals including electronic. Computerized library services include interlibrary loans, database searching, Internet access, and Wi-Fi capability. Special learning facilities include an art gallery, radio station, TV station, and the Museum of American Political Life. **Physically Challenged Students:** Facilities include wheelchair ramps, elevators, special parking, specially equipped restrooms, lowered drinking fountains, lowered telephones, and special housing. **Special:** Cross-registration with the Greater Hartford Consortium, internships in all majors, study abroad, a Washington semester, work-study programs, credit for life experience, non-degree study, and pass/fail options are available. In addition, students may pursue accelerated degrees, B.A.-B.S. degrees, dual majors, or their own individually designed majors. There are interdisciplinary majors in acoustics and music and in experimental studio combining performing, literary, and visual arts. Also available are preprofessional programs in biology/preoptometry with the New England College of Optometry, predentistry with the New York University School of Dentistry, prechiropractic with the New York Chiropractic College, preosteopathic with the University of New England College of Osteopathic Medicine, and prepodiatry with the New York College of Podiatric Medicine. There are 19 national honor societies, a freshman honors program, and 7 departmental honors programs. **Visiting:** There are regularly scheduled orientations for prospective students. There are guides for informal visits, visitors may sit in on classes, and stay overnight. To schedule a visit, contact the Office of Admissions. **Campus Safety and Security:** Measures include 24-hour foot and vehicle patrol, emergency notification system, self-defense education, and security escort services. There are shuttle buses, emergency telephones, lighted pathways/sidewalks, controlled access to dorms/residences, and a bicycle patrol.

REQUIREMENTS: The SAT is required. Applicants should have 16 academic high school credits and 16 Carnegie units, including 4 units in English, 3 in math (3.5 for B.S. candidates), and 2 each in foreign language, science, and social studies. A portfolio and an audition are required for B.F.A. and B.Mus. candidates, respectively. A personal statement is required, and an interview is recommended for all students. AP and CLEP credits are accepted. Important factors in the admissions decision are advanced placement or honors courses, recommendations by school officials, and leadership record. To graduate, students must complete at least 120 credit hours, fulfill the university's core curriculum requirements, and maintain an overall GPA of 2.0. Specific core and course requirements vary with the major. **Procedure:** Freshmen are admitted fall and spring. Entrance exams should be taken in the spring of the junior year or the fall of the senior year. There are deferred admissions and rolling admissions plans. Application deadlines are open. The fall 2017 application fee was $40. Notification is sent on a rolling basis. Applications are accepted on-line. **Transfer Students:** 232 transfer students enrolled in 2016-2017. Transfer students must have a minimum college GPA of 2.25, with 2.5 recommended, and must submit SAT or ACT scores if they have fewer than 30 transferable college-level credits. An interview is also recommended. 30 of 120 credits required for the bachelor's degree must be completed at Hartford. **International Students:** There are 195 international students enrolled. They must take the TOEFL with a minimum score of 550 on the paper-based TOEFL (PBT). The SAT or the ACT is recommended.

ADMISSIONS: 62% of the 2017-2018 applicants were accepted. The SAT scores for the 2017-2018 freshman class were: Critical Reading--46% below 500, 39% between 500 and 599, 14% between 600 and 699, and 1% between 700 and 800. Math-- 44% below 500, 37% between 500 and 599, 17% between 600 and 699, and 2% between 700 and 800. The ACT scores were 38% below 12, 28% between 12 and 17, 20% between 18 and 23, 6% between 24 and 29, and 8% above 30. 12% of the current freshmen were in the top fifth of their class; 27% were in the top two fifths. **Admissions Contact:** Richard A. Zeiser, Dean of Admissions. Email: *admission@hartford.edu* Web: *www.hartford.edu*

FINANCIAL AID: In 2017-2018, 94% of all full-time freshmen received some form of financial aid. 80% of all full-time freshmen received need-based aid. 22% of undergraduate students work part-time. The FAFSA code is 001422. The priority date for freshman financial aid applications for fall entry is February 1. The deadline for filing freshman financial aid applications for fall entry is March 1.

UNIVERSITY OF NEW HAVEN C-3

www.newhaven.edu

West Haven, CT 06516	(203) 931-7354 (800) 342-5864
Fax: (203) 931-6093	Email: admissions@newhaven.edu
Full-time: 2257 men, 2574 women	**Faculty:** n/av
Part-time: 211 men, 174 women	**Ph.D.s:** 81%
Graduate: 919 men, 849 women	**Student/Faculty:** n/av
Year: 4-1-4, summer session	**Tuition:** $38,170
Room & Board: $15,510	**Freshman Class:** 9953 applied, 8735 accepted, 1449 enrolled
SAT EBR-W/M: 562/550 **ACT:** 24	**CEEB CODE:** 3663
Application Deadline: open	**COMPETITIVE**

University of New Haven, founded in 1920, is a private, comprehensive institution recognized as a national leader in experiential education providing students with a unique combination of a liberal arts education and real-world, hands-on career and research opportunities. There are 5 undergraduate schools and 4 graduate schools. In addition to regional accreditation, UNH has baccalaureate program accreditation with ABET, ADA, CAEP, FEPAC, and ACEND. The 82-acre campus is in a suburban area 90 minutes from New York City and approximately 2 1/2 hours from Boston. Including any residence halls, there are 40 buildings.

STUDENT LIFE: 55% of undergraduates are from out of state, mostly the Northeast. Students are from 40 states, 36 foreign countries, and Canada. 61% are White; 6% Foreign; 6% race unknown; 3% Asian American; 12% African American; 12% Hispanic; 1% two or more races. **Female To Male Ratio:** 1.1:1. The average age of freshmen is 18; all undergraduates, 21. 21% do not continue beyond their first year; 60% remain to graduate. **Housing:** 2946 students can be accommodated in college housing, which includes dorms, on-campus apartments, off-campus apartments, and living learning communities. On-campus housing is guaranteed for all 4 years, is available on a first-come, first-served basis, and is available on a lottery system for upperclassmen. 53% of students live on campus. Upperclassmen may keep cars.

FACULTY/CLASSROOMS: 66% of faculty are male; 34% are female. No introductory courses are taught by graduate students.

PROGRAMS OF STUDY: UNH confers B.A., B.S., and B.F.A. degrees. Associate, master's, and doctoral degrees are also awarded. Bachelor's degrees are awarded in BIOLOGICAL SCIENCE (biology/biological science, biotechnology, marine biology, and nutrition), BUSINESS (accounting, banking and finance, business administration and management, hospitality management services, hotel/motel and restaurant management, marketing/retailing/merchandising, sports management, and tourism), COMMUNICATIONS AND THE ARTS (art, audio technology, communications, communications technology, creative writing, design, English, fine arts, fine/studio arts, general, graphic design, literature, music, music business management, music performance, music technology, theatre arts, visual and performing arts, and visual design), COMPUTER AND PHYSICAL SCIENCE (applied mathematics, chemistry, computer management, computer programming, computer science, cyber operations, mathematics, and natural sciences), EDUCATION (global studies and mathematics education), ENGINEERING AND ENVIRONMENTAL DESIGN (chemical engineering, civil engineering, computer engineering, electrical/electronics engineering, engineering, environmental science, fire protection engineering, interior design, mechanical engineering, and systems engineering), HEALTH PROFESSIONS (dental hygiene), SOCIAL SCIENCE (clinical psychology, community psychology, counseling/psychology, criminal justice, criminology, dietetics, economics, family/juvenile justice, fire control and safety technology, fire protection, fire science, fire services administration, forensic studies, history, law enforcement and corrections, legal studies, liberal arts/general studies, political science/government, and psychology). Criminal justice, forensic science, and psychology have the largest enrollments.

ACTIVITIES: There are 140 groups on campus, including art, cheerleading, communications, computers, dance, debate, drama, ethnic, film, forensics, honors, international, LGBT, marching band, newspaper, pep band, photography, political, professional, radio and TV, religious, social, social service, student government, and yearbook. **Sports:** There are 7 intercollegiate sports for men and 9 for women, and 11 intramural sports for men and 11 for women. Facilities include baseball, softball, intramural playing fields, tennis courts, a gym with basketball courts, weight training room, racquetball court, a recreation center, an outdoor stadium for football, soccer, and lacrosse. **Graduates:** From July 1, 2016 to June 30, 2017, 1156 bachelor's degrees were awarded. The most popular majors were criminal justice (24%), forensic science (7%), and psychology (7%). In an average class, 60% graduate in 6 years or less.

SERVICES: Counseling and information services are available, as is tutoring in every subject. There is a reader service for the blind, and remedial math, reading, and writing. There is also campus access services, and centers for academic success and advising. **Library/Resources:** The library contains 383,261 volumes, 412,224 microform items, 1,672 audio/video tapes/CDs/DVDs, and subscribes to 43,197 periodicals including electronic. Computerized library services include interlibrary loans, database searching, Internet access, and Wi-Fi capability. Special learning facilities include an art gallery, radio station, TV station, institute of forensic science, crime scene training & technology center, dental hygiene center, finance and technology center, communication studios, and music and sound recording facilities. **Physically Challenged Students:** Facilities include wheelchair ramps, elevators, special parking, specially equipped restrooms, special class scheduling, lowered drinking fountains, lowered telephones, and special housing. **Special:** The University offers co-op programs in some majors, internships in all majors, work-study programs, interdisciplinary majors, fast-track business programs leading to bachelor's degrees in 3 years, 5-year B.S.-M.S. programs, and non-degree study programs. A vast array of study abroad programs are also available. There is a freshman honors program. **Visiting:** There are regularly scheduled orientations for prospective students, including daily information sessions, open houses, accepted student days, charger days, and summer preview days. There are guides for informal visits, visitors may sit in on classes, and stay overnight. To schedule a visit, contact the Office of Undergraduate Admissions. **Campus Safety and Security:** Measures include 24-hour foot and vehicle patrol, emergency notification system, self-defense education, and security escort services. There are shuttle buses, emergency telephones, lighted pathways/sidewalks, and controlled access to dorms/residences.

REQUIREMENTS: The SAT or ACT is required. Applicants should be graduates of an accredited secondary school. The GED is accepted. An interview is recommended. A letter of recommendation along with a personal essay is also required. AP and CLEP credits are accepted. Important factors in the admissions decision are advanced placement or honors courses, extracurricular activities record, and recommendations by school officials. To graduate, all students must maintain a GPA of 2.0, pass a writing proficiency exam, and complete a total of 120 to 132 credits, depending on the major. Students must complete at least 40 credits from the university core curriculum, including a total of 28 credits in lab science, social sciences, history, literature or philosophy, art, music, or theater, 9 credits in communication skills, and 3 credits each in quantitative skills, computers, and scientific methodology. **Procedure:** Freshmen are admitted fall and spring. Entrance exams should be taken in the fall or winter of the senior year. There are early decision, early admissions, and rolling admissions plans. Application deadlines are open. The fall 2017 application fee was $50. Applications are accepted on-line. **Transfer Students:** 237 transfer students enrolled in 2016-2017. Applicants should have a minimum college GPA of 2.3 and should submit all official transcripts. An interview is recommended, and the SAT is required for students with fewer than 24 college credits. 30 of 120 credits required for the bachelor's degree must be completed at UNH. **International Students:** There are 288 international students enrolled. They must take the TOEFL with a minimum score of 75 on the Internet-based version (iBT). They must also take the SAT or ACT.

ADMISSIONS: 88% of the 2017-2018 applicants were accepted. The SAT scores for the 2017-2018 freshman class were: Math-- 23% below 500, 51% between 500 and 599, 23% between 600 and 699, and 3% between 700 and 800. Evidence-Based Reading/Writing-- 17% below 500, 50% between 500 and 599, 30% between 600 and 699, and 3% between 700 and 800. The ACT scores were 6% between 12 and 17, 45% between 18 and 23, 41% between 24 and 29, and 8% above 30. **Admissions Contact:** Jason Riendeau, Director of Undergraduate Admissions. Email: *admissions@newhaven.edu* Web: *www.newhaven.edu*

FINANCIAL AID: UNH is a member of CSS. The FAFSA code is 001397. Check with the school for current application deadlines.

UNIVERSITY OF SAINT JOSEPH C-2

www.usj.edu

West Hartford, CT 06117	(860) 231-5223 (866) 442-8752 Email: admissions@usj.edu
Full-time: 8 men, 646 women	**Faculty:** 70; IIA, -$
Part-time: 12 men, 144 women	**Ph.D.s:** n/av
Graduate: 280 men, 1315 women	**Student/Faculty:** 9 to 1
Year: semesters, summer session	**Tuition:** $37,974
Room & Board: $11,095	**Freshman Class:** 776 applied, 599 accepted, 134 enrolled
SAT CR/M: 549/520	**CEEB CODE:** 3754
Application Deadline: n/av	**COMPETITIVE**

University of Saint Joseph, is a private institution consisting of an undergraduate women's program (which will be coed beginning Fall 2018), a coed bachelor's degree completion program for adults, a coed graduate program, and a coed School of Pharmacy. There are 4 undergraduate schools and 4 graduate schools. In addition to regional accreditation, USJ has baccalaureate program accreditation with CSWE, ACEND, and ASBMB. The 90-acre campus is in a suburban area 3 miles from Hartford, CT, approximately 2 hours to Boston, MA, and approximately 2.5 hours to New York, NY. Including any residence halls, there are 17 buildings.

STUDENT LIFE: 95% of undergraduates are from Connecticut. Others are from 15 states. 54% are White; 5% Asian American; 15% Hispanic; 14% African American; 11% race unknown; 1% two or more races. **Female To Male Ratio:** 7.0:1. The average age of freshmen is 18; all undergraduates, 23. 23% do not continue beyond their first year; 68% remain to graduate. **Housing:** 403 students can be accommodated in college housing, which includes dorms, and special-interest houses. On-campus housing is available on a first-come, first-served basis, and is available on a lottery system for upperclassmen. 72% of students commute. All students may keep cars.

FACULTY/CLASSROOMS: No introductory courses are taught by graduate students.

PROGRAMS OF STUDY: USJ confers B.A. and B.S. degrees. Master's and doctoral degrees are also awarded. Bachelor's degrees are awarded in BIOLOGICAL SCIENCE (biochemistry, biology/biological science, and nutrition), BUSINESS (accounting and management science), COMMUNICATIONS AND THE ARTS (art history and appreciation, English, and Spanish), COMPUTER AND PHYSICAL SCIENCE (chemistry and mathematics), EDUCATION (special education), HEALTH PROFESSIONS (nursing and public health), SOCIAL SCIENCE (child psychology/development, criminal justice, family/consumer studies, history, international studies, philosophy, psychology, religion, social work, and women's studies). Nursing, and education are the strongest academically. Nursing, social work, and biology have the largest enrollments.

ACTIVITIES: There are no fraternities or sororities. Groups on campus include choir, dance, drama, ethnic, honors, international, LGBT, literary magazine, political, professional, religious, social, social service, and student government. **Sports:** There are 8 intercollegiate sports for women, and 6 intramural sports for women. Facilities include a fitness center, swimming pool, indoor and outdoor tracks, tennis courts, basketball/volleyball court, softball field, lacrosse/soccer field, and dance studio. **Graduates:** From July 1, 2016 to June 30, 2017, 221 bachelor's degrees were awarded. The most popular majors were nursing (39%), social work (13%), and biology (10%). In an average class, 61% graduate in 4 years or less, 68% graduate in 5 years or less, and 68% graduate in 6 years or less.

SERVICES: Counseling and information services are available, as is tutoring in most subjects. **Library/Resources:** The library contains 83,561 volumes, and 2,078 audio/video tapes/CDs/DVDs, and subscribes to 84,839 periodicals including electronic. Computerized library services include interlibrary loans, database searching, Internet access, and Wi-Fi capability. Special learning facilities include an art gallery, a lab school for young children and the Gengras Center. **Physically Challenged Students:** Facilities include wheelchair ramps, elevators, special parking, specially equipped restrooms, special class scheduling, and special housing. **Special:** USJ offers cross-registration for full-time students at member colleges through the Hartford Consortium for Higher Education. Internship opportunities, study abroad, double majors, and student-designed majors are also available. There is a freshman honors program. **Visiting:** There are regularly scheduled orientations for prospective students. There are guides for informal visits, visitors may sit in on classes, and stay overnight.. **Campus Safety and Security:** Measures include 24-hour foot and vehicle patrol, emergency notification system, and security escort services. There are shuttle buses, emergency telephones, lighted pathways/sidewalks, and controlled access to dorms/residences.

REQUIREMENTS: SAT/ACT scores are optional except for a few programs in which it is required. High school transcripts should show a minimum of 16 units (18 units if the SAT/ACT is not submitted). Full requirements are posted at www.usj.edu/admissions-financial-aid/. AP and CLEP credits are accepted. To earn a bachelor's degree: students must have a minimum 2.0 GPA and 120 earned credits which meet requirements in the general education curriculum and the major area of study. **Procedure:** Freshmen are admitted fall and spring. There are deferred admissions and rolling admissions plans. Application deadlines are open. The fall 2017 application fee was $50. Applications are accepted on-line. **Transfer Students:** 96 transfer students enrolled in 2016-2017. 45 of 120 credits required for the bachelor's degree must be completed at USJ. **International Students:** There are 3 international students enrolled. They must take the TOEFL. They must also take the SAT or ACT.

ADMISSIONS: 77% of the 2017-2018 applicants were accepted. The SAT scores for the 2017-2018 freshman class were: Math-- 39% below 500, 48% between 500 and 599, and 13% between 600 and 699. Evidence-Based Reading/Writing-- 39% below 500, 48% between 500 and 599, and 13% between 600 and 699. 46% of the current freshmen were in the top fifth of their class; 72% were in the top two fifths. 2 freshmen graduated first in their class. **Admissions Contact:** Molly Dever, Director of Admissions. Email: *admissions@usj.edu* Web: *www.usj.edu*

FINANCIAL AID: In 2017-2018, 95% of all full-time freshmen received some form of financial aid and need-based aid. The average freshman award was $29,691. Need-based scholarships or need-based grants averaged $25,874; and need-based self-help aid (loans and jobs) averaged $4,660. USJ is a member of CSS. The FAFSA code is 001409. The priority date for freshman financial aid applications for fall entry is March 1.

WESLEYAN UNIVERSITY C-3

www.wesleyan.edu

Middletown, CT 06459	(860) 685-3000
Fax: (860) 685-3001	**Email: admission@wesleyan.edu**
Full-time: 1331 men, 1565 women	**Faculty:** 377; IIA, ++$
Part-time: 45 men, 35 women	**Ph.D.s:** 92%
Graduate: 116 men, 121 women	**Student/Faculty:** 8 to 1
Year: semesters, summer session	**Tuition:** $52,474
Room & Board: $14,466	**Freshman Class:** 12360 applied, 2013 accepted, 761 enrolled
SAT EBR-W/M: 710/690 **ACT:** 31	**CEEB CODE:** 3959
Application Deadline: January 1	**MOST COMPETITIVE**

Wesleyan University, founded in 1831, is a private institution offering programs in the liberal arts and sciences. There is 1 undergraduate school and 1 graduate school. In addition to regional accreditation, WU has baccalaureate program accreditation with NEASE-CIHE. The 316-acre campus is in a suburban area 15 miles south of Hartford, and 2 hours from both Boston and New York City. Including any residence halls, there are 301 buildings.

STUDENT LIFE: 92% of undergraduates are from out of state, mostly the Northeast. Students are from 48 states, 49 foreign countries, and Canada. 52% are from public schools. 8% are Asian American; 7% African American; 53% White; 5% two or more races; 3% race unknown; 12% Foreign; 11% Hispanic. **Female To Male Ratio:** 1.2:1. The average age of freshmen is 18; all undergraduates, 20. 5% do not continue beyond their first year; 94% remain to graduate. **Housing:** 2915 students can be accommodated in college housing, which includes dorms and on-campus apartments. In addition, there are language/international houses, special-interest houses, and fraternity houses. On-campus housing is guaranteed for all 4 years. All students may keep cars.

FACULTY/CLASSROOMS: 55% of faculty are male; 45% are female. All

teach undergraduates and do research. No introductory courses are taught by graduate students. The average class size in an introductory lecture is 21; in a laboratory is 21; and in a regular course is 16.

PROGRAMS OF STUDY: Wesleyan confers B.A. degrees. Master's and doctoral degrees are also awarded. Bachelor's degrees are awarded in AGRICULTURE (environmental studies), BIOLOGICAL SCIENCE (biology/biological science, molecular biology, and neurosciences), COMMUNICATIONS AND THE ARTS (art history and appreciation, classics, dance, dramatic arts, English, English literature, film arts, music, romance languages and literature, and studio art), COMPUTER AND PHYSICAL SCIENCE (astronomy, chemistry, computer science, earth science, mathematics, and physics), SOCIAL SCIENCE (African American studies, American studies, anthropology, archeology, classical/ancient civilization, East Asian studies, economics, French studies, gender studies, German area studies, Hispanic American studies, history, Italian studies, Latin American studies, medieval studies, philosophy, political science/government, psychology, religion, Russian and Slavic studies, science and society, social studies, and sociology). Sciences, economics, and history are the strongest academically. Psychology, chemistry, and music have the largest enrollments.

ACTIVITIES: 4% of men belong to 4 local and 3 national fraternities; 1% of women belong to 1 local sorority. There are 238 groups on campus, including art, band, cheerleading, chess, choir, chorale, chorus, communications, computers, dance, debate, drama, environmental, ethnic, film, honors, international, jazz band, LGBT, literary magazine, musical theater, newspaper, opera, orchestra, pep band, photography, political, professional, radio and TV, religious, social, social service, student government, symphony, and yearbook. Popular campus events include Cultural Shows, and Spring Fling. **Sports:** There are 15 intercollegiate sports for men and 14 for women, and 5 intramural sports for men and 5 for women. Facilities include a stadium, a gym, Olympic-size pool, outdoor track, cross-country trail, hockey arena, strength and fitness center, outdoor tennis courts, squash courts, soccer fields, football practice fields, rugby pitch, boathouse, baseball diamond, softball diamond, and artificial turf fields, a field house featuring indoor track, 4 indoor tennis courts, recreational basketball courts, volleyball courts, and badminton courts. **Graduates:** From July 1, 2016 to June 30, 2017, 764 bachelor's degrees were awarded. The most popular majors were economics (11%), psychology (7%), and government (7%). In an average class, 88% graduate in 4 years or less, 89% graduate in 5 years or less, and 90% graduate in 6 years or less. Of the 2016 graduating class, 13% were enrolled in graduate school within 6 months of graduation, and 71% were employed.

SERVICES: Counseling and information services are available, as is tutoring in most subjects. There is a Peer Advisor Assistance in time management, academic skills development, writing tutors, math tutoring, quantitative skills and quantitative analysis, and supplemental instruction in biology and chemistry. **Library/Resources:** The library contains 1.6 million volumes, 295,898 microform items, and 77,705 audio/video tapes/CDs/DVDs, and subscribes to 75,956 periodicals including electronic. Computerized library services include interlibrary loans, database searching, Internet access, and Wi-Fi capability. Special learning facilities include an art gallery, radio station, and an observatory. **Physically Challenged Students:** 53% of the campus is accessible. Facilities include wheelchair ramps, elevators, special parking, specially equipped restrooms, special class scheduling, lowered drinking fountains, lowered telephones, and special housing. **Special:** Wesleyan offers exchange programs with 11 northeastern colleges, cross-registration with 2 area colleges, study abroad in 45 countries on 6 continents, internships, dual and student-designed majors, and pass/fail options. 3-2 engineering programs with Cal Tech, Columbia University, and Dartmouth College are also available. There are 2 national honor societies, Phi Beta Kappa, and 48 departmental honors programs. **Visiting:** There are regularly scheduled orientations for prospective students, consisting of a hour-long campus tour and group information sessions. There are guides for informal visits, visitors may sit in on classes, and stay overnight. To schedule a visit, contact the Office of Admission. **Campus Safety and Security:** Measures include 24-hour foot and vehicle patrol, emergency notification system, self-defense education, and security escort services. There are shuttle buses, emergency telephones, lighted pathways/sidewalks, and controlled access to dorms/residences.

REQUIREMENTS: Applicants must submit the common application, transcript, and a letter of recommendation. Standardized tests are optional. Students should have a minimum of 20 academic credits, including 4 years each of English, foreign language, math, science, and social studies. AP credits are accepted. Important factors in the admissions decision are advanced placement or honors courses, recommendations by school officials, and personality/intangible qualities. To graduate, all students must complete 128 credit hours. All students are expected, but not required to take courses each in humanities and arts, social and behavioral sciences, and natural science and math. A minimum academic average of 74 must be maintained, with at least 6 semesters of full-time residency. **Procedure:** Freshmen are admitted in the fall. Entrance exams should be taken in the spring of the junior year or the fall of the senior year. There are early decision, early admissions, and deferred admissions plans. Early decision applications should be filed by November 15; regular applications, by January 1 for fall entry. The fall 2017 application fee was $55. Notification of early decision is sent December 15; regular decision, April 1. 427 early decision candidates were accepted for the 2017-2018 class. 1233 applicants were on the 2017 waiting list; 97 were admitted. Applications are accepted on-line. **Transfer Students:** 65 transfer students enrolled in 2016-2017. Applicants need a strong academic record. Standardized tests are optional. An interview is recommended. 76 of 128 credits required for the bachelor's degree must be completed at Wesleyan. **International Students:** There are 338 international students enrolled. They must take the TOEFL with a minimum score of 600 on the paper-based TOEFL (PBT) or 100 on the Internet-based version (iBT). Students must also take the IELTS.

ADMISSIONS: 16% of the 2017-2018 applicants were accepted. The SAT scores for the 2017-2018 freshman class were: Math-- 1% below 500, 12% between 500 and 599, 42% between 600 and 699, and 46% between 700 and 800. Evidence-Based Reading/Writing-- 8% between 500 and 599, 33% between 600 and 699, and 59% between 700 and 800. The ACT scores were 4% between 18 and 23, 24% between 24 and 29, and 72% above 30. 87% of the current freshmen were in the top fifth of their class; 84% were in the top two fifths. **Admissions Contact:** Nancy Hargrave Meislahn, Dean of Admissions and Financial Aid. Email: *admission@wesleyan.edu* Web: *www.wesleyan.edu/admission*

FINANCIAL AID: In 2017-2018, 47% of all full-time freshmen received some form of financial aid. 43% of all full-time freshmen received need-based aid. The average freshman award was $51,412. Need-based scholarships or need-based grants averaged $47,653; and need-based self-help aid (loans and jobs) averaged $4,726. 60% of undergraduate students work part-time. The average financial indebtedness of the 2017 graduate was $16,877. WU is a member of CSS. The CSS/Profile, and parent and student 1040 forms, W-2s, business tax returns are required. The FAFSA code is 001424. The priority date for freshman financial aid applications for fall entry is February 15.

WESTERN CONNECTICUT STATE UNIVERSITY *(The complete profile is made available exclusively on our website, www.barronspac.com)*

YALE UNIVERSITY — C-3

www.yale.edu

New Haven, CT 06511 — **(203) 432-9316**

Fax: (203) 432-9370	**Email:** apply.questions@yale.edu
Full-time: 2812 men, 2696 women	**Faculty:** 1159; I, ++$
Part-time: 16 men, 4 women	**Ph.D.s:** 92%
Graduate: 3455 men, 3398 women	**Student/Faculty:** 6 to 1
Year: semesters, summer session	**Tuition:** $49,480
Room & Board: $15,170	**Freshman Class:** 30236 applied, 2034 accepted, 1364 enrolled
SAT CR/M/W: 760/755/750 **ACT:** 33	**CEEB CODE:** 3987
Application Deadline: January 1	**MOST COMPETITIVE**

Yale University, founded in 1701, is a private liberal arts institution. The figures given in the above capsule and in this profile are approximate. There is 1 undergraduate school and 13 graduate schools. In addition to regional accreditation, Yale has baccalaureate program accreditation with AACSB, ABET, CAHEA, NAAB, NASM, NLN, SAF, ABA, APA, ATS, AMA, CAAHEP, CCNE, LCME, and NEASC. The 342-acre campus is in an urban area 75 miles northeast of New York City. Including any residence halls, there are 440 buildings.

STUDENT LIFE: 93% of undergraduates are from out of state, mostly the West. Students are from 49 states, 74 foreign countries, and Canada.

57% are from public schools. 7% are African American; 53% White; 17% Asian American; 11% Hispanic; 10% Foreign; 1% American Indian/ Alaska Native. **Male To Female Ratio:** 1.0:1. The average age of freshmen is 18; all undergraduates, 20. 1% do not continue beyond their first year; 96% remain to graduate. **Housing:** College-sponsored housing includes dorms, and 12 residential colleges. On-campus housing is guaranteed for the freshman year only and is available on a lottery system for upperclassmen. 84% of students live on campus. All students may keep cars.

FACULTY/CLASSROOMS: 64% of faculty are male; 36% are female. All teach undergraduates. No introductory courses are taught by graduate students.

PROGRAMS OF STUDY: Yale confers B.A. and B.S. degrees. Master's and doctoral degrees are also awarded. Bachelor's degrees are awarded in AGRICULTURE (environmental studies), BIOLOGICAL SCIENCE (biochemistry, biology/biological science, biophysics, evolutionary biology, and molecular biology), COMMUNICATIONS AND THE ARTS (art history, art, Chinese, classics, dramatic arts, East Asian languages and literature, English, film arts, French, Germanic languages and literature, Italian, Japanese, linguistics, literature, music, Portuguese, Russian, Russian languages and literature, Slavic languages, and Spanish), COMPUTER AND PHYSICAL SCIENCE (applied mathematics, applied physics, astronomy, chemistry, computer science, geology, mathematics, mathematics-economics, mathematics-philosophy, physics, and statistics), ENGINEERING AND ENVIRONMENTAL DESIGN (architecture, biomedical engineering, chemical engineering, electrical/electronics engineering, engineering, engineering and applied science, environmental engineering, and mechanical engineering), SOCIAL SCIENCE (African studies, African American studies, American studies, anthropology, archeology, classical/ancient civilization, cognitive science, East Asian studies, Eastern European studies, economics, ethics, politics, and social policy, ethnic studies, German area studies, history, history of science, humanities, international studies, Judaic studies, Latin American studies, Middle Eastern studies, Near Eastern studies, philosophy, political science/government, psychology, religion, Russian and Slavic studies, sociology, South Asian studies, and women's studies). History, political science, and economics have the largest enrollments.

ACTIVITIES: There are 400 groups on campus, including art, band, cheerleading, chess, choir, chorale, chorus, communications, computers, dance, debate, drama, environmental, ethnic, film, honors, international, jazz band, LGBT, literary magazine, marching band, musical theater, newspaper, opera, orchestra, pep band, photography, political, professional, radio and TV, religious, social, social service, student government, symphony, and yearbook. Popular campus events include Freshman Dinner, Spring Fling Concert, Fall Show, Yale Symphony Orchestra Halloween Show, Yale Top Chef Competition, Yale-Harvard Football Game, and special cultural dinners in the residential colleges. **Sports:** There are 16 intercollegiate sports for men and 18 for women, and 25 intramural sports for men and 21 for women. Facilities include a sports complex, a gym, swimming pools, a fitness center, football field, ice rink, squash center, tennis center, golf course, and a sailing center and boathouse. **Graduates:** From July 1, 2016 to June 30, 2017, 1327 bachelor's degrees were awarded. The most popular majors were social sciences (29%), biological/life sciences (10%), area, ethnic, and gender studies, history, and and interdisciplinary studies (7%). In an average class, 97% graduate in 6 years or less. Of the 2016 graduating class, 21% were enrolled in graduate school within 6 months of graduation, and 75% were employed.

SERVICES: Counseling and information services are available, as is tutoring in every subject. There is a reader service for the blind. **Library/ Resources:** The library contains 15.0 million volumes, 10.0 million microform items, and 400,000 audio/video tapes/CDs/DVDs, and subscribes to 450,000 periodicals including electronic. Computerized library services include interlibrary loans, database searching, Internet access, and Wi-Fi capability. Special learning facilities include an art gallery, natural history museum, planetarium, radio station, center for British art, rare book and manuscript library, film study center, center for engineering innovation and design, Botanical gardens and natural preserves, and numerous research centers. **Physically Challenged Students:** Facilities include wheelchair ramps, elevators, special parking, specially equipped restrooms, special class scheduling, lowered drinking fountains, lowered telephones, special housing, and a door-to-door lift-van service. **Special:** The university runs a study abroad program in England and offers opportunities for term-time or summer study in many other countries. It also offers an accelerated degree program, B.A.-B.S. degrees, dual majors, and student-designed majors. Directed Studies, a special freshman program in the humanities, affords outstanding students the opportunity to survey the Western cultural tradition. Perspectives on Science is a special freshmen program for students who are especially strong in science and mathematics. Freshmen Seminars offer the opportunity for first-year students the opportunity to enroll in small classes with some of Yale's most distinguished faculty members. The STARS (Science, Technology and Research Scholars) program offers research opportunities, mentoring and support to students historically under-represented in fields of natural science and quantitative reasoning. There is a chapter of Phi Beta Kappa. **Visiting:** There are regularly scheduled orientations for prospective students, flexible: admissions information sessions, campus tours, in summer Student Forums. There are guides for informal visits and visitors may sit in on classes. To schedule a visit, contact the Receptionist Office at (203) 432-9300. **Campus Safety and Security:** Measures include 24-hour foot and vehicle patrol, emergency notification system, self-defense education, and security escort services. There are shuttle buses, emergency telephones, lighted pathways/sidewalks, and controlled access to dorms/residences.

REQUIREMENTS: Applicants only submitting SAT scores must also take any 2 SAT Subject tests. ACT submitters must take the ACT with Writing. Most successful applicants rank in the top 10% of their high school class. All students must have completed a rigorous high school program encompassing all academic disciplines. 2 essays, 2 teacher recommendations and a counselor letter are required. An interview is recommended. Yale offers a non-binding Single Choice Early Action option (not Early Decision.) AP credits are accepted. Important factors in the admissions decision are leadership record, parents or siblings attended your school, recommendations by alumni, geographical diversity, advanced placement or honors courses, evidence of special talent, personality/intangible qualities, extracurricular activities record, and recommendations by school officials. To graduate, students must complete at least 36 semester courses, including 2 course credits each in the humanities, social sciences, sciences, writing courses, and quantitative reasoning, and courses to further proficiency in a foreign language. All students complete requirements for an academic major. Yale does not have a 'minor' program but students may have two majors. **Procedure:** Freshmen are admitted in the fall. Entrance exams should be taken at any time up to and including the January test date in the year of application. There is a deferred admissions plan. Applications should be filed by January 1 for fall entry. The fall 2017 application fee was $80. Notifications are sent April 1. 1098 applicants were on the 2017 waiting list; 713 were admitted. Applications are accepted on-line. **Transfer Students:** 24 transfer students enrolled in 2016-2017. Applicants must take either the SAT or ACT and have 1 full year of credit. An essay and 3 letters of recommendation are required. Student may transfer in the fall, closing date is March 1, notification date is mid-May, students must reply by late May. 18 of 36 credits required for the bachelor's degree must be completed at Yale. **International Students:** There are 555 international students enrolled. They must take the TOEFL with a minimum score of 600 on the paper-based TOEFL (PBT) or 100 on the Internet-based version (iBT). Students must either take the ELTS or Pearson test of English, the SAT and 2 SAT Subject tests, or the ACT with writing test.

ADMISSIONS: 7% of the 2017-2018 applicants were accepted. The SAT scores for the 2017-2018 freshman class were: Critical Reading-- 3% between 500 and 599, 17% between 600 and 699, and 80% between 700 and 800. Math-- 1% between 500 and 599, 17% between 600 and 699, and 82% between 700 and 800. Writing-- 2% between 500 and 599, 17% between 600 and 699, and 81% between 700 and 800. **Admissions Contact:** Margit A. Dahl, Director of Undergraduate Admissions. Email: *apply.questions@yale.edu* Web: *www.yale.edu*

FINANCIAL AID: 100% of all full-time freshmen received need-based aid. The average freshman award was $52,016. Need-based scholarships or need-based grants averaged $50,359; need-based self-help aid (loans and jobs) averaged $2,266; and other non-need-based awards and non-need-based scholarships averaged $2,272. 56% of undergraduate students work part-time. The average financial indebtedness of the 2017 graduate was $15,521. Yale is a member of CSS. The CSS/Profile, student and parent tax returns, CSS divorced/separated parents statement, and business/farm supplement (if appropriate) are required. The FAFSA code is 001426. The deadline for filing freshman financial aid applications for fall entry is March 1.

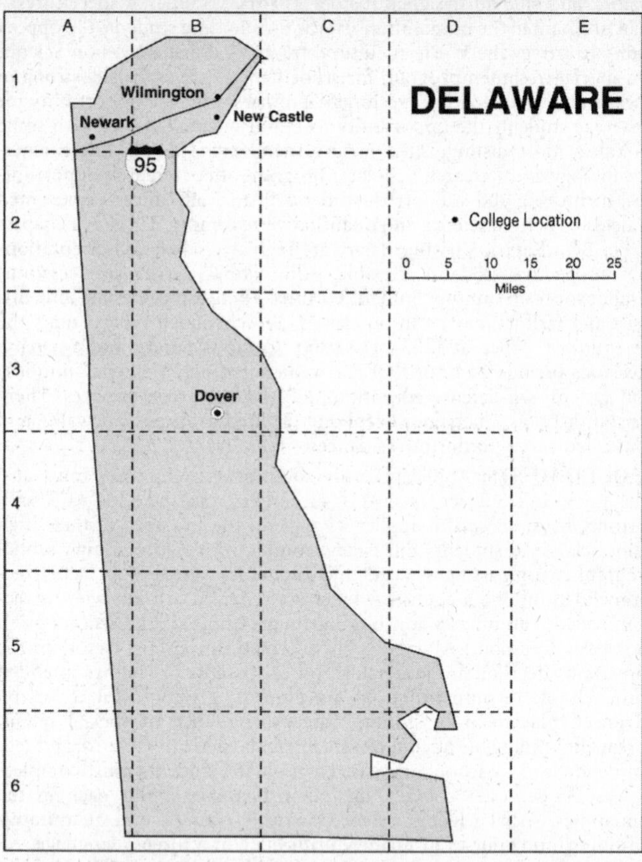

DELAWARE STATE UNIVERSITY *(The complete profile is made available exclusively on our website, www.barronspac.com)*

GOLDEY-BEACOM COLLEGE B-1

www.gbc.edu

Wilmington, DE 19808	**(302) 225-6248** **(800) 833-4877**
Fax: (302) 996-5408	**Email: admissions@gbc.edu**
Full-time: 208 men, 254 women	**Faculty:** 18
Part-time: 70 men, 93 women	**Ph.D.s:** 100%
Graduate: 458 men, 269 women	**Student/Faculty:** 24 to 1
Year: semesters, summer session	**Tuition:** $23,850
Room & Board: $12,188	**Freshman Class:** 717 applied, 385 accepted, 128 enrolled
SAT: required	**CEEB CODE:** 5255
Application Deadline: August 15	**COMPETITIVE**

Goldey-Beacom College, founded in 1886, is a private coeducational college offering programs in psychology, criminal justice, English, economics, and other areas of business. The figures in the above capsule and in this profile are approximate, which is based on 30 undergraduate credit hours. There is 1 undergraduate school and 1 graduate school. In addition to regional accreditation, Goldey-Beacom has baccalaureate program accreditation with ACBSP. The 24-acre campus is in a suburban area in the Pike Creek Valley suburb of Wilmington, Delaware. Including any residence halls, there are 6 buildings.

STUDENT LIFE: 67% of undergraduates are from Delaware. Others are from 19 states, 60 foreign countries, and Canada. 75% are from public schools. 5% are Asian American; 41% White; 4% Hispanic; 28% Foreign; 15% African American. **Male To Female Ratio:** 1.2:1. The average age of freshmen is 19; all undergraduates, 21. 24% do not continue beyond their first year; 62% remain to graduate. **Housing:** 271 students can be accommodated in college housing, which includes on-campus apartments, and special-interest houses. On-campus housing is guaranteed for all 4 years, is available on a first-come, and first-served basis. 64% of students commute. All students may keep cars.

FACULTY/CLASSROOMS: 59% of faculty are male; 41% are female. 89% teach undergraduates. No introductory courses are taught by graduate students. The average class size in an introductory lecture is 28 and in a regular course is 21.

PROGRAMS OF STUDY: Goldey-Beacom confers B.A. and B.S. degrees. Associate and master's degrees are also awarded. Bachelor's degrees are awarded in BUSINESS (accounting, banking and finance, business administration and management, human resources, international business management, management information systems, marketing management, and sports management), COMPUTER AND PHYSICAL SCIENCE (information sciences and systems), SOCIAL SCIENCE (economics and psychology). Accounting, economics, and finance are the strongest academically. Accounting, management, and business administration have the largest enrollments.

ACTIVITIES: There are no fraternities or sororities. There are 14 groups on campus, including computers, drama, ethnic, honors, international, newspaper, professional, religious, social service, and student government. Popular campus events include Spring Fest, Karaoke Night, Casino Night, and Homecoming. **Sports:** There are 4 intercollegiate sports for men and 6 for women. Facilities include soccer and softball fields, tennis and handball courts, a gym with basketball and volleyball courts, and a fitness center. **Graduates:** From July 1, 2016 to June 30, 2017, 119 bachelor's degrees were awarded. The most popular majors were business administration (63%), accounting (26%), and psychology (5%). In an average class, 41% graduate in 6 years or less. Of the 2016 graduating class, 45% were enrolled in graduate school within 6 months of graduation, and 90% were employed.

SERVICES: Counseling and information services are available, as is tutoring in most subjects. There is a reader service for the blind, and remedial math, reading, and writing, and computer-based tutorials. **Library/Resources:** The library contains 191,268 volumes, and 3,793 audio/video tapes/CDs/DVDs, and subscribes to 17,434 periodicals including electronic. Computerized library services include interlibrary loans, database searching, Internet access, and Wi-Fi capability. **Physically Challenged Students:** All of the campus is accessible. Facilities include wheelchair ramps, elevators, special parking, specially equipped restrooms, lowered drinking fountains, and lowered telephones. **Special:** A 5-year B.S/M.B.A degree, dual majors, internships, and work-study programs are available. There is 1 national honor society, a freshman honors program, and 1 departmental honors program. **Visiting:** There are regularly scheduled orientations for prospective students, a meeting with an admissions representative, and tour the campus. Open house is held on Saturdays, twice a year. There are guides for informal visits, visitors may sit in on classes, and stay overnight. To schedule a visit, contact the Admissions Office. **Campus Safety and Security:** Measures include 24-hour foot and vehicle patrol, emergency notification system, self-defense education, and security escort services. There are lighted pathways/sidewalks and controlled access to dorms/residences.

REQUIREMENTS: Applicants must be high school graduates or have a GED and submit their official high school transcripts and SAT scores. AP and CLEP credits are accepted. Important factors in the admissions decision are advanced placement or honors courses, extracurricular activities record, and recommendations by school officials. To graduate, students must complete a minimum of 136 credit hours with an overall GPA of 2.0. Students must also fulfill the college's degree requirements. **Procedure:** Freshmen are admitted to all sessions. There are early admissions, deferred admissions, and rolling admissions plans. Applications should be filed by August 15 for fall entry. Applications are accepted on-line. **Transfer Students:** 77 transfer students enrolled in 2016-2017. Transfer applicants must submit high school and college transcripts. 65 of 136 credits required for the bachelor's degree must be completed at Goldey-Beacom. **International Students:** There are 55 international students enrolled. They must take the TOEFL with a minimum score of 500 on the paper-based TOEFL (PBT) or 60 on the Internet-based version (iBT). Student must take the IELTS. They must also take the SAT or ACT.

ADMISSIONS: 54% of the 2017-2018 applicants were accepted. **Admissions Contact:** Larry Eby, Director of Admissions. Email: *admissions@gbc.edu* Web: *www.gbc.edu*

FINANCIAL AID: In 2017-2018, 100% of all full-time freshmen

received some form of financial aid. 99% of all full-time freshmen received need-based aid. 90% of undergraduate students work part-time. Goldey-Beacom is a member of CSS. The FAFSA code is 001429. The priority date for freshman financial aid applications for fall entry is April 1.

UNIVERSITY OF DELAWARE — A-1

www.udel.edu

Newark, DE 19716 — (302) 831-8123

Fax: (302) 831-8530	**Email:** admissions@udel.edu
Full-time: 7141 men, 9787 women	**Faculty:** 1198; I, +$
Part-time: 337 men, 404 women	**Ph.D.s:** 84%
Graduate: 1825 men, 1969 women	**Student/Faculty:** 13 to 1
Year: 4-1-4, summer session	**Tuition:** $12,830 ($32,250)
Room & Board: $19,384	**Freshman Class:** 24456 applied, 15879 accepted, 3952 enrolled
SAT CR/M/W: 595/600/590 **ACT:** 26	**CEEB CODE:** 5811
Application Deadline: January 15	**VERY COMPETITIVE**

University of Delaware, founded in 1743, was chartered in 1833, is a state-assisted, land-grant, sea-grant, space-grant, Carnegie Research University offering programs in agriculture and natural resources, arts and sciences, business and economics, engineering, health sciences, education and public policy. There are 7 undergraduate schools and 7 graduate schools. In addition to regional accreditation, UD has baccalaureate program accreditation with AACSB, ABET, ADA, APTA, CAHEA, NASM, CAEP, and NLN. The 969-acre campus is in a small town 12 miles southwest of Wilmington. Including any residence halls, there are 347 buildings.

STUDENT LIFE: 62% of undergraduates are from out of state, mostly the Middle Atlantic. Students are from 47 states, 77 foreign countries, and Canada. 8% are Hispanic; 73% White; 5% African American; 5% Asian American; 4% Foreign; 3% two or more races. 36% are Catholic; 26% claim no religious affiliation. **Female To Male Ratio:** 1.3:1. The average age of freshmen is 18; all undergraduates, 20. 10% do not continue beyond their first year; 80% remain to graduate. **Housing:** College-sponsored housing includes married student dorms and on-campus apartments. In addition, there are honors houses, special-interest houses, fraternity houses, sorority houses, alcohol/smoke-free residence halls, women's dorms, gender-neutral, executive apartments in traditional residence halls, and living learning communities. On-campus housing is guaranteed for all 4 years. 60% of students commute. All students may keep cars.

FACULTY/CLASSROOMS: 61% of faculty are male; 39% are female. All teach undergraduates. No introductory courses are taught by graduate students. The average class size in a laboratory is 18 and in a regular course is 35.

PROGRAMS OF STUDY: UD confers B.A., B.S., B.A.E.S., B.A. Liberal Studies, B.C.E., B.Ch.E., B.C.P.E., B.E.E., B.En.E., B.F.A., B.M.E., B.Mus., B.R.N., B.S.Ed., and B.S.N. degrees. Associate, master's, and doctoral degrees are also awarded. Bachelor's degrees are awarded in AGRICULTURE (agricultural business management, agricultural economics, agriculture, animal science, natural resource management, plant science, soil science, and wildlife management), BIOLOGICAL SCIENCE (biochemistry, biology/biological science, biotechnology, entomology, nutrition, and plant pathology), BUSINESS (accounting, banking and finance, business administration and management, hotel/motel and restaurant management, management information systems, management science, marketing/retailing/merchandising, operations management, organizational leadership and management, and sports management), COMMUNICATIONS AND THE ARTS (apparel design, applied music, art, art history and appreciation, communications, comparative literature, English, fine arts, historic preservation, Italian, journalism, languages, music, music theory and composition, theater management, and visual design), COMPUTER AND PHYSICAL SCIENCE (astronomy, chemistry, computer science, geology, information sciences and systems, mathematics, physics, and statistics), EDUCATION (athletic training, early childhood education, education, elementary education, English education, foreign languages education, mathematics education, music education, physical education, psychology education, science education, secondary education, and special education), ENGINEERING AND ENVIRONMENTAL DESIGN (bioengineering, chemical engineering, civil engineering, computer engineering, electrical/electronics engineering, engineering, engineering technology, environmental engineering, environmental science, landscape architecture/design, and mechanical engineering), HEALTH PROFESSIONS (health, health science, medical laboratory technology, and nursing), SOCIAL SCIENCE (anthropology, criminal justice, dietetics, East Asian studies, economics, European studies, family and community services, fashion design and technology, food production/management/services, food science, geography, history, human development, human services, interdisciplinary studies, international relations, Latin American studies, liberal arts/general studies, philosophy, political science/government, psychology, sociology, and women's studies). Biological sciences, psychology, and nursing have the largest enrollments.

ACTIVITIES: 18% of men belong to 20 national fraternities; 23% of women belong to 15 national sororities. Groups on campus include art, band, cheerleading, chess, choir, chorale, chorus, computers, dance, debate, drama, drill team, drum and bugle corps, environmental, ethnic, film, honors, international, jazz band, LGBT, literary magazine, marching band, musical theater, newspaper, opera, orchestra, pep band, political, professional, radio and TV, religious, social service, student government, and symphony. Popular campus events include Greek Week, Convocation, and Commencement. **Sports:** There are 11 intercollegiate sports for men and 12 for women, and 32 intramural sports for men and 32 for women. Facilities include a football stadium, multipurpose gyms, multipurpose fields, outdoor basketball courts, squash court, racquetball courts, tennis courts, indoor and outdoor pools, a universal weight room, basketball arena, a rock-climbing wall, high-ropes challenge course, a student fitness centers, ice arenas, and an outdoor hockey rink. **Graduates:** From July 1, 2016 to June 30, 2017, 4085 bachelor's degrees were awarded. The most popular majors were business/marketing (16%), health professions and related programs (15%), and social science (15%). Of the 2016 graduating class, 15% were enrolled in graduate school within 6 months of graduation, and 75% were employed.

SERVICES: Counseling and information services are available, as is tutoring in every subject. There is a reader service for the blind, and remedial math, reading, and writing. There is also a writing center, a math center, an academic services center for assistance with academic self-management development, critical thinking, and problem solving, as well as individual assistance for learning-disabled students. **Library/Resources:** The library contains 2.8 million volumes, 3.4 million microform items, and 600,000 audio/video tapes/CDs/DVDs, and subscribes to 30,000 periodicals including electronic. Computerized library services include interlibrary loans, database searching, Internet access, and Wi-Fi capability. Special learning facilities include an art gallery, radio station, TV station, a preschool lab, development ice skating science center, computer-controlled greenhouse, nursing practice labs, physical therapy clinic, agricultural research complex, exercise physiology biomechanics labs, foreign language media center, and composite materials center. **Physically Challenged Students:** 95% of the campus is accessible. Facilities include wheelchair ramps, elevators, special parking, specially equipped restrooms, special class scheduling, lowered drinking fountains, lowered telephones, and special housing. **Special:** Students may participate in cooperative programs, internships, study abroad in 55 countries, a Washington semester, and work-study programs. The university offers accelerated degree programs, B.A.and B.S. degrees, dual majors, minors, student-designed majors (Bachelor of Arts in Liberal Studies), and pass/fail options. There are 4-1 degree programs in engineering, and hotel and restaurant management. A non-degree study is available through the Division of Continuing Education. There is an extensive undergraduate research program. Students may earn an enriched degree through the University Honors Program. There are 35 national honor societies, Phi Beta Kappa, and a freshman honors program. **Visiting:** There are regularly scheduled orientations for prospective students, consisting of a 40-minute admissions information session and a 90-minute walking tour of campus. There are guides for informal visits and visitors may sit in on classes. To schedule a visit, contact the Admissions Office. **Campus Safety and Security:** Measures include 24-hour foot and vehicle patrol, emergency notification system, self-defense education, and security escort services. There are shuttle buses, emergency telephones, lighted pathways/sidewalks, controlled access to dorms/residences, ongoing student-awareness programs in the residence halls, community policing, and keycard access to residence halls.

REQUIREMENTS: The SAT or ACT is required. The ACT Optional

Writing test is also required. Applicants should be graduates of an accredited secondary school. The GED is accepted. Students should have completed a minimum of 18 high school academic units, 4 units in English, 3 units each in math, and science with 2 lab units, 2 units each in foreign language, history, social studies, and academic course electives. SAT Subject Tests are recommended, especially for honors program applicants. A writing sample and at least 1 letter of recommendation are required. AP credits are accepted. Important factors in the admissions decision are advanced placement or honors courses, leadership record, evidence of special talent, personality/intangible qualities, extracurricular activities record, and recommendations by school officials. For graduation, students must complete at least 120 credits with a minimum GPA of 2.0. All students must take freshman English and 3 credits of coursework with multicultural, ethnic, and/or gender-related content. Most majors require more than 120 credits. Most degree programs require that half of the courses be in the major field of study. Students must also have 1 incoming semester of First Year Experience (FYE) and 3 credits of Discovery Learning Experience (DLE). **Procedure:** Freshmen are admitted fall and spring. Entrance exams should be taken by the junior year or the beginning of the senior year. There are early admissions and deferred admissions plans. Applications should be filed by January 15 for fall entry; December 15 for spring entry. The fall 2017 application fee was $75. Notifications are sent November 1. Applications are accepted on-line. **Transfer Students:** 393 transfer students enrolled in 2016-2017. Applicants for transfer should have completed at least 24 credits with a minimum GPA of 2.5 for most majors. Some majors require a GPA of 3.0 or better and/or specific coursework. All transfer students must submit high school and college transcripts, an essay, and a statement of good standing from their prior institution. In some cases, an interview and standardized test scores are required. 30 of 120 credits required for the bachelor's degree must be completed at Delaware. **International Students:** There are 716 international students enrolled. They must take the TOEFL with a minimum score of 550 on the paper-based TOEFL (PBT) or 80 on the Internet-based version (iBT), and take the IELTS. They must also take the SAT.

ADMISSIONS: 65% of the 2017-2018 applicants were accepted. The SAT scores for the 2017-2018 freshman class were: Critical Reading-- 8% below 500, 43% between 500 and 599, 35% between 600 and 699, and 14% between 700 and 800. Math-- 7% below 500, 37% between 500 and 599, 44% between 600 and 699, and 12% between 700 and 800. Writing-- 11% below 500, 46% between 500 and 599, 36% between 600 and 699, and 7% between 700 and 800. The ACT scores were 3% between 12 and 17, 26% between 18 and 23, 51% between 24 and 29, and 20% above 30. 97 freshmen graduated first in their class. **Admissions Contact:** Dr. Heather Kelly, Director of Institutional Research. Email: *admissions@udel.edu* Web: *www.udel.edu*

FINANCIAL AID: In 2017-2018, 62% of all full-time freshmen received some form of financial aid. 62% of all full-time freshmen received need-based aid. The average freshman award was $13,812. Need-based scholarships or need-based grants averaged $10,142; need-based self-help aid (loans and jobs) averaged $3,566; non-need-based athletic scholarships averaged $13,553; other non-need-based awards and non-need-based scholarships averaged $3,566; and $3,674 from other forms of aid. The average financial indebtedness of the 2017 graduate was $41,452. The FAFSA code is 001431. The priority date for freshman financial aid applications for fall entry is January 15. The deadline for filing freshman financial aid applications for fall entry is March 15.

WESLEY COLLEGE *(The complete profile is made available exclusively on our website, www.barronspac.com)*

WILMINGTON UNIVERSITY *(The complete profile is made available exclusively on our website, www.barronspac.com)*

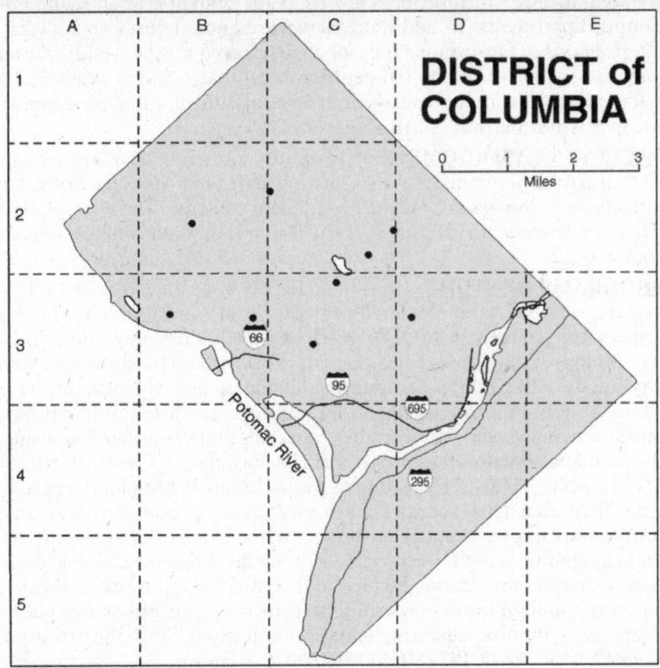

GALLAUDET UNIVERSITY *(The complete profile is made available exclusively on our website, www.barronspac.com)*

GEORGETOWN UNIVERSITY B-3

www.georgetown.edu

Washington, DC 20057 **(202) 687-3600**

Fax: (202) 687-5084
Email: guadmiss@georgetown.edu
Full-time: 3074 men, 3876 women
Faculty: 1017; I, +$
Part-time: 86 men, 88 women
Ph.D.s: 89%
Graduate: 5424 men, 6118 women
Student/Faculty: 11 to 1
Year: semesters, summer session
Tuition: $52,300
Room & Board: $16,670
Freshman Class: 19997 applied, 3369 accepted, 1574 enrolled
SAT CR/M: 710/710 **ACT:** 32
CEEB CODE: 5422
Application Deadline: January 10
MOST COMPETITIVE

Georgetown University, founded in 1789, is a private institution affiliated with the Roman Catholic Church and offers programs in arts and sciences, business administration, foreign service, languages and linguistics, and nursing. The tuition figures in the above capsule are for the Georgetown Undergraduate COL, MSB, and SFS schools. Tuition cost varies for undergraduate NHS and BALS schools. There are 4 undergraduate schools and 3 graduate schools. In addition to regional accreditation, Georgetown has baccalaureate program accreditation with AACSB and CCNE. The 104-acre campus is in an urban area 1.5 miles northwest of downtown Washington D.C. Including any residence halls, there are 64 buildings.

STUDENT LIFE: 99% of undergraduates are from out of state, mostly the Middle Atlantic. Students are from 50 states, 91 foreign countries, and Canada. 46% are from public schools. 6% are African American; 54% White; 5% two or more races; 2% race unknown; 13% Foreign; 10% Asian American; 10% Hispanic. 42% are Catholic; 21% Protestant. **Female To Male Ratio:** 1.2:1. The average age of freshmen is 18; all undergraduates, 21. 4% do not continue beyond their first year; 94% remain to graduate. **Housing:** 5053 students can be accommodated in college housing, which includes dorms and on-campus apartments, wellness housing, and special interest floors. On-campus housing is available on a lottery system for upperclassmen. No one may keep cars.

FACULTY/CLASSROOMS: All teach undergraduates, and all do research. No introductory courses are taught by graduate students.

PROGRAMS OF STUDY: Georgetown confers A.B., B.S., B.A.L.S., B.S.B.A., B.S.F.S., and B.S.N. degrees. Master's and doctoral degrees are also awarded. Bachelor's degrees are awarded in BIOLOGICAL SCIENCE (biochemistry, biology/biological science, and environmental biology), BUSINESS (accounting, banking and finance, business administration and management, finance, international business management, and marketing/retailing/merchandising), COMMUNICATIONS AND THE ARTS (Arabic, art history, art, Chinese, classics, comparative literature, English, fine arts, French, German, Italian, Japanese, linguistics, Portuguese, Russian, and Spanish), COMPUTER AND PHYSICAL SCIENCE (chemistry, computer science, mathematics, and physics), HEALTH PROFESSIONS (health and nursing), SOCIAL SCIENCE (American studies, anthropology, economics, history, interdisciplinary studies, international relations, philosophy, political science/government, psychology, religion, and sociology). International politics, government, and have the largest enrollments.

ACTIVITIES: There are no fraternities or sororities. There are 171 groups on campus, including art, band, cheerleading, chess, choir, chorale, chorus, computers, dance, debate, drama, ethnic, film, honors, international, jazz band, LGBT, literary magazine, musical theater, newspaper, orchestra, pep band, photography, political, professional, radio and TV, religious, social, social service, student government, symphony, and yearbook. Popular campus events include GU Day, Career Week, and Senior Salute. **Sports:** There are 11 intercollegiate sports for men and 12 for women. Facilities include a gym for basketball and volleyball, a sports medicine and training room, a multi-sport field for football and lacrosse, and a sports and recreation facility that houses a swimming pool, basketball courts, aerobics rooms, a weight area, cardiovascular equipment, a wellness center, and racquetball courts. **Graduates:** From July 1, 2016 to June 30, 2017, 1827 bachelor's degrees were awarded. The most popular majors were social science (34%), history (26%), and interdisciplinary studies (6%).

SERVICES: Counseling and information services are available, as is tutoring in some subjects, such as accounting, finance, biological sciences, math, Spanish, French and Arabic. There is a reader service for the blind. **Library/Resources:** The library contains 3.0 million volumes, 4.0 million microform items, and 54,513 audio/video tapes/CDs/DVDs, and subscribes to 61,257 periodicals including electronic. Computerized library services include interlibrary loans, database searching, Internet access, and Wi-Fi capability. Special learning facilities include an art gallery, planetarium, radio station, and TV station. **Physically Challenged Students:** 94% of the campus is accessible. Facilities include wheelchair ramps, elevators, special parking, specially equipped restrooms, special class scheduling, lowered drinking fountains, lowered telephones, and special housing. There is a special map of the campus with accessibility routes, a tactile map of the campus for visually disabled students, and a paratransit vehicle for mobility on the main campus. **Special:** Cross-registration is available with a consortium of universities in the Washington metropolitan area. Opportunities are provided for internships, study abroad in 30 countries, work-study programs, student-designed majors, and dual majors. A liberal studies degree, B.A. and B.S. degrees, non-degree study, credit by examination, and pass/fail options are also offered. There is a chapter of Phi Beta Kappa and a freshman honors program. **Visiting:** There are regularly scheduled orientations for prospective students, throughout the year, including a question and answer period led by an admissions officer, followed by a campus tour led by a student guide. There are guides for informal visits and visitors may sit in on classes. To schedule a visit, contact the Office of Undergraduate Admissions. **Campus Safety and Security:** Measures include 24-hour foot and vehicle patrol, emergency notification system, and security escort services. There are shuttle buses, emergency telephones, lighted pathways/sidewalks, controlled access to dorms/residences, laptop computer registration, bicycle registration, and off-campus security assessments.

REQUIREMENTS: The SAT or ACT is required. Graduation from an accredited secondary school is required, including 4 years of English, a minimum of 2 each of a foreign language, math, and social studies, history, and 1 of natural science. An additional 2 years each of math and science is required for students intending to major in math, science, nursing, or business. SAT subject tests are strongly recommended. AP credits are accepted. Important factors in the admissions decision are leadership record, evidence of special talent, personality/intangible qualities, recommendations by school officials, and extracurricular activities record. Students must complete 120 credits and maintain a minimum

GPA of 2.0. A core of liberal arts courses is required, consisting of 2 courses each in philosophy and theology. Additional requirements are specific to undergraduate school as well as major concentration. **Procedure:** Freshmen are admitted in the fall. Entrance exams should be taken in the junior year and again at the beginning of the senior year. There is a deferred admissions plan. Applications should be filed by January 10 for fall entry. The fall 2017 application fee was $65. Notifications are sent April 1. 1334 applicants were on the 2017 waiting list; 80 were admitted. Applications are accepted on-line. **Transfer Students:** 161 transfer students enrolled in 2016-2017. Transfer students must have successfully completed a minimum of 12 credit hours with a minimum GPA of 3.0. Either the SAT or the ACT is required. An interview is recommended. Transfers must complete their last 2 years at Georgetown. 60 of 120 credits required for the bachelor's degree must be completed at Georgetown. **International Students:** There are 781 international students enrolled. They must take the TOEFL.

ADMISSIONS: 17% of the 2017-2018 applicants were accepted. The SAT scores for the 2017-2018 freshman class were: Critical Reading-- 9% between 500 and 599, 31% between 600 and 699, and 60% between 700 and 800. Math-- 7% between 500 and 599, 35% between 600 and 699, and 57% between 700 and 800. The ACT scores were 2% between 18 and 23, 20% between 24 and 29, and 78% above 30. **Admissions Contact:** Charles A. Deacon, Dean of Admissions. Email: *guadmiss@georgetown.edu* Web: *www.georgetown.edu*

FINANCIAL AID: In 2017-2018, 100% of all full-time freshmen received some form of financial aid. The average freshman award was $48,620. Need-based scholarships or need-based grants averaged $41,492; need-based self-help aid (loans and jobs) averaged $4,454; non-need-based athletic scholarships averaged $20,133; and $2,723 from other forms of aid. The average financial indebtedness of the 2017 graduate was $23,412. Georgetown is a member of CSS. The CSS/Profile, and non-custodial profile, business/farm supplement, and tax returns are required. The FAFSA code is 001445. The priority date for freshman financial aid applications for fall entry is February 1.

HOWARD UNIVERSITY — C-3

www.howard.edu

Washington, DC 20059	**(202) 806-2864** **(800) 822-6363**
Fax: (202) 806-2818	**Email: dkindle@howard.edu**
Full-time: 2071 men, 4341 women	**Faculty:** 746; I, --$
Part-time: 171 men, 300 women	**Ph.D.s:** 73%
Graduate: 1230 men, 1889 women	**Student/Faculty:** 8 to 1
Year: semesters, summer session	**Tuition:** $23,970
Room & Board: $13,646	**Freshman Class:** n/av
SAT or ACT: required	**CEEB CODE:** 5297
Application Deadline: February 15	**COMPETITIVE+**

Howard University, founded in 1867, is the largest predominantly Black university in the United States. As a culturally diverse, comprehensive, nonsectarian, research intensive, and historically Black private university, Howard University provides an educational experience of exceptional quality at the undergraduate, graduate, and professional levels to students of high academic standing and potential, with particular emphasis upon educational opportunities for Black students. With an abiding interest in both domestic and international affairs, the university is committed to continuing to produce leaders for America and the global community. There are 6 undergraduate schools and 12 graduate schools. In addition to regional accreditation, Howard University has baccalaureate program accreditation with AACSB, ABET, ACEJMC, ACPE, ADA, APTA, CSWE, NAAB, NASAD, NASDTEC, NASM, CAEP, ABA, ATS, APA, CCNE, ARL, NAEYC, NCSS, LCME JRCERT, NAACLS, MLA, AALL, ASLHA, ACEI, NASP, ACOTE, CADE, AAHPERD, ACS, NAST, NASPE, CEC, AALS, ARCPA, and AUPHA. The 258-acre campus is in an urban area in Northwest Washington, D.C. Including any residence halls, there are 127 buildings.

STUDENT LIFE: 96% of undergraduates are from out of state, mostly the Middle Atlantic. Students are from 45 states, 38 foreign countries, and Canada. 87% are African American; 5% Foreign; 3% White; 2% Asian American; 2% Hispanic; 1% American Indian/Alaska Native. **Female To Male Ratio:** 1.9:1. The average age of freshmen is 18; all undergraduates, 21. 17% do not continue beyond their first year; 83% remain to graduate. **Housing:** 5748 students can be accommodated in college housing, which includes dorms, on-campus apartments, and off-campus apartments. In addition, there are honors houses and special-interest houses. On-campus housing is guaranteed for the freshman year only, is available on a first-come, first-served basis, and is available on a lottery system for upperclassmen. 56% of students live on campus. Alcohol is not permitted. All students may keep cars.

FACULTY/CLASSROOMS: 55% of faculty are male; 45% are female. 65% teach undergraduates, 35% do research, and 40% do both. No introductory courses are taught by graduate students. The average class size in an introductory lecture is 35; in a laboratory is 20; and in a regular course is 20.

PROGRAMS OF STUDY: Howard confers B.B.A., B.A., B.S. and B.F.A. degrees. Master's and doctoral degrees are also awarded. Bachelor's degrees are awarded in BIOLOGICAL SCIENCE (anatomy, biochemistry, biology/biological science, genetics, microbiology, nutrition, and physiology), BUSINESS (accounting, banking and finance, business administration and management, fashion merchandising, international business management, labor studies, marketing/retailing/merchandising, sports management, and supply chain management), COMMUNICATIONS AND THE ARTS (acting, advertising, art history and appreciation, broadcasting, ceramic art and design, communications, communication science, dance, design, dramatic arts, English, film arts, French, graphic design, jazz, journalism, media arts, music, music business management, music history and appreciation, musical theater, painting, photography, playwriting/screenwriting, printmaking, public relations, sculpture, Spanish, telecommunications, and theatre arts), COMPUTER AND PHYSICAL SCIENCE (atmospheric sciences and meteorology, chemistry, computer engineering technology, computer science, mathematics, physics, and radiological technology), EDUCATION (art education, early childhood education, education, education administration, elementary education, health education, music education, physical education, reading education, school psychology, and secondary education), ENGINEERING AND ENVIRONMENTAL DESIGN (architecture, chemical engineering, civil engineering, computer engineering, electrical/electronics engineering, environmental science, interior design, and mechanical engineering), HEALTH PROFESSIONS (allied health, clinical science, community health work, dental hygiene, health care administration, health science, music therapy, nursing, occupational therapy, pharmaceutical science, pharmacology, pharmacy, physical therapy, physician's assistant, predentistry, premedicine, public health, radiation therapy, radiograph medical technology, speech pathology/audiology, and sports medicine), SOCIAL SCIENCE (African studies, African American studies, anthropology, child psychology/development, classical/ancient civilization, counseling/psychology, criminal justice, economics, fashion design and technology, geography, history, human development, interdisciplinary studies, law, legal studies, philosophy, political science/government, psychology, public administration, public affairs, religion, social work, sociology, Spanish studies, textiles and clothing, urban studies, and women's studies). Chemical engineering, computer engineering, and physics are the strongest academically. Biology, psychology, and political science have the largest enrollments.

ACTIVITIES: 3% of men belong to 10 local fraternities; 5% of women belong to 8 local sororities. There are 155 groups on campus, including entertainment industry clubs, programming boards (residence halls and activities), residence hall councils, step teams, youth/peer mentorship, art, band, cheerleading, chess, choir, chorus, communications, community service, computers, dance, debate, drama, drill team, drum and bugle corps, environmental, ethnic, film, honors, international, jazz band, LGBT, marching band, musical theater, newspaper, opera, orchestra, pep band, photography, political, professional, radio and TV, religious, social, social service, student government, symphony, and yearbook. Popular campus events include Orientation, Freshman Welcome Pep Rally and Pinning Ceremony, Opening Convocation, Charter Day Dinner, Global Community Week, Howard Homecoming, Spring Black Arts Festival (Springfest), MLK Day of Service, and Student Leadership Conference. **Sports:** There are 8 intercollegiate sports for men and 10 for women, and 6 intramural sports for men and 5 for women. Facilities include an outdoor track, fields for football, soccer, and lacrosse, a gymnasium for basketball, a swimming pool, indoor track, a weight room, and cardio fitness center. The recreational center has a bowling alley, a pool, and several practice fields. **Graduates:** From July 1, 2016 to June 30, 2017, 2045 bachelor's degrees were awarded. The most popular majors were biology health professions and related programs (22%), business, management, marketing, and related support services (18%), communication, journalism, and related programs (16%). In an average class, 49% graduate in 4 years or less, 62% graduate in 5 years or less, and 61% graduate in 6 years or less. Of the 2016 graduating class, 54% were enrolled in graduate school within 6 months of graduation, and 65% were employed.

SERVICES: Counseling and information services are available, as is tutoring in most subjects. There is a reader service for the blind, and remedial math, reading, and writing. Tutoring is also available for the following subjects: humanities, research, mathematics, foreign languages, English, science, psychology, statistics. **Library/Resources:** The library contains 2.5 million volumes, 4.2 million microform items, and 194,000 audio/video tapes/CDs/DVDs, and subscribes to 82,758 periodicals including electronic. Computerized library services include interlibrary loans, database searching, Internet access, and Wi-Fi capability. Special learning facilities include an art gallery, radio station, TV station, a history and culture research center, an international center, and a reading room. **Physically Challenged Students:** All of the campus is accessible. Facilities include wheelchair ramps, elevators, special parking, specially equipped restrooms, special class scheduling, lowered drinking fountains, lowered telephones, and special housing. **Special:** Cross-registration is available with the Consortium of Universities in the Washington Metropolitan Area. Opportunities are also provided for internships, work-study, co-op programs, study abroad in 5 countries including Europe and Africa, B.A.-B.S. degrees in engineering and business, student-designed majors, pass/fail options, and accelerated degree programs in medicine and dentistry. There are 20 national honor societies, Phi Beta Kappa, and a freshman honors program. **Visiting:** There are regularly scheduled orientations for prospective students, consisting of a verbal presentation by an admission staff member, followed by a walking guided tour. There are guides for informal visits and visitors may sit in on classes. To schedule a visit, contact the Office of Admissions at (202) 806-2755. **Campus Safety and Security:** Measures include 24-hour foot and vehicle patrol, emergency notification system, self-defense education, and security escort services. There are shuttle buses, emergency telephones, lighted pathways/sidewalks, controlled access to dorms/residences, biweekly checks of calls for service and response time, blue light emergency system, fingerprinting services, town-hall meetings, and a crime prevention program.

REQUIREMENTS: Evaluation of an applicant's qualifications for admission is based on high school coursework, GPA, class rank, test scores, extracurricular activities and letters of recommendation. An essay, audition, portfolio, or interview also may be required. Academic Eligibility; we consider the applicant's secondary school academic record, standardized college entrance exams (SAT or ACT), leadership in school and community activities, unique talents and skills, and educational objectives. For admission consideration, an applicant should have a well-balanced college preparatory program that includes the following course work; 4 years English, 3 years mathematics, 2 years each of social science, science (with lab), and foreign language. A complete application package includes the following credentials; Application for Admission, official high school transcript or GED certificate, SAT or ACT scores, one letter of recommendation from a high school counselor, Guidance Counselor Recommendation Form, one letter of recommendation from a high school teacher, Teacher Recommendation Form, an admission essay, and a resume (optional). A GPA of 3.0 is required. AP and CLEP credits are accepted. Important factors in the admissions decision are leadership record, advanced placement or honors courses, and extracurricular activities record. To graduate, students must complete a total of 120 semester hours, exclusive of courses taken through the Center for Academic Reinforcement (CAR), maintain grades of C or better in all courses used to satisfy the minimum credit-hour requirement for departmental majors, maintain grades higher than C for courses used to satisfy requirements for departmental majors in any department stipulating this requirement, and maintain a cumulative GPA of 2.0 or better in departmental majors, as well as in the minor fields of concentration. **Procedure:** Freshmen are admitted fall, spring, and summer. Entrance exams should be taken by January of senior year. There are early decision, deferred admissions, and rolling admissions plans. Early decision applications should be filed by November 1; regular applications, by February 15 for fall entry; November 1 for spring entry; and April 1 for summer entry. The fall 2017 application fee was $45. Notification of early decision is sent December 20; regular decision, January 15. 636 early decision candidates were accepted for the 2017-2018 class. Applications are accepted on-line. **Transfer Students:** 317 transfer students enrolled in 2016-2017. Admission criteria vary among Howard University's schools and colleges. As a transfer applicant, you must meet the following minimum requirements for admission consideration: 15 transferrable credit hours (30 credit hours for the School of Business) from a regionally accredited postsecondary institution, earned a 2.5 cumulative GPA (3.0 GPA for the School of Business) and received a passing grade of C or better in both a college-level English and college-level math course. additional credentials such as a high school transcript and SAT scores may be requested for admission. 30 of 120 credits required for the bachelor's degree must be completed at Howard. **International Students:** There are 292 international students enrolled. They must take the TOEFL with a minimum score of 550 on the paper-based TOEFL (PBT) or 79 on the Internet-based version (iBT). If TOEFL is not offered in your country, applicants may submit results from IELTS (International English Language). They must also take the SAT or ACT.

ADMISSIONS: 55% of the current freshmen were in the top fifth of their class; 81% were in the top two fifths. **Admissions Contact:** Derek Kindle, Director of Student Financial Services. Email: *dkindle@howard.edu* Web: *www.howard.edu*

FINANCIAL AID: In 2017-2018, 93% of all full-time freshmen received some form of financial aid. 50% of all full-time freshmen received need-based aid. The average freshman award was $17,752. Need-based scholarships or need-based grants averaged $5,729 ($15,188 maximum); need-based self-help aid (loans and jobs) averaged $3,699 ($5,000 maximum); non-need-based athletic scholarships averaged $23,128 ($23,970 maximum); and other non-need-based awards and non-need-based scholarships averaged $27,266 ($41,983 maximum). 10% of undergraduate students work part-time. The average financial indebtedness of the 2017 graduate was $32,071. The FAFSA code is 001448. The priority date for freshman financial aid applications for fall entry is February 1.

THE AMERICAN UNIVERSITY — A-2

www.american.edu

Washington, DC 20016	(202) 885-6000
Fax: (202) 885-1025	**Email:** admissions@american.edu
Full-time: 2928 men, 4836 women	**Faculty:** I, av$
Part-time: 166 men, 193 women	**Ph.D.s:** n/av
Graduate: 2215 men, 3520 women	**Student/Faculty:** n/av
Year: semesters, summer session	**Tuition:** $46,615
Room & Board: $14,702	**Freshman Class:** 18699 applied, 5498 accepted, 1785 enrolled
SAT CR/M/W: 646/616/608 **ACT:** 28	**CEEB CODE:** 5007
Application Deadline: January 15	**HIGHLY COMPETITIVE**

The American University offers five schools for degree-seeking undergraduate study: the School of Public Affairs, the School of International Service, the Kogod School of Business, the School of Communication, the School of Education and the College of Arts and Sciences, the university's liberal arts core and home to distinguished artists and writers, scientists, and presidential and judicial historians. Students may elect to double major, pursue an interdisciplinary program or one of three 3-year bachelor programs, participate in living learning communities and take advantage of AU's extensive study abroad opportunities. In addition to regional accreditation, AU has baccalaureate program accreditation with AACSB, ACEJMC, NASDTEC, NASM, CAEP, NASPAA, and APA. The 84-acre campus is in a suburban area 5 miles northwest of downtown Washington D.C. Including any residence halls, there are 60 buildings.

STUDENT LIFE: 82% of undergraduates are from out of state, mostly the Middle Atlantic. Students are from 50 states, 116 foreign countries, and Canada. 7% are African American; 7% Asian American; 54% White; 4% two or more races; 4% race unknown; 13% Hispanic; 11% Foreign. **Female To Male Ratio:** 1.6:1. The average age of freshmen is 18; all undergraduates, 20. 10% do not continue beyond their first year; 79% remain to graduate. **Housing:** 4283 students can be accommodated in college housing, which includes dorms and off-campus apartments. In addition, there are honors houses, special-interest houses, living learning communities, and community service housing. On-campus housing is guaranteed for the freshman year only, is available on a first-come, and first-served basis. Alcohol is not permitted. Upperclassmen may keep cars.

FACULTY/CLASSROOMS: No introductory courses are taught by graduate students.

PROGRAMS OF STUDY: AU confers B.A., B.F.A., B.S., and B.S.B.A. degrees. Master's, and doctoral degrees are also awarded. Bachelor's degrees are awarded in AGRICULTURE (environmental studies), BIOLOGICAL SCIENCE (biochemistry, biology/biological science, and neurosciences), BUSINESS (business administration and management and international business management), COMMUNICATIONS AND THE ARTS (American literature, Arabic, art, art history and appreciation, audio technology, Chinese, communication studies, communications, creative writing, dramatic arts, film arts, fine arts, French, German, graphic design, Hebrew, Italian, Japanese, journalism, Korean, literature, multimedia, music, musical theater, performing arts, public relations, Russian, Spanish, strategic communication, and studio art), COMPUTER AND PHYSICAL SCIENCE (applied mathematics, chemistry, computer science, mathematics, physics, and statistics), EDUCATION (elementary education, foreign languages education, health education, and secondary education), ENGINEERING AND ENVIRONMENTAL DESIGN (computational sciences and environmental science), HEALTH PROFESSIONS (health promotion and public health), SOCIAL SCIENCE (American studies, anthropology, area studies, criminal justice, economics, government, French studies, gender studies, German area studies, history, interdisciplinary studies, international studies, Judaic studies, Latin American studies, philosophy, political science/government, psychology, religious studies, Russian and Slavic studies, sociology, Spanish studies, and women's studies). International studies, business administration, and political science have the largest enrollments.

ACTIVITIES: There are 200 groups on campus, including art, band, cheerleading, chess, choir, chorale, chorus, computers, dance, debate, drama, environmental, ethnic, film, honors, international, jazz band, LGBT, literary magazine, musical theater, newspaper, opera, orchestra, pep band, photography, political, professional, radio and TV, religious, social, social service, student government, symphony, and yearbook. Popular campus events include Family Weekend, Founders Day Ball, and Campus Beautification Day. **Sports:** There are 6 intercollegiate sports for men and 8 for women. Facilities include a sports arena, swimming pools, hockey and soccer fields, a softball diamond, an all-purpose field, cardiovascular and strength training equipment, weight rooms, courts for tennis, basketball, and volleyball, an aerobics studio, an indoor jogging track, an outdoor 6-lane tartan track, and fitness centers. **Graduates:** From July 1, 2016 to June 30, 2017, 1734 bachelor's degrees were awarded. The most popular majors were international studies (25%), business administration (13%), and political science (7%). In an average class, 7% graduate in 3 years or less, 75% graduate in 4 years or less, 78% graduate in 5 years or less, and 78% graduate in 6 years or less.

SERVICES: Counseling and information services are available, as is tutoring in every subject. There is a reader service for the blind, and remedial math, reading, and writing. Academic Support and Access Center is available to help students develop the tools needed for college success. In addition, a math and statistics tutoring lab, a writing center, and a foreign language resource center are available. **Library/Resources:** The library contains 1,000,000 volumes, 1.1 million microform items, and 66,000 audio/video tapes/CDs/DVDs, and subscribes to 125,650 periodicals including electronic. Computerized library services include interlibrary loans, database searching, Internet access, and Wi-Fi capability. Special learning facilities include an art gallery, radio station, TV station, American University's Washington College of law library, a music library, a language resource center, multimedia design and development labs, science and computer science labs, and well-equipped buildings for art and the performing arts, and National Public Radio station (WAMU 88.5FM). The American University Game Lab serves as a hub for experiential education, persuasive play research, and innovative production in the fields of games for change and rhetorical play. Part of a university-wide commitment to high-impact research, this multidisciplinary initiative combines the expertise of the School of Communication and the College of Arts and Sciences. AU's Kreeger Building is the site of the Audio Technology Program recording studios. **Physically Challenged Students:** 95% of the campus is accessible. Facilities include wheelchair ramps, elevators, special parking, specially equipped restrooms, special class scheduling, lowered drinking fountains, lowered telephones, and special housing. The Academic Support and Access Center is committed to providing access for individuals with disabilities within the university's diverse community. Also, university shuttles are equipped to accommodate students in wheelchairs. **Special:** AU offers co-op programs and internships in all majors, over 100 distinct study abroad programs in more than 45 countries, and the Washington Semester and Gateway programs. Work-study is available on campus and with local community service agencies. Dual majors, interdisciplinary programs, student-designed majors, 3-year B.A. degree programs, 3-2 engineering degrees, and B.A./B.S.degrees are also available. Combined bachelor's/master's programs are available in most majors. Cross-registration may be arranged through the Consortium of Universities of the Washington Metropolitan Area. Credit for life experience, nondegree study, and pass/fail options are available. There are preprofessional programs in engineering, law, and medicine (the medical program is aimed at strengthening credentials for applying to programs in medicine, dentistry, optometry, podiatry, oral survey, veterinary medicine, and public health). There are 12 national honor societies, Phi Beta Kappa, and a freshman honors program. **Visiting:** There are regularly scheduled orientations for prospective students, including student-led daily tours and information sessions, open houses, and overnight programs. There are guides for informal visits, visitors may sit in on classes, and stay overnight. To schedule a visit, contact the Admissions Office Tours and Information Program at admissions@american.edu. **Campus Safety and Security:** Measures include 24-hour foot and vehicle patrol, emergency notification system, self-defense education, and security escort services. There are shuttle buses, emergency telephones, lighted pathways/sidewalks, controlled access to dorms/residences, crime prevention programs, building alarms, video surveillance, posted crime alerts, on-line annual crime reports, escorts, laptop security protocols, RAD courses, emergency preparedness protocols and alerting system.

REQUIREMENTS: Prospective students may apply to American University through our Early or Regular Decision Plan without submitting standardized test scores. Students must have graduated from an accredited secondary school with at least 16 Carnegie units, including at least 4 units in English, 3 units in college preparatory math (including the equivalent of 2 units in algebra), 3 units in science, 2 units each in social sciences, and foreign language(s). Applicants who have satisfactory scores on the GED may also apply. All students must submit an essay and 2 letters of recommendation. American University's test-optional plan is open to all students graduating from a secondary school within the United States. AP and CLEP credits are accepted. Important factors in the admissions decision are advanced placement or honors courses, recommendations by school officials, and extracurricular activities record. To graduate, students must complete 120 credit hours with a minimum GPA of 2.0. In addition, students must complete 31 credit hours of general education requirements in 5 curricular areas and fulfill the school's competency requirements in English composition and mathematics by either passing an exam or taking a course in each area. Please see program specific websites for additional requirements. **Procedure:** Freshmen are admitted to all sessions. Entrance exams should be taken in the spring of the junior year or the fall of the senior year. There are early decision and deferred admissions plans. Early decision applications should be filed by November 15; regular applications, by January 15 for fall entry; and October 1 for spring entry. The fall 2017 application fee was $70. Notification of early decision is sent December 31; regular decision, April 1. Applications are accepted on-line. **Transfer Students:** 175 transfer students enrolled in 2016-2017. Transfer applicants who wish to be considered competitive candidates should have a cumulative GPA of at least 2.5 from all schools attended. All applicants with a cumulative GPA of 2.0 or above will be considered. 45 of 120 credits required for the bachelor's degree must be completed at AU. **International Students:** There are 896 international students enrolled. They must take the TOEFL with a minimum score of 550 on the paper-based TOEFL (PBT) or 80 on the Internet-based version (iBT) and the college's own test. Students may also take the IELTS Composite with a score 6.5 or higher, or the Pearson Test of English with score 53 or higher. Students graduating from a secondary school located outside the United States, please note that neither the SAT or ACT is required for admission.

ADMISSIONS: 29% of the 2017-2018 applicants were accepted. The SAT scores for the 2017-2018 freshman class were: Critical Reading-- 1% below 500, 18% between 500 and 599, 59% between 600 and 699, and 22% between 700 and 800. Math-- 3% below 500, 35% between 500 and 599, 51% between 600 and 699, and 11% between 700 and 800. Writing-- 10% below 500, 33% between 500 and 599, 40% between 600 and 699, and 16% between 700 and 800. The ACT scores were 8% between 18 and 23, 57% between 24 and 29, and 34% above 30. **Admissions Contact:** Andrea Felder, Asst Vice Provost Undergrad Admissions. Email: *admissions@american.edu* Web: *www.american.edu*

FINANCIAL AID: The CSS/Profile is required. The FAFSA code is 001434. The priority date for freshman financial aid applications for fall entry is November 15.

THE CATHOLIC UNIVERSITY OF AMERICA C-2

www.cua.edu

Washington, DC 20064 | (202) 319-5305 | (800) 673-2772

Fax: (202) 319-6533 | **Email:** cua-admissions@cua.edu

Full-time: 1410 men, 1676 women	**Faculty:** 270
Part-time: 52 men, 79 women	**Ph.D.s:** 98%
Graduate: 1258 men, 1468 women	**Student/Faculty:** 10 to 1
Year: semesters, summer session	**Tuition:** $44,060
Room & Board: $14,316	**Freshman Class:** 5926 applied, 4714 accepted, 723 enrolled
SAT CR/M: 575/570 **ACT:** 26	**CEEB CODE:** 5104
Application Deadline: February 15	**VERY COMPETITIVE**

The Catholic University of America, founded in 1887 and affiliated with the Roman Catholic Church, offers undergraduate programs in arts and sciences, engineering, architecture, nursing, philosophy, social service, and music and through the Metropolitan College. CUA's location provides a unique college experience and a wide spectrum of internship opportunities. A student's academic program determines the rate at which tuition is assessed. The figures given in the above capsule and in this profile are approximate. There are 8 undergraduate schools and 12 graduate schools. In addition to regional accreditation, CUA has baccalaureate program accreditation with AACSB, ABET, ACPE, CSWE, NAAB, NASM, NLN, and APA. The 180-acre campus is in an urban area in the heart of the nation's capital, Washington, DC. Including any residence halls, there are 52 buildings.

STUDENT LIFE: 98% of undergraduates are from out of state, mostly the Middle Atlantic. Students are from 50 states, 86 foreign countries, and Canada. 56% are from public schools. 63% are White; 6% African American; 6% Foreign; 5% two or more races; 3% Asian American; 13% Hispanic. 80% are Catholic. **Female To Male Ratio:** 1.2:1. The average age of freshmen is 18; all undergraduates, 21. 20% do not continue beyond their first year; 73% remain to graduate. **Housing:** College-sponsored housing includes dorms and on-campus apartments. In addition, there are honors houses, special-interest houses, a freshman residential college, and a residential college for upperclassmen, living and learning communities based on common interest. On-campus housing is available on a first-come, first-served basis, and is available on a lottery system for upperclassmen. 93% of students live on campus. Upperclassmen may keep cars.

FACULTY/CLASSROOMS: 70% teach undergraduates and 70% do research. No introductory courses are taught by graduate students. The average class size in an introductory lecture is 21; in a laboratory is 20; and in a regular course is 19.

PROGRAMS OF STUDY: CUA confers B.A., B.S., B.A.G.S., B.Arch., B.B.E., B.C.E., B.E.E., B.M., B.M.E., B.S.Arch., B.S.N. and B.S.B.A. degrees. Master's and doctoral degrees are also awarded. Bachelor's degrees are awarded in BIOLOGICAL SCIENCE (biochemistry, biology/biological science, and biotechnology), BUSINESS (accounting, banking and finance, business administration and management, finance, international economics, management science, and marketing and distribution), COMMUNICATIONS AND THE ARTS (art history, art, art history and appreciation, ceramic art and design, classics, communications, dramatic arts, English, English literature, French, German, Greek (classical), Italian, Latin, music, music history and appreciation, music performance, music theory and composition, musical theater, painting, piano/organ, Spanish, studio art, and voice), COMPUTER AND PHYSICAL SCIENCE (chemical physics, chemistry, computer science, mathematics, and physics), EDUCATION (art education, drama education, early childhood education, education, elementary education, English education, mathematics education, music education, and secondary education), ENGINEERING AND ENVIRONMENTAL DESIGN (architecture, biomedical engineering, civil engineering, computer engineering, construction engineering, electrical/electronics engineering, engineering, environmental engineering, environmental science, and mechanical engineering), HEALTH PROFESSIONS (medical laboratory technology, medical technology, nursing, predentistry, premedicine, and preveterinary science), SOCIAL SCIENCE (anthropology, economics, French studies, history, liberal arts/general studies, medieval studies, philosophy, political science/government, prelaw, psychology, religion, social science, social work, sociology, Spanish studies, and theological studies). Politics is the strongest academically. Architecture has the largest enrollment.

ACTIVITIES: 1% of women belong to 1 local and 1 national sororities. There are 90 groups on campus, including art, cheerleading, choir, chorale, chorus, computers, dance, debate, drama, ethnic, film, honors, international, jazz band, literary magazine, musical theater, newspaper, opera, orchestra, pep band, political, professional, religious, social, social service, student government, symphony, and yearbook. Popular campus events include Luaupalooza, Movies on the Mall, Fall Fiesta, Beaux Arts Ball, and Mistletoe Ball. **Sports:** There are 10 intercollegiate sports for men and 11 for women, and 9 intramural sports for men and 9 for women. Facilities include the DuFour Athletic Center which houses basketball and handball/racquetball courts, a swimming pool, a weight training room, an aerobics room, dance studios, an indoor jogging track, and volleyball courts. Outdoor facilities include a stadium FieldTurf, playing fields for baseball and softball, and tennis courts. **Graduates:** From July 1, 2016 to June 30, 2017, 806 bachelor's degrees were awarded. The most popular majors were business/marketing (17%), social sciences (15%), and engineering (14%). In an average class, 62% graduate in 4 years or less and 70% graduate in 6 years or less. Of the 2016 graduating class, 36% were enrolled in graduate school within 6 months of graduation.

SERVICES: Counseling and information services are available, as is tutoring in most subjects. There is a Center for Academic Success: drop-in tutoring, individual tutoring, smart thinking online service, and a writing center. There is a reader service for the blind, and remedial math, reading, and writing. Taped books/scanned books, assistive technology, including reading software and screen readers, test accommodations, and sign language interpreters are available. **Library/Resources:** The library contains 1.6 million volumes, 1.2 million microform items, and 40,697 audio/video tapes/CDs/DVDs, and subscribes to 10,448 periodicals including electronic. Computerized library services include interlibrary loans, database searching, Internet access, and Wi-Fi capability. Special learning facilities include an art gallery. **Physically Challenged Students:** 78% of the campus is accessible. Facilities include wheelchair ramps, elevators, special parking, specially equipped restrooms, special class scheduling, lowered drinking fountains, lowered telephones, and special housing. **Special:** Cross-registration is available with the Consortium of Universities of the Washington Metropolitan Area. Opportunities are also provided for internships, accelerated degree programs, dual majors, B.A.-B.S. degrees, work study, pass/fail options, and study abroad in 13 countries. There are 15 national honor societies, Phi Beta Kappa, and a freshman honors program. **Visiting:** There are regularly scheduled orientations for prospective students, visits include an information session with an admissions counselor and a guided campus tour. There are guides for informal visits, visitors may sit in on classes, and stay overnight. To schedule a visit, contact the Admissions Office. **Campus Safety and Security:** Measures include 24-hour foot and vehicle patrol, emergency notification system, self-defense education, and security escort services. There are shuttle buses, emergency telephones, lighted pathways/sidewalks, controlled access to dorms/residences, fixed security posts, emergency whistles, watch captains in every building, and an access control system.

REQUIREMENTS: Applicants must be graduates of an accredited secondary school. Students should present 18 academic credits, including 4 each in English, social studies, and math, 3 in science with 2 in lab, and foreign language. An essay is required, one letter of recommendation, official high school transcripts, and either an SAT or ACT score. An audition is required for music applicants, and a portfolio for architecture applicants is recommended. A GPA of 3.0 is required. AP credits are accepted. Important factors in the admissions decision are extracurricular activities record, leadership record, and advanced placement or honors courses. To graduate, students must complete 120 credit hours, including 36 to 42 hours in the major, with a minimum GPA of 2.0. Courses must meet distribution requirements in theology and religious studies, philosophy, English composition, humanities, language and literature, math and natural sciences, and social and behavioral sciences. A comprehensive exam is required in most majors. **Procedure:** Freshmen are admitted fall and spring. Entrance exams should be taken by February of the senior year of high school. There are early admissions and deferred admissions plans. Early decision applications should be filed by November 15; regular applications, by February 15 for fall entry. The fall 2017 application fee was $55. Notification of early decision is sent December 20; regular decision, March 15. 538 applicants were on the 2017 waiting list; 94 were admitted. Applications are accepted online. **Transfer Students:** 69 transfer students enrolled in 2016-2017. Applicants must submit a high school transcript, SAT or ACT scores, and a college transcript. A letter of recommendation and an essay are required. Terms of admission are finalized by the dean of the appropriate school. 60 of 120 credits required for the bachelor's degree must be completed at CUA. **International Students:** There are 66 international students enrolled. They must take the TOEFL. They must also take the SAT or ACT.

ADMISSIONS: 80% of the 2017-2018 applicants were accepted. The SAT scores for the 2017-2018 freshman class were: Critical Reading-- 17% below 500, 43% between 500 and 599, 31% between 600 and 699, and 8% between 700 and 800. Math-- 19% below 500, 45% between 500 and 599, 30% between 600 and 699, and 6% between 700 and 800. The ACT scores were 3% between 12 and 17, 27% between 18 and 23, 50% between 24 and 29, and 20% above 30. **Admissions Contact:** Christine Mica, Dean of University Admissions. Email: *cua-admissions@cua.edu* Web: *www.cua.edu*

FINANCIAL AID: In 2017-2018, 90% of all full-time freshmen received some form of financial aid. The average freshman award was $31,783. Need-based scholarships or need-based grants averaged $28,319; need-based self-help aid (loans and jobs) averaged $4,304; other non-need-based awards and non-need-based scholarships averaged $18,182; and $4,326 from other forms of aid. The Catholic University of America is a member of CSS. The FAFSA code is 001437. The priority date for freshman financial aid applications for fall entry is February 1.

THE GEORGE WASHINGTON UNIVERSITY B-3

www.gwu.edu

Washington, DC 20052	(202) 994-6040 (800) 447-3765
Fax: (202) 994-0325	**Email:** gwadm@gwu.edu
Full-time: 4333 men, 6010 women	**Faculty:** 1091; I, +$
Part-time: 495 men, 406 women	**Ph.D.s:** n/av
Graduate: 6337 men, 9318 women	**Student/Faculty:** 13 to 1
Year: semesters, summer session	**Tuition:** $51,329
Room & Board: $17,145	**Freshman Class:** 25488 applied, 10249 accepted, 2525 enrolled
SAT CR/M/W: 640/650/650 **ACT:** 30	**CEEB CODE:** 5246
Application Deadline: n/av	**HIGHLY COMPETITIVE+**

The George Washington University, founded in 1821, is a private institution providing degree programs in arts and sciences, business, engineering, international affairs, health sciences, education, law, and public health. There are 7 undergraduate schools and 10 graduate schools. In addition to regional accreditation, GWU has baccalaureate program accreditation with AACSB, ABET, CAHEA, CSAB, NASAD, NASM, and CAEP. The 37-acre campus is in an urban area 3 blocks west of the White House. Including any residence halls, there are 123 buildings.

STUDENT LIFE: 99% of undergraduates are from out of state, mostly the Middle Atlantic. Students are from 50 states, 137 foreign countries, and Canada. 70% are from public schools. 9% are Hispanic; 7% African American; 54% White; 5% race unknown; 4% two or more races; 11% Foreign; 10% Asian American. **Female To Male Ratio:** 1.4:1. The average age of freshmen is 18; all undergraduates, 21. 7% do not continue beyond their first year; 81% remain to graduate. **Housing:** 8245 students can be accommodated in college housing, which includes dorms and on-campus apartments. In addition, there are special-interest houses, fraternity houses, sorority floors, and theme housing. On-campus housing is available on a lottery system for upperclassmen. 70% of students live on campus. All students may keep cars.

FACULTY/CLASSROOMS: 59% of faculty are male; 41% are female. No introductory courses are taught by graduate students.

PROGRAMS OF STUDY: GWU confers B.A., B.S., B.Accy., B.B.A., B.S.H.S., and B.S.N. degrees. Associate, master's, and doctoral degrees are also awarded. Bachelor's degrees are awarded in BIOLOGICAL SCIENCE (biology/biological science), BUSINESS (accounting, banking and finance, business administration and management, business economics, human resources, international business management, marketing management, and tourism), COMMUNICATIONS AND THE ARTS (art history and appreciation, broadcasting, Chinese, classics, communications, dance, dramatic arts, English, fine arts, French, German, Japanese, journalism, literature, multimedia, music, music performance, public relations, Russian, and Spanish), COMPUTER AND PHYSICAL SCIENCE (applied mathematics, chemistry, computer science, geology, information sciences and systems, mathematics, physics, statistics, and systems analysis), ENGINEERING AND ENVIRONMENTAL DESIGN (civil engineering, computer engineering, electrical/electronics engineering, engineering, environmental science, and mechanical engineering), HEALTH PROFESSIONS (clinical science, emergency medical technologies, medical laboratory technology, nuclear medical technology, physician's assistant, premedicine, radiological science, and speech pathology/audiology), SOCIAL SCIENCE (American studies, anthropology, archeology, criminal justice, East Asian studies, economics, European studies, geography, history, human services, humanities, interdisciplinary studies, international relations, Judaic studies, Latin American studies, liberal arts/general studies, Middle Eastern studies, philosophy, physical fitness/movement, political science/government, psychology, religion, and sociology). Political communication, international affairs, and biological sciences are the strongest academically. International affairs, political science, and economics have the largest enrollments.

ACTIVITIES: 15% of men belong to 11 national fraternities; 26% of women belong to 7 national sororities. There are 257 groups on campus, including folk life club, art, band, cheerleading, chess, choir, chorale, chorus, computers, dance, debate, drama, ethnic, film, forensics, geology, honors, international, jazz band, LGBT, literary magazine, marching band, musical theater, newspaper, opera, orchestra, pep band, photography, political, professional, radio and TV, religious, social, social service, student government, and yearbook. Popular campus events include Spring Fling, Fall Fest, and a Benefit Auction. **Sports:** There are 9 intercollegiate sports for men and 8 for women, and 16 intramural sports for men and 16 for women. Facilities include a gym with auxiliary gyms, a swimming pool, weight rooms, a jogging track, squash and racquetball courts, and fields for soccer and baseball. **Graduates:** From July 1, 2016 to June 30, 2017, 2441 bachelor's degrees were awarded. The most popular majors were social sciences (33%), business/marketing (18%), and health professions and related programs (9%). In an average class, 84% graduate in 6 years or less.

SERVICES: Counseling and information services are available, as is tutoring in every subject. There is a reader service for the blind. **Library/Resources:** Computerized library services include interlibrary loans and database searching. Special learning facilities include an art gallery and radio station. **Physically Challenged Students:** 95% of the campus is accessible. Facilities include wheelchair ramps, elevators, special parking, specially equipped restrooms, special class scheduling, lowered drinking fountains, and lowered telephones. **Special:** Cross-registration is available through the Consortium of Colleges and Universities. There are co-op programs in education, business, engineering, arts and sciences, and international affairs and internships in the Washington metropolitan area. Study abroad in locations throughout the world, work-study programs, dual majors, student-designed majors, and a 3-2 engineering degree program with 8 colleges are also available. Nondegree study, a general studies degree, credit by exam, and pass/fail options are possible. There are 12 national honor societies, Phi Beta Kappa, a freshman honors program, and 21 departmental honors programs. **Visiting:** There are regularly scheduled orientations for prospective students, a group information sessions and campus tours. Class visitation, lunch with current students, and other activities can be arranged. There are guides for informal visits, visitors may sit in on classes, and stay overnight. To schedule a visit, contact the University Visitor Center at (202) 994-6602. **Campus Safety and Security:** Measures include 24-hour foot and vehicle patrol, emergency notification system, self-defense education, and security escort services. There are emergency telephones, lighted pathways/sidewalks, controlled access to dorms/residences, and a bike patrol.

REQUIREMENTS: The SAT or ACT is required. Students must have successfully completed a strong academic program in high school, including 4 of English, 2-4 recommended of math, science (with 1 lab), foreign language, and social studies. SAT: Subject tests are strongly recommended. An essay, 1 teacher recommendation, and 1 counselor recommendation are required. An interview is encouraged. AP and CLEP credits are accepted. Important factors in the admissions decision are advanced placement or honors courses, evidence of special talent, extracurricular activities record, and recommendations by school officials. Students must complete 120 semester hours with a minimum GPA of 2.0 for most majors. Arts and sciences majors must meet general curriculum requirements that include literacy, quantitative and logical reasoning, natural sciences, social and behavioral sciences, creative and performing arts, literature, Western civilization, and foreign languages or culture. Other specific course requirements vary with the different divisions of the university. **Procedure:** Freshmen are admitted to all sessions. Entrance exams should be taken in the junior year and the fall semester of the senior year. There are early decision and deferred admissions plans. Early decision applications should be filed by November 1. The fall 2017 application fee was $75. Notification of early decision is sent December 15. 1616 applicants were on the 2017 waiting list; 170 were admitted. Applications are accepted on-line. **Transfer Students:** 627 transfer students enrolled in 2016-2017. In addition to a record of high grades and exam scores, applicants must submit official transcripts of all postsecondary work. Minimum GPA requirements vary from 2.5 to 3.0, depending on the major. The SAT or ACT is required, and an interview is encouraged. 30 of 120 credits required for the bachelor's degree must be completed at GWU. **International Students:** They must take the TOEFL and the college's own test.

ADMISSIONS: 40% of the 2017-2018 applicants were accepted. The SAT scores for the 2017-2018 freshman class were: Critical Reading-- 5% below 500, 24% between 500 and 599, 46% between 600 and 699, and 25% between 700 and 800. Math-- 3% below 500, 18% between 500 and 599, 51% between 600 and 699, and 27% between 700 and 800. Writing-- 5% below 500, 20% between 500 and 599, 49% between 600 and 699, and 26% between 700 and 800. **Admissions Contact:** Costas Solomou, Dean for Undergraduate Admissions. Email: *gwadm@gwu.edu* Web: *www.gwu.edu*

FINANCIAL AID: The average freshman award was $42,555. Need-based scholarships or need-based grants averaged $28,416; need-based self-help aid (loans and jobs) averaged $5,859; non-need-based athletic scholarships averaged $28,036; other non-need-based awards and non-need-based scholarships averaged $4,674; and $19,477 from other forms of aid. The average financial indebtedness of the 2017 graduate was $33,305. GWU is a member of CSS. The CSS/Profile is required. The FAFSA code is 001444. The deadline for filing freshman financial aid applications for fall entry is February 1.

TRINITY WASHINGTON UNIVERSITY C-2

www.trinitydc.edu

Washington, DC 20017	(202) 884-9407 (800) 492-6882
Fax: (202) 884-9403	Email: admissions@trinitydc.edu
Full-time: 17 men, 841 women	Faculty: 48; IIA, --$
Part-time: 45 men, 488 women	Ph.D.s: 98%
Graduate: 107 men, 515 women	Student/Faculty: 12 to 1
Year: semesters	Tuition: $23,730
Room & Board: $10,096	Freshman Class: n/av
SAT or ACT: recommended	CEEB CODE: 5796
Application Deadline: July 31	COMPETITIVE+

Trinity Washington University, founded in 1897, is a private, women's liberal arts college in the nation's capital. The school year consists of traditional semesters for its College of Arts and Sciences plus accelerated 8-week terms for its graduate and professional programs. The School of Business and Graduate Studies, School of Professional Studies, School of Education and School of Nursing and Health Professions offer coeducational options for adult students seeking an associate's, bachelor's and master's degree with evening, weekend and hybrid class options. A student's academic program determines the rate at which tuition is assessed. The figures given in the above capsule and in this profile are approximate. There are 4 undergraduate schools and 3 graduate schools. In addition to regional accreditation, TWU has baccalaureate program accreditation with NCATE and CCNE. The 26-acre campus is in an urban area 2.5 miles north of the U.S. Capitol. Including any residence halls, there are 8 buildings.

STUDENT LIFE: 51% of undergraduates are from out of state, mostly the Middle Atlantic. Students are from 21 states, and 2 foreign countries. 90% are from public schools. 7% are Hispanic; 68% African American; 6% White; 4% Foreign; 1% Asian American. 52% claim no religious affiliation; 35% Protestant; 12% Catholic. **Female To Male Ratio:** 10.9:1. The average age of freshmen is 18; all undergraduates, 22. 30% do not continue beyond their first year; 50% remain to graduate. **Housing:** 275 students can be accommodated in college housing, which includes dorms. On-campus housing is available on a first-come, first-served basis, and is available on a lottery system for upperclassmen. 75% of students commute. Alcohol is not permitted. All students may keep cars.

FACULTY/CLASSROOMS: 35% of faculty are male; 65% are female. 72% teach undergraduates. No introductory courses are taught by graduate students. The average class size in an introductory lecture is 16; in a laboratory is 16; and in a regular course is 13.

PROGRAMS OF STUDY: TWU confers B.A. and B.S. degrees. Associate and master's degrees are also awarded. Bachelor's degrees are awarded in BIOLOGICAL SCIENCE (biochemistry and biology/biological science), BUSINESS (business administration and management), COMMUNICATIONS AND THE ARTS (communications and English), COMPUTER AND PHYSICAL SCIENCE (chemistry and mathematics), EDUCATION (early childhood education, education, and elementary education), HEALTH PROFESSIONS (exercise science and nursing), SOCIAL SCIENCE (criminal justice, economics, history, human services, international studies, political science/government, psychology, and sociology). Nursing, health services, and biology are the strongest academically. Psychology, business administration, and nursing have the largest enrollments.

ACTIVITIES: There are no fraternities or sororities. There are 23 groups on campus, including choir, computers, dance, debate, drama, ethnic, honors, international, literary magazine, newspaper, political, professional, religious, social, social service, student government, and yearbook. Popular campus events include Founders Day, Class Days, Junior Ring Day, and Cap & Gown. **Sports:** There are 5 intercollegiate sports for women, and 2 intramural sports for women. Facilities include athletic fields for soccer and lacrosse, a fitness center, tennis courts, a sports center with pool, weight room, and courts for basketball and volleyball. **Graduates:** From July 1, 2016 to June 30, 2017, 130 bachelor's degrees were awarded. The most popular majors were psychology (36%), business administration (15%), and English (10%).

SERVICES: Counseling and information services are available, as is tutoring in every subject. There is a reader service for the blind. There is also available signing for hearing-impaired students. **Library/ Resources:** The library contains 215,338 volumes, 6,826 microform items, and 13,797 audio/video tapes/CDs/DVDs, and subscribes to 509 periodicals including electronic. Computerized library services include interlibrary loans, database searching, Internet access, and Wi-Fi capability. Special learning facilities include an art gallery. **Physically Challenged Students:** 85% of the campus is accessible. Facilities include wheelchair ramps, elevators, special parking, and specially equipped restrooms. **Special:** Cross-registration is offered through the Consortium of Universities of the Washington Metropolitan Area. Trinity offers internships in all majors and minors, as well as work-study programs. Students may study in France, Italy, and various other countries by arrangement with their faculty adviser. B.A.-B.S. degrees, a 5-year accelerated degree in teaching, dual and student-designed majors, a general studies degree, credit for life experience, nondegree study, and pass/fail options are also available. There are 7 national honor societies, Phi Beta Kappa, and a freshman honors program. **Visiting:** There are regularly scheduled orientations for prospective students, consisting of a half-day program, including an overview of the college, the curriculum, and financing. There are guides for informal visits, visitors may sit in on classes, and stay overnight. To schedule a visit, contact the Office of Admissions. **Campus Safety and Security:** Measures include 24-hour foot and vehicle patrol, self-defense education, and security escort services. There are shuttle buses, emergency telephones, lighted pathways/sidewalks, and controlled access to dorms/residences.

REQUIREMENTS: The SAT or ACT is recommended. Graduation from an accredited secondary school or satisfactory scores on the GED are required for admission. A total of 16 academic credits is required, including 4 years of English and 3 to 4 years each of a foreign language, history, math, and science. An essay or graded writing sample is required, as are two letters of recommendation from faculty/guidance counselor. An interview is optional, but may be required of some applicants. Standardized tests are not required, but are recommended. A GPA of 2.0 is required. AP and CLEP credits are accepted. Important factors in the admissions decision are leadership record, extracurricular activities record, and recommendations by school officials. To graduate, students must complete a total of 120 credit hours with a minimum GPA of 2.0. Between 42 and 60 hours are required in the major. All students must take the courses required in the general education curriculum and must complete a senior seminar. **Procedure:** Freshmen are admitted fall and spring. Entrance exams should be taken by the junior year. There are deferred admissions and rolling admissions plans. Applications should be filed by July 31 for fall entry. The fall 2017 application fee was $40. Applications are accepted on-line. **Transfer Students:** 130 transfer students enrolled in 2016-2017. Transfer applicants must have a GPA of

2.5. An interview is recommended, and an essay and recommendation are required. 45 of 128 credits required for the bachelor's degree must be completed at Trinity. **International Students:** There are 2 international students enrolled. They must take the TOEFL with a minimum score of 543 on the paper-based TOEFL (PBT) or 76 on the Internet-based version (iBT).

ADMISSIONS: 2 freshmen graduated first in their class. **Admissions Contact:** Iris Escarraman, Executive Director. Email: *admissions@trinitydc.edu* Web: *www.trinitydc.edu*

FINANCIAL AID: In 2017-2018, 98% of all full-time freshmen received some form of financial aid, and need-based aid. TWU is a member of CSS. The FAFSA code is 001460. Check with the school for current application deadlines.

UNIVERSITY OF THE DISTRICT OF COLUMBIA *(The complete profile is made available exclusively on our website, www.barronspac.com)*

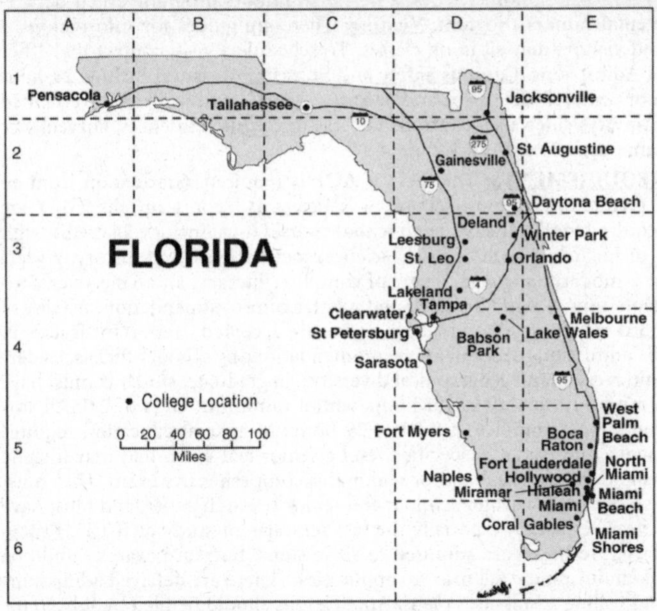

ADVENTIST UNIVERSITY OF HEALTH SCIENCES *(The complete profile is made available exclusively on our website, www.barronspac.com)*

BARRY UNIVERSITY *(The complete profile is made available exclusively on our website, www.barronspac.com)*

BEACON COLLEGE D-3
www.beaconcollege.edu

Leesburg, FL 34748 **(352) 787-7249**

Fax: (352) 787-0721 **Email: admissions@beaconcollege.edu**

Full-time: 120 men, 103 women	**Faculty:** n/av
Part-time: n/av	**Ph.D.s:** 100%
Graduate: n/av	**Student/Faculty:** 12 to 1
Year: semesters, summer session	**Tuition:** $36,172
Room & Board: $10,690	**Freshman Class:** n/av **CEEB CODE:** 3611
Application Deadline: August 20	**COMPETITIVE**

Beacon College, founded in 1989, is a private institution that offers undergraduate degrees in liberal studies, human services, and computer information systems exclusively for students with language-based learning disabilities and or ADHD. The figures given in the above capsule and in this profile are approximate. There is 1 undergraduate school. In addition to regional accreditation, Beacon has baccalaureate program accreditation with SACSCOC. The 2-acre campus is in a small town in the historic downtown Leesburg, approximately 50 miles northwest of Orlando. Including any residence halls, there are 11 buildings.

STUDENT LIFE: 84% of undergraduates are from out of state, mostly the South. Students are from 35 states, and 10 foreign countries. 48% are from public schools. 81% are White; 3% Asian American; 3% Hispanic; 14% African American; 1% Foreign. **Male To Female Ratio:** 1.2:1. The average age of freshmen is 21. 23% do not continue beyond their first year; 76% remain to graduate. **Housing:** College-sponsored housing includes on-campus apartments and off-campus apartments. On-campus housing is guaranteed for all 4 years. Alcohol is not permitted. All students may keep cars.

FACULTY/CLASSROOMS: All teach undergraduates. No introductory courses are taught by graduate students. The average class size in an introductory lecture is 8; in a laboratory is 10; and in a regular course is 8.

PROGRAMS OF STUDY: Beacon confers B.A. and B.S. degrees. Associate degrees are also awarded. Bachelor's degrees are awarded in COMPUTER AND PHYSICAL SCIENCE (information sciences and systems), SOCIAL SCIENCE (human services and liberal arts/general studies). Information sciences & systems, and liberal studies have the largest enrollments.

ACTIVITIES: There are 15 groups on campus, including camping club, graphic novel club, theatre goers club, art, beach goers club, choir, computers, drama, literary magazine, musical theater, newspaper, religious, social, social service, student government, and yearbook. **Sports:** There is no sports program at Beacon.

SERVICES: Counseling and information services are available, as is tutoring in every subject. There is remedial math, reading, and writing. There is an academic mentoring program. **Library/Resources:** The library contains 20,075 volumes, and 554 audio/video tapes/CDs/DVDs, and subscribes to 182 periodicals including electronic. Computerized library services include interlibrary loans, database searching, and Internet access. **Physically Challenged Students:** 90% of the campus is accessible. Facilities include wheelchair ramps, special parking, specially equipped restrooms, special class scheduling, and special housing. **Special:** Internships, B.A.-B.S. degrees, dual majors, and study abroad are possible. **Visiting:** There are regularly scheduled orientations for prospective students. There are guides for informal visits. To schedule a visit, contact the Admissions Office. **Campus Safety and Security:** Measures include 24-hour foot and vehicle patrol, emergency notification system, and security escort services. There are shuttle buses, lighted pathways/sidewalks, parking enforcement, and safety inspections.

REQUIREMENTS: Required testing and documentation include a clear diagnosis of learning disability or ADHD; Wechsler scales (WAIS-III are preferred) with full scale, cluster, and subtest scores; and Woodcock Johnson Test of Achievement with age- or grade-equivalency scores in reading, writing, and math; and average or above average IQ range with diagnosed learning disability. Although ACT and SAT scores are not required, the information is usual for placement and it is highly recommended that students take either the ACT or the SAT. Interviews may be required. CLEP credits are accepted. Important factors in the admissions decision are evidence of special talent, extracurricular activities record, and geographical diversity. To graduate, students must have 120 credit hours, including 33 credit hours of general education and at least 63 credit hours in their major, and a 2.0 GPA. Students in the liberal studies program must write a thesis and take a comprehensive exam. **Procedure:** Freshmen are admitted fall and spring. Entrance exams should be taken within 3 years prior to application. There is a rolling admissions plan. Application deadlines are open. The fall 2017 application fee was $50. **Transfer Students:** Transfer students must meet the same requirements as all incoming students. 60 of 120 credits required for the bachelor's degree must be completed at Beacon. **International Students:** There was 1 international student enrolled. They must take the TOEFL and WAIS subtests with the GLE in reading, writing, and math. SATand/or ACT is recommended.

Admissions Contact: Stephanie Knight, Director of Admissions. Email: *admissions@beaconcollege.edu* Web: *www.beaconcollege.edu*

FINANCIAL AID: The college's own financial statement is required. The FAFSA code is 033733. Check with the school for current application deadlines.

BETHUNE-COOKMAN UNIVERSITY D-2
www.cookman.edu

Daytona Beach, FL 32114 **(386) 481-2600**
(800) 448-0228

Fax: (386) 481-2601 **Email: admissions@cookman.edu**

Full-time: 1305 men, 2013 women	**Faculty:** 183; IIB, -$
Part-time: 101 men, 108 women	**Ph.D.s:** 58%
Graduate: 28 men, 23 women	**Student/Faculty:** 16 to 1
Year: semesters, summer session	**Tuition:** $14,410
Room & Board: $8912	**Freshman Class:** 4707 applied, 3152 accepted, 886 enrolled
SAT or ACT: required	**CEEB CODE:** 5061
Application Deadline: July 30	**COMPETITIVE**

Bethune-Cookman University, founded in 1904, is a private liberal arts institution affiliated with the United Methodist Church. The figures given in the above capsule and in this profile are approximate. There are 6 undergraduate schools and 2 graduate schools. In addition to regional accreditation, Bethune-Cookman has baccalaureate program accreditation with SACS, and CAEP. The 84-acre campus is in a small town 65 miles east of Orlando. Including any residence halls, there are 63 buildings.

STUDENT LIFE: 67% of undergraduates are from Florida. Others are from 39 states, 21 foreign countries, and Canada. 90% are from public schools. 92% are African American; 3% Foreign; 2% Hispanic; 1% White; 1% Asian American; 1% American Indian/Alaska Native. 56% are Protestant; 28% Seventh Day Adventist, Muslim, and Jehovah Witness. **Female To Male Ratio:** 1.5:1. The average age of freshmen is 18; all undergraduates, 21. 31% do not continue beyond their first year; 69% remain to graduate. **Housing:** 1961 students can be accommodated in college housing, which includes dorms. In addition, there are honors houses, leadership house. On-campus housing is guaranteed for the freshman year only, is available on a first-come, and first-served basis. 53% of students commute. Alcohol is not permitted. Upperclassmen may keep cars.

FACULTY/CLASSROOMS: 46% of faculty are male; 54% are female. No introductory courses are taught by graduate students. The average class size in an introductory lecture is 20; in a laboratory is 20; and in a regular course is 25.

PROGRAMS OF STUDY: Bethune-Cookman confers B.A. and B.S. degrees. Master's degrees are also awarded. Bachelor's degrees are awarded in BIOLOGICAL SCIENCE (biology/biological science), BUSINESS (accounting, business administration and management, hotel/motel and restaurant management, and international business management), COMMUNICATIONS AND THE ARTS (communications, dramatic arts, English, modern language, and music), COMPUTER AND PHYSICAL SCIENCE (chemistry, computer science, information sciences and systems, and mathematics), EDUCATION (business education, education, education of the exceptional child, elementary education, English education, music education, physical education, science education, and social science education), ENGINEERING AND ENVIRONMENTAL DESIGN (computer engineering), HEALTH PROFESSIONS (clinical science and nursing), SOCIAL SCIENCE (criminal justice, gerontology, history, international studies, liberal arts/general studies, political science/government, psychology, religion, and sociology). Business administration, education, and nursing are the strongest academically. Criminal justice has the largest enrollment.

ACTIVITIES: 25% of men belong to 5 national fraternities; 35% of women belong to 4 national sororities. There are 60 groups on campus, including band, cheerleading, choir, chorale, computers, dance, drama, drill team, honors, international, jazz band, literary magazine, marching band, newspaper, pep band, political, professional, radio and TV, religious, social, social service, student government, symphony, and yearbook. Popular campus events include Religious Outreach, Career Day, and Founders Day. **Sports:** There are 8 intercollegiate sports for men and 9 for women, and 6 intramural sports for men and 8 for women. Facilities include a gym, weight-rooms, and practice fields. **Graduates:** From July 1, 2016 to June 30, 2017, 561 bachelor's degrees were awarded. The most popular majors were education (15%), criminal justice (14%), and business administration (12%). In an average class, 2% graduate in 3 years or less, 15% graduate in 4 years or less, 31% graduate in 5 years or less, and 37% graduate in 6 years or less. Of the 2016 graduating class, 20% were enrolled in graduate school within 6 months of graduation, and 17% were employed.

SERVICES: Counseling and information services are available, as is tutoring in most subjects. There is remedial math, reading, and writing. **Library/Resources:** The library contains 162,911 volumes, 45,000 microform items, and 6,345 audio/video tapes/CDs/DVDs, and subscribes to 32,767 periodicals including electronic. Computerized library services include interlibrary loans, database searching, Internet access, and Wi-Fi capability. Special learning facilities include an art gallery, radio station, TV station, an observatory and founders' home and gravesite. **Physically Challenged Students:** 35% of the campus is accessible. Facilities include wheelchair ramps, elevators, special parking, specially equipped restrooms, special class scheduling, lowered drinking fountains, and lowered telephones. **Special:** Students may take courses at other institutions with the approval of the area adviser or registrar. B-CU offers cooperative courses in all divisions, internships related to the student's major, work-study programs, an accelerated degree program in business administration, non-degree-study, and 3-2 engineering degrees. Study abroad is available in South Africa, Ghana, Cuba, Brazil and Zimbabwe. There are 11 national honor societies, a freshman honors program, and 1 departmental honors program. **Visiting:** There are guides for informal visits and visitors may sit in on classes. To schedule a visit, contact the Office of Admissions. **Campus Safety and Security:** Measures include 24-hour foot and vehicle patrol and security escort services. There are lighted pathways/sidewalks, controlled access to dorms/residences, surveillance cameras, and auto-lock door.

REQUIREMENTS: The SAT or ACT is required. Graduation from an accredited secondary school or satisfactory scores on the GED are required for admission. High school courses must include 24 credits with 4 of English, 3 each of math, science, social science and history, 2 years of a modern language, 1 year of computer literacy, and 6 electives. Students must submit an essay and a letter of recommendation. A GPA of 2.3 is required. AP and CLEP credits are accepted. Important factors in the admissions decision are recommendations by school officials, leadership record, and geographical diversity. To graduate, students must have a minimum of 120 credit hours with a minimum GPA of 2.0. All students must complete a total of 39 hours in general education requirements, and pass at a specified level a senior exit exam that may include a standardized exam and/or senior area comprehensive exam. They must also complete a senior seminar and senior research paper, and must have 1 year residency, especially the last semester of study at B-CU. **Procedure:** Freshmen are admitted to all sessions. Entrance exams should be taken during the fall prior to application. There are deferred admissions and rolling admissions plans. Applications should be filed by July 30 for fall entry; November 30 for spring entry; and April 30 for summer entry. The fall 2017 application fee was $25. Notification is sent on a rolling basis. **Transfer Students:** 108 transfer students enrolled in 2016-2017. Applicants must submit transcripts from previous institutions attended and a statement of good standing and eligibility to return. A minimum GPA of 2.25 is required. Students having fewer than 24 credit hours must meet the requirements for entering freshmen. 30 of 120 credits required for the bachelor's degree must be completed at B-CC or B-CU. **International Students:** There are 70 international students enrolled. They must take the TOEFL with a minimum score of 550 on the paper-based TOEFL (PBT) or 73 on the Internet-based version (iBT). They must also take the SAT or ACT.

ADMISSIONS: 67% of the 2017-2018 applicants were accepted. **Admissions Contact:** Manicia Finch, Director of Admissions. Email: *admissions@cookman.edu* Web: *www.cookman.edu*

FINANCIAL AID: In 2017-2018, 82% of all full-time freshmen received some form of financial aid. 80% of all full-time freshmen received need-based aid. The average freshman award was $13,190. Need-based scholarships or need-based grants averaged $9,903 ($19,000 maximum); need-based self-help aid (loans and jobs) averaged $3,796 ($5,500 maximum); non-need-based athletic scholarships averaged $10,338 ($22,300 maximum); and other non-need-based awards and non-need-based scholarships averaged $8,380 ($20,000 maximum). 23% of undergraduate students work part-time. The average financial indebtedness of the 2017 graduate was $21,435. The FAFSA code is 001467. The priority date for freshman financial aid applications for fall entry is April 1.

CARLOS ALBIZU UNIVERSITY *(The complete profile is made available exclusively on our website, www.barronspac.com)*

ECKERD COLLEGE — D-4

www.eckerd.edu

St. Petersburg, FL 33711	(727) 864-8331 (800) 456-9009
Fax: (727) 866-2304	**Email:** admissions@eckerd.edu
Full-time: 649 men, 1260 women	**Faculty:** 131
Part-time: 18 men, 30 women	**Ph.D.s:** 96%
Graduate: n/av	**Student/Faculty:** 14 to 1
Year: 4-1-4, summer session	**Tuition:** $43,044
Room & Board: $12,162	**Freshman Class:** 4125 applied, 3291 accepted, 561 enrolled
SAT CR/M: 590/560 **ACT:** 26	**CEEB CODE:** 5223
Application Deadline: April 1	**VERY COMPETITIVE**

Eckerd College, founded in 1958, is a coeducational college of the liberal arts and sciences. The mission of the College is to provide excellent, innovative undergraduate liberal arts education and lifelong learning programs in the unique Florida environment, within the context of a covenant relationship with the Presbyterian Church. There is 1 undergraduate school. In addition to regional accreditation, Eckerd has baccalaureate program accreditation with SACSCOC. The 188-acre campus is in a suburban area 1 1/4 miles of Waterfront, 5 miles south of St. Petersburg. Including any residence halls, there are 88 buildings.

STUDENT LIFE: 79% of undergraduates are from out of state, mostly the South. Students are from 46 states, 42 foreign countries, and Canada. 9% are Hispanic; 78% White; 4% Foreign; 3% African American; 3% two or more races; 2% Asian American; 1% race unknown. **Female To Male Ratio:** 1.9:1. The average age of freshmen is 18; all undergraduates, 20. 19% do not continue beyond their first year; 70% remain to graduate. **Housing:** 1768 students can be accommodated in college housing, which includes dorms and on-campus apartments. In addition, there are language/international houses, community service, pet dorms, and substance-free houses. On-campus housing is guaranteed for the freshman year only, is available on a first-come, first-served basis, and is available on a lottery system for upperclassmen. 87% of students live on campus. All students may keep cars.

FACULTY/CLASSROOMS: All teach undergraduates, and all do research. No introductory courses are taught by graduate students. The average class size in a regular course is 19.

PROGRAMS OF STUDY: Eckerd confers B.A. and B.S. degrees. Bachelor's degrees are awarded in AGRICULTURE (environmental studies), BIOLOGICAL SCIENCE (biochemistry, biology/biological science, and marine science), BUSINESS (business administration and management, international business management, and management science), COMMUNICATIONS AND THE ARTS (communications, comparative literature, creative writing, dramatic arts, French, literature, music, Spanish, and visual and performing arts), COMPUTER AND PHYSICAL SCIENCE (chemistry, computer science, geoscience, mathematics, and physics), HEALTH PROFESSIONS (predentistry and premedicine), SOCIAL SCIENCE (American studies, anthropology, classical/ancient civilization, East Asian studies, economics, history, human development, humanities, international relations, philosophy, political science/government, prelaw, psychology, religion, sociology, and women's studies). Marine science, biology, and environmental studies have the largest enrollments.

ACTIVITIES: There are no fraternities or sororities. There are 105 groups on campus, including art, band, cheerleading, chess, choir, chorale, chorus, communications, computers, dance, drama, environmental, ethnic, film, honors, international, LGBT, literary magazine, newspaper, photography, political, professional, religious, social, social service, student government, and water search and rescue. Popular campus events include Festival of Hope, Festival of Cultures, Springtopia, and Earth Fest. **Sports:** There are 6 intercollegiate sports for men and 8 for women, and 14 intramural sports for men and 14 for women. Facilities include a gym, baseball and softball complex, soccer fields, tennis courts, an open-air multi-purpose sports pavilion, a weight room, beach volleyball courts, fitness room, swimming pool, and waterfront facilities. **Graduates:** From July 1, 2016 to June 30, 2017, 342 bachelor's degrees were awarded. The most popular majors were environmental studies (16%), marine science (11%), and psychology (11%). In an average class, 63% graduate in 4 years or less, 69% graduate in 5 years or less, and 70% graduate in 6 years or less.

SERVICES: Counseling and information services are available, as is tutoring in some subjects, math, sciences, and foreign languages. **Library/Resources:** The library contains 189,909 volumes, 280 microform items, and 3,838 audio/video tapes/CDs/DVDs, and subscribes to 101,999 periodicals including electronic. Computerized library services include interlibrary loans, database searching, and Internet access. Special learning facilities include an art gallery. **Physically Challenged Students:** 95% of the campus is accessible. Facilities include wheelchair ramps, elevators, special parking, specially equipped restrooms, special class scheduling, lowered drinking fountains, lowered telephones, and special housing. **Special:** Eckerd offers internships, study abroad, work-study programs, and dual majors in all subjects, interdisciplinary majors in international relations and environmental studies, student-designed majors, nondegree study, and pass/fail options. Students may earn B.A.-B.S. degrees in biology, chemistry, and marine science. A 3-2 engineering degree is offered with Washington and Columbia Universities, a 3-3 Juris Doctorate degree is offered with Florida State University. There are 8 national honor societies, Phi Beta Kappa, and a freshman honors program. **Visiting:** There are regularly scheduled orientations for prospective students, consisting of an interview and a tour. There are guides for informal visits; visitors may sit in on classes, and stay overnight. To schedule a visit, contact the Admissions Office. **Campus Safety and Security:** Measures include 24-hour foot and vehicle patrol, emergency notification system, and security escort services. There are emergency telephones and lighted pathways/sidewalks.

REQUIREMENTS: The SAT or ACT is required. Graduation from an accredited secondary school or satisfactory scores on the GED are required. High school courses must include 4 years of English, 3 years each of math and science, with 2 units of lab, 2 years each of a foreign language and social studies, and 1 year of history, and 3 academic electives. SAT: Subject tests in writing, literature, and math are recommended. An essay is required and an interview is recommended. A GPA of 2.0 is required. AP and CLEP credits are accepted. Important factors in the admissions decision are advanced placement or honors courses, leadership record, parents or siblings attended your school, evidence of special talent, personality/intangible qualities, and extracurricular activities record. To graduate, students must complete a total of 36 courses or 126 semester hours with a minimum GPA of 2.0. Required courses include 1 each in the arts, humanities, natural and social sciences, and environmental and global perspectives. Students must also demonstrate competencies in writing, speaking, foreign language, computation, and technology and must take a comprehensive exam or submit a thesis or project in the senior year. **Procedure:** Freshmen are admitted fall, winter, and spring. Entrance exams should be taken in October, November, or December. There are early admissions, deferred admissions, and rolling admissions plans. Applications should be filed by April 1 for fall entry; and December 1 for winter entry. The fall 2017 application fee was $40. 95 applicants were on the 2017 waiting list; 1 was admitted. Applications are accepted on-line. **Transfer Students:** 48 transfer students enrolled in 2016-2017. Applicants must have a minimum GPA of 2.5. The SAT or ACT is required. An interview is recommended. A faculty recommendation is required. Students may enroll in the fall, winter, spring, and summer. 63 of 126 credits required for the bachelor's degree must be completed at Eckerd. **International Students:** There are 79 international students enrolled. They must take the TOEFL with a minimum score of 550 on the paper-based TOEFL (PBT) or 79 on the Internet-based version (iBT). They must also take the SAT or ACT.

ADMISSIONS: 80% of the 2017-2018 applicants were accepted. The SAT scores for the 2017-2018 freshman class were: Math-- 6% below 500, 48% between 500 and 599, 40% between 600 and 699, and 7% between 700 and 800. Evidence-Based Reading/Writing-- 15% below 500, 53% between 500 and 599, 26% between 600 and 699, and 5% between 700 and 800. The ACT scores were 1% between 12 and 17, 31% between 18 and 23, 50% between 24 and 29, and 18% above 30. **Admissions Contact:** John Sullivan, Vice President Enrollment Management. Email: *admissions@eckerd.edu* Web: *www.eckerd.edu*

FINANCIAL AID: In 2017-2018, 99% of all full-time freshmen received some form of financial aid. 88% of all full-time freshmen received need-based aid. The average freshman award was $35,564. Need-based scholarships or need-based grants averaged $25,760; need-based self-help aid (loans and jobs) averaged $5,425; non-need-based athletic scholarships averaged $28,381; other non-need-based awards and non-need-based scholarships averaged $16,285; and $3,800 from other forms of aid. The FAFSA code is 001487. The priority date for freshman financial aid applications for fall entry is March 1.

EDWARD WATERS COLLEGE *(The complete profile is made available exclusively on our website, www.barronspac.com)*

EMBRY-RIDDLE AERONAUTICAL UNIVERSITY - DAYTONA BEACH

D-2

http://daytonabeach.erau.edu

Daytona Beach, FL 32114	(386) 226-6100 (800) 862-2416 Email: daytonabeach@erau.edu
Full-time: 4218 men, 1183 women	**Faculty:** IIA, av$
Part-time: 265 men, 63 women	**Ph.D.s:** n/av
Graduate: 442 men, 167 women	**Student/Faculty:** n/av
Year: semesters, summer session	**Tuition:** $34,722
Room & Board: $11,100	**Freshman Class:** 4564 applied, 3419 accepted, 1357 enrolled
SAT EBR-W/M: 600/600 **ACT:** 26	**CEEB CODE:** 5190
Application Deadline: July 1	**VERY COMPETITIVE**

Embry-Riddle Aeronautical University-Daytona Beach offers programs in a wide array of traditional as well as emerging fields. Known as the world's largest and oldest aviation institution, Embry-Riddle offers much more than flight instruction. The strength of our science, technology, engineering, and mathematics programs makes it possible for students to master fields ranging from hybrid electric propulsion and autonomous flying vehicles to the human factors that affect operational efficiency. Embry-Riddle offers its students a wide array of more than 80 undergraduate and graduate degree programs in aviation, aerospace, business, engineering, safety, security and intelligence, transportation, and related high-tech fields. The University also offers Ph.D. degree programs in Aviation, Aerospace Engineering, Aviation, Engineering Physics, Human Factors, Mechanical Engineering, Electrical Engineering & Computer Science, and Aviation Business Administration. There are 4 undergraduate schools and 4 graduate schools. In addition to regional accreditation, ERAU-Daytona Beach has baccalaureate program accreditation with ABET, ACBSP, and AABI. The 289-acre campus is in an urban area 48 miles northeast of Orlando. Including any residence halls, there are 67 buildings.

STUDENT LIFE: 62% of undergraduates are from out of state, mostly the Middle Atlantic. Students are from 51 states, 109 foreign countries, and Canada. 55% are White; 13% Foreign; 7% Hispanic; 7% two or more races; 7% race unknown; 5% African American; 5% Asian American. **Male To Female Ratio:** 3.5:1. The average age of freshmen is 18; all undergraduates, 21. 20% do not continue beyond their first year; 59% remain to graduate. **Housing:** 2328 students can be accommodated in college housing, which includes dorms and off-campus apartments. In addition, there are honors houses. On-campus housing is guaranteed for the freshman year only, is available on a first-come, first-served basis, and is available on a lottery system for upperclassmen. 63% of students commute. All students may keep cars.

FACULTY/CLASSROOMS: No introductory courses are taught by graduate students. The average class size in an introductory lecture is 28; in a laboratory is 15; and in a regular course is 25.

PROGRAMS OF STUDY: ERAU-Daytona Beach confers B.S. degrees. Associate, master's, and doctoral degrees are also awarded. Bachelor's degrees are awarded in BUSINESS (business administration/aviation), COMMUNICATIONS AND THE ARTS (communications), COMPUTER AND PHYSICAL SCIENCE (astronomy and physics, computer science, cyber intelligence/security studies, mathematics/computational, space physics, and software engineering), EDUCATION (global studies), ENGINEERING AND ENVIRONMENTAL DESIGN (aeronautical science, aerospace engineering, air traffic management, aviation business administration, civil engineering, computer engineering, electrical and computer engineering, engineering physics, mechanical engineering, systems engineering, and unmanned aircraft systems), HEALTH PROFESSIONS (electrical engineering), SOCIAL SCIENCE (homeland security and interdisciplinary studies). Aviation, aerospace, and engineering are the strongest academically. Aerospace engineering, aeronautical science, and mechanical engineering have the largest enrollments.

ACTIVITIES: There are 167 groups on campus, including cheerleading, chorale, computers, dance, debate, drama, environmental, ethnic, film, honors, international, LGBT, literary magazine, musical theater, newspaper, pep band, photography, political, professional, radio and TV, religious, social, social service, and student government. Popular campus events include Homecoming, Touch-n-Go events that include Bands, Comedians and Magicians, Movies every Thursday night, Student Activities Fair, and Annual Arts & Letters Shakespeare Production. **Sports:** There are 9 intercollegiate sports for men and 10 for women, and 15 intramural sports for men and 15 for women. The ICI Center is the centerpiece for campus recreation; it offers strength-training equipment, a cardio deck, group fitness classes, an outdoor swimming pool, tennis, basketball courts, racquetball, martial arts, softball, volleyball, soccer, and multipurpose playing fields. **Graduates:** From July 1, 2016 to June 30, 2017, 928 bachelor's degrees were awarded. The most popular majors were aerospace engineering (19%), aeronautical science (17%), and aeronautics (13%). In an average class, 2% graduate in 3 years or less, 29% graduate in 4 years or less, 53% graduate in 5 years or less, and 59% graduate in 6 years or less.

SERVICES: Counseling and information services are available, as is tutoring in some subjects, such as first year math, physics, chemistry and writing (composition). There is remedial math, reading, and writing and lower level engineering courses. **Library/Resources:** The library contains 76,813 volumes, 31,250 microform items, and 3,854 audio/video tapes/CDs/DVDs, and subscribes to 1,196 periodicals, including electronic. Computerized library services include interlibrary loans, database searching, Internet access, and Wi-Fi capability. Special learning facilities include a radio station, Daytona Beach is dedicated to ensuring that its students have the resources they need to excel academically and offers more than two dozen state-of-the-art labs and facilities. In addition, students attending Embry-Riddle Daytona Beach have access to one of the largest and most advanced fleet of training aircraft and simulators available. The Flight Ops Center boasts a dispatch desk, weather monitoring equipment, computer stations for flight planning, and private oral rooms. **Physically Challenged Students:** 95% of the campus is accessible. Facilities include wheelchair ramps, elevators, special parking, specially equipped restrooms, lowered drinking fountains, and lowered telephones. **Special:** ERAU offers co-op programs and internships in all majors, study abroad in 22 countries, work-study programs, accelerated degree programs in aerospace engineering and engineering physics, credit for life experience, and non-degree study. There are 3 national honor societies and a freshman honors program. **Visiting:** There are regularly scheduled orientations for prospective students; tours are available weekdays. All visitors are encouraged to allocate three hours or more for an admission presentation and in-depth tour. There are guides for informal visits and visitors may sit in on classes. To schedule a visit, contact the Admissions Office. **Campus Safety and Security:** Measures include 24-hour foot and vehicle patrol, emergency notification system, self-defense education, and security escort services. There are emergency telephones, lighted pathways/sidewalks, controlled access to dorms/residences, and in-room safes.

REQUIREMENTS: The SAT or ACT is recommended. Students should complete a competitive academic program in high school, including 16 Carnegie units with at least 3 years of math. Admissions decisions are based on the strength of the academic record, rank in class, standardized test scores, recommendations, and the written statement. High school transcript/diploma preferred, GED accepted. AP and CLEP credits are accepted. To graduate, students must complete a total of 120 to 136 credit hours, including 60 in the major, with a minimum GPA of 2.0. All students must complete 36 credits of general education requirements, including courses in communication skills, technical report writing, humanities/social sciences, math, physical science, economics, and computer science. **Procedure:** Freshmen are admitted fall, spring, and summer. Entrance exams should be taken during spring of the junior year or fall of the senior year. There are deferred admissions and rolling admissions plans. Early decision applications should be filed by December 1; regular applications, by July 1 for fall entry; November 1 for spring entry; and April 1 for summer entry. The fall 2017 application fee was $50. Notification is sent on a rolling basis. Applications are accepted online. **Transfer Students:** 403 transfer students enrolled in 2016-2017. A GPA of 2.5 is preferred. 30 of 120 credits required for the bachelor's degree must be completed at ERAU. **International Students:** There are 686 international students enrolled. They must take the TOEFL with a minimum score of 550 on the paper-based TOEFL (PBT) or 79 on the Internet-based version (iBT). Applicants whose native language is not English are required to submit official TOEFL or IELTS scores. SAT 1 reasoning test or ACT is strongly recommended for admission for U.S. citizens and permanent residents.

ADMISSIONS: 75% of the 2017-2018 applicants were accepted. The SAT scores for the 2017-2018 freshman class were: Math-- 8% below 500, 38% between 500 and 599, 40% between 600 and 699, and 14% between 700 and 800. Evidence-Based Reading/Writing-- 8% below 500, 40% between 500 and 599, 43% between 600 and 699, and 9% between 700 and 800. The ACT scores were 4% between 12 and 17, 31% between 18 and 23, 47% between 24 and 29, and 18% above 30. 43% of the current freshmen were in the top fifth of their class; 72% were in the top two fifths. 19 freshmen graduated first in their class. **Admissions Contact:** B.J. Adams, Director for Admissions. Email: *DaytonaBeach@erau.edu* Web: *http:/daytonabeach.erau.edu*

FINANCIAL AID: In 2017-2018, 95% of all full-time freshmen received some form of financial aid. 94% of all full-time freshmen received need-based aid. The average freshman award was $21,034. Need-based scholarships or need-based grants averaged $17,798; need-based self-help aid (loans and jobs) averaged $3,858; and non-need-based athletic scholarships averaged $13,106. 13% of undergraduate students work part-time. The FAFSA code is 001479. The priority date for freshman financial aid applications for fall entry is March 1.

EMBRY-RIDDLE AERONAUTICAL UNIVERSITY - WORLDWIDE

http://worldwide.erau.edu

Daytona Beach, FL 32114 (800) 522-6787

Fax: (386) 226-6984
Full-time: 2500 men, 395 women
Part-time: 7694 men, 1056 women
Graduate: 3272 men, 979 women
Year: other, summer session
Room & Board: $8644
SAT or ACT: recommended
Application Deadline: n/av

Email: worldwide@erau.edu
Faculty: n/av
Ph.D.s: n/av
Student/Faculty: n/av
Tuition: $9076
Freshman Class: n/av

COMPETITIVE

Embry-Riddle Aeronautical University-Worldwide programs are designed specifically to suit demanding schedules. We offer the ultimate experience in flexibility with more than 125 campuses across the globe, more than 90 of which are located on military bases, 12 enrollment dates per year, five modes of learning and coursework that can be completed as it fits into your busy life. There are 3 undergraduate schools and 3 graduate schools. In addition to regional accreditation, ERAU-Worldwide has baccalaureate program accreditation with ACBSP, AABI, and Project Management Institute Global Accreditation. The Worldwide Campus is made up of over 125 locations in the United States, Europe, the Middle East, and Asia.

STUDENT LIFE: 9% are Hispanic; 8% African American; 6% two or more races; 55% White; 4% Asian American; 3% Foreign; 15% race unknown. **Male To Female Ratio:** 5.5:1. The average age of freshmen is 27; all undergraduates, 32.

FACULTY/CLASSROOMS: No introductory courses are taught by graduate students.

PROGRAMS OF STUDY: ERAU-Worldwide confers B.S. degrees. Associate, master's, and doctoral degrees are also awarded. Bachelor's degrees are awarded in BUSINESS (logistics, management information systems, management, and project management), COMMUNICATIONS AND THE ARTS (communications), ENGINEERING AND ENVIRONMENTAL DESIGN (aviation business administration, aviation maintenance management, emergency/disaster science, engineering, engineering technology, and systems engineering), SOCIAL SCIENCE (interdisciplinary studies and safety management). Aeronautics, aeronautical science, and technical management are the strongest academically. Aeronautics, technical management, and master of aeronautical science have the largest enrollments.

ACTIVITIES: There are no fraternities or sororities. **Sports:** There is no sports program at ERAU - Worldwide. **Graduates:** From July 1, 2016 to June 30, 2017, 1612 bachelor's degrees were awarded. The most popular majors were aeronautics (61%), technical management (25%), and aviation business administration (7%).

SERVICES: Library/Resources: Computerized library services include interlibrary loans, database searching, Internet access, and Wi-Fi capability. **Special:** Embry-Riddle Aeronautical University is the world's oldest and largest fully accredited university specializing in aviation and aerospace. With more than 150 campuses, Embry-Riddle Worldwide's online and web-based EagleVision Home courses provide you the flexibility you need to complete your studies no matter where you are, day or night. Members of the military don't have to worry about getting transferred and starting over, they can take their studies with them.

REQUIREMENTS: The SAT or ACT is recommended. Worldwide considers all aspects of a student's qualifications and offers admission to the most competitive applicants building a talented and diverse population of students motivated toward careers in aviation and aerospace. Applications for admission are valid for one year from date received. Admitted students must enroll and maintain enrollment beyond the add/drop period within one year of admission or must reapply. The following documentation is required for consideration of admission for all applicants under the age of 20 that are not active members of the United States military and not a transfer student: an Official High School transcript or GED. Rigor of high school academic program and academic performance will be assessed 2.0 GPA or higher on a 4.0 scale, SAT with a minimum score of 1000 or ACT with a minimum score of 21, 300-500 word essay, 2 letters of recommendation from a school counselor or teacher, an official transcripts from all post-secondary accredited degree-granting institutions with less than 12 college credits earned, if applicable. The university expects all applicants, at a minimum, to have completed by high school graduation the following course work: 4 years of English, 3 years of mathematics, including algebra I or applied math I & II, formal logic or geometry, 2 years of history or social science, 2 years of science in at least two different areas, with at least one lab experience. Applicants age 20 and over that are not classified as a transfer student or have not served in the military must provide the following documentation: Official High School transcript or GED, a 2.0 GPA or higher on a 4.0 scale, an official transcripts from all post-secondary accredited degree-granting institutions attended, and a resume. AP and CLEP credits are accepted. Graduate students are required to complete all graduate course work with ERAU with a maximum of 12 credit hours of transfer work permitted. For undergraduate degree completion, at least 25 percent of semester credit hours must be earned through ERAU instruction. Students pursuing any undergraduate degree must earn a minimum CGPA of 2.0 for all work completed within the degree program at the University. Students pursuing any graduate degree must earn a minimum CGPA of 3.0 for all work completed within the degree program at the University. Students must complete the general graduation requirements as prescribed by the University, as well as all degree requirements specified in the degree program being pursued. Graduation requirements are not subject to petition or waiver. Students must initiate an application for graduation through the student information system, and follow up by completing a Graduation Information Sheet in ERNIE. A qualified student will not be graduated by ERAU until a graduation application and information sheet have been received and processed by the University, and the graduation fee has been remitted. **Procedure:** Freshmen are admitted to all sessions. There are deferred admissions and rolling admissions plans. Application deadlines are open. The fall 2017 application fee was $50. Notification is sent on a rolling basis. Applications are accepted on-line. **Transfer Students:** 3453 transfer students enrolled in 2016-2017. Applicants who graduated from high school and subsequently completed a minimum of 12 semester hours of college level credit from an accredited degree granting institution are considered transfer students. Embry-Riddle considers each application for transfer admission individually, reviewing the student's academic record, grades received in all college-level courses, completion of fundamental studies in English and Mathematics, and the rigor of the student's academic program. To be considered for admission a transfer applicant must have a minimum of a 2.0 CGPA on a 4.0 scale from an accredited degree granting institution. When an applicant has attended more than one institution, a cumulative average for all previous college work attempted will be calculated to determine the overall CGPA, an official transcripts from all colleges and universities (post secondary) accredited degree-granting institutions attended, military documents, if applicable. 30 of 120 credits required for the bachelor's degree must be completed at ERAU-Worldwide. **International Students:** There are 120 international students enrolled. They must take the TOEFL with a minimum score of 550 on the paper-based TOEFL (PBT) or 79 on the Internet-based version (iBT).

Admissions Contact: Admissions Office. Email: *worldwide@erau.edu* Web: *http:/worldwide.erau.edu*

FINANCIAL AID: In 2017-2018, 43% of all full-time freshmen received some form of financial aid. 38% of all full-time freshmen received need-based aid. The average freshman award was $9,150. Need-based scholarships or need-based grants averaged $5,239; and need-based self-help aid (loans and jobs) averaged $3,276. The FAFSA code is 001479. The priority date for freshman financial aid applications for fall entry is March 1.

FLAGLER COLLEGE D-2

www.flagler.edu

St. Augustine, FL 32084 (904) 829-6481 (800) 304-4208

Fax: (904) 819-6466
Full-time: 943 men, 1596 women
Part-time: 28 men, 49 women
Graduate: 6 women
Year: semesters, summer session
Room & Board: $10,120
SAT CR/M/W: 540/510/530 **ACT:** 24
Application Deadline: March 1

Email: admissions@flagler.edu
Faculty: 116
Ph.D.s: 76%
Student/Faculty: 22 to 1
Tuition: $17,500
Freshman Class: 3372 applied, 2529 accepted, 600 enrolled
CEEB CODE: 5235
COMPETITIVE

Flagler College, founded in 1968, is an independent liberal arts college that emphasizes undergraduate education in select liberal studies and preprofessional studies. There is 1 undergraduate school and 1 graduate school. The 49-acre campus is in a small town 35 miles south of Jacksonville and 45 miles north of Daytona Beach. Including any residence halls, there are 36 buildings.

STUDENT LIFE: 57% of undergraduates are from Florida. Others are from 44 states, 45 foreign countries, and Canada. 78% are White; 6% race unknown; 5% Hispanic; 4% African American; 3% Foreign; 2% two or more races; 1% Asian American. **Female To Male Ratio:** 1.7:1. The average age of freshmen is 18; all undergraduates, 22. 29% do not continue beyond their first year; 71% remain to graduate. **Housing:** 1017 students can be accommodated in college housing, which includes dorms. On-campus housing is guaranteed for the freshman year only, is available on a first-come, first-served basis. 63% of students commute. Alcohol is not permitted. All students may keep cars.

FACULTY/CLASSROOMS: 52% of faculty are male; 48% are female. All teach undergraduates. No introductory courses are taught by graduate students. The average class size in an introductory lecture is 18; in a laboratory is 18; and in a regular course is 18.

PROGRAMS OF STUDY: Flagler confers B.A., B.F.A., and B.S. degrees. Master's degrees are also awarded. Bachelor's degrees are awarded in BUSINESS (accounting, business administration and management, and sports management), COMMUNICATIONS AND THE ARTS (art history, communications, dramatic arts, English, fine arts, graphic design, journalism, film and media studies, public relations, Spanish, strategic communication, and theatre arts), EDUCATION (art education, education of the deaf and hearing impaired, education of the exceptional child, elementary education, English education, and social studies secondary school education), ENGINEERING AND ENVIRONMENTAL DESIGN (environmental science), SOCIAL SCIENCE (criminology, economics, history, international studies, Latin American studies, liberal arts/general studies, philosophy and religion, political science/government, psychology, public administration, public history/archives, and sociology). Business administration, psychology, and graphic design are the strongest academically and have the largest enrollments.

ACTIVITIES: There are no fraternities or sororities. There are 45 groups on campus, including art, cheerleading, choir, chorus, dance, deaf awareness club, drama, dive club, environmental, ethnic, film, honors, international, LGBT, literary magazine, musical theater, newspaper, photography, political, professional, radio and TV, religious, social, social service, and student government. Popular campus events include De-Stress Day, Bachelor Bids, Harry Potter Month, Halloween Midnight Breakfast, and Flagler Follies. **Sports:** There are 7 intercollegiate sports for men and 9 for women, and 13 intramural sports for men and 13 for women. Facilities include an athletic complex which includes baseball, softball, soccer, and tennis, a gymnasium that houses a weight room, basketball, and volleyball. **Graduates:** From July 1, 2016 to June 30, 2017, 598 bachelor's degrees were awarded. The most popular majors were business administration (18%), psychology (11%), and public administration (8%). In an average class, 4% graduate in 3 years or less, 46% graduate in 4 years or less, 58% graduate in 5 years or less, and 60% graduate in 6 years or less. Of the 2016 graduating class, 9% were enrolled in graduate school within 6 months of graduation, and 56% were employed.

SERVICES: Counseling and information services are available, as is tutoring in most subjects, such as business, finance, accounting, higher math, economics, natural sciences, study skills, Spanish, and French. There is a reader service for the blind, and remedial math, reading, and writing. **Library/Resources:** The library contains 102,047 volumes, and 4,180 audio/video tapes/CDs/DVDs, and subscribes to 630 periodicals including electronic. Computerized library services include interlibrary loans, database searching, Internet access, and Wi-Fi capability. Special learning facilities include an art gallery, and a radio station. **Physically Challenged Students:** 90% of the campus is accessible. Facilities include wheelchair ramps, elevators, special parking, specially equipped restrooms, special class scheduling, lowered drinking fountains, lowered telephones, and special housing. **Special:** The school offers internships, work-study, and dual majors. Students may participate in study-abroad programs in almost any country. Students majoring in deaf education can work directly with students at the Florida State School for the Deaf and Blind. There is a Student Exchange program with Germany. There are 13 national honor societies and 7 departmental honors programs. **Visiting:** There are regularly scheduled orientations for prospective students, Prospective Student Information Sessions and Tours Monday-Friday (30 minute presentation by an Admissions Representative and tour of campus by a Student Ambassador); Each fall and spring, we offer a day-long Campus Visit Day on a Saturday. There are guides for informal visits and visitors may sit in on classes. To schedule a visit, contact Philadelphia Shoop at pshoop@flagler.edu. **Campus Safety and Security:** Measures include 24-hour foot and vehicle patrol, emergency notification system, self-defense education, and security escort services. There are shuttle buses, emergency telephones, lighted pathways/sidewalks, controlled access to dorms/residences, and a uniformed police officer.

REQUIREMENTS: The SAT or ACT is required. The ACT Optional Writing test is also required. Student must have graduated from an accredited secondary school or have a satisfactory score on the GED. Students must have a total of 19 academic credits. High school courses must include 4 credits of English, 3 credits each of math and science, and 2 credits of a foreign language. An essay is required, and an interview is recommended. A GPA of 3.0 is required. AP and CLEP credits are accepted. Important factors in the admissions decision are advanced placement or honors courses, leadership record, and extracurricular activities record. Completion of 120 semester hours with at least a 2.0 grade point average; completion of at least one major in accordance with the requirements set forth by the academic department; completion of 42 hours in General Education; a grade of C or better in ENG 152 or ENG 172; final 30 credit hours required for the degree must be earned at Flagler College; three semesters as a full-time student; minimum of 45 credit hours completed at Flagler College; completion of institutional and departmental assessments **Procedure:** Freshmen are admitted fall and spring. Entrance exams should be taken during the fall of the senior year at the latest. There are early decision, early admissions, and deferred admissions plans. Early decision applications should be filed by November 1; regular applications, by March 1 for fall entry and December 15 for spring entry. The fall 2017 application fee was $50. Notification of early decision is sent December 15; regular decision, March 31. 251 early decision candidates were accepted for the 2017-2018 class. 1 applicant was on the 2017 waiting list and was admitted. Applications are accepted on-line. **Transfer Students:** 153 transfer students enrolled in 2016-2017. Applicants transferring from another institution must be in good standing with a satisfactory grade point average for all work attempted and must be eligible to return to the institution last attended. Transfer applicants from four-year institutions may receive a maximum of 75 semester hours of credit awarded. Applicants who transfer from junior or community colleges will be allowed no more than 64 semester hours of credit toward the completion of degree requirements at Flagler. The College imposes a minimum testing requirement for students planning to major in Education. All Education majors must have a combined score (Critical Reading plus Mathematics) of at least 1010 on a single administration of the SAT or a composite score of at least 21 on the ACT. 45 of 120 credits required for the bachelor's degree must be completed at Flagler. **International Students:** There are 133 international students enrolled. They must take the TOEFL with a minimum score of 550 on the paper-based TOEFL (PBT) or 75 on the Internet-based version (iBT). Students must take the IELTS. They must also take the SAT or ACT.

ADMISSIONS: 75% of the 2017-2018 applicants were accepted. The SAT scores for the 2017-2018 freshman class were: Critical Reading-- 24% below 500, 51% between 500 and 599, 21% between 600 and 699, and 3% between 700 and 800. Math-- 42% below 500, 43% between 500 and 599, 15% between 600 and 699, and 1% between 700 and 800. Writing-- 31% below 500, 52% between 500 and 599, 15% between 600 and 699, and 2% between 700 and 800. The ACT scores were 47% between 18 and 23, 47% between 24 and 29, and 6% above 30. **Admissions Contact:** Deborah Thompson, Vice President of Enrollment Management. Email: *admissions@flagler.edu* Web: *www.flagler.edu*

FINANCIAL AID: In 2017-2018, 96% of all full-time freshmen received some form of financial aid. 61% of all full-time freshmen received need-based aid. The average freshman award was $15,826. Need-based scholarships or need-based grants averaged $5,393; need-based self-help aid (loans and jobs) averaged $3,517; non-need-based athletic scholarships averaged $7,643; and other non-need-based awards and non-need-based scholarships averaged $10,516. 65% of undergraduate students work part-time. The average financial indebtedness of the 2017 graduate was $25,660. The FAFSA code is 007893. The priority date for freshman financial aid applications for fall entry is March 1.

FLORIDA AGRICULTURAL AND MECHANICAL UNIVERSITY C-1

www.famu.edu

Tallahassee, FL 32307 **(850) 599-3796**

Fax: (850) 599-3069 **Email:** ugradadmissions@famu.edu
Full-time: 2306 men, 4311 women
Part-time: 472 men, 721 women
Graduate: 644 men, 1165 women
Year: semesters, summer session
Room & Board: $10,100
SAT CR/M/W: 515/503/494 **ACT:** 23
Application Deadline: May 15
Faculty: 415; IIA, av$
Ph.D.s: 74%
Student/Faculty: 15 to 1
Tuition: $5785 ($17,725)
Freshman Class: 5198 applied, 1755 accepted, 855 enrolled
CEEB CODE: 5215
COMPETITIVE

Florida Agricultural and Mechanical University, founded in 1887, is a public institution within the state university system of Florida, offers undergraduate programs in agriculture, allied health science, architecture, the arts and sciences, business and industry, education, engineering, journalism, pharmacy and pharmaceutical sciences, upper-level nursing, and technology. There are 12 undergraduate schools and 1 graduate school. In addition to regional accreditation, FAMU has baccalaureate program accreditation with AACSB, ABET, ACEJMC, ACPE, APTA, CSWE, NAAB, CAEP, and NLN. The 422-acre campus is in an urban area 169 miles west of Jacksonville, Florida. Including any residence halls, there are 211 buildings.

STUDENT LIFE: 87% of undergraduates are from Florida. Others are from 45 states, 59 foreign countries, and Canada. 84% are African American; 3% Hispanic; 2% Foreign; 10% White; 1% Asian American. **Female To Male Ratio:** 1.8:1. The average age of freshmen is 19; all undergraduates, 21. 20% do not continue beyond their first year; 40% remain to graduate. **Housing:** 2394 students can be accommodated in college housing, which includes single-sex dorms, on-campus apartments, and married student housing. On-campus housing is guaranteed for the freshman year only, and is available on a first-come, first-served basis. Priority is given to out-of-town students. 73% of students commute. Alcohol is not permitted. Upperclassmen may keep cars.

FACULTY/CLASSROOMS: 54% of faculty are male; 46% are female. 72% teach undergraduates and do research. No introductory courses are taught by graduate students.

PROGRAMS OF STUDY: FAMU confers B.A., B.Arch., B.C.J., B.S., B.S.Arch. and Constr.E.T., B.S.Arch.E.T., B.S.Studies., B.S.C.E., B.S.C.E.T., B.S.Ch.E., B.S.Constr.E.T., B.S.E.E., B.S.Elect.E.T., B.S.H.C.M., B.S.I.E., B.S.J., B.S.M.E., B.S.M.R.A., B.S.N., B.S.Pharm., B.S.P.T., B.S.R.T., B.S.T. and B.S.W. degrees. Associate, master's, and doctoral degrees are also awarded. Bachelor's degrees are awarded in AGRICULTURE (animal science and horticulture), BIOLOGICAL SCIENCE (biology/biological science), BUSINESS (accounting, banking and finance, business administration and management, and business economics), COMMUNICATIONS AND THE ARTS (dramatic arts, English, fine arts, journalism, and music), COMPUTER AND PHYSICAL SCIENCE (actuarial science, chemistry, computer science, mathematics, and physics), EDUCATION (art education, business education, early childhood education, elementary education, industrial arts education, music education, and science education), ENGINEERING AND ENVIRONMENTAL DESIGN (chemical engineering, civil engineering, electrical/electronics engineering, engineering technology, industrial engineering, and mechanical engineering), HEALTH PROFESSIONS (nursing, occupational therapy, pharmacy, physical therapy, predentistry, and premedicine), SOCIAL SCIENCE (criminal justice, economics, history, political science/government, psychology, public administration, social science, social work, and sociology). Business, engineering, and pharmacy are the strongest academically. Business administration, management, and biology/bological sciences have the largest enrollments.

ACTIVITIES: 2% of men belong to 4 national fraternities; 3% of women belong to 4 national sororities. There are 135 groups on campus, including cheerleading, choir, chorus, dance, drama, drill team, ethnic, honors, international, jazz band, marching band, newspaper, orchestra, pep band, political, professional, radio and TV, religious, social, social service, student government, and symphony. Popular campus events include FAMU Essen-Theater, FAMU Orchesis Dance Theater and Ebony Fashion Fair. **Sports:** There are 8 intercollegiate sports for men and 8 for women. Facilities include a 3,300-seat gym, a 1,600-seat auditorium, a 25,559-seat football stadium, swimming pools, baseball diamonds, softball and track fields, tennis courts, a bowling alley, pool hall, a student activities center, and a fitness center. **Graduates:** From July 1, 2015 to June 30, 2016, 1653 bachelor's degrees were awarded. The most popular majors were health (17%), business administration and management (9%), and criminal justice (7%). 76 companies recruited on campus in 2015-2016. In an average class, 13% graduate in 4 years or less, 29% graduate in 5 years or less, and 38% graduate in 6 years or less. Of the 2015 graduating class, 33% were enrolled in graduate school within 6 months of graduation.

SERVICES: Counseling and information services are available, as is tutoring in some subjects, such as math, English, and reading. There is remedial math, reading, and writing. **Library/Resources:** The 4 libraries contain 1.5 million volumes, 515,136 microform items, and 63,067 audio/video tapes/CDs/DVDs, and subscribe to 302,781 periodicals including electronic. Computerized library services include interlibrary loans, database searching, Internet access, and Wi-Fi capability. Special learning facilities include an art gallery, radio station, TV station, an Black Archives, and a observatory. **Physically Challenged Students:** 90% of the campus is accessible. Facilities include wheelchair ramps, elevators, special parking, and specially equipped restrooms. **Special:** Cooperative programs and cross-registration are offered in conjunction with Florida State University. Internships are available either on or off campus. Florida A&M also offers a Washington semester for architecture majors, a B.A.-B.S. degree, credit for life experience, and pass/fail options. Nondegree study is possible. There is a freshman honors program. **Visiting:** There are regularly scheduled orientations for prospective students. There are guides for informal visits and visitors may sit in on classes. To schedule a visit, contact the Admissions Office. **Campus Safety and Security:** Measures include 24-hour foot and vehicle patrol, emergency notification system, self-defense education, and security escort services. There are shuttle buses, emergency telephones, and lighted pathways/sidewalks.

REQUIREMENTS: The SAT or ACT is required, with a satisfactory score on the SAT, or 19 on the ACT. Applicants must be graduates of accredited secondary schools or have earned a GED. The university requires 19 academic credits, including 4 each in English and academic electives, 3 each in math, science, and social studies, and 2 in foreign language. A GPA of 2.5 is required. AP and CLEP credits are accepted. Important factors in the admissions decision are recommendations by school officials, extracurricular activities record, and evidence of special talent. General education requirements include 36 credit hours in English, humanities, social science, natural science, American history, foreign language, and math at the college algebra level or above. In order to graduate, students must complete at least 120 credit hours, including 30 in a major field, with a minimum GPA of 2.0. **Procedure:** Freshmen are admitted to all sessions. Entrance exams should be taken by the fall of the senior year. There are deferred admissions and rolling admissions plans. Applications should be filed by May 15 for fall entry; November 15 for spring entry; and April 1 for summer entry, along with a $30 fee. Applications are accepted on-line. **Transfer Students:** 496 transfer students enrolled in 2015-2016. Applicants must present a minimum GPA of 2.0 in at least 60 semester hours or 90 quarter hours earned. 30 of 120 credits required for the bachelor's degree must be completed at FAMU. **International Students:** There are 80 international students enrolled. They must take the TOEFL with a minimum score of 500 on the paper-based TOEFL (PBT) or 61 on the Internet-based version (iBT). They must also take the SAT or ACT.

ADMISSIONS: 34% of the 2016-2017 applicants were accepted. The SAT scores for the 2016-2017 freshman class were: Critical Reading-- 61% below 500, 27% between 500 and 599, 11% between 600 and 699, and 2% between 700 and 800. Math-- 63% below 500, 28% between 500 and 599, and 9% between 600 and 699. Writing-- 68% below 500, 23% between 500 and 599, and 8% between 600 and 699. The ACT scores were 18% between 12 and 17, 61% between 18 and 23, 19% between 24 and 29, and 2% above 30. **Admissions Contact:** Barbara Cox, Director. Email: *ugradadmissions@famu.edu* Web: *www.famu.edu*

FINANCIAL AID: The FAFSA code is 001480. The priority date for freshman financial aid applications for fall entry is March 1.

FLORIDA ATLANTIC UNIVERSITY E-5

www.fau.edu

Boca Raton, FL 33431	**(561) 297-3040** **(800) 299-4FAU**
Fax: (561) 297-2758	**Email: admissions@fau.edu**
Full-time: 7085 men, 8508 women	**Faculty:** 875; I, --$
Part-time: 3843 men, 5387 women	**Ph.D.s:** 90%
Graduate: 1991 men, 3224 women	**Student/Faculty:** 22 to 1
Year: semesters, summer session	**Tuition:** $5986 ($21,543)
Room & Board: $12,270	**Freshman Class:** 27888 applied, 10876 accepted, 3237 enrolled
SAT CR/M/W: 525/535/520 **ACT:** 23	**CEEB CODE:** 5529
Application Deadline: May 1	**COMPETITIVE**

Florida Atlantic University, founded in 1964, is one of the few universities in the country to offer only upper-division and graduate-level work, on the theory that freshmen and sophomores could be served by the community college system. Today, with its well developed system of distributed campuses and sites that offer students high-quality degree programs at seven locations, FAU serves as a model for America's urban, regional universities. Figures in the above capsule and in this profile are approximate. There are 9 undergraduate schools and 8 graduate schools. In addition to regional accreditation, FAU has baccalaureate program accreditation with AACSB, ABET, CSAB, CSWE, NAAB, NASM, CAEP, NLN, ACS, ASLHA, NAACLS, and NASPAA. The 850-acre campus is in a suburban area 17 miles north of Ft. Lauderdale, 45 miles north of Miami, and 22 miles south of Palm Beach. Including any residence halls, there are 160 buildings.

STUDENT LIFE: 95% of undergraduates are from Florida. Others are from 49 states, 135 foreign countries, and Canada. 73% are from public schools. 50% are White; 4% Asian American; 22% Hispanic; 2% Foreign; 18% African American; 1% American Indian/Alaska Native. **Female To Male Ratio:** 1.3:1. The average age of freshmen is 18; all undergraduates, 24. 22% do not continue beyond their first year; 43% remain to graduate. **Housing:** 3750 students can be accommodated in college housing, which includes dorms and on-campus apartments. In addition, there are honors houses, special-interest houses, living learning communities, and theme housing. On-campus housing is guaranteed for the freshman year only, is available on a first-come, and first-served basis. 94% of students commute. All students may keep cars.

FACULTY/CLASSROOMS: 54% of faculty are male; 46% are female. All teach undergraduates and all do research. No introductory courses are taught by graduate students. The average class size in an introductory lecture is 38; in a laboratory is 21; and in a regular course is 29.

PROGRAMS OF STUDY: FAU confers B.A., B.S., B.A.E., B.Arch., B.B.A., B.E.C.E., B.F.A., B.H.S., B.I.E.T., B.Mus., B.P.M., B.S.C.E., B.S.C.V., B.S.E., B.S.E.E., B.S.G.E., B.S.H.S., B.S.M.E., B.S.M.T., B.S.N., B.S.O.E., B.S.W., and B.U.R.P. degrees. Associate, master's, and doctoral degrees are also awarded. Bachelor's degrees are awarded in BIOLOGICAL SCIENCE (biology/biological science and marine biology), BUSINESS (accounting, banking and finance, business administration and management, business economics, hospitality management services, human resources, international business management, management information systems, marketing/retailing/merchandising, real estate, and small business management), COMMUNICATIONS AND THE ARTS (art, communications, dramatic arts, English, fine arts, French, German, graphic design, Italian, jazz, journalism, linguistics, media arts, multimedia, music, Spanish, and visual and performing arts), COMPUTER AND PHYSICAL SCIENCE (chemistry, computer science, computer security and information assurance, geology, information sciences and systems, mathematics, and physics), EDUCATION (education of the exceptional child, elementary education, English education, foreign languages education, physical education, and special education), ENGINEERING AND ENVIRONMENTAL DESIGN (architecture, civil engineering, computer engineering, electrical/electronics engineering, engineering, mechanical engineering, ocean engineering, and urban planning technology), HEALTH PROFESSIONS (health care administration, health science, medical laboratory technology, and nursing), SOCIAL SCIENCE (anthropology, criminal justice, economics, geography, history, interdisciplinary studies, Judaic studies, liberal arts/general studies, philosophy, political science/government, psychobiology, psychology, public administration, social psychology, social science, social work, and sociology). Engineering, education, and business are the strongest academically. Biological science, psychology, and elementary education have the largest enrollments.

ACTIVITIES: 1% of men belong to 11 national fraternities; 1% of women belong to 8 national sororities. There are 250 groups on campus, including art, band, cheerleading, chess, choir, chorale, chorus, computers, dance, debate, drama, drill team, environmental, ethnic, film, forensics, honors, international, jazz band, LGBT, literary magazine, marching band, musical theater, newspaper, opera, orchestra, pep band, photography, political, professional, radio and TV, religious, social, social service, student government, and symphony. Popular campus events include Luau, African American Festival, Festival of Nations, and Homecoming. **Sports:** There are 8 intercollegiate sports for men and 9 for women, and 10 intramural sports for men and 10 for women. Facilities include weight and training rooms, baseball, softball, and soccer stadiums, arena for volleyball and basketball, cross country and track field, football, aquatic center, tennis courts, a fitness center with cardio, outdoor basketball courts, practice fields, and a football stadium. **Graduates:** From July 1, 2016 to June 30, 2017, 4892 bachelor's degrees were awarded. The most popular majors were business/marketing (23%), education (10%), and social sciences (9%). In an average class, 17% graduate in 4 years or less, 35% graduate in 5 years or less, and 43% graduate in 6 years or less.

SERVICES: Counseling and information services are available, as is tutoring in most subjects. There is a reader service for the blind. Remedial work must be taken at the community college level. **Library/Resources:** The library contains 206,615 volumes, 2.1 million microform items, and 22,414 audio/video tapes/CDs/DVDs, and subscribes to 12,549 periodicals including electronic. Computerized library services include interlibrary loans, database searching, Internet access, and Wi-Fi capability. Special learning facilities include an art gallery, planetarium, radio station, TV station, engineering research labs, a marine sciences research center, a K-12 developmental research school, a nonnative fish research lab, and an environmental sciences center, and medical school. **Physically Challenged Students:** All of the campus is accessible. Facilities include wheelchair ramps, elevators, special parking, specially equipped restrooms, lowered drinking fountains, and lowered telephones. **Special:** FAU offers cooperative programs and internships in most majors. Work-study programs, dual and student-designed majors, a general studies degree, credit for military experience, nondegree study, and pass/fail options are available. The school offers a Washington semester, and study abroad through all state university system of Florida programs. There are 21 national honor societies, a freshman honors program, and 9 departmental honors programs. **Visiting:** There are regularly scheduled orientations for prospective students, consisting of a group tour. There are guides for informal visits. To schedule a visit, contact the Admissions Office. **Campus Safety and Security:** Measures include 24-hour foot and vehicle patrol, emergency notification system, self-defense education, and security escort services. There are shuttle buses, emergency telephones, lighted pathways/sidewalks, and controlled access to dorms/residences.

REQUIREMENTS: The SAT or ACT is required, with a satisfactory score on the SAT Critical Reading and Math sections or on the ACT. In addition, graduation from an accredited secondary school or satisfactory scores on the GED are required. Students must have 19 academic credits, including 4 units of English, 3 each of math (algebra I and higher), science (including 2 with substantial lab work), and social studies, and 2 of a foreign language, plus 4 of electives in computer science, fine arts, or humanities. A portfolio or an audition may be requested by individual departments. An essay and an interview are required. A GPA of 2.0 is required. AP and CLEP credits are accepted. Important factors in the admissions decision are advanced placement or honors courses, evidence of special talent, and recommendations by school officials. All students must take the College Level Academic Skills Test (CLAST) required by the state. To graduate, students must complete a total of 120 credit hours, with a minimum GPA of 2.0. All students must take the required courses in the core curriculum, including 9 credits each of humanities and social sciences, and 6 each of math, communication, and natural sciences, and must demonstrate proficiency in foreign language. **Procedure:** Freshmen are admitted fall, spring, and summer. There are early decision, early admissions, deferred admissions, and rolling admissions plans. Applications should be filed by May 1 for fall entry; October 15 for spring entry; and March 15 for summer entry. The fall 2017 application fee was $30. Applications are accepted on-line. **Transfer Students:** 3678 transfer students enrolled in 2016-2017. Students must have a minimum GPA of 2.0, submit official transcripts from the previous schools attended, and be in good standing at those institutions. Applicants from a community or junior college in Florida with an associate degree are automatically admitted. Students with fewer than 60 transferable hours must meet the same criteria as entering freshmen. 30 credits required for the bachelor's degree must be completed at FAU. **International Students:** There are 268 international students enrolled. They must take the TOEFL with a minimum score of 550 on the paper-based TOEFL (PBT). They must also take the SAT or ACT.

ADMISSIONS: 39% of the 2017-2018 applicants were accepted. The SAT scores for the 2017-2018 freshman class were: Critical Reading-- 30% below 500, 53% between 500 and 599, 15% between 600 and 699, and 3% between 700 and 800. Math-- 27% below 500, 53% between 500 and 599, 18% between 600 and 699, and 2% between 700 and 800. Writing-- 32% below 500, 54% between 500 and 599, 13% between 600 and 699, and 1% between 700 and 800. The ACT scores were 59% between 18 and 23, 37% between 24 and 29, and 3% above 30. 51% of the current freshmen were in the top fifth of their class; 80% were in the top two fifths. **Admissions Contact:** Barbar Pletcher, Director of Admissions. Email: *admissions@fau.edu* Web: *www.fau.edu*

FINANCIAL AID: The average freshman award was $10,684. Need-based scholarships or need-based grants averaged $5,871; need-based self-help aid (loans and jobs) averaged $6,849; non-need-based athletic scholarships averaged $9,892; other non-need-based awards and non-need-based scholarships averaged $6,777; and $2,275 from other forms of aid. The average financial indebtedness of the 2017 graduate was $13,229. FAU is a member of CSS. The FAFSA code is 001481. The priority date for freshman financial aid applications for fall entry is March 1.

FLORIDA GULF COAST UNIVERSITY D-5

www.fgcu.edu

Fort Myers, FL 33965	**(239) 590-7891** **(888) 889-1095**
Fax: (239) 590-7894	**Email: admissions@fgcu.edu**
Full-time: 4743 men, 6066 women	**Faculty:** 463; IIA, -$
Part-time: 1297 men, 1553 women	**Ph.D.s:** 72%
Graduate: 328 men, 656 women	**Student/Faculty:** 22 to 1
Year: semesters, summer session	**Tuition:** $6118
Room & Board: $8620	**Freshman Class:** 10804 applied, 7108 accepted, 2761 enrolled
SAT CR/M/W: 540/530/525 **ACT:** 24	**CEEB CODE:** 5221
Application Deadline: May 1	**COMPETITIVE**

Florida Gulf Coast University, founded in 1991, is part of the State University System of Florida. There are 5 undergraduate schools. In addition to regional accreditation, FGCU has baccalaureate program accreditation with AACSB, APTA, CSWE, NLN, and CAPTE. The 760-acre campus is in a suburban area in southwest Florida in southern Lee County. Including any residence halls, there are 112 buildings.

STUDENT LIFE: 84% of undergraduates are from Florida. Others are from 46 states, 87 foreign countries, and Canada. 65% are White; 20% Hispanic; 10% American Indian/Alaska Native; 7% African American; 3% two or more races; 2% Asian American; 2% Foreign; 1% race unknown. **Female To Male Ratio:** 1.3:1. The average age of freshmen is 18; all undergraduates, 21. **Housing:** 4200 students can be accommodated in college housing, which includes dorms, on-campus apartments, off-campus apartments, and theme housing. On-campus housing is available on a first-come and first-served basis. 78% of students live on campus. Alcohol is not permitted. Some may keep cars.

FACULTY/CLASSROOMS: All teach undergraduates and all do research. No introductory courses are taught by graduate students. The average class size in a regular course is 25.

PROGRAMS OF STUDY: FGCU confers B.A. and B.S. degrees. Associate, master's, and doctoral degrees are also awarded. Bachelor's degrees are awarded in AGRICULTURE (environmental studies), BIOLOGICAL SCIENCE (biology/biological science, biotechnology, and marine science), BUSINESS (accounting, banking and finance, marketing and distribution, and recreational facilities management), COMMUNICATIONS AND THE ARTS (art, communications, English, music, and Spanish), COMPUTER AND PHYSICAL SCIENCE (applied science, chemistry, computer science, and mathematics), EDUCATION (athletic training, early childhood education, elementary education, mathematics education, music education, secondary education, social science education, and special education), ENGINEERING AND ENVIRONMENTAL DESIGN (civil engineering and environmental engineering), HEALTH PROFESSIONS (clinical science, community health work, exercise science, health science, nursing, and occupational therapy), SOCIAL SCIENCE (anthropology, child psychology/development, counseling/psychology, criminal justice, criminology, economics, forensic studies, history, law, liberal arts/general studies, philosophy, political science/government, psychology, social work, and sociology). Management, communication, and psychology have the largest enrollments.

ACTIVITIES: 1% of men belong to 7 national fraternities; 7% of women belong to 5 national sororities. There are 125 groups on campus, including model UN, art, campus ministries, cheerleading, chess, computers, dance, debate, drama, environmental, ethnic, film, honors, international, LGBT, literary magazine, musical theater, newspaper, political, professional, religious, social, social service, and student government. Popular campus events include Eagle Expo and President's Lecture Series. **Sports:** There are 6 intercollegiate sports for men and 8 for women, and 9 intramural sports for men and 9 for women. Facilities include a fitness center, a teaching gym, playing fields, tennis courts, softball, baseball, swimming pool and a recreational pool. **Graduates:** From July 1, 2016 to June 30, 2017, 2334 bachelor's degrees were awarded. The most popular majors were business/marketing, education, and homeland security. In an average class, 47% graduate in 6 years or less.

SERVICES: Counseling and information services are available, as is tutoring in most subjects. **Library/Resources:** The library contains 276,638 volumes, 843,772 microform items, and 319,258 audio/video tapes/CDs/DVDs, and subscribes to 409,967 periodicals including electronic. Computerized library services include interlibrary loans, database searching, Internet access, and Wi-Fi capability. Special learning facilities include an art gallery, TV station, chickee huts, computer labs, and a family resource center. **Physically Challenged Students:** All of the campus is accessible. Facilities include wheelchair ramps, elevators, special parking, specially equipped restrooms, special class scheduling, lowered drinking fountains, lowered telephones, and special housing. **Special:** The university offers cross-registration with the University of Central Florida, study abroad in China, a Washington semester, an accelerated degree in biology, and work-study programs. There is 1 national honor society, Phi Beta Kappa, a freshman honors program, and 1 departmental honors program. **Visiting:** There are regularly scheduled orientations for prospective students. There are guides for informal visits and visitors may sit in on classes. To schedule a visit, contact the Admissions Office. **Campus Safety and Security:** Measures include 24-hour foot and vehicle patrol, self-defense education, and security escort services. There are shuttle buses, emergency telephones, and lighted pathways/sidewalks.

REQUIREMENTS: The SAT is required. The ACT Optional Writing test is also required. In addition, 18 academic high school units are required, 4 units each in English and math, 3 units each in social studies and science (2 must be lab), 2 units each in foreign language and academic electives, and 1 unit in history is recommended. High school diploma is required, and the GED is accepted. A GPA of 2.0 is required. AP and CLEP credits are accepted. Important factors in the admissions decision are advanced placement or honors courses, leadership record, evidence of special talent, and extracurricular activities record. To graduate, students must have a 2.0 minimum GPA and 120 credit hours that include courses in phys ed, computer science, general education, service learning, and university colloquium. **Procedure:** Freshmen are admitted fall, spring, and summer. Entrance exams should be taken in the junior year. There is a deferred admissions plan. Applications should be filed by May 1 for fall entry; November 9 for spring entry; and February 1 for summer entry. The fall 2017 application fee was $30. Notifications are sent February 15. Applications are accepted on-line. **Transfer Students:** 1052 transfer students enrolled in 2016-2017. Lower level transfers must meet the same requirements as regular admissions. Upper level transfers must have a 2.0 GPA and 60 hours of transferable credit, and be in good standing at their last institution. 30 of 120 credits required for the bachelor's degree must be completed at FGCU. **International Students:** There are 206 international students enrolled. They must take the TOEFL with a minimum score of 550 on the paper-based TOEFL (PBT) or 79 on the Internet-based version (iBT). They must also take the SAT or ACT, scoring 440.

ADMISSIONS: 66% of the 2017-2018 applicants were accepted. The SAT scores for the 2017-2018 freshman class were: Critical Reading-- 24% below 500, 58% between 500 and 599, 16% between 600 and 699, and 2% between 700 and 800. Math-- 30% below 500, 55% between 500 and 599, 14% between 600 and 699, and 1% between 700 and 800. Writing-- 33% below 500, 55% between 500 and 599, 11% between 600 and 699, and 1% between 700 and 800. The ACT scores were 1% between 12 and 17, 51% between 18 and 23, 44% between 24 and 29, and 4% above 30. 27% of the current freshmen were in the top fifth of their class; 61% were in the top two fifths. 4 freshmen graduated first in their class. **Admissions Contact:** Marc Maviolette, Director of Admissions. Email: *admissions@fgcu.edu* Web: *www.fgcu.edu*

FINANCIAL AID: In 2017-2018, 57% of all full-time freshmen received some form of financial aid. 36% of all full-time freshmen received need-based aid. The average freshman award was $9,123. Need-based scholarships or need-based grants averaged $4,860; need-based self-help aid (loans and jobs) averaged $7,362; non-need-based athletic scholarships averaged $6,415; other non-need-based awards and non-need-based scholarships averaged $4,312; and $7,369 from other forms of aid. The average financial indebtedness of the 2017 graduate was $24,763. FGCU is a member of CSS. The FAFSA code is 032553. The priority date for freshman financial aid applications for fall entry is March 1. The deadline for filing freshman financial aid applications for fall entry is June 30.

FLORIDA INSTITUTE OF TECHNOLOGY E-4

www.fit.edu

Melbourne, FL 32901	(321) 674-8030 (800) 888-4348
Fax: (321) 674-8004	**Email:** admission@fit.edu
Full-time: 2306 men, 980 women	**Faculty:** 211
Part-time: 230 men, 113 women	**Ph.D.s:** 89%
Graduate: 1714 men, 1108 women	**Student/Faculty:** 15 to 1
Year: semesters, summer session	**Tuition:** $39,696
Room & Board: $13,610	**Freshman Class:** 9503 applied, 5828 accepted, 761 enrolled
SAT CR/M: 556/604 **ACT:** 25	**CEEB CODE:** 5080
Application Deadline: n/av	**VERY COMPETITIVE**

Florida Institute of Technology, founded in 1958, offers undergraduate degrees in engineering, science, business, psychology, liberal arts, and aeronautics. The figures given in the above capsule and in this profile are approximate. There are 6 undergraduate schools and 7 graduate schools. In addition to regional accreditation, FIT has a baccalaureate program accreditation with ABET, CSAB, ACS, APA, and CAA. The 130-acre campus is in a suburban area 65 miles east of Orlando. Including any residence halls, there are 93 buildings.

STUDENT LIFE: 28% of undergraduates are from out of state, mostly the Middle Atlantic. Students are from 48 states, 113 foreign countries, and Canada. 49% are from public schools. 8% are African American; 7% Hispanic; 6% race unknown; 41% White; 33% Foreign; 2% Asian American; 2% two or more races. **Male To Female Ratio:** 1.9:1. The average age of freshmen is 18; all undergraduates, 21. 17% do not continue beyond their first year; 58% remain to graduate. **Housing:** 2127 students can be accommodated in college housing, which includes dorms and on-campus apartments. In addition, there are fraternity houses and sorority houses. On-campus housing is guaranteed for the freshman year only, is available on a first-come, and first-served basis. 56% of students commute. All students may keep cars.

FACULTY/CLASSROOMS: 75% of faculty are male; 25% are female. 10% teach undergraduates, and 36% teach and do research. No introductory courses are taught by graduate students. The average class size in an introductory lecture is 22; in a laboratory is 20; and in a regular course is 21.

PROGRAMS OF STUDY: FIT confers B.A. and B.S. degrees. Master's and doctoral degrees are also awarded. Bachelor's degrees are awarded in AGRICULTURE (conservation and regulation and environmental studies), BIOLOGICAL SCIENCE (biochemistry, biology/biological science, biomathematics, ecology, marine biology, and molecular biology), BUSINESS (accounting, business administration and management, electronic business, international business management, management information systems, marketing management, and sports management), COMMUNICATIONS AND THE ARTS (communications), COMPUTER AND PHYSICAL SCIENCE (applied mathematics, astronomy, astrophysics, atmospheric sciences and meteorology, chemistry, computer science, information sciences and systems, mathematics, oceanography, physics, planetary and space science, and software engineering), EDUCATION (mathematics education, middle school education, and science education), ENGINEERING AND ENVIRONMENTAL DESIGN (aeronautical engineering, aeronautical science, aviation administration/management, aviation computer technology, biomedical engineering, chemical engineering, civil engineering, computer engineering, construction engineering, construction management, electrical/electronics engineering, environmental science, mechanical engineering, military science, and ocean engineering), HEALTH PROFESSIONS (premedicine), SOCIAL SCIENCE (forensic studies, humanities, interdisciplinary studies, prelaw, and psychology). Engineering, science, and aeronautics are the strongest academically. Aerospace engineering, mechanical engineering, and computer science have the largest enrollments.

ACTIVITIES: 3% of men belong to 8 national fraternities; 5% of women belong to 3 national sororities. There are 147 groups on campus, including cheerleading, chess, chorus, computers, dance, drama, drill team, ethnic, film, honors, international, jazz band, LGBT, literary magazine, newspaper, pep band, photography, political, professional, radio and TV, religious, social, social service, and student government. Popular campus events include International Festival, Homecoming, Campus Cleanup, Relay for Life, Engineering Week, and Greek Week. **Sports:** There are 11 intercollegiate sports for men and 11 for women, and 15 intramural sports for men and 15 for women. Facilities include basketball courts, a racquetball court, group fitness rooms, volleyball and badminton courts, weight and fitness area with cardiovascular machines, free weights, and specialized weight equipment. The aquatic facility features a competition pool and a recreation pool with diving boards. **Graduates:** From July 1, 2016 to June 30, 2017, 677 bachelor's degrees were awarded. The most popular majors were mechanical engineering (11%), aerospace engineering (9%), and electrical engineering (6%). In an average class, 2% graduate in 3 years or less, 45% graduate in 4 years or less, 56% graduate in 5 years or less, and 58% graduate in 6 years or less. Of the 2016 graduating class, 35% were enrolled in graduate school within 6 months of graduation, and 59% were employed.

SERVICES: Counseling and information services are available, as is tutoring, in every subject. There is a reader service for the blind, and remedial math, reading, and writing. **Library/Resources:** The library contains 399,275 volumes, 76,388 microform items, and 3,641 audio/video tapes/CDs/DVDs, and subscribes to 46,320 periodicals including electronic. Computerized library services include interlibrary loans, database searching, Internet access, and Wi-Fi capability. Special learning facilities include an art gallery, radio station, TV station, and the Ruth Funk Center for Textile Arts. **Physically Challenged Students:** 90% of the campus is accessible. Facilities include wheelchair ramps, elevators, special parking, specially equipped restrooms, special class scheduling, lowered drinking fountains, and lowered telephones. **Special:** The ProTrack cooperative education program allows students in the College of Engineering to complete three semester-long (amounting to one year) paid work experiences within the four years it takes to earn a bachelor's degree. Students graduate with their employers' names on their final transcripts. The FastTrack accelerated master's degree program allows students to take graduate coursework as undergraduates, so they can complete a master's degree in as little as one additional year of study. Earned scholarships carry over to the fifth year. Florida Tech offers co-op programs in all majors. Students may choose to pursue more than 1 degree by completing degree requirements for each major. Internships are available in the senior year for many majors, including psychology, engineering, and aeronautics. Study abroad and work-study programs are available. There are 8 national honor societies and 1 departmental honors program. **Visiting:** There are regularly scheduled orientations for prospective students, including tours and interviews with admissions staff, faculty, or department heads upon request. There are guides for informal visits and visitors may sit in on classes. To schedule a visit, contact the Office of Undergraduate Admissions at admission@fit.edu. **Campus Safety and Security:** Measures include 24-hour foot and vehicle patrol, emergency notification system, self-defense education, and security escort services. There are shuttle buses, emergency telephones, lighted pathways/sidewalks, and controlled access to dorms/residences.

REQUIREMENTS: The SAT or ACT is required. Applicants must be graduates of an accredited secondary school or have a GED certificate. At least 18 academic credits or Carnegie units are required, including 4 years each of English, math, and science. An experiential essay is required and an interview is recommended. A GPA of 2.8 is required. AP and CLEP credits are accepted. Important factors in the admissions decision are advanced placement or honors courses, recommendations by school officials, and extracurricular activities record. To graduate, students must have a minimum 2.0 GPA and 120 to 135 credit hours. The required number of hours in the major varies. All students must take 9 hours in communication and humanities and 3 in English composition. The core curriculum also requires 6 credit hours each in physical or life sciences and math and 3 hours in computer science and social sciences. **Procedure:** Freshmen are admitted fall, spring, and summer. Entrance exams should be taken during the junior year or the beginning of the senior year of high school. There are deferred admissions and rolling admissions plans. Application deadlines are open. Applications are accepted on-line. **Transfer Students:** 238 transfer students enrolled in 2016-2017. Applicants must have a minimum 2.5 GPA. If transfer students have fewer than 30 semester hours, high school transcripts and SAT or ACT scores are required. A personal statement is recommended. 25 of 120 credits required for the bachelor's degree must be completed at Florida Tech. **International Students:** There are 1084 international students enrolled. They must take the TOEFL with a minimum score of 550 on the paper-based TOEFL (PBT) or 79 on the Internet-based version (iBT), and a math entrance qualifying exam. If students score below the minimum, they must take the language courses on campus.

ADMISSIONS: 61% of the 2017-2018 applicants were accepted. The SAT scores for the 2017-2018 freshman class were: Critical Reading-- 20% below 500, 49% between 500 and 599, 27% between 600 and 699, and 4% between 700 and 800. Math-- 4% below 500, 44% between 500 and 599, 42% between 600 and 699, and 10% between 700 and 800. The ACT scores were 22% between 18 and 23, 56% between 24 and 29, and 22% above 30. 54% of the current freshmen were in the top fifth of their class; 81% were in the top two fifths. 8 freshmen graduated first in their class. **Admissions Contact:** Michael J. Perry, Director, Undergraduate Admissions. Email: *admission@fit.edu* Web: *www.fit.edu*

FINANCIAL AID: In 2017-2018, 60% of all full-time freshmen received some form of financial aid. 60% of all full-time freshmen received need-based aid. The average freshman award was $36,771. Need-based scholarships or need-based grants averaged $25,435; need-based self-help aid (loans and jobs) averaged $5,940; non-need-based athletic scholarships averaged $20,893; and other non-need-based awards and non-need-based scholarships averaged $15,123. 21% of undergraduate students work part-time. The average financial indebtedness of the 2017 graduate was $36,678. The FAFSA code is 001469. The priority date for freshman financial aid applications for fall entry is March 1.

FLORIDA INTERNATIONAL UNIVERSITY E-5

www.fiu.edu

Miami, FL 33199	(305) 348-2363
Fax: (305) 348-3648	Email: admiss@fiu.edu
Full-time: 11,593 men, 15,104 women	**Faculty:** 1275; I, -$
Part-time: 8980 men, 11,909 women	**Ph.D.s:** 87%
Graduate: 3678 men, 5587 women	**Student/Faculty:** n/av
Year: semesters, summer session	**Tuition:** $8038 ($20,437)
Room & Board: $12,090	**Freshman Class:** 15863 applied, 7874 accepted, 2555 enrolled
SAT CR/M/W: 560/550/540 **ACT:** 24	**CEEB CODE:** 5206
Application Deadline: April 15	**COMPETITIVE**

Florida International University is a multi-campus public research university offering a broad array of undergraduate, graduate, and professional programs. FIU offers more than 180 baccalaureate, master's, professional and research doctorate programs, and conducts basic and applied research. Interdisciplinary centers and institutes conduct collaborative research to seek innovative solutions to economic, technological, and social problems. There are 11 undergraduate schools. In addition to regional accreditation, FIU has baccalaureate program accreditation with AACSB, ABET, ACCE, ACEJMC, APTA, ASLA, CSWE, NAAB, NASAD, NASM, NLN, AANA, ACS, ABA, ACOTE, NLNAC, CORPA, NASPAA, CEPH, ASHA, NAST, CIDA, CAPTE, CCNE, CACREP, and CORE. The 582-acre campus is in an urban area in western Miami-Dade County, the Biscayne Bay Campus in northeast Miami-Dade County. Including any residence halls, there are 187 buildings.

STUDENT LIFE: 92% of undergraduates are from Florida. Others are from 50 states, 150 foreign countries, and Canada. 7% are Foreign; 64% Hispanic; 3% Asian American; 2% two or more races; 13% African American; 10% White; 1% race unknown. **Female To Male Ratio:** 1.3:1. The average age of freshmen is 18; all undergraduates, 23. **Housing:** 3710 students can be accommodated in college housing, which includes married student dorms and on-campus apartments. In addition, there are fraternity houses. On-campus housing is available on a first-come and first-served basis. 92% of students commute. All students may keep cars.

FACULTY/CLASSROOMS: 54% of faculty are male; 46% are female. No introductory courses are taught by graduate students.

PROGRAMS OF STUDY: FIU confers B.A., B.S., B.Ac., B.B.A., B.F.A., B.H.S.A., B.M., B.P.A., and B.S.N. degrees. Master's and doctoral degrees are also awarded. Bachelor's degrees are awarded in BIOLOGICAL SCIENCE (biology/biological science, marine biology, and marine science), BUSINESS (accounting, banking and finance, business administration and management, hospitality management services, international business management, management information systems, management, marketing/retailing/merchandising, meeting/special event management, real estate, recreational facilities management, resort management, sports management, sports marketing, and supply chain management), COMMUNICATIONS AND THE ARTS (advertising, art history, art, art history and appreciation, digital media, dramatic arts, English, fine arts, French, Italian, music, music performance, Portuguese, public relations/advertising, radio/TV broadcasting, Spanish, and sports administration), COMPUTER AND PHYSICAL SCIENCE (chemistry, computer science, geology, mathematics, physics, and statistics), EDUCATION (art education, early childhood education, education, elementary education, middle school education, physical education, science education, special education, and specific learning disabilities), ENGINEERING AND ENVIRONMENTAL DESIGN (architecture, biomedical engineering, civil engineering, computer engineering, construction engineering, construction management, construction technology, electrical/electronics engineering, environmental engineering, environmental science, interior architecture, interior design, landscape architecture/design, and mechanical engineering), HEALTH PROFESSIONS (exercise science, health care administration, health services administration, pre-health studies, pre-health biological studies, and premedicine), SOCIAL SCIENCE (African studies, Asian/Oriental studies, criminal justice, dietetics, economics, geography, history, international relations, Latin American studies, liberal arts/general studies, liberal arts, sciences, general studies, humanities, parks and recreation management, philosophy, political science/government, prelaw, psychology, public administration, religion, social work, sociology, and women's studies). Biology, psychology, criminology, international relations, and international business are the strongest academically. Psychology, biology, and business have the largest enrollments.

ACTIVITIES: There are 558 groups on campus, including band, cheerleading, chorus, communications, drama, environmental, ethnic, film, honors, international, jazz band, LGBT, marching band, newspaper, opera, pep band, political, professional, radio and TV, religious, social, social service, student government, and symphony. Popular campus events include Welcome Week, Homecoming, and Dance Marathon. **Sports:** There are 10 intercollegiate sports for men and 10 for women, and 9 intramural sports for men and 9 for women. Facilities include a football stadium, an arena with basketball and racquetball courts, an aquatic center, baseball and soccer fields, a fitness center with Nautilus machines, tennis, and racquetball courts. **Graduates:** From July 1, 2016 to June 30, 2017, 9061 bachelor's degrees were awarded. The most popular majors were business administration (29%), social sciences (12%), and psychology (9%).

SERVICES: Counseling and information services are available, as is tutoring in most subjects. There is a reader service for the blind, and remedial math, reading, and writing. Note taking, adapted testing, and special registration may be arranged for disabled students. **Library/Resources:** The library contains 2.1 million volumes, 4.4 million microform items, and 454,481 audio/video tapes/CDs/DVDs, and subscribes to 108,720 periodicals including electronic. Computerized library services include interlibrary loans, database searching, Internet access, and Wi-Fi capability. Special learning facilities include an art gallery, radio station, including a Frost Art Museum, nature preserve, Biscayne Bay preserve, Jewish Museum of Florida, Aquarius Reef Base, and a Wolfsonian Art Museum. **Physically Challenged Students:** All of the campus is accessible. Facilities include wheelchair ramps, elevators, special parking, specially equipped restrooms, special class scheduling, lowered drinking fountains, and lowered telephones. There is also accessible computer equipment for visually impaired students, including talking and large-print computers. **Special:** FIU offers co-op and work-study programs, and study abroad in 30 countries. Accelerated degree programs, nondegree study, dual majors, and several combined bachelor's-master's programs. There are 31 national honor societies, Phi Beta Kappa, and a freshman honors program. **Visiting:** There are regularly scheduled orientations for prospective students, tours are available on both the Modesto Maidique campus and Biscayne Bay campus. There are guides for informal visits and visitors may sit in on classes. To schedule a visit, contact Undgergraduate Admissions. **Campus Safety and Security:** Measures include 24-hour foot and vehicle patrol, emergency notification system, and a security escort services. There are emergency telephones, lighted pathways/sidewalks, and programs on education, and sexual assault prevention.

REQUIREMENTS: In addition to the application, the following credentials are required: Official secondary school transcripts and appropriate test scores: SAT or ACT. Proof of graduation from an accredited secondary school must be submitted before enrolling. High School diplomas accepted for undergraduate degree-seeking admission to FIU must be completed at a secondary institution accredited by a regional accrediting body or at an institution accredited by a national accrediting agency recognized by the United States Department of Education. 18 academic units in college preparatory courses are required as follows: 4 each in English and mathematics, 3 each in natural science and social science, 2 each in foreign languages and academic electives (see notes). Freshman admission decisions are made based on the student's strong academic preparation. Competition for placement in the freshman class includes a review of all academic credentials and a completed file. Applicants are encouraged to complete the MyMajorMatch assessment to match their interest with FIU majors, find an appropriate major, and explore possible careers. Students who apply to majors in Theatre and Music must meet University academic standards and receive the approval of the respective department through an audition. Students should contact the specific department for audition dates. Notes: (1) Two units in the same foreign language are required, (2) Academic Electives are from the fields of mathematics, English, natural science, social science, and a foreign language. The academic grade point average will be computed only on the units listed above. Grades in honors courses, International Baccalaureate (IB), advanced placement (AP), and dual enrollment courses will be given additional weight. Admission to the University is a selective process and satisfying the general requirements does not guarantee acceptance. A GPA of 2.0 is required. AP and CLEP credits are accepted. Important factors in the admissions decision are advanced placement or honors courses, evidence of special talent, and recommendations by school officials. To graduate, students must complete between 120 and 152 hours with a 2.0 GPA. There are also general education and writing requirements. **Procedure:** Freshmen are admitted fall, spring, and summer. Entrance exams should be taken during the spring of the junior year. There is a rolling admissions plan. Application deadlines are open. The fall 2017 application fee was $30. Applications are accepted on-line. **Transfer Students:** 5135 transfer students enrolled in 2016-2017. Degree-seeking applicants with fewer than 60 semester hours of transfer credits must meet the same requirements as beginning freshmen students. In addition, they must demonstrate satisfactory performance in their college work. Applicants who receive an Associate in Arts (A.A.) degree from a Florida Public Community College or State University in Florida will be considered for admission without restriction except for published limited access programs within the University. Students transferring from independent Florida and out-of-state colleges into the University's upper division must have maintained a minimum 2.0 grade point average using a 4.0 scale (with the exception of some limited access programs). All applicants must meet the criteria published for limited access programs and should consult the specific college and major for requirements. Applicants who meet the above admissions requirements, but who have not completed the University's core curriculum requirements, or the prerequisites of their proposed major, may complete this college work at FIU, or at any other accredited institution. Students may also fulfill general education requirements through the College Level Examination Program (CLEP). Official transcripts from all previous post secondary institutions must be forwarded to the office initiating this request directly from the academic institution. All students seeking admission to the University regardless of whether the student holds an A.A., should have completed two years of credit in one foreign language at the high school level or 8-10 credits in one foreign language at the college level (American Sign Language is acceptable). If a student is admitted to the University without this requirement, the credits must be completed prior to graduation. Students who can demonstrate continuous enrollment in a degree program at an SUS institution or Florida Community College since Fall Term 1989 (continuous enrollment is defined by the state to be the completion of at least one course per academic year) can be exempt from this requirement. Students holding an A.A. degree from a Florida Community College or SUS institution prior to Fall Term 1989 will also be exempt. Students, who are applying to majors in Theatre and Music, in addition to meeting university academic standards, must meet the approval of the respective department through an audition. Students should contact the department for audition dates. Admission to the University is a selective process and satisfying the general requirements does not guarantee acceptance. 30 of 120 credits required for the bachelor's degree must be completed at FIU. **International Students:** There are 1912 international students enrolled. They must take the TOEFL with a minimum score of 550 on the paper-based TOEFL (PBT) or 80 on the Internet-based version (iBT). They must also take the SAT or ACT.

ADMISSIONS: 50% of the 2017-2018 applicants were accepted. The SAT scores for the 2017-2018 freshman class were: Critical Reading-- 10% below 500, 61% between 500 and 599, 27% between 600 and 699, and 2% between 700 and 800. Math-- 16% below 500, 58% between 500 and 599, 24% between 600 and 699, and 2% between 700 and 800. Writing-- 19% below 500, 59% between 500 and 599, 20% between 600 and 699, and 2% between 700 and 800. The ACT scores were 38% between 18 and 23, 55% between 24 and 29, and 7% above 30. **Admissions Contact:** Jody Glassman, Admissions Director. Email: *admiss@fiu.edu* Web: *www.fiu.edu*

FINANCIAL AID: In 2017-2018, 82% of all full-time freshmen received some form of financial aid. 73% of all full-time freshmen received need-based aid. FIU is a member of CSS. The FAFSA code is 009635. The deadline for filing freshman financial aid applications for fall entry is March 1.

FLORIDA MEMORIAL UNIVERSITY *(The complete profile is made available exclusively on our website, www.barronspac.com)*

FLORIDA SOUTHERN COLLEGE — D-3

www.flsouthern.edu

Lakeland, FL 33801	**(863) 680-4131** **(800) 274-4131**
Fax: (863) 680-4120	**Email: fscadm@flsouthern.edu**
Full-time: 843 men, 1521 women	**Faculty:** 139; IIA, -$
Part-time: 72 men, 197 women	**Ph.D.s:** 81%
Graduate: 101 men, 339 women	**Student/Faculty:** 15 to 1
Year: semesters, summer session	**Tuition:** $34,774
Room & Board: $11,204	**Freshman Class:** 5983 applied, 3062 accepted, 722 enrolled
	CEEB CODE: 5218
Application Deadline: May 1	**VERY COMPETITIVE**

Florida Southern College, founded in 1885, is a private, comprehensive college that maintains its commitment to academic excellence through 59 undergraduate programs and distinctive graduate programs in business administration, accounting, education, and nursing. Florida Southern is a national leader in engaged learning, and boasts 29 NCAA Division II National Championships. There are 4 undergraduate schools and 3 graduate schools. In addition to regional accreditation, FSC has baccalaureate program accreditation with AACSB, NASM, and CCNE. The 113-acre campus is in a suburban area 30 miles east of Tampa, 40 miles west of Orlando. Including any residence halls, there are 121 buildings.

STUDENT LIFE: 65% of undergraduates are from Florida. Others are from 50 states, 49 foreign countries, and Canada. 81% are from public schools. 72% are White; 11% Hispanic; 6% African American; 4% Foreign; 2% Asian American; 2% two or more races; 1% American Indian/Alaska Native; 1% race unknown. 38% are Protestant; 22% claim no religious affiliation; 21% Catholic. **Female To Male Ratio:** 2.0:1. The average age of freshmen is 18; all undergraduates, 21. 20% do not continue beyond their first year; 80% remain to graduate. **Housing:** 2125 students can be accommodated in college housing, which includes dorms and off-campus apartments. In addition, there are honors houses, special-interest houses, fraternity houses, and sorority houses. On-campus housing is guaranteed for all 4 years. 89% of students live on campus. Alcohol is not permitted. All students may keep cars.

FACULTY/CLASSROOMS: 46% of faculty are male; 54% are female. All teach undergraduates, 75% do research, and 75% do both. No introductory courses are taught by graduate students. The average class size in an introductory lecture is 18; in a laboratory is 17; and in a regular course is 18.

PROGRAMS OF STUDY: FSC confers B.A., B.S., B.F.A., B.M., B.M.E., and B.S.N. degrees. Master's and doctoral degrees are also awarded. Bachelor's degrees are awarded in AGRICULTURE (agricultural business management, agriculture, environmental studies, and horticulture), BIOLOGICAL SCIENCE (biochemistry, biology/biological science, marine biology, and molecular biology), BUSINESS (accounting and business administration and management), COMMUNICATIONS AND THE ARTS (advertising, art history and appreciation, broadcasting, communications, communication rhetoric/communication, creative writing, dance, digital communications, dramatic arts, English, graphic design, journalism, music, music business management, music performance, musical theater, public relations, Spanish, studio art, theatre acting, theatre arts, and theater design), COMPUTER AND PHYSICAL SCIENCE (chemistry, computer mathematics, computer science, and mathematics), EDUCATION (art education, athletic training, elementary education, music education, and secondary education), ENGINEERING AND ENVIRONMENTAL DESIGN (landscape architecture/design), HEALTH PROFESSIONS (exercise science, nursing, predentistry, premedicine, prepharmacy, and prephysical therapy), SOCIAL SCIENCE (criminology, economics, history, humanities, philosophy, political science/government, psychology, religion, and youth ministry). Biological sciences, nursing, business, and communication are the strongest academically. Business administration, biology, and nursing have the largest enrollments.

ACTIVITIES: 30% of men belong to 7 national fraternities; 33% of women belong to 7 national sororities. There are 102 groups on campus, including and shared interest groups, art, band, cheerleading, chess, choir, chorale, chorus, community service, computers, dance, debate, drama, environmental, ethnic, film, forensics, honors, international, jazz band, LGBT, literary magazine, musical theater, newspaper, opera, orchestra, pep band, photography, political, professional, radio and TV, religious, social, social service, student government, symphony, and yearbook. Popular campus events include Graduating Class Water Dome Splash, Greek Week, Flick 'n' Float movies in the pool, FSC's Got Talent, Flap Jack Fling, annual Winter Carnival, Farewell Festival, Homecoming, Festival of Fine Arts, and Founders Day. **Sports:** There are 10 intercollegiate sports for men and 11 for women, and 25 intramural sports for men and 25 for women. Facilities include a variety of outdoor recreational areas, intramural fields for softball, soccer, lacrosse, flag football, frisbee golf, water-skiing, canoeing, kayaking, and a 3-mile walk/run. The wellness center provides a fully-equipped weight room with personal trainers, aerobics, Pilates and yoga studio, a gymnasium for basketball and volleyball, a swimming pool, and athletic training facilities, baseball, lacrosse, and golf. **Graduates:** From July 1, 2016 to June 30, 2017, 643 bachelor's degrees were awarded. The most popular majors were business/marketing (25%), health professions and related programs (13%), and nursing (12%). In an average class, 57% graduate in 4 years or less, 63% graduate in 5 years or less, and 60% graduate in 6 years or less. Of the 2016 graduating class, 16% were enrolled in graduate school within 6 months of graduation, and 55% were employed.

SERVICES: The Student Solutions Center provides tutoring in various subjects Monday through Friday as well as peer-assisted study sessions in select areas. The center also offers support for navigating financial aid, academic advising, student life, and billing. Additional resources include the Center for English Proficiency and Academic Success to assist international students. **Library/Resources:** The library contains 162,938 volumes, 357 microform items, and 8,077 audio/video tapes/CDs/DVDs, and subscribes to 97,791 periodicals including electronic. Computerized library services include interlibrary loans, database searching, Internet access, and Wi-Fi capability. Special learning facilities include an art gallery, planetarium, radio station, TV station, the Rinker Technology Center, computer labs across campus, including the popular TuTu's Cyber Café, the Christoverson Humanities Building with a film studies theater and modern language lab, the state-of-the-art Blanton Nursing Building with high-tech classrooms and a learning lab featuring a full complement of patient simulators, the McKay Archives Center, which houses the College's original Frank Lloyd Wright drawings and documents, the Florida Citrus Hall of Fame, the Center for Florida History, and the Davis Performing Arts Center, including the nationally renowned Branscomb Auditorium, modern Buckner Theatre, and Melvin Art Gallery. The campus also is home to The Roberts Center for Learning and Literacy and The Roberts Academy, a transitional school for gifted elementary-age students with dyslexia that also serves as a learning lab for education students, the Wynee Warden Dance Studio, and the Barney Barnett School of Business and Free Enterprise. **Physically Challenged Students:** 68% of the campus is accessible. Facilities include wheelchair ramps, elevators, special parking, specially equipped restrooms, special class scheduling, lowered drinking fountains, lowered telephones, and special housing. **Special:** Florida Southern College offers a dynamic, transformational curriculum complemented by a variety of exciting experiential opportunities, including guaranteed internships for all students, numerous travel-study programs, student-faculty research, service learning, and music/theater performances. FSC is the only private college in the state affiliated with the prestigious Washington Center, a D.C.-based internship provider supporting students to study and work in the nation's capital, as well as other major cities around the world. The Honors Program offers innovative curriculum options to talented students seeking extraordinary inter-disciplinary learning opportunities. Honors students receive priority registration and are able to take course overloads without paying additional fees. A self-designed major provides motivated students with the option to create a degree program to suit a unique interest or career path, such as art therapy, politics and justice, and technology management. All FSC students are encouraged to participate in an international or domestic travel-study experience at little to no additional cost as part of their educational journey. Month- and semester-long internships have taken FSC students to England, France, Italy, Spain, China, the Bahamas, Peru, Greece, and Turkey. The College also offers yearlong study through Regent's College in London and a popular modern language school in Spain. The Hollingsworth Scholars program is a full-tuition scholarship offered to select students of extraordinary academic talent and vision. There are 27 national honor societies, a freshman honors program, and 9 departmental honors programs. **Visiting:** There are regularly scheduled orientations for prospective students, including a meeting with faculty, a campus tour, and class visits, as well as special programming for parents with a brief history of Frank Lloyd Wright, and the architect of FSC's West Campus. There are guides for informal visits; visitors may sit in on classes, and stay overnight. To schedule a visit, contact the Admissions Office. **Campus Safety and Security:** Measures include 24-hour foot and vehicle patrol, emergency notification system, self-defense education, and security escort services. There are shuttle buses, emergency telephones, lighted pathways/sidewalks, controlled access to dorms/residences. There are also Safety Key Fobs that students can use in emergency.

REQUIREMENTS: Applicants are expected to have earned credit in at least 18 units of college preparatory courses and to have graduated from an accredited secondary school. It is recommended that students have a 3.0 GPA. An essay is required, and an interview is recommended. Applicants must submit either the SAT or ACT. A GPA of 2.0 is required. AP and CLEP credits are accepted. Important factors in the admissions decision are leadership record, geographical diversity, and recommendations by school officials. To gradate, a student needs a minimum of 124 semester credit hours from Florida Southern College and other regionally accredited colleges or universities. A maximum 62 of the required semester credit hours may have been earned at a junior/community college. After completing 96 hours, a student must finish the remaining credits at Florida Southern College. Some degree programs require more than 124 semester hours. **Procedure:** Freshmen are admitted to all sessions. Entrance exams should be taken starting in the junior year of high school. There are early decision, early admissions, deferred admissions, and rolling admissions plans. Early decision applications should be filed by December 1; regular applications, by May 1 for fall entry; and December 1 for spring entry. Notification of early decision is sent December 15; regular decision, on a rolling basis. 72 early decision candidates were accepted for the 2017-2018 class. Applications are accepted on-line. **Transfer Students:** 102 transfer students enrolled in 2016-2017. Students who have successfully completed work at a regionally accredited college or university may apply for admission to Florida Southern College. Applicants should submit SAT or ACT scores, if available, along with a personal statement indicating the reason for the transfer. Official transcripts are required from each postsecondary institution attended. Transfer students must have a minimum 2.5 GPA in all college work attempted. An associate degree and an interview are recommended. 32 of 124 credits required for the bachelor's degree must be completed at

Florida Southern. **International Students:** There are 95 international students enrolled. They must take the TOEFL with a minimum score of 550 on the paper-based TOEFL (PBT) or 79 on the Internet-based version (iBT). They must also take the SAT or ACT.

ADMISSIONS: 51% of the 2017-2018 applicants were accepted. The SAT scores for the 2017-2018 freshman class were: Math-- 11% below 500, 56% between 500 and 599, 29% between 600 and 699, and 3% between 700 and 800. Writing-- 33% below 500, 50% between 500 and 599, 15% between 600 and 699, and 3% between 700 and 800. Evidence-Based Reading/Writing-- 9% below 500, 48% between 500 and 599, 36% between 600 and 699, and 7% between 700 and 800. The ACT scores were 32% between 18 and 23, 57% between 24 and 29, and 11% above 30. 53% of the current freshmen were in the top fifth of their class; 80% were in the top two fifths. **Admissions Contact:** Arden Mitchell, Director of Admissions. Email: *fscadm@flsouthern.edu* Web: *www.flsouthern.edu*

FINANCIAL AID: In 2017-2018, 99% of all full-time freshmen received some form of financial aid. 74% of all full-time freshmen received need-based aid. The average freshman award was $34,960. Need-based scholarships or need-based grants averaged $25,499 ($49,834 maximum); need-based self-help aid (loans and jobs) averaged $1,902 ($2,754 maximum); non-need-based athletic scholarships averaged $12,934 ($46,778 maximum); and other non-need-based awards and non-need-based scholarships averaged $21,247 ($46,928 maximum). 64% of undergraduate students work part-time. The average financial indebtedness of the 2017 graduate was $25,493. The FAFSA code is 001488. The priority date for freshman financial aid applications for fall entry is March 1.

FLORIDA STATE UNIVERSITY C-1

www.fsu.edu

Tallahassee, FL 32306	(850) 644-6200
Fax: (850) 644-0197	Email: admissions@fsu.edu
Full-time: 12,778 men, 16,407 women	Faculty: 1382; I, av$
Part-time: 1932 men, 1589 women	Ph.D.s: 92%
Graduate: 3660 men, 4464 women	Student/Faculty: 25 to 1
Year: semesters, summer session	Tuition: $6507 ($21,673)
Room & Board: $10,264	Freshman Class: 29828 applied, 16674 accepted, 6100 enrolled
SAT CR/M/W: 623/618/615 ACT: 28	CEEB CODE: 5219
Application Deadline: January 25	HIGHLY COMPETITIVE

Florida State University, a public institution founded in 1851, is a residential university designated as a Doctoral Research (Extensive) University by the Carnegie Foundation for the Advancement of Teaching. There are 15 undergraduate schools and 16 graduate schools. In addition to regional accreditation, FSU has baccalaureate program accreditation with AACSB, ABET, ADA, AHEA, ASLA, CSWE, FIDER, NASAD, NASM, CAEP, NLN, NRPA, NASM, PRSA, and ACS. The 475-acre campus is in a suburban area 163 miles west of Jacksonville. Including any residence halls, there are 260 buildings.

STUDENT LIFE: 93% of undergraduates are from Florida. Others are from 50 states, 143 foreign countries, and Canada. 82% are from public schools. 8% are African American; 64% White; 3% two or more races; 2% Asian American; 19% Hispanic; 1% Foreign; 1% race unknown. **Female To Male Ratio:** 1.2:1. The average age of freshmen is 18; all undergraduates, 21. 8% do not continue beyond their first year; 92% remain to graduate. **Housing:** 6280 students can be accommodated in college housing, which includes married student dorms and on-campus apartments. In addition, there are honors houses, special-interest houses, fraternity houses, sorority houses, living-learning centers, music residence, scholarship houses, academic discipline houses, wellness housing, cooperative living through the southern scholarship foundation, and several private residence halls. On-campus housing is available on a first-come and first-served basis. 81% of students commute. All students may keep cars.

FACULTY/CLASSROOMS: 58% of faculty are male; 42% are female. Graduate students teach 49% of introductory courses. The average class size in an introductory lecture is 40; in a laboratory is 18; and in a regular course is 36.

PROGRAMS OF STUDY: FSU confers B.A., B.S., B.S.N., B.F.A, B.M., and B.M.Ed. degrees. Associate, master's, and doctoral degrees are also awarded. Bachelor's degrees are awarded in AGRICULTURE (environmental studies and plant science), BIOLOGICAL SCIENCE (biochemistry, biology/biological science, cell biology, ecology, evolutionary biology, genetics, marine biology, molecular biology, nutrition, physiology, and zoology), BUSINESS (accounting, banking and finance, business administration and management, entrepreneurial studies, fashion merchandising, hotel/motel and restaurant management, insurance and risk management, international business management, management science, marketing/retailing/merchandising, personnel management, recreation and leisure services, recreational facilities management, small business management, and sports management), COMMUNICATIONS AND THE ARTS (advertising, American literature, apparel design, art history and appreciation, broadcasting, classics, communications, creative writing, dance, dramatic arts, English, fiber/textiles/weaving, film arts, French, German, Greek, Italian, jazz, Latin, linguistics, music, music history and appreciation, music performance, music theory and composition, musical theater, piano/organ, public relations, Russian, Spanish, speech/debate/rhetoric, strings, studio art, theater design, voice, and winds), COMPUTER AND PHYSICAL SCIENCE (actuarial science, applied mathematics, atmospheric sciences and meteorology, chemical technology, chemistry, computer science, geology, information sciences and systems, mathematics, physics, and statistics), EDUCATION (art education, athletic training, early childhood education, education of the emotionally handicapped, education of the mentally handicapped, education of the visually handicapped, elementary education, English education, foreign languages education, health education, home economics education, mathematics education, music education, physical education, reading education, science education, social science education, and specific learning disabilities), ENGINEERING AND ENVIRONMENTAL DESIGN (bioengineering, biomedical engineering, chemical engineering, civil engineering, computer engineering, electrical/electronics engineering, environmental engineering, environmental science, graphic arts technology, industrial engineering, interior design, materials engineering, and mechanical engineering), HEALTH PROFESSIONS (community health work, music therapy, nursing, predentistry, premedicine, preoptometry, prepharmacy, preveterinary science, rehabilitation therapy, speech pathology/audiology, and sports medicine), SOCIAL SCIENCE (American studies, anthropology, Asian/Oriental studies, Caribbean studies, child care/child and family studies, classical/ancient civilization, clothing and textiles management/production/services, criminology, dietetics, Eastern European studies, economics, family/consumer studies, fashion design and technology, food science, geography, history, home economics, humanities, international relations, Latin American studies, philosophy, political science/government, prelaw, psychology, religion, Russian and Slavic studies, social science, social work, sociology, and women's studies). Biology, meteorology, and physics are the strongest academically. Psychology, political science, and business have the largest enrollments.

ACTIVITIES: 19% of men belong to 29 national fraternities; 25% of women belong to 26 national sororities. There are 723 groups on campus, including art, band, cheerleading, chess, choir, chorale, chorus, computers, dance, debate, drama, drill team, ethnic, forensics, honors, international, jazz band, LGBT, literary magazine, marching band, musical theater, newspaper, opera, orchestra, pep band, political, professional, radio and TV, religious, social, social service, student government, and symphony. Popular campus events include Twelve Days of Dance, Parents Weekend, and Seven Days of Opening Nights. **Sports:** There are 9 intercollegiate sports for men and 10 for women, and 27 intramural sports for men and 27 for women. Facilities include a stadium, an aquatic center with outdoor swimming pool, a golf course, track, courts for basketball, tennis, racquetball, and handball, a student recreation center with an indoor swimming pool, racquetball courts, a squash court, multipurpose gym, a jogging track, aerobic exercise machines, and free and fixed weights. **Graduates:** From July 1, 2016 to June 30, 2017, 8421 bachelor's degrees were awarded. The most popular majors were criminal justice/safety studies (6%), psychology, general (6%), English language and literature, and general (5%). In an average class, 62% graduate in 4 years or less, 77% graduate in 5 years or less, and 79% graduate in 6 years or less. Of the 2016 graduating class, 53% were enrolled in graduate school within 6 months of graduation, and 72% were employed.

SERVICES: Counseling and information services are available, as is tutoring in most subjects. There is a reader service for the blind, and remedial math, reading, and writing. **Library/Resources:** The library contains 2.8 million volumes, 9.8 million microform items, and 257,419 audio/video tapes/CDs/DVDs, and subscribes to 119,385 periodicals including electronic. Computerized library services include interlibrary loans, database searching, and Internet access. Special learning facilities include an art gallery, planetarium, radio station, TV station, a nuclear accelerator, X-ray emission lab, marine lab, supercomputers, and the National High Magnetic Field Laboratory. **Physically Challenged Students:** 99% of the campus is accessible. Facilities include wheelchair ramps, elevators, special parking, specially equipped restrooms, special class scheduling, lowered drinking fountains, and lowered telephones. **Special:** Cross-registration with Florida Agricultural and Mechanical University and Tallahassee Community College is possible, as is study at FSU centers in London or Florence, and in programs in Costa Rica, France, Russia, Spain, Switzerland, and Vietnam, among other countries. FSU offers cooperative programs in engineering, computer science, business, and communication, work-study programs, general studies and combined B.A.-B.S. degrees, dual majors, and accelerated degree programs. Internships are required in criminology, human science, education, nursing, business (PMG), and social work. There are preprofessional programs in health and law. There are 35 national honor societies, Phi Beta Kappa, a freshman honors program, and 60 departmental honors programs. **Visiting:** There are regularly scheduled orientations for prospective students, including campus tours several times daily on weekdays. Walking and riding tours are available and tours are coordinated around an 11:00 admissions information session. There are guides for informal visits and visitors may sit in on classes. To schedule a visit, contact the Visitor Services at visitorservices@admin.fsu.edu. **Campus Safety and Security:** Measures include 24-hour foot and vehicle patrol, emergency notification system, self-defense education, and security escort services. There are shuttle buses, emergency telephones, lighted pathways/sidewalks, a full-time police force, a bicycle identification program, a valuables identification program, and a victim advocate program.

REQUIREMENTS: The SAT or ACT is required. It is recommended that in-state students have at least an A-/B+ weighted average and a satisfactory SAT or ACT score. Out-of-state students must meet higher standards. Applicants should have at least the following high school units: 4 units in English and math, 3 units in natural science and social science, and 2 units in a foreign language. Other factors include the number of honors, AP, and IB classes, strength of academic curriculum, class rank, among other requirements. A GPA of 3.9 is required. AP and CLEP credits are accepted. Important factors in the admissions decision are advanced placement or honors courses, evidence of special talent, and recommendations by school officials. Students must satisfy the Florida College-Level Academic Skills (CLAS) requirement or an approved alternative. The required core curriculum includes 6 semester hours in mathematics, 6 semester hours in English composition, 6 to 12 semester hours in history/social science, 5 to 11 semester hours in humanities/fine arts, and 7 in natural sciences. Students must satisfy major requirements of their chosen degree program, including additional requirements set by the college offering the degree. All academic areas require at least 120 semester hours for graduation. Additional information is available in the General Bulletin. **Procedure:** Freshmen are admitted fall, spring, and summer. Entrance exams should be taken beginning in the second semester of the junior year. There is a rolling admissions plan. Applications should be filed by January 25 for fall entry; November 1 for spring entry; and February 13 for summer entry. The fall 2017 application fee was $30. Applications are accepted on-line. **Transfer Students:** 1883 transfer students enrolled in 2016-2017. Transfer applicants should present at least a 3.0 cumulative college GPA unless transferring from a Florida public community college with an associate in arts degree, in which case the minimum college GPA needed varies according to major. Applicants with less than 60 semester hours of transferable credit must also meet freshman admission requirements. All transfers must have completed 2 years of the same foreign language in high school or have 8 semester hours at the college level. Students must pass the Florida CLAST test. 30 of 120 credits required for the bachelor's degree must be completed at FSU. **International Students:** There are 589 international students enrolled. They must take the TOEFL with a minimum score of 550 on the paper-based TOEFL (PBT) or 80 on the Internet-based version (iBT). They must also take the SAT or ACT.

ADMISSIONS: 56% of the 2017-2018 applicants were accepted. The SAT scores for the 2017-2018 freshman class were: Critical Reading-- 2% below 500, 44% between 500 and 599, 46% between 600 and 699, and 8% between 700 and 800. Math-- 3% below 500, 42% between 500 and 599, 48% between 600 and 699, and 6% between 700 and 800. Writing-- 3% below 500, 45% between 500 and 599, 45% between 600 and 699, and 6% between 700 and 800. The ACT scores were 1% between 12 and 17, 19% between 18 and 23, 69% between 24 and 29, and 11% above 30. 76% of the current freshmen were in the top fifth of their class. **Admissions Contact:** Admissions Office Email: *admissions@fsu.edu* Web: *www.fsu.edu*

FINANCIAL AID: In 2017-2018, 90% of all full-time freshmen received some form of financial aid. 45% of all full-time freshmen received need-based aid. The average freshman award was $9,076. Need-based scholarships or need-based grants averaged $6,094; need-based self-help aid (loans and jobs) averaged $3,390; non-need-based athletic scholarships averaged $8,409; and other non-need-based awards and non-need-based scholarships averaged $5,005. 3% of undergraduate students work part-time. The average financial indebtedness of the 2017 graduate was $22,912. The college's own financial statement is required. The FAFSA code is 001489. The priority date for freshman financial aid applications for fall entry is January 15.

HODGES UNIVERSITY *(The complete profile is made available exclusively on our website, www.barronspac.com)*

INTERNATIONAL COLLEGE
(See Hodges University)

JACKSONVILLE UNIVERSITY — D-1
www.ju.edu

Jacksonville, FL 32211	**(904) 256-7000** **(800) 225-2027**
Fax: (904) 256-7012	**Email: admissions@ju.edu**
Full-time: 958 men, 1133 women	**Faculty:** IIA, -$
Part-time: 187 men, 132 women	**Ph.D.s:** 78%
Graduate: 228 men, 1429 women	**Student/Faculty:** n/av
Year: semesters, summer session	**Tuition:** $35,260
Room & Board: $13,950	**Freshman Class:** 2939 applied, 1648 accepted, 400 enrolled
SAT CR/M: 505/505 **ACT:** 22	**CEEB CODE:** 5331
Application Deadline: June 1	**COMPETITIVE**

Jacksonville University, founded in 1934, is a private institution offering undergraduate and graduate degree programs in the arts and sciences, fine arts, and business. The figures given in the above capsule and in this profile are approximate. There are 3 undergraduate schools and 4 graduate schools. In addition to regional accreditation, Jacksonville University has baccalaureate program accreditation with NASAD, NASM, NLN, and CCNE. The 198-acre campus is in a suburban area 10 minutes from downtown Jacksonville, near the St. John's River. Including any residence halls, there are 48 buildings.

STUDENT LIFE: 60% of undergraduates are from Florida. Others are from 48 states, 55 foreign countries, and Canada. 7% are Hispanic; 52% White; 3% Asian American; 2% Foreign; 19% two or more races; 16% African American. 35% claim no religious affiliation; 18% Protestant; 16% Catholic. **Female To Male Ratio:** 2.0:1. The average age of freshmen is 19; all undergraduates, 22. 35% do not continue beyond their first year; 49% remain to graduate. **Housing:** 1342 students can be accommodated in college housing, which includes dorms and on-campus apartments. On-campus housing is guaranteed for the freshman year only, is available on a first-come, first-served basis, and is available on a lottery system for upperclassmen. 59% of students live on campus. All students may keep cars.

FACULTY/CLASSROOMS: 53% of faculty are male; 47% are female. No introductory courses are taught by graduate students. The average class size in an introductory lecture is 18; in a laboratory is 16; and in a regular course is 14.

PROGRAMS OF STUDY: JU confers B.A., B.S., B.B.A., B.F.A., B.G.S., B.Mus., B.Mus.Ed., and B.S.N. degrees. Master's degrees are also awarded. Bachelor's degrees are awarded in BIOLOGICAL SCIENCE (biology/biological science and marine science), BUSINESS (accounting, banking and finance, business administration and management, international business management, and marketing/retailing/merchandising), COMMUNICATIONS AND THE ARTS (art history and appreciation, communications, dance, dramatic arts, English, French, music, music performance, music theory and composition, Spanish, and studio art), COMPUTER AND PHYSICAL SCIENCE (chemistry, computer science, information sciences and systems, mathematics, and physics), EDUCATION (art education, dance education, education of the exceptional child, elementary education, music education, and physical education), ENGINEERING AND ENVIRONMENTAL DESIGN (aviation administration/management, computer graphics, electrical/electronics engineering, engineering physics, environmental science, and mechanical engineering), HEALTH PROFESSIONS (nursing), SOCIAL SCIENCE (economics, geography, history, humanities, international studies, philosophy, political science/government, psychology, and sociology). Business administration, nursing, and biology have the largest enrollments.

ACTIVITIES: 20% of men belong to 8 national fraternities; 15% of women belong to 7 national sororities. There are 100 groups on campus, including art, band, cheerleading, choir, chorale, chorus, computers, dance, debate, drama, drill team, environmental, ethnic, film, honors, international, jazz band, LGBT, literary magazine, musical theater, newspaper, orchestra, pep band, photography, political, professional, radio and TV, religious, social, social service, student government, and symphony. Popular campus events include FIN Fest and campus Movie Fest. **Sports:** There are 8 intercollegiate sports for men and 9 for women. Facilities include a stadium, gym, swimming pool, baseball and softball diamonds, soccer and football fields, and an archery range, tennis, basketball, handball/racquetball, volleyball, and shuffleboard courts, an all-purpose playing field, and a track.

SERVICES: Counseling and information services are available, as is tutoring in most subjects. There is a reader service for the blind, and remedial math, reading, and writing. There also is a writer service for note taking in class. **Library/Resources:** The library contains 385,016 volumes, 253,284 microform items, and 24,919 audio/video tapes/CDs/DVDs, and subscribes to 19,740 periodicals including electronic. Computerized library services include interlibrary loans, database searching, and Internet access. Special learning facilities include an art gallery, a planetarium, a radio station, a TV station, a chemistry research lab, and a marine science center. **Physically Challenged Students:** Facilities include wheelchair ramps, elevators, special parking, specially equipped restrooms, special class scheduling, and lowered drinking fountains. Accommodation for all students regardless of disability. **Special:** Internships and work-study are available, as are student-designed majors and a dual major in music and business. There is a co-op program in art, and a 3-2 engineering degree is available with 7 other universities and technological institutes. There is a Washington semester and study abroad in 12 countries. Credit is granted for military experience. There are 16 national honor societies, Phi Beta Kappa, and a freshman honors program. **Visiting:** There are regularly scheduled orientations for prospective students, consisting of an interview, a campus tour, advisement, area presentations, registration, a parents program, and mock classes. There are guides for informal visits; visitors may sit in on classes, and stay overnight. To schedule a visit, contact the Admissions Office. **Campus Safety and Security:** Measures include 24-hour foot and vehicle patrol, self-defense education, and security escort services. There are emergency telephones and lighted pathways/sidewalks.

REQUIREMENTS: The SAT or ACT is required. Applicants must be graduates of an accredited secondary school and provide an official copy of their secondary school transcripts or have a GED. At least 18 academic credits are required, including 4 in English, 3 each in math, natural science, and social sciences, and 2 of the same foreign language. Art students must submit a portfolio. Music, theater, and dance students must audition. A GPA of 2.0 is required. AP and CLEP credits are accepted. Important factors in the admissions decision are advanced placement or honors courses, extracurricular activities record, and leadership record. All students must complete a core curriculum, which provides the liberal arts foundation for all bachelor's degrees. The core includes 4 hours of lab science and 3 hours each of English composition, world literature, economics, fine arts, global studies, humanities, modern world history, math, philosophy, social science, and technology. The B.A. degree requires completion of a foreign language component in place of 3 hours of global studies. A minimum of 120 credit hours, with a minimum GPA of 2.0, is needed to graduate. **Procedure:** Freshmen are admitted to all sessions. Entrance exams should be taken in the spring of the junior year or the fall or spring of the senior year. There are early admissions, deferred admissions, and rolling admissions plans. Application deadlines are open. The fall 2017 application fee was $30. Applications are accepted on-line. **Transfer Students:** Transfer students must submit official transcripts from all colleges attended. Art students must submit a portfolio; music and dance students must audition. Transfer applicants must have completed at least 1 semester at an accredited college or university, be in good standing at the last institution attended, and have a minimum GPA of 2.0. 30 of 120 credits required for the bachelor's degree must be completed at JU. **International Students:** They must take the TOEFL with a minimum score of 540 on the paper-based TOEFL (PBT) or 76 on the Internet-based version (iBT). They must also take the SAT or ACT.

ADMISSIONS: 56% of the 2017-2018 applicants were accepted. **Admissions Contact:** Lisa Hannasch, Director of Admissions. Email: *admissions@ju.edu* Web: *www.ju.edu*

FINANCIAL AID: JU is a member of CSS. The college's own financial statement, and a federal tax return and W-2 are required. The FAFSA code is 001495. Check with the school for current application deadlines.

JOHNSON & WALES UNIVERSITY/NORTH MIAMI CAMPUS E-5

www.jwu.edu/miami

North Miami, FL 33181	(866) 598-3567
Fax: (305) 892-7020	**Email:** mia@admissions.jwu.edu
Full-time: 545 men, 879 women	**Faculty:** 54
Part-time: 55 men, 74 women	**Ph.D.s:** n/av
Graduate: n/av	**Student/Faculty:** 19 to 1
Year: trimesters	**Tuition:** $31,508
Room & Board: $13,260	**Freshman Class:** 5182 applied, 4392 accepted, 477 enrolled
	CEEB CODE: 3441
Application Deadline: n/av	**COMPETITIVE**

Johnson & Wales University/North Miami Campus, founded in 1992, offers degree programs in its college of culinary arts, college of business, and hospitality college. There are 3 undergraduate schools. In addition to regional accreditation, JWU/North Miami has baccalaureate program accreditation with NEASCE-CIHE. The campus is in a small town in the heart of North Miami, between Miami and Fort Lauderdale. Including any residence halls, there are 13 buildings.

STUDENT LIFE: 51% of undergraduates are from out of state, mostly the South. Students are from 44 states, 54 foreign countries, and Canada. 9% are Foreign; 7% two or more races; 5% race unknown; 34% African American; 22% White; 22% Hispanic; 1% American Indian/Alaska Native. **Female To Male Ratio:** 1.6:1. The average age of freshmen is 18; all undergraduates, 21. **Housing:** 1184 students can be accommodated in college housing, which includes dorms and on-campus apartments, apartments for single students, wellness, and theme housing. On-campus housing is available on a lottery system for upperclassmen. 82% of students live on campus. All students may keep cars.

FACULTY/CLASSROOMS: 61% of faculty are male; 37% are female. No introductory courses are taught by graduate students.

PROGRAMS OF STUDY: JWU/North Miami confers B.S. degrees. Associate degrees are also awarded. Bachelor's degrees are awarded in BUSINESS (accounting, business administration and management, entrepreneurial studies, hospitality management services, hotel/motel and restaurant management, marketing management, marketing/retailing/merchandising, recreation and leisure services, sports management, and tourism), ENGINEERING AND ENVIRONMENTAL DESIGN (electrical/electronics engineering and food services technology), SOCIAL SCIENCE (clothing and textiles management/production/services, criminal justice, food production/management/services, paralegal studies, and parks and recreation management).

ACTIVITIES: Groups on campus include campus ministries, cheerleading, dance, ethnic, honors, international, LGBT, music ensembles, newspaper, pep band, professional, religious, social, and student government. **Sports:** There are 4 intercollegiate sports for men and 4 for women, and 5 intramural sports for men and 5 for women. Facilities include a fitness center equipped with cardio machines, free weights, universal machines, and treadmills. **Graduates:** From July 1, 2016 to June 30, 2017, 357 bachelor's degrees were awarded. The most popular majors were English (41%), family and consumer sciences (38%), and law/legal studies (12%). In an average class, 37% graduate in 6 years or less.

SERVICES: Counseling and information services are available, as is

tutoring in every subject. **Library/Resources:** The library contains 12,525 volumes, and 2,301 audio/video tapes/CDs/DVDs, and subscribes to 232 periodicals including electronic. Computerized library services include interlibrary loans, database searching, Internet access, and Wi-Fi capability. **Physically Challenged Students:** Facilities include wheelchair ramps, elevators, special parking, specially equipped restrooms, special class scheduling, lowered drinking fountains, lowered telephones, and special housing. **Special:** The university offers co-op programs, accelerated degree programs, dual majors, study abroad, and worldwide work-study opportunities in business, hospitality, technology, and culinary arts. Most majors require 11-week internships, **Visiting:** There are regularly scheduled orientations for prospective students, including an introduction to the academic and social aspects of the campus experience through interactive sessions. There are guides for informal visits; visitors may sit in on classes, and stay overnight. To schedule a visit, contact the Admissions Office. **Campus Safety and Security:** Measures include 24-hour foot and vehicle patrol and security escort services. There are shuttle buses and emergency telephones.

REQUIREMENTS: Although SAT and ACT scores are required only for students applying for honors admissions, students who have taken these tests are encouraged to submit their scores. A high school diploma is required the GED is accepted. Student requirements are 4 years of English, 3 years each of mathematics and science, and 2 years of social studies. A GPA of 2.0 is required. AP and CLEP credits are accepted. Important factors in the admissions decision are leadership record, advanced placement or honors courses, extracurricular activities record, evidence of special talent, personality/intangible qualities, and recommendations by school officials. To graduate, students must complete 180 quarter credit hours, including at least 36 in the major, with a minimum GPA of 2.0. Required classes include English, math, history, economics, science, psychology, sociology, and professional development. **Procedure:** Freshmen are admitted to all sessions. There are deferred admissions and rolling admissions plans. Application deadlines are open. **Transfer Students:** 79 transfer students enrolled in 2016-2017. Applicants are required to submit official high school and college transcripts and must have earned a minimum college GPA of 2.0. Students may enroll in the fall, winter, spring and summer. **International Students:** There are 192 international students enrolled. They must take the TOEFL.

ADMISSIONS: 85% of the 2017-2018 applicants were accepted. **Admissions Contact:** George J. Rezendes, Director of Admissions. Email: *mia@admissions.jwu.edu* Web: *www.jwu.edu/miami*

FINANCIAL AID: The average freshman award was $25,819. Need-based scholarships or need-based grants averaged $10,213; need-based self-help aid (loans and jobs) averaged $4,709; other non-need-based awards and non-need-based scholarships averaged $3,371; and $9,280 from other forms of aid. JWU/North Miami is a member of CSS. Check with the school for current application deadlines.

KEISER UNIVERSITY *(The complete profile is made available exclusively on our website, www.barronspac.com)*

LYNN UNIVERSITY *(The complete profile is made available exclusively on our website, www.barronspac.com)*

NEW COLLEGE OF FLORIDA — D-4

www.ncf.edu

Sarasota, FL 34243 — **(941) 487-5000**

Fax: (941) 487-5001	**Email:** admissions@ncf.edu
Full-time: 308 men, 526 women	**Faculty:** 79; IIB, +$
Part-time: n/av	**Ph.D.s:** 98%
Graduate: 15 men, 7 women	**Student/Faculty:** 9 to 1
Year: 4-1-4	**Tuition:** $6916 ($29,944)
Room & Board: $9624	**Freshman Class:** 1353 applied, 933 accepted, 199 enrolled
SAT EBR-W/M: 660/610 **ACT:** 28	**CEEB CODE:** 5506
Application Deadline: February 15	**HIGHLY COMPETITIVE+**

New College of Florida, established in 1960, is an honors college for the liberal arts and sciences of the State University System of Florida. There is 1 undergraduate school and 1 graduate school. The 119-acre campus is in a suburban area 50 miles south of Tampa, Florida on Sarasota Bay. Including any residence halls, there are 61 buildings.

STUDENT LIFE: 80% of undergraduates are from Florida, 20 foreign countries, and Canada. 82% are from public schools. 71% are White; 5% two or more races; 3% Asian American; 2% African American; 18% Hispanic; 1% race unknown. **Female To Male Ratio:** 1.7:1. The average age of freshmen is 18; all undergraduates, 20. 19% do not continue beyond their first year; 71% remain to graduate. **Housing:** 629 students can be accommodated in college housing, which includes gender neutral, single sex, coed dorms and on-campus apartments. Specialized housing options may be arranged in response to student interest. On-campus housing is guaranteed for the freshman year only, is available on a first-come, first-served basis, and is available on a lottery system for upperclassmen. 80% of students live on campus. All students may keep cars.

FACULTY/CLASSROOMS: All teach undergraduates. No introductory courses are taught by graduate students. The average class size in a laboratory is 15 and in a regular course is 13.

PROGRAMS OF STUDY: New College of Florida confers B.A. degrees. Associate and master's degrees are also awarded. Bachelor's degrees are awarded in AGRICULTURE (environmental studies), BIOLOGICAL SCIENCE (biochemistry, biology/biological science, marine biology, and neurosciences), COMMUNICATIONS AND THE ARTS (art, art history and appreciation, Chinese, classics, English, French, Germanic languages and literature, literature, music, Russian languages and literature, and Spanish), COMPUTER AND PHYSICAL SCIENCE (applied mathematics, chemistry, mathematics, natural sciences, and physics), ENGINEERING AND ENVIRONMENTAL DESIGN (computational sciences), SOCIAL SCIENCE (anthropology, economics, French studies, gender studies, German area studies, history, humanities, international studies, Latin American studies, medieval studies, philosophy, political science/government, psychology, public affairs, religion, social science, sociology, Spanish studies, and urban studies). Liberal arts and sciences is the strongest academically. Biology, psychology, and economics have the largest enrollments.

ACTIVITIES: There are no fraternities or sororities. Groups on campus include art, choir, computers, dance, drama, environmental, ethnic, film, international, jazz band, LGBT, literary magazine, newspaper, political, professional, radio and TV, religious, social, social service, and student government. Popular campus events include Salsa Squared, Dance Collective Showcase (spring/fall), NCSA We Serve You, Newstock Food Forest Festival, International Games Day, Turkey Bowl, and New Scripts. **Sports:** There is 1 intercollegiate sport for men and 1 for women, and 6 intramural sports for men and 5 for women. Facilities include a soccer field, a softball diamond, fitness path, outdoor tennis and basketball courts, a volleyball pit, playground equipment, swimming pool, and a fitness center with Cybex equipment and indoor facilities for racquetball, aerobics, dance, and yoga. **Graduates:** From July 1, 2016 to June 30, 2017, 177 bachelor's degrees were awarded. The most popular majors were psychology (13%), anthropology (10%), and biology (9%). In an average class, 1% graduate in 3 years or less, 63% graduate in 4 years or less, 69% graduate in 5 years or less, and 71% graduate in 6 years or less. Of the 2016 graduating class, 19% were enrolled in graduate school within 6 months of graduation, and 35% were employed.

SERVICES: There is a reader service for the blind. A writing resouce center provides assistance in developing writing skills and strategies. A quantitative resource center provides assistance in math and statistics as well as technology needed in these fields. **Library/Resources:** The library contains 225,554 volumes, 198,287 microform items, and 7,171 audio/video tapes/CDs/DVDs, and subscribes to 2,856 periodicals, including electronic. Computerized library services include interlibrary loans, database searching, Internet access, and Wi-Fi capability. Special learning facilities include an art gallery, a radio station, a media and educational technology center, a public archaeology lab, a writing resource center, quantitative resource center, language resource center, marine biology research center, black box theater, fine arts complex, and a living ecosystem teaching and research aquarium. **Physically Challenged Students:** 80% of the campus is accessible. Facilities include wheelchair ramps, elevators, special parking, specially equipped restrooms, special class scheduling, lowered drinking fountains, lowered telephones, and special housing. **Special:** Domestic and international internships, study abroad, accelerated degree programs, student-designed interdisciplinary and dual majors, and independent study are available. There is a freshman honors program. **Visiting:** There are regularly scheduled orientations for prospective students, including a campus tour, admissions information session, and/or class visits, which must be scheduled individually by the student through Admissions. Visitors may sit in on classes. To schedule a visit, contact Carley Ray at admissions@ncf.edu. **Campus Safety and Security:** Measures include 24-hour foot and vehicle patrol, an emergency notification system, self-defense education, and security escort services. There are emergency telephones, lighted pathways/sidewalks, controlled access to dorms/residences, 24-hour dispatch/information services, and fire/smoke alarm systems in all dorms.

REQUIREMENTS: The SAT or ACT is required. The ACT Optional Writing test is also required. Graduation from an accredited secondary school (preferred) or the GED is required. High school students should pursue at least 5 academic courses each year, at the most rigorous level available, with a minimum distribution of 4 years of English and mathematics, 3 years each of sciences and social sciences, 2 consecutive years of the same foreign language, and 3 other academic courses. Application essays must be submitted. AP credits are accepted. Important factors in the admissions decision are advanced placement or honors courses, extracurricular activities record, and personality/intangible qualities. An academic credit system is not used. To qualify for graduation, students must complete 7 semester contracts, which are designed by the student in consultation with faculty; 3 independent study projects completed during January each year, between the fall and spring semesters; a senior thesis, that involves original research or creative work and includes working closely with a faculty committee of the student's choice; and an oral baccalaureate exam, which is primarily a defense of the senior thesis. To fulfill the liberal arts curriculum requirements, students must complete 8 LAC-designated courses, including 1 each in humanities, natural sciences, and social sciences. Exemptions from the LAC requirements are possible through AP exam scores of 3 or above, IB exam scores of 5 to 7, and transferable college course work at the general education level. Students also must use on-line training to sign up for a college e-mail account and complete the College Level Academic Skills Test or be exempted by appropriate college course work or SAT or ACT scores. **Procedure:** Freshmen are admitted in the fall and spring. Entrance exams should be taken in the fall of the senior year. There is a deferred admissions plan. Applications should be filed by February 15 for fall entry; December 1 for spring entry. The fall 2017 application fee was $30. Notifications are sent April 1. Applications are accepted on-line. **Transfer Students:** 24 transfer students enrolled in 2016-2017. Transfers must be in good academic and financial standing with their previous college(s). Transfers with less than 60 semester hours must submit SAT or ACT scores. 72 of 124 credits required for the bachelor's degree must be completed at New College. **International Students:** There are 33 international students enrolled. They must take the TOEFL with a minimum score of 560 on the paper-based TOEFL (PBT) or 83 on the Internet-based version (iBT). They must also take the SAT or ACT.

ADMISSIONS: 69% of the 2017-2018 applicants were accepted. The SAT scores for the 2017-2018 freshman class were: Math-- 1% below 500, 41% between 500 and 599, 39% between 600 and 699, and 19% between 700 and 800. Evidence-Based Reading/Writing-- 14% between 500 and 599, 55% between 600 and 699, and 31% between 700 and 800. The ACT scores were 12% between 18 and 23, 53% between 24 and 29, and 35% above 30. 57% of the current freshmen were in the top fifth of their class; 91% were in the top two fifths. 3 freshmen graduated first in their class. **Admissions Contact:** Jenny Martin, Director of Operations. Email: *admissions@ncf.edu* Web: *www.ncf.edu*

FINANCIAL AID: In 2017-2018, 100% of all full-time freshmen received some form of financial aid. 96% of all full-time freshmen received need-based aid. The average freshman award was $16,754. Need-based scholarships or need-based grants averaged $13,224 ($33,207 maximum); need-based self-help aid (loans and jobs) averaged $4,080 ($18,820 maximum); and other non-need-based awards and non-need-based scholarships averaged $8,926 ($25,500 maximum). The average financial indebtedness of the 2017 graduate was $15,777. The FAFSA code is 039574. The priority date for freshman financial aid applications for fall entry is November 1.

NOVA SOUTHEASTERN UNIVERSITY — E-5

www.nova.edu

Fort Lauderdale, FL 33314

(954) 262-8000
(800) 338-4723
Email: admissions@nova.edu

Full-time: 1062 men, 2132 women
Part-time: 413 men, 1034 women
Graduate: 5699 men, 12,896 women
Year: trimesters, summer session
Room & Board: $10,874

Faculty: n/av
Ph.D.s: 79%
Student/Faculty: 16 to 1
Tuition: $27,760
Freshman Class: 4333 applied, 2567 accepted, 657 enrolled

SAT CR/M: 550/550 **ACT:** 25
Application Deadline: August 1

CEEB CODE: 5514
COMPETITIVE+

Nova Southeastern University, founded in 1964, is an independent institution offering degree programs in liberal arts, sciences, business, health sciences, education, and preprofessional studies. The university also offers graduate and first-professional programs. The figures given in the above capsule and in this profile are approximate. There are 8 undergraduate schools and 14 graduate schools. In addition to regional accreditation, NSEU has baccalaureate program accreditation with APTA, CAHEA, CAEP, CCNE, COATE, and IACBE. The 314-acre campus is in a suburban area 10 miles west of downtown Fort Lauderdale. Including any residence halls, there are 39 buildings.

STUDENT LIFE: 83% of undergraduates are from Florida. Others are from 48 states, 68 foreign countries, and Canada. 9% are Asian American; 5% Foreign; 32% Hispanic; 31% White; 3% race unknown; 2% two or more races; 17% African American. **Female To Male Ratio:** 2.2:1. The average age of freshmen is 19; all undergraduates, 25. 20% do not continue beyond their first year; 44% remain to graduate. **Housing:** 1472 students can be accommodated in college housing, which includes married student dorms and on-campus apartments. In addition, there are fraternity houses, sorority houses, theme housing, leadership, CoED Greek, quiet halls, and international housing. On-campus housing is guaranteed for all 4 years. 77% of students commute. All students may keep cars.

FACULTY/CLASSROOMS: 44% of faculty are male; 56% are female. No introductory courses are taught by graduate students. The average class size in an introductory lecture is 15.

PROGRAMS OF STUDY: NSEU confers B.A., B.H.Sc., B.S., and B.S.N. degrees. Associate, master's, and doctoral degrees are also awarded. Bachelor's degrees are awarded in BIOLOGICAL SCIENCE (biological sciences, marine biology, marine science, and neurosciences), BUSINESS (accounting, business administration and management, finance, and marketing), COMMUNICATIONS AND THE ARTS (art, arts administration/management, communication studies, dance, dramatic arts, fine arts, information technology, music, and theatre acting), COMPUTER AND PHYSICAL SCIENCE (chemistry, computer engineering technology, computer information systems, computer science, mathematics, and software engineering), EDUCATION (athletic training, early childhood education, education, education administration, education of the exceptional child, elementary education, English education, general studies, middle school education, physical education, science education, secondary education, and sports and wellness studies), ENGINEERING AND ENVIRONMENTAL DESIGN (computer engineering and environmental science), HEALTH PROFESSIONS (biology, diagnostic medical sonography, exercise science, health promotion, kinesiology, nursing, recreation therapy, respiratory therapy, and speech pathology/audiology), SOCIAL SCIENCE (anthropology, behavioral science, criminal justice, human development, human services, international relations, legal studies, paralegal studies, philosophy, philosophy and religion, political science/government, psychology, public administration, and sociology). Biology, nursing, and business have the largest enrollments.

ACTIVITIES: 8% of men belong to 6 national fraternities; 7% of women belong to 6 national sororities. There are 316 groups on campus, including band, cheerleading, chorale, chorus, computers, dance, drama, environmental, ethnic, honors, international, LGBT, musical theater, newspaper, orchestra, political, professional, radio and TV, religious, social, social service, and student government. Popular campus events include Homecoming, Sharkapalooza, Student Life Achievement Awards, Cinema Tuesday, and Superbowl Party. **Sports:** There are 7 intercollegiate sports for men and 10 for women, and 7 intramural sports for men and 7 for women. Facilities include baseball and soccer fields and a recreational complex with a swimming pool and basketball and tennis courts. **Graduates:** From July 1, 2016 to June 30, 2017, 1412 bachelor's degrees were awarded. The most popular majors were nursing (17%), biology (premedical) (16%), and business administration (9%). In an average class, 4% graduate in 3 years or less, 31% graduate in 4 years or less, 40% graduate in 5 years or less, and 44% graduate in 6 years or less.

SERVICES: Counseling and information services are available, as is tutoring in some subjects, such as science, math, and writing. **Library/Resources:** The library contains 827,004 volumes, 2.3 million microform items, and 65,295 audio/video tapes/CDs/DVDs, and subscribes to 50,033 periodicals, including electronic. Computerized library services include interlibrary loans, database searching, Internet access, and Wi-Fi capability. Special learning facilities include an art gallery, a radio station, a center of excellence for coral reef ecosystems science, dryland training, the Palm Beach student educational center, nursing simulation labs, the Huizenga Sales Institute, a neuro-immune medicine clinic, health professions division museum, Hall of Fame, a performing arts center, a oceanographic center, a law center, a family village center, and a preschool. **Physically Challenged Students:** All of the campus is accessible. Facilities include wheelchair ramps, elevators, special parking, specially equipped restrooms, special class scheduling, lowered drinking fountains, and special housing. **Special:** NSU offers internships, study abroad, work-study, accelerated degree programs, nondegree study, Washington semester, Undergraduate Honors Program, and undergraduate research experience. Combined bachelor-professional degree programs and a dual admission program are also available. There are 9 national honor societies and a freshman honors program. **Visiting:** There are regularly scheduled orientations for prospective students. There are guides for informal visits and visitors may sit in on classes. **Campus Safety and Security:** Measures include 24-hour foot and vehicle patrol, an emergency notification system, and security escort services. There are shuttle buses, emergency telephones, lighted pathways/sidewalks, and controlled access to dorms/residences.

REQUIREMENTS: The SAT or ACT is required. Applicants must be graduates of an accredited secondary school or have a GED certificate. An interview is recommended. AP and CLEP credits are accepted. Important factors in the admissions decision are advanced placement or honors courses, leadership record, evidence of special talent, and extracurricular activities record. To graduate, all students must complete at least 120 credit hours; at least 30 of the credits must be earned at NSU and at least 50% of the credits in the major area must be earned at NSU. A minimum 2.25 GPA is needed for courses in the major, and a 2.0 for all other courses. **Procedure:** Freshmen are admitted to all sessions. Entrance exams must be taken and received by July for the fall term. There are deferred admissions and rolling admissions plans. Applications should be filed by August 1 for fall entry. The fall 2017 application fee was $50. Notification is sent on a rolling basis. Applications are accepted on-line. **Transfer Students:** 760 transfer students enrolled in 2016-2017. Students transfering in good standing with AA or 60 credits from SACS accredited college are accepted and guaranteed junior standing. 30 of 120 credits required for the bachelor's degree must be completed at NSU. **International Students:** There are 286 international students enrolled. They must take the TOEFL with a minimum score of 550 on the paper-based TOEFL (PBT) or 79 on the Internet-based version (iBT). Students must take the MELAB, the Comprehensive English Language Test, and the college's own test, or take the IELTS or the PTE-Academic.

ADMISSIONS: 59% of the 2017-2018 applicants were accepted. The SAT scores for the 2017-2018 freshman class were: Critical Reading-- 26% below 500, 45% between 500 and 599, 25% between 600 and 699, and 4% between 700 and 800. Math-- 27% below 500, 39% between 500 and 599, 29% between 600 and 699, and 5% between 700 and 800. The ACT scores were 1% between 12 and 17, 39% between 18 and 23, 40% between 24 and 29, and 20% above 30. 51% of the current freshmen were in the top fifth of their class; 79% were in the top two fifths. 4 freshmen graduated first in their class. **Admissions Contact:** Deanna Voss, Dean of Undergraduate Admissions. Email: *admissions@nova.edu* Web: *www.nova.edu*

FINANCIAL AID: The FAFSA code is 001509. Check with the school for current application deadlines.

PALM BEACH ATLANTIC UNIVERSITY E-5

www.pba.edu

West Palm Beach, FL 33416	(561) 803-2100
Fax: (561) 803-2115	**Email:** admit@pba.edu
Full-time: 822 men, 1528 women	**Faculty:** 171; IIB, av$
Part-time: 41 men, 88 women	**Ph.D.s:** 81%
Graduate: 252 men, 580 women	**Student/Faculty:** 12 to 1
Year: semesters, summer session	**Tuition:** $29,950
Room & Board: $9300	**Freshman Class:** 1380 applied, 1344 accepted, 537 enrolled
SAT EBR-W/M: 555/535 **ACT:** 24	**CEEB CODE:** 5553
Application Deadline: n/av	**COMPETITIVE**

Palm Beach Atlantic University, founded in 1968, is an interdenominational Christian university with 51 undergraduate majors. Graduate degrees in business, accounting, leadership, counseling psychology, divinity, Christian studies, pharmacy, global development, and nursing practice are offered. PBAU is an ideal place to grow and explore your faith with young people of many races, nationalities, and creeds. There are 9 undergraduate schools and 6 graduate schools. In addition to regional accreditation, PBAU has baccalaureate program accreditation with ACPE, NASM, IACBE, CCNE, NSCA, CAATE, ACSI, and and NSCA. The 106-acre campus is in an urban area 60 miles north of Miami, 180 miles south of Orlando. Including any residence halls, there are 48 buildings.

STUDENT LIFE: 66% of undergraduates are from Florida. Others are from 46 states, 54 foreign countries, and Canada. 58% are White; 4% two or more races; 3% Asian American; 3% Foreign; 2% race unknown; 17% Hispanic; 13% African American. 75% are Protestant; 16% Catholic. **Female To Male Ratio:** 2.0:1. The average age of freshmen is 18; all undergraduates, 23. 24% do not continue beyond their first year; 51% remain to graduate. **Housing:** 1277 students can be accommodated in college housing, which includes on-campus apartments. In addition, there are honors houses, special-interest houses, apartments for single students, theme housing, all women's dorm and all men's dorm, and coed dorms. On-campus housing is available on a first-come, first-served basis. 50% of students commute. Alcohol is not permitted. All students may keep cars.

FACULTY/CLASSROOMS: 50% of faculty are male; 50% are female. 83% teach undergraduates. No introductory courses are taught by graduate students. The average class size in an introductory lecture is 19; in a laboratory is 15; and in a regular course is 15.

PROGRAMS OF STUDY: PBAU confers B.A., B.G.S., B.S., B.Mus., and B.S.N. degrees. Master's and doctoral degrees are also awarded. Bachelor's degrees are awarded in BIOLOGICAL SCIENCE (biology, ecology and field biology and biology/biological science), BUSINESS (accounting, banking and finance, business administration and management, international business management, management science, marketing management, and organizational leadership and management), COMMUNICATIONS AND THE ARTS (art, communications, dance, English, film arts, graphic design, journalism, music, music performance, music theory and composition, musical theater, piano/organ, theater design, and voice), COMPUTER AND PHYSICAL SCIENCE (chemistry, computer science, and mathematics), EDUCATION (art education, athletic training, elementary education, English education, mathematics education, music education, physical education, science education, and secondary education), HEALTH PROFESSIONS (biology, exercise science, and nursing), SOCIAL SCIENCE (behavioral science, biblical studies, cross-cultural studies, history, interdisciplinary studies, liberal arts/general studies, ministries, philosophy, political science/government, prelaw, and psychology). English, biology, and medicinal and biological chemistry are the strongest academically. Business, pharmacy, and psychology have the largest enrollments.

ACTIVITIES: There are no fraternities or sororities. There are 50 groups on campus, including music ensembles, campus ministries, concert band, international organizations, Army ROTC, art, cheerleading, choir, chorale, chorus, communications, computers, dance, drama, environmental, ethnic, honors, international, jazz band, literary magazine, musical theater, newspaper, orchestra, pep band, political, professional, religious, social, social service, student government, and symphony. Popular campus events include Christival, Sailfish Cup, Paradise Weekend,

Homecoming, and Spring Formal. **Sports:** There are 8 intercollegiate sports for men and 9 for women, and 8 intramural sports for men and 8 for women. Facilities include a sports and recreation facility, an athletic training facility, a fitness center, baseball and softball fields, tennis courts, and soccer fields. **Graduates:** From July 1, 2016 to June 30, 2017, 485 bachelor's degrees were awarded. The most popular majors were business/marketing (16%), health professions and related programs (11%), and psychology (11%). In an average class, 51% graduate in 6 years or less. Of the 2016 graduating class, 16% were enrolled in graduate school within 6 months of graduation, and 31% were employed.

SERVICES: Counseling and information services are available, as is tutoring in some subjects, such as math, sciences, and languages. There is a reader service for the blind, and remedial math and writing, including a center for writing excellence. **Library/Resources:** The library contains 265,125 volumes, and subscribes to 133,228 periodicals including electronic. Computerized library services include interlibrary loans, database searching, Internet access, and Wi-Fi capability. Special learning facilities include an art gallery, center for writing excellence (writing assistance), center for integrated science learning, a center for experiential learning, a center for public policy, a student success center, peer tutoring, first year experience, and ADA accomodations. **Physically Challenged Students:** 60% of the campus is accessible. Facilities include wheelchair ramps, elevators, special parking, specially equipped restrooms, and special class scheduling. **Special:** PBA offers work-study, internships, a student-designed interdisciplinary major, accelerated degree programs in organizational management (evening program only) and ministry, a London semester, study abroad through the Coalition of Christian Colleges and Universities, and teacher certification. There are 11 national honor societies, a freshman honors program, and 1 departmental honors program. **Visiting:** There are regularly scheduled orientations for prospective students, a general open house and a school-specific open house. There are guides for informal visits; visitors may sit in on classes, and stay overnight. To schedule a visit, contact the Admissions Office. **Campus Safety and Security:** Measures include 24-hour foot and vehicle patrol, an emergency notification system, self-defense education, and security escort services. There are emergency telephones, lighted pathways/sidewalks, controlled access to dorms/residences, and closed circuit television system.

REQUIREMENTS: The SAT or ACT is required. Applicants must be graduates of an accredited secondary school or have a GED certificate, and have completed 18 academic credits: 4 in English, 3 each in math and science with lab, 2 recommended in foreign language, and 5 in electives. An essay is required. A portfolio and an interview are required for fine arts students. AP and CLEP credits are accepted. Important factors in the admissions decision are leadership record, advanced placement or honors courses, personality/intangible qualities, evidence of special talent, extracurricular activities record, recommendations by school officials, and recommendations by alumni. Students must complete general education requirements and a minimum of 120 credit hours. The last 32 credit hours must be completed at PBA and a minimum 2.0 GPA is required. **Procedure:** Freshmen are admitted in the fall and spring. Entrance exams should be taken in the junior year of high school. There are deferred admissions and rolling admissions plans. Application deadlines are open. The fall 2017 application fee was $50. Notifications are sent September 1. Applications are accepted online. **Transfer Students:** 201 transfer students enrolled in 2016-2017. Transfer students must have a minimum 2.5 GPA on at least 12 semester hours, 300-500 word essay, and 2 letters of recommendation. Application for admission is in the fall, spring and summer. 32 of 120 credits required for the bachelor's degree must be completed at PBA. **International Students:** There are 107 international students enrolled. They must take the TOEFL with a minimum score of 79 on the Internet-based version (iBT). They must also take the SAT or ACT.

ADMISSIONS: 97% of the 2017-2018 applicants were accepted. The SAT scores for the 2017-2018 freshman class were: Math-- 32% below 500, 45% between 500 and 599, 21% between 600 and 699, and 2% between 700 and 800. Evidence-Based Reading/Writing-- 23% below 500, 43% between 500 and 599, 31% between 600 and 699, and 3% between 700 and 800. The ACT scores were 1% below 12, 8% between 12 and 17, 47% between 18 and 23, 35% between 24 and 29, and 9% above 30. **Admissions Contact:** Joseph Bryan, Assistant. VP for Admission. Email: *admit@pba.edu* Web: *www.pba.edu*

FINANCIAL AID: In 2017-2018, 100% of all full-time freshmen received some form of financial aid. 79% of all full-time freshmen received need-based aid. The average freshman award was $23,523. Need-based scholarships or need-based grants averaged $21,135; need-based self-help aid (loans and jobs) averaged $3,578; non-need-based athletic scholarships averaged $8,766; and other non-need-based awards and non-need-based scholarships averaged $13,237. 20% of undergraduate students work part-time. The average financial indebtedness of the 2017 graduate was $26,907. The state aid form is required. The priority date for freshman financial aid applications for fall entry is May 1.

RINGLING COLLEGE OF ART AND DESIGN *(The complete profile is made available exclusively on our website, www.barronspac.com)*

ROLLINS COLLEGE — D-3

www.rollins.edu

Winter Park, FL 32789 — **(407) 646-2161**

Email: admission@rollins.edu

Full-time: 804 men, 1144 women
Part-time: n/av
Graduate: 249 men, 324 women
Year: semesters
Room & Board: $14,730
Application Deadline: February 15

Faculty: 196; II, --$
Ph.D.s: 92%
Student/Faculty: 10 to 1
Tuition: $48,415
Freshman Class: 4922 applied, 2972 accepted, 493 enrolled
CEEB CODE: 5572
HIGHLY COMPETITIVE

Rollins College, founded in 1885, is a nonsectarian institution, that is focused on excellence and fueled by dedication to pragmatic liberal arts. Students experience small classes led by faculty nationally recognized for innovative teaching and scholarship. The figures given in the above capsule and in this profile are approximate. There are 2 undergraduate schools and 2 graduate schools. In addition to regional accreditation, Rollins College has baccalaureate program accreditation with AACSB, NASM, ACS, AAM, and CACREP. The 80-acre campus is in a suburban area in Winter Park, Florida, adjacent to the city of Orlando.

STUDENT LIFE: 50% of undergraduates are from out of state, mostly the Middle Atlantic. Students are from 41 states, 60 foreign countries, and Canada. 8% are Foreign; 60% White; 6% African American; 4% race unknown; 3% Asian American; 3% two or more races; 16% Hispanic. **Female To Male Ratio:** 1.4:1. The average age of freshmen is 18; all undergraduates, 20. 16% do not continue beyond their first year; 62% remain to graduate. **Housing:** 1320 students can be accommodated in college housing, which includes dorms and on-campus apartments. In addition, there are honors houses, special-interest houses, fraternity houses, and sorority houses. On-campus housing is guaranteed for the freshman year only. 60% of students live on campus. Upperclassmen may keep cars.

FACULTY/CLASSROOMS: 56% of faculty are male; 44% are female. No introductory courses are taught by graduate students.

PROGRAMS OF STUDY: Rollins confers A.B. degrees. Master's degrees are also awarded. Bachelor's degrees are awarded in BIOLOGICAL SCIENCE (biochemistry, biology/biological science, and marine biology), BUSINESS (international business management and organizational behavior), COMMUNICATIONS AND THE ARTS (art history and appreciation, communications, dramatic arts, English, French, media arts, music, music performance, Spanish, studio art, and theatre arts), COMPUTER AND PHYSICAL SCIENCE (chemistry, computer science, mathematics, and physics), EDUCATION (elementary education), ENGINEERING AND ENVIRONMENTAL DESIGN (environmental science), SOCIAL SCIENCE (anthropology, Asian/Oriental studies, classical/ancient civilization, cross-cultural studies, economics, history, humanities, international relations, Latin American studies, philosophy, political science/government, psychology, religion, and sociology). International business, psychology, and communication studies have the largest enrollments.

ACTIVITIES: 38% of men belong to 1 local and 5 national fraternities; 42% of women belong to 1 local and 6 national sororities. There are 110 groups on campus, including art, band, cheerleading, chess, choir, chorale, chorus, computers, dance, debate, drama, drum and bugle corps, environmental, ethnic, film, honors, international, jazz band, LGBT, literary magazine, musical theater, newspaper, orchestra, pep band, photography, political, professional, radio and TV, religious, social, social service, student government, symphony, and yearbook. Popular campus events include Greek Week, Lip Sync, R-Big Event, and Fox Day. **Sports:** There are 11 intercollegiate sports for men and 12 for women, and 9 intramural sports for men and 10 for women. Facilities include an auditorium, a stadium, tennis courts, baseball and soccer fields, a field house with a gym, a weight room, and a swimming pool. **Graduates:** From July 1, 2016 to June 30, 2017, 623 bachelor's degrees were awarded. The most popular majors were international business (12%), communication studies (11%), and economics (10%). In an average class, 64% graduate in 4 years or less, 69% graduate in 5 years or less, and 71% graduate in 6 years or less.

SERVICES: Counseling and information services are available, as is tutoring in every subject. There is a reader service for the blind, and remedial math, reading, and writing. **Library/Resources:** The library contains 259,302 volumes, and 112 microform items. Computerized library services include interlibrary loans, database searching, Internet access, and Wi-Fi capability. Special learning facilities include an art gallery, radio station, TV station, an art museum, theaters, a writing center, and a student resource center. **Physically Challenged Students:** 80% of the campus is accessible. Facilities include wheelchair ramps, elevators, special parking, specially equipped restrooms, special class scheduling, lowered drinking fountains, lowered telephones, and special housing. **Special:** Rollins offers cross-registration with the evening studies division, co-op programs with American University in Washington, D.C., and Duke University School of Forestry and Environmental Studies. Departmental and professional internships, study abroad in 9 countries, and a Washington semester are also options. Also available are an accelerated (3-2) MBA program; a B.A.-B.S. degree in preengineering with Washington University (St. Louis), Auburn, and Columbia Universities; an interdepartmental biochemistry/molecular biology major; dual majors in any combination; and student-designed majors. Nondegree study and pass/fail options are possible. There are 5 national honor societies, a freshman honors program, and 30 departmental honors programs. **Visiting:** There are regularly scheduled orientations for prospective students. There are guides for informal visits and visitors may sit in on classes. To schedule a visit, contact The Office of Admissions. **Campus Safety and Security:** Measures include 24-hour foot and vehicle patrol, emergency notification system, self-defense education, and security escort services. There are shuttle buses, emergency telephones, lighted pathways/sidewalks, controlled access to dorms/residences, and 24-hour locked residential units.

REQUIREMENTS: Applicants must be graduates of an accredited secondary school or have a GED certificate and have completed 4 years of English, 3 years of math, and 2 years each of foreign language, science, and social studies. An essay is required. SAT Subject Tests in writing, math, and foreign language and an interview are recommended. AP and CLEP credits are accepted. Important factors in the admissions decision are advanced placement or honors courses, evidence of special talent, and extracurricular activities record. Students must complete a minimum of 140 semester hours of academic work, of which at least sixty-four semester hours must be outside a single departmental prefix. All students must complete a minimum of sixteen semester hours that are not used to meet either a general education curriculum or major requirement. Students must earn a minimum academic average of 2.0 (C) for all courses taken at Rollins. B>**Procedure:** Freshmen are admitted fall and spring. Entrance exams should be taken by the first semester of the senior year. There are early decision and deferred admissions plans. Early decision applications should be filed by November 15; regular applications, by February 15 for fall entry; and November 1 for spring entry. The fall 2017 application fee was $40. Notification of early decision is sent December 15; regular decision, April 1. 102 applicants were on the 2017 waiting list; 10 were admitted. Applications are accepted online. **Transfer Students:** 69 transfer students enrolled in 2016-2017. Transfer students must satisfy all regular admission requirements and submit official transcripts of college and high school work and SAT or ACT scores. A recommended 3.0 GPA and a year's worth of credit hours earned are required. An interview is recommended. 64 of 140 credits required for the bachelor's degree must be completed at Rollins. **International Students:** There are 173 international students enrolled. They must take the TOEFL with a minimum score of 550 on the paper-based TOEFL (PBT) or 80 on the Internet-based version (iBT). They must also take the SAT or ACT.

ADMISSIONS: 60% of the 2017-2018 applicants were accepted. The SAT scores for the 2017-2018 freshman class were: Critical Reading-- 4% below 500, 41% between 500 and 599, 45% between 600 and 699, and 10% between 700 and 800. Math-- 5% below 500, 43% between 500 and 599, 40% between 600 and 699, and 13% between 700 and 800. Writing-- 8% below 500, 44% between 500 and 599, 39% between 600 and 699, and 10% between 700 and 800. **Admissions Contact:** Office of Admission Email: *admission@rollins.edu* Web: *www.rollins.edu*

FINANCIAL AID: 27% of undergraduate students work part-time. Rollins is a member of CSS. The college's own financial statement is required. The FAFSA code is 001515. The priority date for freshman financial aid applications for fall entry is March 1.

SAINT LEO UNIVERSITY — D-3

http://choose.saintleo.edu

Saint Leo, FL 33574 — (352) 588-8283, (800) 334-5532

Fax: (352) 588-8257 — **Email:** admissions@saintleo.edu

Full-time: 893 men, 1164 women	**Faculty:** 124
Part-time: 34 men, 38 women	**Ph.D.s:** 83%
Graduate: 1310 men, 2118 women	**Student/Faculty:** 17 to 1
Year: semesters, summer session	**Tuition:** $22,280
Room & Board: $10,570	**Freshman Class:** 3320 applied, 2912 accepted, 535 enrolled
SAT CR/M/W: 530/520/470 **ACT:** 22	**CEEB CODE:** 5638
Application Deadline: rolling	**COMPETITIVE**

Saint Leo University was founded in 1889. Undergraduate students benefit from a rewarding, values-based education that integrates caring faculty, state-of-the-art technology, and active learning as they choose from more than 50 outstanding academic programs and endorsements. There are 3 undergraduate schools and 8 graduate schools. In addition to regional accreditation, Saint Leo has baccalaureate program accreditation with ACBSP, CSWE, IACBE, and COSMA. The 215-acre campus is in a rural area 40 miles north of Tampa, Florida. Including any residence halls, there are 32 buildings.

STUDENT LIFE: 69% of undergraduates are from Florida. Others are from 47 states, 71 foreign countries, and Canada. 70% are from public schools. 8% are race unknown; 41% White; 3% two or more races; 20% Hispanic; 2% Asian American; 14% African American; 12% Foreign. 44% claim no religious affiliation; 28% Catholic; 23% Protestant. **Female To Male Ratio:** 1.5:1. The average age of freshmen is 18; all undergraduates, 21. 29% do not continue beyond their first year; 45% remain to graduate. **Housing:** 1577 students can be accommodated in college housing, which includes single-sex and coed dorms and off-campus apartments. In addition, there are honors houses, theme housing, and freshman only housing. On-campus housing is guaranteed for all 4 years. 66% of students live on campus. All students may keep cars.

FACULTY/CLASSROOMS: 53% of faculty are male; 47% are female. All teach undergraduates. No introductory courses are taught by graduate students. The average class size in a laboratory is 14 and in a regular course is 19.

PROGRAMS OF STUDY: Saint Leo confers B.A., B.S, and B.S.W. degrees. Associate, master's, and doctoral degrees are also awarded. Bachelor's degrees are awarded in BIOLOGICAL SCIENCE (biology, ecology and field biology and biology/biological science), BUSINESS (accounting, business communications, hospitality management services, management science, marketing management, and sports management), COMMUNICATIONS AND THE ARTS (English literature, English Writing, multimedia, and theatre arts), COMPUTER AND PHYSICAL SCIENCE (computer information systems, computer security, information sciences and systems, and mathematics), EDUCATION (elementary education, English secondary education, global studies, middle school education, and secondary education), HEALTH PROFESSIONS (biomedical science and health care administration), SOCIAL SCIENCE (applied social science, clinical psychology, criminal justice, developmental psychology, economics, experimental psychology, history, homeland security, political science/government, psychology, religion, social work, and sociology). Biology, English, and accounting are the strongest academically. Biology, management, and criminal justice have the largest enrollments.

ACTIVITIES: 16% of men belong to 1 local and 6 national fraternities; 20% of women belong to 1 local and 6 national sororities. There are 80 groups on campus, including SERVE (organizes service trips during breaks), Caribbean Student Association, Campus Activities Board, cheerleading, chorus, computers, debate, drama, environmental, ethnic, honors, international, jazz band, literary magazine, musical theater, newspaper, political, professional, radio and TV, religious, social, social service, student government, and yearbook. Popular campus events include Spring Fling, Winter Formal, Family Fall Festival, and Halloween Horror Nights Trip. **Sports:** There are 9 intercollegiate sports for men and 10 for women, and 9 intramural sports for men and 9 for women. Facilities include a gym, a fitness center, an outdoor swimming pool, a golf course, soccer, softball, baseball and practice fields, basketball, volleyball, racquetball, tennis courts, a turf field, sailing, and canoeing. **Graduates:** From July 1, 2016 to June 30, 2017, 439 bachelor's degrees were awarded. The most popular majors were sport business (8%), management (8%), and computer information systems/information assurance (7%). In an average class, 34% graduate in 4 years or less, 42% graduate in 5 years or less, and 45% graduate in 6 years or less.

SERVICES: Counseling and information services are available, as is tutoring in most subjects. There is a reader service for the blind, and remedial math and writing. **Library/Resources:** The library contains 500,538 volumes, 21,293 microform items, and 813 audio/video tapes/CDs/DVDs, and subscribes to 171,110 periodicals including electronic. Computerized library services include interlibrary loans, database searching, Internet access, and Wi-Fi capability. Special learning facilities include an art gallery and a radio station. **Physically Challenged Students:** 95% of the campus is accessible. Facilities include wheelchair ramps, elevators, special parking, specially equipped restrooms, lowered drinking fountains, and special housing. Students with disability needs are available on a case-by-case basis with proper documentation. **Special:** Saint Leo offers internships in most majors, study abroad in 11 countries, work-study programs on campus, dual majors, and credit for military experience. There is a prelaw program; preprofessional programs in medicine, dentistry, and veterinary science, and Air Force and Army ROTC programs. Saint Leo also has an ambassador program with the University of St. Augustine for Health Sciences (occupational and physical therapy). There are 20 national honor societies, a freshman honors program, and 1 departmental honors program. **Visiting:** There are regularly scheduled orientations for prospective students, consisting of overnight campus visitation programs. There are guides for informal visits; visitors may sit in on classes, and stay overnight. To schedule a visit, contact the Office of Admissions. **Campus Safety and Security:** Measures include 24-hour foot and vehicle patrol, emergency notification system, and security escort services. There are shuttle buses, emergency telephones, lighted pathways/sidewalks, and controlled access to dorms/residences.

REQUIREMENTS: Applicants for regular admission status are recommended to have successfully completed the following high school courses by the time they enroll at Saint Leo University: 4 years of English, 3 each of mathematics and history/social science, and 2 years each of science, foreign language, and electives. Students must submit an application, official high school transcript, letter of recommendation from a high school guidance counselor or teacher, and standardized test scores if not applying as test optional. AP and CLEP credits are accepted. Important factors in the admissions decision are advanced placement or honors courses, leadership record, and recommendations by school officials. To graduate, all students must complete a minimum of 120 academic credits with 30 to 60 hours in the major, all the requirements of their division and major, and 42 hours in the University Explorations program. The honors program may be substituted for general education requirements. A minimum 2.0 GPA and capstone course are required, and there is a 30-hour residency requirement. **Procedure:** Freshmen are admitted fall and spring. Entrance exams should be taken March 1. There are deferred admissions and rolling admissions plans. Application deadlines are open. Notification is sent on a rolling basis. Applications are accepted online. **Transfer Students:** 142 transfer students enrolled in 2016-2017. Entering transfers are classified according to the number of credits earned at their previous institution (s): freshman (fewer than 30 credits), sophomore (at least 30 and fewer than 60 credits), junior (at least 60 and fewer than 90 credits), and senior (at least 90 credits). Transfer applicants must submit an application along with an official college transcript from each institution attended and a recommendation from the Dean of Students or equivalent. High school transcripts and standardized test scores are required for students transferring with fewer than 24 academic credits. Student must be in good standing at the institution most recently attended. 30 of 120 credits required for the bachelor's degree must be completed at Saint Leo. **International Students:** There are 259 international students enrolled. They must take the TOEFL with a minimum score of 550 on the paper-based TOEFL (PBT) or 78 on the Internet-based version (iBT). Student must take the SAT Verbal (minimum score 450 required). The IELTS with a minimum score of 6 required may be substituted for TOEFL.

ADMISSIONS: 88% of the 2017-2018 applicants were accepted. The SAT scores for the 2017-2018 freshman class were: Critical Reading-- 27% below 500, 51% between 500 and 599, 19% between 600 and 699, and 3% between 700 and 800. Math-- 34% below 500, 49% between 500 and 599, 15% between 600 and 699, and 2% between 700 and 800. Writing-- 54% below 500, 31% between 500 and 599, and 15% between 600 and 699. The ACT scores were 5% between 12 and 17, 61% between 18 and 23, 32% between 24 and 29, and 2% above 30. 18% of the current freshmen were in the top fifth of their class; 34% were in the top two fifths. 2 freshmen graduated first in their class. **Admissions Contact:** Office of Admissions. Email: *admissions@saintleo.edu* Web: *http:/choose.saintleo.edu*

FINANCIAL AID: In 2017-2018, 100% of all full-time freshmen received some form of financial aid. 89% of all full-time freshmen received need-based aid. The average freshman award was $25,756. Need-based scholarships or need-based grants averaged $8,655 ($28,220 maximum); need-based self-help aid (loans and jobs) averaged $4,527 ($8,000 maximum); non-need-based athletic scholarships averaged $13,908 ($33,900 maximum); and other non-need-based awards and non-need-based scholarships averaged $9,224 ($28,940 maximum). 21% of undergraduate students work part-time. The average financial indebtedness of the 2017 graduate was $27,290. Saint Leo is a member of CSS. The FAFSA code is 001526. The priority date for freshman financial aid applications for fall entry is March 1.

SOUTHEASTERN UNIVERSITY *(The complete profile is made available exclusively on our website, www.barronspac.com)*

ST. THOMAS UNIVERSITY *(The complete profile is made available exclusively on our website, www.barronspac.com)*

STETSON UNIVERSITY — D-3

www.stetson.edu

DeLand, FL 32723	(386) 822-7100 (800) 688-0101
Fax: (386) 822-7112	**Email:** admissions@stetson.edu
Full-time: 1295 men, 1749 women	**Faculty:** 219
Part-time: 19 men, 18 women	**Ph.D.s:** 94%
Graduate: 513 men, 674 women	**Student/Faculty:** 13 to 1
Year: semesters, summer session	**Tuition:** $44,490
Room & Board: $12,684	**Freshman Class:** 11732 applied, 7958 accepted, 864 enrolled
SAT CR/M: 611/590 **ACT:** 26	**CEEB CODE:** 5630
Application Deadline: March 15	**VERY COMPETITIVE+**

Stetson University is the oldest private university in the State of Florida. Founded in 1883 by Henry A. DeLand as the DeLand Academy and later renamed Stetson University to honor its benefactor, John B. Stetson, the university has a storied history of leadership, values, and significance. The university is home to many Florida firsts, including the first collegiate newspaper, the first chapter of Phi Beta Kappa (the nation's oldest and most prestigious undergraduate honor society), the oldest schools of business administration and music and the first college of law. Stetson also was Florida's first private university to integrate. Stetson is home to 73 undergraduate academic programs in law, music, arts and sciences, and business with graduate studies offered in business and education. There are 3 undergraduate schools and 2 graduate schools. In addition to regional accreditation, SU has baccalaureate program accreditation with AACSB, NASM, and CAEP. The 159-acre campus is in a small town in DeLand, 35 miles north of Orlando and 25 miles west of Dayton Beach. With a second campus in Gulfport and two satellite campuses, one in Celebration and the other in Tampa. Including any residence halls, there are 92 buildings.

STUDENT LIFE: 68% of undergraduates are from Florida. Others are from 45 states, 64 foreign countries, and Canada. 8% are African American; 7% Foreign; 61% White; 4% two or more races; 2% Asian American; 2% race unknown; 16% Hispanic. 38% claim no religious affiliation;

36% Protestant; 15% Catholic. **Female To Male Ratio:** 1.3:1. The average age of freshmen is 18; all undergraduates, 20. 22% do not continue beyond their first year; 62% remain to graduate. **Housing:** 2051 students can be accommodated in college housing, which includes gender neutral dorms and on-campus apartments. In addition, there are language/international houses, special-interest houses, fraternity houses, sorority houses, family and partnered housing, and animal-friendly options. Themed-Housing Options: First-Year Experience, Women's Leadership, Wellness, and Honors Houses. On-campus housing is guaranteed for all 4 years. 66% of students live on campus. All students may keep cars.

FACULTY/CLASSROOMS: 53% of faculty are male; 47% are female. All teach undergraduates. No introductory courses are taught by graduate students. The average class size in an introductory lecture is 21; in a laboratory is 21; and in a regular course is 18.

PROGRAMS OF STUDY: Stetson confers B.A., B.S., B.B.A., B.M., and B.M.E. degrees. Master's and doctoral degrees are also awarded. Bachelor's degrees are awarded in BIOLOGICAL SCIENCE (biochemistry, biology/biological science, marine biology, and molecular biology), BUSINESS (accounting, banking and finance, business administration and management, business economics, business information systems, business intelligence and analytics, entrepreneurial studies, international business management, marketing/retailing/merchandising, organizational leadership and management, small business management, and sports management), COMMUNICATIONS AND THE ARTS (art history, communications, dramatic arts, English, French, German, guitar, music, music composition, music performance, music technology, music theory and composition, piano/organ, Spanish, studio art, voice, and winds), COMPUTER AND PHYSICAL SCIENCE (applied physics, chemistry, computer science, digital arts/technology, mathematics, and physics), EDUCATION (elementary education, music education, and social science education), ENGINEERING AND ENVIRONMENTAL DESIGN (environmental science), HEALTH PROFESSIONS (health science and public health), SOCIAL SCIENCE (American studies, economics, history, international studies, philosophy, political science/government, prelaw, psychology, public administration, religion, Russian and Slavic studies, and sociology). Biology, environmental science, and finance are the strongest academically. Psychology, business administration, and finance have the largest enrollments.

ACTIVITIES: There are 100 groups on campus, including art, band, cheerleading, chess, choir, chorale, chorus, computers, dance, debate, drama, environmental, ethnic, film, honors, international, jazz band, LGBT, literary magazine, musical theater, newspaper, opera, orchestra, pep band, political, professional, radio and TV, religious, social, social service, student government, and symphony. Popular campus events include Homecoming, Greenfeather (a community fund-raising event coinciding with Homecoming), Hatterpalooza (a live music festival), and Winter Wonderland (snow in Florida). **Sports:** There are 8 intercollegiate sports for men and 10 for women, and 14 intramural sports for men and 14 for women. Facilities include weightroom and exercise facilities, fieldhouse, basketball courts, volleyball courts, tennis courts, handball courts, softball fields, soccer fields, baseball fields, running trail, and swimming pool. **Graduates:** From July 1, 2016 to June 30, 2017, 677 bachelor's degrees were awarded. The most popular majors were psychology (9%), business administration (8%), and health sciences (7%). In an average class, 3% graduate in 3 years or less, 55% graduate in 4 years or less, 62% graduate in 5 years or less, and 62% graduate in 6 years or less. Of the 2016 graduating class, 25% were enrolled in graduate school within 6 months of graduation, and 51% were employed.

SERVICES: Counseling and information services are available, as is tutoring in most subjects. There is a reader service for the blind, and remedial writing. **Library/Resources:** The library contains 448,777 volumes, 266,923 microform items, and 18,676 audio/video tapes/CDs/DVDs, and subscribes to 115,751 periodicals including electronic. Computerized library services include interlibrary loans, database searching, Internet access, and Wi-Fi capability. Special learning facilities include an art gallery, radio station, and a museum of minerals. **Physically Challenged Students:** 80% of the campus is accessible. Facilities include wheelchair ramps, elevators, special parking, specially equipped restrooms, special class scheduling, lowered drinking fountains, and lowered telephones. **Special:** Stetsons curriculum is designed to provide students with a high-quality education that includes high-impact practices such as experiential learning, internships that are available to all students, and community engagement throughout the curriculum. Stetson offers interdisciplinary programs, environmental studies, entrepreneurship, music education, and others. The 3+3 BA/JD program offers accelerated admission to the College of Law. In finance, the Roland George Investments Program gives students the experience of managing over $3.4 million in stocks and bonds. Through the David and Leighan Rinker Center for International Learning, students study throughout the world, including Argentina, Australia, Austria, Belgium, Botswana, Brazil, Cambodia, Cayman Islands, Chile, China, Costa Rica, Cuba, Czech Republic, Denmark, Dominican Republic, Ecuador, England, Finland, France, Germany, Ghana, Greece, Guatemala, Hong Kong, Hungary, Ireland, Italy, Japan, Jordan, Mexico, Morocco, Netherlands, Nicaragua, Peru, Poland, Russia, Scotland, Serbia, Senegal, South Africa, South Korea, Spain, Switzerland, Taiwan, Tanzania, Thailand, and Vietnam. Students in Stetson University's Honors Program take a uniquely integrated curriculum, receive special funding for personal research and travel, may design their major and some courses, and work closely with their advisor to be especially competitive for national scholarships and fellowships. There are 27 national honor societies, Phi Beta Kappa, and a freshman honors program. **Visiting:** There are regularly scheduled orientations for prospective students, consisting of a campus tour and orientation, interviews, class visits, and presentations. There are guides for informal visits; visitors may sit in on classes, and stay overnight. To schedule a visit, contact the Admissions Office. **Campus Safety and Security:** Measures include 24-hour foot and vehicle patrol, emergency notification system, self-defense education, and security escort services. There are emergency telephones, lighted pathways/sidewalks, and controlled access to dorms/residences.

REQUIREMENTS: Applicants must be graduates of an accredited secondary school or have a GED, and have completed 4 years of English, 3 years of math and science, and 2 years each of foreign language, social sciences, and electives. Auditions are required for music students. A GPA of 2.0 is required. AP credits are accepted. Important factors in the admissions decision are advanced placement or honors courses, leadership record, and evidence of special talent. Stetson University provides an integrated, comprehensive learning experience for all students through a combination of courses in the major and general education. General education requirements are based on a set of highly desirable learning outcomes that enable students to succeed academically and in future endeavors. These learning outcomes include communication skills, quantitative reasoning skills, critical thinking, personal and social responsibility, and specific knowledge areas such as the physical world and creative arts. All students at Stetson University accomplish this learning through our First Year Seminars, courses in quantitative reasoning, writing, personal and social responsibility, a selection of knowledge-area courses, the interdisciplinary junior seminar, and senior research capstone courses. Students have a wide range of options from which to select these and other general education courses. To graduate, all students must complete 32 units/courses, and equivalent to 128 credits. **Procedure:** Freshmen are admitted fall, spring, and summer. Entrance exams should be taken spring of the junior year or the fall of the senior year. There are deferred admissions and rolling admissions plans. Application deadlines are open. The fall 2017 application fee was $50. Notification is sent on a rolling basis. Applications are accepted online. **Transfer Students:** 111 transfer students enrolled in 2016-2017. Transfer students must have completed a semester of academic work in good standing at an accredited college with a minimum 2.0 GPA. A 2.75 GPA and an interview (in person or remotely) are encouraged but not required. They must submit college transcripts and also an essay or personal statement at the time of application. High school transcripts may be requested as part of the application process if less than 30 college credits have been earned prior to the time of application. 64 of 128 credits required for the bachelor's degree must be completed at Stetson. **International Students:** There are 209 international students enrolled.

ADMISSIONS: 68% of the 2017-2018 applicants were accepted. Math--7% below 500, 49% between 500 and 599, 36% between 600 and 699, and 8% between 700 and 800. The ACT scores were 1% between 12 and 17, 28% between 18 and 23, 54% between 24 and 29, and 18% above 30. 50% of the current freshmen were in the top fifth of their class; 77% were in the top two fifths. 138 freshmen graduated first in their class. **Admissions Contact:** Director of Admissions. Email: *admissions@stetson.edu* Web: *www.stetson.edu*

FINANCIAL AID: In 2017-2018, 100% of all full-time freshmen received some form of financial aid. 68% of all full-time freshmen received need-based aid. The average freshman award was $39,299. Need-based scholarships or need-based grants averaged $31,065 ($61,086 maximum); need-based self-help aid (loans and jobs) averaged $4,340 ($12,500 maximum); non-need-based athletic scholarships averaged $25,166 ($57,468 maximum); and other non-need-based awards and non-need-based scholarships averaged $26,810. 11% of undergraduate students work part-time. The average financial indebtedness of the 2017 graduate was $34,126. SU is a member of CSS. The FAFSA code is 001531. The priority date for freshman financial aid applications for fall entry is March 15.

UNIVERSITY OF CENTRAL FLORIDA D-3
www.ucf.edu

Orlando, FL 32816	**(407) 823-3000**
Fax: (407) 823-5625	**Email:** admission@ucf.edu
Full-time: 18,222 men, 21,740 women	**Faculty:** I, -$
Part-time: 7821 men, 9189 women	**Ph.D.s:** 84%
Graduate: 3816 men, 5395 women	**Student/Faculty:** 30 to 1
Year: semesters, summer session	**Tuition:** $6368 ($22,467)
Room & Board: $10,011	**Freshman Class:** 37693 applied, 18810 accepted, 6860 enrolled
SAT EBR-W/M: 623/617 **ACT:** 26	**CEEB CODE:** 5233
Application Deadline: May 1	**VERY COMPETITIVE**

University of Central Florida, founded in 1963, is the one of the nation's largest universities and offers 181 bachelor's and master's degrees and 31 doctoral programs. At UCF, the pursuit of excellence is used to solve tomorrow's greatest challenges and to make a better future for the students and society. The Carnegie Foundation for the Advancement of Teaching named UCF a university with "highest research activity." There are 11 undergraduate schools and 11 graduate schools. In addition to regional accreditation, UCF has baccalaureate program accreditation with AACSB, ABET, CSWE, NASM, NAACLS, CCNE, and CAATE. The 1415-acre campus is in a suburban area 13 miles northeast of downtown Orlando. Including any residence halls, there are 180 buildings.

STUDENT LIFE: 94% of undergraduates are from Florida. Others are from 50 states, 153 foreign countries, and Canada. 6% are Asian American; 49% White; 4% two or more races; 3% Foreign; 26% Hispanic; 11% African American; 1% race unknown. **Female To Male Ratio:** 1.2:1. The average age of freshmen is 18; all undergraduates, 22. 10% do not continue beyond their first year; 70% remain to graduate. **Housing:** 11,641 students can be accommodated in college housing, which includes coed dorms, on-campus apartments, and off-campus apartments. In addition, there are honors houses, special-interest houses, fraternity houses, and sorority houses. On-campus housing is available on a first-come, first-served basis, and is available on a lottery system for upperclassmen. 82% of students commute. All students may keep cars.

FACULTY/CLASSROOMS: 54% of faculty are male; 46% are female. 69% teach undergraduates, 67% do research, and 41% do both. Graduate students teach 11% of introductory courses. The average class size in an introductory lecture is 48; in a laboratory is 13; and in a regular course is 47.

PROGRAMS OF STUDY: UCF confers B.A., B.S., B.A.B.A., B.A.S., B.F.A., B.M., B.M.E., B.S.A.E., B.S.B.A., B.S.C.E., B.S.Con.E., B.S.Cp.E., B.S.E.E., B.S.E.E.T., B.S.Env.E., B.S.E.T., B.S.I.E., B.S.M.E., B.S.N., B.Des., B.S.P.S.E., and B.S.W. degrees. Associate, master's, and doctoral degrees are also awarded. Bachelor's degrees are awarded in BIOLOGICAL SCIENCE (biology/biological science, biotechnology, and forensic science), BUSINESS (accounting, banking and finance, business administration and management, business economics, hospitality management services, management science, marketing/retailing/merchandising, and real estate), COMMUNICATIONS AND THE ARTS (advertising, art, broadcasting, communications, dramatic arts, English, film arts, fine arts, French, information technology, journalism, languages, music, music performance, photography, public relations, radio/television technology, Spanish, theatre arts, theatre studies, and writing), COMPUTER AND PHYSICAL SCIENCE (applied science, chemistry, computer science, digital arts/technology, information sciences and systems, mathematics, optics, physics, and statistics), EDUCATION (art education, athletic training, business education, early childhood education, education of the exceptional child, elementary education, English education, foreign languages education, global studies, health information management, mathematics education, music education, science education, social science education, and technical education), ENGINEERING AND ENVIRONMENTAL DESIGN (aeronautical engineering, aerospace studies, architecture, civil engineering, computer engineering, construction engineering, electrical/electronics engineering, environmental engineering, food services technology, industrial engineering, and mechanical engineering), HEALTH PROFESSIONS (biomedical science, exercise science, health care administration, health science, medical laboratory technology, nursing, and speech pathology/audiology), SOCIAL SCIENCE (anthropology, criminal justice, economics, food production/management/services, forensic studies, history, humanities, interdisciplinary studies, international studies, Latin American studies, legal studies, liberal arts/general studies, philosophy, political science/government, psychology, public administration, religion, social science, social work, and sociology). Engineering, business administration, and computer science are the strongest academically. Psychology, biomedical sciences, and health related fields have the largest enrollments.

ACTIVITIES: 6% of men belong to 27 national fraternities; 7% of women belong to 22 national sororities. There are 565 groups on campus, including and sport clubs, pre-professional medical society club, art, band, cheerleading, chess, choir, chorus, communications, computers, dance, debate, drama, drill team, environmental, ethnic, film, forensics, honors, international, jazz band, LGBT, literary magazine, marching band, musical theater, newspaper, opera, orchestra, pep band, photography, political, professional, radio and TV, religious, social, social service, student government, symphony, and volunteer UCF. Popular campus events include Homecoming Events, Spirit Splash, Pegasuspalloza, Symphony Under the Stars, Opening Knight, Knights on the Mall, Concerts, Comedians, and Movies on the Plaza. **Sports:** There are 6 intercollegiate sports for men and 10 for women, and 54 intramural sports for men and 54 for women. Facilities include football, basketball, volleyball, baseball, a weight room, a training room and equipment room, batting cages and pitching mounds, softball, soccer, track, a rowing facility, tennis, a golf facility, climbing tower, group exercise studio, lap pool, disc golf course, and leisure pool.**Graduates:** From July 1, 2016 to June 30, 2017, 13210 bachelor's degrees were awarded. The most popular majors were business (20%), health professions (17%), and psychology (8%). In an average class, 4% graduate in 3 years or less, 40% graduate in 4 years or less, 64% graduate in 5 years or less, and 70% graduate in 6 years or less. Of the 2016 graduating class, 9% were enrolled in graduate school within 6 months of graduation, and 75% were employed.

SERVICES: Counseling and information services are available, as is tutoring in some subjects, such as Biology and Microbiology, Chemistry (Organic and Biochemistry), Genetics, Human Anatomy and Physiology, Accounting, Finance, Programming, Object-oriented Program, Composition English Statics and Dynamics, Thermodynamics, Physics, Electronic Networks, Computer Science, Immunology, Discrete Structures, and Calculus 1 and 2. **Library/Resources:** The library contains 2.0 million volumes, 3.3 million microform items, and 58,583 audio/video tapes/CDs/DVDs, and subscribes to 53,544 periodicals including electronic. Computerized library services include interlibrary loans, database searching, Internet access, and Wi-Fi capability. Special learning facilities include an art gallery, radio station, TV station, University Writing Center, Robinson Observatory, UCF Arboretum, Townes Laser Institute, Siemens Energy Center, Morgridge International Reading Center, Center for Research and Education in Optics and Lasers, Toni Jennings Exceptional Education Institute, Communication Disorders Clinic, Institute for Simulation and Training, Florida Solar Energy Center, Biomolecular Science Center, fine art research facility and non-profit publisher, Florida Space Institute, Community Counseling and Research Center, Florida Photonics Center of Excellence, Institute for Diversity and Ethics in Sport, Blackstone LaunchPad, Business Incubation Program, Center for Entrepreneurship and Innovation, Small Business Development Center, Center for Advanced Turbomachinery and Energy Research, Center for Computer Vision, Interactive Systems and User Experience Research Cluster of Excellence, Dick Pope Sr. Institute for Tourism Studies, Lou Frey Institute of Politics and Government, NanoScience Technology Center, Advanced Materials Processing and Analysis Center, and partnership with the Central Florida Research Park. **Physically Challenged Students:** 97% of the campus is accessible. Facilities include wheelchair ramps, elevators, special parking, specially equipped restrooms, special class scheduling, lowered drinking fountains, and lowered telephones. **Special:** Internships are available in most majors through UCF's extensive partnerships with area businesses and industries such as NASA, Disney, Universal Studios, and AT&T. Students may participate in study abroad and co-op and work-study programs, earn B.A.-B.S. degrees or a liberal studies degree, or pursue dual majors. Nondegree study and pass/fail options are available. There are 22 national honor societies, a freshman honors program, and 63 departmental honors programs. **Visiting:** There are regularly scheduled orientations for prospective students, including tours offered twice a day, Monday through Friday, followed by a group information session or personal interview. There are guides for informal visits and visitors may sit in on classes. To schedule a visit, contact the Undergraduate Admissions Office. **Campus Safety and Security:** Measures include 24-hour foot and vehicle patrol, emergency notification system, self-defense education, and security escort services. There are shuttle buses, emergency telephones, lighted pathways/sidewalks, controlled access to dorms/residences, including a college-sponsored transportation system that buses students to and from apartment complexes within a 2- or 3-mile radius of the school.

REQUIREMENTS: The SAT or ACT is required. GPA and standardized test scores are rated on a sliding scale. A high school diploma or GED is required. Applicants should have completed 4 units of English and math, 3 units of science (with 2 labs) and social studies, and 2 each of foreign language and academic electives. AP and CLEP credits are accepted. Important factors in the admissions decision are advanced placement or honors courses, evidence of special talent, and leadership record. To graduate, students must complete at least 120 semester hours, with 36 hours in general education program courses, including 9 each in communication foundations and cultural and historical foundations and 6 each in math foundations, science foundations, and social foundations. Students must maintain a minimum GPA of 2.0. There is a 30-hour residency requirement, and the last semester is required in residence. **Procedure:** Freshmen are admitted fall, spring, and summer. Entrance exams should be taken during the junior year or the first semester of the senior year. There is a rolling admissions plan. Applications should be filed by May 1 for fall entry; November 1 for spring entry; and March 1 for summer entry. The fall 2017 application fee was $30. Notification is sent on a rolling basis. 2896 applicants were on the 2017 waiting list; 53 were admitted. Applications are accepted on-line. **Transfer Students:** 11605 transfer students enrolled in 2016-2017. A minimum GPA of 2.0 is required. Either the SAT or the ACT is required of applicants with fewer than 30 credit hours. Other transfer requirements vary widely. 30 of 120 credits required for the bachelor's degree must be completed at UCF. **International Students:** There are 1158 international students enrolled. They must take the TOEFL with a minimum score of 550 on the paper-based TOEFL (PBT) or 80 on the Internet-based version (iBT).

ADMISSIONS: 50% of the 2017-2018 applicants were accepted. The SAT scores for the 2017-2018 freshman class were: Math-- 2% below 500, 39% between 500 and 599, 48% between 600 and 699, and 11% between 700 and 800. Evidence-Based Reading/Writing-- 1% below 500, 32% between 500 and 599, 56% between 600 and 699, and 11% between 700 and 800. The ACT scores were 22% between 18 and 23, 59% between 24 and 29, and 19% above 30. 59% of the current freshmen were in the top fifth of their class; 91% were in the top two fifths. 47 freshmen graduated first in their class. **Admissions Contact:** Undergraduate Admissions Email: *admission@ucf.edu* Web: *www.ucf.edu*

FINANCIAL AID: In 2017-2018, 87% of all full-time freshmen received some form of financial aid. 48% of all full-time freshmen received need-based aid. The average freshman award was $9,080. Need-based scholarships or need-based grants averaged $5,994 ($14,265 maximum); need-based self-help aid (loans and jobs) averaged $3,662 ($12,392 maximum); non-need-based athletic scholarships averaged $15,604 ($30,049 maximum); and other non-need-based awards and non-need-based scholarships averaged $3,966 ($52,857 maximum). The average financial indebtedness of the 2017 graduate was $21,818. The FAFSA code is 003954. The priority date for freshman financial aid applications for fall entry is December 1.

UNIVERSITY OF FLORIDA D-2

www.ufl.edu

Gainesville, FL 32611 (352) 294-3683

Email: webrequest@admissions.ufl.edu

Full-time: 13,583 men, 17,800 women	**Faculty:** n/av
Part-time: 1941 men, 1922 women	**Ph.D.s:** 89%
Graduate: 8093 men, 9329 women	**Student/Faculty:** n/av
Year: semesters, summer session	**Tuition:** $6381 ($28,658)
Room & Board: $9910	**Freshman Class:** 32588 applied, 13668 accepted, 6477 enrolled
SAT EBR-W/M: 651/651 **ACT:** 29	**CEEB CODE:** 5812
Application Deadline: November 1	**HIGHLY COMPETITIVE+**

University of Florida, founded in 1853, is a public liberal arts institution that is part of the state university system of Florida. The figures in this profile are approximate. There are 16 undergraduate schools. In addition to regional accreditation, University of Florida has baccalaureate program accreditation with AACSB, ABET, ACCE, ACEJMC, ACPE, ADA, APTA, ASLA, FIDER, NAAB, NASAD, NASM, CAEP, SAF, CEPH, CAATE, and CCNE. The 1955-acre campus is in a suburban area 75 miles from Jacksonville, FL. Including any residence halls, there are 893 buildings.

STUDENT LIFE: 90% of undergraduates are from Florida. Others are from 50 states, 163 foreign countries, and Canada. 9% are Foreign; 7% Asian American; 6% African American; 53% White; 3% two or more races; 3% race unknown; 18% Hispanic. **Female To Male Ratio:** 1.2:1. The average age of freshmen is 18; all undergraduates, 20. **Housing:** 9558 students can be accommodated in college housing, which includes single sex, coed dorms, married student dorms, on-campus apartments, and off-campus apartments. In addition, there are honors houses, language/international houses, special-interest houses, fraternity houses, sorority houses, living learning communities, AIM, ARTS, Black Cultural, engineering, entrepreneurial, Gator Well, Global, Innovation Academy, Leader/Scholar Program, Out of State Gator, Pre-Health, Returning Gators, and ROTC. On-campus housing is available on a first-come, first-served basis. All students may keep cars.

FACULTY/CLASSROOMS: 65% of faculty are male; 35% are female. No introductory courses are taught by graduate students.

PROGRAMS OF STUDY: University of Florida confers B.A. and B.S. degrees. Associate, master's, and doctoral degrees are also awarded. Bachelor's degrees are awarded in AGRICULTURE (agricultural business management, agronomy, animal science, dairy science, forestry and related sciences, horticulture, natural resource management, plant science, and soil science), BIOLOGICAL SCIENCE (botany, entomology, microbiology, wildlife biology, and zoology), BUSINESS (accounting, banking and finance, business administration and management, human resources, insurance, management science, marketing/retailing/merchandising, and recreation and leisure services), COMMUNICATIONS AND THE ARTS (advertising, art, art history and appreciation, creative writing, dance, East Asian languages and literature, English, French, German, graphic design, journalism, linguistics, music, performing arts, photography, Portuguese, public relations, Russian, Spanish, speech/debate/rhetoric, telecommunications, theater design, and visual and performing arts), COMPUTER AND PHYSICAL SCIENCE (astronomy, chemistry, computer science, earth science, geology, information sciences and systems, mathematics, physics, and statistics), EDUCATION (agricultural education, art education, elementary education, health education, and music education), ENGINEERING AND ENVIRONMENTAL DESIGN (aeronautical engineering, agricultural engineering, architecture, chemical engineering, civil engineering, computer engineering, construction engineering, electrical/electronics engineering, emergency/disaster science, engineering and applied science, environmental engineering, industrial engineering technology, interior design, landscape architecture/design, materials engineering, mechanical engineering, nuclear engineering, and nuclear engineering technology), HEALTH PROFESSIONS (allied health, exercise science, health science, nursing, occupational therapy, physical therapy, prepharmacy, rehabilitation therapy, and speech pathology/audiology), SOCIAL SCIENCE (American studies, anthropology, Asian/Oriental studies, classical/ancient civilization, criminology, economics, food science, geography, history, home economics, interdisciplinary studies, Judaic studies, philosophy, physical fitness/movement, political science/government, psychology, religion, and sociology). Biology, finance, and psychology have the largest enrollments.

ACTIVITIES: 22% of men belong to 38 national fraternities; 22% of women belong to 27 national sororities. There are 1052 groups on campus, including art, band, cheerleading, chess, choir, chorale, chorus, computers, dance, debate, drama, environmental, ethnic, film, forensics, honors, international, jazz band, LGBT, literary magazine, marching band, newspaper, opera, orchestra, pep band, photography, political, professional, radio and TV, religious, social, social service, student government, and symphony. Popular campus events include Homecoming Parade, Annual Dance Marathon, Soulfest, Gator Growl Student Run Pep Rally, and Florida Invitational Step Show. **Sports:** There are 9 intercollegiate sports for men and 12 for women, and 42 intramural sports for men and 42 for women. Facilities include a football stadium, a multipurpose facility provides basketball, volleyball, and gymnastics, a practice court, weight rooms, an indoor track, an Olympic pool, dance studio, martial arts studio, baseball, softball, soccer, lacrosse, golf, basketball, tennis, and outdoor climbing wall. **Graduates:** From July 1, 2016 to June 30, 2017, 8240 bachelor's degrees were awarded. The most popular majors were biology (5%), psychology (5%), and finance (4%). In an average class, 4% graduate in 3 years or less, 67% graduate in 4 years or less, 84% graduate in 5 years or less, and 87% graduate in 6 years or less.

SERVICES: Counseling and information services are available, as is tutoring in every subject. There is a reader service for the blind. In addition to a free centralized tutoring service, UF provides subject specific tutoring including a writing center, math tutoring lab, sciences tutoring lab, and others. **Library/Resources:** The library contains 5.6 million volumes, 6.5 million microform items, and 88,388 audio/video tapes/CDs/DVDs, and subscribes to 146,554 periodicals including electronic. Computerized library services include interlibrary loans, database searching, Internet access, and Wi-Fi capability. Special learning facilities include an art gallery, a natural history museum, a radio station, a TV station, a performing arts center, and a teaching hospital. **Physically Challenged Students:** 95% of the campus is accessible. Facilities include wheelchair ramps, elevators, special parking, specially equipped restrooms, special class scheduling, lowered drinking fountains, lowered telephones, and special housing. **Special:** Numerous internships, study abroad, and research opportunities are available to students through the top-ranked UF Career Resource Center, UF International Center, UF Center for Undergraduate Research, and individual colleges and departments. Students can pursue accelerated degree programs and dual degrees and majors, which vary in eligibility and requirements by college and program. Students can pursue Interdisciplinary Studies in the College of Liberal Arts and Sciences. Innovation Academy at UF is a groundbreaking living/learning community that offers a minor in Innovation, a flexible spring-summer cohort, enlightening guest speakers, diverse internship opportunities, and co-curricular environment that emphasizes creativity. UF offers the Washington semester and work-study programs. The Herbert Wertheim College of Engineering administers a 3-2 mathematics-engineering degree program for students from the University of the Virgin Islands. UF enjoys a strong partnership with local Santa Fe College through its support of transfer students and unique academic programs, such as those administered by the Colleges of Engineering and Design, Construction, and Planning, that provide an additional pathway to UF for first-time-in-college students. The International Scholars Program has a graduation medallion program that offers students both a means of organizing and recognition for their international engagement while attending the University of Florida. Students must accomplish the following: complete 12 credits of academic coursework with an international focus; participate in an approved Study Abroad program, other approved international learning experiences, or at least one year of language learning beyond their specific college requirement; attend at least four internationally focused campus life events; and complete an e-portfolio in which students reflect on the role of the international in their broader UF experience. UF Online provides an array of fully online, 4-year undergraduate degree programs. Whether as a transfer or first-time-in-college student, UF Online students earn the same degree with the same faculty as our residential students. Pathway to Campus Enrollment (PaCE) is a hybrid admissions program for select majors that allows first-time-in-college students to complete the first 60 hours of their degree online. Once they have completed their lower division requirements, these students complete the remainder of their degree on campus just like any other residential student. There are 100 national honor societies, Phi Beta Kappa, a freshman honors program, and 100 departmental honors programs. **Visiting:** There are regularly scheduled orientations for prospective students, Refer to the Welcome Center calendar for tour time (www.admissions.ufl.edu/visit.html), as tours are based on the time of the year. There are guides for informal visits; visitors may sit in on classes and stay overnight. To schedule a visit, contact the UF Welcome Center. **Campus Safety and Security:** Measures include 24-hour foot and vehicle patrol, emergency notification system, self-defense education, and security escort services. There are shuttle buses, emergency telephones, lighted pathways/sidewalks, and controlled access to dorms/residences.

REQUIREMENTS: A satisfactory score on the SAT and a minimum score of 19 on the ACT are required. Candidates should have graduated from an accredited secondary school or have a GED, and have completed 4 years each of English, math, and academic electives, 3 years each of science, and social studies, and 2 years of a foreign language. A GPA of 2.5 is required. AP and CLEP credits are accepted. Important factors in the admissions decision are advanced placement or honors courses, extracurricular activities record, and evidence of special talent. Requirements for undergraduate graduation vary depending on the major elected, but all students are required to complete a minimum of 120 credits and maintain a minimum 2.0 GPA, including 36 credits of general education courses. **Procedure:** Freshmen are admitted to all sessions. Entrance exams should be taken in the junior year. Applications should be filed by November 1 for fall entry. The fall 2017 application fee was $30. Notifications are sent February 10. Applications are accepted online. **Transfer Students:** 3733 transfer students enrolled in 2016-2017. Admission requirements for transfer students vary by college. Students must have 60 hours or an A.A. degree. 30 of 120 credits required for the bachelor's degree must be completed at UF. **International Students:** There are 520 international students enrolled. They must take the TOEFL with a minimum score of 550 on the paper-based TOEFL (PBT) or 80 on the Internet-based version (iBT) or take either the MELAB, or IELTS. Freshmen only must take the SAT or ACT.

ADMISSIONS: 42% of the 2017-2018 applicants were accepted. **Admissions Contact:** Zina Evans, Vice President for Enrollment Management. Email: *webrequest@admissions.ufl.edu* Web: *www.ufl.edu*

FINANCIAL AID: In 2017-2018, 97% of all full-time freshmen received some form of financial aid. 32% of all full-time freshmen received need-based aid. The average freshman award was $12,820. Need-based scholarships or need-based grants averaged $7,697; need-based self-help aid (loans and jobs) averaged $4,146; non-need-based athletic scholarships averaged $18,753; and other non-need-based awards and non-need-based scholarships averaged $8,759. 16% of undergraduate students work part-time. The average financial indebtedness of the 2017 graduate was $22,188. The FAFSA code is 001535. The priority date for freshman financial aid applications for fall entry is December 15.

UNIVERSITY OF MIAMI — E-6

www.miami.edu

Coral Gables, FL 33124 — **(305) 284-2211**

Fax: (305) 284-2507	**Email:** admission@miami.edu
Full-time: 4874 men, 5260 women	**Faculty:** 1019; I, av$
Part-time: 210 men, 264 women	**Ph.D.s:** 85%
Graduate: 2980 men, 3191 women	**Student/Faculty:** 12 to 1
Year: semesters, summer session	**Tuition:** $48,484
Room & Board: $16,766	**Freshman Class:** 30634 applied, 10936 accepted, 2211 enrolled
SAT CR/M/W: 640/660/635 **ACT:** 30	**CEEB CODE:** 5815
Application Deadline: January 1	**MOST COMPETITIVE**

University of Miami, founded in 1925, lives are transformed through teaching, research, and service. Students are admitted directly to their major. Whether students seek to make their mark in science, service, or the arts, that passion is nurtured through a curriculum that integrates academic rigor and theory with real-world experience. With the flexibility to choose from more than 180 majors and programs across nine schools and colleges, students are encouraged to design a curriculum that crosses disciplines and is distinctly individualized. There are 9 undergraduate schools and 3 graduate schools. In addition to regional accreditation, University of Miami has baccalaureate program accreditation with AACSB, ABET, ADA, APTA, NAAB, NASM, COA-NA, CAHME, and CCNE. The 239-acre campus is in a suburban area 7 miles from Miami International Airport. Including any residence halls, there are 205 buildings.

STUDENT LIFE: 61% of undergraduates are from out of state, mostly the Middle Atlantic. Students are from 49 states, 118 foreign countries, and Canada. 8% are African American; 5% Asian American; 42% White; 4% race unknown; 3% two or more races; 23% Hispanic; 15% Foreign. 41% are Catholic; 28% Protestant; 17% Jewish. **Female To Male Ratio:** 1.1:1. The average age of freshmen is 18; all undergraduates, 21. 8% do not continue beyond their first year; 92% remain to graduate. **Housing:** 4216 students can be accommodated in college housing, which includes dorms and on-campus apartments. In addition, there are special-interest houses, fraternity houses, freshmen only housing, and theme housing. On-campus housing is guaranteed for the freshman year only, is available on a first-come, first-served basis, and is available on a lottery system for upperclassmen. 61% of students commute. Some may keep cars.

FACULTY/CLASSROOMS: 60% of faculty are male; 40% are female. No introductory courses are taught by graduate students.

PROGRAMS OF STUDY: University of Miami confers A.B., B.A., B.S., B.A.M., B.A.M.A., B.Arch., B.B.A., B.F.A., B.G.S., B.L.A., B.M., B.S.A.E., B.S.A.S.E., B.S.A.T., B.S.B.A., B.S.B.E., B.S.C., B.S.C.E., B.S.Cp.E., B.S.Ed., B.S.E.E., B.S.E.S., B.S.En.E., B.S.Ex.P., B.S.H.S., B.S.I.E., B.S.M.A.S., B.S.M.E., B.S.N., and B.S.P.H. degrees. Master's and doctoral degrees are also awarded. Bachelor's degrees are awarded in BIOLOGICAL SCIENCE (biochemistry, marine affairs, marine biology, marine science, microbiology, and neurosciences), BUSINESS (accounting, business and technology, entrepreneurial studies, finance, human resources/organizational management, international finance, international marketing, management science, marketing, marketing management, real estate, and sports management), COMMUNICATIONS AND THE ARTS (advertising, Africana studies, art history, art, ceramic art and design, classics, communication studies, communications, English, film arts, fine arts, French, German, graphic design, instrumental performance, jazz, journalism, media management, music, music business management, music composition, music performance, music technology, musical theater, painting, photography, printmaking, public relations, sculpture, Spanish, studio art, theatre acting, theatre arts, theater design, theater management, and vocal performance), COMPUTER AND PHYSICAL SCIENCE (atmospheric sciences and meteorology, chemistry, computer science, geology, geoscience, mathematics, physics, and statistics), EDUCATION (athletic training, elementary education, and music education), ENGINEERING AND ENVIRONMENTAL DESIGN (aerospace studies, architectural engineering, architecture, biomedical engineering, civil engineering, computer engineering, computer graphics, electrical/electronics engineering, engineering science, environmental engineering, environmental science, industrial engineering, and mechanical engineering), HEALTH PROFESSIONS (biology, exercise science, health administration and policy, health care administration, health science, music therapy, nursing, prehealth studies, predentistry, premedicine, prepharmacy, prephysical therapy, preveterinary science, and public health), SOCIAL SCIENCE (American studies, anthropology, criminology, economics, gender studies, geography, history, human development, interdisciplinary studies, international studies, Judaic studies, Latin American studies, legal studies, liberal arts/general studies, philosophy, political science/government, prelaw, psychology, religion, religious studies, sociology, and women's studies). Business/marketing, biological/life sciences, and social sciences have the largest enrollments.

ACTIVITIES: 18% of men belong to 17 national fraternities; 20% of women belong to 14 national sororities. There are 285 groups on campus, including art, athletic organization clubs, band, cheerleading, chess, choir, chorale, chorus, computers, dance, debate, drama, environmental, ethnic, film, honors, international, jazz band, LGBT, literary magazine, marching band, musical theater, newspaper, opera, orchestra, pep band, political, professional, radio and TV, religious, social, social service, student government, symphony, and yearbook. Popular campus events include SportsFest, International Week, Homecoming Week (Various Activities), Fun Day, National Gandhi Day of Service, Miami International Film Festival, Black Awareness Month Day of Service, Canefest, Festival Miami, Alumni Weekend, and Hug the Lake. **Sports:** There are 7 intercollegiate sports for men and 10 for women, and 18 intramural sports for men and 18 for women. Facilities include a soccer and track & field facility, basketball courts, an athletic training facility with diagnostic and rehabilitative equipment, baseball stadium, tennis center, swimming pool, and football, a fitness, recreation and wellness facility that includes a fitness room, aerobic classes, indoor track, a gymnasium with basketball, volleyball and badminton courts, racquetball and squash courts, tennis, and a indoor pool. **Graduates:** From July 1, 2016 to June 30, 2017, 2733 bachelor's degrees were awarded. The most popular majors were business/marketing (20%), social science (12%), and health professions and related programs (10%). In an average class, 2% graduate in 3 years or less, 72% graduate in 4 years or less, 82% graduate in 5 years or less, and 84% graduate in 6 years or less. Of the 2016 graduating class, 19% were enrolled in graduate school within 6 months of graduation, and 31% were employed.

SERVICES: Counseling and information services are available, as is tutoring in some subjects. There is a reader service for the blind. **Library/Resources:** The library contains 3.9 million volumes, 4.2 million microform items, and 191,953 audio/video tapes/CDs/DVDs, and subscribes to 114,801 periodicals, including electronic. Computerized library services include interlibrary loans, database searching, Internet access, and Wi-Fi capability. Special learning facilities include an art gallery, a radio station, a TV station, a cinema, an observatory, a palmetum, marine science research vessels, broadcasting studios, a concert hall, an arboretum, performing arts theater, film studios, a sound stage, a museum, a wave machine, a wellness center, and a state-of-the-art student activities center. **Physically Challenged Students:** Facilities include wheelchair ramps, elevators, special parking, specially equipped restrooms, special class scheduling, lowered drinking fountains, lowered telephones, special housing, and lowered elevator controls. **Special:** Internships, work-study programs, and study-abroad programs provide the opportunity for UM students to acquire an expansive perspective in their academic career. Opportunities to learn and grow flourish through our special programs such as our accelerated degree programs as well as our dual degree programs. There are 41 national honor societies, Phi Beta Kappa, and a freshman honors program. **Visiting:** There are regularly scheduled orientations for prospective students, and several open house programs. Daily information sessions are offered on campus as well as walking tours. There are guides for informal visits and visitors may sit in on classes. **Campus Safety and Security:** Measures include 24-hour foot and vehicle patrol, an emergency notification system, self-defense education, and security escort services. There are shuttle buses, emergency telephones, lighted pathways/sidewalks, controlled access to dorms/residences, and a comprehensive crime prevention program.

REQUIREMENTS: The ACT Optional Writing test, the SAT or ACT, and the SAT with Essay component are required. It is recommended that applicants have completed 4 units each of English and mathematics, 3 units of science (with 2 of lab) and social studies, 2 units each of foreign language and history, and 2 units of academic electives with 1 unit being in computer science and 1 unit being in visual/performing arts. Applicants are based on the strength of their high school curriculum and grades earned, standardized test scores, letters of recommendation, essay, extracurricular activities, and awards/achievements. The GED is accepted. Portfolios are required for the arts and architecture programs. Auditions are required for the music and theatre programs. Supplemental applications are required for the Frost School of Music, B.F.A. Theatre, B.F.A. Art, and Architecture, and Dual Degree Programs. AP and CLEP credits are accepted. Important factors in the admissions decision are evidence of special talent, advanced placement or honors courses, personality/intangible qualities, extracurricular activities record, and recommendations by school officials. To receive a Bachelor's degree from the University, the student must earn at least 120 semester hours of credit, more in some schools, with a C average or better, as well as a C average for all work done at the University of Miami. Students must also meet all of the degree requirements of their respective schools and should not expect requirements in composition, mathematics, foreign languages, or other subject areas to be waived for any reason. A student transferring credit hours from a 2-year community or junior college (this being the last school attended) must complete a minimum of 56 credit hours in residence at the University of Miami to earn an undergraduate degree. A student transferring credit hours from a 4-year college or university (this being the last school attended) must complete a minimum of 45 credit hours in residence at the University of Miami to earn an undergraduate degree. In addition, each student must complete at least half of the credit hours specified for his or her major in residence at the University of Miami. Not more than 30 credit hours of correspondence work and extension work combined will be accepted toward a degree, and neither correspondence nor extension work may be credited as a part of the last 45/56 credit hours of the student's program. Not more than 30 credit hours based on military experience will be awarded toward the degree. Credit hours earned in a manner other than by course registration e.g. proficiency examination, CLEP, placement tests, etc. may not be used to meet the final 45/56 credit hour residency requirement however such credit by examination may be earned while the student is enrolled in the courses needed to meet the final 45/56 credit-hour residency requirement. Once a degree has been awarded, no changes will be made to the academic record. **Procedure:** Freshmen are admitted in the fall and spring. Entrance exams should be taken the summer before the senior year in high school. There are early decision, early admissions, and deferred admissions plans. Early decision applications should be filed by November 1; regular applications, by January 1 for fall entry. The fall 2017 application fee was $70. Notification of early decision is sent December 20; regular decision, April 15. 252 early decision candidates were accepted for the 2017-2018 class. 1440 applicants were on the 2017 waiting list; 215 were admitted. Applications are accepted online. **Transfer Students:** 626 transfer students enrolled in 2016-2017. Only credits from a regionally accredited institution are transferable to the University of Miami. The average admitted transfer student has a 3.3 GPA. Courses with a grade lower than a C will not transfer; however, these grades will still be used to compute an admission GPA. If the student has fewer than 30 college credits when submitting the application, official high school transcripts, the Common Application Final Report, and official SAT/ ACT test scores must be submitted in addition to the core application documents. If a student is applying to a special program (Bachelor of Architecture, Art B.F.A., Theatre Arts B.F.A., or the Frost School of Music), a supplemental application, a portfolio, and/or an audition may be required. 45 of 120 credits required for the bachelor's degree must be completed at UM. **International Students:** There are 1613 international students enrolled. They must take the TOEFL with a minimum score of 550 on the paper-based TOEFL (PBT) or 80 on the Internet-based version (iBT). All students whose native language is not English are required to submit official results of the TOEFL or IELTS. The SAT/ ACT is not required and shouldn't be submitted for admission consideration from applicants attending school outside the US.

ADMISSIONS: 44% of the 2017-2018 applicants were accepted. The SAT scores for the 2017-2018 freshman class were: Critical Reading-- 4% below 500, 21% between 500 and 599, 53% between 600 and 699, and 22% between 700 and 800. Math-- 2% below 500, 18% between 500 and 599, 49% between 600 and 699, and 30% between 700 and 800. Writing-- 4% below 500, 26% between 500 and 599, 53% between 600 and 699, and 18% between 700 and 800. The ACT scores were 1% between 12 and 17, 2% between 18 and 23, 39% between 24 and 29, and 58% above 30. 90% of the current freshmen were in the top fifth of their class; 97% were in the top two fifths. 38 freshmen graduated first in their class. **Admissions Contact:** John Haller, Vice President of Enrollment Management. Email: *admission@miami.edu* Web: *www.miami.edu*

FINANCIAL AID: In 2017-2018, 96% of all full-time freshmen received some form of financial aid. 86% of all full-time freshmen received need-based aid. The average freshman award was $46,432. Need-based scholarships or need-based grants averaged $32,486; need-based self-help aid (loans and jobs) averaged $5,241; non-need-based athletic scholarships averaged $77,391; other non-need-based awards and non-need-based scholarships averaged $19,482; other forms of aid averaged $1,600. 56% of undergraduate students work part-time. The average financial indebtedness of the 2017 graduate was $42,292. University of Miami is a member of CSS. The CSS/Profile, noncustodial profile, business/farm supplement, all student/parent W-2's, individual and corporate income tax returns are required. The priority date for freshman financial aid applications for fall entry is January 20.

UNIVERSITY OF NORTH FLORIDA D-1
www.unf.edu

Jacksonville, FL 32224	**(904) 620-2624** **(866) 808-0626**
Fax: (904) 620-2414	**Email: Admissions@unf.edu**
Full-time: 4237 men, 5465 women	**Faculty:** 454; IIA, -$
Part-time: 1873 men, 2271 women	**Ph.D.s:** 92%
Graduate: 687 men, 1229 women	**Student/Faculty:** 19 to 1
Year: semesters, summer session	**Tuition:** $6394 ($20,798)
Room & Board: $9602	**Freshman Class:** 6799 applied, 3397 accepted, 809 enrolled
SAT CR/M: 612/597 **ACT:** 26	**CEEB CODE:** 5490
Application Deadline: August 1	**VERY COMPETITIVE**

University of North Florida, founded in 1965, is a public university that is part of the state university system. There are 5 undergraduate schools and 5 graduate schools. In addition to regional accreditation, UNF has baccalaureate program accreditation with AACSB, ABET, ACCE, APTA, NASM, CAEP, NLN, ACS, CAAHEP, CAATE, CAHME, CoA-NA, FBN, CCNE, CACREP, CADE, CAPTE, COSMA, CED, FDE, ACEND, NASPAA, NASM, NAACLS, ACS, EAC, CAC, and AUPHA. The 1300-acre campus is in an urban area 12 miles southeast of downtown Jacksonville. Including any residence halls, there are 94 buildings.

STUDENT LIFE: 94% of undergraduates are from Florida. Others are from 46 states, 105 foreign countries, and Canada. 67% are White; 5% Asian American; 5% two or more races; 2% Foreign; 10% African American; 10% Hispanic; 1% race unknown. 99% claim no religious affiliation. **Female To Male Ratio:** 1.3:1. The average age of freshmen is 18; all undergraduates, 23. 20% do not continue beyond their first year; 53% remain to graduate. **Housing:** 3500 students can be accommodated in college housing, which includes dorms, on-campus apartments, and off-campus apartments. In addition, there are honors houses, special interest houses, and living learning communities. On-campus housing is guaranteed for the freshman year only, and is available on a first-come, first-served basis. 79% of students commute. All students may keep cars.

FACULTY/CLASSROOMS: 51% of faculty are male; 49% are female. 93% teach undergraduates, 81% do research, and 75% do both. No introductory courses are taught by graduate students. The average class size in an introductory lecture is 35; in a laboratory is 20; and in a regular course is 33.

PROGRAMS OF STUDY: UNF confers B.A., B.S., B.A.E., B.B.A., B.F.A., B.H.A., B.M., B.M.E., B.S.A.T., B.S.E.E., B.S.H., B.S.N., and B.S.W. degrees. Associate, master's, and doctoral degrees are also awarded. Bachelor's degrees are awarded in BIOLOGICAL SCIENCE (biology/ biological science and nutrition), BUSINESS (accounting, banking and finance, business administration and management, business economics, finance, global/general management, international business management, marketing management, sports management, and transportation management), COMMUNICATIONS AND THE ARTS (American Sign Language, art, communications, English, English literature, fine arts, jazz, music, music performance, and Spanish), COMPUTER AND PHYSICAL SCIENCE (applied mathematics, chemistry, computer science, information sciences and systems, mathematics, physics, and statistics), EDUCATION (art education, athletic training, elementary education, English education, mathematics education, middle school education, music education, physical education, science education, secondary education, social studies education, and special education), ENGINEERING AND ENVIRONMENTAL DESIGN (civil engineering, construction engineering, construction management, electrical/ electronics engineering, and mechanical engineering), HEALTH PROFESSIONS (health care administration, health science, mental health/ human services, nursing, and physical therapy), SOCIAL SCIENCE (anthropology, counseling/psychology, criminal justice, dietetics, economics, ethnic studies, French studies, history, interdisciplinary studies, philosophy, political science/government, psychology, public administration, religion, and sociology). Nursing, fine arts, and elementary education are the strongest academically. Psychology, communication, and business management have the largest enrollments.

ACTIVITIES: 3% of men belong to 10 national fraternities; 4% of women belong to 9 national sororities. There are 233 groups on campus, including art, band, cheerleading, choir, chorale, chorus, computers, dance, drama, drum and bugle corps, environmental, ethnic, film, honors, international, jazz band, LGBT, literary magazine, newspaper, photography, political, professional, radio and TV, religious, social, social service, and student government. Popular campus events include Clubfest, Spring Bash, and Earth Music Fest. **Sports:** There are 7 intercollegiate sports for men and 10 for women, and 11 intramural sports for men and 11 for women. Facilities include a baseball stadium, softball, soccer, and multipurpose fields, a soccer stadium, an aquatic center, fitness center, jogging trails, racquetball, basketball, volleyball, and tennis courts, a multipurpose arena, a climbing wall, indoor track, fitness rooms, and weight machines. **Graduates:** From July 1, 2016 to June 30, 2017, 3255 bachelor's degrees were awarded. The most popular majors were psychology (10%), communications (8%), and nursing (6%). In an average class, 2% graduate in 3 years or less, 26% graduate in 4 years or less, 47% graduate in 5 years or less, and 53% graduate in 6 years or less.

SERVICES: Counseling and information services are available, as is tutoring in some subjects, accounting, biology, chemistry, computer science, economics, history, mathematics, physics, psychology, statistics, and world languages. Writing tutoring is available by appointment through the Writing Center. **Library/Resources:** The library contains 860,144 volumes, 1.5 million microform items, and 32,755 audio/video tapes/CDs/DVDs, and subscribes to 38,246 periodicals including electronic. Computerized library services include interlibrary loans, database searching, Internet access, and Wi-Fi capability. Special learning facilities include an art gallery, radio station, TV station, a theater, an auditorium, a nature preserve, and the Museum of Science and History (MOSH). **Physically Challenged Students:** Facilities include wheelchair ramps, elevators, special parking, specially equipped restrooms, special class scheduling, lowered drinking fountains, lowered telephones, special housing. The Disability Resource Center provides specialized assistance and equipment, including priority registration, interpreters for the hearing impaired, and proctored testing. **Special:** There are cooperative programs and internships in most majors and work-study programs with several Jacksonville businesses. Study abroad, an accelerated degree program in nursing, B.A.-B.S. degrees in math, statistics, and psychology, dual majors, and student-designed majors also are available. Credit is given for military experience. There are 6 national honor societies, a freshman honors program, and 14 departmental honors programs. **Visiting:** There are regularly scheduled orientations for prospective students, consisting of open houses which include tours of the campus and housing, a general information session, financial aid sessions, academic advising, and personal interviews by request. There are guides for informal visits. To schedule a visit, contact the Admissions Office. **Campus Safety and Security:** Measures include 24-hour foot and vehicle patrol, emergency notification system, self-defense education, and security escort services. There are shuttle buses, emergency telephones, lighted pathways/sidewalks, and university police presentations at new student orientation.

REQUIREMENTS: The SAT or ACT is required. The Office of Admissions will recalculate a grade point average based on 18 academic units in college preparatory courses. Additional weight is given to grades of C or higher earned in honors, Dual Enrollment, Advanced Placement, IB, or AICE courses. While students may not have completed all the required courses at the time an application is submitted, they are required to complete them prior to high school graduation and entrance into UNF. The State of Florida has implemented new minimum admission standards for freshmen applicants to all state universities. In order to be considered, students must have a minimum 2.5 recalculated GPA, on a 4.0 scale, and meet minimum test score requirements (460 SAT Critical Reading, 460 SAT Math, 440 SAT Writing; or 19 ACT Reading, 19 ACT Math, 18 ACT English/Writing). Please keep in mind that these standards only outline potential eligibility for admission to a state university. UNFs admission criteria depend on the applicant pool and will be higher than these minimums. A GPA of 2.5 is required. AP and CLEP credits are accepted. Important factors in the admissions decision are advanced placement or honors courses, recommendations by school officials, and evidence of special talent. Students are required to take general education distribution requirements, including 9 hours of composition and humanities and 6 each of natural science, math, and social science. There is a core curriculum in Western civilization and cultural diversity. A minimum 2.0 GPA and 120 credit hours, with a minimum of 60 hours in the major, are needed for graduation. **Procedure:** Freshmen are admitted to all sessions. Entrance exams should be taken during the spring of the junior year or the fall of the senior year. There are deferred admissions and rolling admissions plans. Application deadlines are open. The fall 2017 application fee was $30. Notification is sent on a rolling basis. Applications are accepted online. **Transfer Students:** 2671 transfer students enrolled in 2016-2017. Upper-level transfer students are defined as those with at least 60 transferable credit hours or an Associate of Arts degree from a Florida public or postsecondary institution. Admission requirements will vary by major, term, and space-availability. In order to be considered, applicants must meet or exceed a cumulative college GPA of 2.0 or higher, including a C or higher average and good standing status at the most recent college attended. Additional requirements will exist for students applying to limited access/ selective admission programs or as international students. 30 of 120 credits required for the bachelors degree must be completed at UNF. **International Students:** There are 233 international students enrolled. They must take the TOEFL. They must also take the SAT or ACT.

ADMISSIONS: 50% of the 2017-2018 applicants were accepted. The SAT scores for the 2017-2018 freshman class were: Critical Reading-- 3% below 500, 37% between 500 and 599, 52% between 600 and 699, and 8% between 700 and 800. Math-- 2% below 500, 48% between 500 and 599, 47% between 600 and 699, and 3% between 700 and 800. Writing-- 13% below 500, 52% between 500 and 599, 33% between 600 and 699, and 2% between 700 and 800. The ACT scores were 80% between 24 and 29, and 20% above 30. 55% of the current freshmen were in the top fifth of their class; 78% were in the top two fifths. **Admissions Contact:** Karen Lucas, Director of Admissions. Email: *Admissions@unf.edu* Web: *www.unf.edu*

FINANCIAL AID: In 2017-2018, 74% of all full-time freshmen received some form of financial aid. 43% of all full-time freshmen received need-based aid. The average freshman award was $9,649. Need-based scholarships or need-based grants averaged $6,212 ($17,843 maximum); need-based self-help aid (loans and jobs) averaged $2,444 ($13,681 maximum); non-need-based athletic scholarships averaged $11,239 ($25,723 maximum); and other non-need-based awards and non-need-based scholarships averaged $6,229 ($35,806 maximum). 7% of undergraduate students work part-time. The average financial indebtedness of the 2017 graduate was $17,452. The deadline for filing freshman financial aid applications for fall entry is April 1.

UNIVERSITY OF SOUTH FLORIDA ST. PETERSBURG D-4

www.usfsp.edu

St. Petersburg, FL 33701 **(727) 873-4142**

Fax: (727) 873-4525
Email: admissions@usfsp.edu
Full-time: 1134 men, 1654 women
Faculty: 134
Part-time: 462 men, 756 women
Ph.D.s: n/av
Graduate: 155 men, 303 women
Student/Faculty: 24 to 1
Year: semesters, summer session
Tuition: $8412 ($16,736)
Room & Board: $7568
Freshman Class: 1996 applied, 914 accepted, 474 enrolled
SAT CR/M/W: 530/530/510 **ACT:** 23
CEEB CODE: 5828
Application Deadline: March 15
COMPETITIVE

University of South Florida St. Petersburg, founded in 1965, students find an unparalleled depth of academic, professional, and social opportunities, from conducting actual field marine research to leading a local chapter of a national advertising organization and much more. Guided by faculty whose research and scholarship has been awarded by nationally recognized organizations, such as the NIH and NSF, they become the global contributors who lead Fortune 500 companies, make a difference in school districts all over Florida, and go on to advanced study at some of the most prestigious colleges and universities in the world. There are 3 undergraduate schools and 1 graduate school. In addition to regional accreditation, USF St. Petersburg has baccalaureate program accreditation with AACSB, ACEJMC, CAEP, and SACS-COC. The 63-acre campus is in an urban area on Bayboro Harbor in downtown St. Petersburg. Including any residence halls, there are 29 buildings.

STUDENT LIFE: 95% of undergraduates are from Florida. 8% are African American; 74% White; 4% Asian American; 13% Hispanic. **Female To Male Ratio:** 1.5:1. **Housing:** 600 students can be accommodated in college housing, which includes dorms, on-campus apartments, and off-campus apartments. In addition, there are special-interest houses. On-campus housing is guaranteed for the freshman year only. 85% of students commute. Alcohol is not permitted. All students may keep cars.

FACULTY/CLASSROOMS: 48% of faculty are male; 52% are female. No introductory courses are taught by graduate students. The average class size in an introductory lecture is 36; in a laboratory is 23; and in a regular course is 20.

PROGRAMS OF STUDY: USF St. Petersburg confers B.A., B.S., and B.F.A. degrees. Master's degrees are also awarded. Bachelor's degrees are awarded in BIOLOGICAL SCIENCE (biology/biological science and biological sciences), BUSINESS (accounting, business administration and management, entrepreneurial studies, finance, global/general management, management science, and marketing and distribution), COMMUNICATIONS AND THE ARTS (communications, English, and graphic design), COMPUTER AND PHYSICAL SCIENCE (information sciences and systems), EDUCATION (education), ENGINEERING AND ENVIRONMENTAL DESIGN (environmental science), HEALTH PROFESSIONS (health science), SOCIAL SCIENCE (anthropology, criminology, economics, history, political science/government, psychology, and social science). Biology (5 concentrations), business, and education are the strongest academically. Psychology, biology, and business have the largest enrollments.

ACTIVITIES: There are no fraternities or sororities. There are 200 groups on campus, including art, chess, choir, chorus, communications, computers, dance, debate, drama, environmental, ethnic, film, forensics, honors, international, LGBT, literary magazine, musical theater, newspaper, photography, political, professional, radio and TV, religious, social, social service, and student government. Popular campus events include Welcome Week, Homecoming Week, Leadership Retreats, Career and Internship Fairs, and Cardboard Boat Race. **Sports:** There are 5 intramural sports for men and 5 for women. Facilities include a recreation center, an aquatics center, and waterfront activities such as sailing, kayaking, and paddle boarding. **Graduates:** From July 1, 2016 to June 30, 2017,

705 bachelor's degrees were awarded. The most popular majors were accounting (15%), psychology (10%), and general business (10%). In an average class, 11% graduate in 4 years or less, 26% graduate in 5 years or less, and 33% graduate in 6 years or less.

SERVICES: Counseling and information services are available, as is tutoring in most subjects. There is a reader service for the blind, and remedial math, reading, and writing. **Library/Resources:** The library contains 2.6 million volumes, and subscribes to 94,816 periodicals including electronic. Computerized library services include interlibrary loans, database searching, Internet access, and Wi-Fi capability. Special learning facilities include an art gallery, a radio station, TV station, graphic design studios, Marine Science labs, Fish and Wildlife Conservation Commissions, US Geological Survey, Poynter Institute for Media Studies, and National Oceanic and Atmospheric Administration. **Physically Challenged Students:** Facilities include wheelchair ramps, elevators, special parking, specially equipped restrooms, special class scheduling, lowered drinking fountains, lowered telephones, and special housing. **Special:** There are 7 national honor societies, a freshman honors program, and 3 departmental honors programs. **Visiting:** There are regularly scheduled orientations for prospective students, an information session with an admissions counselor, and a walking tour. There are guides for informal visits. To schedule a visit, contact Summer Finck at (727) USF-4802. **Campus Safety and Security:** Measures include 24-hour foot and vehicle patrol, emergency notification system, self-defense education, and security escort services. There are emergency telephones, lighted pathways/sidewalks, and controlled access to dorms/residences.

REQUIREMENTS: The SAT or ACT is required. Academic course units required for admission: 4 units each of English (3 with substantial writing) and mathematics (Algebra I or above), 3 units each in natural sciences (2 with substantial lab) and social sciences, 2 units each in foreign language (same language) and academic electives. AP and CLEP credits are accepted. **Procedure:** Freshmen are admitted fall, spring, and summer. Entrance exams should be taken during the junior year in high school. There are deferred admissions and rolling admissions plans. Applications should be filed by March 15 for fall entry; November 15 for spring entry. The fall 2017 application fee was $30. Notifications are sent October 2. Applications are accepted online. **Transfer Students:** 582 transfer students enrolled in 2016-2017. Requirements include courses taken at a regionally accredited school, minimum GPA of 2.5 (or a GPA of 2.0 if holding an A.A. degree unless applying to a limited access degree). 30 of 120 credits required for the bachelor's degree must be completed at USF St. Petersburg. **International Students:** There are 42 international students enrolled. They must take the TOEFL with a minimum score of 550 on the paper-based TOEFL (PBT) or 79 on the Internet-based version (iBT), IELTS, and PTE-A. They must also take the SAT or ACT, scoring 500/500.

ADMISSIONS: 46% of the 2017-2018 applicants were accepted. 6% of the current freshmen were in the top fifth of their class. **Admissions Contact:** Holly Kickliter, Director, Admissions and Marketing. Email: *admissions@usfsp.edu* Web: *www.usfsp.edu*

FINANCIAL AID: In 2017-2018, 84% of all full-time freshmen received some form of financial aid. 38% of all full-time freshmen received need-based aid. USF St. Petersburg is a member of CSS. The FAFSA code is 009016. The priority date for freshman financial aid applications for fall entry is January 1.

UNIVERSITY OF SOUTH FLORIDA/ TAMPA — D-4

www.usf.edu

Tampa, FL 33620 — (813) 974-4150

Email: dlhenry@usf.edu

Full-time: 10,666 men, 12,937 women	**Faculty:** 1244
Part-time: 3349 men, 3601 women	**Ph.D.s:** n/av
Graduate: 5016 men, 6384 women	**Student/Faculty:** 24 to 1
Year: semesters, summer session	**Tuition:** $6410 ($17,324)
Room & Board: $9700	**Freshman Class:** n/av
SAT or ACT: required	**CEEB CODE:** 5828
Application Deadline: March 15	**VERY COMPETITIVE**

University of South Florida/Tampa, founded in 1956, is a comprehensive public institution and part of the Florida Division of Colleges and Universities, offering programs in liberal and fine arts, business, engineering, health science, and education. USF also maintains campuses at Lakeland, Sarasota, and St. Petersburg. The figures in the above capsule and in this profile are approximate. There are 6 undergraduate schools and 12 graduate schools. In addition to regional accreditation, USF/Tampa has baccalaureate program accreditation with AACSB, ABET, ACEJMC, ASLA, CSAB, CSWE, NAAB, NASAD, NASM, CAEP, and NLN. The 1657-acre campus is in an urban area in Tampa, Florida. Including any residence halls, there are 434 buildings.

STUDENT LIFE: 91% of undergraduates are from Florida. Others are from 50 states, 154 foreign countries, and Canada. 7% are Asian American; 6% Foreign; 50% White; 4% two or more races; 21% Hispanic; 2% race unknown; 10% African American. **Female To Male Ratio:** 1.2:1. The average age of freshmen is 18; all undergraduates, 22. 12% do not continue beyond their first year; 88% remain to graduate. **Housing:** 9297 students can be accommodated in college housing, which includes married student dorms and on-campus apartments. In addition, there are honors houses, special-interest houses, fraternity houses, sorority houses, wellness housing, cooperative housing, and living learning communities. On-campus housing is available on a first-come, first-served basis. 78% of students live on campus. All students may keep cars.

FACULTY/CLASSROOMS: 56% of faculty are male; 44% are female. 61% teach undergraduates, and 18% do research. No introductory courses are taught by graduate students. The average class size in an introductory lecture is 39; in a laboratory is 21; and in a regular course is 26.

PROGRAMS OF STUDY: USF/Tampa confers B.A., B.S., B.F.A., B.I.S., B.M., and B.S.W. degrees. Associate, master's, and doctoral degrees are also awarded. Bachelor's degrees are awarded in BIOLOGICAL SCIENCE (biology/biological science and microbiology), BUSINESS (accounting, banking and finance, business administration and management, business economics, management information systems, management science, and marketing/retailing/merchandising), COMMUNICATIONS AND THE ARTS (classics, communications, dance, dramatic arts, English literature, French, German, Italian, music, Russian, Spanish, and speech/debate/rhetoric), COMPUTER AND PHYSICAL SCIENCE (chemistry, geology, mathematics, physical sciences, and physics), EDUCATION (art education, business education, education, education of the emotionally handicapped, education of the mentally handicapped, elementary education, English education, foreign languages education, mathematics education, music education, physical education, science education, social studies education, special education, and specific learning disabilities), ENGINEERING AND ENVIRONMENTAL DESIGN (chemical engineering, civil engineering, computer engineering, electrical/electronics engineering, engineering, environmental science, industrial engineering, and mechanical engineering), HEALTH PROFESSIONS (medical technology and nursing), SOCIAL SCIENCE (African American studies, American studies, anthropology, criminology, economics, geography, gerontology, history, humanities, international relations, liberal arts/general studies, philosophy, political science/government, psychology, religion, social science, social work, and sociology). Medicine, engineering, and business are the strongest academically. Business, education, and engineering have the largest enrollments.

ACTIVITIES: 10% of men belong to 26 national fraternities; 15% of women belong to 23 national sororities. Groups on campus include art, band, cheerleading, chess, choir, chorale, chorus, computers, dance, drama, drill team, ethnic, film, honors, international, jazz band, LGBT, literary magazine, marching band, musical theater, newspaper, opera, orchestra, pep band, photography, political, professional, radio and TV, religious, social, social service, student government, and symphony. Popular campus events include Minority and International events and the University Lecture Series. **Sports:** There are 9 intercollegiate sports for men and 10 for women, and 19 intramural sports for men and 20 for women. Facilities include a multipurpose arena, pools, tennis and indoor racquetball courts, a jogging course, an indoor recreation center with weight training and aerobics rooms, a soccer stadium, a softball complex, a baseball stadium, a tennis complex, sailing facility, a golf course, cross country, indoor and outdoor track, basketball, volleyball, track and field, and cross country.**Graduates:** From July 1, 2016 to June 30, 2017, 8171 bachelor's degrees were awarded. The most popular majors were health professions and related programs (20%), business/marketing (16%), and social sciences (12%). In an average class, 68% graduate in 6 years or less.

SERVICES: Counseling and information services are available, as is tutoring in most subjects. There is a reader service for the blind. **Library/**

Resources: The library contains 2.6 million volumes. Computerized library services include interlibrary loans, database searching, and Internet access. Special learning facilities include an art gallery, radio station, TV station, an Anthropology Museum, and a Botanical Garden. **Physically Challenged Students:** All of the campus is accessible. Facilities include wheelchair ramps, elevators, special parking, specially equipped restrooms, special class scheduling, lowered drinking fountains, and lowered telephones. **Special:** USF offers co-op programs in business and engineering, study abroad, cross-registration, work-study programs, accelerated degree programs in public health and medicine, internships, a Washington semester, dual and student-designed majors, a liberal arts degree, nondegree study, and pass/fail options for some courses. There are 26 national honor societies, a freshman honors program, and 18 departmental honors programs. **Visiting:** There are regularly scheduled orientations for prospective students, including a 2-day program. There are guides for informal visits and visitors may sit in on classes. To schedule a visit, contact the Admissions Office/New Student Orientation. **Campus Safety and Security:** Measures include 24-hour foot and vehicle patrol, self-defense education, and security escort services. There are shuttle buses, emergency telephones, and lighted pathways/sidewalks.

REQUIREMENTS: The SAT or ACT is required. Candidates for admission should have completed 19 units: 4 units each of English and math, 3 units each of social studies, science, (of those, 2 units must be lab), 2 each of academic electives and foreign language. The GED is accepted. Applicants who do not meet minimum requirements but have important attributes, special talents, or unique circumstances are considered for admission by an academic faculty committee. A GPA of 2.0 is required. AP and CLEP credits are accepted. Important factors in the admissions decision are advanced placement or honors courses, parents or siblings attended your school, evidence of special talent, personality/intangible qualities, extracurricular activities record, geographical diversity, and recommendations by school officials. To graduate, all students are required to complete at least 120 credit hours, including 36 distributed among English, math, science, social science, historical perspectives, fine arts, and humanities and 9 of exit requirements in major works/major issues and literature/writing. The number of hours required for each major varies. Students must maintain a minimum GPA of 2.0. **Procedure:** Freshmen are admitted to all sessions. Entrance exams should be taken at the end of the junior year or the beginning of the senior year. Applications should be filed by March 15 for fall entry. The fall 2017 application fee was $30. Notification of early decision is sent October 1; regular decision, April 15. Applications are accepted on-line. **Transfer Students:** 3575 transfer students enrolled in 2016-2017. Applicants with less than 24 transfer hours are required to submit a personal statement and reviewed by committee. Students with 25-59 hours must have a transfer GPA of 3.0. Florida College System AA degree transfers must have a minimum GPA of 2.0; other transfers with 60+ hours must have a minimum GPA of 2.5. Transfers to limited access major must meet the minimum GPA stated or the GPA for the specified major, whichever is higher. All applicants must be in good standing at their previous institution. 30 of 120 credits required for the bachelor's degree must be completed at USF. **International Students:** There are 1484 international students enrolled. They must take the TOEFL, and the IELTS. They must also take the SAT or ACT.

Admissions Contact: David Lee Henry, Director of Admissions. Email: *dlhenry@usf.edu* Web: *www.usf.edu*

FINANCIAL AID: In 2017-2018, 92% of all full-time freshmen received some form of financial aid. 53% of all full-time freshmen received need-based aid. The average freshman award was $12,007. Need-based scholarships or need-based grants averaged $9,183; need-based self-help aid (loans and jobs) averaged $5,110; non-need-based athletic scholarships averaged $10,046; other non-need-based awards and non-need-based scholarships averaged $3,074; and $4,717 from other forms of aid. The priority date for freshman financial aid applications for fall entry is March 1.

UNIVERSITY OF TAMPA D-4

www.ut.edu

Tampa, FL 33606	(813) 257-1808 (888) 646-2738
Fax: (813) 258-7398	**Email:** admissions@ut.edu
Full-time: 3211 men, 4517 women	**Faculty:** 338; IIA, av$
Part-time: 107 men, 139 women	**Ph.D.s:** 90%
Graduate: 364 men, 501 women	**Student/Faculty:** 17 to 1
Year: semesters, summer session	**Tuition:** $28,426
Room & Board: $10,502	**Freshman Class:** 20495 applied, 10915 accepted, 2140 enrolled
SAT EBR-W/M: 590/590 **ACT:** 24	**CEEB CODE:** 5819
Application Deadline: January 15	**VERY COMPETITIVE**

University of Tampa, founded in 1931, is a comprehensive, independent institution that offers degree programs in more than 200 undergraduate and preprofessional areas of study and graduate and evening programs. There are 4 undergraduate schools and 1 graduate school. In addition to regional accreditation, UT has baccalaureate program accreditation with AACSB, ABET, NASM, and NLN. The 110-acre campus is in an urban area in Tampa, Florida. Including any residence halls, there are 60 buildings.

STUDENT LIFE: 70% of undergraduates are from out of state, mostly the Middle Atlantic. Students are from 50 states, 115 foreign countries, and Canada. 61% are White; 6% race unknown; 5% African American; 3% two or more races; 2% Asian American; 13% Hispanic; 10% Foreign. 55% claim no religious affiliation; 21% Catholic; 21% Christian, Baptist, Presbyterian, Muslim, Methodist, and Episcopal. **Female To Male Ratio:** 1.4:1. The average age of freshmen is 18; all undergraduates, 21. 22% do not continue beyond their first year; 60% remain to graduate. **Housing:** 4262 students can be accommodated in college housing, which includes dorms and on-campus apartments, honors floors, leadership and entrepreneurial themed floors. 53% of students live on campus. All students may keep cars.

FACULTY/CLASSROOMS: 43% of faculty are male; 52% are female. All teach undergraduates. No introductory courses are taught by graduate students. The average class size in an introductory lecture is 25; in a laboratory is 16; and in a regular course is 25.

PROGRAMS OF STUDY: UT confers B.A., B.S., B.F.A., B.L.S., B.M., B.S.A.T., and B.S.N. degrees. Master's degrees are also awarded. Bachelor's degrees are awarded in BIOLOGICAL SCIENCE (biochemistry, biology/biological science, and marine science), BUSINESS (accounting, banking and finance, business administration and management, business economics, entrepreneurial studies, finance enterprise systems, information and communication technology, international business management, management information systems, management, marketing/retailing/merchandising, mathematical programming, and sports management), COMMUNICATIONS AND THE ARTS (advertising, art, communications, creative writing, dance, dramatic arts, English, film arts, graphic design, human performance, journalism, music, music performance, musical theater, new media production, performing arts, Spanish, theatre acting, and writing), COMPUTER AND PHYSICAL SCIENCE (chemistry, computer security, digital arts/technology, mathematics, and physics), EDUCATION (athletic training, elementary education, music education, physical education, and secondary education), ENGINEERING AND ENVIRONMENTAL DESIGN (computer graphics and environmental science), HEALTH PROFESSIONS (allied health, exercise science, nursing, and public health), SOCIAL SCIENCE (criminology, economics, forensic studies, history, international studies, liberal arts/general studies, philosophy, political science/government, psychology, and sociology). Secondary education, performing arts, and elementary education are the strongest academically. Biology, finance, and marketing have the largest enrollments.

ACTIVITIES: 7% of men belong to 15 national fraternities; 13% of women belong to 13 national sororities. There are 154 groups on campus, including academic, art, band, cheerleading, chess, chorale, chorus, computers, dance, debate, drama, environmental, ethnic, film, honors, international, jazz band, LGBT, leadership, literary magazine, media and special interest, musical theater, newspaper, orchestra, pep band, photography, political, professional, radio and TV, religious, social, social service, student government, symphony, and yearbook. Popular campus events include Into the Street (volunteer program),

Campus Movie Fest, Leadership Awards Night, Greek Variety Show, and Spring Concert. **Sports:** There are 8 intercollegiate sports for men and 11 for women, and 22 intramural sports for men and 22 for women. Facilities include a swimming pool, tennis courts, a track, outdoor basketball courts, outdoor sand volleyball courts, a crew training facility (boathouse and dock), a fitness center with exercise rooms, and fields for soccer, baseball, and softball, and a tennis complex. **Graduates:** From July 1, 2016 to June 30, 2017, 1412 bachelor's degrees were awarded. The most popular majors were business/marketing (31%), communications (11%), and social sciences (11%). In an average class, 49% graduate in 4 years or less, 59% graduate in 5 years or less, and 60% graduate in 6 years or less. Of the 2016 graduating class, 22% were enrolled in graduate school within 6 months of graduation, and 91% were employed.

SERVICES: Counseling and information services are available, as is tutoring in most subjects, such as financial accounting, managerial accounting, chemistry & society, general chemistry I & II, organic chemistry, principles of microeconomics & macroeconomics, financial management, human anatomy & physiology I & II, physics, psychology, and statistics. There is a reader service for the blind, and remedial math, reading, and writing. Students can get assistance with any writing assignment at the Writing Center and presentations at the Center for Public Speaking. **Library/Resources:** The library contains 177,545 volumes, 72,665 microform items, and 6,284 audio/video tapes/CDs/DVDs, and subscribes to 74,315 periodicals including electronic. Computerized library services include interlibrary loans, database searching, Internet access, and Wi-Fi capability. Special learning facilities include an art gallery, radio station, TV station, an entrepreneurship center, a fully equipped research vessel for marine science studies, a music facility, writing and language labs, an academic center for excellence, a graphic design studio, a marine science lab, and art studios. **Physically Challenged Students:** All of the campus is accessible. Facilities include wheelchair ramps, elevators, special parking, specially equipped restrooms, lowered drinking fountains, lowered telephones, and special housing. **Special:** Students may participate in internships, independent studies, work-study programs on campus, study abroad in 14 countries, a Washington Center internship, and an Oxford semester program. UT also offers summer marine science courses at the Gulf Coast Research Laboratory, nondegree study, pass/fail options, dual majors, accelerated degree programs, and credit for life, military, and work experience. There are 7 national honor societies and a freshman honors program. **Visiting:** There are regularly scheduled orientations for prospective students, including a campus tour and an interview with an admissions counselor, faculty, and others as requested. There are guides for informal visits; visitors may sit in on classes, and stay overnight. To schedule a visit, contact the Admissions Office. **Campus Safety and Security:** Measures include 24-hour foot and vehicle patrol, emergency notification system, self-defense education, and security escort services. There are shuttle buses, emergency telephones, lighted pathways/sidewalks, controlled access to dorms/residences, and the on-campus security office has a partnership with local law enforcement.

REQUIREMENTS: The SAT or ACT is required. Candidates for admission should have completed 4 credits in English, 3 credits each in math, science, social studies, college-preparatory electives, and science (with 2 units of lab). The GED is accepted. A portfolio or an audition is required for specific art and music programs. A GPA of 2.5 is required. AP and CLEP credits are accepted. Important factors in the admissions decision are recommendations by school officials, evidence of special talent, and extracurricular activities record. To graduate, students must maintain a minimum GPA of 2.0 in at least 124 credit hours, including the 2-year learning community, 11 hours each in humanities/fine arts and social science, 6 in natural science, global issues, non-Western studies, and art/aesthetics as well as writing-intensive course work. The requirements for individual majors vary. **Procedure:** Freshmen are admitted fall, spring, and summer. Entrance exams should be taken by the end of the junior year or early in the senior year. There are deferred admissions and rolling admissions plans. Application deadlines are open. The fall 2017 application fee was $40. Notifications are sent April 1. 1556 applicants were on the 2017 waiting list; 124 were admitted. Applications are accepted online. **Transfer Students:** 547 transfer students enrolled in 2016-2017. Applicants should have earned 17 or more college credits with a minimum GPA of 2.0. 31 of 124 credits required for the bachelor's degree must be completed at UT. **International Students:** There are 800 international students enrolled. They must take the TOEFL with a minimum score of 550 on the paper-based TOEFL (PBT) or 79 on the Internet-based version (iBT).

ADMISSIONS: 53% of the 2017-2018 applicants were accepted. The SAT scores for the 2017-2018 freshman class were: Math-- 8% below 500, 59% between 500 and 599, 31% between 600 and 699, and 3% between 700 and 800. Evidence-Based Reading/Writing-- 7% below 500, 55% between 500 and 599, 35% between 600 and 699, and 4% between 700 and 800. The ACT scores were 43% between 18 and 23, 48% between 24 and 29, and 8% above 30. 36% of the current freshmen were in the top fifth of their class; 72% were in the top two fifths. **Admissions Contact:** Dennis Nostrand, Vice President for Enrollment. Email: *admissions@ut.edu* Web: *www.ut.edu*

FINANCIAL AID: 20% of undergraduate students work part-time. The FAFSA code is 001538. The priority date for freshman financial aid applications for fall entry is February 1.

UNIVERSITY OF WEST FLORIDA — A-1

www.uwf.edu

Pensacola, FL 32514	**(850) 474-2230** **(800) 263-1074**
Fax: (850) 474-3360	**Email: admissions@uwf.edu**
Full-time: 3227 men, 4332 women	**Faculty:** I, --$
Part-time: 1164 men, 1609 women	**Ph.D.s:** n/av
Graduate: 836 men, 1483 women	**Student/Faculty:** 24 to 1
Year: semesters, summer session	**Tuition:** $6360 ($19,260)
Room & Board: $9488	**Freshman Class:** 13623 applied, 8284 accepted, 1797 enrolled
SAT or ACT: required	**CEEB CODE:** 5833
Application Deadline: June 30	**COMPETITIVE**

University of West Florida, founded in 1967, is a public, regional comprehensive institution that is part of the State University System of Florida. The figures in the above capsule and in this profile are approximate. There are 3 undergraduate schools and 3 graduate schools. In addition to regional accreditation, University of West Florida has baccalaureate program accreditation with AACSB, ABET, CSWE, NASM, CAEP, NLN, ACS, NAACLS, and MPAC. The 1600-acre campus is in a suburban area 10 miles north of downtown Pensacola. Including any residence halls, there are 205 buildings.

STUDENT LIFE: 95% of undergraduates are from Florida. Others are from 48 states, 70 foreign countries, and Canada. 8% are Hispanic; 70% White; 3% Asian American; 12% African American; 1% American Indian/Alaska Native; 1% Foreign. **Female To Male Ratio:** 1.4:1. The average age of freshmen is 19; all undergraduates, 24. 16% do not continue beyond their first year; 74% remain to graduate. **Housing:** 1800 students can be accommodated in college housing, which includes dorms and on-campus apartments. In addition, there are honors houses. On-campus housing is available on a first-come, first-served basis. 82% of students commute. All students may keep cars.

FACULTY/CLASSROOMS: 53% of faculty are male; 47% are female. No introductory courses are taught by graduate students. The average class size in an introductory lecture is 34; in a laboratory is 21; and in a regular course is 26.

PROGRAMS OF STUDY: UWF confers B.A., B.S., B.F.A., B.S.B.A., B.S.C.E., B.S.E.E., and B.S.N. degrees. Associate, master's, and doctoral degrees are also awarded. Bachelor's degrees are awarded in BIOLOGICAL SCIENCE (biology/biological science and marine biology), BUSINESS (accounting, banking and finance, business administration and management, business economics, and marketing/retailing/merchandising), COMMUNICATIONS AND THE ARTS (communications, English, music, and studio art), COMPUTER AND PHYSICAL SCIENCE (chemistry, computer science, mathematics, physics, and statistics), EDUCATION (art education, early childhood education, elementary education, health education, middle school education, music education, and secondary education), ENGINEERING AND ENVIRONMENTAL DESIGN (computer engineering and electrical/electronics engineering), HEALTH PROFESSIONS (medical laboratory technology, nursing, predentistry, and premedicine), SOCIAL SCIENCE (criminal justice, history, philosophy, political science/government, prelaw, psychology, religion, social science, and social work). Accounting, communication arts, and management are the strongest academically. Communication arts, psychology, and business have the largest enrollments.

ACTIVITIES: There are 158 groups on campus, including art, band,

cheerleading, chess, choir, chorale, chorus, communications, computers, dance, debate, drama, environmental, ethnic, film, forensics, honors, international, jazz band, LGBT, literary magazine, musical theater, newspaper, orchestra, political, professional, radio and TV, religious, social, social service, student government, and symphony. **Sports:** There are 6 intercollegiate sports for men and 8 for women, and 12 intramural sports for men and 12 for women. Facilities include baseball, track, tennis, racquetball, handball, softball, soccer, swimming, diving, weight lifting, and aerobics. **Graduates:** From July 1, 2016 to June 30, 2017, 2082 bachelor's degrees were awarded. The most popular majors were psychology (8%), nursing (5%), and criminal justice (5%).

SERVICES: Counseling and information services are available, as is tutoring in most subjects. There is remedial math. Remedial courses are offered on campus by the local community college. **Library/Resources:** The library contains 767,633 volumes, 1.2 million microform items, and 5,224 audio/video tapes/CDs/DVDs, and subscribes to 5,056 periodicals including electronic. Computerized library services include interlibrary loans and database searching. Special learning facilities include an art gallery, a radio station, a TV station, and an archeology museum. **Physically Challenged Students:** 80% of the campus is accessible. Facilities include wheelchair ramps, elevators, special parking, specially equipped restrooms, special class scheduling, lowered drinking fountains, and special housing. **Special:** Internships are arranged on an individual basis through a student's major department. The college offers pass/fail options and credit for military experience. A 3-2 engineering degree is also offered. There are 5 national honor societies and a freshman honors program. **Visiting:** There are regularly scheduled orientations for prospective students, including 5 Open House Programs per year. There are guides for informal visits and visitors may sit in on classes. To schedule a visit, contact the Admissions Office. **Campus Safety and Security:** Measures include 24-hour foot and vehicle patrol, emergency notification system, self-defense education, and security escort services. There are emergency telephones, lighted pathways/sidewalks, and a trolley system.

REQUIREMENTS: The SAT or ACT is required. Students must have completed 4 years of English, 3 each of math (algebra 1 and higher), science, and social studies, and 2 of a foreign language. A GPA of 2.0 is required. AP and CLEP credits are accepted. Important factors in the admissions decision are advanced placement or honors courses, evidence of special talent, and geographical diversity. To graduate, students must maintain a 2.0 GPA and complete 120 semester hours with a minimum of 24 hours in the major and 24 hours in upper-division courses. **Procedure:** Freshmen are admitted to all sessions. Entrance exams should be taken by the fall of the senior year. There are early admissions and rolling admissions plans. Early decision applications should be filed by June 30. The fall 2017 application fee was $30. Applications are accepted on-line. **Transfer Students:** Applicants must have a 2.0 GPA and a 2.0 at their last institution. Transfer students with fewer than 60 semester hours of transferable credit must meet freshman admission requirements. 30 of 120 credits required for the bachelor's degree must be completed at UWF. **International Students:** There are 228 international students enrolled. They must take the TOEFL with a minimum score of 525 on the paper-based TOEFL (PBT) or 69 on the Internet-based version (iBT) or take the MELAB. They must also take the SAT or ACT, scoring 970.

ADMISSIONS: 61% of the 2017-2018 applicants were accepted. The SAT scores for the 2017-2018 freshman class were: Critical Reading-- 44% below 500, 44% between 500 and 599, 10% between 600 and 699, and 1% between 700 and 800. Math-- 49% below 500, 41% between 500 and 599, 9% between 600 and 699, and 1% between 700 and 800. Writing-- 60% below 500, 34% between 500 and 599, 5% between 600 and 699, and 1% between 700 and 800. The ACT scores were 8% below 12, 56% between 12 and 17, 32% between 18 and 23, 2% between 24 and 29, and 2% above 30. 4 freshmen graduated first in their class. **Admissions Contact:** Katie Condon, Interim Director of Admissions. Email: *admissions@uwf.edu* Web: *www.uwf.edu*

FINANCIAL AID: In 2017-2018, 23% of all full-time freshmen received some form of financial aid. 15% of all full-time freshmen received need-based aid. The average freshman award was $2,034. Need-based scholarships or need-based grants averaged $1,735 ($4,000 maximum); need-based self-help aid (loans and jobs) averaged $2,352 ($3,500 maximum); non-need-based athletic scholarships averaged $626 ($1,500 maximum); and other non-need-based awards and non-need-based scholarships averaged $2,276 ($10,900 maximum). The college's own financial statement is required. The FAFSA code is 003955. Check with the school for current application deadlines.

WARNER UNIVERSITY — D-4

www.warner.edu

Lake Wales, FL 33859	(863) 638-7212 (800) 309-9563
Fax: (863) 638-7290	**Email:** admissions@warner.edu
Full-time: 340 men, 450 women	**Faculty:** 52
Part-time: 65 men, 235 women	**Ph.D.s:** 42%
Graduate: 40 men, 20 women	**Student/Faculty:** 17 to 1
Year: semesters, summer session	**Tuition:** $20,112
Room & Board: $8104	**Freshman Class:** n/av
SAT or ACT: required	**CEEB CODE:** 5883
Application Deadline: open	**COMPETITIVE**

Warner University is a Christian university in the liberal arts tradition committed to the search for truth in the context of Christian faith and academic excellence. The figures given in the above capsule and in this profile are approximate. There are 2 undergraduate schools and 1 graduate school. In addition to regional accreditation, WU has baccalaureate program accreditation with SACS. The 300-acre campus is in a rural area 5 miles south of Lake Wales, in Polk County, Florida. Including any residence halls, there are 20 buildings.

STUDENT LIFE: 88% of undergraduates are from Florida. Others are from 29 states, 22 foreign countries, and Canada. 8% are Hispanic; 40% African American; 39% White; 2% race unknown; 1% Asian American; 1% American Indian/Alaska Native. 61% are Protestant; 29% claim no religious affiliation. **Female To Male Ratio:** 1.6:1. The average age of freshmen is 19; all undergraduates, 22. 62% do not continue beyond their first year; 50% remain to graduate. **Housing:** 235 students can be accommodated in college housing, which includes dorms and off-campus apartments. On-campus housing is guaranteed for all 4 years. 58% of students commute. Alcohol is not permitted. All students may keep cars.

FACULTY/CLASSROOMS: 52% of faculty are male; 48% are female. All teach undergraduates, 20% do research, and 20% do both. No introductory courses are taught by graduate students. The average class size in an introductory lecture is 28; in a laboratory is 20; and in a regular course is 18.

PROGRAMS OF STUDY: WU confers B.A. degrees. Associate and master's degrees are also awarded. Bachelor's degrees are awarded in BIOLOGICAL SCIENCE (biology/biological science), BUSINESS (accounting, banking and finance, business administration and management, business law, institutional management, marketing management, and sports management), COMMUNICATIONS AND THE ARTS (communications and English), COMPUTER AND PHYSICAL SCIENCE (information sciences and systems), EDUCATION (business education, education of the exceptional child, elementary education, English education, music education, physical education, science education, and social science education), HEALTH PROFESSIONS (exercise science), SOCIAL SCIENCE (biblical studies, history, pastoral studies, psychology, religious music, and social work). Biblical studies, social work, and teacher education are the strongest academically. Organizational management, church ministry, and teacher education have the largest enrollments.

ACTIVITIES: There are no fraternities or sororities. There are 14 groups on campus, including band, cheerleading, choir, chorale, chorus, computers, honors, newspaper, pep band, photography, religious, social, social service, and student government. Popular campus events include Christmas Banquet, Barn Party, and Spring Banquet. **Sports:** There are 7 intercollegiate sports for men and 8 for women, and 4 intramural sports for men and 3 for women. Facilities include baseball, basketball, cross-country, football, golf, softball, soccer, tennis, track and field, volleyball, and sand volleyball. **Graduates:** From July 1, 2016 to June 30, 2017, 368 bachelor's degrees were awarded. The most popular majors were organizational management (63%), elementary education (6%), and business administration (3%). In an average class, 25% graduate in 4 years or less, 32% graduate in 5 years or less, and 35% graduate in 6 years or less.

SERVICES: Counseling and information services are available, as is tutoring in most subjects. There is remedial math, reading, and writing. **Library/Resources:** The library contains 74,000 volumes, 7,267 microform items, and 15,200 audio/video tapes/CDs/DVDs, and subscribes to 178 periodicals including electronic. Computerized library services include interlibrary loans, database searching, and Internet access. **Physi-**

cally Challenged Students: 90% of the campus is accessible. Facilities include wheelchair ramps, special parking, specially equipped restrooms, lowered drinking fountains, and lowered telephones. **Special:** Internships are required in many majors, including teacher education, social work, sports management, and church ministry. An accelerated degree program is available in organizational management. HEART (Hunger Education and Resoure Training) is a missionary training program designed to equip students to serve in missions, community development work, or cross-cultural assignments in developing countries. There are 5 national honor societies and 1 departmental honors program. **Visiting:** There are regularly scheduled orientations for prospective students, consisting of a weekend held in the spring. There are guides for informal visits; visitors may sit in on classes, and stay overnight. To schedule a visit, contact the Admissions Office. **Campus Safety and Security:** Measures include 24-hour foot and vehicle patrol and security escort services. There are shuttle buses, emergency telephones, lighted pathways/sidewalks, special training in CPR/first aid, and emergency response.

REQUIREMENTS: The SAT or ACT is required. A GPA of 2.3 is required. AP and CLEP credits are accepted. To graduate, students must complete 128 credit hours with a GPA of 2.0 to 2.5, depending on the major. 30 to 80 hours are required in the major. 48 hours of upper-division courses are required, as is a computer application course in the major. **Procedure:** Freshmen are admitted fall and spring. Entrance exams should be taken in the junior or senior year. There are early admissions, deferred admissions, and rolling admissions plans. Application deadlines are open. The fall 2017 application fee was $20. Applications are accepted online. **Transfer Students:** 39 transfer students enrolled in 2016-2017. Applicants may transfer 24 or more hours from a regionally accredited school and must present a GPA of 2.0 or higher. 36 of 128 credits required for the bachelor's degree must be completed at Warner. **International Students:** There are 31 international students enrolled. They must take the TOEFL. They must also take the SAT or ACT, scoring 870.

ADMISSIONS: 2 freshmen graduated first in their class. **Admissions Contact:** Jason Roe, Director of Admissions. Email: *admissions@warner.edu* Web: *www.warner.edu*

FINANCIAL AID: In 2017-2018, 98% of all full-time freshmen received some form of financial aid. 98% of all full-time freshmen received need-based aid. 47% of undergraduate students work part-time. The state aid form is required. The FAFSA code is 008848. The priority date for freshman financial aid applications for fall entry is May 10.

WEBBER INTERNATIONAL UNIVERSITY D-4

www.webber.edu

Babson Park, FL 33827	**(863) 638-2927** **(800) 741-1844**
Fax: (863) 638-1591	**Email: admissions@webber.edu**
Full-time: 426 men, 202 women	**Faculty:** 20
Part-time: 16 men, 11 women	**Ph.D.s:** 60%
Graduate: 28 men, 34 women	**Student/Faculty:** 27 to 1
Year: semesters, summer session	**Tuition:** $23,210
Room & Board: $8694	**Freshman Class:** 521 applied, 380 accepted, 263 enrolled
SAT or ACT: required	**CEEB CODE:** 5893
Application Deadline: August 1	**COMPETITIVE**

Webber International University, founded in 1927, is a privately endowed institution offering undergraduate and graduate degrees in business. There is 1 undergraduate school and 1 graduate school. In addition to regional accreditation, WIU has baccalaureate program accreditation with IACBE. The 110-acre campus is in a small town 50 miles east of Tampa and 50 miles south of Orlando. Including any residence halls, there are 12 buildings.

STUDENT LIFE: 69% of undergraduates are from Florida. Others are from 24 states, 41 foreign countries, and Canada. 9% are Hispanic; 41% White; 24% African American; 23% Foreign; 1% Asian American; 1% American Indian/Alaska Native. **Male To Female Ratio:** 1.9:1. The average age of freshmen is 19; all undergraduates, 22. 14% do not continue beyond their first year; 86% remain to graduate. **Housing:** 419 students can be accommodated in college housing, which includes dorms and off-campus apartments. On-campus housing is guaranteed for all 4 years, is guaranteed for the freshman year only, and is available on a first-come, first-served basis. 53% of students live on campus. All students may keep cars.

FACULTY/CLASSROOMS: 56% of faculty are male; 44% are female. All teach undergraduates. No introductory courses are taught by graduate students. The average class size in a regular course is 21.

PROGRAMS OF STUDY: WIU confers B.S. degrees. Associate and master's degrees are also awarded. Bachelor's degrees are awarded in BUSINESS (accounting, banking and finance, business administration and management, business communications, hospitality management services, management science, marketing management, and sports management), COMPUTER AND PHYSICAL SCIENCE (computer security and information assurance and information sciences and systems), SOCIAL SCIENCE (prelaw). General business studies is the strongest academically and has the largest enrollment.

ACTIVITIES: There are no fraternities or sororities. There are 11 groups on campus, including band, cheerleading, debate, honors, international, marching band, newspaper, pep band, photography, political, professional, religious, social, social service, and student government. Popular campus events include Webber Weekend, International Day, and End-of-the-Year Beach Party. **Sports:** There are 9 intercollegiate sports for men and 9 for women, and 6 intramural sports for men and 6 for women. Facilities include a gym, weight rooms, tennis courts, a football practice field, swimming pool, beach volleyball, softball, baseball, and soccer fields. **Graduates:** From July 1, 2016 to June 30, 2017, 131 bachelor's degrees were awarded. The most popular majors were general business (73%), sport management (18%), and communications (1%). In an average class, 1% graduate in 3 years or less, 48% graduate in 4 years or less, 50% graduate in 5 years or less, and 54% graduate in 6 years or less.

SERVICES: Counseling and information services are available, as is tutoring in most subjects. There is remedial math, reading, and writing. **Library/Resources:** The library contains 15,000 volumes, and 200 audio/video tapes/CDs/DVDs, and subscribes to 2 periodicals including electronic. Computerized library services include interlibrary loans, database searching, Internet access, and Wi-Fi capability. **Physically Challenged Students:** 90% of the campus is accessible. Facilities include wheelchair ramps, special parking, specially equipped restrooms, special class scheduling, and special housing. **Special:** Internships, study abroad in 5 countries, work study, and B.S. degrees are offered. Any combination of majors requires an additional 30 credit hours for a total of 150 to graduate. There is a freshman honors program. **Visiting:** There are regularly scheduled orientations for prospective students, including a campus tour and individual attention from admission counselors and other office representatives such as financial aid, coaches, and professors. There are guides for informal visits; visitors may sit in on classes and stay overnight. To schedule a visit, contact Vice President Enrollment Management at PicardRP@webber.edu. **Campus Safety and Security:** Measures include 24-hour foot and vehicle patrol, emergency notification system, self-defense education, and security escort services.

REQUIREMENTS: The SAT or ACT is required. Applicants should be graduates of accredited secondary schools and have completed 3 years each of English, math, and science and 2 years of social studies. An essay is also required. The GED is accepted. A GPA of 2.0 is required. AP and CLEP credits are accepted. To graduate, all students must complete 120 credit hours, including courses in their major, a 36-credit general curriculum, and a 36-credit business core, 18-credit tailored electives, and 30-credit area of concentration. A GPA of 2.0 or better must be maintained. Students must pass the college's required English courses and meet its writing requirements. All students must take at least 3 computer courses. **Procedure:** Freshmen are admitted to all sessions. Entrance exams should be taken during the senior year. There are deferred admissions and rolling admissions plans. Applications should be filed by August 1 for fall entry; December 1 for spring entry; and April 1 for summer entry. The fall 2017 application fee was $35. Applications are accepted on-line. **Transfer Students:** 42 transfer students enrolled in 2016-2017. Applicants must have a minimum GPA of 2.0 with 15 credit hours and leave their previous institution in good academic standing. Students with fewer than 15 credits must meet freshman requirements. 30 of 120 credits required for the bachelor's degree must be completed at Webber. **International Students:** There are 170 international students enrolled. They must take the TOEFL. Webber considers each application on a case-by-case basis.

ADMISSIONS: 73% of the 2017-2018 applicants were accepted. The SAT scores for the 2017-2018 freshman class were: Critical Reading--

68% below 500, 29% between 500 and 599, and 3% between 600 and 699. Math-- 63% below 500, 32% between 500 and 599, 4% between 600 and 699, and 1% between 700 and 800. The ACT scores were 70% below 12, 20% between 12 and 17, and 1% between 24 and 29. **Admissions Contact:** Ryan P. Picard, Director of Admissions. Email: *admissions@webber.edu* Web: *www.webber.edu*

FINANCIAL AID: In 2017-2018, 98% of all full-time freshmen received some form of financial aid. 62% of all full-time freshmen received need-based aid. The average freshman award was $18,697. Need-based scholarships or need-based grants averaged $15,812 ($24,550 maximum); need-based self-help aid (loans and jobs) averaged $3,139 ($11,000 maximum); non-need-based athletic scholarships averaged $3,755 ($12,000 maximum); and other non-need-based awards and non-need-based scholarships averaged $12,973 ($16,000 maximum). 40% of undergraduate students work part-time. The average financial indebtedness of the 2017 graduate was $26,676. WIU is a member of CSS. The FAFSA code is 001540. The priority date for freshman financial aid applications for fall entry is April 1. The deadline for filing freshman financial aid applications for fall entry is August 1.

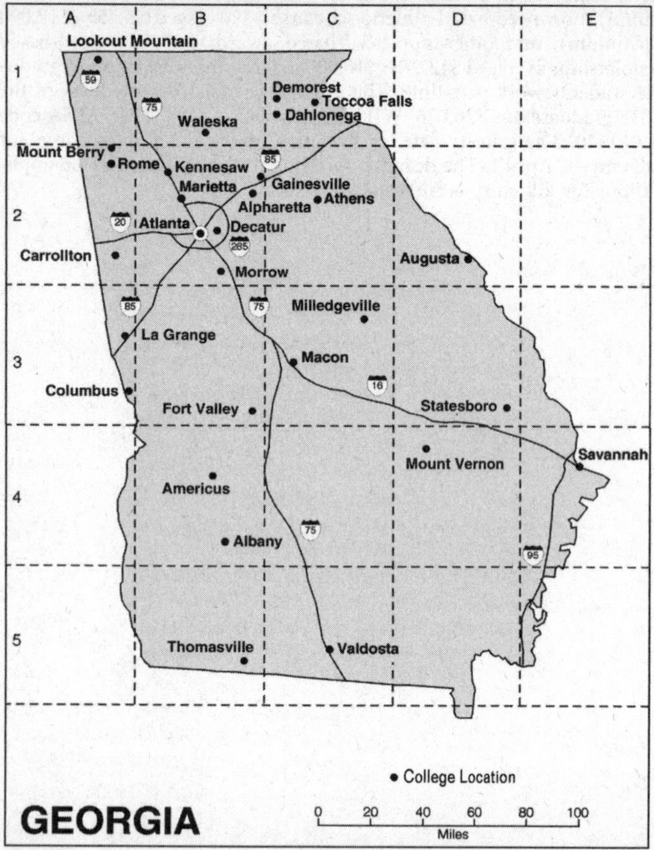

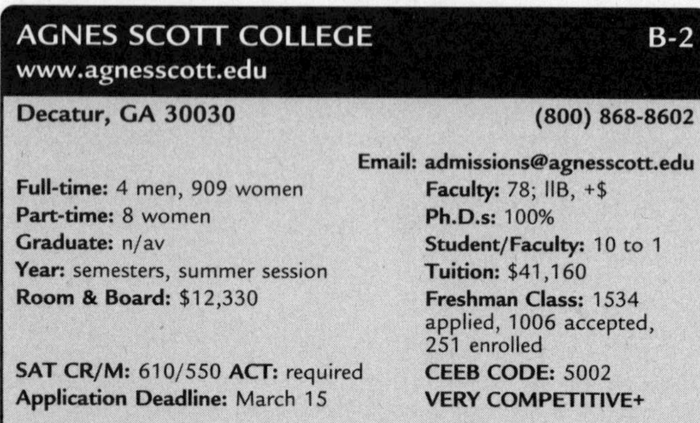

AGNES SCOTT COLLEGE B-2

www.agnesscott.edu

Decatur, GA 30030 **(800) 868-8602**

Email: admissions@agnesscott.edu

Full-time: 4 men, 909 women
Part-time: 8 women
Graduate: n/av
Year: semesters, summer session
Room & Board: $12,330

Faculty: 78; IIB, +$
Ph.D.s: 100%
Student/Faculty: 10 to 1
Tuition: $41,160
Freshman Class: 1534 applied, 1006 accepted, 251 enrolled

SAT CR/M: 610/550 **ACT:** required
Application Deadline: March 15

CEEB CODE: 5002
VERY COMPETITIVE+

Agnes Scott College, founded in 1889, is an independent liberal arts college for women and is affiliated with the Presbyterian Church. There is 1 undergraduate school. In addition to regional accreditation, ASC has baccalaureate program accreditation with SACSCoC. The 100-acre campus is in an urban area 6 miles from downtown Atlanta. Including any residence halls, there are 27 buildings.

STUDENT LIFE: 51% of undergraduates are from Georgia. Others are from 46 states, 34 foreign countries, and Canada. 75% are from public schools. 8% are Foreign; 7% Asian American; 7% two or more races; 35% White; 29% African American; 2% race unknown; 12% Hispanic. **Female To Male Ratio:** 229.3:1. The average age of freshmen is 18; all undergraduates, 20. 13% do not continue beyond their first year; 67% remain to graduate. **Housing:** 847 students can be accommodated in college housing, which includes dorms and on-campus apartments. In addition, there are special-interest houses, and theme housing. On-campus housing is guaranteed for all 4 years. 82% of students live on campus. All students may keep cars.

FACULTY/CLASSROOMS: 33% of faculty are male; 67% are female. All teach undergraduates. No introductory courses are taught by graduate students. The average class size in a regular course is 16.

PROGRAMS OF STUDY: ASC confers B.A. and B.S. degrees. Bachelor's degrees are awarded in BIOLOGICAL SCIENCE (biochemistry, biology/biological science, and neurosciences), BUSINESS (business administration and management), COMMUNICATIONS AND THE ARTS (art history and appreciation, classical languages, creative writing, dance, dramatic arts, English literature, French, German, music, Spanish, and studio art), COMPUTER AND PHYSICAL SCIENCE (astrophysics, chemistry, computer science, mathematics, and physics), ENGINEERING AND ENVIRONMENTAL DESIGN (engineering), HEALTH PROFESSIONS (nursing and public health), SOCIAL SCIENCE (African studies, anthropology, classical/ancient civilization, economics, history, international relations, philosophy, political science/government, psychology, religion, sociology, and women's studies). Psychology, public health, and English literature-creative writing have the largest enrollments.

ACTIVITIES: There are no fraternities or sororities. There are 79 groups on campus, including art, cheerleading, choir, chorale, chorus, communications, dance, drama, environmental, ethnic, honors, international, LGBT, literary magazine, musical theater, newspaper, orchestra, pep band, photography, political, professional, radio and TV, religious, social, social service, student government, symphony, and yearbook. Popular campus events include Black Cat, Spring Fling, Sophomore Ring Ceremony, Opening Convocation, and Senior Investiture. **Sports:** There are 6 intercollegiate sports for women, and 7 intramural sports for women. Facilities include fitness centers, a gym with a regulation basketball court, an 8-lane indoor pool, soccer field, tennis, weight room, track, aerobics room, and dance studios. **Graduates:** From July 1, 2016 to June 30, 2017, 234 bachelor's degrees were awarded. The most popular majors were public health (12%), psychology (9%), and business management (8%). In an average class, 4% graduate in 3 years or less, 62% graduate in 4 years or less, 66% graduate in 5 years or less, and 67% graduate in 6 years or less.

SERVICES: There is a reader service for the blind. There is also a center for writing and speaking, and a resource center for math and science. **Library/Resources:** The library contains 238,754 volumes, and 27,101 audio/video tapes/CDs/DVDs, and subscribes to 94,565 periodicals including electronic. Computerized library services include interlibrary loans, database searching, Internet access, and Wi-Fi capability. Special learning facilities include an art gallery, planetarium, radio station, center for writing and speaking, economics learning center, sociology and anthropology research lab, and science center for women. **Physically Challenged Students:** 90% of the campus is accessible. Facilities include wheelchair ramps, elevators, special parking, specially equipped restrooms, special class scheduling, lowered drinking fountains, lowered telephones, special housing, and lifts. **Special:** All first-year students will be required to participate in first-year travel and leadership immersion experiences. There is cross-registration through ARCHE (a 19-member consortium), and more than 300 credit and noncredit internships are available. There is a 3-2 engineering program with the Georgia Institute of Technology, a Computer Science dual-degree program with Emory University, a 3-2 nursing program with Emory University and the college offers student-designed interdisciplinary majors. Pass/fail options are available. Also offered are a Washington semester, the PLEN Public Policy Semester, the Mills College Exchange, and work-study programs. B.A. degree requirements may be completed in 3 years. There are 11 national honor societies and a chapter of Phi Beta Kappa. **Visiting:** There are regularly scheduled orientations for prospective students, campus tours, interviews, residence hall experiences, and informational sessions. There are guides for informal visits, visitors may sit in on classes, and stay overnight. To schedule a visit, contact the Admissions Office at admission@agnesscott.edu. **Campus Safety and Security:** Measures include 24-hour foot and vehicle patrol, emergency notification system, self-defense education, and security escort services. There are emergency telephones, lighted pathways/sidewalks, and controlled access to dorms/residences.

REQUIREMENTS: US Citizens must submit at least one of the following: SAT/ACT scores; an interview with an Agnes Scott College representative; a graded writing sample. Non-US citizens must submit SAT/ACT scores or complete a video interview. All home-schooled students must submit SAT I or ACT scores and SAT II Subject tests. AP credits are accepted. Important factors in the admissions decision are leadership record, advanced placement or honors courses, and recommendations by school officials. To qualify for a degree, each student must: successfully complete 128 hours of credit, including no more than 10 semester hours of internship credit, with a cumulative grade point average of 2.0 (C average), satisfy the Global Learning, Leadership Development, Intellectual Breadth, SUMMIT Portfolio and depth standards, satisfy the residency requirement. Students must have a cumulative GPA of 2.0 in the major to receive the degree. A student must complete and submit an application for graduation by the first day of course selection in the semester prior to the one in which she intends to graduate. **Procedure:** Freshmen are admitted in the fall. Entrance exams should be taken late in the junior year or by January of the senior year. There are early decision, early admissions, and deferred admissions plans. Early decision applications should be filed by November 1; regular applications, by March 15 for fall entry. Notification of early decision is sent December 1; regular decision, April 15. 22 early decision candidates were accepted for the 2017-2018 class. Applications are accepted on-line. **Transfer Students:** 11 transfer students enrolled in 2016-2017. A minimum college GPA of 3.0 is required, as is an interview and a letter of recommendation from a professor. 64 of 128 credits required for the bachelor's degree must be completed at Agnes Scott. **International Students:** There are 75 international students enrolled. They must take the TOEFL, with a score of 600 recommended. They must also take the SAT or ACT.

ADMISSIONS: 66% of the 2017-2018 applicants were accepted. The SAT scores for the 2017-2018 freshman class were: Critical Reading-- 8% below 500, 33% between 500 and 599, 41% between 600 and 699, and 18% between 700 and 800. Math-- 13% below 500, 48% between 500 and 599, 29% between 600 and 699, and 9% between 700 and 800. Writing-- 8% below 500, 39% between 500 and 599, 44% between 600 and 699, and 9% between 700 and 800. The ACT scores were 19% between 18 and 23, 55% between 24 and 29, and 26% above 30. 60% of the current freshmen were in the top fifth of their class; 90% were in the top two fifths. **Admissions Contact:** Alexa Gaeta, Associate Vice President for Enrollment. Email: *admissions@agnesscott.edu* Web: *www.agnesscott.edu*

FINANCIAL AID: In 2017-2018, 100% of all full-time freshmen received some form of financial aid. The average financial indebtedness of the 2017 graduate was $32,276. Agnes Scott College is a member of CSS. The college's own financial statement, and previous year's tax return are required. The FAFSA code is 001542. The priority date for freshman financial aid applications for fall entry is February 15. The deadline for filing freshman financial aid applications for fall entry is May 1.

ALBANY STATE UNIVERSITY — B-4

www.asurams.edu

Albany, GA 31705 — **(229) 430-4646**

Fax: (229) 430-4105	**Email: admissions@asurams.edu**
Full-time: 855 men, 1610 women	**Faculty:** n/av
Part-time: 150 men, 410 women	**Ph.D.s:** 52%
Graduate: 115 men, 330 women	**Student/Faculty:** n/av
Year: semesters, summer session	**Tuition:** $6470 ($21,550)
Room & Board: $12,992	**Freshman Class:** n/av
SAT or ACT: required	**CEEB CODE:** 5004
Application Deadline: July 1	**COMPETITIVE**

Albany State University, founded in 1903, is a state-supported institution within the University System of Georgia, offering programs in liberal arts, business, health fields, and teacher education. There are 4 undergraduate schools and 1 graduate school. In addition to regional accreditation, ASU has baccalaureate program accreditation with ACBSP, CAEP, and NLN. The 144-acre campus is in an urban area 175 miles south of Atlanta. Including any residence halls, there are 28 buildings.

STUDENT LIFE: 98% of undergraduates are from Georgia. 91% are African American; 8% White; 1% Hispanic. **Female To Male Ratio:** 2.1:1. The average age of all undergraduates is 24. **Housing:** College-sponsored housing includes dorms. On-campus housing is available on a first-come, first-served basis, and is available on a lottery system for upperclassmen. Alcohol is not permitted. All students may keep cars.

FACULTY/CLASSROOMS: 56% of faculty are male; 44% are female. No introductory courses are taught by graduate students.

PROGRAMS OF STUDY: Associate and master's degrees are also awarded. Bachelor's degrees are awarded in BIOLOGICAL SCIENCE (biology/biological science), BUSINESS (accounting, marketing/retailing/merchandising, and office supervision and management), COMMUNICATIONS AND THE ARTS (art, dramatic arts, English, fine arts, French, music, Spanish, and speech/debate/rhetoric), COMPUTER AND PHYSICAL SCIENCE (chemistry, computer science, information sciences and systems, and mathematics), EDUCATION (early childhood education, health education, middle school education, music education, physical education, science education, and special education), HEALTH PROFESSIONS (allied health and nursing), SOCIAL SCIENCE (criminal justice, forensic studies, history, political science/government, psychology, social work, and sociology).

ACTIVITIES: Groups on campus include art, band, cheerleading, choir, chorale, computers, dance, debate, drama, drill team, honors, jazz band, marching band, musical theater, pep band, political, professional, religious, social, social service, student government, and yearbook. Popular campus events include Honors Day, and Founders Day. **Sports:** There are 5 intercollegiate sports for men and 6 for women, and 2 intramural sports for men and 1 for women. Facilities include tennis courts, baseball and softball fields, an Olympic-size pool, a recreation room, and an all-weather track. **Graduates:** From July 1, 2016 to June 30, 2017, 485 bachelor's degrees were awarded. The most popular majors were criminal justice (9%), sociology (7%), and allied health science (6%).

SERVICES: There is remedial math, reading, and writing. **Library/Resources:** The library contains 351,467 volumes, 743,621 microform items, and 3,431 audio/video tapes/CDs/DVDs, and subscribes to 169,097 periodicals including electronic. Computerized library services include interlibrary loans and database searching. **Physically Challenged Students:** 90% of the campus is accessible. Facilities include wheelchair ramps, elevators, special parking, specially equipped restrooms, lowered drinking fountains, and lowered telephones. **Special:** The university offers co-op programs in all majors, 2+2 programs with Darton College, dual majors in social sciences, and 3-2 engineering degrees with the Georgia Institute of Technology. Several work-study programs and a gerontology training program are available. Albany State participates in the Georgian Intern Programs. All language majors are eligible to study abroad. There are 5 national honor societies, a freshman honors program, and 4 departmental honors programs. **Visiting:** There are regularly scheduled orientations for prospective students, consisting of summer and fall orientations and planned campus visitations. There are guides for informal visits and visitors may sit in on classes. To schedule a visit, contact the Office of Student Affairs. **Campus Safety and Security:** Measures include 24-hour foot and vehicle patrol and security escort services. There are emergency telephones and lighted pathways/sidewalks.

REQUIREMENTS: The SAT or ACT is required. Applicants must be graduates of an accredited secondary school and have completed 4 years each of English and math, 3 each of science and social sciences, and 2 of a foreign language. A GED is accepted; however, GED students must take and pass SAT: Subject tests in areas where college-preparatory courses are deficient. A GPA of 2.0 is required. AP and CLEP credits are accepted. To graduate, all students must complete 120 semester hours, including 30 in the major. The core curriculum includes 12 hours of social science, 10 to 11 of science, math and technology, 9 of essential composition and math skills, 6 of humanities and fine arts, 5 of leadership and global awareness, and 3 of phys ed. Most majors require a minimum GPA of 2.25. Students must take a Regents exam to assess English language skills competency, pass a comprehensive exam in their major, and/or score satisfactorily on the aptitude section of the GRE. **Procedure:** Freshmen are admitted to all sessions. Entrance exams should be taken by December of the senior year. There is an early admissions plan. Applications should be filed by July 1 for fall entry; November 1 for spring entry; and April 1 for summer entry. The fall 2017 application fee was $20. **Transfer Students:** Students must provide official transcripts of all previous college work. Students with fewer than 30 transferable semester hours must meet freshman requirements. 30 of 120 credits required for the bachelor's degree must be completed at Albany State. **International Students:** They must take the TOEFL. They must also take the SAT or ACT, scoring 830, and the college's own entrance exam.

Admissions Contact: Cedric Walker, Director of Admissisons. Email: *admissions@asurams.edu* Web: *www.asurams.edu*

FINANCIAL AID: The FAFSA code is 001544. Check with the school for current application deadlines.

ARMSTRONG STATE UNIVERSITY E-4
www.armstrong.edu

Savannah, GA 31419 (912) 344-2503
(800) 633-2349
Fax: (912) 344-3417 **Email:** admissions.info@armstrong.edu

Full-time: 1552 men, 2991 women	**Faculty:** 288
Part-time: 583 men, 1185 women	**Ph.D.s:** n/av
Graduate: 189 men, 571 women	**Student/Faculty:** 16 to 1
Year: semesters, summer session	**Tuition:** $5439 ($15,900)
Room & Board: $10,176	**Freshman Class:** 2047 applied, 1599 accepted, 843 enrolled
SAT EBR-W/M: 543/517 **ACT:** 21	**CEEB CODE:** 5012
Application Deadline: July 15	**COMPETITIVE**

Armstrong State University is "teaching-centered and student-focused, providing diverse learning experiences and professional programs grounded in the liberal arts." Armstrong is governed by the Board of Regents of the University System of Georgia. Armstrong offers more than 100 academic programs and majors. The university grants more than 60 academic credentials including undergraduate and graduate certificates, as well as associate, bachelor, and master's degrees, and Doctor of Physical Therapy degree. There are 4 undergraduate schools and 4 graduate schools. In addition to regional accreditation, ASU has baccalaureate program accreditation with ABET, NASM, CAEP, ACS, NAACLS, CAPTE, CoARC, CAHME, CAA, JRCERT, JRCNMT, CEPH, and CCNE. The 267-acre campus is in a suburban area 250 miles from Atlanta and 150 miles from Jacksonville, FL. Including any residence halls, there are 59 buildings.

STUDENT LIFE: 92% of undergraduates are from Georgia. Others are from 38 states, 64 foreign countries, and Canada. 9% are Hispanic; 54% White; 5% two or more races; 4% Asian American; 26% African American; 2% Foreign. **Female To Male Ratio:** 2.0:1. The average age of freshmen is 20; all undergraduates, 24. 35% do not continue beyond their first year; 32% remain to graduate. **Housing:** 1411 students can be accommodated in college housing, which includes dorms and on-campus apartments. On-campus housing is guaranteed for the freshman year only, is available on a first-come, first-served basis, and is available on a lottery system for upperclassmen. 81% of students commute. Alcohol is not permitted. All students may keep cars.

FACULTY/CLASSROOMS: 39% of faculty are male; 61% are female. No introductory courses are taught by graduate students. The average class size in an introductory lecture is 24; in a laboratory is 20; and in a regular course is 23.

PROGRAMS OF STUDY: ASU confers B.A., B.S., B.F.A., B.H.S., B.I.T., B.L.S., B.M.E., B.S.B.E., B.S.Ed., B.S.M.L.S., B.S.N., B.S.N.C., B.S.P., and B.S.R.S. degrees. Associate, master's, and doctoral degrees are also awarded. Bachelor's degrees are awarded in BIOLOGICAL SCIENCE (biochemistry and biology/biological science), BUSINESS (business economics), COMMUNICATIONS AND THE ARTS (art, English, French, music, music performance, Spanish, theatre arts, and visual and performing arts), COMPUTER AND PHYSICAL SCIENCE (applied mathematics, applied physics, chemistry, computer science, cyber intelligence/security studies, inform, science, systems & tech, and mathematics), EDUCATION (art education, early childhood education, English education, health education, health information management, mathematics education, middle school education, music education, physical education, secondary education, and special education), HEALTH PROFESSIONS (health services administration, health science, medical laboratory science, medical technology, nursing, public health, radiological science, rehabilitation therapy, and respiratory therapy), SOCIAL SCIENCE (child care/child and family studies, communication sciences & disorders, criminal justice, economics, history, liberal arts/general studies, political science/government, psychology, and women & gender studies). Nursing, biology, and rehabilitation sciences have the largest enrollments.

ACTIVITIES: There are 115 groups on campus, including band, cheerleading, choir, chorus, computers, dance, debate, drama, ethnic, honors, international, jazz band, LGBT, literary magazine, musical theater, newspaper, political, professional, religious, social, social service, and student government. Popular campus events include Celebrate Armstrong, International Week and HOLA (Hispanic Outreach and Leadership), and Treasure Savannah. **Sports:** Facilities include volleyball, a recreation center, basketball courts, a multipurpose room, and weight room area. The outdoor field has flag football, softball, baseball and soccer.**Graduates:** From July 1, 2016 to June 30, 2017, 995 bachelor's degrees were awarded. The most popular majors were nursing (15%), liberal studies (7%), and biology (5%). In an average class, 1% graduate in 3 years or less, 13% graduate in 4 years or less, 27% graduate in 5 years or less, and 32% graduate in 6 years or less.

SERVICES: Counseling and information services are available, as is tutoring in most subjects. There is a reader service for the blind, and remedial math, reading, and writing. **Library/Resources:** The library contains 217,793 volumes, 535,080 microform items, and 1,106 audio/video tapes/CDs/DVDs. Computerized library services include interlibrary loans, database searching, Internet access, and Wi-Fi capability. Special learning facilities include an art gallery. **Physically Challenged Students:** Facilities include wheelchair ramps, elevators, special parking, specially equipped restrooms, special class scheduling, lowered drinking fountains, and special housing. **Special:** There are 3 national honor societies and a freshman honors program. **Visiting:** There are regularly scheduled orientations for prospective students, including a tour of the campus and departments. There are guides for informal visits. To schedule a visit, contact Danielle Debien at (912) 344-2503. **Campus Safety and Security:** Measures include 24-hour foot and vehicle patrol, emergency notification system, self-defense education, and security escort services. There are emergency telephones, lighted pathways/sidewalks, and controlled access to dorms/residences.

REQUIREMENTS: The SAT or ACT is required. Applicants should graduate from an accredited secondary school. A GED may be accepted. College preparatory work should include 4 units of English and science, 3 units of math and social studies, and 2 units of foreign language. Art students must submit a portfolio. A GPA of 2.5 is required. AP and CLEP credits are accepted. The core curriculum consists of 60 hours in humanities, math, natural sciences, and social sciences and 3 in phys ed. A minimum GPA of 2.0 overall and a grade of C or better in each major course is required. Each student must complete 123 hours, with 29 hours in the major, and must take a comprehensive exam. **Procedure:** Freshmen are admitted to all sessions. There are deferred admissions and rolling admissions plans. Applications should be filed by July 15 for fall entry; December 1 for spring entry; and April 15 for summer entry. The fall 2017 application fee was $30. Applications are accepted on-line. **Transfer Students:** 569 transfer students enrolled in 2016-2017. Transfer applicants must submit all transcripts and must be in good standing at the last college attended. 30 of 124 credits required for the bachelor's degree must be completed at Armstrong. **International Students:** There are 180 international students enrolled. They must take the TOEFL with a minimum score of 523 on the paper-based TOEFL (PBT) or 70 on the Internet-based version (iBT). They must also take the SAT or ACT.

ADMISSIONS: 78% of the 2017-2018 applicants were accepted. The SAT scores for the 2017-2018 freshman class were: Math-- 35% below 500, 56% between 500 and 599, 8% between 600 and 699, and 1% between 700 and 800. Evidence-Based Reading/Writing-- 23% below 500, 57% between 500 and 599, 19% between 600 and 699, and 1% between 700 and 800. The ACT scores were 14% between 12 and 17, 64% between 18 and 23, 19% between 24 and 29, and 3% above 30. **Admissions Contact:** Tobe Frierson, Director of Admissions. Email: *admissions.info@armstrong.edu* Web: *www.armstrong.edu*

FINANCIAL AID: The FAFSA code is 001546. The priority date for freshman financial aid applications for fall entry is March 15. The deadline for filing freshman financial aid applications for fall entry is April 20.

AUGUSTA UNIVERSITY D-2
www.augusta.edu

Augusta, GA 30912 (706) 737-1632
Email: admissions@augusta.edu

Full-time: 1431 men, 2646 women	**Faculty:** n/av
Part-time: 449 men, 698 women	**Ph.D.s:** 79%
Graduate: 1129 men, 1624 women	**Student/Faculty:** n/av
Year: semesters, summer session	**Tuition:** $4632 ($16,248)
Room & Board: n/app	**Freshman Class:** n/av
SAT or ACT: required	**CEEB CODE:** 5406
Application Deadline: November 15	**COMPETITIVE**

Augusta University is a public comprehensive research institution as well as an academic health center. The figures in the above capsule are for the tuition and fees only. There are 6 undergraduate schools and 3 graduate schools. In addition to regional accreditation, AU has baccalaureate program accreditation with AACSB, CSWE, NASAD, NASM, CAEP, NLN, CODA, CAEP, and CCNE. The campus is in an urban area on the southern banks of the storied Savannah River. Including any residence halls, there are 145 buildings.

STUDENT LIFE: 89% of undergraduates are from Georgia. Others are from 45 states, 40 foreign countries, and Canada. 7% are race unknown; 58% White; 5% Hispanic; 4% Asian American; 3% two or more races; 20% African American; 1% Foreign. **Female To Male Ratio:** 1.7:1. The average age of freshmen is 18; all undergraduates, 24. 69% do not continue beyond their first year; 32% remain to graduate. **Housing:** 825 students can be accommodated in college housing, which includes married student dorms and on-campus apartments. On-campus housing is available on a first-come and first-served basis. 85% of students commute. Alcohol is not permitted. All students may keep cars.

FACULTY/CLASSROOMS: 54% of faculty are male; 46% are female. And 12% do research. No introductory courses are taught by graduate students.

PROGRAMS OF STUDY: AU confers B.A., B.A.F.L, B.S., B.B.A., B.F.A., B.M., B.S.A.I.T., B.S.Ed., B.S.W., B.S.N., B.S.C.L.S, B.S.D.H., B.S.H.I.A., B.S.R.P.T., B.S.R.S. and B.S.K. degrees. Associate, master's, and doctoral degrees are also awarded. Bachelor's degrees are awarded in BIOLOGICAL SCIENCE (biology/biological science, cell biology, and ecology), BUSINESS (accounting, banking and finance, business administration and management, management information systems, and marketing/retailing/merchandising), COMMUNICATIONS AND THE ARTS (art, communications, English, music, and music performance), COMPUTER AND PHYSICAL SCIENCE (chemistry, computer science, information sciences and systems, mathematics, and physics), EDUCATION (elementary education, foreign languages education, health education, health information management, middle school education, music education, and special education), HEALTH PROFESSIONS (dental hygiene, kinesiology, medical laboratory science, medical technology, nuclear medical technology, nursing, radiation therapy, and respiratory therapy), SOCIAL SCIENCE (anthropology, criminal justice, history, political science/government, psychology, social work, and sociology). Chemistry, nursing, and psychology have the largest enrollments.

ACTIVITIES: 1% of men belong to 6 national fraternities; 1% of women belong to 5 national sororities. There are 160 groups on campus, including art, band, cheerleading, choir, chorus, drama, ethnic, film, honors, international, jazz band, LGBT, literary magazine, musical theater, newspaper, orchestra, pep band, photography, political, professional, radio and TV, religious, social, social service, student government, and symphony. Popular campus events include Week of Welcome, Homecoming, Lyceum Series, Family Fun Days, and Pig Out. **Sports:** There are 6 intercollegiate sports for men and 7 for women. Facilities include a gym and fitness center, baseball, soccer, softball fields, a tennis center, an 18-hole golf course, and a fitness center. **Graduates:** From July 1, 2016 to June 30, 2017, 996 bachelor's degrees were awarded. The most popular majors were nursing (17%), communications (6%), and psychology (5%). In an average class, 32% graduate in 6 years or less.

SERVICES: Counseling and information services are available, as is tutoring in most subjects. There is a reader service for the blind, and remedial math. **Library/Resources:** The library contains 619,931 volumes, and 9,888 audio/video tapes/CDs/DVDs, and subscribes to 37,383 periodicals including electronic. Computerized library services include interlibrary loans, database searching, Internet access, and Wi-Fi capability. Special learning facilities include an art gallery and radio station. **Physically Challenged Students:** 95% of the campus is accessible. Facilities include wheelchair ramps, elevators, special parking, specially equipped restrooms, special class scheduling, lowered drinking fountains, and lowered telephones. **Special:** The school offers co-op programs and internships with area companies, work-study programs, dual majors, nondegree study, and cross-registration with Paine College. There is a freshman honors program. **Visiting:** There are regularly scheduled orientations for prospective students, including a meal, campus tour, discussion of schedules, deadlines, and registration. There are guides for informal visits and visitors may sit in on classes. To schedule a visit, contact Erin Smith at emsith35@gru.edu. **Campus Safety and Security:** Measures include 24-hour foot and vehicle patrol, emergency notification system, self-defense education, and security escort services. There are shuttle buses, emergency telephones, lighted pathways/sidewalks, controlled access to dorms/residences, and controlled access to labs after hours.

REQUIREMENTS: The SAT or ACT is required. Applicants must have at least a 2.0 GPA, with a verbal score of 430 and math score of 400 on the SAT or a comparable score on the ACT. Applicants must be graduates of an accredited secondary school. The GED is accepted. Secondary school courses must include 4 units each of English and math, 3 each of science and social science, and 2 of a foreign language. AP and CLEP credits are accepted. Students must complete 125 hours with a minimum GPA of 2.0. All students are required to take 6 courses in phys ed, pass the Regents test in reading and composition, and demonstrate, through course completion or exam, a knowledge of U.S. and Georgia history and their constitutions. **Procedure:** Freshmen are admitted fall, spring, and summer. There are deferred admissions and rolling admissions plans. Applications should be filed by November 15 for fall entry. Applications are accepted on-line. **International Students:** They must take the TOEFL. They must also take the SAT or ACT.

Admissions Contact: Maura Flaschner, Director of Admissions. Email: *admissions@augusta.edu* Web: *www.augusta.edu*

FINANCIAL AID: In 2017-2018, 86% of all full-time freshmen received some form of financial aid. 53% of all full-time freshmen received need-based aid. The average freshman award was $5,692. Need-based scholarships or need-based grants averaged $2,964 ($2,908 maximum); need-based self-help aid (loans and jobs) averaged $1,732 ($2,190 maximum); non-need-based athletic scholarships averaged $3,688 ($4,250 maximum); and other non-need-based awards and non-need-based scholarships averaged $4,069 ($20,000 maximum). 2% of undergraduate students work part-time. The average financial indebtedness of the 2017 graduate was $20,914. The priority date for freshman financial aid applications for fall entry is April 1.

BERRY COLLEGE — A-2
www.berry.edu

Mount Berry, GA 30149 — (706) 236-2215, (800) BERRY GA

Fax: (706) 290-2178 — **Email:** admissions@berry.edu

Full-time: 761 men, 1184 women
Part-time: 17 men, 16 women
Graduate: 45 men, 87 women
Year: semesters, summer session
Room & Board: $12,290
SAT CR/M: 620/590 **ACT:** 26
Application Deadline: January 15

Faculty: 165; IIA, -$
Ph.D.s: 92%
Student/Faculty: 11 to 1
Tuition: $35,176
Freshman Class: 3883 applied, 2392 accepted, 553 enrolled
CEEB CODE: 5059
VERY COMPETITIVE

Berry College, founded in 1902, is a private nonsectarian college offering programs in liberal arts and preprofessional programs in education and business. There are 4 undergraduate schools and 2 graduate schools. In addition to regional accreditation, Berry has baccalaureate program accreditation with AACSB, NASM, SACSCOC, and CCNE. The 27000-acre campus is in a suburban area north of Rome on U.S. 27 in northwest Georgia, 72 miles northwest of Atlanta and 75 miles from Chattanooga, TN. Including any residence halls, there are 47 buildings.

STUDENT LIFE: 67% of undergraduates are from Georgia. Others are from 37 states, 9 foreign countries, and Canada. 72% are from public schools. 80% are White; 7% Hispanic; 5% African American; 3% two or more races; 2% Asian American; 2% race unknown; 1% Foreign. **Female To Male Ratio:** 1.6:1. The average age of freshmen is 19; all undergraduates, 20. 22% do not continue beyond their first year; 64% remain to graduate. **Housing:** 1894 students can be accommodated in college housing, which includes single-sex and coed dorms and on-campus apartments. First-year living learning community and year of service cottages. On-campus housing is guaranteed for all 4 years. 89% of students live on campus. Alcohol is not permitted. All students may keep cars.

FACULTY/CLASSROOMS: 52% of faculty are male; 48% are female. 99% teach undergraduates, and 99% do research. No introductory courses are taught by graduate students. The average class size in an introductory lecture is 19; in a laboratory is 17; and in a regular course is 18.

PROGRAMS OF STUDY: Berry confers B.A., B.S., B.Mus., and B.S.N.

degrees. Master's degrees are also awarded. Bachelor's degrees are awarded in AGRICULTURE (animal science and environmental studies), BIOLOGICAL SCIENCE (biochemistry and biology/biological science), BUSINESS (accounting, business administration and management, finance, international business management, and marketing management), COMMUNICATIONS AND THE ARTS (art, art history and appreciation, communications, creative writing, English, French, German, music, music business management, Spanish, sports administration, studio art, and theatre arts), COMPUTER AND PHYSICAL SCIENCE (applied physics, chemistry, mathematics, and physics), EDUCATION (art education, early childhood education, mathematics education, middle school education, and music education), ENGINEERING AND ENVIRONMENTAL DESIGN (environmental science), HEALTH PROFESSIONS (exercise science and nursing), SOCIAL SCIENCE (anthropology, economics, history, interdisciplinary studies, international studies, philosophy, political science/government, psychology, religion, and sociology). Animal science, psychology, and exercise science have the largest enrollments.

ACTIVITIES: There are no fraternities or sororities. There are 70 groups on campus, including art, cheerleading, chess, choir, chorus, communications, computers, dance, drama, environmental, ethnic, forensics, honors, international, jazz band, literary magazine, musical theater, newspaper, orchestra, pep band, political, professional, religious, social, social service, student government, symphony, Viking Drumline club, and yearbook. Popular campus events include Mountain Day, Conson Wilson Lecture Series, and BCTC Theatre Season. **Sports:** There are 11 intercollegiate sports for men and 12 for women, and 15 intramural sports for men and 15 for women. Facilities include a stadium for football, lacrosse, track and field, an athletic and recreational facility, swimming/diving pool, multipurpose fitness rooms, auxiliary basketball court, racquetball courts, kinesiology lab, fitness/weight facility, an arena for basketball and volleyball, tennis courts, equine center, baseball, softball, and soccer fields, running and biking trails, 18-hole disc golf course, BOLD Challenge Course, four sand volleyball courts, an outdoor basketball court, 60 court tennis facility with six NCAA regulation courts, and three center courts for tournament/collegiate play. **Graduates:** From July 1, 2016 to June 30, 2017, 491 bachelor's degrees were awarded. The most popular majors were biological/life studies (20%), business/marketing (18%), and psychology (9%). In an average class, 1% graduate in 3 years or less, 57% graduate in 4 years or less, 63% graduate in 5 years or less, and 64% graduate in 6 years or less.

SERVICES: Counseling and information services are available, as is tutoring in most subjects. There is a reader service for the blind, and remedial writing. **Library/Resources:** The library contains 1.1 million volumes, 12,600 microform items, and 136,659 audio/video tapes/CDs/DVDs, and subscribes to 56,093 periodicals including electronic. Computerized library services include interlibrary loans, database searching, Internet access, and Wi-Fi capability. Special learning facilities include an art gallery, an observatory, an equine center, a forestry center, beef-and-dairy-cattle operations, BOLD (Berry Outdoor Leadership Development), wildlife management area, and the Longleaf Pine Project. **Physically Challenged Students:** 80% of the campus is accessible. Facilities include wheelchair ramps, elevators, special parking, specially equipped restrooms, lowered drinking fountains, and special housing. **Special:** The college offers internships, study abroad in more than 20 countries, work-study programs, student-designed majors, co-op programs, cross-registration with Shorter College, dual majors, credit by exam, and non-degree study. There are 3-2 engineering degrees and dual-degree programs in several fields with the Georgia Institute of Technology and Kennesaw State University. There is also a dual-degree program in nursing with Emory University. There are 13 national honor societies, a freshman honors program, and 19 departmental honors programs. **Visiting:** There are regularly scheduled orientations for prospective students, including weekdays and Saturday mornings. Students should schedule campus visits in advance. There are guides for informal visits, visitors may sit in on classes, and stay overnight. To schedule a visit, contact the Office of Admissions. **Campus Safety and Security:** Measures include 24-hour foot and vehicle patrol and emergency notification system. There are emergency telephones, lighted pathways/sidewalks, controlled access to dorms/residences, a gated campus, mobile police patrols, and limited access to campus.

REQUIREMENTS: The SAT or ACT is required. Applicants should be graduates of an accredited high school or have a GED. 20 academic credits are required, including 4 units each of English and math (including algebra I, algebra II, and either geometry or trigonometry), 3 units each of science and social studies, and 2 units of foreign language. AP credits are accepted. Important factors in the admissions decision are advanced placement or honors courses, leadership record, and recommendations by school officials. General education requirements include 5 courses in the humanities and fine arts, 3 each in behavioral science, math and natural sciences, communication, and health and phys ed, and 2 in electives. A 2.0 GPA and a total of 124 credits, including at least 30 hours in the major, are required for graduation. All students are also required to attend at least 3 approved cultural events per semester and pass a comprehensive exam or other senior assessment in the major. **Procedure:** Freshmen are admitted to all sessions. Entrance exams should be taken by the fall of the senior year. There are early decision and early admissions plans. Early decision applications should be filed by November 1; regular applications, by January 15 for fall entry; December 11 for spring entry; and April 14 for summer entry. Notification of early decision is sent December 1; regular decision, February 15. 48 early decision candidates were accepted for the 2017-2018 class. 27 applicants were on the 2017 waiting list; 2 were admitted. Applications are accepted on-line. **Transfer Students:** 42 transfer students enrolled in 2016-2017. Applicants must submit official transcripts from all colleges previously attended, have a minimum GPA of 2.5, and be in good standing at the last school attended. 62 of 124 credits required for the bachelor's degree must be completed at Berry. **International Students:** There are 15 international students enrolled. They must take the TOEFL with a minimum score of 550 on the paper-based TOEFL (PBT) or 80 on the Internet-based version (iBT). Student must take the IELTS. They must also take the SAT or ACT if the student is from an English-speaking country.

ADMISSIONS: 62% of the 2017-2018 applicants were accepted. The SAT scores for the 2017-2018 freshman class were: Critical Reading-- 4% below 500, 35% between 500 and 599, 46% between 600 and 699, and 16% between 700 and 800. Math-- 6% below 500, 50% between 500 and 599, 39% between 600 and 699, and 5% between 700 and 800. The ACT scores were 23% between 18 and 23, 60% between 24 and 29, and 17% above 30. 57% of the current freshmen were in the top fifth of their class; 83% were in the top two fifths. 8 freshmen graduated first in their class. **Admissions Contact:** Brett Kennedy, Assistant Vice President of Admissions. Email: *admissions@berry.edu* Web: *www.berry.edu*

FINANCIAL AID: In 2017-2018, 99% of all full-time freshmen received some form of financial aid. 76% of all full-time freshmen received need-based aid. The average freshman award was $32,625. Need-based scholarships or need-based grants averaged $19,886; need-based self-help aid (loans and jobs) averaged $4,087; and other non-need-based awards and non-need-based scholarships averaged $8,652. 83% of undergraduate students work part-time. The average financial indebtedness of the 2017 graduate was $27,378. Berry is a member of CSS. The CSS/Profile and the state aid form are required. The FAFSA code is 001554. The priority date for freshman financial aid applications for fall entry is January 15.

BRENAU UNIVERSITY - WOMEN'S COLLEGE *(The complete profile is made available exclusively on our website, www.barronspac.com)*

BREWTON-PARKER COLLEGE *(The complete profile is made available exclusively on our website, www.barronspac.com)*

CLARK ATLANTA UNIVERSITY *(The complete profile is made available exclusively on our website, www.barronspac.com)*

CLAYTON STATE UNIVERSITY *(The complete profile is made available exclusively on our website, www.barronspac.com)*

COLUMBUS STATE UNIVERSITY *(The complete profile is made available exclusively on our website, www.barronspac.com)*

COVENANT COLLEGE A-1
www.covenant.edu

Lookout Mountain, GA 30750	(706) 820-2398 (888) 451-2683
Fax: (706) 820-0893	**Email:** admissions@covenant.edu
Full-time: 457 men, 525 women	**Faculty:** 64; IIB, av$
Part-time: 2 men, 2 women	**Ph.D.s:** 93%
Graduate: 20 men, 164 women	**Student/Faculty:** 13 to 1
Year: semesters, summer session	**Tuition:** $34,330
Room & Board: $10,260	**Freshman Class:** 692 applied, 659 accepted, 263 enrolled
SAT EBR-W/M: 640/600 **ACT:** 27	**CEEB CODE:** 6124
Application Deadline: February 1	**HIGHLY COMPETITIVE**

Covenant College, founded in 1955, is a private liberal arts college affiliated with the Presbyterian Church in America. At Covenant, we seek to inspire and equip our students to be faithful stewards of their God-given abilities- all of our programs are designed with this in mind. There is 1 undergraduate school and 1 graduate school. In addition to regional accreditation, Covenant has baccalaureate program accreditation with SACS-COC. The 350-acre campus is in a suburban area 12 miles southwest of Chattanooga, Tennessee. Including any residence halls, there are 15 buildings.

STUDENT LIFE: 78% of undergraduates are from out of state, mostly the South. Students are from 48 states, 23 foreign countries, and Canada. 90% are White; 3% African American; 2% Asian American; 2% Hispanic; 2% Foreign; 1% American Indian/Alaska Native. 49% are Protestant. **Female To Male Ratio:** 1.4:1. The average age of freshmen is 18; all undergraduates, 20. 15% do not continue beyond their first year; 58% remain to graduate. **Housing:** 917 students can be accommodated in college housing, which includes dorms and on-campus apartments, and apartments for single students. On-campus housing is guaranteed for all 4 years. 98% of students live on campus. Alcohol is not permitted. All students may keep cars.

FACULTY/CLASSROOMS: 75% of faculty are male; 26% are female. All teach undergraduates. No introductory courses are taught by graduate students. The average class size in an introductory lecture is 19; in a laboratory is 16; and in a regular course is 18.

PROGRAMS OF STUDY: Covenant confers B.A. and B.S. degrees. Master's degrees are also awarded. Bachelor's degrees are awarded in BIOLOGICAL SCIENCE (biology/biological science), BUSINESS (business administration and management), COMMUNICATIONS AND THE ARTS (art, dramatic arts, English, French, music, music performance, and Spanish), COMPUTER AND PHYSICAL SCIENCE (chemistry, computer science, mathematics, and physics), EDUCATION (elementary education, English education, mathematics education, and science education), SOCIAL SCIENCE (biblical studies, economics, history, interdisciplinary studies, philosophy, philosophy and religion, psychology, social science, and sociology). English, history, and sociology have the largest enrollments.

ACTIVITIES: There are no fraternities or sororities. There are 43 groups on campus, including campus ministries, music ensembles and student-run film society, radio station, bagpipe, choir, chorale, concert band, dance, debate, drama, film, honors, international, jazz band, literary magazine, musical theater, newspaper, photography, professional, religious, social, social service, student government, and yearbook. Popular campus events include Madrigal Dinner, Spring Banquet and Kilter Night. **Sports:** There are 6 intercollegiate sports for men and 7 for women, and 9 intramural sports for men and 9 for women. Facilities include a gym, weight room, swimming pool, tennis courts, soccer fields, running trails, an aerobics room, and a wellness room equipped with a variety of fitness machines. **Graduates:** From July 1, 2016 to June 30, 2017, 243 bachelor's degrees were awarded. The most popular majors were social sciences (14%), English (13%), and education (10%).

SERVICES: Counseling and information services are available, as is tutoring in some subjects, such as math and writing. There is remedial math, reading, and writing. **Library/Resources:** The library contains 89,449 volumes, 121,159 microform items, and 4,500 audio/video tapes/CDs/DVDs, and subscribes to 525 periodicals including electronic. Computerized library services include interlibrary loans, database searching, Internet access, and Wi-Fi capability. Special learning facilities include an art gallery. **Physically Challenged Students:** All of the campus is accessible. Facilities include wheelchair ramps, elevators, special parking, specially equipped restrooms, lowered drinking fountains, and lowered telephones. **Special:** Cross-registration is possible with the Council for Christian Colleges and Universities (CCCU). Students may study abroad in 9 countries or spend a semester in Washington. There is a 3-2 engineering program with Georgia Tech, and a cooperative nursing program with Emory, Bridge program for MSN with Vanderbilt. Juniors and seniors may take classes on a pass/fail basis. There are 5 national honor societies and 5 departmental honors programs. **Visiting:** There are regularly scheduled orientations for prospective students, consisting of a campus preview weekend during which high school students stay in dormitories and attend classes, seminars, and other college activities. **Campus Safety and Security:** Measures include 24-hour foot and vehicle patrol, emergency notification system, and security escort services. There are lighted pathways/sidewalks, and a watchman who maintains campus security at night.

REQUIREMENTS: The SAT or ACT is required. Students must submit the following: application for admission, application fee, Christian testimony, official high school transcript, minimum GPA of 2.50, a combined SAT score of at least 1000 (sum of critical reading and math section scores) or composite ACT score of at least 21, academic references, and a church reference. Applicants must graduate from an accredited high school or have a GED. Applicants should have 14 total units, including 4 years of high school English, 3 years of math, and 2 years each of science, and social studies, and academic electives. An essay and an interview are required. A GPA of 2.5 is required. AP and CLEP credits are accepted. Important factors in the admissions decision are advanced placement or honors courses, personality/intangible qualities, recommendations by school officials, leadership record, parents or siblings attended your school, extracurricular activities record, and recommendations by alumni. All students must complete 55 to 63 hours of core and distribution requirements, including coursework in Bible studies, interdisciplinary studies, English composition, cross-cultural experience, language, phys ed, lab science, social science, and history. A minimum total of 126 credits and a GPA of 2.0 are required for graduation. All students must also complete an oral interview and a senior integration project, in which they explore a problem in their major field in light of Christian philosophy. **Procedure:** Freshmen are admitted fall and spring. Entrance exams should be taken by January of the senior year. There is a rolling admissions plan. Applications should be filed by May 1 for fall entry; November 1 for spring entry. The fall 2017 application fee was $35. Notification of early decision is sent August 15. Applications are accepted on-line. **Transfer Students:** 39 transfer students enrolled in 2016-2017. Transfer applicants must take either the SAT, with a minimum satisfactory score, or the ACT, with a minimum composite of 21. Courses with a grade of C or better that apply toward the selected Covenant program will receive transfer credit. 32 of 126 credits required for the bachelor's degree must be completed at Covenant. **International Students:** There are 23 international students enrolled. They must take the TOEFL with a minimum score of 540 on the paper-based TOEFL (PBT) or 76 on the Internet-based version (iBT). Applicants are encouraged to take the SAT or ACT if it is available in their country.

ADMISSIONS: 95% of the 2017-2018 applicants were accepted. The SAT scores for the 2017-2018 freshman class were: Math-- 10% below 500, 38% between 500 and 599, 43% between 600 and 699, and 10% between 700 and 800. Evidence-Based Reading/Writing-- 3% below 500, 31% between 500 and 599, 45% between 600 and 699, and 21% between 700 and 800. The ACT scores were 1% between 12 and 17, 23% between 18 and 23, 47% between 24 and 29, and 29% above 30. 46% of the current freshmen were in the top fifth of their class; 65% were in the top two fifths. **Admissions Contact:** Scott Schindler, Assoc. Director of Admissions. Email: *admissions@covenant.edu* Web: *www.covenant.edu*

FINANCIAL AID: In 2017-2018, 100% of all full-time freshmen received some form of financial aid. 70% of all full-time freshmen received need-based aid. The average freshman award was $21,771. Need-based scholarships or need-based grants averaged $17,722 ($30,430 maximum); need-based self-help aid (loans and jobs) averaged $5,450 ($33,522 maximum); and other non-need-based awards and non-need-based scholarships averaged $12,131 ($27,850 maximum). 56% of undergraduate students work part-time. The average financial indebtedness of the 2017 graduate was $22,208. The state aid form and the college's own financial statement are required. The FAFSA code is 003484. The priority date for freshman financial aid applications for fall entry is March 1.

EMORY UNIVERSITY B-2

www.emory.edu

Atlanta, GA 30322 (404) 727-6036

Email: admission@emory.edu

Full-time: 2754 men, 3960 women	**Faculty:** 710; I, ++$
Part-time: 60 men, 87 women	**Ph.D.s:** 96%
Graduate: 3082 men, 4134 women	**Student/Faculty:** 9 to 1
Year: semesters, summer session	**Tuition:** $49,392
Room & Board: $13,894	**Freshman Class:** 19924 applied, 5039 accepted, 1358 enrolled
SAT CR/M/W: 680/720/700 **ACT:** 31	**CEEB CODE:** 5187
Application Deadline: January 1	**MOST COMPETITIVE**

Emory University, founded in 1836, is a private institution affiliated with the United Methodist Church. There are 5 undergraduate schools and 8 graduate schools. In addition to regional accreditation, Emory has baccalaureate program accreditation with SACS. The 631-acre campus is in a suburban area 5 miles northeast of downtown Atlanta.

STUDENT LIFE: 79% of undergraduates are from out of state, mostly the South. Students are from 50 states, 72 foreign countries, and Canada. 57% are from public schools. 9% are African American; 9% Hispanic; 42% White; 4% two or more races; 2% race unknown; 18% Asian American; 16% Foreign. **Female To Male Ratio:** 1.4:1. The average age of freshmen is 18; all undergraduates, 20. 6% do not continue beyond their first year; 94% remain to graduate. **Housing:** 4703 students can be accommodated in college housing, which includes married student dorms and on-campus apartments. In addition, there are special-interest houses, fraternity houses, sorority houses, and theme housing. On-campus housing is guaranteed for the freshman year only. 64% of students live on campus. Upperclassmen may keep cars.

FACULTY/CLASSROOMS: 60% of faculty are male; 40% are female. No introductory courses are taught by graduate students.

PROGRAMS OF STUDY: Emory confers B.A., B.S., B.B.A., and B.S.N. degrees. Master's and doctoral degrees are also awarded. Bachelor's degrees are awarded in AGRICULTURE (environmental studies), BIOLOGICAL SCIENCE (biology/biological science and neurosciences), BUSINESS (accounting, banking and finance, business administration and management, business economics, and marketing/retailing/merchandising), COMMUNICATIONS AND THE ARTS (art, art history and appreciation, Chinese, classics, comparative literature, creative writing, dance, dramatic arts, English, film arts, fine arts, French, Greek, Italian, Japanese, journalism, Latin, linguistics, music, Russian languages and literature, and Spanish), COMPUTER AND PHYSICAL SCIENCE (chemistry, computer science, mathematics, and physics), HEALTH PROFESSIONS (nursing), SOCIAL SCIENCE (African studies, African American studies, American studies, anthropology, Asian/American studies, Asian/Oriental studies, Caribbean studies, classical/ancient civilization, economics, French studies, German area studies, history, interdisciplinary studies, international studies, Italian studies, Judaic studies, Latin American studies, medieval studies, Middle Eastern studies, philosophy, political science/government, psychology, religion, Russian and Slavic studies, sociology, and women's studies). Business administration, biology, and nursing have the largest enrollments.

ACTIVITIES: 27% of men belong to 16 national fraternities; 33% of women belong to 13 national sororities. There are 220 groups on campus, including art, bagpipe, band, cheerleading, chess, choir, chorale, chorus, computers, dance, debate, drama, ethnic, film, honors, international, jazz band, LGBT, literary magazine, musical theater, newspaper, orchestra, pep band, photography, political, professional, radio and TV, religious, social, social service, student government, symphony, and yearbook. Popular campus events include Heritage Ball, Dooley's Week, and Festival of Nine Lessons. **Sports:** There are 8 intercollegiate sports for men and 8 for women, and 18 intramural sports for men and 18 for women. Facilities include a recreation center, which contains a gym with basketball courts, volleyball courts, an Olympic-size swimming pool, indoor track, Nautilus weight rooms, a sheer rock wall, tennis, racquetball, and squash courts, a soccer field and a 400-meter track. **Graduates:** From July 1, 2016 to June 30, 2017, 1933 bachelor's degrees were awarded. The most popular majors were business administration (15%), biology (8%), and nursing (8%). In an average class, 85% graduate in 4 years or less, 89% graduate in 5 years or less, and 91% graduate in 6 years or less. Of the 2016 graduating class, 31% were enrolled in graduate school within 6 months of graduation, and 42% were employed.

SERVICES: Counseling and information services are available, as is tutoring in most subjects. There is a reader service for the blind. **Library/Resources:** The library contains 3.8 million volumes. Computerized library services include interlibrary loans, database searching, Internet access, and Wi-Fi capability. Special learning facilities include an art gallery, planetarium, radio station, TV station, the Michael C. Carlos museum, and the Carter center. **Physically Challenged Students:** 90% of the campus is accessible. Facilities include wheelchair ramps, elevators, special parking, specially equipped restrooms, special class scheduling, lowered drinking fountains, lowered telephones, and special housing. **Special:** Special academic programs include cross-registration with Atlanta area colleges and universities, departmental internships, work-study programs, dual majors, 3-2 and 4-2 engineering degrees with Georgia Tech, and pass/fail options. A Washington semester and B.A.-B.S. degrees are available, and students may study abroad in many countries. There are accelerated degree programs offered in chemistry, math, and computer science, English, history, philosophy, political science, nursing and sociology. There are 4 national honor societies and a chapter of Phi Beta Kappa. **Visiting:** There are regularly scheduled orientations for prospective students, including a student-led campus tour and an informational focus session led by a member of our Admission staff. Prospective students may also arrange to sit in on classes, as well as meet with faculty or athletic coaches. To schedule a visit, contact the Office of Undergraduate Admission. **Campus Safety and Security:** Measures include 24-hour foot and vehicle patrol, emergency notification system, self-defense education, and security escort services. There are shuttle buses, emergency telephones, and lighted pathways/sidewalks. The campus patrol is a fully accredited police department.

REQUIREMENTS: The SAT or ACT is required. Students must submit a high school transcript. Students may submit SAT results, but they are not required unless a student is home-schooled. A recommendation from a high school counselor and up to 2 additional letters of recommendation are required. The student must have acquired 16 academic credits in secondary school, including 4 years of English, 3 years of math, and 2 years each of history, science, and foreign language. AP credits are accepted. Important factors in the admissions decision are advanced placement or honors courses, recommendations by school officials, and extracurricular activities record. To graduate, students must complete 127 semester hours, including courses during the first 2 years in English, science, math, history, the social sciences, health, and phys ed. Students must maintain at least a C (2.0) average in any major or minor they complete. The number of hours required for the major varies by department. A thesis is required for students in honors or dual B.A.-M.A. or B.S.-M.S. programs. **Procedure:** Freshmen are admitted in the fall. Entrance exams should be taken prior to applying. There are early decision, early admissions, and deferred admissions plans. Early decision applications should be filed by November 1; regular applications, by January 1 for fall entry. The fall 2017 application fee was $75. Notification of early decision is sent December 15; regular decision, April 1. 707 early decision candidates were accepted for the 2017-2018 class. 2150 applicants were on the 2017 waiting list; 61 were admitted. Applications are accepted on-line. **Transfer Students:** 70 transfer students enrolled in 2016-2017. Applicants must have taken the SAT or ACT and completed at least 1 year of college, with a GPA of 3.0. 64 of 127 credits required for the bachelor's degree must be completed at Emory. **International Students:** There are 1146 international students enrolled. They must take the TOEFL with a minimum score of 100 on the Internet-based version (iBT). They must also take the SAT or ACT.

ADMISSIONS: 25% of the 2017-2018 applicants were accepted. The SAT scores for the 2017-2018 freshman class were: Critical Reading-- 1% below 500, 10% between 500 and 599, 48% between 600 and 699, and 41% between 700 and 800. Math-- 5% between 500 and 599, 34% between 600 and 699, and 61% between 700 and 800. Writing-- 1% below 500, 7% between 500 and 599, 42% between 600 and 699, and 51% between 700 and 800. The ACT scores were 22% between 24 and 29, and 78% above 30. **Admissions Contact:** John Latting, Dean of Admissions. Email: *admission@emory.edu* Web: *www.emory.edu*

FINANCIAL AID: In 2017-2018, 50% of all full-time freshmen received some form of financial aid. 46% of all full-time freshmen received need-based aid. The average freshman award was $41,301. Need-based scholarships or need-based grants averaged $38,834; and need-based self-help aid (loans and jobs) averaged $5,324. The average financial indebtedness of the 2017 graduate was $29,217. Emory is a member of CSS. The CSS/

Profile is required. The FAFSA code is 001564. The priority date for freshman financial aid applications for fall entry is February 15.

FORT VALLEY STATE UNIVERSITY B-3

www.fvsu.edu

Fort Valley, GA 31030 **(478) 825-6307**

Fax: (478) 825-6169
Full-time: 1313 men, 1688 women
Part-time: 175 men, 245 women
Graduate: 64 men, 86 women
Year: semesters, summer session
Room & Board: $8508

SAT or ACT: required
Application Deadline: June 15

Email: admissions@fvsu.edu
Faculty: 153
Ph.D.s: 64%
Student/Faculty: 20 to 1
Tuition: $9480 ($18,954)
Freshman Class: 5343 applied, 2161 accepted, 960 enrolled
CEEB CODE: 5220
VERY COMPETITIVE

Fort Valley State University, founded in 1895, is a public land-grant member of the University System of Georgia. The university offers undergraduate programs in the arts and sciences, business, education, agriculture, engineering, and other vocational and technical fields. Graduate programs are offered in early childhood, middle grades education, mental health and rehabilitation counseling, and guidance counseling. The figures given in the above capsule and in this profile are approximate. There are 3 undergraduate schools and 1 graduate school. In addition to regional accreditation, Fort Valley has baccalaureate program accreditation with CAEP. The 1375-acre campus is in a rural area 30 miles southwest of Macon. Including any residence halls, there are 35 buildings.

STUDENT LIFE: 96% of undergraduates are from Georgia. Others are from 29 states, and 5 foreign countries. 92% are African American; 6% White; 1% Asian American; 1% Hispanic. **Female To Male Ratio:** 1.3:1. The average age of freshmen is 19; all undergraduates, 21. 27% do not continue beyond their first year; 39% remain to graduate. **Housing:** 1450 students can be accommodated in college housing, which includes dorms and on-campus apartments. On-campus housing is guaranteed for the freshman year only, is available on a first-come, and first-served basis. 62% of students live on campus. Alcohol is not permitted. All students may keep cars.

FACULTY/CLASSROOMS: 50% of faculty are male; 50% are female. No introductory courses are taught by graduate students. The average class size in a regular course is 25.

PROGRAMS OF STUDY: Fort Valley confers B.A., B.S., B.B.A. and B.S.W. degrees. Associate and master's degrees are also awarded. Bachelor's degrees are awarded in AGRICULTURE (agricultural economics, animal science, horticulture, and plant science), BIOLOGICAL SCIENCE (biology/biological science, nutrition, and zoology), BUSINESS (accounting, business administration and management, marketing/retailing/merchandising, and office supervision and management), COMMUNICATIONS AND THE ARTS (communications and English), COMPUTER AND PHYSICAL SCIENCE (chemistry, computer science, information sciences and systems, and mathematics), EDUCATION (agricultural education, early childhood education, home economics education, mathematics education, middle school education, physical education, and secondary education), ENGINEERING AND ENVIRONMENTAL DESIGN (agricultural engineering technology, commercial art, and electrical/electronics engineering technology), HEALTH PROFESSIONS (veterinary science), SOCIAL SCIENCE (child psychology/development, criminal justice, economics, political science/government, psychology, social work, and sociology).

ACTIVITIES: 5% of men belong to 4 national fraternities; 2% of women belong to 5 national sororities. There are 73 groups on campus, including band, cheerleading, choir, chorus, dance, drama, honors, international, jazz band, marching band, newspaper, opera, orchestra, political, radio and TV, religious, social service, and student government. Popular campus events include Black History month. **Sports:** There are 5 intercollegiate sports for men and 6 for women, and 3 intramural sports for men and 3 for women. Facilities include a stadium, a gym, baseball field, tennis courts, an indoor swimming pool, indoor and outdoor tracks, and shuffleboard courts. **Graduates:** From July 1, 2016 to June 30, 2017, 230 bachelor's degrees were awarded. The most popular majors were mathematics (43%), visual/performing arts (17%), and psychology (10%). In an average class, 13% graduate in 4 years or less, 33% graduate in 5 years or less, and 39% graduate in 6 years or less.

SERVICES: Counseling and information services are available, as is tutoring in most subjects. There is remedial math, reading, and writing. **Library/Resources:** The library contains 250,000 volumes, 172,000 microform items, and subscribes to 1,168 periodicals including electronic. Computerized library services include interlibrary loans and database searching. Special learning facilities include a radio station, TV station, experimental agricultural plots, animal research centers, and a greenhouse complex. **Physically Challenged Students:** All of the campus is accessible. Facilities include wheelchair ramps, elevators, special parking, specially equipped restrooms, and special housing. **Special:** Students may participate in cooperative work-study programs with local industries, cross-register for courses at Robins Residence Center, and study abroad. Fort Valley also offers a 3-2 dual degree program in chemistry, geosciences with University of Oklahoma, in engineering or other technical fields with Georgia Institute of Technology, and a 3-2 engineering degree with University of Nevada, Las Vegas. There are 5 national honor societies and a freshman honors program. **Visiting:** There are regularly scheduled orientations for prospective students, including an overview, an introduction of administration and faculty, and a tour. There are guides for informal visits and visitors may sit in on classes. To schedule a visit, contact the Office of Enrollment Management. **Campus Safety and Security:** Measures include 24-hour foot and vehicle patrol, and emergency telephones.

REQUIREMENTS: The SAT or ACT is required. Applicants must be graduates of an accredited secondary school or have earned a GED. The university requires at least 17 academic units of study, including 4 in English, 3 in social science, 3 each in math and science, and 2 of foreign language. A GPA of 2.7 is required. AP and CLEP credits are accepted. Students must complete a minimum of 120 credit hours, plus 5 additional hours to satisfy requirements for freshmen orientation and for military science or phys ed. General education requirements include courses in humanities, social science, math, science, and courses in the major. The bachelor's degree requires a minimum GPA of 2.0 and no grade below C in the major. **Procedure:** Freshmen are admitted to all sessions. There are early admissions, deferred admissions, and rolling admissions plans. Applications should be filed by June 15 for fall entry; November 1 for spring entry; and April 1 for summer entry. The fall 2017 application fee was $30. Applications are accepted on-line. **Transfer Students:** 135 transfer students enrolled in 2016-2017. In addition to meeting standard admission requirements, transfers must submit transcripts from all colleges previously attended. Transfer credit is accepted based on a 2.0 minimum GPA, and only courses with a C or better will be accepted. 45 of 125 credits required for the bachelor's degree must be completed at Fort Valley. **International Students:** There are 23 international students enrolled. They must take the TOEFL and the college's own test. They must also take the SAT or ACT.

ADMISSIONS: 40% of the 2017-2018 applicants were accepted. **Admissions Contact:** Calandra Wright, Director of Admissions. Email: *admissions@fvsu.edu* Web: *www.fvsu.edu*

FINANCIAL AID: In 2017-2018, 94% of all full-time freshmen received some form of financial aid. 8% of all full-time freshmen received need-based aid. The average freshman award was $2,300. Need-based scholarships or need-based grants averaged $2,300; need-based self-help aid (loans and jobs) averaged $2,425; and other non-need-based awards and non-need-based scholarships averaged $1,850. The FAFSA code is 001566. The deadline for filing freshman financial aid applications for fall entry is March 1.

GEORGIA COLLEGE & STATE UNIVERSITY C-3

www.gcsu.edu

Milledgeville, GA 31061 **(478) 445-1283**

Fax: (478) 445-1914
Full-time: 2026 men, 3416 women
Part-time: 234 men, 311 women
Graduate: 316 men, 649 women
Year: semesters, summer session
Room & Board: $12,538

SAT or ACT: required
Application Deadline: April 1

Email: admissions@gcsu.edu
Faculty: IIA, -$
Ph.D.s: n/av
Student/Faculty: n/av
Tuition: $9346 ($28,060)
Freshman Class: 4089 applied, 3230 accepted, 1443 enrolled
CEEB CODE: 5252
COMPETITIVE+

Georgia College and State University, founded in 1889, is the public liberal arts university of Georgia. There are 4 undergraduate schools and 1 graduate school. In addition to regional accreditation, GCSU has baccalaureate program accreditation with AACSB, NASM, CAEP, NMSA, AMTA, and AEE. The 680-acre campus is in a small town 30 miles from Macon. Including any residence halls, there are 94 buildings.

STUDENT LIFE: 98% of undergraduates are from Georgia. Others are from 24 states, 36 foreign countries, and Canada. 83% are White; 6% African American; 5% Hispanic; 3% two or more races; 2% Asian American; 1% Foreign. **Female To Male Ratio:** 1.7:1. The average age of freshmen is 18; all undergraduates, 20. 16% do not continue beyond their first year; 84% remain to graduate. **Housing:** 2237 students can be accommodated in college housing, which includes dorms and off-campus apartments. In addition, there are honors houses and special-interest houses. On-campus housing is guaranteed for the freshman year only, is available on a first-come, and first-served basis. 67% of students commute. All students may keep cars.

FACULTY/CLASSROOMS: No introductory courses are taught by graduate students.

PROGRAMS OF STUDY: GCSU confers B.A., B.S., B.B.A., B.M.E., B.M.T., and B.S.N. degrees. Master's and doctoral degrees are also awarded. Bachelor's degrees are awarded in BIOLOGICAL SCIENCE (biology/biological science), BUSINESS (accounting, business administration and management, management information systems, marketing and distribution, and recreation and leisure services), COMMUNICATIONS AND THE ARTS (art, English, journalism, music, speech/debate/rhetoric, and theatre arts), COMPUTER AND PHYSICAL SCIENCE (chemistry, computer science, mathematics, and physics), EDUCATION (athletic training, early childhood education, middle school education, music education, and special education), ENGINEERING AND ENVIRONMENTAL DESIGN (environmental science), HEALTH PROFESSIONS (community health work, exercise science, music therapy, and nursing), SOCIAL SCIENCE (criminal justice, economics, geography, history, liberal arts/general studies, philosophy, political science/government, psychology, sociology, and world cultural studies). Exercise science, nursing, and marketing have the largest enrollments.

ACTIVITIES: 22% of men belong to 10 national fraternities; 39% of women belong to 12 national sororities. There are 206 groups on campus, including art, band, cheerleading, choir, chorale, chorus, computers, dance, drama, environmental, ethnic, honors, international, jazz band, LGBT, literary magazine, musical theater, newspaper, photography, political, professional, radio and TV, religious, social, social service, student government, and symphony. Popular campus events include Week of Welcome, Progressive Dinner, and International Week. **Sports:** There are 5 intercollegiate sports for men and 6 for women, and 9 intramural sports for men and 9 for women. Facilities include the wellness and recreation center, and the mind-body-spirit facility that offers a variety of recreation, fitness and sports opportunities as well as Health Services and Counseling Services. **Graduates:** From July 1, 2016 to June 30, 2017, 1259 bachelor's degrees were awarded. The most popular majors were nursing (9%), management (8%), and marketing (8%). In an average class, 50% graduate in 4 years or less, 65% graduate in 5 years or less, and 66% graduate in 6 years or less.

SERVICES: Counseling and information services are available, as is tutoring in some subjects, such as math, biology, chemistry, physics, kinesiology, economics, management, finance, astronomy, computer science, french, geology, psychology, and Spanish. **Library/Resources:** The library contains 206,460 volumes, 22,608 microform items, and 7,200 audio/video tapes/CDs/DVDs, and subscribes to 56,543 periodicals including electronic. Computerized library services include interlibrary loans, database searching, Internet access, and Wi-Fi capability. Special learning facilities include an art gallery, natural history museum, planetarium, radio station, TV station, a campus theatre, and an art deco theatre. **Physically Challenged Students:** 90% of the campus is accessible. Facilities include wheelchair ramps, elevators, special parking, specially equipped restrooms, special class scheduling, lowered drinking fountains, lowered telephones, and special housing. **Special:** Georgia College has study-abroad agreements with institutions worldwide, a Washington semester, co-op programs, internships, work-study programs, dual majors, independent study, and student-designed majors. There is a 3-2 engineering degree program with the Georgia Institute of Technology. There are 3 national honor societies. **Visiting:** There are regularly scheduled orientations for prospective students, including receptions, tours, school meetings, information sessions, academic and cocurricular advising, and registration. There are guides for informal visits and visitors may sit in on classes. **Campus Safety and Security:** Measures include 24-hour foot and vehicle patrol, emergency notification system, self-defense education, and security escort services. There are shuttle buses, emergency telephones, lighted pathways/sidewalks, and controlled access to dorms/residences.

REQUIREMENTS: The SAT or ACT is required. The ACT Optional Writing test is also required. Applicants must be graduates of an accredited or recognized secondary school and must complete the Georgia college preparatory curriculum requirements, including 4 units each of English, math (with math I or algebra I being the minimum level for consideration), and science, (including 2 lab sciences), 3 units of social science, and 2 units of the same foreign language. AP and CLEP credits are accepted. Important factors in the admissions decision are advanced placement or honors courses, extracurricular activities record, and evidence of special talent. To graduate, students must complete at least 120 semester hours, of which 40 must be completed in residence. Complete 21 of the last 30 credit hours at the upper level. All B.A. candidates and some B.S. candidates must demonstrate a foreign language proficiency. All students must pass an exam on the history and Constitution of both the United States and Georgia, and a senior exit exam in the major. They must also earn a C or better in English 1101. **Procedure:** Freshmen are admitted to all sessions. Entrance exams should be taken last chance for regular admission: ACT in February and SAT in March. There are early admissions, deferred admissions, and rolling admissions plans. Application deadlines are open. The fall 2017 application fee was $40. Notification is sent on a rolling basis. 7 applicants were on the 2017 waiting list; 7 were admitted. Applications are accepted on-line. **Transfer Students:** 316 transfer students enrolled in 2016-2017. To transfer applicants must submit official transcripts from all colleges attended and be eligible to return to their previous institution. Those who have completed fewer than 30 semester hours must meet all freshman admissions requirements. 40 of 120 credits required for the bachelor's degree must be completed at GCSU. **International Students:** There are 49 international students enrolled. They must take the TOEFL with a minimum score of 523 on the paper-based TOEFL (PBT) or 69 on the Internet-based version (iBT). Students must take any one of these tests: the SAT Verbal score of 440, ACT English score of 17, or IELTS score of 6.0. To comply with NCAA regulations, international students who will compete in intercollegiate athletics must take either the SAT or ACT.

ADMISSIONS: 79% of the 2017-2018 applicants were accepted. The SAT scores for the 2017-2018 freshman class were: Math-- 8% below 500, 54% between 500 and 599, 34% between 600 and 699, and 4% between 700 and 800. Evidence-Based Reading/Writing-- 3% below 500, 44% between 500 and 599, 47% between 600 and 699, and 7% between 700 and 800. The ACT scores were 35% between 18 and 23, 58% between 24 and 29, and 7% above 30. **Admissions Contact:** Ramon Blakley, Director of Admissions. Email: *admissions@gcsu.edu* Web: *www.gcsu.edu*

FINANCIAL AID: In 2017-2018, 58% of all full-time freshmen received some form of financial aid. 39% of all full-time freshmen received need-based aid. The average freshman award was $11,211. Need-based scholarships or need-based grants averaged $4,394; need-based self-help aid (loans and jobs) averaged $4,233; non-need-based athletic scholarships averaged $3,234; and other non-need-based awards and non-need-based scholarships averaged $2,111. 14% of undergraduate students work part-time. The FAFSA code is 001602. The priority date for freshman financial aid applications for fall entry is March 1.

GEORGIA INSTITUTE OF TECHNOLOGY B-2

www.gatech.edu

Atlanta, GA 30332 **(404) 894-4154**

Fax: (404) 894-9511
Full-time: 9222 men, 5677 women
Part-time: 437 men, 237 women
Graduate: 10,637 men, 3162 women
Year: semesters, summer session
Room & Board: $11,492

SAT CR/M/W: 710/740/670 **ACT:** 32
Application Deadline: January 1

Email: admission@gatech.edu
Faculty: 1075; I, +$
Ph.D.s: 81%
Student/Faculty: 20 to 1
Tuition: $12,418 ($33,014)
Freshman Class: 31485 applied, 7353 accepted, 2859 enrolled
CEEB CODE: 5248
MOST COMPETITIVE

Georgia Institute of Technology, founded in 1885, is a public technological institution offering programs in architecture, management, policy, international affairs, engineering, computing, and science. There are 6 undergraduate schools and 6 graduate schools. In addition to regional accreditation, GIT has baccalaureate program accreditation with AACSB, ABET, ACCE, NASAD, ACS, and RICS. The 400-acre campus is in an urban area in Atlanta, GA. Including any residence halls, there are 244 buildings.

STUDENT LIFE: 60% of undergraduates are from Georgia. Others are from 50 states, 108 foreign countries, and Canada. 7% are African American; 7% Hispanic; 49% White; 4% two or more races; 3% race unknown; 20% Asian American; 10% Foreign. **Male To Female Ratio:** 2.2:1. The average age of freshmen is 18; all undergraduates, 20. 3% do not continue beyond their first year; 86% remain to graduate. **Housing:** 10005 students can be accommodated in college housing, which includes married student dorms and off-campus apartments. In addition, there are honors houses, language/international houses, special-interest houses, fraternity houses, sorority houses, and freshman experience floors. On-campus housing is guaranteed for the freshman year only, is available on a first-come, and first-served basis. 53% of students live on campus. All students may keep cars.

FACULTY/CLASSROOMS: 73% of faculty are male; 27% are female. No introductory courses are taught by graduate students. The average class size in an introductory lecture is 36; in a laboratory is 19; and in a regular course is 32.

PROGRAMS OF STUDY: GIT confers B.S. degrees. Master's and doctoral degrees are also awarded. Bachelor's degrees are awarded in BIOLOGICAL SCIENCE (biochemistry and biology/biological science), BUSINESS (business administration and management and international economics), COMMUNICATIONS AND THE ARTS (digital communications, digital media, and industrial design), COMPUTER AND PHYSICAL SCIENCE (applied mathematics, chemistry, computer science, earth science, mathematics, physics, and science and technology studies), EDUCATION (foreign languages education), ENGINEERING AND ENVIRONMENTAL DESIGN (aerospace engineering, architecture, bioengineering, biomedical engineering, chemical engineering, civil engineering, computer engineering, electrical/electronics engineering, environmental engineering, industrial engineering, materials engineering, materials science, materials science and engineering, mechanical engineering, and nuclear engineering), SOCIAL SCIENCE (economics, history of science, international relations, international studies, psychology, and public affairs). Engineering, computer science, and business administration are the strongest academically. Mechanical engineering, computer science, and industrial engineering have the largest enrollments.

ACTIVITIES: 25% of men belong to 40 national fraternities; 30% of women belong to 16 national sororities. There are 573 groups on campus, including athletic and outdoor clubs, cultural, art, band, cheerleading, chess, choir, chorale, chorus, computers, dance, debate, departmental, drama, drill team, environmental, ethnic, film, honors, international, jazz band, LGBT, literary magazine, marching band, musical theater, newspaper, orchestra, pep band, photography, political, professional, radio and TV, religious, social, social service, student government, symphony, and yearbook. Popular campus events include Team Buzz, Tech Beautification Day, and Dance Marathon. **Sports:** There are 10 intercollegiate sports for men and 9 for women, and 8 intramural sports for men and 4 for women. Facilities include a baseball stadium, football stadium, softball fields, basketball arena, a golf practice facility, football practice facility, a basketball practice center with a weight room, a center for swimming and diving, an eight-lane outdoor track, indoor tennis complex, outdoor tennis courts, outdoor turf field for flag football, recreational fields with outdoor sand volleyball, recreation center with multipurpose indoor courts, racquetball/wallyball/squash courts, a running track, an auxiliary court, a climbing wall, a fitness center with weights and cardio machines, and studios for aerobic fitness. **Graduates:** From July 1, 2016 to June 30, 2017, 3608 bachelor's degrees were awarded. The most popular majors were engineering (63%), business marketing (12%), and computer and information science (11%). In an average class, 41% graduate in 4 years or less, 80% graduate in 5 years or less, and 86% graduate in 6 years or less. Of the 2016 graduating class, 78% were employed within 6 months of graduation.

SERVICES: There is a reader service for the blind, and remedial math, reading, and writing. The Learning Assistance Program has drop-in tutoring sessions for calculus, chemistry, physics, accounting, linear algebra, and computer science. One-to-One Tutoring is offered in addition to success workshops, Peer Led Undergraduate Study (PLUS). We also offer walk-in tutoring and academic coaching. **Library/Resources:** The library contains 1.7 million volumes, 2.2 million microform items, and 40,565 audio/video tapes/CDs/DVDs, and subscribes to 27,533 periodicals including electronic. Computerized library services include interlibrary loans, database searching, Internet access, and Wi-Fi capability. Special learning facilities include an art gallery, radio station, TV station, G. Wayne Clough Undergraduate Learning Commons, Center for Academic Enrichment, Center for Academic Success, Center for the Enhancement of Teaching and Learning, Communication Center, and Center for Career Discovery and Development. **Physically Challenged Students:** 75% of the campus is accessible. Facilities include wheelchair ramps, elevators, special parking, specially equipped restrooms, special class scheduling, lowered drinking fountains, and special housing. **Special:** Extensive co-op programs, cross-registration with other Atlanta-area colleges, internships, and undergraduate research opportunities are available. Numerous study abroad opportunities available. An engineering transfer program is offered within the university system, and a liberal arts-engineering dual degree program serves area colleges and institutions nationwide. Students have access to multidisciplinary and certificate programs outside their major field of study. The College of Engineering offers the opportunity to transfer to Georgia Tech via the Dual Degree Engineering Program (DDEP) and the Regional Engineering Transfer Program (RETP). There are 13 national honor societies, a freshman honors program, and 11 departmental honors programs. **Visiting:** There are regularly scheduled orientations for prospective students. The session is conducted by a counselor from the Office of Undergraduate Admission who discusses the admission process, majors, opportunities outside of the classroom, campus activities, and student life. To schedule a visit, contact the Office of Undergraduate Admissions. **Campus Safety and Security:** Measures include 24-hour foot and vehicle patrol, emergency notification system, self-defense education, and security escort services. There are shuttle buses, emergency telephones, lighted pathways/sidewalks, controlled access to dorms/residences, mobile security patrol, video cameras, K-9 force, and bike and laptop registration.

REQUIREMENTS: The SAT or ACT is required. The ACT Optional Writing test is also required. Candidates for admission must have completed 4 units each of English, science, and math, 3 units of social studies, and 2 units each of lab sciences, and foreign language. An essay is required. AP credits are accepted. Important factors in the admissions decision are parents or siblings attended your school, evidence of special talent, personality/intangible qualities, and geographical diversity. All students must fulfill the core curriculum requirements and maintain a 2.0 GPA for their entire academic program. Core curriculum requirements include 12 hours of science, math, and technology; 12 hours of social sciences, 13 hours of essential skills courses (English composition, calculus, and computing), 6 hours of humanities, and 5 or more hours of electives depending on the major. Other course requirements include an ethics course and a wellness course. **Procedure:** Freshmen are admitted fall and summer. Entrance exams should be taken by the end of the junior year. There are early admissions and deferred admissions plans. Applications should be filed by January 1 for fall entry. The fall 2017 application fee was $75. Notifications are sent March 14. 2267 applicants were on the 2017 waiting list; 470 were admitted. Applications are accepted on-line. **Transfer Students:** 584 transfer students enrolled in 2016-2017. Transfer applicants must have completed a minimum of 30 credit hours of coursework, not including AP/IB/DE, and have a minimum 3.0 cumulative GPA, and have a combined GPA of 3.0 in math and science. All of the specifically required courses on the course requirements chart for the prospective major must be completed. Grades and academic standing must be satisfactory for the last term of enrollment at the prior college. 36 of 122 credits required for the bachelor's degree must be completed at Georgia Tech. **International Students:** There are 1434 international students enrolled. They must also take the SAT or ACT.

ADMISSIONS: 23% of the 2017-2018 applicants were accepted. The SAT scores for the 2017-2018 freshman class were: Critical Reading-- 1% below 500, 4% between 500 and 599, 39% between 600 and 699, and 57% between 700 and 800. Math-- 1% below 500, 3% between 500 and 599, 25% between 600 and 699, and 71% between 700 and 800. Writing-- 3% below 500, 19% between 500 and 599, 42% between 600 and 699, and 35% between 700 and 800. The ACT scores were 2% between 18 and 23, 15% between 24 and 29, and 83% above 30. **Admissions Contact:** Rick Clark, Director of Undergraduate Admissions. Email: *admission@gatech.edu* Web: *www.gatech.edu*

FINANCIAL AID: GIT is a member of CSS. The CSS/Profile and the college's own financial statement are required. The FAFSA code is 001569. Check with the school for current application deadlines.

GEORGIA SOUTHERN UNIVERSITY D-3
www.georgiasouthern.edu

Statesboro, GA 30458 (912) 478-5391

Fax: (912) 478-7240 Email: admissions@georgiasouthern.edu

Full-time: 7791 men, 7964 women	**Faculty:** 699; I, --$
Part-time: 1013 men, 991 women	**Ph.D.s:** 81%
Graduate: 873 men, 1786 women	**Student/Faculty:** 22 to 1
Year: semesters, summer session	**Tuition:** $6890 ($19,022)
Room & Board: $9650	**Freshman Class:** 9202 applied, 6284 accepted, 3508 enrolled
SAT EBR-W/M: 590/570 **ACT:** 23	**CEEB CODE:** 5253
Application Deadline: May 1	**VERY COMPETITIVE**

Georgia Southern University is the state's largest and most comprehensive center of higher education south of Atlanta. With 120-plus degree programs at the baccalaureate, master's and doctoral levels, Georgia Southern has been designated a Carnegie Doctoral-Research university and provides the classic residential campus experience and online learning options. Since 1906, the University's hallmark has been a culture of engagement that bridges theory with practice, extends the learning environment beyond the classroom, and promotes student growth and life success. Central to the University's mission is the faculty's dedication to excellence in teaching and the development of a fertile learning environment exemplified by a free exchange of ideas, high academic expectations, and individual responsibility for academic achievement. There are 7 undergraduate schools and 1 graduate school. In addition to regional accreditation, GSU has baccalaureate program accreditation with AACSB, ABET, NASAD, CAEP, NAEYC, IACS, APA, AAAHC, CACREP, NASP, CAATE, NCACE, CIDA, CCNE, ACEND, COAPRT, CEPH, NASM, NAST, and ACS. The 900-acre campus is in a small town 1 hour from Savannah, 2 hours from Florida, and about 3 hours from metropolitan Atlanta. Including any residence halls, there are 216 buildings.

STUDENT LIFE: 94% of undergraduates are from Georgia. Others are from 50 states, 74 foreign countries, and Canada. 86% are from public schools. 62% are White; 5% Hispanic; 24% African American; 2% Asian American; 2% Foreign; 2% two or more races; 1% race unknown. 98% claim no religious affiliation. **Female To Male Ratio:** 1.1:1. The average age of freshmen is 18; all undergraduates, 21. 20% do not continue beyond their first year; 50% remain to graduate. **Housing:** 4950 students can be accommodated in college housing, which includes dorms, on-campus apartments, and off-campus apartments. In addition, there are honors houses and special-interest houses. On-campus housing is guaranteed for the freshman year only, is available on a first-come, first-served basis, and is available on a lottery system for upperclassmen. 72% of students commute. All students may keep cars.

FACULTY/CLASSROOMS: 50% of faculty are male; 50% are female. 86% teach undergraduates, 66% do research, and 71% do both. Graduate students teach 6% of introductory courses. The average class size in an introductory lecture is 23; in a laboratory is 20; and in a regular course is 35.

PROGRAMS OF STUDY: GSU confers B.A., B.B.A., B.G.S., B.F.A, B.M., B.S., B.S.B., B.S.C.E., B.S.Chem., B.S.Cons., B.S.Ed., B.S.E.E., B.S.GraphCom., B.S.P.H., B.S.I.T., B.S.K., B.S.Mat., B.S.M.E., B.S.N., B.S.M.F.G.E., B.S.A.T., B.S.E.E, B.S.J.S, B.S.M.E, B.S.P., and B.S.P. degrees. Master's and doctoral degrees are also awarded. Bachelor's degrees are awarded in BIOLOGICAL SCIENCE (biology/biological science and nutrition), BUSINESS (accounting, finance, logistics, management science, marketing management, and sports management), COMMUNICATIONS AND THE ARTS (art, communications, English, graphic design, journalism, linguistics, multimedia, music, public relations, and writing), COMPUTER AND PHYSICAL SCIENCE (chemistry, chemistry education, computer science, geology, information science, and physics), EDUCATION (athletic training, early childhood education, health education, health and physical education, mathematics education, middle school education, music education, nursing education, recreation education, and special education), ENGINEERING AND ENVIRONMENTAL DESIGN (civil engineering, construction management, electrical/electronics engineering, manufacturing engineering, and mechanical engineering), HEALTH PROFESSIONS (exercise science), SOCIAL SCIENCE (anthropology, child care/child and family studies, economics, geography, history, international studies, philosophy, political science/government, and psychology). Sport management, computer science, applied economics, WebMAcc, and WebMBA are the strongest academically. Exercise science, biology, and mechanical engineering have the largest enrollments.

ACTIVITIES: 10% of men belong to 48 national fraternities; 15% of women belong to 12 national sororities. There are 280 groups on campus, including art, band, cheerleading, choir, chorale, chorus, communications, computers, dance, drama, environmental, ethnic, film, honors, international, jazz band, LGBT, literary magazine, marching band, musical theater, newspaper, opera, orchestra, pep band, political, professional, radio and TV, religious, social, social service, student government, and symphony. Popular campus events include Homecoming, Concerts, and Final Feast. **Sports:** There are 6 intercollegiate sports for men and 9 for women, and 23 intramural sports for men and 23 for women. Facilities include baseball, football, and softball stadiums, volleyball and basketball field house, natatorium, tennis courts, track/soccer stadium and golf practice facility, and a rifle shooting range. **Graduates:** From July 1, 2016 to June 30, 2017, 3228 bachelor's degrees were awarded. The most popular majors were business/marketing (21%), parks and recreation (9%), and liberal arts/general studies (6%). In an average class, 1% graduate in 3 years or less, 26% graduate in 4 years or less, 45% graduate in 5 years or less, and 50% graduate in 6 years or less.

SERVICES: Counseling and information services are available, as is tutoring in most subjects. There is a reader service for the blind, and remedial math and writing. **Library/Resources:** The library contains 667,972 volumes, 900,843 microform items, and 92,501 audio/video tapes/CDs/DVDs, and subscribes to 86,323 periodicals, including electronic. Computerized library services include interlibrary loans, database searching, Internet access, and Wi-Fi capability. Special learning facilities include an art gallery, natural history museum, planetarium, radio station, Bureau of Business Research and Economic Development, Center for Addiction Recovery, Center for Africana Studies, Karl E. Peace Center for Bio-statistics and Survey, Center for Education Leadership, Center for Entrepreneurial Learning and Leadership, Center for Forensic Studies in Accounting, Center for International Schooling, Center for International Studies, Center for Irish Studies, Center for Retail Studies, Center for Sustainability, Center for Wildlife Education, Center for Women's and Gender Studies, Child Development Center, Graduate Academic Services Center, Instructional Resources Center, Institute for Coastal Plain Science, Magnolia Coastlands AHEC, National Youth-At-Risk Center, Small Business Development Center, Student Success Center, Black Box Theatre, Performing Arts Center, and Garden of the Coastal Plain. **Physically Challenged Students:** 97% of the campus is accessible. Facilities include wheelchair ramps, elevators, special parking, specially equipped restrooms, special class scheduling, lowered drinking fountains, and special housing. **Special:** Co-op programs in: Accounting, finance, construction management, biology, geology, engineering technology (civil, electrical, and mechanical) information technology, industrial management, engineering (electrical, civil, and mechanical), and logistics. A number of academic degree programs require internships as part of the program requirements and offer academic credit for internship experiences. Non-academic internships are offered for all majors through the Office of Career Services. GSU offers a Washington Semester. The Accelerate degree program Dual Enrollment is a state-funded program for public and private high school students that provides dual enrollment tuition assistance in Georgia. The program offers the opportunity to earn dual credit, satisfying high school and college core curriculum requirements. Admissions requirements for Dual Enrollment are: Have earned an academic GPA of 3.0 as recalculated by the Office of Admissions; Submit SAT scores of at least 1010 (math and critical reading only) or ACT 21 composite; Gain permission from their high school guidance counselor and parents by completing the MOWR student participation agreement; Meet all other (non provisional) admissions requirements. Dual majors students may be granted a second baccalaureate degree if the following conditions are met: If the first degree is earned at GSU, a student may seek a second degree if it is different from the first degree, satisfy all major requirements, must complete the history and constitution requirements, take 32-34 additional credit hours at GSU, must earn at least 50% of the credits toward the major at GSU. The student have the option to work on two degrees at the same time.

There is a 3-2 engineering degree with University System of Georgia. The Regents Engineering Pathway Program (REPP) formerly the Regents Engineering Transfer Program – allows students at colleges and universities in the University System of Georgia to study for two years at their home institution, then transfer to Georgia Southern, Georgia Tech, Kennesaw State, Mercer University or the University of Georgia to complete their engineering degrees. Study abroad in: Argentina, Australia, Austria, Belgium, Bolivia, Botswana, Brazil, Bulgaria, Canada, Chile, China, Colombia, Costa Rica, Czech Republic, Denmark, Ecuador, England, Estonia, Fiji, Finland, France, Germany, Ghana, Greece, Honduras, Hungary, India, Indonesia, Ireland, Italy, Japan, Latvia, Lithuania, Malaysia, Malta, Mexico, Morocco, Netherlands, New Zealand, Nicaragua, Norway, Panama, Poland, Portugal, Romania, Russia, Scotland, Senegal, South Africa, South Korea, Spain, Sweden, Switzerland, Thailand, Turkey, United Arab Emirates, Uruguay, and Vietnam. Career Services assists students in relevant work experience through several different formats. Through our Experiential Education program, students can participate in job shadowing, nonacademic internships, and cooperative education assignments. The student's assignments vary based on their majors and interests. B.A. degrees include: Modern Languages, English, Writing and Linguistics, Biology, Philosophy, Chemistry, Geology, Physics, Anthropology, Economics, Geography, International Studies, Political Science, Theatre, Art, Music, and History. B.S. degrees include: Journalism, Multimedia Communication, Public Relations and Organizational Communications, Computer Science, Nutrition and Food Science, Child and Family Development, Fashion Merchandising and Apparel Design, Communication Studies, Mathematics, Recreation, Sport Management, Geology, Psychology, Geography, Political Science, Sociology, Interior Design, and International Trade. There are also Student Designed Majors. There are 17 national honor societies, a freshman honors program, and 32 departmental honors programs. **Visiting:** There are regularly scheduled orientations for prospective students. There are guides for informal visits and visitors may sit in on classes. To schedule a visit, contact Sean Cleary at (912) 478-5851. **Campus Safety and Security:** Measures include 24-hour foot and vehicle patrol, emergency notification system, self-defense education, and security escort services. There are shuttle buses, emergency telephones, lighted pathways/sidewalks, controlled access to dorms/residences, and panic button alarms in all residence hall rooms.

REQUIREMENTS: The SAT or ACT is required. Applicants must have a high school diploma or the equivalent is required. A minimum of 17 credits in college preparatory courses should include 4 each in English, science, and math, 3 in social studies, and 2 in foreign language. AP and CLEP credits are accepted. All students must complete a total of 126-135 semester credit hours, including at least 32-34 semester credit hours in the major, with a minimum GPA of 2.0. Students must complete specific courses in English, math, humanities, science, and social sciences, a healthful living class, two physical activity courses, orientation course and interdisciplinary studies class. **Procedure:** Freshmen are admitted fall, spring, and summer. Entrance exams should be taken during the junior year. There are deferred admissions and rolling admissions plans. Applications should be filed by May 1 for fall entry; December 1 for spring entry; and April 1 for summer entry. The fall 2017 application fee was $30. Notification is sent on a rolling basis. Applications are accepted on-line. **Transfer Students:** 1076 transfer students enrolled in 2016-2017. Applicants must have completed at least 30 semester credit hours of college courses with a minimum GPA of 2.0. Those with fewer than 30 hours must meet freshman requirements. Students transferring with an associate degree must have a minimum GPA of 2.0 in a school with a parallel curriculum. 30 of 126 credits required for the bachelor's degree must be completed at Georgia Southern. **International Students:** There are 285 international students enrolled. They must take the TOEFL with a minimum score of 69 on the Internet-based version (iBT). Students must take the IELTS. If the students native language is not English, they must submit TOEFL or SAT/ACT.

ADMISSIONS: 65% of the 2017-2018 applicants were accepted. The SAT scores for the 2017-2018 freshman class were: Math-- 3% below 500, 67% between 500 and 599, 28% between 600 and 699, and 2% between 700 and 800. Writing-- 48% below 500, 42% between 500 and 599, 9% between 600 and 699, and 1% between 700 and 800. Evidence-Based Reading/Writing-- 2% below 500, 51% between 500 and 599, 45% between 600 and 699, and 2% between 700 and 800. The ACT scores were 1% between 12 and 17, 53% between 18 and 23, 40% between 24 and 29, and 6% above 30. 39% of the current freshmen were in the top fifth of their class; 69% were in the top two fifths. **Admissions Contact:** Amy Smith, Director. Email: *admissions@georgiasouthern.edu* Web: *www.georgiasouthern.edu*

FINANCIAL AID: In 2017-2018, 91% of all full-time freshmen received some form of financial aid. 59% of all full-time freshmen received need-based aid. The average freshman award was $9,952. Need-based scholarships or need-based grants averaged $7,559 ($40,145 maximum); need-based self-help aid (loans and jobs) averaged $4,297 ($33,916 maximum); non-need-based athletic scholarships averaged $11,618 ($31,440 maximum); and other non-need-based awards and non-need-based scholarships averaged $1,652 ($8,215 maximum). The average financial indebtedness of the 2017 graduate was $28,098. GSU is a member of CSS. The FAFSA code is 001572. The priority date for freshman financial aid applications for fall entry is April 20.

GEORGIA SOUTHWESTERN STATE UNIVERSITY *(The complete profile is made available exclusively on our website, www.barronspac.com)*

GEORGIA STATE UNIVERSITY B-2

www.gsu.edu

Atlanta, GA 30302 **(404) 413-2000**

Fax: (404) 413-2002	**Email:** admissions@gsu.edu
Full-time: 8057 men, 11852 women	**Faculty:** 1157
Part-time: 2449 men, 3432 women	**Ph.D.s:** 84%
Graduate: 2725 men, 4333 women	**Student/Faculty:** 23 to 1
Year: semesters, summer session	**Tuition:** $10,858 ($29,432)
Room & Board: $14,392	**Freshman Class:** 18971 applied, 9898 accepted, 4105 enrolled
SAT EBR-W/M: 530/524 **ACT:** 23	**CEEB CODE:** 5251
Application Deadline: March 1	**COMPETITIVE**

Georgia State University, founded in 1913, and a part of the University System of Georgia. GSU is a public research university offering programs in liberal arts and sciences, business administration, education, law, health sciences, and public policy. There are 7 undergraduate schools and 7 graduate schools. In addition to regional accreditation, GSU has baccalaureate program accreditation with AACSB, ADA, APTA, CAHEA, CSWE, NASAD, NASM, NCATE, NLN, ABA, ACS, APA, CADE, CACREP, and CAPTE. The 109-acre campus is in an urban area in downtown Atlanta Including any residence halls, there are 64 buildings.

STUDENT LIFE: 96% of undergraduates are from Georgia. Others are from 49 states, 124 foreign countries, and Canada. 6% are two or more races; 42% African American; 23% White; 2% Foreign; 14% Asian American; 11% Hispanic; 1% race unknown. **Female To Male Ratio:** 1.5:1. The average age of freshmen is 19; all undergraduates, 22. 23% do not continue beyond their first year; 54% remain to graduate. **Housing:** 5567 students can be accommodated in college housing, which includes married student dorms and on-campus apartments. In addition, there are special-interest houses, fraternity houses, and sorority houses. On-campus housing is available on a first-come, first-served basis. 79% of students commute. All students may keep cars.

FACULTY/CLASSROOMS: 53% of faculty are male; 47% are female. No introductory courses are taught by graduate students.

PROGRAMS OF STUDY: GSU confers B.A., B.S., B.B.A., B.F.A., B.I.S., B.M., B.S.Ed., B.M.U., and B.S.W., A.A., A.S., and A.A.S. degrees. Associate, master's, and doctoral degrees are also awarded. Bachelor's degrees are awarded in BIOLOGICAL SCIENCE (biology/biological science and nutrition), BUSINESS (accounting, banking and finance, business administration and management, business economics, hospitality management services, insurance and risk management, management information systems, marketing/retailing/merchandising, office supervision and management, and real estate), COMMUNICATIONS AND THE ARTS (art, art history and appreciation, classics, English, film arts, fine arts, French, German, journalism, music, music business management, Spanish, speech/debate/rhetoric, and studio art), COMPUTER AND PHYSICAL SCIENCE (actuarial science, chemistry, computer science, geology, mathematics, physics, and statistics), EDUCATION (art education, early childhood education, and physical education), HEALTH PROFESSIONS (exercise science, nursing, and respiratory therapy), SOCIAL SCIENCE (African American studies, anthropology, criminal justice, economics, geography, history, interdisciplinary studies, philosophy, political science/government, psychology, religious education, social work, sociology, urban studies, and women's studies). Business is the strongest academically. Biological sciences, computer science, and psychology have the largest enrollments.

ACTIVITIES: 3% of men belong to 10 national fraternities; 4% of women belong to 11 national sororities. There are 456 groups on campus, including art, band, cheerleading, chess, chorale, chorus, computers, dance, debate, drama, environmental, ethnic, film, honors, including an outdoor club, international, jazz band, LGBT, literary magazine, musical theater, newspaper, opera, orchestra, pep band, photography, political, professional, radio and TV, religious, social, social service, and student government. Popular campus events include Welcome Week, Panther Prowl, and Homecoming. **Sports:** There are 6 intercollegiate sports for men and 9 for women, and 19 intramural sports for men and 19 for women. Facilities include a phys ed complex with gyms, a pool and diving well, a weight room, indoor and outdoor tennis courts, a climbing wall, jogging track, exercise rooms, dance studio, and racquetball courts. In addition, the Indian Creek recreation area has a pool, 3 tennis courts, picnic facilities, regular and sand volleyball, basketball courts, a rope challenge course, and athletic fields. **Graduates:** From July 1, 2016 to June 30, 2017, 3973 bachelor's degrees were awarded. The most popular majors were biological science (3%), psychology (3%), and finance (3%). In an average class, 23% graduate in 4 years or less, 47% graduate in 5 years or less, and 54% graduate in 6 years or less.

SERVICES: Counseling and information services are available, as is tutoring in most subjects. There is a reader service for the blind. Programs are available in effective studying, reading comprehension, speed reading, test and note taking, test anxiety, fear of public speaking, and organization and planning. **Library/Resources:** The library contains 2.0 million volumes, 2.3 million microform items, and 7.9 million audio/video tapes/CDs/DVDs, and subscribes to 11,156 periodicals including electronic. Computerized library services include interlibrary loans, database searching, Internet access, and Wi-Fi capability. Special learning facilities include an art gallery, radio station, TV station, a digital arts lab, an observatory, a instructional technology center, and distance learning classrooms. **Physically Challenged Students:** All of the campus is accessible. Facilities include wheelchair ramps, elevators, special parking, specially equipped restrooms, special class scheduling, lowered drinking fountains, and lowered telephones. **Special:** There is cross-registration with the Atlanta Regional Consortium for Higher Education (ARCHE). Internships with numerous employers and government agencies can be arranged. Study abroad is available in various countries. Work-study, an accelerated degree program in nursing, and dual majors are available. There are 8 national honor societies and a freshman honors program. **Visiting:** There are regularly scheduled orientations for prospective students, 45 minute informations session followed by a 90 minute campus Atlanta tour. There are guides for informal visits and visitors may sit in on classes. To schedule a visit, contact the Welcome Center at (404) 651-3900. **Campus Safety and Security:** Measures include 24-hour foot and vehicle patrol, an emergency notification system, self-defense education, and security escort services. There are shuttle buses, emergency telephones, lighted pathways/sidewalks, controlled access to dorms/residences, including a bicycle patrol.

REQUIREMENTS: The SAT or ACT is required. The ACT Optional Writing test is also required. A high school diploma is required. A total of 17 academic units is required, 4 units each in English, mathematics, and science (with 2 units of lab), 3 units in social studies, and 2 units in foreign language. A GPA of 2.8 is required. AP and CLEP credits are accepted. Students must complete core curriculum requirements, including courses in written communication, mathematics, institutional foundations, humanities and fine arts, natural and computational sciences, social science, and lower division major requirements. A minimum of 120 hours must be completed for graduation. **Procedure:** Freshmen are admitted in the fall, spring, and summer. There are early admissions and deferred admissions plans. Applications should be filed by March 1 for fall entry; December 1 for spring entry; and April 1 for summer entry. The fall 2017 application fee was $60. Notifications are sent April 15. Applications are accepted online. **Transfer Students:** 1586 transfer students enrolled in 2016-2017. Transfer applicants must submit official transcripts of all college-level work, have a minimum GPA of 2.5, have earned 30 semester hours, and be in good academic standing. Those with fewer than 30 semester hours earned must meet freshman requirements. 39 of 120 credits required for the bachelor's degree must be completed at GSU. **International Students:** There are 543 international students enrolled. They must take the TOEFL with a minimum score of 550 on the paper-based TOEFL (PBT) or 80 on the Internet-based version (iBT). They must also take the SAT or ACT.

ADMISSIONS: 52% of the 2017-2018 applicants were accepted. The SAT scores for the 2017-2018 freshman class were: Math-- 34% below 500, 44% between 500 and 599, 20% between 600 and 699, and 3% between 700 and 800. Evidence-Based Reading/Writing-- 24% below 500, 58% between 500 and 599, 15% between 600 and 699, and 3% between 700 and 800. The ACT scores were 5% between 12 and 17, 51% between 18 and 23, 36% between 24 and 29, and 8% above 30. **Admissions Contact:** Scott Burke, Assistant VP for Undergraduates. Email: *admissions@gsu.edu* Web: *www.gsu.edu*

FINANCIAL AID: In 2017-2018, 81% of all full-time freshmen received some form of financial aid. 54% of all full-time freshmen received need-based aid. The average freshman award was $12,541. Need-based scholarships or need-based grants averaged $5,276; and need-based self-help aid (loans and jobs) averaged $3,574. The deadline for filing freshman financial aid applications for fall entry is April 1.

KENNESAW STATE UNIVERSITY — B-2

www.kennesaw.edu

Kennesaw, GA 30144 — **(770) 423-6300**

Fax: (470) 578-9169 — **Email:** ksuadmit@kennesaw.edu

Full-time: 12,869 men, 12,000 women	**Faculty:** 1151; IIA, -$
Part-time: 4425 men, 3651 women	**Ph.D.s:** 78%
Graduate: 1183 men, 1718 women	**Student/Faculty:** 20 to 1
Year: semesters, summer session	**Tuition:** $7432 ($21,158)
Room & Board: $11,467	**Freshman Class:** 13,998 applied, 8487 accepted, 5238 enrolled
SAT EBR-W/M: 585/570 **ACT:** 23	**CEEB CODE:** 5359
Application Deadline: April 1	**VERY COMPETITIVE**

A leader in innovative teaching and learning, Kennesaw State University offers more than 150 undergraduate, graduate and doctoral degrees. There are 13 colleges on two metro Atlanta campuses, Kennesaw State is a member of the University System of Georgia and the third-largest university in the state. The university's vibrant campus culture, diverse population, strong global ties and entrepreneurial spirit. A Carnegie-designated doctoral institution, it is one of the 50 largest public institutions in the country. There are 12 undergraduate schools and 10 graduate schools. In addition to regional accreditation, KSU has baccalaureate program accreditation with AACSB, ABET, ACCE, CSWE, NAAB, NASAD, NASM, CAEP, CCNE, National Schools of Theatre, and NAACLS. The 602-acre campus is in a suburban area Kennesaw State University has three instructional sites located in Kennesaw GA, Marietta GA, and Paulding County GA. Including any residence halls, there are 154 buildings.

STUDENT LIFE: 88% of undergraduates are from Georgia. Others are from 54 states, 135 foreign countries, and Canada. 9% are Hispanic; 56% White; 5% Asian American; 5% two or more races; 21% African American; 2% Foreign; 2% race unknown. **Male To Female Ratio:** 1.1:1. The average age of freshmen is 18; all undergraduates, 23. 22% do not continue beyond their first year; 42% remain to graduate. **Housing:** 5213 students can be accommodated in college housing, which includes on-campus apartments. In addition, there are honors houses, language/international houses, special-interest houses, and theme communities. On-campus housing is available on a first-come and first-served basis. 85% of students commute. Alcohol is not permitted. All students may keep cars.

FACULTY/CLASSROOMS: 48% of faculty are male; 52% are female. No introductory courses are taught by graduate students. The average class size in an introductory lecture is 36; in a laboratory is 23; and in a regular course is 36.

PROGRAMS OF STUDY: KSU confers B.A., B.A.R.C.H., B.A.T., B.S., B.B.A., B.F.A., B.M., B.S.N., B.A.S., B.S.C.E., B.S.C.G.D.D., B.S.C.V.E., B.S.E.E., B.S.E.S., B.S.I.T., B.S.M.E., B.S.S.E.N.G., and B.S.S.W.E. degrees. Master's and doctoral degrees are also awarded. Bachelor's degrees are awarded in BIOLOGICAL SCIENCE (biochemistry, biology/biological science, and biotechnology), BUSINESS (accounting, entrepreneurial studies, finance, information & communication technology, integrative studies, international business management, management science, marketing/retailing/merchandising, and sports management), COMMUNICATIONS AND THE ARTS (apparel design, art history, art, communications, dance, English, journalism - news & information, media arts, modern language, music, music performance, public relations, technical communication, telecommunications engineering technology, and theatre arts), COMPUTER AND PHYSICAL SCIENCE (chemistry, computer game design/development, computer science, computer security and information assurance, cyber intelligence/security studies, digital animation & game design, information sciences and systems, mathematics, physics, and software engineering), EDUCATION (art education, Asian studies, childhood education, early childhood education, English education, health education, history education, mathematics education, middle school education, and music education), ENGINEERING AND ENVIRONMENTAL DESIGN (civil engineering, computer engineering, construction engineering, construction management, electrical/electronics engineering, electrical/electronics engineering technology, environmental engineering, environmental science, industrial engineering technology, mechanical engineering, mechanical engineering technology, mechatronics engineering, survey and mapping technology, and systems engineering), HEALTH PROFESSIONS (exercise science, nursing, and public health), SOCIAL SCIENCE (African studies, anthropology, architectural studies, criminal justice, culinary arts, economics, geography, geography information science, history, human services, international studies, philosophy, political science/government, psychology, and sociology). Nursing, biology, and psychology have the largest enrollments.

ACTIVITIES: 5% of men belong to 19 national fraternities; 10% of women belong to 12 national sororities. There are 322 groups on campus, including art, band, cheerleading, chess, choir, chorale, chorus, communications, computers, dance, drama, environmental, ethnic, honors, international, jazz band, LGBT, literary magazine, marching band, musical theater, newspaper, opera, orchestra, pep band, political, professional, radio and TV, religious, social, social service, student government, and symphony. Popular campus events include KSU Day, Week of Welcome Comedian, Week of Welcome Yard Show, Homecoming Lip Sync, KSU LIVE (Homecoming Concert), Pumpkin Launch, Kennesaw Pride Alliance Annual Drag show, International Student Association International Bazaar, and Year of Program. **Sports:** There are 7 intercollegiate sports for men and 9 for women, and 17 intramural sports for men and 17 for women. Facilities include the athletic complex for softball and baseball, a stadium for football, soccer, and lacrosse, indoor golf, indoor basketball and volleyball, outdoor track and field, athletics rehabilitation center, tennis courts, a baseball stadium, sports performance facility, and golf. **Graduates:** From July 1, 2016 to June 30, 2017, 4687 bachelor's degrees were awarded. The most popular majors were management (20%), computer and information sciences (9%), and communication (8%). In an average class, 14% graduate in 4 years or less, 33% graduate in 5 years or less, and 42% graduate in 6 years or less.

SERVICES: Counseling and information services are available, as is tutoring in some subjects, such as math, foreign languages, and English. There is also academic coaching for writing and research skills. There is a reader service for the blind, and remedial math, reading, and writing. **Library/Resources:** The library contains 471,440 volumes, 500,000 microform items, and 5,441 audio/video tapes/CDs/DVDs, and subscribes to 114,022 periodicals including electronic. Computerized library services include interlibrary loans, database searching, Internet access, and Wi-Fi capability. Special learning facilities include an art gallery, radio station, Museum of History and Holocaust Education, The Bentley Rare Book Gallery, Zuckerman Museum of Art, The 3D Center, Alternative Energy Innovation Center, Center for Advanced Materials Research and Education, Center for African and African Diaspora Studies, Center for Information Security Education, Center for Machine Vision and Security Research, Center for Professional Selling, Center for Student Leadership, Entrepreneurship Center, ESL Center, Georgia Pavement and Traffic Research Center, Intensive English Program, Internal Audit Center, Mobile Application Development Center, Visualization and Simulation Research Center, and a Writing Center. **Physically Challenged Students:** All of the campus is accessible. Facilities include wheelchair ramps, elevators, special parking, specially equipped restrooms, special class scheduling, lowered drinking fountains, and lowered telephones. **Special:** Students may register for courses with any of the colleges in the University System of Georgia. Students can participate in Study Abroad, Directed Study, Cooperative Study, Internship, Directed Study, Federal Work-Study, Dual Majors, Online Programs, and Non-degree Programs. Additionally, the Division of Global Affairs offers more than 60 international studies programs, offering more than 100 courses and organizing more than 130 distinct international educational and scholarly events. The Honors College houses the University Honors Program, including the President's Emerging Global Scholars cohort and the Great Books cohort. In addition, it is home to the Dual Enrollment Honors Program, which allows academically talented high school students to take classes at KSU. There are 25 national honor societies and a freshman honors program. **Visiting:** There are regularly scheduled orientations for prospective students. There are guides for informal visits. To schedule a visit, contact the Office of Undergraduate Admissions. **Campus Safety and Security:** Measures include 24-hour foot and vehicle patrol, emergency notification system, self-defense education, and security escort services. There are shuttle buses, emergency telephones, lighted pathways/sidewalks, full-service police department, siren system with messages, pop-up computer notification on the KSU network, telephone emergency message system, email emergency notification, security badges, and intrusion alarms and video surveillance.

REQUIREMENTS: Applications for admission and all required credentials such as transcripts and test scores. The Required High School Curriculum (RHSC) is a key factor considered in freshman admissions decisions. Completion of the University System of Georgia's RHSC requirements at a regionally accredited or USG recognized high school is expected of most successful traditional freshman applicants. The Required Course Emphasis is 4 years each of English, and mathematics, 3 years each of science and social science, and 2 years of foreign language. Completion of the 17 required RHSC units. High School academic GPA of at least a 2.5. All minimum SAT or ACT scores as follow: SAT I Critical Reading and Math Combined-950 (1000 for the Architecture Program), SAT I Critical Reading-No lower than 450, SAT I Math- No lower than 450 or, SAT Taken March 2016 or Later: Redesigned SAT Total Score (on 1600 scale) - 1030 (1080 for the Architecture Program); Redesigned Reading Test Score - No lower than 25; Redesigned Math Test Score - No lower than 490 or ACT-Composite Score-20 (21 for the Architecture Program), ACT-English- No lower than 18. A GPA of 2.5 is required. AP and CLEP credits are accepted. Check with the school for additional requirements. **Procedure:** Freshmen are admitted fall, spring, and summer. Entrance exams should be taken before June 1. There is a rolling admissions plan. Early decision applications should be filed by October 28; regular applications, by May 5 for fall entry; November 4 for spring entry; and March 31 for summer entry. The fall 2017 application fee was $40. Applications are accepted on-line. **Transfer Students:** 2786 transfer students enrolled in 2016-2017. Transfer students must make arrangements with each college previously attended, whether credit was completed or not, to have a complete official transcript forwarded to the Office of Undergraduate Admissions. Transfer students must have completed 30 semester hours of transferable credit with a 2.0 cumulative GPA or above and be in good academic standing at their most recent college. Check with the school for additional transfer requirements. 30 of 123 credits required for the bachelor's degree must be completed at Kennesaw State or KSU. **International Students:** There are 461 international students enrolled. They must take the TOEFL with a minimum score of 550 on the paper-based TOEFL (PBT) or 79 on the Internet-based version (iBT), the IELTS test score of 6.5. They must also take the SAT or ACT, scoring ACT-Composite Score, 20 (21 for Architect Program). SAT I Critical Reading and Math Combined, 950 (1000 for the Architecture Program).

ADMISSIONS: 61% of the 2017-2018 applicants were accepted. The SAT scores for the 2017-2018 freshman class were: Math-- 4% below 500, 63% between 500 and 599, 29% between 600 and 699, and 4% between 700 and 800. Evidence-Based Reading/Writing-- 3% below 500, 54% between 500 and 599, 39% between 600 and 699, and 4% between 700 and 800. The ACT scores were 2% between 12 and 17, 53% between 18 and 23, 38% between 24 and 29, and 7% above 30. **Admissions Contact:** Sam Mahra, Director of Admissions. Email: *ksuadmit@kennesaw.edu* Web: *www.kennesaw.edu*

FINANCIAL AID: Kennesaw State University is a member of CSS. Check with the school for current application deadlines.

LAGRANGE COLLEGE — A-3

www.lagrange.edu

LaGrange, GA 30240	**(706) 880-8005** **(800) 593-2885**
Fax: (706) 880-8010	**Email: admissions@lagrange.edu**
Full-time: 440 men, 447 women	**Faculty:** 73
Part-time: 15 men, 34 women	**Ph.D.s:** 79%
Graduate: 35 men, 77 women	**Student/Faculty:** 12 to 1
Year: 4-1-4, summer session	**Tuition:** $29,480
Room & Board: $11,830	**Freshman Class:** 1548 applied, 879 accepted, 274 enrolled
SAT CR/M: 557/538 **ACT:** 22	**CEEB CODE:** 5362
Application Deadline: n/av	**COMPETITIVE**

LaGrange College, founded in 1831, is a private liberal arts institution affiliated with the United Methodist Church. Major undergraduate programs include business, visual and performing arts, education, biology, psychology, and exercise science. The figures given in the above capsule and in this profile are approximate. There is 1 undergraduate school and 1 graduate school. In addition to regional accreditation, LaGrange College has baccalaureate program accreditation with ACBSP, NLN, and GPSC. The 120-acre campus is in a small town 70 miles southwest of Atlanta. Including any residence halls, there are 27 buildings.

STUDENT LIFE: 84% of undergraduates are from Georgia. Others are from 18 states, and 7 foreign countries. 83% are from public schools. 73% are White; 3% two or more races; 22% African American; 1% Asian American; 1% Hispanic; 1% Foreign. 73% are Protestant; 19% Unknown Religious affiliation. **Female To Male Ratio:** 1.1:1. The average age of freshmen is 18; all undergraduates, 21. 35% do not continue beyond their first year; 41% remain to graduate. **Housing:** 662 students can be accommodated in college housing, which includes married student dorms and on-campus apartments. In addition, there are special-interest houses, fraternity houses, and sorority houses. On-campus housing is guaranteed for all 4 years. 59% of students live on campus. Alcohol is not permitted. All students may keep cars.

FACULTY/CLASSROOMS: 49% of faculty are male; 51% are female. 97% teach undergraduates. No introductory courses are taught by graduate students. The average class size in an introductory lecture is 19 and in a laboratory is 19.

PROGRAMS OF STUDY: LaGrange confers B.A, B.S., B.S.N., B.B.A., and B.M. degrees. Master's degrees are also awarded. Bachelor's degrees are awarded in BIOLOGICAL SCIENCE (biochemistry and biology/biological science), BUSINESS (accounting and business administration and management), COMMUNICATIONS AND THE ARTS (art, English, music, Spanish, and theatre arts), COMPUTER AND PHYSICAL SCIENCE (chemistry, computer science, and mathematics), EDUCATION (early childhood education and education), HEALTH PROFESSIONS (exercise science and nursing), SOCIAL SCIENCE (history, interdisciplinary studies, political science/government, psychology, religion, and sociology). Nursing, business, and exercise science have the largest enrollments.

ACTIVITIES: 29% of men belong to 3 national fraternities; 40% of women belong to 3 national sororities. There are 25 groups on campus, including art, cheerleading, choir, chorale, chorus, drama, environmental, ethnic, honors, international, LGBT, literary magazine, marching band, musical theater, newspaper, orchestra, pep band, political, professional, religious, social, social service, and student government. Popular campus events include Spirit and Traditions Kickoff, Callaway Gardens Beach Bash, Hypnotist, Late Night Study Break Breakfasts, Midnight Madness, Food Trucks, and Vegas on the Hill. **Sports:** There are 8 intercollegiate sports for men and 8 for women, and 10 intramural sports for men and 10 for women. Facilities include a fitness center, indoor and outdoor pools, gyms, tennis courts, softball, baseball stadium, soccer fields, a football practice field, and a football stadium. **Graduates:** From July 1, 2016 to June 30, 2017, 165 bachelor's degrees were awarded. The most popular majors were nursing (16%), business (14%), and exercise science (13%). In an average class, 36% graduate in 4 years or less, 41% graduate in 5 years or less, and 41% graduate in 6 years or less. Of the 2016 graduating class, 34% were enrolled in graduate school within 6 months of graduation, and 57% were employed.

SERVICES: Counseling and information services are available, as is tutoring in most subjects, such as French, Religion, Spanish, chemistry, nursing, political science, American experience, psychology, art history, statistics, problem solving, biology, economics, and history. There is remedial math, reading, and writing. **Library/Resources:** The library contains 493,449 volumes, 268,299 microform items, and 34,148 audio/video tapes/CDs/DVDs, and subscribes to 112 periodicals including electronic. Computerized library services include interlibrary loans, database searching, Internet access, and Wi-Fi capability. Special learning facilities include an art gallery, Lab Science building, 2 music technology labs, an exercise science lab, a performing arts theater, and auditorium. **Physically Challenged Students:** 85% of the campus is accessible. Facilities include wheelchair ramps, elevators, special parking, specially equipped restrooms, special class scheduling, lowered drinking fountains, and special housing. **Special:** Students may participate in an international study tour progam currently offered through the Interim Program in January. A 3-2 engineering degree is offered with Georgia Institute of Technology and Auburn University. A self-designed B.A. in Interdisciplinary Studies is also available to qualifying students. Internships and work-study programs are offered in numerous disciplines. The CHIP program allows students to work and study in Washington, D.C. Cross-registration relationships have been established with postsecondary institutions in Japan. There are 13 national honor societies. **Visiting:** There are regularly scheduled orientations for prospective students. Preview Day consists of a Welcome and Introduction to the college, guided campus tour, and showcase sessions (including major departments and financial aid). There are guides for informal visits, visitors may sit in on classes, and stay overnight. To schedule a visit, contact Holly Phillips at (760) 880-8005. **Campus Safety and Security:** Measures include 24-hour foot and vehicle patrol, emergency notification system, and security escort services. There are emergency telephones, lighted pathways/sidewalks, and controlled access to dorms/residences.

REQUIREMENTS: The SAT or ACT is required. Applicants should be graduates of accredited secondary schools or have a GED certificate. They should have completed a minimum of 4 units of English and math, 3 of social studies, 3 of science (2 with labs), and 2 units of a foreign language is recommended. A GPA of 2.5 is required. AP and CLEP credits are accepted. Important factors in the admissions decision are leadership record, evidence of special talent, personality/intangible qualities, recommendations by alumni, recommendations by school officials, parents or siblings attended your school, and extracurricular activities record. To graduate, all students must complete 120 semester hours. The core curriculum includes First-Year Cornerstone, rhetoric and compostion, math, world languages and culture, laboratory science, problem solving, computer applications, humanities, fine arts, religion, and the American experience. All students must have a minimum GPA of 2.0. **Procedure:** Freshmen are admitted to all sessions. There are early admissions, deferred admissions, and rolling admissions plans. Application deadlines are open. Applications are accepted on-line. **Transfer Students:** 82 transfer students enrolled in 2016-2017. Transfer students must have a minimum 2.0 College GPA and be in good standing with the previous college. Transfer students must also have a minimum high school GPA of 3.0 if less than 30 hours of college credit is transferred. 39 of 120 credits required for the bachelor's degree must be completed at LaGrange. **International Students:** There are 7 international students enrolled. They must take the TOEFL with a minimum score of 500 on the paper-based TOEFL (PBT) or 61 on the Internet-based version (iBT). They must also take the SAT or ACT, scoring 450.

ADMISSIONS: 57% of the 2017-2018 applicants were accepted. The SAT scores for the 2017-2018 freshman class were: Critical Reading-- 14% below 500, 60% between 500 and 599, 23% between 600 and 699, and 3% between 700 and 800. Math-- 24% below 500, 55% between 500 and 599, 16% between 600 and 699, and 2% between 700 and 800. The ACT scores were 1% between 12 and 17, 70% between 18 and 23, 25% between 24 and 29, and 4% above 30. 31% of the current freshmen were in the top fifth of their class; 57% were in the top two fifths. 2 freshmen graduated first in their class. **Admissions Contact:** Holly Phillips, Admissions Services Coordinator. Email: *admissions@lagrange.edu* Web: *www.lagrange.edu*

FINANCIAL AID: In 2017-2018, 99% of all full-time freshmen received some form of financial aid. 85% of all full-time freshmen received need-based aid. The average freshman award was $31,234. Need-based scholarships or need-based grants averaged $5,282 ($21,315 maximum); need-based self-help aid (loans and jobs) averaged $4,478 ($7,950 maximum); other non-need-based awards and non-need-based scholarships averaged $13,833 ($38,700 maximum); and $4,662 from other forms of aid. 38% of undergraduate students work part-time. The average financial indebtedness of the 2017 graduate was $37,318. The college's own financial statement is required. The FAFSA code is 001578. The priority date for freshman financial aid applications for fall entry is March 1.

MERCER UNIVERSITY — C-3

www.mercer.edu

Macon, GA 31207	**(478) 301-2650** **(800) 840-8577**
Fax: (478) 301-2828	**Email: admissions@mercer.edu**
Full-time: 1258 men, 1214 women	**Faculty:** IIA, -$
Part-time: 35 men, 31 women	**Ph.D.s:** 94%
Graduate: 1410 men, 2522 women	**Student/Faculty:** 12 to 1
Year: semesters, summer session	**Tuition:** $34,450
Room & Board: $10,898	**Freshman Class:** 3864 applied, 2666 accepted, 727 enrolled
SAT CR/M/W: 580/590/560 **ACT:** 26	**CEEB CODE:** 5025
Application Deadline: April 1	**VERY COMPETITIVE**

Mercer University, founded in 1833, is a private institution of higher learning that seeks to achieve excellence and scholarly discipline in the fields of liberal learning and professional knowledge. The university offers degree programs in liberal arts, music, business and economics, education, engineering, nursing and professional studies. Mercer also offers a Great Books program as an alternative to the traditional core curriculum. The figures given in the above capsule and in this profile are approximate. There are 5 undergraduate schools and 11 graduate schools. In addition to regional accreditation, Mercer has baccalaureate program accreditation with AACSB, ABET, NASM, CAEP, ACS, CCNE, and NCAA. The 130-acre campus is in a suburban area 85 miles south of Atlanta.

STUDENT LIFE: 83% of undergraduates are from Georgia. Others are from 37 states, 42 foreign countries, and Canada. 7% are Asian American; 59% White; 4% Hispanic; 4% Foreign; 3% two or more races; 3% race unknown; 19% African American. 50% are Protestant; 23% claim no religious affiliation; 11% Catholic. **Female To Male Ratio:** 1.4:1. The average age of freshmen is 18; all undergraduates, 20. 18% do not continue beyond their first year; 61% remain to graduate. **Housing:** 1647 students can be accommodated in college housing, which includes married student dorms, on-campus apartments, and off-campus apartments. In addition, there are special-interest houses and fraternity houses. On-campus housing is available on a first-come, first-served basis, and is available on a lottery system for upperclassmen. 65% of students live on campus. Alcohol is not permitted. All students may keep cars.

FACULTY/CLASSROOMS: 50% of faculty are male; 50% are female. No introductory courses are taught by graduate students. The average class size in a laboratory is 20 and in a regular course is 20.

PROGRAMS OF STUDY: Mercer confers B.A., B.S., B.B.A., B.M., B.M.E., B.S.E., B.S.ED., B.S.M. and B.S.N. degrees. Master's and doctoral degrees are also awarded. Bachelor's degrees are awarded in AGRICULTURE (environmental studies), BIOLOGICAL SCIENCE (biochemistry, biology/biological science, and environmental biology), BUSINESS (accounting, business administration and management, finance, international business management, and marketing management), COMMUNICATIONS AND THE ARTS (art, communications, communication rhetoric/communication, creative writing, dramatic arts, English literature, French, German, journalism, Latin, media arts, music, Spanish, and technical communication), COMPUTER AND PHYSICAL SCIENCE (chemistry, computer science, earth science, information sciences and systems, mathematics, natural sciences, and physics), EDUCATION (early childhood education, education, elementary education, music education, secondary education, and special education), ENGINEERING AND ENVIRONMENTAL DESIGN (computational sciences, engineering, and industrial administration/management), HEALTH PROFESSIONS (predentistry, premedicine, and prepharmacy), SOCIAL SCIENCE (African studies, anthropology, area studies, Christian studies, criminal justice, economics, gender studies, history, philosophy, political science/government, prelaw, psychology, religion, social science, sociology, and women's studies). Engineering, business, and biology have the largest enrollments.

ACTIVITIES: 22% of men belong to 8 national fraternities; 24% of women belong to 7 national sororities. There are 115 groups on campus, including bagpipe, band, cheerleading, choir, chorale, chorus, computers, dance, debate, drama, environmental, ethnic, film, honors, international, jazz band, LGBT, literary magazine, marching band, musical theater, newspaper, opera, orchestra, pep band, photography, political, professional, radio and TV, religious, social, social service, student government, and symphony. Popular campus events include Bearstock (outdoor concert), Pilgrimage to Penfield, Homecoming, and Mercer Madness. **Sports:** There are 8 intercollegiate sports for men and 10 for women, and 10 intramural sports for men and 10 for women. Facilities include gyms, playing fields, a student center, swimming pool, lighted intramural complex, tennis, volleyball, and racquetball courts. **Graduates:** From July 1, 2016 to June 30, 2017, 446 bachelor's degrees were awarded. The most popular majors were business (18%), biology (12%), and engineering (10%). In an average class, 45% graduate in 4 years or less, 59% graduate in 5 years or less, and 61% graduate in 6 years or less.

SERVICES: Counseling and information services are available, as is tutoring in most subjects. There is a reader service for the blind, and remedial math. **Library/Resources:** The library contains 864,793 volumes, 3.4 million microform items, and 70,477 audio/video tapes/CDs/DVDs, and subscribes to 14,491 periodicals including electronic. Computerized library services include interlibrary loans, database searching, and Internet access. Special learning facilities include a radio station, TV station, and a music building. **Physically Challenged Students:** 85% of the campus is accessible. Facilities include wheelchair ramps, elevators, special parking, specially equipped restrooms, special class scheduling, lowered drinking fountains, and lowered telephones. Assistance with registration. **Special:** Mercer offers co-op programs in all majors, cross-registration with Wesleyan and Macon State Colleges, B.A.-B.S. degrees in various science and math fields, internships, student-designed majors, work-study programs, and satisfactory-unsatisfactory options for elective courses. Mercer offers a wide variety of study-abroad opportunities, including independent semester or year-long programs, faculty-led programs, or Mercer on Mission. There are 2 national honor societies, a freshman honors program, and 20 departmental honors programs. **Visiting:** There are regularly scheduled orientations for prospective students. There are guides for informal visits, visitors may sit in on classes, and stay overnight. To schedule a visit, contact the Office of Admissions at (478) 301-2650. **Campus Safety and Security:** Measures include 24-hour foot and vehicle patrol, emergency notification system, self-defense education, and security escort services. There are shuttle buses, emergency telephones, lighted pathways/sidewalks, controlled access to dorms/residences, and external cameras monitored by the police department.

REQUIREMENTS: The SAT or ACT is required. Applicants must be graduates of an accredited secondary school and have completed 16 academic units. Students should submit their transcript and class rank, a recommendation from a guidance counselor, and a list of extracurricular activities, including employment. AP and CLEP credits are accepted. To graduate, all students must complete at least 120 semester hours with a minimum GPA of 2.0. **Procedure:** Freshmen are admitted fall, spring, and summer. Entrance exams should be taken in the spring of the junior year or fall of the senior year. There are deferred admissions and rolling admissions plans. Applications should be filed by April 1 for fall entry. The fall 2017 application fee was $50. Notification is sent on a rolling basis. Applications are accepted on-line. **Transfer Students:** A minimum GPA of 2.0 is required for all transfer students. Applicants with fewer than 9 semester hours must meet freshman entrance requirements. Those with fewer than 20 semester hours must submit a high school transcript and SAT or ACT scores, and those with more than 20 semester hours must submit transcripts from all colleges attended and be in good academic standing at their present school, or present evidence of satisfactory work in a previously attended college. 30 of 120 credits required for the bachelor's degree must be completed at Mercer. **International Students:** There are 103 international students enrolled. They must take the TOEFL, or Mercer's ELI exit examination. They must also take the SAT or ACT.

ADMISSIONS: 69% of the 2017-2018 applicants were accepted. The SAT scores for the 2017-2018 freshman class were: Critical Reading-- 9% below 500, 47% between 500 and 599, 35% between 600 and 699, and 9% between 700 and 800. Math-- 7% below 500, 48% between 500 and 599, 37% between 600 and 699, and 8% between 700 and 800. Writing-- 19% below 500, 46% between 500 and 599, 29% between 600 and 699, and 6% between 700 and 800. **Admissions Contact:** Lael Whiteside, Director of Admissions. Email: *admissions@mercer.edu* Web: *www.mercer.edu*

FINANCIAL AID: In 2017-2018, 99% of all full-time freshmen received some form of financial aid. 81% of all full-time freshmen received need-based aid. The average financial indebtedness of the 2017 graduate was $29,101. The college's own financial statement is required. The FAFSA code is 001580. The deadline for filing freshman financial aid applications for fall entry is April 1.

MOREHOUSE COLLEGE — B-2

www.morehouse.edu

Atlanta, GA 30314	**(404) 215-2632** **(800) 851-1254**
Fax: (404) 572-3668	**Email: admissions@morehouse.edu**
Full-time: 2088 men	**Faculty:** 168; IIB, av$
Part-time: 111 men	**Ph.D.s:** n/av
Graduate: n/av	**Student/Faculty:** 11 to 1
Year: semesters, summer session	**Tuition:** $27,278
Room & Board: $13,557	**Freshman Class:** 2349 applied, 1748 accepted, 617 enrolled
SAT EBR-W/M: 537/520 **ACT:** 20	**CEEB CODE:** 5415
Application Deadline: February 15	**COMPETITIVE**

Morehouse College is the nation's historically black college for men of exceptional ambition and promise. Our students engage with renowned faculty members in an intensive liberal arts and sciences program that inspires intellectual growth, character development and the pursuit of social justice. Morehouse students build their skills and networks through extensive internship opportunities, push their boundaries through a residential experience that spurs lively debate and constant interaction, and hone their leadership capabilities through a wide variety of student-run organizations, formal and informal discussions with nationally known speakers and scholars, and boundless international travel opportunities. In addition to regional accreditation, Morehouse has baccalaureate program accreditation with AACSB, NASM, and ACS. The 66-acre campus is in an urban area in Atlanta, Georgia. Including any residence halls, there are 42 buildings.

STUDENT LIFE: 71% of undergraduates are from out of state, mostly the South. Students are from 42 states, and 17 foreign countries. 81% are from public schools. 95% are African American; 2% Foreign; 2% race unknown; 1% Hispanic. The student base is all male. The average age of freshmen is 18; all undergraduates, 20. 20% do not continue beyond their first year; 51% remain to graduate. **Housing:** 1532 students can be accommodated in college housing, which includes dorms and on-campus apartments. In addition, there are special-interest houses. On-campus housing is available on a first-come and first-served basis. 74% of students live on campus. Alcohol is not permitted. All students may keep cars.

FACULTY/CLASSROOMS: 64% of faculty are male; 36% are female. All teach undergraduates and all do research. No introductory courses are taught by graduate students. The average class size in an introductory lecture is 20 and in a laboratory is 15.

PROGRAMS OF STUDY: Morehouse confers B.A., B.S., and B.S.G.S. degrees. Bachelor's degrees are awarded in BIOLOGICAL SCIENCE (biology/biological science), BUSINESS (business administration and management), COMMUNICATIONS AND THE ARTS (art, dance, dramatic arts, English, film, television and digital media, French, music, and Spanish), COMPUTER AND PHYSICAL SCIENCE (chemistry, computer science, mathematics, and physics), EDUCATION (early childhood education, health and physical education, and physical education), ENGINEERING AND ENVIRONMENTAL DESIGN (engineering physics and engineering science), SOCIAL SCIENCE (African American studies, economics, history, international studies, philosophy, political science/government, psychology, religion, sociology, and urban studies). Business administration, biology, and political science are the strongest academically. Business administration, biology, and dual degree engineering have the largest enrollments.

ACTIVITIES: 3% of men belong to 6 national fraternities. There are 42 groups on campus, including campus alliance for student activities, debate team, glee club, band, cheerleading, chess, choir, chorus, communications, computers, dance, debate, drama, drill team, environmental, ethnic, film, honors, international, jazz band, LGBT, marching band, newspaper, orchestra, pep band, photography, political, professional, radio and TV, religious, social, social service, student government, symphony, and yearbook. Popular campus events include New Student Orientation, Homecoming, Founder's Day, Parent's Weekend, Admitted Students Day, Martin Luther King Jr. Commemoration, and Spring Fest. **Sports:** There are 7 intercollegiate sports for men, and 10 intramural sports for men. Facilities include a swimming pool, a weight room, cardio room, gymnasium/basketball courts, basketball, football stadium, track, and a tennis center. **Graduates:** From July 1, 2016 to June 30, 2017, 286 bachelor's degrees were awarded. The most popular majors were business administration (20%), biology (10%), and economics (8%). In an average class, 51% graduate in 6 years or less.

SERVICES: Counseling and information services are available, as is tutoring in some subjects, such as computer science, French, Spanish, Chinese, biology, physical science, and accounting. There is remedial math, reading, and writing. For those students who are visually impaired, enlarging accessible software is used (zoom text and magnifier). **Library/Resources:** The library contains 352,310 volumes, 841,341 microform items, and 8,425 audio/video tapes/CDs/DVDs, and subscribes to 8,194 periodicals including electronic. Computerized library services include interlibrary loans, database searching, Internet access, and Wi-Fi capability. Special learning facilities include a radio station, Martin Luther King Jr Collection, Ray Charles Performing Arts Center, Martin Luther King Jr International Chapel, African American Hall of Fame, Danforth Chapel, Howard Thurman Meditation Room, and a Chapel for the Inward Journey. **Physically Challenged Students:** All of the campus is accessible. Facilities include wheelchair ramps, elevators, special parking, specially equipped restrooms, lowered drinking fountains, lowered telephones, and special housing. **Special:** Morehouse is a member of the Atlanta University Center and Morehouse students may register for courses at any of the other member institutions (i.e, Clark Atlanta University, Spelman College, and Morehouse School of Medicine). Morehouse students can complete a major (art, drama or early childhood education) at Spelman College. Moreover, through the Atlanta Regional Consortium for Higher Education (ARCHE), students can take courses at Atlanta-area colleges and universities such as Agnes Scott College, Kennesaw State University, Emory University, Georgia Institute of Technology, Georgia State University, and many others. In addition, students may elect to participate in a wide range of study abroad and domestic exchange programs. Morehouse also offers students the option to study engineering through the Dual Degree Engineering Program (DDEP); participating engineering institutions include the University of Michigan, Columbia University, Dartmouth College, Georgia Institute of Technology, Rensselaer Polytechnic Institute, and nine other institutions. Other opportunities that Morehouse students engage in include summer internships, work study, and undergraduate research programs. There are 15 national honor societies, Phi Beta Kappa, a freshman honors program, and 14 departmental honors programs. **Visiting:** There are regularly scheduled orientations for prospective students. There are guides for informal visits and visitors may sit in on classes. To schedule a visit, contact Erica S. Johnson at (404) 653-7736. **Campus Safety and Security:** Measures include 24-hour foot and vehicle patrol, emergency notification system, and security escort services. There are shuttle buses, lighted pathways/sidewalks, controlled access to dorms/residences, emergency call boxes, safety tips, and awareness training.

REQUIREMENTS: The SAT or ACT is required. Students must have a high school diploma or GED. A general college-preparatory high school curriculum is recommended, including 4 units in English, 3 units in math, 2 units each in natural and social sciences. 2 units of foreign language are also recommended. Applicants must write an application essay and are urged to seek an interview. AP and CLEP credits are accepted. Important factors in the admissions decision are advanced placement or honors courses, leadership record, and recommendations by school officials. Students must complete a minimum of 120 semester hours, including 53 hours in the general education core curriculum, plus 8 noncredit hours in Freshman Orientation and Crown Forum. An approved major concentration sequence and at least two years of coursework (a minimum of 60 semester hours) in residence at Morehouse College are required as well. **Procedure:** Freshmen are admitted fall and spring. Entrance exams should be taken by the fall of the senior year. There are early decision, early admissions, and deferred admissions plans. Early decision applications should be filed by November 1; regular applications, by February 15 for fall entry; and November 1 for spring entry. The fall 2017 application fee was $50. Notification of early decision is sent December 15; regular decision, March 15. Applications are accepted on-line. **Transfer Students:** 64 transfer students enrolled in 2016-2017. Transfer applicants must have at least a 2.5 GPA and a minimum of 26 semester hours of credit. Students may enroll in the fall and spring. 60 of 120 credits required for the bachelor's degree must be completed at Morehouse. **International Students:** There are 27 international students enrolled. They must take the TOEFL with a minimum score of 75 on the Internet-based version (iBT). They must also take the SAT or ACT.

ADMISSIONS: 74% of the 2017-2018 applicants were accepted. The SAT scores for the 2017-2018 freshman class were: Math-- 35% below 500, 49% between 500 and 599, 15% between 600 and 699, and 1% between 700 and 800. Evidence-Based Reading/Writing-- 31% below 500, 45% between 500 and 599, 21% between 600 and 699, and 2% between 700 and 800. The ACT scores were 23% between 12 and 17, 57% between 18 and 23, 17% between 24 and 29, and 3% above 30. **Admissions Contact:** Darryl Isom, Director of Admissions and Recruitment. Email: *admissions@morehouse.edu* Web: *www.morehouse.edu*

FINANCIAL AID: In 2017-2018, 97% of all full-time freshmen received some form of financial aid. 90% of all full-time freshmen received need-based aid. The average freshman award was $21,078. Need-based scholarships or need-based grants averaged $13,233 ($47,952 maximum); need-based self-help aid (loans and jobs) averaged $3,379 ($13,000 maximum); non-need-based athletic scholarships averaged $897 ($41,647 maximum); and other non-need-based awards and non-need-based scholarships averaged $3,569 ($44,806 maximum). The average financial indebtedness of the 2017 graduate was $30,739. MC is a member of CSS. The FAFSA code is 001582. The priority date for freshman financial aid applications for fall entry is Febuary 15.

OGLETHORPE UNIVERSITY B-2

www.oglethorpe.edu

Atlanta, GA 30319 (404) 364-8307
(800) 428-8491
Fax: (404) 364-8500 Email: admission@oglethorpe.edu

Full-time: 455 men, 612 women
Part-time: 57 men, 60 women
Graduate: n/av
Year: semesters, summer session
Room & Board: $11,700

SAT CR/M/W: 570/550/550 **ACT:** 24
Application Deadline: open

Faculty: 60
Ph.D.s: n/av
Student/Faculty: n/av
Tuition: $32,500
Freshman Class: 2768 applied, 2172 accepted, 277 enrolled
CEEB CODE: 5521
COMPETITIVE

Oglethorpe University, founded in 1835, is an independent institution offering programs in the liberal arts and science, business, and preprofessional studies. The figures in the above capsule and in this profile are approximate. There are 2 undergraduate schools. The 102-acre campus is in a suburban area 10 miles northeast of downtown Atlanta. Including any residence halls, there are 25 buildings.

STUDENT LIFE: 74% of undergraduates are from Georgia. Others are from 33 states, 36 foreign countries, and Canada. 74% are from public schools. 6% are Foreign; 4% Asian American; 34% White; 3% two or more races; 25% race unknown; 18% African American; 10% Hispanic. **Female To Male Ratio:** 1.3:1. The average age of freshmen is 18; all undergraduates, 21. 28% do not continue beyond their first year; 55% remain to graduate. **Housing:** 803 students can be accommodated in college housing, which includes dorms. In addition, there are fraternity houses and sorority houses. On-campus housing is guaranteed for the freshman year only, is available on a first-come, and first-served basis. 65% of students live on campus. All students may keep cars.

FACULTY/CLASSROOMS: 58% of faculty are male; 42% are female. No introductory courses are taught by graduate students. The average class size in an introductory lecture is 20; in a laboratory is 18; and in a regular course is 15.

PROGRAMS OF STUDY: Oglethorpe confers B.A., B.S., B.A.L.S. and B.B.A. degrees. Bachelor's degrees are awarded in BIOLOGICAL SCIENCE (biology/biological science), BUSINESS (accounting and business administration and management), COMMUNICATIONS AND THE ARTS (art, art history and appreciation, communications, English, French, and Spanish), COMPUTER AND PHYSICAL SCIENCE (chemistry, mathematics, and physics), SOCIAL SCIENCE (American studies, behavioral science, biopsychology, economics, history, international studies, philosophy, political science/government, psychology, social work, and sociology). Biology, business, and pyschology are the strongest academically. Business administration, biology, and communications have the largest enrollments.

ACTIVITIES: 26% of men belong to 5 national fraternities; 22% of women belong to 1 local and 4 national sororities. There are 51 groups on campus, including art, cheerleading, choir, chorale, chorus, computers, dance, drama, ethnic, honors, international, LGBT, literary magazine, newspaper, orchestra, pep band, photography, political, professional, radio and TV, religious, social, social service, student government, and yearbook. Popular campus events include Oglethorpe Day, and Liberal Arts Symposium. **Sports:** There are 8 intercollegiate sports for men and 8 for women, and 6 intramural sports for men and 6 for women. Facilities include a field house and recreation center housing basketball, volleyball, a running track, handball courts, and a weight room. Outdoor facilities include tennis courts, an all-weather track, a sand volleyball court, and fields for soccer, baseball, and intramural. **Graduates:** From July 1, 2016 to June 30, 2017, 154 bachelor's degrees were awarded. The most popular majors were business and accounting (18%), English and communications (14%), and social sciences (14%).

SERVICES: Counseling and information services are available, as is tutoring in most subjects, including all core (general education) courses, English, writing, accounting, and math. **Library/Resources:** The library contains 157,000 volumes, 4,189 microform items, and 6,786 audio/video tapes/CDs/DVDs, and subscribes to 775 periodicals including electronic. Computerized library services include interlibrary loans, database searching, Internet access, and Wi-Fi capability. Special learning facilities include an art gallery, radio station, Atlanta Laboratory for Learning which includes the Center for Civic Engagement, Global Education Opportunities, and Professional Development. Additionally, Oglethorpe has an in-residence, professional theatre program. **Physically Challenged Students:** 80% of the campus is accessible. Facilities include wheelchair ramps, elevators, special parking, specially equipped restrooms, special class scheduling, lowered drinking fountains, and special housing. **Special:** Oglethorpe offers co-op programs in all majors, cross-registration through the Atlanta Regional Consortium for Higher Education, international exchange agreements with several universities in Europe, Asia, and South America, and other study-abroad options. Internships are available in all areas of study for up to 15 credit hours for upperclassmen with a minimum 2.8 GPA, and a Washington semester offers internships with Georgia senators and others. There is a 3-2 engineering program with Georgia Institute of Technology, the Universities of Florida and Southern California, and Auburn University. Accelerated degrees, dual majors, student-designed majors, federal work-study programs, and nondegree study are offered. There are 7 national honor societies, a freshman honors program, and 99 departmental honors programs. **Visiting:** There are regularly scheduled orientations for prospective students, including placement tests, class registration, an activities fair, and group activities. There are guides for informal visits, visitors may sit in on classes, and stay overnight. To schedule a visit, contact the Admissions Office at admissions@oglethorpe.edu. **Campus Safety and Security:** Measures include 24-hour foot and vehicle patrol, emergency notification system, self-defense education, and security escort services. There are lighted pathways/sidewalks, controlled access to dorms/residences. Entrance to residence halls is on an ID card-swipe system.

REQUIREMENTS: The SAT or ACT is required. Students should graduate from an accredited high school or have a GED certificate. They should have completed 4 courses in English, 3 each in science and social studies, and a math sequence of algebra I and II and geometry. A counselor's or teacher's recommendation is required, and an essay is required for a scholarship. An interview is recommended. AP and CLEP credits are accepted. Important factors in the admissions decision are recommendations by school officials, extracurricular activities record, and advanced placement or honors courses. To graduate with a B.A. or B.S., all students must complete at least 128 credit hours (120 for B.B.A. and B.A.L.S.). They must fulfill a major as well as complete the core curriculum and achieve a minimum GPA of 2.0. The core curriculum is a unique 4-year sequence of related interdisciplinary courses, 1 per semester. All freshman must complete the first-year experience program. **Procedure:** Freshmen are admitted to all sessions. Entrance exams should be taken late in the junior year or early in the senior year. There are early decision, early admissions, deferred admissions, and rolling admissions plans. Check with the school for current application deadlines. The fall 2017 application fee was $50. Notification is sent on a rolling basis. Applications are accepted on-line. **Transfer Students:** 42 transfer students enrolled in 2016-2017. Applicants who have completed less than a full year of college work must take the SAT or ACT. All transfers must be in good academic standing with a minimum GPA of 2.5. An interview is recommended. 64 of 128 credits required for the bachelor's degree must be completed at Oglethorpe. **International Students:** There are 66 international students enrolled. They must take the TOEFL with a minimum score of 550 on the paper-based TOEFL (PBT), or demonstrate proficiency in English by other means. They must also take the SAT or ACT.

ADMISSIONS: 78% of the 2017-2018 applicants were accepted. The SAT scores for the 2017-2018 freshman class were: Critical Reading-- 8% below 500, 51% between 500 and 599, 35% between 600 and 699, and 6% between 700 and 800. Math-- 20% below 500, 52% between 500 and 599, 23% between 600 and 699, and 4% between 700 and 800. Writing-- 24% below 500, 49% between 500 and 599, 24% between 600 and 699, and 3% between 700 and 800. The ACT scores were 12% below 12, 30% between 12 and 17, 25% between 18 and 23, 14% between 24 and 29, and 19% above 30. 45% of the current freshmen were in the top fifth of their class; 78% were in the top two fifths. **Admissions Contact:** Lucy Leusch, Vice President for Enrollment. Email: *admission@oglethorpe.edu* Web: *www.oglethorpe.edu*

FINANCIAL AID: In 2017-2018, 98% of all full-time freshmen received some form of financial aid. 73% of all full-time freshmen received need-based aid. The average freshman award was $33,046. Need-based scholarships or need-based grants averaged $7,062; need-based self-help aid (loans and jobs) averaged $3,062; other non-need-based awards and non-need-based scholarships averaged $20,887; and $2,034 from other forms of aid. 12% of undergraduate students work part-time. The average financial indebtedness of the 2017 graduate was $27,650. Oglethorpe is a member of CSS. The FAFSA code is 001586. The priority date for freshman financial aid applications for fall entry is February 15.

PAINE COLLEGE *(The complete profile is made available exclusively on our website, www.barronspac.com)*

PIEDMONT COLLEGE C-1
www.piedmont.edu

Demorest, GA 30535	**(706) 778-3000** **(800) 277-7020**
Fax: (706) 776-6635	**Email: bboonstra@piedmont.edu**
Full-time: 409 men, 751 women	**Faculty:** n/av
Part-time: 25 men, 96 women	**Ph.D.s:** 75%
Graduate: 212 men, 868 women	**Student/Faculty:** 10 to 1
Year: semesters, summer session	**Tuition:** $24,464
Room & Board: $9870	**Freshman Class:** n/av
SAT or ACT: required	**CEEB CODE:** 5537
Application Deadline: August 1	**COMPETITIVE**

Piedmont College is an independent, comprehensive, co-educational liberal arts college that offers bachelors, masters and doctoral degrees. With campuses in Demorest and Athens, GA students are challenged to immerse themselves in discovery, analysis, and communication. The college maintains affiliation with the National Association of Congregational Christian Churches and United Church of Christ. There are 4 undergraduate schools and 2 graduate schools. In addition to regional accreditation, Piedmont has baccalaureate program accreditation with ACBSP and NLN. The 186-acre campus is in a small town 75 miles northeast of Atlanta. Including any residence halls, there are 35 buildings.

STUDENT LIFE: 92% of undergraduates are from Georgia. 8% are Hispanic; 67% White; 14% race unknown; 10% African American; 1% Asian American. **Female To Male Ratio:** 2.7:1. The average age of freshmen is 18; all undergraduates, 23. 34% do not continue beyond their first year; 50% remain to graduate. **Housing:** 705 students can be accommodated in college housing, which includes dorms and on-campus apartments. On-campus housing is guaranteed for all 4 years, is available on a first-come, and first-served basis. 72% of students live on campus. Alcohol is not permitted. All students may keep cars.

FACULTY/CLASSROOMS: 48% of faculty are male; 52% are female. No introductory courses are taught by graduate students. The average class size in a regular course is 12.

PROGRAMS OF STUDY: Piedmont confers B.A., B.S., B.F.A., and B.S.N. degrees. Master's and doctoral degrees are also awarded. Bachelor's degrees are awarded in AGRICULTURE (environmental studies), BIOLOGICAL SCIENCE (biology/biological science, forensic science, and nutritional sciences), BUSINESS (business administration and management), COMMUNICATIONS AND THE ARTS (art, arts administration/management, communications, dramatic arts, English, fine arts, music, musical theater, performing arts, Spanish, theatre arts, and theater design), COMPUTER AND PHYSICAL SCIENCE (applied mathematics, applied physics, chemistry, mathematics, physics, and science), EDUCATION (art education, athletic training, early childhood education, education, English education, mathematics education, middle school education, music education, science education, secondary education, social science education, social studies education, and special education), ENGINEERING AND ENVIRONMENTAL DESIGN (environmental science), HEALTH PROFESSIONS (cardiac sonography, exercise science, nursing, and nutrition and wellness), SOCIAL SCIENCE (criminal justice, history, interdisciplinary studies, philosophy, political science/government, psychology, religion, social science, and sociology). Education, nursing/healthsciences, and business administration have the largest enrollments.

ACTIVITIES: There are no fraternities or sororities. There are 32 groups on campus, including art, cheerleading, choir, chorale, chorus, dance, debate, drama, environmental, film, honors, jazz band, literary magazine, musical theater, newspaper, pep band, photography, professional, radio and TV, religious, social, social service, student government, and yearbook. Popular campus events include Arrendale Amphitheatre Festivals, Bands, Athletic events, Music Recitals & Performances, and Art Museum Receptions. **Sports:** There are 9 intercollegiate sports for men and 10 for women, and 5 intramural sports for men and 5 for women. Facilities include an athletic center, tennis courts, beach volleyball courts, regulation baseball, softball, soccer and lacrosse fields, a fitness center, indoor walking track & intramural basketball court, and a climbing wall. **Graduates:** From July 1, 2016 to June 30, 2017, 277 bachelor's degrees were awarded. The most popular majors were nursing (29%), business (17%), and education (16%). In an average class, 2% graduate in 3 years or less, 45% graduate in 4 years or less, 49% graduate in 5 years or less, and 50% graduate in 6 years or less.

SERVICES: Counseling and information services are available, as is tutoring in most subjects. The Learning Center offers academic support, including accounting, foreign languages, math, science, and writing. **Library/Resources:** The library contains 516,373 volumes, and 73,670 audio/video tapes/CDs/DVDs, and subscribes to 24,272 periodicals including electronic. Computerized library services include interlibrary loans, database searching, Internet access, and Wi-Fi capability. Special learning facilities include an art gallery, radio station, and TV station. **Physically Challenged Students:** 85% of the campus is accessible. Facilities include wheelchair ramps, elevators, special parking, specially equipped restrooms, special class scheduling, and special housing. **Special:** Piedmont College assists students with internships in business, psychology, education, art management, criminal justice, sociology, nursing/health sciences, political science and other areas. Study abroad and interdisciplinary majors are available. There are 4 national honor societies and 1 departmental honors program. **Visiting:** There are regularly scheduled orientations for prospective students, including a campus tour, introduction to student activities, academic overview, admissions counseling, resident orientation, and a financial aid presentation. There are guides for informal visits, visitors may sit in on classes, and stay overnight. To schedule a visit, contact the Undergraduate Admissions Office. **Campus Safety and Security:** Measures include 24-hour foot and vehicle patrol, emergency notification system, self-defense education, and security escort services. There are shuttle buses, emergency telephones, lighted pathways/sidewalks, controlled access to dorms/residences, campus is also patrolled by the local police department. Student security hosts in each residence hall.

REQUIREMENTS: The SAT is required. Applicants must be graduates of an accredited secondary school or have a GED certificate. Students must have completed a minimum of 23 academic units. A portfolio is required for art scholarship applicants and an audition for music scholarship applicants. An interview is recommended for all students. AP and CLEP credits are accepted. To graduate with a bachelor's degree a minimum of 120 credit hours is required. Students must complete credit hours for their major, including general education coursework in the humanities, fine arts, math, natural sciences, social sciences, and in computer science. **Procedure:** Freshmen are admitted to all sessions. There are deferred admissions and rolling admissions plans. Applications should be filed by August 1 for fall entry; January 1 for spring entry; and May 1 for summer entry. Applications are accepted on-line. **Transfer Students:** 132 transfer students enrolled in 2016-2017. Applicants must have a GPA of 2.0 at each institution attended. An interview is recommended. 30 of 120 credits required for the bachelor's degree must be completed at Piedmont. **International Students:** There are 9 international students enrolled. They must take the TOEFL with a minimum score of 550 on the paper-based TOEFL (PBT) or 80 on the Internet-based version (iBT). They must also take the SAT or ACT.

Admissions Contact: Brenda Boonstra, Director of Undergraduate Admissions. Email: *bboonstra@piedmont.edu* Web: *www.piedmont.edu*

FINANCIAL AID: In 2017-2018, 100% of all full-time freshmen received some form of financial aid. 66% of all full-time freshmen received need-based aid. The average freshman award was $24,080. Need-based scholarships or need-based grants averaged $5,462 ($17,207 maximum); need-based self-help aid (loans and jobs) averaged $3,281 ($5,256 maximum); other non-need-based awards and non-need-based scholarships averaged $14,429 ($29,836 maximum); and $6,960 from other forms of aid. 32% of undergraduate students work part-time. The average financial indebtedness of the 2017 graduate was $24,651. The state aid form is required. The FAFSA code is 001588. Check with the school for current application deadlines.

REINHARDT UNIVERSITY B-1
www.reinhardt.edu

Waleska, GA 30183 **(770) 720-5526**

Fax: (770) 720-5899 **Email: admissions@reinhardt.edu**
Full-time: 390 men, 575 women
Part-time: 65 men, 90 women
Graduate: n/av
Year: semesters, summer session
Room & Board: $9022
SAT or ACT: required
Application Deadline: August 15
Faculty: n/av
Ph.D.s: n/av
Student/Faculty: n/av
Tuition: $22,322
Freshman Class: n/av
CEEB CODE: 5568
COMPETITIVE

Reinhardt University, founded in 1883, is a private institution affiliated with the Methodist Church and offering undergraduate degrees. The figures given in the above capsule and in this profile are approximate. There are 4 undergraduate schools. In addition to regional accreditation, Reinhardt University has baccalaureate program accreditation with SACS. The 600-acre campus is in a small town 40 miles north of Atlanta. Including any residence halls, there are 31 buildings.

STUDENT LIFE: 98% of undergraduates are from Georgia. Others are from 4 states, 6 foreign countries, and Canada. 90% are from public schools. 82% are White; 8% African American; 2% Hispanic; 2% Foreign; 1% Asian American; 1% American Indian/Alaska Native. 70% are Protestant; 23% claim no religious affiliation. **Female To Male Ratio:** 1.5:1. The average age of freshmen is 18; all undergraduates, 23. 36% do not continue beyond their first year; 50% remain to graduate. **Housing:** 404 students can be accommodated in college housing, which includes dorms. On-campus housing is guaranteed for all 4 years. 64% of students commute. Alcohol is not permitted. All students may keep cars.

FACULTY/CLASSROOMS: 45% of faculty are male; 55% are female. All teach undergraduates. No introductory courses are taught by graduate students. The average class size in an introductory lecture is 17; in a laboratory is 17; and in a regular course is 17.

PROGRAMS OF STUDY: Reinhardt confers B.A., B.S., B.F.A. and B.S.B.A. degrees. Associate degrees are also awarded. Bachelor's degrees are awarded in BIOLOGICAL SCIENCE (biology/biological science), BUSINESS (business administration and management), COMMUNICATIONS AND THE ARTS (communications), SOCIAL SCIENCE (liberal arts/general studies). Business, and liberal studies have the largest enrollments.

ACTIVITIES: There are no fraternities or sororities. There are 14 groups on campus, including cheerleading, honors, newspaper, professional, radio and TV, religious, social, social service, student government, and yearbook. Popular campus events include Spring Day, Spring Formal, and Diversity Days. **Sports:** There are 5 intercollegiate sports for men and 4 for women, and 4 intramural sports for men and 4 for women. Facilities include jogging trails, outdoor volleyball, golf, cross-country, tennis, and basketball courts, soccer and softball fields, a pool, weight room, bowling alley, and racquetball courts.

SERVICES: Counseling and information services are available, as is tutoring in every subject. **Library/Resources:** The library contains 48,000 volumes, 1,983 microform items, and 3,598 audio/video tapes/CDs/DVDs, and subscribes to 315 periodicals including electronic. Computerized library services include interlibrary loans, database searching, and Internet access. Special learning facilities include an art gallery, natural history museum, radio station, and TV station. **Physically Challenged Students:** 90% of the campus is accessible. Facilities include wheelchair ramps, elevators, special parking, specially equipped restrooms, special class scheduling, and lowered drinking fountains. **Special:** Internships, study abroad, and work-study programs are available. There is an accelerated degree program in organizational leadership. There is 1 national honor society and a freshman honors program. **Visiting:** There are regularly scheduled orientations for prospective students. There are guides for informal visits and visitors may sit in on classes. To schedule a visit, contact the Admissions Office. **Campus Safety and Security:** Measures include 24-hour foot and vehicle patrol and self-defense education. There are lighted pathways/sidewalks.

REQUIREMENTS: The SAT or ACT is required. The GED is accepted and a placement test may be required. A GPA of 2.0 is required. AP and CLEP credits are accepted. Important factors in the admissions decision are recommendations by alumni, recommendations by school officials, and parents or siblings attended your school. To graduate, students must have a core curriculum in the humanities, math and science, social science, language, phys ed, and wellness. A total of 120 semester hours is required, including 65 in the major. A 2.0 GPA must be maintained. **Procedure:** Freshmen are admitted to all sessions. Entrance exams should be taken before acceptance. There are early admissions and rolling admissions plans. Application deadlines are open. The fall 2017 application fee was $25. Applications are accepted on-line. **Transfer Students:** A GPA of 2.0 or better may be considered for transfer applicants. 40 of 120 credits required for the bachelor's degree must be completed at Reinhardt. **International Students:** They must take the TOEFL.

Admissions Contact: Lacy Satterfield, Director of Admissions. Email: *admissions@reinhardt.edu* Web: *www.reinhardt.edu*

FINANCIAL AID: Reinhardt is a member of CSS. The FAFSA code is 001589. Check with the school for current application deadlines.

SAVANNAH COLLEGE OF ART AND DESIGN *(The complete profile is made available exclusively on our website, www.barronspac.com)*

SAVANNAH STATE UNIVERSITY E-4
www.savannahstate.edu

Savannah, GA 31404 **912-358-4338**
(800) 788-0478

Fax: 912-358-3171 **Email: admissions@savannahstate.edu**
Full-time: 1727 men, 2077 women
Part-time: 277 men, 332 women
Graduate: 38 men, 131 women
Year: semesters, summer session
Room & Board: $10,302
SAT or ACT: required
Application Deadline: July 15
Faculty: n/av
Ph.D.s: n/av
Student/Faculty: 23 to 1
Tuition: $6734
Freshman Class: 3374 applied, 2134 accepted, 1104 enrolled
CEEB CODE: 5609
COMPETITIVE

Savannah State University, founded in 1890, is a liberal arts institution that is part of the University System of Georgia. Undergraduate and graduate degrees are offered through the colleges of business, liberal arts and social sciences, and sciences and technology. Preprofessional programs are available. The figures given in the above capsule and in this profile are approximate. There are 3 undergraduate schools and 5 graduate schools. In addition to regional accreditation, SSU has baccalaureate program accreditation with ABET, CSWE, and CAEP. The 165-acre campus is in a suburban area 265 miles southeast of Atlanta. Including any residence halls, there are 45 buildings.

STUDENT LIFE: Students are from 38 states, 33 foreign countries, and Canada. 87% are African American; 6% White; 2% Hispanic; 1% Foreign. **Female To Male Ratio:** 1.2:1. The average age of freshmen is 19; all undergraduates, 21. 28% do not continue beyond their first year; 32% remain to graduate. **Housing:** 2745 students can be accommodated in college housing, which includes married student dorms and on-campus apartments. On-campus housing is available on a first-come and first-served basis. Alcohol is not permitted. All students may keep cars.

FACULTY/CLASSROOMS: 54% of faculty are male; 46% are female. No introductory courses are taught by graduate students.

PROGRAMS OF STUDY: SSU confers B.A., B.S., B.B.A. and B.S.W. degrees. Associate and master's degrees are also awarded. Bachelor's degrees are awarded in BIOLOGICAL SCIENCE (biology/biological science and marine biology), BUSINESS (accounting, business administration and management, management information systems, and marketing/retailing/merchandising), COMMUNICATIONS AND THE ARTS (communications, English, and visual and performing arts), COMPUTER AND PHYSICAL SCIENCE (chemistry, computer science, and mathematics), ENGINEERING AND ENVIRONMENTAL DESIGN (civil engineering, electrical/electronics engineering technology, and environmental science), SOCIAL SCIENCE (African studies, behavioral science, criminal justice, history, homeland security, political science/government, social work, and sociology). Marine science, social work, and computer information systems are the strongest academically. Biology, mass communications, and management have the largest enrollments.

ACTIVITIES: 2% of men belong to 7 national fraternities; 3% of women

belong to 6 national sororities. Groups on campus include art, band, cheerleading, choir, chorale, computers, dance, debate, drama, drill team, ethnic, international, jazz band, literary magazine, marching band, newspaper, political, professional, radio and TV, religious, and student government. Popular campus events include Drama Presentations, a Fine Arts Festival, Christmas Concert, and Spring Concerts. **Sports:** There are 5 intercollegiate sports for men and 4 for women, and 1 intramural sports for men. Facilities include a student center, a gym complex, swimming pool, a stadium, field house, tennis court, and track and field. **Graduates:** From July 1, 2016 to June 30, 2017, 395 bachelor's degrees were awarded. The most popular majors were mass communications (10%), business management (10%), and criminal justice (8%). In an average class, 32% graduate in 6 years or less.

SERVICES: Counseling and information services are available, as is tutoring in every subject. There is remedial math, reading, and writing. **Library/Resources:** The library contains 209,714 volumes, 586,633 microform items, and 3,725 audio/video tapes/CDs/DVDs, and subscribes to 360 periodicals including electronic. Computerized library services include interlibrary loans, database searching, and Internet access. Special learning facilities include a radio station, an arts center, and marine science lab. **Physically Challenged Students:** Facilities include wheelchair ramps, elevators, special parking, specially equipped restrooms, lowered drinking fountains, and special housing. **Special:** The college offers co-op programs, cross-registration with Armstrong Atlantic State University, study abroad, a dual-degree program with Georgia Institute of Technology, the Georgia Legislative Internship Program, and a variety of other internship programs across the curriculum, on- and off-campus work-study programs, correspondence study, credit for military experience, and non-degree study. There is a freshman honors program. **Visiting:** There are guides for informal visits and visitors may sit in on classes. To schedule a visit, contact the Office of Admissions. **Campus Safety and Security:** Measures include 24-hour foot and vehicle patrol and emergency notification system. There are shuttle buses, emergency telephones, lighted pathways/sidewalks. The campus police department is staffed with public safety officers, building attendants, security guards, safety inspectors, and telephone operators.

REQUIREMENTS: A minimum composite score of 830 on the SAT, or 17 on the ACT is required. In addition, applicants must be graduates of an accredited secondary school. Students should have completed 4 units each of English, math and science, 3 units of social science, and 2 units of 1 foreign language. AP and CLEP credits are accepted. To graduate, all students must complete a minimum of 120 credit hours with satisfactory completion of the core curriculum requirements. Students must maintain a minimum 2.0 GPA. Exit competency exams and other requirements may be required. **Procedure:** Freshmen are admitted fall, spring, and summer. Entrance exams should be taken early in the senior year. There are early admissions and deferred admissions plans. Applications should be filed by July 15 for fall entry; November 15 for spring entry; and May 1 for summer entry. The fall 2017 application fee was $20. Notification is sent on a rolling basis. Applications are accepted online. **Transfer Students:** Applicants with at least 45 quarter hours or 30 semester hours of core curriculum credit do not need to submit high school transcripts, but must have a 2.0 average. All transfers must submit college transcripts, standardized test scores, and proof of good standing at the previous institution. 30 of 120 credits required for the bachelor's degree must be completed at Savannah State. **International Students:** There are 50 international students enrolled. They must take the TOEFL with a minimum score of 530 on the paper-based TOEFL (PBT). They must also take the SAT or ACT, and the college's own entrance exam, or the Collegiate Placement Exams.

ADMISSIONS: 63% of the 2017-2018 applicants were accepted. **Admissions Contact:** Brian Dawsey, Director of Admissions. Email: *admissions@savannahstate.edu* Web: *www.savannahstate.edu*

FINANCIAL AID: The CSS/Profile, the college's own financial statement, and the Scholarship Application Form are required. The FAFSA code is 001590. The deadline for filing freshman financial aid applications for fall entry is July 15.

SHORTER UNIVERSITY *(The complete profile is made available exclusively on our website, www.barronspac.com)*

SOUTH UNIVERSITY *(The complete profile is made available exclusively on our website, www.barronspac.com)*

SPELMAN COLLEGE — B-2
www.spelman.edu

Atlanta, GA 30314	(404) 681-3643 (800) 982-2411
Fax: (404) 215-7788	**Email:** admiss@spelman.edu
Full-time: 2125 women	**Faculty:** IIB, av$
Part-time: 64 women	**Ph.D.s:** n/av
Graduate: n/av	**Student/Faculty:** 9 to 1
Year: semesters	**Tuition:** $28,181
Room & Board: $13,461	**Freshman Class:** 7864 applied, 2810 accepted, 533 enrolled
SAT: required **ACT:** 25	**CEEB CODE:** 5628
Application Deadline: February 1	**COMPETITIVE**

Spelman College, founded in 1881, is a private, nonsectarian, liberal arts college for black women. The figures given in the above capsule and in this profile are approximate. There is one undergraduate school. In addition to regional accreditation, SC has baccalaureate program accreditation with NASM and CAEP. The 39-acre campus is in an urban area 3 miles southwest of downtown Atlanta. Including any residence halls, there are 24 buildings.

STUDENT LIFE: 71% of undergraduates are from out of state. Students are from 41 states, 18 foreign countries, and Canada. 86% are from public schools. 96% are African American. The student base is all female. The average age of freshmen is 18; all undergraduates, 20. 10% do not continue beyond their first year; 72% remain to graduate. **Housing:** 1169 students can be accommodated in college housing, which includes dorms. In addition, there are honors houses. On-campus housing is guaranteed for the freshman year only, is available on a first-come, first-served basis, and is available on a lottery system for upperclassmen. 60% of students live on campus. Alcohol is not permitted. Upperclassmen may keep cars.

FACULTY/CLASSROOMS: 36% of faculty are male; 64% are female. No introductory courses are taught by graduate students.

PROGRAMS OF STUDY: Spelman confers B.A. and B.S. degrees. Bachelor's degrees are awarded in BIOLOGICAL SCIENCE (biochemistry and biology/biological science), COMMUNICATIONS AND THE ARTS (art, dramatic arts, English, fine arts, French, music, and Spanish), COMPUTER AND PHYSICAL SCIENCE (chemistry, computer science, mathematics, natural sciences, and physics), EDUCATION (art education), ENGINEERING AND ENVIRONMENTAL DESIGN (engineering), SOCIAL SCIENCE (anthropology, child psychology/development, economics, history, philosophy, political science/government, psychology, religion, sociology, and women's studies). Biology, and engineering are the strongest academically. Psychology, biology, and English have the largest enrollments.

ACTIVITIES: There are no fraternities; 8% of women belong to 4 local and 4 national sororities. There are 60 groups on campus, including art, band, cheerleading, choir, chorus, communications, dance, drama, honors, international, jazz band, LGBT, literary magazine, musical theater, newspaper, political, religious, social, student government, and yearbook. Popular campus events include Founders Day, and Martin Luther King Jr.'s Birthday. **Sports:** There are 4 intercollegiate sports for women, and 6 intramural sports for women. Facilities include a gym, tennis courts, swimming pool, a weight room, dance studios, and bowling lanes.

SERVICES: Counseling and information services are available, as is tutoring in every subject. **Library/Resources:** The library contains 500,000 volumes, 385,538 microform items, and subscribes to 1,439 periodicals including electronic. Special learning facilities include an art gallery, a language lab, a media center, and music and art studios. **Physically Challenged Students:** 25% of the campus is accessible. Facilities include wheelchair ramps, elevators, special parking, and specially equipped restrooms. **Special:** Students may cross-register with Atlanta University Center member institutions. Spelman offers internships, study abroad in several countries, student-designed majors, work-study programs at the school, B.A.-B.S. degrees, and dual majors, as well as a 3-2 engineering degree with Georgia Tech, Rochester Institute of Technology, University of Alabama at Huntsville, Auburn and Boston Universities, and North Carolina Agricultural and Technical State University. The college grants credit for life experience and permits non-degree study. There are 9 national honor societies, Phi Beta Kappa, and a freshman honors program. **Visiting:** There are regularly scheduled orientations for prospective students, including a general information session and a campus tour. There are also high school senior days and junior days. There are guides for informal visits. To schedule a visit, contact the Admissions Office at admiss@spelman.edu. **Campus Safety and Security:** Measures include 24-hour foot and vehicle patrol, self-defense education, and security escort services. There are shuttle buses, emergency telephones, and lighted pathways/sidewalks.

REQUIREMENTS: The SAT or ACT is required. Applicants should be high school graduates or have a GED certificate. Students should have earned at least 12 academic credits, including 4 in English, 2 each in foreign language, math (algebra and geometry), social studies, and science (including a lab science). Students with additional years in math, science, and language and with AP and honors courses are considered more competitive. An essay is required. An audition or portfolio is recommended for art majors. A GPA of 3.7 is required. AP and CLEP credits are accepted. Important factors in the admissions decision are advanced placement or honors courses, leadership record, and recommendations by school officials. To graduate, students must complete 120 semester hours, including at least 30 or more in the major and maintain a GPA of 2.0. Core requirements include 8 credits of African studies, up to 8 of foreign language, 4 of international or women's studies, up to 4 each of English composition, computer literacy, and math, and 2 to 3 of phys ed, plus freshman orientation and sophmore assembly. Students also must complete 4 credits each of divisional requirements in social science, humanities, natural science, and fine arts. A reading course may be required, based on the placement test scores. **Procedure:** Freshmen are admitted in the fall. Entrance exams should be taken by December of the senior year. There are early decision, early admissions, and deferred admissions plans. Early decision applications should be filed by November 15; regular applications, by February 1 for fall entry. The fall 2017 application fee was $35. Notification of early decision is sent December 31; regular decision, April 1. 546 early decision candidates were accepted for the 2017-2018 class. **Transfer Students:** 47 transfer students enrolled in 2016-2017. A 3.0 GPA is recommended, with a minimum 2.0 required. Applicants must submit high school and college transcripts, as well as 2 recommendations from instructors at the last school attended. Students with fewer than 30 semester hours of credit must also submit SAT or ACT scores. 30 of 120 credits required for the bachelor's degree must be completed at Spelman. **International Students:** They must take the TOEFL. They must also take the SAT or ACT.

ADMISSIONS: 36% of the 2017-2018 applicants were accepted. 71% of the current freshmen were in the top fifth of their class; 91% were in the top two fifths. **Admissions Contact:** Tiffany Nelson, Director of Admissions. Email: *admiss@spelman.edu* Web: *www.spelman.edu*

FINANCIAL AID: In 2017-2018, 82% of all full-time freshmen received some form of financial aid. 82% of all full-time freshmen received need-based aid. 20% of undergraduate students work part-time. The average financial indebtedness of the 2017 graduate was $18,000. Spelman is a member of CSS. The college's own financial statement is required. The FAFSA code is 001594. The deadline for filing freshman financial aid applications for fall entry is April 1.

THE ART INSTITUTE OF ATLANTA *(The complete profile is made available exclusively on our website, www.barronspac.com)*

THOMAS UNIVERSITY *(The complete profile is made available exclusively on our website, www.barronspac.com)*

TOCCOA FALLS COLLEGE C-1
www.tfc.edu

Toccoa Falls, GA 30598 (706) 886-6831

Fax: (706) 282-6012	**Email:** admission@tfc.edu
Full-time: 384 men, 392 women	**Faculty:** 49; IIB
Part-time: 51 men, 47 women	**Ph.D.s:** 55%
Graduate: n/av	**Student/Faculty:** 16 to 1
Year: 4-1-4, summer session	**Tuition:** $22,114
Room & Board: $7934	**Freshman Class:** 1008 applied, 556 accepted, 258 enrolled
SAT CR/M: 505/500 **ACT:** required	**CEEB CODE:** 5799
Application Deadline: August 1	**COMPETITIVE**

Toccoa Falls College is a private, interdenominational Christian college founded in 1907 that offers programs in Biblical studies, biology, business administration, counseling, Christian education, communication, education, history, theology, music, philosophy, science, youth ministries, and general studies. The figures given in the above capsule and in this profile are approximate. There are 4 undergraduate schools. In addition to regional accreditation, Toccoa has baccalaureate program accreditation with NASM and ABHE. The 1100-acre campus is in a small town 90 miles northeast of Atlanta. Including any residence halls, there are 45 buildings.

STUDENT LIFE: 55% of undergraduates are from Georgia. Others are from 42 states, 27 foreign countries, and Canada. 61% are from public schools. 9% are Asian American; 83% White; 5% African American; 2% Hispanic; 1% Foreign. 100% are Protestant. **Female To Male Ratio:** 1.0:1. The average age of freshmen is 19; all undergraduates, 22. 32% do not continue beyond their first year; 47% remain to graduate. **Housing:** 616 students can be accommodated in college housing, which includes single-sex and married student dorms and on-campus apartments. On-campus housing is guaranteed for all 4 years. 64% of students live on campus. Alcohol is not permitted. All students may keep cars.

FACULTY/CLASSROOMS: 75% of faculty are male; 25% are female. 94% teach undergraduates. No introductory courses are taught by graduate students. The average class size in an introductory lecture is 23; in a laboratory is 12; and in a regular course is 12.

PROGRAMS OF STUDY: Toccoa confers B.A., B.S. and B.M. degrees. Associate degrees are also awarded. Bachelor's degrees are awarded in BIOLOGICAL SCIENCE (biology/biological science), BUSINESS (business administration and management), COMMUNICATIONS AND THE ARTS (choral music, communications, English, music, and music performance), EDUCATION (early childhood education, middle school education, music education, recreation education, and science education), HEALTH PROFESSIONS (nursing), SOCIAL SCIENCE (biblical studies, Christian studies, counseling/psychology, crosscultural studies, history, ministries, pastoral studies, philosophy, and youth ministry). Counseling/psychology, cross-cultural studies, early childhood education, and nursing are the strongest academically.

ACTIVITIES: There are no fraternities or sororities. There are 19 groups on campus, including outdoor club, band, choir, chorus, drama, environmental, ethnic, international, jazz band, newspaper, orchestra, photography, radio and TV, religious, social, social service, and student government. Popular campus events include Grocery Bingo, Christmas Banquet, Spiritual Emphasis Week, Lecture Series, and World Outreach Conference. **Sports:** There are 5 intercollegiate sports for men and 5 for women, and 5 intramural sports for men and 5 for women. Facilities include a gymnasium with racquetball courts and a weight room, tennis courts, soccer and baseball fields. **Graduates:** From July 1, 2016 to June 30, 2017, 185 bachelor's degrees were awarded. The most popular majors were counseling psychology (18%), cross cultural studies (13%), and early childhood education (8%). In an average class, 1% graduate in 3 years or less, 43% graduate in 4 years or less, 47% graduate in 5 years or less, and 47% graduate in 6 years or less.

SERVICES: Counseling and information services are available, as is tutoring in most subjects. **Library/Resources:** The library contains 151,427 volumes, 6,471 microform items, and 3,008 audio/video tapes/CDs/DVDs, and subscribes to 20,310 periodicals including electronic. Computerized library services include interlibrary loans, database searching, Internet access, and Wi-Fi capability. Special learning facilities include a natural history museum and radio station. **Physically Challenged Students:** 70% of the campus is accessible. Facilities include wheelchair ramps, elevators, special parking, specially equipped restrooms, special class scheduling, lowered drinking fountains, and special housing. **Special:** The college offers dual majors, and B.A.-B.S. degrees are available. An on-campus work-study program and internships for many majors are also provided. There are 2 national honor societies. **Visiting:** There are regularly scheduled orientations for prospective students, including visits to the admissions counselor, school directors, and the financial aid office arranged 2 weeks in advance. There are guides for informal visits, visitors may sit in on classes, and stay overnight. To schedule a visit, contact the Office of Admissions. **Campus Safety and Security:** Measures include 24-hour foot and vehicle patrol, emergency notification system, and security escort services. There are emergency telephones, lighted pathways/sidewalks, and the campus is closed at night with a guard at the entrance.

REQUIREMENTS: The SAT or ACT is required. A high school education or GED certificate is required. A personal reference from the student's pastor and an essay submitted with the student's application are also required. Admission is based on an index found by multiplying high school GPA by the best total standardized test score. A GPA of 2.0 is required. AP and CLEP credits are accepted. Important factors in the admissions decision are personality/intangible qualities, extracurricular activities record, and leadership record. Students must successfully complete at least 126 semester hours, with an average of 42 hours in the major, maintaining a C- or better, to earn a bachelor's degree. All students must also complete a core curriculum of 69 hours, which includes 30 hours of Bible and doctrine. A GPA of at least 2.0 must be maintained. Additional requirements for graduation include 4 semesters of student ministry, and a senior oral comprehensive exam or a thesis in some majors. **Procedure:** Freshmen are admitted to all sessions. Entrance exams should be taken early in the senior year. There are deferred admissions and rolling admissions plans. Applications should be filed by August 1 for fall entry; January 1 for spring entry; and May 15 for summer entry. The fall 2017 application fee was $25. Notification is sent on a rolling basis. Applications are accepted on-line. **Transfer Students:** 66 transfer students enrolled in 2016-2017. Transfer students must have successfully completed 12 semester hours of college credit courses and have maintained a minimum GPA of 2.0. Students must also provide 3 references and write an essay. **International Students:** There are 13 international students enrolled. They must take the TOEFL. They must also take the SAT or ACT.

ADMISSIONS: 55% of the 2017-2018 applicants were accepted. The SAT scores for the 2017-2018 freshman class were: Critical Reading-- 44% below 500, 36% between 500 and 599, and 20% between 600 and 699. Math-- 49% below 500, 41% between 500 and 599, 9% between 600 and 699, and 1% between 700 and 800. The ACT scores were 69% below 12, 18% between 12 and 17, 9% between 18 and 23, 3% between 24 and 29, and 1% above 30. **Admissions Contact:** Ronald Stewart, Director of Admissions. Email: *admission@tfc.edu* Web: *www.tfc.edu*

FINANCIAL AID: In 2017-2018, 99% of all full-time freshmen received some form of financial aid. 65% of all full-time freshmen received need-based aid. The average freshman award was $17,838. Need-based scholarships or need-based grants averaged $13,493; need-based self-help aid (loans and jobs) averaged $3,838; and other non-need-based awards and non-need-based scholarships averaged $10,411. 31% of undergraduate students work part-time. The average financial indebtedness of the 2017 graduate was $17,181. The state aid form and the college's own financial statement are required. The FAFSA code is 001596. The priority date for freshman financial aid applications for fall entry is May 1. The deadline for filing freshman financial aid applications for fall entry is July 15.

UNIVERSITY OF GEORGIA C-2

www.uga.edu

Athens, GA 30602	(706) 542-2112
	Email: adm-info@uga.edu
Full-time: 11,638 men, 15,425 women	**Faculty:** 1770; I, av$
Part-time: 826 men, 861 women	**Ph.D.s:** 88%
Graduate: 3553 men, 5178 women	**Student/Faculty:** 18 to 1
Year: semesters, summer session	**Tuition:** $11,818 ($30,392)
Room & Board: $10,060	**Freshman Class:** 24165 applied, 13052 accepted, 5824 enrolled
SAT or ACT: required	**CEEB CODE:** 5813
Application Deadline: January 15	**HIGHLY COMPETITIVE**

University of Georgia, chartered in 1785 and part of the University System of Georgia, offers degree programs in agricultural and environmental sciences, arts and sciences, business, ecology, education, engineering, environment and design, family and consumer sciences, forestry and natural resources, journalism and mass communication, law, pharmacy, public health, public and international affairs, social work, and veterinary medicine. There are 17 undergraduate schools and 1 graduate school. In addition to regional accreditation, University of Georgia has baccalaureate program accreditation with AACSB, ABET, ACEJMC, ACPE, ADA, ASLA, CSWE, NASAD, NASM, NRPA, SAF, ALA/CoA, APA/CoA, ASHA, AVMA, AAMFT/COAMFTE, CFA, CADE-ADA, CACREP, CIDA, NASD, NASPAA-COPRA, and NAST. The 767-acre campus is in a small town 70 miles northeast of downtown Atlanta. Including any residence halls, there are 475 buildings.

STUDENT LIFE: 82% of undergraduates are from Georgia. Others are from 50 states, 123 foreign countries, and Canada. 9% are Asian American; 8% African American; 67% White; 5% Hispanic; 5% Foreign; 4% two or more races; 1% race unknown. 11% are Protestant. **Female To Male Ratio:** 1.3:1. The average age of freshmen is 18; all undergraduates, 20. 5% do not continue beyond their first year; 84% remain to graduate. **Housing:** 9727 students can be accommodated in college housing, which includes married student dorms and on-campus apartments. In addition, there are honors houses, language/international houses, fraternity houses, sorority houses, theme housing and learning communities within residence halls. On-campus housing is guaranteed for the freshman year only, is available on a first-come, and first-served basis. 70% of students commute. Alcohol is not permitted. All students may keep cars.

FACULTY/CLASSROOMS: 64% of faculty are male; 36% are female. No introductory courses are taught by graduate students.

PROGRAMS OF STUDY: University of Georgia confers A.B., A.B.J., B.B.A., B.F.A., B.L.A., B.Mus., B.S., B.S.A., B.S.A.B., B.S.A.E., B.S.Bch.E., B.S.B.E., B.S.C.E., B.S.Chem., B.S.C.S.E., B.S.Ed., B.S.Env.E., B.S.E.H., B.S.Env., B.S.E.S., B.S.F.C.S., B.S.F.R., B.S.H.P., B.S.M.E., and B.S.W. degrees. Master's and doctoral degrees are also awarded. Bachelor's degrees are awarded in AGRICULTURE (agricultural communications, animal science, dairy science, fishing and fisheries, forestry and related sciences, horticulture, natural resource/environmental economics, poultry science, and turfgrass and landscape management), BIOLOGICAL SCIENCE (avian sciences, biochemistry, biology/biological science, biotechnology, cell biology, cell & molecular biology, ecology, entomology, genetics, microbiology, nutrition, and nutritional sciences), BUSINESS (accounting, fashion merchandising, finance, finance (financial planning), international business, insurance and risk management, management information systems, management, marketing, real estate, recreation and leisure services, and sports management), COMMUNICATIONS AND THE ARTS (advertising, Arabic, art history, art, classical languages, communication studies, communication science, comparative literature, dance, English, film arts, film, television and digital media, French, German, Germanic languages and literature, Greek, Italian, Japanese, journalism, Latin, linguistics, film and media studies, music, music composition, music performance, music theory and composition, public relations, romance languages and literature, Russian, Spanish, studio art, and theatre acting), COMPUTER AND PHYSICAL SCIENCE (astronomy and physics, chemistry, computer networks & systems, computer science, environmental chemistry, geology, mathematics, physics, and statistics), EDUCATION (agricultural education, art education, Asian studies, athletic training, childhood education, classical studies, early childhood education, English education, health education, mathematics education, middle school education, music education, science education, social studies education, special education, and world language education), ENGINEERING AND ENVIRONMENTAL DESIGN (agricultural engineering, bioengineering, civil engineering, computer engineering, electrical/electronics engineering, environmental engineering, environmental science, landscape architecture, and mechanical engineering), HEALTH PROFESSIONS (biology, communicative disorders, environmental health science, exercise science, health promotion, music therapy, and pharmaceutical science), SOCIAL SCIENCE (African American studies, anthropology, child care/child and family studies, Chinese Studies, cognitive science, consumer services, criminal justice, dietetics, economics, family/consumer studies, food production/management/services, food science, geography, history, home furnishings and equipment management/production/services, human development & family studies, interdisciplinary studies, international political science, Latin American studies, philosophy, political science/government, psychology, religion, social work, sociology, water resources, and women's studies). Biology, psychology, and finance have the largest enrollments.

ACTIVITIES: 21% of men belong to 38 national fraternities; 31% of women belong to 28 national sororities. There are 789 groups on campus, including art, band, cheerleading, chess, choir, chorale, chorus, computers, dance, debate, drama, drill team, environmental, ethnic, film, forensics, honors, international, jazz band, LGBT, literary magazine, marching band, musical theater, newspaper, orchestra, pep band, photography, political, professional, radio and TV, religious, social, social service, student government, symphony, and yearbook. Popular campus events include Dance Marathon, Relay for Life and Dawgs after Dark. **Sports:** There are 8 intercollegiate sports for men and 11 for women, and 24 intramural sports for men and 24 for women. Facilities include a stadium for basketball, and tennis, indoor tennis courts, baseball field, football-training facilities, a sports complex, a student center with gyms, swimming pools, a strength/conditioning room, racquetball courts, an indoor track, and a climbing wall. The Women's Athletic Complex hosts women's soccer and softball programs. **Graduates:** From July 1, 2016 to June 30, 2017, 7629 bachelor's degrees were awarded. The most popular majors were finance (8%), psychology (7%), and biology (6%). In an average class, 4% graduate in 3 years or less, 66% graduate in 4 years or less, 84% graduate in 5 years or less, and 85% graduate in 6 years or less. Of the 2016 graduating class, 20% were enrolled in graduate school within 6 months of graduation, and 70% were employed.

SERVICES: Counseling and information services are available, as is tutoring in every subject. There is a reader service for the blind, and remedial math, reading, and writing. Alternate format textbooks and class materials, note takers, modifications for tests and assignments, and counseling and advisement from learning disability specialists are available. There are also sign language interpreters, text type machines, FM/assistive listening devices, and a pilot closed-captioning program. **Library/Resources:** The library contains 5.2 million volumes. Computerized library services include interlibrary loans, database searching, Internet access, and Wi-Fi capability. Special learning facilities include an art gallery and museum, natural history museum, radio station, TV station, bioscience learning center, rare book and manuscript library, performing arts center, Peabody Awards Archives, and Cox Institute for Newspaper Management Studies **Physically Challenged Students:** 90% of the campus is accessible. Facilities include wheelchair ramps, elevators, special parking, specially equipped restrooms, special class scheduling, lowered drinking fountains, lowered telephones, and special housing, wheelchair vans, auxiliary aides, residence hall accommodations, and adaptive technology lab. **Special:** UG offers cross-registration with University Center institutions in urban Atlanta. In the Governor's Intern Program, students may serve a full-time 10-week internship in a state government agency; many other internships are available within the departments, as well as work-study programs within the university and with many area businesses. A Washington semester, an accelerated degree program in business, a general studies degree, student-designed majors, dual degrees and double majors, and nondegree study are also available. There are 25 national honor societies, Phi Beta Kappa, and a freshman honors program. **Visiting:** There are regularly scheduled orientations for prospective students, including walking and driving tours of the campus and meetings with faculty, staff, and students. There are guides for informal visits, visitors may sit in on classes, and stay overnight. To schedule a visit, contact the Visitors Center at (706) 542-0842. **Campus Safety and Security:** Measures include 24-hour foot and vehicle patrol, emergency notification system, self-defense education, and security escort services. There are shuttle buses, emergency telephones, lighted pathways/sidewalks, and controlled access to dorms/residences.

REQUIREMENTS: The SAT or ACT is required. UG admits freshmen primarily on the basis of high school curriculum, grades earned, and college admissions test scores. The university may consider qualitative information to determine a student's potential for success. Applicants should be high school graduates or present a GED certificate. Students should have taken 4 years each of English, math and science (of these 2 must be lab), 3 of social studies, and 2 of a foreign language. Satisfactory scores are required on the SAT or ACT. An audition is required for music majors. AP and CLEP credits are accepted. Students must have a 2.0 GPA to graduate, and must complete a minimum of 120 semester hours. A baccalaureate degree program must require at least, 21 semester hours of upper division courses in the major field and at least, 39 semester hours of upper division work overall. The core curriculum includes 9 credit hours of Foundation courses, 7-8 hours of Sciences, 3-4 hours of Quantitative Reasoning, 12 hours of World Languages and Culture, Humanities and the Arts, 9 hours of Social Sciences. Required specific disciplines are grammar, composition, literature, math, biological sciences, history, American government, and environmental literacy. Specific courses include basic phys ed and English 1101 and 1102. UG also requires all students to pass the Regents Exit Exam, as well as exams on the federal and state constitutions. **Procedure:** Freshmen are admitted fall, spring, and summer. Entrance exams should be taken by January of the senior year. There is a deferred admissions plan. Early decision applications should be filed by October 15; regular applications, by January 15 for fall entry; October 1 for spring entry; and January 15 for summer entry. The fall 2017 application fee was $60. Notification of early decision is sent December 1; regular decision, April 1. 531 applicants were on the 2017 waiting list; 31 were admitted. Applications are accepted online. **Transfer Students:** 1354 transfer students enrolled in 2016-2017. A transfer GPA of 3.2 is required of all sophomores (30-59 hrs) and 2.8 required with 60 hrs or more. These students are admitted based on space availability and there is no minimum GPA that guarantees admission. Students with fewer than 30 transferable hours are not eligible for transfer admission. 45 of 120 credits required for the bachelor's degree must be completed at UG. **International Students:** There are 1153 international students enrolled. They must take the TOEFL with a minimum score of 550 on the paper-based TOEFL (PBT) or 80 on the Internet-based version (iBT). They must also take the SAT or ACT.

ADMISSIONS: 54% of the 2017-2018 applicants were accepted. The SAT scores for the 2017-2018 freshman class were: Math-- 2% below 500, 27% between 500 and 599, 51% between 600 and 699, and 20% between 700 and 800. Evidence-Based Reading/Writing-- 1% below 500, 15% between 500 and 599, 61% between 600 and 699, and 23% between 700 and 800. The ACT scores were 7% between 18 and 23, 48% between 24 and 29, and 45% above 30. **Admissions Contact:** Patrick Winter, Associate Vice President for Admissions and Enrollment. Email: *adm-info@uga.edu* Web: *www.uga.edu*

FINANCIAL AID: In 2017-2018, 45% of all full-time freshmen received some form of financial aid. 44% of all full-time freshmen received need-based aid. The average freshman award was $13,999. Need-based scholarships or need-based grants averaged $10,769; need-based self-help aid (loans and jobs) averaged $3,421; non-need-based athletic scholarships averaged $23,462; and other non-need-based awards and non-need-based scholarships averaged $3,636. The average financial indebtedness of the 2017 graduate was $23,403. UG is a member of CSS. The FAFSA code is 001598. The priority date for freshman financial aid applications for fall entry is March 1.

UNIVERSITY OF NORTH GEORGIA C-1

www.ung.edu

Dahlonega, GA 30597	(706) 864-2886 (800) 498-9581
Fax: (706) 864-1478	**Email:** admissions-dah@ung.edu
Full-time: 5650 men, 6917 women	**Faculty:** 584; IIA, --$
Part-time: 2208 men, 2929 women	**Ph.D.s:** n/av
Graduate: 165 men, 350 women	**Student/Faculty:** 23 to 1
Year: semesters, summer session	**Tuition:** $7178 ($20,720)
Room & Board: $10,138	**Freshman Class:** 10558 applied, 7694 accepted, 4063 enrolled
SAT CR/M/W: 530/530/500 **ACT:** 23	**CEEB CODE:** 5497
Application Deadline: February 15	**COMPETITIVE**

University of North Georgia, formed from the consolidation of North Georgia College and State University and Gainesville State College, is a liberal arts college within the University System of Georgia. UNG is 1 of 6 colleges in the United States classified as military colleges by the Department of the Army. There are 6 undergraduate schools and 1 graduate school. In addition to regional accreditation, University of North Georgia has baccalaureate program accreditation with AACSB, ACBSP, APTA, NASAD, CAEP, NLN, ACEN, ABA, and and ACS. The 212-acre campus is in a small town 60 miles north of Atlanta. Including any residence halls, there are 25 buildings.

STUDENT LIFE: 95% of undergraduates are from Georgia. Others are from 47 states, 94 foreign countries, and Canada. 90% are from public schools. 78% are White; 4% African American; 4% Foreign; 3% Asian American; 3% two or more races; 10% Hispanic; 1% race unknown. **Female To Male Ratio:** 1.3:1. The average age of freshmen is 18; all undergraduates, 22. **Housing:** 2685 students can be accommodated in college housing, which includes dorms and on-campus apartments. On-campus housing is available on a first-come and first-served basis. 85% of students commute. Alcohol is not permitted. All students may keep cars.

FACULTY/CLASSROOMS: 47% of faculty are male; 51% are female. No introductory courses are taught by graduate students. The average class size in an introductory lecture is 23; in a laboratory is 19; and in a regular course is 19.

PROGRAMS OF STUDY: UNG confers B.A., B.A.S., B.S., B.B.A., B.F.A. and B.S.N. degrees. Associate, master's, and doctoral degrees are also awarded. Bachelor's degrees are awarded in BIOLOGICAL SCIENCE (biology/biological science), BUSINESS (accounting, banking and finance, business administration and management, business economics, finance, management, marketing/retailing/merchandising, and recreation and leisure services), COMMUNICATIONS AND THE ARTS (art, arts administration/management, communication studies, English, fine arts, French, modern language, music, and Spanish), COMPUTER AND PHYSICAL SCIENCE (chemistry, computer science, mathematics, and physics), EDUCATION (art education, early childhood education, elementary education, foreign languages education, health education, mathematics education, middle school education, music education, physical education, science education, secondary education, social science education, and special education), ENGINEERING AND ENVIRONMENTAL DESIGN (preengineering and technological management), HEALTH PROFESSIONS (nursing, predentistry, premedicine, prepharmacy, and preveterinary science), SOCIAL SCIENCE (criminal justice, history, human services, international political science, paralegal studies, political science/government, prelaw, psychology, social science, and sociology). Education, and premedicine are the strongest academically. Biology, nursing, and psychology have the largest enrollments.

ACTIVITIES: 2% of men belong to 2 local and 6 national fraternities; 4% of women belong to 6 national sororities. There are 364 groups on campus, including art, band, chess, choir, chorale, chorus, communications, computers, dance, debate, drama, drill team, environmental, ethnic, forensics, honors, international, jazz band, LGBT, literary magazine, marching band, musical theater, newspaper, pep band, political, professional, radio and TV, religious, social, social service, student government, and yearbook. Popular campus events include Fall/Spring Jam, Frisbee Golf, and Military reviews. **Sports:** There are 6 intercollegiate sports for men and 8 for women, and 19 intramural sports for men and 19 for women. Facilities include a student recreation center, swimming pool, track, a fully equipped exercise room, a rappeling tower, a gym, and an arena. **Graduates:** From July 1, 2016 to June 30, 2017, 1796 bachelor's degrees were awarded. The most popular majors were registered nursing (10%), business administration and management (9%), and biology (7%).

SERVICES: Counseling and information services are available, as is tutoring in most subjects. There is a reader service for the blind, and remedial math, reading, and writing. **Library/Resources:** The library contains 270,623 volumes, 774,482 microform items, and 9,889 audio/video tapes/CDs/DVDs, and subscribes to 2,546 periodicals including electronic. Computerized library services include interlibrary loans, database searching, and Internet access. Special learning facilities include an art gallery, planetarium, radio station, math lab, language lab, and writing center. **Physically Challenged Students:** 50% of the campus is accessible. Facilities include wheelchair ramps, elevators, special parking, specially equipped restrooms, and lowered drinking fountains. **Special:** Special academic programs include a co-op program in business, internships, a 3-2 engineering degree with Georgia Institute of Technology, a joint Engineering degree program with Clemson University, study abroad in Europe, South America, and Canada, dual majors, and credit for life, military, or work experience. There are 9 national honor societies, a freshman honors program, and 23 departmental honors programs. **Visiting:** There are regularly scheduled orientations for prospective students, including an admissions video, college overview, tour, and a meeting with an admissions counselor. There are guides for informal visits and visitors may stay overnight. To schedule a visit, contact Admissions Office. **Campus Safety and Security:** Measures include 24-hour foot and vehicle patrol, emergency notification system, and security escort services. There are shuttle buses, emergency telephones, lighted pathways/sidewalks, and controlled access to dorms/residences.

REQUIREMENTS: The SAT or ACT is required. Students must have graduated from a secondary school with 4 years of English, 3 each of math, science, and social science, and 2 of a foreign language. The GED is accepted if granted at least 5 years later than expected high school graduation date. SAT II: Subject tests are required of home-schooled students. A GPA of 2.0 is required. AP and CLEP credits are accepted. Important factors in the admissions decision are leadership record, advanced placement or honors courses, and evidence of special talent. To graduate, students must complete 120 semester credit hours with a minimum GPA of 2.0. English, math, lab sciences, and social sciences are required. **Procedure:** Freshmen are admitted fall, spring, and summer. Entrance exams should be taken in the junior year. There are deferred admissions and rolling admissions plans. Applications should be filed by February 15 for fall entry; December 15 for spring entry; and April 15 for summer entry. The fall 2017 application fee was $30. Applications are accepted on-line. **Transfer Students:** Transfer students must have maintained a C average and a clear conduct record, and be in good academic standing. Those who have not completed 90 semester hours of transferable credit must have completed the approved precollege curriculum and must submit high school transcripts and the SAT or ACT results. 30 of 120 credits required for the bachelor's degree must be completed at UNG. **International Students:** There are 139 international students enrolled. They must take the TOEFL with a minimum score of 550 on the paper-based TOEFL (PBT) or 79 on the Internet-based version (iBT). They must also take the SAT or ACT.

ADMISSIONS: 73% of the 2017-2018 applicants were accepted. The SAT scores for the 2017-2018 freshman class were: Critical Reading-- 33% below 500, 47% between 500 and 599, 18% between 600 and 699, and 2% between 700 and 800. Math-- 30% below 500, 47% between 500 and 599, 21% between 600 and 699, and 2% between 700 and 800. Writing-- 45% below 500, 41% between 500 and 599, 12% between 600 and 699, and 1% between 700 and 800. The ACT scores were 7% between 12 and 17, 50% between 18 and 23, 39% between 24 and 29, and 3% above 30. 18% of the current freshmen were in the top fifth of their class; 40% were in the top two fifths. **Admissions Contact:** Molly Potts, Director of Undergraduate Admissions. Email: *admissions-dah@ung.edu* Web: *www.ung.edu*

FINANCIAL AID: In 2017-2018, 95% of all full-time freshmen received some form of financial aid. 28% of all full-time freshmen received need-based aid. The average freshman award was $1,973. The college's own financial statement is required. The FAFSA code is 001585. Check with the school for current application deadlines.

UNIVERSITY OF WEST GEORGIA *(The complete profile is made available exclusively on our website, www.barronspac.com)*

VALDOSTA STATE UNIVERSITY C-5
www.valdosta.edu

Valdosta, GA 31698 **(229) 333-5791**
(800) 618-1878
Fax: (229) 333-5482 **Email: admissions@valdosta.edu**

Full-time: 2854 men, 4312 women	**Faculty:** 419; I
Part-time: 618 men, 942 women	**Ph.D.s:** 75%
Graduate: 644 men, 1764 women	**Student/Faculty:** 20 to 1
Year: semesters, summer session	**Tuition:** $6297 ($17,866)
Room & Board: $7900	**Freshman Class:** 5108 applied, 3327 accepted, 1422 enrolled
SAT: required **ACT:** 21	**CEEB CODE:** 5855
Application Deadline: July 1	**COMPETITIVE**

Valdosta State University, founded in 1906, and a unit of the University System of Georgia, is a public liberal arts institution offering degrees in arts and sciences, education, business administration, nursing, fine arts, social work, and library. There are 5 undergraduate schools and 1 graduate school. In addition to regional accreditation, VSU has baccalaureate program accreditation with AACSB, NASAD, NASM, CAEP, CCNE, and NAST. The 172-acre campus is in a suburban area in southern Georgia, 3.5 hours from Atlanta and from Orlando, Florida. Including any residence halls, there are 94 buildings.

STUDENT LIFE: 96% of undergraduates are from Georgia. Others are from 45 states, 70 foreign countries, and Canada. 6% are Hispanic; 49% White; 4% two or more races; 37% African American; 3% Foreign; 1% Asian American. **Female To Male Ratio:** 1.7:1. The average age of freshmen is 18; all undergraduates, 22. **Housing:** 2896 students can be accommodated in college housing, which includes dorms and on-campus apartments. In addition, there are honors houses, language/international houses, special-interest houses, wellness, living learning communities, and 24-hour quiet wings in the dorms. On-campus housing is available on a first-come and first-served basis. 74% of students live on campus. All students may keep cars.

FACULTY/CLASSROOMS: 91% teach undergraduates. No introductory courses are taught by graduate students. The average class size in an introductory lecture is 30; in a laboratory is 23; and in a regular course is 18.

PROGRAMS OF STUDY: VSU confers B.A., B.S., B.B.A., B.G.S., B.M., B.S.Ed., B.S.E.P., and B.S.N. degrees. Associate degrees are also awarded. Biology, early childhood education, and nursing have the largest enrollments.

ACTIVITIES: There are 163 groups on campus, including art, band, cheerleading, chess, chorale, chorus, computers, dance, debate, drama, drum and bugle corps, environmental, ethnic, film, honors, international, jazz band, LGBT, literary magazine, marching band, musical theater, newspaper, orchestra, outdoor/recreation clubs, pep band, political, professional, radio and TV, religious, social, social service, student government, and symphony. Popular campus events include Family Day, and the Happening. **Sports:** There are 6 intercollegiate sports for men and 5 for women, and 12 intramural sports for men and 12 for women. Facilities include a phys ed complex for basketball, a health fitness center, a weight training room, a human performance lab, a gym with a weight room, training room, dance studio, auxiliary gym, outdoor pool, a climbing wall, racketball courts, and an indoor track. **Graduates:** From July 1, 2016 to June 30, 2017, 1657 bachelor's degrees were awarded. The most popular majors were business/marketing (22%), communication/journalism, and education (9%), and psychology (8%).

SERVICES: Counseling and information services are available, as is tutoring in some subjects, such as biology, chemistry, physics, math, computer science, foreign languges, social science, and writing. There is a reader service for the blind. **Library/Resources:** The library contains 539,557 volumes, 1.1 million microform items, and 27,582 audio/video tapes/CDs/DVDs, and subscribes to 2,732 periodicals including electronic. Computerized library services include interlibrary loans, database searching, Internet access, and Wi-Fi capability. Special learning facilities include an art gallery, planetarium, radio station, TV station, an herbarium. **Physically Challenged Students:** All of the campus is accessible. Facilities include wheelchair ramps, elevators, special parking, specially equipped restrooms, special class scheduling, lowered drinking fountains, lowered telephones, and special housing. Students registered with the Access Office are able to register for classes on the first day of registration regardless of classification. Also all campus transportation is accessible. **Special:** Valdosta offers co-op programs, internships, study abrod, accelerated degree program in RN to BSN/MSN Nursing program and 3-2 engineering degree with Georgia Institute of Technology. There are 28 national honor societies, Phi Beta Kappa, and a freshman honors program. **Visiting:** There are regularly scheduled orientations for prospective students, including a tour of the campus, information sessions, advising, meal plan selection, fee payment. There are guides for informal visits and visitors may sit in on classes. To schedule a visit, contact the Admissions Office. **Campus Safety and Security:** Measures include 24-hour foot and vehicle patrol, emergency notification system, self-defense education, and security escort services. There are shuttle buses, emergency telephones, lighted pathways/sidewalks, bicycle patrol, security cameras, and electronic key card access to residence halls.

REQUIREMENTS: The SAT or ACT is required. 19 academic high school units are required 4 each in English, math, and science with 2 lab, 3 in social studies, and 2 in history AP and CLEP credits are accepted. To graduate, all students must complete a minimum of 120 semester hours, including 60 in the core curriculm and 21 in a major, with a GPA of 2.0. Reseasonable proficiency in written and spoken English is also required. **Procedure:** There are deferred admissions and rolling admissions plans. Applications should be filed by July 1 for fall entry; December 1 for spring entry; and May 1 for summer entry. The fall 2017 application fee was $40. Notification is sent on a rolling basis. **Transfer Students:** 787 transfer students enrolled in 2016-2017. 30 of 120 credits required for the bachelor's degree must be completed at VSU. **International Students:** There are 200 international students enrolled. They must take the TOEFL with a minimum score of 523 on the paper-based TOEFL (PBT) or 69 on the Internet-based version (iBT). TOEFL can be subsituted with SAT.

ADMISSIONS: 65% of the 2017-2018 applicants were accepted. The SAT scores for the 2017-2018 freshman class were: Critical Reading--51% below 500, 41% between 500 and 599, and 8% between 600 and 699. Math-- 61% below 500, 32% between 500 and 599, and 6% between 600 and 699. Writing-- 65% below 500, 30% between 500 and 599, and 5% between 600 and 699. **Admissions Contact:** Ryan Hogan, Director of Admissions. Email: *admissions@valdosta.edu* Web: *www.valdosta.edu*

FINANCIAL AID: In 2017-2018, 89% of all full-time freshmen received some form of financial aid. 56% of all full-time freshmen received need-based aid. The average freshman award was $16,340. Need-based scholarships or need-based grants averaged $6,862; need-based self-help aid (loans and jobs) averaged $3,390; non-need-based athletic scholarships averaged $5,933; other non-need-based awards and non-need-based scholarships averaged $3,310; and $2,250 from other forms of aid. 6% of undergraduate students work part-time. The average financial indebtedness of the 2017 graduate was $21,117. VSU is a member of CSS. The FAFSA code is 001599. The priority date for freshman financial aid applications for fall entry is April 1.

WESLEYAN COLLEGE C-3

www.wesleyancollege.edu

Macon, GA 31210 (478) 477-1110
(800) 447-6610
Email: admissions@wesleyancollege.edu

Full-time: 435 women	**Faculty:** 57; IIB, --$
Part-time: 12 men, 124 women	**Ph.D.s:** 94%
Graduate: 9 men, 29 women	**Student/Faculty:** 8 to 1
Year: semesters, summer session	**Tuition:** $22,370
Room & Board: $9570	**Freshman Class:** 617 applied, 302 accepted, 135 enrolled
SAT: required **ACT:** 22	**CEEB CODE:** 5895
Application Deadline: August 1	**COMPETITIVE+**

Wesleyan College, founded in 1836, is a private, liberal arts college for women, affiliated with the United Methodist Church. It is the world's first college chartered to grant degrees to women. There is 1 undergraduate school and 2 graduate schools. In addition to regional accreditation, WC has baccalaureate program accreditation with NASM and Georgia Professional Standards Commission. The 200-acre campus is in a suburban area 90 miles south of Atlanta. Including any residence halls, there are 24 buildings.

STUDENT LIFE: 74% of undergraduates are from Georgia. Others are from 14 states, and 17 foreign countries. 90% are from public schools. 5% are Hispanic; 43% White; 3% Asian American; 29% African American; 15% Foreign. 63% are Protestant; 26% claim no religious affiliation. **Female To Male Ratio:** 28.0:1. The average age of freshmen is 18; all undergraduates, 22. 32% do not continue beyond their first year; 57% remain to graduate. **Housing:** 550 students can be accommodated in college housing, which includes dorms and on-campus apartments. On-campus housing is guaranteed for all 4 years. 76% of students live on campus. Alcohol is not permitted. All students may keep cars.

FACULTY/CLASSROOMS: 42% of faculty are male; 58% are female. All teach undergraduates, and 75% do research. No introductory courses are taught by graduate students. The average class size in an introductory lecture is 13; in a laboratory is 12; and in a regular course is 10.

PROGRAMS OF STUDY: WC confers A.B., B.F.A., and B.S.N. degrees. Master's degrees are also awarded. Bachelor's degrees are awarded in AGRICULTURE (environmental studies), BIOLOGICAL SCIENCE (biology/biological science), BUSINESS (accounting, business administration and management, and international business management), COMMUNICATIONS AND THE ARTS (advertising, art history and appreciation, communications, dramatic arts, English, French, music, Spanish, and studio art), COMPUTER AND PHYSICAL SCIENCE (applied mathematics, chemistry, and mathematics), EDUCATION (early childhood education), HEALTH PROFESSIONS (nursing), SOCIAL SCIENCE (economics, history, interdisciplinary studies, international relations, political science/government, psychology, religion, and women & gender studies). Biology, chemistry, and nursing are the strongest academically. Business administration, psychology, and nursing have the largest enrollments.

ACTIVITIES: There are no fraternities or sororities. There are 27 groups on campus, including art, choir, chorus, dance, debate, drama, ethnic, forensics, honors, international, LGBT, literary magazine, political, professional, religious, social, social service, and student government. Popular campus events include Homecoming, Color Rush, Holiday Banquet, A.X.I.S. Dinner, STUNT, and Candle Lighting at Alumnae Weekend. **Sports:** There are 7 intercollegiate sports for women. Facilities include an equestrian arena, softball and soccer fields, indoor pool, a gym, dance studio, weight room, tennis courts, and fitness trail & center. **Graduates:** From July 1, 2016 to June 30, 2017, 113 bachelor's degrees were awarded. The most popular majors were nursing (21%), business administration (12%), and biology (11%). In an average class, 41% graduate in 4 years or less, 44% graduate in 5 years or less, and 45% graduate in 6 years or less. Of the 2016 graduating class, 22% were enrolled in graduate school within 6 months of graduation, and 36% were employed.

SERVICES: Counseling and information services are available, as is

tutoring in some subjects. Free tutors are available upon request, and the Academic Center is available for all students. **Library/Resources:** The library contains 143,071 volumes, 33,438 microform items, and 4,267 audio/video tapes/CDs/DVDs, and subscribes to 615 periodicals including electronic. Computerized library services include interlibrary loans, database searching, Internet access, and Wi-Fi capability. Special learning facilities include an art gallery, a computerized teaching classroom, language and math labs, collaborative research science labs, and an arboretum. **Physically Challenged Students:** 89% of the campus is accessible. Facilities include wheelchair ramps, elevators, special parking, specially equipped restrooms, and special class scheduling. **Special:** Wesleyan offers cross-registration with Mercer University and a 3-2 engineering degree with Georgia Institute of Technology, Auburn University, and Mercer University. Students can pursue a self-designed interdisciplinary major. Wesleyan also offers internships, study abroad programs, work-study programs, credit for life experience, non-degree study, and pass/fail options. There are 11 national honor societies. **Visiting:** There are regularly scheduled orientations for prospective students, including a campus tour, parent/student panels, class visits, admission and financial aid sessions, and meals in the dining hall. There are guides for informal visits, visitors may sit in on classes, and stay overnight. To schedule a visit, contact Mary Ann Steinbach at admissions@wesleyancollege.edu. **Campus Safety and Security:** Measures include 24-hour foot and vehicle patrol, emergency notification system, self-defense education, and security escort services. There are emergency telephones, lighted pathways/sidewalks, controlled access to dorms/residences, and dorm entrances are locked 24 hours a day, 7 days a week.

REQUIREMENTS: The SAT or ACT is required. The ACT Optional Writing test is also required. Each applicant for admission is reviewed on the following: performance in and quality of a college preparatory curriculum, standardized test score, counselor and teacher recommendation, writing ability, and cocurricular involvement. A minimum of 15 Carnegie units is required, including 4 units of English, 3 each of math, natural sciences, and social sciences, and 2 of foreign language. Admitted students must graduate from an accredited secondary school or have a GED certificate. The admission staff does not require but welcomes the opportunity to interview prospective students. Students who wish to be considered for a performance arts scholarship must submit a portfolio or audition. AP and CLEP credits are accepted. Important factors in the admissions decision are advanced placement or honors courses, evidence of special talent, and leadership record. To graduate, students must complete 120 credit hours with a minimum GPA of 2.0. Students must satisfy proficiency in modern foreign language and writing. The General Education Program at Wesleyan College requires 37-38 credit hours and a minimum of 12 courses. Students must also complete the number of hours and the designated courses required for the major selected including an interdisciplinary integrative experience. All major programs consist of at least 27 semester hours. **Procedure:** Freshmen are admitted fall and spring. Entrance exams should be taken by the fall of the senior year. There are early decision, early admissions, deferred admissions, and rolling admissions plans. Early decision applications should be filed by November 15; regular applications, by August 1 for fall entry; and December 1 for spring entry. The fall 2017 application fee was $30. Notification of early decision is sent December 15. 40 early decision candidates were accepted for the 2017-2018 class. Applications are accepted on-line. **Transfer Students:** 5 transfer students enrolled in 2016-2017. Applicants with fewer than 24 transferable semester hours must submit a final high school transcript and record of standardized test scores in addition to their college transcripts. 30 of 120 credits required for the bachelor's degree must be completed at Wesleyan. **International Students:** There are 94 international students enrolled. They must take the TOEFL with a minimum score of 550 on the paper-based TOEFL (PBT) or 80 on the Internet-based version (iBT). They must also take the SAT or ACT.

ADMISSIONS: 49% of the 2017-2018 applicants were accepted. The ACT scores were 36% below 12, 27% between 12 and 17, 25% between 18 and 23, 7% between 24 and 29, and 7% above 30. 49% of the current freshmen were in the top fifth of their class; 72% were in the top two fifths. 3 freshmen graduated first in their class. **Admissions Contact:** Clint Hobbs, Vice President of Enrollment. Email: *admissions@wesleyancollege.edu* Web: *www.wesleyancollege.edu*

FINANCIAL AID: In 2017-2018, 99% of all full-time freshmen received some form of financial aid. 71% of all full-time freshmen received need-based aid. The average freshman award was $13,842. Need-based scholarships or need-based grants averaged $10,116; need-based self-help aid (loans and jobs) averaged $3,064; and other non-need-based awards and non-need-based scholarships averaged $12,230. 40% of undergraduate students work part-time. The average financial indebtedness of the 2017 graduate was $21,872. The college's own financial statement is required. The FAFSA code is 001600. The priority date for freshman financial aid applications for fall entry is March 1. The deadline for filing freshman financial aid applications for fall entry is May 1.

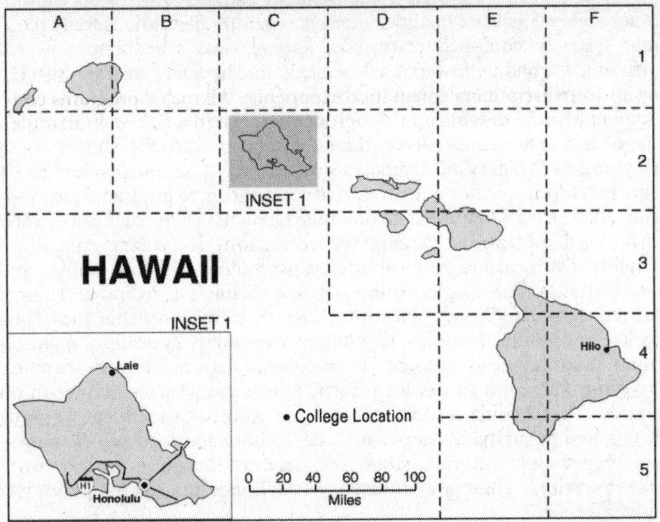

BRIGHAM YOUNG UNIVERSITY/HAWAII C-2

www.byuh.edu

Laie, HI 96762 **(808) 675-3738**

Fax: (808) 675-3211
Full-time: 945 men, 1200 women
Part-time: 99 men, 153 women
Graduate: n/av
Year: semesters, summer session
Room & Board: $6310

SAT: recommended **ACT:** 23
Application Deadline: February 15

Email: admissions@byuh.edu
Faculty: 120
Ph.D.s: 60%
Student/Faculty: 18 to 1
Tuition: $5400 ($10,800)
Freshman Class: 1265 applied, 603 accepted, 297 enrolled
CEEB CODE: 4106
COMPETITIVE

Brigham Young University/Hawaii is a private, comprehensive undergraduate institution. The figures given in the above capsule and in this profile are approximate. There are 5 undergraduate schools. In addition to regional accreditation, BYU has baccalaureate program accreditation with CAEP, CSWE, WASC, and WSCUC. The 200-acre campus is in a rural area 38 miles from Honolulu. Including any residence halls, there are 42 buildings.

STUDENT LIFE: 83% of undergraduates are from out of state, mostly the West. Students are from 41 states, 75 foreign countries, and Canada. 6% are Hispanic; 44% Foreign; 39% White; 29% Asian American; 1% African American; 1% American Indian/Alaska Native. **Female To Male Ratio:** 1.3:1. The average age of freshmen is 21; all undergraduates, 23. 35% do not continue beyond their first year; 47% remain to graduate. **Housing:** 1635 students can be accommodated in college housing, which includes married student dorms and on-campus apartments. On-campus housing is guaranteed for the freshman year only, is available on a first-come, and first-served basis. 62% of students live on campus. Alcohol is not permitted. All students may keep cars.

FACULTY/CLASSROOMS: 80% of faculty are male; 20% are female. All teach undergraduates. No introductory courses are taught by graduate students. The average class size in an introductory lecture is 21; in a laboratory is 17; and in a regular course is 19.

PROGRAMS OF STUDY: BYU confers B.A., B.S., B.F.A., and B.S.W. degrees. Bachelor's degrees are awarded in BIOLOGICAL SCIENCE (biology/biological science), BUSINESS (accounting, hospitality management services, international business management, and tourism), COMMUNICATIONS AND THE ARTS (art, English, fine arts, and music), COMPUTER AND PHYSICAL SCIENCE (computer science, information sciences and systems, and mathematics), EDUCATION (art education, business education, elementary education, English education, mathematics education, science education, social science education, special education, and teaching English as a second/foreign language (TESOL/TEFOL)), HEALTH PROFESSIONS (predentistry and premedicine), SOCIAL SCIENCE (Hawaiian studies, history, interdisciplinary studies, international studies, Pacific area studies, physical fitness/movement, political science/government, psychology, and social work). International business management, accounting, and hospitality and tourism management have the largest enrollments.

ACTIVITIES: There are no fraternities or sororities. There are 41 groups on campus, including art, band, cheerleading, chess, choir, chorale, communications, computers, dance, drama, ethnic, film, honors, international, jazz band, literary magazine, musical theater, newspaper, pep band, political, professional, religious, social, social service, and student government. Popular campus events include International Food Fest, International Cultural Night, and Talent Show. **Sports:** There are 5 intercollegiate sports for men and 6 for women, and 10 intramural sports for men and 10 for women. Facilities include softball fields, soccer fields, a rugby field, tennis and racquetball courts, a swimming pool, water polo, weight room, bowling alley, dance studio, pool tables, golf, cross country, golf, softball, and gyms. **Graduates:** From July 1, 2016 to June 30, 2017, 609 bachelor's degrees were awarded. The most popular majors were international business management (15%), information system (8%), and social work (6%). In an average class, 47% graduate in 6 years or less. Of the 2016 graduating class, 44% were enrolled in graduate school within 6 months of graduation, and 61% were employed.

SERVICES: Counseling and information services are available, as is tutoring in most subjects. There is a reading and writting center available. **Library/Resources:** The library contains 21,004 volumes, 450,000 microform items, and 9,538 audio/video tapes/CDs/DVDs, and subscribes to 17,000 periodicals including electronic. Computerized library services include interlibrary loans, database searching, Internet access, and Wi-Fi capability. Special learning facilities include an art gallery, natural history museum, the nearby Polynesian Cultural Center, which houses an art collection and an artifact collection, computer labs, counseling services, and Church services. **Physically Challenged Students:** 95% of the campus is accessible. Facilities include wheelchair ramps, elevators, special parking, specially equipped restrooms, lowered drinking fountains, and lowered telephones. **Special:** BYU offers work-study programs with the Polynesian Cultural Center, internships, cooperative programs in most majors, non-degree study, student-designed majors in interdisciplinary studies, and pass/fail options. There are 5 national honor societies and a freshman honors program. **Visiting:** There are guides for informal visits. To schedule a visit, contact the University Advancement Office. **Campus Safety and Security:** Measures include 24-hour foot and vehicle patrol and security escort services. There are emergency telephones and lighted pathways/sidewalks.

REQUIREMENTS: The ACT is required. The SAT is recommended. Applicants should be high school graduates. Home-schooled and other non-traditional students should call for more information. A GPA of 2.0 is required. AP and CLEP credits are accepted. Important factors in the admissions decision are geographical diversity, recommendations by alumni, and personality/intangible qualities. Students must complete the 31 to 43 credits in general education curriculum, as well as meet English proficiency, religious education, and exercise science requirements. A total of 120 credit hours, including 40 in the major, must be earned with a minimum GPA of 2.0 for graduation. A thesis is required in certain areas. **Procedure:** Freshmen are admitted to all sessions. Entrance exams should be taken prior to the application deadline. There is a deferred admissions plan. Applications should be filed by February 15 for fall entry; October 1 for winter entry. Notifications are sent April 1. Applications are accepted on-line. **Transfer Students:** 209 transfer students enrolled in 2016-2017. Applicants must have 30 hours of college credit, with a minimum GPA of 2.5. 30 of 120 credits required for the bachelor's degree must be completed at BYU. **International Students:** There are 942 international students enrolled. They must take the TOEFL with a minimum score of 500 on the paper-based TOEFL (PBT). They must also take the ACT.

ADMISSIONS: 48% of the 2017-2018 applicants were accepted. The ACT scores were 26% below 12, 22% between 12 and 17, 24% between 18 and 23, 16% between 24 and 29, and 12% above 30. **Admissions Contact:** Arapata Meha, Dean of Admissions and Records. Email: *admissions@byuh.edu* Web: *www.byuh.edu*

FINANCIAL AID: The FAFSA code is 001606. Check with the school for current application deadlines.

CHAMINADE UNIVERSITY OF HONOLULU
C-2

www.chaminade.edu

Honolulu, HI 96816
(808) 735-8340
(800) 735-3733
Fax: (808) 739-4647
Email: admissions@chaminade.edu

Full-time: 322 men, 804 women
Part-time: 10 men, 21 women
Graduate: 171 men, 391 women
Year: semesters, summer session
Room & Board: $13,100
SAT or ACT: required
Application Deadline: open
Faculty: IIA, -$
Ph.D.s: n/av
Student/Faculty: 12 to 1
Tuition: $24,514
Freshman Class: n/av
CEEB CODE: 4105
COMPETITIVE

Chaminade University of Honolulu, is a private Catholic college, offers a rich educational environment with a dedicated, involved faculty, small class sizes, and a safe, beautiful campus. The figures given in the above capsule and in this profile are approximate. There are 6 undergraduate schools and 4 graduate schools. In addition to regional accreditation, CUH has baccalaureate program accreditation with WASC. The 65-acre campus is in an urban area 4 miles east of downtown Honolulu. Including any residence halls, there are 16 buildings.

STUDENT LIFE: 71% of undergraduates are from Hawaii. Others are from 36 states, and 12 foreign countries. 5% are Hispanic; 4% race unknown; 37% Asian American; 3% African American; 14% White; 10% two or more races; 1% Foreign. 43% are Catholic; 21% Christian; 15% claim no religious affiliation. **Female To Male Ratio:** 2.4:1. The average age of freshmen is 18; all undergraduates, 22. 23% do not continue beyond their first year; 53% remain to graduate. **Housing:** 328 students can be accommodated in college housing, which includes single sex, coed dorms, on-campus apartments, and off-campus apartments. On-campus housing is available on a first-come and first-served basis. 77% of students commute. All students may keep cars.

FACULTY/CLASSROOMS: 54% of faculty are male; 46% are female. All teach undergraduates. No introductory courses are taught by graduate students. The average class size in an introductory lecture is 19; in a laboratory is 14; and in a regular course is 19.

PROGRAMS OF STUDY: CUH confers B.A., B.S., B.S.N., and B.F.A. degrees. Associate and master's degrees are also awarded. Bachelor's degrees are awarded in AGRICULTURE (environmental studies), BIOLOGICAL SCIENCE (biochemistry and biology/biological science), BUSINESS (accounting, business administration and management, and management science), COMMUNICATIONS AND THE ARTS (communications and English), COMPUTER AND PHYSICAL SCIENCE (computer science), EDUCATION (early childhood education, elementary education, and secondary education), ENGINEERING AND ENVIRONMENTAL DESIGN (interior design), HEALTH PROFESSIONS (nursing), SOCIAL SCIENCE (behavioral science, criminal justice, forensic studies, history, humanities, international relations, psychology, religion, and social studies). Forensic sciences, nursing, and biology are the strongest academically. Nursing, criminal justice, and business administration have the largest enrollments.

ACTIVITIES: There are no fraternities or sororities. There are 43 groups on campus, including art, cheerleading, chorale, computers, dance, drama, ethnic, forensics, honors, international, musical theater, newspaper, orchestra, political, professional, radio and TV, religious, social, social service, and student government. Popular campus events include Spring Serendipity, International Extravaganza, and Club Fest. **Sports:** There are 4 intercollegiate sports for men and 6 for women. Facilities include volleyball, tennis, and basketball courts, fitness and weight-training facilities, soccer field, and a student center. **Graduates:** From July 1, 2016 to June 30, 2017, 270 bachelor's degrees were awarded. The most popular majors were nursing (17%), criminology & criminal justice (14%), and business administration (11%). In an average class, 37% graduate in 4 years or less, 50% graduate in 5 years or less, and 53% graduate in 6 years or less.

SERVICES: Counseling and information services are available, as is tutoring in most subjects. There is remedial math, reading, and writing. **Library/Resources:** The library contains 53,239 volumes, 134,000 microform items, and 4,330 audio/video tapes/CDs/DVDs, and subscribes to 273 periodicals including electronic. Computerized library services include interlibrary loans, database searching, Internet access, and Wi-Fi capability. Special learning facilities include a radio station, an observatory and a theater. **Physically Challenged Students:** 95% of the campus is accessible. Facilities include wheelchair ramps, elevators, special parking, specially equipped restrooms, special class scheduling, lowered drinking fountains, lowered telephones, and special housing. **Special:** Internships are available with local companies through the Career Development office. Students may design majors toward a B.A. in humanities. There is a sister university exchange program with the University of Dayton and St. Mary's University. Students may take independent study courses with instructor approval. Accelerated degree programs are available for business administration, management, criminal justice, early childhood education, elementary education, secondary education, English, historical and political studies, psychology, religious studies, and social studies. Distance Learning is also available for business, criminal justice, early childhood education, English, elementary education, historical and political studies, psychology, secondary education, management, and religious studies. There are 8 national honor societies. **Visiting:** There are guides for informal visits and visitors may sit in on classes. To schedule a visit, contact the Admissions Office. **Campus Safety and Security:** Measures include 24-hour foot and vehicle patrol, emergency notification system, self-defense education, and security escort services. There are emergency telephones and lighted pathways/sidewalks.

REQUIREMENTS: The SAT or ACT is required. General Requirements: minimum GPA 2.5, minimum Old SAT 920, New SAT 1000, or ACT 19, high school diploma or equivalent, and a personal statement. Recommendations: 4 years each of English, and college preparatory electives, 3 years of social studies, 3 years of mathematics, and 2 years of science. Nursing Requirements: minimum GPA of 2.75, minimum old SAT 950, new SAT 1030, or ACT 20, 1 year of high school chemistry or equivalent, 1 year of high school biology or equivalent, completion of algebra II, 1-page personal statement, and at least 2 letters of recommendation. A GPA of 2.5 is required. AP and CLEP credits are accepted. Important factors in the admissions decision are leadership record, personality/intangible qualities, and extracurricular activities record. To graduate, students must complete 120 credit hours, including 61 in general education courses and at least 24 in the major at the upper-division level. A 2.0 GPA is required in all majors except criminal justice 2.5, communications 2.5, and education 2.75. Students must complete courses in art, English, history, humanities, mathematics, philosophy, sciences, social studies, and communications. **Procedure:** Freshmen are admitted fall and spring. Entrance exams should be taken during the first semester of the senior year. There are deferred admissions and rolling admissions plans. Application deadlines are open. The fall 2017 application fee was $50. Notification is sent on a rolling basis. Applications are accepted online. **Transfer Students:** 96 transfer students enrolled in 2016-2017. Applicants must have a minimum GPA of 2.00 and write a personal statement. If fewer than 24 college credits, applicants must meet requirements for first-year students. Nursing applicants must have minimum GPA of 2.75, have completed chemistry and college algebra, and meet same requirements of first-year nursing applicants. 30 of 120 credits required for the bachelor's degree must be completed at Chaminade. **International Students:** There are 11 international students enrolled. They must take the TOEFL with a minimum score of 550 on the paper-based TOEFL (PBT) or 79 on the Internet-based version (iBT). They must also take the SAT or ACT.

ADMISSIONS: 41% of the current freshmen were in the top fifth of their class; 78% were in the top two fifths. **Admissions Contact:** Shauna Pimentel-Motooka, Director of Admissions. Email: *admissions@chaminade.edu* Web: *www.chaminade.edu/*

FINANCIAL AID: In 2017-2018, 100% of all full-time freshmen received some form of financial aid. 71% of all full-time freshmen received need-based aid. The average freshman award was $20,785. Need-based scholarships or need-based grants averaged $4,672 ($10,815 maximum); need-based self-help aid (loans and jobs) averaged $3,174 ($6,500 maximum); non-need-based athletic scholarships averaged $6,644 ($28,881 maximum); and other non-need-based awards and non-need-based scholarships averaged $12,892 ($52,100 maximum). CUH is a member of CSS. The FAFSA code is 001605. The priority date for freshman financial aid applications for fall entry is March 1.

HAWAII PACIFIC UNIVERSITY C-2
www.hpu.edu

Honolulu, HI 96813 808-543-8088 (866) 225-5478
Fax: (808) 543-8065 Email: admissions@hpu.edu

Full-time: 1566 men, 2378 women	**Faculty:** 235
Part-time: 1197 men, 1027 women	**Ph.D.s:** 64%
Graduate: 578 men, 717 women	**Student/Faculty:** 17 to 1
Year: semesters, summer session	**Tuition:** $22,440
Room & Board: $10,980	**Freshman Class:** 4129 applied, 2980 accepted, 492 enrolled
SAT CR/M/W: required **ACT:** 21	**CEEB CODE:** 4352
Application Deadline: August 15	**COMPETITIVE**

Hawaii Pacific University, founded in 1965, is a private (non-profit) coeducational institution offering 50 undergraduate and 14 graduate programs in liberal arts, business, natural sciences, nursing, international studies, and communication. The figures given in the above capsule and in this profile are approximate. There is 1 undergraduate school. In addition to regional accreditation, HPU has baccalaureate program accreditation with CSWE, NLN, SATE, and WASC. The 135-acre campus is in an urban area in downtown Honolulu and suburban Kaneohe on the island of Oahu. Including any residence halls, there are 16 buildings.

STUDENT LIFE: 64% of undergraduates are from Hawaii. Others are from 50 states, 80 foreign countries, and Canada. 67% are from public schools. 5% are African American; 29% White; 19% Asian American; 13% Hispanic; 13% Foreign; 1% American Indian/Alaska Native. **Female To Male Ratio:** 1.2:1. The average age of freshmen is 19; all undergraduates, 26. 34% do not continue beyond their first year; 39% remain to graduate. **Housing:** 200 students can be accommodated in college housing, which includes dorms and off-campus apartments. The housing office assists students in finding apartments and other living arrangements in Honolulu. On-campus housing is available on a first-come and first-served basis. 97% of students commute. Alcohol is not permitted. All students may keep cars.

FACULTY/CLASSROOMS: 54% of faculty are male; 46% are female. 91% teach undergraduates, 42% do research, and 42% do both. No introductory courses are taught by graduate students. The average class size in an introductory lecture is 18; in a laboratory is 10; and in a regular course is 18.

PROGRAMS OF STUDY: HPU confers B.A., B.S., B.S.B.A., B.S.N., B.S.W., B.Ed. and B.S.H.S. degrees. Associate and master's degrees are also awarded. Bachelor's degrees are awarded in AGRICULTURE (environmental studies), BIOLOGICAL SCIENCE (biochemistry, biology/biological science, marine biology, marine biology, marine biology, and marine science), BUSINESS (accounting, banking and finance, business administration and management, business economics, entrepreneurial studies, finance, finance, finance, human resources, international business management, management information systems, management information systems, management information systems, management science, marketing management, personnel management, small business management, and tourism), COMMUNICATIONS AND THE ARTS (advertising, communications, English, journalism, multimedia, and public relations), COMPUTER AND PHYSICAL SCIENCE (applied mathematics, chemistry, computer programming, computer science, mathematics, oceanography, and science), EDUCATION (elementary education and teaching English as a second/foreign language (TESOL/TEFOL), ENGINEERING AND ENVIRONMENTAL DESIGN (environmental science and military science), HEALTH PROFESSIONS (nursing, premedicine, and public health), SOCIAL SCIENCE (anthropology, classical/ancient civilization, criminal justice, economics, history, human services, humanities, international relations, international studies, Pacific area studies, political science/government, psychology, public administration, social science, social work, and sociology). Marine biology, nursing, and computer science are the strongest academically. Nursing, computer science, and management have the largest enrollments.

ACTIVITIES: There are no fraternities or sororities. There are 93 groups on campus, including art, band, cheerleading, chorale, computers, dance, debate, drama, environmental, ethnic, film, honors, international, LGBT, literary magazine, musical theater, newspaper, orchestra, pep band, political, professional, religious, social, social service, and student government. Popular campus events include Intercultural Day, Honors Banquet, and Club Carnival. **Sports:** There are 6 intercollegiate sports for men and 6 for women, and 6 intramural sports for men and 6 for women. Facilities include an soccer and softball fields, tennis courts, basketball courts, women's softball team, cheerleading squad and dance team. **Graduates:** From July 1, 2016 to June 30, 2017, 926 bachelor's degrees were awarded. The most popular majors were business administration (33%), nursing (28%), and psychology (7%). In an average class, 4% graduate in 3 years or less, 23% graduate in 4 years or less, 36% graduate in 5 years or less, and 39% graduate in 6 years or less. Of the 2016 graduating class, 40% were enrolled in graduate school within 6 months of graduation, and 69% were employed.

SERVICES: Counseling and information services are available, as is tutoring in most subjects. There is remedial math, reading, and writing. **Library/Resources:** The library contains 175,000 volumes, 415,000 microform items, and 6,300 audio/video tapes/CDs/DVDs, and subscribes to 45,000 periodicals including electronic. Computerized library services include interlibrary loans, database searching, Internet access, and Wi-Fi capability. Special learning facilities include an art gallery, a research vessel. **Physically Challenged Students:** 75% of the campus is accessible. Facilities include wheelchair ramps, elevators, special parking, specially equipped restrooms, special class scheduling, lowered drinking fountains, and lowered telephones. **Special:** Upperclassmen may participate in internships and work-study programs with numerous companies and study abroad in 16 countries. HPU also offers accelerated degree and co-op programs in all majors, B.A.-B.S. degrees in most majors, student-designed majors, dual majors in all business subjects, a 3-2 engineering degree with Washington University in St. Louis and the University of Southern California, credit for military experience, nondegree study, and pass/fail options. There are 18 national honor societies, a freshman honors program, and 7 departmental honors programs. **Visiting:** There are regularly scheduled orientations for prospective students, with an appointment required. There are guides for informal visits and visitors may sit in on classes. To schedule a visit, contact the Admissions Office. **Campus Safety and Security:** Measures include 24-hour foot and vehicle patrol, emergency notification system, and security escort services. There are shuttle buses, emergency telephones, and lighted pathways/sidewalks.

REQUIREMENTS: The SAT or ACT is required. Hawaii Pacific University prefers completion of 20 credits based on 4 years of English, 2 each of math, social studies, history, and science. An essay and an interview are recommended. Certain programs, for example, marine science and nursing, have more specific admission requirements. A GPA of 2.5 is required. AP and CLEP credits are accepted. Important factors in the admissions decision are recommendations by school officials, extracurricular activities record, and evidence of special talent. Seniors who have completed a minimum of 100 semester hours of credit toward their undergraduate degree program and have a cumulative GPA of at least 3.0 may enroll concurrently in certain graduate degree programs. Students enrolled in this program may earn a maximum of 12 semester hours of dual graduate and undergraduate credit while pursuing both degrees. (MA-TESL allows only 6 AL concurrent credits). **Procedure:** Freshmen are admitted to all sessions. Entrance exams should be taken during the spring or summer of the junior year or the fall of the senior year. There are early admissions, deferred admissions, and rolling admissions plans. Applications should be filed by August 15 for fall entry; October 15 for spring entry. The fall 2017 application fee was $50. Applications are accepted on-line. **Transfer Students:** 890 transfer students enrolled in 2016-2017. Applicants must have a GPA of 2.0 in a minimum of 24 credit hours. The SAT or ACT and an interview are recommended. 30 of 124 credits required for the bachelor's degree must be completed at HPU. **International Students:** There are 632 international students enrolled. They must take the TOEFL with a minimum score of 550 on the paper-based TOEFL (PBT) or 80 on the Internet-based version (iBT) and the college's own test, or take the IELTS, scoring a minimum of 6, or the APIEL, scoring a minimum of 3.

ADMISSIONS: 72% of the 2017-2018 applicants were accepted. The ACT scores were 47% below 12, 30% between 12 and 17, 14% between 18 and 23, 5% between 24 and 29, and 5% above 30. 44% of the current freshmen were in the top fifth of their class; 76% were in the top two fifths. 18 freshmen graduated first in their class. **Admissions Contact:** Sara Sato, Assistant V.P. Enrollment Management. Email: *admissions@hpu.edu* Web: *www.hpu.edu*

FINANCIAL AID: 36% of all full-time freshmen received need-based aid. The FAFSA code is 007279. The priority date for freshman financial aid applications for fall entry is March 1.

UNIVERSITY OF HAWAII AT HILO F-4

www.hilo.hawaii.edu

Hilo, HI 96720	**(808) 932-7446** **(800) 897-4456**
Fax: (808) 933-0861	**Email: uhhadm@hawaii.edu**
Full-time: 880 men, 1335 women	**Faculty:** 221; I, -$
Part-time: 235 men, 400 women	**Ph.D.s:** 80%
Graduate: 30 men, 75 women	**Student/Faculty:** 12 to 1
Year: semesters, summer session	**Tuition:** $7620 ($20,580)
Room & Board: $10,418	**Freshman Class:** n/av
SAT or ACT: required	**CEEB CODE:** 4869
Application Deadline: July 1	**VERY COMPETITIVE**

University of Hawaii at Hilo, founded in 1970, is part of the public University of Hawaii and offers degree programs through its Colleges of Agriculture, Arts and Sciences, Business & Economics, Hawaiian language and Pharmacy. As the only university on Hawaii Island, UH at Hilo offers many unique and popular major programs, including business, marine science, volcanology, nursing, astronomy, environmental science, psychology and Hawaiian studies. There are 5 undergraduate schools and 2 graduate schools. In addition to regional accreditation, UH Hilo has baccalaureate program accreditation with NLN. The 115-acre campus is in a small town of Hilo, on Hawaii Island. Including any residence halls, there are 54 buildings.

STUDENT LIFE: 69% of undergraduates are from Hawaii. Others are from 46 states, 32 foreign countries, and Canada. 76% are from public schools. 7% are Foreign; 52% Asian American; 3% Hispanic; 23% White; 2% African American; 14% two or more races; 1% American Indian/Alaska Native. **Female To Male Ratio:** 1.6:1. The average age of all undergraduates is 27. 29% do not continue beyond their first year; 39% remain to graduate. **Housing:** 800 students can be accommodated in college housing, which includes married student dorms, on-campus apartments, and off-campus apartments. In addition, there are special-interest houses, and an educational/recreational enrichment hall. On-campus housing is guaranteed for the freshman year only, is available on a first-come, and first-served basis. 80% of students commute. Alcohol is not permitted. All students may keep cars.

FACULTY/CLASSROOMS: 60% of faculty are male; 40% are female. All teach undergraduates and all do research. No introductory courses are taught by graduate students. The average class size in an introductory lecture is 35; in a laboratory is 20; and in a regular course is 19.

PROGRAMS OF STUDY: UH at Hilo confers B.A., B.S., B.B.A. and B.S.N. degrees. Master's and doctoral degrees are also awarded. Bachelor's degrees are awarded in AGRICULTURE (agriculture), BIOLOGICAL SCIENCE (biology/biological science and marine science), BUSINESS (accounting and business administration and management), COMMUNICATIONS AND THE ARTS (art, art studies, communications, English, Hawaiian, Japanese, linguistics, and music), COMPUTER AND PHYSICAL SCIENCE (astronomy, chemistry, computer science, geology, mathematics, natural sciences, and physics), ENGINEERING AND ENVIRONMENTAL DESIGN (environmental science), HEALTH PROFESSIONS (biology and nursing), SOCIAL SCIENCE (anthropology, criminal justice, geography, Hawaiian studies, history, Japanese studies, liberal arts/general studies, philosophy, political science/government, psychology, and sociology). Business, computer science, marine science, Hawaiian studies, nursing, and biology are the strongest academically. Business, psychology, and marine science have the largest enrollments.

ACTIVITIES: There are no fraternities or sororities. There are 40 groups on campus, including art, band, cheerleading, chess, choir, chorale, chorus, computers, dance, drama, environmental, ethnic, honors, international, jazz band, LGBT, literary magazine, musical theater, newspaper, pep band, political, professional, radio and TV, religious, social, social service, and student government. Popular campus events include International Nights, May Day, and Dances. **Sports:** There are 5 intercollegiate sports for men and 7 for women, and 10 intramural sports for men and 10 for women. Facilities include a student activities center with billiards and game room, an athletic complex with basketball courts and a weight room, fitness rooms, swimming pool, tennis courts, baseball, softball, and soccer fields. **Graduates:** From July 1, 2016 to June 30, 2017, 955 bachelor's degrees were awarded. The most popular majors were psychology (9%), kinesiology & exercise science (8%), and business administration (7%). In an average class, 1% graduate in 3 years or less, 34% graduate in 4 years or less, 53% graduate in 5 years or less, and 60% graduate in 6 years or less.

SERVICES: Counseling and information services are available, as is tutoring in most subjects. There is a reader service for the blind, and remedial math, reading, and writing. **Library/Resources:** The library contains 240,000 volumes, 11,000 microform items, and subscribes to 1,200 periodicals including electronic. Computerized library services include interlibrary loans, database searching, Internet access, and Wi-Fi capability. Special learning facilities include an art gallery, planetarium, and radio station. **Physically Challenged Students:** 95% of the campus is accessible. Facilities include wheelchair ramps, elevators, special parking, specially equipped restrooms, special class scheduling, lowered drinking fountains, and lowered telephones. **Special:** UH Hilo offers cross-registration with Hawaii Community College, a political science legislative internship and other internships in business and psychology, and many work-study programs. Students may study abroad through a variety of programs and other internships in business and psychology. The school permits a student-designed liberal studies major, dual degrees, a 3-2 engineering degree with the University of Hawaii at Manoa, nondegree study, pass/fail options, and credit for military experience. **Visiting:** There are regularly scheduled orientations for prospective students, including a campus tour and a meeting with an admissions counselor. There are guides for informal visits and visitors may sit in on classes. To schedule a visit, contact the Admissions Office. **Campus Safety and Security:** Measures include 24-hour foot and vehicle patrol, emergency notification system, self-defense education, and security escort services. There are emergency telephones and lighted pathways/sidewalks.

REQUIREMENTS: The SAT or ACT is required. Applicants should be high school graduates or present a GED certificate. Students should have earned 22 academic credits, including 4 units of English, 3 each of math, and physical sciences, and 7 of electives. Applications are accepted on-line. A GPA of 2.5 is required. AP and CLEP credits are accepted. Important factors in the admissions decision are advanced placement or honors courses, recommendations by school officials, and evidence of special talent. To graduate, students must earn a minimum of 120 semester hours, including at least 30 in the college from which a degree is sought, with a 2.0 GPA overall and in the major. Students also must complete general education requirements, including 10 semester hours of natural sciences with 1 hour of lab, 9 each of humanities and social sciences, 6 of world cultures, and 3 each of English composition and quantitative reasoning. 3 writing-intensive sourses and 1 Hawaiian/Asian/Pacific course are also required. **Procedure:** Freshmen are admitted fall and spring. Entrance exams should be taken by November of the senior year. There are early admissions and rolling admissions plans. Applications should be filed by July 1 for fall entry; December 1 for spring entry. The fall 2017 application fee was $50. Applications are accepted on-line. **Transfer Students:** 720 transfer students enrolled in 2016-2017. Applicants must have a GPA of 2.0; those with fewer than 24 college credits must submit their high school transcript and SAT I or ACT results. 30 of 120 credits required for the bachelor's degree must be completed at UH at Hilo. **International Students:** There are 311 international students enrolled. They must take the TOEFL and the college's own test. The SAT I or ACT is not required, but it is recommended.

Admissions Contact: Admissions Office Email: *uhhadm@hawaii.edu* Web: *www.hilo.hawaii.edu*

FINANCIAL AID: In 2017-2018, 65% of all full-time freshmen received some form of financial aid. 65% of all full-time freshmen received need-based aid. 70% of undergraduate students work part-time. The average financial indebtedness of the 2017 graduate was $10,698. UH at Hilo is a member of CSS. The college's own financial statement is required. The FAFSA code is 001611. The deadline for filing freshman financial aid applications for fall entry is March 1.

UNIVERSITY OF HAWAII AT MANOA C-2

www.manoa.hawaii.edu

Honolulu, HI 96822 (808) 956-5366
(800) 823-9771
Fax: (808) 956-7115 **Email:** uhmanoa.admissions@hawaii.edu

Full-time: 4759 men, 5917 women
Part-time: 958 men, 1133 women
Graduate: 5825 men, 7307 women
Year: semesters, summer session
Room & Board: $11,529
SAT CR/M/W: 530/550/520 **ACT:** 24
Application Deadline: May 1
Faculty: 1148; I, av$
Ph.D.s: 91%
Student/Faculty: 10 to 1
Tuition: $11,732 ($33,764)
Freshman Class: 7861 applied, 6296 accepted, 1974 enrolled
CEEB CODE: 4867
COMPETITIVE

University of Hawaii at Manoa, founded in 1907, is a public research institution in the University of Hawaii system. The undergraduate programs offered include liberal arts and sciences, business, education, engineering, nursing, tropical agriculture, architecture, travel industry management, physical science, technology, Hawaiian, Asian-Pacific studies, social work, and medicine. Cost of tuition varies by programs chosen by student. There are 14 undergraduate schools and 15 graduate schools. In addition to regional accreditation, UH Manoa has baccalaureate program accreditation with AACSB, ABET, ADA, CSWE, NAAB, NASM, CAEP, NLN, CODA, and NLNAC. The 320-acre campus is in a small town in Manoa, Valley, just outside downtown Honolulu.

STUDENT LIFE: 67% of undergraduates are from Hawaii. Others are from 50 states, 126 foreign countries, and Canada. 68% are from public schools. 40% are Asian American; 20% White; 2% Hispanic; 2% Foreign; 17% American Indian/Alaska Native; 16% two or more races; 1% African American. **Female To Male Ratio:** 1.2:1. The average age of freshmen is 18; all undergraduates, 22. 23% do not continue beyond their first year; 55% remain to graduate. **Housing:** 3696 students can be accommodated in college housing, which includes married student dorms and on-campus apartments. In addition, there are honors houses, language/international houses, special-interest houses, substance free/wellness, first-year experience, technology, and 24-hour quiet halls. On-campus housing is guaranteed for the freshman year only and is available on a lottery system for upperclassmen. 53% of students live on campus. All students may keep cars.

FACULTY/CLASSROOMS: 56% of faculty are male; 44% are female. 81% teach undergraduates. Graduate students teach 20% of introductory courses. The average class size in an introductory lecture is 38; in a laboratory is 15; and in a regular course is 22.

PROGRAMS OF STUDY: UH Manoa confers B.A., B.S., B.B.A., B.Ed., B.F.A., B.Mus., and B.S.W. degrees. Master's and doctoral degrees are also awarded. Bachelor's degrees are awarded in AGRICULTURE (animal science, natural resource management, plant protection (pest management), plant science, and soil science), BIOLOGICAL SCIENCE (biology/biological science, botany, marine biology, microbiology, and zoology), BUSINESS (accounting, banking and finance, business administration and management, human resources, international business management, management information systems, management science, marketing/retailing/merchandising, recreation and leisure services, and tourism), COMMUNICATIONS AND THE ARTS (apparel design, art, Chinese, classics, communications, dance, dramatic arts, English, English as a second/foreign language, French, German, Hawaiian, Japanese, journalism, Korean, linguistics, music, Russian, Spanish, and speech/debate/rhetoric), COMPUTER AND PHYSICAL SCIENCE (atmospheric sciences and meteorology, chemistry, computer science, geology, geophysics and seismology, information sciences and systems, mathematics, and physics), EDUCATION (elementary education, physical education, and secondary education), ENGINEERING AND ENVIRONMENTAL DESIGN (bioengineering, civil engineering, electrical/electronics engineering, environmental science, and mechanical engineering), HEALTH PROFESSIONS (dental hygiene, exercise science, medical laboratory technology, medical technology, nursing, and speech pathology/audiology), SOCIAL SCIENCE (American studies, anthropology, Asian/Oriental studies, economics, ethnic studies, family/consumer resource management, food science, geography, Hawaiian studies, history, interdisciplinary studies, Pacific area studies, peace studies, philosophy, political science/government, psychology, religion, social work, sociology, and women's studies). Biology, art, and business have the largest enrollments.

ACTIVITIES: 1% of men belong to 1 local and 2 national fraternities; 1% of women belong to 1 local and 1 national sorority. There are 100 groups on campus, including art, band, cheerleading, chess, choir, chorale, chorus, dance, drama, drill team, ethnic, film, honors, international, LGBT, literary magazine, marching band, musical theater, newspaper, opera, pep band, photography, political, professional, radio and TV, religious, social, social service, student government, and symphony. Popular campus events include Live Band at Bale, Movie Nights, Sustainable UH, and Recreational Sports Events. **Sports:** There are 9 intercollegiate sports for men and 13 for women, and 24 intramural sports for men and 21 for women. Facilities include an arena that houses basketball, volleyball, and gymnasiums, a weight training and conditioning center, baseball stadium, swimming facilities, a turf field and rubberized track, a softball field, tennis courts, golf, sailing, water polo, cross country, football, and women's soccer. **Graduates:** From July 1, 2016 to June 30, 2017, 3600 bachelor's degrees were awarded. The most popular majors were buisness/marketing (20%), health professions and related programs (8%), social sciences, and biological/life sciences (7%). In an average class, 15% graduate in 4 years or less, 40% graduate in 5 years or less, and 51% graduate in 6 years or less.

SERVICES: Counseling and information services are available, as is tutoring in some subjects. There is a reader service for the blind. **Library/Resources:** The library contains 3.4 million volumes, 2.4 million microform items, and 73,000 audio/video tapes/CDs/DVDs, and subscribes to 59,000 periodicals including electronic. Computerized library services include interlibrary loans, database searching, Internet access, and Wi-Fi capability. Special learning facilities include an art gallery, radio station, TV station, Hamilton houses research collections in: humanities, social sciences and technology, collections for Asia, Hawaii and the Pacific. There are also archived manuscripts and other special collections. **Physically Challenged Students:** 40% of the campus is accessible. Facilities include wheelchair ramps, elevators, special parking, specially equipped restrooms, special class scheduling, lowered drinking fountains, lowered telephones, and special housing. Disability access information is available on request, and auxiliary aids and program adjustments can be arranged on an individual basis. **Special:** Internships are available with a variety of employers, including the state legislature, and through 55 different offices as well as academic departments via career services. Co-op and workstudy programs, dual majors, non-degree study, and pass/fail options are available. The liberal studies program offers student-designed majors. Students may study abroad in any one of 20 countries for a summer, a semester, or a year. There are 9 national honor societies, Phi Beta Kappa, a freshman honors program, and 45 departmental honors programs. **Visiting:** There are regularly scheduled orientations for prospective students, visiting students can meet with an admissions representative and tour the campus with a current Manoa student. To schedule a visit, contact the School and College Services at visituhm@hawaii.edu. **Campus Safety and Security:** Measures include 24-hour foot and vehicle patrol, emergency notification system, and security escort services. There are shuttle buses, emergency telephones, lighted pathways/sidewalks, crime alerts via campuswide e-mail, and a campus security web site.

REQUIREMENTS: The SAT or ACT is required. The ACT Optional Writing test is also required. Applicants must be graduates of an accredited secondary school, and have the minimum required score. The GED is also accepted. UH at Monoa requires 22 Carnegie units or 17 academic credits, including 4 units of English, 3 units each of math, science, and social studies, 4 units of college preparatory courses, and 5 electives. UH at Monoa requires applicants to be in the upper 40% of their class. A GPA of 2.8 is required. AP and CLEP credits are accepted. Important factors in the admissions decision are advanced placement or honors courses, recommendations by school officials, and leadership record. In most disciplines, a minimum GPA of 2.0 and a total of 124 credit hours are required for graduation. The total number of hours required in the major varies according to discipline. All students must fulfill general education core requirements. **Procedure:** Freshmen are admitted fall and spring. Entrance exams should be taken by December of the senior year for fall admission. There is a rolling admissions plan. Applications should be filed by May 1 for fall entry; October 1 for spring entry. The fall 2017 application fee was $70. Notification is sent on a rolling basis. Applications are accepted on-line. **Transfer Students:** 1530 transfer students enrolled in 2016-2017. Applicants must have a total of 24 semester credits with a minimum GPA of 2.5. All college transcripts are required. Student may enroll in the fall and spring. 30 of 124 credits required for the bachelor's degree must be completed at UH Manoa. **International Students:** There are 628 international students enrolled. They must take the TOEFL with a minimum score of 500 on the paper-based TOEFL (PBT) or 100 on the Internet-based version (iBT). They must also take the SAT or ACT, scoring 510.

ADMISSIONS: 80% of the 2017-2018 applicants were accepted. The SAT scores for the 2017-2018 freshman class were: Critical Reading-- 34% below 500, 44% between 500 and 599, 18% between 600 and 699, and 3% between 700 and 800. Math-- 26% below 500, 44% between 500 and 599, 25% between 600 and 699, and 5% between 700 and 800. Writing-- 42% below 500, 43% between 500 and 599, 15% between 600 and 699, and 2% between 700 and 800. The ACT scores were 4% between 12 and 17, 48% between 18 and 23, 40% between 24 and 29, and 8% above 30. 60% of the current freshmen were in the top fifth of their class; 82% were in the top two fifths. 24 freshmen graduated first in their class.
Admissions Contact: Dr. Alan Yang, Interim Director of Admissions and Records. Email: *uhmanoa.admissions@hawaii.edu* Web: *www.manoa.hawaii.edu*

FINANCIAL AID: In 2017-2018, 66% of all full-time freshmen received some form of financial aid. 38% of all full-time freshmen received need-based aid. The average freshman award was $14,790. Need-based scholarships or need-based grants averaged $9,904; need-based self-help aid (loans and jobs) averaged $4,177; non-need-based athletic scholarships averaged $11,092; other non-need-based awards and non-need-based scholarships averaged $3,907; and $21,189 from other forms of aid. 27% of undergraduate students work part-time. The average financial indebtedness of the 2017 graduate was $25,724. The college's own financial statement is required. The FAFSA code is 001610. The deadline for filing freshman financial aid applications for fall entry is March 1.

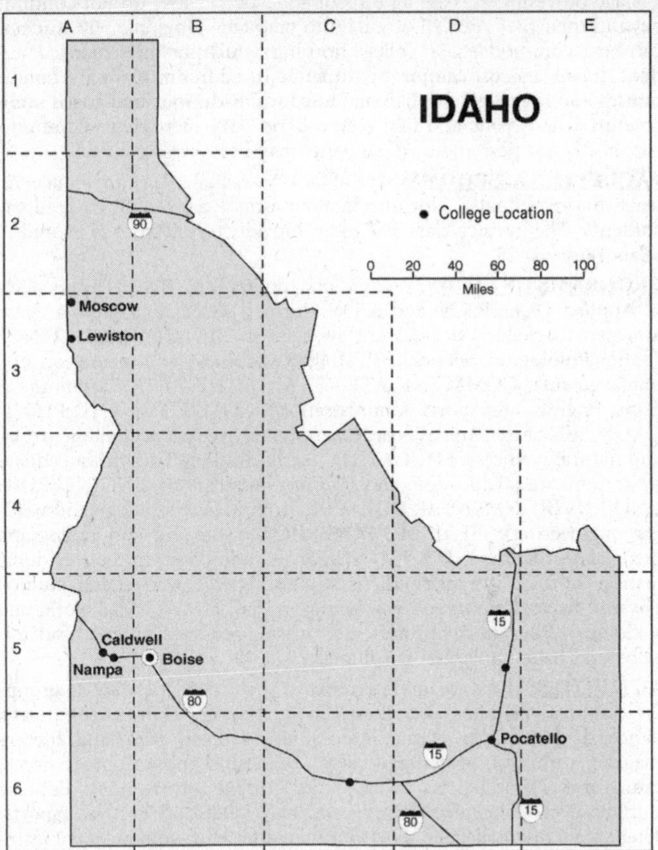

ALBERTSON COLLEGE OF IDAHO
(See The College of Idaho)

BOISE STATE UNIVERSITY — B-5

www.boisestate.edu

Boise, ID 83725	**(208) 426-1156** **(800) 824-7017**
Fax: (208) 426-3765	**Email: bsuinfo@boisestate.edu**
Full-time: 5700 men, 6777 women	**Faculty:** n/av
Part-time: 3499 men, 4791 women	**Ph.D.s:** n/av
Graduate: 1298 men, 2092 women	**Student/Faculty:** n/av
Year: semesters, summer session	**Tuition:** $7326 ($22,642)
Room & Board: $10,042	**Freshman Class:** n/av
SAT or ACT: required	**CEEB CODE:** 4018
Application Deadline: May 15	**COMPETITIVE**

Boise State University, founded in 1932, is a public, metropolitan research university offering an array of undergraduate and graduate degrees in the arts and sciences, business, education, engineering, health science, public affairs, and technology. There are 7 undergraduate schools and 1 graduate school. In addition to regional accreditation, BSU has baccalaureate program accreditation with AACSB, ABET, ACCE, CAHEA, CSWE, NASAD, NASM, NLN, JCERT, EHAC, and CoARC. The 286-acre campus is in an urban area in Boise, Idaho. Including any residence halls, there are 209 buildings.

STUDENT LIFE: 72% of undergraduates are from Idaho. Others are from 50 states, 58 foreign countries, and Canada. 74% are White; 13% Hispanic; 4% two or more races; 3% Foreign; 2% Asian American; 2% race unknown; 1% African American; 1% American Indian/Alaska Native. **Female To Male Ratio:** 1.3:1. The average age of freshmen is 18; all undergraduates, 24. 24% do not continue beyond their first year; 38% remain to graduate. **Housing:** 3158 students can be accommodated in college housing, which includes gender neutral, coed, and married student dorms and on-campus apartments. In addition, there are honors houses, special-interest houses, fraternity houses, and sorority houses. On-campus housing is guaranteed for the freshman year only, is available on a first-come, and first-served basis. 83% of students commute. All students may keep cars.

FACULTY/CLASSROOMS: No introductory courses are taught by graduate students.

PROGRAMS OF STUDY: BSU confers B.A., B.A.S., B.G.S., B.B.A., B.F.A., B.S., and B.Mus. degrees. Associate, master's, and doctoral degrees are also awarded. Bachelor's degrees are awarded in AGRICULTURE (environmental studies), BIOLOGICAL SCIENCE (biology/biological science), BUSINESS (accounting, business administration and management, economics – statistics, finance, international business management, marketing/retailing/merchandising, and supply chain management), COMMUNICATIONS AND THE ARTS (art, communications, dramatic arts, English, English literature, English Writing, fine arts, French, German, music, Spanish, and theatre arts), COMPUTER AND PHYSICAL SCIENCE (chemistry, computer science, geology, geophysics and seismology, geoscience, information sciences and systems, mathematics, physics, and radiological technology), EDUCATION (art education, education, elementary education, English education, music education, physical education, secondary education, social science education, and special education), ENGINEERING AND ENVIRONMENTAL DESIGN (civil engineering, construction management, electrical/electronics engineering, materials science, and mechanical engineering), HEALTH PROFESSIONS (environmental health science, health science, nursing, predentistry, premedicine, prepharmacy, prephysical therapy, preveterinary science, and respiratory therapy), SOCIAL SCIENCE (anthropology, criminal justice, early childhood studies, economics, history, interdisciplinary studies, philosophy, political science/government, psychology, social science, social work, and sociology). Health science studies & nursing, management, and marketing & finance have the largest enrollments.

ACTIVITIES: There are 461 groups on campus, including residence life club, art, band, cheerleading, choir, chorale, communications, computers, dance, debate, drama, drill team, environmental, ethnic, film, health & ability club, honors, international, jazz band, LGBT, literary magazine, marching band, newspaper, orchestra, pep band, political, professional, radio and TV, religious, social, social service, and student government. Popular campus events include Bronco Welcome, Annual Seven Arrows Contest Pow Wow, Homecoming, Annual Spring Fling, Tunnel of Oppression, and Undergraduate Research & Scholarship Conference. **Sports:** There are 7 intercollegiate sports for men and 11 for women, and 24 intramural sports for men and 24 for women. Facilities include a student recreation center, a stadium, indoor arena, aquatic complex, racquetball courts, indoor and outdoor tennis courts, and indoor and outdoor tracks. **Graduates:** From July 1, 2016 to June 30, 2017, 3167 bachelor's degrees were awarded. The most popular majors were registered nursing (9%), health science studies (7%), and communications (6%). In an average class, 15% graduate in 4 years or less, 30% graduate in 5 years or less, and 38% graduate in 6 years or less.

SERVICES: Counseling and information services are available, as is tutoring in some subjects, such as accounting, biology, foreign language, algebra, physics, economics, finance, chemistry, and engineering. There is a reader service for the blind, and remedial math, reading, and writing. **Library/Resources:** The library contains 644,899 volumes, and 14,893 audio/video tapes/CDs/DVDs, and subscribes to 1,889 periodicals including electronic. Computerized library services include interlibrary loans, database searching, Internet access, and Wi-Fi capability. Special learning facilities include an art gallery, radio station, a technology center. **Physically Challenged Students:** 97% of the campus is accessible. Facilities include wheelchair ramps, elevators, special parking, specially equipped restrooms, special class scheduling, lowered drinking fountains, lowered telephones, special housing, and electric doors. **Special:** Boise State offers internships, work-study programs, dual majors, a general studies degree, nondegree study, pass/fail options, and study abroad. There are 7 national honor societies, Phi Beta Kappa, a freshman honors program, and 5 departmental honors programs. **Visiting:** There are regularly scheduled orientations for prospective students, information session, campus tour, workshops, and housing. There are guides for informal visits and visitors may sit in on classes. To schedule a visit, contact the Admissions Office. **Campus Safety and Security:** Measures include 24-hour foot and vehicle patrol, emergency notification system, and security escort services. There are shuttle buses, emergency telephones, lighted pathways/sidewalks, and controlled access to dorms/residences.

REQUIREMENTS: The SAT or ACT is recommended. Students must graduate from an accredited high school and have an appropriate GPA and ACT or SAT test score (as rated by the school's admission index). Students must have completed 4 years of English, 3 each of math (algebra I and higher) and natural science, 2.5 of social science, 1 of humanities or foreign language, and 1.5 in other college-preparatory classes. Students who have not completed all the above classes but meet the other admission requirements will be considered for provisional admission status. AP and CLEP credits are accepted. To graduate, students must complete the number of credits specified for their degree with a minimum GPA of 2.0. Requirements include 6 semester hours in English composition and 12 each in arts and humanities, social sciences, math, and natural sciences. Students must fulfill all Foundation Studies Program requirements. A minimum grade of C is required in all major courses and courses used to meet the core requirements. **Procedure:** Freshmen are admitted fall, spring, and summer. Entrance exams should be taken in mid junior year or early senior year. There is a rolling admissions plan. Applications should be filed by May 15 for fall entry; November 15 for spring entry; and May 15 for summer entry. The fall 2017 application fee was $50. Notification is sent on a rolling basis. Applications are accepted on-line. **Transfer Students:** 1485 transfer students enrolled in 2016-2017. A minimum GPA of 2.0 is required for students with at least 14 college credits. Those students with fewer credits must submit SAT or ACT scores and a high school transcript. 30 of 120 credits required for the bachelor's degree must be completed at Boise State. **International Students:** There are 353 international students enrolled. They must take the TOEFL with a minimum score of 520 on the paper-based TOEFL (PBT) or 68 on the Internet-based version (iBT). They must also take the SAT or ACT.

ADMISSIONS: 37% of the current freshmen were in the top fifth of their class; 73% were in the top two fifths. **Admissions Contact:** Kelly Talbert, Director of Admission. Email: *bsuinfo@boisestate.edu* Web: *www.boisestate.edu*

FINANCIAL AID: The average freshman award was $11,233. Need-based scholarships or need-based grants averaged $5,974; need-based self-help aid (loans and jobs) averaged $3,461; and $3,405 from other forms of aid. The average financial indebtedness of the 2017 graduate was $30,390. BSU is a member of CSS. The FAFSA code is 001616. The priority date for freshman financial aid applications for fall entry is February 15. The deadline for filing freshman financial aid applications for fall entry is May 15.

IDAHO STATE UNIVERSITY *(The complete profile is made available exclusively on our website, www.barronspac.com)*

LEWIS-CLARK STATE COLLEGE — A-3

www.lcsc.edu

Lewiston, ID 83501	**(208) 792-2210** **(800) 933-LCSC**
Fax: (208) 792-2876	**Email: admissions@lcsc.edu**
Full-time: 960 men, 1315 women	**Faculty:** 134; IIB, --$
Part-time: 415 men, 805 women	**Ph.D.s:** 71%
Graduate: n/av	**Student/Faculty:** 17 to 1
Year: semesters, summer session	**Tuition:** $6000 ($17,000)
Room & Board: $8202	**Freshman Class:** n/av
SAT or ACT: required	**CEEB CODE:** 4385
Application Deadline: August 8	**COMPETITIVE**

Lewis-Clark State College, founded in 1893 and part of the Idaho Higher Education System, offers programs in the arts and sciences, business, education, nursing, and preprofessional and technical training. The figures given in the above capsule and in this profile are approximate. There are 8 undergraduate schools. In addition to regional accreditation, Lewis-Clark has baccalaureate program accreditation with AACSB, NASDTEC, CAEP, and NLN. The 44-acre campus is in an urban area 100 miles southeast of Spokane. Including any residence halls, there are 29 buildings.

STUDENT LIFE: 86% of undergraduates are from Idaho. Others are from 20 states, 30 foreign countries, and Canada. 82% are White; 5% American Indian/Alaska Native; 3% Hispanic; 3% Foreign; 1% African American; 1% Asian American. **Female To Male Ratio:** 1.5:1. The average age of freshmen is 21; all undergraduates, 25. 46% do not continue beyond their first year; 28% remain to graduate. **Housing:** 300 students can be accommodated in college housing, which includes married student dorms and off-campus apartments. In addition, there are honors houses and language/international houses. On-campus housing is available on a first-come and first-served basis. 91% of students commute. Alcohol is not permitted. All students may keep cars.

FACULTY/CLASSROOMS: 58% of faculty are male; 42% are female. All teach undergraduates. No introductory courses are taught by graduate students. The average class size in an introductory lecture is 33 and in a laboratory is 25.

PROGRAMS OF STUDY: Lewis-Clark confers B.A., B.S., B. Applied Sc., B. Applied Tech., B.S.N. and B.S.W. degrees. Associate degrees are also awarded. Bachelor's degrees are awarded in BIOLOGICAL SCIENCE (biology/biological science), BUSINESS (business administration and management), COMMUNICATIONS AND THE ARTS (communications, English, and sports administration), COMPUTER AND PHYSICAL SCIENCE (chemistry, computer science, geoscience, mathematics, and natural sciences), EDUCATION (early childhood education, education, elementary education, and secondary education), ENGINEERING AND ENVIRONMENTAL DESIGN (automotive technology and welding engineering), HEALTH PROFESSIONS (nursing and radiograph medical technology), SOCIAL SCIENCE (addiction studies, criminal justice, history, interdisciplinary studies, liberal arts/general studies, physical fitness/movement, psychology, social science, social work, and sociology). Education, business, and nursing are the strongest academically, and have the largest enrollments.

ACTIVITIES: There are no fraternities or sororities. There are 46 groups on campus, including art, chess, choir, chorale, chorus, computers, dance, debate, drama, ethnic, honors, international, jazz band, literary magazine, musical theater, newspaper, orchestra, political, professional, radio and TV, religious, social, and student government. Popular campus events include Artists Series and Dogwood Festival. **Sports:** There are 5 intercollegiate sports for men and 5 for women, and 8 intramural sports for men and 7 for women. Facilities include a gym, indoor tennis courts, and a baseball field. **Graduates:** From July 1, 2016 to June 30, 2017, 299 bachelor's degrees were awarded. The most popular majors were business (25%), justice studies (15%), and nursing (14%). Of the 2016 graduating class, 8% were enrolled in graduate school within 6 months of graduation.

SERVICES: Counseling and information services are available, as is tutoring in every subject. There is a reader service for the blind, and remedial math, reading, and writing. **Library/Resources:** The library contains 253,000 volumes, 53,000 microform items, and 7,000 audio/video tapes/CDs/DVDs, and subscribes to 4,000 periodicals including electronic. Computerized library services include interlibrary loans and database searching. Special learning facilities include an art gallery, planetarium, radio station, TV station, an educational technology center. **Physically Challenged Students:** 99% of the campus is accessible. Facilities include wheelchair ramps, elevators, special parking, specially equipped restrooms, and special class scheduling. **Special:** Lewis-Clark offers cooperative programs and cross-registration with 3 Idaho universities, on-campus internships, work-study programs, student-designed majors, nondegree study, and pass/fail options. The college grants credit for military experience. There are also between-semester and weekend academic programs, and flexible scheduling in a variety of programs. A 3-2 engineering degree is available at Boise or Idaho State Universities. There is 1 national honor society and a freshman honors program. **Visiting:** There are regularly scheduled orientations for prospective students, including STAR (Student Advising and Registration), and Warrior Discovery Day. There are guides for informal visits, visitors may sit in on classes, and stay overnight. To schedule a visit, contact the Office of Recruitment and Retention at (208) 792-2378. **Campus Safety and Security:** Measures include 24-hour foot and vehicle patrol, emergency notification system, self-defense education, and security escort services. There are shuttle buses and lighted pathways/sidewalks.

REQUIREMENTS: The SAT or ACT is required. Lewis-Clark has a liberal admissions policy, but students must be high school graduates or present a GED certificate. They must have fulfilled requirements in English, math, social and natural sciences, fine arts, and speech, with a minimum GPA of 2.0. AP and CLEP credits are accepted. Students must earn between 120 and 128 credit hours depending on program, including 38 to 40 in the core curriculum and 48 in their major, with a minimum GPA of 2.0 to graduate. **Procedure:** Freshmen are admitted to all sessions. Entrance exams should be taken before registration. There are early admissions, deferred admissions, and rolling admissions plans. Application deadlines are open. The fall 2017 application fee was $35. Applications are accepted on-line. **Transfer Students:** 389 transfer students enrolled in 2016-2017. Applicants who do not have a minimum GPA of 2.0 must submit standardized test scores. 32 of 128 credits required for the bachelor's degree must be completed at Lewis-Clark. **International Students:** There are 94 international students enrolled. They must take the TOEFL.

ADMISSIONS: 5 freshmen graduated first in their class. **Admissions Contact:** Steven J. Bussolini, Director of Admission and Market Development. Email: *admissions@lcsc.edu* Web: *www.lcsc.edu*

FINANCIAL AID: In 2017-2018, 94% of all full-time freshmen received some form of financial aid. 52% of all full-time freshmen received need-based aid. The average freshman award was $4,033. Need-based scholarships or need-based grants averaged $2,781; need-based self-help aid (loans and jobs) averaged $2,652; non-need-based athletic scholarships averaged $4,485; and other non-need-based awards and non-need-based scholarships averaged $2,873. 10% of undergraduate students work part-time. Lewis-Clark is a member of CSS. The FAFSA code is 001621. The deadline for filing freshman financial aid applications for fall entry is March 1.

NORTHWEST NAZARENE UNIVERSITY A-5

www.nnu.edu

Nampa, ID 83686 **(208) 467-8950**

Fax: (208) 467-8645	**Email:** admissions@nnu.edu
Full-time: 468 men, 686 women	**Faculty:** 103
Part-time: 63 men, 130 women	**Ph.D.s:** 67%
Graduate: 241 men, 452 women	**Student/Faculty:** 16 to 1
Year: semesters, summer session	**Tuition:** $29,300
Room & Board: $10,950	**Freshman Class:** 956 applied, 910 accepted, 248 enrolled
SAT EBR-W/M: 580/555 **ACT:** required	**CEEB CODE:** 4544
Application Deadline: August 15	**COMPETITIVE**

Northwest Nazarene University, founded in 1913, a comprehensive Christian university, offers over 60 areas of study, 19 master's degrees in seven different disciplines and 1 doctoral degree. The university also offers programs online as well as in Boise, Idaho Falls, McCall, Twin Falls and in cooperation with programs in 10 countries. There is 1 undergraduate school and 1 graduate school. In addition to regional accreditation, NNU has baccalaureate program accreditation with ABET, ACBSP, CSWE, NASM, CAEP, CACREP, CCNE, and NACEP. The 90-acre campus is in a small town 20 miles west of Boise. Including any residence halls, there are 34 buildings.

STUDENT LIFE: 43% of undergraduates are from out of state, mostly the Northwest. Students are from 41 states, 21 foreign countries, and Canada. 73% are White; 7% Hispanic; 7% race unknown; 4% two or more races; 2% African American; 2% Asian American; 1% American Indian/Alaska Native; 1% Foreign. 66% are Protestant; 12% claim no religious affiliation. **Female To Male Ratio:** 1.3:1. The average age of freshmen is 18; all undergraduates, 23. 28% do not continue beyond their first year; 48% remain to graduate. **Housing:** 808 students can be accommodated in college housing, which includes single-sex and married student dorms and on-campus apartments. On-campus housing is guaranteed for all 4 years. 75% of students live on campus. Alcohol is not permitted. All students may keep cars.

FACULTY/CLASSROOMS: 57% of faculty are male; 43% are female. No introductory courses are taught by graduate students.

PROGRAMS OF STUDY: NNU confers B.A. and B.S. degrees. Associate, master's, and doctoral degrees are also awarded. Bachelor's degrees are awarded in BIOLOGICAL SCIENCE (biochemistry and biology/biological science), BUSINESS (accounting, business administration and management, and recreation and leisure services), COMMUNICATIONS AND THE ARTS (art, communications, English, graphic design, music, and Spanish), COMPUTER AND PHYSICAL SCIENCE (chemistry, computer information systems, computer science, mathematics, and physics), EDUCATION (art education, Christian education, education of the exceptional child, elementary education, English education, mathematics education, music education, physical education, recreation education, and secondary education), ENGINEERING AND ENVIRONMENTAL DESIGN (computer graphics, engineering, and engineering physics), HEALTH PROFESSIONS (nursing), SOCIAL SCIENCE (biblical studies, criminal justice, cultural studies/critical theory & analysis, history, international studies, liberal arts/general studies, ministries, philosophy and religion, political science/government, psychology, social work, and youth ministry). Nursing, engineering, and teaching are the strongest academically. Nursing, engineering, and biology/chemistry have the largest enrollments.

ACTIVITIES: There are no fraternities or sororities. There are 50 groups on campus, including art, band, cheerleading, choir, chorale, chorus, computers, debate, drama, environmental, ethnic, film, forensics, honors, international, jazz band, literary magazine, musical theater, newspaper, orchestra, pep band, photography, political, professional, radio and TV, religious, social, social service, student government, symphony, and yearbook. Popular campus events include Welcome Week, and Week One and Spiritual Emphasis. **Sports:** There are 6 intercollegiate sports for men and 6 for women, and 7 intramural sports for men and 7 for women. Facilities include baseball field, soccer fields, outdoor basketball, tennis, sand volleyball courts, track-and-field facility, golf, cross country, field house, park, and a softball field. **Graduates:** From July 1, 2016 to June 30, 2017, 332 bachelor's degrees were awarded. The most popular majors were business/marketing (26%), education (12%), health professions, and related programs (10%). In an average class, 49% graduate in 6 years or less.

SERVICES: Counseling and information services are available, as is tutoring in every subject. There is remedial math, reading, and writing. **Library/Resources:** Computerized library services include interlibrary loans, database searching, Internet access, and Wi-Fi capability. Special learning facilities include an art gallery, radio station, an educational media center. **Physically Challenged Students:** 2% of the campus is accessible. Facilities include wheelchair ramps, elevators, special parking, specially equipped restrooms, special class scheduling, lowered drinking fountains, lowered telephones, and special housing. **Special:** NNU offers cross-registration with other Nazarene schools and study abroad in 14 countries. The university also offers internships, which are required in many majors, a work-study program, a general studies degree, dual and student-designed majors, and credit for military experience (Army ROTC program). Adult and Professional programs are offered in business, education and religion. There are 4 national honor societies, a freshman honors program, and 3 departmental honors programs. **Visiting:** There are regularly scheduled orientations for prospective students, including overnight stay in a dorm, campus tour, class attendance, financial and admission counseling, meetings with professor and coaches, and music and athletic try-outs. To schedule a visit, contact the Campus Visit Coordinator at (208) 467-8000. **Campus Safety and Security:** Measures include 24-hour foot and vehicle patrol, emergency notification system, and security escort services. There are emergency telephones, lighted pathways/sidewalks, controlled access to dorms/residences, a professional security company, student lock-up-unlock and walk-around-campus teams, and a city police substation.

REQUIREMENTS: Applicants should be graduates of an accredited secondary school; the GED may also be accepted. For standard admission, students must fulfill 2 of the 3 following requirements: graduate with a 2.5 (or higher) GPA on a 4.0 scale, rank in the top 50% of their graduating class, or have an ACT composite score of 18 or a combined score of 870 on the math and critical reasoning sections of the SAT. Provisional admission may be available for students who do not meet the above requirements. Applicants should prepare with recommended units of 4 years of English, 3 each of math, science, and 2 of foreign language, 1.5 each of social studies and history. AP and CLEP credits are accepted. All students must complete 124 semester credits, of which 43 must be upper division. Students must show competency in communication and language skills, have a 2.0 GPA, demonstrate math proficiency, complete a major field of study, and take a comprehensive exam. In addition, each student must complete general education requirements, which are divided into three categories: abilities (17 credits of English, communications, kinesiology, math, and humanities courses), contextual disciplines (15 credits of bible, theology, philosophy, and history courses as well as a cross-cultural experience), and explorations (23 credits of upper-division bible literature or theology, humanities, science, and social sciences electives). The number of hours required varies per major, as do senior internships and projects. **Procedure:** Freshmen are admitted fall, spring, and summer. Entrance exams should be taken early in the senior year. There are early admissions and rolling admissions plans. Early decision applications should be filed by December 15; regular applications, by August 15 for fall entry; and December 15 for winter entry. The fall 2017 application fee was $40. Notification is sent on a rolling basis. Applications are accepted on-line. **Transfer Students:** 75 transfer students enrolled in 2016-2017. Students wishing to transfer to NNU must have completed 28 college or university semester credits and have a cumulative GPA of at least 2.0 and be in good academic standing at their previous institution. Students below the required GPA may be accepted provisionally at the discretion of the Admissions Committee. Students who have earned the equivalent of 12 semester credits may be admitted as transfer students. Official transcripts from all colleges previously attended must be submitted. 24 of 124 credits required for the bachelor's degree must be completed at NNU. **International Students:** There are 30 international students enrolled. They must take the TOEFL with a minimum score of 500 on the paper-based TOEFL (PBT) or 61 on the Internet-based version (iBT). They must also take the SAT or ACT, scoring 18.

ADMISSIONS: 95% of the 2017-2018 applicants were accepted. The SAT scores for the 2017-2018 freshman class were: Critical Reading-- 32% below 500, 46% between 500 and 599, 16% between 600 and 699, and 6% between 700 and 800. Math-- 38% below 500, 42% between 500 and 599, 16% between 600 and 699, and 4% between 700 and 800. Writing-- 53% below 500, 25% between 500 and 599, 19% between 600 and 699, and 3% between 700 and 800. 10 freshmen graduated first in their class. **Admissions Contact:** Shawn Blenker, Director of Admissions. Email: *admissions@nnu.edu* Web: *www.nnu.edu*

FINANCIAL AID: In 2017-2018, 99% of all full-time freshmen received some form of financial aid. 99% of all full-time freshmen received need-based aid. The average freshman award was $23,814. Need-based scholarships or need-based grants averaged $19,358; need-based self-help aid (loans and jobs) averaged $7,554; non-need-based athletic scholarships averaged $12,170; other non-need-based awards and non-need-based scholarships averaged $7,554; and $13,992 from other forms of aid. 66% of undergraduate students work part-time. The average financial indebtedness of the 2017 graduate was $23,672. The FAFSA code is 001624. The priority date for freshman financial aid applications for fall entry is January 15.

THE COLLEGE OF IDAHO — A-5

www.collegeofidaho.edu

Caldwell, ID 83605	(208) 459-5834 (800) 224-3246
Fax: (208) 459-5849	Email: admission@collegeofidaho.edu
Full-time: 499 men, 508 women	**Faculty:** 84
Part-time: 11 men, 21 women	**Ph.D.s:** 83%
Graduate: 9 men, 22 women	**Student/Faculty:** 12 to 1
Year: other	**Tuition:** $27,425
Room & Board: $8990	**Freshman Class:** 955 applied, 863 accepted, 201 enrolled
SAT CR/M/W: 510/505/490 **ACT:** 23	**CEEB CODE:** 4060
Application Deadline: July 15	**COMPETITIVE**

The College of Idaho, founded in 1891, is a private institution offering degree programs in liberal arts education and the sciences. The college runs on a 13-4-13 calendar, with a 6-week intercession. The figures given in the above capsule and in this profile are approximate. There is 1 undergraduate school. In addition to regional accreditation, CI has baccalaureate program accreditation with NASDTEC. The 50-acre campus is in a small town 25 miles west of Boise. Including any residence halls, there are 21 buildings.

STUDENT LIFE: 70% of undergraduates are from Idaho. Others are from 26 states, 54 foreign countries, and Canada. 66% are White; 14% Hispanic; 7% Foreign; 5% race unknown; 3% two or more races; 2% African American; 2% Asian American; 1% American Indian/Alaska Native. **Female To Male Ratio:** 1.1:1. The average age of freshmen is 18; all undergraduates, 20. 15% do not continue beyond their first year; 68% remain to graduate. **Housing:** 683 students can be accommodated in college housing, which includes dorms, on-campus apartments, and off-campus apartments. In addition, there are honors houses and special-interest houses. On-campus housing is guaranteed for the freshman year only, is available on a first-come, first-served basis, and is available on a lottery system for upperclassmen. 57% of students live on campus. All students may keep cars.

FACULTY/CLASSROOMS: 53% of faculty are male; 47% are female. All teach undergraduates. No introductory courses are taught by graduate students.

PROGRAMS OF STUDY: CI confers B.A. and B.S. degrees. Master's degrees are also awarded. Bachelor's degrees are awarded in AGRICULTURE (environmental studies), BIOLOGICAL SCIENCE (biology/biological science), BUSINESS (accounting, business administration and management, and international economics), COMMUNICATIONS AND THE ARTS (art, creative writing, literature, music, music theory and composition, Spanish, and theatre arts), COMPUTER AND PHYSICAL SCIENCE (chemistry and mathematics), EDUCATION (education, elementary education, and physical education), ENGINEERING AND ENVIRONMENTAL DESIGN (preengineering), HEALTH PROFESSIONS (clinical science, exercise science, health, nursing, pharmacy, and speech pathology/audiology), SOCIAL SCIENCE (anthropology, history, philosophy, political science/government, psychology, and religion). Biology, business, and psychology have the largest enrollments.

ACTIVITIES: 15% of men belong to 3 national fraternities; 22% of women belong to 1 local and 3 national sororities. There are 33 groups on campus, including math club, art, band, cheerleading, chess, choir, chorale, chorus, Coyote cinemas, dance, debate, drama, environmental, ethnic, forensics, honors, international, jazz band, LGBT, literary magazine, musical theater, newspaper, pep band, political, professional, religious, social, social service, student government, and yearbook. Popular campus events include Spring Fling, Coyote Connection, Taste of Harvest, and Winterfest. **Sports:** There are 8 intercollegiate sports for men and 10 for women, and 7 intramural sports for men and 7 for women. Facilities include basketball and volleyball, activities center features a weight room, athletic training facility, a swimming pool, dance room, and a rock climbing wall. The college has also partnered with the City of Caldwell on Wolfe Field, the only synthetic turf baseball field in Idaho. Home tennis matches are played on campus on the all-weather courts, and softball. **Graduates:** From July 1, 2016 to June 30, 2017, 191 bachelor's degrees were awarded. The most popular majors were business (15%), social sciences (13%), and psychology (12%). In an average class, 55% graduate in 4 years or less, 64% graduate in 5 years or less, and 68% graduate in 6 years or less.

SERVICES: Counseling and information services are available, as is tutoring in most subjects. **Library/Resources:** Computerized library services include interlibrary loans, database searching, Internet access, and Wi-Fi capability. Special learning facilities include an art gallery, natural history museum, planetarium, a rock and mineral collection, and the Robert E. Smylie Archives. **Physically Challenged Students:** 95% of the campus is accessible. Facilities include wheelchair ramps, elevators, special parking, specially equipped restrooms, lowered drinking fountains, special housing, a pool lift, and disability van. **Special:** Co-op Programs: Dual Degree Doctoral Program in Pharmacy (BS/Pharm.D.), Nursing (BS/BS), Medical Laboratory Science (BS/BS), Speech-Language Pathology and Audiology (BS/BS), and Juris Doctor (BA or BS/JD). Study Abroad programs that faculty are leading month-long study courses in Australia, London, and Idaho's Sawtooth Mountains. The College of Idaho offers two types of off-campus study opportunities: study programs led by faculty for our students, and foreign study opportunities for individual students offered by partner, institutions, study tours to such places as Australia, China, Florida, France, Greece, Italy, London, Mexico, and Peru. CI students also can study for a semester or more in more than 57 countries through our partner institutions. Approved Partner Programs for Study Abroad: Arcadia University-Center for Education Abroad, Brethren Colleges Abroad (BCA), Council Study Centers (CIEE), International Studies Abroad, Schiller International University, School for International Training (SIT), University Studies Abroad Consortium, and University of Idaho. **Visiting:** There are regularly scheduled orientations for prospective students, student visits include an overnight stay with student hosts, class visitations, personal appointments with financial aid counselors, professors, and coaches, social events, and a campus tour. Individual tours can also be arranged. To schedule a visit, contact the Visit and Event Coordinator at visitcenter@collegeofidaho.com. **Campus Safety and Security:** Measures include 24-hour foot and vehicle patrol, emergency notification system, self-defense education, and security escort services. There are emergency telephones, lighted pathways/sidewalks, controlled access to dorms/residences, and electronic identification cards to all dorms and certain buildings throughout the campus.

REQUIREMENTS: In order to be considered for admission, students should submit the following materials to the Admission Office; an application for admission, official high school transcript, a transcript of any college work attempted. If you are considered for the Boone Program, you will need an on-campus interview with the Dean of Students and Dean of Enrollment, and official ACT or SAT test scores. Students must complete the following: The First-Year Seminar and pre-modern Civilization. While there is no required pattern of high school study necessary for admission, the following combination is strongly recommended: 4 years each of English, math laboratory science and language, 3 years of history and social science. AP credits are accepted. Important factors in the admissions decision are leadership record, advanced placement or honors courses, evidence of special talent, recommendations by school officials, personality/intangible qualities, extracurricular activities record, recommendations by alumni, geographical diversity, and parents or siblings attended your school. In order to earn the BA or BS degree, students must complete 124 credits, to include at least one major and three minors, covering all four PEAKs: Humanities and Fine Arts, Natural Sciences and Mathematics, Social Sciences and History, Professional Studies and Enhancement. Students are expected to engage in each of the areas listed as part of their academic program: in Writing, History, Mathematics, Natural Science, Foreign Language, Social Science, Literature, Philosophy/Religion, Fine Arts, and Cultural Diversity. GPA of at least 2.0 in The College of Idaho record and in the entire undergraduate record, the major field and in all minors. **Procedure:** Freshmen are admitted fall and spring. Entrance exams should be taken by the fall of the senior year. There are early admissions, deferred admissions, and rolling admissions plans. Early decision applications should be filed by November 15; regular applications, by July 15 for fall entry; December 1 for winter entry; and January 15 for spring entry. Notification of early decision is sent December 15; regular decision, March 15. Applications are accepted on-line. **Transfer Students:** 56 transfer students enrolled in 2016-2017. Students who have already completed at least 28 semester credits or 42 quarter credits of continuous enrollment at accredited colleges or universities will be considered for admission on the basis of that academic record (rather than the secondary school record) provided they have a cumulative GPA of 2.0 or better. Transfer applicants should submit an application for admission and an official high school transcript, as well as official transcripts from all post-secondary institutions attended. A 1-2 page essay/personal statement and faculty evaluation is required. The transfer application deadline is August 1. Any applications submitted after this date will be considered by petition only. 30 of 124 credits required for the bachelor's degree must be completed at CI. **International Students:** There are 74 international students enrolled. They must take the TOEFL with a minimum score of 550 on the paper-based TOEFL (PBT) or 79 on the Internet-based version (iBT), or take the IELTS language proficiency. They must also take the SAT or ACT.

ADMISSIONS: 90% of the 2017-2018 applicants were accepted. The SAT scores for the 2017-2018 freshman class were: Critical Reading-- 40% below 500, 42% between 500 and 599, 16% between 600 and 699, and 2% between 700 and 800. Math-- 41% below 500, 40% between 500 and 599, 16% between 600 and 699, and 3% between 700 and 800. Writing-- 51% below 500, 35% between 500 and 599, 13% between 600 and 699, and 1% between 700 and 800. The ACT scores were 2% between 12 and 17, 53% between 18 and 23, 37% between 24 and 29, and 8% above 30. **Admissions Contact:** Lorna Hunter, Vice President of Enrollment Management. Email: *admission@collegeofidaho.edu* Web: *www.collegeofidaho.edu*

FINANCIAL AID: In 2017-2018, 98% of all full-time freshmen received some form of financial aid. 76% of all full-time freshmen received need-based aid. The average freshman award was $22,793. Need-based scholarships or need-based grants averaged $3,831; need-based self-help aid (loans and jobs) averaged $3,465; and other non-need-based awards and non-need-based scholarships averaged $15,497. The average financial indebtedness of the 2017 graduate was $30,865. The college's own financial statement is required. The FAFSA code is 001617. The priority date for freshman financial aid applications for fall entry is February 15.

UNIVERSITY OF IDAHO — A-3

www.uidaho.edu

Moscow, ID 83844 — **(208) 885-6326** / **(888) 884-3246**

Fax: (208) 885-9119 — **Email:** admissions@uidaho.edu

Full-time: 3744 men, 3422 women	**Faculty:** 679
Part-time: 1224 men, 1495 women	**Ph.D.s:** 82%
Graduate: 1208 men, 979 women	**Student/Faculty:** 14 to 1
Year: semesters, summer session	**Tuition:** $7488 ($23,812)
Room & Board: $8670	**Freshman Class:** 7087 applied, 5180 accepted, 1538 enrolled
SAT EBR-W/M: 570/528 **ACT:** 23	**CEEB CODE:** 4843
Application Deadline: August 1	**COMPETITIVE**

University of Idaho, founded in 1889 as a public institution, offers programs in art, architecture, agriculture, business and economics, education, engineering, letters and social sciences, natural resources, forestry, wildlife, and range sciences. There are 8 undergraduate schools and 1 graduate school. In addition to regional accreditation, UI has baccalaureate program accreditation with AACSB, ABET, ADA, ASLA, CSAB, FIDER, NAAB, NASAD, NASM, NRPA, SAF, and NWCCU. The 810-acre campus is in a small town 90 miles southeast of Spokane, Washington. Including any residence halls, there are 146 buildings.

STUDENT LIFE: 79% of undergraduates are from Idaho. Others are from 50 states, 56 foreign countries, and Canada. 90% are from public schools. 70% are White; 10% Hispanic; 7% race unknown; 6% Foreign; 4% two or more races; 2% Asian American; 1% African American; 1% American Indian/Alaska Native. **Male To Female Ratio:** 1.0:1. The average age of freshmen is 18; all undergraduates, 22. 18% do not continue beyond their first year; 54% remain to graduate. **Housing:** 2019 students can be accommodated in college housing, which includes married student dorms and on-campus apartments. In addition, there are honors houses, special-interest houses, fraternity houses, sorority houses, alcohol-free, smoke-free, and living learning communities. On-campus housing is guaranteed for all 4 years. 64% of students commute. Alcohol is not permitted. All students may keep cars.

FACULTY/CLASSROOMS: 61% of faculty are male; 39% are female. 90% teach undergraduates, and 75% do research. No introductory courses are taught by graduate students. The average class size in an introductory lecture is 29; in a laboratory is 15; and in a regular course is 23.

PROGRAMS OF STUDY: UI confers B.A., B.F.A., B.G.S., B.I.D., B.Mus., B.S., B.S.A.V.S., B.S.Ag.Econ., B.S.Ag.Ed., B.S.Ag.L.S., B.S.Arch., B.S.Art Ed., B.S.B.A.E., B.S.Biochem., B.S.Bus., B.S.C.E., B.S.C.S., B.S.Ch.E., B.S.Comp.E., B.S.Dan., B.S.E.E., B.S.E.S.H., B.S.Ecol.Cons.Biol., B.S.Ed., B.S.Env.S., B.S.Early.Chdhd.Dev.Ed., B.S.F.C.S., B.S.F.S., B.S.Fire.Ecol.Mgmt., B.S.Fish.Res., B.S.Res., B.S.Forestry, B.S.I.S., B.S.L.A., B.S.M.B.B., B.S.M.E., B.S.M.S.E., B.S.Microbiol., B.S.Nat.Resc.Consv., B.S.P.E., B.S.Pl.Sc., B.S.Rangeland Ecol.Mgmt., B.S.Rangeland.Consv., B.S.Rec., B.S.Renew.Mat., B.S.S.W.S., B.S.Tech., and B.S.Wildlife Rescue degrees. Master's and doctoral degrees are also awarded. Bachelor's degrees are awarded in AGRICULTURE (agricultural business management, agricultural communications, agricultural economics, agricultural mechanics, agricultural sciences, agriculture, animal science, dairy science, fish and game management, fishing and fisheries, forestry production and processing, forestry and related sciences, horticulture, natural resources, natural resource management, plant science, range/farm management, soil science, and wildlife management), BIOLOGICAL SCIENCE (biochemistry, bioinformatics, biology/biological science, entomology, microbiology, molecular biology, and neurosciences), BUSINESS (accounting, business administration and management, business economics, finance, human resources, management information systems, marketing management, marketing/retailing/merchandising, operations management, recreation and leisure services, and professional golf management), COMMUNICATIONS AND THE ARTS (advertising, animation, apparel design, applied art, applied music, art, broadcasting, creative writing, dance, design, digital communications, dramatic arts, English, English Writing, fine arts, French, integrated art and design, journalism, modern language, music, music history and appreciation, music performance, music theory and composition, public relations, Spanish, studio art, telecommunications, and theatre arts), COMPUTER

AND PHYSICAL SCIENCE (applied mathematics, chemistry, computer science, digital arts/technology, geology, information sciences and systems, mathematics, physics, and statistics), EDUCATION (agricultural education, art education, career, technical education & training, education, elementary education, foreign languages education, general studies, mathematics education, music education, physical education, science education, secondary education, special education, teaching English as a second/foreign language (TESOL/TEFOL), and technical education), ENGINEERING AND ENVIRONMENTAL DESIGN (architecture, bioengineering, biomedical engineering, chemical engineering, civil engineering, computer engineering, electrical and computer engineering, electrical/electronics engineering, engineering, engineering management, environmental engineering, environmental science, geological engineering, interior design, landscape architecture/design, materials engineering, materials science and engineering, mechanical engineering, metallurgical engineering, nuclear engineering, and technological management), HEALTH PROFESSIONS (exercise science, movement science, rehabilitative and human services, and veterinary science), SOCIAL SCIENCE (anthropology, child care/child and family studies, counseling/psychology, economics, experimental psychology, family/consumer studies, fire science, food science, geography, history, interdisciplinary studies, international relations, international studies, Latin American studies, parks and recreation management, philosophy, political science/government, psychology, public administration, rural economics, sociology, textiles and clothing, and water resources). Engineering, natural resources, and business are the strongest academically. Business, engineering, and psychology have the largest enrollments.

ACTIVITIES: 22% of men belong to 17 national fraternities; 17% of women belong to 10 national sororities. There are 191 groups on campus, including art, band, cheerleading, choir, chorale, chorus, computers, dance, drama, drill team, environmental, ethnic, film, honors, international, jazz band, LGBT, literary magazine, marching band, musical theater, newspaper, opera, orchestra, pep band, photography, political, professional, radio and TV, religious, social, social service, student government, and symphony. Popular campus events include Lionel Hampton Jazz Festival, the Borah Symposium, Palouse fest, Homecoming, and Mom's Weekend and Dad's Weekend. **Sports:** There are 6 intercollegiate sports for men and 8 for women, and 15 intramural sports for men and 16 for women. Facilities include an activity center, a domed stadium for basketball and football, indoor and outdoor tracks, swimming pools, gyms, an auditorium, golf, tennis, racquetball and handball courts, and a student recreation center with a climbing wall. **Graduates:** From July 1, 2016 to June 30, 2017, 1733 bachelor's degrees were awarded. The most popular majors were psychology (7%), mechanical engineering (6%), and educational leadership (5%). In an average class, 2% graduate in 3 years or less, 30% graduate in 4 years or less, 50% graduate in 5 years or less, and 54% graduate in 6 years or less.

SERVICES: Counseling and information services are available, as is tutoring in most subjects. There is a reader service for the blind, and remedial math and writing. **Library/Resources:** The library contains 1.4 million volumes, 2.6 million microform items, and 14,719 audio/video tapes/CDs/DVDs, and subscribes to 43,777 periodicals including electronic. Computerized library services include interlibrary loans, database searching, Internet access, and Wi-Fi capability. Special learning facilities include an art gallery, radio station, TV station, an electron microscopy center, IQ-Station, lab animal facility, research institutes for water resources, geospatial lab, microelectronics, aquaculture, university farms, experimental forests, arboretum and botanical garden. **Physically Challenged Students:** 87% of the campus is accessible. Facilities include wheelchair ramps, elevators, special parking, specially equipped restrooms, special class scheduling, lowered drinking fountains, lowered telephones, special housing, 2 motorized wheelchairs, readers, note takers, sign language interpreters, alternate text, assistive devices, assistive technology computers, priority registration, real-time capturing, enlarged print classroom materials, advocacy, specialized classroom furniture, testing accommodations, and on-campus transportation. **Special:** UI offers cooperative programs and cross-registration with Washington State and Idaho State Universities, internships, extensive study-abroad programs, work-study programs, B.A.-B.S. degrees, dual and student-designed majors, a general studies degree, credit for life and work experience, non-degree study, and pass/fail options. There are 11 national honor societies, Phi Beta Kappa, and a freshman honors program. **Visiting:** There are regularly scheduled orientations for prospective students, scheduled visits include a visit with faculty and financial aid personnel, a tour of campus, Greek houses and a visit to the recreation center. There are guides for informal visits and visitors may sit in on classes. To schedule a visit, contact the Office of Admissions and Campus Visits at (208) 885-6163. **Campus Safety and Security:** Measures include 24-hour foot and vehicle patrol, emergency notification system, and self-defense education. There are shuttle buses, emergency telephones, lighted pathways/sidewalks, controlled access to dorms/residences. There is also a violence prevention programs office.

REQUIREMENTS: The SAT or ACT is required. Students from accredited high schools must have graduated and completed 15 academic units, 4 units in English, 3 units each in math, and science (of those, 1 unit must be lab), 2.5 units in social studies, 1.5 units in academic electives, 1 unit in humanities, and foreign language. Home-schooled students and non-accredited high school students, including GED students, will have their application for admission referred to a committee for a decision. A GPA of 2.2 is required. AP and CLEP credits are accepted. To graduate, students must complete at least 120 credit hours (128 for some majors), including 36 in upper-division courses and 40 in the major, with a minimum GPA of 2.0. The core curriculum requires a total of 33 to 36 credits in the following categories: communication, natural and applied sciences, mathematics, statistics or computer science, humanities, social sciences, one American diversity course, one international course, one lower-division seminar, and one upper-division seminar. **Procedure:** Freshmen are admitted to all sessions. Entrance exams should be taken during the junior or senior year of high school. There are deferred admissions and rolling admissions plans. Applications should be filed by August 1 for fall entry; December 15 for spring entry; and May 1 for summer entry. The fall 2017 application fee was $60. Notification is sent on a rolling basis. Applications are accepted on-line. **Transfer Students:** 601 transfer students enrolled in 2016-2017. Transfer applicants must have completed at least 14 credit hours with a cumulative GPA of at least 2.0. Students transferring from out-of-state schools into the College of Engineering must have a minimum cumulative GPA of 2.8. 32 of 120 credits required for the bachelor's degree must be completed at UI. **International Students:** There are 433 international students enrolled. They must take the TOEFL with a minimum score of 525 on the paper-based TOEFL (PBT) or 70 on the Internet-based version (iBT). They must also take the SAT or ACT.

ADMISSIONS: 73% of the 2017-2018 applicants were accepted. The SAT scores for the 2017-2018 freshman class were: Math-- 38% below 500, 38% between 500 and 599, 18% between 600 and 699, and 6% between 700 and 800. Evidence-Based Reading/Writing-- 18% below 500, 44% between 500 and 599, 31% between 600 and 699, and 7% between 700 and 800. The ACT scores were 10% between 12 and 17, 42% between 18 and 23, 39% between 24 and 29, and 9% above 30. 35% of the current freshmen were in the top fifth of their class; 63% were in the top two fifths. 52 freshmen graduated first in their class. **Admissions Contact:** Director, Admissions Email: *admissions@uidaho.edu* Web: *www.uidaho.edu*

FINANCIAL AID: In 2017-2018, 87% of all full-time freshmen received some form of financial aid. 65% of all full-time freshmen received need-based aid. The average freshman award was $13,930. Need-based scholarships or need-based grants averaged $4,537 ($9,815 maximum); need-based self-help aid (loans and jobs) averaged $5,744 ($11,315 maximum); non-need-based athletic scholarships averaged $21,070 ($37,573 maximum); and other non-need-based awards and non-need-based scholarships averaged $5,608 ($30,394 maximum). 91% of undergraduate students work part-time. The average financial indebtedness of the 2017 graduate was $26,258. UI is a member of CSS. The FAFSA code is 001626. The priority date for freshman financial aid applications for fall entry is December 1. The deadline for filing freshman financial aid applications for fall entry is February 15.

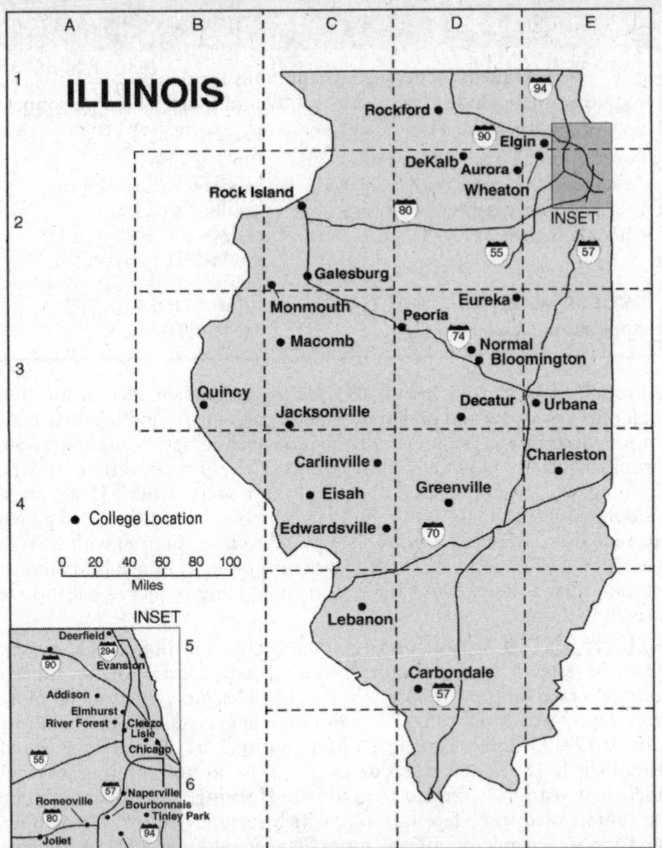

AUGUSTANA COLLEGE C-2

www.augustana.edu

Rock Island, IL 61201	(309) 794-7341 (800) 798-8100
Fax: (309) 794-7422	**Email:** admissions@augustana.edu
Full-time: 1114 men, 1523 women	**Faculty:** 195; IIB, av$
Part-time: 6 men, 4 women	**Ph.D.s:** 92%
Graduate: n/av	**Student/Faculty:** 12 to 1
Year: quarters, summer session	**Tuition:** $40,908
Room & Board: $10,314	**Freshman Class:** 6750 applied, 3980 accepted, 735 enrolled
SAT EBR-W/M: 630/610 **ACT:** 26	**CEEB CODE:** 1025
Application Deadline: open	**VERY COMPETITIVE+**

Augustana College is a private, selective liberal arts college. Augustana's focus on creating a well-rounded experience for students has generated an environment of learning that goes beyond the classroom. From the moment students set foot on campus, the college provides them with tools that will help them be successful now and in the future. In addition to working closely with their professors on special projects and research, students benefit from visiting scholars and lecturers as well as international study opportunities. There is 1 undergraduate school. In addition to regional accreditation, Augustana College has baccalaureate program accreditation with NASM and CAEP. The 115-acre campus is in a suburban area near the Mississippi River in Rock Island, and 165 miles west of Chicago. Including any residence halls, there are 99 buildings.

STUDENT LIFE: 85% of undergraduates are from Illinois. Others are from 32 states, 43 foreign countries, and Canada. 73% are White; 7% Foreign; 4% African American; 3% two or more races; 2% Asian American; 10% Hispanic; 1% race unknown. 30% are Catholic; 26% claim no religious affiliation; 23% 1% listed other non-Christian faiths; 21% Protestant. **Female To Male Ratio:** 1.4:1. The average age of freshmen is 18; all undergraduates, 20. 14% do not continue beyond their first year; 75% remain to graduate. **Housing:** 1897 students can be accommodated in college housing, which includes both single sex and coed dorms, on-campus apartments, and off-campus apartments. In addition, there are special-interest houses, and wellness housing. On-campus housing is guaranteed for the freshman year only. 69% of students live on campus. Alcohol is not permitted. All students may keep cars.

FACULTY/CLASSROOMS: 52% of faculty are male; 48% are female. All teach undergraduates, 59% do research, and 59% do both. No introductory courses are taught by graduate students.

PROGRAMS OF STUDY: Augustana confers B.A. degrees. Bachelor's degrees are awarded in AGRICULTURE (environmental studies), BIOLOGICAL SCIENCE (biochemistry, biology/adolescence education, biology/biological science, and neurosciences), BUSINESS (accounting, business administration and management, and international business management), COMMUNICATIONS AND THE ARTS (Africana studies, art, art history and appreciation, classics, communication studies, creative writing, English, English Writing, French, German, graphic design, multimedia, music, music performance, Scandinavian languages, Spanish, and theatre arts), COMPUTER AND PHYSICAL SCIENCE (applied mathematics, chemistry, chemistry/adolescence education, computer science, earth science/adolescence education, geology, mathematics, physics secondary education, and physics), EDUCATION (art education, elementary education, English education, French studies K-12 education, history education, mathematics education, music education, secondary education, and Spanish adolescense education), ENGINEERING AND ENVIRONMENTAL DESIGN (engineering physics), HEALTH PROFESSIONS (premedicine and public health), SOCIAL SCIENCE (anthropology, Asian/Oriental studies, communication sciences & disorders, economics, geography, history, philosophy, political science/government, psychology, religion, social work, sociology, and women's studies). Education, pre-medicine, and neuroscience are the strongest academically. Business/accounting, biology, and psychology have the largest enrollments.

ACTIVITIES: 23% of men belong to 7 local fraternities; 39% of women belong to 7 local sororities. There are 110 groups on campus, including art, band, cheerleading, choir, chorale, chorus, communications, computers, dance, debate, drama, environmental, ethnic, film, honors, international, jazz band, LGBT, literary magazine, musical theater, newspaper, opera, orchestra, pep band, photography, political, professional, religious, social, social service, student government, and symphony. Popular campus events include Symposium Day, and Slough Fest. **Sports:** There are 12 intercollegiate sports for men and 11 for women, and 28 intramural sports for men and 27 for women. The PepsiCo Recreation Center has a 6-lane 200-meter track, courts for basketball, volleyball, badminton, tennis, cardio and a weight room facility. The athletic building has courts for basketball, volleyball and badminton, weight and physical conditioning rooms, golf practice area, wrestling facilities, a swimming pool, a lighted synthetic turf field and an all-weather track for football and track and field, lacrosse and soccer, a baseball field, outdoor tennis courts, and a dance studio. **Graduates:** From July 1, 2016 to June 30, 2017, 501 bachelor's degrees were awarded. The most popular majors were biology/life science (19%), business/marketing (19%), and premedicine (10%). In an average class, 65% graduate in 4 years or less, 73% graduate in 5 years or less, and 75% graduate in 6 years or less. Of the 2016 graduating class, 24% were enrolled in graduate school within 6 months of graduation, and 74% were employed.

SERVICES: Counseling and information services are available, as is tutoring in all subjects. There is a reader service for the blind, and remedial math. **Library/Resources:** The library contains 131,497 volumes, 2,700 microform items, and 8,541 audio/video tapes/CDs/DVDs, and subscribes to 122,827 periodicals, including electronic. Computerized library services include interlibrary loans, database searching, Internet access, and Wi-Fi capability. Special learning facilities include an art gallery, a natural history museum, a center for communicative disorders, a geology museum, a planetarium and observatory, a U.S. geological survey map repository, a Swedish immigration research center, 3 outdoor environmental labs, a 3D printer, and a spectrometer. **Physically Challenged Students:** 75% of the campus is accessible. Facilities include wheelchair ramps, elevators, special parking, specially equipped restrooms, lowered drinking fountains, lowered telephones, and special housing. **Special:** Coordinated degree programs (3-2, 3-3, 3-4) are offered in Accounting (Wake Forest University), Engineering (Northern Illinois University, Washington University and Columbia University), Environmental Management and Forestry (Duke University), Landscape

Architecture (University of Illinois), Occupational Therapy (Washington University), Optometry (Illinois College of Optometry), Pre-Law (Capital University Law School), Nursing (Trinity College of Nursing and Health Sciences), Physical Therapy (Washington University), and Veterinary Medicine (University of Illinois). Domestic and international internships are offered in London, New York, Sydney, Denver, Washington, D.C., and New Zealand. Study abroad programs travel to France, Ecuador, Germany, Nicaragua, Brazil, England, Norway, Guatemala, Greece, Botswana, Hong Kong, Japan, Sweden, India, Italy, Spain, China, Australia, Switzerland, Austria, Ghana, Senegal, and Jamaica. There are 16 national honor societies, Phi Beta Kappa, a freshman honors program, and 1 departmental honors program. **Visiting:** There are regularly scheduled orientations for prospective students, including information sessions with speakers, exhibits, campus tours, meetings with faculty, counselors, and students, and social activities. There are guides for informal visits; visitors may sit in on classes, and stay overnight. To schedule a visit, contact Karen Dahlstrom at karendahlstrom@augustana.edu. **Campus Safety and Security:** Measures include 24-hour foot and vehicle patrol, emergency notification system, self-defense education, and security escort services. There are shuttle buses, emergency telephones, lighted pathways/sidewalks, and controlled access to dorms/residences.

REQUIREMENTS: The SAT or ACT is recommended. Applicants should be graduates of an accredited secondary school with 16 academic credits, including 3-4 each in English, math, and science (with 2 labs), and 1 each in social studies, foreign language, and history, plus 4 recommended in academic electives. An audition for music majors and an interview are recommended. The GED is accepted. Students who choose not to submit ACT or SAT scores must interview and submit a photocopy of a graded high school paper. AP credits are accepted. Important factors in the admissions decision are advanced placement or honors courses, evidence of special talent, and recommendations by school officials. A total of 123 credits with a minimum GPA of 2.0 is required to graduate. Courses in foreign language, religion, writing, physical ed, fine arts, humanities, literature, and the sciences must be completed. **Procedure:** Freshmen are admitted fall, winter, and spring. Entrance exams should be taken by fall of the senior year. There are early decision, early admissions, deferred admissions, and rolling admissions plans. Application deadlines are open. Notification of early decision is sent November 15; regular decision, on a rolling basis. 32 early decision candidates were accepted for the 2017-2018 class. Applications are accepted on-line. **Transfer Students:** 56 transfer students enrolled in 2016-2017. A minimum GPA of 2.0 is required. SAT or ACT scores and an interview are recommended. Students may enroll in the fall, winter, and spring. 60 of 123 credits required for the bachelor's degree must be completed at Augustana. **International Students:** There are 192 international students enrolled. They must take the TOEFL with a minimum score of 550 on the paper-based TOEFL (PBT) or 80 on the Internet-based version (iBT).

ADMISSIONS: 59% of the 2017-2018 applicants were accepted. The SAT scores for the 2017-2018 freshman class were: Math-- 9% below 500, 34% between 500 and 599, 43% between 600 and 699, and 14% between 700 and 800. Evidence-Based Reading/Writing-- 2% below 500, 34% between 500 and 599, 48% between 600 and 699, and 16% between 700 and 800. The ACT scores were 1% between 12 and 17, 28% between 18 and 23, 55% between 24 and 29, and 16% above 30. 57% of the current freshmen were in the top fifth of their class; 83% were in the top two fifths. 8 freshmen graduated first in their class. **Admissions Contact:** Kent Brands, Executive Vice President for External Relations. Email: *admissions@augustana.edu* Web: *www.augustana.edu*

FINANCIAL AID: In 2017-2018, 100% of all full-time freshmen received some form of financial aid. 77% of all full-time freshmen received need-based aid. The average freshman award was $32,193. Need-based scholarships or need-based grants averaged $26,317; and need-based self-help aid (loans and jobs) averaged $5,438. 61% of undergraduate students work part-time. AC is a member of CSS. The college's own financial statement is required. The FAFSA code is 001633. The priority date for freshman financial aid applications for fall entry is February 1.

AURORA UNIVERSITY D-2

www.aurora.edu

Aurora, IL 60506 (630) 844-5533
(800) 742-5281

Fax: (630) 844-5535
Email: admission@aurora.edu

Full-time: 1278 men, 2183 women	**Faculty:** IIA, -$
Part-time: 116 men, 356 women	**Ph.D.s:** 71%
Graduate: 433 men, 1467 women	**Student/Faculty:** 36 to 1
Year: semesters, summer session	**Tuition:** $23,520
Room & Board: $11,470	**Freshman Class:** 3105 applied, 2675 accepted, 801 enrolled
SAT EBR-W/M: 510/510 **ACT:** 21	**CEEB CODE:** 1027
Application Deadline: n/av	**COMPETITIVE**

Aurora University, founded in 1893, is a private, independent institution that offers graduate and undergraduate degrees in arts and sciences, education, accounting, business, information technology, communication, criminal justice, nursing, health sciences, physical education, athletic training, recreation, special education, and social work. There are 6 undergraduate schools and 4 graduate schools. In addition to regional accreditation, AU has baccalaureate program accreditation with CSWE, CCNE, CAATE, and CAEP. The 70-acre campus is in a suburban area 40 miles from downtown Chicago. Including any residence halls, there are 28 buildings.

STUDENT LIFE: 88% of undergraduates are from Illinois. Others are from 40 states, 4 foreign countries, and Canada. 8% are African American; 6% race unknown; 50% White; 30% Hispanic; 3% two or more races; 2% Asian American. 47% claim no religious affiliation; 31% Protestant; 17% Catholic. **Female To Male Ratio:** 2.2:1. The average age of freshmen is 18; all undergraduates, 23. 27% do not continue beyond their first year; 53% remain to graduate. **Housing:** 737 students can be accommodated in college housing, which includes dorms. On-campus housing is available on a first-come, first-served basis. 75% of students commute. Alcohol is not permitted. All students may keep cars.

FACULTY/CLASSROOMS: 47% of faculty are male; 53% are female. 96% teach undergraduates. No introductory courses are taught by graduate students. The average class size in an introductory lecture is 26; in a laboratory is 25; and in a regular course is 26.

PROGRAMS OF STUDY: AU confers B.A., B.S., B.S.N., and B.S.W. degrees. Master's and doctoral degrees are also awarded. Bachelor's degrees are awarded in BIOLOGICAL SCIENCE (biology/biological science), BUSINESS (accounting, business administration and management, finance, marketing, organizational leadership and management, recreation and leisure services, and sustainable management), COMMUNICATIONS AND THE ARTS (art, communications, English, music, musical theater, Spanish, and theatre studies), COMPUTER AND PHYSICAL SCIENCE (actuarial science, computer science, and mathematics), EDUCATION (athletic training, early childhood education, elementary education, physical education, secondary education, and special education), ENGINEERING AND ENVIRONMENTAL DESIGN (environmental science), HEALTH PROFESSIONS (biology, disabilities studies, exercise science, health science, and nursing), SOCIAL SCIENCE (criminal justice, history, liberal arts/general studies, parks and recreation management, philosophy, political science/government, psychology, religion, social work, and sociology). Nursing, health sciences, and education are the strongest academically. Social work, nursing, and education have the largest enrollments.

ACTIVITIES: 1% of men belong to 1 national fraternity; 1% of women belong to 1 local and 4 national sororities. There are 58 groups on campus, including art, cheerleading, choir, chorale, computers, dance, debate, drama, environmental, ethnic, forensics, honors, jazz band, LGBT, literary magazine, musical theater, newspaper, pep band, photography, political, professional, radio and TV, religious, social, social service, and student government. Popular campus events include Spring Fling, Homecoming Week, Arts and Ideas Series, and Student Organization Events. **Sports:** There are 12 intercollegiate sports for men and 12 for women, and 22 intramural sports for men and 22 for women. Facilities include soccer, lacrosse, softball, football fields, a fitness center, weight room, gym, racquetball, multi-use room for yoga, cycling, and batting cages. **Graduates:** From July 1, 2016 to June 30, 2017, 1004 bachelor's degrees were awarded. The most popular majors were health professions and related services (27%), business (22%), and social work

(12%). In an average class, 38% graduate in 4 years or less, 51% graduate in 5 years or less, and 53% graduate in 6 years or less.

SERVICES: Counseling and information services are available, as is tutoring in most subjects. There are professional and peer tutors, workshops, and computer-based tutorials. **Library/Resources:** The library contains 36,274 volumes, and 4,560 audio/video tapes/CDs/DVDs, and subscribes to 46,481 periodicals, including electronic. Computerized library services include interlibrary loans, database searching, Internet access, and Wi-Fi capability. Special learning facilities include a natural history museum, a radio station, a Native American museum. The Jenks Memorial collection of Adventual Materials, and the Doris K. Colby Memorial Archives. **Physically Challenged Students:** 98% of the campus is accessible. Facilities include wheelchair ramps, elevators, special parking, specially equipped restrooms, special class scheduling, lowered drinking fountains, and special housing. **Special:** AU offers cross-registration with North Central College and Benedictine University, field-related job experience, work-study programs, study abroad in a number of countries and travel programs during the Summer-May term. Internships and an MBA/MSW dual major are available. There are 7 national honor societies. **Visiting:** There are regularly scheduled orientations for prospective students, including meeting with an admission representative, a campus tour with students, and classroom and/or faculty visits . There are guides for informal visits; visitors may sit in on classes and stay overnight. To schedule a visit, contact Melody Ulin at mulin@aurora.edu. **Campus Safety and Security:** Measures include 24-hour foot and vehicle patrol, an emergency notification system, self-defense education, and security escort services. There are emergency telephones and lighted pathways/sidewalks.

REQUIREMENTS: The ACT is required. Applicants must be graduates of an accredited secondary school or have earned the GED. Secondary school academic units must include a minimum of 4 years of English and 3 years each of mathematics, social studies, science, and electives. An interview is recommended but not required. A GPA of 2.0 is required. AP and CLEP credits are accepted. Important factors in the admissions decision are advanced placement or honors courses, extracurricular activities record, and leadership record. To graduate, students must complete a minimum of 120 semester hours with a GPA of at least 2.0 on a 4.0 scale, including at least 52 semester hours at a senior college. Completion at Aurora University requires at least 30 semester hours, including the last 24 semester hours in the degree, and including at least 18 semester hours in the major. A minimum of 30 semester hours of which 15 semester hours must lie within the major and 15 additional semester hours must be completed at AU. Completion of the approved major requirements and general education program requirements (must have no grades lower than C). **Procedure:** Freshmen are admitted in the fall and spring. Entrance exams should be taken by late in the junior year or early in the senior year. There is a rolling admissions plan. Application deadlines are open. Notifications are sent September 1. Applications are accepted on-line. **Transfer Students:** 462 transfer students enrolled in 2016-2017. Applicants are required to have a minimum GPA of 2.0 and must have completed at least 15 semester hours at the post-secondary level. 30 of 120 credits required for the bachelor's degree must be completed at AU. **International Students:** There are 10 international students enrolled. They must take the TOEFL with a minimum score of 550 on the paper-based TOEFL (PBT) or 79 on the Internet-based version (iBT).

ADMISSIONS: 86% of the 2017-2018 applicants were accepted. The SAT scores for the 2017-2018 freshman class were: Math-- 39% below 500, 46% between 500 and 599, and 15% between 600 and 699. Evidence-Based Reading/Writing-- 39% below 500, 49% between 500 and 599, 11% between 600 and 699, and 1% between 700 and 800. The ACT scores were 9% between 12 and 17, 68% between 18 and 23, 21% between 24 and 29, and 2% above 30. **Admissions Contact:** Tracy Phillippe, Director of Enrollment Systems. Email: *admission@aurora.edu* Web: *www.aurora.edu*

FINANCIAL AID: In 2017-2018, 100% of all full-time freshmen received some form of financial aid. 83% of all full-time freshmen received need-based aid. The average freshman award was $22,277. Need-based scholarships or need-based grants averaged $17,908 ($31,388 maximum); need-based self-help aid (loans and jobs) averaged $4,328 ($6,500 maximum); and other non-need-based awards and non-need-based scholarships averaged $12,464 ($23,260 maximum). The average financial indebtedness of the 2017 graduate was $27,117. The FAFSA code is 001634. The priority date for freshman financial aid applications for fall entry is October 1.

BENEDICTINE UNIVERSITY E-2

www.ben.edu

Lisle, IL 60532 **(630) 829-6300**

Fax: (630) 829-6301	**Email:** admissions@ben.edu
Full-time: 1046 men, 1358 women	**Faculty:** IIA, -$
Part-time: 243 men, 293 women	**Ph.D.s:** 89%
Graduate: 655 men, 1711 women	**Student/Faculty:** 18 to 1
Year: semesters, summer session	**Tuition:** $29,700
Room & Board: $8600	**Freshman Class:** 2558 applied, 1974 accepted, 486 enrolled
ACT: 23	**CEEB CODE:** 1707
Application Deadline: March 30	**COMPETITIVE**

Benedictine University, founded in 1887, is a private, Roman Catholic liberal arts and sciences institution. There are 4 undergraduate schools and 4 graduate schools. In addition to regional accreditation, Benedictine University has baccalaureate program accreditation with ADA, HLC, and CCLN. The 108-acre campus is in a suburban area 25 miles west of Chicago. Including any residence halls, there are 11 buildings.

STUDENT LIFE: 94% of undergraduates are from Illinois. Others are from 50 states, 10 foreign countries, and Canada. 7% are Hispanic; 45% White; 21% Asian American; 2% Foreign; 12% African American; 12% race unknown; 1% American Indian/Alaska Native. **Female To Male Ratio:** 1.7:1. The average age of freshmen is 18; all undergraduates, 25. 27% do not continue beyond their first year; 52% remain to graduate. **Housing:** 756 students can be accommodated in college housing, which includes dorms and on-campus apartments. On-campus housing is available on a first-come, first-served basis. All students may keep cars.

FACULTY/CLASSROOMS: 49% of faculty are male; 51% are female. All teach undergraduates, and all do research. No introductory courses are taught by graduate students. The average class size in an introductory lecture is 21; in a laboratory is 17; and in a regular course is 19.

PROGRAMS OF STUDY: Benedictine confers B.A., B.S., B.B.A. and B.S.N. degrees. Associate, master's, and doctoral degrees are also awarded. Bachelor's degrees are awarded in BIOLOGICAL SCIENCE (biochemistry, biology/biological science, molecular biology, and nutrition), BUSINESS (accounting, banking and finance, business administration and management, business economics, international business management, management information systems, marketing management, marketing/retailing/merchandising, and organizational behavior), COMMUNICATIONS AND THE ARTS (arts administration/management, communications, creative writing, fine arts, literature, music, publishing, Spanish, and studio art), COMPUTER AND PHYSICAL SCIENCE (chemistry, computer science, mathematics, and physics), EDUCATION (elementary education and special education), ENGINEERING AND ENVIRONMENTAL DESIGN (engineering and applied science and environmental science), HEALTH PROFESSIONS (clinical science, health care administration, health science, nuclear medical technology, nursing, and radiation therapy), SOCIAL SCIENCE (economics, history, international studies, philosophy, political science/government, psychology, social science, sociology, and theological studies). Management, health science, and psychology have the largest enrollments.

ACTIVITIES: There are no fraternities or sororities. There are 46 groups on campus, including art, band, cheerleading, choir, chorus, computers, dance, debate, ethnic, honors, international, jazz band, literary magazine, musical theater, newspaper, pep band, political, professional, radio and TV, religious, social, social service, and student government. Popular campus events include Relay for Life, Quad Day, and Spring Ball. **Sports:** There are 8 intercollegiate sports for men and 9 for women, and 11 intramural sports for men and 11 for women. Facilities include a recreation center housing the main arena, a weight room, a dance room, racquetball and tennis courts, a sports complex that includes football/soccer/track, and a stadium for baseball and softball. **Graduates:** From July 1, 2016 to June 30, 2017, 723 bachelor's degrees were awarded. The most popular majors were health science (12%), accounting (7%), and management (7%).

SERVICES: Counseling and information services are available, as is tutoring in most subjects. There is a reader service for the blind, and remedial math, reading, and writing. **Library/Resources:** The library contains 274,635 volumes, 23,377 microform items, and 51,032 audio/

video tapes/CDs/DVDs, and subscribes to 66,295 periodicals, including electronic. Computerized library services include interlibrary loans, database searching, Internet access, and Wi-Fi capability. Special learning facilities include an art gallery, a natural history museum, a radio station, and a TV station. **Physically Challenged Students:** All of the campus is accessible. Facilities include wheelchair ramps, elevators, special parking, specially equipped restrooms, and lowered drinking fountains. **Special:** There is cross-registration with North Central College, Aurora University, and the Illinois Institute of Technology. Benedictine offers study abroad in 9 countries, and exchange programs can be arranged through other colleges. There are 3-2 pre-engineering degrees with Marquette University and the Universities of Illinois, Detroit, and Notre Dame, and an engineering degree with the Illinois Institute of Technology. Pre-professional programs including pre-podiatry, pre-physical therapy, and pre-nursing are offered. Work-study programs with a number of surrounding firms, internships, an accelerated degree program in management, credit for work and life experience, and dual majors are also offered. There are 11 national honor societies and a freshman honors program. **Visiting:** There are regularly scheduled orientations for prospective students, student visits include a regularly scheduled visit day and open houses each semester. There are guides for informal visits; visitors may sit in on classes and stay overnight. To schedule a visit, contact the Enrollment Center. **Campus Safety and Security:** Measures include 24-hour foot and vehicle patrol, self-defense education, and security escort services. There are emergency telephones and lighted pathways/sidewalks.

REQUIREMENTS: The ACT is required. Students must complete 4 years of English, 3 years each of social studies, math, and science with lab, and 2 years of foreign language. The GED is accepted. Benedictine requires applicants to be in the upper 50% of their class. AP and CLEP credits are accepted. To graduate, students must complete 120 semester hours, including 36 in their majors, and maintain a minimum GPA of 2.0. They must complete 12 hours in the arts and humanities, 9 each in social sciences, natural sciences, and cultural heritage; 6 in rhetoric; and 3 each in speech, math, and freshman seminar. A thesis, capstone course or project, or comprehensive exam is required in specific departments. **Procedure:** Freshmen are admitted in the fall and spring. There is a rolling admissions plan. Application deadlines are open. The fall 2017 application fee was $40. Applications are accepted online. **Transfer Students:** 449 transfer students enrolled in 2016-2017. Applicants must have a C average. A minimum GPA of 2.0 is necessary, and an interview is required in some cases. Students who have completed fewer than 20 semester hours must submit ACT or SAT scores. 30 of 120 credits required for the bachelor's degree must be completed at Benedictine. **International Students:** There are 50 international students enrolled. They must take the TOEFL with a minimum score of 550 on the paper-based TOEFL (PBT) or 79 on the Internet-based version (iBT).

ADMISSIONS: 77% of the 2017-2018 applicants were accepted. The ACT scores were 30% below 12, 27% between 12 and 17, 26% between 18 and 23, 9% between 24 and 29, and 8% above 30. 28% of the current freshmen were in the top fifth of their class; 59% were in the top two fifths. 3 freshmen graduated first in their class. **Admissions Contact:** Robert A. Stanley, Ed.D., Vice President Office of the Provost. Email: *admissions@ben.edu* Web: *www.ben.edu*

FINANCIAL AID: In 2017-2018, 98% of all full-time freshmen received some form of financial aid. 70% of all full-time freshmen received need-based aid. The average freshman award was $24,046. Need-based scholarships or need-based grants averaged $7,689 ($14,450 maximum); need-based self-help aid (loans and jobs) averaged $5,542 ($8,500 maximum); and other non-need-based awards and non-need-based scholarships averaged $16,585 ($36,600 maximum). 13% of undergraduate students work part-time. The average financial indebtedness of the 2017 graduate was $27,110. The FAFSA code is 001767. The priority date for freshman financial aid applications for fall entry is March 1.

BLACKBURN COLLEGE *(The complete profile is made available exclusively on our website, www.barronspac.com)*

BRADLEY UNIVERSITY — D-3

www.bradley.edu

Peoria, IL 61625 — **(309) 677-1000**

Fax: (309) 677-2797	**Email:** admissions@bradley.edu
Full-time: 2227 men, 2285 women	**Faculty:** 355; IIA, av$
Part-time: 68 men, 69 women	**Ph.D.s:** 80%
Graduate: 361 men, 834 women	**Student/Faculty:** 12 to 1
Year: varies, summer session	**Tuition:** $32,930
Room & Board: $10,310	**Freshman Class:** 10232 applied, 7303 accepted, 1265 enrolled
SAT: required **ACT:** 25	**CEEB CODE:** 1070
Application Deadline: February 1	**VERY COMPETITIVE**

Bradley University is a mid-sized university providing students the opportunities and resources of a larger university and the personal attention of a smaller university. Bradley offers more than 185 undergraduate and graduate academic programs in business, communications, education, engineering, fine arts, health sciences, liberal arts and sciences, and technology. There are 5 undergraduate schools and 1 graduate school. In addition to regional accreditation, BU has baccalaureate program accreditation with AACSB, ABET, ACCE, CSWE, NASAD, NASM, CCNE, NAEYC, and NAST. The 85-acre campus is in a suburban area in Peoria, Illinois, 3 hours from Chicago, Indianapolis, and St. Louis. Including any residence halls, there are 77 buildings.

STUDENT LIFE: 82% of undergraduates are from Illinois. Others are from 36 states, 39 foreign countries, and Canada. 73% are White; 7% African American; 4% Asian American; 2% Foreign; 2% two or more races; 2% race unknown; 10% Hispanic. **Female To Male Ratio:** 1.2:1. The average age of freshmen is 18; all undergraduates, 20. 13% do not continue beyond their first year; 73% remain to graduate. **Housing:** 3290 students can be accommodated in college housing, which includes coed dorms and on-campus apartments. In addition, there are fraternity houses, sorority houses, an honors floor and an international interest floor in the residence hall. On-campus housing is guaranteed for all 4 years. 62% of students live on campus. All students may keep cars.

FACULTY/CLASSROOMS: 52% of faculty are male; 48% are female. No introductory courses are taught by graduate students.

PROGRAMS OF STUDY: BU confers B.A., B.F.A., B.Mus., B.S., B.S.Civil Eng., B.S.Constr., B.S.E.E., B.S.I.E., B.S.M.E., B.S.Mfg.E., B.S.Mfg.E.Tech., and B.S.N. degrees. Master's and doctoral degrees are also awarded. Bachelor's degrees are awarded in BIOLOGICAL SCIENCE (biology, ecology, and field biology, biochemistry, biology/biological science, and cell and molecular biology), BUSINESS (accounting, business administration and management, business economics, business information systems, entrepreneurial studies, finance, hospitality management services, human resources/organizational management, international business, management information systems, marketing, management and strategic leadership, organizational leadership and management, retailing, and supply chain management), COMMUNICATIONS AND THE ARTS (advertising, animation, art, art history and appreciation, communications, drawing, English, game design and development, journalism, music, music business management, music composition, music industry, music performance, Spanish, sports communication, studio art graphic design, television and digital media production, theatre arts, and visual effects), COMPUTER AND PHYSICAL SCIENCE (actuarial science, chemistry, computer information systems, computer security, computer science, mathematics, physics, statistics, and web technology), EDUCATION (art education, early childhood education, education, education of the emotionally handicapped, education of the exceptional child, education of the mentally handicapped, education of the physically handicapped, elementary education, middle school education, music education, and secondary education), ENGINEERING AND ENVIRONMENTAL DESIGN (civil engineering, construction, electrical and computer engineering, electrical/electronics engineering, engineering physics, environmental science, industrial engineering, manufacturing engineering, manufacturing technology, and mechanical engineering), HEALTH PROFESSIONS (community health work, health science, medical laboratory science, medical technology, nursing, nutrition and dietetics, and premedicine), SOCIAL SCIENCE (criminal justice, economics, family/consumer studies, French studies, history, international studies, legal studies, liberal arts, sciences, general studies, humanities, philosophy, political science/government, prelaw, psychology, religious studies, social work, and sociology). Business, engineering, and health have the largest enrollments.

ACTIVITIES: 32% of men belong to 17 national fraternities; 31% of women belong to 12 national sororities. There are 240 groups on campus, including art, band, cheerleading, chess, choir, chorale, chorus, computers, dance, drama, drill team, environmental, ethnic, film, forensics, honors, international, jazz band, LGBT, literary magazine, musical theater, newspaper, orchestra, pep band, photography, political, professional, radio and TV, religious, social, social service, student government, and symphony. Popular campus events include Late Night BU, Student Activities Fair, and Taste of Bradley. **Sports:** There are 6 intercollegiate sports for men and 7 for women, and 14 intramural sports for men and 14 for women. Facilities include tennis courts, intramural playing fields, a softball field, baseball field, outdoor lighted basketball courts, a student recreation center with a pool, indoor track, weights, cardio machines, spinning room, practice courts, a climbing wall, and racquetball courts. Students have access to the local civic center for basketball, and hockey at the local skating center. **Graduates:** From July 1, 2016 to June 30, 2017, 1138 bachelor's degrees were awarded. The most popular majors were engineering (20%), business, management, related support services (19%), and health professions and related programs (11%). In an average class, 1% graduate in 3 years or less, 50% graduate in 4 years or less, 19% graduate in 5 years or less, and 2% graduate in 6 years or less.

SERVICES: Counseling and information services are available, as is tutoring in most subjects, such as introductory subjects and selected higher-level classes. There is remedial math and writing. **Library/Resources:** The library contains 548,000 volumes, 84,300 microform items, 14,764 audio/video tapes/CDs/DVDs, and subscribes to 55,411 periodicals, including electronic. Computerized library services include interlibrary loans, database searching, Internet access, and Wi-Fi capability. Special learning facilities include an art gallery, a radio station, and a TV station. **Physically Challenged Students:** 75% of the campus is accessible. Facilities include wheelchair ramps, elevators, special parking, specially equipped restrooms, special class scheduling, and lowered drinking fountains. **Special:** Special academic programs include an honors program, co-op programs, internships, a Washington semester, a Hollywood semester, work-study programs, study abroad in 30 countries, B.A.-B.S. degrees in most majors, dual and student-designed majors, independent study, distance learning, certificate programs, four 3-2 programs and two 4-1 programs and leadership fellowships. There are 15 national honor societies, a freshman honors program, and 16 departmental honors programs. **Visiting:** There are regularly scheduled orientations for prospective students, including class visits, campus tours, admissions information, financial assistance seminars, lunch, and student and parent meetings. There are guides for informal visits; visitors may sit in on classes and stay overnight. To schedule a visit, contact the Office of Undergraduate Admissions. **Campus Safety and Security:** Measures include 24-hour foot and vehicle patrol, an emergency notification system, self-defense education, and security escort services. There are shuttle buses, emergency telephones, lighted pathways/sidewalks, and controlled access to dorms/residences.

REQUIREMENTS: The SAT or ACT is required. Applicants must have a high school diploma or GED. Students should have completed 16 academic credits: 4 in English, 3 in mathematics, and 2 each in science with lab, and social studies. Recommended academic credits are 5 in English, 4 in mathematics, and 3 in science with 2 lab, social studies, foreign language, and history. An audition is required for music and theatre, and test scores are waived for students who have not attended high school in a year. AP and CLEP credits are accepted. To graduate, the students must complete the university's core curriculum. Overall, the university requires 124 total credit hours, with 32 hours in the students major and a minimum of 40 semester hours in junior and senior courses (those numbered 300 or above). A minimum of 30 semester hours must be earned in residence, and 24 of the last 30 semester hours must be earned in residence. Additionally, students must have a minimum GPA of 2.0. **Procedure:** Freshmen are admitted in the fall, spring, and summer. Entrance exams should be taken in the spring of the junior year or the fall of the senior year. There are deferred admissions and rolling admissions plans. The fall 2017 application fee was $35. Notifications are sent October 15. Applications are accepted online. **Transfer Students:** 243 transfer students enrolled in 2016-2017. Transfer students must have a minimum GPA of 2.0. Those with fewer than 15 hours of college credit must submit their ACT or SAT scores and a high school transcript. Additionally, college transcripts and a statement of good standing from prior institution(s) are required of all; an interview is recommended and an essay or personal statement required for some. 30 of 124 credits required for the bachelors degree must be completed at BU. **International Students:** There are 84 international students enrolled. They must take the TOEFL with a minimum score of 550 on the paper-based TOEFL (PBT) or 79 on the Internet-based version (iBT). The SAT or ACT is recommended.

ADMISSIONS: 71% of the 2017-2018 applicants were accepted. The ACT scores were 37% between 18 and 23, 50% between 24 and 29, and 13% above 30. 28% of the current freshmen were in the top fifth of their class; 45% were in the top two fifths. 23 freshmen graduated first in their class. **Admissions Contact:** Dr. Justin Ball, Associate Vice President for Enrollment. Email: *admissions@bradley.edu* Web: *www.bradley.edu*

FINANCIAL AID: BU is a member of CSS. The FAFSA code is 001641. The priority date for freshman financial aid applications for fall entry is December 1.

CHICAGO STATE UNIVERSITY — E-2

www.csu.edu

Chicago, IL 60628	(773) 995-2513 (800) 278-3011
Fax: (773) 995-3820	**Email:** ug-admissions@csu.edu
Full-time: 917 men, 2092 women	**Faculty:** n/av
Part-time: 392 men, 1211 women	**Ph.D.s:** 62%
Graduate: 467 men, 1022 women	**Student/Faculty:** n/av
Year: other, summer session	**Tuition:** $24,172 ($20,706)
Room & Board: $17,448	**Freshman Class:** n/av
ACT: required	**CEEB CODE:** 1118
Application Deadline: July 15	**COMPETITIVE**

Chicago State University, founded in 1867, is a public commuter and residential institution controlled by the State of Illinois. It offers day and evening undergraduate programs through the colleges of arts and sciences, health sciences, business administration, education, and nontraditional programs. The figures given in the above capsule and in this profile are approximate. There are 5 undergraduate schools and 2 graduate schools. In addition to regional accreditation, CSU has baccalaureate program accreditation with AACSB, ACPE, ADA, CAHEA, CAEP, and NLN. The 161-acre campus is in an urban area Southside of Chicago, 12 miles south of downtown Chicago. Including any residence halls, there are 13 buildings.

STUDENT LIFE: 98% of undergraduates are from Illinois. Others are from 24 states, 21 foreign countries, and Canada. 80% are African American; 7% Hispanic; 10% White; 1% Asian American. **Female To Male Ratio:** 2.4:1. The average age of freshmen is 21; all undergraduates, 29. **Housing:** 360 students can be accommodated in college housing, which includes dorms. On-campus housing is available on a first-come, first-served basis. 97% of students commute. Alcohol is not permitted. All students may keep cars.

FACULTY/CLASSROOMS: 99% teach undergraduates. No introductory courses are taught by graduate students. The average class size in an introductory lecture is 60; in a laboratory is 26; and in a regular course is 35.

PROGRAMS OF STUDY: CSU confers B.A., B.S., B.M.E., and B.S.Ed. degrees. Master's and doctoral degrees are also awarded. Bachelor's degrees are awarded in BIOLOGICAL SCIENCE (biochemistry and biology/biological science), BUSINESS (accounting, banking and finance, business administration and management, management science, marketing/retailing/merchandising, and recreation and leisure services), COMMUNICATIONS AND THE ARTS (art, broadcasting, English, music, Spanish, and speech/debate/rhetoric), COMPUTER AND PHYSICAL SCIENCE (chemistry, computer science, information sciences and systems, mathematics, and physics), EDUCATION (art education, bilingual/bicultural education, business education, early childhood education, elementary education, industrial arts education, music education, physical education, secondary education, and vocational education), HEALTH PROFESSIONS (health, health care administration, health science, nursing, predentistry, and premedicine), SOCIAL SCIENCE (African American studies, criminal justice, economics, geography, history, political science/government, prelaw, psychology, and sociology). Business administration and computer science are the strongest academically. Elementary education and nursing have the largest enrollments.

ACTIVITIES: There are 72 groups on campus, including cheerleading, chess, choir, dance, honors, international, jazz band, literary magazine, newspaper, political, professional, radio and TV, religious, social, social service, and student government. Popular campus events include Welcome Week activities, Black Writers Conference, and Hispanic Heritage Month. **Sports:** There are 6 intercollegiate sports for men and 6 for women, and 4 intramural sports for men and 2 for women. Facilities include tennis courts, indoor/outdoor tracks, an Olympic-size swimming pool, weight rooms, basketball courts, a fitness center, a dance studio, a baseball field, and a convocation center. **Graduates:** From July 1, 2016 to June 30, 2017, 839 bachelor's degrees were awarded. The most popular majors were general studies (26%), business administration (13%), and criminal justice (6%). In an average class, 7% graduate in 4 years or less and 22% graduate in 6 years or less.

SERVICES: Counseling and information services are available, as is tutoring in some subjects. There is remedial math, reading, and writing. **Library/Resources:** The library contains 26,000 volumes, 388,028 microform items, and subscribes to 1,734 periodicals, including electronic. Computerized library services include interlibrary loans, database searching, and Internet access. Special learning facilities include an art gallery, a radio station, and a TV studio. **Physically Challenged Students:** All of the campus is accessible. Facilities include wheelchair ramps, elevators, special parking, specially equipped restrooms, lowered drinking fountains, and lowered telephones. **Special:** Chicago State offers a combined B.A.-B.S. degree, a board of governors degree program, a University Without Walls Program, and an individualized curriculum program. Study abroad in Liberia and life experience credits are also provided. There is a freshman honors program. **Visiting:** There are regularly scheduled orientations for prospective students, including a tour of campus, admissions overview, and financial aid information. To schedule a visit, contact the Office of Admissions. **Campus Safety and Security:** Measures include 24-hour foot and vehicle patrol and security escort services. There are emergency telephones and lighted pathways/sidewalks.

REQUIREMENTS: The ACT is required; scores need not be submitted if the applicant is over 25 years of age. Graduation from an accredited secondary school is required; a GED will be accepted. Minimum credits submitted should include 4 units of English, 3 of math, 3 of science, and 3 of social sciences. A GPA of 2.5 is required. AP and CLEP credits are accepted. All students must complete 120 credit hours, including 40 hours in the major, maintain a 2.0 GPA, and fulfill the foreign language requirement. They must complete a 39-hour core curriculum as well as examinations in English, math, reading, and the U.S. Constitution. **Procedure:** Freshmen are admitted to all sessions. There is a rolling admissions plan. Applications should be filed by July 15 for fall entry; November 15 for spring entry; and May 1 for summer entry. The fall 2017 application fee was $25. Notification is sent on a rolling basis. Applications are accepted online. **Transfer Students:** Transfer students must have a minimum GPA of 2.0, and those with fewer than 24 hours must also meet freshman admission requirements. 30 of 120 credits required for the bachelor's degree must be completed at CSU. **International Students:** There are 26 international students enrolled. They must take the TOEFL with a minimum score of 525 on the paper-based TOEFL (PBT) or 69 on the Internet-based version (iBT) and the college's own test, or take the IELTS. They must also take the SAT or ACT.

Admissions Contact: Stephen Powenski, Interim Director. Email: *ug-admissions@csu.edu* Web: *www.csu.edu*

FINANCIAL AID: In 2017-2018, 97% of all full-time freshmen received some form of financial aid. 97% of all full-time freshmen received need-based aid. The average freshman award was $16,154. Need-based scholarships or need-based grants averaged $7,263 ($9,540 maximum); need-based self-help aid (loans and jobs) averaged $3,473 ($7,000 maximum); non-need-based athletic scholarships averaged $10,575 ($17,010 maximum); and other non-need-based awards and non-need-based scholarships averaged $6,898 ($19,522 maximum). 5% of undergraduate students work part-time. The average financial indebtedness of the 2017 graduate was $28,955. The FAFSA code is 001694. The priority date for freshman financial aid applications for fall entry is February 1. The deadline for filing freshman financial aid applications for fall entry is April 15.

COLUMBIA COLLEGE CHICAGO — E-2

www.colum.edu

Chicago, IL 60605 — **(312) 369-7130**

Email: admissions@colum.edu

Full-time: 2663 men, 3773 women
Part-time: 271 men, 320 women
Graduate: 98 men, 187 women
Year: semesters, summer session
Room & Board: $13,630
ACT: 23
Application Deadline: n/av

Faculty: n/av
Ph.D.s: n/av
Student/Faculty: n/av
Tuition: $26,474
Freshman Class: 8120 applied, 7439 accepted, 1443 enrolled
CEEB CODE: 1135
COMPETITIVE

Columbia College Chicago is a private, nonprofit college offering a distinctive curriculum that blends creative and media arts, liberal arts, and business and more than 100 undergraduate and graduate degree programs. Dedicated to academic excellence and long-term career success, Columbia creates a dynamic, challenging, and collaborative space for students who experience the world through a creative lens. There are 3 undergraduate schools and 3 graduate schools. The campus is in an urban area in Chicago, IL.

STUDENT LIFE: 53% of undergraduates are from Illinois. Others are from 50 states, 53 foreign countries, and Canada. 54% are White; 5% Foreign; 5% race unknown; 4% Asian American; 4% two or more races; 14% Hispanic; 13% African American. **Female To Male Ratio:** 1.4:1. 34% do not continue beyond their first year; 41% remain to graduate. **Housing:** College-sponsored housing includes gender-neutral dorms, and honors houses. On-campus housing is available on a first-come, first-served basis. 67% of students commute. Alcohol is not permitted. All students may keep cars.

FACULTY/CLASSROOMS: No introductory courses are taught by graduate students.

PROGRAMS OF STUDY: Columbia confers B.A., B.F.A., B.S., and B.Mus degrees. Master's degrees are also awarded. Bachelor's degrees are awarded in BUSINESS (fashion merchandising, management, marketing, and sports management), COMMUNICATIONS AND THE ARTS (acting, advertising, American Sign Language, animation, art history, arts administration/management, audio technology, communications, creative writing, dance, digital communications, digital media, dramatic arts, fashion studies, film arts, film, television and digital media, fine arts, game design and development, game programming, graphic design, illustration, intermedia/multimedia, interdisciplinary art, journalism, media management, film and media studies, music, music business management, music composition, music performance, music technology, musical theater, performing arts, photography, playwriting/screenwriting, public relations, radio/television technology, theatre arts, theater design, and writing), COMPUTER AND PHYSICAL SCIENCE (computer programming, computer game design/development, and digital animation and game design), EDUCATION (early childhood education and general studies), ENGINEERING AND ENVIRONMENTAL DESIGN (interior design), SOCIAL SCIENCE (cross-cultural studies and fashion design and technology). Audio design and production, cinema art and science, comedy writing and performance, and game development are the strongest academically. Cinema art and science, audio design and production, and fashion business have the largest enrollments.

ACTIVITIES: There are no fraternities or sororities. There are 85 groups on campus, including art, chorale, chorus, communications, computers, dance, drama, environmental, ethnic, film, honors, international, jazz band, LGBT, literary magazine, musical theater, newspaper, orchestra, photography, political, professional, a radio station, a TV station, religious, social, social service, student government, symphony, and yearbook. Popular campus events include Manifest, New Student Convocation, Wabash Arts Corridor (WAC) Crawl, African Heritage, Dr. Martin Luther King Jr.'s Birthday, and Women in the Arts. **Sports:** **Graduates:** From July 1, 2016 to June 30, 2017, 1849 bachelor's degrees were awarded. The most popular majors were cinema art and science (17%), music business management (6%), and fashion business (6%). In an average class, 33% graduate in 4 years or less, 42% graduate in 5 years or less, and 44% graduate in 6 years or less.

SERVICES: Counseling and information services are available, as is

tutoring in most subjects. There is a reader service for the blind, and remedial math, reading, and writing. **Library/Resources:** Computerized library services include interlibrary loans, database searching, Internet access, and Wi-Fi capability. Special learning facilities include an art gallery, a radio station, a TV station, Museum of Contemporary Photography, Center for Black Music Research, ShopColumbia, Big Mouth open mic, Averill and Bernard Leviton Gallery, C33 Gallery, Center for Book, Paper and Print, Fashion Studies Exhibition Windows, Fashion Study Collection, Glass Curtain Gallery, Hokin Project, Project Room, The Arcade, Efroymson Art + Design Resource Center, Anchor Graphics, Fashion Lab, Media Production Center, Digital Music Lab, Music MFA Lab, Digital Photography Lab, and The Loft. **Physically Challenged Students:** Facilities include wheelchair ramps, elevators, specially equipped restrooms, special class scheduling, lowered drinking fountains, lowered telephones, and special housing. **Special:** Columbia offers study abroad in many countries, independent study, internships, work-study programs, an honors program, a semester in LA program, a comedy studies program, a student-designed majors, and a general studies degree. There is a freshman honors program. **Visiting:** There are regularly scheduled orientations for prospective students. There are guides for informal visits and visitors may sit in on classes. To schedule a visit, contact the Undergraduate Admissions Office. **Campus Safety and Security:** Measures include 24-hour foot and vehicle patrol, an emergency notification system, self-defense education, and security escort services. There are emergency telephones, lighted pathways/sidewalks, and controlled access to dorms/residences.

REQUIREMENTS: The following are required: essay (250-650 words), official high school transcripts/GED test results/home-school transcript, application fee, and if English is not your country's primary language, you must prove English language proficiency. While test scores are not required for admission, you're welcome to submit ACT, SAT, AP, or IB scores to further demonstrate your preparedness for college-level work. Submitting a portfolio or audition makes you eligible for the Faculty Recognition Award, and the Columbia's competitive talent-based scholarship. This scholarship is renewable up to four years. We recommend that students submit at least one letter of recommendation. AP and CLEP credits are accepted. In addition to Liberal Arts and Sciences Core Curriculum (LAS Core) requirements, the B.A., B.Mus., B.S., and B.F.A. programs may include core requirements and specialized concentrations of courses that enable students to prepare for particular careers. General academic requirements for graduation: a minimum total of earned credits (120 or 128); minimum 2.0 cumulative GPA; completion of the LAS Core; two 200-level LAS courses; one global awareness course (GA); one US Pluralism course (PL); one writing intensive course (WI); and successful completion of a major. **Procedure:** Freshmen are admitted to all sessions. There are deferred admissions and rolling admissions plans. Check with the school for current application deadlines. The fall 2017 application fee was $50. Applications are accepted online. **Transfer Students:** 873 transfer students enrolled in 2016-2017. The following are required: essay (250-650 words), official transcripts from high school/any college previously attended, application fee, and if English is not your country's primary language, you must prove English language proficiency. While test scores are not required for admission, you're welcome to submit ACT, SAT, AP, or IB scores to further demonstrate your preparedness for college-level work. Submitting a portfolio or audition makes you eligible for the Faculty Recognition Award, and Columbia's competitive talent-based scholarship. This scholarship is renewable up to four years. We recommend that students submit at least one letter of recommendation. 45 of 120 credits required for the bachelor's degree must be completed at Columbia. **International Students:** There are 323 international students enrolled.

ADMISSIONS: 92% of the 2017-2018 applicants were accepted. The ACT scores were 11% between 12 and 17, 45% between 18 and 23, 37% between 24 and 29, and 7% above 30. **Admissions Contact:** Derek Brinkley, Senior Director Admissions and Recruitment. Email: *admissions@colum.edu* Web: *www.colum.edu*

FINANCIAL AID: In 2017-2018, 91% of all full-time freshmen received some form of financial aid. The average freshman award was $18,669. The FAFSA code is 001665. Check with the school for current application deadlines.

CONCORDIA UNIVERSITY, CHICAGO E-2

www.curf.edu

River Forest, IL 60305 **(708) 209-3101**

Fax: (708) 209-3473	**Email:** admission@cuchicago.edu
Full-time: 351 men, 610 women	**Faculty:** 74
Part-time: 21 men, 50 women	**Ph.D.s:** 65%
Graduate: 428 men, 1323 women	**Student/Faculty:** 13 to 1
Year: semesters, summer session	**Tuition:** $32,074
Room & Board: $9448	**Freshman Class:** 680 applied, 628 accepted, 210 enrolled
ACT: required	**CEEB CODE:** 1140
Application Deadline: n/av	**COMPETITIVE**

Concordia University, Chicago, founded in 1864, is a private liberal arts institution affiliated with the Lutheran Church, Missouri Synod. The figures given in the above capsule, and in this profile are approximate. There are 4 undergraduate schools and 1 graduate school. In addition to regional accreditation, CUC has baccalaureate program accreditation with CAEP and NLN. The 40-acre campus is in a suburban area 10 miles west of downtown Chicago. Including any residence halls, there are 24 buildings.

STUDENT LIFE: 65% of undergraduates are from Illinois. Others are from 21 states, 1 foreign country, and Canada. 66% are from public schools. 51% are White; 5% Hispanic; 10% African American; 1% Asian American. 59% are undeclared denomination; 31% Protestant; 13% Catholic. **Female To Male Ratio:** 2.5:1. The average age of freshmen is 18; all undergraduates, 22. 27% do not continue beyond their first year; 53% remain to graduate. **Housing:** 775 students can be accommodated in college housing, which includes married student dorms. On-campus housing is guaranteed for all 4 years. 65% of students live on campus. Alcohol is not permitted. All students may keep cars.

FACULTY/CLASSROOMS: 50% of faculty are male; 50% are female. 82% teach undergraduates, and 82% do research. No introductory courses are taught by graduate students. The average class size in an introductory lecture is 20; in a laboratory is 18; and in a regular course is 25.

PROGRAMS OF STUDY: CUC confers B.A., B.Mus., and B.Mus.Ed. degrees. Master's and doctoral degrees are also awarded. Bachelor's degrees are awarded in BIOLOGICAL SCIENCE (biology/biological science), BUSINESS (accounting and business administration and management), COMMUNICATIONS AND THE ARTS (art, communications, English, and music), COMPUTER AND PHYSICAL SCIENCE (chemistry, computer programming, computer science, mathematics, natural sciences, and physical sciences), EDUCATION (computer education, early childhood education, elementary education, middle school education, music education, physical education, science education, and secondary education), HEALTH PROFESSIONS (premedicine), SOCIAL SCIENCE (geography, history, physical fitness/movement, political science/government, prelaw, psychology, religion, social science, social work, sociology, and theological studies). Elementary education, exercise science, and theology are the strongest academically. Elementary education, business, and psychology have the largest enrollments.

ACTIVITIES: There are no fraternities or sororities. There are 43 groups on campus, including band, cheerleading, choir, chorale, chorus, communications, dance, drama, ethnic, honors, jazz band, literary magazine, musical theater, newspaper, pep band, professional, religious, social, social service, student government, symphony, and yearbook. Popular campus events include Orientation Week, Campus Awareness Day, and Family Weekend. **Sports:** There are 7 intercollegiate sports for men and 7 for women, and 12 intramural sports for men and 12 for women. Facilities include gyms, an indoor swimming pool, a weight training room, a human performance lab, football and soccer fields, tennis courts, baseball and softball fields, and track. **Graduates:** From July 1, 2016 to June 30, 2017, 216 bachelor's degrees were awarded. The most popular majors were education (34%), business (8%), and sociology/social work (4%). In an average class, 36% graduate in 4 years or less, 41% graduate in 5 years or less, and 41% graduate in 6 years or less. Of the 2016 graduating class, 23% were enrolled in graduate school within 6 months of graduation, and 98% were employed.

SERVICES: Counseling and information services are available, as is tutoring in every subject. There is remedial math, reading, and writing.

Library/Resources: The library contains 140,000 volumes, 480,000 microform items, 2,250 audio/video tapes/CDs/DVDs, and subscribes to 235 periodicals, including electronic. Computerized library services include interlibrary loans, database searching, Internet access, and Wi-Fi capability. Special learning facilities include an art gallery, natural history museum, a TV station, a early childhood resource center, a human performance lab, a language lab, computer center, and a weather station. **Physically Challenged Students:** 74% of the campus is accessible. Facilities include wheelchair ramps, elevators, special parking, specially equipped restrooms, special class scheduling, lowered drinking fountains, and lowered telephones. **Special:** Cross-registration is possible with Dominican University and the Chicago Consortium of Colleges. Concordia also offers internships for liberal arts majors in the Chicago area, which provides numerous opportunities, study abroad in England, and pass/fail options. Work-study is possible, as is an accelerated degreee program in organizational management. There are 3 national honor societies, including Phi Beta Kappa, and a freshman honors program. **Visiting:** There are regularly scheduled orientations for prospective students consisting of daily planned activities during orientation in the first week of the fall semester. There are guides for informal visits; visitors may sit in on classes, and stay overnight. To schedule a visit, contact the Office of Admission. **Campus Safety and Security:** Measures include 24-hour foot and vehicle patrol, self-defense education, and security escort services. There are shuttle buses, emergency telephones, and lighted pathways/sidewalks.

REQUIREMENTS: The ACT is required. Applicants should have 15 units of credit, with 11 units in college preparatory courses, including English, math, lab science, and social studies. A letter of recommendation is required, as is a minimum GPA of 2.0 in the college preparatory subjects and a ranking in the top half of their graduating class. AP and CLEP credits are accepted. Important factors in the admissions decision are advanced placement or honors courses, recommendations by school officials, and leadership record. All students are required to take 2 years of liberal arts, including humanities, English, science, religion, and social science, and 5 quarter hours of physical education. A 2.0 to 2.25 GPA and a total of 128 to 150 quarter hours are required. The number of hours required for the major varies by program. **Procedure:** Freshmen are admitted to all sessions. Entrance exams should be taken in the spring of the junior year or fall of the senior year. There is a rolling admissions plan. Application deadlines are open. Applications are accepted online. **Transfer Students:** 90 transfer students enrolled in 2016-2017. A cumulative GPA of 2.0 or higher at all previous colleges plus a letter of recommendation are required. 48 of 128 credits required for the bachelor's degree must be completed at CUC. **International Students:** There are 5 international students enrolled. They must take the TOEFL or MELAB, or successfully complete Level 109 at an ELS language center.

ADMISSIONS: 92% of the 2017-2018 applicants were accepted. The ACT scores were 36% below 12, 23% between 12 and 17, 20% between 18 and 23, 9% between 24 and 29, and 12% above 30. 30% of the current freshmen were in the top fifth of their class; 41% were in the top two fifths. **Admissions Contact:** Rosa Reiber, Associate Director of Admissions. Email: *admission@cuchicago.edu* Web: *www.curf.edu*

FINANCIAL AID: In 2017-2018, 93% of all full-time freshmen received some form of financial aid. 85% of all full-time freshmen received need-based aid. The average freshman award was $12,000. The average financial indebtedness of the 2017 graduate was $12,000. The college's own financial statement, and student and parent 1040 U.S. tax forms are required. Check with the school for current application deadlines.

DEPAUL UNIVERSITY — E-2

www.depaul.edu

Chicago, IL 60604 — **(312) 362-8300**, **(800) 4-DEPAUL**

Fax: (312) 362-5749 — **Email: admission@depaul.edu**

Full-time: 6123 men, 6763 women	**Faculty:** 769
Part-time: 918 men, 1012 women	**Ph.D.s:** 85%
Graduate: 3686 men, 4267 women	**Student/Faculty:** 16 to 1
Year: quarters, summer session	**Tuition:** $39,010
Room & Board: $13,797	**Freshman Class:** 21613 applied, 15506 accepted, 2542 enrolled
SAT CR/M: 610/590 **ACT:** 25	**CEEB CODE:** 1165
Application Deadline: February 1	**VERY COMPETITIVE**

DePaul University is the nation's largest Catholic university. Its partnerships throughout Chicago enable DePaul to provide an exceptional educational experience that is vibrant, pragmatic, and socially engaged. Classes are small and are taught by knowledgeable and experienced faculty members who take full advantage of Chicago's resources. DePaul's mission to provide a quality education to students from a broad range of backgrounds has resulted in one of the nation's most diverse student bodies. With ten colleges and schools, DePaul has campuses in the heart of Chicago's Loop and Lincoln Park neighborhoods. In addition to regional accreditation, DePaul University has baccalaureate program accreditation with AACSB, NASM, and ACS (American Chemical Society). The 38-acre campus is in an urban area in Chicago, Illinois. Including any residence halls, there are 46 buildings.

STUDENT LIFE: 75% of undergraduates are from Illinois. Others are from 48 states, 97 foreign countries, and Canada. 80% are from public schools. 8% are African American; 53% White; 4% two or more races; 3% Foreign; 3% race unknown; 19% Hispanic; 10% Asian American. 30% are Catholic; 15% claim no religious affiliation. **Female To Male Ratio:** 1.1:1. The average age of freshmen is 18; all undergraduates, 23. 16% do not continue beyond their first year; 71% remain to graduate. **Housing:** 2684 students can be accommodated in college housing, which includes dorms, on-campus apartments, and off-campus apartments. In addition, there are honors houses, language/international houses, private studios and apartments, and traditional residence-style units. On-campus housing is available on a first-come, first-served basis, and is available on a lottery system for upperclassmen. 82% of students commute. All students may keep cars.

FACULTY/CLASSROOMS: 53% of faculty are male; 47% are female. 86% do both. Graduate students teach 2% of introductory courses.

PROGRAMS OF STUDY: DePaul confers B.A., B.S., B.F.A., B.M., B.S.B., and B.S.P.E. degrees. Master's and doctoral degrees are also awarded. Bachelor's degrees are awarded in AGRICULTURE (environmental studies), BIOLOGICAL SCIENCE (biochemistry, biology/biological science, and neurosciences), BUSINESS (accounting, banking and finance, business administration and management, business administration, business economics, finance, hospitality management services, human resources, business management, management information systems, management science, marketing management, organizational behavior, and real estate), COMMUNICATIONS AND THE ARTS (acting, animation, Arabic, art history, art, art and design, Chinese, communication studies, communications, composition, creative writing, dramatic arts, English, film, television and digital media, fine arts, French, game design and development, game programming, German, graphic design, information technology, Italian, jazz, journalism, media arts, music, music business management, music performance, music theory and composition, organizational communication, performing arts, playwriting/screenwriting, public relations, public relations/advertising, scenic and lighting design, Spanish, speech/debate/rhetoric, theatre arts, theater design, theater management, and writing and rhetoric), COMPUTER AND PHYSICAL SCIENCE (actuarial science, applied mathematics, chemistry, computer programming, computer game design/development, computer science, computer security and information assurance, cyber intelligence/security studies, digital arts/technology, information sciences and systems, mathematics, network and computer security, physical sciences, and physics), EDUCATION (art education, early childhood education, education, education administration, elementary education, foreign languages education, health education, middle level education, music education, physical education, secondary education, special education, and world language education), ENGINEERING AND ENVIRONMENTAL DESIGN (architectural history, computational sciences, computer graphics, computer technology, environmental science, and history of architecture/urban development), HEALTH PROFESSIONS (art therapy, biology, clinical science, exercise science, health science, and nursing), SOCIAL SCIENCE (African studies, American studies, anthropology, community services, criminology, East Asian studies, economics, geography, history, humanities, international studies, Islamic studies, Japanese studies, Judaic studies, Latin American studies, peace studies, philosophy, political science/government, psychology, public administration, public affairs, public policy, religion, social science, social studies, sociology, urban studies, women and gender studies, and womens studies). Accounting, finance, and film and television have the largest enrollments.

ACTIVITIES: 5% of men belong to 13 national fraternities; 11% of women belong to 16 national sororities. There are 320 groups on campus, including art, band, cheerleading, chess, choir, chorale, chorus, communications, computers, dance, debate, drama, environmental, ethnic, film, honors, international, jazz band, LGBT, literary magazine, musical theater, newspaper, opera, orchestra, pep band, photography, political, professional, radio and TV, religious, social, social service, student government, and symphony. Popular campus events include FEST (University Festival), Blue Demon Week, Welcome Week, Vincentian Service Day, New Student Service Day, DemonTHON (DePaul's Dance Marathon), VinnyFEST, and Fall Involvement Fair. **Sports:** There are 6 intercollegiate sports for men and 7 for women, and 31 intramural sports for men and 33 for women. Facilities include a fitness and recreation center offering a strength and conditioning area with over 100 pieces of cardio equipment, selectorized equipment, free weights, a swimming pool, a gymnasium for basketball, volleyball, and badminton, racquetball courts, 1/8 mile banked jogging track, over 65 group fitness classes, aquatics, yoga, dance, Pilates, martial arts, fitness training, safety training, personal training, and massage therapy. **Graduates:** From July 1, 2016 to June 30, 2017, 3735 bachelor's degrees were awarded. The most popular majors were accounting (8%), public relations and advertising (7%), and finance (7%). In an average class, 2% graduate in 3 years or less, 59% graduate in 4 years or less, 68% graduate in 5 years or less, and 71% graduate in 6 years or less.

SERVICES: There is a reader service for the blind, and remedial reading and writing. The Center for Students with Disabilities offers clinician services, which includes remediation of skills for time management, organizational skills, reading strategies, and writing skills. The University provides free tutoring services across a range of departments and subjects area: University Writing Center, Quantitative Reasoning Lab, Math Department, College of Science/Health, computer software (Word, Excel, etc.), Computer Programming, and Accounting, amongst others. **Library/Resources:** The library contains 1.1 million volumes, 242,339 microform items, and 32,765 audio/video tapes/CDs/DVDs, and subscribes to 80,875 periodicals, including electronic. Computerized library services include interlibrary loans, database searching, Internet access, and Wi-Fi capability. Special learning facilities include an art gallery, a radio station, a LEED-certified environmental science, and chemistry building with greenhouse and green roof, a digital cinema laboratory with motion-capture system, a green-screen studio, converged newsroom, 10 specialized computer research labs including artificial intelligence, biomedics informatics and mobile e-commerce, a theatre, and art museum. **Physically Challenged Students:** 97% of the campus is accessible. Facilities include wheelchair ramps, elevators, special parking, specially equipped restrooms, special class scheduling, lowered drinking fountains, lowered telephones, and special housing. The Center for Students with Disabilities coordinates DePaul University's provision of accommodations and other services to students with documented disabilities in accordance with the Americans with Disabilities Act and Section 504 of the Rehabilitation Act. All CSD programs and services are free of charge with the exception of a modest fee for students requesting weekly clinician services for academic support strategies. CSD works with the range of all documented disabilities, e.g., LD, AD/HD, medical conditions, chronic illness, psychiatric illness, physical/visual/hearing impaired, etc. Students may be full time, part-time, and undergraduate or graduate. CSD students are enrolled in university-wide colleges and schools such as Education, Business, Science and Health, Cinema Digital Media (CDM), Communication, Law, Music, Theatre, Liberal Arts and social Sciences, and the School for New Learning (SNL) with declared majors across a wide spectrum of career tracks. **Special:** There are 17 national honor societies and a freshman honors program. **Visiting:** There are regularly scheduled orientations for prospective students, freshmen orientation, DePaul Premiere, Transfer and Adult student orientation and provide academic advising, assessment testing, course registration, and information on social activities and residence life. There are guides for informal visits; visitors may sit in on classes, and stay overnight. To schedule a visit, contact the Office of Admission. **Campus Safety and Security:** Measures include 24-hour foot and vehicle patrol, an emergency notification system, self-defense education, and security escort services. There are emergency telephones, lighted pathways/sidewalks, and controlled access to dorms/residences.

REQUIREMENTS: DePaul has adopted a test-optional alternative for freshman admission. Students applying for freshman admission can choose whether or not to submit ACT or SAT scores as part of the application. Students who do not submit test scores will be required to send responses to several short essay questions. All Music School applicants and Theatre School applicants are required to schedule an audition or interview. Applicants to the Acting Program must submit a prescreen video and some Music applicants must submit a prescreen recording. A GPA of 2.3 is required. AP and CLEP credits are accepted. Important factors in the admissions decision are advanced placement or honors courses, leadership record, and personality/intangible qualities. In order to graduate, undergraduate students must have fulfilled all of the following requirements: 1. The student must have completed a minimum of 192 quarter hours or a minimum of 50 competencies for the School for New Learning competency-based programs 2. The student must have a minimum of 2.0 cumulative GPA. 3. The student must have completed all requirements for his or her degree by the last day of the term for which he or she is applying for degree conferral. 4. The student must have earned grades of C- or better in all major and minor classes. Please note that the cumulative GPA in each of these areas must be greater than or equal to 2.0. 5. The student must have fulfilled the residency requirement; i.e., he or she must have completed the following work at DePaul University: for the final 60 quarter hours of credit, one-half of the credit must be earned in the major area of concentration. 6. A formal application for graduation must be filed by a candidate. Application for graduation may be made only by classified degree-seeking students. The student must complete the online degree conferral application in Campus Connect by the designated deadline date. **Procedure:** Freshmen are admitted to all sessions. Entrance exams should be taken and scores need to be submitted by February 1. There are early admissions, deferred admissions, and rolling admissions plans. Early decision applications should be filed by November 15; regular applications, by February 1 for fall entry; November 1 for winter entry; March 1 for spring entry; and May 1 for summer entry. Notification of early decision is sent January 15; regular decision, March 15. Applications are accepted online. **Transfer Students:** 2093 transfer students enrolled in 2016-2017. A 2.0 GPA is required for most programs; a 2.5 GPA is required for Driehaus College of Business, College of Education, and School of Music. Applicants with fewer than 30 semester hours or 44 quarter hours should submit high school transcripts and SAT or ACT scores. An audition is required for music and theater majors. 60 of 192 credits required for the bachelor's degree must be completed at DePaul. **International Students:** There are 472 international students enrolled. They must take the TOEFL with a minimum score of 80 on the Internet-based version (iBT). Students must take the International English Language Testing Systems, SAT/ACT, or PTE Academic.

ADMISSIONS: 72% of the 2017-2018 applicants were accepted. The SAT scores for the 2017-2018 freshman class were: Critical Reading-- 5% below 500, 37% between 500 and 599, 44% between 600 and 699, and 14% between 700 and 800. Math-- 9% below 500, 46% between 500 and 599, 39% between 600 and 699, and 6% between 700 and 800. The ACT scores were 2% between 12 and 17, 32% between 18 and 23, 49% between 24 and 29, and 17% above 30. **Admissions Contact:** Carlene Klaas-Kennelly, Dean of Undergraduate Admission. Email: *admission@depaul.edu* Web: *www.depaul.edu*

FINANCIAL AID: In 2017-2018, 71% of all full-time freshmen received some form of financial aid. 63% of all full-time freshmen received need-based aid. The average freshman award was $25,812. Need-based scholarships or need-based grants averaged $11,045; need-based self-help aid (loans and jobs) averaged $3,318; non-need-based athletic scholarships averaged $30,048; and other non-need-based awards and non-need-based scholarships averaged $16,447. 12% of undergraduate students work part-time. The average financial indebtedness of the 2017 graduate was $30,115. The FAFSA code is 001671. The priority date for freshman financial aid applications for fall entry is December 1.

DOMINICAN UNIVERSITY — E-2

www.dom.edu

River Forest, IL 60305	**(708) 524-6795** **(800) 828-8475**
Fax: (708) 524-6864	**Email: domadmis@dom.edu**
Full-time: 688 men, 1326 women	**Faculty:** 139; IIA, -$
Part-time: 32 men, 125 women	**Ph.D.s:** 86%
Graduate: 188 men, 768 women	**Student/Faculty:** 11 to 1
Year: semesters, summer session	**Tuition:** $32,530
Room & Board: $9942	**Freshman Class:** 4697 applied, 3052 accepted, 441 enrolled
SAT CR/M: 620/470 **ACT:** 23	**CEEB CODE:** 1667
Application Deadline: July 1	**COMPETITIVE+**

Dominican University, founded in 1901, is an independent liberal arts institution. It ranks among the top 20 of Midwest regional universities, according to U.S. News & World Report which also cited Dominican as one of three Illinois schools offering a "best value" in college education. Small by design, Dominican is rich in resources and opportunities. There are 6 undergraduate schools and 6 graduate schools. In addition to regional accreditation, Dominican has baccalaureate program accreditation with AACSB, ADA, CSWE, CAEP, ALA, and ARC-PA. The 37-acre campus is in a suburban area 10 miles west of downtown Chicago. Including any residence halls, there are 13 buildings.

STUDENT LIFE: 94% of undergraduates are from Illinois. Others are from 29 states, 16 foreign countries, and Canada. 8% are African American; 8% race unknown; 43% White; 34% Hispanic; 3% Asian American; 3% Foreign; 1% two or more races. 38% are Catholic; 36% claim no religious affiliation. **Female To Male Ratio:** 2.4:1. The average age of freshmen is 19; all undergraduates, 22. 19% do not continue beyond their first year; 62% remain to graduate. **Housing:** 610 students can be accommodated in college housing, which includes single-sex, coed, and married student dorms and off-campus apartments. On-campus housing is available on a first-come, first-served basis. 74% of students commute. All students may keep cars.

FACULTY/CLASSROOMS: 37% of faculty are male; 63% are female. 79% teach undergraduates. No introductory courses are taught by graduate students. The average class size in an introductory lecture is 17 and in a regular course is 17.

PROGRAMS OF STUDY: Dominican confers B.A., B.S., B.S.N, B.L.S., B.H.S., B.B.A, and B.M.S. degrees. Master's and doctoral degrees are also awarded. Bachelor's degrees are awarded in BIOLOGICAL SCIENCE (biochemistry, biology/biological science, neurosciences, and nutrition), BUSINESS (accounting, apparel and accessories marketing, business administration and management, fashion merchandising, finance, information and communication technology, international business management, and marketing management), COMMUNICATIONS AND THE ARTS (apparel design, art history, communications, dramatic arts, English, film arts, fine arts, French, graphic design, Italian, journalism, music, painting, performing arts, photography, Spanish, and theatre arts), COMPUTER AND PHYSICAL SCIENCE (chemistry, computer science, digital arts/technology, mathematics, and natural sciences), EDUCATION (early childhood education, education, elementary education, and secondary education), ENGINEERING AND ENVIRONMENTAL DESIGN (engineering and environmental science), HEALTH PROFESSIONS (nursing, predentistry, premedicine, and prepharmacy), SOCIAL SCIENCE (American studies, criminal justice, dietetics, economics, fashion design and technology, food production/management/services, food science, gender studies, history, international relations, legal studies, ministries, philosophy, political science/government, prelaw, psychology, religion, social science, sociology, theological studies, and women's studies). Business administration, nursing, psychology, nutrition, and fashion design and merchandising are the strongest academically. Business administration, nursing, and psychology have the largest enrollments.

ACTIVITIES: There are no fraternities or sororities. There are 45 groups on campus, including art, band, cheerleading, choir, chorus, communications, computers, dance, drama, environmental, ethnic, honors, fashion club, international, LGBT, literary magazine, musical theater, newspaper, photography, political, professional, religious, social, Social Justice Advocates, social service, and student government. Popular campus events include the Caritas Veritas Symposium. **Sports:** There are 7 intercollegiate sports for men and 6 for women, and 6 intramural sports for men and 6 for women. Facilities include a gym, an indoor running track, a weight room, a training room, a fitness center, dance room, racquetball courts, and soccer fields. **Graduates:** From July 1, 2016 to June 30, 2017, 533 bachelor's degrees were awarded. The most popular majors were business administration (11%), psychology (8%), and medical studies (7%). In an average class, 51% graduate in 4 years or less, 58% graduate in 5 years or less, and 62% graduate in 6 years or less. Of the 2016 graduating class, 24% were enrolled in graduate school within 6 months of graduation, and 89% were employed.

SERVICES: Counseling and information services are available, as is tutoring in most subjects. There is remedial math and writing. **Library/Resources:** The library contains 250,000 volumes, 50,000 microform items, and 5,000 audio/video tapes/CDs/DVDs, and subscribes to 35,000 periodicals, including electronic. Computerized library services include interlibrary loans, database searching, Internet access, and Wi-Fi capability. Special learning facilities include an art gallery, a language lab, and a writing center. **Physically Challenged Students:** All of the campus is accessible. Facilities include wheelchair ramps, elevators, special parking, specially equipped restrooms, special class scheduling, lowered drinking fountains, and special housing. **Special:** Co-op programs in nursing with Rush University, cross-registration with Concordia University, internships, study abroad in 11 countries, and a Washington semester are offered. Student-designed majors and interdisciplinary majors, including computer information systems, math and computer science, and environmental science; credit for prior learning; and pass/fail options are possible. There is an accelerated degree program in organizational leadership, a joint B.A.-B.S. in engineering with the Illinois Institute of Technology, and a dual admission program with Midwestern University for pharmacy. There are 19 national honor societies, a freshman honors program, and 1 departmental honors program. **Visiting:** There are regularly scheduled orientations for prospective students, including visiting day and open house programs, which consist of faculty and student presentations, tours, and an academic and co-curricular fair. Special events are also held during the summer. There are guides for informal visits; visitors may sit in on classes and stay overnight. To schedule a visit, contact the Office of Undergraduate Admissions. **Campus Safety and Security:** Measures include 24-hour foot and vehicle patrol, an emergency notification system, self-defense education, and security escort services. There are shuttle buses, emergency telephones, lighted pathways/sidewalks, controlled access to dorms/residences, and door alarms.

REQUIREMENTS: The ACT is required. Graduation from an accredited secondary school or satisfactory scores on the GED are required for admission. The school requires 14 academic credits or 16 Carnegie units. High school courses should include English, math, foreign language, social science, and lab science. An essay is required and an interview is recommended. A GPA of 2.5 is required. AP and CLEP credits are accepted. Important factors in the admissions decision are advanced placement or honors courses, recommendations by school officials, and leadership record. To graduate, students must complete 124 credit hours with a minimum GPA of 2.0. A total of 30 to 56 hours is required in the major. All students must demonstrate proficiency through a placement exam or the completion of specified courses in English composition, math, computer competency, and library skills. In addition, students must take 1 interdisciplinary seminar at each academic level and 1 course each in natural sciences, history, fine arts and literature, social sciences, theology, and philosophy. 1 course must meet the multicultural requirement. **Procedure:** Freshmen are admitted in the fall and spring. Entrance exams should be taken in the junior year. There are deferred admissions and rolling admissions plans. Application deadlines are open. The fall 2017 application fee was $25. Notification is sent on a rolling basis. Applications are accepted online. **Transfer Students:** 166 transfer students enrolled in 2016-2017. A college transcript is required. Applicants must have a minimum of 12 credit hours with a GPA of 2.5. An interview is recommended. The high school record will be evaluated if GPA is below 2.5 at the previous college. 34 of 124 credits required for the bachelor's degree must be completed at Dominican. **International Students:** There are 51 international students enrolled. They must take the TOEFL with a minimum score of 550 on the paper-based TOEFL (PBT) or 79 on the Internet-based version (iBT). They must also take the SAT or ACT.

ADMISSIONS: 65% of the 2017-2018 applicants were accepted. The SAT scores for the 2017-2018 freshman class were: Critical Reading-- 19% below 500, 47% between 500 and 599, and 34% between 600 and 699. Math-- 25% below 500, 59% between 500 and 599, and 16% between 600 and 699. The ACT scores were 6% between 12 and 17, 59% between 18 and 23, 30% between 24 and 29, and 5% above 30. 55% of the current freshmen were in the top fifth of their class; 80% were in the top two fifths. **Admissions Contact:** Glenn Hamilton, Assistant Vice President for Enrollment. Email: *domadmis@dom.edu* Web: *www.dom.edu*

FINANCIAL AID: In 2017-2018, 100% of all full-time freshmen received some form of financial aid. 90% of all full-time freshmen received need-based aid. The average freshman award was $24,562. Need-based scholarships or need-based grants averaged $20,734; need-based self-help aid (loans and jobs) averaged $4,038; and other non-need-based awards and non-need-based scholarships averaged $9,404. 27% of undergraduate students work part-time. The average financial indebtedness of the 2017 graduate was $25,966. Dominican is a member of CSS. The FAFSA code is 001750. The priority date for freshman financial aid applications for fall entry is November 15.

EASTERN ILLINOIS UNIVERSITY E-4

www.eiu.edu

Charleston, IL 61920	(217) 581-2223
Fax: (217) 581-7060	Email: admissions@eiu.edu
Full-time: 1754 men, 2565 women	Faculty: IIA, av$
Part-time: 495 men, 754 women	Ph.D.s: n/av
Graduate: 534 men, 928 women	Student/Faculty: n/av
Year: semesters, summer session	Tuition: $11,678 ($13,868)
Room & Board: $9736	Freshman Class: 6965 applied, 3588 accepted, 634 enrolled
ACT: 21	CEEB CODE: 1199
Application Deadline: August 15	COMPETITIVE

Eastern Illinois University is a public comprehensive university that offers superior, accessible undergraduate and graduate education. Students learn the methods and results of free and rigorous inquiry in the arts, humanities, sciences, and professions, guided by a faculty known for its excellence in teaching, research, creative activity, and service. The University community is committed to diversity and inclusion and fosters opportunities for student-faculty scholarship and applied learning experiences within a student-centered campus culture. Throughout their education, students refine their abilities to reason and to communicate clearly so as to become responsible citizens and leaders. There are 5 undergraduate schools and 1 graduate school. In addition to regional accreditation, EIU has baccalaureate program accreditation with AACSB, ACEJMC, NASAD, NASM, NCATE, NRPA, AAFCS, ACS, ACTFL, NASPE, NCTM, NASP, CTTE, SABPAC, NAST, CAA-ASHA, ELCC, ACEI, NCTE, AAHE, NSTA, NAEYC, CACREP, ATMAE, CCNE, NCSS, CEC, HLC, and CAATE. The 320-acre campus is in a small town 110 miles from Indianapolis, Indiana and 147 miles from St. Louis, Missouri. Including any residence halls, there are 80 buildings.

STUDENT LIFE: 94% of undergraduates are from Illinois. Others are from 36 states, 44 foreign countries, and Canada. 8% are Hispanic; 64% White; 6% Foreign; 2% Asian American; 2% two or more races; 2% race unknown; 16% African American. **Female To Male Ratio:** 1.5:1. The average age of freshmen is 18; all undergraduates, 22. 25% do not continue beyond their first year; 57% remain to graduate. **Housing:** 5425 students can be accommodated in college housing, which includes married student dorms and on-campus apartments. In addition, there are honors houses, special-interest houses, fraternity houses, and sorority houses. On-campus housing is guaranteed for the freshman year only, and is available on a first-come, first-served basis. 62% of students commute. All students may keep cars.

FACULTY/CLASSROOMS: No introductory courses are taught by graduate students. The average class size in a regular course is 15.

PROGRAMS OF STUDY: EIU confers B.A., B.F.A., B.Mus., B.S., B.S.Bus., and B.S.Ed. degrees. Master's degrees are also awarded. Bachelor's degrees are awarded in BIOLOGICAL SCIENCE (biology/biological science), BUSINESS (accounting, business administration and management, finance, management information systems, marketing, and organizational leadership and management), COMMUNICATIONS AND THE ARTS (Africana studies, art, communication studies, English, foreign language, journalism, music, recreation administration, and theatre arts), COMPUTER AND PHYSICAL SCIENCE (chemistry, clinical laboratory science, computer science, geology, mathematics, and physics), EDUCATION (athletic training, early childhood education, elementary education, general studies, middle school education, science education, social science education, special education, and technical education), ENGINEERING AND ENVIRONMENTAL DESIGN (engineering and industrial engineering technology), HEALTH PROFESSIONS (health, kinesiology, and nursing), SOCIAL SCIENCE (communication sciences and disorders, economics, family/consumer studies, geography, history, philosophy, political science/government, psychology, and sociology). Communication disorders science is the strongest academically. Kinesiology and sports studies, psychology and general studies have the largest enrollments.

ACTIVITIES: 18% of men belong to 13 national fraternities; 15% of women belong to 12 national sororities. There are 216 groups on campus, including art, band, cheerleading, chess, choir, chorale, chorus, communications, dance, drama, drill team, environmental, ethnic, film, honors, international, jazz band, LGBT, literary magazine, marching band, musical theater, newspaper, orchestra, pep band, political, professional, radio and TV, religious, social, social service, student government, symphony, and yearbook. Popular campus events include Homecoming, Family Weekend, Greek Week, PantherPalooza, Panther Service Day, Prowl, and Prowlin with the Prez. **Sports:** There are 10 intercollegiate sports for men and 10 for women, and 21 intramural sports for men and 21 for women. Facilities include a gym, a swimming pool, a student recreation center, a track, tennis courts, racquetball courts, a jogging trail, baseball field, softball field, football field, basketball courts, a soccer field, and a rugby field. **Graduates:** From July 1, 2016 to June 30, 2017, 1703 bachelor's degrees were awarded. The most popular majors were kinesiology and sports studies (9%), general studies (8%), and communication studies (8%). In an average class, 34% graduate in 4 years or less, 53% graduate in 5 years or less, and 57% graduate in 6 years or less.

SERVICES: Counseling and information services are available, as is tutoring in every subject, such as biology, business, chemistry, writing (all subjects), economics, foreign language, geology/geography, history, mathematics, physics, and psychology. There is remedial math, reading, and writing, student success center for help on study skills, test-taking, and time management. **Library/Resources:** The library contains 1.8 million volumes, 578,049 microform items, 76,151 audio/video tapes/CDs/DVDs, and subscribes to 39,134 periodicals, including electronic. Computerized library services include interlibrary loans, database searching, Internet access, and Wi-Fi capability. Special learning facilities include an art gallery, a radio station, a TV station, an observatory, a scanning electron microscope, and Thut Greenhouse. **Physically Challenged Students:** 80% of the campus is accessible. Facilities include wheelchair ramps, elevators, special parking, specially equipped restrooms, lowered drinking fountains, and special housing. **Special:** EIU offers a B.S. in Engineering Cooperative with the University of Illinois at Champaign-Urbana or Southern Illinois University at Carbondale. Internships, study abroad, and double major options are available. Credit for life experience may be granted through the General Studies program and the Organizational and Professional Development program. There are 44 national honor societies, a freshman honors program, and 24 departmental honors programs. **Visiting:** There are regularly scheduled orientations for prospective students, including a tour of the campus and residence halls; sessions on financial aid, housing, admission process, tips for academic success, steps to take after admission, and transfer admission,; and an academic and student services fair. There are guides for informal visits and visitors may sit in on classes. To schedule a visit, contact Brittany Tierney at (217) 581-2223. **Campus Safety and Security:** Measures include 24-hour foot and vehicle patrol, an emergency notification system, and self-defense education. There are shuttle buses, emergency telephones, lighted pathways/sidewalks, controlled access to dorms/residences, student patrols, alert EIU, and warning sirens.

REQUIREMENTS: All applicants must submit ACT or SAT scores and meet one of the following: rank in the top quarter of their high school class based on 6 or more semesters or have a GPA of 3.0 and have an ACT composite of at least 18 (SAT 860); or rank in the top one half of their high school class based on 6 or more semesters or have a GPA of 2.5 and have an ACT composite score of at least 19 (SAT 910); or rank in the top three quarters of their high school class based on 6 or more semesters or have a GPA of 2.25 and an ACT composite score of at least 22 (SAT 1020). Applicants must be graduates of an accredited secondary school or have passed the GED. 15 academic credits are required and should include 4 years of English and 3 years each of math, science, and social studies, 2 years of electives; and 2 years foreign language are recommended. EIU requires applicants to be in the upper 75% of their class. A GPA of 2.3 is required. AP and CLEP credits are accepted. A total of 120 credit hours, with a minimum of 40 hours in upper-division courses, must be completed for graduation. The minimum GPA required for graduation is 2.0 (2.65 in education). A core curriculum of 40 hours includes courses in language, humanities and fine arts, math, social and behavioral science, scientific awareness, and senior seminar. **Procedure:** Freshmen are admitted in the fall, spring, and summer. There are deferred admissions and rolling admissions plans. Applications should be filed by August 15 for fall entry; January 8 for spring entry; and June 10 for summer entry. The fall 2017 application fee was $30. Notification is sent on a rolling basis. Applications are accepted online. **Transfer Students:** 1178 transfer students enrolled in 2016-2017. Applicants with 30 or more college-level semester hours must have a cumulative GPA of 2.0 on a 4.0 grading scale based on all college-level work attempted and a 2.0 cumulative GPA on a 4.0 scale from the last institution attended. Applicants with 24 or more college-level semester hours must have a cumulative GPA of 2.5 on a 4.0 grading scale based on all college-level work attempted and a 2.0 cumulative GPA on a 4.0 scale from the last institution attended. Applicants with fewer than the required number of hours of earned credit must have at least a 2.0 GPA on a 4.0 scale based on all college-level work attempted, a 2.0 GPA on a 4.0 scale from the last institution attended, and meet the freshman admission criteria. 42 of 120 credits required for the bachelor's degree must be completed at EIU. **International Students:** There are 112 international students enrolled. They must take the TOEFL with a minimum score of 500 on the paper-based TOEFL (PBT) or 61 on the Internet-based version (iBT). Student must take the MELAB or IELTS.

ADMISSIONS: 52% of the 2017-2018 applicants were accepted. The ACT scores were 15% between 12 and 17, 58% between 18 and 23, 23% between 24 and 29, and 4% above 30. 25% of the current freshmen were in the top fifth of their class; 54% were in the top two fifths. **Admissions Contact:** Kelly Miller, Director of Admissions. Email: *admissions@eiu.edu* Web: *www.eiu.edu*

FINANCIAL AID: In 2017-2018, 78% of all full-time freshmen received some form of financial aid. 62% of all full-time freshmen received need-based aid. The average freshman award was $13,760. Need-based scholarships or need-based grants averaged $9,503; need-based self-help aid (loans and jobs) averaged $3,542; non-need-based athletic scholarships averaged $8,423; and other non-need-based awards and non-need-based scholarships averaged $4,575. 31% of undergraduate students work part-time. The average financial indebtedness of the 2017 graduate was $30,695. The FAFSA code is 001674. The priority date for freshman financial aid applications for fall entry is March 1.

ELMHURST COLLEGE — E-2

www.elmhurst.edu

Elmhurst, IL 60126	(630) 617-3400 (800) 697-1871
Fax: (630) 617-5501	Email: admit@elmhurst.edu
Full-time: 1072 men, 1660 women	Faculty: 138
Part-time: 51 men, 92 women	Ph.D.s: 82%
Graduate: 201 men, 405 women	Student/Faculty: 20 to 1
Year: 4-1-4, summer session	Tuition: $36,370
Room & Board: $10,144	Freshman Class: 3645 applied, 2571 accepted, 497 enrolled
SAT CR/M/W: 460/520/530 ACT: 23	CEEB CODE: 1204
Application Deadline: n/av	COMPETITIVE

Elmhurst College is a premier, private, liberal arts college. Among Elmhurst's specialties is its synergy of two indispensable elements of a quality college experience: professional preparation and liberal learning. For 143 years, EC has sought to prepare students superbly, both for their first jobs and for fulfilling lives. EC offers students of many backgrounds purposeful learning for the whole of life. There are 2 undergraduate schools and 1 graduate school. In addition to regional accreditation, EC has baccalaureate program accreditation with CCNE. The 48-acre campus is in a suburban area 15 miles west of Chicago. Including any residence halls, there are 23 buildings.

STUDENT LIFE: 91% of undergraduates are from Illinois. Others are from 33 states, 30 foreign countries, and Canada. 89% are from public schools. 62% are White; 5% African American; 5% Asian American; 4% two or more races; 4% race unknown; 20% Hispanic. 31% are Catholic; 26% claim no religious affiliation. **Female To Male Ratio:** 1.6:1. The average age of freshmen is 18; all undergraduates, 22. 25% do not continue beyond their first year; 64% remain to graduate. **Housing:** 958 students can be accommodated in college housing, which includes dorms, on-campus apartments, and off-campus apartments. 69% of students commute. Some may keep cars.

FACULTY/CLASSROOMS: 39% of faculty are male; 61% are female. 90% teach undergraduates and all do research. No introductory courses are taught by graduate students. The average class size in an introductory lecture is 19; in a laboratory is 15; and in a regular course is 18.

PROGRAMS OF STUDY: EC confers B.A., B.F.A, B.S., B.L.S., and B.Mus. degrees. Master's degrees are also awarded. Bachelor's degrees are awarded in BIOLOGICAL SCIENCE (biology/biological science), BUSINESS (accounting, business administration and management, finance, international business management, management science, marketing/retailing/merchandising, sports management, and supply chain management), COMMUNICATIONS AND THE ARTS (art, arts administration/management, communications, communication science, English, French, German, graphic design, information technology, jazz, music, music business management, music performance, music theory and composition, Spanish, and theatre arts), COMPUTER AND PHYSICAL SCIENCE (actuarial science, chemistry, computer game design/development, computer science, information sciences and systems, mathematics, and physics), EDUCATION (art education, early childhood education, elementary education, mathematics education, music education, physical education, secondary education, and special education), ENGINEERING AND ENVIRONMENTAL DESIGN (environmental science and preengineering), HEALTH PROFESSIONS (exercise science, nursing, pre-health studies, pre-health biological studies, premedicine, prephysical therapy, preveterinary science, and speech pathology/audiology), SOCIAL SCIENCE (American studies, communication sciences and disorders, criminal justice, economics, geography, geography information science, history, liberal arts/general studies, philosophy, political science/government, psychology, religion, sociology, theological studies, and urban studies). Biology, English, nursing, and education are the strongest academically. Business, health professions, and education-related programs have the largest enrollments.

ACTIVITIES: 9% of men belong to 3 national fraternities; 14% of women belong to 4 national sororities. There are 119 groups on campus, including art, band, cheerleading, chess, choir, chorale, chorus, communications, computers, dance, drama, environmental, ethnic, film, honors, international, jazz band, LGBT, literary magazine, musical theater, newspaper, orchestra, pep band, political, professional, radio and TV, religious, social, social service, student government, symphony, and yearbook. Popular campus events include Elmhurst College Jazz Festival, Lecture Series, Theater Performances, Summer Extravaganza, and Performances by Elmhurst College Ensembles. **Sports:** There are 10 intercollegiate sports for men and 10 for women, and 7 intramural sports for men and 7 for women. Facilities include a physical education center, weight rooms, courts for tennis, racquetball, and handball, and an athletic field for football, soccer, track and field. **Graduates:** From July 1, 2016 to June 30, 2017, 712 bachelor's degrees were awarded. The most popular majors were business (21%), health sciences (16%), and psychology (10%). In an average class, 1% graduate in 3 years or less, 53% graduate in 4 years or less, 63% graduate in 5 years or less, and 64% graduate in 6 years or less. Of the 2016 graduating class, 15% were enrolled in graduate school within 6 months of graduation, and 83% were employed.

SERVICES: Counseling and information services are available, as is tutoring in most subjects. There is remedial math, reading, and writing. **Library/Resources:** The library contains 237,539 volumes, 49,798 microform items, 49,413 audio/video tapes/CDs/DVDs, and subscribes to 24,245 periodicals, including electronic. Computerized library services include interlibrary loans, database searching, Internet access, and Wi-Fi capability. Special learning facilities include an art gallery, a radio station, a recording studio that offers recording and control room spaces with grand piano and isolation booth and a digital 24-track hard drive Otari Radar system with automated status console; the SimBaby, a life-size, robotic model of an infant and SimMan, an adult patient simulator, an electron microscopy lab, and a accelerator lab. **Physically Challenged Students:** 95% of the campus is accessible. Facilities include wheelchair ramps, elevators, special parking, specially equipped restrooms, lowered drinking fountains, and lowered telephones. **Special:** There are cooperative programs in all majors. In keeping with the hallmarks of the Elmhurst experience, self-formation and early professional preparation, career education starts early-on in most students' academic experience. The Center for Professional Excellence provides experiential opportunities for career exploration to majors in 23 academic departments, e.g., internships, informational interviews, career shadowing, and connections to professional mentors. Internships varying from 1 month to 1 term are available in approximately 20 major fields. Students may study abroad in over 40 countries. Elmhurst also offers a Washington and Chicago semester and a 3-2 engineering degree with the Illinois Institute of Technology, Washington University, and the Universities of Illinois and Southern California. There are accelerated degree programs in business administration, organizational leadership and communication, information technology, and preclinical psychology. Credit for life, military, and work experience, and nondegree study and pass/fail options, are possible. There are 23 national honor societies, a freshman honors program, and 25 departmental honors programs. **Visiting:** There are regularly scheduled orientations for prospective students, including an admissions interview, a campus tour, and faculty meetings if desired. There are guides for informal visits; visitors may sit in on classes and stay overnight. To schedule a visit, contact Francesca Garza at (630) 617-3400. **Campus Safety and Security:** Measures include 24-hour foot and vehicle patrol, an emergency notification system, and security escort services. There are shuttle buses, emergency telephones, lighted pathways/sidewalks, and controlled access to dorms/residences.

REQUIREMENTS: The SAT is required, with the ACT preferred. Candidates for admission must have completed 16 academic units of credit, including at least 4 units in English and 2 units each of math, social science, and natural science lab courses. AP and CLEP credits are accepted. Important factors in the admissions decision are advanced placement or honors courses, leadership record, and extracurricular activities record. The following are required for graduation: complete all aspects of the Integrated Curriculum or General Education program; complete all the requirements for a major; earn a minimum of 32.00 course credits; complete at least 10.00 course credits at the 300/400 level at a four-year institution; achieve a minimum combined and institutional GPA of 2.0 (some majors require a higher GPA); Earn one's final 8.00 course credits at Elmhurst College (residency requirement). **Procedure:** Freshmen are admitted in the fall and spring. Entrance exams should be taken by the spring of the senior year. There are deferred admissions and rolling admissions plans. Applications should be filed by January 15 for spring entry. Notification is sent on a rolling basis. Applications are accepted online. **Transfer Students:** 372 transfer students enrolled in 2016-2017. Qualified applicants should show evidence of their ability to successfully complete college-level work, based on their good standing at the last college or university attended. 32 of 128 credits required for the bachelor's degree must be completed at EC. **International Students:** There are 37 international students enrolled. They must take the TOEFL with a minimum score of 550 on the paper-based TOEFL (PBT) or 79 on the Internet-based version (iBT), or take the MELAB.

ADMISSIONS: 71% of the 2017-2018 applicants were accepted. The SAT scores for the 2017-2018 freshman class were: Critical Reading-- 67% below 500 and 33% between 500 and 599. Math-- 33% below 500, 56% between 500 and 599, and 11% between 600 and 699. Writing-- 44% below 500, 45% between 500 and 599, and 11% between 600 and 699. The ACT scores were 8% between 12 and 17, 49% between 18 and 23, 37% between 24 and 29, and 6% above 30. 38% of the current freshmen were in the top fifth of their class; 67% were in the top two fifths. 1 freshman graduated first in the class. **Admissions Contact:** Stephanie Levenson, Director of Admissions. Email: *admit@elmhurst.edu* Web: *www.elmhurst.edu*

FINANCIAL AID: The FAFSA code is 001676. The priority date for freshman financial aid applications for fall entry is Februray 1.

EUREKA COLLEGE — D-3

www.eureka.edu

Eureka, IL 61530	(309) 467-6350
Fax: (309) 467-6576	**Email:** admissions@eureka.edu
Full-time: 340 men, 350 women	**Faculty:** 44
Part-time: 10 women	**Ph.D.s:** 85%
Graduate: n/av	**Student/Faculty:** 13 to 1
Year: semesters, summer session	**Tuition:** $25,390
Room & Board: $9370	**Freshman Class:** 900 applied, 600 accepted, 140 enrolled
SAT: required **ACT:** 23	**CEEB CODE:** 1206
Application Deadline: August 1	**COMPETITIVE**

Eureka College, founded in 1855, is a small, private, liberal arts college affiliated with the Christian Church (Disciples of Christ), welcoming students of all background and faiths. The figures given in the above capsule and in this profile are approximate. There is 1 undergraduate school. In addition to regional accreditation, Eureka College has baccalaureate program accreditation with CAEP. The 100-acre campus is in a small town 20 minutes east of Peoria, 20 minutes west of Bloomington, and 2 hours south of Chicago. Including any residence halls, there are 24 buildings.

STUDENT LIFE: 90% of undergraduates are from Illinois. Others are from 17 states, and 3 foreign countries. 80% are from public schools. 87% are White; 6% African American; 2% Hispanic; 2% Foreign; 1% Asian American. 37% claim no religious affiliation; 31% Protestant; 28% Catholic. **Female To Male Ratio:** 1.1:1. The average age of freshmen is 18; all undergraduates, 21. 25% do not continue beyond their first year; 65% remain to graduate. **Housing:** 550 students can be accommodated in college housing, which includes dorms. In addition, there are fraternity houses and sorority houses. On-campus housing is guaranteed for all 4 years. 80% of students live on campus. All students may keep cars.

FACULTY/CLASSROOMS: 64% of faculty are male; 36% are female. All teach undergraduates. No introductory courses are taught by graduate students. The average class size in an introductory lecture is 15; in a laboratory is 10; and in a regular course is 15.

PROGRAMS OF STUDY: EC confers B.A. and B.S. degrees. Bachelor's degrees are awarded in BIOLOGICAL SCIENCE (biology/biological science), BUSINESS (accounting, business administration and management, business economics, and management information systems), COMMUNICATIONS AND THE ARTS (communications, dramatic arts, English, fine arts, and music), COMPUTER AND PHYSICAL SCIENCE (chemistry, computer science, mathematics, and physical sciences), EDUCATION (athletic training, education, elementary education, music education, physical education, science education, and secondary education), HEALTH PROFESSIONS (medical laboratory technology), SOCIAL SCIENCE (child care/child and family studies, history, liberal arts/general studies, philosophy, physical fitness/movement, political science/government, psychology, religion, social science, and sociology). Chemistry, biology, and business administration are the strongest academically. Business administration, education, and psychology have the largest enrollments.

ACTIVITIES: 35% of men belong to 3 national fraternities; 35% of women belong to 1 local and 2 national sororities. There are 41 groups on campus, including art, band, cheerleading, choir, chorale, chorus, communications, computers, dance, drama, ethnic, honors, international, literary magazine, musical theater, newspaper, pep band, photography, political, professional, religious, social, social service, student government, and yearbook. Popular campus events include Pride Day, Tree Lighting Ceremony, and Ivy Ceremony. **Sports:** There are 8 intercollegiate sports for men and 8 for women, and 6 intramural sports for men and 6 for women. Facilities include a gym, a swimming pool, a weight room, tennis and basketball courts, cross country, soccer, swimming and diving, track and field, football, softball, and baseball fields, and a wellness center. **Graduates:** From July 1, 2016 to June 30, 2017, 131 bachelor's degrees were awarded. The most popular majors were education (24%), business (23%), and psychology (15%). In an average class, 2% graduate in 3 years or less, 58% graduate in 4 years or less, and 5% graduate in 5 years or less. Of the 2016 graduating class, 20% were enrolled in graduate school within 6 months of graduation, and 75% were employed.

SERVICES: Counseling and information services are available, as is tutoring in most subjects. There is remedial reading and writing. There is a writing center and math lab located within the Learning Center. **Library/Resources:** The library contains 85,000 volumes, 4,989 microform items, and 977 audio/video tapes/CDs/DVDs, and subscribes to 343 periodicals including electronic. Computerized library services include interlibrary loans, database searching, and Internet access. Special learning facilities include an art gallery, and the Ronald Reagan Museum. **Physically Challenged Students:** 50% of the campus is accessible. Facilities include wheelchair ramps, elevators, special parking, and specially equipped restrooms. **Special:** Cooperative programs include a 3-2 engineering degree with Washington University in St. Louis and Illinois Institute of Technology, a 2-2 B.S.N. with Mennonite College of Nursing or St. Francis College of Nursing, and a 3-1 clinical lab science degree with St. Francis or St. John's School of Clinical Laboratory Science. Students may study abroad in most countries. Professional programs in arts management, art therapy, communications, prelaw, premedicine, preministry, and teacher education are offered. An interdisciplinary major in arts and letters combines visual, performing, and literary arts. Internships, student-designed, and dual majors are offered in various areas. A Washington semester is available. There are 7 national honor societies, a freshman honors program, and 100 departmental honors programs. **Visiting:** There are regularly scheduled orientations for prospective students, including visits with admissions and financial aid advisers, observing student panels, meetings with faculty and coaches, and campus tours. There are guides for informal visits, visitors may sit in on classes, and stay overnight. To schedule a visit, contact the Office of Admissions. **Campus Safety and Security:** There are lighted pathways/sidewalks, a city officer provides campus security in the evenings and on weekends.

REQUIREMENTS: The SAT or ACT is required. Applicants should be graduates of accredited secondary schools or have a GED. EC requires applicants to be in the upper 50% of their class. A GPA of 2.3 is required. AP and CLEP credits are accepted. Important factors in the admissions decision are recommendations by school officials, extracurricular activities record, and leadership record. All students must take English composition, biological and physical sciences, general studies, math, physical education, Western civilization, 3 humanities courses, 3 social science courses, and a global awareness component. A total of at least 124 hours is required for graduation, including 32 hours in the major. A minimum GPA of 2.0 is required. **Procedure:** Freshmen are admitted to all sessions. Entrance exams should be taken by December of the senior year. There are deferred admissions and rolling admissions plans. Applications should be filed by August 1 for fall entry. Notification is sent on a rolling basis. Applications are accepted online. **Transfer Students:** 90 transfer students enrolled in 2016-2017. Applicants must have at least a 2.0 GPA in previous college work. Those with fewer than 30 hours of transferable credit must submit high school transcripts and ACT scores. Courses with grades below C are not accepted. 30 of 124 credits required for the bachelor's degree must be completed at EC. **International Students:** There are 12 international students enrolled. They must take the TOEFL.

ADMISSIONS: 67% of the 2017-2018 applicants were accepted. 35% of the current freshmen were in the top fifth of their class; 65% were in the top two fifths. **Admissions Contact:** Dr. Brian Sajko, Dean of Admissions and Financial Aid. Email: *admissions@eureka.edu* Web: *www.eureka.edu*

FINANCIAL AID: In 2017-2018, 98% of all full-time freshmen received some form of financial aid. 30% of all full-time freshmen received need-based aid. The average freshman award was $4,000. 49% of undergraduate students work part-time. The average financial indebtedness of the 2017 graduate was $8,500. Eureka is a member of CSS. The FAFSA code is 001678. The priority date for freshman financial aid applications for fall entry is April 1. The deadline for filing freshman financial aid applications for fall entry is August 1.

GREENVILLE COLLEGE *(The complete profile is made available exclusively on our website, www.barronspac.com)*

ILLINOIS COLLEGE C-3

www.ic.edu

Jacksonville, IL 62650 (217) 245-3030
(866) 464-5265

Fax: (217) 245-3034 **Email: info@mail.ic.edu**

Full-time: 449 men, 500 women	**Faculty:** 71; IIB, -$
Part-time: 1 men, 2 women	**Ph.D.s:** 80%
Graduate: 2 women	**Student/Faculty:** 14 to 1
Year: semesters	**Tuition:** $32,140
Room & Board: $9190	**Freshman Class:** 4462 applied, 2411 accepted, 293 enrolled
SAT or ACT: required	**CEEB CODE:** 1315
Application Deadline: rolling	**VERY COMPETITIVE**

Illinois College, founded in 1829, is a private liberal arts institution with historical ties to the Presbyterian Church and the United Church of Christ. The figures given in the above capsule are approximate. The 62-acre campus is in a small town 30 miles west of Springfield. Including any residence halls, there are 36 buildings.

STUDENT LIFE: 88% of undergraduates are from Illinois. Others are from 22 states, and 15 foreign countries. 9% are Hispanic; 69% White; 4% Foreign; 4% two or more races; 12% African American. 62% are Protestant; 25% Catholic; 12% claim no religious affiliation. **Female To Male Ratio:** 1.1:1. The average age of freshmen is 18; all undergraduates, 20. 20% do not continue beyond their first year; 60% remain to graduate. **Housing:** 742 students can be accommodated in college housing, which includes dorms and on-campus apartments. In addition, there are honors houses, language/international houses, special-interest houses, and theme housing. On-campus housing is guaranteed for all 4 years. 95% of students live on campus. All students may keep cars.

FACULTY/CLASSROOMS: 57% of faculty are male; 43% are female. All teach undergraduates. No introductory courses are taught by graduate students. The average class size in an introductory lecture is 40; in a laboratory is 20; and in a regular course is 16.

PROGRAMS OF STUDY: Illinois confers B.A. and B.S. degrees. Bachelor's degrees are awarded in BIOLOGICAL SCIENCE (biochemistry and biology/biological science), BUSINESS (accounting and business administration and management), COMMUNICATIONS AND THE ARTS (communications, dramatic arts, English, fine arts, French, German, music, Spanish, and speech/debate/rhetoric), COMPUTER AND PHYSICAL SCIENCE (chemistry, computer science, information sciences and systems, mathematics, and physics), EDUCATION (elementary education, foreign languages education, science education, and secondary education), ENGINEERING AND ENVIRONMENTAL DESIGN (environmental science), HEALTH PROFESSIONS (exercise science and medical laboratory technology), SOCIAL SCIENCE (American studies, economics, history, international relations, philosophy, political science/government, prelaw, psychology, religion, and sociology). Life sciences is the strongest academically. Business management, education, and biology have the largest enrollments.

ACTIVITIES: There are no fraternities or sororities. There are 72 groups on campus, including art, band, cheerleading, chess, choir, chorale, communications, computers, dance, debate, drama, ethnic, forensics, honors, international, jazz band, LGBT, literary magazine, music ensembles, newspaper, photography, political, professional, radio and TV, religious, social, social service, student government, symphony, and yearbook. Popular campus events include the Osage Orange Picnic, Honors Retreat, and McGaw Fine Arts Series. **Sports:** There are 10 intercollegiate sports for men and 10 for women, and 7 intramural sports for men and 7 for women. Facilities include a fitness center with a swimming pool, gyms, a weight and exercise room, an aerobics room, basketball courts, volleyball courts, an indoor track, an outdoor track, and playing fields for soccer and football that have an artifical turf surface, a baseball field, an all-weather track, and tennis courts. **Graduates:** From July 1, 2016 to June 30, 2017, 168 bachelor's degrees were awarded. The most popular majors were biological/life sciences (18%), interdisciplinary studies (16%), and education (13%). In an average class, 1% graduate in 3 years or less and 62% graduate in 4 years or less. Of the 2016 graduating class, 20% were enrolled in graduate school within 6 months of graduation, and 80% were employed.

SERVICES: Counseling and information services are available, as is tutoring in every subject. There is a reader service for the blind. Note takers, scribes, and test readers are also available. **Library/Resources:** The library contains 183,172 volumes, 8,049 microform items, and 4,041 audio/video tapes/CDs/DVDs, and subscribes to 631 periodicals including electronic. Computerized library services include interlibrary loans, database searching, Internet access, and Wi-Fi capability. Special learning facilities include an art gallery, a radio station, a theater, and an observatory. **Physically Challenged Students:** 35% of the campus is accessible. Facilities include wheelchair ramps, elevators, special parking, specially equipped restrooms, special class scheduling, lowered drinking fountains, lowered telephones, and special housing. **Special:** The college offers study abroad in various countries, on- and off-campus work-study programs, and internships through the departments of communication, computer science and information systems, economics and business administration, English, political science, and sociology. Also available are student-designed and dual majors; B.A.-B.S. degrees; a 3-2 engineering degree with the University of Illinois, Washington University, or Southern Illinois University-Edwardsville; and a 3-2 occupational therapy program with Washington University. A 3-1 cytotechnology program with Mayo School of Health-related Sciences, a 3-1 program in Medical Technology with St. John's Hospital in Springfield, an Intercultural Exchange Program with Ritsumeikan University in Kyoto, Japan, Model United Nations simulations, and the Urban Studies Program of Associated Colleges of the Midwest in Chicago are offered. The College also offers opportunities for collaborative student/faculty research. There are 12 national honor societies, Phi Beta Kappa, and 12 departmental honors programs. **Visiting:** There are regularly scheduled orientations for prospective students, including general information sessions with a member of the admissions staff, meeting with faculty, a campus tour, and lunch. There are guides for informal visits and visitors may sit in on classes. To schedule a visit, contact the Admissions Office. **Campus Safety and Security:** Measures include 24-hour foot and vehicle patrol, self-defense education, and security escort services. There are shuttle buses, emergency telephones, and lighted pathways/sidewalks.

REQUIREMENTS: The SAT or ACT is required. The ACT Optional Writing test is also required. Applicants must be graduates of an accredited secondary school or have a GED certificate. Students should have completed at least 16 academic credits: 4 in English, 3 each in math and academic electives, 2 in science with lab, 1 each in history, and social studies. Also required are 1 recommendation and 1 essay or 2 letters of recommendation. A GPA of 2.5 is required. AP and CLEP credits are accepted. Important factors in the admissions decision are advanced placement or honors courses, personality/intangible qualities, evidence of special talent, and extracurricular activities record. To graduate, all students must fulfill general graduation and convocation requirements and complete at least 120 semester hours, including 24 hours of electives outside of the major discipline. Other requirements include 1 unit each in public speaking, writing, library research methods, and a first-year seminar. To meet the convocation requirement, students must attend 30 cultural, artistic, or public affairs events. A 2.0 GPA is required. **Procedure:** Freshmen are admitted to all sessions. Entrance exams should be taken in the spring of the junior year or fall of the senior year of high school. There is a rolling admissions plan. Application deadlines are open. Notifications are sent September 15. Applications are accepted online. **Transfer Students:** 34 transfer students enrolled in 2016-2017. Transfer students must have graduated from an accredited four year high school. A minimum of 2.0 for their most recent full-time semester of college level work and a minimum cumulative 2.0 GPA for all college work attempted are required. If 24 credits have not been completed, these student's high school record will be reviewed. 36 of 120 credits required for the bachelor's degree must be completed at IC. **International Students:** There are 24 international students enrolled. They must take the TOEFL.

ADMISSIONS: 54% of the 2017-2018 applicants were accepted. 13 freshmen graduated first in their class. **Admissions Contact:** Barbara J. Lundberg, Vice President for Enrollment. Email: *info@mail.ic.edu* Web: *www.ic.edu*

FINANCIAL AID: In 2017-2018, 99% of all full-time freshmen received some form of financial aid. 73% of all full-time freshmen received need-based aid. 55% of undergraduate students work part-time. The average financial indebtedness of the 2017 graduate was $23,156. The FAFSA code is 001688. The priority date for freshman financial aid applications for fall entry is March 1.

ILLINOIS INSTITUTE OF TECHNOLOGY E-2

www.iit.edu

Chicago, IL 60616	(312) 567-3000 (800) 448-2329
Fax: (312) 567-6939	**Email:** admission@iit.edu
Full-time: 2013 men, 907 women	**Faculty:** I, +$
Part-time: 101 men, 25 women	**Ph.D.s:** 88%
Graduate: 2831 men, 1819 women	**Student/Faculty:** 13 to 1
Year: semesters, summer session	**Tuition:** $45,214
Room & Board: $11,612	**Freshman Class:** 3559 applied, 1801 accepted, 440 enrolled
SAT CR/M/W: 580/690/580 **ACT:** 28	**CEEB CODE:** 1318
Application Deadline: open	**HIGHLY COMPETITIVE+**

Illinois Institute of Technology, founded in 1890, is a Ph.D.-granting university in engineering, sciences, architecture, psychology, design, humanities, business, and law. IITs interprofessional, technology-focused curriculum is designed to advance knowledge through research and scholarship, to cultivate invention improving the human condition, and to prepare students from throughout the world for a life of professional achievement, service to society, and individual fulfillment. There are 6 undergraduate schools and 8 graduate schools. In addition to regional accreditation, IIT has baccalaureate program accreditation with ABET and NAAB. The 120-acre campus is in an urban area 3 miles south of downtown Chicago. Including any residence halls, there are 33 buildings.

STUDENT LIFE: 57% of undergraduates are from Illinois. Others are from 47 states, 83 foreign countries, and Canada. 83% are from public schools. 7% are Hispanic; 50% White; 4% African American; 16% Foreign; 14% Asian American. **Male To Female Ratio:** 1.8:1. The average age of freshmen is 18; all undergraduates, 22. 15% do not continue beyond their first year. **Housing:** 1184 students can be accommodated in college housing, which includes single-sex and coed dorms, on-campus apartments, and married student housing. In addition, there are fraternity houses and sorority houses. On-campus housing is guaranteed for all 4 years. 62% of students live on campus. All students may keep cars.

FACULTY/CLASSROOMS: No introductory courses are taught by graduate students. The average class size in an introductory lecture is 24; in a laboratory is 22; and in a regular course is 15.

PROGRAMS OF STUDY: IIT confers B.A. and B.S. degrees. Master's and doctoral degrees are also awarded. Bachelor's degrees are awarded in BIOLOGICAL SCIENCE (biochemistry, biology/biological science, biophysics, and molecular biology), COMMUNICATIONS AND THE ARTS (technical and business writing), COMPUTER AND PHYSICAL SCIENCE (applied mathematics, chemistry, computer science, information sciences and systems, physics, and Web technology), ENGINEERING AND ENVIRONMENTAL DESIGN (aeronautical engineering, architectural engineering, architecture, chemical engineering, civil engineering, computer engineering, electrical/electronics engineering, engineering management, industrial administration/management, manufacturing technology, materials science, mechanical engineering, and metallurgical engineering), SOCIAL SCIENCE (humanities, political science/government, and psychology). Architecture, engineering, and science and letters have the largest enrollments.

ACTIVITIES: 13% of men belong to 7 national fraternities; 15% of women belong to 2 local and 1 national sororities. There are 100 groups on campus, including a union club, art, chess, choir, chorus, commuter club, computers, dance, drama, environmental, ethnic, film, honors, international, LGBT, musical theater, newspaper, photography, professional, radio and TV, religious, social, social service, student government, and yearbook. Popular campus events include International Fest, Greek Week, and Spring Formal. **Sports:** There are 5 intercollegiate sports for men and 5 for women, and 10 intramural sports for men and 10 for women. Facilities include tennis, basketball, volleyball, racquetball, and squash courts, soccer and softball fields, a swimming pool, exercise room, weight room, bowling alley, and a game room. **Graduates:** From July 1, 2015 to June 30, 2016, 587 bachelor's degrees were awarded. The most popular majors were engineering (51%), natural resources and conservation (17%), and computer and information sciences (10%). In an average class, 3% graduate in 3 years or less, 38% graduate in 4 years or less, 62% graduate in 5 years or less, and 67% graduate in 6 years or less.

SERVICES: Counseling and information services are available, as is tutoring in some subjects, such as math, electrical and computer engineering, chemistry, biology, mechanical engineering, materials and aerospace engineering, physics, computer science, and writing courses. There is a reader service for the blind. **Library/Resources:** The 3 libraries contain 1.3 million volumes, and 4,256 audio/video tapes/CDs/DVDs, and subscribe to 24,596 periodicals, including electronic. Computerized library services include interlibrary loans, database searching, Internet access, and Wi-Fi capability. Special learning facilities include an art gallery and a radio station. **Physically Challenged Students:** 90% of the campus is accessible. Facilities include wheelchair ramps, elevators, special parking, specially equipped restrooms, lowered drinking fountains, and special housing. **Special:** Co-op programs and internships are available to all majors. All countries are eligible for study abroad. Dual majors may include a variety of majors. Cross-registration is available. There are 3 national honor societies. **Visiting:** There are regularly scheduled orientations for prospective students, including special events and open houses. Open houses include a brief welcome, tours of Main Campus, academic exploration sessions with faculty members, discussion panels with current students, and staff from numerous student service departments on hand to answer questions. There are guides for informal visits; visitors may sit in on classes and stay overnight. To schedule a visit, contact the Office of Undergraduate Admission. **Campus Safety and Security:** Measures include 24-hour foot and vehicle patrol, an emergency notification system, and security escort services. There are shuttle buses, emergency telephones, lighted pathways/sidewalks, and controlled access to dorms/residences.

REQUIREMENTS: Graduation from an accredited secondary school is required for admission including 17 academic credits: 4 units each of English and math, 3 units of science (of those; 2 units must be laboratory science), 2 units each of social studies, foreign language, and 2 units of history (recommended), and 1 unit each of computer science, and visual/performing arts. AP credits are accepted. Important factors in the admissions decision are leadership record, parents or siblings attended your school, evidence of special talent, recommendations by school officials, advanced placement or honors courses, personality/intangible qualities, extracurricular activities record, and recommendations by alumni. To graduate, all degree-seeking undergraduate students must complete the departmental curriculum, credit hour requirements as appropriate to the various curricula (a minimum of 126 hours total, with a minimum of 45 hours taken at IIT), general education requirements and a minimum major GPA of 2.0. General education requirements include 5 credit hours of mathematics, 2 credit hours in computer science, 21 credit hours in humanities and social or behavioral sciences, 11 credit hours in natural science or engineering, 2 credit hours of Introduction to the Profession, and 6 credit hours of Interprofessional Projects (IPRO). **Procedure:** Freshmen are admitted in the fall, spring, and summer. There are deferred admissions and rolling admissions plans. Application deadlines are open. Notification is sent on a rolling basis. Applications are accepted on-line. **Transfer Students:** 232 transfer students enrolled in 2015-2016. Good academic standing at previous postsecondary institution, and a minimum 3.0 cumulative GPA is required. 45 credits required for the bachelor's degree must be completed at IIT. **International Students:** There are 388 international students enrolled. The school actively recruits these students. They must take the TOEFL with a minimum score of 550 on the paper-based TOEFL (PBT) or 80 on the Internet-based version (iBT).

ADMISSIONS: 51% of the 2016-2017 applicants were accepted. The SAT scores for the 2016-2017 freshman class were: Critical Reading-- 13% below 500, 44% between 500 and 599, 32% between 600 and 699, and 11% between 700 and 800. Math-- 8% between 500 and 599, 44% between 600 and 699, and 48% between 700 and 800. Writing-- 12% below 500, 40% between 500 and 599, 41% between 600 and 699, and 7% between 700 and 800. The ACT scores were 11% below 12, 53% between 18 and 23, and 37% above 30. 61% of the current freshmen were in the top fifth of their class; 87% were in the top two fifths. 2 freshmen graduated first in their class. **Admissions Contact:** Gerald Doyle, Associate Vice President, Undergraduate Admissions. Email: *admission@iit.edu* Web: *www.iit.edu*

FINANCIAL AID: In 2016-2017, 58% of all full-time freshmen received some form of financial aid. 56% of all full-time freshmen received need-based aid. The average freshman award was $35,649. Need-based scholarships or need-based grants averaged $28,262; need-based self-help aid (loans and jobs) averaged $5,870; other non-need-based awards and non-need-based scholarships averaged $4,918; and $19,854 from other forms of aid. The average financial indebtedness of the 2016 graduate was $31,907. IIT is a member of CSS. The FAFSA code is 001691. The priority date for freshman financial aid applications for fall entry is February 1.

ILLINOIS STATE UNIVERSITY D-3

www.illinoisstate.edu

Normal, IL 61761 (309) 438-2181 (800) 366-2478

Fax: (309) 438-3932 **Email:** Admissions@IllinoisState.edu

Full-time: 7689 men, 9465 women	**Faculty:** 877; I, --$
Part-time: 623 men, 650 women	**Ph.D.s:** 65%
Graduate: 845 men, 1535 women	**Student/Faculty:** 20 to 1
Year: semesters, summer session	**Tuition:** $13,664 ($21,480)
Room & Board: $9754	**Freshman Class:** n/av
ACT: 24	**CEEB CODE:** 1319
Application Deadline: April 1	**VERY COMPETITIVE**

Illinois State University, founded in 1857, is a public institution offering instruction through schools of applied science and technology, arts and sciences, business, education, fine arts, and nursing. There are 6 undergraduate schools and 1 graduate school. In addition to regional accreditation, ISU has baccalaureate program accreditation with AACSB, ABET, ACCE, CSWE, NASAD, NASM, CAEP, and NRPA. The 1100-acre campus is in an urban area 137 miles southwest of Chicago and 164 miles northeast of St. Louis. Including any residence halls, there are 191 buildings.

STUDENT LIFE: 97% of undergraduates are from Illinois. Others are from 43 states, 67 foreign countries, and Canada. 9% are Hispanic; 77% White; 7% African American; 3% two or more races; 2% Asian American; 2% Foreign. **Female To Male Ratio:** 1.3:1. The average age of freshmen is 19; all undergraduates, 21. 18% do not continue beyond their first year; 73% remain to graduate. **Housing:** 6046 students can be accommodated in college housing, which includes married student dorms and on-campus apartments. In addition, there are honors houses and special-interest houses. On-campus housing is available on a first-come, first-served basis. 67% of students commute. Alcohol is not permitted. All students may keep cars.

FACULTY/CLASSROOMS: 45% of faculty are male; 55% are female. All teach undergraduates. Graduate students teach 33% of introductory courses. The average class size in an introductory lecture is 51 and in a laboratory is 22.

PROGRAMS OF STUDY: ISU confers B.S., B.A., B.S. Ed., B.S.W., B.S./M.P.A., B.F.A, B.M.E., B.M. and B.S.N. degrees. Master's and doctoral degrees are also awarded. Bachelor's degrees are awarded in AGRICULTURE (agricultural business management and agriculture), BIOLOGICAL SCIENCE (biochemistry, biology/biological science, and molecular biology), BUSINESS (accounting, business administration and management, business information systems, finance, insurance, international business, and marketing), COMMUNICATIONS AND THE ARTS (art, communication studies, dramatic arts, English, French, German, graphic communications, journalism, media arts, music, music performance, public relations, Spanish, speech/debate/rhetoric, telecommunications, and theatre acting), COMPUTER AND PHYSICAL SCIENCE (chemistry, computer science, digital arts/technology, geology, information sciences and systems, mathematics, and physics), EDUCATION (business education, early childhood education, elementary education, health education, health information management, middle school education, music education, social science education, special education, and technical education), ENGINEERING AND ENVIRONMENTAL DESIGN (construction management, energy management technology, and industrial engineering technology), HEALTH PROFESSIONS (environmental health science, exercise science, health care administration, medical laboratory technology, nursing, and speech pathology/audiology), SOCIAL SCIENCE (anthropology, criminal justice, economics, family/consumer studies, fashion design and technology, geography, history, home economics, interdisciplinary studies, legal studies, parks and recreation management, philosophy, political science/government, psychology, safety management, social science, social work, and sociology). Elementary education, special education, and business administration have the largest enrollments.

ACTIVITIES: 9% of men belong to 18 national fraternities; 16% of women belong to 18 national sororities. There are 380 groups on campus, including art, band, cheerleading, chess, choir, chorale, chorus, communications, computers, dance, debate, drama, drill team, ethnic, film, forensics, honors, international, jazz band, LGBT, literary magazine, marching band, musical theater, newspaper, opera, orchestra, pep band, photography, political, professional, radio and TV, religious, social, social service, student government, and symphony. Popular campus events include Festival ISU, International Fair, Madrigal Dinners, Family Weekend, and Homecoming. **Sports:** There are 7 intercollegiate sports for men and 10 for women, and 29 intramural sports for men and 29 for women. Facilities include a student recreational building, a basketball arena, a football stadium, a field house, baseball diamonds, tennis courts, swimming pools, an 18-hole golf course, a soccer and softball field, field area that is devoted to intramurals and sport clubs, and a bowling and billiards center. **Graduates:** From July 1, 2016 to June 30, 2017, 4322 bachelor's degrees were awarded. The most popular majors were elementary education (5%), marketing (4%), and nursing (4%). In an average class, 48% graduate in 4 years or less, 70% graduate in 5 years or less, and 73% graduate in 6 years or less.

SERVICES: Counseling and information services are available, as is tutoring in most subjects, such as 100 level courses. There is a reader service for the blind, and remedial math. **Library/Resources:** The library contains 1.6 million volumes, 84,905 microform items, 38,797 audio/video tapes/CDs/DVDs, and subscribes to 52,249 periodicals, including electronic. Computerized library services include interlibrary loans, database searching, Internet access, and Wi-Fi capability. Special learning facilities include an art gallery, a planetarium, a radio station, a TV station, an distance-learning classrooms, a farm, and Japanese gardens. **Physically Challenged Students:** All of the campus is accessible. Facilities include wheelchair ramps, elevators, special parking, specially equipped restrooms, special class scheduling, lowered drinking fountains, lowered telephones, and special housing. **Special:** There are numerous cooperative programs and internships, dual majors, student-designed majors, and work-study programs both on campus and with nonprofit organizations. There is also a general studies degree, a 3-2 engineering program with the University of Illinois or Bradley University, a B.S./M.P.A., and study abroad in 32 countries. Pass/fail options are available. Credit is given for military experience. ISU is part of the National Student Exchange, enabling qualifying juniors and seniors to study for up to 1 year at one of several hundred colleges around the country. There are 24 national honor societies, a freshman honors program, and 1 departmental honors program. **Visiting:** There are regularly scheduled orientations for prospective students, While attending Preview, students will have the opportunity to meet with their academic advisor, register for classes, meet current Illinois State students and their future classmates, interact with faculty and staff from various academic departments. There are guides for informal visits; visitors may sit in on classes, and stay overnight. To schedule a visit, contact the Admissions Office. **Campus Safety and Security:** Measures include 24-hour foot and vehicle patrol, emergency notification system, self-defense education, and security escort services. There are shuttle buses, emergency telephones, lighted pathways/sidewalks, and controlled access to dorms/residences.

REQUIREMENTS: The ACT is required. Admission is based on a combination of factors including rigor of secondary school record, academic GPA, standardized test scores, and application essay. AP and CLEP credits are accepted. Students must complete 39 hours of General Education and a total of 120 credit hours with a minimum GPA of 2.0. In addition, the senior college hours must total at least 42 hours. Every student must have successfully completed a course designated as a course in the cultures and traditions of societies or peoples from Asia, the Middle East, Africa, Latin America, or Indigenous Peoples of the World. **Procedure:** Freshmen are admitted in the fall, spring, and summer. Entrance exams should be taken in the spring of junior year. There are deferred admissions and rolling admissions plans. Applications should be filed by April 1 for fall entry. The fall 2017 application fee was $50. Notifications are sent September 1. 139 applicants were on the 2017 waiting list; 11 were admitted. Applications are accepted online. **Transfer Students:** 1882 transfer students enrolled in 2016-2017. ISU requires transfer students to provide official transcripts from all colleges and universities attended. Transfer students must be in good academic standing at the last institution attended. Many programs have required courses and minimum GPA requirements. Transfer students with a minimum 2.4 cumulative transfer GPA may be admitted to the University as undeclared if program prerequisites were not met or if space is not available in the preferred major. Students with 75 or more semester hours completed will not be admitted as undeclared. Transfer requirements by program can be found at http:/admissions.illinoisstate.edu/transfer/apply/transfer_requirements/. 30 of 120 credits required for the bachelor's degree must be completed at ISU. **International Students:** There are 117 international students enrolled. They must take the TOEFL with a minimum score of 550 on the paper-based TOEFL (PBT) or 79 on the Internet-based version (iBT). They must also take the SAT or ACT.

ADMISSIONS: The ACT scores for 2017-2018 were 1% between 12 and 17, 54% between 18 and 23, 37% between 24 and 29, and 4% above 30. **Admissions Contact:** Ryan Smith, Director of Institutional Research. Email: *Admissions@IllinoisState.edu* Web: *www.illinoisstate.edu*

FINANCIAL AID: The CCS/Profile, FAFSA, FFS, and SFS are required. The FAFSA code is 001692. The deadline for filing freshman financial aid applications for fall entry is March 1.

ILLINOIS WESLEYAN UNIVERSITY D-3

www.iwu.edu

Bloomington, IL 61702

(309) 556-3031
(800) 332-2498
Email: iwuadmit@iwu.edu

Full-time: 745 men, 895 women	**Faculty:** 142; IIB, av$
Part-time: 1 man, 1 woman	**Ph.D.s:** 70%
Graduate: n/av	**Student/Faculty:** 10 to 1
Year: other	**Tuition:** $45,856
Room & Board: $10,574	**Freshman Class:** 3697 applied, 2250 accepted, 378 enrolled
SAT: required **ACT:** 27	**CEEB CODE:** 1320
Application Deadline: March 1	**VERY COMPETITIVE+**

Illinois Wesleyan University, founded in 1850, is a private institution offering major programs in liberal arts, fine arts, and nursing. There are 5 undergraduate schools. In addition to regional accreditation, IWU has baccalaureate program accreditation with NASM and CCNE. The 80-acre campus is in a suburban area 130 miles from Chicago and 160 miles from St. Louis, Missouri. Including any residence halls, there are 54 buildings.

STUDENT LIFE: 83% of undergraduates are from Illinois. Others are from 32 states, and 24 foreign countries. 80% are from public schools. 8% are Hispanic; 8% Foreign; 69% White; 6% Asian American; 5% African American; 2% two or more races; 1% race unknown. **Female To Male Ratio:** 1.2:1. The average age of freshmen is 18; all undergraduates, 20. 7% do not continue beyond their first year; 83% remain to graduate. **Housing:** 1229 students can be accommodated in college housing, which includes dorms and on-campus apartments. In addition, there are honors houses, language/international houses, special-interest houses, fraternity houses, sorority houses, and theme housing communities. On-campus housing is guaranteed for all 4 years. All students may keep cars.

FACULTY/CLASSROOMS: 58% of faculty are male; 42% are female. All teach undergraduates and all do research. No introductory courses are taught by graduate students. The average class size in a laboratory is 13 and in a regular course is 17.

PROGRAMS OF STUDY: IWU confers B.A., B.S., B.F.A., B.Mus., B.Mus.Ed. and B.S.N. degrees. Bachelor's degrees are awarded in AGRICULTURE (environmental studies), BIOLOGICAL SCIENCE (biology/biological science), BUSINESS (accounting, business administration and management, insurance and risk management, and international business management), COMMUNICATIONS AND THE ARTS (art, classics, English, French, German, guitar, music, music performance, music theory and composition, musical theater, performing arts, piano/organ, theater design, theater management, and voice), COMPUTER AND PHYSICAL SCIENCE (chemistry, computer science, and physics), EDUCATION (education and music education), HEALTH PROFESSIONS (nursing), SOCIAL SCIENCE (American studies, anthropology, economics, history, interdisciplinary studies, international studies, philosophy, political science/government, psychology, religion, sociology, and women and gender studies). Business administration/accounting, biology, and psychology have the largest enrollments.

ACTIVITIES: 33% of men belong to 6 national fraternities; 26% of women belong to 1 local and 4 national sororities. There are 185 groups on campus, including art, band, cheerleading, choir, chorale, chorus, computers, dance, drama, ethnic, film, honors, international, jazz band, LGBT, literary magazine, musical theater, newspaper, opera, orchestra, pep band, political, professional, radio and TV, religious, social, social service, student government, symphony, and yearbook. Popular campus events include Family Days, Comedy Clubs, and International Festivals. **Sports:** There are 9 intercollegiate sports for men and 9 for women, and 15 intramural sports for men and 13 for women. Facilities include a fitness center with weight/exercise equipment and racquetball courts, a swimming pool with diving boards, an activity center, an indoor track, tennis, basketball, volleyball courts, a separate gym for intercollegiate and other activities, an outdoor track, softball, baseball, and soccer fields. **Graduates:** From July 1, 2016 to June 30, 2017, 437 bachelor's degrees were awarded. The most popular majors were business/marketing (30%), social sciences (10%), and health professions and related programs (10%). In an average class, 78% graduate in 4 years or less, 82% graduate in 5 years or less, and 83% graduate in 6 years or less. Of the 2016 graduating class, 21% were enrolled in graduate school within 6 months of graduation, and 72% were employed.

SERVICES: Counseling and information services are available, as is tutoring in every subject. There is a reader service for the blind. There is also assistance in writing and study skills; but not at the remedial level. **Library/Resources:** The library contains 315,166 volumes, and 20,239 audio/video tapes/CDs/DVDs. Computerized library services include interlibrary loans, database searching, Internet access, and Wi-Fi capability. Special learning facilities include an art gallery, a radio station, a TV station, an observatory, a multicultural center, an action research center, a center for human rights, and a peace garden. **Physically Challenged Students:** 90% of the campus is accessible. Facilities include wheelchair ramps, elevators, special parking, specially equipped restrooms, special class scheduling, lowered drinking fountains, lowered telephones, and special housing. **Special:** There are several combined degree programs, including a 3-2 degree in forestry and environmental studies with Duke University and a 2-2 engineering degree with the University of Illinois. Students may study abroad in many locations throughout the world through the Institute for the International Education of Students (IES), Pembroke College, Keio University, University of Oxford, Arcadia University Center for Study Abroad, and other programs. Illinois Wesleyan also offers its own semester-long programs in London and Barcelona. The university also offers on-campus work-study, both credit and noncredit internships, Washington and United Nations semesters, B.A.-B.S. degrees, dual and student-designed majors, pass/fail options, and an honors research program for upperclass students. There are 25 national honor societies, Phi Beta Kappa, and 44 departmental honors programs. **Visiting:** There are regularly scheduled orientations for prospective students, including a 1 to 1-1/2 hour guided tour in small groups, and with advance scheduling, interviews with an admissions counselor and faculty members in the fields of the students interest. Accepted applicants may visit classes or stay overnight. There are guides for informal visits; visitors may sit in on classes and stay overnight. To schedule a visit, contact the Admissions Office. **Campus Safety and Security:** Measures include 24-hour foot and vehicle patrol, an emergency notification system, self-defense education, and security escort services. There are shuttle buses, emergency telephones, lighted pathways/sidewalks, controlled access to dorms/residences, an emergency response team of key executives and staff members, and policies and procedures for natural disasters and other crises.

REQUIREMENTS: The SAT or ACT is required. Applicants should graduate from an accredited secondary school; a GED may be accepted. 15 academic credits are recommended. It is strongly recommended that these units include 4 units of English, 3 each of natural science with 2 lab, math, and foreign language, and 2 units of social studies. An audition is required for theater and music majors and a portfolio is required for art majors. A GPA of 3.0 is required. AP credits are accepted. Important factors in the admissions decision are advanced placement or honors courses, evidence of special talent, personality/intangible qualities, and extracurricular activities record. For B.A., B.S., B.S.N., and B.F.A. degrees, a total of 32 course units (128 semester hours) is required for the bachelor's degree with a 2.0 GPA. General education requirements include 2 course units in natural sciences and 1 each in literature, English, intellectual traditions, formal reasoning, cultural and historical change, contemporary social institutions, the arts, history, humanities, math, social science, analysis of values, and Gateway Colloquium, plus demonstrated proficiency in a foreign language. 2 additional writing-intensive courses are required, as is coursework focusing on U.S. and global diversity issues. 2 degree programs (B.M.Ed.and B.M.) require more than 32 course units due to additional requirements in the major. Physical ed is a noncredit graduation requirement. **Procedure:** Freshmen are admitted in the fall and spring. Entrance exams should be taken in the spring of the junior year. There are early admissions, deferred admissions, and rolling admissions plans. Early decision applications should be filed by November 1; regular applications, by March 1 for fall entry; and November 1 for spring entry. Notifications are sent January 15. 38 applicants were on the 2017 waiting list; 9 were admitted. Applications are accepted online. **Transfer Students:** 30 transfer students enrolled in 2016-2017. Applicants must submit all high school and college transcripts. A GPA of at least 2.0 is required. An essay or personal statement is required, as well as standardized test scores. 16 of 32 credits required for the bachelor's degree must be completed at IWU. **International Students:** There are 170 international students enrolled. They must take the TOEFL with a minimum score of 550 on the paper-based TOEFL (PBT) or 80 on the Internet-based version (iBT). They must also take the SAT or ACT.

ADMISSIONS: 61% of the 2017-2018 applicants were accepted. The ACT scores were 13% between 18 and 23, 63% between 24 and 29, and 24% above 30. **Admissions Contact:** Bob Geraty, Interim Dean of Admissions. Email: *iwuadmit@iwu.edu* Web: *www.iwu.edu*

FINANCIAL AID: In 2017-2018, 71% of all full-time freshmen received some form of financial aid and need-based aid. The average freshman award was $34,845. Need-based scholarships or need-based grants averaged $28,592; need-based self-help aid (loans and jobs) averaged $6,505; other non-need-based awards and non-need-based scholarships averaged $21,219; and $4,620 from other forms of aid. The average financial indebtedness of the 2017 graduate was $37,841. IWU is a member of CSS. The CSS/Profile and the college's own financial statement are required. The FAFSA code is 001696. The priority date for freshman financial aid applications for fall entry is March 1.

JUDSON UNIVERSITY — E-1

www.judsonu.edu

Elgin, IL 60123 — (847) 628-2521, (800) 879-5376

Fax: (847) 695-0216 — Email: admissions@judsonu.edu

Full-time: 394 men, 521 women
Part-time: 106 men, 174 women
Graduate: 27 men, 23 women
Year: semesters
Room & Board: $9740
Application Deadline: open

Faculty: 54
Ph.D.s: 86%
Student/Faculty: 10 to 1
Tuition: $29,434
Freshman Class: 626 applied, 484 accepted, 221 enrolled
CEEB CODE: 1351
COMPETITIVE

Judson University is an evangelical Christian college of the liberal arts, sciences, and professions. The figures in the above capsule and in this profile is approximate. There are 2 undergraduate schools and 1 graduate school. In addition to regional accreditation, Judson has baccalaureate program accreditation with NAAB. The 90-acre campus is in a suburban area 45 miles northwest of Chicago. Including any residence halls, there are 15 buildings.

STUDENT LIFE: 65% of undergraduates are from Illinois. Others are from 30 states, 25 foreign countries, and Canada. 71% are White; 5% Hispanic; 4% African American; 4% Foreign; 1% Asian American. 80% are Protestant. **Female To Male Ratio:** 1.4:1. The average age of freshmen is 18; all undergraduates, 20. 22% do not continue beyond their first year; 50% remain to graduate. **Housing:** 670 students can be accommodated in college housing, which includes married student dorms and on-campus apartments. On-campus housing is guaranteed for all 4 years. 65% of students live on campus. Alcohol is not permitted. All students may keep cars.

FACULTY/CLASSROOMS: 66% of faculty are male; 34% are female. 80% teach undergraduates, 20% do research, and 20% do both. No introductory courses are taught by graduate students. The average class size in an introductory lecture is 28; in a laboratory is 9; and in a regular course is 16.

PROGRAMS OF STUDY: Judson confers B.A. degrees. Master's degrees are also awarded. Bachelor's degrees are awarded in BIOLOGICAL SCIENCE (biology/biological science), BUSINESS (accounting, business administration and management, international business management, and sports management), COMMUNICATIONS AND THE ARTS (art and design, communications, dramatic arts, English, fine arts, media arts, and music), COMPUTER AND PHYSICAL SCIENCE (chemistry, computer science, and mathematics), EDUCATION (early childhood education, education, elementary education, mathematics education, music education, physical education, science education, and secondary education), ENGINEERING AND ENVIRONMENTAL DESIGN (architecture and preengineering), HEALTH PROFESSIONS (medical laboratory technology, nursing, predentistry, and premedicine), SOCIAL SCIENCE (anthropology, biblical studies, history, political science/government, prelaw, psychology, sociology, and youth ministry). Architecture, visual communications/graphic design, and education are the strongest academically. Business, youth ministry, and worship arts have the largest enrollments.

ACTIVITIES: There are no fraternities or sororities. There are 23 groups on campus, including art, band, business, cheerleading, choir, chorale, chorus, computers, drama, ethnic, honors, international, literary magazine, newspaper, orchestra, photography, political, radio and TV, religious, social, social service, and student government. Popular campus events include Spiritual Enrichment Week, Fall Orientation, and Christmas by Candlelight. **Sports:** There are 3 intercollegiate sports for men and 4 for women, and 9 intramural sports for men and 8 for women. Facilities include a fitness center, a gym, a soccer field, baseball and softball fields, tennis courts, racquetball and handball courts, indoor and outdoor running tracks, and a Nautilus and free-weight room. **Graduates:** From July 1, 2016 to June 30, 2017, 339 bachelor's degrees were awarded. In an average class, 46% graduate in 4 years or less and 48% graduate in 5 years or less.

SERVICES: Counseling and information services are available, as is tutoring in some subjects. There is remedial math, reading, and writing. **Library/Resources:** The library contains 92,000 volumes, 27,000 microform items, and 17,000 audio/video tapes/CDs/DVDs, and subscribes to

470 periodicals including electronic. Computerized library services include interlibrary loans, database searching, and Internet access. Special learning facilities include an art gallery and a radio station. **Physically Challenged Students:** 80% of the campus is accessible. Facilities include wheelchair ramps, elevators, special parking, specially equipped restrooms, special class scheduling, lowered drinking fountains, lowered telephones, and special housing. **Special:** The college has co-op programs with North Park College, Rush University, and the Mennonite College of Nursing; cross-registration with the Christian College Coalition; and work-study programs with many businesses. Students may serve internships in art and business, take a Washington semester, take a film studies semester in Hollywood, take an ecology studies semester at Sable Institute in Michigan, or study abroad in numerous external programs recognized by Judson College. The college allows dual majors, student-designed majors, and accelerated degrees in business leadership and management, human services, human resource management, and criminal justice management. There is 1 national honor society, a freshman honors program, and 2 departmental honors programs. **Visiting:** There are regularly scheduled orientations for prospective students, including a tour, class visits, individual meetings with professors, coaches, the choir and-or band director, and other select campus administrators if requested. In addition, lunch or dinner in the cafeteria and the opportunity to meet with current students and the opportunity to stay a night in the dorms are offered. To schedule a visit, contact the Enrollment Services Office/Admissions. **Campus Safety and Security:** Measures include 24-hour foot and vehicle patrol and security escort services. There are emergency telephones and lighted pathways/sidewalks.

REQUIREMENTS: The ACT with a minimum score of 18 or SAT with a minimum score of 840 is required. Applicants need to be in the upper 50% of their class. A GPA of 2.0 is required. AP and CLEP credits are accepted. Most students must have a GPA of 2.0; education majors must have a 2.5. Students must complete at least 126 credit hours, including 45 to 66 in the major, and take the college's core courses of Bible study, writing, speech, literature, math, science, history, fine arts, human relations, and physical education, as well as a course in either psychology or sociology. **Procedure:** Freshmen are admitted to all sessions. Entrance exams should be taken in the spring of the junior year or the fall of the senior year. There are deferred admissions and rolling admissions plans. Application deadlines are open. The fall 2017 application fee was $35. Notification is sent on a rolling basis. Applications are accepted on-line. **Transfer Students:** 86 transfer students enrolled in 2016-2017. Students with fewer than 28 hours of college credit must submit high school transcripts showing a GPA of at least 2.0, as well as ACT results with a composite score of at least 18 or 840 on the SAT. Transfer students with more than 28 hours must have a GPA of at least 2.0. 30 of 126 credits required for the bachelor's degree must be completed at Judson. **International Students:** There are 44 international students enrolled. They must take the TOEFL or MELAB. They must also take the SAT or ACT, scoring 18.

ADMISSIONS: 77% of the 2017-2018 applicants were accepted. **Admissions Contact:** Nate McNeely, Director of Admissions. Email: *admissions@judsonu.edu* Web: *www.judsonu.edu*

FINANCIAL AID: In 2017-2018, 90% of all full-time freshmen received some form of financial aid, and received need-based aid. The college's own financial statement is required. The FAFSA code is 001700. Check with the school for current application deadlines.

KENDALL COLLEGE E-2

www.kendall.edu

Chicago, IL 60642	**(312) 752-2240** **(877) 588-8860**
Fax: (312) 752-2241	**Email: info@kendall.edu**
Full-time: 498 men, 982 women	**Faculty:** 41
Part-time: 162 men, 903 women	**Ph.D.s:** 11%
Graduate: n/av	**Student/Faculty:** 35 to 1
Year: quarters, summer session	**Tuition:** $22,125
Room & Board: $10,485	**Freshman Class:** n/av **CEEB CODE:** 1366
Application Deadline: rolling	**COMPETITIVE**

Kendall College, part of Laureate Internationl Universities, was founded in 1934 and is a private institution committed to cultivating extraordinary talent for the global business, hospitality, culinary, and education fields. Kendall offers 4 schools of study: Culinary Arts, Business, Hospitality Management, and Education. Figures in the above capsule and in this profile are approximate. Tuition figures vary for each academic program chosen by students. There are 4 undergraduate schools. The campus is in an urban area in Chicago. Including any residence halls, there is 1 building.

STUDENT LIFE: 73% of undergraduates are from Illinois. Others are from 35 states, 62 foreign countries, and Canada. 6% are Foreign; 51% White; 4% Asian American; 20% African American; 12% Hispanic. **Female To Male Ratio:** 2.9:1. The average age of freshmen is 21; all undergraduates, 31. 46% do not continue beyond their first year; 37% remain to graduate. **Housing:** 180 students can be accommodated in college housing, which includes off-campus apartments. On-campus housing is available on a first-come, first-served basis. 89% of students commute. Alcohol is not permitted. No one may keep cars.

FACULTY/CLASSROOMS: 50% of faculty are male; 50% are female. 91% teach undergraduates. No introductory courses are taught by graduate students. The average class size in an introductory lecture is 25; in a laboratory is 18; and in a regular course is 20.

PROGRAMS OF STUDY: Kendall confers B.A. degrees. Associate degrees are also awarded. Bachelor's degrees are awarded in BUSINESS (business administration and management, hospitality management services, and hotel/motel and restaurant management), EDUCATION (early childhood education), SOCIAL SCIENCE (culinary arts). Culinary arts and education have the largest enrollments.

ACTIVITIES: There are no fraternities or sororities. There are 10 groups on campus, including chorus, computers, dance, environmental, ethnic, honors, international, LGBT, professional, social, social service, and student government. Popular campus events include Fright Fest, African American History Community Dinner, and Monthly Birthday Celebrations. **Sports:** There is no sports program at Kendall. **Graduates:** From July 1, 2016 to June 30, 2017, 185 bachelor's degrees were awarded. The most popular majors were hospitality management (89%) and early childhood education (75%). In an average class, 2% graduate in 3 years or less, 33% graduate in 4 years or less, and 43% graduate in 5 years or less. Of the 2016 graduating class, 92% were employed within 6 months of graduation.

SERVICES: Counseling and information services are available, as is tutoring in every subject. There is remedial math, reading, and writing. **Library/Resources:** The library contains 36,293 volumes, 453 audio/video tapes/CDs/DVDs, and subscribes to 187 periodical, including electronic. Computerized library services include interlibrary loans, database searching, and Internet access. **Physically Challenged Students:** All of the campus is accessible. Facilities include wheelchair ramps, elevators, special parking, specially equipped restrooms, special class scheduling, lowered drinking fountains, and lowered telephones. **Special:** All majors require internships. Study abroad in 8 countries and work-study programs are available. An accelerated degree in culinary arts and B.A.-B.S. degrees are also possible. There are 2 national honor societies. **Visiting:** There are regularly scheduled orientations for prospective students, including program overviews, financial aid information, and campus tours. There are guides for informal visits and visitors may sit in on classes. To schedule a visit, contact the Admissions Office. **Campus Safety and Security:** Measures include 24-hour foot and vehicle patrol and emergency notification system. There are lighted pathways/sidewalks and controlled access to dorms/residences.

REQUIREMENTS: Applicants need to submit a high school transcript with a minimum 2.0 GPA or a GED, and a personal statement. ACT or SAT scores are required for all applicants who have graduated within 5 years of the intended start date and have a GPA below 2.5. An interview with an Enrollment Advisor is required and a campus tour is recommended. A GPA of 2.0 is required. AP and CLEP credits are accepted. Students must complete 180 credit hours and meet all major requirements as well as the residency requirement. A 2.0 GPA is required to graduate. **Procedure:** Freshmen are admitted to all sessions. There are deferred admissions and rolling admissions plans. Application deadlines are open. The fall 2017 application fee was $50. Applications are accepted on-line. **Transfer Students:** 217 transfer students enrolled in 2016-2017. Students must submit an official college transcript with at least 12 earned semester credits (or 18 quarter credits) with a cumulative GPA of at least 2.0. An interview and a personal statement are required. A campus tour is recommended. 45 of 180 credits required for the bachelor's degree must be completed at Kendall. **International Students:** There are 180 international students enrolled. They must take the TOEFL with a minimum score of 525 on the paper-based TOEFL (PBT) or 71 on the Internet-based version (iBT), or take the IELTS.

Admissions Contact: Richard Kriofsky, Director of Admissions. Email: *info@kendall.edu* Web: *www.kendall.edu*

FINANCIAL AID: In 2017-2018, 84% of all full-time freshmen received some form of financial aid. 71% of all full-time freshmen received need-based aid. The average freshman award was $6,659. Need-based scholarships or need-based grants averaged $1,136 ($10,990 maximum); need-based self-help aid (loans and jobs) averaged $1,927 ($4,000 maximum); and other non-need-based awards and non-need-based scholarships averaged $3,596 ($32,000 maximum). 8% of undergraduate students work part-time. The average financial indebtedness of the 2017 graduate was $11,801. The college's own financial statement is required. The FAFSA code is 001703. Check with the school for current application deadlines.

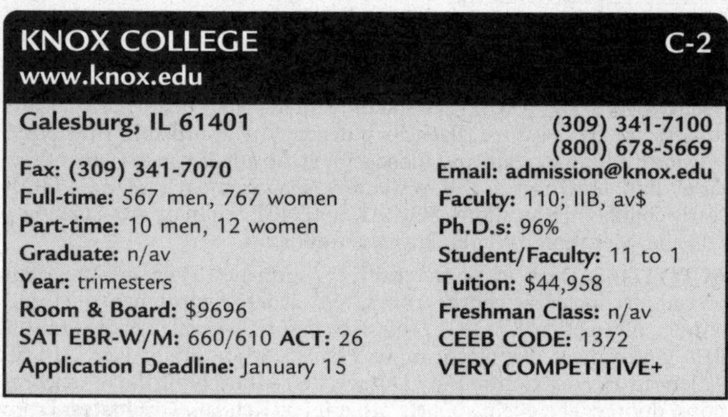

KNOX COLLEGE C-2

www.knox.edu

Galesburg, IL 61401	(309) 341-7100 (800) 678-5669
Fax: (309) 341-7070	Email: admission@knox.edu
Full-time: 567 men, 767 women	Faculty: 110; IIB, av$
Part-time: 10 men, 12 women	Ph.D.s: 96%
Graduate: n/av	Student/Faculty: 11 to 1
Year: trimesters	Tuition: $44,958
Room & Board: $9696	Freshman Class: n/av
SAT EBR-W/M: 660/610 ACT: 26	CEEB CODE: 1372
Application Deadline: January 15	VERY COMPETITIVE+

Knox College, founded in 1837, is a nationally ranked, private, residential liberal arts college. The 82-acre campus is in a small town just an hour from the Mississippi River in the heart of Western Illinois. Including any residence halls, there are 55 buildings.

STUDENT LIFE: 55% of undergraduates are from out of state, mostly the Midwest. Students are from 46 states, 46 foreign countries, and Canada. 77% are from public schools. 8% are African American; 6% two or more races; 5% Asian American; 47% White; 2% race unknown; 17% Foreign; 15% Hispanic. **Female To Male Ratio:** 1.4:1. The average age of freshmen is 18; all undergraduates, 20. 13% do not continue beyond their first year; 76% remain to graduate. **Housing:** 1225 students can be accommodated in college housing, which includes dorms and on-campus apartments. In addition, there are language/international houses, special-interest houses, fraternity houses, cultural centers, and ABLE (Allied Blacks for Liberty and Equality) housing. On-campus housing is guaranteed for all 4 years and is available on a lottery system for upperclassmen. 87% of students live on campus. All students may keep cars.

FACULTY/CLASSROOMS: 58% of faculty are male; 42% are female. All teach undergraduates and all do research. No introductory courses are taught by graduate students. The average class size in an introductory lecture is 25; in a laboratory is 13; and in a regular course is 14.

PROGRAMS OF STUDY: Knox confers B.A. degrees. Bachelor's degrees are awarded in AGRICULTURE (environmental studies), BIOLOGICAL SCIENCE (biochemistry, biology/biological science, and neurosciences), COMMUNICATIONS AND THE ARTS (Africana studies, art history and appreciation, classics, creative writing, dramatic arts, English literature, French, German, Greek (classical), Latin, modern language, music, Spanish, studio art, and theatre arts), COMPUTER AND PHYSICAL SCIENCE (chemistry, computer science, mathematics, and physics), EDUCATION (elementary education, secondary education, and social science education), SOCIAL SCIENCE (American studies, anthropology, Asian/Oriental studies, economics, history, international relations, international studies, Latin American studies, philosophy, political science/government, psychology, sociology, and women and gender studies). Creative writing, computer science, and psychology are the strongest academically. Economics, biology, and creative writing have the largest enrollments.

ACTIVITIES: 32% of men belong to 1 local and 5 national fraternities; 18% of women belong to 4 national sororities. There are 90 groups on campus, including band, chess, choir, communications, computers, dance, drama, drill team, environmental, ethnic, film, international, jazz band, LGBT, literary magazine, newspaper, orchestra, photography, political, professional, radio and TV, religious, social, social service, student government, and symphony. Popular campus events include International Fair, Rootabaga Jazz Festival, Lincoln Fest (local band all-day festival), and Pause for Paws (finals stress relief program with visiting canines). **Sports:** There are 10 intercollegiate sports for men and 10 for women, and 3 intramural sports for men and 3 for women. Facilities include a fitness center with cardio and selectorized equipment, a fitness studio with free weights, a six-lane track, gymnasium, natatorium, fields for football, softball, soccer, and baseball, an outdoor track, and tennis courts. **Graduates:** From July 1, 2016 to June 30, 2017, 309 bachelor's degrees were awarded. The most popular majors were psychology (11%), creative writing (10%), and economics (8%). In an average class, 3% graduate in 3 years or less, 64% graduate in 4 years or less, 75% graduate in 5 years or less, and 76% graduate in 6 years or less. Of the 2016 graduating class, 21% were enrolled in graduate school within 6 months of graduation, and 30% were employed.

SERVICES: Counseling and information services are available, as is tutoring in most subjects. The Center for Teaching and Learning provides academic support to students in most subjects, particularly development of writing skills. **Library/Resources:** The library contains 342,751 volumes, 98,729 microform items, and 13,632 audio/video tapes/CDs/DVDs, and subscribes to 15,463 periodicals including electronic. Computerized library services include interlibrary loans, database searching, Internet access, and Wi-Fi capability. Special learning facilities include a radio station, Green Oaks Biological Field Station Green Oaks, a 760–acre biological field station, consisting of tallgrass prairie, forest, and aquatic habitat. Every other year, 12 students have the opportunity to participate in Green Oaks Term, a 10-week immersive term during which students take interdisciplinary courses in ecology, anthropology, nature writing, nature and art, utopian societies, regional natural history, and sustainability and live at the field station. The Knox Farm consisting of an acre of outdoor growing area and two season-extending "high tunnel" structures, produces food for on-campus use and for sharing with the greater community. Old Main, is the only remaining building from the 1858 Lincoln-Douglas Debates; features dozens of documents, maps, and photographs drawn from the College's 178-year history. The Whitcomb Heritage Center, features exhibits that vividly illustrate the historical context local, regional and national for the Lincoln-Douglas Debate at Knox in 1858. **Physically Challenged Students:** 85% of the campus is accessible. Facilities include wheelchair ramps, elevators, special parking, specially equipped restrooms, lowered drinking fountains, and special housing. **Special:** Knox offers all incoming students a Power of Experience Grant, which provides up to $2,000 to support a qualifying experiential learning opportunity during their junior or senior year. The grant helps to fund the additional expenses that are often associated with research or creative work, internships, community service, or study abroad. Knox offers six immersive terms Clinical Psychology Term, Green Oaks Term, Japan Term, Open Studio, Repertory Theatre Term, and StartUp Term that provide students with a focused, hands-on exploration of a single field of study over the course of an entire term. Cooperative programs are offered with Washington University in St. Louis in architecture and engineering; Columbia University in engineering and law; University of Illinois at Urbana-Champaign and Rensselaer Polytechnic Institute in engineering; Rush University in nursing and medical technology; Duke University in forestry and environmental management; and University of Chicago in law and social work. A cooperative program with the George Washington University School of Medicine and Health Sciences means guaranteed admission for selected sophomores. A Direct Admission Program with University of Rochester Simon School of Business allows highly qualified juniors and seniors to apply for an M.B.A. with this graduate program. The Knox College Law Scholars Program helps graduates pursue an affordable legal education at Indiana University Maurer School of Law. Individuals who are selected for the program will receive a scholarship that reduces the cost of tuition at the Maurer School of Law by about 50%. Students also will participate in a mentorship program and other opportunities through the law school. Knox is the first college or university in the country to have an official Peace Corps Preparatory Program, designed to prepare students for the Peace Corps or other international service programs. Study abroad is available in more than 90 countries. Other off-campus study programs include a Washington semester, an urban studies semester, science and library research programs, work-study programs, and numerous internships. Knox participates in the Kemper Scholars Program, which provides students with scholarships, practical experience, and opportunities to explore careers.

Self-designed majors and minors may be pursued by students when they have an interest in an intellectual issue that is best studied through an integrative approach based in multiple academic disciplines. A self-designed major/minor has the same characteristics of an established major/minor. There are 13 national honor societies, Phi Beta Kappa, and 39 departmental honors programs. **Visiting:** There are regularly scheduled orientations for prospective students, Open houses for prospective students are offered in July, October, November, January and May, and offer campus tours, class visits, lunch with students and professors, and informational sessions. Interviews are available on request. To schedule a visit, contact Sarah Bainter at (800) 678-KNOX. **Campus Safety and Security:** Measures include 24-hour foot and vehicle patrol, emergency notification system, self-defense education, and security escort services. There are emergency telephones, lighted pathways/sidewalks, and controlled access to dorms/residences.

REQUIREMENTS: Successful applicants have excelled in a challenging college preparatory course of study, including at least 4 years of English, 3-4 years each of mathematics, science, and social studies, and 2-3 years of a second language. An essay is required and an interview is strongly recommended. Submission of ACT or SAT scores is optional for most applicants; scores will be considered if submitted. Auditions or portfolio presentations are required for scholarship consideration only. AP credits are accepted. Important factors in the admissions decision are advanced placement or honors courses, personality/intangible qualities, and recommendations by school officials. Knox works on a 3-3 academic schedule 3 terms per year, 3 courses per term. The academic program is structured by four goals, or guideposts: an understanding of five broad areas of human inquiry (Foundations); developing expertise in a field of study (Specialization); acquiring competencies in key areas required for personal and professional success in the new century (Key Competencies); and applying classroom learning through hands-on experience (Experiential Learning). The advising system engages students in a four-year dialogue with faculty through which they a develop a personalized educational plan, addressing these four goals, but tailored to their own unique aspirations, values, and talents. Breadth requirements include 1 course each in the 5 areas of arts, humanities, quantitative reasoning, natural and physical sciences, and social sciences. An additional minor or major, not in the department of the first major, and a 2.0 GPA, overall and in each major and minor, are required. All first-year students participate in the First-Year Experience (FYE), which is an integrated orientation, common reading, first-year preceptorial, residential curriculum, and academic advising experience. Students can also choose to participate in a living-learning community, in which first-year preceptorial faculty engage with students both in the classroom and in the residence halls. **Procedure:** Freshmen are admitted in the fall. Entrance exams should be taken by December of the senior year. There are early admissions and deferred admissions plans. Early decision applications should be filed by November 1; regular applications, by January 15 for fall entry. The fall 2017 application fee was $50. Notification of early decision is sent November 15; regular decision, March 15. 139 applicants were on the 2017 waiting list; 2 were admitted. Applications are accepted on-line. **Transfer Students:** 23 transfer students enrolled in 2016-2017. A 3.0 college GPA is expected. An interview is recommended. 14 of 36 credits required for the bachelor's degree must be completed at Knox. **International Students:** There are 227 international students enrolled. They must take the TOEFL with a minimum score of 550 on the paper-based TOEFL (PBT) or 80 on the Internet-based version (iBT). Student must take the IELTS.

ADMISSIONS: The SAT scores for the 2017-2018 freshman class were: Math-- 5% below 500, 35% between 500 and 599, 37% between 600 and 699, and 23% between 700 and 800. Evidence-Based Reading/Writing-- 4% below 500, 32% between 500 and 599, 51% between 600 and 699, and 13% between 700 and 800. The ACT scores were 1% between 12 and 17, 26% between 18 and 23, 48% between 24 and 29, and 26% above 30. 62% of the current freshmen were in the top fifth of their class; 86% were in the top two fifths. 5 freshmen graduated first in their class. **Admissions Contact:** Paul Steenis, Dean of Admission. Email: *admission@knox.edu* Web: *www.knox.edu*

FINANCIAL AID: In 2017-2018, 100% of all full-time freshmen received some form of financial aid. 85% of all full-time freshmen received need-based aid. The average freshman award was $39,800. Need-based scholarships or need-based grants averaged $33,000; and need-based self-help aid (loans and jobs) averaged $6,800. 68% of undergraduate students work part-time. The average financial indebtedness of the 2017 graduate was $26,508. Knox is a member of CSS. The college's own financial statement is required. The FAFSA code is 001704. The priority date for freshman financial aid applications for fall entry is November 1.

LAKE FOREST COLLEGE — E-1

www.lakeforest.edu

Lake Forest, IL 60045 — (847) 735-5000, (800) 828-4751

Fax: (847) 735-6271 — **Email:** admissions@lakeforest.edu

Full-time: 676 men, 913 women	**Faculty:** 101; IIB, +$
Part-time: 12 men, 6 women	**Ph.D.s:** 98%
Graduate: 4 men, 15 women	**Student/Faculty:** 15 to 1
Year: semesters, summer session	**Tuition:** $41,172
Room & Board: $9480	**Freshman Class:** 3451 applied, 1905 accepted, 416 enrolled
	CEEB CODE: 1392
Application Deadline: February 15	**VERY COMPETITIVE**

Lake Forest College, founded in 1857, is a private liberal arts institution offering an innovative and challenging curriculum with abundant internship and research opportunities. There is 1 undergraduate school. In addition to regional accreditation, Lake Forest has baccalaureate program accreditation with HLC. The 107-acre campus is in a suburban area 30 miles north of Chicago. Including any residence halls, there are 43 buildings.

STUDENT LIFE: 54% of undergraduates are from Illinois. Others are from 43 states, 73 foreign countries, and Canada. 73% are from public schools. 9% are Foreign; 7% African American; 57% White; 5% Asian American; 4% two or more races; 3% race unknown; 15% Hispanic. **Female To Male Ratio:** 1.3:1. The average age of freshmen is 18; all undergraduates, 20. 15% do not continue beyond their first year; 85% remain to graduate. **Housing:** 1270 students can be accommodated in college housing, which includes dorms and on-campus apartments. In addition, there are special-interest houses, an international house, and themed/special interest suites within residence halls. On-campus housing is guaranteed for the freshman year only and is available on a lottery system for upperclassmen. 75% of students live on campus. Upperclassmen may keep cars.

FACULTY/CLASSROOMS: 52% of faculty are male; 48% are female. All teach undergraduates, and all do research. No introductory courses are taught by graduate students.

PROGRAMS OF STUDY: Lake Forest confers B.A. degrees. Master's degrees are also awarded. Bachelor's degrees are awarded in BIOLOGICAL SCIENCE (biology/biological science and neurosciences), BUSINESS (business economics and finance), COMMUNICATIONS AND THE ARTS (art, communications, English, French, music, Spanish, and theatre arts), COMPUTER AND PHYSICAL SCIENCE (chemistry, computer science, mathematics, and physics), EDUCATION (education and music education), ENGINEERING AND ENVIRONMENTAL DESIGN (environmental science), SOCIAL SCIENCE (American studies, anthropology, area studies, Asian/Oriental studies, economics, history, international relations, Latin American studies, philosophy, political science/government, psychology, religion, and sociology). Business, communication, and biology have the largest enrollments.

ACTIVITIES: 12% of men belong to 3 national fraternities; 16% of women belong to 4 national sororities. There are 66 groups on campus, including art, band, cheerleading, chess, choir, chorus, computers, dance, debate, drama, environmental, ethnic, film, honors, international, jazz band, LGBT, literary magazine, musical theater, newspaper, orchestra, pep band, photography, political, professional, radio and TV, religious, social, social service, and student government. Popular campus events include Homecoming, Global Fest, Gates Day of Service, and Spring Concert. **Sports:** There are 9 intercollegiate sports for men and 10 for women, and 16 intramural sports for men and 16 for women. Facilities include the sports and recreation center, a gymnasium, a training room, a weight room, a cardio suite, a dance studio, basketball courts, racquetball and handball courts, batting/golf cages, suspended track, a pool, an indoor hockey rink, outdoor sand volleyball courts, tennis courts, and baseball, football, soccer, and intramural fields. **Graduates:** From July 1, 2016 to June 30, 2017, 348 bachelor's degrees were awarded. The most popular majors were communication (15%), economics (9%), and psychology (8%). In an average class, 64% graduate in 4 years or less, 72% graduate in 5 years or less, and 73% graduate in 6 years or less. Of the 2016 graduating class, 77% were employed within 6 months of graduation.

SERVICES: Counseling and information services are available, as is tutoring in most subjects. **Library/Resources:** The library contains 360,848 volumes, 111,460 microform items, and 10,324 audio/video tapes/CDs/DVDs, and subscribes to 16,980 periodicals, including electronic. Computerized library services include interlibrary loans, database searching, Internet access, and Wi-Fi capability. Special learning facilities include an art gallery, a radio station, a multimedia language lab, an electronic music studio with practice rooms, a technology resource center equipped with high-end computing hardware and software, and rhetoric and production room. **Physically Challenged Students:** 75% of the campus is accessible. Facilities include wheelchair ramps, elevators, special parking, specially equipped restrooms, special class scheduling, lowered drinking fountains, lowered telephones, and special housing. **Special:** Lake Forest offers cross-registration with Associated Colleges of the Midwest, an extensive internship program, a student-designed Independent Scholar major, and extensive off-campus study opportunities in 15+ countries with international internships available. Lake Forest has a number of accelerated and dual-degree programs including a 3-3 program in cooperation with a number of law schools whereby a student can earn a BA and J.D. in six years instead of seven. Students at Lake Forest can choose to earn a B.A. degree in communication or philosophy in just three years. The college also offers accelerated and dual degree programs in engineering, international studies, pharmacy, and nursing. There are 14 national honor societies, Phi Beta Kappa, a freshman honors program, and 14 departmental honors programs. **Visiting:** There are regularly scheduled orientations for prospective students. Visits include class visitation, panel presentations, tours, and individual appointments with faculty, coaches, and/or admission officers. There are guides for informal visits and visitors may sit in on classes. To schedule a visit, contact the Admissions Office. **Campus Safety and Security:** Measures include 24-hour foot and vehicle patrol, an emergency notification system, self-defense education, and security escort services. There are shuttle buses, emergency telephones, lighted pathways/sidewalks, and controlled access to dorms/residences.

REQUIREMENTS: Applicants are advised to complete a minimum of 16 academic credits, including 4 in English, 3 in math, 2 to 4 each in social and natural sciences, and study in 1 or more foreign languages. A GED is accepted. An interview is encouraged. AP credits are accepted. Important factors in the admissions decision are personality/intangible qualities, advanced placement or honors courses, and extracurricular activities record. All students are required to complete 32 courses with a minimum GPA of 2.0. General education requirements include 2 courses in natural science or math, 2 cultural diversity courses, and 1 course each in freshman studies, freshman writing, humanities, social science, and senior studies. **Procedure:** Freshmen are admitted in the fall and spring. Entrance exams should be taken in the junior or senior year. There are early decision and deferred admissions plans. Early decision applications should be filed by November 15; regular applications, by February 15 for fall entry; and December 1 for spring entry. Notification of early decision is sent December 15; regular decision, March 20. 70 early decision candidates were accepted for the 2017-2018 class. Applications are accepted online. **Transfer Students:** 74 transfer students enrolled in 2016-2017. Transfer applicants should have a minimum C average in all college work and should be in good standing with their previous institution. High school and college transcripts and a letter of recommendation from the academic dean or a teacher at the most recent college attended are required. 16 of 32 credits required for the bachelor's degree must be completed at Lake Forest. **International Students:** There are 242 international students enrolled. They must take the TOEFL with a minimum score of 550 on the paper-based TOEFL (PBT) or 83 on the Internet-based version (iBT). They must also take the SAT or ACT.

ADMISSIONS: 55% of the 2017-2018 applicants were accepted. **Admissions Contact:** Irene Rarliff, Director of Communications. Email: *admissions@lakeforest.edu* Web: *www.lakeforest.edu*

FINANCIAL AID: 100% of undergraduate students work part-time. Lake Forest is a member of CSS. The FAFSA code is 001706. The priority date for freshman financial aid applications for fall entry is February 15. The deadline for filing freshman financial aid applications for fall entry is May 1.

LEWIS UNIVERSITY — E-2

www.lewisu.edu

Romeoville, IL 60446 — (815) 838-0500, (800) 897-9000

Fax: (815) 836-5002 — **Email:** admissions@lewisu.edu

Full-time: 1715 men, 1972 women	**Faculty:** 223; IIA, av$
Part-time: 418 men, 401 women	**Ph.D.s:** 80%
Graduate: 684 men, 1316 women	**Student/Faculty:** 13 to 1
Year: semesters, summer session	**Tuition:** $31,250
Room & Board: $10,460	**Freshman Class:** 5447 applied, 2932 accepted, 609 enrolled
SAT CR/M: 546/548 **ACT:** 23	**CEEB CODE:** 1404
Application Deadline: open	**COMPETITIVE**

Lewis University is a Catholic university offering distinctive undergraduate and graduate programs to 6,500 traditional and adult students. Lewis offers multiple campus locations, online degree programs, and a variety of formats that provide accessibility and convenience to students. Sponsored by the De La Salle Christian Brothers, Lewis prepares intellectually engaged, ethically grounded, globally aware, and socially responsible graduates. Lewis provides a well-rounded liberal and professional education in fields including business, education, nursing, criminal/social justice, and aviation. The Lewis Flyers compete in NCAA Division II athletics and are members of the GLVC Conference with a multipurpose athletic and recreation complex. There are 5 undergraduate schools and 12 graduate schools. In addition to regional accreditation, LU has baccalaureate program accreditation with ACBSP, CSWE, CAEP, CCNE, FAA, and CAATE. The 410-acre campus is in a suburban area 30 miles southwest of downtown Chicago. Including any residence halls, there are 68 buildings.

STUDENT LIFE: 90% of undergraduates are from Illinois. Others are from 33 states, 26 foreign countries, and Canada. 8% are race unknown; 58% White; 5% African American; 4% Asian American; 3% two or more races; 20% Hispanic; 2% Foreign. 49% are Catholic; 44% majority of other Christian religions; 18% of population did not report religious preference. **Female To Male Ratio:** 1.3:1. The average age of freshmen is 18; all undergraduates, 23. 20% do not continue beyond their first year; 67% remain to graduate. **Housing:** 1444 students can be accommodated in college housing, which includes coed dorms. In addition, there are special-interest houses, living-learning communities, and suite style accommodations. On-campus housing is guaranteed for the freshman year only, and is available on a first-come, first-served basis. 78% of students commute. All students may keep cars.

FACULTY/CLASSROOMS: 49% of faculty are male; 51% are female. No introductory courses are taught by graduate students.

PROGRAMS OF STUDY: LU confers B.A., B.S., B.E.S., and B.S.N. degrees. Associate, master's, and doctoral degrees are also awarded. Bachelor's degrees are awarded in BIOLOGICAL SCIENCE (biochemistry), BUSINESS (accounting, business administration and management, finance, human resource management, international business, management information systems, management, marketing, organizational leadership and management, sports management, and professional studies), COMMUNICATIONS AND THE ARTS (broadcasting, computer graphic design, drawing, English, general art studio, illustration, interactive media, journalism, music, music business management, organizational communication, painting, public relations/advertising, radio/TV broadcasting, social media marketing, and theatre studies), COMPUTER AND PHYSICAL SCIENCE (chemistry, computer science, information security and risk management, information technology management, mathematics, and physics), EDUCATION (athletic training, early childhood education, elected studies, elementary education, middle level education, secondary education, and special education), ENGINEERING AND ENVIRONMENTAL DESIGN (air traffic control management, aviation administration/management, aviation and aerospace technology, aviation flight management, aviation maintenance management, computer engineering, environmental science, nuclear medicine technology, preengineering, transportation administration, and unmanned aircraft systems), HEALTH PROFESSIONS (biology, biomedical science, dental hygiene, diagnostic medical sonography, exercise and movement science, health care leadership, nursing, predentistry, premedicine, preoptometry, preoccupational therapy, preosteopathy, prepharmacy, prephysician assistant, prephysical therapy, prepodiatry, preveterinary science, radiation therapy, and radiography), SOCIAL SCIENCE (criminal justice, economics, forensic criminal investigation, foreign language instruction, history, international relations, liberal arts/general studies, paralegal studies, philosophy, philosophy of law, political science/government, prelaw, psychology, public policy, social work, sociology, Spanish language and culture, and theology). Aviation, biology, business, computer science, criminal justice, education, nursing, and psychology are the strongest academically. Nursing, criminal justice, and business administration have the largest enrollments.

ACTIVITIES: 2% of men belong to 8 national fraternities; 4% of women belong to 1 local and 4 national sororities. There are 100 groups on campus, including Teachers of Tomorrow, Mock Trial, Student Nurses Association, art, band, cheerleading, chess, choir, chorale, chorus, computers, dance, debate, drama, environmental, ethnic, film, flight team, forensics, honors, international, jazz band, LGBT, literary magazine, musical theater, newspaper, orchestra, pep band, photography, political, professional, radio and TV, religious, social, social service, student government, and symphony. Popular campus events include Fall and Spring Formals, Homecoming, Founders Week events, and International Student Food Festival. **Sports:** There are 9 intercollegiate sports for men and 9 for women, and 22 intramural sports for men and 22 for women. The Student Recreation and Fitness Center contains a field house with multipurpose courts, a weight room, aerobics studio, group exercise room, a swimming pool, an indoor track, an arena for basketball and volleyball, and fields for soccer and track and field. The Powerhouse Flex and Fitness Center provides weightlifting, exercise and workouts. Outdoor facilities include baseball and softball fields, tennis courts, disc golf course, sand volleyball courts, a bags area, intramural/rugby fields, and cross country course and trail. **Graduates:** From July 1, 2016 to June 30, 2017, 1266 bachelor's degrees were awarded. The most popular majors were criminal social justice (9%), nursing (8%), and psychology (6%). In an average class, 48% graduate in 4 years or less, 64% graduate in 5 years or less, and 67% graduate in 6 years or less.

SERVICES: Counseling and information services are available, as is tutoring in most subjects. The University Success Program provides assistance to those students who do not meet the outright scholastic requirements. **Library/Resources:** The library contains 120,468 volumes, 141,287 microform items, and 14,382 audio/video tapes/CDs/DVDs, and subscribes to 152,807 periodicals including electronic. Computerized library services include interlibrary loans, database searching, Internet access, and Wi-Fi capability. Special learning facilities include an art gallery, a radio station, and a TV station. Lewis aviation programs utilize the University Airport, Harold E. White Aviation Center, and Brother Neil Kieffe FSC Aviation Building. Lewis aviation students use a Boeing 737 jet for clinical experiences. The Oremus Fine Arts Center houses a Black Box Theatre, Brent & Jean Wadsworth Family Gallery, Caterpillar Gallery, Ives Recital Hall, art studios and music performance facilities. The Brother James Miller FSC Chapel, James A. LaGrippe Pastoral Center with D'Arcy Great Room and Lewis Family Room, the Sancta Alberta Chapel with Blessed Sacrament Chapel and Miguel Center for University Ministry are available to students for ministry and spiritual uses. Academic facilities include buildings for College of Arts and Sciences classrooms, labs and computer labs, a LEED-certified Science Center, St. Charles Borromeo Center for College of Business programs, Convocation Hall, Lowell Stahl Center for Entrepreneurship and Real Estate, and De La Salle Hall for College of Education programs. South Hall for College of Nursing and Health Professions programs features new nursing simulation labs including SimMan mannequins. The Brother Paul French FSC Learning Resource Center houses Career Services, Library, Writing Center, and the Center for Academic Success and Enrichment (CASE). CASE provides Academic Services (Tutoring, Disability Services, Success Program, ESL support), Community Engaged Learning, Study Abroad, and Military Education Resource Center. Additionally there is the Brother Raymond McManaman FSC Center for Student Organizations and Cultural Resources, and a Student Recreation and Fitness Center. **Physically Challenged Students:** 95% of the campus is accessible. Facilities include wheelchair ramps, elevators, special parking, specially equipped restrooms, special class scheduling, lowered drinking fountains, lowered telephones, and special housing. **Special:** LU offers an honors program, undergraduate research opportunities, study abroad options in a number of locations, work-study programs, service members opportunities, student-designed majors, continuing education, distance learning, evening courses, and weekend courses. There are joint programs with a number of colleges in the Allied Health areas including Midwest University for pharmacy and Logan Chiropractic College. There are accelerated-degree programs for adults that include business administration, information security and risk management, information technology management, management, social media marketing, aviation maintenance management, computer science, criminal social justice, human resource management, organizational leadership, paralegal studies, psychology, healthcare leadership, RN-BSN completion, B.A.C. to B.S.N., and professional studies. The aviation program permits graduates to qualify for the FAA Airframe and Powerplant certificate, air traffic control, and flight certifications. There is a freshman honors program. **Visiting:** There are regularly scheduled orientations for prospective students consisting of 1 day sessions (parent orientation included) followed by welcome week activities before the first class day in the fall. There are guides for informal visits; visitors may sit in on classes and stay overnight. To schedule a visit, contact the Admission Office. **Campus Safety and Security:** Measures include 24-hour foot and vehicle patrol, an emergency notification system, self-defense education, and security escort services. There are shuttle buses, emergency telephones, lighted pathways/sidewalks, and controlled access to dorms/residences.

REQUIREMENTS: The SAT or ACT is required. Applicants must have graduated from an approved high school with a combination of grade point average, class rank, and test scores that indicate a strong likelihood of success in university studies. Students should have completed 18 units consisting of 3 in English and 15 in other college preparatory subjects. The GED is accepted. A GPA of 2.0 is required. AP and CLEP credits are accepted. Important factors in the admissions decision are advanced placement or honors courses, leadership record, and extracurricular activities record. All students must earn 128 credit hours in courses acceptable for graduation, with about one-third of these courses in the core curriculum-science, mathematics, fine arts, writing, human communications, literature, Western civilization, philosophy, ethics, theology, economics, and social sciences. Students must maintain a minimum cumulative GPA that varies depending upon the academic program selected. At least 4 upper-division courses must be taken in the major and the final 32 hours must be completed at LU. Requirements for practicums, capstone courses, internships, major field tests, and student portfolios vary depending on academic program selected. **Procedure:** Freshmen are admitted in the fall and spring. Entrance exams should be taken prior to enrollment. There are deferred admissions and rolling admissions plans. Application deadlines are open. The fall 2017 application fee was $40. Notification is sent on a rolling basis. Applications are accepted online. **Transfer Students:** 521 transfer students enrolled in 2016-2017. Biology, chemistry, education, and nursing programs require a minimum 2.75 cumulative transfer GPA. Air traffic control, allied health, and computer engineering programs require a minimum 3.0 cumulative transfer GPA. Preprofessional biology programs require a 3.25 minimum biology course and cumulative transfer GPA (based on a 4.0 grading scale), and a 2.0 GPA in transferable course work of at least 12 semester hours for admission to other programs. Transfer students should submit official transcripts from all colleges attended, and be in good standing at the previous institution. 32 of 128 credits required for the bachelor's degree must be completed at LU. **International Students:** There are 68 international students enrolled. They must take the TOEFL with a minimum score of 79 on the Internet-based version (iBT). They must also take the SAT or ACT.

ADMISSIONS: 54% of the 2017-2018 applicants were accepted. The SAT scores for the 2017-2018 freshman class were: Critical Reading--37% below 500, 33% between 500 and 599, 22% between 600 and 699, and 8% between 700 and 800. Math-- 33% below 500, 33% between 500 and 599, 30% between 600 and 699, and 4% between 700 and 800. The ACT scores were 3% between 12 and 17, 53% between 18 and 23, 38% between 24 and 29, and 6% above 30. 39% of the current freshmen were in the top fifth of their class; 66% were in the top two fifths. 4 freshmen graduated first in their class. **Admissions Contact:** Ryan Cockerill, Director of Admission. Email: *admissions@lewisu.edu* Web: *www.lewisu.edu*

FINANCIAL AID: In 2017-2018, 99% of all full-time freshmen received some form of financial aid. The average freshman award was $27,000. The FAFSA code is 001707. The priority date for freshman financial aid applications for fall entry is October 31.

LOYOLA UNIVERSITY CHICAGO E-2

www.luc.edu

Chicago, IL 60660	**(773) 508-3075** **(800) 262-2373**
Fax: (773) 508-8926	**Email: admission@luc.edu**
Full-time: 3591 men, 7090 women	**Faculty:** I, av$
Part-time: 265 men, 474 women	**Ph.D.s:** 93%
Graduate: 1826 men, 3427 women	**Student/Faculty:** 14 to 1
Year: semesters, summer session	**Tuition:** $43,078
Room & Board: $14,080	**Freshman Class:** 22712 applied, 16482 accepted, 2622 enrolled
SAT CR/M/W: 580/570/570 **ACT:** 26	**CEEB CODE:** 1412
Application Deadline: May 1	**VERY COMPETITIVE**

Loyola University of Chicago, founded in 1870, is a private Roman Catholic (Jesuit) university offering undergraduate curricula in the arts and sciences, business, communication, nursing, social work, and education. There are 8 undergraduate schools and 7 graduate schools. In addition to regional accreditation, LUC has baccalaureate program accreditation with AACSB, ACPE, CSWE, NLN, ACS, NAST, CCNE, and NCA-HLC. The 105-acre campus is in an urban area in Chicago, Illinois. Including any residence halls, there are 76 buildings.

STUDENT LIFE: 64% of undergraduates are from Illinois. Others are from 50 states, 105 foreign countries, and Canada. 66% are from public schools. 6% are African American; 55% White; 5% Foreign; 4% two or more races; 2% race unknown; 16% Hispanic; 12% Asian American. 59% are Catholic; 22% Orthodox Hindu, Buddhist, and Islam; 17% Protestant. **Female To Male Ratio:** 1.9:1. The average age of freshmen is 18; all undergraduates, 21. 18% do not continue beyond their first year; 75% remain to graduate. **Housing:** 4728 students can be accommodated in college housing, which includes dorms, on-campus apartments, and off-campus apartments. In addition, there are honors houses, fraternity houses, sorority houses, and living learning community floors. On-campus housing is available on a lottery system for upperclassmen. 60% of students commute. All students may keep cars.

FACULTY/CLASSROOMS: 53% of faculty are male; 47% are female. 92% teach undergraduates, and all do research. No introductory courses are taught by graduate students. The average class size in a laboratory is 19.

PROGRAMS OF STUDY: LUC confers B.A., B.S., B.A.Classics., B.B.A., B.F.A., B.G., B.S.Ed., B.S.N., and B.S.W. degrees. Associate, master's, and doctoral degrees are also awarded. Bachelor's degrees are awarded in BIOLOGICAL SCIENCE (biochemistry, bioinformatics, biology/biological science, and biophysics), BUSINESS (accounting, business administration and management, business economics, entrepreneurial studies, finance, human resources, international business management, management information systems, marketing/retailing/merchandising, organizational leadership and management, and sports management), COMMUNICATIONS AND THE ARTS (advertising, art history, communications, dance, digital communications, English, fine arts, French, Greek, Greek (classical), Italian, journalism, Latin, media arts, music, Spanish, studio art, theatre arts, and visual design), COMPUTER AND PHYSICAL SCIENCE (chemistry, clinical laboratory science, computer engineering technology, computer science, computer security and information assurance, information sciences and systems, mathematics, mathematics/computational, physics, software engineering, and statistics), EDUCATION (bilingual/bicultural education, early childhood education, elementary education, health information management, mathematics education, science education, secondary education, and special education), ENGINEERING AND ENVIRONMENTAL DESIGN (bioengineering, engineering science, environmental engineering, environmental engineering technology, and environmental science), HEALTH PROFESSIONS (clinical science, exercise science, and nursing), SOCIAL SCIENCE (African studies, African American studies, anthropology, applied psychology, classical/ancient civilization, criminal justice, criminology, economics, forensic studies, history, human services, international studies, paralegal studies, pastoral studies, philosophy, political science/government, psychology, religious education, social work, sociology, theological studies, and womens studies). Biology, psychology, and nursing have the largest enrollments.

ACTIVITIES: 8% of men belong to 7 national fraternities; 17% of women belong to 10 national sororities. There are 250 groups on campus, including art, band, chess, choir, chorus, dance, debate, drama, environmental, ethnic, film, honors, international, jazz band, LGBT, literary magazine, newspaper, photography, political, professional, radio and TV, religious, social, social service, student government, and waterpolo. Popular campus events include New Year's Festival, President's Ball, Department of Programming Concert, and Mainstage Events. **Sports:** There are 7 intercollegiate sports for men and 8 for women, and 20 intramural sports for men and 20 for women. Facilities include soccer fields, an athletics complex and center, a sports medicine facility, strength and conditioning equipment, a swimming pool, 3 basketball courts, an indoor track, dance studios, and racquetball courts. **Graduates:** From July 1, 2016 to June 30, 2017, 2178 bachelor's degrees were awarded. The most popular majors were biology (15%), nursing (13%), and psychology (10%). In an average class, 1% graduate in 3 years or less, 65% graduate in 4 years or less, 74% graduate in 5 years or less, and 75% graduate in 6 years or less.

SERVICES: Counseling and information services are available, as is tutoring in some subjects, such as general education courses. A writing center is also available for student use as well as small group tutoring, tutor-led study halls, academic skills workshop, and language learning center. **Library/Resources:** The library contains 1.9 million volumes, 1.6 million microform items, and 15,027 audio/video tapes/CDs/DVDs, and subscribes to 58,387 periodicals, including electronic. Computerized library services include interlibrary loans, database searching, Internet access, and Wi-Fi capability. Special learning facilities include an art gallery, a radio station, theaters, art museums, digital media labs, a convergence media studio, a language learning resource center, neuroscience labs, a clean energy lab, a mock trial room, performance and specialized fine arts rooms, a clinical simulation nursing laboratory, a geothermal system, an ecodome greenhouse, an aquaponics system showcase, an artificial stream research facility, a retreat and ecology campus, a biodiesel lab, an ecology research lab, and green roofs. **Physically Challenged Students:** 90% of the campus is accessible. Facilities include wheelchair ramps, elevators, specially equipped restrooms, special class scheduling, lowered drinking fountains, and lowered telephones. Selected dorms are wheelchair accessible. **Special:** There are study abroad service learning opportunities in Vietnam, Peru, El Salvador, South Africa, Chile, Spain, and India. Dual majors in math education/secondary education and physics/engineering, nondegree study, and pass/fail options are available. The school also offers a B.A.-B.S. degree in chemistry and a 3-2 engineering degree with Columbia and Washington Universities. There are 5-year programs and combination bachelor's/master's available. LUC also offers engineering majors: bioengineering, computer engineering, and environmental health engineering. There are 9 national honor societies, Phi Beta Kappa, and a freshman honors program. **Visiting:** There are regularly scheduled orientations for prospective students, including interviews and tours; students may attend classes if previous arrangements have been made. There are guides for informal visits and visitors may stay overnight. To schedule a visit, contact the Undergraduate Admissions Office. **Campus Safety and Security:** Measures include 24-hour foot and vehicle patrol, emergency notification system, self-defense education, and security escort services. There are shuttle buses, an emergency telephones, lighted pathways/sidewalks, Hot Spot tours, a bicycle safety U-lock program, and an active shooter event reference guide.

REQUIREMENTS: The SAT or ACT is required. Graduation from an accredited secondary school or satisfactory scores on the GED are required for admission. 15 academic credits are required. Secondary school courses should include 4 credits of English and 3 each of math, science, and social studies. AP and CLEP credits are accepted. Important factors in the admissions decision are advanced placement or honors courses, leadership record, and extracurricular activities record. To graduate, students must have a total of 120 credit hours with a minimum GPA of 2.0. There is a core requirement. The Core includes a total of 15 courses (45 credit hours of coursework), primarily from the arts and sciences, which develop important college-level skills and integrate an understanding of values through 10 required areas of knowledge. Important skills on which the Core focuses are communication, critical thinking, ethical awareness, information literacy, quantitativeand qualitative analysis, research methods, and technological literacy. The 10 required areas of knowledge include a college writing seminar, artistic knowledge and experience, historical knowledge, literary knowledge, quantitative analysis, scientific literacy, societal and cultural knowledge, philosophical knowledge, theological and religious studies, and ethics For the core requirement, all students must take 9 hours each of theology, philosophy, and social sciences and 6 hours each of English composition and humanities. **Procedure:** Freshmen are admitted to all sessions. Entrance exams should be taken as early as possible, normally in the spring of the junior year. There is a rolling admissions plan. Applications should be filed by May 1 for fall entry. Applications are accepted on-line. **Transfer Students:** 519 transfer students enrolled in 2016-2017. Transfer students must have 20 transferable semester hours of credit, with a minimum GPA of 2.0 for the schools of arts and sciences and education. A minimum GPA of 2.5 is required for the schools of nursing and business administration. If transfers have fewer then 20 hours, students must meet the same requirements as entering freshmen. 45 of 120 credits required for the bachelor's degree must be completed at Loyola. **International Students:** There are 551 international students enrolled. They must take the TOEFL with a minimum score of 550 on the paper-based TOEFL (PBT) or 79 on the Internet-based version (iBT). They must also take the SAT or ACT.

ADMISSIONS: 73% of the 2017-2018 applicants were accepted. The SAT scores for the 2017-2018 freshman class were: Critical Reading-- 17% below 500, 40% between 500 and 599, 34% between 600 and 699, and 9% between 700 and 800. Math-- 18% below 500, 44% between 500 and 599, 32% between 600 and 699, and 6% between 700 and 800. Writing-- 20% below 500, 41% between 500 and 599, 32% between 600 and 699, and 7% between 700 and 800. The ACT scores were 22% between 18 and 23, 57% between 24 and 29, and 21% above 30. 60% of the current freshmen were in the top fifth of their class; 87% were in the top two fifths. 17 freshmen graduated first in their class. **Admissions Contact:** Erin Moriarty, Director for Undergraduate Admissions. Email: *admission@luc.edu* Web: *www.luc.edu*

FINANCIAL AID: In 2017-2018, 98% of all full-time freshmen received some form of financial aid. 61% of all full-time freshmen received need-based aid. The average freshman award was $27,511. Need-based scholarships or need-based grants averaged $10,609 ($36,398 maximum); need-based self-help aid (loans and jobs) averaged $5,289 ($10,500 maximum); non-need-based athletic scholarships averaged $23,671 ($56,722 maximum); and other non-need-based awards and non-need-based scholarships averaged $18,980 ($59,447 maximum). 29% of undergraduate students work part-time. The average financial indebtedness of the 2017 graduate was $33,319. The FAFSA code is 001710. The deadline for filing freshman financial aid applications for fall entry is March 1.

MACMURRAY COLLEGE C-3
www.mac.edu

Jacksonville, IL 62650	**(217) 479-7056** **(800) 252-7485**
Fax: (217) 291-0702	**Email: admiss@mac.edu**
Full-time: 267 men, 375 women	**Faculty:** 45; IIB, --$
Part-time: 15 men, 44 women	**Ph.D.s:** 62%
Graduate: n/av	**Student/Faculty:** 13 to 1
Year: semesters, summer session	**Tuition:** $26,100
Room & Board: $8925	**Freshman Class:** 1421 applied, 806 accepted, 186 enrolled
SAT: required **ACT:** 21	**CEEB CODE:** 1435
Application Deadline: rolling	**COMPETITIVE**

MacMurray College, founded in 1846, is a private liberal arts general education institution affiliated with the United Methodist Church. The figures given in the above capsule and in this profile are approximate. There are 2 undergraduate schools. In addition to regional accreditation, MacMurray has baccalaureate program accreditation with CSWE, CCNE, and NCACS. The 60-acre campus is in a small town in Jacksonville, Illinois, easy driving distance to St. Louis and Chicago.

STUDENT LIFE: 88% of undergraduates are from Illinois. Others are from 17 states, 3 foreign countries, and Canada. 90% are from public schools. 79% are White; 3% Hispanic; 11% African American; 1% American Indian/Alaska Native; 1% Foreign. 78% are Protestant; 18% Catholic. **Female To Male Ratio:** 1.5:1. The average age of freshmen is 19; all undergraduates, 22. 40% do not continue beyond their first year; 56% remain to graduate. **Housing:** 725 students can be accommodated in college housing, which includes dorms. On-campus housing is guaranteed for all 4 years. 54% of students live on campus. All students may keep cars.

FACULTY/CLASSROOMS: 42% of faculty are male; 58% are female. All teach undergraduates. No introductory courses are taught by graduate students. The average class size in an introductory lecture is 41; in a laboratory is 14; and in a regular course is 17.

PROGRAMS OF STUDY: MacMurray confers B.A., B.S., B.S.N., and B.S.W. degrees. Associate degrees are also awarded. Bachelor's degrees are awarded in BIOLOGICAL SCIENCE (biology/biological science), BUSINESS (accounting, business administration and management, management information systems, marketing/retailing/merchandising, and sports management), COMMUNICATIONS AND THE ARTS (art, dramatic arts, English, music, and Spanish), COMPUTER AND PHYSICAL SCIENCE (chemistry, computer science, mathematics, and physics), EDUCATION (education of the deaf and hearing impaired, elementary education, music education, physical education, science education, secondary education, and special education), ENGINEERING AND ENVIRONMENTAL DESIGN (preengineering), HEALTH PROFESSIONS (nursing, predentistry, premedicine, and preveterinary science), SOCIAL SCIENCE (criminal justice, history, interpreter for the deaf, liberal arts/general studies, philosophy, political science/government, prelaw, psychology, religion, social work, and youth ministry). Nursing, criminal justice, and homeland security are the strongest academically.

ACTIVITIES: 9% of men belong to 1 local and 2 national fraternities; 15% of women belong to 3 local sororities. There are 31 groups on campus, including art, bagpipe, band, cheerleading, choir, chorale, chorus, dance, drama, ethnic, international, LGBT, literary magazine, musical theater, newspaper, orchestra, pep band, photography, professional, religious, social, social service, student government, and yearbook. Popular campus events include Spring Formal, Sigma Tau Gamma Day, and Midnight Breakfasts. **Sports:** There are 9 intercollegiate sports for men and 8 for women, and 15 intramural sports for men and 15 for women. Facilities include a gym, basketball and volleyball courts, football and soccer fields, golf, tennis and outdoor basketball courts, a swimming pool, a weight room, wrestling room, and dance studios. **Graduates:** From July 1, 2016 to June 30, 2017, 115 bachelor's degrees were awarded. The most popular majors were social work (12%), nursing (10%), and psychology (10%). In an average class, 36% graduate in 4 years or less, 45% graduate in 5 years or less, and 52% graduate in 6 years or less. Of the 2016 graduating class, 15% were enrolled in graduate school within 6 months of graduation, and 90% were employed.

SERVICES: Counseling and information services are available, as is tutoring in every subject. There is remedial math, reading, and writing. The college provides services to visually and hearing impaired students through interpreters, readers, and note takers. **Library/Resources:** The library contains 1.8 million volumes, 28,093 microform items, and 1,085 audio/video tapes/CDs/DVDs, and subscribes to 130 periodicals, including electronic. Computerized library services include interlibrary loans, database searching, Internet access, and Wi-Fi capability. Special learning facilities include an art gallery. **Physically Challenged Students:** 90% of the campus is accessible. Facilities include wheelchair ramps, elevators, special parking, specially equipped restrooms, special class scheduling, and special housing. **Special:** The school has co-op programs in modern languages and international studies and cross-registration with 5 colleges through the West Central Illinois Foreign Language Consortium. A 3-2 engineering degree with Washington and Columbia Universities, a Washington semester, internships in all majors, work-study programs, dual majors, and pass/fail options are available. Students may study abroad in England, Germany, Japan, or Russia. There are 4 national honor societies, a freshman honors program, and 5 departmental honors programs. **Visiting:** There are regularly scheduled orientations for prospective students, including a financial aid conference, a tour, and faculty appointments. There are guides for informal visits; visitors may sit in on classes, and stay overnight. To schedule a visit, contact the Office of Admissions. **Campus Safety and Security:** Measures include security escort services. There are emergency telephones, lighted pathways/sidewalks, evening patrols, and evening sign-in at dorms.

REQUIREMENTS: The SAT or ACT is required. Applicants must be graduates of an accredited secondary school. The GED is accepted. Secondary school courses should include 4 years of English, 3 years of math, and 2 years each of science, foreign language, and social studies. MacMurray requires applicants to be in the upper 50% of their class. A GPA of 2.5 is required. AP and CLEP credits are accepted. Important factors in the admissions decision are advanced placement or honors courses, extracurricular activities record, and leadership record. To graduate, students must complete 120 semester hours with a minimum GPA of 2.0. All students must take 3 courses in rhetorical skills and a 3-course sequence on major ideas in Western civilization, as well as a course in

Diversity and the American Experience; and satisfy the requirements of the breadth component, a 16-hour distribution of nonmajor courses. They also must pass a proficiency exam in writing, given when students attain junior standing. **Procedure:** Freshmen are admitted to all sessions. Entrance exams should be taken in the spring of the junior year. There are deferred admissions and rolling admissions plans. Application deadlines are open. Notification is sent on a rolling basis. Applications are accepted online. **Transfer Students:** 101 transfer students enrolled in 2016-2017. Transfer students must have a minimum GPA of 2.0 in at least 28 transferable semester credits. Nursing applicants must have a GPA of 2.75 and a minimum score of 20 on the ACT. 30 of 120 credits required for the bachelor's degree must be completed at MacMurray. **International Students:** There are 8 international students enrolled. They must take the TOEFL. Some may be required to take the SAT or ACT with a minimum score of 950 (SAT) or 20 (ACT).

ADMISSIONS: 57% of the 2017-2018 applicants were accepted. The ACT scores were 50% below 12, 28% between 12 and 17, 15% between 18 and 23, 4% between 24 and 29, and 3% above 30. 28% of the current freshmen were in the top fifth of their class; 50% were in the top two fifths. 3 freshmen graduated first in their class. **Admissions Contact:** Kathryn Hall, Director of Admissions. Email: *admiss@mac.edu* Web: *www.mac.edu*

FINANCIAL AID: In 2017-2018, 98% of all full-time freshmen received some form of financial aid. 98% of all full-time freshmen received need-based aid. MacMurray College is a member of CSS. The FAFSA code is 001717. The deadline for filing freshman financial aid applications for fall entry is open.

MCKENDREE UNIVERSITY C-5

www.mckendree.edu

Lebanon, IL 62254 **(618) 537-6833**

Fax: (618) 537-6496	**Email:** inquiry@mckendree.edu
Full-time: 883 men, 937 women	**Faculty:** 105; IIA, --$
Part-time: 195 men, 327 women	**Ph.D.s:** 85%
Graduate: 208 men, 445 women	**Student/Faculty:** 14 to 1
Year: semesters, summer session	**Tuition:** $28,740
Room & Board: $9200	**Freshman Class:** 1904 applied, 1209 accepted, 362 enrolled
ACT: 24	**CEEB CODE:** 1456
Application Deadline: rolling	**COMPETITIVE+**

McKendree University, founded in 1828, is the oldest college in Illinois. It is a private liberal arts institution affiliated with the United Methodist Church, offering 54 majors, 46 minors, 6 graduate programs, and 2 doctorate programs. The figures given in the above capsule and in this profile are approximate. There are 4 undergraduate schools and 4 graduate schools. In addition to regional accreditation, MU has baccalaureate program accreditation with CAEP, NLN, IACBE, and CAAHEP. The 235-acre campus is in a suburban area in Lebanon, Illinois, 23 miles east of St. Louis.

STUDENT LIFE: 82% of undergraduates are from Illinois. Others are from 41 states, 24 foreign countries, and Canada. 68% are White; 13% African American; 7% race unknown; 4% Hispanic; 3% Foreign; 3% two or more races; 1% Asian American; 1% American Indian/Alaska Native. **Female To Male Ratio:** 1.3:1. The average age of freshmen is 18; all undergraduates, 20. 29% do not continue beyond their first year; 71% remain to graduate. **Housing:** 1200 students can be accommodated in college housing, which includes dorms and on-campus apartments. In addition, there are special-interest houses, residence halls, and apartment-style living. On-campus housing is guaranteed for all 4 years. 73% of students live on campus. Alcohol is not permitted. All students may keep cars.

FACULTY/CLASSROOMS: 41% of faculty are male; 59% are female. All teach undergraduates. No introductory courses are taught by graduate students. The average class size in an introductory lecture is 20; in a laboratory is 17; and in a regular course is 14.

PROGRAMS OF STUDY: McKendree confers B.A., B.S., B.B.A., B.F.A., B.M.E., B.S.Ed., and B.S.N. degrees. Master's and doctoral degrees are also awarded. Bachelor's degrees are awarded in AGRICULTURE (environmental studies), BIOLOGICAL SCIENCE (biology/biological science), BUSINESS (accounting, banking and finance, business administration and management, and marketing/retailing/merchandising), COMMUNICATIONS AND THE ARTS (art, dramatic arts, English, music, music business management, music history and appreciation, music performance, public relations, and speech/debate/rhetoric), COMPUTER AND PHYSICAL SCIENCE (chemistry, computer information systems, computer science, information sciences and systems, and mathematics), EDUCATION (art education, athletic training, business education, elementary education, global studies, middle school education, music education, physical education, and special education), HEALTH PROFESSIONS (health, medical laboratory technology, nursing, and occupational therapy), SOCIAL SCIENCE (biopsychology, criminal justice, economics, gerontology, history, international relations, international studies, philosophy, political science/government, psychology, religion, religious studies, religious music, social science, social work, and sociology). Business, education, and psychology are the strongest academically. Business, education, and nursing have the largest enrollments.

ACTIVITIES: 4% of men belong to 2 local and 1 national fraternities; 20% of women belong to 2 local and 1 national sororities. There are 86 groups on campus, including art, band, cheerleading, choir, chorale, chorus, communications, computers, dance, debate, drama, environmental, ethnic, film, forensics, honors, international, jazz band, LGBT, literary magazine, marching band, musical theater, newspaper, pep band, photography, political, professional, religious, social, social service, and student government. Popular campus events include Academic Excellence Celebration, Homecoming, McKendree Idol, Fall Festival, Model United Nations, and Midnight Breakfast. **Sports:** There are 17 intercollegiate sports for men and 16 for women. Facilities include a gym, an intramural gym, a fitness center, tennis courts, a student center with table tennis and billiards, an all-weather track, a football stadium, and playing fields for baseball, softball, basketball, bowling, cross country, fencing, golf, hockey, powerlifting, soccer, volleyball, wrestling, lacrosse, and co-ed bass fishing. The Sports and Permormance Center and Wrestling Center contain weight lifting equipment and a full-time strength and conditioning coach. The Rec Plex contains ice rinks, an aquatic center, an indoor walking track, workout space, and multiple group exercise rooms. **Graduates:** From July 1, 2016 to June 30, 2017, 701 bachelor's degrees were awarded. The most popular majors were business (34%), health professions/nursing (22%), and psychology (7%). In an average class, 33% graduate in 4 years or less, 52% graduate in 5 years or less, and 56% graduate in 6 years or less. Of the 2016 graduating class, 18% were enrolled in graduate school within 6 months of graduation, and 72% were employed.

SERVICES: Counseling and information services are available, as is tutoring in every subject. There is a reader service for the blind, and remedial reading and writing. **Library/Resources:** The library contains 140,000 volumes, 43,234 microform items, and 30,000 audio/video tapes/CDs/DVDs, and subscribes to 9,000 periodicals, including electronic. Computerized library services include interlibrary loans, database searching, Internet access, and Wi-Fi capability. Special learning facilities include an art gallery, the Russel E. and Fern M. Hettenhausen Center for the Arts, the Bothwell Chapel, and the McKendree Metro Rec Plex. **Physically Challenged Students:** Facilities include wheelchair ramps, elevators, special parking, specially equipped restrooms, special class scheduling, and lowered drinking fountains. **Special:** McKendree offers internships, work-study programs, study abroad in over 120 different locations across the globe, dual and student-designed majors, and nondegree study, as well as a 3-2 program in occupational therapy with Washington University in St. Louis. There are 12 national honor societies, a freshman honors program, and 1 departmental honors program. **Visiting:** There are regularly scheduled orientations for prospective students consisting of Preview Days, where faculty members and personnel from several departments answer questions. Student-led tours of the campus and various other events are also available. There are guides for informal visits; visitors may sit in on classes and stay overnight. To schedule a visit, contact the Admissions Office. **Campus Safety and Security:** Measures include 24-hour foot and vehicle patrol, an emergency notification system, and security escort services. There are shuttle buses, emergency telephones, lighted pathways/sidewalks, and controlled access to dorms/residences.

REQUIREMENTS: The ACT is required. Students must be high school graduates or submit the GED certificate. Completion of at least 15 units of high school work is recommended. A recommendation from the secondary school counselor is recommended. McKendree requires applicants to be in the upper 50% of their class. A GPA of 2.5 is required. AP and CLEP credits are accepted. Important factors in the admissions decision are advanced placement or honors courses, leadership record, and evidence of special talent. To graduate, students must complete 120 semester hours, with a minimum GPA of 2.0. The 51-credit-hour core curriculum includes 9 credits of social science; 7 of science; 6 of freshman English; 3 each of speech, math, ethics, philosophy or religion, history, cross-cultural studies, literature, fine or performing arts, and computer competency; and 1 to 2 of physical education. In addition, 2 writing-intensive courses must be taken. A thesis is required for biology majors seeking a B.S. degree. **Procedure:** Freshmen are admitted to all sessions. Entrance exams should be taken in the junior year. There is a rolling admissions plan. Application deadlines are open. Applications are accepted online. **Transfer Students:** Applicants must have a minimum 2.0 GPA from all colleges previously attended. 30 of 120 credits required for the bachelor's degree must be completed at MU. **International Students:** There are 30 international students enrolled. They must take the TOEFL with a minimum score of 520 on the paper-based TOEFL (PBT) or 70 on the Internet-based version (iBT). They must also take the SAT or ACT, scoring 20.

ADMISSIONS: 63% of the 2017-2018 applicants were accepted. The SAT scores for the 2017-2018 freshman class were: Critical Reading-- 56% below 500 and 44% between 500 and 599. Math-- 41% below 500, 54% between 500 and 599, and 5% between 600 and 699. Writing-- 79% below 500, 15% between 500 and 599, and 5% between 600 and 699. The ACT scores were 27% below 12, 34% between 12 and 17, 27% between 18 and 23, 4% between 24 and 29, and 7% above 30. 34% of the current freshmen were in the top fifth of their class; 71% were in the top two fifths. 97 freshmen graduated first in their class. **Admissions Contact:** Chris Hall, Vice President for Admission and Financial Aid. Email: *inquiry@mckendree.edu* Web: *www.mckendree.edu*

FINANCIAL AID: In 2017-2018, 100% of all full-time freshmen received some form of financial aid. 94% of all full-time freshmen received need-based aid. The average freshman award was $25,062. Need-based scholarships or need-based grants averaged $20,705; need-based self-help aid (loans and jobs) averaged $4,926; non-need-based athletic scholarships averaged $11,910; and other non-need-based awards and non-need-based scholarships averaged $12,956. 23% of undergraduate students work part-time. The average financial indebtedness of the 2017 graduate was $27,378. The FAFSA code is 001722. The priority date for freshman financial aid applications for fall entry is March 1.

MILLIKIN UNIVERSITY — D-3

www.millikin.edu

Decatur, IL 62522 — (217) 424-6210, (800) 373-7733

Fax: (217) 425-4669 — **Email:** admis@millikin.edu

Full-time: 786 men, 1039 women	**Faculty:** 141; IIB, --$
Part-time: 39 men, 107 women	**Ph.D.s:** 80%
Graduate: 32 men, 53 women	**Student/Faculty:** 13 to 1
Year: semesters, summer session	**Tuition:** $31,824
Room & Board: $10,334	**Freshman Class:** 3431 applied, 2216 accepted, 474 enrolled
SAT: required **ACT:** 23	**CEEB CODE:** 1470
Application Deadline: rolling	**COMPETITIVE**

Millikin University is an independent, four-year university with undergraduate offering undergraduate programs in arts and sciences, fine arts, professional studies and business, graduate studies in business administration and nursing, accelerated adult learning programs, and master's and doctorate degree programs. The signature of a Millikin University education is a unique experience called Performance Learning. When James Millikin founded the university in 1901, he did so based upon the idea of combining theory and practice. While this was a radical idea at the time, today, we know that practice is not enough. Today's students must perform their knowledge in order to be truly prepared for life after college. Millikin's students participate in various classes, programs, projects and performances to gain experience and the confidence to succeed. There are 4 undergraduate schools and 2 graduate schools. In addition to regional accreditation, MU has baccalaureate program accreditation with ACBSP, NASM, CANAEP, CCNE, and CAATE. The 75-acre campus is in a suburban area 180 miles southwest of Chicago and 130 miles northeast of St. Louis. Including any residence halls, there are 31 buildings.

STUDENT LIFE: 84% of undergraduates are from Illinois. Others are from 33 states, 24 foreign countries, and Canada. 91% are from public schools. 71% are White; 6% Hispanic; 4% two or more races; 3% Foreign; 14% African American; 1% Asian American; 1% race unknown. **Female To Male Ratio:** 1.4:1. The average age of freshmen is 18; all undergraduates, 21. 28% do not continue beyond their first year; 61% remain to graduate. **Housing:** 1083 students can be accommodated in college housing, which includes married student dorms and on-campus apartments. In addition, there are special-interest houses, fraternity houses, sorority houses, living-learning communities, and single-gender floors. On-campus housing is available on a first-come and first-served basis. 58% of students live on campus. Upperclassmen may keep cars.

FACULTY/CLASSROOMS: 46% of faculty are male; 54% are female. All teach undergraduates. No introductory courses are taught by graduate students. The average class size in an introductory lecture is 21; in a laboratory is 13; and in a regular course is 17.

PROGRAMS OF STUDY: MU confers B.A., B.S., B.F.A., B.M., and B.S.N. degrees. Master's and doctoral degrees are also awarded. Bachelor's degrees are awarded in AGRICULTURE (environmental studies), BIOLOGICAL SCIENCE (biochemistry, biology/adolescence education, biology/biological science, and molecular biology), BUSINESS (accounting, business administration and management, entrepreneurial studies, international business management, management science, marketing/retailing/merchandising, organizational leadership and management, recreational facilities management, and sports management), COMMUNICATIONS AND THE ARTS (acting, art, communications, digital media, dramatic arts, English, journalism, music, music business management, music performance, musical theater, performing arts, piano/organ, public relations, Spanish, sports communication, studio art, theatre arts, theater design, theatre production, theater management, visual and performing arts, and voice), COMPUTER AND PHYSICAL SCIENCE (actuarial mathematics, chemistry, chemistry/adolescence education, information sciences and systems, mathematics, and physics), EDUCATION (art education, athletic training, early childhood education, education, elementary education, English education, foreign languages education, mathematics education, music education, physical education, secondary education, and social science education), ENGINEERING AND ENVIRONMENTAL DESIGN (commercial art, computer graphics, and preengineering), HEALTH PROFESSIONS (allied health, art therapy, health and physical activity, nursing, predentistry, premedicine, preoptometry, prepharmacy, pre-physician assistant, prephysical therapy, and preveterinary science), SOCIAL SCIENCE (ethics, politics, social policy, history, human services, interdisciplinary studies, philosophy, political science/government, prelaw, psychology, and sociology). Music, and theater are the strongest academically. Nursing, music, and theater have the largest enrollments.

ACTIVITIES: 23% of men belong to 5 national fraternities; 27% of women belong to 6 national sororities. There are 90 groups on campus, including art, band, cheerleading, chess, choir, chorale, chorus, computers, dance, debate, drama, drill team, environmental, ethnic, film, honors, international, jazz band, LGBT, literary magazine, musical theater, newspaper, opera, orchestra, pep band, photography, political, professional, radio and TV, religious, social, social service, student government, and symphony. Popular campus events include Homecoming, Fall Family Weekend, Millipalooza, University Event (big name entertainment), Halloween in the Halls, and Cookie Party. **Sports:** There are 10 intercollegiate sports for men and 9 for women, and 8 intramural sports for men and 8 for women. Facilities include indoor sports center with a track, and soccer, basketball/volleyball courts, batting cages, golf practice area, a climbing wall, aerobic and dance areas, and a fitness/wellness center, a pool, a field house with regulation-sized basketball courts, a football field encircled by 8-lane all-weather track, outdoor soccer fields, practice fields, and tennis courts.**Graduates:** From July 1, 2016 to June 30, 2017, 453 bachelor's degrees were awarded. The most popular majors were business/marketing (24%), visual and performing arts (17%), and health professions (12%). In an average class, 49% graduate in 4 years or less, 59% graduate in 5 years or less, and 60% graduate in 6 years or less. Of the 2016 graduating class, 19% were enrolled in graduate school within 6 months of graduation, and 79% were employed.

SERVICES: Counseling and information services are available, as is tutoring in most subjects. There is a reader service for the blind. Math and writing centers, workshops on various topics are available. **Library/ Resources:** The library contains 167,802 volumes, 9,000 microform items, and 11,690 audio/video tapes/CDs/DVDs, and subscribes to 53,000 periodicals including electronic. Computerized library services include interlibrary loans, database searching, Internet access, and Wi-Fi capability. Special learning facilities include a radio station, 32-track recording studio, computer imaging center, art museum and galleries, observatory with 20" reflecting telescope, 280-seat proscenium theater, 90-seat experimental space for student-directed productions, 3D arts building; student-owned and operated art gallery, business incubator, printing press, record label and music publishing company, and a theatre company. **Physically Challenged Students:** 66% of the campus is accessible. Facilities include wheelchair ramps, elevators, special parking, specially equipped restrooms, special class scheduling, lowered drinking fountains, and special housing. **Special:** Millikin offers internships, a Washington semester through American University, study abroad in 28 countries, student-designed majors, 3-2 engineering dual degrees with Washington University and University of Missouri-Kansas City, credit by exam, and pass/fail options. Students may study multiple majors of their choice; including dual degree programs. There are preprofessional programs in engineering, law, optometry, dentistry, medicine, veterinary science, occupational therapy, medical technology, physical therapy, chiropractic, physician's assistant, and pharmacy. Students are also offered a United Nations semester at Drew University and can benefit from affiliate agreements with programs such as the Institute for the International Education of Students, Paris School of Business, International Teacher-Scholars Program, Tunghai University and the Chicago Center for Urban Life and Culture semester. There are 13 national honor societies, a freshman honors program, and 20 departmental honors programs. **Visiting:** There are regularly scheduled orientations for prospective students, including meet with students, faculty, coaches, and staff, tour the campus facilities, and curriculum, honors, housing, and financial aid discussions/presentations. There is also an opportunity for students to audition or have portfolios reviewed. There are guides for informal visits, visitors may sit in on classes, and stay overnight. To schedule a visit, contact the Office of Admission. **Campus Safety and Security:** Measures include 24-hour foot and vehicle patrol, emergency notification system, and security escort services. There are shuttle buses, emergency telephones, lighted pathways/sidewalks, and controlled access to dorms/ residences.

REQUIREMENTS: The SAT or ACT is required. Applicants should be graduates of an accredited secondary school or have a GED. They should be prepared with 4 units of English, 3 units each of math and science, and 2 units each of foreign language, social studies, and history. An audition is required for music-theater, music, or theater majors. A portfolio is required for art majors. Millikin requires applicants to be in the upper 50% of their class. A GPA of 2.5 is required. AP and CLEP credits are accepted. Important factors in the admissions decision are recommendations by school officials, advanced placement or honors courses, and leadership record. Requirements for graduation include courses in writing, math, fine arts, natural sciences, and oral communication. Sequential interdisciplinary requirements include first-year seminar, critical writing, reading, and research 1 and 2, U.S. culture studies, U.S. social structures, and global issues. Nonsequential requirements include quantitative reasoning, natural science with a lab, oral communication, creative arts, and 2 courses in international cultures and structures. The minimum GPA is 2.0 (higher for some programs); additional requirements for specific programs must be met. Students must complete a minimum of 124 credits (or more for some programs) with a minimum of 39 credits earned in courses numbered 300 or above; at least 12 credits must be in the major department or area. **Procedure:** Freshmen are admitted fall, spring, and summer. Entrance exams should be taken by May 1. There are deferred admissions and rolling admissions plans. Application deadlines are open. Notification is sent on a rolling basis. Applications are accepted on-line. **Transfer Students:** 122 transfer students enrolled in 2016-2017. Applicants are required to provide official transcripts from previous institutions and asked to submit ACT/SAT scores. Applicants who are in good standing at the previous institution and who have earned at least a C average in all college study previously attempted will be favorably considered for admission (additional requirements for specific programs). 33 of 124 credits required for the bachelor's degree must be completed at Millikin. **International Students:** There are 52 international students enrolled. They must take the TOEFL with a minimum score of 550 on the paper-based TOEFL (PBT) or 79 on the Internet-based version (iBT).

ADMISSIONS: 64% of the 2017-2018 applicants were accepted. The ACT scores were 12% between 12 and 17, 49% between 18 and 23, 32% between 24 and 29, and 7% above 30. 30% of the current freshmen were in the top fifth of their class; 57% were in the top two fifths. 9 freshmen graduated first in their class. **Admissions Contact:** Kevin McIntyre, Dean of Admission. Email: *admis@millikin.edu* Web: *www.millikin.edu*

FINANCIAL AID: In 2017-2018, 100% of all full-time freshmen received some form of financial aid. 88% of all full-time freshmen received need-based aid. The average freshman award was $24,230. Need-based scholarships or need-based grants averaged $9,192; need-based self-help aid (loans and jobs) averaged $4,533; and other non-need-based awards and non-need-based scholarships averaged $13,705. 48% of undergraduate students work part-time. The average financial indebtedness of the 2017 graduate was $34,225. The FAFSA code is 001724. The priority date for freshman financial aid applications for fall entry is January 6.

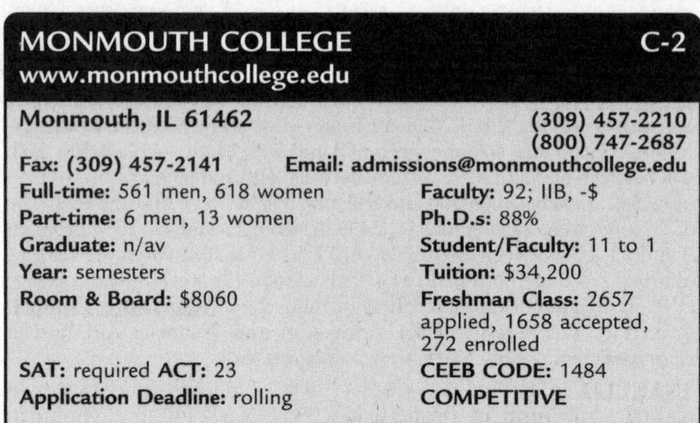

MONMOUTH COLLEGE C-2

www.monmouthcollege.edu

Monmouth, IL 61462 (309) 457-2210
(800) 747-2687
Fax: (309) 457-2141 Email: admissions@monmouthcollege.edu

Full-time: 561 men, 618 women	**Faculty:** 92; IIB, -$
Part-time: 6 men, 13 women	**Ph.D.s:** 88%
Graduate: n/av	**Student/Faculty:** 11 to 1
Year: semesters	**Tuition:** $34,200
Room & Board: $8060	**Freshman Class:** 2657 applied, 1658 accepted, 272 enrolled
SAT: required **ACT:** 23	**CEEB CODE:** 1484
Application Deadline: rolling	**COMPETITIVE**

Monmouth College, founded in 1853, is a selective, residential, private liberal arts and sciences college. In addition to regional accreditation, MC has baccalaureate program accreditation with ACS. The 112-acre campus is in a small town in west-central Illinois, 20 miles east of the Mississippi River, and 45 miles south of Rock Island and Moline. Including any residence halls, there are 39 buildings.

STUDENT LIFE: 89% of undergraduates are from Illinois. Others are from 26 states, 22 foreign countries, and Canada. 61% are White; 13% Hispanic; 9% African American; 7% Foreign; 5% race unknown; 2% Asian American; 2% two or more races; 1% American Indian/Alaska Native. 53% claim no religious affiliation; 30% Protestant; 17% Catholic. **Female To Male Ratio:** 1.1:1. The average age of freshmen is 18; all undergraduates, 20. 26% do not continue beyond their first year; 56% remain to graduate. **Housing:** 1435 students can be accommodated in college housing, which includes dorms and on-campus apartments. In addition, there are honors houses, special-interest houses, fraternity houses, and sorority houses. On-campus housing is guaranteed for all 4 years. 92% of students live on campus. All students may keep cars.

FACULTY/CLASSROOMS: 56% of faculty are male; 44% are female. All teach undergraduates, and all do research. No introductory courses are taught by graduate students. The average class size in an introductory lecture is 22; in a laboratory is 12; and in a regular course is 15.

PROGRAMS OF STUDY: MC confers B.A. degrees. Bachelor's degrees are awarded in BIOLOGICAL SCIENCE (biochemistry and biology/ biological science), BUSINESS (accounting, business administration and management, and international business management), COMMUNICATIONS AND THE ARTS (art, classics, communications, dramatic arts, English, French, Greek, Latin, music, and Spanish), COMPUTER AND PHYSICAL SCIENCE (chemistry, computer programming, computer science, mathematics, and physics), EDUCATION (elementary education, physical education, and secondary education), ENGINEERING AND ENVIRONMENTAL DESIGN (environmental science), HEALTH PROFESSIONS (exercise science), SOCIAL SCIENCE (anthropology, biopsychology, economics, history, international studies, philosophy, political science/government, psychology, religion, and sociology). English, classics (Greek and Latin), and history are the strongest academically. Business, communications, and psychology have the largest enrollments.

ACTIVITIES: 18% of men belong to 4 national fraternities; 34% of women belong to 3 national sororities. There are 70 groups on campus, including art, bagpipe, band, cheerleading, chess, choir, chorale, chorus, computers, dance, debate, drama, environmental, ethnic, film, forensics, honors, international, jazz band, LGBT, literary magazine, marching band, musical theater, newspaper, orchestra, pep band, photography, political, professional, radio and TV, religious, social, social service, and student government. Popular campus events include Homecoming, Scots Day (Founders Day), and Parents Weekend. **Sports:** There are 11 intercollegiate sports for men and 11 for women, and 14 intramural sports for men and 14 for women. Facilities include the athletic center, a gym, indoor and outdoor track, all-purpose indoor courts, indoor batting cages, tennis courts, a weight room, fitness/wellness center, a dance studio, football and soccer fields, baseball and softball fields, sand volleyball court, and a climbing wall. **Graduates:** From July 1, 2016 to June 30, 2017, 269 bachelor's degrees were awarded. The most popular majors were business management (20%), communication/journalism (14%), and social sciences (10%). In an average class, 48% graduate in 4 years or less, 55% graduate in 5 years or less, and 56% graduate in 6 years or less. Of the 2016 graduating class, 26% were enrolled in graduate school within 6 months of graduation, and 74% were employed.

SERVICES: Counseling and information services are available, as is tutoring in most subjects, such as accounting, biology, chemistry, education, math/statistics, Spanish, French, business/economics, psychology, and sociology/anthropology. There is a reader service for the blind, and remedial math, reading, and writing. Individualized academic-support services to students who seek, assistance include one-on-one tutoring and small-group and group tutoring **Library/Resources:** The library contains 356,564 volumes, 237,283 microform items, and 12,511 audio/video tapes/CDs/DVDs, and subscribes to 28,190 periodicals, including electronic. Computerized library services include interlibrary loans, database searching, Internet access, and Wi-Fi capability. Special learning facilities include an art gallery, a planetarium, a radio station, a TV station, a prairie-habitat biology field station, Spring Grove Prairie, a freshwater pond for field research on amphibians and reptiles, an educational garden, a 16.5-acre Le Suer Nature Preserve, the James Christie Shields Collection of Art and Antiquities collection housed in the Len G. Everett Galleries, the Lewis L. Gould U.S. First Ladies letter collection, the regions largest collection of Western Illinois Native American artifacts and archeology lab, and the Hewes Library which holds the federal government documents repository. **Physically Challenged Students:** 98% of the campus is accessible. Facilities include wheelchair ramps, elevators, special parking, specially equipped restrooms, special class scheduling, lowered drinking fountains, lowered telephones, and special housing. **Special:** Monmouth has agreements with Rush University, Chicago, for nursing, occupational therapy, and medical technology; and 5- and 6-year coordinated degree partnerships (master's) with Case Western Reserve (engineering), the University of Southern California (engineering), and Creighton University (atmospheric science). Students have the opportunity to study in more than 25 countries in Europe, Asia, Central and South America, and Africa, as well as in programs within the United States. All Associated Colleges of the Midwest (ACM) programs, as well as internships, a Washington semester, and dual and student-designed majors, are available. There are 13 national honor societies, a freshman honors program, and 20 departmental honors programs. **Visiting:** There are regularly scheduled orientations for prospective students, including tours, admissions and financial aid discussions, faculty appointments, lunch and entertainment, and a talk with the president. There are guides for informal visits; visitors may sit in on classes and stay overnight. To schedule a visit, contact Maria Godina in Admissions. **Campus Safety and Security:** Measures include 24-hour foot and vehicle patrol, an emergency notification system, self-defense education, and security escort services. There are shuttle buses, emergency telephones, lighted pathways/sidewalks, and controlled access to dorms/residences, key cards are required for entrance to all residence halls.

REQUIREMENTS: The SAT or ACT is required. A score of at least 22 on the ACT is highly recommended. Applicants must be graduates of accredited high schools with a GPA of 2.5. We strongly recommend that applicants have completed 4 years of English, 2 years each of math, social studies, foreign language, and science, 1 year of lab, and history. The GED is accepted. AP credits are accepted. Important factors in the admissions decision are advanced placement or honors courses, evidence of special talent, and extracurricular activities record. To graduate, all students must complete 32 course credits (equivalent to 128 credit hours) with a minimum GPA of 2.0. A major program must be completed with a minimum of C in all courses. Students must also fulfill 9 courses within the general education program, including an art course, a science course with lab and language course (s). Students must successfully complete the integrated studies curriculum (1 course per year) within the general education program. A topical major (of the students design) is also possible. **Procedure:** Freshmen are admitted in the fall and spring. Entrance exams should be taken by the spring of the junior year. There are early admissions, deferred admissions, and rolling admissions plans. Application deadlines are open. Notification is sent on a rolling basis. Applications are accepted online. **Transfer Students:** Students must have a minimum GPA of 2.5. A satisfactory score of at least 19 on the ACT is recommended. 64 of 128 credits required for the bachelor's degree must be completed at MC. **International Students:** There are 54 international students enrolled. They must also take the SAT or ACT.

ADMISSIONS: 62% of the 2017-2018 applicants were accepted. The ACT scores were 5% between 12 and 17, 55% between 18 and 23, 33% between 24 and 29, and 7% above 30. 27% of the current freshmen were in the top fifth of their class; 56% were in the top two fifths. **Admissions Contact:** Trent Gilbert, VP Enrollment Management. Email: *admissions@monmouthcollege.edu* Web: *www.monmouthcollege.edu*

FINANCIAL AID: In 2017-2018, 100% of all full-time freshmen received some form of financial aid. 94% of all full-time freshmen received need-based aid. The average freshman award was $34,600. Need-based scholarships or need-based grants averaged $26,884; need-based self-help aid (loans and jobs) averaged $4,777; other non-need-based awards and non-need-based scholarships averaged $3,241; and $2,485 from other forms of aid. 51% of undergraduate students work part-time. The average financial indebtedness of the 2017 graduate was $29,238. The FAFSA code is 001725. The priority date for freshman financial aid applications for fall entry is February 1. The deadline for filing freshman financial aid applications for fall entry is May 1.

NATIONAL LOUIS UNIVERSITY *(The complete profile is made available exclusively on our website, www.barronspac.com)*

NORTH CENTRAL COLLEGE — E-2

www.northcentralcollege.edu

Naperville, IL 60540	**(630) 637-5800** **(800) 411-1861**
Fax: (630) 637-5819	**Email: admissions@noctrl.edu**
Full-time: 1091 men, 1469 women	**Faculty:** 130; IIA, av$
Part-time: 90 men, 105 women	**Ph.D.s:** 89%
Graduate: 140 men, 147 women	**Student/Faculty:** 20 to 1
Year: quarters, summer session	**Tuition:** $37,054
Room & Board: $11,658	**Freshman Class:** 3987 applied, 2401 accepted, 552 enrolled
ACT: 24	**CEEB CODE:** 1555
Application Deadline: February 20	**COMPETITIVE+**

North Central College, founded in 1861, is a private comprehensive liberal arts institution affiliated with the United Methodist Church. The college is highly selective, primarily residential, and primarily full-time undergraduate. There is 1 undergraduate school and 1 graduate school. In addition to regional accreditation, NCC has baccalaureate program accreditation with CAATE and ACS. The 64-acre campus is in a suburban area 30 miles west of Chicago. Including any residence halls, there are 42 buildings.

STUDENT LIFE: 93% of undergraduates are from Illinois. Others are from 30 states, 22 foreign countries, and Canada. 90% are from public schools. 8% are Hispanic; 79% White; 4% African American; 2% Asian American; 1% Foreign. 56% are Protestant; 34% Catholic. **Female To Male Ratio:** 1.3:1. The average age of freshmen is 18; all undergraduates, 21. 20% do not continue beyond their first year; 66% remain to graduate. **Housing:** 1537 students can be accommodated in college housing, which includes dorms, on-campus apartments, off-campus apartments, and substance free housing. On-campus housing is available on a lottery system for upperclassmen. 54% of students live on campus. All students may keep cars.

FACULTY/CLASSROOMS: 53% of faculty are male; 47% are female. All teach undergraduates. No introductory courses are taught by graduate students. The average class size in an introductory lecture is 24; in a laboratory is 20; and in a regular course is 22.

PROGRAMS OF STUDY: NCC confers B.A. and B.S. degrees. Master's degrees are also awarded. Bachelor's degrees are awarded in BIOLOGICAL SCIENCE (biochemistry and biology/biological science), BUSI-

NESS (accounting, business administration and management, finance, human resources, international business management, marketing/retailing/merchandising, and sports management), COMMUNICATIONS AND THE ARTS (art history, art, broadcasting, Chinese, communications, English, English literature, English writing, French, German, Japanese, jazz, journalism, music, Spanish, speech/debate/rhetoric, studio art, and theatre arts), COMPUTER AND PHYSICAL SCIENCE (actuarial science, applied mathematics, chemistry, computer science, mathematics, and physics), EDUCATION (art education, athletic training, elementary education, music education, and secondary education), ENGINEERING AND ENVIRONMENTAL DESIGN (graphic arts technology and preengineering), HEALTH PROFESSIONS (exercise science, nuclear medical technology, predentistry, premedicine, preveterinary science, and radiation therapy), SOCIAL SCIENCE (anthropology, classical/ancient civilization, East Asian studies, economics, history, philosophy, political science/government, prelaw, psychology, religion, social science, and sociology). Business and education have the largest enrollment.

ACTIVITIES: There are no fraternities or sororities. There are 60 groups on campus, including art, band, cheerleading, choir, chorale, chorus, dance, drama, environmental, ethnic, forensics, honors, international, jazz band, LGBT, literary magazine, musical theater, newspaper, pep band, photography, political, professional, radio and TV, religious, social, social service, and student government. Popular campus events include Springfest, Winter Comedy Series, and Honors Day. **Sports:** There are 10 intercollegiate sports for men and 10 for women, and 12 intramural sports for men and 12 for women. Facilities include indoor and outdoor tracks, a recreation center, a weight room, football and baseball stadiums, soccer fields, an swimming pool, tennis courts, an athletic training facility, and a human performance lab. **Graduates:** From July 1, 2016 to June 30, 2017, 582 bachelor's degrees were awarded. The most popular majors were psychology (7%), marketing (6%), and elementary education (6%). In an average class, 1% graduate in 3 years or less, 57% graduate in 4 years or less, 66% graduate in 5 years or less, and 68% graduate in 6 years or less.

SERVICES: Counseling and information services are available, as is tutoring in most subjects. There is a reader service for the blind, and remedial math. **Library/Resources:** The library contains 138,968 volumes, 105,494 microform items, and 4,405 audio/video tapes/CDs/DVDs, and subscribes to 11,821 periodicals, including electronic. Computerized library services include interlibrary loans, database searching, and Internet access. Special learning facilities include an art gallery, aradio station, a foreign language lab, an academic support services center, and a writing center. **Physically Challenged Students:** 90% of the campus is accessible. Facilities include wheelchair ramps, elevators, special parking, specially equipped restrooms, special class scheduling, lowered drinking fountains, lowered telephones, and special housing. **Special:** North Central offers co-op programs in radiation therapy, nuclear medicine technology, and chemical microscopy; cross-registration with Benedictine University and Aurora University; a Washington semester; and study abroad. Internships in most subject areas, a 3-2 engineering degree with the Universities of Minnesota and Illinios at Urbana-Champaign, experiential credit, and nondegree study are available. Dual majors, student-designed majors, and 5-year integrated bachelors/masters degree programs are available. There are 18 national honor societies, a freshman honors program, and 14 departmental honors programs. **Visiting:** There are regularly scheduled orientations for prospective students, including the opportunity to hear a presentation about academic programs, student life, admission guidelines, and financial aid. Campus tours, faculty presentations, and coaches are also available. There are guides for informal visits,; visitors may sit in on classes and stay overnight. To schedule a visit, contact the Office of Admissions. **Campus Safety and Security:** Measures include 24-hour foot and vehicle patrol, emergency notification system, self-defense education, and security escort services. There are emergency telephones, lighted pathways/sidewalks, and controlled access to dorms/residences.

REQUIREMENTS: The SAT or ACT is required, with a minimum of 20 or 940 on the SAT. Minimum requirements also include a GPA of at least 2.5 and involvement in the school and/or community. An admission essay and/or admission interview may be recommended. The GED is accepted. The recommended secondary school courses are 4 years of English and 3 years each of math, science, social science, and foreign language. AP and CLEP credits are accepted. All students must complete a general education core, including 9 hours in humanities and fine arts, 9 hours in social sciences, 6.5 hours in life and physical sciences, 3 to 6 hours in composition, and 3 hours each in speech communication and math. All freshman must complete an interdisciplinary course. In addition, all students take an intercultural seminar, a leadership, ethics, and values seminar, and a course in religion and ethics. A GPA of 2.0 and a total of 120 credit hours are required for graduation, with 27 to 51 credits taken in the major. Students in the College Scholars program must complete an Honor Thesis. **Procedure:** Freshmen are admitted to all sessions. Entrance exams should be taken in the spring of the junior year or the fall of the senior year. There are deferred admissions and rolling admissions plans. The fall 2017 application fee was $25. Applications are accepted online. **Transfer Students:** 360 transfer students enrolled in 2016-2017. Applicants need a minimum 2.5 transferable GPA or better and 27 transferrable semester hours. If they have not earned 27 transferrable hours, their high school transcripts and ACT/SAT scores are also considered. Students can be considered for admission with a college grade point average of 2.25 or above. 30 of 120 credits required for the bachelor's degree must be completed at NCC. **International Students:** There are 28 international students enrolled. They must take the TOEFL with a minimum score of 520 on the paper-based TOEFL (PBT) or 68 on the Internet-based version (iBT). Students must take the IELTS.

ADMISSIONS: 60% of the 2017-2018 applicants were accepted. The ACT scores were 11% below 12, 30% between 12 and 17, 31% between 18 and 23, 15% between 24 and 29, and 13% above 30. 47% of the current freshmen were in the top fifth of their class; 78% were in the top two fifths. 5 freshmen graduated first in their class. **Admissions Contact:** Marty Sauer, Dean of Admission and Financial Aid. Email: *admissions@noctrl.edu* Web: *www.northcentralcollege.edu*

FINANCIAL AID: In 2017-2018, 99% of all full-time freshmen received some form of financial aid. 80% of all full-time freshmen received need-based aid. The average freshman award was $28,066. Need-based scholarships or need-based grants averaged $6,140; need-based self-help aid (loans and jobs) averaged $2,418; other non-need-based awards and non-need-based scholarships averaged $12,966; and $6,542 from other forms of aid. The average financial indebtedness of the 2017 graduate was $25,644. The college's own financial statement is required. The FAFSA code is 001734. Check with the school for current application deadlines.

NORTH PARK UNIVERSITY — E-2

www.northpark.edu

Chicago, IL 60625

(773) 244-5500
(800) 888-6728
Email: admissions@northpark.edu

Full-time: 699 men, 1070 women	**Faculty:** 108
Part-time: 158 men, 297 women	**Ph.D.s:** 90%
Graduate: 322 men, 683 women	**Student/Faculty:** 18 to 1
Year: semesters, summer session	**Tuition:** $27,090
Room & Board: $8770	**Freshman Class:** 1864 applied, 1618 accepted, 425 enrolled
SAT CR/M: 530/500 **ACT:** 22	**CEEB CODE:** 1556
Application Deadline: June 1	**COMPETITIVE**

North Park University, founded in 1891, is a private comprehensive university affiliated with the Evangelical Covenant Church offering undergraduate and graduate education liberal arts and professional and theological programs. There are 6 undergraduate schools and 5 graduate schools. In addition to regional accreditation, North Park has baccalaureate program accreditation with NLN, ATS, CCNE, IACBE, and NASM. The 30-acre campus is in an urban area 10 miles northwest of downtown Chicago. Including any residence halls, there are 30 buildings.

STUDENT LIFE: 66% of undergraduates are from Illinois. Others are from 40 states, 28 foreign countries, and Canada. 8% are African American; 6% Asian American; 6% Foreign; 58% White; 11% Hispanic. 33% are Protestant; 20% Catholic; 20% claim no religious affiliation. **Female To Male Ratio:** 1.7:1. The average age of freshmen is 18; all undergraduates, 21. 23% do not continue beyond their first year; 58% remain to graduate. **Housing:** 1130 students can be accommodated in college housing, which includes dorms, on-campus apartments, and off-campus apartments. In addition, there are special-interest houses. On-campus housing is guaranteed for all 4 years. 50% of students commute. Alcohol is not permitted. Upperclassmen may keep cars.

FACULTY/CLASSROOMS: 47% of faculty are male; 53% are female. All

teach undergraduates. No introductory courses are taught by graduate students. The average class size in an introductory lecture is 25; in a laboratory is 25; and in a regular course is 18.

PROGRAMS OF STUDY: North Park confers B.A., B.S., B.Mus., B.S.N., B.G.S., and B.M.E. degrees. Master's and doctoral degrees are also awarded. Bachelor's degrees are awarded in BIOLOGICAL SCIENCE (biology/biological science), BUSINESS (accounting, banking and finance, business administration and management, international business management, and marketing/retailing/merchandising), COMMUNICATIONS AND THE ARTS (advertising, communications, English, French, music, music theory and composition, Scandinavian languages, and Spanish), COMPUTER AND PHYSICAL SCIENCE (chemistry, mathematics, and physics), EDUCATION (athletic training, early childhood education, elementary education, and secondary education), ENGINEERING AND ENVIRONMENTAL DESIGN (environmental science), HEALTH PROFESSIONS (exercise science, medical laboratory technology, nursing, physical therapy, predentistry, and premedicine), SOCIAL SCIENCE (African studies, anthropology, biblical studies, criminal justice, economics, French studies, history, international relations, philosophy, political science/government, prelaw, psychology, sociology, and youth ministry). Sciences, nursing, and education are the strongest academically. Business has the largest enrollment.

ACTIVITIES: There are no fraternities or sororities. There are 25 groups on campus, including art, band, cheerleading, choir, chorale, chorus, communications, computers, drama, environmental, ethnic, honors, international, jazz band, literary magazine, musical theater, newspaper, opera, orchestra, pep band, photography, political, professional, religious, social, social service, student government, symphony, and yearbook. Popular campus events include dances, concerts, and film festivals. **Sports:** There are 7 intercollegiate sports for men and 8 for women, and 5 intramural sports for men and 5 for women. Facilities include football, baseball, track, and soccer fields, tennis courts, a weight room, a gym, and a fitness center. **Graduates:** From July 1, 2016 to June 30, 2017, 481 bachelor's degrees were awarded. The most popular majors were business and marketing (23%), health and related programs (22%), and communication (8%). In an average class, 39% graduate in 4 years or less, 52% graduate in 5 years or less, and 58% graduate in 6 years or less.

SERVICES: Counseling and information services are available, as is tutoring in every subject. There is a reader service for the blind, and remedial math, reading, and writing. An extended orientation program is available. **Library/Resources:** The library contains 225,000 volumes, 93,000 microform items, and 6,500 audio/video tapes/CDs/DVDs, and subscribes to 995 periodicals, including electronic. Computerized library services include interlibrary loans, database searching, Internet access, and Wi-Fi capability. Special learning facilities include an art gallery. **Physically Challenged Students:** 90% of the campus is accessible. Facilities include wheelchair ramps, elevators, special parking, specially equipped restrooms, lowered drinking fountains, lowered telephones, and special housing. **Special:** Opportunities are provided for a co-op program in occupational therapy, internships, work-study, a Washington semester, 3-2 engineering degrees, accelerated degree programs in organization management and nursing, credit by examination, dual majors, student-designed majors, B.A.-B.S. degrees, pass/fail options, and study abroad. There are 6 national honor societies, a freshman honors program, and 5 departmental honors programs. **Visiting:** There are regularly scheduled orientations for prospective students. There are guides for informal visits; visitors may sit in on classes and stay overnight. To schedule a visit, contact the Campus Visit Counselor at (773) 244-5511. **Campus Safety and Security:** Measures include 24-hour foot and vehicle patrol, an emergency notification system, self-defense education, and security escort services. There are emergency telephones, lighted pathways/sidewalks, and controlled access to dorms/residences.

REQUIREMENTS: The SAT or ACT and ACT Writing Test are recommended. Graduation from an accredited secondary school is required; a GED will be accepted. Students should have completed coursework in a foreign language, 4 years of English, and 3 years each of math, science, and social studies. A recommendation from a teacher is required. An essay is required. An interview is recommended and sometimes required. A GPA of 2.8 is required. AP and CLEP credits are accepted. Important factors in the admissions decision are evidence of special talent, personality/intangible qualities, and extracurricular activities record. Students must successfully complete 120 semester hours with a minimum 2.0 GPA. The required number of hours in the major varies. Students must meet a general education requirement of 46 semester hours. **Procedure:** Freshmen are admitted in the fall and winter. Entrance exams should be taken during the spring of the junior year or fall of the senior year. There is a rolling admissions plan. Applications should be filed by June 1 for fall entry. The fall 2017 application fee was $40. Applications are accepted on-line. **Transfer Students:** 300 transfer students enrolled in 2016-2017. To be eligible for transfer admission, students must submit 1 letter of recommendation and official transcripts from the previous college and must have maintained a minimum GPA of 2.5. An interview is also recommended. 30 of 120 credits required for the bachelor's degree must be completed at North Park. **International Students:** There are 100 international students enrolled. They must take the TOEFL with a minimum score of 550 on the paper-based TOEFL (PBT) or 80 on the Internet-based version (iBT) and the college's own test.

ADMISSIONS: 87% of the 2017-2018 applicants were accepted. The SAT scores for the 2017-2018 freshman class were: Critical Reading-- 33% below 500, 49% between 500 and 599, 17% between 600 and 699, and 1% between 700 and 800. Math-- 40% below 500, 43% between 500 and 599, 14% between 600 and 699, and 3% between 700 and 800. The ACT scores were 41% below 12, 25% between 12 and 17, 16% between 18 and 23, 9% between 24 and 29, and 9% above 30. 32% of the current freshmen were in the top fifth of their class; 61% were in the top two fifths. **Admissions Contact:** Mark Olson, Acting Director of Undergraduate Admission. Email: *admissions@northpark.edu* Web: *www.northpark.edu*

FINANCIAL AID: In 2017-2018, 98% of all full-time freshmen received some form of financial aid. 79% of all full-time freshmen received need-based aid. 20% of undergraduate students work part-time. The average financial indebtedness of the 2017 graduate was $28,467. The FAFSA code is 001735. The priority date for freshman financial aid applications for fall entry is March 1.

NORTHEASTERN ILLINOIS UNIVERSITY *(The complete profile is made available exclusively on our website, www.barronspac.com)*

NORTHERN ILLINOIS UNIVERSITY D-2
www.niu.edu

DeKalb, IL 60115	(815) 753-0446
Fax: (815) 753-1783	**Email:** admissions@niu.edu
Full-time: 8044 men, 8308 women	**Faculty:** 922; I
Part-time: 900 men, 1025 women	**Ph.D.s:** 83%
Graduate: 2635 men, 3512 women	**Student/Faculty:** 18 to 1
Year: semesters, summer session	**Tuition:** $10,588 ($17,440)
Room & Board: $9588	**Freshman Class:** 17787 applied, 10409 accepted, 3033 enrolled
ACT: 22	**CEEB CODE:** 1559
Application Deadline: August 1	**COMPETITIVE**

Northern Illinois University, founded in 1895, is a publicly funded institution offering undergraduate and graduate programs in a comprehensive range of disciplines. There are 6 undergraduate schools and 2 graduate schools. The figures in the above capsule and in this profile are approximate. In addition to regional accreditation, NIU has baccalaureate program accreditation with AACSB, ABET, ACEJMC, APTA, ASLA, CAHEA, NASAD, NASM, CAEP, and NLN. The 755-acre campus is in a small town 65 miles west of Chicago. Including any residence halls, there are 55 buildings.

STUDENT LIFE: 95% of undergraduates are from Illinois. Others are from 50 states, 95 foreign countries, and Canada. 84% are from public schools. 73% are White; 7% Hispanic; 6% Asian American; 13% African American; 1% Foreign. **Female To Male Ratio:** 1.1:1. The average age of freshmen is 18; all undergraduates, 22. 22% do not continue beyond their first year; 78% remain to graduate. **Housing:** 5800 students can be accommodated in college housing, which includes single-sex and coed dorms, on-campus apartments, and married student housing. In addition, there are honors houses, language houses, and special-interest houses, such as computer science, law, music, political science, and health professions. On-campus housing is guaranteed for the freshman year only, and is available on a first-come, first-served basis. 67% of students live on campus; of those, 60% remain on campus on weekends. All students may keep cars.

FACULTY/CLASSROOMS: 54% of faculty are male; 46% are female.

Graduate students teach 20% of introductory courses. The average class size in an introductory lecture is 37; in a laboratory is 17; and in a regular course is 30.

PROGRAMS OF STUDY: NIU confers B.A., B.S., B.F.A., B.G.S., B.M., and B.S.Ed. degrees. Master's and doctoral degrees are also awarded. Bachelor's degrees are awarded in BIOLOGICAL SCIENCE (biology/biological science and nutrition), BUSINESS (accounting, banking and finance, business administration and management, and marketing/retailing/merchandising), COMMUNICATIONS AND THE ARTS (art, art history and appreciation, communications, dramatic arts, English, French, German, journalism, music, Russian, Spanish, and studio art), COMPUTER AND PHYSICAL SCIENCE (atmospheric sciences and meteorology, chemistry, computer science, geology, geoscience, information sciences and systems, mathematics, and physics), EDUCATION (art education, early childhood education, elementary education, health education, music education, physical education, and special education), ENGINEERING AND ENVIRONMENTAL DESIGN (electrical/electronics engineering, industrial engineering, mechanical engineering, and technological management), HEALTH PROFESSIONS (clinical science, community health work, health science, nursing, and speech pathology/audiology), SOCIAL SCIENCE (anthropology, child care/child and family studies, dietetics, early childhood studies, economics, geography, history, liberal arts/general studies, philosophy, physical fitness/movement, political science/government, psychology, sociology, and textiles and clothing). Business, engineering, and sciences are the strongest academically. Business, education, and communications have the largest enrollments.

ACTIVITIES: 15% of men belong to 22 national fraternities; 11% of women belong to 15 national sororities. There are 200 groups on campus, including art, band, cheerleading, chess, choir, chorale, chorus, computers, dance, drama, drill team, ethnic, film, honors, international, jazz band, LGBT, literary magazine, marching band, musical theater, newspaper, orchestra, pep band, photography, political, professional, radio and TV, religious, social, social service, student government, and symphony. Popular campus events include Unity in Diversity Week, Greek Week, and Springfest. **Sports:** There are 8 intercollegiate sports for men and 8 for women, and 15 intramural sports for men and 15 for women. Facilities include a sports stadium, a recreation center, a field house with facilities for basketball, volleyball, badminton, table tennis, tennis, racquetball/handball, and weight training, and swimming pools. **Graduates:** From July 1, 2015 to June 30, 2016, 4027 bachelor's degrees were awarded. The most popular majors were teacher education (7%), communication studies (6%), and accountancy (6%). 800 companies recruited on campus in 2015-2016. In an average class, 47% graduate in 5 years or less and 48% graduate in 6 years or less. Of the 2015 graduating class, 19% were enrolled in graduate school within 6 months of graduation.

SERVICES: Formal tutoring is provided for eligible students. **Library/Resources:** The 4 libraries contain 2.2 million volumes, 3.6 million microform items, and 59,076 audio/video tapes/CDs/DVDs, and subscribe to 32,722 periodicals including electronic. Computerized library services include interlibrary loans and database searching. Special learning facilities include an art gallery, a radio station, a TV station, and an anthropology museum. **Physically Challenged Students:** 85% of the campus is accessible. Facilities include wheelchair ramps, elevators, special parking, specially equipped restrooms, special class scheduling, lowered drinking fountains, lowered telephones, and special housing. **Special:** NIU offers internships in several areas. Students may study abroad in 30 countries. A physics/engineering degree is offered in cooperation with the University of Illinois. Either a B.A. or a B.S. may be obtained in the social science programs. Work-study programs, a general studies degree, co-op programs, pass/fail options, and student-designed majors are available. There are 5 national honor societies, a freshman honors program, and 18 departmental honors programs. **Visiting:** There are regularly scheduled orientations for prospective students, including open house programs, bus tours, faculty meetings, residence hall tours, and department receptions. There are guides for informal visits; visitors may sit in on classes and stay overnight. To schedule a visit, contact the Office of Orientation and Student Assistance at (815) 753-1535. **Campus Safety and Security:** Measures include 24-hour foot and vehicle patrol, self-defense education, and security escort services. There are shuttle buses, emergency telephones, lighted pathways/sidewalks, and a bicycle patrol.

REQUIREMENTS: Students must have a minimum score of 19 on the ACT and be in the top half of their class, or have an ACT score of 23 and be in the upper two-thirds of their class. Graduation from an accredited secondary school or satisfactory scores on the GED are required for admission. Secondary school courses must include 4 years of English and 2 to 3 years each of math, science, and social studies. In addition, students must have completed 1 to 2 years of art, film, foreign language, music, or theater. NIU requires applicants to be in the upper 50% of their class. AP and CLEP credits are accepted. To graduate, students must have a minimum of 124 credit hours and a minimum GPA of 2.0. All students must take English 103 and 104 and Communication Studies 100. In addition, they must take Math 101 or obtain at least a C in Math 155, 201, 206, 210, 211, or 229. The school also requires that students complete 29 hours in distributive studies areas, consisting of 9 to 12 hours in the humanities and arts, 7 to 11 hours in science and math, 6 to 9 hours in social science, and 3 to 6 hours in interdisciplinary studies. **Procedure:** Freshmen are admitted to all sessions. Entrance exams should be taken during the junior year. There is a rolling admissions plan. Applications should be filed by August 1 for fall entry. The fall 2016 application fee was $30. Applications are accepted online. **Transfer Students:** 2248 transfer students enrolled in 2015-2016. Transfer students with 24 or more credit hours must have a minimum GPA of 2.0. The core competency requirement in English, math, and speech must be satisfied by all transfer students. 30 of 124 credits required for the bachelor's degree must be completed at NIU. **International Students:** They must take the TOEFL with a minimum score of 527 on the paper-based TOEFL (PBT) or 71 on the Internet-based version (iBT).

ADMISSIONS: 59% of the 2016-2017 applicants were accepted. The ACT scores were 37% below 12, 30% between 12 and 17, 21% between 18 and 23, 7% between 24 and 29, and 5% above 30. 23% of the current freshmen were in the top fifth of their class; 54% were in the top two fifths. **Admissions Contact:** Brandon Lagana, Director of Admissions. Email: *admissions@niu.edu* Web: *www.niu.edu*

FINANCIAL AID: In 2016-2017, 85% of all full-time freshmen and 75% of continuing full-time students received some form of financial aid. 67% of all full-time freshmen and 58% of continuing full-time students received need-based aid. 12% of undergraduate students work part-time. Average annual earnings from campus work are $1722. The average financial indebtedness of the 2016 graduate was $16,838. The college's own financial statement is required. The FAFSA code is 001737. The priority date for freshman financial aid applications for fall entry is March 1.

NORTHWESTERN UNIVERSITY — E-2

www.northwestern.edu

Evanston, IL 60208 — **(847) 491-7271**

Email: ug-admission@northwestern.edu

Full-time: 4108 men, 4108 women	**Faculty:** I, ++$
Part-time: 63 men, 74 women	**Ph.D.s:** 100%
Graduate: 6910 men, 5945 women	**Student/Faculty:** 7 to 1
Year: quarters, summer session	**Tuition:** $52,678
Room & Board: $16,047	**Freshman Class:** 35100 applied, 3743 accepted, 1985 enrolled
SAT or ACT: required	**CEEB CODE:** 1565
Application Deadline: January 1	**MOST COMPETITIVE**

Northwestern University combines innovative teaching and pioneering research in a highly collaborative environment that transcends traditional academic boundaries. It provides students and faculty exceptional opportunities for intellectual, personal, and professional growth in three richly unique settings: Chicago, Evanston, and Doha, Qatar. Northwestern is committed to excellent teaching, innovative research, and the personal and intellectual growth of its students in a diverse academic community. There are 6 undergraduate schools and 7 graduate schools. In addition to regional accreditation, NU has baccalaureate program accreditation with AACSB, ABET, ACEJMC, APTA, and NASM. The 240-acre campus is in a suburban area 12 miles north of Chicago on the shores of Lake Michigan. Including any residence halls, there are 180 buildings.

STUDENT LIFE: Students are from 50 states, 78 foreign countries, and Canada. 6% are African American; 5% two or more races; 48% White; 2% race unknown; 17% Asian American; 12% Hispanic; 10% Foreign.

Male To Female Ratio: 1.1:1. The average age of freshmen is 18; all undergraduates, 20. 94% remain to graduate. **Housing:** College-sponsored housing includes gender neutral dorms and off-campus apartments. In addition, there are special-interest houses, fraternity houses, and sorority houses. On-campus housing is guaranteed for the freshman year only. 53% of students live on campus. Alcohol is not permitted. Upperclassmen may keep cars.

FACULTY/CLASSROOMS: 63% of faculty are male; 37% are female. All teach undergraduates, and all do research. No introductory courses are taught by graduate students.

PROGRAMS OF STUDY: NU confers B.A., B.S., B.A.C.M.N., B.A.Mus., B.M.E., B.Mus., B.Ph., B.P.H.C., B.S.A.M., B.S.B.M., B.S.C.H., B.S.C.I., B.S.C.M.N., B.S.C.O., B.S.C.S., B.S.Ed., B.S.E.E., B.S.E.N., B.S.E.S., B.S.G.E., B.S.G.S., B.S.I.E., B.S.J., B.S.M., B.S.M.D., B.S.M.E., B.S.M.F., B.S.M.T., B.S.S.E., and B.S.S.P. degrees. Master's and doctoral degrees are also awarded. Bachelor's degrees are awarded in BIOLOGICAL SCIENCE (biology/biological science, ecology, molecular biology, and neurosciences), BUSINESS (organizational behavior), COMMUNICATIONS AND THE ARTS (art, art history and appreciation, classics, communications, communications technology, comparative literature, dance, dramatic arts, English, fine arts, French, German, Italian, jazz, journalism, linguistics, music, music performance, music technology, music theory and composition, percussion, performing arts, piano/organ, radio/television technology, Slavic languages, Spanish, strings, voice, and winds), COMPUTER AND PHYSICAL SCIENCE (applied mathematics, astronomy, chemistry, computer science, geology, information sciences and systems, mathematics, physics, and statistics), EDUCATION (education, mathematics education, music education, and secondary education), ENGINEERING AND ENVIRONMENTAL DESIGN (biomedical engineering, chemical engineering, civil engineering, computer engineering, electrical/electronics engineering, engineering, environmental engineering, environmental science, industrial engineering, manufacturing engineering, materials engineering, materials science, and mechanical engineering), HEALTH PROFESSIONS (premedicine and speech pathology/audiology), SOCIAL SCIENCE (African American studies, American studies, anthropology, cognitive science, economics, ethics, politics, and social policy, European studies, gender studies, geography, history, human development, international studies, philosophy, political science/government, psychology, religion, science and society, sociology, and urban studies). Economics, political science, and engineering have the largest enrollments.

ACTIVITIES: 34% of men belong to 17 local fraternities; 39% of women belong to 12 local sororities. There are 400 groups on campus, including art, band, cheerleading, chess, choir, chorale, chorus, communications, dance, debate, drama, ethnic, film, honors, international, jazz band, LGBT, literary magazine, marching band, musical theater, newspaper, opera, orchestra, pep band, photography, political, professional, radio and TV, religious, social, social service, student government, symphony, and yearbook. Popular campus events include Dillo Day Music Festival, Dance Marathon, Wildcat Welcome, Family Weekend, and Homecoming. **Sports:** Facilities include a sailing center, a sports pavilion,an aquatics center, a tennis center, and a gymnasium. **Graduates:** From July 1, 2016 to June 30, 2017, 2933 bachelor's degrees were awarded. The most popular majors were social sciences (23%), communication/journalism (17%), and engineering (12%). In an average class, 86% graduate in 4 years or less, 93% graduate in 5 years or less, and 94% graduate in 6 years or less.

SERVICES: Counseling and information services are available, as is tutoring in most subjects. There are peer mentoring, and study groups, and one-on-one tutoring. **Library/Resources:** The library contains 6.0 million volumes. Computerized library services include interlibrary loans, database searching, Internet access, and Wi-Fi capability. Special learning facilities include an art gallery, planetarium, a radio station, a TV station, and an observatory. **Physically Challenged Students:** All of the campus is accessible. Facilities include wheelchair ramps, elevators, special parking, specially equipped restrooms, special class scheduling, lowered drinking fountains, lowered telephones, and special housing. **Special:** The university offers cooperative engineering programs throughout the country; many off-campus field studies and research opportunities; internships in the arts, journalism, and teaching; study abroad in 50 countries; a Washington semester, and numerous work-study programs both on and off campus. There is an accelerated degree program in medical education, and B.A.-B.S. degrees in liberal arts and engineering, liberal arts and music, and music and engineering. An integrated science program, an interdisciplinary study in mathematical methods in social sciences and numerous other interdisciplinary majors, a variety of dual and student-designed majors, and pass/fail options are offered. Teaching media programs are also available. There are 23 national honor societies, Phi Beta Kappa, a freshman honors program, and 40 departmental honors programs. **Visiting:** There are regularly scheduled orientations for prospective students, and daily information sessions and campus tours Monday through Friday. There are guides for informal visits; visitors may sit in on classes and stay overnight. To schedule a visit, contact Justin Clarke at justin.clarke@northwestern.edu. **Campus Safety and Security:** Measures include 24-hour foot and vehicle patrol, an emergency notification system, self-defense education, and security escort services. There are shuttle buses, emergency telephones, lighted pathways/sidewalks, controlled access to dorms/residences, and a security keycard system in residence halls.

REQUIREMENTS: The SAT or ACT is required. Applicants must be graduates of an accredited secondary school or have a GED certificate, and have completed a minimum of 16 units, including 4 units of English, 3 units of math, 2 or 3 units each of a foreign language and history, and 2 units of lab sciences. SAT II: Subject tests are required for the accelerated honors program in medical education and the integrated science program. Auditions are required for applicants to the Bienen School of Music. AP credits are accepted. Important factors in the admissions decision are leadership record, advanced placement or honors courses, evidence of special talent, personality/intangible qualities, recommendations by school officials, parents or siblings attended the school, extracurricular activities record, recommendations by alumni, and geographical diversity. Requirements for graduation vary by school and degree program. Students must maintain a minimum 2.0 GPA and complete a total of 45 to 48 quarter units (courses). **Procedure:** Freshmen are admitted in the fall. Entrance exams should be taken by December of the senior year. There are early decision and deferred admissions plans. Early decision applications should be filed by November 1; regular applications, by January 1 for fall entry. The fall 2017 application fee was $75. Notification of early decision is sent December 15; regular decision, April 1. 2752 applicants were on the 2017 waiting list; 9 were admitted. Applications are accepted on-line. **Transfer Students:** 111 transfer students enrolled in 2016-2017. We require a minimum of one full year of college coursework for a student to be eligible to transfer. This is usually equivalent to 24 semester hours or 36 quarter hours. Our minimum GPA requirement is a 3.0, but most successful applicants have at least a 3.5. We do not have any course prerequisites for transfer applicants. 24 of 45 credits required for the bachelor's degree must be completed at NU. **International Students:** There are 818 international students enrolled. They must take the TOEFL. They must also take the SAT or ACT.

ADMISSIONS: 11% of the 2017-2018 applicants were accepted. The SAT scores for the 2017-2018 freshman class were: Critical Reading-- 4% between 500 and 599, 26% between 600 and 699, and 70% between 700 and 800. Math-- 2% between 500 and 599, 18% between 600 and 699, and 80% between 700 and 800. The ACT scores were 1% between 18 and 23, 12% between 24 and 29, and 87% above 30. **Admissions Contact:** Christopher Watson, AVP Student Outreach & Dean Undergraduate Admissions. Email: *ug-admission@northwestern.edu* Web: *www.northwestern.edu*

FINANCIAL AID: In 2017-2018, 46% of all full-time freshmen received some form of financial aid. 45% of all full-time freshmen received need-based aid. The average freshman award was $48,603. Need-based scholarships or need-based grants averaged $42,976; and need-based self-help aid (loans and jobs) averaged $3,281. NU is a member of CSS. The CSS/Profile, noncustodial profile, and parent and student tax forms are required. The FAFSA code is 001739. The priority date for freshman financial aid applications for fall entry is March 5.

OLIVET NAZARENE UNIVERSITY E-2

www.olivet.edu

Bourbonnais, IL 60914 (815) 939-5203
(800) 648-1463

Fax: (815) 935-4998 **Email: admissions@olivet.edu**

Full-time: 1253 men, 1766 women	**Faculty:** 137
Part-time: 98 men, 241 women	**Ph.D.s:** 70%
Graduate: 304 men, 1245 women	**Student/Faculty:** 16 to 1
Year: semesters, summer session	**Tuition:** $33,940
Room & Board: $7900	**Freshman Class:** 4132 applied, 3047 accepted, 704 enrolled
ACT: 24	**CEEB CODE:** 1596
Application Deadline: August 1	**VERY COMPETITIVE**

Olivet Nazarene University is a private, Christian liberal arts university with a strong emphasis on academic excellence and Christ-centered living. The campus atmosphere and world-class facilities support the University's mission to provide high-quality academic instruction for the purpose of personal development, career and professional readiness, and preparation of individuals for lives of service to God and humanity. There are 7 undergraduate schools and 1 graduate school. In addition to regional accreditation, ONU has baccalaureate program accreditation with ABET, ADA, CSWE, NASM, CAEP, CCNE, CAATE, and IACBE. The 275-acre campus is in a suburban area 50 miles south of Chicago. Including any residence halls, there are 53 buildings.

STUDENT LIFE: 64% of undergraduates are from Illinois. Others are from 43 states, 23 foreign countries, and Canada. 80% are White; 7% African American; 7% Hispanic; 3% two or more races; 2% Asian American; 1% Foreign. 56% are Protestant. **Female To Male Ratio:** 2.0:1. The average age of freshmen is 18; all undergraduates, 20. 22% do not continue beyond their first year; 61% remain to graduate. **Housing:** 2400 students can be accommodated in college housing, which includes married student dorms and on-campus apartments. In addition, there are honors houses. On-campus housing is guaranteed for all 4 years. 80% of students live on campus. Alcohol is not permitted. All students may keep cars.

FACULTY/CLASSROOMS: 56% of faculty are male; 44% are female. All teach undergraduates. No introductory courses are taught by graduate students. The average class size in an introductory lecture is 30 and in a laboratory is 22.

PROGRAMS OF STUDY: ONU confers B.A., B.B.A., B.M., B.S., B.S.N., and B.S.W. degrees. Associate, master's, and doctoral degrees are also awarded. Bachelor's degrees are awarded in BIOLOGICAL SCIENCE (biology/biological science, biological sciences, and zoology), BUSINESS (accounting, business administration and management, business communications, fashion merchandising, finance, finance (financial planning), international business management, leadership, marketing management, recreation and leisure services, and sports management), COMMUNICATIONS AND THE ARTS (art, communication studies, communications, digital communications, dramatic arts, drawing, English, English as a second/foreign language, information technology, journalism, media arts, music, music performance, music theory and composition, musical theater, public relations, Spanish, and strategic communication), COMPUTER AND PHYSICAL SCIENCE (actuarial science, chemistry, chemistry education, chemistry/forensic chemistry, computer science, digital arts/technology, geology, geoscience, information sciences and systems, mathematics, and physical sciences), EDUCATION (art education, athletic training, Christian education, early childhood education, education, elementary education, English education, general studies, history education, mathematics education, music education, physical education, physical education teacher education, science education, social science education, and teaching English as a second/foreign language (TESOL/TEFOL), ENGINEERING AND ENVIRONMENTAL DESIGN (architectural engineering, chemical engineering, civil engineering, computer engineering, engineering, environmental design, environmental science, geological engineering, industrial engineering, interior design, mechanical engineering, and military science), HEALTH PROFESSIONS (biology, electrical engineering, exercise science, nursing, predentistry, premedicine, preoptometry, prepharmacy, prephysical therapy, and preveterinary science), SOCIAL SCIENCE (biblical languages, biblical studies, child psychology/development, criminal justice, cross cultural studies, dietetics, economics, family/consumer studies, geography, history, ministries, missions, pastoral studies, philosophy, political science/government, prelaw, psychology, public affairs, religion, religious studies, religious music, social science, social work, sociology, Spanish studies, and youth ministry). Engineering, nursing, and premedicine are the strongest academically. Engineering, nursing, and business have the largest enrollments.

ACTIVITIES: There are no fraternities or sororities. There are 90 groups on campus, including art, band, cheerleading, choir, chorale, chorus, communications, computers, debate, drama, environmental, ethnic, film, honors, international, jazz band, literary magazine, marching band, musical theater, newspaper, orchestra, pep band, photography, political, professional, radio and TV, religious, social, social service, student government, symphony, and yearbook. Popular campus events include concerts, revival services, chapel, and Ollies Follies (Class Olympics). **Sports:** There are 9 intercollegiate sports for men and 9 for women, and 19 intramural sports for men and 19 for women. Facilities include basketball, volleyball and racquetball courts, gymnasium, weight-lifting room, turf football field, athletic park with softball, baseball and soccer fields, jogging track, track and field facilities, and tennis courts. The Student Life and Recreation Center has swimming pools, basketball courts, 8-lane indoor track, workout facilities, gaming area and four-story rock climbing wall. **Graduates:** From July 1, 2016 to June 30, 2017, 796 bachelor's degrees were awarded. The most popular majors were nursing (31%), business administration (8%), and psychology (4%). In an average class, 4% graduate in 3 years or less, 51% graduate in 4 years or less, 59% graduate in 5 years or less, and 61% graduate in 6 years or less.

SERVICES: Counseling and information services are available, as is tutoring in every subject. There is a reader service for the blind, and remedial math, reading, and writing. **Library/Resources:** The library contains 529,092 volumes, 312,729 microform items, and 7,703 audio/video tapes/CDs/DVDs, and subscribes to 12,100 periodicals; including electronic. Computerized library services include interlibrary loans, database searching, Internet access, and Wi-Fi capability. Special learning facilities include an art gallery, radio station, Strickler Planetarium, one of only a few planetaria in the state of Illinois with digital projection capabilities, Reed Hall of Science Engineering wing, featuring state-of-the-art lab space, a tech shop and additive manufacturing lab, iLearn@Olivet using iPad technology, Greer Botanical Greenhouse, solar telescope, a television studio, an ROTC training facility, Mac labs for design students, music labs, and a lab where students are able to compose, arrange and transcribe music. **Physically Challenged Students:** 99% of the campus is accessible. Facilities include wheelchair ramps, elevators, special parking, specially equipped restrooms, special class scheduling, lowered drinking fountains, lowered telephones, and special housing. **Special:** Special academic programs include a work-study program, which can be arranged with other institutions, and a general studies degree. A 4-year engineering program (ABET) is available. There are 6 national honor societies, a freshman honors program, and 5 departmental honors programs. **Visiting:** There are regularly scheduled orientations for prospective students, class/faculty/athletic visits, financial aid appointments, campus tour, and an entrance interview. There are guides for informal visits, visitors may sit in on classes, and stay overnight. To schedule a visit, contact Admissions Office, Jean Milton. **Campus Safety and Security:** Measures include 24-hour foot and vehicle patrol, emergency notification system, self-defense education, and security escort services. There are shuttle buses, emergency telephones, lighted pathways/sidewalks, and controlled access to dorms/residences.

REQUIREMENTS: SAT or ACT test scores are required. The minimum ACT score required is 18. Olivet requires graduation from an accredited secondary school. Olivet does not have any specific high school course requirements, but there are some suggestions for high school courses. College preparatory courses completed with a C or above are recommended. In general, students should have 3 years of English and 2 years each of math, foreign language, and natural or social science. To enroll in the nursing program, students need a year of biology and a year of chemistry. In choosing high school courses, students should also take into consideration the career/major they intend to pursue. The GED is accepted. AP and CLEP credits are accepted. To graduate, students must complete 128 semester hours of credit, with 32 to 70 in a major and a minimum of 40 hours of credit in upper-division courses, and maintain a minimum GPA of 2.0. The required general education studies, 50 to 61 hours, include 12 credit hours of Christianity, 9 to 10 of communication, 9 of natural science and math, 6 of social sciences, 6 to 8 of international culture, 6 of literature and the arts, and 3 of wellness/nutrition. **Procedure:** Freshmen are admitted to all sessions. Entrance exams should be taken in the spring of junior year, or fall of senior year. There are deferred admissions and rolling admissions plans. Applications should be filed by August 1 for fall entry; December 1 for spring entry. The fall 2017 application fee was $25. Notification is sent on a rolling basis. Applications are accepted online. **Transfer Students:** 268 transfer students enrolled in 2016-2017. Application and transcripts of all college work must be submitted. 30 of 128 credits required for the bachelor's degree must be completed at ONU. **International Students:** There are 26 international students enrolled. They must take the TOEFL with a minimum score of 500 on the paper-based TOEFL (PBT) or 61 on the Internet-based version (iBT). They must also take the ACT, scoring 18.

ADMISSIONS: 74% of the 2017-2018 applicants were accepted. The ACT scores were 3% between 12 and 17, 46% between 18 and 23, 41% between 24 and 29, and 10% above 30. **Admissions Contact:** Susan Wolff, Dean of Undergraduate Admissions. Email: *admissions@olivet.edu* Web: *www.olivet.edu*

FINANCIAL AID: In 2017-2018, 99% of all full-time freshmen received

some form of financial aid. 83% of all full-time freshmen received need-based aid. The average freshman award was $30,000. 36% of undergraduate students work part-time. The FAFSA code is 001741. The priority date for freshman financial aid applications for fall entry is November 15.

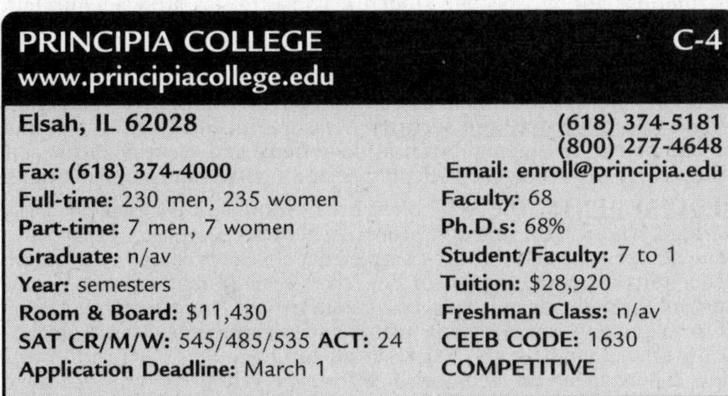

PRINCIPIA COLLEGE C-4
www.principiacollege.edu

Elsah, IL 62028	(618) 374-5181 (800) 277-4648
Fax: (618) 374-4000	Email: enroll@principia.edu
Full-time: 230 men, 235 women	Faculty: 68
Part-time: 7 men, 7 women	Ph.D.s: 68%
Graduate: n/av	Student/Faculty: 7 to 1
Year: semesters	Tuition: $28,920
Room & Board: $11,430	Freshman Class: n/av
SAT CR/M/W: 545/485/535 ACT: 24	CEEB CODE: 1630
Application Deadline: March 1	COMPETITIVE

Principia College, founded in 1910, is a private liberal arts and sciences college for Christian Scientists. It is the only college in the world strictly for Christian Scientists. There is 1 undergraduate school. In addition to regional accreditation, PC has baccalaureate program accreditation with CAEP. The 2600-acre campus is in a rural area 30 miles northeast of St. Louis. Including any residence halls, there are 33 buildings.

STUDENT LIFE: 90% of undergraduates are from out of state, mostly the Midwest. Students are from 36 states, 30 foreign countries, and Canada. 45% are from public schools. 73% are White; 4% Hispanic; 2% African American; 2% Asian American; 17% Foreign; 1% two or more races; 1% race unknown. 100% are Christian Scientist. **Female To Male Ratio:** 1.0:1. The average age of freshmen is 19; all undergraduates, 21. 13% do not continue beyond their first year; 79% remain to graduate. **Housing:** 555 students can be accommodated in college housing, which includes married student dorms, on-campus apartments, and abroad group dorms. On-campus housing is guaranteed for all 4 years. 98% of students live on campus. Alcohol is not permitted. All students may keep cars.

FACULTY/CLASSROOMS: 56% of faculty are male; 44% are female. All teach undergraduates. No introductory courses are taught by graduate students. The average class size in an introductory lecture is 14; in a laboratory is 10; and in a regular course is 16.

PROGRAMS OF STUDY: PC confers B.A. and B.S. degrees. Bachelor's degrees are awarded in BIOLOGICAL SCIENCE (biology/biological science), BUSINESS (business administration and management and sports management), COMMUNICATIONS AND THE ARTS (communications, dramatic arts, English, fine arts, French, languages, music, Spanish, and studio art), COMPUTER AND PHYSICAL SCIENCE (chemistry, computer science, mathematics, and physics), EDUCATION (elementary education), ENGINEERING AND ENVIRONMENTAL DESIGN (environmental science), SOCIAL SCIENCE (economics, history, international relations, philosophy, political science/government, religion, and sociology). Political science, computer science, history, and philosophy are the strongest academically. Education studies, business administration, and mass communication have the largest enrollments.

ACTIVITIES: There are no fraternities or sororities. There are 45 groups on campus, including art, cheerleading, choir, chorus, computers, dance, debate, drama, environmental, ethnic, film, honors, international, jazz band, LGBT, literary magazine, musical theater, newspaper, orchestra, photography, political, radio and TV, religious, social, social service, student government, and yearbook. Popular campus events include athletic events, and drama and dance performances. **Sports:** There are 9 intercollegiate sports for men and 10 for women, and 3 intramural sports for men and 3 for women. Facilities include gyms, a 6-lane track, a pool, indoor and outdoor tennis courts, a racquetball court, basketball/volleyball courts, a dance studio, a weight room, and baseball, football, soccer, and practice fields. **Graduates:** From July 1, 2016 to June 30, 2017, 117 bachelor's degrees were awarded. The most popular majors were education studies (22%), business administration (20%), and mass communications (10%). In an average class, 1% graduate in 3 years or less, 79% graduate in 4 years or less, 98% graduate in 5 years or less, and 100% graduate in 6 years or less.

SERVICES: Counseling and information services are available, as is tutoring in most subjects. There is remedial reading and writing. Assistance in study skills is available. **Library/Resources:** The library contains 170,040 volumes, 19 microform items, and 5,326 audio/video tapes/CDs/DVDs, and subscribes to 85,782 periodicals, including electronic. Computerized library services include interlibrary loans, database searching, Internet access, and Wi-Fi capability. Special learning facilities include an art gallery, a planetarium, a radio station, and TV station. **Physically Challenged Students:** 85% of the campus is accessible. Facilities include wheelchair ramps, elevators, special parking, specially equipped restrooms, and lowered drinking fountains. **Special:** Students may design their own majors, study abroad, or pursue a B.A.-B.S. degree. Internships, student-planned with a professor, independent study, work-study, and an interdisciplinary major, global studies, are available. An accredited engineering degree is offered as part of a dual-degree program with a few other institutions. **Visiting:** There are regularly scheduled orientations for prospective students, including a visit to classes, meeting professors, living in a dorm, and meeting students (3-day weekend). There are guides for informal visits; visitors may sit in on classes and stay overnight. To schedule a visit, contact Amber McCartt at (618) 374-5175. **Campus Safety and Security:** Measures include 24-hour foot and vehicle patrol and emergency notification system. There are emergency telephones, lighted pathways/sidewalks, and controlled access to dorms/residences.

REQUIREMENTS: SAT or ACT is required. The SAT Subject Tests in foreign language and math are recommended. High school preparation should include 4 years of English, 3 years of math (including algebra II), 2-3 years of foreign languages, natural sciences, history or social sciences, including electives. An essay is also required. AP and CLEP credits are accepted. Important factors in the admissions decision are advanced placement or honors courses, recommendations by school officials, and leadership record. All students must complete a minimum of 120 semester hours, with 30 to 71 semester hours in the major (10 to 19 courses) and at least a 2.0 overall GPA. Courses in Arts, Humanities, Math, Natural Sciences, Social Sciences, and Bible are also required. In addition, students must be certified as proficient in written English, take a second (foreign) language, pass a moral reasoning seminar, and earn 2 credits in individual or team physical education activities. **Procedure:** Freshmen are admitted in the fall and spring. Entrance exams should be taken in the spring of the junior year and again in the fall of the senior year. There are deferred admissions and rolling admissions plans. Applications should be filed by March 1 for fall entry; November 1 for winter entry. Notification of early decision is sent December 1; regular decision, March 15. Applications are accepted online. **Transfer Students:** 15 transfer students enrolled in 2016-2017. Applicants must be in good standing at their previous college or university and have a 2.3 GPA. 45 of 180 credits required for the bachelor's degree must be completed at PC. **International Students:** There are 82 international students enrolled. They must take the TOEFL with a minimum score of 80 on the Internet-based version (iBT). They must also take the SAT or ACT, scoring 1010-SAT, 19-ACT.

ADMISSIONS: The SAT scores for the 2017-2018 freshman class were: Critical Reading-- 22% below 500, 45% between 500 and 599, 27% between 600 and 699, and 6% between 700 and 800. Math-- 59% below 500, 22% between 500 and 599, 14% between 600 and 699, and 5% between 700 and 800. Writing-- 22% below 500, 45% between 500 and 599, 27% between 600 and 699, and 6% between 700 and 800. The ACT scores were 12% between 12 and 17, 35% between 18 and 23, 43% between 24 and 29, and 10% above 30. 44% of the current freshmen were in the top fifth of their class; 61% were in the top two fifths. 1 freshman graduated first in the class. **Admissions Contact:** Tami Gavaletz, Director of Admissions and Financial Aid. Email: *enroll@principia.edu* Web: *www.principiacollege.edu*

FINANCIAL AID: In 2017-2018, 98% of all full-time freshmen received some form of financial aid. 68% of all full-time freshmen received need-based aid. The average freshman award was $32,058. Need-based scholarships or need-based grants averaged $30,527 ($39,750 maximum); need-based self-help aid (loans and jobs) averaged $5,837 ($6,000 maximum); and other non-need-based awards and non-need-based scholarships averaged $25,691 ($39,780 maximum). 63% of undergraduate students work part-time. The average financial indebtedness of the 2017 graduate was $20,949. PC is a member of CSS. The CSS/Profile is required. The deadline for filing freshman financial aid applications for fall entry is March 1.

QUINCY UNIVERSITY *(The complete profile is made available exclusively on our website, www.barronspac.com)*

ROCKFORD UNIVERSITY D-1

www.rockford.edu

Rockford, IL 61108	**(815) 226-3383** **(800) 892-2984**
Fax: (815) 226-2822	**Email: admissions@rockford.edu**
Full-time: 299 men, 454 women	**Faculty:** 69
Part-time: 46 men, 70 women	**Ph.D.s:** 71%
Graduate: 176 men, 295 women	**Student/Faculty:** 11 to 1
Year: semesters, summer session	**Tuition:** $30,150
Room & Board: $8420	**Freshman Class:** n/av
ACT: 22	**CEEB CODE:** 1665
Application Deadline: August 15	**COMPETITIVE**

Rockford University, founded in 1847, is a private coeducational institution offering undergraduate and graduate instruction in liberal arts and professional programs. There is 1 undergraduate school and 2 graduate schools. In addition to regional accreditation, RU has baccalaureate program accreditation with NLN, ACS, and IACBE. The 135-acre campus is in a suburban area 90 miles west of Chicago. Including any residence halls, there are 27 buildings.

STUDENT LIFE: 91% of undergraduates are from Illinois. Others are from 26 states and 2 foreign countries. 73% are White; 7% African American; 6% Hispanic; 2% Asian American. **Female To Male Ratio:** 1.6:1. The average age of freshmen is 18; all undergraduates, 24. **Housing:** 356 students can be accommodated in college housing, which includes dorms. In addition, there are special-interest houses, first-year student housing, substance-free housing, 24-hour quiet housing, and health and science housing. On-campus housing is guaranteed for all 4 years. 65% of students commute. All students may keep cars.

FACULTY/CLASSROOMS: 56% of faculty are male; 44% are female. All teach undergraduates. No introductory courses are taught by graduate students. The average class size in an introductory lecture is 18; in a laboratory is 11; and in a regular course is 15.

PROGRAMS OF STUDY: RU confers B.A., B.S., B.F.A. and B.S.N. degrees. Master's degrees are also awarded. Bachelor's degrees are awarded in BIOLOGICAL SCIENCE (biochemistry and biology/biological science), BUSINESS (accounting, business administration and management, and management information systems), COMMUNICATIONS AND THE ARTS (art, art history and appreciation, classics, dramatic arts, English, French, German, Latin, music, music performance, romance languages and literature, and Spanish), COMPUTER AND PHYSICAL SCIENCE (chemistry, computer science, mathematics, and science), EDUCATION (elementary education, physical education, and special education), HEALTH PROFESSIONS (nursing), SOCIAL SCIENCE (anthropology, economics, history, humanities, international studies, philosophy, political science/government, psychology, social science, and sociology). Business, education, and nursing have the largest enrollments.

ACTIVITIES: There are no fraternities or sororities. There are 21 groups on campus, including senior club, Anime, Black Student Union, RAGE, Rockford Paranormal Society, Alpha Helix, art, band, cheerleading, chess, choir, chorale, dance, drama, environmental, ethnic, honors, international, LGBT, literary magazine, musical theater, opera, orchestra, pep band, political, professional, religious, social, social service, and student government. Popular campus events include Snowball Dance, International Food Fair, and Black History Month Events. **Sports:** There are 9 intercollegiate sports for men and 8 for women, and 7 intramural sports for men and 7 for women. Facilities include a swimming pool, athletic fields, tennis courts, and a fitness center. **Graduates:** From July 1, 2016 to June 30, 2017, 224 bachelor's degrees were awarded. The most popular majors were education (28%), business (22%), and nursing (10%). In an average class, 44% graduate in 5 years or less and 44% graduate in 6 years or less.

SERVICES: Counseling and information services are available, as is tutoring in most subjects. There is a reader service for the blind, and remedial math and reading. Diagnostic testing is available. **Library/Resources:** The library contains 146,829 volumes, 8,430 microform items, and 2,819 audio/video tapes/CDs/DVDs, and subscribes to 389 periodicals; including electronic. Computerized library services include interlibrary loans, database searching, and Internet access. Special learning facilities include an art gallery. **Physically Challenged Students:** Facilities include wheelchair ramps, elevators, special parking, specially equipped restrooms, special class scheduling, lowered drinking fountains, lowered telephones, and special housing. **Special:** RC offers a variety of special academic opportunities including community-based learning, liberal arts honors program, internships, study abroad, and Washington semester. In addition to our traditional undergraduate programs, RC offers English as a second language and an accelerated bachelor's degree in management studies. There are 6 national honor societies and a chapter of Phi Beta Kappa. **Visiting:** There are regularly scheduled orientations for prospective students, consisting of an academic fair, opportunities to meet with social/athletic staff members, and administrative offices, admission presentation, a campus tour, and meetings with current students. There are guides for informal visits; visitors may sit in on classes and stay overnight. To schedule a visit, contact the Admissions Office. **Campus Safety and Security:** Measures include 24-hour foot and vehicle patrol, emergency notification system, and security escort services. There are emergency telephones and lighted pathways/sidewalks.

REQUIREMENTS: The ACT is required. Admission is based primarily on high school GPA and test scores (GED also accepted). Prospective students are expected to have completed a college preparatory program of 15 units including 4 years of English; 3 years of mathematics (introductory through advanced algebra, geometry and trigonometry); 3 years of social sciences (emphasizing history and government); 3 years of laboratory science; and 2 years of electives chosen from music, art and/or foreign language at an accredited secondary school. Home schooled students should also meet the unit requirements. Auditions are required for performing arts students. requires applicants to be in the upper 50% of their class. A GPA of 2.7 is required. AP and CLEP credits are accepted. To graduate, students must have a total of at least 124 credit hours and a minimum GPA of 2.0 (nursing 2.75). The required hours for each major varies. Students are required to take 12 hours of social sciences, 8 to 12 of science, mathematics, and computer science, 8 of language and literature, 11 of rhetoric, 6 of art, and 2 hours of physical education. All students must complete a senior seminar or project. **Procedure:** Freshmen are admitted to all sessions. There are early admissions, deferred admissions, and rolling admissions plans. The fall 2017 application fee was $35. Notifications are sent September 15. Applications are accepted online. **Transfer Students:** 164 transfer students enrolled in 2016-2017. In order to be considered for transfer admission, prospective students must have completed at least 12 credit hours of college-level work (at the 100-level or higher). Students transferring from other colleges must be in good academic standing in order to be considered for standard admission. High school transcripts and standardized test scores (ACT/SAT) also may be requested. 30 of 124 credits required for the bachelor's degree must be completed at RU. **International Students:** There are 4 international students enrolled. They must take the TOEFL with a minimum score of 550 on the paper-based TOEFL (PBT) or 79 on the Internet-based version (iBT). RC will also accept the IELTS test. They must also take the SAT or ACT.

ADMISSIONS: The SAT scores for the 2017-2018 freshman class were: The ACT scores were 43% below 12, 26% between 12 and 17, 24% between 18 and 23, and 3% between 24 and 29. 28% of the current freshmen were in the top fifth of their class; 55% were in the top two fifths. **Admissions Contact:** Jennifer Nordstrom, Associate Vice President for Undergraduate Admissions and Strategy. Email: *admissions@rockford.edu* Web: *www.rockford.edu*

FINANCIAL AID: In 2017-2018, 100% of all full-time freshmen received some form of financial aid. 81% of all full-time freshmen received need-based aid. The average freshman award was $24,895. Need-based scholarships or need-based grants averaged $8,332 ($13,468 maximum); need-based self-help aid (loans and jobs) averaged $3,768 ($11,600 maximum); and other non-need-based awards and non-need-based scholarships averaged $14,970 ($35,660 maximum). 24% of undergraduate students work part-time. The average financial indebtedness of the 2017 graduate was $26,000. The FAFSA code is 001748. The priority date for freshman financial aid applications for fall entry is March 15.

ROOSEVELT UNIVERSITY E-2

www.roosevelt.edu

Chicago, IL 60605	**(847) 619-8620** **(877) APPLYRU**
Fax: (847) 619-8636	**Email: admission@roosevelt.edu**
Full-time: 680 men, 1180 women	**Faculty:** 190; IIA, -$
Part-time: 745 men, 1695 women	**Ph.D.s:** 85%
Graduate: 1035 men, 2205 women	**Student/Faculty:** 10 to 1
Year: semesters, summer session	**Tuition:** $28,963
Room & Board: $12,927	**Freshman Class:** n/av
SAT or ACT: required	**CEEB CODE:** 1666
Application Deadline: rolling	**VERY COMPETITIVE**

Roosevelt University, founded in 1945, is an independent, comprehensive university. The figures given in the above capsule and in this profile are approximate. There are 5 undergraduate schools and 5 graduate schools. In addition to regional accreditation, RU has baccalaureate program accreditation with AACSB, NASM, and CAEP. The campus is in an urban area in downtown Chicago. Including any residence halls, there are 2 buildings.

STUDENT LIFE: 90% of undergraduates are from Illinois. Others are from 24 states, 70 foreign countries, and Canada. 44% are White; 4% Asian American; 27% African American; 12% Hispanic; 10% Foreign; 1% American Indian/Alaska Native. **Female To Male Ratio:** 2.1:1. The average age of freshmen is 21; all undergraduates, 27. **Housing:** 300 students can be accommodated in college housing, which includes dorms. On-campus housing is available on a first-come, first-served basis. 94% of students commute.

FACULTY/CLASSROOMS: All teach undergraduates. No introductory courses are taught by graduate students.

PROGRAMS OF STUDY: RU confers B.A., B.S., B.A.Comp.Sci., B.A.Ed., B.F.A.Mus.Theater, B.G.S., B.M., B.S.B.A., B.S. in Hospitality Mgt. and B.S.Telecomm. degrees. Master's and doctoral degrees are also awarded. Bachelor's degrees are awarded in BIOLOGICAL SCIENCE (biology/biological science), BUSINESS (accounting, banking and finance, business administration and management, hotel/motel and restaurant management, insurance, insurance and risk management, management science, marketing/retailing/merchandising, and personnel management), COMMUNICATIONS AND THE ARTS (advertising, art history and appreciation, broadcasting, communications, dramatic arts, English, French, guitar, jazz, journalism, languages, literature, media arts, music, music history and appreciation, music performance, music theory and composition, musical theater, percussion, performing arts, piano/organ, public relations, Spanish, strings, telecommunications, theater design, theater management, voice, and winds), COMPUTER AND PHYSICAL SCIENCE (actuarial science, chemistry, computer science, information sciences and systems, mathematics, and statistics), EDUCATION (early childhood education, elementary education, music education, and secondary education), ENGINEERING AND ENVIRONMENTAL DESIGN (electrical/electronics engineering technology and environmental science), HEALTH PROFESSIONS (allied health, medical technology, nuclear medical technology, predentistry, premedicine, prepharmacy, and preveterinary science), SOCIAL SCIENCE (African American studies, American studies, economics, history, international studies, liberal arts/general studies, philosophy, political science/government, prelaw, psychology, public administration, social science, sociology, urban studies, and women's studies). Journalism, accounting, and psychology are the strongest academically.

ACTIVITIES: 1% of men belong to 1 local fraternity; 1% of women belong to 1 local sorority. There are 45 groups on campus, including model United Nations, band, choir, chorale, chorus, computers, cultural, drama, ethnic, honors, international, jazz band, literary magazine, musical theater, newspaper, opera, orchestra, political, professional, radio and TV, religious, social service, student government, and symphony. **Sports:** There is 1 intramural sport for men and 1 for women. Facilities include a fitness center and a recreational gym for basketball, volleyball, soccer, and intramural activities.

SERVICES: Counseling and information services are available, as is tutoring in most subjects. There is remedial math, reading, and writing. There is arranged counseling, and testing when needed. Emphasis is placed on individual program planning. **Library/Resources:** The library contains 405,022 volumes, 130,233 microform items, and 10,000 audio/video tapes/CDs/DVDs, and subscribes to 1,601 periodicals; including electronic. Computerized library services include interlibrary loans and database searching. Special learning facilities include a radio station. **Physically Challenged Students:** All of the campus is accessible. Facilities include wheelchair ramps, elevators, specially equipped restrooms, special class scheduling, and lowered telephones. **Special:** Roosevelt offers internships in approximately 20 subject areas, on-campus work-study, study abroad in 4 countries, dual and student-designed majors, pass/fail options, and noncredit courses. Adults older than 25 years of age may earn a Bachelor of General Studies through an accelerated degree program. Credit for life, military, and work experience is available in some majors through continuing education. The Roosevelt Scholars Program is offered. There are 4 national honor societies, a freshman honors program, and 20 departmental honors programs. **Visiting:** There are regularly scheduled orientations for prospective students, including open houses and Transfer Days. There are guides for informal visits and visitors may sit in on classes. To schedule a visit, contact the Undergraduate Admissions Office. **Campus Safety and Security:** There are shuttle buses and lighted pathways/sidewalks.

REQUIREMENTS: The SAT or ACT is required. Students must have completed 15 academic units, including 4 of English, 3 of math, 2 each of science, social studies, and foreign language, and 1 each of history and electives. An interview is recommended for all applicants, and an audition is required for music and theater candidates. AP and CLEP credits are accepted. Important factors in the admissions decision are advanced placement or honors courses, evidence of special talent, and extracurricular activities record. For graduation, students must complete 120 credit hours, including 54 in the major, with a minimum GPA of 2.0, or 2.5 in the College of Education. The core curriculum consists of courses in the social sciences, natural sciences, humanities, and English 101 and 102. The last 54 hours must be from a 4-year school. **Procedure:** Freshmen are admitted to all sessions. There are early decision, early admissions, deferred admissions, and rolling admissions plans. Application deadlines are open. The fall 2017 application fee was $25. Notification is sent on a rolling basis. Applications are accepted on-line. **Transfer Students:** 732 transfer students enrolled in 2016-2017. Applicants must have earned a minimum GPA of 2.0 in all accredited college course work. Official transcripts must be received from each college where coursework was attempted. 30 of 120 credits required for the bachelor's degree must be completed at RU. **International Students:** They must take the college's own test.

Admissions Contact: Gwen Kanelos, Assistant Vice President for Enrollment Services. Email: *admission@roosevelt.edu* Web: *www.roosevelt.edu*

FINANCIAL AID: In 2017-2018, 85% of all full-time freshmen received some form of financial aid. 75% of all full-time freshmen received need-based aid. The average freshman award was $10,500. Need-based scholarships or need-based grants averaged $7,725; need-based self-help aid (loans and jobs) averaged $7,170; and other non-need-based awards and non-need-based scholarships averaged $5,220. The college's own financial statement is required. The FAFSA code is 001749. Check with the school for current application deadlines.

SAINT XAVIER UNIVERSITY — E-2

www.sxu.edu

Chicago, IL 60655	**(773) 298-3050** **(800) 462-9288**
Fax: (773) 298-3076	**Email: admissions@sxu.edu**
Full-time: 705 men, 1630 women	**Faculty:** IIA, --$
Part-time: 170 men, 565 women	**Ph.D.s:** 86%
Graduate: 510 men, 1995 women	**Student/Faculty:** n/av
Year: semesters, summer session	**Tuition:** $33,380
Room & Board: $11,060	**Freshman Class:** n/av
ACT: required	**CEEB CODE:** 1708
Application Deadline: May 1	**COMPETITIVE**

Saint Xavier University is a private institution founded by the Sisters of Mercy in 1846 and affiliated with the Roman Catholic Church. The figures given in the above capsule and in this profile are approximate. There are 4 undergraduate schools and 4 graduate schools. In addition to regional accreditation, SXU has baccalaureate program accreditation with AACSB, ACBSP, NASM, NLN, CAEP, and CCNE. The 70-acre campus is in an urban area 15 miles southwest of Chicago's Loop. Including any residence halls, there are 16 buildings.

STUDENT LIFE: 96% of undergraduates are from Illinois. Others are from 21 states and 4 foreign countries. 50% are from public schools. 49% are White; 3% Asian American; 15% African American; 11% Hispanic. 80% are Catholic; 16% Protestant. **Female To Male Ratio:** 3.0:1. The average age of freshmen is 18; all undergraduates, 23. 24% do not continue beyond their first year. **Housing:** 630 students can be accommodated in college housing, which includes dorms. On-campus housing is guaranteed for all 4 years. 81% of students commute. Alcohol is not permitted. All students may keep cars.

FACULTY/CLASSROOMS: 44% of faculty are male; 56% are female. All teach undergraduates. No introductory courses are taught by graduate students. The average class size in an introductory lecture is 20; in a laboratory is 15; and in a regular course is 16.

PROGRAMS OF STUDY: SXU confers B.A., B.S., and B.M. degrees.

Master's degrees are also awarded. Bachelor's degrees are awarded in BIOLOGICAL SCIENCE (biology/biological science), BUSINESS (accounting, banking and finance, business administration and management, international business management, and marketing/retailing/merchandising), COMMUNICATIONS AND THE ARTS (communications, English, French, music, and Spanish), COMPUTER AND PHYSICAL SCIENCE (chemistry, computer science, and mathematics), EDUCATION (art education, early childhood education, elementary education, foreign languages education, middle school education, music education, science education, and secondary education), HEALTH PROFESSIONS (nursing, predentistry, premedicine, prepharmacy, and speech pathology/audiology), SOCIAL SCIENCE (criminal justice, history, philosophy, political science/government, prelaw, psychology, religion, social science, and sociology). Business, nursing, and education are the strongest academically and have the largest enrollments.

ACTIVITIES: There are no fraternities or sororities. There are 37 groups on campus, including art, band, cheerleading, choir, chorus, computers, drama, ethnic, honors, international, jazz band, literary magazine, marching band, musical theater, newspaper, pep band, political, professional, radio and TV, religious, social service, student government, and yearbook. Popular campus events include Xavierfest, Boat Bash, and Octoberfest. **Sports:** There are 4 intercollegiate sports for men and 5 for women, and 4 intramural sports for men and women. Facilities include baseball and softball fields, an outdoor sports facility, and a football field. The Convocation and Athletic Center hosts competition courts, racquetball courts, an indoor running track, training rooms, and a health and fitness center.

SERVICES: Counseling and information services are available, as is tutoring in every subject. There are reading and language clinics and a center for learning disabilities. **Library/Resources:** The library contains 172,104 volumes, 10,519 microform items, and 2,282 audio/video tapes/CDs/DVDs, and subscribes to 798 periodicals, including electronic. Computerized library services include interlibrary loans, database searching, and Internet access. Special learning facilities include an art gallery and a radio station. **Physically Challenged Students:** 98% of the campus is accessible. Facilities include wheelchair ramps, elevators, special parking, specially equipped restrooms, special class scheduling, lowered drinking fountains, and lowered telephones. **Special:** The university offers internships and study abroad in England, Ireland, and Italy. There is a freshman honors program. **Visiting:** There are regularly scheduled orientations for prospective students. There are guides for informal visits; visitors may sit in on classes and stay overnight. To schedule a visit, contact the Director of Admissions. **Campus Safety and Security:** Measures include 24-hour foot and vehicle patrol, self-defense education, and security escort services. There are shuttle buses, emergency telephones, and lighted pathways/sidewalks.

REQUIREMENTS: The ACT is required. Students must be graduates of an accredited secondary school and have earned 16 specific academic credits, including 4 years each of English and the natural and social sciences, 3 each of math and academic electives, and 2 years of a foreign language. The GED is accepted. AP and CLEP credits are accepted. To graduate, the student must complete 120 credit hours, including the school's 57-semester-hour core curriculum, and earn a GPA of 2.0. The credit hours required in the student's major vary by subject. **Procedure:** Freshmen are admitted in the fall and spring. Entrance exams should be taken during the spring of the junior year. There are deferred admissions and rolling admissions plans. Applications should be filed by May 1 for fall entry. The fall 2017 application fee was $25. Notification is sent on a rolling basis. Applications are accepted online. **Transfer Students:** 471 transfer students enrolled in 2016-2017. Applicants must have completed 12 semester hours with a GPA of 2.25. An interview is recommended. 30 of 120 credits required for the bachelor's degree must be completed at SXU. **International Students:** They must take the TOEFL.

Admissions Contact: Beth Gierach, Director of Enrollment Services. Email: *admissions@sxu.edu* Web: *www.sxu.edu*

FINANCIAL AID: In 2017-2018, 96% of all full-time freshmen received some form of financial aid, and need-based aid. Check with the school for current application deadlines.

SCHOOL OF THE ART INSTITUTE OF CHICAGO *(The complete profile is made available exclusively on our website, www.barronspac.com)*

SOUTHERN ILLINOIS UNIVERSITY CARBONDALE D-5

www.siu.edu

Carbondale, IL 62901 **(618) 536-4405**

Email: admissions@siu.edu

Full-time: 5000 men, 4455 women
Part-time: 887 men, 645 women
Graduate: 1798 men, 1769 women
Year: semesters, summer session
Room & Board: $10,622

SAT CR/M: 490/530 **ACT:** 22
Application Deadline: May 1

Faculty: 715; I, --$
Ph.D.s: 77%
Student/Faculty: 14 to 1
Tuition: $13,932
Freshman Class: 7961 applied, 6051 accepted, 1319 enrolled
CEEB CODE: 1726
COMPETITIVE

Southern Illinois University Carbondale is a comprehensive public institution founded in 1869. It is a multicampus doctoral-research university offering undergraduate and graduate programs in agricultural sciences, business, education, health and human services, the humanities and social sciences, media and performing arts, and the sciences. The university also includes schools of law and medicine, graduate school, and university college. In addition to regional accreditation, SIUC has baccalaureate program accreditation with AACSB, ABET, ABFSE, ACEJMC, ADA, APTA, CSWE, NAAB, NASAD, NASM, CAEP, SAF, AAAHC, ACPHA, ACEND, ARC-PA, AAM, ABA, ACAIL, ACS, APA, AAALAC, AALS, LCME, AMA, AAMC, ATMAE, AABI, COLA, NAST, NATEF, NAEYC, NASPAA, CAAHEP, CARF, CEA, and CIDA. The 1136-acre campus is in a small town 100 miles southeast of St. Louis, Missouri. Including any residence halls, there are 242 buildings.

STUDENT LIFE: 84% of undergraduates are from Illinois. Others are from 46 states, 46 foreign countries, and Canada. 9% are Hispanic; 65% White; 4% Foreign; 3% two or more races; 2% Asian American; 17% African American. **Male To Female Ratio:** 1.1:1. The average age of freshmen is 19; all undergraduates, 23. 32% do not continue beyond their first year; 45% remain to graduate. **Housing:** 4492 students can be accommodated in college housing, which includes married student dorms and on-campus apartments. In addition, there are honors houses, special-interest houses, theme and wellness housing, and living learning communities. On-campus housing is guaranteed for the freshman year only, and is available on a first-come, first-served basis. 78% of students commute. All students may keep cars.

FACULTY/CLASSROOMS: 63% of faculty are male; 37% are female. 83% teach undergraduates, 58% do research, and 49% do both. Graduate students teach 26% of introductory courses. The average class size in an introductory lecture is 24.

PROGRAMS OF STUDY: SIUC confers B.A., B.S., B.F.A., and B.Mus. degrees. Associate, master's, and doctoral degrees are also awarded. Bachelor's degrees are awarded in AGRICULTURE (agricultural economics, agriculture, animal science, forestry and related sciences, horticulture, plant science, and soil science), BIOLOGICAL SCIENCE (biology/adolescence education, biology/biological science, botany, microbiology, physiology, and zoology), BUSINESS (accounting, banking and finance, business administration and management, business economics, fashion merchandising, funeral home services, hospitality management services, management science, marketing/retailing/merchandising, and recreation and leisure services), COMMUNICATIONS AND THE ARTS (Africana studies, art, classical languages, design, dramatic arts, English literature, film arts, fine arts, foreign language, French language and literature, Germanic languages and literature, information technology, journalism, linguistics, music, radio/television technology, Russian languages and literature, Spanish language and literature, speech/debate/rhetoric, and sports administration), COMPUTER AND PHYSICAL SCIENCE (chemistry, computer science, geology, information sciences and systems, mathematics, physics, and radiological technology), EDUCATION (early childhood education, elementary education, health education, health information management, mathematics education, physical education, social science education, special education, trade and industrial education, and vocational education), ENGINEERING AND ENVIRONMENTAL DESIGN (architecture, automotive technology, aviation administration/management, aviation maintenance technology, civil engineering, computer engineering, electrical/electronics engineering, electrical/electronics engineering technology, engineering technology, industrial engineering technology, interior design, mechanical engineering, mining and mineral engineering, and technological management), HEALTH PROFESSIONS (dental hygiene, health care administration, kinesiology, physician's assistant, and rehabilitation therapy), SOCIAL SCIENCE (anthropology, clothing and textiles management/production/services, communication sciences and disorders, criminal justice, criminology, dietetics, economics, fire protection, geography, history, international studies, liberal arts/general studies, paralegal studies, philosophy, political science/government, psychology, social science, social work, and sociology). Accounting, biological sciences, and psychology have the largest enrollments.

ACTIVITIES: 9% of men belong to 24 national fraternities; 9% of women belong to 11 national sororities. There are 331 groups on campus, including art, band, cheerleading, choir, chorale, chorus, communications, computers, dance, debate, drama, drill team, environmental, ethnic, film, forensics, honors, international, jazz band, LGBT, literary magazine, marching band, musical theater, newspaper, opera, pep band, photography, political, professional, radio and TV, religious, social, social service, student government, symphony, and yearbook. Popular campus events include Cardboard Boat Regatta, International Festival, Heritage Celebration Months, and Homecoming. **Sports:** There are 8 intercollegiate sports for men and 8 for women, and 16 intramural sports for men and 16 for women. Facilities include a football stadium, basketball arena, softball stadium, a gym, volleyball, track & field complex, swimming and diving, tennis, baseball, and a student-athlete academic center and weight room.**Graduates:** From July 1, 2016 to June 30, 2017, 3240 bachelor's degrees were awarded. The most popular majors were education (11%), business/marketing (9%), and engineering technologies (9%). In an average class, 2% graduate in 3 years or less, 24% graduate in 4 years or less, 37% graduate in 5 years or less, and 40% graduate in 6 years or less.

SERVICES: Counseling and information services are available, as is tutoring in most subjects, such as 100 and 200 level general education courses. There is a reader service for the blind. Through SIUCs Center for Learning Support Services, students can receive one-on-one tutoring, group study sessions, peer mentoring, and academic coaching. **Library/ Resources:** The library contains 3.0 million volumes, 2.3 million microform items, and 25,244 audio/video tapes/CDs/DVDs, and subscribes to 58,875 periodicals including electronic. Computerized library services include interlibrary loans, database searching, Internet access, and Wi-Fi capability. Special learning facilities include an art gallery, student-run newspaper and broadcast programs, farms and timberlands, greenhouses, livestock facilities, archaeological center, aviation program, a crime study center, a wildlife lab, engineering and science labs, simulated commodity and financial trading floor, child development laboratories, international programs and services, broadcasting division that operates public television and radio stations, a dental lab, and a craft shop and museum. **Physically Challenged Students:** 98% of the campus is accessible. Facilities include wheelchair ramps, elevators, special parking, specially equipped restrooms, special class scheduling, lowered drinking fountains, lowered telephones, and special housing, paratransit services, classroom accommodations, and disability support services. **Special:** SIUs academic offerings extend from the classroom and the lab to students residence hall and overseas. SIUs University Honors Program is an enriching, rewarding experience much like that of a private college. The UHP courses are more exclusive than others students will take at SIUs small, limited to UHP students, and taught by our faculty. Scholarship, leadership, mentorship, and other benefits are unlimited if students push themselves. Hands-on research opportunities are available for all students undergraduate and graduate. REACH (Research-Enriched Academic Challenge) is just one program that offers undergraduates small grants and other opportunities to gain research expertise by working alongside faculty mentors. Study abroad fulfills student desires for a multidimensional education by going beyond the classroom and seeing how the world works firsthand. SIU offers a variety of university-level, international study abroad experiences through semester or year-abroad programs, short-term travel/study programs, and educational exchanges. At SIU, you also have access to internships/co-ops, service learning, and writing in the disciplines. There are 8 national honor societies, a freshman honors program, and 11 departmental honors programs. **Visiting:** There are regularly scheduled orientations for prospective students. Open House events include campus and residence hall tours, meetings with admissions counselors, Academic College Fair, information sessions on a variety of topics, academic showcases and more. There are guides for informal visits. To schedule a visit, contact Campus Visit Program- Amber Rivers at (618) 453-7141. **Campus Safety and Security:** Measures include 24-hour foot and vehicle patrol, an emergency notification system, self-defense education, and security escort services. There are shuttle buses, emergency telephones, lighted pathways/sidewalks, controlled access to dorms/residences, and a student patrol program in addition to campus police officers.

REQUIREMENTS: First-time students will be admitted if they have earned: a 23 ACT/1130 SAT and 2.0 high school GPA (as calculated by SIU) or an 18 ACT/940 SAT and 3.0 high school GPA. All other students' applications are holistically reviewed. SIU considers GPA, high school course pattern, class rank, sub-scores, absences, a personal statement (optional), activities, extracurricular participation, and other features of the application. SIU does not require a foreign language in high school. However, SIU does require 2 years of electives whether that be music, P.E., art, or foreign language. SIU requires 4 years of English, 3 years each of math (4 years strongly suggested), science with lab, and social studies/ science. AP and CLEP credits are accepted. All students must complete at least 120 semester hours of credit, which can include credit for work experience, CLEP, AP, military credit, and proficiency examination credit, with at least 42 semester hours in courses at the 300 level or above, earned or awarded through proficiency examination from an accredited, senior-level institution. Students must also meet the requirements of the academic unit, the major, and when appropriate, the minor. In addition, they must achieve at least a C average for all work taken at SIUC, and at least a C average for all major work taken at SIUC, with exceptions granted by the forgiveness policy and the repeated grade policy. All students must complete the last 30 semester hours or a total of 90 semester hours, in residence at SIUC. Finally, students must complete the university core curriculum requirements. **Procedure:** Freshmen are admitted in the fall, spring, and summer. Entrance exams should be taken during spring of the junior year. There are deferred admissions and rolling admissions plans. Applications should be filed by May 1 for fall entry. The fall 2017 application fee was $40. Notification is sent on a rolling basis. Applications are accepted online. **Transfer Students:** 2184 transfer students enrolled in 2016-2017. Transfer students must have 26 transferable semester hours or 39 quarter hours and a GPA of 2.0 on a 4.0 scale (as calculated by SIUC grading policies). If less than 26 transferable hours are acquired, transfer students must have a 2.0 GPA on a 4.0 scale (as calculated by SIUC grading policies) and also meet freshman admission requirements. 30 of 120 credits required for the bachelor's degree must be completed at SIUC. **International Students:** There are 433 international students enrolled. They must take the TOEFL with a minimum score of 520 on the paper-based TOEFL (PBT) or 68 on the Internet-based version (iBT). Students must take the IELTS with a score of 6 and iTEP with a score of 4. They must also take the SAT or ACT.

ADMISSIONS: 76% of the 2017-2018 applicants were accepted. The SAT scores for the 2017-2018 freshman class were: Critical Reading-- 58% below 500, 26% between 500 and 599, and 16% between 600 and 699. Math-- 32% below 500, 42% between 500 and 599, and 26% between 600 and 699. The ACT scores were 7% between 12 and 17, 53% between 18 and 23, 33% between 24 and 29, and 7% above 30. 21% of the current freshmen were in the top fifth of their class; 40% were in the top two fifths. 15 freshmen graduated first in their class. **Admissions Contact:** Terri Harfst, Interim Director of Undergrad Admissions. Email: *admissions@siu.edu* Web: *www.siu.edu*

FINANCIAL AID: 47% of undergraduate students work part-time. The FAFSA code is 001758. The priority date for freshman financial aid applications for fall entry is March 1.

SOUTHERN ILLINOIS UNIVERSITY EDWARDSVILLE C-4

www.siue.edu

Edwardsville, IL 62026 **(618) 650-3705**

Fax: (618) 650-5013
Full-time: 4729 men, 5179 women
Part-time: 785 men, 1027 women
Graduate: 965 men, 1457 women
Year: semesters, summer session
Room & Board: $9180

ACT: 23
Application Deadline: May 1

Email: admissions@siue.edu
Faculty: 556; IIA, -$
Ph.D.s: 79%
Student/Faculty: 15 to 1
Tuition: $11,008 ($23,986)
Freshman Class: 7660 applied, 6272 accepted, 2075 enrolled
CEEB CODE: 1759
COMPETITIVE

Southern Illinois University Edwardsville, founded in 1957, is part of the Southern Illinois University system and offers undergraduate programs in business, education, engineering, arts and sciences, and nursing. Graduate programs also are offered in 34 subject areas, including professional programs in pharmacy and dental medicine. There are 5 undergraduate schools and 1 graduate school. In addition to regional accreditation, SIUE has baccalaureate program accreditation with AACSB, ABET, ACCE, ACEJMC, CSWE, NASM, CAEP, CCNE, ASHA, and NAST. The 2660-acre campus is in a suburban area 18 miles northeast of downtown St. Louis, Missouri. Including any residence halls, there are 25 buildings.

STUDENT LIFE: 84% of undergraduates are from Illinois. Others are from 41 states, 61 foreign countries, and Canada. 70% are White; 4% Hispanic; 3% two or more races; 2% Asian American; 2% Foreign; 2% race unknown; 13% African American. **Female To Male Ratio:** 1.2:1. The average age of all undergraduates is 21. 26% do not continue beyond their first year; 52% remain to graduate. **Housing:** 3524 students can be accommodated in college housing, which includes married student dorms and on-campus apartments, honors wings, and special-interest wings. On-campus housing is available on a first-come, first-served basis. 74% of students commute. All students may keep cars.

FACULTY/CLASSROOMS: 51% of faculty are male; 49% are female. 84% teach undergraduates. Graduate students teach 4% of introductory courses.

PROGRAMS OF STUDY: SIUE confers B.A., B.S., B.F.A., B.L.S., B.M., B.S.A., and B.S.W. degrees. Master's and doctoral degrees are also awarded. Bachelor's degrees are awarded in BIOLOGICAL SCIENCE (biochemistry, biology/biological science, ecology, and genetics), BUSINESS (accounting, business administration and management, business economics, entrepreneurial studies, human resources, international business management, management information systems, and marketing and distribution), COMMUNICATIONS AND THE ARTS (American literature, art, art history and appreciation, communications, dance, dramatic arts, English, French, German, journalism, languages, media arts, music, music business management, music history and appreciation, music performance, music theory and composition, musical theater, public relations, radio/television technology, Spanish, speech/debate/rhetoric, studio art, and theater design), COMPUTER AND PHYSICAL SCIENCE (actuarial science, applied mathematics, chemistry, computer management, computer science, earth science, mathematics, physics, and statistics), EDUCATION (art education, early childhood education, elementary education, health education, health information management, mathematics education, music education, physical education, science education, social science education, and special education), ENGINEERING AND ENVIRONMENTAL DESIGN (civil engineering, computer engineering, construction management, electrical/electronics engineering, industrial engineering, manufacturing engineering, and mechanical engineering), HEALTH PROFESSIONS (community health work, exercise science, medical technology, medical science, nursing, and speech pathology/audiology), SOCIAL SCIENCE (anthropology, criminal justice, economics, forensic studies, geography, gerontology, history, liberal arts/general studies, philosophy, political science/government, psychology, social work, and sociology). Pharmacy is the strongest academically. Nursing, biological sciences, and business administration have the largest enrollments.

ACTIVITIES: 7% of men belong to 13 national fraternities; 5% of women belong to 8 national sororities. There are 240 groups on campus, including art, band, cheerleading, choir, chorale, chorus, dance, drama, environmental, ethnic, honors, international, jazz band, LGBT, literary magazine, musical theater, newspaper, opera, orchestra, pep band, photography, political, professional, radio and TV, recreational, religious, social, social service, student government, and symphony. Popular campus events include Welcome Week, Arts and Issues Series, International Week, and Homecoming. **Sports:** There are 8 intercollegiate sports for men and 8 for women, and 17 intramural sports for men and 17 for women. Facilities include the Vadalabene Center and student fitness center; racquetball, basketball, aquatics, volleyball, indoor track, exercise and weight training. The University Center has billiards, a bowling alley, and a swimming pool. There is an outdoor track-and-field and a soccer stadium, fields for baseball, softball, and soccer, walking and biking trails, and a Frisbee course. **Graduates:** From July 1, 2016 to June 30, 2017, 2223 bachelor's degrees were awarded. The most popular majors were business administration (20%), education (19%), and engineering (10%). In an average class, 1% graduate in 3 years or less, 28% graduate in 4 years or less, 45% graduate in 5 years or less, and 50% graduate in 6 years or less.

SERVICES: Counseling and information services are available, as is tutoring in most subjects. There is a reader service for the blind, and remedial math, reading, and writing. **Library/Resources:** The library contains 810,537 volumes, 1.7 million microform items, and 33,438 audio/video tapes/CDs/DVDs, and subscribes to 32,858 periodicals, including electronic. Computerized library services include interlibrary loans, database searching, and Internet access. Special learning facilities include an art gallery, radio station, TV station, a recording studio, engineering labs, an anthropology museum, a greenhouse, an arboretum, and a nursing psychomotor skills lab. **Physically Challenged Students:** All of the campus is accessible. Facilities include wheelchair ramps, elevators, special parking, specially equipped restrooms, special class scheduling, lowered drinking fountains, lowered telephones, Visualtek large-screen TV, Kurzweil readers, test-taking facilities, accessible weight-training equipment, and a swimming pool. **Special:** 2+2 programs with various regional community colleges, integrative studies programs, co-op programs, internships, work-study programs, dual majors, B.A.-B.S. degrees, study abroad throughout the world, a liberal studies degree, and a 5-year (3+2) program in dental medicine. There are 20 national honor societies, a freshman honors program, and 15 departmental honors programs. **Visiting:** There are regularly scheduled orientations for prospective students, including visits before the semester starts. There are guides for informal visits and visitors may sit in on classes. To schedule a visit, contact the Office of Admissions. **Campus Safety and Security:** Measures include 24-hour foot and vehicle patrol, an emergency notification system, self-defense education, and security escort services. There are shuttle buses, emergency telephones, lighted pathways/sidewalks, and emergency blue lights located throughout campus.

REQUIREMENTS: The ACT is required. Applicants must be graduates of an accredited secondary school or have a GED certificate. They must have completed 15 academic credits, based on 4 years of English, 3 each of math and lab science, 2 years of any combination of art, foreign language, music, and vocational education, at least 2 years of government and/or history, plus 1 more year of social studies. A GPA of 2.5 is required. AP and CLEP credits are accepted. To graduate, students must complete a total of 124 semester hours with a minimum GPA of 2.0. Students must fulfill general education requirements, including 9 hours of math/science, and complete a senior project. **Procedure:** Freshmen are admitted to all sessions. Entrance exams should be taken before high school graduation. There is a rolling admissions plan. Applications should be filed by May 1 for fall entry; December 15 for spring entry; and May 3 for summer entry. The fall 2017 application fee was $30. Notification is sent on a rolling basis. Applications are accepted online. **Transfer Students:** 1242 transfer students enrolled in 2016-2017. Applicants must have a minimum 2.0 GPA in at least 30 semester hours earned. 30 of 124 credits required for the bachelor's degree must be completed at SIUE. **International Students:** There are 320 international students enrolled. They must take the TOEFL with a minimum score of 550 on the paper-based TOEFL (PBT) or 80 on the Internet-based version (iBT).

ADMISSIONS: 82% of the 2017-2018 applicants were accepted. The ACT scores were 31% below 12, 30% between 12 and 17, 22% between 18 and 23, 9% between 24 and 29, and 8% above 30. 33% of the current freshmen were in the top fifth of their class; 64% were in the top two fifths. **Admissions Contact:** Office of Admissions. Email: *admissions@siue.edu* Web: *www.siue.edu*

FINANCIAL AID: In 2017-2018, 75% of all full-time freshmen received some form of financial aid. 70% of all full-time freshmen received need-based aid. The average freshman award was $11,620. Need-based scholarships or need-based grants averaged $8,827; need-based self-help aid (loans and jobs) averaged $8,130; and non-need-based athletic scholarships averaged $10,660. 27% of undergraduate students work part-time. The average financial indebtedness of the 2017 graduate was $25,998. The FAFSA code is 001759. The deadline for filing freshman financial aid applications for fall entry is March 1.

TRINITY CHRISTIAN COLLEGE E-2
www.trnty.edu

Palos Heights, IL 60463	**(708) 597-3000** **(800) 748-0085**
Fax: (708) 385-5665	**Email: admissions@trnty.edu**
Full-time: 365 men, 716 women	**Faculty:** 79
Part-time: 112 men, 257 women	**Ph.D.s:** 67%
Graduate: n/av	**Student/Faculty:** 11 to 1
Year: semesters, summer session	**Tuition:** $26,190
Room & Board: $9390	**Freshman Class:** 625 applied, 536 accepted, 201 enrolled
SAT CR/M: 543/552 **ACT:** 23	**CEEB CODE:** 1820
Application Deadline: November 1	**COMPETITIVE**

Trinity Christian College, founded in 1959, is a private college offering programs in arts and sciences, business, health science, liberal arts, music, religion, and teacher preparation. There is 1 undergraduate school and 1 graduate school. In addition to regional accreditation, TCC has baccalaureate program accreditation with AACSB, CSWE, and CCNE. The 170-acre campus is in a suburban area 20 miles southwest of the Chicago Loop. Including any residence halls, there are 22 buildings.

STUDENT LIFE: 71% of undergraduates are from Illinois. Others are from 34 states, 3 foreign countries, and Canada. 52% are from public schools. 9% are African American; 80% White; 7% Hispanic; 2% Asian American; 2% Foreign. 86% are Protestant; 14% Catholic. **Female To Male Ratio:** 2.0:1. The average age of freshmen is 18; all undergraduates, 21. 27% do not continue beyond their first year; 58% remain to graduate. **Housing:** 726 students can be accommodated in college housing, which includes dorms and off-campus apartments. On-campus housing is guaranteed for all 4 years. 61% of students live on campus. Alcohol is not permitted. All students may keep cars.

FACULTY/CLASSROOMS: 60% of faculty are male; 40% are female. All teach undergraduates, and all do research. No introductory courses are taught by graduate students. The average class size in an introductory lecture is 25; in a laboratory is 18; and in a regular course is 18.

PROGRAMS OF STUDY: TCC confers B.A., B.S., B.S.N., B.F.A. and B.S.W. degrees. Master's degrees are also awarded. Bachelor's degrees are awarded in BIOLOGICAL SCIENCE (biochemistry, bioinformatics, and biology/biological science), BUSINESS (accounting and business administration and management), COMMUNICATIONS AND THE ARTS (applied music, art, communications, English, music, music production/recording technology, music performance, Spanish, and studio art), COMPUTER AND PHYSICAL SCIENCE (chemistry, computer science, digital arts/technology, information sciences and systems, and mathematics), EDUCATION (art education, education, elementary education, music education, special education, and sports studies), HEALTH PROFESSIONS (nursing, predentistry, premedicine, and preoptometry), SOCIAL SCIENCE (biblical studies, criminal justice, history, ministries, philosophy, prelaw, psychology, social work, sociology, and theological studies). Business, education, and nursing are the strongest academically and have the largest enrollments.

ACTIVITIES: There are no fraternities or sororities. There are 18 groups on campus, including art, band, cheerleading, choir, chorale, chorus, dance, drama, ethnic, honors, jazz band, literary magazine, newspaper, pep band, photography, political, professional, religious, social, social service, student government, and yearbook. Popular campus events include the Opus Fine Arts Festival and the Trollstock Concert. **Sports:** There are 6 intercollegiate sports for men and women, and 7 intramural sports for men and women. Facilities include a gym, track, stadium, baseball diamond, and softball and soccer fields. **Graduates:** From July 1, 2016 to June 30, 2017, 303 bachelor's degrees were awarded. The most popular majors were elementary education (38%), business (17%), and nursing (13%). In an average class, 54% graduate in 4 years or less, 58% graduate in 5 years or less, and 59% graduate in 6 years or less. Of the 2016 graduating class, 10% were enrolled in graduate school within 6 months of graduation, and 82% were employed.

SERVICES: Counseling and information services are available, as is tutoring in every subject. **Library/Resources:** The library contains 75,298 volumes, 54,158 microform items, and 1,841 audio/video tapes/CDs/DVDs, and subscribes to 16,711 periodicals, including electronic. Computerized library services include interlibrary loans, database searching, Internet access, and Wi-Fi capability. Special learning facilities include an art gallery and a Dutch heritage collection. **Physically Challenged Students:** 95% of the campus is accessible. Facilities include wheelchair ramps, elevators, special parking, specially equipped restrooms, and lowered drinking fountains. **Special:** Students may have various part-time or full-time internships in their major field. There are study abroad programs in Spain, Nicaragua, Ecuador, and South Korea. Pass/fail options exist. Dual majors are offered. There is 1 national honor society and a freshman honors program. **Visiting:** There are regularly scheduled orientations for prospective students, including a tour, an interview, a seminar, and class visits. There are guides for informal visits; visitors may sit in on classes and stay overnight. To schedule a visit, contact the Admissions Office. **Campus Safety and Security:** Measures include 24-hour foot and vehicle patrol, self-defense education, and security escort services. There are emergency telephones and lighted pathways/sidewalks.

REQUIREMENTS: The ACT is recommended. Applicants should graduate from an accredited high school or have a GED. They should prepare with 3 or 4 years of high school English, 3 years of math, science, and social studies, or 2 years each of a combination of 2 subject areas chosen among foreign language, math, science, or social studies. An interview is required. A GPA of 2.0 is required. AP and CLEP credits are accepted. Important factors in the admissions decision are advanced placement or honors courses, leadership record, and recommendations by school officials. All students must take 9 credits in English, 6 each in philosophy, history, and theology, as well as distribution requirements in cross-cultural studies, natural sciences, social sciences, fine arts, math, and physical education. Students must complete 125 credit hours and maintain a minimum GPA of 2.0 to graduate. **Procedure:** Freshmen are admitted in the fall and spring. Entrance exams should be taken during the last semester of the junior year. There is a rolling admissions plan. Applications should be filed by November 1 for fall entry; January 15 for spring entry. The fall 2017 application fee was $20. Notification is sent on a rolling basis. **Transfer Students:** 218 transfer students enrolled in 2016-2017. Applicants must have 24 hours of acceptable credits and a minimum 2.3 GPA. Associate degrees are recognized for transfer. 45 of 125 credits required for the bachelor's degree must be completed at TCC. **International Students:** There are 36 international students enrolled. They must take the TOEFL. They must also take the SAT or ACT.

ADMISSIONS: 86% of the 2017-2018 applicants were accepted. The SAT scores for the 2017-2018 freshman class were: Critical Reading--32% below 500, 52% between 500 and 599, 11% between 600 and 699, and 5% between 700 and 800. Math-- 37% below 500, 47% between 500 and 599, and 16% between 600 and 699. The ACT scores were 35% below 12, 22% between 12 and 17, 14% between 18 and 23, 13% between 24 and 29, and 16% above 30. 36% of the current freshmen were in the top fifth of their class; 60% were in the top two fifths. 3 freshmen graduated first in their class. **Admissions Contact:** Pete Hamstra, Vice President for Admissions. Email: *admissions@trnty.edu* Web: *www.trnty.edu*

FINANCIAL AID: In 2017-2018, 98% of all full-time freshmen received some form of financial aid and need-based aid. The FAFSA code is 001771. The deadline for filing freshman financial aid applications for fall entry is February 15.

TRINITY COLLEGE OF NURSING AND HEALTH SCIENCES *(The complete profile is made available exclusively on our website, www.barronspac.com)*

TRINITY INTERNATIONAL UNIVERSITY E-2
www.tiu.edu

Deerfield, IL 60015	**(847) 317-7000** **(800) 822-3225**
Fax: (847) 317-7081	**Email: admissions@tiu.edu**
Full-time: 445 men, 590 women	**Faculty:** IIA, --$
Part-time: 45 men, 185 women	**Ph.D.s:** 85%
Graduate: 1080 men, 550 women	**Student/Faculty:** n/av
Year: semesters, summer session	**Tuition:** $23,370
Room & Board: $7700	**Freshman Class:** n/av
SAT or ACT: required	**CEEB CODE:** 1810
Application Deadline: open	**VERY COMPETITIVE**

Trinity International University, established in 1897 by the Evangelical Free Church, is a Christian liberal arts institution offering undergraduate, graduate, and doctoral programs. There are 8 undergraduate schools and 3 graduate schools. In addition to regional accreditation, TIU has baccalaureate program accreditation with ATS and CAAHEP. The 111-acre campus is in a suburban area 25 miles north of Chicago. Including any residence halls, there are 34 buildings.

STUDENT LIFE: 52% of undergraduates are from Illinois. Others are from 48 states, 46 foreign countries, and Canada. 69% are from public schools. 8% are African American; 77% White; 4% Asian American; 4% Hispanic; 2% Foreign. 96% are Protestant. **Male To Female Ratio:** 1.2:1. The average age of freshmen is 18; all undergraduates, 21. 22% do not continue beyond their first year; 47% remain to graduate. **Housing:** 700 students can be accommodated in college housing, which includes married student dorms and on-campus apartments. On-campus housing is guaranteed for all 4 years. 58% of students live on campus. Alcohol is not permitted. All students may keep cars.

FACULTY/CLASSROOMS: 68% of faculty are male; 32% are female. 56% teach undergraduates. No introductory courses are taught by graduate students. The average class size in an introductory lecture is 40; in a laboratory is 20; and in a regular course is 15.

PROGRAMS OF STUDY: TIU confers B.A. degrees. Master's and doctoral degrees are also awarded. Bachelor's degrees are awarded in BIOLOGICAL SCIENCE (biology/biological science), BUSINESS (accounting, business administration and management, human resources, international business management, marketing/retailing/merchandising, and sports management), COMMUNICATIONS AND THE ARTS (communications, digital communications, digital media, English, graphic design, graphic design and media, media arts, and music), COMPUTER AND PHYSICAL SCIENCE (chemistry and mathematics), EDUCATION (athletic training, elementary education, music education, physical education, and secondary education), HEALTH PROFESSIONS (physical therapy, premedicine, prephysical therapy, and sports medicine), SOCIAL SCIENCE (biblical studies, Christian studies, criminal justice, family and community services, history, human services, humanities, liberal arts/general studies, philosophy, psychology, social science, and youth ministry). Music, education, and Biblical studies are the strongest academically. Business, Christian ministries, and education have the largest enrollments.

ACTIVITIES: There are no fraternities or sororities. There are 36 groups on campus, including art, band, cheerleading, choir, chorale, computers, debate, drama, ethnic, gospel choir, handbell choir, honors, international, jazz band, literary magazine, newspaper, orchestra, pep band, political, religious, social service, student government, symphony, and yearbook. Popular campus events include Santa Lucia Festival, Fine Arts Series, Day of Prayer, and Mr. TIU. **Sports:** There are 5 intercollegiate sports for men and women, and 6 intramural sports for men and women. Facilities include a student center, sports complex, football and soccer fields. Students have access to a nearby indoor tennis and racquetball club. **Graduates:** From July 1, 2016 to June 30, 2017, 168 bachelor's degrees were awarded. The most popular majors were business (21%), Christian ministries (16%), and elementary education (12%). In an average class, 33% graduate in 4 years or less, 9% graduate in 5 years or less, and 4% graduate in 6 years or less. Of the 2016 graduating class, 21% were enrolled in graduate school within 6 months of graduation, and 55% were employed.

SERVICES: Counseling and information services are available, as is tutoring in every subject. There is a reader service for the blind, and remedial math, reading, and writing. **Library/Resources:** The library contains 247,650 volumes, 110,503 microform items, and 6,741 audio/video tapes/CDs/DVDs, and subscribes to 1,091 periodicals including electronic. Computerized library services include interlibrary loans, database searching, Internet access, and Wi-Fi capability. **Physically Challenged Students:** 75% of the campus is accessible. Facilities include wheelchair ramps, elevators, special parking, specially equipped restrooms, and special class scheduling. **Special:** Students can cross-register with the Christian College Consortium and at Trinity Evangelical Divinity School. Trinity offers 3 levels of internships, study abroad in 7 countries, and an opportunity through the American Studies Program to spend a semester in Washington. Dual majors, a general studies degree, and nondegree study are offered. There are 2 national honor societies, a freshman honors program, and 15 departmental honors programs. **Visiting:** There are regularly scheduled orientations for prospective students, including class visits, and meetings with professors and admission counselors. There are guides for informal visits, and visitors may stay overnight. To schedule a visit, contact the Campus Visit Coordinator at visits@tiu.edu. **Campus Safety and Security:** Measures include 24-hour foot and vehicle patrol, self-defense education, and security escort services. There are emergency telephones and lighted pathways/sidewalks.

REQUIREMENTS: A satisfactory score on the SAT or ACT is required. Applicants should be graduates of an accredited high school and have completed 15 academic credits in art, a foreign language, math, music, science, social studies, and English. A GED is accepted. Recommendations from a pastor must be submitted. A GPA of 2.5 is required. AP and CLEP credits are accepted. Important factors in the admissions decision are personality/intangible qualities, leadership record, and advanced placement or honors courses. To graduate, all students must complete 126 semester hours, including 58 general education hours and a variable 36 to 54 hours in the major. A GPA of 2.0 is required. Chapel attendance, Christian service, Bible study, and science are also required. **Procedure:** Freshmen are admitted in the fall and spring. Entrance exams should be taken during spring of the junior year or fall of the senior year. There is a rolling admissions plan. Application deadlines are open. The fall 2017 application fee was $25. Applications are accepted online. **Transfer Students:** 90 transfer students enrolled in 2016-2017. Applicants must submit college transcripts and have a cumulative college GPA of 2.0 or higher. 30 of 126 credits required for the bachelor's degree must be completed at TIU. **International Students:** They must take the TOEFL with a minimum score of 580 on the paper-based TOEFL (PBT). They must also take the SAT or ACT, scoring 19.

ADMISSIONS: 6 freshmen graduated first in their class. **Admissions Contact:** Jordan Bryant, Director of Undergraduate Admissions. Email: *admissions@tiu.edu* Web: *www.tiu.edu*

FINANCIAL AID: In 2017-2018, 90% of all full-time freshmen received some form of financial aid. 63% of all full-time freshmen received need-based aid. The average freshman award was $17,895. Need-based scholarships or need-based grants averaged $8,442 ($12,000 maximum); need-based self-help aid (loans and jobs) averaged $5,513 ($5,625 maximum); and non-need-based athletic scholarships averaged $9,389 ($22,980 maximum). 53% of undergraduate students work part-time. The average financial indebtedness of the 2017 graduate was $20,621. TIU is a member of CSS. The FAFSA code is 001772. Check with the school for current application deadlines.

UNIVERSITY OF CHICAGO — E-2

www.uchicago.edu

Chicago, IL 60637 — **(773) 702-8650**

Fax: (773) 834-5297 — **Email:** collegeadmissions@uchicago.edu

Full-time: 3190 men, 3052 women	**Faculty:** 1403; I, ++$
Part-time: 9 men, 13 women	**Ph.D.s:** 100%
Graduate: 4360 men, 3112 women	**Student/Faculty:** 5 to 1
Year: quarters, summer session	**Tuition:** $54,825
Room & Board: $15,726	**Freshman Class:** 27694 applied, 2419 accepted, 1736 enrolled
SAT EBR-W/M: 755/775 **ACT:** 34	**CEEB CODE:** 1832
Application Deadline: January 1	**MOST COMPETITIVE**

University of Chicago, founded in 1890, is a private liberal arts institution offering undergraduate and graduate programs with emphasis on interdisciplinary studies and rigorous theoretical inquiry, performed through open discussions between faculty and students. There is 1 undergraduate school and 12 graduate schools. In addition to regional accreditation, University of Chicago has baccalaureate program accreditation with CAEP. The 217-acre campus is in an urban area in Chicago, Illinois. Including any residence halls, there are 164 buildings.

STUDENT LIFE: 82% of undergraduates are from out of state, mostly the Midwest. Students are from 50 states, 73 foreign countries, and Canada. 5% are African American; 5% two or more races; 42% White; 2% race unknown; 18% Asian American; 13% Foreign; 12% Hispanic. **Male To Female Ratio:** 1.2:1. The average age of freshmen is 18; all undergraduates, 20. 93% remain to graduate. **Housing:** College-sponsored housing includes married student dorms and on-campus apartments. On-campus housing is guaranteed for all 4 years, is available on a first-come, first-served basis, and is available on a lottery system for upperclassmen. 54% of students live on campus. Upperclassmen may keep cars.

FACULTY/CLASSROOMS: 68% of faculty are male; 32% are female. No introductory courses are taught by graduate students.

PROGRAMS OF STUDY: University of Chicago confers B.A. and B.S. degrees. Master's and doctoral degrees are also awarded. Bachelor's degrees are awarded in BIOLOGICAL SCIENCE (biochemistry and biology/biological science), COMMUNICATIONS AND THE ARTS (art history and appreciation, classics, comparative literature, East Asian languages and literature, English, film arts, German, linguistics, media arts, music, romance languages and literature, Russian, Slavic languages, theatre studies, and visual and performing arts), COMPUTER AND PHYSICAL SCIENCE (applied mathematics, chemistry, computer science, geoscience, mathematics, physics, and statistics), ENGINEERING AND ENVIRONMENTAL DESIGN (environmental science), HEALTH PROFESSIONS (biology and medical science), SOCIAL SCIENCE (African American studies, anthropology, classical/ancient civilization, economics, gender studies, geography, history, human development, humanities, interdisciplinary studies, international studies, Judaic studies, Latin American studies, law, medieval studies, Near Eastern studies, philosophy, political science/government, psychology, public affairs, religion, religious studies, social science, sociology, South Asian studies, and theological studies). Economics, biological sciences, and mathematics have the largest enrollments.

ACTIVITIES: 8% of men belong to 10 national fraternities; 12% of women belong to 8 national sororities. There are 405 groups on campus, including College Bowl, improv groups, art, band, cheerleading, chess, choir, chorale, chorus, computers, dance, debate, drama, ethnic, film, honors, international, jazz band, LGBT, literary magazine, Model UN, musical theater, newspaper, orchestra, photography, political, professional, radio and TV, religious, social, social service, student government, and symphony. Popular campus events include Scavenger Hunt, Summer Breeze Festival, Kuviasungnerk Winter Festival, and Festival of the Arts. **Sports:** There are 10 intercollegiate sports for men and 9 for women, and 13 intramural sports for men and women. Facilities include a field house, a stadium, an outdoor track, baseball and softball fields, an arena, indoor basketball and squash courts, an indoor track, weight and wrestling rooms, aerobic machines, and an indoor swimming pool. **Graduates:** From July 1, 2016 to June 30, 2017, 1397 bachelor's degrees were awarded. The most popular majors were economics (21%), mathematics (13%), and biological sciences (9%). In an average class, 88% graduate in 4 years or less and 93% graduate in 6 years or less.

SERVICES: Counseling and information services are available, as is tutoring in some subjects. There is a reader service for the blind. **Library/Resources:** The library contains 1.3 million volumes, 3.2 million microform items, and 88,092 audio/video tapes/CDs/DVDs, and subscribes to 124,682 periodicals, including electronic. Computerized library services include interlibrary loans, database searching, Internet access, and Wi-Fi capability. Special learning facilities include an art gallery, radio station, accessible high-quality computer labs, state of the art research laboratories, multiple buildings dedicated to fine arts and performance (practice rooms, performance halls, and studio space), on campus museums (Oriental Institute, Renaissance Society), and daily tutor/mentor services. **Physically Challenged Students:** Facilities include wheelchair ramps, elevators, special parking, specially equipped restrooms, lowered drinking fountains, lowered telephones, and special housing. **Special:** Special academic programs include Careers In programs that emphasize pre-professional skills, and study abroad programs in 18 countries, as well as many on-campus research and internship opportunities. B.A.-B.S. and general studies degrees are offered, as are student-designed majors. Bachelor's-master's joint programs are offered in many fields. Professional options in Public Policy Studies, Social Service Administration, and early admission to the University of Chicago Pritzker School of Medicine are available. Nondegree study and pass/fail options are also possible. There are 2 national honor societies and a chapter of Phi Beta Kappa. **Visiting:** There are regularly scheduled orientations for prospective students, and daily tours, and information sessions with admissions counselors, and prospective students can sit in on classes, meet faculty, and current students. Interviews and overnight visits are available upon appointment. There are guides for informal visits; visitors may sit in on classes and stay overnight. To schedule a visit, contact the Office of College Admissions. **Campus Safety and Security:** Measures include 24-hour foot and vehicle patrol, emergency notification system, self-defense education, and security escort services. There are shuttle buses, emergency telephones, lighted pathways/sidewalks, and controlled access to dorms/residences.

REQUIREMENTS: The SAT or ACT is required. Admissions criteria include a recommended secondary school curriculum of 4 years each of English, mathematics, and science, 3 years of foreign language, and 2 years each of history and social studies. The GED is accepted. Complete applications consist of test scores, a high school transcript, a school report, letters of recommendation, and essays. Interviews are optional. AP credits are accepted. To graduate, students must complete 42 quarter courses, including 9 to 13 courses in the major, with an overall GPA of at least 1.75 and at least 2.0 in the major. The core curriculum includes diverse sequences in humanities, social sciences, biological and physical sciences, civilization studies, and foreign languages; these sequences vary in length and content depending on the students, requests. Also required are 2 quarters of math and 1 of art, music, or drama. Students are free to shape and schedule this curriculum according to their interests. **Procedure:** Freshmen are admitted in the fall. Entrance exams should be taken during the junior or senior year. There are early decision, early admissions, and deferred admissions plans. Early decision applications should be filed by November 1; regular applications, by January 1 for fall entry. The fall 2017 application fee was $75. Notification of early decision is sent December 18; regular decision, April 1. 531 early decision candidates were accepted for the 2017-2018 class. Applications are accepted on-line. **Transfer Students:** 36 transfer students enrolled in 2016-2017. Proven ability and interest in liberal arts education is considered. Essay, broad coursework, and solid performance at the home institution is considered critical. Recommendations are required from secondary school instructors, and the dean of previous institution, and a 2-year residency is a requirement. **International Students:** They must take the TOEFL with a minimum score of 100 on the Internet-based version (iBT). Students must take the IELTS, with a minimum overall score of 7. They must also take the SAT or ACT.

ADMISSIONS: 9% of the 2017-2018 applicants were accepted. The SAT scores for the 2017-2018 freshman class were: Math-- 8% between 600 and 699 and 92% between 700 and 800. Evidence-Based Reading/Writing-- 8% between 600 and 699 and 92% between 700 and 800. The ACT scores were 5% between 24 and 29, and 95% above 30. 100% of the current freshmen were in the top fifth of their class; 100% were in the top two fifths. **Admissions Contact:** Amanda Fijal, Senior Executive Director. Email: *collegeadmissions@uchicago.edu* Web: *www.uchicago.edu*

FINANCIAL AID: In 2017-2018, 54% of all full-time freshmen received some form of financial aid. The average freshman award was $54,438. Need-based scholarships or need-based grants averaged $48,113; and need-based self-help aid (loans and jobs) averaged $3,000. The average financial indebtedness of the 2017 graduate was $23,401. University of Chicago is a member of CSS. The CSS/Profile, the college's own financial statement, and a federal tax return are required. The FAFSA code is 001774. The priority date for freshman financial aid applications for fall entry is February 15.

UNIVERSITY OF ILLINOIS AT CHICAGO E-2

www.uic.edu

Chicago, IL 60607 **(312) 996-4366**

Fax: (312) 413-7628 **Email: uicadmit@uic.edu**

Full-time: 8805 men, 9156 women
Part-time: 826 men, 661 women
Graduate: 4752 men, 6339 women
Year: semesters, summer session
Room & Board: $10,960

SAT EBR-W/M: 589/616 **ACT:** 23
Application Deadline: January 15

Faculty: 1147; av$
Ph.D.s: n/av
Student/Faculty: n/av
Tuition: $13,704 ($26,560)
Freshman Class: 18768 applied, 14467 accepted, 4337 enrolled

CEEB CODE: 1851
VERY COMPETITIVE

University of Illinois at Chicago provides undergraduate and graduate programs in liberal arts, fine arts, business, engineering, architecture, health sciences, music, teacher preparation, social work, and professional training in dentistry, medicine, and pharmacy. There are 9 undergraduate schools and 14 graduate schools. In addition to regional accreditation, UIC has baccalaureate program accreditation with AACSB, ABET, ACPE, APTA, CAHEA, CSAB, CSWE, NAAB, APA, AOTA, and ACME. The 244-acre campus is in an urban area just west of downtown Chicago. Including any residence halls, there are 180 buildings.

STUDENT LIFE: 92% of undergraduates are from Illinois. Others are from 49 states, 105 foreign countries, and Canada. 79% are from public schools. 34% are White; 25% Hispanic; 19% Asian American; 12% Foreign; 8% African American; 3% two or more races; 1% race unknown. **Female To Male Ratio:** 1.1:1. The average age of freshmen is 18; all undergraduates, 21. 20% do not continue beyond their first year; 57% remain to graduate. **Housing:** 3718 students can be accommodated in college housing, which includes dorms and on-campus apartments. In addition, there are honors houses, special-interest houses, the President's Award House, and special-interest floors. On-campus housing is available on a first-come, first-served basis. 85% of students commute. All students may keep cars.

FACULTY/CLASSROOMS: No introductory courses are taught by graduate students.

PROGRAMS OF STUDY: UIC confers B.A., B.B.A., B.Des., B.Mus., B.S.N., B.S., and B.F.A. degrees. Master's and doctoral degrees are also awarded. Bachelor's degrees are awarded in AGRICULTURE (environmental studies), BIOLOGICAL SCIENCE (biochemistry, biology/biological science, biophysics, forensic science, neurosciences, nutrition, and nutritional sciences), BUSINESS (accounting, banking and finance, business administration and management, business economics, business information systems, entrepreneurial studies, finance, management science, marketing/retailing/merchandising, and real estate), COMMUNICATIONS AND THE ARTS (applied music, art history, art history and appreciation, art studies, communications, dramatic arts, English, English literature, film arts, film, television and digital media, fine arts, French, French and Francophone studies, German, Germanic languages and literature, graphic design, graphic design and media, industrial design, Italian, jazz, music, music performance, painting, photography, Polish, Russian, Russian languages and literature, sculpture, Slavic languages, Spanish, studio art, theatre acting, theatre arts, theater design, theatre production, theatre studies, and visual and performing arts), COMPUTER AND PHYSICAL SCIENCE (chemistry, computer mathematics, computer science, digital arts/technology, earth science, environmental geology, geoenvironmental studies, information sciences and systems, mathematics, mathematics/computational, physics, science of earth systems, and statistics), EDUCATION (art education, early childhood education, elementary education, English education, health education, health information management, learner designed area of study, mathematics education, museum studies, nutrition education, physical education, secondary education, and sports and wellness studies), ENGINEERING AND ENVIRONMENTAL DESIGN (architecture, bioengineering, chemical engineering, civil engineering, computer engineering, electrical/electronics engineering, energy systems technology, engineering, engineering physics, history of architecture/urban development, industrial engineering technology, materials engineering, and mechanical engineering), HEALTH PROFESSIONS (allied health, exercise science, nursing, occupational therapy, pharmacology, pharmacy, physical therapy, pre-health studies, predentistry, premedicine, prepharmacy, and public health), SOCIAL SCIENCE (African American studies, anthropology, applied psychology, architectural studies, classical/ancient civilization, criminal justice, criminology, economics, ethnic studies, forensic studies, French studies, gender studies, German area studies, history, humanities, Italian studies, Latin American studies, law enforcement and corrections, philosophy, physical fitness/movement, political science/government, psychology, public administration, public affairs, Russian and Slavic studies, sociology, Spanish studies, urban studies, and women and gender studies). Math, history, and fine arts are the strongest academically. Psychology, biological science, and computer science have the largest enrollments.

ACTIVITIES: 4% of men belong to 18 national fraternities; 5% of women belong to 15 national sororities. There are 285 groups on campus, including American medical and dental student association clubs, Indian Graduate Student Association, Muslim Student Association, accounting club, art, band, cheerleading, chess, choir, chorus, communications, computers, dance, drama, environmental, ethnic, honors, international, jazz band, LGBT, literary magazine, musical theater, newspaper, orchestra, pep band, political, professional, radio and TV, religious, social, social service, student government, and symphony. Popular campus events include Fun Fair, Meet the Greeks, New Student Convocation, Spark in the Park, and LOL @ UIC. **Sports:** There are 9 intercollegiate sports for men and 10 for women, and 52 intramural sports for men and 42 for women. Facilities include a stadium, sports and fitness centers, a recreation center, a gym, pools, racquetball and tennis courts, baseball, softball, and soccer fields, bowling, indoor and outdoor tracks, and weight rooms. **Graduates:** From July 1, 2016 to June 30, 2017, 3912 bachelor's degrees were awarded. The most popular majors were business/marketing (15%), biological sciences (14%), and psychology (13%). In an average class, 34% graduate in 4 years or less, 55% graduate in 5 years or less, and 58% graduate in 6 years or less.

SERVICES: Counseling and information services are available, as is tutoring in most subjects, such as a writing center, and academic skills classes. There is a reader service for the blind, and remedial math, reading, and writing. **Library/Resources:** The library contains 2.3 million volumes, 532,379 microform items, and 27,000 audio/video tapes/CDs/DVDs, and subscribes to 61,000 periodicals, including electronic. Computerized library services include interlibrary loans, database searching, Internet access, and Wi-Fi capability. Special learning facilities include an art gallery, radio station, a Jane Addams Hull House; which is a restored settlement house, and the James Woodworth Prairie Reserve. **Physically Challenged Students:** 80% of the campus is accessible. Facilities include wheelchair ramps, elevators, special parking, specially equipped restrooms, special class scheduling, lowered drinking fountains, and lowered telephones. **Special:** Special academic programs include a wide variety of co-op and program internships, work-study with some 70 on- and off-campus employers, and study abroad opportunities at accredited foreign universities, as well as special programs in France, Italy, Canada, Austria, Spain, and Mexico. Interdisciplinary majors are offered in architectural studies, communications and theater, math and computer science, bioengineering, and information and decision sciences. Up to 4 semester hours of credit may be granted for military experience. Dual and student-designed majors, nondegree study, and pass/fail options are available. There are 4 national honor societies, Phi Beta Kappa, a freshman honors program, and 90 departmental honors programs. **Visiting:** There are regularly scheduled orientations for prospective students, consisting of a general meeting, a college meeting, and campus tours. There are guides for informal visits; visitors may sit in on classes and stay overnight. To schedule a visit, contact Robert M. Moranetz at (312) 413-7628. **Campus Safety and Security:** Measures include 24-hour foot and vehicle patrol, an emergency notification system, self-defense education, and security escort services. There are shuttle buses, emergency telephones, lighted pathways/sidewalks, controlled access to dorms/residences, and emergency call buttons across campus.

REQUIREMENTS: The ACT, SAT or SAT-I are required. Applicants should be graduates of an accredited secondary school the GED is accepted. The recommended secondary school curriculum varies according to the college program chosen, but 15 high school credits are required as follows: 4 in English, 3 each in math and science, 2 each in foreign language and social studies. AP and CLEP credits are accepted. Important factors in the admissions decision are leadership record, advanced placement or honors courses, and extracurricular activities record. Students must demonstrate proficiency in written English through either course work or testing and complete 24 hours of general education, including at least 1 course in each of the general education categories: Analyzing the Natural World, Understanding the Individual and Society, Understanding the Past, Understanding the Creative Arts, Exploring the World Cultures, and Understanding U.S. Society. A minimum overall GPA of 2.0 is required. The total number of hours to graduate varies by major but is always at least 120. **Procedure:** Freshmen are admitted in the fall. Entrance exams should be taken in the spring of the junior year or the fall of the senior year. There is a rolling admissions plan. Applications should be filed by January 15 for fall entry. The fall 2017 application fee was $50. Notification is sent on a rolling basis. Applications are accepted online. **Transfer Students:** 2189 transfer students enrolled in 2016-2017. Transferable hours and minimum GPA vary according to program. 30 of 120 credits required for the bachelor's degree must be completed at UIC. **International Students:** There are 566 international students enrolled. They must take the TOEFL with a minimum score of 550 on the paper-based TOEFL (PBT) or 80 on the Internet-based version (iBT). They must also take the SAT or ACT. Freshmen minimum required scores depend on the specific college.

ADMISSIONS: 77% of the 2017-2018 applicants were accepted. The SAT scores for the 2017-2018 freshman class were: Math-- 10% below 500, 32% between 500 and 599, 39% between 600 and 699, and 19% between 700 and 800. Evidence-Based Reading/Writing-- 14% below 500, 38% between 500 and 599, 39% between 600 and 699, and 9% between 700 and 800. The ACT scores were 4% between 12 and 17, 50% between 18 and 23, 37% between 24 and 29, and 8% above 30. 48% of the current freshmen were in the top fifth of their class; 79% were in the top two fifths. **Admissions Contact:** Malinda Lorkovich, Managing Director of Admissions. Email: *uicadmit@uic.edu* Web: *www.uic.edu*

FINANCIAL AID: In 2017-2018, 61% of all full-time freshmen received

some form of financial aid. 61% of all full-time freshmen received need-based aid. The average freshman award was $14,869. Need-based scholarships or need-based grants averaged $13,795; need-based self-help aid (loans and jobs) averaged $3,637; non-need-based athletic scholarships averaged $22,513; and other non-need-based awards and non-need-based scholarships averaged $6,086. 18% of undergraduate students work part-time. The average financial indebtedness of the 2017 graduate was $23,076. UIC is a member of CSS. The FAFSA code is 001776. The priority date for freshman financial aid applications for fall entry is March 15.

UNIVERSITY OF ILLINOIS AT URBANA-CHAMPAIGN E-3

www.illinois.edu

Urbana, IL 61801 **(217) 333-0302**

Email: admissions@illinois.edu

Full-time: 17,685 men, 13,831 women	**Faculty:** I, +$
Part-time: 770 men, 409 women	**Ph.D.s:** 92%
Graduate: 6343 men, 5904 women	**Student/Faculty:** 19 to 1
Year: semesters, summer session	**Tuition:** $15,698 ($30,796)
Room & Board: $11,308	**Freshman Class:** n/av
SAT or ACT: required	**CEEB CODE:** 1836
Application Deadline: December 1	**HIGHLY COMPETITIVE**

University of Illinois at Urbana-Champaign, founded in 1867, is the oldest and largest campus in the University of Illinois system, offering some 150 undergraduate and more than 100 graduate degree programs. There are 18 undergraduate schools. In addition to regional accreditation, UIUC has baccalaureate program accreditation with AACSB, AALE, ABET, ACEJMC, ADA, ASLA, CSAB, CSWE, NAAB, NASAD, NASM, CAEP, NRPA, SAF, ABA, ACS, APA, CAAHEP, CADE, NASD, and NAST. The 4938-acre campus is in a small town 140 miles south of Chicago, 125 miles west of Indianapolis, and 180 miles northeast of St. Louis. Including any residence halls, there are 705 buildings.

STUDENT LIFE: 76% of undergraduates are from Illinois. Others are from 50 states, 115 foreign countries, and Canada. 7% are African American; 7% Hispanic; 66% White; 6% Foreign; 13% Asian American; 1% American Indian/Alaska Native. **Male To Female Ratio:** 1.2:1. The average age of freshmen is 18; all undergraduates, 20. 7% do not continue beyond their first year; 83% remain to graduate. **Housing:** 11,034 students can be accommodated in college housing, which includes married student dorms and on-campus apartments. In addition, there are language/international houses, special-interest houses, privately owned university-approved residence halls, and fraternity and sorority houses. On-campus housing is guaranteed for all 4 years. 50% of students commute. All students may keep cars.

FACULTY/CLASSROOMS: 67% of faculty are male; 33% are female. 95% teach undergraduates, and 95% do research. Graduate students teach 38% of introductory courses. The average class size in an introductory lecture is 19; in a laboratory is 22; and in a regular course is 29.

PROGRAMS OF STUDY: UIUC confers A.B., B.S., B.A.U.P., B.F.A., B.Land.Arch., B.Mus., B.S.Ed., B.S.J., B.S.W., and B.V.M. degrees. Master's and doctoral degrees are also awarded. Bachelor's degrees are awarded in AGRICULTURE (agricultural business management, agricultural communications, agricultural economics, agricultural mechanics, agronomy, animal science, forestry and related sciences, horticulture, natural resource management, range/farm management, and wildlife management), BIOLOGICAL SCIENCE (biology/biological science, biophysics, biotechnology, botany, cell biology, entomology, microbiology, molecular biology, nutrition, physiology, plant physiology, and wildlife biology), BUSINESS (accounting, banking and finance, entrepreneurial studies, hospitality management services, human resources, insurance, labor studies, logistics, management information systems, management science, marketing and distribution, marketing management, marketing/retailing/merchandising, operations research, organizational behavior, personnel management, purchasing/inventory management, real estate, and recreation and leisure services), COMMUNICATIONS AND THE ARTS (advertising, art history and appreciation, broadcasting, classics, communications, comparative literature, crafts, dance, dramatic arts, East Asian languages and literature, English, English literature, film arts, fine arts, French, Germanic languages and literature, graphic design, Hebrew, industrial design, Italian, journalism, linguistics, media arts, music, music history and appreciation, music performance, music theory and composition, painting, photography, Portuguese, Russian languages and literature, sculpture, Spanish, speech/debate/rhetoric, and voice), COMPUTER AND PHYSICAL SCIENCE (actuarial science, astronomy, chemistry, computer management, computer mathematics, computer programming, geology, mathematics, physics, and statistics), EDUCATION (agricultural education, art education, athletic training, computer education, early childhood education, education, education of the multiply handicapped, elementary education, English education, foreign languages education, mathematics education, music education, physical education, science education, secondary education, and vocational education), ENGINEERING AND ENVIRONMENTAL DESIGN (aeronautical engineering, agricultural engineering, airline piloting and navigation, architectural engineering, architecture, aviation administration/management, bioengineering, ceramic engineering, chemical engineering, city/community/regional planning, civil engineering, computational sciences, computer engineering, computer technology, electrical/electronics engineering, engineering, engineering mechanics, engineering physics, geological engineering, industrial administration/management, industrial engineering, landscape architecture/design, materials engineering, materials science, mechanical engineering, metallurgical engineering, nuclear engineering, and plastics engineering), HEALTH PROFESSIONS (biomedical science, community health work, exercise science, health care administration, preveterinary science, public health, and rehabilitation therapy), SOCIAL SCIENCE (anthropology, child psychology/development, dietetics, East Asian studies, economics, family/consumer studies, food production/management/services, food science, geography, history, human development, humanities, international studies, Latin American studies, liberal arts/general studies, parks and recreation management, philosophy, political science/government, prelaw, psychology, religion, Russian and Slavic studies, sociology, textiles and clothing, and women's studies). Engineering, computer science, and business are the strongest academically. Psychology, biology, and electrical and computer engineering have the largest enrollments.

ACTIVITIES: 21% of men belong to 3 local and 59 national fraternities; 21% of women belong to 2 local and 34 national sororities. There are 1000 groups on campus, including art, band, cheerleading, chess, choir, chorale, chorus, computers, dance, debate, drama, drill team, environmental, ethnic, film, forensics, honors, international, jazz band, LGBT, literary magazine, marching band, musical theater, newspaper, opera, orchestra, pep band, photography, political, professional, radio and TV, religious, social, social service, student government, symphony, and yearbook. Popular campus events include Quad Day to introduce Campus Organizations, Homecoming, Dad's Weekend, and Mom's Weekend. **Sports:** There are 10 intercollegiate sports for men and 12 for women, and 21 intramural sports for men and 21 for women. Facilities include an indoor recreation space, an outdoor recreation space for students' fitness and wellness needs, all major varsity sport facilities, and numerous student union facilities from bowling to exercise facilities. **Graduates:** The most popular majors were business, engineering, and social sciences/engineering technology.

SERVICES: Counseling and information services are available, as is tutoring in every subject. There is a reader service for the blind, and remedial math, reading, and writing. Transportation and rehabilitation services are offered, as well as interpreters, note taking, taped lectures, and priority registration. **Library/Resources:** The library contains 11.0 million volumes and 1,000,000 audio/video tapes/CDs/DVDs. Computerized library services include interlibrary loans, database searching, Internet access, and Wi-Fi capability. Special learning facilities include an art gallery, natural history museum, a planetarium, radio station, TV station, a language learning lab, performing arts center, a graphic technologies lab, world history and cultural museum, a rehabilitation-education center, a center for American music, Japan House and Gardens, and rare books and special collections libraries. **Physically Challenged Students:** All of the campus is accessible. Facilities include wheelchair ramps, elevators, special parking, specially equipped restrooms, special class scheduling, lowered drinking fountains, lowered telephones, and special housing. **Special:** Illinois offers numerous academic opportunities to students outside of the classroom. Students can participate in research with a faculty member, work in Research Park, take a trip on one of our 400 study abroad programs taking them to every continent except Antarctica, and engage in a flexible curriculum that prepares them for life after Illinois. There are 89 national honor societies, including Phi Beta Kappa, a freshman honors program, and 99 departmental honors programs. **Visiting:** There are regularly scheduled orientations for prospective students consisting of a university overview and admission presentation followed by a student-led campus tour. There are guides for informal visits and visitors may sit in on classes. To schedule a visit, contact Campus Visits at (217) 333-0824. **Campus Safety and Security:** Measures include 24-hour foot and vehicle patrol, emergency notification system, self-defense education, and security escort services. There are shuttle buses, emergency telephones, lighted pathways/sidewalks, controlled access to dorms/residences, saferides program, safety presentations, and evaluations by campus police.

REQUIREMENTS: The SAT or ACT is required. The ACT Optional Writing test is also required. Applicants should be graduates of accredited secondary schools or have the GED. Advanced placement tests are encouraged and accepted. High school preparation must include 4 years of English, 3 or more of math, 2 each of lab science and social studies, 2 of the same foreign language, and 2 of flexible academic units. A personal and professional essay is required. Visual arts applicants must submit a portfolio; performing arts applicants are required to audition. AP credits are accepted. Important factors in the admissions decision are advanced placement or honors courses, evidence of special talent, and geographical diversity. All students must demonstrate satisfactory proficiency in the use of English and 6 hours each in approved composition classes, Western/non-Western cultural studies, arts and humanities, social sciences/behavior, natural sciences/technology, and quantitative reasoning. Successful completion of either the third or fourth year (depending on the college) of a language other than the student's primary language is required. Students must maintain a minimum GPA of 2.0 while completing 120 to 132 credit hours (depending on the major) in order to graduate. **Procedure:** Freshmen are admitted in the fall. Applications should be filed by December 1 for fall entry. The fall 2017 application fee was $50. Notifications are sent February 13. Applications are accepted online. **Transfer Students:** 1343 transfer students enrolled in 2016-2017. Transfer application requirements differ by degree program. Transfer requirements by program can be viewed in the Transfer Handbook on the Admissions website. Admission is also subject to the number of places available. 30 of 132 credits required for the bachelor's degree must be completed at UIUC. **International Students:** There are 5031 international students enrolled. They must take the TOEFL with a minimum score of 550 on the paper-based TOEFL (PBT) or 79 on the Internet-based version (iBT), or take the IELTS. They must also take the SAT and ACT if they have attended a U.S. institution for 2 or more years.

ADMISSIONS: 9 freshmen graduated first in their class. **Admissions Contact:** Mike Drish, Director of Undergraduate Admissions. Email: *admissions@illinois.edu* Web: *www.illinois.edu*

FINANCIAL AID: The FAFSA code is 001775. Check with the school for current application deadlines.

UNIVERSITY OF ST. FRANCIS — E-2

www.stfrancis.edu

Joliet, IL 60435 — **(815) 740-3400**, **(800) 735-7500**

Fax: (815) 740-5032 — **Email: admissions@stfrancis.edu**

Full-time: 484 men, 789 women	**Faculty:** 80; IIA, -$
Part-time: 28 men, 70 women	**Ph.D.s:** 76%
Graduate: 236 men, 872 women	**Student/Faculty:** 12 to 1
Year: semesters, summer session	**Tuition:** $31,470
Room & Board: $9358	**Freshman Class:** 1560 applied, 806 accepted, 230 enrolled
SAT: required **ACT:** 23	**CEEB CODE:** 1130
Application Deadline: August 1	**COMPETITIVE**

University of St. Francis, founded as a college in 1920, is a private liberal arts and professional institution affiliated with the Roman Catholic Church. There are 4 undergraduate schools and 4 graduate schools. In addition to regional accreditation, USF has baccalaureate program accreditation with ACBSP, CSWE, CAEP, NRPA, ARCPA, and CCNE. The 34-acre campus is in a suburban area 35 miles southwest of Chicago. Including any residence halls, there are 7 buildings.

STUDENT LIFE: 95% of undergraduates are from Illinois. Others are from 20 states and 14 foreign countries. 88% are from public schools. 8% are African American; 60% White; 4% Foreign; 4% two or more races; 22% Hispanic; 2% Asian American. 48% are Catholic; 25% Protestant. **Female To Male Ratio:** 2.3:1. The average age of freshmen is 18; all undergraduates, 22. 20% do not continue beyond their first year; 63% remain to graduate. **Housing:** 455 students can be accommodated in college housing, which includes dorms and on-campus apartments. On-campus housing is guaranteed for the freshman year only, is available on a first-come, first-served basis, and is available on a lottery system for upperclassmen. 75% of students commute. All students may keep cars.

FACULTY/CLASSROOMS: 38% of faculty are male; 62% are female. 68% teach undergraduates. No introductory courses are taught by graduate students. The average class size in a laboratory is 13 and in a regular course is 16.

PROGRAMS OF STUDY: USF confers B.A., B.S., B.B.A., B.S.N., and B.S.W. degrees. Master's and doctoral degrees are also awarded. Bachelor's degrees are awarded in BIOLOGICAL SCIENCE (biology/biological science), BUSINESS (accounting, banking and finance, business administration and management, entrepreneurial studies, international business management, logistics, management science, marketing/retailing/merchandising, organizational leadership and management, and recreational facilities management), COMMUNICATIONS AND THE ARTS (art and design, communications, English, journalism, music, music performance, and visual and performing arts), COMPUTER AND PHYSICAL SCIENCE (computer programming, computer science, information sciences and systems, mathematics, and web technology), EDUCATION (art education, elementary education, music education, secondary education, and special education), ENGINEERING AND ENVIRONMENTAL DESIGN (computer technology and environmental science), HEALTH PROFESSIONS (allied health, health administration and policy, health care administration, medical technology, nuclear medical technology, nursing, predentistry, premedicine, preoptometry, prepharmacy, prephysical therapy, preveterinary science, radiation therapy, and radiograph medical technology), SOCIAL SCIENCE (addiction studies, counseling/psychology, criminal justice, history, liberal arts/general studies, political science/government, psychology, social work, and theological studies). Biology, education, and nursing are the strongest academically. Business, nursing, and biology have the largest enrollments.

ACTIVITIES: 1% of men belong to 1 national fraternity; 2% of women belong to 1 national sorority. There are 64 groups on campus, including Saints Ambassador Corps, business, nursing, education, art, cheerleading, choir, chorale, chorus, communications, computers, dance, drama, environmental, ethnic, honors, international, LGBT, literary magazine, musical theater, newspaper, opera, orchestra, pep band, political, professional, radio and TV, religious, social, social service, student government, and symphony. Popular campus events include Homecoming Competition, Glow Paint Party, and Outdoor Activities. **Sports:** There are 10 intercollegiate sports for men and women, and 10 intramural sports for men and women. Facilities include a football/soccer stadium, a baseball stadium, a softball complex, golf courses, soccer fields, indoor/outdoor tennis complex, a gymnasium, racquetball court, a golf hitting studio, and a fitness center. **Graduates:** From July 1, 2016 to June 30, 2017, 336 bachelor's degrees were awarded. The most popular majors were nursing (32%), business/marketing (17%), and education (8%). In an average class, 41% graduate in 4 years or less, 59% graduate in 5 years or less, and 63% graduate in 6 years or less. Of the 2016 graduating class, 19% were enrolled in graduate school within 6 months of graduation, and 85% were employed.

SERVICES: Counseling and information services are available, as is tutoring in most subjects. There is a reader service for the blind. **Library/Resources:** The library contains 143,887 volumes, 1,767 microform items, 9,573 audio/video tapes/CDs/DVDs, and subscribes to 21,237 periodicals, including electronic. Computerized library services include interlibrary loans, database searching, Internet access, and Wi-Fi capability. Special learning facilities include an art gallery, radio station, TV station, wireless and multimedia classrooms, numerous science laboratories, testing centers, private music practice and instruction rooms, digital audio and recording arts studio, 2D/3D design labs and equipment, medical and skills simulation labs, a cadaver lab, a mock trial courtroom, a business incubator, an art design complex with studio spaces for senior students, an international student center, a golf studio, a greenhouse, numerous multipurpose spaces, on-campus beehives, and an outdoor challenge course. **Physically Challenged Students:** All of the campus is accessible. Facilities include wheelchair ramps, elevators, special parking, specially equipped restrooms, special class scheduling, lowered drinking fountains, and special housing. **Special:** Internships, on-

and off-campus, paid and unpaid, are available in most majors. USF is the only school in Illinois that offers a B.A. in Substance Abuse Counseling. Dual and interdisciplinary majors, a pass/fail option, a Washington semester, study abroad, cross-registration with OCICU (Online Consortium of Independent Colleges and Universities), CIC (Council of Independent Colleges), and credit for life, military, and work experience are available. Individualized major, study abroad in Brazil, France, Ireland, Spain, India, Italy, England, Austria, Sweden, Bolivia, China, Finland, Costa Rica and Iceland are available. There are 19 national honor societies and a freshman honors program. **Visiting:** There are regularly scheduled orientations for prospective students, visiting students can participate in an orientation, meet faculty, take a tour, and listen to student presentations. There are guides for informal visits; visitors may sit in on classes and stay overnight. To schedule a visit, contact the Welcome Center, Emily Ellis at (815) 740-2270. **Campus Safety and Security:** Measures include 24-hour foot and vehicle patrol, an emergency notification system, and security escort services. There are shuttle buses, emergency telephones, lighted pathways/sidewalks, controlled access to dorms/residences, and routine fire inspections.

REQUIREMENTS: The SAT or ACT is required. Applicants must take 4 years of English, 3 years each of art, music, foreign language, or computer science, and math (including geometry), 2 years each of science (with 1 lab), and social studies, and 3 electives. USF requires applicants to be in the upper 50% of their class. A GPA of 2.5 is required. AP and CLEP credits are accepted. Important factors in the admissions decision are leadership record, advanced placement or honors courses, and personality/intangible qualities. Candidates for the bachelor's degree must complete the following: complete the Application for Graduation available in the Registrar's Office or through the MyUSF portal (consult the Academic Calendar for specific deadlines); earn a minimum of 120 semester hours of college credit; complete the residency requirement of a minimum of 32 semester hours of approved undergraduate credit. All students must complete a minimum of 15 hours of upper division (300-400) coursework, in the major, in residence at USF. In addition, 30 of the last 36 hours taken before graduation must be USF courses. (Note: individual colleges may have additional residency requirements). Complete all requirements with respect to the major program, support courses, liberal education, electives, achieve a cumulative GPA of 2.0 or higher at USF, earn grades of C or higher in all courses required by the major and any minor programs, and satisfy all financial requirements with the Business and Financial Aid Offices. It is the responsibility of the student to see that all graduation requirements are met. If a student withdraws for more than 1 semester, the catalog and regulations in effect at the time of their return will apply. Students completing a double major must select which degree they wish to receive since the University only awards one degree at graduation (however, the second major will appear on the transcript). If a student returns to complete a second major, they may apply for a second degree only if the new major leads to a different degree and they have met the current general education requirements in place at the time of awarding. **Procedure:** Freshmen are admitted in the fall and spring. Entrance exams should be taken in the spring of the junior year or the fall of the senior year. There are deferred admissions and rolling admissions plans. Applications should be filed by August 1 for fall entry. Notifications are sent September 15. Applications are accepted on-line. **Transfer Students:** 176 transfer students enrolled in 2016-2017. Transfer students must have a GPA of 2.5 and must submit transcripts from colleges previously attended. Applicants with fewer than 30 semester hours must also submit high school transcripts. Applicants must have taken English at the college level, and math at the intermediate algebra level. 32 of 120 credits required for the bachelor's degree must be completed at USF. **International Students:** There are 55 international students enrolled. They must take the TOEFL with a minimum score of 550 on the paper-based TOEFL (PBT) or 79 on the Internet-based version (iBT). They must also take the SAT or ACT, scoring 20.

ADMISSIONS: 52% of the 2017-2018 applicants were accepted. The SAT scores for the 2017-2018 freshman class were: Math-- 7% below 500, 57% between 500 and 599, 29% between 600 and 699, and 7% between 700 and 800. Evidence-Based Reading/Writing-- 29% below 500, 21% between 500 and 599, 50% between 600 and 699, and 0% between 700 and 800. The ACT scores were: 3% between 12 and 17, 61% between 18 and 23, 32% between 24 and 29, and 4% above 30. 28% of the current freshmen were in the top fifth of their class; 69% were in the top two fifths. **Admissions Contact:** Eric Ruiz, Director of Freshman Admissions. Email: *admissions@stfrancis.edu* Web: *www.stfrancis.edu*

FINANCIAL AID: In 2017-2018, 100% of all full-time freshmen received some form of financial aid. 76% of all full-time freshmen received need-based aid. The average freshman award was $27,256. Need-based scholarships or need-based grants averaged $23,833; need-based self-help aid (loans and jobs) averaged $4,400; non-need-based athletic scholarships averaged $24,790; and other non-need-based awards and non-need-based scholarships averaged $13,904. 14% of undergraduate students work part-time. The average financial indebtedness of the 2017 graduate was $32,838. The college's own financial statement is required. The FAFSA code is 001664. The priority date for freshman financial aid applications for fall entry is February 15.

VANDERCOOK COLLEGE OF MUSIC *(The complete profile is made available exclusively on our website, www.barronspac.com)*

WESTERN ILLINOIS UNIVERSITY C-3

www.wiu.edu

Macomb, IL 61455 **(309) 298-3157**

Fax: (309) 298-3111	**Email:** admissions@wiu.edu
Full-time: 3256 men, 3412 women	**Faculty:** 504; IIA, -$
Part-time: 497 men, 434 women	**Ph.D.s:** 73%
Graduate: 793 men, 1049 women	**Student/Faculty:** 14 to 1
Year: semesters, summer session	**Tuition:** $11,267
Room & Board: $9630	**Freshman Class:** 9767 applied, 5857 accepted, 1206 enrolled
SAT: required **ACT:** 21	**CEEB CODE:** 1900
Application Deadline: May 15	**COMPETITIVE**

Western Illinois University-Macomb, founded in 1902, is a traditional, residential four-year campus. WIU-Quad Cities, an urban, non-residential campus and the only public university in the Quad Cities, has been providing educational opportunities to the region for more than 50 years. There are 5 undergraduate schools and 1 graduate school. In addition to regional accreditation, WIU has baccalaureate program accreditation with AACSB, ABET, ADA, ASLA, CSWE, NASAD, NASM, CAEP, NRPA, ATMAE, ACCGC, and NAST. The 1050-acre campus is in a rural area 76 miles from Peoria, Illinois, 83 miles from Springfield, Illinois and 151 miles from St. Louis, Missouri. Including any residence halls, there are 60 buildings.

STUDENT LIFE: 89% of undergraduates are from Illinois. Others are from 38 states, 61 foreign countries, and Canada. 91% are from public schools. 60% are White; 5% Foreign; 3% two or more races; 2% race unknown; 19% African American; 11% Hispanic; 1% Asian American. **Female To Male Ratio:** 1.1:1. The average age of freshmen is 18; all undergraduates, 22. 32% do not continue beyond their first year; 68% remain to graduate. **Housing:** 4400 students can be accommodated in college housing, which includes coed and married student dorms and on-campus apartments. In addition, there are honors houses, language/international houses, special-interest houses, academic majors, honors, and wellness floors in residence halls. On-campus housing is guaranteed for all 4 years. 56% of students commute. Alcohol is not permitted. All students may keep cars.

FACULTY/CLASSROOMS: 55% of faculty are male; 45% are female. 89% teach undergraduates, 52% do research, and 56% do both. No introductory courses are taught by graduate students. The average class size in an introductory lecture is 25; in a laboratory is 19; and in a regular course is 17.

PROGRAMS OF STUDY: WIU confers B.A., B.B., B.F.A, B.M., B.S., B.S.Ed., B.L.A.S., B.S.N., and B.S.W. degrees. Master's and doctoral degrees are also awarded. Bachelor's degrees are awarded in AGRICULTURE (agriculture and animal science), BIOLOGICAL SCIENCE (forensic science and nutrition), BUSINESS (accounting, apparel and accessories marketing, business administration and management, business administration marketing, finance, hospitality management services, human resources/organizational management, marketing, and supply chain management), COMMUNICATIONS AND THE ARTS (art, broadcasting, communications, English, foreign language, graphic communications, journalism, music, musical theater, and theatre arts), COMPUTER AND PHYSICAL SCIENCE (chemistry, clinical laboratory science, computer science, cyber intelligence/security studies, geology, information sciences and systems, mathematics, and physics), EDUCA-

TION (agricultural education, art education, athletic training, bilingual/bicultural education, elementary education, foreign languages education, general studies, middle school education, physical education, and special education), ENGINEERING AND ENVIRONMENTAL DESIGN (construction management, emergency/disaster science, engineering, engineering technology, and mechanical engineering), HEALTH PROFESSIONS (biology, exercise science, health administration and policy, nursing, and public health), SOCIAL SCIENCE (anthropology, communication sciences and disorders, dietetics, economics, fire protection, geography, history, history and political science, interdisciplinary studies, law enforcement and corrections, liberal arts, sciences, general studies, humanities, parks and recreation management, psychology, social work, and sociology). Agriculture, accountancy, biology, engineering, and forensic chemistry are the strongest academically. Law enforcement and justice administration, biology, and psychology have the largest enrollments.

ACTIVITIES: 14% of men belong to 16 national fraternities; 14% of women belong to 11 national sororities. There are 263 groups on campus, including art, band, cheerleading, chess, choir, chorale, chorus, communications, computers, dance, drama, drill team, environmental, ethnic, film, honors, international, jazz band, LGBT, literary magazine, marching band, musical theater, newspaper, opera, orchestra, pep band, photography, political, professional, radio and TV, religious, social, social service, student government, and symphony. Popular campus events include Balloon Rally, Family Weekend, Homecoming Weekend, and International Bazaar. **Sports:** There are 9 intercollegiate sports for men and 10 for women, and 40 intramural sports for men and 40 for women. Facilities include an 18-hole golf course, tennis courts, basketball court, swimming pool, recreation center, softball, soccer, and football fields. **Graduates:** From July 1, 2016 to June 30, 2017, 2081 bachelor's degrees were awarded. The most popular majors were law enforcement and justice administration (19%), business/marketing (14%), and general studies (10%). In an average class, 30% graduate in 4 years or less, 47% graduate in 5 years or less, and 50% graduate in 6 years or less. Of the 2016 graduating class, 37% were enrolled in graduate school within 6 months of graduation, and 61% were employed.

SERVICES: Counseling and information services are available, as is tutoring in some subjects, such as business, art, English, computer science, science, social sciences, and humanities There is a reader service for the blind, and remedial math and writing. **Library/Resources:** The library contains 1.0 million volumes, 113,426 microform items, 25,775 audio/video tapes/CDs/DVDs, and subscribes to 5,410 periodicals, including electronic. Computerized library services include interlibrary loans, database searching, Internet access, and Wi-Fi capability. Special learning facilities include an art gallery, a natural history museum, radio station, TV station, an international studies center, and a multicultural center. **Physically Challenged Students:** 95% of the campus is accessible. Facilities include wheelchair ramps, elevators, special parking, specially equipped restrooms, special class scheduling, lowered drinking fountains, and lowered telephones. Special housing needs assessed/accommodated on an individual basis. **Special:** WIU offers internships in business, law enforcement, and physical training to name a few; study abroad group and exchange programs; and dual programs in engineering, clinical laboratory science, law, and chiropractic. Student-designed majors and independent study are available through the General Studies and Interdisciplinary Studies programs. The General Studies degree program offers credit for work experience. Also available are a field campus and a life science station on the Mississippi River. There are 11 national honor societies, a freshman honors program, and 36 departmental honors programs. **Visiting:** There are regularly scheduled orientations for prospective students consisting of registration, continental breakfast, university fair, program and Q/A, tours, meeting with an advisor, lunch and residence hall tour, and financial aid session. There are guides for informal visits; visitors may sit in on classes and stay overnight. To schedule a visit, contact the Admissions Office. **Campus Safety and Security:** Measures include 24-hour foot and vehicle patrol, emergency notification system, self-defense education, and security escort services. There are shuttle buses, emergency telephones, lighted pathways/sidewalks, a beacon/call box system, and student patrols.

REQUIREMENTS: The SAT or ACT is required. Students must have 4 years of English, 3 years each of math, science, and social studies, and 2 electives in art, film, foreign language, music, speech, theater, journalism, religion, philosophy, or vocational education. Academic Services is a program for selected students who do not meet regular admission requirements. A GPA of 2.2 is required. AP and CLEP credits are accepted. To graduate, all students must complete at least 120 credit hours, with at least 32 hours in the major, and have a minimum 2.0 GPA. Students must take 43 hours in the fields of basic skills, well-being, natural science, math, historical and social foundations, and humanities. **Procedure:** Freshmen are admitted in the fall, spring, and summer. Entrance exams should be taken by April of the senior year. There are deferred admissions and rolling admissions plans. Applications should be filed by May 15 for fall entry. The fall 2017 application fee was $30. Applications are accepted on-line. **Transfer Students:** 968 transfer students enrolled in 2016-2017. Students transferring fewer than 24 semester credits or 36 quarter credits must meet freshman admissions standards, have a combined C average for all hours attempted, and be in good standing at their previous college. 30 of 120 credits required for the bachelor's degree must be completed at WIU. **International Students:** There are 86 international students enrolled. They must take the TOEFL with a minimum score of 533 on the paper-based TOEFL (PBT) or 73 on the Internet-based version (iBT), or successfully complete WIUs ESL program.

ADMISSIONS: 60% of the 2017-2018 applicants were accepted. The ACT scores were 13% between 12 and 17, 61% between 18 and 23, 21% between 24 and 29, and 5% above 30. 22% of the current freshmen were in the top fifth of their class; 54% were in the top two fifths. **Admissions Contact:** Office of Admissions Email: *admissions@wiu.edu* Web: *www.wiu.edu*

FINANCIAL AID: In 2017-2018, 94% of all full-time freshmen received some form of financial aid. 77% of all full-time freshmen received need-based aid. The average freshman award was $16,008. Need-based scholarships or need-based grants averaged $6,989; need-based self-help aid (loans and jobs) averaged $2,598; non-need-based athletic scholarships averaged $354; other non-need-based awards and non-need-based scholarships averaged $2,557; and $3,511 from other forms of aid. 18% of undergraduate students work part-time. The average financial indebtedness of the 2017 graduate was $26,200. The FAFSA code is 001780. The priority date for freshman financial aid applications for fall entry is November 15.

WHEATON COLLEGE E-2

www.wheaton.edu

Wheaton, IL 60187	(630) 752-5005 (800) 222-2419
Fax: (630) 752-5285	**Email:** admissions@wheaton.edu
Full-time: 1046 men, 1264 women	**Faculty:** IIB, +$
Part-time: 51 men, 30 women	**Ph.D.s:** 95%
Graduate: 222 men, 287 women	**Student/Faculty:** n/av
Year: semesters, summer session	**Tuition:** $35,190
Room & Board: $9806	**Freshman Class:** 1693 applied, 1439 accepted, 580 enrolled
SAT EBR-W/M: 680/650 **ACT:** 29	**CEEB CODE:** 1905
Application Deadline: January 10	**MOST COMPETITIVE**

Wheaton College, founded in 1860, is a private nondenominational institution committed to providing students with a Christian education. A liberal arts school, it offers undergraduate programs in the sciences, business, the arts and fine arts, music, teacher preparation, and religious and biblical studies. There is 1 undergraduate school and 1 graduate school. In addition to regional accreditation, WC has baccalaureate program accreditation with NASM and NCATE. The 80-acre campus is in a suburban area 25 miles west of Chicago. Including any residence halls, there are 69 buildings.

STUDENT LIFE: 73% of undergraduates are from out of state, mostly the Midwest. Students are from 50 states, 40 foreign countries, and Canada. 48% are from public schools. 9% are Asian American; 74% White; 6% Hispanic; 4% two or more races; 3% African American; 3% Foreign; 1% race unknown. 99% are Protestant. **Female To Male Ratio:** 1.2:1. The average age of freshmen is 18; all undergraduates, 20. 7% do not continue beyond their first year; 89% remain to graduate. **Housing:** 2161 students can be accommodated in college housing, which includes both single sex and coed and married student dorms, on-campus apartments, and off-campus apartments. In addition, the college owns and rents houses to groups of students. On-campus housing is guaranteed for all 4 years, is available on a first-come, first-served basis, and is available on a lottery system for upperclassmen. 89% of students live on campus. Alcohol is not permitted. Upperclassmen may keep cars.

FACULTY/CLASSROOMS: 60% of faculty are male; 40% are female. All teach and do research. No introductory courses are taught by graduate students. The average class size in an introductory lecture is 19; in a laboratory is 17; and in a regular course is 18.

PROGRAMS OF STUDY: WC confers B.A., B.S., B.M., and B.M.E. degrees. Master's and doctoral degrees are also awarded. Bachelor's degrees are awarded in BIOLOGICAL SCIENCE (biology/biological science), BUSINESS (business economics), COMMUNICATIONS AND THE ARTS (art, classical languages, communications, English, French, German, music, and Spanish), COMPUTER AND PHYSICAL SCIENCE (applied mathematics, chemistry, computer science, geology, mathematics, and physics), EDUCATION (Christian education, elementary education, music education, and secondary education), ENGINEERING AND ENVIRONMENTAL DESIGN (engineering and environmental science), HEALTH PROFESSIONS (health science and nursing), SOCIAL SCIENCE (anthropology, archeology, biblical studies, economics, history, interdisciplinary studies, international relations, philosophy, political science/government, psychology, social science, sociology, and urban studies). Business/economics, biology, and applied health science have the largest enrollments.

ACTIVITIES: There are no fraternities or sororities. There are 91 groups on campus, including art, band, cheerleading, chess, choir, chorale, chorus, communications, computers, dance, debate, drama, environmental, ethnic, film, international, jazz band, literary magazine, musical theater, newspaper, opera, orchestra, pep band, political, professional, religious, social, social service, student government, and symphony. Popular campus events include New Student Orientation, College Union Concerts, and Talent Show. **Sports:** There are 11 intercollegiate sports for men and 10 for women, and 11 intramural sports for men and 10 for women. Facilities include a sports and recreation complex that features a weight room, gyms, an elevated jogging track, a climbing wall, a natatorium, and an arena. **Graduates:** From July 1, 2016 to June 30, 2017, 627 bachelor's degrees were awarded. The most popular majors were business economics (10%), English (8%), and applied health science (7%). In an average class, 80% graduate in 4 years or less, 88% graduate in 5 years or less, and 89% graduate in 6 years or less. Of the 2016 graduating class, 21% were enrolled in graduate school within 6 months of graduation, and 68% were employed.

SERVICES: Counseling and information services are available, as is tutoring in most subjects. There is a reader service for the blind. There is a writing center, and other services are provided as needed. **Library/Resources:** The library contains 611,357 volumes, 93,982 microform items, and 85,386 audio/video tapes/CDs/DVDs, and subscribes to 6,571 periodicals, including electronic. Computerized library services include interlibrary loans, database searching, Internet access, and Wi-Fi capability. Special learning facilities include an art gallery, a special collection of British authors' books and papers, an evangelical museum with document archives, and the Center for Applied Christian Ethics. The Science Building includes a unique, interactive atrium museum featuring the Perry Mastodon, a geology exhibit, a natural history exhibit, a Foucault pendulum, and additional exhibits. **Physically Challenged Students:** 97% of the campus is accessible. Facilities include wheelchair ramps, elevators, special parking, specially equipped restrooms, lowered drinking fountains, lowered telephones, and special housing. **Special:** Pre-Professional Programs - Health Professions and Pre-Law, Liberal Arts/Nursing 3-2 program (Emory University, Indiana Wesleyan University), and Liberal Arts/Engineering 3-2 program (Illinois Institute of Technology). There are 12 national honor societies and 15 departmental honors programs. **Visiting:** There are regularly scheduled orientations for prospective students, consisting of presentations by faculty, administrators, students, and financial aid, and admissions staff, as well as social activities. There are guides for informal visits; visitors may sit in on classes and stay overnight. **Campus Safety and Security:** Measures include 24-hour foot and vehicle patrol, an emergency notification system, self-defense education, and security escort services. There are shuttle buses, emergency telephones, lighted pathways/sidewalks, and controlled access to dorms/residences.

REQUIREMENTS: The SAT or ACT is required. A high school diploma is required and the GED is accepted. Wheaton requires a general college preparatory program of 15 units, including 4 units of English, 3 to 4 units of math, science, and social studies, and 2 to 3 units of a foreign language. AP credits are accepted. Important factors in the admissions decision are recommendations by school officials, advanced placement or honors courses, and personality/intangible qualities. To graduate, students must complete 124 semester hours, with 36 in upper-division courses and a minimum of 32 in a major, and maintain at least a 2.0 GPA. Students must satisfactorily meet all general education requirements in the areas of competency, a shared core requiring Bible and Theology and Integrative Studies courses, and a Thematic Core requiring 10 areas of study, including the arts, humanities, social science and science courses. A senior capstone is also required. **Procedure:** Freshmen are admitted in the fall and spring. Entrance exams should be taken in October of the senior year (early action) and December. There are early admissions and deferred admissions plans. Applications should be filed by January 10 for fall entry. The fall 2017 application fee was $50. Notifications are sent April 1. 28 applicants were on the 2017 waiting list; 15 were admitted. Applications are accepted online. **Transfer Students:** 64 transfer students enrolled in 2016-2017. Applicants must have completed 15 semester hours with a 3.0 average and present a high school transcripts, a college transcript, and an essay or personal statement. 48 of 124 credits required for the bachelor's degree must be completed at WC. **International Students:** There are 72 international students enrolled. They must take the TOEFL with a minimum score of 587 on the paper-based TOEFL (PBT) or 95 on the Internet-based version (iBT). Students must take the TSE or TWE. They must also take the SAT or ACT.

ADMISSIONS: 85% of the 2017-2018 applicants were accepted. The SAT scores for the 2017-2018 freshman class were: Math-- 3% below 500, 20% between 500 and 599, 53% between 600 and 699, and 25% between 700 and 800. Evidence-Based Reading/Writing-- 1% below 500, 9% between 500 and 599, 48% between 600 and 699, and 42% between 700 and 800. The ACT scores were 7% between 18 and 23, 45% between 24 and 29, and 48% above 30. 69% of the current freshmen were in the top fifth of their class; 88% were in the top two fifths. 27 freshmen graduated first in their class. **Admissions Contact:** Jason Kircher, Interim Director of Admissions. Email: *admissions@wheaton.edu* Web: *www.wheaton.edu*

FINANCIAL AID: In 2017-2018, 84% of all full-time freshmen received some form of financial aid. 59% of all full-time freshmen received need-based aid. The average freshman award was $27,369. Need-based scholarships or need-based grants averaged $23,361 ($45,444 maximum); need-based self-help aid (loans and jobs) averaged $5,176 ($11,500 maximum); and other non-need-based awards and non-need-based scholarships averaged $13,965 ($46,626 maximum). 45% of undergraduate students work part-time. The average financial indebtedness of the 2017 graduate was $27,543. WC is a member of CSS. The FAFSA code is 001781. The priority date for freshman financial aid applications for fall entry is November 10.

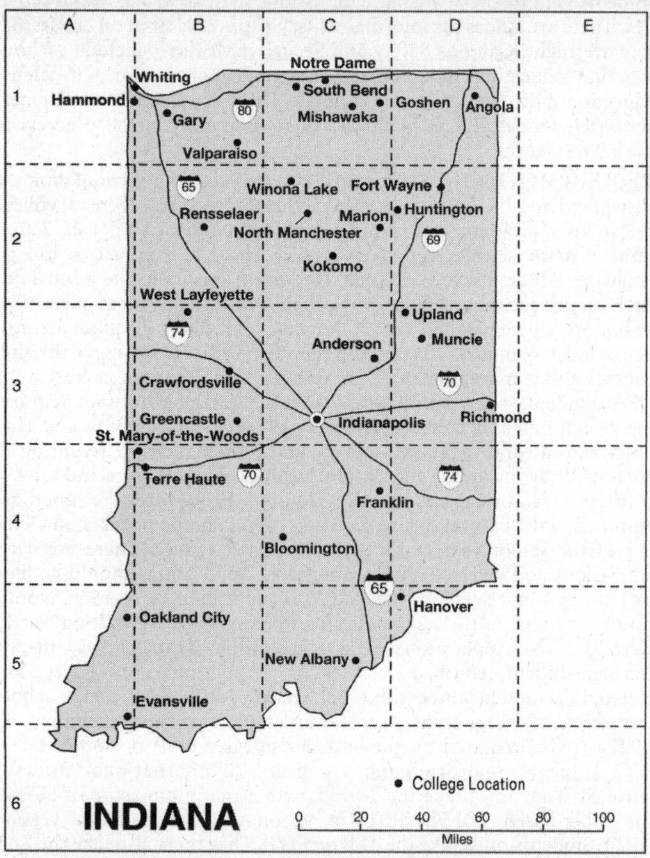

ANDERSON UNIVERSITY C-3

www.anderson.edu

Anderson, IN 46012	**(765) 641-4080**
	(800) 428-6414
Fax: (765) 641-4091	**Email: info@anderson.edu**
Full-time: 591 men, 840 women	**Faculty:** 116
Part-time: 54 men, 81 women	**Ph.D.s:** 85%
Graduate: 177 men, 133 women	**Student/Faculty:** 11 to 1
Year: semesters, summer session	**Tuition:** $29,710
Room & Board: $9740	**Freshman Class:** 2236 applied, 1459 accepted, 348 enrolled
SAT CR/M: 512/519 **ACT:** 23	**CEEB CODE:** 1016
Application Deadline: open	**COMPETITIVE**

Anderson University, founded in 1917, is a private liberal arts institution affiliated with the Church of God. The university offers programs in theoretical and applied science, social and professional studies, the arts, culture, and religion. There are 6 undergraduate schools and 4 graduate schools. In addition to regional accreditation, AU has baccalaureate program accreditation with ACBSP, CSWE, NASM, CAEP, and NLN. The 163-acre campus is in a suburban area 40 miles northeast of Indianapolis. Including any residence halls, there are 36 buildings.

STUDENT LIFE: 80% of undergraduates are from Indiana. Others are from 39 states, 18 foreign countries, and Canada. 90% are from public schools. 81% are White; 10% African American; 2% Hispanic; 2% Foreign; 2% race unknown; 1% Asian American; 1% American Indian/Alaska Native; 1% two or more races. 49% claim no religious affiliation; 46% Protestant. **Female To Male Ratio:** 1.3:1. The average age of freshmen is 18; all undergraduates, 21. 22% do not continue beyond their first year; 59% remain to graduate. **Housing:** 1157 students can be accommodated in college housing, which includes married student dorms, on-campus apartments, and off-campus apartments. On-campus housing is guaranteed for all 4 years. 65% of students live on campus. Alcohol is not permitted. All students may keep cars.

FACULTY/CLASSROOMS: 62% of faculty are male; 38% are female. 95% teach undergraduates. No introductory courses are taught by graduate students. The average class size in an introductory lecture is 19; in a laboratory is 17; and in a regular course is 16.

PROGRAMS OF STUDY: AU confers B.A., B.S., B.Mus., and B.S.N. degrees. Associate, master's, and doctoral degrees are also awarded. Bachelor's degrees are awarded in BIOLOGICAL SCIENCE (biochemistry and biology/biological science), BUSINESS (accounting, banking and finance, business administration and management, finance, management, management science, marketing, marketing/retailing/merchandising, and sports management), COMMUNICATIONS AND THE ARTS (communications, dance, dramatic arts, English, fine arts, French, graphic design, instrumental performance, film and media studies, music business management, music performance, Spanish, and vocal performance), COMPUTER AND PHYSICAL SCIENCE (chemistry, computer information systems, computer science, mathematics, and physics), EDUCATION (athletic training, elementary education, foreign languages education, general studies, health education, music education, physical education, science education, and social studies education), ENGINEERING AND ENVIRONMENTAL DESIGN (mechanical engineering), HEALTH PROFESSIONS (electrical engineering, exercise science, medical laboratory technology, and nursing), SOCIAL SCIENCE (criminal justice, economics, family/consumer studies, history, political science/government, psychology, religion, social work, sociology, and youth ministry). Physical sciences is the strongest academically. Business, education, and nursing have the largest enrollments.

ACTIVITIES: There are no fraternities or sororities. There are 41 groups on campus, including art, band, cheerleading, choir, chorale, dance, debate, drama, ethnic, film, honors, international, jazz band, literary magazine, musical theater, newspaper, opera, orchestra, photography, political, professional, radio and TV, religious, social, social service, student government, and symphony. Popular campus events include Heritage Week, Spiritual Emphasis Week, and Candles and Carols Christmas Performance. **Sports:** There are 9 intercollegiate sports for men and 9 for women, and 7 intramural sports for men and 7 for women. Facilities include gyms, football, baseball/softball, and soccer fields, an 8-lane all-weather track, tennis courts, bowling, a game room, a stadium, and indoor gym. **Graduates:** From July 1, 2016 to June 30, 2017, 393 bachelor's degrees were awarded. The most popular majors were business/marketing (21%), education (13%), and health professions and related programs (12%). In an average class, 44% graduate in 4 years or less, 52% graduate in 5 years or less, and 54% graduate in 6 years or less.

SERVICES: Counseling and information services are available, as is tutoring in most subjects. There is a reader service for the blind, and remedial math, reading, and writing. **Library/Resources:** The library contains 580,041 volumes, 38,706 microform items, 133,199 audio/video tapes/CDs/DVDs, and subscribes to 457 periodicals including electronic. Computerized library services include interlibrary loans and database searching. Special learning facilities include an art gallery, radio station, Museum of the Bible and the Ancient Near East. **Physically Challenged Students:** 97% of the campus is accessible. Facilities include wheelchair ramps, elevators, special parking, specially equipped restrooms, special class scheduling, lowered drinking fountains, and lowered telephones. **Special:** AU offers co-op programs with Purdue University, internships, study abroad in 25 countries through the International Studies Program, and a Washington semester. Also available are credit for military experience and pass/fail options. Courses in electronic engineering may be taken through the Purdue Anderson campus. Preprofessional programs are offered in medical, podiatry, dentistry, law, engineering, seminary, and several allied health fields. There are 16 national honor societies, a freshman honors program, and 10 departmental honors programs. **Visiting:** There are regularly scheduled orientations for prospective students, including a campus tour, an academic overview, financial aid and athletics overview, and appointments with professors and departmental chairs. There are guides for informal visits; visitors may sit in on classes and stay overnight. To schedule a visit, contact the Admissions Office. **Campus Safety and Security:** Measures include 24-hour foot and vehicle patrol, emergency notification system, self-defense education, and security escort services. There are emergency telephones, and lighted pathways/sidewalks. The Indiana state police academy graduates are AU security officers.

REQUIREMENTS: The SAT or ACT is required. Applicants must be graduates of an accredited secondary school or have a GED certificate and submit a photograph, references, and a health form. AP and CLEP credits are accepted. Important factors in the admissions decision are leadership record, recommendations by alumni, and personality/intangible qualities. Requirements for graduation include 120 credit hours with 40 to 58 hours in the general education core and at least 36 hours in the major. A minimum 2.0 GPA overall and in the major is required. All students must complete a liberal arts seminar. The last 24 credit hours must be taken in residence. **Procedure:** Freshmen are admitted in the fall and spring. Entrance exams should be taken in the fall of the junior year. There is a rolling admissions plan. Application deadlines are open. The fall 2017 application fee was $25. Applications are accepted online. **Transfer Students:** 78 transfer students enrolled in 2016-2017. Applicants must have a minimum 2.0 GPA, satisfactory SAT or ACT scores, and transcripts for all previously attended colleges. 24 of 120 credits required for the bachelor's degree must be completed at AU. **International Students:** There are 28 international students enrolled. They must take the TOEFL with a minimum score of 547 on the paper-based TOEFL (PBT) or 78 on the Internet-based version (iBT). They must also take the SAT.

ADMISSIONS: 65% of the 2017-2018 applicants were accepted. The SAT scores for the 2017-2018 freshman class were: Critical Reading-- 39% below 500, 37% between 500 and 599, 12% between 600 and 699, and 5% between 700 and 800. Math-- 44% below 500, 34% between 500 and 599, 20% between 600 and 699, and 2% between 700 and 800. The ACT scores were 15% between 12 and 17, 41% between 18 and 23, 38% between 24 and 29, and 6% above 30. 36% of the current freshmen were in the top fifth of their class; 60% were in the top two fifths. 10 freshmen graduated first in their class. **Admissions Contact:** Kynan Simison, Director of Admissions. Email: *info@anderson.edu* Web: *www.anderson.edu*

FINANCIAL AID: AU is a member of CSS. The FAFSA code is 001785. Check with the school for current application deadlines.

BALL STATE UNIVERSITY — D-3

www.bsu.edu

Muncie, IN 47306	**(765) 285-8287** **(800) 482-4BSU**
Fax: (765) 285-1632	**Email: askus@bsu.edu**
Full-time: 6211 men, 8992 women	**Faculty:** I, --$
Part-time: 670 men, 1131 women	**Ph.D.s:** n/av
Graduate: 1341 men, 4168 women	**Student/Faculty:** n/av
Year: semesters, summer session	**Tuition:** $9774 ($25,942)
Room & Board: $10,034	**Freshman Class:** 24221 applied, 15031 accepted, 3985 enrolled
SAT CR/M: 589/572 **ACT:** 23	**CEEB CODE:** 1051
Application Deadline: August 10	**COMPETITIVE+**

Ball State University, founded in 1918, is a public university offering undergraduate and graduate programs through 7 academic colleges in architecture and planning, business, communication, information, and media, fine arts, sciences and humanities, health, and teachers education. There are 7 undergraduate schools and 1 graduate school. In addition to regional accreditation, BSU has baccalaureate program accreditation with AACSB, ABET, ACBSP, ACEJMC, ADA, AHEA, ASLA, CAHEA, CSAB, CSWE, NAAB, NASAD, NASM, CEAP, and NLN. The 1140-acre campus is in a suburban area 56 miles northwest of Indianapolis. Including any residence halls, there are 106 buildings.

STUDENT LIFE: 85% of undergraduates are from Indiana. Others are from 50 states, 70 foreign countries, and Canada. 8% are African American; 78% White; 5% Hispanic; 3% two or more races; 3% race unknown; 2% Foreign; 1% Asian American. **Female To Male Ratio:** 1.7:1. The average age of freshmen is 18; all undergraduates, 21. 21% do not continue beyond their first year; 62% remain to graduate. **Housing:** College-sponsored housing includes married student dorms and on-campus apartments. In addition, there are honors houses, special-interest houses, and sorority houses. On-campus housing is guaranteed for the freshman year only. 56% of students commute. Alcohol is not permitted. All students may keep cars.

FACULTY/CLASSROOMS: No introductory courses are taught by graduate students.

PROGRAMS OF STUDY: BSU confers B.A., B.A.T., B.F.A., B.S., B.ARCH., B.G.S., B.L.A., B.M., B.S.W., and B.U.P.D. degrees. Associate, master's, and doctoral degrees are also awarded. Bachelor's degrees are awarded in AGRICULTURE (natural resource management), BIOLOGICAL SCIENCE (biology/biological science), BUSINESS (accounting, business administration and management, business administration - international, business economics, economics – statistics, finance, human resources, marketing, operations management, and sports management), COMMUNICATIONS AND THE ARTS (acting, advertising, animation, art, Chinese, classical languages, classics, dance, digital media, English, French, German, Greek, Japanese, journalism, Latin, literature, film and media studies, music, Spanish, and sports administration), COMPUTER AND PHYSICAL SCIENCE (actuarial science, applied mathematics, applied physics, astronomy, chemistry, computer science, data processing, geology, mathematics, and physics), EDUCATION (early childhood education, elementary education, health education, home economics education, industrial arts education, physical education, reading education, science education, and special education), ENGINEERING AND ENVIRONMENTAL DESIGN (architecture, city/community/regional planning, environmental design, environmental science, graphic arts technology, industrial engineering technology, landscape architecture/design, preengineering, and urban planning technology), HEALTH PROFESSIONS (health science, medical technology, nursing, predentistry, premedicine, preoptometry, preveterinary science, respiratory therapy, and speech pathology/audiology), SOCIAL SCIENCE (anthropology, criminal justice, dietetics, economics, family/consumer studies, geography, history, home economics, international studies, liberal arts/general studies, philosophy, political science/government, prelaw, psychology, religion, social science, social work, sociology, and women's studies). Architecture, business, TCOM, and education are the strongest academically. Elementary education, business, and radio and television have the largest enrollments.

ACTIVITIES: 15% of men belong to 18 national fraternities; 17% of women belong to 15 national sororities. There are 390 groups on campus, including art, band, cheerleading, chess, choir, chorale, chorus, computers, dance, debate, drama, drill team, ethnic, film, forensics, honors, international, jazz band, LGBT, literary magazine, marching band, musical theater, newspaper, opera, orchestra, pep band, photography, political, professional, radio and TV, religious, social, social service, student government, and symphony. Popular campus events include Late Night Carnival, Unity Week, and Family Weekend. **Sports:** Facilities include the student recreation/wellness facility, has an fitness center with an elevated jogging track, basketball/volleyball gym, a climbing wall, indoor turf field including batting cages, an auxiliary gym, a game room, racquetball/handball and wallyball courts, competitive pool, and a field sports building. **Graduates:** The most popular majors were business/marketing (17%), communication/journalism (14%), and health professions and related programs (10%).

SERVICES: Counseling and information services are available, as is tutoring in most subjects. There is a reader service for the blind. **Library/Resources:** The library contains 1.1 million volumes, 1.0 million microform items, and 77,911 audio/video tapes/CDs/DVDs, and subscribes to 104,066 periodicals including electronic. Computerized library services include interlibrary loans, database searching, Internet access, and Wi-Fi capability. Special learning facilities include an art gallery, planetarium, radio station, TV station, research centers in solar energy, a human performance lab, and international programs. **Physically Challenged Students:** 95% of the campus is accessible. Facilities include wheelchair ramps, elevators, special parking, specially equipped restrooms, special class scheduling, lowered drinking fountains, lowered telephones, and special housing. A special resource guide, an accessibility map (including tactile), and text telephones (TDD) in all key offices are also available. **Special:** Nearly all undergraduate disciplines offer internships, and work study is available. Study abroad is possible at the university's London center and in 20 other programs; students may also spend a semester in Washington, D.C. Most disciplines offer dual majors, and accelerated degrees are available. There is a B.A.-B.S. degree in elementary/special education, 3-2 program in engineering, an award-winning program in entrepreneurship, a general studies degree, nondegree study, and pass/fail options. There are 35 national honor societies and a freshman honors program. **Visiting:** There are regularly scheduled orientations for prospective students, consisting of twice-a-day presentations and tours . There are guides for informal visits and visitors may sit in on classes. To schedule a visit, contact the Welcome Center at (765) 285-5683. **Campus Safety and Security:** Measures include 24-hour foot and vehicle patrol, emergency notification system, self-defense education, and security escort services. There are shuttle buses, emergency telephones, lighted pathways/sidewalks, and controlled access to dorms/residences.

REQUIREMENTS: Admission is a holistic review based on strength of applicants' curriculum, grades in English, math, lab sciences, social sciences, and foreign language, curricula patterns and grade trends, and the SAT or ACT scores. AP and CLEP credits are accepted. All students must take at least 120 credits and maintain a 2.0 GPA for graduation, and required hours in the major vary by program. Required courses are in English composition, math, speech, history, personal finance, physical sciences, social or behavioral sciences, humanities or fine arts, global studies, and 2 hours of phys ed. In addition, all juniors must pass a writing proficiency exam. **Procedure:** Freshmen are admitted in the fall, spring, and summer. Entrance exams should be taken during the spring of the junior year or early in the senior year. There are deferred admissions and rolling admissions plans. Applications should be filed by August 10 for fall entry. The fall 2017 application fee was $55. Notification is sent on a rolling basis. 3061 applicants were on the 2017 waiting list; 787 were admitted. Applications are accepted on-line. **Transfer Students:** 796 transfer students enrolled in 2016-2017. Applicants are considered if they have earned a minimum cumulative GPA of 2.0 on a 4.0 scale for all transferable coursework attempted. Courses from remedial programs, vocational and technical schools, and colleges and universities that are not regionally accredited cannot be transferred. Accrediting associations include: Middle States Commission on Higher Education, Higher Learning Commission, New England Association, Northwest Commission on Colleges and Universities, Southern Association, and Western Association. Admissions decisions will be based upon your academic records at all educational institutions you've attended. Students must be in good academic standing and eligible to return immediately to the last institution you attended. If you apply for transfer admission to Ball State while you're enrolled at another college or university, you may be considered for admission on the basis of your current college or university cumulative GPA. If you're admitted to BSU while enrolled at another college or university (referred to as "admit with conditions"), your cumulative GPA must remain above 2.0. Admission granted under such circumstances may be withdrawn if your cumulative GPA falls below 2.0. 30 of 120 credits required for the bachelor's degree must be completed at BSU. **International Students:** There are 244 international students enrolled. They must take the TOEFL with a minimum score of 550 on the paper-based TOEFL (PBT) or 79 on the Internet-based version (iBT). The SAT or ACT is recommended.

ADMISSIONS: 62% of the 2017-2018 applicants were accepted. The SAT scores for the 2017-2018 freshman class were: Critical Reading-- 7% below 500, 58% between 500 and 599, 31% between 600 and 699, and 4% between 700 and 800. Math-- 13% below 500, 62% between 500 and 599, 23% between 600 and 699, and 2% between 700 and 800. The ACT scores were 2% between 12 and 17, 56% between 18 and 23, 36% between 24 and 29, and 6% above 30. 55% of the current freshmen were in the top fifth of their class; 68% were in the top two fifths. 35 freshmen graduated first in their class. **Admissions Contact:** Chris Munchel, Associate VP of Enrollment and Director of Admissions. Email: *askus@bsu.edu* Web: *www.bsu.edu*

FINANCIAL AID: BSU is a member of CSS. The FAFSA code is 001786. The priority date for freshman financial aid applications for fall entry is March 15.

BETHEL COLLEGE — C-1
www.bethelcollege.edu

Mishawaka, IN 46545	(574) 807-7600 (800) 422-4101
Fax: (574) 807-7650	Email: admissions@BethelCollege.edu
Full-time: 410 men, 623 women	**Faculty:** 67; IIB, --$
Part-time: 62 men, 199 women	**Ph.D.s:** 55%
Graduate: 81 men, 138 women	**Student/Faculty:** 13 to 1
Year: semesters, summer session	**Tuition:** $28,030
Room & Board: $8800	**Freshman Class:** 1058 applied, 949 accepted, 226 enrolled
SAT EBR-W/M: 530/520 **ACT:** 23	**CEEB CODE:** 1079
Application Deadline: rolling	**COMPETITIVE**

Bethel College, founded in 1947, is a private institution affiliated with the Missionary Church, offering undergraduate and master's degree programs with a Christian perspective. There is 1 undergraduate school and 1 graduate school. In addition to regional accreditation, BC has baccalaureate program accreditation with NASM, CAEP, and ACEN. The 80-acre campus is in a suburban area of Northern Indiana, adjacent to South Bend, 90 miles east of Chicago. Including any residence halls, there are 52 buildings.

STUDENT LIFE: 73% of undergraduates are from Indiana. Others are from 29 states, and 15 foreign countries. 78% are from public schools. 8% are Hispanic; 72% White; 5% two or more races; 2% Asian American; 2% Foreign; 10% African American; 1% race unknown. 71% are Protestant; 21% claim no religious affiliation. **Female To Male Ratio:** 1.7:1. The average age of freshmen is 18; all undergraduates, 24. 22% do not continue beyond their first year; 64% remain to graduate. **Housing:** 781 students can be accommodated in college housing, which includes single-sex and married student dorms, on-campus apartments, and off-campus apartments. In addition, there are special-interest houses, urban ministries house. On-campus housing is guaranteed for all 4 years. 52% of students live on campus. Alcohol is not permitted. Upperclassmen may keep cars.

FACULTY/CLASSROOMS: 54% of faculty are male; 46% are female. All teach undergraduates. No introductory courses are taught by graduate students. The average class size in an introductory lecture is 25; in a laboratory is 12; and in a regular course is 17.

PROGRAMS OF STUDY: BC confers B.A., B.S. and B.S.N. degrees. Associate and master's degrees are also awarded. Bachelor's degrees are awarded in BIOLOGICAL SCIENCE (biochemistry and biology/biological science), BUSINESS (accounting, business administration and management, business economics, financial services, and sports management), COMMUNICATIONS AND THE ARTS (American Sign Language, communications, dramatic arts, English Writing, graphic design, music, music performance, studio art, and theatre arts), COMPUTER AND PHYSICAL SCIENCE (chemistry, mathematics, and physical sciences), EDUCATION (art education, early childhood education, education, elementary education, English secondary education, mathematics education, music education, physical education, science education, secondary education, social studies education, and sports studies), ENGINEERING AND ENVIRONMENTAL DESIGN (engineering management, engineering physics, and preengineering), HEALTH PROFESSIONS (exercise science and nursing), SOCIAL SCIENCE (behavioral science, biblical studies, Christian studies, criminal justice, economics, history, human services, interdisciplinary studies, international studies, interpreter for the deaf, liberal arts/general studies, ministries, missions, pastoral studies, philosophy, philosophy and religion, political science/government, psychology, religion, and sociology). Psychology, religion/philosophy, and nursing are the strongest academically. Business, nursing, and elementary education have the largest enrollments.

ACTIVITIES: There are no fraternities or sororities. There are 15 groups on campus, including art, band, cheerleading, choir, chorale, chorus, drama, ethnic, honors, international, jazz band, musical theater, newspaper, pep band, political, professional, radio and TV, religious, social, student government, and yearbook. Popular campus events include All-Campus Christmas Party, BABE and Dude Week, Spiritual Emphasis Week, Service Day, Midnight Breakfast, Leadership Weekend, and World Christian Action Conference. **Sports:** There are 9 intercollegiate sports for men and 10 for women, and 7 intramural sports for men and 5 for women. Facilities include gyms, weight rooms, exercise rooms, indoor baseball training facilities, baseball, softball, soccer fields, tennis courts, and a practice track. **Graduates:** From July 1, 2016 to June 30, 2017, 338 bachelor's degrees were awarded. The most popular majors were business (21%), nursing (14%), and education (10%). In an average class, 1% graduate in 3 years or less, 59% graduate in 4 years or less, 63% graduate in 5 years or less, and 64% graduate in 6 years or less. Of the 2016 graduating class, 15% were enrolled in graduate school within 6 months of graduation, and 90% were employed.

SERVICES: Counseling and information services are available, as is tutoring in most subjects. There is remedial math, reading, and writing. **Library/Resources:** The library contains 305,090 volumes, 4,577 microform items, 1,698 audio/video tapes/CDs/DVDs, and subscribes to 1,971 periodicals including electronic. Computerized library services include interlibrary loans, database searching, Internet access, and Wi-Fi capability. Special learning facilities include an art gallery and radio station. **Physically Challenged Students:** 80% of the campus is accessible. Facilities include wheelchair ramps, elevators, special parking, specially equipped restrooms, lowered drinking fountains, and special housing. **Special:** Students may cross-register for courses at various local colleges including Northern Indiana Consortium for Education (NICE). Also available are a 3-2 engineering degree with the University of Notre Dame and Trine University (Angola), a liberal arts degree, degree programs for nontraditional students, and online degree programs. BC also offers a pass/fail course option, student teaching, internships, and study abroad in several countries. Army and Air Force ROTC programs are available. There is 1 national honor society and a freshman honors program. **Visiting:** There are regularly scheduled orientations for prospective students, including an interview, chapel visit, tour, lunch, and a class or professor visit as requested. There are guides for informal visits; visitors may sit in on classes and stay overnight. To schedule a visit, contact the Office of Admission. **Campus Safety and Security:** Measures include 24-hour foot and vehicle patrol, emergency notification system, self-defense education, and security escort services. There are emergency telephones, lighted pathways/sidewalks, and controlled access to dorms/residences.

REQUIREMENTS: The SAT or ACT is required. Applicants should be graduates of a secondary school program or have the GED. BC recommends that 17 academic units in secondary school include 4 in English, 3 in math, 2 in history and foreign language, and 1 each in lab science and social science. An audition is required of music program applicants. AP and CLEP credits are accepted. To graduate, students must complete 120 credits, including 24 to 52 in the major, with a minimum 2.0 GPA. Also required 9 credits in Bible and religion, courses in communication, social science, history, fine arts, humanities, natural sciences, mathematics, fitness, and physical activity. The last 30 hours of a bachelor's degree must be completed at Bethel. **Procedure:** Freshmen are admitted to all sessions. Entrance exams should be taken as early as possible in the junior or senior year. There are early admissions, deferred admissions, and rolling admissions plans. Application deadlines are open. Applications are accepted on-line. **Transfer Students:** 194 transfer students enrolled in 2016-2017. Grades of C or better are eligible for transfer; students without a minimum GPA of 2.0 may be admitted on probation. Other admission requirements are the same as for entering freshmen. 30 of 120 credits required for the bachelor's degree must be completed at BC. **International Students:** There are 13 international students enrolled. They must take the TOEFL with a minimum score of 540 on the paper-based TOEFL (PBT) or 76 on the Internet-based version (iBT). Student must take the IELTS.

ADMISSIONS: 90% of the 2017-2018 applicants were accepted. The SAT scores for the 2017-2018 freshman class were: Math-- 35% below 500, 46% between 500 and 599, 15% between 600 and 699, and 4% between 700 and 800. Evidence-Based Reading/Writing-- 31% below 500, 44% between 500 and 599, 21% between 600 and 699, and 4% between 700 and 800. The ACT scores were 17% between 12 and 17, 43% between 18 and 23, 36% between 24 and 29, and 4% above 30. 32% of the current freshmen were in the top fifth of their class; 62% were in the top two fifths. 2 freshmen graduated first in their class. **Admissions Contact:** Stephanie Hochstetler, Director of Admission. Email: *admissions@BethelCollege.edu* Web: *www.bethelcollege.edu*

FINANCIAL AID: In 2017-2018, 99% of all full-time freshmen received some form of financial aid. 77% of all full-time freshmen received need-based aid. The average freshman award was $24,360. Need-based scholarships or need-based grants averaged $9,517; need-based self-help aid (loans and jobs) averaged $3,532; non-need-based athletic scholarships averaged $4,291; and other non-need-based awards and non-need-based scholarships averaged $13,319. 30% of undergraduate students work part-time. The average financial indebtedness of the 2017 graduate was $34,200. BC is a member of CSS. The FAFSA code is 001787. The priority date for freshman financial aid applications for fall entry is March 1.

BUTLER UNIVERSITY C-3

www.butler.edu

Indianapolis, IN 46208 (317) 940-8100
(888) 940-8100

Fax: (317) 940-8150
Email: admission@butler.edu

Full-time: 1736 men, 2689 women	**Faculty:** 365; IIA, -$
Part-time: 27 men, 27 women	**Ph.D.s:** 80%
Graduate: 215 men, 405 women	**Student/Faculty:** 12 to 1
Year: semesters, summer session	**Tuition:** $38,920
Room & Board: $13,020	**Freshman Class:** 14636 applied, 9531 accepted, 1064 enrolled
SAT CR/M: 614/609 **ACT:** 27	**CEEB CODE:** 1073
Application Deadline: February 1	**VERY COMPETITIVE+**

Butler University, founded in 1855, is an independent, private institution offering programs in liberal arts and sciences, business, communications, fine and performing arts, pharmacy and health sciences, and education. Butler emphasizes experiential learning (including internships, service learning, and research) and job placement outcomes. There are 6 undergraduate schools and 5 graduate schools. In addition to regional accreditation, BU has baccalaureate program accreditation with AACSB, ACPE, NASAD, NASM, CAEP, ARCPA, ACS, CACREP, IDOE, NASD, and NAST. The 295-acre campus is in a suburban area in the city of Indianapolis, approximately five miles north of downtown, near the Broad Ripple cultural district. Including any residence halls, there are 39 buildings.

STUDENT LIFE: 56% of undergraduates are from out of state, mostly the Midwest. Students are from 50 states, 27 foreign countries, and Canada. 83% are White; 4% African American; 4% Hispanic; 3% Asian American; 3% two or more races; 3% race unknown; 1% Foreign. **Female To Male Ratio:** 1.6:1. The average age of freshmen is 18; all undergraduates, 20. 8% do not continue beyond their first year; 74% remain to graduate. **Housing:** 2368 students can be accommodated in college housing, which includes dorms, on-campus apartments, and off-campus apartments. In addition, there are fraternity houses and sorority houses. On-campus housing is guaranteed for all 4 years and is available on a lottery system for upperclassmen. 77% of students live on campus. Alcohol is not permitted. All students may keep cars.

FACULTY/CLASSROOMS: 50% of faculty are male; 50% are female. No introductory courses are taught by graduate students. The average class size in an introductory lecture is 23; in a laboratory is 19; and in a regular course is 22.

PROGRAMS OF STUDY: BU confers B.A., B.S., B.F.A., B.M., B.S.H.S., and B.S.E. degrees. Associate, master's, and doctoral degrees are also awarded. Bachelor's degrees are awarded in BIOLOGICAL SCIENCE (biochemistry and biology/biological science), BUSINESS (accounting, banking and finance, international business management, management information systems, and marketing/retailing/merchandising), COMMUNICATIONS AND THE ARTS (advertising, art, arts administration/management, communications, dance, dramatic arts, English, French, German, Greek (classical), jazz, journalism, Latin, media arts, music, music performance, music theory and composition, performing arts, public relations, Spanish, speech/debate/rhetoric, strategic communication, theatre arts, and voice), COMPUTER AND PHYSICAL SCIENCE (actuarial science, chemistry, computer science, mathematics, physics, and software engineering), EDUCATION (elementary education, middle school education, music education, secondary education, and special education), ENGINEERING AND ENVIRONMENTAL DESIGN (biomedical engineering and engineering), HEALTH PROFESSIONS (health science, pharmacy, and speech pathology/audiology), SOCIAL SCIENCE (anthropology, criminal justice, economics, gender studies, history, international studies, philosophy, political science/government, psychology, religion, science and society, and sociology). Pharmacy, marketing, and biology have the largest enrollments.

ACTIVITIES: 17% of men belong to 5 national fraternities; 26% of women belong to 9 national sororities. There are 155 groups on campus, including college mentors for kids, philanthropic club, strategic games club, veterans, art, band, cheerleading, chess, choir, chorale, chorus, computers, dance, debate, drama, drill team, emerging leaders, environmental, ethnic, film, honors, international, jazz band, LGBT, literary magazine, marching band, musical theater, newspaper, opera, orchestra, pep band, photography, political, professional, radio and TV, religious, social, social service, student government, symphony, and yearbook. Popular campus events include Bulldogs Into the Streets, Homecoming, Dance Marathon, ButlerPalooza, and Spring Sports Spectacular. **Sports:** There are 9 intercollegiate sports for men and 11 for women, and 16 intramural sports for men and 16 for women. Facilities include a field house, football stadium, tennis courts, indoor and outdoor tracks, a weight-training room, an aerobics/exercise room, intramural fields, baseball, softball, and soccer fields. The Health Education and Recreation Complex, provides counseling and consultation services. **Graduates:** From July 1, 2016 to June 30, 2017, 838 bachelor's degrees were awarded. The most popular majors were marketing (11%), finance (8%), and health sciences (6%). In an average class, 51% graduate in 4 years or less, 65% graduate in 5 years or less, and 74% graduate in 6 years or less. Of the 2016 graduating class, 20% were enrolled in graduate school within 6 months of graduation, and 55% were employed.

SERVICES: Counseling and information services are available, as is tutoring in every subject, such as math, most sciences, and the Core curriculum. There is a reader service for the blind. The Writer's Studio offers assistance in all areas of the writing process. **Library/Resources:** The library contains 238,728 volumes, 12,260 microform items, and 20,132 audio/video tapes/CDs/DVDs, and subscribes to 61,114 periodicals including electronic. Computerized library services include interlibrary loans, database searching, Internet access, and Wi-Fi capability. Special learning facilities include a planetarium, and the Holcomb Observatory and Planetarium. **Physically Challenged Students:** All of the campus is accessible. Facilities include wheelchair ramps, elevators, special parking, specially equipped restrooms, special class scheduling, and lowered drinking fountains. **Special:** BU offers co-op programs in business administration, internships in most academic programs, extensive study abroad programs, a Washington learning semester, and work study programs. Also available is a 3-2 degree program in engineering with Indiana University Purdue University in Indianapolis, as well as cross registration with the 6 other members of the Consortium for Urban Education, which includes Franklin College, University of Indianapolis, Indiana University Purdue University Indianapolis, Indiana Vocational Technical College, Marian University, and Martin University. In addition to numerous majors offered for a Bachelor of Arts or Bachelor of Science degree, BU offers several dual majors, including a sociology major combined with criminology, majors in philosophy, anthropology, criminology, sociology and political science combined with psychology, a history major combined with anthropology or political science, and a religion major combined with anthropology or philosophy. Other offerings include student designed majors, a general studies associate degree, pass/fail options, and non-degree study. Also offered are graduate non-degree certificate programs in college and career readiness, wellness and sport leadership, International Baccalaureate teaching and learning, licensed mental health counselor, and teachers of the visually impaired, and an alternative graduate initial licensure program, as well as an accelerated alternative certificate for licensure in Mild Interventions. There are 9 national honor societies, Phi Beta Kappa, and a freshman honors program. **Visiting:** There are regularly scheduled orientations for prospective students, Traditional prospective student visits include an admission and financial aid presentation followed by a campus tour. There are guides for informal visits and visitors may sit in on classes. To schedule a visit, contact the Office of Admission. **Campus Safety and Security:** Measures include 24-hour foot and vehicle patrol, emergency notification system, self-defense education, and security escort services. There are shuttle buses, emergency telephones, lighted pathways/sidewalks, and controlled access to dorms/residences.

REQUIREMENTS: The SAT or ACT is required. Applicants must be slated to graduate from an accredited secondary school, and/or have demonstrated successful completion of all required academic units. Applicants must be on track to earn at least 17 core academic units, including 4 years of English, 3 each of math and lab science, 2 each of the same foreign language, and 2 each of history/social science; the balance of coursework may include electives or advanced coursework in core academic courses. In addition to submitting the Common Application or BU Application, a separate application and audition or interview is required for all candidates applying for admission to the Jordan College of the Arts. AP and CLEP credits are accepted. Important factors in the admissions decision are advanced placement or honors courses, extracurricular activities record, and recommendations by school officials. Complementing students' majors, the BU Core Curriculum emphasizes the development of key skills that transfer directly into careers post-graduation. Employers are seeking flexible, creative, and critical thinkers who can demonstrate competencies in strong written and oral communication, information fluency, intercultural awareness, and analytical and ethical reasoning skills. Through direct experience working in the Indianapolis community, study abroad opportunities, and rich cultural experiences in the Core Curriculum, BU students also engage central issues of our increasingly globalized world, including diversity, personal and social responsibility, and social justice. In these varied ways, the Core Curriculum prepares BU students to enter the workforce as successful professionals and well-rounded individuals. **Procedure:** Freshmen are admitted to all sessions. Entrance exams should be taken during the junior year or early the senior year. There are early admissions and deferred admissions plans. Early decision applications should be filed by November 1; regular applications, by February 1 for fall entry; and November 1 for spring entry. Notification of early decision is sent December 15; regular decision, February 15. Applications are accepted online. **Transfer Students:** 72 transfer students enrolled in 2016-2017. Applicants who have completed more than 11 hours of college work following graduation from an accredited secondary school must present transcripts from all previous college attended, indicating good standing and a minimum GPA of 2.5, and an official high school transcript showing a posted date of graduation. Those students with fewer than 20 hours must also, submit SAT or ACT scores. Students wishing to transfer into pharmacy must apply through PharmCAS; and students applying to the professional phase of physician assistant program must apply through CASPA. Transfer credits for classes taken online may be restricted. 45 of 120 credits required for the bachelor's degree must be completed at BU. **International Students:** There are 95 international students enrolled. They must take the TOEFL with a minimum score of 550 on the paper-based TOEFL (PBT) or 79 on the Internet-based version (iBT). Students must complete level 5 at the American Language Academy on Butler's campus.

ADMISSIONS: 65% of the 2017-2018 applicants were accepted. The SAT scores for the 2017-2018 freshman class were: Critical Reading-- 3% below 500, 38% between 500 and 599, 48% between 600 and 699, and 12% between 700 and 800. Math-- 4% below 500, 40% between 500 and 599, 48% between 600 and 699, and 9% between 700 and 800. Writing-- 14% between 500 and 599, 6% between 600 and 699, and 1% between 700 and 800. The ACT scores were 16% between 18 and 23, 54% between 24 and 29, and 30% above 30. **Admissions Contact:** Delorean Menifee, Director of Admissions. Email: *admission@butler.edu* Web: *www.butler.edu*

FINANCIAL AID: In 2017-2018, 97% of all full-time freshmen received some form of financial aid. 61% of all full-time freshmen received need-based aid. The average freshman award was $25,981. Need-based scholarships or need-based grants averaged $21,726; need-based self-help aid (loans and jobs) averaged $3,658; non-need-based athletic scholarships averaged $24,534; and other non-need-based awards and non-need-based scholarships averaged $15,614. The average financial indebtedness of the 2017 graduate was $40,393. BU is a member of CSS. The FAFSA code is 001788. The priority date for freshman financial aid applications for fall entry is March 1.

CALUMET COLLEGE OF ST. JOSEPH — B-1
www.ccsj.edu

Whiting, IN 46394	(219) 473-4739 (877) 700-9100
Fax: (219) 473-4259	**Email:** admissions@ccsj.edu
Full-time: 160 men, 310 women	**Faculty:** IIA
Part-time: 345 men, 385 women	**Ph.D.s:** 50%
Graduate: 100 men, 40 women	**Student/Faculty:** n/av
Year: semesters, summer session	**Tuition:** $17,135
Room & Board: $5600	**Freshman Class:** n/av
SAT or ACT: recommended	**CEEB CODE:** 1776
Application Deadline: open	**COMPETITIVE**

Calumet College of St. Joseph, founded in 1951, is a private Catholic institution offering commuting students a liberal arts education in a Christian environment. The figures given in the above capsule and in this profile are approximate. There are 2 undergraduate schools. The 256-acre campus is in a small town 15 miles southeast of Chicago in northwest Indiana. Including any residence halls, there is 1 building.

STUDENT LIFE: 70% of undergraduates are from Indiana. Others are from 2 states. 65% are from public schools. 46% are White; 33% African American; 19% Hispanic. 45% are Catholic. **Female To Male Ratio:** 1.2:1. The average age of freshmen is 21; all undergraduates, 35. 42% do not continue beyond their first year; 58% remain to graduate. **Housing:** Alcohol is not permitted. All students may keep cars.

FACULTY/CLASSROOMS: 75% of faculty are male; 25% are female. All teach undergraduates. No introductory courses are taught by graduate students. The average class size in an introductory lecture is 25; in a laboratory is 20; and in a regular course is 20.

PROGRAMS OF STUDY: CCSJ confers B.A., B.S., B.S.Ed. and B.S.M.T. degrees. Associate and master's degrees are also awarded. Bachelor's degrees are awarded in BUSINESS (accounting, business administration and management, and institutional management), COMMUNICATIONS AND THE ARTS (English and media arts), COMPUTER AND PHYSICAL SCIENCE (information sciences and systems), EDUCATION (elementary education and secondary education), HEALTH PROFESSIONS (health care administration), SOCIAL SCIENCE (criminal justice, human services, law enforcement and corrections, liberal arts/

general studies, paralegal studies, psychology, religion, theological studies, and urban studies). Management, accounting, and criminal justice are the strongest academically. Management, human services, and education have the largest enrollments.

ACTIVITIES: There are no fraternities or sororities. There are 15 groups on campus, including cheerleading, drama, ethnic, literary magazine, musical theater, newspaper, photography, professional, religious, social, social service, and student government. Popular campus events include Thanksgiving Ethnicfest and Student Appreciation Week. **Sports:** There is 1 intramural sport for men.

SERVICES: Counseling and information services are available, as is tutoring in most subjects. There is remedial math, reading, and writing. **Library/Resources:** The library contains 93,055 volumes, 3,035 microform items, and 6,412 audio/video tapes/CDs/DVDs, and subscribes to 354 periodicals including electronic. Computerized library services include interlibrary loans and database searching. Special learning facilities include an art gallery. **Physically Challenged Students:** All of the campus is accessible. Facilities include wheelchair ramps, elevators, special parking, and specially equipped restrooms. **Special:** The college offers a cooperative 3-1 baccalaureate degree in medical technology with the schools of St. Margaret-Mercy Hospital in Indiana, where students complete their study and a clinical internship. Accelerated degree programs in organizational management, health-care management, and law enforcement management are possible. The LEAP program offers credit for life experience. Study abroad, internships, work-study programs, a general studies degree, pass/fail options, and nondegree study are possible. **Visiting:** There are regularly scheduled orientations for prospective students. There are guides for informal visits and visitors may sit in on classes. To schedule a visit, contact the Director of Admissions. **Campus Safety and Security:** There are emergency telephones and lighted pathways/sidewalks.

REQUIREMENTS: The SAT or ACT is recommended. Applicants should have completed 4 years of high school English, 3 to 4 of math, 2 to 3 of science, and 2 of social studies. The GED is accepted. An essay and an interview are recommended. The Vocabulary and Reading Assessment Test is required. A GPA of 2.0 is required. AP and CLEP credits are accepted. Important factors in the admissions decision are extracurricular activities record, leadership record, and evidence of special talent. All students must complete 42 semester hours of general education courses, including English composition, economics, speech, theology, philosophy, communication and fine arts, science and math, and social and behavioral science. A total of 124 semester hours with a minimum GPA of 2.0 is required to graduate. **Procedure:** Freshmen are admitted to all sessions. There are deferred admissions and rolling admissions plans. Application deadlines are open. Applications are accepted on-line. **Transfer Students:** A 2.0 GPA is required. An interview is recommended. The Vocabulary and Reading Assessment Test is required. 30 of 124 credits required for the bachelor's degree must be completed at CCSJ. **International Students:** They must take the TOEFL.

Admissions Contact: Carl Cutton, Director of Admissions and Financial Aid. Email: *admissions@ccsj.edu* Web: *www.ccsj.edu*

FINANCIAL AID: CCSJ is a member of CSS. The college's own financial statement is required. The FAFSA code is 001834. Check with the school for current application deadlines.

DEPAUW UNIVERSITY — B-3

www.depauw.edu

Greencastle, IN 46135	**(765) 658-4006** **(800) 447-2495**
Fax: (765) 658-4007	**Email: admission@depauw.edu**
Full-time: 1046 men, 1179 women	**Faculty:** 224; IIB, ++$
Part-time: n/av	**Ph.D.s:** 91%
Graduate: n/av	**Student/Faculty:** 10 to 1
Year: 4-1-4	**Tuition:** $46,448
Room & Board: $12,240	**Freshman Class:** 4913 applied, 3023 accepted, 578 enrolled
SAT CR/M/W: 580/600/580 **ACT:** 27	**CEEB CODE:** 1166
Application Deadline: March 1	**VERY COMPETITIVE**

DePauw University, founded in 1837, is a private institution offering programs in the fields of liberal arts and music. There are 2 undergraduate schools. In addition to regional accreditation, DePauw has baccalaureate program accreditation with NASM, CAEP, ACS, and CAAHEP. The 695-acre campus is in a rural area 45 miles west of Indianapolis. Including any residence halls, there are 81 buildings.

STUDENT LIFE: 64% of undergraduates are from out of state, mostly the Midwest. Students are from 49 states, and 30 foreign countries. 88% are from public schools. 75% are White; 7% Foreign; 6% African American; 4% Hispanic; 3% Asian American. 45% are Protestant; 20% Catholic. **Female To Male Ratio:** 1.1:1. The average age of freshmen is 19; all undergraduates, 20. 10% do not continue beyond their first year; 83% remain to graduate. **Housing:** 1490 students can be accommodated in college housing, which includes dorms, on-campus apartments, and off-campus apartments. In addition, there are special-interest houses, fraternity houses, sorority houses, and international student housing. On-campus housing is guaranteed for all 4 years. 99% of students live on campus. All students may keep cars.

FACULTY/CLASSROOMS: 55% of faculty are male; 45% are female. All teach undergraduates, and 82% do research. No introductory courses are taught by graduate students. The average class size in an introductory lecture is 20; in a laboratory is 14; and in a regular course is 18.

PROGRAMS OF STUDY: DePauw confers B.A., B.M.A., B.M.E., and B.Mu. degrees. Bachelor's degrees are awarded in AGRICULTURE (natural resource management), BIOLOGICAL SCIENCE (biochemistry and biology/biological science), COMMUNICATIONS AND THE ARTS (art history and appreciation, classical languages, communications, English, English literature, French, German, Greek, Latin, linguistics, literature, music, music business management, music performance, music theory and composition, romance languages and literature, Spanish, and studio art), COMPUTER AND PHYSICAL SCIENCE (chemistry, computer science, earth science, geology, mathematics, and physics), EDUCATION (elementary education, foreign languages education, and music education), ENGINEERING AND ENVIRONMENTAL DESIGN (environmental science and preengineering), HEALTH PROFESSIONS (health), SOCIAL SCIENCE (African American studies, anthropology, classical/ancient civilization, East Asian studies, economics, gender studies, geography, history, interdisciplinary studies, peace studies, philosophy, physical fitness/movement, political science/government, psychology, religion, Russian and Slavic studies, sociology, and women's studies). English, economics, and communications have the largest enrollments.

ACTIVITIES: 78% of men belong to 12 national fraternities; 64% of women belong to 10 national sororities. There are 80 groups on campus, including art, band, cheerleading, chess, choir, chorale, chorus, computers, dance, debate, drama, ethnic, film, forensics, honors, international, jazz band, LGBT, literary magazine, musical theater, newspaper, opera, orchestra, pep band, political, professional, radio and TV stations, religious, social, social service, student government, and symphony. Popular campus events include Little 5 Track Meet, Monon Bell Football Game, and Old Gold Day. **Sports:** There are 17 intercollegiate sports for men and 16 for women, and 14 intramural sports for men and 12 for women. Facilities include a recreation center, a stadium, baseball, soccer, and field hockey fields, basketball courts, indoor/outdoor tennis courts and tracks, a pool, a fitness center, volleyball and badminton courts, and a gym. **Graduates:** From July 1, 2016 to June 30, 2017, 499 bachelor's degrees were awarded. The most popular majors were English, communication/theatre, and music. In an average class, 79% graduate in 4 years or less and 81% graduate in 5 years or less.

SERVICES: Counseling and information services are available, as is tutoring in most subjects. There is a reader service for the blind. **Library/Resources:** The library contains 818,618 volumes, 381,066 microform items, and 34,325 audio/video tapes/CDs/DVDs, and subscribes to 29,188 periodicals including electronic. Computerized library services include interlibrary loans, database searching, and Internet access. Special learning facilities include an art gallery, natural history museum, an observatory, an arboretum, a digital video studio, the Institute for Ehtics, and a digital media lab. **Physically Challenged Students:** 85% of the campus is accessible. Facilities include wheelchair ramps, elevators, special parking, specially equipped restrooms, special class scheduling, lowered drinking fountains, and lowered telephones. **Special:** DePauw offers dual majors in any 2 disciplines, student-designed majors, internships for honors programs and winter-term projects, unlimited study-abroad options through cooperative arrangements with other universities, a Washington semester, pass/fail options, and credit by departmental examination. Also available are 3-2 engineering degrees with Case Western Reserve, Columbia, and Washington Universities and a 3-2 nursing program with Rush University Hospital in Chicago. The Media Fellows, Management Fellows, and Science Research Fellows programs offer majors in any discipline, plus a semester-long internship. There are 13 national honor societies, Phi Beta Kappa, a freshman honors program, and 12 departmental honors programs. **Visiting:** There are regularly scheduled orientations for prospective students, consisting of day-long student/parent programs that include campus tours, faculty viewpoints, conversations with students, admissions information, financial aid and career planning sessions, and a meal in a residence hall. There are guides for informal visits; visitors may sit in on classes and stay overnight. To schedule a visit, contact the Admission Program and Visit Coordinator at (765) 658-4006. **Campus Safety and Security:** Measures include 24-hour foot and vehicle patrol, emergency notification system, self-defense education, and security escort services. There are shuttle buses, emergency telephones, and lighted pathways/sidewalks.

REQUIREMENTS: The SAT or ACT is required. Graduation from an accredited secondary school or a GED is required for admission. Course distribution should include 4 each in English and math, 3 to 4 each in social studies, and science (2 or more with lab), and 2 to 4 in a foreign language. An essay is required, and an interview is strongly recommended. Applicants for the School of Music must audition. AP credits are accepted. Important factors in the admissions decision are advanced placement or honors courses, recommendations by school officials, and personality/intangible qualities. Students must demonstrate competence in oral communications, quantitative reasoning, and writing. Successful completion of 124 semester hours, including 32 to 40 in the major, is required for graduation. In addition, students must fulfill distribution requirements in natural sciences, social and behavioral sciences, literature and the arts, historical and philosophical understanding, foreign language, and self-expression. A comprehensive exam, thesis, or seminar is required for each major. **Procedure:** Freshmen are admitted in the fall and spring. Entrance exams should be taken as early as possible. There are early decision, early admissions, and deferred admissions plans. Early decision applications should be filed by November 1; regular applications, by March 1 for fall entry; and December 1 for spring entry. The fall 2017 application fee was $40. Notification of early decision is sent January 1; regular decision, April 1. 50 early decision candidates were accepted for the 2017-2018 class. 216 applicants were on the 2017 waiting list; 112 were admitted. Applications are accepted on-line. **Transfer Students:** 21 transfer students enrolled in 2016-2017. Applicants must submit either SAT or ACT scores. High school and college transcripts are required, and a minimum GPA on previous college work of 3.0 is preferred. 60 of 124 credits required for the bachelor's degree must be completed at DePauw. **International Students:** There are 185 international students enrolled. They must take the TOEFL with a minimum score of 560 on the paper-based TOEFL (PBT) or 83 on the Internet-based version (iBT), or take the IELTS. They must also take the SAT or ACT.

ADMISSIONS: 62% of the 2017-2018 applicants were accepted. The SAT scores for the 2017-2018 freshman class were: Critical Reading-- 14% below 500, 40% between 500 and 599, 35% between 600 and 699, and 10% between 700 and 800. Math-- 8% below 500, 36% between 500 and 599, 41% between 600 and 699, and 14% between 700 and 800. Writing-- 13% below 500, 42% between 500 and 599, 37% between 600 and 699, and 7% between 700 and 800. **Admissions Contact:** Becca Moore, Senior Associate. of Admissions. Email: *admission@depauw.edu* Web: *www.depauw.edu*

FINANCIAL AID: DePauw is a member of CSS. The CSS/Profile and the college's own financial statement are required. The FAFSA code is 001792. The priority date for freshman financial aid applications for fall entry is February 15.

EARLHAM COLLEGE — D-3
www.earlham.edu

Richmond, IN 47374	**(765) 983-1600** **(800) 327-5426**
Fax: (765) 983-1560	**Email: admission@earlham.edu**
Full-time: 467 men, 584 women	**Faculty:** 101; IIB, av$
Part-time: 7 men, 2 women	**Ph.D.s:** 97%
Graduate: 19 men, 47 women	**Student/Faculty:** 10 to 1
Year: semesters	**Tuition:** $45,750
Room & Board: $9920	**Freshman Class:** 2799 applied, 1452 accepted, 287 enrolled
SAT EBR-W/M: 640/630 **ACT:** 27	**CEEB CODE:** 1195
Application Deadline: February 15	**HIGHLY COMPETITIVE**

Recognized as one of the nation's finest liberal arts colleges, Earlham College offers the highest quality liberal arts education distinguished by the Earlham Plan for Integrative Collaboration (EPIC) and the opportunities provided by the EPIC Advantage. The EPIC Advantage is a funded summer internship or faculty-student research experience for every interested student. These opportunities match students academic and personal interests, on campus, within the United States and in other countries around the world. There is 1 undergraduate school and 2 graduate schools. In addition to regional accreditation, EC has baccalaureate program accreditation with ACS and ATS. The 800-acre campus is in a small town 70 miles east of Indianapolis and 40 miles west of Dayton. Including any residence halls, there are 64 buildings.

STUDENT LIFE: 82% of undergraduates are from out of state, mostly the Midwest. Students are from 45 states, 59 foreign countries, and Canada. 65% are from public schools. 49% are White; 23% Foreign; 12% African American; 7% Hispanic; 5% Asian American; 2% race unknown; 1% American Indian/Alaska Native; 1% two or more races. 41% claim no religious affiliation; 40% Quaker, Christian, Buddhist, Hindu, and Muslim; 11% Protestant. **Female To Male Ratio:** 1.3:1. The average age of freshmen is 18; all undergraduates, 20. 17% do not continue beyond their first year; 70% remain to graduate. **Housing:** 1050 students can be accommodated in college housing, which includes dorms. In addition, there are language/international houses, special-interest houses, service learning house, Jewish cultural center, an African American cultural center, international cultural center, and LBGTQ. On-campus housing is guaranteed for all 4 years. 96% of students live on campus. All students may keep cars.

FACULTY/CLASSROOMS: 49% of faculty are male; 51% are female. All teach undergraduates. No introductory courses are taught by graduate students. The average class size in an introductory lecture is 48; in a laboratory is 15; and in a regular course is 12.

PROGRAMS OF STUDY: EC confers B.A. degrees. Master's degrees are also awarded. Bachelor's degrees are awarded in AGRICULTURE (environmental studies), BIOLOGICAL SCIENCE (biochemistry, biology/biological science, and neurosciences), BUSINESS (business administration and management), COMMUNICATIONS AND THE ARTS (art, dramatic arts, English, French, German, languages, linguistics, music, and Spanish), COMPUTER AND PHYSICAL SCIENCE (chemistry, computer science, geology, mathematics, and physics), ENGINEERING AND ENVIRONMENTAL DESIGN (environmental science), HEALTH PROFESSIONS (premedicine), SOCIAL SCIENCE (African American studies, anthropology, classical/ancient civilization, economics, history, human development, international studies, Japanese studies, Latin American studies, peace studies, philosophy, political science/government, psychology, religion, sociology, and women's studies). Life sciences (pre-medical), and psychology are the strongest academically. Biology, psychology, and business non-profit management have the largest enrollments.

ACTIVITIES: There are no fraternities or sororities. There are 63 groups on campus, including art, cheerleading, choir, chorale, chorus, computers, dance, drama, environmental, ethnic, film, honors, international, jazz band, LBGT, literary magazine, newspaper, orchestra, photography, political, professional, radio and TV, religious, social, social service, student government, and symphony. Popular campus events include Student Research Conference, International Festival, Dance Alloy student performance, and Homecoming Dance. **Sports:** There are 9 intercollegiate sports for men and 9 for women, and 8 intramural sports for men and 8 for women. Facilities include a fitness center with cardiovascular equipment and weights, group fitness and dance rooms, a field house with courts for tennis, volleyball, and basketball, racquetball courts, golf, an indoor climbing wall, indoor running track, 25-meter pool, and a performance gym, baseball stadium, soccer, football, field hockey and lacrosse, an equestrian center (with indoor and outdoor riding areas), an all-weather tennis courts, basketball courts, and outdoor areas (for cross-country running, skiing or hiking). **Graduates:** From July 1, 2016 to June 30, 2017, 178 bachelor's degrees were awarded. The most popular majors were social sciences (21%), biology/life sciences (18%), and interdisciplinary studies (16%). In an average class, 1% graduate in 3 years or less, 60% graduate in 4 years or less, 67% graduate in 5 years or less, and 69% graduate in 6 years or less. Of the 2016 graduating class, 18% were enrolled in graduate school within 6 months of graduation, and 66% were employed.

SERVICES: Counseling and information services are available, as is tutoring in most subjects, such as most 100-and 200-level courses and some 300 level courses, and a writing center. There is a reader service for the blind. **Library/Resources:** The library contains 380,360 volumes, 151,115 microform items, 9,670 audio/video tapes/CDs/DVDs, and subscribes to 74,422 periodicals including electronic. Computerized library services include interlibrary loans, database searching, Internet access, and Wi-Fi capability. Special learning facilities include an art gallery, natural history museum, planetarium, Center for Science and Technology (CST) and a Center for the Visual and Performing Arts. Other notable facilities include the Landrum Bolling Center, which features the Center for Career and Community Engagement and the Center for Global Education, the CoLab (dedicated to collaborative learning), theme residential houses, an observatory, herbarium, and a greenhouse. **Physically Challenged Students:** 80% of the campus is accessible. Facilities include wheelchair ramps, elevators, special parking, specially equipped restrooms, lowered drinking fountains, lowered telephones, and special housing. **Special:** The Earlham Plan for Integrative Collaboration (EPIC) is the College's distinctive approach to the liberal arts, collaborative academic inquiry and integrative learning. In order to offer the richest possible undergraduate experience, EPIC purposefully links the College's academic program with exceptional experiential learning opportunities through the Center for Career and Community Engagement and the Center for Global Education as well as research and study opportunities through Earlham's three Interdisciplinary Academic Centers: Global Health, Entrepreneurship and Innovation, and Social Justice. There are 2 national honor societies and a chapter of Phi Beta Kappa. **Visiting:** There are regularly scheduled orientations for prospective students, including class visitation, an admissions interview, a tour, and special appointments with faculty. There are guides for informal visits, visitors may sit in on classes, and stay overnight. To schedule a visit, contact the Admissions Office at (765) 983-1600. **Campus Safety and Security:** Measures include 24-hour foot and vehicle patrol, emergency notification system, self-defense education, and security escort services. There are shuttle buses, emergency telephones, lighted pathways/sidewalks, and controlled access to dorms/residences.

REQUIREMENTS: The SAT or ACT is required. Graduation from an accredited secondary school is required. The GED is accepted. Students must have completed at least 15 academic credits, including 4 years of English, 3 of math, and 2 each of science, history or social studies, and foreign language. Students are required to submit an essay and letters of recommendation from a teacher and guidance counselor. An interview is recommended. A GPA of 2.5 is required. AP credits are accepted. Important factors in the admissions decision are advanced placement or honors courses, evidence of special talent, and extracurricular activities record. To graduate, all students must complete core requirements, featuring a global seminar, courses in cultural diversity, and an integrated pathway tailored to students' academic passions and pre-professional interests. Every student also has multiple immersive learning opportunities, such as a research experience, internship, or off-campus study. The EPIC Advantage is funded and offered to every 3rd and 4th-year student. It provides an opportunity for an internship or research experience. Students must also maintain a minimum GPA of 2.0 and complete a total of 122 semester hours, including 32 semester hours in the major and at least 36-upper level semester hours and 40 outside the major division. A senior capstone experience is required. **Procedure:** Freshmen are admitted fall and spring. Entrance exams should be taken during the spring of the junior year or early fall of the senior year. There are early decision, early admissions, and deferred admissions plans. Early decision applications should be filed by November 1; regular applications, by February 15 for fall entry; and November 1 for winter entry. Notification of early decision is sent December 1; regular decision, February 15. 10 early decision candidates were accepted for the 2017-2018 class. 336 applicants were on the 2017 waiting list; 60 were admitted. Applications are accepted on-line. **Transfer Students:** 14 transfer students enrolled in 2016-2017. Applicants must have a minimum GPA of 2.5 in college coursework. An interview is recommended. High school and college transcripts, an essay, and a statement of good standing from the prior institution are required. 62 of 122 credits required for the bachelor's degree must be completed at EC. **International Students:** There are 216 international students enrolled. They must take the TOEFL with a minimum score of 550 on the paper-based TOEFL (PBT) or 80 on the Internet-based version (iBT).

ADMISSIONS: 52% of the 2017-2018 applicants were accepted. The SAT scores for the 2017-2018 freshman class were: Math-- 2% below 500, 27% between 500 and 599, 45% between 600 and 699, and 26% between 700 and 800. Evidence-Based Reading/Writing-- 3% below 500, 18% between 500 and 599, 53% between 600 and 699, and 26% between 700 and 800. The ACT scores were 17% between 18 and 23, 57% between 24 and 29, and 26% above 30. 64% of the current freshmen were in the top fifth of their class; 88% were in the top two fifths. 7 freshmen graduated first in their class. **Admissions Contact:** Priscilla Alicea, VP of Enrollment Management. Email: *admission@earlham.edu* Web: *www.earlham.edu*

FINANCIAL AID: In 2017-2018, 98% of all full-time freshmen received some form of financial aid. 89% of all full-time freshmen received need-based aid. The average freshman award was $43,032. Need-based scholarships or need-based grants averaged $38,564; need-based self-help aid (loans and jobs) averaged $3,717; and other non-need-based awards and non-need-based scholarships averaged $25,203. 70% of undergraduate students work part-time. The average financial indebtedness of the 2017 graduate was $27,830. EC is a member of CSS. The FAFSA code is 001793. The priority date for freshman financial aid applications for fall entry is March 1.

FRANKLIN COLLEGE — C-4

www.franklincollege.edu

Franklin, IN 46131 — (317) 738-8758, (800) 852-0232

Fax: (317) 738-8274 — **Email:** admissions@franklincollege.edu

Full-time: 460 men, 502 women	**Faculty:** 71; IIB, -$
Part-time: 23 men, 31 women	**Ph.D.s:** 88%
Graduate: 5 men, 13 women	**Student/Faculty:** 13 to 1
Year: 4-1-4, summer session	**Tuition:** $30,920
Room & Board: $9630	**Freshman Class:** 2003 applied, 1447 accepted, 267 enrolled
SAT: required **ACT:** 22	**CEEB CODE:** 1228
Application Deadline: open	**COMPETITIVE**

Franklin College, founded in 1834, provides a liberal arts and sciences education that fosters independent thinking, innovation, leadership and action for ever-changing professions and a globally connected world. With an emphasis on engaged learning opportunities, FC offers a Bachelor of Arts degree in more than 50 majors and a Master of Science degree in athletic training. The college values collaboration and upholds common values that benefit communities and inspire students. FC is historically related to the American Baptist Churches. There is 1 undergraduate school and 1 graduate school. In addition to regional accreditation, Franklin College has baccalaureate program accreditation with CAEP and CAATE. The 207-acre campus is in a small town 25 miles south of downtown Indianapolis. Including any residence halls, there are 23 buildings.

STUDENT LIFE: 92% of undergraduates are from Indiana. Others are from 17 states, and 3 foreign countries. 87% are White; 4% African American; 3% two or more races; 2% Hispanic; 2% race unknown; 1% Asian American; 1% Foreign. 52% are Protestant; 29% claim no religious affiliation; 12% Catholic. **Female To Male Ratio:** 1.1:1. The average age of freshmen is 19; all undergraduates, 21. 25% do not continue beyond their first year; 66% remain to graduate. **Housing:** 712 students can be accommodated in college housing, which includes single sex and coed dorms. In addition, there are language/international houses, special-interest houses, fraternity houses, and a substance/alcohol-free residence hall. On-campus housing is available on a first-come, first-served basis, and is available on a lottery system for upperclassmen. 72% of students live on campus. All students may keep cars.

FACULTY/CLASSROOMS: 55% of faculty are male; 45% are female. All teach undergraduates. No introductory courses are taught by graduate students. The average class size in an introductory lecture is 18; in a laboratory is 15; and in a regular course is 14.

PROGRAMS OF STUDY: FC confers B.A. degrees. Master's degrees are also awarded. Bachelor's degrees are awarded in BIOLOGICAL SCIENCE (biology ecology and field biology, biology/biological science, and life science secondary school education), BUSINESS (accounting, business administration and management, business administration - international, and business administration marketing), COMMUNICATIONS AND THE ARTS (art history, creative writing, English, French, journalism, multimedia, music, public relations, Spanish, studio art, studio art graphic design, studio art painting, and theatre arts), COMPUTER AND PHYSICAL SCIENCE (applied mathematics, chemistry, computer programming, computer science, and mathematics), EDUCATION (elementary education, English education, mathematics education, physical education, secondary education, and social studies education), HEALTH PROFESSIONS (biology and exercise science), SOCIAL SCIENCE (economics, history, philosophy, political science/government, psychology, religion, and sociology). Biology, business, and psychology are the strongest academically. Biology, business, and education have the largest enrollments.

ACTIVITIES: 25% of men belong to 5 national fraternities; 46% of women belong to 3 national sororities. There are 55 groups on campus, including art, band, cheerleading, choir, chorus, drama, drum and bugle corps, environmental, ethnic, film, honors, international, LGBT, literary magazine, newspaper, pep band, photography, political, professional, radio and TV, religious, social, social service, and student government. Popular campus events include Homecoming, Grizzly Grand Prix, and Greek Week. **Sports:** There are 9 intercollegiate sports for men and 10 for women, and 6 intramural sports for men and 6 for women. Facilities include athletic and soccer fields, track, tennis courts, athletic center including basketball, fitness and racquetball, and a fitness center including indoor athletic practice facilities. **Graduates:** From July 1, 2016 to June 30, 2017, 193 bachelor's degrees were awarded. The most popular majors were exercise science (12%), education (11%), and biology (10%). In an average class, 56% graduate in 4 years or less, 60% graduate in 5 years or less, and 61% graduate in 6 years or less. Of the 2016 graduating class, 18% were enrolled in graduate school within 6 months of graduation, and 75% were employed.

SERVICES: Counseling and information services are available, as is tutoring in most subjects. There is a reader service for the blind, and remedial math, reading, and writing. **Library/Resources:** The library contains 108,212 volumes, 310,676 microform items, and 6,060 audio/video tapes/CDs/DVDs, and subscribes to 33,498 periodicals including electronic. Computerized library services include interlibrary loans, database searching, Internet access, and Wi-Fi capability. **Physically Challenged Students:** All of the campus is accessible. Facilities include wheelchair ramps, elevators, special parking, specially equipped restrooms, special class scheduling, lowered drinking fountains, lowered telephones, and special housing. **Special:** Cooperative programs are available in Biology and Chemistry (health-related professions). A 3-2 Accelerated Masters in Public Health, and a 3-2 engineering degree with Indiana University-Purdue University in Indianapolis are available. Also available are fall, winter, spring, and summer internships, as well as study abroad in various countries and cross-registration with 7 Indiana universities and colleges (Consortium for Urban Education). There are 10 national honor societies. **Visiting:** There are regularly scheduled orientations for prospective students. There are guides for informal visits; visitors may sit in on classes and stay overnight. To schedule a visit, contact Visit Coordinator at visits@franklincollege.edu. **Campus Safety and Security:** Measures include 24-hour foot and vehicle patrol, emergency notification system, and security escort services. There are emergency telephones, lighted pathways/sidewalks, and controlled access to dorms/residences.

REQUIREMENTS: The SAT or ACT is required. A complete application file includes: a submitted Franklin College application, official transcript submitted by the guidance office or via parchment. For Guidance Offices that use PrepHQ, Franklin College is able to accept transcripts through the ConnectEDU system. Official SAT Code: 1228, ACT Code: 1194. Other items we take into consideration for admission include: Academic achievements: grade point average, official high school transcript, the student's course load and class rank, and standardized test scores (SAT or ACT); remember that the writing section of either test is required Personal Statement/Essay (optional). Extracurricular involvement and leadership experience: such as athletic, literary, artistic, social service, church and community involvement, and employment are also considered as well as the quality of a student's high school. If a school no longer ranks students, our admission team may call to ask for an estimated class rank for scholarship purposes. Students must receive at least an Indiana Core 40 degree to be considered for admission to Franklin College. AP credits are accepted. Important factors in the admissions decision are advanced placement or honors courses, leadership record, and recommendations by school officials. Requirements for graduation include 80 hours outside the major, including general education, and 120 total credit hours. Students must demonstrate proficiency in a foreign language at the 111 level. Each student must maintain a minimum GPA of 2.0 and must pass the Senior Competency Exam, which is administered by the department in which the student completes a major. **Procedure:** Freshmen are admitted to all sessions. Entrance exams should be taken in spring of the junior year or fall of the senior year. There is a rolling admissions plan. Application deadlines are open. Notification is sent on a rolling basis. Applications are accepted on-line. **Transfer Students:** 33 transfer students enrolled in 2016-2017. Transfer students must have at least a 2.0 cumulative GPA. Required materials: Official high school transcript or GED certificatefranklin_0410_-2007, official college transcripts from all previously attended institutions. The Transfer Student Recommendation Form (pdf) is required for all applicants who have attended another institution since completing high school, along with a SAT or ACT score, and a written personal statement (one or two pages typed) and should address why you have chosen to transfer to Franklin College. Your personal statement may be submitted online via the Transfer Student Application or via email to admissions@franklincollege.edu. Students who have been removed from high school for more than five years are not required to submit a transcript or SAT/ACT scores. 48 of 120 credits required for the bachelor's degree must be completed at Franklin College. **International Students:** There are 3 international students enrolled. They must take the TOEFL with a minimum score of 550 on the paper-based TOEFL (PBT). Completion of level 109 in an English language service (ELS) center is necessary. They must also take the SAT or ACT.

ADMISSIONS: 72% of the 2017-2018 applicants were accepted. The SAT scores for the 2017-2018 freshman class were: Critical Reading-- 58% below 500, 32% between 500 and 599, 5% between 600 and 699, and 5% between 700 and 800. Math-- 46% below 500, 42% between 500 and 599, 10% between 600 and 699, and 2% between 700 and 800. Writing-- 58% below 500, 32% between 500 and 599, 8% between 600 and 699, and 2% between 700 and 800. The ACT scores were 18% between 12 and 17, 50% between 18 and 23, 27% between 24 and 29, and 5% above 30. 3 freshmen graduated first in their class. **Admissions Contact:** Tara Evans, Director of Admissions. Email: *admissions@franklincollege.edu* Web: *www.franklincollege.edu*

FINANCIAL AID: 88% of all full-time freshmen received need-based aid. The average freshman award was $26,401. Need-based scholarships or need-based grants averaged $23,014; need-based self-help aid (loans and jobs) averaged $4,102; and other non-need-based awards and non-need-based scholarships averaged $15,338. 31% of undergraduate students work part-time. The average financial indebtedness of the 2017 graduate was $34,884. The college's own financial statement is required. The FAFSA code is 001798. The priority date for freshman financial aid applications for fall entry is Dec 1.

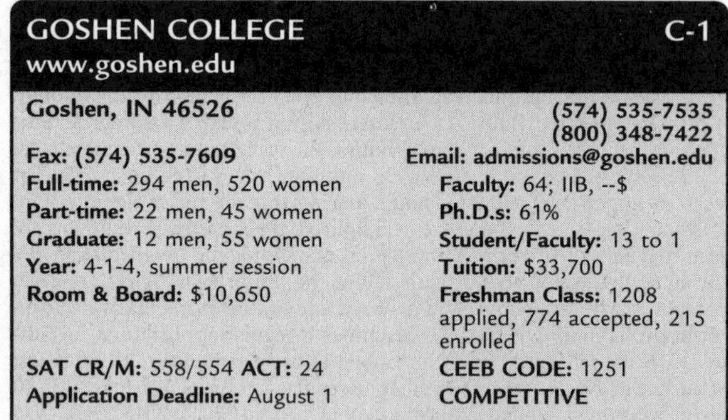

GOSHEN COLLEGE — C-1

www.goshen.edu

Goshen, IN 46526	(574) 535-7535 (800) 348-7422
Fax: (574) 535-7609	**Email:** admissions@goshen.edu
Full-time: 294 men, 520 women	**Faculty:** 64; IIB, --$
Part-time: 22 men, 45 women	**Ph.D.s:** 61%
Graduate: 12 men, 55 women	**Student/Faculty:** 13 to 1
Year: 4-1-4, summer session	**Tuition:** $33,700
Room & Board: $10,650	**Freshman Class:** 1208 applied, 774 accepted, 215 enrolled
SAT CR/M: 558/554 **ACT:** 24	**CEEB CODE:** 1251
Application Deadline: August 1	**COMPETITIVE**

Goshen College, founded in 1894, is a private, Christian, liberal arts institution affiliated with the Mennonite Church offering bachelor's and master's degrees in a variety of fields. The figures given in the above capsule and in this profile are approximate. There are 3 undergraduate schools and 1 graduate school. In addition to regional accreditation, GC has baccalaureate program accreditation with CSWE and CAEP. The 135-acre campus is in a small town approximately 120 miles east of Chicago, and 30 miles southeast of South Bend, IN. Including any residence halls, there are 25 buildings.

STUDENT LIFE: 63% of undergraduates are from Indiana. Others are from 35 states, 22 foreign countries, and Canada. 80% are from public schools. 7% are Foreign; 64% White; 4% African American; 20% Hispanic; 2% Asian American; 2% two or more races; 1% race unknown. 28% are Protestant; 20% claim no religious affiliation; 13% Catholic. **Female To Male Ratio:** 1.9:1. The average age of freshmen is 18; all undergraduates, 23. 22% do not continue beyond their first year; 73% remain to graduate. **Housing:** 700 students can be accommodated in college housing, which includes married student dorms, on-campus apartments, and off-campus apartments. In addition, there are special-interest houses. On-campus housing is guaranteed for all 4 years. 51% of students live on campus. Alcohol is not permitted. All students may keep cars.

FACULTY/CLASSROOMS: 47% of faculty are male; 53% are female. 98% teach undergraduates. No introductory courses are taught by graduate students. The average class size in an introductory lecture is 26; in a laboratory is 19; and in a regular course is 22.

PROGRAMS OF STUDY: GC confers B.A., B.S., and B.S.N. degrees. Master's and doctoral degrees are also awarded. Bachelor's degrees are awarded in AGRICULTURE (environmental studies), BIOLOGICAL SCIENCE (biochemistry, biology/biological science, ecology, and molecular biology), BUSINESS (accounting, business administration and management, institutional management, information & communication technology, and marketing management), COMMUNICATIONS AND THE ARTS (American Sign Language, art, broadcasting, communications, creative writing, dramatic arts, English, English Writing, film, television and digital media, journalism, music, public relations, Spanish, theatre arts, and writing), COMPUTER AND PHYSICAL SCIENCE (chemistry, computer science, information sciences and systems, mathematics, and physics), EDUCATION (art education, business education, early childhood education, elementary education, English education, environmental education, foreign languages education, health education, mathematics education, middle school education, music education, physical education, science education, secondary education, and teaching English as a second/foreign language (TESOL/TEFOL), ENGINEERING AND ENVIRONMENTAL DESIGN (environmental science and preengineering), HEALTH PROFESSIONS (nursing, predentistry, premedicine, prepharmacy, and preveterinary science), SOCIAL SCIENCE (biblical studies, economics, history, interdisciplinary studies, peace studies, psychology, religion, social work, and sociology). Nursing, elementary education, and biology have the largest enrollments.

ACTIVITIES: There are no fraternities or sororities. There are 24 groups on campus, including art, choir, chorale, chorus, drama, environmental, ethnic, international, jazz band, literary magazine, musical theater, newspaper, opera, orchestra, photography, professional, religious, social, social service, student government, and yearbook. Popular campus events include Kick Off (student talent show), Martin Luther King Jr Day, and Homecoming. **Sports:** There are 8 intercollegiate sports for men and 8 for women, and 3 intramural sports for men and 3 for women. Facilities include a fitness center with an indoor track, a weight room, basketball courts, racquetball courts, and workout equipment. Athletic facilities include a soccer field, tennis courts, a sand volleyball court, an all-weather track, and baseball and softball diamonds. **Graduates:** From July 1, 2016 to June 30, 2017, 204 bachelor's degrees were awarded. The most popular majors were nursing (27%), biology (10%), and environmental science (6%). In an average class, 3% graduate in 3 years or less, 52% graduate in 4 years or less, 66% graduate in 5 years or less, and 73% graduate in 6 years or less. Of the 2016 graduating class, 5% were enrolled in graduate school within 6 months of graduation, and 77% were employed.

SERVICES: Counseling and information services are available, as is tutoring in every subject. There is a reader service for the blind, and remedial math, reading, and writing. **Library/Resources:** The library contains 106,765 volumes, 140,000 microform items, and 2,261 audio/video tapes/CDs/DVDs, and subscribes to 212 periodicals including electronic. Computerized library services include interlibrary loans, database searching, Internet access, and Wi-Fi capability. Special learning facilities include an art gallery, radio station, and TV station. **Physically Challenged Students:** All of the campus is accessible. Facilities include wheelchair ramps, elevators, special parking, specially equipped restrooms, special class scheduling, lowered drinking fountains, and lowered telephones. **Special:** A semester-abroad in the required Study Service Term is possible in Cambodia, Morocco, Peru, Tanzania, Nicaragua, China and Senegal. **Visiting:** There are regularly scheduled orientations for prospective students, a campus tour, parents session, talks with professors, a financial aid session, visiting classes, an overnight stay in residence halls, a student panel, and a campus interview. **Campus Safety and Security:** Measures include 24-hour foot and vehicle patrol, emergency notification system, and security escort services. There are lighted pathways/sidewalks and controlled access to dorms/residences.

REQUIREMENTS: The SAT or ACT is required. Applicants should be graduates of an accredited secondary school or have a GED equivalent, including 4 years of high school English, 2 to 4 years of math, and 2 years each of foreign language, science, history, and social studies. A GPA of 2.6 is required. AP and CLEP credits are accepted. Important factors in the admissions decision are advanced placement or honors courses, leadership record, and recommendations by school officials. All students must complete the general education program, including courses in literature and communication, fine arts, Bible, religion, philosophy, natural science, math, social science, and history, and 12 hours of international education in the Study Service Term and 1 hour of phys ed. A total of 120 credit hours with a minimum GPA of 2.0 is required to graduate. **Procedure:** Freshmen are admitted to all sessions. Entrance exams should be taken by fall of the senior year. There are deferred admissions and rolling admissions plans. Applications should be filed by August 1 for fall entry. The fall 2017 application fee was $25. Notification is sent on a rolling basis. Applications are accepted online. **Transfer Students:** 55 transfer students enrolled in 2016-2017. A GPA of 2.0 or higher is required on previous college work. 30 of 120 credits required for the bachelor's degree must be completed at GC. **International Students:** There are 66 international students enrolled. They must take the TOEFL with a minimum score of 550 on the paper-based TOEFL (PBT) or 79 on the Internet-based version (iBT). They must also take the SAT or ACT.

ADMISSIONS: 64% of the 2017-2018 applicants were accepted. The SAT scores for the 2017-2018 freshman class were: Critical Reading-- 26% below 500, 41% between 500 and 599, 28% between 600 and 699, and 6% between 700 and 800. Math-- 29% below 500, 37% between 500 and 599, 30% between 600 and 699, and 4% between 700 and 800. The ACT scores were 13% between 12 and 17, 37% between 18 and 23, 40% between 24 and 29, and 10% above 30. 40% of the current freshmen were in the top fifth of their class; 72% were in the top two fifths. 4 freshmen graduated first in their class. **Admissions Contact:** Adela Hufford, Dean of Admissions. Email: *admissions@goshen.edu* Web: *www.goshen.edu*

FINANCIAL AID: In 2017-2018, 100% of all full-time freshmen received some form of financial aid. 85% of all full-time freshmen received need-based aid. The average freshman award was $35,107. Need-based scholarships or need-based grants averaged $9,408 ($24,640 maximum); need-based self-help aid (loans and jobs) averaged $4,091 ($22,758 maximum); non-need-based athletic scholarships averaged $1,962 ($27,200 maximum); and other non-need-based awards and non-need-based scholarships averaged $19,647 ($44,900 maximum). 91% of undergraduate students work part-time. The average financial indebtedness of the 2017 graduate was $18,545. GC is a member of CSS. The FAFSA code is 001799. The deadline for filing freshman financial aid applications for fall entry is March 10.

GRACE COLLEGE AND SEMINARY — C-2

www.grace.edu

Winona Lake, IN 46590	**(574) 372-5100**
Fax: (574) 372-5120	**Email: enroll@grace.edu**
Full-time: 633 men, 888 women	**Faculty:** 49
Part-time: 217 men, 196 women	**Ph.D.s:** 63%
Graduate: 217 men, 182 women	**Student/Faculty:** 20 to 1
Year: semesters, summer session	**Tuition:** $23,120
Room & Board: $8404	**Freshman Class:** 4199 applied, 3298 accepted, 454 enrolled
SAT CR/M: 519/512 **ACT:** required	**CEEB CODE:** 1252
Application Deadline: March 1	**COMPETITIVE**

Grace College and Seminary, founded in 1948, is a Christian liberal arts institution affiliated with the Fellowship of Grace Brethren Churches. There are 5 undergraduate schools and 2 graduate schools. In addition to regional accreditation, GCS has baccalaureate program accreditation with CAEP, ATS, and CACREP. The 150-acre campus is in a small town 40 miles west of Fort Wayne. Including any residence halls, there are 25 buildings.

STUDENT LIFE: 74% of undergraduates are from Indiana. Others are from 32 states, 12 foreign countries, and Canada. 74% are from public schools. 79% are White; 7% race unknown; 6% Hispanic; 5% African American; 2% two or more races; 1% Asian American. **Female To Male**

Ratio: 1.2:1. The average age of freshmen is 18; all undergraduates, 21. 17% do not continue beyond their first year; 67% remain to graduate. **Housing:** 850 students can be accommodated in college housing, which includes dorms and on-campus apartments. On-campus housing is guaranteed for the freshman year only, and is available on a first-come, first-served basis, and is available on a lottery system for upperclassmen. 75% of students live on campus. Alcohol is not permitted. All students may keep cars.

FACULTY/CLASSROOMS: 57% of faculty are male; 43% are female. All teach undergraduates, 10% do research, and 10% do both. No introductory courses are taught by graduate students. The average class size in an introductory lecture is 48; in a laboratory is 14; and in a regular course is 17.

PROGRAMS OF STUDY: GCS confers B.A. and B.S. degrees. Associate, master's, and doctoral degrees are also awarded. Bachelor's degrees are awarded in BIOLOGICAL SCIENCE (biology/biological science), BUSINESS (accounting, business administration and management, and management information systems), COMMUNICATIONS AND THE ARTS (art, communications, English, French, German, graphic design, journalism, music, and Spanish), COMPUTER AND PHYSICAL SCIENCE (mathematics and science), EDUCATION (art education, business education, elementary education, English education, foreign languages education, journalism education, mathematics education, music education, physical education, science education, and special education), HEALTH PROFESSIONS (predentistry and premedicine), SOCIAL SCIENCE (biblical studies, counseling/psychology, criminal justice, prelaw, psychology, religion, social work, sociology, and youth ministry). Biology, psychology, and business are the strongest academically. Psychology, elementary education, and business have the largest enrollments.

ACTIVITIES: There are no fraternities or sororities. There are 14 groups on campus, including band, cheerleading, choir, chorale, communications, drama, honors, international, musical theater, newspaper, orchestra, pep band, religious, social, student government, and yearbook. Popular campus events include Fall Fest, Heart of the Holidays, Missionary Conference, Day of Prayer, and MLK day. **Sports:** There are 7 intercollegiate sports for men and 8 for women, and 3 intramural sports for men and 3 for women. Facilities include gym, soccer fields, tennis courts, softball and baseball diamonds, and a recreation center with basketball courts, indoor & outdoor track, and weight and exercise rooms. **Graduates:** From July 1, 2016 to June 30, 2017, 362 bachelor's degrees were awarded. The most popular majors were business/marketing (30%), psychology (20%), and education (13%). In an average class, 28% graduate in 3 years or less, 66% graduate in 4 years or less, 66% graduate in 5 years or less, and 67% graduate in 6 years or less.

SERVICES: Counseling and information services are available, as is tutoring in most subjects. There is a reader service for the blind, and remedial math, reading, and writing. **Library/Resources:** The library contains 150,843 volumes, 26,000 microform items, and 3,714 audio/video tapes/CDs/DVDs, and subscribes to 19,360 periodicals including electronic. Computerized library services include interlibrary loans, database searching, Internet access, and Wi-Fi capability. Special learning facilities include an art gallery, and the Winona History Center. **Physically Challenged Students:** 80% of the campus is accessible. Facilities include wheelchair ramps, elevators, special parking, specially equipped restrooms, and special class scheduling. **Special:** Students may study abroad in 5 countries. A B.A.-B.S. degree is available in all majors except languages, English, and biblical studies. Dual majors are offered in psychology, sociology, communication, business, accounting, youth ministries, and management information technology. There is 1 national honor society and a freshman honors program. **Visiting:** There are regularly scheduled orientations for prospective students, including tours, class visits, and meetings with professors. There are guides for informal visits, visitors may sit in on classes, and stay overnight. To schedule a visit, contact the Visitors Center at (574) 372-5100. **Campus Safety and Security:** Measures include 24-hour foot and vehicle patrol, emergency notification system, and security escort services. There are emergency telephones, lighted pathways/sidewalks, and controlled access to dorms/residences.

REQUIREMENTS: The SAT or ACT is recommended. Applicants must have completed 15 Carnegie units, including 4 of English, 3 each of math and science, 2 each of a foreign language and social studies, and 1 of history. A GED is accepted. Grace requires applicants to be in the upper 50% of their class. A GPA of 2.3 is required. AP and CLEP credits are accepted. Important factors in the admissions decision are advanced placement or honors courses, leadership record, and personality/intangible qualities. **Procedure:** Freshmen are admitted to all sessions. Entrance exams should be taken in October, December, or February. There are deferred admissions and rolling admissions plans. Applications should be filed by March 1 for fall entry. The fall 2017 application fee was $25. Notification is sent on a rolling basis. Applications are accepted on-line. **Transfer Students:** Transfer applicants should have a minimum 2.0 GPA in addition to fulfilling freshman entrance requirements. 60 of 124 credits required for the bachelor's degree must be completed at Grace. **International Students:** There are 9 international students enrolled. They must take the TOEFL. They must also take the SAT or ACT.

ADMISSIONS: 79% of the 2017-2018 applicants were accepted. The SAT scores for the 2017-2018 freshman class were: Critical Reading-- 40% below 500, 41% between 500 and 599, 17% between 600 and 699, and 2% between 700 and 800. Math-- 40% below 500, 39% between 500 and 599, 19% between 600 and 699, and 2% between 700 and 800. The ACT scores were 6% between 12 and 17, 34% between 18 and 23, 50% between 24 and 29, and 10% above 30. 2% of the current freshmen were in the top fifth of their class; 10% were in the top two fifths. **Admissions Contact:** Cynthia Sisson, VP of Enrollment Management and Marketing. Email: *enroll@grace.edu* Web: *www.grace.edu*

FINANCIAL AID: The FAFSA code is 001800. Check with the school for current application deadlines.

HANOVER COLLEGE — D-5

www.hanover.edu

Hanover, IN 47243 — (812) 866-7021, (800) 213-2178

Fax: (812) 866-7098 — **Email: admission@hanover.edu**

Full-time: 463 men, 621 women	**Faculty:** 87; IIB, av$
Part-time: 4 men, 2 women	**Ph.D.s:** 94%
Graduate: n/av	**Student/Faculty:** 12 to 1
Year: 4-1-4	**Tuition:** $35,514
Room & Board: $10,850	**Freshman Class:** n/av
SAT or ACT: required	**CEEB CODE:** 1290
Application Deadline: March 1	**COMPETITIVE+**

Hanover College, founded in 1827 and the oldest private college in Indiana, is a liberal arts school affiliated with the United Presbyterian Church. There is 1 undergraduate school. In addition to regional accreditation, HC has baccalaureate program accreditation with CAEP. The 650-acre campus is in a rural area 45 miles northeast of Louisville, KY, 70 miles southwest of Cincinnati, and 90 miles south of Indianapolis. Including any residence halls, there are 36 buildings.

STUDENT LIFE: 67% of undergraduates are from Indiana. Others are from 28 states, and 26 foreign countries. 81% are from public schools. 80% are White; 5% African American; 5% race unknown; 4% Foreign; 3% Hispanic; 1% Asian American; 1% American Indian/Alaska Native; 1% two or more races. **Female To Male Ratio:** 1.3:1. The average age of freshmen is 18; all undergraduates, 19. 18% do not continue beyond their first year; 69% remain to graduate. **Housing:** 1150 students can be accommodated in college housing, which includes dorms and on-campus apartments. In addition, there are honors houses, special-interest houses, fraternity houses, sorority houses, and a multicultural center. On-campus housing is guaranteed for all 4 years. 93% of students live on campus. All students may keep cars.

FACULTY/CLASSROOMS: 59% of faculty are male; 41% are female. All teach undergraduates. No introductory courses are taught by graduate students. The average class size in an introductory lecture is 16; in a laboratory is 15; and in a regular course is 16.

PROGRAMS OF STUDY: HC confers B.A. and B.S. degrees. Bachelor's degrees are awarded in BIOLOGICAL SCIENCE (biochemistry, biology/biological science, and environmental biology), COMMUNICATIONS AND THE ARTS (art, art history and appreciation, classics, communications, dramatic arts, English, French, music, and Spanish), COMPUTER AND PHYSICAL SCIENCE (chemistry, computer science, environmental geology, geology, mathematics, and physics), EDUCATION (elementary education), ENGINEERING AND ENVIRONMENTAL DESIGN (environmental science), HEALTH PROFESSIONS (health and physical activity and kinesiology), SOCIAL SCIENCE (anthropology, economics, gender studies, history, international studies, medieval studies, philosophy, political science/government, psychology, sociology, and theological studies). Arts & sciences, and interdisciplinary studies are the strongest academically. Psychology, kinesiology, and integrative physiology have the largest enrollments.

ACTIVITIES: 42% of men belong to 4 national fraternities; 32% of women belong to 4 national sororities. There are 60 groups on campus, including art, band, cheerleading, choir, chorus, communications, computers, dance, debate, drama, environmental, ethnic, film, honors, international, jazz band, LGBT, literary magazine, marching band, musical theater, newspaper, orchestra, pep band, photography, political, professional, radio and TV, religious, social, social service, student government, and yearbook. Popular campus events include Hanover Enrichment Series, Wiffleball Tournament, and MLK Marade. **Sports:** There are 9 intercollegiate sports for men and 9 for women, and 10 intramural sports for men and 10 for women. Facilities include a health and recreation center consisting of a performance gym, a multisports forum, a suspended running track, racquetball and squash courts, a weight room, a training room, and a physiology lab. There also is an outdoor athletic complex consisting of a football/track stadium, baseball, softball and soccer facilities, tennis courts, and a lacrosse field. **Graduates:** From July 1, 2016 to June 30, 2017, 276 bachelor's degrees were awarded. The most popular majors were psychology (9%), economics (7%), and communication (7%). In an average class, 67% graduate in 4 years or less, 70% graduate in 5 years or less, and 71% graduate in 6 years or less.

SERVICES: Counseling and information services are available, as is tutoring in most subjects, and writing. **Library/Resources:** The library contains 299,841 volumes, 53,006 microform items, 7,501 audio/video tapes/CDs/DVDs, and subscribes to 45,968 periodicals including electronic. Computerized library services include interlibrary loans, database searching, Internet access, and Wi-Fi capability. Special learning facilities include an art gallery, planetarium, radio station, TV station, and a geology museum. **Physically Challenged Students:** 75% of the campus is accessible. Facilities include wheelchair ramps, elevators, special parking, specially equipped restrooms, special class scheduling, lowered drinking fountains, lowered telephones, and special housing. **Special:** B.S. and B.A. degrees; Internships, study abroad in Australia, Belgium, France, Turkey, City Semester programs in Philadelphia, Washington, D.C., and Chicago, and self-designed majors including 2 or more disciplines, are offered. The Business Scholars Program provides preparation for a career in business, built on a liberal arts foundation, where everyone in the program completes a paid internship. There are 8 national honor societies and 8 departmental honors programs. **Visiting:** There are regularly scheduled orientations for prospective students. There are guides for informal visits, visitors may sit in on classes, and stay overnight. To schedule a visit, contact Lyn Lyon at (800) 213-2178. **Campus Safety and Security:** Measures include 24-hour foot and vehicle patrol, emergency notification system, self-defense education, and security escort services. There are shuttle buses, emergency telephones, lighted pathways/sidewalks, and controlled access to dorms/residences.

REQUIREMENTS: The SAT or ACT is required. Admission is competitive, based on the applicant pool. The college requires 18 academic credits, including 4 years of English and 2 each of foreign language, math, science, and either history or social studies. The GED is accepted. The college also requires a foreign language achievement test for those who wish to meet their world language requirement in the language they studied in high school, as well as an essay; an interview is recommended. AP credits are accepted. Important factors in the admissions decision are recommendations by school officials, advanced placement or honors courses, and extracurricular activities record. To graduate, students must complete 36 units of credit, including 8 to 12 in the major, LADRs or CCRs/ACEs (12 to 13 units of general degree requirements), maintain a GPA of 2.0 overall and in the major, pass a comprehensive exam, and participate in a culminating experience in the major. **Procedure:** Freshmen are admitted in the fall and winter. Entrance exams should be taken late in the spring of the junior year. There are deferred admissions and rolling admissions plans. Early decision applications should be filed by December 1; regular applications, by March 1 for fall entry. Applications are accepted on-line. **Transfer Students:** 19 transfer students enrolled in 2016-2017. Transfer students must submit transcripts from all colleges attended and must have performed successfully. SAT or ACT scores and high school record may also be taken into consideration. 17 of 36 credits required for the bachelor's degree must be completed at HC. **International Students:** There are 45 international students enrolled. They must take the TOEFL with a minimum score of 550 on the paper-based TOEFL (PBT) or 80 on the Internet-based version (iBT). They must also take the SAT or ACT.

ADMISSIONS: 45% of the current freshmen were in the top fifth of their class; 81% were in the top two fifths. 8 freshmen graduated first in their class. **Admissions Contact:** Victoria Hidalgo, Director of Admission. Email: *admission@hanover.edu* Web: *www.hanover.edu*

FINANCIAL AID: In 2017-2018, 99% of all full-time freshmen received some form of financial aid. 63% of all full-time freshmen received need-based aid. The average freshman award was $25,651. HC is a member of CSS. The FAFSA code is 001801. The deadline for filing freshman financial aid applications for fall entry is March 1.

HUNTINGTON UNIVERSITY D-2
www.huntington.edu

Huntington, IN 46750 (260) 358-4016 (800) 642-6493

Fax: (260) 358-3699 **Email:** admissions@huntington.edu
Full-time: 378 men, 515 women
Part-time: 75 men, 111 women
Graduate: 67 men, 175 women
Year: 4-1-4, summer session
Room & Board: $8456
Faculty: 54; IIB, --$
Ph.D.s: 76%
Student/Faculty: 13 to 1
Tuition: $25,540
Freshman Class: 747 applied, 732 accepted, 218 enrolled
SAT CR/M: 490/507 **ACT:** 22
CEEB CODE: 1304
Application Deadline: open
COMPETITIVE

Huntington University, founded in 1897 is a comprehensive Christian college, by the Church of the United Brethren in Christ offering graduate and undergraduate programs in more than 70 academic concentrations. The university is a member of the Council for Christian Colleges and Universities. There are 2 undergraduate schools and 1 graduate school. In addition to regional accreditation, HU has baccalaureate program accreditation with CSWE, NASM, NCATE, NCA-HLC, CAEP, and CCNE. The 170-acre campus is in a small town 20 miles southwest of Fort Wayne. Including any residence halls, there are 25 buildings.

STUDENT LIFE: 63% of undergraduates are from Indiana. Others are from 37 states, 26 foreign countries, and Canada. 84% are White; 5% Hispanic; 4% Foreign; 3% African American; 3% two or more races. 73% are Protestant; 23% Non-denominational. **Female To Male Ratio:** 1.5:1. The average age of freshmen is 18; all undergraduates, 20. 19% do not continue beyond their first year; 68% remain to graduate. **Housing:** 831 students can be accommodated in college housing, which includes single-sex, married student dorms, on-campus apartments, and off-campus apartments. In addition, there are language/international houses, and special-interest houses. On-campus housing is guaranteed for all 4 years. 75% of students live on campus. Alcohol is not permitted. All students may keep cars.

FACULTY/CLASSROOMS: 58% of faculty are male; 42% are female. 85% teach undergraduates. No introductory courses are taught by graduate students. The average class size in an introductory lecture is 25; in a laboratory is 15; and in a regular course is 20.

PROGRAMS OF STUDY: HU confers B.A., B.S., B.Mus., B.S.Sc., and B.S.N. degrees. Associate, master's, and doctoral degrees are also awarded. Bachelor's degrees are awarded in AGRICULTURE (agricultural business management, agricultural sciences, and agriculture), BIOLOGICAL SCIENCE (biology/biological science and biological sciences), BUSINESS (accounting, business administration and management, business administration marketing, entrepreneurial studies, marketing management, nonprofit/public organization management, organizational behavior, small business management, and sports management), COMMUNICATIONS AND THE ARTS (acting, animation, art, broadcasting, communications, creative writing, digital communications, digital media, dramatic arts, English, English as a second/foreign language, English literature, film arts, fine arts, graphic design, journalism, media arts, music business management, music performance, music theory and composition, performing arts, public relations, studio art, theatre arts, and theater design), COMPUTER AND PHYSICAL SCIENCE (actuarial science, actuarial mathematics, chemistry, chemistry/chemical biology, computer science, information sciences and systems, mathematics, and physics), EDUCATION (agricultural education, art education, education, elementary education, English education, mathematics education, music education, physical education, science education, secondary education, social studies education, sports studies, and teaching English as a second/foreign language (TESOL/TEFOL), ENGINEERING AND

ENVIRONMENTAL DESIGN (computational sciences), HEALTH PROFESSIONS (biology, exercise science, nursing, premedicine, prepharmacy, prephysical therapy, and recreation therapy), SOCIAL SCIENCE (area studies, biblical studies, counseling/psychology, criminal justice, economics, history, ministries, parks and recreation management, philosophy, prelaw, psychology, religion, religious music, social work, sociology, and youth ministry). Film, animation, and nursing are the strongest academically. Business, animation, and psychology have the largest enrollments.

ACTIVITIES: There are no fraternities or sororities. There are 35 groups on campus, including art, band, cheerleading, choir, chorale, chorus, communications, computers, dance, drama, environmental, ethnic, film, Friesen Center for Volunteer Service, honors, international, jazz band, literary magazine, musical theater, newspaper, orchestra, pep band, political, professional, radio and TV, religious, social, social service, student government, and symphony. Popular campus events include Olympiad, Forester Night, Chapel Series, and Hoe Down. **Sports:** There are 8 intercollegiate sports for men and 8 for women, and 9 intramural sports for men and 9 for women. Facilities include a fieldhouse with an indoor running track, basketball courts, outdoor basketball court, indoor and outdoor tennis courts, softball and baseball diamonds, an outdoor track, soccer and intramural fields, a weight room and aerobic facility, and a gym. **Graduates:** From July 1, 2016 to June 30, 2017, 210 bachelor's degrees were awarded. The most popular majors were business (9%), nursing (9%), and elementary and special education (5%). In an average class, 55% graduate in 4 years or less and 68% graduate in 6 years or less.

SERVICES: Counseling and information services are available, as is tutoring in most subjects, such as English, and math. There is a reader service for the blind, and remedial math and writing. **Library/Resources:** The library contains 356,206 volumes, 11,803 microform items, and 7,566 audio/video tapes/CDs/DVDs, and subscribes to 30,230 periodicals including electronic. Computerized library services include interlibrary loans, database searching, Internet access, and Wi-Fi capability. Special learning facilities include an art gallery, radio and TV stations, a writing center and an Enterprise Resource Center which helps students with internships, resumes, job training and practicum; herbarium, nature preserve, an arboretum, a greenhouse, studio theatre, exercise science training facilities (including a BODPOD), and the historical archives (United Brethren Historical Center). **Physically Challenged Students:** 64% of the campus is accessible. Facilities include wheelchair ramps, elevators, special parking, specially equipped restrooms, lowered drinking fountains, and special housing. **Special:** Companies in the area offer a number of internships to students in concentrations such as business, sociology, social work, ministry and missions, education, graphic design, digital media arts, music business, and sport and recreation management. Students may study abroad in a number of countries. A Washington semester, a Hollywood semester, dual majors, correspondence courses with other schools, and an accelerated degree program in organizational management, business administration, accounting, nursing, marketing, human resource management, and organizational management are available. There are 11 national honor societies, a freshman honors program, and 6 departmental honors programs. **Visiting:** There are regularly scheduled orientations for prospective students, available on 3 days notice. There are guides for informal visits; visitors may sit in on classes and stay overnight. To schedule a visit, contact Carlene Peters at (260) 359-4020. **Campus Safety and Security:** Measures include 24-hour foot and vehicle patrol, emergency notification system, and security escort services. There are emergency telephones, lighted pathways/sidewalks, and controlled access to dorms/residences.

REQUIREMENTS: The SAT or ACT is required. Applicants must have 4 years of English, 3 years of social studies, and 2 years of college-preparatory math. AP and CLEP credits are accepted. Important factors in the admissions decision are recommendations by school officials, recommendations by alumni, and personality/intangible qualities. Students must complete a minimum of 128 credit hours including 36 in the major, and maintain a GPA of 2.0 overall and a major GPA of at least 2.0 (higher for some programs). Students must complete a program in general education, and take 36 hours in upper-division courses numbered 300 or above, 3 hours of math or computer science and religion courses are required. **Procedure:** Freshmen are admitted to all sessions. Entrance exams should be taken before or during the fall semester of the senior year. There are deferred admissions and rolling admissions plans. Application deadlines are open. The fall 2017 application fee was $20. Applications are accepted online. **Transfer Students:** 46 transfer students enrolled in 2016-2017. Transfer applicants should be in good standing at the college previously attended and have maintained a GPA of 2.0., and are also able to transfer courses with a grade C or better. All transcripts and an essay are required. 30 of 128 credits required for the bachelor's degree must be completed at HU. **International Students:** There are 49 international students enrolled. They must take the TOEFL with a minimum score of 525 on the paper-based TOEFL (PBT) or 65 on the Internet-based version (iBT). They must also take the SAT or ACT.

ADMISSIONS: 89% of the 2017-2018 applicants were accepted. The SAT scores for the 2017-2018 freshman class were: Critical Reading-- 34% below 500, 45% between 500 and 599, 20% between 600 and 699, and 1% between 700 and 800. Math-- 36% below 500, 47% between 500 and 599, 15% between 600 and 699, and 2% between 700 and 800. The ACT scores were 13% between 12 and 17, 54% between 18 and 23, 31% between 24 and 29, and 2% above 30. 2 freshmen graduated first in their class. **Admissions Contact:** Daniel Solms, VP for Enrollment Management. Email: *admissions@huntington.edu* Web: *www.huntington.edu*

FINANCIAL AID: In 2017-2018, 100% of all full-time freshmen received some form of financial aid. 51% of all full-time freshmen received need-based aid. The average freshman award was $22,983. Need-based scholarships or need-based grants averaged $13,992; need-based self-help aid (loans and jobs) averaged $7,009; and non-need-based athletic scholarships averaged $4,764. 10% of undergraduate students work part-time. The average financial indebtedness of the 2017 graduate was $34,625. The college's own financial statement is required. The FAFSA code is 001803. The priority date for freshman financial aid applications for fall entry is March 10.

INDIANA INSTITUTE OF TECHNOLOGY *(The complete profile is made available exclusively on our website, www.barronspac.com)*

INDIANA STATE UNIVERSITY *(The complete profile is made available exclusively on our website, www.barronspac.com)*

INDIANA UNIVERSITY BLOOMINGTON C-4

www.iub.edu

Bloomington, IN 47405 **(812) 855-0661**

Fax: (812) 855-5102	**Email:** iuadmit@indiana.edu
Full-time: 16,234 men, 15,978 women	**Faculty:** 2114; I, av$
Part-time: 660 men, 557 women	**Ph.D.s:** 84%
Graduate: 5575 men, 4706 women	**Student/Faculty:** 17 to 1
Year: semesters, summer session	**Tuition:** $10,533 ($34,845)
Room & Board: $10,258	**Freshman Class:** 41939 applied, 31878 accepted, 8001 enrolled
SAT EBR-W/M: 620/626 **ACT:** 28	**CEEB CODE:** 1324
Application Deadline: February 1	**HIGHLY COMPETITIVE**

Bloomington is the flagship residential, doctoral-extensive campus of Indiana University. Its mission is to create, disseminate, preserve, and apply knowledge. It does so through its commitments to cutting-edge research, scholarship, arts, and creative activity; to challenging and inspired undergraduate, graduate, professional, and lifelong education; to culturally diverse and international educational programs and communities; to first-rate library and museum collections; to economic development in the state and region; and to meaningful experiences outside the classroom. The Bloomington campus is committed to full diversity, academic freedom, and meeting the changing educational and research needs of the state, the nation, and the world. There are 16 undergraduate schools and 16 graduate schools. In addition to regional accreditation, IU-Bloomington has baccalaureate program accreditation with AACSB, ACEJMC, CSWE, NASAD, NASM, CAEP, ACOE, CCNE, and CIDA. The 1939-acre campus is in a small town 50 miles southwest of Indianapolis. Including any residence halls, there are 564 buildings.

STUDENT LIFE: 59% of undergraduates are from Indiana. Others are from 50 states, 147 foreign countries, and Canada. 66% are White; 6% Hispanic; 5% Asian American; 4% African American; 4% two or more races; 14% Foreign; 1% race unknown. **Male To Female Ratio:** 1.1:1. The average age of freshmen is 18; all undergraduates, 20. 9% do not continue beyond their first year. **Housing:** 12872 students can be accommodated in college housing, which includes coed, married student dorms, on-campus apartments, and off-campus apartments. In addition, there are honors houses, language/international houses, special-interest houses, living learning centers, an international center, a center for women, a wellness center, freshman interest groups (FIGs), and thematic communities. On-campus housing is guaranteed for the freshman year only, and is available on a first-come, first-served basis. 64% of students commute. Alcohol is not permitted. All students may keep cars.

FACULTY/CLASSROOMS: 60% of faculty are male; 40% are female. No introductory courses are taught by graduate students.

PROGRAMS OF STUDY: IU-Bloomington confers B.A., B.A.J., B.F.A., B.G.S., B.L.S., B.M., B.M.E., B.M.Ed., B.S., B.S.B., B.S.Ed., B.S.E.S., B.S.N., B.S.P.A., B.S.P.H., B.S.R., and B.S.W. degrees. Associate, master's, and doctoral degrees are also awarded. Bachelor's degrees are awarded in AGRICULTURE (animal science and environmental studies), BIOLOGICAL SCIENCE (biochemistry, biotechnology, human biology, health, and society, microbiology, and neurosciences), BUSINESS (business administration and management, labor studies, management, organizational leadership and management, and recreation and leisure services), COMMUNICATIONS AND THE ARTS (apparel design, art history, arts administration/management, audio technology, ballet, communication studies, comparative literature, dance, East Asian languages and literature, English, fashion studies, fine arts, folklore and mythology, French, game design and development, Germanic languages and literature, Greek (classical), Italian, journalism, linguistics, media arts, music, music composition, music performance, music theory and composition, musical theater, Portuguese, recreation administration, Slavic languages, Spanish, studio art, telecommunications, theatre arts, theatre studies, and visual and performing arts), COMPUTER AND PHYSICAL SCIENCE (applied science, astronomy, astrophysics, chemistry, chemistry/adolescence education, computer science, earth and space science, geoscience, informatics and computer science, mathematics, physics secondary education, physics, and statistics), EDUCATION (Asian studies, athletic training, classical studies, early childhood education, elementary education, general studies, health information management, journalism education, mathematics education, music education, recreation education, secondary education, social studies education, special education, and world language education), ENGINEERING AND ENVIRONMENTAL DESIGN (computational sciences, environmental science, interior design, and systems engineering), HEALTH PROFESSIONS (biology, environmental health science, health care administration, kinesiology, nursing, optometry, public health, and speech pathology/audiology), SOCIAL SCIENCE (African studies, African American studies, American studies, anthropology, Asian/American studies, Asian/Oriental studies, classical/ancient civilization, classical and near eastern civilization, cognitive science, criminal justice, East Asian studies, Eastern European studies, economics, gender studies, geography, history, international studies, Judaic studies, liberal arts/general studies, Near Eastern studies, philosophy, political science/government, psychology, public affairs, religious studies, social studies, social work, and sociology). Business, music, and law are the strongest academically. Business/commerce, public administration, and general studies have the largest enrollments.

ACTIVITIES: 24% of men belong to 40 national fraternities; 21% of women belong to 32 national sororities. There are 797 groups on campus, including art, band, cheerleading, chess, choir, chorale, chorus, communications, computers, dance, debate, drama, drill team, drum and bugle corps, environmental, ethnic, film, honors, international, jazz band, LGBT, literary magazine, marching band, musical theater, newspaper, opera, orchestra, pep band, photography, political, professional, radio and TV stations, religious, social, social service, student government, and symphony. Popular campus events include Little 500, Founder's Day, Homecoming Parade, IU Dance Marathon, and Welcome Week. **Sports:** There are 10 intercollegiate sports for men and 12 for women, and 20 intramural sports for men and women. Facilities include Student Recreational Sports Center features multi-sport gyms, strength and conditioning area with cardiovascular and weight-training equipment, an elevated running track, basketball/volleyball courts, a track, squash courts, a pool, tennis courts, a fieldhouse for track & field, softball and baseball complex with hitting cages, stadiums for soccer, football, basketball, field hockey, golf, a cross-country course, and a rowing center.**Graduates:** From July 1, 2016 to June 30, 2017, 7553 bachelor's degrees were awarded. The most popular majors were business/marketing (24%), parks and recreation (8%), and biological/life sciences (8%). In an average class, 63% graduate in 4 years or less, 75% graduate in 5 years or less, and 77% graduate in 6 years or less.

SERVICES: Counseling and information services are available, as is tutoring in most subjects. There is a reader service for the blind, remedial math, reading, and writing. Skills workshops are also offered. **Library/Resources:** The library contains 8.8 million volumes. Computerized library services include interlibrary loans, database searching, Internet access, and Wi-Fi capability. Special learning facilities include an art gallery, an arboretum, museum of world cultures, natural history museum, an observatory, a garden and nature center, musical arts center, auditorium and theaters, and more than 200 research centers and institutes. **Physically Challenged Students:** 95% of the campus is accessible. Facilities include wheelchair ramps, elevators, special parking, specially equipped restrooms, special class scheduling, lowered drinking fountains, lowered telephones, and scheduled transportation. **Special:** IU offers cooperative programs with universities in many countries, a variety of internships, and study abroad. A Washington semester, work-study programs, B.A.-B.S. degrees in the sciences and liberal arts, dual majors, online degrees and the general studies degree are available. Student-designed majors through the Individualized Major Program, credit for military experience, nondegree study and pass/fail options are also available. There are 18 national honor societies, Phi Beta Kappa, and a freshman honors program. **Visiting:** There are regularly scheduled orientations for prospective students, admissions counseling and answers to students' questions. There are guides for informal visits, visitors may sit in on classes, and stay overnight. To schedule a visit, contact Office of Admissions. **Campus Safety and Security:** Measures include 24-hour foot and vehicle patrol, emergency notification system, self-defense education, and security escort services. There are shuttle buses, emergency telephones, lighted pathways/sidewalks, controlled access to dorms/residences, and safety awareness education.

REQUIREMENTS: The SAT or ACT is required. Applicants must be graduates of an accredited secondary high school or have a GED certificate. Indiana residents must be on track to complete Core 40 curriculum, Core 40 academic curriculum, or the equivalent as a condition of admission. SAT: Subject tests are recommended for credit and placement. Auditions for music majors are required. An interview is recommended for information purposes. AP and CLEP credits are accepted. Important factors in the admissions decision are advanced placement or honors courses, parents or siblings attended your school, and recommendations by school officials. The general requirements for graduation include courses in English and writing, math, foreign language, arts and humanities, social and behavioral sciences, natural sciences, and culture studies. Students must complete 120 credit hours, with approximately 36 hours in the major. Many degrees have intensive writing requirements, and the minimum GPA requirement varies by department. Liberal arts requirements are common throughout all degree programs. **Procedure:** Freshmen are admitted to all sessions. Entrance exams should be taken late in the junior year or early in the senior year. There are deferred admissions and rolling admissions plans. Applications should be filed by February 1 for fall entry; November 1 for spring entry. The fall 2017 application fee was $65. Applications are accepted on-line. **Transfer Students:** 770 transfer students enrolled in 2016-2017. Admission for transfers is selective. Decisions are based on high school background, college curriculum, grade trends, choice of major, and overall performance. If transferring with fewer than 26 credit hours, student must also meet freshman guidelines. 2.3 GPA required for residents; 2.5 GPA for nonresidents for consideration. 60 of 120 credits required for the bachelor's degree must be completed at IU. **International Students:** There are 3349 international students enrolled. They must take the TOEFL with a minimum score of 550 on the paper-based TOEFL (PBT) or 79 on the Internet-based version (iBT). They must also take the SAT or ACT.

ADMISSIONS: 76% of the 2017-2018 applicants were accepted. The SAT scores for the 2017-2018 freshman class were: Math-- 4% below 500, 33% between 500 and 599, 43% between 600 and 699, and 20% between 700 and 800. Evidence-Based Reading/Writing-- 4% below 500, 32% between 500 and 599, 50% between 600 and 699, and 14% between 700 and 800. The ACT scores were 1% between 12 and 17, 16% between 18 and 23, 47% between 24 and 29, and 36% above 30. 70% of the current freshmen were in the top fifth of their class; 95% were in the top two fifths. **Admissions Contact:** Sacha Thieme, Executive Director of Admissions. Email: *iuadmit@indiana.edu* Web: *www.iub.edu*

FINANCIAL AID: In 2017-2018, 77% of all full-time freshmen received some form of financial aid. 44% of all full-time freshmen received need-based aid. The average freshman award was $13,765. Need-based scholarships or need-based grants averaged $12,633 ($48,666 maximum); need-based self-help aid (loans and jobs) averaged $5,694 ($42,892 maximum); non-need-based athletic scholarships averaged $19,362 ($51,460 maximum); and other non-need-based awards and non-need-based scholarships averaged $8,490 ($52,629 maximum). 21% of undergraduate students work part-time. The average financial indebtedness of the 2017 graduate was $28,792. IUB is a member of CSS. The FAFSA code is 001809. The priority date for freshman financial aid applications for fall entry is March 1.

INDIANA UNIVERSITY EAST D-3

www.iue.edu

Richmond, IN 47374	**(765) 973-8208** **(800) 959-4485**
Fax: (765) 973-8209	**Email: applyiue@indiana.edu**
Full-time: 656 men, 1231 women	**Faculty:** 117; IIA, --$
Part-time: 545 men, 860 women	**Ph.D.s:** 76%
Graduate: 40 men, 158 women	**Student/Faculty:** 14 to 1
Year: semesters, summer session	**Tuition:** $7207 ($19,038)
Room & Board: n/app	**Freshman Class:** 1279 applied, 891 accepted, 396 enrolled
SAT EBR-W/M: 521/510 **ACT:** 21	**CEEB CODE:** 1194
Application Deadline: open	**COMPETITIVE**

Indiana University East, a regional campus of Indiana University, offers a broad range of bachelor's degrees and selected master's degrees and certificates through its traditional main campus in Richmond, off-campus sites, and online program options. IUEast challenges students to grow intellectually and personally in a supportive and scholarly environment where faculty teaching skills and participation in the creation and dissemination of new knowledge and artistic work enhance learning opportunities for all. There are 8 undergraduate schools and 6 graduate schools. In addition to regional accreditation, IUEast has baccalaureate program accreditation with ACBSP, CSWE, CAEP, CAEP, and ACEN. The 182-acre campus is in a small town 45 miles west of Dayton, Ohio. Including any residence halls, there are 10 buildings.

STUDENT LIFE: 75% of undergraduates are from Indiana. Others are from 43 states, 46 foreign countries, and Canada. 84% are White; 5% African American; 4% Hispanic; 3% two or more races; 1% Asian American; 1% Foreign; 1% race unknown. **Female To Male Ratio:** 1.8:1. The average age of freshmen is 18; all undergraduates, 27. 34% do not continue beyond their first year. Alcohol is not permitted. All students commute. All students may keep cars.

FACULTY/CLASSROOMS: 37% of faculty are male; 63% are female. No introductory courses are taught by graduate students.

PROGRAMS OF STUDY: IUEast confers B.A., B.A.S., B.F.A., B.G.S., B.S., B.S.Ed., B.S.N and B.S.W. degrees. Associate and master's degrees are also awarded. Bachelor's degrees are awarded in BIOLOGICAL SCIENCE (biochemistry, biotechnology, and life science), BUSINESS (business administration and management), COMMUNICATIONS AND THE ARTS (communication studies, English, fine arts, and Spanish), COMPUTER AND PHYSICAL SCIENCE (applied science, informatics and computer science, mathematics, and natural sciences/mathematics), EDUCATION (elementary education, general studies, and secondary education), HEALTH PROFESSIONS (biology, health science, and nursing), SOCIAL SCIENCE (criminal justice, history, humanities, international studies, political science/government, psychology, social work, and sociology). Business, nursing, and general studies have the largest enrollments.

ACTIVITIES: There are 39 groups on campus, including art, communications, computers, dance, drama, environmental, ethnic, honors, international, LGBT, newspaper, political, professional, radio and TV, religious, social, social service, and student government. Popular campus events include Homecoming, and Spirit of Philanthropy. **Sports:** There are 6 intercollegiate sports for men and 7 for women. Facilities include a recreation and fitness center, a softball field, tennis and sand volleyball courts, and a field house. **Graduates:** From July 1, 2016 to June 30, 2017, 777 bachelor's degrees were awarded. The most popular majors were business, management, marketing (25%), health professions and related programs (18%), and psychology (11%). In an average class, 17% graduate in 4 years or less, 31% graduate in 5 years or less, and 36% graduate in 6 years or less.

SERVICES: Counseling and information services are available, as is tutoring in some subjects, such as in several freshman-level courses. There is a reader service for the blind, and remedial math, reading, and writing. **Library/Resources:** The library contains 431,441 volumes. Computerized library services include interlibrary loans, database searching, Internet access, and Wi-Fi capability. Special learning facilities include an art gallery and radio station. **Physically Challenged Students:** 98% of the campus is accessible. Facilities include wheelchair ramps, elevators, special parking, lowered drinking fountains, and lowered telephones. There is also special testing accommodations and note taking. **Special:** IUEast offers a cooperative program in criminal justice with Indiana University-Purdue University and an organizational leadership program through Purdue's Statewide Technology program. IUEast also offers online degrees, cross-registration with Earlham College, dual majors, independent study, an internship in social work, pass/fail options, study abroad through Indiana University Bloomington, and credit for life experience. Nondegree study is possible. There are 8 national honor societies and a freshman honors program. **Visiting:** There are regularly scheduled orientations for prospective students, including tours, counseling, registration, and financial aid sessions. There are guides for informal visits and visitors may sit in on classes. To schedule a visit, contact the Admissions Office. **Campus Safety and Security:** Measures include emergency notification system and security escort services. There are emergency telephones, lighted pathways/sidewalks, and a 14-hour foot and vehicle patrol.

REQUIREMENTS: The SAT is required, and the ACT is recommended. Recent high school graduates from Indiana are expected to complete the Core 40 curriculum. Out-of-state students are expected to complete a minimum of 28 semester hours of college prep courses listed above. The 4 units of academic electives include additional math, lab science, social science, computer science, and foreign language, or other college-prep courses. Recent high school graduates should rank in the upper half of their graduating class. AP and CLEP credits are accepted. To graduate, students must satisfactorily complete the General Education Curriculum (30 credit hours) which applies to all IUEast students admitted effective in the Summer. This includes a Written Communication Competency, Speaking and Listening Competency, Quantitative Reasoning Competency, Natural Sciences Competency, (must include at least 1 course with laboratory), Humanistic Artistic Competency, (must include at least 2 different disciplines), Social-Behavioral Competency, (must include at least 2 different disciplines). Students must complete a minimum of 120 semester hours (30 hours taken at IUEast) with a GPA of at least 2.0. **Procedure:** Freshmen are admitted to all sessions. Entrance exams should be taken during the junior or senior year. There are early admissions, deferred admissions, and rolling admissions plans. Application deadlines are open. The fall 2017 application fee was $35. Applications are accepted online. **Transfer Students:** 368 transfer students enrolled in 2016-2017. Applicants must be high school graduates, or equivalent completed 12 or more semester hours at an accredited university or college (including junior and community colleges), with a GPA of 2.0 (2.5 for out-of-state transfer applicants) and submit college transcripts. Grades of C or better transfer for credit. 30 of 120 credits required for the bachelor's degree must be completed at IUEast. **International Students:** There are 15 international students enrolled. They must take the TOEFL with a minimum score of 550 on the paper-based TOEFL (PBT) or 79 on the Internet-based version (iBT).

ADMISSIONS: 70% of the 2017-2018 applicants were accepted. The SAT scores for the 2017-2018 freshman class were: Math-- 40% below 500, 50% between 500 and 599, 9% between 600 and 699, and 1% between 700 and 800. Evidence-Based Reading/Writing-- 38% below 500, 47% between 500 and 599, 14% between 600 and 699, and 1% between 700 and 800. The ACT scores were 18% between 12 and 17, 59% between 18 and 23, 21% between 24 and 29, and 2% above 30. 30% of the current freshmen were in the top fifth of their class; 71% were in the top two fifths. **Admissions Contact:** Molly Vanderpool, Executive Director Admissions. Email: *applyiue@indiana.edu* Web: *www.iue.edu*

FINANCIAL AID: In 2017-2018, 95% of all full-time freshmen received some form of financial aid. 74% of all full-time freshmen received need-based aid. The average freshman award was $8,638. Need-based scholarships or need-based grants averaged $7,319 ($19,244 maximum); need-based self-help aid (loans and jobs) averaged $3,970 ($15,500 maximum); non-need-based athletic scholarships averaged $2,588 ($15,610 maximum); and other non-need-based awards and non-need-based scholarships averaged $3,901 ($13,000 maximum). 5% of undergraduate students work part-time. The average financial indebtedness of the 2017 graduate was $22,392. The college's own financial statement is required.

The FAFSA code is 001811. The priority date for freshman financial aid applications for fall entry is March 1.

INDIANA UNIVERSITY KOKOMO C-2

www.iuk.edu

Kokomo, IN 46902	**(765) 455-9217** **(888) 875-4485**
Fax: (765) 455-9537	**Email: iuadmis@iuk.edu**
Full-time: 797 men, 1418 women	**Faculty:** 123; IIB, -$
Part-time: 226 men, 435 women	**Ph.D.s:** 61%
Graduate: 60 men, 93 women	**Student/Faculty:** 16 to 1
Year: semesters, summer session	**Tuition:** $7207 ($19,038)
Room & Board: n/app	**Freshman Class:** 1770 applied, 1244 accepted, 605 enrolled
SAT EBR-W/M: 527/515 **ACT:** required	**CEEB CODE:** 1337
Application Deadline: August 24	**COMPETITIVE**

Indiana University Kokomo, a regional campus of Indiana University, providing a wide range of bachelor's degrees, and a limited number of master's and associate degrees. IUK is further dedicated to enhancing research, creative work, and other scholarly activity and to strengthening the economic and cultural vitality of the region through a variety of partnerships and programs. There are 8 undergraduate schools and 8 graduate schools. In addition to regional accreditation, IUK has baccalaureate program accreditation with AACSB, CCNE, JRCERT, and CAEP. The 52-acre campus is in a small town 53 miles north of Indianapolis. Including any residence halls, there are 13 buildings.

STUDENT LIFE: 98% of undergraduates are from Indiana. Others are from 13 states, 32 foreign countries, and Canada. 81% are White; 5% Hispanic; 4% African American; 3% two or more races; 3% race unknown; 2% Foreign; 1% Asian American. **Female To Male Ratio:** 1.8:1. The average age of freshmen is 19; all undergraduates, 23. 40% do not continue beyond their first year. Alcohol is not permitted. All students commute. All students may keep cars.

FACULTY/CLASSROOMS: 39% of faculty are male; 61% are female. No introductory courses are taught by graduate students.

PROGRAMS OF STUDY: IUK confers B.A., B.A.S., B.S., B.F.A., B.G.S., B.S.B., B.S.Ed., B.S.N., and B.S.P.A. degrees. Associate and master's degrees are also awarded. Bachelor's degrees are awarded in BIOLOGICAL SCIENCE (biochemistry and biology/biological science), BUSINESS (business administration and management, sports management, and tourism), COMMUNICATIONS AND THE ARTS (communications, English, fine arts, media arts, and new media production), COMPUTER AND PHYSICAL SCIENCE (applied science, chemistry, chemistry/chemical biology, information sciences and systems, informatics and computer science, mathematics, and physical sciences), EDUCATION (early childhood education, elementary education, general studies, and secondary education), HEALTH PROFESSIONS (biology, health science, medical imaging, nursing, and radiation therapy), SOCIAL SCIENCE (criminal justice, history and political science, humanities, psychology, public administration, and sociology). Nursing, business, and general studies have the largest enrollments.

ACTIVITIES: There are no fraternities; 1% of women belong to 1 national sorority. There are 42 groups on campus, including cheerleading, choir, chorale, communications, computers, dance, drama, environmental, ethnic, honors, international, LGBT, newspaper, political, professional, religious, social, social service, and student government. Popular campus events include Campus Fall Kick-off BBQ, Campus Beautification Day, Dance-a-Thon, and Take Back the Night. **Sports:** There are 5 intercollegiate sports for men and 6 for women. **Graduates:** From July 1, 2016 to June 30, 2017, 560 bachelor's degrees were awarded. The most popular majors were health professions (41%), business, management, marketing, and related support services (14%), liberal arts and sciences, and general studies and humanities (11%). In an average class, 18% graduate in 4 years or less, 34% graduate in 5 years or less, and 39% graduate in 6 years or less.

SERVICES: Counseling and information services are available, as is tutoring in most subjects. There is remedial math, reading, and writing. Students who do not meet regular admissions standards can be admitted under the Guided Study Program, which includes courses in basic skills as needed, counseling and tutoring, and a seminar on studying. **Library/Resources:** The library contains 1.2 million volumes. Computerized library services include interlibrary loans, database searching, and Internet access. **Physically Challenged Students:** All of the campus is accessible. Facilities include wheelchair ramps, elevators, special parking, specially equipped restrooms, special class scheduling, lowered drinking fountains, and lowered telephones. **Special:** Student-designed majors, a general studies degree, internships, study abroad, joint programs with other Indiana University campuses and with Purdue University, pass/fail options, nondegree study, credit for military experience and by exam, as well as online degrees are available. There are 3 national honor societies and a freshman honors program. **Visiting:** There are regularly scheduled orientations for prospective students. There are guides for informal visits and visitors may sit in on classes. To schedule a visit, contact the Admissions Office. **Campus Safety and Security:** Measures include emergency notification system and security escort services. There are emergency telephones, lighted pathways/sidewalks, and campus police are on duty.

REQUIREMENTS: The SAT or ACT is required. Students that have not earned an Academic Honors or Core 40 high school diploma, your high school preparation should include a minimum of at least the 40 college preparatory courses. The academic electives include foreign language, mathematics, laboratory science, social science, computer science or other college preparatory courses. AP and CLEP credits are accepted. Important factors in the admissions decision are recommendations by school officials and advanced placement or honors courses. All students must maintain a minimum GPA of 2.0 while taking 120 credit hours. The following general education curriculum is required of each student who is granted a baccalaureate degree at the Kokomo campus. Total credit hours will typically consist of 42 or 44, if a student takes more than the required number of courses within a section, the course (s) with the highest grade (s) will be used in the GPA calculation. Additional departments and/or schools may have specific general education requirements rather than the general ones listed here. Students should consult with their advisor for more information. General education curriculum: Communication Skills Requirement – 3 required courses (9 hours); Information Literacy; Quantitative Literacy (4 – 8 hours); Critical Thinking (3 hours); Cultural Diversity (3 hours); Ethics and Civic Engagement (3 hours); Social and Behavioral Sciences - two 3 credit hour courses, each from a different area (6 hours); Humanities and Arts - two 3 credit hour courses, each from a different area (6 hours); Physical and Life Sciences - one 5 credit hour course with a lab and one 3 credit hour course from a different area (8 hours). All students must complete coursework in English, computer, and math. **Procedure:** Freshmen are admitted to all sessions. Entrance exams should be taken prior to registration. There are deferred admissions and rolling admissions plans. Applications should be filed by August 24 for fall entry; January 12 for spring entry; and May 18 for summer entry. The fall 2017 application fee was $35. Applications are accepted on-line. **Transfer Students:** 271 transfer students enrolled in 2016-2017. Transfer applicants must have at least 13 credits with a minimum GPA of 2.0 and clear records of conduct from previously attended colleges. Transcripts are required. Transfers are considered on a case-by-case basis. 30 of 120 credits required for the bachelor's degree must be completed at IUK. **International Students:** There are 25 international students enrolled. They must take the TOEFL with a minimum score of 513 on the paper-based TOEFL (PBT) or 65 on the Internet-based version (iBT).

ADMISSIONS: 70% of the 2017-2018 applicants were accepted. The SAT scores for the 2017-2018 freshman class were: Math-- 37% below 500, 52% between 500 and 599, 10% between 600 and 699, and 1% between 700 and 800. Evidence-Based Reading/Writing-- 32% below 500, 54% between 500 and 599, 13% between 600 and 699, and 1% between 700 and 800. The ACT scores were 28% between 12 and 17, 55% between 18 and 23, 16% between 24 and 29, and 1% above 30. 28% of the current freshmen were in the top fifth of their class; 70% were in the top two fifths. **Admissions Contact:** Angie Siders, Director of Admissions. Email: *iuadmis@iuk.edu* Web: *www.iuk.edu*

FINANCIAL AID: In 2017-2018, 86% of all full-time freshmen received some form of financial aid. 67% of all full-time freshmen received need-based aid. The average freshman award was $7,898. Need-based scholarships or need-based grants averaged $6,998 ($17,587 maximum); need-based self-help aid (loans and jobs) averaged $4,104 ($10,500 maximum); non-need-based athletic scholarships averaged $960 ($1,500 maximum); and other non-need-based awards and non-need-based scholarships averaged $3,710 ($19,916 maximum). 9% of undergraduate students work part-time. The average financial indebtedness of the 2017 graduate was $23,664. The FAFSA code is 001814. The priority date for freshman financial aid applications for fall entry is March 1.

INDIANA UNIVERSITY NORTHWEST *(The complete profile is made available exclusively on our website, www.barronspac.com)*

INDIANA UNIVERSITY SOUTH BEND C-1

www.iusb.edu

South Bend, IN 46615 **(574) 520-4839** **(877) GO-2-IUSB**

Fax: (574) 520-4834 **Email: admissions@iusb.edu**

Full-time: 1431 men, 2336 women
Part-time: 431 men, 678 women
Graduate: 162 men, 347 women
Year: semesters, summer session
Room & Board: $8850
SAT EBR-W/M: 524/510 **ACT:** 21
Application Deadline: August 1

Faculty: 258; IIA, --$
Ph.D.s: 79%
Student/Faculty: 13 to 1
Tuition: $7207 ($19,038)
Freshman Class: 2580 applied, 2005 accepted, 982 enrolled
CEEB CODE: 1339
COMPETITIVE

Indiana University South Bend is the comprehensive undergraduate and graduate regional campus of Indiana University that is committed to serving north central Indiana and southwestern Michigan. Its mission is to create, disseminate, preserve, and apply knowledge. The campus is committed to excellence in teaching, learning, research, and creative activity; to strong liberal arts and sciences programs and professional disciplines; to acclaimed programs in the arts and nursing/health professions; and to diversity, civic engagement, and a global perspective. South Bend supports student learning, access and success for a diverse residential and nonresidential student body that includes underrepresented and international students. There are 7 undergraduate schools and 6 graduate schools. In addition to regional accreditation, IUSouth Bend has baccalaureate program accreditation with AACSB, CSWE, NASM, CCNE, CODA, and CAEP. The 104-acre campus is in a suburban area 95 miles east of Chicago. Including any residence halls, there are 31 buildings.

STUDENT LIFE: 94% of undergraduates are from Indiana. Others are from 20 states, 70 foreign countries, and Canada. 8% are African American; 71% White; 4% two or more races; 3% Foreign; 2% Asian American; 11% Hispanic; 1% race unknown. **Female To Male Ratio:** 1.7:1. The average age of freshmen is 19; all undergraduates, 23. 34% do not continue beyond their first year. **Housing:** 396 students can be accommodated in college housing, which includes on-campus apartments, off-campus apartments, and special housing for international students. On-campus housing is available on a first-come, first-served basis. 92% of students commute. Alcohol is not permitted. All students may keep cars.

FACULTY/CLASSROOMS: 49% of faculty are male; 51% are female. No introductory courses are taught by graduate students.

PROGRAMS OF STUDY: IUSouth Bend confers B.A., B.S., B.A.S., B.F.A, B.G.S., B.M., B.S.Ed., B.S.M.I.T., B.S.N., and B.S.W. degrees. Associate and master's degrees are also awarded. Bachelor's degrees are awarded in BIOLOGICAL SCIENCE (biochemistry, biology/adolescence education, and biology/biological science), BUSINESS (business administration and management and labor studies), COMMUNICATIONS AND THE ARTS (communication studies, English, fine arts, French, German, music, new media production, Spanish, and theatre arts), COMPUTER AND PHYSICAL SCIENCE (actuarial science, applied science, chemistry, chemistry/adolescence education, clinical laboratory science, computer science, informatics and computer science, mathematics, physics secondary education, and physics), EDUCATION (art education, elementary education, English education, general studies, French studies K-12 education, mathematics education, music education, science education, secondary education, social studies education, Spanish education K-12, and special education), HEALTH PROFESSIONS (dental hygiene, health care administration, health science, medical imaging, and nursing), SOCIAL SCIENCE (anthropology, criminal justice, economics, history, philosophy, political science/government, psychology, social work, sociology, and women and gender studies). Business, nursing, and general studies have the largest enrollments.

ACTIVITIES: There are 129 groups on campus, including art, cheerleading, choir, communications, dance, debate, drama, environmental, ethnic, film, honors, international, LGBT, musical theater, newspaper, political, professional, religious, social, social service, and student government. Popular campus events include Titan Fest, Red and White Dance, Mini University Welcome Week, and Alternative Spring Break Trips. **Sports:** There are 5 intercollegiate sports for men and 6 for women, and 11 intramural sports for men and 11 for women. Facilities include Student Activities Center features: basketball, volleyball courts, racquetball and vallyball courts, indoor running tracks (1/8 mile), group exercise and aerobic room, table tennis, billiards tables, and a wellness center, free-weight equipment, cardiovascular machines, and weight training machines.**Graduates:** From July 1, 2016 to June 30, 2017, 808 bachelor's degrees were awarded. The most popular majors were business, management, marketing (21%), health professions (13%), and education (11%). In an average class, 9% graduate in 4 years or less, 22% graduate in 5 years or less, and 30% graduate in 6 years or less.

SERVICES: Counseling and information services are available, as is tutoring in most subjects. There is remedial math, reading, and writing. Taped texts, note takers, and interpreters or transcription services are also available. **Library/Resources:** The library contains 1.6 million volumes. Computerized library services include interlibrary loans, database searching, Internet access, and Wi-Fi capability. Special learning facilities include an art gallery, science labs, studios for fine and performing arts, instructional media services, and an academic resource center. **Physically Challenged Students:** 95% of the campus is accessible. Facilities include wheelchair ramps, elevators, special parking, specially equipped restrooms, special class scheduling, lowered drinking fountains, and lowered telephones. **Special:** Cross-registration with Northern Indiana Consortium for education (NICE), internships, study abroad, accelerated degree programs, online degrees and dual majors are possible. There are 4 national honor societies and a freshman honors program. **Visiting:** There are regularly scheduled orientations for prospective students, including a visit to the admissions office, a campus tour, professor meetings, and information on financial aid. There are guides for informal visits, visitors may sit in on classes, and stay overnight. To schedule a visit, contact the Admissions Office. **Campus Safety and Security:** Measures include 24-hour foot and vehicle patrol, emergency notification system, and security escort services. There are emergency telephones and lighted pathways/sidewalks.

REQUIREMENTS: The SAT or ACT is required. Indiana high school graduates are expected to complete the Core 40 curriculum and are strongly encouraged to earn the Academic Honors Diploma. Out-of-state students are expected to complete a comparable college-prep curriculum. CLEP credits are accepted. Important factors in the admissions decision are advanced placement or honors courses, extracurricular activities record, and leadership record. All students must complete the campus-wide general education curriculum which is composed of three elements and requires a total of between 33 and 39 credit hours of course work. These include: I. Fundamental Literacies Courses (13-19 cr.) Writing, Critical Thinking, Oral Communication, Visual Literacy, Quantitative Reasoning, Information Literacy and Computer Literacy. II. Common Core Courses (12 cr.) The Natural World, Human Behavior and Social Institutions, Literary and Intellectual Traditions, Art, Aesthetics, and Creativity. III. Contemporary Social Values Courses (8 cr.) Non-Western Cultures, Diversity in U.S. Society, Health and Wellness. A total of 120 semester hours, with a minimum GPA of 2.0, is required to graduate. **Procedure:** Freshmen are admitted to all sessions. Entrance exams should be taken 1 year to 6 months before entering the university. There are deferred admissions and rolling admissions plans. Application deadlines are open. The fall 2017 application fee was $35. Applications are accepted on-line. **Transfer Students:** 337 transfer students enrolled in 2016-2017. A 2.0 GPA is required. College transcripts must be submitted. 30 of 120 credits required for the bachelor's degree must be completed at IUSouthBend. **International Students:** There are 109 international students enrolled. They must take the TOEFL with a minimum score of 530 on the paper-based TOEFL (PBT) or 71 on the Internet-based version (iBT).

ADMISSIONS: 78% of the 2017-2018 applicants were accepted. The SAT scores for the 2017-2018 freshman class were: Math-- 44% below 500, 45% between 500 and 599, 10% between 600 and 699, and 1% between 700 and 800. Evidence-Based Reading/Writing-- 38% below 500, 45% between 500 and 599, 15% between 600 and 699, and 2% between 700 and 800. The ACT scores were 20% between 12 and 17, 53% between 18 and 23, 24% between 24 and 29, and 3% above 30. 25% of the current freshmen were in the top fifth of their class; 66% were in the top two fifths. **Admissions Contact:** Constance Peterson-Miller, Director of Admissions. Email: *admissions@iusb.edu* Web: *www.iusb.edu*

FINANCIAL AID: In 2017-2018, 87% of all full-time freshmen received some form of financial aid. 69% of all full-time freshmen received need-based aid. The average freshman award was $8,295. Need-based scholarships or need-based grants averaged $7,127 ($25,498 maximum); need-based self-help aid (loans and jobs) averaged $4,105 ($13,399 maximum); non-need-based athletic scholarships averaged $2,530 ($6,000 maximum); and other non-need-based awards and non-need-based scholarships averaged $4,241 ($16,872 maximum). 9% of undergraduate students work part-time. The average financial indebtedness of the 2017 graduate was $25,780. The FAFSA code is 001816. The priority date for freshman financial aid applications for fall entry is March 1.

INDIANA UNIVERSITY SOUTHEAST C-5

www.ius.edu

New Albany, IN 47150 (812) 941-2212
(800) 852-8835
Fax: (812) 941-2595 Email: admissions@ius.edu

Full-time: 1245 men, 1973 women
Part-time: 684 men, 921 women
Graduate: 161 men, 254 women
Year: semesters, summer session
Room & Board: $9724
Faculty: 214; IIA, -$
Ph.D.s: 79%
Student/Faculty: 14 to 1
Tuition: $7207 ($19,038)
Freshman Class: 2273 applied, 1881 accepted, 927 enrolled
SAT EBR-W/M: 530/509 **ACT:** required
CEEB CODE: 1314
Application Deadline: August 12
COMPETITIVE

Indiana University Southeast is the regional campus of Indiana University that serves southern Indiana and the greater Louisville metropolitan area. As a public comprehensive university, its mission is to provide high-quality educational programs and services that promote student learning and prepare students for productive citizenship in a diverse society, and to contribute to the intellectual, cultural, and economic development of the region. Its academic programs include a comprehensive array of baccalaureate degrees, a limited number of associate degrees, and a selected set of master's programs. The campus is committed to offering educational programs and services which promote and support diversity in all its aspects. The faculty engage in research and creative activities which strengthen teaching and learning through inquiry into both the content and the pedagogy of the disciplines and create opportunities for students to engage in applied learning. There are 8 undergraduate schools and 4 graduate schools. In addition to regional accreditation, IUSE has baccalaureate program accreditation with AACSB, CCNE, CAEP, and ACS. The 180-acre campus is in a suburban area 10 miles northwest of Louisville, Kentucky, and 114 miles south of Indianapolis. Including any residence halls, there are 55 buildings.

STUDENT LIFE: 69% of undergraduates are from Indiana. Others are from 21 states, 46 foreign countries, and Canada. 83% are White; 7% African American; 4% Hispanic; 3% two or more races; 1% Asian American; 1% Foreign; 1% race unknown. **Female To Male Ratio:** 1.5:1. The average age of freshmen is 19; all undergraduates, 24. 41% do not continue beyond their first year. **Housing:** 399 students can be accommodated in college housing, which includes on-campus apartments. On-campus housing is available on a first-come, first-served basis. 92% of students commute. Alcohol is not permitted. All students may keep cars.

FACULTY/CLASSROOMS: 43% of faculty are male; 57% are female. No introductory courses are taught by graduate students.

PROGRAMS OF STUDY: IUSE confers B.A., B.A.S., B.F.A., B.G.S., B.S., B.S.Ed., and B.S.N. degrees. Associate and master's degrees are also awarded. Bachelor's degrees are awarded in BIOLOGICAL SCIENCE (biology/adolescence education and neurosciences), BUSINESS (business administration and management), COMMUNICATIONS AND THE ARTS (communications, English, fine arts, French, German, journalism, music, and Spanish), COMPUTER AND PHYSICAL SCIENCE (applied science, chemistry, clinical laboratory science, computer science, geoscience, informatics and computer science, mathematics, and physics), EDUCATION (elementary education, general studies, health information management, mathematics education, secondary education, social studies education, and special education), HEALTH PROFESSIONS (biology and nursing), SOCIAL SCIENCE (criminal justice, criminology, economics, history, humanities, international studies, philosophy, political science/government, psychology, and sociology). Business, general studies, and nursing have the largest enrollments.

ACTIVITIES: There are 133 groups on campus, including art, band, cheerleading, choir, chorus, communications, computers, dance, debate, drama, environmental, ethnic, honors, international, jazz band, LGBT, literary magazine, newspaper, pep band, political, professional, religious, social, social service, and student government. Popular campus events include International Festival, Wares of the World, Common Experience, and Hunger Banquet. **Sports:** There are 3 intercollegiate sports for men and 4 for women, and 12 intramural sports for men and 11 for women. Facilities include the campus fitness center, which has strength machines, a free weight area, a variety of cardiovascular exercise equipment that includesÂ treadmills, bikes, elliptical, stairmaster and cros-strainers, a basketball court, facilities for jogging, badminton, volleyball, gymnastics, tennis courts, baseball and softball fields and playing fields. **Graduates:** From July 1, 2016 to June 30, 2017, 858 bachelor's degrees were awarded. The most popular majors were business, management, marketing (21%), health professions (13%), and education (10%). In an average class, 14% graduate in 4 years or less, 27% graduate in 5 years or less, and 32% graduate in 6 years or less.

SERVICES: Counseling and information services are available, as is tutoring in most subjects. There is a reader service for the blind, and remedial math, reading, and writing. The service coordinator provides information and coordination of needs to student with disabilities. **Library/Resources:** The library contains 1.5 million volumes. Computerized library services include interlibrary loans, database searching, Internet access, and Wi-Fi capability. Special learning facilities include an art gallery. **Physically Challenged Students:** All of the campus is accessible. Facilities include wheelchair ramps, elevators, special parking, specially equipped restrooms, lowered drinking fountains, lowered telephones, and special accommodations as needed. **Special:** Cross-registration with Metroversity is possible, and opportunities are provided for study abroad, internships, work-study programs, dual majors, a general studies degree, credit by exam, nondegree study, online degree, accelerated degree programs, and pass/fail options. There are 9 national honor societies. **Visiting:** There are regularly scheduled orientations for prospective students, including an opportunity for students to apply for admission, financial aid, and scholarships, a faculty perspective, a student perspective, and a campus tour. There are guides for informal visits and visitors may sit in on classes. To schedule a visit, contact the Office of Admissions. **Campus Safety and Security:** Measures include 24-hour foot and vehicle patrol, emergency notification system, and self-defense education. There are emergency telephones and lighted pathways/sidewalks.

REQUIREMENTS: High school graduates from Indiana are expected to complete the Core 40 curriculum. Out-of-state students are expected to complete a minimum of 28 semester hours of college preparatory courses. Scores from either the SAT or ACT are required for those applicants who graduated from high school within the past two years or who completed a GED and are 19 years of age or younger. Students who have been out of high school for over two years and do not meet the minimum requirements listed for traditional students may be asked to arrange for an interview with an admissions counselor to demonstrate intention through maturity and experience. AP and CLEP credits are accepted. Students must complete 120 credit hours, with 30 in upper-level courses and at least 25 in the major, and must maintain a minimum cumulative GPA of 2.0. **Procedure:** Freshmen are admitted to all sessions. Entrance exams should be taken late junior, early senior year. There are early admissions, deferred admissions, and rolling admissions plans. Applications should be filed by August 12 for fall entry; December 31 for spring entry. The fall 2017 application fee was $35. Notification is sent on a rolling basis. Applications are accepted on-line. **Transfer Students:** 408 transfer students enrolled in 2016-2017. A GPA of 2.0 is required for Indiana residents, 2.5 for out-of-state applicants. If the student has earned less than 26 hours of college transfer credit, high school transcripts or GED test scores are required as well as SAT or ACT scores if you have been out of high school less than 2 years. Transfer students are required to submit official transcripts from all previously attended colleges. 30 of 120 credits required for the bachelor's degree must be completed at IUS. **International Students:** There are 18 international students enrolled. They must take the TOEFL with a minimum score of 530 on the paper-based TOEFL (PBT) or 71 on the Internet-based version (iBT).

ADMISSIONS: 83% of the 2017-2018 applicants were accepted. The SAT scores for the 2017-2018 freshman class were: Math-- 36% below

500, 54% between 500 and 599, 9% between 600 and 699, and 1% between 700 and 800. Evidence-Based Reading/Writing-- 31% below 500, 51% between 500 and 599, 16% between 600 and 699, and 2% between 700 and 800. The ACT scores were 29% between 12 and 17, 52% between 18 and 23, 17% between 24 and 29, and 2% above 30. 32% of the current freshmen were in the top fifth of their class; 70% were in the top two fifths. **Admissions Contact:** Christopher Crews, Director of Recruitment and Admission. Email: *admissions@ius.edu* Web: *www.ius.edu*

FINANCIAL AID: In 2017-2018, 84% of all full-time freshmen received some form of financial aid. 64% of all full-time freshmen received need-based aid. The average freshman award was $7,732. Need-based scholarships or need-based grants averaged $6,942 ($19,990 maximum); need-based self-help aid (loans and jobs) averaged $4,343 ($14,463 maximum); non-need-based athletic scholarships averaged $1,348 ($3,000 maximum); and other non-need-based awards and non-need-based scholarships averaged $3,942 ($20,840 maximum). 8% of undergraduate students work part-time. The average financial indebtedness of the 2017 graduate was $23,845. The FAFSA code is 001817. The priority date for freshman financial aid applications for fall entry is March 1.

INDIANA UNIVERSITY-PURDUE UNIVERSITY FORT WAYNE D-2

www.ipfw.edu

Fort Wayne, IN 46805	(260) 481-6812 (866) 597-0010
Fax: (260) 481-5450	Email: ASK@ipfw.edu
Full-time: 2636 men, 3277 women	Faculty: 372; IIA, -$
Part-time: 1770 men, 2274 women	Ph.D.s: 85%
Graduate: 210 men, 247 women	Student/Faculty: 16 to 1
Year: semesters, summer session	Tuition: $8330 ($20,005)
Room & Board: $9345	Freshman Class: 4754 applied, 4500 accepted, 1562 enrolled
SAT or ACT: required	CEEB CODE: 1336
Application Deadline: August 1	COMPETITIVE

Indiana University-Purdue University Fort Wayne, founded in 1917, joined Purdue University at Fort Wayne, founded in 1944. The combined school, a state-controlled institution, offers programs in liberal arts, science, business, education, health sciences, engineering, technology, public affairs, and visual and performing arts. There are 8 undergraduate schools and 5 graduate schools. In addition to regional accreditation, Fort Wayne has baccalaureate program accreditation with AACSB, ABET, ADA, NASAD, NASM, CAEP, NLN, ACS, AMTA, CAC, CODA, EAC, NASPAA, TAC, and NAST. The 688-acre campus is in a suburban area 113 miles north of Indianapolis. Including any residence halls, there are 51 buildings.

STUDENT LIFE: 93% of undergraduates are from Indiana. Others are from 39 states, 38 foreign countries, and Canada. 80% are White; 6% Hispanic; 5% African American; 3% Asian American; 3% two or more races; 2% Foreign; 1% race unknown. **Female To Male Ratio:** 1.3:1. The average age of freshmen is 20; all undergraduates, 22. 37% do not continue beyond their first year; 25% remain to graduate. **Housing:** 1204 students can be accommodated in college housing, which includes on-campus apartments. On-campus housing is available on a first-come and first-served basis. 93% of students commute. Alcohol is not permitted. All students may keep cars.

FACULTY/CLASSROOMS: 57% of faculty are male; 43% are female. All teach undergraduates, and 92% do research. Graduate students teach 3% of introductory courses. The average class size in an introductory lecture is 20; in a laboratory is 19; and in a regular course is 20.

PROGRAMS OF STUDY: IU-Purdue University Fort Wayne confers B.A., B.S., B.F.A., B.G.S, B.Mus., B.Mus.Ed., B.S.B., B.S.C., B.S.C.E., B.S.Cp.E., B.S.Ed., B.S.E.E., B.S.G., B.S.M.E., B.S.P.A., B.S.L.S., and B.S.M.T. degrees. Associate, master's, and doctoral degrees are also awarded. Bachelor's degrees are awarded in BIOLOGICAL SCIENCE (biochemistry and biology/biological science), BUSINESS (accounting, banking and finance, business administration and management, business economics, hospitality management services, labor studies, management science, marketing/retailing/merchandising, and organizational leadership and management), COMMUNICATIONS AND THE ARTS (communications, crafts, dramatic arts, drawing, English, English literature, fine arts, French, German, graphic design, music, music performance, painting, percussion, photography, piano/organ, printmaking, sculpture, Spanish, speech/debate/rhetoric, strings, technical and business writing, telecommunications, visual design, and voice), COMPUTER AND PHYSICAL SCIENCE (actuarial science, chemistry, computer programming, computer science, earth science, geology, information sciences and systems, mathematics, physical sciences, physics, and statistics), EDUCATION (art education, computer education, early childhood education, elementary education, English education, foreign languages education, mathematics education, middle school education, music education, science education, and secondary education), ENGINEERING AND ENVIRONMENTAL DESIGN (civil engineering, computer engineering, computer graphics, electrical/electronics engineering, electrical/electronics engineering technology, engineering, engineering technology, industrial engineering technology, interior design, mechanical engineering, and mechanical engineering technology), HEALTH PROFESSIONS (health care administration, medical technology, music therapy, nursing, predentistry, premedicine, preoptometry, prepharmacy, preveterinary science, and speech pathology/audiology), SOCIAL SCIENCE (anthropology, criminal justice, economics, history, human services, liberal arts/general studies, philosophy, political science/government, prelaw, psychology, public administration, public affairs, social science, sociology, and women's studies). Engineering, and biology are the strongest academically. Business, education, and engineering have the largest enrollments.

ACTIVITIES: There are 120 groups on campus, including art, band, cheerleading, chess, choir, chorus, dance, debate, drama, ethnic, film, forensics, honors, international, jazz band, LGBT, literary magazine, musical theater, newspaper, opera, orchestra, pep band, political, professional, radio and TV, religious, social, social service, student government, and symphony. Popular campus events include Mastodon Roast, and Freshmen Fest. **Sports:** There are 6 intercollegiate sports for men and 7 for women, and 18 intramural sports for men and 18 for women. Facilities include a physical fitness center with a gym, basketball courts, an indoor track, a weight room, racquetball courts, wallyball court, dance room, baseball and soccer fields, and an indoor soccer facility. **Graduates:** From July 1, 2016 to June 30, 2017, 1376 bachelor's degrees were awarded. The most popular majors were general studies (10%), nursing (7%), and psychology (6%). In an average class, 7% graduate in 4 years or less, 19% graduate in 5 years or less, and 25% graduate in 6 years or less.

SERVICES: Counseling and information services are available, as is tutoring in most subjects. There is a reader service for the blind, and remedial math, reading, and writing. **Library/Resources:** The library contains 224,862 volumes, 241,033 microform items, 7,849 audio/video tapes/CDs/DVDs, and subscribes to 90,000 periodicals including electronic. Computerized library services include interlibrary loans, database searching, Internet access, and Wi-Fi capability. Special learning facilities include an art gallery, radio station, and TV station. **Physically Challenged Students:** All of the campus is accessible. Facilities include wheelchair ramps, elevators, special parking, specially equipped restrooms, special class scheduling, lowered drinking fountains, lowered telephones, and special housing. **Special:** There are continuing education, co-op, and work-study programs, as well as study abroad in 5 countries. An accelerated general studies degree, cross-registration with other Fort Wayne colleges, B.A.-B.S. degrees, dual majors, a Washington semester for public affairs students, internships, and credit for military experience are available. Nondegree study and pass/fail options are possible. An accelerated MBA degree is also offered. There are 16 national honor societies and a freshman honors program. **Visiting:** There are regularly scheduled orientations for prospective students. There are guides for informal visits and visitors may sit in on classes. To schedule a visit, contact the Admissions Office. **Campus Safety and Security:** Measures include 24-hour foot and vehicle patrol, emergency notification system, self-defense education, and security escort services. There are shuttle buses, emergency telephones, lighted pathways/sidewalks, and controlled access to dorms/residences.

REQUIREMENTS: The SAT or ACT is required, with a minimum composite score of 1420 on the SAT or a minimum composite score of 20 on the ACT. Indiana Core 40, Academic Honors, or Technical Honors Diploma. Out-of-state students must complete a college prep curriculum A GPA of 2.8 is required. AP and CLEP credits are accepted. Important factors in the admissions decision are recommendations by school officials, evidence of special talent, and advanced placement or honors courses. All bachelor's degree students must complete 120 credits, including 33 general education hours, with a GPA of 2.0, and take English composition, speech communication, and math to graduate. Students must take 32 credit hours at the 200 level or above (including 15 credit hours at the 300 level or above) in their major. **Procedure:** Freshmen are admitted in the fall, spring, and summer. Entrance exams should be taken in the senior year of high school. There are deferred admissions and rolling admissions plans. Applications should be filed by August 1 for fall entry; December 15 for spring entry; and May 1 for summer entry. The fall 2017 application fee was $50. Notification is sent on a rolling basis. Applications are accepted on-line. **Transfer Students:** Transfer applicants must have a minimum GPA of 2.0. Grades of C or better transfer for credit. 32 of 120 credits required for the bachelor's degree must be completed at Fort Wayne. **International Students:** There are 181 international students enrolled. They must take the TOEFL with a minimum score of 550 on the paper-based TOEFL (PBT) or 77 on the Internet-based version (iBT), or pass level 112 of an ESL program. They may also take the ACT or SAT.

ADMISSIONS: 95% of the 2017-2018 applicants were accepted. The SAT scores for the 2017-2018 freshman class were: The ACT scores were 19% between 12 and 17, 50% between 18 and 23, 24% between 24 and 29, and 7% above 30. 20% of the current freshmen were in the top fifth of their class; 45% were in the top two fifths. 12 freshmen graduated first in their class. **Admissions Contact:** Kenneth Christmon, Director of Admissions. Email: *ASK@ipfw.edu* Web: *www.ipfw.edu*

FINANCIAL AID: In 2017-2018, 75% of all full-time freshmen received some form of financial aid. 47% of all full-time freshmen received need-based aid. The average freshman award was $8,500. Need-based scholarships or need-based grants averaged $5,600 ($13,000 maximum); need-based self-help aid (loans and jobs) averaged $3,170 ($26,400 maximum); non-need-based athletic scholarships averaged $12,770 ($39,800 maximum); and other non-need-based awards and non-need-based scholarships averaged $4,000 ($24,900 maximum). 1% of undergraduate students work part-time. The average financial indebtedness of the 2017 graduate was $25,000. IU-PU-Fort Wayne is a member of CSS. The FAFSA code is 001828. The priority date for freshman financial aid applications for fall entry is March 10.

INDIANA UNIVERSITY-PURDUE UNIVERSITY INDIANAPOLIS C-3

www.iupui.edu

Indianapolis, IN 46202 **(317) 274-4591**

Fax: (317) 278-1862
Email: apply@iupui.edu
Full-time: 7469 men, 10,052 women
Part-time: 1958 men, 2131 women
Graduate: 3637 men, 4544 women
Year: semesters, summer session
Room & Board: $9618
SAT EBR-W/M: 554/545 **ACT:** 23
Application Deadline: May 1
Faculty: 2414; I, --$
Ph.D.s: 85%
Student/Faculty: 17 to 1
Tuition: $9344 ($29,806)
Freshman Class: 11091 applied, 8834 accepted, 4093 enrolled
CEEB CODE: 1325
COMPETITIVE

Indiana University–Purdue University Indianapolis, a partnership between Indiana and Purdue Universities, is Indiana's urban research and academic health sciences campus. IUPUI's mission is to advance the State of Indiana and the intellectual growth of its citizens to the highest levels nationally and internationally through research and creative activity, teaching and learning, and civic engagement. By offering a distinctive range of bachelor's, master's, professional, and Ph.D. degrees, IUPUI promotes the educational, cultural, and economic development of central Indiana and beyond through innovative collaborations, external partnerships, and a strong commitment to diversity. There are 20 undergraduate schools and 18 graduate schools. In addition to regional accreditation, IUPUI has baccalaureate program accreditation with AACSB, ABET, CSWE, NASAD, NASM, CAEP, FEPAC, CAAHEP, and CODA. The 534-acre campus is in an urban area near downtown Indianapolis. Including any residence halls, there are 129 buildings.

STUDENT LIFE: 93% of undergraduates are from Indiana. Others are from 49 states, 145 foreign countries, and Canada. 9% are African American; 7% Hispanic; 7% Foreign; 68% White; 5% Asian American; 4% two or more races; 1% race unknown. **Female To Male Ratio:** 1.3:1. The average age of freshmen is 18; all undergraduates, 23. 25% do not continue beyond their first year. **Housing:** 2398 students can be accommodated in college housing, which includes married student dorms, on-campus apartments, and off-campus apartments. In addition, there are honors houses, special-interest houses, an international house, women in science house, and a sustainability house. On-campus housing is available on a first-come and first-served basis. 88% of students commute. Alcohol is not permitted. All students may keep cars.

FACULTY/CLASSROOMS: 53% of faculty are male; 47% are female. No introductory courses are taught by graduate students.

PROGRAMS OF STUDY: IUPUI confers B.A., B.S., B.S.B., B.A.E.D., B.F.A., B.G.S., B.S.CE., B.S. Ch., B.S.CJ., B.S.E., B.S.ED., B.S.EE., B.S.HSM., B.S.ME., B.S.MT., B.S.N., B.S.PA., B.S.PH. and B.S.W. degrees. Associate, master's, and doctoral degrees are also awarded. Bachelor's degrees are awarded in BIOLOGICAL SCIENCE (biotechnology, forensic science, and neurosciences), BUSINESS (business administration and management, labor studies, organizational leadership and management, and tourism), COMMUNICATIONS AND THE ARTS (Africana studies, American Sign Language, art history, communication studies, English, fine arts, French, German, journalism, media arts, music technology, Spanish, and technical communication), COMPUTER AND PHYSICAL SCIENCE (chemistry, clinical laboratory science, computer engineering technology, computer information technology, computer science, energy science, geology, informatics and computer science, mathematics, and physics), EDUCATION (art education, elementary education, English education, general studies, health information management, social studies education, and Spanish education K-12), ENGINEERING AND ENVIRONMENTAL DESIGN (biomedical engineering, computer engineering, computer graphics, electrical/electronics engineering, electrical/electronics engineering technology, engineering technology, environmental science, interior design, mechanical engineering, mechanical engineering technology, and nuclear medicine technology), HEALTH PROFESSIONS (biology, cytotechnology, dental hygiene, health care administration, health science, health services technology, medical imaging, kinesiology, nursing, premedicine, pre-occupational therapy, prepharmacy, pre-physician assistant, prephysical therapy, preveterinary science, public health, radiation therapy, and respiratory therapy), SOCIAL SCIENCE (anthropology, criminal justice, economics, geography, history, interdisciplinary studies, international studies, law, philosophy, political science/government, prelaw, psychology, public affairs, religious studies, social work, and sociology). Engineering and medicine are the strongest academically. Business, nursing, and general studies have the largest enrollment.

ACTIVITIES: There are 515 groups on campus, including art, band, cheerleading, chess, choir, communications, computers, dance, debate, drama, environmental, ethnic, film, forensics, honors, international, LGBT, literary magazine, newspaper, orchestra, pep band, photography, political, professional, religious, social, social service, and student government. Popular campus events include Weeks of Welcome, Spring Dance, InternationalFest, Jag-A-Palooza, Cultural Heritage Months, IUPUI Regatta, and FountainFest. **Sports:** There are 7 intercollegiate sports for men and 9 for women, and 11 intramural sports for men and 11 for women. Facilities include a gymnasium that features basketball and volleyball courts, a soccer stadium that has FIFA regulated game fields, a competition pool, instructional pool and diving well, softball complex, and track and field. The fitness and sport facility provides an indoor track, free weights, Cybex and cardio equipment, pilates studio, indoor batting nets, and half size basketball courts.**Graduates:** From July 1, 2016 to June 30, 2017, 4185 bachelor's degrees were awarded. The most popular majors were health professions (19%), business, management and marketing (16%), and engineering (7%). In an average class, 21% graduate in 4 years or less, 39% graduate in 5 years or less, and 45% graduate in 6 years or less.

SERVICES: Counseling and information services are available, as is tutoring in most subjects. There is a reader service for the blind, and remedial math, reading, and writing. **Library/Resources:** The library contains 2.3 million volumes. Computerized library services include interlibrary loans, database searching, Internet access, and Wi-Fi capability. Special learning facilities include an art gallery, an 85-acre medical center, 100 research centers, 27 signature centers, the IU Research and Technology Corporation. **Physically Challenged Students:** All of the campus is accessible. Facilities include wheelchair ramps, elevators, special parking, specially equipped restrooms, special class scheduling, lowered drinking fountains, lowered telephones, classroom aids, and sign language interpreters. **Special:** There is a metropolitan studies program for career work in the city and cross-registration with the Consortium for Urban Education. IUPUI also offers study abroad, combined B.A.-B.S. degree programs, internships, work-study programs, dual and student-designed majors, online degrees, nondegree study, nontraditional programs for adult learners, and interdisciplinary majors such as business economics and public policy, health occupations education, and interdisciplinary engineering. There are 21 national honor societies and a freshman honors program. **Visiting:** There are regularly scheduled orientations for prospective students, consisting of a campus tour and talks with students. There are guides for informal visits; visitors may sit in on classes. To schedule a visit, contact the Office of Admissions. **Campus Safety and Security:** Measures include 24-hour foot and vehicle patrol, emergency notification system, self-defense education, and security escort services. There are shuttle buses, emergency telephones, and lighted pathways/sidewalks.

REQUIREMENTS: The SAT or ACT is required. Indiana high school graduates are expected to complete the Core 40 curriculum, and are strongly encouraged to earn the Academic Honors Diploma. Out-of-state students are expected to complete the required core of classes listed above to be considered for admission. The units of academic electives can be a combination of additional mathematics, laboratory science, social science, computer science, foreign language, or other courses of college preparatory nature. Some IUPUI schools require additional courses. Rank in upper half of high school class or show above average on the GED. SAT or ACT scores for Indiana residents should be at or above the Indiana median. Student who have been out of high school for more than 1 year are nor required to submit. AP and CLEP credits are accepted. All students must complete 120 to 126 credits required for the bachelor's degree. Most schools also require grades of C or higher in major courses. All beginning first-year students at Indiana University–Purdue University Indianapolis will complete 30 hours of general education course work (the IUPUI General Education Core) prior to graduation with either an associate degree a baccalaureate degree. Course work is divided into the broad domains of Foundational Intellectual Skills (core communication, analytical reasoning, and cultural understanding) and course work that promotes Intellectual Breadth and Adaptiveness (life and physical sciences, and arts, humanities, and social sciences). **Procedure:** Freshmen are admitted to all sessions. Entrance exams should be taken by the end of junior year or fall of senior year. There are deferred admissions and rolling admissions plans. Application deadlines are open. The fall 2017 application fee was $65. Notification is sent on a rolling basis. Applications are accepted on-line. **Transfer Students:** 1421 transfer students enrolled in 2016-2017. Transfers who are Indiana residents must present a minimum GPA of 2.0 in all previous college work; out-of-state residents need a minimum 2.5. All applicants must be in good standing at their former schools. 30 of 120 credits required for the bachelor's degree must be completed at IU-PUI. **International Students:** There are 756 international students enrolled. They must take the TOEFL with a minimum score of 550 on the paper-based TOEFL (PBT) or 60 on the Internet-based version (iBT).

ADMISSIONS: 80% of the 2017-2018 applicants were accepted. The SAT scores for the 2017-2018 freshman class were: Math-- 25% below 500, 51% between 500 and 599, 20% between 600 and 699, and 4% between 700 and 800. Evidence-Based Reading/Writing-- 22% below 500, 50% between 500 and 599, 25% between 600 and 699, and 3% between 700 and 800. The ACT scores were 13% between 12 and 17, 43% between 18 and 23, 37% between 24 and 29, and 7% above 30. 43% of the current freshmen were in the top fifth of their class; 84% were in the top two fifths. **Admissions Contact:** Yohlunda Mosley, Director of Undergraduate Admissions. Email: *apply@iupui.edu* Web: *www.iupui.edu*

FINANCIAL AID: In 2017-2018, 90% of all full-time freshmen received some form of financial aid. 69% of all full-time freshmen received need-based aid. The average freshman award was $12,489. Need-based scholarships or need-based grants averaged $10,412 ($42,842 maximum); need-based self-help aid (loans and jobs) averaged $4,958 ($23,172 maximum); non-need-based athletic scholarships averaged $10,704 ($50,468 maximum); and other non-need-based awards and non-need-based scholarships averaged $7,262 ($45,847 maximum). 10% of undergraduate students work part-time. The average financial indebtedness of the 2017 graduate was $29,065. The FAFSA code is 001813. The priority date for freshman financial aid applications for fall entry is March 1.

INDIANA WESLEYAN UNIVERSITY C-2

www.indwes.edu

Marion, IN 46953 **(765) 677-1677**

Email: admissions@indwes.edu

Full-time: 887 men, 1731 women
Part-time: 69 men, 95 women
Graduate: 73 men, 185 women
Year: semesters, summer session
Room & Board: $8148
SAT CR/M/W: 525/535/515 **ACT:** 24
Application Deadline: n/av

Faculty: IIA, --$
Ph.D.s: 67%
Student/Faculty: 14 to 1
Tuition: $25,526
Freshman Class: 3323 applied, 2455 accepted, 683 enrolled
CEEB CODE: 1446
COMPETITIVE

Indiana Wesleyan University, founded in 1920, is a private, evangelical Christian, liberal arts university. IWU is a Christ-centered academic community committed to changing the world by developing students in character, scholarship, and leadership. There are 6 undergraduate schools and 3 graduate schools. In addition to regional accreditation, IWU has baccalaureate program accreditation with CSWE, NASM, CAEP, CCNE, CACREP, and CAATE. The 320-acre campus is in a small town in north-central Indiana, 70 miles north of Indianapolis, 50 miles south of Fort Wayne. Including any residence halls, there are 64 buildings.

STUDENT LIFE: 53% of undergraduates are from Indiana. Others are from 46 states, 7 foreign countries, and Canada. 91% are White; 3% Hispanic; 2% African American; 1% Asian American; 1% American Indian/Alaska Native; 1% Foreign; 1% two or more races. 92% are Protestant. **Female To Male Ratio:** 2.0:1. The average age of freshmen is 18; all undergraduates, 20. 26% do not continue beyond their first year; 70% remain to graduate. **Housing:** 2801 students can be accommodated in college housing, which includes married student dorms, on-campus apartments, and special-interest houses. On-campus housing is guaranteed for all 4 years, is available on a first-come, and first-served basis. 82% of students live on campus. Alcohol is not permitted. All students may keep cars.

FACULTY/CLASSROOMS: 60% of faculty are male; 40% are female. 98% teach undergraduates, 20% do research, and 20% do both. No introductory courses are taught by graduate students. The average class size in an introductory lecture is 50; in a laboratory is 15; and in a regular course is 18.

PROGRAMS OF STUDY: IWU confers A.B., B.A., B.S.N., B.S.M., and M.A. degrees. Associate, master's, and doctoral degrees are also awarded. Bachelor's degrees are awarded in BIOLOGICAL SCIENCE (biology/biological science), BUSINESS (accounting, banking and finance, business administration and management, management science, marketing/retailing/merchandising, and recreational facilities management), COMMUNICATIONS AND THE ARTS (applied music, art, ceramic art and design, communications, creative writing, English, illustration, music, music theory and composition, painting, photography, printmaking, Spanish, and studio art), COMPUTER AND PHYSICAL SCIENCE (chemistry, computer science, information sciences and systems, mathematics, and science), EDUCATION (art education, athletic training, elementary education, English education, mathematics education, music education, nursing education, physical education, science education, secondary education, social studies education, and special education), ENGINEERING AND ENVIRONMENTAL DESIGN (computer graphics and interior design), HEALTH PROFESSIONS (health, medical laboratory technology, nursing, and premedicine), SOCIAL SCIENCE (addiction studies, biblical studies, criminal justice, economics, history, law enforcement and corrections, liberal arts/general studies, ministries, political science/government, prelaw, psychology, religion, religious education, religious music, social studies, social work, and sociology). Nursing, education, and premedicine are the strongest academically. Nursing, education, and business have the largest enrollments.

ACTIVITIES: There are no fraternities or sororities. There are 35 groups on campus, including art, band, cheerleading, choir, chorale, chorus, computers, drama, environmental, ethnic, film, honors, international, jazz band, literary magazine, musical theater, newspaper, opera, orchestra, pep band, photography, political, professional, radio and TV, religious, social, social service, student government, symphony, and yearbook. Popular campus events include Spotted Cow Music Festival,

Friday Night Live, and Taste of Marion. **Sports:** There are 9 intercollegiate sports for men and 9 for women, and 21 intramural sports for men and women. The Recreation and Wellness Center has fitness rooms, weight rooms, a swimming pool, athletic training center, indoor track, practice/intramural gym, and a basketball gymnasium. Outdoor fields: include soccer, baseball, softball, track and field, tennis courts. The Indoor Sports Complex: has long/triple jump pits, pole vault area, indoor weight throw, 8 lane 200 meter track, and a competition area. **Graduates:** From July 1, 2016 to June 30, 2017, 635 bachelor's degrees were awarded. The most popular majors were nursing (18%), elementary education (8%), and psychology (6%). In an average class, 56% graduate in 4 years or less, 68% graduate in 5 years or less, and 70% graduate in 6 years or less.

SERVICES: Counseling and information services are available, as is tutoring in most subjects. There is a reader service for the blind, and remedial math, reading, and writing. External testing, a note-taker service, and advocacy are also available. **Library/Resources:** The library contains 276,070 volumes, 315,162 microform items, and 11,479 audio/video tapes/CDs/DVDs, and subscribes to 106,118 periodicals including electronic. Computerized library services include interlibrary loans, database searching, Internet access, and Wi-Fi capability. Special learning facilities include an art gallery, radio station, TV station, a globe theatre, and the daily planet. **Physically Challenged Students:** 95% of the campus is accessible. Facilities include wheelchair ramps, elevators, special parking, specially equipped restrooms, special class scheduling, lowered drinking fountains, lowered telephones, and special housing. **Special:** Students may study abroad in 20 countries. IWU also offers business, pastoral, nursing, and social work internships, cross-registration with CCCU, a Washington semester, work-study programs with the Economic Growth Council, pass/fail options, and nondegree study. Accelerated degree programs are available in accounting, business administration, business information, management, and nursing. Students may earn a B.A.-B.S. degree in management, business, and education. Dual majors and student-designed majors are available. Adult learners may earn credit for life experience toward bachelor's degrees in business. There are 6 national honor societies, a freshman honors program, and 12 departmental honors programs. **Visiting:** There are regularly scheduled orientations for prospective students, who may visit with the admissions counselors and professors, and take a campus tour. There are guides for informal visits; visitors may sit in on classes and stay overnight. To schedule a visit, contact the Admissions Office **Campus Safety and Security:** Measures include 24-hour foot and vehicle patrol, emergency notification system, self-defense education, and security escort services. There are emergency telephones, lighted pathways/sidewalks, and controlled access to dorms/residences.

REQUIREMENTS: Student are required to have completed an application, high school transcript, an essay, score form either the SAT or ACT, a recommendation, and a community values contract that are necessary for an admission decision. A tuition deposit is required before registration and is fully refundable until May 1. The admission decision may be made with a high school transcript at the end of the junior year. It is to be followed later by the full four-year record and certification of graduation. A student should have a minimum of the following academic courses: 8 credits in language arts; 6-8 credits in mathematics; 6 credits each in science and social studies; 4 credits in foreign language; 2 credits in health, physical education, and safety; and 4-6 credits from other academic courses offered. Regular admission requires that applicants have at least a 2.6 cumulative high school GPA on a 4.0 scale and a 880 SAT (math and critical reading) or 18 ACT score. Applicants who do not meet the requirements for regular admission may request special consideration. AP and CLEP credits are accepted. Important factors in the admissions decision are advanced placement or honors courses, parents or siblings attended your school, evidence of special talent, personality/intangible qualities, extracurricular activities record, recommendations by alumni, recommendations by school officials, leadership record, and geographical diversity. A 52-credit general education core includes 12 credit hours of humanities, 10 of math and science, 9 each of English and history or social studies, 6 of biblical literature, and 3 each of intercultural experience and phys ed. foreign language courses are required for the B.A., computer literacy courses for the B.S. To graduate, students must complete at least 124 semester hours, including 40 to 60 in a major field of study, with a minimum GPA of 2.0 overall and 2.25 in the major. A thesis is required for the honors college. **Procedure:** Freshmen are admitted to all sessions. Entrance exams should be taken during their junior year, or early in their senior year. There are early decision, deferred admissions, and rolling admissions plans. Application deadlines are open. Applications are accepted on-line. **Transfer Students:** 106 transfer students enrolled in 2016-2017. Addition to standard admissions requirements, transfers must submit transcripts of all previous college work and be in good standing at their former school. 30 credits required for the bachelor's degree must be completed at IWU. **International Students:** There are 111 international students enrolled. They must take the TOEFL with a minimum score of 550 on the paper-based TOEFL (PBT) or 79 on the Internet-based version (iBT). They must also take the SAT or ACT.

ADMISSIONS: 74% of the 2017-2018 applicants were accepted. The SAT scores for the 2017-2018 freshman class were: Critical Reading-- 36% below 500, 40% between 500 and 599, 20% between 600 and 699, and 4% between 700 and 800. Math-- 36% below 500, 424% between 500 and 599, 19% between 600 and 699, and 3% between 700 and 800. Writing-- 44% below 500, 37% between 500 and 599, 17% between 600 and 699, and 2% between 700 and 800. The ACT scores were 7% between 12 and 17, 37% between 18 and 23, 45% between 24 and 29, and 11% above 30. 57% of the current freshmen were in the top fifth of their class; 85% were in the top two fifths. **Admissions Contact:** Tracy Curfman, Admissions Administrative Assistant. Email: *admissions@indwes.edu* Web: *www.indwes.edu*

FINANCIAL AID: In 2017-2018, 99% of all full-time freshmen received some form of financial aid. 73% of all full-time freshmen received need-based aid. The average freshman award was $21,377. Need-based scholarships or need-based grants averaged $13,847; need-based self-help aid (loans and jobs) averaged $7,446; non-need-based athletic scholarships averaged $6,994; and other non-need-based awards and non-need-based scholarships averaged $5,185. 51% of undergraduate students work part-time. The average financial indebtedness of the 2017 graduate was $31,482. The college's own financial statement is required. The FAFSA code is 001822. The deadline for filing freshman financial aid applications for fall entry is March 1.

MANCHESTER UNIVERSITY C-2

www.manchester.edu

North Manchester, IN 46962	(260) 982-5055 (800) 852-3648
Fax: (260) 982-5239	**Email:** admitinfo@manchester.edu
Full-time: 600 men, 600 women	**Faculty:** IIB, -$
Part-time: 5 men, 10 women	**Ph.D.s:** n/av
Graduate: n/av	**Student/Faculty:** n/av
Year: 4-1-4, summer session	**Tuition:** $31,660
Room & Board: $9880	**Freshman Class:** n/av
SAT or ACT: required	**CEEB CODE:** 1440
Application Deadline: open	**COMPETITIVE**

Manchester University, established in 1889, is a private liberal arts college affiliated with the Church of the Brethren offering undergraduate programs in accounting, business and economics, premedicine, education, psychology, the social sciences, and the humanities. The figures given in the above capsule and in this profile are approximate. There are 3 undergraduate schools and 1 graduate school. In addition to regional accreditation, MU has baccalaureate program accreditation with CSWE and CAEP. The 124-acre campus is in a small town 35 miles west of Fort Wayne, Indiana. Including any residence halls, there are 44 buildings.

STUDENT LIFE: 90% of undergraduates are from Indiana. Others are from 21 states, 20 foreign countries, and Canada. 99% are from public schools. 89% are White; 4% Foreign; 3% African American; 3% Hispanic; 1% Asian American. 36% are Protestant; 15% Catholic. **Female To Male Ratio:** 1.0:1. The average age of freshmen is 18; all undergraduates, 20. 30% do not continue beyond their first year; 55% remain to graduate. **Housing:** 995 students can be accommodated in college housing, which includes married student dorms, on-campus apartments, and off-campus apartments. In addition, there are special-interest houses, and theme housing. On-campus housing is guaranteed for all 4 years. 79% of students live on campus. Alcohol is not permitted. All students may keep cars.

FACULTY/CLASSROOMS: 53% of faculty are male; 47% are female. All teach undergraduates, 20% do research, and 20% do both. No introductory courses are taught by graduate students. The average class size in an introductory lecture is 30; in a laboratory is 15; and in a regular course is 20.

PROGRAMS OF STUDY: MU confers B.A. and B.S. degrees. Associate degrees are also awarded. Bachelor's degrees are awarded in AGRICULTURE (environmental studies), BIOLOGICAL SCIENCE (biochemistry and biology/biological science), BUSINESS (accounting, banking and finance, and business administration and management), COMMUNICATIONS AND THE ARTS (art, communications, English, French, German, music, and Spanish), COMPUTER AND PHYSICAL SCIENCE (chemistry, computer science, mathematics, and physics), EDUCATION (art education, elementary education, health education, middle school education, and secondary education), ENGINEERING AND ENVIRONMENTAL DESIGN (engineering), HEALTH PROFESSIONS (medical laboratory technology), SOCIAL SCIENCE (economics, history, interdisciplinary studies, peace studies, philosophy, political science/government, prelaw, psychology, religion, social work, and sociology). Education, accounting, and biology-chemistry are the strongest academically. Education, accounting, and communication studies have the largest enrollments.

ACTIVITIES: There are no fraternities or sororities. There are 53 groups on campus, including band, cheerleading, choir, chorale, chorus, computers, dance, drama, environmental, ethnic, honors, international, jazz band, LGBT, literary magazine, musical theater, newspaper, opera, orchestra, pep band, photography, political, professional, radio and TV, religious, social, social service, student government, symphony, and yearbook. Popular campus events include Parents Weekend, Sibling Weekend, International Fair, and May Day Weekend. **Sports:** There are 9 intercollegiate sports for men and 8 for women, and 13 intramural sports for men and 12 for women. Facilities include a gym, racquetball courts, a fitness center, tennis courts, cross-country and an all-weather track, athletic fields for baseball, softball, soccer, and football. **Graduates:** From July 1, 2016 to June 30, 2017, 198 bachelor's degrees were awarded. The most popular majors were business (27%), education (17%), and health sciences (12%). In an average class, 42% graduate in 4 years or less, 52% graduate in 5 years or less, and 52% graduate in 6 years or less. Of the 2016 graduating class, 18% were enrolled in graduate school within 6 months of graduation, and 75% were employed.

SERVICES: Counseling and information services are available, as is tutoring in every subject. There is a reader service for the blind. There is also a learning center with an academic assistance program, a seminar to enhance study and learning skills, and time and project management. **Library/Resources:** The library contains 174,078 volumes, 23,014 microform items, and 5,258 audio/video tapes/CDs/DVDs, and subscribes to 973 periodicals including electronic. Computerized library services include interlibrary loans, database searching, and Internet access. Special learning facilities include an art gallery, planetarium, radio station, a 100-acre nature preserve. **Physically Challenged Students:** 50% of the campus is accessible. Facilities include wheelchair ramps, elevators, special parking, specially equipped restrooms, special class scheduling, lowered drinking fountains, lowered telephones, and special housing. **Special:** The college offers cooperative programs in nursing and engineering science. The Brethren Colleges Abroad program allows study abroad in 13 countries, including Ecuador, China, England, France, Germany, Ireland, Japan, Mexico, and Spain. Manchester also offers B.A.-B.S. degrees, internships, work-study programs, dual majors, student-designed majors, a 3-2 engineering program, pass/fail options, and non-degree study. Other special academic features include independent study, required study in non-Western culture, and interdisciplinary programs in both peace studies and environmental studies. A January interterm permits internships, travel abroad, and concentrated classes on campus. There are 6 national honor societies, a freshman honors program, and 5 departmental honors programs. **Visiting:** There are regularly scheduled orientations for prospective students, visits include advice on financial aid, meetings with faculty and admissions, and campus tours. Visitors may also eat meals on campus, sit in on classes, and meet with current students. To schedule a visit, contact the Campus Visit Coordinator. **Campus Safety and Security:** Measures include 24-hour foot and vehicle patrol, emergency notification system, and security escort services. There are emergency telephones and lighted pathways/sidewalks.

REQUIREMENTS: The SAT or ACT is required. Applicants must have a minimum SAT I composite of 900, with 450 on each part, or an ACT composite of 18. The GED is accepted. For high school students, the college recommends completion of 28 academic credits, based on 4 years each of English, math, and science, and 2 years each of foreign language, history, and social studies. A GPA of 2.3 is required. AP and CLEP credits are accepted. Important factors in the admissions decision are advanced placement or honors courses, leadership record, and recommendations by school officials. Students must complete a core curriculum, including requirements in humanities, social sciences, and natural sciences, as well as specific courses in English composition, public communication, Western civilization, and physical fitness. In order to graduate, students must complete a minimum of 128 semester hours, including 26 to 52 hours in a major field, with a GPA of at least 2.0 (2.5 for the education and athletic training majors). A comprehensive exam in the major is also required. A thesis for honors students is optional. **Procedure:** Freshmen are admitted to all sessions. Entrance exams should be taken by November of the senior year. There are deferred admissions and rolling admissions plans. Application deadlines are open. The fall 2017 application fee was $20. Notification is sent on a rolling basis. Applications are accepted online. **Transfer Students:** 29 transfer students enrolled in 2016-2017. Transfer students must present a minimum GPA of 2.0 in all previous college work. 96 of 128 credits required for the bachelor's degree must be completed at Manchester. **International Students:** There are 41 international students enrolled. They must take the TOEFL with a minimum score of 550 on the paper-based TOEFL (PBT).

Admissions Contact: Adam Hohman, Associate Director of Admissions. Email: *admitinfo@manchester.edu* Web: *www.manchester.edu*

FINANCIAL AID: In 2017-2018, 100% of all full-time freshmen received some form of financial aid. The average freshman award was $18,110. 40% of undergraduate students work part-time. The average financial indebtedness of the 2017 graduate was $16,333. The FAFSA code is 001820. The deadline for filing freshman financial aid applications for fall entry is rolling.

MARIAN UNIVERSITY — C-3

www.marian.edu

Indianapolis, IN 46222	**(317) 955-6306** **(800) 772-7264**
Fax: (317) 955-6401	**Email: lbrames@marian.edu**
Full-time: 784 men, 1177 women	**Faculty:** 149
Part-time: 97 men, 253 women	**Ph.D.s:** 63%
Graduate: 505 men, 621 women	**Student/Faculty:** 17 to 1
Year: semesters, summer session	**Tuition:** $33,000
Room & Board: $10,206	**Freshman Class:** 2247 applied, 1320 accepted, 336 enrolled
SAT CR/M: 518/516 **ACT:** 22	**CEEB CODE:** 1442
Application Deadline: August 1	**COMPETITIVE**

Marian University is a private institution founded in 1851 by the Sisters of St. Francis, and affiliated with the Roman Catholic Church. The college offers undergraduate programs and graduate programs, as well as a doctorate in osteopathic medicine and one in nursing practice with two tracks--that of a nurse anesthetist and that of a family nurse practitioner. There are 4 undergraduate schools and 8 graduate schools. In addition to regional accreditation, MU has baccalaureate program accreditation with AHEA, CAEP, NLN, CCNE, IACBE, and COCA. The 114-acre campus is in a suburban area 6 miles from downtown Indianapolis. Including any residence halls, there are 21 buildings.

STUDENT LIFE: 77% of undergraduates are from Indiana. Others are from 36 states, 18 foreign countries, and Canada. 78% are from public schools. 70% are White; 10% African American; 5% Asian American; 5% Hispanic; 5% race unknown; 4% two or more races; 1% Foreign. 38% are Catholic; 37% Buddhism, Islam, Hinduism, Eastern Orthodox, and Unknown ; 23% Protestant. **Female To Male Ratio:** 1.5:1. The average age of freshmen is 18.2; all undergraduates, 20.1. 22% do not continue beyond their first year; 56% remain to graduate. **Housing:** 894 students can be accommodated in college housing, which includes dorms, on-campus apartments, and special-interest houses. On-campus housing is guaranteed for all 4 years. 61% of students live on campus. Alcohol is not permitted. All students may keep cars.

FACULTY/CLASSROOMS: 45% of faculty are male; 55% are female. 74% teach undergraduates. No introductory courses are taught by graduate students. The average class size in an introductory lecture is 19; in a laboratory is 15; and in a regular course is 18.

PROGRAMS OF STUDY: MU confers B.A., B.S., and B.S.N. degrees. Associate, master's, and doctoral degrees are also awarded. Bachelor's degrees are awarded in BIOLOGICAL SCIENCE (biology/biological science), BUSINESS (accounting, business administration and management, business intelligence and analytics, finance, management science, marketing, and sports management), COMMUNICATIONS AND THE ARTS (communications, English, instrumental performance, instrumental music education, music, music ministry, Spanish, studio art, vocal performance, and vocal music education), COMPUTER AND PHYSICAL SCIENCE (chemistry, clinical laboratory science, and mathematics), EDUCATION (education, education of the exceptional child, educational studies, elementary education, health and physical education, secondary education, and special education), ENGINEERING AND ENVIRONMENTAL DESIGN (engineering), HEALTH PROFESSIONS (exercise science, health services administration, nursing, and public health), SOCIAL SCIENCE (history, pastoral studies, philosophy, political science/government, psychology, religious education, religious studies, sociology, and theology). Nursing, business management, biology are the strongest academically and the largest enrollments.

ACTIVITIES: There are no fraternities or sororities. There are 42 groups on campus, including art, band, cheerleading, choir, chorale, chorus, computers, dance, debate, departmental clubs, drama, drill team, ethnic, forensics, honors, international, jazz band, literary magazine, marching band, musical theater, newspaper, pep band, photography, political, professional, religious, social, social service, student government, and yearbook. Popular campus events include Homecoming, Fall and Spring Formals, and Coffeehouse and Open Mic Series. **Sports:** There are 11 intercollegiate sports for men and 11 for women, and 6 intramural sports for men and 6 for women. Facilities include varsity and intramural gyms, a stadium, a cycling center, racquetball courts, a fitness center, a weight-training room, and a phys ed assessment lab. **Graduates:** From July 1, 2016 to June 30, 2017, 511 bachelor's degrees were awarded. The most popular majors were nursing (46%), business and related fields (24%), and exercise and sport science (5%). In an average class, 1% graduate in 3 years or less, 34% graduate in 4 years or less, 53% graduate in 5 years or less, and 56% graduate in 6 years or less. Of the 2016 graduating class, 22% were enrolled in graduate school within 6 months of graduation, and 71% were employed.

SERVICES: Counseling and information services are available, as is tutoring in most subjects. There is a reader service for the blind, and remedial math, reading, and writing. Study skills training and peer tutoring are also available. **Library/Resources:** The library contains 80,118 volumes, 150 microform items, 3,828 audio/video tapes/CDs/DVDs, and subscribes to 108,559 periodicals including electronic. Computerized library services include interlibrary loans, database searching, Internet access, and Wi-Fi capability. Special learning facilities include an art gallery, and a 55-acre Wetlands Ecology Laboratory. **Physically Challenged Students:** 95% of the campus is accessible. Facilities include wheelchair ramps, elevators, special parking, specially equipped restrooms, special class scheduling, and lowered drinking fountains. **Special:** Co-op programs in accounting, finance, business administration, chemistry, management information systems, and sociology and cross-registration through the Consortium for Urban Education are offered. A dual degree program in math and engineering, and accelerated degrees in nursing and business administration are also offered. Internships, study abroad, work-study, and independent study options are available. There are 11 national honor societies, a freshman honors program, and 6 departmental honors programs. **Visiting:** There are regularly scheduled orientations for prospective students, including a campus tour, visits with faculty and coaches, and financial aid information. There are guides for informal visits, visitors may sit in on classes, and stay overnight. To schedule a visit, contact Matt Cramer at (317 955-6300. **Campus Safety and Security:** Measures include 24-hour foot and vehicle patrol, emergency notification system, self-defense education, and security escort services. There are shuttle buses, emergency telephones, lighted pathways/sidewalks, and controlled access to dorms/residences.

REQUIREMENTS: The SAT or ACT is required. Applicants must be graduates of an accredited secondary school or have a GED. Marian requires 20 academic units, including 8 credits in English, 4 credits in math, of which algebra and geometry are recommended, and 4 credits each in a lab science and social studies. A GPA of 2.3 is required. AP and CLEP credits are accepted. Important factors in the admissions decision are recommendations by school officials, recommendations by alumni, and leadership record. To graduate, students must complete 128 semester hours, including 30 to 40 in the major, with a minimum GPA of 2.0 overall and in the major. General education requirements include 9 to 10 semester hours in cultural awareness and language, 7 to 13 in scientific and quantitative reasoning, 9 in written and oral communication, 6 in faith and ethics, 6 to 12 in individual and social understanding, and 12-26 in broad integrative knowledge. **Procedure:** Freshmen are admitted to all sessions. Entrance exams should be taken at the end of the junior year or the beginning of the senior year. There are deferred admissions and rolling admissions plans. Applications should be filed by August 1 for fall entry; December 10 for spring entry; and April 15 for summer entry. The fall 2017 application fee was $35. Notification is sent on a rolling basis. Applications are accepted on-line. **Transfer Students:** 116 transfer students enrolled in 2016-2017. In addition to meeting standard admissions requirements, applicants must submit transcripts of all college work and be in good standing at their former school. Students transferring must have a 2.0 GPA. 30 of 128 credits required for the bachelor's degree must be completed at Marian. **International Students:** There are 27 international students enrolled. They must take the TOEFL with a minimum score of 550 on the paper-based TOEFL (PBT) or 80 on the Internet-based version (iBT). They must also take the SAT or ACT.

ADMISSIONS: 59% of the 2017-2018 applicants were accepted. The SAT scores for the 2017-2018 freshman class were: Critical Reading-- 23% below 500, 50% between 500 and 599, 25% between 600 and 699, and 2% between 700 and 800. Math-- 20% below 500, 49% between 500 and 599, 24% between 600 and 699, and 3% between 700 and 800. The ACT scores were 9% between 12 and 17, 52% between 18 and 23, 34% between 24 and 29, and 5% above 30. 35% of the current freshmen were in the top fifth of their class; 65% were in the top two fifths. 2 freshmen graduated first in their class. **Admissions Contact:** Luann Brames, Director of Freshman Admissions. Email: *lbrames@marian.edu* Web: *www.marian.edu*

FINANCIAL AID: 11% of undergraduate students work part-time. The average financial indebtedness of the 2017 graduate was $27,022. The college's own financial statement is required. The FAFSA code is 001821. The priority date for freshman financial aid applications for fall entry is April 15.

MARTIN UNIVERSITY *(The complete profile is made available exclusively on our website, www.barronspac.com)*

OAKLAND CITY UNIVERSITY *(The complete profile is made available exclusively on our website, www.barronspac.com)*

PURDUE UNIVERSITY NORTHWEST B-1

www.pnw.edu

Hammond, IN 46323	**(219) 989-2213** **(800) HI PURDUE**
Fax: (219) 989-2775	**Email: admissions@pnw.edu**
Full-time: 3072 men, 3100 women	**Faculty:** n/av
Part-time: 1714 men, 3248 women	**Ph.D.s:** n/av
Graduate: 362 men, 575 women	**Student/Faculty:** n/av
Year: semesters, summer session	**Tuition:** $7581 ($17,129)
Room & Board: $7597	**Freshman Class:** n/av
SAT EBR-W/M: 540/479 **ACT:** 22	**CEEB CODE:** 1638
Application Deadline: August 1	**COMPETITIVE**

Purdue University Northwest, part of the Purdue University system, offers 70 programs at the undergraduate, master's, and doctoral levels, and is distinguished by its commitment to hands-on, experiential learning, including undergraduate research. PNW students also enjoy numerous opportunities to interact one-on-one with faculty members in learning activities. In addition to helping qualified, ambitious students persist successfully to graduation, PNW strategically advances positive change and economic growth within northwest Indiana through outreach institutes and centers. There are 6 undergraduate schools and 2 graduate schools. In addition to regional accreditation, PNW has baccalaureate program accreditation with AACSB, ABET, ACEN, ATMAE, and COAMFTE. The 441-acre campus is in an urban area 29 miles southeast of Chicago. Including any residence halls, there are 34 buildings.

STUDENT LIFE: 81% of undergraduates are from Indiana. Others are from 32 states, 44 foreign countries, and Canada. 9% are African American; 62% White; 6% Foreign; 2% Asian American; 2% two or more races; 17% Hispanic; 1% race unknown. **Female To Male Ratio:** 1.3:1. The average age of freshmen is 20; all undergraduates, 25. **Housing:** 749 students can be accommodated in college housing, which includes on-campus apartments. On-campus housing is guaranteed for all 4 years, and is available on a first-come, first-served basis. Alcohol is not permitted. All students may keep cars.

FACULTY/CLASSROOMS: No introductory courses are taught by graduate students.

PROGRAMS OF STUDY: PNW confers B.A., B.A.B., B.L.S., B.S., B.S.A., B.S.B., B.S.C.E., B.S.CH., B.S.CMP.E., B.S.E., B.S.E.E., B.S.M.E., and B.S.N. degrees. Associate, master's, and doctoral degrees are also awarded. Bachelor's degrees are awarded in BIOLOGICAL SCIENCE (biology/biological science, biotechnology, ecology, forensic science, and microbiology), BUSINESS (accounting, business economics, business intelligence and analytics, finance, hotel/motel and restaurant management, human resources, human resources/organizational management, leadership, management, marketing/retailing/merchandising, and organizational leadership and management), COMMUNICATIONS AND THE ARTS (advertising, broadcasting, communication design , communications, English, English literature, English Writing, French, journalism, public relations, Spanish, and visual communication), COMPUTER AND PHYSICAL SCIENCE (chemistry, computer programming, computer science, information sciences and systems, mathematics, physical sciences, and physics), EDUCATION (early childhood education, elementary education, English education, foreign languages education, mathematics education, science education, secondary education, and social studies education), ENGINEERING AND ENVIRONMENTAL DESIGN (civil engineering, computer engineering, computer graphics, computer technology, construction technology, electrical/electronics engineering technology, engineering, engineering mechanics, engineering physics, engineering technology, industrial engineering technology, materials science, mechanical engineering, mechanical engineering technology, mechatronics engineering, and survey and mapping technology), HEALTH PROFESSIONS (electrical engineering, environmental health science, health science, medical laboratory technology, nursing, and physical therapy), SOCIAL SCIENCE (behavioral science, criminal justice, food production/management/services, history, human development & family studies, liberal arts/general studies, philosophy, political science/government, psychology, social work, and sociology). Nursing, and engineering are the strongest academically. Nursing, business, and psychology have the largest enrollments.

ACTIVITIES: 1% of men belong to 1 local and 2 national fraternities; 1% of women belong to 1 local and 1 national sorority. There are 86 groups on campus, including art, cheerleading, chorus, dance, drama, environmental, ethnic, honors, international, LGBT, newspaper, orchestra, pep band, political, professional, radio and TV, religious, social, social service, and student government. Popular campus events include Welcome Week (Fall), Haunted Hall - Halloween Event, Homecoming, Alternative Spring Break Program, Play Day (Stress-Free Week), Sham-Rock It Out (Battle of the Bands), Blacklight Dance, Movie on the Lawn, Chinese Moon Festival, and Global Groove. **Sports:** There are 6 intercollegiate sports for men and 7 for women, and 42 intramural sports for men and 42 for women. Facilities include a gym, racquetball courts, an outdoor volleyball court, an indoor running track, a weight room, and a total fitness center. **Graduates:** From July 1, 2016 to June 30, 2017, 2056 bachelor's degrees were awarded. The most popular majors were nursing (39%), business (4%), and psychology (4%).

SERVICES: Counseling and information services are available, as is tutoring in some subjects. **Library/Resources:** The library contains 269,648 volumes, 764,621 microform items, and 998 audio/video tapes/CDs/DVDs, and subscribes to 228 periodicals including electronic. Computerized library services include interlibrary loans, database searching, and Internet access. Special learning facilities include an art gallery, radio station, a computer education building, and an educational media laboratory. **Physically Challenged Students:** All of the campus is accessible. Facilities include wheelchair ramps, elevators, special parking, specially equipped restrooms, special class scheduling, lowered drinking fountains, and lowered telephones. **Special:** Purdue Northwest offers cross-registration in philosophy, with programs that include trips to Cuba, South Korea, Canada, and Spain among other countries. There is also credit for military experience, as well as nondegree study, and pass/fail options. Some cooperative programs, internships, and work-study programs are also available. There are 6 national honor societies and a freshman honors program. **Visiting:** There are regularly scheduled orientations for prospective students. There are guides for informal visits and visitors may sit in on classes. To schedule a visit, contact the Office of Admissions and Recruitment. **Campus Safety and Security:** Measures include 24-hour foot and vehicle patrol, emergency notification system, self-defense education, and security escort services. There are shuttle buses, emergency telephones, lighted pathways/sidewalks, and controlled access to dorms/residences.

REQUIREMENTS: The SAT or ACT is required. Applicants must be graduates of an accredited secondary school. The GED is accepted. 33 Carnegie units are required for admission. Required courses vary, depending on the curriculum, and include 3 or 4 years of English, 2 or 3 years of math, 2 years of foreign language (for some majors), and 2 years of history or social studies. A GPA of 2.0 is required. AP and CLEP credits are accepted. Graduation requirements vary depending on the program. The total number of credit hours required for a degree varies from 126 to 136, with 24 to 73 in the major. All students must take English composition and 36 hours of general education courses and maintain a C average. **Procedure:** Freshmen are admitted in the fall, spring, and summer. Entrance exams should be taken during their junior and/or senior year, as early as possible. There is a rolling admissions plan. Applications should be filed by August 1 for fall entry; December 20 for spring entry; and June 1 for summer entry. The fall 2017 application fee was $25. Applications are accepted on-line. **Transfer Students:** 517 transfer students enrolled in 2016-2017. Must have completed at least 12 college level credits with a minimum cumulative GPA of 2.0 for admission to university. Some programs have higher requirements. 32 of 120 credits required for the bachelor's degree must be completed at PUW. **International Students:** There are 390 international students enrolled. They must take the TOEFL with a minimum score of 550 on the paper-based TOEFL (PBT) or 79 on the Internet-based version (iBT).

ADMISSIONS: The SAT scores for the 2017-2018 freshman class were: Math-- 63% below 500, 30% between 500 and 599, 6% between 600 and 699, and 1% between 700 and 800. Evidence-Based Reading/Writing-- 26% below 500, 53% between 500 and 599, 20% between 600 and 699, and 1% between 700 and 800. The ACT scores were 16% between 12 and 17, 53% between 18 and 23, 28% between 24 and 29, and 3% above 30. 29% of the current freshmen were in the top fifth of their class; 63% were in the top two fifths. 7 freshmen graduated first in their class. **Admissions Contact:** Karen Stachyra, Executive Director, Undergraduate Admissions. Email: *admissions@pnw.edu* Web: *www.pnw.edu*

FINANCIAL AID: In 2017-2018, 77% of all full-time freshmen received some form of financial aid. 61% of all full-time freshmen received need-based aid. PUN is a member of CSS. The FAFSA code is 001827. The priority date for freshman financial aid applications for fall entry is April 15. The deadline for filing freshman financial aid applications for fall entry is June 30.

PURDUE UNIVERSITY/WEST LAFAYETTE B-3

www.purdue.edu

West Lafayette, IN 47907 **(765) 494-1776**

Fax: (765) 494-0544 **Email: admissions@purdue.edu**

Full-time: 16,558 men, 12,168 women	**Faculty:** n/av
Part-time: 755 men, 562 women	**Ph.D.s:** 97%
Graduate: 5903 men, 4505 women	**Student/Faculty:** 12 to 1
Year: semesters, summer session	**Tuition:** $10,002 ($28,804)
Room & Board: $10,030	**Freshman Class:** 48776 applied, 27227 accepted, 7243 enrolled
SAT CR/M/W: 570/680/570 **ACT:** 29	**CEEB CODE:** 1631
Application Deadline: February 1	**MOST COMPETITIVE**

Purdue University/West Lafayette, founded in 1869, is a publicly supported institution offering degree programs with an emphasis on engineering, business, communications, arts, social sciences, allied health, and technology. There are 12 undergraduate schools and 1 graduate school. In addition to regional accreditation, PWL has baccalaureate program accreditation with AACSB, ABET, ACCE, ACPE, ADA, ASLA, FIDER, NASM, CAEP, NLN, SAF, ACS, APA, AVMA, CACREP, and CCNE. The 2595-acre campus is in a suburban area 65 miles northwest of Indianapolis. Including any residence halls, there are 376 buildings.

STUDENT LIFE: 53% of undergraduates are from Indiana. Others are from 50 states, 122 foreign countries, and Canada. 7% are Asian American; 63% White; 5% Hispanic; 3% African American; 3% race unknown; 2% two or more races; 17% Foreign. **Male To Female Ratio:** 1.3:1. The average age of freshmen is 18; all undergraduates, 20. 8% do not continue beyond their first year; 77% remain to graduate. **Housing:** 11284 students can be accommodated in college housing, which includes married student dorms and on-campus apartments. In addition, there are honors houses, fraternity houses, sorority houses, and living learning communities. On-campus housing is guaranteed for all 4 years. 62% of students commute. Alcohol is not permitted. Upperclassmen may keep cars.

FACULTY/CLASSROOMS: 65% of faculty are male; 35% are female. No introductory courses are taught by graduate students. The average class size in an introductory lecture is 45; in a laboratory is 24; and in a regular course is 39.

PROGRAMS OF STUDY: PWL confers B.A., B.F.A., B.S., B.S.A.A.E., B.S.A.G.E., B.S.B.E., B.S.B.M.E., B.S.C.E., B.S.C.H., B.S.C.H.E., B.S.C.M.P.E., B.S.C.N.E., B.S.E., B.S.E.E., B.S.E.E.E., B.S.E.H., B.S.F.O.R., B.S.I.E., B.S.I.M., B.S.L.A., B.S.M.E., B.S.M.S.E., B.S.N., and B.S.N.E., degrees. Associate, master's, and doctoral degrees are also awarded. Bachelor's degrees are awarded in AGRICULTURE (agricultural business management, agricultural communications, agricultural economics, agriculture, agronomy, animal science, fishing and fisheries, forestry and related sciences, horticulture, natural resource management, plant protection (pest management), plant science, soil science, and wood science), BIOLOGICAL SCIENCE (biochemistry, biology/biological science, cell biology, ecology, entomology, genetics, microbiology, molecular biology, nutrition, plant genetics, plant physiology, and wildlife biology), BUSINESS (accounting, banking and finance, entrepreneurial studies, fashion merchandising, hospitality management services, human resources, marketing management, marketing/retailing/merchandising, organizational leadership and management, retailing, and tourism), COMMUNICATIONS AND THE ARTS (advertising, apparel design, art history and appreciation, audio technology, broadcasting, classics, communications, comparative literature, creative writing, dramatic arts, English, film arts, fine arts, French, German, graphic design, industrial design, Japanese, journalism, Latin, Latin, linguistics, photography, public relations, Russian, Spanish, and visual and performing arts), COMPUTER AND PHYSICAL SCIENCE (actuarial science, applied mathematics, applied physics, atmospheric sciences and meteorology, chemistry, computer science, earth science, geology, information sciences and systems, mathematics, physics, radiological technology, science, software engineering, and statistics), EDUCATION (agricultural education, art education, athletic training, early childhood education, education, elementary education, English education, foreign languages education, health education, mathematics education, science education, secondary education, social studies education, special education, and technical education), ENGINEERING AND ENVIRONMENTAL DESIGN (aeronautical engineering, aeronautical technology, agricultural engineering, air traffic control, airline piloting and navigation, aviation administration/management, aviation computer technology, bioengineering, biomedical engineering, chemical engineering, chemical engineering technology, civil engineering, computational sciences, computer engineering, computer graphics, computer technology, construction engineering, construction management, construction technology, electrical/electronics engineering, electrical/electronics engineering technology, engineering management, environmental science, food services technology, industrial administration/management, industrial engineering, industrial engineering technology, interior design, landscape architecture/design, manufacturing engineering, manufacturing technology, materials science, mechanical engineering, mechanical engineering technology, nuclear engineering, occupational safety and health, and surveying engineering), HEALTH PROFESSIONS (clinical science, environmental health science, exercise science, health science, medical laboratory technology, nursing, pharmaceutical science, radiological science, and speech pathology/audiology), SOCIAL SCIENCE (African American studies, anthropology, Asian/American studies, Asian/Oriental studies, behavioral science, criminal justice, dietetics, economics, family and community services, family/consumer studies, fashion design and technology, food production/management/services, food science, French studies, history, Italian studies, Japanese studies, Judaic studies, liberal arts/general studies, medieval studies, philosophy, physical fitness/movement, political science/government, psychology, religion, Russian and Slavic studies, social studies, social work, sociology, Spanish studies, and women's studies). Engineering, actuarial science, and industrial management are the strongest academically. Management, preengineering, and mechanical engineering have the largest enrollments.

ACTIVITIES: 24% of men belong to 5 local and 50 national fraternities; 26% of women belong to 7 local and 33 national sororities. There are 983 groups on campus, including band, cheerleading, chess, choir, chorale, chorus, computers, dance, debate, drama, ethnic, film, forensics, honors, international, jazz band, LGBT, literary magazine, marching band, newspaper, orchestra, pep band, photography, political, professional, radio and TV, religious, social, social service, student government, and symphony. Popular campus events include Grand Prix Race, Old Masters, Gala week, Mortar Board Leadership Conference, Purdue University Dance Marathon, Martin Luther King Day of Service, Industrial Round Table, Big Man on Campus, Diwali, Relay for Life, B-Involved Fair, and Starry Night. **Sports:** There are 10 intercollegiate sports for men and 10 for women, and 40 intramural sports for men and 40 for women. Facilities include a football stadium, basketball arena, volleyball and wrestling gymnasium, indoor football practice facility, a field house, track & field complex, golf courses, Olympic-size competition pool and diving well, baseball, softball and soccer stadiums, fitness and recreational pools, weight rooms/cardio equipment rooms, outdoor intramural playing fields, outdoor tennis courts, outdoor sand volleyball courts, outdoor basketball courts, 18-hole disc golf, climbing areas, trap and skeet range, and crew boathouse. **Graduates:** From July 1, 2016 to June 30, 2017, 6834 bachelor's degrees were awarded. The most popular majors were management (6%), mechanical engineering (5%), and accounting (3%). In an average class, 1% graduate in 3 years or less, 49% graduate in 4 years or less, 71% graduate in 5 years or less, and 74% graduate in 6 years or less. Of the 2016 graduating class, 63% were employed within 6 months of graduation.

SERVICES: Counseling and information services are available, as is tutoring in every subject. There is a reader service for the blind, and remedial math, reading, and writing. **Library/Resources:** The library contains 3.8 million volumes, 2.7 million microform items, 10,182 audio/video tapes/CDs/DVDs, and subscribes to 59,223 periodicals, including electronic. Computerized library services include interlibrary loans, database searching, Internet access, and Wi-Fi capability. Special learning facilities include an art gallery and radio station. **Physically Challenged Students:** 90% of the campus is accessible. Facilities include wheelchair ramps, elevators, special parking, specially equipped restrooms, special class scheduling, lowered drinking fountains, lowered telephones, and special housing. **Special:** Cooperative programs are available in engineering, technology, agriculture, science, and health and human sciences. Cross-registration with Purdue's regional campuses, numerous internships, study abroad in 60+ countries, dual majors, student-designed majors, nondegree study, and pass/fail options are also offered. There are 33 national honor societies, Phi Beta Kappa, a freshman honors program, and 10 departmental honors programs. **Visiting:** There are regularly scheduled orientations for prospective students, including fall and spring preview days, which consist of admission, financial aid, housing, and school sessions, a campus tour, and dormitory visits. The Summer Visit Program consists of a counselors' orientation and campus and residence hall visits. There are guides for informal visits and visitors may sit in on classes. To schedule a visit, contact the Office of Admissions. **Campus Safety and Security:** Measures include 24-hour foot and vehicle patrol, emergency notification system, self-defense education, and security escort services. There are shuttle buses, emergency telephones, lighted pathways/sidewalks, and public transportation routes throughout campus.

REQUIREMENTS: The SAT or ACT is required. The ACT Optional Writing test is also required. Purdue requires that most students have 8 semesters each of English and math, 6 semesters each of social studies, lab sciences (for engineering, nursing, pharmacy and veterinary technology, 4 semesters of foreign language, and 2 semesters must be chemistry; nursing also requires 2 semesters of biology). The GED is also accepted. AP and CLEP credits are accepted. Important factors in the admissions decision are advanced placement or honors courses, extracurricular activities record, and geographical diversity. To graduate, students must be enrolled for at least 2 semesters and complete 32 semester hours of course work, complete approximately 128 hours and earn a minimum GPA of 2.0. In most majors, students must take courses in English, math, science, computer science, and social sciences. **Procedure:** Freshmen are admitted to all sessions. Entrance exams should be taken at the end of the junior year. There is a rolling admissions plan. Applications should be filed by February 1 for fall entry. The fall 2017 application fee was $60. Applications are accepted online. **Transfer Students:** 676 transfer students enrolled in 2016-2017. Requirements for transfer students vary greatly depending on each students unique situation, including academic background and intended major. For this reason, we encourage prospective students to visit our website and read in depth about the requirements that pertain to your specific situation. 32 of 120 credits required for the bachelor's degree must be completed at Purdue University. **International Students:** There are 4904 international students enrolled. They must take the TOEFL with a minimum score of 570 on the paper-based TOEFL (PBT) or 88 on the Internet-based version (iBT). Students must take the IELTS, SAT, or the ACT.

ADMISSIONS: 56% of the 2017-2018 applicants were accepted. The SAT scores for the 2017-2018 freshman class were: Critical Reading-- 16% below 500, 44% between 500 and 599, 32% between 600 and 699, and 9% between 700 and 800. Math-- 7% below 500, 27% between 500 and 599, 37% between 600 and 699, and 28% between 700 and 800. Writing-- 16% below 500, 43% between 500 and 599, 33% between 600 and 699, and 7% between 700 and 800. The ACT scores were 8% below 12, 16% between 12 and 17, 23% between 18 and 23, 13% between 24 and 29, and 41% above 30. 70% of the current freshmen were in the top fifth of their class; 94% were in the top two fifths. 101 freshmen graduated first in their class. **Admissions Contact:** Pamela Horne, Dean of Admissions/Assistant VP for Enrollment. Email: *admissions@purdue.edu* Web: *www.purdue.edu*

FINANCIAL AID: In 2017-2018, 73% of all full-time freshmen received some form of financial aid. 48% of all full-time freshmen received need-based aid. The average freshman award was $10,723. Need-based scholarships or need-based grants averaged $4,145; need-based self-help aid (loans and jobs) averaged $2,651; non-need-based athletic scholarships averaged $303; and other non-need-based awards and non-need-based scholarships averaged $3,624. 31% of undergraduate students work part-time. The average financial indebtedness of the 2017 graduate was $27,530. The priority date for freshman financial aid applications for fall entry is March 1.

ROSE-HULMAN INSTITUTE OF TECHNOLOGY — B-4

www.rose-hulman.edu

Terre Haute, IN 47803	(812) 877-8892 (800) 248-7448
Fax: (812) 877-8941	Email: admissions@rose-hulman.edu
Full-time: 1612 men, 535 women	**Faculty:** 190; IIB, ++$
Part-time: 18 men, 3 women	**Ph.D.s:** 99%
Graduate: 57 men, 20 women	**Student/Faculty:** 11 to 1
Year: quarters, summer session	**Tuition:** $45,762
Room & Board: $14,061	**Freshman Class:** 4473 applied, 2726 accepted, 558 enrolled
SAT CR/M/W: 600/660/570 **ACT:** 30	**CEEB CODE:** 1668
Application Deadline: February 1	**MOST COMPETITIVE**

Rose-Hulman Institute of Technology, founded in 1874, is a private college emphasizing engineering, science, and math. There is 1 undergraduate school. In addition to regional accreditation, RHIT has baccalaureate program accreditation with ABET. The 200-acre campus is in a suburban area on the east side of Terre Haute. Including any residence halls, there are 37 buildings.

STUDENT LIFE: 69% of undergraduates are from out of state, mostly the Midwest. Students are from 48 states, and 11 foreign countries. 68% are White; 5% Asian American; 5% Hispanic; 5% two or more races; 3% African American; 15% Foreign; 1% race unknown. **Male To Female Ratio:** 3.0:1. The average age of freshmen is 18; all undergraduates, 20. 9% do not continue beyond their first year; 91% remain to graduate. **Housing:** 1299 students can be accommodated in college housing, which includes dorms and on-campus apartments. In addition, there are fraternity houses, sorority houses, and sophomore residence hall. On-campus housing is guaranteed for the freshman year only, is available on a first-come, first-served basis. 58% of students live on campus. All students may keep cars.

FACULTY/CLASSROOMS: 75% of faculty are male; 25% are female. All teach undergraduates, and 20% do research. No introductory courses are taught by graduate students. The average class size in an introductory lecture is 19; in a laboratory is 20; and in a regular course is 19.

PROGRAMS OF STUDY: RHIT confers B.S. degrees. Master's degrees are also awarded. Bachelor's degrees are awarded in BIOLOGICAL SCIENCE (biochemistry and biology/biological science), COMPUTER AND PHYSICAL SCIENCE (chemistry, computer science, mathematics, physics, and software engineering), ENGINEERING AND ENVIRONMENTAL DESIGN (biomedical engineering, chemical engineering, civil engineering, computer engineering, electrical/electronics engineering, engineering physics, mechanical engineering, and optical engineering), SOCIAL SCIENCE (economics). Engineering, science, and mathematics are the strongest academically. Mechanical engineering, chemical engineering, and computer science have the largest enrollments.

ACTIVITIES: 36% of men belong to 8 national fraternities; 34% of women belong to 3 national sororities. There are 104 groups on campus, including art, band, cheerleading, chess, chorale, chorus, computers, dance, debate, drama, drill team, environmental, ethnic, film, honors, international, jazz band, LGBT, literary magazine, musical theater, newspaper, orchestra, pep band, photography, political, professional, radio and TV, religious, social, social service, and student government. Popular campus events include student run drama productions, and diversity speakers. **Sports:** There are 10 intercollegiate sports for men and 10 for women, and 24 intramural sports for men and 24 for women. Facilities include a field house, recreational center, swimming pool, tennis courts, and intramural fields. **Graduates:** From July 1, 2016 to June 30, 2017, 526 bachelor's degrees were awarded. The most popular majors were mechanical engineering (34%), chemical engineering (17%), and computer science (9%). In an average class, 3% graduate in 3 years or less, 68% graduate in 4 years or less, 80% graduate in 5 years or less, and 81% graduate in 6 years or less. Of the 2016 graduating class, 19% were enrolled in graduate school within 6 months of graduation, and 74% were employed.

SERVICES: Counseling and information services are available, as is tutoring in most subjects. **Library/Resources:** The library contains 317,821 volumes, 1,514 audio/video tapes/CDs/DVDs, and subscribes to 76,352 periodicals including electronic. Computerized library services include interlibrary loans, database searching, and Internet access. Special learning facilities include an art gallery, planetarium, and radio station. **Physically Challenged Students:** 95% of the campus is accessible. Facilities include wheelchair ramps, elevators, special parking, specially equipped restrooms, special class scheduling, and lowered drinking fountains. **Special:** The institute offers co-op programs, independent study, cross-registration with Indiana State University and Saint Mary-of-the-Woods College, summer industrial internships, study abroad, and dual majors. Pass/fail options are also available. There are 7 national honor societies and 3 departmental honors programs. **Visiting:** There are regularly scheduled orientations for prospective students, interviews, campus tours, and academic meetings. There are guides for informal visits; visitors may sit in on classes and stay overnight. To schedule a visit, contact Kelli Lloyd at (800) 248-7448. **Campus Safety and Security:** Measures include 24-hour foot and vehicle patrol, emergency notification system, self-defense education, and security escort services. There are emergency telephones, lighted pathways/sidewalks, controlled access to dorms/residences, medical transports, and free traffic assistance.

REQUIREMENTS: The SAT or ACT is required. Candidates should have at least 16 units of credit, including 4 units in English, 2 units in social sciences, and 1 unit each in math, chemistry, physics, biology and electives. An essay is required. Rose-Hulman requires applicants to be in the upper 25% of their class. AP credits are accepted. Important factors in the admissions decision are advanced placement or honors courses, recommendations by school officials, and extracurricular activities record. All students must complete at least 192 to 195 quarter hours with a minimum GPA of 2.0 and 36 hours in the humanities and social sciences. Freshmen are required to take math, biology, chemistry, or physics. The total number of hours required in the major varies. **Procedure:** Freshmen are admitted in the fall. Entrance exams should be taken in the fall of the senior year or spring of the junior year. There is a deferred admissions plan. Regular decision applications should be filed by February 1 for fall entry. The fall 2017 application fee was $40. Notification of early decision is sent December 15; regular decision, March 15. 379 applicants were on the 2017 waiting list; 39 were admitted. Applications are accepted on-line. **Transfer Students:** 19 transfer students enrolled in 2016-2017. Applicants need 1 year each of calculus, physics, biology, and chemistry and a minimum GPA of 3.0. 45 of 192 credits required for the bachelor's degree must be completed at Rose-Hulman. **International Students:** There are 312 international students enrolled. They must take the TOEFL with a minimum score of 88 on the Internet-based version (iBT). They must also take the SAT or ACT, scoring 550.

ADMISSIONS: 61% of the 2017-2018 applicants were accepted. The SAT scores for the 2017-2018 freshman class were: Critical Reading-- 6% below 500, 41% between 500 and 599, 39% between 600 and 699, and

13% between 700 and 800. Math-- 3% below 500, 25% between 500 and 599, 45% between 600 and 699, and 27% between 700 and 800. Writing-- 8% below 500, 46% between 500 and 599, 32% between 600 and 699, and 4% between 700 and 800. The ACT scores were 4% between 18 and 23, 44% between 24 and 29, and 53% above 30. 84% of the current freshmen were in the top fifth of their class; 99% were in the top two fifths. 35 freshmen graduated first in their class. **Admissions Contact:** Lisa Norton, Dean of Admissions. Email: *admissions@rose-hulman.edu* Web: *www.rose-hulman.edu*

FINANCIAL AID: In 2017-2018, 99% of all full-time freshmen received some form of financial aid. 61% of all full-time freshmen received need-based aid. The average freshman award was $28,846. Need-based scholarships or need-based grants averaged $28,736 ($64,828 maximum); need-based self-help aid (loans and jobs) averaged $12,857 ($50,500 maximum); and other non-need-based awards and non-need-based scholarships averaged $12,101 ($62,104 maximum). 35% of undergraduate students work part-time. The average financial indebtedness of the 2017 graduate was $45,520. RHIT is a member of CSS. The FAFSA code is 001830. The priority date for freshman financial aid applications for fall entry is March 1.

SAINT MARY-OF-THE-WOODS COLLEGE *(The complete profile is made available exclusively on our website, www.barronspac.com)*

SAINT MARY'S COLLEGE — C-1

www.saintmarys.edu

Notre Dame, IN 46556 — **(574) 284-4587** / **(800) 551-7621**

Fax: (574) 284-4841 — **Email: admission@saintmarys.edu**

Full-time: 1581 women	**Faculty:** 133; IIB, av$
Part-time: 13 women	**Ph.D.s:** 87%
Graduate: 10 men, 66 women	**Student/Faculty:** 10 to 1
Year: semesters, summer session	**Tuition:** $38,880
Room & Board: $11,720	**Freshman Class:** 1771 applied, 1446 accepted, 432 enrolled
SAT CR/M/W: 545/529/543 **ACT:** 25	**CEEB CODE:** 1702
Application Deadline: February 15	**COMPETITIVE**

Saint Mary's College, established in 1844, was founded and sponsored by the Congregation of the Sisters of the Holy Cross. It continues to be a Catholic comprehensive college for women in the liberal arts tradition. There is 1 undergraduate school and 1 graduate school. In addition to regional accreditation, SMC has baccalaureate program accreditation with CSWE, NASAD, NASM, CAEP, and CCNE. The 100-acre campus is in a suburban area in South Bend, IN and 90 miles east of Chicago. Including any residence halls, there are 20 buildings.

STUDENT LIFE: 73% of undergraduates are from out of state, mostly the Midwest. Students are from 43 states, 10 foreign countries, and Canada. 51% are from public schools. 77% are White; 3% two or more races; 3% race unknown; 2% African American; 2% Asian American; 2% Foreign; 11% Hispanic. 76% are Catholic; 11% Protestant. **Female To Male Ratio:** 166.0:1. The average age of freshmen is 18; all undergraduates, 20. 13% do not continue beyond their first year; 73% remain to graduate. **Housing:** 1350 students can be accommodated in college housing, which includes dorms and on-campus apartments. On-campus housing is guaranteed for all 4 years, and is available on a first-come, first-served basis. 86% of students live on campus. All students may keep cars.

FACULTY/CLASSROOMS: 31% of faculty are male; 69% are female. All teach undergraduates and do research. No introductory courses are taught by graduate students. The average class size in an introductory lecture is 20; in a laboratory is 15; and in a regular course is 15.

PROGRAMS OF STUDY: SMC confers B.A., B.S., B.S.W., B.B.A., B.F.A., and B.Mus. degrees. Master's and doctoral degrees are also awarded. Bachelor's degrees are awarded in BIOLOGICAL SCIENCE (biology/biological science), BUSINESS (accounting, business administration and management, and management information systems), COMMUNICATIONS AND THE ARTS (art, communications, creative writing, English literature, English Writing, fine arts, music, Spanish, and visual and performing arts), COMPUTER AND PHYSICAL SCIENCE (actuarial mathematics, applied mathematics, chemistry, mathematics, mathematics/computational, physics, and statistics), EDUCATION (elementary education and global studies), HEALTH PROFESSIONS (nursing and speech pathology/audiology), SOCIAL SCIENCE (communication sciences & disorders, economics, history, humanities, international studies, philosophy, political science/government, psychology, religion, social work, sociology, and women & gender studies). Nursing, psychology, and business administration have the largest enrollments.

ACTIVITIES: There are no fraternities or sororities. There are 75 groups on campus, including art, band, cheerleading, choir, chorale, chorus, dance, drama, environmental, ethnic, honors, international, LGBT, literary magazine, marching band, musical theater, newspaper, opera, orchestra, pep band, photography, political, professional, radio and TV, religious, social, social service, student government, and yearbook. Popular campus events include Back to School Dance, School Formal, and Dance Marathon. **Sports:** There are 8 intercollegiate and 8 intramural sports for women. Facilities include an athletic facility, outdoor tennis and volleyball courts, and soccer, lacrosse and softball fields. **Graduates:** From July 1, 2016 to June 30, 2017, 359 bachelor's degrees were awarded. The most popular majors were nursing (14%), business administration (9%), and biology (9%). In an average class, 71% graduate in 4 years or less, 76% graduate in 5 years or less, and 77% graduate in 6 years or less. Of the 2016 graduating class, 29% were enrolled in graduate school within 6 months of graduation, and 74% were employed.

SERVICES: Counseling and information services are available, as is tutoring in most subjects. There is a writing center, math center, and a student success program. **Library/Resources:** The library contains 244,651 volumes, 18,729 microform items, and 3,539 audio/video tapes/CDs/DVDs, and subscribes to 30,704 periodicals including electronic. Computerized library services include interlibrary loans, database searching, Internet access, and Wi-Fi capability. Special learning facilities include an art gallery, radio station, and TV station. **Physically Challenged Students:** All of the campus is accessible. Facilities include wheelchair ramps, elevators, special parking, specially equipped restrooms, lowered drinking fountains, and special housing. **Special:** Cross-registration is permitted with the University of Notre Dame and a consortium of 6 northern Indiana colleges. Opportunities are provided for internships, a Washington semester, dual and student-designed majors, a 3-2 engineering degree with the University of Notre Dame, non-degree study, pass/fail options, and study abroad in more than 20 countries. All students must complete a senior comprehensive project or exam and demonstrate proficiency in writing before graduating. There are 14 national honor societies. **Visiting:** There are regularly scheduled orientations for prospective students, including campus tours and visits with admissions and financial aid counselors and faculty and athletic staff. There are guides for informal visits; visitors may sit in on classes and stay overnight. To schedule a visit, contact Campus Visit Coordinator in Admissions. **Campus Safety and Security:** Measures include 24-hour foot and vehicle patrol, emergency notification system, self-defense education, and security escort services. There are shuttle buses, emergency telephones, lighted pathways/sidewalks, controlled access to dorms/residences, and key cards for controlled residence hall entry.

REQUIREMENTS: The SAT or ACT is required. Graduation from an accredited secondary school is required; a GED will be accepted. Applicants must have completed 16 academic credits, including 4 in English, 3 in math, and 2 in foreign language, history or social studies, and lab science with the remainder from college preparatory electives in the above areas. An essay is required. AP and CLEP credits are accepted. Important factors in the admissions decision are extracurricular activities record, advanced placement or honors courses, and recommendations by school officials. Students must successfully complete 128 credits, with at least 24 in the major, and must maintain a minimum GPA of 2.0. Students must complete the Sophia Program, a learning outcomes based general education curriculum promoting integration with majors and minors. Advanced proficiency in composition within the student's major must also be demonstrated, and a comprehensive exam in the major area is required by the end of the senior year. **Procedure:** Freshmen are admitted in the fall and spring. Entrance exams should be taken between March of the junior year and December of senior year. There are early decision, deferred admissions, and rolling admissions plans. Early decision applications should be filed by November 15; regular applications, by February 15 for fall entry; and November 15 for spring entry. Notification of early decision is sent December 15; regular decision, January 15. 56 early decision candidates were accepted for the 2017-2018 class. Applications are accepted on-line. **Transfer Students:** 32

transfer students enrolled in 2016-2017. Students must submit a transcript from high school and each previous college attended, along with an essay, a recommendation from a college adviser, and SAT or ACT test scores if the student has fewer than 24 semester hours of transferable credit. All transfer applicants must have maintained a minimum GPA of 2.75. An informational meeting with a counselor is recommended. Syllabi or course description is required for credit evaluation. 60 of 128 credits required for the bachelor's degree must be completed at SMC. **International Students:** There are 25 international students enrolled. They must take the TOEFL with a minimum score of 500 on the paper-based TOEFL (PBT) or 80 on the Internet-based version (iBT). Students must take the IELTS. They must also take the SAT or ACT.

ADMISSIONS: 82% of the 2017-2018 applicants were accepted. The SAT scores for the 2017-2018 freshman class were: Critical Reading-- 25% below 500, 51% between 500 and 599, 22% between 600 and 699, and 3% between 700 and 800. Math-- 33% below 500, 47% between 500 and 599, 17% between 600 and 699, and 3% between 700 and 800. Writing-- 28% below 500, 46% between 500 and 599, 24% between 600 and 699, and 1% between 700 and 800. The ACT scores were 1% between 12 and 17, 35% between 18 and 23, 52% between 24 and 29, and 11% above 30. 48% of the current freshmen were in the top fifth of their class; 82% were in the top two fifths. 6 freshmen graduated first in their class. **Admissions Contact:** Sarah Gallagher Dvorak, Director of Admissions. Email: *admission@saintmarys.edu* Web: *www.saintmarys.edu*

FINANCIAL AID: In 2017-2018, 100% of all full-time freshmen received some form of financial aid. 75% of all full-time freshmen received need-based aid. The average freshman award was $29,550. Need-based scholarships or need-based grants averaged $24,872; need-based self-help aid (loans and jobs) averaged $4,457; and other non-need-based awards and non-need-based scholarships averaged $13,429. 83% of undergraduate students work part-time. The average financial indebtedness of the 2017 graduate was $31,986. SMC is a member of CSS. The FAFSA code is 001836. The priority date for freshman financial aid applications for fall entry is March 1.

TAYLOR UNIVERSITY — D-3

www.taylor.edu

Upland, IN 46989	**(765) 998-5565** **(800) 882-3456**
Fax: (765) 998-4925	**Email: admissions@taylor.edu**
Full-time: 819 men, 1021 women	**Faculty:** 131; IIB, -$
Part-time: 107 men, 163 women	**Ph.D.s:** 88%
Graduate: 18 men, 17 women	**Student/Faculty:** 13 to 1
Year: 4-1-4, summer session	**Tuition:** $32,885
Room & Board: $9245	**Freshman Class:** 1673 applied, 1452 accepted, 449 enrolled
SAT EBR-W/M: 590/570 **ACT:** 26	**CEEB CODE:** 1802
Application Deadline: December 1	**VERY COMPETITIVE**

Taylor University, founded in 1846, is a private Christian interdenominational liberal arts institution that integrates faith, living and learning. There are 3 undergraduate schools and 1 graduate school. In addition to regional accreditation, TU has baccalaureate program accreditation with ABET, ACBSP, CSWE, NASM, CAEP, and CELP. The 952-acre campus is in a rural area 70 miles north of Indianapolis and 45 miles south of Fort Wayne. Including any residence halls, there are 43 buildings.

STUDENT LIFE: 60% of undergraduates are from out of state, mostly the Midwest. Students are from 45 states, 36 foreign countries, and Canada. 83% are White; 6% Foreign; 4% Hispanic; 3% African American; 3% Asian American; 1% American Indian/Alaska Native. 98% are Protestant. **Female To Male Ratio:** 1.3:1. The average age of freshmen is 19; all undergraduates, 21. 10% do not continue beyond their first year; 79% remain to graduate. **Housing:** 1768 students can be accommodated in college housing, which includes married student dorms, on-campus apartments, and off-campus apartments. On-campus housing is guaranteed for all 4 years. 89% of students live on campus. Alcohol is not permitted. Upperclassmen may keep cars.

FACULTY/CLASSROOMS: 70% of faculty are male; 30% are female. 98% teach undergraduates. No introductory courses are taught by graduate students. The average class size in an introductory lecture is 20; in a laboratory is 10; and in a regular course is 21.

PROGRAMS OF STUDY: TU confers B.A., B.B.A., B.Mus., B.F.A., and B.S. degrees. Associate and master's degrees are also awarded. Bachelor's degrees are awarded in AGRICULTURE (environmental studies), BIOLOGICAL SCIENCE (biochemistry and biology/biological science), BUSINESS (accounting, banking and finance, business administration and management, business administration marketing, finance, international business, international business management, marketing, sports management, and sustainable management), COMMUNICATIONS AND THE ARTS (art, art and design, communications, communications technology, digital media, dramatic arts, English, English as a second/foreign language, English literature, English Writing, film arts, film, television and digital media, fine arts, journalism, media arts, English and Professional Communication, music, music performance, music theory and composition, musical theater, public relations, Spanish, studio art, technical and business writing, theatre arts, visual and performing arts, vocal performance, and writing), COMPUTER AND PHYSICAL SCIENCE (chemistry, computer networks & systems, computer security, computer science, mathematics, natural sciences, physics, and web services), EDUCATION (art education, childhood education, Christian education, early childhood education, education, elementary education, English education, foreign languages education, health education, mathematics education, music education, physical education, science education, secondary education, social studies education, social studies secondary school education, and teaching English as a second/foreign language (TESOL/TEFOL), ENGINEERING AND ENVIRONMENTAL DESIGN (computer engineering, computer graphics, engineering physics, environmental engineering, environmental science, and systems engineering), HEALTH PROFESSIONS (biology, exercise science, health science, kinesiology, music therapy, premedicine, and public health), SOCIAL SCIENCE (biblical studies, Christian studies, development economics, economics, geography, history, humanities, interdisciplinary studies, international relations, international studies, liberal arts/general studies, liberal arts, sciences, general studies, humanities, ministries, philosophy, philosophy and religion, political science/government, psychology, social work, and sociology). Engineering physics, and biology are the strongest academically. Business, kinesiology, communication, and education have the largest enrollments.

ACTIVITIES: There are no fraternities or sororities. There are 65 groups on campus, including art, band, cheerleading, choir, chorale, chorus, communications, computers, dance, debate, drama, ethnic, film, honors, international, jazz band, literary magazine, musical theater, newspaper, opera, orchestra, pep band, photography, political, professional, radio and TV, religious, social, social service, student government, and symphony. Popular campus events include Taylathon, AirBand, Silent Night and Spiritual Renewal, and Emphasis Weeks. **Sports:** There are 9 intercollegiate sports for men and 8 for women, and 9 intramural sports for men and women. Facilities include indoor and outdoor track, multipurpose athletic courts, a fitness center with swimming/lap pool. A field house that provides a football stadium, practice fields with artificial turf, tennis and racquetball courts, multiple baseball and softball fields, and a soccer field. **Graduates:** From July 1, 2016 to June 30, 2017, 462 bachelor's degrees were awarded. The most popular majors were elementary education (9%), psychology (7%), and exercise science (6%). In an average class, 2% graduate in 3 years or less, 71% graduate in 4 years or less, 78% graduate in 5 years or less, and 79% graduate in 6 years or less. Of the 2016 graduating class, 18% were enrolled in graduate school within 6 months of graduation, and 73% were employed.

SERVICES: Counseling and information services are available, as is tutoring in most subjects. There is a reader service for the blind, and remedial math, reading, and writing. **Library/Resources:** The library contains 257,400 volumes, 30,679 microform items, 11,064 audio/video tapes/CDs/DVDs, and subscribes to 19,460 periodicals including electronic. Computerized library services include interlibrary loans, database searching, Internet access, and Wi-Fi capability. Special learning facilities include an art gallery, radio station, TV station, environmental study laboratory, NASA-approved clean room, particle accelerator, NASA project space research equipment, 65-acre arboretum, C. S. Lewis Collection, observatory room, 10 kW Photo-Voltaic Solar Array and two 50 kW Wind Turbines available for student data collection. **Physically Challenged Students:** 95% of the campus is accessible. Facilities include wheelchair ramps, elevators, special parking, specially equipped restrooms, special class scheduling, lowered drinking fountains, and lowered telephones. **Special:** Opportunities are provided for internships, cooperative programs, a Washington semester, study abroad program in over 35 countries, work-study programs, dual majors, student-designed majors, and B.A., B.S., B.M. and B.F.A. degrees. There is cross-registration with the other members of the Council for Christian Colleges and Universities, and the Christian College Consortium. There are 7 national honor societies, Phi Beta Kappa, a freshman honors program, and 23 departmental honors programs. **Visiting:** There are regularly scheduled orientations for prospective students, including a campus tour, lunch, class meetings, faculty meetings, a financial aid session, and an admissions interview. There are guides for informal visits, visitors may sit in on classes, and stay overnight. To schedule a visit, contact Amy Barnett at (765) 998-5134. **Campus Safety and Security:** Measures include 24-hour foot and vehicle patrol, emergency notification system, self-defense education, and security escort services. There are lighted pathways/sidewalks.

REQUIREMENTS: The SAT or ACT and ACT Writing Test are recommended. Graduation from an accredited secondary school is required; a GED will be accepted. It is recommended that applicants complete 4 years of English, 3 to 4 each of math and lab science, 2 each of social studies and a foreign language, and course work in computing, typing/keyboarding, and the arts. The applications includes 1 essay. Either ACT or SAT scores are required in most cases. High school transcripts and recommendation forms from a guidance counselor and pastor are also required. An interview is recommended for all students, and an audition is required for music majors. A GPA of 2.5 is required. AP and CLEP credits are accepted. Important factors in the admissions decision are recommendations by school officials, extracurricular activities record, and leadership record. Students must complete at least 128 total hours of which at least 42 must be upper division (300/400). To graduate, students must have a minimum cumulative GPA of 2.0 and a 2.3 GPA (2.5 in social work) in all majors and minors and demonstrate proficiency in writing, math, science, and reading. Students must also complete a senior paper, exam, or project in their major(s). General education requirements include courses in spiritual formation, speech, expository writing, fine arts, computer science, literature, science, history, math, social science, and a course designated as cross-cultural. The B.A. degree requires the equivalency of 2 years of 1 foreign language. Most B.S. degrees must be combined with systems analysis curriculum. **Procedure:** Freshmen are admitted in the fall, winter, and spring. Entrance exams should be taken during the spring of the junior year or fall of the senior year. There are early admissions and deferred admissions plans. Early decision applications should be filed by November 1; regular applications, by December 1 for fall entry; February 1 for winter entry; and April 1 for spring entry. The fall 2017 application fee was $25. Notification of early decision is sent November 20; regular decision, Applications are accepted on-line. **Transfer Students:** 64 transfer students enrolled in 2016-2017. Applicants must have maintained a minimum GPA of 2.5 and have completed at least 12 credit hours at the previous college. An interview is recommended. 64 of 128 credits required for the bachelor's degree must be completed at TU. **International Students:** There are 104 international students enrolled. They must take the TOEFL with a minimum score of 550 on the paper-based TOEFL (PBT). The school will accept the TOEFL in lieu of the SAT or the ACT.

ADMISSIONS: 87% of the 2017-2018 applicants were accepted. The SAT scores for the 2017-2018 freshman class were: Math-- 16% below 500, 48% between 500 and 599, 31% between 600 and 699, and 11% between 700 and 800. Evidence-Based Reading/Writing-- 11% below 500, 40% between 500 and 599, 43% between 600 and 699, and 13% between 700 and 800. The ACT scores were 5% between 12 and 17, 28% between 18 and 23, 47% between 24 and 29, and 20% above 30. 57% of the current freshmen were in the top fifth of their class; 81% were in the top two fifths. **Admissions Contact:** Amy Barnett, Executive Director of Admissions. Email: *admissions@taylor.edu* Web: *www.taylor.edu*

FINANCIAL AID: In 2017-2018, 99% of all full-time freshmen received some form of financial aid. 54% of all full-time freshmen received need-based aid. The average freshman award was $23,246. Need-based scholarships or need-based grants averaged $3,116 ($16,000 maximum); need-based self-help aid (loans and jobs) averaged $3,343 ($7,400 maximum); non-need-based athletic scholarships averaged $1,143 ($32,640 maximum); and other non-need-based awards and non-need-based scholarships averaged $15,644 ($32,640 maximum). 64% of undergraduate students work part-time. The average financial indebtedness of the 2017 graduate was $28,889. Taylor University is a member of CSS. The FAFSA code is 001838. The priority date for freshman financial aid applications for fall entry is February 15. The deadline for filing freshman financial aid applications for fall entry is March 10.

TRINE UNIVERSITY — D-1

www.trine.edu

Angola, IN 46703	**(260) 665-4149** **(800) 347-4878**
Fax: (260) 665-4578	**Email: admit@trine.edu**
Full-time: 1245 men, 484 women	**Faculty:** 116
Part-time: 47 men, 18 women	**Ph.D.s:** 64%
Graduate: 283 men, 75 women	**Student/Faculty:** 13 to 1
Year: semesters, summer session	**Tuition:** $30,960
Room & Board: $10,350	**Freshman Class:** n/av
SAT CR/M: 510/540 **ACT:** 23	**CEEB CODE:** 1811
Application Deadline: August 1	**COMPETITIVE**

Trine University, founded in 1884, is a private, independent university. There are 4 undergraduate schools and one graduate school. In addition to regional accreditation, TU has baccalaureate program accreditation with ABET, CAEP, and ACBSP. The 400-acre campus is in a small town 40 miles north of Ft. Wayne. Including any residence halls, there are 35 buildings.

STUDENT LIFE: 71% of undergraduates are from Indiana. Others are from 31 states, 20 foreign countries, and Canada. 80% are from public schools. 84% are White; 4% Foreign; 4% race unknown; 3% Hispanic; 2% African American; 2% two or more races. **Male To Female Ratio:** 2.7:1. The average age of freshmen is 18; all undergraduates, 21. 24% do not continue beyond their first year; 51% remain to graduate. **Housing:** 1241 students can be accommodated in college housing, which includes dorms and on-campus apartments, and honors houses. On-campus housing is guaranteed for all 4 years. 90% of students live on campus. Alcohol is not permitted. All students may keep cars.

FACULTY/CLASSROOMS: 62% of faculty are male; 38% are female. All teach undergraduates, 10% do research, and 10% do both. No introductory courses are taught by graduate students. The average class size in an introductory lecture is 25; in a laboratory is 16; and in a regular course is 18.

PROGRAMS OF STUDY: TU confers B.A. and B.S. degrees. Associate, master's, and doctoral degrees are also awarded. Bachelor's degrees are awarded in BIOLOGICAL SCIENCE (biology/biological science), BUSINESS (accounting, banking and finance, business administration and management, management information systems, management science, marketing/retailing/merchandising, recreation and leisure services, recreational facilities management, and sports management), COMMUNICATIONS AND THE ARTS (communications), COMPUTER AND PHYSICAL SCIENCE (chemistry, computer science, cyber intelligence/security studies, information sciences and systems, mathematics, and physical sciences), EDUCATION (elementary education, English education, mathematics education, physical education, science education, secondary education, and social science education), ENGINEERING AND ENVIRONMENTAL DESIGN (chemical engineering, civil engineering, computer engineering, drafting and design technology, electrical/electronics engineering, engineering management, environmental science, industrial administration/management, and mechanical engineering), HEALTH PROFESSIONS (physical therapy and premedicine), SOCIAL SCIENCE (criminal justice, forensic studies, psychology, and social science). Engineering, math/computer science, and science are the strongest academically. Engineering, psychology, and business have the largest enrollments.

ACTIVITIES: 26% of men belong to 8 national fraternities; 20% of women belong to 5 local and 2 national sororities. There are 35 groups on campus, including band, cheerleading, choir, chorus, communications, computers, dance, drama, environmental, ethnic, forensics, honors, international, jazz band, marching band, newspaper, pep band, professional, radio and TV, religious, social, social service, student government, and yearbook. Popular campus events include Homecoming, Bingo for Bucks, and Moonlight Breakfast. **Sports:** There are 10 intercollegiate sports for men and 9 for women, and 6 intramural sports for men and 5 for women. Facilities include an athletic stadium for football, a weight room and sports medicine area, an athletic and recreation center that is a multi purpose-sports complex with an indoor 200-meter track, tennis courts, volleyball, baseball/softball cages, basketball, indoor soccer, and lacrosse, a gym, basketball and racquetball courts, an 18-hole championship golf course, tennis courts, and practice and playing fields. **Graduates:** From July 1, 2016 to June 30, 2017, 264 bachelor's degrees were awarded. The most popular majors were engineering (33%), business (19%), and education (9%). In an average class, 35% graduate in 4 years or less, 50% graduate in 5 years or less, and 51% graduate in 6 years or less. Of the 2016 graduating class, 25% were enrolled in graduate school within 6 months of graduation, and 97% were employed.

SERVICES: Counseling and information services are available, as is tutoring in some subjects, such as math, business, engineering, accounting, science, and English. There is also remedial math. **Library/Resources:** The library contains 154,527 volumes, 668 microform items, and 19,216 audio/video tapes/CDs/DVDs, and subscribes to 31,993 periodicals including electronic. Computerized library services include interlibrary loans, database searching, Internet access, and Wi-Fi capability. Special learning facilities include a radio station. **Physically Challenged Students:** 98% of the campus is accessible. Facilities include wheelchair ramps, elevators, special parking, specially equipped restrooms, special class scheduling, lowered drinking fountains, lowered telephones, and special housing. **Special:** Cooperative education programs are available in engineering and business. Opportunities exist for internships and work-study programs with the university and many companies. Study abroad is offered in more than 31 countries. There are 12 national honor societies and a freshman honors program. **Visiting:** There are regularly scheduled orientations for prospective students, including meetings with faculty, administrators, financial aid personnel, a coach (if the student is an athlete), and a campus tour. There are guides for informal visits, visitors may sit in on classes, and stay overnight. To schedule a visit, contact the Admissions Office. **Campus Safety and Security:** Measures include 24-hour foot and vehicle patrol, emergency notification system, self-defense education, and security escort services. There are emergency telephones and lighted pathways/sidewalks.

REQUIREMENTS: The SAT or ACT is required. Candidates for admission should be graduates of accredited secondary schools. The GED is accepted. Students should have 4 years of English and 3 years each of science, social studies, and math. A GPA of 2.5 is required. AP and CLEP credits are accepted. Important factors in the admissions decision are advanced placement or honors courses, recommendations by school officials, and leadership record. Candidates for graduation must complete 120 semester hours, satisfying the general education program and major requirements and maintaining a minimum overall GPA of 2.0. Required courses vary by degree sought. All students must complete a general education curriculum including science, math, American studies, social science, global studies, English composition, humanistics, computer literacy, and oral communication course work. Some majors have senior design projects. The number of hours in the major varies from 40 to 60. **Procedure:** Freshmen are admitted to all sessions. Entrance exams should be taken in the junior or senior year. There are deferred admissions and rolling admissions plans. Applications should be filed by August 1 for fall entry. Notifications are sent August 15. Applications are accepted on-line. **Transfer Students:** 27 transfer students enrolled in 2016-2017. In addition to meeting the university's requirements for freshmen, applicants must have satisfactory records from previous institutions. 30 of 120 credits required for the bachelor's degree must be completed at Trine. **International Students:** There are 179 international students enrolled. They must take the TOEFL with a minimum score of 550 on the paper-based TOEFL (PBT) or 79 on the Internet-based version (iBT). Applicants not transferring credits in math or English must be tested in those subjects.

ADMISSIONS: The SAT scores for the 2017-2018 freshman class were: Critical Reading-- 42% below 500, 38% between 500 and 599, 17% between 600 and 699, and 3% between 700 and 800. Math-- 27% below 500, 40% between 500 and 599, 29% between 600 and 699, and 4% between 700 and 800. The ACT scores were 8% between 12 and 17, 45% between 18 and 23, 38% between 24 and 29, and 9% above 30. 37% of the current freshmen were in the top fifth of their class; 73% were in the top two fifths. 8 freshmen graduated first in their class. **Admissions Contact:** Scott Goplin, Vice President, Enrollment Management. Email: *admit@trine.edu* Web: *www.trine.edu*

FINANCIAL AID: In 2017-2018, 84% of all full-time freshmen received some form of financial aid, and need-based aid. The average freshman award was $27,189. Need-based scholarships or need-based grants averaged $5,796 ($7,000 maximum); need-based self-help aid (loans and jobs) averaged $5,721 ($5,500 maximum); and other non-need-based awards and non-need-based scholarships averaged $11,230 ($17,000 maximum). 56% of undergraduate students work part-time. The average financial indebtedness of the 2017 graduate was $32,641. The FAFSA code is 001839. The priority date for freshman financial aid applications for fall entry is March 1.

UNIVERSITY OF EVANSVILLE — A-5

www.evansville.edu

Evansville, IN 47722 (812) 488-2468 (800) 423-8633

Fax: (812) 488-4076 **Email: admission@evansville.edu**

Full-time: 960 men, 1122 women
Part-time: 63 men, 89 women
Graduate: 43 men, 121 women
Year: semesters, summer session
Room & Board: $11,240

Faculty: 169; IIA, -$
Ph.D.s: 85%
Student/Faculty: 13 to 1
Tuition: $32,946
Freshman Class: 3916 applied, 2765 accepted, 515 enrolled

SAT CR/M/W: 560/570/535 **ACT:** required
CEEB CODE: 1208
Application Deadline: n/av
COMPETITIVE+

University of Evansville, founded in 1854, is a private institution affiliated with the United Methodist Church, that offers undergraduate degree programs in arts and sciences, business administration, education and health sciences, and engineering and computer science. There are 4 undergraduate schools and 4 graduate schools. In addition to regional accreditation, Evansville has baccalaureate program accreditation with AACSB, ABET, APTA, NASM, CAEP, NLN, and CAATE. The 75-acre campus is in an urban area 180 miles southwest of Indianapolis, 170 miles east of St. Louis, and 120 miles west of Louisville. Including any residence halls, there are 54 buildings.

STUDENT LIFE: 60% of undergraduates are from Indiana. Others are from 41 states, 47 foreign countries, and Canada. 72% are White; 3% African American; 3% Hispanic; 3% race unknown; 2% Asian American; 2% two or more races; 15% Foreign. 57% are Protestant; 33% Catholic. **Female To Male Ratio:** 1.2:1. The average age of freshmen is 18; all undergraduates, 20. 19% do not continue beyond their first year; 69% remain to graduate. **Housing:** 1919 students can be accommodated in college housing, which includes dorms and on-campus apartments. In addition, there are honors houses, fraternity houses, International connection, and housing for students in math and sciences. On-campus housing is guaranteed for the freshman year only, is available on a first-come, first-served basis, and is available on a lottery system for upperclassmen. 63% of students live on campus. Alcohol is not permitted. All students may keep cars.

FACULTY/CLASSROOMS: 52% of faculty are male; 48% are female. All teach undergraduates. No introductory courses are taught by graduate students.

PROGRAMS OF STUDY: Evansville confers B.A., B.S., B.F.A. and B.M. degrees. Associate, master's, and doctoral degrees are also awarded. Bachelor's degrees are awarded in AGRICULTURE (environmental studies), BIOLOGICAL SCIENCE (biochemistry, biology/biological science, and neurosciences), BUSINESS (accounting, business administration and management, finance, international business, marketing, and sports management), COMMUNICATIONS AND THE ARTS (art history, art, communications, creative writing, dramatic arts, French, German, graphic design, literature, music, music business management, music performance, Spanish, and theater management), COMPUTER AND PHYSICAL SCIENCE (chemistry, clinical laboratory science, computer science, mathematics, and physics), EDUCATION (art education, athletic training, drama education, elementary education, English education, foreign languages education, mathematics education, music education, science education, social studies education, and special education), ENGINEERING AND ENVIRONMENTAL DESIGN (civil engineering, computer engineering, electrical/electronics engineering, environmental science, and mechanical engineering), HEALTH PROFESSIONS (exercise science, health care administration, music therapy, nursing, predentistry, premedicine, preoptometry, prepharmacy, preveterinary science, and public health), SOCIAL SCIENCE (archeology, biblical studies, classical/ancient civilization, cognitive science, criminal justice, economics, history, interdisciplinary studies, international studies, liberal arts/general studies, philosophy, political science/government, prelaw, psychology, sociology, and theological studies). Theater, engineering, and physical therapy are the strongest academically. Exercise science, mechanical engineering, and theatre have the largest enrollments.

ACTIVITIES: 30% of men belong to 6 national fraternities; 29% of women belong to 1 local and 4 national sororities. There are 144 groups on campus, including art, band, cheerleading, choir, chorale, chorus, computers, dance, drama, drill team, environmental, ethnic, film, honors, international, jazz band, LGBT, literary magazine, musical theater, newspaper, opera, orchestra, pep band, political, professional, radio and TV, religious, social, social service, student government, symphony, and yearbook. Popular campus events include Labor Day Picnic and Student Organization Fair, Bike Race, and Sunset Concert. **Sports:** There are 6 intercollegiate sports for men and 8 for women, and 17 intramural sports for men and 17 for women. Facilities include a stadium for softball, baseball, a pool, a conditioning room, an aerobics room, free weight rooms, an indoor track, eight outdoor tennis courts, a 1/2-mile security lighted jogging trail, basketball, racquetball, and volleyball courts. **Graduates:** From July 1, 2016 to June 30, 2017, 562 bachelor's degrees were awarded. The most popular majors were health professions and related programs (14%), business/marketing (13%), and parks and recreation (10%). In an average class, 58% graduate in 4 years or less, 67% graduate in 5 years or less, and 69% graduate in 6 years or less.

SERVICES: There is remedial writing and tutoring for most subjects. **Library/Resources:** The library contains 282,262 volumes, 474,391 microform items, and 14,597 audio/video tapes/CDs/DVDs, and subscribes to 50 periodicals including electronic. Computerized library services include interlibrary loans, database searching, Internet access, and Wi-Fi capability. Special learning facilities include an art gallery and radio station. **Physically Challenged Students:** 87% of the campus is accessible. Facilities include wheelchair ramps, elevators, special parking, specially equipped restrooms, special class scheduling, lowered drinking fountains, and special housing. **Special:** Students may study abroad at the University of Evansville British campus, Harlaxton College, and many places throughout the world. There is also an Israeli archeological excavation program, an accelerated bachelor of science in global leadership degree, combined bachelor's/graduate degrees, cooperative education (business administration, chemistry, engineering, environmental studies), dual enrollment of high school students, ESL, and teacher certification, as well as honors, independent study programs, internships, and student-designed majors. There are 15 national honor societies and a freshman honors program. **Visiting:** There are regularly scheduled orientations for prospective students, including a campus tour, faculty academic sessions, financial aid and admission appointments, and study abroad and honors program sessions. There are guides for informal visits, visitors may sit in on classes, and stay overnight. To schedule a visit, contact Carla Hachem at (800) 423-8633. **Campus Safety and Security:** Measures include 24-hour foot and vehicle patrol, emergency notification system, self-defense education, and security escort services. There are emergency telephones and lighted pathways/sidewalks.

REQUIREMENTS: The SAT or ACT and the ACT Optional Writing test are required. In addition, to be competitive for admission, students should submit a minimum SAT composite score of 1500 (math, critical reading, and writing) or ACT composite of 21. Applicants must be graduates of accredited secondary schools; applicants who have been homeschooled are also considered. The University requires completion of 4 years of college preparatory English, 3 years each of math, science, and social studies, and 2 years of foreign language are recommended. An interview is recommended but not required. AP and CLEP credits are accepted. Important factors in the admissions decision are extracurricular activities record, personality/intangible qualities, and advanced placement or honors courses. To graduate, students must complete at least 120 semester hours with a minimum GPA of 2.0 cumulative and in their major. All students must complete a 41-hour general education program. A demonstration of writing proficiency, a capstone course in the major, and a demonstration of foreign language proficiency are required for graduation. Students must complete at least 39 credit hours in courses numbered 300 or above, at least 48 credit hours in residence at UE, and at least 51 percent of coursework in their major at UE. **Procedure:** Freshmen are admitted fall and spring. Entrance exams should be taken by fall of senior year. There is a deferred admissions plan. Early decision applications should be filed by December 1. Notification of early decision is sent December 15; regular decision, Applications are accepted on-line. **Transfer Students:** 75 transfer students enrolled in 2016-2017. Applicants must submit official transcripts from each college from which they earned credit and must have a minimum GPA of 2.5 in all previous college work. High school transcripts, standardized test scores, and comments from the Dean of Students Recommendation Form are optional but considered if submitted with the application. 48 of 120 credits required for the bachelor's degree must be completed at UE. **International Students:** There are 296 international students enrolled. They must take the TOEFL with a minimum score of 61 on the Internet-based version (iBT).

ADMISSIONS: 71% of the 2017-2018 applicants were accepted. The SAT scores for the 2017-2018 freshman class were: Critical Reading-- 21% below 500, 46% between 500 and 599, 25% between 600 and 699, and 8% between 700 and 800. Math-- 20% below 500, 43% between 500 and 599, 31% between 600 and 699, and 6% between 700 and 800. Writing-- 29% below 500, 46% between 500 and 599, 21% between 600 and 699, and 4% between 700 and 800. The ACT scores were 2% between 12 and 17, 27% between 18 and 23, 49% between 24 and 29, and 22% above 30. 57% of the current freshmen were in the top fifth of their class; 85% were in the top two fifths. 23 freshmen graduated first in their class. **Admissions Contact:** Scott Henne, Dean of Admission. Email: *admission@evansville.edu* Web: *www.evansville.edu*

FINANCIAL AID: In 2017-2018, 93% of all full-time freshmen received some form of financial aid. 71% of all full-time freshmen received need-based aid. The average freshman award was $29,342. Need-based scholarships or need-based grants averaged $24,275 ($31,900 maximum); need-based self-help aid (loans and jobs) averaged $8,217 ($25,025 maximum); and non-need-based athletic scholarships averaged $18,943 ($49,760 maximum). 18% of undergraduate students work part-time. The average financial indebtedness of the 2017 graduate was $31,013. UE is a member of CSS. The FAFSA code is 001795. The deadline for filing freshman financial aid applications for fall entry is March 10.

UNIVERSITY OF INDIANAPOLIS C-3

www.uindy.edu

Indianapolis, IN 46227	**(317) 788-3216** **(800) 232-8634**
Fax: (317) 788-3300	**Email: admissions@uindy.edu**
Full-time: 1319 men, 2131 women	**Faculty:** IIA, --$
Part-time: 168 men, 507 women	**Ph.D.s:** 77%
Graduate: 300 men, 967 women	**Student/Faculty:** 11 to 1
Year: semesters, summer session	**Tuition:** $26,550
Room & Board: $9930	**Freshman Class:** 7216 applied, 5297 accepted, 961 enrolled
SAT or ACT: required	**CEEB CODE:** 1321
Application Deadline: open	**VERY COMPETITIVE**

University of Indianapolis, established in 1902, is a private liberal arts school affiliated with the United Methodist Church that provides undergraduate and graduate studies with an emphasis on education, business, nursing, and arts and sciences. There are 8 undergraduate schools and 8 graduate schools. In addition to regional accreditation, University of Indianapolis has baccalaureate program accreditation with ACBSP, ACEJMC, CSWE, NASAD, NASM, CAEP, NLN, and APA. The 65-acre campus is in a suburban area on the south side of Indianapolis. Including any residence halls, there are 32 buildings.

STUDENT LIFE: 93% of undergraduates are from Indiana. Others are from 44 states, and Canada. 9% are Foreign; 8% African American; 71% White; 4% Hispanic; 4% race unknown; 3% two or more races; 2% Asian American. 43% claim no religious affiliation; 42% Protestant. **Female To Male Ratio:** 2.0:1. The average age of freshmen is 20; all undergraduates, 23. 23% do not continue beyond their first year; 50% remain to graduate. **Housing:** 1432 students can be accommodated in college housing, which includes married student dorms, on-campus apartments, off-campus apartments, and honors houses. On-campus housing is guaranteed for all 4 years. 63% of students commute. Alcohol is not permitted. All students may keep cars.

FACULTY/CLASSROOMS: 42% of faculty are male; 58% are female. No introductory courses are taught by graduate students. The average class size in a regular course is 18.

PROGRAMS OF STUDY: University of Indianapolis confers B.A., B.S., B.S.N., B.S.W., B.S.A.T., B.M., B.L.S. and B.F.A. degrees. Associate, master's, and doctoral degrees are also awarded. Bachelor's degrees are awarded in BIOLOGICAL SCIENCE (biology/biological science), BUSINESS (accounting, banking and finance, business administration and management, business communications, business economics, entrepreneurial studies, international business management, management information systems, marketing/retailing/merchandising, and sports management), COMMUNICATIONS AND THE ARTS (art, broadcasting, communications, digital communications, digital media, dramatic arts, English, French, German, journalism, music, music performance, musical theater, public relations, Spanish, studio art, and theatre studies), COMPUTER AND PHYSICAL SCIENCE (actuarial science, chemistry, computer information systems, computer science, earth science, mathematics, and physics), EDUCATION (art education, athletic training, drama education, elementary education, English education, foreign languages education, mathematics education, middle school education, music education, physical education, science education, secondary education, and social studies education), ENGINEERING AND ENVIRONMENTAL DESIGN (commercial art, electrical/electronics engineering, environmental science, and mechanical engineering), HEALTH PROFESSIONS (art therapy, exercise science, medical laboratory technology, nursing, and respiratory therapy), SOCIAL SCIENCE (anthropology, archeology, criminal justice, economics, history, international relations, philosophy, political science/government, psychology, religion, social science, social work, and sociology). Nursing, science (biology/chemistry), exercise science, and psychology are the strongest academically. Business, nursing, and health sciences have the largest enrollments.

ACTIVITIES: There are no fraternities or sororities. There are 45 groups on campus, including academic clubs, art, cheerleading, chess, choir, chorale, chorus, computers, dance, debate, drama, ethnic, forensics, honors, international, jazz band, LGBT, literary magazine, musical theater, newspaper, orchestra, pep band, photography, political, professional, radio and TV, religious, social, social service, and student government. Popular campus events include Winter and Spring Formals, Ceremony of Flags, and Midnight Breakfast. **Sports:** There are 12 intercollegiate sports for men and 11 for women, and 8 intramural sports for men and 7 for women. Facilities include a health and fitness center, a gym, a swimming pool, racquetball courts, a weight room, and a dance studio. **Graduates:** From July 1, 2016 to June 30, 2017, 771 bachelor's degrees were awarded. In an average class, 1% graduate in 3 years or less, 41% graduate in 4 years or less, 53% graduate in 5 years or less, and 54% graduate in 6 years or less.

SERVICES: Counseling and information services are available, as is tutoring in every subject. There is remedial math and writing. There is also a special learning disabled program (BUILD). **Library/Resources:** The library contains 197,419 volumes, 19,841 microform items, and 6,775 audio/video tapes/CDs/DVDs, and subscribes to 401 periodicals including electronic. Computerized library services include interlibrary loans, database searching, Internet access, and Wi-Fi capability. Special learning facilities include an art gallery, planetarium, radio station, TV station, and an archeology and forensics lab. **Physically Challenged Students:** 95% of the campus is accessible. Facilities include wheelchair ramps, elevators, special parking, specially equipped restrooms, special class scheduling, lowered drinking fountains, and lowered telephones. **Special:** Cross-registration is offered in conjunction with 6 area colleges. Cooperative programs, internships, various work-study programs, study abroad, dual and student-designed majors, accelerated programs in liberal studies and organizational leadership, pass/fail options, and a 3-2 engineering degree with Indiana University-Purdue University Indianapolis are available. A fleximester, which is a 3-week spring term, is also offered. There are 14 national honor societies and a freshman honors program. **Visiting:** There are regularly scheduled orientations for prospective students, including campus visits and tours. There are guides for informal visits, visitors may sit in on classes, and stay overnight. To schedule a visit, contact the Admissions Office. **Campus Safety and Security:** Measures include 24-hour foot and vehicle patrol, emergency notification system, self-defense education, and security escort services. There are emergency telephones, lighted pathways/sidewalks, and controlled access to dorms/residences.

REQUIREMENTS: The SAT or ACT is required. Each applicant should complete a college preparatory curriculum with 15 to 20 academic credits from English/language arts, social studies, science, math, and world languages. The GED is accepted. An interview is recommended. UIndy requires applicants to be in the upper 50% of their class. A GPA of 2.5 is required. AP and CLEP credits are accepted. Important factors in the admissions decision are leadership record, recommendations by school officials, and advanced placement or honors courses. All undergraduates must complete at least 120 hours, including 24 hours or more in the major with a GPA of 2.0 or better. Requirements include a core curriculum in which 4 learning goals must be met. Students must also take a health and phys ed course and 1 spring term, and attend lecture/performance events. Specific courses include math, history, modern language, science, global/local, writing and speaking, communication, philosophy/ethics, religion, English composition and literature. **Procedure:** Freshmen are admitted to all sessions. There are deferred admissions and rolling admissions plans. Application deadlines are open. 63 applicants were on the 2017 waiting list; 39 were admitted. Applications are accepted on-line. **Transfer Students:** 212 transfer students enrolled in 2016-2017. ACT or SAT is not needed if applicants have a GPA of C and 20 semester hours of credit. 30 of 120 credits required for the bachelor's degree must be completed at UIndy. **International Students:** They must take the TOEFL with a minimum score of 500 on the paper-based TOEFL (PBT) or 61 on the Internet-based version (iBT) or take the MELAB, or Cambridge Examinations IELTS, CPE, or CAE. They must also take the SAT or ACT.

ADMISSIONS: 73% of the 2017-2018 applicants were accepted. 48% of the current freshmen were in the top fifth of their class; 73% were in the top two fifths. **Admissions Contact:** Ron Wilks, Director of Admissions. Email: *admissions@uindy.edu* Web: *www.uindy.edu*

FINANCIAL AID: In 2017-2018, 93% of all full-time freshmen received some form of financial aid. 50% of all full-time freshmen received need-based aid. The average freshman award was $23,460. Need-based scholarships or need-based grants averaged $8,500; need-based self-help aid (loans and jobs) averaged $3,250; non-need-based athletic scholarships averaged $1,510 ($39,530 maximum); and other non-need-based awards and non-need-based scholarships averaged $10,000. 16% of undergraduate students work part-time. The average financial indebtedness of the 2017 graduate was $35,480. University of Indianapolis is a member of CSS. The college's own financial statement is required. The FAFSA code is 001804. The priority date for freshman financial aid applications for fall entry is March 10.

UNIVERSITY OF NOTRE DAME — C-1

www.nd.edu

Notre Dame, IN 46556 — **(574) 631-7505**

Fax: (574) 631-8865	**Email: admissions@nd.edu**
Full-time: 4493 men, 4064 women	**Faculty:** 1188; I, +$
Part-time: 10 men, 9 women	**Ph.D.s:** 91%
Graduate: 2259 men, 1632 women	**Student/Faculty:** 10 to 1
Year: semesters, summer session	**Tuition:** $53,391
Room & Board: $15,410	**Freshman Class:** 19564 applied, 3702 accepted, 2051 enrolled
SAT EBR-W/M: 720/770 **ACT:** 34	**CEEB CODE:** 1841
Application Deadline: January 1	**MOST COMPETITIVE**

University of Notre Dame, founded in 1842, is a comprehensive Catholic research university offering programs through the Colleges of Arts and Letters, Engineering, Science, Business, and the School of Architecture. There are 5 undergraduate schools and 6 graduate schools. In addition to regional accreditation, UND has baccalaureate program accreditation with AACSB, ABET, and NAAB. The 1250-acre campus is in a suburban area 90 miles east of Chicago. Including any residence halls, there are 159 buildings.

STUDENT LIFE: 92% of undergraduates are from out of state, mostly the Midwest. Students are from 50 states, 72 foreign countries, and Canada. 44% are from public schools. 7% are Foreign; 69% White; 5% Asian American; 4% African American; 4% two or more races; 11% Hispanic. **Male To Female Ratio:** 1.2:1. The average age of freshmen is 18; all undergraduates, 20. 2% do not continue beyond their first year; 98% remain to graduate. **Housing:** 6929 students can be accommodated in college housing, which includes dorms. On-campus housing is guaranteed for the freshman year only, and is available on a first-come, first-served basis. 75% of students live on campus. Upperclassmen may keep cars.

FACULTY/CLASSROOMS: 69% of faculty are male; 31% are female. No introductory courses are taught by graduate students.

PROGRAMS OF STUDY: UND confers B.A., B.S., B.Arch., B.B.A., and B.F.A. degrees. Master's and doctoral degrees are also awarded. Bachelor's degrees are awarded in BIOLOGICAL SCIENCE (biochemistry, biological sciences, environmental earth resources, and neurosciences), BUSINESS (accounting, finance, international economics, management, and marketing), COMMUNICATIONS AND THE ARTS (Africana studies, Arabic, art history, Chinese, design, English, film, television and digital media, French, German, Greek, information technology, Italian, Japanese, music, romance languages and literature, Russian, Spanish, and studio art), COMPUTER AND PHYSICAL SCIENCE (applied mathematics, chemistry, computer science, environmental geology, mathematics, physics, science, and statistics), EDUCATION (classical studies and science education), ENGINEERING AND ENVIRONMENTAL DESIGN (aerospace engineering, architecture, chemical engineering, civil engineering, computer engineering, electrical/electronics engineering, environmental engineering, environmental science, and mechanical engineering), SOCIAL SCIENCE (American studies, anthropology, economics, gender studies, history, liberal arts/general studies, medieval studies, philosophy, philosophy and religion, political science/government, psychology, sociology, and theology). Engineering, theology, and business are the strongest academically. Finance, psychology, and economics have the largest enrollments.

ACTIVITIES: There are no fraternities or sororities. There are 465 groups on campus, including art, bagpipe, band, cheerleading, chess, choir, chorale, chorus, computers, dance, debate, drama, drill team, ethnic, film, forensics, honors, international, jazz band, literary magazine, marching band, musical theater, newspaper, orchestra, pep band, photography, political, professional, radio club, religious, social, social service, student government, symphony, and yearbook. Popular campus events include Spring Festival, Home Football Weekends, and Collegiate Jazz Festival. **Sports:** There are 13 intercollegiate sports for men and 13 for women, and 16 intramural sports for men and 13 for women. Facilities include indoor and outdoor tennis, swimming pools, golf courses, several outdoor general recreational fields, an indoor 100-yard general facility with track, fitness and recreation centers, varsity softball/baseball stadiums, football stadium, basketball/volleyball arena, a track, soccer stadium, lacrosse stadium, hockey arena, a fencing gym, volleyball practice area, varsity rowing erg gym, and varsity football practice fields. **Graduates:** From July 1, 2016 to June 30, 2017, 2146 bachelor's degrees were awarded. The most popular majors were finance (13%), accountancy (8%), and finance (7%). In an average class, 90% graduate in 4 years or less, 95% graduate in 5 years or less, and 95% graduate in 6 years or less. Of the 2016 graduating class, 22% were enrolled in graduate school within 6 months of graduation, and 64% were employed.

SERVICES: There is a reader service for the blind. **Library/Resources:** Computerized library services include interlibrary loans, database searching, Internet access, and Wi-Fi capability. Special learning facilities include an art gallery, an art museum and performing arts center. **Physically Challenged Students:** 95% of the campus is accessible. Facilities include wheelchair ramps, elevators, special parking, specially equipped restrooms, special class scheduling, lowered drinking fountains, lowered telephones, and special housing. **Special:** Cross-registration is offered with Saint Mary's College. Study abroad is possible in 20 countries. A 5-year arts and letters/engineering B.A.-B.S. degree is offered. There is a program of liberal studies, centered on the discussion of great books. Internships, an accelerated degree program, a Washington semester, dual majors, 3-2 engineering degrees, and pass/fail options are available. There are 16 national honor societies, Phi Beta Kappa, and 24 departmental honors programs. **Visiting:** There are regularly scheduled orientations for prospective students, including small group sessions for students, larger sessions for parents, and tours for all. Visitors may sit in on classes and stay overnight. To schedule a visit, contact the Admissions Office. **Campus Safety and Security:** Measures include 24-hour foot and vehicle patrol, an emergency notification system, self-defense education, and security escort services. There are shuttle buses, emergency telephones, lighted pathways/sidewalks, controlled access to dorms/residences, controlled access to vehicle, property registration, lost and found, and monthly electronic safety newsletter.

REQUIREMENTS: The SAT or ACT is required. Applicants should be graduates of an accredited secondary school with 16 Carnegie credits completed, including 4 years of English, 3 years of math, and 2 years each of science, foreign language, and history. The SAT subject test in foreign language is recommended. An essay is required. An audition or a portfolio is recommended for some majors. AP credits are accepted. All students must complete courses in English, philosophy, science, history, theology, math, social science, and phys ed. A total of 125 semester hours with a minimum GPA of 2.0 is required to graduate. **Procedure:** Freshmen are admitted in the fall. Entrance exams should be taken by fall of the senior year. There is a deferred admissions plan. Applications should be filed by January 1 for fall entry. The fall 2017 application fee was $75. Notifications are sent April 1. Applications are accepted online. **Transfer Students:** 184 transfer students enrolled in 2016-2017. Applicants should have completed at least 27 semester hours of transferable credit and maintained a 3.3 GPA in all courses. Admission depends on openings in each undergraduate college. 60 of 120 credits required for the bachelor's degree must be completed at UND. **International Students:** There are 574 international students enrolled. They must take the TOEFL with a minimum score of 110 on the Internet-based version (iBT). They must also take the SAT or ACT.

ADMISSIONS: 19% of the 2017-2018 applicants were accepted. The SAT scores for the 2017-2018 freshman class were: Math-- 3% between 500 and 599, 27% between 600 and 699, and 70% between 700 and 800. Evidence-Based Reading/Writing-- 1% below 500, 3% between 500 and 599, 31% between 600 and 699, and 65% between 700 and 800. The ACT scores were % below 12, % between 12 and 17, 1% between 18 and 23, 10% between 24 and 29, and 89% above 30. **Admissions Contact:** Donald Bishop, Assistant Vice President for Undergraduate Enrollment. Email: *admissions@nd.edu* Web: *www.nd.edu*

FINANCIAL AID: In 2017-2018, 71% of all full-time freshmen received some form of financial aid. 96% of all full-time freshmen received need-based aid. The average freshman award was $47,455. Need-based scholarships or need-based grants averaged $38,673; need-based self-help aid (loans and jobs) averaged $5,036; non-need-based athletic scholarships averaged $38,072; and other non-need-based awards and non-need-based scholarships averaged $25,299. The average financial indebtedness of the 2017 graduate was $29,254. University of UND is a member of CSS. The CSS/Profile, and Federal Tax form (s), and W-2 forms is required. The FAFSA code is 001840. The priority date for freshman financial aid applications for fall entry is February 15.

UNIVERSITY OF SAINT FRANCIS D-2

www.sf.edu

Fort Wayne, IN 46808	(260) 399-8000 (800) 729-4732 Email: admis@sf.edu
Full-time: 500 men, 1023 women	**Faculty:** 116
Part-time: 49 men, 334 women	**Ph.D.s:** 40%
Graduate: 124 men, 292 women	**Student/Faculty:** 13 to 1
Year: semesters, summer session	**Tuition:** $29,430
Room & Board: $9090	**Freshman Class:** 1249 applied, 1233 accepted, 454 enrolled
SAT EBR-W/M: 530/520 **ACT:** 21	**CEEB CODE:** 1693
Application Deadline: n/av	**COMPETITIVE**

University of Saint Francis is a private, Catholic university enrolling students in majors ranging from the liberal arts, to the creative arts, to the health sciences. With small class sizes, personal attention, and the freedom to explore your options, a USF education has a lot to offer. There are 4 undergraduate schools and 1 graduate school. In addition to regional accreditation, University of Saint Francis has baccalaureate program accreditation with ACBSP, CAHEA, CSWE, NASAD, CAEP, NLN, ACEN, ACEND, and ARC-PA. The 100-acre campus is in an urban area in Fort Wayne, Indiana, 125 miles north of Indianapolis and 150 miles east of Chicago IL. Including any residence halls, there are 26 buildings.

STUDENT LIFE: 90% of undergraduates are from Indiana. Others are from 17 states, 7 foreign countries, and Canada. 81% are from public schools. 79% are White; 7% African American; 7% Hispanic; 3% two or more races; 2% Asian American; 2% race unknown; 1% Foreign. 46% are Protestant; 28% Catholic; 21% 20% Unknown; 1% Buddhist, Muslim, Other. **Female To Male Ratio:** 2.5:1. The average age of freshmen is 18; all undergraduates, 23. 28% do not continue beyond their first year; 72% remain to graduate. **Housing:** 409 students can be accommodated in college housing, which includes dorms and on-campus apartments. On-campus housing is guaranteed for the freshman year only, and is available on a first-come, first-served basis. 80% of students commute. Alcohol is not permitted. All students may keep cars.

FACULTY/CLASSROOMS: 34% of faculty are male; 66% are female. 95% teach undergraduates. No introductory courses are taught by graduate students. The average class size in an introductory lecture is 19; in a laboratory is 15; and in a regular course is 16.

PROGRAMS OF STUDY: USF confers B.A., B.F.A., B.S., B.S.Ed., B.S.N., and B.S.W. degrees. Associate and master's degrees are also awarded. Bachelor's degrees are awarded in BIOLOGICAL SCIENCE (biology/biological science and nutrition), BUSINESS (accounting, business administration and management, finance, insurance and risk management, management, and marketing), COMMUNICATIONS AND THE ARTS (animation, art history, communications, dance, English, graphic design, music technology, and studio art), COMPUTER AND PHYSICAL SCIENCE (chemistry, clinical laboratory science, chemistry/forensic chemistry, computer game design/development, computer information systems, computer security, mathematics, and science and management), EDUCATION (art education, educational studies, elementary education, museum studies, and special education), ENGINEERING AND ENVIRONMENTAL DESIGN (environmental science), HEALTH PROFESSIONS (art therapy, exercise science, health services administration, nursing, predentistry, premedicine, prephysician assistant, and preveterinary science), SOCIAL SCIENCE (criminal justice, history, liberal arts/general studies, ministries, philosophy, political science/government, psychology, social work, sociology, and theology). Nursing is the strongest academically. Nursing, exercise science, and business administration have the largest enrollments.

ACTIVITIES: There are no fraternities or sororities. There are 45 groups on campus, including TRIO Navigators, art, cheerleading, chorale, communications, dance, drama, environmental, ethnic, film, gaming club, honors, jazz band, literary magazine, marching band, musical theater, newspaper, pep band, photography, professional, religious, social, social service, and student government. Popular campus events include Homecoming Week, Casino Night, Ultimate Road Trip, SOCA Art Openings, Legacy Seasonal Conferences, Spring Fling Week, and Football and Basketball Games. **Sports:** There are 8 intercollegiate sports for men and 8 for women, and 7 intramural sports for men and 7 for women. Facilities include an athletic center, a gym with basketball or volleyball courts, a fitness center, exercise studio, football stadium and training center, and fields for soccer, baseball and softball. **Graduates:** From July 1, 2016 to June 30, 2017, 317 bachelor's degrees were awarded. The most popular majors were nursing (41%), health & exercise science (8%), and business administration (8%). In an average class, 1% graduate in 3 years or less, 40% graduate in 4 years or less, 54% graduate in 5 years or less, and 56% graduate in 6 years or less. Of the 2016 graduating class, 10% were enrolled in graduate school within 6 months of graduation, and 79% were employed.

SERVICES: Counseling and information services are available, as is tutoring in every subject. There is a reader service for the blind, and remedial math, reading, and writing. **Library/Resources:** The library contains 258,619 volumes, 14,300 microform items, 29,300 audio/video tapes/CDs/DVDs, and subscribes to 38,832 periodicals including electronic. Computerized library services include interlibrary loans, database searching, Internet access, and Wi-Fi capability. Special learning facilities include an art gallery, School of Health Sciences Simulation Lab, North Campus Auditorium, Performing Arts Center, music technology digital recording studio, School of Creative Arts specialized facilities and studios, and nature preserve. **Physically Challenged Students:** Facilities include wheelchair ramps, elevators, special parking, specially equipped restrooms, and lowered drinking fountains. **Special:** Cross-registration available with the Fort Wayne Higher Education Consortium, dual majors available with A.S. in Physical Therapist Assistant and B.S. in Exercise Science, A.S. in Radiologic Technology and B.S. in Health Services, A.S. in Surgical Technology and B.S. in Health Services, internship available in many academic programs, co-operative education program available to business majors, media entrepreneurship training in the arts, and student-designed major There are 6 national honor societies, a freshman honors program, and 1 departmental honors program. **Visiting:** There are regularly scheduled orientations for prospective students, student tours and meetings with faculty and staff. There are guides for informal visits and visitors may sit in on classes. To schedule a visit, contact Aaron West at (260) 434-3279. **Campus Safety and Security:** Measures include 24-hour foot and vehicle patrol, emergency notification system, and security escort services. There are shuttle buses, emergency telephones, lighted pathways/sidewalks, and controlled access to dorms/residences.

REQUIREMENTS: Incoming students should meet the following requirements: graduate from an accredited high school; rank in the upper half of the high school graduation class; have a 2.3 GPA on a 4.0 scale; earn a SAT score of 1000 or above (verbal/critical reading and math combined) or ACT composite score of 21 or above USF requires applicants to be in the upper 50% of their class. AP and CLEP credits are accepted. To complete a bachelor's degree at the University of Saint Francis, students must meet the following criteria: Complete the general education requirements; a minimum of 120 semester hours of credit earned as required by the academic program curriculum; a major of at least 30 hours, with no fewer than 12 hours earned from the University of Saint Francis; a year's residence, that is, at least 30 semester hours of credit earned at the University of Saint Francis; a cumulative GPA of at least 2.0 on a 4.0 scale; satisfactory completion of a comprehensive examination or senior project as specified by the department; completion of the academic advising file audit with a representative of Academic Affairs. **Procedure:** Freshmen are admitted in the fall, spring, and summer. Entrance exams should be taken Spring of the junior year or fall of the senior year. There are deferred admissions and rolling admissions plans. Application deadlines are open. Notification is sent on a rolling basis. Applications are accepted on-line. **Transfer Students:** 287 transfer students enrolled in 2016-2017. To be considered for admission to the USF, a transfer student must: request that an official copy of the final high school transcript (must include date of graduation) and/or GED score, and request that official transcripts from all colleges and universities attended be sent directly to the Office of Admissions, and students who have earned a CGPA of 2.3 or better will be considered for admission 30 of 120 credits required for the bachelor's degree must be completed at USF. **International Students:** There are 9 international students enrolled. They must take the TOEFL with a minimum score of 550 on the paper-based TOEFL (PBT) or 80 on the Internet-based version (iBT). They must also take the SAT or ACT, scoring 21 ACT.

ADMISSIONS: 99% of the 2017-2018 applicants were accepted. The SAT scores for the 2017-2018 freshman class were: Math-- 31% below 500, 54% between 500 and 599, and 15% between 600 and 699. Evidence-Based Reading/Writing-- 31% below 500, 49% between 500 and 599, 19% between 600 and 699, and 2% between 700 and 800. The ACT scores were 15% between 12 and 17, 55% between 18 and 23, 26% between 24 and 29, and 4% above 30. 31% of the current freshmen were in the top fifth of their class; 67% were in the top two fifths. 5 freshmen graduated first in their class. **Admissions Contact:** Joel Wincowski, Interim Vice President, Enrollment Management. Email: *admis@sf.edu* Web: *www.sf.edu*

FINANCIAL AID: In 2017-2018, 100% of all full-time freshmen received some form of financial aid. 89% of all full-time freshmen received need-based aid. 11% of undergraduate students work part-time. The average financial indebtedness of the 2017 graduate was $37,167. The FAFSA code is 001832. The priority date for freshman financial aid applications for fall entry is March 10.

UNIVERSITY OF SOUTHERN INDIANA A-5

www.usi.edu

Evansville, IN 47712	**(812) 464-1765** **(800) 467-1965**
Fax: (812) 465-7154	**Email: enroll@usi.edu**
Full-time: 2478 men, 4060 women	**Faculty:** 328; IIA, --$
Part-time: 435 men, 733 women	**Ph.D.s:** 71%
Graduate: 424 men, 884 women	**Student/Faculty:** 20 to 1
Year: semesters, summer session	**Tuition:** $7970 ($18,626)
Room & Board: $8838	**Freshman Class:** 4569 applied, 4277 accepted, 1722 enrolled
SAT EBR-W/M: 540/533 **ACT:** 22	**CEEB CODE:** 1335
Application Deadline: August 15	**COMPETITIVE**

University of Southern Indiana, founded in 1965, offering programs through the College of Liberal Arts, College of Nursing and Health Professions, Romain College of Business, and the Pott College of Science, Engineering, and Education. There are 6 undergraduate schools and 1 graduate school. In addition to regional accreditation, USI has baccalaureate program accreditation with AACSB, ABET, CSWE, NASAD, CAEP, ACS, ACEND, ACOTE, CCNE, CDA/ADA, CARC, JRCERT, NACEP, NAEYC, NCTE, CELPA, and CSMA. The 1400-acre campus is in a suburban area in Evansville, IN and within 150 miles of Indianapolis, IN, St. Louis, MO and Nashville, TN. Including any residence halls, there are 89 buildings.

STUDENT LIFE: 87% of undergraduates are from Indiana. Others are from 32 states, and 44 foreign countries. 86% are White; 5% African American; 3% Hispanic; 2% Foreign; 2% two or more races; 1% Asian American; 1% American Indian/Alaska Native. **Female To Male Ratio:** 1.7:1. The average age of freshmen is 18; all undergraduates, 22. 29% do not continue beyond their first year; 26% remain to graduate. **Housing:**

2800 students can be accommodated in college housing, which includes dorms and on-campus apartments. In addition, there are honors houses, language/international houses, special-interest houses, fraternity houses, and sorority houses. On-campus housing is available on a first-come, first-served basis. 68% of students commute. Alcohol is not permitted. All students may keep cars.

FACULTY/CLASSROOMS: 40% of faculty are male; 60% are female. All teach undergraduates. No introductory courses are taught by graduate students. The average class size in an introductory lecture is 25; in a laboratory is 26; and in a regular course is 25.

PROGRAMS OF STUDY: USI confers B.A., B.S., B.P.S., B.S.E., B.S.N., BSHIIM, B.S.M.E., B.S.M.F.E. and B.S.W. degrees. Associate, master's, and doctoral degrees are also awarded. Bachelor's degrees are awarded in BIOLOGICAL SCIENCE (biochemistry, biology/biological science, biophysics, and nutrition), BUSINESS (accounting, business administration and management, finance, management information systems, marketing/retailing/merchandising, and sports management), COMMUNICATIONS AND THE ARTS (advertising, art, broadcasting, communications, English, French, German, journalism, performing arts, public relations, radio/television technology, Spanish, and theatre arts), COMPUTER AND PHYSICAL SCIENCE (chemistry, computer science, geology, mathematics, and physics), EDUCATION (early childhood education, elementary education, English education, health information management, mathematics education, physical education, science education, secondary education, social science education, and special education), ENGINEERING AND ENVIRONMENTAL DESIGN (civil engineering technology, electrical/electronics engineering technology, engineering, environmental science, industrial administration/management, manufacturing technology, mechanical engineering technology, and mining and mineral engineering), HEALTH PROFESSIONS (dental hygiene, dental laboratory technology, exercise science, health care administration, nursing, occupational therapy, radiological science, and respiratory therapy), SOCIAL SCIENCE (anthropology, criminal justice, economics, history, international studies, philosophy, political science/government, psychology, public administration, social science, social work, and sociology). Nursing is the strongest academically. Nursing, general studies, and psychology have the largest enrollments.

ACTIVITIES: 8% of men belong to 6 national fraternities; 7% of women belong to 7 national sororities. There are 137 groups on campus, including art, cheerleading, chess, choir, chorale, chorus, communications, computers, dance, drama, environmental, ethnic, film, honors, international, jazz band, LGBT, literary magazine, musical theater, newspaper, pep band, photography, political, professional, radio and TV, religious, social, social service, and student government. Popular campus events include Welcome Week, Cinema USI, Springfest, Dance Marathon, and International Food Festival. **Sports:** There are 7 intercollegiate sports for men and 8 for women, and 12 intramural sports for men and 12 for women. Facilities include cardio and weight machine area, treadmills, elliptical machines, stationary bikes, Nu-step, stretching and ab area, free weight room, multipurpose courts, indoor track, a climbing center, group exercise rooms, and a game room. **Graduates:** From July 1, 2016 to June 30, 2017, 1685 bachelor's degrees were awarded. The most popular majors were nursing (30%), biology (16%), and health services (15%). In an average class, 20% graduate in 4 years or less, 35% graduate in 5 years or less, and 39% graduate in 6 years or less. Of the 2016 graduating class, 25% were enrolled in graduate school within 6 months of graduation, and 86% were employed.

SERVICES: Counseling and information services are available, as is tutoring in most subjects. There is a reader service for the blind, and remedial math, reading, and writing. **Library/Resources:** The library contains 472,554 volumes, 325,144 microform items, and 8,534 audio/video tapes/CDs/DVDs, and subscribes to 142,796 periodicals including electronic. Computerized library services include interlibrary loans, database searching, Internet access, and Wi-Fi capability. Special learning facilities include an art gallery, radio station, and TV station. **Physically Challenged Students:** 95% of the campus is accessible. Facilities include wheelchair ramps, elevators, special parking, specially equipped restrooms, special class scheduling, lowered drinking fountains, and lowered telephones. **Special:** Students may participate in cooperative programs, internships and work-study programs. Study abroad, dual majors, pass/fail options, accelerated degree programs, and B.A.-B.S. degrees are possible. There are 16 national honor societies and a freshman honors program. **Visiting:** There are regularly scheduled orientations for prospective students, Tour campus and housing and hear about the USI experience and admission process. Meetings with faculty members can be arranged upon request. There are guides for informal visits, visitors may sit in on classes, and stay overnight. To schedule a visit, contact Cindy Braker at (800) 467-1965. **Campus Safety and Security:** Measures include 24-hour foot and vehicle patrol, emergency notification system, self-defense education, and security escort services. There are shuttle buses, emergency telephones, and lighted pathways/sidewalks.

REQUIREMENTS: The SAT or ACT is required. Applicants must be graduates of an accredited secondary school, with a minimum GPA of 2.0. The GED is accepted. An interview is recommended if the student is below admissions standards. AP and CLEP credits are accepted. Important factors in the admissions decision are advanced placement or honors courses, evidence of special talent, and leadership record. A student must have a 2.0 (C) minimum grade-point average on all University courses counted for graduation requirements. Some curricula, such as teacher education programs, require a higher grade point average. Students must have a minimum of 120 semester hours of credit for a baccalaureate degree. If all specified requirements are completed with fewer than 120 semester hours, a student must elect sufficient work to total at least 120 hours. Some curricula or combination of fields require more. Students must have a minimum of 60 semester hours of credit for an associate degree. If all specified requirements are completed with fewer than 60 semester hours, a student must elect sufficient work to total at least 60 hours. Some curricula or combination of fields requires more. All students must complete a minimum of 39 semester hours at the 300- and 400-level to complete a baccalaureate degree. A student must complete the minimum University Core Curriculum program. Specific requirements for the University Core Curriculum component of each degree program are noted in the sections of the bulletin describing each of the academic programs. Incomplete grades should be resolved at least six weeks before the end of the term of graduation. Course requirements for graduation in the student's degree program (s) may be those in effect at the time of matriculation into the program or at graduation, but not a combination of both. **Procedure:** Freshmen are admitted in the fall, spring, and summer. There are deferred admissions and rolling admissions plans. Applications should be filed by August 15 for fall entry. The fall 2017 application fee was $40. Applications are accepted on-line. **Transfer Students:** 499 transfer students enrolled in 2016-2017. Grades of C and above will transfer for credit. 30 of 120 credits required for the bachelor's degree must be completed at USI. **International Students:** There are 136 international students enrolled. They must take the TOEFL with a minimum score of 525 on the paper-based TOEFL (PBT) or 71 on the Internet-based version (iBT). They must also take the SAT or ACT.

ADMISSIONS: 94% of the 2017-2018 applicants were accepted. The SAT scores for the 2017-2018 freshman class were: Math-- 29% below 500, 54% between 500 and 599, 15% between 600 and 699, and 2% between 700 and 800. Evidence-Based Reading/Writing-- 28% below 500, 50% between 500 and 599, 20% between 600 and 699, and 2% between 700 and 800. The ACT scores were 12% between 12 and 17, 52% between 18 and 23, 32% between 24 and 29, and 4% above 30. 28% of the current freshmen were in the top fifth of their class; 60% were in the top two fifths. 10 freshmen graduated first in their class. **Admissions Contact:** Rashad Smith, Director of Undergraduate Admissions. Email: *enroll@usi.edu* Web: *www.usi.edu*

FINANCIAL AID: In 2017-2018, 67% of all full-time freshmen received some form of financial aid. 60% of all full-time freshmen received need-based aid. The average freshman award was $9,908. Need-based scholarships or need-based grants averaged $7,997; need-based self-help aid (loans and jobs) averaged $3,267; non-need-based athletic scholarships averaged $4,627; and other non-need-based awards and non-need-based scholarships averaged $3,847. 12% of undergraduate students work part-time. The average financial indebtedness of the 2017 graduate was $22,262. The college's own financial statement is required. The FAFSA code is 001808. The deadline for filing freshman financial aid applications for fall entry is March 10.

VALPARAISO UNIVERSITY — B-1

www.valpo.edu

Valparaiso, IN 46383	(219) 464-5011 (888) GO-VALPO
Fax: (219) 464-6898	**Email:** undergrad.admission@valpo.edu
Full-time: 1428 men, 1752 women	**Faculty:** IIA, -$
Part-time: 34 men, 41 women	**Ph.D.s:** n/av
Graduate: 369 men, 433 women	**Student/Faculty:** n/av
Year: semesters, summer session	**Tuition:** $38,760
Room & Board: $11,400	**Freshman Class:** n/av
SAT or ACT: required	**CEEB CODE:** 1874
Application Deadline: rolling	**VERY COMPETITIVE**

Valparaiso University, founded in 1859, is an independent institution affiliated with the Lutheran Church and offering degree programs in arts and sciences, business, engineering, nursing and health professions, and law. There are 5 undergraduate schools and 4 graduate schools. In addition to regional accreditation, VU has baccalaureate program accreditation with AACSB, ABET, CSWE, NASM, CAEP, ABA, AALS, ACS, CCNE, and CACREP. The 350-acre campus is in a small town 55 miles southeast of Chicago. Including any residence halls, there are 60 buildings.

STUDENT LIFE: 55% of undergraduates are from out of state, mostly the Midwest. Students are from 42 states, 27 foreign countries, and Canada. 71% are White; 6% African American; 5% Foreign; 3% two or more races; 3% race unknown; 2% Asian American; 10% Hispanic. 39% are Protestant; 23% Catholic. **Female To Male Ratio:** 1.2:1. The average age of freshmen is 18; all undergraduates, 20. 17% do not continue beyond their first year; 72% remain to graduate. **Housing:** 2154 students can be accommodated in college housing, which includes dorms and on-campus apartments. In addition, there are language/international houses, fraternity houses, and sorority houses. On-campus housing is guaranteed for all 4 years. 60% of students live on campus. Alcohol is not permitted. Upperclassmen may keep cars.

FACULTY/CLASSROOMS: No introductory courses are taught by graduate students. The average class size in an introductory lecture is 23; in a laboratory is 24; and in a regular course is 23.

PROGRAMS OF STUDY: VU confers B.A., B.L.P.S., B.Mus., B.Mus.Ed., B.S., B.S.Acc., B.S.Bus.Adm., B.S.C.E., B.S.Comp.Eng., B.S.Ed., B.S.E.E., B.S.H.C.L., B.S.M.E., B.S.N., B.S.P.E., and B.S.W. degrees. Associate, master's, and doctoral degrees are also awarded. Bachelor's degrees are awarded in BIOLOGICAL SCIENCE (biochemistry and biology/biological science), BUSINESS (accounting, banking and finance, business administration and management, business intelligence and analytics, finance, international economics, management science, marketing/retailing/merchandising, and sports management), COMMUNICATIONS AND THE ARTS (art, classics, communications, creative writing, digital communications, dramatic arts, English, English Writing, French, German, music, music performance, music theory and composition, Spanish, technical and business writing, theatre arts, and voice), COMPUTER AND PHYSICAL SCIENCE (actuarial science, astronomy, atmospheric sciences and meteorology, chemistry, computer science, applied data science analytics, geology, mathematics, physics, and statistics), EDUCATION (art education, elementary education, English education, foreign languages education, global studies, mathematics education, music education, physical education, psychology education, science education, secondary education, social science education, and social studies education), ENGINEERING AND ENVIRONMENTAL DESIGN (civil engineering, computer engineering, computer technology, electrical/electronics engineering, environmental science, and mechanical engineering), HEALTH PROFESSIONS (exercise science, health care administration, health science, nursing, pre-health studies, premedicine, and public health), SOCIAL SCIENCE (American studies, criminology, East Asian studies, economics, geography, history, humanities, interdisciplinary studies, international public service, international relations, ministries, philosophy, political science/government, prelaw, psychology, religion, religious music, social science, social work, sociology, and theological studies). Nursing, business, and engineering have the largest enrollments.

ACTIVITIES: 26% of men belong to 9 national fraternities; 26% of women belong to 6 national sororities. There are 100 groups on campus, including art, band, cheerleading, choir, chorale, chorus, dance, debate, drama, environmental, ethnic, film, honors, international, jazz band, LGBT, literary magazine, musical theater, newspaper, orchestra, pep band, photography, political, professional, religious, social, social service, student government, symphony, and yearbook. Popular campus events include Christmas Concert, Martin Luther King Day Celebration, and Jazz Festival. **Sports:** There are 9 intercollegiate sports for men and 10 for women, and 20 intramural sports for men and women. Facilities include an arena, swimming pool, a track and field facility, racquetball/handball courts, a fitness center, a football stadium, tennis complex, soccer, softball, baseball fields, and indoor batting facilities. **Graduates:** From July 1, 2016 to June 30, 2017, 902 bachelor's degrees were awarded. The most popular majors were nursing (14%), mechanical engineering (7%), and finance (5%). In an average class, 1% graduate in 3 years or less, 63% graduate in 4 years or less, 71% graduate in 5 years or less, and 72% graduate in 6 years or less. Of the 2016 graduating class, 18% were enrolled in graduate school within 6 months of graduation, and 78% were employed.

SERVICES: Counseling and information services are available, as is tutoring in most subjects. There is a reader service for the blind. The writing center provides assistance, and the Academic Success Center coordinates all academic support services and resources, including tutoring, advising, and support groups. **Library/Resources:** The library contains 673,544 volumes, 418,809 microform items, and 15,717 audio/video tapes/CDs/DVDs, and subscribes to 112,792 periodicals including electronic. Computerized library services include interlibrary loans, database searching, Internet access, and Wi-Fi capability. Special learning facilities include an art gallery, planetarium, radio station, TV station, observatory, weather station, center for visual and performing arts, virtual nursing learning center, solar energy research facility, and scientific visualization laboratory. **Physically Challenged Students:** 59% of the campus is accessible. Facilities include wheelchair ramps, elevators, special parking, specially equipped restrooms, lowered drinking fountains, and special housing. **Special:** There is cross-registration with Indiana University Northwest at the undergraduate level in geology. Off-campus study programs in the United States include a Washington semester programs, a Chicago urban semester, a Chicago arts semester, and a Chicago Business, Entrepreneurship, and Society program. Students may also study abroad in 26 countries including Greece, England, Spain, China, Japan, Namibia, France, Germany, Mexico, India, Thailand, Costa Rica, Chile, Israel, Ireland, Hungary, Nicaragua, Italy, New Zealand, Australia, Argentina, Czech Republic, Ecuador, Oman, Peru, and South Africa. Co-op programs, internships, the B.A.-B.S. degree, work-study programs, dual and student-designed majors, an accelerated degree program in numerous majors, pass/fail options, and non-degree study are also available. Other special academic features include Christ College, which is the honors college. There are 8 national honor societies, Phi Beta Kappa, a freshman honors program, and 27 departmental honors programs. **Visiting:** There are regularly scheduled orientations for prospective students, includes a campus tour conducted by a current student, an interview with a counselor, the option to meet with professors, attend a class, and meet with a coach. There are guides for informal visits; visitors may sit in on classes and stay overnight. To schedule a visit, contact the Office of Admission. **Campus Safety and Security:** Measures include 24-hour foot and vehicle patrol, emergency notification system, and security escort services. There are shuttle buses, emergency telephones, lighted pathways/sidewalks, and controlled access to dorms/residences.

REQUIREMENTS: The SAT or ACT is required. VU requires completion of 4 years of English, 3 to 4 years of math, 2 to 3 years of lab science, 2 years each of history and foreign language, and 3 years of additional academic courses. An application essay is required and an interview is recommended for all applicants; an audition is required for music majors. AP and CLEP credits are accepted. Important factors in the admissions decision are advanced placement or honors courses, extracurricular activities record, and evidence of special talent. General education requirements include the 10-credit Valpo core plus 2 courses in theology, courses in natural sciences, humanities, cultural diversity, and social sciences, 1 course in quantitative analysis, and 1 credit hour in physical education. Requirements may vary by degree program, particularly in the professional colleges. To graduate, students must complete at least 124 credit hours, including a minimum of 27 in the major, with a GPA of at least 2.0. **Procedure:** Freshmen are admitted fall, spring, and summer. Entrance exams should be taken prior to the senior year. There are deferred admissions and rolling admissions plans. Application deadlines are open. Notifications are sent October 1. Applications are accepted on-line. **Transfer Students:** 227 transfer students enrolled in 2016-2017. Applicants must submit official transcripts from all colleges attended. To be considered for admission, a minimum 2.0 cumulative GPA in college coursework is required for most programs. However, some programs require a minimum 3.0 GPA for transfer students. If the applicant has completed fewer than 24 credit hours, entrance exam scores and a high school transcript are required. A completed transfer evaluation form from the Dean of Students of the current institution must also be submitted. An interview is recommended. 30 of 124 credits required for the bachelor's degree must be completed at VU. **International Students:** There are 154 international students enrolled. They must take the TOEFL with a minimum score of 550 on the paper-based TOEFL (PBT) or 80 on the Internet-based version (iBT). Students must take any one of the IELTS, GCE, GCSE English Exam or IB Higher Level English Exam. They must also take the SAT or ACT.

ADMISSIONS: 30% of the current freshmen were in the top fifth of their class; 47% were in the top two fifths. 18 freshmen graduated first in their class. **Admissions Contact:** David Fevig, Assistant. Vice President, Enrollment. Email: *undergrad.admission@valpo.edu* Web: *www.valpo.edu*

FINANCIAL AID: In 2017-2018, 98% of all full-time freshmen received some form of financial aid. 82% of all full-time freshmen received need-based aid. The average freshman award was $32,327. Need-based scholarships or need-based grants averaged $28,268; need-based self-help aid (loans and jobs) averaged $4,059; non-need-based athletic scholarships averaged $12,646; and other non-need-based awards and non-need-based scholarships averaged $17,669. 38% of undergraduate students work part-time. The average financial indebtedness of the 2017 graduate was $36,815. VU is a member of CSS. The FAFSA code is 001842. The priority date for freshman financial aid applications for fall entry is March 1.

WABASH COLLEGE B-3
www.wabash.edu

Crawfordsville, IN 47933 (765) 361-6225 (800) 345-5385

Fax: (765) 361-6437 **Email: admissions@wabash.edu**

Full-time: 864 men	**Faculty:** 82; IIB, +$
Part-time: n/av	**Ph.D.s:** 100%
Graduate: n/av	**Student/Faculty:** 10 to 1
Year: semesters	**Tuition:** $42,250
Room & Board: $9850	**Freshman Class:** 1304 applied, 821 accepted, 232 enrolled
SAT CR/M/W: 585/598/557 **ACT:** 25	**CEEB CODE:** 1895
Application Deadline: January 15	**VERY COMPETITIVE**

Wabash College, founded in 1832, is a private liberal arts college that educates men to think critically, act responsibly, lead effectively, and live humanely. There is 1 undergraduate school. The 94-acre campus is in a small town 45 miles northwest of Indianapolis. Including any residence halls, there are 63 buildings.

STUDENT LIFE: 78% of undergraduates are from Indiana. Others are from 28 states, and 18 foreign countries. 88% are from public schools. 8% are Hispanic; 73% White; 7% Foreign; 6% African American; 3% two or more races; 2% race unknown; 1% Asian American. The student base is all male. The average age of freshmen is 19; all undergraduates, 20. 13% do not continue beyond their first year; 77% remain to graduate. **Housing:** 924 students can be accommodated in college housing, which includes dorms and on-campus apartments, and fraternity houses. On-campus housing is guaranteed for the freshman year only, ans is available on a first-come, first-served basis. 97% of students live on campus. All students may keep cars.

FACULTY/CLASSROOMS: 61% of faculty are male; 39% are female. All teach undergraduates, 83% do research, and 83% do both. No introductory courses are taught by graduate students.

PROGRAMS OF STUDY: WC confers A.B. degrees. Bachelor's degrees are awarded in BIOLOGICAL SCIENCE (biochemistry and biology/biological science), BUSINESS (finance), COMMUNICATIONS AND THE ARTS (art, classics, dramatic arts, English, French, German, Greek, Latin, music, Spanish, and speech/debate/rhetoric), COMPUTER AND PHYSICAL SCIENCE (chemistry, mathematics, and physics), SOCIAL SCIENCE (economics, Hispanic American studies, history, philosophy, political science/government, psychology, and religion). French, biochemistry, chemistry, math, and physics are the strongest academically. Economics, biology, and political science have the largest enrollments.

ACTIVITIES: 63% of men belong to 10 national fraternities. There are no sororities. There are 54 groups on campus, including art, band, chess, choir, chorale, chorus, communications, computers, dance, debate, drama, environmental, ethnic, film, forensics, honors, international, jazz band, LGBT, literary magazine, musical theater, newspaper, orchestra, pep band, photography, political, professional, radio and TV, religious, social, social service, student government, symphony, and yearbook. Popular campus events include Homecoming, Pan-Hel Weekend, Monon Bell, Scarlet Honors Weekend, National Act, Oktoberfest, and Chapel Sing. **Sports:** There are 12 intercollegiate sports for men, and 6 intramural sports for men. Facilities include a football stadium with FieldTurf Dura-spine Pro surface, indoor and outdoor tennis courts, baseball stadium, soccer stadium, natatorium, indoor track, all-weather outdoor track, wrestling practice facility, basketball arena, racquetball courts, aerobics room, and a wellness center. **Graduates:** From July 1, 2016 to June 30, 2017, 189 bachelor's degrees were awarded. The most popular majors were mathematics (15%), biology (10%), and political science (9%). In an average class, 69% graduate in 4 years or less and 77% graduate in 6 years or less. Of the 2016 graduating class, 24% were enrolled in graduate school within 6 months of graduation, and 52% were employed.

SERVICES: Counseling and information services are available, as is tutoring in some subjects, such as economics, math, physics, biology, chemistry, rhetoric, and Spanish. There is a reader service for the blind. There is also a quantitative skills center as well as a writing center where, under professional supervision, students help each other. **Library/Resources:** The library contains 199,887 volumes, 18,420 microform items, and 19,452 audio/video tapes/CDs/DVDs, and subscribes to 34,732 periodicals including electronic. Computerized library services include interlibrary loans, database searching, Internet access, and Wi-Fi capability. Special learning facilities include an art gallery, radio station, an archival center, the Wabash Center for the teaching of theology and religion, center of inquiry in the liberal arts, and two biological field stations. **Physically Challenged Students:** 60% of the campus is accessible. Facilities include wheelchair ramps, elevators, special parking, specially equipped restrooms, special class scheduling, lowered drinking fountains, special housing. There is also Braille signage in several buildings, a theater equipped for hearing-impared patrons, and some laboratory rooms with lowered work stations. **Special:** Wabash offers internships with off-campus organizations, study abroad in approximately 40 countries, a Washington semester with American University, dual majors, and a 3-2 engineering program with Purdue University, Columbia University and Washington University in St. Louis. Wabash also has a pipeline program that will guide students through the prerequisites for admission to the Master of Science in Accounting (MSA) degree program and give privileged access to Wabash students so that they may enroll at IU immediately upon graduation. Wabash has a new major in Financial Economics, and interdisciplinary minors in Hispanic Studies, Asian Studies, Multicultural American Studies, International Studies, and Gender Studies. There are 9 national honor societies and a chapter of Phi Beta Kappa. **Visiting:** There are regularly scheduled orientations for prospective students, consisting of a tour, an opportunity to meet faculty, coaches, and alumni, and panel discussions on academics, extracurricular activities, and financial aid. There are guides for informal visits, visitors may sit in on classes, and stay overnight. To schedule a visit, contact Mary Towell at (800) 345-5385. **Campus Safety and Security:** Measures include 24-hour foot and vehicle patrol, emergency notification system, and security escort services. There are lighted pathways/sidewalks and controlled access to dorms/residences.

REQUIREMENTS: The SAT or ACT is required. Wabash recommends applicants to have 4 high school courses in English, 3 in math (4 recommended), and 2 each in foreign language, lab science, and social studies. An essay is required, and an interview is recommended. AP credits are accepted. Important factors in the admissions decision are advanced placement or honors courses, leadership record, and extracurricular activities record. All students must complete at least 3 courses each in literature/fine arts, behavioral science, and natural science/math, 2 in history, philosophy, or religion, and 1 in quantitative skills. To graduate, students must maintain a minimum 2.0 GPA for 136 credit hours (34 courses), which include a freshman tutorial and the all-freshmen course Enduring Questions. The student must pass a written comprehensive exam in the major as well as a senior oral exam and must demonstrate proficiency in English and proficiency in a foreign language at a level equivalent to 2 college courses. **Procedure:** Freshmen are admitted in the fall and spring. Entrance exams should be taken by the spring of the junior year or fall of the senior year. There are early decision, early admissions, deferred admissions, and rolling admissions plans. Early decision applications should be filed by October 15; regular applications, by January 15 for fall entry. The fall 2017 application fee was $50. Notification of early decision is sent November 16; regular decision, on a rolling basis. 22 early decision candidates were accepted for the 2017-2018 class. 173 applicants were on the 2017 waiting list; 46 were admitted. Applications are accepted online. **Transfer Students:** 8 transfer students enrolled in 2016-2017. Applicants must submit official transcripts of all college courses attended. Wabash strongly considers the overall high school and college background of applicants. Courses must be liberal arts in nature with a minimum GPA of 2.0 to transfer. Recommendations from the college adviser and dean of students at the previous college attended and a personal written statement are required, with an interview strongly recommended. 24 of 34 credits required for the bachelor's degree must be completed at WC. **International Students:** There are 59 international students enrolled. They must take the TOEFL with a minimum score of 550 on the paper-based TOEFL (PBT) or 80 on the Internet-based version (iBT). They must also take the SAT or ACT.

ADMISSIONS: 63% of the 2017-2018 applicants were accepted. The SAT scores for the 2017-2018 freshman class were: Critical Reading-- 10% below 500, 45% between 500 and 599, 35% between 600 and 699, and 7% between 700 and 800. Math-- 6% below 500, 44% between 500 and 599, 37% between 600 and 699, and 13% between 700 and 800. Writing-- 39% below 500, 38% between 500 and 599, 21% between 600 and 699, and 2% between 700 and 800. The ACT scores were 3% between 12 and 17, 37% between 18 and 23, 45% between 24 and 29, and 15% above 30. 56% of the current freshmen were in the top fifth of their class; 85% were in the top two fifths. 4 freshmen graduated first in their class. **Admissions Contact:** Heidi Carl, and Chip Timmons, Associate Deans of Enrollment Management. Email: *admissions@wabash.edu* Web: *www.wabash.edu*

FINANCIAL AID: In 2017-2018, 99% of all full-time freshmen received some form of financial aid. 81% of all full-time freshmen received need-based aid. The average freshman award was $41,702. Need-based scholarships or need-based grants averaged $27,588; need-based self-help aid (loans and jobs) averaged $3,743; other non-need-based awards and non-need-based scholarships averaged $7,535; and $2,836 from other forms of aid. 44% of undergraduate students work part-time. The average financial indebtedness of the 2017 graduate was $35,726. The FAFSA code is 001844. The priority date for freshman financial aid applications for fall entry is January 15. The deadline for filing freshman financial aid applications for fall entry is March 1.

ALLEN COLLEGE *(The complete profile is made available exclusively on our website, www.barronspac.com)*

BRIAR CLIFF UNIVERSITY B-2

www.briarcliff.edu

Sioux City, IA 51104 **(712) 279-5200** **(800) 662-3303**

Fax: (712) 279-1632 **Email: admissions@briarcliff.edu**

Full-time: 355 men, 365 women
Part-time: 31 men, 194 women
Graduate: 86 men, 155 women
Year: trimesters, summer session
Room & Board: $8348

ACT: 21
Application Deadline: open

Faculty: 61
Ph.D.s: 75%
Student/Faculty: 13 to 1
Tuition: $28,608
Freshman Class: 1774 applied, 1035 accepted, 237 enrolled
CEEB CODE: 6046
COMPETITIVE

Briar Cliff University, founded in 1930, is a private Roman Catholic-Franciscan liberal arts institution. There are 2 undergraduate schools and 1 graduate school. In addition to regional accreditation, BCU has baccalaureate program accreditation with AACSB, CSWE, and NLN. The 70-acre campus is in a suburban area minutes from downtown Sioux City. Including any residence halls, there are 13 buildings.

STUDENT LIFE: 54% of undergraduates are from Iowa. Others are from 42 states, and 16 foreign countries. 65% are White; 2% Asian American; 15% Hispanic; 10% African American; 1% American Indian/ Alaska Native. 58% are Catholic; 26% claim no religious affiliation. **Female To Male Ratio:** 1.5:1. **Housing:** 577 students can be accommodated in college housing, which includes dorms and special-interest houses. On-campus housing is guaranteed for the freshman year only. All students may keep cars.

FACULTY/CLASSROOMS: 48% of faculty are male; 52% are female. All teach undergraduates. No introductory courses are taught by graduate students. The average class size in an introductory lecture is 20; in a laboratory is 18; and in a regular course is 20.

PROGRAMS OF STUDY: BCU confers B.A., B.S., B.S.N., and B.S.W. degrees. Associate and master's degrees are also awarded. Bachelor's degrees are awarded in BIOLOGICAL SCIENCE (biology/biological science), BUSINESS (accounting, business administration and management, and human resources), COMMUNICATIONS AND THE ARTS (art, communications, dramatic arts, English, graphic design, journalism, media arts, music, and Spanish), COMPUTER AND PHYSICAL SCIENCE (chemistry, computer science, information sciences and systems, mathematics, and radiological technology), EDUCATION (elementary education, health education, and secondary education), ENGINEERING AND ENVIRONMENTAL DESIGN (environmental science), HEALTH PROFESSIONS (medical technology, nursing, and sports medicine), SOCIAL SCIENCE (criminal justice, history, political science/government, psychology, social work, sociology, and theological studies). Biology, business administration, and education are the strongest academically. Nursing has the largest enrollment.

ACTIVITIES: BCU has no fraternities or sororities. There are 44 groups on campus, including art, cheerleading, choir, chorale, chorus, computers, dance, drama, ethnic, film, honors, jazz band, literary magazine, musical theater, newspaper, pep band, photography, professional, radio and TV, religious, social, social service, and student government. Popular campus events include Texas Hold 'em Tournaments, Welcome Week, and Theater Productions. **Sports:** **Graduates:** From July 1, 2016 to June 30, 2017, 204 bachelor's degrees were awarded. The most popular majors were business/ marketing (33%), health professions and related sciences (11%), and biological/ life sciences (8%). In an average class, 43% graduate in 4 years or less, 53% graduate in 5 years or less, and 55% graduate in 6 years or less. Of the 2016 graduating class, 37% were enrolled in graduate school within 6 months of graduation.

SERVICES: Counseling and information services are available, as is tutoring in most subjects. There is remedial math, reading, and writing. **Library/Resources:** The library contains 82,007 volumes, 21,664 microform items, and 1,244 audio/video tapes/CDs/DVDs. Computerized library services include interlibrary loans, database searching, Internet access, and Wi-Fi capability. Special learning facilities include an art gallery, radio station, TV station, an integrated multimedia center, a nursing simulation lab, a human anatomy/cadaver lab, and a entrepreneurship lab. **Physically Challenged Students:** Facilities include wheelchair ramps, elevators, special parking, specially equipped restrooms, lowered drinking fountains, and lowered telephones. **Special:** Internships, study abroad, dual majors, work-study programs, accelerated degree programs in business administration, human resource management, and professional studies, student-designed interdisciplinary majors, and pass/fail options are available. Students may earn a 3-2 engineering degree with Iowa State University. There are 4 national honor societies, a freshman honors program, and 3 departmental honors programs. **Visiting:** There are regularly scheduled orientations for prospective students, including a presidential welcome, a meeting with faculty and student panels, a luncheon, campus tours, a slide show, and financial aid information. There are guides for informal visits, visitors may sit in on classes, and stay overnight. To schedule a visit, contact the Admissions Office. **Campus Safety and Security:** Measures include 24-hour foot and vehicle patrol, emergency notification system, and security escort services. There are emergency telephones, lighted pathways/ sidewalks, and controlled access to dorms/residences.

REQUIREMENTS: The SAT is accepted, but the ACT is preferred, and a score of 18 qualifies for automatic acceptance review. Applicants need not be graduates of an accredited secondary school. The GED is accepted. Admission to freshman standing requires 4 years each of English and math, 3 of science, 2 of history, and 1 of social studies, and 2 years of foreign language is recommended. A GPA of 2.0 is required. AP and CLEP credits are accepted. Important factors in the admissions decision are leadership record, extracurricular activities record, and advanced placement or honors courses. To graduate, students must complete a minimum of 124 semester hours, maintain a GPA of 2.0 with no more than 1 D in the major, complete the three components of Briar Cliff's general educational program, and complete a major field of concentration. **Procedure:** Freshmen are admitted to all sessions. Entrance exams should be taken by October for scholarship consideration, and by April for admission. There is a rolling admissions plan. Application deadlines are open. The fall 2017 application fee was $20. Notification is sent on a rolling basis. Applications are accepted on-line. **Transfer Students:** 37 transfer students enrolled in 2016-2017. Applicants must have a minimum GPA of 2.0 with at least 10 credit hours earned and satisfactory dismissal from the previous institution. Grades of D or better transfer for credit. 31 of 124 credits required for the bachelor's degree must be completed at BCU. **International Students:** There are 6 international students enrolled. They must take the TOEFL or MELAB. Students may be required to have a telephone interview with an ESL advisor.

ADMISSIONS: 58% of the 2017-2018 applicants were accepted. The ACT scores were 40% below 12, 28% between 12 and 17, 20% between 18 and 23, 9% between 24 and 29, and 3% above 30. 25% of the current freshmen were in the top fifth of their class; 50% were in the top two fifths. 2 freshmen graduated first in their class. **Admissions Contact:** Adam Cory, Assistant Director of Admissions. Email: *admissions@briarcliff.edu* Web: *www.briarcliff.edu*

FINANCIAL AID: In 2017-2018, 100% of all full-time freshmen received some form of financial aid. 73% of all full-time freshmen received need-based aid. The average freshman award was $12,250. Need-based scholarships or need-based grants averaged $3,900; need-based self-help aid (loans and jobs) averaged $7,255; and non-need-based athletic scholarships averaged $5,109. 23% of undergraduate students work part-time. The average financial indebtedness of the 2017 graduate was $30,100. The FAFSA code is 001846. The priority date for freshman financial aid applications for fall entry is March 1.

BUENA VISTA UNIVERSITY B-2

www.bvu.edu

Storm Lake, IA 50588	(712) 749-2078 (800) 383-9600
Fax: (712) 749-2035	Email: admissions@bvu.edu
Full-time: 385 men, 399 women	Faculty: 82; IIB, av$
Part-time: 5 men, 6 women	Ph.D.s: 77%
Graduate: 5 men, 29 women	Student/Faculty: 10 to 1
Year: 4-1-4, summer session	Tuition: $32,210
Room & Board: $9304	Freshman Class: 1256 applied, 800 accepted, 183 enrolled
ACT: 22	CEEB CODE: 6047
Application Deadline: open	COMPETITIVE

Buena Vista University, founded in 1891, is a private institution affiliated with the Presbyterian Church. The university offers undergraduate degree programs in business, education, communication and arts, science, social science, philosophy, and religion, and an accredited master's program in education. Programs emphasize career education with a liberal arts foundation. There are 5 undergraduate schools and 1 graduate school. In addition to regional accreditation, BVU has baccalaureate program accreditation with CSWE and CAATE. The 60-acre campus is in a small town 65 miles east of Sioux City. Including any residence halls, there are 16 buildings.

STUDENT LIFE: 79% of undergraduates are from Iowa. Others are from 27 states, and 15 foreign countries. 90% are from public schools. 74% are White; 7% Hispanic; 6% Foreign; 4% two or more races; 4% race unknown; 3% African American; 2% Asian American. **Female To Male Ratio:** 1.1:1. The average age of freshmen is 18; all undergraduates, 20. 27% do not continue beyond their first year; 53% remain to graduate. **Housing:** 1012 students can be accommodated in college housing, which includes coed dorms, and special-interest houses. On-campus housing is guaranteed for all 4 years. 90% of students live on campus. All students may keep cars.

FACULTY/CLASSROOMS: 45% of faculty are male; 55% are female. All teach undergraduates. No introductory courses are taught by graduate students. The average class size in an introductory lecture is 25; in a laboratory is 20; and in a regular course is 14.

PROGRAMS OF STUDY: BVU confers B.A., B.S., B.A.S., and B.A.Sc. degrees. Master's degrees are also awarded. Bachelor's degrees are awarded in BIOLOGICAL SCIENCE (biochemistry and biology/biological science), BUSINESS (accounting, banking and finance, business administration and management, business economics, marketing/retailing/merchandising, and sports management), COMMUNICATIONS AND THE ARTS (animation, art, arts administration/management, communications, digital media, English, graphic design, music, music production/recording technology, Spanish, and theatre arts), COMPUTER AND PHYSICAL SCIENCE (chemistry, computer science, mathematics, physics, and science), EDUCATION (art education, athletic training, business education, elementary education, music education, science education, secondary education, and special education), ENGINEERING AND ENVIRONMENTAL DESIGN (environmental science), HEALTH PROFESSIONS (art therapy, biomedical science, and exercise science), SOCIAL SCIENCE (criminal justice, history, interdisciplinary studies, physical fitness/movement, political science/government, psychology, and social work). Biology, mathematics, and business are the strongest academically. Biology, education, and business have the largest enrollments.

ACTIVITIES: There are no fraternities or sororities. There are 60 groups on campus, including art, band, cheerleading, choir, chorale, chorus, communications, computers, dance, drama, drill team, environmental, ethnic, honors, international, jazz band, LGBT, musical theater, newspaper, photography, political, professional, radio and TV, religious, social, social service, and student government. Popular campus events include Academic and Cultural Events Series, Buenafication Day, American Heritage Lecture Series, Scholars Day, and the All-Campus Christmas Dinner. **Sports:** There are 9 intercollegiate sports for men and 8 for women, and 10 intramural sports for men and 10 for women. Facilities include a stadium, a field house with a gym, basketball, volleyball, racquetball, tennis courts, football, softball, baseball fields, a track, weight training, an indoor pool, and a game room. **Graduates:** From July 1, 2015 to June 30, 2016, 173 bachelor's degrees were awarded. The most popular majors were business (14%), biology (13%), and exercise science (8%).

SERVICES: Counseling and information services are available, as is tutoring in most subjects, a reader service for the blind, and remedial math, reading, and writing. **Library/Resources:** The library contains 5,000 volumes, 41,372 microform items, 6,000 audio/video tapes/CDs/DVDs, and subscribes to 639 periodicals including electronic. Computerized library services include interlibrary loans, database searching, Internet access, and Wi-Fi capability. Special learning facilities include an art gallery, radio station, TV station, a student newspaper desktop production lab. **Physically Challenged Students:** Facilities include wheelchair ramps, elevators, special parking, specially equipped restrooms, special class scheduling, lowered drinking fountains, and lowered telephones. **Special:** Special academic offerings include a 3-2 engineering degree program with Washington University School of Engineering and Applied Science in St. Louis. Buena Vista has also partnered with the University of Iowa College of Law and the Creighton University School of Law in a 3+3 Accelerated Law School Entry Program. Students may study abroad in Japan, Taiwan, Australia, and Europe. Buena Vista offers dual and student-designed majors, credit for life experience, and pass/fail options in courses outside the major field. Nondegree study is possible. Internships are required in many majors and encouraged in most. The J. Leslie Rollins Fellowship allows 1 or 2 students each year to design an internship anywhere in the world. There are 6 national honor societies and a freshman honors program. **Visiting:** There are regularly scheduled orientations for prospective students, campus tour and meetings with an admissions counselor, faculty representatives, coaches, and activity representatives in the student's areas of interest. There are guides for informal visits, visitors may sit in on classes, and stay overnight. To schedule a visit, contact Deb Willer at (712) 749-2078. **Campus Safety and Security:** Measures include 24-hour foot and vehicle patrol, emergency notification system, self-defense education, and security escort services. There are also shuttle buses, emergency telephones, lighted pathways/sidewalks, controlled access to dorms/residences, and an enhanced 911 system on campus.

REQUIREMENTS: The ACT is required. The SAT scores may be submitted. Applicants must be graduates of an accredited secondary school or have earned a GED. The college requires 13 academic credits, including 4 of English and 3 each of math, social studies, and science. Campus visits and an interview are recommended. AP and CLEP credits are accepted. Important factors in the admissions decision are advanced placement or honors courses, leadership record, and recommendations by school officials. All students must complete 12 semester hours of humanities, 9 semester hours each of natural sciences and social sciences, and 3 semester hours of fine arts. In addition, students must successfully complete requirements in intellectual foundation courses in mathematics and communication. Students must also participate in the Academic and Cultural Events Series, through which they attend lectures and performances by national and world leaders. The bachelor's degree requires a minimum of 128 semester hours, including 32 to 64 hours in the major, with a GPA of at least 2.0, or higher for some majors. **Procedure:** Freshmen are admitted in the fall, winter, and spring. Entrance exams should be taken during the spring of the junior year or October of the senior year. There are deferred admissions and rolling admissions plans. Application deadlines are open. Notification is sent on a rolling basis. Application fees are waived if application is completed on-line. **Transfer Students:** 33 transfer students enrolled in 2015-2016. A high school diploma and a minimum GPA of 2.5 from the applicant's college are required. 30 of 128 credits required for the bachelor's degree must be completed at BVU. **International Students:** There are 44 international students enrolled. The school actively recruits these students. They must take the TOEFL with a minimum score of 500 on the paper-based TOEFL (PBT) or 59 on the Internet-based version (iBT), and the college's own test.

ADMISSIONS: 64% of the 2016-2017 applicants were accepted. The

ACT scores were 12% between 12 and 17, 49% between 18 and 23, 34% between 24 and 29, and 5% above 30. 31% of the current freshmen were in the top fifth of their class; 63% were in the top two fifths. 7 freshmen graduated first in their class. **Admissions Contact:** Michael Fox, Director of Admissions. Email: *admissions@bvu.edu* Web: *www.bvu.edu*

FINANCIAL AID: In 2016-2017, 99% of all full-time freshmen and 98% of continuing full-time students received some form of financial aid. The college's own financial statement is required. The FAFSA code is 001847. The deadline for filing freshman financial aid applications for fall entry is June 1.

CENTRAL COLLEGE D-3

www.central.edu

Pella, IA 50219	(641) 628-7637 (877) 462-3687
Fax: (641) 628-5316	Email: admission@central.edu
Full-time: 580 men, 624 women	**Faculty:** 97; IIB, -$
Part-time: 13 men, 31 women	**Ph.D.s:** 94%
Graduate: n/av	**Student/Faculty:** 12 to 1
Year: semesters, summer session	**Tuition:** $34,612
Room & Board: $9980	**Freshman Class:** n/av
SAT M/W: required	**CEEB CODE:** 6087
Application Deadline: August 15	**COMPETITIVE**

Central College, founded in 1853, is a private, residential four-year liberal arts college known for its academic rigor and strength in global experiential learning, STEM (science, technology, engineering and math), sustainability education, athletics success and tradition, and leadership and service. Central continues to value its long-standing relationship with the Reformed Church in America. The college participates in NCAA Division III athletics and is a member of the Iowa Conference. There is 1 undergraduate school. In addition to regional accreditation, Central College has baccalaureate program accreditation with NASM, CAEP, ACS, and CAATE. The 169-acre campus is in a small town 45 miles southeast of Des Moines. Including any residence halls, there are 58 buildings.

STUDENT LIFE: 75% of undergraduates are from Iowa. Others are from 26 states, and 7 foreign countries. 95% are from public schools. 89% are White; 5% race unknown; 4% Hispanic; 2% African American; 2% Asian American; 2% two or more races; 1% Foreign. 62% are Protestant; 22% claim no religious affiliation; 16% Catholic. **Female To Male Ratio:** 1.1:1. The average age of freshmen is 18; all undergraduates, 20. 21% do not continue beyond their first year; 65% remain to graduate. **Housing:** 1405 students can be accommodated in college housing, which includes dorms and on-campus apartments. In addition, there are language/international houses, special-interest houses, fraternity houses, and sorority houses. On-campus housing is guaranteed for all 4 years. 94% of students live on campus. Alcohol is not permitted. All students may keep cars.

FACULTY/CLASSROOMS: 51% of faculty are male; 49% are female. All teach and do research. No introductory courses are taught by graduate students. The average class size in an introductory lecture is 19; in a laboratory is 19; and in a regular course is 16.

PROGRAMS OF STUDY: Central confers B.A. and B.S. degrees. Bachelor's degrees are awarded in BIOLOGICAL SCIENCE (biochemistry and biology/biological science), BUSINESS (accounting and business administration and management), COMMUNICATIONS AND THE ARTS (art, communications, dramatic arts, English, French, German, linguistics, music, Spanish, and theatre arts), COMPUTER AND PHYSICAL SCIENCE (actuarial science, chemistry, computer science, mathematics, natural sciences, and physics), EDUCATION (athletic training, elementary education, and music education), ENGINEERING AND ENVIRONMENTAL DESIGN (engineering and environmental science), HEALTH PROFESSIONS (exercise science), SOCIAL SCIENCE (anthropology, economics, history, international studies, philosophy, political science/government, psychology, religion, and sociology). Exercise science, business management, and biology have the largest enrollments.

ACTIVITIES: 4% of men belong to 5 local fraternities; 3% of women belong to 2 local sororities. There are 100 groups on campus, including art, band, cheerleading, choir, chorale, chorus, communications, dance, drama, entrepreneurship, environmental, ethnic, honors, international, jazz band, LGBT, literary magazine, mock trial, musical theater, orchestra, pep band, political, professional, religious, social, social service, student government, and sustainability. Popular campus events include Lemming Race, Breakfast of Champions, Candlelight Christmas Concert, and Charity Ball. **Sports:** There are 9 intercollegiate sports for men and 9 for women, and 8 intramural sports for men and 8 for women. Facilities include a field house with a gym, indoor track, tennis, a fitness center for strength/conditioning, football/track stadium, competition and practice soccer fields, golf practice facility, cross country course, baseball and softball fields, and a fitness center. **Graduates:** From July 1, 2016 to June 30, 2017, 280 bachelor's degrees were awarded. The most popular majors were biology (11%), elementary education (11%), and business management (10%). In an average class, 58% graduate in 4 years or less, 64% graduate in 5 years or less, and 65% graduate in 6 years or less. Of the 2016 graduating class, 20% were enrolled in graduate school within 6 months of graduation, and 75% were employed.

SERVICES: Counseling and information services are available, as is tutoring in every subject. **Library/Resources:** The library contains 150,877 volumes, 2,085 microform items, and 4,143 audio/video tapes/CDs/DVDs, and subscribes to 204 periodicals including electronic. Computerized library services include interlibrary loans, database searching, Internet access, and Wi-Fi capability. Special learning facilities include an art gallery. **Physically Challenged Students:** 90% of the campus is accessible. Facilities include wheelchair ramps, elevators, special parking, specially equipped restrooms, special class scheduling, lowered drinking fountains, lowered telephones, and special housing. **Special:** Central College offers a B.S. in engineering degree and a partnership program with Allen College whereby students receive a B.A. from Central and a BSN from Allen College. About 50% of Central students participate in study abroad in Vienna, London, Granada, Merida, Bangor, and Budapest. 76% of students complete at least one internship, including the Washington semester and the Chicago semester as well as opportunities abroad. 30% of students participate in music ensembles. There is a freshman honors program and 10 departmental honors programs. **Visiting:** There are regularly scheduled orientations for prospective students, consisting of registration session with academic advisor, and presentations by the academic dean, student life dean, financial aid director, registrar and admission staff. There are guides for informal visits, visitors may sit in on classes, and stay overnight. To schedule a visit, contact Sue Cerwinske in Admissions. **Campus Safety and Security:** Measures include 24-hour foot and vehicle patrol, emergency notification system, self-defense education, and security escort services. There are emergency telephones, lighted pathways/sidewalks, and controlled access to dorms/residences.

REQUIREMENTS: The ACT is required. All applicants must be graduates of an accredited secondary school or have earned a GED. Candidates who have an ACT composite score of 20 or above (940-970 SAT critical reading and mathematics combined), have a 2.70 cumulative high school GPA, rank in the top half of their secondary school graduating class and have met the recommended college-preparatory curriculum are typically admitted. Central College requires applicants to be in the upper 50% of their class. A GPA of 2.7 is required. AP and CLEP credits are accepted. Important factors in the admissions decision are advanced placement or honors courses, extracurricular activities record, and leadership record. Students are required to complete 120 semester hours, including at least 20 hours of 300-level or above, with a minimum 2.0 cumulative and major GPA. Core requirements include courses in integrative studies, disciplinary studies, global sustainability, global perspective, and writing intensive. **Procedure:** Freshmen are admitted fall, spring, and summer. Entrance exams should be taken Spring junior year of high school. There are deferred admissions and rolling admissions plans. Applications should be filed by August 15 for fall entry; January 1 for spring entry; and May 1 for summer entry. The fall 2017 application fee was $25. Notification is sent on a rolling basis. Applications are accepted on-line. **Transfer Students:** 31 transfer students enrolled in 2016-2017. Each transfer student is considered individually. Interviews are encouraged. 45 of 120 credits required for the bachelor's degree must be completed at Central College. **International Students:** There are 10 international students enrolled. They must take the TOEFL with a minimum score of 530 on the paper-based TOEFL (PBT) or 71 on the Internet-based version (iBT). They must also take the SAT or ACT.

ADMISSIONS: 17% of the current freshmen were in the top fifth of their class; 80% were in the top two fifths. **Admissions Contact:** Chevy Frieburger, Director of Admission. Email: *admission@central.edu* Web: *www.central.edu*

FINANCIAL AID: In 2017-2018, 100% of all full-time freshmen

received some form of financial aid. 86% of all full-time freshmen received need-based aid. The average freshman award was $32,165. Need-based scholarships or need-based grants averaged $21,485 ($34,612 maximum); need-based self-help aid (loans and jobs) averaged $3,144 ($7,500 maximum); other non-need-based awards and non-need-based scholarships averaged $4,787 ($34,612 maximum); and $2,749 from other forms of aid. 57% of undergraduate students work part-time. The average financial indebtedness of the 2017 graduate was $29,590. Central is a member of CSS. The FAFSA code is 001850. The priority date for freshman financial aid applications for fall entry is January 15.

CLARKE UNIVERSITY — E-2
www.clarke.edu

Dubuque, IA 52001	**(563) 588-6436** **(800) 383-2345**
Fax: (563) 588-6789	**Email: admissions@clarke.edu**
Full-time: 253 men, 455 women	**Faculty:** 83; IIB, --$
Part-time: 23 men, 36 women	**Ph.D.s:** 84%
Graduate: 62 men, 209 women	**Student/Faculty:** 10 to 1
Year: semesters, summer session	**Tuition:** $31,950
Room & Board: $9400	**Freshman Class:** 1149 applied, 728 accepted, 162 enrolled
SAT CR/M: 507/520 **ACT:** 23	**CEEB CODE:** 6099
Application Deadline: open	**COMPETITIVE**

Clarke University, established in 1843, is a private Catholic institution where strong liberal arts core is integrated into all majors and preprofessional programs. There is 1 undergraduate school and 1 graduate school. In addition to regional accreditation, CU has baccalaureate program accreditation with APTA, CSWE, NASM, NCATE, NLN, CAPTE, COSW, CCNE, CAATE, and the Iowa Department of Education. The 55-acre campus is in a small town 150 miles west of Chicago. Including any residence halls, there are 14 buildings.

STUDENT LIFE: 63% of undergraduates are from Iowa. Others are from 32 states, 8 foreign countries, and Canada. 80% are from public schools. 80% are White; 7% Hispanic; 6% African American; 2% two or more races; 1% Asian American; 1% American Indian/Alaska Native; 1% Foreign; 1% race unknown. 59% claim no religious affiliation; 25% Catholic; 15% Protestant. **Female To Male Ratio:** 2.1:1. The average age of freshmen is 18; all undergraduates, 21. 25% do not continue beyond their first year; 63% remain to graduate. **Housing:** 572 students can be accommodated in college housing, which includes dorms and on-campus apartments. In addition, there are honors houses, a residence hall reserved for upperclassmen, and an apartment residence building reserved for juniors and seniors. On-campus housing is guaranteed for all 4 years. 62% of students live on campus. All students may keep cars.

FACULTY/CLASSROOMS: 33% of faculty are male; 67% are female. 91% teach undergraduates, and all do research. No introductory courses are taught by graduate students. The average class size in an introductory lecture is 24; in a laboratory is 11; and in a regular course is 14.

PROGRAMS OF STUDY: CU confers B.A., B.S., B.A.S., B.F.A., B.S.W., and B.S.N. degrees. Associate, master's, and doctoral degrees are also awarded. Bachelor's degrees are awarded in AGRICULTURE (environmental studies), BIOLOGICAL SCIENCE (biochemistry and biology/biological science), BUSINESS (accounting, business administration and management, and sports management), COMMUNICATIONS AND THE ARTS (art history and appreciation, communications, dramatic arts, English, graphic design, musical theater, Spanish, and studio art), COMPUTER AND PHYSICAL SCIENCE (chemistry, computer information systems, computer science, and mathematics), EDUCATION (art education, athletic training, elementary education, music education, secondary education, and special education), ENGINEERING AND ENVIRONMENTAL DESIGN (environmental science), HEALTH PROFESSIONS (nursing and physical therapy), SOCIAL SCIENCE (food science, history, liberal arts/general studies, philosophy, psychology, religion, and social work). Physical therapy, biology, and chemistry are the strongest academically. Business administration, nursing, and psychology have the largest enrollments.

ACTIVITIES: There are no fraternities or sororities. There are 26 groups on campus, including art, cheerleading, choir, chorale, chorus, computers, dance, drama, environmental, ethnic, honors, international, jazz band, LGBT, literary magazine, musical theater, newspaper, pep band, photography, political, professional, religious, social, social service, and student government. Popular campus events include Family Weekend, New Year's Dance, Homecoming Activities, Christmas Dinner, and Midnight Pancake Breakfast. **Sports:** There are 10 intercollegiate sports for men and 10 for women, and 7 intramural sports for men and 7 for women. Facilities include a gym, an arena, indoor track, a soccer field, basketball, volleyball, tennis, and racquetball courts, a fitness trail, weight and aerobics rooms, indoor batting cage/pitching mound area, baseball/softball fields, a municipal golf course. **Graduates:** From July 1, 2016 to June 30, 2017, 203 bachelor's degrees were awarded. The most popular majors were nursing (30%), philosophy (14%), and education (9%). In an average class, 49% graduate in 4 years or less, 66% graduate in 5 years or less, and 68% graduate in 6 years or less. Of the 2016 graduating class, 31% were enrolled in graduate school within 6 months of graduation, and 69% were employed.

SERVICES: Counseling and information services are available, as is tutoring in most subjects. There is a reader service for the blind, and remedial math, reading, and writing. **Library/Resources:** The library contains 76,525 volumes, 6,700 microform items, 1,570 audio/video tapes/CDs/DVDs, and subscribes to 104,625 periodicals, including electronic. Computerized library services include interlibrary loans, database searching, Internet access, and Wi-Fi capability. Special learning facilities include an art gallery, planetarium, an art slide library, electronic music studio, and several computer-integrated specialized departmental labs. **Physically Challenged Students:** 90% of the campus is accessible. Facilities include wheelchair ramps, elevators, special parking, specially equipped restrooms, special class scheduling, lowered drinking fountains, and lowered telephones. **Special:** There are 4 national honor societies, a freshman honors program, and 3 departmental honors programs. **Visiting:** There are regularly scheduled orientations for prospective students, including admissions presentation and tour, and faculty appointments. There are guides for informal visits, visitors may sit in on classes, and stay overnight. To schedule a visit, contact Julie Cirks at julie.cirks@clarke.edu. **Campus Safety and Security:** Measures include 24-hour foot and vehicle patrol, emergency notification system, and security escort services. There are emergency telephones, lighted pathways/sidewalks, and controlled access to dorms/residences.

REQUIREMENTS: The SAT or ACT is required. The high school transcript should include 4 years of English, 3 each of math, history/social science, and science (4 for human biology and physical therapy majors), 2 of the same foreign language, and 5 of electives. A GPA of 2.0 is required. AP and CLEP credits are accepted. To graduate, all students must complete 124 semester hours, with 30 to 70 in the major, and maintain a GPA of 2.0 (2.5 for education majors or 3.25 for physical therapy majors). Students must complete Cornerstone I and II, a Capstone course, and 6 hours each in religious studies, philosophy, fine arts, humanities, math, and natural sciences, and social sciences **Procedure:** Freshmen are admitted to all sessions. Entrance exams should be taken in the spring of the junior year or the fall of the senior year. There are deferred admissions and rolling admissions plans. Application deadlines are open. The fall 2017 application fee was $25. Applications are accepted on-line. **Transfer Students:** 65 transfer students enrolled in 2016-2017. Applicants must submit a transcript and a recommendation from the dean of students for each college attended. Students with fewer than 24 completed semester hours must also submit a high school transcript and SAT or ACT scores. 30 of 124 credits required for the bachelor's degree must be completed at CU. **International Students:** There are 7 international students enrolled. They must take the TOEFL with a minimum score of 527 on the paper-based TOEFL (PBT) or 71 on the Internet-based version (iBT). They must also take the SAT or ACT.

ADMISSIONS: 72% of the 2017-2018 applicants were accepted. The SAT scores for the 2017-2018 freshman class were: Critical Reading-- 43% below 500, 43% between 500 and 599, and 14% between 600 and 699. Math-- 48% below 500, 33% between 500 and 599, 14% between 600 and 699, and 5% between 700 and 800. The ACT scores were 4% between 12 and 17, 56% between 18 and 23, 37% between 24 and 29, and 3% above 30. 40% of the current freshmen were in the top fifth of their class; 70% were in the top two fifths. **Admissions Contact:** Julie Cirks, Associate Director of Admissions. Email: *admissions@clarke.edu* Web: *www.clarke.edu*

FINANCIAL AID: In 2017-2018, 100% of all full-time freshmen received some form of financial aid. 87% of all full-time freshmen received need-based aid. The average freshman award was $27,301.

Need-based scholarships or need-based grants averaged $6,157; need-based self-help aid (loans and jobs) averaged $3,648; non-need-based athletic scholarships averaged $2,513; and other non-need-based awards and non-need-based scholarships averaged $12,582. 35% of undergraduate students work part-time. The average financial indebtedness of the 2017 graduate was $30,594. The FAFSA code is 001852. The priority date for freshman financial aid applications for fall entry is April 15. The deadline for filing freshman financial aid applications for fall entry is rolling.

COE COLLEGE E-3

www.coe.edu

Cedar Rapids, IA 52402	**(319) 399-8046** **(877) CALL-COE**
Fax: (319) 399-8816	**Email: admission@coe.edu**
Full-time: 563 men, 780 women	**Faculty:** 96; IIB, -$
Part-time: 39 men, 26 women	**Ph.D.s:** 91%
Graduate: n/av	**Student/Faculty:** 8 to 1
Year: semesters, summer session	**Tuition:** $42,430
Room & Board: $9140	**Freshman Class:** 6173 applied, 3249 accepted, 362 enrolled
SAT CR/M/W: 580/570/545 **ACT:** 25	**CEEB CODE:** 6101
Application Deadline: March 1	**VERY COMPETITIVE**

Coe College, founded in 1851, offers superb academics and exciting social opportunities in a thriving urban setting that allows students to grow and succeed. There is 1 undergraduate school. In addition to regional accreditation, CC has baccalaureate program accreditation with NASM, CAAHEP, CCNE, CAATE, and ACS. The 53-acre campus is in the heart of the Cedar Rapids community, 225 miles west of Chicago. Including any residence halls, there are 32 buildings.

STUDENT LIFE: 55% of undergraduates are from out of state, mostly the Midwest. Students are from 38 states, 18 foreign countries, and Canada. 9% are Hispanic; 70% White; 6% African American; 6% Foreign; 4% race unknown; 3% two or more races; 2% Asian American. **Female To Male Ratio:** 1.3:1. The average age of freshmen is 18; all undergraduates, 20. 25% do not continue beyond their first year; 67% remain to graduate. **Housing:** 1150 students can be accommodated in college housing, which includes dorms and on-campus apartments. In addition, there are honors houses, special-interest houses, and a living-learning community. On-campus housing is guaranteed for all 4 years. 86% of students live on campus. All students may keep cars.

FACULTY/CLASSROOMS: 48% of faculty are male; 50% are female. All teach undergraduates, and 95% do research. No introductory courses are taught by graduate students. The average class size in an introductory lecture is 17; in a laboratory is 12; and in a regular course is 11.

PROGRAMS OF STUDY: CC confers B.A., B.M., and B.S.N. degrees. Bachelor's degrees are awarded in AGRICULTURE (environmental studies), BIOLOGICAL SCIENCE (biochemistry, biology/biological science, molecular biology, and neurosciences), BUSINESS (accounting, business administration and management, and organizational behavior), COMMUNICATIONS AND THE ARTS (art, art history and appreciation, communications, creative writing, English, film arts, French, German, literature, music, public relations, Spanish, theatre arts, and writing), COMPUTER AND PHYSICAL SCIENCE (chemistry, computer science, mathematics, physics, and science), EDUCATION (athletic training, elementary education, music education, physical education, and secondary education), ENGINEERING AND ENVIRONMENTAL DESIGN (environmental science and preengineering), HEALTH PROFESSIONS (nursing, physical therapy, predentistry, premedicine, prephysical therapy, and preveterinary science), SOCIAL SCIENCE (African American studies, American studies, Asian/Oriental studies, economics, French studies, gender studies, German area studies, history, industrial and organizational psychology, interdisciplinary studies, philosophy, political science/government, prelaw, psychology, religion, sociology, Spanish studies, and women's studies). Biology, physics, and psychology are the strongest academically. Business administration, psychology, and biology have the largest enrollments.

ACTIVITIES: 24% of men belong to 5 national fraternities; 26% of women belong to 3 national sororities. There are 80 groups on campus, including art, band, cheerleading, choir, chorale, chorus, communications, computers, dance, drama, environmental, ethnic, film, honors, international, jazz band, LGBT, literary magazine, musical theater, newspaper, orchestra, pep band, photography, political, professional, radio and TV, religious, social, social service, student government, and symphony. Popular campus events include Coe Olympics, International Student Banquet and Cultural Show, Flunk Day, and Prez Ball. **Sports:** There are 11 intercollegiate sports for men and 10 for women, and 8 intramural sports for men and 6 for women. Facilities include indoor and outdoor tennis courts, racquetball courts, squash courts, indoor track and a field house with natatorium, wrestling, a fitness center, a rock-climbing wall, courts for basketball and volleyball, and batting cages for baseball and softball, outdoor track, softball diamond, and football/soccer field. **Graduates:** From July 1, 2016 to June 30, 2017, 286 bachelor's degrees were awarded. The most popular majors were business administration (18%), psychology (16%), and physical education (8%). In an average class, 60% graduate in 4 years or less, 66% graduate in 5 years or less, and 67% graduate in 6 years or less.

SERVICES: Counseling and information services are available, as is tutoring in most subjects, such as sciences, math, business, and foreign languages. There is a reader service for the blind, and remedial math, reading, and writing. A writing center, speaking center, and an academic achievement program are available. **Library/Resources:** The library contains 550,116 volumes, 5,979 microform items, and 12,664 audio/video tapes/CDs/DVDs, and subscribes to 4,031 periodicals including electronic. Computerized library services include interlibrary loans, database searching, Internet access, and Wi-Fi capability. Special learning facilities include an art gallery, radio station, an ornithological wing. **Physically Challenged Students:** 80% of the campus is accessible. Facilities include wheelchair ramps, elevators, special parking, specially equipped restrooms, special class scheduling, lowered drinking fountains, lowered telephones, and special housing. **Special:** Coe offers cross-registration with nearby Mount Mercy University and the University of Iowa. 31 Off-campus programs are offered; 8 domestic and 23 international in 19 countries. Nondegree study, dual majors and student-designed majors also are possible. Practicum experience is required for graduation. Core course instructors serve as students' academic advisors. There are 8 national honor societies, Phi Beta Kappa, and a freshman honors program. **Visiting:** There are regularly scheduled orientations for prospective students, consisting of tours, a luncheon, and informational sessions on admission, financial aid, and student life. There are guides for informal visits, visitors may sit in on classes, and stay overnight. To schedule a visit, contact Larimer Porter or Maggie St. Clair at (319) 399-8500. **Campus Safety and Security:** Measures include 24-hour foot and vehicle patrol, emergency notification system, and security escort services. There are emergency telephones, lighted pathways/sidewalks, and controlled access to dorms/residences.

REQUIREMENTS: The SAT or ACT is required. Coe recommends that applicants have 4 years in English, 3 each in math, history, science, and social studies, and 2 in foreign language. All students must submit an essay. The GED is accepted. A GPA of 3.0 is required. AP credits are accepted. Important factors in the admissions decision are advanced placement or honors courses, recommendations by school officials, and extracurricular activities record. All students must take 5 writing-emphasis courses, a first-year seminar, and a distribution of courses in fine arts, humanities, natural sciences and mathematics, social sciences, and diverse cultural perspectives. A minimum of 32 course credits, including 9 to 12 in the major, and a 2.0 GPA are required for graduation. All students are required to do a practicum experience including an internship, independent research project, or off-campus study program. Students in the honors program must submit a thesis. **Procedure:** Freshmen are admitted fall and spring. Entrance exams should be taken in the spring of the junior year or the fall of the senior year. There are deferred admissions and rolling admissions plans. Applications should be filed by March 1 for fall entry. The fall 2017 application fee was $30. Notification is sent on a rolling basis. Applications are accepted on-line. **Transfer Students:** 42 transfer students enrolled in 2016-2017. Applicants must be high school graduates, have a minimum GPA of 2.5, and submit either SAT or ACT scores. An associate degree and an interview also are recommended. 8 of 32 credits required for the bachelor's degree must be completed at CC. **International Students:** There are 79 international students enrolled. They must take the TOEFL with a minimum score of 520 on the paper-based TOEFL (PBT) or 68 on the Internet-based version (iBT). Student must take the IELTS. They must also take the SAT or ACT.

ADMISSIONS: 53% of the 2017-2018 applicants were accepted. The

SAT scores for the 2017-2018 freshman class were: Critical Reading-- 13% below 500, 48% between 500 and 599, 23% between 600 and 699, and 16% between 700 and 800. Math-- 16% below 500, 42% between 500 and 599, 29% between 600 and 699, and 13% between 700 and 800. Writing-- 40% below 500, 25% between 500 and 599, 30% between 600 and 699, and 5% between 700 and 800. The ACT scores were 1% between 12 and 17, 37% between 18 and 23, 46% between 24 and 29, and 16% above 30. 53% of the current freshmen were in the top fifth of their class; 79% were in the top two fifths. 9 freshmen graduated first in their class. **Admissions Contact:** Julie Staker, Dean of Admission. Email: *admission@coe.edu* Web: *www.coe.edu*

FINANCIAL AID: In 2017-2018, 99% of all full-time freshmen received some form of financial aid. 87% of all full-time freshmen received need-based aid. The average freshman award was $38,065. Need-based scholarships or need-based grants averaged $8,650 ($31,000 maximum); need-based self-help aid (loans and jobs) averaged $6,950 ($8,800 maximum); and other non-need-based awards and non-need-based scholarships averaged $26,200 ($40,670 maximum). 51% of undergraduate students work part-time. The average financial indebtedness of the 2017 graduate was $35,782. The FAFSA code is 001854. The priority date for freshman financial aid applications for fall entry is March 1.

CORNELL COLLEGE — E-4

www.cornellcollege.edu

Mount Vernon, IA 52314 — **(319) 895-4215**, **(800) 747-1112**

Fax: (319) 895-4451 — **Email: admission@cornellcollege.edu**

Full-time: 507 men, 493 women	**Faculty:** 78; IIB, -$
Part-time: 3 men, 3 women	**Ph.D.s:** 98%
Graduate: 3 men	**Student/Faculty:** 11 to 1
Year: other	**Tuition:** $40,880
Room & Board: $9110	**Freshman Class:** 2276 applied, 1480 accepted, 300 enrolled
SAT EBR-W/M: 610/610 **ACT:** 26	**CEEB CODE:** 6119
Application Deadline: March 1	**VERY COMPETITIVE**

Cornell College, founded in 1853, is a private college affiliated with the United Methodist Church, that emphases the liberal arts and on student service, and leadership. Cornell has a one-course-at-a-time calendar in which the year is divided into eight 3 1/2 week terms. There is 1 undergraduate school. In addition to regional accreditation, Cornell has baccalaureate program accreditation with ACS. The 130-acre campus is in a small town 15 miles east of Cedar Rapids and 3 hours west of Chicago. Including any residence halls, there are 61 buildings.

STUDENT LIFE: 79% of undergraduates are from out of state, mostly the Midwest. Students are from 44 states, and 18 foreign countries. 70% are White; 9% Hispanic; 6% African American; 5% Foreign; 4% race unknown; 3% Asian American; 2% two or more races; 1% American Indian/Alaska Native. **Male To Female Ratio:** 1.0:1. The average age of freshmen is 18; all undergraduates, 20. 19% do not continue beyond their first year; 90% remain to graduate. **Housing:** 1060 students can be accommodated in college housing, which includes gender neutral, single sex, coed dorms and on-campus apartments. In addition, there are special-interest houses, and living learning communities. On-campus housing is guaranteed for all 4 years, and is available on a first-come, first-served basis, and is available on a lottery system for upperclassmen. 88% of students live on campus. All students may keep cars.

FACULTY/CLASSROOMS: 45% of faculty are male; 55% are female. All teach undergraduates and 50% do research. No introductory courses are taught by graduate students. The average class size in an introductory lecture is 18; in a laboratory is 18; and in a regular course is 16.

PROGRAMS OF STUDY: Cornell confers B.A., B.Mus., B.S. in Engineering, B.F.A, and B.S.S. degrees. Bachelor's degrees are awarded in BIOLOGICAL SCIENCE (biochemistry and biology/biological science), BUSINESS (business economics, business intelligence and analytics, business systems analysis, and management), COMMUNICATIONS AND THE ARTS (art history and appreciation, English, English literature, English writing, French, German, music, Russian, Spanish, studio art, and theatre studies), COMPUTER AND PHYSICAL SCIENCE (chemistry, computer science, geology, mathematics, and physics), EDUCATION (elementary education, foreign languages education, music education, and secondary education), ENGINEERING AND ENVIRONMENTAL DESIGN (engineering, engineering science, and environmental science), SOCIAL SCIENCE (classical/ancient civilization, economics, ethnic studies, gender studies, history, international relations, Latin American studies, philosophy, political science/government, psychology, religion, Russian and Slavic studies, sociology, and women & gender studies). Biochemistry and molecular biology, psychology, and economics and business are the strongest academically. Biochemistry and molecular biology, kinesiology, and economics and business have the largest enrollments.

ACTIVITIES: 21% of men belong to 8 local fraternities; 39% of women belong to 8 local sororities. There are 78 groups on campus, including art, band, cheerleading, chess, choir, chorale, chorus, communications, computers, dance, debate, drama, environmental, ethnic, honors, international, jazz band, leadership development, LGBT, literary magazine, mock trial, musical theater, newspaper, opera, orchestra, photography, political, professional, radio and TV, religious, social, social service, steel drum band, student government, and yearbook. Popular campus events include Music Mondays. **Sports:** There are 10 intercollegiate sports for men and 9 for women, and 15 intramural sports for men and 15 for women. Facilities include a multisport center for basketball and volleyball, a sports fitness and training facilities, indoor track, a wrestling room, multipurpose courts for tennis, basketball, and volleyball, batting cages, golf hitting nets, a football and track stadium, baseball, soccer, softball, and football practice fields, outdoor tennis courts, and ultimate frisbee. **Graduates:** From July 1, 2016 to June 30, 2017, 213 bachelor's degrees were awarded. The most popular majors were economics and business (10%), psychology (10%), and kinesiology (8%). In an average class, 63% graduate in 4 years or less, 80% graduate in 5 years or less, and 71% graduate in 6 years or less. Of the 2016 graduating class, 16% were enrolled in graduate school within 6 months of graduation, and 77% were employed.

SERVICES: Counseling and information services are available, as is tutoring in most subjects. There is a Quantitative Reasoning Studio, and a Center for Teaching and Learning for writing, research, academic technology, and careers. **Library/Resources:** The library contains 232,914 volumes, 69,348 microform items, 9,467 audio/video tapes/CDs/DVDs, and subscribes to 491 periodicals including electronic. Computerized library services include interlibrary loans, database searching, Internet access, and Wi-Fi capability. Special learning facilities include an art gallery, natural history museum, and radio station. **Physically Challenged Students:** 25% of the campus is accessible. Facilities include wheelchair ramps, elevators, special parking, specially equipped restrooms, special class scheduling, lowered drinking fountains, lowered telephones, and special housing. **Special:** Special academic programs include study abroad in 25 to 30 countries, internships including a Washington semester, student-designed majors, and interdisciplinary majors. Degree programs in combination with professional schools in environmental management, forestry, law, medical technology, and dentistry. Preprofessional advising programs in architecture, education, engineering, law, medicine, physical therapy, social work/human services, and theology. There are 16 national honor societies, Phi Beta Kappa, and 22 departmental honors programs. **Visiting:** There are regularly scheduled orientations for prospective students, including campus tours and meetings with an informational panel, a student panel, financial aid staff, and faculty and coaches as requested. There are guides for informal visits, visitors may sit in on classes, and stay overnight. To schedule a visit, contact Danielle Grimm at (800) 747-1112. **Campus Safety and Security:** Measures include 24-hour foot and vehicle patrol, emergency notification system, self-defense education, and security escort services. There are emergency telephones, lighted pathways/sidewalks, and controlled access to dorms/residences.

REQUIREMENTS: Applicants are required to submit a ACT, SAT or personal portfolio with responses to two short answer questions. Applicants should be graduates of an accredited secondary school, with a recommended 4 years each of English, 3 or more years of math and science, and social studies, 2 or more years of a foreign language. An essay and a secondary school report are required, and an interview is advised. The GED is accepted. AP credits are accepted. Important factors in the admissions decision are advanced placement or honors courses, evidence of special talent, and leadership record. Students choosing the BA degree must complete 31 course credits (124 semester hours), with at least a 2.0 cumulative GPA. B.A. candidates must complete the requirements of a faculty approved major usually 8 to 15 courses in the major and distribution requirements including: a first year seminar, a first year writing course, 2 courses in humanities, 1 course each in the natural sciences, social sciences, fine arts and math, and 1 to 4 courses in a foreign language. **Procedure:** Freshmen are admitted in the fall. There are early decision, early admissions, and deferred admissions plans. Early decision applications should be filed by November 1; regular applications, by March 1 for fall entry. Notification of early decision is sent December 15; regular decision, April 1. 27 early decision candidates were accepted for the 2017-2018 class. Applications are accepted on-line. **Transfer Students:** 35 transfer students enrolled in 2016-2017. Applicants must provide all items required of traditional students; in addition, they must submit official college transcripts from all other institutions they have attended. 15 of 31 credits required for the bachelor's degree must be completed at Cornell. **International Students:** There are 48 international students enrolled. They must take the TOEFL with a minimum score of 550 on the paper-based TOEFL (PBT) or 79 on the Internet-based version (iBT). Students must take either the IELTS, STEP, SAT or ACT.

ADMISSIONS: 65% of the 2017-2018 applicants were accepted. The SAT scores for the 2017-2018 freshman class were: Math-- 7% below 500, 43% between 500 and 599, 34% between 600 and 699, and 16% between 700 and 800. Writing-- 38% below 500, 38% between 500 and 599, and 25% between 600 and 699. Evidence-Based Reading/Writing-- 7% below 500, 32% between 500 and 599, 43% between 600 and 699, and 18% between 700 and 800. The ACT scores were 2% between 12 and 17, 30% between 18 and 23, 47% between 24 and 29, and 22% above 30. 2% of the current freshmen were in the top fifth of their class; 2% were in the top two fifths. 8 freshmen graduated first in their class. **Admissions Contact:** Marie Schofer, Director of Admissions. Email: *admission@cornellcollege.edu* Web: *www.cornellcollege.edu*

FINANCIAL AID: In 2017-2018, 100% of all full-time freshmen received some form of financial aid. 70% of all full-time freshmen received need-based aid. The average freshman award was $32,978. Need-based scholarships or need-based grants averaged $27,868 ($47,520 maximum); need-based self-help aid (loans and jobs) averaged $4,339 ($7,000 maximum); and other non-need-based awards and non-need-based scholarships averaged $19,307 ($50,500 maximum). 51% of undergraduate students work part-time. The average financial indebtedness of the 2017 graduate was $33,827. Cornell is a member of CSS. The FAFSA code is 001856. The priority date for freshman financial aid applications for fall entry is March 1.

DORDT COLLEGE — B-2
www.dordt.edu

Sioux Center, IA 51250	**(712) 722-6080** **(800) 34-DORDT**
Fax: (712) 722-1967	**Email: admissions@dordt.edu**
Full-time: 728 men, 658 women	**Faculty:** 80; IIB, -$
Part-time: 44 men, 41 women	**Ph.D.s:** 85%
Graduate: 25 men, 29 women	**Student/Faculty:** 15 to 1
Year: semesters	**Tuition:** $29,130
Room & Board: $8730	**Freshman Class:** 1355 applied, 1022 accepted, 381 enrolled
SAT: required **ACT:** 25	**CEEB CODE:** 6171
Application Deadline: August 1	**COMPETITIVE+**

Dordt College, founded in 1955, is a private institution affiliated with the Christian Reformed Church. The curriculum, which is designed to reflect the principles of the Christian faith, leads to degrees in liberal arts, agriculture, art, music, business, engineering, and teaching preparation. The figures given in the above capsule and in this profile are approximate. There are 4 undergraduate schools. In addition to regional accreditation, DC has baccalaureate program accreditation with ABET and CSWE. The 120-acre campus is in a rural area 42 miles north of Sioux City. Including any residence halls, there are 25 buildings.

STUDENT LIFE: 60% of undergraduates are from out of state, mostly the Midwest. Students are from 34 states, 26 foreign countries, and Canada. 40% are from public schools. 88% are White; 3% African American; 3% Asian American; 3% Hispanic; 3% Foreign. 99% are Protestant. **Male To Female Ratio:** 1.1:1. The average age of freshmen is 18; all undergraduates, 21. 15% do not continue beyond their first year; 68% remain to graduate. **Housing:** 1300 students can be accommodated in college housing, which includes dorms, on-campus apartments, and off-campus apartments. On-campus housing is guaranteed for all 4 years. 90% of students live on campus. Alcohol is not permitted. All students may keep cars.

FACULTY/CLASSROOMS: 85% of faculty are male; 15% are female. All teach undergraduates. No introductory courses are taught by graduate students. The average class size in an introductory lecture is 30; in a laboratory is 20; and in a regular course is 25.

PROGRAMS OF STUDY: DC confers B.A., B.S., B.S.N., and B.S.W. degrees. Associate and master's degrees are also awarded. Bachelor's degrees are awarded in AGRICULTURE (agricultural business management, agriculture, and animal science), BIOLOGICAL SCIENCE (biology/biological science), BUSINESS (accounting, banking and finance, business administration and management, business economics, management information systems, marketing management, recreational facilities management, secretarial studies/office management, and sports management), COMMUNICATIONS AND THE ARTS (advertising, art history, art, broadcasting, church music, communications, dramatic arts, English as a second/foreign language, film, television and digital media, fine arts, German, graphic design, journalism, languages, literature, music performance, music theory and composition, Spanish, speech/debate/rhetoric, theatre acting, theatre arts, visual and performing arts, and vocal music education), COMPUTER AND PHYSICAL SCIENCE (actuarial science, chemistry, computer programming, computer science, information sciences and systems, mathematics, physical sciences, and physics), EDUCATION (agricultural education, art education, athletic training, business education, childhood education, early childhood education, education, elementary education, English education, foreign languages education, mathematics education, middle school education, music education, physical education, physical science secondary school education, science education, secondary education, social science education, and special education), ENGINEERING AND ENVIRONMENTAL DESIGN (architectural engineering, bioengineering, chemical engineering, civil engineering, computer engineering, construction management, electrical/electronics engineering, engineering, environmental science, and mechanical engineering), HEALTH PROFESSIONS (exercise science, health science, medical laboratory technology, nursing, predentistry, premedicine, preoptometry, prepharmacy, prephysical therapy, and preveterinary science), SOCIAL SCIENCE (criminal justice, economics, history, ministries, missions, philosophy, philosophy and religion, political science/government, prelaw, psychology, public administration, religion, religious studies, social science, social work, sociology, and youth ministry). Engineering, business administration, and social work are the strongest academically. Education has the largest enrollment.

ACTIVITIES: There are no fraternities or sororities. There are 25 groups on campus, including band, choir, chorale, chorus, computers, dance, debate, drama, drill team, environmental, film, forensics, international, jazz band, literary magazine, newspaper, opera, orchestra, pep band, photography, PLIA (Putting Love into Action), political, professional, radio and TV, religious, social, social service, student government, symphony, and yearbook. Popular campus events include Parents Day in October. **Sports:** There are 7 intercollegiate sports for men and 7 for women, and 10 intramural sports for men and 10 for women. Facilities include a gym with courts, a recreation center with indoor track, basketball, volleyball, and tennis, racquetball courts, weight-lifting and exercise equipment rooms, golf simulation, an outdoor track, tennis courts, soccer, softball, and baseball fields, an indoor pool, and an ice arena. **Graduates:** From July 1, 2016 to June 30, 2017, 290 bachelor's degrees were awarded. The most popular majors were business, education, and engineering. In an average class, 68% graduate in 4 years or less. Of the 2016 graduating class, 15% were enrolled in graduate school within 6 months of graduation, and 96% were employed.

SERVICES: Counseling and information services are available, as is tutoring in every subject. There is a reader service for the blind, and remedial math, reading, and writing. **Library/Resources:** The library contains 185,000 volumes, 14,819 microform items, 5,000 audio/video tapes/CDs/DVDs, and subscribes to 700 periodicals including electronic. Computerized library services include interlibrary loans. Special learning facilities include a planetarium, radio station, and 2 observatories, as well as a 160-acre agriculture stewardship center just north of the campus. **Physically Challenged Students:** All of the campus is accessible. Facilities include wheelchair ramps, elevators, special parking, specially equipped restrooms, special class scheduling, lowered drinking fountains, lowered telephones, and special housing. **Special:** Students may study abroad in 10 countries. Dordt also offers a Washington semester, a Chicago Metro semester, a joint nursing degree program with St. Luke's School of Nursing, a B.S.N. with Briar Cliff University, B.A.-B.S. degrees in engineering and agriculture, and numerous internships in all majors. Dual majors, student-designed majors, and pass/fail options are available. There is a freshman honors program. **Visiting:** There are regularly scheduled orientations for prospective students, including tours, class visits, personal visits with professors and coaches, and a financial aid session. There are guides for informal visits, visitors may sit in on classes, and stay overnight. To schedule a visit, contact the Admissions Office. **Campus Safety and Security:** Measures include 24-hour foot and vehicle patrol, and lighted pathways/sidewalks.

REQUIREMENTS: The SAT or ACT is required. Applicants must be graduates of accredited secondary schools or have earned a GED. The college requires 18 academic credits, including 4 in English and 2 each in foreign language, math, science, and social studies. A GPA of 2.3 is required. AP and CLEP credits are accepted. Important factors in the admissions decision are advanced placement or honors courses, evidence of special talent, and leadership record. All students must complete a college introductory course and a distribution of 14 other courses in the various academic disciplines, including General Education 300. Proficiency requirements must be met in English, math, and phys ed. To graduate, students must complete a minimum of 126 credits with a 2.0 GPA. **Procedure:** Freshmen are admitted fall and spring. Entrance exams should be taken by October of the senior year and no later than April. There is a rolling admissions plan. Applications should be filed by August 1 for fall entry; December 1 for spring entry. Applications are accepted on-line. **Transfer Students:** 60 transfer students enrolled in 2016-2017. Transfer students must have a GPA of 2.0. 62 of 126 credits required for the bachelor's degree must be completed at DC. **International Students:** There are 60 international students enrolled. They must take the TOEFL with a minimum score of 72 on the Internet-based version (iBT). They must also take the SAT or ACT, scoring 19.

ADMISSIONS: 75% of the 2017-2018 applicants were accepted. The SAT scores for the 2017-2018 freshman class were: Critical Reading-- 47% below 500, 29% between 500 and 599, 21% between 600 and 699, and 3% between 700 and 800. Math-- 22% below 500, 45% between 500 and 599, 30% between 600 and 699, and 3% between 700 and 800. Writing-- 43% below 500, 40% between 500 and 599, and 17% between 600 and 699. The ACT scores were 15% below 12, 25% between 12 and 17, 36% between 18 and 23, 20% between 24 and 29, and 15% above 30. 62% of the current freshmen were in the top fifth of their class; 75% were in the top two fifths. **Admissions Contact:** Jim Bos, Registrar and Director/Institutional Research. Email: *jim.bos@dordt.edu* Web: *www.dordt.edu*

FINANCIAL AID: In 2017-2018, 98% of all full-time freshmen received some form of financial aid. 85% of all full-time freshmen received need-based aid. The average freshman award was $21,900. Need-based scholarships or need-based grants averaged $4,000 ($6,000 maximum); need-based self-help aid (loans and jobs) averaged $8,000 ($12,000 maximum); non-need-based athletic scholarships averaged $6,000 ($9,000 maximum); and other non-need-based awards and non-need-based scholarships averaged $7,000 ($12,500 maximum). 70% of undergraduate students work part-time. The average financial indebtedness of the 2017 graduate was $22,400. DC is a member of CSS. The college's own financial statement is required. The FAFSA code is 001859. Check with the school for current application deadlines.

DRAKE UNIVERSITY — C-3

www.drake.edu

Des Moines, IA 50311 — (515) 271-3181, (800) 44-DRAKE

Fax: (515) 271-2831 — Email: admission@drake.edu

Full-time: 1252 men, 1703 women	**Faculty:** IIA, --$
Part-time: 72 men, 71 women	**Ph.D.s:** 92%
Graduate: 599 men, 1207 women	**Student/Faculty:** 12 to 1
Year: semesters, summer session	**Tuition:** $39,062
Room & Board: $10,158	**Freshman Class:** 5596 applied, 3839 accepted, 758 enrolled
ACT: 27	**CEEB CODE:** 6168
Application Deadline: March 1	**HIGHLY COMPETITIVE**

Drake University, founded in 1881, is a private institution offering undergraduate and graduate programs in arts and sciences, business and public administration, pharmacy and health sciences, journalism and mass communication, education, fine arts, and law. There are 5 undergraduate schools and 4 graduate schools. In addition to regional accreditation, DU has baccalaureate program accreditation with ACEJMC, ACPE, NASAD, and NASM. The 120-acre campus is in an urban area in Des Moines. Including any residence halls, there are 49 buildings.

STUDENT LIFE: 70% of undergraduates are from out of state, mostly the Midwest. Students are from 45 states, 37 foreign countries, and Canada. 78% are White; 6% Foreign; 5% African American; 5% Hispanic; 3% Asian American; 3% two or more races; 1% race unknown. **Female To Male Ratio:** 1.6:1. The average age of freshmen is 18; all undergraduates, 20. 13% do not continue beyond their first year; 79% remain to graduate. **Housing:** 1787 students can be accommodated in college housing, which includes dorms and off-campus apartments. In addition, there are fraternity houses and sorority houses. On-campus housing is guaranteed for the freshman year only, is available on a first-come, first-served basis, and is available on a lottery system for upperclassmen. 70% of students live on campus. All students may keep cars.

FACULTY/CLASSROOMS: 49% of faculty are male; 51% are female. No introductory courses are taught by graduate students. The average class size in an introductory lecture is 29; in a laboratory is 14; and in a regular course is 27.

PROGRAMS OF STUDY: DU confers B.A., B.S., B.A.Journ/Mass Comm., B.F.A., B.Mus., B.Mus.Ed., B.S.B.A., and B.S.Ed. degrees. Master's and doctoral degrees are also awarded. Bachelor's degrees are awarded in BIOLOGICAL SCIENCE (biology/biological science and neurosciences), BUSINESS (accounting, banking and finance, business administration and management, international business management, management science, and marketing management), COMMUNICATIONS AND THE ARTS (advertising, art history and appreciation, broadcasting, communications, dramatic arts, English, graphic design, journalism, music, music business management, music performance, printmaking, public relations, speech/debate/rhetoric, and studio art), COMPUTER AND PHYSICAL SCIENCE (actuarial science, chemistry, computer science, information sciences and systems, mathematics, and physics), EDUCATION (elementary education, mathematics education, music education, and secondary education), ENGINEERING AND ENVIRONMENTAL DESIGN (environmental science), HEALTH PROFESSIONS (pharmacy), SOCIAL SCIENCE (economics, ethics, politics, and social policy, history, international relations, philosophy, political science/government, psychology, religion, and sociology). Actuarial science, pharmacy, and physics/astronomy are the strongest academically. Pharmacy, marketing, and actuarial science have the largest enrollments.

ACTIVITIES: 36% of men belong to 9 national fraternities; 29% of women belong to 5 national sororities. There are 160 groups on campus, including art, band, cheerleading, chess, choir, chorale, chorus, computers, dance, drama, drill team, ethnic, film, honors, international, jazz band, LGBT, literary magazine, marching band, musical theater, newspaper, opera, orchestra, pep band, photography, political, professional, radio and TV, religious, social, social service, student government, and symphony. Popular campus events include Drake Relays, Supreme Court Days, and Iowa Caucuses. **Sports:** There are 8 intercollegiate sports for men and 10 for women, and 24 intramural sports for men and 24 for women. Facilities include a football stadium, indoor swimming pool, aerobics room, weight rooms, basketball, volleyball, and badminton courts, indoor tracks, and an outdoor track, racquetball courts, indoor and outdoor tennis courts, and a recreation and sports facility. **Graduates:** From July 1, 2016 to June 30, 2017, 975 bachelor's degrees were awarded. The most popular majors were business/marketing (31%), communication/journalism (11%), and education (8%). In an average class, 74% graduate in 4 years or less, 78% graduate in 5 years or less, and 79% graduate in 6 years or less.

SERVICES: There is a reader service for the blind. The Student Disability Service works with Recordings for the Blind Dyslexic students. **Library/Resources:** The library contains 558,044 volumes, 936,863 microform items, 3,609 audio/video tapes/CDs/DVDs, and subscribes to 74,473 periodicals including electronic. Computerized library services include interlibrary loans, database searching, Internet access, and Wi-Fi capability. Special learning facilities include an art gallery, radio station, TV station, an observatory, and the Henry G. Harmon Fine Arts Center. **Physically Challenged Students:** 90% of the campus is accessible. Facilities include wheelchair ramps, elevators, special parking, specially equipped restrooms, special class scheduling, lowered drinking fountains, lowered telephones. an IBM-compatible computer and scanner that includes a voice and screen enlargement program, closed-caption television, and TDD at multiple locations. **Special:** Study abroad is available in 60 countries and at sea. The university offers cross-registration with Des Moines area colleges, including Grand View, internships, a Washington semester, cooperative programs in computer science, and work-study programs. Dual majors, B.A.-B.S. degrees, a 3-2 engineering degree with Washington University, student-designed majors, credit for military experience, and nondegree study are also possible. Students may take a maximum of 12 hours of course work on a credit/no credit basis. There are 25 national honor societies, Phi Beta Kappa, a freshman honors program, and 19 departmental honors programs. **Visiting:** There are regularly scheduled orientations for prospective students, including an opportunity for students and parents to confer with professors, meet with current students, and attend information sessions on academic programs, financial aid, housing, the Drake campus, and a walking tour. There are guides for informal visits and stay overnight. To schedule a visit, contact the Office of Admission. **Campus Safety and Security:** Measures include 24-hour foot and vehicle patrol, emergency notification system, self-defense education, and security escort services. There are shuttle buses, emergency telephones, and lighted pathways/sidewalks.

REQUIREMENTS: Applicants must be graduates of an accredited secondary school. The GED is accepted. Students should have completed 4 years of English, 3 years of math, and 9 other units to be selected from English, foreign languages, social studies, math, lab sciences, and others. A portfolio is required for art majors and for those seeking scholarship consideration. An audition is necessary for admission to the music and theatre programs. Tapes are accepted. A GPA of 3.3 is required. AP and CLEP credits are accepted. Important factors in the admissions decision are advanced placement or honors courses, recommendations by school officials, and extracurricular activities record. Undergraduates must take a first-year seminar and general education courses and satisfy 11 areas of inquiry requirements that include writing, critical thinking, artistic experience, historical consciousness, information and technical literacy, multicultural experience, scientific and quantitative literacy, values and ethics, and the engaged citizen. A capstone demonstration is required. For graduation, 124 credit hours are required with 27 to 36 hours in the major. The minimum GPA is 2.0. **Procedure:** Freshmen are admitted to all sessions. Entrance exams should be taken during the spring of the junior year or early fall of the senior year. There are deferred admissions and rolling admissions plans. Applications should be filed by March 1 for fall entry. The fall 2017 application fee was $25. Applications are accepted on-line. **Transfer Students:** Applicants must have a minimum GPA of 2.0 and have completed 24 credit hours for evaluation. Grades of C or better transfer for credit. There is no assurance that all courses transferred will apply toward the major requirement. The final 30 hours must be completed in residence. Transfer students are admitted in the fall, spring, and summer. 30 of 124 credits required for the bachelor's degree must be completed at DU. **International Students:** There are 173 international students enrolled. They must take the TOEFL with a minimum score of 550 on the paper-based TOEFL (PBT) or 79 on the Internet-based version (iBT). They must also take the SAT or ACT.

ADMISSIONS: 69% of the 2017-2018 applicants were accepted. The SAT scores for the 2017-2018 freshman class were: Critical Reading-- 18% below 500, 33% between 500 and 599, 38% between 600 and 699, and 10% between 700 and 800. Math-- 10% below 500, 40% between 500 and 599, 32% between 600 and 699, and 18% between 700 and 800. The ACT scores were 13% between 18 and 23, 58% between 24 and 29, and 29% above 30. **Admissions Contact:** Anne Kremer, Dean of Admissions. Email: *admission@drake.edu* Web: *www.drake.edu*

FINANCIAL AID: In 2017-2018, 97% of all full-time freshmen received some form of financial aid. 76% of all full-time freshmen received need-based aid. The average freshman award was $26,153. Need-based scholarships or need-based grants averaged $20,124; need-based self-help aid (loans and jobs) averaged $4,887; non-need-based athletic scholarships averaged $21,525; and other non-need-based awards and non-need-based scholarships averaged $16,178. DU is a member of CSS. The FAFSA code is 001860. Check with the school for current application deadlines.

GRACELAND UNIVERSITY — C-4

www.graceland.edu

Lamoni, IA 50140 — (641) 784-5196, (800) 833-0524

Fax: (641) 784-5058 — **Email:** admissions@graceland.edu

Full-time: 579 men, 664 women	**Faculty:** IIB, -$
Part-time: 104 men, 209 women	**Ph.D.s:** 47%
Graduate: 105 men, 631 women	**Student/Faculty:** 15 to 1
Year: trimesters, summer session	**Tuition:** $27,010
Room & Board: $8280	**Freshman Class:** 1031 accepted, 290 enrolled
SAT or ACT: required	**CEEB CODE:** 6249
Application Deadline: n/av	**COMPETITIVE**

Graceland University, established in 1895, is a private liberal arts college sponsored by the Community of Christ. Graceland also maintains a campus in Independence, Missouri. There are 4 undergraduate schools and 4 graduate schools. In addition to regional accreditation, GU has baccalaureate program accreditation with CAEP, NLN, CCNE, and CAATE. The 170-acre campus is in a small town 80 miles south of Des Moines. Including any residence halls, there are 28 buildings.

STUDENT LIFE: **Female To Male Ratio:** 1.9:1. The average age of freshmen is 18; all undergraduates, 20. **Housing:** 815 students can be accommodated in college housing, which includes married student dorms and on-campus apartments. On-campus housing is guaranteed for all 4 years. 70% of students live on campus. Alcohol is not permitted. All students may keep cars.

FACULTY/CLASSROOMS: 47% of faculty are male; 53% are female. 93% teach undergraduates, and 10% do research. No introductory courses are taught by graduate students. The average class size in an introductory lecture is 24; in a laboratory is 24; and in a regular course is 11.

PROGRAMS OF STUDY: GU confers B.A., B.S., and B.S.N. degrees. Master's and doctoral degrees are also awarded. Bachelor's degrees are awarded in BIOLOGICAL SCIENCE (biology/biological science), BUSINESS (accounting, business administration and management, international business management, recreation and leisure services, and recreational facilities management), COMMUNICATIONS AND THE ARTS (communications, dramatic arts, English, German, graphic design, literature, modern language, music, Spanish, speech/debate/rhetoric, and studio art), COMPUTER AND PHYSICAL SCIENCE (chemistry, computer science, information sciences and systems, mathematics, and science), EDUCATION (athletic training, elementary education, music education, and physical education), ENGINEERING AND ENVIRONMENTAL DESIGN (commercial art), HEALTH PROFESSIONS (health, medical laboratory technology, nursing, predentistry, premedicine, and preveterinary science), SOCIAL SCIENCE (addiction studies, criminal justice, economics, history, human services, international studies, liberal arts/general studies, philosophy, psychology, religion, social science, and sociology). Business administration, education, and nursing have the largest enrollments.

ACTIVITIES: There are no fraternities or sororities. There are 54 groups on campus, including art, band, cheerleading, chess, choir, chorale, chorus, computers, dance, drama, drill team, entrepreneurial, ethnic, honors, international, jazz band, LGBT, literary magazine, musical theater, newspaper, orchestra, pep band, political, professional, radio and TV, religious, social, social service, student government, symphony, and yearbook. Popular campus events include Renaissance Week, Multicultural Week, and New Year's in November. **Sports:** There are 9 intercollegiate sports for men and 8 for women, and 17 intramural sports for men and 17 for women. Facilities include a sports complex with an all-weather track, soccer and football fields, a phys ed center with an indoor pool, a gym, an indoor track, a weight room, and courts for racquetball, basketball, volleyball, and tennis, an intramural sports complex, tennis, and a golf. **Graduates:** The most popular majors were health professons and related programs (23%), education (21%), and business (16%).

SERVICES: Counseling and information services are available, as is tutoring in most subjects. There is a reader service for the blind, and remedial math, reading, and writing. **Library/Resources:** The library contains 199,447 volumes, 914 microform items, 3,658 audio/video tapes/CDs/DVDs, and subscribes to 624 periodicals including electronic. Computerized library services include interlibrary loans, database searching, Internet access, and Wi-Fi capability. Special learning facilities include an art gallery and radio station. **Physically Challenged Students:** 86% of the campus is accessible. Facilities include wheelchair ramps, elevators, special parking, specially equipped restrooms, special class scheduling, lowered drinking fountains, and lowered telephones. **Special:** Internships are required in business, education, recreation, communications, and publication design. Graceland offers study abroad, cross-registration, B.A.-B.S. degrees, work-study, dual and student-designed majors, and a general studies degree. Credit for life, military, or work experience is possible. A pass/fail option is available for 2 courses each semester. The university also offers nondegree study, home study in addiction studies and nursing, a program for students with learning disabilities, an accelerated degree program in nursing, and a 3-2 engineering degree with the University of Iowa and the University of Missouri-Rolla. There is a freshman honors program. **Visiting:** There are regularly scheduled orientations for prospective students, including a campus tour and opportunities to meet students, faculty, and campus personnel. There are guides for informal visits, visitors may sit in on classes, and stay overnight. To schedule a visit, contact the Admissions Office. **Campus Safety and Security:** Measures include 24-hour foot and vehicle patrol, emergency notification system, and security escort services. There are emergency telephones, lighted pathways/sidewalks, controlled access to dorms/residences, and night security personnel.

REQUIREMENTS: Graceland requires applicants to meet 2 of the following 3 criteria: rank in the upper 50% of their class, a GPA of 2.5, or a minimum score on the SAT or ACT. Applicants must be graduates of an accredited secondary school. The GED is accepted. A GPA of 2.5 is required. AP and CLEP credits are accepted. Important factors in the admissions decision are advanced placement or honors courses, evidence of special talent, and leadership record. To graduate, students must complete 128 credit hours, including 39 in upper-division courses and an average of 40 in the major, and maintain a minimum GPA of 2.0 overall and in the major. General education requirements include studies in humanities, social sciences, natural sciences, behavioral sciences, ethics, math, computer science, leadership, thinking skills, human diversity, and the arts. **Procedure:** Freshmen are admitted to all sessions. Entrance exams should be taken in the junior or senior year. There is a rolling admissions plan. Check with the school for current application deadlines. The fall 2017 application fee was $50. Applications are accepted on-line. **Transfer Students:** 191 transfer students enrolled in 2016-2017. Applicants must submit official transcripts from all colleges attended and from high school. The required GPA varies by the number of hours of college study completed. Transfer students are admitted every term. 32 of 128 credits required for the bachelor's degree must be completed at GU. **International Students:** They must take the TOEFL.

ADMISSIONS: The SAT scores for the 2017-2018 freshman class were: Critical Reading-- 87% below 500, 11% between 500 and 599, and 2% between 600 and 699. Math-- 78% below 500, 16% between 500 and 599, 5% between 600 and 699, and 1% between 700 and 800. The ACT scores were 18% between 12 and 17, 55% between 18 and 23, 24% between 24 and 29, and 3% above 30. **Admissions Contact:** Kevin Brown, Director of Admissions. Email: *admissions@graceland.edu* Web: *www.graceland.edu*

FINANCIAL AID: The FAFSA code is 001866. Check with the school for current application deadlines.

GRAND VIEW UNIVERSITY C-3

www.grandview.edu

Des Moines, IA 50316 **(515) 263-2810** **(800) 444-6083**

Fax: (515) 263-2974	**Email:** admissions@grandview.edu
Full-time: 766 men, 962 women	**Faculty:** 95
Part-time: 117 men, 251 women	**Ph.D.s:** 68%
Graduate: 11 men, 22 women	**Student/Faculty:** 18 to 1
Year: semesters, summer session	**Tuition:** $24,394
Room & Board: $7908	**Freshman Class:** n/av
SAT or ACT: required	**CEEB CODE:** 6251
Application Deadline: August 15	**COMPETITIVE**

Grand View University, founded in 1896, is a private liberal arts college affiliated with the Evangelical Lutheran Church in America, that focuses on connecting liberal arts with career preparation. There are 2 undergraduate schools and 1 graduate school. In addition to regional accreditation, GVU has baccalaureate program accreditation with NLN. The 25-acre campus is in an urban area in a residential area of Des Moines. Including any residence halls, there are 27 buildings.

STUDENT LIFE: 87% of undergraduates are from Iowa. Others are from 34 states, 16 foreign countries, and Canada. 80% are White; 8% African American; 4% two or more races; 3% Hispanic; 2% Asian American; 1% American Indian/Alaska Native; 1% Foreign. 15% are Catholic; 13% Protestant. **Female To Male Ratio:** 1.4:1. The average age of freshmen is 18; all undergraduates, 22. 31% do not continue beyond their first year; 49% remain to graduate. **Housing:** 900 students can be accommodated in college housing, which includes dorms, on-campus apartments, and special-interest houses. On-campus housing is available on a first-come, first-served basis, and is available on a lottery system for upperclassmen. 63% of students commute. All students may keep cars.

FACULTY/CLASSROOMS: 39% of faculty are male; 61% are female. All teach undergraduates. No introductory courses are taught by graduate students. The average class size in an introductory lecture is 20; in a laboratory is 10; and in a regular course is 15.

PROGRAMS OF STUDY: GVU confers B.A. and B.S.N. degrees. Master's degrees are also awarded. Bachelor's degrees are awarded in BIOLOGICAL SCIENCE (biochemistry, biology/biological science, and biotechnology), BUSINESS (accounting, business administration and management, management information systems, and sports management), COMMUNICATIONS AND THE ARTS (broadcasting, communications, English, graphic design, journalism, music, and visual and performing arts), COMPUTER AND PHYSICAL SCIENCE (computer science and mathematics), EDUCATION (art education, elementary education, music education, physical education, and secondary education), HEALTH PROFESSIONS (nursing), SOCIAL SCIENCE (criminal justice, human services, political science/government, and psychology). Art, nursing, and education are the strongest academically. Business, nursing, and biology have the largest enrollments.

ACTIVITIES: There are no fraternities or sororities. There are 43 groups on campus, including art, band, cheerleading, choir, chorale, chorus, computers, dance, departmental, drama, drill team, ethnic, honors, international, jazz band, LGBT, literary magazine, newspaper, pep band, political, professional, radio and TV, religious, social service, student government, and yearbook. **Sports:** There are 12 intercollegiate sports for men and 12 for women, and 8 intramural sports for men and 8 for women. Facilities include a wellness facilities for varsity athletics and recreation programs and an athletic field. **Graduates:** From July 1, 2016 to June 30, 2017, 460 bachelor's degrees were awarded. The most popular majors were business administration (23%), nursing (14%), and education (10%). In an average class, 39% graduate in 4 years or less, 47% graduate in 5 years or less, and 49% graduate in 6 years or less. Of the 2016 graduating class, 8% were enrolled in graduate school within 6 months of graduation, and 90% were employed.

SERVICES: Counseling and information services are available, as is tutoring in every subject. There is a reader service for the blind, and remedial math, reading, and writing. **Library/Resources:** The library contains 135,448 volumes, 11,386 microform items, 3,875 audio/video tapes/CDs/DVDs, and subscribes to 27,077 periodicals including electronic. Computerized library services include interlibrary loans, database searching, and Internet access. Special learning facilities include an art gallery, radio station, and TV station. **Physically Challenged Students:** 90% of the campus is accessible. Facilities include wheelchair ramps, elevators, special parking, specially equipped restrooms, special class scheduling, lowered drinking fountains, and lowered telephones. The Support Service is for disabled students. **Special:** Co-op programs, cross-registration with Drake University and Des Moines Area Community College, student-designed majors, study abroad, and internships for most majors are available. Dual majors, a B.A.-B.S. degree, a Washington semester, work-study programs, and an accelerated degree program in business administration are offered. Nondegree study, a liberal arts degree, a certificate in art therapy, and pass/fail options are possible. There are 10 national honor societies, a freshman honors program, and 1 departmental honors program. **Visiting:** There are regularly scheduled orientations for prospective students, including placement tests, a financial aid session, lunch, advisor meetings, and a registration session. There are guides for informal visits, visitors may sit in on classes, and stay overnight. To schedule a visit, contact the Admissions Office. **Campus Safety and Security:** Measures include 24-hour foot and vehicle patrol, emergency notification system, and security escort services. There are emergency telephones, lighted pathways/sidewalks, and controlled access to dorms/residences.

REQUIREMENTS: The SAT and ACT Writing Test are recommended, with a minimum recommended score of 18 on the ACT or the equivalent on the SAT. Students must be graduates of an accredited secondary school. The GED is also accepted. Grand View recommends that students should have completed 4 courses in English, 3 courses each in math, science, and social science, and 2 courses in a foreign language. AP and CLEP credits are accepted. Students must complete core requirements, including courses in English, public speaking, liberal arts, integrating seminar, other culture encounter, religion or philosophy, history or other humanities, lab science, and social science. Students must complete at least 124 hours of work, including 60 hours in courses other than the major and 24 hours in the major. They must also maintain an overall GPA of 2.0 and a 2.2 GPA in the major, and demonstrate computer proficiency. **Procedure:** Freshmen are admitted in the fall, spring, and summer. Entrance exams should be taken during the second semester of the junior year. There are deferred admissions and rolling admissions plans. Applications should be filed by August 15 for fall entry. Applications are accepted on-line. **Transfer Students:** 303 transfer students enrolled in 2016-2017. Applicants must submit transcripts from each college attended. Students who are not transferring in with an associate or bachelor's degree must submit a high school transcript. Those with less than 24 college credits must also submit ACT or SAT test results. 30 of 124 credits required for the bachelor's degree must be completed at GVU. **International Students:** There are 35 international students enrolled. They must take the TOEFL with a minimum score of 550 on the paper-based TOEFL (PBT) or 77 on the Internet-based version (iBT). They must also take the SAT or ACT, scoring 18.

ADMISSIONS: 8 freshmen graduated first in their class. **Admissions Contact:** Diane Schafer Johnson, Director of Admissions. Email: *admissions@grandview.edu* Web: *www.grandview.edu*

FINANCIAL AID: In 2017-2018, 99% of all full-time freshmen received some form of financial aid. 90% of all full-time freshmen received need-based aid. The average financial indebtedness of the 2017 graduate was $36,794. The FAFSA code is 001867. The deadline for filing freshman financial aid applications for fall entry is April 15.

GRINNELL COLLEGE — D-3

www.grinnell.edu

Grinnell, IA 50112	(641) 269-3600 (800) 247-0113
Fax: (641) 269-4800	Email: admission@grinnell.edu
Full-time: 744 men, 914 women	Faculty: 171; IIB, ++$
Part-time: 26 men, 15 women	Ph.D.s: 98%
Graduate: n/av	Student/Faculty: 9 to 1
Year: semesters	Tuition: $48,758
Room & Board: $11,980	Freshman Class: 3979 applied, 1395 accepted, 423 enrolled
SAT CR/M: 685/710 ACT: 32	CEEB CODE: 6252
Application Deadline: January 15	MOST COMPETITIVE

Grinnell College, founded in 1846, is a private institution that offers undergraduate degree programs in the arts and sciences. There is 1 undergraduate school. The 120-acre campus is in a small town 55 miles east of Des Moines. Including any residence halls, there are 64 buildings.

STUDENT LIFE: 77% of undergraduates are from out of state, mostly the Midwest. Students are from 49 states, 42 foreign countries, and Canada. 65% are from public schools. 8% are Asian American; 8% Hispanic; 6% African American; 52% White; 5% two or more races; 5% race unknown; 18% Foreign. **Female To Male Ratio:** 1.2:1. The average age of freshmen is 18; all undergraduates, 20. 7% do not continue beyond their first year; 86% remain to graduate. **Housing:** 1340 students can be accommodated in college housing, which includes dorms and on-campus apartments. In addition, there are language/international houses, special-interest houses, theme housing, wellness housing, and cooperative housing. On-campus housing is guaranteed for all 4 years. 88% of students live on campus. All students may keep cars.

FACULTY/CLASSROOMS: 55% of faculty are male; 45% are female. All teach undergraduates, and all do research. No introductory courses are taught by graduate students. The average class size in an introductory lecture is 20; in a laboratory is 13; and in a regular course is 17.

PROGRAMS OF STUDY: Grinnell confers B.A. degrees. Bachelor's degrees are awarded in BIOLOGICAL SCIENCE (biochemistry and biology/biological science), COMMUNICATIONS AND THE ARTS (art history and appreciation, Chinese, classics, English, French, German, music, Russian, Spanish, studio art, and theatre arts), COMPUTER AND PHYSICAL SCIENCE (chemistry, computer science, mathematics, physics, and science), SOCIAL SCIENCE (anthropology, economics, gender studies, history, philosophy, political science/government, psychology, religion, and sociology). Economics, psychology, and political science have the largest enrollments.

ACTIVITIES: There are no fraternities or sororities. There are 130 groups on campus, including art, chess, choir, chorale, chorus, computers, dance, debate, drama, environmental, ethnic, film, forensics, honors, international, jazz band, LGBT, literary magazine, musical theater, newspaper, orchestra, photography, political, radio and TV, religious, social, social service, student government, and yearbook. Popular campus events include the Titular Head Student Film Festival and Grinnell Relays. **Sports:** There are 10 intercollegiate sports for men and 10 for women, and 16 intramural sports for men and 16 for women. Facilities include recreation and athletic complex with a gymnasium, a fieldhouse, a natatorium, an auxillary practice gymnasium, climbing and bouldering walls, racquetball courts, sports fields, an outdoor track, and intramural fields. **Graduates:** From July 1, 2016 to June 30, 2017, 375 bachelor's degrees were awarded. The most popular majors were economics (13%), biology (11%), and computer science (10%). In an average class, 78% graduate in 4 years or less, 86% graduate in 5 years or less, and 86% graduate in 6 years or less. Of the 2016 graduating class, 19% were enrolled in graduate school within 6 months of graduation, and 52% were employed.

SERVICES: Counseling and information services are available, as is tutoring in every subject. There is a reader service for the blind. There are also reading, writing, math, and science labs. **Library/Resources:** The library contains 768,671 volumes, 416,593 microform items, 34,144 audio/video tapes/CDs/DVDs, and subscribes to 22,059 periodicals including electronic. Computerized library services include interlibrary loans, database searching, Internet access, and Wi-Fi capability. Special learning facilities include an art gallery, radio station, an observatory, physics museum, a print and drawing study room. **Physically Challenged Students:** 85% of the campus is accessible. Facilities include wheelchair ramps, elevators, special parking, specially equipped restrooms, special class scheduling, lowered drinking fountains, lowered telephones, and special housing. **Special:** Students may participate in 63 study-abroad programs in 33 countries or in off-campus study at selected locations in the United States. Grinnell offers cooperative programs in architecture with Washington University in St. Louis and a 3-2 engineering program with California Institute of Technology, Columbia University, Washington University, and Rensselaer Polytechnic Institute. There is also an extensive internship program, a Washington semester, a general studies degree in science, student-designed majors, and S/D/F grading options in selected courses. Grinnell's special "plus-2" option permits students to add 2 credits to a regular course through independent study. Students may pursue one of 11 interdisciplinary concentrations in addition to their major. Accelerated degree programs of 6 to 7 semesters may be approved on an individual basis. There are 2 national honor societies and a chapter of Phi Beta Kappa. **Visiting:** There are regularly scheduled orientations for prospective students, including a campus tour, an interview with a member of the admissions staff, an opportunity to attend classes, and presentations/discussions with students and faculty from a number of academic departments. There are guides for informal visits; visitors may sit in on classes and stay overnight. To schedule a visit, contact the Admissions Office. **Campus Safety and Security:** Measures include 24-hour foot and vehicle patrol, emergency notification system, self-defense education, and security escort services. There are emergency telephones, lighted pathways/sidewalks, controlled access to dorms/residences, fire drills, and a committee on personal safety education.

REQUIREMENTS: The SAT or ACT is required. Applicants must be graduates of accredited secondary schools. The college recommends 20 Carnegie units, 4 each in English and math, 3/4 years each in lab science, social studies or history, and a foreign language. An essay is required and an interview is recommended. AP credits are accepted. Important factors in the admissions decision are advanced placement or honors courses, extracurricular activities record, and leadership record. All students are required to take a tutorial in the first semester focusing on writing. All students must also complete a major field, which includes between 32 and 48 credits in most departments. Of the total 124 credits needed for the bachelor's degree, no more than 48 may be earned in any one department or 92 in any one division, and a minimum 2.0 GPA must be maintained. **Procedure:** Freshmen are admitted in the fall. Entrance exams should be taken during the second semester of the junior year or early in the fall semester of the senior year. There are early decision, early admissions, and deferred admissions plans. Early decision applications should be filed by November 15; regular applications, by January 15 for fall entry; and November 1 for spring entry. The fall 2017 application fee was $30. Notification of early decision is sent December 15; regular decision, April 1. 137 early decision candidates were accepted for the 2017-2018 class. 1266 applicants were on the 2017 waiting list; 8 were admitted. Applications are accepted on-line. **Transfer Students:** 14 transfer students enrolled in 2016-2017. Students must have a 3.0 GPA and submit all high school transcripts, college transcripts, an essay or personal statement, standardized test scores, and a statement of good standing from prior institutions. Students may enroll in the fall, and spring. 62 of 124 credits required for the bachelor's degree must be completed at Grinnell. **International Students:** There are 304 international students enrolled. They must take the TOEFL with a minimum score of 550 on the paper-based TOEFL (PBT) or 80 on the Internet-based version (iBT). They must also take the SAT or ACT.

ADMISSIONS: 35% of the 2017-2018 applicants were accepted. The SAT scores for the 2017-2018 freshman class were: Critical Reading-- 12% between 500 and 599, 44% between 600 and 699, and 43% between 700 and 800. Math-- 1% between 500 and 599, 9% between 600 and 699, and 37% between 700 and 800. 70% of the current freshmen were in the top fifth of their class; 92% were in the top two fifths. **Admissions Contact:** Joseph P. Bagnoli Jr., Vice President for Enrollment, Dean of A. Email: *admission@grinnell.edu* Web: *www.grinnell.edu*

FINANCIAL AID: In 2017-2018, 89% of all full-time freshmen received some form of financial aid. 73% of all full-time freshmen received need-based aid. The average freshman award was $42,392. Need-based scholarships or need-based grants averaged $36,762; need-based self-help aid (loans and jobs) averaged $4,974; and other non-need-based awards and non-need-based scholarships averaged $656. The average financial indebtedness of the 2017 graduate was $16,570. Grinnell is a member of CSS. The CSS/Profile, and a noncustodial profile is required. The FAFSA code is 001868. The deadline for filing freshman financial aid applications for fall entry is February 8.

IOWA STATE UNIVERSITY — C-3

www.iastate.edu

Ames, IA 50011	(515) 294-5836 (800) 262-3810
Fax: (515) 294-2592	**Email:** admissions@iastate.edu
Full-time: 17,494 men, 12,912 women	**Faculty:** I, av$
Part-time: n/av	**Ph.D.s:** 88%
Graduate: 2968 men, 2023 women	**Student/Faculty:** n/av
Year: semesters, summer session	**Tuition:** $8636 ($22,472)
Room & Board: $8546	**Freshman Class:** n/av
SAT or ACT: required	**CEEB CODE:** 6306
Application Deadline: rolling	**COMPETITIVE**

Iowa State University, established in 1858, is a public land-grant institution offering undergraduate and graduate programs in agriculture, business, design, engineering, human sciences, liberal arts and sciences, and veterinary medicine. There are 7 undergraduate schools and 1 graduate school. In addition to regional accreditation, ISU has baccalaureate program accreditation with AACSB, ABET, ACEJMC, ADA, AHEA, ASLA, CSAB, FIDER, NAAB, NASM, SAF, ACS, and APA. The 1813-acre campus is in an urban area in Ames, Iowa, 30 minutes north of Des Moines. Including any residence halls, there are 284 buildings.

STUDENT LIFE: 55% of undergraduates are from Iowa. Others are from 50 states, 128 foreign countries, and Canada. 11% are Foreign. **Male To Female Ratio:** 1.4:1. The average age of freshmen is 18; all undergraduates, 21. 14% do not continue beyond their first year. **Housing:** 12000 students can be accommodated in college housing, which includes married student dorms, on-campus apartments, and off-campus apartments. In addition, there are honors houses, special-interest houses, fraternity houses, sorority houses, nonalcoholic houses, cross-cultural houses, nonsmoking houses, quiet houses, academic learning communities, and adult undergraduate housing. On-campus housing is guaranteed for all 4 years. All students may keep cars.

FACULTY/CLASSROOMS: 60% of faculty are male; 40% are female. 85% teach undergraduates, and 85% do research. Graduate students teach 15% of introductory courses. The average class size in a laboratory is 18 and in a regular course is 33.

PROGRAMS OF STUDY: ISU confers B.A, B.S., B.Arch., B.B.A., B.F.A., B.L.A., B.L.S. and B.Mus. degrees. Master's and doctoral degrees are also awarded. Bachelor's degrees are awarded in AGRICULTURE (agricultural business management, agriculture international, agriculture, agronomy, animal science, dairy science, forestry and related sciences, horticulture, plant protection (pest management), and plant science), BIOLOGICAL SCIENCE (biochemistry, biology/biological science, biophysics, entomology, genetics, microbiology, nutrition, and plant pathology), BUSINESS (accounting, banking and finance, business administration and management, fashion merchandising, hotel/motel and restaurant management, international business management, management science, marketing/retailing/merchandising, and transportation management), COMMUNICATIONS AND THE ARTS (advertising, communications, creative writing, design, English, fine arts, French, German, graphic design, journalism, linguistics, music, Russian, Spanish, and speech/debate/rhetoric), COMPUTER AND PHYSICAL SCIENCE (atmospheric sciences and meteorology, chemistry, computer science, earth science, geology, mathematics, physics, and statistics), EDUCATION (agricultural education, early childhood education, elementary education, health education, industrial arts education, music education, physical education, and secondary education), ENGINEERING AND ENVIRONMENTAL DESIGN (aeronautical engineering, agricultural engineering, architecture, chemical engineering, city/community/regional planning, civil engineering, computer engineering, construction engineering, electrical/electronics engineering, engineering, engineering technology, environmental science, industrial engineering technology, interior design, landscape architecture/design, materials engineering, and mechanical engineering), SOCIAL SCIENCE (anthropology, child care/child and family studies, child psychology/development, dietetics, economics, family/consumer resource management, family/consumer studies, fashion design and technology, food science, history, international relations, liberal arts/general studies, philosophy, political science/government, psychology, religion, sociology, and textiles and clothing). Engineering, agriculture, and statistics are the strongest academically. Engineering, business, and agriculture have the largest enrollments.

ACTIVITIES: 13% of men belong to 1 local and 29 national fraternities; 12% of women belong to 1 local and 17 national sororities. There are 850 groups on campus, including art, band, cheerleading, chess, choir, chorale, chorus, computers, dance, debate, drama, drum and bugle corps, ethnic, film, forensics, honoraries, honors, international, jazz band, LGBT, literary magazine, marching band, musical theater, newspaper, opera, orchestra, pep band, photography, political, professional, radio and TV, religious, social, social service, special interest, student government, and symphony. Popular campus events include Homecoming. **Sports:** There are 7 intercollegiate sports for men and 11 for women, and 43 intramural sports for men and 43 for women. Facilities include a coliseum, a stadium/field, a baseball and softball complex, a track complex, a tennis complex, multipurpose gyms, swimming pools, an ice center, a phys ed building, recreation centers, multipurpose intramural-recreation fields, and a competitive soccer site.

SERVICES: Counseling and information services are available, as is tutoring in most subjects. There is a reader service for the blind, and remedial math and writing. A Kurzweil and Arkanstone reader, enlargement services, talking and braille text from the Iowa Commission for the Blind, a braille printer, loaner computers, steno-captioning service, a TTY telecommunications device, FM listeners, and sign interpreters are also available. **Library/Resources:** The library contains 2.9 million volumes, 3.5 million microform items, and 64,524 audio/video tapes/CDs/DVDs, and subscribes to 112,491 periodicals including electronic. Computerized library services include interlibrary loans, database searching, Internet access, and Wi-Fi capability. Special learning facilities include an art gallery, natural history museum, planetarium, radio station, and TV station. **Physically Challenged Students:** 95% of the campus is accessible. Facilities include wheelchair ramps, elevators, special parking, specially equipped restrooms, special class scheduling, lowered drinking fountains, lowered telephones, and special housing. **Special:** Iowa State offers cooperative programs in engineering, forestry, agronomy, chemistry, computer science, economics, agricultural systems technology, business administration, industrial technology, and performing arts and cross-registration with the Universities of Iowa and Northern Iowa. Internships, study abroad in 38 countries, dual majors, the B.A.-B.S.

degree, student-designed majors, and accelerated degree programs are available. Interdisciplinary studies include agricultural biochemistry, agricultural systems technology, animal ecology, public service and administration in agriculture, and engineering operations. There are work-study programs, a Washington semester, nondegree study, and pass/no pass options. There are 16 national honor societies, Phi Beta Kappa, and a freshman honors program. **Visiting:** There are regularly scheduled orientations for prospective students, including presentations on academics, admissions, residence hall living, fraternity and sorority life, and financial aid. There is also a group session with an adviser and a tour of the campus. There are guides for informal visits, visitors may sit in on classes, and stay overnight. To schedule a visit, contact Office of Admissions. **Campus Safety and Security:** Measures include 24-hour foot and vehicle patrol, self-defense education, and security escort services. There are shuttle buses, emergency telephones, lighted pathways/sidewalks, controlled access to dorms/residences, and an SafeRide ISU app.

REQUIREMENTS: The SAT or ACT is required. Students will be admitted based upon their Regent Admission Index (RAI) score. There are two mathematical formulas for computing student's RAI scores, the primary RAI formula (for students whose high school provides class rank) and the Alternative RAI formula (for students whose high school does not provide class rank). Students must meet the minimum high school course requirements for admission, 4 years of English/Language Arts, 3 years each of math, and science, and 2 years of social studies. Iowa State requires applicants to be in the upper 50% of their class. AP and CLEP credits are accepted. A minimum of 120 1/2 to 169 1/2 credit hours, depending on the major, and a GPA of 2.0 are required for graduation. The total number of credits required in the major varies. All students must take freshman English, library instruction, 3 credits in U.S. diversity, and 3 credits in internationalization. **Procedure:** Freshmen are admitted to all sessions. Entrance exams should be taken during the spring of the junior year or the fall of the senior year. There are deferred admissions and rolling admissions plans. Check with the school for current application deadlines. The fall 2017 application fee was $40. Applications are accepted on-line. **Transfer Students:** Applicants must have a minimum GPA of 2.0 and at least 24 semester credits of acceptable transfer course work. They must also submit standardized test scores and provide a statement of good standing from prior institutions. 32 of 125 credits required for the bachelor's degree must be completed at ISU. **International Students:** There are 4131 international students enrolled. They must take the TOEFL and the college's own test.

Admissions Contact: Phil Caffrey, Associate Director of Admissions. Email: *admissions@iastate.edu* Web: *www.iastate.edu*

FINANCIAL AID: The FAFSA code is 001869. Check with the school for current application deadlines.

IOWA WESLEYAN UNIVERSITY E-4
www.iw.edu

Mount Pleasant, IA 52641 — **(319) 385-6230**, **(800) 582-2383**

Fax: (319) 385-6240 — **Email: admit@iw.edu**

Full-time: 250 men, 273 women	**Faculty:** n/av
Part-time: n/av	**Ph.D.s:** 85%
Graduate: n/av	**Student/Faculty:** 10 to 1
Year: semesters, summer session	**Tuition:** $30,500
Room & Board: $10,500	**Freshman Class:** 5449 applied, 2773 accepted, 169 enrolled
SAT: required **ACT:** 22	**CEEB CODE:** 0608
Application Deadline: open	**COMPETITIVE**

Iowa Wesleyan University, founded in 1842, is a fully accredited, coeducational liberal arts university with a rich history of innovation in education, the sciences, and educational opportunities for women and service-learning. Seven female Iowa Wesleyan students founded the P.E.O. Sisterhood on campus in 1869. The academic program at Iowa Wesleyan combines a liberal arts foundation with education in a specific career field, including art, business, English, music, nursing, psychology, and teacher education. Service-learning is integrated into the curriculum, ensuring that all students connect classroom learning with service to others. Internships and other field experience opportunities are part of every major, giving students hands-on professional experience before graduation. There is 1 undergraduate school. In addition to regional accreditation, IWU has baccalaureate program accreditation with Iowa Department of Education, ACEN, and University Senate of the United Methodist Church. The 60-acre campus is in a small town 45 miles south of Iowa City in the Southeastern region of Iowa. Including any residence halls, there are 15 buildings.

STUDENT LIFE: 60% of undergraduates are from out of state, mostly the Midwest. Students are from 25 states, 22 foreign countries, and Canada. 90% are from public schools. 6% are Foreign; 45% White; 36% African American; 2% Asian American; 13% Hispanic. 46% claim no religious affiliation. **Female To Male Ratio:** 1.1:1. The average age of freshmen is 15; all undergraduates, 21. 47% do not continue beyond their first year; 38% remain to graduate. **Housing:** 493 students can be accommodated in college housing, which includes dorms. On-campus housing is guaranteed for all 4 years. 75% of students live on campus. All students may keep cars.

FACULTY/CLASSROOMS: 59% of faculty are male; 41% are female. All teach undergraduates. No introductory courses are taught by graduate students. The average class size in an introductory lecture is 22; in a laboratory is 24; and in a regular course is 11.

PROGRAMS OF STUDY: IWU confers B.A., B.S., B.M.E., and B.S.N. degrees. Bachelor's degrees are awarded in BIOLOGICAL SCIENCE (biology ecology and field biology and biology/biological science), BUSINESS (accounting, business administration and management, business administration marketing, management & strategic leadership, and sports management), COMMUNICATIONS AND THE ARTS (digital media, fine arts, music, stage management, and visual communication), COMPUTER AND PHYSICAL SCIENCE (chemistry), EDUCATION (early childhood education, elementary education, music education, physical education, physical ed teacher education, and secondary education), HEALTH PROFESSIONS (biology, environmental health science, nursing, predentistry, premedicine, preoptometry, prephysical therapy, and preveterinary science), SOCIAL SCIENCE (Christian studies, criminal justice, prelaw, psychology, religion, and sociology). Nursing, and education are the strongest academically. Business, elementary education, nursing, and criminal justice have the largest enrollments.

ACTIVITIES: 6% of men belong to 1 national fraternity; 12% of women belong to 2 local and 1 national sororities. There are 35 groups on campus, including art, band, cheerleading, choir, chorus, dance, ethnic, film, international, jazz band, literary magazine, newspaper, orchestra, pep band, photography, political, professional, religious, social, social service, student government, symphony, and yearbook. Popular campus events include Forum, Winterfest, and Spring Thing. **Sports:** There are 5 intercollegiate sports for men and 5 for women, and 6 intramural sports for men and 6 for women. Facilities include a complex with baseball, softball, and football fields and an all-weather quarter-mile track, basketball/volleyball courts, an athletic training room, a walking/jogging track, and a fitness/wellness center.

SERVICES: Counseling and information services are available, as is tutoring in every subject. There is remedial math, reading, and writing. **Library/Resources:** The library contains 83,244 volumes, 25,305 microform items, 27,259 audio/video tapes/CDs/DVDs, and subscribes to 11,460 periodicals including electronic. Computerized library services include interlibrary loans, database searching, Internet access, and Wi-Fi capability. Special learning facilities include an art gallery. **Physically Challenged Students:** 77% of the campus is accessible. Facilities include wheelchair ramps, elevators, special parking, and special class scheduling. **Special:** The Office of Internships at Iowa Wesleyan University supports the mission of the institution by combining the values of a liberal education with those of professional preparation. Internships are a key component of how our programs provide opportunities to acquire the necessary theoretical and applied knowledge, which permits students to function effectively in professional life and a changing global community. Working with practicing professionals provides students the opportunity to integrate theory with practical learning. As part of a student's participation in the internship process, they will be evaluated in the workplace regarding the Institutional Learning Outcomes of Communication, Critical Reasoning, and Civic Engagement. While participating in experiential learning programs, students will face challenges and issues which they will continue to encounter throughout their professional careers There are 5 national honor societies and 2 departmental honors programs. **Visiting:** There are regularly scheduled orientations for prospective students, including meetings with admissions, financial aid, and academic staff, as well as social activities. There are guides for informal visits, visitors may sit in on classes, and stay overnight. To schedule a visit, contact the Admissions Office. **Campus Safety and Security:** Measures include 24-hour foot and vehicle patrol, emergency notification system, self-defense education, and security escort services. There are emergency telephones, lighted pathways/sidewalks, and controlled access to dorms/residences.

REQUIREMENTS: The SAT or ACT and ACT Writing Test are recommended. Applicants must be graduates of accredited secondary schools or have earned a GED. A GPA of 2.5 is required. AP and CLEP credits are accepted. Important factors in the admissions decision are geographical diversity, extracurricular activities record, and evidence of special talent. General education requirements of 35 to 40 hours include 6 of English, 4 of science, and 3 each of computer science, math, communication, civic issues, fine arts, religion, English literature, and global issues. Students must complete English 102 with a minimum of C-, satisfy a safety and survival requirement, and complete 6 semester hours of service learning and 6 to 14 semester hours of a field experience in the major. A minimum of 124 semester hours is required for the bachelor's degree, 28 or more must be in the major. **Procedure:** Freshmen are admitted in the fall and spring. Entrance exams should be taken in April of the junior year or in June, October, or December of the senior year. There are deferred admissions and rolling admissions plans. Application deadlines are open. Applications are accepted on-line. **Transfer Students:** 51 transfer students enrolled in 2016-2017. A minimum cumulative college GPA of 2.0 is required. 30 of 124 credits required for the bachelor's degree must be completed at IWU. **International Students:** There are 70 international students enrolled. They must take the TOEFL with a minimum score of 500 on the paper-based TOEFL (PBT).

ADMISSIONS: 51% of the 2017-2018 applicants were accepted. The ACT scores were 2% between 12 and 17, 75% between 18 and 23, 22% between 24 and 29, and 1% above 30. **Admissions Contact:** Jeremy Hommowun, Associate Director of Admissions. Email: *admit@iw.edu* Web: *www.iw.edu*

FINANCIAL AID: In 2017-2018, 100% of all full-time freshmen received some form of financial aid and need-based aid. The average freshman award was $24,000. Other non-need-based awards and non-need-based scholarships averaged $14,000 ($20,000 maximum). IWU is a member of CSS. The college's own financial statement is required. The FAFSA code is 001871. The priority date for freshman financial aid applications for fall entry is April.

LORAS COLLEGE E-2

www.loras.edu

Dubuque, IA 52001	(563) 588-7236 (800) 245-6727
Fax: (563) 588-7119	Email: admission@loras.edu
Full-time: 694 men, 641 women	**Faculty:** 100; IIB, --$
Part-time: 33 men, 29 women	**Ph.D.s:** 97%
Graduate: 31 men, 39 women	**Student/Faculty:** 14 to 1
Year: other, summer session	**Tuition:** $32,886
Room & Board: $7840	**Freshman Class:** 1161 applied, 1104 accepted, 337 enrolled
SAT: required **ACT:** 23	**CEEB CODE:** 0670
Application Deadline: open	**COMPETITIVE**

Loras College enables students to thrive and discover paths they're excited to follow through its challenging academic programs, co-curricular offerings, and a faith tradition that inspires responsibility, excellence, service and respect. Relating the rich liberal arts tradition to a changing world, Loras strives to develop active learners, reflective thinkers, ethical decision makers, and responsible contributors in their diverse professional, social, and religious roles. There is 1 undergraduate school and 1 graduate school. In addition to regional accreditation, LC has baccalaureate program accreditation with ABET, CSWE, ACS, and CAATE. The 64-acre campus is in a small town 180 miles west of Chicago and 250 miles south of Minneapolis. Including any residence halls, there are 23 buildings.

STUDENT LIFE: 59% of undergraduates are from out of state, mostly the Midwest. Students are from 24 states, 9 foreign countries, and Canada. 64% are from public schools. 80% are White; 8% Hispanic; 5% race unknown; 2% African American; 2% Foreign; 2% two or more races; 1% Asian American. 62% are Catholic; 18% Protestant. **Male To Female Ratio:** 1.1:1. The average age of freshmen is 18; all undergraduates, 20. 24% do not continue beyond their first year; 68% remain to graduate. **Housing:** 1037 students can be accommodated in college housing, which includes dorms, on-campus apartments, and off-campus apartments. On-campus housing is guaranteed for all 4 years and is available on a lottery system for upperclassmen. 65% of students live on campus. All students may keep cars.

FACULTY/CLASSROOMS: 54% of faculty are male; 46% are female. All teach undergraduates. No introductory courses are taught by graduate students. The average class size in a regular course is 16.

PROGRAMS OF STUDY: LC confers B.A. and B.S. degrees. Associate and master's degrees are also awarded. Bachelor's degrees are awarded in BIOLOGICAL SCIENCE (biochemistry and neurosciences), BUSINESS (accounting, business administration and management, finance, management information systems, management science, marketing, and sports management), COMMUNICATIONS AND THE ARTS (communication studies, creative writing, English literature, music, public relations, and Spanish), COMPUTER AND PHYSICAL SCIENCE (chemistry, computer science, and mathematics), EDUCATION (athletic training, elementary education, and music education), ENGINEERING AND ENVIRONMENTAL DESIGN (engineering physics), HEALTH PROFESSIONS (biology and exercise science), SOCIAL SCIENCE (criminal justice, economics, history, international relations, philosophy, political science/government, psychology, religion, social work, and sociology). Business/marketing, education, and parks and recreation have the largest enrollments.

ACTIVITIES: There are 56 groups on campus, including drumline club, band, cheerleading, choir, chorus, computers, dance, debate, drama, environmental, ethnic, film, forensics, honors, international, jazz band, LGBT, literary magazine, musical theater, newspaper, photography, political, professional, programming board, radio and TV, religious, social, social service, student government, and yearbook. Popular campus events include Campus Fest, Homecoming, and Family Weekend. **Sports:** There are 12 intercollegiate sports for men and 11 for women, and 7 intramural sports for men and 6 for women. Facilities include an athletic wellness facility, a sports center with a gym, a swimming pool, racquetball courts, and an 8-lane Olympic indoor/outdoor track, outdoor tennis courts, a field house for basketball games, a football field, a soccer field, and a softball field. **Graduates:** From July 1, 2016 to June 30, 2017, 321 bachelor's degrees were awarded. The most popular majors were business/marketing (20%), communication/journalism (10%), and biological/life science (9%). In an average class, 60% graduate in 4 years or less, 68% graduate in 5 years or less, and 68% graduate in 6 years or less.

SERVICES: Counseling and information services are available, as is tutoring in every subject. There is a reader service for the blind, and remedial math and writing. **Library/Resources:** The library contains 270,111 volumes, 77,700 microform items, 2,862 audio/video tapes/CDs/DVDs, and subscribes to 146 periodicals, including electronic. Computerized library services include interlibrary loans, database searching, Internet access, and Wi-Fi capability. Special learning facilities include a planetarium, radio station, TV station, a center for Dubuque history, and an observatory. **Physically Challenged Students:** 63% of the campus is accessible. Facilities include wheelchair ramps, elevators, special parking, specially equipped restrooms, special class scheduling, lowered drinking fountains, lowered telephones, and special housing. **Special:** The college offers 3+2 programs in athletic training and business analytics, paid internships for needy students, and a first generation scholars program. We offer study abroad through both Loras College and affiliate programs, along with internships, work-study programs, a Washington semester, and pre-professional programs. There are 3 national honor societies and a freshman honors program. **Visiting:** There are regularly scheduled orientations for prospective students, meet with faculty, tour campus, meet with admission representative. There are guides for informal visits, visitors may sit in on classes, and stay overnight. To schedule a visit, contact Kristie Arthofer at kristie.arthofer@loras.edu. **Campus Safety and Security:** Measures include 24-hour foot and vehicle patrol, emergency notification system, and security escort services. There are emergency telephones and lighted pathways/sidewalks.

REQUIREMENTS: The SAT or ACT is required. Applicants must be graduates of an accredited secondary school or have a GED certificate and have completed 4 units each of English and math, 3 units of science with 2 units of lab, 3 units of social studies, and 2 units of academic electives. A GPA of 2.5 is required. AP and CLEP credits are accepted. To earn any degree students must complete a total of 120 hours with a minimum GPA of 2.0 and 35 to 36 hours of general education. All students must complete and present a student portfolio for review. A thesis and/or comprehensive exam is required for some majors. **Procedure:** Freshmen are admitted in the fall and spring. Entrance exams should be taken in April or June before the senior year or October of the senior year. There are deferred admissions and rolling admissions plans. Application deadlines are open. Notification is sent on a rolling basis. Applications are accepted on-line. **Transfer Students:** 72 transfer students enrolled in 2016-2017. Transfer students must have a minimum 2.5 GPA and submit transcripts from all previous educational institutions as well as ACT or SAT scores. Students may apply in the fall, winter, spring and summer. 30 of 120 credits required for the bachelor's degree must be completed at LC. **International Students:** There are 23 international students enrolled. They must take the TOEFL with a minimum score of 550 on the paper-based TOEFL (PBT) or 79 on the Internet-based version (iBT).

ADMISSIONS: 95% of the 2017-2018 applicants were accepted. The ACT scores were 3% between 12 and 17, 54% between 18 and 23, 39% between 24 and 29, and 4% above 30. 44% of the current freshmen were in the top fifth of their class; 61% were in the top two fifths. **Admissions Contact:** Kyle Klapatauskas, Admission Director. Email: *admission@loras.edu* Web: *www.loras.edu*

FINANCIAL AID: In 2017-2018, 100% of all full-time freshmen received some form of financial aid. 82% of all full-time freshmen received need-based aid. The average freshman award was $30,985. Need-based scholarships or need-based grants averaged $22,697 ($40,120 maximum); need-based self-help aid (loans and jobs) averaged $5,741 ($13,500 maximum); other non-need-based awards and non-need-based scholarships averaged $8,914 ($37,888 maximum); and $13,605 from other forms of aid. 22% of undergraduate students work part-time. The average financial indebtedness of the 2017 graduate was $34,156. The FAFSA code is 001873. The priority date for freshman financial aid applications for fall entry is March 1.

LUTHER COLLEGE E-1

www.luther.edu

Decorah, IA 52101	(563) 387-1287 (800) 458-8437
Fax: (563) 387-2159	Email: admissions@luther.edu
Full-time: 952 men, 1179 women	Faculty: 168; IIB, av$
Part-time: 18 men, 20 women	Ph.D.s: 95%
Graduate: n/av	Student/Faculty: 11 to 1
Year: 4-1-4, summer session	Tuition: $41,020
Room & Board: $8970	Freshman Class: 4288 applied, 2791 accepted, 517 enrolled
SAT EBR-W/M: 575/590 ACT: 26	CEEB CODE: 6375
Application Deadline: n/av	VERY COMPETITIVE

Luther College, founded in 1861 is a residential, liberal arts institution affiliated with the Evangelical Lutheran Church. One of the outstanding undergraduate institutions in the Midwest, Luther offers more than 60 majors, minors, pre-professional and special programs leading to the bachelor of arts degree. There is 1 undergraduate school. In addition to regional accreditation, Luther has baccalaureate program accreditation with CSWE, NASM, CAEP, and NLN. The 200-acre campus is in a small town in Northeast Iowa at the intersection of State Highway 9 and U.S. Route 52, and is 70 miles southeast of Rochester, Minnesota, and 56 miles southwest of La Crosse, Wisconsin. Including any residence halls, there are 35 buildings.

STUDENT LIFE: 71% of undergraduates are from out of state, mostly the Midwest. Students are from 38 states, 68 foreign countries, and Canada. 90% are from public schools. 82% are White; 7% Foreign; 5% Hispanic; 2% African American; 2% Asian American; 2% two or more races. 53% are Protestant; 17% Catholic. **Female To Male Ratio:** 1.2:1. The average age of freshmen is 18; all undergraduates, 20. 15% do not continue beyond their first year; 79% remain to graduate. **Housing:** 2017 students can be accommodated in college housing, which includes married student dorms, on-campus apartments, and off-campus apartments. In addition, there are special-interest houses, sustainability house, dialogue floors, and wellness floors. On-campus housing is guaranteed for all 4 years and is available on a lottery system for upperclassmen. 89% of students live on campus. All students may keep cars.

FACULTY/CLASSROOMS: 48% of faculty are male; 52% are female. All teach undergraduates. No introductory courses are taught by graduate students. The average class size in an introductory lecture is 17; in a laboratory is 11; and in a regular course is 17.

PROGRAMS OF STUDY: Luther confers B.A. degrees. Bachelor's degrees are awarded in AGRICULTURE (environmental studies), BIOLOGICAL SCIENCE (biology/biological science and neurosciences), BUSINESS (accounting and management science), COMMUNICATIONS AND THE ARTS (art, classical languages, communications, dance, English, French, German, music, Russian, Spanish, and theatre arts), COMPUTER AND PHYSICAL SCIENCE (chemistry, computer science, computer science & informatics, mathematics, physics, and statistics), EDUCATION (athletic training, elementary education, and physical education), HEALTH PROFESSIONS (health and nursing), SOCIAL SCIENCE (African American studies, anthropology, biblical languages, economics, history, international studies, philosophy, political science/government, psychology, religion, social work, sociology, and women's studies). Biology, music, and English are the strongest academically. Biology, management, and music have the largest enrollments.

ACTIVITIES: 1% of men belong to 3 local fraternities; 2% of women belong to 3 local sororities. There are 99 groups on campus, including art, band, cheerleading, choir, chorale, chorus, communications, computers, dance, debate, drama, drill team, environmental, ethnic, forensics, honors, international, jazz band, LGBT, literary magazine, musical theater, newspaper, opera, orchestra, pep band, photography, political, professional, radio and TV, religious, social, social service, student government, and symphony. Popular campus events include Christmas at Luther, Ethnic Arts Fair, Dance Marathon, and Family Weekend. **Sports:** There are 10 intercollegiate sports for men and 9 for women, and 45 intramural sports for men and 45 for women. Facilities include basketball courts, an aquatic center, batting cages, a fitness center, climbing wall, soccer fields, golf driving range, dance studio, a stadium and gym, racquetball courts, indoor and outdoor tracks, and outdoor tennis courts. **Graduates:** From July 1, 2016 to June 30, 2017, 562 bachelor's degrees were awarded. The most popular majors were biology (17%), management (13%), and music (9%). In an average class, 72% graduate in 4 years or less, 78% graduate in 5 years or less, and 79% graduate in 6 years or less. Of the 2016 graduating class, 16% were enrolled in graduate school within 6 months of graduation, and 62% were employed.

SERVICES: Counseling and information services are available, as is tutoring in every subject. There is a reader service for the blind, and remedial math, reading, and writing. A drop in tutoring service is available for mathematics, writing, speech/debate, accounting, chemistry, music theory, modern languages, and physics. There is also reading machines, tape recorders, note taking, and a Learning Center. **Library/Resources:** The library contains 565,593 volumes, 24,839 microform items, 69,881 audio/video tapes/CDs/DVDs, and subscribes to 30,000 periodicals, including electronic. Computerized library services include interlibrary loans, database searching, and Internet access. Special learning facilities include an art gallery, a natural history museum, a planetarium, and a radio station. **Physically Challenged Students:** 95% of the campus is accessible. Facilities include wheelchair ramps, elevators, special parking, specially equipped restrooms, special class scheduling, lowered drinking fountains, lowered telephones, and special housing. **Special:** Internships in most disciplines, study away opportunities both domestically and in many countries (e.g. Malta, Germany, England, France, Ireland, Italy, South Africa, Tanzania, China, Ecuador, Switzerland, Austria, Ireland, Norway, Netherlands, Belgium, Denmark, Sweden, Jamaica, Chile, Cambodia, Czech Republic, Poland, Japan, Belize, Peru, Dominican Republic, Ukraine, Vietnam, Cuba, Spain), a Washington semester, student-designed and dual majors, and 3-2 engineering degrees with Washington University in St. Louis and the University of Minnesota are available, on-campus work-study programs. There are 17 national honor societies, Phi Beta Kappa, and a freshman honors program. **Visiting:** There are regularly scheduled orientations for prospective students. There are guides for informal visits, visitors may sit in on classes, and stay overnight. To schedule a visit, contact the Admissions Office. **Campus Safety and Security:** Measures include 24-hour foot and vehicle patrol, emergency notification system, self-defense education, and security escort services. There are shuttle buses, emergency telephones, lighted pathways/sidewalks, controlled access to dorms/

residences. There are also personal safety education, safety alerts, security cameras, and shelter areas in residence halls known as SHIP (Shelter Here Inside Phone).

REQUIREMENTS: The SAT or ACT is required. In order to be considered for admission, the applicant should be within 2 semesters of graduation from an accredited high school and complete the following college preparatory coursework: 4 years of English, which may include 1 year of speech, communications, or journalism, 3 years each of math, social science, 2 years each of natural science, including 1 year of lab science and foreign language study are recommended. Applicants who do not meet these standards will be considered for admission if they submit above-average ACT or SAT scores. A GPA of 2.5 is required. AP and CLEP credits are accepted. Important factors in the admissions decision are advanced placement or honors courses, evidence of special talent, and extracurricular activities record. Students must complete 128 credit hours for a B.A. with a cumulative grade-point average of 2.0 (C) or higher. The 128 hours must include the following: 30 fall/spring full courses or their equivalents. A full course is equivalent to 4 credit hours; other courses offered are equivalent to 2 credit hours or 1 credit hour. Including 2-January terms, these 2 month-long terms must include a first-year seminar, and one of the following types of experiences: study away, directed readings, student-initiated project. At least 20 course equivalents outside the student's major discipline. 64 credit hours completed in residence. All-college requirements: Common ground; Fields of inquiry; Integrative understanding; Perspectives and skills. **Procedure:** Freshmen are admitted in the fall, winter, and spring. Entrance exams should be taken by the fall of the senior year. There are deferred admissions and rolling admissions plans. Application deadlines are open. Notifications are sent September 1. Applications are accepted on-line. **Transfer Students:** 27 transfer students enrolled in 2016-2017. Applicants must meet the same high school standards and the SAT or ACT requirements as entering freshmen, with a minimum GPA of 2.5 in parallel college course work. 64 of 128 credits required for the bachelor's degree must be completed at Luther. **International Students:** There are 146 international students enrolled. They must take the TOEFL with a minimum score of 550 on the paper-based TOEFL (PBT) or 80 on the Internet-based version (iBT). Students must take the IELTS.

ADMISSIONS: 65% of the 2017-2018 applicants were accepted. The SAT scores for the 2017-2018 freshman class were: Math-- 17% below 500, 35% between 500 and 599, 31% between 600 and 699, and 17% between 700 and 800. Evidence-Based Reading/Writing-- 24% below 500, 31% between 500 and 599, 31% between 600 and 699, and 14% between 700 and 800. The ACT scores were 3% between 12 and 17, 29% between 18 and 23, 48% between 24 and 29, and 20% above 30. 47% of the current freshmen were in the top fifth of their class; 75% were in the top two fifths. 17 freshmen graduated first in their class. **Admissions Contact:** Scot Schaeffer, Vice President for Enrollment Management. Email: *admissions@luther.edu* Web: *www.luther.edu*

FINANCIAL AID: In 2017-2018, 100% of all full-time freshmen received some form of financial aid. 83% of all full-time freshmen received need-based aid. The average freshman award was $37,684. Need-based scholarships or need-based grants averaged $26,547; and need-based self-help aid (loans and jobs) averaged $7,030. 67% of undergraduate students work part-time. The average financial indebtedness of the 2017 graduate was $26,476. Luther is a member of CSS. The college's own financial statement, and student family tax returns are required. The FAFSA code is 001874. The priority date for freshman financial aid applications for fall entry is March 1.

MAHARISHI UNIVERSITY OF MANAGEMENT — E-3

www.mum.edu

Fairfield, IA 52557	(641) 472-1110 (800) 369-6480
Fax: (641) 472-1179	**Email:** admissions@mum.edu
Full-time: 120 men, 80 women	**Faculty:** n/av
Part-time: 10 men, 10 women	**Ph.D.s:** 100%
Graduate: 610 men, 145 women	**Student/Faculty:** n/av
Year: semesters	**Tuition:** $27,530
Room & Board: $7400	**Freshman Class:** n/av **CEEB CODE:** 4497
Application Deadline: open	**VERY COMPETITIVE**

Maharishi University of Management, established in 1971, is a private institution offering undergraduate and graduate programs in a broad range of disciplines. The University provides consciousness-based education and incorporates the group practice of the Maharishi Transcendental Meditation technique into a traditional academic program. There are 5 undergraduate schools and 5 graduate schools. The 272-acre campus is in a small town 114 miles southeast of Des Moines and 60 miles southwest of Iowa City. Including any residence halls, there are 50 buildings.

STUDENT LIFE: 61% of undergraduates are from out of state, mostly the Midwest. Students are from 21 states, 29 foreign countries, and Canada. 74% are White; 5% Asian American; 2% African American; 2% Hispanic; 17% Foreign. **Male To Female Ratio:** 3.1:1. 39% do not continue beyond their first year; 46% remain to graduate. **Housing:** 350 students can be accommodated in college housing, which includes married student dorms and on-campus apartments. In addition, there are special-interest houses, privately owned, and on-campus family housing for students with families. On-campus housing is guaranteed for all 4 years. 70% of students live on campus. Alcohol is not permitted. All students may keep cars.

FACULTY/CLASSROOMS: 80% of faculty are male; 20% are female. All teach undergraduates, 20% do research, and 20% do both. No introductory courses are taught by graduate students. The average class size in an introductory lecture is 35 and in a regular course is 10.

PROGRAMS OF STUDY: MUM confers B.A., B.S., and B.F.A. degrees. Master's and doctoral degrees are also awarded. Bachelor's degrees are awarded in BUSINESS (management science), COMMUNICATIONS AND THE ARTS (dramatic arts, fine arts, and literature), COMPUTER AND PHYSICAL SCIENCE (computer science and mathematics), EDUCATION (education). Sustainable living, Maharishi Vedic science, and business have the largest enrollments.

ACTIVITIES: There are no fraternities or sororities. There are 15 groups on campus, including art, chess, chorale, chorus, dance, drama, ecology, entrepreneurial, environmental, ethnic, international, musical theater, newspaper, permaculture, photography, political, professional, radio and TV, religious, social, social service, student government, and yearbook. Popular campus events include Sports Festivals, Seasonal Celebrations, and International Cultural Exchange Festival. **Sports:** There are 2 intercollegiate sports for men and 1 for women, and 5 intramural sports for men and 5 for women. Facilities include outdoor and indoor tennis, basketball, and volleyball courts, a gym, a weight-training room, a field house, swimming pool, table tennis room, batting and golf driving cages, a golf putting range, an indoor jogging track, a dance studio, and a rock-climbing wall.

SERVICES: Counseling and information services are available, as is tutoring in every subject. There is remedial math, reading, and writing. **Library/Resources:** The library contains 150,294 volumes, 59,851 microform items, 21,291 audio/video tapes/CDs/DVDs, and subscribes to 23,345 periodicals including electronic. Computerized library services include interlibrary loans, database searching, and Internet access. Special learning facilities include an art gallery, radio station, a psychophysiology, electronic engineering, visual technology, and physics labs, a scanning electron microscope, and domes for practicing the Transcendental Meditation Sidhi program. **Physically Challenged Students:** 95% of the campus is accessible. Facilities include wheelchair ramps, special parking, specially equipped restrooms, and lowered telephones. **Special:** Opportunities are provided for internships, study abroad, and nondegree study. Systematic programs are offered in the Science of Creative Intelligence, by which students apply knowledge to practical professional values. There are several 1-month blocks a year during which students may study, art in Italy, literature in Switzerland, or business in China. There are a freshman honors program. **Visiting:** There are regularly scheduled orientations for prospective students, including campus tours, visits to classes, interviews, student panels, and informal dinners. There are guides for informal visits, visitors may sit in on classes, and stay overnight. To schedule a visit, contact the Admissions Office. **Campus Safety and Security:** Measures include 24-hour foot and vehicle patrol and security escort services. There are emergency telephones and lighted pathways/sidewalks.

REQUIREMENTS: Applicants must graduate from an accredited secondary school or have a GED. An essay and 2 personal recommendations are required. An interview is also recommended. A GPA of 2.5 is required. AP and CLEP credits are accepted. Important factors in the admissions decision are personality/intangible qualities, recommendations by school officials, and leadership record. Students must complete 166 credit units with a minimum of 60 credits in the major and must also complete the core curriculum of 18 units as well as 20 units in a distribution of academic fields. All students must maintain a minimum GPA of 2.0. Requirements include health and fitness courses, the Science of Creative Intelligence course with its applied aspect, the Transcendental Meditation program, and courses in math and writing. The 42-week school year and block scheduling system allow students to take 1 course at a time. **Procedure:** Freshmen are admitted in the fall and spring. Entrance exams should be taken in the fall of the senior year or spring of the junior year. There are early admissions, deferred admissions, and rolling admissions plans. Application deadlines are open. Applications are accepted on-line. **Transfer Students:** Students must have a 2.5 GPA and acceptable recommendations as well as meet all standards set by the university. 66 of 166 credits required for the bachelor's degree must be completed at MUM. **International Students:** They must take the TOEFL and the college's own test.

Admissions Contact: Barbara Rainbow, Associate Dean of Admissions. Email: *admissions@mum.edu* Web: *www.mum.edu*

FINANCIAL AID: The FAFSA code is 011113. Check with the school for current application deadlines.

MERCY COLLEGE OF HEALTH SCIENCES *(The complete profile is made available exclusively on our website, www.barronspac.com)*

MORNINGSIDE COLLEGE — B-2

www.morningside.edu

Sioux City, IA 51106	(712) 274-5511 (800) 831-0806
Fax: (712) 274-5101	Email: mscadm@morningside.edu
Full-time: 590 men, 662 women	**Faculty:** 70; IIB, -$
Part-time: 32 men, 38 women	**Ph.D.s:** 74%
Graduate: 245 men, 1221 women	**Student/Faculty:** 18 to 1
Year: semesters, summer session	**Tuition:** $30,390
Room & Board: $9390	**Freshman Class:** 4603 applied, 2540 accepted, 354 enrolled
ACT: 22	**CEEB CODE:** 6415
Application Deadline: open	**COMPETITIVE**

Morningside College, founded in 1894, is a private college affiliated with the United Methodist Church. Its curriculum includes the liberal arts and pre-professional and professional programs of study. There is 1 undergraduate school and 2 graduate schools. In addition to regional accreditation, MC has baccalaureate program accreditation with NASM, NCATE, and HLC. The 69-acre campus is in a suburban area 100 miles north of Omaha at the convergence of the states of South Dakota, Iowa, and Nebraska. Including any residence halls, there are 25 buildings.

STUDENT LIFE: 54% of undergraduates are from Iowa. Others are from 29 states, 19 foreign countries, and Canada. 76% are White; 8% Hispanic; 5% Foreign; 4% race unknown; 3% two or more races; 2% African American; 1% Asian American; 1% American Indian/Alaska Native. 49% claim no religious affiliation; 32% Protestant; 12% Catholic. **Female To Male Ratio:** 2.2:1. The average age of freshmen is 18; all undergraduates, 21. 30% do not continue beyond their first year; 56% remain to graduate. **Housing:** 912 students can be accommodated in college housing, which includes married student dorms and on-campus apartments. In addition, there are fraternity houses, sorority houses, freshman halls, upperclassman leadership-themed, and apartment-style residence hall. On-campus housing is guaranteed for all 4 years. 60% of students live on campus. All students may keep cars.

FACULTY/CLASSROOMS: 47% of faculty are male; 53% are female. 60% teach undergraduates. No introductory courses are taught by graduate students. The average class size in an introductory lecture is 27; in a laboratory is 16; and in a regular course is 20.

PROGRAMS OF STUDY: MC confers B.A., B.S., B.Mus., B.Mus.Ed., and B.S.N. degrees. Master's degrees are also awarded. Bachelor's degrees are awarded in AGRICULTURE (agricultural business management and agricultural sciences), BIOLOGICAL SCIENCE (biology/biological science), BUSINESS (business administration and management, management information systems, and organizational leadership and management), COMMUNICATIONS AND THE ARTS (advertising, art, communications, dramatic arts, English, graphic design, music, photography, and Spanish), COMPUTER AND PHYSICAL SCIENCE (chemistry, computer science, mathematics, and physics), EDUCATION (art education, education, elementary education, English education, mathematics education, music education, science education, social studies education, and special education), HEALTH PROFESSIONS (medical technology and nursing), SOCIAL SCIENCE (history, international relations, philosophy, political science/government, psychology, and religion). biology, business, and nursing have the largest enrollments.

ACTIVITIES: 4% of men belong to 2 national fraternities; 2% of women belong to 1 national sorority. There are 41 groups on campus, including art, band, cheerleading, choir, chorale, chorus, computers, dance, drama, drill team, environmental, ethnic, honors, international, jazz band, literary magazine, marching band, newspaper, orchestra, pep band, photography, political, professional, radio and TV, religious, social, and student government. Popular campus events include Homecoming, Friday is Writing Day, and Christmas at Morningside. **Sports:** There are 11 intercollegiate sports for men and 10 for women, and 13 intramural sports for men and 13 for women. Facilities include a stadium, football field, a campus recreation center with basketball, volleyball, and racquetball/handball courts, an elevated track, a weight room, and a pool. **Graduates:** From July 1, 2016 to June 30, 2017, 272 bachelor's degrees were awarded. The most popular majors were business (23%), biology (22%), and nursing (10%). In an average class, 1% graduate in 3 years or less, 56% graduate in 4 years or less, 50% graduate in 5 years or less, and 56% graduate in 6 years or less. Of the 2016 graduating class, 17% were enrolled in graduate school within 6 months of graduation.

SERVICES: Counseling and information services are available, as is tutoring in most subjects. There is a reader service for the blind, and remedial math, reading, and writing. **Library/Resources:** The library contains 53,081 volumes, 123 microform items, 1,590 audio/video tapes/CDs/DVDs, and subscribes to 152 periodicals, including electronic. Computerized library services include interlibrary loans, database searching, and Internet access. Special learning facilities include an art gallery, radio station, TV station, and a theater. **Physically Challenged Students:** 80% of the campus is accessible. Facilities include wheelchair ramps, elevators, special parking, specially equipped restrooms, special class scheduling, lowered drinking fountains, and lowered telephones. **Special:** There is a co-op program in medical technology. Internships are available in all departments. Study abroad in over 15 countries, a Washington semester, work-study programs, both on campus and with 20 nonprofit agencies, and student-designed majors are available. There are 15 national honor societies and a freshman honors program. **Visiting:** There are regularly scheduled orientations for prospective students, consists of a campus tour, appointments with faculty and financial aid, and an interview with an admissions counselor. There are guides for informal visits, visitors may sit in on classes, and stay overnight. To schedule a visit, contact the Office of Admissions. **Campus Safety and Security:** Measures include emergency notification system, self-defense education, and security escort services. There are emergency telephones, lighted pathways/sidewalks, and controlled access to dorms/residences.

REQUIREMENTS: The ACT is required. Applicants must be graduates of an accredited secondary school. The GED is accepted. A portfolio is required for all studio art majors and an audition for performing music majors. Applicants graduating from high school 5 years or more prior to entering college are exempted from submitting the ACT scores. Those entering from a home-schooled environment must submit a completed Home School Credit Evaluation form, which may be obtained in the Office of Admissions. Morningside requires applicants to be in the upper 50% of their class. A GPA of 2.5 is required. AP and CLEP credits are accepted. Important factors in the admissions decision are recommendations by school officials, evidence of special talent, and advanced placement or honors courses. The total number of credit hours required for graduation is 124 with 44 hours of core curriculum in liberal arts and 30 hours minimum in the major. Students must have a minimum GPA of 2.0 to graduate. **Procedure:** Freshmen are admitted to all sessions. Entrance exams should be taken in the junior year. There is a rolling admissions plan. Application deadlines are open. Applications are accepted on-line. **Transfer Students:** 56 transfer students enrolled in 2016-2017. Transfer applicants must take the ACT and have an interview. They must have 24 semester hours with a 2.25 or above cumulative GPA. They must present official transcripts of previous collegiate records. 30 of 124 credits required for the bachelor's degree must be completed at MC. **International Students:** There are 64 international students enrolled. They must take the TOEFL with a minimum score of 500 on the paper-based TOEFL (PBT) or 61 on the Internet-based version (iBT). They must also take the ACT.

ADMISSIONS: 55% of the 2017-2018 applicants were accepted. The

ACT scores were 7% between 12 and 17, 58% between 18 and 23, 30% between 24 and 29, and 5% above 30. 29% of the current freshmen were in the top fifth of their class; 58% were in the top two fifths. 2 freshmen graduated first in their class. **Admissions Contact:** Terri Curry, Vice President Admissions. Email: *mscadm@morningside.edu* Web: *www.morningside.edu*

FINANCIAL AID: In 2017-2018, 100% of all full-time freshmen received some form of financial aid. 72% of all full-time freshmen received need-based aid. The average freshman award was $32,110. Need-based scholarships or need-based grants averaged $6,526 ($16,570 maximum); need-based self-help aid (loans and jobs) averaged $5,278 ($10,000 maximum); non-need-based athletic scholarships averaged $4,546 ($10,000 maximum); other non-need-based awards and non-need-based scholarships averaged $15,728 ($34,414 maximum); and $7,567 from other forms of aid. 45% of undergraduate students work part-time. The average financial indebtedness of the 2017 graduate was $36,427. The FAFSA code is 001879. The priority date for freshman financial aid applications for fall entry is March 1.

MOUNT MERCY UNIVERSITY E-3

www.mtmercy.edu

Cedar Rapids, IA 52402 (319) 368-6460
(800) 248-4504

Fax: (319) 363-5270 **Email:** admission@.mtmercy.edu

Full-time: 371 men, 712 women	**Faculty:** 83
Part-time: 119 men, 315 women	**Ph.D.s:** 68%
Graduate: 110 men, 221 women	**Student/Faculty:** 15 to 1
Year: 4-1-4, summer session	**Tuition:** $30,382
Room & Board: $9166	**Freshman Class:** 1457 applied, 834 accepted, 238 enrolled
SAT: recommended **ACT:** 22	**CEEB CODE:** 6417
Application Deadline: August 14	**COMPETITIVE**

The men and women who make up our student body come from all over Iowa and the world. They choose Mount Mercy for our small, hands-on classes, meaningful faculty interaction, vibrant student life and our commitment to leadership and compassionate service. There are 5 undergraduate schools and 5 graduate schools. In addition to regional accreditation, MMU has baccalaureate program accreditation with CSWE and NLN. The 40-acre campus is in an urban area in Cedar Rapids in eastern Iowa. Including any residence halls, there are 19 buildings.

STUDENT LIFE: 85% of undergraduates are from Iowa. Others are from 28 states, 33 foreign countries, and Canada. 79% are White; 7% African American; 4% Foreign; 4% race unknown; 2% Asian American; 2% two or more races; 1% American Indian/Alaska Native; 1% Hispanic. 65% are Protestant; 30% Catholic; 11% claim no religious affiliation. **Female To Male Ratio:** 2.1:1. The average age of freshmen is 18; all undergraduates, 25. 26% do not continue beyond their first year; 58% remain to graduate. **Housing:** 604 students can be accommodated in college housing, which includes dorms and on-campus apartments. In addition, there are special-interest houses, and themed living learning communities. On-campus housing is guaranteed for all 4 years and is available on a lottery system for upperclassmen. 54% of students commute. All students may keep cars.

FACULTY/CLASSROOMS: 37% of faculty are male; 63% are female. 94% teach undergraduates, 2% do research, and 2% do both. No introductory courses are taught by graduate students. The average class size in an introductory lecture is 24; in a laboratory is 14; and in a regular course is 25.

PROGRAMS OF STUDY: MMU confers B.A., B.A.A., B.A.S., B.B.A., B.S., and B.S.N. degrees. Master's degrees are also awarded. Bachelor's degrees are awarded in AGRICULTURE (conservation and regulation), BIOLOGICAL SCIENCE (biology/biological science), BUSINESS (accounting, business administration and management, finance, human resources, management information systems, and marketing/retailing/merchandising), COMMUNICATIONS AND THE ARTS (art, communications, English, graphic design, journalism, and music), COMPUTER AND PHYSICAL SCIENCE (actuarial science, computer science, and mathematics), EDUCATION (early childhood education, elementary education, middle school education, and secondary education), HEALTH PROFESSIONS (health care administration, medical laboratory technology, and nursing), SOCIAL SCIENCE (criminal justice, history, international studies, philosophy, political science/government, psychology, religion, social work, and sociology). Business, nursing, and education have the largest enrollments.

ACTIVITIES: There are no fraternities or sororities. There are 34 groups on campus, including academic club, art, band, cheerleading, choir, chorale, chorus, computers, dance, drama, drill team, environmental, ethnic, film, honors, international, jazz band, LGBT, literary magazine, musical theater, newspaper, pep band, political, professional, religious, social, social service, and student government. Popular campus events include Octoberfest, Bingo Nights, and Vegas Night. **Sports:** There are 9 intercollegiate sports for men and 9 for women, and 15 intramural sports for men and 15 for women. The recreation center offers practice facilities, a weight room, fully-equipped training room, a cardio and weight area, group exercise rooms, equipment and spaces for a variety of cardiovascular and muscle-building workout.**Graduates:** From July 1, 2016 to June 30, 2017, 443 bachelor's degrees were awarded. The most popular majors were nursing (32%), business (19%), and criminal justice (7%). In an average class, 1% graduate in 3 years or less, 53% graduate in 4 years or less, 56% graduate in 5 years or less, and 58% graduate in 6 years or less. Of the 2016 graduating class, 20% were enrolled in graduate school within 6 months of graduation, and 96% were employed.

SERVICES: Counseling and information services are available, as is tutoring in most subjects, such as communication skills. There is a reader service for the blind, and remedial math, reading, and writing. **Library/Resources:** The library contains 124,017 volumes, 54,945 microform items, 9,196 audio/video tapes/CDs/DVDs, and subscribes to 3,972 periodicals including electronic. Computerized library services include interlibrary loans, database searching, Internet access, and Wi-Fi capability. Special learning facilities include an art gallery, all of the classrooms are "smart" technology classrooms. **Physically Challenged Students:** 95% of the campus is accessible. Facilities include wheelchair ramps, elevators, special parking, specially equipped restrooms, special class scheduling, and lowered drinking fountains. **Special:** Mount Mercy offers internships in most majors, study abroad opportunities, work-study programs on campus, several adult accelerated business majors, an accelerated degree completion program for RNs, and student-designed, interdisciplinary majors. Credit for prior experiential learning may be granted, and pass/fail options are available. There are 3 national honor societies, a freshman honors program, and 10 departmental honors programs. **Visiting:** There are regularly scheduled orientations for prospective students, consisting of a presidential welcome, campus tour, student panel, faculty academic fair, presentations on college selection and admission requirements, and student evaluation. There are guides for informal visits, visitors may sit in on classes, and stay overnight. To schedule a visit, contact the Admissions Office. **Campus Safety and Security:** Measures include emergency notification system, self-defense education, and security escort services. There are emergency telephones, lighted pathways/sidewalks, controlled access to dorms/residences, Safety personnel who are on duty 24-hours-a-day, 365-days-a-year, with regularly scheduled patrols, extensive video monitoring of building entrances building exits, and most parking facilities. Surveillance is monitored and recorded after hours, use of residence elevators and entry to student room corridors require a resident-only passkey.

REQUIREMENTS: The SAT or ACT is recommended. Strong consideration will be given to applicants with the following: cumulative GPA of 2.75 (on a 4.0 scale), composite ACT score of 20 (940 SAT) with subscores of 17 or higher, and class rank in the top half of their graduating class. While specific courses are not required for admission, students applying to Mount Mercy are encouraged to complete the following high school coursework: 4 years of English, 3 years each of mathematics, social studies, and science. A GPA of 2.5 is required. AP and CLEP credits are accepted. Important factors in the admissions decision are leadership record, extracurricular activities record, and geographical diversity. To graduate, students must complete 123 semester hours, have a minimum cumulative GPA of at least 2.0, a minimum cumulative GPA in all credits taken, completion of the core curriculum requirements, completions of a major program of study, at least 12 semester hours, above course number 200, completed in the major, a minimum of 30 semester hours completed, and a minimum of 30 consecutive semester hours completed immediately preceding graduation. **Procedure:** Freshmen are admitted to all sessions. Entrance exams should be taken in the junior year or the fall of the senior year. There are deferred admissions and rolling admissions plans. Applications should be filed by August 14 for fall entry. Notification is sent on a rolling basis. Applications are accepted online. **Transfer Students:** 154 transfer students enrolled in 2016-2017. Mount Mercy evaluates all files on an individual basis. While specific courses are not required for admission, the transcripts will be evaluated to ensure that strong college curriculum has been successfully completed. Strong consideration will be given to applicants with a cumulative transfer GPA of 2.50 (on a 4.0 scale). Students looking to transfer with two semesters or less will be reviewed by the Admission Committee. Transfer students must submit an application for admission, and official high school transcripts. For applicants who have not earned an associates degree or higher from an accredited college or university official transcripts from all previous colleges attended are required. For applicants who have earned an associates degree or higher from an accredited college or university, updated copies of college transcripts will need to be sent prior to enrollment for students who apply for admission while enrolled at another college. 30 of 123 credits required for the bachelor's degree must be completed at MMU. **International Students:** There are 60 international students enrolled. They must take the TOEFL with a minimum score of 550 on the paper-based TOEFL (PBT) or 79 on the Internet-based version (iBT). Students must take the ICHS 6.5; Step EIKEN Grade 1; IELTS (6.5); ACT (20); SAT (940).

ADMISSIONS: 57% of the 2017-2018 applicants were accepted. The ACT scores were 12% between 12 and 17, 55% between 18 and 23, 28% between 24 and 29, and 5% above 30. 37% of the current freshmen were in the top fifth of their class; 72% were in the top two fifths. 2 freshmen graduated first in their class. **Admissions Contact:** Terri Crumley, Dean of Admissions. Email: *admission@.mtmercy.edu* Web: *www.mtmercy.edu*

FINANCIAL AID: In 2017-2018, 100% of all full-time freshmen received some form of financial aid. 81% of all full-time freshmen received need-based aid. The average freshman award was $19,302. 41% of undergraduate students work part-time. The average financial indebtedness of the 2017 graduate was $25,739. The FAFSA code is 001880. The priority date for freshman financial aid applications for fall entry is March 1.

NORTHWESTERN COLLEGE OF IOWA — B-2

www.nwciowa.edu

Orange City, IA 51041 — (712) 707-7114, (800) 747-4757

Fax: (712) 707-7164 — **Email:** admissions@nwciowa.edu

Full-time: 438 men, 559 women	**Faculty:** 83; IIB, --$
Part-time: 18 men, 33 women	**Ph.D.s:** 83%
Graduate: 22 men, 180 women	**Student/Faculty:** 12 to 1
Year: semesters, summer session	**Tuition:** $29,500 ($30,200)
Room & Board: $9000	**Freshman Class:** 1965 applied, 1340 accepted, 281 enrolled
SAT CR/M: 540/540 **ACT:** 24	**CEEB CODE:** 6490
Application Deadline: August 15	**COMPETITIVE**

Northwestern College of Iowa, is a Christian academic community engaging students in courageous and faithful learning and living that empowers them to follow Christ and pursue God's redeeming work in the world. There is 1 undergraduate school and 1 graduate school. In addition to regional accreditation, NWCI has baccalaureate program accreditation with CSWE, CAEP, CAATE, IACBE, and CCNE. The 100-acre campus is in a small town 40 miles northeast of Sioux City, and 75 miles southeast of Sioux Falls, South Dakota. Including any residence halls, there are 33 buildings.

STUDENT LIFE: 55% of undergraduates are from Iowa. Others are from 31 states, 21 foreign countries, and Canada. 71% are from public schools. 83% are White; 5% race unknown; 4% Hispanic; 3% Foreign; 2% two or more races; 1% African American; 1% Asian American; 1% American Indian/Alaska Native. 84% are Protestant. **Female To Male Ratio:** 1.6:1. The average age of freshmen is 18; all undergraduates, 20. 22% do not continue beyond their first year; 68% remain to graduate. **Housing:** 1045 students can be accommodated in college housing, which includes dorms and on-campus apartments. On-campus housing is guaranteed for all 4 years. 84% of students live on campus. Alcohol is not permitted. All students may keep cars.

FACULTY/CLASSROOMS: 58% of faculty are male; 42% are female. All teach undergraduates, 80% do research, and 80% do both. No introductory courses are taught by graduate students. The average class size in an introductory lecture is 22; in a laboratory is 15; and in a regular course is 15.

PROGRAMS OF STUDY: NWCI confers B.A., B.A.A.T., and B.S.N. degrees. Master's degrees are also awarded. Bachelor's degrees are awarded in AGRICULTURE (agricultural business management), BIOLOGICAL SCIENCE (biochemistry, biology/biological science, and genetics), BUSINESS (accounting, business administration and management, and business economics), COMMUNICATIONS AND THE ARTS (dramatic arts, graphic design, journalism, literature, music, public relations, and Spanish), COMPUTER AND PHYSICAL SCIENCE (actuarial science, chemistry, computer science, and mathematics), EDUCATION (art education, athletic training, business education, Christian education, early childhood education, elementary education, foreign languages education, middle school education, music education, physical education, science education, secondary education, and special education), HEALTH PROFESSIONS (medical laboratory technology, nursing, predentistry, and premedicine), SOCIAL SCIENCE (criminal justice, economics, history, philosophy, physical fitness/movement, political science/government, prelaw, psychology, religion, religious music, social work, sociology, and youth ministry). Biology, education, and religion are the strongest academically. Business, education, and kinesiology have the largest enrollments.

ACTIVITIES: There are no fraternities or sororities. There are 50 groups on campus, including art, band, cheerleading, choir, chorus, communications, computers, dance, drama, drill team, environmental, ethnic, honors, international, jazz band, literary magazine, musical theater, newspaper, orchestra, pep band, photography, political, professional, religious, social, social service, student government, symphony, and yearbook. Popular campus events include Clash of the Classes competition, Airband competition, Coly Christmas Bash, Raider Days Homecoming, NC/DC singing competition, RUSH Student Dance Exhibition, and Winter Formal. **Sports:** There are 8 intercollegiate sports for men and 8 for women, and 21 intramural sports for men and 21 for women. Facilities include athletic facilities include a gymnasium for basketball and volleyball, an outdoor stadium with a turf football field surrounded by an eight-lane polyurethane track, practice football fields, soccer fields, indoor practice facility for intercollegiate baseball, softball, football, and track, weight room and training, wrestling room, a one-tenth-mile/six-lane indoor track, handball/racquetball courts, basketball and volleyball courts, indoor tennis courts, and a fitness center with free weights and fitness equipment. **Graduates:** From July 1, 2016 to June 30, 2017, 256 bachelor's degrees were awarded. The most popular majors were business administration (16%), elementary education (9%), and nursing (9%). In an average class, 2% graduate in 3 years or less, 58% graduate in 4 years or less, 67% graduate in 5 years or less, and 68% graduate in 6 years or less. Of the 2016 graduating class, 14% were enrolled in graduate school within 6 months of graduation, and 82% were employed.

SERVICES: Counseling and information services are available, as is tutoring in most subjects. There is remedial math, reading, and writing. **Library/Resources:** The library contains 80,000 volumes, 3,000 audio/video tapes/CDs/DVDs, and subscribes to 500 periodicals including electronic. Computerized library services include interlibrary loans, database searching, Internet access, and Wi-Fi capability. Special learning facilities include an art gallery. **Physically Challenged Students:** 90% of the campus is accessible. Facilities include wheelchair ramps, elevators, special parking, specially equipped restrooms, lowered drinking fountains, and special housing. **Special:** Northwestern offers cross-registration with Dordt College, student-designed majors, numerous internships, off-campus semester programs in Chicago, Washington, D.C., and Denver, and study abroad in over 20 countries, including China, Oman, Romania, Egypt, Spain, France, and the Netherlands. There are 2 national honor societies, a freshman honors program, and 23 departmental honors programs. **Visiting:** There are regularly scheduled orientations for prospective students, campus tour, meet with financial aid and admissions personnel, attend chapel, meet with a faculty member and attend a class in the student's area of interest. There are guides for informal visits; visitors may sit in on classes, and stay overnight. To schedule a visit, contact Laura De Boer at (712) 707-7142. **Campus Safety and Security:** Measures include an emergency notification system. There are emergency telephones, lighted pathways/sidewalks, and controlled access to dorms/residences.

REQUIREMENTS: Applicants with a minimum ACT composite of 19, in the top half of their high school class, and with a 2.4 GPA are generally accepted. Applicants should be graduates of an accredited secondary school. The suggested distribution of high school courses is 4 years of English, 3 years each of math, foreign language, and social studies, and 2 of natural science. The GED is accepted. A GPA of 2.0 is required. AP and CLEP credits are accepted. All students are required to take an integrated general education core curriculum, including a first-year seminar, eight credits of Christian story and tradition courses, between 31 and 44 credits in a variety of disciplines, and a senior seminar. Students must maintain a 2.0 GPA for 124 total credits and pass both writing and math competency levels. **Procedure:** Freshmen are admitted to all sessions. Entrance exams should be taken spring semester of the junior year of high school. There is a rolling admissions plan. Application deadlines are open. Notifications are sent November 1. Applications are accepted online. **Transfer Students:** 53 transfer students enrolled in 2016-2017. Transfer applicants must submit a transcript and letter of recommendation. A minimum college GPA of 2.0 is required. 30 of 124 credits required for the bachelor's degree must be completed at NWCI. **International Students:** There are 34 international students enrolled. They must take the TOEFL with a minimum score of 475 on the paper-based TOEFL (PBT) or 53 on the Internet-based version (iBT).

ADMISSIONS: 68% of the 2017-2018 applicants were accepted. The SAT scores for the 2017-2018 freshman class were: Critical Reading-- 26% below 500, 50% between 500 and 599, 24% between 600 and 699, and 0% between 700 and 800. Math-- 23% below 500, 46% between 500 and 599, 23% between 600 and 699, and 8% between 700 and 800. The ACT scores were 3% between 12 and 17, 42% between 18 and 23, 40% between 24 and 29, and 15% above 30. 48% of the current freshmen were in the top fifth of their class; 73% were in the top two fifths. 18 freshmen graduated first in their class. **Admissions Contact:** Jackie Davis, Director of Admissions. Email: *admissions@nwciowa.edu* Web: *www.nwciowa.edu*

FINANCIAL AID: In 2017-2018, 100% of all full-time freshmen received some form of financial aid. 89% of all full-time freshmen received need-based aid. The average freshman award was $29,913. Need-based scholarships or need-based grants averaged $5,906 ($22,570 maximum); need-based self-help aid (loans and jobs) averaged $4,310 ($9,820 maximum); non-need-based athletic scholarships averaged $6,010 ($18,000 maximum); and other non-need-based awards and non-need-based scholarships averaged $18,033 ($42,250 maximum). 85% of undergraduate students work part-time. The average financial indebtedness of the 2017 graduate was $29,595. The FAFSA code is 001883. The priority date for freshman financial aid applications for fall entry is April 1.

SIMPSON COLLEGE — C-3

www.simpson.edu

Indianola, IA 50125 — **(515) 961-1624**

Fax: (515) 961-1870	**Email: admiss@simpson.edu**
Full-time: 587 men, 693 women	**Faculty:** 105
Part-time: 62 men, 89 women	**Ph.D.s:** 86%
Graduate: 15 men, 32 women	**Student/Faculty:** 12 to 1
Year: other, summer session	**Tuition:** $37,663
Room & Board: $7963	**Freshman Class:** 1243 applied, 1042 accepted, 296 enrolled
ACT: 24	**CEEB CODE:** 6650
Application Deadline: rolling	**VERY COMPETITIVE**

Simpson College, founded in 1860, is a private institution affiliated with the United Methodist Church that combines the best of a liberal arts education with outstanding career preparation and extracurricular programs. More than 80 majors, minors, and pre-professional programs are offered. Extra-curricular activities at Simpson are designed to supplement and reinforce the academic program and contribute toward a total learning experience. Activities range from award-winning fine arts programs to nationally recognized NCAA Division III teams. There are 3 undergraduate schools and 1 graduate school. In addition to regional accreditation, Simpson has baccalaureate program accreditation with NASM and CAATE. The 80-acre campus is in a small town 12 miles south of Des Moines, Iowa's capital city. Including any residence halls, there are 45 buildings.

STUDENT LIFE: 81% of undergraduates are from Iowa. Others are from 29 states, and 9 foreign countries. 82% are White; 7% race unknown; 4% Hispanic; 2% African American; 2% Asian American; 2% two or more races; 1% Foreign. 42% are Protestant; 23% Unknown, Agnostic, Muslim, Buddhist, and Atheist; 16% Catholic. **Female To Male Ratio:** 1.2:1. The average age of freshmen is 18; all undergraduates, 23. 20% do not continue beyond their first year; 68% remain to graduate. **Housing:** 1268 students can be accommodated in college housing, which includes dorms and on-campus apartments. In addition, there are special-interest houses, fraternity houses, sorority houses, and theme houses. On-campus housing is guaranteed for all 4 years. 87% of students live on campus. All students may keep cars.

FACULTY/CLASSROOMS: 53% of faculty are male; 47% are female. All teach undergraduates. No introductory courses are taught by graduate students. The average class size in an introductory lecture is 25; in a laboratory is 22; and in a regular course is 17.

PROGRAMS OF STUDY: Simpson confers B.A. and B.Mus. degrees. Master's degrees are also awarded. Bachelor's degrees are awarded in BIOLOGICAL SCIENCE (biochemistry, biology/biological science, and neurosciences), BUSINESS (accounting, business administration and management, international business management, management information systems, marketing management, and sports management), COMMUNICATIONS AND THE ARTS (art, communications, dramatic arts, English, French, German, graphic design, journalism, multimedia, music, music performance, public relations, Spanish, sports communication, and studio art), COMPUTER AND PHYSICAL SCIENCE (actuarial science, chemistry, computer science, information sciences and systems, mathematics, and physics), EDUCATION (elementary education, music education, physical education, and secondary education), ENGINEERING AND ENVIRONMENTAL DESIGN (environmental science and preengineering), HEALTH PROFESSIONS (exercise science, predentistry, premedicine, preoptometry, prepharmacy, prephysical therapy, and preveterinary science), SOCIAL SCIENCE (criminal justice, economics, forensic studies, history, interdisciplinary studies, international relations, philosophy, political science/government, prelaw, psychology, religion, and sociology). Education, sciences, and music are the strongest academically. Management, psychology, and education have the largest enrollments.

ACTIVITIES: 24% of men belong to 1 local and 3 national fraternities; 24% of women belong to 3 national sororities. There are 75 groups on campus, including art, band, campus activities board, cheerleading, choir, chorale, computers, dance, debate, drama, drill team, environmental, ethnic, honors, international, jazz band, LGBT, literary magazine, musical theater, newspaper, opera, orchestra, pep band, political, professional, radio and TV, religious, social, social service, student government, and yearbook. Popular campus events include Back to School Stand-Around, Homecoming Yell Like Hell Pep Rally, Campus Day, and Lessons and Carols Christmas Concert. **Sports:** There are 10 intercollegiate sports for men and 9 for women, and 50 intramural sports for men and 50 for women. Facilities include a gym, a wrestling practice room, weight room/workout facility, training facility, racquetball courts, a field house for volleyball, basketball, and wrestling, football and soccer stadium with track, tennis courts, baseball field, softball complex, practice and intramural fields, outdoor basketball, and sand volleyball courts. There is a pool and diving facility at the YMCA for student to use. **Graduates:** From July 1, 2016 to June 30, 2017, 420 bachelor's degrees were awarded. The most popular majors were business, management (11%), elementary education (8%), and criminal justice (7%). In an average class, 63% graduate in 4 years or less, 68% graduate in 5 years or less, and 68% graduate in 6 years or less. Of the 2016 graduating class, 22% were enrolled in graduate school within 6 months of graduation, and 75% were employed.

SERVICES: Counseling and information services are available, as is tutoring in every subject. There is a reader service for the blind. **Library/Resources:** The library contains 134,098 volumes, 8,539 microform items, and 4,621 audio/video tapes/CDs/DVDs, and subscribes to 87,887 periodicals including electronic. Computerized library services include interlibrary loans, database searching, Internet access, and Wi-Fi capability. Special learning facilities include an art gallery, radio station, Avery O. Craven antebellum period collection, the George Washington Carver papers, the Iowa History Center, the John C. Culver Center for Public Policy Studies, an education lab, and a cadaver lab. **Physically Challenged Students:** All of the campus is accessible. Facilities include wheelchair ramps, elevators, special parking, specially equipped restrooms, special class scheduling, lowered drinking fountains, and special housing. **Special:** Internships, study abroad, a Washington semester, and work-study are all available. Dual and student-designed majors are possible. There are several preprofessional programs in health related areas, and 3-2 engineering degrees are offered with Washington University at St. Louis, Iowa State University, and Institute of Technology (University of Minnesota). We also offer a 3 + 3 Law program with Drake University, and a 3 + 2 Nursing program in conjunction with Allen College of Nursing. There are 15 national honor societies, a freshman honors program, and 5 departmental honors programs. **Visiting:** There are regularly scheduled orientations for prospective students, Orientation is scheduled 4 times throughout the summer to allow incoming students to meet with an academic advisor, register for classes, and participate in activity information sessions. Parents are encouraged to attend. There are guides for informal visits, visitors may sit in on classes, and stay overnight. To schedule a visit, contact Gail Fennelly at admiss@simpson.edu. **Campus Safety and Security:** Measures include 24-hour foot and vehicle patrol, emergency notification system, and security escort services. There are emergency telephones, lighted pathways/sidewalks, and controlled access to dorms/residences.

REQUIREMENTS: Applicants must be graduates of an accredited secondary school; however, the GED is accepted. ACT or SAT test scores, counselor recommendations, GPA, college prep course grades, and class rank are all considered in a selective admissions process. The college strongly recommends that applicants complete 4 years of English, 3 each of math, lab science, social science, and foreign language. A visit to the campus and speak with an admissions representative is also recommended. AP and CLEP credits are accepted. Students must satisfactorily complete the Engaged Citizenship curriculum including a first-year colloquium, a senior capstone course, complete two May term courses, and complete a major course load. **Procedure:** Freshmen are admitted to all sessions. Entrance exams should be taken during the junior or senior year. There are deferred admissions and rolling admissions plans. Application deadlines are open. Notification is sent on a rolling basis. Applications are accepted on-line. **Transfer Students:** 58 transfer students enrolled in 2016-2017. In addition to freshman requirements, transfer applicants are considered on the basis of college work taken and grades received. It is recommended that applicants take either the SAT or ACT. The recommended GPA is 2.5, and grades of 2.0 and above transfer for credit. 32 of 128 credits required for the bachelor's degree must be completed at Simpson. **International Students:** There are 9 international students enrolled. They must take the TOEFL with a minimum score of 550 on the paper-based TOEFL (PBT) or 79 on the Internet-based version (iBT). They must also take the SAT and ACT.

ADMISSIONS: 84% of the 2017-2018 applicants were accepted. The ACT scores were 2% between 12 and 17, 41% between 18 and 23, 46% between 24 and 29, and 11% above 30. **Admissions Contact:** Deborah Tierney, Vice President for Enrollment. Email: *admiss@simpson.edu* Web: *www.simpson.edu*

FINANCIAL AID: In 2017-2018, 100% of all full-time freshmen received some form of financial aid. 86% of all full-time freshmen received need-based aid. The average freshman award was $31,851. Need-based scholarships or need-based grants averaged $26,115; need-based self-help aid (loans and jobs) averaged $4,660; and other non-need-based awards and non-need-based scholarships averaged $22,897. 60% of undergraduate students work part-time. The average financial indebtedness of the 2017 graduate was $24,422. The FAFSA code is 001887. The priority date for freshman financial aid applications for fall entry is February 1.

ST. AMBROSE UNIVERSITY E-3

www.sau.edu

Davenport, IA 52803

(563) 333-6306
(800) 383-2627
Email: admit@sau.edu

Full-time: 981 men, 1234 women	**Faculty:** 175
Part-time: 62 men, 93 women	**Ph.D.s:** 86%
Graduate: 230 men, 518 women	**Student/Faculty:** 13 to 1
Year: semesters, summer session	**Tuition:** $30,016
Room & Board: $10,164	**Freshman Class:** 5359 applied, 3246 accepted, 550 enrolled
ACT: 23	**CEEB CODE:** 6617
Application Deadline: n/av	**COMPETITIVE**

St. Ambrose University, founded in 1882 and affiliated with the Diocese of Davenport, is independent, coeducational, and Catholic. It is recognized as a leading Midwestern university, consistently rated among the top universities in the region by major national ranking publications. The University offers more than 60 areas of study leading to bachelor's degrees, as well as graduate programs granting master's and doctoral degrees. Robust academic and co-curricular programs are offered in the liberal arts and sciences, education, business, the health sciences, and increasingly in STEM fields. There are 3 undergraduate schools and 3 graduate schools. In addition to regional accreditation, SAU has baccalaureate program accreditation with ABET, ACBSP, APTA, CSWE, CAEP, ACOTE, AOTA, CAPTE, ARC-PA, NAEYC, CCNE, and and ASHA. The 123-acre campus is in an urban area St. Ambrose University is located 180 miles west of Chicago in Davenport, Iowa. Including any residence halls, there are 33 buildings.

STUDENT LIFE: 62% of undergraduates are from out of state, mostly the Midwest. Students are from 28 states, and 24 foreign countries. 65% are from public schools. 8% are Hispanic; 74% White; 5% African American; 5% Foreign; 4% race unknown; 3% two or more races; 1% Asian American. 38% are Catholic; 38% claim no religious affiliation; 17% Protestant. **Female To Male Ratio:** 1.4:1. The average age of freshmen is 18; all undergraduates, 22. 78% do not continue beyond their first year; 63% remain to graduate. **Housing:** 1700 students can be accommodated in college housing, which includes gender neutral dorms, on-campus apartments, and off-campus apartments. In addition, there are honors houses, special-interest houses, and townhouse residences for upper-division students. On-campus housing is guaranteed for the freshman year only, and is available on a lottery system for upperclassmen. 66% of students live on campus. All students may keep cars.

FACULTY/CLASSROOMS: 49% of faculty are male; 51% are female. 86% teach undergraduates. No introductory courses are taught by graduate students. The average class size in an introductory lecture is 17; in a laboratory is 13; and in a regular course is 13.

PROGRAMS OF STUDY: SAU confers B.A., B.S., B.A.M.T., B.B.A., B.M.E., B.S.I.E., B.S.N., B.A.IS, and B.Ed degrees. Master's and doctoral degrees are also awarded. Bachelor's degrees are awarded in BIOLOGICAL SCIENCE (biology/ gen science secondary education), BUSINESS (business administration and management, business administration marketing, business economics, finance, international business, integrative studies, management, organizational leadership and management, and sports management), COMMUNICATIONS AND THE ARTS (art history, English, foreign language, graphic design, painting, printmaking, radio/television technology, Spanish, speech and theatre education, theatre acting, voice, and vocal music education), COMPUTER AND PHYSICAL SCIENCE (chemistry, chemistry education, computer networks & systems, computer security, computer science, and mathematics), EDUCATION (art education, business education, childhood education, mathematics education, music education, secondary education, Spanish education K-12, and special education), ENGINEERING AND ENVIRONMENTAL DESIGN (industrial engineering), HEALTH PROFESSIONS (biology, kinesiology, nursing, occupational therapy, physician's assistant, public health, and speech pathology/audiology), SOCIAL SCIENCE (area studies, gender studies, history, international studies, pastoral studies, philosophy, political science/government, prelaw, psychology, social work, sociology, theological studies, and women & gender studies). Allied health fields, nursing, and speech path are the strongest academically. Exercise science, nursing, psychology, and biology have the largest enrollments.

ACTIVITIES: There are no fraternities or sororities. There are 82 groups on campus, including Ambrosians for Peace and Justice, art, band, cheerleading, choir, chorale, chorus, computers, dance, Dance Marathon, debate, drama, environmental, ethnic, honors, international, jazz band, LGBT, literary magazine, marching band, musical theater, newspaper, pep band, photography, political, professional, radio and TV, religious, social, social service, and student government. Popular campus events include Homecoming, Dance Marathon, Multicultural Week, Mission Week, and Brother/Sister Weekend. **Sports:** There are 12 intercollegiate sports for men and 12 for women, and 12 intramural sports for men and 12 for women. The Wellness and Recreation Center provides cardio workout and weight rooms, multipurpose group exercise room, an exercise physiology lab, 200-meter competition track, pole vault areas, long- and triple-jump pits, 4 basketball/volleyball courts, and a club room. **Graduates:** From July 1, 2016 to June 30, 2017, 647 bachelor's degrees were awarded. The most popular majors were nursing (14%), psychology (11%), and exercise science (8%). In an average class,

53% graduate in 4 years or less, 63% graduate in 5 years or less, and 63% graduate in 6 years or less. Of the 2016 graduating class, 19% were enrolled in graduate school within 6 months of graduation, and 61% were employed.

SERVICES: Counseling and information services are available, as is tutoring in most subjects, such as biology, psychology, and chemistry. There is a reader service for the blind, and remedial math, reading, and writing. **Library/Resources:** The library contains 182,763 volumes, 7,191 microform items, 4,494 audio/video tapes/CDs/DVDs, and subscribes to 463,852 periodicals including electronic. Computerized library services include interlibrary loans, database searching, Internet access, and Wi-Fi capability. Special learning facilities include an art gallery, radio station, TV station, and an observatory. **Physically Challenged Students:** 96% of the campus is accessible. Facilities include wheelchair ramps, elevators, special parking, specially equipped restrooms, special class scheduling, lowered drinking fountains, and special housing. **Special:** The university offers credit for life, military, work experience, and nondegree study, pass/fail options are available, and students can design their own integrative major. Six bachelor's degrees are offered at an accelerated pace that is both convenient and affordable. There are over 400 work-study positions available to students through the University, as well as the opportunity to study abroad in over 40 countries including: Australia, Belize, China, Czech Republic, Ecuador, England, France, Germany, India, Ireland, Italy, Morocco, the Netherlands, South Africa, Greece, Spain, Israel and Palestine. With the support of both faculty and the Career Center, students can earn academic credit for internships both locally and afar. Transfer students may earn an associate's degree at their community college and then continue to St. Ambrose to finish their bachelor's degree with the seamless transition of the Dual Admissions Program. Students currently enrolled at community colleges not only save money by attending a community college for their first two years, but are granted academic advising, scholarship funds, a student ID, access to the library and other student faciliies at SAU prior to enrolling. There are 15 national honor societies, Phi Beta Kappa, and a freshman honors program. **Visiting:** There are regularly scheduled orientations for prospective students, Institutional welcome and overview, advising and registration, financial aid counseling, campus tour, presentations from student service offices, and overnight stay. There are guides for informal visits, visitors may sit in on classes, and stay overnight. To schedule a visit, contact the Admissions Office. **Campus Safety and Security:** Measures include 24-hour foot and vehicle patrol, emergency notification system, self-defense education, and security escort services. There are emergency telephones, lighted pathways/sidewalks, and controlled access to dorms/residences.

REQUIREMENTS: Individuals are eligible for admission to St. Ambrose University as a First Year student if they meet the following requirements: have a cumulative grade point average of 2.5 or above (on a 4.0 scale) from an accredited high school and either have a composite score of 20 or above on the American College Testing Program (ACT), or a 950 or above on the Scholastic Aptitude Test (SAT) of the College Board. Students who graduated from high school five or more years ago do not need to supply ACT or SAT scores. The writing portion of the ACT is optional for admission to St. Ambrose University. Students may also have an ACT composite score of 18 or 19 (or an SAT score between 870 and 950) and graduate in the upper half of their senior class. AP and CLEP credits are accepted. To graduate, all students must complete at least 120 credit hours, including 45 outside the major and 30 in upper-level courses. A minimum GPA of 2.0 is required. Students must also demonstrate proficiency in English composition, math, public speaking, and library skills, among other requirements. Selections of courses must include those that provide an opportunity to develop specific skills, content knowledge, and exposure to attitude and value development. **Procedure:** Freshmen are admitted to all sessions. Entrance exams should be taken in the spring of the junior year of high school. There is a rolling admissions plan. Application deadlines are open. Applications are accepted on-line. **Transfer Students:** 250 transfer students enrolled in 2016-2017. Transfer students are eligible for admission if they meet the following requirements: Have completed 12 college transferable credits of academic work from a fully accredited institution of higher education, and maintained a 2.0 GPA or above (on a 4.0 scale). Students must submit transcripts of all prior work at higher education levels. With less than 12 transferable semester credits of college work, admission will be based on high school GPA and test scores. 30 of 120 credits required for the bachelor's degree must be completed at SAU. **International Students:** There are 114 international students enrolled. They must take the TOEFL with a minimum score of 550 on the paper-based TOEFL (PBT) or 79 on the Internet-based version (iBT).

ADMISSIONS: 61% of the 2017-2018 applicants were accepted. The ACT scores were 1% between 12 and 17, 60% between 18 and 23, 34% between 24 and 29, and 5% above 30. 35% of the current freshmen were in the top fifth of their class; 63% were in the top two fifths. 10 freshmen graduated first in their class. **Admissions Contact:** Allie Conklin, Director of First Year Admissions. Email: *admit@sau.edu* Web: *www.sau.edu*

FINANCIAL AID: In 2017-2018, 99% of all full-time freshmen received some form of financial aid. 58% of all full-time freshmen received need-based aid. The average freshman award was $21,354. Need-based scholarships or need-based grants averaged $3,376 ($11,970 maximum); need-based self-help aid (loans and jobs) averaged $4,997 ($29,502 maximum); non-need-based athletic scholarships averaged $3,088 ($18,736 maximum); and other non-need-based awards and non-need-based scholarships averaged $8,219 ($29,736 maximum). 33% of undergraduate students work part-time. The average financial indebtedness of the 2017 graduate was $39,973. SAU is a member of CSS. The FAFSA code is 001889. The priority date for freshman financial aid applications for fall entry is March 15.

UNIVERSITY OF DUBUQUE — E-2
www.dbq.edu

Dubuque, IA 52001	(563) 589-3214 (800) 722-5583
Fax: (563) 589-3690	Email: admssns@dbq.edu
Full-time: 710 men, 410 women	Faculty: n/av
Part-time: 30 men, 35 women	Ph.D.s: 80%
Graduate: 170 men, 110 women	Student/Faculty: n/av
Year: semesters, summer session	Tuition: $28,700
Room & Board: $9124	Freshman Class: n/av
SAT or ACT: required	CEEB CODE: 6869
Application Deadline: August 15	COMPETITIVE

University of Dubuque, established in 1852, is a private, liberal arts institution affiliated with the Presbyterian Church. Strengths in the undergraduate curriculum include environmental science, business, aviation, education, and computer graphics/interactive media. There are 3 undergraduate schools and 2 graduate schools. The 56-acre campus is in a suburban area 180 miles northwest of Chicago. Including any residence halls, there are 24 buildings.

STUDENT LIFE: 60% of undergraduates are from out of state, mostly the Midwest. Students are from 35 states, and 21 foreign countries. 90% are from public schools. 79% are White; 4% Hispanic; 2% American Indian/Alaska Native; 12% African American; 1% Asian American; 1% Foreign. 50% are Catholic; 40% Protestant; 35% claim no religious affiliation. **Male To Female Ratio:** 1.6:1. The average age of freshmen is 18; all undergraduates, 22. 12% do not continue beyond their first year; 59% remain to graduate. **Housing:** 600 students can be accommodated in college housing, which includes married student dorms, on-campus apartments, and special-interest houses. On-campus housing is guaranteed for all 4 years. 30% of students commute. Alcohol is not permitted. All students may keep cars.

FACULTY/CLASSROOMS: 55% of faculty are male; 45% are female. All teach undergraduates. No introductory courses are taught by graduate students. The average class size in an introductory lecture is 25; in a laboratory is 16; and in a regular course is 17.

PROGRAMS OF STUDY: UD confers B.A., B.S. and B.B.A. degrees. Associate, master's, and doctoral degrees are also awarded. Bachelor's degrees are awarded in BIOLOGICAL SCIENCE (biology/biological science), BUSINESS (accounting and business administration and management), COMMUNICATIONS AND THE ARTS (English and speech/debate/rhetoric), COMPUTER AND PHYSICAL SCIENCE (computer science), EDUCATION (education and physical education), ENGINEERING AND ENVIRONMENTAL DESIGN (aviation administration/management, computer graphics, and environmental science), HEALTH PROFESSIONS (nursing), SOCIAL SCIENCE (philosophy, psychology, religion, and sociology). Nursing, computer graphics, and business are the strongest academically. Business, aviation management/flight operations, and computer graphics have the largest enrollments.

ACTIVITIES: 11% of men belong to 5 local fraternities; 10% of women belong to 3 local sororities. There are 50 groups on campus, including art, cheerleading, choir, chorale, chorus, computers, dance, drama, ecology club, ethnic, honors, international, musical theater, newspaper, pep band, political, professional, religious, social, social service, and student government. Popular campus events include Founder's Day Ball, Annual Gala, and Family Weekend. **Sports:** There are 10 intercollegiate sports for men and 9 for women, and 13 intramural sports for men and 13 for women. Facilities include a sports center with basketball and volleyball courts, racquetball courts, a wrestling room, and an athletic training room, a football field and track, baseball and softball fields, and a practice football/intramural field, and a cardiovascular workout center.

SERVICES: Counseling and information services are available, as is tutoring in some subjects, such as English, math, economics, accounting, and computer literacy. There is remedial math, reading, and writing. **Library/Resources:** The library contains 164,859 volumes, 20,739 microform items, 2,180 audio/video tapes/CDs/DVDs, and subscribes to 801 periodicals including electronic. Computerized library services include interlibrary loans, database searching, and Internet access. Special learning facilities include an art gallery and planetarium. **Physically Challenged Students:** 50% of the campus is accessible. Facilities include wheelchair ramps, elevators, special parking, specially equipped restrooms, special class scheduling, and lowered drinking fountains. **Special:** UD offers cross-registration with Loras and Clarke Colleges, internships, study abroad through the Maastricht Center for Transatlantic Studies, work-study programs, accelerated degree programs, B.A.-B.S. degrees, dual and student-designed majors, credit for life, military, and work experience, nondegree study, and pass/fail options. B.A.-M.A. programs are offered in conjunction with the university's theological seminary. Adult degree programs and an environmental field trip to Colorado and New Mexico are available. There are 8 national honor societies and 2 departmental honors programs. **Visiting:** There are regularly scheduled orientations for prospective students, including a campus tour and visits with coaches, faculty, admissions, and financial aid advisers. There are guides for informal visits, visitors may sit in on classes, and stay overnight. To schedule a visit, contact the Admission Director. **Campus Safety and Security:** Measures include 24-hour foot and vehicle patrol, self-defense education, and security escort services. There are shuttle buses, emergency telephones, lighted pathways/sidewalks, and security-locked residence halls.

REQUIREMENTS: The SAT or ACT is required. Applicants must graduate from an accredited secondary school with a minimum of 4 years in English and 3 each in math, social sciences, and natural sciences. Other academic areas, such as foreign languages, business courses, computer programming, and the fine and performing arts, are also considered. The GED is accepted. Essays and recommendations are required. Auditions are required for music scholarship candidates. A GPA of 2.5 is required. AP and CLEP credits are accepted. Important factors in the admissions decision are leadership record, recommendations by school officials, and extracurricular activities record. As part of our mission, the University aims to prepare students for successful, professional careers and fulfilling lives by providing them with an education that encourages their growth as whole persons. A total of 120 credits must be earned, with a minimum GPA of 2.0 (2.5 for education majors) for graduation. At UD, we combine professional preparation and the liberal arts to create programs that serve our students. **Procedure:** Freshmen are admitted in the fall and spring. Entrance exams should be taken before the senior year. There are deferred admissions and rolling admissions plans. Applications should be filed by August 15 for fall entry; December 1 for spring entry. The fall 2017 application fee was $25. Applications are accepted on-line. **Transfer Students:** A minimum GPA of 2.0 is required. The applicant must be in good standing at all previously attended institutions. 30 of 120 credits required for the bachelor's degree must be completed at UD. **International Students:** They must take the TOEFL and the college's own test.

ADMISSIONS: 10 freshmen graduated first in their class. **Admissions Contact:** Jesse L. James, Admission Director. Email: *admssns@dbq.edu* Web: *www.dbq.edu*

FINANCIAL AID: The FAFSA code is 001891. Check with the school for current application deadlines.

UNIVERSITY OF IOWA — E-3

www.uiowa.edu

Iowa City, IA 52242 — **(319) 335-3847**

Fax: (319) 335-1535	**Email: admissions@uiowa.edu**
Full-time: 9981 men, 11241 women	**Faculty:** I, av$
Part-time: 1581 men, 1700 women	**Ph.D.s:** 96%
Graduate: 4529 men, 4532 women	**Student/Faculty:** 16 to 1
Year: semesters, summer session	**Tuition:** $8965 ($30,609)
Room & Board: $10,450	**Freshman Class:** 27734 applied, 23862 accepted, 5027 enrolled
SAT EBR-W/M: 623/631 **ACT:** 26	**CEEB CODE:** 6681
Application Deadline: April 1	**HIGHLY COMPETITIVE**

University of Iowa is one of the nation's top public research universities, a member of the Big Ten conference since 1899, and an Association of American Universities member since 1909. Iowa is known around the world for its balanced commitment to the arts, sciences, and humanities. It's home to one of the nation's largest academic medical centers, the pioneering Iowa Writers' Workshop, and hundreds of options for affordable, accessible education. The University delivers the energy and opportunity of a leading university, but remains one of the smallest and most affordable universities among its peer institutions. There are 5 undergraduate schools and 11 graduate schools. In addition to regional accreditation, UI has baccalaureate program accreditation with AACSB, ABET, ACEJMC, ACPE, ADA, APTA, CSWE, NASM, NRPA, CACREP, ISBE, and ACEJ. The 1700-acre campus is in a small town 110 miles east of Des Moines and 220 miles west of Chicago. Including any residence halls, there are 582 buildings.

STUDENT LIFE: 58% of undergraduates are from Iowa. Others are from 50 states, 59 foreign countries, and Canada. 91% are from public schools. 67% are White; 10% Foreign; 7% Hispanic; 5% race unknown; 4% Asian American; 4% two or more races; 3% African American; 1% American Indian/Alaska Native. **Female To Male Ratio:** 1.1:1. The average age of freshmen is 18; all undergraduates, 21. 14% do not continue beyond their first year; 74% remain to graduate. **Housing:** 6964 students can be accommodated in college housing, which includes gender neutral, coed, and married student dorms, on-campus apartments, and off-campus apartments. In addition, there are honors houses, special-interest houses, and living learning communities. On-campus housing is available on a first-come, first-served basis. 72% of students commute. Alcohol is not permitted. All students may keep cars.

FACULTY/CLASSROOMS: 60% of faculty are male; 40% are female. Graduate students teach 13% of introductory courses. The average class size in an introductory lecture is 105; in a laboratory is 16; and in a regular course is 18.

PROGRAMS OF STUDY: UI confers B.A., B.S., B.A.S., B.B.A., B.F.A., B.L.S., B.M., B.S.E., and B.S.N. degrees. Master's and doctoral degrees are also awarded. Bachelor's degrees are awarded in BIOLOGICAL SCIENCE (biochemistry, biology/biological science, and microbiology), BUSINESS (accounting, banking and finance, business administration and management, business economics, management science, marketing management, recreation and leisure services, and recreational facilities management), COMMUNICATIONS AND THE ARTS (art, art history and appreciation, ceramic art and design, Chinese, classics, communications, comparative literature, dance, dramatic arts, drawing, English, film arts, fine arts, French, German, graphic design, Greek, Italian, Japanese, jazz, journalism, Latin, linguistics, metal/jewelry, music, painting, percussion, performing arts, photography, piano/organ, Portuguese, printmaking, Russian, sculpture, Spanish, speech/debate/rhetoric, strings, theatre arts, and voice), COMPUTER AND PHYSICAL SCIENCE (actuarial science, applied physics, astronomy, chemistry, computer science, geology, information sciences and systems, mathematics, physics, and statistics), EDUCATION (art education, athletic training, elementary education, foreign languages education, health education, mathematics education, middle school education, music education, science education, secondary education, and sports studies), ENGINEERING AND ENVIRONMENTAL DESIGN (biomedical engineering, chemical engineering, civil engineering, electrical/electronics engineering, engineering, environmental science, industrial administration/management, industrial engineering, and mechanical engineering), HEALTH PROFESSIONS (medical laboratory science, medical laboratory technology, music therapy, nuclear medical technology, nursing, pharmacy, predentistry, premedicine, preoptometry, prepharmacy, prephysical therapy, prepodiatry, preveterinary science, radiological science, recreation therapy, and speech pathology/audiology), SOCIAL SCIENCE (African American studies, American studies, anthropology, Asian/Oriental studies, classical/ancient civilization, economics, gender studies, geography, history, international studies, liberal arts/general studies, parks and recreation management, philosophy, political science/government, prelaw, psychology, religion, Russian and Slavic studies, Sanskrit and Indian studies, social science, social work, sociology, and women's studies). Business, engineering, and creative writing are the strongest academically. Business, engineering, and psychology have the largest enrollments.

ACTIVITIES: 14% of men belong to 27 national fraternities; 19% of women belong to 23 national sororities. There are 500 groups on campus, including art, bagpipe, band, cheerleading, chess, choir, chorale, chorus, communications, computers, dance, debate, drama, drill team, environmental, ethnic, film, forensics, honors, international, jazz band, LGBT, literary magazine, marching band, musical theater, newspaper, opera, orchestra, pep band, photography, political, professional, radio and TV stations, religious, social, social service, student government, and symphony. Popular campus events include Dance Marathon, Riverfest, RiverRun, and Cultural Diversity Festivals. **Sports:** There are 10 intercollegiate sports for men and 12 for women, and 36 intramural sports for men and 32 for women. Facilities include a campus recreation and wellness center that features a climbing wall, competitive swimming pool, deep diving well, a leisure pool, basketball/volleyball courts, a multiactivity gym, football, an arena, softball and baseball stadiums, an 18-hole golf course, racquetball and handball courts, outdoor and indoor tennis courts, jogging and running tracks, weight and fitness rooms, a hockey stadium, fields for hiking, cross-country skiing, and soccer. **Graduates:** From July 1, 2016 to June 30, 2017, 5379 bachelor's degrees were awarded. The most popular majors were finance (7%), psychology (5%), and health and human physiology (5%). In an average class, 2% graduate in 3 years or less, 54% graduate in 4 years or less, 71% graduate in 5 years or less, and 74% graduate in 6 years or less. Of the 2016 graduating class, 18% were enrolled in graduate school within 6 months of graduation, and 72% were employed.

SERVICES: Counseling and information services are available, as is tutoring in most subjects. There is a reader service for the blind, and remedial math, reading, and writing. **Library/Resources:** The library contains 6.9 million volumes. Computerized library services include interlibrary loans, database searching, Internet access, and Wi-Fi capability. Special learning facilities include an art gallery, natural history museum, UI hospitals and clinics, the Iowa Center for the Arts, Oakdale Research Center, Iowa Lakeside lab, and a driving simulator. **Physically Challenged Students:** 98% of the campus is accessible. Facilities include wheelchair ramps, elevators, special parking, specially equipped restrooms, special class scheduling, lowered drinking fountains, lowered telephones, special housing, and transportation service when needed. **Special:** The University offers a wide array of internships and experience-based learning opportunities, combined degree programs, 3+3 program with College of Law, joint bachelors/master programs, 3+2 program with College of Public Health, 22 certificate programs including Aging Studies, American Indian and Native Studies, American Sign Language and Deaf Studies, Critical Cultural Competence, Disability Studies, Entrepreneurial Management, Fundraising and Philanthropy Communication, Global Health Studies, Human Rights, International Business, Latin American Studies, Leadership Studies, Medieval Studies, Museum Studies, Nonprofit Management, Performing Arts Entrepreneurship, Public Health, Risk Management and Insurance, Sustainability, Technological Entrepreneurship, Writing, and Wind Energy. Iowa's Study Abroad Program includes studies in 75 countries worldwide. There are 18 national honor societies, Phi Beta Kappa, a freshman honors program, and 52 departmental honors programs. **Visiting:** There are regularly scheduled orientations for prospective students, including information sessions, campus tours, lunch, and visits to departments and residence halls. There are guides for informal visits and visitors may sit in on classes. To schedule a visit, contact the Admission Visitors Center. **Campus Safety and Security:** Measures include 24-hour foot and vehicle patrol, emergency notification system, self-defense education, and security escort services. There are shuttle buses, emergency telephones, lighted pathways/sidewalks, controlled access to dorms/residences, code blue phones, defense courses, and a WhistleSAFE program.

REQUIREMENTS: The SAT or ACT is required. All applicants must have completed 4 years of high school English, 3 years each of social studies, science, and math (including 2 years of algebra and 1 of geometry), and 2 years of a single world language. Students in music and dance students must audition. AP and CLEP credits are accepted. To graduate, students must complete at least 120 semester hours, with a GPA of 2.0. The general education program includes rhetoric, historical perspectives, world language, quantitative and formal reasoning, international and global issues, values, society and diversity, and natural and social sciences. **Procedure:** Freshmen are admitted to all sessions. Entrance exams should be taken in the junior year. There are deferred admissions and rolling admissions plans. Applications should be filed by April 1 for fall entry; November 15 for spring entry. The fall 2017 application fee was $40. Notification is sent on a rolling basis. Applications are accepted online. **Transfer Students:** 1265 transfer students enrolled in 2016-2017. For the College of Liberal Arts, a GPA of at least 2.5 is required for applicants with 24 or more semester hours of credit. Those with fewer credits are considered on the same criteria as freshmen. 30 of 120 credits required for the bachelor's degree must be completed at UI. **International Students:** There are 1884 international students enrolled.

ADMISSIONS: 86% of the 2017-2018 applicants were accepted. The SAT scores for the 2017-2018 freshman class were: Math-- 5% below 500, 33% between 500 and 599, 37% between 600 and 699, and 24% between 700 and 800. Evidence-Based Reading/Writing-- 6% below 500, 28% between 500 and 599, 45% between 600 and 699, and 20% between 700 and 800. The ACT scores were 1% between 12 and 17, 30% between 18 and 23, 50% between 24 and 29, and 19% above 30. 51% of the current freshmen were in the top fifth of their class; 83% were in the top two fifths. 141 freshmen graduated first in their class. **Admissions Contact:** Brent Gage, Associate VP for Enrollment Management. Email: *admissions@uiowa.edu* Web: *www.uiowa.edu*

FINANCIAL AID: In 2017-2018, 84% of all full-time freshmen received some form of financial aid. 59% of all full-time freshmen received need-based aid. The average freshman award was $13,439. Need-based scholarships or need-based grants averaged $8,087; need-based self-help aid (loans and jobs) averaged $6,339; non-need-based athletic scholarships averaged $12,545; and other non-need-based awards and non-need-based scholarships averaged $4,972. 44% of undergraduate students work part-time. The average financial indebtedness of the 2017 graduate was $23,316. The FAFSA code is 001892. The priority date for freshman financial aid applications for fall entry is March 1.

UNIVERSITY OF NORTHERN IOWA — D-2

www.uni.edu

Cedar Falls, IA 50614	**(319) 273-2281** **(800) 772-2037**
Fax: (319) 273-2885	**Email: admissions@uni.edu**
Full-time: 3796 men, 5304 women	**Faculty:** 478
Part-time: 466 men, 439 women	**Ph.D.s:** 79%
Graduate: 506 men, 1396 women	**Student/Faculty:** 19 to 1
Year: semesters, summer session	**Tuition:** $8699 ($19,241)
Room & Board: $8781	**Freshman Class:** 5195 applied, 4290 accepted, 1834 enrolled
ACT: 23	**CEEB CODE:** 6307
Application Deadline: August 15	**COMPETITIVE**

University of Northern Iowa, established in 1876, is a public institution offering degree programs in business administration, education, humanities, arts, sciences, and social and behavioral sciences. There are 4 undergraduate schools and 1 graduate school. In addition to regional accreditation, UNI has baccalaureate program accreditation with AACSB, ABET, CSWE, NASM, NRPA, ACS, ASHA, ATMAE, CAATE, CACREP, CEA, NCFR, NASP, and and NAST. The 908-acre campus is in a small town in Cedar Falls, Iowa, about 60 miles northwest of Cedar Rapids. Including any residence halls, there are 106 buildings.

STUDENT LIFE: 89% of undergraduates are from Iowa. Others are from 37 states, 68 foreign countries, and Canada. 93% are from public schools. 82% are White; 5% Foreign; 4% Hispanic; 4% race unknown; 3% African American; 2% two or more races; 1% Asian American. **Female To Male Ratio:** 1.5:1. The average age of freshmen is 18; all undergraduates, 21. 19% do not continue beyond their first year; 65% remain to graduate. **Housing:** 4766 students can be accommodated in college housing, which includes gender neutral, coed, married student dorms, and on-campus apartments. In addition, there are honors houses and special-interest houses. On-campus housing is guaranteed for all 4 years, is available on a first-come, first-served basis, and is available on a lottery system for upperclassmen. 61% of students commute. All students may keep cars.

FACULTY/CLASSROOMS: 49% of faculty are male; 51% are female. 84% teach undergraduates and do research. Graduate students teach 5% of introductory courses. The average class size in an introductory lecture is 33; in a laboratory is 27; and in a regular course is 33.

PROGRAMS OF STUDY: UNI confers B.A., B.A.S., B.S., B.F.A., B.L.S., and B.Mus. degrees. Master's and doctoral degrees are also awarded. Bachelor's degrees are awarded in BIOLOGICAL SCIENCE (biochemistry, bioinformatics, biology/biological science, biotechnology, microbiology, and nutrition), BUSINESS (accounting, banking and finance, management information systems, management science, marketing/retailing/merchandising, real estate, recreation and leisure services, and supply chain management), COMMUNICATIONS AND THE ARTS (art history, communications, digital media, dramatic arts, English, fine arts, graphic design, music, music performance, music theory and composition, public relations, Spanish, speech/debate/rhetoric, studio art, and theatre arts), COMPUTER AND PHYSICAL SCIENCE (actuarial science, chemistry, computer management, computer science, earth science, geology, information sciences and systems, mathematics, physics, and science), EDUCATION (art education, athletic training, business education, early childhood education, elementary education, foreign languages education, health education, middle school education, music education, physical education, science education, social science education, special education, teaching English as a second/foreign language (TESOL/TEFOL), and technical education), ENGINEERING AND ENVIRONMENTAL DESIGN (computer technology, construction management, electrical/electronics engineering technology, energy management technology, environmental science, industrial engineering technology, and manufacturing technology), HEALTH PROFESSIONS (communicative disorders, exercise science, health promotion, and speech pathology/audiology), SOCIAL SCIENCE (anthropology, clothing and textiles management/production/services, criminal justice, criminology, economics, family and community services, geography, geography information science, gerontology, history, humanities, liberal arts/general studies, philosophy, political science/government, psychology, public administration, religion, social work, sociology, and world cultural studies). Teaching majors, biology, communication, and accounting are the strongest academically. Elementary education, management, and accounting have the largest enrollments.

ACTIVITIES: 3% of men belong to 4 national fraternities; 6% of women belong to 5 national sororities. There are 258 groups on campus, including Alumni clubs, art, band, cheerleading, chess, choir, chorale, chorus, communications, computers, dance, debate, drama, drill team, environmental, ethnic, film, forensics, honors, international, jazz band, LGBT, literary magazine, marching band, musical theater, newspaper, opera, orchestra, pep band, political, professional, radio and TV stations, religious, social, social service, student government, and symphony. Popular campus events include UNI NOW! Welcome Week, Relay for Life, Dance Marathon, and Homecoming. **Sports:** There are 7 intercollegiate sports for men and 10 for women, and 41 intramural sports for men and 37 for women. Facilities include a domed stadium, a field house, basketball arena, tennis courts, multi purpose play fields, a track, wellness/recreation center with an 8-lane swimming pool, handball/racquetball courts, a climbing wall, weight rooms, basketball courts, and a fitness center with exercise rooms. **Graduates:** From July 1, 2016 to June 30, 2017, 2126 bachelor's degrees were awarded. The most popular majors were elementary education (7%), psychology (4%), and accounting (4%). In an average class, 3% graduate in 3 years or less, 40% graduate in 4 years or less, 64% graduate in 5 years or less, and 67% graduate in 6 years or less. Of the 2016 graduating class, 12% were enrolled in graduate school within 6 months of graduation, and 82% were employed.

SERVICES: Counseling and information services are available, as is tutoring in some subjects, such as liberal arts core and major courses in humanities, biology, chemistry, physics, earth science, economics, calculus, statistics, research methods, music, management, finance, accounting, plus writing and reading assistance. There is a reader service for the blind, and remedial math, reading, and writing. In additional there are Supplemental Instruction in Calculus I, Statistics, Anatomy & Physiology I, Macroeconomics, College Success Workshops, Supportive Seminars in Humanities I-III, and Art History. **Library/Resources:** The library contains 786,247 volumes, 822,055 microform items, and 29,028 audio/video tapes/CDs/DVDs, and subscribes to 1,323 periodicals including electronic. Computerized library services include interlibrary loans, database searching, Internet access, and Wi-Fi capability. Special learning facilities include an art gallery, natural history museum, and a planetarium. The university sponsors the Native Roadside Vegetation Center, the Iowa Center for Immigrant Leadership and Integration, a waste reduction center, a performing arts center, and several research institutes. **Physically Challenged Students:** 95% of the campus is accessible. Facilities include wheelchair ramps, elevators, special parking, specially equipped restrooms, special class scheduling, lowered drinking fountains, lowered telephones, and special housing. **Special:** Internships and co-op programs are offered through all colleges of the university. Students may study abroad in 28 countries and participate in a Washington semester. Interdisciplinary majors include safety education, chemistry/marketing, design/human environment, and natural history interpretation. Cross-registration, work-study programs, a general studies degree, dual and student-designed majors, nondegree study, and pass/fail options are also available. There are 25 national honor societies and a freshman honors program. **Visiting:** There are regularly scheduled orientations for prospective students, including a student panel, a campus tour, and presentations by admissions, financial aid, housing, and academic departments. There are guides for informal visits and visitors may sit in on classes. To schedule a visit, contact Kara Hadley Shakya in Admissions **Campus Safety and Security:** Measures include 24-hour foot and vehicle patrol, emergency notification system, self-defense education, and security escort services. There are shuttle buses, emergency telephones, lighted pathways/sidewalks, and controlled access to dorms/residences.

REQUIREMENTS: A Regents Admissions Index (RAI) score of 245 guarantees admission. High school requirements include 4 years of English, 3 years each of math, social studies, and science, and 2 years or more of electives, which may include foreign language and fine arts. The GED with a minimum standard score average of 57, and no score below 500, is accepted. The HiSET is also accepted. AP and CLEP credits are accepted. Important factors in the admissions decision are advanced placement or honors courses, evidence of special talent, and recommendations by school officials. Degree requirements include completion of 120 to 130 credits, with 30 to 60 in the major. Liberal arts majors must maintain a minimum GPA of 2.0 (2.5 for business, communication, and education majors). Liberal arts core requirements include 11 hours of civilizations and cultures, 9 each of natural science/technology, social science, and communication, 6 of arts/literature/philosophy/religion, and 3 of personal wellness. Students must meet requirements in foreign language and complete a capstone course. Education students must complete a 32-credit professional sequence. **Procedure:** Freshmen are admitted to all sessions. Entrance exams should be taken by October of the senior year. There is a rolling admissions plan. Applications should be filed by August 15 for fall entry; December 31 for spring entry; and May 15 for summer entry. The fall 2017 application fee was $40. Applications are accepted on-line. **Transfer Students:** 895 transfer students enrolled in 2016-2017. Applicants must have a minimum GPA of 2.0 to 2.5, depending on the number of credits they wish to transfer. A small number of applicants may be admitted on academic probation. 32 of 120 credits required for the bachelor's degree must be completed at UNI. **International Students:** There are 373 international students enrolled. They must take the TOEFL with a minimum score of 550 on the paper-based TOEFL (PBT) or 79 on the Internet-based version (iBT) or take the MELAB. Student must also take the Comprehensive English Language Test, and the college's own test.

ADMISSIONS: 83% of the 2017-2018 applicants were accepted. The ACT scores were 5% between 12 and 17, 53% between 18 and 23, 36% between 24 and 29, and 6% above 30. 37% of the current freshmen were in the top fifth of their class; 69% were in the top two fifths. 44 freshmen graduated first in their class. **Admissions Contact:** Kara M. Hadley-Shakya, Director of Admissions. Email: *admissions@uni.edu* Web: *www.uni.edu*

FINANCIAL AID: In 2017-2018, 95% of all full-time freshmen received some form of financial aid. 51% of all full-time freshmen received need-based aid. The average freshman award was $11,911. Need-based scholarships or need-based grants averaged $4,962 ($17,328 maximum); need-based self-help aid (loans and jobs) averaged $2,719 ($5,500 maximum); non-need-based athletic scholarships averaged $6,629 ($29,882 maximum); and other non-need-based awards and non-need-based scholarships averaged $3,046 ($15,000 maximum). 34% of undergraduate students work part-time. The average financial indebtedness of the 2017 graduate was $22,372. The FAFSA code is 001890.

UPPER IOWA UNIVERSITY *(The complete profile is made available exclusively on our website, www.barronspac.com)*

WARTBURG COLLEGE D-2
www.wartburg.edu

Waverly, IA 50677 (319) 352-8264
(800) 772-2085
Fax: (319) 352-8579 **Email: admissions@wartburg.edu**
Full-time: 688 men, 786 women
Part-time: 33 men, 20 women
Graduate: n/av
Year: other, summer session
Room & Board: $9748
Faculty: 94; IIB, -$
Ph.D.s: 88%
Student/Faculty: 11 to 1
Tuition: $39,730
Freshman Class: 4342 applied, 3339 accepted, 451 enrolled
SAT or ACT: required
Application Deadline: May 1
CEEB CODE: 6926
COMPETITIVE

Wartburg College is a selective liberal arts institution of the ELCA, internationally recognized for community engagement. Wartburg is dedicated to challenging and nurturing students for lives of leadership and service as a spirited expression of their faith and learning. Opportunities for service-learning, leadership, undergraduate research, global and multicultural studies, and participation in co-curricular activities enrich the academic experience. Wartburg helps students discover their life's purpose through meaning and vocational discernment. There are 3 undergraduate schools. In addition to regional accreditation, WC has baccalaureate program accreditation with CSWE, NASM, and CAEP. The 118-acre campus is in a small town 15 miles north of Waterloo/Cedar Falls, Iowa. Including any residence halls, there are 37 buildings.

STUDENT LIFE: 63% of undergraduates are from Iowa. Others are from 30 states, and 55 foreign countries. 8% are Foreign; 75% White; 5% African American; 5% Hispanic; 3% two or more races; 3% race unknown; 1% Asian American. 65% are Protestant; 26% Catholic. **Female To Male Ratio:** 1.1:1. The average age of freshmen is 18; all undergraduates, 20. 21% do not continue beyond their first year; 65% remain to graduate. **Housing:** 1410 students can be accommodated in college housing, which includes single sex dorms, coed dorms and on-campus apartments. In addition, there are honors houses, language/international houses, and special-interest houses. On-campus housing is guaranteed for all 4 years. 87% of students live on campus. All students may keep cars.

FACULTY/CLASSROOMS: 53% of faculty are male; 47% are female. All teach undergraduates, and 89% do research. No introductory courses are taught by graduate students. The average class size in a laboratory is 17 and in a regular course is 19.

PROGRAMS OF STUDY: WC confers B.A., B.A.A., B.A.S., B.M., and B.M.E. degrees. Bachelor's degrees are awarded in BIOLOGICAL SCIENCE (biochemistry, biology/general science secondary education, and neurosciences), BUSINESS (accounting, business administration and management, business administration - international, business administration marketing, finance, and business management), COMMUNICATIONS AND THE ARTS (applied music, art, communication studies, English, film, television and digital media, German, German studies, graphic design, journalism, multimedia, music, music performance, public relations, Spanish, and vocal music education), COMPUTER AND PHYSICAL SCIENCE (actuarial science, chemistry, clinical laboratory science, chemistry/gen science second education, chemistry secondary education, computer information systems, computer science, mathematics, physics/gen science secondary education, and physics), EDUCATION (art education, education, elementary education, English secondary education, foreign languages education, history education, journalism education, mathematics education, music education, physical education, psychology education, science education, secondary education, social science education, social studies secondary school education, and Spanish education K-12), ENGINEERING AND ENVIRONMENTAL DESIGN (engineering science, environmental science, and preengineering), HEALTH PROFESSIONS (biology, fitness management, medical laboratory technology, music therapy, occupational therapy, predentistry, premedicine, preoptometry, preoccupational therapy, prepharmacy, prephysician assistant, prephysical therapy, and public health), SOCIAL SCIENCE (criminology, economics, government, history, interdisciplinary studies, international relations, peace studies, philosophy, political science/government, prelaw, psychology, religion, religious music, social work, and sociology). Biology, engineering, music education, and business are the strongest academically. Business, biology, and journalism/communications have the largest enrollments.

ACTIVITIES: There are no fraternities or sororities. There are 89 groups on campus, including art, band, cheerleading, chess, choir, chorale, chorus, communications, computers, dance, debate, drama, drum and bugle corps, environmental, ethnic, forensics, honors, international, jazz band, LGBT, literary magazine, musical theater, newspaper, opera, orchestra, pep band, political, professional, radio and TV stations, religious, social, social service, student government, symphony, and yearbook. Popular campus events include Homecoming and Family Weekend, Culture Week, Martin Luther King Week, St. Elizabeth's Week, and Outfly. **Sports:** There are 11 intercollegiate sports for men and 11 for women, and 4 intramural sports for men and 4 for women. Facilities include indoor pool, 200-meter track, racquetball courts, batting cages, golf putting area, tennis/badminton/volleyball courts, weight rooms, a fitness area with a 30-foot climbing wall. Outdoor amenities include a football stadium with an all-weather track, baseball, soccer, softball, and lacrosse fields, a cross country course and outdoor tennis courts. **Graduates:** From July 1, 2016 to June 30, 2017, 306 bachelor's degrees were awarded. The most popular majors were business administration (18%), biology (16%), and communication arts (8%). In an average class, 2% graduate in 3 years or less, 58% graduate in 4 years or less, 67% graduate in 5 years or less, and 65% graduate in 6 years or less. Of the 2016 graduating class, 24% were enrolled in graduate school within 6 months of graduation, and 69% were employed.

SERVICES: Counseling and information services are available, as is tutoring in most subjects. There is remedial math, reading and writing. There is a comprehensive academic support center, a supplemental instruction program, and assistance with mathematics, and speech writing and delivery. **Library/Resources:** The library contains 238,298 volumes, 374 microform items, and 6,487 audio/video tapes/CDs/DVDs, and subscribes to 61,929 periodicals including electronic. Computerized library services include interlibrary loans, database searching, Internet access, and Wi-Fi capability. Special learning facilities include an art gallery, a planetarium, a multipurpose classroom, a small movie theater, innovation studio, media-creation computer lab, a business center, classroom technology center, fine arts center, journalism lab, symbolic computation lab, music computer lab, center for community engagement, an institute for leadership education, and six acres of native grasses and prairie plants. **Physically Challenged Students:** 85% of the campus is accessible. Facilities include wheelchair ramps, elevators, special parking, specially equipped restrooms, special class scheduling, lowered drinking fountains, lowered telephones, and special housing. **Special:** Special academic programs at Wartburg include those in leadership education and global and multicultural studies. Internships are available in all majors and there are internship programs in Denver, Washington, D.C. Study abroad in 65 countries, on and off campus work-study, dual majors in any combination, and individualized majors are possible. 3-1 degrees are possible in clinical laboratory science and occupational therapy, as well as 3-1 and 2-2 degrees in nursing. A deferred admit program with the University of Iowa College of Dentistry is offered, as is an array of experiential learning opportunities. There are 17 national honor societies, a freshman honors program, and 1 departmental honors program. **Visiting:** There are regularly scheduled orientations for prospective students, including an introduction to academic and student life conducted by administrators, faculty, and students. There are guides for informal visits; visitors may sit in on classes and stay overnight. To schedule a visit, contact the Admissions Office. **Campus Safety and Security:** Measures include 24-hour foot and vehicle patrol, emergency notification system, and security escort services. There are emergency telephones, lighted pathways/sidewalks, controlled access to dorms/residences, 24-hour patrol, and student escort service.

REQUIREMENTS: The SAT is required, with a minimum score of 910 or 19 on the ACT is expected. Candidates for admission must be graduates of an accredited secondary school, having completed 4 years of English, 3 each of math and science, 2 each of social studies and foreign language, and 1 of introduction to computers. The GED is accepted, with an average of 50 or above. A GPA of 2.2 is required. AP and CLEP credits are accepted. Important factors in the admissions decision are advanced placement or honors courses, recommendations by school officials, and leadership record. Degree requirements include a minimum cumulative and major GPA of 2.0 and completion of 36 course credits (128 semester hours), including 4 May term course credits. All students must complete the Wartburg Plan of Essential Education, an integrative and interdisciplinary program of study, based on course work in thinking strategies, reasoning skills, faith and reflection, health and wellness, and literacy in writing, diversity, and a foreign lanaguage. Students must also demonstrate proficiency in information systems and in oral communication and must complete a Capstone course. Inquiry Studies 101/201 are required of all students. **Procedure:** Freshmen are admitted in the fall and winter. Entrance exams should be taken before the senior year. There are early admissions and rolling admissions plans. Applications should be filed by May 1 for fall entry. Notification is sent on a rolling basis. Applications are accepted on-line. **Transfer Students:** 23 transfer students enrolled in 2016-2017. Applicants must have earned an associate degree or have maintained a minimum GPA of 2.0 in previous college work for 1 year. The ACT or the SAT must be taken; the minimum acceptable ACT score is 19. Students must submit official transcripts from all colleges attended. 7 of 36 credits required for the bachelor's degree must be completed at WC. **International Students:** There are 121 international students enrolled. They must take the TOEFL with a minimum score of 480 on the paper-based TOEFL (PBT) or 55 on the Internet-based version (iBT). SAT or ACT scores are not required but are useful in admissions decisions and for placement.

ADMISSIONS: 77% of the 2017-2018 applicants were accepted. The SAT scores for the 2017-2018 freshman class were: Math-- 32% below 500, 37% between 500 and 599, 26% between 600 and 699, and 5% between 700 and 800. The ACT scores were 5% between 12 and 17, 48% between 18 and 23, 37% between 24 and 29, and 10% above 30. 42% of the current freshmen were in the top fifth of their class; 74% were in the top two fifths. 12 freshmen graduated first in their class. **Admissions Contact:** Todd Coleman, Assistant Vice President for Admissions. Email: *admissions@wartburg.edu* Web: *www.wartburg.edu*

FINANCIAL AID: In 2017-2018, 100% of all full-time freshmen received some form of financial aid. 76% of all full-time freshmen received need-based aid. The average freshman award was $39,335. Need-based scholarships or need-based grants averaged $12,503 ($38,120 maximum); need-based self-help aid (loans and jobs) averaged $6,238 ($10,620 maximum); and other non-need-based awards and non-need-based scholarships averaged $27,842 ($52,500 maximum). 63% of undergraduate students work part-time. The average financial indebtedness of the 2017 graduate was $30,659. The FAFSA code is 001896.

WILLIAM PENN UNIVERSITY D-3

www.wmpenn.edu

Oskaloosa, IA 52577 (641) 673-1012
(800) 779-7366

Fax: (641) 673-2113 **Email:** admissions@wmpenn.edu

Full-time: 900 men, 750 women	**Faculty:** n/av
Part-time: 70 men, 115 women	**Ph.D.s:** n/av
Graduate: 40 men, 45 women	**Student/Faculty:** n/av
Year: varies, summer session	**Tuition:** $20,000
Room & Board: $6000	**Freshman Class:** n/av
ACT: required	**CEEB CODE:** 6943
Application Deadline: open	**COMPETITIVE**

William Penn University, founded in 1873, is a private liberal arts institution affiliated with the Society of Friends (Quakers). There are 2 undergraduate schools and 1 graduate school. In addition to regional accreditation, WPU has baccalaureate program accreditation with CAEP and CCNE. The 53-acre campus is in a rural area 58 miles southeast of Des Moines. Including any residence halls, there are 14 buildings.

STUDENT LIFE: 73% of undergraduates are from Iowa. Others are from 40 states, 10 foreign countries, and Canada. 90% are from public schools. 83% are White; 3% Hispanic; 10% African American; 1% Asian American; 1% American Indian/Alaska Native; 1% Foreign. 44% are Protestant; 39% claim no religious affiliation; 13% Catholic. **Male To Female Ratio:** 1.1:1. The average age of freshmen is 19; all undergraduates, 25. 35% do not continue beyond their first year; 35% remain to graduate. **Housing:** 500 students can be accommodated in college housing, which includes married student dorms and on-campus apartments. On-campus housing is guaranteed for all 4 years. 55% of students commute. Alcohol is not permitted. All students may keep cars.

FACULTY/CLASSROOMS: 57% of faculty are male; 43% are female. All teach undergraduates. No introductory courses are taught by graduate students. The average class size in an introductory lecture is 25.

PROGRAMS OF STUDY: WPU confers B.A., B.S., and B.S.N. degrees. Associate and master's degrees are also awarded. Bachelor's degrees are awarded in BIOLOGICAL SCIENCE (biology/biological science and biotechnology), BUSINESS (accounting, business administration and management, recreation and leisure services, and sports management), COMMUNICATIONS AND THE ARTS (communications, digital communications, English, fine arts, journalism, and public relations), COMPUTER AND PHYSICAL SCIENCE (computer science), EDUCATION (elementary education, health education, physical education, science education, secondary education, and special education), ENGINEERING AND ENVIRONMENTAL DESIGN (environmental science, industrial administration/management, and industrial engineering technology), SOCIAL SCIENCE (criminology, history, human services, political science/government, psychology, and sociology). Elementary and secondary education, industrial technology, and business are the strongest academically. Education and business have the largest enrollments.

ACTIVITIES: 5% of men belong to 2 local fraternities; 5% of women belong to 2 local and 1 national sororities. There are 25 groups on campus, including art, band, cheerleading, choir, chorale, chorus, computers, dance, drama, drum and bugle corps, ethnic, honors, international, jazz band, literary magazine, marching band, musical theater, newspaper, pep band, photography, political, professional, radio and TV, religious, social, social service, student government, and yearbook. Popular campus events include Multicultural Day, and Campus Beautification Day. **Sports:** There are 8 intercollegiate sports for men and 7 for women, and 6 intramural sports for men and 6 for women. Facilities include a gym, wrestling and weight training rooms, baseball and softball fields, tennis courts, football and soccer practice fields, a 300 meter walking/jogging track, basketball/volleyball courts, and aerobic fitness area. **Graduates:** From July 1, 2016 to June 30, 2017, 220 bachelor's degrees were awarded. The most popular majors were business management (61%), elementary education (9%), and psychology (5%). In an average class, 56% graduate in 4 years or less, 90% graduate in 5 years or less, and 98% graduate in 6 years or less. Of the 2016 graduating class, 15% were enrolled in graduate school within 6 months of graduation, and 75% were employed.

SERVICES: Counseling and information services are available, as is tutoring in most subjects. There is remedial math, reading, and writing. **Library/Resources:** The library contains 64,974 volumes, 1,733 audio/video tapes/CDs/DVDs, and subscribes to 31,974 periodicals including electronic. Computerized library services include interlibrary loans, database searching, Internet access, and Wi-Fi capability. Special learning facilities include an art gallery, radio station, and Mideast collection. **Physically Challenged Students:** 70% of the campus is accessible. Facilities include wheelchair ramps, elevators, special parking, specially equipped restrooms, special class scheduling, and lowered drinking fountains. **Special:** William Penn offers internships, work-study programs with local businesses, dual majors, nondegree study, pass/fail options, and 3-2 engineering degree programs with Iowa State and Washington Universities. Preprofessional studies, driver and safety education, and endorsements in numerous secondary education subjects are also offered. There are 2 national honor societies and a chapter of Phi Beta Kappa. **Visiting:** There are regularly scheduled orientations for prospective students, including a 1-day visit comprised of meetings with faculty, student services, financial aid, personnel, and people who share students' interests. To schedule a visit, contact the Visitor Coordinater. **Campus Safety and Security:** Measures include 24-hour foot and vehicle patrol, emergency notification system, and self-defense education. There are emergency telephones, lighted pathways/sidewalks, and controlled access to dorms/residences.

REQUIREMENTS: The ACT is required of traditional undergraduates only. Applicants must be graduates of an accredited secondary and should have completed 15 high school units. The GED is accepted. Working adults does not require ACT scores. AP and CLEP credits are accepted. Important factors in the admissions decision are evidence of special talent, extracurricular activities record, and leadership record. To graduate, students must complete 124 hours, with 30 to 75 hours in the major. A GPA of 2.0 overall and in major and minor courses is required. Leadership core requirements total 47 hours in English/

communications, math, natural science, social science, religion, fine arts, and philosophy. **Procedure:** Freshmen are admitted to all sessions. Entrance exams should be taken late in the junior year or early in the senior year. There are early admissions, deferred admissions, and rolling admissions plans. Application deadlines are open. The fall 2017 application fee was $20. Applications are accepted on-line. **Transfer Students:** 189 transfer students enrolled in 2016-2017. Applicants must be in good standing at their previous institution and submit official transcripts from previously attended schools. 30 of 124 credits required for the bachelor's degree must be completed at WPU. **International Students:** There are 20 international students enrolled. They must take the TOEFL with a minimum score of 500 on the paper-based TOEFL (PBT).

ADMISSIONS: 2 freshmen graduated first in their class. **Admissions Contact:** Kerra Strong, Director of Admissions. Email: *admissions@wmpenn.edu* Web: *www.wmpenn.edu*

FINANCIAL AID: In 2017-2018, 99% of all full-time freshmen received some form of financial aid. 96% of all full-time freshmen received need-based aid. The average freshman award was $18,373. 70% of undergraduate students work part-time. The average financial indebtedness of the 2017 graduate was $18,600. The FAFSA code is 001900.

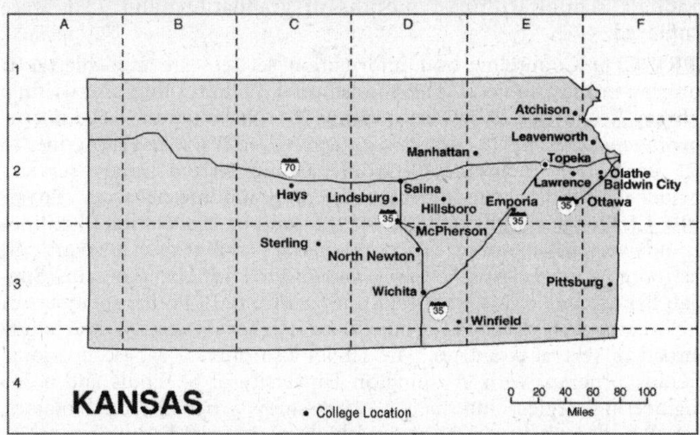

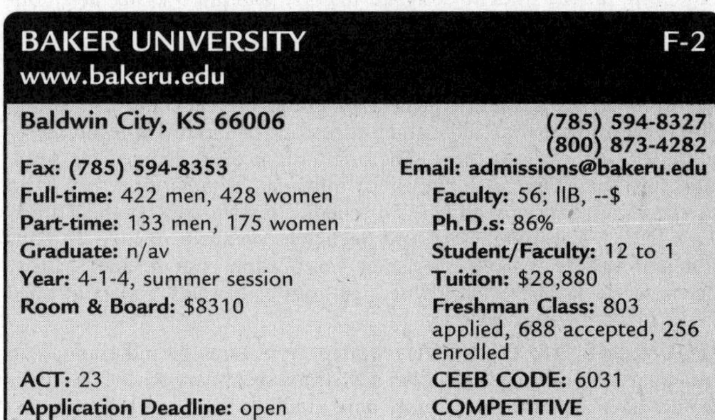

BAKER UNIVERSITY F-2
www.bakeru.edu

Baldwin City, KS 66006 (785) 594-8327
(800) 873-4282

Fax: (785) 594-8353	**Email:** admissions@bakeru.edu
Full-time: 422 men, 428 women	**Faculty:** 56; IIB, --$
Part-time: 133 men, 175 women	**Ph.D.s:** 86%
Graduate: n/av	**Student/Faculty:** 12 to 1
Year: 4-1-4, summer session	**Tuition:** $28,880
Room & Board: $8310	**Freshman Class:** 803 applied, 688 accepted, 256 enrolled
ACT: 23	**CEEB CODE:** 6031
Application Deadline: open	**COMPETITIVE**

Baker University, founded in 1858, is a private liberal arts institution affiliated with the United Methodist Church. There are 3 undergraduate schools and 2 graduate schools. In addition to regional accreditation, Baker has baccalaureate program accreditation with ACBSP, NASM, CAEP, and CCNE. The 26-acre campus is in a rural area 50 miles southwest of Kansas City and 15 miles south of Lawrence. Including any residence halls, there are 26 buildings.

STUDENT LIFE: 76% of undergraduates are from Kansas. Others are from 29 states, 18 foreign countries, and Canada. 95% are from public schools. 74% are White; 8% African American; 6% Hispanic; 5% two or more races; 2% Asian American; 2% Foreign; 2% race unknown; 1% American Indian/Alaska Native. **Female To Male Ratio:** 1.1:1. The average age of freshmen is 18; all undergraduates, 20. 32% do not continue beyond their first year; 61% remain to graduate. **Housing:** 576 students can be accommodated in college housing, which includes single sex dorms, coed dorms and on-campus apartments. In addition, there are fraternity houses and sorority houses. On-campus housing is guaranteed for all 4 years. 83% of students live on campus. Alcohol is not permitted. All students may keep cars.

FACULTY/CLASSROOMS: 52% of faculty are male; 48% are female. All teach undergraduates. No introductory courses are taught by graduate students. The average class size in an introductory lecture is 17; in a laboratory is 11; and in a regular course is 16.

PROGRAMS OF STUDY: Baker confers B.A., B.M.E., and B.S. degrees. Bachelor's degrees are awarded in BIOLOGICAL SCIENCE (biochemistry and biology/biological science), BUSINESS (accounting and business administration and management), COMMUNICATIONS AND THE ARTS (communications, English, French, German, media arts, music, Spanish, sports administration, studio art, and theatre studies), COMPUTER AND PHYSICAL SCIENCE (chemistry, computer science, mathematics, and physics), EDUCATION (elementary education, mathematics education, music education, physical education, and secondary education), HEALTH PROFESSIONS (exercise science, human biology, nursing, and public health), SOCIAL SCIENCE (economics, history, international studies, philosophy, psychology, religion, and sociology). Business, exercise science, and biology have the largest enrollments.

ACTIVITIES: 44% of men belong to 1 local and 3 national fraternities; 47% of women belong to 4 national sororities. There are 75 groups on campus, including art, band, cheerleading, choir, chorale, chorus, communications, computers, dance, drama, environmental, ethnic, honors, international, jazz band, LGBT, literary magazine, newspaper, orchestra, pep band, photography, professional, radio and TV, religious, social, social service, and student government. Popular campus events include Maple Leaf Festival, International Education Week, and Springfest Week. **Sports:** There are 10 intercollegiate sports for men and 10 for women, and 5 intramural sports for men and 5 for women. Facilities include a football/track stadium, a gym, a baseball stadium, practice and varsity fields for football, track, soccer, softball and baseball, basketball courts, racquetball courts, tennis courts, a jogging track, a wellness facility, and a weight room. **Graduates:** From July 1, 2016 to June 30, 2017, 175 bachelor's degrees were awarded. The most popular majors were business (20%), exercise science (11%), and sports administration (10%). In an average class, 1% graduate in 3 years or less, 41% graduate in 4 years or less, 55% graduate in 5 years or less, and 57% graduate in 6 years or less.

SERVICES: Counseling and information services are available, as is tutoring in most subjects. There is a reader service for the blind, and remedial math, reading, and writing. **Library/Resources:** The library contains 221,646 volumes, and 6,093 audio/video tapes/CDs/DVDs, and subscribes to 1,822 periodicals including electronic. Computerized library services include interlibrary loans, database searching, Internet access, and Wi-Fi capability. Special learning facilities include an art gallery, radio station, TV station, a greenhouse, and wetlands. **Physically Challenged Students:** 90% of the campus is accessible. Facilities include wheelchair ramps, elevators, special parking, specially equipped restrooms, special class scheduling, lowered drinking fountains, lowered telephones, and special housing. **Special:** Internships are encouraged for students in most majors. Baker also offers study abroad, work-study, B.A.-B.S. degrees, accelerated degrees, and dual and student-designed majors. A 3-2 engineering degree may be earned in conjunction with Washington University in St. Louis, the University of Kansas, and University of Missouri in Kansas City. There are 13 national honor societies, a freshman honors program, and 7 departmental honors programs. **Visiting:** There are regularly scheduled orientations for prospective students, including Preview Days scheduled for both freshman and transfers in spring and fall. Individual visits are scheduled daily. There are guides for informal visits, visitors may sit in on classes, and stay overnight. To schedule a visit, contact the Admissions Office. **Campus Safety and Security:** Measures include 24-hour foot and vehicle patrol, emergency notification system, and security escort services. There are lighted pathways/sidewalks and controlled access to dorms/residences.

REQUIREMENTS: The ACT is required. Candidates for admission must graduate from an accredited secondary school or earn a GED. High school coursework in English, foreign language, social studies, math, and natural science is recommended. Applications of students not meeting these requirements will be reviewed, and students may be invited for an on-campus interview, as necessary. AP and CLEP credits are accepted. To graduate, all students must complete 128 credit hours, including 24 to 36 hours in the major, a cornerstone liberal arts core, 6 core liberal studies courses, 4 exploratory courses in disciplines, and a minimal level of proficiency in written and oral communication and math. A minimum GPA of 2.0 is required. **Procedure:** Freshmen are admitted to all sessions. Entrance exams should be taken in the fall of the senior year. There is a rolling admissions plan. Application deadlines are open. Applications are accepted on-line. **Transfer Students:** 52 transfer students enrolled in 2016-2017. Transfer applicants must supply a recommendation form, available from the Baker Admissions Office. The ACT or the SAT score, official high school transcript, and official transcripts of all college courses are required. The minimum GPA is 2.3. 31 of 128 credits required for the bachelor's degree must be completed at Baker. **International Students:** There are 26 international students enrolled. They must take the TOEFL with a minimum score of 525 on the paper-based TOEFL (PBT) or 69 on the Internet-based version (iBT). They must also take the SAT or ACT.

ADMISSIONS: 86% of the 2017-2018 applicants were accepted. The ACT scores were 4% between 12 and 17, 48% between 18 and 23, 44% between 24 and 29, and 4% above 30. 30% of the current freshmen were in the top fifth of their class; 57% were in the top two fifths. 15 freshmen graduated first in their class. **Admissions Contact:** Cheryl McCrary, Director of Admissions. Email: *admissions@bakeru.edu* Web: *www.bakeru.edu*

FINANCIAL AID: The college's own financial statement is required. The

FAFSA code is 001903. The priority date for freshman financial aid applications for fall entry is March 1.

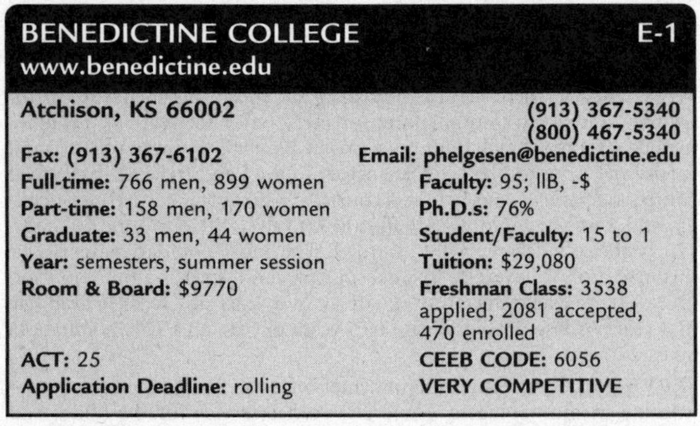

BENEDICTINE COLLEGE E-1
www.benedictine.edu

Atchison, KS 66002	**(913) 367-5340** **(800) 467-5340**
Fax: (913) 367-6102	**Email: phelgesen@benedictine.edu**
Full-time: 766 men, 899 women	**Faculty:** 95; IIB, -$
Part-time: 158 men, 170 women	**Ph.D.s:** 76%
Graduate: 33 men, 44 women	**Student/Faculty:** 15 to 1
Year: semesters, summer session	**Tuition:** $29,080
Room & Board: $9770	**Freshman Class:** 3538 applied, 2081 accepted, 470 enrolled
ACT: 25	**CEEB CODE:** 6056
Application Deadline: rolling	**VERY COMPETITIVE**

Benedictine College, established in 1971 by a merger of St. Benedict's College and Mount Saint Scholastics College, is a liberal arts, Catholic, Benedictine institution. The figures given in the above capsule and in this profile are approximate. There is 1 undergraduate school and 2 graduate schools. In addition to regional accreditation, BC has baccalaureate program accreditation with NASM, CAEP, CAATE, and CCNE. The 225-acre campus is in a small town 45 miles north of Kansas City. Including any residence halls, there are 27 buildings.

STUDENT LIFE: 75% of undergraduates are from out of state, mostly the Midwest. Students are from 48 states, 12 foreign countries, and Canada. 55% are from public schools. 84% are White; 5% Hispanic; 3% African American; 1% Asian American; 1% American Indian/Alaska Native; 1% Foreign. 89% are Catholic. **Female To Male Ratio:** 1.2:1. The average age of freshmen is 18; all undergraduates, 20. 20% do not continue beyond their first year; 55% remain to graduate. **Housing:** 1240 students can be accommodated in college housing, which includes dorms. On-campus housing is guaranteed for all 4 years. 77% of students live on campus. All students may keep cars.

FACULTY/CLASSROOMS: 66% of faculty are male; 34% are female. All teach undergraduates, 40% do research, and 40% do both. No introductory courses are taught by graduate students. The average class size in an introductory lecture is 25; in a laboratory is 20; and in a regular course is 20.

PROGRAMS OF STUDY: BC confers B.A., B.S., and B.Mus.Ed degrees. Associate and master's degrees are also awarded. Bachelor's degrees are awarded in BIOLOGICAL SCIENCE (biochemistry and biology/biological science), BUSINESS (accounting and business administration and management), COMMUNICATIONS AND THE ARTS (art, dramatic arts, English, French, journalism, music, Spanish, and theater management), COMPUTER AND PHYSICAL SCIENCE (astronomy, chemistry, computer science, mathematics, natural sciences, and physics), EDUCATION (athletic training, elementary education, music education, physical education, secondary education, and special education), ENGINEERING AND ENVIRONMENTAL DESIGN (engineering), HEALTH PROFESSIONS (nursing), SOCIAL SCIENCE (economics, history, liberal arts/general studies, philosophy, political science/government, psychology, religion, social science, sociology, and youth ministry). Biology, engineering, and education are the strongest academically. Business, and theology have the largest enrollments.

ACTIVITIES: There are no fraternities or sororities. There are 35 groups on campus, including band, cheerleading, choir, chorale, computers, dance, drama, drill team, ethnic, honors, international, jazz band, literary magazine, musical theater, newspaper, orchestra, pep band, photography, political, professional, religious, social, social service, student government, and symphony. Popular campus events include Discovery Week, Parents Weekend, and All School Mass. **Sports:** There are 7 intercollegiate sports for men and 8 for women, and 7 intramural sports for men and 7 for women. Facilities include a gym, weight rooms, a football and track stadium, baseball, softball, track fields, lacrosse, rugby, wrestling, volleyball, cheer and dance, and an isometrics training room. **Graduates:** From July 1, 2016 to June 30, 2017, 336 bachelor's degrees were awarded. The most popular majors were business (20%), education (10%), and theology/youth ministry (6%). In an average class, 42% graduate in 4 years or less, 46% graduate in 5 years or less, and 53% graduate in 6 years or less. Of the 2016 graduating class, 15% were enrolled in graduate school within 6 months of graduation, and 75% were employed.

SERVICES: Counseling and information services are available, as is tutoring in most subjects. There is remedial math, reading, and writing. **Library/Resources:** The library contains 231,796 volumes, 10,803 microform items, and 52,593 audio/video tapes/CDs/DVDs, and subscribes to 425 periodicals including electronic. Computerized library services include interlibrary loans, database searching, and Internet access. **Physically Challenged Students:** 80% of the campus is accessible. Facilities include wheelchair ramps, elevators, special parking, specially equipped restrooms, special class scheduling, and lowered drinking fountains. **Special:** Benedictine offers cross-registration with the 14 other members of the Kansas City Regional Council for Higher Education and study abroad in several countries. The school also offers a 3-2 occupational therapy program with Washington University of St. Louis and a 3-2 engineering degree. Internships, work-study programs, dual majors, B.A.-B.S. degrees in chemistry and biology, an interdisciplinary music marketing major, student-designed majors, pass/fail options, and non-degree study are also available. There are 4 national honor societies, a freshman honors program, and 4 departmental honors programs. **Visiting:** There are regularly scheduled orientations for prospective students, consisting of an advanced placement exam, preregistration, meetings with the dean, student affairs, and business office and financial aid representatives, and campus tours. The orientations are scheduled for April, June, and July. There are guides for informal visits, visitors may sit in on classes, and stay overnight. To schedule a visit, contact the Admissions Office. **Campus Safety and Security:** Measures include 24-hour foot and vehicle patrol, emergency notification system, and security escort services. There are lighted pathways/sidewalks and controlled access to dorms/residences.

REQUIREMENTS: The ACT is required. Applicants should graduate in the upper 50% of their class at an accredited secondary school. Students should have 16 academic units, 4 in English, 3 in math (4 recommended), 2 in foreign language and science (4 recommended), 2 in social science, and 1 in history. An interview is recommended. Counselor recommendations are required. A GPA of 2.0 is required. AP and CLEP credits are accepted. Important factors in the admissions decision are advanced placement or honors courses, recommendations by school officials, and recommendations by alumni. To graduate, students must complete 128 semester hours, pass a comprehensive exam in their major, and earn a minimum GPA of 2.0 overall and in the major. Curriculum requirements include 9 hours each in philosophy and religious studies, 8 hours each in English, natural science, and foreign language, 6 each in Western civilization and social science, 4 in math, 3 in fine arts, and 2 each in speech communication and physical education. A dean's colloquium and a comprehensive exam are also required. **Procedure:** Freshmen are admitted to all sessions. Entrance exams should be taken before the July following graduation from high school. There are deferred admissions and rolling admissions plans. Application deadlines are open. The fall 2017 application fee was $25. Notification is sent on a rolling basis. Applications are accepted on-line. **Transfer Students:** 78 transfer students enrolled in 2016-2017. Applicants must submit transcripts from all colleges attended, a statement of courses in progress, and, if transferring with less than 60 hours, a high school transcript and ACT score. A minimum GPA of 2.0 is required. 30 of 128 credits required for the bachelor's degree must be completed at BC. **International Students:** There are 21 international students enrolled. They must take the TOEFL with a minimum score of 533 on the paper-based TOEFL (PBT) or 72 on the Internet-based version (iBT). Student must take the MELAB. They must also take the SAT or ACT.

ADMISSIONS: 59% of the 2017-2018 applicants were accepted. 47% of the current freshmen were in the top fifth of their class; 70% were in the top two fifths. **Admissions Contact:** Pete Helgesen, Dean of Enrollment Management. Email: *phelgesen@benedictine.edu* Web: *www.benedictine.edu*

FINANCIAL AID: In 2017-2018, 100% of all full-time freshmen received some form of financial aid. 64% of all full-time freshmen received need-based aid. The average freshman award was $21,132. Need-based scholarships or need-based grants averaged $4,015 ($8,550 maximum); need-based self-help aid (loans and jobs) averaged $3,880 ($5,234 maximum); non-need-based athletic scholarships averaged $14,444 ($28,900 maximum); other non-need-based awards and non-need-based scholarships averaged $12,426 ($20,000 maximum); and $2,828 from other forms of aid. 28% of undergraduate students work part-time. The average financial indebtedness of the 2017 graduate was $27,303. BC is a member of CSS. The college's own financial statement is required. The FAFSA code is 010256. The priority date for freshman financial aid applications for fall entry is April 1.

BETHANY COLLEGE *(The complete profile is made available exclusively on our website, www.barronspac.com)*

BETHEL COLLEGE D-3

www.bethelks.edu

North Newton, KS 67117 (316) 284-5339 (800) 522-1887

Fax: (316) 284-5870 **Email:** admissions@bethelks.edu

Full-time: 230 men, 259 women	**Faculty:** 38
Part-time: 7 men, 7 women	**Ph.D.s:** 66%
Graduate: n/av	**Student/Faculty:** 10 to 1
Year: 4-1-4, summer session	**Tuition:** $27,720
Room & Board: $8720	**Freshman Class:** 886 applied, 493 accepted, 140 enrolled
ACT: required	**CEEB CODE:** 6037
Application Deadline: rolling	**COMPETITIVE**

Bethel College, established in 1887, is a private liberal arts institution affiliated with the Mennonite Church. There is 1 undergraduate school. In addition to regional accreditation, BC has baccalaureate program accreditation with CSWE, CAEP, CCNE, and and CAATE. The 90-acre campus is in a suburban area 25 miles north of Wichita. Including any residence halls, there are 21 buildings.

STUDENT LIFE: 64% of undergraduates are from Kansas. Others are from 28 states, 5 foreign countries, and Canada. 92% are from public schools. 8% are Hispanic; 71% White; 5% two or more races; 14% African American; 1% Asian American; 1% American Indian/Alaska Native. 38% are unknown denominations; 37% claim no religious affiliation. **Female To Male Ratio:** 1.1:1. The average age of freshmen is 18; all undergraduates, 22. 23% do not continue beyond their first year; 53% remain to graduate. **Housing:** 427 students can be accommodated in college housing, which includes dorms, coed dorms, and special housing for international students. On-campus housing is guaranteed for all 4 years. 68% of students live on campus. Alcohol is not permitted. All students may keep cars.

FACULTY/CLASSROOMS: 42% of faculty are male; 58% are female. All teach undergraduates, 50% do research, and 50% do both. No introductory courses are taught by graduate students. The average class size in an introductory lecture is 21; in a laboratory is 11; and in a regular course is 18.

PROGRAMS OF STUDY: BC confers B.A., B.S., and B.S.N. degrees. Bachelor's degrees are awarded in BIOLOGICAL SCIENCE (biology/biological science), BUSINESS (business administration and management), COMMUNICATIONS AND THE ARTS (art, communications, English, graphic design, and music), COMPUTER AND PHYSICAL SCIENCE (chemistry, mathematics, and natural sciences), EDUCATION (athletic training, elementary education, and health and physical education), HEALTH PROFESSIONS (nursing), SOCIAL SCIENCE (history, psychology, religion, and social work). Business, biology, and psychology are the strongest academically. Nursing, business, and fine arts have the largest enrollments.

ACTIVITIES: There are no fraternities or sororities. There are 30 groups on campus, including choral groups, theater and music ensembles, band, campus ministries, cheerleading, chess, choir, chorale, chorus, computers, debate, drama, environmental, ethnic, forensics, international, jazz band, LGBT, literary magazine, newspaper, orchestra, political, professional, radio and TV, religious, social, social service, student government, symphony, and yearbook. Popular campus events include Fall Festival, Christmas Gala, and Spring Fling. **Sports:** There are 7 intercollegiate sports for men and 7 for women, and 18 intramural sports for men and 18 for women. Facilities include gyms, weight rooms, cardio-exercise room, tennis courts, soccer practice fields, all-weather track, outdoor stadium complex for football, soccer, an 8-lane track, artificial field turf, football field, outdoor basketball court, and an outdoor sand volleyball court. **Graduates:** From July 1, 2016 to June 30, 2017, 98 bachelor's degrees were awarded. The most popular majors were nursing (31%), business (19%), and fine arts (12%). In an average class, 35% graduate in 4 years or less and 15% graduate in 5 years or less.

SERVICES: Counseling and information services are available, as is tutoring in most subjects. There is a reader service for the blind, and remedial math, reading, and writing. **Library/Resources:** The library contains 147,965 volumes, 14,377 microform items, and 7,113 audio/video tapes/CDs/DVDs, and subscribes to 32,765 periodicals including electronic. Computerized library services include interlibrary loans, database searching, Internet access, and Wi-Fi capability. Special learning facilities include an art gallery, natural history museum, radio station, TV station, and an observatory. **Physically Challenged Students:** 75% of the campus is accessible. Facilities include wheelchair ramps, elevators, special parking, specially equipped restrooms, special class scheduling, lowered drinking fountains, and special housing. **Special:** Students may cross-register with Associated Colleges of Central Kansas institutions and Hesston College. Internships are required in many majors. Work-study programs, study abroad, dual majors, and a Washington semester are available. The college offers a 3-2 engineering degree with University of Kansas, Kansas State University, and Wichita State University. **Visiting:** There are regularly scheduled orientations for prospective students, including a campus tour, classroom observations, visits with faculty, an interview with an admissions counselor, and lunch, and overnight residence hall lodging. There are guides for informal visits, visitors may sit in on classes, and stay overnight. To schedule a visit, contact the Admissions Office. **Campus Safety and Security:** Measures include emergency notification system. There are emergency telephones and lighted pathways/sidewalks.

REQUIREMENTS: Applicants should present a satisfactory score for SAT and ACT, with a minimum GPA of 2.5 for automatic admission. The GED is accepted. Auditions are required of candidates applying for some scholarships, and interviews are recommended for all applicants. Specific departmental requirements may vary. CLEP, AP, and International Baccalaureate credit may be awarded. A GPA of 2.0 is required. AP and CLEP credits are accepted. Important factors in the admissions decision are evidence of special talent, recommendations by alumni, and parents or siblings attended your school. To graduate, students must earn a total of 124 credits, including 24 to 50 in the major, 12 to 50 of those in upper-level courses, with a GPA of 2.0. Students must also meet general education requirements that include demonstrating competency in writing, math, speech, and foreign language. Additional core requirements include convocation, religious studies, cross-cultural learning, and peace, justice, and conflict studies. Distribution requirements include at least six hours in each division: arts and humanities, science and mathematics, and social sciences. **Procedure:** Freshmen are admitted to all sessions. Entrance exams should be taken by the fall of the senior year. There is a rolling admissions plan. Application deadlines are open. Notification is sent on a rolling basis. Applications are accepted on-line. **Transfer Students:** 84 transfer students enrolled in 2016-2017. A high school transcript (or GED), or official college transcript (minimum 2.0 GPA), ACT or SAT scores (waived if the student has more than 24 hours accepted in transfer to Bethel College), and a transfer recommendation are required. Automatic admission requires a cumulative GPA of 2.0 and satisfactory ACT or SAT scores. 30 of 124 credits required for the bachelor's degree must be completed at BC. **International Students:** There are 7 international students enrolled. They must take the TOEFL with a minimum score of 540 on the paper-based TOEFL (PBT) or 76 on the Internet-based version (iBT). They must also take the SAT or ACT.

ADMISSIONS: 56% of the 2017-2018 applicants were accepted. The ACT scores were 2% between 12 and 17, 68% between 18 and 23, 28% between 24 and 29, and 2% above 30. **Admissions Contact:** Andy Johnson, Vice President for Amissions. Email: *admissions@bethelks.edu* Web: *www.bethelks.edu*

FINANCIAL AID: In 2017-2018, 100% of all full-time freshmen received some form of financial aid. 87% of all full-time freshmen received need-based aid. The average freshman award was $26,000. Need-based scholarships or need-based grants averaged $4,910; need-based self-help aid (loans and jobs) averaged $7,083; non-need-based athletic scholarships averaged $5,125; other non-need-based awards and non-need-based scholarships averaged $5,933; and $9,631 from other forms of aid. 45% of undergraduate students work part-time. The average financial indebtedness of the 2017 graduate was $24,132. The FAFSA code is 001905. The priority date for freshman financial aid applications for fall entry is August 15.

EMPORIA STATE UNIVERSITY E-2

www.emporia.edu

Emporia, KS 66801 **(620) 341-5465**

Fax: (620) 341-5599	**Email:** go2esu@emporia.edu
Full-time: 1255 men, 2085 women	**Faculty:** 282; IIA, --$
Part-time: 102 men, 163 women	**Ph.D.s:** 76%
Graduate: 662 men, 1465 women	**Student/Faculty:** 17 to 1
Year: semesters, summer session	**Tuition:** $6345 ($19,918)
Room & Board: $8684	**Freshman Class:** 2041 applied, 1053 accepted, 606 enrolled
ACT: required	**CEEB CODE:** 6335
Application Deadline: open	**COMPETITIVE**

Emporia State University, founded in 1863, is a comprehensive university and a progressive student-centered learning community that fosters student success through engagement in academic excellence, community and global involvement, and the pursuit of personal and professional fulfillment. There are 3 undergraduate schools and 1 graduate school. In addition to regional accreditation, ESU has baccalaureate program accreditation with AACSB, NASAD, NASM, CAEP, NLN, CAAHEP, and ACS. The 207-acre campus is in a small town 110 miles from Kansas City. Including any residence halls, there are 20 buildings.

STUDENT LIFE: 84% of undergraduates are from Kansas. Others are from 47 states, 62 foreign countries, and Canada. 8% are Foreign; 60% White; 5% Hispanic; 5% two or more races; 3% African American; 17% race unknown; 1% Asian American. **Female To Male Ratio:** 1.8:1. The average age of freshmen is 18; all undergraduates, 22. 27% do not continue beyond their first year; 44% remain to graduate. **Housing:** 809 students can be accommodated in college housing, which includes dorms and on-campus apartments. In addition, there are honors houses, special-interest houses, fraternity houses, and sorority houses. On-campus housing is guaranteed for the freshman year only, and is available on a first-come, first-served basis. 76% of students commute. All students may keep cars.

FACULTY/CLASSROOMS: 50% of faculty are male; 50% are female. 96% teach undergraduates. Graduate students teach 9% of introductory courses. The average class size in an introductory lecture is 18; in a laboratory is 10; and in a regular course is 21.

PROGRAMS OF STUDY: ESU confers B.A., B.S., B.F.A., B.I.S., B Mus., B.Mus.Ed., B.S.Bus., B.S.Ed. and B.S.N. degrees. Master's and doctoral degrees are also awarded. Bachelor's degrees are awarded in BIOLOGICAL SCIENCE (biochemistry and biology/biological science), BUSINESS (accounting, business administration and management, marketing/retailing/merchandising, and recreation and leisure services), COMMUNICATIONS AND THE ARTS (art, communications, dramatic arts, English, modern language, music, and theatre arts), COMPUTER AND PHYSICAL SCIENCE (chemistry, computer science, earth science, information sciences and systems, mathematics, physical sciences, and physics), EDUCATION (art education, athletic training, business education, elementary education, foreign languages education, health education, music education, physical education, and secondary education), HEALTH PROFESSIONS (health care administration, health science, nursing, and rehabilitation therapy), SOCIAL SCIENCE (criminal justice, economics, history, liberal arts/general studies, political science/government, psychology, social science, and sociology). Teacher education elementary and secondary education is the strongest academically. Elementary education, business administration, and biology have the largest enrollments.

ACTIVITIES: 16% of men belong to 8 national fraternities; 12% of women belong to 6 national sororities. There are 130 groups on campus, including art, band, cheerleading, choir, chorale, chorus, computers, debate, drama, drill team, environmental, ethnic, film, honors, international, jazz band, LGBT, literary magazine, marching band, musical theater, newspaper, opera, orchestra, pep band, political, professional, religious, social, social service, student government, symphony, and yearbook. Popular campus events include Family Day, International Student Festival, and Homecoming. **Sports:** There are 7 intercollegiate sports for men and 8 for women, and 12 intramural sports for men and 12 for women. Facilities include a stadium, a student recreation center, an Olympic-size pool, gyms, handball courts, dance rooms, a sports complex with softball fields and a baseball diamond, and an all-weather 8-lane track. **Graduates:** From July 1, 2016 to June 30, 2017, 696 bachelor's degrees were awarded. The most popular majors were education (27%), business administration (17%), and health fields (11%). In an average class, 26% graduate in 4 years or less, 41% graduate in 5 years or less, and 45% graduate in 6 years or less. Of the 2016 graduating class, 20% were enrolled in graduate school within 6 months of graduation, and 22% were employed.

SERVICES: Counseling and information services are available, as is tutoring in most subjects. There is a reader service for the blind, and remedial math, reading, and writing. **Library/Resources:** The library contains 527,389 volumes. Computerized library services include interlibrary loans, database searching, Internet access, and Wi-Fi capability. Special learning facilities include an art gallery, natural history museum, planetarium, theaters, geology museum, and Great Plains study center. **Physically Challenged Students:** All of the campus is accessible. Facilities include wheelchair ramps, elevators, special parking, specially equipped restrooms, special class scheduling, lowered drinking fountains, lowered telephones, and special housing. **Special:** ESU offers internships in many majors, study abroad in 34 countries, work-study programs, on-campus and on-line general studies degrees, B.A.-B.S. degrees, dual and student-designed majors, 3-2 engineering degrees with Kansas State University, Wichita State University, and the University of Kansas, credit for military experience, non-degree study, independent study, evening and Saturday classes, and pass/no credit options. There are 22 national honor societies and a freshman honors program. **Visiting:** There are regularly scheduled orientations for prospective students, visits include campus and residence hall tours, meetings with admissions and financial aid personnel, and appointments with academic and extracurricular personnel. There are guides for informal visits and visitors may sit in on classes. To schedule a visit, contact the Admissions Office. **Campus Safety and Security:** Measures include 24-hour foot and vehicle patrol, emergency notification system, self-defense education, and security escort services. There are emergency telephones, lighted pathways/sidewalks, motorist-assist programs, safety and self-awareness programs for students and parents, 24-hour residence hall monitoring, and smoke detectors in residence halls.

REQUIREMENTS: Applicants must meet 1 of these 3 criteria: an ACT score of 21 or above, class rank in the top third, or a 2.0 GPA in the Kansas core curriculum in-state and a 2.5 for out-of-state applicants. Students should have completed 4 units of English, 3 each of natural science, math, and social science, and 1 of computer technology. Applicants may also be admitted through an exceptions window and are encouraged to apply. A GPA of 2.0 is required. AP and CLEP credits are accepted. To graduate, all students must complete at least 124 credit hours, including 40 in upper-division courses, with a minimum GPA of 2.0. Students must complete the general education program for their field of study, which includes courses in math, physical and applied science, humanities, history, speech, cultural diversity, and fitness and physical education. **Procedure:** Freshmen are admitted to all sessions. Entrance exams should be taken during October or December of the senior year. There are deferred admissions and rolling admissions plans. Application deadlines are open. The fall 2017 application fee was $30. Applications are accepted on-line. **Transfer Students:** 349 transfer students enrolled in 2016-2017. Applicants must submit official transcripts of all previous college work. The minimum GPA depends on the number of semester hours earned. Physical activity requirements must be met. 30 of 124 credits required for the bachelor's degree must be completed at ESU. **International Students:** There are 444 international students enrolled. They must take the TOEFL with a minimum score of 520 on the paper-based TOEFL (PBT) or 68 on the Internet-based version (iBT). They must also take the ACT.

ADMISSIONS: 33% of the current freshmen were in the top fifth of their class; 69% were in the top two fifths. 32 freshmen graduated first in their class. **Admissions Contact:** Dr. Shelly Gehrke, Assistant Provost Enrollment Management. Email: *go2esu@emporia.edu* Web: *www.emporia.edu*

FINANCIAL AID: In 2017-2018, 95% of all full-time freshmen received some form of financial aid. 67% of all full-time freshmen received need-based aid. The average freshman award was $8,900. Need-based scholarships or need-based grants averaged $5,755 ($34,378 maximum); need-based self-help aid (loans and jobs) averaged $2,131 ($6,250 maximum); non-need-based athletic scholarships averaged $3,890 ($28,261 maximum); and other non-need-based awards and non-need-based scholarships averaged $8,106 ($30,968 maximum). 15% of undergraduate students work part-time. The average financial indebtedness of the 2017 graduate was $20,433. The state aid form is required. The FAFSA code is 001927. The priority date for freshman financial aid applications for fall entry is February 2.

FORT HAYS STATE UNIVERSITY C-2

www.fhsu.edu

Hays, KS 67601	**(785) 628-5666** **(800) 628-FHSU**
Fax: (785) 628-4014	**Email: tigers@fhsu.edu**
Full-time: 2270 men, 3248 women	**Faculty:** IIA, --$
Part-time: 2205 men, 3575 women	**Ph.D.s:** 77%
Graduate: 746 men, 1176 women	**Student/Faculty:** n/av
Year: semesters, summer session	**Tuition:** $5008 ($14,831)
Room & Board: $7669	**Freshman Class:** 3199 applied, 2887 accepted, 2185 enrolled
ACT: 21	**CEEB CODE:** 6218
Application Deadline: open	**COMPETITIVE**

Fort Hays State University, established in 1902, is a public liberal arts institution offering programs in arts and sciences, business and entrepreneurship, education, health and life sciences, and pre-professional study. The figures given in the above capsule and in this profile are approximate. There are 4 undergraduate schools and 1 graduate school. In addition to regional accreditation, FHSU has baccalaureate program accreditation with AACSB, NASM, CAEP, and NLN. The 200-acre campus is in a small town 180 miles northwest of Wichita. Including any residence halls, there are 44 buildings.

STUDENT LIFE: 93% of undergraduates are from Kansas. Others are from 36 states, 32 foreign countries, and Canada. 95% are from public schools. 87% are White; 2% Asian American; 2% Hispanic; 1% African American; 1% American Indian/Alaska Native. **Female To Male Ratio:** 1.5:1. The average age of freshmen is 18; all undergraduates, 23. 61% do not continue beyond their first year; 40% remain to graduate. **Housing:** 1000 students can be accommodated in college housing, which includes married student dorms and on-campus apartments. In addition, there are fraternity houses, sorority houses, apartments for students with families, and apartments for nontraditional-age students. 82% of students commute. All students may keep cars.

FACULTY/CLASSROOMS: 59% of faculty are male; 41% are female. All teach undergraduates. No introductory courses are taught by graduate students. The average class size in an introductory lecture is 17; in a laboratory is 17; and in a regular course is 18.

PROGRAMS OF STUDY: FHSU confers B.A., B.S., B.B.A., B.F.A., B.G.S., B.M. and B.S.W. degrees. Associate and master's degrees are also awarded. Bachelor's degrees are awarded in AGRICULTURE (agricultural business management and agriculture), BIOLOGICAL SCIENCE (biology/biological science), BUSINESS (accounting, banking and finance, business administration and management, management information systems, marketing/retailing/merchandising, and office supervision and management), COMMUNICATIONS AND THE ARTS (art, communications, English, fine arts, French, German, modern language, music, music performance, music theory and composition, Spanish, and telecommunications), COMPUTER AND PHYSICAL SCIENCE (chemistry, computer science, geology, information sciences and systems, mathematics, physical sciences, physics, radiological technology, and science), EDUCATION (art education, elementary education, music education, physical education, and technical education), HEALTH PROFESSIONS (nursing and speech pathology/audiology), SOCIAL SCIENCE (criminal justice, economics, history, liberal arts/general studies, philosophy, political science/government, psychology, social work, and sociology). Speech pathology is the strongest academically. Interdisciplinary studies, teacher education, and business administration have the largest enrollments.

ACTIVITIES: 1% of men belong to 3 national fraternities; 1% of women belong to 3 national sororities. There are 85 groups on campus, including art, band, cheerleading, choir, chorale, chorus, computers, dance, debate, drama, drill team, ethnic, film, honors, international, jazz band, LGBT, literary magazine, marching band, musical theater, newspaper, opera, orchestra, pep band, photography, political, professional, radio and TV, religious, social, social service, student government, symphony, and yearbook. Popular campus events include Octoberfest and Parents Day. **Sports:** There are 8 intercollegiate sports for men and 7 for women, and 40 intramural sports for men and 40 for women. Facilities include a stadium, tennis courts, and a coliseum containing a basketball arena, a track, and wrestling and training rooms. **Graduates:** From July 1, 2016 to June 30, 2017, 2572 bachelor's degrees were awarded. The most popular majors were business/marketing (49%), liberal arts/general studies (13%), and education (11%).

SERVICES: Counseling and information services are available, as is tutoring in most subjects. There is remedial math and reading. **Library/Resources:** The library contains 300,000 volumes, 500,000 microform items, and 1,480 audio/video tapes/CDs/DVDs, and subscribes to 3,100 periodicals including electronic. Computerized library services include interlibrary loans, database searching, Internet access, and Wi-Fi capability. Special learning facilities include an art gallery, radio station, TV station, and an English lab. **Physically Challenged Students:** 95% of the campus is accessible. Facilities include wheelchair ramps, elevators, special parking, specially equipped restrooms, special class scheduling, lowered drinking fountains, and lowered telephones. **Special:** Students may, with approval, earn their degrees through a cooperative program with FHSU and another accredited institution, or a correspondence or extension school. Cross-registration with several community colleges, internships, study abroad, work-study programs, a 3-2 engineering degree with Kansas State University, B.A.-B.S. degrees, a general studies degree, and pass/fail options are available. There are 21 national honor societies and a freshman honors program. **Visiting:** There are regularly scheduled orientations for prospective students. There are guides for informal visits, visitors may sit in on classes, and stay overnight. To schedule a visit, contact Campus Tour Coordinator. **Campus Safety and Security:** Measures include 24-hour foot and vehicle patrol and security escort services. There are emergency telephones and lighted pathways/sidewalks.

REQUIREMENTS: The ACT is recommended. 14 total high school units are recommended, 4 in English, 3 in math and science, 2 in social studies, and 1 in history and computer science A GPA of 2.0 is required. AP and CLEP credits are accepted. To graduate, students must earn an overall minimum GPA of 2.0 or higher in some departments for 124 credit hours, including 40 hours in upper-level study, and 30 hours minimum in the major. The 55-hour liberal arts general education curriculum includes courses addressing personal wellness, analysis and communication, international studies, humanities, math, and natural, social, and behavioral sciences. **Procedure:** Freshmen are admitted fall, spring, and summer. Entrance exams should be taken in the senior year. There is a rolling admissions plan. Application deadlines are open. The fall 2017 application fee was $30. Applications are accepted on-line. **Transfer Students:** Applicants must have a minimum college GPA of 2.0 and submit official college transcripts from all institutions previously attended. 30 of 124 credits required for the bachelor's degree must be completed at FHSU. **International Students:** They must take the TOEFL.

ADMISSIONS: 90% of the 2017-2018 applicants were accepted. **Admissions Contact:** Tricia Cline, Director of Admissions. Email: *tigers@fhsu.edu* Web: *www.fhsu.edu*

FINANCIAL AID: The average freshman award was $7,207. Need-based scholarships or need-based grants averaged $5,074; need-based self-help aid (loans and jobs) averaged $3,154; non-need-based athletic scholarships averaged $3,716; other non-need-based awards and non-need-based scholarships averaged $1,406; and $2,953 from other forms of aid. The FFS and the college's own financial statement are required. The FAFSA code is 001915. Check with the school for current application deadlines.

FRIENDS UNIVERSITY D-3

www.friends.edu

Wichita, KS 67213	**(316) 295-5000** **(800) 794-6945**
Fax: (316) 295-5101	**Email: admissions@friends.edu**
Full-time: 434 men, 486 women	**Faculty:** n/av
Part-time: 120 men, 152 women	**Ph.D.s:** n/av
Graduate: 192 men, 378 women	**Student/Faculty:** n/av
Year: semesters, summer session	**Tuition:** $26,730
Room & Board: $11,270	**Freshman Class:** 737 applied, 399 accepted, 159 enrolled
ACT: required	**CEEB CODE:** 6224
Application Deadline: open	**COMPETITIVE**

Friends University, established in 1898, is a nondenominational, independent Christian university that incorporates liberal arts instruction and professional studies into a high-quality undergraduate and graduate education. There are 2 undergraduate schools and 1 graduate school. In addition to regional accreditation, Friends has baccalaureate program accreditation with NASM and CAEP. The 54-acre campus is in an urban area in the heart of Wichita, Kansas adjacent to highway 54, approximately 200 miles southwest of Kansas City. Including any residence halls, there are 19 buildings.

STUDENT LIFE: 70% of undergraduates are from Kansas. Others are from 39 states, 11 foreign countries, and Canada. 81% are from public schools. 70% are White; 2% Asian American; 2% American Indian/Alaska Native; 11% African American; 11% Hispanic; 1% Foreign. 66% are Protestant; 37% claim no religious affiliation; 12% Catholic. **Female To Male Ratio:** 1.4:1. The average age of freshmen is 18; all undergraduates, 21. 40% do not continue beyond their first year; 60% remain to graduate. **Housing:** 423 students can be accommodated in college housing, which includes dorms, on-campus apartments, and off-campus apartments. On-campus housing is available on a first-come and first-served basis. 56% of students commute. Alcohol is not permitted. All students may keep cars.

FACULTY/CLASSROOMS: 92% teach undergraduates. No introductory courses are taught by graduate students. The average class size in an introductory lecture is 35; in a laboratory is 18; and in a regular course is 25.

PROGRAMS OF STUDY: Friends confers B.A., B.S., B.B.A., B.F.A. and B.Mus. degrees. Associate and master's degrees are also awarded. Bachelor's degrees are awarded in BIOLOGICAL SCIENCE (biology/biological science, wildlife biology, and zoology), BUSINESS (accounting, banking and finance, business administration and management, business economics, human resources, international business management, and management information systems), COMMUNICATIONS AND THE ARTS (art, ballet, communications, English, fine arts, music, music performance, musical theater, performing arts, and Spanish), COMPUTER AND PHYSICAL SCIENCE (chemistry, computer science, information sciences and systems, mathematics, and radiological technology), EDUCATION (art education, business education, drama education, education, elementary education, English education, foreign languages education, health education, music education, recreation education, science education, secondary education, and social science education), ENGINEERING AND ENVIRONMENTAL DESIGN (environmental science), HEALTH PROFESSIONS (health science, premedicine, and radiological science), SOCIAL SCIENCE (Christian studies, counseling/psychology, criminal justice, forensic studies, history, human services, liberal arts/general studies, philosophy and religion, political science/government, psychology, and religion). Science is the strongest academically. Business, and education have the largest enrollments.

ACTIVITIES: There are no fraternities or sororities. There are 24 groups on campus, including Zoo science, psychology club, Spanish club, art, band, cheerleading, choir, chorale, chorus, communications, computers, dance, drama, ethnic, honors, international, jazz band, literary magazine, musical theater, newspaper, orchestra, pep band, photography, political, professional, religious, Singing Quakers, social, social service, student government, symphony, and yearbook. Popular campus events include Homecoming Week, Cherry Carnival, and Chili Cookoff. **Sports:** There are 8 intercollegiate sports for men and 10 for women, and 8 intramural sports for men and 8 for women. Facilities include a stadium that is equipped with turf for football and soccer, a track, tennis courts, and a gymnasium for basketball and volleyball, indoor practice facility for baseball, softball, racquetball courts, weight rooms, and the athletic training and sports medicine facilities. **Graduates:** The most popular majors were business/marketing (51%), computer and information sciences (9%), and psychology (7%).

SERVICES: Counseling and information services are available, as is tutoring in most subjects. There is a reader service for the blind. **Library/Resources:** Computerized library services include interlibrary loans, database searching, Internet access, and Wi-Fi capability. Special learning facilities include an art gallery, an observatory. **Physically Challenged Students:** 95% of the campus is accessible. Facilities include wheelchair ramps, elevators, special parking, specially equipped restrooms, special class scheduling, lowered drinking fountains, and lowered telephones. **Special:** Students may cross-register with Newman University at no additional charge. Oportunity to participate in a long-standing study-abroad program is available in Cancun, Mexico, several other study-abroad programs of both shorter and longer duration have occurred in London, Paris, Italy, Cuba, Germany, and Scotland. Friends University offers several accelerated degree completion programs for the adult student in the College of Adult and Professional Studies. Friends also offers credit for life, military, and work experience. There is 1 national honor society, a freshman honors program, and 1 departmental honors program. **Visiting:** There are regularly scheduled orientations for prospective students, including half-day classroom visits, individual instructor visits, discussion with current students, a tour of the campus, and a financial aid session. There are guides for informal visits, visitors may sit in on classes, and stay overnight. To schedule a visit, contact the Admissions Office. **Campus Safety and Security:** Measures include 24-hour foot and vehicle patrol, emergency notification system, and security escort services. There are lighted pathways/sidewalks and controlled access to dorms/residences.

REQUIREMENTS: Candidates for admission must graduate from an accredited secondary school or earn a GED, having completed 4 courses in English, 2 each in history and math, and 1 each in science and social studies. The composite ACT score or converted SAT score is multiplied by the high school GPA. A result of 45 is the minimum for full admission, students scoring lower may be admitted provisionally. Transfer students with at least 15 transferrable hours and adult students aged 23 or older are not required to submit test scores. A GPA of 2.0 is required. AP and CLEP credits are accepted. To graduate, students must complete 124 credit hours, including 33 to 54 in general education (varies by degree sought) and 24 to 45 in the major, with a minimum GPA of 2.0. Distribution requirements include coursework in humanities, fine arts, religion and philosophy, behavioral science, and natural science. **Procedure:** Freshmen are admitted fall and spring. Entrance exams should be taken in the spring of the junior year or fall of the senior year. There is a rolling admissions plan. Application deadlines are open. Notification is sent on a rolling basis. Applications are accepted on-line. **Transfer Students:** 121 transfer students enrolled in 2016-2017. Applicants with fewer than 15 semester hours must submit ACT or SAT I scores and high school and college transcripts. 30 of 124 credits required for the bachelor's degree must be completed at Friends. **International Students:** There are 12 international students enrolled. They must take the TOEFL with a minimum score of 52 on the Internet-based version (iBT), unless they are either native speakers of English or non-native speakers who attended an English-speaking high school. SAT or ACT scores may be submited in place of TOEFL scores.

ADMISSIONS: 54% of the 2017-2018 applicants were accepted. The ACT scores were 6% between 12 and 17, 57% between 18 and 23, 30% between 24 and 29, and 7% above 30. 24% of the current freshmen were in the top fifth of their class; 50% were in the top two fifths. 7 freshmen graduated first in their class. **Admissions Contact:** Brandon Pierce, Senior Director of Admissions. Email: *admissions@friends.edu* Web: *www.friends.edu*

FINANCIAL AID: In 2017-2018, 100% of all full-time freshmen received some form of financial aid. 52% of all full-time freshmen received need-based aid. The average freshman award was $24,142. Need-based scholarships or need-based grants averaged $2,190; need-based self-help aid (loans and jobs) averaged $3,438; non-need-based athletic scholarships averaged $4,784; other non-need-based awards and non-need-based scholarships averaged $11,086; and $2,644 from other forms of aid. The average financial indebtedness of the 2017 graduate was $13,418. The FAFSA code is 001918. The priority date for freshman financial aid applications for fall entry is March 15.

KANSAS STATE UNIVERSITY E-2
www.k-state.edu

Manhattan, KS 66506 **(785) 532-6250**

Fax: (785) 532-6393	**Email: k-state@k-state.edu**
Full-time: 9388 men, 8547 women	**Faculty:** I, --$
Part-time: 960 men, 964 women	**Ph.D.s:** 84%
Graduate: 1917 men, 2370 women	**Student/Faculty:** 19 to 1
Year: semesters, summer session	**Tuition:** $9350 ($23,429)
Room & Board: $8430	**Freshman Class:** 9178 applied, 8712 accepted, 3624 enrolled
ACT: 25	**CEEB CODE:** 6334
Application Deadline: open	**VERY COMPETITIVE**

Kansas State University, established in 1863, is a land-grant institution offering degree programs in agriculture, arts and sciences, business, engineering, human ecology, architecture, education, veterinary medicine, technology and aviation. There are 9 undergraduate schools and 1 graduate school. In addition to regional accreditation, K-State has baccalaureate program accreditation with AACSB, ABET, ACCE, ACEJMC, AHEA, CSWE, FIDER, NAAB, NASAD, NASM, CAEP, NRPA, LAAB, CEA, CIDA, CAATE, CAA, CADE, NASPAA, CADE, NAEYC, ACPHA, AVMA, AABI, and NAST. The 668-acre campus is in a suburban area in Manhattan, Kansas, 125 miles west of Kansas City. Including any residence halls, there are 96 buildings.

STUDENT LIFE: 77% of undergraduates are from Kansas. Others are from 50 states, 110 foreign countries, and Canada. 75% are White; 8% Foreign; 6% Hispanic; 3% African American; 3% two or more races; 2% Asian American; 2% race unknown; 1% American Indian/Alaska Native. **Male To Female Ratio:** 1.0:1. The average age of freshmen is 18; all undergraduates, 21. 16% do not continue beyond their first year; 63% remain to graduate. **Housing:** 4319 students can be accommodated in college housing, which includes married student dorms and on-campus apartments. In addition, there are honors houses and special-interest houses. On-campus housing is available on a first-come and first-served basis. 77% of students commute. All students may keep cars.

FACULTY/CLASSROOMS: 56% of faculty are male; 44% are female. No introductory courses are taught by graduate students. The average class size in a regular course is 30.

PROGRAMS OF STUDY: K-State confers B.A., B.S., B.F.A., B.M. and B.M.E. degrees. Associate, master's, and doctoral degrees are also awarded. Bachelor's degrees are awarded in AGRICULTURE (agricultural business management, agricultural communications, agricultural economics, agronomy, animal science, fish and game management, horticulture, milling science, and wildlife management), BIOLOGICAL SCIENCE (biochemistry, biology/biological science, life science, microbiology, nutrition, and wildlife biology), BUSINESS (accounting, apparel and accessories marketing, banking and finance, business administration and management, entrepreneurial studies, hotel/motel and restaurant management, management information systems, marketing/retailing/merchandising, and personal financial planning), COMMUNICATIONS AND THE ARTS (apparel design, applied music, art, communications, dramatic arts, English, journalism, modern language, and music), COMPUTER AND PHYSICAL SCIENCE (chemistry, computer science, geology, information sciences and systems, mathematics, physical sciences, physics, and statistics), EDUCATION (agricultural education, art education, athletic training, early childhood education, elementary education, music education, and secondary education), ENGINEERING AND ENVIRONMENTAL DESIGN (aeronautical technology, agricultural engineering, agricultural engineering technology, airline piloting and navigation, architectural engineering, architecture, chemical engineering, civil engineering, computer engineering, construction management, electrical/electronics engineering, electrical/electronics engineering technology, engineering management, engineering technology, industrial engineering, interior design, landscape architecture/design, manufacturing engineering, and mechanical engineering), HEALTH PROFESSIONS (exercise science, medical technology, preveterinary science, and speech pathology/audiology), SOCIAL SCIENCE (anthropology, child care/child and family studies, dietetics, economics, ethnic studies, family and community services, family/consumer studies, food science, geography, history, human ecology, humanities, parks and recreation management, philosophy, physical fitness/movement, political science/government, psychology, social science, social work, sociology, textiles and clothing, and women's studies). Architecture, engineering, and accounting are the strongest academically. Business administration, mechanical engineering, and animal sciences have the largest enrollments.

ACTIVITIES: There are 478 groups on campus, including student society of America, band, cheerleading, chess, choir, chorale, chorus, computers, dance, debate, drama, drill team, environmental, ethnic, honors, international, jazz band, LGBT, literary magazine, marching band, musical theater, newspaper, orchestra, pep band, photography, political, prenursing club, professional, radio and TV, religious, social, social service, student government, symphony, and yearbook. Popular campus events include Family Weekend, K-State Open House, and the Festival of Nations. **Sports:** There are 6 intercollegiate sports for men and 8 for women, and 49 intramural sports for men and 49 for women. Facilities include indoor and outdoor tracks, baseball fields, tennis courts, basketball courts, swimming pools, a football stadium, and an indoor practice field. **Graduates:** From July 1, 2016 to June 30, 2017, 3887 bachelor's degrees were awarded. The most popular majors were business and marketing (17%), agriculture and engineering (13%), and social sciences (7%). In an average class, 31% graduate in 4 years or less, 56% graduate in 5 years or less, and 62% graduate in 6 years or less. Of the 2016 graduating class, 21% were enrolled in graduate school within 6 months of graduation, and 73% were employed.

SERVICES: Counseling and information services are available, as is tutoring in every subject. There is a reader service for the blind, and remedial math, reading, and writing. **Library/Resources:** The library contains 3.2 million volumes, 1.6 million microform items, and 209,055 audio/video tapes/CDs/DVDs, and subscribes to 107,980 periodicals including electronic. Computerized library services include interlibrary loans, database searching, and Internet access. Special learning facilities include an art gallery, planetarium, radio station, TV station, a nuclear reactor, laser center, a cancer research center, and telecommunications satellite teaching. **Physically Challenged Students:** 90% of the campus is accessible. Facilities include wheelchair ramps, elevators, special parking, specially equipped restrooms, special class scheduling, lowered drinking fountains, lowered telephones, special housing, and campus shuttle service. **Special:** K-State offers co-op programs, internships, and dual degrees and majors through most of its colleges. Study abroad is available in more than 100 countries. Concurrent bachelor's/master's degree programs are available in 11 major areas. There are 78 national honor societies, Phi Beta Kappa, a freshman honors program, and 7 departmental honors programs. **Visiting:** There are regularly scheduled orientations for prospective students, including campus tours and visits with academic advisers and admissions representatives. There are guides for informal visits, visitors may sit in on classes, and stay overnight. To schedule a visit, contact the Office of Admissions. **Campus Safety and Security:** Measures include 24-hour foot and vehicle patrol, emergency notification system, self-defense education, and security escort services. There are shuttle buses, emergency telephones, lighted pathways/sidewalks, controlled access to dorms/residences, televised monitors in parking lots, CPR classes, and vehicle assistance devices.

REQUIREMENTS: Applicants must have earned a 2.0 GPA in the Kansas high school core curriculum or equivalent. It is recommended that students complete 4 units of English, 3 each of natural science, math, and social studies, 1.5 of history, and 1 of computer technology. The GED is accepted. In addition, applicants must meet 1 of these 2 criteria: an ACT score of 21 or above OR class rank in the top third of their high school graduating class. AP and CLEP credits are accepted. Bachelor's degree programs require a minimum of 120 or more semester credit hours for completion. All undergraduates must complete 6 credit hours of expository writing and 2 credit hours of public speaking. Other requirements vary by college and program. **Procedure:** Freshmen are admitted to all sessions. Entrance exams should be taken in the junior and senior years. There is a rolling admissions plan. Application deadlines are open. The fall 2017 application fee was $30. Notification is sent on a rolling basis. Applications are accepted on-line. **Transfer Students:** 1474 transfer students enrolled in 2016-2017. Applicants must have a minimum of 24 transfer credit hours and a college GPA of 2.0 or otherwise must meet freshman requirements. Students must submit official transcripts from previous colleges attended. 30 of 120 credits required for the bachelor's degree must be completed at K-State. **International Students:** There are 1269 international students enrolled. They must take the TOEFL with a minimum score of 550 on the paper-based TOEFL (PBT) or 79 on the Internet-based version (iBT). Student must present acceptable scores on the SAT or the ACT. Student must also take the English proficiency test given at the university.

ADMISSIONS: 95% of the 2017-2018 applicants were accepted. The ACT scores were 3% between 12 and 17, 37% between 18 and 23, 44% between 24 and 29, and 16% above 30. **Admissions Contact:** Larry Moeder, Assistant VP for Student Life/Director Admissions & Financial Aid. Email: *k-state@k-state.edu* Web: *www.k-state.edu*

FINANCIAL AID: In 2017-2018, 84% of all full-time freshmen received some form of financial aid. 40% of all full-time freshmen received need-based aid. The average freshman award was $13,462. Need-based scholarships or need-based grants averaged $4,623 ($9,925 maximum); need-based self-help aid (loans and jobs) averaged $3,839 ($11,000 maximum); non-need-based athletic scholarships averaged $18,890 ($36,210 maximum); and other non-need-based awards and non-need-based scholarships averaged $6,869 ($40,154 maximum). The average financial indebtedness of the 2017 graduate was $24,993. K-State is a member of CSS. The FAFSA code is 001928. The priority date for freshman financial aid applications for fall entry is March 1.

KANSAS WESLEYAN UNIVERSITY D-2
www.kwu.edu

Salina, KS 67401	**(785) 827-5541** **(800) 874-1154**
Fax: (785) 827-0927	**Email: admissions@kwu.edu**
Full-time: 310 men, 380 women	**Faculty:** n/av
Part-time: 40 men, 70 women	**Ph.D.s:** n/av
Graduate: 45 men, 30 women	**Student/Faculty:** 14 to 1
Year: semesters, summer session	**Tuition:** $28,980
Room & Board: $8950	**Freshman Class:** n/av
SAT or ACT: required	**CEEB CODE:** 6337
Application Deadline: open	**COMPETITIVE**

Kansas Wesleyan University, founded in 1886, is affiliated with the United Methodist Church. The college offers undergraduate programs in the arts and sciences, business, and education. The figures given in the above capsule and in this profile are approximate. There are 3 undergraduate schools and 1 graduate school. In addition to regional accreditation, KWU has baccalaureate program accreditation with CAEP and NLN. The 28-acre campus is in an urban area 85 miles north of Wichita. Including any residence halls, there are 12 buildings.

STUDENT LIFE: 61% of undergraduates are from Kansas. Others are from 14 states, 12 foreign countries, and Canada. 92% are from public schools. 85% are White; 7% African American; 3% Hispanic; 2% Asian American; 1% American Indian/Alaska Native. 48% are Protestant; 39% claim no religious affiliation; 13% Catholic. **Female To Male Ratio:** 1.2:1. The average age of freshmen is 20; all undergraduates, 24. 33% do not continue beyond their first year. **Housing:** 450 students can be accommodated in college housing, which includes married student dorms and on-campus apartments. On-campus housing is guaranteed for all 4 years. 65% of students live on campus. Alcohol is not permitted. All students may keep cars.

FACULTY/CLASSROOMS: All teach undergraduates, 65% do research, and 65% do both. No introductory courses are taught by graduate students. The average class size in an introductory lecture is 24; in a laboratory is 7; and in a regular course is 13.

PROGRAMS OF STUDY: KWU confers B.A., B.S. and B.S.N. degrees. Associate and master's degrees are also awarded. Bachelor's degrees are awarded in BIOLOGICAL SCIENCE (biology/biological science), BUSINESS (accounting and business economics), COMMUNICATIONS AND THE ARTS (communications, dramatic arts, English, music, Spanish, speech/debate/rhetoric, and studio art), COMPUTER AND PHYSICAL SCIENCE (chemistry, computer science, mathematics, and physics), EDUCATION (art education, music education, physical education, secondary education, and special education), HEALTH PROFESSIONS (nursing), SOCIAL SCIENCE (addiction studies, criminal justice, history, prelaw, psychology, religion, religious education, and sociology). Premedicine, nursing, and preengineering are the strongest academically. Education, nursing, and business have the largest enrollments.

ACTIVITIES: There are no fraternities or sororities. There are 38 groups on campus, including art, band, cheerleading, choir, chorale, chorus, computers, dance, departmental clubs, drama, ethnic, film, honors, international, literary magazine, musical theater, newspaper, pep band, photography, professional, radio and TV, religious, social, social service, student government, and yearbook. Popular campus events include Lilac Fete, Sweetheart Dance, and Family Weekend. **Sports:** There are 7 intercollegiate sports for men and 7 for women, and 8 intramural sports for men and 6 for women. Facilities include a student activities center, a gym, a sand volleyball court, football practice and game fields, a multipurpose courtyard, a track and a weight room. **Graduates:** In an average class, 24% graduate in 4 years or less.

SERVICES: Counseling and information services are available, as is tutoring in most subjects. There is remedial reading and writing. **Library/Resources:** The library contains 76,621 volumes, 33,505 microform items, and 984 audio/video tapes/CDs/DVDs, and subscribes to 421 periodicals including electronic. Computerized library services include interlibrary loans, database searching, and Internet access. Special learning facilities include an art gallery, planetarium, radio station, and TV station. **Physically Challenged Students:** 90% of the campus is accessible. Facilities include wheelchair ramps, elevators, special parking, specially equipped restrooms, special class scheduling, lowered drinking fountains, and lowered telephones. **Special:** Cross-registration is available with other members of the Associated Colleges of Central Kansas and the Salina College Consortium. Cooperative degree programs are offered in agriculture, cytotechnology, engineering, environmental studies, and medical technology. Kansas Wesleyan also offers January interterm study trips throughout the United States and abroad, Washington, D.C., and UN semesters, internships, dual majors, student designed majors, credit for life experience, and nondegree study. A 3-2 engineering degree is offered with Columbia University and Washington University at St. Louis. There are 4 national honor societies and a freshman honors program. **Visiting:** There are regularly scheduled orientations for prospective students. There are guides for informal visits, visitors may sit in on classes, and stay overnight. To schedule a visit, contact the Admissions Office. **Campus Safety and Security:** Measures include self-defense education and security escort services. There are lighted pathways/sidewalks, random security checks and private service security guards.

REQUIREMENTS: The SAT or ACT is required. Applicants must be graduates of accredited secondary schools or have earned a GED. An interview is recommended. A GPA of 2.5 is required. AP and CLEP credits are accepted. Students must demonstrate proficiency in English and math and must fulfill distribution requirements in 15 liberal arts components, including environmental awareness, biblical heritage, and lifetime recreation. Courses in phys ed and computers are required. To graduate, students must complete at least 126 credit hours, including 30 to 40 in a major field of study, with a minimum GPA of 2.0. **Procedure:** Freshmen are admitted to all sessions. Entrance exams should be taken as early as possible. There are deferred admissions and rolling admissions plans. Application deadlines are open. The fall 2017 application fee was $20. Notification is sent on a rolling basis. **Transfer Students:** Transfers must submit transcripts from all colleges previously attended. Those students transferring fewer than 15 credit hours must submit ACT scores and a high school transcript. A minimum GPA of 2.0 is recommended. 63 of 126 credits required for the bachelor's degree must be completed at KWU. **International Students:** They must take the TOEFL.

Admissions Contact: Esteban Paredes, Admissions Office. Email: *admissions@kwu.edu* Web: *www.kwu.edu*

FINANCIAL AID: In 2017-2018, 99% of all full-time freshmen received some form of financial aid. 99% of all full-time freshmen received need-based aid. The FAFSA code is 001929. Check with the school for current application deadlines.

MCPHERSON COLLEGE D-2
www.mcpherson.edu

McPherson, KS 67460	**(620) 241-0731** **(800) 365-7402**
Fax: (620) 241-8443	**Email: admiss@mcpherson.edu**
Full-time: 365 men, 234 women	**Faculty:** IIA
Part-time: 18 men, 15 women	**Ph.D.s:** 72%
Graduate: 5 men, 7 women	**Student/Faculty:** 14 to 1
Year: 4-1-4, summer session	**Tuition:** $27,823
Room & Board: $8311	**Freshman Class:** n/av
SAT or ACT: required	**CEEB CODE:** 6404
Application Deadline: August 1	**COMPETITIVE**

McPherson College, founded in 1887 and affiliated with the Church of the Brethren, is a private institution offering undergraduate programs in the arts and sciences, business, and education. There is 1 undergraduate school and 1 graduate school. In addition to regional accreditation, McPherson has baccalaureate program accreditation with CAEP. The 27-acre campus is in a small town in central Kansas, 50 miles north of Wichita. Including any residence halls, there are 16 buildings.

STUDENT LIFE: 53% of undergraduates are from Kansas. Others are from 29 states, and 2 foreign countries. 99% are from public schools. 80% are White; 6% Hispanic; 2% American Indian/Alaska Native; 13% African American; 1% Asian American; 1% Foreign. 43% claim no religious affiliation; 13% Catholic. **Male To Female Ratio:** 1.5:1. The average age of freshmen is 18; all undergraduates, 23. **Housing:** 392 students can be accommodated in college housing, which includes dorms and on-campus apartments. On-campus housing is guaranteed for all 4 years. 79% of students live on campus. Alcohol is not permitted. All students may keep cars.

FACULTY/CLASSROOMS: 72% of faculty are male; 28% are female. All teach undergraduates. No introductory courses are taught by graduate

students. The average class size in an introductory lecture is 30; in a laboratory is 12; and in a regular course is 15.

PROGRAMS OF STUDY: McPherson confers B.A., and B.S. degrees. Master's degrees are also awarded. Bachelor's degrees are awarded in BIOLOGICAL SCIENCE (biology/biological science), BUSINESS (business administration and management), COMMUNICATIONS AND THE ARTS (art, communications, dramatic arts, English, music, Spanish, and speech/debate/rhetoric), COMPUTER AND PHYSICAL SCIENCE (chemistry and mathematics), EDUCATION (elementary education, physical education, secondary education, and special education), SOCIAL SCIENCE (history, philosophy, psychology, religion, and sociology). Business, education, and technology have the largest enrollments.

ACTIVITIES: There are no fraternities or sororities. There are 18 groups on campus, including art, band, cheerleading, choir, chorus, computers, drama, ethnic, honors, international, LGBT, musical theater, newspaper, orchestra, pep band, professional, religious, social service, and student government. Popular campus events include Family Weekend. **Sports:** There are 5 intercollegiate sports for men and 6 for women, and 6 intramural sports for men and 6 for women. Facilities include a sports center with basketball/volleyball courts, a racquetball court, and a fitness center with an open weight-training room, football/track stadium, practice fields, and tennis courts. **Graduates:** From July 1, 2016 to June 30, 2017, 105 bachelor's degrees were awarded.

SERVICES: Counseling and information services are available, as is tutoring in most subjects. There is remedial reading and writing. **Library/Resources:** The library contains 98,214 volumes, 60,799 microform items, and 4,626 audio/video tapes/CDs/DVDs, and subscribes to 26,828 periodicals including electronic. Computerized library services include interlibrary loans, database searching, Internet access, and Wi-Fi capability. Special learning facilities include an art gallery, natural history museum, and an automobile restoration center. **Physically Challenged Students:** 95% of the campus is accessible. Facilities include wheelchair ramps, elevators, special parking, specially equipped restrooms, special class scheduling, lowered drinking fountains, and special housing. **Special:** Cross-registration with other colleges is available through the Associated Colleges of Central Kansas. McPherson also offers internships, study abroad in 10 countries, co-op programs, credit by exam, a general studies degree, student-designed majors, and pass/fail options. There are preprofessional programs in health, engineering, law, forestry, veterinary medicine, nursing and medicine, optometry, and dentistry. There are 3 national honor societies, Phi Beta Kappa, and 3 departmental honors programs. **Visiting:** There are regularly scheduled orientations for prospective students, consisting of campus tours, meetings with admissions personnel, and class attendance. There are guides for informal visits, visitors may sit in on classes, and stay overnight. To schedule a visit, contact the Admissions Office. **Campus Safety and Security:** Measures include emergency notification system. There are emergency telephones and lighted pathways/sidewalks.

REQUIREMENTS: The SAT or ACT is required. The GED is accepted. A GPA of 2.0 is required. AP and CLEP credits are accepted. Important factors in the admissions decision are recommendations by school officials, evidence of special talent, and parents or siblings attended your school. To graduate, students must complete 124 credits, including 32 in the major, with a GPA of 2.0. All students must fulfill general education requirements in the following areas: written and oral communication, aesthetics, history, society, natural sciences, technology and culture, and religion/beliefs/values. Students must also participate in an integrative seminar and a service experience, and must complete a global/intercultural experience, which may include intercultural studies courses or modern language courses. **Procedure:** Freshmen are admitted fall, winter, and spring. Entrance exams should be taken in the junior year of high school. There are deferred admissions and rolling admissions plans. Applications should be filed by August 1 for fall entry. The fall 2017 application fee was $25. Notification is sent on a rolling basis. Applications are accepted on-line. **Transfer Students:** 288 transfer students enrolled in 2016-2017. Applicants must have satisfactorily completed 12 credit hours of college course work covering 3 academic areas with a 2.0 GPA. 32 of 124 credits required for the bachelor's degree must be completed at McPherson. **International Students:** There are 12 international students enrolled. They must take the TOEFL. They must also take the ACT.

Admissions Contact: Carol Williams, Director of Admissions and Financial Aid. Email: *admiss@mcpherson.edu* Web: *www.mcpherson.edu*

FINANCIAL AID: In 2017-2018, 99% of all full-time freshmen received some form of financial aid. 99% of all full-time freshmen received need-based aid. The FAFSA code is 001933. Check with the school for current application deadlines.

MIDAMERICA NAZARENE UNIVERSITY F-2

www.mnu.edu

Olathe, KS 66062	**(913) 791-3380** **(800) 800-8887**
Fax: (913) 791-3487	**Email: admissions@mnu.edu**
Full-time: n/av	**Faculty:** 67
Part-time: n/av	**Ph.D.s:** 64%
Graduate: n/av	**Student/Faculty:** 12 to 1
Year: semesters, summer session	**Tuition:** $57,390
Room & Board: $8138	**Freshman Class:** 957 applied, 628 accepted, 223 enrolled
SAT or ACT: required	**CEEB CODE:** 6437
Application Deadline: August 1	**COMPETITIVE**

MidAmerica Nazarene University is a private, Christian, liberal arts university founded in 1966. Offering 35 traditional undergraduate majors, the university is also known for its accelerated professional and graduate programs, including undergraduate degrees in business and nursing and graduate degrees in business, education, nursing, and counseling, and postgraduate certificates. Online offerings include classes in education, nursing, business and associates-level studies. Study abroad as well as service-learning experiences are encouraged through MNU's Go Global and ServiceCorps programs. The campus in Liberty, Missouri, is for professional and graduate programs. There are 5 undergraduate schools and 4 graduate schools. In addition to regional accreditation, MNV has baccalaureate program accreditation with ACBSP, NASM, CAEP, NLN, HLC, CCLN, CAATE, KSBE, and and CACREP. The 105-acre campus is in a suburban area 19 miles southwest of downtown Kansas City, Missouri. Including any residence halls, there are 22 buildings.

STUDENT LIFE: Housing: 699 students can be accommodated in college housing, which includes single-sex dorms. On-campus housing is guaranteed for all 4 years. Alcohol is not permitted. All students may keep cars.

FACULTY/CLASSROOMS: 53% of faculty are male; 47% are female. No introductory courses are taught by graduate students.

PROGRAMS OF STUDY: MidAmerica Nazarene confers B.A.,B.S., B.M.Ed., and B.S.N. degrees. Associate and master's degrees are also awarded. Bachelor's degrees are awarded in BIOLOGICAL SCIENCE (biology/general science/environment science second education), BUSINESS (accounting, business administration and management, international business management, marketing/retailing/merchandising, organizational leadership and management, recreation and leisure services, and sports management), COMMUNICATIONS AND THE ARTS (communications, English, graphic design, music, and speech and theatre education), COMPUTER AND PHYSICAL SCIENCE (chemistry, mathematics, and physics), EDUCATION (athletic training, elementary education, English education, health education, mathematics education, music education, physical education, science education, and social studies education), HEALTH PROFESSIONS (biology, kinesiology, and nursing), SOCIAL SCIENCE (criminal justice, cultural studies/critical theory & analysis, history, interdisciplinary studies, ministries, psychology, religious studies, sociology, and youth ministry). Nursing, and business are the strongest academically. Nursing, business administration, and behavioral science have the largest enrollments.

ACTIVITIES: There are no fraternities or sororities. There are 43 groups on campus, including cheerleading, choir, chorale, chorus, computers, drama, ethnic, honors, Improv club, international, jazz band, musical theater, newspaper, orchestra, pep band, political, professional, religious, student government, and yearbook. Popular campus events include White Light Event, Root Beer Fest, Homecoming Hoe Down, and Welcome Week. **Sports:** There are 7 intercollegiate sports for men and 7 for women, and 7 intramural sports for men and 7 for women. Facilities include a weight room, basketball/volleyball arena, a gym, a track, tennis and sand volleyball courts, softball, baseball, and soccer fields. **Graduates:** From July 1, 2016 to June 30, 2017, 423 bachelor's degrees were awarded.

SERVICES: Counseling and information services are available, as is

tutoring in most subjects, such as nursing, business, psychology, sociology, history, music, chemistry, biology, and physics. There is a reader service for the blind, and remedial math, reading, and writing. There are also test-taking accommodations, interpreters for the hearing impaired, and note takers for the blind, hearing impaired, and learning disabled. **Library/Resources:** Computerized library services include interlibrary loans, database searching, Internet access, and Wi-Fi capability. **Physically Challenged Students:** Facilities include wheelchair ramps, elevators, special parking, specially equipped restrooms, special class scheduling, and lowered drinking fountains. **Special:** MNU, offers non-degree study, cross-registration with the Christian College Coalition, study abroad in 4 countries, internships, and a Washington semester. There are accelerated degree programs in management and human relations and in nursing. There are 4 national honor societies, a freshman honors program, and 4 departmental honors programs. **Visiting:** There are regularly scheduled orientations for prospective students, including an academic fair, advising, class visitation, informational meetings, social activities, and experiencing residential life. There are guides for informal visits, visitors may sit in on classes, and stay overnight. To schedule a visit, contact Jean Kilber at jlkilber@mnu.edu. **Campus Safety and Security:** Measures include 24-hour foot and vehicle patrol, emergency notification system, self-defense education, and security escort services. There are emergency telephones, lighted pathways/sidewalks, and controlled access to dorms/residences.

REQUIREMENTS: Recommended composite score of 18 on the ACT or a satisfactory score on the SAT. Candidates for admission should be graduates of an accredited secondary school. The GED is accepted. Students should have completed 15 units of study, including 4 units of English and 3 each of natural science, social studies, and math. An essay is optional. AP and CLEP credits are accepted. All students must meet core curriculum requirements in humanities-communications, natural sciences-math, social sciences, religion-philosophy, and phys ed. Students must maintain a minimum GPA of 2.0 and complete 126 semester hours to graduate. **Procedure:** Freshmen are admitted to all sessions. Entrance exams should be taken during the junior or senior year. There are deferred admissions and rolling admissions plans. Applications should be filed by August 1 for fall entry; January 1 for spring entry. Applications are accepted on-line. **Transfer Students:** 90 transfer students enrolled in 2016-2017. Transfer applicants should have earned 24 or more hours at an accredited institution and not be on academic or disciplinary probation. ACT or SAT scores are required. 30 of 126 credits required for the bachelor's degree must be completed at MidAmerica Nazarene. **International Students:** They must take the TOEFL with a minimum score of 76 on the Internet-based version (iBT). Students must take the ACT and/or SAT where English is the official first language. Incoming freshman students must take the placement tests.

ADMISSIONS: 66% of the 2017-2018 applicants were accepted. The ACT scores were 1% below 12, 17% between 12 and 17, 48% between 18 and 23, 29% between 24 and 29, and 5% above 30. **Admissions Contact:** Derry Ebert, Vice President and Dean for Traditional Undergraduate. Email: *admissions@mnu.edu* Web: *www.mnu.edu*

FINANCIAL AID: The FAFSA code is 007032. The priority date for freshman financial aid applications for fall entry is March 1.

NEWMAN UNIVERSITY D-3

www.newmanu.edu

Wichita, KS 67213 **(316) 942-4291**

Fax: (316) 942-4483	**Email:** admissions@newmanu.edu
Full-time: 394 men, 727 women	**Faculty:** 74
Part-time: 668 men, 1006 women	**Ph.D.s:** 61%
Graduate: 219 men, 722 women	**Student/Faculty:** 17 to 1
Year: semesters, summer session	**Tuition:** $29,360
Room & Board: $8022	**Freshman Class:** 2378 applied, 1050 accepted, 165 enrolled
SAT CR/M/W: 509/548/487 **ACT:** 24	**CEEB CODE:** 6615
Application Deadline: open	**COMPETITIVE**

Newman University, founded in 1933, is a private, liberal arts institution affiliated with the Roman Catholic Church. Tuition in the above capsule is based on 16 credit hours. There are 3 undergraduate schools and 3 graduate schools. In addition to regional accreditation, NU has baccalaureate program accreditation with CSWE, CAEP, ACOTE, CoARC, ARRT, KS Dept of Ed, CCNE, and COA. The 61-acre campus is in an urban area in Wichita west of downtown. Including any residence halls, there are 12 buildings.

STUDENT LIFE: 91% of undergraduates are from Kansas. Others are from 28 states, 30 foreign countries, and Canada. 54% are from public schools. 74% are White; 10% Hispanic; 5% Asian American; 4% African American; 2% American Indian/Alaska Native; 2% Foreign; 2% two or more races; 1% race unknown. 59% are Catholic. **Female To Male Ratio:** 1.9:1. The average age of freshmen is 18; all undergraduates, 21. 24% do not continue beyond their first year; 52% remain to graduate. **Housing:** 406 students can be accommodated in college housing, which includes married student dorms, on-campus apartments, and special-interest houses. On-campus housing is guaranteed for the freshman year only, and is available on a first-come, first-served basis. 75% of students commute. Alcohol is not permitted. All students may keep cars.

FACULTY/CLASSROOMS: 33% of faculty are male; 67% are female. 94% teach undergraduates, 25% do research, and 25% do both. No introductory courses are taught by graduate students. The average class size in an introductory lecture is 22; in a laboratory is 16; and in a regular course is 19.

PROGRAMS OF STUDY: NU confers B.A., B.B.A., B.S. and B.S.N. degrees. Associate and master's degrees are also awarded. Bachelor's degrees are awarded in BIOLOGICAL SCIENCE (biochemistry and biology/biological science), BUSINESS (accounting, business administration and management, and management information systems), COMMUNICATIONS AND THE ARTS (art, communications, English, and sports media), COMPUTER AND PHYSICAL SCIENCE (chemistry, information sciences and systems, and mathematics), EDUCATION (early childhood education, elementary education, and secondary education), HEALTH PROFESSIONS (health science, nursing, and ultrasound technology), SOCIAL SCIENCE (counseling/psychology, criminal justice, forensic studies, history, interdisciplinary studies, liberal arts/general studies, pastoral studies, philosophy, psychology, sociology, and theological studies). Nursing, allied health and pre-med, and biology are the strongest academically. Nursing, biology, and education have the largest enrollments.

ACTIVITIES: There are no fraternities or sororities. There are 26 groups on campus, including art, cheerleading, choir, chorale, chorus, communications, computers, dance, drama, environmental, ethnic, honors, international, literary magazine, musical theater, newspaper, pep band, photography, political, professional, religious, social, social service, and student government. Popular campus events include Family Weekend, Newman Week, Homecoming, Weeks of Welcome/Welcome Back Bash, and Gerber Institute Activities. **Sports:** There are 8 intercollegiate sports for men and 9 for women, and 10 intramural sports for men and 9 for women. Facilities include baseball and softball fields, soccer fields, a gym with 1 main basketball court, a weight room, aerobics room, and wrestling room. **Graduates:** From July 1, 2016 to June 30, 2017, 266 bachelor's degrees were awarded. The most popular majors were nursing (18%), education (14%), and biology (11%). In an average class, 36% graduate in 4 years or less and 52% graduate in 6 years or less. Of the 2016 graduating class, 17% were enrolled in graduate school within 6 months of graduation, and 76% were employed.

SERVICES: Counseling and information services are available, as is tutoring in most subjects. There is a reader service for the blind, and remedial math and writing. **Library/Resources:** The library contains 90,129 volumes, 143,723 microform items, and 2,300 audio/video tapes/CDs/DVDs, and subscribes to 7,015 periodicals including electronic. Computerized library services include interlibrary loans, database searching, Internet access, and Wi-Fi capability. Special learning facilities include an art gallery, a allied health and nursing labs, and ITV studio facilities. **Physically Challenged Students:** All of the campus is accessible. Facilities include wheelchair ramps, elevators, special parking, specially equipped restrooms, special class scheduling, and lowered drinking fountains. **Special:** Newman University offers co-op placements in most majors, internships, dual majors, and study abroad in England, Europe, and Latin America. Majors in counseling, business studies, education, RN to BSN, and interdisciplinary studies can be satisfied through evening, weekend and online classes. There are 11 national honor societies and a freshman honors program. **Visiting:** There are regularly scheduled orientations for prospective students, include meetings with faculty, athletic coaches, co-curricular sponsors, financial aid counselors, admissions counselors, and a campus tour. There are guides for informal visits, visitors may sit in on classes, and stay overnight. To schedule a visit, contact the Admissions Office. **Campus Safety and Security:** Measures include 24-hour foot and vehicle patrol, emergency notification system, self-defense education, and security escort services. There are emergency telephones, lighted pathways/sidewalks, and controlled access to dorms/residences.

REQUIREMENTS: Criteria for admissions: cumulative grade point average of at least 2.0 on a 4.0 scale or an average GED score of 450 with no individual score below 410, ACT composite score of 18 or a combined verbal, math and writing SAT score of 1290. The recommended high school curriculum is 4 units English, 3 units each of math, science and social science. AP and CLEP credits are accepted. Important factors in the admissions decision are leadership record, advanced placement or honors courses, evidence of special talent, personality/intangible qualities, recommendations by alumni, recommendations by school officials, parents or siblings attended your school, extracurricular activities record, and geographical diversity. Degree requirements include completion of 124 credit hours, 40 of which must be upper division and 30 resident. The number of credits required in the major varies. A minimum GPA of 2.0 is required for graduation, and students must fulfill the university's Newman Studies Program requirements which include skills, general education and core courses. **Procedure:** Freshmen are admitted fall, spring, and summer. Entrance exams should be taken during the spring of the junior year or fall of the senior year. There are deferred admissions and rolling admissions plans. Application deadlines are open. The fall 2017 application fee was $20. Notification is sent on a rolling basis. Applications are accepted on-line. **Transfer Students:** 309 transfer students enrolled in 2016-2017. A minimum GPA of 2.0 is required. 30 of 124 credits required for the bachelor's degree must be completed at NU. **International Students:** There are 73 international students enrolled. They must take the TOEFL with a minimum score of 530 on the paper-based TOEFL (PBT) or 74 on the Internet-based version (iBT).

ADMISSIONS: 45% of the current freshmen were in the top fifth of their class; 68% were in the top two fifths. 10 freshmen graduated first in their class. **Admissions Contact:** Kristen English, Director of Undergraduate Admissions. Email: *admissions@newmanu.edu* Web: *www.newmanu.edu*

FINANCIAL AID: In 2017-2018, 99% of all full-time freshmen received some form of financial aid. 68% of all full-time freshmen received need-based aid. The average freshman award was $11,344. Need-based scholarships or need-based grants averaged $2,777 ($6,448 maximum); need-based self-help aid (loans and jobs) averaged $1,574 ($2,750 maximum); non-need-based athletic scholarships averaged $3,870 ($10,714 maximum); and other non-need-based awards and non-need-based scholarships averaged $9,641 ($17,863 maximum). 10% of undergraduate students work part-time. The average financial indebtedness of the 2017 graduate was $25,936. The FAFSA code is 001939. The priority date for freshman financial aid applications for fall entry is March 1.

OTTAWA UNIVERSITY — E-2

www.ottawa.edu

Ottawa, KS 66067	(785) 242-5200
Fax: (785) 229-1008	**Email:** admiss@ottawa.edu
Full-time: 350 men, 200 women	**Faculty:** IIB, --$
Part-time: 15 men, 20 women	**Ph.D.s:** n/av
Graduate: n/av	**Student/Faculty:** n/av
Year: semesters, summer session	**Tuition:** $30,210
Room & Board: $9770	**Freshman Class:** n/av
ACT: required	**CEEB CODE:** 6547
Application Deadline: open	**VERY COMPETITIVE**

Ottawa University, founded in 1865 and affiliated with the American Baptist Churches, is a private institution offering programs through the divisions of arts and humanities, natural sciences, and social and behavioral sciences. The figures given in the above capsule and in this profile are approximate. There is 1 undergraduate school. The 64-acre campus is in a small town 45 miles southwest of Kansas City. Including any residence halls, there are 15 buildings.

STUDENT LIFE: 55% of undergraduates are from Kansas. Others are from 18 states, 5 foreign countries, and Canada. 99% are from public schools. 77% are White; 7% Foreign; 4% Hispanic; 2% American Indian/Alaska Native; 11% African American; 1% Asian American. 64% are Protestant; 20% claim no religious affiliation; 13% Catholic. **Male To Female Ratio:** 1.7:1. The average age of freshmen is 19; all undergraduates, 22. 25% do not continue beyond their first year; 30% remain to graduate. **Housing:** 428 students can be accommodated in college housing, which includes married student dorms and on-campus apartments. On-campus housing is guaranteed for all 4 years. 58% of students live on campus. Alcohol is not permitted. All students may keep cars.

FACULTY/CLASSROOMS: 60% of faculty are male; 40% are female. All teach undergraduates. No introductory courses are taught by graduate students. The average class size in a laboratory is 12.

PROGRAMS OF STUDY: Ottawa confers B.A. degrees. Bachelor's degrees are awarded in BIOLOGICAL SCIENCE (biology/biological science), BUSINESS (accounting, business administration and management, and management information systems), COMMUNICATIONS AND THE ARTS (art, communications, dramatic arts, English, and music), COMPUTER AND PHYSICAL SCIENCE (chemistry, information sciences and systems, and mathematics), EDUCATION (elementary education and physical education), SOCIAL SCIENCE (history, human services, political science/government, psychology, religion, and sociology). English, business, and math are the strongest academically. Business, teacher education, and human services have the largest enrollments.

ACTIVITIES: There are no fraternities or sororities. There are 35 groups on campus, including cheerleading, choir, chorale, chorus, computers, dance, debate, drama, ethnic, forensics, honors, international, jazz band, musical theater, newspaper, orchestra, pep band, photography, professional, radio and TV, religious, social, social service, student government, and yearbook. Popular campus events include Family Day, Charter Day, and Christmas Feast. **Sports:** There are 7 intercollegiate sports for men and 7 for women, and 12 intramural sports for men and 12 for women. Facilities include a field, a sports complex, an athletic center, and a gym with a wellness center. Men's sports include baseball, basketball, cross country, football, golf, lacrosse, soccer, tennis, track & field, volleyball, and wrestling. Women's sports include basketball, cross-country, golf, lacrosse, soccer, softball, tennis, track & field, volleyball, and wrestling.

SERVICES: Counseling and information services are available, as is tutoring in most subjects. There is remedial math, reading, and writing. **Library/Resources:** The library contains 90,000 volumes, and subscribes to 400 periodicals including electronic. Computerized library services include interlibrary loans and database searching. Special learning facilities include an art gallery and radio station. **Physically Challenged Students:** 50% of the campus is accessible. Facilities include wheelchair ramps, elevators, special parking, specially equipped restrooms, and special class scheduling. **Special:** Internships are available, especially in business, human services, and teacher education. Student-designed majors are an option. 3/2 engineering degrees with Kansas state and the University of Kansas, 3 +1 degree in medical technology, and preprofessional programs in premedicine, predentistry, prelaw, and preministry are available. Work-study programs are also offered. There are 2 national honor societies. **Visiting:** There are regularly scheduled orientations for prospective students, including Discovery Day in the early spring, which gives prospective students a chance to meet faculty, students, and staff and to learn more about Ottawa University, the admissions process, and financial aid. There are guides for informal visits, visitors may sit in on classes, and stay overnight. To schedule a visit, contact the Admissions Office. **Campus Safety and Security:** Measures include self-defense education and security escort services. There are lighted pathways/sidewalks, controlled access to dorms/residences, nighttime security guard.

REQUIREMENTS: The ACT is required. The GED is accepted. There are no specific high school courses required, but a sound college preparatory curriculum is highly recommended. A GPA of 2.5 is required. AP and CLEP credits are accepted. Important factors in the admissions decision are parents or siblings attended your school, recommendations by alumni, and recommendations by school officials. To graduate, students must complete 9 courses in 8 academic areas with a minimum GPA of 2.0. The university requires students to complete 124 semester hours, with 24 to 40 in the major. Three interdisciplinary general education seminars must be completed. In addition, students must attend 10 University Program events each semester for 6 semesters. **Procedure:** Freshmen are admitted to all sessions. Entrance exams should be taken as early as possible. There is a rolling admissions plan. Application deadlines are open. The fall 2017 application fee was $15. **Transfer Students:** Transfer applicants must submit transcripts from all colleges attended and must have a 2.0 GPA and 12 hours of college credit, or else they must meet freshman requirements. 30 of 124 credits required for the bachelor's degree must be completed at Ottawa. **International Students:** They must take the TOEFL or MELAB.

Admissions Contact: Tim Albers, Director of Admissions. Email: *admiss@ottawa.edu* Web: *www.ottawa.edu*

FINANCIAL AID: The college's own financial statement is required. The FAFSA code is 001937. Check with the school for current application deadlines.

PITTSBURG STATE UNIVERSITY F-3
www.pittstate.edu

Pittsburg, KS 66762	**(620) 235-4251** **(800) 854-PITT**
Fax: (620) 235-6003	**Email: psuadmit@pittstate.edu**
Full-time: 2776 men, 2471 women	**Faculty:** 323
Part-time: 147 men, 142 women	**Ph.D.s:** 77%
Graduate: 438 men, 759 women	**Student/Faculty:** 17 to 1
Year: semesters, summer session	**Tuition:** $6910 ($17,662)
Room & Board: $7572	**Freshman Class:** 503 applied, 2186 accepted, 973 enrolled
ACT: 22	**CEEB CODE:** 6336
Application Deadline: open	**COMPETITIVE**

Pittsburg State University, founded in 1903, is a state-supported institution offering programs in arts and sciences, business, education, and technology. There are 4 undergraduate schools and 1 graduate school. In addition to regional accreditation, Pitt State has baccalaureate program accreditation with AACSB, ABET, CSWE, NASM, CAEP, NRPA, and CCNE. The 630-acre campus is in a small town 120 miles south of Kansas City. Including any residence halls, there are 84 buildings.

STUDENT LIFE: 70% of undergraduates are from Kansas. Others are from 38 states, 47 foreign countries, and Canada. 79% are White; 6% two or more races; 5% Hispanic; 4% African American; 3% Foreign; 1% American Indian/Alaska Native. **Female To Male Ratio:** 1.0:1. The average age of freshmen is 19; all undergraduates, 22. 27% do not continue beyond their first year; 50% remain to graduate. **Housing:** 1342 students can be accommodated in college housing, which includes married student dorms, wellness, theme, and academic excellence floors. On-campus housing is available on a first-come and first-served basis. 81% of students commute. Alcohol is not permitted. All students may keep cars.

FACULTY/CLASSROOMS: 54% of faculty are male; 46% are female. 94% teach undergraduates. Graduate students teach 10% of introductory courses. The average class size in an introductory lecture is 33; in a laboratory is 21; and in a regular course is 22.

PROGRAMS OF STUDY: Pitt State confers B.B.A., B.F.A., B.A.S., B.S.T., B.A., B.M.T., B.S., B.S.E., B.S.E.T., B.M., B.M.E., B.S.N., B.I.S. and B.G.S. degrees. Associate, master's, and doctoral degrees are also awarded. Bachelor's degrees are awarded in AGRICULTURE (wood science), BIOLOGICAL SCIENCE (biochemistry and biology/biological science), BUSINESS (accounting, banking and finance, business administration and management, business economics, international business management, and recreation and leisure services), COMMUNICATIONS AND THE ARTS (art, communications, English, and music), COMPUTER AND PHYSICAL SCIENCE (chemistry, information sciences and systems, mathematics, physics, and polymer science), EDUCATION (early childhood education, education, elementary education, English education, home economics education, mathematics education, music education, physical education, psychology education, secondary education, social studies education, technical education, and vocational education), ENGINEERING AND ENVIRONMENTAL DESIGN (automotive technology, construction management, construction technology, electrical/electronics engineering technology, graphic arts technology, graphic and printing production, manufacturing technology, mechanical engineering technology, plastics technology, and technological management), HEALTH PROFESSIONS (medical technology, nursing, premedicine, preoptometry, prepharmacy, prephysical therapy, preveterinary science, and recreation therapy), SOCIAL SCIENCE (counseling/psychology, criminal justice, family/consumer studies, geography, history, international studies, liberal arts/general studies, political science/government, psychology, safety management, social work, and sociology). Education, nursing, and business have the largest enrollments.

ACTIVITIES: 7% of men belong to 7 national fraternities; 8% of women belong to 3 national sororities. There are 120 groups on campus, including academic and special interest, recreational, art, band, cheerleading, choir, chorale, chorus, computers, dance, debate, drama, drill team, environmental, ethnic, film, forensics, honors, housing, international, jazz band, LGBT, literary magazine, marching band, newspaper, opera, orchestra, pep band, photography, political, professional, radio and TV, religious, social, social service, student government, symphony, and yearbook. Popular campus events include Greek Week, Multicultural Month, Homecoming, and Apple Day. **Sports:** There are 5 intercollegiate sports for men and 5 for women, and 20 intramural sports for men and 20 for women. Facilities include a football stadium, indoor and outdoor tracks, basketball arena and outdoor courts, softball diamonds, baseball field, weight room, Olympic-size pool, volleyball, racquetball, and badminton courts, tennis courts, sand volleyball courts, a recreation center, gyms, cardio and strength fitness center with a 1/10-mile track, and dance studio. **Graduates:** From July 1, 2016 to June 30, 2017, 1179 bachelor's degrees were awarded. The most popular majors were business/marketing (19%), engineering technology (14%), and education (13%). In an average class, 4% graduate in 3 years or less, 26% graduate in 4 years or less, 48% graduate in 5 years or less, and 51% graduate in 6 years or less. Of the 2016 graduating class, 76% were employed within 6 months of graduation.

SERVICES: Counseling and information services are available, as is tutoring in most subjects, such as accounting, biology, chemistry, elementary education, English, modern language/Spanish, math, music, computers, physics, psychology, reading/study, art, sociology, and writing. There is a reader service for the blind. There are also counseling services, a center for student accommodations, and a writing center. **Library/Resources:** The library contains 698,731 volumes, 90,500 microform items, and 10,225 audio/video tapes/CDs/DVDs, and subscribes to 35,485 periodicals including electronic. Computerized library services include interlibrary loans, database searching, Internet access, and Wi-Fi capability. Special learning facilities include an art gallery, planetarium, radio station, TV station, a dedicated channel on local cable TV, a nature reach, an herbarium, an observatory, a field biology reserve, a technology center, a mammal collection, a greenhouse, a polymer research lab, a broadcasting lab, and a cadaver lab. **Physically Challenged Students:** 70% of the campus is accessible. Facilities include wheelchair ramps, elevators, special parking, specially equipped restrooms, special class scheduling, lowered drinking fountains, and lowered telephones. **Special:** Co-op and work-study programs by arrangement, internships, general studies degree, B.A.-B.S. degrees, dual majors, credit by exam, student-designed majors, and pass/fail options are available. Pitt State has student exchange programs with 20 countries. There are 4 national honor societies, a freshman honors program, and 22 departmental honors programs. **Visiting:** There are regularly scheduled orientations for prospective students, meet with current students, other offices on campus, tours. There are guides for informal visits and visitors may sit in on classes. To schedule a visit, contact the Admission Office. **Campus Safety and Security:** Measures include 24-hour foot and vehicle patrol, emergency notification system, and security escort services. There are shuttle buses, emergency telephones, lighted pathways/sidewalks, controlled access to dorms/residences, crime prevention programs, an engraving program for valuables, a crisis management plan and procedures, e-mail, text, and phone alerts.

REQUIREMENTS: The ACT is required. Applicants must meet 1 of these 4 criteria: an ACT score of 21 or above, class rank in the top third, a 2.0 GPA in the Kansas core curriculum (2.5 GPA for out-of-state students), or have 24 or more transferable college credit hours with at least a 2.0 GPA. Candidates may also be accepted through an exceptions window. The GED is accepted. Pitt State requires applicants to be in the upper 33% of their class. AP and CLEP credits are accepted. To graduate, students must complete at least 124 semester hours, including 36 to 60 hours in the major, with a minimum GPA of 2.0. General education requirements total 46 to 57 hours (up to 54 for education majors) and include courses in English, speech, math, sciences, producing and consuming, cultural studies, fine arts, human heritage (history, literature, philosophy), political and social studies and health/well-being. **Procedure:** Freshmen are admitted fall, spring, and summer. Entrance exams should be taken before the first semester of the freshman year of college.

There is a rolling admissions plan. Application deadlines are open. The fall 2017 application fee was $30. Applications are accepted on-line. **Transfer Students:** 497 transfer students enrolled in 2016-2017. Applicants must have 24 credit hours and a college GPA of 2.0 or else meet freshman admissions requirements. 30 of 124 credits required for the bachelor's degree must be completed at Pitt State. **International Students:** There are 289 international students enrolled. They must take the TOEFL with a minimum score of 520 on the paper-based TOEFL (PBT) or 68 on the Internet-based version (iBT). Student must take the IELTS.

ADMISSIONS: 45% of the 2017-2018 applicants were accepted. The ACT scores were 12% between 12 and 17, 57% between 18 and 23, 28% between 24 and 29, and 3% above 30. 40% of the current freshmen were in the top fifth of their class; 63% were in the top two fifths. 38 freshmen graduated first in their class. **Admissions Contact:** Melinda Roelfs, Director of Admission. Email: *psuadmit@pittstate.edu* Web: *www.pittstate.edu*

FINANCIAL AID: In 2017-2018, 91% of all full-time freshmen received some form of financial aid. 56% of all full-time freshmen received need-based aid. The average freshman award was $6,091. Need-based scholarships or need-based grants averaged $4,710; need-based self-help aid (loans and jobs) averaged $3,312; other non-need-based awards and non-need-based scholarships averaged $3,312; and $3,019 from other forms of aid. The average financial indebtedness of the 2017 graduate was $24,384. The FAFSA code is 001926. The priority date for freshman financial aid applications for fall entry is March 1.

SOUTHWESTERN COLLEGE *(The complete profile is made available exclusively on our website, www.barronspac.com)*

STERLING COLLEGE *(The complete profile is made available exclusively on our website, www.barronspac.com)*

TABOR COLLEGE — D-2

www.tabor.edu

Hillsboro, KS 67063	(620) 947-3121
Fax: (620) 947-6276	**Email:** admissions@tabor.edu
Full-time: 307 men, 216 women	**Faculty:** 36
Part-time: 52 men, 95 women	**Ph.D.s:** 21%
Graduate: 28 men, 29 women	**Student/Faculty:** 12 to 1
Year: 4-1-4	**Tuition:** $26,590
Room & Board: $9280	**Freshman Class:** 836 applied, 442 accepted, 203 enrolled
ACT: 21	**CEEB CODE:** 6815
Application Deadline: August 1	**COMPETITIVE**

Tabor College, established in 1908, is a private liberal arts facility affiliated with the Mennonite Brethren Church. The mission of Tabor College is to prepare people for a life of learning, work and service for Christ and His Kingdom. The vision of Tabor College is to be the college of choice for students who seek a life-transforming, academically excellent, globally relevant, and decidedly Christian education. There is 1 undergraduate school and 1 graduate school. In addition to regional accreditation, TC has baccalaureate program accreditation with CSWE, NASM, CAEP, CCNE, and and CAATE. The 86-acre campus is in a small town is located in Hillsboro, Kansas, about 50 miles north of Wichita. Including any residence halls, there are 43 buildings.

STUDENT LIFE: 55% of undergraduates are from out of state, mostly the West. Students are from 32 states, 14 foreign countries, and Canada. 9% are African American; 67% White; 4% Foreign; 4% two or more races; 3% race unknown; 12% Hispanic; 1% American Indian/Alaska Native. 64% are Protestant; 24% claim no religious affiliation. **Male To Female Ratio:** 1.1:1. The average age of freshmen is 18; all undergraduates, 23. 38% do not continue beyond their first year; 48% remain to graduate. **Housing:** 590 students can be accommodated in college housing, which includes dorms and off-campus apartments, and theme housing. On-campus housing is guaranteed for all 4 years. 86% of students live on campus. Alcohol is not permitted. All students may keep cars.

FACULTY/CLASSROOMS: 47% of faculty are male; 53% are female. 87% teach undergraduates. No introductory courses are taught by graduate students. The average class size in an introductory lecture is 22; in a laboratory is 14; and in a regular course is 13.

PROGRAMS OF STUDY: TC confers B.A., B.S. and B.S.N degrees. Associate and master's degrees are also awarded. Bachelor's degrees are awarded in BIOLOGICAL SCIENCE (biochemistry and biology/biological science), BUSINESS (accounting and business administration and management), COMMUNICATIONS AND THE ARTS (applied art, communications, English, graphic design, music, studio art, and theatre arts), COMPUTER AND PHYSICAL SCIENCE (chemistry and mathematics), EDUCATION (athletic training, educational studies, elementary education, general studies, health education, music education, physical education, physical education/ exercise science, physical ed teacher education, and secondary education), HEALTH PROFESSIONS (nursing), SOCIAL SCIENCE (behavioral science, biblical studies, Christian studies, criminal justice, history, international studies, liberal arts/general studies, ministries, psychology, religion, and social work). Science, business and education are the strongest academically. Elementary education, psychology, and business have the largest enrollments.

ACTIVITIES: There are no fraternities or sororities. There are 18 groups on campus, including art, band, Campus Ministries, cheerleading, choir, chorale, chorus, computers, drama, drill team, ethnic, honors, international, jazz band, math and business clubs, musical theater, newspaper, pep band, photography, religious, social, social service, student government, and yearbook. Popular campus events include Service Emphasis Week, Mission Emphasis Week, Taborstock, Sadie Hawkins Event, and Winter Banquet. **Sports:** There are 9 intercollegiate sports for men and 9 for women, and 8 intramural sports for men and 8 for women. Facilities include a Campus Recreation Center and an athletic stadium, tennis courts, racquetball courts, football and baseball fields, practice fields, a soccer field, a curbed metric all-weather track, a gym with playing floors, a practice/intramural gym, an indoor soccer court, aerobic exercise, athletic training, and weight rooms. **Graduates:** The most popular majors were business (13%), psychology (9%), and elementary education (8%). In an average class, 80% graduate in 4 years or less, 11% graduate in 5 years or less, and 9% graduate in 6 years or less.

SERVICES: Counseling and information services are available, as is tutoring in most subjects. Tutoring in writing is available for all students through the campus Writing Center. The Student Support Services serves students who need additional academic support. Life-skills courses and individualized help sessions are also available. **Library/Resources:** The library contains 61,171 volumes, 435 microform items, and 1,640 audio/video tapes/CDs/DVDs, and subscribes to 21 periodicals including electronic. Computerized library services include interlibrary loans, database searching, Internet access, and Wi-Fi capability. **Physically Challenged Students:** 75% of the campus is accessible. Facilities include wheelchair ramps, elevators, special parking, and specially equipped restrooms. **Special:** Cross-registration is offered within the Associated Colleges of Central Kansas. Dual majors, student-designed majors, internships, and semester-long study-abroad opportunities are available. There is a freshman honors program and 1 departmental honors program. **Visiting:** There are regularly scheduled orientations for prospective students, Visits to the Tabor College campus include a campus tour, admissions interview, and faculty, class, and financial aid visits. If requested, an audition or tryout will be scheduled. There are guides for informal visits, visitors may sit in on classes, and stay overnight. To schedule a visit, contact Brenda Hamm at brendah@tabor.edu. **Campus Safety and Security:** Measures include emergency notification system. There are lighted pathways/sidewalksActive-Shooter Training is provided to all students and staff.

REQUIREMENTS: Applicants with a minimum ACT composite score of 18 (SAT score of 860 or 940, based on Evidence-Based Reading/Writing and Mathematics Composite scores) will be considered for admission. AP and CLEP credits are accepted. TC has Core Curriculum requirements which include Tabor Distinctives, courses which must be taken at Tabor College. Students must complete 124 degree-applicable credit hours to graduate, of which the last 33 hours must be completed through TC. Credit-hours per major must be met as well as a minimum GPA of 2.0 in all required courses; individual majors may require a higher GPA in content-specific coursework. **Procedure:** Freshmen are admitted to all sessions. Entrance exams should be taken Early in senior year of high school. There is a rolling admissions plan. Applications should be filed by August 1 for fall entry. The fall 2017 application fee was $50. Applications are accepted on-line. **Transfer Students:** 119 transfer students enrolled in 2016-2017. A minimum 2.0 GPA is required and an interview is recommended. 33 of 124 credits required for the bachelor's degree must be completed at TC. **International Students:** There are 29 international students enrolled. They must take the TOEFL with a minimum score of 525 on the paper-based TOEFL (PBT) or 70 on the Internet-based version (iBT). They must also take the SAT or ACT.

Admissions Contact: Kelly Dugger, Interim Director of Admissions. Email: *admissions@tabor.edu* Web: *www.tabor.edu*

FINANCIAL AID: The FAFSA code is 001946. Check with the school for current application deadlines.

UNIVERSITY OF KANSAS — E-2

www.ku.edu

Lawrence, KS 66045	**(785) 864-3911**
Fax: (785) 864-5017	**Email: adm@ku.edu**
Full-time: 8378 men, 8773 women	**Faculty:** 1431
Part-time: 1053 men, 1134 women	**Ph.D.s:** 90%
Graduate: 3628 men, 4659 women	**Student/Faculty:** 12 to 1
Year: semesters, summer session	**Tuition:** $10,824 ($26,592)
Room & Board: $10,060	**Freshman Class:** 14538 applied, 13576 accepted, 4153 enrolled
SAT: required **ACT:** 26	**CEEB CODE:** 6871
Application Deadline: n/av	**VERY COMPETITIVE**

University of Kansas, founded in 1865, is a public, comprehensive research institution. Its undergraduate and graduate programs emphasize the liberal arts, architecture, business, engineering, fine arts, health professions, journalism, law, medicine, music, nursing, pharmacy, social welfare, and teacher preparation. UK is a member of the highly prestigious Association of American Universities and has a national cancer institute designation. There are 11 undergraduate schools and 3 graduate schools. In addition to regional accreditation, UK has baccalaureate program accreditation with AACSB, ABET, ACEJMC, ACPE, CSWE, NAAB, NASAD, NASM, CAAHEP, CAHIIM, CoARC, CCNE, CAEP, NAACLS, AMTA, caATe, and CEA. The 1000-acre campus is in a suburban area 30 miles west of Kansas City. Including any residence halls, there are 200 buildings.

STUDENT LIFE: 64% of undergraduates are from Kansas. Others are from 50 states, 76 foreign countries, and Canada. 71% are White; 8% Hispanic; 6% Foreign; 5% Asian American; 5% two or more races; 4% African American; 1% race unknown. **Female To Male Ratio:** 1.1:1. The average age of freshmen is 18; all undergraduates, 21. 17% do not continue beyond their first year; 63% remain to graduate. **Housing:** 5160 students can be accommodated in college housing, which includes single sex dorms, coed dorms, and on-campus apartments. In addition, there are honors houses, special-interest floors, and a residence hall with fine arts emphasis. On-campus housing is available on a first-come and first-served basis. 74% of students commute. Alcohol is not permitted. All students may keep cars.

FACULTY/CLASSROOMS: 58% of faculty are male; 42% are female. 98% teach undergraduates, and 98% do research. Graduate students teach 16% of introductory courses. The average class size in a laboratory is 15 and in a regular course is 25.

PROGRAMS OF STUDY: UK confers B.A., B.S., B.A.E., B.A.S., B.B.A., B.F.A., B.G.S., B.M., B.M.E., B.S.B., B.S.E., B.S.J., B.S.N., B.S.P.S., and B.S.W. degrees. Master's and doctoral degrees are also awarded. Bachelor's degrees are awarded in AGRICULTURE (environmental studies), BIOLOGICAL SCIENCE (biochemistry, biology/biological science, biotechnology, microbiology, and molecular biology), BUSINESS (accounting, business administration and management, business administration, business information systems, business intelligence and analytics, entrepreneurial studies, finance, management information systems, marketing/retailing/merchandising, sports management, and supply chain management), COMMUNICATIONS AND THE ARTS (art history, art, ceramic art and design, choral music, classical languages, communication studies, dance, design, dramatic arts, East Asian languages and literature, English, fiber/textiles/weaving, film, television and digital media, fine arts, French, German, Germanic languages and literature, graphic design, illustration, industrial design, information technology, journalism, linguistics, film and media studies, metal/jewelry, music, music composition, music history and appreciation, music performance, music theory and composition, musicology/ethnomusicology, painting, percussion, piano/organ, printmaking, sculpture, Slavic languages, Spanish, speech/debate/rhetoric, strings, theatre arts, theater design, voice, and winds), COMPUTER AND PHYSICAL SCIENCE (astronomy, atmospheric sciences and meteorology, chemistry, computer science, geology, information sciences and systems, mathematics, and physics), EDUCATION (art education, athletic training, early childhood education, elementary education, global studies, health education, health information management, middle school education, music education, physical ed teacher education, and secondary education), ENGINEERING AND ENVIRONMENTAL DESIGN (aerospace engineering, architectural engineering, architecture, chemical engineering, civil engineering, computer engineering, electrical and computer engineering, electrical/electronics engineering, engineering physics, interior design, mechanical engineering, and petroleum/natural gas engineering), HEALTH PROFESSIONS (communicative disorders, community health work, cytotechnology, exercise science, human biology, medical laboratory technology, music therapy, nursing, occupational therapy, pharmacy, respiratory therapy, and sports medicine), SOCIAL SCIENCE (African studies, African American studies, American studies, anthropology, archeology, architectural studies, behavioral science, classical/ancient civilization, economics, European studies, gender studies, geography, history, humanities, international studies, Judaic studies, Latin American studies, legal studies, liberal arts/general studies, philosophy, political science/government, psychology, public administration, religion, Russian and Slavic studies, social work, sociology, women & gender studies, and women's studies). Pharmacy, and engineering are the strongest academically. Business/accounting, engineering, and biological sciences have the largest enrollments.

ACTIVITIES: 18% of men belong to 30 national fraternities; 25% of women belong to 17 national sororities. There are 540 groups on campus, including art, band, cheerleading, chess, choir, chorale, chorus, communications, computers, dance, debate, drama, environmental, ethnic, film, honors, international, jazz band, LGBT, literary magazine, marching band, musical theater, newspaper, opera, orchestra, pep band, photography, political, professional, radio and TV, religious, social, social service, student government, and symphony. Popular campus events include Late Night in the Phog (basketball season kickoff), Homecoming, Rock Chalk Revue, Hawk Week, and basketball and football games. **Sports:** There are 7 intercollegiate sports for men and 11 for women, and 30 intramural sports for men and 30 for women. Facilities include a basketball arena, football stadium, a sports pavilion with an indoor football field and indoor track, a health and phys ed center with indoor pools, handball and racquetball courts, gyms, tennis and sand volleyball courts, lacrosse, cricket, and rugby fields, a tennis center, a student recreation center containing an indoor climbing wall, a suspended jogging track, racquetball courts, a free weight/cardiovascular area, aerobic and martial arts studios, multipurpose courts, and golf simulator, a rowing boathouse, an athletic center with volleyball and basketball courts, a football complex, a softball stadium, a baseball park with clubhouse, a soccer stadium, a track and field stadium, a strength center, a golf training center, cross country training farm, and an outdoor education center/challenge course. **Graduates:** From July 1, 2016 to June 30, 2017, 4046 bachelor's degrees were awarded. The most popular majors were business (18%), engineering (9%), and journalism (7%). In an average class, 2% graduate in 3 years or less, 48% graduate in 4 years or less, 62% graduate in 5 years or less, and 63% graduate in 6 years or less. Of the 2016 graduating class, 29% were enrolled in graduate school within 6 months of graduation, and 67% were employed.

SERVICES: Counseling and information services are available, as is tutoring in most subjects, including how-to sessions on study and organizational skills and a workshop. There is a reader service for the blind, and remedial math, and writing. **Library/Resources:** The library contains 4.7 million volumes. Computerized library services include interlibrary loans, database searching, Internet access, and Wi-Fi capability. Special learning facilities include a natural history museum, radio station, TV station, art museum, classics museum, entomology museum, invertebrate paleontology collection, film studio, space technology center, performing arts center, organ recital hall, institute of politics, and a center for the humanities. **Physically Challenged Students:** 95% of the campus is accessible. Facilities include wheelchair ramps, elevators, special parking, specially equipped restrooms, special class scheduling, lowered drinking fountains, and lowered telephones. **Special:** Special academic programs include Honors program, internships, study abroad has over 130 programs in over 70 countries, a Washington semester, and work-study programs with the university. A cooperative program in engineering is offered, as are B.A.-B.S. degrees in many combinations, interdisciplinary majors, and dual majors in any approved combination.

General studies degrees are available in many areas, and student-designed majors are possible. Nondegree study and pass/fail options are offered. There are 16 national honor societies, Phi Beta Kappa, and a freshman honors program. **Visiting:** There are regularly scheduled orientations for prospective students, consisting of a summer orientation program that includes a 1-day campus visit. There are guides for informal visits, visitors may sit in on classes, and stay overnight. To schedule a visit, contact the Visitor Center at (785) 864-3911. **Campus Safety and Security:** Measures include 24-hour foot and vehicle patrol, emergency notification system, and security escort services. There are shuttle buses, emergency telephones, lighted pathways/sidewalks, and controlled access to dorms/residences.

REQUIREMENTS: Admissions Curriculum includes 4 units of English, 3 of college preparatory math and meet the ACT/SAT college readiness math benchmark (22+ ACT/550+ SAT on math section) or complete 4 units of math, with one taken in the graduating year, 3 of natural science (1 must be chemistry or physics), 3 of social sciences (includes history), and 3 electives. Kansas residents must complete the Kansas Qualified Admissions Curriculum with 2.0+ GPA, have an overall 3.0 GPA and 24+ ACT (1160+ SAT), or 3.25 overall GPA and 21+ ACT (1060+ SAT). Nonresidents must meet the above criteria with a 2.5+ GPA, have an overall 3.0+ GPA and 24+ ACT (1160+ SAT), or 3.25+ overall GPA and 21+ ACT (1060+ SAT). Students who don't meet these criteria will be asked to answer two to four short answer questions on the application. Their application will be individually reviewed on these factors: cumulative high school GPA, ACT or SAT scores, GPA in the core curriculum, and strength of classes. A GPA of 2.0 is required. AP and CLEP credits are accepted. To graduate with a B.A., B.S., or B.G.S. degree, all students must complete at least 120 credit hours, including 30 to 50 credit hours in the major, and maintain a GPA of at least 2.0. These, as well as curricula and distribution requirements, vary according to the school and the major. **Procedure:** Freshmen are admitted to all sessions. Entrance exams should be taken by the end of the junior year. There is a rolling admissions plan. Application deadlines are open. The fall 2017 application fee was $40. Applications are accepted on-line. **Transfer Students:** 1082 transfer students enrolled in 2016-2017. Entrance to the College of Liberal Arts and Sciences, and transfer students must meet minimum GPA of 2.0 in-state or 2.5 out-of-state and freshman admissions requirements, if the student is transferring with less than 24 credit hours. The criteria vary widely within the other KU schools, some of which may also consider the ACT score and coursework. 30 of 120 credits required for the bachelor's degree must be completed at UK. **International Students:** There are 1190 international students enrolled. They must take the TOEFL, and the IELTS.

ADMISSIONS: 93% of the 2017-2018 applicants were accepted. The ACT scores were 1% between 12 and 17, 30% between 18 and 23, 50% between 24 and 29, and 18% above 30. **Admissions Contact:** Lisa Pinamonti Kress, Director of Admissions. Email: *adm@ku.edu* Web: *www.ku.edu*

FINANCIAL AID: In 2017-2018, 80% of all full-time freshmen received some form of financial aid. 45% of all full-time freshmen received need-based aid. The average freshman award was $16,455. Need-based scholarships or need-based grants averaged $8,743; need-based self-help aid (loans and jobs) averaged $3,664; non-need-based athletic scholarships averaged $18,619; and other non-need-based awards and non-need-based scholarships averaged $6,643. 15% of undergraduate students work part-time. The average financial indebtedness of the 2017 graduate was $28,462. The FAFSA code is 001948. The priority date for freshman financial aid applications for fall entry is November 1.

UNIVERSITY OF SAINT MARY *(The complete profile is made available exclusively on our website, www.barronspac.com)*

WASHBURN UNIVERSITY — E-2

www.washburn.edu

Topeka, KS 66621	**(785) 670-1030** **(877) 281-2637**
Fax: (785) 670-1113	**Email: admissions@washburn.edu**
Full-time: 1610 men, 2256 women	**Faculty:** 260; IIA, --$
Part-time: 723 men, 1191 women	**Ph.D.s:** 84%
Graduate: 333 men, 523 women	**Student/Faculty:** 13 to 1
Year: semesters, summer session	**Tuition:** $8300 ($18,620)
Room & Board: $7527	**Freshman Class:** 1678 applied, 1671 accepted, 908 enrolled
ACT: 22	**CEEB CODE:** 6928
Application Deadline: August 1	**COMPETITIVE**

Washburn University, founded in 1865, is publicly funded, independently governed, and state-coordinated university. WU offers more than 200 programs leading to certification, associate, bachelor, master, professional, and juris doctor degrees through the college of arts and sciences and the schools of law, business, nursing, and applied studies. There are 4 undergraduate schools and 5 graduate schools. In addition to regional accreditation, WU has baccalaureate program accreditation with AACSB, CAHEA, CSWE, NASAD, NASM, CAEP, ACS, CAAHEP, and CAATE. The 160-acre campus is in an urban area 60 miles west of Kansas City. Including any residence halls, there are 30 buildings.

STUDENT LIFE: 89% of undergraduates are from Kansas. Others are from 39 states, 28 foreign countries, and Canada. 91% are from public schools. **Female To Male Ratio:** 1.5:1. The average age of freshmen is 19; all undergraduates, 24. 28% do not continue beyond their first year; 36% remain to graduate. **Housing:** 986 students can be accommodated in college housing, which includes dorms and on-campus apartments. On-campus housing is available on a first-come and first-served basis. Alcohol is not permitted. All students may keep cars.

FACULTY/CLASSROOMS: 41% of faculty are male; 59% are female. 91% teach undergraduates. No introductory courses are taught by graduate students.

PROGRAMS OF STUDY: WU confers B.A., B.A.S., B.B.A., B.Ed., B.F.A., B.H.S., B.I.S., B.L.S., B.M., B.P.A., B.S., B.S.C.J., B.S.N. and B.S.W. degrees. Associate, master's, and doctoral degrees are also awarded. Bachelor's degrees are awarded in BIOLOGICAL SCIENCE (biochemistry, biology/biological science, and molecular biology), BUSINESS (accounting, banking and finance, business administration and management, business economics, entrepreneurial studies, finance, international business management, and marketing/retailing/merchandising), COMMUNICATIONS AND THE ARTS (art, art history and appreciation, communications, dramatic arts, English, French, German, media arts, music, music performance, Spanish, speech/debate/rhetoric, and theater design), COMPUTER AND PHYSICAL SCIENCE (chemistry, computer science, mathematics, physics, and science), EDUCATION (art education, athletic training, early childhood education, education, elementary education, music education, physical education, physical ed teacher education, and secondary education), ENGINEERING AND ENVIRONMENTAL DESIGN (technological management), HEALTH PROFESSIONS (clinical science, health care administration, kinesiology, nursing, prepharmacy, and ultrasound technology), SOCIAL SCIENCE (anthropology, corrections, criminal justice, economics, forensic studies, history, human services, interdisciplinary studies, law enforcement and corrections, liberal arts/general studies, paralegal studies, philosophy, political science/government, psychology, public administration, religion, social work, and sociology). Business administration, criminal justice, and nursing have the largest enrollments.

ACTIVITIES: There are 78 groups on campus, including art, band, campus activities board, and peer educators, cheerleading, chess, choir, chorus, computers, dance, debate, drama, drill team, drum and bugle corps, environmental, ethnic, forensics, honors, international, jazz band, LGBT, literary magazine, marching band, musical theater, newspaper, orchestra, pep band, political, professional, radio and TV, religious, social, social service, student government, symphony, and yearbook. Popular campus events include Greek Week, Student Activities Fair, and the Annual Sunflower Music Festival. **Sports:** There are 7 intercollegiate sports for men and 7 for women, and 15 intramural sports for men and 15 for women. Facilities include a recreation and wellness center with a rock-climbing wall, indoor track, gym, cardiovascular and resistance training area, and wellness suite, a field house for indoor sports, a stadium for intercollegiate football, and a health center with a 6-lane swimming pool. **Graduates:** From July 1, 2016 to June 30, 2017, 841 bachelor's degrees were awarded. The most popular majors were nursing/health professions (26%), business (18%), and education (7%). In an average class, 36% graduate in 6 years or less.

SERVICES: Counseling and information services are available, as is tutoring in most subjects. There is a reader service for the blind, and remedial math and writing. **Library/Resources:** The library contains 451,534 volumes, 88,198 microform items, and 4,612 audio/video tapes/CDs/DVDs, and subscribes to 87,358 periodicals including electronic. Computerized library services include interlibrary loans, database searching, Internet access, and Wi-Fi capability. Special learning facilities include an art gallery, planetarium, radio station, and TV station. **Physically Challenged Students:** 95% of the campus is accessible. Facilities include wheelchair ramps, elevators, special parking, specially equipped restrooms, special class scheduling, lowered drinking fountains, lowered telephones, and special housing. **Special:** Washburn offers a co-op program in computer information science, engineering, social/behavioral science, education, and health profession, internships in numerous departments and study abroad in 20 countries. Dual and student-designed majors, B.A.-B.S. degrees, an integrated studies degree, credit by examination, nondegree study, and pass/fail options are also available. A 3-2 engineering degree is possible in conjunction with the University of Kansas and Kansas State University. There are 11 national honor societies and a freshman honors program. **Visiting:** There are regularly scheduled orientations for prospective students, students will get to learn expectations of the classroom environment, meet with current students over our free lunch, register for their first semester courses, explore the MyWashburn online portal, attend meetings about activities and organizations. There are guides for informal visits, visitors may sit in on classes, and stay overnight. To schedule a visit, contact Office of Admissions. **Campus Safety and Security:** Measures include 24-hour foot and vehicle patrol, emergency notification system, self-defense education, and security escort services. There are emergency telephones, lighted pathways/sidewalks, sexual assault reduction program & bystander skill building intervention, bicycle patrol, fire safety programs for residential living facilities.

REQUIREMENTS: The ACT is required. Applicants should be graduates of an accredited secondary school or have the GED. AP and CLEP credits are accepted. **Procedure:** Freshmen are admitted to all sessions. Entrance exams should be taken during the junior year. There is a rolling admissions plan. Applications should be filed by August 1 for fall entry; January 2 for spring entry; and May 12 for summer entry. The fall 2017 application fee was $20. Applications are accepted on-line. **Transfer Students:** 611 transfer students enrolled in 2016-2017. Applicants must meet the same requirements as incoming freshmen. 30 of 120 credits required for the bachelor's degree must be completed at WU. **International Students:** There are 226 international students enrolled. They must take the TOEFL with a minimum score of 72 on the Internet-based version (iBT).

ADMISSIONS: 100% of the 2017-2018 applicants were accepted. The ACT scores were 15% between 12 and 17, 51% between 18 and 23, 32% between 24 and 29, and 2% above 30. 27% of the current freshmen were in the top fifth of their class; 54% were in the top two fifths. 29 freshmen graduated first in their class. **Admissions Contact:** Kris Klima, Director of Admissions. Email: *admissions@washburn.edu* Web: *www.washburn.edu*

FINANCIAL AID: In 2017-2018, 60% of all full-time freshmen received some form of financial aid. 36% of all full-time freshmen received need-based aid. The average freshman award was $9,616. Need-based scholarships or need-based grants averaged $4,850; need-based self-help aid (loans and jobs) averaged $4,081; non-need-based athletic scholarships averaged $5,670; and other non-need-based awards and non-need-based scholarships averaged $3,611. The average financial indebtedness of the 2017 graduate was $24,665. WU is a member of CSS. The FAFSA code is 001949. The priority date for freshman financial aid applications for fall entry is February 15.

WICHITA STATE UNIVERSITY — D-3

www.wichita.edu

Wichita, KS 67260	**(316) 978-3085** **(800) 362-2594**
Fax: (316) 978-3174	**Email: admissions@wichita.edu**
Full-time: 3999 men, 4567 women	**Faculty:** 526; I, --$
Part-time: 1169 men, 1302 women	**Ph.D.s:** n/av
Graduate: 1249 men, 1402 women	**Student/Faculty:** 19 to 1
Year: semesters, summer session	**Tuition:** $7895 ($16,634)
Room & Board: $9878	**Freshman Class:** 6306 applied, 6067 accepted, 1476 enrolled
SAT CR/M: 530/538 **ACT:** 24	**CEEB CODE:** 6884
Application Deadline: rolling	**COMPETITIVE**

Wichita State University, established in 1895, is a public institution offering programs in the liberal arts and sciences, business, engineering, education, and health professions. There are 6 undergraduate schools and 1 graduate school. In addition to regional accreditation, WSU has baccalaureate program accreditation with AACSB, ABET, ADA, APTA, CAHEA, CSWE, NASM, CAEP, and NLN. The 330-acre campus is in an urban area in the metropolitan Wichita area. Including any residence halls, there are 61 buildings.

STUDENT LIFE: 85% of undergraduates are from Kansas. Others are from 49 states, 88 foreign countries, and Canada. 7% are Asian American; 7% Foreign; 61% White; 6% African American; 4% two or more races; 2% race unknown; 11% Hispanic. **Female To Male Ratio:** 1.1:1. The average age of freshmen is 18; all undergraduates, 24. 27% do not continue beyond their first year; 43% remain to graduate. **Housing:** 1453 students can be accommodated in college housing, which includes married student dorms and on-campus apartments. In addition, there are honors houses, fraternity houses, sorority houses, theme housing, and living learning communities. On-campus housing is available on a first-come and first-served basis. 54% of students commute. All students may keep cars.

FACULTY/CLASSROOMS: No introductory courses are taught by graduate students. The average class size in an introductory lecture is 23; in a laboratory is 20; and in a regular course is 15.

PROGRAMS OF STUDY: WSU confers B.A., B.A.Ed., BAES, BASM, B.B.A., B.F.A., B.G.S., B.M., B.M.E., B.S., BSASE, B.S.CPE, B.S.E.E., B.S.H.S., B.S.I.E., B.S.M.E., BSMFE. and B.S.N. degrees. Associate, master's, and doctoral degrees are also awarded. Bachelor's degrees are awarded in BIOLOGICAL SCIENCE (biology/biological science), BUSINESS (accounting, banking and finance, business administration and management, economics – statistics, entrepreneurial studies, finance, human resources, international business management, management science, marketing/retailing/merchandising, and sports management), COMMUNICATIONS AND THE ARTS (art, art history and appreciation, audio technology, communications, creative writing, dance, English, French, graphic design, Latin, music, music business management, music composition, music history and appreciation, Spanish, studio art, theatre arts, and visual and performing arts), COMPUTER AND PHYSICAL SCIENCE (chemistry, computer science, earth science/adolescence education, geology, mathematics, and physics), EDUCATION (art education, elementary education, general studies, music education, physical education, secondary education, and special education), ENGINEERING AND ENVIRONMENTAL DESIGN (aeronautical engineering, computer engineering, electrical/electronics engineering, industrial engineering, manufacturing engineering, and mechanical engineering), HEALTH PROFESSIONS (dental education, health, health care administration, health services technology, medical laboratory technology, nursing, physician's assistant, and speech pathology/audiology), SOCIAL SCIENCE (anthropology, criminal justice, economics, ethnic studies, gerontology, history, liberal arts/general studies, philosophy, political science/government, psychology, social work, sociology, women & gender studies, and women's studies). Engineering programs, and physics & chemistry are the strongest academically. Psychology, nursing, and elementary education have the largest enrollments.

ACTIVITIES: 4% of men belong to 10 national fraternities; 3% of women belong to 8 national sororities. There are 200 groups on campus, including art, band, cheerleading, chess, choir, chorus, computers, dance, debate, drama, environmental, ethnic, film, honors, international, jazz band, LGBT, literary magazine, Model UN, musical theater, newspaper, opera, orchestra, pep band, photography, political, professional, religious, social, social service, student government, and symphony. Popular campus events include Hippodrome, International Week, and ShocktoberFest. **Sports:** There are 14 intercollegiate sports for men and 12 for women, and 30 intramural sports for men and 30 for women. Facilities include an arena, stadiums, an 18-hole golf course, a baseball field, a tennis complex, and a recreation and sports center. **Graduates:** From July 1, 2016 to June 30, 2017, 2145 bachelor's degrees were awarded. The most popular majors were buisness/marketing (19%), health professions and related programs (15%), and engineering (13%).

SERVICES: Counseling and information services are available, as is tutoring in most subjects. There is a reader service for the blind, and remedial math, reading, and writing. Group and individual psychological services are available for students and their families. **Library/Resources:** The library contains 1.9 million volumes, 1.2 million microform items, and 200,973 audio/video tapes/CDs/DVDs, and subscribes to 61,010 periodicals including electronic. Computerized library services include interlibrary loans, database searching, Internet access, and Wi-Fi capability. Special learning facilities include an art gallery, natural history museum, TV station, an electronic classroom, telecourses, the National Institute for Aviation Research, museum of art, and public observatory.

Physically Challenged Students: 98% of the campus is accessible. Facilities include wheelchair ramps, elevators, special parking, specially equipped restrooms, special class scheduling, lowered drinking fountains, lowered telephones, wheelchairs, and braille typewriters. Interpreters for the hearing impaired, note taking, and typing services are also offered. **Special:** WSU offers accelerated programs, co-op programs, cross registration, internships, study abroad, work-study programs, and a Washington semester. Dual and student-designed majors, a general studies degree, credit by exam, nondegree study, and pass/fail options are also available. There are 14 national honor societies and a freshman honors program. **Visiting:** There are regularly scheduled orientations for prospective students. There are guides for informal visits, visitors may sit in on classes, and stay overnight. To schedule a visit, contact the Admissions Office. **Campus Safety and Security:** Measures include 24-hour foot and vehicle patrol, self-defense education, and security escort services. There are shuttle buses, emergency telephones, lighted pathways/sidewalks, and bicycle patrol.

REQUIREMENTS: Applicants must submit a minimum composite ACT score of 21 or a satisfactory SAT score, rank in the top one third of their high school graduating class, and have a 2.0 GPA (nonresidents, 2.5). Requirements needed are 4 years of English, 3 each of math, sciences, (1 unit must be lab), social studies, and academic electives. Recommended units are 3 years of foreign language, and computer science. AP and CLEP credits are accepted. To graduate, students need at least 124 credit hours, with a GPA of 2.0 to 2.5, depending on the major. Specific distribution requirements, as well as department requirements, must also be met. The core curriculum consists of 14 courses (42 hours) in general education. Students must have a minimum of 45 credit hours in courses numbered 300 or above. **Procedure:** Freshmen are admitted to all sessions. There are deferred admissions and rolling admissions plans. Application deadlines are open. The fall 2017 application fee was $30. Applications are accepted on-line. **Transfer Students:** 1399 transfer students enrolled in 2016-2017. Applicants must have a minimum GPA of 2.0 to 2.5, depending on the WSU college they wish to enter. Including all college transcripts. 30 of 60 credits required for the bachelor's degree must be completed at WSU. **International Students:** They must take the TOEFL with a minimum score of 530 on the paper-based TOEFL (PBT) or 72 on the Internet-based version (iBT).

ADMISSIONS: 96% of the 2017-2018 applicants were accepted. The SAT scores for the 2017-2018 freshman class were: Critical Reading--41% below 500, 33% between 500 and 599, 18% between 600 and 699, and 7% between 700 and 800. Math-- 22% below 500, 47% between 500 and 599, 15% between 600 and 699, and 16% between 700 and 800. The ACT scores were 8% between 12 and 17, 43% between 18 and 23, 40% between 24 and 29, and 9% above 30. 20% of the current freshmen were in the top fifth of their class; 80% were in the top two fifths. **Admissions Contact:** Bobby Gandu, Director of Admissions. Email: *admissions@wichita.edu* Web: *www.wichita.edu*

FINANCIAL AID: In 2017-2018, 68% of all full-time freshmen received some form of financial aid. 58% of all full-time freshmen received need-based aid. The average freshman award was $7,347. Need-based scholarships or need-based grants averaged $4,340; need-based self-help aid (loans and jobs) averaged $2,220; non-need-based athletic scholarships averaged $4,924; other non-need-based awards and non-need-based scholarships averaged $1,349; and $2,044 from other forms of aid. The average financial indebtedness of the 2017 graduate was $22,580. The FAFSA code is 001950. The priority date for freshman financial aid applications for fall entry is March 1.

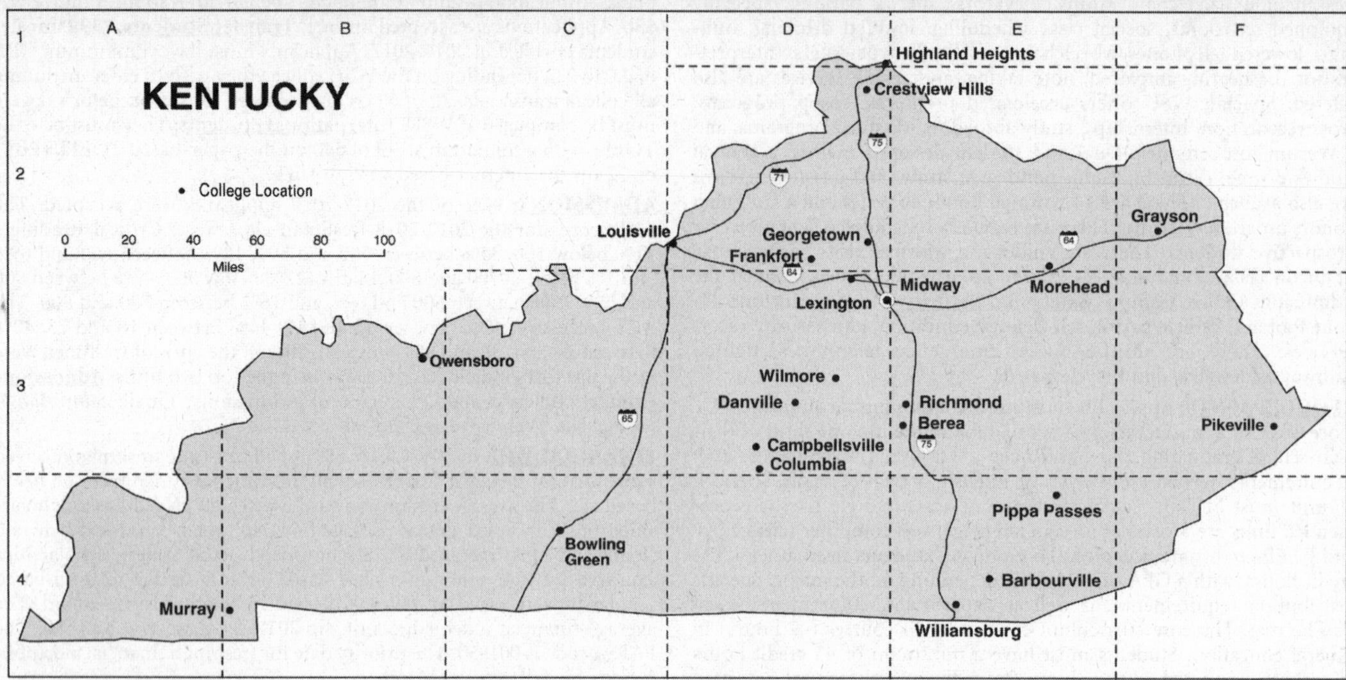

ALICE LLOYD COLLEGE *(The complete profile is made available exclusively on our website, www.barronspac.com)*

ASBURY UNIVERSITY D-3
www.asbury.edu

Wilmore, KY 40390	**(859) 858-3511** **(800) 888-1818**
Fax: (859) 858-3921	**Email: admissions@asbury.edu**
Full-time: 517 men, 809 women	**Faculty:** 87
Part-time: 90 men, 116 women	**Ph.D.s:** 74%
Graduate: 54 men, 196 women	**Student/Faculty:** 12 to 1
Year: semesters, summer session	**Tuition:** $29,500
Room & Board: $6950	**Freshman Class:** 1211 applied, 796 accepted, 322 enrolled
SAT CR/M: 568/558 **ACT:** 24	**CEEB CODE:** 1019
Application Deadline: open	**COMPETITIVE+**

Asbury University is an independent liberal arts university, providing undergraduate and graduate educational programs guided by the classical tradition of orthodox Christian thought. The figures given in the above capsule and in this profile are approximate. There are 4 undergraduate schools and 4 graduate schools. In addition to regional accreditation, AU has baccalaureate program accreditation with CSWE, NASM, and CAEP. The 65-acre campus is in a small town 20 minutes south of Lexington, KY. Including any residence halls, there are 30 buildings.

STUDENT LIFE: 52% of undergraduates are from Kentucky. Others are from 44 states, 17 foreign countries, and Canada. 67% are from public schools. 85% are White; 5% two or more races; 2% African American; 2% Hispanic; 2% Foreign; 2% race unknown; 1% Asian American. 83% are Protestant; 15% Unknown denominations. **Female To Male Ratio:** 1.7:1. The average age of freshmen is 18; all undergraduates, 20. 17% do not continue beyond their first year; 68% remain to graduate. **Housing:** 1168 students can be accommodated in college housing, which includes married student dorms, on-campus apartments, off-campus apartments, and language/international houses. On-campus housing is guaranteed for all 4 years. 85% of students live on campus. Alcohol is not permitted. All students may keep cars.

FACULTY/CLASSROOMS: 51% of faculty are male; 49% are female. 94% teach undergraduates, and 1% do research. No introductory courses are taught by graduate students. The average class size in an introductory lecture is 20; in a laboratory is 16; and in a regular course is 18.

PROGRAMS OF STUDY: AU confers B.A. and B.S. degrees. Associate and master's degrees are also awarded. Bachelor's degrees are awarded in AGRICULTURE (equine science), BIOLOGICAL SCIENCE (biochemistry and biology/biological science), BUSINESS (accounting, business administration and management, recreation and leisure services, and sports management), COMMUNICATIONS AND THE ARTS (art, classical languages, communications, creative writing, dramatic arts, English, film, television and digital media, French, journalism, music, Spanish, and theatre acting), COMPUTER AND PHYSICAL SCIENCE (actuarial mathematics, applied mathematics, chemistry, mathematics, and physical sciences), EDUCATION (art education, Christian education, elementary education, English education, foreign languages education, mathematics education, middle school education, music education, physical education, science education, secondary education, and social studies education), ENGINEERING AND ENVIRONMENTAL DESIGN (preengineering), HEALTH PROFESSIONS (exercise science, health science, pre-health studies, and prephysical therapy), SOCIAL SCIENCE (biblical languages, biblical studies, criminal justice, history, ministries, missions, philosophy, political science/government, psychology, religion, social work, sociology, and youth ministry). Media communications and communication arts, teacher education, and business have the largest enrollments.

ACTIVITIES: There are no fraternities or sororities. There are 45 groups on campus, including art, band, cheerleading, choir, chorale, chorus, computers, debate, drama, ethnic, film, forensics, honors, international, jazz band, literary magazine, musical theater, newspaper, opera, orchestra, photography, political, professional, radio and TV, religious, social service, student government, and yearbook. Popular campus events include High Bridge Film Festival, Homecoming, Fall Revival, and Missions Conference. **Sports:** There are 8 intercollegiate sports for men and 9 for women, and 7 intramural sports for men and 7 for women. Facilities include a gym, athletic fields, lacrosse, volleyball, golf, cross-country, tennis courts, an indoor swimming pool, indoor/outdoor basketball courts, indoor horseback riding arena, and student center. **Graduates:** From July 1, 2016 to June 30, 2017, 323 bachelor's degrees were awarded. The most popular majors were media communication (16%), education (13%), and business management (9%). In an average class, 2% graduate in 3 years or less, 56% graduate in 4 years or less, 63% graduate in 5 years or less, and 64% graduate in 6 years or less.

SERVICES: Counseling and information services are available, as is tutoring in most subjects. There is remedial writing. For students on academic probation, there are special classes and mentors who provide help in such areas as time management and test-taking skills. There is some help available for the visually impaired, such as tapes and agencies that offer aid. **Library/Resources:** The library contains 184,084 volumes,

13,238 microform items, and 7,188 audio/video tapes/CDs/DVDs, and subscribes to 299 periodicals including electronic. Computerized library services include interlibrary loans, database searching, Internet access, and Wi-Fi capability. Special learning facilities include an art gallery, radio station, TV station, and a blackbox theatre. The Equine Center houses classrooms, stables, and a riding arena. **Physically Challenged Students:** 80% of the campus is accessible. Facilities include wheelchair ramps, elevators, special parking, specially equipped restrooms, special class scheduling, lowered drinking fountains, lowered telephones, and special housing. **Special:** For-credit internships are available in several academic areas as are opportunities for study abroad in 14 countries. 3-2 engineering degrees are offered with the University of Kentucky. There are 6 national honor societies. **Visiting:** There are regularly scheduled orientations for prospective students, including visits, scheduled individually or during planned visitation weekends, in which students stay overnight in dorms, visit classes, attend departmental open houses and financial aid sessions, and participate in chapel and campus events. To schedule a visit, contact the Admissions Visit Coordinators at visit@asbury.edu. **Campus Safety and Security:** Measures include 24-hour foot and vehicle patrol, emergency notification system, and security escort services. There are lighted pathways/sidewalks, controlled access to dorms/residences. There are planning forums and a student parking and safety committee.

REQUIREMENTS: The SAT or ACT is required. An official high school transcript or the GED is required for all new students. Applicants should have completed 15 high school academic credits, including 4 units of English, 3 of math, and 2 each of lab science, social studies, and a foreign language. A GPA of 2.5 is required. AP and CLEP credits are accepted. To graduate with a bachelor's degree, students must complete a minimum of 124 cumulative semester hours, fulfill any liberal arts core requirements, and meet all requirements for at least one chosen major (50% of which must be completed at Asbury University), plus maintain a minimum GPA of 2.0. Traditional undergraduates earning a Bachelor of Arts degree must demonstrate proficiency in foreign language through the third semester college level. Students must complete 12 of their final 21 credit hours with Asbury. **Procedure:** Freshmen are admitted to all sessions. Entrance exams should be taken in the junior year or in the first semester of the senior year. There are early admissions, deferred admissions, and rolling admissions plans. Application deadlines are open. Notification is sent on a rolling basis. Applications are accepted on-line. **Transfer Students:** 52 transfer students enrolled in 2016-2017. Applicants with 18 quarter hours or 12 semester hours of college work or more are considered transfers. They must have an overall minimum GPA of 2.5 and be in good standing at each previous institution attended. Transfers with fewer than 30 semester hours of college work must submit a high school transcript. 49 of 124 credits required for the bachelor's degree must be completed at AU. **International Students:** There are 25 international students enrolled. They must take the TOEFL with a minimum score of 550 on the paper-based TOEFL (PBT) or 80 on the Internet-based version (iBT).

ADMISSIONS: 66% of the 2017-2018 applicants were accepted. The SAT scores for the 2017-2018 freshman class were: Critical Reading-- 21% below 500, 41% between 500 and 599, 33% between 600 and 699, and 5% between 700 and 800. Math-- 24% below 500, 40% between 500 and 599, 32% between 600 and 699, and 4% between 700 and 800. The ACT scores were 17% below 12, 27% between 12 and 17, 26% between 18 and 23, 11% between 24 and 29, and 19% above 30. 47% of the current freshmen were in the top fifth of their class; 75% were in the top two fifths. 9 freshmen graduated first in their class. **Admissions Contact:** Brandon Combs, Director of Undergraduate Admissions. Email: *admissions@asbury.edu* Web: *www.asbury.edu*

FINANCIAL AID: In 2017-2018, 79% of all full-time freshmen received some form of financial aid. 79% of all full-time freshmen received need-based aid. The average freshman award was $19,835. Need-based scholarships or need-based grants averaged $14,781; need-based self-help aid (loans and jobs) averaged $4,117; non-need-based athletic scholarships averaged $5,261; and other non-need-based awards and non-need-based scholarships averaged $13,764. The average financial indebtedness of the 2017 graduate was $27,916. The college's own financial statement is required. The priority date for freshman financial aid applications for fall entry is February 1.

BELLARMINE UNIVERSITY D-2

www.bellarmine.edu

Louisville, KY 40205 (502) 272-8131 (800) 274-4723

Fax: (502) 272-8002 **Email:** admissions@bellarmine.edu

Full-time: 875 men, 1584 women
Part-time: 38 men, 74 women
Graduate: 217 men, 493 women
Year: semesters, summer session
Room & Board: $12,182
Faculty: 176
Ph.D.s: 82%
Student/Faculty: 12 to 1
Tuition: $40,350
Freshman Class: 6212 applied, 5122 accepted, 636 enrolled
SAT CR/M/W: 540/530/500 **ACT:** required
CEEB CODE: 1056
Application Deadline: August 15
COMPETITIVE

Bellarmine University, founded in 1950, is an independent Catholic university offering undergraduate and graduate programs in the liberal arts and professional studies. There are 6 undergraduate schools and 6 graduate schools. In addition to regional accreditation, Bellarmine has baccalaureate program accreditation with AACSB, CAEP, CAAHEP, CAPTE, CCNE, CoARC, and NAACLS. The 144-acre campus is in a suburban area in Louisville, Kentucky. Including any residence halls, there are 42 buildings.

STUDENT LIFE: 72% of undergraduates are from Kentucky. Others are from 29 states, 20 foreign countries, and Canada. 63% are from public schools. 82% are White; 4% African American; 4% race unknown; 3% Hispanic; 3% two or more races; 2% Asian American; 2% Foreign. 49% are Catholic; 25% Protestant. **Female To Male Ratio:** 1.9:1. The average age of freshmen is 18; all undergraduates, 21. 22% do not continue beyond their first year; 63% remain to graduate. **Housing:** 1127 students can be accommodated in college housing, which includes dorms and on-campus apartments. In addition, there are honors houses, language/international houses, special-interest houses, fraternity houses, sorority houses, theme housing, apartments for students 21 and over, and suites for upperclassmen. When possible international students are housed with U.S. students. On-campus housing is available on a first-come, first-served basis, and is available on a lottery system for upperclassmen. 67% of students live on campus. Alcohol is not permitted. All students may keep cars.

FACULTY/CLASSROOMS: 47% of faculty are male; 53% are female. 85% teach undergraduates, 75% do research, and 75% do both. No introductory courses are taught by graduate students. The average class size in an introductory lecture is 21; in a laboratory is 17; and in a regular course is 21.

PROGRAMS OF STUDY: Bellarmine confers B.A., B.S., B.S.H.S. and B.S.N. degrees. Master's and doctoral degrees are also awarded. Bachelor's degrees are awarded in BIOLOGICAL SCIENCE (biochemistry, biology/biological science, biophysics, and molecular biology), BUSINESS (accounting, banking and finance, and business administration and management), COMMUNICATIONS AND THE ARTS (arts administration/management, communications, English, fine arts, languages, music, music technology, Spanish, speech/debate/rhetoric, and studio art), COMPUTER AND PHYSICAL SCIENCE (actuarial science, chemistry, computer science, mathematics, and physics), EDUCATION (elementary education, middle school education, and special education), ENGINEERING AND ENVIRONMENTAL DESIGN (computer engineering, computer technology, and preengineering), HEALTH PROFESSIONS (clinical science, exercise science, medical technology, nursing, predentistry, premedicine, prephysical therapy, preveterinary science, and respiratory therapy), SOCIAL SCIENCE (criminal justice, economics, history, interdisciplinary studies, international studies, liberal arts/general studies, philosophy, political science/government, psychology, sociology, and theological studies). Preprofessional programs, nursing, and accounting are the strongest academically.

ACTIVITIES: 1% of men belong to 3 national fraternities; 1% of women belong to 1 national sorority. There are 50 groups on campus, including wind ensemble, art, band, cheerleading, chess, choir, chorale, chorus, computers, dance, debate, drama, ethnic, honors, international, jazz band, LGBT, literary magazine, mock trial team, musical theater, newspaper, opera, pep band, photography, political, professional, radio and TV, religious, social, social service, and student government. Popular campus events include Hillside Concerts, Midnight Breakfast, and Ball on the Belle (Halloween Cruise). **Sports:** There are 9 intercollegiate sports for men and 10 for women, and 8 intramural sports for men and 8 for women. Facilities include basketball, volleyball arena, soccer, field hockey, lacrosse, a track stadium with an artificial turf field. **Graduates:** From July 1, 2016 to June 30, 2017, 573 bachelor's degrees were awarded. The most popular majors were health professions and related sciences (27%), business/marketing (13%), and psychology (12%). In an average class, 1% graduate in 3 years or less, 51% graduate in 4 years or less, 65% graduate in 5 years or less, and 66% graduate in 6 years or less. Of the 2016 graduating class, 23% were enrolled in graduate school within 6 months of graduation, and 90% were employed.

SERVICES: Counseling and information services are available, as is tutoring in every subject. The Academic Resource Center provides one-on-one or group tutoring for all 100- and 200-level courses. Disability Services provides note takers, distraction-reduced testing environments, extended time, books on tape, and scribe services. **Library/Resources:** The library contains 128,772 volumes, 316,810 microform items, and 4,964 audio/video tapes/CDs/DVDs, and subscribes to 105,441 periodicals including electronic. Computerized library services include interlibrary loans, database searching, Internet access, and Wi-Fi capability. Special learning facilities include an art gallery, radio station, the Thomas Merton Center is the official repository of the collection of materials by and about Thomas Merton (1915-1968 writer and Trappist Monk at Our Lady of Gethsemani Abbey in Kentucky). **Physically Challenged Students:** 85% of the campus is accessible. Facilities include wheelchair ramps, elevators, special parking, specially equipped restrooms, special class scheduling, lowered drinking fountains, lowered telephones, and special housing. **Special:** Cross-registration may be arranged through Kentuckiana Metroversity, a consortium of colleges in Kentucky and southern Indiana. Bellarmine also offers study abroad in more than 50 countries, internships in most majors, a Washington semester, a liberal studies degree, dual majors, accelerated degree programs, credit for life experience, pass/fail options during the junior and senior years, and a marine biology program in the Bahamas. There is also an honors program and the Brown Leadership Program. There are 5 national honor societies and a freshman honors program. **Visiting:** There are regularly scheduled orientations for prospective students, including admissions and financial aid session, a campus tour, interviews with faculty, and participation in a student panel. There are guides for informal visits, visitors may sit in on classes, and stay overnight. To schedule a visit, contact the Office of Admissions. **Campus Safety and Security:** Measures include 24-hour foot and vehicle patrol, self-defense education, and security escort services. There are shuttle buses, emergency telephones, lighted pathways/sidewalks, controlled access to dorms/residences, security alert bulletins, CPR-certified security, and security cameras in residence halls and in the parking lot.

REQUIREMENTS: The SAT or ACT is required. Student should have completed 22 high school course; 4 years of English, 3-4 years each of math and science with 2 units of lab, 2 years of foreign language, 2 of social studies (3 years recommended), 1-2 years of history, and 5-7 of academic electives. The GED is accepted. An essay may be requested. A GPA of 2.5 is required. AP and CLEP credits are accepted. Important factors in the admissions decision are personality/intangible qualities, recommendations by school officials, leadership record, advanced placement or honors courses, and extracurricular activities record. In order to graduate, students must complete a minimum of 126 credit hours with a minimum GPA of 2.0. Between 24 and 52 hours are required in the major. All students must fulfill 49 credit hours of core requirements, including English, philosophy, theology, math, social sciences, natural sciences, fine arts, and Western civilization. Required freshman, sophomore, junior, and senior seminars focus on the American experience, transcultural experience, and Catholic social justice. Students in the honors program must complete a senior honors thesis. **Procedure:** Freshmen are admitted fall, spring, and summer. Entrance exams should be taken by December of the senior year. There is a deferred admissions plan. Applications should be filed by August 15 for fall entry. The fall 2017 application fee was $25. Notifications are sent September 1. Applications are accepted on-line. **Transfer Students:** 88 transfer students enrolled in 2016-2017. Applicants should have a minimum college GPA of 2.0 and submit transcripts from all postsecondary schools attended. If English is your second language you are required to take the TOEFL, IELTS, or MELAB. No limit on the number of credits which may be transferred, but each student must meet the BU degree requirements. 36 of 126 credits required for the bachelor's degree must be completed at Bellarmine. **International Students:** There are 51 international students enrolled. They must take the TOEFL with a minimum score of 550 on the paper-based TOEFL (PBT) or 80 on the Internet-based version (iBT). Student must take the MELAB. The SAT or ACT can be used in lieu of the TOEFL. Students must fill out and complete the international application.

ADMISSIONS: 82% of the 2017-2018 applicants were accepted. The SAT scores for the 2017-2018 freshman class were: Critical Reading-- 27% below 500, 49% between 500 and 599, 23% between 600 and 699, and 1% between 700 and 800. Math-- 31% below 500, 54% between 500 and 599, and 15% between 600 and 699. Writing-- 62% below 500, 24% between 500 and 599, 9% between 600 and 699, and 5% between 700 and 800. The ACT scores were 40% between 18 and 23, 47% between 24 and 29, and 11% above 30. 50% of the current freshmen were in the top fifth of their class; 80% were in the top two fifths. 10 freshmen graduated first in their class. **Admissions Contact:** Timothy Sturgeon, Dean of Admissions. Email: *admissions@bellarmine.edu* Web: *www.bellarmine.edu*

FINANCIAL AID: In 2017-2018, 100% of all full-time freshmen received some form of financial aid. 77% of all full-time freshmen received need-based aid. The average freshman award was $32,099. Need-based scholarships or need-based grants averaged $24,796; need-based self-help aid (loans and jobs) averaged $5,755; non-need-based athletic scholarships averaged $6,733; other non-need-based awards and non-need-based scholarships averaged $3,468; and $25,298 from other forms of aid. 65% of undergraduate students work part-time. The average financial indebtedness of the 2017 graduate was $27,164. The FAFSA code is 001954. The priority date for freshman financial aid applications for fall entry is November 1.

BEREA COLLEGE E-3

www.berea.edu

Berea, KY 40404	**(859) 985-3500** **(800) 326-5948**
Fax: (859) 985-3512	**Email: hodsonl@berea.edu**
Full-time: 681 men, 934 women	**Faculty:** 136; IIB, av$
Part-time: 25 men, 30 women	**Ph.D.s:** 92%
Graduate: n/av	**Student/Faculty:** 10 to 1
Year: semesters, summer session	**Tuition:** see profile
Room & Board: $6534	**Freshman Class:** 1712 applied, 600 accepted, 432 enrolled
SAT CR/M/W: 547/554/530 **ACT:** 24	**CEEB CODE:** 1060
Application Deadline: April 30	**COMPETITIVE**

Berea College, founded in 1855, is a private liberal arts institution. All students admitted to Berea receive our Tuition Promise Scholarship. This scholarship is combined with financial aid you may receive as well as any other scholarship you may be awarded by outside parties or organizations to cover 100% of tuition costs. For most Berea students, the Tuition Promise Scholarship amounts to nearly $100,000 over four years. Students are required to pay student fees only in the amount of $560.00. There is 1 undergraduate school. In addition to regional accreditation, BC has baccalaureate program accreditation with CAEP, and CCNE. The 140-acre campus is in a suburban area 40 miles south of Lexington, KY. Including any residence halls, there are 48 buildings.

STUDENT LIFE: 52% of undergraduates are from out of state, mostly the South. Students are from 42 states, and 76 foreign countries. 8% are Foreign; 7% two or more races; 56% White; 2% Asian American; 15% African American; 11% Hispanic; 1% race unknown. **Female To Male Ratio:** 1.4:1. The average age of freshmen is 18; all undergraduates, 20. 20% do not continue beyond their first year; 80% remain to graduate. **Housing:** 1500 students can be accommodated in college housing, which includes gender neutral, married student dorms, and on-campus apartments. In addition, there are special-interest houses, Ecovillage and a green sustainable living hall. On-campus housing is guaranteed for all 4 years. 89% of students live on campus. Alcohol is not permitted. Some may keep cars.

FACULTY/CLASSROOMS: 51% of faculty are male; 49% are female. All teach undergraduates. No introductory courses are taught by graduate students. The average class size in a laboratory is 20 and in a regular course is 20.

PROGRAMS OF STUDY: BC confers B.A. and B.S. degrees. Bachelor's degrees are awarded in AGRICULTURE (agriculture and environmental studies), BIOLOGICAL SCIENCE (biology/biological science), BUSINESS (business administration and management), COMMUNICATIONS AND THE ARTS (art, communications, dramatic arts, English, French, German, music, Spanish, and theatre arts), COMPUTER AND PHYSICAL SCIENCE (applied mathematics, chemistry, computer science, mathematics, and physics), EDUCATION (education, elementary education, and physical education), ENGINEERING AND ENVIRONMENTAL DESIGN (industrial engineering technology), HEALTH PROFESSIONS (nursing), SOCIAL SCIENCE (African studies, African American studies, Asian/Oriental studies, child care/child and family studies, economics, history, peace studies, philosophy, political science/government, psychology, religion, sociology, and women's studies). Business administration, technology and applied design, and child and family studies have the largest enrollments.

ACTIVITIES: There are no fraternities or sororities. There are 75 groups on campus, including art, band, cheerleading, chess, choir, chorus, communications, dance, debate, drama, environmental, ethnic, honors, international, jazz band, LGBT, literary magazine, newspaper, orchestra, pep band, photography, political, professional, radio and TV, religious, social, social service, student government, and yearbook. Popular campus events include Mountain Day and Labor Day. **Sports:** There are 7 intercollegiate sports for men and 7 for women, and 9 intramural sports for men and 9 for women. Facilities include an indoor swimming pool, racquetball courts, tennis courts, playing fields, a dance studio, indoor walking track, all-weather track, and weight training and cardiovascular exercise rooms. **Graduates:** From July 1, 2016 to June 30, 2017, 319 bachelor's degrees were awarded. The most popular majors were biology (10%), computer and information sciences (9%), and business administration (8%). In an average class, 55% graduate in 4 years or less, 61% graduate in 5 years or less, and 66% graduate in 6 years or less.

SERVICES: Counseling and information services are available, as is tutoring in some subjects. There is a reader service for the blind, and remedial math, reading, and writing. The Center for Teaching and Learning supports research, writing, and public speaking across the curriculum, valuing writing in all disciplines including the spoken and written word. **Library/Resources:** The library contains 350,474 volumes, 149,900 microform items, and 16,431 audio/video tapes/CDs/DVDs, and subscribes to 28,828 periodicals including electronic. Computerized library services include interlibrary loans, database searching, Internet access, and Wi-Fi capability. Special learning facilities include an art gallery, planetarium, radio station, a geology museum. **Physically Challenged Students:** 53% of the campus is accessible. Facilities include wheelchair ramps, elevators, special parking, specially equipped restrooms, special class scheduling, lowered drinking fountains, lowered telephones, electronic doors, and a lift chair for the indoor pool. **Special:** Students may study abroad in many countries. They can also participate in internships, independent and team-initiated studies. Student-designed majors are available. A 3-2 engineering degree is offered with the University of Kentucky. All students must participate in an on-campus work program 10 to 15 hours per week. There are 19 national honor societies. **Visiting:** There are regularly scheduled orientations for prospective students, student visits consist of an introductory session, a tour of campus and residence halls, a private interview and/or conversation with an admissions representative. To schedule a visit, contact Denessa McPherson in Admissions. **Campus Safety and Security:** Measures include 24-hour foot and vehicle patrol, emergency notification system, self-defense education, and security escort services. There are emergency telephones, lighted pathways/sidewalks, ongoing programs on campus safety, theft prevention, assault and rape prevention, fire prevention, defensive driving, and occupational safety working with hazardous materials.

REQUIREMENTS: The ACT or SAT is required. Applicants should be graduates of an accredited secondary school. The GED is accepted. Home-schooled students are also encouraged to apply. Financial need is a requirement for admission. Berea recommends 4 units in English, 3 in math, and 2 each in foreign language, science, and social studies. AP and CLEP credits are accepted. Important factors in the admissions decision are geographical diversity and advanced placement or honors courses. Berea's curriculum offers the advantage of interdisciplinary general study coupled with intensive study in 33 major fields (some of which have multiple concentrations) and 34 minor fields of study. In all academic disciplines, students acquire knowledge and deepen their understanding of the subject area, while gaining competency in applying the content and methods of inquiry to daily life. A degree is conferred upon the completion of both the General Education curriculum and the curriculum of a selected major, provided the student has earned the minimum number of credits (including 20 outside the major), and has earned a cumulative GPA of 2.0 or higher in all courses, as well as in the major coursework. (Please be aware that some academic departments require a GPA higher than the college requirement of 2.0.) A minimum of 32 earned course credits (typically 34 in Nursing) is required for graduation, with at least 20 credits taken outside the major discipline. **Procedure:** Freshmen are admitted in the fall. Entrance exams should be taken during the junior year or early in the senior year. There is a rolling admissions plan. Application deadlines are open. Notifications are sent November 1. Applications are accepted on-line. **Transfer Students:** 53 transfer students enrolled in 2016-2017. Applicants must be in good standing at the last college attended, and have a minimum GPA of 2.0. 8 of 32 credits required for the bachelor's degree must be completed at Berea. **International Students:** There are 122 international students enrolled. They must take the TOEFL with a minimum score of 500 on the paper-based TOEFL (PBT) or 61 on the Internet-based version (iBT). Student must also take the IELTS, scoring 5 overall and 5 in each exam area; and either the SAT, scoring 1210 (430 Critical Reading); or ACT, scoring 17.

ADMISSIONS: 35% of the 2017-2018 applicants were accepted. The SAT scores for the 2017-2018 freshman class were: Critical Reading-- 27% below 500, 50% between 500 and 599, 18% between 600 and 699, and 5% between 700 and 800. Math-- 30% below 500, 43% between 500 and 599, 23% between 600 and 699, and 5% between 700 and 800. Writing-- 34% below 500, 48% between 500 and 599, 14% between 600 and 699, and 5% between 700 and 800. The ACT scores were 47% between 18 and 23, 47% between 24 and 29, and 6% above 30. 49% of the current freshmen were in the top fifth of their class; 85% were in the top two fifths. 14 freshmen graduated first in their class. **Admissions Contact:** Luke Hodson, Director of Admissions. Email: *hodsonl@berea.edu* Web: *www.berea.edu*

FINANCIAL AID: In 2017-2018, 100% of all full-time freshmen received some form of financial aid. 100% of all full-time freshmen received need-based aid. The average freshman award was $34,366. Need-based scholarships or need-based grants averaged $31,803; and need-based self-help aid (loans and jobs) averaged $1,825. 100% of undergraduate students work part-time. The average financial indebtedness of the 2017 graduate was $7,891. The FAFSA code is 001955. The priority date for freshman financial aid applications for fall entry is February 1.

BRESCIA UNIVERSITY — B-3
www.brescia.edu

Owensboro, KY 42301 — (270) 685-3131, (877) BRESCIA
Email: admissions@brescia.edu

Full-time: 196 men, 515 women	**Faculty:** 53
Part-time: 148 men, 314 women	**Ph.D.s:** 70%
Graduate: 17 men, 39 women	**Student/Faculty:** 11 to 1
Year: semesters, summer session	**Tuition:** $20,390
Room & Board: $9500	**Freshman Class:** 4565 applied, 2135 accepted, 128 enrolled
SAT or ACT: required	**CEEB CODE:** 1071
Application Deadline: open	**VERY COMPETITIVE**

Brescia University, founded in 1925 as a women's junior college, became a 4-year, coeducational liberal arts institution in 1950. It is a private school affiliated with the Roman Catholic Church. The university offers certificates, associate, baccalaureate, and master's degrees through on-ground and online classes. There are 7 undergraduate schools and 3 graduate schools. In addition to regional accreditation, BU has baccalaureate program accreditation with CSWE and CAEP. The 6-acre campus is in an urban area in Downtown Owensboro, KY, 32 miles southeast of Evansville, Indiana, and 125 miles from both Louisville and Nashville. Including any residence halls, there are 20 buildings.

STUDENT LIFE: 58% of undergraduates are from Kentucky. Others are from 42 states, 8 foreign countries, and Canada. 89% are White; 4% African American; 4% Foreign; 1% American Indian/Alaska Native; 1% Hispanic. 39% are Catholic; 32% Protestant; 27% claim no religious affiliation. **Female To Male Ratio:** 2.4:1. The average age of freshmen is

19; all undergraduates, 26. 33% do not continue beyond their first year. **Housing:** 224 students can be accommodated in college housing, which includes dorms and on-campus apartments. In addition, there are honors houses and special-interest houses. On-campus housing is available on a first-come, first-served basis, and is available on a lottery system for upperclassmen. 60% of students commute. Alcohol is not permitted. All students may keep cars.

FACULTY/CLASSROOMS: 40% of faculty are male; 60% are female. All teach undergraduates. No introductory courses are taught by graduate students. The average class size in an introductory lecture is 14; in a laboratory is 10; and in a regular course is 12.

PROGRAMS OF STUDY: BU confers B.A., B.S., and B.S.W. degrees. Associate and master's degrees are also awarded. Bachelor's degrees are awarded in BIOLOGICAL SCIENCE (biochemistry and biology/biological science), BUSINESS (accounting, banking and finance, business administration and management, business economics, and human resources), COMMUNICATIONS AND THE ARTS (art, English, graphic design, and Spanish), COMPUTER AND PHYSICAL SCIENCE (chemistry, computer science, mathematics, and physical sciences), EDUCATION (art education, early childhood education, education of the mentally handicapped, elementary education, and special education), HEALTH PROFESSIONS (medical laboratory technology, medical technology, and speech pathology/audiology), SOCIAL SCIENCE (history, liberal arts/general studies, pastoral studies, psychology, religion, social studies, and social work). Education, business, and social work are the strongest academically. Business, social work, and education have the largest enrollments.

ACTIVITIES: There are no fraternities or sororities. There are 25 groups on campus, including Z.E.S.T. (Zombie emergency survival team), black student union, clay club, habitat for humanity, philosophy club, art, choir, chorus, communications, computers, creative writing, drama, honors, international, literary magazine, musical theater, newspaper, pep band, political, professional, religious, social, social service, and student government. Popular campus events include Homecoming, Opening Year Mass, Founders Convocation, and Inaugural Ball. **Sports:** There are 7 intercollegiate sports for men and 9 for women, and 5 intramural sports for men and 6 for women. Facilities include a gym, tennis courts, a weight room, a cardiovascular workout room, a racquetball court, a batting cage, a baseball field, and soccer field. **Graduates:** From July 1, 2016 to June 30, 2017, 87 bachelor's degrees were awarded. The most popular majors were social work (25%), business (16%), and communication sciences and disorders (10%). In an average class, 17% graduate in 4 years or less, 27% graduate in 5 years or less, and 32% graduate in 6 years or less.

SERVICES: Counseling and information services are available, as is tutoring in most subjects. There is remedial math, reading, and writing. **Library/Resources:** The library contains 65,597 volumes, 2,513 microform items, and 3,320 audio/video tapes/CDs/DVDs, and subscribes to 35,766 periodicals including electronic. Computerized library services include interlibrary loans, database searching, Internet access, and Wi-Fi capability. Special learning facilities include an art gallery, and a clay studio. **Physically Challenged Students:** 95% of the campus is accessible. Facilities include wheelchair ramps, elevators, special parking, specially equipped restrooms, lowered drinking fountains, and lowered telephones. **Special:** Brescia offers a combined engineering degree with the University of Kentucky and the University of Louisville. Work-study programs, student-designed majors, nondegree study, dual majors, study abroad in Mexico, an internship in professional writing, pass/fail options and cross-registration with Kentucky Wesleyan are available. There are 2 national honor societies, a freshman honors program, and 2 departmental honors programs. **Visiting:** There are regularly scheduled orientations for prospective students, including spring and fall open houses for freshmen and a spring transfer open house. There are guides for informal visits, visitors may sit in on classes, and stay overnight. To schedule a visit, contact the Office of Admissions. **Campus Safety and Security:** Measures include emergency notification system and security escort services. There are emergency telephones, lighted pathways/sidewalks, and night security.

REQUIREMENTS: The SAT or ACT is required. High school units should include 4 of English, 3 of math, and 2 each in social studies, science, foreign language, fine arts, and computer science. Applications are accepted on-line at the university's web site. A GPA of 2.5 is required. AP and CLEP credits are accepted. Important factors in the admissions decision are advanced placement or honors courses and recommendations by school officials. All students must earn 128 credit hours, including 42 upper-division hours, and 30 or more hours in the major, while maintaining an overall GPA of 2.0 and 2.5 in the major. Distribution requirements include 18 hours in aesthetics, language, and literature, 12 in social science, 9 each in fine arts, science, and math, 6 in religious studies, and 3 in philosophy. Students must also demonstrate computer competency. **Procedure:** Freshmen are admitted to all sessions. Entrance exams should be taken at the end of the junior year. There is a rolling admissions plan. Application deadlines are open. The fall 2017 application fee was $25. Applications are accepted on-line. **Transfer Students:** 106 transfer students enrolled in 2016-2017. Transfer students must have a minimum GPA of 2.0. 42 of 128 credits required for the bachelor's degree must be completed at BU. **International Students:** They must take the TOEFL and either take the SAT or ACT.

ADMISSIONS: 47% of the 2017-2018 applicants were accepted. The SAT scores for the 2017-2018 freshman class were: Math-- 53% below 500 and 47% between 500 and 599. The ACT scores were 20% below 12, 45% between 12 and 17, 17% between 18 and 23, 15% between 24 and 29, and 3% above 30. **Admissions Contact:** Christy Rohner, Assistant Director of Admissions. Email: *admissions@brescia.edu* Web: *www.brescia.edu*

FINANCIAL AID: 100% of undergraduate students work part-time. BU is a member of CSS. The FAFSA code is 001958. The deadline for filing freshman financial aid applications for fall entry is March 1.

CAMPBELLSVILLE UNIVERSITY D-3

www.campbellsville.edu

Campbellsville, KY 42718	(270) 789-5220 (800) 264-6014
Fax: (270) 789-5071	**Email:** admissions@campbellsville.edu
Full-time: 927 men, 1192 women	**Faculty:** 188
Part-time: 732 men, 1246 women	**Ph.D.s:** 68%
Graduate: 2767 men, 1178 women	**Student/Faculty:** 15 to 1
Year: semesters, summer session	**Tuition:** $25,400
Room & Board: $8000	**Freshman Class:** 2784 applied, 1904 accepted, 541 enrolled
ACT: 21	**CEEB CODE:** 1097
Application Deadline: August 1	**COMPETITIVE**

Campbellsville University is a comprehensive, Christian institution that offers pre-professional, undergraduate and graduate programs. The university is dedicated to academic excellence solidly grounded in the liberal arts that fosters personal growth, integrity and professional preparation within a caring environment. The university prepares students as Christian servant leaders for life-long learning, continued scholarship, and active participation in a diverse, and global society. There are 7 undergraduate schools and 6 graduate schools. In addition to regional accreditation, CU has baccalaureate program accreditation with CSWE, NASM, CAEP, and IACBE. The 90-acre campus is in a small town 85 miles southwest of Lexington and 85 miles southeast of Louisville. Including any residence halls, there are 56 buildings.

STUDENT LIFE: 87% of undergraduates are from Kentucky. Others are from 46 states, and 57 foreign countries. 6% are African American; 47% White; 41% Foreign; 2% Hispanic; 2% race unknown; 1% Asian American; 1% two or more races. 56% claim no religious affiliation; 23% Protestant. **Male To Female Ratio:** 1.2:1. The average age of freshmen is 19; all undergraduates, 21. 36% do not continue beyond their first year; 42% remain to graduate. **Housing:** 1044 students can be accommodated in college housing, which includes married student dorms, on-campus apartments, and off-campus apartments. On-campus housing is guaranteed for all 4 years. 23% of students commute. Alcohol is not permitted. All students may keep cars.

FACULTY/CLASSROOMS: 40% of faculty are male; 60% are female. No introductory courses are taught by graduate students.

PROGRAMS OF STUDY: CU confers B.A., B.S., B.M., B.S.B.A., and B.S.W. degrees. Associate, master's, and doctoral degrees are also awarded. Bachelor's degrees are awarded in BIOLOGICAL SCIENCE (biology/biological science), BUSINESS (accounting, business administration and management, business economics, marketing management, office supervision and management, and sports management), COMMUNICATIONS AND THE ARTS (art, communications, English, music, music performance, theatre arts, and voice), COMPUTER AND

PHYSICAL SCIENCE (chemistry, computer science, information sciences and systems, and mathematics), EDUCATION (early childhood education, elementary education, health education, middle school education, music education, physical education, recreation education, social science education, and teaching English as a second/foreign language (TESOL/TEFOL), ENGINEERING AND ENVIRONMENTAL DESIGN (preengineering), HEALTH PROFESSIONS (exercise science, medical laboratory technology, nursing, predentistry, premedicine, prepharmacy, and sports medicine), SOCIAL SCIENCE (biblical studies, Christian studies, criminal justice, economics, history, political science/government, prelaw, psychology, religious education, religious music, social work, sociology, and youth ministry). Nursing, social work, biology, and music are the strongest academically. Social work, criminal justice, and nursing have the largest enrollments.

ACTIVITIES: There are no fraternities or sororities. There are 45 groups on campus, including art, band, cheerleading, choir, chorale, chorus, computers, dance, drama, environmental, ethnic, film, honors, international, jazz band, literary magazine, marching band, musical theater, newspaper, opera, orchestra, pep band, photography, political, professional, radio and TV, religious, social, social service, student government, and symphony. Popular campus events include Valentine Banquet, Christmas Tapestry, Homecoming, and Family Weekend. **Sports:** There are 13 intercollegiate sports for men and 12 for women, and 10 intramural sports for men and 10 for women. Facilities include a swimming pool, a gym, football stadium, baseball field, an intramural activities center with skating facilities, softball and soccer fields, and an indoor practice field. **Graduates:** From July 1, 2016 to June 30, 2017, 339 bachelor's degrees were awarded. The most popular majors were business (18%), criminal justice/homeland security (9%), and nursing (8%). In an average class, 25% graduate in 4 years or less, 34% graduate in 5 years or less, and 36% graduate in 6 years or less.

SERVICES: Counseling and information services are available, as is tutoring in every subject. There is remedial math, reading, and writing. There is also a study skills program. **Library/Resources:** The library contains 404,600 volumes, 12,000 microform items, and 689 audio/video tapes/CDs/DVDs, and subscribes to 78 periodicals including electronic. Computerized library services include interlibrary loans, database searching, and Internet access. Special learning facilities include an art gallery, radio station, TV station, a teacher resource center, the Kentuckiana Collection, and Clay Hill Memorial Forest. **Physically Challenged Students:** 85% of the campus is accessible. Facilities include wheelchair ramps, elevators, special parking, specially equipped restrooms, special class scheduling, lowered drinking fountains, and lowered telephones. **Special:** Legislative and public administration internships, a Washington semester, and federal work-study programs are available. The university also offers a semester in London program, a 3-2 engineering degree with the University of Kentucky, dual majors, credit by exam, credit for life, military, and work experience, non-degree study, and pass/fail options. There is a freshman honors program. **Visiting:** There are regularly scheduled orientations for prospective students, consisting of visitation days held in May, June, July, and August. There are guides for informal visits and visitors may sit in on classes. To schedule a visit, contact Office of Enrollment and Admissions. **Campus Safety and Security:** Measures include 24-hour foot and vehicle patrol, emergency notification system, self-defense education, and security escort services. There are emergency telephones, lighted pathways/sidewalks, and controlled access to dorms/residences.

REQUIREMENTS: The SAT may be substituted for the ACT. Applicants must be graduates of an accredited secondary school with a GPA of 2.0. The GED is accepted. An interview is recommended. AP and CLEP credits are accepted. Important factors in the admissions decision are evidence of special talent, leadership record, and advanced placement or honors courses. All candidates must be of good moral character. All students must complete a minimum of 128 semester hours, including 30 in the major, 21 in the minor, and 51 in general education courses. The minimum GPA is 2.5 for education majors, 2.1 for all others. All students must fulfill an English composition requirement. **Procedure:** Freshmen are admitted fall and spring. Entrance exams should be taken no later than February of the senior year. There are deferred admissions and rolling admissions plans. Application deadlines are open. The fall 2017 application fee was $20. Applications are accepted on-line. **Transfer Students:** 286 transfer students enrolled in 2016-2017. Of the 120 credits needed to graduate, all students must complete one third of the credits required for the major and the minor at the university. The last year must be completed in residence. 30 of 120 credits required for the bachelor's degree must be completed at CU. **International Students:** There are 178 international students enrolled. They must take the TOEFL with a minimum score of 500 on the paper-based TOEFL (PBT) or 61 on the Internet-based version (iBT). Student must take the IELTS. They must also take the SAT or ACT, scoring 19.

ADMISSIONS: 68% of the 2017-2018 applicants were accepted. The SAT scores for the 2017-2018 freshman class were: Math-- 38% below 500, 51% between 500 and 599, and 11% between 600 and 699. The ACT scores were 20% between 12 and 17, 53% between 18 and 23, 24% between 24 and 29, and 3% above 30. **Admissions Contact:** Paula Caldwell, Director of Undergraduate Admissions. Email: *admissions@campbellsville.edu* Web: *www.campbellsville.edu*

FINANCIAL AID: The FAFSA code is 001959. The priority date for freshman financial aid applications for fall entry is October 1.

CENTRE COLLEGE D-3

www.centre.edu

Danville, KY 40422	(859) 238-5350 (800) 423-6236
Fax: (859) 238-5373	Email: admission@centre.edu
Full-time: 708 men, 741 women	**Faculty:** 128; IIB, av$
Part-time: 1 men	**Ph.D.s:** 98%
Graduate: n/av	**Student/Faculty:** 10 to 1
Year: 4-1-4	**Tuition:** $40,500
Room & Board: $10,180	**Freshman Class:** 2454 applied, 1873 accepted, 401 enrolled
SAT EBR-W/M: 636/656 **ACT:** 29	**CEEB CODE:** 1109
Application Deadline: January 15	**MOST COMPETITIVE**

Centre College is a small, independent, and selective educational community dedicated to study in the liberal arts as the means to develop the intellectual, personal, and moral potential of its students. Centre nurtures in its students the ability to think logically and critically, to work creatively, to analyze and compare values, and to write and speak with clarity and grace. It acquaints students with the range of accomplishments of the human mind and spirit in a variety of arts and theoretical disciplines. It enables students to choose and fulfill significant responsibilities in society. The Centre Commitment guarantees students who meet the college's academic and social expectations an internship or (beginning with the class of 2017) a research opportunity, study abroad, and graduation in four years. If a student is unable to secure the components of the Centre Commitment within four consecutive years of enrollment, the college will provide up to an additional year of study tuition-free. There is 1 undergraduate school. In addition to regional accreditation, CC has baccalaureate program accreditation with NASDTEC and CAEP. The 160-acre campus is in a small town 35 miles southwest of Lexington and 80 miles southeast of Louisville. Including any residence halls, there are 85 buildings.

STUDENT LIFE: 66% of undergraduates are from Kentucky. Others are from 47 states, 17 foreign countries, and Canada. 68% are from public schools. 8% are Foreign; 73% White; 6% Hispanic; 5% African American; 5% Asian American; 3% two or more races; 1% race unknown. 37% are Protestant; 35% claim no religious affiliation; 19% Catholic. **Female To Male Ratio:** 1.0:1. The average age of freshmen is 18; all undergraduates, 20. 9% do not continue beyond their first year; 86% remain to graduate. **Housing:** 1461 students can be accommodated in college housing, which includes single sex coed, married student dorms, and on-campus apartments. In addition, there are special-interest houses, fraternity houses, sorority houses, and theme housing. On-campus housing is guaranteed for all 4 years. 98% of students live on campus. All students may keep cars.

FACULTY/CLASSROOMS: 55% of faculty are male; 45% are female. All teach undergraduates and all do research. No introductory courses are taught by graduate students. The average class size in an introductory lecture is 25; in a laboratory is 15; and in a regular course is 19.

PROGRAMS OF STUDY: CC confers B.A. and B.S. degrees. Bachelor's degrees are awarded in AGRICULTURE (environmental studies), BIOLOGICAL SCIENCE (biochemistry, biology/biological science, and molecular biology), BUSINESS (finance), COMMUNICATIONS AND THE ARTS (art history and appreciation, dramatic arts, English, fine arts, French, German, music, and Spanish), COMPUTER AND PHYSI-

CAL SCIENCE (chemical physics, chemistry, computer science, mathematics, physical chemistry, and physics), SOCIAL SCIENCE (anthropology, classical/ancient civilization, economics, history, international relations, philosophy, political science/government, psychobiology, psychology, religion, and sociology). Biochemistry and molecular biology, chemistry, and economics and finance are the strongest academically. Biology, economics and finance, and history have the largest enrollments.

ACTIVITIES: 45% of men belong to 6 national fraternities; 45% of women belong to 5 national sororities. There are 70 groups on campus, including art, band, cheerleading, choir, chorale, chorus, communications, computers, dance, debate, drama, environmental, ethnic, film, honors, international, jazz band, LGBT, literary magazine, musical theater, newspaper, orchestra, pep band, photography, political, professional, radio and TV, religious, social, social service, and student government. Popular campus events include Carnival, Homecoming, Homelessness and Poverty Week, International Dinner, Green Week, CARE Trick or Treat, the Honors Convocation, and the Honor Walk. **Sports:** There are 10 intercollegiate sports for men and 11 for women, and 8 intramural sports for men and 8 for women. Facilities include a complex with a gym, basketball courts, volleyball courts, training room, weight room, fitness center, racquetball/handball courts, a stadium, tennis courts, playing fields for football, a track, baseball, softball, soccer, a swimming pool, golf teams, outdoor turf fields support lacrosse, football, and field hockey. **Graduates:** From July 1, 2016 to June 30, 2017, 327 bachelor's degrees were awarded. The most popular majors were social sciences (27%), psychology (13%), and biological/life sciences (9%). In an average class, 86% graduate in 4 years or less, 86% graduate in 5 years or less, and 86% graduate in 6 years or less. Of the 2016 graduating class, 30% were enrolled in graduate school within 6 months of graduation, and 68% were employed.

SERVICES: Counseling and information services are available, as is tutoring in most subjects. There is a reader service for the blind, and remedial writing. **Library/Resources:** The library contains 231,820 volumes, 31,034 microform items, and 6,584 audio/video tapes/CDs/DVDs, and subscribes to 112,943 periodicals including electronic. Computerized library services include interlibrary loans, database searching, Internet access, and Wi-Fi capability. Special learning facilities include an art gallery, natural history museum, radio station, a center for teaching and learning, a hot glass studio, digital media editing lab, and a performing arts center. **Physically Challenged Students:** 70% of the campus is accessible. Facilities include wheelchair ramps, elevators, special parking, specially equipped restrooms, special class scheduling, lowered drinking fountains, lowered telephones, and special housing. **Special:** Centre offers internships, study abroad in 12 countries, a Washington semester through American University, work-study, and a 3-2 engineering degree with Vanderbilt University, Washington University at St. Louis, Columbia University, and the University of Kentucky. Student-designed majors, interdisciplinary majors including chemical physics, secondary education certification, pre-law, pre-business, pre-medicine programs, and pass/fail options. There are 8 national honor societies and a chapter of Phi Beta Kappa. **Visiting:** There are regularly scheduled orientations for prospective students, including a campus tour, an interview, pre-tour, and faculty appointments. There are guides for informal visits, visitors may sit in on classes, and stay overnight. To schedule a visit, contact Bob Nesmith at bob.nesmith@centre.edu. **Campus Safety and Security:** Measures include 24-hour foot and vehicle patrol, emergency notification system, self-defense education, and security escort services. There are emergency telephones, lighted pathways/sidewalks, controlled access to dorms/residences, and a working relationship with outside agencies.

REQUIREMENTS: The SAT or ACT and ACT Writing Test are recommended. No minimum test scores are required. Students should have completed 13 academic credits (20 recommended), including 4 years each in English, 3-4 years of math, 2-4 years each in science (with 2 years of lab), 2-4 years in foreign language, 2 years recommended of social studies, 2 years of history, and 1 year in an art or music related course. An essay is required, and an interview is strongly recommended. AP credits are accepted. Important factors in the admissions decision are leadership record, advanced placement or honors courses, recommendations by school officials, parents or siblings attended your school, evidence of special talent, personality/intangible qualities, extracurricular activities record, recommendations by alumni, and geographical diversity. All students must earn an overall GPA of 2.0 and complete a minimum of 110 credit hours. Students also must demonstrate competency in writing, foreign language, and mathematics plus 1 course beyond basic skills in mathematics, foreign language, or computer science. A first-year humanities program and a freshman seminar must be completed. Core curriculum requirements include 2 courses each in the humanities or art from the aesthetic context, the scientific/technological context, the social context, and the fundamental questions context. **Procedure:** Freshmen are admitted fall. Entrance exams should be taken by January of the senior year. There are early decision, early admissions, and deferred admissions plans. Early decision applications should be filed by November 15; regular applications, by January 15 for fall entry. Notification of early decision is sent December 15; regular decision, March 15. 67 early decision candidates were accepted for the 2017-2018 class. 107 applicants were on the 2017 waiting list; 4 were admitted. Applications are accepted on-line. **Transfer Students:** 4 transfer students enrolled in 2016-2017. Applicants for transfer must have all previous college transcripts on file and a recommendation from the dean of the most recent college attended. If the student has completed fewer than 2 years of college work, high school records must also be submitted. Students may enroll in the fall, winter, and spring. An interview is recommended. 45 of 111 credits required for the bachelor's degree must be completed at CC. **International Students:** There are 110 international students enrolled. They must take the TOEFL with a minimum score of 90 on the Internet-based version (iBT). Students may submit SAT or ACT scores.

ADMISSIONS: 76% of the 2017-2018 applicants were accepted. The SAT scores for the 2017-2018 freshman class were: Math-- 33% between 500 and 599, 31% between 600 and 699, and 36% between 700 and 800. Evidence-Based Reading/Writing-- 1% below 500, 25% between 500 and 599, 25% between 600 and 699, and 20% between 700 and 800. The ACT scores were 8% between 18 and 23, 47% between 24 and 29, and 45% above 30. 76% of the current freshmen were in the top fifth of their class; 94% were in the top two fifths. 24 freshmen graduated first in their class. **Admissions Contact:** Bob Nesmith, Dean of Admission and Financial Aid. Email: *admission@centre.edu* Web: *www.centre.edu*

FINANCIAL AID: In 2017-2018, 99% of all full-time freshmen received some form of financial aid. 65% of all full-time freshmen received need-based aid. The average freshman award was $34,441. Need-based scholarships or need-based grants averaged $31,901 ($41,700 maximum); need-based self-help aid (loans and jobs) averaged $4,523 ($7,300 maximum); other non-need-based awards and non-need-based scholarships averaged $23,084; and $3,412 from other forms of aid. 31% of undergraduate students work part-time. The average financial indebtedness of the 2017 graduate was $24,917. The college's own financial statement is required. The FAFSA code is 001961. The priority date for freshman financial aid applications for fall entry is January 31.

EASTERN KENTUCKY UNIVERSITY — E-3

www.eku.edu

Richmond, KY 40475	**(859) 622-2106** **(800) 465-9191**
Fax: (859) 622-3024	**Email: admissions@eku.edu**
Full-time: 6171 men, 8121 women	**Faculty:** 687; IIA, --$
Part-time: n/av	**Ph.D.s:** 66%
Graduate: n/av	**Student/Faculty:** 16 to 1
Year: semesters, summer session	**Tuition:** $9366 ($19,144)
Room & Board: $8376	**Freshman Class:** n/av
ACT: required	**CEEB CODE:** 1200
Application Deadline: August 1	**COMPETITIVE**

Eastern Kentucky University, established in 1906, is a public, state-supported institution offering degree programs in the arts and sciences, business, environmental studies, health fields, justice and safety, education, and public service occupations. There are 6 undergraduate schools and 1 graduate school. In addition to regional accreditation, EKU has baccalaureate program accreditation with AACSB, ACCE, ADA, AHEA, CSWE, FIDER, NASM, CAEP, NLN, NRPA, ACEN, ACEND, ACOTE, ACS, CAHIIM, CACREP, CAEP, CCNE, CCIE, CAATE, and CAEP. The 628-acre campus is in a small town 20 miles south of Lexington. Including any residence halls, there are 98 buildings.

STUDENT LIFE: 87% of undergraduates are from Kentucky. Others are from 50 states, 36 foreign countries, and Canada. 90% are from public schools. 82% are White; 5% African American; 3% race unknown; 2% Hispanic; 2% two or more races; 1% Asian American; 1% Foreign. **Female To Male Ratio:** 1.3:1. The average age of freshmen is 19; all undergraduates, 23. 35% do not continue beyond their first year; 37% remain to graduate. **Housing:** 5260 students can be accommodated in college housing, which includes coed and married student dorms and on-campus apartments. In addition, there are honors houses. On-campus housing is guaranteed for all 4 years. 71% of students commute. Alcohol is not permitted. All students may keep cars.

FACULTY/CLASSROOMS: 49% of faculty are male; 51% are female. 98% teach undergraduates, 25% do research, and 25% do both. No introductory courses are taught by graduate students. The average class size in an introductory lecture is 30; in a laboratory is 15; and in a regular course is 25.

PROGRAMS OF STUDY: EKU confers B.A., B.S., B.B.A., B.F.A., B.I.S., B.M., B.M.Ed., B.S.N., and B.S.W. degrees. Associate, master's, and doctoral degrees are also awarded. Bachelor's degrees are awarded in AGRICULTURE (agriculture, horticulture, and wildlife management), BIOLOGICAL SCIENCE (biology/biological science and microbiology), BUSINESS (accounting, banking and finance, business administration and management, and marketing/retailing/merchandising), COMMUNICATIONS AND THE ARTS (apparel design, art, broadcasting, dramatic arts, English, French, journalism, music, performing arts, public relations, Spanish, and speech/debate/rhetoric), COMPUTER AND PHYSICAL SCIENCE (chemistry, computer programming, computer science, geology, mathematics, and statistics), EDUCATION (art education, business education, education of the deaf and hearing impaired, elementary education, foreign languages education, health education, home economics education, industrial arts education, middle school education, music education, physical education, secondary education, special education, and technical education), ENGINEERING AND ENVIRONMENTAL DESIGN (airline piloting and navigation, construction technology, environmental science, interior design, and manufacturing technology), HEALTH PROFESSIONS (environmental health science, health care administration, nursing, and occupational therapy), SOCIAL SCIENCE (anthropology, child care/child and family studies, corrections, dietetics, economics, fire protection, forensic studies, geography, history, paralegal studies, philosophy, political science/government, psychology, social work, and sociology). Occupational therapy, psychology, and nursing are the strongest academically. Education, nursing, and law enforcement have the largest enrollments.

ACTIVITIES: There are 230 groups on campus, including art, band, cheerleading, choir, chorale, chorus, computers, dance, debate, drama, drill team, ethnic, film, honors, international, jazz band, LGBT, marching band, musical theater, newspaper, orchestra, pep band, photography, political, professional, radio and TV, religious, social service, student government, and symphony. Popular campus events include International Month, and Fraternity/Sorority Competitions. **Sports:** There are 8 intercollegiate sports for men and 9 for women, and 12 intramural sports for men and 12 for women. Facilities include a dance studio, gyms, outdoor and indoor swimming pools, outdoor hard-courts and indoor tennis courts, handball and racquetball courts, training rooms, martial arts room, wellness center, basketball arena, a stadium, an 8-lane outdoor track, a field hockey area, an 18-hole golf course, fields for baseball, softball, and soccer, weight facilities, and a conditioning center. **Graduates:** From July 1, 2016 to June 30, 2017, 2532 bachelor's degrees were awarded. The most popular majors were criminal justice and police studies (9%), nursing (9%), and curriculum and instruction (9%).

SERVICES: Counseling and information services are available, as is tutoring in some subjects, such as math, English, and reading. There is a reader service for the blind, and remedial math, reading, and writing. **Library/Resources:** The library contains 764,662 volumes, 1.3 million microform items, and 12,209 audio/video tapes/CDs/DVDs, and subscribes to 19,033 periodicals including electronic. Computerized library services include interlibrary loans, database searching, Internet access, and Wi-Fi capability. Special learning facilities include an art gallery, planetarium, radio station, TV station, a law enforcement complex that includes a training tank for underwater rescue and recovery. **Physically Challenged Students:** 85% of the campus is accessible. Facilities include wheelchair ramps, elevators, special parking, specially equipped restrooms, special class scheduling, lowered drinking fountains, and lowered telephones. **Special:** EKU offers cooperative programs with all academic colleges, internships, study abroad in various European countries, and a 3-2 engineering degree with the University of Kentucky or Auburn University. Students may opt for credit by exam, non-degree study, pass/fail options, student-designed and dual majors, and a general studies degree. There are 23 national honor societies, Phi Beta Kappa, a freshman honors program, and 1 departmental honors programs. **Visiting:** There are regularly scheduled orientations for prospective students, consisting of a 1-day program during the summer prior to fall enrollment. There are guides for informal visits, visitors may sit in on classes, and stay overnight. To schedule a visit, contact the Admissions Office. **Campus Safety and Security:** Measures include 24-hour foot and vehicle patrol, emergency notification system, self-defense education, and security escort services. There are shuttle buses, emergency telephones, lighted pathways/sidewalks, and 16 crime-prevention programs.

REQUIREMENTS: The ACT is required. A GPA of 2.0 is required. AP and CLEP credits are accepted. All students must complete 51 credit hours of general education requirements, including courses in phys ed, health, English, natural science, social science, math, and the humanities. Students must complete a total of 128 credit hours, including 45 to 60 credits in the major, with a minimum GPA of 2.0. **Procedure:** Freshmen are admitted to all sessions. Entrance exams should be taken prior to enrollment. There is a rolling admissions plan. Applications should be filed by August 1 for fall entry. The fall 2017 application fee was $35. Applications are accepted on-line. **Transfer Students:** 1075 transfer students enrolled in 2016-2017. Applicants must have a 2.0 cumulative GPA from all accredited institutions previously attended and must not have been dismissed. 30 of 120 credits required for the bachelor's degree must be completed at EKU. **International Students:** There are 159 international students enrolled. They must take the TOEFL with a minimum score of 530 on the paper-based TOEFL (PBT) or 71 on the Internet-based version (iBT). They must also take the ACT, scoring 21 or the SAT for those applicants from states where the SAT is dominant.

Admissions Contact: Stephanie L. Whaley, Director of Admissions. Email: *admissions@eku.edu* Web: *www.eku.edu*

FINANCIAL AID: EKU is a member of CSS. The CSS/Profile and the college's own financial statement are required. The FAFSA code is 001963. The deadline for filing freshman financial aid applications for fall entry is April 15.

GEORGETOWN COLLEGE D-2
www.georgetowncollege.edu

Georgetown, KY 40324 (502) 863-8204 (800) 788-9985
Fax: (502) 868-7733 **Email: admissions@georgetowncollege.edu**

Full-time: 438 men, 469 women	**Faculty:** 76; IIB, --$
Part-time: 26 men, 51 women	**Ph.D.s:** 96%
Graduate: 87 men, 293 women	**Student/Faculty:** 10 to 1
Year: semesters, summer session	**Tuition:** $32,960
Room & Board: $8480	**Freshman Class:** 2145 applied, 1452 accepted, 282 enrolled
SAT CR/M: 494/511 **ACT:** 23	**CEEB CODE:** 1249
Application Deadline: August 1	**COMPETITIVE**

Georgetown College, dating back to 1787 and chartered in 1829, is a small residential liberal arts college distinguished by a combination of respected, rigorous undergraduate and graduate programs, an array of opportunities for involvement and leadership, a commitment to Christian values and its distinctive heritage. There is 1 undergraduate school and 1 graduate school. In addition to regional accreditation, GC has baccalaureate program accreditation with CAEP, ACS, and CAATE. The 104-acre campus is in a suburban area 12 miles north of Lexington just off I-75. It is about an hour from Louisville and Cincinnati. Including any residence halls, there are 42 buildings.

STUDENT LIFE: 74% of undergraduates are from Kentucky. Others are from 30 states, and 11 foreign countries. 85% are from public schools. 79% are White; 3% Hispanic; 3% race unknown; 2% Foreign; 2% two or more races; 10% African American; 1% Asian American. 81% are Protestant; 11% Catholic. **Female To Male Ratio:** 1.5:1. The average age of freshmen is 18; all undergraduates, 20. 28% do not continue beyond their first year; 57% remain to graduate. **Housing:** 1325 students can be accommodated in college housing, which includes married student dorms and on-campus apartments. In addition, there are fraternity houses and sorority houses. On-campus housing is guaranteed for all 4 years. 91% of students live on campus. Alcohol is not permitted. All students may keep cars.

FACULTY/CLASSROOMS: 50% of faculty are male; 50% are female. 92% teach undergraduates, 20% do research, and 20% do both. No introductory courses are taught by graduate students. The average class size in an introductory lecture is 14 and in a regular course is 12.

PROGRAMS OF STUDY: GC confers B.A. and B.S. degrees. Master's degrees are also awarded. Bachelor's degrees are awarded in BIOLOGICAL SCIENCE (biochemistry and biology/biological science), BUSINESS (accounting, banking and finance, business administration and management, business economics, international business management, management information systems, marketing/retailing/merchandising, and sports management), COMMUNICATIONS AND THE ARTS (art, communications, creative writing, dramatic arts, English, fine/studio arts, general, French, music, performing arts, and Spanish), COMPUTER AND PHYSICAL SCIENCE (chemistry, mathematics, and physics), EDUCATION (athletic training, elementary education, English education, foreign languages education, history education, mathematics education, middle school education, secondary education, and social studies secondary school education), ENGINEERING AND ENVIRONMENTAL DESIGN (environmental science and preengineering), HEALTH PROFESSIONS (exercise science, predentistry, premedicine, prepharmacy, and prephysical therapy), SOCIAL SCIENCE (American studies, economics, European studies, family/juvenile justice, history, interdisciplinary studies, justice and society, liberal arts/general studies, philosophy, political science/government, prelaw, psychology, religion, safety and security technology, and sociology). Biology, chemistry, and psychology are the strongest academically. Kinesiology, psychology, and education have the largest enrollments.

ACTIVITIES: 27% of men belong to 1 local and 4 national fraternities; 35% of women belong to 5 national sororities. There are 98 groups on campus, including Christian leadership scholars, equine scholars, art, band, cheerleading, choir, chorale, chorus, communications, computers, dance, drama, environmental, ethnic, forensics, honors, international, jazz band, literary magazine, musical theater, newspaper, pep band, photography, political, professional, radio and TV, religious, social, social service, and student government. Popular campus events include Songfest, Chapel Day/Bid Day, Belle of the Blue, Midnight Brunch, Grubfest, Family Weekend, and Hanging of the Green. **Sports:** There are 8 intercollegiate sports for men and 11 for women, and 11 intramural sports for men and 11 for women. Facilities include a stadium, tennis courts, soccer, baseball, football, softball and intramural fields, a gym, racquetball courts, a training room, and a fitness center housing a Nautilus area, a weight lifting area, and basketball courts. **Graduates:** From July 1, 2016 to June 30, 2017, 224 bachelor's degrees were awarded. The most popular majors were business/marketing (13%), biological/life sciences (12%), and communication and media studies (12%). In an average class, 51% graduate in 4 years or less, 60% graduate in 5 years or less, and 67% graduate in 6 years or less.

SERVICES: Counseling and information services are available, as is tutoring in every subject. **Library/Resources:** The library contains 150,279 volumes, 238,214 microform items, and 11,204 audio/video tapes/CDs/DVDs, and subscribes to 43,132 periodicals including electronic. Computerized library services include interlibrary loans, database searching, Internet access, and Wi-Fi capability. Special learning facilities include an art gallery, planetarium, radio station, center for civic engagement, center for solids analysis and a writing lab. **Physically Challenged Students:** 70% of the campus is accessible. Facilities include wheelchair ramps, elevators, special parking, specially equipped restrooms, special class scheduling, and lowered drinking fountains. **Special:** Georgetown offers an innovative Spanish Immersion program, and cross-registration with the University of Kentucky for Army and Air Force ROTC for aerospace studies. A 3-2 engineering degree and nursing degree are available with the University of Kentucky. Internships, co-op programs in math, political science and other areas, and study abroad in 28 countries, a dual degree at Oxford University, work-study programs, student-designed majors, and pass/fail options are available. Interdisciplinary majors of all kinds, frequently including business administration, communication arts, psychology and religion combinations among others are designed by students. A dual BA/BTh degree is offered in religion with Regents Park College of Oxford University. There are 20 national honor societies and a freshman honors program. **Visiting:** There are regularly scheduled orientations for prospective students, consisting of campus tours and information on admissions, financial assistance, student life, academic programs, and meetings with faculty. There are guides for informal visits, visitors may sit in on classes, and stay overnight. To schedule a visit, contact Terri Hulette at (800) 788-9985. **Campus Safety and Security:** Measures include 24-hour foot and vehicle patrol, emergency notification system, self-defense education, and security escort services. There are shuttle buses, emergency telephones, lighted pathways/sidewalks, and controlled access to dorms/residences.

REQUIREMENTS: ACT or SAT required. Applicants should have completed 4 high school credits in English, 3 each in math and science, 2 in a foreign language, and 1 each in social studies and history, with additional credits in electives strongly encouraged. A student essay is required; Kentucky high school applicants may substitute a writing portfolio entry. A GPA of 2.0 is required. AP and CLEP credits are accepted. Important factors in the admissions decision are advanced placement or honors courses, evidence of special talent, extracurricular activities record, and leadership record. All students are required to complete the Foundations and Core curriculum, a general education program including courses from several disciplines across campus emphasizing writing, quantitative skills, world languages, wellness, science and inquiry, religion, and culture. A minimum of 120 semester hours, including 24 to 42 in the major, with a minimum GPA of 2.0, is required to graduate, as is successful completion of a comprehensive exam in the major. **Procedure:** Freshmen are admitted to all sessions. Entrance exams should be taken during December of the junior year through October of the senior year. There are early decision and rolling admissions plans. Early decision applications should be filed by October 15; regular applications, by August 1 for fall entry. Notification is sent on a rolling basis. Applications are accepted on-line. **Transfer Students:** 46 transfer students enrolled in 2016-2017. Applicants must be in good standing at the school most recently attended and must submit official college and sometimes high school transcripts. 30 of 120 credits required for the bachelor's degree must be completed at GC. **International Students:** There are 14 international students enrolled. They must take the TOEFL with a minimum score of 520 on the paper-based TOEFL (PBT) or 68 on the Internet-based version (iBT).

ADMISSIONS: 68% of the 2017-2018 applicants were accepted. The SAT scores for the 2017-2018 freshman class were: Critical Reading--57% below 500, 29% between 500 and 599, and 14% between 600 and 699. Math-- 43% below 500, 46% between 500 and 599, and 11% between 600 and 699. The ACT scores were 4% between 12 and 17, 50% between 18 and 23, 39% between 24 and 29, and 7% above 30. 40% of the current freshmen were in the top fifth of their class; 69% were in the top two fifths. 10 freshmen graduated first in their class. **Admissions Contact:** Jonathan Sands Wise, Vice President for Enrollment Management. Email: *admissions@georgetowncollege.edu* Web: *www.georgetowncollege.edu*

FINANCIAL AID: In 2017-2018, 100% of all full-time freshmen received some form of financial aid. 86% of all full-time freshmen received need-based aid. The average freshman award was $29,516. Need-based scholarships or need-based grants averaged $26,011 ($41,290 maximum); need-based self-help aid (loans and jobs) averaged $2,799 ($8,500 maximum); non-need-based athletic scholarships averaged $7,089 ($29,147 maximum); and other non-need-based awards and non-need-based scholarships averaged $13,174 ($38,690 maximum). 61% of undergraduate students work part-time. The average financial indebtedness of the 2017 graduate was $31,267. The FAFSA code is 001964. The priority date for freshman financial aid applications for fall entry is February 1.

KENTUCKY CHRISTIAN UNIVERSITY *(The complete profile is made available exclusively on our website, www.barronspac.com)*

KENTUCKY STATE UNIVERSITY *(The complete profile is made available exclusively on our website, www.barronspac.com)*

KENTUCKY WESLEYAN COLLEGE *(The complete profile is made available exclusively on our website, www.barronspac.com)*

LINDSEY WILSON COLLEGE D-3

www.lindsey.edu

Columbia, KY 42728 (270) 384-8100
(800) 264-0138

Fax: (270) 384-8591
Email: admissions@lindsey.edu

Full-time: 759 men, 1159 women	**Faculty:** 88
Part-time: 48 men, 101 women	**Ph.D.s:** 52%
Graduate: 97 men, 399 women	**Student/Faculty:** 22 to 1
Year: semesters, summer session	**Tuition:** $24,246
Room & Board: $9300	**Freshman Class:** n/av
ACT: required	**CEEB CODE:** 1409
Application Deadline: open	**COMPETITIVE**

Lindsey Wilson College, founded in 1903, is a private liberal arts college affiliated with the United Methodist Church, offering undergraduate programs in arts and sciences, business administration, education, human services, and pre-health. There are 3 undergraduate schools and 1 graduate school. In addition to regional accreditation, LWC has baccalaureate program accreditation with CAEP. The 45-acre campus is in a small town 100 miles southeast of Louisville. Including any residence halls, there are 45 buildings.

STUDENT LIFE: 84% of undergraduates are from Kentucky. Others are from 30 states, 34 foreign countries, and Canada. 8% are African American; 63% White; 26% race unknown; 1% Asian American; 1% Hispanic; 1% two or more races. 50% are Protestant. **Female To Male Ratio:** 1.8:1. The average age of freshmen is 18; all undergraduates, 22. 43% do not continue beyond their first year; 33% remain to graduate. **Housing:** 1150 students can be accommodated in college housing, which includes dorms and on-campus apartments. In addition, there are honors houses. On-campus housing is guaranteed for all 4 years, is available on a first-come, first-served basis, and is available on a lottery system for upperclassmen. 50% of students commute. Alcohol is not permitted. All students may keep cars.

FACULTY/CLASSROOMS: 42% of faculty are male; 58% are female. All teach undergraduates. No introductory courses are taught by graduate students. The average class size in an introductory lecture is 20; in a laboratory is 20; and in a regular course is 20.

PROGRAMS OF STUDY: LWC confers B.A., B.S.N., and B.S. degrees. Associate, master's, and doctoral degrees are also awarded. Bachelor's degrees are awarded in BIOLOGICAL SCIENCE (biology/biological science), BUSINESS (accounting, business administration and management, and recreation and leisure services), COMMUNICATIONS AND THE ARTS (art, communications, English, media arts, and theatre studies), COMPUTER AND PHYSICAL SCIENCE (mathematics), EDUCATION (art education, elementary education, music education, and secondary education), HEALTH PROFESSIONS (nursing), SOCIAL SCIENCE (American studies, criminal justice, history, human services, liberal arts/general studies, ministries, psychobiology, psychology, and social science). Human services and biology are the strongest academically. Human services, business, and education have the largest enrollments.

ACTIVITIES: There are no fraternities or sororities. There are 40 groups on campus, including art, band, cheerleading, choir, chorale, chorus, computers, dance, drama, environmental, film, honors, international, jazz band, literary magazine, marching band, musical theater, newspaper, pep band, photography, political, professional, religious, social, social service, and student government. Popular campus events include Founders Day and Malvina Farkle Day (community service). **Sports:** There are 10 intercollegiate sports for men and 13 for women, and 10 intramural sports for men and 10 for women. Facilities include a sports center with a gym, health and wellness center with a weight-training room, competition swimming pool, and a sand volleyball court. **Graduates:** From July 1, 2016 to June 30, 2017, 475 bachelor's degrees were awarded. The most popular majors were human services and counseling (49%), business administration (10%), and criminal justice (7%). In an average class, 1% graduate in 3 years or less, 27% graduate in 4 years or less, 32% graduate in 5 years or less, and 33% graduate in 6 years or less.

SERVICES: Counseling and information services are available, as is tutoring in every subject. There is remedial math, reading, and writing. **Library/Resources:** The library contains 105,000 volumes, 16,000 microform items, and 5,250 audio/video tapes/CDs/DVDs, and subscribes to 16,000 periodicals including electronic. Computerized library services include interlibrary loans, database searching, Internet access, and Wi-Fi capability. Special learning facilities include an art gallery. **Physically Challenged Students:** 95% of the campus is accessible. Facilities include wheelchair ramps, elevators, special parking, specially equipped restrooms, special class scheduling, lowered drinking fountains, and special housing. **Special:** Human services majors are offered a social services practicum in their field of study. Internships, work-study programs, a Washington semester, a general studies degree, student-designed majors, and pass/fail options in some courses are available. Study abroad is possible through Lindsey in London and the Northern Ireland Exchange. There are 3 national honor societies and a freshman honors program. **Visiting:** There are regularly scheduled orientations for prospective students. There are guides for informal visits, visitors may sit in on classes, and stay overnight. To schedule a visit, contact the Admissions Office. **Campus Safety and Security:** Measures include 24-hour foot and vehicle patrol, emergency notification system, and security escort services. There are lighted pathways/sidewalks and controlled access to dorms/residences.

REQUIREMENTS: The ACT is required. Applicants should have completed 20 academic high school credits or the GED equivalent. A GPA of 2.5 is required. AP and CLEP credits are accepted. Important factors in the admissions decision are geographical diversity, recommendations by alumni, and recommendations by school officials. All students must complete 45 hours of general education core requirements, including courses in communication of ideas, math, natural science, religion, humanities, fine arts, social behavioral science, and phys ed, as well as a 1-hour personal development career seminar. A total of 120 semester hours, with a minimum GPA of 2.0, is required to graduate. **Procedure:** Freshmen are admitted to all sessions. Entrance exams should be taken during the junior year. There is a rolling admissions plan. Application deadlines are open. Applications are accepted on-line. **Transfer Students:** 68 transfer students enrolled in 2016-2017. Transfer applicants are required to submit an official transcript from schools previously attended. An interview is recommended. 120 of 120 credits required for the bachelor's degree must be completed at LWC. **International Students:** There are 87 international students enrolled. They must take the TOEFL with a minimum score of 450 on the paper-based TOEFL (PBT) or 45 on the Internet-based version (iBT). They must also take the SAT or ACT.

ADMISSIONS: 7 freshmen graduated first in their class. **Admissions Contact:** Charity Ferguson, Director of Admissions. Email: *admissions@lindsey.edu* Web: *www.lindsey.edu*

FINANCIAL AID: In 2017-2018, 100% of all full-time freshmen received some form of financial aid, and need-based aid. The average freshman award was $25,889. Need-based scholarships or need-based grants averaged $21,869 ($37,272 maximum); and need-based self-help aid (loans and jobs) averaged $6,528 ($28,289 maximum). LWC is a member of CSS. The FAFSA code is 001972. The priority date for freshman financial aid applications for fall entry is November 1.

MIDWAY UNIVERSITY *(The complete profile is made available exclusively on our website, www.barronspac.com)*

MOREHEAD STATE UNIVERSITY *(The complete profile is made available exclusively on our website, www.barronspac.com)*

MURRAY STATE UNIVERSITY — B-4

www.murraystate.edu

Murray, KY 42071 — **(270) 809-3750**, **(800) 272-4678**

Fax: (270) 809-3780 — **Email: msu.admissions@murraystate.edu**

Full-time: 2749 men, 3862 women	**Faculty:** 412; IIA, --$
Part-time: 731 men, 1294 women	**Ph.D.s:** 79%
Graduate: 515 men, 866 women	**Student/Faculty:** 16 to 1
Year: semesters, summer session	**Tuition:** $8820 ($23,820)
Room & Board: $8906	**Freshman Class:** 6900 applied, 5980 accepted, 1443 enrolled
SAT CR/M: 525/565 **ACT:** 24	**CEEB CODE:** 1494
Application Deadline: August 17	**COMPETITIVE+**

Murray State University, founded in 1922, is a regionally accredited, four-year public institution that places its highest priority on student learning and excellence in teaching in order to afford students the range of educational opportunities experienced at research institutions while maintaining the nurturing student-teacher environment of a smaller university. Comprised of 4 colleges and 2 schools, MSU offers 126 programs in the broad areas of agriculture, business, education and human service, humanities and fine arts, science, engineering and technology, nursing, and health professions. In addition to regional accreditation, MSU has baccalaureate program accreditation with AACSB, ABET, ACEJMC, CSWE, NASAD, NASM, CAEP, ACEND, ACS, AVMA, CAATE, CAEP, CAAHEP, CCNE, CACREP, COA, MPCAC, CAA, and NAST. The 253-acre campus is in a small town 115 miles northwest of Nashville, Tennessee in Murray, Kentucky. Including any residence halls, there are 92 buildings.

STUDENT LIFE: 69% of undergraduates are from Kentucky. Others are from 47 states, 55 foreign countries, and Canada. 82% are White; 6%

African American; 3% Foreign; 3% two or more races; 3% race unknown; 2% Hispanic; 1% Asian American. **Female To Male Ratio:** 1.5:1. The average age of freshmen is 18; all undergraduates, 22. 26% do not continue beyond their first year; 74% remain to graduate. **Housing:** 2938 students can be accommodated in college housing, which includes single-sex, coed, married student dorms, on-campus apartments, and honors houses. On-campus housing is guaranteed for all 4 years, and is available on a first-come, first-served basis. 67% of students commute. Alcohol is not permitted. All students may keep cars.

FACULTY/CLASSROOMS: 53% of faculty are male; 47% are female. 98% teach undergraduates. No introductory courses are taught by graduate students.

PROGRAMS OF STUDY: MSU confers B.A., B.S., B.A.B., B.S.B., B.F.A., B.I.S., B.M., B.S.A., B.S.N., B.S.E., and B.S.W. degrees. Associate, master's, and doctoral degrees are also awarded. Bachelor's degrees are awarded in AGRICULTURE (agricultural business management, agricultural mechanics, agricultural sciences, agronomy, equine science, and horticulture), BIOLOGICAL SCIENCE (biology/adolescence education, biology/biological science, forensic science, marine biology, molecular biology, nutrition, and wildlife biology), BUSINESS (accounting, business administration and management, business communications, business intelligence and analytics, entrepreneurial studies, finance, finance (financial planning), human resources/organizational management, international business, integrative studies, management science, marketing, nonprofit/public organization management, recreation and leisure services, and supply chain management), COMMUNICATIONS AND THE ARTS (advertising, art history, creative writing, English literature, French, German, graphic design & media, instrumental music education, Japanese, journalism, keyboard - piano concentration, music, music business management, music composition, music performance, public relations, radio/television technology, Spanish, studio art, telecommunications systems management, theatre arts, and vocal music education), COMPUTER AND PHYSICAL SCIENCE (applied mathematics, applied physics, chemistry, chemistry/adolescence education, chemistry/chemical biology, computer information systems, computer science, earth science, earth science/adolescence education, environmental geology, mathematics, mathematics-actuarial concentration, physics, and polymer science), EDUCATION (agricultural education, art education, athletic training, early childhood education, elementary education, English education, foreign languages education, health information management, health and physical education, history education, home economics education, industrial arts education, marketing and distribution education, mathematics education, middle school education, physical science secondary school education, social studies secondary school education, Spanish education K-12, specific learning disabilities, teaching English as a second/foreign language (TESOL/TEFOL), and technical education), ENGINEERING AND ENVIRONMENTAL DESIGN (agricultural engineering technology, architectural technology, civil engineering technology, construction technology, electrical/electronics engineering technology, engineering graphics & design, engineering physics, environmental engineering technology, interior design, manufacturing technology, and occupational safety and health), HEALTH PROFESSIONS (biomedical science, community health work, exercise science, nursing, nutrition and dietetics, pre-health studies, predentistry, premedicine, preoptometry, pre-occupational therapy, prepharmacy, pre-physician assistant, prephysical therapy, preveterinary science, speech pathology/audiology, and veterinary technology), SOCIAL SCIENCE (archeology, criminal justice, economics, food production/management/services, geography information science, history, international studies, liberal arts, sciences, general studies, humanities, philosophy, philosophy (aesthetics/media writing), philosophy (history/contemporary thought), philosophy (political thought), philosophy and religion, political science/government, psychology, public administration, social work, and sociology). Telecommunications systems management, occupational safety and health, and accounting are the strongest academically. Nursing, animal health technology, and agriculture have the largest enrollments.

ACTIVITIES: 17% of men belong to 12 national fraternities; 16% of women belong to 11 national sororities. There are 162 groups on campus, including Student Ambassadors, art, band, cheerleading, chess, choir, chorale, chorus, communications, computers, dance, debate, drama, drill team, environmental, ethnic, film, forensics, honors, international, jazz band, LGBT, literary magazine, marching band, musical theater, newspaper, opera, orchestra, pep band, photography, political, professional, radio and TV, religious, social, social service, student government, symphony, and Veteran Student Organization. Popular campus events include Presidential Lecture Series, All-Campus Sing, Campus Lights, Alpha Phi Alpha Step-Off, Mr. MSU, Miss MSU, Homecoming and Related Festivities, Take Back the Night, Alliance Drag Show, and NPHC Step Show. **Sports:** There are 6 intercollegiate sports for men and 9 for women, and 15 intramural sports for men and 15 for women. Facilities include a recreation and wellness center that includes a 5 lane pool, 3 full-size basketball courts, 2 racquetball courts, indoor track, cardio and weight areas, 3 dance/aerobic studios, group fitness classes, and a fitness assessment center. Athletic and recreation facilities include a football stadium, a sports arena and special events center, an exposition center, golf course, soccer fields, baseball fields, rifle range, volleyball courts, basketball courts, tennis courts, and a fitness trail. **Graduates:** From July 1, 2016 to June 30, 2017, 1699 bachelor's degrees were awarded. The most popular majors were integrated studies (7%), nursing (7%), and agriculture (6%). In an average class, 25% graduate in 4 years or less, 43% graduate in 5 years or less, and 49% graduate in 6 years or less.

SERVICES: Counseling and information services are available, as is tutoring in most subjects. There is a reader service for the blind, and remedial math, reading, and writing. Student tutoring/mentoring program available for students with documented learning and/or physical disabilities. **Library/Resources:** The library contains 525,804 volumes, 38 microform items, and 16,082 audio/video tapes/CDs/DVDs, and subscribes to 974 periodicals including electronic. Computerized library services include interlibrary loans, database searching, Internet access, and Wi-Fi capability. Special learning facilities include an art gallery, radio station, TV station, writing center, oral communications center, mathematical studies and career center, speech and hearing clinic, voice and swallowing research clinic, gifted studies, environmental education, counseling and assessment center, curriculum materials center, Kentucky Academy of Technology Education, Kentucky Center for School Safety, recruitment and retention center, student success center, teacher education services, teacher quality institute, musculoskeletal evaluation lab, therapeutic interventions lab, an arboretum, Hancock Biological Station, watershed studies institute, mapping application and resource center, Wrather West Kentucky Museum, Robert E. Johnson Theatre, the performing arts hall, center for economic education, 4 agricultural research farms, greenhouses, farm shop, rodeo barn, swine unit, animal health technology center, Cherry Agricultural Exposition Center, and MSU Equine Center. **Physically Challenged Students:** Facilities include wheelchair ramps, elevators, special parking, specially equipped restrooms, special class scheduling, lowered drinking fountains, lowered telephones, and special housing. Accommodations and services for students are provided by the Office of Student Disability Services. Accommodations for faculty, staff, and students are facilitated by the Office of Institutional Diversity, Equity, and Access. **Special:** Students can pursue double majors in any bachelors degree programs, and design interdisciplinary majors in the Liberal Arts and Integrated Studies programs. MSU emphasizes experiential learning opportunities, including internships, co-ops, service learning, student teaching, and study abroad courses in several countries. Cross-registration is available through the National Student Exchange. Work-study opportunities are also available. There are 22 national honor societies and a freshman honors program. **Visiting:** There are regularly scheduled orientations for prospective students, students are invited to attend sessions planned before all academic terms for which they are first enrolling. These sessions contain both academic and social orientation. There are guides for informal visits and visitors may sit in on classes. To schedule a visit, contact Shawn Smee at ssmee@murraystate.edu. **Campus Safety and Security:** Measures include 24-hour foot and vehicle patrol, emergency notification system, self-defense education, and security escort services. There are shuttle buses, emergency telephones, lighted pathways/sidewalks, controlled access to dorms/residences, and LiveSafe app (a mobile app that allows students to contact campus police to report crimes, request an escort, or report emergencies).

REQUIREMENTS: Each applicant must have an official high school transcript that includes a minimum of 6 semesters of coursework, a list of senior-year courses, and the student's class rank mailed/sent as a PDF file by email or submitted through Parchment.com. Transcript must include the date of graduation, all courses and grades, and the student's final class rank. If your high school does not rank, then the applicant's admissions status will be based on GPA and Standardized Test Scores. For unconditional admission to a baccalaureate program, students must meet the following criteria: scored at least 18 on the ACT or at least 870 on the SAT; completed pre-college high school curriculum requirements; ranked in top half of high school class or earned a GPA of 3.0 or greater; and requires no developmental courses. Those individuals who have not graduated from accredited high schools may be required to have a GED. Applicants who have attended any college (s) other than Murray State while in high school must also have official college transcripts mailed or sent electronically and must have a minimum cumulative GPA of a 2.0 on a 4.0 scale. MSU requires applicants to be in the upper 50% of their class. A GPA of 3.0 is required. AP and CLEP credits are accepted. All students must complete University Studies (general education) requirements, including courses in Oral and Written Communications, Global Awareness/Cultural Diversity/World's Artistic Traditions, Scientific Inquiry/Methodologies/Quantitative Skills, Social and Self-Awareness/Responsible Citizenship, World's Historical/Literary/Philosophical Traditions, University Studies Approved Electives, and, for the BA degree, Foreign Languages. Programs require at least 120 semester hours, with a minimum of 40 hours earned in residence (32 hours for the Bachelor of Integrated Studies). 42 of the 120 hours must be earned in courses at the 300-level or above (39 for the Bachelor of Integrated Studies). Students must complete either an area; a major plus a minor; a major plus a second major; a major plus an area. A minimum of 9 hours in the major (s), 6 hours in the minor (s), and 15 hours in the area (s), must be in upper-level courses. The baccalaureate degree candidate must have a GPA of at least 2.0: in all credits presented for graduation whether earned at Murray State or elsewhere (cumulative GPA); in all credits completed at Murray State; and in the courses for each major, minor or area. Some programs may require a cumulative GPA higher than 2.0 for graduation. **Procedure:** Freshmen are admitted to all sessions. Entrance exams should be taken before January of the enrollment year. There are early admissions, deferred admissions, and rolling admissions plans. Applications should be filed by August 17 for fall entry; January 19 for spring entry. The fall 2017 application fee was $40. Applications are accepted on-line. **Transfer Students:** 906 transfer students enrolled in 2016-2017. A student who has 24 semester hours or more of transferable degree credit, with a minimum of a 2.0 cumulative GPA on all previous courses, is eligible for admission. Applicants must be in good standing academically and financially at all previous schools attended. Students who have less than 24 hours of credit must present official copies of high school transcript and either the ACT or SAT. 40 of 120 credits required for the bachelor's degree must be completed at MSU. **International Students:** There are 285 international students enrolled. They must take the TOEFL with a minimum score of 527 on the paper-based TOEFL (PBT) or 71 on the Internet-based version (iBT). Students must take the IELTS. They must also take the SAT or ACT.

ADMISSIONS: 87% of the 2017-2018 applicants were accepted. The SAT scores for the 2017-2018 freshman class were: Critical Reading-- 31% below 500, 57% between 500 and 599, 6% between 600 and 699, and 6% between 700 and 800. Math-- 19% below 500, 56% between 500 and 599, and 25% between 600 and 699. The ACT scores were 1% between 12 and 17, 44% between 18 and 23, 43% between 24 and 29, and 12% above 30. 44% of the current freshmen were in the top fifth of their class; 71% were in the top two fifths. 66 freshmen graduated first in their class. **Admissions Contact:** Lesa Harris, Associate Director, Admissions. Email: *msu.admissions@murraystate.edu* Web: *www.murraystate.edu*

FINANCIAL AID: In 2017-2018, 96% of all full-time freshmen received some form of financial aid. 72% of all full-time freshmen received need-based aid. The average freshman award was $13,484. Need-based scholarships or need-based grants averaged $11,790 ($41,259 maximum); need-based self-help aid (loans and jobs) averaged $5,975 ($29,181 maximum); non-need-based athletic scholarships averaged $10,885 ($37,202 maximum); and other non-need-based awards and non-need-based scholarships averaged $7,227 ($35,931 maximum). 24% of undergraduate students work part-time. The average financial indebtedness of the 2017 graduate was $27,033. The college's own financial statement, and International Student's Certification of Finances are required. The FAFSA code is 001977. The priority date for freshman financial aid applications for fall entry is February 1.

NORTHERN KENTUCKY UNIVERSITY D-1

www.nku.edu

Highland Heights, KY 41099 — (859) 572-5220, (800) 637-9948

Fax: (859) 572-6665 — **Email:** admitnku@nku.edu

Full-time: 4332 men, 5064 women
Part-time: 1034 men, 1221 women
Graduate: 797 men, 1398 women
Year: semesters, summer session
Room & Board: $7750
SAT CR/M/W: 505/505/480 **ACT:** 23
Application Deadline: August 18

Faculty: IIA, --$
Ph.D.s: 72%
Student/Faculty: 19 to 1
Tuition: $8736 ($17,472)
Freshman Class: 6957 applied, 6489 accepted, 2193 enrolled
CEEB CODE: 1574
COMPETITIVE

Northern Kentucky University, founded in 1968, is a publicly controlled institution offering undergraduate and graduate programs in arts and sciences, business, health professions, informatics, and education and human services. The figures given in the above capsule and in this profile are approximate. There are 5 undergraduate schools and 6 graduate schools. In addition to regional accreditation, NKU has baccalaureate program accreditation with AACSB, ABET, ACCE, CSWE, NASM, CAEP, NLN, NASPAA, CAATE, and JRCERT. The 424-acre campus is in a suburban area in Highland Heights, Kentucky, 7 miles southeast of Cincinnati, Ohio. Including any residence halls, there are 41 buildings.

STUDENT LIFE: 69% of undergraduates are from Kentucky. Others are from 45 states, 59 foreign countries, and Canada. 82% are White; 7% African American; 4% Foreign; 2% Hispanic; 2% two or more races; 2% race unknown; 1% Asian American. **Female To Male Ratio:** 1.2:1. The average age of freshmen is 19; all undergraduates, 13. 33% do not continue beyond their first year. **Housing:** 1820 students can be accommodated in college housing, which includes dorms and on-campus apartments, honors houses, and theme housing. On-campus housing is available on a first-come and first-served basis. 84% of students commute. Alcohol is not permitted. All students may keep cars.

FACULTY/CLASSROOMS: 54% of faculty are male; 46% are female. No introductory courses are taught by graduate students.

PROGRAMS OF STUDY: NKU confers B.A., B.S., B.M., B.S.N., B.F.A., B.H.S. and B.S.W. degrees. Associate, master's, and doctoral degrees are also awarded. Bachelor's degrees are awarded in BIOLOGICAL SCIENCE (biology/adolescence education and biology/biological science), BUSINESS (accounting, business administration and management, business information systems, entrepreneurial studies, finance, human resources, labor studies, marketing and distribution, organizational leadership and management, and sports management), COMMUNICATIONS AND THE ARTS (communications, dramatic arts, English, fine arts, French, German, Japanese, journalism, music, music composition, music performance, public relations, radio/television technology, Spanish, speech/debate/rhetoric, studio art, and theatre arts), COMPUTER AND PHYSICAL SCIENCE (chemistry, chemistry/adolescence education, computer engineering technology, computer information technology, computer science, geology, information sciences and systems, mathematics, physics, radiological technology, science, and statistics), EDUCATION (athletic training, business education, early childhood education, elementary education, English education, industrial arts education, mathematics education, middle school education, music education, physical education, secondary education, Spanish adolescense education, and special education), ENGINEERING AND ENVIRONMENTAL DESIGN (architectural engineering, construction management, construction technology, electrical/electronics engineering technology, environmental science, manufacturing engineering, manufacturing technology, and mechanical engineering technology), HEALTH PROFESSIONS (exercise science, health science, medical technology, mental health/human services, nursing, predentistry, premedicine, preoptometry, prepharmacy, prephysical therapy, and preveterinary science), SOCIAL SCIENCE (anthropology, criminal justice, economics, forensic studies, geography, history, liberal arts/general studies, philosophy, political science/government, prelaw, psychology, public administration, public history/archives, social science, social studies, social work, sociology, and women's studies). Organizational leadership, computer information technology, and nursing have the largest enrollments.

ACTIVITIES: 7% of men belong to 7 national fraternities; 10% of

women belong to 7 national sororities. There are 221 groups on campus, including mock trial club, leadership, recreational, special interest, art, cheerleading, choir, chorale, chorus, computers, cultural, dance, drama, drill team, environmental, ethnic, film, honors, international, jazz band, LGBT, literary magazine, musical theater, newspaper, pep band, photography, political, professional, radio and TV, religious, social, social service, and student government. Popular campus events include Welcome Week, Freshfusion, Pumpkin Bust, Feast4Finals and Homecoming. **Sports:** There are 8 intercollegiate sports for men and 9 for women, and 12 intramural sports for men and 13 for women. Facilities include a gym, baseball and soccer fields, tennis and racquetball courts, a track, weight room, and swimming pool. **Graduates:** From July 1, 2016 to June 30, 2017, 2143 bachelor's degrees were awarded. The most popular majors were business/marketing (26%), health professions and related programs (12%), communication/journalism, and education (9%). In an average class, 14% graduate in 4 years or less, 31% graduate in 5 years or less, and 38% graduate in 6 years or less.

SERVICES: Counseling and information services are available, as is tutoring in most subjects. There is a reader service for the blind, and remedial math, reading, and writing. There are also developmental education courses. **Library/Resources:** The library contains 925,652 volumes, 620,179 microform items, 20,088 audio/video tapes/CDs/DVDs, and subscribes to 51,986 periodicals including electronic. Computerized library services include interlibrary loans, database searching, Internet access, and Wi-Fi capability. Special learning facilities include an art gallery, planetarium, radio station, TV station, a digitorium, herbarium, and the anthropology museum. **Physically Challenged Students:** All of the campus is accessible. Facilities include wheelchair ramps, elevators, special parking, specially equipped restrooms, special class scheduling, lowered drinking fountains, lowered telephones, and special housing. **Special:** A 3-2 engineering degree is offered with the University of Kentucky. Cross-registration is possible through the Greater Cincinnati Area Consortium of colleges and universities. Study abroad in 34 countries, a Washington semester, on-campus work-study programs, an accelerated degree program, an interdisciplinary honors program, B.A.-B.S. degrees, dual majors, student designed majors credit for work experience, and pass/fail options are offered. There are co-op programs in most majors. Non-degree study is possible. There are 14 national honor societies, a freshman honors program, and 9 departmental honors programs. **Visiting:** There are regularly scheduled orientations for prospective students, consisting of a 1-day program with sessions on student services and financial aid, activities, a campus tour, and academic information, advising, and registration. There are guides for informal visits, visitors may sit in on classes, and stay overnight. To schedule a visit, contact the Office of Admissions. **Campus Safety and Security:** Measures include 24-hour foot and vehicle patrol, emergency notification system, and security escort services. There are shuttle buses, emergency telephones, lighted pathways/sidewalks, controlled access to dorms/residences, and ALICE training.

REQUIREMENTS: The SAT or ACT is required. 16 academic units are required, 24 is recommended including 4 in English, 3 each in math, and science, (with 1 unit of lab), and social studies, 2 in foreign language, recommended units are 5 in academic electives, 1 each in history, computer science, and visual/performing arts. A GPA of 2.0 is required. AP and CLEP credits are accepted. Important factors in the admissions decision are leadership record, advanced placement or honors courses, recommendations by alumni, and recommendations by school officials. All students must complete 37 semester hours of general studies, including communication--written and oral, mathematics/statistics, natural sciences, culture, self & society, and global viewpoints, along with major and minor requirements. A total of 120 semester hours, with a minimum GPA of 2.0, is required to graduate. **Procedure:** Freshmen are admitted fall, spring, and summer. Entrance exams should be taken prior to enrollment. There are deferred admissions and rolling admissions plans. Early decision applications should be filed by February 1; regular applications, by August 18 for fall entry. The fall 2017 application fee was $40. Applications are accepted on-line. **Transfer Students:** 671 transfer students enrolled in 2016-2017. Students must be eligible to return to their previous institution. College transcripts from previous institutions are required. 30 of 120 credits required for the bachelor's degree must be completed at NKU. **International Students:** There are 504 international students enrolled. They must take the TOEFL with a minimum score of 86 on the Internet-based version (iBT).

ADMISSIONS: 93% of the 2017-2018 applicants were accepted. The SAT scores for the 2017-2018 freshman class were: Critical Reading-- 47% below 500, 38% between 500 and 599, 12% between 600 and 699, and 4% between 700 and 800. Math-- 46% below 500, 36% between 500 and 599, 14% between 600 and 699, and 3% between 700 and 800. Writing-- 55% below 500, 34% between 500 and 599, 7% between 600 and 699, and 4% between 700 and 800. **Admissions Contact:** Melissa Gorbrandt, Director of Admissions. Email: *admitnku@nku.edu* Web: *www.nku.edu*

FINANCIAL AID: In 2017-2018, 71% of all full-time freshmen received some form of financial aid and need-based aid. The average freshman award was $11,120. Need-based scholarships or need-based grants averaged $5,869; need-based self-help aid (loans and jobs) averaged $4,139; non-need-based athletic scholarships averaged $12,510; other non-need-based awards and non-need-based scholarships averaged $5,334; and $3,388 from other forms of aid. The average financial indebtedness of the 2017 graduate was $27,594. The college's own financial statement is required. The FAFSA code is 009275. The priority date for freshman financial aid applications for fall entry is March 1.

SPALDING UNIVERSITY D-2

www.spalding.edu

Louisville, KY 40203 — **(502) 873-4177** **(800) 896-8941**

Fax: (502) 992-2418 — **Email: admissions@spalding.edu**

Full-time: 254 men, 666 women	**Faculty:** n/av
Part-time: 130 men, 266 women	**Ph.D.s:** n/av
Graduate: 201 men, 805 women	**Student/Faculty:** n/av
Year: other, summer session	**Tuition:** $24,338
Room & Board: $7600	**Freshman Class:** 1469 applied, 736 accepted, 196 enrolled
SAT or ACT: required	**CEEB CODE:** 1552
Application Deadline: n/av	**COMPETITIVE**

Spalding University, established in 1814, is a private institution affiliated with the Roman Catholic Church. Today this urban, co-educational institution offers over 24 degree programs at the bachelor's, master's and doctoral level, providing quality, real-world learning in liberal and professional studies. There are 11 undergraduate schools and 9 graduate schools. In addition to regional accreditation, SU has baccalaureate program accreditation with ACBSP, CSWE, CAEP, NLN, APA, AACD, and CCNE. The 24-acre campus is in an urban area in downtown Louisville, KY. Including any residence halls, there are 14 buildings.

STUDENT LIFE: 80% of undergraduates are from Kentucky. Others are from 41 states, 3 foreign countries, and Canada. 60% are White; 3% Hispanic; 3% two or more races; 17% African American; 16% race unknown; 1% Asian American. **Female To Male Ratio:** 3.0:1. The average age of freshmen is 21; all undergraduates, 25. 27% do not continue beyond their first year; 47% remain to graduate. **Housing:** 340 students can be accommodated in college housing, which includes dorms. On-campus housing is available on a first-come and first-served basis. 88% of students commute. Alcohol is not permitted. All students may keep cars.

FACULTY/CLASSROOMS: No introductory courses are taught by graduate students.

PROGRAMS OF STUDY: SU confers B.A., B.S., B.S.N. and B.F.A. degrees. Associate, master's, and doctoral degrees are also awarded. Bachelor's degrees are awarded in BUSINESS (accounting, business administration and management, human resources, and marketing), COMMUNICATIONS AND THE ARTS (communication rhetoric/communication, creative writing, media arts, and studio art), COMPUTER AND PHYSICAL SCIENCE (natural sciences), EDUCATION (education, elementary education, middle school education, and secondary education), HEALTH PROFESSIONS (health science, nursing, and occupational therapy), SOCIAL SCIENCE (humanities and social science, liberal arts/general studies, psychology, social science, and social work). Nursing, art, and business have the largest enrollments.

ACTIVITIES: There are 25 groups on campus, including art, chorale, dance, ethnic, honors, LGBT, literary magazine, professional, religious, social, social service, and student government. Popular campus events include Annual Running of the Rodents, Scholarship and Learning Day, HOOPLA, Pelican Ball, and UAM Halloween Party. **Sports:** There are 7 intercollegiate sports for men and 9 for women. Facilities include a gym with an exercise room. **Graduates:** From July 1, 2016 to June 30, 2017, 221 bachelor's degrees were awarded. The most popular majors were nursing (7%), art (6%), and business (6%).

SERVICES: Counseling and information services are available, as is tutoring in every subject. There is remedial math, reading, and writing. **Library/Resources:** The library contains 473,838 volumes, and 76,469 audio/video tapes/CDs/DVDs, and subscribes to 19,300 periodicals including electronic. Computerized library services include interlibrary loans, database searching, Internet access, and Wi-Fi capability. Special learning facilities include an art gallery, a writing center and mathematics lab. **Physically Challenged Students:** 90% of the campus is accessible. Facilities include wheelchair ramps, elevators, special parking, specially equipped restrooms, special class scheduling, lowered drinking fountains. **Special:** Internships, study abroad, B.A. - B.S. degrees, dual majors, work-study programs, and accelerated degree programs in business, psychology, and nursing are available. The Adult Accelerated Program enables students to earn a bachelor's degree by attending classes on weekends and evenings. Credit is given for military experience and pass/fail options are available. Cross-registration is offered with the Kentuckiana Metroversity Consortium. There are 8 national honor societies. **Visiting:** There are regularly scheduled orientations for prospective students, New Student Orientation, AAP Orientation, Graduate Program Specific Orientation. There are guides for informal visits, visitors may sit in on classes, and stay overnight. To schedule a visit, contact the Office of University Admission at (502) 585-7111. **Campus Safety and Security:** Measures include 24-hour foot and vehicle patrol, emergency notification system, and security escort services. There are emergency telephones, lighted pathways/sidewalks, controlled access to dorms/residences, emergency call boxes, camera surveillance in campus buildings and parking lots, and direct access to campus security from campus phones.

REQUIREMENTS: The SAT or ACT is required. Applicants must be graduates of an accredited secondary school and should have completed 4 years of high school English and 2 years each of a foreign language, math, science, and social studies. A GED may be substituted for the high school degree. A GPA of 2.5 is required. AP and CLEP credits are accepted. Important factors in the admissions decision are advanced placement or honors courses, recommendations by school officials, and extracurricular activities record. To graduate, students must earn 120 credits and a minimum overall GPA of 2.0. All students must complete a university studies requirement (average 51 credits) in humanities, social sciences, communication, natural sciences and math, religious studies, and one general introduction course to the college. **Procedure:** Freshmen are admitted to all sessions. There are early admissions, deferred admissions, and rolling admissions plans. Application deadlines are open. The fall 2017 application fee was $20. Notification is sent on a rolling basis. Applications are accepted on-line. **Transfer Students:** 110 transfer students enrolled in 2016-2017. It is preferred that applicants have a 2.5 GPA. Anyone wishing to transfer to Spalding University from another college or university must submit the following documents to the Admissions Office: the completed application with the nonrefundable $20 application fee; proof of high school graduation (or official GED test score report); an official transcript from each college and/or university previously attended; a scan or photocopy of the applicant's state-issued driver's license or state-issued identification card. 30 of 120 credits required for the bachelor's degree must be completed at SU. **International Students:** There are 3 international students enrolled. They must take the TOEFL with a minimum score of 535 on the paper-based TOEFL (PBT) or 75 on the Internet-based version (iBT). They must also take the SAT or ACT, scoring 20.

ADMISSIONS: 50% of the 2017-2018 applicants were accepted. **Admissions Contact:** Matthew Elder, Director of Undergraduate Admissions. Email: *admissions@spalding.edu* Web: *www.spalding.edu*

FINANCIAL AID: The FAFSA code is 001960. The deadline for filing freshman financial aid applications for fall entry is January 1.

THOMAS MORE COLLEGE *(The complete profile is made available exclusively on our website, www.barronspac.com)*

TRANSYLVANIA UNIVERSITY — D-3
www.transy.edu

Lexington, KY 40508 — (859) 233-8242, (800) 872-6798

Fax: (859) 233-8797 — **Email:** admissions@transy.edu

Full-time: 381 men, 578 women	**Faculty:** 82; IIB, av$
Part-time: 3 men, 1 women	**Ph.D.s:** 96%
Graduate: n/av	**Student/Faculty:** 11 to 1
Year: 4-1-4, summer session	**Tuition:** $37,290
Room & Board: $10,160	**Freshman Class:** 1567 applied, 1496 accepted, 283 enrolled
SAT CR/M: 647/621 **ACT:** 27	**CEEB CODE:** 1808
Application Deadline: February 1	**HIGHLY COMPETITIVE+**

Transylvania University, founded in 1780, is an independent liberal arts institution affiliated with the Christian Church (Disciples of Christ). Through an engagement with the liberal arts, Transylvania prepares its students for a humane and fulfilling personal and public life by cultivating independent thinking, open-mindedness, creative expression, and commitment to lifelong learning and social responsibility in a diverse world. There is 1 undergraduate school. The 70-acre campus is in an urban area in the historic district of downtown Lexington. Including any residence halls, there are 33 buildings.

STUDENT LIFE: 78% of undergraduates are from Kentucky. Others are from 30 states, and 7 foreign countries. 85% are from public schools. 79% are White; 5% Hispanic; 4% African American; 4% two or more races; 4% race unknown; 3% Foreign; 1% Asian American. 25% are Protestant; 24% Christian, Mormon, Muslim, Orthodox, and Buddhist; 18% claim no religious affiliation; 16% Catholic. **Female To Male Ratio:** 1.5:1. The average age of freshmen is 18; all undergraduates, 20. 16% do not continue beyond their first year; 75% remain to graduate. **Housing:** 925 students can be accommodated in college housing, which includes dorms and on-campus apartments. On-campus housing is guaranteed for all 4 years. 76% of students live on campus. All students may keep cars.

FACULTY/CLASSROOMS: 54% of faculty are male; 46% are female. All teach undergraduates. No introductory courses are taught by graduate students. The average class size in an introductory lecture is 18; in a laboratory is 14; and in a regular course is 18.

PROGRAMS OF STUDY: TU confers B.A. degrees. Bachelor's degrees are awarded in BIOLOGICAL SCIENCE (biochemistry, biology/biological science, and neurosciences), BUSINESS (accounting and business administration and management), COMMUNICATIONS AND THE ARTS (art history, art, classics, dramatic arts, English, French, Germanic languages and literature, music, music technology, Spanish, studio art, and theatre arts), COMPUTER AND PHYSICAL SCIENCE (chemistry, computer science, mathematics, and physics), EDUCATION (education, elementary education, and middle school education), HEALTH PROFESSIONS (exercise science), SOCIAL SCIENCE (anthropology, economics, history, philosophy, political science/government, psychology, religion, and sociology). Exercise science, business, and psychology have the largest enrollments.

ACTIVITIES: 50% of men belong to 4 national fraternities; 54% of women belong to 4 national sororities. There are 60 groups on campus, including art, band, cheerleading, choir, chorale, chorus, computers, dance, debate, drama, environmental, ethnic, forensics, honors, international, jazz band, LGBT, literary magazine, musical theater, newspaper, opera, orchestra, pep band, political, professional, radio and TV, religious, social, social service, student government, and yearbook. **Sports:** There are 12 intercollegiate sports for men and 15 for women, and 10 intramural sports for men and 10 for women. Facilities include a performance gym, a fitness center with an indoor jogging track, a swimming pool, basketball courts, tennis courts, and athletic fields for baseball, field hockey, lacrosse, soccer, softball, and track/field. **Graduates:** From July 1, 2016 to June 30, 2017, 216 bachelor's degrees were awarded. The most popular majors were exercise science (10%), business (9%), and psychology (9%). In an average class, 1% graduate in 3 years or less, 66% graduate in 4 years or less, 74% graduate in 5 years or less, and 76% graduate in 6 years or less. Of the 2016 graduating class, 36% were enrolled in graduate school within 6 months of graduation, and 50% were employed.

SERVICES: Counseling and information services are available, as is

tutoring in every subject. Academic Center for Excellence (ACE) provides additional help for students when needed. **Library/Resources:** The library contains 334,492 volumes, 59 microform items, 3,976 audio/video tapes/CDs/DVDs, and subscribes to 19,000 periodicals including electronic. Computerized library services include interlibrary loans, database searching, Internet access, and Wi-Fi capability. Special learning facilities include an art gallery, a natural history museum, and a radio station. **Physically Challenged Students:** 90% of the campus is accessible. Facilities include wheelchair ramps, elevators, special parking, specially equipped restrooms, special class scheduling, lowered drinking fountains. Arrangements are made according to individual needs. **Special:** 3-2 engineering degrees with the University of Kentucky and Vanderbilt University are offered, along with a pre-engineering partnership with the University of Kentucky. Internships, study abroad, work-study programs, a Washington semester, dual majors, and student-designed majors are available. There are 9 national honor societies. **Visiting:** There are regularly scheduled orientations for prospective students, consisting of campus open houses in fall and winter for high school juniors and seniors, including a welcome program, an academic information fair, campus tours, a luncheon, a financial aid session, and a faculty session. There are guides for informal visits, visitors may sit in on classes, and stay overnight. To schedule a visit, contact Office of Admissions. **Campus Safety and Security:** Measures include 24-hour foot and vehicle patrol, emergency notification system, self-defense education, and security escort services. There are shuttle buses, emergency telephones, lighted pathways/sidewalks, and controlled access to dorms/residences.

REQUIREMENTS: Transylvania is Test Optional. Applicants are required to be in the upper 50% of their class. A GPA of 2.0 is required. AP credits are accepted. Important factors in the admissions decision are advanced placement or honors courses, recommendations by school officials, and extracurricular activities record. The university believes that all students, no matter what career or vocation they choose, benefit from liberal education; and so the college encourages the free search for knowledge and understanding drawn from the natural and social sciences, the humanities, and the arts. The university strives to empower students to develop lifelong habits of learning and intelligent, respectful discussion. Therefore, students must fulfill requirements in five general areas: Area I Introduction to Critical Skills, Area II Approaches to Learning, Area III Cultural Traditions, Area IV Upper-level Liberal Arts (2+2), and Area V Writing Intensive Courses. **Procedure:** Freshmen are admitted to all sessions. Entrance exams should be taken during the junior year and no later than December of the senior year for scholarship consideration or February for general admission. There are early admissions, deferred admissions, and rolling admissions plans. Early decision applications should be filed by October 15; regular applications, by February 1 for fall entry; and December 1 for winter entry. Notification of early decision is sent December 1; regular decision, March 15. Applications are accepted on-line. **Transfer Students:** 13 transfer students enrolled in 2016-2017. Applicants must have a minimum college GPA of 2.75 and should submit official copies of all college transcripts, 2 recommendations, and 1 essay. A high school transcript or GED is required. 18 of 36 credits required for the bachelor's degree must be completed at TU. **International Students:** There are 26 international students enrolled. They must take the TOEFL and either the SAT or ACT.

ADMISSIONS: 95% of the 2017-2018 applicants were accepted. The SAT scores for the 2017-2018 freshman class were: Critical Reading-- 4% below 500, 15% between 500 and 599, 56% between 600 and 699, and 26% between 700 and 800. Math-- 4% below 500, 33% between 500 and 599, 44% between 600 and 699, and 19% between 700 and 800. The ACT scores were 13% between 18 and 23, 55% between 24 and 29, and 32% above 30. 61% of the current freshmen were in the top fifth of their class; 85% were in the top two fifths. **Admissions Contact:** Holly Sheilley, VP for Enrollment and Student Affairs. Email: *admissions@transy.edu* Web: *www.transy.edu*

FINANCIAL AID: In 2017-2018, 99% of all full-time freshmen received some form of financial aid. 78% of all full-time freshmen received need-based aid. The average freshman award was $29,177. Need-based scholarships or need-based grants averaged $25,956 ($47,450 maximum); need-based self-help aid (loans and jobs) averaged $4,167 ($9,500 maximum); and other non-need-based awards and non-need-based scholarships averaged $17,309 ($47,450 maximum). 50% of undergraduate students work part-time. The average financial indebtedness of the 2017 graduate was $30,595. TU is a member of CSS. The FAFSA code is 001987. The priority date for freshman financial aid applications for fall entry is October 1.

UNION COLLEGE — E-4

www.unionky.edu

Barbourville, KY 40906	**(606) 546-1612** **(800) 489-8646**
Fax: (606) 546-1667	**Email: enrollme@unionky.edu**
Full-time: 455 men, 398 women	**Faculty:** 50
Part-time: 18 men, 41 women	**Ph.D.s:** 46%
Graduate: 76 men, 147 women	**Student/Faculty:** 17 to 1
Year: semesters, summer session	**Tuition:** $25,060
Room & Board: $7250	**Freshman Class:** 1389 applied, 925 accepted, 263 enrolled
SAT or ACT: required	**CEEB CODE:** 1825
Application Deadline: open	**COMPETITIVE**

Union College, founded in 1879, is a private liberal arts institution affiliated with the United Methodist Church. There are 4 undergraduate schools and 1 graduate school. In addition to regional accreditation, UC has baccalaureate program accreditation with CAEP, CCNE, and and CAATE. The 100-acre campus is in a small town 95 miles south of Lexington, Kentucky and 85 miles north of Knoxville, Tennessee. Including any residence halls, there are 20 buildings.

STUDENT LIFE: 66% of undergraduates are from Kentucky. Others are from 35 states, 17 foreign countries, and Canada. 70% are White; 6% Foreign; 4% two or more races; 3% Hispanic; 15% African American; 1% race unknown. **Female To Male Ratio:** 1.1:1. The average age of freshmen is 20; all undergraduates, 22. 36% do not continue beyond their first year; 32% remain to graduate. **Housing:** 472 students can be accommodated in college housing, which includes married student dorms, on-campus apartments, and off-campus apartments. On-campus housing is guaranteed for all 4 years, and is available on a first-come, first-served basis. 52% of students live on campus. Alcohol is not permitted. All students may keep cars.

FACULTY/CLASSROOMS: 56% of faculty are male; 44% are female. 90% teach undergraduates. No introductory courses are taught by graduate students. The average class size in an introductory lecture is 25 and in a regular course is 20.

PROGRAMS OF STUDY: UC confers B.A. and B.S. degrees. Master's degrees are also awarded. Bachelor's degrees are awarded in BIOLOGICAL SCIENCE (biology/biological science), BUSINESS (accounting, business administration and management, international business management, marketing management, organizational leadership and management, recreational facilities management, and sports management), COMMUNICATIONS AND THE ARTS (communications, dramatic arts, English, and fine arts), COMPUTER AND PHYSICAL SCIENCE (chemistry and mathematics), EDUCATION (athletic training, education, elementary education, middle school education, physical education, science education, secondary education, social studies education, and special education), ENGINEERING AND ENVIRONMENTAL DESIGN (computer technology), HEALTH PROFESSIONS (exercise science, health, and nursing), SOCIAL SCIENCE (criminal justice, history, Latin American studies, ministries, psychology, religion, social work, and sociology). Education, business, and nursing are the strongest academically and have the largest enrollments.

ACTIVITIES: There are no fraternities or sororities. There are 31 groups on campus, including cheerleading, choir, chorale, chorus, computers, drama, ethnic, honors, international, LGBT, literary magazine, pep band, professional, radio and TV, religious, social, social service, student government, and yearbook. Popular campus events include Springfest, Student Holiday Dinner, and CIRCLES Ceremony. **Sports:** There are 14 intercollegiate sports for men and 13 for women, and 5 intramural sports for men and 3 for women. Facilities include a campus stadium, a gym, an indoor pool, tennis courts, a weight-training center, an athletic training center, baseball stadium with batting cages and a practice infield, a soccer field, softball field, and practice fields for football and soccer. **Graduates:** From July 1, 2016 to June 30, 2017, 133 bachelor's degrees were awarded. The most popular majors were education (13%), health professions and related programs (13%), and business (8%). In an average class, 1% graduate in 3 years or less, 16% graduate in 4 years or less, 28% graduate in 5 years or less, and 32% graduate in 6 years or less.

SERVICES: Counseling and information services are available, as is tutoring in most subjects. There is a reader service for the blind, and remedial math, reading, and writing. There is a tutoring lab with computer support. **Library/Resources:** The library contains 108,583 volumes, 123,928 microform items, and 3,432 audio/video tapes/CDs/DVDs, and subscribes to 365,525 periodicals including electronic. Computerized library services include interlibrary loans, database searching, Internet access, and Wi-Fi capability. Special learning facilities include a radio station. **Physically Challenged Students:** 85% of the campus is accessible. Facilities include wheelchair ramps, elevators, special parking, specially equipped restrooms, special class scheduling, and lowered drinking fountains. **Special:** Work-study programs, study abroad in 7 countries, an accelerated business degree completion program, and internships in business, sociology, psychology, recreational management, and mass communications are available. There are 2 national honor societies and a freshman honors program. **Visiting:** There are regularly scheduled orientations for prospective students, consisting of advising and registration, parent sessions, and break-out sessions. There are guides for informal visits, visitors may sit in on classes, and stay overnight. To schedule a visit, contact Sam Lee at slee@unionky.edu. **Campus Safety and Security:** Measures include 24-hour foot and vehicle patrol, emergency notification system, self-defense education, and security escort services. There are emergency telephones, lighted pathways/sidewalks, controlled access to dorms/residences, The campus web site has a notification system (alert system) that provides information about recent crimes on campus.

REQUIREMENTS: The SAT or ACT is required. Standardized text scores are not required for students 25 of older. All first-year students should have completed a pre-college high school curriculum that includes 4 units of English, 3 of math, 2 each of lab science and social science, and the study of a foreign language. An official, sealed high school transcript or an official GED score report is also required. A GPA of 2.0 is required. AP and CLEP credits are accepted. Important factors in the admissions decision are evidence of special talent, geographical diversity, and advanced placement or honors courses. All students are required to complete 43 credits in a liberal education core, including 21 hours in humanities, 7 to 8 of general science, 6 of social science, and 3 each of wellness, math, and cultural studies. **Procedure:** Freshmen are admitted to all sessions. Entrance exams should be taken by January of the senior year. There are deferred admissions and rolling admissions plans. Application deadlines are open. The fall 2017 application fee was $10. Notification is sent on a rolling basis. Applications are accepted on-line. **Transfer Students:** 92 transfer students enrolled in 2016-2017. Applicants should have a minimum GPA of 2.0. 32 of 120 credits required for the bachelor's degree must be completed at UC. **International Students:** There are 58 international students enrolled. They must take the TOEFL with a minimum score of 550 on the paper-based TOEFL (PBT) and the college's own test, and complete an ELS program at level 109. They must also take the SAT or ACT, scoring 18.

ADMISSIONS: 67% of the 2017-2018 applicants were accepted. The ACT scores were 22% between 12 and 17, 61% between 18 and 23, 16% between 24 and 29, and 1% above 30. **Admissions Contact:** Meghann Chestnut, Director of Undergraduate Enrollment. Email: *enrollme@unionky.edu* Web: *www.unionky.edu*

FINANCIAL AID: In 2017-2018, 100% of all full-time freshmen received some form of financial aid. 84% of all full-time freshmen received need-based aid. The average freshman award was $22,100. Need-based scholarships or need-based grants averaged $18,282; need-based self-help aid (loans and jobs) averaged $3,550; and other non-need-based awards and non-need-based scholarships averaged $5,587. The average financial indebtedness of the 2017 graduate was $22,348. Union is a member of CSS. The CSS/Profile is required. The FAFSA code is 001988. The priority date for freshman financial aid applications for fall entry is November 15.

UNIVERSITY OF KENTUCKY D-3

www.uky.edu

Lexington, KY 40506 **(859) 257-2000**

Fax: (859) 257-3823
Full-time: 9420 men, 11352 women
Part-time: 755 men, 717 women
Graduate: 3069 men, 3744 women
Year: semesters, summer session
Room & Board: $12,858

SAT CR/M/W: 560/565/545 **ACT:** 26
Application Deadline: February 15

Email: admissions@uky.edu
Faculty: 1388; I, -$
Ph.D.s: 92%
Student/Faculty: 17 to 1
Tuition: $11,942 ($28,046)
Freshman Class: 20480 applied, 18593 accepted, 5117 enrolled
CEEB CODE: 1837
COMPETITIVE+

University of Kentucky, founded in 1865, is a public land-grant institution offering undergraduate and graduate programs in a variety of areas. There are 13 undergraduate schools and 1 graduate school. In addition to regional accreditation, UK has baccalaureate program accreditation with AACSB, ABET, ACEJMC, ACPE, ADA, AHEA, APTA, ASLA, CAHEA, CSWE, FIDER, NAAB, NASAD, NASM, CAEP, NLN, NRPA, and SAF. The 764-acre campus is in a suburban area 75 miles south of Cincinnati. Including any residence halls, there are 335 buildings.

STUDENT LIFE: 62% of undergraduates are from Kentucky. Others are from 49 states, 114 foreign countries, and Canada. 8% are African American; 79% White; 4% Hispanic; 4% two or more races; 3% Asian American; 3% Foreign; 3% race unknown. **Female To Male Ratio:** 1.2:1. The average age of freshmen is 18; all undergraduates, 21. 19% do not continue beyond their first year; 58% remain to graduate. **Housing:** 6166 students can be accommodated in college housing, which includes married student dorms and on-campus apartments. In addition, there are honors houses, language/international houses, special-interest houses, fraternity houses, and sorority houses. On-campus housing is available on a first-come and first-served basis. 74% of students commute. Alcohol is not permitted. All students may keep cars.

FACULTY/CLASSROOMS: 60% of faculty are male; 40% are female. No introductory courses are taught by graduate students.

PROGRAMS OF STUDY: UK confers B.A., B.S., B.Arch., B.B.A., B.F.A., B.H.S. and B.M. degrees. Master's and doctoral degrees are also awarded. Bachelor's degrees are awarded in AGRICULTURE (agricultural economics, agriculture, animal science, and forestry and related sciences), BIOLOGICAL SCIENCE (biology/biological science, botany, and zoology), BUSINESS (accounting, banking and finance, business economics, hotel/motel and restaurant management, and marketing/retailing/merchandising), COMMUNICATIONS AND THE ARTS (advertising, art history and appreciation, arts administration/management, communications, dramatic arts, English, French, German, Italian, journalism, linguistics, music, music performance, Russian, Spanish, and telecommunications), COMPUTER AND PHYSICAL SCIENCE (chemistry, computer science, geology, mathematics, and physics), EDUCATION (agricultural education, art education, business education, early childhood education, elementary education, foreign languages education, health education, mathematics education, middle school education, music education, physical education, science education, secondary education, social studies education, and special education), ENGINEERING AND ENVIRONMENTAL DESIGN (chemical engineering, civil engineering, electrical/electronics engineering, landscape architecture/design, materials engineering, mechanical engineering, and mining and mineral engineering), HEALTH PROFESSIONS (nursing, physical therapy, and physician's assistant), SOCIAL SCIENCE (anthropology, economics, food science, geography, history, Latin American studies, philosophy, political science/government, psychology, social work, sociology, and textiles and clothing). Pharmacy, architecture, and allied health are the strongest academically. Finance, accounting, and marketing have the largest enrollments.

ACTIVITIES: 16% of men belong to 24 national fraternities; 25% of women belong to 19 national sororities. There are 272 groups on campus, including band, cheerleading, chess, choir, chorale, chorus, computers, dance, debate, drama, drill team, environmental, ethnic, honors, international, jazz band, LGBT, literary magazine, marching band, musical theater, newspaper, orchestra, pep band, photography, political, professional, radio and TV, religious, social, social service, student government, symphony, and yearbook. Popular campus events include Little Kentucky Derby, Cultural Diversity Week, and Spotlight Jazz Series. **Sports:** There are 11 intercollegiate sports for men and 12 for women, and 22 intramural sports for men and 22 for women. Facilities include a football stadium, an arena for basketball and other activities, an aquatic center and swimming pool, baseball fields, a training center, indoor tennis courts, and a field house. **Graduates:** From July 1, 2016 to June 30, 2017, 4540 bachelor's degrees were awarded. The most popular majors were business/marketing, and interdisciplinary studies (33%), communication/journalism (12%), and engineering (11%). In an average class, 64% graduate in 6 years or less.

SERVICES: There is a reader service for the blind, and remedial math. **Library/Resources:** The library contains 2.8 million volumes, 5.9 million microform items, and 73,600 audio/video tapes/CDs/DVDs, and subscribes to 26,539 periodicals including electronic. Computerized library services include database searching. Special learning facilities include an art gallery, natural history museum, radio station, and TV station. **Physically Challenged Students:** 90% of the campus is accessible. Facilities include wheelchair ramps, elevators, special parking, specially equipped restrooms, special class scheduling, lowered drinking fountains, and lowered telephones. **Special:** Co-op programs are offered in engineering, business, computer science, math, and agriculture. The Academic Common Market allows students in 14 southern states to study outside the university. Internships in a variety of fields, study abroad in 36 countries, work-study programs with the university and local businesses, and credit for life experience are available. An accelerated degree program, B.A.-B.S. degrees, dual and double majors, a general studies degree, student-designed majors, a 3-2 engineering degree with several smaller schools in Kentucky, non-degree study, and pass/fail options are also offered. There are 12 national honor societies, Phi Beta Kappa, and a freshman honors program. **Visiting:** There are regularly scheduled orientations for prospective students, including a campus tour and information on admissions, housing, financial aid, and campus activities. There are guides for informal visits and visitors may sit in on classes. **Campus Safety and Security:** Measures include 24-hour foot and vehicle patrol, emergency notification system, self-defense education, and security escort services. There are shuttle buses, emergency telephones, lighted pathways/sidewalks, and controlled access to dorms/residences.

REQUIREMENTS: The SAT or ACT is required. Applicants must complete 24 high school units, 4 units in English, 3 each in math, social studies, and science (with 1 unit of lab), 2 units in foreign language, 7 in academic electives, 1 in visual/performing arts, and 1 of any other. A portfolio is required for art studio courses, and an audition is required for music performance. An application essay is also required. A GPA of 2.0 is required. AP and CLEP credits are accepted. Important factors in the admissions decision are advanced placement or honors courses and recommendations by school officials. All students must maintain a minimum 2.0 GPA and complete at least 120 credit hours. Students must demonstrate competency in math, foreign language, writing, and oral communications. Required studies include courses in basic skills, inference, and communicative skills, along with disciplinary and cross-disciplinary studies. **Procedure:** Freshmen are admitted to all sessions. Entrance exams should be taken before December of the senior year. There is a rolling admissions plan. Applications should be filed by February 15 for fall entry. The fall 2017 application fee was $50. **Transfer Students:** 897 transfer students enrolled in 2016-2017. Transfer students need a minimum GPA of 2.0. If they have fewer than 24 credit hours, they must meet freshmen admission standards. With 24 credits or more, the SAT I or ACT is not required. College transcripts and a statement of good standing from prior institution (s). 30 of 120 credits required for the bachelor's degree must be completed at UK. **International Students:** There are 366 international students enrolled. They must take the TOEFL.

ADMISSIONS: 91% of the 2017-2018 applicants were accepted. The SAT scores for the 2017-2018 freshman class were: Critical Reading-- 23% below 500, 42% between 500 and 599, 24% between 600 and 699, and 11% between 700 and 800. Math-- 22% below 500, 39% between 500 and 599, 27% between 600 and 699, and 12% between 700 and 800. Writing-- 28% below 500, 44% between 500 and 599, 21% between 600 and 699, and 7% between 700 and 800. **Admissions Contact:** Steven Barnett, Associate Director for Admissions. Email: *admissions@uky.edu* Web: *www.uky.edu*

FINANCIAL AID: 32% of all full-time freshmen received need-based aid. The average freshman award was $6,007. UK is a member of CSS. The FAFSA code is 001989. The deadline for filing freshman financial aid applications for fall entry is February 15.

UNIVERSITY OF LOUISVILLE — D-2
www.louisville.edu

Louisville, KY 40292	**(502) 852-6531** **(800) 334-8635**
Fax: (502) 852-4476	**Email: admitme@louisville.edu**
Full-time: 5694 men, 6372 women	**Faculty:** 1814; I, -$
Part-time: 1989 men, 1684 women	**Ph.D.s:** 71%
Graduate: 2800 men, 3124 women	**Student/Faculty:** 16 to 1
Year: semesters, summer session	**Tuition:** $11,264 ($26,286)
Room & Board: $8428	**Freshman Class:** 10992 applied, 8252 accepted, 2661 enrolled
SAT CR/M: 543/546 **ACT:** required	**CEEB CODE:** 1838
Application Deadline: n/av	**COMPETITIVE**

University of Louisville is a state supported research university. The Health Sciences Center is situated in downtown Louisville's medical complex and houses the university's health related programs and the University of Louisville Hospital. There are 8 undergraduate schools and 12 graduate schools. In addition to regional accreditation, UL has baccalaureate program accreditation with AACSB, ABET, ACCE, ADA, CSWE, NASM, ABA, CCNE, CEPH, CIDA, COAES, COSMA, NAST, CAEP, and ACS. The 1183-acre campus is in an urban area of Louisville, KY. Including any residence halls, there are 206 buildings.

STUDENT LIFE: 80% of undergraduates are from Kentucky. Others are from 50 states, 59 foreign countries, and Canada. 82% are from public schools. 72% are White; 5% Hispanic; 5% two or more races; 4% Asian American; 3% Foreign; 11% African American. **Female To Male Ratio:** 1.1:1. The average age of freshmen is 18; all undergraduates, 24. 19% do not continue beyond their first year; 79% remain to graduate. **Housing:** 7044 students can be accommodated in college housing, which includes single sex, coed dorms, married student dorms, on-campus apartments, and off-campus apartments. In addition, there are honors houses, special-interest houses, living learning communities and themed communities. On-campus housing is guaranteed for the freshman year only. 83% of students commute. All students may keep cars.

FACULTY/CLASSROOMS: 56% of faculty are male; 44% are female. No introductory courses are taught by graduate students.

PROGRAMS OF STUDY: UL confers B.A., B.M., B.S., B.S.B., B.S.N., and B.S.W degrees. Associate, master's, and doctoral degrees are also awarded. Bachelor's degrees are awarded in AGRICULTURE (equine science), BIOLOGICAL SCIENCE (biology/biological science), BUSINESS (accounting, banking and finance, business administration and management, business economics, entrepreneurial studies, management science, marketing/retailing/merchandising, and sports management), COMMUNICATIONS AND THE ARTS (American Sign Language, art history, art, art history and appreciation, communications, dramatic arts, English, French, linguistics, music, Spanish, and theatre arts), COMPUTER AND PHYSICAL SCIENCE (atmospheric sciences and meteorology, chemistry, computer science, information sciences and systems, mathematics, and physics), EDUCATION (art education, Asian studies, business education, early childhood education, elementary education, foreign languages education, middle school education, music education, physical education, science education, secondary education, and teaching English as a second/foreign language (TESOL/TEFOL), ENGINEERING AND ENVIRONMENTAL DESIGN (bioengineering, chemical engineering, civil engineering, computer engineering, electrical/electronics engineering, engineering, engineering management, industrial engineering, and mechanical engineering), HEALTH PROFESSIONS (dental hygiene, health, medical laboratory technology, medical science, music therapy, nursing, and public health), SOCIAL SCIENCE (anthropology, clinical psychology, criminal justice, geography, history, humanities, liberal arts/general studies, paralegal studies, philosophy, political science/government, psychology, public administration, social work, sociology, and women's studies). Engineering, health professional, and business management are the strongest academically. Arts and sciences, education and human development, and engineering have the largest enrollments.

ACTIVITIES: 20% of men belong to 19 national fraternities; 18% of women belong to 14 national sororities. There are 458 groups on campus, including art, band, cheerleading, chess, choir, chorale, chorus, computers, dance, debate, ethnic, honors, international, jazz band, LGBT, literary magazine, marching band, newspaper, opera, orchestra, pep band, photography, political, professional, radio and TV, religious, social, social service, student government, and symphony. Popular campus events include Homecoming, Welcome Week, International Fashion Show, and Fryberger Greek Sing. **Sports:** There are 10 intercollegiate sports for men and 13 for women, and 37 intramural sports for men and 37 for women. Facilities include a football stadium, soccer, volleyball, basketball, weight training facility, indoor practice courts for basketball, football, and volleyball, tennis center, golf course, track & field, softball, baseball, a rowing center, lacrosse, a Student Recreation Center that provides an exercise and weight facility, basketball courts, a multi-activity court, jogging track, aerobics studio, and fitness labs. **Graduates:** From July 1, 2016 to June 30, 2017, 3010 bachelor's degrees were awarded. The most popular majors were communication (7%), psychology (6%), and nursing (6%). In an average class, 1% graduate in 3 years or less, 31% graduate in 4 years or less, 49% graduate in 5 years or less, and 54% graduate in 6 years or less.

SERVICES: Counseling and information services are available, as is

tutoring in most subjects. There is a reader service for the blind, and remedial math, reading, and writing. **Library/Resources:** The library contains 2.2 million volumes, 2.3 million microform items, and 63,988 audio/video tapes/CDs/DVDs, and subscribes to 92,972 periodicals including electronic. Computerized library services include interlibrary loans, database searching, Internet access, and Wi-Fi capability. Special learning facilities include an art gallery, planetarium, and radio station. **Physically Challenged Students:** 90% of the campus is accessible. Facilities include wheelchair ramps, elevators, special parking, specially equipped restrooms, special class scheduling, lowered drinking fountains, lowered telephones, and special housing. **Special:** The university offers cross-registration with other schools, study abroad in 5 countries (China, Panama, Portugal, Trinidad, Canada), work-study programs, and B.A.-B.S. degrees. A general studies degree, nondegree study, and pass/fail options are available. Co-op programs in engineering and business and internships are also possible. There are 16 national honor societies, a freshman honors program, and 4 departmental honors programs. **Visiting:** There are regularly scheduled orientations for prospective students, admissions presentation, campus tour, and optional faculty appointments. There are guides for informal visits. To schedule a visit, contact Shelby Eisenback at shelby.eisenback@louisville.edu. **Campus Safety and Security:** Measures include 24-hour foot and vehicle patrol, emergency notification system, self-defense education, and security escort services. There are shuttle buses, emergency telephones, lighted pathways/sidewalks, and controlled access to dorms/residences.

REQUIREMENTS: The SAT or ACT is required. Applicants must be graduates from an accredited high school or have received a GED, must have completed a precollege curriculum with a GPA of 2.5, and must have at least 1 of the following: a composite ACT score of 20 or a satisfactory SAT score; completion of the University of Louisville enhanced precollege curriculum (PCC) with a minimum GPA of 2.5; or a rank in the top 15% of the high school graduating class. AP and CLEP credits are accepted. Requirements include at least 6 hours each in social sciences, natural sciences, the history of world civilizations, and humanities. Freshmen are required to take college writing or advanced composition and 2 phys ed courses. A total of 123 semester hours, including 46 to 60 hours in the major, with a minimum GPA of 2.5, 2.0 in education, 2.75 in engineering. **Procedure:** Freshmen are admitted to all sessions. Entrance exams should be taken no later than December of the senior year. There is a rolling admissions plan. Application deadlines are open. The fall 2017 application fee was $25. Applications are accepted on-line. **Transfer Students:** 1174 transfer students enrolled in 2016-2017. Transfer students must have a minimum GPA of 2.0. 30 of 123 credits required for the bachelor's degree must be completed at UL. **International Students:** There are 217 international students enrolled. They must take the TOEFL with a minimum score of 550 on the paper-based TOEFL (PBT) or 79 on the Internet-based version (iBT). Student must take the IELTS. Some programs may require proof of Calculus readiness.

ADMISSIONS: 75% of the 2017-2018 applicants were accepted. The SAT scores for the 2017-2018 freshman class were: Critical Reading-- 39% below 500, 32% between 500 and 599, 16% between 600 and 699, and 13% between 700 and 800. Math-- 27% below 500, 46% between 500 and 599, 20% between 600 and 699, and 7% between 700 and 800. The ACT scores were 1% between 12 and 17, 38% between 18 and 23, 42% between 24 and 29, and 19% above 30. **Admissions Contact:** Jenny Sawyer, Executive Director of Admissions. Email: *admitme@louisville .edu* Web: *www.louisville.edu*

FINANCIAL AID: In 2017-2018, 96% of all full-time freshmen received some form of financial aid. 48% of all full-time freshmen received need-based aid. The average freshman award was $7,772. Need-based scholarships or need-based grants averaged $1,313 ($6,472 maximum); need-based self-help aid (loans and jobs) averaged $1,696 ($2,250 maximum); non-need-based athletic scholarships averaged $2,110 ($15,046 maximum); other non-need-based awards and non-need-based scholarships averaged $2,064 ($15,000 maximum); and $2,913 from other forms of aid. The average financial indebtedness of the 2017 graduate was $27,357. The FAFSA code is 001999. The priority date for freshman financial aid applications for fall entry is February 15.

UNIVERSITY OF PIKEVILLE F-3

www.upike.edu

Pikeville, KY 41501	(606) 218-5251 (866) 232-7700
Fax: (606) 218-5255	**Email:** wewantyou@upike.edu
Full-time: 513 men, 536 women	**Faculty:** 65
Part-time: 14 men, 25 women	**Ph.D.s:** 66%
Graduate: 392 men, 384 women	**Student/Faculty:** 16 to 1
Year: semesters, summer session	**Tuition:** $20,338
Room & Board: $7500	**Freshman Class:** 2299 applied, 2299 accepted, 279 enrolled
ACT: 21	**CEEB CODE:** 1901
Application Deadline: August 15	**COMPETITIVE**

University of Pikeville is the leading higher education institution of Central Appalachia. The university enhances intellectual, cultural, and economic opportunities through educational excellence as well as involvement in community service, research, humanitarian efforts, and global outreach. There are 3 undergraduate schools and 4 graduate schools. In addition to regional accreditation, Pikeville has baccalaureate program accreditation with CSWE, ACEN, and EPSB. The 25-acre campus is in a small town 20 miles north of the Virginia border, in the eastern Kentucky hills. Including any residence halls, there are 21 buildings.

STUDENT LIFE: 80% of undergraduates are from Kentucky. Others are from 28 states, 14 foreign countries, and Canada. 98% are from public schools. 9% are African American; 86% White; 3% Foreign; 1% Asian American; 1% Hispanic. 73% are Protestant. **Female To Male Ratio:** 1.0:1. The average age of freshmen is 18; all undergraduates, 21. 43% do not continue beyond their first year; 31% remain to graduate. **Housing:** 580 students can be accommodated in college housing, which includes dorms, on-campus apartments, and off-campus apartments. On-campus housing is available on a first-come and first-served basis. 50% of students commute. Alcohol is not permitted. All students may keep cars.

FACULTY/CLASSROOMS: 49% of faculty are male; 51% are female. All teach undergraduates. No introductory courses are taught by graduate students. The average class size in an introductory lecture is 20; in a laboratory is 16; and in a regular course is 17.

PROGRAMS OF STUDY: Pikeville confers B.A., B.S., and B.B.A. degrees. Associate, master's, and doctoral degrees are also awarded. Bachelor's degrees are awarded in BIOLOGICAL SCIENCE (biology/biological science), BUSINESS (business administration and management), COMMUNICATIONS AND THE ARTS (art, communications, English, film, television and digital media, and Spanish), COMPUTER AND PHYSICAL SCIENCE (chemistry, computer science, and mathematics), EDUCATION (elementary education, middle school education, and secondary education), HEALTH PROFESSIONS (nursing), SOCIAL SCIENCE (criminal justice, history, interdisciplinary studies, political science/government, psychology, religion, social work, and sociology). English, religion, and biology are the strongest academically. Business, biology, and nursing have the largest enrollments.

ACTIVITIES: There are no fraternities or sororities. There are 25 groups on campus, including art, cheerleading, choir, dance, debate, drama, honors, newspaper, pep band, political, professional, religious, social, social service, and student government. Popular campus events include Homecoming. **Sports:** There are 10 intercollegiate sports for men and 10 for women, and 4 intramural sports for men and 4 for women. Facilities include East Kentucky Expo center, Hoops training facility, gymnasium, basketball and volleyball courts, softball and baseball fields, and a football stadium. **Graduates:** From July 1, 2016 to June 30, 2017, 211 bachelor's degrees were awarded. The most popular majors were business (22%), biology (15%), and psychology (13%). In an average class, 17% graduate in 4 years or less, 29% graduate in 5 years or less, and 31% graduate in 6 years or less. Of the 2016 graduating class, 36% were enrolled in graduate school within 6 months of graduation, and 79% were employed.

SERVICES: Counseling and information services are available, as is tutoring in most subjects, such as English, biology, math, all physical sciences, computers, accounting, social sciences, and Spanish. There is a reader service for the blind, and remedial math, reading, and writing. **Library/Resources:** The library contains 86,637 volumes, 44,680 microform items, and 2,893 audio/video tapes/CDs/DVDs, and subscribes to

117,412 periodicals including electronic. Computerized library services include interlibrary loans, database searching, Internet access, and Wi-Fi capability. Special learning facilities include an art gallery. **Physically Challenged Students:** 99% of the campus is accessible. Facilities include wheelchair ramps, elevators, special parking, specially equipped restrooms, and lowered drinking fountains. **Special:** The faculty at the University of Pikeville are committed to student engagement and learning outside the classroom. There is a constantly evolving global studies initiative on campus. The undergraduate programs continue to send students to professional conferences, immerse them in fieldwork, and place them in internships. There are 6 national honor societies and 5 departmental honors programs. **Visiting:** There are guides for informal visits, visitors may sit in on classes, and stay overnight. To schedule a visit, contact John Yancey at (606) 218-5251. **Campus Safety and Security:** Measures include 24-hour foot and vehicle patrol, emergency notification system, self-defense education, and security escort services. There are lighted pathways/sidewalks and controlled access to dorms/residences.

REQUIREMENTS: The ACT is required. Applicants must graduate from an accredited secondary school or have a GED. AP and CLEP credits are accepted. All students must complete core courses in humanities, English, social sciences, natural sciences, and math, as well as 2 courses each in religion, phys ed, and history and 1 course in computer science. Additional requirements include 6 hours in a foreign language for the B.A. degree and 2 lab science courses for the B.S. degree. An overall GPA of 2.0 is required. To graduate, students must complete 120 semester hours, with 30 to 60 hours in the major. **Procedure:** Freshmen are admitted fall, spring, and summer. There are deferred admissions and rolling admissions plans. Applications should be filed by August 15 for fall entry; January 10 for spring entry; and June 4 for summer entry. Notification is sent on a rolling basis. Applications are accepted on-line. **Transfer Students:** 109 transfer students enrolled in 2016-2017. Transfer students are required to submit official transcripts from all colleges previously attended by the designated document deadline. Admission to the university will be based on the overall GPA achieved. Applicants with a cumulative 2.0 GPA or higher (on 0-4 quality point scale) will be admitted in good standing. Transfer applicants with less than a 2.0 GPA will be reviewed for admission to the university. 30 of 120 credits required for the bachelor's degree must be completed at Pikeville. **International Students:** There are 27 international students enrolled. They must take the TOEFL. They must also take the ACT.

ADMISSIONS: 100% of the 2017-2018 applicants were accepted. The ACT scores were 22% between 12 and 17, 54% between 18 and 23, 22% between 24 and 29, and 2% above 30. 28% of the current freshmen were in the top fifth of their class; 48% were in the top two fifths. 14 freshmen graduated first in their class. **Admissions Contact:** John Yancey, Admissions Director. Email: *wewantyou@upike.edu* Web: *www.upike.edu*

FINANCIAL AID: In 2017-2018, 100% of all full-time freshmen received some form of financial aid and need-based aid. The average freshman award was $20,100. Need-based scholarships or need-based grants averaged $18,081; and need-based self-help aid (loans and jobs) averaged $2,019. 18% of undergraduate students work part-time. The average financial indebtedness of the 2017 graduate was $23,876. The FAFSA code is 001980. The priority date for freshman financial aid applications for fall entry is February 15.

UNIVERSITY OF THE CUMBERLANDS *(The complete profile is made available exclusively on our website, www.barronspac.com)*

WESTERN KENTUCKY UNIVERSITY C-4

www.wku.edu

Bowling Green, KY 42101	**(270) 745-2551** **(800) 495-8463**
Fax: (270) 745-6133	**Email: admission@wku.edu**
Full-time: 5567 men, 7352 women	**Faculty:** 754
Part-time: 1729 men, 3008 women	**Ph.D.s:** 86%
Graduate: 888 men, 1713 women	**Student/Faculty:** 18 to 1
Year: semesters, summer session	**Tuition:** $10,202 ($25,512)
Room & Board: $8350	**Freshman Class:** 9804 applied, 9358 accepted, 3116 enrolled
SAT CR/M: 510/510 **ACT:** 23	**CEEB CODE:** 1901
Application Deadline: August 1	**COMPETITIVE**

Western Kentucky University prepares students of all backgrounds to be productive, engaged, and socially responsible citizen-leaders of a global society. The university provides research, service and lifelong learning opportunities for its students, faculty, and other constituents. WKU enriches the quality of life for those within its reach. There are 6 undergraduate schools and 1 graduate school. In addition to regional accreditation, WKU has baccalaureate program accreditation with AACSB, ABET, ACEJMC, ADA, CSWE, NASAD, NASM, ACEN, ACEND, AUPHA, CAA, CAHIIM, CODA, CACREP, COAPRT, CEPH, EAC, EPSB, NAB, NASD, NAST, NASPAA, and ATMAE. The 200-acre campus is in a suburban area 65 miles north of Nashville, Tennessee and 110 miles south of Louisville, Kentucky. Including any residence halls, there are 88 buildings.

STUDENT LIFE: 79% of undergraduates are from Kentucky. Others are from 48 states, 55 foreign countries, and Canada. 8% are African American; 78% White; 4% Foreign; 3% Hispanic; 3% two or more races; 2% Asian American; 1% race unknown. **Female To Male Ratio:** 1.5:1. The average age of freshmen is 18; all undergraduates, 21. 30% do not continue beyond their first year; 50% remain to graduate. **Housing:** 5298 students can be accommodated in college housing, which includes single sex, coed dorms and on-campus apartments. In addition, there are honors houses, language/international houses, special-interest houses, and special housing for Gatton Academy students. On-campus housing is available on a first-come and first-served basis. 67% of students commute. Alcohol is not permitted. All students may keep cars.

FACULTY/CLASSROOMS: 47% of faculty are male; 53% are female. No introductory courses are taught by graduate students.

PROGRAMS OF STUDY: WKU confers B.S., B.A., B.F.A., B.I.S., B.M., B.S.N., and B.S.W. degrees. Associate, master's, and doctoral degrees are also awarded. Bachelor's degrees are awarded in AGRICULTURE (agricultural mechanics, agriculture, agronomy, dairy science, environmental studies, and horticulture), BIOLOGICAL SCIENCE (biochemistry, biology/biological science, biophysics, and genetics), BUSINESS (accounting, banking and finance, business administration and management, business (dual major program), business administration - international, business administration marketing, business communications, business economics, entrepreneurial studies, environment & national resource economics, hospitality management services, management engineering, management information systems, management science, marketing, marketing and distribution, nonprofit/public organization management, and recreation and leisure services), COMMUNICATIONS AND THE ARTS (acting, advertising, Arabic, art history, broadcasting, Chinese, classics, communication studies, communications, communications technology, dance, design, dramatic arts, English, English as a second/foreign language, film arts, fine arts, French, German, graphic design & media, journalism, language arts, literature, film and media studies, music, performing arts, public relations, Spanish, and visual and performing arts), COMPUTER AND PHYSICAL SCIENCE (actuarial science, astronomy, astronomy and physics, atmospheric sciences and meteorology, chemistry, computer science, geology, industrial technology, mathematics, and physics), EDUCATION (agricultural education, art education, Asian studies, athletic training, business education, childhood education, early childhood education, education of the exceptional child, elementary education, English secondary education, general studies, home economics education, marketing and distribution education, middle school education, physical education, physical education/exercise science, technical education, and vocational education), ENGINEERING AND ENVIRONMENTAL DESIGN (aerospace studies, agricultural engineering technology, chemical engineering, city/community/regional planning, civil engineering, civil engineering technology, computational sciences, construction management, construction mgmt/commercial/industrial, electrical/electronics engineering, electromechanical technology, industrial engineering technology, manufacturing technology, mechanical engineering, occupational safety and health, and technology and public affairs), HEALTH PROFESSIONS (allied health, biology, communicative disorders, dental hygiene, environmental health science, exercise science, health care administration, medical technology, nursing, public health, and speech pathology/audiology), SOCIAL SCIENCE (African American studies, anthropology, archeology, clinical psychology, communication sciences & disorders, criminology, crosscultural studies, cultural anthropology, economics, family and community services, family/consumer studies, geography, history, human development & family studies, liberal arts/general studies, Middle Eastern studies, paralegal studies, philosophy, political science/government, psychology, religion, social studies, social work, sociology, and textiles and clothing). Education, nursing, and business have the largest enrollments.

ACTIVITIES: There are 400 groups on campus, including art, band, cheerleading, chess, choir, chorale, chorus, communications, computers, dance, debate, drama, drill team, environmental, ethnic, film, forensics, forensics club, honors, international, jazz band, LGBT, literary magazine, marching band, musical theater, newspaper, opera, orchestra, pep band, photography, political, professional, radio and TV, religious, social, social service, student government, symphony, and yearbook. Popular campus events include Homecoming, and Cultural Enhancement Series. **Sports:** There are 6 intercollegiate sports for men and 9 for women, and 13 intramural sports for men and 13 for women. Facilities include a football stadium, a basketball arena, baseball fields, softball fields, a soccer complex, tennis courts, a weight room, a fitness room, a gym, a dance studio, racquetball courts, a swimming pool, an outdoor recreation and adventure center, and a health and fitness lab. **Graduates:** From July 1, 2016 to June 30, 2017, 2851 bachelor's degrees were awarded. The most popular majors were business/marketing (18%), health professions and related programs, and education (12%), social sciences, and communication/journalism (11%).

SERVICES: Counseling and information services are available, as is tutoring in every subject. The Student Support Services Center ensures each student has the opportunity to succeed in the classroom with the help of tutoring. There is a reader service for the blind, and remedial math, reading, and writing. **Library/Resources:** The library contains 869,321 volumes, 1.9 million microform items, and 32,047 audio/video tapes/CDs/DVDs, and subscribes to 44,000 periodicals including electronic. Computerized library services include interlibrary loans, database searching, Internet access, and Wi-Fi capability. Special learning facilities include an art gallery, planetarium, radio station, TV station, Kentucky Museum, Agriculture Research and Education Center, Biotechnology Center, Social Science Research Center, Center for Research and Development, Institute for Combustion Science and Environmental Technology Labs. **Physically Challenged Students:** 75% of the campus is accessible. Facilities include wheelchair ramps, elevators, special parking, specially equipped restrooms, special class scheduling, lowered drinking fountains, lowered telephones, and special housing. **Special:** Internships, study abroad, work-study programs, cooperative programs, and accelerated degree programs are available. There are 36 national honor societies and a freshman honors program. **Visiting:** There are regularly scheduled orientations for prospective students, campus tours, informational sessions, presentations, departmental visits, residence hall visits, and a video. There are guides for informal visits and visitors may sit in on classes. To schedule a visit, contact the Admissions Office. **Campus Safety and Security:** Measures include 24-hour foot and vehicle patrol, emergency notification system, self-defense education, and security escort services. There are shuttle buses, emergency telephones, lighted pathways/sidewalks, and controlled access to dorms/residences.

REQUIREMENTS: Students must meet one of the following requirements for admission: ACT composite of 20 or greater, SAT (math + critical reading) of 940 or higher, unweighted high school GPA of 2.50 or higher, or the required Composite Admission Index (CAI) score. AP and CLEP credits are accepted. To graduate, all students must complete at least 120 semester hours, with a varying number of hours in the major, and maintain a minimum GPA of 2.0. Curricula must meet general education requirements and meet the requirements of each student's major. **Procedure:** Freshmen are admitted to all sessions. Entrance exams should be taken by fall of the senior year. There are early admissions, deferred admissions, and rolling admissions plans. Applications should be filed by August 1 for fall entry; January 1 for spring entry; and May 1 for summer entry. The fall 2017 application fee was $45. Notification is sent on a rolling basis. Applications are accepted on-line. **Transfer Students:** 1033 transfer students enrolled in 2016-2017. Transfer students must have a minimum GPA 2.0 for the last semester or term of full-time work, a cumulative GPA of 2.0, and be in good standing at the institution from which they are transferring. Students with fewer that 24 hours earned are required to have completed the pre-college curriculum. **International Students:** There are 588 international students enrolled. They must take the TOEFL or MELAB. They must also take the SAT or ACT.

ADMISSIONS: 95% of the 2017-2018 applicants were accepted. The SAT scores for the 2017-2018 freshman class were: Critical Reading-- 41% below 500, 47% between 500 and 599, 10% between 600 and 699, and 2% between 700 and 800. Math-- 37% below 500, 47% between 500 and 599, 12% between 600 and 699, and 4% between 700 and 800. The ACT scores were 15% between 12 and 17, 42% between 18 and 23, 33% between 24 and 29, and 10% above 30. 38% of the current freshmen were in the top fifth of their class; 62% were in the top two fifths. 73 freshmen graduated first in their class. **Admissions Contact:** Dr. Jace Lux, Director of Recruitment and Admissions. Email: *admission@wku.edu* Web: *www.wku.edu*

FINANCIAL AID: In 2017-2018, 65% of all full-time freshmen received some form of financial aid. 39% of all full-time freshmen received need-based aid. The average freshman award was $13,586. Need-based scholarships or need-based grants averaged $5,387; and need-based self-help aid (loans and jobs) averaged $3,078. The average financial indebtedness of the 2017 graduate was $28,081. WKU is a member of CSS. The FAFSA code is 002002. The priority date for freshman financial aid applications for fall entry is February 15.

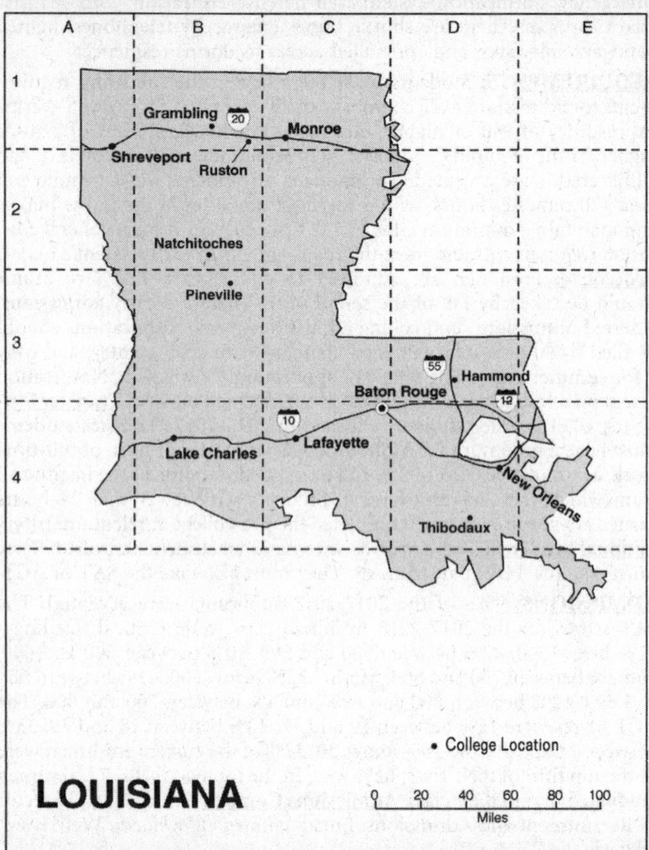

CENTENARY COLLEGE OF LOUISIANA A-1

www.centenary.edu

Shreveport, LA 71104 **(318) 869-5131**
(800) 234-4448

Fax: (318) 869-5005 **Email: admission@centenary.edu**

Full-time: 231 men, 293 women
Part-time: 3 men, 6 women
Graduate: n/av
Year: semesters, summer session
Room & Board: $13,150

SAT or ACT: required
Application Deadline: August 1

Faculty: 57; IIB, -$
Ph.D.s: 96%
Student/Faculty: 8 to 1
Tuition: $35,900
Freshman Class: 886 applied, 569 accepted, 130 enrolled
CEEB CODE: 6082
COMPETITIVE+

Centenary College of Louisiana, founded in 1825 is a private, four-year arts and sciences college affiliated with the United Methodist Church. Centenary is the oldest chartered liberal arts college west of the Mississippi River. In addition to regional accreditation, CCL has baccalaureate program accreditation with NASM and ACS. The 65-acre campus is in an urban area in the Shreveport/Bossier City located in the northwest corner of Louisiana near the Texas and Arkansas borders. Including any residence halls, there are 23 buildings.

STUDENT LIFE: 56% of undergraduates are from Louisiana. Others are from 23 states, and 9 foreign countries. 63% are White; 5% two or more races; 3% Asian American; 2% Foreign; 16% African American; 10% Hispanic; 1% American Indian/Alaska Native. **Female To Male Ratio:** 1.3:1. The average age of freshmen is 18; all undergraduates, 20. **Housing:** College-sponsored housing includes dorms, fraternity houses, and sorority houses. On-campus housing is guaranteed for all 4 years, and is available on a first-come, first-served basis. 89% of students live on campus. Alcohol is not permitted. All students may keep cars.

FACULTY/CLASSROOMS: 63% of faculty are male; 37% are female. No introductory courses are taught by graduate students. The average class size in an introductory lecture is 12 and in a laboratory is 11.

PROGRAMS OF STUDY: CCL confers B.A. and B.S. degrees. Master's degrees are also awarded. Bachelor's degrees are awarded in BIOLOGICAL SCIENCE (biochemistry, biology/biological science, biophysics, and neurosciences), BUSINESS (business administration and management and business economics), COMMUNICATIONS AND THE ARTS (art, communications, dance, dramatic arts, English, French, German, Latin, music, music performance, Spanish, and studio art), COMPUTER AND PHYSICAL SCIENCE (chemistry, geology, mathematics, and physics), ENGINEERING AND ENVIRONMENTAL DESIGN (environmental science), SOCIAL SCIENCE (economics, history, interdisciplinary studies, liberal arts/general studies, philosophy, political science/government, psychology, religion, religious music, and sociology). Biological/life sciences, business and marketing, and visual and performing arts have the largest enrollments.

ACTIVITIES: There are 60 groups on campus, including cheerleading, choir, chorale, communications, drama, environmental club, film, honors, international, jazz band, LGBT, literary magazine, musical theater, newspaper, opera, photography, political, professional, radio station, religious, social, social service, student government, symphony, and yearbook. Popular campus events include Spring Fling, President's Convocation, and Freak Week. **Sports:** There are 8 intercollegiate sports for men and 9 for women. Facilities include a gym, weight rooms, basketball, racquetball, volleyball, and tennis courts, baseball, soccer, and softball fields, a fitness center with aerobic exercise and strengthening equipment, and a natatorium. **Graduates:** From July 1, 2016 to June 30, 2017, 119 bachelor's degrees were awarded. The most popular majors were biological/life sciences (18%), business and marketing (17%), and visual and performing arts (16%). In an average class, 1% graduate in 3 years or less, 59% graduate in 4 years or less, and 55% graduate in 6 years or less.

SERVICES: Counseling and information services are available, as is tutoring in most subjects. **Library/Resources:** The library contains 155,940 volumes, and 711,952 audio/video tapes/CDs/DVDs, and subscribes to 323 periodicals including electronic. Computerized library services include interlibrary loans, database searching, and Internet access. Special learning facilities include an art gallery, a theater, and an art museum. **Physically Challenged Students:** 95% of the campus is accessible. Facilities include wheelchair ramps, elevators, special parking, specially equipped restrooms, special class scheduling, lowered drinking fountains, lowered telephones. **Special:** Centenary offers study abroad in 7 countries, cross-registration with Associated Colleges of the South, internships in all majors, a Washington semester, and a work-study program within the college. A 3-1 communications disorders degree with Louisiana State University Medical Center is possible, as is a 3-2 engineering degree with Washington University in St. Louis, University of Southern California, and Columbia University, Texas A&M University, and Case Western Reserve Universities. A 3-2 applied science preprofessional degree combines with health administration or medical school. Pre-veterinary studies, general studies and interdisciplinary degrees, and student-designed majors are available. There are 7 national honor societies and 15 departmental honors programs. **Visiting:** There are regularly scheduled orientations for prospective students, consisting of information sessions with a counselor, tour of the campus, and visit to a class or with faculty. To schedule a visit, contact Nora Fradin at nfradin@centenary.edu. **Campus Safety and Security:** Measures include 24-hour foot and vehicle patrol and security escort services. There are emergency telephones and lighted pathways/sidewalks.

REQUIREMENTS: The SAT or ACT is required. Applicants should be high school graduates. The GED is accepted. Secondary school preparation should include 15 academic credits, including 4 of English, 3 each of math and science and history, and 2 of a foreign language. Music students must audition; art students are advised to present a portfolio. A GPA of 2.0 is required. AP credits are accepted. Important factors in the admissions decision are leadership record, advanced placement or honors courses, extracurricular activities record, and personality/intangible qualities. To graduate, all students must complete 124 semester hours, with a maximum of 45 in a non-interdisciplinary major and a minimum of 30 at the upper-division level, including a writing and speaking class in the major at the junior level, and maintain a minimum GPA of 2.0. There are 48 to 52 hours of distribution requirements. Core curriculum requirements include courses in the humanities, social sciences, hard sciences, and math. In addition, freshmen must take a first year experience course. All students must complete a Trek component, study or live in a different culture, or study abroad, and fulfill career explorations. **Procedure:** Freshmen are admitted fall, spring, and summer. Entrance exams should be taken by the fall of the senior year. There are early decision, early admissions, and rolling admissions plans. Early decision applications should be filed by December 15; regular applications, by August 1 for fall entry. The fall 2017 application fee was $30. Notifications are sent September 1. Applications are accepted on-line. **Transfer Students:** 14 transfer students enrolled in 2016-2017. Transfer applicants must have a minimum GPA of 2.0 and demonstrate good performance in a liberal arts curriculum. 45 credits required for the bachelor's degree must be completed at CCL. **International Students:** There are 16 international students enrolled. They must take the TOEFL with a minimum score of 550 on the paper-based TOEFL (PBT) or 79 on the Internet-based version (iBT).

ADMISSIONS: 64% of the 2017-2018 applicants were accepted. **Admissions Contact:** Thomas Newton, Director of Admissions. Email: *admission@centenary.edu* Web: *www.centenary.edu*

FINANCIAL AID: In 2017-2018, 99% of all full-time freshmen received some form of financial aid. 77% of all full-time freshmen received need-based aid. The average freshman award was $22,432. Need-based scholarships or need-based grants averaged $19,469; need-based self-help aid (loans and jobs) averaged $4,759; other non-need-based awards and non-need-based scholarships averaged $3,403; and $17,544 from other forms of aid. 32% of undergraduate students work part-time. The average financial indebtedness of the 2017 graduate was $51,018. The FAFSA code is 002003. The priority date for freshman financial aid applications for fall entry is February 15.

DILLARD UNIVERSITY D-4

www.dillard.edu

New Orleans, LA 70122	(504) 816-4632 (800) 216-6637
Fax: 504-816-4895	Email: dpage@dillard.edu
Full-time: 624 men, 625 women	Faculty: 82
Part-time: n/av	Ph.D.s: 56%
Graduate: n/av	Student/Faculty: n/av
Year: semesters, summer session	Tuition: $15,250
Room & Board: $5690	Freshman Class: n/av
SAT or ACT: recommended	CEEB CODE: 6164
Application Deadline: n/av	VERY COMPETITIVE

Dillard University, established in 1869, is an independent, nonsectarian, liberal arts institution, affiliated with the United Church of Christ and the United Methodist Church. It offers undergraduate programs, 19 baccalaureate degrees in the colleges of arts of sciences, professional studies, and general studies. There are 2 undergraduate schools. In addition to regional accreditation, DU has baccalaureate program accreditation with NLN. The 55-acre campus is in an urban area in New Orleans. Including any residence halls, there are 21 buildings.

STUDENT LIFE: 67% of undergraduates are from Louisiana. Others are from 29 states, 12 foreign countries, and Canada. 98% are African American. **Female To Male Ratio:** 1.0:1. 28% do not continue beyond their first year. **Housing:** College-sponsored housing includes dorms, on-campus apartments, and off-campus apartments. On-campus housing is guaranteed for the freshman year only, and is available on a first-come, first-served basis, and is available on a lottery system for upperclassmen. 30% of students commute. Alcohol is not permitted. All students may keep cars.

FACULTY/CLASSROOMS: 43% of faculty are male; 57% are female. All teach undergraduates. No introductory courses are taught by graduate students. The average class size in an introductory lecture is 30.

PROGRAMS OF STUDY: DU confers B.A., B.S. and B.S.N. degrees. Bachelor's degrees are awarded in BIOLOGICAL SCIENCE (biology/biological science), BUSINESS (accounting and business administration and management), COMMUNICATIONS AND THE ARTS (art, communications, English, music, music business management, and music performance), COMPUTER AND PHYSICAL SCIENCE (chemistry, computer science, and physics), HEALTH PROFESSIONS (nursing and public health), SOCIAL SCIENCE (economics, history, political science/government, psychology, sociology, and urban studies). Biological sciences has the largest enrollment.

ACTIVITIES: 4% of men belong to 5 national fraternities; 11% of women belong to 4 national sororities. There are 64 groups on campus, including art, cheerleading, chess, choir, chorus, dance, drama, ethnic, honors, professional, religious, social service, student government, and yearbook. Popular campus events include Coronation, Avenue of the Oaks Gala, and Founder's Day. **Sports:** There are 3 intercollegiate sports for men and 3 for women. Facilities include a gym, swimming pool, nautilus room, tennis courts, dance facility, and game room. **Graduates:** From July 1, 2016 to June 30, 2017, 278 bachelor's degrees were awarded. The most popular majors were public health (16%), biology (13%), and mass communications (9%). Of the 2016 graduating class, 45% were enrolled in graduate school within 6 months of graduation, and 45% were employed.

SERVICES: Counseling and information services are available, as is tutoring in every subject. There is remedial math, reading, and writing. **Library/Resources:** The library contains 104,615 volumes, 21,638 microform items, and 426 audio/video tapes/CDs/DVDs, and subscribes to 295 periodicals including electronic. Computerized library services include interlibrary loans and database searching. Special learning facilities include an art gallery and TV station. **Physically Challenged Students:** 70% of the campus is accessible. Facilities include wheelchair ramps, elevators, special parking, specially equipped restrooms, and special class scheduling. **Special:** Opportunities are provided for internships, work-study programs, credit by exam, nondegree study, and pass/fail options. All social science majors are encouraged to pursue a double major. There is a 4-year co-op degree in music therapy with Loyola University, a clinical public health curriculum with Howard University, a 5-year joint degree in urban studies with Columbia University, and pre-engineering dual degree programs with the Georgia Institute of Technology and Auburn and Columbia Universities. There are 3 national honor societies. **Visiting:** There are regularly scheduled orientations for prospective students, scheduled on individual basis. There are guides for informal visits, visitors may sit in on classes, and stay overnight. To schedule a visit, contact Office of Admissions. **Campus Safety and Security:** Measures include 24-hour foot and vehicle patrol and emergency notification system. There are shuttle buses and lighted pathways/sidewalks.

REQUIREMENTS: The SAT or ACT is recommended. Graduation from an accredited secondary school is required; a GED will be accepted. Applicants must submit an academic record of 20 units, distributed as follows: 4 units in English, 3 each in math and natural sciences, 2 in social studies, and 8 in other academic electives. Recommendations from a high school teacher and the principal or a student counselor are required. A GPA of 2.5 is required. AP credits are accepted. Important factors in the admissions decision are recommendations by school officials, leadership record, and personality/intangible qualities. Students must successfully complete 125 semester hours and maintain a minimum overall GPA of 2.0 and a GPA of 2.0 or better in all courses in the major. In addition, all students must complete 35 semester hours in the core curriculum, which includes courses in English composition, world literature, English literature, math, natural sciences, world history, political science, economics, university assembly, phys ed, and academic orientation. Additionally, each student must engage in a minimum of 120 clock hours of volunteer service in the community. **Procedure:** Freshmen are admitted spring. Entrance exams should be taken between April of the junior year and December of the senior year. There are early admissions, deferred admissions, and rolling admissions plans. Applications should be filed by December 1 for spring entry. The fall 2017 application fee was $36. Notification is sent on a rolling basis. Applications are accepted on-line. **Transfer Students:** 46 transfer students enrolled in 2016-2017. Applicants for transfer must submit a secondary school record or equivalent, transcripts from previous colleges showing an average grade of C, and personal recommendations. No more than 60 semester hours may be submitted for transfer credit. 65 of 125 credits required for the bachelor's degree must be completed at DU. **International Students:** There are 12 international students enrolled. They must take the TOEFL with a minimum score of 550 on the paper-based TOEFL (PBT). They must also take the SAT or ACT.

Admissions Contact: David Page, VP for Enrollment Management. Email: *dpage@dillard.edu* Web: *www.dillard.edu*

FINANCIAL AID: In 2017-2018, 99% of all full-time freshmen received some form of financial aid. 93% of all full-time freshmen received need-based aid. 25% of undergraduate students work part-time. The average financial indebtedness of the 2017 graduate was $26,250. DU is a member of CSS. The college's own financial statement is required. The FAFSA code is 002004. The deadline for filing freshman financial aid applications for fall entry is March 1.

GRAMBLING STATE UNIVERSITY B-1

www.gram.edu

Grambling, LA 71245 (318) 274-6423
(888) 863-3655
Fax: (318) 274-3292 Email: admissions@gram.edu

Full-time: 1529 men, 2069 women	**Faculty:** n/av
Part-time: 122 men, 163 women	**Ph.D.s:** n/av
Graduate: 264 men, 716 women	**Student/Faculty:** n/av
Year: semesters, summer session	**Tuition:** $7063 ($16,086)
Room & Board: $8638	**Freshman Class:** 6366 applied, 1372 accepted, 865 enrolled
SAT or ACT: required	**CEEB CODE:** 6250
Application Deadline: July 1	**COMPETITIVE**

Grambling State University, founded in 1901, is a constituent member of the University of Louisiana System, and a historically and predominantly black comprehensive university, offering degrees ranging from associate to doctorate. There are 4 undergraduate schools and one graduate school. In addition to regional accreditation, GSU has baccalaureate program accreditation with AACSB, ABET, ACEJMC, CSAB, CSWE, NASAD, NASM, CAEP, NLN, NRPA, NASPAA, ACS, and NAST. The 590-acre campus is in a small town 60 miles from Shreveport. Including any residence halls, there are 147 buildings.

STUDENT LIFE: 69% of undergraduates are from Louisiana. Others are from 41 states, 27 foreign countries, and Canada. 91% are African American; 4% Foreign; 1% White; 1% Hispanic; 1% two or more races; 1% race unknown. **Female To Male Ratio:** 1.5:1. The average age of freshmen is 20; all undergraduates, 22. **Housing:** 2581 students can be accommodated in college housing, which is guaranteed for all 4 years. All students may keep cars. Alcohol is not permitted.

FACULTY/CLASSROOMS: No introductory courses are taught by graduate students.

PROGRAMS OF STUDY: GSU confers B.A., B.S., B.S.W. and B.P.A. degrees. Associate, master's, and doctoral degrees are also awarded. Bachelor's degrees are awarded in BIOLOGICAL SCIENCE (biology/biological science), BUSINESS (accounting, business administration and management, business economics, hotel/motel and restaurant management, marketing/retailing/merchandising, and recreation and leisure services), COMMUNICATIONS AND THE ARTS (communications, English, music, and visual and performing arts), COMPUTER AND PHYSICAL SCIENCE (chemistry, computer science, information sciences and systems, mathematics, and physics), EDUCATION (early childhood education, elementary education, English education, mathematics education, physical education, secondary education, social studies education, and special education), ENGINEERING AND ENVIRONMENTAL DESIGN (engineering technology), HEALTH PROFESSIONS (nursing), SOCIAL SCIENCE (criminal justice, economics, history, political science/government, psychology, public administration, social work, and sociology). Criminal justice, and biology are the strongest academically. Criminal justice has the largest enrollment.

ACTIVITIES: 2% of men belong to 3 national fraternities; 2% of women belong to 4 national sororities. There are 62 groups on campus, including art, band, cheerleading, choir, chorus, communications, computers, dance, drama, honors, international, jazz band, marching band, newspaper, orchestra, political, professional, radio and TV, religious, social, social service, student government, symphony, and yearbook. Popular campus events include Candlelight and Pinning Ceremony, Founder's Day/Week, Black History Month, and Springfest. **Sports:** There are 5 intercollegiate sports for men and 8 for women, and 4 intramural sports for men and 4 for women. Facilities include a gymnasium, a stadium, intramural center, park and field-baseball complex, softball field, and tennis courts. **Graduates:** From July 1, 2016 to June 30, 2017, 686 bachelor's degrees were awarded. The most popular majors were criminal justice (17%), social work (10%), and nursing (8%).

SERVICES: Counseling and information services are available, as is tutoring in some subjects, such as biology, English, chemistry, history, math and physics. There is remedial math, reading, and writing. **Library/Resources:** The library contains 1.6 million volumes, 122,298 microform items, and 6,394 audio/video tapes/CDs/DVDs, and subscribes to 109,517 periodicals including electronic. Computerized library services include interlibrary loans, database searching, Internet access, and Wi-Fi capability. Special learning facilities include an art gallery, radio station, TV station, and student technology labs. **Physically Challenged Students:** Facilities include wheelchair ramps, elevators, special parking, specially equipped restrooms, special class scheduling, lowered drinking fountains, and lowered telephones. **Special:** Special training programs available in the Department of Biological Sciences are designed to: encourage and assist biology majors interested in medicine, dentistry or allied health professions to apply for summer programs conducted by medical/dental schools at major universities throughout the nation; prepare students for graduate schools to earn Ph.D. or MD/Ph.D. degrees and pursue research careers in biomedical sciences; and increase the number and quality of students earning baccalaureate and doctoral degrees in the areas of science, engineering, and mathematic. The College of Business faculty members have partnered with various organizations and/or economic programs to provide students with economic development activities. Industry-based internships are available in accounting and finance, housekeeping, recreation, banquet/catering, front office, restaurants, culinary and pastry arts, human resources, and sales. Through an agreement with Southern University at Shreveport their students are enabled to engage in a military science curriculum at Grambling State University. The university-wide Honors College provides unique intellectual and educational experiences for academically talented students to extend their academic, personal, and social development while completing requirements in their chosen majors. There are 5 national honor societies and a freshman honors program. **Visiting:** There are guides for informal visits. To schedule a visit, contact the Office of Admissions. **Campus Safety and Security:** Measures include 24-hour foot and vehicle patrol and emergency notification system. There are shuttle buses, emergency telephones, and lighted pathways/sidewalks.

REQUIREMENTS: The SAT or ACT is required. All applicants must submit the general admissions documents, complete 19 units from Core 4 Curriculum, have a minimum 2.0 overall GPA (on 4.0 scale), need no more than one developmental course, and, either a minimum 2.0 GPA on Core 4 Curriculum or ACT Composite 20 or SAT 940 (reading & math combined). Admission to the university is conditional until evidence of graduation from high school and completion of required core units are received. Applicants with Certificate of Achievement diplomas and General Equivalency Diplomas (GED) are not eligible for admission to Grambling; however, assistance is provided with a referral to the BPCC at GSU Program where requirements for admission to Grambling State University can be completed. A GPA of 2.0 is required. AP and CLEP credits are accepted. In order to graduate and be awarded a bachelor's degree from Grambling State University, students must: Complete all course requirements in an academic major, with no grades lower than C; complete all academic requirements in the General Education Program; complete at least 125 credit hours of coursework. Pass examinations required for the chosen major; pass the Rising Junior Examination. Have a minimum grade point average of 2.0. Earn at least 25 percent of the required credit hours for graduation in residence. **Procedure:** Freshmen are admitted fall, spring, and summer. There is a rolling admissions plan. Applications should be filed by July 1 for fall entry; December 1 for spring entry; and May 1 for summer entry. The fall 2017 application fee was $20. Applications are accepted on-line. **Transfer Students:** 262 transfer students enrolled in 2016-2017. Transfer applicants must submit an application fee (check with the school for fee), submit proof of immunization, submit official transcript from each regionally, accredited institution attended, regardless if credits appear on another transcript, have earned at least 18 semester hours of college-level coursework (excluding developmental courses). Students must have completed a college-level English and math course designed to fulfill general education requirement, have earned a cumulative GPA of at least 2.0 on college-level courses, and be in good standing and eligible to return to the last college or university of attendance. 30 of 120 credits required for the bachelor's degree must be completed at GSU. **International Students:** There are 173 international students enrolled. They must take the TOEFL with a minimum score of 500 on the paper-based TOEFL (PBT) or 62 on the Internet-based version (iBT). They must also take the SAT or ACT, scoring 24.

ADMISSIONS: 22% of the 2017-2018 applicants were accepted. The SAT scores for the 2017-2018 freshman class were: Critical Reading-- 86% below 500 and 14% between 500 and 599. Math-- 80% below 500, 19% between 500 and 599, and 1% between 600 and 699. Writing-- 91% below 500 and 10% between 500 and 599. The ACT scores 41% between 12 and 17, 54% between 18 and 23, and 14% between 24 and 29. **Admissions Contact:** Chemia Herron, Assistant Director of Admissions/Recruitment. Email: *admissions@gram.edu* Web: *www.gram.edu*

FINANCIAL AID: In 2017-2018, 98% of all full-time freshmen received

some form of financial aid. 94% of all full-time freshmen received need-based aid. The average freshman award was $18,031. Need-based scholarships or need-based grants averaged $6,027 ($4,357,523 maximum); need-based self-help aid (loans and jobs) averaged $3,898 ($3,047,976 maximum); non-need-based athletic scholarships averaged $11,063 ($531,002 maximum); and other non-need-based awards and non-need-based scholarships averaged $9,137 ($7,263,502 maximum). 24% of undergraduate students work part-time. The college's own financial statement is required. The FAFSA code is 002006. The priority date for freshman financial aid applications for fall entry is April 1.

LOUISIANA COLLEGE B-3

www.lacollege.edu

Pineville, LA 71359 **(318) 487-7259** **(800) 487-1906**

Fax: (318) 487-7550 **Email: admissions@lacollege.edu**

Full-time: 436 men, 420 women	**Faculty:** 60
Part-time: 67 men, 133 women	**Ph.D.s:** 60%
Graduate: n/av	**Student/Faculty:** 14 to 1
Year: semesters, summer session	**Tuition:** $17,630
Room & Board: $4256	**Freshman Class:** 549 applied, 429 accepted, 246 enrolled
SAT: required **ACT:** 22	**CEEB CODE:** 6371
Application Deadline: August 15	**COMPETITIVE**

Louisiana College, founded in 1906, is a private liberal arts college affiliated with the Southern Baptist Churches of Louisiana offering more than 80 majors, minors, and pre-professional programs of study, and is one of the most recognized colleges in the South. There are 5 undergraduate schools. In addition to regional accreditation, LC has baccalaureate program accreditation with AACSB, ACBSP, CSWE, NASM, and NLN. The 81-acre campus is in a small town in the heart of Louisiana, 1 mile northeast of Alexandria, VA. Including any residence halls, there are 25 buildings.

STUDENT LIFE: 92% of undergraduates are from Louisiana. Others are from 16 states, 5 foreign countries, and Canada. 88% are White; 8% African American; 1% Asian American; 1% American Indian/Alaska Native; 1% Hispanic; 1% Foreign. 66% are Protestant; 18% claim no religious affiliation; 13% Catholic. **Female To Male Ratio:** 1.1:1. The average age of freshmen is 18; all undergraduates, 22. 36% do not continue beyond their first year; 43% remain to graduate. **Housing:** 726 students can be accommodated in college housing, which includes married student dorms and on-campus apartments. On-campus housing is guaranteed for all 4 years. 54% of students live on campus. Alcohol is not permitted. All students may keep cars.

FACULTY/CLASSROOMS: 57% of faculty are male; 43% are female. All teach undergraduates. No introductory courses are taught by graduate students. The average class size in an introductory lecture is 30; in a laboratory is 20; and in a regular course is 18.

PROGRAMS OF STUDY: LC confers B.A., B.S., B.G.S., B.M., B.S.N., and B.S.W. degrees. Associate degrees are also awarded. Bachelor's degrees are awarded in BIOLOGICAL SCIENCE (biology/biological science), BUSINESS (business administration and management), COMMUNICATIONS AND THE ARTS (communications, dramatic arts, English, French, graphic design, journalism, languages, multimedia, music, speech/debate/rhetoric, and studio art), COMPUTER AND PHYSICAL SCIENCE (chemistry and mathematics), EDUCATION (art education, athletic training, business education, elementary education, English education, health education, mathematics education, music education, science education, secondary education, social studies education, and special education), HEALTH PROFESSIONS (exercise science, medical laboratory technology, music therapy, nursing, predentistry, premedicine, preoptometry, and preveterinary science), SOCIAL SCIENCE (criminal justice, economics, history, philosophy, prelaw, psychology, public administration, religion, religious education, religious music, social work, and sociology). Education, biology, and business have the largest enrollments.

ACTIVITIES: 5% of men belong to 4 local fraternities; 15% of women belong to 4 local sororities. There are 57 groups on campus, including and Union Board (campus programming), art, band, Breaking All Barriers (Diversity), cheerleading, choir, chorale, chorus, communications, debate, drama, honors, international, jazz band, literary magazine, marching band, musical theater, newspaper, opera, pep band, political, professional, radio and TV, religious, social, social service, student government, symphony, and yearbook. Popular campus events include Gala Christmas, Sanders Lecture Series, and Miss LC Pageant. **Sports:** There are 5 intercollegiate sports for men and 5 for women, and 11 intramural sports for men and 11 for women. Facilities include a field house for basketball, a baseball field, a fitness/wellness center, a jogging trail, tennis courts, an intramural/soccer/football field, an outdoor beach volleyball court, softball field, and a practice football field. **Graduates:** From July 1, 2016 to June 30, 2017, 159 bachelor's degrees were awarded. The most popular majors were nursing (9%), biology (9%), and social work (8%). In an average class, 24% graduate in 4 years or less, 41% graduate in 5 years or less, and 45% graduate in 6 years or less.

SERVICES: Counseling and information services are available, as is tutoring in most subjects. There is a reader service for the blind, and remedial math and writing. PASS (Program to Assist Student Success) offers services for students with documented learning disabilities. **Library/Resources:** The library contains 138,985 volumes, 126,266 microform items, and 2,500 audio/video tapes/CDs/DVDs, and subscribes to 19,993 periodicals including electronic. Computerized library services include interlibrary loans, database searching, and Internet access. Special learning facilities include an art gallery, a radio station, and a performing arts center. **Physically Challenged Students:** 95% of the campus is accessible. Facilities include wheelchair ramps, elevators, special parking, specially equipped restrooms, and lowered telephones. **Special:** Study abroad in London and Hong Kong, interdisciplinary studies, work-study programs, non-degree study, internships, dual majors, and pass/fail options are offered. There are 13 national honor societies and a freshman honors program. **Visiting:** There are regularly scheduled orientations for prospective students, consisting of spring and fall campus preview days and a 2-day orientation and pre-registration in June. There are guides for informal visits; visitors may sit in on classes and stay overnight. To schedule a visit, contact the Office of Admissions. **Campus Safety and Security:** Measures include 24-hour foot and vehicle patrol, self-defense education, and security escort services. There are lighted pathways/sidewalks.

REQUIREMENTS: The SAT or ACT is required. Candidates for admission must have completed 17 units, which include 4 of English, 3 each of math (algebra I, II, and geometry), social studies, and science (2 with lab). Graduates of accredited high schools must meet one of the following requirements for unconditional admission: (1) Score at least 20 composite on ACT or satisfactorily on the SAT and possess a GPA of 2.0 on a 4.0 scale; or (2) Possess an academic GPA of 2.0 on a 4.0 scale and rank in the upper 50% of their graduating class with an acceptable ACT or SAT score. AP and CLEP credits are accepted. Important factors in the admissions decision are extracurricular activities record, leadership record, and advanced placement or honors courses. To graduate, students must complete 127 total credit hours, 42 of which must be junior-senior level, including a central core of 56 hours in all degree programs, and maintain a minimum GPA of 2.0, and a 2.25 in the major. They must also complete Cultural/Intellectual and Spiritual Enrichment requirements and earn at least 25% of credit applied toward degree through instruction offered by LC. They must complete the last 30 hours of coursework at LC, and take 3 hours each of phys ed and computer applications. **Procedure:** Freshmen are admitted fall, spring, and summer. Entrance exams should be taken during the junior or senior year. There is a rolling admissions plan. The fall 2017 application fee was $25. Notification is sent on a rolling basis. Applications are accepted on-line. **Transfer Students:** Applicants must have an overall minimum GPA of 2.0 and finish all remedial course work prior to transfer. 30 of 127 credits required for the bachelor's degree must be completed at LC. **International Students:** The TOEFL is waived for students taking the SAT who earn 480 on the verbal section. They must take the SAT or ACT.

ADMISSIONS: 78% of the 2017-2018 applicants were accepted. The ACT scores were 38% below 12, 29% between 12 and 17, 16% between 18 and 23, 9% between 24 and 29, and 8% above 30. **Admissions Contact:** Renee Melder, Director of Admissions. Email: *admissions@lacollege.edu* Web: *www.lacollege.edu*

FINANCIAL AID: 19% of undergraduate students work part-time. The FFS and the college's own financial statement are required. The FAFSA code is 002007. The priority date for freshman financial aid applications for fall entry is March 15.

LOUISIANA STATE UNIVERSITY AND A&M COLLEGE C-4

www.lsu.edu

Baton Rouge, LA 70803 **(225) 578-1175**

Fax: (225) 578-4433
Email: admissions@lsu.edu
Full-time: 10,979 men, 11,832 women
Faculty: 1053; I, -$
Part-time: 1101 men, 1011 women
Ph.D.s: 89%
Graduate: 2713 men, 2842 women
Student/Faculty: 22 to 1
Year: semesters, summer session
Tuition: $7873 ($25,790)
Room & Board: $10,804
Freshman Class: 16005 applied, 12002 accepted, 5501 enrolled
SAT CR/M: 559/577 **ACT:** 26
CEEB CODE: 6373
Application Deadline: April 15
VERY COMPETITIVE

Louisiana State University and A&M College, a public institution founded in 1860, and part of the Louisiana State University System, offers programs in the colleges of agriculture, humanities and social sciences, business administration, coast and environment, art and design, human sciences and education, engineering, music and dramatic arts, mass communication, and science. The figures given in the above capsule and in this profile are approximate. There are 11 undergraduate schools and 2 graduate schools. In addition to regional accreditation, LSU and A&M has baccalaureate program accreditation with AACSB, ABET, ACCE, ACEJMC, ASLA, CSWE, FIDER, NAAB, NASAD, NASM, CAEP, SAF, and ADA. The 2000-acre campus is in an urban area in Baton Rouge, Louisiana. Including any residence halls, there are 250 buildings.

STUDENT LIFE: 80% of undergraduates are from Louisiana. Others are from 49 states, 81 foreign countries, and Canada. 52% are from public schools. 76% are White; 5% Hispanic; 3% Asian American; 2% Foreign; 2% two or more races; 11% African American. 40% are Catholic; 33% Protestant; 23% claim no religious affiliation. **Female To Male Ratio:** 1.1:1. The average age of freshmen is 19; all undergraduates, 21. 18% do not continue beyond their first year; 69% remain to graduate. **Housing:** 7450 students can be accommodated in college housing, which includes married student dorms, and on-campus apartments. In addition, there are and honors houses, special-interest houses, fraternity houses, and sorority houses. 75% of students commute. All students may keep cars.

FACULTY/CLASSROOMS: 64% of faculty are male; 36% are female. 89% teach undergraduates. Graduate students teach 17% of introductory courses. The average class size in an introductory lecture is 52; in a laboratory is 25; and in a regular course is 38.

PROGRAMS OF STUDY: LSU and A&M confers B.A., B.S., B.A.M.C., B.Arch., B.F.A., B.I.S., B.I.D., B.L.A., B.M., B.M.Ed., B.S.B.E., B.S.C.E., B.S.Ch.E., B.S.E.E., B.S.Env.E., B.S.C.M., B.S.F., B.S.I.E., B.S. in Coastal Environmental Science, B.S. in Geol., B.S.M.E. and B.S.P.E. degrees. Master's and doctoral degrees are also awarded. Bachelor's degrees are awarded in AGRICULTURE (agricultural business management, animal science, environmental studies, forestry and related sciences, natural resource management, and plant science), BIOLOGICAL SCIENCE (biochemistry, biology/biological science, microbiology, and nutrition), BUSINESS (accounting, banking and finance, business administration and management, human resources, international economics, management science, marketing/retailing/merchandising, and sports management), COMMUNICATIONS AND THE ARTS (communications, dramatic arts, English, French, journalism, music, Spanish, and studio art), COMPUTER AND PHYSICAL SCIENCE (chemistry, computer science, geology, information sciences and systems, mathematics, and physics), EDUCATION (agricultural education, athletic training, early childhood education, elementary education, music education, and special education), ENGINEERING AND ENVIRONMENTAL DESIGN (architecture, bioengineering, chemical engineering, civil engineering, computer engineering, construction management, electrical/electronics engineering, environmental engineering, environmental science, industrial engineering, interior design, landscape architecture/design, mechanical engineering, and petroleum/natural gas engineering), HEALTH PROFESSIONS (speech pathology/audiology), SOCIAL SCIENCE (anthropology, child care/child and family studies, economics, geography, history, interdisciplinary studies, international studies, liberal arts/general studies, philosophy, physical fitness/movement, political science/government, psychology, sociology, and textiles and clothing). Biological sciences, chemistry, and civil & environmental engineering are the strongest academically. Biological sciences, mass communication, and kinesiology have the largest enrollments.

ACTIVITIES: 17% of men belong to 23 national fraternities; 26% of women belong to 16 national sororities. There are 300 groups on campus, including art, band, cheerleading, choir, chorus, communications, computers, dance, debate, drama, environmental, ethnic, film, honors, international, jazz band, LGBT, literary magazine, marching band, musical theater, newspaper, opera, orchestra, pep band, political, professional, radio and TV, religious, social, social service, student government, symphony, and yearbook. Popular campus events include Fall Fest, Home Football Games, and Groovin on the Grounds. **Sports:** There are 9 intercollegiate sports for men and 11 for women, and 23 intramural sports for men and 23 for women. Facilities include a football stadium, a domed sports center, baseball stadium, a track, a natatorium with an pool and diving well, an indoor track, and courts for handball, badminton, volleyball, and tennis. The campus recreation facility provides a multifaceted program that includes aquatics, sports clubs, informal recreation, fitness classes, instructional sports, personal training, intramural sports, outdoor recreation, challenge course, climbing wall, and special-events activities. There is also an indoor practice facility for football, a soccer field, and a softball stadium. **Graduates:** From July 1, 2016 to June 30, 2017, 4529 bachelor's degrees were awarded. The most popular majors were biological sciences (7%), kinesiology (6%), and mass communication (6%). In an average class, 40% graduate in 4 years or less, 65% graduate in 5 years or less, and 69% graduate in 6 years or less. Of the 2016 graduating class, 22% were enrolled in graduate school within 6 months of graduation, and 58% were employed.

SERVICES: Counseling and information services are available, as is tutoring in some subjects, such as English, math, foreign languages, and sciences. There is remedial reading and writing. **Library/Resources:** The library contains 3.8 million volumes, 2.3 million microform items, and 26,938 audio/video tapes/CDs/DVDs, and subscribes to 337,837 periodicals including electronic. Computerized library services include interlibrary loans, database searching, Internet access, and Wi-Fi capability. Special learning facilities include an art gallery, natural history museum, radio station, TV station, 3 herbaria, and museums of natural science, natural history, geoscience, rural life, and art. **Physically Challenged Students:** 85% of the campus is accessible. Facilities include wheelchair ramps, elevators, special parking, specially equipped restrooms, special class scheduling, lowered drinking fountains, lowered telephones, and special housing. **Special:** Co-op programs in all areas of engineering and landscape architecture, cross-registration with Southern University and Baton Rouge Community College, study abroad, and work-study programs are offered. B.A.-B.S. degrees, dual majors, a general studies degree, non-degree study, an evening school, a program of study for adult learners, and pass/fail options are available. There are 23 national honor societies, Phi Beta Kappa, and a freshman honors program. **Visiting:** There are regularly scheduled orientations for prospective students, including an information session and a tour of campus. Department appointments can be arranged. There are guides for informal visits. To schedule a visit, contact the Office of Enrollment Management at (225) 578-6908. **Campus Safety and Security:** Measures include 24-hour foot and vehicle patrol, emergency notification system, self-defense education, and security escort services. There are shuttle buses, emergency telephones, lighted pathways/sidewalks, controlled access to dorms/residences, and specialized crime prevention programs.

REQUIREMENTS: The SAT or ACT is required. Applicants must be graduates of an accredited secondary school. GED certificates may be accepted in unusual circumstances. Students must have completed 19 units, including 4 credits in English, 4 each in specific math, science, and social studies courses, 2 credits in a foreign language, and one additional credit from certain courses in the visual and performing arts. A GPA of 3.0 is required. AP and CLEP credits are accepted. Important factors in the admissions decision are advanced placement or honors courses, extracurricular activities record, and evidence of special talent. To graduate, all students must have a minimum overall 2.0 GPA in 120 to 162 credit hours. They must complete a general education component of 39 semester hours in approved courses in 6 major areas, including humanities, natural sciences, English composition, analytical reasoning, social sciences, and the arts. Students must earn at least 25% of required hours for their degree at LSU and meet college residency requirements. **Procedure:** Freshmen are admitted to all sessions. Entrance exams should be taken in spring of the junior year or fall of the senior year. There are early admissions, deferred admissions, and rolling admissions plans. Applications should be filed by April 15 for fall entry; December 1 for spring entry. The fall 2017 application fee was $40. Notification is sent on a rolling basis. Applications are accepted on-line. **Transfer Students:** 866 transfer students enrolled in 2016-2017. Transfer students must submit an official transcript from each previously attended school. Requirements are 30 or more semester hours with a minimum 2.5 GPA, and college level English and math courses. 30 of 120 credits required for the bachelor's degree must be completed at LSU and A&M. **International Students:** There are 442 international students enrolled. They must take the TOEFL with a minimum score of 550 on the paper-based TOEFL (PBT) or 79 on the Internet-based version (iBT), or take the IELTS (minimum score of 6.5). They must also take the SAT or ACT.

ADMISSIONS: 75% of the 2017-2018 applicants were accepted. The SAT scores for the 2017-2018 freshman class were: Critical Reading-- 22% below 500, 51% between 500 and 599, 24% between 600 and 699, and 4% between 700 and 800. Math-- 15% below 500, 44% between 500 and 599, 35% between 600 and 699, and 6% between 700 and 800. The ACT scores were 5% below 12, 27% between 12 and 17, 31% between 18 and 23, 17% between 24 and 29, and 21% above 30. 44% of the current freshmen were in the top fifth of their class; 73% were in the top two fifths. 355 freshmen graduated first in their class. **Admissions Contact:** David Kurpius, Associate Enrollment Management. Email: *admissions@lsu.edu* Web: *www.lsu.edu*

FINANCIAL AID: In 2017-2018, 93% of all full-time freshmen received some form of financial aid. 38% of all full-time freshmen received need-based aid. The average freshman award was $12,800. Need-based scholarships or need-based grants averaged $7,300; need-based self-help aid (loans and jobs) averaged $3,400; non-need-based athletic scholarships averaged $19,500; and other non-need-based awards and non-need-based scholarships averaged $6,600. 27% of undergraduate students work part-time. The average financial indebtedness of the 2017 graduate was $21,613. The college's own financial statement is required. The priority date for freshman financial aid applications for fall entry is April 1.

LOUISIANA STATE UNIVERSITY IN SHREVEPORT — A-1
www.lsus.edu

Shreveport, LA 71115 — **(318) 797-5061**

Fax: (318) 797-5286
Full-time: 722 men, 1128 women
Part-time: 390 men, 579 women
Graduate: 570 men, 994 women
Year: semesters, summer session
Room & Board: n/app
SAT CR/M: 500/530 **ACT:** 22
Application Deadline: July 15

Email: admissions@lsus.edu
Faculty: 127
Ph.D.s: 79%
Student/Faculty: 20 to 1
Tuition: $6902 ($20,057)
Freshman Class: 695 applied, 621 accepted, 345 enrolled
CEEB CODE: 6355
COMPETITIVE

Louisiana State University in Shreveport, established in 1965, is a state-supported, primarily commuter institution offering undergraduate and graduate programs through the colleges of liberal arts, business, education, and sciences. There are 4 undergraduate schools and 4 graduate schools. In addition to regional accreditation, LSUS has baccalaureate program accreditation with AACSB, ABET, CAEP, and ACS. The 258-acre campus is in an urban area 7 miles south of downtown Shreveport. Including any residence halls, there are 18 buildings.

STUDENT LIFE: 92% of undergraduates are from Louisiana. Others are from 47 states, 25 foreign countries, and Canada. 95% are from public schools. 53% are White; 23% African American; 13% race unknown; 4% Hispanic; 3% Asian American; 3% two or more races; 2% Foreign; 1% American Indian/Alaska Native. **Female To Male Ratio:** 1.6:1. The average age of freshmen is 18; all undergraduates, 23. 35% do not continue beyond their first year; 30% remain to graduate. **Housing:** 480 students can be accommodated in college housing. Housing is available on a first-come and first-served basis. All students may keep cars.

FACULTY/CLASSROOMS: 59% of faculty are male; 41% are female. 80% teach undergraduates, 70% do research, and 70% do both. No introductory courses are taught by graduate students. The average class size in an introductory lecture is 30; in a laboratory is 18; and in a regular course is 19.

PROGRAMS OF STUDY: LSUS confers B.A., B.S., B.C.J. and B.G.S. degrees. Master's and doctoral degrees are also awarded. Bachelor's degrees are awarded in BIOLOGICAL SCIENCE (biochemistry and biology/biological science), BUSINESS (accounting, banking and finance, business administration and management, management science, and marketing/retailing/merchandising), COMMUNICATIONS AND THE ARTS (communications, English, and fine arts), COMPUTER AND PHYSICAL SCIENCE (chemistry, computer science, mathematics, and physics), EDUCATION (elementary education and secondary education), HEALTH PROFESSIONS (community health work), SOCIAL SCIENCE (history, liberal arts/general studies, psychology, and sociology). Biology, computer science, and chemistry are the strongest academically. Psychology, and biology have the largest enrollments.

ACTIVITIES: 5% of men belong to 6 national fraternities; 2% of women belong to 4 national sororities. There are 70 groups on campus, including computers, dance, debate, drama, ethnic, film, forensics, honors, international, literary magazine, photography, political, professional, religious, social, social service, student activities board, student government, and yearbook. Popular campus events include Fall Fest, Spring Fling, and Welcome Back Bash. **Sports:** There are 3 intercollegiate sports for men and 3 for women. Facilities include tennis and racquetball courts, sand or volleyball courts, a swimming pool, gym, weight room, dance studio, football fields, softball diamonds, and a soccer field. **Graduates:** From July 1, 2016 to June 30, 2017, 639 bachelor's degrees were awarded. The most popular majors were business/marketing (23%), general studies (14%), and biology (11%). In an average class, 30% graduate in 6 years or less.

SERVICES: Counseling and information services are available, as is tutoring in some subjects, such as math and English. There is remedial math and writing. **Library/Resources:** The library contains 915,751 volumes, 396,114 microform items, and 4,508 audio/video tapes/CDs/DVDs, and subscribes to 2,000 periodicals including electronic. Computerized library services include interlibrary loans, database searching, and Internet access. Special learning facilities include an art gallery, natural history museum, a pioneer heritage center, and a museum of life sciences. **Physically Challenged Students:** All of the campus is accessible. Facilities include wheelchair ramps, elevators, special parking, specially equipped restrooms, special class scheduling, lowered drinking fountains, lowered telephones, and special housing. **Special:** Opportunities are provided internships, a Washington semester, a general studies degree, credit for military service schools, non-degree study, and pass/fail options. There are 12 national honor societies and a freshman honors program. **Visiting:** There are regularly scheduled orientations for prospective students, including a preview program during the spring semester for high school juniors and seniors, students may stay overnight for this scheduled visit. There are guides for informal visits. **Campus Safety and Security:** Measures include 24-hour foot and vehicle patrol, self-defense education, and security escort services. There are emergency telephones, lighted pathways/sidewalks, and commissioned university police officers.

REQUIREMENTS: The ACT is required. Students must have a minimum composite score of 20. Graduation from an accredited secondary school is required with the 19 State approved core courses. A GPA of 2.0 is required. AP and CLEP credits are accepted. A minimum of 120 semester hours, with a minimum GPA of 2.0, is required for the bachelor's degree. **Procedure:** Freshmen are admitted to all sessions. Entrance exams should be taken at least 2 months before start of the current semester. There is a rolling admissions plan. Applications should be filed by July 15 for fall entry; December 1 for spring entry; and May 1 for summer entry. The fall 2017 application fee was $20. Notification is sent on a rolling basis. **Transfer Students:** Transfers must be in good academic standing, with 18 transferable hours and a GPA of 2.0. They must be eligible to continue at the last institution attended. 30 of 120 credits required for the bachelor's degree must be completed at LSUS. **International Students:** There are 43 international students enrolled. They must take the TOEFL with a minimum score of 173 on the paper-based TOEFL (PBT) or 61 on the Internet-based version (iBT). They must also take the SAT or ACT.

ADMISSIONS: 89% of the 2017-2018 applicants were accepted. The SAT scores for the 2017-2018 freshman class were: Critical Reading-- 40% below 500 and 60% between 500 and 599. Math-- 17% below 500 and 83% between 500 and 599. The ACT scores were 30% below 12, 32% between 12 and 17, 24% between 18 and 23, 6% between 24 and 29, and 5% above 30. **Admissions Contact:** Lauren M Wood, Assistant Director of Admissions. Email: *admissions@lsus.edu* Web: *www.lsus.edu*

FINANCIAL AID: 90% of undergraduate students work part-time. The

FAFSA code is 002013. The deadline for filing freshman financial aid applications for fall entry is June 1.

LOUISIANA TECH UNIVERSITY B-1
www.latech.edu

Ruston, LA 71272	(318) 257-3036
Fax: (318) 257-2499	**Email:** bulldog@latech.edu
Full-time: 5700 men, 3300 women	**Faculty:** 397; I, --$
Part-time: 800 men, 1000 women	**Ph.D.s:** 80%
Graduate: 820 men, 1410 women	**Student/Faculty:** 23 to 1
Year: trimesters, summer session	**Tuition:** $7302 ($18,411)
Room & Board: $4120	**Freshman Class:** n/av
ACT: 24	**CEEB CODE:** 4633
Application Deadline: January 15	**VERY COMPETITIVE**

Louisiana Tech University, founded in 1894, is a public institution offering programs in arts and sciences, business, agriculture, engineering, health science, education, fine and liberal arts, and human ecology. There are 5 undergraduate schools and 5 graduate schools. In addition to regional accreditation, LTU has baccalaureate program accreditation with AACSB, ABET, ADA, AHEA, ASLA, CAHEA, FIDER, NAAB, NASAD, NASM, CAEP, NLN, SAF, CIDA, CAA, CAHIIM, and NAEYC. The 260-acre campus is in a small town 30 miles west of Monroe and 90 miles east of Shreveport, Louisiana. Including any residence halls, there are 146 buildings.

STUDENT LIFE: 85% of undergraduates are from Louisiana. Others are from 44 states, 65 foreign countries, and Canada. 70% are White; 6% Foreign; 16% African American; 1% Asian American; 1% American Indian/Alaska Native; 1% Hispanic. 51% are Protestant; 12% Catholic. **Male To Female Ratio:** 1.3:1. The average age of freshmen is 19; all undergraduates, 20. 22% do not continue beyond their first year; 49% remain to graduate. **Housing:** 3067 students can be accommodated in college housing, which includes married student dorms. In addition, there are honors houses. On-campus housing is guaranteed for all 4 years. 74% of students commute. Alcohol is not permitted. All students may keep cars.

FACULTY/CLASSROOMS: 65% of faculty are male; 35% are female. 95% teach undergraduates, 75% do research, and 75% do both. Graduate students teach 2% of introductory courses. The average class size in an introductory lecture is 40; in a laboratory is 20; and in a regular course is 26.

PROGRAMS OF STUDY: LTU confers B.A., B.S., B. Arch., B.F.A. and B.G.S. degrees. Associate, master's, and doctoral degrees are also awarded. Bachelor's degrees are awarded in AGRICULTURE (agricultural business management, animal science, forestry and related sciences, and wildlife management), BIOLOGICAL SCIENCE (biology/biological science), BUSINESS (accounting, banking and finance, business administration and management, business economics, business systems analysis, management science, marketing/retailing/merchandising, and personnel management), COMMUNICATIONS AND THE ARTS (English, fine arts, French, journalism, music, music performance, Spanish, and speech/debate/rhetoric), COMPUTER AND PHYSICAL SCIENCE (chemistry, computer science, geology, mathematics, and physics), EDUCATION (art education, early childhood education, elementary education, foreign languages education, music education, physical education, secondary education, and special education), ENGINEERING AND ENVIRONMENTAL DESIGN (airline piloting and navigation, architecture, aviation administration/management, biomedical engineering, chemical engineering, civil engineering, construction engineering, electrical/electronics engineering technology, environmental science, industrial engineering, and mechanical engineering), HEALTH PROFESSIONS (medical laboratory technology, medical records administration/services, and speech pathology/audiology), SOCIAL SCIENCE (dietetics, geography, history, liberal arts/general studies, political science/government, psychology, and sociology). Business, and engineering are the strongest academically, and have the largest enrollments.

ACTIVITIES: 7% of men belong to 9 national fraternities; 11% of women belong to 5 national sororities. There are 121 groups on campus, including art, band, cheerleading, choir, chorale, chorus, computers, dance, debate, drama, drill team, drum and bugle corps, ethnic, film, honors, international, jazz band, marching band, musical theater, newspaper, opera, orchestra, pep band, photography, political, professional, radio and TV, religious, social, social service, student government, symphony, and yearbook. Popular campus events include International Student Festival, Spring Fling, and Little Theater Concerts. **Sports:** There are 5 intercollegiate sports for men and 5 for women, and 10 intramural sports for men and 10 for women. Facilities include a football stadium, a coliseum, an intramural complex, natatorium, golf, and lighted tennis courts. **Graduates:** From July 1, 2016 to June 30, 2017, 1401 bachelor's degrees were awarded. The most popular majors were business (22%), engineering (17%), and education (11%). In an average class, 29% graduate in 4 years or less, 49% graduate in 5 years or less, and 55% graduate in 6 years or less.

SERVICES: Counseling and information services are available, as is tutoring in some subjects. There is a reader service for the blind, and remedial math, reading, and writing. **Library/Resources:** The library contains 1.1 million volumes, 2.1 million microform items, and 511 audio/video tapes/CDs/DVDs, and subscribes to 2,932 periodicals including electronic. Computerized library services include interlibrary loans and database searching. Special learning facilities include an art gallery, natural history museum, planetarium, and radio station. **Physically Challenged Students:** 95% of the campus is accessible. Facilities include wheelchair ramps, elevators, special parking, specially equipped restrooms, lowered drinking fountains, and lowered telephones. **Special:** Co-op programs are available in engineering and applied and natural sciences, and cross-registration with Grambling State University is offered. Internships in agriculture, engineering, dietetics, and human ecology are offered. Study abroad, work-study programs, dual majors, a general studies degree, non-degree study, and pass/fail options are available. There is a chapter of Phi Beta Kappa, a freshman honors program, and 20 departmental honors programs. **Visiting:** There are regularly scheduled orientations for prospective students. There are guides for informal visits and visitors may stay overnight. To schedule a visit, contact the Admissions Office. **Campus Safety and Security:** Measures include 24-hour foot and vehicle patrol, self-defense education, and security escort services. There are emergency telephones and lighted pathways/sidewalks.

REQUIREMENTS: The ACT is required. Applicants must be graduates of an accredited secondary school or have a GED. Students must have graduated in the upper half of their class. A GPA of 2.3 is required. AP credits are accepted. All students must complete 45 quarter hours of general education courses, including 12 hours in humanities, 9 each in natural and social sciences, 6 each in English and math, and 3 in arts or computer literacy. A total of 120 to 142 quarter hours, with a minimum GPA of 2.0, is required to graduate. **Procedure:** Freshmen are admitted to all sessions. There is a rolling admissions plan. Applications should be filed by January 15 for fall entry. The fall 2017 application fee was $20. **Transfer Students:** 526 transfer students enrolled in 2016-2017. Transfer applicants should have a 2.0 GPA and be eligible to enroll in the school from which they are transferring. 30 of 120 credits required for the bachelor's degree must be completed at LTU. **International Students:** There are 139 international students enrolled. They must take the TOEFL.

Admissions Contact: Jan Albritton, Admissions Office. Email: *bulldog@latech.edu* Web: *www.latech.edu*

FINANCIAL AID: In 2017-2018, 71% of all full-time freshmen received some form of financial aid. 71% of all full-time freshmen received need-based aid. 27% of undergraduate students work part-time. The FAFSA code is 002008. The deadline for filing freshman financial aid applications for fall entry is July 16.

LOYOLA UNIVERSITY NEW ORLEANS D-4
www.loyno.edu

New Orleans, LA 70118	(504) 865-3240
Fax: (504) 865-3383	**Email:** admit@loyno.edu
Full-time: 918 men, 1528 women	**Faculty:** 186; IIA, av$
Part-time: 68 men, 88 women	**Ph.D.s:** 91%
Graduate: 369 men, 788 women	**Student/Faculty:** 12 to 1
Year: semesters, summer session	**Tuition:** $39,242
Room & Board: $13,214	**Freshman Class:** 5112 applied, 3533 accepted, 803 enrolled
SAT or ACT: required	**CEEB CODE:** 6374
Application Deadline: February 20	**VERY COMPETITIVE**

Loyola University New Orleans, founded in 1912, is a private, Catholic, Jesuit university that serves undergraduate, graduate, professional, and continuing education students. There are 4 undergraduate schools and 3 graduate schools. In addition to regional accreditation, LUNO has baccalaureate program accreditation with AACSB, ACEJMC, NASM, NLN, AALS, ABA, APT, ACS, CACREP, CCNE, LSBN, NASM, NLNAC, and CEPR. The 26-acre campus is in a suburban area in the Uptown university district of New Orleans. Including any residence halls, there are 29 buildings.

STUDENT LIFE: 57% of undergraduates are from out of state, mostly the South. Students are from 48 states, 42 foreign countries, and Canada. 55% are from public schools. 51% are White; 17% Hispanic; 15% African American; 5% two or more races; 3% Asian American; 3% Foreign; 1% American Indian/Alaska Native; 1% race unknown. 47% are Catholic; 21% Baptist, Buddhist, Episcopalian, Hindu, Lutheran, Methodist, Muslim, and Presbyterian; 20% claim no religious affiliation. **Female To Male Ratio:** 1.8:1. The average age of freshmen is 18; all undergraduates, 20. 20% do not continue beyond their first year; 56% remain to graduate. **Housing:** 1332 students can be accommodated in college housing, which includes dorms and on-campus apartments. In addition, there are honors houses, special-interest houses, theme housing, wellness housing, LEAD community, and SPARK community. On-campus housing is guaranteed for the freshman year only, is available on a first-come, and first-served basis. 54% of students live on campus. All students may keep cars.

FACULTY/CLASSROOMS: 58% of faculty are male; 42% are female. 79% teach undergraduates, and 90% do research. No introductory courses are taught by graduate students. The average class size in an introductory lecture is 25; in a laboratory is 14; and in a regular course is 17.

PROGRAMS OF STUDY: LUNO confers B.A., B.S., B.Acc., B.B.A., B.C.J., B.F.A., B.Mus., B.Mus.Ed., B.Mus. Therapy, B.S.N., B.A. Music, B.S. Mus. Industry, and B.Design. degrees. Master's and doctoral degrees are also awarded. Bachelor's degrees are awarded in AGRICULTURE (environmental studies), BIOLOGICAL SCIENCE (biology/biological science and biological sciences), BUSINESS (accounting, banking and finance, business administration and management, business (dual major program), business intelligence and analytics, international business management, management science, and marketing/retailing/merchandising), COMMUNICATIONS AND THE ARTS (acting, advertising, art, classics, communications, creative writing, design, digital media, dramatic arts, English literature, film, television and digital media, fine arts, fine/studio arts, French, game programming, graphic design, Greek (classical), guitar, jazz, journalism, languages, music, music business management, music composition, music industry, music performance, music theory and composition, piano/organ, Spanish, studio art, visual and performing arts, and voice), COMPUTER AND PHYSICAL SCIENCE (chemistry, computer game design/development, computer information systems, mathematics, mathematics/computational, and physics), EDUCATION (music education), ENGINEERING AND ENVIRONMENTAL DESIGN (environmental science and preengineering), HEALTH PROFESSIONS (biology, music therapy, nursing, predentistry, premedicine, and preveterinary science), SOCIAL SCIENCE (classical/ancient civilization, criminal justice, economics, food production/management/services, forensic studies, history, humanities, Latin American studies, liberal arts/general studies, philosophy, political science/government, psychology, religion, religious education, social science, and sociology). Music industry studies, business, communications, psychology, and biological sciences have the largest enrollments.

ACTIVITIES: 11% of men belong to 4 national fraternities; 20% of women belong to 7 national sororities. There are 129 groups on campus, including art, band, cheerleading, chess, choir, chorale, chorus, communications, computers, dance, debate, drama, environmental, ethnic, film, forensics, honors, international, jazz band, LGBT, literary magazine, musical theater, newspaper, opera, orchestra, pep band, photography, political, professional, radio and TV, religious, social, social service, student government, symphony, and yearbook. Popular campus events include Take Back the Night, Maroon and Gold, Senior Crawfish Boil, Sneaux, Family Weekend, Mass and Pancakes, Get to NOLA Excursions, and New Student Convocation. **Sports:** There are 8 intercollegiate sports for men and 8 for women, and 8 intramural sports for men and 8 for women. Facilities include a sports complex with an arena, multipurpose courts for basketball, tennis, volleyball, badminton, floor hockey, racquetball courts, an Olympic style natatorium, a jogging track, and weight lifting and conditioning area. There are off campus facilities for baseball, tennis, cross country, track/field, and golf. **Graduates:** From July 1, 2016 to June 30, 2017, 559 bachelor's degrees were awarded. The most popular majors were music industry (12%), psychology (9%), and mass communication (8%). In an average class, 49% graduate in 4 years or less, 59% graduate in 5 years or less, and 56% graduate in 6 years or less. Of the 2016 graduating class, 25% were enrolled in graduate school within 6 months of graduation, and 70% were employed.

SERVICES: Counseling and information services are available, as is tutoring in most subjects. There is remedial math and writing. Peer tutoring is available in all introductory common curriculum courses. A reader service for the blind is provided for all exams and for coursework if books on tape are not sufficient. **Library/Resources:** The library contains 584,939 volumes, 1.4 million microform items, 17,352 audio/video tapes/CDs/DVDs, and subscribes to 169,032 periodicals including electronic. Computerized library services include interlibrary loans, database searching, Internet access, and Wi-Fi capability. Special learning facilities include an art gallery, radio and TV stations, Monroe Hall with a 3-D printing machine, a greenhouse, specialized science labs and exhibit spaces; multimedia classrooms throughout campus; The Maroon newsroom with in-house TV studio and digital communications laboratory; College of Business; Collins C. Diboll Art Gallery; The Brand Lab; Center for Nonprofit Communications; audio recording/video editing studio; Center for International Education; University Sports Complex with suspended pool; Career Development Center; Jesuit Social Research Institute; Business Portfolio Program; Office of Service Learning; the Pan-American Life Student Success Center; and an auditorium used for performances. **Physically Challenged Students:** 99% of the campus is accessible. Facilities include wheelchair ramps, elevators, special parking, specially equipped restrooms, lowered drinking fountains, lowered telephones, special housing, and special class relocation to provide accessibility. **Special:** Cross-registration is available with, Our Lady of Holy Cross, Xavier University, Notre Dame Seminary, the University of New Orleans, Tulane University, and Southern University of New Orleans. Internships with the New Orleans business community are also available. Study abroad in over 40 countries, dual and student-designed majors, nondegree studies, an accelerated B.S.N. to D.N.P nursing program, and a general studies degree are offered. A Washington semester through American University. There are 13 national honor societies, a freshman honors program, and 8 departmental honors programs. **Visiting:** There are regularly scheduled orientations for prospective students, including class and department visits, a student panel, a tour, a financial aid session, a campus support panel, and meetings with faculty members. There are guides for informal visits, visitors may sit in on classes, and stay overnight. To schedule a visit, contact the Admissions Office. **Campus Safety and Security:** Measures include 24-hour foot, an emergency notification system, self-defense education, and security escort services. There are shuttle buses, emergency telephones, lighted pathways/sidewalks, controlled access to dorms/residences, CCTV coverage, card access control, ID cards issued, intrusion alarm monitoring, first aid medical assistance, bicycle registration, fingerprinting service, crime prevention services, multiple vehicle patrols. Off-campus police patrols, Silent Witness program (which allows students to anonymously report criminal activity via the internet); RAVE Guardian Campus Safety App.(Panic Button, Tip Texting and Personal Guardian); direct radio communication with city police (NOPD), adjoining Tulane University police and other police departments during a local area or in-state emergencies; officers are trained in active shooter response and a Special Emergency Response Team. All officers are trained in First-Aid/CPR/AED. LUPD serves on several university committees as well as off-campus organizations: Emergency Management Team, Threat Assessment Team, Care & Concern Committee, Tobacco Free Committee, Loyola/Tulane Transportation Advisory Board, Maple St. Quality of Life Committee, Women Resource Center Advisory Committee, Advocate Training Committee, Sexual Assault Committee, Bias-Incident Related Committee, New Orleans Anti-Terrorism Advisory Council (ATAC), and NOPD Compstat and NONPAC organizations.

REQUIREMENTS: The SAT or ACT is required. Candidates for admission must be graduates of an accredited secondary school or have a GED. Units recommended: 4 units in English and 3 each in math, and science (of those; 1 must be a lab), 2 each in foreign language, history, and social studies, and 1 academic elective. A portfolio is required for fine arts students, an audition for music majors. An interview is recommended for scholarship consideration. Home schooled students require proof of high school graduation or its equivalent. AP and CLEP credits are accepted. Important factors in the admissions decision are advanced placement or honors courses, evidence of special talent, extracurricular activities record, recommendations by school officials, personality/intangible qualities, recommendations by alumni, and geographical diversity. All students must complete a core curriculum that includes courses in English composition and literature, math, philosophy, science, global history, social science and religious studies; the number of credit hours varies by college. At least 120 credit hours, with at least 30 in the major, and a minimum GPA of 2.0 are required to graduate. **Procedure:** Freshmen are admitted fall, spring, and summer. Entrance exams should be taken during the junior or senior year. There are early admissions, deferred admissions, and rolling admissions plans. Application deadlines are open. Applications are accepted online. **Transfer Students:** 90 transfer students enrolled in 2016-2017. Transfers must submit the application for admission, an essay, a letter of recommendation, a resume, and two official transcripts from each institution previously attended. Students attempting less than 12 semester hours of credit should also submit the high school transcript and the results of the ACT or SAT. 30 of 120 credits required for the bachelor's degree must be completed at Loyola. **International Students:** There are 85 international students enrolled. They must take the TOEFL with a minimum score of 550 on the paper-based TOEFL (PBT) or 79 on the Internet-based version (iBT) and the college's own test. Scores are minimum score for a student to be admitted through the LIEP Pilot Program. They must also take the SAT or ACT.

ADMISSIONS: 69% of the 2017-2018 applicants were accepted. 60% of the current freshmen were in the top fifth of their class; 87% were in the top two fifths. 1 freshman graduated first in the class. **Admissions Contact:** John D. Head, VP of Enrollment Management. Email: *admit@loyno.edu* Web: *www.loyno.edu*

FINANCIAL AID: In 2017-2018, 89% of all full-time freshmen received some form of financial aid. 89% of all full-time freshmen received need-based aid. The average freshman award was $35,842. Need-based scholarships or need-based grants averaged $32,173; need-based self-help aid (loans and jobs) averaged $4,299; non-need-based athletic scholarships averaged $11,370; other non-need-based awards and non-need-based scholarships averaged $18,586; and $3,182 from other forms of aid. 25% of undergraduate students work part-time. The FAFSA code is 002016. The priority date for freshman financial aid applications for fall entry is March 1.

MCNEESE STATE UNIVERSITY B-4

www.mcneese.edu

Lake Charles, LA 70609 **(337) 475-5504** **(800) 622-3352**

Fax: (337) 475-5151 **Email: admissions@mcneese.edu**

Full-time: 2300 men, 3659 women	**Faculty:** IIA, --$
Part-time: 582 men, 960 women	**Ph.D.s:** 66%
Graduate: 270 men, 578 women	**Student/Faculty:** 21 to 1
Year: semesters, summer session	**Tuition:** $7838 ($11,075)
Room & Board: n/app	**Freshman Class:** n/av **CEEB CODE:** 6403
Application Deadline: August 1	**COMPETITIVE**

McNeese State University, founded in 1939, and part of the University of Louisiana System, is a public institution offering programs in business, engineering, education, science, liberal arts, and nursing. The figures given in the above capsule and in this profile are approximate. There are 7 undergraduate schools and one graduate school. In addition to regional accreditation, McNeese State University has baccalaureate program accreditation with AACSB, ADA, CAHEA, CSAB, NASAD, NASM, CAEP, AAFCS, ACS, EAC/ABET, CAATE, CADE, CCNE, CAC/ABET, NAACLS, NLNAC, JRCET, and TAC/ABET. The 121-acre campus is in a suburban area 130 miles west of Baton Rouge and 150 miles east of Houston, Texas. Including any residence halls, there are 88 buildings.

STUDENT LIFE: 90% of undergraduates are from Louisiana. Others are from 34 states, 49 foreign countries, and Canada. 73% are White; 4% Foreign; 2% Hispanic; 2% two or more races; 18% African American; 1% Asian American; 1% American Indian/Alaska Native. **Female To Male Ratio:** 1.6:1. The average age of freshmen is 20; all undergraduates, 23. 31% do not continue beyond their first year. **Housing:** 975 students can be accommodated in college housing, which includes dorms and on-campus apartments. On-campus housing is guaranteed for all 4 years, is available on a first-come, and first-served basis. Alcohol is not permitted. All students may keep cars.

FACULTY/CLASSROOMS: 48% of faculty are male; 52% are female. No introductory courses are taught by graduate students.

PROGRAMS OF STUDY: McNeese confers B.A., B.S., B.S.N. and B.G.S. degrees. Associate and master's degrees are also awarded. Bachelor's degrees are awarded in AGRICULTURE (agriculture and natural resource management), BIOLOGICAL SCIENCE (biology/biological science and nutritional sciences), BUSINESS (accounting, business administration and management, marketing, and organizational leadership and management), COMMUNICATIONS AND THE ARTS (art, communications, English, languages, and music), COMPUTER AND PHYSICAL SCIENCE (chemistry, computer science, mathematics, and radiological technology), EDUCATION (athletic training, early childhood education, elementary education, and health education), ENGINEERING AND ENVIRONMENTAL DESIGN (engineering and engineering technology), HEALTH PROFESSIONS (clinical science and nursing), SOCIAL SCIENCE (criminal justice, gender studies, history, liberal arts/general studies, political science/government, psychology, and sociology). Nursing, engineering, and education have the largest enrollments.

ACTIVITIES: Groups on campus include art, band, cheerleading, choir, chorale, chorus, computers, dance, debate, drama, drill team, ethnic, honors, international, jazz band, marching band, musical theater, newspaper, orchestra, pep band, political, professional, religious, social, social service, student government, symphony, and yearbook. Popular campus events include Homecoming, and Spring Fling. **Sports:** Facilities include a football stadium, softball and intramural fields, an indoor/outdoor track, a 50-meter pool, baseball complex, outdoor tennis courts, weight room, racquetball courts, basketball courts, golf, cross country, volleyball, and soccer. **Graduates:** From July 1, 2016 to June 30, 2017, 1177 bachelor's degrees were awarded. The most popular majors were general studies (15%), nursing (14%), and engineering (6%).

SERVICES: Counseling and information services are available, as is tutoring in some subjects. **Library/Resources:** Computerized library services include interlibrary loans, database searching, Internet access, and Wi-Fi capability. Special learning facilities include an art gallery, planetarium, a 503- acre farm, a vertebrate museum, a community health care clinic, a meat processing plant, and the Southwest Louisiana Entrepreneurial and Economic Development Center. **Physically Challenged Students:** Facilities include wheelchair ramps, elevators, special parking, specially equipped restrooms, and lowered drinking fountains. There is also an academic planning and registration assistance including classroom and testing accommodations. **Special:** MSU offers co-op programs in engineering, internships in clinical lab sciences, radiologic science, business and education, dual majors, a general studies degree, nondegree study, and credit for military experience. Innovation program available. There is a freshman honors program. **Visiting:** There are regularly scheduled orientations for prospective students. There are guides for informal visits, visitors may sit in on classes, and stay overnight. To schedule a visit, contact the Admissions Office. **Campus Safety and Security:** Measures include 24-hour foot and vehicle patrol, emergency notification system, and security escort services. There are emergency telephones and lighted pathways/sidewalks.

REQUIREMENTS: First-time freshmen who are graduates of state-approved Louisiana high schools must meet the following admission criteria: Completion of the Regents' high school Core 4 Curriculum; Need no developmental courses; and have a minimum high school overall GPA of 2.35; and one of the following: Minimum high school core GPA of 2.0 on a 4.0 scale as reported by the Department of Education or ACT composite score of 20 or greater (SAT combined mathematics and critical reading score of 940). AP and CLEP credits are accepted. McNeese State University's general education curriculum consists of coursework from 6 broad disciplinary areas: 6 hours each in writing, mathematics, natural sciences, and fine arts; 9 hours in humanities, social and behavioral sciences, and 3 hours in fine arts. The mission of this core curriculum is to provide students with a foundation of knowledge, skills, and methods of inquiry that support advanced study in their chosen degree program and constitute the characteristics of an informed, college-educated citizen. **Procedure:** Freshmen are admitted to all sessions. There are early admissions and rolling admissions plans. Applications should be filed by August 1 for fall entry. The fall 2017 application fee was $20. Applications are accepted on-line. **Transfer Students:** Transfer students who have earned 18 or more college-level academic credit hours must either have earned a transferable associate degree or higher from a regionally accredited institution or meet the following admission standards: Cumulative GPA of at least 2.0 on all college-level academic courses; Be eligible to return to the institution from which they are transferring; and have completed a college-level English and mathematics course designed to fulfill general education requirements. Transfer students who have a cumulative GPA of at least 2.0 on all college-level academic courses, but who have earned less than 18 college-level academic hours, must meet first-time freshman admission standards. 30 of 120 credits required for the bachelor's degree must be completed at MSU. **International Students:** There are 292 international students enrolled. They must take the TOEFL with a minimum score of 500 on the paper-based TOEFL (PBT). They must also take the SAT or ACT.

ADMISSIONS: The ACT scores were 36% below 12, 37% between 12 and 17, 17% between 18 and 23, 5% between 24 and 29, and 5% above 30. **Admissions Contact:** Kara Smith, Director of Admissions and Recruiting. Email: *admissions@mcneese.edu* Web: *www.mcneese.edu*

FINANCIAL AID: The FFS and the college's own financial statement are required. The FAFSA code is 002017. Check with the school for current application deadlines.

NICHOLLS STATE UNIVERSITY D-4

www.nicholls.edu

Thibodaux, LA 70310	(985) 448-4507 (877) 642-4655
Fax: (985) 448-4929	**Email:** nicholls@nicholls.edu
Full-time: 1673 men, 2912 women	**Faculty:** 255
Part-time: 241 men, 461 women	**Ph.D.s:** 58%
Graduate: 108 men, 461 women	**Student/Faculty:** 17 to 1
Year: semesters, summer session	**Tuition:** $7641 ($18,572)
Room & Board: $7318	**Freshman Class:** 2734 applied, 2260 accepted, 1138 enrolled
ACT: 22	**CEEB CODE:** 6221
Application Deadline: August 15	**COMPETITIVE**

Nicholls State University, established in 1948, and part of the University of Louisiana System, is a public liberal arts institution offering instruction in health sciences, fine arts, business, teacher preparation, and agricultural and technical disciplines. There are 6 undergraduate schools and 4 graduate schools. In addition to regional accreditation, NSU has baccalaureate program accreditation with AACSB, ACEJMC, ADA, CSAB, NASAD, NASM, CAEP, NLN, AAFCS, CAAHEP, and CCNE. The 210-acre campus is in a small town 50 miles southwest of New Orleans and 60 miles southeast of Baton Rouge. Including any residence halls, there are 48 buildings.

STUDENT LIFE: 97% of undergraduates are from Louisiana. Others are from 32 states, 45 foreign countries, and Canada. 69% are from public schools. 75% are White; 2% American Indian/Alaska Native; 2% Hispanic; 18% African American; 1% Asian American. 37% are Catholic; 18% Protestant. **Female To Male Ratio:** 1.9:1. The average age of freshmen is 18; all undergraduates, 22. 34% do not continue beyond their first year; 26% remain to graduate. **Housing:** 1503 students can be accommodated in college housing, which includes married student dorms, and single student apartments. On-campus housing is guaranteed for the freshman year only, and is available on a first-come, first-served basis. 54% of students commute. Alcohol is not permitted. All students may keep cars.

FACULTY/CLASSROOMS: 46% of faculty are male; 54% are female. Graduate students teach 1% of introductory courses.

PROGRAMS OF STUDY: NSU confers B.A., B.S., B.G.S., B.M.E. and B.S.N. degrees. Associate and master's degrees are also awarded. Bachelor's degrees are awarded in AGRICULTURE (agricultural business management), BIOLOGICAL SCIENCE (biology/biological science), BUSINESS (accounting, banking and finance, business administration and management, marketing/retailing/merchandising, and personnel management), COMMUNICATIONS AND THE ARTS (art, communications, English, French, journalism, and music), COMPUTER AND PHYSICAL SCIENCE (chemistry, computer science, information sciences and systems, and mathematics), EDUCATION (business education, elementary education, music education, secondary education, and special education), ENGINEERING AND ENVIRONMENTAL DESIGN (manufacturing technology and petroleum/natural gas engineering), HEALTH PROFESSIONS (health science, nursing, and speech pathology/audiology), SOCIAL SCIENCE (dietetics, family/consumer studies, food production/management/services, history, political science/government, psychology, and sociology). Languages, literature, and biological sciences are the strongest academically. Nursing, general studies, and teacher education have the largest enrollments.

ACTIVITIES: 13% of men belong to 7 national fraternities; 16% of women belong to 7 national sororities. Groups on campus include art, band, cheerleading, choir, chorale, chorus, computers, dance, debate, drama, drill team, ethnic, honors, international, jazz band, LGBT, literary magazine, marching band, musical theater, newspaper, pep band, photography, political, professional, radio and TV, religious, social, social service, student government, symphony, and yearbook. Popular campus events include Midterm Exam Week Breakfast, Family Day, and Crawfish Boil. **Sports:** There are 6 intercollegiate sports for men and 8 for women, and 4 intramural sports for men and 4 for women. Facilities include a stadium, gyms, tennis and racquetball courts, a soccer field, swimming pool, baseball and softball fields, and a weight room. **Graduates:** From July 1, 2016 to June 30, 2017, 875 bachelor's degrees were awarded. The most popular majors were business/marketing (26%), health professions and related programs (19%), and interdisciplinary studies (14%). In an average class, 9% graduate in 4 years or less, 20% graduate in 5 years or less, and 47% graduate in 6 years or less.

SERVICES: Counseling and information services are available, as is tutoring in most subjects. There is a reader service for the blind, and remedial math and writing. Tutoring is available in math, English, computer science, biology, chemistry, physics, and foreign languages. **Library/Resources:** Computerized library services include interlibrary loans, database searching, and Internet access. Special learning facilities include an art gallery, radio station, TV station, a culinary institute, a rural development institute, and centers for the study of dyslexia, women and government, and economic education. **Physically Challenged Students:** Facilities include wheelchair ramps, elevators, special parking, specially equipped restrooms, special class scheduling, lowered drinking fountains, and lowered telephones. **Special:** Internships are offered in business areas, government, home economics, computer science, and psychology. A Washington semester congressional internship and dual majors in education are available. Cross-registration with Fletcher Community College and River Parishes Community College and study abroad in 5 countries are offered. There are 12 national honor societies, a freshman honors program, and 1 departmental honors programs. **Visiting:** There are regularly scheduled orientations for prospective students, consisting of general information, advising, and registration. There are guides for informal visits, visitors may sit in on classes, and stay overnight. To schedule a visit, contact the Admissions Office. **Campus Safety and Security:** Measures include 24-hour foot and vehicle patrol, emergency notification system, self-defense education, and security escort services. There are emergency telephones and lighted pathways/sidewalks.

REQUIREMENTS: The ACT is recommended. Applicants must be graduates of an accredited secondary school or have the GED. 19 High school units required 4 each in English, math, and science, 2 each in foreign language, social studies, and history, and 1 in visual/performing arts. Nicholls requires applicants to be in the upper 50% of their class. A GPA of 2.0 is required. AP and CLEP credits are accepted. All students must complete general education requirements, including 9 hours each in English, natural sciences, and humanities, 6 hours each in social sciences and math, 3 hours in the arts, and student development, freshman and computer science course. At least 120 total credit hours, plus a minimum of 24 hours in the major, with a minimum GPA of 2.0, are required to graduate. Students also take a general education competency test before graduation. **Procedure:** Freshmen are admitted to all sessions. Entrance exams should be taken as early as possible. There are deferred admissions and rolling admissions plans. Application deadlines are open. The fall 2017 application fee was $20. Notification is sent on a rolling basis. Applications are accepted on-line. **Transfer Students:** 268 transfer students enrolled in 2016-2017. Transfer applicants must be eligible to return to the institution from which they are transferring, must have earned a minimum of 12 college-level hours, have a GPA of 2.0 on college-level courses, and require not more than 1 developmental course. 30 of 120 credits required for the bachelor's degree must be completed at NSU. **International Students:** There are 42 international students enrolled. They must take the TOEFL with a minimum score of 500 on the paper-based TOEFL (PBT) or 61 on the Internet-based version (iBT).

ADMISSIONS: 83% of the 2017-2018 applicants were accepted. The

ACT scores were 50% between 12 and 17, 40% between 18 and 23, and 10% between 24 and 29. 31% of the current freshmen were in the top fifth of their class; 58% were in the top two fifths. 43 freshmen graduated first in their class. **Admissions Contact:** Becky L. Durocher, Director of Admissions. Email: *nicholls@nicholls.edu* Web: *www.nicholls.edu*

FINANCIAL AID: In 2017-2018, 84% of all full-time freshmen received some form of financial aid. 46% of all full-time freshmen received need-based aid. The average freshman award was $11,512. Need-based scholarships or need-based grants averaged $8,557; need-based self-help aid (loans and jobs) averaged $2,810; non-need-based athletic scholarships averaged $6,980; other non-need-based awards and non-need-based scholarships averaged $2,683; and $3,580 from other forms of aid. 9% of undergraduate students work part-time. The average financial indebtedness of the 2017 graduate was $16,710. The FAFSA code is 002005. The priority date for freshman financial aid applications for fall entry is April 15.

NORTHWESTERN STATE UNIVERSITY OF LOUISIANA *(The complete profile is made available exclusively on our website, www.barronspac.com)*

SOUTHEASTERN LOUISIANA UNIVERSITY D-3
www.southeastern.edu

Hammond, LA 70402	**(985) 549-5910** **(800) 222-7358**
Fax: (985) 549-5632	**Email: admissions@southeastern.edu**
Full-time: 3465 men, 5555 women	**Faculty:** 423; IIA
Part-time: 1669 men, 2870 women	**Ph.D.s:** 65%
Graduate: 251 men, 689 women	**Student/Faculty:** 21 to 1
Year: semesters, summer session	**Tuition:** $7773 ($20,251)
Room & Board: $8464	**Freshman Class:** 3949 applied, 3534 accepted, 2474 enrolled
ACT: 22	**CEEB CODE:** 6656
Application Deadline: August 1	**COMPETITIVE**

Southeastern Louisiana University, founded in 1925, is a public university offering more than 60 undergraduate and graduate degree programs. There are 5 undergraduate schools. In addition to regional accreditation, SELU has baccalaureate program accreditation with AACSB, ABET, CSWE, NASAD, NASM, ACS, CCNE, AAFCS, CACREP, ATMAE, CAATE, CAAASLP, and CAEP. The 365-acre campus is in a small town 60 miles northwest of New Orleans and 50 miles east of Baton Rouge. Including any residence halls, there are 101 buildings.

STUDENT LIFE: 95% of undergraduates are from Louisiana. Others are from 38 states, 51 foreign countries, and Canada. 7% are Hispanic; 7% race unknown; 61% White; 5% two or more races; 2% Asian American; 2% Foreign; 18% African American. **Female To Male Ratio:** 1.7:1. The average age of freshmen is 18; all undergraduates, 21. 37% do not continue beyond their first year; 39% remain to graduate. **Housing:** 2387 students can be accommodated in college housing, which includes dorms and on-campus apartments. In addition, there are honors houses, fraternity houses, and sorority houses. On-campus housing is available on a first-come and first-served basis. 82% of students commute. All students may keep cars.

FACULTY/CLASSROOMS: 42% of faculty are male; 58% are female. 92% teach undergraduates, 41% do research, and 41% do both. No introductory courses are taught by graduate students. The average class size in an introductory lecture is 32; in a laboratory is 18; and in a regular course is 18.

PROGRAMS OF STUDY: SELU confers B.A., B.S., B.B.A., B.G.S., B.S.N. and B.M. degrees. Associate, master's, and doctoral degrees are also awarded. Bachelor's degrees are awarded in BIOLOGICAL SCIENCE (biology/biological science), BUSINESS (accounting, business administration and management, finance, management, marketing, sports management, and supply chain management), COMMUNICATIONS AND THE ARTS (art, communications, English, information technology, music, and Spanish), COMPUTER AND PHYSICAL SCIENCE (chemistry, computer science, mathematics, and physics), EDUCATION (athletic training, early childhood education, elementary education, English education, health education, middle school education, physical education, social science education, and special education), ENGINEERING AND ENVIRONMENTAL DESIGN (engineering technology, industrial engineering technology, and occupational safety and health), HEALTH PROFESSIONS (health, kinesiology, nursing, and occupational hygiene & safety), SOCIAL SCIENCE (communication sciences & disorders, criminal justice, family/consumer resource management, history, liberal arts/general studies, political science/government, psychology, social work, and sociology). Nursing, biology, and kinesiology have the largest enrollments.

ACTIVITIES: 2% of men belong to 11 national fraternities; 4% of women belong to 9 national sororities. There are 94 groups on campus, including art, band, cheerleading, choir, computers, dance, environmental, ethnic, film, honors, international, jazz band, LGBT, marching band, musical theater, newspaper, orchestra, photography, political, professional, radio and TV, religious, social, social service, student government, and yearbook. Popular campus events include Fanfare (cultural events monthly), Strawberry Jubilee, and Gumbo Ya Ya. **Sports:** There are 6 intercollegiate sports for men and 7 for women, and 20 intramural sports for men and 20 for women. Facilities include a weight, fitness, and aerobics rooms, an indoor elevated track, basketball, volleyball, badminton, tennis, and racquetball courts, multipurpose fields, a pool, gym, a football stadium, baseball and soccer fields. **Graduates:** From July 1, 2016 to June 30, 2017, 1760 bachelor's degrees were awarded. The most popular majors were general studies (12%), nursing (8%), and management (8%). In an average class, 18% graduate in 4 years or less, 17% graduate in 5 years or less, and 39% graduate in 6 years or less.

SERVICES: Counseling and information services are available, as is tutoring in some subjects, such as math, English, biology, physics, chemistry, foreign languages, accounting, economics, and computer science. There is remedial math and reading. **Library/Resources:** The library contains 366,589 volumes, 682,166 microform items, and 43,921 audio/video tapes/CDs/DVDs, and subscribes to 1,579 periodicals including electronic. Computerized library services include interlibrary loans, database searching, Internet access, and Wi-Fi capability. Special learning facilities include an art gallery, radio station, and TV station. **Physically Challenged Students:** 90% of the campus is accessible. Facilities include wheelchair ramps, elevators, special parking, specially equipped restrooms, special class scheduling, special housing. **Special:** Through a special adult learning initiative known as CALL (Center for Adult Learning in Louisiana), Southeastern is now offering registered nurses who are graduates of associate or diploma programs the opportunity to earn their bachelor of science degree in nursing completely online. The Turtle Cove Environmental Research Station is the environmental research, education, outreach, and restoration facility for Southeastern Louisiana University. The Institute for Biodiversity and Interdisciplinary Studies (IBIS). The mission of IBIS is to increase our understanding of the ecosystems of the Gulf Coast and the Lake Pontchartrain drainage basin in particular with an emphasis on fostering interdisciplinary understanding for students and other participants that will allow a generation to address environmental and biodiversity issues in a more comprehensive and inclusive manner. The University also offers summer abroad programs. There are 16 national honor societies, a freshman honors program, and 18 departmental honors programs. **Visiting:** There are regularly scheduled orientations for prospective students, includes a 1-day program of academic advising, class registration, social programs, and session presentations. There are guides for informal visits, visitors may sit in on classes, and stay overnight. To schedule a visit, contact the Admissions Office at admissions@selu.edu. **Campus Safety and Security:** Measures include 24-hour foot and vehicle patrol, emergency notification system, self-defense education, and security escort services. There are shuttle buses, emergency telephones, lighted pathways/sidewalks, controlled access to dorms/residences, community policing, bicycle patrols, and video cameras.

REQUIREMENTS: The ACT is required. Applicants should have completed the Louisiana Regents High School core curriculum, no developmental course requirement, have a minimum high school GPA of 2.35 (ACT 21 or a core GPA of 2.0). A GPA of 2.4 is required. AP and CLEP credits are accepted. To graduate, students must complete one of the curricula, including demonstrated profiency in English and math and have a cumulative degree GPA of 2.0 (2.5 in some majors). **Procedure:** Freshmen are admitted fall, spring, and summer. Entrance exams should be taken prior to registering for classes. There are deferred admissions and rolling admissions plans. Applications should be filed by August 1 for fall entry; December 1 for spring entry; and May 1 for summer entry. The fall 2017 application fee was $20. Applications are accepted on-line. **Transfer Students:** 599 transfer students enrolled in 2016-2017. Option

1 - Transferrable associates degree or higher from regionally accredited institution & cumulative GPA of 2.0 or higher. Option 2 - Cumulative GPA of 2.0 or higher on all college work, college-level English and Math credits earned, must be eligible to return to last institution attended. 30 of 120 credits required for the bachelor's degree must be completed at SELU. **International Students:** There are 174 international students enrolled. They must take the TOEFL with a minimum score of 500 on the paper-based TOEFL (PBT) or 61 on the Internet-based version (iBT). They must also take the ACT, scoring 21.

ADMISSIONS: 89% of the 2017-2018 applicants were accepted. The ACT scores were 4% between 12 and 17, 64% between 18 and 23, 30% between 24 and 29, and 2% above 30. 28% of the current freshmen were in the top fifth of their class; 59% were in the top two fifths. 42 freshmen graduated first in their class. **Admissions Contact:** Mike Rivault, Interim Director of Admissions. Email: *admissions@southeastern.edu* Web: *www.southeastern.edu*

FINANCIAL AID: The average financial indebtedness of the 2017 graduate was $23,536. SELU is a member of CSS. The FAFSA code is 002024. The priority date for freshman financial aid applications for fall entry is May 1.

SOUTHERN UNIVERSITY AND A&M COLLEGE *(The complete profile is made available exclusively on our website, www.barronspac.com)*

SOUTHERN UNIVERSITY AT NEW ORLEANS *(The complete profile is made available exclusively on our website, www.barronspac.com)*

TULANE UNIVERSITY D-4

www.tulane.edu

New Orleans, LA 70118 **(504) 865-5731** **(800) 873-9283**

Fax: (504) 862-8715 **Email: undergrad.admission@tulane.edu**

Full-time: 2672 men, 3868 women	**Faculty:** 859; I, av$
Part-time: 15 men, 16 women	**Ph.D.s:** 91%
Graduate: 2046 men, 2631 women	**Student/Faculty:** 7 to 1
Year: semesters, summer session	**Tuition:** $52,960
Room & Board: $14,536	**Freshman Class:** 35622 applied, 7657 accepted, 1905 enrolled
SAT CR/M: 710/710 **ACT:** 31	**CEEB CODE:** 6832
Application Deadline: January 15	**MOST COMPETITIVE**

Tulane University is one of the country's most respected universities, with top-ranked programs in the academic and professional schools, and research and educational partnerships that span the globe. Tulane University offers an unparalleled educational experience. Founded in 1834, Tulane is home to schools and colleges offering undergraduate, graduate, and professional degrees in architecture, business, science and engineering, law, liberal arts, medicine, public health and tropical medicine, and social work. There are 6 undergraduate schools and 8 graduate schools. In addition to regional accreditation, TU has baccalaureate program accreditation with AACSB, ABET, CSAB, CSWE, NAAB, and ACS. The 110-acre campus is in an urban area of Uptown New Orleans. Including any residence halls, there are 92 buildings.

STUDENT LIFE: 77% of undergraduates are from out of state, mostly the Northeast. Students are from 50 states, 100 foreign countries, and Canada. 57% are from public schools. 73% are White; 7% Hispanic; 5% Asian American; 5% Foreign; 4% African American; 4% two or more races; 1% race unknown. **Female To Male Ratio:** 1.4:1. The average age of freshmen is 18; all undergraduates, 22. **Housing:** 4056 students can be accommodated in college housing, which includes coed and married student dorms and on-campus apartments. In addition, there are honors houses, special-interest houses, fraternity houses, sorority houses, and special-interest floors. On-campus housing is available on a lottery system for upperclassmen. 52% of students commute. Upperclassmen may keep cars.

FACULTY/CLASSROOMS: 59% of faculty are male; 41% are female. No introductory courses are taught by graduate students.

PROGRAMS OF STUDY: TU confers B.A., B.A.R., B.B.S., B.F.A., B.G.S., B.M.T., B.P.A., B.P.E., B.P.H., B.S., B.S.E., B.S.M., B.S.W., and M.Arch degrees. Associate, master's, and doctoral degrees are also awarded. Bachelor's degrees are awarded in BIOLOGICAL SCIENCE (biochemistry, cell biology, ecology, environmental biology, evolutionary biology, molecular biology, and neurosciences), BUSINESS (accounting, banking and finance, business administration and management, entrepreneurial studies, finance, management science, and marketing management), COMMUNICATIONS AND THE ARTS (art history and appreciation, classics, communications, dance, dramatic arts, English, film arts, French, German, Greek (modern), Italian, jazz, journalism, linguistics, media arts, music, music composition, Portuguese, Russian, Spanish, studio art, and theater design), COMPUTER AND PHYSICAL SCIENCE (chemistry, digital arts/technology, earth science, geology, information sciences and systems, mathematics, physics, science, and web technology), EDUCATION (early childhood education, global studies, health education, and psychology education), ENGINEERING AND ENVIRONMENTAL DESIGN (architecture, biomedical engineering, chemical engineering, computer technology, engineering physics, and environmental science), HEALTH PROFESSIONS (community health work and public health), SOCIAL SCIENCE (African studies, American studies, anthropology, Asian/Oriental studies, cognitive science, economics, gender studies, history, homeland security/emergency preparedness, humanities, Judaic studies, Latin American studies, legal studies, liberal arts/general studies, medieval studies, paralegal studies, philosophy, political science/government, psychology, religion, Russian and Slavic studies, social science, social studies, social work, sociology, and women's studies). Environmental sciences, political economy, and pre-professional programs. are the strongest academically. Liberal arts, business, and science have the largest enrollments.

ACTIVITIES: 29% of men belong to 12 national fraternities; 50% of women belong to 12 national sororities. There are 344 groups on campus, including art, band, cheerleading, chess, choir, chorale, chorus, communications, computers, dance, debate, drama, drill team, drum and bugle corps, environmental, ethnic, film, honors, international, jazz band, LGBT, literary magazine, marching band, musical theater, newspaper, orchestra, pep band, photography, political, professional, radio and TV, religious, social, social service, student government, symphony, and yearbook. Popular campus events include Crawfest, Wave Good-Bye, Technology Expo, and Homecoming. **Sports:** There are 6 intercollegiate sports for men and 7 for women, and 24 intramural sports for men and 24 for women. Facilities include a baseball diamond, a track complex, tennis facility, a recreation center with indoor and outdoor pools, indoor track, squash and racquetball courts, gymnastics area, weight room, exercise rooms and equipment, basketball and volleyball facilities, and football. **Graduates:** From July 1, 2016 to June 30, 2017, 1753 bachelor's degrees were awarded. The most popular majors were business/marketing (26%), social science (16%), and health professions and related programs (10%).

SERVICES: Counseling and information services are available, as is tutoring in most subjects, such as high-demand math, science classes and some languages. There is a reader service for the blind. **Library/Resources:** The library contains 4.6 million volumes, 2.5 million microform items, and 162,872 audio/video tapes/CDs/DVDs, and subscribes to 72,300 periodicals including electronic. Computerized library services include interlibrary loans, database searching, Internet access, and Wi-Fi capability. Special learning facilities include an art gallery, natural history museum, radio station, TV station, an observatory, Middle American Research Institute, Amistad Research Center, Tulane Jazz Archives, Latin American Library, and Tulane Center for Research on Women, Koch Herbarium, Tulane Museum of Natural History, Newcomb Art Gallery, and the ByWater Institute. **Physically Challenged Students:** 60% of the campus is accessible. Facilities include wheelchair ramps, elevators, special parking, specially equipped restrooms, lowered drinking fountains, lowered telephones, and special housing. **Special:** Students may pursue cross-registration with Loyola and Xavier Universities, numerous internships, study abroad in 23 countries, work-study programs, a Washington semester, and B.A.-B.S. degrees in liberal arts, engineering, and architecture. Tulane also offers accelerated joint degrees with its schools of medicine, law, business, and public health; student-designed, dual, and interdisciplinary majors, including art and biology, Greek and Latin, mathematical economics, political economy, and cognitive studies; a 3-2 engineering degree with Xavier University of Louisiana, joint graduate/professional programs, and 4+1 programs. There are 37 national honor societies, Phi Beta Kappa, a freshman honors program, and 37 departmental honors programs. **Visiting:** There are regularly scheduled orientations for prospective students, including 3 on-campus Saturday programs in the fall, daily information sessions, and tours Monday through Friday and Saturday mornings during the academic year. In the spring semester, more structured programs are available daily. There are guides for informal visits, visitors may sit in on classes, and stay overnight. To schedule a visit, contact the Office of Undergraduate Admissions. **Campus Safety and Security:** Measures include 24-hour foot and vehicle patrol, emergency notification system, self-defense education, and security escort services. There are shuttle buses, emergency telephones, lighted pathways/sidewalks, controlled access to dorms/residences. There are trained student patrols, and programs about living safely off campus. Victim resources include academic assistance, legal counseling, emergency housing, and security review of home and personal security habits. In addition, there are bike patrols, limited dorm access, smoke detectors in dorms, and surveillance cameras.

REQUIREMENTS: The SAT or ACT is required. A GPA of 3.6 is required. AP credits are accepted. Important factors in the admissions decision are advanced placement or honors courses, recommendations by school officials, and extracurricular activities record. All students in the liberal arts and sciences must meet proficiency requirements in English, foreign language, and math. They must take a distribution component including courses in humanities and fine arts, social sciences, and sciences and math. A total of 120 credits, including at least 24 in the major, with a minimum cumulative GPA of 2.0, is required to graduate. **Procedure:** Freshmen are admitted fall and spring. Entrance exams should be taken during spring of the junior year or fall of the senior year. There is a deferred admissions plan. Early decision applications should be filed by November 1; regular applications, by January 15 for fall entry; and November 1 for spring entry. Notification of early decision is sent December 15; regular decision, April 1. 5596 applicants were on the 2017 waiting list. Applications are accepted on-line. **Transfer Students:** 94 transfer students enrolled in 2016-2017. Applicants must submit SAT or ACT scores, high school transcripts, proof of good standing at previously attended institutions, and transcripts (with course descriptions) from all colleges or universities attended. A minimum 2.50 GPA is recommended. 60 of 120 credits required for the bachelor's degree must be completed at TU. **International Students:** There are 390 international students enrolled. They must take the TOEFL with a minimum score of 550 on the paper-based TOEFL (PBT) or 88 on the Internet-based version (iBT). They must also take the SAT or ACT.

ADMISSIONS: 21% of the 2017-2018 applicants were accepted. The SAT scores for the 2017-2018 freshman class were: Math-- 3% below 500, 3% between 500 and 599, 35% between 600 and 699, and 59% between 700 and 800. Evidence-Based Reading/Writing-- 2% below 500, 5% between 500 and 599, 32% between 600 and 699, and 61% between 700 and 800. The ACT scores were 2% between 18 and 23, 20% between 24 and 29, and 79% above 30. **Admissions Contact:** Satyajit Dattagupta, Vice President of Enrollment & Dean of Undergraduate Admission. Email: *undergrad.admission@tulane.edu* Web: *www.tulane.edu*

FINANCIAL AID: In 2017-2018, 36% of all full-time freshmen received some form of financial aid. 37% of all full-time freshmen received need-based aid. 55% of undergraduate students work part-time. The average financial indebtedness of the 2017 graduate was $33,717. Tulane University is a member of CSS. The CSS/Profile, and the noncustodial profile and the business/farm supplement (if applicable) are required. The FAFSA code is 002029. The priority date for freshman financial aid applications for fall entry is February 15.

UNIVERSITY OF HOLY CROSS *(The complete profile is made available exclusively on our website, www.barronspac.com)*

UNIVERSITY OF LOUISIANA AT LAFAYETTE — C-4

www.louisiana.edu

Lafayette, LA 70504 — **(337) 482-6473**

Fax: (337) 482-6195	**Email:** admissions@louisiana.edu
Full-time: 5000 men, 7000 women	**Faculty:** 666
Part-time: 920 men, 1640 women	**Ph.D.s:** 79%
Graduate: 700 men, 930 women	**Student/Faculty:** 18 to 1
Year: semesters, summer session	**Tuition:** $8256 ($19,364)
Room & Board: $6260	**Freshman Class:** n/av
SAT or ACT: required	**CEEB CODE:** 6672
Application Deadline: open	**COMPETITIVE**

University of Louisiana at Lafayette, founded in 1898, is a public institution offering degree programs in liberal arts, fine arts, business, agriculture, technical disciplines, health science, engineering, and teacher preparation. Figures in the above capsule and in this profile are approximate. There are 9 undergraduate schools and one graduate school. In addition to regional accreditation, UL Lafayette has baccalaureate program accreditation with AACSB, ABET, ACEJMC, ADA, AHEA, ASLA, CAHEA, CSAB, FIDER, NAAB, NASM, NCATE, and NLN. The 1375-acre campus is in an urban area 129 miles west of New Orleans. Including any residence halls, there are 239 buildings.

STUDENT LIFE: 95% of undergraduates are from Louisiana. Others are from 48 states, 102 foreign countries, and Canada. 74% are White; 4% Foreign; 2% Asian American; 17% African American; 1% American Indian/Alaska Native; 1% Hispanic. 50% are Catholic; 31% claim no religious affiliation; 12% Protestant. **Female To Male Ratio:** 1.4:1. The average age of freshmen is 19; all undergraduates, 24. 28% do not continue beyond their first year; 30% remain to graduate. **Housing:** 1860 students can be accommodated in college housing, which includes single-sex dorms, on-campus apartments, and married student housing. Residence halls for athletes and for Pan-Hellenic groups available. On-campus housing is guaranteed for all 4 years. 89% of students commute. All students may keep cars.

FACULTY/CLASSROOMS: 59% of faculty are male; 41% are female. No introductory courses are taught by graduate students.

PROGRAMS OF STUDY: UL Lafayette confers B.A., B.S., B.A.M., B.F.A., B.G.S., B.M.E., B.M.P., B.M.P.P., B.S.A., B.S.A.E., B.S.B.A., B.S.C.E., B.S.C.I.E., B.S.E.E., B.S.I.T., B.S.M.E., B.S.N., and B.S.P.E. degrees. Master's and doctoral degrees are also awarded. Bachelor's degrees are awarded in BUSINESS (accounting, banking and finance, business administration and management, fashion merchandising, hotel/motel and restaurant management, management science, marketing/retailing/merchandising, and personnel management), COMMUNICATIONS AND THE ARTS (advertising, broadcasting, communications, dance, dramatic arts, English, fine arts, French, music, public relations, Spanish, and telecommunications), COMPUTER AND PHYSICAL SCIENCE (chemistry, computer science, geology, mathematics, physics, and statistics), EDUCATION (agricultural education, art education, elementary education, English education, foreign languages education, health education, home economics education, industrial arts education, mathematics education, music education, science education, secondary education, social studies education, and special education), ENGINEERING AND ENVIRONMENTAL DESIGN (chemical engineering, civil engineering, computer engineering, electrical/electronics engineering, industrial engineering, interior design, land use management and reclamation, mechanical engineering, and petroleum/natural gas engineering), HEALTH PROFESSIONS (nursing and speech pathology/audiology), SOCIAL SCIENCE (anthropology, criminal justice, dietetics, economics, history, philosophy, political science/government, psychology, and sociology). Computer science, engineering, and math are the strongest academically. Nursing, elementary education, and business administration have the largest enrollments.

ACTIVITIES: 5% of women belong to 8 national sororities. There are 200 groups on campus, including wakeboard club, camping club, band, cheerleading, choir, chorus, computers, dance, debate, drama, drum and bugle corps, ethnic, forensics, honors, international, jazz band, LGBT, marching band, musical theater, newspaper, opera, orchestra, photography, political, powerlifting club, professional, radio and TV, religious, social, social service, student government, and yearbook. Popular campus events include Rajun Roar, Welcome Week, Homecoming Week, Mardi Gras Parade and Celebration, and Freshman First Down. **Sports:** There are 8 intercollegiate sports for men and 7 for women, and 16 intramural sports for men and 16 for women. Facilities include a stadium, basketball arena, gym, track, a softball park, tennis courts, various playing fields, and a health and phys ed complex. Recreation such as fishing, ice hockey, lacrosse, soccer, bowling, sport shooting, and volleyball offered. **Graduates:** From July 1, 2015 to June 30, 2016, 2494 bachelor's degrees were awarded. The most popular majors were business (20%), general studies (14%), and education (14%). 114 companies recruited on campus in 2015-2016. In an average class, 7% graduate in 4 years or less, 21% graduate in 5 years or less, and 29% graduate in 6 years or less.

SERVICES: Counseling and information services are available, as is tutoring in most subjects. There is remedial math, reading, and writing. Entering freshman can only be in 1 remedial course. **Library/Resources:** The library contains 873,173 volumes, 1.8 million microform items, and 255,992 audio/video tapes/CDs/DVDs, and subscribes to 4,965 periodicals including electronic. Computerized library services include interlibrary loans and database searching. Special learning facilities include an art gallery, radio station, and numerous research centers for environmental, business, science, computer, and business studies. **Physically Challenged Students:** 90% of the campus is accessible. Facilities include wheelchair ramps, elevators, special parking, specially equipped restrooms, and special class scheduling. **Special:** Various internships are available, including a Washington semester. Students may study in France, Canada, Belgium, Japan, and Mexico. UL Lafayette also offers an accelerated degree program in nursing, B.A.-B.S. degrees, and dual majors. There are 6 national honor societies and a freshman honors program. **Visiting:** There are regularly scheduled orientations for prospective students, including campus tours. There are guides for informal visits. To schedule a visit, contact the Admissions Office. **Campus Safety and Security:** Measures include 24-hour foot and vehicle patrol and security escort services. There are shuttle buses, emergency telephones, and lighted pathways/sidewalks.

REQUIREMENTS: The SAT or ACT is required. Admissions criteria are based on a sliding scale of standardized test scores and GPA. Students should be graduates of accredited secondary schools or have the GED. UL Lafayette requires that students have at least 4 units in English, 3 each in math, science, and social studies, and 4 1/2 in electives, recommended to include 2 in foreign language, 1 each in fine arts and speech, and 1/2 in computer studies. A GPA of 2.0 is required. AP and CLEP credits are accepted. Students are required to complete 42 semester hours of general education courses in the arts, literature, history, math, sciences, behavioral sciences, and composition. Phys ed is required in all but engineering and nursing programs. A minimum of 124 semester hours, with at least 33 in the major, is required for graduation. A minimum GPA of 2.0 is needed; some majors require higher GPAs. **Procedure:** Freshmen are admitted to all sessions. There are early admissions, deferred admissions, and rolling admissions plans. Application deadlines are open. Application fee is $20. **Transfer Students:** 740 transfer students enrolled in 2015-2016. A cumulative GPA of 2.0 is required. 30 of 124 credits required for the bachelor's degree must be completed at UL Lafayette. **International Students:** There are 259 international students enrolled. The school actively recruits these students. They must take the TOEFL. They must also take the SAT or ACT.

Admissions Contact: Leroy Broussard, Director of Admissions. Email: *admissions@louisiana.edu* Web: *www.louisiana.edu*

FINANCIAL AID: 30% of undergraduate students work part-time. Average annual earnings from campus work are $1250. UL Lafayette is a member of CSS. The FAFSA code is 002031. The deadline for filing freshman financial aid applications for fall entry is March 1.

UNIVERSITY OF LOUISIANA AT MONROE C-1

www.ulm.edu

Monroe, LA 71209	(318) 342-5259
	Email: schmeer@ulm.edu
Full-time: 1856 men, 3352 women	**Faculty:** n/av
Part-time: 985 men, 1585 women	**Ph.D.s:** n/av
Graduate: 413 men, 847 women	**Student/Faculty:** n/av
Year: semesters, summer session	**Tuition:** $8282 ($20,382)
Room & Board: $7688	**Freshman Class:** 3944 applied, 3551 accepted, 1430 enrolled
SAT CR/M: 500/570 **ACT:** 22	**CEEB CODE:** 6482
Application Deadline: open	**COMPETITIVE**

University of Louisiana at Monroe, founded in 1931, is a public institution offering programs in business, education, liberal arts, pharmacy and health sciences, and pure and applied science. There are 3 undergraduate schools and 1 graduate school. In addition to regional accreditation, ULM has baccalaureate program accreditation with AACSB, ABET, ACCE, ACPE, CSWE, NASM, CAEP, ACOTE, CNNE, CODA, CAEP, JRCERT, and NAACLS. The 238-acre campus is in an urban area in Northeast Louisiana, 90 miles east of Shreveport on I-20. Including any residence halls, there are 97 buildings.

STUDENT LIFE: 88% of undergraduates are from Louisiana. Others are from 48 states, 55 foreign countries, and Canada. 65% are White; 4% Foreign; 22% African American; 2% Asian American; 2% Hispanic; 2% two or more races; 2% race unknown. **Female To Male Ratio:** 1.8:1. The average age of freshmen is 18; all undergraduates, 21. **Housing:** 1862 students can be accommodated in college housing, which includes dorms and on-campus apartments, and a scholastic residence hall. On-campus housing is available on a first-come and first-served basis. 76% of students commute. Alcohol is not permitted. All students may keep cars.

FACULTY/CLASSROOMS: No introductory courses are taught by graduate students.

PROGRAMS OF STUDY: ULM confers B.A., B.S., B.B.A., B.F.A., B.G.S., B.M., and B.S.N. degrees. Associate, master's, and doctoral degrees are also awarded. Bachelor's degrees are awarded in AGRICULTURE (agricultural business management), BIOLOGICAL SCIENCE (biological sciences and toxicology), BUSINESS (accounting, business administration and management, finance, insurance, marketing, management & strategic leadership, and organizational leadership and management), COMMUNICATIONS AND THE ARTS (art, communications, English, foreign language, modern language, and music), COMPUTER AND PHYSICAL SCIENCE (computer information systems, computer science, mathematics, and radiological technology), EDUCATION (education, elementary education, secondary education, and special education), ENGINEERING AND ENVIRONMENTAL DESIGN (aviation business administration and construction management), HEALTH PROFESSIONS (dental hygiene, exercise science, health science, kinesiology, medical laboratory science, nursing, occupational therapy, pharmaceutical science, pharmacy, and speech pathology/audiology), SOCIAL SCIENCE (criminal justice, history, political science/government, psychology, and social work). Pharmacy, nursing, and health sciences are the strongest academically. Pharmacy, nursing, and kinesiology have the largest enrollments.

ACTIVITIES: 9% of men belong to 7 national fraternities; 11% of women belong to 8 national sororities. There are 108 groups on campus, including art, band, cheerleading, choir, chorale, chorus, computers, dance, debate, drama, drill team, drum and bugle corps, ethnic, film, forensics, honors, international, jazz band, literary magazine, marching band, musical theater, newspaper, opera, orchestra, pep band, political, professional, radio and TV, religious, social, social service, student government, symphony, and yearbook. Popular campus events include Week of Welcome, Lyceum Series, Spring Fever, and Casino Night. **Sports:** There are 7 intercollegiate sports for men and 10 for women, and 28 intramural sports for men and 28 for women. Facilities include a coliseum, stadiums, tennis courts, a softball complex, an activity center, a baseball complex, and outdoor volleyball courts. **Graduates:** From July 1, 2016 to June 30, 2017, 1023 bachelor's degrees were awarded. The most popular majors were political science (9%), general studies (8%), and kinesiology (7%).

SERVICES: Counseling and information services are available, as is tutoring in most subjects. There is remedial math, reading, and writing. **Library/Resources:** The library contains 1.1 million volumes, 578,611 microform items, and subscribes to 83,979 periodicals including electronic. Computerized library services include interlibrary loans, database searching, Internet access, and Wi-Fi capability. Special learning facilities include an art gallery, natural history museum, planetarium, radio station, a herbarium, state poison control center, and state tumor registry. **Physically Challenged Students:** 98% of the campus is accessible. Facilities include wheelchair ramps, elevators, special parking, specially equipped restrooms, special class scheduling, lowered drinking fountains, and specially equipped dorm rooms. **Special:** ULM offers cross registration with selected other institutions as well as internships across a wide variety of academic disciplines. There are 30 national honor societies, a freshman honors program, and 23 departmental honors programs. **Visiting:** There are regularly scheduled orientations for prospective students, visiting students may participate in the mandatory PREP program, which includes campus tours, meetings with deans/advisers, class registration, and placement examinations. There are guides for informal visits and visitors may sit in on classes. To schedule a visit, contact the Office of Recruitment and Admissions. **Campus Safety and Security:** Measures include 24-hour foot and vehicle patrol, emergency notification system, self-defense education, and security escort services. There are emergency telephones, lighted pathways/sidewalks, and controlled access to dorms/residences.

REQUIREMENTS: The ACT is required. Applicants must be graduates of an accredited high school or have a GED. CLEP credits are accepted. 1 hour university seminar, 6 hours English composition, 6 hours mathematics, 9 hours natural/physical sciences, 9 hours humanities, 3 hours fine arts, 6 hours social/behavioral sciences. Overall minimum GPA of 2.0 required for graduation, plus variable total hours earned dependent upon program required. **Procedure:** Freshmen are admitted to all sessions. Entrance exams should be taken by April 1. There is a rolling admissions plan. Application deadlines are open. The fall 2017 application fee was $20. Applications are accepted on-line. **Transfer Students:** Applicants must have a minimum overall GPA of 2.0 from a regionally accredited institution and at least 12 semester hours of college-level credit above the remedial level, including a math and an English course. Students who have completed fewer than 12 semester hours of college credit must meet ULM freshman admission requirements. 30 credits required for the bachelor's degree must be completed at ULM. **International Students:** There are 282 international students enrolled. They must take the TOEFL with a minimum score of 61 on the Internet-based version (iBT). They must also take the SAT or ACT.

ADMISSIONS: 90% of the 2017-2018 applicants were accepted. The SAT scores for the 2017-2018 freshman class were: Critical Reading-- 50% below 500, 34% between 500 and 599, 14% between 600 and 699, and 2% between 700 and 800. Math-- 32% below 500, 27% between 500 and 599, 27% between 600 and 699, and 14% between 700 and 800. The ACT scores were 6% between 12 and 17, 58% between 18 and 23, 54% between 24 and 29, and 5% above 30. **Admissions Contact:** Mary Schmeer, Director of Enrollment and Scholarships. Email: *schmeer@ulm.edu* Web: *www.ulm.edu*

FINANCIAL AID: The FAFSA code is 002020. Check with the school for current application deadlines.

UNIVERSITY OF NEW ORLEANS D-4

www.uno.edu

New Orleans, LA 70148	**(504) 280-6595**
Fax: (504) 280-5522	**Email: admissions@uno.edu**
Full-time: 3104 men, 3400 women	**Faculty:** 326; I
Part-time: 974 men, 1175 women	**Ph.D.s:** 67%
Graduate: 1116 men, 1594 women	**Student/Faculty:** 20 to 1
Year: semesters, summer session	**Tuition:** $7600 ($11,175)
Room & Board: $5240	**Freshman Class:** 1767 applied, 1430 accepted, 1119 enrolled
SAT CR/M/W: 550/550/540 **ACT:** 21	**CEEB CODE:** 6379
Application Deadline: July 25	**COMPETITIVE**

University of New Orleans, founded in 1958, is a public liberal arts institution. Figures in the above capsule and in this profile are approxiate. There are 6 undergraduate schools. In addition to regional accreditation, UNO has baccalaureate program accreditation with AACSB, ABET, NASM, NCATE, NAST, CACREP, and NLN. The 195-acre campus is in an urban area on the southern shore of Lake Pontchartrain, 15 minutes from the French Quarter. Including any residence halls, there are 34 buildings.

STUDENT LIFE: 70% of undergraduates are from Louisiana. Others are from 42 states, 74 foreign countries, and Canada. 62% are from public schools. 7% are Hispanic; 60% White; 6% Asian American; 6% Foreign; 19% African American; 1% American Indian/Alaska Native. 67% claim no religious affiliation; 19% Catholic. **Female To Male Ratio:** 1.2:1. The average age of freshmen is 19; all undergraduates, 24. 31% do not continue beyond their first year. **Housing:** 1426 students can be accommodated in college housing, which includes coed dorms and married student housing. On-campus housing is available on a first-come, first-served basis. 95% of students commute. All students may keep cars.

FACULTY/CLASSROOMS: 59% of faculty are male; 41% are female. No introductory courses are taught by graduate students.

PROGRAMS OF STUDY: UNO confers B.A., B.S. and B.G.S. degrees. Master's and doctoral degrees are also awarded. Bachelor's degrees are awarded in BIOLOGICAL SCIENCE (biology/biological science), BUSINESS (accounting, banking and finance, business administration and management, hotel/motel and restaurant management, marketing/retailing/merchandising, and tourism), COMMUNICATIONS AND THE ARTS (art, art history and appreciation, communications, dramatic arts, English, fine arts, French, music, Spanish, and studio art), COMPUTER AND PHYSICAL SCIENCE (chemistry, computer science, earth science, geology, geophysics and seismology, mathematics, and physics), EDUCATION (early childhood education, elementary education, English education, foreign languages education, mathematics education, music education, physical education, and secondary education), ENGINEERING AND ENVIRONMENTAL DESIGN (civil engineering, electrical/electronics engineering, environmental science, marine engineering, mechanical engineering, and naval architecture and marine engineering), HEALTH PROFESSIONS (health, medical technology, premedicine, and preveterinary science), SOCIAL SCIENCE (anthropology, economics, geography, history, international studies, philosophy, political science/government, psychology, sociology, and urban studies). Business administration, general studies, and film have the largest enrollments.

ACTIVITIES: 1% of men belong to 8 national fraternities; 1% of women belong to 8 national sororities. There are 108 groups on campus, including art, band, choir, chorale, chorus, computers, dance, drama, ethnic, film, honors, international, jazz band, LGBT, literary magazine, newspaper, opera, orchestra, pep band, political, professional, radio and TV, religious, social, social service, and student government. Popular campus events include International Night, Privateer Plunge for New Students, Homecoming, Holi a Hindu Celebration, Krewe of UNO Parade, Swampball, Behind the Scenes, and Commencement Celebration. **Sports:** There are 3 intercollegiate sports for men and 3 for women, and 10 intramural sports for men and 10 for women. Facilities include a lakefront arena, a Privateer Park, 1/10 mile indoor jogging/walking track, various group exercise classes such as indoor cycling, yoga and step aerobics, 2 dry saunas, 2 racquetball courts, 3 basketball courts, snack bar, outdoor deck adjacent to pool, and natatorium (25-yard/4-lane lap pool) for water group exercise and lap/recreational swimming. **Graduates:** From July 1, 2015 to June 30, 2016, 1368 bachelor's degrees were awarded. The most popular majors were business (16%), psychology (5%), and film, theater, and communication arts (5%). 284 companies recruited on campus in 2015-2016. In an average class, 47% graduate in 4 years or less, 64% graduate in 5 years or less, and 88% graduate in 6 years or less.

SERVICES: Counseling and information services are available, as is tutoring in most subjects. There is a reader service for the blind, and remedial math, reading, and writing. **Library/Resources:** The library contains 896,000 volumes, 12.4 million microform items, and 22,775 audio/video tapes/CDs/DVDs, and subscribes to 4,950 periodicals including electronic. Computerized library services include interlibrary loans, database searching, and Internet access. Special learning facilities include an art gallery and radio station. **Physically Challenged Students:** 80% of the campus is accessible. Facilities include wheelchair ramps, elevators, special parking, specially equipped restrooms, lowered drinking fountains, lowered telephones, and special housing. **Special:** Students may participate in co-op programs and may cross-register with Southern University in New Orleans, Elaine P. Nunez Community College, and Delgado Community College. Internships are available, and work-study programs are available with various federal agencies and private companies. Students may study abroad in 14 countries or participate in a Washington semester. UNO also offers dual majors, B.A.-B.S. and degrees, pre-professional programs in cardiopulmonary science, dental hygiene, dentistry, medical technology, medicine, nursing, occupational therapy, opthhalmic medical technology, pharmacy, physical therapy, physician's assistant, rehabilitation counseling, and veterinary medicine. 3-2 engineering degrees with Xavier University, Southern University in New Orleans, Loyola University New Orleans, and Dillard University are offered. There are 12 national honor societies, a freshman honors program, and 29 departmental honors programs. **Visiting:** There are guides for informal visits. To schedule a visit, contact Privateer Enrollment Center at leverink@uno.edu. **Campus Safety and Security:** Measures include 24-hour foot and vehicle patrol, emergency notification system, self-defense education, and security escort services. There are emergency telephones, lighted pathways/sidewalks, and monitored parking.

REQUIREMENTS: Students who graduate from state-approved high schools must complete the Louisiana Board of Regents Core Curriculum and require no more than one developmental/remedial course and meet one of the following criteria: ACT composite score of 23 or greater (SAT 1060) or high school cumulative GPA of 2.5 or greater with an ACT (SAT equivalent) of 18 or greater on the English and or Math sub scores OR, high school graduation rank top 25% of class. UNO requires applicants to be in the upper 25% of their class. A GPA of 2.5 is required. AP and CLEP credits are accepted. Important factors in the admissions decision are advanced placement or honors courses, recommendations by school officials, and evidence of special talent. Requirements for graduation include completion of courses in English, literature, math, humanities and art, science, social science, and computer literacy. Students must complete 120 hours with a minimum GPA of 2.0. **Procedure:**

Freshmen are admitted to all sessions. Entrance exams should be taken at least 6 months prior to enrollment. There are early admissions, deferred admissions, and rolling admissions plans. Applications should be filed by July 25 for fall entry; November 15 for spring entry; and May 1 for summer entry, along with a $40 fee. Applications are accepted online. **Transfer Students:** A student must have completed at least 18 hours of non-remedial course-work, have a 2.25 GPA from an accredited college or university, and completed all developmental course-work before transferring. Students who have not earned at least 18 hours of non-remedial course work, are required to submit an official high school transcript and official ACT or SAT test scores. 30 of 120 credits required for the bachelor's degree must be completed at UNO. **International Students:** There are 267 international students enrolled. The school actively recruits these students. They must take the TOEFL with a minimum score of 525 on the paper-based TOEFL (PBT) or 71 on the Internet-based version (iBT). If they do not have the TOEFL, they must submit the ACT or SAT.

ADMISSIONS: 81% of the 2016-2017 applicants were accepted. The SAT scores for the 2016-2017 freshman class were: Critical Reading-- 35% below 500, 31% between 500 and 599, 30% between 600 and 699, and 4% between 700 and 800. Math-- 32% below 500, 34% between 500 and 599, 29% between 600 and 699, and 5% between 700 and 800. Writing-- 35% below 500, 40% between 500 and 599, 22% between 600 and 699, and 3% between 700 and 800. The ACT scores were 37% below 12, 35% between 12 and 17, 18% between 18 and 23, 6% between 24 and 29, and 4% above 30. **Admissions Contact:** Office of Admissions Email: *admissions@uno.edu* Web: *www.uno.edu*

FINANCIAL AID: In 2016-2017, 71% of all full-time freshmen and 67% of continuing full-time students received some form of financial aid. 46% of all full-time freshmen and 45% of continuing full-time students received need-based aid. The average freshman award was $6,830. UNO is a member of CSS. The deadline for filing freshman financial aid applications for fall entry is May 15.

XAVIER UNIVERSITY OF LOUISIANA D-4

www.xula.edu

New Orleans, LA 70125 **(504) 520-7388**

Fax: (504) 520-7941
Email: apply@xula.edu
Full-time: 577 men, 1620 women
Faculty: 221
Part-time: 34 men, 62 women
Ph.D.s: 96%
Graduate: 191 men, 479 women
Student/Faculty: 14 to 1
Year: semesters, summer session
Tuition: $23,166
Room & Board: $8523
Freshman Class: 6640 applied, 4084 accepted, 764 enrolled
SAT CR/M/W: 509/494/476 **ACT:** required
CEEB CODE: 6975
Application Deadline: July 1
COMPETITIVE

Xavier University of Louisiana, founded by Saint Katharine Drexel and the Sisters of the Blessed Sacrament, is Catholic and historically Black. The ultimate purpose of the University is to contribute to the promotion of a more just and humane society by preparing its students to assume roles of leadership and service in a global society. This preparation takes place in a diverse learning and teaching environment that incorporates all relevant educational means, including research and community service. There is 1 undergraduate school and 1 graduate school. In addition to regional accreditation, XUL has baccalaureate program accreditation with ACBSP, ACPE, NASM, and CAEP. The 29-acre campus is in an urban area 2 miles from downtown New Orleans. Including any residence halls, there are 65 buildings.

STUDENT LIFE: 60% of undergraduates are from Louisiana. Others are from 40 states, and 12 foreign countries. 20% are from public schools. 9% are Asian American; 78% African American; 3% White; 3% Hispanic; 3% two or more races. 30% are Baptist; 25% Catholic. **Female To Male Ratio:** 2.7:1. The average age of freshmen is 18; all undergraduates, 20. 28% do not continue beyond their first year; 41% remain to graduate. **Housing:** 1433 students can be accommodated in college housing, which includes dorms and on-campus apartments. In addition, there are honors houses, and wellness housing. On-campus housing is available on a first-come and first-served basis. 52% of students commute. Alcohol is not permitted. All students may keep cars.

FACULTY/CLASSROOMS: 52% of faculty are male; 48% are female. No introductory courses are taught by graduate students. The average class size in an introductory lecture is 25; in a laboratory is 21; and in a regular course is 21.

PROGRAMS OF STUDY: XUL confers B.A., B.S., and B.M. degrees. Master's and doctoral degrees are also awarded. Bachelor's degrees are awarded in BIOLOGICAL SCIENCE (biochemistry and biology/biological science), BUSINESS (accounting, business administration and management, and business economics), COMMUNICATIONS AND THE ARTS (communications, English, fine arts, French, languages, music, music performance, and Spanish), COMPUTER AND PHYSICAL SCIENCE (chemistry, computer science, mathematics, physics, and statistics), EDUCATION (art education, elementary education, English education, mathematics education, middle school education, music education, science education, and social studies education), HEALTH PROFESSIONS (premedicine and speech pathology/audiology), SOCIAL SCIENCE (history, philosophy, political science/government, psychology, sociology, and theological studies). Science, education, and English are the strongest academically. Pharmacy, biology, and business have the largest enrollments.

ACTIVITIES: 1% of men belong to 4 national fraternities; 2% of women belong to 4 national sororities. There are 80 groups on campus, including art, band, cheerleading, chess, choir, chorus, communications, computers, dance, debate, drill team, ethnic, honors, international, jazz band, literary magazine, newspaper, opera, pep band, political, professional, radio and TV, religious, social, social service, student government, symphony, and yearbook. Popular campus events include Wellness Week, Octoberfest, Homecoming, Neophyte Show, and Culturefest. **Sports:** There are 4 intercollegiate sports for men and 3 for women, and 12 intramural sports for men and 12 for women. Facilities include a health and fitness center. **Graduates:** From July 1, 2016 to June 30, 2017, 353 bachelor's degrees were awarded. The most popular majors were biological/life sciences (37%), physical sciences (14%), and psychology (11%). In an average class, 29% graduate in 4 years or less, 40% graduate in 5 years or less, and 43% graduate in 6 years or less. Of the 2016 graduating class, 31% were enrolled in graduate school within 6 months of graduation, and 14% were employed.

SERVICES: Counseling and information services are available, as is tutoring in every subject. There is a reader service for the blind, and remedial math, reading, and writing. **Library/Resources:** The library contains 261,000 volumes, 779,654 microform items, and 6,074 audio/video tapes/CDs/DVDs, and subscribes to 1,624 periodicals including electronic. Computerized library services include interlibrary loans, database searching, Internet access, and Wi-Fi capability. Special learning facilities include an art gallery, radio station, and TV station. The Confucius Institute, and Xavier University of Louisiana Confucius Institute, in partnering with Hebei University in China, is the first Confucius Institute among the nation's HBCUs and in the State of Louisiana. The Confucius Institute helps prepare students to become global leaders, and to teach Chinese language, culture, and economic development courses to Xavier students and the surrounding communities, including local groups, government agencies, and businesses. It also aims to facilitate research activities in the above areas and promote increased understanding between the United States and China. **Physically Challenged Students:** 99% of the campus is accessible. Facilities include wheelchair ramps, elevators, special parking, specially equipped restrooms, special class scheduling, lowered drinking fountains, lowered telephones, and special housing. **Special:** The university offers cooperative programs in any major and 3-2 engineering degrees with Tulane, Louisiana State, Morgan State, and Southern Universities as well as the Universities of Wisconsin, Maryland, New Orleans, and Detroit, and Georgia Institute of Technology. In addition, students may cross-register at colleges of the New Orleans Consortium. Internships are available in legal, political, and pharmaceutical areas. Students may earn an accelerated degree in biology, chemistry, psychology, or political science, pursue dual majors in engineering and biostatistics, opt for non-degree study, and earn a B.A.-B.S. degree in almost any combination. Students may study abroad in 6 countries or participate in an exchange program with Notre Dame University. There are 7 national honor societies, a freshman honors program, and 7 departmental honors programs. **Visiting:** There are guides for informal visits, visitors may sit in on classes, and stay overnight. To schedule a visit, contact the Admissions Office. **Campus Safety and Security:** Measures include 24-hour foot and vehicle patrol, emergency notification system, and security escort services. There are shuttle buses, emergency telephones, and lighted pathways/sidewalks.

REQUIREMENTS: The SAT or ACT is required. Applicants must have earned a high school diploma or the GED. Candidates must also have completed 16 academic units; 4 units of English, 2-4 of math, and 2-3 science, 1 unit of social studies, and 7 of academic electives, and recommended 1 each of foreign language and history. A GPA of 2.0 is required. AP and CLEP credits are accepted. Important factors in the admissions decision are advanced placement or honors courses and recommendations by school officials. Requirements for graduation include 9 semester hours in English, 6 each in history, social science, language, theology, philosophy, and natural sciences, 3 each in speech, math, and the arts, and 1 in health and phys ed. Students must complete 128 to 132 total credit hours, including 24 to 54 total hours in the major. Students must maintain a minimum GPA of 2.0, take Introduction to African American History/Culture, pass a comprehensive exam, and by the beginning of the junior year declare a minor in an academic discipline other than the major. **Procedure:** Freshmen are admitted fall, spring, and summer. Entrance exams should be taken in the spring of the junior year or the fall of the senior year. Early decision applications should be filed by March 1; regular applications, by July 1 for fall entry. Notification of early decision is sent October 15; regular decision, April 15. 100 applicants were on the 2017 waiting list. Applications are accepted on-line. **Transfer Students:** 128 transfer students enrolled in 2016-2017. Applicants must submit college transcripts. High school transcripts are required of applicants with fewer than 30 transferable credits. Enrollment for Admissions are in the fall and spring. 30 of 128 credits required for the bachelor's degree must be completed at XUL. **International Students:** There are 33 international students enrolled. They must take the TOEFL. They must also take the SAT or ACT.

ADMISSIONS: 29% of the current freshmen were in the top fifth of their class; 55% were in the top two fifths. **Admissions Contact:** Winston D. Brown, Dean of Admissions. Email: *apply@xula.edu* Web: *www.xula.edu*

FINANCIAL AID: In 2017-2018, 93% of all full-time freshmen received some form of financial aid. 86% of all full-time freshmen received need-based aid. The average freshman award was $22,835. Need-based scholarships or need-based grants averaged $5,773; need-based self-help aid (loans and jobs) averaged $5,417; non-need-based athletic scholarships averaged $14,963; other non-need-based awards and non-need-based scholarships averaged $12,833; and $4,698 from other forms of aid. The average financial indebtedness of the 2017 graduate was $26,106. XUL is a member of CSS. The FAFSA code is 002032. The priority date for freshman financial aid applications for fall entry is January 1.

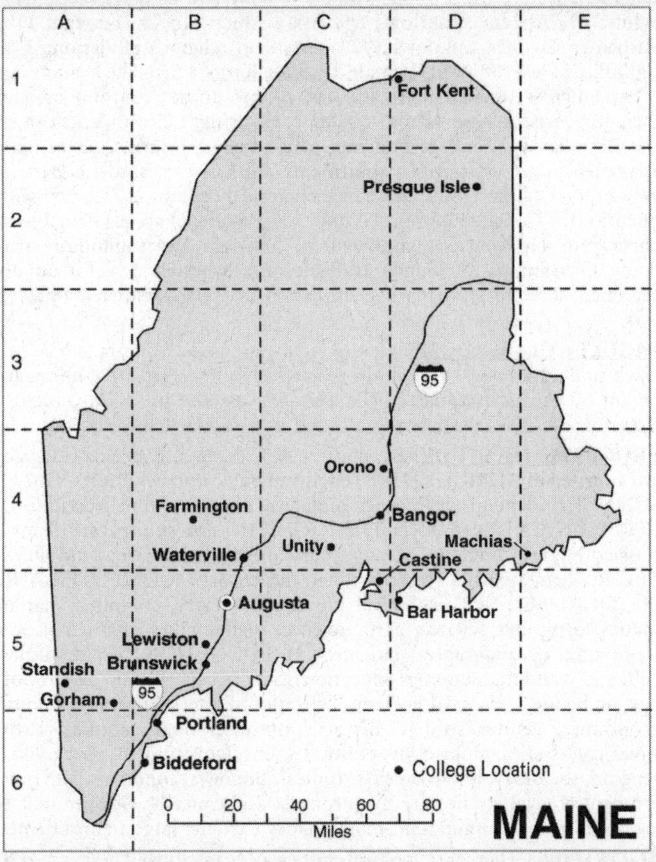

BATES COLLEGE B-5

www.bates.edu

Lewiston, ME 04240 (207) 786-6000 (855) 228-3755

Fax: (207) 786-6025
Email: admission@bates.edu
Full-time: 881 men, 899 women
Faculty: 190; IIB, ++$
Part-time: n/av
Ph.D.s: 93%
Graduate: n/av
Student/Faculty: 10 to 1
Year: other
Tuition: $50,310
Room & Board: $14,190
Freshman Class: 5356 applied, 1213 accepted, 484 enrolled
SAT CR/M/W: 630/640/630 **ACT:** required
CEEB CODE: 3076
Application Deadline: January 1
HIGHLY COMPETITIVE

Bates College is a private, highly selective, residential college devoted to undergraduate study in the liberal arts. Bates has always stood firmly for the ideals of academic rigor, intellectual curiosity, egalitarianism, social justice and freedom. Bates is recognized for its inclusive social character and progressive tradition, and is rightly celebrated as one of the first U.S. institutions of higher learning to admit women and people of color. A Bates education fosters intellectual inquiry and reflection, personal growth, and a commitment to the world beyond oneself. There is 1 undergraduate school. In addition to regional accreditation, BC has baccalaureate program accreditation with CFAT and ACS. The 133-acre campus is in a small town 35 miles north of Portland. Including any residence halls, there are 170 buildings.

STUDENT LIFE: 91% of undergraduates are from out of state, mostly the Northeast. Students are from 43 states, 59 foreign countries, and Canada. 55% are from public schools. 9% are Hispanic; 70% White; 7% Foreign; 6% African American; 4% Asian American; 4% two or more races. **Female To Male Ratio:** 1.0:1. The average age of freshmen is 19; all undergraduates, 20. 5% do not continue beyond their first year; 88% remain to graduate. **Housing:** 1714 students can be accommodated in college housing, which includes dorms. In addition, there are special-interest houses, chemical-free housing, quiet/study housing, and themed-based housing (by application; ex. sustainability, arts). On-campus housing is guaranteed for all 4 years. 90% of students live on campus. All students may keep cars.

FACULTY/CLASSROOMS: 48% of faculty are male; 52% are female. All teach undergraduates, and all do research. No introductory courses are taught by graduate students.

PROGRAMS OF STUDY: BC confers B.A. and B.S. degrees. Bachelor's degrees are awarded in AGRICULTURE (environmental studies), BIOLOGICAL SCIENCE (biochemistry, biology/biological science, and neurosciences), COMMUNICATIONS AND THE ARTS (Chinese, English, French and Francophone studies, German, Japanese, music, Russian, Spanish, speech/debate/rhetoric, and theatre acting), COMPUTER AND PHYSICAL SCIENCE (chemistry, geology, mathematics, and physics), EDUCATION (Asian studies), SOCIAL SCIENCE (African American studies, American studies, anthropology, classical/ancient civilization, East Asian studies, economics, European studies, history, interdisciplinary studies, Latin American studies, medieval studies, philosophy, political science/government, psychology, religious studies, sociology, and women & gender studies). Economics, politics, and psychology have the largest enrollments.

ACTIVITIES: There are no fraternities or sororities. There are 110 groups on campus, including art, chess, choir, chorale, chorus, computers, dance, debate, drama, environmental, ethnic, film, honors, international, jazz band, LGBT, literary magazine, musical theater, newspaper, orchestra, pep band, photography, political, professional, radio and TV, religious, social, social service, student government, symphony, and yearbook. Popular campus events include Parents and Family Weekend, Homecoming, Mount David Summit, Winter Carnival, Reunion Weekend, International Dinners, and Ocean Clambakes. **Sports:** There are 21 intercollegiate sports for men and 22 for women, and 12 intramural sports for men and 12 for women. Facilities include a pool, a field house, indoor and outdoor tracks, indoor and outdoor tennis courts, basketball courts, volleyball courts, dance and fencing space, squash and racquetball courts, training rooms, a rock-climbing wall, a winter sports arena, a weight room and football, soccer, baseball, softball, and lacrosse fields. **Graduates:** From July 1, 2016 to June 30, 2017, 462 bachelor's degrees were awarded. The most popular majors were economics (13%), politics (13%), and psychology (11%). In an average class, 84% graduate in 4 years or less, 87% graduate in 5 years or less, and 88% graduate in 6 years or less.

SERVICES: Counseling and information services are available, as is tutoring in every subject. There is a reader service for the blind, and remedial math and writing. **Library/Resources:** The library contains 602,011 volumes, 183,300 microform items, and 36,544 audio/video tapes/CDs/DVDs, and subscribes to 85,988 periodicals including electronic. Computerized library services include interlibrary loans, database searching, Internet access, and Wi-Fi capability. Special learning facilities include a planetarium, radio station, a learning research center, art gallery, radio station, television studio, a 654-acre mountain conservation area, an observatory, a language resource center, and the Edmund S. Muskie archives. **Physically Challenged Students:** 69% of the campus is accessible. Facilities include wheelchair ramps, elevators, special parking, specially equipped restrooms, special class scheduling, lowered drinking fountains, and lowered telephones. **Special:** Bates College offers Co-op programs in engineering, internships, research apprenticeships, work-study programs, study abroad, and a Washington semester. Student-designed, and interdisciplinary majors, and a dual-degree 3-2 engineering degree with Columbia University, Dartmouth College, Case Western Reserve University, Rensselaer Polytechnic Institute, and Washington University in St. Louis are available. Students in any major may graduate in 3 years. Students may also participate in the Williams-Mystic Seaport program in marine biology and maritime history, and exchanges with Spelman College, Morehouse College, Washington and Lee University, and McGill University are possible. There are 2 national honor societies, Phi Beta Kappa, and 32 departmental honors programs. **Visiting:** There are guides for informal visits, visitors may sit in on classes, and stay overnight. To schedule a visit, contact the Office of Admission. **Campus Safety and Security:** Measures include 24-hour foot and vehicle patrol, emergency notification system, self-defense education, and security escort services. There are shuttle buses, emergency telephones, lighted pathways/sidewalks, controlled access to dorms/residences, electronic access control in residence halls and all major buildings on campus, automated 911 telephone system, and emergency public address system.

REQUIREMENTS: Candidates for admission should have completed at least 4 years of English, 3 each of math, social science, and a foreign language, and 2 of lab science. Essays are required and an interview on or off campus is strongly recommended. The submission of test scores is optional. AP credits are accepted. Important factors in the admissions decision are advanced placement or honors courses, evidence of special talent, and leadership record. Requirements for graduation include one major plus two general education concentrations (which are comprised of four courses and may alternatively be satisfied by another major(s) or minor(s) or a combination thereof); three writing attentive courses; and three courses focused on scientific reasoning, laboratory experience, and quantitative literacy. The total number of hours in the major varies by department, but students should take at least 32 courses, plus 2 short terms, and maintain a minimum GPA of 2.0. All majors require a senior thesis or capstone project. **Procedure:** Freshmen are admitted fall and winter. There are early decision and deferred admissions plans. Early decision applications should be filed by November 15; regular applications, by January 1 for fall entry; and November 1 for winter entry. The fall 2017 application fee was $60. Notification of early decision is sent December 20; regular decision, April 1. 273 early decision candidates were accepted for the 2017-2018 class. 1536 applicants were on the 2017 waiting list; 11 were admitted. Applications are accepted on-line. **Transfer Students:** 5 transfer students enrolled in 2016-2017. More weight is given to the student's college record than to high school credentials. Applicants must submit official college and final high school transcripts, a statement of good standing, 3 letters of recommendation, and an essay. An interview is strongly recommended. 16 of 32 credits required for the bachelor's degree must be completed at Bates. **International Students:** There are 122 international students enrolled. They must take the TOEFL.

ADMISSIONS: 23% of the 2017-2018 applicants were accepted. The SAT scores for the 2017-2018 freshman class were: Critical Reading-- 5% below 500, 28% between 500 and 599, 45% between 600 and 699, and 22% between 700 and 800. Math-- 5% below 500, 27% between 500 and 599, 42% between 600 and 699, and 26% between 700 and 800. Writing-- 6% below 500, 24% between 500 and 599, 47% between 600 and 699, and 23% between 700 and 800. The ACT scores were 1% between 12 and 17, 9% between 18 and 23, 36% between 24 and 29, and 54% above 30. 79% of the current freshmen were in the top fifth of their class; 92% were in the top two fifths. **Admissions Contact:** Leigh Weisenburger, Dean of Admission and Financial Aid. Email: *admission@bates.edu* Web: *www.bates.edu*

FINANCIAL AID: In 2017-2018, 49% of all full-time freshmen received some form of financial aid. 42% of all full-time freshmen received need-based aid. The average freshman award was $46,647. Need-based scholarships or need-based grants averaged $43,506; and need-based self-help aid (loans and jobs) averaged $3,232. Bates is a member of CSS. The CSS/Profile, and FAFSA, parent and student tax returns and W-2 forms is required. The FAFSA code is 002036. The deadline for filing freshman financial aid applications for fall entry is February 15.

BOWDOIN COLLEGE B-5

www.bowdoin.edu/admissions

Brunswick, ME 04011 **(207) 725-3100**

Fax: (207) 725-3101	**Email:** admissions@bowdoin.edu
Full-time: 907 men, 906 women	**Faculty:** 194; IIB, ++$
Part-time: 1 men, 2 women	**Ph.D.s:** 99%
Graduate: n/av	**Student/Faculty:** 9 to 1
Year: semesters	**Tuition:** $51,848
Room & Board: $14,132	**Freshman Class:** 7251 applied, 988 accepted, 501 enrolled
SAT EBR-W/M: 710/700 **ACT:** 32	**CEEB CODE:** 3089
Application Deadline: January 1	**MOST COMPETITIVE**

Bowdoin College, established in 1794, is a private liberal arts institution. In addition to regional accreditation, BC has baccalaureate program accreditation with ACS. The 207-acre campus is in a small town 25 miles northeast of Portland. Including any residence halls, there are 120 buildings.

STUDENT LIFE: 90% of undergraduates are from out of state, mostly the Northeast. Students are from 48 states, 32 foreign countries, and Canada. 50% are from public schools. 7% are two or more races; 64% White; 6% African American; 6% Asian American; 5% Foreign; 11% Hispanic; 1% race unknown. 42% claim no religious affiliation; 23% Catholic; 21% Protestant. **Female To Male Ratio:** 1.0:1. The average age of freshmen is 18; all undergraduates, 20. 6% do not continue beyond their first year; 94% remain to graduate. **Housing:** 1756 students can be accommodated in college housing, which includes dorms, on-campus apartments, and off-campus apartments. All first-year students participate in the College House System; their residence floor is affiliated with one of eight College Houses. All upperclass students are also eligible to participate. Housing is guaranteed for first-year and sophomore students. On-campus housing is available on a lottery system for upperclassmen. 88% of students live on campus. Upperclassmen may keep cars.

FACULTY/CLASSROOMS: 49% of faculty are male; 51% are female. All teach undergraduates, and all do research. No introductory courses are taught by graduate students. The average class size in an introductory lecture is 28; in a laboratory is 12; and in a regular course is 16.

PROGRAMS OF STUDY: BC confers A.B. degrees. Bachelor's degrees are awarded in AGRICULTURE (environmental studies), BIOLOGICAL SCIENCE (biochemistry, biology/biological science, and neurosciences), COMMUNICATIONS AND THE ARTS (Africana studies, art history, classics, English, French, German, music, romance languages and literature, Russian, Spanish, studio art, and theatre arts), COMPUTER AND PHYSICAL SCIENCE (chemical physics, chemistry, computer mathematics, computer science, earth science, mathematics, mathematics – economics, oceanography, and physics), EDUCATION (Asian studies, education, and mathematics education), SOCIAL SCIENCE (anthropology, archeology, classical/ancient civilization, Eastern European studies, economics, gender studies, history, interdisciplinary studies, Latin American studies, philosophy, political science/government, psychology, religion, sociology, and women's studies). Biology, economics, and government & legal studies are the strongest academically. Government & legal studies, economics, and mathematics have the largest enrollments.

ACTIVITIES: There are no fraternities or sororities. There are 120 groups on campus, including Students for Justice in Palestine, alpine ski, club sports, equestrian club, cultural clubs, curling club, environmental awareness groups, fencing club, J Street U, Jiu Jitsu, literary society, Ultimate Frisbee and water polo, men's Rugby, mock trial, organic garden club, outing club, peer counseling and advising, robocup, science clubs, ski and ride, slam poets society, women's clubs, art, cheerleading, chess, choir, chorus, communications, dance, drama, environmental, ethnic, film, honors, Improvisational comedy, international, jazz band, LGBT, literary magazine, musical theater, newspaper, political, professional, radio and TV, religious, social, social service, and student government. Popular campus events include Common Good Day, Ivies Weekend, Winter Weekend, Asia Week, Student Night at the Museum of Art, Student Night at the Arctic Museum, Junior/Senior Ball, First-Year/Sophomore Semi Formal, Common Hour, Spring Gala, and Bowdoin-Colby Ice Hockey Games. **Sports:** There are 15 intercollegiate sports for men and 17 for women, and 6 intramural sports for men and 6 for women. Facilities include a field house, an ice arena, swimming pool, gyms, indoor and outdoor track, tennis and squash courts, a climbing wall, crew boathouse, an outdoor leadership center, cross-country ski trails, a fitness center with cardiovascular equipment, weight machines, free weights, rowing machines, and fitness classes. There are playing fields for football, baseball, softball, lacrosse, field hockey, soccer, rugby, and ultimate frisbee. **Graduates:** From July 1, 2016 to June 30, 2017, 461 bachelor's degrees were awarded. The most popular majors were government and legal studies (19%), economics (13%), and biology (8%). In an average class, 89% graduate in 4 years or less, 94% graduate in 5 years or less, and 94% graduate in 6 years or less. Of the 2016 graduating class, 9% were enrolled in graduate school within 6 months of graduation.

SERVICES: Counseling and information services are available, as is tutoring in most subjects. There is a reader service for the blind. A counselor is available to assist students with accommodations as needed. Tutoring is available through the Quantitative Reasoning Program and the Writing Project. **Library/Resources:** The library contains 1.5 million volumes, 33,052 microform items, and 29,736 audio/video tapes/CDs/DVDs, and subscribes to 64,688 periodicals including electronic. Computerized library services include interlibrary loans, database searching, Internet access, and Wi-Fi capability. Special learning facilities include an art gallery, radio station, TV station, museum of art, arctic museum, language media center, women's resource center, electronic classroom, coastal studies center and marine laboratory, individual and group screening rooms, production studios, multimedia lab, African American center, crafts center, ceramics studio, photography darkroom, printmaking studio, woodworking studio, sculpture studio, dance studio, scientific station located in the Bay of Fundy, educational research and development program, theaters, music halls, recording studio, community service resource center, environmental studies center, and visual arts center. **Physically Challenged Students:** 72% of the campus is accessible. Facilities include wheelchair ramps, elevators, special parking, specially equipped restrooms, special class scheduling, lowered drinking fountains, lowered telephones, and special housing. All buildings are built to ADA compliance standards. **Special:** A.B. degrees in 43 majors (including nine interdisciplinary majors), with single, coordinate, double and self-designed major options. Plus (+) and minus (-) grading system, with credit/D/fail option. Dean's list, Latin Honors and departmental honors awarded. First-year seminars, intermediate and advanced independent study, student research, and close work with faculty advisors strongly emphasized. Study abroad during the junior year encouraged. Washington semester. Academic support programs include the Baldwin Program for Academic Development, Quantitative Reasoning Program, Writing Project, Office of Student Fellowships and Research, Health Professions Advising. Dual-degree programs offered in Engineering (3-2 with California Institute of Tech., Columbia University, Dartmouth College, and University of Maine, Orono) and Law (3-3 with Columbia University). Teacher Certification program. There is 1 national honor society and a chapter of Phi Beta Kappa. **Visiting:** There are regularly scheduled orientations for prospective students, The Admissions Office offers student-led campus tours, one-hour information sessions with an Admissions representative, and personal interviews. There are guides for informal visits, visitors may sit in on classes, and stay overnight. To schedule a visit, contact the Admissions Office. **Campus Safety and Security:** Measures include 24-hour foot and vehicle patrol, emergency notification system, self-defense education, and security escort services. There are shuttle buses, emergency telephones, lighted pathways/sidewalks. Residences are locked 24 hours a day, and a staffed communications center is available around the clock.

REQUIREMENTS: Applicants for admission will have had 4 years each of English, social studies, foreign language, and math, 3 to 4 years of laboratory sciences, and one course each in art, music, and history. A high school record, two teacher recommendations, an advisor's estimate of the applicant's character and accomplishments, and an essay are required. Applicants must submit the Common Application as well as the Bowdoin Supplement to be considered for admission. AP credits are accepted. Important factors in the admissions decision are advanced placement or honors courses, recommendations by school officials, and extracurricular activities record. To qualify for the bachelor of arts degree, a student must have: successfully passed thirty-two full-credit courses (or the equivalent), completed a first-year seminar, completed at least one full-credit course (or the equivalent) in each of the following five distribution areas mathematical, computational, or statistical reasoning, inquiry in the natural sciences, exploring social differences, international perspectives, and visual & performing arts, completed at least one full-credit course (or the equivalent) in natural sciences and mathematics, social & behavioral sciences, and humanities (in addition to the required course in the visual and performing arts), and completed an approved major. **Procedure:** Freshmen are admitted fall. Entrance exams should be taken by the late summer before the freshman year. There are early decision and deferred admissions plans. Early decision applications should be filed by November 15; regular applications, by January 1 for fall entry. The fall 2017 application fee was $65. Notification of early decision is sent December 15; regular decision, March 20. 237 early decision candidates were accepted for the 2017-2018 class. Applications are accepted on-line. **Transfer Students:** 1 transfer students enrolled in 2016-2017. College grades of "B" or better are required to transfer. Applicants should submit high school and college transcripts, a dean's or advisor's statement from the most recent college attended, and two recommendations from recent professors. Transfer applicants must submit the Common Application, transfer essay and Bowdoin Supplement to be considered for admission. 16 of 32 credits required for the bachelor's degree must be completed at BC. **International Students:** There are 87 international students enrolled. They must take the TOEFL with a minimum score of 600 on the paper-based TOEFL (PBT) or 100 on the Internet-based version (iBT). SAT scores are not required for admission but must be submitted at matriculation for counseling and placement.

ADMISSIONS: 14% of the 2017-2018 applicants were accepted. The SAT scores for the 2017-2018 freshman class were: Math-- 1% below 500, 8% between 500 and 599, 36% between 600 and 699, and 55% between 700 and 800. Evidence-Based Reading/Writing-- 8% between 500 and 599, 36% between 600 and 699, and 56% between 700 and 800. The ACT scores were 3% between 18 and 23, 19% between 24 and 29, and 78% above 30. 94% of the current freshmen were in the top fifth of their class; 98% were in the top two fifths. 29 freshmen graduated first in their class. **Admissions Contact:** Whitney W. Soule, Dean of Admissions and Financial Aid. Email: *admissions@bowdoin.edu* Web: *www.bowdoin.edu/admissions*

FINANCIAL AID: In 2017-2018, 54% of all full-time freshmen received some form of financial aid. 52% of all full-time freshmen received need-based aid. The average freshman award was $43,895. Need-based scholarships or need-based grants averaged $42,165 ($61,540 maximum); need-based self-help aid (loans and jobs) averaged $1,819 ($1,900 maximum); and other non-need-based awards and non-need-based scholarships averaged $1,000 ($1,000 maximum). 63% of undergraduate students work part-time. The average financial indebtedness of the 2017 graduate was $23,174. BC is a member of CSS. The CSS/Profile, noncustodial profile, and business/farm supplement are required. The FAFSA code is 002038. The deadline for filing freshman financial aid applications for fall entry is February 15.

COLBY COLLEGE B-4

www.colby.edu

Waterville, ME 04901	**(207) 859-4818** **(800) 723-3032**
Fax: (207) 859-4828	**Email: admissions@colby.edu**
Full-time: 894 men, 985 women	**Faculty:** 185; IIB, ++$
Part-time: n/av	**Ph.D.s:** 99%
Graduate: n/av	**Student/Faculty:** 10 to 1
Year: 4-1-4	**Tuition:** $50,960
Room & Board: $13,100	**Freshman Class:** 9833 applied, 1840 accepted, 510 enrolled
SAT CR/M/W: 680/680/680 **ACT:** 31	**CEEB CODE:** 3280
Application Deadline: January 1	**MOST COMPETITIVE**

Colby College, founded in 1813, is a private liberal arts college. There is 1 undergraduate school. In addition to regional accreditation, CC has baccalaureate program accreditation with ACS. The 714-acre campus is in a small town 75 miles north of Portland. Including any residence halls, there are 60 buildings.

STUDENT LIFE: 90% of undergraduates are from out of state, mostly the Northeast. Students are from 45 states, 75 foreign countries, and Canada. 51% are from public schools. 9% are Foreign; 60% White; 6% Asian American; 6% Hispanic; 5% two or more races; 3% African American; 11% race unknown. **Female To Male Ratio:** 1.1:1. The average age of freshmen is 18; all undergraduates, 20. 7% do not continue beyond their first year; 90% remain to graduate. **Housing:** 1779 students can be accommodated in college housing, which includes dorms and on-campus apartments. In addition, there are special-interest houses, substance-free halls, theme housing, wellness housing, green, chem-free, quiet housing, and residence halls and apartments for seniors. On-campus housing is guaranteed for all 4 years. 96% of students live on campus. All students may keep cars.

FACULTY/CLASSROOMS: 54% of faculty are male; 46% are female. All teach undergraduates and all do research. No introductory courses are taught by graduate students. The average class size in an introductory lecture is 27; in a laboratory is 16; and in a regular course is 16.

PROGRAMS OF STUDY: CC confers B.A. degrees. Bachelor's degrees are awarded in AGRICULTURE (environmental studies), BIOLOGICAL SCIENCE (biochemistry, biology/biological science, environmental biology, and neurosciences), COMMUNICATIONS AND THE ARTS (art history, art, classics, creative writing, English, Germanic languages and literature, music, Russian languages and literature, Spanish, studio art, and theatre arts), COMPUTER AND PHYSICAL SCIENCE (applied mathematics, astronomy, chemistry, computer science, geology, geoscience, mathematics, physics, and science technology), EDUCATION (global studies), SOCIAL SCIENCE (African American studies, American studies, anthropology, classical/ancient civilization, East Asian studies, economics, French studies, history, Latin American studies, philosophy, political science/government, psychology, religion, sociology, and women's studies). Economics, biology, and government have the largest enrollments.

ACTIVITIES: There are no fraternities or sororities. There are 120 groups on campus, including coed woodsmen's team, outdoor, art, band, choir, chorale, chorus, communications, computers, dance, debate, drama, environmental, ethnic, film, honors, human rights, international, jazz band, LGBT, literary magazine, musical theater, newspaper, orchestra, photography, political, professional, religious, social, social service, student government, symphony, and yearbook. Popular campus events include Winter Carnival, Foss Arts Festival, and International Extravaganza. **Sports:** There are 16 intercollegiate sports for men and 17 for women, and 8 intramural sports for men and 8 for women. Facilities include an athletic center with fitness, weight training, yoga and exercise areas, a gym with badminton, volleyball, and basketball courts, a hockey and skating rink, a field house for track and field, climbing wall, soccer, baseball, softball, tennis, lacrosse, golf, a swimming pool, physical therapy and athletic training center, squash, and handball courts. Outdoor playing fields includes 2 artificial-turf fields, tennis courts, an all-weather track, cross-country skiing, and running trails. A Woodsmen's area for lumberjack events and competition. **Graduates:** From July 1, 2016 to June 30, 2017, 491 bachelor's degrees were awarded. The most popular majors were social sciences (25%), interdisciplinary studies (11%), and biology/life sciences (10%). In an average class, 94% graduate in 6 years or less. Of the 2016 graduating class, 24% were enrolled in graduate school within 6 months of graduation, and 87% were employed.

SERVICES: Counseling and information services are available, as is tutoring in every subject. There is a reader service for the blind. There is also a writing center and a support program for students needs. **Library/Resources:** The library contains 1.6 million volumes, 300,500 microform items, and 26,052 audio/video tapes/CDs/DVDs, and subscribes to 19,877 periodicals including electronic. Computerized library services include interlibrary loans, database searching, Internet access, and Wi-Fi capability. Special learning facilities include an art gallery, an astronomy observatory and classroom, 128-acre arboretum, electronic-research classroom, MIDI studio/electronic-music lab, language resource center, proscenium-style theater, research greenhouses, world-class collection in Maine's largest art museum. **Physically Challenged Students:** 93% of the campus is accessible. Facilities include wheelchair ramps, elevators, special parking, specially equipped restrooms, special class scheduling, lowered drinking fountains, and lowered telephones. **Special:** Colby incorporates research in majors across the curriculum and showcases research results at its annual Colby Liberal Arts Symposium. Study abroad is accessible through more than 200 programs in more than 60 countries, and two thirds of students participate during their time at Colby. The college offers opportunities to study or intern in Washington, D.C, on-campus work-study, exchange programs with the Claremont Colleges and Howard University, 3-2 engineering degree programs with Dartmouth College and Columbia University, and a semester-in-residence program working with research scientists at the Bigelow Laboratory for Ocean Sciences. Students, with approval, may pursue independent majors. Colby offers combined and interdisciplinary majors including four that combine interdisciplinary computation with biology, environmental studies, music, and theater and dance. The Jan Plan, offers a month-long term for internships or focused study on or off campus. There are 9 national honor societies, Phi Beta Kappa, and 26 departmental honors programs. **Visiting:** There are regularly scheduled orientations for prospective students, including panel discussions, tours, class visits, complimentary meals, interviews, and information sessions. There are guides for informal visits, visitors may sit in on classes, and stay overnight. To schedule a visit, contact the Admissions Office. **Campus Safety and Security:** Measures include 24-hour foot and vehicle patrol, emergency notification system, self-defense education, and security escort services. There are shuttle buses, emergency telephones, lighted pathways/sidewalks, controlled access to dorms/residences, radical attack defense classes for women, fire safety with drills and inspections, ID program for bikes, computers, party checks, and alcohol education programs.

REQUIREMENTS: Student must submit either SAT, ACT, or 3 SAT Subject Tests. Candidates should be high school graduates with a recommended academic program of 16 units in 4 years of English, 3 units each of foreign language and math, and 2 units each of science, (of those, 2 units must be lab work), social studies, and other college-preparatory courses. AP credits are accepted. Important factors in the admissions decision are personality/intangible qualities, advanced placement or honors courses, evidence of special talent, extracurricular activities record, leadership record, parents or siblings attended your school, recommendations by alumni, geographical diversity, and recommendations by school officials. To graduate, all students must take English composition and fulfill a three-semester foreign language requirement. They must also take 2 courses in the natural sciences and 1 course each in the arts, historical studies, literature, quantitative reasoning, the social sciences, and human or cultural diversity, and meet Colby's wellness requirement by attending 8 lectures. Students must complete a total of 128 credit hours, including 3 January term courses, and maintain a GPA of 2.0. **Procedure:** Freshmen are admitted fall and spring. Entrance exams should be taken by January of the senior year. There are early decision and deferred admissions plans. Early decision applications should be filed by November 15; regular applications, by January 1 for fall entry. Notification of early decision is sent December 15; regular decision, April 1. 259 early decision candidates were accepted for the 2017-2018 class. 634 applicants were on the 2017 waiting list; 42 were admitted. Applications are accepted on-line. **Transfer Students:** 8 transfer students enrolled in 2016-2017. Applicants must have a minimum GPA of 3.0 and, as a rule, have earned enough credit hours to qualify for at least sophomore standing. They must be in good academic and social standing and should submit references from a faculty member and a dean of their current school. If the SAT or ACT has been taken, the results may be submitted as well. Students may enroll in the fall and spring. 64 of 128 credits required for the bachelor's degree must be completed at Colby. **International Students:** There are 153 international students enrolled. They must take the TOEFL, or IELTS if English is neither your first language nor your current language of instruction. SAT or ACT or three SAT Subject Tests of your choice, sent by the testing agency.

ADMISSIONS: 19% of the 2017-2018 applicants were accepted. The SAT scores for the 2017-2018 freshman class were: Critical Reading-- 1% below 500, 11% between 500 and 599, 50% between 600 and 699, and 38% between 700 and 800. Math-- 1% below 500, 11% between 500 and 599, 45% between 600 and 699, and 44% between 700 and 800. Writing-- 2% below 500, 10% between 500 and 599, 50% between 600 and 699, and 38% between 700 and 800. The ACT scores were 25% between 24 and 29, and 75% above 30. 90% of the current freshmen were in the top fifth of their class; 98% were in the top two fifths. 4 freshmen graduated first in their class. **Admissions Contact:** Randi Arsenault, Associate Dean and Director of Admissions. Email: *admissions@colby.edu* Web: *www.colby.edu*

FINANCIAL AID: In 2017-2018, 33% of all full-time freshmen received some form of financial aid. 32% of all full-time freshmen received need-based aid. The average freshman award was $42,991. Need-based scholarships or need-based grants averaged $43,762; need-based self-help aid (loans and jobs) averaged $2,357; and $2,925 from other forms of aid. 67% of undergraduate students work part-time. The average financial indebtedness of the 2017 graduate was $21,958. CC is a member of CSS. The CSS/Profile and the college's own financial statement, current tax returns to finalize aid awards, and business or farm supplement are required. The FAFSA code is 002039. The priority date for freshman financial aid applications for fall entry is November 15.

COLLEGE OF THE ATLANTIC — D-5

www.coa.edu

Bar Harbor, ME 04609	**(207) 288-5015** **(800) 528-0025**
Fax: (207) 288-4126	**Email: inquiry@coa.edu**
Full-time: 81 men, 231 women	**Faculty:** 25
Part-time: 10 men, 15 women	**Ph.D.s:** 96%
Graduate: 1 men, 6 women	**Student/Faculty:** 12 to 1
Year: trimesters	**Tuition:** $43,542
Room & Board: $9747	**Freshman Class:** 485 applied, 314 accepted, 79 enrolled
SAT CR/M/W: 650/550/600 **ACT:** 28	**CEEB CODE:** 3305
Application Deadline: February 1	**HIGHLY COMPETITIVE+**

College of the Atlantic was founded in 1969 on the premise that education should go beyond understanding the world as it is, to enabling students to actively shape its future. A leader in experiential education and environmental stewardship, COA has pioneered a distinctive interdisciplinary approach to learning human ecology that develops the kinds of creative thinkers and doers needed by all sectors of society in addressing the compelling and growing needs of our world. There is 1 undergraduate school and 1 graduate school. In addition to regional accreditation, COA has baccalaureate program accreditation with NEASC. The 35-acre campus is in a small town 45 miles southeast of Bangor, on the coast of Maine's Mount Desert Island adjacent to Acadia National Park. Including any residence halls, there are 20 buildings.

STUDENT LIFE: 75% of undergraduates are from out of state, mostly the Northeast. Students are from 36 states, 46 foreign countries, and Canada. 51% are from public schools. 66% are White; 5% Hispanic; 3% Asian American; 3% race unknown; 21% Foreign; 1% African American; 1% two or more races. **Female To Male Ratio:** 2.7:1. The average age of freshmen is 19; all undergraduates, 21. 16% do not continue beyond their first year; 65% remain to graduate. **Housing:** 153 students can be accommodated in college housing, which includes dorms, substance-free housing, and green housing. On-campus housing is guaranteed for the freshman year only, is available on a first-come, first-served basis, and is available on a lottery system for upperclassmen. 50% of students commute. Alcohol is not permitted. All students may keep cars.

FACULTY/CLASSROOMS: 54% of faculty are male; 46% are female. All teach undergraduates, 80% do research, and 80% do both. No introductory courses are taught by graduate students. The average class size in an introductory lecture is 12; in a laboratory is 12; and in a regular course is 12.

PROGRAMS OF STUDY: COA confers B.A. degrees. Master's degrees are also awarded. Bachelor's degrees are awarded in SOCIAL SCIENCE (human ecology). Human ecology, is the strongest academically and has the largest enrollment.

ACTIVITIES: There are no fraternities or sororities. There are 20 groups on campus, including an outing club, art, chess, chorus, computers, dance, drama, environmental, film, international, jazz band, LGBT, literary magazine, newspaper, orchestra, photography, political, social, social service, student government, and yearbook. Popular campus events include Bar Island Swim, Fandango Talent Show, Earth Day, and Aurora Ball-ealis (winter dance), Spanish Festival, Human Ecology Forums, Fall Community Show. **Sports:** There is no sports program at COA. All students have memberships to the local YMCA and may use its pool, equipment, and volleyball and basketball facilities, as well as nearby tennis courts, outdoor program, with camping and outdoor equipment and canoes, sea kayaks, sailboats and lessons, and wilderness first responder class. There are yoga and martial arts classes, a bouldering wall, and an ice-skating rink in winter. SCUBA instruction is offered using the Y facilities. Dance instruction is also available. **Graduates:** From July 1, 2016 to June 30, 2017, 80 bachelor's degrees were awarded. The most popular majors were human ecology (100%). In an average class, 53% graduate in 4 years or less, 66% graduate in 5 years or less, and 69% graduate in 6 years or less. Of the 2016 graduating class, 26% were enrolled in graduate school within 6 months of graduation, and 54% were employed.

SERVICES: Counseling and information services are available, as is tutoring in some subjects, such as writing, math, language, photography and computer use. There is remedial math and writing. **Library/Resources:** The library contains 60,000 volumes, 37,000 microform items, and 3,300 audio/video tapes/CDs/DVDs, and subscribes to 30,000 periodicals including electronic. Computerized library services include interlibrary loans, database searching, Internet access, and Wi-Fi capability. Special learning facilities include an art gallery, natural history museum, writing center, taxidermy lab, sculpture, painting, graphic design, animation and ceramics studios, marine mammal research center, greenhouses, community garden on campus, two organic farms, sustainable enterprise hatchery, ocean-going vessels and two offshore island research centers. **Physically Challenged Students:** 80% of the campus is accessible. Facilities include wheelchair ramps, elevators, special parking, specially equipped restrooms, lowered drinking fountains, and lowered telephones. **Special:** Students may cross-register with the University of Maine. As part of the EcoLeague consortium, students may do exchange terms at Dickinson College, Green Mountain College, Prescott College, Northland College, or Alaska Pacific University. Students may also spend a term on exchange at The New School, NOLS, or Sea-Mester. COA offers regular study abroad programs in Mexico and France, and supports other study abroad programs as well as independent residencies abroad. A 10-week internship is a requirement of graduation; students are assisted in finding internships in the US and abroad in an area of interest, and we have several guaranteed internship slots at The Jackson Laboratory, a genetics research facility. All students design their own major as part of our B.A. in human ecology. **Visiting:** There are regularly scheduled orientations for prospective students. We offer a Fall Open House on Columbus Day Weekend. Students attend classes, stay in student housing, and are invited to join outings at Acadia National Park. To schedule a visit, contact Donna McFarland at (207) 288-5015. **Campus Safety and Security:** Measures include 24-hour foot and vehicle patrol and security escort services. There are shuttle buses, emergency telephones, and lighted pathways/sidewalks.

REQUIREMENTS: Candidates for admission must be high school graduates who have completed 4 years of English, 3-4 years of math, 2-3 years of science, (with 2 units of lab), 2 years recommended of a foreign language, 2 years recommended of history/social studies, and 1 academic elective. AP credits are accepted. Important factors in the admissions decision are personality/intangible qualities, extracurricular activities record, and recommendations by school officials. All students major in human ecology, which serves as a focus for a self-designed pathway to understanding the relationships between humans and our environment. Students complete a total of 36 COA credits, including an interdisciplinary core course, two courses each in environmental science, human studies, and arts and design, along with a history, writing, and quantitative reasoning course. Also required are a 450-hour internship, a human ecology essay, community service, and a culminating 3-credit senior/capstone project. **Procedure:** Freshmen are admitted fall, winter, and spring. Entrance exams should be taken in the junior or senior year. There are early decision and deferred admissions plans. Early decision applications should be filed by December 1; regular applications, by February 1 for fall entry; and November 1 for winter entry. The fall 2017 application fee was $50. Notification of early decision is sent December 15; regular decision, April 1. 30 early decision candidates were accepted for the 2017-2018 class. Applications are accepted on-line. **Transfer Students:** 29 transfer students enrolled in 2016-2017. Only coursework for which the student has received a grade of "C" (2.0) or better will be accepted for transfer credit. Transfer students may enroll in the fall, winter, or spring trimesters. 18 of 36 credits required for the bachelor's degree must be completed at COA. **International Students:** There are 56 international students enrolled. They must take the TOEFL, or submit SAT scores or the IB English exam score.

ADMISSIONS: 65% of the 2017-2018 applicants were accepted. The SAT scores for the 2017-2018 freshman class were: Critical Reading-- 6% below 500, 24% between 500 and 599, 49% between 600 and 699, and 21% between 700 and 800. Math-- 15% below 500, 58% between 500 and 599, and 27% between 600 and 699. Writing-- 3% below 500, 42% between 500 and 599, 46% between 600 and 699, and 9% between 700 and 800. The ACT scores were 6% between 18 and 23, 63% between 24 and 29, and 31% above 30. 60% of the current freshmen were in the top fifth of their class; 90% were in the top two fifths. **Admissions Contact:** Heather Albert-Knopp, Dean of Admission. Email: *inquiry@coa.edu* Web: *www.coa.edu*

FINANCIAL AID: In 2017-2018, 97% of all full-time freshmen received some form of financial aid. 90% of all full-time freshmen received need-based aid. The average freshman award was $43,006. Need-based scholarships or need-based grants averaged $39,592 ($54,969 maximum); need-based self-help aid (loans and jobs) averaged $5,668 ($8,000 maximum); other non-need-based awards and non-need-based scholarships averaged $16,279 ($20,000 maximum); and $3,000 from other forms of aid. 74% of undergraduate students work part-time. The average financial indebtedness of the 2017 graduate was $26,723. The college's own financial statement is required. The FAFSA code is 011385. The priority date for freshman financial aid applications for fall entry is February 1.

HUSSON UNIVERSITY C-4

www.husson.edu

Bangor, ME 04401 — **(207) 941-7175** **(800) 448-7766**

Fax: (207) 941-7935 — **Email: admit@husson.edu**

Full-time: 1069 men, 1229 women	**Faculty:** 112
Part-time: 160 men, 305 women	**Ph.D.s:** 68%
Graduate: 308 men, 569 women	**Student/Faculty:** 20 to 1
Year: semesters, summer session	**Tuition:** $17,010
Room & Board: $9498	**Freshman Class:** 2476 applied, 2136 accepted, 577 enrolled
SAT CR/M: 530/520 **ACT:** 22	**CEEB CODE:** 3440
Application Deadline: August 1	**COMPETITIVE**

Husson University was founded in 1898 and is a private institution offering BS and graduate degrees in business (MBA), criminal justice and health careers (nursing, physical therapy and occupational therapy, clinical mental health and school counseling, human relations), a doctorate in pharmacy, as well a bachelor's degree in business administration, elementary and secondary education, English, biology, biochemistry, criminal justice, data analytics, environmental science, exercise science, forensic science and health sciences, psychology and health care studies. There are 9 undergraduate schools and 7 graduate schools. In addition to regional accreditation, HU has baccalaureate program accreditation with ACPE, NEASC, ACOTE, CAPTE, CCNE, IACBE, and NBCC. The 208-acre campus is in a suburban area in the city of Bangor. Including any residence halls, there are 13 buildings.

STUDENT LIFE: 76% of undergraduates are from Maine. Others are from 29 states, 28 foreign countries, and Canada. 84% are from public schools. 86% are White; 4% African American; 4% Foreign; 2% Hispanic; 2% two or more races; 1% Asian American; 1% race unknown. **Female To Male Ratio:** 1.4:1. The average age of freshmen is 18; all undergraduates, 23. 24% do not continue beyond their first year; 54% remain to graduate. **Housing:** 1156 students can be accommodated in college housing, which includes dorms and on-campus apartments. In addition, there are special-interest houses, upper level undergraduates and graduate student suite housing. On-campus housing is guaranteed for all 4 years, and is available on a first-come, first-served basis. 61% of students commute. All students may keep cars.

FACULTY/CLASSROOMS: 52% of faculty are male; 48% are female. 79% teach undergraduates, and 75% do both. No introductory courses are taught by graduate students. The average class size in an introductory lecture is 22; in a laboratory is 17; and in a regular course is 20.

PROGRAMS OF STUDY: HU confers B.S. degrees. Associate, master's, and doctoral degrees are also awarded. Bachelor's degrees are awarded in BIOLOGICAL SCIENCE (biochemistry and biology/biological science), BUSINESS (accounting, banking and finance, business administration and management, business intelligence and analytics, business systems analysis, hospitality management services, information & communication technology, marketing/retailing/merchandising, and sports management), COMMUNICATIONS AND THE ARTS (English), COMPUTER AND PHYSICAL SCIENCE (computer information systems, data processing, and software engineering), EDUCATION (elementary education, English education, physical education, and science education), ENGINEERING AND ENVIRONMENTAL DESIGN (environmental science), HEALTH PROFESSIONS (exercise science, health, health care administration, nursing, occupational therapy, pharmacy, physical therapy, and prepharmacy), SOCIAL SCIENCE (counseling/psychology, criminal justice, forensic studies, paralegal studies, and psychology). Physical therapy, pharmacy, and nursing are the strongest academically. Business administration, criminal justice, and nursing have the largest enrollments.

ACTIVITIES: 3% of men belong to 1 local and 1 national fraternities; 4% of women belong to 3 local sororities. There are 51 groups on campus, including cheerleading, choir, chorus, communications, computers, dance, drama, environmental, ethnic, film, forensics, international, LGBT, literary magazine, musical theater, newspaper, pep band, political, professional, radio and TV, religious, social, social service, and student government. Popular campus events include Spring Fling, Winter Carnival, and Greek Alumni Weekend. **Sports:** There are 10 intercollegiate sports for men and 12 for women, and 5 intramural sports for men and 5 for women. Facilities include a gym, a swimming pool, weight training, a health and fitness center, outdoor basketball, volleyball and tennis courts, baseball and softball complexes, and a turf soccer field. **Graduates:** From July 1, 2016 to June 30, 2017, 512 bachelor's degrees were awarded. The most popular majors were business administration (18%), criminal justice (12%), and communications technology (11%). In an average class, 33% graduate in 4 years or less and 54% graduate in 6 years or less. Of the 2016 graduating class, 15% were enrolled in graduate school within 6 months of graduation, and 84% were employed.

SERVICES: Counseling and information services are available, as is tutoring in most subjects. There is remedial math and writing. **Library/Resources:** The library contains 41,743 volumes, 16,050 microform items, and 469 audio/video tapes/CDs/DVDs, and subscribes to 38,175 periodicals including electronic. Computerized library services include interlibrary loans, database searching, Internet access, and Wi-Fi capability. Special learning facilities include an art gallery, radio station, and a theatre with teaching sound room. **Physically Challenged Students:** All of the campus is accessible. Facilities include wheelchair ramps, elevators, special parking, specially equipped restrooms, lowered drinking fountains, lowered telephones, and special housing. **Special:** Experiential learning is part of the core curriculum in all majors. Internships are incorporated in accounting, sports management, hospitality management, nursing, physical therapy, occupational therapy, health care studies, international business, and family business. Co-op programs, internships, practicums or clinicals are included in the curriculum in all majors. Business and health care students can do a fifth year and obtain a master's in business administration. An accelerated degree program, dual majors, and student-designed majors are also available. There are 10 national honor societies. **Visiting:** There are regularly scheduled orientations for prospective students, including an interview, several information sessions by different groups, and a campus tour. There are guides for informal visits, visitors may sit in on classes, and stay overnight. To schedule a visit, contact the Admissions Office. **Campus Safety and Security:** Measures include 24-hour foot and vehicle patrol, emergency notification system, self-defense education, and security escort services. There are lighted pathways/sidewalks and controlled access to dorms/residences.

REQUIREMENTS: The SAT is required. The ACT and ACT Writing Test are recommended. Applicants must be graduates of an accredited secondary school or have earned a GED. A recommendation from a high school counselor/teacher/non-family member, high school transcript, SAT or ACT scores, and a 250 word essay are required. A GPA of 2.0 is required. AP and CLEP credits are accepted. Important factors in the admissions decision are advanced placement or honors courses, recommendations by school officials, and leadership record. The minimum requirement is a total of 120 credit hours with a GPA of 2.0 or higher. **Procedure:** Freshmen are admitted to all sessions. Entrance exams should be taken prior to enrollment. There are deferred admissions and rolling admissions plans. Applications should be filed by August 1 for fall entry. The fall 2017 application fee was $40. Notification is sent on a rolling basis. Applications are accepted on-line. **Transfer Students:** 331 transfer students enrolled in 2016-2017. Applicants must have a 2.0 GPA. Courses with a C grade or better transfer. 30 of 120 credits required for the bachelor's degree must be completed at HU. **International Students:** There are 64 international students enrolled. They must take the TOEFL with a minimum score of 500 on the paper-based TOEFL (PBT) or 75 on the Internet-based version (iBT). They must also take the SAT or ACT.

ADMISSIONS: 86% of the 2017-2018 applicants were accepted. The SAT scores for the 2017-2018 freshman class were: Critical Reading-- 34% below 500, 49% between 500 and 599, 16% between 600 and 699, and 1% between 700 and 800. Math-- 35% below 500, 49% between 500 and 599, 15% between 600 and 699, and 1% between 700 and 800. The ACT scores were 8% between 12 and 17, 59% between 18 and 23, 31% between 24 and 29, and 2% above 30. 25% of the current freshmen were in the top fifth of their class; 54% were in the top two fifths. 5 freshmen graduated first in their class. **Admissions Contact:** John Champoli, Director of Undergraduate Admissions. Email: *admit@husson.edu* Web: *www.husson.edu*

FINANCIAL AID: In 2017-2018, 95% of all full-time freshmen received some form of financial aid. 81% of all full-time freshmen received need-based aid. The average freshman award was $17,190. Need-based scholarships or need-based grants averaged $10,317 ($13,914 maximum); need-based self-help aid (loans and jobs) averaged $4,817 ($5,800 maximum); and other non-need-based awards and non-need-based scholarships averaged $5,677 ($18,458 maximum). 46% of undergraduate students work part-time. The average financial indebtedness of the 2017 graduate was $28,656. HU is a member of CSS. The FAFSA code is 002043. The priority date for freshman financial aid applications for fall entry is April 15.

MAINE COLLEGE OF ART *(The complete profile is made available exclusively on our website, www.barronspac.com)*

MAINE MARITIME ACADEMY C-5
www.mainemaritime.edu

Castine, ME 04420	(207) 326-2215 (800) 227-8465
Fax: (207) 326-2515	**Email:** jeff.wright@mma.edu
Full-time: 750 men, 175 women	**Faculty:** n/av
Part-time: 5 men, 5 women	**Ph.D.s:** n/av
Graduate: 10 men, 10 women	**Student/Faculty:** n/av
Year: semesters	**Tuition:** $12,988 ($25,572)
Room & Board: $9548	**Freshman Class:** n/av
SAT or ACT: required	**CEEB CODE:** 3505
Application Deadline: May 1	**COMPETITIVE**

Maine Maritime Academy, founded in 1941, is a public institution offering 18 degree programs in ocean and marine-oriented studies with emphasis on engineering, transportation, business management, and ocean sciences, to prepare graduates for private and public sector careers and the uniformed services of the United States. The academic calendar consists of 2 semesters plus a 2- to 3- month annual training cruise for the USCG Unlimited license majors and summer internships for others. There are 4 undergraduate schools and 1 graduate school. In addition to regional accreditation, MMA has baccalaureate program accreditation with ABET, NEASC, USCG, and STCW. The 50-acre campus is in a small town 38 miles south of Bangor on the east coast of Penobscot Bay. Including any residence halls, there are 14 buildings.

STUDENT LIFE: 69% of undergraduates are from Maine. Others are from 40 states, 7 foreign countries, and Canada. 90% are from public schools. 98% are White; 1% Asian American; 1% Hispanic. **Male To Female Ratio:** 4.0:1. The average age of freshmen is 19; all undergraduates, 24. 12% do not continue beyond their first year; 75% remain to graduate. **Housing:** 625 students can be accommodated in college housing, which includes dorms and on-campus apartments. On-campus housing is guaranteed for all 4 years. 85% of students live on campus. Alcohol is not permitted. All students may keep cars.

FACULTY/CLASSROOMS: 75% of faculty are male; 25% are female. All teach undergraduates. No introductory courses are taught by graduate students. The average class size in an introductory lecture is 30; in a laboratory is 15; and in a regular course is 25.

PROGRAMS OF STUDY: MMA confers B.S. degrees. Associate and master's degrees are also awarded. Bachelor's degrees are awarded in BUSINESS (international business management), COMPUTER AND PHYSICAL SCIENCE (oceanography), ENGINEERING AND ENVIRONMENTAL DESIGN (engineering, engineering technology, marine engineering, maritime science, and transportation technology). Marine systems engineering is the strongest academically. Marine transportation, and marine engineering degree programs have the largest enrollments.

ACTIVITIES: 10% of men belong to 1 national fraternity. There are no sororities. There are 30 groups on campus, including martial arts, billiards, chess, engineering, hockey, outing, rugby, sailing, scuba, social, amateur radio, bagpipe, band, chess, chorale, drama, drill team, drum and bugle corps, environmental, ethnic, international, newspaper, pep band, photography, professional, social, social service, student government, and yearbook. Popular campus events include GSA Weekend, BSA Klondike Derby, and Veterans Day. **Sports:** There are 6 intercollegiate sports for men and 6 for women, and 10 intramural sports for men and 10 for women. Facilities include Olympic pool, weight rooms, field house with climbing walls, a gym, racquetball/squash courts, aerobics room, a weight/workout room on the training ship, and synthetic multi sport athletic field. **Graduates:** From July 1, 2016 to June 30, 2017, 160 bachelor's degrees were awarded. The most popular majors were marine engineering (30%), marine transportation (30%), and power engineering (15%).

SERVICES: Counseling and information services are available, as is tutoring in most subjects. There is a reader service for the blind, and remedial math, reading, and writing. **Library/Resources:** The library contains 88,490 volumes, 5,000 microform items, and 808 audio/video tapes/CDs/DVDs, and subscribes to 1,311 periodicals including electronic. Computerized library services include interlibrary loans, database searching, Internet access, and Wi-Fi capability. Special learning facilities include a natural history museum, planetarium, more than 60 vessels, a bridge simulator, radar sims, power plant sims, cargo system simulators, and multiple sophisticated training vessels. **Physically Challenged Students:** All of the campus is accessible. Facilities include wheelchair ramps, elevators, special parking, specially equipped restrooms, and special housing. **Special:** The 2-month freshman and junior year training cruises give students practical experience aboard the academy's 500-foot ship. Cadet shipping co-ops on assigned merchant ships for 65 to 90 days. Co-op programs and internships for all programs are offered, as is study abroad through special agreements with other maritime colleges worldwide. Dual and student-designed majors are possible. **Visiting:** There are regularly scheduled orientations for prospective students, consisting of 3 open houses per year; campus visits are available weekdays throughout the year. Visitors may sit in on classes and stay overnight. To schedule a visit, contact Admissions office at admissions@mma.edu. **Campus Safety and Security:** Measures include 24-hour foot and vehicle patrol and self-defense education. There are emergency telephones, lighted pathways/sidewalks, controlled access to dorms/residences, on-campus medical and counseling services, and locked dorms.

REQUIREMENTS: The SAT or ACT is required. Candidates for admission must have completed 4 years of English, 3 years of math, and 2 years of lab science. Courses must include algebra I, algebra II, trigonometry, geometry, and either chemistry or physics with a lab. A GPA of 2.0 is required. AP and CLEP credits are accepted. Important factors in the admissions decision are advanced placement or honors courses, evidence of special talent, and leadership record. A minimum GPA of 2.0 in an average of 140 total credit hours is required for graduation. GPA in the major must be at least 2.25. A senior thesis is required for some majors and a comprehensive exam is required for USCG license candidates. **Procedure:** Freshmen are admitted fall and spring. Entrance exams should be taken as early as possible in the senior year. There are early decision, deferred admissions, and rolling admissions plans. Early decision applications should be filed by December 31; regular applications, by May 1 for fall entry; and November 1 for spring entry. The fall 2017 application fee was $15. Applications are accepted on-line. **Transfer Students:** 16 transfer students enrolled in 2016-2017. Applicants must have a minimum 2.0 GPA in previous college work and meet the same prerequisites as entering freshmen. **International Students:** They must take the TOEFL.

Admissions Contact: Jeff Wright, Director of Admissions. Email: *jeff.wright@mma.edu* Web: *www.mainemaritime.edu*

FINANCIAL AID: The FAFSA code is 002044. Check with the school for current application deadlines.

SAINT JOSEPH'S COLLEGE OF MAINE A-5
www.sjcme.edu

Standish, ME 04084	(207) 893-7746 (800) 338-7057
Fax: (207) 893-7862	**Email:** admission@sjcme.edu
Full-time: 300 men, 600 women	**Faculty:** 63
Part-time: 9 men, 21 women	**Ph.D.s:** 98%
Graduate: n/av	**Student/Faculty:** 15 to 1
Year: semesters, summer session	**Tuition:** $34,610
Room & Board: $13,280	**Freshman Class:** n/av
SAT: required **ACT:** 21	**CEEB CODE:** 3755
Application Deadline: August 1	**COMPETITIVE**

Saint Joseph's College of Maine, founded in 1912, is a private, Roman Catholic institution offering liberal arts and pre-professional programs. The figures given in the above capsule and in this profile are approximate. There are 5 undergraduate schools. In addition to regional accreditation, SJCM has baccalaureate program accreditation with CCNE. The 350-acre campus is in a rural area 18 miles west of Portland. Including any residence halls, there are 20 buildings.

STUDENT LIFE: 60% of undergraduates are from Maine. Others are from 15 states, 3 foreign countries, and Canada. 82% are White; 1% African American; 1% Asian American; 1% American Indian/Alaska Native; 1% Hispanic; 1% Foreign. **Female To Male Ratio:** 2.0:1. The average age of freshmen is 18; all undergraduates, 20. 18% do not continue beyond their first year; 59% remain to graduate. **Housing:** 829 students can be accommodated in college housing, which includes dorms, and substance free housing. On-campus housing is guaranteed for all 4 years. 83% of students live on campus. All students may keep cars.

FACULTY/CLASSROOMS: 48% of faculty are male; 52% are female. All teach undergraduates. No introductory courses are taught by graduate

students. The average class size in an introductory lecture is 25; in a laboratory is 12; and in a regular course is 18.

PROGRAMS OF STUDY: SJCM confers B.A., B.S., B.S.B.A. and B.S.N. degrees. Associate degrees are also awarded. Bachelor's degrees are awarded in BIOLOGICAL SCIENCE (biology/biological science), BUSINESS (business administration and management), COMMUNICATIONS AND THE ARTS (communications and English), COMPUTER AND PHYSICAL SCIENCE (chemistry and mathematics), EDUCATION (elementary education and physical education), ENGINEERING AND ENVIRONMENTAL DESIGN (environmental science), HEALTH PROFESSIONS (nursing and prepharmacy), SOCIAL SCIENCE (criminal justice, history, philosophy, psychology, sociology, and theological studies). Business, nursing, and biology are the strongest academically. Elementary education, business, and nursing have the largest enrollments.

ACTIVITIES: There are no fraternities or sororities. There are 28 groups on campus, including campus cheerleading, choir, chorale, computers, dance, drama, ethnic, Habitat for Humanity, honors, international, literary magazine, musical theater, newspaper, pep band, photography, political, professional, radio and TV, religious, social, social service, student government, and yearbook. Popular campus events include Family Weekend, Christmas Benefit Concert, and Spring Fling. **Sports:** There are 5 intercollegiate sports for men and 6 for women, and 12 intramural sports for men and 12 for women. Facilities include a multipurpose facility housing, a gym, workout room with free weights, Nautilus and other weight-training equipment, a cardiovascular workout room, dance aerobics rooms, climbing wall, 25-meter pool, and an elevated jogging track, soccer and field hockey fields, lighted athletic fields for baseball and softball, cross-country running and ski trails, and a low ropes course. **Graduates:** From July 1, 2016 to June 30, 2017, 213 bachelor's degrees were awarded. The most popular majors were education (20%), business (20%), and nursing (12%). In an average class, 54% graduate in 4 years or less, 60% graduate in 5 years or less, and 61% graduate in 6 years or less. Of the 2016 graduating class, 15% were enrolled in graduate school within 6 months of graduation, and 89% were employed.

SERVICES: Counseling and information services are available, as is tutoring in every subject. There is a reader service for the blind. **Library/Resources:** The library contains 98,626 volumes, 29,010 microform items, and 1,000 audio/video tapes/CDs/DVDs, and subscribes to 11,461 periodicals including electronic. Computerized library services include interlibrary loans, database searching, and Internet access. Special learning facilities include a radio station, and a telescope observatory. **Physically Challenged Students:** 75% of the campus is accessible. Facilities include wheelchair ramps, elevators, special parking, specially equipped restrooms, special class scheduling, and lowered drinking fountains. **Special:** Saint Joseph's offers internships, cross-registration with 4 southern Maine colleges, study abroad in 5 countries a semester at sea, dual majors, work-study programs, and non-degree study. There are 2 national honor societies, a freshman honors program, and 6 departmental honors programs. **Visiting:** There are regularly scheduled orientations for prospective students, including application and acceptance day programs, visits on Saturdays, and during the summer. There are guides for informal visits, visitors may sit in on classes, and stay overnight. **Campus Safety and Security:** Measures include 24-hour foot and vehicle patrol, self-defense education, and security escort services. There are emergency telephones, lighted pathways/sidewalks, and round-the-clock security officers.

REQUIREMENTS: The SAT or ACT is required. Candidates for admission must be high school graduates who have completed a college preparatory curriculum with a recommended 4 units in English, 3 to 4 in math, 2 in foreign language, and 1 to 3 each in history, science, and social studies. A GPA of 2.0 is required. AP and CLEP credits are accepted. Important factors in the admissions decision are advanced placement or honors courses, recommendations by school officials, and extracurricular activities record. To graduate, students must complete 128 credit hours with a minimum GPA of 2.0, including 8 hours of English, history, theology, and a foreign language, 4 each of science and math, and 8 of electives. **Procedure:** Freshmen are admitted fall and spring. Entrance exams should be taken by January of the senior year. There are early admissions, deferred admissions, and rolling admissions plans. Applications should be filed by August 1 for fall entry. The fall 2017 application fee was $40. Notifications are sent December 18. 45 applicants were on the 2017 waiting list; 25 were admitted. Applications are accepted online. **Transfer Students:** 40 transfer students enrolled in 2016-2017. Transfer students should have a minimum GPA of 2.0. 32 of 128 credits required for the bachelor's degree must be completed at SJCM. **International Students:** There are 3 international students enrolled. For non-English speaking students we require the TOEFL exam.

ADMISSIONS: 2 freshmen graduated first in their class. **Admissions Contact:** Vincent Kloskowski, Dean of Admissions. Email: *admission@sjcme.edu* Web: *www.sjcme.edu*

FINANCIAL AID: In 2017-2018, 99% of all full-time freshmen received some form of financial aid. 80% of all full-time freshmen received need-based aid. The average freshman award was $17,086. Need-based scholarships or need-based grants averaged $12,302 ($25,700 maximum); need-based self-help aid (loans and jobs) averaged $5,772 ($6,625 maximum); and other non-need-based awards and non-need-based scholarships averaged $13,398 ($20,390 maximum). 35% of undergraduate students work part-time. The average financial indebtedness of the 2017 graduate was $16,020. SSCM is a member of CSS. The college's own financial statement is required. The FAFSA code is 002051. The priority date for freshman financial aid applications for fall entry is March 1.

THOMAS COLLEGE *(The complete profile is made available exclusively on our website, www.barronspac.com)*

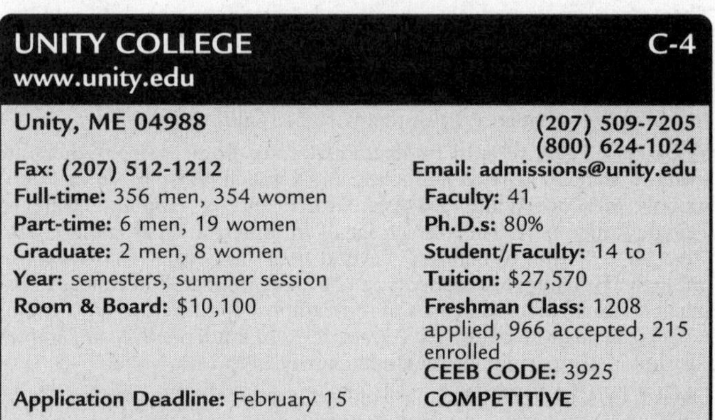

UNITY COLLEGE C-4

www.unity.edu

Unity, ME 04988 (207) 509-7205 (800) 624-1024

Fax: (207) 512-1212 Email: admissions@unity.edu

Full-time: 356 men, 354 women
Part-time: 6 men, 19 women
Graduate: 2 men, 8 women
Year: semesters, summer session
Room & Board: $10,100
Application Deadline: February 15

Faculty: 41
Ph.D.s: 80%
Student/Faculty: 14 to 1
Tuition: $27,570
Freshman Class: 1208 applied, 966 accepted, 215 enrolled
CEEB CODE: 3925
COMPETITIVE

Unity College is a small, private college in rural Maine that provides dedicated, engaged students with a liberal arts education that emphasizes the environment and natural resources. Unity graduates are prepared to be environmental stewards, effective leaders, and responsible citizens through active learning experiences within a supportive community. There is 1 undergraduate school and 1 graduate school. The 225-acre campus is in a small town in mid-coast Maine. Including any residence halls, there are 30 buildings.

STUDENT LIFE: 70% of undergraduates are from out of state, mostly the Northeast. Students are from 32 states, and 1 foreign country. 97% are from public schools. 89% are White; 3% Hispanic; 3% two or more races; 2% Asian American; 1% African American; 1% American Indian/Alaska Native; 1% Foreign. **Female To Male Ratio:** 1.0:1. The average age of freshmen is 19; all undergraduates, 20. 28% do not continue beyond their first year; 53% remain to graduate. **Housing:** 570 students can be accommodated in college housing, which includes dorms and on-campus apartments. On-campus housing is guaranteed for all 4 years and is available on a lottery system for upperclassmen. 71% of students live on campus. All students may keep cars.

FACULTY/CLASSROOMS: 51% of faculty are male; 49% are female. All teach undergraduates, 45% do research, and 45% do both. No introductory courses are taught by graduate students. The average class size in an introductory lecture is 22; in a laboratory is 14; and in a regular course is 20.

PROGRAMS OF STUDY: Unity confers B.A. and B.S. degrees. Associate and master's degrees are also awarded. Bachelor's degrees are awarded in AGRICULTURE (agriculture, animal science, conservation and regulation, environmental studies, natural resource management, range/farm management, and wildlife management), BIOLOGICAL SCIENCE (biology/biological science, ecology, marine biology, and wildlife biology), BUSINESS (recreation and leisure services), COMMUNICATIONS AND THE ARTS (art), COMPUTER AND PHYSICAL SCIENCE (natural sciences), EDUCATION (education and secondary education), ENGINEERING AND ENVIRONMENTAL DESIGN (environmental science and land use management and reclamation), HEALTH PROFESSIONS (recreation therapy), SOCIAL SCIENCE (ethics, politics, social policy, law enforcement and corrections officer, and parks and recreation management). Biology, earth & environmental science, and sustainable agriculture are the strongest academically. Conservation law enforcement, captive wildlife care & education, and wildlife biology have the largest enrollments.

ACTIVITIES: There are no fraternities or sororities. There are 36 groups on campus, including art, band, chorus, drama, environmental, honors, LGBT, literary magazine, outdoor and environmental clubs, photography, and student government. Popular campus events include Community Weekend in late September, Regional Woodsman's Meet in October, and Earth Day Activities. **Sports:** There are 3 intercollegiate sports for men and 4 for women, and 10 intramural sports for men and 10 for women. Facilities include a gym, weight training room, playing fields, indoor climbing wall, nature trails, and game rooms. **Graduates:** From July 1, 2016 to June 30, 2017, 121 bachelor's degrees were awarded. The most popular majors were conservation law enforcement (20%), captive wildlife care and education (17%), and wildlife biology/management (16%). In an average class, 5% graduate in 3 years or less, 45% graduate in 4 years or less, 53% graduate in 5 years or less, and 53% graduate in 6 years or less. Of the 2016 graduating class, 22% were enrolled in graduate school within 6 months of graduation, and 72% were employed.

SERVICES: Counseling and information services are available, as is tutoring in most subjects. There is a reader service for the blind, and remedial math, reading, and writing. A full-time learning disability specialist is on staff. **Library/Resources:** The library contains 53,340 volumes, and 2,649 audio/video tapes/CDs/DVDs, and subscribes to 1,932 periodicals including electronic. Computerized library services include interlibrary loans, database searching, Internet access, and Wi-Fi capability. Special learning facilities include an art gallery, farm research station, organic gardens, greenhouses, and performing art center. **Physically Challenged Students:** Facilities include wheelchair ramps, special parking, specially equipped restrooms, and special housing. **Special:** Unity College offers credit-bearing internships, study abroad, a partnership with the Washington Semester, work-study programs, accelerated degree programs, dual majors, and an honors program. **Visiting:** There are guides for informal visits, visitors may sit in on classes, and stay overnight. To schedule a visit, contact Kristina Dube at (800) 624-1024. **Campus Safety and Security:** Measures include 24-hour foot and vehicle patrol and emergency notification system. There are emergency telephones, lighted pathways/sidewalks, and controlled access to dorms/residences.

REQUIREMENTS: Applicants must be graduates of an accredited secondary school with a minimum GPA of 2.3. A GED is accepted. SAT or ACT scores, though not required, should be submitted, if available for placement purposes. An interview and campus visit are recommended. A GPA of 2.3 is required. AP and CLEP credits are accepted. Important factors in the admissions decision are extracurricular activities record, advanced placement or honors courses, and leadership record. General education requirements include 38 credits. Included are composition and communication, math, computer science proficiency, life science, physical science, humanities, art, community-based learning, and environmental studies. Students must complete 120 credit hours with a minimum GPA of 2.0. A capstone course is required in all bachelor's degree programs. A minimum of 30 credits must be earned at the junior and senior level. **Procedure:** Freshmen are admitted fall and spring. Entrance exams should be taken in the junior or senior year. There are early decision, early admissions, and deferred admissions plans. Early decision applications should be filed by December 15; regular applications, by February 15 for fall entry; and November 1 for spring entry. Notification of early decision is sent January 2; regular decision, March 1. 47 early decision candidates were accepted for the 2017-2018 class. Applications are accepted on-line. **Transfer Students:** 59 transfer students enrolled in 2016-2017. Applicants must submit: an application for admission, all college/university transcripts (and a high school transcript, if you earned fewer than 15 credits in college), and one letter of recommendation. 30 of 120 credits required for the bachelor's degree must be completed at Unity. **International Students:** There is 1 international student enrolled. They must take the TOEFL with a minimum score of 550 on the paper-based TOEFL (PBT) or 80 on the Internet-based version (iBT).

ADMISSIONS: 80% of the 2017-2018 applicants were accepted. 20% of the current freshmen were in the top fifth of their class; 55% were in the top two fifths. **Admissions Contact:** Joe Saltalamachia, Director of Admission. Email: *admissions@unity.edu* Web: *www.unity.edu*

FINANCIAL AID: In 2017-2018, 99% of all full-time freshmen received some form of financial aid. 91% of all full-time freshmen received need-based aid. The average freshman award was $27,943. Need-based scholarships or need-based grants averaged $15,799 ($24,405 maximum); need-based self-help aid (loans and jobs) averaged $5,390 ($6,700 maximum); and other non-need-based awards and non-need-based scholarships averaged $6,754 ($22,659 maximum). 59% of undergraduate students work part-time. The average financial indebtedness of the 2017 graduate was $40,320. The FAFSA code is 006858. The priority date for freshman financial aid applications for fall entry is March.

UNIVERSITY OF MAINE — C-4

www.umaine.edu

Orono, ME 04469 — (207) 581-1622, (877) 486-2364

Fax: (207) 581-1213 — **Email:** umaineadmissions@maine.edu

Full-time: 4370 men, 3834 women	**Faculty:** IIB, +$
Part-time: 530 men, 545 women	**Ph.D.s:** 87%
Graduate: 660 men, 1301 women	**Student/Faculty:** n/av
Year: semesters, summer session	**Tuition:** $10,902 ($30,282)
Room & Board: $10,136	**Freshman Class:** 13231 applied, 12207 accepted, 2299 enrolled
SAT EBR-W/M: 581/571 **ACT:** 24	**CEEB CODE:** 3916
Application Deadline: February 1	**VERY COMPETITIVE**

University of Maine, established in 1865, is Maine's land grant and sea grant institution. It is the largest public university in the state and the flagship campus of the University of Maine System. UMaine has 5 colleges Engineering; Natural Sciences, Forestry, and Agriculture; Liberal Arts and Sciences; Education and Human Development; Honors, and the Maine Business School. In addition to regional accreditation, UMaine has baccalaureate program accreditation with AACSB, ABET, ADA, CSAB, CSWE, NASAD, NASM, CAEP, SAF, ACS, APA, SAF, ASHA, SWST, CCNE, and NAEYC. The 660-acre campus is in a small town 5 miles north of Bangor. Including any residence halls, there are 202 buildings.

STUDENT LIFE: 65% of undergraduates are from Maine. Others are from 47 states, 40 foreign countries, and Canada. 82% are White; 4% Hispanic; 4% race unknown; 3% two or more races; 2% African American; 2% Asian American; 2% Foreign; 1% American Indian/Alaska Native. **Female To Male Ratio:** 1.0:1. The average age of freshmen is 18; all undergraduates, 21. 25% do not continue beyond their first year. **Housing:** 3650 students can be accommodated in college housing, which includes married student dorms, on-campus apartments, and off-campus apartments. In addition, there are honors houses, language/international houses, and special-interest houses. Learning Communities include engineering and technology; outdoor adventure; healthy living; education students; science students; substance free; and green living. Also offered: first-year residential experience and graduate family housing. On-campus housing is guaranteed for the freshman year only, and is available on a first-come, first-served basis. 62% of students commute. All students may keep cars.

FACULTY/CLASSROOMS: 53% of faculty are male; 47% are female. Graduate students teach 13% of introductory courses. The average class size in an introductory lecture is 49; in a laboratory is 16; and in a regular course is 34.

PROGRAMS OF STUDY: UMaine confers B.A., B.S., B.F.A. and B.M.E. degrees. Master's and doctoral degrees are also awarded. Bachelor's degrees are awarded in AGRICULTURE (agriculture, animal science, forest engineering, forestry and related sciences, horticulture, wildlife management, and wood science), BIOLOGICAL SCIENCE (biochemistry, biology/biological science, botany, marine science, microbiology, molecular biology, nutrition, and zoology), BUSINESS (accounting, business administration and management, business administration marketing, business economics, and finance), COMMUNICATIONS AND THE ARTS (art history, communications, dramatic arts, English, French, journalism, media arts, modern language, music, music performance, Spanish, and studio art), COMPUTER AND PHYSICAL SCIENCE (chemistry, computer science, earth science, mathematics, and physics), EDUCATION (art education, athletic training, elementary education, music education, physical education, secondary education, and university studies), ENGINEERING AND ENVIRONMENTAL DESIGN (bioengineering, chemical engineering, civil engineering, computer engineering, construction technology, electrical/electronics engineering, electrical/electronics engineering technology, engineering physics, environmental science, mechanical engineering, mechanical engineering technology, paper and pulp science, and surveying engineering), HEALTH PROFESSIONS (kinesiology, medical laboratory technology, nursing, speech pathology/audiology, and veterinary science), SOCIAL SCIENCE (anthropology, child care/child and family studies, economics, food science, history, interdisciplinary studies, international studies, parks and recreation management, philosophy, political science/government, psychology, social work, sociology, and women & gender studies). Engineering, forest resources, and marine sciences are the strongest academically. Psychology, nursing, and mechanical engineering have the largest enrollments.

ACTIVITIES: There are 183 groups on campus, including art, band, cheerleading, chess, choir, chorale, chorus, computers, dance, debate, drama, drill team, environmental, ethnic, film, forensics, honors, international, jazz band, LGBT, literary magazine, marching band, musical theater, newspaper, opera, orchestra, pep band, photography, political, professional, radio and TV, religious, social, social service, student government, symphony, and yearbook. Popular campus events include Black Bear Marathon and Half Marathon; Career Fair; Culturefest; Division I Athletics games; Family and Friends Weekend; Homecoming; International Dance Festival; Maine Day; Maine Hello and Welcome Weekend; Dance Marathon. **Sports:** There are 8 intercollegiate sports for men and 9 for women, and 30 intramural sports for men and 26 for women. Facilities include an arena for ice hockey, a field house, swimming and diving center, football stadium, track and field, indoor climbing center, student recreation center, a swimming pool, a weight room, indoor track, dance studio, basketball, volleyball, badminton, squash, tennis and racquetball courts, baseball, softball, soccer, field hockey, football fields, and sports dome. **Graduates:** From July 1, 2016 to June 30, 2017, 1681 bachelor's degrees were awarded. The most popular majors were mechanical engineering (6%), pyschology (5%), and management (5%). In an average class, 38% graduate in 4 years or less, 55% graduate in 5 years or less, and 58% graduate in 6 years or less.

SERVICES: Counseling and information services are available, as is tutoring in some subjects, such as 100- and 200-level courses. There is a reader service for the blind. **Library/Resources:** The library contains 3.6 million volumes, 1.7 million microform items, and 184,907 audio/video tapes/CDs/DVDs, and subscribes to 117,000 periodicals including electronic. Computerized library services include interlibrary loans, database searching, Internet access, and Wi-Fi capability. Special learning facilities include an art gallery, planetarium, radio station, astronomy center, a museum, media center, research and commercialization, recital hall, a pavilion, ornamentals trial garden, a farm, manufacturing center, student innovation, laboratory for surface science and technology, and the advanced structures and composites center. **Physically Challenged Students:** 90% of the campus is accessible. Facilities include wheelchair ramps, elevators, special parking, specially equipped restrooms, special class scheduling, lowered drinking fountains, lowered telephones, and a transport van. **Special:** Cross-registration at other University of Maine campuses, internships at the upper level, a Washington semester, work-study programs both on- and off-campus, dual majors, a general studies degree, and pass/fail options are available. Students may study abroad in 78 countries. Cooperative programs are available in most majors, and accelerated degrees may be arranged. Innovate for Maine Fellows program connects the best and brightest Maine college students with Maine's most exciting, growing companies and business leaders in an effort to help grow and create jobs across Maine. There are 10 national honor societies, Phi Beta Kappa, and a freshman honors program. **Visiting:** There are regularly scheduled orientations for prospective students, includes an opening welcome, campus tours, registration, department tours, a student panel, admissions, financial aid and student life sessions, a performing arts presentation, and music auditions. There are guides for informal visits and visitors may sit in on classes. To schedule a visit, contact Silverio Barrera at silverio.barrerajr@maine.edu. **Campus Safety and Security:** Measures include 24-hour foot and vehicle patrol, emergency notification system, self-defense education, and security escort services. There are emergency telephones, lighted pathways/sidewalks, controlled access to dorms/residences, and a text and email emergency communication system.

REQUIREMENTS: The SAT or ACT is required. The GED is accepted. The number of academic or Carnegie credits required varies according to the program. The required secondary school courses also vary with each program but should include 4 credits of English, 3 units each of math and academic electives, 2 units each of lab science, social studies, and foreign language. Guidance counselor recommendation is required for high school students. An essay is required. An audition is required for music majors. An essay is also required. A GPA of 2.0 is required. AP and CLEP credits are accepted. Important factors in the admissions decision are advanced placement or honors courses, recommendations by school officials, and extracurricular activities record. To graduate, students must complete a minimum of 120 credit hours, including at least 48 in the major, with a GPA of 2.0 or higher. 40 credits in approved courses must be taken. General education requirements include 18 credits in human values and social context, 6 credits in math/statistics/computer science, 2 courses in science, and at least 1 course in ethics. English composition is required. Students must demonstrate writing competency and complete a capstone. **Procedure:** Freshmen are admitted fall and spring. Entrance exams should be taken by October of the senior year. There are early admissions and deferred admissions plans. Applications should be filed by February 1 for fall entry. The fall 2017 application fee was $40. Applications are accepted on-line. **Transfer Students:** 585 transfer students enrolled in 2016-2017. Applicants must submit transcripts of all college and high school records. A minimum GPA of 2.0 is required. Some majors specify a higher cumulative GPA. 30 of 120 credits required for the bachelor's degree must be completed at UMaine. **International Students:** There are 192 international students enrolled. They must take the TOEFL with a minimum score of 550 on the paper-based TOEFL (PBT) or 79 on the Internet-based version (iBT).

ADMISSIONS: 92% of the 2017-2018 applicants were accepted. The SAT scores for the 2017-2018 freshman class were: Math-- 14% below 500, 52% between 500 and 599, 28% between 600 and 699, and 6% between 700 and 800. Evidence-Based Reading/Writing-- 11% below 500, 48% between 500 and 599, 36% between 600 and 699, and 5% between 700 and 800. The ACT scores were 4% between 12 and 17, 38% between 18 and 23, 47% between 24 and 29, and 11% above 30. 35% of the current freshmen were in the top fifth of their class; 64% were in the top two fifths. 28 freshmen graduated first in their class. **Admissions Contact:** Whitney Yorston, Director of Communications. Email: *umaineadmissions@maine.edu* Web: *www.umaine.edu*

FINANCIAL AID: In 2017-2018, 99% of all full-time freshmen received some form of financial aid. 71% of all full-time freshmen received need-based aid. The average freshman award was $15,811. Need-based scholarships or need-based grants averaged $7,591; need-based self-help aid (loans and jobs) averaged $4,500; non-need-based athletic scholarships averaged $16,532; and other non-need-based awards and non-need-based scholarships averaged $8,288. 29% of undergraduate students work part-time. The average financial indebtedness of the 2017 graduate was $34,741. The FAFSA code is 002053. The priority date for freshman financial aid applications for fall entry is March 1.

UNIVERSITY OF MAINE AT AUGUSTA — B-5

www.uma.edu

Augusta, ME 04430 — **(207) 621-3465**

Fax: (207) 621-3333	**Email:** umaadm@maine.edu
Full-time: 639 men, 1260 women	**Faculty:** 104; IIB, av$
Part-time: 772 men, 2319 women	**Ph.D.s:** 54%
Graduate: n/av	**Student/Faculty:** 15 to 1
Year: semesters, summer session	**Tuition:** $7812 ($19,332)
Room & Board: n/app	**Freshman Class:** 875 applied, 817 accepted, 512 enrolled
	CEEB CODE: 3929
Application Deadline: August 15	**COMPETITIVE**

University of Maine at Augusta, founded in 1965, offers both associate and baccalaureate degrees and is part of the University of Maine System. There are 3 undergraduate schools. In addition to regional accreditation, UM at Augusta has baccalaureate program accreditation with ADA, NLN, and NEASC. The 159-acre campus is in a small town 50 miles north of Portland. Including any residence halls, there are 15 buildings.

STUDENT LIFE: 97% of undergraduates are from Maine. Others are from 35 states, 3 foreign countries, and Canada. 99% are from public schools. 73% are White; 3% American Indian/Alaska Native; 1% African

American; 1% Asian American; 1% Hispanic. **Female To Male Ratio:** 2.5:1. The average age of freshmen is 27; all undergraduates, 32. 46% do not continue beyond their first year; 30% remain to graduate. **Housing:** Alcohol is not permitted. All students commute. All students may keep cars.

FACULTY/CLASSROOMS: 43% of faculty are male; 47% are female. All teach undergraduates. No introductory courses are taught by graduate students. The average class size in an introductory lecture is 20; in a laboratory is 16; and in a regular course is 18.

PROGRAMS OF STUDY: UM at Augusta confers B.A., B.A.S., B. Mus. and B.S. degrees. Associate degrees are also awarded. Bachelor's degrees are awarded in BIOLOGICAL SCIENCE (biology/biological science), BUSINESS (accounting and business administration and management), COMMUNICATIONS AND THE ARTS (art, English, and jazz), COMPUTER AND PHYSICAL SCIENCE (applied science and information sciences and systems), EDUCATION (library science), ENGINEERING AND ENVIRONMENTAL DESIGN (architecture), HEALTH PROFESSIONS (dental hygiene, mental health/human services, and nursing), SOCIAL SCIENCE (interdisciplinary studies, law enforcement and corrections, liberal arts/general studies, public administration, and social science). Mental health, and human services have the largest enrollments.

ACTIVITIES: There are no fraternities or sororities. There are 17 groups on campus, including music ensembles, art, drama, honors, international, jazz band, LGBT, literary magazine, newspaper, pep band, professional, religious, social, social service, student government, and theater. Popular campus events include Mile of Art, Jazz Week, and Plunkett Poetry Festival. **Sports:** There are 2 intercollegiate sports for men and 3 for women, and 4 intramural sports for men and 4 for women. Facilities include the UMA Community Outdoor Leisure Center, which provide for seasonal activities and features a running and cross-country skiing trail, tennis courts, a soccer field, and a softball field. Indoor facilities include a small gym, a racquetball court, and a small fitness center. **Graduates:** From July 1, 2016 to June 30, 2017, 362 bachelor's degrees were awarded. The most popular majors were health professions (29%), liberal arts/general studies (20%), and business/marketing (17%).

SERVICES: Counseling and information services are available, as is tutoring in some subjects, such as developmental and introductory level courses. There is remedial math and writing. There are also workshops on a variety of student success skills, such as effective learning and reducing test anxiety. **Library/Resources:** The library contains 93,897 volumes, 4,676 microform items, and 4,783 audio/video tapes/CDs/DVDs, and subscribes to 493 periodicals including electronic. Computerized library services include interlibrary loans, database searching, Internet access, and Wi-Fi capability. Special learning facilities include an art gallery, and an interactive television system. **Physically Challenged Students:** 95% of the campus is accessible. Facilities include wheelchair ramps, elevators, special parking, specially equipped restrooms, special class scheduling, lowered drinking fountains, and lowered telephones. **Special:** Work-study and internship programs with local employers, study abroad in Germany, and a student-designed interdisciplinary studies major are available. Cross-registration is offered with University of Maine System campuses. There is 1 national honor society. **Visiting:** There are regularly scheduled orientations for prospective students, during the month before the beginning of a semester. There are guides for informal visits and visitors may sit in on classes. To schedule a visit, contact the Admissions Office. **Campus Safety and Security:** Measures include emergency notification system and security escort services. There are emergency telephones and lighted pathways/sidewalks.

REQUIREMENTS: Students are encouraged to submit SAT scores for placement only. Applicants should have a high school diploma or the GED. Recommended secondary preparation varies according to the degree program. Applicants for the B.M. program must audition. UMA requires applicants to be in the upper 25% of their class. AP and CLEP credits are accepted. All students must complete at least 120 hours, including 30 to 40 in the major, with a minimum GPA of 2.0. All degree programs require courses in communications, humanities, college writing, and fine arts. 6 credits of writing-intensive coursework is required. **Procedure:** Freshmen are admitted fall, spring, and summer. There are deferred admissions and rolling admissions plans. Applications should be filed by August 15 for fall entry; October 15 for spring entry. The fall 2017 application fee was $40. Notification is sent on a rolling basis. Applications are accepted on-line. **Transfer Students:** 625 transfer students enrolled in 2016-2017. High school/college transcripts and a statement of good standing from prior institutions are required. Standardized test scores are required for some students, and an interview is recommended. 30 of 120 credits required for the bachelor's degree must be completed at UM at Augusta. **International Students:** There are 42 international students enrolled. They must take the TOEFL with a minimum score of 500 on the paper-based TOEFL (PBT).

ADMISSIONS: 93% of the 2017-2018 applicants were accepted. 12% of the current freshmen were in the top fifth of their class; 63% were in the top two fifths. **Admissions Contact:** Kathy Trask, Associate Director of Admissions. Email: *umaadm@maine.edu* Web: *www.uma.edu*

FINANCIAL AID: In 2017-2018, 90% of all full-time freshmen received some form of financial aid. 84% of all full-time freshmen received need-based aid. The average freshman award was $8,026. Need-based scholarships or need-based grants averaged $5,816 ($6,640 maximum); need-based self-help aid (loans and jobs) averaged $6,164 ($7,500 maximum); non-need-based athletic scholarships averaged $2,850; and other non-need-based awards and non-need-based scholarships averaged $6,156 ($2,600 maximum). 5% of undergraduate students work part-time. The average financial indebtedness of the 2017 graduate was $24,353. The FAFSA code is 006760. The priority date for freshman financial aid applications for fall entry is March 1.

UNIVERSITY OF MAINE AT FARMINGTON B-4

www.umf.maine.edu

Farmington, ME 04938 — **(207) 778-7050**

Fax: (207) 778-8182
Email: umfadmit@maine.edu
Full-time: 567 men, 1106 women
Part-time: 42 men, 96 women
Graduate: 48 men, 221 women
Year: semesters, summer session
Room & Board: $9334
SAT EBR-W/M: 548/522 **ACT:** 23
Application Deadline: rolling
Faculty: 110; IIB, -$
Ph.D.s: 88%
Student/Faculty: 14 to 1
Tuition: $9458 ($19,026)
Freshman Class: 1939 applied, 1601 accepted, 437 enrolled
CEEB CODE: 3506
COMPETITIVE

University of Maine at Farmington, founded in 1863 and part of the University of Maine System, is a public liberal arts institution offering programs in arts and sciences, teacher education, and human services. There is 1 undergraduate school and 1 graduate school. In addition to regional accreditation, UMF has baccalaureate program accreditation with CAEP. The 55-acre campus is in a small town 38 miles northwest of Augusta, and 80 miles north of Portland. Including any residence halls, there are 43 buildings.

STUDENT LIFE: 83% of undergraduates are from Maine. Others are from 32 states, 6 foreign countries, and Canada. 88% are from public schools. 87% are White; 5% race unknown; 2% African American; 2% Hispanic; 2% two or more races; 1% Asian American; 1% Foreign. **Female To Male Ratio:** 2.2:1. The average age of freshmen is 18; all undergraduates, 21. 28% do not continue beyond their first year; 55% remain to graduate. **Housing:** 1034 students can be accommodated in college housing, which includes gender neutral, single-sex, and coed dorms, honors dormitories and interest-based themes floors available in residence halls. On-campus housing is guaranteed for all 4 years. 52% of students live on campus. All students may keep cars.

FACULTY/CLASSROOMS: 37% of faculty are male; 63% are female. All teach undergraduates, 80% do research, and 80% do both. No introductory courses are taught by graduate students. The average class size in an introductory lecture is 38; in a laboratory is 18; and in a regular course is 17.

PROGRAMS OF STUDY: UMF confers B.A., B.S., B.F.A. and B.G.S. degrees. Master's degrees are also awarded. Bachelor's degrees are awarded in AGRICULTURE (environmental studies), BIOLOGICAL SCIENCE (biology/biological science), BUSINESS (business administration and management, business economics, and recreation and leisure services), COMMUNICATIONS AND THE ARTS (art, creative writing, English, media arts, and visual and performing arts), COMPUTER AND PHYSICAL SCIENCE (actuarial science, computer science, geology, and mathematics), EDUCATION (early childhood education, elementary education, health education, health information management, secondary education, and special education), ENGINEERING AND ENVIRONMENTAL DESIGN (environmental science), HEALTH PROFESSIONS (community health work and rehabilitation therapy), SOCIAL SCIENCE (anthropology, geography, history, interdisciplinary studies, international studies, liberal arts/general studies, philosophy and religion, political science/government, psychology, and sociology). Creative writing, actuarial science, and secondary education are the strongest academically. Education, psychology, and community health education have the largest enrollments.

ACTIVITIES: There are no fraternities or sororities. There are 65 groups on campus, including anime, campus residence council, improvisation, poetry, table gaming, art, band, cheerleading, choir, chorus, communications, computers, dance, drama, environmental, ethnic, film, honors, international, LGBT, literary magazine, musical theater, newspaper, orchestra, political, professional, radio and TV, religious, social, social service, Student Education Association of Maine, student government, symphony, and yearbook. Popular campus events include Parents and Alumni weekends, Excursions to Boston & other destinations, Outdoor Recreation Excursions, Michael D. Wilson Symposium Day, Spring Fling, Sustainability Carnival & Sledding Event, Skating Under the Stars, and Days of Service. **Sports:** There are 8 intercollegiate sports for men and 9 for women, and 10 intramural sports for men and 10 for women. Facilities include a gymnasium, with a comprehensive training room, baseball field, a skinned softball field with dugouts, field hockey, lacrosse, soccer fields, a rugby pitch, ultimate Frisbee and intramural field, a field house with an indoor jogging track, multipurpose courts, a group fitness area and a cardio and strength area, a free weight area and a 25 yard swimming pool. The track and field teams have access to the local high school's facility. **Graduates:** From July 1, 2016 to June 30, 2017, 361 bachelor's degrees were awarded. The most popular majors were education (34%), psychology (13%), and community health (13%). In an average class, 36% graduate in 4 years or less, 51% graduate in 5 years or less, and 54% graduate in 6 years or less.

SERVICES: Counseling and information services are available, as is tutoring in every subject. There is a reader service for the blind, and remedial math, reading, and writing. Math and writing are available for drop-in tutoring; tutoring in all other subjects is available upon request. **Library/Resources:** The library contains 58,690 volumes, 15,471 microform items, and 5,998 audio/video tapes/CDs/DVDs, and subscribes to 78,109 periodicals including electronic. Computerized library services include interlibrary loans, database searching, Internet access, and Wi-Fi capability. Special learning facilities include an art gallery, radio station, an astronomy observatory, Alice James books poetry journal, assistive learning center, and on-site nursery school and day care as a teaching environment. **Physically Challenged Students:** 95% of the campus is accessible. Facilities include wheelchair ramps, elevators, special parking, specially equipped restrooms, special class scheduling, lowered drinking fountains, special housing, a swimming pool, and TDD. **Special:** Many opportunities for travel courses to countries such as Costa Rica, Italy, St. Johns, Ireland, Peru, Spain and more. Semester-long study abroad programs in China or France are available, as well as numerous other countries through co-operative arrangements with other universities. There are opportunities to participate in the National Student Exchange program. Student teaching is required of all education majors. Internships are required in rehabilitation and health and are also available in other disciplines under the sponsorship of the Partnership for Civic Advancement. There are multiple opportunities for student employment, including positions funded by the President's Work Initiative, which are available to all students. There are eight interdisciplinary majors offered, and individualized, student-designed majors are available and encouraged. UMF also offers 3+2 programs in Engineering and in Counseling. There are 13 national honor societies, a freshman honors program, and 9 departmental honors programs. **Visiting:** There are regularly scheduled orientations for prospective students, sessions on financial aid, majors, student life, the admissions process, and special opportunities such as study abroad, and tours of the campus. There are guides for informal visits and visitors may sit in on classes. To schedule a visit, contact the UM at Farmington Admissions Office. **Campus Safety and Security:** Measures include 24-hour foot and vehicle patrol, emergency notification system, self-defense education, and security escort services. There are shuttle buses, emergency telephones, lighted pathways/sidewalks, controlled access to dorms/residences, and safety whistles.

REQUIREMENTS: Applicants are required to have 4 credits in English, 3 each in math, sciences (2 that are labs), and social sciences. An essay and a counselor recommendation are required, and an interview is recommended for some. The GED is accepted for highly motivated students. AP and CLEP credits are accepted. Important factors in the admissions decision are advanced placement or honors courses, recommendations by school officials, and extracurricular activities record. All students must maintain a minimum GPA of 2.0 while earning 128 semester hours, including 40 or more credits in their majors, and at least 40 credits in General Education. Core requirements include first-year seminar, English composition, mathematics, two courses in natural sciences, two courses in social sciences, humanities, fine arts, and a physical activity requirement. **Procedure:** Freshmen are admitted fall and spring. There are early admissions, deferred admissions, and rolling admissions plans. Application deadlines are open. Notification is sent on a rolling basis. Applications are accepted on-line. **Transfer Students:** 107 transfer students enrolled in 2016-2017. Applicants must have a minimum GPA of 2.0 (2.5 or 2.75 for some majors). Submission of passing Praxis Core scores are required of all students seeking transfer into teacher education programs leading to certification. 32 of 128 credits required for the bachelor's degree must be completed at UMF. **International Students:** There are 11 international students enrolled. They must take the TOEFL with a minimum score of 550 on the paper-based TOEFL (PBT) or 79 on the Internet-based version (iBT), and take the IELTS. The SAT is optional for admittance, but recommended for placement of matriculating first-year students.

ADMISSIONS: 80% of the 2017-2018 applicants were accepted. The SAT scores for the 2017-2018 freshman class were: Math-- 34% below 500, 51% between 500 and 599, 14% between 600 and 699, and 1% between 700 and 800. Evidence-based Reading/Writing-- 23% below 500, 48% between 500 and 599, 26% between 600 and 699, and 2% between 700 and 800. 35% of the current freshmen were in the top fifth of their class; 67% were in the top two fifths. 3 freshmen graduated first in their class. **Admissions Contact:** Admissions Office, Email: *umfadmit@maine.edu* Web: *www.umf.maine.edu*

FINANCIAL AID: In 2017-2018, 82% of all full-time freshmen received some form of financial aid. 79% of all full-time freshmen received need-based aid. The average freshman award was $14,568. Need-based scholarships or need-based grants averaged $8,916; need-based self-help aid (loans and jobs) averaged $6,237; and other non-need-based awards and non-need-based scholarships averaged $3,026. 47% of undergraduate students work part-time. The average financial indebtedness of the 2017 graduate was $30,517. The FAFSA code is 002040. The priority date for freshman financial aid applications for fall entry is March 1.

UNIVERSITY OF MAINE AT FORT KENT *(The complete profile is made available exclusively on our website, www.barronspac.com)*

UNIVERSITY OF MAINE AT MACHIAS — E-4

www.machias.edu

Machias, ME 04654	**(207) 255-1318** **(888) 468-6866**
Fax: (207) 255-1363	**Email: ummadmissions@maine.edu**
Full-time: 200 men, 300 women	**Faculty:** 31; IIB, --$
Part-time: 145 men, 542 women	**Ph.D.s:** 71%
Graduate: n/av	**Student/Faculty:** 15 to 1
Year: semesters, summer session	**Tuition:** $14,960 ($38,600)
Room & Board: $8000	**Freshman Class:** 374 applied, 312 accepted, 120 enrolled
SAT: recommended **ACT:** 22	**CEEB CODE:** 3956
Application Deadline: August 15	**COMPETITIVE**

University of Maine at Machias, founded in 1909, is a publicly funded liberal arts institution in the University of Maine system. There are 4 undergraduate schools. In addition to regional accreditation, UM at Machias has baccalaureate program accreditation with NRPA. The 243-acre campus is in a rural area 85 miles east of Bangor. Including any residence halls, there are 8 buildings.

STUDENT LIFE: 82% of undergraduates are from Maine. Others are from 26 states, 16 foreign countries, and Canada. 98% are from public schools. 90% are White; 4% American Indian/Alaska Native; 4% Foreign; 1% African American; 1% Hispanic. **Female To Male Ratio:** 2.4:1. The average age of freshmen is 20; all undergraduates, 29. 28% do not continue beyond their first year; 45% remain to graduate. **Housing:** 353 students can be accommodated in college housing, which includes dorms. On-campus housing is guaranteed for all 4 years. 76% of students commute. All students may keep cars.

FACULTY/CLASSROOMS: 54% of faculty are male; 46% are female. All teach undergraduates. No introductory courses are taught by graduate students. The average class size in an introductory lecture is 21; in a laboratory is 16; and in a regular course is 17.

PROGRAMS OF STUDY: UM at Machias confers B.A., B.S. and B.C.S. degrees. Associate degrees are also awarded. Bachelor's degrees are awarded in AGRICULTURE (agricultural business management, agricultural sciences, environmental studies, fish and game management, fishing and fisheries, and natural resources), BIOLOGICAL SCIENCE (biology ecology and field biology, biology/biological science, biological sciences, marine biology, marine science, wildlife conservation biology, and wildlife biology), BUSINESS (accounting, business administration and management, business administration marketing, entrepreneurial studies, environment & national resource economics, marketing/retailing/merchandising, recreation and leisure services, recreational facilities management, small business management, sports management, sustainable management, and tourism), COMMUNICATIONS AND THE ARTS (creative writing, English, fine arts, fine/studio arts, general, printmaking, recreation administration, sport & lifestyle studies, and writing), EDUCATION (business education, elementary education, English education, general studies, physical education, physical science secondary school education, recreation education, social studies education, social studies secondary school education, special education, and sports and wellness studies), ENGINEERING AND ENVIRONMENTAL DESIGN (environmental science and survey and mapping technology), HEALTH PROFESSIONS (allied health, biology, exercise science, mental health/human services, preallied health, predentistry, premedicine, prephysician assistant, and preveterinary science), SOCIAL SCIENCE (behavioral science, criminal justice, human services, interdisciplinary studies, liberal arts/general studies, liberal arts, sciences, general studies, humanities, parks and recreation management, and psychology). Elementary education, marine biology, and environmental studies are the strongest academically. Elementary education, business administration, and behavioral science have the largest enrollments.

ACTIVITIES: 7% of men belong to 2 local and 2 national fraternities; 3% of women belong to 1 local and 3 national sororities. There are 34 groups on campus, including pop band, art, band, chorale, chorus, communications, computers, dance, drama, ethnic, honors, international, LGBT, literary magazine, musical theater, outing club, photography, professional, radio and TV, religious, social service, and student government. Popular campus events include Winter Carnival, Spring Weekend, Homecoming Weekend, and Greek Week. **Sports:** There are 2 intercollegiate sports for men and 3 for women, and 10 intramural sports for men and 10 for women. Facilities include gyms, weight/exercise rooms, handball/raquetball courts, a pool, and a recreational center. **Graduates:** From July 1, 2016 to June 30, 2017, 100 bachelor's degrees were awarded. The most popular majors were behavioral science (15%), business administration (13%), and recreation management (13%). In an average class, 19% graduate in 4 years or less, 42% graduate in 5 years or less, and 46% graduate in 6 years or less.

SERVICES: Counseling and information services are available, as is tutoring in every subject. There is remedial math, reading, and writing. The Student Services Coordinator provides one-on-one services, including learning strategies, study skills, and assistance with papers and learning styles. **Library/Resources:** The library contains 82,000 volumes, 5,000 microform items, and 3,000 audio/video tapes/CDs/DVDs, and subscribes to 320 periodicals including electronic. Computerized library services include interlibrary loans, database searching, Internet access, and Wi-Fi capability. Special learning facilities include an art gallery, radio station, aquariums for marine and aquaculture studies. **Physically Challenged Students:** 85% of the campus is accessible. Facilities include wheelchair ramps, elevators, special parking, specially equipped restrooms, lowered drinking fountains, and automatic doors. **Special:** Co-op programs in all majors except education, cross-registration, internships, work-study programs, a B.A.-B.S. degree, study abroad in England and Wales, and a student designed concentration in environmental science are available. UM at Machias also offers a Bachelor of College Studies program, credit for prior learning, nondegree study, and a pass/fail option in certain courses. There is a freshman honors program. **Visiting:** There are regularly scheduled orientations for prospective students, consisting of traditional orientations prior to the fall and spring semesters, which include programming to guide students in all aspects of starting college—academic, student services and activities, and administrative. UM at Machias also offers two summer student orientations, which include aspects of the fall orientations plus a parent orientation. There are guides for informal visits and visitors may sit in on classes. To schedule a visit, contact the Admissions Office. **Campus Safety and Security:** Measures include emergency notification system, self-defense education, and security escort services. There are lighted pathways/sidewalks, controlled access to dorms/residences, a keyless entry system for residence halls, and security patrol daily.

REQUIREMENTS: The SAT or ACT is recommended. All candidates must be graduates of an accredited secondary school, although the GED/HiSET is accepted. UM at Machias recommends that students place in the top half of their graduating class and that composite SAT scores be satisfactory. UM at Machias also recommends completion of 4 units of English, 3 units of math, and electives, 2 each of lab science, social science/history, and fine arts or foreign language. An essay is required and an interview is strongly recommended. UMM requires applicants to be in the upper 50% of their class. AP and CLEP credits are accepted. Important factors in the admissions decision are extracurricular activities record, leadership record, and recommendations by school officials. To graduate, students must complete a minimum of 120 credit hours with a GPA of 2.0. The environmental core curriculum consists of 40-43 hours in the areas of communication skills, science and math, humans in social context, fine arts, historical and cultural perspectives, and lifetime fitness. **Procedure:** Freshmen are admitted fall, spring, and summer. There are early admissions, deferred admissions, and rolling admissions plans. Applications should be filed by August 15 for fall entry. The fall 2017 application fee was $40. Notification is sent on a rolling basis. Applications are accepted on-line. **Transfer Students:** 36 transfer students enrolled in 2016-2017. A minimum college GPA of 2.0 and evidence of good standing are required of transfer applicants. 30 of 120 credits required for the bachelor's degree must be completed at UM at Machias. **International Students:** There are 10 international students enrolled. They must take the TOEFL with a minimum score of 5 on the paper-based TOEFL (PBT) or 5 on the Internet-based version (iBT).

ADMISSIONS: 83% of the 2017-2018 applicants were accepted. The ACT scores were 43% below 12, 14% between 12 and 17, 29% between 18 and 23, 7% between 24 and 29, and 7% above 30. 23% of the current freshmen were in the top fifth of their class; 53% were in the top two fifths. **Admissions Contact:** PJ Singh, Admissions Counselor. Email: *ummadmissions@maine.edu* Web: *www.machias.edu*

FINANCIAL AID: In 2017-2018, 88% of all full-time freshmen received some form of financial aid. 78% of all full-time freshmen received need-based aid. The average freshman award was $8,488. Need-based scholarships or need-based grants averaged $5,884; need-based self-help aid (loans and jobs) averaged $3,439; and other non-need-based awards and non-need-based scholarships averaged $6,420. The FAFSA code is 002055. The deadline for filing freshman financial aid applications for fall entry is March 1.

UNIVERSITY OF MAINE AT PRESQUE ISLE *(The complete profile is made available exclusively on our website, www.barronspac.com)*

UNIVERSITY OF NEW ENGLAND B-6

www.une.edu

Biddeford, ME 04005	**(800) 477-4863** **(800) 477-4863**
Fax: (207) 602-4900	**Email: admissions@une.edu**
Full-time: 686 men, 1639 women	**Faculty:** n/av
Part-time: 12 men, 23 women	**Ph.D.s:** n/av
Graduate: 1138 men, 2690 women	**Student/Faculty:** n/av
Year: semesters, summer session	**Tuition:** $36,530
Room & Board: $13,580	**Freshman Class:** 5087 applied, 4107 accepted, 651 enrolled
SAT EBR-W/M: 567/556 **ACT:** 24	**CEEB CODE:** 3751
Application Deadline: February 15	**COMPETITIVE**

University of New England is leading the transformation of global health sciences education. Beyond mere "training," we provide a full and integrated education preparing our graduates for evolving health care professions. In addition to our 27 health sciences disciplines, the full range of liberal arts classes and majors makes UNE a unique participatory, educational environment. No matter what degree or profession you are pursuing, the interdisciplinary learning turns out scholars and professionals who can adapt and prosper. In Dental Medicine, Pharmacy, Medicine, Nursing and 11 allied health programs, UNE prepares future health care professionals to practice comprehensive and collaborative team-based care the new gold standard. We have three beautiful campuses: in Portland and Biddeford, Maine, and in Tangier, Morocco. This newest campus in Tangier allows UNE students to experience the world while staying on track for their majors. It gives our future professionals a unique understanding of the world they will lead. There are 3 undergraduate schools and 6 graduate schools. In addition to regional accreditation, University of New England has baccalaureate program accreditation with ACBSP, ADA, APTA, CSWE, NLN, CAAHEP, AOA, CAATE, and NLNAC. The 623-acre campus is in a small town on the banks of the Saco River and the shore of the Atlantic Ocean in Biddeford, ME. Including any residence halls, there are 61 buildings.

STUDENT LIFE: 70% of undergraduates are from out of state, mostly the Northeast. Students are from 38 states, 6 foreign countries, and Canada. 88% are White; 5% race unknown; 3% Asian American; 2% two or more races; 1% African American. **Female To Male Ratio:** 2.4:1. The average age of freshmen is 18; all undergraduates, 20. 12% do not continue beyond their first year; 78% remain to graduate. **Housing:** 1525 students can be accommodated in college housing, which includes dorms. In addition, there are special-interest houses. On-campus housing is guaranteed for the freshman year only. 65% of students commute. All students may keep cars.

FACULTY/CLASSROOMS: No introductory courses are taught by graduate students. The average class size in a laboratory is 17 and in a regular course is 20.

PROGRAMS OF STUDY: UNE confers B.A., B.S., B.S.W., and B.S.N. degrees. Master's and doctoral degrees are also awarded. Bachelor's degrees are awarded in AGRICULTURE (animal science, aquaculture & fishery technology, and environmental studies), BIOLOGICAL SCIENCE (biochemistry, biology/biological science, marine affairs, marine science, neurosciences, and nutrition), BUSINESS (business administration and management and sports management), COMMUNICATIONS AND THE ARTS (art and design, communications, English, and recreation administration), COMPUTER AND PHYSICAL SCIENCE (applied mathematics, chemistry, and oceanography), EDUCATION (art education, athletic training, education, elementary education, and secondary education), ENGINEERING AND ENVIRONMENTAL DESIGN (environmental science), HEALTH PROFESSIONS (biomedical science, dental hygiene, exercise science, medical laboratory science, nursing, occupational therapy, predentistry, prepharmacy, pre-physician assistant, and public health), SOCIAL SCIENCE (applied social science, history, liberal arts/general studies, political science/government, psychology, social work, and sociology). Medical biology/medical sciences, nursing, and applied exercise science have the largest enrollments.

ACTIVITIES: There are no fraternities or sororities. There are 70 groups on campus, including skiing, surfing, art, cheerleading, communications, dance, debate, drama, environmental, ethnic, honors, international, LGBT, literary magazine, musical theater, newspaper, pep band, political, professional, religious, sailing, social, social service, student government, and yearbook. Popular campus events include Welcome Week, Family and Friends Weekend, and Full Leadership Retreat. **Sports:** There are 7 intercollegiate sports for men and 6 for women, and 14 intramural sports for men and 13 for women. Facilities include an ice hockey arena, a performance court, a fitness center, athletic training rooms, a turf field, indoor track, fitness center, a pool, a racquetball court. **Graduates:** From July 1, 2016 to June 30, 2017, 542 bachelor's degrees were awarded. The most popular majors were nursing (18%), applied exercise science (10%), and health wellness occupational studies (10%). In an average class, 54% graduate in 4 years or less, 59% graduate in 5 years or less, and 60% graduate in 6 years or less. Of the 2016 graduating class, 28% were enrolled in graduate school within 6 months of graduation, and 54% were employed.

SERVICES: Counseling and information services are available, as is tutoring in most subjects. There is a reader service for the blind, and remedial math, reading, and writing. **Library/Resources:** The library contains 135,000 volumes, 536 microform items, and 18,000 audio/video tapes/CDs/DVDs, and subscribes to 130,000 periodicals including electronic. Computerized library services include interlibrary loans, database searching, Internet access, and Wi-Fi capability. Special learning facilities include an art gallery, institutes for research and scholarship. These University-wide centers build on existing strengths of the institution in interprofessional education, marine science, neuroscience, public health, global humanities, and biomedical research. **Physically Challenged Students:** 85% of the campus is accessible. Facilities include wheelchair ramps, elevators, special parking, specially equipped restrooms, special class scheduling, lowered drinking fountains, lowered telephones, special housing, and stair climbers. **Special:** UNE offers cross-registration with the Greater Portland Alliance of Colleges and Universities, internships in all majors, work-study programs, study abroad and dual majors in all departments. There are transfer articulation agreements with the following community colleges: Central Maine Community College and Great Bay Community College. Additionally, the University offers several premedical tracks for students interested in pursuing a medical field as a graduate student, including several accelerated programs: social work, health/wellness/occupational studies, pre-pharmacy, physician assistant, medicine and dental medicine all offer undergrad/grad level tracks. There are 2 national honor societies. **Visiting:** There are regularly scheduled orientations for prospective students, includes a tour and information session. There are guides for informal visits and visitors may sit in on classes. To schedule a visit, contact the Office of Undergraduate Admissions. **Campus Safety and Security:** Measures include 24-hour foot and vehicle patrol, emergency notification system, self-defense education, and security escort services. There are shuttle buses, emergency telephones, lighted pathways/sidewalks, controlled access to dorms/residences, and a safe-ride program provides drivers for students.

REQUIREMENTS: Applicants should be high school graduates with 4 years of English, 3 years each of math and science, and 2 years each of history and social studies. The GED is accepted. SAT or ACT scores are required (students do not need to submit scores from both exams.) AP and CLEP credits are accepted. Important factors in the admissions decision are recommendations by school officials, geographical diversity, and advanced placement or honors courses. A total of at least 120 credits with a minimum GPA of 2.0 is required for graduation. Some programs require more than 120 credits. Students must take 43 credits in a liberal arts core curriculum of humanities, sciences, and social sciences. Most majors require 1-semester internships. Courses in English composition, human traditions, environmental studies, lab science, creative arts, and math are required. **Procedure:** Freshmen are admitted fall and spring. Entrance exams should be taken during the spring of the junior year or the fall of the senior year. There are early admissions and deferred admissions plans. Early decision applications should be filed by December 1; regular applications, by February 15 for fall entry; and December 1 for spring entry. The fall 2017 application fee was $40. Notification is sent on a rolling basis. Applications are accepted on-line. **Transfer Students:** 158 transfer students enrolled in 2016-2017. Transfer applicants should present a GPA of at least 2.5 in prior college work. 30 of 120 credits required for the bachelor's degree must be completed at UNE. **International Students:** There are 8 international students enrolled. They must take the TOEFL with a minimum score of 550 on the paper-based TOEFL (PBT) or 79 on the Internet-based version (iBT). They must also take the SAT or ACT.

ADMISSIONS: 81% of the 2017-2018 applicants were accepted. The SAT scores for the 2017-2018 freshman class were: Math-- 18% below 500, 54% between 500 and 599, 24% between 600 and 699, and 3% between 700 and 800. Evidence-Based Reading/Writing-- 14% below 500, 53% between 500 and 599, 31% between 600 and 699, and 3% between 700 and 800. The ACT scores were 2% between 12 and 17, 45% between 18 and 23, 43% between 24 and 29, and 9% above 30. **Admissions Contact:** Scott Steinberg, Dean of University Admission. Email: *admissions@une.edu* Web: *www.une.edu*

FINANCIAL AID: In 2017-2018, 100% of all full-time freshmen received some form of financial aid. The average freshman award was $34,306. 36% of undergraduate students work part-time. The FAFSA code is 002050. The deadline for filing freshman financial aid applications for fall entry is May 1.

UNIVERSITY OF SOUTHERN MAINE — A-5

www.usm.maine.edu

Gorham, ME 04038 — **(207) 780-5670** **(800) 800-4876**

Fax: (207) 780-5640 — **Email: admitusm@maine.edu**

Full-time: 2166 men, 2665 women
Part-time: 1128 men, 1659 women
Graduate: 686 men, 1351 women
Year: semesters, summer session
Room & Board: $9400
SAT CR/M/W: 500/500/490 **ACT:** 21
Application Deadline: February 15

Faculty: IIB, +$
Ph.D.s: 74%
Student/Faculty: n/av
Tuition: $8920 ($21,280)
Freshman Class: 3819 applied, 3676 accepted, 924 enrolled
CEEB CODE: 3691
COMPETITIVE

University of Southern Maine, founded in 1878, is a publicly funded, multi-campus, comprehensive, residential, liberal arts institution serving the University of Maine system. There are 5 undergraduate schools and 8 graduate schools. In addition to regional accreditation, USM has baccalaureate program accreditation with AACSB, ABET, CSAB, CSWE, NASM, NCATE, NLN, and NRPA. The 144-acre campus is in an urban area 110 miles north of Boston, MA. Including any residence halls, there are 66 buildings.

STUDENT LIFE: 90% of undergraduates are from Maine. Others are from 35 states, 27 foreign countries, and Canada. 97% are White; 1% African American; 1% Asian American; 1% American Indian/Alaska Native; 1% Hispanic. **Female To Male Ratio:** 1.4:1. The average age of freshmen is 19; all undergraduates, 25. **Housing:** 1835 students can be accommodated in college housing, which includes married student dorms and on-campus apartments. In addition, there are honors houses, special-interest houses, and a fine arts house. On-campus housing is guaranteed for all 4 years. 81% of students commute. All students may keep cars.

FACULTY/CLASSROOMS: 53% of faculty are male; 47% are female. 80% teach undergraduates and do research. No introductory courses are taught by graduate students. The average class size in an introductory lecture is 50; in a laboratory is 20; and in a regular course is 22.

PROGRAMS OF STUDY: USM confers B.A., B.S., B.F.A. and B.M. degrees. Associate, master's, and doctoral degrees are also awarded. Bachelor's degrees are awarded in BIOLOGICAL SCIENCE (biology/biological science), BUSINESS (accounting and business administration and management), COMMUNICATIONS AND THE ARTS (communications, dramatic arts, English, fine arts, French, music, and music performance), COMPUTER AND PHYSICAL SCIENCE (chemistry, computer science, geology, geoscience, mathematics, and physics), EDUCATION (music education and technical education), ENGINEERING AND ENVIRONMENTAL DESIGN (electrical/electronics engineering, environmental science, and industrial engineering technology), HEALTH PROFESSIONS (environmental health science, health science, nursing, recreation therapy, and sports medicine), SOCIAL SCIENCE (anthropology, economics, geography, history, philosophy, political science/government, psychology, social work, sociology, and women's studies). Electrical engineering, computer science, and nursing are the strongest academically. Business administration, nursing, and psychology have the largest enrollments.

ACTIVITIES: 2% of men belong to 1 local and 3 national fraternities; 2% of women belong to 2 local and 2 national sororities. There are 100 groups on campus, including art, band, cheerleading, chess, choir, chorale, chorus, computers, dance, drama, ethnic, honors, international, jazz band, LGBT, literary magazine, musical theater, opera, orchestra, outing, photography, political, professional, religious, social, social service, and student government. Popular campus events include Winter Weekend, Spring Fling, and Comedy Nights. **Sports:** There are 12 intercollegiate sports for men and 13 for women, and 14 intramural sports for men and 14 for women. Facilities include gyms, tennis courts, athletic fields, racquetball and squash courts, cross-country ski trails, two weight-training and fitness facilities, an ice arena, a field house, and an indoor track. **Graduates:** From July 1, 2016 to June 30, 2017, 1101 bachelor's degrees were awarded. The most popular majors were health professions (20%), social sciences (19%), and business (13%).

SERVICES: Counseling and information services are available, as is tutoring in most subjects. There is a reader service for the blind, and remedial math, reading, and writing. **Library/Resources:** The library contains 455,129 volumes, 731,755 microform items, and 5,288 audio/video tapes/CDs/DVDs, and subscribes to 3,249 periodicals including electronic. Computerized library services include interlibrary loans and database searching. Special learning facilities include an art gallery, planetarium, TV station, cartography collections. **Physically Challenged Students:** All of the campus is accessible. Facilities include wheelchair ramps, elevators, special parking, specially equipped restrooms, special class scheduling, lowered drinking fountains, and lowered telephones. **Special:** Cross-registration within the University of Maine system and 4 Greater Portland colleges, a Washington semester, and study abroad in more than 12 countries are offered. Internships, co-op and work-study programs, a B.A.-B.S. degree, dual and student-designed majors, a 2-2 engineering program with the University of Maine, credit for life experience, nondegree study, and pass/fail options are also available. There is a January intersession. There are 2 national honor societies, a freshman honors program, and 1 departmental honors program. **Visiting:** There are regularly scheduled orientations for prospective students, including regularly scheduled campus tours and group information sessions, as well as special events such as fall open houses. Interviews are also available on request. There are guides for informal visits and visitors may sit in on classes. To schedule a visit, contact the Admissions Office. **Campus Safety and Security:** Measures include 24-hour foot and vehicle patrol, self-defense education, and security escort services. There are shuttle buses, emergency telephones, lighted pathways/sidewalks, and preventive programs within residence halls.

REQUIREMENTS: The SAT or ACT is required. Applicants must be graduates of an accredited secondary school. The GED is accepted. Either 41 academic credits or 20.5 Carnegie units are required. Secondary school courses should include 4 years of English, 3 of math, 2 each of a foreign language and lab science, and 1 each of history and social studies. An essay is required, as are auditions for music applicants and interviews for applicants to the School of Applied Science. Guidance counselor recommendations are required for those students applying during their senior year. A GPA of 2.0 is required. AP and CLEP credits are accepted. Important factors in the admissions decision are advanced placement or honors courses, recommendations by school officials, and extracurricular activities record. A total of 120 hours, of which 36 to 94 are in the major, and a minimum GPA of 2.0 are required for graduation. All students must fulfill the distribution requirements of the 3-part core curriculum: basic competence, methods of inquiry/ways of knowing, and interdisciplinary studies. **Procedure:** Freshmen are admitted fall and spring. Entrance exams should be taken by May of the junior year or January of the senior year. There are deferred admissions and rolling admissions plans. Applications should be filed by February 15 for fall entry; December 1 for spring entry. The fall 2017 application fee was $40. Applications are accepted on-line. **Transfer Students:** 848 transfer students enrolled in 2016-2017. Applicants must have a minimum GPA of 2.0 or 2.75 for those from non-regionally accredited institutions. Students who have been out of high school for less than 3 years must submit SAT scores. 30 of 120 credits required for the bachelor's degree must be completed at USM. **International Students:** They must take the TOEFL.

ADMISSIONS: 96% of the 2017-2018 applicants were accepted. The SAT scores for the 2017-2018 freshman class were: Critical Reading-- 47% below 500, 39% between 500 and 599, 12% between 600 and 699, and 2% between 700 and 800. Math-- 50% below 500, 40% between 500 and 599, 9% between 600 and 699, and 1% between 700 and 800. Writing-- 51% below 500, 37% between 500 and 599, 11% between 600 and 699, and 1% between 700 and 800. The ACT scores were 45% below 12, 32% between 12 and 17, 15% between 18 and 23, 3% between 24 and 29, and 5% above 30. 22% of the current freshmen were in the top fifth of their class; 51% were in the top two fifths. **Admissions Contact:** Scott Steinberg, Dean of Undergraduate Admission. Email: *admitusm@maine.edu* Web: *www.usm.maine.edu*

FINANCIAL AID: The FAFSA code is 009762. The priority date for freshman financial aid applications for fall entry is February 15. The deadline for filing freshman financial aid applications for fall entry is March 1.

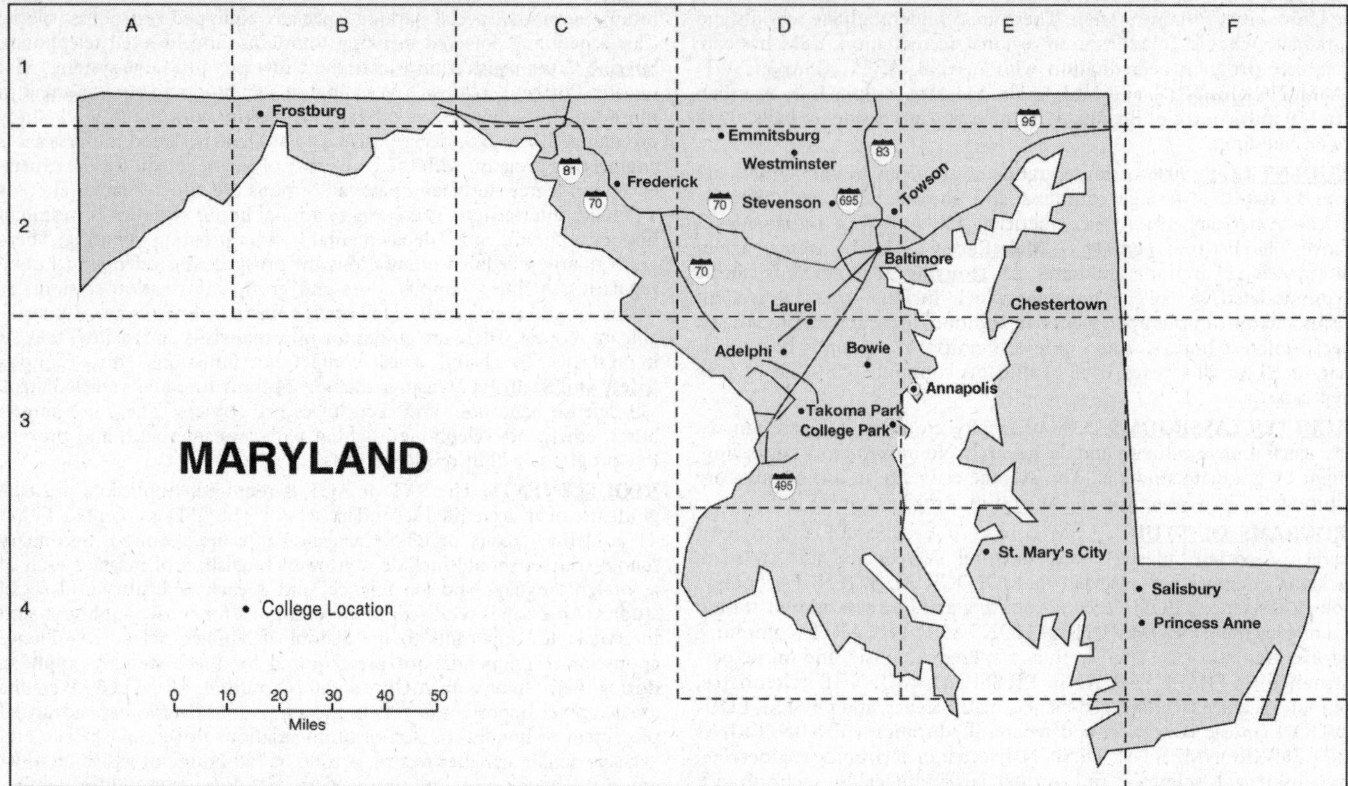

BOWIE STATE UNIVERSITY *(The complete profile is made available exclusively on our website, www.barronspac.com)*

CAPITOL TECHNOLOGY UNIVERSITY *(The complete profile is made available exclusively on our website, www.barronspac.com)*

COPPIN STATE UNIVERSITY — D-2

www.coppin.edu

Baltimore, MD 21216	**(410) 951-3600** **(800) 635-3674**
Fax: (410) 523-7351	**Email: admissions@coppin.edu**
Full-time: 554 men, 1935 women	**Faculty:** 143; IIA, -$
Part-time: 137 men, 616 women	**Ph.D.s:** 55%
Graduate: 174 men, 516 women	**Student/Faculty:** 17 to 1
Year: semesters, summer session	**Tuition:** $4468 ($10,616)
Room & Board: $9603	**Freshman Class:** 5593 applied, 1988 accepted, 632 enrolled
SAT or ACT: required	**CEEB CODE:** 5122
Application Deadline: July 15	**VERY COMPETITIVE**

Coppin State University, founded in 1900 and part of the University System of Maryland, offers undergraduate programs in liberal arts, teacher education, and nursing. There are 8 undergraduate schools and 1 graduate school. In addition to regional accreditation, CSU has baccalaureate program accreditation with ACBSP, CAEP, NLN, and NCSWE. The 65-acre campus is in an urban area in Baltimore, Maryland. Including any residence halls, there are 13 buildings.

STUDENT LIFE: 90% of undergraduates are from Maryland. Others are from 10 states, 5 foreign countries, and Canada. 90% are from public schools. 86% are African American; 4% Foreign; 3% Asian American; 2% Hispanic; 1% White; 1% American Indian/Alaska Native. **Female To Male Ratio:** 3.5:1. The average age of freshmen is 19; all undergraduates, 23. **Housing:** 600 students can be accommodated in college housing, which includes dorms. On-campus housing is available on a first-come and first-served basis. 79% of students commute. Alcohol is not permitted. Upperclassmen may keep cars.

FACULTY/CLASSROOMS: 55% of faculty are male; 45% are female. No introductory courses are taught by graduate students. The average class size in a regular course is 25.

PROGRAMS OF STUDY: CSU confers B.A., B.S. and B.S.N. degrees. Master's degrees are also awarded. Bachelor's degrees are awarded in BIOLOGICAL SCIENCE (biology/biological science), BUSINESS (accounting, business administration and management, management science, and sports management), COMMUNICATIONS AND THE ARTS (English and visual and performing arts), COMPUTER AND PHYSICAL SCIENCE (chemistry, computer science, and mathematics), EDUCATION (elementary education, health information management, and special education), HEALTH PROFESSIONS (health, nursing, and rehabilitation therapy), SOCIAL SCIENCE (applied psychology, criminal justice, history, interdisciplinary studies, international studies, liberal arts/general studies, political science/government, psychology, social science, social work, and urban studies). Business, psychology, and criminal justice, and nursing are the strongest academically and have the largest enrollments.

ACTIVITIES: 20% of men belong to 5 national fraternities; 27% of women belong to 4 national sororities. There are 35 groups on campus, including art, cheerleading, choir, chorus, computers, dance, drama, ethnic, film, honors, international, marching band, musical theater, newspaper, political, professional, religious, social, social service, and student government. Popular campus events include The Lyceum Series, Honors Program, and Black History Month. **Sports:** There are 7 intercollegiate sports for men and 7 for women, and 5 intramural sports for men and 5 for women. Facilities include a gym, an Olympic-size indoor swimming pool, handball and racquetball courts, a soccer field, dance studio, weight room, an outdoor track, softball field, and tennis courts. **Graduates:** From July 1, 2016 to June 30, 2017, 484 bachelor's degrees were awarded. The most popular majors were nursing (16%), criminal justice (12%), and applied psychology (10%).

SERVICES: Counseling and information services are available, as is tutoring in every subject. There is remedial math, reading, and writing. **Library/Resources:** The library contains 200,000 volumes, 233,000 microform items, and subscribes to 715 periodicals including electronic. Computerized library services include interlibrary loans, database searching, and Internet access. Special learning facilities include an art gallery. **Physically Challenged Students:** 95% of the campus is accessible. Facilities include wheelchair ramps, elevators, special parking, specially equipped restrooms, lowered drinking fountains, and lowered telephones. Individual attention for students requiring specialized materials, equipment, or instructional style accommodation. **Special:** Internships are available in Business, as are B.A.-B.S. degrees in all majors. Student-designed majors are possible with approval. There are 3 national honor societies, a chapter of Phi Beta Kappa, and a freshman honors program. **Visiting:** There are regularly scheduled orientations for prospective students, consisting of open houses. There are guides for informal visits and visitors may sit in on classes. To schedule a visit, contact the Office of Admissions. **Campus Safety and Security:** Measures include 24-hour foot and vehicle patrol, emergency notification system, and security escort services. There are shuttle buses, emergency telephones, lighted pathways/sidewalks, and controlled access to dorms/residences.

REQUIREMENTS: The SAT or ACT is required. Applicants must be graduates of an accredited secondary school with a minimum GPA of 2.0 or have a GED certificate. Students must have completed 4 courses in English, 2 courses each in history, math, science, and social studies, and 1 course in foreign language. Up to 15% of a freshman class may be admitted conditionally without these requirements, and those students who graduated high school more than 5 years ago will be reviewed individually. A GPA of 2.5 is required. AP and CLEP credits are accepted. Important factors in the admissions decision are advanced placement or honors courses, extracurricular activities record, and evidence of special talent. To graduate, all students must have a minimum 2.0 GPA and complete a minimum of 120 credit hours (varies by program of study), with 36 to 40 hours in the major. Students must complete about 50 hours of liberal arts courses in English, math, speech, history, health, physical education, natural and social sciences, and philosophy. All seniors must take a standardized exit exam relevant to their major. **Procedure:** Freshmen are admitted to all sessions. There is a rolling admissions plan. Applications should be filed by July 15 for fall entry; December 15 for spring entry. The fall 2017 application fee was $50. Applications are accepted on-line. **Transfer Students:** Transfer students must have a minimum 2.0 GPA and be in good academic standing at their former institutions. Applicants with fewer than 25 credits must meet freshman requirements. 30 of 120 credits required for the bachelor's degree must be completed at CSU. **International Students:** They must take the TOEFL with a minimum score of 500 on the paper-based TOEFL (PBT). They must also take the SAT or ACT.

ADMISSIONS: 36% of the 2017-2018 applicants were accepted. **Admissions Contact:** Michelle Gross, Director of Admissions. Email: *admissions@coppin.edu* Web: *www.coppin.edu*

FINANCIAL AID: CSU is a member of CSS. The college's own financial statement is required. The FAFSA code is 002068. The priority date for freshman financial aid applications for fall entry is March 1.

FROSTBURG STATE UNIVERSITY *(The complete profile is made available exclusively on our website, www.barronspac.com)*

GOUCHER COLLEGE — D-2
www.goucher.edu

Baltimore, MD 21204	**(410) 337-6100** **(800) 468-2437**
Fax: (410) 337-6354	**Email: admissions@goucher.edu**
Full-time: 452 men, 982 women	**Faculty:** 133; IIB, av$
Part-time: 5 men, 16 women	**Ph.D.s:** 92%
Graduate: 144 men, 554 women	**Student/Faculty:** 10 to 1
Year: semesters	**Tuition:** $43,440
Room & Board: $12,670	**Freshman Class:** 3443 applied, 2728 accepted, 440 enrolled
SAT EBR-W/M: 610/500 **ACT:** 25	**CEEB CODE:** 5257
Application Deadline: February 1	**VERY COMPETITIVE**

Goucher College, established in 1885, is an innovative liberal arts college and graduate school preparing students for 21st-century careers and where every undergraduate studies abroad. With its new undergraduate curriculum (Fall 2017), the college expects all students to pursue a common set of learning experiences, but also allows students to customize their education within its more than 30 majors and several interdisciplinary areas. Undergraduate students can also continue their education at Goucher's graduate school, The Welch Center for Graduate and Professional Studies, which offers 12 graduate programs and certificate programs, including: Master of Arts and Master of Fine Arts degrees, a post-baccalaureate premedical program, and professional development certificates. These programs are led by industry leaders who will help strengthen students' skills and add to their knowledge base. There is 1 undergraduate school and 1 graduate school. The 287-acre campus is in a suburban area 8 miles north of downtown Baltimore. Including any residence halls, there are 22 buildings.

STUDENT LIFE: 65% of undergraduates are from out of state, mostly the Middle Atlantic. Students are from 46 states, 53 foreign countries, and Canada. 65% are from public schools. 9% are Hispanic; 59% White; 5% two or more races; 4% Asian American; 4% race unknown; 3% Foreign; 14% African American. **Female To Male Ratio:** 2.6:1. The average age of freshmen is 18; all undergraduates, 20. 21% do not continue beyond their first year; 79% remain to graduate. **Housing:** 1229 students can be accommodated in college housing, which includes dorms and on-campus apartments. In addition, there are language/international houses, special-interest houses, healthy living house, peace house, art and music house, and gaming house. On-campus housing is guaranteed for all 4 years and is available on a lottery system for upperclassmen. 93% of students live on campus. All students may keep cars.

FACULTY/CLASSROOMS: 40% of faculty are male; 60% are female. All teach undergraduates. No introductory courses are taught by graduate students. The average class size in an introductory lecture is 17 and in a laboratory is 14.

PROGRAMS OF STUDY: Goucher confers B.A. degrees. Master's degrees are also awarded. Bachelor's degrees are awarded in AGRICULTURE (environmental studies), BIOLOGICAL SCIENCE (biochemistry and biology/biological science), BUSINESS (business administration and management), COMMUNICATIONS AND THE ARTS (art history, art, communications, dance, English, French, music, Russian, Spanish, and theatre arts), COMPUTER AND PHYSICAL SCIENCE (chemistry, computer science, mathematics, and physics), EDUCATION (education and special education), SOCIAL SCIENCE (American studies, anthropology, economics, history, interdisciplinary studies, international relations, peace studies, philosophy, political science/government, psychology, religion, sociology, and women's studies). Dance, political science, biology, chemistry, and psychology are the strongest academically. Psychology, business management, and English have the largest enrollments.

ACTIVITIES: There are no fraternities or sororities. There are 60 groups on campus, including art, campus agricultural co-op, choir, chorale, chorus, communications, computers, dance, debate, drama, environmental, ethnic, film, honors, international, jazz band, LGBT, literary magazine, musical theater, newspaper, opera, orchestra, political, professional, radio and TV, religious, social, social service, student government, symphony, and yearbook. Popular campus events include Get into Goucher Day, Gala, Opening Celebration, Ashanti talent show, Umoja fashion show, International Night, Rocky Horror Picture Show, Winter Carnival, Humans vs. Zombies, Breakfast After Dark, Relaxation Stations, intercollegiate home games. **Sports:** There are 9 intercollegiate sports for men and 11 for women, and 4 intramural sports for men and 3 for women. Facilities include 2 gyms, indoor swimming pool, strength and conditioning center, training room, cardio fitness center, racquetball court, squash, and 8 outdoor tennis courts, indoor and outdoor equestrian facilities, outdoor track, outdoor volleyball court, and disc golf, a turf field 3 other fields. **Graduates:** From July 1, 2016 to June 30, 2017, 327 bachelor's degrees were awarded. The most popular majors were psychology (12%), English (8%), and communications (7%). In an average class, 52% graduate in 4 years or less, 68% graduate in 5 years or less, and 72% graduate in 6 years or less.

SERVICES: Many academic support options are available through the college's Academic Center for Excellence (ACE). **Library/Resources:** The library contains 568,594 volumes, 22,268 microform items, and 6,188 audio/video tapes/CDs/DVDs, and subscribes to 98,000 periodicals including electronic. Computerized library services include interlibrary loans, database searching, Internet access, and Wi-Fi capability. Special learning facilities include an art gallery, radio station, Sanford J. Ungar Athenaeum (library) features a forum for public events and classrooms, and an art gallery. The Academic Center for Excellence offers study-skills workshops, peer-led supplemental instruction, and yoga, meditation, and Reiki sessions. Goucher also has a radio station, TV studio, three multi-purpose performance spaces, a robotics lab, a rooftop observatory, advanced teaching labs for physics, neuroscience, and computer science, research labs for math, physics, and psychology, a technology/learning center, international technology and media center, and centers for writing, math, and politics. **Physically Challenged Students:** 70% of the campus is accessible. Facilities include wheelchair ramps, elevators, special parking, specially equipped restrooms, special class scheduling, lowered drinking fountains, and special housing. **Special:** Goucher offers internships in Baltimore and Washington, D.C., study abroad in 40 countries, and other off-campus experiences. Goucher participates in the Baltimore Student Exchange Program (BSEP), which allows qualified students to take undergraduate courses offered at other colleges during fall and spring semesters. Students may cross-register with Johns Hopkins University, Towson University, Peabody Institute, Stevenson University, Coppin State University, University of Baltimore, University of Maryland Baltimore County, Loyola University Maryland, the Community College of Baltimore County, Maryland Institute College of Art, Notre Dame of MD University, and Morgan State University. 3-2 engineering degrees with Johns Hopkins University and Columbia University are offered. Dual majors and student-designed, interdisciplinary majors are an option. There is 1 national honor society and a chapter of Phi Beta Kappa. **Visiting:** There are regularly scheduled orientations for prospective students, a full day experience introducing students to Goucher, academic life, and the campus community. There are guides for informal visits, visitors may sit in on classes, and stay overnight. To schedule a visit, contact Office of Admissions. **Campus Safety and Security:** Measures include 24-hour foot and vehicle patrol, emergency notification system, self-defense education, and security escort services. There are shuttle buses, emergency telephones, lighted pathways/sidewalks, controlled access to dorms/residences, an officer-manned gatehouse 24/7 during academic sessions, green dot program, 12 on-campus AEDs, all officers trained first responders, and overnight officer coverage of 24-hour library.

REQUIREMENTS: Applicants should be graduates of an accredited high school or have earned the GED. A personal essay is required, and an interview is recommended. Prospective performing or visual arts majors are urged to seek an audition or submit a portfolio through our Fine and Performing Arts Scholarship program. As an alternative to the traditional Common Application, Goucher has created the Goucher Video Application. AP credits are accepted. Important factors in the admissions decision are extracurricular activities record, recommendations by school officials, and advanced placement or honors courses. For students starting Goucher fall 2017 and forward, the General Education Requirements is referred to as Goucher Commons Requirements (GCRs). The listing of those overall requirements is as follows: Completion of a Major, Completion of 120+ overall credits (at least 60 of which must be in Goucher "credits"), Cumulative GPA of 2.0 or higher, First Year Experience course, Physical Education Activity. (Unless student is over 25 years of age), Completion of all GCRs including: First Year Seminar course (if coming to Goucher as first-year student. Not required for transfer students), Center Pair Exploration courses. 1-3 courses depending on transfer credit, College Writing Proficiency, Data Analytics (2 course requirement), Foreign Language, Race, Power, and Perspective, Environmental Sustainability, Study Abroad Experience, and Reflection Portfolio and Capstone Experience/Signature Project. **Procedure:** Freshmen are admitted fall and spring. Entrance exams should be taken in spring of the junior year or fall of the senior year. There are early decision, early admissions, and deferred admissions plans. Early decision applications should be filed by November 15; regular applications, by February 1 for fall entry; and December 1 for spring entry. The fall 2017 application fee was $55. Notification of early decision is sent December 15; regular decision, April 1. 25 early decision candidates were accepted for the 2017-2018 class. 54 applicants were on the 2017 waiting list; 11 were admitted. Applications are accepted on-line. **Transfer Students:** 31 transfer students enrolled in 2016-2017. Common Application with personal essay, recommendation from college professor or academic teacher and final high school transcript (if a student has attempted less than 30 credits) 60 of 120 credits required for the bachelor's degree must be completed at Goucher. **International Students:** There are 55 international students enrolled. They must take the TOEFL with a minimum score of 550 on the paper-based TOEFL (PBT) or 80 on the Internet-based version (iBT).

ADMISSIONS: 79% of the 2017-2018 applicants were accepted. The SAT scores for the 2017-2018 freshman class were: Math-- 22% below 500, 51% between 500 and 599, 23% between 600 and 699, and 4% between 700 and 800. Evidence-Based Reading/Writing-- 13% below 500, 32% between 500 and 599, 45% between 600 and 699, and 10% between 700 and 800. The ACT scores were 3% between 12 and 17, 26% between 18 and 23, 51% between 24 and 29, and 20% above 30. 42% of the current freshmen were in the top fifth of their class; 76% were in the top two fifths. 2 freshmen graduated first in their class. **Admissions Contact:** Carlton E. Surbeck, Director of Admissions. Email: *admissions@goucher.edu* Web: *www.goucher.edu*

FINANCIAL AID: In 2017-2018, 100% of all full-time freshmen received some form of financial aid. 73% of all full-time freshmen received need-based aid. The average freshman award was $37,562. Need-based scholarships or need-based grants averaged $33,996 ($47,500 maximum); need-based self-help aid (loans and jobs) averaged $4,102 ($5,500 maximum); and other non-need-based awards and non-need-based scholarships averaged $19,581 ($24,000 maximum). 33% of undergraduate students work part-time. The average financial indebtedness of the 2017 graduate was $25,287. Goucher is a member of CSS. The CSS/Profile and the college's own financial statement are required. The FAFSA code is 002073. The priority date for freshman financial aid applications for fall entry is February 1.

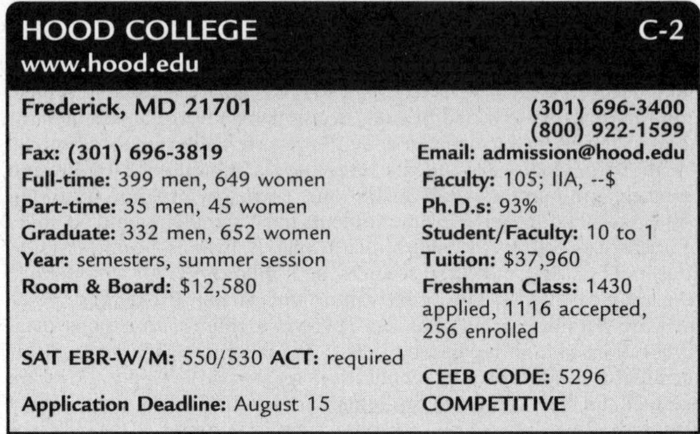

HOOD COLLEGE — C-2
www.hood.edu

Frederick, MD 21701 — (301) 696-3400, (800) 922-1599

Fax: (301) 696-3819 — **Email:** admission@hood.edu
Full-time: 399 men, 649 women — **Faculty:** 105; IIA, --$
Part-time: 35 men, 45 women — **Ph.D.s:** 93%
Graduate: 332 men, 652 women — **Student/Faculty:** 10 to 1
Year: semesters, summer session — **Tuition:** $37,960
Room & Board: $12,580 — **Freshman Class:** 1430 applied, 1116 accepted, 256 enrolled
SAT EBR-W/M: 550/530 **ACT:** required — **CEEB CODE:** 5296
Application Deadline: August 15 — **COMPETITIVE**

Hood College, founded in 1893, is an independent, comprehensive college that offers an integration of the liberal arts and professional preparation, as well as undergraduate majors in the natural sciences. There is 1 undergraduate school and 1 graduate school. In addition to regional accreditation, HC has baccalaureate program accreditation with ABET, ACBSP, CSWE, CAEP, and CCNE. The 50-acre campus is in a suburban area 50 miles northwest of Washington, D.C. and 45 miles west of Baltimore. Including any residence halls, there are 38 buildings.

STUDENT LIFE: 74% of undergraduates are from Maryland. Others are from 29 states, and 17 foreign countries. 79% are from public schools. 6% are two or more races; 58% White; 4% race unknown; 3% Asian American; 2% Foreign; 17% African American; 11% Hispanic. 36% are Islam, Buddhism, and Greek Orthodox; 29% Protestant; 18% Catholic. **Female To Male Ratio:** 1.8:1. The average age of freshmen is 18; all undergraduates, 21. 22% do not continue beyond their first year; 60% remain to graduate. **Housing:** 823 students can be accommodated in college housing, which includes dorms. In addition, there are honors houses, language/international houses, freshman dorms, special-interest floors in the residence halls include a community service floor. On-campus housing is guaranteed for all 4 years, is available on a first-come, first-served basis, and is available on a lottery system for upperclassmen. 52% of students live on campus. All students may keep cars.

FACULTY/CLASSROOMS: 39% of faculty are male; 61% are female. All teach undergraduates, and all do research. No introductory courses are taught by graduate students. The average class size in an introductory lecture is 15; in a laboratory is 12; and in a regular course is 12.

PROGRAMS OF STUDY: HC confers B.A., B.S., and B.S.N degrees. Master's and doctoral degrees are also awarded. Bachelor's degrees are awarded in BIOLOGICAL SCIENCE (biochemistry and biology/biological science), BUSINESS (accounting, business administration and management, business administration marketing, and marketing), COMMUNICATIONS AND THE ARTS (art, communications, English, French, German, music, and Spanish), COMPUTER AND PHYSICAL SCIENCE (chemistry, computer science, and mathematics), EDUCATION (early childhood education, elementary education, English education, foreign languages education, global studies, mathematics education, science education, secondary education, and special education), ENGINEERING AND ENVIRONMENTAL DESIGN (computational sciences and environmental science), HEALTH PROFESSIONS (nursing), SOCIAL SCIENCE (archeology, economics, history, international studies, Latin American studies, law, Middle Eastern studies, philosophy, political science/government, psychology, religion, social work, and sociology). Computer science, social work, and psychology are the strongest academically. Business administration, education, and biology have the largest enrollments.

ACTIVITIES: There are no fraternities or sororities. There are 50 groups on campus, including art, band, cheerleading, choir, chorale, chorus, communications, computers, dance, drama, environmental, ethnic, film, honors, international, jazz band, LGBT, literary magazine, musical theater, newspaper, orchestra, political, professional, radio and TV, religious, social, social service, and student government. Popular campus events include Ring Formal, Liberation Weekend, Fall Frenzy, May Madness, and Crab Fest. **Sports:** There are 9 intercollegiate sports for men and 11 for women, and 5 intramural sports for men and 4 for women. Facilities include an arena for basketball and volleyball, a fitness center equipped with weight training and cardio equipment, athletic training room, indoor swimming pool, softball field, tennis complex with regulation courts, and multi use turf fields for field hockey, soccer, and lacrosse. **Graduates:** From July 1, 2016 to June 30, 2017, 282 bachelor's degrees were awarded. The most popular majors were business administration (17%), communications (11%), and education (9%). In an average class, 2% graduate in 3 years or less, 50% graduate in 4 years or less, 63% graduate in 5 years or less, and 65% graduate in 6 years or less. Of the 2016 graduating class, 36% were enrolled in graduate school within 6 months of graduation, and 80% were employed.

SERVICES: Counseling and information services are available, as is tutoring in some subjects. There are readers for the blind and interpreters for the hearing impaired, and remedial math and writing. There are also services for students with learning disabilities, a language lab, and courses in time management and study skills. **Library/Resources:** The library contains 172,311 volumes, and 7,398 audio/video tapes/CDs/DVDs. Computerized library services include interlibrary loans, database searching, Internet access, and Wi-Fi capability. Special learning facilities include an art gallery, radio station, TV station, aquatic center, a child development lab, an observatory, information technology center, mock trial court room, and financial trading room. **Physically Challenged Students:** 55% of the campus is accessible. Facilities include wheelchair ramps, elevators, special parking, specially equipped restrooms, special class scheduling, and special housing. **Special:** The college offers a Washington semester with American University, dual majors, student-designed majors, credit for life experience, nondegree study, pass/fail options, and cross-registration with area colleges and the Duke University Marine Sciences Education Consortium. Internships of up to 15 credits are available in all majors at more than 100 sites throughout the United States and abroad. Students may study abroad in the Dominican Republic, Japan, Spain, France, and other countries. There is a 4-year honors program featuring 1 interdisciplinary course per semester and special co-curricular activities. There are 16 national honor societies, a freshman honors program, and 10 departmental honors programs. **Visiting:** There are regularly scheduled orientations for prospective students, including tours and meetings with faculty, students and administrators, and admissions interviews. There are guides for informal visits, visitors may sit in on classes, and stay overnight. To schedule a visit, contact Elizabeth Gomer at admission@hood.edu. **Campus Safety and Security:** Measures include 24-hour foot and vehicle patrol, emergency notification system, self-defense education, and security escort services. There are emergency telephones, lighted pathways/sidewalks, and controlled access to dorms/residences.

REQUIREMENTS: The SAT or ACT is recommended. Applicants should be graduates of an accredited secondary school. The GED is accepted. Hood recommends the completion of at least 16 academic credits in high school, including courses in English, social studies, natural sciences, foreign languages, and math. A GPA of 2.5 is required. AP and CLEP credits are accepted. Important factors in the admissions decision are advanced placement or honors courses, leadership record, and extracurricular activities record. To graduate, students must complete a total of 124 credit hours, with a minimum GPA of 2.0, and a 2.0 GPA in the major. 24 to 52 credits are required in a student's major. All students must complete 41 to 45 credits in the core curriculum, which includes First-Year Seminar, English, math, language courses, and courses in methods of inquiry. Phys ed courses are also required. Enrollment in the final 30 credits must be on the Hood Campus as a degree candidate. **Procedure:** Freshmen are admitted fall and spring. Entrance exams should be taken in spring of the junior year or fall of the senior year. There is a rolling admissions plan. Application deadlines are open. Notifications are sent October 15. Applications are accepted on-line. **Transfer Students:** 93 transfer students enrolled in 2016-2017. Applicants must have at least 13 college credits and a minimum GPA of 2.0. A maximum of 62 credits may be awarded for freshman/sophomore level work completed elsewhere. Although there is no limit for junior/senior level coursework, students will be awarded no more than a total of 94 credits for all college-level work completed. 30 of 124 credits required for the bachelor's degree must be completed at HC. **International Students:** There are 22 international students enrolled. They must take the TOEFL with a minimum score of 550 on the paper-based TOEFL (PBT) or 79 on the Internet-based version (iBT). Students must take the IELTS. They must also take the SAT or ACT. The SAT scores may be substituted for the TOEFL.

ADMISSIONS: 78% of the 2017-2018 applicants were accepted. The SAT scores for the 2017-2018 freshman class were: Math-- 32% below 500, 42% between 500 and 599, 25% between 600 and 699, and 1% between 700 and 800. Evidence-Based Reading/Writing-- 23% below 500, 42% between 500 and 599, 33% between 600 and 699, and 2% between 700 and 800. 29% of the current freshmen were in the top fifth of their class; 57% were in the top two fifths. 1 freshman graduated first in the class. **Admissions Contact:** William J. Brown, Vice President for Enrollment Management. Email: *admission@hood.edu* Web: *www.hood.edu*

FINANCIAL AID: In 2017-2018, 97% of all full-time freshmen received some form of financial aid. 85% of all full-time freshmen received need-based aid. The average freshman award was $34,663. Need-based scholarships or need-based grants averaged $30,793; need-based self-help aid (loans and jobs) averaged $4,593; and other non-need-based awards and non-need-based scholarships averaged $18,253. 40% of undergraduate students work part-time. The average financial indebtedness of the 2017 graduate was $35,823. HC is a member of CSS. The FAFSA code is 002076. The priority date for freshman financial aid applications for fall entry is February 15.

JOHNS HOPKINS UNIVERSITY D-2

www.apply.jhu.edu

Baltimore, MD 21218 **(410) 516-8171**

Email: gotojhu@jhu.edu

Full-time: 2641 men, 2712 women	**Faculty:** 708; I, +$
Part-time: 8 men, 5 women	**Ph.D.s:** 93%
Graduate: 1460 men, 703 women	**Student/Faculty:** 7 to 1
Year: 4-1-4, summer session	**Tuition:** $52,670
Room & Board: $15,410	**Freshman Class:** 26578 applied, 3116 accepted, 1349 enrolled
SAT CR/M/W: 730/750/730 **ACT:** 34	**CEEB CODE:** 5532
Application Deadline: January 3	**MOST COMPETITIVE**

Johns Hopkins University, founded in 1876, is a private multicampus institution offering undergraduate degrees at the Homewood campus through the Krieger School of Arts and Sciences, the Whiting School of Engineering, and the Peabody Institute of music. There are 3 undergraduate schools and 9 graduate schools. In addition to regional accreditation, JHU has baccalaureate program accreditation with ABET. The 140-acre campus is in a suburban area in a residential setting in northern Baltimore. Including any residence halls, there are 46 buildings.

STUDENT LIFE: 88% of undergraduates are from out of state, mostly the Middle Atlantic. Students are from 50 states, 60 foreign countries, and Canada. 60% are from public schools. 6% are African American; 5% two or more races; 4% race unknown; 37% White; 25% Asian American; 14% Hispanic; 10% Foreign. **Male To Female Ratio:** 1.2:1. The average age of freshmen is 18; all undergraduates, 20. 3% do not continue beyond their first year; 94% remain to graduate. **Housing:** 2800 students can be accommodated in college housing, which includes dorms, on-campus apartments, and off-campus apartments. In addition, there are special-interest houses, non-university-sponsored fraternity and sorority houses. On-campus housing is available on a lottery system for upperclassmen. 48% of students commute. Upperclassmen may keep cars.

FACULTY/CLASSROOMS: 68% of faculty are male; 32% are female. No introductory courses are taught by graduate students.

PROGRAMS OF STUDY: JHU confers B.A. and B.S. degrees. Master's and doctoral degrees are also awarded. Bachelor's degrees are awarded in BIOLOGICAL SCIENCE (biology/biological science, biophysics, molecular biology, and neurosciences), COMMUNICATIONS AND THE ARTS (Africana studies, art history and appreciation, classics, creative writing, English, French, German, Germanic languages and literature, Italian, media arts, music composition, romance languages and literature, Spanish, and writing & rhetoric), COMPUTER AND PHYSICAL SCIENCE (applied mathematics, chemistry, computer science, earth science, mathematics, natural sciences, and physics), EDUCATION (music education), ENGINEERING AND ENVIRONMENTAL DESIGN (biomedical engineering, chemical engineering, civil engineering, computer engineering, electrical/electronics engineering, engineering, engineering mechanics, environmental engineering, materials engineering, materials science, mechanical engineering, and systems engineering), HEALTH PROFESSIONS (public health), SOCIAL SCIENCE (anthropology, archeology, behavioral science, cognitive science, East Asian studies, economics, history, history of science, humanities, interdisciplinary studies, international studies, Latin American studies, Near Eastern studies, philosophy, political science/government, psychology, social science, and sociology). Engineering, public health, sciences, and international studies are the strongest academically. Biomedical engineering, public health studies, and neuroscience have the largest enrollments.

ACTIVITIES: 17% of men belong to 13 national fraternities; 26% of women belong to 21 national sororities. There are 300 groups on campus, including art, band, cheerleading, chess, choir, chorale, chorus, clubs for volunteer organizations, computers, dance, debate, drama, environmental, ethnic, film, forensics, honors, international, jazz band, LGBT, literary magazine, marching band, musical theater, newspaper, opera, orchestra, pep band, photography, political, professional, radio and TV, religious, social, social service, student government, and symphony. Popular campus events include Fall Fest, Hoptoberfest, Spring Fair, Homecoming, Milton S. Eisenhower Symposium, and Foreign Affairs Symposium. **Sports:** There are 12 intercollegiate sports for men and 10 for women, and 20 intramural sports for men and 20 for women. Facilities include a recreation center with a swimming pool and diving pool, wrestling and fencing rooms, a varsity weight room, a fitness center, a climbing wall, an indoor jogging track, multipurpose rooms, and courts for basketball, badminton, squash, volleyball and handball, a stadium, outdoor playing fields, and tennis courts. **Graduates:** From July 1, 2016 to June 30, 2017, 1049 bachelor's degrees were awarded. The most popular majors were public health studies (9%), biomedical engineering (8%), and neuroscience (7%). In an average class, 88% graduate in 4 years or less, 93% graduate in 5 years or less, and 94% graduate in 6 years or less. Of the 2016 graduating class, 35% were enrolled in graduate school within 6 months of graduation, and 51% were employed.

SERVICES: Counseling and information services are available, as is tutoring in most subjects. There is a reader service for the blind. **Library/Resources:** The library contains 2.6 million volumes, 4.1 million microform items, and 9,707 audio/video tapes/CDs/DVDs, and subscribes to 30,120 periodicals including electronic. Computerized library services include interlibrary loans, database searching, Internet access, and Wi-Fi capability. Special learning facilities include an art gallery, radio station, space telescope science institute, Digital Media Center, Archaeological Museum, Undergraduate Teaching Labs. **Physically Challenged Students:** Facilities include wheelchair ramps, elevators, special parking, specially equipped restrooms, special class scheduling, lowered drinking fountains, and lowered telephones. JHU works with all individuals to ensure access to all programs. Also, existing housing is accommodated as needed. **Special:** Internships, dual majors in music and arts and sciences/engineering, cross-registration with Baltimore-area colleges and Johns Hopkins divisions, a cooperative double degree with Peabody Conservatory of Music, a cooperative film center with the Maryland Institute College of Arts (MICA), a student-designed semester at the Johns Hopkins School of International Studies in Washington, D.C., and various multidisciplinary programs are offered. Students may enroll at Johns Hopkins in Bologna, Italy, or Nanjing, China, or arrange programs in Europe, South America, the Far East, or Australia. Combined BA/BS-MA/MS programs are available in many departments. Direct Matriculation Program in International Studies in partnership with the Johns Hopkins School of International Studies in Washington, D.C. and Direct Matriculation Program in Global Health Studies in partnership with the Bloomberg School of Public Health. There are 4 national honor societies, Phi Beta Kappa, and 25 departmental honors programs. **Visiting:** There are regularly scheduled orientations for prospective students, including scheduled open house programs, campus tours led by current students, and group information sessions offered weekday mornings and afternoons. There are guides for informal visits, visitors may sit in on classes, and stay overnight. To schedule a visit, contact Office of Undergraduate Admissions at gotojhu@jhu.edu. **Campus Safety and Security:** Measures include 24-hour foot and vehicle patrol, emergency notification system, self-defense education, and security escort services. There are shuttle buses, emergency telephones, lighted pathways/sidewalks, and controlled access to dorms/residences.

REQUIREMENTS: The SAT Reasoning Test or the ACT is required for all first-year applicants. The writing section of the ACT is optional. The essay section of the redesigned SAT is optional. Applicants may also choose to submit SAT Subject Tests in one or more areas of interest as a way to demonstrate an academic strength. Johns Hopkins will consider the two highest Subject Test scores when reviewing applications, but your application will not be negatively affected if you choose not to submit Subject Test scores. The university encourages applicants interested in an engineering major to submit scores from the Mathematics Level 2 SAT Subject Test and at least one science SAT Subject Test as a way to demonstrate their strengths in relevant subject areas. In addition, applicants should be graduates of an accredited secondary school or have the GED. The university recommends that secondary preparation include 4 years each of English and math, 2 (prefer 3) of social science or history and lab science, and 3 to 4 of a foreign language, and 2 for engineering majors. Two personal essays are required, and interviews are available but not required. AP credits are accepted. Important factors in the admissions decision are advanced placement or honors courses, extracurricular activities record, and personality/intangible qualities. The B.A. requires a total of 120 hours; the B.S. in engineering requires 120 to 128 hours, depending on the major. A GPA of at least 2.0 is required for graduation. All students must take at least 4 courses (2 for engineers) with a writing-intensive component to graduate. **Procedure:** Freshmen are admitted in the fall. There are early decision and deferred admissions plans. Early decision applications should be filed by November 1; regular applications, by January 3 for fall entry. The fall 2017 application fee was $70. Notification of early decision is sent December 15; regular decision, March 15. 589 early decision candidates were accepted for the 2017-2018 class. Applications are accepted on-line. **Transfer Students:** 165 transfer students enrolled in 2016-2017. Transfer students from two- and four-year colleges and universities may apply for admission into the Johns Hopkins sophomore and junior classes in the fall semester only. Applicants must have completed more than 12 semester based credits (either matriculated or not) with a minimum cumulative grade point average of 3.0. Applications must include a written essay and at least 1 letter of recommendation. High school records are also required. 60 of 120 credits required for the bachelor's degree must be completed at JHC. **International Students:** There are 511 international students enrolled. They must also take the SAT or ACT.

ADMISSIONS: 12% of the 2017-2018 applicants were accepted. The SAT scores for the 2017-2018 freshman class were: Critical Reading-- 1% between 500 and 599, 16% between 600 and 699, and 84% between 700 and 800. Math-- 1% between 500 and 599, 8% between 600 and 699, and 92% between 700 and 800. Writing-- 1% below 500, 1% between 500 and 599, 15% between 600 and 699, and 83% between 700 and 800. The ACT scores were 2% between 24 and 29, and 98% above 30. 98% of the current freshmen were in the top fifth of their class; 99% were in the top two fifths. 67 freshmen graduated first in their class. **Admissions Contact:** Chelsea Ryder, Office of Undergraduate Admissions. Email: *gotojhu@jhu.edu* Web: *www.jhu.edu*

FINANCIAL AID: The average freshman award was $38,946. The average financial indebtedness of the 2017 graduate was $24,702. JHU is a member of CSS. The CSS/Profile is required. The FAFSA code is 002077. The deadline for filing freshman financial aid applications for fall entry is February 1.

LOYOLA UNIVERSITY MARYLAND — D-2

www.loyola.edu

Baltimore, MD 21210

(410) 617-5012
(800) 221-9107
Email: admission@loyola.edu

Full-time: 1638 men, 2248 women	**Faculty:** 368; IIA, +$
Part-time: 19 men, 19 women	**Ph.D.s:** 86%
Graduate: 546 men, 1313 women	**Student/Faculty:** 11 to 1
Year: semesters, summer session	**Tuition:** $47,560
Room & Board: $14,150	**Freshman Class:** 11600 applied, 8733 accepted, 1021 enrolled
SAT CR/M/W: 595/595/595 **ACT:** 27	**CEEB CODE:** 5379
Application Deadline: January 15	**VERY COMPETITIVE**

Loyola University Maryland, is a Catholic, Jesuit comprehensive university. Loyola University Maryland is committed to the ideals of liberal education and the development of the whole person, a university dedicated to inspiring its students to learn, lead and serve in a diverse and changing world. This mission is embraced through an undergraduate curriculum, rooted in the Jesuit tradition of the liberal arts, which prepares students for success in wide-ranging professional pursuits and graduate studies. Loyola's undergraduate experience is complemented by its graduate programs, the region's leaders in professional education. There are 3 undergraduate schools and 3 graduate schools. In addition to regional accreditation, LUM has baccalaureate program accreditation with AACSB, ABET, CSAB, NASDTEC, CAEP, and MSHEC. The 89-acre campus is in an urban area 3 miles from downtown Baltimore. Including any residence halls, there are 51 buildings.

STUDENT LIFE: 81% of undergraduates are from out of state, mostly the Middle Atlantic. 77% are White; 5% African American; 4% Asian American; 3% two or more races; 10% Hispanic. **Female To Male Ratio:** 1.6:1. **Housing:** 3291 students can be accommodated in college housing, which includes dorms and on-campus apartments. In addition, there are honors houses, special-interest houses, theme and wellness housing. On-campus housing is guaranteed for the freshman year only, is available on a first-come, first-served basis, and is available on a lottery system for upperclassmen. 97% of students live on campus. Upperclassmen may keep cars.

FACULTY/CLASSROOMS: 50% of faculty are male; 50% are female. All teach undergraduates. No introductory courses are taught by graduate students.

PROGRAMS OF STUDY: LUM confers B.A., B.S., B.B.A., and B.S.E. degrees. Master's and doctoral degrees are also awarded. Bachelor's degrees are awarded in BIOLOGICAL SCIENCE (biology/biological science), BUSINESS (accounting and business administration and management), COMMUNICATIONS AND THE ARTS (communications, creative writing, English, fine arts, French, German, Latin, and Spanish), COMPUTER AND PHYSICAL SCIENCE (chemistry, computer science, mathematics, and physics), EDUCATION (elementary education), ENGINEERING AND ENVIRONMENTAL DESIGN (engineering), HEALTH PROFESSIONS (speech pathology/audiology), SOCIAL SCIENCE (classical/ancient civilization, economics, history, philosophy, political science/government, psychology, sociology, and theological studies). General business, communication and social sciences have the largest enrollments.

ACTIVITIES: There are no fraternities or sororities. There are 201 groups on campus, including art, band, cheerleading, chess, choir, chorale, chorus, computers, dance, drama, ethnic, film, honors, international, jazz band, LGBT, literary magazine, musical theater, newspaper, orchestra, pep band, photography, political, professional, radio and TV, religious, social, social service, student government, symphony, and yearbook. Popular campus events include Modern Masters Series, Humanities Symposium, Loyolapalooza, International Festival, Evergreen Players, ChordBusters, Luna Fest, Poisened Cup Players, and Bull and Oyster Roast. **Sports:** There are 8 intercollegiate sports for men and 9 for women, and 8 intramural sports for men and 8 for women. Facilities include lacrosse and soccer teams, practice field, training facilities, natatorium, aquatic center, a climbing wall, a fitness center, an elevated indoor track, racquetball and squash courts, areobic/martial arts studios, a three-court gymnasium and a multi-activity court with rounded corners and plexi-glass walls for indoor soccer and floor hockey. **Graduates:** From July 1, 2016 to June 30, 2017, 665 bachelor's degrees were awarded. The most popular majors were business/marketing (39%), communications/journalism, and social studies (11%), and social science (10%).

SERVICES: Counseling and information services are available, as is tutoring in most subjects. There is a reader service for the blind, and remedial math. **Library/Resources:** The library contains 1.1 million volumes, 691 microform items, and 19,086 audio/video tapes/CDs/DVDs, and subscribes to 56,888 periodicals including electronic. Computerized library services include interlibrary loans, database searching, and Internet access. Special learning facilities include an art gallery, radio station, and TV station. **Physically Challenged Students:** 99% of the campus is accessible. Facilities include wheelchair ramps, elevators, special parking, specially equipped restrooms, special class scheduling, lowered drinking fountains, and lowered telephones. **Special:** Loyola offers cross-registration with Johns Hopkins, Towson, and Morgan State Universities, Goucher College, the College of Notre Dame, Maryland Art Institute, and Peabody Conservatory. Credit-bearing internships are available in most majors and study abroad is possible in 27 countries. Work-study programs and dual majors are also offered. There is a chapter of Phi Beta Kappa and a freshman honors program. **Visiting:** There are regularly scheduled orientations for prospective students, the visit includes a group information session, a campus tour, and an interview (optional). There are guides for informal visits and visitors may sit in on classes. To schedule a visit, contact the Admission Office. **Campus Safety and Security:** Measures include 24-hour foot and vehicle patrol, emergency notification system, self-defense education, and security escort services. There are shuttle buses, emergency telephones, lighted pathways/sidewalks, and controlled access to dorms/residences.

REQUIREMENTS: LUM is Test Optional. SAT and ACT are considered if submitted. All applicants should have graduated from an accredited secondary school or have earned the GED. Secondary preparation should include 4 years of English, 3-4 years each of math, foreign language, natural science (with lab), and classical or modern foreign language, and 2-3 each of social studies, and history. Recommended 1 each of computer science and visual/performing arts AP and CLEP credits are accepted. Important factors in the admissions decision are advanced placement or honors courses, personality/intangible qualities, evidence of special talent, and extracurricular activities record. All students must complete 120 hours, including 36 in the major, with at least a 2.0 GPA. The required core curriculum includes 2 courses each in history, language (at the second-year level), literature, philosophy, social sciences, and theology, 1 course each in composition, ethics, fine arts, math, humanities, and natural sciences, and 1 additional course in math, natural science, or computer science. **Procedure:** Freshmen are admitted fall, spring, and summer. Entrance exams should be taken by December of the senior year. There are early admissions, deferred admissions, and rolling admissions plans. Early decision applications should be filed by November 1; regular applications, by January 15 for fall entry. The fall 2017 application fee was $50. Notification of early decision is sent December 15; regular decision, March 15. 476 applicants were on the 2017 waiting list; 161 were admitted. Applications are accepted on-line. **Transfer Students:** 47 transfer students enrolled in 2016-2017. Applying for transfer admissions, students must submit high school transcript, college transcript (s), an essay or personal review, and statement from prior institution (s). 60 of 120 credits required for the bachelor's degree must be completed at LUM. **International Students:** There are 31 international students enrolled. They must take the TOEFL with a minimum score of 550 on the paper-based TOEFL (PBT) or 79 on the Internet-based version (iBT).

ADMISSIONS: 75% of the 2017-2018 applicants were accepted. The SAT scores for the 2017-2018 freshman class were: Critical Reading-- 3% below 500, 31% between 500 and 599, 58% between 600 and 699, and 8% between 700 and 800. Math-- 4% below 500, 44% between 500 and 599, 45% between 600 and 699, and 7% between 700 and 800. The ACT scores were 9% between 18 and 23, 62% between 24 and 29, and 29% above 30. **Admissions Contact:** Office of Admission Email: *admission@loyola.edu* Web: *www.loyola.edu*

FINANCIAL AID: The average freshman award was $32,616. Need-based scholarships or need-based grants averaged $21,593; need-based self-help aid (loans and jobs) averaged $5,873; non-need-based athletic scholarships averaged $34,649; other non-need-based awards and non-need-based scholarships averaged $6,010; and $17,165 from other forms of aid. LUM is a member of CSS. The CSS/Profile, and if applicable, a noncustodial parent's profile is required. The FAFSA code is 002078. The priority date for freshman financial aid applications for fall entry is January 15.

MARYLAND INSTITUTE COLLEGE OF ART *(The complete profile is made available exclusively on our website, www.barronspac.com)*

MCDANIEL COLLEGE — D-2
www.mcdaniel.edu

Westminster, MD 21157 — (410) 857-2230, (800) 638-5005

Fax: (410) 857-2757	**Email:** admissions@mcdaniel.edu
Full-time: 759 men, 784 women	**Faculty:** 121; IIB, av$
Part-time: 22 men, 25 women	**Ph.D.s:** 89%
Graduate: 245 men, 1023 women	**Student/Faculty:** 11 to 1
Year: 4-1-4, summer session	**Tuition:** $41,800
Room & Board: $11,110	**Freshman Class:** 2814 applied, 2392 accepted, 450 enrolled
SAT CR/M: 584/565 **ACT:** 25	**CEEB CODE:** 5898
Application Deadline: February 1	**VERY COMPETITIVE**

McDaniel College, founded in 1867, is a four-year independent college of the liberal arts and sciences offering more than 70 undergraduate programs of study, including dual and student-designed majors, plus highly regarded graduate and professional studies programs. McDaniel College is the only American college with a European campus in Budapest, Hungary. There is 1 undergraduate school and 1 graduate school. In addition to regional accreditation, McDaniel has baccalaureate program accreditation with CSWE, CAEP, and ACS. The 160-acre campus is in a suburban area 30 miles from Baltimore's Inner Harbor, and 60 miles from Washington, D.C. Including any residence halls, there are 73 buildings.

STUDENT LIFE: 66% of undergraduates are from Maryland. Others are from 38 states, 12 foreign countries, and Canada. 79% are from public schools. 65% are White; 6% Hispanic; 4% Foreign; 4% two or more races; 4% race unknown; 3% Asian American; 14% African American. **Female To Male Ratio:** 1.8:1. The average age of freshmen is 18; all undergraduates, 20. 19% do not continue beyond their first year; 71% remain to graduate. **Housing:** 1349 students can be accommodated in college housing, which includes single sex dorms, coed dorms, and on-campus apartments. In addition, there are honors houses, language/international houses, special-interest houses, fraternity houses, and sorority houses. On-campus housing is guaranteed for all 4 years. 82% of students live on campus. Some may keep cars.

FACULTY/CLASSROOMS: 46% of faculty are male; 54% are female. All teach undergraduates, and all do research. No introductory courses are taught by graduate students. The average class size in an introductory lecture is 18; in a laboratory is 17; and in a regular course is 16.

PROGRAMS OF STUDY: McDaniel confers B.A. degrees. Master's degrees are also awarded. Bachelor's degrees are awarded in BIOLOGICAL SCIENCE (biology/biological science), BUSINESS (accounting and business administration and management), COMMUNICATIONS AND THE ARTS (art history, art, communications, dramatic arts, English, film, television and digital media, fine arts, French, German, music, and Spanish), COMPUTER AND PHYSICAL SCIENCE (chemistry, computer science, mathematics, and physics), EDUCATION (Asian studies, education, and physical education), ENGINEERING AND ENVIRONMENTAL DESIGN (environmental science), SOCIAL SCIENCE (economics, history, Middle Eastern studies, philosophy, political science/government, psychology, religion, social work, and sociology). Kinesiology, psychology, and business administration have the largest enrollments.

ACTIVITIES: 15% of men belong to 1 local and 3 national fraternities; 19% of women belong to 1 local and 5 national sororities. There are 100 groups on campus, including Green Terror Productions, Heroes Helping Hopkins, various ethnic and cultural student organizations, art, band, Canine Companions for Independence, cheerleading, choir, chorale, chorus, communications, computers, dance, drama, environmental, ethnic, film, forensics, honors, international, jazz band, LGBT, literary magazine, musical theater, newspaper, opera, orchestra, pep band, photography, political, professional, radio and TV, religious, social, social service, student government, symphony, and yearbook. Popular campus events include Homecoming, Late Night Carnival, Fall Fest, Midnight Madness, Cultural dinners, Spring Fling, Relay for Life, and Improv performances. **Sports:** There are 12 intercollegiate sports for men and 12 for women, and 12 intramural sports for men and 12 for women. Facilities include a stadium for football, field hockey, lacrosse, and track includes a synthetic turf field, and competition track, an aerobic conditioning area, a selectorized machine area, and a power/free weight room, basketball and volleyball, multi-purpose synthetic courts, a wrestling room, exercise science labs, classrooms and meeting rooms, a sports medicine center with equipment, baseball, a softball and training facility, a soccer complex, a practice/intramural field venues and a track throwing area, swimming pool, a squash/racquetball court, golf course and training facility, and tennis. **Graduates:** From July 1, 2016 to June 30, 2017, 376 bachelor's degrees were awarded. The most popular majors were kinesiology (14%), psychology (11%), and business administration (7%). In an average class, 59% graduate in 4 years or less, 66% graduate in 5 years or less, and 68% graduate in 6 years or less.

SERVICES: Counseling and information services are available, as is tutoring in most subjects. There is a reader service for the blind, and remedial math, reading, and writing. **Library/Resources:** The library contains 445,893 volumes, 1.4 million microform items, and 48,219 audio/video tapes/CDs/DVDs, and subscribes to 66,237 periodicals including electronic. Computerized library services include interlibrary loans, database searching, Internet access, and Wi-Fi capability. Special learning facilities include an art gallery, radio station, TV station, an observatory, human performance lab, video production lab, photography studio, graphics lab, and student research science labs. **Physically Challenged Students:** 85% of the campus is accessible. Facilities include wheelchair ramps, elevators, special parking, specially equipped restrooms, special class scheduling, lowered drinking fountains, lowered telephones, and special housing. **Special:** The Center for Experience and Opportunity (CEO) provides students with experiences including volunteer and internship opportunities, career services, scholarships and fellowships, plus study abroad at McDaniel's campus in Budapest, Hungary, one of our exchange programs or one of many affiliated programs. Global Initiatives offers special academic programming and activities to help students find their place as global citizens. McDaniel's Encompass Distinction builds a new generation of innovators and entrepreneurs. There is a Washington semester in conjunction with American University and a Gallaudet Visiting Student Program for juniors and seniors wishing to complete the requirements for the ASL and Deaf Studies minor. The college offers dual and student-designed majors, credit by exam (in foreign languages), and pass/fail options. McDaniel College offers 5-year B.A./M.S. programs, pre-professional programs, and teaching certification in elementary and secondary education. The college also offers advanced standing for international baccalaureate recipients. There are 20 national honor societies, Phi Beta Kappa, a freshman honors program, and 24 departmental honors programs. **Visiting:** There are regularly scheduled orientations for prospective students, an information session conducted by a counselor and/or the Director or Dean of Admissions and a student-led tour of campus. Individual visits and fall visit days include a class visit and lunch. To schedule a visit, contact the Office of Admissions. **Campus Safety and Security:** Measures include 24-hour foot and vehicle patrol, emergency notification system, and security escort services. There are shuttle buses, emergency telephones, lighted pathways/sidewalks, and controlled access to dorms/residences.

REQUIREMENTS: The SAT or ACT is required. Applicants must be graduates of an accredited secondary school or have a GED. A minimum of 16 academic credits are required, including 4 years of English, 3 each of foreign language, math, and social studies, and 3 of a lab science. SAT Subject Tests and an interview are recommended. An essay and academic recommendations are required. AP and CLEP credits are accepted. Important factors in the admissions decision are advanced placement or honors courses, recommendations by alumni, leadership record, parents or siblings attended your school, recommendations by school officials, evidence of special talent, personality/intangible qualities, and extracurricular activities record. All students are required to complete the McDaniel Plan, which provides a liberal arts education combining a comprehensive program of general education and a rigorous program in the major, complemented by electives and a range of special opportunities. For the B.A. degree, students must complete at least 128 credit hours distributed among the requirements of the McDaniel Plan, including a First Year Seminar, introduction to college writing, Global Citizenship, second language study, departmental writing, critical inquiries in the liberal arts, at least one two-credit January Term course, two physical activity and wellness courses, up to 50 credit hours of required coursework in the major, and electives. The minimum GPA for graduation is 2.0. **Procedure:** Freshmen are admitted fall and spring. Entrance exams should be taken at the end of the junior year. There are early admissions and deferred admissions plans. Early decision applications should be filed by November 1; regular applications, by February 1 for fall entry. The fall 2017 application fee was $50. Notifications are sent in rolling. 22 early decision candidates were accepted for the 2017-2018 class. 81 applicants were on the 2017 waiting list; 1 was admitted. Applications are accepted on-line. **Transfer Students:** 60 transfer students enrolled in 2016-2017. A minimum college GPA of 2.5 is required. 32 of 128 credits required for the bachelor's degree must be completed at McDaniel. **International Students:** There are 55 international students enrolled. They must take the TOEFL with a minimum score of 550 on the paper-based TOEFL (PBT) or 80 on the Internet-based version (iBT). They must also take the SAT.

ADMISSIONS: 85% of the 2017-2018 applicants were accepted. The SAT scores for the 2017-2018 freshman class were: Math-- 16% below 500, 52% between 500 and 599, 27% between 600 and 699, and 5% between 700 and 800. Evidence-Based Reading/Writing-- 9% below 500, 51% between 500 and 599, 33% between 600 and 699, and 7% between 700 and 800. The ACT scores were 48% between 18 and 23, 35% between 24 and 29, and 17% above 30. **Admissions Contact:** Florence W. Hines, VP, Dean of Admissions. Email: *admissions@mcdaniel.edu* Web: *www.mcdaniel.edu*

FINANCIAL AID: In 2017-2018, 85% of all full-time freshmen received

some form of financial aid. 85% of all full-time freshmen received need-based aid. The average freshman award was $39,191. Need-based scholarships or need-based grants averaged $35,998; need-based self-help aid (loans and jobs) averaged $8,563; and other non-need-based awards and non-need-based scholarships averaged $21,775. The college's own financial statement is required. The FAFSA code is 002109. The priority date for freshman financial aid applications for fall entry is November 15.

MORGAN STATE UNIVERSITY *(The complete profile is made available exclusively on our website, www.barronspac.com)*

MOUNT ST. MARY'S UNIVERSITY D-2
www.msmary.edu

Emmitsburg, MD 21727 **(301) 447-5214**
(800) 448-4347
Fax: (301) 447-5860 **Email: admissions@msmary.edu**

Full-time: 804 men, 892 women	**Faculty:** 114; IIA, -$
Part-time: 65 men, 56 women	**Ph.D.s:** 90%
Graduate: 304 men, 202 women	**Student/Faculty:** 12 to 1
Year: semesters, summer session	**Tuition:** $40,550
Room & Board: $12,830	**Freshman Class:** 6162 applied, 3954 accepted, 524 enrolled
SAT CR/M/W: 500/510/480 **ACT:** 21	**CEEB CODE:** 5421
Application Deadline: March 1	**COMPETITIVE**

Mount St. Mary's University, founded in 1808, is a private liberal arts institution affiliated with the Roman Catholic Church. There are 5 undergraduate schools. In addition to regional accreditation, MSMU has baccalaureate program accreditation with NASDTEC, CAEP, and IACBE. The 1500-acre campus is in a rural area 60 miles northwest of Washington, D.C., and 50 miles west of Baltimore. Including any residence halls, there are 32 buildings.

STUDENT LIFE: 59% of undergraduates are from Maryland. Others are from 38 states, 10 foreign countries, and Canada. 63% are from public schools. 63% are White; 4% two or more races; 3% Asian American; 17% African American; 11% Hispanic; 1% Foreign; 1% race unknown. 62% are Catholic; 26% Protestant. **Male To Female Ratio:** 1.0:1. The average age of freshmen is 18; all undergraduates, 21. 25% do not continue beyond their first year; 68% remain to graduate. **Housing:** 1459 students can be accommodated in college housing, which includes dorms and on-campus apartments. In addition, there are special-interest houses, wellness floors, and quiet floors. On-campus housing is guaranteed for all 4 years. 80% of students live on campus. All students may keep cars.

FACULTY/CLASSROOMS: 57% of faculty are male; 43% are female. 87% teach undergraduates, 50% do research, and 50% do both. No introductory courses are taught by graduate students. The average class size in an introductory lecture is 20; in a laboratory is 10; and in a regular course is 19.

PROGRAMS OF STUDY: MSMU confers B.A. and B.S. degrees. Master's degrees are also awarded. Bachelor's degrees are awarded in BIOLOGICAL SCIENCE (biochemistry and biology/biological science), BUSINESS (accounting, business administration and management, and sports management), COMMUNICATIONS AND THE ARTS (communications, English, fine arts, French, German, and Spanish), COMPUTER AND PHYSICAL SCIENCE (chemistry, computer science, cyber intelligence/security studies, information sciences and systems, and mathematics), EDUCATION (elementary education), ENGINEERING AND ENVIRONMENTAL DESIGN (environmental science), HEALTH PROFESSIONS (health science), SOCIAL SCIENCE (criminal justice, economics, history, human services, interdisciplinary studies, international studies, philosophy, political science/government, psychology, social studies, sociology, and theological studies). Business, biology, and criminal justice have the largest enrollments.

ACTIVITIES: There are no fraternities or sororities. There are 70 groups on campus, including art, band, cheerleading, chess, choir, chorale, computers, dance, debate, drama, environmental, ethnic, honors, international, literary magazine, musical theater, newspaper, pep band, political, professional, radio and TV, religious, social, social service, student government, and yearbook. Popular campus events include Acoustic Battle, Christmas Dance, Crab Feast, Homecoming, and Special Olympics. **Sports:** There are 8 intercollegiate sports for men and 9 for women, and 25 intramural sports for men and 25 for women. Facilities include multipurpose indoor courts, a track, pool, aerobics, weight room, basketball, tennis courts, and playing fields. **Graduates:** From July 1, 2016 to June 30, 2017, 383 bachelor's degrees were awarded. The most popular majors were business (24%), criminal justice (13%), and accounting (7%). In an average class, 2% graduate in 3 years or less, 65% graduate in 4 years or less, 70% graduate in 5 years or less, and 71% graduate in 6 years or less. Of the 2016 graduating class, 16% were enrolled in graduate school within 6 months of graduation, and 89% were employed.

SERVICES: Counseling and information services are available, as is tutoring in every subject. There is a reader service for the blind, and remedial math. There is also a study skills and language lab, and writing center. Closed-caption TV and software for sight-impaired students are also available. **Library/Resources:** The library contains 149,524 volumes, 0 microform items, and 5,369 audio/video tapes/CDs/DVDs, and subscribes to 27,516 periodicals including electronic. Computerized library services include interlibrary loans, database searching, Internet access, and Wi-Fi capability. Special learning facilities include an art gallery, radio station, and TV station. **Physically Challenged Students:** 85% of the campus is accessible. Facilities include wheelchair ramps, elevators, special parking, specially equipped restrooms, special class scheduling, lowered drinking fountains, and lowered telephones. **Special:** Mount St. Mary's offers cross-registration with an area community college, study abroad in the U.K., Europe, and South America, and secondary teacher certification in English, foreign languages, math, and social studies. Dual majors, interdisciplinary majors in biopsychology, American culture, and classical studies, a general studies degree, 3 dual degree programs, and non-degree and accelerated study are possible. A number of independently designed internships, work-study programs, and pass/fail options are available. The Core curriculum is a common 4 year curriculum integrated with every academic major. There are 20 national honor societies and a freshman honors program. **Visiting:** There are regularly scheduled orientations for prospective students, including campus tours and information sessions on academic programs, community life, admissions, and financial aid. There are guides for informal visits, visitors may sit in on classes, and stay overnight. To schedule a visit, contact the Admissions Office. **Campus Safety and Security:** Measures include 24-hour foot and vehicle patrol, emergency notification system, and security escort services. There are emergency telephones, lighted pathways/sidewalks, and controlled access to dorms/residences.

REQUIREMENTS: The SAT is required. Applicants should be graduates of an accredited secondary school or hold the GED. Secondary preparation should include 4 years of English, 3 each of math, history, natural science, and social sciences, and 2 of a foreign language. An interview is recommended. AP and CLEP credits are accepted. Important factors in the admissions decision are recommendations by school officials, advanced placement or honors courses, and extracurricular activities record. Students are required to take a 4-year, 49 credit core curriculum in liberal arts (a number of which will overlap with/contribute to a student's major). The common educational experience includes a liberal arts symposium, a Western civilization sequence including art and literature, and courses in philosophy, theology, foreign language, math, American culture, and ethics. Graduation requirements include 120 credits, with most majors requiring 36 credits (30 to 36 in the major) and a minimum GPA of 2.0. **Procedure:** Freshmen are admitted fall and spring. Entrance exams should be taken by January of the senior year. There are early admissions, deferred admissions, and rolling admissions plans. Application deadlines are open. The fall 2017 application fee was $45. Applications are accepted on-line. **Transfer Students:** 63 transfer students enrolled in 2016-2017. Transfer applicants should have at least a 2.0 GPA in previous college work, be in good academic and disciplinary standing, and account for all time elapsed since graduation from high school. 30 of 120 credits required for the bachelor's degree must be completed at MSMU. **International Students:** There are 12 international students enrolled. They must take the TOEFL with a minimum score of 550 on the paper-based TOEFL (PBT) or 83 on the Internet-based version (iBT). They must also take the SAT or ACT.

ADMISSIONS: 64% of the 2017-2018 applicants were accepted. 24% of the current freshmen were in the top fifth of their class; 51% were in the top two fifths. 1 freshman graduated first in the class. **Admissions Contact:** Michael Post, VP for Enrollment Management. Email: *admissions@msmary.edu* Web: *www.msmary.edu*

FINANCIAL AID: In 2017-2018, 99% of all full-time freshmen received some form of financial aid. 78% of all full-time freshmen received need-based aid. The average freshman award was $27,021. Need-based schol-

arships or need-based grants averaged $3,000 ($18,850 maximum); need-based self-help aid (loans and jobs) averaged $5,570 ($7,030 maximum); non-need-based athletic scholarships averaged $1,340 ($51,610 maximum); and other non-need-based awards and non-need-based scholarships averaged $16,050 ($37,700 maximum). 42% of undergraduate students work part-time. The average financial indebtedness of the 2017 graduate was $33,894. The FAFSA code is 002086. The priority date for freshman financial aid applications for fall entry is December 1.

NOTRE DAME OF MARYLAND UNIVERSITY D-2

www.ndm.edu

Baltimore, MD 21210 **(410) 532-5330**
(800) 435-0200

Fax: (410) 532-6287 **Email: admiss@ndm.edu**

Full-time: 650 women	**Faculty:** 74; IIA, -$
Part-time: 90 men, 880 women	**Ph.D.s:** 65%
Graduate: 270 men, 1190 women	**Student/Faculty:** 8 to 1
Year: 4-1-4, summer session	**Tuition:** $36,070
Room & Board: $11,500	**Freshman Class:** n/av
SAT or ACT: required	**CEEB CODE:** 5114
Application Deadline: open	**VERY COMPETITIVE**

Notre Dame of Maryland University, founded in 1873, is a private liberal arts institution primarily for women and affiliated with the Catholic Church. The figures given in the above capsule and in this profile are approximate. There are 4 undergraduate schools and 1 graduate school. In addition to regional accreditation, NDMU has baccalaureate program accreditation with NLN. The 58-acre campus is in a suburban area 10 miles north of Baltimore. Including any residence halls, there are 11 buildings.

STUDENT LIFE: 70% of undergraduates are from Maryland. Others are from 21 states. **Female To Male Ratio:** 7.6:1. **Housing:** 450 students can be accommodated in college housing, which includes dorms. On-campus housing is guaranteed for all 4 years. 65% of students live on campus. Alcohol is not permitted. All students may keep cars.

FACULTY/CLASSROOMS: 30% of faculty are male; 70% are female. All teach undergraduates. No introductory courses are taught by graduate students. The average class size in an introductory lecture is 30; in a laboratory is 20; and in a regular course is 20.

PROGRAMS OF STUDY: NDMU confers B.A. and B.S. degrees. Master's degrees are also awarded. Bachelor's degrees are awarded in BIOLOGICAL SCIENCE (biology/biological science), BUSINESS (accounting, banking and finance, business administration and management, international business management, and marketing/retailing/merchandising), COMMUNICATIONS AND THE ARTS (art history and appreciation, classics, communications, English, graphic design, modern language, music, photography, and studio art), COMPUTER AND PHYSICAL SCIENCE (chemistry, computer science, information sciences and systems, mathematics, and physics), EDUCATION (art education, early childhood education, elementary education, foreign languages education, music education, science education, secondary education, and special education), ENGINEERING AND ENVIRONMENTAL DESIGN (preengineering), HEALTH PROFESSIONS (nursing, predentistry, premedicine, and prepharmacy), SOCIAL SCIENCE (economics, history, interdisciplinary studies, international relations, liberal arts/general studies, political science/government, prelaw, psychology, and religion). Business, education, and communication arts are the strongest academically.

ACTIVITIES: There are no fraternities or sororities. There are 24 groups on campus, including art, choir, dance, drama, ethnic, honors, international, literary magazine, newspaper, political, professional, radio and TV, religious, social, social service, student government, and yearbook. Popular campus events include Honors Convocation, Antostal Day, and Multicultural Awareness Week. **Sports:** Facilities include a sports/activities complex that houses racquetball courts, a dance studio, a fitness center, an indoor walking track, a game room, an activities resource center, and a basketball court.

SERVICES: Counseling and information services are available, as is tutoring in most subjects. **Library/Resources:** The library contains 290,000 volumes, 378,138 microform items, and 24,000 audio/video tapes/CDs/DVDs, and subscribes to 2,000 periodicals including electronic. Computerized library services include database searching. Special learning facilities include an art gallery, planetarium, radio station, TV station, a graphic arts studio, roof-top greenhouse, and cultural center. **Physically Challenged Students:** 98% of the campus is accessible. Facilities include wheelchair ramps, elevators, special parking, specially equipped restrooms, and lowered drinking fountains. **Special:** The college offers cross-registration with Johns Hopkins, Towson State, and Morgan State Universities; Coppin State, Goucher, and Loyola Colleges; and the Maryland Institute College of Art. Study abroad, internships, dual bachelor's degrees in nursing and engineering, 3-2 engineering degrees with Johns Hopkins University and the University of Maryland, and pass/fail options are available. Notre Dame's Weekend College offers bachelor's degree programs for employed adults. There are 8 national honor societies, a freshman honors program, and 4 departmental honors programs. **Visiting:** There are regularly scheduled orientations for prospective students, consisting of programs in June and January, each of which includes a stay in the dormitory, registration, and advisement. There are guides for informal visits and visitors may sit in on classes. To schedule a visit, contact the Office of Admissions. **Campus Safety and Security:** Measures include 24-hour foot and vehicle patrol, self-defense education, and security escort services. There are lighted pathways/sidewalks.

REQUIREMENTS: The SAT or ACT is required. For scholarship purposes, applicants should be graduates of an accredited secondary school. 18 academic credits are required, including 4 units of English, 3 each of math and a foreign language, and 2 each of history and science, plus 4 electives. An essay is required and an interview is recommended. A GPA of 2.5 is required. AP credits are accepted. Important factors in the admissions decision are recommendations by school officials, advanced placement or honors courses, and leadership record. To graduate, students must complete a total of 128 credit hours with a minimum GPA of 2.0 (2.5 in many majors). All students must fulfill the distribution requirements in the general education core, the major, and electives, and must demonstrate proficiency in writing, public speaking, computer literacy, and library research. In most majors, a minimum of 42 hours is required. All students must take a speech course and 2 courses in phys ed, and some majors require senior practicums. **Procedure:** Freshmen are admitted fall and spring. Entrance exams should be taken no later than January of the senior year. There are early decision, early admissions, deferred admissions, and rolling admissions plans. Application deadlines are open. Notification is sent on a rolling basis. Applications are accepted on-line. **Transfer Students:** NDUM requires a minimum GPA of 2.5 for transfer students but recommends a GPA of 3.0. A combined score of 800 is required for the SAT I and 18 for the ACT. Students must also submit a letter of recommendation and an essay. 60 of 128 credits required for the bachelor's degree must be completed at NDMU. **International Students:** They must take the TOEFL for placement purposes.

Admissions Contact: Sharon Bogdan, Director of Admissions. Email: *admiss@ndm.edu* Web: *www.ndm.edu*

FINANCIAL AID: In 2017-2018, 85% of all full-time freshmen received some form of financial aid. 80% of all full-time freshmen received need-based aid. The average freshman award was $20,796. Need-based scholarships or need-based grants averaged $15,600 ($22,750 maximum); need-based self-help aid (loans and jobs) averaged $4,011 ($6,125 maximum); and other non-need-based awards and non-need-based scholarships averaged $9,202 ($18,700 maximum). NDMU is a member of CSS. The CSS/Profile is required. The FAFSA code is 002065. Check with the school for current application deadlines.

SALISBURY UNIVERSITY F-4

www.salisbury.edu

Salisbury, MD 21801 **(410) 543-6161**
(800) 543-0148

Fax: (410) 546-6016 **Email: admissions@salisbury.edu**

Full-time: 3158 men, 4033 women	**Faculty:** 435; IIA, -$
Part-time: 272 men, 319 women	**Ph.D.s:** 85%
Graduate: 194 men, 738 women	**Student/Faculty:** 17 to 1
Year: 4-1-4, summer session	**Tuition:** $9582 ($18,622)
Room & Board: $11,550	**Freshman Class:** 8171 applied, 5313 accepted, 1328 enrolled
SAT CR/M/W: 596/584/560 **ACT:** required	**CEEB CODE:** 5403
Application Deadline: January 15	**VERY COMPETITIVE**

Salisbury University, founded in 1925, is a member of the University System of Maryland, and a regionally accredited four-year comprehensive institution offering 60 distinct graduate and undergraduate programs. There are 5 undergraduate schools and 1 graduate school. In addition to regional accreditation, SU has baccalaureate program accreditation with AACSB, CSWE, NASM, NCATE, ACS-CPT, CoARC, CAAHEP, CAATE, CCNE, NAACLS, and CAEP. The 185-acre campus is in a rural area on the historic Eastern Shore of Maryland, 30 miles from Ocean City and 2.5 hours from Baltimore and Washington, D.C. Including any residence halls, there are 80 buildings.

STUDENT LIFE: 85% of undergraduates are from Maryland. Others are from 32 states, 59 foreign countries, and Canada. 80% are from public schools. 71% are White; 14% African American; 4% Hispanic; 3% Asian American; 3% two or more races; 3% race unknown; 1% American Indian/Alaska Native; 1% Foreign. **Female To Male Ratio:** 1.4:1. The average age of freshmen is 18; all undergraduates, 21. 18% do not continue beyond their first year; 68% remain to graduate. **Housing:** 3151 students can be accommodated in college housing, which includes dorms, on-campus apartments, and off-campus apartments. In addition, there are special-interest houses, international, and living-learning community. On-campus housing is available on a first-come and first-served basis. 69% of students commute. All students may keep cars.

FACULTY/CLASSROOMS: 43% of faculty are male; 58% are female. 91% teach undergraduates, 20% do research, and 18% do both. Graduate students teach 2% of introductory courses. The average class size in an introductory lecture is 31; in a laboratory is 21; and in a regular course is 26.

PROGRAMS OF STUDY: SU confers B.A., B.S., B.A.S.W., and B.F.A. degrees. Master's and doctoral degrees are also awarded. Bachelor's degrees are awarded in AGRICULTURE (environmental studies), BIOLOGICAL SCIENCE (biology/biological science), BUSINESS (accounting, business administration and management, business economics, finance, international business, management science, and marketing), COMMUNICATIONS AND THE ARTS (art, communications, English, English as a second/foreign language, fine arts, French, music, Spanish, and theatre arts), COMPUTER AND PHYSICAL SCIENCE (chemistry, computer science, earth science, information sciences and systems, mathematics, and physics), EDUCATION (athletic training, early childhood education, elementary education, physical education, and physical education/exercise science), HEALTH PROFESSIONS (community health work, medical laboratory technology, nursing, and respiratory therapy), SOCIAL SCIENCE (economics, geography, history, international studies, liberal arts/general studies, peace studies, philosophy, political science/government, psychology, social work, sociology, and urban and regional studies). Communication arts, psychology, and social work are the strongest academically. Nursing, biology, and communication arts have the largest enrollments.

ACTIVITIES: There are 106 groups on campus, including art, band, cheerleading, choir, chorale, chorus, communications, computers, dance, debate, drama, environmental, ethnic, film, honors, international, jazz band, LGBT, literary magazine, musical theater, newspaper, opera, orchestra, pep band, photography, political, professional, radio and TV, religious, social, social service, student government, and symphony. Popular campus events include Gullfest, Homecoming Week, and The Big Event and I Love Salisbury (Community Service Projects). **Sports:** There are 10 intercollegiate sports for men and 11 for women, and 14 intramural sports for men and 14 for women. Facilities include a stadium, gym, multipurpose gym, swimming pool, indoor climbing walls, dance studio, racquetball courts, indoor and outdoor tennis courts, baseball diamond, varsity fields, practice fields, all-weather track, fitness center, strength rooms, lighted intramural fields, outdoor sand volleyball courts. **Graduates:** From July 1, 2016 to June 30, 2017, 2026 bachelor's degrees were awarded. The most popular majors were exercise science (9%), communication arts (8%), and psychology (7%). In an average class, 47% graduate in 4 years or less, 66% graduate in 5 years or less, and 68% graduate in 6 years or less.

SERVICES: Counseling and information services are available, as is tutoring in most subjects, such as biology, business, chemistry, economics, exercise science, history, math, physics, psychology, praxis, reading, Spanish, and writing. There is a reader service for the blind. **Library/Resources:** The library contains 264,146 volumes, 7,631 microform items, and 2,207 audio/video tapes/CDs/DVDs, and subscribes to 842 periodicals including electronic. Computerized library services include interlibrary loans, database searching, Internet access, and Wi-Fi capability. Special learning facilities include an art gallery, radio station, TV station, Nabb Research Center for Delmarva History & Culture, Scarborough Student Leadership Center, Center for Conflict Resolution, Richard A Henson Medical Simulation Center, Ward Museum of Wildfowl Art, Center for Integrated Media, Guerrieri University Center, BEACON, Small Business Development Center, Franklin P Perdue Museum of Business and Entrepreneurship; Guerrieri Academic Commons. **Physically Challenged Students:** 95% of the campus is accessible. Facilities include wheelchair ramps, elevators, special parking, specially equipped restrooms, special class scheduling, lowered drinking fountains, lowered telephones, and special housing. **Special:** Cross-registration with schools in the University System of Maryland and study abroad in numerous countries are offered. SU also offers an Annapolis semester, a Washington semester, internships, work-study programs, accelerated degree programs in dentistry, optometry, podiatric medicine, and pharmacy, dual majors in biology/environmental marine science, social work/sociology, and physical engineering, interdisciplinary and student-designed majors including physics/microelectronics, a 3-2 engineering degree with the University of Maryland at College Park, Old Dominion University, and Widener University, a co-op program in electrical engineering, and pass/fail options. There are 26 national honor societies and a freshman honors program. **Visiting:** There are regularly scheduled orientations for prospective students, presentations, tours, meetings with faculty and staff, additional scheduled Saturday open house programs. There are guides for informal visits and visitors may sit in on classes. To schedule a visit, contact the Admissions Office. **Campus Safety and Security:** Measures include 24-hour foot and vehicle patrol, emergency notification system, self-defense education, and security escort services. There are shuttle buses, emergency telephones, lighted pathways/sidewalks, controlled access to dorms/residences, 24-hour university police protection, video surveillance system, information meetings/discussions, student patrols, pamphlets/posters/fliers, and 911 Shield app.

REQUIREMENTS: Applicants must be graduates of accredited secondary schools or have earned a GED. The university requires 15 academic credits, including 4 in English, 3 each in math, social studies and science (2 with labs), and 2 in foreign language. Auditions are required for admission into the music and B.F.A. programs once admission to the university is granted. Essays are recommended but not required. A campus visit is recommended for all students. The SAT is not required for any enrolling student with a 3.5 or greater GPA. A GPA of 2.0 is required. AP and CLEP credits are accepted. Important factors in the admissions decision are leadership record, extracurricular activities record, and advanced placement or honors courses. Students must successfully complete at least 120 credit hours of coursework with a cumulative GPA of 2.0 or higher. Students must take 30 of the last 37 credit hours at SU (special cooperative programs are exempt). Students completing their course requirements through an approved study abroad program are exempt from this policy. Complete at least 30 credit hours at SU by direct classroom instruction and/or lab experience and not through credit by examination. Complete at least 30 credit hours at the 300/400 level with grades of C or better. Transfer students must complete at least 15 hours of their 30 upper-level credits at SU (note: other than field-based courses in the Seidel School of Education & Professional Studies, courses taken on a PS/F basis do not satisfy this requirement). Satisfy the General Education requirements. Satisfy the requirements in at least one major program of study including the major's required GPA. Earn grades of C or better in English 101, 102 or 103. **Procedure:** Freshmen are admitted fall and spring. Entrance exams should be taken Fall of Junior High School year. There are early decision, early admissions, and deferred admissions plans. Early decision applications should be filed by November 15; regular applications, by January 15 for fall entry. The fall 2017 application fee was $50. Notification of early decision is sent December 15; regular decision, March 15. 195 early decision candidates were accepted for the 2017-2018 class. Applications are accepted on-line. **Transfer Students:** 1259 transfer students enrolled in 2016-2017. Applicants must present a minimum GPA of 2.0 with at least 24 transferable credit hours earned from a regionally accredited community college or 4-year college or university. Contractural admission is extended to individuals who complete 12 credit hours of transferable coursework and present a minimum GPA of 2.5 Students with fewer than 24 credit hours must be eligible for freshman admission in addition to maintaining at least a 2.0 GPA in college courses. 30 of 120 credits required for the bachelor's degree must be completed at SU. **International Students:** There are 100 international students enrolled. They must take the TOEFL with a minimum score of 550 on the paper-based TOEFL (PBT) or 79 on the Internet-based version (iBT), SAT or ACT, IELTS, Cambridge English, Elken, ELI (SU) Completer, other approved proof of English competency. Test optional admission for eligible applicants with GPA if 3.5 or higher (on 4.0 scale).

ADMISSIONS: 65% of the 2017-2018 applicants were accepted. The SAT scores for the 2017-2018 freshman class were: Critical Reading-- 5% below 500, 43% between 500 and 599, 48% between 600 and 699, and 4% between 700 and 800. Math-- 6% below 500, 52% between 500 and 599, 39% between 600 and 699, and 3% between 700 and 800. The ACT scores were 9% between 12 and 17, 49% between 18 and 23, 38% between 24 and 29, and 4% above 30. 42% of the current freshmen were in the top fifth of their class; 74% were in the top two fifths. **Admissions Contact:** Elizabeth Skoglund, Director of Admissions. Email: *admissions@salisbury.edu* Web: *www.salisbury.edu*

FINANCIAL AID: In 2017-2018, 88% of all full-time freshmen received some form of financial aid. 62% of all full-time freshmen received need-based aid. The average freshman award was $14,092. Need-based scholarships or need-based grants averaged $7,172 ($24,716 maximum); need-based self-help aid (loans and jobs) averaged $12,585 ($33,128 maximum); and other non-need-based awards and non-need-based scholarships averaged $3,618 ($18,864 maximum). The average financial indebtedness of the 2017 graduate was $27,038. SU is a member of CSS. The FAFSA code is 002091. The priority date for freshman financial aid applications for fall entry is February 15.

ST. JOHN'S COLLEGE AT ANNAPOLIS E-3

www.sjc.edu

Annapolis, MD 21401	(410) 626-2522 (800) 727-9238
Fax: (410) 269-7916	**Email:** annapolis.admissions@sjc.edu
Full-time: 244 men, 215 women	**Faculty:** 56
Part-time: n/av	**Ph.D.s:** 86%
Graduate: 35 men, 20 women	**Student/Faculty:** 8 to 1
Year: semesters	**Tuition:** $51,670
Room & Board: $11,678	**Freshman Class:** 790 applied, 435 accepted, 138 enrolled
SAT CR/M: 688/675 **ACT:** 29	**CEEB CODE:** 5598
Application Deadline: January 15	**MOST COMPETITIVE**

St. John's College at Annapolis is a liberal arts college with a distinct purpose: reading and discussing the great books of Western civilization. Alongside names such as Plato, Shakespeare, Euclid, Nietzsche, Einstein, and Austen, Johnnies wrestle with ideas in interdisciplinary seminars with two faculty and fewer than 20 students. Johnnies are original and unconventional, love big questions and discussion, and debate the ideas of thinkers, authors, scientists, philosophers, musicians, mathematicians, politicians, and more who changed our world. St. John's, was founded in 1696 and chartered in 1784, but Johnnies explore the great books on two different campuses one in Annapolis, Maryland, and the other in Santa Fe, New Mexico. There is 1 undergraduate school and 1 graduate school. The 36-acre campus is in a small town in the heart of Annapolis, Maryland, near the Chesapeake Bay, 35 miles east of Washington, D.C., and 32 miles south of Baltimore. Including any residence halls, there are 18 buildings.

STUDENT LIFE: 88% of undergraduates are from out of state, mostly the Middle Atlantic. Students are from 42 states, 29 foreign countries, and Canada. 64% are White; 6% Hispanic; 4% Asian American; 3% two or more races; 22% Foreign; 2% African American. **Male To Female Ratio:** 1.2:1. The average age of freshmen is 19; all undergraduates, 20. 13% do not continue beyond their first year; 87% remain to graduate. **Housing:** 375 students can be accommodated in college housing, which includes dorms. On-campus housing is guaranteed for the freshman year only and is available on a lottery system for upperclassmen. 82% of students live on campus. Upperclassmen may keep cars.

FACULTY/CLASSROOMS: 71% of faculty are male; 29% are female. All teach undergraduates. No introductory courses are taught by graduate students. The average class size in a laboratory is 15 and in a regular course is 15.

PROGRAMS OF STUDY: St. John's confers B.A. in Liberal Arts degrees. Master's degrees are also awarded. Bachelor's degrees are awarded in BIOLOGICAL SCIENCE (biology/biological science), COMMUNICATIONS AND THE ARTS (languages, literature, and music), COMPUTER AND PHYSICAL SCIENCE (chemistry, mathematics, and physics), SOCIAL SCIENCE (economics, history, history of science, liberal arts/general studies, liberal arts, sciences, general studies, humanities, philosophy, political science/government, psychobiology, theological studies, Western European studies, and Western civilization/culture). Liberal arts is the strongest academically.

ACTIVITIES: There are no fraternities or sororities. There are 40 groups on campus, including Christian fellowship, community garden, fencing and Jewish fellowship, vegetarian, waltz and swing, woodshop, art, band, choir, chorale, chorus, communications, dance, debate, drama, ethnic, film, international, jazz band, LGBT, literary magazine, newspaper, orchestra, photography, poetry, political, professional, religious, social, social service, student government, and symphony. Popular campus events include Reality Weekend, Senior Prank, homecoming, waltz parties, and St. John's/Naval Academy croquet match. **Sports:** There are 4 intercollegiate sports for men and 4 for women, and 19 intramural sports for men and 19 for women. Facilities include a gym with a weight room, cardio room, and indoor running track, tennis courts, a boathouse for sailing and crew, and playing fields, martial arts and yoga, rafting, skiing, and rock climbing. **Graduates:** From July 1, 2016 to June 30, 2017, 93 bachelor's degrees were awarded. The most popular majors were liberal arts (100%). In an average class, 70% graduate in 4 years or less, 76% graduate in 5 years or less, and 76% graduate in 6 years or less. Of the 2016 graduating class, 20% were enrolled in graduate school within 6 months of graduation, and 70% were employed.

SERVICES: Counseling and information services are available, as is tutoring in some subjects, such as Greek, French, math, and writing. There is remedial math and writing. **Library/Resources:** The library contains 133,000 volumes, 2,000 microform items, and 5,000 audio/video tapes/CDs/DVDs, and subscribes to 240 periodicals including electronic. Computerized library services include interlibrary loans, database searching, Internet access, and Wi-Fi capability. Special learning facilities include an art gallery, planetarium, soundproof music practice rooms, dark room, an art gallery and a music library. **Physically Challenged Students:** 70% of the campus is accessible. Facilities include wheelchair ramps, elevators, special parking, specially equipped restrooms, special class scheduling, lowered drinking fountains, lowered telephones, and special housing. **Special:** Career Services helps connect students to internship opportunities and provides funding for otherwise unpaid summer internships. Informal study abroad opportunities are arranged by the college in the summer, and a new study abroad program in Aix-en-Provence, France is available during junior year. **Visiting:** There are regularly scheduled orientations for prospective students, including information session, tour, class observations, overnight, interview, and/or meals in the dining hall. To schedule a visit, contact the Admission Office at annapolis.admissions@sjc.edu. **Campus Safety and Security:** Measures include 24-hour foot and vehicle patrol, emergency notification system, self-defense education, and security escort services. There are emergency telephones, lighted pathways/sidewalks, and controlled access to dorms/residences.

REQUIREMENTS: Applicants must submit either the Common Application or St. John's application, including the writing supplement, secondary school report, two letters of recommendation, and transcripts. Most international students, homeschooled students, and students not receiving a high school diploma should submit test scores. Important factors in the admissions decision are personality/intangible qualities, advanced placement or honors courses, and recommendations by school officials. All students have the same requirements for graduation: completion of the great books curriculum, which is the equivalent of 132 credits, covering a range of subjects including literature, philosophy, history, politics, economics, law, math, science, language, music, and more. All classes (four or five each semester) are discussion-based with 20 students or fewer. During junior and senior year, students have the choice of an elective class each year. Assessment by faculty includes class participation and regular essays and tests; students take oral exams each semester and submit annual essays. Sophomores also take a math exam and seniors an oral exam that admits them to degree candidacy. Seniors also present a final essay to the faculty and take a 1-hour public oral exam. **Procedure:** Freshmen are admitted in the fall. There are early admissions, deferred admissions, and rolling admissions plans. Early decision applications should be filed by November 15; regular applications, by January 15 for fall entry. Notification of early decision is sent December 15; regular decision, February 15. Applications are accepted on-line. **Transfer Students:** 15 transfer students enrolled in 2016-2017. Transfer students enter as freshmen and complete the entire four-year program at St. John's. The admissions criteria are the same as for first-year students. 132 of 132 credits required for the bachelor's degree must be completed at St. John's. **International Students:** There are 102 international students enrolled. They must take the TOEFL, and take the IELTS. They must also take the SAT and ACT.

ADMISSIONS: 55% of the 2017-2018 applicants were accepted. The SAT scores for the 2017-2018 freshman class were: Critical Reading-- 0% below 500, 7% between 500 and 599, 43% between 600 and 699, and 50% between 700 and 800. Math-- 3% below 500, 25% between 500 and 599, 45% between 600 and 699, and 28% between 700 and 800. Evidence-Based Reading/Writing-- 13% between 500 and 599, 37% between 600 and 699, and 48% between 700 and 800. The ACT scores were 13% between 18 and 23, 33% between 24 and 29, and 54% above 30. **Admissions Contact:** Benjamin Baum, Director of Admissions. Email: *annapolis.admissions@sjc.edu* Web: *www.sjc.edu*

FINANCIAL AID: In 2017-2018, 97% of all full-time freshmen received some form of financial aid. 81% of all full-time freshmen received need-based aid. The average freshman award was $49,897. Need-based scholarships or need-based grants averaged $16,807 ($51,200 maximum); need-based self-help aid (loans and jobs) averaged $3,484 ($6,200 maximum); and other non-need-based awards and non-need-based scholarships averaged $14,441 ($29,000 maximum). 44% of undergraduate students work part-time. The average financial indebtedness of the 2017 graduate was $16,700. St. John's is a member of CSS. The FAFSA code is 002092. The priority date for freshman financial aid applications for fall entry is February 15.

ST. MARY'S COLLEGE OF MARYLAND E-4

www.smcm.edu

St. Marys City, MD 20686	**(240) 895-5000** **(800) 492-7181**
Fax: (240) 895-5001	**Email: admissions@smcm.edu**
Full-time: 636 men, 880 women	**Faculty:** 143; IIB, +$
Part-time: 29 men, 25 women	**Ph.D.s:** 99%
Graduate: 8 men, 20 women	**Student/Faculty:** 11 to 1
Year: semesters, summer session	**Tuition:** $14,496 ($29,948)
Room & Board: $12,816	**Freshman Class:** 1655 applied, 1364 accepted, 342 enrolled
SAT EBR-W/M: 596/573 **ACT:** 25	**CEEB CODE:** 5601
Application Deadline: February 15	**VERY COMPETITIVE**

St. Mary's College of Maryland, founded in 1840, is a small public liberal arts college designated by law as the Maryland public honors college in 1992. There is 1 undergraduate school and 1 graduate school. In addition to regional accreditation, St. Mary's has baccalaureate program accreditation with ACS, ASBMB, and MSDE. The 361-acre campus is in a rural area 70 miles southeast of Washington, D.C. Including any residence halls, there are 55 buildings.

STUDENT LIFE: 93% of undergraduates are from Maryland. Others are from 27 states, and 12 foreign countries. 80% are from public schools. 9% are African American; 8% Hispanic; 70% White; 5% two or more races; 4% Asian American; 2% race unknown; 1% Foreign. **Female To Male Ratio:** 1.4:1. The average age of freshmen is 18; all undergraduates, 20. 13% do not continue beyond their first year; 78% remain to graduate. **Housing:** 1507 students can be accommodated in college housing, which includes gender neutral, single sex and coed, and on-campus apartments. In addition, there are special-interest houses. On-campus housing is guaranteed for all 4 years, is available on a first-come, and first-served basis. 82% of students live on campus. All students may keep cars.

FACULTY/CLASSROOMS: 50% of faculty are male; 50% are female. All teach undergraduates, and all do research. No introductory courses are taught by graduate students. The average class size in an introductory lecture is 17 and in a laboratory is 17.

PROGRAMS OF STUDY: St. Mary's confers B.A. and B.S. degrees. Master's degrees are also awarded. Bachelor's degrees are awarded in AGRICULTURE (environmental studies), BIOLOGICAL SCIENCE (biochemistry and biology/biological science), COMMUNICATIONS AND THE ARTS (art, art history and appreciation, dramatic arts, English, film arts, languages, and music), COMPUTER AND PHYSICAL SCIENCE (chemistry, computer science, mathematics, natural sciences, and physics), SOCIAL SCIENCE (anthropology, Asian/Oriental studies, economics, history, philosophy, political science/government, psychology, public affairs, religion, and sociology). Biology, psychology, and economics have the largest enrollments.

ACTIVITIES: There are no fraternities or sororities. There are 101 groups on campus, including academic, outdoors, art, cheerleading, chess, choir, chorale, chorus, dance, drama, drum and bugle corps, environmental, ethnic, honors, international, jazz band, LGBT, literary magazine, newspaper, orchestra, performance, photography, political, professional, radio and TV, religious, social, social service, student government, symphony, and yearbook. Popular campus events include World Carnival, Dance Club Shows, Relay for Life, River Concert Series, the Great Bamboo-Boat Race, Burlesque Club Shows, A Capella Group Shows. **Sports:** There are 9 intercollegiate sports for men and 10 for women, and 7 intramural sports for men and 7 for women. Facilities include a 50 meter pool, a swimming pool, a climbing wall, basketball and volleyball arena, health and fitness center, weight room, training room, exercise room, gymnasiums, varsity practice fields, a track, lighted tennis courts, an outdoor stadium, rowing center, and baseball facilities. **Graduates:** From July 1, 2016 to June 30, 2017, 414 bachelor's degrees were awarded. The most popular majors were economics (13%), psychology (13%), and biology (10%). In an average class, 69% graduate in 4 years or less, 77% graduate in 5 years or less, and 78% graduate in 6 years or less.

SERVICES: Counseling and information services are available, as is tutoring in some subjects, such as biology, chemistry, computer science, English, foreign languages, history, mathematics, physics, psychology, sociology, and writing. There is a reader service for the blind. **Library/Resources:** The library contains 149,367 volumes, 18,731 microform items, and 7,283 audio/video tapes/CDs/DVDs, and subscribes to 477 periodicals including electronic. Computerized library services include interlibrary loans, database searching, Internet access, and Wi-Fi capability. Special learning facilities include an art gallery, radio station, Historic archaeological site, and estuarine research facilities. **Physically Challenged Students:** 95% of the campus is accessible. Facilities include wheelchair ramps, elevators, special parking, specially equipped restrooms, special class scheduling, lowered drinking fountains, lowered telephones, special housing, and living suites that meet ADA standards. **Special:** A B.S. degree is available in biology, biochemistry, chemistry, computer science, physics, and psychology. A B.A. degree is available in all other fields. St. Mary's offers internships, study abroad, national and international exchange programs, work-study, and both dual and student-designed majors. Credit bearing internships offered by St. Mary's include a Computer Science co-op program and the Washington Program in Political Science. St. Mary's has an MOU with the George Washington University's Semester in Washington program. Non-degree study and pass/fail options are possible. There are 12 national honor societies and a chapter of Phi Beta Kappa. **Visiting:** There are regularly scheduled orientations for prospective students, Student visits include personal interviews, group presentations, open house programs, meetings with faculty and students, and campus tours. To schedule a visit, contact Jessica Blofsky at (800) 492-7181. **Campus Safety and Security:** Measures include emergency notification system, self-defense education, and security escort services. There are emergency telephones, lighted pathways/sidewalks, controlled access to dorms/residences, Student security-assistant foot patrols, and nighthawk program.

REQUIREMENTS: The SAT or ACT is required. As an honors college, the admission process is competitive, the admissions committee takes great pride in the careful review of all required credentials as it strives to admit and enroll an entering class that meets institutional goals. A student's academic record carries the greatest weight with careful attention also paid to co-curricular activities, essays, letters of recommendation, and standardized test scores as the committee strives to determine a student's fit with the advantages of a St. Mary's education. AP and CLEP credits are accepted. Important factors in the admissions decision are advanced placement or honors courses, leadership record, and recommendations by school officials. Students must complete core curriculum requirements, which include a liberal arts seminar, a foreign language course, six breadth categories, and an academic experience that takes students outside the classroom (e.g., study abroad, internships, service-learning). There is also a St. Mary's Project or a senior capstone experience. Students must meet additional requirements in their major fields and complete at least 128 semester hours, with at least 44 upper division credits and at least a 2.0 GPA. **Procedure:** Freshmen are admitted fall and spring. Entrance exams should be taken by January of the senior year. There are early admissions and deferred admissions plans. Applications should be filed by February 15 for fall entry; November 1 for spring entry. The fall 2017 application fee was $50. Notifications are sent February 15. Applications are accepted on-line. **Transfer Students:** 110 transfer students enrolled in 2016-2017. St. Mary's College of Maryland admissions committee takes pride in reviewing applications holistically, and we consider many facets of a student's application when making admissions decisions. A student's success at their prior institution is most important to us, with careful attention paid to co-curricular activities (including work and family responsibilities), writing, and recommendations. A competitive candidate has completed at least 12 hours of credit with a minimum grade point average of 2.75 in all college courses and has earned a high school diploma or satisfactory score on the General Education Development (GED) examination. 38 of 128 credits required for the bachelor's degree must be completed at St. Mary's. **International Students:** There are 17 international students enrolled. They must take the TOEFL with a minimum score of 550 on the paper-based TOEFL (PBT) or 90 on the Internet-based version (iBT). They must also take the SAT or ACT.

ADMISSIONS: 82% of the 2017-2018 applicants were accepted. The SAT scores for the 2017-2018 freshman class were: Math-- 13% below 500, 50% between 500 and 599, 31% between 600 and 699, and 6% between 700 and 800. Evidence-Based Reading/Writing-- 11% below 500, 35% between 500 and 599, 44% between 600 and 699, and 10% between 700 and 800. The ACT scores were 6% between 12 and 17, 35% between 18 and 23, 39% between 24 and 29, and 20% above 30. 5 freshmen graduated first in their class. **Admissions Contact:** David Hautanen, Jr., Vice President for Enrollment Management. Email: *admissions@smcm.edu* Web: *www.smcm.edu*

FINANCIAL AID: In 2017-2018, 92% of all full-time freshmen received some form of financial aid. 57% of all full-time freshmen received need-based aid. The average freshman award was $16,829. Need-based scholarships or need-based grants averaged $9,087 ($22,758 maximum); need-based self-help aid (loans and jobs) averaged $3,234 ($5,200 maximum); and other non-need-based awards and non-need-based scholarships averaged $3,646 ($15,000 maximum). 23% of undergraduate students work part-time. The average financial indebtedness of the 2017 graduate was $20,223. The FAFSA code is 002095. The priority date for freshman financial aid applications for fall entry is February 15.

STEVENSON UNIVERSITY D-2

www.stevenson.edu

Stevenson, MD 21153 (410) 486-7001
(877) 468-6852

Fax: (443) 352-4440 Email: admissions@stevenson.edu

Full-time: 1049 men, 1877 women	**Faculty:** 128
Part-time: 104 men, 367 women	**Ph.D.s:** 76%
Graduate: 121 men, 358 women	**Student/Faculty:** 22 to 1
Year: semesters, summer session	**Tuition:** $35,490
Room & Board: $12,922	**Freshman Class:** n/av
SAT EBR-W/M: 559/548 **ACT:** 22	**CEEB CODE:** 5856
Application Deadline: March 1	**COMPETITIVE**

Stevenson University, founded as Villa Julie College in 1947, is the third-largest independent university in Maryland and offers more than 25 undergraduate degree programs. Stevenson is committed to providing career-focused programs based in theory, practice, and mentoring whereby students develop a deep knowledge coupled with practical application and mastery in their major areas. There are 6 undergraduate schools and 1 graduate school. In addition to regional accreditation, SU has baccalaureate program accreditation with NLN, NAEYC, CCNE, MBON, CSHSE, and CAEP. The 173-acre campus is in a suburban area 12 miles from downtown Baltimore. Including any residence halls, there are 43 buildings.

STUDENT LIFE: 77% of undergraduates are from Maryland. Others are from 33 states, 5 foreign countries, and Canada. 6% are Hispanic; 55% White; 5% two or more races; 4% Asian American; 3% race unknown; 28% African American; 1% Foreign. **Female To Male Ratio:** 2.0:1. The average age of freshmen is 18; all undergraduates, 23. 54% remain to graduate. **Housing:** 2000 students can be accommodated in college housing, which includes dorms and on-campus apartments. On-campus housing is available on a first-come, first-served basis, and is available on a lottery system for upperclassmen. 61% of students live on campus. All students may keep cars.

FACULTY/CLASSROOMS: 49% of faculty are male; 51% are female. 99% teach undergraduates. No introductory courses are taught by graduate students. The average class size in an introductory lecture is 19; in a laboratory is 24; and in a regular course is 17.

PROGRAMS OF STUDY: SU confers B.A. and B.S. degrees. Master's degrees are also awarded. Bachelor's degrees are awarded in BIOLOGICAL SCIENCE (biochemistry, biology/biological science, biotechnology, and forensic science), BUSINESS (accounting, apparel and accessories marketing, business administration and management, business communications, business information systems, business systems analysis, fashion merchandising, and marketing management), COMMUNICATIONS AND THE ARTS (apparel design, applied art, art and design, communication design, dramatic arts, English literature, film arts, film, television and digital media, theatre arts, theatre production, theatre studies, video, and visual design), COMPUTER AND PHYSICAL SCIENCE (applied mathematics, chemistry, computer information systems, computer security and information assurance, information sciences and systems, and mathematics), EDUCATION (early childhood education, elementary education, and middle school education), ENGINEERING AND ENVIRONMENTAL DESIGN (environmental science), HEALTH PROFESSIONS (medical laboratory technology and nursing), SOCIAL SCIENCE (criminal justice, fashion design and technology, forensic studies, human services, interdisciplinary studies, legal studies, paralegal studies, psychology, and public history/archives). Sciences, and education are the strongest academically. Nursing, business administration, and business communication have the largest enrollments.

ACTIVITIES: There are no fraternities; 4% of women belong to 2 national sororities. There are 60 groups on campus, including an active minds club, It's on Us, PhiBeta lambda, art, band, cheerleading, choir, chorale, computers, dance, drama, environmental, ethnic, film, forensics, health & wellness, honors, international, LGBT, marching band, musical theater, newspaper, pep band, political, professional, radio and TV, religious, social, social service, and student government. Popular campus events include Homecoming, Rockland Blow Out, Food Truck Rally, Wet & Wild Field Day, Soul Food Sunday, Fashion Show, Fall Carnival, TEDxStevensonU, Relay for Life. **Sports:** There are 13 intercollegiate sports for men and 14 for women, and 8 intramural sports for men and 8 for women. Facilities include 2 full-sized collegiate gymnasiums, 6 tennis courts, an intramural field, volleyball courts, a stadium with a field for football, field hockey, soccer and lacrosse, racquetball court, 3 fitness/workout centers, basketball court, and 1 competition eSports room. **Graduates:** From July 1, 2016 to June 30, 2017, 835 bachelor's degrees were awarded. The most popular majors were nursing (23%), business administration (10%), and business communication (7%). In an average class, 42% graduate in 4 years or less, 53% graduate in 5 years or less, and 56% graduate in 6 years or less. Of the 2016 graduating class, 10% were enrolled in graduate school within 6 months of graduation, and 76% were employed.

SERVICES: Counseling and information services are available, as is tutoring in most subjects, Tutoring is available for most freshman subject and select upper class courses. There is a reader service for the blind, and remedial math, reading, and writing. Free individual tutoring by a peer or professional tutor in the Academic Link. **Library/Resources:** The library contains 71,975 volumes, 199,324 microform items, and 3,465 audio/video tapes/CDs/DVDs, and subscribes to 72,885 periodicals including electronic. Computerized library services include interlibrary loans, database searching, Internet access, and Wi-Fi capability. Special learning facilities include an art gallery, radio station, TV station, a theater, video studio, academic link for tutoring/testing, and a center for student success. **Physically Challenged Students:** 80% of the campus is accessible. Facilities include wheelchair ramps, elevators, special parking, specially equipped restrooms, special class scheduling, lowered drinking fountains, lowered telephones, and special housing. **Special:** Most majors require internships in the field of study. In addition, study abroad, service learning, field placements, independent study and research, and other experiential learning opportunities are offered as part of classes. Cross-registration, work study, accelerated degree programs for Forensic Studies and Forensic Science, student-designed majors, interdisciplinary studies, and the Baltimore Student Exchange are all available at Stevenson. There are 20 national honor societies and a freshman honors program. **Visiting:** There are regularly scheduled orientations for prospective students, a general overview, information on how to apply and how to finance a college education, special academic presentations, tours, meetings with faculty and students, and lunch. There are guides for informal visits, visitors may sit in on classes, and stay overnight. To schedule a visit, contact Admissions Office. **Campus Safety and Security:** Measures include an emergency notification system, and security escort services. There are shuttle buses, emergency telephones, lighted pathways/sidewalks, controlled access to dorms/residences, closed circuit TV, controlled vehicle access to Owings Mills campus between 8pm-4 am, additional security in suite style residence halls.

REQUIREMENTS: The SAT or ACT is required. Applicants must be graduates of an accredited secondary school. Although a secondary transcript is required, particular secondary preparation is not stipulated for all programs. Some degree programs do require specific high school courses. Stevenson requires 17 units of 4 in English, 3 each in math, and science (with 2 units of lab), 2 units in social studies, and 1 unit in history, and 4 units in other academic areas. An essay is required. A GPA of 2.0 is required. AP and CLEP credits are accepted. Important factors in the admissions decision are advanced placement or honors courses, personality/intangible qualities, recommendations by alumni, recommendations by school officials, and extracurricular activities record. In order to obtain a bachelor's degree from Stevenson University, a student must earn a minimum of 120 credits, which must include a minimum of 15 credits at the 300- or 400-level, and complete the core curriculum for a bachelor's degree. Successfully complete the courses required by the major. Clear all "incomplete" from the student's record. Achieve a CGPA of at least 2.00; the GPA is calculated on the basis of work done at Stevenson only. Earn a minimum CGPA in the major of 2.0. Majors may have additional grade or GPA requirements. Earn at least 30 credits at Stevenson University. Comply with the general regulations of the University. File the official Application for Graduation in accordance with deadlines. **Procedure:** Freshmen are admitted fall and spring. Entrance exams should be taken by December of the senior year in high school. There are deferred admissions and rolling admissions plans. Application deadlines are open. The fall 2017 application fee was $40. Applications are accepted on-line. **Transfer Students:** 154 transfer students enrolled in 2016-2017. Transfer applicants must provide all college transcripts and have a minimum 2.5 GPA. Transfer students with a 2.0 cumulative GPA and other program accomplishments or experience may be granted conditional admission to the college. The nursing program has additional requirements for transfer applicants. 30 of 120 credits required for the bachelor's degree must be completed at Stevenson. **International Students:** There are 13 international students enrolled. They must take the TOEFL with a minimum score of 550 on the paper-based TOEFL (PBT) or 80 on the Internet-based version (iBT). They must also take the SAT or ACT.

ADMISSIONS: The SAT scores for the 2017-2018 freshman class were: Math-- 23% below 500, 54% between 500 and 599, 21% between 600 and 699, and 3% between 700 and 800. Evidence-Based Reading/ Writing-- 17% below 500, 54% between 500 and 599, 25% between 600 and 699, and 3% between 700 and 800. The ACT scores were 13% between 12 and 17, 57% between 18 and 23, 26% between 24 and 29, and 4% above 30. 38% of the current freshmen were in the top fifth of their class; 68% were in the top two fifths. **Admissions Contact:** Mark J. Hergan, Vice President for Enrollment Management. Email: *admissions@stevenson.edu* Web: *www.stevenson.edu*

FINANCIAL AID: In 2017-2018, 91% of all full-time freshmen received some form of financial aid. 91% of all full-time freshmen received need-based aid. 21% of undergraduate students work part-time. The average financial indebtedness of the 2017 graduate was $30,672. SU is a member of CSS. The FAFSA code is 002107. The priority date for freshman financial aid applications for fall entry is February 1.

TOWSON UNIVERSITY D-2

www.towson.edu

Towson, MD 21252 **(410) 704-2113**

Fax: (410) 704-3030	**Email:** admissions@towson.edu
Full-time: n/av	**Faculty:** 899
Part-time: n/av	**Ph.D.s:** 79%
Graduate: n/av	**Student/Faculty:** 17 to 1
Year: semesters, summer session	**Tuition:** $9694 ($22,140)
Room & Board: $12,184	**Freshman Class:** 11897 applied, 8773 accepted, 2755 enrolled
SAT CR/M/W: 535/535/530 **ACT:** 23	**CEEB CODE:** 5404
Application Deadline: January 17	**COMPETITIVE**

Towson University, founded in 1866, is part of the University System of Maryland and offers undergraduate and graduate programs in liberal arts and sciences, allied health sciences, education, fine arts, communication, and business and economics. There are 7 undergraduate schools and 1 graduate school. In addition to regional accreditation, TU has baccalaureate program accreditation with AACSB, CAHEA, NASDTEC, NASM, NLN, ACOTE, AOTA, and CAAHEP. The 328-acre campus is in a suburban area 8 miles north of Baltimore City's Inner Harbor. Including any residence halls, there are 56 buildings.

STUDENT LIFE: 85% of undergraduates are from Maryland. Others are from 50 states, 12 foreign countries, and Canada. 6% are Hispanic; 59% White; 5% Asian American; 4% two or more races; 4% race unknown; 2% Foreign; 18% African American. The average age of freshmen is 18; all undergraduates, 21. 14% do not continue beyond their first year. **Housing:** 5051 students can be accommodated in college housing, which includes gender neutral dorms and on-campus apartments. In addition, there are honors houses, language/international houses, special-interest houses, separate floors that are alcohol-free, smoke-free, and substance-free, leadership and quiet floors, and SAGE community, and STEM housing. On-campus housing is available on a first-come, first-served basis, and is available on a lottery system for upperclassmen. 33% of students commute. Upperclassmen may keep cars.

FACULTY/CLASSROOMS: 44% of faculty are male; 56% are female. No introductory courses are taught by graduate students. The average class size in an introductory lecture is 24; in a laboratory is 24; and in a regular course is 24.

PROGRAMS OF STUDY: TU confers B.A., B.S., B.F.A. and B.M. degrees. Master's and doctoral degrees are also awarded. Bachelor's degrees are awarded in BIOLOGICAL SCIENCE (biology/biological science and molecular biology), BUSINESS (accounting, business administration and management, and sports management), COMMUNICATIONS AND THE ARTS (art, communications, dance, English, French, German, media arts, music, Spanish, and theater design), COMPUTER AND PHYSICAL SCIENCE (chemistry, computer science, earth science, geology, geoscience, information sciences and systems, mathematics, and physics), EDUCATION (art education, athletic training, dance education, early childhood education, education, education of the deaf and hearing impaired, elementary education, music education, physical education, and special education), ENGINEERING AND ENVIRONMENTAL DESIGN (environmental science), HEALTH PROFESSIONS (exercise science, health care administration, health science, medical laboratory technology, nursing, occupational therapy, speech pathology/audiology, and sports medicine), SOCIAL SCIENCE (anthropology, crosscultural studies, economics, family/consumer studies, geography, gerontology, history, interdisciplinary studies, international studies, law, philosophy, political science/government, psychology, religion, social science, sociology, and women's studies). Fine arts, business, and education are the strongest academically. Business disciplines, mass communications, and psychology have the largest enrollments.

ACTIVITIES: 8% of men belong to 13 national fraternities; 15% of women belong to 11 national sororities. There are 300 groups on campus, including art, band, cheerleading, chess, choir, chorale, chorus, communications, computers, dance, debate, drama, drill team, environmental, ethnic, film, forensics, honors, international, jazz band, LGBT, literary magazine, marching band, musical theater, newspaper, opera, orchestra, pep band, photography, political, professional, radio and TV, religious, ROTC Army and Air Force, social, social service, student government, and symphony. Popular campus events include Fraternity and Sorority Dances, Ethics Forum, and Tiger Fest. **Sports:** There are 7 intercollegiate sports for men and 12 for women. Facilities include an athletic center, a stadium, baseball and softball fields, tennis courts, a pool, a soccer field, and practice fields, gyms, a weight room, a pool, lighted playing fields, and an indoor climbing wall. **Graduates:** From July 1, 2016 to June 30, 2017, 4428 bachelor's degrees were awarded. The most popular majors were business marketing (14%), health professions and related programs (13%), and social sciences (11%).

SERVICES: Counseling and information services are available, as is tutoring in most subjects. There is a reader service for the blind, and remedial math, reading, and writing. There are also note takers, English language and tutorial services centers, a writing lab, and signers for the hearing impaired. **Library/Resources:** The library contains 364,468 volumes, 830,286 microform items, and 14,174 audio/video tapes/CDs/ DVDs, and subscribes to 2,164 periodicals including electronic. Computerized library services include interlibrary loans, database searching, and Internet access. Special learning facilities include an art gallery, planetarium, radio station, TV station, an curriculum center, a herbarium, animal museum, observatory, and greenhouse. **Physically Challenged Students:** 85% of the campus is accessible. Facilities include wheelchair ramps, elevators, special parking, specially equipped restrooms, special class scheduling, lowered drinking fountains, lowered telephones, and special housing. Automatic doors, assistive listening devices in theaters and concert halls, and interior and exterior signage. **Special:** Towson University offers cooperative programs with other institutions in the University System of Maryland and at Loyola College, the College of Notre Dame, and Johns Hopkins University, cross-registration at more than 80 colleges through the National Student Exchange, and study abroad. Students may pursue a dual major in physics and engineering, an interdisciplinary studies degree, which allows them to design their own majors, a 3-2 engineering program with the University of Maryland at College Park and Penn State, or nondegree study. There are pass/fail options, extensive evening offerings, and opportunities to earn credits between semesters. Internships are available in most majors, and work-study programs are offered both on and off campus. There are 20 national honor societies, a freshman honors program, and 12 departmental honors programs. **Visiting:** There are regularly scheduled orientations for prospective students, including campus tours, a session for parents, a session on the admissions process for transfers and freshmen, and a roundtable discussion. There are guides for informal visits and visitors may sit in on classes. To schedule a visit, contact Lauren Bottcher at admissions@towson.edu. **Campus Safety and Security:** Measures include 24-hour foot and vehicle patrol, emergency notification system, self-defense education, and security escort services. There are shuttle buses, emergency telephones, lighted pathways/sidewalks, controlled access to dorms/residences, Operation ID and a police dog on campus.

REQUIREMENTS: The SAT or ACT is required. Applicants should have graduated from an accredited secondary school or earned the GED. Secondary preparation should include 4 units each of English and math, 3 units each of social studies and science (of these, 2 units must be labs), 2 units of foreign language, and 6 academic electives. Prospective music and dance majors must audition. AP and CLEP credits are accepted. Important factors in the admissions decision are advanced placement or honors courses, recommendations by school officials, leadership record, parents or siblings attended your school, and evidence of special talent. Students must complete coursework in the arts, English, humanities, math, biological or physical science, social science, information technology, and global awareness. **Procedure:** Freshmen are admitted fall and spring. Entrance exams should be taken in the junior or senior year. There are early admissions, deferred admissions, and rolling admissions plans. Applications should be filed by January 17 for fall entry; October 15 for spring entry. The fall 2017 application fee was $45. Notifications are sent December 1. Applications are accepted on-line. **Transfer Students:** 2432 transfer students enrolled in 2016-2017. Transfer applicants should have earned at least 30 academic credits. For those with fewer than 30 attempted, freshmen requirements must be met. Minimum GPA requirements range from 2.0 to 2.5, depending on the number of credits completed. Transcripts are required. 30 of 120 credits required for the bachelor's degree must be completed at Towson. **International Students:** There are 463 international students enrolled. They must take the TOEFL and the college's own test, The TOEFL is required at preadmission; a college test is required at postadmission. They must also take the SAT or ACT, scoring 550. The school accepts the TOEFL as a substitute for the verbal SAT.

ADMISSIONS: 74% of the 2017-2018 applicants were accepted. The SAT scores for the 2017-2018 freshman class were: Critical Reading-- 29% below 500, 53% between 500 and 599, 16% between 600 and 699, and 2% between 700 and 800. Math-- 28% below 500, 52% between 500 and 599, 18% between 600 and 699, and 2% between 700 and 800. Writing-- 30% below 500, 55% between 500 and 599, 14% between 600 and 699, and 1% between 700 and 800. The ACT scores were 3% between 12 and 17, 56% between 18 and 23, 37% between 24 and 29, and 4% above 30. 9 freshmen graduated first in their class. **Admissions Contact:** Louise Shulack, Director of Admissions. Email: *admissions@towson.edu* Web: *www.towson.edu*

FINANCIAL AID: In 2017-2018, 72% of all full-time freshmen received some form of financial aid. 27% of all full-time freshmen received need-based aid. The average financial indebtedness of the 2017 graduate was $17,750. The FAFSA code is 002099. The priority date for freshman financial aid applications for fall entry is January 17.

UNITED STATES NAVAL ACADEMY E-3

www.usna.edu

Annapolis, MD 21402	**(410) 293-4361** **(888) 249-7707**
Fax: (410) 293-4348	**Email: inquire@usna.edu**
Full-time: 3334 men, 1153 women	**Faculty:** 592; IIB, +$
Part-time: n/av	**Ph.D.s:** 66%
Graduate: n/av	**Student/Faculty:** 8 to 1
Year: semesters, summer session	**Tuition:** see profile
Room & Board: n/app	**Freshman Class:** 17043 applied, 1355 accepted, 1177 enrolled
SAT CR/M: 620/643 **ACT:** required	**CEEB CODE:** 5809
Application Deadline: January 31	**HIGHLY COMPETITIVE**

United States Naval Academy, founded in 1845, is a national military service college offering undergraduate degree programs and professional training in aviation, surface ships, submarines, and various military, maritime, and technical fields. The U.S. Navy pays tuition, room and board, medical and dental care, and a monthly stipend to all Naval Academy students. Graduates earn a Bachelor of Science degree and a commission in the United States Navy or the United States Marine Corps and have a five year obligation of active military service. There is 1 undergraduate school. In addition to regional accreditation, USNA has baccalaureate program accreditation with ABET and ACS. The 338-acre campus is in a small town on the Chesapeake Bay 30 miles southeast of Baltimore, Maryland and 32 miles east of Washington, D.C. Including any residence halls, there are 343 buildings.

STUDENT LIFE: 94% of undergraduates are from out of state, mostly the Middle Atlantic. Students are from 50 states, and 29 foreign countries. 64% are White; 11% Hispanic; 8% two or more races; 7% African American; 7% Asian American; 1% American Indian/Alaska Native; 1% Foreign; 1% race unknown. **Male To Female Ratio:** 2.9:1. The average age of freshmen is 18; all undergraduates, 20. 3% do not continue beyond their first year; 89% remain to graduate. **Housing:** 4650 students can be accommodated in college housing, which includes dorms. On-campus housing is guaranteed for all 4 years. Some may keep cars.

FACULTY/CLASSROOMS: 71% of faculty are male; 29% are female. All teach undergraduates, 67% do research, and 67% do both. No introductory courses are taught by graduate students. The average class size in an introductory lecture is 20; in a laboratory is 18; and in a regular course is 18.

PROGRAMS OF STUDY: USNA confers B.S. degrees. Bachelor's degrees are awarded in BUSINESS (operations research), COMMUNICATIONS AND THE ARTS (Arabic, Chinese, and English), COMPUTER AND PHYSICAL SCIENCE (chemistry, computer science, cyber operations, information sciences and systems, mathematics, oceanography, physics, and science), ENGINEERING AND ENVIRONMENTAL DESIGN (aerospace engineering, computer engineering, electrical/electronics engineering, engineering, marine engineering, mechanical engineering, naval architecture and marine engineering, nuclear engineering, ocean engineering, and systems engineering), SOCIAL SCIENCE (economics, history, and political science/government).

ACTIVITIES: There are no fraternities or sororities. There are 100 groups on campus, including bagpipe, band, cheerleading, chess, choir, chorale, chorus, communications, computers, dance, debate, drama, drill team, drum and bugle corps, ethnic, honors, international, jazz band, LGBT, literary magazine, marching band, Military Professional, musical theater, orchestra, pep band, photography, professional, radio and TV, religious, social, social service, student government, and yearbook. Popular campus events include Induction Day, Commissioning Week, which includes the Plebe Recognition Ceremony, Ring Dance, Graduation, and Army/Navy sporting events. **Sports:** There are 33 intercollegiate sports for men and 23 for women, and 15 intramural sports for men and 15 for women. Facilities include a stadium, basketball arena, Olympic pool with a diving well, a wrestling arena, hydraulically banked indoor track, outdoor track, indoor ice rink, nautilus and weight rooms, facilities for gymnastics, boxing, volleyball, swimming, water polo, racquetball, basketball and personal conditioning, squash courts, climbing wall, baseball stadium, a crew house, 18 hole golf course, soccer facility, a sailing center, indoor and outdoor tennis courts, and athletic field houses. **Graduates:** From July 1, 2016 to June 30, 2017, 1084 bachelor's degrees were awarded. The most popular majors were political science

(11%), systems engineering (10%), and economics (10%). In an average class, 91% graduate in 4 years or less. Of the 2016 graduating class, 6% were enrolled in graduate school within 6 months of graduation, and 100% were employed.

SERVICES: Counseling and information services are available, as is tutoring in some subjects, such as mathematics, chemistry, physics, and cybersecurity. **Library/Resources:** The library contains 682,396 volumes, 614 microform items, and 8,518 audio/video tapes/CDs/DVDs, and subscribes to 68,224 periodicals including electronic. Computerized library services include interlibrary loans, database searching, Internet access, and Wi-Fi capability. Special learning facilities include a planetarium, radio station, propulsion lab, wind tunnels-both subsonic and supersonic, flight simulator, space environment simulators, clean room to assemble space parts, vibration lab, oceanographic research vessel, field laboratory which includes NOAA tide guide guage and equipment for biogeochemical analysis, rotating wave tank laboratory, weather and oceanographic monitoring equipment, autonomous surface and underwater vehicles, high capacity server which provides access to near-realtime and archived geoscience data and forecast model output available to the university community, a Volt Pellatron Accelerator, state of the art liquid crystal laboratory, state of the art dielectrics lab, acoustics lab with two anechoic chambers, robotic 20 inch Cassegrain telescope, 2 warship bridge simulators, fleet of Yard Patrol Craft, fleet of 44 foot keelboats, fleet of 26 foot keelboats, fleet of 20 foot dinghies, fleet of lasers, fleet of 420's, 380 foot towing tank, 120 foot towing tank, recirculating water channel, ballasting tank, circular water basin, 2-D wave tank, ship structures lab, autonomous surface vessels lab, naval history museum, 50 yard rifle range, 15 yard pistol range, trap and skeet range, 200 yard rifle range, and a 50 foot indoor shooting range. **Physically Challenged Students:** All of the campus is accessible. Facilities include wheelchair ramps, elevators, special parking, and specially equipped restrooms. **Special:** A voluntary graduate program is available for those midshipmen who complete academic graduation requirements by the end of their seventh semester and are selected to begin master's work at nearby universities. Midshipmen selected as Trident Scholars spend their senior year in independent research at the Naval Academy. Study abroad for one semester is available in countries around the world. Honors programs are available in selected majors. There are 8 national honor societies and 10 departmental honors programs. **Visiting:** There are regularly scheduled orientations for prospective students, visitation weekends for highly competitive candidates for admission, and summer seminar weeks for rising high school seniors. There are guides for informal visits, visitors may sit in on classes, and stay overnight. To schedule a visit, contact USNA Admissions. **Campus Safety and Security:** Measures include 24-hour foot and vehicle patrol, emergency notification system, and self-defense education. There are emergency telephones, lighted pathways/sidewalks, controlled access to dorms/residences, gate guards, and dorm room lockers.

REQUIREMENTS: The SAT or ACT is required. Candidates must be unmarried with no dependents, U.S. citizens of good moral character, and between 17 and 22 years of age. Candidates should have a solid secondary school background, including 4 years each of English and math, 2 years of a foreign language, and 1 year each of U.S. history, world or European history, chemistry, physics, and computer literacy. Candidates must obtain an official nomination from congressional or military sources. An interview is conducted, and medical and physical aptitude exams must be passed to qualify for admission. AP credits are accepted. Students must complete approximately 140 semester hours, including core requirements in mathematics, engineering, natural sciences, humanities, cybersecurity, and social sciences. Professional Development courses and Physical Education are required during all 4 years. Physical readiness test must be passed semi-annually. During required summer training sessions, students train aboard U.S. Navy ships, submarines, and aircraft and with units of the U.S. Marine Corps. Graduates are obligated to serve at least 5 years on active duty as commissioned officers of the United States Navy or United States Marine Corps. **Procedure:** Freshmen are admitted summer. Entrance exams should be taken December of the junior year in high school. There are early admissions and rolling admissions plans. Applications should be filed by January 31 for fall entry. Notifications are sent April 15. Applications are accepted on-line. **Transfer Students:** All students enter as freshmen/plebes and must complete the entire 47 month program. 140 of 140 credits required for the bachelor's degree must be completed at Navy; Annapolis. **International Students:** There are 56 international students enrolled. They must take the TOEFL. They must also take the SAT or ACT.

ADMISSIONS: 8% of the 2017-2018 applicants were accepted. The SAT scores for the 2017-2018 freshman class were: Critical Reading-- 5% below 500, 37% between 500 and 599, 38% between 600 and 699, and 20% between 700 and 800. Math-- 2% below 500, 25% between 500 and 599, 41% between 600 and 699, and 40% between 700 and 800. 78% of the current freshmen were in the top fifth of their class; 91% were in the top two fifths. 177 freshmen graduated first in their class. **Admissions Contact:** USNA Admissions Office Email: *webmail@usna.edu* Web: *www.usna.edu*

FINANCIAL AID: Check with the school for current application deadlines.

UNIVERSITY OF MARYLAND UNIVERSITY COLLEGE *(The complete profile is made available exclusively on our website, www.barronspac.com)*

UNIVERSITY OF MARYLAND/BALTIMORE COUNTY D-2

www.umaryland.edu

Baltimore, MD 21250	(410) 455-2291
Fax: (410) 455-1094	**Email:** admissions@umbc.edu
Full-time: 5260 men, 4214 women	**Faculty:** I, +$
Part-time: 851 men, 700 women	**Ph.D.s:** 85%
Graduate: 1312 men, 1186 women	**Student/Faculty:** 19 to 1
Year: 4-1-4, summer session	**Tuition:** $11,518 ($25,654)
Room & Board: $11,486	**Freshman Class:** 10812 applied, 6144 accepted, 1538 enrolled
SAT CR/M/W: 600/620/580 **ACT:** 27	**CEEB CODE:** 5835
Application Deadline: February 1	**VERY COMPETITIVE**

University of Maryland/Baltimore County, is a dynamic public research university integrating teaching, research and service to benefit the citizens of Maryland. As an Honors University, the campus offers academically talented students a strong undergraduate liberal arts foundation that prepares them for graduate and professional study, entry into the workforce, and community service and leadership. UMBC emphasizes science, engineering, information technology, human services and public policy at the graduate level. There are 6 undergraduate schools and 4 graduate schools. In addition to regional accreditation, UMBC has baccalaureate program accreditation with ABET, CSWE, and CAEP. The 500-acre campus is in a suburban area 5 miles southwest of Baltimore and 35 miles north of Washington, D.C. Including any residence halls, there are 50 buildings.

STUDENT LIFE: 93% of undergraduates are from Maryland. Others are from 45 states, 104 foreign countries, and Canada. 7% are Hispanic; 43% White; 4% Foreign; 4% two or more races; 4% race unknown; 21% Asian American; 18% African American. **Male To Female Ratio:** 1.2:1. The average age of freshmen is 18; all undergraduates, 22. 13% do not continue beyond their first year; 86% remain to graduate. **Housing:** 5000 students can be accommodated in college housing, which includes gender neutral dorms and on-campus apartments. In addition, there are honors houses, language/international houses, special-interest houses, wellness and quiet-study floors, and living learning communities. On-campus housing is guaranteed for the freshman year only, is available on a first-come, and first-served basis. 74% of students live on campus. Alcohol is not permitted. All students may keep cars.

FACULTY/CLASSROOMS: 61% of faculty are male; 39% are female. No introductory courses are taught by graduate students. The average class size in an introductory lecture is 41; in a laboratory is 28; and in a regular course is 30.

PROGRAMS OF STUDY: UMBC confers B.A., B.S., B.F.A. and B.S.E. degrees. Master's and doctoral degrees are also awarded. Bachelor's degrees are awarded in AGRICULTURE (environmental studies), BIOLOGICAL SCIENCE (biology ecology and field biology, biochemistry, bioinformatics, biology/biological science, biological sciences, and cell & molecular biology), BUSINESS (entrepreneurial studies), COMMUNICATIONS AND THE ARTS (acting, Africana studies, applied art, art history, art, art and design, art history and appreciation, art studies, arts administration/management, communications, dance, design, dramatic arts, English, fine arts, French, German, linguistics, modern language, music, Russian, Spanish, theater design, and visual and performing arts),

COMPUTER AND PHYSICAL SCIENCE (applied physics, chemistry, computer science, cybernetics, cyber operations, cyber intelligence/security studies, information sciences and systems, mathematics, physics, and statistics), EDUCATION (art education and childhood education), ENGINEERING AND ENVIRONMENTAL DESIGN (chemical engineering, computer engineering, environmental science, and mechanical engineering), HEALTH PROFESSIONS (allied health, biology, emergency medical technologies, and health science), SOCIAL SCIENCE (African American studies, American studies, anthropology, classical/ancient civilization, cultural studies/critical theory & analysis, cultural anthropology, economics, gender studies, geography, history, interdisciplinary studies, philosophy, political science/government, psychology, social work, sociology, women & gender studies, and women's studies). Biological & biomedical sciences, computer & information sciences, and support services are the strongest academically. Information systems, computer science, and biological sciences have the largest enrollments.

ACTIVITIES: 4% of men belong to 11 national fraternities; 5% of women belong to 8 national sororities. There are 268 groups on campus, including art, band, cheerleading, chess, choir, chorale, chorus, computers, dance, debate, drama, environmental, ethnic, film, forensics, honors, international, jazz band, LGBT, literary magazine, Model United Nations, musical theater, newspaper, opera, orchestra, pep band, photography, political, professional, radio and TV, religious, social, social service, student government, and symphony. Popular campus events include Quadmania, Welcome Week, and Homecoming. **Sports:** There are 8 intercollegiate sports for men and 9 for women, and 16 intramural sports for men and 16 for women. Facilities include a multipurpose arena, an aquatic center, a fitness center, tennis courts, a stadium, playing and practice fields, an indoor track, an outdoor cross-country course, a golf driving range, a track and field complex, and a soccer stadium. **Graduates:** From July 1, 2016 to June 30, 2017, 2521 bachelor's degrees were awarded. The most popular majors were computer information systems, and biological/life sciences (17%), psychology, and social sciences (12%), and visual and perorming arts (6%). In an average class, 1% graduate in 3 years or less, 21% graduate in 5 years or less, and 64% graduate in 6 years or less. Of the 2016 graduating class, 7% were enrolled in graduate school within 6 months of graduation, and 83% were employed.

SERVICES: Counseling and information services are available, as is tutoring in every subject. There is a reader service for the blind, and remedial math, reading, and writing. Other services include notetakers, readers, mobility training, American Sign Language interpreters, and scribes for students who have a need based on a manual or learning disability. **Library/Resources:** The library contains 1.0 million volumes, 1.1 million microform items, and 1.9 million audio/video tapes/CDs/DVDs, and subscribes to 33,000 periodicals including electronic. Computerized library services include interlibrary loans, database searching, and Internet access. Special learning facilities include an art gallery, radio station, the Imaging Research Center, the Howard Hughes Medical Institute, and a telescope, a center for Art Design and Visual Culture and the Albin O Kuhn library, and 2 professional dance companies. **Physically Challenged Students:** 95% of the campus is accessible. Facilities include wheelchair ramps, elevators, special parking, specially equipped restrooms, special class scheduling, and lowered drinking fountains, and lowered telephones. Braille writer, tape recorders, talking book machines, TTY, talking calculators, Optacon and information on the talking computer. **Special:** Dual and student-designed majors, cooperative education programs in all majors, a Washington semester, the Sondheim Public Affairs Scholars Program, cross-registration with University of Maryland schools and Johns Hopkins University, internships, both paid and nonpaid, in public, private, and nonprofit organizations, study abroad in 19 countries, work-study programs, B.A.-B.S. degrees, pass/fail options, and nondegree study are available. UMBC also offers various opportunities in interdisciplinary studies and in such fields as artificial intelligence and optical communications. There are 15 national honor societies, Phi Beta Kappa, a freshman honors program, and 17 departmental honors programs. **Visiting:** There are regularly scheduled orientations for prospective students, including a group information session with an admissions counselor followed by a student-guided walking tour of campus. Saturday information sessions and 4 campus open houses are also scheduled each fall. Summer preview days are in July and August. There are two transfer open houses. There are guides for informal visits, visitors may sit in on classes, and stay overnight. To schedule a visit, contact the Office of Undergraduate Admissions. **Campus Safety and Security:** Measures include 24-hour foot and vehicle patrol, emergency notification system, self-defense education, and security escort services. There are shuttle buses, emergency telephones, lighted pathways/sidewalks, controlled access to dorms/residences, a 24-hour police department, and a campus risk management department.

REQUIREMENTS: The SAT or ACT is required. Minimum high school preparation should include 4 years of English and math including algebra I and II and geometry, 3 of science, social studies and history, and 2 of foreign language. An essay is required of all freshman applicants. UMBC requires applicants to be in the upper 50% of their class. A GPA of 3.0 is required. AP and CLEP credits are accepted. Important factors in the admissions decision are advanced placement or honors courses, recommendations by school officials, and leadership record. To graduate, students are required to complete at least 120 credits, including 45 at the upper-division level, with a minimum GPA of 2.0. The core curriculum includes courses in arts and humanities, social sciences, math and natural sciences, phys ed, and modern or classical language and culture. Students must pass an English composition course with a C or better. **Procedure:** Freshmen are admitted to all sessions. Entrance exams should be taken by fall of the senior year. There is an early admissions plan. Early decision applications should be filed by November 1; regular applications, by February 1 for fall entry. The fall 2017 application fee was $50. Notifications are sent February 15. 234 applicants were on the 2017 waiting list; 188 were admitted. Applications are accepted on-line. **Transfer Students:** 1187 transfer students enrolled in 2016-2017. A 2.5 cumulative GPA for all previous college work is recommended. Applicants with fewer than 30 semester hours should submit SAT scores and the high school transcript; they must also meet freshman admission requirements. 30 of 120 credits required for the bachelor's degree must be completed at UMBC. **International Students:** There are 1042 international students enrolled. They must take the TOEFL with a minimum score of 550 on the paper-based TOEFL (PBT) or 80 on the Internet-based version (iBT).

ADMISSIONS: 57% of the 2017-2018 applicants were accepted. The SAT scores for the 2017-2018 freshman class were: Critical Reading-- 8% below 500, 43% between 500 and 599, 37% between 600 and 699, and 12% between 700 and 800. Math-- 4% below 500, 33% between 500 and 599, 48% between 600 and 699, and 15% between 700 and 800. Writing-- 12% below 500, 47% between 500 and 599, 33% between 600 and 699, and 8% between 700 and 800. The ACT scores were 2% below 12, 1% between 12 and 17, 18% between 18 and 23, 55% between 24 and 29, and 24% above 30. 25% of the current freshmen were in the top fifth of their class; 54% were in the top two fifths. **Admissions Contact:** Dale Bittinger, Director of Admissions. Email: *admissions@umbc.edu* Web: *www.umaryland.edu*

FINANCIAL AID: In 2017-2018, 57% of all full-time freshmen received some form of financial aid. 54% of all full-time freshmen received need-based aid. The average freshman award was $10,402. Need-based scholarships or need-based grants averaged $9,300; need-based self-help aid (loans and jobs) averaged $3,329; non-need-based athletic scholarships averaged $10,016; other non-need-based awards and non-need-based scholarships averaged $10,180; and $3,248 from other forms of aid. 100% of undergraduate students work part-time. The average financial indebtedness of the 2017 graduate was $27,953. The priority date for freshman financial aid applications for fall entry is February 14.

UNIVERSITY OF MARYLAND/COLLEGE PARK D-3

www.umd.edu

College Park, MD 20742	**(301) 314-8385** **(800) 422-5867**
Fax: (301) 314-9693	**Email: ApplyMaryland@umd.edu**
Full-time: 13,906 men, 12,444 women	**Faculty:** 1803; I, +$
Part-time: 1240 men, 882 women	**Ph.D.s:** 91%
Graduate: 5521 men, 5090 women	**Student/Faculty:** 15 to 1
Year: semesters, summer session	**Tuition:** $10,180 ($32,044)
Room & Board: $11,758	**Freshman Class:** 30272 applied, 14538 accepted, 4553 enrolled
SAT or ACT: required	**CEEB CODE:** 5814
Application Deadline: January 20	**HIGHLY COMPETITIVE**

University of Maryland/College Park, founded in 1856, is a land-grant institution, the flagship campus of the state's university system, offering undergraduate and graduate degrees. There are 12 undergraduate schools and 13 graduate schools. In addition to regional accreditation, UMCP has baccalaureate program accreditation with AACSB, ABET, ACEJMC, ASLA, NASM, CAEP, and CADE. The 1339-acre campus is in a suburban area 3 miles northeast of Washington, D.C., and 35 miles south of Baltimore. Including any residence halls, there are 253 buildings.

STUDENT LIFE: 79% of undergraduates are from Maryland. Others are from 48 states, 57 foreign countries, and Canada. 50% are White; 5% Foreign; 4% two or more races; 2% race unknown; 16% Asian American; 13% African American; 10% Hispanic. **Male To Female Ratio:** 1.1:1. The average age of freshmen is 18; all undergraduates, 21. 5% do not continue beyond their first year; 87% remain to graduate. **Housing:** 12525 students can be accommodated in college housing, which includes dorms and on-campus apartments. In addition, there are honors houses, language/international houses, special-interest houses, fraternity houses, and sorority houses. On-campus housing is guaranteed for the freshman year only and is available on a lottery system for upperclassmen. 60% of students commute. All students may keep cars.

FACULTY/CLASSROOMS: 62% of faculty are male; 38% are female. 57% teach undergraduates, and 43% do research. Graduate students teach 12% of introductory courses. The average class size in an introductory lecture is 37; in a laboratory is 21; and in a regular course is 35.

PROGRAMS OF STUDY: UMCP confers B.A., B.S., B.L.A., B.M. and B.M.E. degrees. Master's and doctoral degrees are also awarded. Bachelor's degrees are awarded in AGRICULTURE (agricultural business management, agricultural economics, agriculture, animal science, natural resource management, and plant science), BIOLOGICAL SCIENCE (biochemistry, biology/biological science, microbiology, and nutrition), BUSINESS (accounting, business administration and management, finance, international business management, logistics, management information systems, marketing, operations management, and supply chain management), COMMUNICATIONS AND THE ARTS (Arabic, art history and appreciation, Chinese, classics, communications, dance, dramatic arts, English, English literature, film arts, foreign language, French, Germanic languages and literature, Japanese, journalism, linguistics, music, music performance, music theory and composition, romance languages and literature, Russian, Spanish, studio art, and theatre arts), COMPUTER AND PHYSICAL SCIENCE (astronomy, atmospheric sciences and meteorology, chemistry, computer science, geology, information sciences and systems, mathematics, physical sciences, and physics), EDUCATION (art education, drama education, early childhood education, education, elementary education, middle school education, music education, physical education, secondary education, and special education), ENGINEERING AND ENVIRONMENTAL DESIGN (aerospace engineering, architecture, bioengineering, chemical engineering, civil engineering, computer engineering, electrical/electronics engineering, engineering, environmental science, fire protection engineering, landscape architecture/design, materials engineering, and mechanical engineering), HEALTH PROFESSIONS (community health work, predentistry, preveterinary science, public health, speech pathology/audiology, and veterinary science), SOCIAL SCIENCE (African American studies, American studies, anthropology, criminal justice, criminology, early childhood studies, economics, family/consumer studies, geography, history, interdisciplinary studies, Italian studies, Judaic studies, philosophy, political science/government, prelaw, psychology, Russian and Slavic studies, sociology, and women's studies). Engineering, computer science, and business are the strongest academically. Biological sciences, economics, and psychology have the largest enrollments.

ACTIVITIES: 13% of men belong to 21 national fraternities; 14% of women belong to 24 national sororities. There are 675 groups on campus, including art, band, cheerleading, chess, choir, chorale, chorus, computers, dance, debate, drama, drill team, environmental, ethnic, film, forensics, honors, international, jazz band, LGBT, literary magazine, marching band, musical theater, newspaper, opera, orchestra, pep band, photography, political, professional, radio and TV, religious, social, social service, student government, symphony, and yearbook. Popular campus events include Art Attack, Union All-Niter, and Maryland Day. **Sports:** There are 8 intercollegiate sports for men and 11 for women, and 16 intramural sports for men and 16 for women. Facilities include indoor and outdoor swimming pools, intramural fields, tennis, squash, racquetball, volleyball, and basketball courts, a fitness center including weight rooms, aerobic rooms, martial arts rooms, and an indoor track, a bowling alley, golf course, an outdoor artificial turf field, a stadium, a gym, and indoor and outdoor artificial turf practice fields.

Graduates: From July 1, 2016 to June 30, 2017, 7253 bachelor's degrees were awarded. The most popular majors were engineering (14%), biological sciences (7%), and economics (5%). In an average class, 70% graduate in 4 years or less, 83% graduate in 5 years or less, and 87% graduate in 6 years or less.

SERVICES: Counseling and information services are available, as is tutoring in most subjects, such as 100- and 200-level courses. There is a reader service for the blind, and remedial math. **Library/Resources:** The library contains 4.8 million volumes, 519,086 microform items, and 445,966 audio/video tapes/CDs/DVDs, and subscribes to 155,601 periodicals including electronic. Computerized library services include interlibrary loans, database searching, Internet access, and Wi-Fi capability. Special learning facilities include an art gallery, radio station, TV station, and an observatory. **Physically Challenged Students:** 95% of the campus is accessible. Facilities include wheelchair ramps, elevators, special parking, specially equipped restrooms, special class scheduling, lowered drinking fountains, and lowered telephones. Special shuttle service, and electronic doors. **Special:** Each of the 12 undergraduate schools offers special programs, and there is a campus-wide co-op education program offering engineering and other majors. In addition, the university offers cross-registration with other colleges in the Consortium of Universities of the Washington Metropolitan area, several living-learning programs for undergraduates, the B.A./B.S. degree in most majors, dual and student-designed majors, non-degree study, an accelerated veterinary medicine program, varied study abroad opportunities, work-study programs with government and nonprofit organizations, and internship opportunities with federal and state legislators, the local media, and various federal agencies. There are 49 national honor societies, Phi Beta Kappa, a freshman honors program, and 39 departmental honors programs. **Visiting:** There are regularly scheduled orientations for prospective students, consisting of 3 fall and 4 spring open house programs for admitted students, as well as regularly scheduled information sessions followed by a campus tour. There are guides for informal visits, visitors may sit in on classes, and stay overnight. To schedule a visit, contact the Office of Undergraduate Admissions. **Campus Safety and Security:** Measures include 24-hour foot and vehicle patrol, emergency notification system, self-defense education, and security escort services. There are shuttle buses, emergency telephones, lighted pathways/sidewalks, controlled access to dorms/residences, video surveillance.

REQUIREMENTS: The SAT or ACT is required. The ACT Optional Writing test is also required. The university evaluates exam scores along with GPA, curriculum, and other criteria. Applicants should be graduates of accredited secondary schools or have the GED. Secondary preparation should include 4 years of English, 3 of history or social sciences, 2 of algebra and 1 of plane geometry, and 2 of lab sciences. An essay and counselor recommendation are required. Music majors must also audition. Applicants who submit the ACT rather than the SAT must submit the ACT Writing Test. AP and CLEP credits are accepted. Important factors in the admissions decision are advanced placement or honors courses, recommendations by school officials, parents or siblings attended your school, evidence of special talent, extracurricular activities record, and geographical diversity. Most programs require a minimum of 120 credits for graduation; the number of hours required in the major varies. All students are required to complete a set of General Education courses. **Procedure:** Freshmen are admitted fall, spring, and summer. Entrance exams should be taken at the end of the junior year or the beginning of the senior year. There are deferred admissions and rolling admissions plans. Early decision applications should be filed by November 1; regular applications, by January 20 for fall entry; and December 1 for spring entry. The fall 2017 application fee was $75. Notification of early decision is sent February 15; regular decision, April 1. Applications are accepted on-line. **Transfer Students:** 2197 transfer students enrolled in 2016-2017. Transfer applicants from regionally accredited institutions should have attempted at least 12 credits and have earned at least a 2.0 GPA, although this requirement varies depending on space available. Applicants from Maryland community colleges may be given special consideration. 30 of 120 credits required for the bachelor's degree must be completed at UMCP. **International Students:** There are 1238 international students enrolled. They must take the TOEFL with a minimum score of 100 on the Internet-based version (iBT). Students must take the IELTS. They must also take the SAT or ACT.

ADMISSIONS: 48% of the 2017-2018 applicants were accepted. The SAT scores for the 2017-2018 freshman class were: Critical Reading-- 5% below 500, 22% between 500 and 599, 49% between 600 and 699, and 24% between 700 and 800. Math-- 4% below 500, 15% between 500 and

599, 43% between 600 and 699, and 38% between 700 and 800. The ACT scores were 7% between 18 and 23, 35% between 24 and 29, and 58% above 30. **Admissions Contact:** Admissions Officer Email: *ApplyMaryland@umd.edu* Web: *www.umd.edu*

FINANCIAL AID: In 2017-2018, 86% of all full-time freshmen received some form of financial aid. 37% of all full-time freshmen received need-based aid. The average freshman award was $14,586. Need-based scholarships or need-based grants averaged $11,040; need-based self-help aid (loans and jobs) averaged $5,194; non-need-based athletic scholarships averaged $20,282; and other non-need-based awards and non-need-based scholarships averaged $6,577. 19% of undergraduate students work part-time. The average financial indebtedness of the 2017 graduate was $26,818. The FAFSA code is 002103. The priority date for freshman financial aid applications for fall entry is February 15.

UNIVERSITY OF MARYLAND/EASTERN SHORE *(The complete profile is made available exclusively on our website, www.barronspac.com)*

WASHINGTON ADVENTIST UNIVERSITY *(The complete profile is made available exclusively on our website, www.barronspac.com)*

WASHINGTON COLLEGE — E-2

www.washcoll.edu

Chestertown, MD 21620
(410) 778-7700
(800) 422-1782
Email: wc_admissions@washcoll.edu

Full-time: 639 men, 819 women	**Faculty:** 117; IIB, av$
Part-time: 9 men, 12 women	**Ph.D.s:** 98%
Graduate: n/av	**Student/Faculty:** 12 to 1
Year: semesters	**Tuition:** $43,850
Room & Board: $10,612	**Freshman Class:** 6847 applied, 3702 accepted, 391 enrolled
SAT CR/M: 590/590	**CEEB CODE:** 5888
Application Deadline: February 15	**VERY COMPETITIVE**

Washington College, founded in 1782, is an independent college offering programs in the liberal arts and sciences, business management, and teacher preparation. There are 4 undergraduate schools. The 112-acre campus is in a small town 75 miles from Baltimore, Washington DC, and Philadelphia. Including any residence halls, there are 75 buildings.

STUDENT LIFE: 59% of undergraduates are from out of state, mostly the Middle Atlantic. Students are from 37 states, 31 foreign countries, and Canada. 67% are from public schools. 72% are White; 11% Foreign; 5% African American; 5% race unknown; 3% Hispanic; 2% Asian American; 2% two or more races; 1% American Indian/Alaska Native. **Female To Male Ratio:** 1.3:1. The average age of freshmen is 18; all undergraduates, 20. 17% do not continue beyond their first year; 75% remain to graduate. **Housing:** 1226 students can be accommodated in college housing, which includes single-sex and coed dorms, on-campus apartments, special-interest houses, fraternity houses, International house, a science house. There is also substance-free housing, theme housing, and wellness housing. On-campus housing is guaranteed for the freshman year only and is available on a lottery system for upperclassmen. 85% of students live on campus; of those, 65% remain on campus on weekends. All students may keep cars.

FACULTY/CLASSROOMS: 56% of faculty are male; 44% are female. All teach undergraduates. No introductory courses are taught by graduate students. The average class size in an introductory lecture is 15; in a laboratory is 16; and in a regular course is 15.

PROGRAMS OF STUDY: WC confers B.A. and B.S. degrees. Master's degrees are also awarded. Bachelor's degrees are awarded in AGRICULTURE (environmental studies), BIOLOGICAL SCIENCE (biology/biological science), BUSINESS (business administration and management), COMMUNICATIONS AND THE ARTS (art, dramatic arts, English, fine arts, French, German, music, and Spanish), COMPUTER AND PHYSICAL SCIENCE (chemistry, computer science, mathematics, and physics), ENGINEERING AND ENVIRONMENTAL DESIGN (environmental science), SOCIAL SCIENCE (American studies, anthropology, economics, history, humanities, interdisciplinary studies, international studies, liberal arts, sciences, general studies, humanities, philosophy, political science/government, psychology, and sociology). Biology, business management, and psychology have the largest enrollments.

ACTIVITIES: 8% of men belong to 3 national fraternities; 14% of women belong to 3 national sororities. There are 100 groups on campus, including band, chorale, chorus, computers, dance, debate, drama, environmental, ethnic, honors, international, jazz band, LGBT, literary magazine, minority and human rights, newspaper, orchestra, photography, political, professional, radio and TV, religious, social, social service, student government, and yearbook. Popular campus events include Fall and Spring Convocations, George Washington Birthday Ball, War on the Shore, and May Day. **Sports:** There are 8 intercollegiate sports for men and 10 for women, and 12 intramural sports for men and 11 for women. Facilities include a stadium, swim center, gym, field house, squash and racquetball courts, fitness center, playing and practice fields, and a boathouse. **Graduates:** From July 1, 2015 to June 30, 2016, 340 bachelor's degrees were awarded. The most popular majors were social sciences (20%), business and marketing (15%), and biological and life sciences (11%). 75 companies recruited on campus in 2015-2016. In an average class, 2% graduate in 3 years or less, 72% graduate in 4 years or less, 74% graduate in 5 years or less, and 76% graduate in 6 years or less. Of the 2015 graduating class, 15% were enrolled in graduate school within 6 months of graduation, and 75% were employed.

SERVICES: Counseling and information services are available, as is tutoring in every subject, and remedial math and writing. **Library/Resources:** The library contains 325,000 volumes, 100,635 microform items, 8,750 audio/video tapes/CDs/DVDs, and subscribes to 28,300 periodicals including electronic. Computerized library services include interlibrary loans, database searching, Internet access, and Wi-Fi capability. Special learning facilities include an art gallery, and radio station. The Center for the American Experience, the Center for Environment and Society, the Kohl Gallery, the Rose O'Neill Literary House, the Geographic Information Systems (GIS) laboratory, and the Chester River Watershed Observatory. **Physically Challenged Students:** 95% of the campus is accessible. Facilities include wheelchair ramps, elevators, special parking, specially equipped restrooms, special class scheduling, lowered drinking fountains, lowered telephones, motorized carts, and curb cuts. **Special:** A program that provides internships, externships, and job shadowing during all four years is available in all majors. There is study abroad in 26 countries and a Washington, DC semester. The college offers a 3-2 nursing program with Johns Hopkins University and a 3-2 pharmacology program, along with an option for a student-designed interdisciplinary major. There are 19 national honor societies and a chapter of Phi Beta Kappa. **Visiting:** Regularly scheduled orientations are available for prospective students consisting of weekday visits. There are also guides for informal visits and visitors may sit in on classes. To schedule a visit, contact the Admissions Office. **Campus Safety and Security:** Measures include 24-hour foot and vehicle patrol, emergency notification system, security escort services, emergency telephones, lighted pathways/sidewalks, controlled access to dorms/residences, and peer education through student groups.

REQUIREMENTS: Applicants must be graduates of an accredited secondary school or have a GED. 16 Carnegie units are required; 20 are recommended. Applicants should take high school courses in English, foreign language, history, math, science, and social studies. An essay is required, and an interview is recommended. Either the SAT or the ACT is required. AP and CLEP credits are accepted. Important factors in the admissions decision are advanced placement or honors courses, recommendations by school officials, and leadership record. All students are required to take a freshman Global Perspective seminar and courses distributed among the social sciences, natural sciences, humanities, quantitative studies, foreign languages, and a writing requirement. The Senior Capstone Experience consists of a comprehensive exam, thesis, or independent project. Students must complete 128 credit hours, including at least 32 in the major, to graduate. A minimum GPA of 2.0 is required. **Procedure:** Freshmen are admitted in the fall and spring. Entrance exams should be taken in the spring of the junior year or fall of the senior year. There are early decision, deferred admissions, and rolling admissions plans. Early decision applications should be filed by November 1; regular applications, by February 15 for fall entry; and December 1 for spring entry, along with a $50 fee. Notification is sent on a rolling basis. 64 early decision candidates were accepted for the 2016-2017 class. 384 applicants were on the 2016 waiting list; 2 were admitted. Applications are accepted online. **Transfer Students:** 36 transfer students enrolled in 2015-2016. Requirements for students are a minimum GPA of 2.3, a high school transcript, college transcript (s) and essay or personal statement.

An interview and standardized test scores are recommended. 56 of 128 credits required for the bachelor's degree must be completed at WC. **International Students:** There are 136 international students enrolled. The school actively recruits these students. They must take the TOEFL with a minimum score of 550 on the paper-based TOEFL (PBT) or 79 on the Internet-based version (iBT). They must also take the SAT or ACT.

ADMISSIONS: 54% of the 2016-2017 applicants were accepted. The SAT scores for the 2016-2017 freshman class were: Critical Reading-- 7% below 500, 42% between 500 and 599, 43% between 600 and 699, and 8% between 700 and 800. Math-- 11% below 500, 41% between 500 and 599, 42% between 600 and 699, and 6% between 700 and 800. 55% of the current freshmen were in the top fifth of their class; 82% were in the top two fifths. **Admissions Contact:** Satyajit Dattagupta, Vice President of Enrollment Management. Email: *wc_admissions@washcoll.edu* Web: *www.washcoll.edu*

FINANCIAL AID: In 2016-2017, 92% of all full-time freshmen and 90% of continuing full-time students received some form of financial aid. 100% of all full-time freshmen and 98% of continuing full-time students received need-based aid. The average freshman award was $31,250. Need-based scholarships or need-based grants averaged $27,166; need-based self-help aid (loans and jobs) averaged $4,723; other non-need-based awards and non-need-based scholarships averaged $16,766; and $4,472 from other forms of aid. 40% of undergraduate students work part-time. Average annual earnings from campus work are $1000. The average financial indebtedness of the 2016 graduate was $36,911. WC is a member of CSS. The college's own financial statement, signed copies of the student's and parents' federal tax returns, and W2s are required. The FAFSA code is 002108. The deadline for filing freshman financial aid applications for fall entry is February 15.

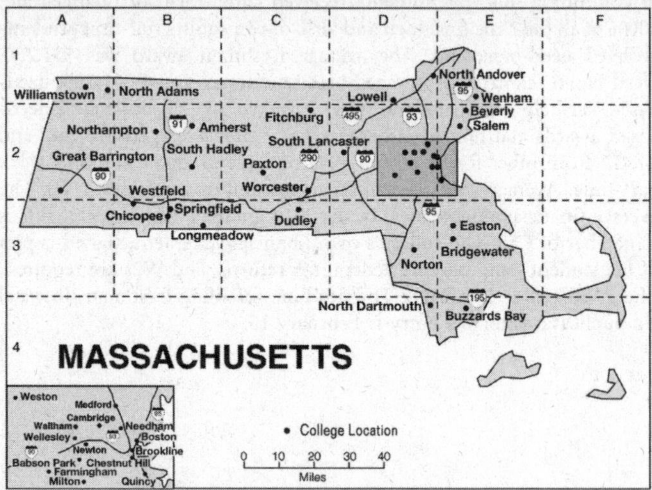

AMERICAN INTERNATIONAL COLLEGE *(The complete profile is made available exclusively on our website, www.barronspac.com)*

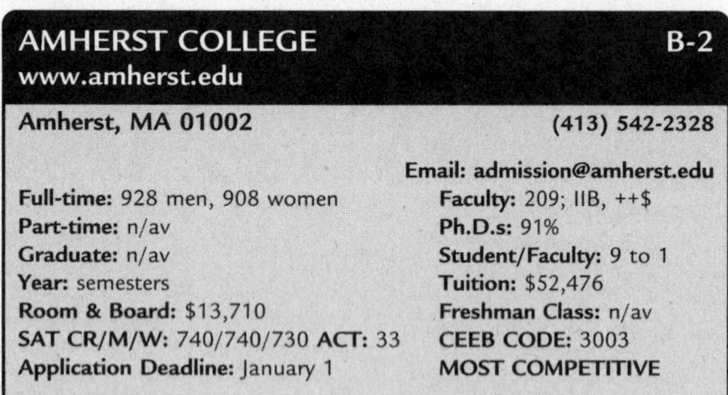

AMHERST COLLEGE — B-2

www.amherst.edu

Amherst, MA 01002 — **(413) 542-2328**

Email: admission@amherst.edu

Full-time: 928 men, 908 women	**Faculty:** 209; IIB, ++$
Part-time: n/av	**Ph.D.s:** 91%
Graduate: n/av	**Student/Faculty:** 9 to 1
Year: semesters	**Tuition:** $52,476
Room & Board: $13,710	**Freshman Class:** n/av
SAT CR/M/W: 740/740/730 **ACT:** 33	**CEEB CODE:** 3003
Application Deadline: January 1	**MOST COMPETITIVE**

Amherst College, founded in 1821, is a private liberal arts institution. In addition to regional accreditation, AC has baccalaureate program accreditation with NEASC-CIHE. The 1015-acre campus is in a small town 90 miles west of Boston. Including any residence halls, there are 75 buildings.

STUDENT LIFE: 87% of undergraduates are from out of state, mostly the Middle Atlantic. 9% are Foreign; 5% two or more races; 43% White; 3% race unknown; 14% Asian American; 14% Hispanic; 12% African American. **Female To Male Ratio:** 1.0:1. The average age of freshmen is 22; all undergraduates, 20. 2% do not continue beyond their first year; 95% remain to graduate. **Housing:** College-sponsored housing includes dorms. In addition, there are language/international houses, special-interest houses, and cooperative houses. On-campus housing is guaranteed for all 4 years. 98% of students live on campus. Upperclassmen may keep cars.

FACULTY/CLASSROOMS: 52% of faculty are male; 48% are female. All teach undergraduates, 77% do research, and 77% do both. No introductory courses are taught by graduate students. The average class size in an introductory lecture is 26; in a laboratory is 17; and in a regular course is 17.

PROGRAMS OF STUDY: AC confers B.A. degrees. Bachelor's degrees are awarded in AGRICULTURE (environmental studies), BIOLOGICAL SCIENCE (biochemistry, biology/biological science, biophysics, and neurosciences), COMMUNICATIONS AND THE ARTS (art history, art studies, classics, dance, English, film, television and digital media, fine arts, French, German, music, Russian, Spanish, and theatre studies), COMPUTER AND PHYSICAL SCIENCE (astronomy, chemistry, computer science, geology, mathematics, physics, and statistics), EDUCATION (Asian studies), SOCIAL SCIENCE (African American studies, American studies, anthropology, architectural studies, economics, European studies, history, interdisciplinary studies, law, philosophy, political science/government, psychology, religion, sociology, and women & gender studies). Economics, English, and political science have the largest enrollments.

ACTIVITIES: There are no fraternities or sororities. There are 150 groups on campus, including art, band, cheerleading, chess, choir, chorale, chorus, communications, computers, dance, debate, drama, environmental, ethnic, film, honors, international, jazz band, LGBT, literary magazine, musical theater, newspaper, opera, orchestra, photography, political, professional, radio and TV, religious, social, social service, student government, symphony, and yearbook. Popular campus events include Fall Festival, Harlem Renaissance, and Spring Weekend Concert. **Sports:** There are 13 intercollegiate sports for men and 14 for women, and 6 intramural sports for men and 6 for women. Facilities include a pool, field house, gyms, a hockey rink, an outdoor track, a fitness center, international squash courts, an indoor jogging track, indoor and outdoor tennis courts, baseball and softball diamonds, a golf course, and playing fields. **Graduates:** From July 1, 2016 to June 30, 2017, 432 bachelor's degrees were awarded. The most popular majors were economics (17%), mathematics (14%), and psychology (13%). In an average class, 86% graduate in 4 years or less, 92% graduate in 5 years or less, and 93% graduate in 6 years or less.

SERVICES: Counseling and information services are available, as is tutoring in every subject. There is a reader service for the blind. A quantitative skills center and a writing center are also available. **Library/Resources:** The library contains 1.5 million volumes, 448,680 microform items, and 60,547 audio/video tapes/CDs/DVDs, and subscribes to 16,069 periodicals including electronic. Computerized library services include interlibrary loans, database searching, Internet access, and Wi-Fi capability. Special learning facilities include an art gallery, natural history museum, planetarium, radio station, an observatory, the Emily Dickinson Museum, the Amherst Center for Russian Culture, and the Center for Humanistic Inquiry. **Physically Challenged Students:** Facilities include wheelchair ramps, elevators, special parking, specially equipped restrooms, special class scheduling, lowered drinking fountains, lowered telephones, and special housing. **Special:** Students may cross-register through the Five College Consortium, the other members of which are all within 10 miles of Amherst, or through the Twelve College Exchange Program. A number of Interterm and summer internships are available, as is study-abroad in 40 countries. Dual majors, triple majors, student-designed interdisciplinary majors based on independent study as of junior or senior year, and work-study programs are possible. There are limited pass/fail options. There are 2 national honor societies, Phi Beta Kappa, and 38 departmental honors programs. **Visiting:** There are regularly scheduled orientations for prospective students, dean-led information sessions and student-led tours. There are guides for informal visits, visitors may sit in on classes, and stay overnight. To schedule a visit, contact the Admission Office. **Campus Safety and Security:** Measures include 24-hour foot and vehicle patrol, emergency notification system, self-defense education, and security escort services. There are emergency telephones, lighted pathways/sidewalks, controlled access to dorms/residences, Amherst College Emergency Medical Service, and access code pad security to dorms.

REQUIREMENTS: Amherst recommends that applicants take 4 years each of English, and math, 3 or 4 years of a foreign language, 2 years each of history and social science, 3 years of natural science (with at least one lab science). Required application materials include: Application, Writing Supplement, SAT or ACT scores. Recommendations (1 counselor and 2 teacher) and high school transcript. To earn the B.A., all students must complete 32 courses, equivalent to 128 credits, 8 to 14 of which are in the major, with at least a C average. Other than a 1-semester freshman seminar in liberal studies, there are no specific course requirements. A thesis or comparable work is required for honors candidates. **Procedure:** Freshmen are admitted fall. Entrance exams should be taken no later than December of the senior year. There are early decision and deferred admissions plans. Early decision applications should be filed by November 15; regular applications, by January 1 for fall entry. The fall 2017 application fee was $60. Notification of early decision is sent December 15; regular decision, April 1. 180 early decision candidates were accepted for the 2017-2018 class. 582 applicants were on the 2017 waiting list; 3 were admitted. Applications are accepted on-line. **Transfer Students:** 15 transfer students enrolled in 2016-2017. Applicants must have full sophomore standing prior to applying and a minimum 3.0 GPA in previous college work. Transfers are accepted for the sophomore and junior classes only, and Amherst recommends that they submit SAT or ACT scores, plus high school and college transcripts, and seek a personal interview. 64 of 128 credits required for the bachelor's degree must be completed at Amherst. **International Students:** There are 175 international students enrolled. They must take the TOEFL with a minimum score of 600 on the paper-based TOEFL (PBT) or 100 on the Internet-based version (iBT). Students must take the MELAB, or the SAT: ELAP if English is not the applicant's first language.

ADMISSIONS: 14% of the 2017-2018 applicants were accepted. The SAT scores for the 2017-2018 freshman class were: Critical Reading-- 1% between 500 and 599, 31% between 600 and 699, and 68% between 700 and 800. Math-- 1% between 500 and 599, 32% between 600 and 699, and 67% between 700 and 800. Writing-- 3% between 500 and 599, 27% between 600 and 699, and 70% between 700 and 800. The ACT scores were 11% between 24 and 29, and 89% above 30. 95% of the current freshmen were in the top fifth of their class; 99% were in the top two fifths. **Admissions Contact:** Katharine L. Fretwell, Dean of Admission and Financial Aid. Email: *admission@amherst.edu* Web: *www.amherst.edu*

FINANCIAL AID: In 2017-2018, 52% of all full-time freshmen received some form of financial aid. 52% of all full-time freshmen received need-based aid. The average freshman award was $52,877. Need-based scholarships or need-based grants averaged $51,513; need-based self-help aid (loans and jobs) averaged $1,976 ($2,200 maximum); and other non-need-based awards and non-need-based scholarships averaged $2,000 ($2,000 maximum). 60% of undergraduate students work part-time. The average financial indebtedness of the 2017 graduate was $18,662. AC is a member of CSS. The CSS/Profile is required. The FAFSA code is 002115. The priority date for freshman financial aid applications for fall entry is February 15.

ANNA MARIA COLLEGE C-2

www.annamaria.edu

Paxton, MA 01612 — **(508) 849-3306**, **(800) 344-4586**

Fax: (508) 849-3362 — **Email: jhamel@annamaria.edu**

Full-time: 349 men, 516 women	**Faculty:** 41
Part-time: 144 men, 109 women	**Ph.D.s:** 61%
Graduate: 166 men, 147 women	**Student/Faculty:** 11 to 1
Year: semesters, summer session	**Tuition:** $37,130
Room & Board: $13,890	**Freshman Class:** 2089 applied, 1655 accepted, 272 enrolled
SAT CR/M/W: 509/500/492 **ACT:** required	**CEEB CODE:** 3005
Application Deadline: March 15	**COMPETITIVE**

Anna Maria College is a private, Catholic, co-educational institution founded in 1946 by the Sisters of Saint Anne. The college prides itself on providing a values-based, service-focused liberal arts education offering a variety of undergraduate majors, as well as many graduate and certificate programs, both on-ground and online. Anna Maria offers more than 30 undergraduate degree programs with popular majors including Business, Criminal Justice, Education, Fire Science, Health Science, Music and Art Therapy, Nursing, Social Work and Sport Management. There are 5 undergraduate schools and 1 graduate school. In addition to regional accreditation, AMC has baccalaureate program accreditation with CSWE, NASM, NLN, CAEP, ACEN, and AMTA. The 192-acre campus is in a small town 8 miles northwest of Worcester. Including any residence halls, there are 13 buildings.

STUDENT LIFE: 73% of undergraduates are from Massachusetts. Others are from 28 states, 2 foreign countries, and Canada. 8% are race unknown; 64% White; 2% Asian American; 13% African American; 11% Hispanic; 1% two or more races. **Female To Male Ratio:** 1.2:1. The average age of freshmen is 19; all undergraduates, 20. 32% do not continue beyond their first year; 49% remain to graduate. **Housing:** 711 students can be accommodated in college housing, which includes dorms, and substance-free housing. On-campus housing is guaranteed for the freshman year only, is available on a first-come, first-served basis, and is available on a lottery system for upperclassmen. 63% of students live on campus. All students may keep cars.

FACULTY/CLASSROOMS: 50% of faculty are male; 50% are female. All teach undergraduates. No introductory courses are taught by graduate students. The average class size in an introductory lecture is 20; in a laboratory is 20; and in a regular course is 13.

PROGRAMS OF STUDY: AMC confers B.A., B.S., B.M., and B.S.N. degrees. Master's degrees are also awarded. Bachelor's degrees are awarded in BUSINESS (business administration and management and sports management), COMMUNICATIONS AND THE ARTS (art, English, graphic design, media arts, modern language, music, music performance, studio art, and visual and performing arts), COMPUTER AND PHYSICAL SCIENCE (computer science), EDUCATION (early childhood education, elementary education, health education, and music education), ENGINEERING AND ENVIRONMENTAL DESIGN (environmental science), HEALTH PROFESSIONS (art therapy, emergency medical services, music therapy, and nursing), SOCIAL SCIENCE (counseling/psychology, criminal justice, fire science, history, human development, humanities, liberal arts/general studies, paralegal studies, political science/government, psychology, public administration, religion, social science, social work, and sociology). Nursing, health science, criminal justice, business, fire science, paramedic science, art and music therapy are the strongest academically. Nursing, criminal justice, fire science, and business have the largest enrollments.

ACTIVITIES: There are no fraternities or sororities. There are 32 groups on campus, including art, band, cheerleading, choir, chorus, computers, dance, drama, ethnic, honors, international, jazz band, LGBT, marching band, musical theater, newspaper, political, professional, religious, social, social service, student government, and yearbook. Popular campus events include Highlighter Party, Sporting Events, Dances, Skating, the Annual Pig Roast/Spring Weekend, and traveling Broadway shows. **Sports:** There are 6 intercollegiate sports for men and 7 for women, and 3 intramural sports for men and 3 for women. Facilities include field hockey, soccer and lacrosse, football, a synthetic turf field, basketball, volleyball, and a fitness center for aerobics and weight training. Our exercise equipment includes treadmills, exercycles, and stair climbers, along with free weights and a complete universal machine, women's tennis program, indoor courts and outdoor courts, riding lessons, boarding and competitive equestrian competitions. **Graduates:** From July 1, 2016 to June 30, 2017, 268 bachelor's degrees were awarded. The most popular majors were nursing (35%), fire science (21%), and criminal justice (12%). In an average class, 36% graduate in 4 years or less and 41% graduate in 6 years or less.

SERVICES: Counseling and information services are available, as is tutoring in every subject. There is a reader service for the blind, and remedial math, reading, and writing. **Library/Resources:** The library contains 58,957 volumes, and 774 audio/video tapes/CDs/DVDs, and subscribes to 102 periodicals including electronic. Computerized library services include interlibrary loans, database searching, Internet access, and Wi-Fi capability. Special learning facilities include an art gallery, music facilities/labs, and audiovisual center. The Trinity Hall East offers placement testing, workshops on writing and study skills, and directs a peer-tutoring program supporting courses in mathematics, business, English, languages, and science. **Physically Challenged Students:** 80% of the campus is accessible. Facilities include wheelchair ramps, elevators, special parking, specially equipped restrooms, special class scheduling, lowered drinking fountains, and special housing. **Special:** Cross-registration with the Higher Education Consortium of Central Massachusetts, and internships in all majors are available. The college offers study abroad, a Washington semester, student-designed majors, accelerated degree programs, a general studies degree, credit by exam, work-study programs, and 5-year advanced degree programs in business, counseling psychology, criminal justice, education, and public administration. There are 7 national honor societies and a freshman honors program. **Visiting:** There are regularly scheduled orientations for prospective students, including on-campus interviews, campus tours, day visitation program by appointment, and a fall open house. There are guides for informal visits, visitors may sit in on classes, and stay overnight. To schedule a visit, contact Nancy Dowd at ndowd@annamaria.edu. **Campus Safety and Security:** Measures include 24-hour foot and vehicle patrol, emergency notification system, and security escort services. There are shuttle buses, emergency telephones, and lighted pathways/sidewalks.

REQUIREMENTS: A GED is accepted. 16 academic units are recommended, including 4 years of English, 2 years each of foreign language, history or social studies, math, and sciences. An interview is recommended. When applicable, an audition and portfolio are required. An essay and one letter of recommendation are required. A GPA of 2.0 is required. AP and CLEP credits are accepted. Important factors in the admissions decision are advanced placement or honors courses, evidence of special talent, and recommendations by school officials. The 54-credit core curriculum consists of classes in English, literature, math, natural science, foreign language, fine arts, history, philosophy, social/behavioral sciences, and religious studies. A total of 120 credits is required for graduation, with a minimum of 30 in the major and a 2.0 GPA. **Procedure:** Freshmen are admitted fall and spring. There are early admissions, deferred admissions, and rolling admissions plans. Early decision applications should be filed by November 15; regular applications, by March 15 for fall entry; and November 15 for spring entry. The fall 2017 application fee was $25. Notification is sent on a rolling basis. Applications are accepted on-line. **Transfer Students:** 61 transfer students enrolled in 2016-2017. Transfers with a minimum GPA of 2.0 are accepted for upper-division work. High school and college transcripts are required. An essay or personal statement and a statement of good standing from prior institutions are also required. 45 of 120 credits required for the bachelor's degree must be completed at AMC. **International Students:** There is 1 international students enrolled. They must take the TOEFL, IELTS, or Testing with an International School Partner. Nursing students will be required to submit the SAT or the ACT or the TEAS test.

Admissions Contact: John Hamel, Vice President for Enrollment Management. Email: *jhamel@annamaria.edu* Web: *www.annamaria.edu*

FINANCIAL AID: In 2017-2018, 100% of all full-time freshmen received some form of financial aid. 81% of all full-time freshmen received need-based aid. The average freshman award was $27,703. Need-based scholarships or need-based grants averaged $8,261; and need-based self-help aid (loans and jobs) averaged $5,571. 22% of undergraduate students work part-time. The state aid form is required. International students interested in receiving consideration for FA should submit International financial aid form. The FAFSA code is 002117. Check with the school for current application deadlines.

ASSUMPTION COLLEGE C-2

www.assumption.edu

Worcester, MA 01609 (508) 767-7285 (866) 477-7776

Fax: (508) 799-4412 **Email:** admiss@assumption.edu

Full-time: 815 men, 1110 women	**Faculty:** 143; IIA, -$
Part-time: 3 men, 1 women	**Ph.D.s:** 91%
Graduate: 100 men, 294 women	**Student/Faculty:** 11 to 1
Year: semesters, summer session	**Tuition:** $36,260
Room & Board: $12,195	**Freshman Class:** 4508 applied, 3561 accepted, 492 enrolled
SAT EBR-W/M: 586/579 **ACT:** 26	**CEEB CODE:** 3009
Application Deadline: February 15	**VERY COMPETITIVE**

Assumption College, a Catholic institution sponsored by the Augustinians of the Assumption and rooted in the Catholic intellectual tradition, strives to form graduates known for critical intelligence, thoughtful citizenship and compassionate service. We pursue these ambitious goals through a curriculum grounded in the liberal arts and extending to the domain of professional studies. Enlivened by the Catholic affirmation of the harmony of faith and reason, we aim, by the pursuit of the truth, to transform the minds and hearts of students. Assumption favors diversity and ecumenically welcomes all who share its goals. There is 1 undergraduate school and 1 graduate school. In addition to regional accreditation, Assumption College has baccalaureate program accreditation with CRE and ACS. The 180-acre campus is in a suburban area 45 miles west of Boston in New England's second-largest city, Worcester, MA. Including any residence halls, there are 51 buildings.

STUDENT LIFE: 65% of undergraduates are from Massachusetts. Others are from 29 states, 21 foreign countries, and Canada. 69% are from public schools. 77% are White; 7% Hispanic; 5% African American; 4% race unknown; 3% Asian American; 2% Foreign; 2% two or more races; 1% American Indian/Alaska Native. **Female To Male Ratio:** 1.5:1. The average age of freshmen is 18; all undergraduates, 20. 18% do not continue beyond their first year; 71% remain to graduate. **Housing:** 1879 students can be accommodated in college housing, which includes dorms and on-campus apartments. In addition, there are special-interest houses, freshman dorms, substance-free dorms, first-year experience dorm, and a living/learning center. On-campus housing is guaranteed for all 4 years. 85% of students live on campus. Upperclassmen may keep cars.

FACULTY/CLASSROOMS: 56% of faculty are male; 44% are female. All teach undergraduates. No introductory courses are taught by graduate students. The average class size in a laboratory is 16 and in a regular course is 20.

PROGRAMS OF STUDY: Assumption College confers B.A. degrees. Master's degrees are also awarded. Bachelor's degrees are awarded in BIOLOGICAL SCIENCE (biology/biological science and molecular biology), BUSINESS (accounting, business administration and management, international business management, marketing management, and organizational behavior), COMMUNICATIONS AND THE ARTS (English, graphic design, music, and Spanish), COMPUTER AND PHYSICAL SCIENCE (actuarial science, chemistry, computer science, data analytics, and mathematics), EDUCATION (education), ENGINEERING AND ENVIRONMENTAL DESIGN (environmental science), HEALTH PROFESSIONS (health science), SOCIAL SCIENCE (criminology, economics, history, human services, international studies, Latin American studies, philosophy, political science/government, psychology, sociology, and theological studies). Business studies, natural sciences, and English have the largest enrollments.

ACTIVITIES: There are no fraternities or sororities. There are 60 groups on campus, including art, band, cheerleading, choir, chorale, chorus, computers, dance, drama, environmental, ethnic, film, honors, international, jazz band, literary magazine, musical theater, newspaper, orchestra, pep band, photography, political, professional, radio and TV, religious, social, social service, student government, and yearbook. Popular campus events include Midnight Madness Basketball Kickoff, Campus Concert, and Duck Day. **Sports:** There are 10 intercollegiate sports for men and 11 for women, and 8 intramural sports for men and 8 for women. Facilities include a multisport stadium, a gym, baseball and softball diamonds, a field hockey area, a soccer field, tennis courts, a 6-lane swimming pool, jogging/walking track, racquetball courts, an aerobics/dance studio, a multi-purpose room with TRX equipment, fully equipped bodymaster and free-weight rooms, a fitness center, a varsity weight room, and a field house with multipurpose courts for basketball, volleyball, and floor hockey. **Graduates:** From July 1, 2016 to June 30, 2017, 404 bachelor's degrees were awarded. The most popular majors were human services and rehabilitation studies (13%), marketing (9%), and management (8%). In an average class, 1% graduate in 3 years or less, 68% graduate in 4 years or less, 70% graduate in 5 years or less, and 71% graduate in 6 years or less. Of the 2016 graduating class, 23% were enrolled in graduate school within 6 months of graduation, and 62% were employed.

SERVICES: Counseling and information services are available, as is tutoring in most subjects. There is a reader service for the blind. There is signing for the deaf, and technology services for the disabled. **Library/Resources:** The library contains 291,240 volumes, 8,619 microform items, and 26,000 audio/video tapes/CDs/DVDs, and subscribes to 47,526 periodicals including electronic. Computerized library services include interlibrary loans, database searching, Internet access, and Wi-Fi capability. Special learning facilities include a radio station and TV station. **Physically Challenged Students:** 69% of the campus is accessible. Facilities include wheelchair ramps, elevators, special parking, specially equipped restrooms, special class scheduling, lowered drinking fountains, lowered telephones, and special housing. **Special:** Co-op program in marine studies. Cross-registration with the Higher Education Consortium of Central Massachusetts is offered. The college has its own study abroad campus in Rome, and study abroad is available through other providers as well. The college offers internships, a Washington semester, student-designed and dual majors, credit by exam, and credit for military experience. The college offers 6-in-5 programs in accounting (BA/MBA), special education(BA/MA), school counseling (BA/MA), and rehabilitation counseling (BA/MA); a 3/-2 program in engineering with the University of Notre Dame, and multiple combined degree programs with other institutions. There are 12 national honor societies and a freshman honors program. **Visiting:** There are regularly scheduled orientations for prospective students, consisting of new student orientation, meetings with future classmates, choosing roommates, registration, testing, conferences with academic advisers, and discussions of aspects of college life. There are guides for informal visits and visitors may sit in on classes. To schedule a visit, contact Maureen Langhammer at (866) 477-7776. **Campus Safety and Security:** Measures include 24-hour foot and vehicle patrol, emergency notification system, self-defense education, and security escort services. There are shuttle buses, emergency telephones, lighted pathways/sidewalks, controlled access to dorms/residences, and gated entrance.

REQUIREMENTS: Applicants must graduate from an accredited secondary school or have a GED. 18 academic units are required, including 4 years of English, 3 of math, and 2 each of history, science, and foreign language. An essay and an interview are recommended. AP and CLEP credits are accepted. Important factors in the admissions decision are advanced placement or honors courses, leadership record, and recommendations by school officials. Assumption College's core curriculum centers around three reading and writing intensive seminar sequences in English, Philosophy, and Theology taken in the first and second years. From these seminars four areas of skill or expertise branch: Scientific and Quantitative Reasoning, comprising courses in mathematics and laboratory science; Person and Society, comprising courses in history and a wide range of the social sciences; Culture and Expression, comprising courses in the fine arts and foreign language, and The Great Conversation, comprising further coursework in literature, political science, philosophy, or theology. A global awareness requirement ensures all students experience non-Western traditions. The baccalaureate degree is completed with 120 credit hours, and a grade point average of 2.0. **Procedure:** Freshmen are admitted fall and spring. Entrance exams should be taken in May of the junior year or November of the senior year. There are early decision, early admissions, and deferred admissions plans. Early decision applications should be filed by November 1; regular applications, by February 15 for fall entry; and December 15 for spring entry. The fall 2017 application fee was $50. Notification of early decision is sent December 1; regular decision, March 15. 24 early decision candidates were accepted for the 2017-2018 class. 39 applicants were on the 2017 waiting list; 14 were admitted. Applications are accepted on-line. **Transfer Students:** 42 transfer students enrolled in 2016-2017. Transfer students must have maintained a minimum 2.5 GPA at their previous college. SAT scores and high school and college transcripts are required. 60 of 120 credits required for the bachelor's degree must be completed at Assumption. **International Students:** There are 43 international students enrolled. They must take the TOEFL with a minimum score of 550 on the paper-based TOEFL (PBT) or 80 on the Internet-based version (iBT).

ADMISSIONS: 79% of the 2017-2018 applicants were accepted. The SAT scores for the 2017-2018 freshman class were: Math-- 7% below 500, 55% between 500 and 599, 34% between 600 and 699, and 4% between 700 and 800. Evidence-Based Reading/Writing-- 7% below 500, 50% between 500 and 599, 37% between 600 and 699, and 6% between 700 and 800. The ACT scores were 31% between 18 and 23, 51% between 24 and 29, and 18% above 30. 36% of the current freshmen were in the top fifth of their class; 66% were in the top two fifths. **Admissions Contact:** Evan E. Lipp, Vice President for Enrollment Management. Email: *admiss@assumption.edu* Web: *www.assumption.edu*

FINANCIAL AID: In 2017-2018, 99% of all full-time freshmen received some form of financial aid. 82% of all full-time freshmen received need-based aid. The average freshman award was $26,850. Need-based scholarships or need-based grants averaged $23,496 ($48,621 maximum); need-based self-help aid (loans and jobs) averaged $3,910 ($10,342 maximum); non-need-based athletic scholarships averaged $14,220 ($51,846 maximum); and other non-need-based awards and non-need-based scholarships averaged $16,748 ($39,350 maximum). The FAFSA code is 002118. The priority date for freshman financial aid applications for fall entry is February 15.

ATLANTIC UNION COLLEGE D-2

www.atlanticuc.edu

South Lancaster, MA 01561	(978) 368-2239 (800) 282-2030
Fax: (978) 368-2517	Email: enroll@atlanticuc.edu
Full-time: 150 men, 250 women	**Faculty:** n/av
Part-time: 20 men, 30 women	**Ph.D.s:** 42%
Graduate: 5 men, 10 women	**Student/Faculty:** n/av
Year: semesters, summer session	**Tuition:** $17,998
Room & Board: $9230	**Freshman Class:** n/av
SAT or ACT: required	**CEEB CODE:** 3010
Application Deadline: August 1	**COMPETITIVE**

Atlantic Union College, established in 1882, is a private liberal arts institution associated with the Seventh-Day Adventist church and offers limited professional and pre-professional programs. There is 1 undergraduate school. In addition to regional accreditation, AUC has baccalaureate program accreditation with NASM. The 135-acre campus is in a small town 50 miles west of Boston. Including any residence halls, there are 54 buildings.

STUDENT LIFE: 55% of undergraduates are from out of state, mostly the Northeast. Students are from 14 states, 21 foreign countries, and Canada. 53% are African American; 22% Hispanic; 20% White; 15% Foreign; 1% Asian American; 1% American Indian/Alaska Native. **Female To Male Ratio:** 1.7:1. The average age of freshmen is 21; all undergraduates, 23. 27% do not continue beyond their first year. **Housing:** 469 students can be accommodated in college housing, which includes married student dorms and on-campus apartments. On-campus housing is guaranteed for all 4 years. 56% of students live on campus. Alcohol is not permitted. All students may keep cars.

FACULTY/CLASSROOMS: 45% of faculty are male; 55% are female. All teach undergraduates, 10% do research, and 10% do both. No introductory courses are taught by graduate students. The average class size in an introductory lecture is 18; in a laboratory is 30; and in a regular course is 16.

PROGRAMS OF STUDY: AUC confers B.A., B.S. and B.M. degrees. Associate and master's degrees are also awarded. Bachelor's degrees are awarded in BIOLOGICAL SCIENCE (biology/biological science and life science), BUSINESS (accounting and business administration and management), COMMUNICATIONS AND THE ARTS (art, English, and music), COMPUTER AND PHYSICAL SCIENCE (computer science, information sciences and systems, and mathematics), EDUCATION (early childhood education, elementary education, and music education), HEALTH PROFESSIONS (nursing), SOCIAL SCIENCE (culinary arts, history, liberal arts/general studies, ministries, psychology, religion, social work, and theological studies). Nursing, business, and psychology are the strongest academically. Nursing, business, and education have the largest enrollments.

ACTIVITIES: There are no fraternities or sororities. There are 13 groups on campus, including art, band, choir, chorale, drama, ethnic, honors, newspaper, orchestra, religious, social, student government, and yearbook. Popular campus events include Fall Picnic, Cultural Heritage Weeks, and Fine Arts Week. **Sports:** There are 7 intramural sports for men and 7 for women. Facilities include a gym and field house with a weight room and tennis/volleyball/badminton, racquetball/handball, and basketball courts, a swimming pool, and athletic fields for flag football, soccer, softball, and baseball.

SERVICES: Counseling and information services are available, as is tutoring in most subjects. There is remedial math, reading, and writing. Additional services are provided upon request. **Library/Resources:** The library contains 139,000 volumes, 17,336 microform items, and 4,754 audio/video tapes/CDs/DVDs, and subscribes to 469 periodicals including electronic. Computerized library services include interlibrary loans, database searching, Internet access, and Wi-Fi capability. **Physically Challenged Students:** 73% of the campus is accessible. Facilities include wheelchair ramps, elevators, special parking, specially equipped restrooms, special class scheduling, and lowered drinking fountains. **Special:** There is cross-registration with Mount Wachusett Community College and the Colleges of Worcester Consortium. Students may study abroad in 6 countries. AUC also offers newspaper and biology research internships, cooperative programs in several majors, pass/fail options, and nondegree study. The Summer Advantage in New England program offers precollege credit to high school honor students. There is also an adult degree program, in which most study is done at home and student-designed majors are permited. Dual majors, an accelerated degree in management and professional studies, a 1-3 engineering degree with Walla Walla College, and preprofessional curricula in dentistry, dental hygiene, medicine, respiratory therapy, radiologic technology, and veterinary medicine in conjunction with Loma Linda University are offered. There are 3 national honor societies, a freshman honors program, and 4 departmental honors programs. **Visiting:** There are regularly scheduled orientations for prospective students, including campus tours, class visits, and financial aid and admissions information sessions. There are guides for informal visits, visitors may sit in on classes, and stay overnight. **Campus Safety and Security:** Measures include self-defense education and security escort services. There are lighted pathways/sidewalks.

REQUIREMENTS: The SAT or ACT is required. Applicants should be graduates of an accredited secondary school. The GED is accepted with a minimum score of 250. Required academic credits include 4 years of high school English and 2 years each of a foreign language, math, history, and science. A GPA of 2.2 is required. AP and CLEP credits are accepted. Important factors in the admissions decision are recommendations by school officials, recommendations by alumni, and personality/intangible qualities. Students must complete 9 hours each in humanities, science, and social science and 12 hours in religion/ethics. Foreign language proficiency, a phys ed requirement, 40 hours of community service, and a course in college writing must also be completed. AUC requires 128 to 143 credit hours for the bachelor's degree, with 30 to 60 in the major, and a 2.0 GPA. **Procedure:** Freshmen are admitted fall and spring. Entrance exams should be taken during the senior year of high school. There is a rolling admissions plan. Applications should be filed by August 1 for fall entry; January 2 for spring entry. The fall 2017 application fee was $25. Notification is sent on a rolling basis. Applications are accepted on-line. **Transfer Students:** Applicants who have completed at least 24 semester hours are not required to submit SAT or ACT scores. Applicants from junior colleges may receive credit for up to 72 semester hours. Only a grade of C or better transfers for credit. 30 of 128 credits required for the bachelor's degree must be completed at AUC. **International Students:** They must take the TOEFL. They must also take the ACT, scoring 17.

Admissions Contact: Rosita Lashley, Director of Admissions. Email: *enroll@atlanticuc.edu* Web: *www.atlanticuc.edu*

FINANCIAL AID: AUC is a member of CSS. Check with the school for current application deadlines.

BABSON COLLEGE D-2
www.babson.edu

Babson Park, MA 02457 (781) 239-5522 (800) 488-3696

Fax: (781) 239-4135	**Email:** ugradadmission@babson.edu
Full-time: 1070 men, 730 women	**Faculty:** IIB
Part-time:	**Ph.D.s:** 72%
Graduate: 1200 men, 440 women	**Student/Faculty:** n/av
Year: semesters, summer session	**Tuition:** $48,288
Room & Board: $15,376	**Freshman Class:** n/av
SAT or ACT: required	**CEEB CODE:** 3075
Application Deadline: January 4	**HIGHLY COMPETITIVE**

Babson College, founded in 1919, is a private business school. All students start their own businesses during their freshman year with money loaned by the college. There are 4 undergraduate schools and 1 graduate school. In addition to regional accreditation, Babson College has baccalaureate program accreditation with AACSB. The 370-acre campus is in a suburban area in Wellesley MA, 14 miles west of Boston. Including any residence halls, there are 53 buildings.

STUDENT LIFE: 70% of undergraduates are from out of state, mostly the Northeast. Students are from 47 states, 60 foreign countries, and Canada. 50% are from public schools. 8% are Hispanic; 44% White; 4% African American; 18% Foreign; 11% Asian American. **Male To Female Ratio:** 1.9:1. The average age of freshmen is 18; all undergraduates, 20. 5% do not continue beyond their first year; 85% remain to graduate. **Housing:** 1441 students can be accommodated in college housing, which includes married student dorms and on-campus apartments. In addition, there are special-interest houses, substance-free living, fraternity and sorority towers, and a cultural house. On-campus housing is guaranteed for all 4 years. 85% of students live on campus. All students may keep cars.

FACULTY/CLASSROOMS: 69% of faculty are male; 31% are female. No introductory courses are taught by graduate students. The average class size in an introductory lecture is 34; in a laboratory is 20; and in a regular course is 27.

PROGRAMS OF STUDY: Babson confers B.S.M. degrees. Master's degrees are also awarded. Bachelor's degrees are awarded in BUSINESS (business administration and management).

ACTIVITIES: 10% of men belong to 7 national fraternities; 12% of women belong to 3 national sororities. There are 60 groups on campus, including art, band, cappella group, cheerleading, choir, chorus, dance, drama, ethnic, honors, international, jazz band, LGBT, literary magazine, musical theater, newspaper, photography, political, professional, radio and TV, religious, social, social service, student government, and yearbook. Popular campus events include multicultural week. **Sports:** There are 11 intercollegiate sports for men and 11 for women, and 11 intramural sports for men and 11 for women. Facilities include a sports complex with an indoor swimming pool/diving, an indoor track, a field house, a gym with basketball courts, squash and racquetball courts, a fitness center, a dance aerobics studio, a sports medicine facility, archery, badminton, baseball, softball, cricket, golf, lacrosse, rugby, table tennis, ultimate disk, ice hockey, alpine skiing, cross county, yoga, and volleyball. **Graduates:** From July 1, 2016 to June 30, 2017, 424 bachelor's degrees were awarded. In an average class, 80% graduate in 4 years or less, 85% graduate in 5 years or less, and 85% graduate in 6 years or less. Of the 2016 graduating class, 3% were enrolled in graduate school within 6 months of graduation, and 92% were employed.

SERVICES: Counseling and information services are available, as is tutoring in most subjects. There are writing/speech skills and math/science skills centers. **Library/Resources:** The library contains 132,024 volumes, 346,941 microform items, and 4,645 audio/video tapes/CDs/DVDs, and subscribes to 511 periodicals including electronic. Computerized library services include interlibrary loans, database searching, and Internet access. Special learning facilities include an art gallery, radio station, performing arts theater, and centers for entrepreneurial studies, management, language and culture, writing, math, visual arts, executive education, and women's leadership. **Physically Challenged Students:** 75% of the campus is accessible. Facilities include wheelchair ramps, elevators, special parking, specially equipped restrooms, special class scheduling, lowered drinking fountains, and special housing. **Special:** There is cross-registration with Brandeis University, Wellesley College, and F.W. Olin College of Engineering. Internships and study abroad in 27 countries are available. There is a freshman honors program and 10 departmental honors programs. **Visiting:** There are regularly scheduled orientations for prospective students, including an open house each year, personal interviews, campus tours, group information sessions and fall preview days on selected Saturdays. To schedule a visit, contact the Admission Office. **Campus Safety and Security:** Measures include 24-hour foot and vehicle patrol, self-defense education, and security escort services. There are shuttle buses, emergency telephones, lighted pathways/sidewalks, a motorist assist program, a transportation service for the cross-registration program. Vans are also available to students for school activities, and crime prevention programs.

REQUIREMENTS: The SAT or ACT is required. Applicants must be graduates of an accredited secondary school or have a GED. 16 academic courses are required, including 4 credits of English, 3 of math, 2 of social studies, and 1 of science. A fourth year of math is strongly recommended. Essays are required. SAT Subject tests in math are recommended. AP credits are accepted. Important factors in the admissions decision are advanced placement or honors courses, evidence of special talent, and leadership record. Students must complete a curriculum of general management and liberal arts, with 50% in management and 50% in liberal arts. A total of 128 semester hours is required for graduation. A minimum GPA of 2.0 is required. **Procedure:** Freshmen are admitted in the fall. Entrance exams should be taken prior to application (SAT or ACT). There are early decision, early admissions, and deferred admissions plans. Early decision applications should be filed by November 1; regular applications, by January 4 for fall entry. The fall 2017 application fee was $60. Notification of early decision is sent December 15; regular decision, March 20. Applications are accepted on-line. **Transfer Students:** Transfer applicants are expected to demonstrate solid academic performance at their prior institution and must submit 1 essay and 1 recommendation from a college teacher or administrator, in addition to a high school transcript and SAT scores. They must also submit course descriptions and syllabi for any courses they have taken. 64 of 128 credits required for the bachelor's degree must be completed at Babson. **International Students:** There are 318 international students enrolled. They must take the TOEFL with a minimum score of 600 on the paper-based TOEFL (PBT) or 100 on the Internet-based version (iBT). Students must take the English Language Proficiency Test. They must also take the SAT or ACT.

Admissions Contact: Grant Gosselin, Dean of Undergraduate Admission. Email: *ugradadmission@babson.edu* Web: *www.babson.edu*

FINANCIAL AID: In 2017-2018, 4% of all full-time freshmen received some form of financial aid. 45% of all full-time freshmen received need-based aid. The average freshman award was $26,171. Need-based scholarships or need-based grants averaged $29,787; and need-based self-help aid (loans and jobs) averaged $5,013. 32% of undergraduate students work part-time. The average financial indebtedness of the 2017 graduate was $24,900. The CSS/Profile, and tax returns are required. The FAFSA code is 002121. The deadline for filing freshman financial aid applications for fall entry is April 15.

BARD COLLEGE AT SIMON'S ROCK A-2

www.simons-rock.edu

Great Barrington, MA 01230 (413) 528-7228 (800) 235-7186
Fax: (413) 541-0081 Email: admit@simons-rock.edu

Full-time: 140 men, 219 women	**Faculty:** 51
Part-time: 2 men, 1 women	**Ph.D.s:** 90%
Graduate: n/av	**Student/Faculty:** 6 to 1
Year: semesters	**Tuition:** $51,735
Room & Board: $14,060	**Freshman Class:** 304 applied, 272 accepted, 143 enrolled
SAT CR/M/W: 692/656/661 **ACT:** 28	**CEEB CODE:** 3795
Application Deadline: n/av	**MOST COMPETITIVE**

Bard College at Simon's Rock is the only four-year college in the United States specifically designed to allow bright, highly motivated adolescents to fully realize their intellectual and creative potential by beginning college immediately after the tenth or eleventh grade. Offering students both significant autonomy and appropriate support, Simon's Rock fosters a diverse community of intellectual and chronological peers. Under the guidance of talented and dedicated faculty, students learn to formulate and defend their own ideas, to engage with the ideas of others, and to become innovative thinkers who contribute with purpose to the world around them. There is 1 undergraduate school. The 210-acre campus is in a small town, Berkshire Hills of Western MA, approximately 2 hours from New York City and Boston. Including any residence halls, there are 47 buildings.

STUDENT LIFE: 77% of undergraduates are from out of state, mostly the Middle Atlantic. Students are from 37 states, and 16 foreign countries. 65% are from public schools. 57% are White; 16% Foreign; 9% race unknown; 6% Asian American; 5% African American; 4% Hispanic; 3% two or more races; 1% American Indian/Alaska Native. **Female To Male Ratio:** 1.5:1. The average age of freshmen is 16; all undergraduates, 18. 17% do not continue beyond their first year; 75% remain to graduate. **Housing:** 347 students can be accommodated in college housing, which includes dorms and on-campus apartments, and senior only housing. On-campus housing is guaranteed for all 4 years. 93% of students live on campus. Alcohol is not permitted. Upperclassmen may keep cars.

FACULTY/CLASSROOMS: 51% of faculty are male; 49% are female. All teach undergraduates, and all do research. No introductory courses are taught by graduate students. The average class size in an introductory lecture is 14; in a laboratory is 10; and in a regular course is 12.

PROGRAMS OF STUDY: BCSR confers B.A. degrees. Associate degrees are also awarded. Bachelor's degrees are awarded in AGRICULTURE (environmental studies), BIOLOGICAL SCIENCE (biology/biological science), COMMUNICATIONS AND THE ARTS (art history and appreciation, creative writing, dance, dramatic arts, drawing, intermedia/multimedia, linguistics, literature, music, studio art ceramics, and studio art painting), COMPUTER AND PHYSICAL SCIENCE (chemistry, computer science, mathematics, physics, and quantitative methods), EDUCATION (global studies), ENGINEERING AND ENVIRONMENTAL DESIGN (preengineering), HEALTH PROFESSIONS (premedicine), SOCIAL SCIENCE (African American studies, Asian/Oriental studies, crosscultural studies, cultural studies/critical theory & analysis, French studies, gender studies, geography, German area studies, history, philosophy, political science/government, psychology, and Spanish studies). Pre-engineering is the strongest academically. Literary studies, music, and politics have the largest enrollments.

ACTIVITIES: There are no fraternities or sororities. There are 29 groups on campus, including astronomy club, Black Student Union, math club, Model UN, QueerSA, Anime, art, choir, chorus, computers, dance, debate, drama, environmental, ethnic, film, international, jazz band, LGBT, literary magazine, musical theater, newspaper, orchestra, photography, political, religious, social, social service, and student government. Popular campus events include Mayfest, Spring Formal, Dance Concert, Rock the Community Day of Service, Chinese New Year, Bollywood, Dolly Drag, and Black Student Union Ball. **Sports:** There are 3 intercollegiate sports for men and 3 for women, and 6 intramural sports for men and 6 for women. Facilities include a swimming pool, multicourt gym, racquetball courts, an elevated running track, fitness, weight-training center, rock-climbing wall, soccer field, tennis courts, and hiking trails. **Graduates:** From July 1, 2016 to June 30, 2017, 51 bachelor's degrees were awarded. The most popular majors were mathematics (10%), creative writing (8%), and pre-engineering (8%). In an average class, 1% graduate in 3 years or less, 69% graduate in 4 years or less, 18% graduate in 5 years or less, and 1% graduate in 6 years or less. Of the 2016 graduating class, 31% were enrolled in graduate school within 6 months of graduation, and 60% were employed.

SERVICES: Counseling and information services are available, as is tutoring in most subjects. There is a reader service for the blind, and remedial writing. There is also study skills. **Library/Resources:** The library contains 69,517 volumes, 3,896 microform items, and 6,425 audio/video tapes/CDs/DVDs, and subscribes to 43,313 periodicals including electronic. Computerized library services include interlibrary loans, database searching, Internet access, and Wi-Fi capability. Special learning facilities include an art gallery. **Physically Challenged Students:** 75% of the campus is accessible. Facilities include wheelchair ramps, elevators, special parking, specially equipped restrooms, special class scheduling, lowered drinking fountains, lowered telephones, and special housing. **Special:** 3-2 BA/BS engineering degree programs with Columbia University and Dartmouth University. 3-2 BA/MS program in environmental science with Bard College's Center for Environmental Policy. Articulated junior-year study abroad agreements with two colleges at Oxford University (Lincoln College and St. Catherine's College), the University of Manchester's Center for New Writing, Qingdao University in China, the University of Glasgow in Scotland, the London Dramatic Academy in London, Eastern Carolina University's Italy Intensives abroad, and the Umbra Institute, Perugia, Italy. There are also domestic study away opportunities with the Bard Globalization and International Affairs (BGIA) program in NYC, the Eugene O'Neil Theater in CT, the Washington Center in Washington DC, and the International Center of Photography in NYC. Internships may be completed for course credit through the Extended Campus Project program, and students are encouraged to work with the Director of Career Development to develop internships for credit or personal development that connect with their academic and career interests. Most Simon's Rock BA graduates complete more than one of the college's BA concentrations and students have the option of creating a self-designed 2nd concentration. Work-study opportunities are available on campus, as well as with several nonprofit organizations and schools in the community. **Visiting:** There are regularly scheduled orientations for prospective students, includes a sample class, a campus tour, and an interview. To schedule a visit, contact the Office of Admission. **Campus Safety and Security:** Measures include 24-hour foot and vehicle patrol, emergency notification system, and security escort services. There are shuttle buses, lighted pathways/sidewalks, and controlled access to dorms/residences.

REQUIREMENTS: Applicants are required to submit an application form, parent statement, 3 letters of recommendation, personal interview, high school transcript and school report, and application essays. Test scores are optional, but will be considered if submitted. Important factors in the admissions decision are personality/intangible qualities, recommendations by school officials, advanced placement or honors courses, evidence of special talent, recommendations by alumni, leadership record, parents or siblings attended your school, extracurricular activities record, and geographical diversity. AA degree requirements: Writing and Thinking Workshop; General Education Seminars; courses in Intercultural Perspectives, Arts course; Mathematics, Natural Sciences and World Languages. Students in the BA program must complete: at least one BA Concentration, a tutorial, internship, independent study and/or study abroad, and a Senior Thesis. **Procedure:** Freshmen are admitted fall and spring. There is a rolling admissions plan. Application deadlines are open. Notification is sent on a rolling basis. Applications are accepted on-line. **Transfer Students:** 2 transfer students enrolled in 2016-2017. Transfer students must be evaluated by Admission, although review of transfer credit is done by the Dean of Academic Affairs and the Registrar. 60 of 120 credits required for the bachelor's degree must be completed at BCSR. **International Students:** There are 51 international students enrolled. They must take the TOEFL with a minimum score of 600 on the paper-based TOEFL (PBT) or 100 on the Internet-based version (iBT). Students must also take the IELTS.

ADMISSIONS: 89% of the 2017-2018 applicants were accepted. The SAT scores for the 2017-2018 freshman class were: Critical Reading-- 4% between 500 and 599, 41% between 600 and 699, and 52% between 700 and 800. Math-- 22% between 500 and 599, 48% between 600 and 699, and 30% between 700 and 800. Writing-- 11% between 500 and 599, 26% between 600 and 699, and 19% between 700 and 800. The ACT scores were 14% between 18 and 23, 57% between 24 and 29, and 14%

above 30. 75% of the current freshmen were in the top fifth of their class; 83% were in the top two fifths. **Admissions Contact:** Office of Admission Email: *admit@simons-rock.edu* Web: *www.simons-rock.edu*

FINANCIAL AID: In 2017-2018, 99% of all full-time freshmen received some form of financial aid. 68% of all full-time freshmen received need-based aid. The average freshman award was $30,220. Need-based scholarships or need-based grants averaged $32,929; need-based self-help aid (loans and jobs) averaged $6,252; and other non-need-based awards and non-need-based scholarships averaged $13,897. The average financial indebtedness of the 2017 graduate was $27,544. BCSR is a member of CSS. The CSS/Profile is required. The FAFSA code is 009645. The priority date for freshman financial aid applications for fall entry is February 1. The deadline for filing freshman financial aid applications for fall entry is May 1.

BAY PATH UNIVERSITY — B-3

www.baypath.edu

Longmeadow, MA 01106 — (413) 565-6806, (800) 782-7284

Fax: (413) 565-1336 — **Email:** kamartin@baypath.edu

Full-time: 1367 women	**Faculty:** 41
Part-time: 580 women	**Ph.D.s:** 63%
Graduate: 182 men, 1169 women	**Student/Faculty:** 13 to 1
Year: semesters	**Tuition:** $33,557
Room & Board: $12,799	**Freshman Class:** 1470 applied, 924 accepted, 144 enrolled
	CEEB CODE: 3078
Application Deadline: n/av	**COMPETITIVE**

Bay Path University, founded in 1897, is a comprehensive, private college offering innovative undergraduate programs for women only and graduate programs for men and women. There are 3 undergraduate schools and 1 graduate school. In addition to regional accreditation, BPU has baccalaureate program accreditation with ABA, Mass. Dept. of Education & Secondary Education, and ACOTE. The 48-acre campus is in a suburban area in Longmeadow MA, 90-minutes to Boston and 2 hours to New York City. Including any residence halls, there are 17 buildings.

STUDENT LIFE: 64% of undergraduates are from Massachusetts. Others are from 27 states, and 5 foreign countries. 94% are from public schools. 7% are race unknown; 62% White; 2% Asian American; 2% two or more races; 14% Hispanic; 12% African American; 1% Foreign. **Female To Male Ratio:** 17.1:1. The average age of freshmen is 18; all undergraduates, 21. 30% do not continue beyond their first year; 70% remain to graduate. **Housing:** 411 students can be accommodated in college housing, which includes dorms, themed floors in residence halls. On-campus housing is guaranteed for all 4 years, is available on a first-come, first-served basis, and is available on a lottery system for upperclassmen. 56% of students commute. Alcohol is not permitted. All students may keep cars.

FACULTY/CLASSROOMS: 22% of faculty are male; 78% are female. 57% teach undergraduates. No introductory courses are taught by graduate students. The average class size in a laboratory is 18 and in a regular course is 13.

PROGRAMS OF STUDY: BPU confers B.A. and B.S. degrees. Associate and master's degrees are also awarded. Bachelor's degrees are awarded in BIOLOGICAL SCIENCE (biochemistry, biology/biological science, biology/general science/environmental science second education, biotechnology, forensic psychology, forensic science, and neurosciences), BUSINESS (accounting, business administration and management, business administration marketing, human resources/organizational mgmt, marketing/retailing/merchandising, and small business management), COMMUNICATIONS AND THE ARTS (communications and writing), COMPUTER AND PHYSICAL SCIENCE (cyber intelligence/security studies), EDUCATION (early childhood education, educational studies, and elementary education), ENGINEERING AND ENVIRONMENTAL DESIGN (interior design), HEALTH PROFESSIONS (biomedical science, medical science, and pre-occupational therapy), SOCIAL SCIENCE (child psychology/development, criminal justice, forensic studies, legal studies, liberal arts/general studies, paralegal studies, and psychology). Medical science, cybersecurity, and business are the strongest academically. Pre-OT, psychology, and forensic science have the largest enrollments.

ACTIVITIES: There are no fraternities or sororities. There are 32 groups on campus, including Diverse Step Sisters, Habitat for Humanity, Wellness Wildcats, Women of Cultures, cheerleading, chorale, computers, dance, drama, ethnic, forensics, honors, international, LGBT, musical theater, political, professional, religious, social, social service, student government, and Tactical Team. Popular campus events include Campus Awakening, Generations Banquets, Karaoke Unplugged, and Dinner with the President. **Sports:** There are 8 intercollegiate sports for women. Facilities include a fitness center that houses a weight-training room, a dance studio, and an aerobics room and a nearby 12-acre playing field for soccer and softball, a walking/jogging track, and a field house. **Graduates:** From July 1, 2016 to June 30, 2017, 438 bachelor's degrees were awarded. The most popular majors were business (20%), psychology (15%), and liberal studies (11%). In an average class, 53% graduate in 4 years or less, 60% graduate in 5 years or less, and 61% graduate in 6 years or less.

SERVICES: Counseling and information services are available, as is tutoring in every subject. **Library/Resources:** The library contains 367,343 volumes, and 35,000 audio/video tapes/CDs/DVDs, and subscribes to 49,120 periodicals including electronic. Computerized library services include interlibrary loans, database searching, and Internet access. **Physically Challenged Students:** 90% of the campus is accessible. Facilities include wheelchair ramps, elevators, special parking, and specially equipped restrooms. **Special:** Cross-registration is possible with other member schools of the Cooperating Colleges of Greater Springfield Consortium. Bay Path's capital of the world program allows students to visit a different world center during each spring break. Most academic programs require an internship or other experiential learning opportunity. There are 4 national honor societies, a freshman honors program, and 2 departmental honors programs. **Visiting:** There are regularly scheduled orientations for prospective students. There are guides for informal visits, visitors may sit in on classes, and stay overnight. To schedule a visit, contact Dawn Bryden at dbryden@baypath.edu. **Campus Safety and Security:** Measures include 24-hour foot and vehicle patrol, emergency notification system, self-defense education, and security escort services. There are shuttle buses, emergency telephones, lighted pathways/sidewalks, controlled access to dorms/residences, fire, vehicle, and driving safety education programs.

REQUIREMENTS: Applicants should have completed at least 4 academic courses each year, including 4 years of English, 3 of math, at least 2 each of social studies and lab sciences, and 2 of a foreign language. An essay is required, as are letters of recommendation from a guidance counselor and a teacher. An interview is strongly recommended. A GPA of 2.0 is required. AP and CLEP credits are accepted. To graduate, students must complete at least 120 credits with a minimum GPA of 2.0. The 46-hour core curriculum includes course work in communication, science, social science, math, and fine and performing arts. **Procedure:** Freshmen are admitted fall and spring. Entrance exams should be taken in the spring of the junior year or by December of the senior year. There are deferred admissions and rolling admissions plans. Application deadlines are open. Applications are accepted on-line. **Transfer Students:** 84 transfer students enrolled in 2016-2017. Applicants must be in good standing at their previous school and are encouraged to arrange for an interview at Bay Path. Students who have earned fewer than 12 credits must submit SAT or ACT scores. 30 of 120 credits required for the bachelor's degree must be completed at Bay Path. **International Students:** There are 10 international students enrolled. They must take the TOEFL with a minimum score of 76 on the Internet-based version (iBT). Students must the IELTS.

ADMISSIONS: 63% of the 2017-2018 applicants were accepted. The SAT scores for the 2017-2018 freshman class were: Critical Reading--55% below 500, 33% between 500 and 599, 11% between 600 and 699, and 1% between 700 and 800. Math-- 63% below 500, 32% between 500 and 599, and 5% between 600 and 699. Writing-- 60% below 500, 34% between 500 and 599, 5% between 600 and 699, and 1% between 700 and 800. The ACT scores were 19% between 12 and 17, 48% between 18 and 23, 26% between 24 and 29, and 7% above 30. 19% of the current freshmen were in the top fifth of their class; 66% were in the top two fifths. **Admissions Contact:** Kathleen Martin, Vice Provost. Email: *kamartin@baypath.edu* Web: *www.baypath.edu*

FINANCIAL AID: In 2017-2018, 97% of all full-time freshmen received some form of financial aid. 92% of all full-time freshmen received need-based aid. The average freshman award was $30,290. Need-based scholarships or need-based grants averaged $14,176 ($18,843 maximum); need-based self-help aid (loans and jobs) averaged $5,571 ($5,746 maximum); and other non-need-based awards and non-need-based scholarships averaged $14,515 ($18,500 maximum). 40% of undergraduate students work part-time. The average financial indebtedness of the 2017 graduate was $28,120. BPU is a member of CSS. The college's own financial statement, and parent and student income tax forms are required. The FAFSA code is 002122. Check with the school for current application deadlines.

BECKER COLLEGE *(The complete profile is made available exclusively on our website, www.barronspac.com)*

BENJAMIN FRANKLIN INSTITUTE OF TECHNOLOGY *(The complete profile is made available exclusively on our website, www.barronspac.com)*

BENTLEY UNIVERSITY — D-2
www.bentley.edu

Waltham, MA 02452	**(781) 891-2244** **(800) 523-2354**
Fax: (781) 891-3414	**Email: ugadmission@bentley.edu**
Full-time: 2452 men, 1719 women	**Faculty:** 291; IIA, ++$
Part-time: 58 men, 43 women	**Ph.D.s:** 81%
Graduate: 540 men, 731 women	**Student/Faculty:** 11 to 1
Year: semesters, summer session	**Tuition:** $48,000
Room & Board: $15,720	**Freshman Class:** 8867 applied, 3915 accepted, 1018 enrolled
SAT EBR-W/M: 630/665 **ACT:** 29	**CEEB CODE:** 3096
Application Deadline: January 7	**MOST COMPETITIVE**

Bentley University is one of the nation's leading business schools, dedicated to preparing a new kind of business leader, one with the deep technical skills, the broad global perspective and the high ethical standards required to make a difference in an ever-changing world. To achieve our goal, we infuse our advanced business curriculum with the richness of a liberal arts education. The results are graduates who are making an impact in their chosen fields and turning their passions into success stories. More students are considering business as the foundation of their higher education experience, and considering Bentley in the process. Students interested in business professions choose from a wide range of programs that address all functional areas including accountancy, finance, marketing, management and liberal arts   all anchored in technology. There is 1 undergraduate school and 1 graduate school. In addition to regional accreditation, Bentley has baccalaureate program accreditation with AACSB and EQUIS. The 163-acre campus is in a suburban area in Waltham, Massachusetts. Including any residence halls, there are 46 buildings.

STUDENT LIFE: 58% of undergraduates are from out of state, mostly the Middle Atlantic. Students are from 44 states, 77 foreign countries, and Canada. 67% are from public schools. 8% are Asian American; 7% Hispanic; 61% White; 4% race unknown; 3% African American; 2% two or more races; 15% Foreign. **Male To Female Ratio:** 1.2:1. The average age of freshmen is 18; all undergraduates, 20. 8% do not continue beyond their first year; 91% remain to graduate. **Housing:** College-sponsored housing includes dorms and on-campus apartments. Honors floors and other special interest floors are also available. On-campus housing is guaranteed for all 4 years. 78% of students live on campus. Upperclassmen may keep cars.

FACULTY/CLASSROOMS: 59% of faculty are male; 41% are female. 94% teach undergraduates, 69% do research, and 67% do both. No introductory courses are taught by graduate students. The average class size in an introductory lecture is 33; in a laboratory is 20; and in a regular course is 28.

PROGRAMS OF STUDY: Bentley confers B.A. and B.S. degrees. Master's and doctoral degrees are also awarded. Bachelor's degrees are awarded in AGRICULTURE (environmental studies), BUSINESS (accounting, business administration and management, business (dual major program), business communications, business economics, business information systems, business and technology, finance, information & communication technology, business management, marketing, and sustainable management), COMMUNICATIONS AND THE ARTS (English, foreign language, and media arts), COMPUTER AND PHYSICAL SCIENCE (actuarial science, computer information systems, and mathematics), EDUCATION (global studies), HEALTH PROFESSIONS (health), SOCIAL SCIENCE (economics, history, interdisciplinary studies, liberal arts/general studies, philosophy, public administration, and Spanish studies). Marketing, accounting, finance, and management are the strongest academically. Finance, accounting, and economics-finance have the largest enrollments.

ACTIVITIES: 16% of men belong to 2 local and 6 national fraternities; 19% of women belong to 3 national sororities. There are 110 groups on campus, including art, band, cheerleading, chess, choir, chorus, computers, dance, debate, drama, environmental, ethnic, film, honors, international, jazz band, LGBT, literary magazine, musical theater, newspaper, orchestra, photography, political, professional, radio and TV, religious, social, social service, student government, and yearbook. Popular campus events include Spring Day, Back2Bentley Concert, Halloween Dance Party, Homecoming, Diwali, Culturefest, Football Games, and Take Back the Night. **Sports:** There are 12 intercollegiate sports for men and 11 for women, and 7 intramural sports for men and 7 for women. Facilities include a multipurpose facility, a field house, fitness center for varsity athletics, a swimming pool, athletic training rooms and rehabilitation area. **Graduates:** From July 1, 2016 to June 30, 2017, 1040 bachelor's degrees were awarded. The most popular majors were finance (20%), economics-finance (16%), and marketing (15%). In an average class, 87% graduate in 4 years or less, 91% graduate in 5 years or less, and 91% graduate in 6 years or less. Of the 2016 graduating class, 10% were enrolled in graduate school within 6 months of graduation, and 87% were employed.

SERVICES: Counseling and information services are available, as is tutoring in most subjects. There is a reader service for the blind, and remedial math, reading, and writing. There is a natural reader, and additional assistive programs available upon request. **Library/Resources:** The library contains 187,590 volumes, 9,079 microform items, and 43,461 audio/video tapes/CDs/DVDs, and subscribes to 87,163 periodicals including electronic. Computerized library services include interlibrary loans, database searching, Internet access, and Wi-Fi capability. Special learning facilities include an art gallery, radio station, media and culture lab, accounting center for electronic learning and business, center for languages and international collaboration, a trading room, center for service learning and civic engagement center, center for women and business, academic technology center, UX lab, center for marketing technology, center for business ethics, and arts and sciences.**Physically Challenged Students:** 80% of the campus is accessible. Facilities include wheelchair ramps, elevators, special parking, specially equipped restrooms, special class scheduling, and special housing. **Special:** 89% of Bentley seniors report that they complete at least one professional internship and 63% have two or more internships. Internships can be paid, for-credit and not-for-credit. Bentley offers more than 50 study abroad programs in 26 countries as well as Semester at Sea. In addition, Bentley offers Faculty-lead international courses which are 3-credit intensive study abroad experiences offered during semester breaks. During these courses, a Bentley professor leads students on an immersive learning experience in a multitude of world regions offering students the opportunity to combine cultural activities with business, NGO, or other relevant site visits. Corporate Partnerships pair students with leaders from top companies to work on real-world issues. Every student participates in this hands-on learning experience usually in their junior year. A fourth credit option is available. Work-study is offered through various departments throughout campus. Students can access available openings through an on campus employment website. There are 14 Bachelor of Science majors and 10 Bachelor of Arts majors in addition to 35 minors and multiple concentrations. Bentley offers a Liberal Studies second (dual) major in American Studies, Diversity and Society, Earth, Environment and Global Sustainability, Ethics and Social Responsibility, Global Perspectives, Health and Industry, Media Arts and Society and Quantitative Perspectives. Through our Falcon Fast Track program, students can combine any of the university's undergraduate degrees in Business or the Arts and Sciences with a choice of masters programs offered at the Bentley Graduate School of Business. Starting graduate study in their fourth year at Bentley enables students to trim the typical time commitment for earning the two degrees. Possible graduate majors include the Emerging Leaders MBA or 1 of eight MS programs: Master of Science in Accountancy, Master of Science in Business Analytics, Master of Science in Finance, Master of Science in Financial Planning, Master of Science in Human Factors in Information Design, Master of Science in Information Technology, Master of Science in Marketing Analytics, and Master of Science in Taxation. There are 5 national honor societies, a freshman honors program, and 17 departmental honors programs. **Visiting:** There are regularly scheduled orientations for prospective students, fall, spring, and summer open house programs; Interviews are arranged by appointment. Campus tours and group information sessions take place regularly throughout the year. Visits are available during the week and some selected Saturdays. There are guides for informal visits and visitors may sit in on classes. To schedule a visit, contact the Office of Undergraduate Admission. **Campus Safety and Security:** Measures include 24-hour foot and vehicle patrol, emergency notification system, self-defense education, and security escort services. There are shuttle buses, emergency telephones, lighted pathways/sidewalks, controlled access to dorms/residence, and crime reporting through website Emergency Response Guidebook (flipbooks) in all classrooms.

REQUIREMENTS: The ACT Optional Writing test is required. All students need to submit the Common Application, official secondary school transcript, standardized test scores (either the SAT or ACT), 2 letters of recommendation. AP credits are accepted. Important factors in the admissions decision are advanced placement or honors courses, extracurricular activities record, and recommendations by school officials. All undergraduate students complete general education courses in areas such as IT, writing and literature, mathematics, government, economics, history, philosophy, and social science. Students in B.S. programs take a common core of nine courses covering areas such as business law, accounting, finance, marketing, organizational behavior business statistics and strategic management. BA students except for Liberal arts are required to do a minor or major in business studies which contains many of the courses that students in the BS program take in the common core. All students that entered as a first year student take elective courses that fulfill diversity, international and communication intensive requirements. A total of 122 credit hours for students beginning as freshmen, 121 for transfer students. All students are required to have a minimum GPA of 2.0 overall and 2.0 in the major are required for graduation. All first year students must take a first-year seminar. Majors are anywhere from 24-30 credit hours. **Procedure:** Freshmen are admitted fall and spring. Entrance exams should be taken scores must be received by February 15. There are early decision and deferred admissions plans. Early decision applications should be filed by November 15; regular applications, by January 7 for fall entry. The fall 2017 application fee was $75. Notification of early decision is sent December 22; regular decision, March 30. 206 early decision candidates were accepted for the 2017-2018 class. 2082 applicants were on the 2017 waiting list. Applications are accepted on-line. **Transfer Students:** 101 transfer students enrolled in 2016-2017. Transfer application, personal statement, official transcripts, mid-year progress report and two letters of recommendation, transfer college report, standardized test scores 60 of 121 credits required for the bachelor's degree must be completed at Bentley. **International Students:** There are 638 international students enrolled. They must take the TOEFL with a minimum score of 577 on the paper-based TOEFL (PBT) or 90 on the Internet-based version (iBT) and the Comprehensive English Language Test, and take the IELTS. They must also take the SAT or ACT.

ADMISSIONS: 44% of the 2017-2018 applicants were accepted. The SAT scores for the 2017-2018 freshman class were: Math-- 1% below 500, 14% between 500 and 599, 53% between 600 and 699, and 32% between 700 and 800. Evidence-Based Reading/Writing-- 1% below 500, 25% between 500 and 599, 62% between 600 and 699, and 12% between 700 and 800. The ACT scores were 3% between 18 and 23, 60% between 24 and 29, and 37% above 30. 63% of the current freshmen were in the top fifth of their class; 90% were in the top two fifths. 7 freshmen graduated first in their class. **Admissions Contact:** Mario Silva-Rosa, Director of Undergraduate Admission. Email: *ugadmission@bentley.edu* Web: *www.bentley.edu*

FINANCIAL AID: In 2017-2018, 75% of all full-time freshmen received some form of financial aid. 50% of all full-time freshmen received need-based aid. The average freshman award was $35,924. Need-based scholarships or need-based grants averaged $31,621; need-based self-help aid (loans and jobs) averaged $4,891; non-need-based athletic scholarships averaged $30,217; and other non-need-based awards and non-need-based scholarships averaged $18,050. Bentley is a member of CSS. The CSS/Profile, and federal tax returns, including all schedules for parents and student are required. The FAFSA code is 002124. The priority date for freshman financial aid applications for fall entry is January 7.

BERKLEE COLLEGE OF MUSIC *(The complete profile is made available exclusively on our website, www.barronspac.com)*

BOSTON ARCHITECTURAL COLLEGE *(The complete profile is made available exclusively on our website, www.barronspac.com)*

BOSTON COLLEGE — E-2

www.bc.edu

Chestnut Hill, MA 02467 — (617) 552-3100, (800) 360-2522

Fax: (617) 552-0798

Full-time: 4308 men, 5001 women	**Faculty:** I, +$
Part-time: n/av	**Ph.D.s:** 94%
Graduate: 1970 men, 2572 women	**Student/Faculty:** 12 to 1
Year: semesters, summer session	**Tuition:** $53,346
Room & Board: $14,142	**Freshman Class:** 28956 applied, 9017 accepted, 2359 enrolled
SAT CR/M/W: 670/690/685 **ACT:** 32	**CEEB CODE:** 3083
Application Deadline: January 1	**MOST COMPETITIVE**

Boston College, founded in 1863, is an independent institution affiliated with the Roman Catholic Church and the Jesuit Order. It offers undergraduate programs in the arts and sciences, business, nursing, and education, and graduate and professional programs. There are 4 undergraduate schools and 7 graduate schools. In addition to regional accreditation, BC has baccalaureate program accreditation with AACSB, CSWE, CAEP, and NLN. The 338-acre campus is in a suburban area 6 miles west of Boston. Including any residence halls, there are 151 buildings.

STUDENT LIFE: 75% of undergraduates are from out of state, mostly the Northeast. Students are from 49 states, 59 foreign countries, and Canada. 45% are from public schools. 7% are Foreign; 63% White; 4% African American; 4% race unknown; 3% two or more races; 10% Asian American; 10% Hispanic. **Female To Male Ratio:** 1.2:1. The average age of freshmen is 18; all undergraduates, 21. 5% do not continue beyond their first year; 95% remain to graduate. **Housing:** 7638 students can be accommodated in college housing, which includes dorms and on-campus apartments. In addition, there are honors houses, special-interest houses, community and multicultural housing, quiet residences, single-sex freshman halls, perspectives academic program housing, and a substance-free residence. On-campus housing is guaranteed for the freshman year only and is available on a lottery system for upperclassmen. 85% of students live on campus. Upperclassmen may keep cars.

FACULTY/CLASSROOMS: 52% of faculty are male; 48% are female. All teach undergraduates and all do research. Graduate students teach 14% of introductory courses. The average class size in a laboratory is 15 and in a regular course is 30.

PROGRAMS OF STUDY: BC confers B.A. and B.S. degrees. Master's and doctoral degrees are also awarded. Bachelor's degrees are awarded in BIOLOGICAL SCIENCE (biochemistry and biology/biological science), BUSINESS (accounting, banking and finance, business administration and management, business economics, human resources, management science, marketing/retailing/merchandising, and operations research), COMMUNICATIONS AND THE ARTS (art history and appreciation, classics, communications, dramatic arts, English, film arts, French, Italian, linguistics, music, romance languages and literature, and studio art), COMPUTER AND PHYSICAL SCIENCE (chemistry, computer science, geology, geophysics and seismology, information sciences and systems, mathematics, and physics), EDUCATION (early childhood education, elementary education, secondary education, and special education), ENGINEERING AND ENVIRONMENTAL DESIGN (environmental science), HEALTH PROFESSIONS (nursing), SOCIAL SCIENCE (applied psychology, classical/ancient civilization, developmental psychology, economics, German area studies, Hispanic American studies, history, human development, philosophy, political science/government, psychology, Russian and Slavic studies, sociology, and theological studies). Finance, economics, and chemistry are the strongest academically. Economics, finance, and biology have the largest enrollments.

ACTIVITIES: There are no fraternities or sororities. There are 230 groups on campus, including art, band, cheerleading, chess, choir, chorale, chorus, communications, computers, dance, debate, drama, environmental, ethnic, film, honors, international, jazz band, LGBT, literary magazine, marching band, musical theater, newspaper, orchestra, pep band, photography, political, professional, radio and TV, religious, social, social service, student government, symphony, and yearbook. Popular campus events include Middlemarch Ball, Senior Week, and Sporting Events. **Sports:** There are 12 intercollegiate sports for men and 15 for women, and 38 intramural sports for men and 30 for women. Facilities include a stadium, basketball, ice hockey, soccer fields, baseball fields, and a track, a student recreation complex with: equipment for cardio, weight, strength training, dozens of group exercise class options including spinning, yoga, pilates, an indoor pool diving, swimming, and dedicated indoor courts for basketball, racquetball, squash, tennis and volleyball. **Graduates:** From July 1, 2016 to June 30, 2017, 2315 bachelor's degrees were awarded. The most popular majors were economics (12%), finance (11%), and biology (8%). In an average class, 89% graduate in 4 years or less and 93% graduate in 6 years or less. Of the 2016 graduating class, 18% were enrolled in graduate school within 6 months of graduation, and 70% were employed.

SERVICES: Counseling and information services are available, as is tutoring in most subjects. There is a reader service for the blind, and academic development center that serves all students. **Library/Resources:** The library contains 3.2 million volumes, 4.3 million microform items, and subscribes to 45,837 periodicals including electronic. Computerized library services include interlibrary loans, database searching, and Internet access. Special learning facilities include an art gallery, radio station, and TV station. **Physically Challenged Students:** 95% of the campus is accessible. Facilities include wheelchair ramps, elevators, special parking, specially equipped restrooms, special class scheduling, lowered drinking fountains, lowered telephones, and special housing. **Special:** There are internship programs in management and in arts and sciences. Students may cross-register with Boston University, Brandeis University, Hebrew College, Hellenic College, Pine Manor College, Regis College, or Tufts University. BC also offers a Washington semester in cooperation with American University, work-study programs with nonprofit agencies, study abroad, and dual and student-designed majors. Students may pursue a 3-2 engineering program with Boston University and accelerated 5-year programs in social work and education. There are 12 national honor societies, Phi Beta Kappa, a freshman honors program, and 4 departmental honors programs. **Visiting:** There are regularly scheduled orientations for prospective students, group information sessions and campus tours Monday through Friday. There are guides for informal visits and visitors may sit in on classes. To schedule a visit, contact Office of Undergraduate Admission. **Campus Safety and Security:** Measures include 24-hour foot and vehicle patrol, emergency notification system, self-defense education, and security escort services. There are shuttle buses, emergency telephones, lighted pathways/sidewalks, controlled access to dorms/residences, safety seminars and safety walking tours are offered for incoming students during orientation. A fire safety awareness week is held every year with a mock dorm room burning demonstration, distribution of fire safety education materials, and drills. Students and faculty/staff members can also opt into an emergency alert system that can send emergency messages from the college to cell phones.

REQUIREMENTS: Students may submit either the newly designed SAT Test or ACT test or the old SAT test with Writing or the ACT test with Writing. Applicants must be graduates of an accredited high school completing 4 units each of English, foreign language, science, and math. Those students applying to the school of nursing must complete at least 2 years of a lab science including 1 unit of chemistry. Applicants to the school of management are strongly encouraged to take 4 years of college preparatory math. An essay is required. AP credits are accepted. Core requirements include 2 courses each in natural science, social science, history, philosophy, and theology; 1 course each in literature, writing, math, and cultural diversity; and proficiency in a foreign language for College of Arts and Science students. To graduate, students must complete 120 credits (or 117 for nursing majors) including at least 30 in the major with a minimum GPA. Computer science is required for management majors, and a freshman writing seminar for all students except honors and AP students. Students in the honors program may elect to take courses in lieu of a thesis. Scholars of the college must complete a scholar's project before graduation. **Procedure:** Freshmen are admitted fall and spring. Entrance exams should be taken no later than January of the senior year. There are early admissions and deferred admissions plans. Early decision applications should be filed by November 1; regular applications, by January 1 for fall entry; and November 1 for spring entry. The fall 2017 application fee was $75. Notification of early decision is sent December 25; regular decision, April 15. 5689 applicants were on the 2017 waiting list; 112 were admitted. Applications are accepted on-line. **Transfer Students:** 153 transfer students enrolled in 2016-2017. Applicants must have a current GPA of at least 3.0 and must have earned a minimum of 9 semester hours. High school transcripts, letters of recommendation, and SAT or ACT scores are required. 60 of 120 credits required for the bachelor's degree must be completed at BC. **International Students:** There are 609 international students enrolled. They must take the TOEFL with a minimum score of 600 on the paper-based TOEFL (PBT) or 100 on the Internet-based version (iBT). TOEFL requirement will be waived if student scores 600+ on SAT Critical Reading or 27+ on ACT English.

ADMISSIONS: 31% of the 2017-2018 applicants were accepted. The SAT scores for the 2017-2018 freshman class were: Critical Reading-- 2% below 500, 13% between 500 and 599, 50% between 600 and 699, and 34% between 700 and 800. Math-- 1% below 500, 10% between 500 and 599, 44% between 600 and 699, and 44% between 700 and 800. Writing-- 2% below 500, 12% between 500 and 599, 41% between 600 and 699, and 44% between 700 and 800. The ACT scores were 2% between 18 and 23, 15% between 24 and 29, and 83% above 30. 95% of the current freshmen were in the top fifth of their class; 99% were in the top two fifths. **Admissions Contact:** John L. Mahoney Jr., Director Undergraduate Admission. Web: *www.bc.edu*

FINANCIAL AID: 40% of all full-time freshmen received need-based aid. The average freshman award was $41,768. Need-based scholarships or need-based grants averaged $38,238; need-based self-help aid (loans and jobs) averaged $4,855; non-need-based athletic scholarships averaged $54,189; and other non-need-based awards and non-need-based scholarships averaged $20,287. 26% of undergraduate students work part-time. The average financial indebtedness of the 2017 graduate was $20,481. BC is a member of CSS. The CSS/Profile, federal IRS income tax form, W-2s, divorced/separated statement (when applicable) are required. The FAFSA code is 002128. The deadline for filing freshman financial aid applications for fall entry is February 1.

BOSTON UNIVERSITY E-2

www.bu.edu

Boston, MA 02215 **(617) 353-2300**

Fax: (617) 353-9695 **Email:** admissions@bu.edu
Full-time: 6601 men, 10,238 women
Part-time: 616 men, 625 women
Graduate: 6615 men, 8660 women
Year: semesters, summer session
Room & Board: $15,270
Faculty: 1226; I, +$
Ph.D.s: 89%
Student/Faculty: 10 to 1
Tuition: $52,082
Freshman Class: 60825 applied, 15273 accepted, 3498 enrolled
SAT EBR-W/M: 690/690 **ACT:** 31
Application Deadline: January 2
CEEB CODE: 3087
MOST COMPETITIVE

Boston University is a private teaching and research university committed to excellence in undergraduate education. BU offers students more than 250 programs of study, internships in the US and abroad, one of the nations's most extensive study abroad programs, and cutting-edge research with faculty mentors. Students experience the city of Boston as an extension of the campus for study, internships, employment, and cultural and recreational activities. There are 10 undergraduate schools and 14 graduate schools. In addition to regional accreditation, BU has baccalaureate program accreditation with AACSB, ABET, and NASM. The 134-acre campus is in an urban area on the Charles River in Boston's Back Bay. Including any residence halls, there are 321 buildings.

STUDENT LIFE: 75% of undergraduates are from out of state, mostly the Northeast. Students are from 50 states, 118 foreign countries, and Canada. 61% are from public schools. 40% are White; 4% African American; 4% two or more races; 4% race unknown; 22% Foreign; 15% Asian American; 11% Hispanic. **Female To Male Ratio:** 1.4:1. The average age of freshmen is 19; all undergraduates, 20. 7% do not continue beyond their first year; 87% remain to graduate. **Housing:** 11096 students can be accommodated in college housing, which includes married student dorms, on-campus apartments, and off-campus apartments. In addition, there are honors houses, language/international houses, special-interest houses, international floors, and gender neutral floors. On-campus housing is guaranteed for all 4 years. 75% of students live on campus. All students may keep cars.

FACULTY/CLASSROOMS: 58% of faculty are male; 42% are female. 61% teach undergraduates. No introductory courses are taught by grad-

uate students. The average class size in an introductory lecture is 80; in a laboratory is 17; and in a regular course is 16.

PROGRAMS OF STUDY: BU confers B.A., B.S., B.F.A., B.L.S., Mus.B., and B.S.B.A. degrees. Master's and doctoral degrees are also awarded. Bachelor's degrees are awarded in AGRICULTURE (environmental studies), BIOLOGICAL SCIENCE (biochemistry, biology/biological science, ecology, environmental biology, marine science, neurosciences, nutrition, and physiology), BUSINESS (business administration and management, hospitality management services, and hotel/motel and restaurant management), COMMUNICATIONS AND THE ARTS (acting, art history and appreciation, Chinese, classical languages, classics, communications, dramatic arts, English, film arts, French, Germanic languages and literature, graphic design, Greek (classical), guitar, journalism, Latin, linguistics, film and media studies, music, music composition, music history and appreciation, music performance, music theory and composition, organ performance, painting, percussion, performing arts, piano performance, printmaking, Russian languages and literature, scenic and lighting design, sculpture, Spanish, stage management, theatre arts, theater design, theatre production, theater management, and voice), COMPUTER AND PHYSICAL SCIENCE (astronomy, astronomy and physics, astrophysics, chemistry, chemistry education, computer science, earth science, geophysics and seismology, mathematics, mathematics – philosophy, physics, and planetary and space science), EDUCATION (art education, Asian studies, athletic training, bilingual/bicultural education, early childhood education, education, education of the deaf and hearing impaired, elementary education, English education, foreign languages education, mathematics education, music education, physical education, science education, social studies education, and special education), ENGINEERING AND ENVIRONMENTAL DESIGN (architectural history, biomedical engineering, computer engineering, electrical/electronics engineering, engineering, manufacturing engineering, and mechanical engineering), HEALTH PROFESSIONS (biomedical science, health science, medical science, occupational therapy, physical therapy, predentistry, and speech pathology/audiology), SOCIAL SCIENCE (American studies, anthropology, archeology, architectural studies, classical/ancient civilization, criminal justice, economics, European studies, French studies, geography, Hispanic American studies, history, interdisciplinary studies, international relations, Italian studies, Japanese studies, Latin American studies, Middle Eastern studies, philosophy, philosophy and religion, political science/government, psychology, religion, sociology, and urban studies). Medical & dental programs, and engineering are the strongest academically. Communications, business, and engineering have the largest enrollments.

ACTIVITIES: 3% of men belong to 1 local and 8 national fraternities; 5% of women belong to 10 national sororities. There are 500 groups on campus, including sports club, art, band, cheerleading, chess, choir, chorale, chorus, communications, computers, dance, debate, drama, environmental, ethnic, film, honors, international, jazz band, LGBT, literary magazine, marching band, multicultural club, musical theater, newspaper, opera, orchestra, pep band, photography, political, professional, radio and TV, religious, social, social service, student government, and yearbook. Popular campus events include Fall Welcome (Splash), World Fair and Culture Fest, Fringe Festival, Lobster Night, Pumpkin Drop, and Head of the Charles River Regatta. **Sports:** There are 9 intercollegiate sports for men and 13 for women, and 16 intramural sports for men and 16 for women. Facilities include multipurpose fields, softball field, indoor track, tennis center and outdoor tennis courts, ice rinks, competition pool, recreational pools, a rock wall, multipurpose gymnasium, squash/racquetball courts, dance studio, fitness center, boathouse and sailing pavilion.**Graduates:** From July 1, 2016 to June 30, 2017, 4495 bachelor's degrees were awarded. The most popular majors were management (18%), communications (12%), and engineering (8%). In an average class, 4% graduate in 3 years or less, 81% graduate in 4 years or less, 85% graduate in 5 years or less, and 87% graduate in 6 years or less. Of the 2016 graduating class, 12% were enrolled in graduate school within 6 months of graduation, and 69% were employed.

SERVICES: Counseling and information services are available, as is tutoring in most subjects, such as liberal arts, science, engineering, management, and writing. There is a reader service for the blind. Comprehensive learning strategy for learning disabled is available. **Library/Resources:** The library contains 5.7 million volumes. Computerized library services include interlibrary loans, database searching, Internet access, and Wi-Fi capability. Special learning facilities include an art gallery, planetarium, radio station, TV station, over 2,000 research laboratories, 3 supercomputers that are available for student use, and 4 specialized high-performance computer labs, an astronomy observatory, 20th-century archives, a theater, language lab, a speech language, and hearing clinic, a performance center, a multi-media center, the Life Sciences and Engineering building, the Engineering Product Innovation Center and the Photonics Center which houses laboratories for developing new light-based technologies. **Physically Challenged Students:** 90% of the campus is accessible. Facilities include wheelchair ramps, elevators, special parking, specially equipped restrooms, special class scheduling, lowered drinking fountains, lowered telephones, special housing, on-campus transportation, relocation of classes/events for access, tactile and access maps, visual fire alarms for the deaf, adaptive computers, and readers, notetakers and ASL interpreters. **Special:** The Kilachand Honors College is a university-wide honors program, BU's Seven-Year Accelerated Medical and Dental Programs, allow highly motivated students to complete their bachelor's degree and medical or dental doctorate in seven years, and the MMEDIC/ENGMEDIC integrated curriculums students to begin their medical studies as undergraduates. BU's Dual Degree program enables students to earn two degrees simultaneously. Combined bachelors and masters programs are also available in many disciplines. Students conduct research with faculty or independently though our Undergraduate Research Opportunities Program and Work for Distinction. Students have many opportunities to intern in the US and abroad, and participate in more than 100 BU study abroad programs around the world. There are 10 national honor societies, Phi Beta Kappa, and a freshman honors program. **Visiting:** There are regularly scheduled orientations for prospective students, admissions at the Alan & Sherry Leventhal center is open Mon.-Fri., and some Saturdays during the academic year. Appointments can be made in the Admissions office for class visits or lunch with current students. Campus tours and information sessions are also offered. **Campus Safety and Security:** Measures include 24-hour foot and vehicle patrol, emergency notification system, self-defense education, and security escort services. There are shuttle buses, emergency telephones, lighted pathways/sidewalks, controlled access to dorms/residences, mountain bicycle patrol system. There is a uniformed safety/security assistant on duty 24 hours a day in large residence halls and there are 60 academy-trained officers in the university police department.

REQUIREMENTS: The SAT or ACT is required. The ACT Optional Writing test is also required. Applicants are evaluated on an individual basis. For most BU programs, the recommended curriculum includes 4 years of English, 3 to 4 years each of math (pre-calculus/calculus recommended), lab sciences, and history/social science, and 2 to 4 years of a foreign language. Students applying to the accelerated medical or dental programs are required to submit Subject Tests in chemistry, math (level 2), and a foreign language (recommended). Candidates for the College of Fine Arts are not required to submit standardized test scores, but must present a portfolio or participate in an audition. BU does not require the optional essay on the new SAT test. For students applying for fall 2018, BU will accept only the new SAT or the ACT. You can find more information about the new SAT on the College Board website. AP and CLEP credits are accepted. Important factors in the admissions decision are advanced placement or honors courses, recommendations by school officials, and extracurricular activities record. All students are required to complete at least 128 credit hours to qualify for graduation from Boston University. The individual schools and colleges within BU have specific academic requirements and standards for determining satisfactory completion of a program of study such as grades, majors, concentrations, divisional studies, or internships. **Procedure:** Freshmen are admitted fall and spring. Entrance exams should be taken in the junior year or early in the senior year. There are early decision, early admissions, and deferred admissions plans. Early decision applications should be filed by November 1; regular applications, by January 3 for fall entry. The fall 2017 application fee was $80. Notification of early decision is sent December 15; regular decision, April 1. 1098 early decision candidates were accepted for the 2017-2018 class. 4107 applicants were on the 2017 waiting list. Applications are accepted on-line. **Transfer Students:** 575 transfer students enrolled in 2016-2017. College transcript and secondary school transcripts, including proof of high school graduation (or GED), must be submitted. Recommendations, Transfer College Report, and an essay are also required. **International Students:** There are 3595 international students enrolled. They must take the TOEFL with a minimum score of 90 on the Internet-based version (iBT). Students must take the IELTS. They must also take the SAT or ACT.

ADMISSIONS: 25% of the 2017-2018 applicants were accepted. The SAT scores for the 2017-2018 freshman class were: Math-- 8% between

500 and 599, 44% between 600 and 699, and 48% between 700 and 800. Evidence-Based Reading/Writing-- 5% between 500 and 599, 49% between 600 and 699, and 46% between 700 and 800. The ACT scores were 1% between 18 and 23, 32% between 24 and 29, and 67% above 30. 87% of the current freshmen were in the top fifth of their class; 98% were in the top two fifths. 45 freshmen graduated first in their class. **Admissions Contact:** Kelly Walter, Associate Vice President & Executive Director of Undergraduate Admissions. Email: *admissions@bu.edu* Web: *www.bu.edu*

FINANCIAL AID: In 2017-2018, 54% of all full-time freshmen received some form of financial aid. 39% of all full-time freshmen received need-based aid. The average freshman award was $36,848. Need-based scholarships or need-based grants averaged $35,594 ($71,366 maximum); need-based self-help aid (loans and jobs) averaged $5,730 ($9,500 maximum); non-need-based athletic scholarships averaged $45,742 ($70,259 maximum); and other non-need-based awards and non-need-based scholarships averaged $22,204 ($57,000 maximum). 35% of undergraduate students work part-time. The average financial indebtedness of the 2017 graduate was $41,098. BU is a member of CSS. The CSS/Profile is required. The FAFSA code is 002130. The deadline for filing freshman financial aid applications for fall entry is February 1.

BRANDEIS UNIVERSITY D-2

www.brandeis.edu

Waltham, MA 02453 (781) 736-3500 / (800) 622-0622

Fax: (781) 736-3536 **Email: admissions@brandeis.edu**

Full-time: 1476 men, 2144 women	**Faculty:** 333
Part-time: 4 men, 11 women	**Ph.D.s:** 95%
Graduate: 902 men, 1185 women	**Student/Faculty:** 10 to 1
Year: semesters, summer session	**Tuition:** $53,537
Room & Board: $14,906	**Freshman Class:** 11721 applied, 4011 accepted, 858 enrolled
SAT EBR-W/M: 690/680 **ACT:** 31	**CEEB CODE:** 3092
Application Deadline: January 1	**MOST COMPETITIVE**

Brandeis University is a highly competitive private liberal arts and research university. Founded in 1948 by the American Jewish community and named for Supreme Court Justice Louis D. Brandeis, Brandeis embraces the values of academic excellence, critical thinking, openness to all, and making the world a better place. Brandeis is a member of the Association of American Universities, which represents the 62 leading research universities in the United States and Canada. There is 1 undergraduate school and 4 graduate schools. The 235-acre campus is in a suburban area 10 miles west of Boston. Including any residence halls, there are 94 buildings.

STUDENT LIFE: 71% of undergraduates are from out of state, mostly the Middle Atlantic. Students are from 47 states, 98 foreign countries, and Canada. 7% are Hispanic; 5% African American; 47% White; 3% two or more races; 3% race unknown; 21% Foreign; 13% Asian American. **Female To Male Ratio:** 1.4:1. The average age of freshmen is 18; all undergraduates, 20. 3% do not continue beyond their first year; 90% remain to graduate. **Housing:** 2900 students can be accommodated in college housing, which includes coed dorms and on-campus apartments. Leader Scholar Communities for first-year students and Common Cause Communities for upperclassmen. On-campus housing is guaranteed for the freshman year only, is available on a first-come, first-served basis, and is available on a lottery system for upperclassmen. 75% of students live on campus. Upperclassmen may keep cars.

FACULTY/CLASSROOMS: 54% of faculty are male; 46% are female. No introductory courses are taught by graduate students.

PROGRAMS OF STUDY: Brandeis confers B.A. and B.S. degrees. Master's and doctoral degrees are also awarded. Bachelor's degrees are awarded in AGRICULTURE (environmental studies), BIOLOGICAL SCIENCE (biochemistry, biology/biological science, biophysics, and neurosciences), BUSINESS (business administration and management), COMMUNICATIONS AND THE ARTS (art history, classics, comparative literature, creative writing, English, film arts, French, German, linguistics, music, Russian languages and literature, Spanish, studio art, and theatre arts), COMPUTER AND PHYSICAL SCIENCE (chemistry, computer science, mathematics, and physics), EDUCATION (education), HEALTH PROFESSIONS (health science), SOCIAL SCIENCE (African American studies, American studies, anthropology, East Asian studies, economics, European studies, history, interdisciplinary studies, international studies, Islamic studies, Judaic studies, Latin American studies, Middle Eastern studies, Near Eastern studies, philosophy, political science/government, psychology, sociology, and women's studies). Economics, biology, and business have the largest enrollments.

ACTIVITIES: There are no fraternities or sororities. There are 246 groups on campus, including BEMCO (EMTs), Student Events (programming board), Triskelion (GLBTQIA organization), art, band, cheerleading, chess, choir, chorale, chorus, computers, dance, debate, drama, environmental, ethnic, film, honors, international, jazz band, LGBT, literary magazine, musical theater, newspaper, orchestra, pep band, photography, political, professional, radio and TV, religious, social, social service, student government, symphony, Waltham Group, and yearbook. Popular campus events include Library Party, MELA, Concerts, Night for Africa, Culture X, SpringFest, Speakers, Festival of the Arts, Deis Impact, Liquid Latex Show, Purim. **Sports:** There are 9 intercollegiate sports for men and 10 for women, and 30 intramural sports for men and 30 for women. Facilities include a field house, basketball arena, indoor tennis courts, indoor basketball courts, squash courts, indoor track, several multipurpose rooms for aerobics, dance, group fitness, fencing room, weight room, turf soccer field, baseball and softball diamonds, outdoor tennis courts, indoor pool, and outdoor track. **Graduates:** From July 1, 2016 to June 30, 2017, 904 bachelor's degrees were awarded. The most popular majors were economics (11%), biology (10%), and business (9%). In an average class, 1% graduate in 3 years or less, 83% graduate in 4 years or less, 88% graduate in 5 years or less, and 90% graduate in 6 years or less. Of the 2016 graduating class, 36% were enrolled in graduate school within 6 months of graduation, and 58% were employed.

SERVICES: Counseling and information services are available, as is tutoring in most subjects. We produce Alt-Format Text for our blind students. Students with disabilities access the peer tutoring program available to all students. **Library/Resources:** The library contains 2.1 million volumes, 960,912 microform items, and 195,089 audio/video tapes/CDs/DVDs, and subscribes to 38,001 periodicals including electronic. Computerized library services include interlibrary loans, database searching, Internet access, and Wi-Fi capability. Special learning facilities include an art gallery, radio station, TV station, a spatial orientation laboratory, an astronomical observatory, an emotion laboratory, a cultural center, a treasure hall, an art museum, and an audiovisual center. **Physically Challenged Students:** 85% of the campus is accessible. Facilities include wheelchair ramps, elevators, special parking, specially equipped restrooms, special class scheduling, lowered drinking fountains, lowered telephones, special housing. Libraries, student centers, several other buildings, sports facilities, and the majority of residence halls are accessible. **Special:** Students may pursue interdepartmental programs in 18 different fields. Students may cross-register with Boston, Wellesley, Babson, Bentley and Olin Colleges and Boston and Tufts Universities. Study abroad is possible in 69 countries. Internships are available in virtually every field, and work-study is also available. Dual and student-designed majors can be arranged. Brandeis University and the Fu Foundation School of Engineering and Applied Science of Columbia University have established a dual degree program whereby students complete three years of course work at Brandeis, then spend two years at Columbia University to complete the requirements for an engineering degree. The university also offers credit by exam, non-degree study, and pass/fail options. Opportunities for early acceptance to area medical schools are offered to Brandeis students. There is 1 national honor society and a chapter of Phi Beta Kappa. **Visiting:** There are regularly scheduled orientations for prospective students, and most weekdays we offer morning and afternoon information sessions led by admissions counselors and followed by student-led tours. To schedule a visit, contact the Office of Admissions. **Campus Safety and Security:** Measures include 24-hour foot and vehicle patrol, emergency notification system, self-defense education, and security escort services. There are shuttle buses, emergency telephones, lighted pathways/sidewalks, controlled access to dorms/residences, extensive closed circuit television system on campus, a student EMT division that responds to medical calls during the academic year, and a personal Safety Committee with student involvement.

REQUIREMENTS: Brandeis has a test-flexible policy and no longer requires that citizens and permanent residents of the US or Canada submit SAT or ACT scores for the purposes of admission. Eligible applicants can choose one of the following three submission options: Option

1: Submit SAT or ACT, Option 2: Submit a combination of three SAT Subject Tests and/or AP tests (or IB exams), Option 3: Submit an academic portfolio through the Common Application including: One graded analytical paper from 11th or 12th grade and a second academic Teacher Evaluation. Home-schooled applicants and candidates applying from secondary schools that provide written evaluations rather than grades are required to submit the SAT or the ACT test with the writing section. AP credits are accepted. Important factors in the admissions decision are advanced placement or honors courses, recommendations by school officials, and personality/intangible qualities. All candidates for a bachelor's degree must satisfactorily complete 128 credits, a major, a writing requirement, a foreign language requirement, a group of courses designed to provide a strong foundation in general education, and the physical education requirement. Oral communication, quantitative reasoning, and non-Western and comparative studies requirements also must be met. **Procedure:** Freshmen are admitted fall, spring, and summer. Entrance exams should be taken by January of the senior year. There are early decision and deferred admissions plans. Early decision applications should be filed by November 1; regular applications, by January 1 for fall entry; and November 1 for spring entry. The fall 2017 application fee was $80. Notification of early decision is sent December 15; regular decision, April 1. 322 early decision candidates were accepted for the 2017-2018 class. 1826 applicants were on the 2017 waiting list; 8 were admitted. Applications are accepted on-line. **Transfer Students:** 46 transfer students enrolled in 2016-2017. Major consideration is given to the quality of college-level work completed, the secondary school record, professors' and deans' evaluations as well as the students fit for our institution. Because there is a 2-year residence requirement, students should apply before entering their junior year. 64 of 128 credits required for the bachelor's degree must be completed at Brandeis. **International Students:** There are 761 international students enrolled. They must take the TOEFL with a minimum score of 600 on the paper-based TOEFL (PBT) or 100 on the Internet-based version (iBT). Student must take the IELTS. They must also take the SAT or ACT.

ADMISSIONS: 34% of the 2017-2018 applicants were accepted. The SAT scores for the 2017-2018 freshman class were: Math-- 13% between 500 and 599, 48% between 600 and 699, and 39% between 700 and 800. Evidence-Based Reading/Writing-- 11% between 500 and 599, 41% between 600 and 699, and 47% between 700 and 800. The ACT scores were 1% between 18 and 23, 25% between 24 and 29, and 74% above 30. 84% of the current freshmen were in the top fifth of their class; 98% were in the top two fifths. 17 freshmen graduated first in their class. **Admissions Contact:** Jennifer Walker, Dean of Admissions. Email: *admissions@brandeis.edu* Web: *www.brandeis.edu*

FINANCIAL AID: In 2017-2018, 60% of all full-time freshmen received some form of financial aid. 47% of all full-time freshmen received need-based aid. The average freshman award was $42,400. Need-based scholarships or need-based grants averaged $39,010 ($67,500 maximum); need-based self-help aid (loans and jobs) averaged $3,390 ($8,500 maximum); and other non-need-based awards and non-need-based scholarships averaged $12,850 ($17,500 maximum). 58% of undergraduate students work part-time. The average financial indebtedness of the 2017 graduate was $29,452. BU is a member of CSS. The CSS/Profile, and copies of student and parent tax returns are required. The FAFSA code is 002133. The priority date for freshman financial aid applications for fall entry is January 1.

BRIDGEWATER STATE UNIVERSITY E-3
www.bridgew.edu

Bridgewater, MA 02325 **(508) 531-1237**

Fax: (508) 531-1746
Email: admissions@bridgew.edu
Full-time: 3226 men, 4632 women
Faculty: n/av
Part-time: 715 men, 985 women
Ph.D.s: 95%
Graduate: 403 men, 1063 women
Student/Faculty: 19 to 1
Year: semesters, summer session
Tuition: $10,012 ($16,152)
Room & Board: $12,750
Freshman Class: 6338 applied, 5094 accepted, 1506 enrolled
SAT EBR-W/M: 538/523 **ACT:** 22
CEEB CODE: 3517
Application Deadline: February 15
COMPETITIVE

Bridgewater State University provides a broad range of baccalaureate degree programs through its College of Humanities and Social Sciences, Bartlett College of Science and Mathematics, College of Education and Allied Studies and its Ricciardi College of Business. BSU offers 32 undergraduate academic programs with 90 different areas of concentration as well as internships, research programs, study abroad and honors programs. There are 5 undergraduate schools and 1 graduate school. In addition to regional accreditation, BSU has baccalaureate program accreditation with CSWE, NASAD, NASDTEC, NASM, CAEP, ACS, FAA, CAATE, NASPAA, and CACREP. The 278-acre campus is in a suburban area 28 miles from Boston. Including any residence halls, there are 44 buildings.

STUDENT LIFE: 95% of undergraduates are from Massachusetts. Others are from 29 states, 24 foreign countries, and Canada. 74% are White; 7% Hispanic; 4% two or more races; 2% Asian American; 2% race unknown; 10% African American. **Female To Male Ratio:** 1.5:1. The average age of freshmen is 18; all undergraduates, 23. 24% do not continue beyond their first year; 59% remain to graduate. **Housing:** 3295 students can be accommodated in college housing, which includes dorms and on-campus apartments, break housing for athletes, student teachers, visiting lecturers, international students, and special housing for disabled students. On-campus housing is available on a first-come and first-served basis. 58% of students commute. Alcohol is not permitted. Upperclassmen may keep cars.

FACULTY/CLASSROOMS: 46% of faculty are male; 54% are female. No introductory courses are taught by graduate students.

PROGRAMS OF STUDY: BSU confers B.A., B.S. and B.S.Ed. degrees. Master's degrees are also awarded. Bachelor's degrees are awarded in BIOLOGICAL SCIENCE (biology/biological science), BUSINESS (accounting, finance, and management science), COMMUNICATIONS AND THE ARTS (art, art history and appreciation, English, fine arts, music, Spanish, and speech/debate/rhetoric), COMPUTER AND PHYSICAL SCIENCE (chemistry, computer science, earth science, geochemistry, mathematics, and physics), EDUCATION (art education, athletic training, dance education, drama education, early childhood education, elementary education, health education, music education, physical education, and special education), ENGINEERING AND ENVIRONMENTAL DESIGN (aeronautical science), SOCIAL SCIENCE (anthropology, criminal justice, economics, geography, philosophy, political science/government, psychology, social work, and sociology). Counselor education, special education, and business are the strongest academically. Early childhood and elementary education, management, and psychology have the largest enrollments.

ACTIVITIES: 5% of men belong to 6 local fraternities; 6% of women belong to 4 local sororities. There are 90 groups on campus, including art, band, chorale, communications, computers, dance, drama, environmental, ethnic, forensics, honors, international, jazz band, LGBT, musical theater, newspaper, political, professional, religious, social, social service, student government, and yearbook. Popular campus events include Homecoming, Springfest, and Campus Movie Fest. **Sports:** There are 10 intercollegiate sports for men and 11 for women, and 7 intramural sports for men and 7 for women. Facilities include a competition court with NCAA regulation basketball and volleyball venue, multipurpose courts for basketball, badminton, tennis, 1/8 mile three lane track, cardiovascular machines, selectorized weight machines, a plate-loaded equipment, free-weights, and Olympic lifting platforms, large and small gyms, a pool, athletic complex for football, field hockey, soccer, and softball. **Graduates:** From July 1, 2016 to June 30, 2017, 1994 bachelor's degrees were awarded. The most popular majors were education (18%), business/marketing (17%), and psychology (13%). In an average class, 32% graduate in 4 years or less, 53% graduate in 5 years or less, and 59% graduate in 6 years or less. Of the 2016 graduating class, 19% were enrolled in graduate school within 6 months of graduation, and 87% were employed.

SERVICES: Counseling and information services are available, as is tutoring in most subjects. There is a reader service for the blind, and remedial math, reading, and writing. There are recorded texts, classroom interpreters, scribes and note takers, testing accommodations, and a speech/hearing/language center. **Library/Resources:** Computerized library services include interlibrary loans, database searching, Internet access, and Wi-Fi capability. Special learning facilities include an art gallery, planetarium, an observatory, and a greenhouse. **Physically Challenged Students:** 95% of the campus is accessible. Facilities include wheelchair ramps, elevators, special parking, specially equipped restrooms, special class scheduling, lowered drinking fountains, lowered telephones, and special housing. **Special:** Opportunities are provided for cross-registration with other Massachusetts Colleges and Universities, internships available in most majors, double majors, joint/dual degree in B.S. & M.S. in Criminal Justice and B.S.Ed. in Elementary Education & M.Ed. in Special Education, core curriculum requirements, non-degree study, and study abroad programs. BSU participates in The Washington Center Internship Program, National Student Exchange, Southeastern Association for Cooperation in Higher Education, and the College Academic Program Sharing. Accelerated degree program available for MSW and some post-bacs. There is a chapter of Phi Beta Kappa, a freshman honors program, and 27 departmental honors programs. **Visiting:** There are regularly scheduled orientations for prospective students, campus tours for prospective students Monday through Thursday at 11 a.m. and 3 p.m. when college is in session and 10 a.m. and 2 p.m. during summer months. BSU also offers prospective students and their families participation in an interactive open. To schedule a visit, contact Gregg Meyer at (508) 531-1237. **Campus Safety and Security:** Measures include 24-hour foot and vehicle patrol, emergency notification system, self-defense education, and security escort services. There are shuttle buses, emergency telephones, lighted pathways/sidewalks, controlled access to dorms/residences, BSU police department, and a safety-escort van 7 days a week.

REQUIREMENTS: Graduation from an accredited secondary school is required; SAT or ACT scores required, a GED will be accepted. Applicants must have successfully completed 17 Carnegie units, including 4 units of English, 4 units of mathematics, 3 units of science with 2 lab units, 2 units of a foreign language, 2 units of social studies, and 2 in other college preparatory electives. An essay is recommended. AP and CLEP credits are accepted. Students are required to complete a minimum of 120 semester hours. Students must maintain a minimum GPA of 2.0. **Procedure:** Freshmen are admitted fall and spring. There are early admissions and deferred admissions plans. Applications should be filed by February 15 for fall entry; November 1 for spring entry. The fall 2017 application fee was $50. Notifications are sent April 15. Applications are accepted on-line. **Transfer Students:** 1103 transfer students enrolled in 2016-2017. Transfer students must have maintained a minimum GPA of 2.5 from 1 to 23 credits or 2.0 from more than 24 credits at a previous institution. College transcripts and an essay are required of all transfer students; some students must submit high school transcripts and standardized test scores. 30 of 120 credits required for the bachelor's degree must be completed at BSU. **International Students:** There are 37 international students enrolled. They must take the TOEFL with a minimum score of 500 on the paper-based TOEFL (PBT) or 61 on the Internet-based version (iBT). Student must take the IELTS. They must also take the SAT or ACT.

ADMISSIONS: 80% of the 2017-2018 applicants were accepted. The SAT scores for the 2017-2018 freshman class were: Math-- 30% below 500, 57% between 500 and 599, 13% between 600 and 699, and 1% between 700 and 800. Evidence-Based Reading/Writing-- 27% below 500, 52% between 500 and 599, 20% between 600 and 699, and 1% between 700 and 800. The ACT scores were 15% between 12 and 17, 55% between 18 and 23, 27% between 24 and 29, and 3% above 30. **Admissions Contact:** Gregg A. Meyer, Dean of University Admissions. Email: *admissions@bridgew.edu* Web: *www.bridgew.edu*

FINANCIAL AID: In 2017-2018, 76% of all full-time freshmen received some form of financial aid. 72% of all full-time freshmen received need-based aid. The average freshman award was $8,523. Need-based scholarships or need-based grants averaged $6,095; need-based self-help aid (loans and jobs) averaged $3,431; other non-need-based awards and non-need-based scholarships averaged $5,322; and $3,188 from other forms of aid. The average financial indebtedness of the 2017 graduate was $34,146. The FAFSA code is 002183. The priority date for freshman financial aid applications for fall entry is March 1.

CAMBRIDGE COLLEGE *(The complete profile is made available exclusively on our website, www.barronspac.com)*

CLARK UNIVERSITY C-2

www.clarku.edu

Worcester, MA 01610	(508) 793-7431 (800) 462-5275
Fax: (508) 793-8821	Email: admissions@clarku.edu
Full-time: 846 men, 1353 women	**Faculty:** 212; I, -$
Part-time: 23 men, 18 women	**Ph.D.s:** 95%
Graduate: 384 men, 529 women	**Student/Faculty:** 9 to 1
Year: semesters, summer session	**Tuition:** $44,400
Room & Board: $8860	**Freshman Class:** 8355 applied, 4701 accepted, 615 enrolled
SAT EBR-W/M: 645/630 **ACT:** 29	**CEEB CODE:** 3279
Application Deadline: January 15	**HIGHLY COMPETITIVE+**

Clark University, founded in 1887, is a liberal arts-based research university that prides itself on being a diverse and welcoming community. There are 2 undergraduate schools and 3 graduate schools. In addition to regional accreditation has baccalaureate program accreditation with AACSB and NASDTEC. The 50-acre campus is in an urban area within an hour of Boston and Providence and about 3 hours from New York City. Including any residence halls, there are 79 buildings.

STUDENT LIFE: 62% of undergraduates are from out of state, mostly the Northeast. Students are from 41 states, 67 foreign countries, and Canada. 73% are from public schools. 8% are Asian American; 8% Hispanic; 6% race unknown; 58% White; 4% African American; 2% two or more races; 14% Foreign. 24% claim no religious affiliation; 15% Protestant; 13% Catholic. **Female To Male Ratio:** 1.5:1. The average age of freshmen is 19; all undergraduates, 20. 14% do not continue beyond their first year; 83% remain to graduate. **Housing:** 1739 students can be accommodated in college housing, which includes single sex, coed dorms, on-campus apartments, and off-campus apartments. In addition, there are special-interest houses, wellness, and quiet houses. On-campus housing is guaranteed for the freshman year only and is available on a lottery system for upperclassmen. 67% of students live on campus. All students may keep cars.

FACULTY/CLASSROOMS: 54% of faculty are male; 46% are female. All teach undergraduates and all do research. No introductory courses are taught by graduate students. The average class size in an introductory lecture is 25; in a laboratory is 13; and in a regular course is 20.

PROGRAMS OF STUDY: Clark confers B.A. and B.S. degrees. Master's and doctoral degrees are also awarded. Bachelor's degrees are awarded in BIOLOGICAL SCIENCE (biochemistry and biology/biological science), BUSINESS (business administration and management), COMMUNICATIONS AND THE ARTS (art history and appreciation, communications, comparative literature, dramatic arts, English, film arts, fine arts, French, languages, music, romance languages and literature, Spanish, studio art, and visual and performing arts), COMPUTER AND PHYSICAL SCIENCE (chemistry, computer science, mathematics, and physics), ENGINEERING AND ENVIRONMENTAL DESIGN (environmental science), HEALTH PROFESSIONS (predentistry and premedicine), SOCIAL SCIENCE (Asian/Oriental studies, classical/ancient civilization, economics, geography, history, international relations, international studies, philosophy, political science/government, prelaw, psychology, sociology, and women's studies). Psychology, and geography are the strongest academically. Psychology, biology/biochemistry, and political science have the largest enrollments.

ACTIVITIES: There are no fraternities or sororities. There are 132 groups on campus, including art, band, chess, choir, chorale, chorus, computers, dance, debate, drama, environmental, ethnic, film, honors, international, jazz band, LGBT, literary magazine, musical theater, newspaper, orchestra, political, professional, radio and TV, religious, social, social service, student government, symphony, and yearbook. Popular campus events include GALA, Spree Day, Haunted Jonas Clark, Clark Con, Rocky Horror Picture Show, Eid Diwali Dinner, Eid Dinner, Isa Journey, SAB's Bingo & Trivia Nights, Shabbat Dinner, Lunar New Year, Kwanzaa Celebration, Improv. Shows, Vagina Monologues. **Sports:** There are 8 intercollegiate sports for men and 9 for women, and 12 intramural sports for men and 12 for women. Facilities include a gym, pool, racquetball and squash courts; a fitness center; a field house with basketball/tennis courts; outdoor tennis courts; two turf fields for baseball, soccer, field hockey and lacrosse; and a softball field. **Graduates:** From July 1, 2016 to June 30, 2017, 567 bachelor's degrees were awarded.

The most popular majors were psychology (19%), biology and biochemistry (13%), and political science (8%). In an average class, 1% graduate in 3 years or less, 76% graduate in 4 years or less, 82% graduate in 5 years or less, and 83% graduate in 6 years or less. Of the 2016 graduating class, 40% were enrolled in graduate school within 6 months of graduation, and 50% were employed.

SERVICES: Counseling and information services are available, as is tutoring in some subjects, such as biology, chemistry, economics, management, math, and writing. For students with learning disabilities, the university provides early orientation, alternative test-taking accommodations, and a learning specialist. **Library/Resources:** The library contains 669,664 volumes, 61,417 microform items, and 2,489 audio/video tapes/CDs/DVDs, and subscribes to 2,115 periodicals including electronic. Computerized library services include interlibrary loans, database searching, Internet access, and Wi-Fi capability. Special learning facilities include an art gallery and radio station. **Physically Challenged Students:** 95% of the campus is accessible. Facilities include wheelchair ramps, elevators, special parking, specially equipped restrooms, special class scheduling, lowered drinking fountains, lowered telephones, and special housing. **Special:** For-credit internships are available in all disciplines with private corporations and small businesses, medical centers, not-for-profits, and government agencies. There is cross-registration with members of the Higher Education Consortium of Central Massachusetts, including 9 other colleges and universities. Clark also offers study abroad in 27 countries, a Washington semester with American University, work-study programs, accelerated degree programs, dual and student-designed majors, pass/no-record options, and a 3-2 engineering program in partnership with Columbia University. There are 10 national honor societies, Phi Beta Kappa, and 21 departmental honors programs. **Visiting:** There are regularly scheduled orientations for prospective students, consisting of open houses during fall and spring semesters, which include tours, information sessions, and talks with faculty, administration, and coaches. There are guides for informal visits and visitors may sit in on classes. To schedule a visit, contact Clark Admissions Office. **Campus Safety and Security:** Measures include 24-hour foot and vehicle patrol, emergency notification system, self-defense education, and security escort services. There are shuttle buses, emergency telephones, lighted pathways/sidewalks, and controlled access to dorms/residences.

REQUIREMENTS: SAT or ACT are optional. Applicants must graduate from an accredited secondary school or have a GED. 16 Carnegie units are required, including 4 years of English, 3 each of math and science, and 2 each of foreign languages and social studies, including history. AP credits are accepted. Each student is required to complete 2 critical thinking courses, one in verbal expression and one in formal analysis, and 6 perspective courses, one each in the categories of aesthetics, comparative, historical, language and culture, science, and values. The university also has a diversity and inclusion requirement and a capstone requirement. A student must receive passing grades in a minimum of 32 full courses, with a C- or better in at least 24 of those courses, and maintain a minimum 2.0 GPA to graduate. **Procedure:** Freshmen are admitted fall and spring. Entrance exams should be taken by November of the senior year. There are early decision, early admissions, and deferred admissions plans. Early decision applications should be filed by November 1; regular applications, by January 15 for fall entry; and November 15 for spring entry. The fall 2017 application fee was $60. Notification of early decision is sent December 15; regular decision, April 1. 40 early decision candidates were accepted for the 2017-2018 class. 590 applicants were on the 2017 waiting list; 8 were admitted. Applications are accepted on-line. **Transfer Students:** 42 transfer students enrolled in 2016-2017. Applicants should have a minimum GPA of about 2.8. At least one full semester of college coursework is required. High school and college transcripts, recent SAT or ACT test scores, a statement of good standing from previous institutions attended, and a transfer statement are required. Grades of C or better in comparable course work transfer for credit. 16 of 32 credits required for the bachelor's degree must be completed at Clark. **International Students:** There are 304 international students enrolled. They must take the TOEFL with a minimum score of 550 on the paper-based TOEFL (PBT) or 80 on the Internet-based version (iBT), and take the IELTS, scoring 6.5.

ADMISSIONS: 56% of the 2017-2018 applicants were accepted. The SAT scores for the 2017-2018 freshman class were: Math-- 3% below 500, 29% between 500 and 599, 48% between 600 and 699, and 20% between 700 and 800. Evidence-Based Reading/Writing-- 3% below 500, 22% between 500 and 599, 49% between 600 and 699, and 26% between 700 and 800. The ACT scores were 6% between 18 and 23, 53% between 24 and 29, and 41% above 30. 63% of the current freshmen were in the top fifth of their class; 91% were in the top two fifths. 5 freshmen graduated first in their class. **Admissions Contact:** Donald Honeman, Dean of Admissions. Email: *admissions@clarku.edu* Web: *www.clarku.edu*

FINANCIAL AID: In 2017-2018, 93% of all full-time freshmen received some form of financial aid. 54% of all full-time freshmen received need-based aid. The average freshman award was $28,876. Need-based scholarships or need-based grants averaged $25,252; and need-based self-help aid (loans and jobs) averaged $6,028. 75% of undergraduate students work part-time. The average financial indebtedness of the 2017 graduate was $32,866. CU is a member of CSS. The CSS/Profile is required. The FAFSA code is 002139. The priority date for freshman financial aid applications for fall entry is January 15. The deadline for filing freshman financial aid applications for fall entry is February 1.

COLLEGE OF ART AND DESIGN AT LESLEY UNIVERSITY *(The complete profile is made available exclusively on our website, www.barronspac.com)*

COLLEGE OF THE HOLY CROSS — C-2

www.holycross.edu

Worcester, MA 01610 — **(508) 793-2443**, **(800) 442-2421**

Fax: (508) 793-3888	**Email: admissions@holycross.edu**
Full-time: 1452 men, 1568 women	**Faculty:** 278; IIB, ++$
Part-time: 10 men, 21 women	**Ph.D.s:** 95%
Graduate: n/av	**Student/Faculty:** 11 to 1
Year: semesters	**Tuition:** $50,630
Room & Board: $13,690	**Freshman Class:** 6622 applied, 2622 accepted, 819 enrolled
SAT EBR-W/M: 669/665 **ACT:** 30	**CEEB CODE:** 3282
Application Deadline: January 15	**MOST COMPETITIVE**

College of the Holy Cross is the only liberal arts college that embraces a Catholic, Jesuit identity, and of the 28 Jesuit colleges and universities in the United States, Holy Cross stands alone in its exclusive commitment to undergraduate education. Students enjoy a full array of athletic facilities, fitness and wellness centers, and outstanding arts spaces. There is 1 undergraduate school. In addition to regional accreditation, CHC has baccalaureate program accreditation with NAST. The 174-acre campus is in a suburban area 45 miles west of Boston. Including any residence halls, there are 35 buildings.

STUDENT LIFE: 59% of undergraduates are from out of state, mostly the Northeast. Students are from 47 states, 24 foreign countries, and Canada. 50% are from public schools. 70% are White; 5% Asian American; 4% African American; 4% two or more races; 3% Foreign; 3% race unknown; 11% Hispanic. 64% are Catholic; 18% Unknown denominations. **Female To Male Ratio:** 1.1:1. The average age of freshmen is 18; all undergraduates, 20. 5% do not continue beyond their first year; 92% remain to graduate. **Housing:** 2522 students can be accommodated in college housing, which includes dorms and on-campus apartments. In addition, there are special-interest houses, substance-free housing, and first-year living learning housing. On-campus housing is guaranteed for all 4 years. 91% of students live on campus. Upperclassmen may keep cars.

FACULTY/CLASSROOMS: 53% of faculty are male; 47% are female. All teach undergraduates, and all do research. No introductory courses are taught by graduate students. The average class size in a regular course is 18.

PROGRAMS OF STUDY: CHC confers A.B. degrees. Bachelor's degrees are awarded in AGRICULTURE (environmental studies), BIOLOGICAL SCIENCE (biology/biological science), BUSINESS (accounting), COMMUNICATIONS AND THE ARTS (art history and appreciation, Chinese, classics, English, French, German, Italian, literature, music, Russian, Spanish, studio art, and theatre arts), COMPUTER AND PHYSICAL SCIENCE (chemistry, computer science, mathematics, and physics), SOCIAL SCIENCE (anthropology, architectural studies, Asian/Oriental studies, economics, history, international studies, Latin American studies, philosophy, political science/government, psychology, religion, and sociology). Economics, psychology, and political science have the largest enrollments.

ACTIVITIES: There are no fraternities or sororities. There are 104

groups on campus, including art, band, cheerleading, choir, chorale, chorus, computers, dance, debate, drama, environmental, ethnic, film, honors, international, jazz band, LGBT, literary magazine, marching band, musical theater, newspaper, orchestra, pep band, photography, political, professional, religious, social, social service, student government, symphony, and yearbook. Popular campus events include Family Weekend, Purple Pride Day, Winter Homecoming, and Spring Weekend. **Sports:** There are 13 intercollegiate sports for men and 14 for women, and 9 intramural sports for men and 8 for women. Facilities include baseball, football, soccer fields and stadiums, indoor and outdoor running tracks, a swimming pool, ice rink, indoor crew tanks, basketball arena, weight and exercise rooms, wellness centers, tennis, squash, and racquetball courts. **Graduates:** From July 1, 2016 to June 30, 2017, 667 bachelor's degrees were awarded. The most popular majors were economics (16%), psychology (13%), and political science (11%). In an average class, 87% graduate in 4 years or less, 91% graduate in 5 years or less, and 92% graduate in 6 years or less. Of the 2016 graduating class, 14% were enrolled in graduate school within 6 months of graduation, and 74% were employed.

SERVICES: Counseling and information services are available, as is tutoring in some subjects, such as calculus, biology, chemistry, Spanish, physics, economics, accounting, and statistics. **Library/Resources:** The library contains 649,119 volumes, 16,599 microform items, and 31,280 audio/video tapes/CDs/DVDs, and subscribes to 15,637 periodicals including electronic. Computerized library services include interlibrary loans, database searching, Internet access, and Wi-Fi capability. Special learning facilities include an art gallery, greenhouses, research-level laboratories and equipment, and multimedia resource center. **Physically Challenged Students:** 85% of the campus is accessible. Facilities include wheelchair ramps, elevators, special parking, specially equipped restrooms, special class scheduling, lowered drinking fountains, lowered telephones, and special housing. **Special:** Academic internships are available through the Center for Interdisciplinary Studies. The Internship program includes a student-managed large-cap investment portfolio. Student-designed majors, dual majors, Washington semester, New York City semester, and study abroad in approximately 15 countries are possible. The college also offers several 4- to 6-week programs in locations such as Jerusalem, Kenya, London, Luxembourg, Moscow, Paris, Rome and South Africa. There is a 3-2 engineering program in conjunction with Columbia University, internships, and an accelerated degree program. Students may also cross-register with 10 other colleges and universities in a local higher education consortium. There are 2 national honor societies, Phi Beta Kappa, and 8 departmental honors programs. **Visiting:** There are regularly scheduled orientations for prospective students, open houses in October and November consist of informational panels on academics, admissions, financial aid, and student life, as well as tours of the facilities. To schedule a visit, contact the Admissions Office. **Campus Safety and Security:** Measures include 24-hour foot and vehicle patrol, emergency notification system, self-defense education, and security escort services. There are shuttle buses, emergency telephones, lighted pathways/sidewalks, controlled access to dorms/residences, and card access control system.

REQUIREMENTS: Applicants should be graduates of an accredited secondary school or hold the GED. Recommended preparatory courses include English, foreign language, history, math, and science. An essay is required. Students have the option to submit standardized test scores if they believe the results represent a fuller picture of their achievements and potential; students who opt not to submit scores will not be at any disadvantage in admissions decisions. An interview is recommended. AP credits are accepted. Important factors in the admissions decision are extracurricular activities record, recommendations by school officials, and advanced placement or honors courses. Distribution requirements include social science, natural and mathematical science, cross-cultural studies, religious and philosophical studies, historical studies and the arts, and literature. In addition, students must demonstrate competence in a classical or modern language or American sign language. A total of 32 courses worth at least 1 unit each is required for graduation, with 10 to 14 courses in the major. The minimum GPA for graduation is 2.0. **Procedure:** Freshmen are admitted fall. Entrance exams should be taken no later than February 1st of the senior year. There are early decision and deferred admissions plans. Early decision applications should be filed by December 15; regular applications, by January 15 for fall entry. The fall 2017 application fee was $60. Notification of early decision is sent January 15; regular decision, April 1. 345 early decision candidates were accepted for the 2017-2018 class. 444 applicants were on the 2017 waiting list. Applications are accepted on-line. **Transfer Students:** 16 transfer students enrolled in 2016-2017. Standardized test scores are not required but applicants must provide transcripts and 2 professor recommendations. Personal interviews are highly recommended. 64 of 128 credits required for the bachelor's degree must be completed at CHC. **International Students:** There are 97 international students enrolled. They must take the TOEFL with a minimum score of 600 on the paper-based TOEFL (PBT) or 100 on the Internet-based version (iBT).

ADMISSIONS: 40% of the 2017-2018 applicants were accepted. The SAT scores for the 2017-2018 freshman class were: Math-- 12% between 500 and 599, 58% between 600 and 699, and 30% between 700 and 800. Evidence-Based Reading/Writing-- 9% between 500 and 599, 57% between 600 and 699, and 34% between 700 and 800. The ACT scores were 1% between 18 and 23, 43% between 24 and 29, and 56% above 30. **Admissions Contact:** Ann McDermott, Director. Email: *admissions@holycross.edu* Web: *www.holycross.edu*

FINANCIAL AID: In 2017-2018, 66% of all full-time freshmen received some form of financial aid. 58% of all full-time freshmen received need-based aid. The average freshman award was $40,451. Need-based scholarships or need-based grants averaged $36,511; need-based self-help aid (loans and jobs) averaged $6,105; non-need-based athletic scholarships averaged $34,987; and other non-need-based awards and non-need-based scholarships averaged $23,008. 47% of undergraduate students work part-time. The average financial indebtedness of the 2017 graduate was $26,258. CHC is a member of CSS. The CSS/Profile, student and parent federal tax returns, business/farm supplement, are required if applicable. The FAFSA code is 002141. The deadline for filing freshman financial aid applications for fall entry is January 15.

CURRY COLLEGE — E-2

www.curry.edu

Milton, MA 02186	**(617) 333-2210** **(800) 669-0686**
Fax: (617) 333-2114	**Email: adm@curry.edu**
Full-time: 925 men, 1134 women	**Faculty:** 119; IIB, ++$
Part-time: 108 men, 398 women	**Ph.D.s:** 82%
Graduate: 101 men, 133 women	**Student/Faculty:** 18 to 1
Year: semesters, summer session	**Tuition:** $38,596
Room & Board: $14,735	**Freshman Class:** 6031 applied, 5431 accepted, 660 enrolled
SAT CR/M: 515/504	**CEEB CODE:** 3285
Application Deadline: April 1	**COMPETITIVE**

Curry College, founded in 1879, is a private, four-year, liberal arts-based institution. Curry extends its educational programs to a continuing education branch campus in Plymouth, MA. Curry offers 25 undergraduate majors, as well as graduate degrees in business, education, criminal justice and nursing. There is 1 undergraduate school and 1 graduate school. In addition to regional accreditation, Curry College has baccalaureate program accreditation with CCNE, PCIPP, and IACBE. The 131-acre campus is in a suburban area 7 miles south of downtown Boston. Including any residence halls, there are 47 buildings.

STUDENT LIFE: 74% of undergraduates are from Massachusetts. Others are from 29 states, 21 foreign countries, and Canada. 78% are from public schools. 8% are race unknown; 7% Hispanic; 66% White; 2% Asian American; 2% Foreign; 2% two or more races; 11% African American. **Female To Male Ratio:** 1.5:1. The average age of freshmen is 18; all undergraduates, 20. 32% do not continue beyond their first year; 53% remain to graduate. **Housing:** 1573 students can be accommodated in college housing, which includes dorms. On-campus housing is available on a first-come, first-served basis, and is available on a lottery system for upperclassmen. 75% of students live on campus. Upperclassmen may keep cars.

FACULTY/CLASSROOMS: 35% of faculty are male; 65% are female. All teach undergraduates. No introductory courses are taught by graduate students. The average class size in an introductory lecture is 18; in a laboratory is 13; and in a regular course is 18.

PROGRAMS OF STUDY: Curry confers B.A. and B.S. degrees. Master's degrees are also awarded. Bachelor's degrees are awarded in BIOLOGICAL SCIENCE (biochemistry and biology/biological science), BUSINESS (accounting and business administration and management), COMMUNICATIONS AND THE ARTS (communications, English, graphic design, and visual and performing arts), COMPUTER AND PHYSICAL SCIENCE (computer programming, information sciences and systems, and software production & management), EDUCATION (early childhood education, education, elementary education, health education, and special education), HEALTH PROFESSIONS (nursing and public health), SOCIAL SCIENCE (criminal justice, history, liberal arts/general studies, philosophy, political science/government, psychology, and sociology). Nursing, and communication are the strongest academically. Nursing, business, and criminal justice have the largest enrollments.

ACTIVITIES: There are no fraternities or sororities. There are 34 groups on campus, including art, cheerleading, chorale, dance, drama, ethnic, film, honors, international, LGBT, musical theater, newspaper, photography, political, professional, radio and TV, religious, social, social service, student government, and yearbook. Popular campus events include Dances, Late Night Programs, and Theater Productions. **Sports:** There are 7 intercollegiate sports for men and 7 for women, and 9 intramural sports for men and 9 for women. The Athletic and Recreational facilities include a gymnasium, fitness center, dance studio, and athletic weight room. Outdoor facilities include tennis courts, a pool, grass athletic fields, a turf stadium, and a cross-country trail. **Graduates:** From July 1, 2016 to June 30, 2017, 689 bachelor's degrees were awarded. The most popular majors were nursing (40%), business (13%), and criminal justice (12%). In an average class, 46% graduate in 4 years or less, 52% graduate in 5 years or less, and 53% graduate in 6 years or less.

SERVICES: Counseling and information services are available, as is tutoring in most subjects. There is a reader service for the blind, and remedial math, reading, and writing. General development courses in writing, reading, and math are designed to develop the student's basic skills. **Library/Resources:** The library contains 284,646 volumes, and 3,441 audio/video tapes/CDs/DVDs, and subscribes to 51,584 periodicals including electronic. Computerized library services include interlibrary loans, database searching, Internet access, and Wi-Fi capability. Special learning facilities the Curry communication radio station WMLN-FM 91.5, and the Hirsh Communication Center and our television station CC8. TV and film students can garner real-word experience through the Semester in Los Angeles, New York City, and Washington D.C. programs which allow students to complete internships with leading industry employers. Curry nursing clinical placements begin in the sophomore year, differentiated from many nursing programs which begin in the junior year. The Program for Advancement of Learning (PAL) provides academically focused assistance to bright, college-able students with specific language-based learning disabilities, executive function disorders, and/or AD/HD. Curry College offers English for Speakers of Other Languages (ESOL) coursework for both domestic and international students. **Physically Challenged Students:** 80% of the campus is accessible. Facilities include wheelchair ramps, elevators, special parking, specially equipped restrooms, special class scheduling, and special housing. **Special:** Curry College provides rigorous and relevant academic programs to undergraduate and graduate students, and our rich blend of liberal arts and career-directed programs is enhanced by practical field experiences and co-curricular activities. There are 6 national honor societies and a freshman honors program. **Visiting:** There are regularly scheduled orientations for prospective students, student visits consist of interviews with an admissions counselor and tours with a student. There are guides for informal visits and visitors may sit in on classes. To schedule a visit, contact the Admissions Office. **Campus Safety and Security:** Measures include 24-hour foot and vehicle patrol, emergency notification system, self-defense education, and security escort services. There are shuttle buses, emergency telephones, lighted pathways/sidewalks, controlled access to dorms/residences, and campus safety offices.

REQUIREMENTS: The college's Program for the Advancement of Learning does not require nor does it consider SAT or ACT scores during the admission process. AP and CLEP credits are accepted. Important factors in the admissions decision are recommendations by school officials, leadership record, and extracurricular activities record. Successful completion of the liberal arts core curriculum and a total of 120 semester hours, completion of a major, and a minimum 2.0 GPA, are required for graduation. Transfer students have modified liberal arts requirements. **Procedure:** Freshmen are admitted fall and spring. Entrance exams should be taken during the junior year or in November of the senior year. There are early admissions, deferred admissions, and rolling admissions plans. Applications should be filed by April 1 for fall entry; December 1 for spring entry. The fall 2017 application fee was $50. Notification is sent on a rolling basis. 83 applicants were on the 2017 waiting list; 28 were admitted. Applications are accepted on-line. **Transfer Students:** 57 transfer students enrolled in 2016-2017. Transfer applicants must be in good academic and judicial standing at their previous colleges, with a minimum GPA of 2.0. 30 of 120 credits required for the bachelor's degree must be completed at Curry. **International Students:** There are 47 international students enrolled. They must take the TOEFL with a minimum score of 525 on the paper-based TOEFL (PBT) or 71 on the Internet-based version (iBT).

ADMISSIONS: 90% of the 2017-2018 applicants were accepted. The SAT scores for the 2017-2018 freshman class were: Math-- 41% below 500, 51% between 500 and 599, and 7% between 600 and 699. Evidence-Based Reading/Writing-- 32% below 500, 50% between 500 and 599, and 9% between 600 and 699. The ACT scores were 19% between 12 and 17, 58% between 18 and 23, 23% between 24 and 29, and 2% above 30. 20% of the current freshmen were in the top fifth of their class; 40% were in the top two fifths. **Admissions Contact:** Jane Fidler, VP of Admission & Dean of Undergraduate Admissions. Email: *adm@curry.edu* Web: *www.curry.edu*

FINANCIAL AID: In 2017-2018, 99% of all full-time freshmen received some form of financial aid. 74% of all full-time freshmen received need-based aid. The average freshman award was $30,772. Need-based scholarships or need-based grants averaged $27,851 ($33,820 maximum); need-based self-help aid (loans and jobs) averaged $5,014 ($9,500 maximum); and other non-need-based awards and non-need-based scholarships averaged $19,845 ($28,500 maximum). 26% of undergraduate students work part-time. The average financial indebtedness of the 2017 graduate was $45,947. The FAFSA code is 002143. The priority date for freshman financial aid applications for fall entry is March 1.

EASTERN NAZARENE COLLEGE E-2

www.enc.edu

Quincy, MA 02170	(617) 745-3711 (800) 883-6288
Fax: (617) 745-3980	Email: admissions@enc.edu
Full-time: 245 men, 355 women	Faculty: n/av
Part-time: 15 men, 25 women	Ph.D.s: 57%
Graduate: 30 men, 140 women	Student/Faculty: n/av
Year: 4-1-4, summer session	Tuition: $31,780
Room & Board: $9334	Freshman Class: n/av CEEB CODE: 3365
Application Deadline: September 1	COMPETITIVE

Eastern Nazarene College, founded in 1918, is a private college affiliated with the Church of the Nazarene. It offers a program in the liberal arts. The figures given in the above capsule and in this profile are approximate. There are 5 undergraduate schools and 1 graduate school. In addition to regional accreditation, ENC has baccalaureate program accreditation with CSWE. The 15-acre campus is in a suburban area 6 miles south of Boston. Including any residence halls, there are 16 buildings.

STUDENT LIFE: 55% of undergraduates are from out of state, mostly the Northeast. Students are from 27 states, 24 foreign countries, and Canada. 88% are White; 5% African American; 4% Asian American; 3% Foreign; 1% Hispanic. 88% are Protestant. **Female To Male Ratio:** 1.8:1. The average age of freshmen is 18; all undergraduates, 20. 25% do not continue beyond their first year; 60% remain to graduate. **Housing:** 638 students can be accommodated in college housing, which includes married student dorms. On-campus housing is guaranteed for all 4 years. 75% of students live on campus. Alcohol is not permitted. All students may keep cars.

FACULTY/CLASSROOMS: 72% of faculty are male; 28% are female. 83% teach undergraduates. No introductory courses are taught by graduate students. The average class size in an introductory lecture is 75; in a laboratory is 20; and in a regular course is 22.

PROGRAMS OF STUDY: ENC confers B.A. and B.S. degrees. Associate and master's degrees are also awarded. Bachelor's degrees are awarded in BIOLOGICAL SCIENCE (biology/biological science and marine biology), BUSINESS (accounting and business administration and management), COMMUNICATIONS AND THE ARTS (advertising, broadcasting, communications, dramatic arts, English, French, journalism, literature, music, music performance, Spanish, and speech/debate/rhetoric), COMPUTER AND PHYSICAL SCIENCE (chemistry, computer science, mathematics, physics, and science), EDUCATION (athletic training, education, elementary education, music education, science education, and social science education), ENGINEERING AND ENVIRONMENTAL DESIGN (computer engineering, engineering physics, and environmental science), HEALTH PROFESSIONS (sports medicine), SOCIAL SCIENCE (child psychology/development, Christian studies, clinical psychology, history, ministries, physical fitness/movement, psychology, religion, religious music, social studies, social work, and sociology). Chemistry, physics, and history are the strongest academically. Education, business, and psychology have the largest enrollments.

ACTIVITIES: There are no fraternities or sororities. There are 34 groups on campus, including band, cheerleading, choir, chorale, chorus, drama, jazz band, literary magazine, musical theater, newspaper, pep band, photography, professional, radio and TV, religious, social service, student government, and yearbook. Popular campus events include Freshmen Breakout, All-School Outing, and Junior/Senior Banquet. **Sports:** There are 5 intercollegiate sports for men and 5 for women, and 4 intramural sports for men and 5 for women. Facilities include a phys ed center equipped with basketball, a batting cage, and playing courts.

SERVICES: Counseling and information services are available, as is tutoring in most subjects. There is remedial math, reading, and writing. **Library/Resources:** The library contains 115,000 volumes, and subscribes to 600 periodicals including electronic. Computerized library services include interlibrary loans and database searching. Special learning facilities include a radio station. **Physically Challenged Students:** 65% of the campus is accessible. Facilities include wheelchair ramps, elevators, special parking, and specially equipped restrooms. **Special:** Internships are available in the metropolitan Boston area. Study abroad in Costa Rica, a Washington semester, a 3-2 engineering degree with Boston University, and a cooperative program with the Massachusetts College of Pharmacy are offered. Work-study programs, dual majors, credit for life, military, and work experience, and pass/fail options are available. An off-campus degree-completion program for adults in business administration is offered. There is 1 national honor society. **Visiting:** There are regularly scheduled orientations for prospective students. There are guides for informal visits, visitors may sit in on classes, and stay overnight. To schedule a visit, contact the Office of Admissions. **Campus Safety and Security:** Measures include 24-hour foot and vehicle patrol, self-defense education, and security escort services. There are emergency telephones and lighted pathways/sidewalks.

REQUIREMENTS: Applicants must be graduates of an accredited secondary school or have a GED. They must have a minimum of 16 academic credits, 4 years of English, 2 years each of history, social science, 3 years each of language, mathematics, and 2-3 years of sciences. Music students must audition. An essay and interview are recommended. First-time freshman applicants who present a minimum of 540 for Evidence-Based Reading and Writing and 510 for Math on the SAT or a minimum composite score of 20 on the ACT are eligible for full admission to the college. Students that do not meet the minimum admission requirements, may be considered for admission through the Bridge Program at Eastern Nazarene College. A GPA of 2.3 is required. AP and CLEP credits are accepted. Important factors in the admissions decision are advanced placement or honors courses, recommendations by school officials, and leadership record. All students must complete the core curriculum of writing and rhetoric, biblical history, social science, science or math, symbolic systems and intercultural awareness, philosophy and religion, and phys ed. A total of 130 credits is required for the B.A. or B.S., with 32 to 40 in the major. Minimum GPA for graduation is 2.0. **Procedure:** Freshmen are admitted to all sessions. Entrance exams should be taken in the spring of the junior year. There are deferred admissions and rolling admissions plans. Applications should be filed by September 1 for fall entry. The fall 2017 application fee was $25. **Transfer Students:** A minimum 2.0 GPA is required. An interview is recommended. 60 of 130 credits required for the bachelor's degree must be completed at ENC. **International Students:** They must take the TOEFL.

Admissions Contact: Rodney Rogers, Director of Admissions. Email: *admissions@enc.edu* Web: *www.enc.edu*

FINANCIAL AID: ENC is a member of CSS. The college's own financial statement is required. The FAFSA code is 002145. The priority date for freshman financial aid applications for fall entry is January 1.

ELMS COLLEGE — B-3

www.elms.edu

Chicopee, MA 01013 — (413) 592-3189, (800) 255-ELMS

Fax: (413) 594-2781	**Email:** admissions@elms.edu
Full-time: 65 men, 360 women	**Faculty:** n/av
Part-time: 25 men, 190 women	**Ph.D.s:** 76%
Graduate: 20 men, 80 women	**Student/Faculty:** n/av
Year: semesters	**Tuition:** $33,410
Room & Board: $16,192	**Freshman Class:** n/av
SAT or ACT: required	**CEEB CODE:** 3283
Application Deadline: open	**VERY COMPETITIVE**

Elms College, founded in 1928 as College of Our Lady of the Elms, is a Roman Catholic institution offering undergraduate degrees in liberal arts and sciences and graduate degrees in liberal arts, education, and theology. The figures given in the above capsule and in this profile are approximate. There are 4 undergraduate schools. In addition to regional accreditation, EC has baccalaureate program accreditation with CSWE and NLN. The 32-acre campus is in a suburban area 2 miles north of Springfield and 90 miles west of Boston. Including any residence halls, there are 11 buildings.

STUDENT LIFE: 85% of undergraduates are from Massachusetts. Others are from 9 states, and 10 foreign countries. 74% are from public schools. 80% are White; 4% African American; 4% Hispanic; 1% Asian American; 1% Foreign. 60% are Catholic. **Female To Male Ratio:** 5.7:1. The average age of freshmen is 20; all undergraduates, 22. 11% do not continue beyond their first year. **Housing:** 315 students can be accommodated in college housing, which includes dorms. On-campus housing is guaranteed for all 4 years. 60% of students commute. All students may keep cars.

FACULTY/CLASSROOMS: 35% of faculty are male; 65% are female. 90% teach undergraduates and do research. No introductory courses are taught by graduate students. The average class size in an introductory lecture is 13; in a laboratory is 8; and in a regular course is 11.

PROGRAMS OF STUDY: EC confers B.A. and B.S. degrees. Associate and master's degrees are also awarded. Bachelor's degrees are awarded in BIOLOGICAL SCIENCE (biology/biological science), BUSINESS (accounting, business administration and management, international business management, and marketing/retailing/merchandising), COMMUNICATIONS AND THE ARTS (English, fine arts, and Spanish), COMPUTER AND PHYSICAL SCIENCE (chemistry, computer science, mathematics, and natural sciences), EDUCATION (bilingual/bicultural education, early childhood education, elementary education, foreign languages education, middle school education, science education, secondary education, special education, and teaching English as a second/foreign language (TESOL/TEFOL), HEALTH PROFESSIONS (health science, medical laboratory technology, nursing, predentistry, premedicine, and speech pathology/audiology), SOCIAL SCIENCE (American studies, international studies, paralegal studies, prelaw, psychology, religion, social work, and sociology). Nursing, education, and biology are the strongest academically. Education, business, and nursing have the largest enrollments.

ACTIVITIES: There are no fraternities or sororities. There are 41 groups on campus, including art, choir, chorale, chorus, computers, dance, drama, ethnic, honors, international, literary magazine, musical theater, newspaper, photography, professional, radio and TV, religious, social, social service, student government, and yearbook. Popular campus events include Soph Show, Cap and Gown, and Ring Ceremony. **Sports:** There are 6 intercollegiate sports for men and 9 for women, and 6 intramural sports for men and 6 for women. Facilities include a fitness and athletic center housing a suspended indoor track, a 25-meter, 6-lane pool, a weight and aerobics room, a multipurpose arena, a basketball court, and a volleyball court.

SERVICES: Counseling and information services are available, as is tutoring in every subject. There is a reader service for the blind, and remedial math, reading, and writing. There also is an academic advising and resource center, a counseling service office, career services, wellness services, student activities, a campus ministry office, and resident advisers. **Library/Resources:** The library contains 103,136 volumes, 77,784 microform items, and 2,208 audio/video tapes/CDs/DVDs, and subscribes to 695 periodicals including electronic. Computerized library services include interlibrary loans and database searching. Special learning facilities include an art gallery, radio station, TV station, and a rare book collections. **Physically Challenged Students:** 40% of the campus is accessible. Facilities include wheelchair ramps, elevators, special parking, specially equipped restrooms, special class scheduling, lowered drinking fountains, and lowered telephones. **Special:** Students may cross-register at any of the Cooperating Colleges of Greater Springfield or Consortium of Sisters of St. Joseph Colleges. Internships are available with local hospitals, businesses, and schools. Study abroad, student-designed interdepartmental majors, accelerated degree programs, work-study, dual majors, nondegree study, and pass/fail options are offered. There are 5 national honor societies, Phi Beta Kappa, and a freshman honors program. **Visiting:** There are regularly scheduled orientations for prospective students, including tours and interviews scheduled weekdays, and 2 open houses in the fall and 1 in the spring. There are guides for informal visits, visitors may sit in on classes, and stay overnight. To schedule a visit, contact the Admission Office. **Campus Safety and Security:** Measures include 24-hour foot and vehicle patrol, self-defense education, and security escort services. There are emergency telephones, lighted pathways/sidewalks. A safety and security manual is published each year, and there is a safety and security committee of administrators, students, faculty, and staff.

REQUIREMENTS: The SAT or ACT is required. Applicants should be graduates of accredited high schools or have earned the GED. Secondary preparation should include 4 units of English, 3 each of math and science, and 2 each of foreign language, history, and social studies. A personal essay is required; an interview is recommended. A GPA of 2.5 is required. AP and CLEP credits are accepted. Important factors in the admissions decision are advanced placement or honors courses, recommendations by school officials, and extracurricular activities record. To graduate, all students must complete 120 hours with a 2.0 GPA. 54 hours are required in courses in rhetoric, computer science, history, religion, phys ed, philosophy, sociology, fine arts, humanities, foreign language, math, senior seminar, and service learning experience. **Procedure:** Freshmen are admitted fall and spring. Entrance exams should be taken no later than November of the senior year. There are early admissions, deferred admissions, and rolling admissions plans. Application deadlines are open. The fall 2017 application fee was $30. Applications are accepted on-line. **Transfer Students:** Applicants must have a minimum 2.0 GPA. 45 of 120 credits required for the bachelor's degree must be completed at EC.

Admissions Contact: Joseph P. Wagner, Director of Admission. Email: *admissions@elms.edu* Web: *www.elms.edu*

FINANCIAL AID: EC is a member of CSS. The college's own financial statement is required. The FAFSA code is 002140. Check with the school for current application deadlines.

EMERSON COLLEGE — E-2

www.emerson.edu

Boston, MA 02116 — **(617) 824-8600**

Fax: (617) 824-8609	**Email:** admission@emerson.edu
Full-time: 1522 men, 2226 women	**Faculty:** 201; IIA, +$
Part-time: 24 men, 40 women	**Ph.D.s:** 71%
Graduate: 170 men, 483 women	**Student/Faculty:** 13 to 1
Year: semesters, summer session	**Tuition:** $44,832
Room & Board: $16,992	**Freshman Class:** 10360 applied, 4772 accepted, 932 enrolled
SAT CR/M: 660/620 **ACT:** 28	**CEEB CODE:** 3367
Application Deadline: January 15	**HIGHLY COMPETITIVE+**

Emerson College, founded in 1880, is the premier college in the United States for the study of communication and the arts. There are 2 undergraduate schools and 2 graduate schools. The 8-acre campus is in an urban area downtown Boston on Boston Common in the Theater District. Including any residence halls, there are 14 buildings.

STUDENT LIFE: 78% of undergraduates are from out of state, mostly the Middle Atlantic. Students are from 50 states, 30 foreign countries, and Canada. 75% are from public schools. 65% are White; 12% Hispanic; 9% Foreign; 5% Asian American; 4% two or more races; 3% African American; 2% race unknown. **Female To Male Ratio:** 1.6:1. The average age of freshmen is 18; all undergraduates, 20. 13% do not continue beyond their first year; 80% remain to graduate. **Housing:** 2000 students can be accommodated in college housing, which includes dorms, and living/learning communities such as a writers' block and digital culture floors. On-campus housing is guaranteed for the freshman year only, is available on a first-come, first-served basis, and is available on a lottery system for upperclassmen. 58% of students live on campus. No one may keep cars.

FACULTY/CLASSROOMS: 54% of faculty are male; 46% are female. All teach undergraduates. Graduate students teach 4% of introductory courses. The average class size in an introductory lecture is 35; in a laboratory is 18; and in a regular course is 24.

PROGRAMS OF STUDY: EC confers B.A., B.S. and B.F.A. degrees. Master's and doctoral degrees are also awarded. Bachelor's degrees are awarded in BUSINESS (marketing management), COMMUNICATIONS AND THE ARTS (advertising, broadcasting, communications, creative writing, dramatic arts, film arts, journalism, media arts, musical theater, performing arts, public relations, publishing, radio/television technology, speech/debate/rhetoric, theater design, and theater management), HEALTH PROFESSIONS (speech pathology/audiology), SOCIAL SCIENCE (interdisciplinary studies). Visual & media arts, writing, and literature & publishing are the strongest academically. Visual & media arts, performing arts, and communication have the largest enrollments.

ACTIVITIES: 2% of men belong to 2 local and 1 national fraternities; 3% of women belong to 2 local and 1 national sororities. There are 80 groups on campus, including chorale, computers, debate, drama, environmental, ethnic, film, forensics, honors, international, LGBT, literary magazine, musical theater, newspaper, photography, political, professional, religious, social, social service, student government, theatre troupes, and yearbook. Popular campus events include Evvy's Award Show, Emerson Recognition and Achievement Awards. **Sports:** There are 7 intercollegiate sports for men and 8 for women. Facilities include a gymnasium, a fitness center, and a lighted athletic field. **Graduates:** From July 1, 2016 to June 30, 2017, 960 bachelor's degrees were awarded. The most popular majors were communication/journalism (36%), visual and performing arts (30%), and business/marketing (15%). In an average class, 77% graduate in 4 years or less, 80% graduate in 5 years or less, and 81% graduate in 6 years or less.

SERVICES: Counseling and information services are available, as is tutoring in most subjects. There is remedial math, reading, and writing. **Library/Resources:** The library contains 380,203 volumes, 9,414 microform items, and 29,558 audio/video tapes/CDs/DVDs, and subscribes to 57,169 periodicals including electronic. Computerized library services include interlibrary loans, database searching, Internet access, and Wi-Fi capability. Special learning facilities include an art gallery, TV station, sound-treated television studios, film production facilities and digital production labs, speech-language-hearing clinics, several theaters, 2 radio stations, marketing research suite, and digital newsroom. **Physically Challenged Students:** 85% of the campus is accessible. Facilities include wheelchair ramps, elevators, specially equipped restrooms, special class scheduling, and special housing. **Special:** Student-designed, interdisciplinary, and dual majors are available. Cross-registration is offered with the 6-member Boston ProArts consortium. Studying is available in Emerson facilities in the Netherlands and Los Angeles with additional programs in Spain and Washington, DC. Nearly 800 internships are possible, 600 in Boston and 200 in Los Angeles. Internships bear credit and are graded. There is 1 national honor society and a freshman honors program. **Visiting:** There are regularly scheduled orientations for prospective students, including an information session with an admission representative and a tour lead by a current student. To schedule a visit, contact the Admissions Office. **Campus Safety and Security:** Measures include 24-hour foot and vehicle patrol, emergency notification system, self-defense education, and security escort services. There are shuttle buses, emergency telephones, lighted pathways/sidewalks, and controlled access to dorms/residences.

REQUIREMENTS: Emerson is a member of the Common Application and requires an Application Supplement. Candidates must have graduated from high school (or have a GED) and present 4 years of English and 3 years each in science, social studies, foreign language, and math. Candidates for performing arts programs are required to submit a theatre-related resume and either audition or interview, or submit a portfolio or an essay. Candidates for film are required to submit either a 5-8 minute video sample and statement, or a 5-10 page script. Beginning in Fall 2018, standardized testing will be optional for new first-year students. AP and CLEP credits are accepted. Important factors in the admissions decision are advanced placement or honors courses, evidence of special talent, and recommendations by school officials. All students must complete 128 credit hours, with 40 to 64 in their major and a minimum GPA of 2.0. The general education curriculum consists of 4 foundations courses (oral and written communication and quantitative reasoning), 7 perspectives courses (liberal arts humanities), and 2 global/U.S. diversity courses. **Procedure:** Freshmen are admitted fall and spring. Entrance exams should be taken before December of the senior year. There are early admissions and deferred admissions plans. Early decision applications should be filed by November 1; regular applications, by January 15 for fall entry; and November 1 for spring entry. The fall 2017 application fee was $65. Notification of early decision is sent December 15; regular decision, April 1. 1080 applicants were on the 2017 waiting list; 19 were admitted. Applications are accepted on-line. **Transfer Students:** 167 transfer students enrolled in 2016-2017. Requirements for transfer students are the same as for all students. 48 of 128 credits required for the bachelor's degree must be completed at Emerson. **International Students:** There are 344 international students enrolled. They must take the TOEFL with a minimum score of 550 on the paper-based TOEFL (PBT) or 80 on the Internet-based version (iBT). Students must take the IELTS.

ADMISSIONS: 46% of the 2017-2018 applicants were accepted. The SAT scores for the 2017-2018 freshman class were: Critical Reading-- 14% between 500 and 599, 60% between 600 and 699, and 26% between 700 and 800. Math-- 1% below 500, 35% between 500 and 599, 50% between 600 and 699, and 14% between 700 and 800. The ACT scores were 11% between 18 and 23, 56% between 24 and 29, and 33% above 30. 57% of the current freshmen were in the top fifth of their class; 89% were in the top two fifths. 8 freshmen graduated first in their class. **Admissions Contact:** Michael Lynch, Director of Undergraduate Admission. Email: *admission@emerson.edu* Web: *www.emerson.edu*

FINANCIAL AID: In 2017-2018, 76% of all full-time freshmen received some form of financial aid. 52% of all full-time freshmen received need-based aid. The average freshman award was $22,315. Need-based scholarships or need-based grants averaged $26,064 ($53,204 maximum); need-based self-help aid (loans and jobs) averaged $4,195 ($9,000 maximum); and other non-need-based awards and non-need-based scholarships averaged $14,249 ($34,000 maximum). 61% of undergraduate students work part-time. The average financial indebtedness of the 2017 graduate was $23,639. The CSS/Profile is required. The FAFSA code is 002146. The priority date for freshman financial aid applications for fall entry is March 1.

EMMANUEL COLLEGE — E-2

www.emmanuel.edu

Boston, MA 02115 — **(617) 735-9715**

Fax: (617) 735-9801	**Email: enroll@emmanuel.edu**
Full-time: 498 men, 1306 women	**Faculty:** 90; IIB, +$
Part-time: 24 men, 119 women	**Ph.D.s:** 88%
Graduate: 23 men, 113 women	**Student/Faculty:** 13 to 1
Year: semesters, summer session	**Tuition:** $38,844
Room & Board: $14,628	**Freshman Class:** 5965 applied, 4354 accepted, 474 enrolled
	CEEB CODE: 3368
Application Deadline: February 15	**COMPETITIVE+**

Emmanuel College is a co-educational, residential institution, providing boundless opportunities for students to expand their worldview through rigorous coursework, significant internship and career opportunities throughout the Boston area and beyond, collaborations with distinguished and dedicated faculty, and participation in a dynamic campus community. Emmanuel's more than 60 programs in the sciences, liberal arts, business, nursing, and education foster spirited discourse and substantive learning experiences that honor the college's Catholic educational mission to educate the whole person and provide an ethical and relevant 21st-century education. In addition to regional accreditation, Emmanuel College has baccalaureate program accreditation with CCNE. The 17-acre campus is in an urban area in the city of Boston. Including any residence halls, there are 12 buildings.

STUDENT LIFE: 58% of undergraduates are from Massachusetts. Others are from 32 states, 51 foreign countries, and Canada. 75% are from public schools. 71% are White; 5% African American; 4% Asian American; 4% two or more races; 4% race unknown; 10% Hispanic; 1% Foreign. **Female To Male Ratio:** 2.8:1. The average age of freshmen is 18; all undergraduates, 20. 22% do not continue beyond their first year; 78% remain to graduate. **Housing:** 1209 students can be accommodated in college housing, which includes coed dorms, and theme housing. On-campus housing is guaranteed for all 4 years and is available on a lottery system for upperclassmen. 68% of students live on campus. Alcohol is not permitted. No one may keep cars.

FACULTY/CLASSROOMS: 39% of faculty are male; 61% are female. All teach undergraduates. No introductory courses are taught by graduate students. The average class size in an introductory lecture is 24; in a laboratory is 17; and in a regular course is 22.

PROGRAMS OF STUDY: Emmanuel confers B.A., B.F.A., and B.S. degrees. Master's degrees are also awarded. Bachelor's degrees are awarded in BIOLOGICAL SCIENCE (biochemistry, biology/biological science, biomathematics, neurosciences, and physiology), BUSINESS (accounting, business administration and management, finance, marketing, and sports management), COMMUNICATIONS AND THE ARTS (communications, English, Spanish, and studio art), COMPUTER AND PHYSICAL SCIENCE (chemistry, chemistry/forensic chemistry, and mathematics), EDUCATION (elementary education and secondary education), ENGINEERING AND ENVIRONMENTAL DESIGN (graphic arts technology), HEALTH PROFESSIONS (art therapy, health psychology, and health science), SOCIAL SCIENCE (American studies, counseling/psychology, criminology, developmental psychology, economics, government, history, human services, interdisciplinary studies, international relations, international studies, justice and society, liberal arts/general studies, philosophy, political science/government, psychology, religion, and sociology). Psychology, biology, business, and economics have the largest enrollments.

ACTIVITIES: There are no fraternities or sororities. There are 66 groups on campus, including art, band, choir, chorus, communications, computers, dance, debate, drama, ethnic, honors, jazz band, LGBT, literary magazine, musical theater, newspaper, orchestra, pep band, photography, political, professional, religious, social, social service, and student government. Popular campus events include Big Man On Campus, Latin Explosion, Emmanuel College Dance Marathon, Clamless Bake, Cinema Sundays, Chinese New Year, Afro-Caribbean Night, 12 Days of Christmas, Tip Off Tournament, EC Madness, and Spirit Week. **Sports:** There are 8 intercollegiate sports for men and 8 for women, and 18 intramural sports for men and 26 for women. The gymnasium includes one NCAA regulation court or practice courts for volleyball and basketball, a fitness center and training room, a turf field for practice and games for softball, soccer, lacrosse, and a track. **Graduates:** From July 1, 2016 to June 30, 2017, 421 bachelor's degrees were awarded. The most popular majors were psychology with concentration in counseling and health psychology (11%), management (9%), and communication and media studies (8%). In an average class, 2% graduate in 3 years or less, 58% graduate in 4 years or less, 64% graduate in 5 years or less, and 66% graduate in 6 years or less. Of the 2016 graduating class, 12% were enrolled in graduate school within 6 months of graduation, and 73% were employed.

SERVICES: Counseling and information services are available, as is tutoring in most subjects. There is a reader service for the blind. **Library/Resources:** The library contains 64,408 volumes, and 1,585 audio/video tapes/CDs/DVDs, and subscribes to 3,275 periodicals including electronic. Computerized library services include interlibrary loans, database searching, Internet access, and Wi-Fi capability. Special learning facilities include an art gallery. **Physically Challenged Students:** All of the campus is accessible. Facilities include elevators, special parking, specially equipped restrooms, special class scheduling, lowered drinking fountains, and special housing. **Special:** Students can cross-register at Massachusetts College of Art and Design, Massachusetts College of Pharmacy and Health Sciences, Simmons College, Wentworth Institute of Technology, and Wheelock College. The college offers internships, study abroad, a Washington semester, work-study programs on campus and in Boston-area organizations, dual and student-designed majors, and pre-law/pre-health preparation. There are 17 national honor societies, a freshman honors program, and 13 departmental honors programs. **Visiting:** There are regularly scheduled orientations for prospective students. The Fall Open Houses are weekday and weekend information sessions. There are guides for informal visits and visitors may sit in on classes. To schedule a visit, contact the Office of Admissions. **Campus Safety and Security:** Measures include 24-hour foot and vehicle patrol, emergency notification system, self-defense education, and security escort services. There are shuttle buses, emergency telephones, lighted pathways/sidewalks, controlled access to dorms/residences, 24-hour staffed residence hall desks and security office, closed-circuit surveillance in public areas, off-campus escorts, bike patrol, first responders program, a Rape Aggression Defense program, and a mass notification system.

REQUIREMENTS: Applicants must be graduates of an accredited secondary school or have a GED. A total of 16 academic credits are required, including 4 years of English, 3 years each of math, science (with 2 units of lab), foreign language, and social studies. An interview is encouraged but not required. AP credits are accepted. Important factors in the admissions decision are recommendations by school officials, advanced placement or honors courses, and leadership record. Students must complete a minimum of 128 credit hours and maintain a GPA of 2.0 in order to graduate. Degree requirements are comprised of four components: Foundation skills competency, Domains of knowledge program (minimum 44 credits), Major program (minimum 40 credits), and Capstone experience (4 credits). **Procedure:** Freshmen are admitted fall and spring. There are early admissions and deferred admissions plans. Applications should be filed by February 15 for fall entry. Notifications are sent December 15. Applications are accepted on-line. **Transfer Students:** 29 transfer students enrolled in 2016-2017. Students must submit their high school and college transcripts, essays, and a letter of recommendation. There is a $60 fee to process a paper application. 64 of 128 credits required for the bachelor's degree must be completed at Emmanuel. **International Students:** There are 22 international students enrolled. They must take the TOEFL with a minimum score of 550 on the paper-based TOEFL (PBT) or 79 on the Internet-based version (iBT), and take the IELTS.

ADMISSIONS: 73% of the 2017-2018 applicants were accepted. The SAT scores for the 2017-2018 freshman class were: Math-- 7% below 500, 56% between 500 and 599, 34% between 600 and 699, and 3% between 700 and 800. Evidence-Based Reading/Writing-- 3% below 500, 43% between 500 and 599, 50% between 600 and 699, and 4% between 700 and 800. The ACT scores were 17% between 18 and 23, 66% between 24 and 29, and 17% above 30. **Admissions Contact:** Sandra Robbins, Dean of Enrollment. Email: *enroll@emmanuel.edu* Web: *www.emmanuel.edu*

FINANCIAL AID: In 2017-2018, 100% of all full-time freshmen received some form of financial aid. 84% of all full-time freshmen received need-based aid. The average freshman award was $29,383. Need-based scholarships or need-based grants averaged $25,226; need-based self-help aid (loans and jobs) averaged $4,660; and $18,271 from other forms of aid. 34% of undergraduate students work part-time. The FAFSA code is 002147. The priority date for freshman financial aid applications for fall entry is February 15.

ENDICOTT COLLEGE — E-2

www.endicott.edu

Beverly, MA 01915	**(978) 921-1000** **(800) 325-1114**
Fax: (978) 232-2520	**Email: admissio@endicott.edu**
Full-time: 1187 men, 1893 women	**Faculty:** 105; IIB, +$
Part-time: 156 men, 254 women	**Ph.D.s:** 72%
Graduate: 395 men, 994 women	**Student/Faculty:** 27 to 1
Year: 4-1-4, summer session	**Tuition:** $32,154
Room & Board: $14,900	**Freshman Class:** 3623 applied, 2949 accepted, 781 enrolled
SAT CR/M: 576/567 **ACT:** 23	**CEEB CODE:** 3369
Application Deadline: February 15	**COMPETITIVE+**

Endicott College, founded in 1939, offers doctoral, master's, bachelor and associate degree programs in the professional and liberal arts. Endicott provides an education built upon a combination of theory and practice, which is tested through internships and work experience. There are 8 undergraduate schools and 1 graduate school. In addition to regional accreditation, Endicott has baccalaureate program accreditation with NASAD, NLN, NASAD, CIDA, and AHPCA. The 235-acre campus is in a suburban area 20 miles north of Boston. Including any residence halls, there are 56 buildings.

STUDENT LIFE: 51% of undergraduates are from out of state, mostly the Northeast. Students are from 34 states, 33 foreign countries, and Canada. 80% are from public schools. 86% are White; 3% Hispanic; 3% Foreign; 3% race unknown; 2% two or more races; 1% African American; 1% Asian American; 1% American Indian/Alaska Native. **Female To Male Ratio:** 1.8:1. The average age of freshmen is 18; all undergraduates, 19. 16% do not continue beyond their first year; 75% remain to graduate. **Housing:** 2539 students can be accommodated in college housing, which includes gender neutral, single-sex, coed dorms, on-campus apartments, and off-campus apartments. In addition, there are honors houses, special-interest houses, single-parent, international, academic themed, and healthy living. On-campus housing is guaranteed for the freshman year only, is available on a first-come, first-served basis, and is available on a lottery system for upperclassmen. 91% of students live on campus. Upperclassmen may keep cars.

FACULTY/CLASSROOMS: 44% of faculty are male; 56% are female. No introductory courses are taught by graduate students. The average class size in an introductory lecture is 17 and in a laboratory is 14.

PROGRAMS OF STUDY: Endicott confers B.A., B.S. and B.F.A. degrees. Associate, master's, and doctoral degrees are also awarded. Bachelor's degrees are awarded in BIOLOGICAL SCIENCE (biotechnology), BUSINESS (accounting, business administration and management, entrepreneurial studies, finance, hospitality management services, hotel/motel and restaurant management, international business management, marketing management, and sports management), COMMUNICATIONS AND THE ARTS (communications, digital communications, English, graphic design, photography, and studio art), COMPUTER AND PHYSICAL SCIENCE (applied mathematics, computer science, and mathematics), EDUCATION (athletic training, education, and physical education), ENGINEERING AND ENVIRONMENTAL DESIGN (bioengineering, environmental science, and interior design), HEALTH PROFESSIONS (art therapy, exercise science, and nursing), SOCIAL SCIENCE (criminal justice, history, international studies, liberal arts/general studies, political science/government, and psychology). Business management, nursing, and sport management have the largest enrollments.

ACTIVITIES: There are no fraternities or sororities. There are 60 groups on campus, including fitness, outdoor adventure, art, band, cheerleading, chorale, chorus, computers, crew, dance, debate, drama, environmental, ethnic, film, honors, international, jazz band, LGBT, literary magazine, musical theater, newspaper, pep band, photography, political, professional, radio and TV, religious, social, social service, student government, and yearbook. Popular campus events include Family/Homecoming Weekend, Annual Regatta, Festival of Lights, Performing Arts Events, and Ice Skating. **Sports:** There are 13 intercollegiate sports for men and 15 for women, and 12 intramural sports for men and 12 for women. Outdoor facilities include a multi-purpose turf stadium with an athletic support building, a turf baseball/soccer field, outdoor tennis courts, a softball stadium, and cross country courses (5k and 8k). Indoor facilities include a gym, racquetball, indoor tennis and basketball courts, weight, fitness, and group fitness rooms, indoor track, rock climbing wall, a field house and an ice arena. **Graduates:** From July 1, 2016 to June 30, 2017, 603 bachelor's degrees were awarded. The most popular majors were nursing (13%), business management (10%), and liberal studies/education (8%). In an average class, 71% graduate in 4 years or less, 74% graduate in 5 years or less, and 75% graduate in 6 years or less. Of the 2016 graduating class, 27% were enrolled in graduate school within 6 months of graduation, and 75% were employed.

SERVICES: Counseling and information services are available, as is tutoring in every subject. There is a reader service for the blind. **Library/Resources:** The library contains 114,891 volumes, 6,987 microform items, and 1,867 audio/video tapes/CDs/DVDs, and subscribes to 154,585 periodicals including electronic. Computerized library services include interlibrary loans, database searching, Internet access, and Wi-Fi capability. Special learning facilities include an art gallery, radio station, TV station, nursing and science labs, several fine art studios (interior design, graphic design, photography, painting, ceramics, etc.) recital hall, black box theater, nature trails, private beaches and marshland, a student-run restaurant, and an archives museum. **Physically Challenged Students:** 99% of the campus is accessible. Facilities include wheelchair ramps, elevators, special parking, specially equipped restrooms, special class scheduling, and lowered drinking fountains. **Special:** Three internships are required of most undergraduates. Students may study abroad. There are accelerated degree programs in Business Administration, Hospitality Management, Liberal Studies, Liberal Studies/Education, Nursing and Psychology. Cross-registration available through NECCUM.

Five-year bachelor/master's programs available. There are 16 national honor societies, a freshman honors program, and 1 departmental honors program. **Visiting:** There are regularly scheduled orientations for prospective students, includes testing, preregistration, and an introduction to general student life. There are guides for informal visits, visitors may sit in on classes, and stay overnight. To schedule a visit, contact the Office of Admission. **Campus Safety and Security:** Measures include 24-hour foot and vehicle patrol, emergency notification system, self-defense education, and security escort services. There are shuttle buses, emergency telephones, lighted pathways/sidewalks, controlled access to dorms/residences, security cameras, property identification, crime prevention workshops, and alcohol safety programs.

REQUIREMENTS: The SAT or ACT is recommended. Essays and two science and math recommendations are required for Nursing (including chemistry) and Athletic Training majors. AP and CLEP credits are accepted. All undergraduates complete a senior thesis and three internships. Core requirements for undergraduate students include the areas of writing and academic inquiry. General education requirements include completing at least 3 credits in each of the College's eight thematic categories. **Procedure:** Freshmen are admitted fall and spring. Entrance exams should be taken in fall of the senior year. Applications should be filed by February 15 for fall entry; December 15 for spring entry. The fall 2017 application fee was $50. 49 applicants were on the 2017 waiting list; 14 were admitted. Applications are accepted on-line. **Transfer Students:** 101 transfer students enrolled in 2016-2017. Official high school and college transcripts and a letter of recommendation are required. 24 of 124 credits required for the bachelor's degree must be completed at Endicott. **International Students:** There are 76 international students enrolled. They must take the TOEFL with a minimum score of 550 on the paper-based TOEFL (PBT) or 79 on the Internet-based version (iBT). The SAT or ACT is optional.

ADMISSIONS: 81% of the 2017-2018 applicants were accepted. The SAT scores for the 2017-2018 freshman class were: Math-- 12% below 500, 57% between 500 and 599, 28% between 600 and 699, and 3% between 700 and 800. Evidence-Based Reading/Writing-- 8% below 500, 60% between 500 and 599, 30% between 600 and 699, and 2% between 700 and 800. The ACT scores were 2% between 12 and 17, 48% between 18 and 23, 48% between 24 and 29, and 2% above 30. **Admissions Contact:** Thomas J. Redman, Vice President Admissions. Email: *admissio@endicott.edu* Web: *www.endicott.edu*

FINANCIAL AID: In 2017-2018, 94% of all full-time freshmen received some form of financial aid. 54% of all full-time freshmen received need-based aid. The average freshman award was $19,903. 36% of undergraduate students work part-time. The average financial indebtedness of the 2017 graduate was $44,159. Endicott College is a member of CSS. The college's own financial statement is required. The FAFSA code is 002148. The priority date for freshman financial aid applications for fall entry is March 15.

FITCHBURG STATE UNIVERSITY *(The complete profile is made available exclusively on our website, www.barronspac.com)*

FRAMINGHAM STATE UNIVERSITY D-2
www.framingham.edu

Framingham, MA 01701 **(508) 626-4500**

Fax: (508) 626-4017 **Email:** admissions@framingham.edu
Full-time: 1471 men, 2088 women
Part-time: 215 men, 353 women
Graduate: 319 men, 1246 women
Year: semesters, summer session
Room & Board: $11,820
Faculty: 197
Ph.D.s: 89%
Student/Faculty: 14 to 1
Tuition: $9920 ($16,000)
Freshman Class: 6041 applied, 4115 accepted, 765 enrolled
SAT EBR-W/M: 526/517 **ACT:** 22
Application Deadline: February 15
CEEB CODE: 3518
COMPETITIVE

Framingham State University, founded in 1839, is a comprehensive public institution offering degree programs based on a liberal arts foundation that includes unique career programs. There are 4 undergraduate schools and 1 graduate school. In addition to regional accreditation, FSU has baccalaureate program accreditation with ADA and NLN. The 78-acre campus is in a suburban area 20 miles west of Boston. Including any residence halls, there are 23 buildings.

STUDENT LIFE: 95% of undergraduates are from Massachusetts. 68% are White; 4% two or more races; 3% Asian American; 3% race unknown; 14% Hispanic; 11% African American; 1% Foreign. **Female To Male Ratio:** 1.8:1. The average age of freshmen is 18; all undergraduates, 22. 24% do not continue beyond their first year; 54% remain to graduate. **Housing:** 1978 students can be accommodated in college housing, which includes dorms. On-campus housing is available on a first-come and first-served basis. 54% of students live on campus. Alcohol is not permitted. Upperclassmen may keep cars.

FACULTY/CLASSROOMS: 42% of faculty are male; 58% are female. All teach undergraduates. No introductory courses are taught by graduate students.

PROGRAMS OF STUDY: FSU confers B.A., B.S. and B.S.Ed. degrees. Master's degrees are also awarded. Bachelor's degrees are awarded in BIOLOGICAL SCIENCE (biochemistry, biology/biological science, and nutrition), BUSINESS (accounting, business administration and management, business and technology, fashion merchandising, finance, management, and marketing), COMMUNICATIONS AND THE ARTS (American Sign Language, art history and appreciation, communications, English, modern language, Spanish, and studio art), COMPUTER AND PHYSICAL SCIENCE (chemistry, computer science, and mathematics), EDUCATION (early childhood education, elementary education, and global studies), ENGINEERING AND ENVIRONMENTAL DESIGN (environmental science), HEALTH PROFESSIONS (nursing), SOCIAL SCIENCE (criminology, economics, fashion design and technology, food science, geography, history, interdisciplinary studies, political science/government, psychology, sociology, and textiles and clothing). Psychology, management, and criminology have the largest enrollments.

ACTIVITIES: There are no fraternities or sororities. There are 50 groups on campus, including art, cheerleading, chorus, computers, dance, drama, environmental, ethnic, honors, international, LGBT, literary magazine, musical theater, newspaper, political, professional, radio and TV, religious, social, social service, and student government. Popular campus events include Sandbox Festival, Homecoming and Family Weekend, and Semi-Formal Dance. **Sports:** There are 6 intercollegiate sports for men and 7 for women, and 9 intramural sports for men and 9 for women. Facilities include an athletic and recreation center, a gym, all-weather turf fields for soccer, football, field hockey, softball, women's lacrosse and intramural sports. **Graduates:** From July 1, 2016 to June 30, 2017, 969 bachelor's degrees were awarded. The most popular majors were psychology (9%), food and nutrition (8%), and management (7%). In an average class, 35% graduate in 4 years or less, 52% graduate in 5 years or less, and 54% graduate in 6 years or less. Of the 2016 graduating class, 16% were enrolled in graduate school within 6 months of graduation, and 88% were employed.

SERVICES: Counseling and information services are available, as is tutoring in most subjects. There is a reader service for the blind, and remedial math, reading, and writing. There is a Center for Academic Success and Achievement. **Library/Resources:** The library contains 216,902 volumes, 4,288 audio/video tapes/CDs/DVDs, and subscribes to 163 periodicals including electronic. Computerized library services include interlibrary loans, database searching, Internet access, and Wi-Fi capability. Special learning facilities include an art gallery, planetarium, greenhouse, radio station, Center for Global Education, Center for Social Research, Metrowest Economic Research Center, McAuliffe Center for Education and Teaching Excellence, Challenger Learning Center, NASA Educator Resource Center, Metrowest STEM Education Network, Child Development Laboratory, Education Curriculum Library, Entrepreneur Innovation Center, John C. Stalker Institute for Food and Nutrition, and Framingham State/Boston Children's Hospital Food Study. **Physically Challenged Students:** 95% of the campus is accessible. Facilities include wheelchair ramps, elevators, special parking, specially equipped restrooms, special class scheduling, lowered drinking fountains, and lowered telephones. **Special:** The university offers a 2-3 preengineering program in cooperation with the University of Massachusetts at Amherst, Lowell, and Dartmouth. Study abroad in 8 countries, a Washington semester, and various internships are available. Pass/fail options are limited to 2 courses. There are 17 national honor societies, a freshman honors program, and 8 departmental honors programs. **Visiting:** There are regularly scheduled orientations for prospective students, include campus tours, advising, and information sessions (majors, computing, campus life and resources). There are guides for informal visits and visitors may sit in on classes. To schedule a visit, contact the Office of Undergraduate Admissions. **Campus Safety and Security:** Measures include 24-hour foot and vehicle patrol, emergency notification system, self-defense education, and security escort services. There are shuttle buses, emergency telephones, lighted pathways/sidewalks, controlled access to dorms/residences, and security cameras.

REQUIREMENTS: The SAT is required. Applicants must have a high school diploma or the GED. Secondary preparation must total 17 college-preparatory credits, including 4 years of English, 4 years of math, and 3 years of science (3 with lab), and 2 each of foreign language and social science. The required 2 years of electives may include additional academic subjects or art, music, or computer courses. Prospective studio art majors must submit a portfolio. AP and CLEP credits are accepted. Important factors in the admissions decision are advanced placement or honors courses, leadership record, and recommendations by school officials. The university's goal-based general education model includes writing, math, language, literature or philosophy, visual or performing arts, physical science, life science, historical studies, social and behavioral sciences, forces in the United States, study of Constitutions, gender, class, and race, and non-Western studies. Every student must take 12 general education courses and fulfill all required goals. A total of 128 credits (32 courses), including 40 to 68 credits in the major, and a 2.0 GPA are required to graduate. **Procedure:** Freshmen are admitted fall and spring. Entrance exams should be taken in the spring of the junior year or fall of the senior year. There are early admissions, deferred admissions, and rolling admissions plans. Applications should be filed by February 15 for fall entry; December 1 for spring entry. The fall 2017 application fee was $50. Notification is sent on a rolling basis. Applications are accepted on-line. **Transfer Students:** 424 transfer students enrolled in 2016-2017. Applicants with more than 24 transferable college credits must present a college GPA between 2.00-2.50 for admission consideration; those with fewer than 24 transferable credits must also meet freshman admission requirements. Official transcripts must be submitted from all colleges previously attended at the time of application. 32 of 128 credits required for the bachelor's degree must be completed at FSU. **International Students:** They must take the TOEFL with a minimum score of 550 on the paper-based TOEFL (PBT) or 79 on the Internet-based version (iBT). They must also take the SAT or ACT.

ADMISSIONS: 68% of the 2017-2018 applicants were accepted. The SAT scores for the 2017-2018 freshman class were: Math-- 37% below 500, 51% between 500 and 599, 11% between 600 and 699, and 1% between 700 and 800. Evidence-Based Reading/Writing-- 34% below 500, 51% between 500 and 599, 14% between 600 and 699, and 1% between 700 and 800. The ACT scores were 10% between 12 and 17, 65% between 18 and 23, 23% between 24 and 29, and 2% above 30. **Admissions Contact:** Shayna Eddy, Director of Undergraduate Admissions. Email: *admissions@framingham.edu* Web: *www.framingham.edu*

FINANCIAL AID: In 2017-2018, 86% of all full-time freshmen received some form of financial aid. 70% of all full-time freshmen received need-based aid. The average freshman award was $10,993. Need-based scholarships or need-based grants averaged $3,991; need-based self-help aid (loans and jobs) averaged $2,328; and other non-need-based awards and non-need-based scholarships averaged $4,674. 60% of undergraduate students work part-time. The average financial indebtedness of the 2017 graduate was $29,493. FSU is a member of CSS. The FAFSA code is 002185. The priority date for freshman financial aid applications for fall entry is March 1.

FRANKLIN W. OLIN COLLEGE OF ENGINEERING *(The complete profile is made available exclusively on our website, www.barronspac.com)*

GORDON COLLEGE E-1

www.gordon.edu

Wenham, MA 01984	(978) 867-4218 (866) 464-6736
Fax: (978) 867-4682	**Email:** admissions@gordon.edu
Full-time: 565 men, 963 women	**Faculty:** 94; IIB, +$
Part-time: 27 men, 36 women	**Ph.D.s:** 85%
Graduate: 77 men, 295 women	**Student/Faculty:** 16 to 1
Year: semesters, summer session	**Tuition:** $36,740
Room & Board: $11,000	**Freshman Class:** n/av
SAT CR/M/W: 596/572/549 **ACT:** 25	**CEEB CODE:** 3417
Application Deadline: August 1	**VERY COMPETITIVE**

The mission of Gordon College is to graduate men and women distinguished by intellectual maturity and Christian character, dedicated to lives of service and prepared for leadership worldwide. Gordon combines an exceptional liberal arts education with an informed Christian faith. Three pillars undergird this mission: stretch the mind, deepen the faith and elevate the contribution. Gordon offers more than 90 areas of undergraduate study, as well as several graduate programs. There is 1 undergraduate school and 3 graduate schools. In addition to regional accreditation, Gordon College has baccalaureate program accreditation with CSWE, NASDTEC, NASM, DECM, MBHE, and NEASC. The 485-acre campus is in a suburban area 25 miles north of Boston. Including any residence halls, there are 40 buildings.

STUDENT LIFE: 68% of undergraduates are from out of state, mostly the Northeast. Students are from 44 states, 52 foreign countries, and Canada. 64% are from public schools. 9% are Foreign; 8% Hispanic; 68% White; 6% African American; 5% Asian American; 3% two or more races; 1% race unknown. 92% are Protestant. **Female To Male Ratio:** 1.9:1. The average age of freshmen is 18; all undergraduates, 20. 17% do not continue beyond their first year; 70% remain to graduate. **Housing:** 1448 students can be accommodated in college housing, which includes single-sex and married student dorms and on-campus apartments. In addition, there are special-interest houses. On-campus housing is guaranteed for all 4 years. 88% of students live on campus. Alcohol is not permitted. All students may keep cars.

FACULTY/CLASSROOMS: 47% of faculty are male; 53% are female. 15% teach undergraduates, and 85% do both. No introductory courses are taught by graduate students. The average class size in an introductory lecture is 38; in a laboratory is 15; and in a regular course is 16.

PROGRAMS OF STUDY: Gordon confers B.A., B.S. and B.Mu. degrees. Master's degrees are also awarded. Bachelor's degrees are awarded in BIOLOGICAL SCIENCE (biology/biological science), BUSINESS (accounting, business administration and management, finance, and recreation and leisure services), COMMUNICATIONS AND THE ARTS (art, communications, English, French, languages, linguistics, music, music performance, Spanish, and theatre acting), COMPUTER AND PHYSICAL SCIENCE (chemistry, computer science, mathematics, and physics), EDUCATION (early childhood education, elementary education, middle school education, music education, and secondary education), SOCIAL SCIENCE (biblical studies, economics, history, philosophy, political science/government, psychology, social work, and sociology). Biology, biblical studies, psychology, education, music, and art are the strongest academically. Business administration, psychology, and biology have the largest enrollments.

ACTIVITIES: There are no fraternities or sororities. There are 120 groups on campus, including band, choir, chorale, chorus, computers, dance, debate, drama, environmental, student outreach clubs, film, honors, international, jazz band, literary magazine, musical theater, newspaper, orchestra, photography, political, professional, radio and TV, religious, social, social service, student government, symphony, and yearbook. Popular campus events include Golden Goose, Gordon Globes, Senior Formal, Winter Ball, Gordon's Got Talent, Gordon's Amazing Race, Founders Ball, Christmas Gala, and Highland Games. **Sports:** There are 8 intercollegiate sports for men and 10 for women, and 14 intramural sports for men and 14 for women. Facilities include a gym, weight rooms, tennis courts, athletic fields, training room, indoor swimming pool, climbing wall, racquetball courts, aerobics room, ski/running trails, outdoor ropes course, indoor walking track, outdoor track and field facilities. **Graduates:** From July 1, 2016 to June 30, 2017, 369 bachelor's degrees were awarded. The most popular majors were psychology (8%), business administration (7%), and biology (5%). In an average class, 61% graduate in 4 years or less and 70% graduate in 6 years or less. Of the 2016 graduating class, 17% were enrolled in graduate school within 6 months of graduation, and 72% were employed.

SERVICES: There is a reader service for the blind. There are writing and academic support centers, and tutors in many subjects. **Library/Resources:** The library contains 130,608 volumes, 154 microform items, and 6,060 audio/video tapes/CDs/DVDs, and subscribes to 1,603 periodicals including electronic. Computerized library services include interlibrary loans, database searching, Internet access, and Wi-Fi capability. Special learning facilities include an art gallery, radio station, theaters, an electron microscope and gene sequencing machine, human anatomy and physiology cadaver lab, and a pre-fabrication lab, a music center, and biomechanics laboratory containing a 6-camera Vicon Motion Capture System. **Physically Challenged Students:** 84% of the campus is accessible. Facilities include wheelchair ramps, elevators, special parking, specially equipped restrooms, special class scheduling, lowered drinking fountains, lowered telephones, and special housing. **Special:** Gordon offers a variety of internship experiences, including a package of global internship opportunities for students. The college permits cross-registration with other institutions in the Northeast Consortium of Colleges and Universities in Massachusetts. There is a 3-2 engineering program with the University of Southern California. B.A.- B.S. degrees, dual majors, student-designed majors, nondegree study, and pass/fail options are available. Off-campus study opportunities include a Washington semester, the Christian College Consortium Visitor Program, the LaVida Wilderness Expedition, and study abroad in Europe and Asia. Center for Entrepreneurial Leadership offers practical, creative, cross-disiplinary programs, and seeks to promote entrepreneurial thinking. There are 8 national honor societies, a freshman honors program, and 13 departmental honors programs. **Visiting:** There are guides for informal visits, visitors may sit in on classes, and stay overnight. To schedule a visit, contact Kristy Walker at (866) 464-6736. **Campus Safety and Security:** Measures include 24-hour foot and vehicle patrol, emergency notification system, self-defense education, and security escort services. There are shuttle buses, emergency telephones, lighted pathways/sidewalks, controlled access to dorms/residences, a gated entrance, active treat training, and video surveillance.

REQUIREMENTS: The SAT or ACT is required. Applicants must graduate from an accredited secondary school or have a GED. Home-schooled students are not required to provide a GED. A minimum of 17 Carnegie units is required, including 4 English courses and 2 courses each in math, science and social studies. Foreign language is a recommended elective. A personal statement, a personal reference, and an interview are required. Music majors must audition. Art majors must submit a portfolio for acceptance to the program. A GPA of 3.0 is required. AP and CLEP credits are accepted. Important factors in the admissions decision are advanced placement or honors courses, evidence of special talent, personality/intangible qualities, extracurricular activities record, leadership record, and recommendations by alumni. All students must demonstrate competency in writing, and foreign language. The common core curriculum consists of 36 credits - 8 credits each in biblical studies and language studies, 4 credits each in theology, social science, natural sciences, humanities, and in a freshman seminar, and 3 physical and outdoor education courses. The general core consists of 12-16 credits (depending on foreign language fulfillment). 4 credits in natural science and 2-4 credits in each division (social science, fine arts, and literature). A total of 124 credits is required for graduation, with 20 or more Gordon credits in a major and a minimum cumulative GPA of 2.0. **Procedure:** Freshmen are admitted fall and spring. Entrance exams should be taken in spring of the junior year and the fall of the senior year. There are deferred admissions and rolling admissions plans. Applications should be filed by August 1 for fall entry; December 15 for spring entry. The fall 2017 application fee was $50. Notifications are sent August 15. 28 applicants were on the 2017 waiting list. Applications are accepted on-line. **Transfer Students:** 45 transfer students enrolled in 2016-2017. Applicants must have a minimum GPA of 2.00. College transcripts, a reference from a college official and an interview is required. If the applicant has completed less than 1 year of full time study, high school transcripts and SAT or ACT scores are required in addition. 32 of 124 credits required for the bachelor's degree must be completed at Gordon. **International Students:** There are 147 international students enrolled. They must take the TOEFL with a minimum score of 85 on the Internet-based version (iBT). Student must take any one of these tests: the IELTS, SAT or ACT.

ADMISSIONS: The SAT scores for the 2017-2018 freshman class were: Critical Reading-- 11% below 500, 39% between 500 and 599, 38% between 600 and 699, and 12% between 700 and 800. Math-- 19% below 500, 44% between 500 and 599, 27% between 600 and 699, and 10% between 700 and 800. Writing-- 4% below 500, 6% between 500 and 599, 3% between 600 and 699, and 1% between 700 and 800. The ACT scores were 6% between 12 and 17, 30% between 18 and 23, 43% between 24 and 29, and 21% above 30. 46% of the current freshmen were in the top fifth of their class; 72% were in the top two fifths. 29 freshmen graduated first in their class. **Admissions Contact:** June Bodoni, Associate Vice President for Enrollment. Email: *admissions@gordon.edu* Web: *www.gordon.edu*

FINANCIAL AID: In 2017-2018, 100% of all full-time freshmen received some form of financial aid. 63% of all full-time freshmen received need-based aid. The average freshman award was $27,296. Need-based scholarships or need-based grants averaged $23,035; need-based self-help aid (loans and jobs) averaged $4,867; and other non-need-based awards and non-need-based scholarships averaged $16,886. 66% of undergraduate students work part-time. The average financial indebtedness of the 2017 graduate was $36,943. GC is a member of CSS. The FAFSA code is 002153. The priority date for freshman financial aid applications for fall entry is March 1.

HAMPSHIRE COLLEGE — B-2

www.hampshire.edu

Amherst, MA 01002 — **(413) 559-5752**

Email: admissions@hampshire.edu

Full-time: 494 men, 811 women	**Faculty:** 123; IIB, +$
Part-time: n/av	**Ph.D.s:** 93%
Graduate: n/av	**Student/Faculty:** 10 to 1
Year: 4-1-4	**Tuition:** $51,608
Room & Board: $13,606	**Freshman Class:** 2347 applied, 1511 accepted, 331 enrolled
	CEEB CODE: 3447
Application Deadline: January 15	**MOST COMPETITIVE**

Hampshire College, founded in 1965, is a private institution offering a liberal arts education with an emphasis on independent research, creative work, and multidisciplinary study. There are 5 undergraduate schools. The 800-acre campus is in a rural area in Amherst, Massachusetts. Including any residence halls, there are 30 buildings.

STUDENT LIFE: 78% of undergraduates are from out of state, mostly the Northeast. Students are from 46 states, and Canada. 65% are from public schools. 66% are White; 10% Hispanic; 7% two or more races; 6% African American; 6% Foreign; 4% race unknown; 2% Asian American; 1% American Indian/Alaska Native. **Female To Male Ratio:** 1.6:1. The average age of freshmen is 18; all undergraduates, 20. 18% do not continue beyond their first year; 74% remain to graduate. **Housing:** 1400 students can be accommodated in college housing, which includes dorms and on-campus apartments. In addition, there are special-interest houses, living/learning communities plus various themed housing options, wellness housing, and LGBT housing. On-campus housing is guaranteed for all 4 years. 99% of students live on campus. All students may keep cars.

FACULTY/CLASSROOMS: All teach undergraduates. No introductory courses are taught by graduate students. The average class size in a regular course is 14.

PROGRAMS OF STUDY: HC confers B.A. degrees. Bachelor's degrees are awarded in AGRICULTURE (agriculture and animal science), BIOLOGICAL SCIENCE (biology/biological science, botany, ecology, marine biology, nutrition, and physiology), COMMUNICATIONS AND THE ARTS (art history and appreciation, communications, comparative literature, creative writing, dance, dramatic arts, film arts, fine arts, journalism, linguistics, literature, media arts, music, performing arts, photography, and video), COMPUTER AND PHYSICAL SCIENCE (chemistry, computer science, geology, mathematics, physics, and science), EDUCATION (education), ENGINEERING AND ENVIRONMENTAL DESIGN (architecture, environmental design, and environmental science), HEALTH PROFESSIONS (health science and premedicine), SOCIAL SCIENCE (African studies, African American studies, American studies, anthropology, Asian/Oriental studies, cognitive science, crosscultural studies, economics, family/consumer studies, geography, history, humanities, international relations, international studies, Judaic studies, Latin American studies, law, Middle Eastern studies, peace studies, philosophy, political science/government, psychology, religion, sociology, urban studies, and women's studies). Film, photography, and video are the strongest academically. Social sciences has the largest enrollment.

ACTIVITIES: There are no fraternities or sororities. There are 100 groups on campus, including art, chorus, computers, dance, drama, environmental, ethnic, film, international, LGBT, literary magazine, musical theater, newspaper, orchestra, photography, political, radio and TV, religious, social, social service, and student government. Popular campus events include Div Days, Hampshire Halloween, and Spring Jam. **Sports:** There are 3 intercollegiate sports for men and 3 for women, and 18 intramural sports for men and 18 for women. Facilities include

2 multipurpose sports centers housing a swimming pool, a 30-feet climbing wall, a weight-lifting area, indoor tennis courts, a jogging track, soccer fields, outdoor tennis courts, softball diamonds, and a 2-mile nature trail. **Graduates:** From July 1, 2016 to June 30, 2017, 342 bachelor's degrees were awarded. The most popular majors were visual and performing arts (30%), social science (9%), and biological/life sciences (8%).

SERVICES: Counseling and information services are available, as is tutoring in most subjects. There is a reader service for the blind. There is also an advising center, a writing and reading program, and a lab quantitative skills program. **Library/Resources:** The library contains 129,804 volumes, 4,534 microform items, and 9,134 audio/video tapes/CDs/DVDs, and subscribes to 53,366 periodicals including electronic. Computerized library services include interlibrary loans, database searching, Internet access, and Wi-Fi capability. Special learning facilities include an art gallery, multimedia center, farm center, music and dance studios, optics lab, electronics shop, integrated greenhouse and aquaculture facility, fabrication shop, performing arts center, and a living laboratory. **Physically Challenged Students:** 90% of the campus is accessible. Facilities include wheelchair ramps, elevators, special parking, specially equipped restrooms, special class scheduling, lowered drinking fountains, lowered telephones, and special housing. The college provides a variety of support services to meet individual special needs. **Special:** Cross-registration is possible with other members of the Five College Consortium (Amherst College, the University of Massachusetts, Smith College, and Mount Holyoke). Internships, multidisciplinary dual majors, and study abroad (in the ISEP program, Tibetan Center, or a Costa Rica semester) are offered. All majors are student-designed. Students may complete their programs in fewer than 4 years. **Visiting:** There are regularly scheduled orientations for prospective students, including interviews, information sessions, campus tours, Discover Hampshire Days, Campus Visitation Days, and an overnight program. There are guides for informal visits, visitors may sit in on classes, and stay overnight. To schedule a visit, contact the Admissions Office. **Campus Safety and Security:** Measures include 24-hour foot and vehicle patrol and security escort services. There are lighted pathways/sidewalks, EMT on-call program, and dorm doors accessible by students only.

REQUIREMENTS: Applicants must submit all transcripts from 9th grade on or GED/state equivalency exam results. Students are required to submit a personal statement and an analytic essay or academic paper. An interview is recommended. Also required 16 Carnegie academic units 4 in English, 3-4 each in math, science (with 2 lab), foreign language, and history. AP credits are accepted. Important factors in the admissions decision are personality/intangible qualities, evidence of special talent, extracurricular activities record, and recommendations by school officials. All students must complete 3 divisions of study. In Division I: Basic Studies, students complete courses in cognitive science, humanities, arts and cultural studies, natural science, interdisciplinary arts, and social science and must complete 2 courses or the Division I exam project. In Division II: Concentration, students explore their field or fields of emphasis through individually designed internships or field studies. In Division III: Advanced Studies, students complete a major independent study project centered on a specific topic, question, or idea. Students must also partcipate in service to the college or the surrounding community and consider some aspect of their work from a non-Western perspective. **Procedure:** Freshmen are admitted fall and spring. There are early decision, early admissions, and deferred admissions plans. Early decision applications should be filed by November 15; regular applications, by January 15 for fall entry; and November 1 for spring entry. Notification of early decision is sent December 15; regular decision, April 1. 106 applicants were on the 2017 waiting list; 70 were admitted. Applications are accepted on-line. **Transfer Students:** 56 transfer students enrolled in 2016-2017. A proposed program of study, high school and college transcripts, and 1 recommendation must be submitted. Students can transfer in the fall, and spring. **International Students:** They must take the TOEFL.

ADMISSIONS: 64% of the 2017-2018 applicants were accepted. **Admissions Contact:** Meredith Twombly, Dean of Enrollment and Retention. Email: *mtwombly@hampshire.edu* Web: *www.hampshire.edu*

FINANCIAL AID: In 2017-2018, 61% of all full-time freshmen received some form of financial aid. 61% of all full-time freshmen received need-based aid. The average freshman award was $42,087. Need-based scholarships or need-based grants averaged $37,941; need-based self-help aid (loans and jobs) averaged $4,576; other non-need-based awards and non-need-based scholarships averaged $8,854; and $3,026 from other forms of aid. HC is a member of CSS. The CSS/Profile and the college's own financial statement, and noncustodial parent statement are required. The FAFSA code is 004661. The priority date for freshman financial aid applications for fall entry is February 1.

HARVARD COLLEGE/HARVARD UNIVERSITY D-2

www.college.harvard.edu

Cambridge, MA 02138	(617) 495-1551
Fax: (617) 495-8821	**Email:** college@harvard.edu
Full-time: 3503 men, 3196 women	**Faculty:** 973; I
Part-time: 1 men, 1 women	**Ph.D.s:** 86%
Graduate: 7850 men, 8250 women	**Student/Faculty:** 7 to 1
Year: semesters, summer session	**Tuition:** $48,949
Room & Board: $16,660	**Freshman Class:** 39506 applied, 2037 accepted, 1687 enrolled
SAT CR/M/W: 750/750/740 **ACT:** 33	**CEEB CODE:** 3434
Application Deadline: January 1	**MOST COMPETITIVE**

Harvard College, founded in 1636, is the undergraduate liberal arts college of Harvard University. There are 4 undergraduate schools and 10 graduate schools. In addition to regional accreditation, Harvard College has baccalaureate program accreditation with ABET. The 380-acre campus is in an urban area across the Charles River from Boston. Including any residence halls, there are 400 buildings.

STUDENT LIFE: 81% of undergraduates are from out of state, mostly the Middle Atlantic. Students are from 50 states, 118 foreign countries, and Canada. 67% are from public schools. 8% are African American; 8% Hispanic; 7% Foreign; 43% White; 17% Asian American; 1% American Indian/Alaska Native. **Male To Female Ratio:** 1.1:1. The average age of freshmen is 18; all undergraduates, 20. 96% remain to graduate. **Housing:** 6325 students can be accommodated in college housing, which includes dorms and on-campus apartments. On-campus housing is guaranteed for all 4 years. 97% of students live on campus. All students may keep cars.

FACULTY/CLASSROOMS: 98% teach undergraduates, 97% do research, and 95% do both. No introductory courses are taught by graduate students. The average class size in a regular course is 25.

PROGRAMS OF STUDY: Harvard College confers A.B. and S.B. degrees. Master's and doctoral degrees are also awarded. Bachelor's degrees are awarded in BIOLOGICAL SCIENCE (biochemistry, biology/biological science, and biophysics), COMMUNICATIONS AND THE ARTS (art history and appreciation, Chinese, classics, creative writing, English, fine arts, folklore and mythology, French, German, Greek, Hebrew, Italian, Japanese, Latin, linguistics, literature, music, Portuguese, Russian, and Spanish), COMPUTER AND PHYSICAL SCIENCE (applied mathematics, astronomy, chemistry, computer science, geology, geophysics and seismology, mathematics, physical sciences, physics, and statistics), ENGINEERING AND ENVIRONMENTAL DESIGN (engineering, environmental design, environmental science, and preengineering), SOCIAL SCIENCE (African American studies, American studies, anthropology, Asian/Oriental studies, economics, European studies, history, humanities, Middle Eastern studies, philosophy, political science/government, psychology, religion, Russian and Slavic studies, Sanskrit and Indian studies, social science, social studies, sociology, and women's studies). Economics, government, and biology have the largest enrollments.

ACTIVITIES: There are no fraternities or sororities. There are 250 groups on campus, including art, band, cheerleading, chess, choir, chorale, chorus, computers, dance, debate, drama, ethnic, film, honors, international, jazz band, LGBT, literary magazine, marching band, musical theater, newspaper, opera, orchestra, pep band, photography, political, professional, radio and TV, religious, social, social service, student government, symphony, and yearbook. Popular campus events include Harvard/Yale Football, Head of the Charles Crew Regatta, and Cultural Rhythms Festival. **Sports:** There are 21 intercollegiate sports for men and 20 for women, and 16 intramural sports for men and 16 for women. Facilities include several gyms and athletic centers, swimming pools, a track, sailing center with boat house, hockey rink, various courts, and playing fields.

SERVICES: There is a reader service for the blind. Tutoring is available in all subjects. **Library/Resources:** The library contains 15.0 million volumes, and subscribes to 100,000 periodicals including electronic. Computerized library services include interlibrary loans and database searching. Special learning facilities include an art gallery, natural history museum, planetarium, and radio station. **Physically Challenged Students:** Facilities include wheelchair ramps, elevators, special parking, specially equipped restrooms, special class scheduling, lowered drinking fountains, and lowered telephones. **Special:** Students may cross-register with MIT and with other schools within the university and may design their own concentrations or enroll for nondegree study. Internships and study abroad may be arranged. Accelerated degree programs, dual majors, a 3-2 engineering degree, and a combined A.B.-S.B. in engineering are offered. There are pass/fail options. There is a chapter of Phi Beta Kappa. **Visiting:** There are regularly scheduled orientations for prospective students, consisting of group information sessions and tours. There are guides for informal visits, visitors may sit in on classes, and stay overnight. To schedule a visit, contact the Undergraduate Admissions Office. **Campus Safety and Security:** Measures include 24-hour foot and vehicle patrol, self-defense education, and security escort services. There are shuttle buses, emergency telephones, and lighted pathways/sidewalks.

REQUIREMENTS: The SAT or ACT is required, as well as 3 SAT Subject tests. Applicants need not be high school graduates but are expected to be well prepared academically. An essay and an interview are required, in addition to a transcript, a counselor report, and 2 teacher recommendations from academic disciplines. AP credits are accepted. Important factors in the admissions decision are evidence of special talent, personality/intangible qualities, and recommendations by school officials. In 8 semesters, students must pass a minimum of 32 1-semester courses. The average course load is 4 courses per semester, but the course rate may be varied for special reasons. A typical balanced program devotes about one-fourth of its courses to core curriculum requirements, one-half to the concentration (or major field), and the remaining one-fourth to electives. **Procedure:** Freshmen are admitted fall. Entrance exams should be taken by January of the senior year. There is a deferred admissions plan. Early decision applications should be filed by November 1; regular applications, by January 1 for fall entry. The fall 2017 application fee was $65. Notification of early decision is sent December 1; regular decision, March 15. Applications are accepted on-line. **Transfer Students:** Transfer applicants must have completed at least 1 full year of daytime study in a degree-granting program at 1 institution. Students are required to submit the SAT or ACT, 2 letters of recommendation, high school and college transcripts with a dean's report, and several essays. 16 of 32 credits required for the bachelor's degree must be completed at Harvard College. **International Students:** They must also take the SAT or ACT.

ADMISSIONS: 5% of the 2017-2018 applicants were accepted. The SAT scores for the 2017-2018 freshman class were: Math-- 1% between 500 and 599, 11% between 600 and 699, and 88% between 700 and 800. Evidence-Based Reading/Writing-- 1% between 500 and 599, 11% between 600 and 699, and 88% between 700 and 800. The ACT scores were 7% between 24 and 29, and 93% above 30. 99% of the current freshmen were in the top fifth of their class; 100% were in the top two fifths. **Admissions Contact:** Marlyn McGrath, Director of Admissions. Email: *college@harvard.edu* Web: *www.college.harvard.edu*

FINANCIAL AID: Harvard College is a member of CSS. The CSS/Profile, the college's own financial statement, and federal tax forms are required. The FAFSA code is E00468. Check with the school for current application deadlines.

HELLENIC COLLEGE/HOLY CROSS GREEK ORTHODOX SCHOOL OF THEOLOGY D-2

www.hchc.edu

Brookline, MA 02445	**(617) 850-1285** **(866) 424-2338**
Fax: (617) 850-1460	**Email: gfloor@hchc.edu**
Full-time: 61 men, 38 women	**Faculty:** 13
Part-time: n/av	**Ph.D.s:** 90%
Graduate: 125 men, 16 women	**Student/Faculty:** 9 to 1
Year: semesters	**Tuition:** $23,714
Room & Board: $16,192	**Freshman Class:** 64 applied, 52 accepted, 38 enrolled
SAT CR/M/W: required **ACT:** 22	**CEEB CODE:** 3449
Application Deadline: August 1	**COMPETITIVE**

Hellenic College Holy Cross Greek Orthodox School of Theology, founded in 1968, is a private college affiliated with the Greek Orthodox Church. It offers programs in the classics, elementary education, religious studies, human development, management and leadership, and literature and history. The figures given in the above capsule and in this profile are approximate. There is 1 undergraduate school and 1 graduate school. In addition to regional accreditation, HCHC has baccalaureate program accreditation with NASDTEC. The 59-acre campus is in an urban area 4 miles southwest of Boston. Including any residence halls, there are 7 buildings.

STUDENT LIFE: 90% of undergraduates are from out of state, mostly the Midwest. Students are from 25 states, 9 foreign countries, and Canada. 90% are from public schools. 95% are White; 5% Hispanic; 13% Foreign. 95% are Eastern Orthodox. **Male To Female Ratio:** 3.4:1. The average age of freshmen is 20; all undergraduates, 22. 5% do not continue beyond their first year; 95% remain to graduate. **Housing:** 220 students can be accommodated in college housing, which includes married student dorms and on-campus apartments. On-campus housing is available on a first-come and first-served basis. 90% of students live on campus. Alcohol is not permitted. All students may keep cars.

FACULTY/CLASSROOMS: 70% of faculty are male; 30% are female. No introductory courses are taught by graduate students. The average class size in an introductory lecture is 20; in a laboratory is 20; and in a regular course is 15.

PROGRAMS OF STUDY: HCHC confers B.A. degrees. Master's degrees are also awarded. Bachelor's degrees are awarded in BUSINESS (business administration and management), COMMUNICATIONS AND THE ARTS (classics and literature), EDUCATION (elementary education), SOCIAL SCIENCE (history, human development, and religion). Religious studies, and elementary education are the strongest academically. Religious studies, and human development have the largest enrollments.

ACTIVITIES: There are no fraternities or sororities. Groups on campus include choir, ethnic, religious, social, social service, and student government. Popular campus events include Feast of the Holy Cross, Matriculation Day, and Campus Christmas Party. **Sports:** There are 4 intramural sports for men and 3 for women. Facilities include a gym, tennis, basketball, racquetball courts, and a soccer field. **Graduates:** From July 1, 2016 to June 30, 2017, 12 bachelor's degrees were awarded. The most popular majors were religious studies (50%), management and leadership (25%), and human development (25%). In an average class, 97% graduate in 4 years or less. Of the 2016 graduating class, 60% were enrolled in graduate school within 6 months of graduation, and 30% were employed.

SERVICES: Counseling and information services are available, as is tutoring in some subjects, such as Greek and music writing and composition. There is remedial math, reading, and writing. **Library/Resources:** The library contains 63,374 volumes, 883 microform items, and 3,015 audio/video tapes/CDs/DVDs, and subscribes to 720 periodicals including electronic. Computerized library services include interlibrary loans, database searching, and Internet access. **Physically Challenged Students:** 10% of the campus is accessible. Facilities include wheelchair ramps, elevators, special parking, specially equipped restrooms, and lowered drinking fountains. **Special:** The college offers cross-registration with Boston Theological Institute, Newbury College, and Boston College, credit by examination, and study abroad in Greece. There is a freshman honors program. **Visiting:** There are regularly scheduled orientations for prospective students, including observation of classroom and student life. To schedule a visit, contact the Office of Admissions at admissions@hchc.edu. **Campus Safety and Security:** There are shuttle buses, lighted pathways/sidewalks, and 16-hour security patrol.

REQUIREMENTS: The SAT or ACT is required. Applicants should graduate from an accredited secondary school or have a GED. 15 academic credits are required, including 4 units of English, 2 each of math, foreign language, and social studies, and 1 of science. An essay is required. A GPA of 2.5 is required. AP and CLEP credits are accepted. Important factors in the admissions decision are recommendations by school officials, advanced placement or honors courses, and recommendations by alumni. To graduate, students must complete 129 credits, with 39 in the major, and maintain a minimum overall GPA of 2.0. General education requirements include 72 credits, with courses in English language and literature, music, history, science, philosophy, and social science. **Procedure:** Freshmen are admitted fall and spring. There are deferred admissions and rolling admissions plans. Early decision applications should be filed by December 1; regular applications, by August 1 for fall entry; and December 1 for spring entry. The fall 2017 application fee was $50. Notification of early decision is sent February 1; regular decision, June 15. **Transfer Students:** 11 transfer students enrolled in 2016-2017. An essay, college transcripts, recommendation letters, an interview, and a health certificate are required. SAT or ACT scores and high school transcripts are waived if the student has 24 or more college credit hours. 60 of 129 credits required for the bachelor's degree must be completed at HCHC. **International Students:** There are 5 international students enrolled. They must take the TOEFL with a minimum score of 500 on the paper-based TOEFL (PBT) or 61 on the Internet-based version (iBT).

ADMISSIONS: 81% of the 2017-2018 applicants were accepted. The SAT scores for the 2017-2018 freshman class were: Critical Reading-- 30% below 500, 35% between 500 and 599, 30% between 600 and 699, and 5% between 700 and 800. Math-- 55% below 500, 35% between 500 and 599, 5% between 600 and 699, and 5% between 700 and 800. Writing-- 45% below 500, 35% between 500 and 599, and 20% between 600 and 699. The ACT scores were 20% below 12, 60% between 12 and 17, and 20% between 18 and 23. **Admissions Contact:** Gregory Floor, Director for Admissions. Email: *gfloor@hchc.edu* Web: *www.hchc.edu*

FINANCIAL AID: In 2017-2018, 95% of all full-time freshmen received some form of financial aid and need-based aid. The average financial indebtedness of the 2017 graduate was $31,000. The college's own financial statement is required. The FAFSA code is 002154. Check with the school for current application deadlines.

LASELL COLLEGE — D-2

www.lasell.edu

Newton, MA 02466	**(617) 243-2225** **(888) LASELL-4**
Fax: (617) 243-2380	**Email: info@lasell.edu**
Full-time: 606 men, 1063 women	**Faculty:** 93; IIA, -$
Part-time: 12 men, 15 women	**Ph.D.s:** 81%
Graduate: 121 men, 248 women	**Student/Faculty:** 19 to 1
Year: semesters, summer session	**Tuition:** $34,600
Room & Board: $14,800	**Freshman Class:** 3493 applied, 2862 accepted, 411 enrolled
SAT CR/M/W: 500/500/480 **ACT:** 21	**CEEB CODE:** 3481
Application Deadline: September 1	**COMPETITIVE**

An innovator in education for over 160 years, Lasell College today is a comprehensive coeducational college offering professionally oriented bachelor's and masters degree programs. Lasell encourages students to explore new ideas and shared interests through high impact learning experiences including internships, service learning, international study and a collaborative, problem based learning approach that engages students in the work of their field. The college offers over 40 undergraduate majors and minors. There is 1 undergraduate school and 1 graduate school. In addition to regional accreditation, LC has baccalaureate program accreditation with ACBSP, CAEP, CAATE, CAHE, and COSMA. The 53-acre campus is in a suburban area in Newton, MA, at the interchange of Route 95 and the Massachusetts Turnpike, 8 miles west of Boston. Including any residence halls, there are 51 buildings.

STUDENT LIFE: 54% of undergraduates are from Massachusetts. Others are from 29 states, and 22 foreign countries. 80% are from public schools. 8% are Hispanic; 69% White; 5% African American; 5% Foreign; 4% race unknown; 2% Asian American; 2% two or more races. **Female To Male Ratio:** 1.8:1. The average age of freshmen is 18.5; all undergraduates, 20.5. 27% do not continue beyond their first year; 54% remain to graduate. **Housing:** 1325 students can be accommodated in college housing, which includes dorms and on-campus apartments. In addition, there are special-interest houses, and community service housing. On-campus housing is guaranteed for all 4 years, is available on a first-come, first-served basis, and is available on a lottery system for upperclassmen. 74% of students live on campus. Upperclassmen may keep cars.

FACULTY/CLASSROOMS: 42% of faculty are male; 58% are female. All teach undergraduates. No introductory courses are taught by graduate students. The average class size in a regular course is 17.

PROGRAMS OF STUDY: LC confers B.A. and B.S. degrees. Master's degrees are also awarded. Bachelor's degrees are awarded in AGRICULTURE (environmental studies), BUSINESS (accounting, business administration and management, entrepreneurial studies, fashion merchandising, finance, hospitality management services, international business management, marketing/retailing/merchandising, meeting/special event management, resort management, and sports management), COMMUNICATIONS AND THE ARTS (arts administration/management, communications, English, and graphic design), COMPUTER AND PHYSICAL SCIENCE (applied mathematics, information and technology, and information and technology), EDUCATION (athletic training, early childhood education, education, elementary education, IDS curriculum and instruction, and secondary education), HEALTH PROFESSIONS (allied health, exercise science, fitness management, and health science), SOCIAL SCIENCE (criminal justice, fashion design and technology, history, human services, humanities, interdisciplinary studies, law, legal studies, psychology, and sociology). Athletic training, fashion design, and management are the strongest academically. Fashion, communication, sport management, and psychology have the largest enrollments.

ACTIVITIES: There are no fraternities or sororities. There are 74 groups on campus, including art, cheerleading, chorale, chorus, dance, drama, environmental, ethnic, honors, international, jazz band, LGBT, literary magazine, newspaper, political, professional, radio and TV, religious, social, social service, student government, and yearbook. Popular campus events include River Day, Torchlight Parade, Awards Night, and Rugby. **Sports:** There are 7 intercollegiate sports for men and 8 for women, and 3 intramural sports for men and 3 for women. Facilities include an athletic center with basketball courts, volleyball court, an indoor track, dance studio, tennis courts, fitness centers, and athletic fields. **Graduates:** From July 1, 2016 to June 30, 2017, 421 bachelor's degrees were awarded. The most popular majors were communication (20%), fashion and retail merchandising (9%), and Sport and Fitness Administration/Management (7%). In an average class, 50% graduate in 4 years or less, 53% graduate in 5 years or less, and 54% graduate in 6 years or less. Of the 2016 graduating class, 10% were enrolled in graduate school within 6 months of graduation, and 86% were employed.

SERVICES: Counseling and information services are available, as is tutoring in most subjects. There is remedial math and writing. The Academic Achievement Center offers individual assistance in math, accounting, and many other subjects, as well as in techniques for writing, coaching on presentation skills, and improving reading comprehension, and provides special resources for students with documented learning disabilities. **Library/Resources:** The library contains 41,816 volumes, and 4,842 audio/video tapes/CDs/DVDs, and subscribes to 43,705 periodicals including electronic. Computerized library services include interlibrary loans, database searching, Internet access, and Wi-Fi capability. Special learning facilities include an art gallery, radio station, Academic Achievement Center, Lasell Village (continuing care retirement community), the center for Community-Based Learning, the center for teaching and learning, two child study centers, a cultural center, and a fashion collection. **Physically Challenged Students:** Facilities include wheelchair ramps, elevators, special parking, specially equipped restrooms, special class scheduling, and lowered drinking fountains. **Special:** All academic programs require at least one internship, and student employment options are available on campus. Student-designed majors are possible, as is a 5th year master's degree option. Over 25% of Lasell graduates have a college sponsored international learning experience, including study abroad (over 90 options), international service and departmental trips. Over 90% of graduates participated in service learning programs. Multiple programs can be completed in three years under guidance from professional advisor. All programs feature connected learning, which is an ongoing practical application of classroom theory. Additionally, the college has cross registration with Regis College and participates in the Washington semester program at American University. There are 4 national honor societies and a freshman honors program. **Visiting:** There are regularly scheduled orientations for prospective students, consisting of the president's welcome, faculty presentations, tours, and student panels. There are guides for informal visits, visitors may sit in on classes, and stay overnight. To schedule a visit, contact the Office of Undergraduate Admission. **Campus Safety and Security:** Measures include 24-hour foot and vehicle patrol, emergency notification system, self-defense education, and security escort services. There are shuttle buses, emergency telephones, lighted pathways/sidewalks, and controlled access to dorms/residences.

REQUIREMENTS: Applicants should have completed 16 Carnegie units of high school study. The GED is accepted. Two letters of recommendation and a personal essay are required, and an interview is recommended. AP and CLEP credits are accepted. Important factors in the admissions decision are advanced placement or honors courses, personality/intangible qualities, and leadership record. A graduate of Lasell receives the degree of Bachelor of Arts or Bachelor of Science. Specific requirements of the various curricula are described under each major. In order to graduate, each student must earn a minimum of 120 credits of academic work; out of these 120 credits, students must complete a minimum of 42 credits in the arts and sciences. Most degree programs at the college require between 120 and 127 credits to graduate. Lasell College allows a maximum of 90 transferable credits, the final semester of which must be at Lasell. Students must attain a GPA of 2.0 or higher, complete a major degree program, and meet Lasell's Core Curriculum competencies. All degree programs have additional requirements described in the catalog. **Procedure:** Freshmen are admitted fall and spring. There are early admissions, deferred admissions, and rolling admissions plans. Applications should be filed by September 1 for fall entry. The fall 2017 application fee was $40. Notifications are sent December 1. Applications are accepted on-line. **Transfer Students:** 67 transfer students enrolled in 2016-2017. Applicants must submit an application, final secondary school transcript (if <24 college credits), official college/university transcripts, official SAT/ACT scores (if <24 college credits), personal statement or essay, 2 recommendations (1 must be academic), and if English is not the native language, applicants must submit TOEFL or other English proficiency exam score. 30 of 120 credits required for the bachelor's degree must be completed at Lasell. **International Students:** There are 113 international students enrolled. They must take the TOEFL with a minimum score of 525 on the paper-based TOEFL (PBT) or 71 on the Internet-based version (iBT), and take the IELTS.

ADMISSIONS: 82% of the 2017-2018 applicants were accepted. **Admissions Contact:** James M. Tweed, AVP Enroll Management, Dean Undergraduate Admissions & Financial Aid. Email: *info@lasell.edu* Web: *www.lasell.edu*

FINANCIAL AID: In 2017-2018, 98% of all full-time freshmen received some form of financial aid. 85% of all full-time freshmen received need-based aid. The average freshman award was $31,893. Need-based scholarships or need-based grants averaged $27,185 ($34,100 maximum); need-based self-help aid (loans and jobs) averaged $6,921 ($7,500 maximum); and other non-need-based awards and non-need-based scholarships averaged $12,168 ($34,600 maximum). 30% of undergraduate students work part-time. The average financial indebtedness of the 2017 graduate was $40,629. LC is a member of CSS. The FAFSA code is 002158. The priority date for freshman financial aid applications for fall entry is March 1.

LESLEY UNIVERSITY — D-2

www.lesley.edu

Cambridge, MA 02138	(617) 349-8800 (800) 999-1959
Fax: (617) 349-8810	**Email:** admissions@lesley.edu
Full-time: 331 men, 1019 women	**Faculty:** 80; IIA, av$
Part-time: 19 men, 49 women	**Ph.D.s:** 85%
Graduate: 444 men, 2641 women	**Student/Faculty:** 20 to 1
Year: semesters, summer session	**Tuition:** $26,250
Room & Board: $15,300	**Freshman Class:** 3115 applied, 2135 accepted, 379 enrolled
SAT CR/M/W: 545/520/540 **ACT:** 23	**CEEB CODE:** 3483
Application Deadline: February 15	**COMPETITIVE**

Lesley University, founded in 1909, is a private undergraduate institution, offering degree programs in education, human services, and the arts. Expanded resources, course work, and opportunities are available to students through the larger coeducational Lesley University system, including cross-registration with the Lesley University College of Art and Design. Tuition and fees, varies by undergraduate and graduate programs. There are 2 undergraduate schools and 2 graduate schools. In addition to regional accreditation, Lesley has baccalaureate program accreditation with NASAD, CAEP, AACTE, and CACREP. The 5-acre campus is in an urban area outside of Harvard Square in Cambridge, MA. Including any residence halls, there are 53 buildings.

STUDENT LIFE: 57% of undergraduates are from out of state, mostly the Northeast. Students are from 33 states, 24 foreign countries, and Canada. 84% are from public schools. 71% are White; 7% Hispanic; 4% Asian American; 4% Foreign; 4% two or more races; 2% African American; 12% race unknown. **Female To Male Ratio:** 4.7:1. The average age of freshmen is 18; all undergraduates, 20. 27% do not continue beyond their first year; 73% remain to graduate. **Housing:** 803 students can be accommodated in college housing, which includes single-sex and coed dorms. In addition, there are special-interest houses, theme housing, and wellness housing. There are also Victorian houses, and suite-style residence. On-campus housing is available on a first-come and first-served basis. 60% of students live on campus. All students may keep cars.

FACULTY/CLASSROOMS: 44% of faculty are male; 56% are female. All teach undergraduates, and all do research. No introductory courses are taught by graduate students. The average class size in an introductory lecture is 20; in a laboratory is 14; and in a regular course is 14.

PROGRAMS OF STUDY: Lesley confers B.S. and B.F.A. degrees. Associate, master's, and doctoral degrees are also awarded. Bachelor's degrees are awarded in BUSINESS (management science), COMMUNICATIONS AND THE ARTS (creative writing and visual and performing arts), COMPUTER AND PHYSICAL SCIENCE (natural sciences), EDUCATION (early childhood education, elementary education, middle school education, and special education), SOCIAL SCIENCE (human services, humanities, psychology, and social science). Education, counseling, and photography & art therapy have the largest enrollments.

ACTIVITIES: There are no fraternities or sororities. There are 25 groups on campus, including Third Wave (a women's group), choir, chorus, dance, drama, ethnic, international, LGBT, literary magazine, musical theater, newspaper, photography, political, professional, religious, Second Start, social, social service, and student government. Popular campus events include Family and Friends Weekend, Quad Fest, and World Fest. **Sports:** There are 7 intercollegiate sports for men and 7 for women, and 3 intramural sports for men and 5 for women. Facilities include outdoor tennis courts, and a fitness center with Nautilus circuit, free weights and cardiovascular equipment. At a nearby school students may also use an Olympic-size swimming, the indoor and outdoor facilities, two full-size basketball courts, two racquetball courts, a rowing tank, a softball court, an indoor track and a lighted outdoor soccer field. **Graduates:** From July 1, 2015 to June 30, 2016, 453 bachelor's degrees were awarded. The most popular majors were visual and performing arts (25%), psychology (19%), and education (13%). 100 companies recruited on campus in 2015-2016. In an average class, 33% graduate in 4 years or less, 10% graduate in 5 years or less, and 3% graduate in 6 years or less.

SERVICES: Counseling and information services are available, as is tutoring in most subjects. There is a reader service for the blind, and remedial math. **Library/Resources:** The 2 libraries contain 124,022 volumes, 878,938 microform items, and 42,680 audio/video tapes/CDs/DVDs, and subscribe to 861 periodicals including electronic. Computerized library services include interlibrary loans, database searching, Internet access, and Wi-Fi capability. Special learning facilities include an art gallery, center for teaching resources, media production facility, and instructional computing and math achievement center. **Physically Challenged Students:** 85% of the campus is accessible. Facilities include wheelchair ramps, elevators, special parking, specially equipped restrooms, special class scheduling, and lowered drinking fountains. The Disability Services Office provides document review and arranges for reasonable accommodations for special needs students. **Special:** Study abroad in Cuba, England, and Sweden, and 6 others by arrangement, a Washington Justice semester, and on-campus work-study programs are offered. All students participate in at least 3 field placement experiences, beginning in their freshman year. There are combined accelerated degree programs in management, counseling, and education majors. Dual majors and student-designed majors are also available. Accelerated and weekend course programs as well as cross-registration with AIB are offered for Adult Baccalaureate College and School of Education. There is a freshman honors program and 2 departmental honors programs. **Visiting:** There are regularly scheduled orientations for prospective students, which includes personal interviews with professional staff, student campus tours, information sessions, class visits, and meetings with financial aid. There are guides for informal visits, visitors may sit in on classes, and stay overnight. To schedule a visit, contact the Admissions Office. **Campus Safety and Security:** Measures include 24-hour foot and vehicle patrol, self-defense education, and security escort services. There are shuttle buses, emergency telephones, lighted pathways/sidewalks, and watch tours.

REQUIREMENTS: It is recommended that students complete 20 academic units in high school, including 4 in English, 3 each in science, with 2 units in lab, and math, and 1 each in history, and social studies, and 4 in academic electives. SAT or ACT scores, a writing sample, and 2 recommendations are also required as part of the application, and a personal interview is recommended. Applicants must have a high school diploma from an accredited secondary school or a GED. AP and CLEP credits are accepted. Important factors in the admissions decision are evidence of special talent, personality/intangible qualities, recommendations by school officials, and advanced placement or honors courses. Students must complete 45 hours of general education requirements, including 15 of humanities, 12 of natural science, 9 of social science, 6 of multicultural perspectives, and 3 of first-year seminar. Emphasis is given to cross-curriculum components in writing, critical and quantitative reasoning, global perspectives, and leadership and ethics. Art Institute of Boston students must also complete a foundation year. To graduate, students need 128 total credit hours, including 30 to 33 in the liberal arts majors or 41 to 43 in professional majors. **Procedure:** Freshmen are admitted fall and spring. Entrance exams should be taken by February 15. There are deferred admissions and rolling admissions plans. Early decision applications should be filed by December 1; regular applications, by February 15 for fall entry; and November 1 for spring entry, along with a $50 fee. Notification of early decision is sent January 1; regular decision, on a rolling basis. 2 applicants were on the 2016 waiting list. Applications are accepted on-line. **Transfer Students:** 124 transfer students enrolled in 2015-2016. Applicants must have a minimum 2.5 GPA. They must provide high school and college transcripts, complete an essay or personal statement, and have a statement of good standing from prior institution. An interview is recommended for all Lesley College students and required of all Art Institute of Boston students. 45 of 124 credits required for the bachelor's degree must be completed at Lesley. **International Students:** There are 32 international students enrolled. The school actively recruits these students. They must take the TOEFL with a minimum score of 500 on the paper-based TOEFL (PBT).

ADMISSIONS: The SAT scores for the 2016-2017 freshman class were: Critical Reading-- 26% below 500, 48% between 500 and 599, 22% between 600 and 699, and 3% between 700 and 800. Math-- 37% below 500, 46% between 500 and 599, and 16% between 600 and 699. Writing-- 29% below 500, 47% between 500 and 599, 22% between 600 and 699, and 2% between 700 and 800. The ACT scores were 5% between 12 and 17, 36% between 18 and 23, 54% between 24 and 29, and 5% above 30. 40% of the current freshmen were in the top fifth of their class; 75% were in the top two fifths. **Admissions Contact:** Deb Kocar, Director of Admissions. Email: *admissions@lesley.edu* Web: *www.lesley.edu*

FINANCIAL AID: In 2016-2017, 75% of all full-time freshmen and 70% of continuing full-time students received some form of financial aid. 75% of all full-time freshmen and 71% of continuing full-time students received need-based aid. The average freshman award was $14,886. Need-based scholarships or need-based grants averaged $8,614; need-based self-help aid (loans and jobs) averaged $4,996; other non-need-based awards and non-need-based scholarships averaged $10,553; and $3,805 from other forms of aid. 25% of undergraduate students work part-time. Average annual earnings from campus work are $1400. The average financial indebtedness of the 2016 graduate was $18,000. The college's own financial statement, and parent and student federal tax returns are required. The FAFSA code is 002160. The priority date for freshman financial aid applications for fall entry is February 15.

MASSACHUSETTS COLLEGE OF ART AND DESIGN *(The complete profile is made available exclusively on our website, www.barronspac.com)*

MASSACHUSETTS COLLEGE OF LIBERAL ARTS — A-1

www.mcla.edu

North Adams, MA 01247 — (413) 662-5410

Fax: (413) 662-5179
Full-time: 466 men, 735 women
Part-time: 72 men, 134 women
Graduate: 138 men, 110 women
Year: semesters, summer session
Room & Board: $10,524
SAT or ACT: required
Application Deadline: open

Email: admissions@mcla.edu
Faculty: 91
Ph.D.s: 86%
Student/Faculty: 12 to 1
Tuition: $10,135 ($19,080)
Freshman Class: n/av
CEEB CODE: 3521
COMPETITIVE

Massachusetts College of Liberal Arts delivers a high-quality, affordable education that provides students with the critical thinking and communication skills of greatest value to their development, their community, and their future employers. As the public liberal arts college of the Commonwealth, MCLA is committed to preparing students for success at work and in life. MCLA provides unmatched, hands-on growth opportunities early, and often, in an inspiring, creative community. In addition to regional accreditation, MCLA has baccalaureate program accreditation with CAATE. The 80-acre campus is in a rural area 45 miles east of Albany, NY. Including any residence halls, there are 20 buildings.

STUDENT LIFE: 76% of undergraduates are from Massachusetts. Others are from 23 states, and 3 foreign countries. 8% are African American; 73% White; 9% Hispanic; 4% race unknown; 2% Asian American; 2% two or more races. **Male To Female Ratio:** 5.6:1. The average age of freshmen is 18; all undergraduates, 22. 22% do not continue beyond their first year; 52% remain to graduate. **Housing:** 1020 students can be accommodated in college housing, which includes single-sex and coed dorms and on-campus apartments. In addition, there are special-interest houses. On-campus housing is guaranteed for all 4 years. 60% of students live on campus. All students may keep cars.

FACULTY/CLASSROOMS: 48% of faculty are male; 52% are female. No introductory courses are taught by graduate students.

PROGRAMS OF STUDY: MCLA confers B.A. and B.S. degrees. Master's degrees are also awarded. Bachelor's degrees are awarded in AGRICULTURE (environmental studies), BIOLOGICAL SCIENCE (biology/biological science), BUSINESS (accounting and business administration and management), COMMUNICATIONS AND THE ARTS (art, arts administration/management, communications, English, English literature, English Writing, fine arts, performing arts, and visual and performing arts), COMPUTER AND PHYSICAL SCIENCE (chemistry, computer science, mathematics, and physics), EDUCATION (athletic training, childhood education, education, mathematics education, middle school education, and secondary education), HEALTH PROFESSIONS (allied health, cytotechnology, and pre-health studies), SOCIAL SCIENCE (history, interdisciplinary studies, liberal arts/general studies, philosophy, philosophy and religion, political science/government, psychology, public administration, and sociology).

ACTIVITIES: There are 50 groups on campus, including band, cheerleading, choir, chorale, chorus, computers, dance, drama, environmental, ethnic, honors, international, jazz band, LGBT, literary magazine, musical theater, newspaper, photography, political, professional, radio and TV, religious, social, social service, student government, and yearbook. **Sports:** There are 6 intercollegiate sports for men and 7 for women. Facilities include a campus center with a swimming pool, weight rooms, a fitness center, handball, squash, and racquetball courts. The campus also features an outdoor complex with tennis courts and soccer, baseball, and softball fields, a 1,750-seat gym, and a 5-mile cross-country running trail. **Graduates:** From July 1, 2015 to June 30, 2016, 354 bachelor's degrees were awarded. The most popular majors were business (18%), English (13%), and biology (11%). In an average class, 38% graduate in 4 years or less, 50% graduate in 5 years or less, and 53% graduate in 6 years or less.

SERVICES: Counseling and information services are available, as is tutoring in some subjects. There is remedial math, reading, and writing. **Library/Resources:** The library contains 170,000 volumes, 290,000 microform items, and 6,300 audio/video tapes/CDs/DVDs, and subscribes to 70 periodicals including electronic. Computerized library services include interlibrary loans, database searching, and Internet access. Special learning facilities include an art gallery, radio station, and TV station. **Physically Challenged Students:** 98% of the campus is accessible. Facilities include wheelchair ramps, elevators, special parking, specially equipped restrooms, and special class scheduling. **Special:** There are 8 national honor societies, a freshman honors program, and 7 departmental honors programs. **Visiting:** There are regularly scheduled orientations for prospective students. There are guides for informal visits and visitors may sit in on classes. To schedule a visit, contact Admissions Office. **Campus Safety and Security:** Measures include 24-hour foot and vehicle patrol, emergency notification system, self-defense education, and security escort services. There are emergency telephones and lighted pathways/sidewalks.

REQUIREMENTS: MCLA's admission criteria can be described as moderately selective with a strong emphasis placed on a student's academic performance in high school. Successful candidates for admission should meet MCLA's sliding scale which correlates high school GPA with SAT or ACT scores. Secondly, applicants should demonstrate completion of

17 Carnegie units, including 4 courses in English, 4 each in science and math, and 2 each in foreign language, history/social science, and electives. The GED is also accepted. A GPA of 2.0 is required. AP and CLEP credits are accepted. All students must complete at least 120 credits, including 40 in the core curriculum, and maintain a GPA of at least 2.0. **Procedure:** Freshmen are admitted fall and spring. Entrance exams should be taken by January of the senior year. There are early decision, early admissions, deferred admissions, and rolling admissions plans. Application deadlines are open. The fall 2016 application fee was $40. Notification is sent on a rolling basis. Applications are accepted on-line. **Transfer Students:** 144 transfer students enrolled in 2015-2016. MCLA's transfer policy is highly dependent on a student's performance at their previous college (s). A minimum GPA of 2.5 is expected for admission. Students applying without an earned Associate's degree must submit official high school transcript and standardized test scores as well. 45 of 120 credits required for the bachelor's degree must be completed at MCLA. **International Students:** There are 7 international students enrolled. The school actively recruits these students. They must take the TOEFL with a minimum score of 550 on the paper-based TOEFL (PBT). They must also take the SAT.

Admissions Contact: Gina Puc, Director of Admissions. Email: *admissions@mcla.edu* Web: *www.mcla.edu*

FINANCIAL AID: In 2016-2017, 80% of all full-time freshmen and 81% of continuing full-time students received some form of financial aid. 70% of all full-time freshmen and 69% of continuing full-time students received need-based aid. The average freshman award was $15,549. Need-based scholarships or need-based grants averaged $6,942; and need-based self-help aid (loans and jobs) averaged $3,540. The average financial indebtedness of the 2016 graduate was $29,933. MCLA is a member of CSS. The priority date for freshman financial aid applications for fall entry is March 1.

MASSACHUSETTS INSTITUTE OF TECHNOLOGY — D-2

web.mit.edu

Cambridge, MA 02139 — **(617) 253-3400**

Fax: (617) 258-8304	**Email:** admissions@mit.edu
Full-time: 2426 men, 2066 women	**Faculty:** 1022; I, ++$
Part-time: 19 men, 16 women	**Ph.D.s:** 97%
Graduate: 4539 men, 2265 women	**Student/Faculty:** 4 to 1
Year: 4-1-4, summer session	**Tuition:** $46,704
Room & Board: $13,730	**Freshman Class:** 18,306 applied, 1519 accepted, 1107 enrolled
SAT CR/M/W: 730/780/740 **ACT:** 34	**CEEB CODE:** 3514
Application Deadline: January 1	**MOST COMPETITIVE**

MIT, founded in 1861, is a private, independent institution offering programs in architecture and planning, engineering, humanities, arts, social sciences, management, science, health sciences, and technology. There are 5 undergraduate schools and 5 graduate schools. In addition to regional accreditation, MIT has baccalaureate program accreditation with AACSB, ABET, CSAB, and ACS. The 168-acre campus is in an urban area 1 mile north of Boston. Including any residence halls, there are 158 buildings.

STUDENT LIFE: 90% of undergraduates are from out of state, mostly the Middle Atlantic. Students are from 50 states, 96 foreign countries, and Canada. 6% are African American; 6% two or more races; 36% White; 25% Asian American; 2% race unknown; 15% Hispanic; 11% Foreign. **Male To Female Ratio:** 1.6:1. The average age of freshmen is 19; all undergraduates, 20. 2% do not continue beyond their first year; 98% remain to graduate. **Housing:** 3420 students can be accommodated in college housing, which includes single-sex and coed dorms, on-campus apartments, and married student housing. In addition, there are language houses, special-interest houses, fraternity houses, sorority houses, off-campus independent living groups, and non-Greek cooperative houses. On-campus housing is guaranteed for all 4 years. 74% of students live on campus. Some may keep cars.

FACULTY/CLASSROOMS: 78% of faculty are male; 22% are female. All teach undergraduates, and all do research. No introductory courses are taught by graduate students.

PROGRAMS OF STUDY: MIT confers B.S. degrees. Master's and doctoral degrees are also awarded. Bachelor's degrees are awarded in BIOLOGICAL SCIENCE (biology/biological science and neurosciences), BUSINESS (management science), COMMUNICATIONS AND THE ARTS (creative writing, digital communications, linguistics, literature, media arts, and music), COMPUTER AND PHYSICAL SCIENCE (chemistry, computer science, earth science, mathematics, physics, and science technology), ENGINEERING AND ENVIRONMENTAL DESIGN (aeronautical engineering, aerospace studies, architecture, bioengineering, biomedical engineering, chemical engineering, civil engineering, electrical/electronics engineering, engineering, environmental engineering, materials engineering, materials science, mechanical engineering, nuclear engineering, and ocean engineering), SOCIAL SCIENCE (anthropology, archeology, cognitive science, economics, history, humanities, interdisciplinary studies, philosophy, political science/government, and urban studies). Engineering, science, and management & social science programs are the strongest academically. Engineering has the largest enrollment.

ACTIVITIES: 32% of women belong to 6 national sororities. There are 400 groups on campus including art, band, cheerleading, chess, choir, chorale, chorus, computers, dance, debate, drama, environmental, ethnic, film, honors, international, jazz band, LGBT, literary magazine, marching band, musical theater, newspaper, orchestra, photography, political, professional, radio and TV, religious, social, social service, student government, symphony, and yearbook. Popular campus events include Independent Activities Period, and Spring Weekend. **Sports:** There are 16 intercollegiate sports for men and 15 for women, and 20 intramural sports for men and 20 for women. Facilities include an athletic complex with 10 buildings and 26 acres of playing fields. **Graduates:** From July 1, 2015 to June 30, 2016, 1011 bachelor's degrees were awarded. The most popular majors were computer science and engineering (9%), mechanical engineering 2-A (7%), and electrical engineering/computer science (7%). 307 companies recruited on campus in 2015-2016. In an average class, 84% graduate in 4 years or less, 91% graduate in 5 years or less, and 93% graduate in 6 years or less. Of the 2015 graduating class, 33% were enrolled in graduate school within 6 months of graduation, and 58% were employed.

SERVICES: Counseling and information services are available, as is tutoring in most subjects. There is a reader service for the blind. Accommodations for students with documented disabilities are determined on an individual basis. **Library/Resources:** The 5 libraries contain 2.9 million volumes, 2.4 million microform items, and 49,480 audio/video tapes/CDs/DVDs. Computerized library services include interlibrary loans, database searching, Internet access, and Wi-Fi capability. Special learning facilities include an art gallery, radio station, and TV station. **Physically Challenged Students:** Facilities include wheelchair ramps, elevators, special parking, specially equipped restrooms, special class scheduling, lowered drinking fountains, lowered telephones, wheelchair lifts, and automatic doors. An assistive technology lab and assistance with library services are available, upon determination of need. **Special:** MIT offers cross-registration with Harvard, Wellesley, the Massachusetts College of Art and Design, and the School of the Museum of Fine Arts. Internships are offered in a number of programs. Short and long-term study abroad options are offered. The Undergraduate Research Opportunities Program (UROP) cultivates and supports research partnerships between MIT undergraduates and faculty. There are 10 national honor societies and a chapter of Phi Beta Kappa. **Visiting:** There are regularly scheduled orientations for prospective students, including daily tours (Monday through Friday) preceded by an information session with admissions staff. Visitors may sit in on classes and stay overnight. To schedule a visit, contact the Office of Admissions. **Campus Safety and Security:** Measures include 24-hour foot and vehicle patrol, emergency notification system, self-defense education, and security escort services. There are shuttle buses, emergency telephones, lighted pathways/sidewalks, and automated external defibrillators (AEDs) are stationed across campus.

REQUIREMENTS: The SAT or ACT is required. The ACT Optional Writing test is also required. In addition, 2 SAT Subject Tests, including 1 each of math and science, are required. 16 academic units are recommended, including 4 each of English, math, and science, 2 each of social studies, and foreign language. The GED is accepted. Essays, 2 teacher evaluations, an official transcript, and a guidance counselor report are required. An interview is strongly recommended. AP credits are accepted. To graduate, students must fulfill the General Institute Requirements, as well as communication and physical education requirements, and fulfill departmental program requirements. The General Institute Requirements consist of 6 courses in science, 1 in lab science, 2 in restricted science and technology electives, and 8 in humanities, arts, and social sciences for a total of 17 courses. **Procedure:** Freshmen are admitted in the fall. Entrance exams should be taken by the January test date. There are early admissions and deferred admissions plans. Applications should be filed by January 1 for fall entry, along with a $75 fee. Notifications are sent March 20. 652 applicants were on the 2016 waiting list; 52 were admitted. Applications are accepted on-line. **Transfer Students:** 16 transfer students enrolled in 2015-2016. In order to apply, applicant must have minimum of 2 semesters of college, but not more than 5 semesters, at the time they would enroll. Transfer credit is assessed by each academic department on a course by course basis. Enrolling transfer students are required to complete at least 3 semesters at MIT to earn a bachelors degree. For entry in the spring semester, only U.S. citizens and permanent residents may apply. Applicants who are not U.S. citizens or permanent residents must apply for entry in the fall semester. **International Students:** There are 484 international students enrolled. The school actively recruits these students. Non-English speakers may substitute the TOEFL for the SAT or ACT.

ADMISSIONS: 8% of the 2016-2017 applicants were accepted. The SAT scores for the 2016-2017 freshman class were: Critical Reading-- 4% between 500 and 599, 27% between 600 and 699, and 69% between 700 and 800. Math-- 5% between 600 and 699 and 95% between 700 and 800. Writing-- 2% between 500 and 599, 27% between 600 and 699, and 71% between 700 and 800. The ACT scores were 3% between 24 and 29, and 97% above 30. 100% of the current freshmen were in the top fifth of their class. 208 freshmen graduated first in their class. **Admissions Contact:** Stuart Schmill, Dean of Admissions. Email: *admissions@mit.edu* Web: *web.mit.edu*

FINANCIAL AID: MIT is a member of CSS. The CSS/Profile, parent W-2s, 1040s, and the business tax form are required. The FAFSA code is 002178. The deadline for filing freshman financial aid applications for fall entry is February 15.

MASSACHUSETTS MARITIME ACADEMY E-4

www.maritime.edu

Buzzards Bay, MA 02532

(508) 830-5000
(800) 544-3411
Email: admissions@maritime.edu

Full-time: 1416 men, 191 women	**Faculty:** n/av
Part-time: 49 men, 32 women	**Ph.D.s:** n/av
Graduate: 71 men, 21 women	**Student/Faculty:** n/av
Year: semesters, summer session	**Tuition:** $8398 ($25,824)
Room & Board: $12,306	**Freshman Class:** 838 applied, 697 accepted, 392 enrolled
SAT EBR-W/M: 560/560 **ACT:** 23	**CEEB CODE:** 3515
Application Deadline: n/av	**COMPETITIVE**

Massachusetts Maritime Academy, founded in 1891, is the oldest continuously operating maritime academy in the country. Cooperative educational learning and leadership training opportunities prepare graduates for professional positions within private industry or, if opted, military commissions. There is 1 undergraduate school and 1 graduate school. In addition to regional accreditation, MMA has baccalaureate program accreditation with ABET and IACBE. The 54-acre campus is in a small town 60 miles south of Boston. Including any residence halls, there are 12 buildings.

STUDENT LIFE: 80% of undergraduates are from Massachusetts. Others are from 32 states, and 3 foreign countries. 86% are White; 4% Hispanic; 3% two or more races; 3% race unknown; 1% African American; 1% Asian American; 1% Foreign. **Male To Female Ratio:** 6.3:1. The average age of freshmen is 18; all undergraduates, 20. **Housing:** 1615 students can be accommodated in college housing, which includes dorms. On-campus housing is guaranteed for all 4 years. 97% of students live on campus. Alcohol is not permitted. Upperclassmen may keep cars.

FACULTY/CLASSROOMS: No introductory courses are taught by graduate students.

PROGRAMS OF STUDY: MMA confers B.S. degrees. Master's degrees are also awarded. Bachelor's degrees are awarded in BIOLOGICAL SCIENCE (marine science), BUSINESS (international business management), ENGINEERING AND ENVIRONMENTAL DESIGN (engineering, engineering mechanical, EMP energy system focus, marine engineering, and marine transportation), SOCIAL SCIENCE (homeland security/emergency preparedness). Marine engineering is the strongest academically. Marine engineering and marine transportation have the largest enrollments.

ACTIVITIES: There are no fraternities or sororities. There are 20 groups on campus, including regimental leadership, band, communications, drama, international, intramurals, jazz band, LGBT, literary magazine, marching band, pep band, professional, social service, student government, and yearbook. Popular campus events include Ring Dance, Emory Rice Day, and Change of Command. **Sports:** There are 8 intercollegiate sports for men and 8 for women. Facilities include a multi-purpose stadium for football, soccer & lacrosse, baseball & softball fields, sailing center to accommodate co-ed sailing and rowing programs, an Olympic-size swimming pool, weight rooms, cardiovascular center, and an indoor gymnasium. **Graduates:** From July 1, 2016 to June 30, 2017, 344 bachelor's degrees were awarded. The most popular majors were marine engineering (33%), marine transportation (21%), and facilities engineering (17%). In an average class, 61% graduate in 4 years or less, 73% graduate in 5 years or less, and 76% graduate in 6 years or less. Of the 2016 graduating class, 2% were enrolled in graduate school within 6 months of graduation, and 81% were employed.

SERVICES: Counseling and information services are available, as is tutoring in most subjects. **Library/Resources:** Computerized library services include interlibrary loans, database searching, Internet access, and Wi-Fi capability. **Physically Challenged Students:** 90% of the campus is accessible. Facilities include wheelchair ramps, elevators, special parking, specially equipped restrooms, special class scheduling, and lowered drinking fountains. **Special:** Spring semester study abroad opportunities are available via exchange programs with Dalian Maritime University, Shanghai Maritime University, and Metropolitan University College (Denmark). Students with a minimum cumulative GPA of 3.0 may enroll in a dual-degree program with the permission of the department chairperson of each program. Interested students may pursue dual-degree combinations by presenting their proposals for approval by the chairperson of each department. In order to officially declare a dual major before the end of the third semester, a student must have completed either Calculus I or Applied Calculus. **Visiting:** There are regularly scheduled orientations for prospective students, campus tours, admissions interviews, and overnight visits can be arranged. There are also Open House programs. To schedule a visit, contact the Admissions Office. **Campus Safety and Security:** Measures include 24-hour foot and vehicle patrol and emergency notification system. There are emergency telephones, lighted pathways/sidewalks, controlled access to dorms/residences, and late night transport/escort service when available.

REQUIREMENTS: The SAT or ACT is required. Applicants must have graduated from an accredited secondary school or hold a GED certificate. They should have completed 17 Carnegie units, including 4 each in English, math, and science (with 3 in lab), 2 in a foreign language, 1 in social studies, and history, and 2 in academic electives. An essay, official school transcripts, copy of passport/birth certificate, and two letters of recommendation are also required. An interview is strongly recommended. AP and CLEP credits are accepted. Important factors in the admissions decision are advanced placement or honors courses, leadership record, and extracurricular activities record. A major program at MMA includes approximately 128 credits of academic semester courses plus sea terms, experiential learning, and/or cooperative programs. Within each program the academic courses are designated in the categories of major courses, general education courses, and support courses. Each major program includes at least two free electives. Students may choose to add more free elective courses or a minor or concentration sequence of elective courses. During August orientation, all first-year students are required to participate in a freshman mini-cruise. Students in license majors (marine engineering and marine transportation) are required to participate in four seagoing experiences, three aboard the USTS Kennedy (freshman, sophomore and senior years) and one aboard a commercial vessel (junior year). Students enrolled in shore-side majors must complete cooperative education placements as required by the program. Depending upon the major, students completing a non-license degree program may be required to complete experiential learning opportunities. **Procedure:** Freshmen are admitted fall. There are early admissions and rolling admissions plans. Application deadlines are open. The fall 2017 application fee was $50. Notifications are sent December 31. 24 applicants were on the 2017 waiting list; 17 were admitted. Applications are accepted on-line. **Transfer Students:** Minimum number of credits completed for transfer admissions must be 12 to 23 transferable credits with a 2.5 minimum college GPA or 24 or more transferable credits with a 2.0 minimum college GPA. Transfer students must have successfully completed college-level algebra, college-level English composition, and Chemistry I with lab. 30 credits required for the bachelor's degree must be completed at MMA. **International Students:** There are 14 international students enrolled. They must also take the SAT or ACT.

ADMISSIONS: 83% of the 2017-2018 applicants were accepted. The SAT scores for the 2017-2018 freshman class were: Math-- 10% below 500, 62% between 500 and 599, 24% between 600 and 699, and 4% between 700 and 800. Evidence-Based Reading/Writing-- 14% below 500, 58% between 500 and 599, 26% between 600 and 699, and 2% between 700 and 800. The ACT scores were 3% between 12 and 17, 50% between 18 and 23, 40% between 24 and 29, and 7% above 30. **Admissions Contact:** Captain Elizabeth Stevenson, VP of Enrollment Management & External Affairs. Email: *admissions@maritime.edu* Web: *www.maritime.edu*

FINANCIAL AID: The FAFSA code is 002181. Check with the school for current application deadlines.

MCPHS UNIVERSITY *(The complete profile is made available exclusively on our website, www.barronspac.com)*

MERRIMACK COLLEGE — D-1

www.merrimack.edu

North Andover, MA 01845 — **(978) 837-5100**

Fax: (978) 837-5133
Email: admissions@merrimack.edu
Full-time: 1621 men, 1725 women
Faculty: 175; IIA, -$
Part-time: 101 men, 68 women
Ph.D.s: 87%
Graduate: 220 men, 436 women
Student/Faculty: 14 to 1
Year: semesters, summer session
Tuition: $40,190
Room & Board: $15,225
Freshman Class: 8656 applied, 7058 accepted, 855 enrolled
CEEB CODE: 3525
Application Deadline: February 15
COMPETITIVE

Merrimack College, founded in 1947, by the Order of St. Augustine, is a private, selective college offering over 90 undergraduate programs in liberal arts, science and engineering, business, and education, and 15 graduate programs in business, criminology, education, engineering, health sciences, and public affairs, as well as part-time degree completion and certificate programs. There are 5 undergraduate schools and 1 graduate school. In addition to regional accreditation, Merrimack has baccalaureate program accreditation with ABET, CAATE, and ACS. The 220-acre campus is in a suburban area 25 miles north of Boston.

STUDENT LIFE: 69% of undergraduates are from Massachusetts. Others are from 34 states, 27 foreign countries, and Canada. 79% are White; 7% Hispanic; 6% race unknown; 4% African American; 2% Foreign; 1% Asian American; 1% two or more races. **Female To Male Ratio:** 1.1:1. The average age of freshmen is 18; all undergraduates, 20. 20% do not continue beyond their first year. **Housing:** 2346 students can be accommodated in college housing, which includes dorms and on-campus apartments. In addition, there are honors houses, language/international houses, special-interest houses, and living learning communities. On-campus housing is guaranteed for all 4 years. 69% of students live on campus. Upperclassmen may keep cars.

FACULTY/CLASSROOMS: No introductory courses are taught by graduate students. The average class size in an introductory lecture is 25; in a laboratory is 15; and in a regular course is 15.

PROGRAMS OF STUDY: Merrimack confers B.A. and B.S. degrees. Master's degrees are also awarded. Bachelor's degrees are awarded in BIOLOGICAL SCIENCE (biochemistry, biology/biological science, and nutritional sciences), BUSINESS (accounting, business administration and management, finance, financial planning, human resource management, international business management, and marketing/retailing/merchandising), COMMUNICATIONS AND THE ARTS (art history, communications, English, French language and literature, information technology, romance languages and literature, Spanish, sports administration, and theatre acting), COMPUTER AND PHYSICAL SCIENCE (chemistry, computer science, mathematics, and physics), EDUCATION (athletic training, early childhood education, education, elementary education, secondary education, and special education), ENGINEERING AND ENVIRONMENTAL DESIGN (civil engineering, computer engineering, electrical/electronics engineering, environmental science, and mechanical engineering), HEALTH PROFESSIONS (exercise science, health science, public health, and sports medicine), SOCIAL SCIENCE (criminal justice, economics, gender studies, history, human development & family studies, Italian studies, liberal arts/general studies, philosophy, political science/government, psychology, religious studies, sociology, and theology). Science, engineering, and business are the strongest academically. Human development, business, and exercise science have the largest enrollments.

ACTIVITIES: 1% of men belong to 2 national fraternities; 3% of women belong to 2 national sororities. There are 60 groups on campus, including art, cheerleading, choir, chorale, chorus, communications, computers, dance, drama, environmental, ethnic, film, honors, international, jazz band, LGBT, musical theater, newspaper, pep band, photography, political, professional, radio and TV, religious, social, social service, student government, and yearbook. Popular campus events include Spring Weekend, Mr. Merrimack, Cram Jam, Merrimack Survivor, and Relay for Life. **Sports:** There are 9 intercollegiate sports for men and 13 for women, and 10 intramural sports for men and 10 for women. Facilities include an athletic complex, ice rink, basketball court, aerobics studio, exercise room, tennis courts, football stadium, softball, soccer, lacrosse, field hockey fields, and a turf field. **Graduates:** From July 1, 2016 to June 30, 2017, 754 bachelor's degrees were awarded. The most popular majors were business marketing, health professions and related programs, and human development. In an average class, 51% graduate in 4 years or less.

SERVICES: Counseling and information services are available, as is tutoring in every subject. There is a reader service for the blind. Math and writing resource centers are available to all students. **Library/Resources:** Computerized library services include interlibrary loans, database searching, Internet access, and Wi-Fi capability. Special learning facilities include an art gallery, planetarium, radio station, TV station, astronomy dome and telescope, Rogers Center for the Arts, Diversity Education Center, Center for Augustinian Study & Legacy, Center for Biotechnology and Biomedical Sciences, Center for the Study of Jewish-Christian-Muslim Relations, RFID (Radio Frequency Identification), Mucci Capital Markets Lab, Behavior Research Lab, Memory and Sleep Lab, and writers house. **Physically Challenged Students:** 95% of the campus is accessible. Facilities include wheelchair ramps, elevators, special parking, specially equipped restrooms, special class scheduling, lowered drinking fountains, lowered telephones, and special housing. **Special:** Merrimack offers cooperative programs across all majors through the Northeast Consortium, internships in all arts and science programs, study abroad in 20 countries, and a Washington semester at American University. Work-study programs, a 5-year combined B.A.-B.S. degree in many major fields, and dual and self-designed majors are available. General studies, nondegree study, and pass/fail options are possible. **Visiting:** There are regularly scheduled orientations for prospective students. In the fall, admission offers 2 Open Houses and 3 Academic Preview Days. In the Spring we have 3 Admitted Student Days as well as special programming for juniors and seniors, such as shadow days. We also offer daily info sessions and campus tours. There are guides for informal visits and visitors may sit in on classes. To schedule a visit, contact Amy Vachon at (978) 837-5000. **Campus Safety and Security:** Measures include 24-hour foot and vehicle patrol, emergency notification system, self-defense education, and security escort services. There are shuttle buses, emergency telephones, lighted pathways/sidewalks, controlled access to dorms/residences. Rape Aggressive Defense is available through police services.

REQUIREMENTS: High school requirements: 4 years of business administration, humanities, and social sciences and English, 3-4 years of mathematics, 2-3 years of history, government and social sciences, and science (with lab), 2-4 years of foreign language and 1 of electives (health science, biology, chemistry, computer science, engineering, mathematics, physics, and exercise science) Mathematics subject matter should include the equivalent of Algebra I, II and Geometry. An additional, advanced mathematics course is required of all Science and Engineering applicants. Prospective Engineering students must have three units in the sciences including physics. AP and CLEP credits are accepted. Important factors in the admissions decision are personality/intangible qualities, extracurricular activities record, and recommendations by school officials. Students in all bachelor's degree programs must complete a minimum of

124 credits, with a final GPA of 2.00 or better. All students matriculating at the college must complete the requirements for the Core Curriculum in Liberal Studies. The Core Curriculum consists of (11) Course Requirements and (5) Area Requirements. **Procedure:** Freshmen are admitted fall and spring. Entrance exams should be taken during the spring of the junior year and the fall of the senior year. There are early decision, early admissions, and deferred admissions plans. Early decision applications should be filed by November 15; regular applications, by February 15 for fall entry. Notification of early decision is sent December 15; regular decision, March 15. 38 early decision candidates were accepted for the 2017-2018 class. Applications are accepted on-line. **Transfer Students:** 92 transfer students enrolled in 2016-2017. Applicants must have maintained a minimum 2.5 GPA; some programs require a higher GPA. Transfer students must complete the transfer application and essay and must submit official college/university transcript (from each college/university attended), course descriptions of all courses completed from each college/university (needed for evaluation and determination of transfer credit), and a letter of recommendation. Student must not be under disciplinary censure and must be eligible to return to previous institution. A high school transcript is required if the student has less than 30 semester hours of college-level credit completed at the time of application. 48 of 124 credits required for the bachelor's degree must be completed at Merrimack. **International Students:** There are 81 international students enrolled. They must take the TOEFL with a minimum score of 550 on the paper-based TOEFL (PBT) or 79 on the Internet-based version (iBT).

ADMISSIONS: 82% of the 2017-2018 applicants were accepted. **Admissions Contact:** Darren Conine, Associate Vice President for Enrollment. Email: *admissions@merrimack.edu* Web: *www.merrimack.edu*

FINANCIAL AID: 65% of all full-time freshmen received need-based aid. The average freshman award was $24,754. Need-based scholarships or need-based grants averaged $21,091; need-based self-help aid (loans and jobs) averaged $3,445; non-need-based athletic scholarships averaged $24,179; other non-need-based awards and non-need-based scholarships averaged $14,176; and $3,412 from other forms of aid. Merrimack is a member of CSS. The FAFSA code is 002120. The priority date for freshman financial aid applications for fall entry is February 15.

MONTSERRAT COLLEGE OF ART *(The complete profile is made available exclusively on our website, www.barronspac.com)*

MOUNT HOLYOKE COLLEGE — B-2
www.mtholyoke.edu

South Hadley, MA 01075 — **(413) 538-2023**

Fax: (413) 538-2409	**Email: admission@mtholyoke.edu**
Full-time: 2095 women	**Faculty:** 186; IIB, +$
Part-time: 1 men, 30 women	**Ph.D.s:** 98%
Graduate: 12 men, 77 women	**Student/Faculty:** 10 to 1
Year: semesters, summer session	**Tuition:** $43,886
Room & Board: $12,860	**Freshman Class:** n/av
SAT or ACT: required	**CEEB CODE:** 3529
Application Deadline: January 15	**MOST COMPETITIVE**

Mount Holyoke College, founded in 1837, is an independent liberal arts college and the oldest institution of higher learning for women in the United States. The 800-acre campus is in a small town 90 miles west of Boston and 160 miles north of New York City. Including any residence halls, there are 68 buildings.

STUDENT LIFE: 75% of undergraduates are from out of state, mostly the Middle Atlantic. Students are from 44 states, 69 foreign countries, and Canada. 65% are from public schools. 8% are Hispanic; 6% African American; 45% White; 4% two or more races; 27% Foreign; 10% Asian American; 1% race unknown. **Female To Male Ratio:** 169.4:1. The average age of freshmen is 18; all undergraduates, 20. 10% do not continue beyond their first year; 85% remain to graduate. **Housing:** 2111 students can be accommodated in college housing, which includes single-sex dorms, on-campus apartments, and special accommodations. On-campus housing is guaranteed for all 4 years. 95% of students live on campus; of those, 70% remain on campus on weekends. All students may keep cars.

FACULTY/CLASSROOMS: 42% of faculty are male; 58% are female. All teach undergraduates and all do research. No introductory courses are taught by graduate students. The average class size in an introductory lecture is 20; in a laboratory is 12; and in a regular course is 15.

PROGRAMS OF STUDY: MHC confers A.B. degrees. Master's degrees are also awarded. Bachelor's degrees are awarded in AGRICULTURE (environmental studies), BIOLOGICAL SCIENCE (biochemistry, biology/biological science, and neurosciences), COMMUNICATIONS AND THE ARTS (Africana studies, art history and appreciation, classics, dance, dramatic arts, English, film arts, French, Greek, Italian, Latin, music, romance languages and literature, Spanish, and studio art), COMPUTER AND PHYSICAL SCIENCE (astronomy, chemistry, computer science, geology, mathematics, physics, and statistics), EDUCATION (psychology education), ENGINEERING AND ENVIRONMENTAL DESIGN (architecture), SOCIAL SCIENCE (anthropology, Asian/Oriental studies, classical/ancient civilization, East Asian studies, economics, gender studies, geography, German area studies, history, international relations, Latin American studies, medieval studies, Middle Eastern studies, philosophy, political science/government, psychology, religion, Russian and Slavic studies, sociology, and South Asian studies). Sciences, social sciences, and international relations are the strongest academically. Psychology, biology, and economics have the largest enrollments.

ACTIVITIES: There are no fraternities or sororities. There are 130 groups on campus, including art, band, cheerleading, choir, chorale, chorus, computers, dance, debate, drama, environmental, ethnic, film, honors, international, jazz band, LGBT, literary magazine, newspaper, orchestra, photography, political, professional, radio and TV, religious, social, social service, student government, symphony, and yearbook. Popular campus events include Nightfest, Mountain Day, Fall Fest, No Study Zone, Pangy Day, Cultural Nights, and Spring Weekend. **Sports:** There are 14 intercollegiate sports for women. Facilities include indoor athletic and recreational facilities housed in the Kendall Sports & Dance Complex, fitness center, gymnasium, natatorium, field house, turf & track complex, soccer field, activity field and tennis courts. Also in close proximity are the college's Canoe House and a scenic one-mile loop around Upper Lake for running, walking, or riding a horse, and the Mount Holyoke College Equestrian Center. **Graduates:** From July 1, 2015 to June 30, 2016, 628 bachelor's degrees were awarded. The most popular majors were psychology (10%), economics (9%), and English (8%). 87 companies recruited on campus in 2015-2016. In an average class, 78% graduate in 4 years or less, 84% graduate in 5 years or less, and 85% graduate in 6 years or less. Of the 2015 graduating class, 22% were enrolled in graduate school within 6 months of graduation, and 85% were employed.

SERVICES: Counseling and information services are available, as is tutoring in every subject. There is a writing center available to all students at all levels, a reader service for the blind, and an adaptive technology lab. Special testing accommodations, diagnostic testing services, note-taking services, as well as readers and tutors. **Library/Resources:** The 2 libraries contain 1.4 million volumes, 24,481 microform items, and 12,030 audio/video tapes/CDs/DVDs, and subscribe to 7,525 periodicals including electronic. Computerized library services include interlibrary loans, database searching, Internet access, and Wi-Fi capability. Special learning facilities include an art gallery, radio station, an observatory, a child study center, a botanical garden and greenhouse, an equestrian center, a conference center, and centers for global initiatives, leadership, and the environment. **Physically Challenged Students:** Facilities include wheelchair ramps, elevators, special parking, specially equipped restrooms, special class scheduling, lowered drinking fountains, and special housing. **Special:** Mount Holyoke offers students cross-registration through the Five-College Consortium. Other opportunities include the 12-College Exchange Program, science and international studies internships, study abroad in over 50 countries (semester or full-year), a Washington semester, work-study, student-designed majors, dual majors, accelerated degrees, nondegree study, and pass/fail options. A teacher licensure program is available. Mount Holyoke's "The Lynk" Program enables students to meaningfully link their liberal arts education with their career goals through internships, research projects, and summer employment. There are 5 national honor societies and a chapter of Phi Beta Kappa. **Visiting:** There are regularly scheduled orientations for prospective students, including tours, on-campus interviews, overnight stays, and meetings with professors and coaches. There are guides for informal visits, visitors may sit in on classes, and stay overnight. To schedule a visit, contact the Admission Office. **Campus Safety and Security:** Measures include 24-hour foot and vehicle patrol, emergency notification system, self-defense education, and security escort services. There are shuttle buses, emergency telephones, lighted pathways/sidewalks, and controlled access to dorms/residences.

REQUIREMENTS: The school recommends that applicants have 4 years each of English and foreign language, 3 each of math and science, and 2 of social studies. An essay is required and an interview is strongly recommended. AP credits are accepted. Important factors in the admissions decision are advanced placement or honors courses, leadership record, and recommendations by school officials. Students must complete 128 total credits with a final GPA of 2.0. Students must complete a first-year seminar and a major (generally 32-56 credits). At least 68 credits must be earned from course work outside the major department. Students must complete one course each in the humanities, science/math, and social sciences. Students must also complete a foreign language course, a multicultural perspectives course, and 4 units (2 semesters) of physical education courses. While not required, students may also elect to complete any number (or none) of the following: a second major, a minor (but not both a second major and a minor), a Five College certificate, or a Nexus program. At least 64 of the student's 128 credits must be earned at Mount Holyoke over a minimum of 4 semesters during the student's sophomore, junior and senior years. **Procedure:** Freshmen are admitted fall and spring. Entrance exams should be taken before the application deadline. There are early decision and deferred admissions plans. Early decision applications should be filed by November 15; regular applications, by January 15 for fall entry, along with a $60 fee. Notification of early decision is sent January 1; regular decision, April 1. 161 early decision candidates were accepted for the 2016-2017 class. 459 applicants were on the 2016 waiting list; 7 were admitted. Applications are accepted on-line. Application fees are waived if application is completed on-line. **Transfer Students:** 77 transfer students enrolled in 2015-2016. A statement of good standing, transcripts of secondary school or college-level work, and an essay are required of transfer applicants. An interview is recommended. SAT scores will be considered if submitted but are not required. 64 of 128 credits required for the bachelor's degree must be completed at Mount Holyoke. **International Students:** There are 564 international students enrolled. The school actively recruits these students. They must take the TOEFL with a minimum score of 100 on the Internet-based version (iBT).

ADMISSIONS: 50% of the 2016-2017 applicants were accepted. 81% of the current freshmen were in the top fifth of their class; 96% were in the top two fifths. 14 freshmen graduated first in their class. **Admissions Contact:** Gail Berson, Vice President of Enrollment and Dean of Admissions. Email: *admission@mtholyoke.edu* Web: *www.mtholyoke.edu*

FINANCIAL AID: In 2016-2017, 79% of all full-time freshmen and 78% of continuing full-time students received some form of financial aid. 66% of all full-time freshmen and 65% of continuing full-time students received need-based aid. The average freshman award was $36,894. Need-based scholarships or need-based grants averaged $32,332; need-based self-help aid (loans and jobs) averaged $5,360; and other non-need-based awards and non-need-based scholarships averaged $19,312. 64% of undergraduate students work part-time. Average annual earnings from campus work are $1152. MHC is a member of CSS. The CSS/Profile, parent and student tax returns, and noncustodial parent form are required. The FAFSA code is 002192. The priority date for freshman financial aid applications for fall entry is February 15.

MOUNT IDA COLLEGE — D-2

www.mountida.edu

Newton, MA 02459 — (617) 928-4553

Fax: (617) 928-4507	**Email:** admissions@mountida.edu
Full-time: 400 men, 700 women	**Faculty:** 56; IIB, -$
Part-time: 10 men, 20 women	**Ph.D.s:** 61%
Graduate: n/av	**Student/Faculty:** 19 to 1
Year: semesters, summer session	**Tuition:** $33,820
Room & Board: $13,000	**Freshman Class:** n/av
SAT or ACT: required	**CEEB CODE:** 3530
Application Deadline: August 15	**COMPETITIVE**

Mount Ida College, founded in 1899, is an independent baccalaureate college that prepares students for a profession through a curriculum that emphasizes career studies integrated with liberal learning. The figures in the above capsule and in this profile are approximate. There are 5 undergraduate schools. In addition to regional accreditation, Mount Ida has baccalaureate program accreditation with ABFSE, ADA, FIDER, and NASAD. The 72-acre campus is in a suburban area 8 miles west of downtown Boston. Including any residence halls, there are 18 buildings.

STUDENT LIFE: 54% of undergraduates are from Massachusetts. Others are from 23 states, 33 foreign countries, and Canada. 80% are from public schools. 7% are Hispanic; 63% White; 3% Asian American; 16% African American; 10% Foreign; 1% American Indian/Alaska Native. **Female To Male Ratio:** 1.8:1. The average age of freshmen is 19; all undergraduates, 21. **Housing:** 803 students can be accommodated in college housing, which includes single-sex and coed dorms. In addition, there are honors houses, and housing for students over age 21. On-campus housing is guaranteed for all 4 years. 60% of students live on campus. Upperclassmen may keep cars.

FACULTY/CLASSROOMS: 46% of faculty are male; 54% are female. All teach undergraduates. No introductory courses are taught by graduate students. The average class size in an introductory lecture is 25; in a laboratory is 16; and in a regular course is 20.

PROGRAMS OF STUDY: Mount Ida confers B.A., B.S. and B.L.S. degrees. Associate degrees are also awarded. Bachelor's degrees are awarded in AGRICULTURE (equine science), BUSINESS (business administration and management, fashion merchandising, funeral home services, hospitality management services, marketing/retailing/merchandising, retailing, and small business management), COMMUNICATIONS AND THE ARTS (American literature, art and design, communications, English, graphic design, journalism, media arts, and radio/television technology), EDUCATION (early childhood education and history education), ENGINEERING AND ENVIRONMENTAL DESIGN (interior design), HEALTH PROFESSIONS (veterinary science), SOCIAL SCIENCE (American studies, child psychology/development, criminal justice, fashion design and technology, law, liberal arts/general studies, and sociology). Veterinary technology, dental hygiene, and funeral service are the strongest academically. Business and veterinary technology have the largest enrollments.

ACTIVITIES: There are no fraternities or sororities. There are 25 groups on campus, including art, cheerleading, chess, choir, dance, drama, ethnic, fashion, honors, international, LGBT, literary magazine, newspaper, photography, professional, radio and TV, religious, social, social service, student government, and yearbook. Popular campus events include Welcome Week, Spring Fling, and Senior Week. **Sports:** There are 7 intercollegiate sports for men and 6 for women, and 8 intramural sports for men and 10 for women. Facilities include a gym, playing fields, a fitness center, tennis courts, an outdoor swimming pool, athletic fields, and an athletic center. **Graduates:** From July 1, 2015 to June 30, 2016, 128 bachelor's degrees were awarded. The most popular majors were criminal justice (16%), graphic design (13%), and management (11%).

SERVICES: Counseling and information services are available, as is tutoring in most subjects. There is remedial math, reading, and writing. There is a program for learning-disabled students, for which a fee is charged. Studies skills courses are also available. The Learning Circle is another innovative campuswide initiative that provides a professional learning specialist to assist students and monitor their academic progress. **Library/Resources:** The library contains 62,500 volumes, 68 microform items, and 2,000 audio/video tapes/CDs/DVDs, and subscribes to 530 periodicals including electronic. Computerized library services include interlibrary loans, database searching, and Internet access. Special learning facilities include an art gallery, radio station, TV station, communication lab, darkroom, sewing rooms, blueprint-making facility, and dental labs. **Physically Challenged Students:** 75% of the campus is accessible. Facilities include wheelchair ramps, elevators, special parking, specially equipped restrooms, special class scheduling, lowered drinking fountains, lowered telephones, and special housing. **Special:** Internships in the form of work experience are available in each department. Work-study provided by the college, student-designed majors, study abroad in 14 countries, exchange program with Strasbourg, France, a general studies degree, an interdisciplinary major in legal studies, nondegree study, and an accelerated degree program in funeral service are also available. There are 4 national honor societies, a freshman honors program, and 4 departmental honors programs. **Visiting:** There are regularly scheduled orientations for prospective students, consisting of fall and spring open houses, Saturday sessions, and weekday appointments. There are guides for informal visits, visitors may sit in on classes, and stay overnight. To schedule a visit, contact the Admissions Office. **Campus Safety and Security:** Measures include 24-hour foot and vehicle patrol, self-defense education, and security escort services. There are shuttle buses, emergency telephones, and lighted pathways/sidewalks.

REQUIREMENTS: The SAT or ACT is required. Applicants are required to have 4 units of English, 2 of social studies, and 3 each of math and science. A portfolio is recommended for certain programs, while an interview is recommended for all applicants. The GED is accepted. AP and CLEP credits are accepted. Important factors in the admissions decision are advanced placement or honors courses, evidence of special talent, and recommendations by school officials. Candidates for a bachelor's degree require 128 credits with a 2.0 GPA. The distribution requirement varies for each major. 1 phys ed course is required. The all-college curriculum includes these common experiences for all students: a college success course, a junior year interdisciplinary seminar, and a senior capstone project. **Procedure:** Freshmen are admitted fall and spring. Entrance exams should be taken as early as possible by the junior year. There are early admissions, deferred admissions, and rolling admissions plans. Applications should be filed by August 15 for fall entry, along with a $35 fee. Applications are accepted on-line. **Transfer Students:** 144 transfer students enrolled in 2015-2016. Applicants need a minimum GPA of C and must submit college and high school transcripts. 32 of 120 credits required for the bachelor's degree must be completed at Mount Ida. **International Students:** There are 93 international students enrolled. The school actively recruits these students. They must take the TOEFL. They must also take the SAT or ACT.

Admissions Contact: Matthew Morrison, Director of Admissions. Email: *admissions@mountida.edu* Web: *www.mountida.edu*

FINANCIAL AID: 70% of undergraduate students work part-time. Average annual earnings from campus work are $1500. The average financial indebtedness of the 2016 graduate was $19,268. Mount Ida is a member of CSS. The FAFSA code is 002193. The priority date for freshman financial aid applications for fall entry is May 1.

NEW ENGLAND CONSERVATORY OF MUSIC *(The complete profile is made available exclusively on our website, www.barronspac.com)*

NEWBURY COLLEGE — D-2

www.newbury.edu

Brookline, MA 02445 — **(617) 730-7007**

Fax: (617) 731-9618	**Email:** admissions@newbury.edu
Full-time: 293 men, 390 women	**Faculty:** 28
Part-time: 25 men, 43 women	**Ph.D.s:** n/av
Graduate: n/av	**Student/Faculty:** 26 to 1
Year: semesters, summer session	**Tuition:** $32,750
Room & Board: $14,200	**Freshman Class:** n/av
SAT or ACT: recommended	**CEEB CODE:** 3639
Application Deadline: n/av	**COMPETITIVE**

Newbury College, founded in 1962, is a private institution offering career-relevant degree programs in business, graphic design, legal studies, computer science, interior design, communication, culinary arts, hotel and restaurant management, and psychology. The figures in the above capsule and in this profile are approximate. There are 4 undergraduate schools. In addition to regional accreditation, Newbury has baccalaureate program accreditation with NEASC. The 10-acre campus is in a suburban area 3 miles west of Boston. Including any residence halls, there are 10 buildings.

STUDENT LIFE: 75% of undergraduates are from Massachusetts. Others are from 24 states, 12 foreign countries, and Canada. 7% are Asian American; 37% White; 36% African American; 3% Foreign; 16% Hispanic; 1% race unknown. **Female To Male Ratio:** 1.4:1. The average age of freshmen is 19; all undergraduates, 21. 42% do not continue beyond their first year; 40% remain to graduate. **Housing:** College-sponsored housing includes coed dorms. In addition, there are special-interest houses. On-campus housing is guaranteed for all 4 years, and is available on a first-come, first-served basis, and is available on a lottery system for upperclassmen. Priority is given to out-of-town students. 63% of students commute. Alcohol is not permitted. Some may keep cars.

FACULTY/CLASSROOMS: All teach undergraduates. No introductory courses are taught by graduate students. The average class size in a regular course is 20.

PROGRAMS OF STUDY: Newbury confers B.S. and B.A. degrees. Associate degrees are also awarded. Bachelor's degrees are awarded in BUSINESS (accounting, business administration and management, fashion merchandising, hotel/motel and restaurant management, international business management, marketing management, and sports management), COMMUNICATIONS AND THE ARTS (communications and graphic design), COMPUTER AND PHYSICAL SCIENCE (computer science), ENGINEERING AND ENVIRONMENTAL DESIGN (interior design), HEALTH PROFESSIONS (health care administration), SOCIAL SCIENCE (criminal justice, food production/management/services, legal studies, and psychology). Psychology, and legal studies are the strongest academically. Psychology, criminal justice, and business management have the largest enrollments.

ACTIVITIES: There are no fraternities or sororities. There are 20 groups on campus, including choir, chorus, communications, dance, ethnic, honors, international, LGBT, professional, radio and TV, religious, social, social service, and student government. Popular campus events include Multicultural Week, Spring Fling and Fall Fest. **Sports:** There are 6 intercollegiate sports for men and 6 for women, and 9 intramural sports for men and 9 for women. Facilities include an off-site gym and a cardiovascular/weight room. **Graduates:** From July 1, 2015 to June 30, 2016, 152 bachelor's degrees were awarded. The most popular majors were psychology (17%), culinary management (10%), and criminal justice (7%). 60 companies recruited on campus in 2015-2016. In an average class, 37% graduate in 4 years or less, 41% graduate in 5 years or less, and 42% graduate in 6 years or less.

SERVICES: Counseling and information services are available, as is tutoring in every subject. There is a reader service for the blind, and remedial math, reading, and writing. **Library/Resources:** The library contains 61,529 volumes, and 311 audio/video tapes/CDs/DVDs, and subscribes to 18,200 periodicals including electronic. Computerized library services include interlibrary loans, database searching, Internet access, and Wi-Fi capability. Special learning facilities include an art gallery, radio station, and TV station. **Physically Challenged Students:** 80% of the campus is accessible. Facilities include wheelchair ramps, elevators, special parking, specially equipped restrooms, special class scheduling, and lowered drinking fountains. **Special:** Internships are part of the bachelor's degree program. Dual majors are available. Credits earned for associate degrees in professional areas can be applied toward the college's bachelor's degree programs. There are 4 national honor societies, a freshman honors program, and 4 departmental honors programs. **Visiting:** There are regularly scheduled orientations for prospective students, including fall and spring open houses, daily interviews, and campus tours. There are guides for informal visits and visitors may sit in on classes. To schedule a visit, contact the Office of Admissions. **Campus Safety and Security:** Measures include 24-hour foot and vehicle patrol, emergency notification system, and security escort services. There are shuttle buses and lighted pathways/sidewalks.

REQUIREMENTS: The SAT or ACT is recommended. Applicants must submit an application, 2 letters of recommendation, high school transcripts, and an essay. AP and CLEP credits are accepted. Important factors in the admissions decision are leadership record, recommendations by alumni, and extracurricular activities record. Candidates for a bachelor's degree must earn 120 credits or 60 credits beyond the associate degree, with a 2.0 GPA. Distribution requirements include courses in math, lab science, literature, and social science, as well as 3 additional credits in arts and sciences. A minimum of 45 credits as well as a minimum of 50% of the courses in the major must be taken at Newbury College. **Procedure:** Freshmen are admitted fall and spring. Entrance exams should be taken following acceptance. There are deferred admissions and rolling admissions plans. Application deadlines are open. Application fee is $25. Notification is sent on a rolling basis. Applications are accepted on-line. Application fees are waived if application is completed on-line. **Transfer Students:** 43 transfer students enrolled in 2015-2016. Transfer students must submit an application, 1 recommendation, high school and college transcripts, and an essay. 60 of 120 credits required for the bachelor's degree must be completed at Newbury. **International Students:** There are 16 international students enrolled. The school actively recruits these students. They must take the TOEFL with a minimum score of 71 on the Internet-based version (iBT).

Admissions Contact: Yavuz Kiremit, Director of Admissions. Email: *admissions@newbury.edu* Web: *www.newbury.edu*

FINANCIAL AID: In 2016-2017, 84% of all full-time freshmen and 85% of continuing full-time students received some form of financial aid. 98% of all full-time freshmen and 98% of continuing full-time students received need-based aid. The average freshman award was $28,610.

Need-based scholarships or need-based grants averaged $14,813 ($13,759 maximum); need-based self-help aid (loans and jobs) averaged $3,460 ($5,500 maximum); and other non-need-based awards and non-need-based scholarships averaged $6,064 ($18,000 maximum). 22% of undergraduate students work part-time. Average annual earnings from campus work are $1472. The average financial indebtedness of the 2016 graduate was $30,875. Newbury is a member of CSS. The FAFSA code is 007484. The priority date for freshman financial aid applications for fall entry is March 1. The deadline for filing freshman financial aid applications for fall entry is May 1.

NICHOLS COLLEGE *(The complete profile is made available exclusively on our website, www.barronspac.com)*

NORTHEASTERN UNIVERSITY E-2

www.northeastern.edu

Boston, MA 02115 **(617) 373-2200**

Fax: (617) 373-8780	**Email: admissions@neu.edu**
Full-time: 8778 men, 9017 women	**Faculty:** 1261; I, +$
Part-time: none	**Ph.D.s:** 95%
Graduate: 4133 men, 3410 women	**Student/Faculty:** 14 to 1
Year: semesters, summer session	**Tuition:** $49,628
Room & Board: $15,724	**Freshman Class:** n/av
SAT or ACT: required	**CEEB CODE:** 3667
Application Deadline: January 1	**MOST COMPETITIVE**

Northeastern University, founded in 1898, is a private research university located in the heart of Boston. Northeastern is the leader in worldwide experiential learning, urban engagement, and interdisciplinary research that meets global and societal needs. Our broad mix of experience-based education programs our signature cooperative education program, as well as student research, service learning, and global learning build the connections that enable students to transform their lives. The university offers a comprehensive range of undergraduate and graduate programs leading to degrees. There are 7 undergraduate schools and 9 graduate schools. In addition to regional accreditation, NU has baccalaureate program accreditation with AACSB, ABET, ACPE, NAAB, CAATE, CCNE, and ACS. The 73-acre campus is in an urban area in the heart of Boston, on Huntington Avenue, known as the Avenue of the Arts. Including any residence halls, there are 88 buildings.

STUDENT LIFE: 76% of undergraduates are from out of state, mostly the Northeast. Students are from 48 states, 119 foreign countries, and Canada. 7% are Hispanic; 5% race unknown; 48% White; 4% African American; 4% two or more races; 19% Foreign; 13% Asian American. **Male To Female Ratio:** 1.0:1. The average age of freshmen is 19; all undergraduates, 21. **Housing:** 8354 students can be accommodated in college housing, which includes dorms, on-campus apartments, and off-campus apartments. In addition, there are honors houses, special-interest houses, academic/college-based, innovation, single singles housing, global perspective, leadership, creative expression, and green living housing. On-campus housing is guaranteed for the freshman year only, is available on a first-come, first-served basis, and is available on a lottery system for upperclassmen. 99% of students live on campus. Upperclassmen may keep cars.

FACULTY/CLASSROOMS: No introductory courses are taught by graduate students.

PROGRAMS OF STUDY: NU confers B.A., B.S., B.F.A. and B.L.A. degrees. Master's and doctoral degrees are also awarded. Bachelor's degrees are awarded in AGRICULTURE (environmental studies), BIOLOGICAL SCIENCE (biochemistry, biology/biological science, marine biology, and neurosciences), BUSINESS (accounting, business administration and management, international business management, and management information systems), COMMUNICATIONS AND THE ARTS (American Sign Language, art, communications, dramatic arts, English, film arts, graphic design, journalism, languages, linguistics, multimedia, music, music technology, studio art, and theatre arts), COMPUTER AND PHYSICAL SCIENCE (applied physics, chemistry, computer programming, computer science, digital arts/technology, earth science, information sciences and systems, mathematics, and physics), ENGINEERING AND ENVIRONMENTAL DESIGN (architecture, chemical engineering, civil engineering, computer engineering, electrical/electronics engineering, environmental science, industrial engineering, landscape architecture/design, and mechanical engineering), HEALTH PROFESSIONS (health science, nursing, pharmaceutical science, pharmacy, physical therapy, and speech pathology/audiology), SOCIAL SCIENCE (African American studies, anthropology, Asian/Oriental studies, criminal justice, economics, history, interdisciplinary studies, Judaic studies, philosophy, philosophy and religion, political science/government, psychology, religion, and sociology). Business administration, engineering, and sciences have the largest enrollments.

ACTIVITIES: 5% of men belong to 18 national fraternities; 8% of women belong to 11 national sororities. Groups on campus include ROTC Navy and Air Force, art, band, cheerleading, chess, chorale, chorus, computers, dance, debate, drama, environmental, ethnic, film, honors, international, jazz band, LGBT, literary magazine, musical theater, orchestra, pep band, political, professional, radio and TV, religious, resident student association, social, social service, student government, symphony, and yearbook. Popular campus events include Springfest, Senior Week, Welcome Week, and Carnevale. **Sports:** There are 7 intercollegiate sports for men and 9 for women, and 31 intramural sports for men and 31 for women. Facilities include outdoor and indoor tracks, indoor hockey arena, swimming pool, indoor and outdoor tennis courts, racquetball, squash, volleyball, basketball courts, and fitness centers. **Graduates:** From July 1, 2016 to June 30, 2017, 3999 bachelor's degrees were awarded. The most popular majors were business/marketing (26%), engineering (17%), and health professions and related programs (13%). In an average class, 86% graduate in 6 years or less.

SERVICES: Counseling and information services are available, as is tutoring in most subjects. There is remedial math, reading, and writing. **Library/Resources:** The library contains 896,213 volumes, 1.3 million microform items, and 18,210 audio/video tapes/CDs/DVDs, and subscribes to 128,027 periodicals including electronic. Computerized library services include interlibrary loans, database searching, Internet access, and Wi-Fi capability. Special learning facilities include an art gallery, radio station, architecture studio, TV production suite, and various research labs. **Physically Challenged Students:** 95% of the campus is accessible. Facilities include wheelchair ramps, elevators, special parking, specially equipped restrooms, special class scheduling, lowered drinking fountains, lowered telephones, and special housing. Specially equipped labs, and a tunnel system connecting the major administrative and academic buildings. **Special:** Northeastern offers a variety of experiential learning opportunities; Co-op, research, global experience, and service-learning in Boston, throughout the U.S., and around the world to integrate classroom instruction with professional experience. Northeastern takes a flexible student-centered approach to academics that allows you to create the education that best suits your goals and aspirations. We offer four- and five-year programs, combined degree programs, interdisciplinary study options, study abroad in dozens of countries, undergraduate research opportunities, an Honors Program, work-study through the university and in neighboring public and private agencies, and student-designed majors. There are 14 national honor societies and a freshman honors program. **Visiting:** There are regularly scheduled orientations for prospective students. There are guides for informal visits. To schedule a visit, contact the Office of Undergraduate Admissions Office. **Campus Safety and Security:** Measures include 24-hour foot and vehicle patrol, emergency notification system, self-defense education, and security escort services. There are shuttle buses, emergency telephones, lighted pathways/sidewalks, controlled access to dorms/residences, and in-room safes.

REQUIREMENTS: The SAT or ACT is required. The ACT Optional Writing test is also required. Northeastern requires that applicants have 17 academic units, including 4 in English, 3 each in math, 2 units each in science with lab, social studies, foreign language, and history. An essay is required. AP credits are accepted. Important factors in the admissions decision are advanced placement or honors courses, leadership record, evidence of special talent, and extracurricular activities record. Although each college has its own requirements, students must generally complete at least 128 semester hours with a minimum GPA of 2.0. Students must also fulfill the university-wide general education requirement. **Procedure:** Freshmen are admitted in the fall. Entrance exams should be taken from May of the junior year through December of the senior year. There are early admissions and deferred admissions plans. Early decision applications should be filed by November 1; regular applications, by January 1 for fall entry. The fall 2017 application fee was $75. Notification of early decision is sent December 15; regular decision, April 1. 889 early decision candidates were accepted for the 2017-2018 class. Applications are accepted on-line. **Transfer Students:** 587 transfer students enrolled in 2016-2017. The most successful transfer students have earned a cumulative GPA of 3.3. Students have also completed the introductory-level courses for their intended majors. Transfer students with less than 24 semester hours of college-level credit must also submit their high school transcripts and SAT or ACT scores. **International Students:** There are 2881 international students enrolled. They must take the TOEFL with a minimum score of 92 on the Internet-based version (iBT).

ADMISSIONS: 29% of the 2017-2018 applicants were accepted. 94% of the current freshmen were in the top fifth of their class; 99% were in the top two fifths. **Admissions Contact:** Dewayne Clacher, Director of Admissions. Email: *admissions@neu.edu* Web: *www.northeastern.edu*

FINANCIAL AID: In 2017-2018, 100% of all full-time freshmen received some form of financial aid, and need-based aid. The average freshman award was $39,320. Need-based scholarships or need-based grants averaged $34,803; non-need-based athletic scholarships averaged $37,703; other non-need-based awards and non-need-based scholarships averaged $19,869; and $4,281 from other forms of aid. The CSS/Profile is required. The FAFSA code is 002199. The priority date for freshman financial aid applications for fall entry is February 15.

PINE MANOR COLLEGE *(The complete profile is made available exclusively on our website, www.barronspac.com)*

REGIS COLLEGE *(The complete profile is made available exclusively on our website, www.barronspac.com)*

SALEM STATE UNIVERSITY *(The complete profile is made available exclusively on our website, www.barronspac.com)*

SIMMONS COLLEGE — E-2

www.simmons.edu

Boston, MA 02115	**(617) 521-2515** **(800) 345-8468**
Fax: (617) 521-3190	**Email: ugadm@simmons.edu**
Full-time: 1553 women	**Faculty:** 148
Part-time: 186 women	**Ph.D.s:** 68%
Graduate: 545 men, 3999 women	**Student/Faculty:** 10 to 1
Year: semesters, summer session	**Tuition:** $39,600
Room & Board: $14,800	**Freshman Class:** 2969 applied, 2105 accepted, 405 enrolled
SAT EBR-W/M: 630/604 **ACT:** 27	**CEEB CODE:** 3761
Application Deadline: February 1	**HIGHLY COMPETITIVE**

Simmons College, founded in 1899, is a private institution with an undergraduate college for women that offers a comprehensive education combining the arts, sciences, and humanities with preprofessional training. All graduate programs are co-ed, with the exception of the women-only MBA program. There are 5 undergraduate schools and 5 graduate schools. In addition to regional accreditation, Simmons College has baccalaureate program accreditation with AACSB, APTA, CSWE, ACS, CCNE, and ACEND. The 12-acre campus is in an urban area in Boston. Including any residence halls, there are 17 buildings.

STUDENT LIFE: 60% of undergraduates are from Massachusetts. Others are from 43 states, 53 foreign countries, and Canada. 64% are White; 6% African American; 6% Hispanic; 5% Foreign; 5% two or more races; 3% race unknown; 10% Asian American. **Female To Male Ratio:** 10.5:1. The average age of freshmen is 19; all undergraduates, 21. 18% do not continue beyond their first year; 73% remain to graduate. **Housing:** 1111 students can be accommodated in college housing, which includes dorms and off-campus apartments. In addition, there are special-interest houses, theme housing, wellness housing, cooperative housing, women's dorms, and non-traditional students with dependents. On-campus housing is guaranteed for the freshman year only, is available on a first-come, first-served basis, and is available on a lottery system for upperclassmen. 63% of students live on campus. No one may keep cars.

FACULTY/CLASSROOMS: 24% of faculty are male; 76% are female. 69% teach undergraduates. No introductory courses are taught by graduate students. The average class size in an introductory lecture is 15; in a laboratory is 11; and in a regular course is 14.

PROGRAMS OF STUDY: Simmons confers B.A., B.S., and B.S.W. degrees. Master's and doctoral degrees are also awarded. Bachelor's degrees are awarded in AGRICULTURE (environmental studies), BIOLOGICAL SCIENCE (biochemistry, biology/biological science, and biometrics and biostatistics), BUSINESS (business administration and management, finance, management information systems, marketing and distribution, and retailing), COMMUNICATIONS AND THE ARTS (arts administration/management, communications, English, French, information technology, music, and Spanish), COMPUTER AND PHYSICAL SCIENCE (chemistry, computer science, mathematics, and physics), EDUCATION (education, elementary education, health information management, secondary education, special education, and teaching English as a second/foreign language (TESOL/TEFOL)), HEALTH PROFESSIONS (exercise science, nursing, physical therapy, and public health), SOCIAL SCIENCE (African American studies, biopsychology, dietetics, East Asian studies, economics, food production/management/services, food science, history, interdisciplinary studies, international relations, philosophy, political science/government, psychobiology, psychology, social work, sociology, and women's studies). Nursing has the largest enrollment.

ACTIVITIES: There are no fraternities or sororities. There are 66 groups on campus, including art, choir, chorale, chorus, communications, dance, drama, ethnic, film, honors, international, jazz band, LGBT, literary magazine, model UN, newspaper, orchestra, political, professional, radio and TV, religious, social service, student government, symphony, and yearbook. Popular campus events include Connections Carnival - the Simmons Student Organization and Involvement Fair, Winter Wonderland, and Almost Midnight Breakfast. **Sports:** There are 10 intercollegiate sports for women. Facilities include an 8-lane pool, racquetball and squash courts, rowing tanks, fitness rooms, a dance studio, an indoor running area, volleyball courts, and a basketball court. **Graduates:** From July 1, 2016 to June 30, 2017, 491 bachelor's degrees were awarded. The most popular majors were nursing (35%), biology (6%), and kinesiology and exercise science (5%). In an average class, 1% graduate in 3 years or less, 67% graduate in 4 years or less, 72% graduate in 5 years or less, and 73% graduate in 6 years or less. Of the 2016 graduating class, 22% were enrolled in graduate school within 6 months of graduation, and 69% were employed.

SERVICES: Counseling and information services are available, as is tutoring in every subject. There is a reader service for the blind, remedial writing, and a writing center and lab. **Library/Resources:** The library contains 280,302 volumes, 13,580 microform items, and 3,460 audio/video tapes/CDs/DVDs, and subscribes to 3,825 periodicals including electronic. Computerized library services include interlibrary loans, database searching, Internet access, and Wi-Fi capability. Special learning facilities include an art gallery, radio station, a writing center, tutoring, and disability services. **Physically Challenged Students:** 95% of the campus is accessible. Facilities include wheelchair ramps, elevators, special parking, specially equipped restrooms, special class scheduling, and lowered drinking fountains. **Special:** Cross-registration is available with the New England Conservatory of Music, Hebrew, Emmanuel, and Wheelock Colleges, Massachusetts College of Art, Massachusetts College of Pharmacy and Health Sciences, and Wentworth Institute of Technology. Simmons offers study abroad in Europe through the Institute of European studies. A Washington semester at American University, accelerated degree programs, profit and nonprofit internship programs, a B.A.-B.S. degree, dual majors, interdisciplinary majors, student-designed majors, work-study programs, and pass/fail options are also offered. There is a dual-degree program in chemistry, pharmacy, and physician's assistant with Massachusetts College of Pharmacy. There are 9 national honor societies, a freshman honors program, and 12 departmental honors programs. **Visiting:** There are regularly scheduled orientations for prospective students. There are guides for informal visits, visitors may sit in on classes, and stay overnight. To schedule a visit, contact Alie Wilkins at (800) 345-8468. **Campus Safety and Security:** Measures include 24-hour foot and vehicle patrol, emergency notification system, self-defense education, and security escort services. There are emergency telephones, lighted pathways/sidewalks, and controlled access to dorms/residences.

REQUIREMENTS: The SAT or ACT is required. Simmons recommends that applicants have 4 years of English, math, foreign language, and social studies, 3 years each of science and history. An essay is required, and an interview is strongly recommended. AP and CLEP credits are accepted. Important factors in the admissions decision are leadership record, advanced placement or honors courses, parents or siblings attended your school, evidence of special talent, personality/intangible qualities, extracurricular activities record, recommendations by alumni, geographical diversity, and recommendations by school officials. To graduate, students must complete 128 semester hours, including 24 to 48 in the major, and maintain a minimum GPA of 2.0. Eight semester hours in a supervised independent learning experience or an internship are also required. Students must also fulfill foreign language, math competency, and technology competency requirements. In addition to completing the multidisciplinary core courses, students must complete 1 course from each of the following 6 modes of inquiry categories: creative and performing arts, language, literature, and culture, quantitative analysis and reasoning, scientific inquiry, social and historical perspectives, and psychological and ethical development. A thesis is optional. **Procedure:** Freshmen are admitted fall and spring. There are early admissions and deferred admissions plans. Applications should be filed by February 1 for fall entry; November 1 for spring entry. The fall 2017 application fee was $55. Notification of early decision is sent December 15; regular decision, March 15. Applications are accepted on-line. **Transfer Students:** 48 transfer students enrolled in 2016-2017. Applicants should have a GPA of 2.8, at least 17 college-level credit hours, official transcripts from all colleges attended, and a faculty recommendation and dean's report from the previous college attended. 48 of 128 credits required for the bachelor's degree must be completed at Simmons. **International Students:** There are 43 international students enrolled. They must take the TOEFL with a minimum score of 83 on the Internet-based version (iBT). Students may take the IELTS or SAT/ACT.

ADMISSIONS: 71% of the 2017-2018 applicants were accepted. The SAT scores for the 2017-2018 freshman class were: Math-- 5% below 500, 39% between 500 and 599, 48% between 600 and 699, and 8% between 700 and 800. Evidence-Based Reading/Writing-- 29% between 500 and 599, 55% between 600 and 699, and 16% between 700 and 800. The ACT scores were 25% between 18 and 23, 56% between 24 and 29, and 19% above 30. 64% of the current freshmen were in the top fifth of their class; 93% were in the top two fifths. 4 freshmen graduated first in their class. **Admissions Contact:** Ellen Johnson, Director. Email: *ugadm@simmons.edu* Web: *www.simmons.edu*

FINANCIAL AID: In 2017-2018, 100% of all full-time freshmen received some form of financial aid. 86% of all full-time freshmen received need-based aid. The average freshman award was $32,611. Need-based scholarships or need-based grants averaged $24,749 ($60,020 maximum); need-based self-help aid (loans and jobs) averaged $3,666 ($6,000 maximum); and other non-need-based awards and non-need-based scholarships averaged $4,171 ($58,910 maximum). 30% of undergraduate students work part-time. Simmons is a member of CSS. The college's own financial statement, and federal tax returns, and an institutional form are required. The FAFSA code is 002208. The priority date for freshman financial aid applications for fall entry is December 1.

SMITH COLLEGE — B-2

www.smith.edu

Northampton, MA 01063 — **(413) 585-2500**

Fax: (413) 585-2527	**Email:** admission@smith.edu
Full-time: 2503 women	**Faculty:** 270; IIB, ++$
Part-time: 16 women	**Ph.D.s:** 99%
Graduate: 55 men, 341 women	**Student/Faculty:** 9 to 1
Year: semesters	**Tuition:** $50,044
Room & Board: $16,730	**Freshman Class:** 5432 applied, 1731 accepted, 639 enrolled
SAT CR/M: 695/695 **ACT:** 32	**CEEB CODE:** 3762
Application Deadline: January 15	**MOST COMPETITIVE**

Smith College, founded in 1871, is an independent women's college, offering liberal arts education. There is 1 undergraduate school and 1 graduate school. In addition to regional accreditation, SC has baccalaureate program accreditation with ABET. The 156-acre campus is in a small town 90 miles west of Boston. Including any residence halls, there are 118 buildings.

STUDENT LIFE: 81% of undergraduates are from out of state, mostly the Northeast. Students are from 48 states, 72 foreign countries, and Canada. 64% are from public schools. 9% are Asian American; 7% African American; 5% two or more races; 5% race unknown; 48% White; 15% Foreign; 11% Hispanic. 40% are Hindu, Buddhist, Muslim, Unitarian, and Christian Scientists; 20% Protestant; 18% claim no religious affiliation; 14% Catholic. **Female To Male Ratio:** 52.0:1. The average age of freshmen is 18; all undergraduates, 20. 9% do not continue beyond their first year; 86% remain to graduate. **Housing:** There are language/international houses, special-interest houses, non-smoking houses, 2 cooperative houses, an apartment complex for a limited number of juniors and seniors, non-traditional students with dependents, and women's dorms. On-campus housing is guaranteed for all 4 years. Upperclassmen may keep cars.

FACULTY/CLASSROOMS: 44% of faculty are male; 56% are female. All teach undergraduates and do research. No introductory courses are taught by graduate students. The average class size in an introductory lecture is 25; in a laboratory is 13; and in a regular course is 20.

PROGRAMS OF STUDY: SC confers A.B. and B.S.Eng. degrees. Master's and doctoral degrees are also awarded. Bachelor's degrees are awarded in BIOLOGICAL SCIENCE (biochemistry, biology/biological science, and neurosciences), COMMUNICATIONS AND THE ARTS (art history and appreciation, classics, comparative literature, creative writing, dance, dramatic arts, East Asian languages and literature, English, film arts, French, Germanic languages and literature, Greek, Italian, Latin, music, Russian, Spanish, and studio art), COMPUTER AND PHYSICAL SCIENCE (astronomy, chemistry, computer science, geology, mathematics, and physics), EDUCATION (early childhood education, education, and elementary education), ENGINEERING AND ENVIRONMENTAL DESIGN (architecture, engineering, and environmental science), HEALTH PROFESSIONS (exercise science), SOCIAL SCIENCE (African studies, African American studies, American studies, anthropology, classical/ancient civilization, cognitive science, economics, ethics, politics, and social policy, European studies, French studies, history, international relations, Japanese studies, Judaic studies, Latin American studies, Luso-Brazilian studies, medieval studies, Middle Eastern studies, philosophy, political science/government, psychology, religion, Russian and Slavic studies, sociology, urban studies, and women's studies). Art, economics, and government have the largest enrollments.

ACTIVITIES: There are no fraternities or sororities. There are 127 groups on campus, including art, cheerleading, chess, chorus, computers, dance, debate, drama, environmental, ethnic, honors, international, jazz band, LGBT, literary magazine, musical theater, newspaper, photography, political, professional, radio and TV, religious, social, social service, student government, symphony, and yearbook. Popular campus events include International Student Day, Spring and Winter Weekends, and Rally Day. **Sports:** There are 14 intercollegiate sports for women, and 4 intramural sports for women. Facilities include indoor and outdoor tracks, tennis courts, riding rings, gyms, a climbing wall, an indoor swimming pool with diving boards, weight-training rooms, a dance studio, athletic training rooms, a human performance lab, squash courts, and field hockey, soccer, lacrosse, and softball fields. **Graduates:** From July 1, 2016 to June 30, 2017, 632 bachelor's degrees were awarded. The most popular majors were social sciences (23%), biological/life sciences, and psychology (10%), foreign languages, literatures, and linguistics (8%). In an average class, 82% graduate in 4 years or less, 85% graduate in 5 years or less, and 89% graduate in 6 years or less.

SERVICES: Counseling and information services are available, as is tutoring in every subject. There is a reader service for the blind. Numerous services are provided for learning-disabled students, including note taking, oral tests, readers, tutors, books on tape, reading software, voice recognition, tape recorders, extended-timed tests, and writing counselors. **Library/Resources:** The library contains 1.5 million volumes, 149,402 microform items, and 76,662 audio/video tapes/CDs/DVDs, and subscribes to 60,916 periodicals including electronic. Computerized library services include interlibrary loans, database searching, Internet access, and Wi-Fi capability. Special learning facilities include an art gallery, radio station, TV station, astronomy observatories, center for foreign languages and culture, digital design studio, plant and horticultural labs, art studios with casting, printmaking, and darkroom facilities, and specialized libraries for science, music, and art, the Quantitative Learning Center, and the Jacobson Center for writing, teaching and learning. **Physically Challenged Students:** 85% of the campus is accessible. Facilities include wheelchair ramps, elevators, special parking, specially equipped restrooms, special class scheduling, lowered drinking fountains, lowered telephones, and accessible van service. **Special:** Smith offers study abroad in more than 50 countries including the Smith College programs in Italy, France, Germany, and Switzerland, affiliated programs in India, Japan, Russia, China, South Africa, Peru, Brazil, and Spain. Other opportunities include cross-registration with 5 area colleges, a Washington semester, Smithsonian internships, exchanges with historically black colleges and other liberal arts colleges, and at BioSphere2. A 3-2 engineering degree is offered with Dartmouth College. Support for nontraditional-age students and for international students is provided, and funding for a summer internship is available for every undergraduate. Accelerated degree programs, student-designed majors, dual majors, and non-degree study are offered. There are 3 national honor societies and a chapter of Phi Beta Kappa. **Visiting:** There are regularly scheduled orientations for prospective students, including student-guided tours available 4 times a day, Monday through Friday, when school is in full session and on Saturday mornings from September to January. Interviews may also be scheduled during these times. Information sessions are offered twice daily most of the year. There are guides for informal visits, visitors may sit in on classes, and stay overnight. To schedule a visit, contact the Office of Admissions. **Campus Safety and Security:** Measures include 24-hour foot and vehicle patrol, emergency notification system, self-defense education, and security escort services. There are shuttle buses, emergency telephones, and lighted pathways/sidewalks. First-year students are required to attend panel discussions on campus safety. Specialized personal safety presentations, including self defense and sexual assault information, are provided to various houses and organizations. There are crime prevention programs including bicycle registration.

REQUIREMENTS: Smith highly recommends that applicants have 4 years of English, 3 years each of math, science with lab, and foreign language, 2 years of history, and 1 year of academic electives. SAT and ACT are considered but not required. Interviews are recommended. The GED is accepted. AP credits are accepted. Important factors in the admissions decision are personality/intangible qualities, evidence of special talent, extracurricular activities record, parents or siblings attended your school, and recommendations by school officials. All students plan individual programs in consultation with faculty advisers and take 64 credits outside their major and 36 to 64 credits in the major. Students must maintain a minimum 2.0 GPA in all academic work and during the senior year. A total of 128 credits is needed to graduate. A writing-intensive course is required for first-year students. A thesis is required for departmental honors programs. Distribution requirements are necessary for Latin honors eligibility. **Procedure:** Freshmen are admitted fall. Entrance exams should be taken before January of the senior year. There are early decision, early admissions, and deferred admissions plans. Early decision applications should be filed by November 15; regular applications, by January 15 for fall entry. The fall 2017 application fee was $60. Notification of early decision is sent December 15; regular decision, April 1. 158 early decision candidates were accepted for the 2017-2018 class. 471 applicants were on the 2017 waiting list; 19 were admitted. Applications are accepted on-line. **Transfer Students:** 45 transfer students enrolled in 2016-2017. Criteria for transfer students are similar to those for entering freshmen, with more emphasis on the college record. Students may apply in the fall (February 1) and spring (November 15). 64 credits required for the bachelor's degree must be completed at Smith. **International Students:** They must take the TOEFL with a minimum score of 600 on the paper-based TOEFL (PBT) or 95 on the Internet-based version (iBT). They must also take the SAT or ACT if the language of instruction is English.

ADMISSIONS: 32% of the 2017-2018 applicants were accepted. The SAT scores for the 2017-2018 freshman class were: Critical Reading-- 7% between 500 and 599, 43% between 600 and 699, and 49% between 700 and 800. Math-- 11% between 500 and 599, 44% between 600 and 699, and 45% between 700 and 800. The ACT scores were 3% between 18 and 23, 20% between 24 and 29, and 77% above 30. **Admissions Contact:** Debra Shaver, Director of Admissions. Email: *admission@smith.edu* Web: *www.smith.edu*

FINANCIAL AID: In 2017-2018, 67% of all full-time freshmen received some form of financial aid. 58% of all full-time freshmen received need-based aid. The average freshman award was $50,844. Need-based scholarships or need-based grants averaged $48,185; need-based self-help aid (loans and jobs) averaged $4,167; other non-need-based awards and non-need-based scholarships averaged $16,095; and $3,023 from other forms of aid. The average financial indebtedness of the 2017 graduate was $41,115. Smith is a member of CSS. The CSS/Profile and the college's own financial statement, noncustodial profile, and parent and student federal tax returns are required. The FAFSA code is 002209. The priority date for freshman financial aid applications for fall entry is January 25. The deadline for filing freshman financial aid applications for fall entry is February 15.

SPRINGFIELD COLLEGE — B-3

www.springfieldcollege.edu

Springfield, MA 01109	**(413) 748-3136** **(800) 343-1257**
Fax: (413) 748-3694	**Email: admissions@spfldcol.edu**
Full-time: 1109 men, 1071 women	**Faculty:** 210; IIA, -$
Part-time: 14 men, 10 women	**Ph.D.s:** 82%
Graduate: 296 men, 708 women	**Student/Faculty:** 12 to 1
Year: semesters, summer session	**Tuition:** $36,535
Room & Board: $12,240	**Freshman Class:** 3770 applied, 2635 accepted, 660 enrolled
SAT EBR-W/M: 558/560 **ACT:** 23	**CEEB CODE:** 3763
Application Deadline: n/av	**COMPETITIVE**

The mission of Springfield College is to educate the whole person in spirit, mind, and body for leadership in service to others. There are 3 undergraduate schools and 4 graduate schools. In addition to regional accreditation, SC has baccalaureate program accreditation with APTA, CAHEA, and NRPA. The 182-acre campus is in a suburban area 26 miles north of Hartford, CT. Including any residence halls, there are 45 buildings.

STUDENT LIFE: 61% of undergraduates are from out of state, mostly the Northeast. Students are from 33 states, 12 foreign countries, and Canada. 8% are Hispanic; 75% White; 6% African American; 4% race unknown; 2% Asian American; 2% Foreign; 2% two or more races. **Female To Male Ratio:** 1.3:1. The average age of freshmen is 18; all undergraduates, 21. 13% do not continue beyond their first year; 74% remain to graduate. **Housing:** 1980 students can be accommodated in college housing, which includes coed and married student dorms, on-campus apartments, and off-campus apartments. In addition, there are special-interest houses, and living learning communities. On-campus housing is guaranteed for all 4 years. 85% of students live on campus. Alcohol is not permitted. Upperclassmen may keep cars.

FACULTY/CLASSROOMS: 48% of faculty are male; 52% are female. No introductory courses are taught by graduate students.

PROGRAMS OF STUDY: Springfield confers B.A. and B.S. degrees. Master's and doctoral degrees are also awarded. Bachelor's degrees are awarded in BIOLOGICAL SCIENCE (biochemistry, biology/biological science, and biotechnology), BUSINESS (business administration and management and sports management), COMMUNICATIONS AND THE ARTS (English and fine arts), COMPUTER AND PHYSICAL SCIENCE (chemistry, information sciences and systems, and mathematics), EDUCATION (early childhood education, elementary education, health education, middle school education, physical education, science education, and secondary education), ENGINEERING AND ENVIRONMENTAL DESIGN (computer graphics), HEALTH PROFESSIONS (art therapy, emergency medical technologies, environmental health science, health care administration, predentistry, premedicine, recreation therapy, and rehabilitation therapy), SOCIAL SCIENCE (gerontology, history, human services, parks and recreation management, physical fitness/movement, political science/government, prelaw, psychology, and sociology). Physical therapy, and athletic training are the strongest academically. Physical education has the largest enrollment.

ACTIVITIES: There are no fraternities or sororities. There are 58 groups on campus, including art, band, cheerleading, choir, chorus, club sports, communications, computers, dance, drama, ethnic, film, honors, international, jazz band, LGBT, literary magazine, musical theater, newspaper, pep band, professional, radio and TV, religious, social, social service, student government, and yearbook. Popular campus events include Parents Weekend, and Stepping Up Day. **Sports:** There are 13 intercollegiate sports for men and 11 for women, and 10 intramural sports for men and 10 for women. Facilities include a stadium, a gym, superturf fields for football, soccer, lacrosse, and field hockey, tennis courts, and baseball and softball fields, and free weight and Nautilus rooms. **Graduates:** From July 1, 2016 to June 30, 2017, 479 bachelor's degrees were awarded. The most popular majors were physical therapy (9%), applied exercise science (8%), and movement and sports studies (8%). In an average class, 68% graduate in 4 years or less, 73% graduate in 5 years or less, and 74% graduate in 6 years or less.

SERVICES: Counseling and information services are available, as is tutoring in every subject. There is remedial math and writing. **Library/Resources:** The library contains and subscribes to 66,644 periodicals including electronic. Computerized library services include interlibrary loans, database searching, Internet access, and Wi-Fi capability. Special learning facilities include an art gallery, radio station, an outdoor center. **Physically Challenged Students:** 75% of the campus is accessible. Facilities include wheelchair ramps, elevators, special parking, specially equipped restrooms, special class scheduling, and lowered drinking fountains. **Special:** There is a co-op program and cross-registration with cooperating colleges in the greater Springfield area. Internships are required in most majors, and there is limited study abroad. There are 2 national honor societies. **Visiting:** There are guides for informal visits, visitors may sit in on classes, and stay overnight. To schedule a visit, contact the Admissions Office. **Campus Safety and Security:** Measures include 24-hour foot and vehicle patrol, self-defense education, and security escort services. There are shuttle buses, emergency telephones, and lighted pathways/sidewalks.

REQUIREMENTS: The SAT or ACT is required. Applicants must be graduates of an accredited secondary school and have completed 4 years of English and 3 years each of history, math, and science. The school accepts the GED. An essay is required and an interview is recommended. Applications are accepted on-line. AP and CLEP credits are accepted. Important factors in the admissions decision are advanced placement or honors courses, leadership record, and extracurricular activities record. To graduate, students must complete a total of 130 credits with a 2.0 GPA. Core requirements include 50 semester hours in English, social and natural sciences, health, religion, philosophy, and art, and 4 credits in phys ed. **Procedure:** Freshmen are admitted fall and spring. Entrance exams should be taken by November of the senior year. There are early decision, early admissions, deferred admissions, and rolling admissions plans. Early decision applications should be filed by December 1. The fall 2017 application fee was $40. Notification of early decision is sent February 1; regular decision, March 15. Applications are accepted on-line. **Transfer Students:** 62 transfer students enrolled in 2016-2017. Grades of 2.0 transfer for credit. Transfer students are admitted in the fall and spring. **International Students:** There are 52 international students enrolled. They must take the TOEFL. They must also take the SAT or ACT.

ADMISSIONS: 70% of the 2017-2018 applicants were accepted. The SAT scores for the 2017-2018 freshman class were: Math-- 17% below 500, 48% between 500 and 599, 32% between 600 and 699, and 3% between 700 and 800. Evidence-Based Reading/Writing-- 18% below 500, 52% between 500 and 599, 29% between 600 and 699, and 2% between 700 and 800. The ACT scores were 8% between 12 and 17, 42% between 18 and 23, 44% between 24 and 29, and 6% above 30. **Admissions Contact:** Mary N. DeAngelo, Director of Admissions. Email: *admissions@spfldcol.edu* Web: *www.springfieldcollege.edu*

FINANCIAL AID: The average freshman award was $28,265. Need-based scholarships or need-based grants averaged $23,785; and need-based self-help aid (loans and jobs) averaged $5,027. The FAFSA code is 002211. The deadline for filing freshman financial aid applications for fall entry is March 15.

STONEHILL COLLEGE — E-3

www.stonehill.edu

Easton, MA 02357 — **(508) 565-1373**

Fax: (508) 565-1545
Email: admissions@stonehill.edu
Full-time: 984 men, 1471 women
Faculty: 163; IIB, +$
Part-time: 11 men, 6 women
Ph.D.s: 90%
Graduate: n/av
Student/Faculty: 12 to 1
Year: semesters, summer session
Tuition: $39,900
Room & Board: $15,230
Freshman Class: 6362 applied, 4639 accepted, 734 enrolled
SAT CR/M/W: 550/555/550 **ACT:** required
CEEB CODE: 3770
Application Deadline: January 15
COMPETITIVE

Stonehill College is a selective Catholic college with a welcoming community and beautiful campus. Dedicated, supportive faculty mentor students in 80+ academic programs in the liberal arts, sciences, and business. Nearly 90% of students participate in internships, study abroad, research, practicum, and field work. Stonehill is a vibrant community where students learn to live lives that make a difference. There are 4 undergraduate schools. In addition to regional accreditation, SC has baccalaureate program accreditation with ACS and AUPHA. The 384-acre campus is in a suburban area 22 miles south of Boston. Including any residence halls, there are 65 buildings.

STUDENT LIFE: 59% of undergraduates are from Massachusetts. Others are from 29 states, and 10 foreign countries. 83% are White; 5% African American; 5% Hispanic. 71% are Catholic; 13% claim no religious affiliation. **Female To Male Ratio:** 1.5:1. The average age of freshmen is 18; all undergraduates, 20. 8% do not continue beyond their first year; 85% remain to graduate. **Housing:** College-sponsored housing includes dorms. In addition, there are honors houses, special-interest houses, substance-free/wellness housing, theme, and community service housing, house of justice, mindful living and ACE housing. On-campus housing is guaranteed for all 4 years. 93% of students live on campus. Upperclassmen may keep cars.

FACULTY/CLASSROOMS: All teach undergraduates, and all do research. No introductory courses are taught by graduate students. The average class size in an introductory lecture is 21.

PROGRAMS OF STUDY: SC confers B.A., B.S., and B.S.B.A. degrees. Bachelor's degrees are awarded in AGRICULTURE (environmental studies), BIOLOGICAL SCIENCE (biochemistry, biology/biological science, and neurosciences), BUSINESS (accounting, banking and finance, business administration and management, international business management, and marketing/retailing/merchandising), COMMUNICATIONS AND THE ARTS (art history and appreciation, communications, English, fine arts, French, music, and Spanish), COMPUTER AND PHYSICAL SCIENCE (chemistry, computer science, mathematics, and physics), EDUCATION (education), HEALTH PROFESSIONS (health care administration), SOCIAL SCIENCE (American studies, Christian studies, criminology, economics, gender studies, history, interdisciplinary studies, international studies, philosophy, political science/government, psychology, public administration, religion, and sociology). Business, biology, and psychology have the largest enrollments.

ACTIVITIES: There are no fraternities or sororities. There are 77 groups on campus, including art, band, cheerleading, choir, chorale, chorus, computers, dance, drama, environmental, ethnic, film, honors, international, LGBT, literary magazine, musical theater, newspaper, pep band, photography, political, professional, radio and TV, religious, social, social service, student government, and yearbook. Popular campus events include Skyhawk Weekend, Spring Weekend, and Halloween Mixer. **Sports:** There are 9 intercollegiate sports for men and 11 for women, and 20 intramural sports for men and 20 for women. Facilities include a stadium for football, field hockey, soccer, and lacrosse, a gym with basketball and volleyball courts, weight and cardiovascular fitness areas, a recreational and intramural sports complex, tennis courts, baseball, softball, and field hockey fields, a regulation beach volleyball court, and recreational fields for intramural and club sports. **Graduates:** From July 1, 2016 to June 30, 2017, 515 bachelor's degrees were awarded. The most popular majors were business/marketing (22%), social sciences (17%), and biological/life sciences (13%). In an average class, 80% graduate in 4 years or less, 84% graduate in 5 years or less, and 87% graduate in 6 years or less. Of the 2016 graduating class, 41% were enrolled in graduate school within 6 months of graduation, and 71% were employed.

SERVICES: Counseling and information services are available, as is tutoring in most subjects. A learning disability specialist and free diagnostic testing are available as are auxiliary aids for hearing impaired students, note takers, and other resources based on need. There is a reader service for the blind, and remedial writing. **Library/Resources:** The library contains 243,500 volumes, 150,431 microform items, and 9,593 audio/video tapes/CDs/DVDs, and subscribes to 13,111 periodicals including electronic. Computerized library services include interlibrary loans, database searching, Internet access, and Wi-Fi capability. Special learning facilities include an art gallery, radio station, an observatory, an institute for the study of law and society, and several archives and special collections. **Physically Challenged Students:** All of the campus is accessible. Facilities include wheelchair ramps, elevators, special parking, specially equipped restrooms, special class scheduling, lowered drinking fountains, lowered telephones, and special housing. **Special:** Stonehill offers cross registration, double major, duel enrollment, exchange student program (domestic), honors program and independent study, internships liberal arts/career combination, student-designed major, study abroad, and teachers certification program. There are fall-semester international internship sites in Belgrade, Dublin, London, Madrid, Paris and Yerevan. Stonehill also offers BA/BS programs with the University of Notre Dame, Indiana, Los Angeles semester, New York semester, Washington DC semester, and SEA semester, and the Stonehill undergraduate research experience (SURE) program. There are 20 national honor societies and a freshman honors program. **Visiting:** There are regularly scheduled orientations for prospective students, consisting of group information sessions and guided campus tours available by appointment throughout the year. Visitors may sit in on classes. To schedule a visit, contact the Admissions Office. **Campus Safety and Security:** Measures include 24-hour foot and vehicle patrol, emergency notification system, self-defense education, and security escort services. There are emergency telephones, lighted pathways/sidewalks, controlled access to dorms/residences, bicycle patrols, and a weekend guest sign-in policy.

REQUIREMENTS: Applicants should be graduates of an accredited high school or have earned the GED. Secondary preparation should include 4 units of English, 3 units of foreign language, 3-4 units of math, 3-4 units of science (with 3 units of lab), and 3-4 history. An essay, school report, 2 teacher evaluations, and a completed common application sent with a Stonehill Supplemental Information Form are required. SAT or ACT not required but will be considered if submitted. AP credits are accepted. Important factors in the admissions decision are advanced placement or honors courses, evidence of special talent, leadership record, extracurricular activities record, recommendations by alumni, and recommendations by school officials. All students must complete a cornerstone program, which consists of 4 common courses within history/literature and philosophy/religious studies; a learning community consisting of 2 linked courses and a 3rd integrated course; a moral inquiry course; and a senior capstone experience within the major. Distribution requirements include 2 semesters of a foreign language and 1 course each in in natural scientific inquiry, social scientific inquiry, and statistical reasoning. Students must complete 3- to 4-credit courses while maintaining a minimum GPA of 2.0. **Procedure:** Freshmen are admitted fall and spring. There are early decision, early admissions, and deferred admissions plans. Early decision applications should be filed by December 1; regular applications, by January 15 for fall entry; and November 1 for spring entry. The fall 2017 application fee was $60. Notification of early decision is sent December 31; regular decision, March 15. 44 early decision candidates were accepted for the 2017-2018 class. 231 applicants were on the 2017 waiting list; 26 were admitted. Applications are accepted on-line. **Transfer Students:** 26 transfer students enrolled in 2016-2017. Applicants must have a minimum GPA of 2.0. Official high school transcripts and college transcripts along with catalogs with course descriptions from all colleges attended are required. An essay and 2 recommendations are required, and an interview is recommended. Application for transfer admission is in the fall and spring. 62 of 120 credits required for the bachelor's degree must be completed at SC. **International Students:** There are 12 international students enrolled. They must take the TOEFL.

ADMISSIONS: 58% of the current freshmen were in the top fifth of their class; 90% were in the top two fifths. 7 freshmen graduated first in their class. **Admissions Contact:** Emma Brown, Assistant Dean of Admissions. Email: *admissions@stonehill.edu* Web: *www.stonehill.edu*

FINANCIAL AID: In 2017-2018, 78% of all full-time freshmen received some form of financial aid. The average freshman award was $28,147. Need-based scholarships or need-based grants averaged $23,248; need-based self-help aid (loans and jobs) averaged $5,088; non-need-based athletic scholarships averaged $15,419; other non-need-based awards and non-need-based scholarships averaged $23,248; and $18,770 from other forms of aid. 47% of undergraduate students work part-time. The average financial indebtedness of the 2017 graduate was $31,622. Stonehill is a member of CSS. The CSS/Profile, noncustodial profile and business/farm supplement are required. The FAFSA code is 002217. The deadline for filing freshman financial aid applications for fall entry is February 1.

SUFFOLK UNIVERSITY — E-2

www.suffolk.edu

Boston, MA 02108 — **(617) 573-8460**

Fax: (617) 742-4291
Email: admission@suffolk.edu
Full-time: 2199 men, 2650 women
Faculty: 275; IIA, ++$
Part-time: 138 men, 130 women
Ph.D.s: 90%
Graduate: 889 men, 1282 women
Student/Faculty: 19 to 1
Year: semesters, summer session
Tuition: $37,128
Room & Board: $15,046
Freshman Class: 8237 applied, 6867 accepted, 1087 enrolled
SAT EBR-W/M: 546/538 **ACT:** 24
CEEB CODE: 3771
Application Deadline: Feb 15
COMPETITIVE

Suffolk University, founded in 1906, offers students experiential learning, a campus set amid Boston's world-renowned landmarks, and enviable access to top employers. Thanks to small classes, students work closely with their professors experts in their fields who mentor and connect them with career-shaping internships. Our students gain global insights at Suffolk's campus in Madrid, Spain, and partner institutions around the world. Suffolk strongly emphasizes on hands-on learning and equips students to define and successfully pursue their professional careers upon graduation. There are 2 undergraduate schools and 3 graduate schools. In addition to regional accreditation, Suffolk University has baccalaureate program accreditation with AACSB, ABET, FIDER, NASAD, NASPAA, CAHME, and NEASC. The 2-acre campus is in an urban area in the heart of downtown Boston. Including any residence halls, there are 11 buildings.

STUDENT LIFE: 68% of undergraduates are from Massachusetts. Others are from 47 states, 98 foreign countries, and Canada. 64% are from public schools. 8% are Asian American; 6% African American; 47% White; 4% race unknown; 22% Foreign; 2% two or more races; 12% Hispanic. **Female To Male Ratio:** 1.3:1. The average age of freshmen is 18; all undergraduates, 22. 23% do not continue beyond their first year; 77% remain to graduate. **Housing:** 1299 students can be accommodated in college housing, which includes dorms. On-campus housing is available on a first-come, first-served basis, and is available on a lottery system for upperclassmen. Alcohol is not permitted. No one may keep cars.

FACULTY/CLASSROOMS: 55% of faculty are male; 45% are female. 80% teach undergraduates. No introductory courses are taught by graduate students. The average class size in an introductory lecture is 22 and in a laboratory is 16.

PROGRAMS OF STUDY: Suffolk confers B.A., B.S., B.F.A., B.S.B.A., B.S.G.S. and B.S.J. degrees. Associate, master's, and doctoral degrees are also awarded. Bachelor's degrees are awarded in AGRICULTURE (environmental studies), BIOLOGICAL SCIENCE (biochemistry, biology/biological science, biotechnology, life science, and marine science), BUSINESS (accounting, banking and finance, entrepreneurial studies, international business management, international economics, management science, and marketing/retailing/merchandising), COMMUNICATIONS AND THE ARTS (advertising, art history and appreciation, broadcasting, communications, creative writing, dramatic arts, English, film arts, fine arts, French, graphic design, journalism, media arts, music history and appreciation, performing arts, public relations, Spanish, and speech/debate/rhetoric), COMPUTER AND PHYSICAL SCIENCE (chemistry, computer programming, computer science, information sciences and systems, mathematics, and physics), EDUCATION (business education, English education, mathematics education, and science education), ENGINEERING AND ENVIRONMENTAL DESIGN (computer engineering, electrical/electronics engineering, environmental engineering, environmental science, and interior design), HEALTH PROFESSIONS (medical laboratory technology and radiological science), SOCIAL SCIENCE (African American studies, American studies, criminal justice, economics, European studies, German area studies, history, human development, human services, humanities, international relations, paralegal studies, philosophy, political science/government, psychology, social science, sociology, and women's studies). Business, sociology, and communications are the strongest academically. Finance, communication & journalism, and marketing have the largest enrollments.

ACTIVITIES: There are 75 groups on campus, including art, choir, chorale, chorus, computers, dance, debate, drama, ethnic, film, forensics, honors, international, jazz band, LGBT, literary magazine, musical theater, newspaper, orientation, photography, political, professional, radio and TV, religious, social, social service, and student government. Popular campus events include Fallfest Talent Show, Temple Street Fair, and Diversity Services-Coffee Hour. **Sports:** There are 7 intercollegiate sports for men and 6 for women, and 2 intramural sports for men and 2 for women. Facilities include a basketball, volleyball, and aerobics facility, intramurals, and indoor baseball/softball practice and a fully equipped fitness center. **Graduates:** From July 1, 2016 to June 30, 2017, 1178 bachelor's degrees were awarded. The most popular majors were communications (13%), finance (10%), and marketing (10%). In an average class, 1% graduate in 3 years or less, 42% graduate in 4 years or less, 58% graduate in 5 years or less, and 60% graduate in 6 years or less. Of the 2016 graduating class, 14% were enrolled in graduate school within 6 months of graduation, and 74% were employed.

SERVICES: Counseling and information services are available, as is tutoring in every subject. There is a reader service for the blind, and remedial math, reading, and writing. **Library/Resources:** The library contains 159,014 volumes, 199,622 microform items, and 1,904 audio/video tapes/CDs/DVDs, and subscribes to 478 periodicals including electronic. Computerized library services include interlibrary loans, database searching, Internet access, and Wi-Fi capability. Special learning facilities include an art gallery, radio station, and TV station. **Physically Challenged Students:** Facilities include wheelchair ramps, elevators, specially equipped restrooms, special class scheduling, lowered drinking fountains, and lowered telephones. **Special:** There are 15 national honor societies, a freshman honors program, and 11 departmental honors programs. **Visiting:** There are regularly scheduled orientations for prospective students. Students visits include a general presentation and an overview panel presentation of student life, career and co-op opportunities, learning center services, athletics and academic department meetings, and campus tours. To schedule a visit, contact the Admissions Office. **Campus Safety and Security:** Measures include 24-hour foot and vehicle patrol, emergency notification system, self-defense education, and security escort services. There are emergency telephones and lighted pathways/sidewalks.

REQUIREMENTS: The SAT or ACT is required. The ACT Optional Writing test is also required. Applicants should have a high school diploma or the GED. Recommended secondary preparation includes 4 years of English, 3 of math, 2 each of a foreign language and science, and 1 of American history. Exact requirements differ by degree program. A personal essay is required, and an interview is recommended. A GPA of 2.0 is required. AP and CLEP credits are accepted. Important factors in the admissions decision are advanced placement or honors courses, recommendations by school officials, and leadership record. All students must complete their semester hours with at least a 2.0 GPA. Distribution requirements vary by degree program. **Procedure:** Freshmen are admitted fall, spring, and summer. Entrance exams should be taken by December of the senior year. There are early admissions and deferred admissions plans. Early decision applications should be filed by November 15; regular applications, by Feb 15 for fall entry; and December 15 for spring entry. The fall 2017 application fee was $50. Notification of early decision is sent December 14; regular decision, March 30. Applications are accepted on-line. **Transfer Students:** 447 transfer students enrolled in 2016-2017. Applicants should have a minimum 2.5 GPA from an accredited college. If the applicant has not achieved an associate's degree by the time of applying for transfer, they need to submit their final high school transcript or proof of high school graduation 30 of 124 credits required for the bachelor's degree must be completed at Suffolk. **International Students:** There are 1101 international students enrolled. They must take the TOEFL with a minimum score of 550 on the paper-based TOEFL (PBT) or 80 on the Internet-based version (iBT). They must also take the SAT or ACT, and the college's own entrance exam.

ADMISSIONS: 83% of the 2017-2018 applicants were accepted. The SAT scores for the 2017-2018 freshman class were: Math-- 24% below 500, 57% between 500 and 599, 18% between 600 and 699, and 1% between 700 and 800. Evidence-Based Reading/Writing-- 23% below 500, 51% between 500 and 599, 25% between 600 and 699, and 2% between 700 and 800. The ACT scores were 6% between 12 and 17, 42% between 18 and 23, 47% between 24 and 29, and 5% above 30. 28% of the current freshmen were in the top fifth of their class; 59% were in the top two fifths. 1 freshman graduated first in the class. **Admissions Contact:** Donna Grand Director of Undergraduate Admissions. Email: *admission@suffolk.edu* Web: *www.suffolk.edu*

FINANCIAL AID: In 2017-2018, 95% of all full-time freshmen received some form of financial aid. 71% of all full-time freshmen received need-based aid. The average freshman award was $27,446. Need-based scholarships or need-based grants averaged $7,703 ($37,128 maximum); need-based self-help aid (loans and jobs) averaged $4,472 ($9,000 maximum); and other non-need-based awards and non-need-based scholarships averaged $23,937 ($59,403 maximum). 11% of undergraduate students work part-time. The average financial indebtedness of the 2017 graduate was $25,348. The university's own financial statement, and verification of income are required. The FAFSA code is 002218. The deadline for filing freshman financial aid applications for fall entry is February 15.

THE BOSTON CONSERVATORY AT BERKLEE *(The complete profile is made available exclusively on our website, www.barronspac.com)*

TUFTS UNIVERSITY D-2

www.tufts.edu

Medford, MA 02155 **(617) 627-3170**

Fax: (617) 627-3860 **Email:** undergraduate.admissions@tufts.edu
Full-time: 2701 men, 2734 women
Part-time: 33 men, 40 women
Graduate: 2392 men, 3589 women
Year: semesters, summer session
Room & Board: $14,054
SAT CR/M/W: 680/710/690 **ACT:** 32
Application Deadline: January 1
Faculty: 543; I, +$
Ph.D.s: 93%
Student/Faculty: 8 to 1
Tuition: $53,506
Freshman Class: 20223 applied, 2889 accepted, 1338 enrolled
CEEB CODE: 3901
MOST COMPETITIVE

Tufts University, founded in 1852, is a private institution offering undergraduate programs in liberal arts and sciences, engineering, and fine arts. There are 3 undergraduate schools and 9 graduate schools. In addition to regional accreditation, TU has baccalaureate program accreditation with ABET, ADA, CAHEA, NASAD, and MA Dept of Elementary and Secondary Education. The 150-acre campus is in a suburban area 5 miles northwest of Boston. Including any residence halls, there are 135 buildings.

STUDENT LIFE: 74% of undergraduates are from out of state, mostly the Northeast. Students are from 50 states, 76 foreign countries, and Canada. 59% are from public schools. 7% are Hispanic; 6% race unknown; 56% White; 5% two or more races; 4% African American; 12% Asian American; 10% Foreign. **Female To Male Ratio:** 1.2:1. The average age of freshmen is 18; all undergraduates, 20. 4% do not continue beyond their first year; 92% remain to graduate. **Housing:** 3372 students can be accommodated in college housing, which includes dorms and on-campus apartments. In addition, there are language/international houses, special-interest houses, fraternity houses, sorority houses, theme, and wellness houses. On-campus housing is available on a lottery system for upperclassmen. 62% of students live on campus. Upperclassmen may keep cars.

FACULTY/CLASSROOMS: 53% of faculty are male; 47% are female. All teach undergraduates, and all do research. No introductory courses are taught by graduate students. The average class size in a regular course is 20.

PROGRAMS OF STUDY: TU confers B.A., B.S.(Engineering options), and B.F.A. degrees. Master's and doctoral degrees are also awarded. Bachelor's degrees are awarded in BIOLOGICAL SCIENCE (biochemistry, biology/biological science, biophysics, and biotechnology), COMMUNICATIONS AND THE ARTS (Africana studies, Arabic, art history, Chinese, classics, dramatic arts, English, French, German, Greek, interdisciplinary art, Italian, Japanese, Latin, film and media studies, music, Russian, and Spanish), COMPUTER AND PHYSICAL SCIENCE (applied mathematics, applied physics, astrophysics, chemistry, computer science, geology, mathematics, and physics), EDUCATION (education), ENGINEERING AND ENVIRONMENTAL DESIGN (architecture, biomedical engineering, chemical engineering, civil engineering, computer engineering, electrical/electronics engineering, engineering, engineering and applied science, engineering physics, environmental engineering, environmental science, and mechanical engineering), HEALTH PROFESSIONS (biology, biomedical science, and community health work), SOCIAL SCIENCE (American studies, anthropology, archeology, Asian/Oriental studies, biopsychology, child psychology/development, cognitive science, economics, German area studies, history, interdisciplinary studies, international relations, Judaic studies, Latin American studies, Middle Eastern studies, peace studies, philosophy, political science/government, psychology, religion, Russian and Slavic studies, sociology, urban studies, and women & gender studies). International relations, engineering, and philosophy are the strongest academically. International relations, computer science, and biology have the largest enrollments.

ACTIVITIES: 16% of men belong to 3 local and 6 national fraternities; 17% of women belong to 4 national sororities. There are 325 groups on campus, including an outdoors mountain club, art, band, cheerleading, chess, choir, chorale, chorus, communications, computers, dance, debate, drama, environmental, ethnic, film, forensics, honors, international, jazz band, LGBT, literary magazine, musical theater, newspaper, opera, orchestra, pep band, photography, political, professional, radio and TV, religious, social, social service, student government, symphony, and yearbook. Popular campus events include Tuftonia's Day, Fan the Fire Athletics Event, Student and Faculty Arts Performances, Fall Gala, Winter Bash, Spring Fling, and the EPIIC International Symposium. **Sports:** There are 15 intercollegiate sports for men and 16 for women, and 7 intramural sports for men and 7 for women. Facilities include sports and fitness center, a football stadium, gyms, an 8-lane all-weather track, tennis courts, a field house, indoor cage, indoor track, squash courts, a swimming pool, multiple dance rooms, a weight room, spin studio, yoga studio, a sailing center, an exercise center, baseball, softball, soccer, lacrosse, field hockey, and playing fields. **Graduates:** From July 1, 2016 to June 30, 2017, 1374 bachelor's degrees were awarded. The most popular majors were social sciences (27%), engineering (10%), and biological/life sciences (8%). In an average class, 87% graduate in 4 years or less and 92% graduate in 6 years or less. Of the 2016 graduating class, 14% were enrolled in graduate school within 6 months of graduation, and 80% were employed.

SERVICES: Counseling and information services are available, as is tutoring in every subject, as needed through the Academic Resources Center with weekly standing tutoring sessions for larger (typically introductory) classes. There is a reader service for the blind. **Library/Resources:** The library contains 1.2 million volumes, 1.3 million microform items, and 61,809 audio/video tapes/CDs/DVDs. Computerized library services include interlibrary loans, database searching, Internet access, and Wi-Fi capability. Special learning facilities include an art gallery, radio station, TV station, a recital hall, theater in the round, and a center for scientific visualization. **Physically Challenged Students:** 90% of the campus is accessible. Facilities include wheelchair ramps, elevators, special parking, specially equipped restrooms, special class scheduling, lowered drinking fountains, lowered telephones, and special housing. **Special:** The university offers cross-registration at Boston University, Boston College, and Brandeis University, a Washington semester, domestic exchanges with Swarthmore College, and study abroad in England, Spain, France, Chile, Japan, Ghana, China, Hong Kong, and Germany. Many internships are available. Double majors in the liberal arts are common; student-designed majors are possible. There is a 5-year B.A./M.A. or B.S./M.S. program in liberal arts or engineering, a 5-year B.A.-B.F.A. program with the School of the Museum of Fine Arts, and a B.A.-B.M. program with the New England Conservatory of Music. There are 5 national honor societies and a chapter of Phi Beta Kappa. **Visiting:** There are regularly scheduled orientations for prospective students. There are guides for informal visits and visitors may sit in on classes. To schedule a visit, contact the Admissions Office. **Campus Safety and Security:** Measures include 24-hour foot and vehicle patrol, emergency notification system, self-defense education, and security escort services. There are shuttle buses, emergency telephones, lighted pathways/sidewalks, and controlled access to dorms/residences.

REQUIREMENTS: The university accepts either the SAT Reasoning Test and the results of 2 SAT: Subject tests or the ACT. Liberal arts applicants should take two SAT: Subject test of their choice, engineering applicants should take a math level I or II, and either physics or chemistry. Students applying for the Bachelors of Fine Arts do not need to submit subject tests but are required to provide a portfolio. In addition, all applicants should be high school graduates or hold the GED. Academic preparation is expected to include 4 years each of English, foreign language, social studies, math, and natural sciences. For the Class of 2022, we will be accepting the old or new SAT and will not be requiring the Writing section for the ACT. AP credits are accepted. Important factors in the admissions decision are leadership record, advanced placement or honors courses, evidence of special talent, extracurricular activities record, recommendations by school officials, parents or siblings attended your school, personality/intangible qualities, recommendations by alumni, and geographical diversity. Liberal arts students must complete 34 courses, 10 of them in the area of concentration. Requirements include foundation courses in writing, quantitative reasoning, and foreign language or culture and courses in humanities, arts, social sciences, math, and natural sciences. Requirements for engineering students include a total of 38 courses, 10 are engineering introduction courses, 8 are engineering foundation courses, 12 of them in the area of concentration, and distribution requirements in English, humanities, arts, and social sciences. Students in the Bachelors of Fine Arts program at the School of the Museum of Fine Arts must complete 14 academic courses in addition to 76 credits of studio art to complete their degree in Interdisciplinary Art. **Procedure:** Freshmen are admitted in the fall. Entrance exams should be taken by January of the senior year unless applying Early Decision. There are early decision and deferred admissions plans. Early decision applications should be filed by November 1; regular applications, by January 1 for fall entry. The fall 2017 application fee was $75. Notification of early decision is sent December 15; regular decision, April 1. Applications are accepted on-line. **Transfer Students:** 67 transfer students enrolled in 2016-2017. Primary consideration is given to college and secondary school achievement and record of personal involvement. Transfer students must submit the Common Application for Transfer Students, the Tufts Supplement, transcripts from both high school and college, a college official's report, letters of recommendation, as well as either the SAT or the ACT with Writing. **International Students:** There are 570 international students enrolled. They must take the TOEFL with a minimum score of 650 on the paper-based TOEFL (PBT) or 100 on the Internet-based version (iBT). The IELTS exam is also accepted. The ACT or SAT with two Subject Tests (portfolio is required in lieu of Subject Tests for BFA applicants).

ADMISSIONS: 14% of the 2017-2018 applicants were accepted. The SAT scores for the 2017-2018 freshman class were: Critical Reading-- 4% between 500 and 599, 32% between 600 and 699, and 64% between 700 and 800. Math-- 2% between 500 and 599, 25% between 600 and 699, and 73% between 700 and 800. Writing-- 1% below 500, 2% between 500 and 599, 31% between 600 and 699, and 66% between 700 and 800. The ACT scores were 1% between 18 and 23, 10% between 24 and 29, and 89% above 30. **Admissions Contact:** Karen Richardson, Dean of Admissions. Email: *undergraduate.admissions@tufts.edu* Web: *www.tufts.edu*

FINANCIAL AID: In 2017-2018, 38% of all full-time freshmen received some form of financial aid. 36% of all full-time freshmen received need-based aid. The average freshman award was $43,518. Need-based scholarships or need-based grants averaged $42,971; need-based self-help aid (loans and jobs) averaged $3,772; and other non-need-based awards and non-need-based scholarships averaged $500. The average financial indebtedness of the 2017 graduate was $24,267. Tufts University is a member of CSS. The CSS/Profile, and parent and student federal income tax forms are required. The deadline for filing freshman financial aid applications for fall entry is February 15.

UNIVERSITY OF MASSACHUSETTS AMHERST — B-2

www.umass.edu

Amherst, MA 01003 — **(413) 545-0222**

Fax: (413) 545-4312 — **Email:** mail@admissions.umass.edu

Full-time: 10,958 men, 10,523 women
Part-time: 601 men, 928 women
Graduate: 3200 men, 3165 women
Year: semesters, summer session
Room & Board: $12,258

Faculty: 1351
Ph.D.s: 94%
Student/Faculty: 16 to 1
Tuition: $15,411 ($33,477)
Freshman Class: 41922 applied, 24102 accepted, 4714 enrolled

SAT CR/M: 630/640 **ACT:** 28
Application Deadline: January 15

CEEB CODE: 0917
HIGHLY COMPETITIVE

University of Massachusetts Amherst, established in 1863, is a public research, land-grant institution offering over 100 bachelor's degree programs. There are 9 undergraduate schools and 9 graduate schools. In addition to regional accreditation, UMass Amherst has baccalaureate program accreditation with AACSB, ABET, ASLA, FIDER, NASAD, NASM, SAF, ACPHA, ACS, APA, ACEND, CCNE, and CEPH. The 1463-acre campus is in a small town 90 miles west of Boston and 60 miles north of Hartford, Connecticut. Including any residence halls, there are 334 buildings.

STUDENT LIFE: 76% of undergraduates are from Massachusetts. Others are from 50 states, 77 foreign countries, and Canada. 64% are White; 6% Hispanic; 6% Foreign; 6% race unknown; 4% African American; 3% two or more races; 10% Asian American. **Male To Female Ratio:** 1.0:1. The average age of freshmen is 18; all undergraduates, 21. 9% do not continue beyond their first year; 77% remain to graduate. **Housing:** 13594 students can be accommodated in college housing, which includes single sex, coed, and married student on-campus apartments. In addition, there are honors houses, language/international houses, special-interest houses, fraternity houses, sorority houses, housing for first-year students, women's dorm, men's dorm, and theme housing. On-campus housing is guaranteed for the freshman year only and is available on a lottery system for upperclassmen. 61% of students live on campus. All students may keep cars.

FACULTY/CLASSROOMS: 56% of faculty are male; 44% are female. All teach undergraduates, and all do research. No introductory courses are taught by graduate students.

PROGRAMS OF STUDY: UMass Amherst confers B.A., B.S., B.B.A., B.F.A., B.G.S., and B.Mus. degrees. Associate, master's, and doctoral degrees are also awarded. Bachelor's degrees are awarded in AGRICULTURE (agricultural economics, animal science, natural resource management, plant science, soil science, and wood science), BIOLOGICAL SCIENCE (biochemistry, biology/biological science, microbiology, and nutrition), BUSINESS (accounting, banking and finance, business administration and management, hospitality management services, marketing management, operations management, and sports management), COMMUNICATIONS AND THE ARTS (art history and appreciation, Chinese, classics, communications, comparative literature, dance, dramatic arts, English, Germanic languages and literature, Japanese, journalism, linguistics, music, music performance, Portuguese, Spanish, and studio art), COMPUTER AND PHYSICAL SCIENCE (astronomy, chemistry, computer science, earth science, geology, mathematics, physics, and science), EDUCATION (education), ENGINEERING AND ENVIRONMENTAL DESIGN (architecture, bioengineering, chemical engineering, civil engineering, computer engineering, construction technology, electrical/electronics engineering, environmental design, environmental science, industrial engineering, landscape architecture/design, and mechanical engineering), HEALTH PROFESSIONS (exercise science, nursing, predentistry, premedicine, preveterinary science, public health, and speech pathology/audiology), SOCIAL SCIENCE (African American studies, anthropology, economics, food science, French studies, gender studies, geography, history, interdisciplinary studies, Italian studies, Judaic studies, law, liberal arts/general studies, Middle Eastern studies, philosophy, political science/government, psychology, Russian and Slavic studies, sociology, and women's studies). Psychology, biology, and computer science have the largest enrollments.

ACTIVITIES: There are 488 groups on campus, including art, band, cheerleading, chess, choir, chorale, chorus, communications, computers, dance, debate, drama, environmental, ethnic, film, honors, international, jazz band, LGBT, literary magazine, marching band, musical theater, newspaper, opera, orchestra, pep band, photography, political, professional, radio and TV, religious, social, social service, student government, student-owned business club, and symphony. Popular campus events include Fall Activities Expo, First Week, Festival of the Arts, Multicultural Film Festival, Cultural Night, Jazz in July, and Fine Arts Center Series Events. **Sports:** There are 9 intercollegiate sports for men and 10 for women, and 25 intramural sports for men and 28 for women. Facilities include multipurpose fields, softball and soccer fields, a football stadium, a track, and tennis courts. The indoor facilities include a recreation center with weight and fitness equipment, a gym, a wellness center, elevated jogging track, swimming pools, handball/squash, racquetball courts, dance studios, and basketball/volleyball/badminton courts. The indoor sports arena has Olympic-sized ice sheets. **Graduates:** From July 1, 2016 to June 30, 2017, 6111 bachelor's degrees were awarded. The most popular majors were psychology (7%), finance (4%), and biology (4%). In an average class, 1% graduate in 3 years or less, 67% graduate in 4 years or less, 76% graduate in 5 years or less, and 77% graduate in 6 years or less. Of the 2016 graduating class, 19% were enrolled in graduate school within 6 months of graduation.

SERVICES: Counseling and information services are available, as is tutoring in most subjects. There is a reader service for the blind. **Library/Resources:** The library contains 4.3 million volumes, 2.6 million microform items, and 49,481 audio/video tapes/CDs/DVDs, and subscribes to 120,877 periodicals including electronic. Computerized library services include interlibrary loans, database searching, Internet access, and Wi-Fi capability. Special learning facilities include an art gallery, radio station, TV station, including botanical gardens, an astronomical observatory, and learning commons. **Physically Challenged Students:** All of the campus is accessible. Facilities include wheelchair ramps, elevators, special parking, specially equipped restrooms, special class scheduling, lowered drinking fountains, lowered telephones, and special housing. All programs are made accessible through accommodations. **Special:** Cross-registration is possible with Smith, Mount Holyoke, Hampshire, and Amherst Colleges. Co-op programs, internships in every major, study abroad in more than 70 countries, domestic exchange, a Washington semester, work-study programs, dual majors, and B.A.-B.S. degrees are available. Accelerated degrees are currently offered in 26 programs, including Engineering, Public Health, Economics and Political Science. The Bachelor's Degree with Individual Concentration (BDIC) is also available. The Commonwealth Honors College welcomes honor students who meet entrance requirements. There are also teacher certification, distance learning, independent study, and ESL programs. There are 48 national honor societies, Phi Beta Kappa, a freshman honors program, and 77 departmental honors programs. **Visiting:** There are regularly scheduled orientations for prospective students. There are 3 guided tours on weekdays, and 2 tours on weekends. Information sessions are offered twice daily. There are guides for informal visits and visitors may sit in on classes. **Campus Safety and Security:** Measures include 24-hour foot and vehicle patrol, emergency notification system, self-defense education, and security escort services. There are shuttle buses, emergency telephones, lighted pathways/sidewalks, controlled access to dorms/residences, project protect valuable registration.

REQUIREMENTS: The SAT or ACT is required. Applicants must be graduates of an accredited secondary school or have the GED. The university recommends that students complete 17 Carnegie units including 4 years each of English and math (including math during their senior year and a minimum of Algebra II), 3 of science (including 2 years lab), and 2 years each of foreign language, social studies and academic electives. Students must present a portfolio for admission to the art program and must audition for admission to music and dance. A GPA of 2.0 is required. AP and CLEP credits are accepted. Important factors in the admissions decision are advanced placement or honors courses, parents or siblings attended your school, evidence of special talent, personality/intangible qualities, and extracurricular activities record. Students must complete 120 credit hours and maintain a minimum GPA of 2.0 overall and in the major. For the general education requirement, students must take 4 courses in social world, 2 courses each in social & cultural diversity, biological & physical world, and writing (one in the first year and one in the junior year), and 1 course each in basic math skills, integrative experience, and analytic reasoning. **Procedure:** Freshmen are admitted fall and spring. Entrance exams should be taken at the end of the junior year or the beginning of the senior year. There are early admissions, deferred admissions, and rolling admissions plans. Applications should be filed by January 15 for fall entry; October 1 for spring entry. The fall 2017 application fee was $80. Notifications are sent March 1. 1557 applicants were on the 2017 waiting list; 44 were admitted. Applications are accepted on-line. **Transfer Students:** 1603 transfer students enrolled in 2016-2017. Transfer applicants must submit transcripts from all colleges or universities attended and an essay. Those with fewer than 27 credits must submit high school transcripts and SAT scores. Priority is given to students with an associate degree. Grades of C- or better in comparable coursework transfer for credit. Students completing an approved Mass-Transfer associate degree program with a 2.5 or higher cumulative GPA, who are in good academic, financial, and disciplinary status at all previously attended colleges, are guaranteed admission. Some UMass Amherst majors may require a higher GPA and/or prerequisite coursework. 45 of 120 credits required for the bachelor's degree must be completed at UMass Amherst. **International Students:** There are 1232 international students enrolled. They must take the TOEFL with a minimum score of 80 on the Internet-based version (iBT). Students must take the IELTS. They must also take the SAT or ACT.

ADMISSIONS: 57% of the 2017-2018 applicants were accepted. The SAT scores for the 2017-2018 freshman class were: Math-- 1% below 500, 27% between 500 and 599, 50% between 600 and 699, and 22% between 700 and 800. Evidence-Based Reading/Writing-- 2% below 500, 27% between 500 and 599, 55% between 600 and 699, and 15% between

700 and 800. The ACT scores were 10% between 18 and 23, 52% between 24 and 29, and 38% above 30. 62% of the current freshmen were in the top fifth of their class; 93% were in the top two fifths. **Admissions Contact:** James Roche, Vice Provost for Enrollment Management. Email: *mail@admissions.umass.edu* Web: *www.umass.edu*

FINANCIAL AID: In 2017-2018, 89% of all full-time freshmen received some form of financial aid. 51% of all full-time freshmen received need-based aid. The average freshman award was $16,906. Need-based scholarships or need-based grants averaged $10,986; need-based self-help aid (loans and jobs) averaged $4,124; non-need-based athletic scholarships averaged $23,179; and other non-need-based awards and non-need-based scholarships averaged $4,848. The average financial indebtedness of the 2017 graduate was $31,860. UMass Amherst is a member of CSS. The FAFSA code is 002221. The priority date for freshman financial aid applications for fall entry is March 1.

UNIVERSITY OF MASSACHUSETTS BOSTON E-2

www.umb.edu

Boston, MA 02125 **(617) 287-6100**

Fax: (617) 287-5999 **Email: undergrad.admissions@umb.edu**

Full-time: 4563 men, 5011 women	**Faculty:** 700; I, av$
Part-time: 1378 men, 1708 women	**Ph.D.s:** 98%
Graduate: 1225 men, 2530 women	**Student/Faculty:** 17 to 1
Year: semesters, summer session	**Tuition:** $13,828 ($32,985)
Room & Board: n/app	**Freshman Class:** 10607 applied, 7896 accepted, 1881 enrolled
SAT CR/M: 560/560 **ACT:** required	**CEEB CODE:** 3924
Application Deadline: March 1	**COMPETITIVE**

University of Massachusetts Boston, established in 1964, is a public research institution offering undergraduate studies in arts and sciences and in preprofessional training. There are 10 undergraduate schools and 11 graduate schools. In addition to regional accreditation, UMass Boston has baccalaureate program accreditation with AACSB, ABET, AACTE, ACS, APA, CCNE, and AACSB. The 120-acre campus is in an urban area 5 miles south of downtown Boston. Including any residence halls, there are 9 buildings.

STUDENT LIFE: 95% of undergraduates are from Massachusetts. Others are from 48 states, 141 foreign countries, and Canada. 7% are race unknown; 38% White; 3% two or more races; 15% African American; 14% Hispanic; 12% Foreign; 11% Asian American. **Female To Male Ratio:** 1.3:1. The average age of freshmen is 19; all undergraduates, 24. 23% do not continue beyond their first year; 48% remain to graduate. All students commute. All students may keep cars.

FACULTY/CLASSROOMS: 46% of faculty are male; 54% are female. All teach undergraduates. No introductory courses are taught by graduate students. The average class size in an introductory lecture is 26; in a laboratory is 16; and in a regular course is 26.

PROGRAMS OF STUDY: UMass Boston confers B.A. and B.S. degrees. Master's and doctoral degrees are also awarded. Bachelor's degrees are awarded in BIOLOGICAL SCIENCE (biochemistry and biology/biological science), BUSINESS (labor studies and management science), COMMUNICATIONS AND THE ARTS (art, classical languages, classics, communications, dramatic arts, English, French, information technology, Italian, music, and Spanish), COMPUTER AND PHYSICAL SCIENCE (chemistry, computer science, earth science, information sciences and systems, mathematics, and physics), EDUCATION (Asian studies and early childhood education), ENGINEERING AND ENVIRONMENTAL DESIGN (electrical and computer engineering, engineering, engineering physics, and environmental science), HEALTH PROFESSIONS (exercise science, medical technology, and nursing), SOCIAL SCIENCE (African American studies, American studies, anthropology, community services, criminal justice, economics, ethics, politics, and social policy, geography, gerontology, Hispanic American studies, history, human services, paralegal studies, philosophy, physical fitness/movement, political science/government, psychology, sociology, and women & gender studies). Management, nursing, and psychology have the largest enrollments.

ACTIVITIES: There are no fraternities or sororities. There are 100 groups on campus, including model UN, music ensembles, art, band, campus ministries, cheerleading, chess, choir, chorale, chorus, computers, dance, drama, ethnic, film, honors, international, jazz band, LGBT, literary magazine, musical theater, newspaper, orchestra, photography, political, professional, religious, social, social service, and student government. Popular campus events include Convocation Day, Seasonal Festivals, and Lecture Series. **Sports:** There are 8 intercollegiate sports for men and 8 for women, and 12 intramural sports for men and 12 for women. Facilities include an athletic center with a gym, basketball and volleyball courts, an ice rink, a Olympic-size swimming pool with high-dive area, a multipurpose weight room, a sports medicine area, an 8-lane, 400-meter track, tennis courts, a softball diamond, multipurpose fields for soccer and lacrosse, and a fitness center with strength-training equipment. **Graduates:** From July 1, 2016 to June 30, 2017, 2658 bachelor's degrees were awarded. The most popular majors were business/marketing (17%), health professions and related programs (14%), and psychology (12%). In an average class, 21% graduate in 4 years or less, 42% graduate in 5 years or less, and 48% graduate in 6 years or less.

SERVICES: Counseling and information services are available, as is tutoring in every subject. There is a reader service for the blind, and remedial math, reading, and writing. There are also reading study skills workshops and a math resource center available. **Library/Resources:** The library contains 1.0 million volumes. Computerized library services include interlibrary loans, database searching, Internet access, and Wi-Fi capability. Special learning facilities include an art gallery, planetarium, tropical greenhouse, observatory, adaptive computer lab, languages lab, and applied language and math center. **Physically Challenged Students:** All of the campus is accessible. Facilities include wheelchair ramps, elevators, special parking, specially equipped restrooms, special class scheduling, lowered drinking fountains, lowered telephones, amplified phones, powered doors, indoor-connected building access, an accessible shuttle bus, an adaptive computer lab, and a center for students with disabilities. **Special:** Students may cross-register with Boston Public Colleges, Massachusetts College of Art, Bunker Hill Community College, Roxbury Community College, and Hebrew College. UMass Boston also offers cooperative programs, internships, study abroad, work-study programs, student-designed majors, B.A.-B.S. degrees, nondegree study, pass/fail options, and dual and interdisciplinary majors, anthropology/history, biology/medical technology, philosophy/public policy, and psychology/sociology. Also available are 3-1 and 2-2 engineering programs with various area institutions. The College of Public and Community Service provides social-oriented education. There are 3 national honor societies and a freshman honors program. **Visiting:** There are regularly scheduled orientations for prospective students, including general information sessions about the university and the admissions process and a tour of the campus. There are guides for informal visits and visitors may sit in on classes. To schedule a visit, contact the Office of Undergraduate Admissions. **Campus Safety and Security:** Measures include 24-hour foot and vehicle patrol, emergency notification system, self-defense education, and security escort services. There are shuttle buses, emergency telephones, lighted pathways/sidewalks, Operation ID, motorist assistance, and crime prevention programs.

REQUIREMENTS: The SAT or ACT is required. Applicants should be graduates of an accredited secondary school. The GED is accepted. The university requires the completion of 17 Carnegie units, including 4 years each of English and math, 3 of college preparatory math and science, 2 each of a foreign language and 1 of social studies, and 2 electives in the above academic areas or in humanities, arts, or computer science. A GPA of 3.0 is required. AP and CLEP credits are accepted. For graduation, students must complete 120 credit hours (123 hours in the College of Nursing) and maintain a minimum GPA of 2.0. Distribution requirements vary by college. All students must demonstrate writing proficiency. **Procedure:** Freshmen are admitted fall and spring. Entrance exams should be taken by the fall of the senior year. There are deferred admissions and rolling admissions plans. Applications should be filed by March 1 for fall entry. The fall 2017 application fee was $60. Notification is sent on a rolling basis. Applications are accepted on-line. **Transfer Students:** 1535 transfer students enrolled in 2016-2017. Applicants with fewer than 24 credits must meet freshman requirements. To transfer, students must have a minimum college GPA of 2.5. Grades of C- or better transfer for credit. 30 of 120 credits required for the bachelor's degree must be completed at UMass Boston. **International Students:** There are 1324 international students enrolled. They must take the TOEFL with a minimum score of 550 on the paper-based TOEFL (PBT) or 79 on the Internet-based version (iBT). They must also take the SAT or ACT if the language of instruction is English.

ADMISSIONS: 74% of the 2017-2018 applicants were accepted. The

SAT scores for the 2017-2018 freshman class were: Critical Reading-- 15% below 500, 53% between 500 and 599, 28% between 600 and 699, and 4% between 700 and 800. Math-- 11% below 500, 57% between 500 and 599, 28% between 600 and 699, and 4% between 700 and 800. The ACT scores were 3% between 12 and 17, 48% between 18 and 23, 44% between 24 and 29, and 5% above 30. **Admissions Contact:** Corey Ford, Director of Undergraduate Admissions. Email: *undergrad.admissions@umb.edu* Web: *www.umb.edu*

FINANCIAL AID: The FAFSA code is 002222. The priority date for freshman financial aid applications for fall entry is March 1.

UNIVERSITY OF MASSACHUSETTS DARTMOUTH D-4
www.umassd.edu

North Dartmouth, MA 02747 **(508) 999-8605**

Fax: (508) 999-8755 **Email: admissions@umassd.edu**
Full-time: 3079 men, 2711 women
Part-time: 395 men, 578 women
Graduate: 764 men, 879 women
Year: semesters, summer session
Room & Board: $12,936
Faculty: 366; I, av$
Ph.D.s: 89%
Student/Faculty: 16 to 1
Tuition: $13,571 ($28,285)
Freshman Class: 7959 applied, 6707 accepted, 1333 enrolled
SAT EBR-W/M: 550/540 **ACT:** 22
Application Deadline: open
CEEB CODE: 3786
COMPETITIVE

University of Massachusetts Dartmouth, founded in 1895, is a public institution that provides undergraduate and graduate programs in the liberal and creative arts and sciences and in professional training. There are 5 undergraduate schools and 3 graduate schools. In addition to regional accreditation, UMass Dartmouth has baccalaureate program accreditation with AACSB, ABET, NASAD, NASDTEC, ACS, NAACLS, and CCNE. The 710-acre campus is in a suburban area 60 miles south of Boston and 28 miles east of Providence, Rhode Island. Including any residence halls, there are 35 buildings.

STUDENT LIFE: 91% of undergraduates are from Massachusetts. Others are from 45 states, 60 foreign countries, and Canada. 88% are from public schools. 9% are Hispanic; 60% White; 6% Foreign; 5% race unknown; 4% Asian American; 3% two or more races; 13% African American. **Male To Female Ratio:** 1.0:1. The average age of freshmen is 18.6; all undergraduates, 22.7. 26% do not continue beyond their first year; 47% remain to graduate. **Housing:** 4494 students can be accommodated in college housing, which includes dorms and on-campus apartments. In addition, there are honors houses, special-interest houses, quiet housing, substance awareness housing, apartments and townhouses for upperclassmen. On-campus housing is guaranteed for the freshman year only, is available on a first-come, first-served basis, and is available on a lottery system for upperclassmen. 52% of students live on campus. All students may keep cars.

FACULTY/CLASSROOMS: 50% of faculty are male; 50% are female. All teach undergraduates, 60% do research, and 60% do both. Graduate students teach 1% of introductory courses. The average class size in an introductory lecture is 35; in a laboratory is 23; and in a regular course is 29.

PROGRAMS OF STUDY: UMass Dartmouth confers B.A., B.S. and B.F.A. degrees. Master's and doctoral degrees are also awarded. Bachelor's degrees are awarded in BIOLOGICAL SCIENCE (biochemistry, biology/biological science, and marine biology), BUSINESS (accounting, business administration and management, finance, management information systems, management, marketing/retailing/merchandising, and operations management), COMMUNICATIONS AND THE ARTS (art history and appreciation, ceramic art and design, drawing with printmaking focus, English literature, English Writing, fiber/textiles/weaving, French, graphic design, illustration, metal/jewelry, music, painting, photography, Portuguese, sculpture, Spanish, and visual design), COMPUTER AND PHYSICAL SCIENCE (astronomy and physics, chemistry, computer science, mathematics, physics, and software engineering), EDUCATION (art education), ENGINEERING AND ENVIRONMENTAL DESIGN (bioengineering, civil engineering, computer engineering, electrical/electronics engineering, and mechanical engineering), HEALTH PROFESSIONS (clinical science, cytotechnology, medical laboratory science, and nursing), SOCIAL SCIENCE (anthropology, criminal justice, economics, history, interdisciplinary studies, liberal arts/general studies, philosophy, political science/government, psychology, sociology, and women & gender studies). Engineering, physical/life sciences, and nursing are the strongest academically. Nursing, psychology, and biology have the largest enrollments.

ACTIVITIES: 1% of men belong to 4 local and 2 national fraternities; 1% of women belong to 3 local and 3 national sororities. There are 170 groups on campus, including art, band, cheerleading, choir, chorale, chorus, computers, dance, drama, ethnic, film, honors, international, jazz band, LGBT, musical theater, newspaper, orchestra, photography, political, professional, religious, social, social service, student government, symphony, and yearbook. Popular campus events include Welcome Back Week, Homecoming Weekend, and Family Fall Weekend. **Sports:** There are 11 intercollegiate sports for men and 12 for women, and 7 intramural sports for men and 7 for women. Facilities include a gym, football stadium, an aquatic sports center, tennis courts, a fitness center, a running track, soccer, softball, and intramural fields. **Graduates:** From July 1, 2016 to June 30, 2017, 1421 bachelor's degrees were awarded. The most popular majors were psychology (8%), accounting (8%), and nursing (7%).

SERVICES: Counseling and information services are available, as is tutoring in most subjects, such as writing/reading, science/engineering, math/business, and academic resource centers. There is a reader service for the blind, and remedial math. **Library/Resources:** The library contains 431,678 volumes, and 7,921 audio/video tapes/CDs/DVD. Computerized library services include interlibrary loans, database searching, Internet access, and Wi-Fi capability. Special learning facilities include an art gallery, an observatory, marine research vessels, and a number of cultural and research centers. **Physically Challenged Students:** 97% of the campus is accessible. Facilities include wheelchair ramps, elevators, special parking, specially equipped restrooms, special class scheduling, lowered drinking fountains, and special housing. **Special:** The university permits cross-registration through the SACHEM Consortium of 9 schools in Massachusetts. Study abroad in 9 countries, an engineering or business co-op program, a Washington semester, internships, numerous work-study programs, dual majors, service learning opportunities and student-designed majors are available. Non degree study, pass/fail options, B.S. to M.S. degrees in chemistry, nursing, computer science, electrical engineering, civil engineering, computer engineering, and mechanical engineering, a B.A.-M.A. in psychology, a English B.A. to Professional Writing Master's, a BA-MAT in several fields, along with MPP-JD and MBA-JD programs. There is a freshman honors program. **Visiting:** There are regularly scheduled orientations for prospective students, including scheduled campus tours Monday through Friday and most Saturdays. There are guides for informal visits and visitors may sit in on classes. To schedule a visit, contact Joshua Sylvester at jsylvester@umassd.edu. **Campus Safety and Security:** Measures include 24-hour foot and vehicle patrol, emergency notification system, self-defense education, and security escort services. There are shuttle buses, emergency telephones, lighted pathways/sidewalks, controlled access to dorms/residences, and bicycle patrol.

REQUIREMENTS: The SAT is required. Applicants should have 4 years each of English and math, 3 of Science, 2 each of the same foreign language, social science which includes 1 in US History, and college-preparatory electives. The GED is accepted. An audition is necessary for music majors, and a portfolio is recommended for studio arts and design applicants. All applicants must submit an essay. A GPA of 3.0 is required. AP and CLEP credits are accepted. Important factors in the admissions decision are recommendations by school officials, advanced placement or honors courses, and evidence of special talent. Each student must complete the requirements of the 5 clusters that comprise the University Studies curriculum: Cluster 1 Foundations for Engagement, Cluster 2 the Natural World, Cluster 3 the Cultural World, Cluster 4 the Social World and Cluster 5 the Educated and Engaged Citizen. A freshman English composition course is required. Colleges set some additional distribution course requirements. The B.A. requires foreign language study. To graduate, students must complete 120 to 132 credit hours and maintain a 2.0 GPA. **Procedure:** Freshmen are admitted fall and spring. Entrance exams should be taken spring of the junior year or early fall of the senior year. There are deferred admissions and rolling admissions plans. Application deadlines are open. The fall 2017 application fee was $60. Notification is sent on a rolling basis. Applications are accepted on-line. **Transfer Students:** 636 transfer students enrolled in 2016-2017. Applicants must submit all official college transcripts and must take the SAT unless they graduated from high school more than 3 years prior to applying. Those with fewer than 24 transferable credits may need to submit high school records. 45 of 120 credits required for the bachelor's degree must be completed at UMass Dartmouth. **International Students:** There are 166 international students enrolled. They must take the TOEFL with a minimum score of 550 on the paper-based TOEFL (PBT) or 79 on the Internet-based version (iBT). They must also take the SAT or ACT.

ADMISSIONS: 84% of the 2017-2018 applicants were accepted. The SAT scores for the 2017-2018 freshman class were: Math-- 25% below 500, 51% between 500 and 599, 21% between 600 and 699, and 3% between 700 and 800. Evidence-Based Reading/Writing-- 23% below 500, 51% between 500 and 599, 24% between 600 and 699, and 2% between 700 and 800. The ACT scores were 9% between 12 and 17, 49% between 18 and 23, 32% between 24 and 29, and 10% above 30. **Admissions Contact:** Hanan Khamis, Director of Admissions. Email: *admissions@umassd.edu* Web: *www.umassd.edu*

FINANCIAL AID: The FAFSA code is 002210. The priority date for freshman financial aid applications for fall entry is March 1.

UNIVERSITY OF MASSACHUSETTS LOWELL — D-1

www.uml.edu

Lowell, MA 01854 — **(978) 934-3931**

Fax: (978) 934-3086	**Email: admissions@uml.edu**
Full-time: 6275 men, 3744 women	**Faculty:** 576; I, av$
Part-time: 2156 men, 1464 women	**Ph.D.s:** 92%
Graduate: 2355 men, 1860 women	**Student/Faculty:** 17 to 1
Year: semesters, summer session	**Tuition:** $14,682 ($31,250)
Room & Board: $12,073	**Freshman Class:** 11231 applied, 6771 accepted, 1685 enrolled
SAT CR/M/W: 571/601/546 **ACT:** 26	**CEEB CODE:** 3911
Application Deadline: February 1	**VERY COMPETITIVE**

University of Massachusells Lowell, founded in 1895, is a public institution offering undergraduate programs through the colleges of fine arts and social sciences, sciences, engineering, health, and management, as well as a graduate school in education. There are 5 undergraduate schools and 1 graduate school. In addition to regional accreditation, UMass Lowell has baccalaureate program accreditation with AACSB, ABET, NASAD, NASM, CCNE, CAEP, CAPTE, EHAC, CAMPEP, NAACL, and ASAC. The 125-acre campus is in an urban area 30 miles northwest of Boston. Including any residence halls, there are 47 buildings.

STUDENT LIFE: 89% of undergraduates are from Massachusetts. Others are from 36 states, 68 foreign countries, and Canada. 9% are Asian American; 63% White; 6% African American; 4% Foreign; 4% race unknown; 3% two or more races; 11% Hispanic. **Male To Female Ratio:** 1.5:1. The average age of freshmen is 18; all undergraduates, 22. 15% do not continue beyond their first year; 56% remain to graduate. **Housing:** 4238 students can be accommodated in college housing, which includes dorms, on-campus apartments, and off-campus apartments. In addition, there are honors houses, special-interest houses, theme housing, wellness housing, and living learning communities. On-campus housing is available on a first-come, first-served basis, and is available on a lottery system for upperclassmen. 63% of students commute. All students may keep cars.

FACULTY/CLASSROOMS: 57% of faculty are male; 43% are female. No introductory courses are taught by graduate students.

PROGRAMS OF STUDY: UMass Lowell confers B.A., B.F.A., B.L.A., B.M., B.S., B.S.B.A., B.S.E., B.S.E.T. and B.S.I.T degrees. Associate, master's, and doctoral degrees are also awarded. Bachelor's degrees are awarded in AGRICULTURE (environmental studies), BIOLOGICAL SCIENCE (biology/biological science and nutritional sciences), BUSINESS (business administration and management), COMMUNICATIONS AND THE ARTS (English, fine arts, information technology, modern language, music, music business management, and music performance), COMPUTER AND PHYSICAL SCIENCE (applied mathematics, chemistry, clinical laboratory science, computer science, earth science, industrial technology, inform, science, systms & tech, information sciences and systems, mathematics, and physics), ENGINEERING AND ENVIRONMENTAL DESIGN (biomedical engineering, chemical engineering, civil engineering, computer engineering, electrical/electronics engineering, electrical/electronics engineering technology, environmental science, mechanical engineering, mechanical engineering technology, and plastics engineering), HEALTH PROFESSIONS (community health work, environmental health science, exercise science, nursing, and public health), SOCIAL SCIENCE (American studies, criminal justice, economics, history, liberal arts/general studies, peace studies, philosophy, political science/government, psychology, and sociology). Business administration, mechanical engineering, and criminal justice have the largest enrollments.

ACTIVITIES: There are 200 groups on campus, including art, band, cheerleading, chess, choir, chorale, communications, computers, dance, drama, environmental, ethnic, film, honors, international, LGBT, literary magazine, marching band, newspaper, orchestra, pep band, photography, political, professional, radio and TV, religious, social, social service, student government, and yearbook. Popular campus events include Homecoming Weekend, Spring Carnival, Battle of the Bands, Concrete Canoe Competition, Fox Hall Common Events, Athletic Events, Club Sports. **Sports:** There are 7 intercollegiate sports for men and 8 for women, and 28 intramural sports for men and 28 for women. Facilities include a recreational facility, fitness center, fields for hockey, lacrosse, and soccer, basketball, and baseball. **Graduates:** From July 1, 2016 to June 30, 2017, 2333 bachelor's degrees were awarded. The most popular majors were business/marketing (18%), engineering (18%), and health professions and related programs (12%). In an average class, 32% graduate in 4 years or less, 52% graduate in 5 years or less, and 56% graduate in 6 years or less. Of the 2016 graduating class, 35% were enrolled in graduate school within 6 months of graduation, and 60% were employed.

SERVICES: Counseling and information services are available, as is tutoring in most subjects. There is a reader service for the blind, and remedial writing. **Library/Resources:** The library contains 382,599 volumes, 91,022 microform items, and 14,353 audio/video tapes/CDs/DVDs, and subscribes to 32,744 periodicals including electronic. Computerized library services include interlibrary loans, database searching, Internet access, and Wi-Fi capability. Special learning facilities include an art gallery, natural history museum, and radio station. The Health & Social Sciences building provides simulation laboratories, observation rooms, a demonstration hospital wing, and true-to-life exam room in the nursing facilities. **Physically Challenged Students:** 90% of the campus is accessible. Facilities include wheelchair ramps, elevators, special parking, specially equipped restrooms, special class scheduling, lowered drinking fountains, and lowered telephones. **Special:** Cross-registration, co-op, and work-study programs are available, as are opportunities for internships, undergraduate research, and study abroad. The university offers a combined B.S.-M.S. degree in multiple majors, dual majors, nondegree study, and pass/fail options. There are 8 national honor societies, Phi Beta Kappa, and a freshman honors program. **Visiting:** There are regularly scheduled orientations for prospective students, campus tours are offered on a daily basis throughout the school year. There are guides for informal visits. **Campus Safety and Security:** Measures include 24-hour foot and vehicle patrol, emergency notification system, and self-defense education. There are shuttle buses, emergency telephones, and lighted pathways/sidewalks.

REQUIREMENTS: The university recommends that secondary preparation includes a solid college preparatory curriculum made up of at least 4 years of English and math, 3 in science with 1 lab, 2 each in history (1 focused on U.S. History), foreign language, and 2 elective courses. The university now offers a No Test option and students may select at the time of application whether or not they wish their tests scores be used in their evaluation. Please note that prospective music majors must successfully complete an audition upon acceptance, and art majors must submit a portfolio as part of the application process. AP and CLEP credits are accepted. Important factors in the admissions decision are advanced placement or honors courses, personality/intangible qualities, and extracurricular activities record. All students must complete a minimum of 120 credits with a 2.0 GPA. Core requirements are 36 credits: 2 College Writing Courses, 3 Arts and Humanities Perspective Courses, 3 Social Sciences Perspective Courses, 2 Sciences with Lab Perspective Courses, 1 Mathematics Perspective Course, and 1 Science, Technology, Engineering and Mathematics Perspective Course. **Procedure:** Freshmen are admitted fall and spring. Entrance exams should be taken during the spring of junior year and fall of senior year. There are early admissions and deferred admissions plans. Applications should be filed by February

1 for fall entry; December 1 for spring entry. The fall 2017 application fee was $60. Notification of early decision is sent December 10; regular decision, March 10. 1183 applicants were on the 2017 waiting list; 42 were admitted. Applications are accepted on-line. **Transfer Students:** 1159 transfer students enrolled in 2016-2017. Transfer applicants must present at least a 2.0 GPA in previous college work. Those with fewer than 30 credits must meet freshman admission requirements. Students may enroll in the fall or spring. 30 of 120 credits required for the bachelor's degree must be completed at UMass Lowell. **International Students:** There are 452 international students enrolled. They must take the TOEFL with a minimum score of 79 on the Internet-based version (iBT). Student must take either the Pearson's Academic (PTE), or IELTS. International freshman applicants may use the no-test option and waive the SAT or ACT.

ADMISSIONS: 60% of the 2017-2018 applicants were accepted. The SAT scores for the 2017-2018 freshman class were: Critical Reading-- 14% below 500, 51% between 500 and 599, 29% between 600 and 699, and 6% between 700 and 800. Math-- 5% below 500, 42% between 500 and 599, 43% between 600 and 699, and 9% between 700 and 800. Writing-- 24% below 500, 51% between 500 and 599, 22% between 600 and 699, and 2% between 700 and 800. The ACT scores were 1% between 12 and 17, 23% between 18 and 23, 59% between 24 and 29, and 17% above 30. 46% of the current freshmen were in the top fifth of their class; 79% were in the top two fifths. 4 freshmen graduated first in their class. **Admissions Contact:** Christine Bryan, Senior Associate Director of Admissions. Email: *admissions@uml.edu* Web: *www.uml.edu*

FINANCIAL AID: The FAFSA code is 002161. The priority date for freshman financial aid applications for fall entry is March 1.

WELLESLEY COLLEGE — D-2

www.wellesley.edu

Wellesley, MA 02481 — **(781) 283-2270**

Fax: (781) 283-3678	**Email: admission@wellesley.edu**
Full-time: 2201 women	**Faculty:** 293; IIB, ++$
Part-time: 11 women	**Ph.D.s:** 98%
Graduate: n/av	**Student/Faculty:** 7 to 1
Year: semesters, summer session	**Tuition:** $51,148
Room & Board: $15,836	**Freshman Class:** 5703 applied, 1251 accepted, 605 enrolled
SAT CR/M/W: 694/703/696 **ACT:** 31	**CEEB CODE:** 3957
Application Deadline: January 15	**MOST COMPETITIVE**

Wellesley College, ranked among the United States top liberal arts and sciences colleges, has a deep tradition of educating women who will make a difference in the world. Living and learning on a campus, just outside of Boston, full of self-directed and intellectually curious women helps students develop the skills needed to succeed in all professional fields, including those traditionally dominated by men. Every resource at the college is devoted to undergraduate women. Students have extraordinary opportunities to cultivate their leadership abilities and gain lifelong access to a legendary network of accomplished Wellesley alumnae. There is 1 undergraduate school. The 500-acre campus is in a suburban area 12 miles west of Boston. Including any residence halls, there are 64 buildings.

STUDENT LIFE: 84% of undergraduates are from out of state, mostly the West. Students are from 50 states, 88 foreign countries, and Canada. 58% are from public schools. 6% are African American; 6% two or more races; 4% race unknown; 39% White; 24% Asian American; 12% Foreign; 11% Hispanic. The student base is all female. The average age of freshmen is 18; all undergraduates, 20. 4% do not continue beyond their first year; 91% remain to graduate. **Housing:** 2211 students can be accommodated in college housing, which includes dorms. In addition, there are language/international houses, special-interest houses, and Co-op housing. On-campus housing is guaranteed for all 4 years. 98% of students live on campus. Upperclassmen may keep cars.

FACULTY/CLASSROOMS: 43% of faculty are male; 57% are female. All teach undergraduates and all do research. No introductory courses are taught by graduate students. The average class size in an introductory lecture is 25 and in a regular course is 18.

PROGRAMS OF STUDY: WC confers B.A. degrees. Bachelor's degrees are awarded in AGRICULTURE (environmental studies), BIOLOGICAL SCIENCE (biochemistry, biology/biological science, biological sciences, and neurosciences), COMMUNICATIONS AND THE ARTS (American literature, Arabic, art history, art, art history and appreciation, art studies, China Asia-Pacific studies, Chinese, classical languages, classics, comparative literature, creative writing, dramatic arts, East Asian languages and literature, English, English literature, English Writing, film arts, fine/studio arts, general, French, French and Francophone studies, German, German studies, Greek, Greek (classical), Hebrew, Italian, Japanese, Korean, Latin, linguistics, literature, media arts, film and media studies, music, Portuguese, Russian, Russian languages and literature, Spanish, studio art, studio art graphic design, studio art painting, and theatre arts), COMPUTER AND PHYSICAL SCIENCE (astronomy, astrophysics, chemistry, computer science, geology, mathematics, and physics), EDUCATION (childhood education, classical studies, early childhood education, elementary education, and secondary education), ENGINEERING AND ENVIRONMENTAL DESIGN (architecture and preengineering), HEALTH PROFESSIONS (biology, predentistry, premedicine, preoptometry, pre-physician assistant, prepodiatry, and preveterinary science), SOCIAL SCIENCE (African American studies, American studies, anthropology, archeology, Asian/American studies, Asian/Oriental studies, biopsychology, child psychology/development, Chinese Studies, classical/ancient civilization, cognitive science, economics, government, French studies, gender studies, German area studies, Hispanic American studies, history, international relations, Italian studies, Japanese studies, Judaic studies, Latin American studies, law, liberal arts/general studies, liberal arts, sciences, general studies, humanities, liberal arts/engineering studies, medieval studies, Middle Eastern studies, peace studies, philosophy, political science/government, prelaw, psychobiology, psychology, religion, sociology, women & gender studies, and women's studies). Economics, psychology, and political science have the largest enrollments.

ACTIVITIES: There are no fraternities or sororities. There are 160 groups on campus, including art, cheerleading, chess, choir, chorale, chorus, communications, computers, dance, debate, drama, environmental, ethnic, film, honors, international, jazz band, LGBT, literary magazine, musical theater, newspaper, orchestra, photography, political, professional, radio and TV, religious, social, social service, student government, symphony, and yearbook. Popular campus events include Lake Day, Marathon Monday/Scream Tunnel, and Spring Concert. **Sports:** There are 13 intercollegiate sports for women, and 21 intramural sports for women. Facilities include an indoor pool, dance studios, a weight room, an indoor track, golf course, courts for racquetball, squash, tennis, and volleyball. **Graduates:** From July 1, 2016 to June 30, 2017, 581 bachelor's degrees were awarded. The most popular majors were economics (15%), psychology (10%), and computer science (9%). In an average class, 86% graduate in 4 years or less, 90% graduate in 5 years or less, and 91% graduate in 6 years or less. Of the 2016 graduating class, 17% were enrolled in graduate school within 6 months of graduation, and 74% were employed.

SERVICES: Counseling and information services are available, as is tutoring in every subject. There is a reader service for the blind. **Library/Resources:** The library contains 1.1 million volumes, 313 microform items, and 33,536 audio/video tapes/CDs/DVDs, and subscribes to 414,382 periodicals including electronic. Computerized library services include interlibrary loans, database searching, Internet access, and Wi-Fi capability. Special learning facilities include an art gallery, radio station, a science center, a botanic greenhouse, an observatory, a center for child developmental studies, centers for research on women, and a media and technology center. **Physically Challenged Students:** 85% of the campus is accessible. Facilities include wheelchair ramps, elevators, special parking, specially equipped restrooms, special class scheduling, lowered drinking fountains, lowered telephones, special housing, and signage in braille. **Special:** Students may cross-register at MIT, Brandeis University, or Babson College. Exchange programs are available with Spelman College in Georgia and Mills College in California, with members of the Twelve College Exchange Program, with Williams College's maritime studies program, and with Connecticut College's National Theater Institute. Study abroad is possible through Wellesley-administered programs in France and Germany, exchange programs in Argentina, Japan, Korea, and the United Kingdom, and other programs in Italy, Japan, Spain, South Africa, and China. There are more than 150 approved study abroad programs available. There are summer internship programs in Boston and Washington, D.C. Dual majors, student-designed majors, non-degree study, and pass/fail options are possible. A 3-2 program with MIT, Dartmouth, and Columbia awards a B.A.-B.S. degree. There are 2 national honor societies, Phi Beta Kappa, and 51 departmental honors programs. **Visiting:** There are regularly scheduled orientations for prospective students, information session followed by campus tour. There are guides for informal visits, visitors may sit in on classes, and stay overnight. To schedule a visit, contact the Admission Office. **Campus Safety and Security:** Measures include 24-hour foot and vehicle patrol, emergency notification system, self-defense education, and security escort services. There are shuttle buses, emergency telephones, lighted pathways/sidewalks, and controlled access to dorms/residences.

REQUIREMENTS: The SAT or ACT is required. The ACT Optional Writing test is also required. The SAT Reasoning Test, or the ACT with Writing are required. Wellesley College does not require a fixed plan of secondary school course preparation. Entering students normally have completed 4 years of college preparatory studies in secondary school that include training in clear and coherent writing and interpreting literature; history; principles of math (typically 4 years); competence in at least 1 foreign language, ancient or modern (usually 4 years of study); and experience in at least 2 lab sciences. An essay is required, and an interview is recommended. AP credits are accepted. Important factors in the admissions decision are advanced placement or honors courses, extracurricular activities record, and leadership record. All students must complete 32 units, at least 8 of which are in the major field, with a minimum 2.0 GPA. Requirements include 3 courses each in humanities, social science, and natural science and math, 1 multicultural course, 1 semester of expository writing in any department, and 2 credits in phys ed. Students must also possess proficiency in a modern or ancient foreign language. A thesis is required for departmental honors. A quantitative reasoning requirement must be satisfied by all students. **Procedure:** Freshmen are admitted fall. Entrance exams should be taken spring of the junior year or fall of the senior year. There are early decision and deferred admissions plans. Early decision applications should be filed by November 1; regular applications, by January 15 for fall entry. Notification of early decision is sent December 15; regular decision, April 1. 166 early decision candidates were accepted for the 2017-2018 class. 957 applicants were on the 2017 waiting list; 23 were admitted. Applications are accepted on-line. **Transfer Students:** 11 transfer students enrolled in 2016-2017. Applicants must provide high school and college transcripts, SAT or ACT scores if they submitted them to their current institution, a personal statement, and a statement of good standing from institutions previously attended. 16 of 32 credits required for the bachelor's degree must be completed at Wellesley. **International Students:** There are 293 international students enrolled. They must also take the SAT or ACT.

ADMISSIONS: 22% of the 2017-2018 applicants were accepted. The SAT scores for the 2017-2018 freshman class were: Critical Reading-- 8% between 500 and 599, 34% between 600 and 699, and 58% between 700 and 800. Math-- 9% between 500 and 599, 42% between 600 and 699, and 49% between 700 and 800. Writing-- 9% between 500 and 599, 34% between 600 and 699, and 57% between 700 and 800. The ACT scores were 1% between 18 and 23, 23% between 24 and 29, and 76% above 30. 97% of the current freshmen were in the top fifth of their class; 100% were in the top two fifths. **Admissions Contact:** Board of Admission Email: *admission@wellesley.edu* Web: *www.wellesley.edu*

FINANCIAL AID: In 2017-2018, 60% of all full-time freshmen received some form of financial aid. 60% of all full-time freshmen received need-based aid. The average freshman award was $48,404. Need-based scholarships or need-based grants averaged $47,355; and need-based self-help aid (loans and jobs) averaged $3,359. 63% of undergraduate students work part-time. The average financial indebtedness of the 2017 graduate was $13,415. WC is a member of CSS. The CSS/Profile, and the most recent income tax returns of parents and student are required. The FAFSA code is 002224. The priority date for freshman financial aid applications for fall entry is March 1.

WENTWORTH INSTITUTE OF TECHNOLOGY — E-2

www.wit.edu

Boston, MA 02115 — (617) 989-4009, (800) 556-0610

Fax: (617) 989-4910

Full-time: 3098 men, 806 women	**Faculty:** 158
Part-time: 297 men, 61 women	**Ph.D.s:** n/av
Graduate: 141 men, 51 women	**Student/Faculty:** 24 to 1
Year: semesters, summer session	**Tuition:** $34,977
Room & Board: $13,833	**Freshman Class:** 8395 applied, 5931 accepted, 1130 enrolled
SAT EBR-W/M: 575/599 **ACT:** 24	**CEEB CODE:** 3958
Application Deadline: February 15	**VERY COMPETITIVE**

Wentworth Institute of Technology (WIT) is a nationally-recognized, private, coeducational, university offering master's, baccalaureate, associate degrees, and certificate programs in the disciplines of computer science, computer networking, computer information systems, architecture, design, engineering, management, applied math, biomedical engineering, and engineering technology. Wentworth's mission is to empower, inspire and innovate through experiential learning and offering baccalaureate programs in a variety of engineering and design-related fields in a cooperative education format during the day and in a part-time format through the College of Professional and Continuing Education (CPCE). There are 4 undergraduate schools and 2 graduate schools. In addition to regional accreditation, WIT has baccalaureate program accreditation with ABET, ACCE, FIDER, NAAB, NASAD, IACBE, IFMA, and CIDA. The 31-acre campus is in an urban area in the Fenway area of Boston Massachusetts. Including any residence halls, there are 27 buildings.

STUDENT LIFE: 62% of undergraduates are from Massachusetts. Others are from 36 states, 60 foreign countries, and Canada. 8% are Foreign; 7% Asian American; 7% race unknown; 64% White; 6% two or more races; 5% African American; 3% Hispanic. **Male To Female Ratio:** 3.9:1. The average age of freshmen is 19; all undergraduates, 21. 16% do not continue beyond their first year; 66% remain to graduate. **Housing:** 2162 students can be accommodated in college housing, which includes gender neutral, single sex, coed dorms and on-campus apartments. On-campus housing is guaranteed for all 4 years. 52% of students live on campus. Alcohol is not permitted. Upperclassmen may keep cars.

FACULTY/CLASSROOMS: 68% of faculty are male; 32% are female. All teach undergraduates. No introductory courses are taught by graduate students.

PROGRAMS OF STUDY: WIT confers B.S. degrees. Associate and master's degrees are also awarded. Bachelor's degrees are awarded in BUSINESS (business management), COMMUNICATIONS AND THE ARTS (industrial design), COMPUTER AND PHYSICAL SCIENCE (applied mathematics, computer networks & systems, computer information systems, computer science, and information sciences and systems), ENGINEERING AND ENVIRONMENTAL DESIGN (architecture, biomedical engineering, civil engineering, computer engineering, construction management, electrical/electronics engineering, electromechanical technology, engineering, industrial administration/management, interior design, and technological management). Computer science and all engineering majors are the strongest academically. Architecture, construction management, and computer science have the largest enrollments.

ACTIVITIES: There are no fraternities or sororities. There are 58 groups on campus, including band, cheerleading, chess, choir, chorale, chorus, communications, computers, dance, debate, drama, ethnic, honors, international, jazz band, LGBT, literary magazine, musical theater, newspaper, orchestra, pep band, political, professional, radio and TV, religious, social, social service, and student government. Popular campus events include Black and Gold Week, Parent and Alumni Weekend. **Sports:** There are 11 intercollegiate sports for men and 6 for women, and 13 intramural sports for men and 13 for women. Facilities include an athletic field and campus recreation center with basketball and volleyball courts, batting cage, weight room, and a fitness center. The university's athletic teams also have access to a nearby hockey rink and baseball stadium. **Graduates:** From July 1, 2016 to June 30, 2017, 817 bachelor's degrees were awarded. The most popular majors were architecture (13%), construction management (10%), and mechanical engineering (9%). In an average class, 53% graduate in 4 years or less, 65% graduate in 5 years or less, and 67% graduate in 6 years or less. Of the 2016 graduating class, 11% were enrolled in graduate school within 6 months of graduation, and 93% were employed.

SERVICES: Counseling and information services are available, as is tutoring in every subject. There is remedial math and writing. Free tutoring is available to all students through the Center of Academic Excellence. **Library/Resources:** The library contains 254,690 volumes, 25,308 audio/video tapes/CDs/DVDs, and subscribes to 28,114 periodicals including electronic. Computerized library services include interlibrary loans, database searching, and Internet access. Special learning facilities include a radio station, Design Studios, Flanagan Campus Center, Computer Networking Lab, Center for Sciences and Biomedical Engineering. **Physically Challenged Students:** 30% of the campus is accessible. Facilities include wheelchair ramps, elevators, special parking, specially equipped restrooms, special class scheduling, lowered drinking fountains, and lowered telephones. **Special:** Wentworth offers extensive cooperative programs, cross-registration with other members of the Colleges of the Fenway Consortium, and study abroad. Most students at the bachelor's level attend school in the summer, as most cooperative work occurs during the academic year. There are 5 national honor societies and a chapter of Phi Beta Kappa. **Visiting:** There are regularly scheduled orientations for prospective students, including daily tours and information programs, Monday to Friday. To schedule a visit, contact Carlo Fierimonte at fierimontec@wit.edu. **Campus Safety and Security:** Measures include 24-hour foot and vehicle patrol, emergency notification system, self-defense education, and security escort services. There are emergency telephones, lighted pathways/sidewalks, controlled access to dorms/residences, and all campus police officers have emergency medical training.

REQUIREMENTS: The SAT or ACT is required. Wentworth has two primary criteria for evaluating all applicants: academic achievement and personal qualities. Applicants are asked to submit an official transcript, letter of recommendation, personal statement, standardized test scores for SAT or ACT, and TOEFL if applicable, as well as a portfolio for certain majors. The recommended prerequisite course of study varies by major. AP and CLEP credits are accepted. Important factors in the admissions decision are advanced placement or honors courses, leadership record, and extracurricular activities record. For a bachelor's degree, students must complete a total of 136 to 176 hours, depending on the major, with a minimum GPA of 2.0 overall and 2.5 in the major. An introductory computer course is required of all students. All full-time bachelor's degree candidates must complete 2 semesters of co-op, beginning after the first 2 years of study. **Procedure:** Freshmen are admitted fall and spring. Entrance exams should be taken in the spring of the junior year or the fall of the senior year. There are deferred admissions and rolling admissions plans. Applications should be filed by February 15 for fall entry. The fall 2017 application fee was $50. Notification is sent on a rolling basis. Applications are accepted on-line. **Transfer Students:** 151 transfer students enrolled in 2016-2017. Requirements for transfer students vary by program. All applicants must submit official college and high school transcripts. Portfolios and faculty reviews are recommended of applicants to industrial design, interior design, and architecture programs. Grades of C or better transfer for credit. Transfer students must take 50% of the coursework in their degree program at Wentworth to graduate. 68 of 136 credits required for the bachelor's degree must be completed at Wentworth. **International Students:** There are 330 international students enrolled. They must take the TOEFL with a minimum score of 550 on the paper-based TOEFL (PBT) or 79 on the Internet-based version (iBT). Student must take the IELTS or Pearson Test of English, and the SAT or ACT. They must also have 3 or more years at an English based high school.

ADMISSIONS: 71% of the 2017-2018 applicants were accepted. The SAT scores for the 2017-2018 freshman class were: Math-- 5% below 500, 45% between 500 and 599, 42% between 600 and 699, and 8% between 700 and 800. Evidence-Based Reading/Writing-- 12% below 500, 49% between 500 and 599, 34% between 600 and 699, and 5% between 700 and 800. The ACT scores were 6% between 12 and 17, 40% between 18 and 23, 40% between 24 and 29, and 13% above 30. **Admissions Contact:** Maureen Dischino, Executive Director of Admissions. Web: *www.wit.edu*

FINANCIAL AID: In 2017-2018, 100% of all full-time freshmen received some form of financial aid. 70% of all full-time freshmen received need-based aid. The average freshman award was $17,668. Need-based scholarships or need-based grants averaged $5,848; need-based self-help aid (loans and jobs) averaged $4,313; and other non-need-based awards and non-need-based scholarships averaged $10,914. 38% of undergraduate students work part-time. The FAFSA code is 002225. The priority date for freshman financial aid applications for fall entry is March 1.

WESTERN NEW ENGLAND UNIVERSITY B-3

www.wne.edu

Springfield, MA 01119	(413) 782-1321 (800) 325-1122
Fax: (413) 782-1777	Email: learn@wne.edu
Full-time: 1646 men, 967 women	**Faculty:** 188
Part-time: 75 men, 48 women	**Ph.D.s:** 86%
Graduate: 438 men, 639 women	**Student/Faculty:** 12 to 1
Year: semesters, summer session	**Tuition:** $35,740
Room & Board: $13,442	**Freshman Class:** 6645 applied, 5363 accepted, 770 enrolled
SAT CR/M: 525/550 **ACT:** 24	**CEEB CODE:** 3962
Application Deadline: open	**COMPETITIVE**

Western New England University, founded in 1919, is a private nonsectarian institution offering undergraduate programs in business, engineering and arts and sciences. There are 3 undergraduate schools and 6 graduate schools. In addition to regional accreditation, WNE has baccalaureate program accreditation with AACSB, ABET, ACPE, CSWE, ABA, and ABAI. The 215-acre campus is in a suburban area 90 miles west of Boston, MA, 30 miles from Hartford, CT, and 150 miles from New York City. Including any residence halls, there are 26 buildings.

STUDENT LIFE: 51% of undergraduates are from Massachusetts. Others are from 26 states, 22 foreign countries, and Canada. 73% are White; 9% Hispanic; 6% African American; 3% Asian American; 3% Foreign; 3% race unknown; 2% two or more races; 1% American Indian/Alaska Native. 97% claim no religious affiliation. **Male To Female Ratio:** 1.3:1. The average age of freshmen is 18; all undergraduates, 20. 24% do not continue beyond their first year; 61% remain to graduate. **Housing:** 2000 students can be accommodated in college housing, which includes coed and married student dorms and on-campus apartments, academic interest areas or theme housing. On-campus housing is guaranteed for all 4 years. 61% of students live on campus. All students may keep cars.

FACULTY/CLASSROOMS: 59% of faculty are male; 41% are female. Graduate students teach 1% of introductory courses. The average class size in an introductory lecture is 20; in a laboratory is 17; and in a regular course is 19.

PROGRAMS OF STUDY: WNE confers B.A., B.S., B.B.A., B.A.L.S., B.S.B.A., B.S.B.E., B.S.C.J., B.S.E.E., B.S.H.S., B.S.I.E., B.S.M.E., B.S.W., B.S.B.M.E., and B.S.C.E.. degrees. Associate, master's, and doctoral degrees are also awarded. Bachelor's degrees are awarded in BIOLOGICAL SCIENCE (biology/biological science and neurosciences), BUSINESS (accounting, business administration and management, entrepreneurial studies, finance, international business, management science, marketing, and sports management), COMMUNICATIONS AND THE ARTS (advertising, communications, creative writing, English, and public relations), COMPUTER AND PHYSICAL SCIENCE (actuarial science, chemistry, chemistry/forensic chemistry, computer information systems, computer science, information sciences and systems, and mathematics), EDUCATION (elementary education and secondary education), ENGINEERING AND ENVIRONMENTAL DESIGN (biomedical engineering, civil engineering, computer engineering, electrical/electronics engineering, industrial engineering, mechanical engineering, and preengineering), HEALTH PROFESSIONS (health science, premedicine, preoptometry, prepharmacy, and pre-physician assistant), SOCIAL SCIENCE (American studies, criminal justice, economics, forensic studies, history, international studies, law, liberal arts/general studies, liberal arts, sciences, general studies, humanities, philosophy, political science/government, psychology, social work, and sociology). Engineering is the strongest academically. Criminal justice, sports management, and mechanical engineering have the largest enrollments.

ACTIVITIES: There are no fraternities or sororities. There are 70 groups on campus, including art, band, cheerleading, chorus, computers, dance, drama, environmental, ethnic, film, forensics, honors, international, jazz band, LGBT, literary magazine, musical theater, newspaper, pep band, photography, political, professional, radio and TV, religious, social, social service, student government, and yearbook. Popular campus events include Spring Week, Family and Friends Weekend, Midnight Madness and Mr. University. **Sports:** There are 10 intercollegiate sports for men and 9 for women, and 13 intramural sports for men and 13 for women. Facilities include basketball, wrestling, racquetball, squash, aerobics, fitness, and volleyball, a weight room, an 8-lane pool, indoor track, football, field hockey, lacrosse, tennis courts, baseball and softball fields, and soccer field. **Graduates:** From July 1, 2016 to June 30, 2017, 593 bachelor's degrees were awarded. The most popular majors were mechanical engineering (10%), accounting (7%), and criminal justice (6%). In an average class, 1% graduate in 3 years or less, 56% graduate in 4 years or less, 62% graduate in 5 years or less, and 61% graduate in 6 years or less.

SERVICES: Counseling and information services are available, as is tutoring in most subjects. There is a reader service for the blind. **Library/Resources:** The library contains 106,500 volumes, 116,644 microform items, and 10,176 audio/video tapes/CDs/DVDs, and subscribes to 328 periodicals including electronic. Computerized library services include interlibrary loans, database searching, Internet access, and Wi-Fi capability. Special learning facilities include an art gallery, radio station, TV station, math, writing and science centers. **Physically Challenged Students:** Facilities include wheelchair ramps, elevators, special parking, specially equipped restrooms, special class scheduling, lowered drinking fountains, lowered telephones, and special housing. **Special:** Students may cross-register with cooperating colleges of Greater Springfield. The college offers internships, study abroad, a Washington semester, work-study programs, B.A.-B.S. degrees, an accelerated degree program, and dual and student-designed majors. The 3+3 law program offers qualified students the opportunity to earn a J.D. in 6 years. There is also a 6-year biomedical engineering/law program, a 5-year Bachelor/M.B.A., a 5-year Bachelor/Masters in Organizational Leadership, a 5-year accounting/M.S.A., a 5-year B.S./M.S. in Engineering Management and Electrical Engineering and Mechanical Engineering and Industrial Engineering and Civil Engineering. There are 14 national honor societies and a freshman honors program. **Visiting:** There are regularly scheduled orientations for prospective students, including multiple open houses. There are guides for informal visits, visitors may sit in on classes, and stay overnight. To schedule a visit, contact the Undergraduate Admissions Office. **Campus Safety and Security:** Measures include 24-hour foot and vehicle patrol, emergency notification system, self-defense education, and security escort services. There are emergency telephones, lighted pathways/sidewalks, controlled access to dorms/residences, security cameras, medical response, fire response, and a comprehensive public safety awareness program.

REQUIREMENTS: Applicants must be graduates of an approved secondary school and must have completed 4 years of high school English, 2 or more years of math, 1 or more years of science, and 1 year of history and social science. An interview is recommended. ACT is accepted in lieu of SAT. AP and CLEP credits are accepted. Important factors in the admissions decision are advanced placement or honors courses, extracurricular activities record, and recommendations by school officials. To graduate, students must complete 122 credit hours, with a minimum GPA of 2.0. Requirements include 2 courses each in English, math, lab science, and phys ed, and 1 course each in history, culture, and computers. A first-year seminar is also required for freshmen. Each student needs to complete two Learning Beyond the Classroom experiences to be eligible for graduation. These are to help them make connections between coursework and applied learning experiences. Other requirements vary according to the major. **Procedure:** Freshmen are admitted fall and spring. Entrance exams should be taken in the spring of the junior year or fall of the senior year. There are early admissions, deferred admissions, and rolling admissions plans. Application deadlines are open. The fall 2017 application fee was $40. Notification is sent on a rolling basis. Applications are accepted on-line. **Transfer Students:** 106 transfer students enrolled in 2016-2017. Applicants must have a minimum GPA of 2.3. Grades of C- or better transfer for credit. The university admits transfer students in the fall and spring. 30 of 122 credits required for the bachelor's degree must be completed at WNE. **International Students:** There are 89 international students enrolled. They must take the TOEFL with a minimum score of 550 on the paper-based TOEFL (PBT) or 79 on the Internet-based version (iBT). They must also take the SAT or ACT only for certain programs.

ADMISSIONS: 81% of the 2017-2018 applicants were accepted. The SAT scores for the 2017-2018 freshman class were: Critical Reading-- 29% below 500, 60% between 500 and 599, 10% between 600 and 699, and 1% between 700 and 800. Math-- 22% below 500, 50% between 500 and 599, 26% between 600 and 699, and 2% between 700 and 800. The ACT scores were 1% between 12 and 17, 40% between 18 and 23, 50% between 24 and 29, and 9% above 30. 30% of the current freshmen were in the top fifth of their class; 62% were in the top two fifths. **Admissions Contact:** Bryan Gross, Vice President for Enrollment Management. Email: *learn@wne.edu* Web: *www.wne.edu*

FINANCIAL AID: In 2017-2018, 99% of all full-time freshmen received some form of financial aid. 84% of all full-time freshmen received need-based aid. The average freshman award was $31,672. Need-based scholarships or need-based grants averaged $19,116. 40% of undergraduate students work part-time. The FAFSA code is 002226. The priority date for freshman financial aid applications for fall entry is rolling.

WESTFIELD STATE UNIVERSITY — B-3

www.westfield.ma.edu

Westfield, MA 01086 — (413) 572-5218

Fax: (413) 572-0520	**Email:** admissions@westfield.ma.edu
Full-time: 2207 men, 2599 women	**Faculty:** 229
Part-time: 377 men, 380 women	**Ph.D.s:** 89%
Graduate: 205 men, 480 women	**Student/Faculty:** 21 to 1
Year: semesters, summer session	**Tuition:** $9715 ($15,795)
Room & Board: $10,689	**Freshman Class:** 5132 applied, 4427 accepted, 1011 enrolled
SAT EBR-W/M: 540/530 **ACT:** 22	**CEEB CODE:** 3523
Application Deadline: March 1	**COMPETITIVE**

Westfield State University, founded in 1839, is a public university with liberal arts and sciences, teacher preparation programs, and professional training in business, nursing and allied health fields. There is 1 undergraduate school and 1 graduate school. In addition to regional accreditation, WSU has baccalaureate program accreditation with ABET, CSWE, NASM, CAAHEP, and CCNE. The 256-acre campus is in a suburban area in western Massachusetts, 15 miles west of Springfield, 100 miles west of Boston. Including any residence halls, there are 26 buildings.

STUDENT LIFE: 93% of undergraduates are from Massachusetts. Others are from 22 states, 18 foreign countries, and Canada. 74% are White; 5% African American; 4% two or more races; 4% race unknown; 2% Asian American; 10% Hispanic. **Female To Male Ratio:** 1.2:1. The average age of freshmen is 19; all undergraduates, 22. 22% do not continue beyond their first year; 65% remain to graduate. **Housing:** 2881 students can be accommodated in college housing, which includes dorms, on-campus apartments, and off-campus apartments. In addition, there are honors houses, special-interest houses, special housing for disabilities students, and special housing for international students. On-campus housing is available on a first-come and first-served basis. 51% of students live on campus. Upperclassmen may keep cars.

FACULTY/CLASSROOMS: 50% of faculty are male; 50% are female. 99% teach undergraduates. No introductory courses are taught by graduate students. The average class size in a laboratory is 15 and in a regular course is 21.

PROGRAMS OF STUDY: WSU confers B.A., B.S., B.S.E., B.S.N. and B.S.W. degrees. Master's degrees are also awarded. Bachelor's degrees are awarded in BIOLOGICAL SCIENCE (biology/biological science), BUSINESS (business administration and management), COMMUNICATIONS AND THE ARTS (art, communications, English, music, Spanish, and theatre arts), COMPUTER AND PHYSICAL SCIENCE (chemistry, computer science, information sciences and systems, mathematics, and science), EDUCATION (athletic training, early childhood education, elementary education, special education, and vocational education), ENGINEERING AND ENVIRONMENTAL DESIGN (city/community/regional planning and environmental science), HEALTH PROFESSIONS (nursing), SOCIAL SCIENCE (criminal justice, economics, ethnic studies, history, liberal arts/general studies, physical fitness/movement, political science/government, psychology, social work, and sociology). Business management, education, and criminal justice have the largest enrollments.

ACTIVITIES: There are no fraternities or sororities. There are 94 groups on campus, including art, band, choir, chorale, chorus, communications, computers, dance, drama, environmental, ethnic, honors, international, jazz band, LGBT, literary magazine, musical theater, newspaper, orchestra, pep band, political, professional, radio and TV, religious, social, social service, student government, and symphony. Popular campus events include Homecoming, Spring Weekend, and Comedy Night. **Sports:** There are 8 intercollegiate sports for men and 10 for women, and 9 intramural sports for men and 8 for women. Facilities include a track, baseball and softball fields, a gym, and a stadium. **Graduates:** From July 1, 2016 to June 30, 2017, 1143 bachelor's degrees were awarded. The most popular majors were criminal justice (16%), liberal studies (15%), and business management (13%). In an average class, 50% graduate in 4 years or less, 62% graduate in 5 years or less, and 65% graduate in 6 years or less.

SERVICES: Counseling and information services are available, as is tutoring in every subject. There is a reader service for the blind. **Library/Resources:** The library contains 129,289 volumes, 481,154 microform items, and 4,995 audio/video tapes/CDs/DVDs, and subscribes to 1,984 periodicals including electronic. Computerized library services include interlibrary loans, database searching, Internet access, and Wi-Fi capability. Special learning facilities include an art gallery, natural history museum, radio station, TV station, a geology museum, a greenhouse, and a science center. **Physically Challenged Students:** 75% of the campus is accessible. Facilities include wheelchair ramps, elevators, special parking, specially equipped restrooms, special class scheduling, and special housing. **Special:** Students may cross-register through College Academic Program Sharing, National Student Exchange, and Cooperating Colleges of Greater Springfield. Internships are for credit only in conjunction with all major programs. The university offers international exchange programs in China, Ireland and Poland and hundreds of study abroad programs in over 35 countries, a Washington semester for political science, criminal justice, and psychology majors, an internship program with Walt Disney World, dual majors, student-designed majors, some credit for military experience and has a multi-department Honors Program. There are 16 national honor societies and a freshman honors program. **Visiting:** There are regularly scheduled orientations for prospective students, including a campus tour, classroom observation, academic department presentations, lunch with faculty, staff, and students, and a question-and-answer session moderated by a panel of administrators. There are guides for informal visits. To schedule a visit, contact the Admissions Office. **Campus Safety and Security:** Measures include 24-hour foot and vehicle patrol, emergency notification system, self-defense education, and security escort services. There are shuttle buses, emergency telephones, lighted pathways/sidewalks, and controlled access to dorms/residences.

REQUIREMENTS: Applicants must achieve a minimum 3.0 GPA in academic subjects. Students who have between a 2.0 and a 3.0 GPA may be accepted via a sliding scale, contingent upon the SAT or ACT scores. They must be graduates of an accredited secondary school and must have completed 4 years of college preparatory level English, 4 years of math (algebra I and II and geometry), 2 years of social sciences (including 1 year of U.S history), 3 years of sciences, including 2 with lab, 2 foreign language, and 2 years of electives. The GED is accepted. A portfolio is required for admission to the art program, and an audition is necessary for admission to the music program. All applicants must submit either SAT or ACT scores unless they have a documented learning disability. AP and CLEP credits are accepted. Students must complete a total of 120 credit hours, with 43 or more credits in 9 specified areas and 30 to 40 hours in the major. The college requires a 2.0 GPA overall and 2.0 in major courses. U.S. history or government and diversity awareness courses are required. **Procedure:** Freshmen are admitted fall and spring. Entrance exams should be taken in the spring of the junior year and fall of the senior year. There are deferred admissions and rolling admissions plans. Applications should be filed by March 1 for fall entry; December 1 for spring entry. The fall 2017 application fee was $50. Notifications are sent March 15. Applications are accepted on-line. **Transfer Students:** 465 transfer students enrolled in 2016-2017. Transfer students must have 24 transferable credits with a minimum cumulative GPA of 2.0 (higher for some majors). A grade of C- or better with a 2.0 GPA will transfer for credit. Transfer students are admitted in the fall and spring. For students transferring from a Massachusetts Community College, a D may be transferred for credit. 30 of 120 credits required for the bachelor's degree must be completed at WSU. **International Students:** There are 29 international students enrolled. They must take the TOEFL with a minimum score of 550 on the paper-based TOEFL (PBT) or 79 on the Internet-based version (iBT). Student must take the IELTS. They must also take the SAT or ACT.

ADMISSIONS: 86% of the 2017-2018 applicants were accepted. The SAT scores for the 2017-2018 freshman class were: Math-- 30% below 500, 57% between 500 and 599, 13% between 600 and 699, and 1% between 700 and 800. Evidence-Based Reading/Writing-- 24% below 500, 57% between 500 and 599, 18% between 600 and 699, and 1% between 700 and 800. The ACT scores were 7% between 12 and 17, 54% between 18 and 23, 32% between 24 and 29, and 7% above 30. **Admissions Contact:** Kelly Hart, Director of Admissions. Email: *admissions@westfield.ma.edu.* Web: *www.westfield.ma.edu*

FINANCIAL AID: WSU is a member of CSS. The FAFSA code is 002189. The deadline for filing freshman financial aid applications for fall entry is March 1.

WHEATON COLLEGE — D-3

wheatoncollege.edu

Norton, MA 02766	**(508) 286-8251** **(800) 394-6003**
Fax: (508) 286-8271	**Email: admission@wheatoncollege.edu**
Full-time: 646 men, 1029 women	**Faculty:** n/av
Part-time: 6 men, 7 women	**Ph.D.s:** n/av
Graduate: n/av	**Student/Faculty:** n/av
Year: semesters	**Tuition:** $50,850
Room & Board: $12,968	**Freshman Class:** 6089 applied, 2916 accepted, 502 enrolled
SAT CR/M: 620/590 **ACT:** 26	**CEEB CODE:** 3963
Application Deadline: January 1	**VERY COMPETITIVE**

Wheaton College, established in 1834, is an independent liberal arts institution. There is 1 undergraduate school. The 478-acre campus is in a suburban area 35 miles south of Boston and 20 miles north of Providence. Including any residence halls, there are 81 buildings.

STUDENT LIFE: 66% of undergraduates are from out of state, mostly the Northeast. Students are from 38 states, 78 foreign countries, and Canada. 8% are Hispanic; 65% White; 6% African American; 5% Asian American; 3% two or more races; 2% race unknown; 10% Foreign. **Female To Male Ratio:** 1.6:1. The average age of freshmen is 18; all undergraduates, 20. 12% do not continue beyond their first year; 78% remain to graduate. **Housing:** 1625 students can be accommodated in college housing, which includes gender neutral, single-sex, and coed dorms. In addition, there are language/international houses and special-interest houses. On-campus housing is guaranteed for all 4 years and is available on a lottery system for upperclassmen. 96% of students live on campus. All students may keep cars.

FACULTY/CLASSROOMS: No introductory courses are taught by graduate students.

PROGRAMS OF STUDY: Wheaton confers B.A. degrees. Bachelor's degrees are awarded in BIOLOGICAL SCIENCE (biochemistry, bioinformatics, and neurosciences), BUSINESS (business administration and management), COMMUNICATIONS AND THE ARTS (art history, art, classics, creative writing, English, German, German studies, Greek, Latin, film and media studies, music, Russian, Russian languages and literature, studio art, and theatre/dance), COMPUTER AND PHYSICAL SCIENCE (astronomy and physics, chemistry, computer mathematics, computer science, mathematics, mathematics – economics, and physics), EDUCATION (early childhood education, education, and secondary education), ENGINEERING AND ENVIRONMENTAL DESIGN (environmental science), HEALTH PROFESSIONS (biology and multidisciplinary studies), SOCIAL SCIENCE (African studies, African American studies, American studies, anthropology, classical/ancient civilization, economics, French studies, Hispanic American studies, history, international relations, Italian studies, philosophy, political science/government, psychology, religion, sociology, and women & gender studies). Arts and sciences is the strongest academically. Business & management, psychology and biology have the largest enrollments.

ACTIVITIES: There are no fraternities or sororities. There are 120 groups on campus, including academic/educational, culture & identity, community service, a capella singing groups, art, band, cheerleading, choir, chorale, chorus, communications, computers, dance, debate, drama, ethnic, film, honors, international, jazz band, LGBT, literary magazine, newspaper, orchestra, photography, political, professional, radio and TV, religious, social, social service, student government, symphony, and yearbook. Popular campus events include Head of the Peacock (boat races), Candle Lighting, Spring Weekend, HOLI, and Vespers & Luminaria. **Sports:** There are 8 intercollegiate sports for men and 11 for women, and 4 intramural sports for men and 4 for women. Facilities include an 8-lane stretch pool, a field house with tennis courts, outdoor and indoor basketball courts, 200-meter track, golf/archery range and batting cage, a gym, outdoor tennis courts, running course, baseball stadium, athletic fields, softball field, artificial turf field, aerobics/dance studio, and a fitness center. **Graduates:** From July 1, 2016 to June 30, 2017, 359 bachelor's degrees were awarded. The most popular majors were psychology (16%), economics (10%), and business and management (9%). In an average class, 74% graduate in 4 years or less, 77% graduate in 5 years or less, and 78% graduate in 6 years or less.

SERVICES: Counseling and information services are available, as is

tutoring in most subjects. There is a reader service for the blind. **Library/Resources:** The library contains 343,662 volumes, 108,137 microform items, and 9,756 audio/video tapes/CDs/DVDs, and subscribes to 32,143 periodicals including electronic. Computerized library services include interlibrary loans, database searching, Internet access, and Wi-Fi capability. Special learning facilities include an art gallery, planetarium, radio station, observatory, greenhouse, GIS lab, Imaging Center for Undergraduate Collaboration (ICUC), Graphics Design lab, Wheaton Autonomous Learning Lab (WHALE), nursery school, early childhood lab. **Physically Challenged Students:** Facilities include wheelchair ramps, elevators, special parking, specially equipped restrooms, and special housing. **Special:** Students may cross-register with Brown University as well as with colleges in the Southeastern Association for Cooperation in Higher Education in Massachusetts (SACHEM), with schools participating in the 12 College Exchange Program, and with member schools of the Boston Marine Studies Consortium. Wheaton offers study abroad in 49 countries, internship programs, nondegree study, dual majors, student-designed majors, and interdisciplinary majors, including math and economics, and physics and astronomy. Dual-degree programs exist with the following institutions: Thayer School of Engineering, Dartmouth College (B.S. Engineering), Emerson College (M.A. Integrated Marketing Communication), Andover-Newton Theological School (M.A. Religion), New England School of Optometry (Doctor of Optometry), and Clark University Graduate School of Management (M.B.A.). There are 10 national honor societies, Phi Beta Kappa, and a freshman honors program. **Visiting:** There are regularly scheduled orientations for prospective students, campus visits may include campus tours, class visits, interviews, faculty & coach visits, and overnight resident hall stays. To schedule a visit, contact the Admissions Office. **Campus Safety and Security:** Measures include 24-hour foot and vehicle patrol, emergency notification system, self-defense education, and security escort services. There are emergency telephones, lighted pathways/sidewalks, and controlled access to dorms/residences.

REQUIREMENTS: Applicants must be graduates of an accredited secondary school. Recommended courses include English with emphasis on composition skills, 4 years each of foreign language, math, social studies, 3 years of history, 2 years of science with lab (recommended 3 years). Wheaton requires an essay and strongly recommends an interview. AP credits are accepted. Among the requirements for graduation are 32 course units (4 semester hours each), with a minimum of 9 courses in the major, at least 3 of which must be at 300-level or above. The requirements for each major are determined by the department (some majors require more than 9 courses). The core classes consist of First-Year Seminar, Writing, Quantitative Analysis, Foreign Language, and a non-Western course. Students must maintain a minimum GPA of 2.0 (C-) in all courses to remain in good academic standing. **Procedure:** Freshmen are admitted fall and spring. Entrance exams should be taken in October or November. There are early decision, early admissions, and deferred admissions plans. Early decision applications should be filed by November 1; regular applications, by January 1 for fall entry; and November 1 for spring entry. The fall 2017 application fee was $60. Notification of early decision is sent December 1; regular decision, March 31. 120 early decision candidates were accepted for the 2017-2018 class. 96 applicants were on the 2017 waiting list; 7 were admitted. Applications are accepted on-line. **Transfer Students:** 71 transfer students enrolled in 2016-2017. Transfer students are encouraged to present a strong B average in their college work to date. Preference will be given to college over high school work. The college transcript is evaluated. High school and college transcripts, an essay or personal statement, a statement of good standing, instructor recommendation, and a midterm evaluation are required. 16 of 32 credits required for the bachelor's degree must be completed at Wheaton. **International Students:** There are 176 international students enrolled. They must take the TOEFL with a minimum score of 580 on the paper-based TOEFL (PBT) or 90 on the Internet-based version (iBT).

ADMISSIONS: 48% of the 2017-2018 applicants were accepted. The SAT scores for the 2017-2018 freshman class were: Critical Reading-- 6% below 500, 29% between 500 and 599, 51% between 600 and 699, and 14% between 700 and 800. Math-- 11% below 500, 44% between 500 and 599, 37% between 600 and 699, and 8% between 700 and 800. The ACT scores were 2% between 12 and 17, 26% between 18 and 23, 46% between 24 and 29, and 27% above 30. 49% of the current freshmen were in the top fifth of their class; 78% were in the top two fifths. 3 freshmen graduated first in their class. **Admissions Contact:** Grant Gosselin, VP for Enrollment and Dean of Admissions & Student Aid. Email: *admission@wheatoncollege.edu* Web: *wheatoncollege.edu*

FINANCIAL AID: In 2017-2018, 98% of all full-time freshmen received some form of financial aid. 68% of all full-time freshmen received need-based aid. The average freshman award was $35,357. Need-based scholarships or need-based grants averaged $36,772 ($66,200 maximum); need-based self-help aid (loans and jobs) averaged $6,638 ($11,500 maximum); and other non-need-based awards and non-need-based scholarships averaged $21,284 ($30,000 maximum). 51% of undergraduate students work part-time. The average financial indebtedness of the 2017 graduate was $34,240. Wheaton College is a member of CSS. The CSS/Profile, noncustodial profile, and business/farm supplement are required. The FAFSA code is 002227. The deadline for filing freshman financial aid applications for fall entry is February 1.

WHEELOCK COLLEGE *(The complete profile is made available exclusively on our website, www.barronspac.com)*

WILLIAMS COLLEGE — A-1

www.williams.edu

Williamstown, MA 01267	**(413) 597-2211**
	Email: admission@williams.edu
Full-time: 1070 men, 948 women	**Faculty:** 291; IIB, ++$
Part-time: 17 men, 26 women	**Ph.D.s:** 97%
Graduate: 24 men, 32 women	**Student/Faculty:** 7 to 1
Year: 4-1-4	**Tuition:** $53,550
Room & Board: $14,150	**Freshman Class:** 8593 applied, 1253 accepted, 548 enrolled
SAT EBR-W/M: 750/750 **ACT:** 33	**CEEB CODE:** 3965
Application Deadline: January 1	**MOST COMPETITIVE**

Williams College, founded in 1793, is a private institution offering undergraduate degrees in liberal arts and graduate degrees in art history and development economics. There are 5 undergraduate schools and 2 graduate schools. The 450-acre campus is in a small town 150 miles north of New York City and west of Boston. Including any residence halls, there are 97 buildings.

STUDENT LIFE: 87% of undergraduates are from out of state, mostly the Northeast. Students are from 46 states, 53 foreign countries, and Canada. 8% are African American; 8% Foreign; 6% two or more races; 49% White; 13% Hispanic; 12% Asian American. **Female To Male Ratio:** 1.0:1. The average age of freshmen is 19; all undergraduates, 20. 2% do not continue beyond their first year; 95% remain to graduate. **Housing:** College-sponsored housing includes dorms, on-campus apartments, and cooperative housing, in which students prepare their own meals. On-campus housing is guaranteed for all 4 years and is available on a lottery system for upperclassmen. Upperclassmen may keep cars.

FACULTY/CLASSROOMS: 56% of faculty are male; 44% are female. No introductory courses are taught by graduate students.

PROGRAMS OF STUDY: Williams confers B.A. degrees. Master's degrees are also awarded. Bachelor's degrees are awarded in BIOLOGICAL SCIENCE (biology/biological science), COMMUNICATIONS AND THE ARTS (Arabic, art, art history and appreciation, classics, dramatic arts, English, fine arts, French, German, literature, music, Russian, and Spanish), COMPUTER AND PHYSICAL SCIENCE (astronomy, astrophysics, chemistry, computer science, geology, mathematics, physics, and statistics), SOCIAL SCIENCE (American studies, anthropology, Asian/Oriental studies, economics, history, philosophy, political science/government, psychology, religion, sociology, and women's studies).

ACTIVITIES: There are no fraternities or sororities. There are 150 groups on campus, including capella singing groups, handbell choir, art, band, chess, choir, chorale, chorus, comedy group, communications, computers, dance, debate, drama, environmental, ethnic, film, honors, international, jazz band, LGBT, literary magazine, marching band, musical theater, newspaper, opera, orchestra, pep band, photography, political, professional, radio and TV, religious, social, social service, student government, symphony, and yearbook. Popular campus events include Winter Carnival, Mountain Day, Claiming Williams, and First Fridays. **Sports:** There are 16 intercollegiate sports for men and 16 for women, and 17 intramural sports for men and 17 for women. Facilities include gyms, fitness centers, a pool, a dance studio, a weight room, rowing tanks, a boathouse, a golf course, playing fields, artificial turf field, ice hockey rink, indoor and outdoor tracks, hiking trails, and courts for tennis, squash, and paddle tennis. **Graduates:** From July 1, 2016 to June 30, 2017, 525 bachelor's degrees were awarded. The most popular majors were economics (20%), mathematics (13%), and English (12%). In an average class, 86% graduate in 4 years or less, 92% graduate in 5 years or less, and 94% graduate in 6 years or less.

SERVICES: Counseling and information services are available, as is tutoring in every subject. There is a reader service for the blind, and remedial math, reading, and writing. **Library/Resources:** Computerized library services include interlibrary loans, database searching, Internet access, and Wi-Fi capability. Special learning facilities include an art gallery, planetarium, radio station, a 2500-acre experimental forest, an environmental studies center, a center for foreign languages, literatures, and cultures, a rare book library, a studio art center, and a three-stage center for the performing arts. **Physically Challenged Students:** Facilities include wheelchair ramps, elevators, special parking, specially equipped restrooms, special class scheduling, lowered drinking fountains, lowered telephones, and special housing. **Special:** Students may cross-register at Bennington or Massachusetts College of Liberal Arts and study abroad in Madrid, Oxford, Cairo, Beijing, and Kyoto, or any approved program with another college or university. Teaching and medical field experiences, dual and student-designed majors, internships, and a 3-2 engineering program with Columbia University is offered. There are pass/fail options during the winter term. Each department offers Oxford-style tutorials where students meet with the professor weekly in groups of 2-3. There are 2 national honor societies and a chapter of Phi Beta Kappa. **Visiting:** There are regularly scheduled orientations for prospective students, including panels, forums, class visits, and campus tours. There are guides for informal visits, visitors may sit in on classes, and stay overnight. To schedule a visit, contact the Admission Office. **Campus Safety and Security:** Measures include 24-hour foot and vehicle patrol, emergency notification system, self-defense education, and security escort services. There are emergency telephones, lighted pathways/sidewalks, and controlled access to dorms/residences. Services also include a peer health program, rape and sexual assault hotline, and 10-1 counseling service.

REQUIREMENTS: Williams requires the following standardized tests: SAT or ACT with Writing, and Two SAT Subject Tests. Applicants to Williams should pursue the strongest program of study offered by their secondary schools. Competitive candidates typically study English, math, natural science, foreign language and social studies in four-year sequences and present a distinguished record throughout their secondary school career. AP credits are accepted. All students must complete 4 winter study courses and 32 regular semester courses, 9 of which are in the major field, with a C- or higher. Requirements include 3 semester-long courses in each of 3 academic divisions: languages and arts, social sciences, and science and math. **Procedure:** Freshmen are admitted in the fall. There are early decision and deferred admissions plans. Early decision applications should be filed by November 15; regular applications, by January 1 for fall entry. The fall 2017 application fee was $65. Notification of early decision is sent December 15; regular decision, 244 early decision candidates were accepted for the 2017-2018 class. 573 applicants were on the 2017 waiting list; 53 were admitted. Applications are accepted on-line. **Transfer Students:** Transfer applicants should present a 3.5 GPA in previous college work and must submit either SAT or ACT scores. 16 of 32 credits required for the bachelor's degree must be completed at Williams. **International Students:** There are 161 international students enrolled. They must take the TOEFL, if English is not the applicant's first language they must take the SAT or ACT.

ADMISSIONS: 15% of the 2017-2018 applicants were accepted. The SAT scores for the 2017-2018 freshman class were: Math-- 4% between 500 and 599, 24% between 600 and 699, and 73% between 700 and 800. Evidence-Based Reading/Writing-- 1% between 500 and 599, 21% between 600 and 699, and 78% between 700 and 800. The ACT scores were 13% between 24 and 29, and 87% above 30. **Admissions Contact:** Richard Nesbitt, Director of Admission. Email: *admission?@williams?.edu* Web: *www.williams.edu*

FINANCIAL AID: In 2017-2018, 52% of all full-time freshmen received some form of financial aid. 52% of all full-time freshmen received need-based aid. The average freshman award was $56,486. Need-based scholarships or need-based grants averaged $53,866; and need-based self-help aid (loans and jobs) averaged $2,620. 63% of undergraduate students work part-time. The average financial indebtedness of the 2017 graduate was $16,230. WC is a member of CSS. The CSS/Profile, and noncustodial profile, and signed copy of parents' and student's federal tax returns are required. The FAFSA code is 002229. The deadline for filing freshman financial aid applications for fall entry is February 1.

WORCESTER POLYTECHNIC INSTITUTE C-2
www.wpi.edu

Worcester, MA 01609	(508) 831-5286
Fax: (508) 831-5875	**Email:** admissions@wpi.edu
Full-time: 2740 men, 1561 women	**Faculty:** 389
Part-time: 91 men, 43 women	**Ph.D.s:** 92%
Graduate: 1517 men, 690 women	**Student/Faculty:** 13 to 1
Year: semesters, summer session	**Tuition:** $48,628
Room & Board: $14,218	**Freshman Class:** 10331 applied, 5009 accepted, 1124 enrolled
SAT EBR-W/M: 660/690 **ACT:** 30	**CEEB CODE:** 3969
Application Deadline: February 1	**MOST COMPETITIVE**

Worcester Polytechnic Institute, founded in 1865 as one of the nation's earliest technological universities, is known for its project-based curriculum and Global Perspective Program, through which students complete projects at more than 25 sites on five continents. WPI's 14 academic departments offer more than 50 undergraduate and graduate programs in the arts and sciences, business, and engineering, while its interdisciplinary research programs advance fields as diverse as the life sciences, energy, information security, and robotics. There is 1 undergraduate school and 1 graduate school. In addition to regional accreditation, WPI has baccalaureate program accreditation with AACSB, ABET, CSAB, ACS, and ASBMB. The 95-acre campus is in a suburban area 40 miles west of Boston. Including any residence halls, there are 65 buildings.

STUDENT LIFE: 62% of undergraduates are from out of state, mostly the Northeast. Students are from 44 states, 70 foreign countries, and Canada. 9% are Hispanic; 9% race unknown; 62% White; 3% African American; 3% Asian American; 2% two or more races; 11% Foreign. **Male To Female Ratio:** 1.9:1. The average age of freshmen is 18; all undergraduates, 20. 5% do not continue beyond their first year; 95% remain to graduate. **Housing:** 2117 students can be accommodated in college housing, which includes coed dorms and on-campus apartments. In addition, there are special-interest houses, fraternity houses, and sorority houses. On-campus housing is guaranteed for the freshman year only and is available on a lottery system for upperclassmen. 59% of students live on campus. Upperclassmen may keep cars.

FACULTY/CLASSROOMS: 70% of faculty are male; 30% are female. No introductory courses are taught by graduate students. The average class size in an introductory lecture is 100; in a laboratory is 20; and in a regular course is 20.

PROGRAMS OF STUDY: WPI confers B.A. and B.S. degrees. Master's and doctoral degrees are also awarded. Bachelor's degrees are awarded in AGRICULTURE (environmental studies), BIOLOGICAL SCIENCE (biochemistry, bioinformatics, and biotechnology), BUSINESS (business administration and management, management engineering, and management information systems), COMMUNICATIONS AND THE ARTS (interactive media), COMPUTER AND PHYSICAL SCIENCE (chemistry, computer science, mathematics, and physics), ENGINEERING AND ENVIRONMENTAL DESIGN (architectural engineering, chemical engineering, civil engineering, electrical and computer engineering, environmental engineering, industrial engineering, mechanical engineering, and robotic & mechatronic systems engineering), HEALTH PROFESSIONS (biology), SOCIAL SCIENCE (economics, humanities, international studies, liberal arts/engineering studies, and psychology). Mechanical engineering, computer science, and biomedical engineering have the largest enrollments.

ACTIVITIES: There are 216 groups on campus, including design teams, art, band, cheerleading, chess, choir, chorale, chorus, communications, computers, dance, debate, drama, environmental, ethnic, forensics, honors, international, jazz band, LGBT, literary magazine, musical theater, newspaper, orchestra, pep band, photography, political, professional, radio and TV, religious, robotics, social, social service, student government, symphony, and yearbook. Popular campus events include Campus Tradition Days, Community Service Day, Cultural Festival, Diya, Greek Week, Homecoming, International Dinner, Night of the Dragon, Quad Fest, Relay for Life, Semi-Formal, Spring Concert, Take Back the Night, Winter Carnival, Work on Worcester. **Sports:** There are 10 intercollegiate sports for men and 10 for women, and 7 intramural sports for men and 7 for women. Facilities include an aerobics area, softball fields, an 8-lane synthetic surface track, a fitness center, a crew center, a playing field with artificial turf, basketball, tennis, racquetball, squash courts, a gym, an indoor track, fitness space, a rowing tank, and a 25-meter competition pool. **Graduates:** From July 1, 2016 to June 30, 2017, 1028 bachelor's degrees were awarded. The most popular majors were mechanical engineering (19%), computer science (12%), and electrical & computer engineering (10%). In an average class, 2% graduate in 3 years or less, 82% graduate in 4 years or less, 87% graduate in 5 years or less, and 89% graduate in 6 years or less. Of the 2016 graduating class, 70% were employed within 6 months of graduation.

SERVICES: Counseling and information services are available, as is tutoring in most subjects, such as math, physics, chemistry, and computer science. **Library/Resources:** The library contains 249,084 volumes, 189,960 microform items, and 5,279 audio/video tapes/CDs/DVDs, and subscribes to 76,238 periodicals including electronic. Computerized library services include interlibrary loans, database searching, Internet access, and Wi-Fi capability. Special learning facilities include an art gallery, and radio station. Laboratories in all science and engineering research departments, including: two atomic-force microscopes, medical imaging lab, fire science lab, laser holography lab, and computer music lab, and life sciences and Bioengineering Center at Gateway Park. **Physically Challenged Students:** 96% of the campus is accessible. Facilities include wheelchair ramps, elevators, special parking, specially equipped restrooms, special class scheduling, and lowered drinking fountains. **Special:** Students may cross-register with 10 other colleges in the Higher Education Consortium of Central Massachusetts. Co-op programs in all majors, internships, work-study programs, dual majors in every subject, student-designed majors, non-degree study, and pass/fail options and an accelerated 5 year BS/MS degree program are all available. There is also a distinctive Global Projects Program with over 40 project centers in 25 countries where students complete immersive 7-week experiences that benefit communities and organizations around the world. There are 14 national honor societies. **Visiting:** There are regularly scheduled orientations for prospective students, daily information sessions & student-led tours; large-scale open house events in fall & spring. There are guides for informal visits, visitors may sit in on classes, and stay overnight. To schedule a visit, contact Barbara Hassett in Admissions. **Campus Safety and Security:** Measures include 24-hour foot and vehicle patrol, emergency notification system, self-defense education, and security escort services. There are shuttle buses, emergency telephones, lighted pathways/sidewalks, controlled access to dorms/residences, and student-run emergency medical service supervised by the campus police department.

REQUIREMENTS: Applicants must have completed 4 years of math, including precalculus, 4 years of English, and 2 lab sciences. An essay is required and a letter of recommendation from either a math or science teacher and the guidance counselor. Those opting for Flex Path will submit academic work in place of the SAT or ACT. AP credits are accepted. For a B.S. degree, WPI requires that students in science and engineering complete an individual project in the humanities. Students must also complete 2 major team projects. Distribution requirements vary according to the major, and all students must take courses in social sciences and phys ed. **Procedure:** Freshmen are admitted in the fall. Entrance exams should be taken between April and January. There are early admissions and deferred admissions plans. Applications should be filed by February 1 for fall entry. The fall 2017 application fee was $65. Notifications are sent April 1. 1093 applicants were on the 2017 waiting list; 102 were admitted. Applications are accepted on-line. **Transfer Students:** 26 transfer students enrolled in 2016-2017. Grades of B or better transfer for credit. A high school transcript or GED is required. Students who have been out of school for a year or more must present a resume or personal biography, and 2 academic recommendations. Also they must have completed a calculus course and 2 lab sciences courses. 72 of 135 credits required for the bachelor's degree must be completed at WPI. **International Students:** There are 457 international students enrolled. They must take the TOEFL with a minimum score of 550 on the paper-based TOEFL (PBT) or 80 on the Internet-based version (iBT). Student must take the MELAB, and any one of these tests: the IELTS, GCSE, or Pearson's Test of English.

ADMISSIONS: 48% of the 2017-2018 applicants were accepted. The SAT scores for the 2017-2018 freshman class were: Math-- 6% between 500 and 599, 45% between 600 and 699, and 49% between 700 and 800. Evidence-Based Reading/Writing-- 1% below 500, 14% between 500 and 599, 55% between 600 and 699, and 30% between 700 and 800. The ACT scores were 2% between 18 and 23, 37% between 24 and 29, and 61% above 30. 88% of the current freshmen were in the top fifth of their class; 99% were in the top two fifths. 45 freshmen graduated first in their class. **Admissions Contact:** Jennifer Cluett, Director of Admissions. Email: *admissions@wpi.edu* Web: *www.wpi.edu*

FINANCIAL AID: In 2017-2018, 97% of all full-time freshmen received some form of financial aid. 54% of all full-time freshmen received need-based aid. WPI is a member of CSS. The CSS/Profile is required. The FAFSA code is 002233. The deadline for filing freshman financial aid applications for fall entry is February 1.

WORCESTER STATE UNIVERSITY C-2

www.worcester.edu

Worcester, MA 01602 **(508) 929-8040**
(866) 972-2255
Fax: (508) 929-8183 **Email: admissions@worcester.edu**

Full-time: 1670 men, 2363 women	**Faculty:** 208; IIA, +$
Part-time: 507 men, 841 women	**Ph.D.s:** 80%
Graduate: 223 men, 867 women	**Student/Faculty:** 20 to 1
Year: semesters, summer session	**Tuition:** $9202 ($15,282)
Room & Board: $11,775	**Freshman Class:** 789 enrolled
SAT CR/M: 501/509 **ACT:** 23	**CEEB CODE:** 3524
Application Deadline: May 1	**COMPETITIVE**

Worcester State University, established in 1874, is part of the Massachusetts public higher education system, and offers undergraduate and graduate programs. A liberal arts core is emphasized, as are selected areas of science, the health professions, education, business, and management. There are 2 undergraduate schools and 1 graduate school. In addition to regional accreditation, WSU has baccalaureate program accreditation with ASHA, ACOTE, JRCEP, NASP, CAEP, CCNE, MACN, and CEC. The 58-acre campus is in an urban area on the west side of Worcester, Massachusetts, 45 miles west of Boston. Including any residence halls, there are 12 buildings.

STUDENT LIFE: 96% of undergraduates are from Massachusetts. Others are from 24 states, 27 foreign countries, and Canada. 8% are African American; 7% race unknown; 67% White; 4% Asian American; 3% two or more races; 10% Hispanic; 1% Foreign. **Female To Male Ratio:** 1.7:1. The average age of freshmen is 19; all undergraduates, 25. **Housing:** 1577 students can be accommodated in college housing, which includes single-sex and coed dorms and on-campus apartments. In addition, there are honors houses, special-interest houses, and Eco-House (students interested in sustainability and green living). On-campus housing is available on a first-come and first-served basis. Priority is given to out-of-town students. 73% of students commute. Alcohol is not permitted. All students may keep cars.

FACULTY/CLASSROOMS: 41% of faculty are male; 59% are female. No introductory courses are taught by graduate students.

PROGRAMS OF STUDY: WSU confers B.A. and B.S. degrees. Master's degrees are also awarded. Bachelor's degrees are awarded in BIOLOGICAL SCIENCE (biology/biological science and biotechnology), BUSINESS (business administration and management), COMMUNICATIONS AND THE ARTS (communications, English, Spanish, and visual and performing arts), COMPUTER AND PHYSICAL SCIENCE (chemistry, computer science, mathematics, and natural sciences), EDUCATION (early childhood education, elementary education, and health education), ENGINEERING AND ENVIRONMENTAL DESIGN (environmental science), HEALTH PROFESSIONS (nursing, occupational therapy, public health, and speech pathology/audiology), SOCIAL SCIENCE (criminal justice, economics, geography, history, liberal arts/general studies, psychology, sociology, and urban studies). Occupational therapy, and nursing are the strongest academically. Business administration, psychology, and criminal justice have the largest enrollments.

ACTIVITIES: There are no fraternities or sororities. There are 40 groups on campus, including cheerleading, chess, chorale, computers, dance, drama, environmental, ethnic, honors, LGBT, newspaper, political, professional, radio and TV, religious, social, social service, student government, and yearbook. Popular campus events include Multicultural Festival, Homecoming, SGA Auction to Benefit Homeless and Lecture Series. **Sports:** There are 9 intercollegiate sports for men and 10 for women, and 10 intramural sports for men and 10 for women. Facilities include the John Coughlin stadium, a weight room, softball and baseball fields, and ice rink. **Graduates:** From July 1, 2015 to June 30, 2016, 1115 bachelor's degrees were awarded. The most popular majors were business administration (17%), psychology (12%), and criminal justice (9%).

SERVICES: Counseling and information services are available, as is tutoring in most subjects. There is a reader service for the blind, and remedial math, reading, and writing. **Library/Resources:** The library contains 144,910 volumes, and 4,213 audio/video tapes/CDs/DVDs, and subscribes to 198,507 periodicals including electronic. Computerized library services include interlibrary loans, database searching, Internet access, and Wi-Fi capability. Special learning facilities include a radio station, photographic labs, an audiovisual center, multimedia classrooms with satellite connectivity, discipline-specific computer labs, and a speech, language, and hearing clinic. **Physically Challenged Students:** All of the campus is accessible. Facilities include wheelchair ramps, elevators, special parking, specially equipped restrooms, lowered drinking fountains, lowered telephones, and special housing. **Special:** Cross-registration with the Worcester Consortium for Higher Education is available, as are internships, study abroad (more than 60 countries), a Washington semester, work-study, non-degree study, and a pass/fail option. There are 20 national honor societies, a freshman honors program, and 16 departmental honors programs. **Visiting:** There are regularly scheduled orientations for prospective students, including a campus tour and review of campus life and organizations, success in college, special opportunities, and available services. To schedule a visit, contact Admissions Office. **Campus Safety and Security:** Measures include 24-hour foot and vehicle patrol, emergency notification system, self-defense education, and security escort services. There are shuttle buses, emergency telephones, lighted pathways/sidewalks, controlled access to dorms/residences, and crime prevention programs offered throughout the year to both students and faculty/staff.

REQUIREMENTS: For students with a GPA of 2.9 or above, a minimum SAT or ACT score may be required. For students whose GPA is below 2.9, a minimum SAT or ACT score is applied according to a scale established by WSU. Applicants must graduate from an accredited secondary school. They should have completed 4 years of English, 3 of math, 2 each of a foreign language, a lab science, and social studies, including 1 year of U.S. history and government, and 2 electives. The College Board Student Descriptive questionnaire must be submitted. AP and CLEP credits are accepted. Candidates for a baccalaureate degree must complete 120 semester-hour credits with a 2.0 GPA and a minimum of 2.0 GPA or higher in the departmental and ancillary courses of the major field of concentration. To receive a baccalaureate degree from WSU, a student must complete 30 of the last 40 credits at WSU, earn a majority of credits in the major at Worcester State University and earn a majority of credits in the minor (if elected) at the university. **Procedure:** Freshmen are admitted fall, spring, and summer. Entrance exams should be taken in spring of the junior year or fall of the senior year. There is a rolling admissions plan. Applications should be filed by May 1 for fall entry, along with a $50 fee. Notifications are sent in rolling. Applications are accepted on-line. **Transfer Students:** 522 transfer students enrolled in 2015-2016. Transfer applicants must have earned a minimum of 12 college credits with a minimum 2.5 GPA or 13 to 23 credits with a minimum 2.0 GPA. Students with fewer than 24 transfer credits may be admitted under the same criteria as first-time freshmen. 30 of 120 credits required for the bachelor's degree must be completed at WSU. **International Students:** There are 36 international students enrolled. They must take the TOEFL with a minimum score of 79 on the Internet-based version (iBT). They must also take the SAT.

ADMISSIONS: The SAT scores for the 2016-2017 freshman class were: Critical Reading-- 50% below 500, 39% between 500 and 599, 11% between 600 and 699, and 1% between 700 and 800. Math-- 44% below 500, 44% between 500 and 599, 11% between 600 and 699, and 1% between 700 and 800. The ACT scores were 5% between 12 and 17, 48% between 18 and 23, 43% between 24 and 29, and 3% above 30. **Admissions Contact:** Joseph DiCarlo, Director of Admissions. Email: *admissions@worcester.edu* Web: *www.worcester.edu*

FINANCIAL AID: WSU is a member of CSS. The college's own financial statement is required. The FAFSA code is 002190. The priority date for freshman financial aid applications for fall entry is March 1.

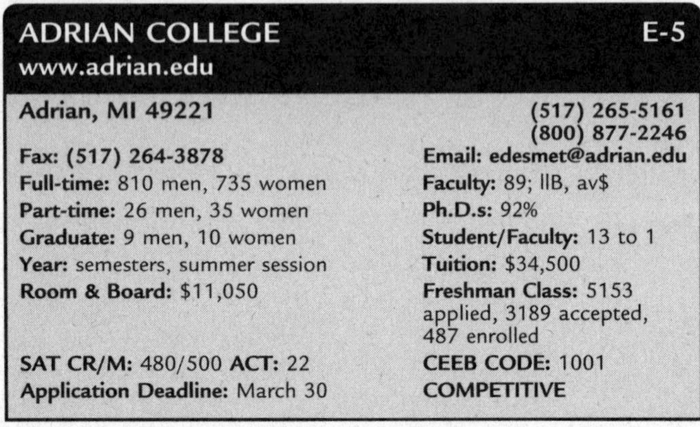

ADRIAN COLLEGE E-5

www.adrian.edu

Adrian, MI 49221

(517) 265-5161
(800) 877-2246

Fax: (517) 264-3878
Email: edesmet@adrian.edu

Full-time: 810 men, 735 women
Part-time: 26 men, 35 women
Graduate: 9 men, 10 women
Year: semesters, summer session
Room & Board: $11,050

Faculty: 89; IIB, av$
Ph.D.s: 92%
Student/Faculty: 13 to 1
Tuition: $34,500
Freshman Class: 5153 applied, 3189 accepted, 487 enrolled

SAT CR/M: 480/500 **ACT:** 22
Application Deadline: March 30

CEEB CODE: 1001
COMPETITIVE

Adrian College, founded in 1859, is a private liberal arts institution affiliated with the United Methodist Church. There is 1 undergraduate school and 4 graduate schools. In addition to regional accreditation, Adrian has baccalaureate program accreditation with CSWE, CAEP, and CAATE. The 132-acre campus is in a small town 35 miles southwest of Ann Arbor. Including any residence halls, there are 41 buildings.

STUDENT LIFE: 75% of undergraduates are from Michigan. 9% are African American; 80% White; 5% race unknown; 4% two or more races; 3% Foreign; 2% Hispanic; 1% Asian American. 48% claim no religious affiliation; 23% Protestant; 18% Catholic. **Male To Female Ratio:** 1.1:1. 46% remain to graduate. **Housing:** 1600 students can be accommodated in college housing, which includes dorms, on-campus apartments, and off-campus apartments. In addition, there are honors houses, special-interest houses, fraternity houses, substance-free, smoke-free, extended quiet hours, upperclassmen only residence halls, and theme housing. On-campus housing is guaranteed for all 4 years. All students may keep cars.

FACULTY/CLASSROOMS: 52% of faculty are male; 48% are female. All teach undergraduates. No introductory courses are taught by graduate students. The average class size in an introductory lecture is 19; in a laboratory is 15; and in a regular course is 12.

PROGRAMS OF STUDY: Adrian confers B.A., B.S., B.B.A., B.F.A., B.M., B.M.E. and B.S.W. degrees. Associate and master's degrees are also awarded. Bachelor's degrees are awarded in AGRICULTURE (environmental studies), BIOLOGICAL SCIENCE (biology/biological science), BUSINESS (accounting, business administration and management, international business management, marketing management, and sports management), COMMUNICATIONS AND THE ARTS (arts administration/management, communications, dramatic arts, English, French, German, journalism, literature, music, music performance, musical theater, Spanish, and studio art), COMPUTER AND PHYSICAL SCIENCE (chemistry, earth science, mathematics, and physics), EDUCATION (elementary education, physical education, and secondary education), ENGINEERING AND ENVIRONMENTAL DESIGN (environmental science and interior design), HEALTH PROFESSIONS (exercise science), SOCIAL SCIENCE (criminal justice, economics, history, international studies, Japanese studies, philosophy, political science/government, psychology, religion, social work, and sociology). Accounting & business administration, and exercise science have the largest enrollments.

ACTIVITIES: 18% of men belong to 4 national fraternities; 19% of women belong to 3 national sororities. There are 79 groups on campus, including art, band, cheerleading, choir, chorale, chorus, computers, dance, drama, environmental, ethnic, feminist empowerment movement, honors, international, jazz band, LGBT, literary magazine, marching band, musical theater, newspaper, orchestra, pep band, photography, political, professional, radio and TV, religious, social, social service, student government, symphony, and yearbook. Popular campus events include Family Weekend, International Week, Dance Marathon, One-Act Plays, Sadie Hawkins Dance, and Sibs 'n' Kids Weekend. **Sports:** There are 13 intercollegiate sports for men and 18 for women, and 6 intramural sports for men and 6 for women. Facilities include a sport and fitness center featuring a multipurpose forum with courts for basketball, volleyball, and tennis, indoor track, racquetball courts, a weight room, a performance gym, football stadium, baseball and softball fields, soccer fields, tennis courts, a 400-meter track, and numerous intramural fields. **Graduates:** From July 1, 2016 to June 30, 2017, 314 bachelor's degrees were awarded. The most popular majors were business and accounting (22%), exercise science and athletic training (11%), and biology (10%). In an average class, 54% graduate in 6 years or less. Of the 2016 graduating class, 20% were enrolled in graduate school within 6 months of graduation, and 22% were employed.

SERVICES: Counseling and information services are available, as is tutoring in most subjects. There is a reader service for the blind, and remedial math, reading, and writing. **Library/Resources:** The library contains 163,727 volumes, 51,188 microform items, and 4,032 audio/video tapes/CDs/DVDs, and subscribes to 10,373 periodicals including electronic. Computerized library services include interlibrary loans, database searching, Internet access, and Wi-Fi capability. Special learning facilities include an art gallery, planetarium, radio station, a solar greenhouse, palatinate lab, and an observatory. **Physically Challenged Students:** Facilities include wheelchair ramps, elevators, special parking, specially equipped restrooms, lowered drinking fountains, lowered telephones, and special housing. There are also diagnostic testing, learning services, note-taking services, oral testing, extended time, priority seating, readers, tape recording, texts on tape, tutors, student and psychological support groups. **Special:** Adrian offers preprofessional programs in architecture, engineering, health sciences, law, ministry, medical technology, and art therapy. Study abroad in 16 countries and a Washington Semester. There are also student-designed majors and internships in more than 450 locations, and a 3-2 engineering degree with Washington University in St. Louis and the University of Detroit Mercy. There are 15 national honor societies and a freshman honors program. **Visiting:** There are regularly scheduled orientations for prospective students, including a student-guided campus tour and visits with an admissions counselor, professors from the student's area of interest, and an athletics coach. There are guides for informal visits, visitors may sit in on classes, and stay overnight. To schedule a visit, contact the Office of Admissions at visitac@adrian.edu. **Campus Safety and Security:** Measures include 24-hour foot and vehicle patrol, self-defense education, and security escort services. There are emergency telephones and lighted pathways/sidewalks.

REQUIREMENTS: The SAT or ACT is required. Applicants must be graduates of an accredited secondary school. The GED is accepted. Each student is reviewed individually based on GPA and test scores. Adrian requires applicants to be in the upper 50% of their class. AP and CLEP credits are accepted. Important factors in the admissions decision are advanced placement or honors courses, leadership record, and extracurricular activities record. To graduate, students must maintain a 2.0 GPA average over 124 credit hours, 30 of which must be in upper-division courses. 22 hours of distribution requirements and 21 of basic educational proficiency are required, including 2 semesters of foreign language and 1 each of communication, English, fine arts, fitness, humanities, math, natural or physical science, religion or philosophy, and social science. **Procedure:** Freshmen are admitted fall and spring. Entrance exams should be taken during the spring of the junior year or fall of the senior year. There are deferred admissions and rolling admissions plans. Application deadlines are open. Applications are accepted on-line. **Transfer Students:** 65 transfer students enrolled in 2016-2017. Applicants must have an above-average GPA and provide final high school transcripts. If the student has completed fewer than 24 semester hours, ACT or SAT test scores are also required. Grades of 2.0 and above transfer for credit. The college admits transfer students every semester. 34 of 124 credits required for the bachelor's degree must be completed at Adrian. **International Students:** There are 69 international students enrolled. They must take the TOEFL with a minimum score of 500 on the paper-based TOEFL (PBT) or 73 on the Internet-based version (iBT). They must also take the SAT or ACT.

ADMISSIONS: 62% of the 2017-2018 applicants were accepted. The SAT scores for the 2017-2018 freshman class were: Critical Reading-- 55% below 500 and 45% between 500 and 599. Math-- 41% below 500, 52% between 500 and 599, and 7% between 600 and 699. The ACT scores were 38% below 12, 34% between 12 and 17, 16% between 18 and 23, 6% between 24 and 29, and 6% above 30. 11 freshmen graduated first in their class. **Admissions Contact:** Erin DeSmet, Executive Director of Enrollment & Marketing. Email: *edesmet@adrian.edu* Web: *www.adrian.edu*

FINANCIAL AID: In 2017-2018, 99% of all full-time freshmen received some form of financial aid. 83% of all full-time freshmen received need-based aid. The average freshman award was $33,831. Need-based scholarships or need-based grants averaged $22,666 ($38,806 maximum); need-based self-help aid (loans and jobs) averaged $12,008 ($45,500 maximum); and other non-need-based awards and non-need-based scholarships averaged $15,472 ($31,870 maximum). 39% of undergraduate students work part-time. The average financial indebtedness of the 2017 graduate was $41,000. Adrian is a member of CSS. The FAFSA code is 002234. The priority date for freshman financial aid applications for fall entry is March 1.

ALBION COLLEGE D-5

www.albion.edu

Albion, MI 49224	**(517) 629-0321** **(800) 858-6770**
Fax: (517) 629-0569	**Email: admission@albion.edu**
Full-time: 737 men, 817 women	**Faculty:** 110; IIB, av$
Part-time: 6 men, 8 women	**Ph.D.s:** 78%
Graduate: n/av	**Student/Faculty:** 14 to 1
Year: semesters, summer session	**Tuition:** $43,050
Room & Board: $12,210	**Freshman Class:** 3884 applied, 2742 accepted, 515 enrolled
SAT CR/M: 557/542 **ACT:** 23	**CEEB CODE:** 1007
Application Deadline: open	**COMPETITIVE**

Albion College, established in 1835, is a nationally-ranked private institution affiliated with the United Methodist Church offering undergraduate degrees in liberal arts curricula. There is 1 undergraduate school. In addition to regional accreditation, Albion has baccalaureate program accreditation with NASM, ACS, and CAATE. The 574-acre campus is in a small town in south central Michigan, 65 miles from Detroit. Including any residence halls, there are 94 buildings.

STUDENT LIFE: 77% of undergraduates are from Michigan. Others are from 28 states, 18 foreign countries, and Canada. 9% are Hispanic; 65% White; 5% race unknown; 3% Asian American; 3% two or more races; 2% Foreign; 13% African American. 87% claim no religious affiliation. **Female To Male Ratio:** 1.1:1. The average age of freshmen is 18; all undergraduates, 19. 21% do not continue beyond their first year; 57% remain to graduate. **Housing:** 1681 students can be accommodated in college housing, which includes married student dorms and on-campus apartments. In addition, there are fraternity houses. On-campus housing is guaranteed for all 4 years. 95% of students live on campus. All students may keep cars.

FACULTY/CLASSROOMS: 53% of faculty are male; 47% are female. All teach undergraduates, 97% do research, and 97% do both. No introductory courses are taught by graduate students. The average class size in an introductory lecture is 22; in a laboratory is 15; and in a regular course is 20.

PROGRAMS OF STUDY: Albion confers B.A. and B.F.A. degrees. Bachelor's degrees are awarded in AGRICULTURE (environmental studies and forestry and related sciences), BIOLOGICAL SCIENCE (biochemistry and biology/biological science), BUSINESS (accounting, business administration and management, and finance), COMMUNICATIONS AND THE ARTS (art, art history and appreciation, communication studies, creative writing, English, French, German, music, music performance, Spanish, theatre arts, and visual and performing arts), COMPUTER AND PHYSICAL SCIENCE (actuarial mathematics, astronomy and physics, chemistry, earth science, geology, mathematics, and physics), EDUCATION (English education and music education), ENGINEERING AND ENVIRONMENTAL DESIGN (engineering, engineering physics, and environmental science), HEALTH PROFESSIONS (exercise science), SOCIAL SCIENCE (anthropology, economics, ethnic studies, gender studies, history, international studies, philosophy, political science/government, psychology, public affairs, religion, sociology, and women's studies). Biology, psychology, and economics & management have the largest enrollments.

ACTIVITIES: 37% of men belong to 6 national fraternities; 30% of women belong to 6 national sororities. There are 110 groups on campus, including art, band, cheerleading, chess, choir, chorale, chorus, computers, dance, drama, environmental, ethnic, film, honors, international, jazz band, LGBT, literary magazine, marching band, musical theater, newspaper, opera, orchestra, pep band, photography, political, professional, radio and TV, religious, social, social service, student government, symphony, and yearbook. Popular campus events include Briton Bash, Day of Woden and The Big Show: National Concert/Comedy Artist Performance. **Sports:** There are 12 intercollegiate sports for men and 12 for women, and 4 intramural sports for men and 4 for women. Facilities include a competition facility for soccer, lacrosse, baseball and softball, aquatic center, a cardiovascular fitness room, individual and group sports activities, physical conditioning, and health and wellness programs, 1/9-mile track, racquetball courts, a weight room, tennis, and Equestrian center, indoor golf practice facility, football field, outdoor track, 4 indoor basketball courts (one for intercollegiate competition), 6 outdoor tennis courts, and 4 indoor tennis courts.**Graduates:** From July 1, 2016 to June 30, 2017, 288 bachelor's degrees were awarded. The most popular majors were economics & management (16%), biology (13%), and psychological sciences (12%). In an average class, 47% graduate in 4 years or less, 55% graduate in 5 years or less, and 57% graduate in 6 years or less. Of the 2016 graduating class, 30% were enrolled in graduate school within 6 months of graduation, and 57% were employed.

SERVICES: Counseling and information services are available, as is tutoring in most subjects. There is a reader service for the blind. The Quantitative Studies Center, and the Writing Center for students are available when needed. **Library/Resources:** The library contains 355,879 volumes, 31,100 microform items, and 9,983 audio/video tapes/CDs/DVDs, and subscribes to 76,782 periodicals including electronic. Computerized library services include interlibrary loans, database searching, Internet access, and Wi-Fi capability. Special learning facilities include an art gallery, planetarium, radio station, a nature center, an equestrian center, and Dow analytical science laboratory. **Physically Challenged Students:** 90% of the campus is accessible. Facilities include wheelchair ramps, elevators, special parking, specially equipped restrooms, special class scheduling, lowered drinking fountains, lowered telephones, and special housing. **Special:** Albion offers study abroad in 40 countries, and study/internship programs in New York City, Philadelphia, Washington, D.C., Oak Ridge, and Chicago. Students may earn a dual engineering degree in conjunction with Columbia University, Michigan Technological University, or the University of Michigan. Student-designed majors and interdisciplinary majors in fields including environmental science, ethnic studies, international studies, and women's and gender studies are available. There are 6 national honor societies, Phi Beta Kappa, a freshman honors program, and 13 departmental honors programs. **Visiting:**

There are regularly scheduled orientations for prospective students, SOAR (Student Orientation, Advising & Registration): consists of 4 programs held in early June and 1 in August for students and parents. There are guides for informal visits, visitors may sit in on classes, and stay overnight. To schedule a visit, contact Martha Bunde at (517) 629-0769. **Campus Safety and Security:** Measures include 24-hour foot and vehicle patrol, emergency notification system, self-defense education, and security escort services. There are shuttle buses, emergency telephones, lighted pathways/sidewalks, and controlled access to dorms/residences.

REQUIREMENTS: The SAT or ACT is required. Applicants must graduate from an accredited secondary school or earn a GED. Completion of 15 Carnegie credits is required. A strong background in English, math, and the lab and social sciences is recommended as the best preparation for academic success. The Admission Committee will consider courses taken, grades earned, the academic rigor of the program and SAT/ACT scores as corroborative evidence. Applications are accepted on-line at the Albion web site and through the Common App. AP and CLEP credits are accepted. Important factors in the admissions decision are advanced placement or honors courses, extracurricular activities record, and personality/intangible qualities. Requirements for graduation are: 32 units (128 semester hours) a minimum of the last 12 units must be taken at Albion College. A minimum of one major, completion of the core, and pass the Writing Competence Exam. Have a minimum of 2.0 cumulative GPA. Submission of an Application for Degree. The CORE Requirement; at Albion, the general education requirement is referred to as "the core." Students begin to fulfill the core in their first semester with Liberal Arts 101; some will be able to complete much of the core requirement by the end of their first year. Liberal Arts 101 (First-Year Seminar, 1 unit), Modes of Inquiry (1 unit in each) - Textual Analysis, Artistic Creation and Analysis, Scientific Analysis, Modeling and Analysis, Historical and Cultural Analysis. Category Requirements (1 unit in each) - Environmental Studies, Ethnicity Studies, Gender Studies, and Global Studies. Distribution Requirement: 1 unit in fine arts (art and art history, music, theatre, honors), 2 units in humanities (English, foreign languages, philosophy, religious studies, honors), 2 units in mathematics or natural sciences (biology, chemistry, computer science, geological sciences, mathematics, physics, honors), 2 units in social science (anthropology and sociology, economics and management, history, political science, psychology, speech communication, honors). **Procedure:** Freshmen are admitted fall and spring. Entrance exams should be taken in April or June of the junior year. There are early admissions, deferred admissions, and rolling admissions plans. Application deadlines are open. Notification is sent on a rolling basis. Applications are accepted on-line. **Transfer Students:** 46 transfer students enrolled in 2016-2017. Transfer applicants must submit official college transcripts. Grades of 2.0 or better are considered for transfer credit. Albion evaluates the applicant's coursework before conferring transfer credit. 48 of 128 credits required for the bachelor's degree must be completed at Albion. **International Students:** There are 30 international students enrolled. They must take the TOEFL with a minimum score of 550 on the paper-based TOEFL (PBT) or 79 on the Internet-based version (iBT). Student must take the IELTS. They must also take the SAT or ACT.

ADMISSIONS: 71% of the 2017-2018 applicants were accepted. The SAT scores for the 2017-2018 freshman class were: Math-- 24% below 500, 53% between 500 and 599, 19% between 600 and 699, and 4% between 700 and 800. Evidence-Based Reading/Writing-- 20% below 500, 50% between 500 and 599, 27% between 600 and 699, and 3% between 700 and 800. The ACT scores were 4% between 12 and 17, 52% between 18 and 23, 37% between 24 and 29, and 7% above 30. **Admissions Contact:** Mandy Dubiel, Director of Admissions. Email: *admission@albion.edu* Web: *www.albion.edu*

FINANCIAL AID: In 2017-2018, 100% of all full-time freshmen received some form of financial aid. 86% of all full-time freshmen received need-based aid. The average freshman award was $44,400. Need-based scholarships or need-based grants averaged $40,200 ($56,750 maximum); and need-based self-help aid (loans and jobs) averaged $4,200 ($6,000 maximum). 54% of undergraduate students work part-time. The average financial indebtedness of the 2017 graduate was $44,140. The FAFSA code is 002235. The priority date for freshman financial aid applications for fall entry is December 1.

ALMA COLLEGE — D-4

www.alma.edu

Alma, MI 48801-1599 — **(989) 463-7139**

Fax: (989) 463-7057 — **Email: admissions@alma.edu**

Full-time: 591 men, 785 women	**Faculty:** 99; IIB, av$
Part-time: 24 men, 26 women	**Ph.D.s:** 83%
Graduate: n/av	**Student/Faculty:** 12 to 1
Year: other	**Tuition:** $38,768
Room & Board: $10,642	**Freshman Class:** 4729 applied, 3043 accepted, 408 enrolled
SAT CR/M: 574/556 **ACT:** 24	**CEEB CODE:** 1010
Application Deadline: open	**VERY COMPETITIVE**

Alma College, a selective, residential college, offers a personalized education with multiple paths and experiences leading to success. Strong academic programs and a deep regard for students as individuals are fundamental to an Alma education, with small classes and many opportunities for one-on-one collaboration with dedicated faculty. In addition to regional accreditation, Alma has baccalaureate program accreditation with NASM, ACS, and CCNE. The 128-acre campus is in a small town Alma, Michigan, about 50 miles north of Lansing. Including any residence halls, there are 29 buildings.

STUDENT LIFE: 90% of undergraduates are from Michigan. Others are from 29 states, 10 foreign countries, and Canada. 8% are race unknown; 77% White; 5% Hispanic; 3% African American; 3% two or more races; 2% Asian American; 2% Foreign. 37% are Protestant; 17% Catholic; 13% claim no religious affiliation. **Female To Male Ratio:** 1.3:1. The average age of freshmen is 18; all undergraduates, 20. 20% do not continue beyond their first year; 67% remain to graduate. **Housing:** 1369 students can be accommodated in college housing, which includes dorms, on-campus apartments, special-interest houses, fraternity houses, sorority houses, and an international house. On-campus housing is guaranteed for all 4 years. 88% of students live on campus. All students may keep cars.

FACULTY/CLASSROOMS: 54% of faculty are male; 46% are female. All teach undergraduates and do research. No introductory courses are taught by graduate students. The average class size in an introductory lecture is 18; in a laboratory is 12; and in a regular course is 17.

PROGRAMS OF STUDY: Alma confers B.A., B.S., B.M., B.S.N. and B.F.A. degrees. Bachelor's degrees are awarded in AGRICULTURE (environmental studies), BIOLOGICAL SCIENCE (biochemistry, biology/biological science, biotechnology, and neurosciences), BUSINESS (accounting, business administration and management, finance, international business management, and marketing), COMMUNICATIONS AND THE ARTS (art, communications, dance, English, French, German, music, Spanish, and theatre arts), COMPUTER AND PHYSICAL SCIENCE (chemistry, computer science, mathematics, and physics), EDUCATION (early childhood education, educational studies, elementary education, secondary education, and special education), HEALTH PROFESSIONS (exercise science, health care administration, health science, and nursing), SOCIAL SCIENCE (anthropology, economics, history, philosophy, political science/government, psychology, religion, and sociology). Media studies, environmental studies, integrative physiology, business administration, and nursing are the strongest academically. Education, business administration, and nursing have the largest enrollments.

ACTIVITIES: 22% of men belong to 2 local and 4 national fraternities; 18% of women belong to 1 local and 4 national sororities. There are 80 groups on campus, including art, bagpipe, band, cheerleading, chess, choir, chorale, chorus, communications, computers, dance, drama, environmental, ethnic, film, honors, international, jazz band, LGBT, literary magazine, marching band, newspaper, orchestra, photography, political, professional, religious, social, social service, student government, symphony, and yearbook. Popular campus events include Homecoming, Songfest, and Honors Day. **Sports:** There are 12 intercollegiate sports for men and 12 for women, and 16 intramural sports for men and 16 for women. Facilities include a recreation center with a climbing wall, a fitness center, suspended 3-lane track, an indoor gym, a pool, an outdoor sports complex with an artificial turf playing field, an 8-lane track, baseball, soccer, softball fields, a weight training room, racquetball and tennis courts. **Graduates:** From July 1, 2016 to June 30, 2017, 318 bachelor's degrees were awarded. The most popular majors were education (14%), nursing (9%), and integrative physiology and health science (8%). In an average class, 1% graduate in 3 years or less, 68% graduate in 4 years or less, 62% graduate in 5 years or less, and 68% graduate in 6 years or less. Of the 2016 graduating class, 26% were enrolled in graduate school within 6 months of graduation, and 63% were employed.

SERVICES: Counseling and information services are available, as is tutoring in every subject. There are individual and group tutoring available. There is also a reader service for the blind. **Library/Resources:** The library contains 245,000 volumes, 247,000 microform items, and 14,520 audio/video tapes/CDs/DVDs, and subscribes to 1,000 periodicals including electronic. Computerized library services include interlibrary loans, database searching, Internet access, and Wi-Fi capability. Special learning facilities include an art gallery, planetarium, Writing lab, Digital Media Commons, Dow Digital Science Center, and Human Performance Laboratory. **Physically Challenged Students:** 75% of the campus is accessible. Facilities include wheelchair ramps, elevators, special parking, specially equipped restrooms, special class scheduling, lowered drinking fountains, 2 residence halls with private baths, and several small housing units. **Special:** Alma offers internships in many fields, study abroad in 18 countries, and an experiential learning program at the Philadelphia Center. There are work-study programs, dual majors, and student-designed majors in a wide variety of subjects. The college confers 3-2 engineering degrees in conjunction with the University of Michigan and Kettering University. Non-degree study may be pursued, and students have a pass/fail grading option. A 4-week spring term provides intensive study in 1 course, often combined with travel. There are 3 national honor societies, Phi Beta Kappa, a freshman honors program, and 19 departmental honors programs. **Visiting:** There are regularly scheduled orientations for prospective students, faculty talks, campus tours, a meal on campus, financial aid information, admissions sessions. There are guides for informal visits, visitors may sit in on classes, and stay overnight. To schedule a visit, contact the Admissions Office at (800) 321-2562. **Campus Safety and Security:** Measures include 24-hour foot and vehicle patrol, emergency notification system, and security escort services. There are emergency telephones, lighted pathways/sidewalks, controlled access to dorms/residences, and ID card access to residence halls.

REQUIREMENTS: Either the SAT or the ACT is required. Applicants must have graduated from an accredited secondary school and have earned 16 Carnegie units, including 4 years of English and 3 each of math, science, and social studies, with 2 of a foreign language recommended. Alma prefers applicants in the upper 25% of their class. Portfolio and audition are required for performing arts scholarships. AP credits are accepted. Important factors in the admissions decision are advanced placement or honors courses, leadership record, and recommendations by school officials. Degree requirements include completion of a minimum of 136 credit hours; 148 hours are required for the B.F.A. degree, 136 to 156 for the B.M. degree. Students must attain a minimum GPA of 2.0, or 3.0 for fine arts majors. All students must demonstrate proficiency in English, second language/international awareness, communication, and computation, and they must complete distribution requirements, which include 12 fine arts and humanities credits and 12 each of social science and natural science credits. The total number of program credits is 36 for a departmental major, 56 for an interdepartmental major, and 56 to 68 for self-directed majors. **Procedure:** Freshmen are admitted fall and winter. Entrance exams should be taken in the spring of the junior year or as late as the winter of the senior year. There are deferred admissions and rolling admissions plans. Application deadlines are open. The fall 2017 application fee was $25. Notification is sent on a rolling basis. Applications are accepted on-line. **Transfer Students:** 43 transfer students enrolled in 2016-2017. Students wishing to transfer to Alma must have a minimum GPA of 2.0 from other colleges attended. 34 of 136 credits required for the bachelor's degree must be completed at Alma. **International Students:** There are 26 international students enrolled. They must take the TOEFL with a minimum score of 550 on the paper-based TOEFL (PBT) or 79 on the Internet-based version (iBT). The SAT or ACT is required if the TOEFL is not submitted.

ADMISSIONS: 64% of the 2017-2018 applicants were accepted. The SAT scores for the 2017-2018 freshman class were: Math-- 17% below 500, 55% between 500 and 599, 26% between 600 and 699, and 2% between 700 and 800. Evidence-Based Reading/Writing-- 14% below 500, 47% between 500 and 599, 33% between 600 and 699, and 6% between 700 and 800. The ACT scores were 2% between 12 and 17, 54% between 18 and 23, 37% between 24 and 29, and 7% above 30. 46% of the current freshmen were in the top fifth of their class; 69% were in the top two fifths. **Admissions Contact:** Craig Aimar, Director of Admissions. Email: *admissions@alma.edu* Web: *www.alma.edu*

FINANCIAL AID: In 2017-2018, 99% of all full-time freshmen received some form of financial aid. 92% of all full-time freshmen received need-based aid. The average freshman award was $24,698. Need-based scholarships or need-based grants averaged $27,547. 33% of undergraduate students work part-time. The FAFSA code is 002236. The priority date for freshman financial aid applications for fall entry is March 1.

ANDREWS UNIVERSITY C-5

www.andrews.edu

Berrien Springs, MI 49104 (616) 471-6343 (800) 253-2874

Fax: (616) 471-3228 **Email:** undergraduate@andrews.edu

Full-time: 783 men, 931 women	**Faculty:** 148
Part-time: 107 men, 143 women	**Ph.D.s:** 72%
Graduate: 1097 men, 528 women	**Student/Faculty:** 12 to 1
Year: semesters, summer session	**Tuition:** $34,872
Room & Board: $6860	**Freshman Class:** 1809 applied, 879 accepted, 377 enrolled
SAT: required **ACT:** 23	**CEEB CODE:** 1030
Application Deadline: open	**COMPETITIVE**

Andrews University, established in 1874, is a private institution affiliated with the Seventh-day Adventist Church that offers undergraduate degrees in business, education, arts and sciences, architecture, and technology. There are 5 undergraduate schools and 6 graduate schools. In addition to regional accreditation, Andrews has baccalaureate program accreditation with AACSB, ABET, ADA, AHEA, APTA, CAHEA, CSWE, NAAB, NASM, NLN, and IACBE. The 1600-acre campus is in a rural area 10 miles south of Benton Harbor. Including any residence halls, there are 51 buildings.

STUDENT LIFE: 56% of undergraduates are from out of state, mostly the Middle Atlantic. Students are from 46 states, 51 foreign countries, and Canada. 23% are from public schools. 42% are White; 25% African American; 12% Foreign; 10% Asian American; 10% Hispanic; 1% American Indian/Alaska Native. 89% are Protestant; 12% Unknown denominations. **Male To Female Ratio:** 1.2:1. The average age of freshmen is 18; all undergraduates, 22. 21% do not continue beyond their first year; 58% remain to graduate. **Housing:** 1500 students can be accommodated in college housing, which includes married student dorms and on-campus apartments. On-campus housing is available on a first-come and first-served basis. 54% of students live on campus. Alcohol is not permitted. All students may keep cars.

FACULTY/CLASSROOMS: 64% of faculty are male; 36% are female. No introductory courses are taught by graduate students. The average class size in a laboratory is 16 and in a regular course is 18.

PROGRAMS OF STUDY: Andrews confers B.A., B.S., B.B.A., B.F.A., B.Mus., B.S.D., B.S.Educ., B.S.El.Ed., B.S.Eng., B.S.W. and B.T. degrees. Associate, master's, and doctoral degrees are also awarded. Bachelor's degrees are awarded in AGRICULTURE (agriculture, animal science, and horticulture), BIOLOGICAL SCIENCE (anatomy, biochemistry, biology/biological science, biophysics, botany, molecular biology, nutrition, and zoology), BUSINESS (accounting, banking and finance, business administration and management, business economics, management information systems, and marketing/retailing/merchandising), COMMUNICATIONS AND THE ARTS (art, ceramic art and design, communications, creative writing, design, English, French, graphic design, journalism, literature, music, music performance, painting, photography, public relations, Spanish, and visual and performing arts), COMPUTER AND PHYSICAL SCIENCE (applied mathematics, chemistry, computer science, information sciences and systems, mathematics, and physics), EDUCATION (art education, elementary education, English education, mathematics education, music education, science education, secondary education, social studies education, and teaching English as a second/foreign language (TESOL/TEFOL), ENGINEERING AND ENVIRONMENTAL DESIGN (aeronautical technology, aircraft mechanics, architecture, aviation administration/management, aviation computer technology, biomedical equipment technology, computer graphics, computer technology, electrical/electronics engineering, engineering, environmental science, graphic arts technology, and landscape architecture/design), HEALTH PROFESSIONS (allied health, art therapy, biomedical science, medical laboratory technology, nursing, preveterinary science, public health, and speech pathology/audiology), SOCIAL SCIENCE (anthropology, behavioral science, crosscultural studies, dietetics, economics, family/consumer studies, history, human development, interdisciplinary studies, pastoral studies, political science/government, psychology, religion, religious education, social studies, social work, sociology, theological studies, and youth ministry). Health sciences, business, and architecture have the largest enrollments.

ACTIVITIES: There are 30 groups on campus, including band, choir, chorale, chorus, computers, drama, ethnic, honors, international, newspaper, professional, religious, social, social service, and student government. Popular campus events include Alumni Weekend, and International Food Fair. **Sports:** There are 6 intramural sports for men and 4 for women. Facilities include a gym, pool, and racquetball courts. **Graduates:** From July 1, 2016 to June 30, 2017, 341 bachelor's degrees were awarded. The most popular majors were health professions (20%), business (10%), and biology/life science (8%). In an average class, 34% graduate in 4 years or less, 51% graduate in 5 years or less, and 58% graduate in 6 years or less.

SERVICES: Counseling and information services are available, as is tutoring in most subjects. There are math, writing, and reading. There are also learning, and assessment centers. **Library/Resources:** The library contains 747,764 volumes, 83,520 microform items, and 48,447 audio/video tapes/CDs/DVDs, and subscribes to 2,874 periodicals including electronic. Computerized library services include interlibrary loans, database searching, and Internet access. Special learning facilities include an art gallery, natural history museum, an archeological museum. **Physically Challenged Students:** 50% of the campus is accessible. Facilities include wheelchair ramps, elevators, special parking, specially equipped restrooms, special class scheduling, lowered drinking fountains, lowered telephones, and special housing. A special committee handles needs as they arise. **Special:** Students may pursue a second major in business administration. Study abroad, student-designed majors, nondegree study, and pass/fail options are available. There is a freshman honors program. **Visiting:** There are regularly scheduled orientations for prospective students, consisting of tours, meetings with faculty, and social activities. There are guides for informal visits, visitors may sit in on classes, and stay overnight. To schedule a visit, contact the Admissions Office. **Campus Safety and Security:** Measures include 24-hour foot and vehicle patrol and security escort services. There are lighted pathways/sidewalks, and CPR training.

REQUIREMENTS: The SAT or ACT is required. Candidates for admission must graduate from an accredited secondary school or earn a GED. 10 Carnegie units are required, and students must have completed 4 courses in English and 2 courses each in history, math, and science. Interviews are recommended for all applicants. A GPA of 2.3 is required. CLEP credits are accepted. Important factors in the admissions decision are advanced placement or honors courses, recommendations by school officials, and evidence of special talent. Students must complete a minimum of 124 semester credits. Specific course requirements include religion, English, behavioral sciences, fine arts, and phys ed. **Procedure:** Freshmen are admitted fall, spring, and summer. Entrance exams should be taken as early as possible. There are deferred admissions and rolling admissions plans. Application deadlines are open. The fall 2017 application fee was $30. **Transfer Students:** 131 transfer students enrolled in 2016-2017. Transfer applicants must submit a high school transcript and transcripts from all colleges attended. A maximum of 70 semester credits from a 2-year school or 90 semester credits from a 4-year school may be transferred toward a bachelor's degree. Credits should be relevant to the student's major at Andrews University. The minimum GPA is 2.25, and the ACT is preferred. Students must meet freshman entrance requirements if they are transferring with less than sophomore standing from an accredited college. 30 of 124 credits required for the bachelor's degree must be completed at Andrews. **International Students:** There are 230 international students enrolled. They must take the TOEFL with a minimum score of 550 on the paper-based TOEFL (PBT). They must also take the SAT or ACT.

ADMISSIONS: 49% of the 2017-2018 applicants were accepted. The ACT scores were 34% below 12, 26% between 12 and 17, 21% between 18 and 23, 11% between 24 and 29, and 8% above 30. 32% of the current freshmen were in the top fifth of their class; 55% were in the top two fifths. **Admissions Contact:** Shanna Leak, Undergraduate Admissions Supervisor. Email: *undergraduate@andrews.edu* Web: *www.andrews.edu*

FINANCIAL AID: The FAFSA code is 002238. The priority date for freshman financial aid applications for fall entry is open.

AQUINAS COLLEGE - MICHIGAN — D-4

www.aquinas.edu

Grand Rapids, MI 49506 — (616) 632-2860, (800) 678-9593

Fax: (616) 732-4469 — **Email:** admissions@aquinas.edu

Full-time: 515 men, 802 women	**Faculty:** 86; IIA
Part-time: 97 men, 137 women	**Ph.D.s:** 80%
Graduate: 32 men, 130 women	**Student/Faculty:** 11 to 1
Year: semesters, summer session	**Tuition:** $31,244
Room & Board: $9070	**Freshman Class:** n/av
ACT: required	**CEEB CODE:** 5750
Application Deadline: open	**VERY COMPETITIVE**

Aquinas College-Michigan was established in 1866, is a private liberal arts institution affiliated with the Roman Catholic Church and offers undergraduate and graduate degrees through day and evening programs. There is 1 undergraduate school and 3 graduate schools. In addition to regional accreditation, ACM has baccalaureate program accreditation with CAEP and CAATE. The 117-acre campus is in a suburban area east of downtown Grand Rapids, MI. Including any residence halls, there are 35 buildings.

STUDENT LIFE: 94% of undergraduates are from Michigan. Others are from 26 states, 21 foreign countries, and Canada. 8% are race unknown; 76% White; 7% Hispanic; 4% African American; 2% Foreign; 2% two or more races; 1% Asian American. 47% are Catholic; 28% Unknown Non-denominational; 21% Protestant. **Female To Male Ratio:** 1.7:1. The average age of freshmen is 18; all undergraduates, 21. 23% do not continue beyond their first year; 52% remain to graduate. **Housing:** 909 students can be accommodated in college housing, which includes dorms, on-campus apartments, special-interest houses, and service learning houses. On-campus housing is available on a first-come, first-served basis, and is available on a lottery system for upperclassmen. 50% of students commute. All students may keep cars.

FACULTY/CLASSROOMS: 54% of faculty are male; 46% are female. All teach undergraduates. No introductory courses are taught by graduate students. The average class size in an introductory lecture is 20; in a laboratory is 20; and in a regular course is 16.

PROGRAMS OF STUDY: ACM confers A.A., A.S., B.A., B.S., B.F.A, B.M., B.M.Ed., B.P.A, B.S.B.A., B.S.S.B., M.A.C., M.A.T., M.Ed., and M.M. degrees. Associate and master's degrees are also awarded. Bachelor's degrees are awarded in AGRICULTURE (environmental studies), BIOLOGICAL SCIENCE (biology/biological science and environmental biology), BUSINESS (accounting, business administration and management, business administration - international, business administration marketing, business communications, business economics, human resources, information & communication technology, international business management, management information systems, marketing and distribution, marketing management, nonprofit/public organization management, recreation and leisure services, recreational facilities management, and sports management), COMMUNICATIONS AND THE ARTS (art history, art, art history and appreciation, arts administration/management, ceramic art and design, communications, drawing, English, English literature, English writing, fine arts, French, German, jazz, journalism, keyboard - piano concentration, language arts, literature, modern language, music, music business management, music history and appreciation, music performance, music theory and composition, musical theater, painting, performing arts, photography, piano performance, printmaking, sculpture, Spanish, theatre arts, theatre production, theatre studies, theater management, visual and performing arts, vocal performance, voice, vocal music education, and writing), COMPUTER AND PHYSICAL SCIENCE (chemistry, information sciences and systems, mathematics, mathematics/computational, mathematics/theoretical, and physical chemistry), EDUCATION (athletic training, early childhood education, education, education of the multiply handicapped, education of the physically handicapped, elementary education, English education, general studies, global studies, health education, health and education science, health and physical education, mathematics education, music education, physical education, physical science secondary school education, science education, secondary education, social science education, social studies education, social studies secondary school education, Spanish education K-12, special education, specific learning disabilities, sports and wellness studies, and teaching English as a second/foreign language (TESOL/TEFOL), ENGINEERING

AND ENVIRONMENTAL DESIGN (environmental science and preengineering), HEALTH PROFESSIONS (health, health and physical activity, kinesiology, pre-health studies, predentistry, premedicine, and sports medicine), SOCIAL SCIENCE (community services, economics, French studies, geography, history, human services, interdisciplinary studies, international relations, international studies, Japanese studies, liberal arts/general studies, liberal arts, sciences, general studies, humanities, philosophy, political science/government, prelaw, psychology, public administration, religion, religious studies, religious music, social science, social studies, sociology, theology, theological studies, women & gender studies, and women's studies). Accounting, communication, and prehealth sciences are the strongest academically. Business administration, biology, and psychology have the largest enrollments.

ACTIVITIES: There are no fraternities or sororities. There are 40 groups on campus, including art, band, cheerleading, choir, chorale, chorus, computers, dance, drama, environmental, ethnic, honors, international, Irish dance club, jazz band, LGBT, literary magazine, musical theater, newspaper, pep band, photography, political, professional, radio and TV, religious, social, social service, and student government. Popular campus events include Spring Fling, Moose Cafe, Refresh Yourself, and AQ Idol. **Sports:** There are 11 intercollegiate sports for men and 13 for women, and 4 intramural sports for men and 4 for women. Facilities include a health and fitness center with volleyball and basketball competition courts, classrooms, athletic training, artificial turf soccer, lacrosse field, and indoor track. **Graduates:** From July 1, 2016 to June 30, 2017, 356 bachelor's degrees were awarded. The most popular majors were business administration (10%), biology (10%), and psychology (6%). In an average class, 34% graduate in 4 years or less, 51% graduate in 5 years or less, and 52% graduate in 6 years or less. Of the 2016 graduating class, 11% were enrolled in graduate school within 6 months of graduation, and 79% were employed.

SERVICES: Counseling and information services are available, as is tutoring in most subjects. There is a reader service for the blind, and remedial math, reading, and writing. **Library/Resources:** The library contains 283,187 volumes, 36,972 microform items, and 4,773 audio/video tapes/CDs/DVDs, and subscribes to 234 periodicals including electronic. Computerized library services include interlibrary loans, database searching, Internet access, and Wi-Fi capability. Special learning facilities include an art gallery, radio station, a theatre, greenhouse, observatory, and nature trails. **Physically Challenged Students:** 95% of the campus is accessible. Facilities include wheelchair ramps, elevators, special parking, specially equipped restrooms, special class scheduling, lowered drinking fountains, lowered telephones, and special housing. **Special:** Students may cross-register with the Dominican Consortium and may study abroad in Ireland, Germany, France, Spain, Costa Rica, Italy, or Japan. Co-op programs and internships are available in all majors, and work-study programs are also available. Students may pursue dual majors in business administration and accounting, sports management, communication arts, or art, and B.A.-B.S. degrees in business, geography, or psychology. Student-designed majors can be arranged. ACM offers a general studies degree and may confer credit for life, military experience. A pass/fail grading option is available. Preengineering, prehealth, and teacher certification programs are all available in conjunction with majors offered at ACM. There are 5 national honor societies, a freshman honors program, and 5 departmental honors programs. **Visiting:** There are regularly scheduled orientations for prospective students, consisting of a tour of the campus and presentations by financial aid personnel, program directors, coaches, and faculty. There are guides for informal visits, visitors may sit in on classes, and stay overnight. To schedule a visit, contact the Admissions Office. **Campus Safety and Security:** Measures include 24-hour foot and vehicle patrol, emergency notification system, self-defense education, and security escort services. There are emergency telephones, lighted pathways/sidewalks, and controlled access to dorms/residences.

REQUIREMENTS: The ACT is required. Candidates for admission must graduate from an accredited secondary school. Students must have completed 15 Carnegie units including 4 years of English and social studies, 3 to 4 years each of math and science. A GPA of 2.5 is required. AP and CLEP credits are accepted. Important factors in the admissions decision are advanced placement or honors courses, leadership record, and extracurricular activities record. To graduate, students must complete 120 semester hours, with 30 to 48 in the major, and maintain a minimum GPA of 2.0. The general education program consists of a core of 18 to 30 hours, which includes, from the first to the fourth year, foreign language, a yearlong integrated skills course, and courses in the humanities, religion, and global perspectives; and distribution requirements of 30 to 33 hours, which include courses in cultural diversity, mythology and spirituality, natural sciences, the fine arts, and quantitative reasoning and technology. **Procedure:** Freshmen are admitted fall and winter. Entrance exams should be taken during the spring of the junior year. There is a rolling admissions plan. Application deadlines are open. Applications are accepted on-line. **Transfer Students:** 59 transfer students enrolled in 2016-2017. Transfer applicants must have earned at least 12 credits in academic course work from an accredited junior or 4-year college with a minimum GPA of 2.0. Interviews are recommended. 30 of 124 credits required for the bachelor's degree must be completed at ACM. **International Students:** There are 39 international students enrolled. They must take the TOEFL with a minimum score of 550 on the paper-based TOEFL (PBT). They must also take the ACT.

ADMISSIONS: The ACT scores were 2% between 12 and 17, 45% between 18 and 23, 47% between 24 and 29, and 7% above 30. **Admissions Contact:** Angela Schlosser Bacon, Director of Admissions. Email: *admissions@aquinas.edu* Web: *www.aquinas.edu*

FINANCIAL AID: In 2017-2018, 100% of all full-time freshmen received some form of financial aid. 83% of all full-time freshmen received need-based aid. The average freshman award was $23,572. Need-based scholarships or need-based grants averaged $21,588; need-based self-help aid (loans and jobs) averaged $1,984; non-need-based athletic scholarships averaged $2,906; and other non-need-based awards and non-need-based scholarships averaged $16,026. 35% of undergraduate students work part-time. The average financial indebtedness of the 2017 graduate was $32,047. The FAFSA code is 002239. The priority date for freshman financial aid applications for fall entry is March 1.

BAKER COLLEGE OF FLINT *(The complete profile is made available exclusively on our website, www.barronspac.com)*

CALVIN COLLEGE — D-4
www.calvin.edu

Grand Rapids, MI 49546	**(616) 526-6106** **(800) 688-0122**
Fax: (616) 526-6777	**Email: admissions@calvin.edu**
Full-time: 1599 men, 1925 women	**Faculty:** 246; IIA, +$
Part-time: 141 men, 81 women	**Ph.D.s:** 90%
Graduate: n/av	**Student/Faculty:** 13 to 1
Year: 4-1-4, summer session	**Tuition:** $33,100
Room & Board: $9990	**Freshman Class:** 3221 applied, 2689 accepted, 889 enrolled
SAT EBR-W/M: 627/609 **ACT:** 27	**CEEB CODE:** 1095
Application Deadline: August 15	**HIGHLY COMPETITIVE**

Calvin College, established in 1876, is a private institution affiliated with the Christian Reformed Church, offering undergraduate and graduate degrees in liberal arts and in some professional programs. Calvin is perhaps best known for the integration of learning and Christian faith. In every aspect of college life teaching and learning, athletics and the arts, campus life and community activities Calvin offers an outstanding education of the mind and heart. There is 1 undergraduate school and 3 graduate schools. In addition to regional accreditation, Calvin has baccalaureate program accreditation with ABET, CSWE, NASM, CAEP, ACS, and CCNE. The 390-acre campus is in a suburban area 7 miles southeast of downtown Grand Rapids. Including any residence halls, there are 40 buildings.

STUDENT LIFE: 58% of undergraduates are from Michigan. Others are from 46 states, 59 foreign countries, and Canada. 49% are from public schools. 71% are White; 5% Asian American; 5% Hispanic; 3% African American; 3% two or more races; 2% race unknown; 12% Foreign. 59% are Protestant. **Female To Male Ratio:** 1.2:1. The average age of freshmen is 18; all undergraduates, 20. 13% do not continue beyond their first year; 72% remain to graduate. **Housing:** 2400 students can be accommodated in college housing, which includes dorms, on-campus apartments, and off-campus apartments. In addition, there are honors houses, language/international houses, and special-interest houses. The college offers residence halls with living learning floors that are focused on outdoor recreation, environmental care, race and ethnicity, and honors living. There are also five off-campus urban houses with a community/

urban focus. On-campus housing is available on a lottery system for upperclassmen. 58% of students live on campus. Alcohol is not permitted. All students may keep cars.

FACULTY/CLASSROOMS: 66% of faculty are male; 34% are female. All teach undergraduates and all do research. No introductory courses are taught by graduate students. The average class size in an introductory lecture is 28; in a laboratory is 20; and in a regular course is 25.

PROGRAMS OF STUDY: Calvin confers B.A., B.S., B.A.S.P.A., B.C.S., B.F.A., B.M.E., B.S.A., B.S.E., B.S.N., B.S.P.A., B.S.R. and B.S.W. degrees. Master's degrees are also awarded. Bachelor's degrees are awarded in AGRICULTURE (environmental studies), BIOLOGICAL SCIENCE (biochemistry and biology/biological science), BUSINESS (accounting, business administration and management, business communications, finance, human resources, management information systems, marketing management, small business management, and sports management), COMMUNICATIONS AND THE ARTS (American literature, art, art and design, art studies, Chinese, communications, creative writing, digital communications, English, English literature, English Writing, film arts, film, television and digital media, fine arts, French, German studies, graphic design, information technology, Japanese, language arts, linguistics, literature, media arts, film and media studies, music, music history and appreciation, music performance, music theory and composition, piano/organ, Spanish, strategic communication, video, voice, vocal music education, and writing), COMPUTER AND PHYSICAL SCIENCE (actuarial science, chemistry, computer programming, computer science, data science, digital arts/technology, earth science, environmental geology, geology, information sciences and systems, mathematics, natural sciences, physics, and statistics), EDUCATION (art education, Asian studies, early childhood education, education, elementary education, English secondary education, English education, mathematics education, music education, physical education, science education, secondary education, and special education), ENGINEERING AND ENVIRONMENTAL DESIGN (chemical engineering, civil engineering, computer engineering, electrical/electronics engineering, engineering, environmental science, and mechanical engineering), HEALTH PROFESSIONS (biology, exercise science, kinesiology, nursing, occupational therapy, predentistry, premedicine, preoptometry, pre-occupational therapy, prepharmacy, prephysical therapy, preveterinary science, public health, recreation therapy, and speech pathology/audiology), SOCIAL SCIENCE (area studies, Asian/Oriental studies, classical and near eastern civilization, development economics, economics, geography, history, interdisciplinary studies, international relations, international studies, philosophy, political science/government, prelaw, psychology, public administration, religion, religious music, social work, sociology, theology, and theological studies). Nursing, biology, accounting, English and philosophy are the strongest academically. Business, engineering, and education have the largest enrollments.

ACTIVITIES: There are no fraternities or sororities. There are 80 groups on campus, including art, band, chess, choir, chorale, chorus, computers, dance, drama, environmental, ethnic, film, honors, international, jazz band, LGBT, literary magazine, musical theater, newspaper, orchestra, pep band, political, professional, radio and TV, religious, social, social service, student government, symphony, and yearbook. Popular campus events include Festival of Faith and Writing, Festival of Faith and Music, Sem Pond Jump, Rangeela, The January Series, Dance Guild, Cardboard Canoe Contest, and The Rivalry: Calvin vs. Hope. **Sports:** There are 10 intercollegiate sports for men and 10 for women. Facilities include a fitness center, arena, a 40-foot climbing wall, Olympic-size pool, basketball courts, a dance studio, indoor track, indoor tennis courts, a soccer facility, baseball and softball diamonds, an 8K cross-country course, an eight-lane, 400-meter polyurethane track, a weight-training/exercise room, outdoor tennis courts, sand beach volleyball courts, and ice skating rink. **Graduates:** From July 1, 2016 to June 30, 2017, 889 bachelor's degrees were awarded. The most popular majors were engineering (11%), business (9%), and nursing (7%). In an average class, 1% graduate in 3 years or less, 59% graduate in 4 years or less, 71% graduate in 5 years or less, and 72% graduate in 6 years or less. Of the 2016 graduating class, 27% were enrolled in graduate school within 6 months of graduation, and 73% were employed.

SERVICES: Counseling and information services are available, as is tutoring in most subjects. There is a reader service for the blind, and remedial math, reading, and writing. There is a braille print service for the blind, books on tape, note taking, interpreting, diagnostic testing, special advising, and early registration. **Library/Resources:** The library contains 1.1 million volumes, 598,135 microform items, and 16,520 audio/video tapes/CDs/DVDs, and subscribes to 33,709 periodicals including electronic. Computerized library services include interlibrary loans, database searching, Internet access, and Wi-Fi capability. Special learning facilities include an art gallery, radio station, TV studio, an ecosystem preserve, an interpretive center, an integrated scientific research experimental laboratory, an observatory with a 16-inch telescope, a greenhouse, a human performance lab, two community gardens and an audiology and speech pathology clinic. **Physically Challenged Students:** 95% of the campus is accessible. Facilities include wheelchair ramps, elevators, special parking, specially equipped restrooms, special class scheduling, lowered drinking fountains, lowered telephones, special housing. **Special:** Dual and student-designed majors are available. Students may study off-campus in semester-long programs in China, Hungary, Britain, France, Ghana, Honduras, Peru, Spain and Washington, D.C. In addition, Calvin's January Interim takes students to more than 30 countries. The college also offers cooperative programs in a variety of majors and locations around the world. Calvin also offers a master's degree in speech pathology and audiology (SPAUD), accounting and education. Experiential learning opportunities are a staple at Calvin as well. In the college's most recent Career Outcomes Report, 85% of 2016 grads reported completing at least one internship/practicum while at Calvin. The college also recently launched Calvin LifeWork, an incentivized, four-year, co-curricular program that helps students prepare for life and work after graduation. The voluntary program is comprised of modules, seminars, online videos and mentorship opportunities emphasizing vocation, career readiness, financial literacy and life skills, and leadership development. Students who complete three years of the program are eligible for a $3,000 scholarship during their fourth year at Calvin. There are 6 national honor societies, a freshman honors program, and 26 departmental honors programs. **Visiting:** There are regularly scheduled orientations for prospective students and their families are invited to explore Calvin firsthand by scheduling an individual visit through the admissions. **Campus Safety and Security:** Measures include 24-hour foot and vehicle patrol, emergency notification system, self-defense education, and security escort services. There are emergency telephones, lighted pathways/sidewalks, controlled access to dorms/residences, a crime alert bulletin, and reports in the school newspaper.

REQUIREMENTS: Either the ACT, SAT or CLT are acceptable. In selecting students for admission, Calvin looks for evidence of a student's Christian commitment and his or her capacity and desire to learn. Students who are interested in the Christian perspective and curriculum of Calvin, and who show interest in its aims, are eligible for consideration. Although the prospect of academic success is of primary consideration, the aspirations of the applicant, the recommendation of a high school teacher, and the ability of Calvin to be of service, will also be considered. AP and CLEP credits are accepted. Important factors in the admissions decision are recommendations by school officials, leadership record, and extracurricular activities record. Degree requirements include completion of 124 credit hours, with 28 credits in the major. All students must complete specific course work in English, religion, history, science, math, communication, fine arts, psychology or sociology, economics or political science, philosophy, kinesiology, research and information technology, foreign language and cross-cultural engagement. A minimum GPA of 2.0 is required. **Procedure:** Freshmen are admitted fall and spring. Entrance exams should be taken during the spring of the junior year or fall of the senior year. There are deferred admissions and rolling admissions plans. Applications should be filed by August 15 for fall entry; January 15 for spring entry. The fall 2017 application fee was $35. Applications are accepted on-line. **Transfer Students:** 76 transfer students enrolled in 2016-2017. Applicants from 4-year colleges are required to have a minimum GPA of 2.0; from 2-year colleges, 2.5. The SAT minimum requirements are 510 on the critical reading section and 510 on the math section. A minimum score of 20 is required on the ACT. 32 of 124 credits required for the bachelor's degree must be completed at Calvin. **International Students:** There are 449 international students enrolled. They must take the TOEFL with a minimum score of 550 on the paper-based TOEFL (PBT) or 80 on the Internet-based version (iBT). Students must take the MELAB if they scored low on the TOEFL. They must also take the SAT or ACT, scoring 20. Exceptions are made for strong students without easy access to standardized exams.

ADMISSIONS: 83% of the 2017-2018 applicants were accepted. The SAT scores for the 2017-2018 freshman class were: Math-- 4% below 500, 42% between 500 and 599, 42% between 600 and 699, and 12% between 700 and 800. Evidence-Based Reading/Writing-- 1% below 500, 31% between 500 and 599, 52% between 600 and 699, and 16% between 700 and 800. The ACT scores were 22% between 18 and 23, 47% between

24 and 29, and 31% above 30. 53% of the current freshmen were in the top fifth of their class; 80% were in the top two fifths. 22 freshmen graduated first in their class. **Admissions Contact:** Ben Arendt, Director of Admissions. Email: *admissions@calvin.edu* Web: *www.calvin.edu*

FINANCIAL AID: In 2017-2018, 99% of all full-time freshmen received some form of financial aid. 66% of all full-time freshmen received need-based aid. The average freshman award was $21,860. Need-based scholarships or need-based grants averaged $20,150 ($26,000 maximum); need-based self-help aid (loans and jobs) averaged $5,500 ($5,500 maximum); and other non-need-based awards and non-need-based scholarships averaged $15,400 ($32,000 maximum). 85% of undergraduate students work part-time. The average financial indebtedness of the 2017 graduate was $31,478. Calvin is a member of CSS. The college's own financial statement is required. The FAFSA code is 002241. The priority date for freshman financial aid applications for fall entry is January 15.

CENTRAL MICHIGAN UNIVERSITY D-4

www.cmich.edu

Mount Pleasant, MI 48859	**(989) 774-3076** **(888) 292-5366**
Fax: (989) 774-7267	**Email: cmuadmit@cmich.edu**
Full-time: 8465 men, 10,946 women	**Faculty:** 629; I, --$
Part-time: 1159 men, 1669 women	**Ph.D.s:** 81%
Graduate: 2568 men, 3767 women	**Student/Faculty:** 21 to 1
Year: semesters, summer session	**Tuition:** $11,550 ($23,670)
Room & Board: $8780	**Freshman Class:** 18025 applied, 12565 accepted, 3733 enrolled
ACT: 23	**CEEB CODE:** 1106
Application Deadline: open	**COMPETITIVE**

Central Michigan University, founded in 1892, is a public university offering programs in liberal arts, business, and health, education, and human services. There are 8 undergraduate schools and 1 graduate school. In addition to regional accreditation, CMU has baccalaureate program accreditation with AACSB, ABET, ACEJMC, CSWE, NASAD, NASM, NRPA, and CADE. The 480-acre campus is in a small town 70 miles north of Lansing, MI. Including any residence halls, there are 56 buildings.

STUDENT LIFE: 93% of undergraduates are from Michigan. Others are from 50 states, 71 foreign countries, and Canada. 70% are from public schools. 73% are White; 5% Foreign; 4% race unknown; 3% Hispanic; 2% Asian American; 12% African American; 1% American Indian/Alaska Native. **Female To Male Ratio:** 1.3:1. The average age of freshmen is 19; all undergraduates, 23. 23% do not continue beyond their first year; 60% remain to graduate. **Housing:** 7529 students can be accommodated in college housing, which includes married student dorms and on-campus apartments. In addition, there are honors houses, special interest housing for colleges for business, education, human services, health professions, science and technology, and music. On-campus housing is guaranteed for all 4 years. 67% of students commute. Alcohol is not permitted. All students may keep cars.

FACULTY/CLASSROOMS: 56% of faculty are male; 44% are female. All teach undergraduates. Graduate students teach 2% of introductory courses. The average class size in an introductory lecture is 39 and in a laboratory is 22.

PROGRAMS OF STUDY: CMU confers B.A., B.S., B.A.A., B.F.A., B.Indiv.S., B.Mus., B.S.B.A., B.S.E. and B.S.E.T. degrees. Master's and doctoral degrees are also awarded. Bachelor's degrees are awarded in AGRICULTURE (environmental studies and natural resource management), BIOLOGICAL SCIENCE (biochemistry, biology/biological science, and neurosciences), BUSINESS (accounting, business administration and management, entrepreneurial studies, hospitality management services, human resources, international business management, logistics, management information systems, management science, marketing and distribution, marketing management, marketing/retailing/merchandising, purchasing/inventory management, real estate, recreational facilities management, and retailing), COMMUNICATIONS AND THE ARTS (advertising, apparel design, art, broadcasting, communications, design, dramatic arts, English, French, German, graphic design, journalism, language arts, music, music history and appreciation, music performance, music theory and composition, musical theater, photography, piano/organ, public relations, Spanish, speech/debate/rhetoric, theater design, visual and performing arts, and voice), COMPUTER AND PHYSICAL SCIENCE (actuarial science, chemistry, computer science, earth science, geology, information sciences and systems, mathematics, oceanography, physical sciences, physics, science, and statistics), EDUCATION (athletic training, education, elementary education, foreign languages education, music education, and physical education), ENGINEERING AND ENVIRONMENTAL DESIGN (computer technology, electrical/electronics engineering, engineering technology, environmental science, industrial administration/management, interior design, manufacturing technology, mechanical engineering, and mechanical engineering technology), HEALTH PROFESSIONS (biomedical science, community health work, health, health care administration, public health, recreation therapy, rehabilitation therapy, speech pathology/audiology, and sports medicine), SOCIAL SCIENCE (anthropology, child psychology/development, cognitive science, community services, criminal justice, dietetics, early childhood studies, economics, ethics, politics, and social policy, European studies, family/consumer studies, food production/management/services, geography, history, interdisciplinary studies, law, parks and recreation management, philosophy, psychology, religion, social science, social studies, social work, sociology, and women's studies). Psychology, marketing, and accounting have the largest enrollments.

ACTIVITIES: 5% of men belong to 14 national fraternities; 10% of women belong to 14 national sororities. There are 400 groups on campus, including art, band, cheerleading, choir, chorus, communications, computers, dance, drama, environmental, ethnic, forensics, honors, international, jazz band, LGBT, literary magazine, marching band, musical theater, orchestra, pep band, photography, political, professional, religious, social, social service, student government, and symphony. Popular campus events include Homecoming, Michigan Story Festival, and Native American Pow Wow. **Sports:** There are 6 intercollegiate sports for men and 10 for women, and 21 intramural sports for men and 21 for women. Facilities include a football stadium, softball fields, a field hockey complex, indoor athletic complex, indoor and outdoor track, soccer field, baseball stadium, an arena, and student activity center. **Graduates:** From July 1, 2016 to June 30, 2017, 4063 bachelor's degrees were awarded. The most popular majors were business (23%), teacher education (11%), and fitness and exercise science (9%). In an average class, 1% graduate in 3 years or less, 18% graduate in 4 years or less, 45% graduate in 5 years or less, and 57% graduate in 6 years or less. Of the 2016 graduating class, 15% were enrolled in graduate school within 6 months of graduation, and 80% were employed.

SERVICES: Counseling and information services are available, as is tutoring in most subjects. There is a reader service for the blind, and remedial math, reading, and writing. **Library/Resources:** The library contains 1.5 million volumes, 1.4 million microform items, and 23,061 audio/video tapes/CDs/DVDs, and subscribes to 2,731 periodicals including electronic. Computerized library services include interlibrary loans, database searching, Internet access, and Wi-Fi capability. Special learning facilities include an art gallery, natural history museum, TV station, Clarke Historical Library, Gerald L. Poor School Museum, an astronomical observatory, leadership institute, and a multicultural education center. **Physically Challenged Students:** 95% of the campus is accessible. Facilities include wheelchair ramps, elevators, special parking, specially equipped restrooms, special class scheduling, lowered drinking fountains, lowered telephones, special housing, and the Student Disability Services. **Special:** CMU offers internships in business administration, study abroad in 43 countries, and dual majors in chemistry/physics and computer science/math. Student-designed majors are available for a bachelor of individualized studies, and there is credit for life, military, and work experience. Students may take up to 25 hours for pass/fail grades. CMU off-campus programs offers external degree programs in which students can get degrees without attending classes on campus. There are 13 national honor societies, a freshman honors program, and 21 departmental honors programs. **Visiting:** There are guides for informal visits, visitors may sit in on classes, and stay overnight. To schedule a visit, contact the Admissions Office. **Campus Safety and Security:** Measures include emergency notification system and security escort services. There are shuttle buses, emergency telephones, lighted pathways/sidewalks, and a blue light phone system.

REQUIREMENTS: The ACT is required. Applicants must be high school graduates or hold a GED. The university strongly recommends 4 years each of English and math, 3 each of science and social studies, and 2 of foreign language, as well as 1 course each in computer science and fine arts. AP and CLEP credits are accepted. Students must complete 124 credit hours, including 30 in the major, with a GPA of 2.0. They must fulfill the requirements in the University Program (27-30 semester hours of coursework in humanities, natural science, social science, an integrative and area studies), and fulfill university competency requirements in written English (Freshmen and Advanced Composition), oral English, and math. **Procedure:** Freshmen are admitted to all sessions. Entrance exams should be taken during the junior or senior year of high school. There are deferred admissions and rolling admissions plans. Application deadlines are open. The fall 2017 application fee was $35. Applications are accepted on-line. **Transfer Students:** 1091 transfer students enrolled in 2016-2017. Transfer students must have a GPA of 2.0. 30 of 124 credits required for the bachelor's degree must be completed at CMU. **International Students:** There are 527 international students enrolled. They must take the TOEFL with a minimum score of 550 on the paper-based TOEFL (PBT) or 79 on the Internet-based version (iBT).

ADMISSIONS: 70% of the 2017-2018 applicants were accepted. The ACT scores were 29% below 12, 34% between 12 and 17, 22% between 18 and 23, 9% between 24 and 29, and 6% above 30. 33% of the current freshmen were in the top fifth of their class; 62% were in the top two fifths. 59 freshmen graduated first in their class. **Admissions Contact:** Krista Casey, Assistant Director of Admissions. Email: *cmuadmit@cmich.edu* Web: *www.cmich.edu*

FINANCIAL AID: In 2017-2018, 66% of all full-time freshmen received some form of financial aid. 56% of all full-time freshmen received need-based aid. The average freshman award was $13,814. Need-based scholarships or need-based grants averaged $8,069; need-based self-help aid (loans and jobs) averaged $6,249; non-need-based athletic scholarships averaged $15,110; and other non-need-based awards and non-need-based scholarships averaged $4,161. 25% of undergraduate students work part-time. The average financial indebtedness of the 2017 graduate was $33,545. The FAFSA code is 002243. The priority date for freshman financial aid applications for fall entry is March 1.

COLLEGE FOR CREATIVE STUDIES *(The complete profile is made available exclusively on our website, www.barronspac.com)*

CONCORDIA UNIVERSITY, ANN ARBOR E-5

www.cuaa.edu

Ann Arbor, MI 48105	(734) 995-7311 (800) 253-0680
Fax: (734) 995-4610	**Email:** admissions@cuaa.edu
Full-time: 186 men, 242 women	**Faculty:** 39
Part-time: 53 men, 40 women	**Ph.D.s:** 60%
Graduate: 154 men, 400 women	**Student/Faculty:** 11 to 1
Year: semesters, summer session	**Tuition:** $28,330
Room & Board: $10,548	**Freshman Class:** 429 applied, 281 accepted, 94 enrolled
SAT CR/M/W: 575/550/560 **ACT:** 22	**CEEB CODE:** 1094
Application Deadline: August 15	**COMPETITIVE+**

Concordia University, Ann Arbor, established in 1963, is a private institution affiliated with the Missouri Synod of the Lutheran Church, offering undergraduate and graduate degrees in the arts and sciences, business, education, and human services. The figures given in the above capsule and in this profile are approximate. There are 4 undergraduate schools and 2 graduate schools. The 187-acre campus is in a suburban area 40 miles west of Detroit. Including any residence halls, there are 30 buildings.

STUDENT LIFE: 83% of undergraduates are from Michigan. Others are from 20 states, 6 foreign countries, and Canada. 85% are White; 8% African American; 2% Asian American; 2% American Indian/Alaska Native; 2% Hispanic; 1% Foreign. 30% are Protestant. **Female To Male Ratio:** 1.7:1. The average age of freshmen is 18; all undergraduates, 23. 31% do not continue beyond their first year; 47% remain to graduate. **Housing:** 436 students can be accommodated in college housing, which includes married student dorms. On-campus housing is guaranteed for all 4 years. 57% of students live on campus. Alcohol is not permitted. All students may keep cars.

FACULTY/CLASSROOMS: 47% of faculty are male; 53% are female. All teach undergraduates. No introductory courses are taught by graduate students. The average class size in an introductory lecture is 24; in a laboratory is 12; and in a regular course is 11.

PROGRAMS OF STUDY: CUAA confers B.A. degrees. Associate and master's degrees are also awarded. Bachelor's degrees are awarded in BIOLOGICAL SCIENCE (biology/biological science), BUSINESS (accounting, business administration and management, finance, hospitality management services, and human resources), COMMUNICATIONS AND THE ARTS (art, communications, dramatic arts, English, Greek, journalism, language arts, music, and Spanish), COMPUTER AND PHYSICAL SCIENCE (chemistry, computer science, mathematics, physical sciences, physics, and science), EDUCATION (early childhood education, elementary education, health education, physical education, and secondary education), ENGINEERING AND ENVIRONMENTAL DESIGN (preengineering), HEALTH PROFESSIONS (predentistry and premedicine), SOCIAL SCIENCE (biblical languages, criminal justice, family/consumer studies, history, humanities, justice and society, philosophy, psychology, religion, religious studies, religious music, safety management, social science, social studies, and sociology). Education, business, and family life are the strongest academically. Business administration, teacher education, and English have the largest enrollments.

ACTIVITIES: There are no fraternities or sororities. There are 21 groups on campus, including band, choir, chorale, communications, computers, dance, debate, drama, ethnic, jazz band, musical theater, newspaper, pep band, religious, social, social service, student government, and yearbook. Popular campus events include Boar's Head Festival, Servant Events, and a Fall Carnival. **Sports:** There are 5 intercollegiate sports for men and 5 for women, and 10 intramural sports for men and 10 for women. Facilities include a soccer field, baseball and softball diamonds, sand volleyball courts, a gym, and an open field for intramurals. **Graduates:** From July 1, 2016 to June 30, 2017, 112 bachelor's degrees were awarded. The most popular majors were teacher education (21%), business (21%), and criminal justice (10%). In an average class, 1% graduate in 3 years or less, 19% graduate in 4 years or less, 35% graduate in 5 years or less, and 37% graduate in 6 years or less.

SERVICES: Counseling and information services are available, as is tutoring in every subject. There is remedial math. There is also a writing lab with consultants. **Library/Resources:** The library contains 117,000 volumes, 300,000 microform items, and 1,400 audio/video tapes/CDs/DVDs, and subscribes to 660 periodicals including electronic. Computerized library services include interlibrary loans, database searching, Internet access, and Wi-Fi capability. Special learning facilities include an art gallery. **Physically Challenged Students:** 90% of the campus is accessible. Facilities include wheelchair ramps, elevators, special parking, specially equipped restrooms, and lowered drinking fountains. **Special:** Internships are available in most academic majors. Cross-registration is available with Eastern Michigan and Kettering Universities, Schoolcraft College, Henry Ford Community College, Michigan State Police Training Division, and Michigan Academy of Emergency Services. Students may study abroad in 6 countries. Accelerated degree programs are available in business administration, criminal justice administration, communication, hospitality management, and public safety. The college confers credit for life, military, and work experience through the School of Adult and Continuing Education. Nondegree study, dual majors in many combinations, student-designed majors, a 3-2 engineering degree with Kettering University, and a pass/fail grading option are available. **Visiting:** There are regularly scheduled orientations for prospective students, including several preview days such as Senior Day, Junior Day, Art Day, Music Day, and Theatre Day. Individual tours are arranged by appointment. There are guides for informal visits, visitors may sit in on classes, and stay overnight. To schedule a visit, contact the Admissions Office. **Campus Safety and Security:** Measures include 24-hour foot and vehicle patrol and security escort services. There are lighted pathways/sidewalks and controlled access to dorms/residences.

REQUIREMENTS: The SAT or ACT is required. Applicants must graduate from an accredited secondary school or have the GED. 20 Carnegie units are recommended, including 4 units in English, 3 in math, and 2 each in science, social studies, and foreign language. AP and CLEP credits are accepted. Important factors in the admissions decision are leadership record, advanced placement or honors courses, and evidence of special talent. Degree requirements include completion of 128 credit hours, with at least 30 in the major, and up to 49 credit hours of general studies, and a minimum GPA of 2.0. The student must also demonstrate proficiency in foreign language, writing, speech, and math. Required courses include upper-level general studies, writing-intensive courses, a freshman seminar, physical activities, computer applications, religion, humanities, social science, language/communication, and science. A senior project is required. Education students must take the Michigan Test for Teacher Certification. **Procedure:** Freshmen are admitted fall and spring. There are deferred admissions and rolling admissions plans. Applications should be filed by August 15 for fall entry. The fall 2017 application fee was $25. Notification is sent on a rolling basis. Applications are accepted on-line. **Transfer Students:** 91 transfer students enrolled in 2016-2017. A GPA of 2.0 is required for transfer students; a GPA of 2.5 is required for admittance to the teacher education program. Transfer students who have earned 12 or more credits are not required to take the ACT. Interviews are recommended. 30 of 128 credits required for the bachelor's degree must be completed at CUAA. **International Students:** There are 7 international students enrolled. They must take the TOEFL with a minimum score of 520 on the paper-based TOEFL (PBT) or 68 on the Internet-based version (iBT) or take the MELAB. They must also take the SAT or ACT.

ADMISSIONS: 66% of the 2017-2018 applicants were accepted. The SAT scores for the 2017-2018 freshman class were: Critical Reading-- 36% below 500, 21% between 500 and 599, 21% between 600 and 699, and 22% between 700 and 800. Math-- 28% below 500, 43% between 500 and 599, and 29% between 600 and 699. Writing-- 43% below 500, 7% between 500 and 599, 29% between 600 and 699, and 21% between 700 and 800. The ACT scores were 36% below 12, 20% between 12 and 17, 27% between 18 and 23, 11% between 24 and 29, and 6% above 30. **Admissions Contact:** Amy Becher, Executive Director of Enrollment Services. Email: *admissions@cuaa.edu* Web: *www.cuaa.edu*

FINANCIAL AID: In 2017-2018, 100% of all full-time freshmen received some form of financial aid. 65% of all full-time freshmen received need-based aid. The average freshman award was $18,392. Need-based scholarships or need-based grants averaged $5,047 ($13,505 maximum); need-based self-help aid (loans and jobs) averaged $7,766 ($9,000 maximum); non-need-based athletic scholarships averaged $8,274 ($17,500 maximum); and other non-need-based awards and non-need-based scholarships averaged $6,500 ($19,700 maximum). 42% of undergraduate students work part-time. The average financial indebtedness of the 2017 graduate was $25,000. The college's own financial statement is required. The deadline for filing freshman financial aid applications for fall entry is March 1.

CORNERSTONE UNIVERSITY — D-4
www.cornerstone.edu

Grand Rapids, MI 49525 — (616) 222-1426, (800) 787-9778

Fax: (616) 222-1418 — **Email:** admissions@cornerstone.edu

Full-time: 542 men, 821 women
Part-time: 159 men, 268 women
Graduate: 280 men, 311 women
Year: semesters, summer session
Room & Board: $9030
SAT CR/M/W: 505/495/490 **ACT:** 22
Application Deadline: August 15
Faculty: 55
Ph.D.s: 40%
Student/Faculty: 21 to 1
Tuition: $27,520
Freshman Class: 1962 applied, 1834 accepted, 322 enrolled
CEEB CODE: 1253
COMPETITIVE

Cornerstone University, founded in 1941, is a private liberal arts college and graduate seminary educating students from a Christian perspective. Major undergraduate programs include business, media studies, teacher education and religion. There are 3 undergraduate schools and 2 graduate schools. In addition to regional accreditation, Cornerstone has baccalaureate program accreditation with CSWE, NASM, ATS, NASM, and CSWE. The 132-acre campus is in a suburban area on the northeast side of Grand Rapids, MI. Including any residence halls, there are 37 buildings.

STUDENT LIFE: 85% of undergraduates are from Michigan. Others are from 37 states, 30 foreign countries, and Canada. 62% are from public schools. 77% are White; 4% Hispanic; 3% Foreign; 13% African American; 1% Asian American. 66% are Protestant. **Female To Male Ratio:** 1.4:1. The average age of freshmen is 18; all undergraduates, 20. 22% do not continue beyond their first year; 48% remain to graduate. **Housing:** 880 students can be accommodated in college housing, which includes married student dorms and on-campus apartments. In addition, there are honors houses, and apartments for single students. On-campus housing is guaranteed for the freshman year only, is available on a first-come, and first-served basis. 65% of students live on campus. Alcohol is not permitted. All students may keep cars.

FACULTY/CLASSROOMS: 67% of faculty are male; 33% are female. All teach undergraduates, 50% do research, and 50% do both. No introductory courses are taught by graduate students. The average class size in an introductory lecture is 60; in a laboratory is 24; and in a regular course is 21.

PROGRAMS OF STUDY: Cornerstone confers B.A., B.Mus., and B.S. degrees. Associate and master's degrees are also awarded. Bachelor's degrees are awarded in BIOLOGICAL SCIENCE (biology/biological science), BUSINESS (accounting, business administration and management, international business management, international economics, marketing/retailing/merchandising, and sports management), COMMUNICATIONS AND THE ARTS (advertising, applied music, audio technology, communications, English, English Writing, fine arts, graphic design, literature, media arts, music, music performance, musical theater, speech/debate/rhetoric, and video), COMPUTER AND PHYSICAL SCIENCE (chemistry), EDUCATION (education, elementary education, English education, middle school education, music education, physical education, science education, and secondary education), HEALTH PROFESSIONS (exercise science, pre-health studies, predentistry, premedicine, and preveterinary science), SOCIAL SCIENCE (biblical studies, Christian studies, family/consumer studies, history, humanities, interdisciplinary studies, liberal arts/general studies, philosophy, psychology, religion, religious education, social work, and youth ministry). English, music, and education are the strongest academically. Education, business, psychology, and media/film have the largest enrollments.

ACTIVITIES: There are no fraternities or sororities. There are 23 groups on campus, including band, cheerleading, choir, chorale, chorus, dance, drama, environmental, ethnic, honors, international, jazz band, musical theater, newspaper, orchestra, pep band, photography, political, professional, religious, social, social service, and student government. Popular campus events include Sibling Weekends, Friends Weekend, and Variety Show. **Sports:** There are 5 intercollegiate sports for men and 5 for women, and 4 intramural sports for men and 4 for women. Facilities include a basketball/volleyball arena, a field house for tennis, volleyball, basketball, a baseball diamond, soccer fields/intramural fields, softball field, sand volleyball court, fitness center, human performance labs, and racquetball courts. **Graduates:** From July 1, 2016 to June 30, 2017, 475 bachelor's degrees were awarded. The most popular majors were business (45%), psychology (12%), and education (8%). In an average class, 30% graduate in 4 years or less, 43% graduate in 5 years or less, and 48% graduate in 6 years or less. Of the 2016 graduating class, 8% were enrolled in graduate school within 6 months of graduation, and 91% were employed.

SERVICES: Counseling and information services are available, as is tutoring in every subject. There is also a Learning Center with a computer lab and special adaptive software that specialize in writing and math. Tutoring is by appointment in the residence halls, test-taking assistance, and readers and typists as needed. There is a reader service for the blind, and remedial math and writing. **Library/Resources:** The library contains 375,000 volumes, 276,107 microform items, and 5,226 audio/video tapes/CDs/DVDs, and subscribes to 39,500 periodicals including electronic. Computerized library services include interlibrary loans, database searching, Internet access, and Wi-Fi capability. **Physically Challenged Students:** All of the campus is accessible. Facilities include wheelchair ramps, elevators, special parking, specially equipped restrooms, special class scheduling, special housing, large computer monitors for the visually impaired, and soundproof rooms for using tape recorders that read books-on-tape. **Special:** All students choose a student-ministries assignment each semester. Cornerstone requires internships in many areas of study. Study abroad programs, accelerated degrees in organizational leadership, management, business administration, ministry leadership, and education, and a Washington semester are available. There are 3 national honor societies, Phi Beta Kappa, a freshman honors program, and 3 departmental honors programs. **Visiting:** There are regularly scheduled orientations for prospective students, including admissions and financial aid presentations, class visits, meeting with a faculty member, and course preregistration. There are guides for informal visits, visitors may sit in on classes, and stay overnight. To schedule a visit, contact Admissions Office. **Campus Safety and Security:** Measures include 24-hour foot and vehicle patrol, emergency notification system, self-defense education, and security escort services. There are emergency telephones, lighted pathways/sidewalks, and controlled access to dorms/residences.

REQUIREMENTS: SAT or ACT is required, and an official high school transcript or GED certificate with a minimum 2.5 high school GPA. A reference from a pastor or other Christian leader is also required. Auditions are required for music scholarships. In addition, the following program is recommended for college preparation: 17 Carnegie units, 4 years of English, 3 each of math, history, and social sciences, 2 each of science and foreign language. AP and CLEP credits are accepted. Important factors in the admissions decision are advanced placement or honors courses and recommendations by school officials. To graduate, students must complete 120 to 129 credit hours depending on the degree, including 46 in the liberal arts core. The number of hours in the major varies. The student must have an overall GPA of 2.0, 2.5 in the major, 2.0 in the minor, and pass a comprehensive exam in his or her field. **Procedure:** Freshmen are admitted to all sessions. Entrance exams should be taken during the junior or senior year of high school. There are deferred admissions and rolling admissions plans. Applications should be filed by August 15 for fall entry; January 15 for spring entry. The fall 2017 application fee was $25. Notification is sent on a rolling basis. Applications are accepted on-line. **Transfer Students:** 509 transfer students enrolled in 2016-2017. The college requires official college transcript (s) from students (minimum college GPA of 2.0), as well as a reference from a pastor or other Christian leader. In addition, if the applicant has fewer than 24 hours of college credit, an official high school transcript is required (minimum high school GPA of 2.5) and official ACT or SAT scores. 32 of 120 credits required for the bachelor's degree must be completed at Cornerstone. **International Students:** There are 49 international students enrolled. They must take the TOEFL with a minimum score of 500 on the paper-based TOEFL (PBT) or 61 on the Internet-based version (iBT). They must also take the SAT or ACT, scoring 900.

ADMISSIONS: 93% of the 2017-2018 applicants were accepted. The SAT scores for the 2017-2018 freshman class were: Critical Reading-- 26% below 500, 37% between 500 and 599, 26% between 600 and 699, and 11% between 700 and 800. Math-- 48% below 500, 21% between 500 and 599, and 32% between 600 and 699. Writing-- 42% below 500, 37% between 500 and 599, 16% between 600 and 699, and 5% between 700 and 800. 31% of the current freshmen were in the top fifth of their class; 64% were in the top two fifths. 5 freshmen graduated first in their class. **Admissions Contact:** Lisa Link, Director of Admissions. Email: *admissions@cornerstone.edu* Web: *www.cornerstone.edu*

FINANCIAL AID: In 2017-2018, 100% of all full-time freshmen received some form of financial aid. 85% of all full-time freshmen received need-based aid. The average freshman award was $23,811. Need-based scholarships or need-based grants averaged $15,028 ($36,098 maximum); need-based self-help aid (loans and jobs) averaged $2,366 ($5,500 maximum); non-need-based athletic scholarships averaged $1,069 ($15,000 maximum); and other non-need-based awards and non-need-based scholarships averaged $5,348 ($20,306 maximum). 34% of undergraduate students work part-time. The average financial indebtedness of the 2017 graduate was $27,919. The priority date for freshman financial aid applications for fall entry is March 1.

DAVENPORT UNIVERSITY *(The complete profile is made available exclusively on our website, www.barronspac.com)*

EASTERN MICHIGAN UNIVERSITY D-5

www.emich.edu

Ypsilanti, MI 48197 **(734) 487-3060**

Fax: (734) 487-6559 Email: undergraduate.admissions@emich.edu

Full-time: 5276 men, 7795 women	**Faculty:** 773; I, -$
Part-time: 2026 men, 2683 women	**Ph.D.s:** 75%
Graduate: 1395 men, 2459 women	**Student/Faculty:** 17 to 1
Year: semesters, summer session	**Tuition:** $10,417 ($27,712)
Room & Board: $9344	**Freshman Class:** 14228 applied, 10639 accepted, 2888 enrolled
SAT: required **ACT:** 22	**CEEB CODE:** 1201
Application Deadline: August 30	**COMPETITIVE**

Eastern Michigan University, founded in 1849, is a public institution offering programs in arts and sciences, business, education, health and human services, and technology. There are 6 undergraduate schools and 1 graduate school. In addition to regional accreditation, EMU has baccalaureate program accreditation with AACSB, ACCE, CSWE, NASM, CAEP, ACPHA, ACOTE, ABA, ACS, APA, ASHA, CCNE, CADE, CAAHEP, CAAT, CIDA, HLC, MDOE, NAACLS, NASPAA, CNSS, and PAB. The 460-acre campus is in a suburban area 8 miles east of Ann Arbor. Including any residence halls, there are 120 buildings.

STUDENT LIFE: 88% of undergraduates are from Michigan. Others are from 49 states, 30 foreign countries, and Canada. 90% are from public schools. 65% are White; 5% Hispanic; 4% two or more races; 3% Asian American; 2% Foreign; 2% race unknown; 19% African American. **Female To Male Ratio:** 1.5:1. The average age of freshmen is 18; all undergraduates, 23. 25% do not continue beyond their first year; 40% remain to graduate. **Housing:** 3688 students can be accommodated in college housing, which includes married student dorms and on-campus apartments. In addition, there are honors houses, special-interest houses, sorority houses, community of scholars, upper-class halls, and first-year center for freshman students. On-campus housing is available on a first-come and first-served basis. 78% of students commute. All students may keep cars.

FACULTY/CLASSROOMS: 46% of faculty are male; 54% are female. 95% teach undergraduates. Graduate students teach 2% of introductory courses.

PROGRAMS OF STUDY: EMU confers B.A., B.S., B.A.E., B.A. in Language and World Business, B.B.A., B.B.E., B.F.A., B.M.E., B.M.T., B.M.U., B.S.N. and B.S.W. degrees. Master's and doctoral degrees are also awarded. Bachelor's degrees are awarded in BIOLOGICAL SCIENCE (biochemistry, biology/biological science, and nutrition), BUSINESS (accounting, apparel and accessories marketing, banking and finance, business administration and management, business data processing, business economics, business systems analysis, entrepreneurial studies, fashion merchandising, hospitality management services, hotel/motel and restaurant management, international business management, labor studies, management information systems, management science, marketing management, marketing/retailing/merchandising, office supervision and management, personnel management, supply chain management, tourism, and trade and industrial supervision and management), COMMUNICATIONS AND THE ARTS (advertising, American literature, animation, applied music, art, art history and appreciation, arts administration/management, classical languages, communications, communications technology, creative writing, dance, design, dramatic arts, English, English literature, film arts, fine arts, French, German, graphic design, historic preservation, Japanese, journalism, language arts, linguistics, literature, media arts, music, music performance, percussion, performing arts, piano/organ, public relations, Spanish, speech/debate/rhetoric, strings, technical and business writing, telecommunications, visual and performing arts, voice, and winds), COMPUTER AND PHYSICAL SCIENCE (actuarial science, applied mathematics, astronomy, chemistry, computer programming, computer science, computer security and information assurance, earth science, geology, hydrogeology, information sciences and systems, mathematics, physics, polymer science, science, and statistics), EDUCATION (art education, athletic training, bilingual/bicultural education, business education, computer education, drama education, early childhood education, education, education of the deaf and hearing impaired, education of the emotionally handicapped, education of the mentally handicapped, education of the multiply handicapped, education of the physically handicapped, education of the visually handicapped, educational media, elementary education, English education, foreign languages education, health education, industrial arts education, mathematics education, middle school education, music education, physical education, psychology education, reading education, school psychology, science education, secondary education, social foundations, social studies education, special education, technical education, and trade and industrial education), ENGINEERING AND ENVIRONMENTAL DESIGN (airline piloting and navigation, applied aviation, aviation administration/management, city/community/regional planning, computer engineering, computer graphics, computer technology, construction management, electrical/electronics engineering technology, engineering physics, engineering technology, interior design, land use management and reclamation, manufacturing engineering, manufacturing technology, mechanical engineering technology, military science, plastics technology, and urban planning technology), HEALTH PROFESSIONS (allied health, exercise science, health care administration, medical laboratory science, medical laboratory technology, music therapy, nursing, occupational therapy, recreation therapy, speech pathology/audiology, and sports medicine), SOCIAL SCIENCE (African studies, African American studies, anthropology, area studies, Asian/Oriental studies, child care/child and family studies, clothing and textiles management/production/services, counseling/psychology, criminal justice, dietetics, economics, gender studies, geography, gerontology, history, interdisciplinary studies, international relations, Latin American studies, Middle Eastern studies, paralegal studies, philosophy, political science/government, psychology, public administration, Russian and Slavic studies, social studies, social work, sociology, textiles and clothing, urban studies, and women's studies). Education, business, and health/nursing are the strongest academically. Elementary education, arts/sciences, and business have the largest enrollments.

ACTIVITIES: 4% of men belong to 1 local and 10 national fraternities; 4% of women belong to 1 local and 11 national sororities. There are 300 groups on campus, including art, band, cheerleading, chess, choir, chorale, chorus, computers, dance, debate, drama, drill team, environmental, ethnic, film, forensics, honors, international, jazz band, LGBT, literary magazine, marching band, musical theater, newspaper, opera, orchestra, pep band, photography, political, professional, radio and TV, religious, social, social service, student government, and symphony. Popular campus events include Martin Luther King Birthday Celebration, and Family Weekend. **Sports:** There are 12 intercollegiate sports for men and 15 for women, and 20 intramural sports for men and 20 for women. Facilities include a stadium, outdoor playing fields, a field house, a student recreation and intramural center, basketball courts, volleyball courts, pools, softball and soccer fields, weight rooms, and aerobic studio. **Graduates:** From July 1, 2016 to June 30, 2017, 3321 bachelor's degrees were awarded. The most popular majors were business/marketing (20%), health professions and related programs (15%), and education (11%). In an average class, 1% graduate in 3 years or less, 13% graduate in 4 years or less, 27% graduate in 5 years or less, and 37% graduate in 6 years or less.

SERVICES: Counseling and information services are available, as is tutoring in every subject. There is a reader service for the blind, and remedial math, reading, and writing. Notetakers and interpreters are provided for the handicapped. **Library/Resources:** The library contains 1.1 million volumes, 994,057 microform items, and 37,078 audio/video tapes/CDs/DVDs, and subscribes to 28,034 periodicals including electronic. Computerized library services include interlibrary loans, database searching, Internet access, and Wi-Fi capability. Special learning facilities include an art gallery, radio station, and TV station. **Physically Challenged Students:** 93% of the campus is accessible. Facilities include wheelchair ramps, elevators, special parking, specially equipped restrooms, special class scheduling, lowered drinking fountains, lowered telephones, and special housing. **Special:** EMU offers internships, work-study programs, a Washington semester in public administration, and co-op programs and cross-registration with the University of Michigan at Ann Arbor, Concordia College, and Washtenaw Community College. Students may study abroad in more than 23 countries. EMU allows dual majors, nondegree study, B.A.-B.S. degrees in all majors, student-designed majors, and accelerated degree programs, and confers a general studies degree, as well as a B.A.-B.B.A. degree in language and world business. Students may receive credit for life, military, and work experience, and pass/fail options are open. There are 9 national honor societies, a freshman honors program, and 36 departmental honors programs. **Visiting:** There are regularly scheduled orientations for prospective students, including tours scheduled every morning and afternoon, as well as Saturday morning, with trained student tour guides. To schedule a visit, contact the Admissions On-Campus Programs. **Campus Safety and Security:** Measures include 24-hour foot and vehicle patrol, emergency notification system, self-defense education, and security escort services. There are shuttle buses, emergency telephones, lighted pathways/sidewalks, controlled access to dorms/residences, bicycle patrols, a crime prevention officer, area police officers in dorms, an anonymous tip line, operation identification, vehicle glass etching, a bike lock lease program, and surveillance cameras.

REQUIREMENTS: A minimum composite of 17 on the ACT, or a satisfactory score on the SAT is required. Applicants should be high school graduates or hold a GED. The university recommends that students complete 21 academic credits in high school, consisting of 4 credits each in English, math, and science, 2 credits each in foreign language and social studies, 1 credit in history, and 4 credits in other traditional college-preparatory courses. A portfolio is required for applicants to the art program, and an audition is required for music students. AP and CLEP credits are accepted. To graduate, students must have a GPA of 2.0, and complete a minimum of 124 semester hours, including usually 30 in the major, 20 in the minor (or 50 in a comprehensive major), and 40 in General Education. In addition to distribution requirements, students must have a course in global awareness, a course in U.S. diversity, and satisfy requirements for learning beyond the classroom. **Procedure:** Freshmen are admitted to all sessions. Entrance exams should be taken by November of the senior year of high school. There are early admissions and rolling admissions plans. Applications should be filed by August 30 for fall entry; January 2 for winter entry; April 25 for spring entry; and June 21 for summer entry. The fall 2017 application fee was $35. Notification is sent on a rolling basis. Applications are accepted on-line. **Transfer Students:** 1697 transfer students enrolled in 2016-2017. Transfer students must have at least 12 semester hours of college credit, with a GPA of 2.0. 30 of 124 credits required for the bachelor's degree must be completed at EMU. **International Students:** There are 360 international students enrolled. They must take the TOEFL with a minimum score of 500 on the paper-based TOEFL (PBT) or 61 on the Internet-based version (iBT), or take the MELAB or IELTS.

ADMISSIONS: 75% of the 2017-2018 applicants were accepted. The SAT scores for the 2017-2018 freshman class were: Critical Reading-- 47% below 500, 26% between 500 and 599, 14% between 600 and 699, and 3% between 700 and 800. Math-- 41% below 500, 40% between 500 and 599, 17% between 600 and 699, and 2% between 700 and 800. Writing-- 57% below 500, 33% between 500 and 599, 9% between 600 and 699, and 1% between 700 and 800. The ACT scores were 11% between 12 and 17, 54% between 18 and 23, 32% between 24 and 29, and 3% above 30. 22 freshmen graduated first in their class. **Admissions Contact:** Brian Selfridge, Freshmen Admissions. Email: *undergraduate.admissions@emich.edu* Web: *www.emich.edu*

FINANCIAL AID: In 2017-2018, 97% of all full-time freshmen received some form of financial aid. 61% of all full-time freshmen received need-based aid. The average freshman award was $13,104. Need-based scholarships or need-based grants averaged $6,283 ($9,061 maximum); need-based self-help aid (loans and jobs) averaged $3,533 ($5,500 maximum); non-need-based athletic scholarships averaged $17,719 ($34,795 maximum); and other non-need-based awards and non-need-based scholarships averaged $7,919 ($28,128 maximum). 16% of undergraduate students work part-time. The average financial indebtedness of the 2017 graduate was $24,402. The FAFSA code is 002259. The priority date for freshman financial aid applications for fall entry is February 1.

FERRIS STATE UNIVERSITY — D-4

www.ferris.edu

Big Rapids, MI 49307 — **(231) 591-2100**

Fax: (231) 591-3944	**Email:** admissions@ferris.edu
Full-time: 4299 men, 4170 women	**Faculty:** 582; IIA, av$
Part-time: 1640 men, 2395 women	**Ph.D.s:** 46%
Graduate: 469 men, 825 women	**Student/Faculty:** 16 to 1
Year: semesters, summer session	**Tuition:** $11,564 ($18,570)
Room & Board: $9894	**Freshman Class:** 9926 applied, 7361 accepted, 1822 enrolled
SAT: required **ACT:** 22	**CEEB CODE:** 1222
Application Deadline: August 1	**COMPETITIVE**

Ferris State University, established in 1884, is a public institution offering day and evening courses through its Schools of Arts and Sciences, Education and Human Services, Health Professions, Engineering Technology, Business, Pharmacy, MI College of Optometry, and Kendall College of Art and Design. There are 7 undergraduate schools and 6 graduate schools. In addition to regional accreditation, FSU has baccalaureate program accreditation with ABET, ACBSP, ACCE, ACPE, and CSWE. The 941-acre campus is in a small town 55 miles north of Grand Rapids. Including any residence halls, there are 109 buildings.

STUDENT LIFE: 92% of undergraduates are from Michigan. Others are from 46 states, 49 foreign countries, and Canada. 77% are White; 7% African American; 5% Hispanic; 4% two or more races; 3% race unknown; 2% Asian American; 2% Foreign; 1% American Indian/Alaska Native. **Female To Male Ratio:** 1.2:1. The average age of freshmen is 19;

all undergraduates, 24. 21% do not continue beyond their first year. **Housing:** 3275 students can be accommodated in college housing, which includes coed and married student dorms and on-campus apartments. In addition, there are honors houses, language/international houses, special-interest houses, substance free, 1st year experience, quiet house, graphic design housing, and sophomore leadership. On-campus housing is guaranteed for all 4 years. 74% of students commute. All students may keep cars.

FACULTY/CLASSROOMS: 54% of faculty are male; 45% are female. All teach undergraduates. No introductory courses are taught by graduate students. The average class size in an introductory lecture is 27; in a laboratory is 17; and in a regular course is 25.

PROGRAMS OF STUDY: FSU confers B.A., B.S., B.F.A., B.S.N., B.S.W. and B.A.S. degrees. Associate, master's, and doctoral degrees are also awarded. Bachelor's degrees are awarded in BIOLOGICAL SCIENCE (biochemistry, biology/biological science, biology/general science secondary education, and biotechnology), BUSINESS (accounting, business administration w/legal studies, business administration and management, business administration/aviation, business data processing, collaborative design, facilities management, finance, hospitality management services, hotel/motel and restaurant management, human resources, insurance, integrative studies, marketing, operations management, resort management, professional golf management, and professional tennis management), COMMUNICATIONS AND THE ARTS (art history, art history and appreciation, communications, digital media, digital media software engineering, drawing, English, fashion studies, graphic communications management, graphic design, illustration, industrial design, journalism & technical communications, metal/jewelry, music industry, painting, photography, printing management, public relations, sculpture, sports communication, technical communication, and television & digital media production), COMPUTER AND PHYSICAL SCIENCE (actuarial science, applied mathematics, chemistry, chemistry education, computer networks & systems, computer information technology, computer information systems, digital animation & game design, digital arts/technology, industrial technology, and information security & risk management), EDUCATION (art education, business education, early childhood education, elementary education, English education, health information management, history education, mathematics education, social studies education, and technical education), ENGINEERING AND ENVIRONMENTAL DESIGN (automotive technology, construction management, construction mgmt/commercial/industrial, electrical/electronics engineering technology, energy systems technology, engineering technology, heavy equip service engineering, manufacturing engineering, mechanical engineering technology, plastics engineering, product design engineering technology, surveying engineering, and welding engineering), HEALTH PROFESSIONS (allied health, biology, dental hygiene, health care administration, healthcare marketing, medical laboratory science, molecular diagnostics, nuclear medical technology, nursing, pre-health studies, pre-health biological studies, predentistry, preoptometry, prephysical therapy, public health, and respiratory therapy), SOCIAL SCIENCE (criminal justice, early childhood studies, ethics, politics, and social policy, history, political science/government, psychology, social work, sociology, and Spanish studies). Pharmacy, and optometry are the strongest academically. Pharmacy/pre pharmacy, nursing, and criminal justice have the largest enrollments.

ACTIVITIES: 1% of men belong to 8 national fraternities; 1% of women belong to 7 national sororities. There are 234 groups on campus, including art, band, cheerleading, chess, choir, chorus, communications, computers, dance, debate, drama, environmental, ethnic, film, forensics, honors, international, jazz band, LGBT, musical theater, newspaper, orchestra, pep band, photography, political, professional, radio and TV, religious, social, social service, student government, and symphony. Popular campus events include Music Takes Action, Family & Friends Weekend, 5 Star Lectures, Bulldawg Beginnings, Homecoming, Big Event, Spring Concert, and Bulldawg Weekends. **Sports:** There are 7 intercollegiate sports for men and 8 for women, and 27 intramural sports for men and 24 for women. Facilities include a golf course, racquetball and fitness club, an ice arena, a stadium, student recreation center with a pool, and tennis courts. **Graduates:** From July 1, 2016 to June 30, 2017, 2557 bachelor's degrees were awarded. The most popular majors were criminal justice (4%), nursing (2%), and business administration (2%). In an average class, 12% graduate in 3 years or less, 29% graduate in 4 years or less, 42% graduate in 5 years or less, and 50% graduate in 6 years or less.

SERVICES: Counseling and information services are available, as is tutoring in most subjects. There is a reader service for the blind, and remedial math, reading, and writing. **Library/Resources:** The library contains 267,897 volumes, 288,577 microform items, and 2,180 audio/video tapes/CDs/DVDs, and subscribes to 160,936 periodicals including electronic. Computerized library services include interlibrary loans, database searching, Internet access, and Wi-Fi capability. Special learning facilities include an art gallery, natural history museum, radio station, TV station, and the Jim Crow Museum. **Physically Challenged Students:** 98% of the campus is accessible. Facilities include wheelchair ramps, elevators, special parking, specially equipped restrooms, special class scheduling, lowered drinking fountains, lowered telephones, and special housing. **Special:** FSU offers co-op programs in automotive service technology, internships, study abroad, work-study programs, accelerated degrees, dual and student-designed majors, and credit for life, military, and work experience. There are 19 national honor societies and a freshman honors program. **Visiting:** There are regularly scheduled orientations for prospective students, day begins with an admission's presentation, lunch and a campus tour. There are guides for informal visits. To schedule a visit, contact the Admissions Office. **Campus Safety and Security:** Measures include 24-hour foot and vehicle patrol, emergency notification system, self-defense education, and security escort services. There are shuttle buses, emergency telephones, lighted pathways/sidewalks, and controlled access to dorms/residences.

REQUIREMENTS: The SAT or ACT is required. Applicants must graduate from an accredited secondary school or earn a GED. Academic requirements are 4 years each of English and math, 3 years each of science (with 2 lab) and social studies, 2 years of foreign language, 1 visual/performing arts, and 1 unit in physical education/health. AP and CLEP credits are accepted. Important factors in the admissions decision are personality/intangible qualities, leadership record, and advanced placement or honors courses. Degree requirements include a minimum 2.0 GPA. The total number of credit hours required varies. General education courses required include English, speech, math, humanities, social science, cultural enrichment, and natural science subjects. **Procedure:** Freshmen are admitted fall, spring, and summer. Entrance exams should be taken before course registration. There is a rolling admissions plan. Applications should be filed by August 1 for fall entry. Applications are accepted on-line. **Transfer Students:** 1279 transfer students enrolled in 2016-2017. A GPA of at least 2.0 is required, as are college transcripts, and a statement of good standing from previously attended institutions. Some students may need to submit high school transcripts and test scores. 30 of 120 credits required for the bachelor's degree must be completed at FSU. **International Students:** There are 326 international students enrolled. They must take the TOEFL with a minimum score of 61 on the Internet-based version (iBT). They must also take the SAT or ACT, scoring 17 or 900 or a supplemental math exam.

ADMISSIONS: 74% of the 2017-2018 applicants were accepted. The SAT scores for the 2017-2018 freshman class were: Math-- 35% below 500, 46% between 500 and 599, 16% between 600 and 699, and 3% between 700 and 800. Evidence-Based Reading/Writing-- 32% below 500, 43% between 500 and 599, 22% between 600 and 699, and 3% between 700 and 800. The ACT scores were 15% between 12 and 17, 48% between 18 and 23, 29% between 24 and 29, and 8% above 30. **Admissions Contact:** Kristen Salomonson, Dean of Enrollment Services & Director of Admissions. Email: *admissions@ferris.edu* Web: *www.ferris.edu*

FINANCIAL AID: In 2017-2018, 97% of all full-time freshmen received some form of financial aid. 70% of all full-time freshmen received need-based aid. The average freshman award was $15,742. Need-based scholarships or need-based grants averaged $3,724 ($5,510 maximum); need-based self-help aid (loans and jobs) averaged $2,028 ($4,480 maximum); non-need-based athletic scholarships averaged $320 ($9,990 maximum); and other non-need-based awards and non-need-based scholarships averaged $9,670. 21% of undergraduate students work part-time. The average financial indebtedness of the 2017 graduate was $21,988. FSU is a member of CSS. The FAFSA code is 002260. The priority date for freshman financial aid applications for fall entry is December 1.

GRACE BIBLE COLLEGE D-4
www.gbcol.edu

Grand Rapids, MI 49509	**(616) 538-2330** **(800) 968-1887**
Fax: (616) 538-2330	**Email: graceadmissions@gbcol.edu**
Full-time: 145 men, 144 women	**Faculty:** 7
Part-time: 6 men, 8 women	**Ph.D.s:** 43%
Graduate: n/av	**Student/Faculty:** 26 to 1
Year: semesters	**Tuition:** $17,850
Room & Board: $7400	**Freshman Class:** 234 applied, 217 accepted, 110 enrolled
SAT CR/M/W: 560/540/500 **ACT:** 21	**CEEB CODE:** 0809
Application Deadline: n/av	**COMPETITIVE**

Grace Bible College, founded in 1939, is a private institution affiliated with the Grace Gospel Fellowship. Its mission is to provide a curriculum that integrates general education and biblical studies and prepares students for service in their career, church, and society. There is 1 undergraduate school and 1 graduate school. In addition to regional accreditation, GBC has baccalaureate program accreditation with ABHES and AABC. The 21-acre campus is in a suburban area on the southwest side of Grand Rapids. Including any residence halls, there are 21 buildings.

STUDENT LIFE: 80% of undergraduates are from Michigan. Others are from 15 states, and 2 foreign countries. 93% are White; 3% African American; 1% Asian American; 1% Hispanic. 97% are Protestant. **Female To Male Ratio:** 1.0:1. The average age of freshmen is 19; all undergraduates, 21. 21% do not continue beyond their first year; 60% remain to graduate. **Housing:** 240 students can be accommodated in college housing, which includes dorms, on-campus apartments, and off-campus apartments. On-campus housing is guaranteed for all 4 years. 60% of students live on campus. Alcohol is not permitted. All students may keep cars.

FACULTY/CLASSROOMS: 72% of faculty are male; 28% are female. All teach undergraduates. No introductory courses are taught by graduate students. The average class size in an introductory lecture is 60 and in a regular course is 16.

PROGRAMS OF STUDY: GBC confers B.S., B.Mus., B.R.E. and B.Th. degrees. Associate and master's degrees are also awarded. Bachelor's degrees are awarded in BUSINESS (business administration and management), COMMUNICATIONS AND THE ARTS (music), EDUCATION (elementary education and secondary education), SOCIAL SCIENCE (biblical studies, criminal justice, early childhood studies, human services, interdisciplinary studies, missions, pastoral studies, religious education, and youth ministry). Youth ministry, worship arts, and human services have the largest enrollments.

ACTIVITIES: There are no fraternities or sororities. Groups on campus include cheerleading, choir, drama, jazz band, musical theater, religious, and student government. Popular campus events include Winter Formal, Missions Conference, and Campus Service Days. **Sports:** There are 3 intercollegiate sports for men and 4 for women. Facilities include a soccer field and an athletic center with a gym for basketball and volleyball, a racquetball court, and exercise and weight room. **Graduates:** From July 1, 2016 to June 30, 2017, 31 bachelor's degrees were awarded. The most popular majors were education (33%), youth and pastoral ministries (17%), and visual performing arts and digital media (17%). In an average class, 20% graduate in 3 years or less, 46% graduate in 4 years or less, 62% graduate in 5 years or less, and 75% graduate in 6 years or less.

SERVICES: Counseling and information services are available, as is tutoring in most subjects. There is remedial writing. **Library/Resources:** The library contains 42,867 volumes, 53 microform items, and 2,582 audio/video tapes/CDs/DVDs, and subscribes to 54,292 periodicals including electronic. Computerized library services include interlibrary loans, database searching, Internet access, and Wi-Fi capability. **Physically Challenged Students:** 85% of the campus is accessible. Facilities include wheelchair ramps, elevators, special parking, specially equipped restrooms, and lowered drinking fountains. **Special:** Cross-registration is available with Cornerstone and Davenport Universities. GBC offers 6-month internships for theology majors. Most 4-year degree programs require a semester practicum. **Visiting:** There are regularly scheduled orientations for prospective students, consisting of 7 Friday programs a year that include workshops, class visits, and campus tours. There are guides for informal visits, visitors may sit in on classes, and stay overnight. To schedule a visit, contact Lizz Niles at lniles@gbcol.edu. **Campus Safety and Security:** Measures include emergency notification system and security escort services. There are lighted pathways/sidewalks, controlled access to dorms/residences, an evening and overnight foot patrol.

REQUIREMENTS: The ACT is required. Applicants must be graduates of accredited secondary schools or have earned a GED. The application must show involvement in Christian activities and personal salvation through Jesus Christ. GBC requires applicants to be in the upper 50% of their class. AP and CLEP credits are accepted. To graduate, students must complete 126 to 158 credits, depending on the major, with a minimum GPA of 2.0 and must be considered worthy in character and conduct by the faculty. Coursework is required in arts and sciences, ministry studies, Bible/theology, math/computer science, lab science, and phys ed. Attendance is expected at worship services twice a week. **Procedure:** Freshmen are admitted fall and spring. There is a rolling admissions plan. Application deadlines are open. Applications are accepted on-line. **Transfer Students:** 20 transfer students enrolled in 2016-2017. Applicants must present a GPA of 2.0 and be in good standing at their previous school. Those with fewer than 24 college credit hours must submit high school records. 63 of 126 credits required for the bachelor's degree must be completed at GBC. **International Students:** They must take the TOEFL.

ADMISSIONS: 93% of the 2017-2018 applicants were accepted. The SAT scores for the 2017-2018 freshman class were: Critical Reading-- 35% below 500 and 66% between 500 and 599. Math-- 34% below 500 and 66% between 500 and 599. Writing-- 34% below 500, 33% between 500 and 599, and 33% between 600 and 699. The ACT scores were 20% between 12 and 17, 70% between 18 and 23, 7% between 24 and 29, and 3% above 30. 32% of the current freshmen were in the top fifth of their class; 41% were in the top two fifths. **Admissions Contact:** Kevin Gilliam, Associate Vice President of Enrollment. Email: *graceadmissions@gbcol.edu* Web: *www.gbcol.edu*

FINANCIAL AID: In 2017-2018, 98% of all full-time freshmen received some form of financial aid. 74% of all full-time freshmen received need-based aid. The average freshman award was $7,780. Need-based scholarships or need-based grants averaged $3,383 ($5,350 maximum); need-based self-help aid (loans and jobs) averaged $2,063 ($3,500 maximum); and other non-need-based awards and non-need-based scholarships averaged $3,946 ($4,500 maximum). 43% of undergraduate students work part-time. The average financial indebtedness of the 2017 graduate was $16,689. The FAFSA code is 002265. The priority date for freshman financial aid applications for fall entry is February 1.

GRAND VALLEY STATE UNIVERSITY D-4
www.gvsu.edu

Allendale, MI 49401	**(616) 331-5000** **(800) 748-0246**
Fax: (616) 331-2000	**Email: admissions@gvsu.edu**
Full-time: 7699 men, 10,964 women	**Faculty:** 1069; IIA, av$
Part-time: 1136 men, 1432 women	**Ph.D.s:** 78%
Graduate: 1102 men, 2235 women	**Student/Faculty:** 17 to 1
Year: semesters, summer session	**Tuition:** $12,290 ($17,352)
Room & Board: $9150	**Freshman Class:** 17880 applied, 14596 accepted, 3966 enrolled
SAT: required **ACT:** 24	**CEEB CODE:** 1258
Application Deadline: May 1	**COMPETITIVE+**

Grand Valley State University, founded in 1960, is a comprehensive public institution offering graduate and undergraduate liberal arts and professional education. The figures in the above capsule and in this profile are approximate. There are 8 undergraduate schools and 7 graduate schools. In addition to regional accreditation, GVSU has baccalaureate program accreditation with AACSB, ABET, APTA, CSWE, NASAD, NASM, CAEP, and NLN. The 1342-acre campus is in a small town 12 miles west of Grand Rapids. Including any residence halls, there are 72 buildings.

STUDENT LIFE: 95% of undergraduates are from Michigan. Others are from 40 states, 73 foreign countries, and Canada. 75% are from public schools. 91% are White; 7% African American; 4% Hispanic; 4% two or more races; 3% Asian American; 2% American Indian/Alaska Native; 1% Foreign; 1% race unknown. **Female To Male Ratio:** 1.5:1. The average age of freshmen is 18; all undergraduates, 21. 18% do not continue beyond their first year; 56% remain to graduate. **Housing:** 5820 students can be accommodated in college housing, which includes married student dorms, on-campus apartments, and off-campus apartments. In addition, there are honors houses, language/international houses, special-interest houses, fraternity houses, and sorority houses. On-campus housing is guaranteed for the freshman year only, is available on a first-come, first-served basis, and is available on a lottery system for upperclassmen. 73% of students commute. Alcohol is not permitted. All students may keep cars.

FACULTY/CLASSROOMS: 51% of faculty are male; 49% are female. 97% teach undergraduates. No introductory courses are taught by graduate students. The average class size in an introductory lecture is 37; in a laboratory is 21; and in a regular course is 27.

PROGRAMS OF STUDY: GVSU confers B.A., B.S., B.B.A., B.F.A., B.M., B.M.E., B.S.E., B.S.N. and B.S.W. degrees. Master's and doctoral degrees are also awarded. Bachelor's degrees are awarded in AGRICULTURE (natural resource management), BIOLOGICAL SCIENCE (biology/biological science and cell biology), BUSINESS (accounting, banking and finance, business administration and management, business economics, hotel/motel and restaurant management, international business management, management science, marketing/retailing/merchandising, and personnel management), COMMUNICATIONS AND THE ARTS (advertising, art, art history and appreciation, broadcasting, Chinese, classics, communications, creative writing, dance, design, dramatic arts, English, film arts, fine arts, French, German, journalism, languages, music, photography, and Spanish), COMPUTER AND PHYSICAL SCIENCE (chemistry, computer science, earth science, geochemistry, geology, information sciences and systems, mathematics, physics, science, and statistics), EDUCATION (art education, athletic training, elementary education, foreign languages education, middle school education, music education, science education, secondary education, and special education), ENGINEERING AND ENVIRONMENTAL DESIGN (engineering, industrial engineering technology, and occupational safety and health), HEALTH PROFESSIONS (biomedical science, clinical science, exercise science, health science, medical laboratory technology, nursing, physical therapy, physician's assistant, predentistry, premedicine, and recreation therapy), SOCIAL SCIENCE (anthropology, behavioral science, biopsychology, criminal justice, economics, geography, history, international relations, law, liberal arts/general studies, philosophy, political science/government, prelaw, psychology, public administration, Russian and Slavic studies, social science, social work, and sociology). Health sciences, English, and psychology have the largest enrollments.

ACTIVITIES: There are 250 groups on campus, including art, band, cheerleading, chess, choir, chorale, chorus, computers, dance, drama, environmental, ethnic, film, honors, international, jazz band, LGBT, literary magazine, marching band, musical theater, newspaper, opera, orchestra, pep band, photography, political, professional, radio and TV, religious, social, social service, student government, and symphony. Popular campus events include Family Day, Hispanic Awareness Week, and Black History Month. **Sports:** There are 9 intercollegiate sports for men and 10 for women, and 26 intramural sports for men and 26 for women. Facilities include a football stadium, a baseball field, basketball arena, swimming and diving pools, an indoor track, weight room, fitness building/intramural center, outdoor cross-country track, and an outdoor soccer field. **Graduates:** From July 1, 2016 to June 30, 2017, 4301 bachelor's degrees were awarded. The most popular majors were business/marketing (16%), biological/life sciences (9%), and health sciences (8%). In an average class, 30% graduate in 4 years or less, 56% graduate in 5 years or less, and 63% graduate in 6 years or less. Of the 2016 graduating class, 25% were enrolled in graduate school within 6 months of graduation, and 79% were employed.

SERVICES: Counseling and information services are available, as is tutoring in most subjects. There is a reader service for the blind, and remedial math, reading, and writing. **Library/Resources:** The library contains 708,000 volumes, 868,850 microform items, and 19,804 audio/video tapes/CDs/DVDs, and subscribes to 73,759 periodicals including electronic. Computerized library services include interlibrary loans, database searching, Internet access, and Wi-Fi capability. Special learning facilities include an art gallery, radio station, TV station, a cadaver lab, 2 Great Lakes research vessels, a performance auditorium, and dance studios. **Physically Challenged Students:** 98% of the campus is accessible. Facilities include wheelchair ramps, elevators, special parking, specially equipped restrooms, special class scheduling, lowered drinking fountains, and lowered telephones. **Special:** Many programs offer dual majors and internships, and most majors qualify for B.A.-B.S. degrees. There is an engineering cooperative program, a student-designed major in liberal studies, and many work-study programs. Outside opportunities include study abroad in 10 countries and a Washington semester. There are 14 national honor societies, a freshman honors program, and 12 departmental honors programs. **Visiting:** There are regularly scheduled orientations for prospective students, including registration activities. There are guides for informal visits, visitors may sit in on classes, and stay overnight. To schedule a visit, contact the Admissions Office. **Campus Safety and Security:** Measures include 24-hour foot and vehicle patrol, emergency notification system, self-defense education, and security escort services. There are shuttle buses, emergency telephones, and lighted pathways/sidewalks.

REQUIREMENTS: Michigan residents must submit ACT test scores, nonresidents either ACT or SAT scores. High school transcripts should indicate 4 years of English with 1 composition course, 3 each of math (including 2 years of algebra), science (including 1 lab), and social studies, and 2 of a foreign language. Applicants who graduated from high school more than 3 years ago need not show test results. The GED is accepted. A GPA of 3.0 is required. AP and CLEP credits are accepted. Important factors in the admissions decision are extracurricular activities record, recommendations by school officials, and advanced placement or honors courses. To graduate, students must have earned 30 credits in general education, composed of 10 courses selected from specific groups, and have completed the university's required courses in English and math, as well as the upper-division writing course. A total of 120 credits, with 36 to 60 in the major, and a GPA of 2.0, are required to graduate. **Procedure:** Freshmen are admitted to all sessions. Entrance exams should be taken during the junior year. There is a rolling admissions plan. Applications should be filed by May 1 for fall entry. The fall 2017 application fee was $30. Notification is sent on a rolling basis. Applications are accepted on-line. **Transfer Students:** 1800 transfer students enrolled in 2016-2017. Transfer students must have a minimum of 30 college credits with a 2.0 GPA. They must submit previous college transcripts and a statement of good standing from prior institutions. 30 of 120 credits required for the bachelor's degree must be completed at GVSU. **International Students:** There are 272 international students enrolled. They must take the TOEFL with a minimum score of 550 on the paper-based TOEFL (PBT) or 80 on the Internet-based version (iBT) or take the MELAB and the Comprehensive English Language Test. They must also take the SAT or ACT.

ADMISSIONS: 82% of the 2017-2018 applicants were accepted. The ACT scores were 19% below 12, 31% between 12 and 17, 28% between 18 and 23, 12% between 24 and 29, and 10% above 30. 45% of the current freshmen were in the top fifth of their class; 80% were in the top two fifths. 18 freshmen graduated first in their class. **Admissions Contact:** Jodi Chycinski, Director of Admissions. Email: *admissions@gvsu.edu* Web: *www.gvsu.edu*

FINANCIAL AID: In 2017-2018, 67% of all full-time freshmen received some form of financial aid. 60% of all full-time freshmen received need-based aid. The average freshman award was $10,949. Need-based scholarships or need-based grants averaged $7,469; and need-based self-help aid (loans and jobs) averaged $4,937. 12% of undergraduate students work part-time. The average financial indebtedness of the 2017 graduate was $24,876. GVSU is a member of CSS. The FAFSA code is 002268. The deadline for filing freshman financial aid applications for fall entry is February 15.

HILLSDALE COLLEGE — D-5

www.hillsdale.edu

Hillsdale, MI 49242 — **(517) 607-2327**

Fax: (517) 607-2223	**Email:** admissions@hillsdale.edu
Full-time: 745 men, 718 women	**Faculty:** 137
Part-time: 25 men, 24 women	**Ph.D.s:** 94%
Graduate: 31 men, 13 women	**Student/Faculty:** 11 to 1
Year: semesters, summer session	**Tuition:** $26,560
Room & Board: $10,610	**Freshman Class:** 2080 applied, 863 accepted, 372 enrolled
SAT CR/M: 689/661 **ACT:** 30	**CEEB CODE:** 1295
Application Deadline: April 1	**MOST COMPETITIVE**

Hillsdale College distinguishes itself from most other academic institutions by its rigorous, traditional, liberal arts core curriculum and its principled determination never to accept federal taxpayer funding. Hillsdale's core curriculum contains the essence of the classical liberal arts education. Through it, our students are introduced to the history, the philosophical and theological ideas, the works of literature, and the scientific discoveries that set Western Civilization apart. As explained in the Hillsdale mission statement, the college considers itself a trustee of modern man's intellectual and spiritual inheritance from the Judeo-Christian faith and Greco-Roman culture, a heritage finding its clearest expression in the American experiment of self-government under law. There is 1 undergraduate school and 1 graduate school. The 400-acre campus is in a small town 120 miles southwest of Detroit. Including any residence halls, there are 75 buildings.

STUDENT LIFE: 66% of undergraduates are from out of state, mostly the Midwest. Students are from 49 states, 14 foreign countries, and Canada. 45% are from public schools. **Male To Female Ratio:** 1.1:1. The average age of freshmen is 18; all undergraduates, 20. 8% do not continue beyond their first year; 85% remain to graduate. **Housing:** 1068 students can be accommodated in college housing, which includes dorms and on-campus apartments. In addition, there are honors houses, fraternity houses, and sorority houses. On-campus housing is guaranteed for all 4 years. 69% of students live on campus. Alcohol is not permitted. All students may keep cars.

FACULTY/CLASSROOMS: All teach undergraduates. No introductory courses are taught by graduate students. The average class size in an introductory lecture is 31; in a laboratory is 13; and in a regular course is 18.

PROGRAMS OF STUDY: Hillsdale confers B.A. and B.S. degrees. Master's and doctoral degrees are also awarded. Bachelor's degrees are awarded in BIOLOGICAL SCIENCE (biochemistry and biology/biological science), BUSINESS (accounting, finance, international business management, marketing/retailing/merchandising, and sports management), COMMUNICATIONS AND THE ARTS (art, classics, comparative literature, English, French, German, Greek, Latin, music, Spanish, speech/debate/rhetoric, and theatre arts), COMPUTER AND PHYSICAL SCIENCE (applied mathematics, chemistry, mathematics, and physics), EDUCATION (physical education), HEALTH PROFESSIONS (exercise science and sports psychology), SOCIAL SCIENCE (American studies, Christian studies, economics, European studies, history, philosophy, philosophy and religion, political science/government, psychology, religion, and sociology). Economics, history, and English have the largest enrollments.

ACTIVITIES: 24% of men belong to 4 national fraternities; 34% of women belong to 3 national sororities. There are 124 groups on campus, including art, band, cheerleading, chess, choir, chorale, chorus, communications, computers, dance, debate, drama, ethnic, film, forensics, honors, international, jazz band, literary magazine, musical theater, newspaper, opera, orchestra, pep band, photography, political, professional, radio and TV, religious, social, social service, student government, symphony, and yearbook. Popular campus events include Centralhallapalooza, President's Ball, Mock Rock, Garden Party, Welcome Party, Kickoff Cookout, Homecoming Spirit Week. **Sports:** There are 13 intercollegiate sports for men and 10 for women, and 9 intramural sports for men and 9 for women. Facilities include an athletic complex with an artificial turf football field, a swimming pool, a 200-meter indoor track and tennis facility, basketball arena, weight room, outdoor Olympic track, an exercise/physiology room, volleyball, handball, racquetball, wallyball courts, and a gym. **Graduates:** From July 1, 2016 to June 30, 2017, 313 bachelor's degrees were awarded. The most popular majors were Economics (13%), History (12%), and English (9%). In an average class, 1% graduate in 3 years or less, 71% graduate in 4 years or less, 84% graduate in 5 years or less, and 85% graduate in 6 years or less. Of the 2016 graduating class, 23% were enrolled in graduate school within 6 months of graduation, and 75% were employed.

SERVICES: Counseling and information services are available, as is tutoring in every subject. **Library/Resources:** The library contains 252,517 volumes, 484,174 microform items, and 22,331 audio/video tapes/CDs/DVDs, and subscribes to 30,570 periodicals including electronic. Computerized library services include interlibrary loans, database searching, Internet access, and Wi-Fi capability. Special learning facilities include an art gallery, natural history museum, radio station, an auditorium, greenhouse, a music hall, media center, K-8 private academy, an arboretum, rare books library, science building, and a preschool. **Physically Challenged Students:** 85% of the campus is accessible. Facilities include wheelchair ramps, elevators, special parking, specially equipped restrooms, lowered drinking fountains, and special housing according to individual needs. **Special:** Special academic programs include the Washington Journalism Internship at the National Journalism Center and the Washington-Hillsdale Intern Program (WHIP), which places students in congressional or government offices. Students may study abroad in France, Germany, or Spain, and qualified students are chosen to attend Oxford University for a year. A business internship is offered in London at Regents College. The Thomas Professional Sales Intern program is also available. The college offers an accelerated degree; interdisciplinary majors, including political economy combining economics, history, and political science; 3-2 and 2-2 engineering degrees; and work-study programs at the city radio station WCSR and the city newspaper, and the Hillsdale Daily News. There are 28 national honor societies and 26 departmental honors programs. **Visiting:** There are regularly scheduled orientations for prospective students, agenda is customized based on visitor request; almost all visits include a campus tour and meeting with an Admissions Representative. Visitors may sit in on classes and stay overnight. To schedule a visit, contact Margaret Braman in Admissions. **Campus Safety and Security:** Measures include 24-hour foot and vehicle patrol, emergency notification system, self-defense education, and security escort services. There are shuttle buses, emergency telephones, lighted pathways/sidewalks, and controlled access to dorms/residences.

REQUIREMENTS: Student must be a high school graduate or have earned a GED, and must have completed 4 years of English, 3 each of math and science, and 2 each of history, social studies, and foreign language. ACT or SAT is required. The college requires 2 letters of recommendation and an essay. An interview is also recommended. For music majors, an audition is required for a scholarship. For art majors, a portfolio must be submitted for review. The school recommends taking SAT: Subject tests, but they are not required. Some AP/CLEP credits do count as college credit. Important factors in the admissions decision are advanced placement or honors courses, extracurricular activities record, and leadership record. To graduate, the student must complete 124 semester hours with a GPA of 2.0. Required courses include 1 year each of English, and science, 1 semester of each of Western Heritage and American Heritage, and political science, 15 hours of the humanities, 12 of the natural sciences and math, 12 of the social sciences, and 2 of phys ed. Students must also enroll in 2 seminars at the school's Center for Constructive Alternatives. 12 credit hours in a foreign language for a B.A. degree and 34 credit hours in math and science for a B.S. degree are also required. **Procedure:** Freshmen are admitted fall and spring. Entrance exams should be taken spring of junior year, fall of senior year. There is a early decision plan, applications should be filed by November 1; April 1 for fall entry; December 1 for spring. The fall 2017 application fee was $35. Notification of early decision is sent December 1; regular decision, on a rolling basis. 100 early decision candidates were accepted for the 2017-2018 class. Applications are accepted on-line. **Transfer Students:** 21 transfer students enrolled in 2016-2017. High school transcript, college transcripts, essay or personal statement, standardized test scores, statement of good standing from prior institution are required. **International Students:** There are 14 international students enrolled. They must also take the SAT or ACT.

ADMISSIONS: 41% of the 2017-2018 applicants were accepted. The SAT scores for the 2017-2018 freshman class were: Critical Reading-- 0% below 500, 7% between 500 and 599, 45% between 600 and 699, and 48% between 700 and 800. Math-- 17% between 500 and 599, 51% between 600 and 699, and 32% between 700 and 800. The ACT scores were 1% between 18 and 23, 33% between 24 and 29, and 66% above 30. **Admissions Contact:** Doug Banbury, Associate VP of Admissions. Email: *admissions@hillsdale.edu* Web: *www.hillsdale.edu*

FINANCIAL AID: In 2017-2018, 98% of all full-time freshmen received some form of financial aid. 34% of all full-time freshmen received need-based aid. The average freshman award was $19,880. Need-based scholarships or need-based grants averaged $6,724 ($12,770 maximum); need-based self-help aid (loans and jobs) averaged $5,635 ($8,000 maximum); non-need-based athletic scholarships averaged $12,683 ($38,552 maximum); other non-need-based awards and non-need-based scholarships averaged $15,611 ($37,352 maximum); and $4,267 from other forms of aid. 49% of undergraduate students work part-time. The average financial indebtedness of the 2017 graduate was $28,394. Hillsdale is a member of CSS. The CSS/Profile and the college's own financial statement are required. The priority date for freshman financial aid applications for fall entry is rolling.

HOPE COLLEGE C-4

www.hope.edu

Holland, MI 49422	**(616) 395-7850** **(800) 968-7850**
Fax: (616) 395-7130	**Email: admissions@hope.edu**
Full-time: 1166 men, 1852 women	**Faculty:** 237; IIB, +$
Part-time: 58 men, 74 women	**Ph.D.s:** 76%
Graduate: n/av	**Student/Faculty:** 11 to 1
Year: semesters, summer session	**Tuition:** $32,780
Room & Board: $10,060	**Freshman Class:** 4377 applied, 3223 accepted, 738 enrolled
SAT CR/M: 608/602 **ACT:** 26	**CEEB CODE:** 1301
Application Deadline: open	**VERY COMPETITIVE**

Hope College, founded by Dutch pioneers in 1866, is a private liberal arts institution affiliated with the Reformed Church in America. There are 4 undergraduate schools. In addition to regional accreditation, HC has baccalaureate program accreditation with ABET, CSWE, NASAD, NASM, ACS, CCNE, NASD, NAST, and CAATE. The 120-acre campus is in an urban area 26 miles southwest of Grand Rapids and 5 miles east of Lake Michigan. Including any residence halls, there are 133 buildings.

STUDENT LIFE: 70% of undergraduates are from Michigan. Others are from 36 states, 27 foreign countries, and Canada. 77% are from public schools. 82% are White; 8% Hispanic; 3% African American; 3% Foreign; 2% Asian American; 2% two or more races. 30% are Protestant; 26% Unknown denominations; 19% Catholic; 17% claim no religious affiliation. **Female To Male Ratio:** 1.6:1. The average age of freshmen is 18; all undergraduates, 20. 10% do not continue beyond their first year; 80% remain to graduate. **Housing:** 2456 students can be accommodated in college housing, which includes married student dorms and on-campus apartments. In addition, there are language/international houses, special-interest houses, fraternity houses, sorority houses, and student cottages. On-campus housing is guaranteed for all 4 years. 78% of students live on campus. Alcohol is not permitted. All students may keep cars.

FACULTY/CLASSROOMS: 56% of faculty are male; 44% are female. All teach undergraduates. No introductory courses are taught by graduate students. The average class size in an introductory lecture is 21; in a laboratory is 17; and in a regular course is 19.

PROGRAMS OF STUDY: HC confers B.A., B.S., B.Mus. and B.S.N. degrees. Bachelor's degrees are awarded in BIOLOGICAL SCIENCE (biochemistry, biology/adolescence education, biology/biological science, and cell biology), BUSINESS (accounting and business administration and management), COMMUNICATIONS AND THE ARTS (art, art history and appreciation, classical languages, communications, creative writing, dance, dramatic arts, English, fine arts, French, German, language arts, Latin, music, music performance, piano/organ, piano performance, Spanish, theatre arts, and vocal music education), COMPUTER AND PHYSICAL SCIENCE (chemistry, chemistry education, computer science, geology, mathematics, and physics), EDUCATION (art education, athletic training, dance education, elementary education, English education, foreign languages education, history education, music education, science education, secondary education, and special education), ENGINEERING AND ENVIRONMENTAL DESIGN (engineering), HEALTH PROFESSIONS (exercise science and nursing), SOCIAL SCIENCE (economics, history, international studies, Japanese studies, philosophy, physical fitness/movement, political science/government, psychology, religion, social work, sociology, and women's studies). Chemistry, biological sciences, and psychology are the strongest academically. Management, psychology and biology have the largest enrollments.

ACTIVITIES: 12% of men belong to 7 local and 1 national fraternities; 14% of women belong to 7 local and 1 national sororities. There are 78 groups on campus, including art, band, cheerleading, chess, choir, chorale, chorus, computers, dance, drama, environmental, ethnic, honors, international, jazz band, literary magazine, musical theater, newspaper, orchestra, pep band, political, professional, radio and TV, religious, social, social service, student government, symphony, and yearbook. Popular campus events include The Pull, Spring Festival, and Nykerk Cup Competition. **Sports:** There are 11 intercollegiate sports for men and 11 for women, and 14 intramural sports for men and 15 for women. Facilities include athletic fields, soccer fields, softball and baseball stadium, an outdoor track and field area, a 6-court indoor tennis center, a health and phys ed center that contains basketball/volleyball courts, a running track, swimming and diving pool, exercise rooms, dance studios, racquetball courts, and weight training and cardiovascular equipment. **Graduates:** From July 1, 2016 to June 30, 2017, 733 bachelor's degrees were awarded. The most popular majors were management (14%), psychology (9%), and speech (8%). In an average class, 1% graduate in 3 years or less, 69% graduate in 4 years or less, 79% graduate in 5 years or less, and 80% graduate in 6 years or less. Of the 2016 graduating class, 25% were enrolled in graduate school within 6 months of graduation, and 72% were employed.

SERVICES: Counseling and information services are available, as is tutoring in most subjects. There is a reader service for the blind. **Library/Resources:** The library contains 404,019 volumes, 376,577 microform items, and 16,233 audio/video tapes/CDs/DVDs, and subscribes to 44,039 periodicals including electronic. Computerized library services include interlibrary loans, database searching, Internet access, and Wi-Fi capability. Special learning facilities include an art gallery, planetarium, radio station, TV station, an academic support center, and a modern and classical language lab. **Physically Challenged Students:** 95% of the campus is accessible. Facilities include wheelchair ramps, elevators, special parking, specially equipped restrooms, special class scheduling, lowered drinking fountains, and special housing. **Special:** The college offers internships in all academic areas as well as on-campus work-study programs, student-designed majors, duel majors, study abroad in more than 57 countries, and Washington, Chicago, New York, and Philadelphia semesters. There are 20 national honor societies, Phi Beta Kappa, and 1 departmental honors program. **Visiting:** There are regularly scheduled orientations for prospective students, including campus tours, lunch with a current student, and appointments with professors. There are guides for informal visits, visitors may sit in on classes, and stay overnight. To schedule a visit, contact the Admissions Office. **Campus Safety and Security:** Measures include 24-hour foot and vehicle patrol and security escort services. There are shuttle buses, emergency telephones, and lighted pathways/sidewalks.

REQUIREMENTS: All applicants must submit either an ACT or SAT score. The college requires a high school transcript, which must include 4 years of English, 2 each of math, a foreign language, and social science, and 1 year of a lab science, as well as 5 other academic courses. The college requires submission of an essay and recommends an interview. A portfolio or audition is required for certain majors. The GED is considered. AP and CLEP credits are accepted. Important factors in the admissions decision are advanced placement or honors courses, evidence of special talent, and leadership record. To graduate with a B.A. or B.S. degree, students must complete 126 semester hours with a 2.0 GPA. All students must take 56 hours of the general education program, including a first-year seminar, 10 hours of math and natural science, 8 of cultural heritage, 6 each of social science, performing and fine arts, and religion, 4 each of language and writing, senior seminar, and cultural diversity courses, and 2 hours of health dynamics. **Procedure:** Freshmen are admitted fall and spring. Entrance exams should be taken during spring of the junior year or fall of the senior year. There are deferred admissions and rolling admissions plans. Application deadlines are open. The fall 2017 application fee was $35. Notifications are sent December 3. 409 applicants were on the 2017 waiting list; 19 were admitted. Applications are accepted on-line. **Transfer Students:** 58 transfer students enrolled in 2016-2017. Transfer students must have a GPA of 2.0 in at least 1 year of liberal arts courses. 30 of 126 credits required for the bachelor's degree must be completed at Hope. **International Students:** There are 80 international students enrolled. They must take the TOEFL with a minimum score of 79 on the Internet-based version (iBT). They must also take the SAT or ACT.

ADMISSIONS: 74% of the 2017-2018 applicants were accepted. The SAT scores for the 2017-2018 freshman class were: Critical Reading-- 5% below 500, 37% between 500 and 599, 47% between 600 and 699, and 11% between 700 and 800. Math-- 6% below 500, 41% between 500 and 599, 43% between 600 and 699, and 10% between 700 and 800. The ACT scores were 24% between 18 and 23, 53% between 24 and 29, and 22% above 30. 55% of the current freshmen were in the top fifth of their class; 93% were in the top two fifths. **Admissions Contact:** William C. Vanderbilt, Vice President for Admissions. Email: *admissions@hope.edu* Web: *www.hope.edu*

FINANCIAL AID: In 2017-2018, 98% of all full-time freshmen received some form of financial aid. 68% of all full-time freshmen received need-based aid. The average freshman award was $21,237. Need-based schol-

arships or need-based grants averaged $13,393; need-based self-help aid (loans and jobs) averaged $2,696; and other non-need-based awards and non-need-based scholarships averaged $5,148. The average financial indebtedness of the 2017 graduate was $25,583. HC is a member of CSS. The college's own financial statement is required. The FAFSA code is 002273. The priority date for freshman financial aid applications for fall entry is March 1.

KALAMAZOO COLLEGE D-5

www.kzoo.edu

Kalamazoo, MI 49006 (269) 337-7166 (800) 253-3602

Fax: (269) 337-7390 **Email:** admissions@kzoo.edu

Full-time: 640 men, 978 women

Part-time: 2 men, 3 women

Graduate: n/av

Year: quarters

Room & Board: $9174

SAT CR/M/W: 610/640/610 **ACT:** 28

Application Deadline: January 15

Faculty: 103

Ph.D.s: 91%

Student/Faculty: 13 to 1

Tuition: $44,418

Freshman Class: 3469 applied, 2377 accepted, 348 enrolled

CEEB CODE: 1365

HIGHLY COMPETITIVE

Kalamazoo College, founded in 1833, as a highly selective, nationally renowned, and internationally oriented four-year college of arts and sciences. "K" College is among the 100 oldest colleges and universities in the nation. There are 5 undergraduate schools. The 60-acre campus is in a suburban area 140 miles from the Detroit and Chicago area. Including any residence halls, there are 30 buildings.

STUDENT LIFE: 61% of undergraduates are from Michigan. Others are from 43 states, and 30 foreign countries. 81% are from public schools. **Female To Male Ratio:** 1.5:1. The average age of freshmen is 18; all undergraduates, 20. 8% do not continue beyond their first year. **Housing:** 875 students can be accommodated in college housing, which includes dorms. In addition, there are special-interest houses, and a wellness house. On-campus housing is available on a lottery system for upperclassmen. 66% of students live on campus. Upperclassmen may keep cars.

FACULTY/CLASSROOMS: 48% of faculty are male; 52% are female. All teach undergraduates. No introductory courses are taught by graduate students. The average class size in an introductory lecture is 26; in a laboratory is 14; and in a regular course is 22.

PROGRAMS OF STUDY: K-College confers B.A. degrees. Bachelor's degrees are awarded in BIOLOGICAL SCIENCE (biochemistry, biology/biological science, and neurosciences), BUSINESS (business economics), COMMUNICATIONS AND THE ARTS (art, art history and appreciation, dramatic arts, English, film, television and digital media, French, German, music, and Spanish), COMPUTER AND PHYSICAL SCIENCE (chemistry, computer science, mathematics, and physics), EDUCATION (physical education), ENGINEERING AND ENVIRONMENTAL DESIGN (engineering and environmental science), HEALTH PROFESSIONS (health science and pre-health studies), SOCIAL SCIENCE (African studies, anthropology, classical/ancient civilization, East Asian studies, economics, ethnic studies, history, human development, interdisciplinary studies, international studies, philosophy, political science/government, psychology, public administration, religion, and sociology). Foreign languages, international studies, and commerce are the strongest academically. Public administration, physical sciences, and biological sciences have the largest enrollments.

ACTIVITIES: There are no fraternities or sororities. There are 70 groups on campus, including art, cheerleading, chess, choir, chorus, computers, dance, drama, environmental, ethnic, film, honors, international, jazz band, LGBT, literary magazine, musical theater, newspaper, orchestra, photography, political, professional, radio and TV, religious, social, social service, student government, and symphony. Popular campus events include Homecoming, pep rally, Monte Carlo-Casino night games and dancing, K-Fest-Student Involvement, and outdoor movies. **Sports:** There are 9 intercollegiate sports for men and 9 for women, and 8 intramural sports for men and 7 for women. Facilities include a field house that houses a gym, basketball and volleyball courts, weight-training rooms, and a dance studio, 11-court tennis stadium, racquetball courts, a natatorium, an athletic field complex and field house, turf football and soccer/lacrosse fields as well as natural turf baseball and softball fields, and athletic training facility. **Graduates:** From July 1, 2016 to June 30, 2017, 348 bachelor's degrees were awarded. The most popular majors were social sciences (18%), biological/life sciences (12%), and psychology (12%). In an average class, 76% graduate in 4 years or less, 81% graduate in 5 years or less, and 83% graduate in 6 years or less.

SERVICES: Counseling and information services are available, as is tutoring in most subjects. There is a writing center, language labs, and supplemental instruction. **Library/Resources:** The library contains 397,384 volumes, 15,025 microform items, and 7,523 audio/video tapes/CDs/DVDs, and subscribes to 1,364 periodicals including electronic. Computerized library services include interlibrary loans, database searching, Internet access, and Wi-Fi capability. Special learning facilities include an art gallery, radio station, and TV station. **Physically Challenged Students:** 25% of the campus is accessible. Facilities include wheelchair ramps, elevators, special parking, specially equipped restrooms, special class scheduling, and special housing. **Special:** The Center for International Programs currently sends students to 59 programs in 25 countries on 6 continents. Over the past four years, the K-College graduate participation rate in our study abroad programs is 80% to 85% and the school allows dual and interdisciplinary majors, and has Inter-Institutional enrollment with Western Michigan University. A 3-2 engineering degree is offered with Washington University and the University of Michigan. There are 3 national honor societies and a chapter of Phi Beta Kappa. **Visiting:** There are regularly scheduled orientations for prospective students, including interviews, tours, and overnight and class visits as requested. Special preview events include formal presentation of the unique curriculum and financial aid seminars. There are guides for informal visits, visitors may sit in on classes, and stay overnight. To schedule a visit, contact Sharayl Moore at (877) 557-9755. **Campus Safety and Security:** Measures include 24-hour foot and vehicle patrol, emergency notification system, self-defense education, and security escort services. There are emergency telephones, lighted pathways/sidewalks, and controlled access to dorms/residences.

REQUIREMENTS: The college requires a high school transcript, an essay, supplement, and teacher and counselor recommendations, and an interview is recommended. Applications are online only. The college is a Common Application exclusive member. AP credits are accepted. Important factors in the admissions decision are recommendations by school officials, leadership record, and advanced placement or honors courses. To graduate, students must complete 36 academic units, including a minimum of 8 units in the major, with a minimum 2.0 GPA. The college requires sophomore and senior seminars and completion of a senior individualized project. The student must also take 5 noncredit courses in phys ed and show proficiency in writing as well as in a foreign language. **Procedure:** Freshmen are admitted in the fall. Entrance exams should be taken by December of the senior year. There are early decision, early admissions, and deferred admissions plans. Early decision applications should be filed by November 1; regular applications, by January 15 for fall entry. Notification of early decision is sent December 1; regular decision, April 1. 27 early decision candidates were accepted for the 2017-2018 class. 317 applicants were on the 2017 waiting list; 65 were admitted. Applications are accepted on-line. **Transfer Students:** 14 transfer students enrolled in 2016-2017. In addition to the Transfer Application, we require the College Official's Report, Instructor Evaluation, official high school and college transcripts. While an interview is not required, it is strongly recommended. In most cases, successful transfer applicants present grades of a B average or better in their current courses. 18 of 36 credits required for the bachelor's degree must be completed at Kalamazoo. **International Students:** There are 132 international students enrolled. They must take the TOEFL with a minimum score of 550 on the paper-based TOEFL (PBT) or 84 on the Internet-based version (iBT). Students must take the SAT. They must also take the IELTS, or IB Programs.

ADMISSIONS: 69% of the 2017-2018 applicants were accepted. The SAT scores for the 2017-2018 freshman class were: Critical Reading-- 16% below 500, 29% between 500 and 599, 33% between 600 and 699, and 22% between 700 and 800. Math-- 9% below 500, 22% between 500 and 599, 37% between 600 and 699, and 31% between 700 and 800. Writing-- 13% below 500, 28% between 500 and 599, 39% between 600 and 699, and 19% between 700 and 800. The ACT scores were 2% between 12 and 17, 13% between 18 and 23, 48% between 24 and 29, and 37% above 30. 9 freshmen graduated first in their class. **Admissions Contact:** Eric P. Staab, Dean of Admission. Email: *admissions@kzoo.edu* Web: *www.kzoo.edu*

FINANCIAL AID: In 2017-2018, 98% of all full-time freshmen received

some form of financial aid. 74% of all full-time freshmen received need-based aid. The average freshman award was $36,012. Need-based scholarships or need-based grants averaged $29,445; need-based self-help aid (loans and jobs) averaged $6,481; and other non-need-based awards and non-need-based scholarships averaged $20,273. The average financial indebtedness of the 2017 graduate was $28,764. The college's own financial statement is required. The FAFSA code is 002275. The priority date for freshman financial aid applications for fall entry is February 15.

KETTERING UNIVERSITY — E-4

www.kettering.edu

Flint, MI 48504 — **(810) 762-9500** / **(800) 955-4464**

Fax: (810) 762-9837 — **Email: admissions@kettering.edu**

Full-time: 1468 men, 338 women	**Faculty:** 114; IIA, av$
Part-time: 43 men, 13 women	**Ph.D.s:** 68%
Graduate: 295 men, 89 women	**Student/Faculty:** 15 to 1
Year: semesters, summer session	**Tuition:** $39,790
Room & Board: $7780	**Freshman Class:** 1931 applied, 1358 accepted, 371 enrolled
SAT EBR-W/M: 620/650 **ACT:** 27	**CEEB CODE:** 1246
Application Deadline: rolling	**HIGHLY COMPETITIVE**

Kettering University, founded in 1919, is a private college. Students in the undergraduate program alternate 11-week terms of full-time classes with 12-week terms of full-time paid professional cooperative education (Co-op) work experience in industry. Students typically begin Co-op during their freshman year. There are 3 undergraduate schools and 1 graduate school. In addition to regional accreditation, Kettering has baccalaureate program accreditation with ABET and ACBSP. The 85-acre campus is in a suburban area 60 miles north of Detroit. Including any residence halls, there are 10 buildings.

STUDENT LIFE: 89% of undergraduates are from Michigan. Others are from 49 states, 18 foreign countries, and Canada. 85% are from public schools. 76% are White; 5% Hispanic; 5% race unknown; 4% Asian American; 4% Foreign; 3% African American; 3% two or more races. **Male To Female Ratio:** 4.1:1. The average age of freshmen is 18; all undergraduates, 21. 86% do not continue beyond their first year; 64% remain to graduate. **Housing:** 623 students can be accommodated in college housing, which includes coed dorms and on-campus apartments. In addition, there are fraternity houses, sorority houses, and theme housing. On-campus housing is guaranteed for the freshman year only and is available on a lottery system for upperclassmen. 60% of students commute. Alcohol is not permitted. All students may keep cars.

FACULTY/CLASSROOMS: 72% of faculty are male; 28% are female. All teach undergraduates, 16% do research, and 16% do both. No introductory courses are taught by graduate students. The average class size in an introductory lecture is 40; in a laboratory is 14; and in a regular course is 20.

PROGRAMS OF STUDY: Kettering confers B.S. degrees. Master's degrees are also awarded. Bachelor's degrees are awarded in BIOLOGICAL SCIENCE (biochemistry), COMPUTER AND PHYSICAL SCIENCE (applied mathematics, applied physics, chemistry, and computer science), ENGINEERING AND ENVIRONMENTAL DESIGN (computer engineering, electrical/electronics engineering, engineering physics, industrial engineering, and mechanical engineering). Mechanical, electrical, and computer engineering have the largest enrollments.

ACTIVITIES: 39% of men belong to 13 national fraternities; 32% of women belong to 6 national sororities. There are 43 groups on campus, including art, band, computers, dance, drama, environmental, ethnic, honors, international, LGBT, literary magazine, newspaper, photography, political, professional, radio and TV, religious, social, social service, student government, and yearbook. Popular campus events include Greek Week, Diversity Week, and Student and Alumni Industry Speaker Series. **Sports:** There is no sports program at Kettering. Facilities include a recreation center with basketball/volleyball, tennis/basketball/volleyball courts, racquetball and squash courts, a one-eighth mile track, an Olympic-size pool, free weight, Nautilus, fitness and group exercise room. The sports and recreation complex includes softball, multipurpose fields, golf, a 1 km outdoor track, and sand volleyball courts. **Graduates:** From July 1, 2016 to June 30, 2017, 320 bachelor's degrees were awarded. The most popular majors were engineering (86%), computer and information sciences (5%), and business/marketing (4%). In an average class, 53% graduate in 6 years or less. Of the 2016 graduating class, 40% were enrolled in graduate school within 6 months of graduation, and 96% were employed.

SERVICES: Counseling and information services are available, as is tutoring in most subjects. Tutoring is routinely available for most subjects in the Academic Support Center, in the residence hall, and with faculty, supplemental tutoring is coordinated through the Academic Services Department. Math and writing labs are available. A Strategies for Academic Success program is also available. **Library/Resources:** The library contains 133,210 volumes, 35,000 microform items, and 800 audio/video tapes/CDs/DVDs, and subscribes to 400 periodicals including electronic. Computerized library services include interlibrary loans, database searching, and Internet access. Special learning facilities include an art gallery, radio station, and industrial history archives. **Physically Challenged Students:** All of the campus is accessible. Facilities include wheelchair ramps, elevators, special parking, specially equipped restrooms, special class scheduling, lowered drinking fountains, lowered telephones, and special housing. **Special:** All undergraduate students participate in paid professional cooperative education work experience. Students may pursue a dual major in any degree combination. Accelerated degree programs in engineering are available in most majors, as is study abroad in 3 countries. There are 8 national honor societies. **Visiting:** There are regularly scheduled orientations for prospective students, including 2 open house programs for prospective students. There are guides for informal visits, visitors may sit in on classes, and stay overnight. To schedule a visit, contact the Admissions Office. **Campus Safety and Security:** Measures include 24-hour foot and vehicle patrol, self-defense education, and security escort services. There are emergency telephones, lighted pathways/sidewalks, and controlled access to dorms/residences. After-hours access (e.g., to the academic building) is secure via the tunnel from the residence hall and campus center.

REQUIREMENTS: The SAT or ACT is required. Applicants must graduate from an accredited secondary school with a minimum of 10.5 academic credits (21 recommended). Applicants must have completed 3-4 years of English, and math, and 2-3 years of science with lab, 2 years of social studies and history, and 1 year recommended of academic electives. AP credits are accepted. Important factors in the admissions decision are extracurricular activities record, advanced placement or honors courses, evidence of special talent, and recommendations by school officials. Degree requirements include completion of 160 credit hours, with 60 in the major. All students must take specific courses in math, chemistry, physics, written and oral communication, humanities, and economics, and complete at least 5 terms of co-op experience in industry plus 2 work terms designated for a senior thesis project. A minimum grade average of 80 on a scale of 100 is required for graduation. The GPA is determined by a formula combining the numerical grades achieved and the number of credits attempted. Students must complete a thesis. **Procedure:** Freshmen are admitted fall, winter, and summer. Entrance exams should be taken during the spring of the junior year and fall of the senior year. There are deferred admissions and rolling admissions plans. Application deadlines are open. Applications are accepted on-line. **Transfer Students:** 46 transfer students enrolled in 2016-2017. Transfer applicants must present the same minimum preparation as freshmen in math and science and must submit both high school and college transcripts and SAT or ACT scores. Required courses can be taken in high school or college. A minimum GPA of 3.0 in English, math, and science is expected. Transfers who present less than 30 credits of full-time study will be judged on both their college and high school record and test scores. 88 of 160 credits required for the bachelor's degree must be completed at Kettering. **International Students:** There are 33 international students enrolled. They must take the TOEFL or MELAB.

ADMISSIONS: 70% of the 2017-2018 applicants were accepted. The SAT scores for the 2017-2018 freshman class were: Evidence-Based Reading/Writing-- 1% below 500, 37% between 500 and 599, 50% between 600 and 699, and 11% between 700 and 800. The ACT scores were 15% between 18 and 23, 60% between 24 and 29, and 25% above 30. 64% of the current freshmen were in the top fifth of their class; 94% were in the top two fifths. 18 freshmen graduated first in their class. **Admissions Contact:** Barbara Sosin, Director of Admissions. Email: *admissions@kettering.edu* Web: *www.kettering.edu*

FINANCIAL AID: In 2017-2018, 89% of all full-time freshmen received some form of financial aid. 79% of all full-time freshmen received need-based aid. The average freshman award was $24,353. Need-based schol-

arships or need-based grants averaged $21,737; need-based self-help aid (loans and jobs) averaged $3,709; other non-need-based awards and non-need-based scholarships averaged $17,436; and $3,445 from other forms of aid. The college's own financial statement is required. The FAFSA code is 002262. The priority date for freshman financial aid applications for fall entry is March 1.

LAKE SUPERIOR STATE UNIVERSITY D-2

www.lssu.edu

Sault Sainte Marie, MI 49783	**(906) 635-2231** **(888) 800-5778**
Fax: (906) 635-6696	**Email: admissions@lssu.edu**
Full-time: 897 men, 910 women	**Faculty:** 99
Part-time: 176 men, 239 women	**Ph.D.s:** n/av
Graduate: 1 men, 1 women	**Student/Faculty:** 23 to 1
Year: semesters, summer session	**Tuition:** $11,019
Room & Board: $9442	**Freshman Class:** n/av
SAT CR/M/W: 470/500/480 **ACT:** 21	**CEEB CODE:** 1421
Application Deadline: August 15	**COMPETITIVE**

Lake Superior State University, founded in 1946, is a public university that provides a blend of liberal and technical studies, offering undergraduate degrees in 45 areas of study. There are 12 undergraduate schools. In addition to regional accreditation, LSSU has baccalaureate program accreditation with ABET, ACBSP, NLN, CAAHEP, CAATE, HEHPAC, ABA, and AAMC. The 115-acre campus is in a small town of Michigan's Upper Peninsula, 45 minutes north of the Mackinac Bridge. Including any residence halls, there are 37 buildings.

STUDENT LIFE: 99% of undergraduates are from Michigan. Others are from 29 states, 11 foreign countries, and Canada. 79% are White; 9% American Indian/Alaska Native; 7% Foreign; 2% African American; 2% Hispanic; 1% Asian American; 1% two or more races; 1% race unknown. **Female To Male Ratio:** 1.1:1. The average age of freshmen is 18; all undergraduates, 22. 30% do not continue beyond their first year; 48% remain to graduate. **Housing:** 900 students can be accommodated in college housing, which includes dorms and on-campus apartments. In addition, there are honors houses, fraternity houses, sorority houses, and theme housing. On-campus housing is guaranteed for the freshman year only, is available on a first-come, first-served basis, and is available on a lottery system for upperclassmen. 66% of students commute. All students may keep cars.

FACULTY/CLASSROOMS: 51% of faculty are male; 49% are female. All teach undergraduates. No introductory courses are taught by graduate students. The average class size in an introductory lecture is 23; in a laboratory is 15; and in a regular course is 27.

PROGRAMS OF STUDY: LSSU confers B.A. and B.S. degrees. Associate degrees are also awarded. Bachelor's degrees are awarded in AGRICULTURE (aquaculture & fishery technology, fish and game management, and wildlife management), BIOLOGICAL SCIENCE (biochemistry, biology/biological science, and wildlife conservation biology), BUSINESS (accounting, banking and finance, business administration and management, business administration - international, business administration marketing, international business, international business management, and marketing/retailing/merchandising), COMMUNICATIONS AND THE ARTS (communications, creative writing, fine arts, and literature), COMPUTER AND PHYSICAL SCIENCE (actuarial mathematics, chemistry, clinical laboratory science, chemistry/forensic chemistry, chemistry secondary education, computer management, computer networks & systems, computer science, environmental chemistry, environmental geology, geology, and mathematics), EDUCATION (athletic training, early childhood education, elementary education, general studies, and secondary education), ENGINEERING AND ENVIRONMENTAL DESIGN (computer engineering, electrical/electronics engineering, engineering, engineering management, engineering technology, environmental engineering technology, environmental science, fire protection science, manufacturing technology, and mechanical engineering), HEALTH PROFESSIONS (clinical science, emergency medical services, environmental health science, exercise science, medical laboratory technology, nursing, predentistry, premedicine, prepharmacy, and recreation therapy), SOCIAL SCIENCE (criminal justice, economics, fire science, forensic studies, French studies, history, homeland security, human services, law enforcement and corrections, parks and recreation management, political science/government, prelaw, psychology, social science, and sociology). Engineering, biological science, and nursing are the strongest academically. Criminal justice, and business have the largest enrollments.

ACTIVITIES: There are 60 groups on campus, including art, band, choir, chorale, chorus, computers, dance, drama, environmental, ethnic, honors, jazz band, LGBT, newspaper, pep band, political, professional, radio and TV, religious, social, social service, and student government. Popular campus events include Winter Carnival, Spring Fling, and Great Lake State Weekend. **Sports:** There are 5 intercollegiate sports for men and 6 for women. Facilities include an ice arena, a gym, swimming and diving pools, handball/squash courts, a weight-training and isometric room, a dance studio, and a training room. **Graduates:** From July 1, 2016 to June 30, 2017, 402 bachelor's degrees were awarded. The most popular majors were nursing (11%), accounting (6%), and criminal justice generalist (6%). In an average class, 3% graduate in 3 years or less, 27% graduate in 4 years or less, 53% graduate in 5 years or less, and 59% graduate in 6 years or less. Of the 2016 graduating class, 13% were enrolled in graduate school within 6 months of graduation, and 83% were employed.

SERVICES: Counseling and information services are available, as is tutoring in every subject, on request and free of charge. There is a reader service for the blind, and remedial math, reading, and writing. There are also math, reading, and writing labs. **Library/Resources:** The library contains 106,618 volumes, 810 audio/video tapes/CDs/DVDs, and subscribes to 950 periodicals including electronic. Computerized library services include interlibrary loans, database searching, Internet access, and Wi-Fi capability. Special learning facilities include an art gallery, natural history museum, planetarium, radio station, fish hatchery and aquatics lab, SIM Lab, and firing range. **Physically Challenged Students:** Facilities include wheelchair ramps, elevators, special parking, specially equipped restrooms, special class scheduling, lowered drinking fountains, and lowered telephones. **Special:** LSSU offers internships in criminal justice, medical science lab, human services, and natural resources technology, work-study programs, co-op programs in engineering technology, and cross-registration with the Canadian Colleges of Sault and Algoma and Bridge International Consortium. Study abroad and student-designed majors are available, as are B.A.-B.S. degrees, dual majors, and distance learning. There is a freshman honors program. **Visiting:** There are regularly scheduled orientations for prospective students. There are guides for informal visits and visitors may sit in on classes. To schedule a visit, contact the Admissions Office. **Campus Safety and Security:** Measures include 24-hour foot and vehicle patrol, emergency notification system, self-defense education, and security escort services. There are lighted pathways/sidewalks.

REQUIREMENTS: The ACT is required. Applicants should be high school graduates with 4 years of English, 3 each of math and science, 2 each of a foreign language and social studies, and 1 of history, and should have a GPA of 2.4. The GED is accepted. Students with below a 2.4 GPA and 19 ACT (or equivalent SAT) will go through a pending process and be evaluated on a case by case basis. AP and CLEP credits are accepted. Important factors in the admissions decision are advanced placement or honors courses, recommendations by school officials, and recommendations by alumni. To graduate, students must complete 124 semester hours with a GPA of 2.0. The core curriculum includes coursework in computer literacy, English, oral communications, aesthetics, critical thinking, humanities, math, science, social science, ethics, and cultural diversity. At least 30 of the final credits, and 50% of all upper-level courses, must be taken in residence at LSSU. **Procedure:** Freshmen are admitted to all sessions. There are deferred admissions and rolling admissions plans. Applications should be filed by August 15 for fall entry. The fall 2017 application fee was $35. Applications are accepted on-line. **Transfer Students:** 137 transfer students enrolled in 2016-2017. Applicants must be eligible to return to the last institution attended and must have an overall college GPA of 2.0. High school transcripts, ACT scores, and/or GED scores are required if transferring with fewer than 19 semester hours of credit. 30 of 124 credits required for the bachelor's degree must be completed at LSSU. **International Students:** There are 20 international students enrolled. They must take the TOEFL with a minimum score of 500 on the paper-based TOEFL (PBT) or 61 on the Internet-based version (iBT).

ADMISSIONS: The SAT scores for the 2017-2018 freshman class were: Critical Reading-- 67% below 500, 22% between 500 and 599, and 11% between 600 and 699. Math-- 45% below 500 and 55% between 500 and 599. Writing-- 55% below 500, 33% between 500 and 599, and 11%

between 600 and 699. The ACT scores were 1% below 12, 12% between 12 and 17, 59% between 18 and 23, 20% between 24 and 29, and 1% above 30. **Admissions Contact:** Michelle Markstrom, Assistant Director of Admissions. Email: *admissions@lssu.edu* Web: *www.lssu.edu*

FINANCIAL AID: In 2017-2018, 73% of all full-time freshmen received some form of financial aid. 61% of all full-time freshmen received need-based aid. The average freshman award was $8,519. Need-based scholarships or need-based grants averaged $4,984 ($5,477 maximum); need-based self-help aid (loans and jobs) averaged $7,394 ($13,882 maximum); non-need-based athletic scholarships averaged $3,489 ($12,762 maximum); and other non-need-based awards and non-need-based scholarships averaged $7,418 ($1,400 maximum). 18% of undergraduate students work part-time. The FAFSA code is 002293. The priority date for freshman financial aid applications for fall entry is March 1.

LAWRENCE TECHNOLOGICAL UNIVERSITY — E-5

www.ltu.edu

Southfield, MI 48075 — (248) 204-3160

Fax: (248) 204-3188	Email: admissions@ltu.edu
Full-time: 1223 men, 449 women	**Faculty:** 121
Part-time: 394 men, 125 women	**Ph.D.s:** 69%
Graduate: 648 men, 230 women	**Student/Faculty:** 14 to 1
Year: semesters, summer session	**Tuition:** $32,130
Room & Board: $9500	**Freshman Class:** 2173 applied, 1296 accepted, 373 enrolled
SAT EBR-W/M: 580/590 **ACT:** 24	**CEEB CODE:** 1399
Application Deadline: n/av	**VERY COMPETITIVE**

Lawrence Technological University, founded in 1932 as Lawrence Institute of Technology, is a private institution housing colleges of engineering, management, arts and sciences, and architecture and design. There are 4 undergraduate schools and 4 graduate schools. In addition to regional accreditation, LTU has baccalaureate program accreditation with AACSB, ABET, ACBSP, FIDER, NAAB, NASAD, CIDA, ASC, and IACBE. The 107-acre campus is in a suburban area 30 minutes north of downtown Detroit. Including any residence halls, there are 20 buildings.

STUDENT LIFE: 90% of undergraduates are from Michigan. Others are from 39 states, 38 foreign countries, and Canada. 60% are White; 6% African American; 3% Asian American; 3% Hispanic; 2% two or more races; 14% Foreign; 12% race unknown. **Male To Female Ratio:** 2.8:1. The average age of freshmen is 18; all undergraduates, 21. 18% do not continue beyond their first year; 53% remain to graduate. **Housing:** 785 students can be accommodated in college housing, which includes on-campus apartments and off-campus apartments. On-campus housing is available on a first-come and first-served basis. 64% of students commute. All students may keep cars.

FACULTY/CLASSROOMS: 70% of faculty are male; 30% are female. 96% teach undergraduates. No introductory courses are taught by graduate students. The average class size in an introductory lecture is 15; in a laboratory is 12; and in a regular course is 15.

PROGRAMS OF STUDY: LTU confers B.A., B.S., B.F.A. and B.F.M. degrees. Associate, master's, and doctoral degrees are also awarded. Bachelor's degrees are awarded in BIOLOGICAL SCIENCE (biochemistry, biotechnology, and molecular biology), BUSINESS (business administration and management and international business management), COMMUNICATIONS AND THE ARTS (animation, audio technology, communications, English, game design and development, illustration, industrial design, information technology, media arts, and technical and business writing), COMPUTER AND PHYSICAL SCIENCE (chemistry, computer science, environmental chemistry, information sciences and systems, mathematics, mathematics/computational, and physics), ENGINEERING AND ENVIRONMENTAL DESIGN (architectural engineering, architecture, biomedical engineering, civil engineering, computer engineering, computer graphics, construction management, electrical/electronics engineering, engineering, engineering technology, industrial administration/management, industrial engineering, interior architecture, interior design, mechanical engineering, technological management, and transportation engineering), SOCIAL SCIENCE (architectural studies, humanities, and psychology). Mathematics, computer science, and engineering are the strongest academically. Engineering, computer science, and architecture have the largest enrollments.

ACTIVITIES: 7% of men belong to 1 local and 5 national fraternities; 16% of women belong to 2 local and 2 national sororities. There are 45 groups on campus, including fishing club, math, cheerleading, chorus, communications, computers, dance, international, LGBT, literary magazine, newspaper, pep band, photography, professional, religious, robotics, social, social service, and student government. Popular campus events include Discovery Days, New Student Convocation, Welcome Back Picnic, Homecoming, Winterfest, Chinese New Year, International Fest, and Greek Week. **Sports:** There are 11 intercollegiate sports for men and 9 for women, and 11 intramural sports for men and 11 for women. The indoor recreation/athletic facility has cardio equipment, treadmills, ellipticles and bikes, weight rooms with free weights and weight machines, a track, basketball, racquetball courts, table tennis, heavy bag, turf field used for flag football, soccer, and ultimate Frisbee. **Graduates:** From July 1, 2016 to June 30, 2017, 362 bachelor's degrees were awarded. The most popular majors were engineering (43%), architecture (21%), and computer science (9%). In an average class, 43% graduate in 4 years or less, 51% graduate in 5 years or less, and 53% graduate in 6 years or less. Of the 2016 graduating class, 13% were enrolled in graduate school within 6 months of graduation, and 86% were employed.

SERVICES: Counseling and information services are available, as is tutoring in most subjects. There is a reader service for the blind, and remedial math, reading, and writing. There is also an Academic Achievement Center. **Library/Resources:** The library contains 77,821 volumes, 49,750 microform items, and 2,282 audio/video tapes/CDs/DVDs, and subscribes to 45,663 periodicals including electronic. Computerized library services include interlibrary loans, database searching, Internet access, and Wi-Fi capability. **Physically Challenged Students:** 97% of the campus is accessible. Facilities include wheelchair ramps, elevators, special parking, specially equipped restrooms, special class scheduling, lowered drinking fountains, lowered telephones, and special housing. **Special:** There are co-op programs in a number of majors, internships, study abroad in 8 countries and dual majors available. There is 1 national honor society and 2 departmental honors programs. **Visiting:** There are regularly scheduled orientations for prospective students. There are guides for informal visits, visitors may sit in on classes, and stay overnight. To schedule a visit, contact the Admissions Office. **Campus Safety and Security:** Measures include 24-hour foot and vehicle patrol, emergency notification system, and security escort services. There are shuttle buses, emergency telephones, lighted pathways/sidewalks, and a closed-circuit camera.

REQUIREMENTS: The ACT is required. The SAT is recommended. Students must have a high school diploma and a GPA of no lower than 2.5, at least 2.0 in each subject area pertaining to their major. Applicants should have taken 4 years each of math, science, and English, and 3 years of social science. The GED is accepted. An interview is recommended. AP and CLEP credits are accepted. Important factors in the admissions decision are advanced placement or honors courses, personality/intangible qualities, and leadership record. To graduate, students must have completed, depending on the major, 120 to 131 semester credit hours, with a GPA no lower than 2.0. Senior projects are required in most degree programs. **Procedure:** Freshmen are admitted to all sessions. Entrance exams should be taken in the semester preceding entry. There are deferred admissions and rolling admissions plans. Application deadlines are open. The fall 2017 application fee was $30. Notification is sent on a rolling basis. Applications are accepted on-line. **Transfer Students:** 183 transfer students enrolled in 2016-2017. Admission is based on the college GPA, which must be 2.0 or higher, with 30 or more semester hours. If less than 30 hours have been completed, admission is based on high school transcripts. 30 of 120 credits required for the bachelor's degree must be completed at LTU. **International Students:** There are 262 international students enrolled. They must take the TOEFL with a minimum score of 550 on the paper-based TOEFL (PBT) or 79 on the Internet-based version (iBT) or take the MELAB and the Comprehensive English Language Test. Placement exams are for incoming freshman students only.

ADMISSIONS: 60% of the 2017-2018 applicants were accepted. The SAT scores for the 2017-2018 freshman class were: Critical Reading-- 16% below 500, 44% between 500 and 599, 36% between 600 and 699, and 4% between 700 and 800. Math-- 12% below 500, 44% between 500 and 599, 36% between 600 and 699, and 8% between 700 and 800. The ACT scores were 10% between 12 and 17, 31% between 18 and 23, 47%

between 24 and 29, and 12% above 30. **Admissions Contact:** Jane Rohrback, Admissions Director. Email: *admissions@ltu.edu* Web: *www.ltu.edu*

FINANCIAL AID: In 2017-2018, 90% of all full-time freshmen received some form of financial aid. 72% of all full-time freshmen received need-based aid. The average freshman award was $35,553. Need-based scholarships or need-based grants averaged $4,701 ($23,040 maximum); need-based self-help aid (loans and jobs) averaged $6,607 ($13,500 maximum); non-need-based athletic scholarships averaged $11,326 ($34,500 maximum); and other non-need-based awards and non-need-based scholarships averaged $15,219 ($36,560 maximum). 85% of undergraduate students work part-time. The average financial indebtedness of the 2017 graduate was $37,352. LTU is a member of CSS. The deadline for filing freshman financial aid applications for fall entry is April 1.

MADONNA UNIVERSITY *(The complete profile is made available exclusively on our website, www.barronspac.com)*

MARYGROVE COLLEGE *(The complete profile is made available exclusively on our website, www.barronspac.com)*

MICHIGAN STATE UNIVERSITY D-4

www.msu.edu

East Lansing, MI 48824 **(517) 355-8332**

Fax: (517) 353-1647	**Email: admissions.msu.edu**
Full-time: 17,386 men, 18,018 women	**Faculty:** 2519; I, +$
Part-time: 1906 men, 1686 women	**Ph.D.s:** 90%
Graduate: 4901 men, 6122 women	**Student/Faculty:** 16 to 1
Year: semesters, summer session	**Tuition:** $14,516 ($39,461)
Room & Board: $10,026	**Freshman Class:** 36143 applied, 25860 accepted, 8066 enrolled
SAT: required **ACT:** 26	**CEEB CODE:** 1465
Application Deadline: May 1	**VERY COMPETITIVE**

Michigan State University, founded in 1855 as a land-grant university, began as a bold experiment that democratized higher education and helped bring science and innovation into everyday life. The university is one of the top research universities in the world and one of the biggest, greenest campuses in the nation. It is home to a diverse community of dedicated students and scholars, athletes and artists, scientists and leaders. There are 17 undergraduate schools and 17 graduate schools. In addition to regional accreditation, MSU has baccalaureate program accreditation with AACSB, ABET, ACCE, ACEJMC, ASLA, CAHEA, CSWE, FIDER, NASM, NLN, and SAF. The 5200-acre campus is in a suburban area in East Lansing, three miles east of Michigan's capitol in Lansing. Including any residence halls, there are 545 buildings.

STUDENT LIFE: 75% of undergraduates are from Michigan. Others are from 50 states, 130 foreign countries, and Canada. 7% are African American; 67% White; 5% Asian American; 4% Hispanic; 3% two or more races; 11% Foreign; 1% American Indian/Alaska Native. **Female To Male Ratio:** 1.1:1. The average age of freshmen is 18; all undergraduates, 20. 9% do not continue beyond their first year; 78% remain to graduate. **Housing:** 18,000 students can be accommodated in college housing, which includes married student dorms and on-campus apartments. In addition, there are honors houses, special-interest houses, residential colleges, living learning communities, quiet floors, and substance-free environments. On-campus housing is guaranteed for all 4 years. 60% of students commute. Upperclassmen may keep cars.

FACULTY/CLASSROOMS: 57% of faculty are male; 43% are female. No introductory courses are taught by graduate students. The average class size in an introductory lecture is 100; in a laboratory is 30; and in a regular course is 30.

PROGRAMS OF STUDY: MSU confers B.A., B.S., B.F.A., B.Land.Arch., B.Mus. and B.S. in nursing degrees. Master's and doctoral degrees are also awarded. Bachelor's degrees are awarded in AGRICULTURE (agricultural business management, agriculture, animal science, environmental studies, fishing and fisheries, forestry and related sciences, horticulture, natural resource management, soil science, and wildlife management), BIOLOGICAL SCIENCE (biochemistry, bioinformatics, biology/biological science, biological sciences, biotechnology, botany, entomology, environmental biology, microbiology, neurosciences, nutrition, physiology, plant pathology, and zoology), BUSINESS (accounting, banking and finance, business administration and management, finance, hospitality management services, human resources, human resources/organizational mgmt, management, marketing, marketing management, marketing/retailing/merchandising, personnel management, supply chain management, and tourism), COMMUNICATIONS AND THE ARTS (advertising, Arabic, art history and appreciation, Chinese, communications, composition, dramatic arts, East Asian languages and literature, English, film arts, French, German, graphic design, jazz, journalism, Latin, linguistics, music, music performance, music theory and composition, Russian, Spanish, studio art, telecommunications, and theatre studies), COMPUTER AND PHYSICAL SCIENCE (actuarial science, astrophysics, chemical physics, chemistry, computer science, earth science, geology, geophysics and seismology, geoscience, information sciences and systems, mathematics, natural sciences, physical sciences, physics, and statistics), EDUCATION (agricultural education, art education, education, music education, physical education, and special education), ENGINEERING AND ENVIRONMENTAL DESIGN (chemical engineering, city/community/regional planning, civil engineering, computational sciences, computer engineering, construction management, electrical/electronics engineering, engineering, engineering mechanics, environmental engineering technology, interior design, landscape architecture, landscape architecture/design, manufacturing engineering, materials engineering, materials science and engineering, mechanical engineering, packaging science, textile technology, and urban planning technology), HEALTH PROFESSIONS (clinical science, human biology, medical laboratory technology, music therapy, nursing, predentistry, preveterinary science, speech pathology/audiology, and veterinary science), SOCIAL SCIENCE (American studies, anthropology, child psychology/development, classical/ancient civilization, criminal justice, dietetics, economics, family and community services, family/consumer resource management, family/consumer studies, food production/management/services, food science, geography, history, human development & family studies, humanities, interdisciplinary studies, international relations, parks and recreation management, philosophy, political science/government, prelaw, psychology, public administration, religion, social science, social work, sociology, and women's studies). Education, business, and physics are the strongest academically. Business, social science, and natural science have the largest enrollments.

ACTIVITIES: There are 900 groups on campus, including art, band, cheerleading, chess, choir, chorale, chorus, communications, computers, dance, debate, drama, drill team, environmental, ethnic, film, forensics, honors, international, jazz band, LGBT, literary magazine, marching band, musical theater, newspaper, opera, orchestra, pep band, photography, political, professional, radio and TV, religious, social, social service, student government, symphony, and yearbook. Popular campus events include Athletic Events (football, basketball, and hockey), Welcome Week, and Homecoming. **Sports:** There are 12 intercollegiate sports for men and 13 for women, and 10 intramural sports for men and 10 for women. Facilities include a stadium, a gym and field house, an ice arena, a multipurpose student events center, an indoor football practice facility, intramural facilities, indoor and outdoor tennis courts, ball fields, a running track, golf courses, swimming pools, and Olympic-size outdoor pool. **Graduates:** The most popular majors were business (17%), communications (12%), and social science (12%). In an average class, 78% graduate in 6 years or less.

SERVICES: Counseling and information services are available, as is tutoring in most subjects. There is a reader service for the blind, and remedial math, reading, and writing. There are also tape recorders, videotaped classes, reading machines, readers and note takers. **Library/Resources:** The library contains 4.5 million volumes, 1.2 million microform items, and 40,000 audio/video tapes/CDs/DVDs, and subscribes to 33,000 periodicals including electronic. Computerized library services include interlibrary loans, database searching, Internet access, and Wi-Fi capability. Special learning facilities include an art gallery, natural history museum, planetarium, radio station, TV station, a botanical garden, a superconducting cyclotron lab, environmental toxicology center, pesticide research center, a center for the performing arts, a center for computer-aided and engineering and manufacturing. **Physically Challenged Students:** Facilities include wheelchair ramps, elevators, special parking, specially equipped restrooms, special class scheduling, lowered drinking fountains, lowered telephones, and special housing. **Special:** Special academic programs include an engineering co-op program with business and industry, internships in business, education, political science, agriculture, and communication arts, study abroad in more than 70 countries, on-campus work-study programs, and at sea semester. An accelerated degree program in all majors and student-designed majors are offered at the Honors College. Nondegree study, pass/fail options in some courses, and dual majors are possible. Educationally disadvantaged students may avail themselves of the College Achievement Admissions Program (CAAP). Cross-registration with the Committee on Institutional Cooperation schools is available. There are 48 national honor societies, Phi Beta Kappa, and a freshman honors program. **Visiting:** There are regularly scheduled orientations for prospective students, including a presentation and a tour of the campus. There are guides for informal visits and visitors may sit in on classes. To schedule a visit, contact the Office of Admissions. **Campus Safety and Security:** Measures include 24-hour foot and vehicle patrol, emergency notification system, self-defense education, and security escort services. There are shuttle buses, emergency telephones, lighted pathways/sidewalks, controlled access to dorms/residences, and regional/campus bus service.

REQUIREMENTS: The SAT or ACT is required. Applicants must be graduates of an accredited secondary school and have completed 4 years of English, 3 years each of math and social studies, 2 years each of science and a single foreign language. A personal statement is strongly recommended. The GED is accepted. Music majors must audition. AP and CLEP credits are accepted. To graduate, students must complete a freshman writing course and a writing course specified by the major and degree program. Students must complete the 26-credit University Integrative Studies requirement consisting of 8 credits each of arts and humanities, social, behavioral, economic sciences, and general science, and 3 of a transcollegiate course. Students must also complete a math requirement determined by each undergraduate college (minimum of college algebra plus trigonometry/finite math/statistics.) A minimum 2.0 GPA and 120 semester hours are required. **Procedure:** Freshmen are admitted fall, spring, and summer. Entrance exams should be taken during the junior year of high school. There are deferred admissions and rolling admissions plans. Applications should be filed by May 1 for fall entry; December 1 for spring entry; and April 15 for summer entry. The fall 2017 application fee was $65. Applications are accepted on-line. **Transfer Students:** 1669 transfer students enrolled in 2016-2017. To transfer, a minimum GPA of 2.0 is required, (prefer 3.0 overall GPA). MSU Integrative Studies requirement should be fulfilled (28 general graduation credits), and college algebra completed. 30 of 120 credits required for the bachelor's degree must be completed at MSU. **International Students:** There are 4463 international students enrolled. They must take the TOEFL with a minimum score of 550 on the paper-based TOEFL (PBT) or 79 on the Internet-based version (iBT) or take the MELAB. Student must also take the college's own test, and the MSUELT.

ADMISSIONS: 72% of the 2017-2018 applicants were accepted. The SAT scores for the 2017-2018 freshman class were: Math-- 6% below 500, 40% between 500 and 599, 40% between 600 and 699, and 13% between 700 and 800. Evidence-Based Reading/Writing-- 7% below 500, 41% between 500 and 599, 43% between 600 and 699, and 9% between 700 and 800. The ACT scores were 2% between 12 and 17, 24% between 18 and 23, 56% between 24 and 29, and 18% above 30. 67% of the current freshmen were in the top fifth of their class; 95% were in the top two fifths. **Admissions Contact:** James Cotter, Director of Admissions. Email: *admissions.msu.edu* Web: *www.msu.edu*

FINANCIAL AID: In 2017-2018, 45% of all full-time freshmen received some form of financial aid. 35% of all full-time freshmen received need-based aid. The average freshman award was $13,208. Need-based scholarships or need-based grants averaged $10,138; need-based self-help aid (loans and jobs) averaged $3,802; non-need-based athletic scholarships averaged $28,376; and other non-need-based awards and non-need-based scholarships averaged $9,915. The average financial indebtedness of the 2017 graduate was $25,724. The FAFSA code is 002290. The priority date for freshman financial aid applications for fall entry is October 1.

MICHIGAN TECHNOLOGICAL UNIVERSITY — B-2

www.mtu.edu

Houghton, MI 49931	**(906) 487-2335** **(888) 688-1885**
Fax: (906) 487-2125	**Email: mtu4u@mtu.edu**
Full-time: 4039 men, 1478 women	**Faculty:** 416; I, -$
Part-time: 279 men, 121 women	**Ph.D.s:** 89%
Graduate: 1018 men, 384 women	**Student/Faculty:** 13 to 1
Year: semesters, summer session	**Tuition:** $15,074 ($32,318)
Room & Board: $10,477	**Freshman Class:** 5469 applied, 4074 accepted, 1323 enrolled
SAT EBR-W/M: 610/630 **ACT:** 27	**CEEB CODE:** 1464
Application Deadline: n/av	**VERY COMPETITIVE+**

Michigan Technological University is a leading public research university, and its mission is preparing students to create the future. The university's world-class faculty conducts research and develops new technologies to help build a prosperous and sustainable world. Michigan Tech's five colleges and schools offer more than 120 undergraduate and graduate degree programs in engineering, forest resources, computing, technology, business and economics, natural, physical and environmental sciences, arts, humanities, and social sciences. In addition to regional accreditation, MTU has baccalaureate program accreditation with AACSB, ABET, ACCE, SAF, ACS, NAACLS, and CELPA. The 925-acre campus is in a small town 325 miles north of Milwaukee, Wisconsin. Including any residence halls, there are 42 buildings.

STUDENT LIFE: 76% of undergraduates are from Michigan. Others are from 43 states, 35 foreign countries, and Canada. 88% are White; 3% Foreign; 3% two or more races; 2% Asian American; 2% Hispanic; 2% race unknown; 1% African American. **Male To Female Ratio:** 2.7:1. The average age of freshmen is 18; all undergraduates, 21. 17% do not continue beyond their first year; 67% remain to graduate. **Housing:** 3175 students can be accommodated in college housing, which includes married student dorms and on-campus apartments. In addition, there are honors houses and special-interest houses. On-campus housing is guaranteed for the freshman year only, is available on a first-come, and first-served basis. 55% of students commute. All students may keep cars.

FACULTY/CLASSROOMS: 69% of faculty are male; 31% are female. All teach undergraduates, 76% do research, and 76% do both. Graduate students teach 7% of introductory courses. The average class size in an introductory lecture is 79; in a laboratory is 26; and in a regular course is 32.

PROGRAMS OF STUDY: MTU confers B.A. and B.S. degrees. Associate, master's, and doctoral degrees are also awarded. Bachelor's degrees are awarded in AGRICULTURE (forestry and related sciences, natural resource management, and wildlife management), BIOLOGICAL SCIENCE (biochemistry, bioinformatics, biology/biological science, and ecology), BUSINESS (accounting, finance, management engineering, management information systems, management science, marketing, and sports management), COMMUNICATIONS AND THE ARTS (audio technology, communications, English, technical and business writing, theater design, and theatre studies), COMPUTER AND PHYSICAL SCIENCE (applied physics, chemistry, computer information systems, computer science, geology, geophysics and seismology, mathematics, physics, software engineering, and statistics), EDUCATION (secondary education), ENGINEERING AND ENVIRONMENTAL DESIGN (biomedical engineering, chemical engineering, civil engineering, computer engineering, construction management, electrical/electronics engineering, electrical/electronics engineering technology, engineering, environmental engineering, environmental science, geological engineering, materials engineering, mechanical engineering, mechanical engineering technology, and surveying engineering), HEALTH PROFESSIONS (exercise science, medical laboratory science, pharmaceutical chemistry, predentistry, premedicine, prepharmacy, and prephysical therapy), SOCIAL SCIENCE (anthropology, economics, history, liberal arts/general studies, psychology, and social science). Engineering and the sciences, are the strongest academically. Mechanical engineering, chemical engineering, and electrical engineering have the largest enrollments.

ACTIVITIES: 11% of men belong to 3 local and 9 national fraternities; 14% of women belong to 3 local and 4 national sororities. There are 229 groups on campus, including art, band, cheerleading, chess, choir, chorale, chorus, communications, computers, dance, drama, environmental, ethnic, film, honors, international, jazz band, LGBT, literary magazine, musical theater, newspaper, orchestra, pep band, photography, political, professional, radio and TV, religious, social, social service, student government, and symphony. Popular campus events include Winter Carnival, K-Day, Homecoming, Spring Fling, Make a Difference Day, International Night, Parade of Nations, Safe House Halloween, Division I Hockey, Design Expo, LeaderShape Institute, and Afternoon on the Town. **Sports:** There are 7 intercollegiate sports for men and 7 for women, and 24 intramural sports for men and 24 for women. Facilities include ice arena, a fitness center, swimming and diving pools, a multipurpose room, a climbing wall, varsity gym, a studio, a shooting range, a hockey education center, outdoor softball fields and sand volleyball courts, football and soccer fields, several practice fields, a 9-hole disc golf course, cross-country skiing, recreation for cyclists, alpine ski hill for skiers, tennis courts, and 18 hole golf course. **Graduates:** From July 1, 2016 to June 30, 2017, 1066 bachelor's degrees were awarded. The most popular majors were mechanical engineering (21%), electrical engineering (9%), and chemical engineering (8%). In an average class, 28% graduate in 4 years or less, 60% graduate in 5 years or less, and 67% graduate in 6 years or less.

SERVICES: Counseling and information services are available, as is tutoring in most subjects. There is a reader service for the blind. **Library/Resources:** The library contains 504,555 volumes, 442,383 microform items, and 828 audio/video tapes/CDs/DVDs, and subscribes to 62,346 periodicals including electronic. Computerized library services include interlibrary loans, database searching, Internet access, and Wi-Fi capability. Special learning facilities include an art gallery, radio station, A.E. Seaman Mineral Museum, a center for the performing arts, a theater, 4,000-acre forest, cosmic ray observatory, X-ray fluorescence spectrometer, Operations Lab and Process Simulation and Control Center, Earth, Planetary and Space Sciences Institute, computer-aided engineering lab, microfabrication facility, the Great Lakes Research Center, academic success coaches, Biological Sciences Learning Center, Business and Economics Tidwell Learning Center, Career Services Learning Center, Chemical Engineering Learning Center, Chemistry Learning Center, Civil and Environmental Engineering Learning Center, Computer Science Learning Center, Electrical and Computer Engineering Learning Center, First-Year Engineering Learning Center, Forestry Learning Center, Materials Science and Engineering Learning Center, mathematics learning center, Multiliteracies Center, and Physics Learning Center. **Physically Challenged Students:** 80% of the campus is accessible. Facilities include wheelchair ramps, elevators, special parking, specially equipped restrooms, special class scheduling, lowered drinking fountains, and special housing. **Special:** Accelerated Master's Degrees are available in nearly 20 areas. Over 460 companies visit campus annually to recruit students for co-ops, internships, and full-time jobs. The Pavlis Honors College provides opportunities for students to participate in the Enterprise Program (teams of students working on large-scale government- and industry-sponsored projects), the Pavlis Institute for Global Technological Leadership, Research Scholars Program, and more. Students may also participate in industry-sponsored senior design or international senior design. Study abroad opportunities exist in over 40 countries. Undergraduate research is also available, last year, students spent over 126,000 hours working on paid undergraduate research. Michigan Tech offers dual degrees, double majors, minors, and certificate programs. Students looking to enroll in professional health programs will find an early assurance program with Michigan State University for medical school and Central Michigan University for physical therapy (DPT), and agreements for 3+2 programs with many institutions in the Midwest are also offered. There are 16 national honor societies and 23 departmental honors programs. **Visiting:** There are regularly scheduled orientations for prospective students, campus tours are at 8:30 AM and 12:30 PM Monday through Friday. Separate interviews are available with academic department advisors, admissions counselors, and financial aid. There are guides for informal visits, visitors may sit in on classes, and stay overnight. To schedule a visit, contact Admissions Office. **Campus Safety and Security:** Measures include 24-hour foot and vehicle patrol, emergency notification system, self-defense education, and security escort services. There are shuttle buses, emergency telephones, lighted pathways/sidewalks, controlled access to dorms/residences, and emergency medical services.

REQUIREMENTS: First-year applicants are required to submit an official high school transcript with grades through the junior year, and official ACT or SAT scores. Scores may be sent directly from the testing agency, or reported on the official high school transcript or on MTU Counselor Information Page. Applicants to programs in the Visual and Performing Arts Department must provide essay responses; select majors must submit examples of creative work. We encourage GED and home school applicants to apply. A GPA of 2.8 is required. AP and CLEP credits are accepted. To graduate, students must complete 120 to 145 credit hours and maintain a minimum GPA (both cumulative and in the major department) of 2.0. The general education curriculum, required for all baccalaureate students and included in the 120-145 credits, consists of 4 core courses, a 12 credit hour distribution requirement, physical education, and a 15 credit hour science/math requirement. Students must take 30 credit hours of upper-level courses at MTU that apply to the degree requirements, and 30 of the last 36 credit hours, regardless of level, must be completed at MTU. **Procedure:** Freshmen are admitted to all sessions. Entrance exams scores will be accepted until time of enrollment. There are deferred admissions and rolling admissions plans. Application deadlines are open. Notifications are sent June 15. Applications are accepted on-line. **Transfer Students:** 199 transfer students enrolled in 2016-2017. Transfer students must have a minimum GPA of 2.75 on a 4.0 scale; grades of B or better are expected in math and science courses. Some selected programs require a 2.5 cumulative transfer GPA. Transfer student applicants are required to submit official college transcripts from all institutions previously attended. An official high school transcript is required for transfer applicants who have not earned an Associate's degree or higher at time of application to MTU. 30 of 120 credits required for the bachelor's degree must be completed at MTU. **International Students:** There are 139 international students enrolled. They must take the TOEFL with a minimum score of 550 on the paper-based TOEFL (PBT) or 79 on the Internet-based version (iBT), and also take any one of these tests, the IELTS, Pearson Test of English, or SAT 1.

ADMISSIONS: 74% of the 2017-2018 applicants were accepted. The SAT scores for the 2017-2018 freshman class were: Math-- 1% below 500, 31% between 500 and 599, 51% between 600 and 699, and 17% between 700 and 800. Evidence-Based Reading/Writing-- 4% below 500, 35% between 500 and 599, 51% between 600 and 699, and 10% between 700 and 800. The ACT scores were 17% between 18 and 23, 54% between 24 and 29, and 29% above 30. 55% of the current freshmen were in the top fifth of their class; 82% were in the top two fifths. 55 freshmen graduated first in their class. **Admissions Contact:** Allison Carter, Director of Admissions. Email: *mtu4u@mtu.edu* Web: *www.mtu.edu*

FINANCIAL AID: 23% of undergraduate students work part-time. The FAFSA code is 002292. The priority date for freshman financial aid applications for fall entry is March 1.

NORTHERN MICHIGAN UNIVERSITY C-2

www.nmu.edu

Marquette, MI 49855	**(906) 227-2650** **(800) 682-9797**
Fax: (906) 227-1747	**Email: admissions@nmu.edu**
Full-time: 2848 men, 3359 women	**Faculty:** 294; IIA, -$
Part-time: 346 men, 465 women	**Ph.D.s:** 75%
Graduate: 199 men, 395 women	**Student/Faculty:** 22 to 1
Year: semesters, summer session	**Tuition:** $10,240 ($15,736)
Room & Board: $10,328	**Freshman Class:** 6173 applied, 4591 accepted, 1501 enrolled
ACT: 22	**CEEB CODE:** 1560
Application Deadline: open	**COMPETITIVE**

Northern Michigan University, founded in 1899, is the university of choice in the Midwest for students seeking quality academic programs in a high-tech learning environment. There are 4 undergraduate schools and 1 graduate school. In addition to regional accreditation, NMU has baccalaureate program accreditation with AACSB, ABET, ADA, CSWE, NASAD, NASM, CAEP, NLN, NRPA, CAAHEP, and CCNE. The 360-acre campus is in an urban area on the southern shores of Lake Superior. Including any residence halls, there are 55 buildings.

STUDENT LIFE: 81% of undergraduates are from Michigan. Others are from 46 states, 39 foreign countries, and Canada. 84% are White; 3% Hispanic; 3% two or more races; 3% race unknown; 2% African American; 2% American Indian/Alaska Native; 2% Foreign; 1% Asian American. **Female To Male Ratio:** 1.2:1. The average age of freshmen is 18; all undergraduates, 22. 28% do not continue beyond their first year; 49% remain to graduate. **Housing:** 3250 students can be accommodated in college housing, which includes coed, married student dorms, and on-campus apartments. In addition, there are honors houses, special-interest houses, smoke-free and chemical-free houses. On-campus housing is guaranteed for all 4 years, is available on a first-come, and first-served basis. 58% of students commute. All students may keep cars.

FACULTY/CLASSROOMS: 49% of faculty are male; 51% are female. All teach undergraduates, 41% do research, and 41% do both. Graduate students teach 1% of introductory courses. The average class size in an introductory lecture is 30; in a laboratory is 17; and in a regular course is 23.

PROGRAMS OF STUDY: NMU confers B.A., B.S., B.F.A., B.M.Ed., B.S.N., B.S.W. and D.N.P. degrees. Associate, master's, and doctoral degrees are also awarded. Bachelor's degrees are awarded in AGRICULTURE (environmental studies, fishing and fisheries, and wildlife management), BIOLOGICAL SCIENCE (biochemistry, biology/biological science, biology/gen sci/envir sci second ed, botany, ecology, forensic science, genetics, microbiology, physiology, and zoology), BUSINESS (accounting, banking and finance, business administration and management, entrepreneurial studies, finance, and marketing/retailing/merchandising), COMMUNICATIONS AND THE ARTS (art and design, broadcasting, communications, design, English, fine arts, French, language arts, music, public relations, Spanish, speech/debate/rhetoric, and theatre arts), COMPUTER AND PHYSICAL SCIENCE (chemistry, computer programming, computer science, cyber intelligence/security studies, earth science, information sciences and systems, mathematics, and physics), EDUCATION (art education, business education, computer education, elementary education, health education, industrial arts education, music education, physical education, science education, and secondary education), ENGINEERING AND ENVIRONMENTAL DESIGN (construction management, electrical/electronics engineering technology, furniture design, industrial engineering technology, and manufacturing technology), HEALTH PROFESSIONS (clinical science, exercise science, medical laboratory technology, nursing, physician's assistant, predentistry, premedicine, preveterinary science, speech pathology/audiology, and speech therapy), SOCIAL SCIENCE (criminal justice, economics, gender studies, geography, history, international studies, parks and recreation management, philosophy, physical fitness/movement, political science/government, prelaw, psychology, public administration, social work, sociology, Spanish studies, and water resources). Nursing, and construction management are the strongest academically. Nursing, art & design, and biology have the largest enrollments.

ACTIVITIES: 1% of men belong to 2 national fraternities; 1% of women belong to 1 local and 2 national sororities. There are 318 groups on campus, including health, philosophy, art, band, cheerleading, chess, choir, chorale, chorus, communications, computers, dance, drama, drill team, environmental, ethnic, film, honors, international, international dance club, jazz band, LGBT, literary magazine, marching band, musical theater, newspaper, orchestra, pep band, photography, political, professional, radio and TV, religious, social, social service, student government, and symphony. Popular campus events include Winterfest, Homecoming, and U.P. 200 Dog Sled Race. **Sports:** There are 7 intercollegiate sports for men and 9 for women, and 12 intramural sports for men and 12 for women. Facilities include indoor and outdoor playing fields, an aerobic and fitness training area, an ice rink, swimming pool with diving tank, a field house, a stadium, basketball, hockey arena, a rock-climbing wall, golf stimulator and racquetball courts. **Graduates:** From July 1, 2016 to June 30, 2017, 1766 bachelor's degrees were awarded. The most popular majors were business (11%), tech/occupational studies (10%), and biology (8%). In an average class, 5% graduate in 3 years or less, 22% graduate in 4 years or less, 41% graduate in 5 years or less, and 47% graduate in 6 years or less. Of the 2016 graduating class, 25% were enrolled in graduate school within 6 months of graduation, and 60% were employed.

SERVICES: Counseling and information services are available, as is tutoring in most subjects. There is a reader service for the blind, and remedial math, reading, and writing. **Library/Resources:** The library contains 750,000 volumes, 131,919 microform items, and 5,641 audio/video tapes/CDs/DVDs, and subscribes to 35,686 periodicals including electronic. Computerized library services include interlibrary loans, database searching, Internet access, and Wi-Fi capability. Special learning facilities include an art gallery, radio station, and TV station. Special learning facilities on campus include a learning resource center, computing help desk, regional heritage center, and an observatory. **Physically Challenged Students:** All of the campus is accessible. Facilities include wheelchair ramps, elevators, special parking, specially equipped restrooms, lowered drinking fountains, lowered telephones, and special housing. **Special:** NMU offers internships, a co-op program in business, study abroad in a number of countries, a Washington semester, dual majors in computer information and accounting and student-designed majors in individual studies and liberal arts. There are 7 national honor societies, a freshman honors program, and 1 departmental honors program. **Visiting:** There are regularly scheduled orientations for prospective students, including an admissions interview, a tour and a faculty visit. Visitors may sit in on classes and stay overnight. To schedule a visit, contact Campus Visit at https:/www.nmu.edu/admissions/visit-register. **Campus Safety and Security:** Measures include 24-hour foot and vehicle patrol, emergency notification system, self-defense education, and security escort services. There are shuttle buses, emergency telephones, lighted pathways/sidewalks, controlled access to dorms/residences, and a crime prevention program.

REQUIREMENTS: NMU requires a GPA of 2.25 and a minimum composite score of 980 for the SAT and 19 for the ACT. Applicants must be graduates of accredited secondary schools or have earned a GED. Requirements are 12 to 16 Carnegie units including 4 years of English, 3 each of math, history, social studies, foreign language, and science, 2 of fine arts or performing arts, and 1 of computer instruction. Students seeking art scholarships must submit a portfolio. Students seeking music and theater scholarships must audition. AP and CLEP credits are accepted. Students must earn 40 semester credits in liberal studies, including courses in humanities, composition, natural sciences/math, social sciences, communications and visual and performing arts. Graduation requirements vary by degree program, but at the minimum, students must earn 124 semester credits, including 32 in a major field, with a GPA of 2.0. Courses in phys ed/health and world culture are also required. **Procedure:** Freshmen are admitted to all sessions. Entrance exams should be taken the year prior to enrollment. There are deferred admissions and rolling admissions plans. Application deadlines are open. The fall 2017 application fee was $35. Notification is sent on a rolling basis. Applications are accepted on-line. **Transfer Students:** 407 transfer students enrolled in 2016-2017. Applicants must present a minimum GPA of 2.0 in at least 12 semester credits of college-level work. 32 of 124 credits required for the bachelor's degree must be completed at NMU. **International Students:** There are 105 international students enrolled. They must take the TOEFL with a minimum score of 500 on the paper-based TOEFL (PBT) or 61 on the Internet-based version (iBT). They must also take the SAT or ACT, scoring 19.

ADMISSIONS: 74% of the 2017-2018 applicants were accepted. **Admissions Contact:** Gerri Daniels, Director of Admissions. Email: *admissions@nmu.edu* Web: *www.nmu.edu*

FINANCIAL AID: In 2017-2018, 94% of all full-time freshmen received some form of financial aid. 59% of all full-time freshmen received need-based aid. The average freshman award was $11,978. Need-based scholarships or need-based grants averaged $5,282 ($10,000 maximum); need-based self-help aid (loans and jobs) averaged $4,195 ($9,500 maximum); non-need-based athletic scholarships averaged $9,240 ($26,363 maximum); and other non-need-based awards and non-need-based scholarships averaged $7,597 ($26,463 maximum). 31% of undergraduate students work part-time. The average financial indebtedness of the 2017 graduate was $25,500. The FAFSA code is 002301. The priority date for freshman financial aid applications for fall entry is March 1.

NORTHWOOD UNIVERSITY - MICHIGAN *(The complete profile is made available exclusively on our website, www.barronspac.com)*

OAKLAND UNIVERSITY — E-4
www.oakland.edu

Rochester, MI 48309 — **(248) 370-3360**

Email: visit@oakland.edu

Full-time: 5344 men, 7543 women	**Faculty:** I, --$
Part-time: 1962 men, 2312 women	**Ph.D.s:** n/av
Graduate: 1519 men, 2031 women	**Student/Faculty:** n/av
Year: semesters, summer session	**Tuition:** $11,513 ($23,873)
Room & Board: $9250	**Freshman Class:** 12152 applied, 7551 accepted, 2464 enrolled
ACT: 22	**CEEB CODE:** 1497
Application Deadline: March 24	**COMPETITIVE**

Oakland University, established in 1957, is a comprehensive state-supported institution serving a primarily commuter student body. There are 7 undergraduate schools and 7 graduate schools. In addition to regional accreditation, OU has baccalaureate program accreditation with AACSB, ABET, CSWE, NASM, NASPAA, NAST, NASD, ACS, CCNE, CACREP, and CAPTE. The 1444-acre campus is in a suburban area 25 miles north of Detroit. Including any residence halls, there are 46 buildings.

STUDENT LIFE: 97% of undergraduates are from Michigan. Others are from 39 states, 45 foreign countries, and Canada. 8% are African American; 75% White; 4% Asian American; 4% race unknown; 3% Hispanic; 3% two or more races; 2% Foreign. **Female To Male Ratio:** 1.3:1. The average age of freshmen is 19; all undergraduates, 23. 24% do not continue beyond their first year. **Housing:** College-sponsored housing includes married student dorms and on-campus apartments. In addition, there are honors houses, special-interest houses, fraternity houses, sorority houses, living learning communities, international, eco interest, pre-business, pre-nursing, and scholars tower. On-campus housing is guaranteed for all 4 years. All students may keep cars.

FACULTY/CLASSROOMS: 54% of faculty are male; 46% are female. No introductory courses are taught by graduate students.

PROGRAMS OF STUDY: OU confers B.A., B.S., B.F.A., B.I.S., B.Mus., B.S.E., B.S.N. and B.S.W. degrees. Master's and doctoral degrees are also awarded. Bachelor's degrees are awarded in BIOLOGICAL SCIENCE (biochemistry and biology/biological science), BUSINESS (accounting, banking and finance, business administration and management, business economics, human resources, management information systems, marketing/retailing/merchandising, operations management, and personnel management), COMMUNICATIONS AND THE ARTS (art history and appreciation, Chinese, communications, dance, dramatic arts, English, film arts, French, German, Japanese, journalism, linguistics, music, performing arts, Spanish, and studio art), COMPUTER AND PHYSICAL SCIENCE (chemistry, computer science, information sciences and systems, mathematics, medical physics, physics, and statistics), EDUCATION (elementary education and music education), ENGINEERING AND ENVIRONMENTAL DESIGN (computer engineering, electrical/electronics engineering, engineering chemistry, engineering physics, environmental science, industrial engineering, mechanical engineering, and occupational safety and health), HEALTH PROFESSIONS (allied health, health science, medical laboratory science, nursing, and preventive/wellness health care), SOCIAL SCIENCE (African American studies, anthropology, East Asian studies, economics, history, international relations, Latin American studies, liberal arts/general studies, philosophy, political science/government, psychology, public administration, Russian and Slavic studies, social work, sociology, South Asian studies, and women's studies). Business, health sciences, and engineering have the largest enrollments.

ACTIVITIES: 2% of men belong to 6 national fraternities; 2% of women belong to 6 national sororities. There are 258 groups on campus, including art, band, cheerleading, choir, chorale, chorus, computers, dance, drama, environmental, ethnic, film, forensics, honors, international, jazz band, LGBT, musical theater, newspaper, orchestra, pep band, political, professional, radio and TV, religious, social, social service, student government, and symphony. Popular campus events include Welcome Week, Hispanic Celebration, and Week of Champions at Oakland. **Sports:** There are 7 intercollegiate sports for men and 9 for women, and 18 intramural sports for men and 18 for women. Facilities include a recreation and athletic center that includes softball and baseball diamonds, an indoor track, soccer and touch football, a pool, basketball, weight training, dance, fencing, handball, squash, racquetball, and golf. **Graduates:** From July 1, 2016 to June 30, 2017, 2345 bachelor's degrees were awarded. The most popular majors were nursing (14%), business (13%), and education (8%).

SERVICES: Counseling and information services are available, as is tutoring in most subjects, such as 100 and 200 level classes. There is a reader service for the blind, and remedial math, reading, and writing. There is also a mentorship program. **Library/Resources:** The library contains 851,190 volumes, 1.2 million microform items, and 29,868 audio/video tapes/CDs/DVDs, and subscribes to 43,501 periodicals including electronic. Computerized library services include interlibrary loans, database searching, Internet access, and Wi-Fi capability. Special learning facilities include an art gallery, radio station, and TV station. There is also the Product Development and Manufacturing Center, the Historical House Museum, and the Lean-Learning Institute. **Physically Challenged Students:** 99% of the campus is accessible. Facilities include wheelchair ramps, elevators, special parking, specially equipped restrooms, special class scheduling, lowered drinking fountains, lowered telephones, special housing, and automatic door openers. **Special:** Special academic programs include internships, cooperative programs for most disciplines, and many work-study opportunities. There are organized programs for study abroad in 8 countries; independent programs can be arranged. Oakland also offers a B.A. or B.S. degree in biology and economics, a general studies program, dual majors, a student-designed major, cross-registration with Macomb Community College, and preprofessional studies in medicine, dentistry, optometry, and veterinary medicine. There are 12 national honor societies and a freshman honors program. **Visiting:** There are regularly scheduled orientations for prospective students, including a review of services, academic advising, and course registration. There are guides for informal visits, visitors may sit in on classes, and stay overnight. To schedule a visit, contact the Admissions Office. **Campus Safety and Security:** Measures include 24-hour foot and vehicle patrol, emergency notification system, self-defense education, and security escort services. There are shuttle buses, emergency telephones, lighted pathways/sidewalks, controlled access to dorms/residences, and text alert.

REQUIREMENTS: The ACT is required. Admissions requirements include graduation from an accredited secondary school and high school level college preparatory work, including 4 years of English and 3 years each of math, science, and social studies. 2 years of foreign language is recommended as well. Music and dance majors must audition. A GPA of 2.5 is required. AP and CLEP credits are accepted. To graduate, students must complete 124 credit hours (153 to 161 for the B.Mus. or 128 for the B.S.Env.Health). All students must complete 40 credits of general education requirements, including at least 1 course (3 or more credits) from the list of approved courses in each of the 10 knowledge areas: writing, formal reasoning, arts, foreign language and culture, global perspective, literature, natural science and technology, social science, Western civilization, and knowledge application. A GPA of 2.0 is required. **Procedure:** Freshmen are admitted to all sessions. Entrance exams should be taken during the spring of the junior year or early fall of the senior year. There are deferred admissions and rolling admissions plans. Applications should be filed by March 24 for fall entry. Notification is sent on a rolling basis. Applications are accepted on-line. **Transfer Students:** 1891 transfer students enrolled in 2016-2017. Applicants must have at least a 2.5 GPA; a higher GPA is required in some majors. 32 of 124 credits required for the bachelor's degree must be completed at Oakland. **International Students:** They must take the TOEFL with a minimum score of 550 on the paper-based TOEFL (PBT) or 79 on the Internet-based version (iBT). Student must take the MELAB. They must also take the ACT.

ADMISSIONS: 62% of the 2017-2018 applicants were accepted. **Admissions Contact:** Eleanor Reynolds, Assistant Vice President Student Affairs Admissions. Email: *visit@oakland.edu* Web: *www.oakland.edu*

FINANCIAL AID: The average freshman award was $12,885. Need-based scholarships or need-based grants averaged $5,645; need-based self-help aid (loans and jobs) averaged $3,173; and non-need-based athletic scholarships averaged $11,515. The FAFSA code is 002307. The priority date for freshman financial aid applications for fall entry is January 1.

OLIVET COLLEGE *(The complete profile is made available exclusively on our website, www.barronspac.com)*

ROCHESTER COLLEGE *(The complete profile is made available exclusively on our website, www.barronspac.com)*

SAGINAW VALLEY STATE UNIVERSITY D-4

www.svsu.edu

University Center, MI 48710	**(989) 964-4200** **(800) 968-9500**
Fax: (989) 790-0180	**Email: admissions@svsu.edu**
Full-time: 2668 men, 3933 women	**Faculty:** 291; IIA, -$
Part-time: 563 men, 729 women	**Ph.D.s:** 88%
Graduate: 199 men, 566 women	**Student/Faculty:** 23 to 1
Year: semesters, summer session	**Tuition:** $9819 ($23,062)
Room & Board: $9465	**Freshman Class:** 6457 applied, 4768 accepted, 1230 enrolled
SAT: required **ACT:** 23	**CEEB CODE:** 1766
Application Deadline: December 1	**COMPETITIVE**

Saginaw Valley State University, founded in 1963, is a state-supported institution offering undergraduate and graduate degrees in arts and behavioral sciences, business and management, education, nursing and health sciences, science, engineering, and technology. There are 5 undergraduate schools and 5 graduate schools. In addition to regional accreditation, SVSU has baccalaureate program accreditation with AACSB, ABET, CSWE, NASM, ACS, NAACLS, ACOTE, CCNE, and CAATE. The 782-acre campus is in a suburban area 5 miles north of Saginaw. Including any residence halls, there are 90 buildings.

STUDENT LIFE: 92% of undergraduates are from Michigan. Others are from 20 states, 43 foreign countries, and Canada. 95% are from public schools. 8% are African American; 72% White; 7% Foreign; 5% race unknown; 4% Hispanic; 3% two or more races; 1% Asian American. **Female To Male Ratio:** 1.5:1. The average age of freshmen is 18; all undergraduates, 23. 26% do not continue beyond their first year; 74% remain to graduate. **Housing:** 2736 students can be accommodated in college housing, which includes dorms, on-campus apartments, healthy life-style floors, and freshman first-year suites. On-campus housing is available on a first-come and first-served basis. 70% of students commute. All students may keep cars.

FACULTY/CLASSROOMS: 54% of faculty are male; 46% are female. All teach undergraduates. No introductory courses are taught by graduate students. The average class size in an introductory lecture is 25 and in a laboratory is 17.

PROGRAMS OF STUDY: SVSU confers B.A., B.S., B.A.S., B.B.A., B.F.A., B.P.A., B.S.E.E., B.S.M.E., B.S.N. and B.S.W. degrees. Master's and doctoral degrees are also awarded. Bachelor's degrees are awarded in BIOLOGICAL SCIENCE (biochemistry and biology/biological science), BUSINESS (accounting, banking and finance, business administration and management, business economics, finance, international business management, and marketing management), COMMUNICATIONS AND THE ARTS (art, communications, creative writing, design, dramatic arts, English, fine arts, French, music, Spanish, and technical and business writing), COMPUTER AND PHYSICAL SCIENCE (applied mathematics, applied science, chemical physics, chemistry, computer science, information sciences and systems, mathematics, optics, and physics), EDUCATION (art education, athletic training, drama education, elementary education, English education, foreign languages education, mathematics education, music education, physical education, science education, social studies education, and special education), ENGINEERING AND ENVIRONMENTAL DESIGN (electrical/electronics engineering, engineering technology, industrial administration/management, mechanical engineering, and preengineering), HEALTH PROFESSIONS (exercise science, health science, medical laboratory science, medical technology, nursing, predentistry, premedicine, and prephysical therapy), SOCIAL SCIENCE (criminal justice, economics, geography, history, interdisciplinary studies, international studies, political science/government, prelaw, psychology, public administration, social work, and sociology). Nursing, education, and kinesiology have the largest enrollments.

ACTIVITIES: 3% of men belong to 7 national fraternities; 3% of women belong to 1 local and 3 national sororities. There are 165 groups on campus, including art, band, cheerleading, chess, choir, chorus, computers, dance, drama, environmental, ethnic, film, honors, international, jazz band, LGBT, literary magazine, marching band, musical theater, newspaper, orchestra, pep band, photography, political, professional, radio and TV, religious, social, social service, and student government. Popular campus events include Battle of the Valleys, Cards Party, and International Food Festival. **Sports:** There are 8 intercollegiate sports for men and 8 for women, and 16 intramural sports for men and 16 for women. Facilities include a health and phys ed complex with an Olympic-size pool, indoor track, basketball courts, badminton courts, volleyball courts, racquetball courts, fitness center, tennis courts, intramural, baseball, softball, soccer fields, archery range, fitness trail, football stadium, golf driving range, putting green, and horse shoe pits. **Graduates:** From July 1, 2016 to June 30, 2017, 1487 bachelor's degrees were awarded. The most popular majors were nursing (12%), social work (7%), and criminal justice (6%). In an average class, 12% graduate in 4 years or less, 32% graduate in 5 years or less, and 40% graduate in 6 years or less. Of the 2016 graduating class, 24% were enrolled in graduate school within 6 months of graduation, and 87% were employed.

SERVICES: Counseling and information services are available, as is tutoring in most subjects. There is a reader service for the blind, and remedial math, reading, and writing. **Library/Resources:** The library contains 368,865 volumes, 354,265 microform items, and 27,210 audio/video tapes/CDs/DVDs, and subscribes to 50,291 periodicals including electronic. Computerized library services include interlibrary loans, database searching, Internet access, and Wi-Fi capability. Special learning facilities include an art gallery, radio station, and an observatory. **Physically Challenged Students:** 99% of the campus is accessible. Facilities include wheelchair ramps, elevators, special parking, specially equipped restrooms, special class scheduling, lowered drinking fountains, lowered telephones, special housing, electronically opened doors, and special access to the library. **Special:** Study abroad in 53 countries, internships, and Michigan Work Study and Federal College Work Study job opportunities within several on-campus departments. There are 4 national honor societies. **Visiting:** There are regularly scheduled orientations for prospective students, including tours, help with schedules, basic information and counseling. There are guides for informal visits. To schedule a visit, contact the Office of Admissions. **Campus Safety and Security:** Measures include 24-hour foot and vehicle patrol, emergency notification system, self-defense education, and security escort services. There are emergency telephones, lighted pathways/sidewalks, and the SVSU public safety department has commissioned police officers.

REQUIREMENTS: Applicants must submit a completed undergraduate application for admission, an official high school transcript or GED, and ACT or SAT results. SVSU recommends high school students take a rigorous college preparatory curriculum prior to enrolling at SVSU: 4 years of English, 3 years each of math, natural sciences, and social sciences, and 2 years of the same foreign language. AP and CLEP credits are accepted. Students must complete a minimum of 124 credits, satisfy basic skills and general education requirements, and maintain a minimum GPA of 2.0. The General Education Program consists of 35 credit hours in 10 categories. **Procedure:** Freshmen are admitted to all sessions. There are deferred admissions and rolling admissions plans. Application deadlines are open. The fall 2017 application fee was $30. Applications are accepted on-line. **Transfer Students:** 524 transfer students enrolled in 2016-2017. Transfer students with fewer than 24 credits from a previous college must submit high school and college transcripts. ACT or SAT scores must be submitted. A minimum GPA of 2.0 is needed. An interview may be required. 31 of 124 credits required for the bachelor's degree must be completed at SVSU. **International Students:** There are 546 international students enrolled. They must take the TOEFL with a minimum score of 500 on the paper-based TOEFL (PBT) or 61 on the Internet-based version (iBT).

ADMISSIONS: 74% of the 2017-2018 applicants were accepted. The SAT scores for the 2017-2018 freshman class were: Math-- 26% below 500, 53% between 500 and 599, 19% between 600 and 699, and 2% between 700 and 800. Evidence-Based Reading/Writing-- 23% below 500, 48% between 500 and 599, 27% between 600 and 699, and 2% between 700 and 800. The ACT scores were 8% between 12 and 17, 50% between 18 and 23, 35% between 24 and 29, and 7% above 30. **Admissions Contact:** Jennifer Pahl, Director of Admissions. Email: *admissions@svsu.edu* Web: *www.svsu.edu*

FINANCIAL AID: In 2017-2018, 95% of all full-time freshmen received some form of financial aid. 64% of all full-time freshmen received need-based aid. The average freshman award was $9,078. The FAFSA code is 002314. Check with the school for current application deadlines.

SIENA HEIGHTS UNIVERSITY — E-5

www.sienaheights.edu

Adrian, MI 49221

(517) 264-7180
(800) 521-0009
Email: admissions@sienaheights.edu

Full-time: 604 men, 723 women	**Faculty:** IIA
Part-time: 388 men, 692 women	**Ph.D.s:** 77%
Graduate: 58 men, 175 women	**Student/Faculty:** 12 to 1
Year: semesters, summer session	**Tuition:** $25,932
Room & Board: $10,390	**Freshman Class:** 1800 applied, 1291 accepted, 293 enrolled
	CEEB CODE: 1719
Application Deadline: August 1	**COMPETITIVE**

Siena Heights University, founded in 1919, is a Catholic university sponsored by the Adrian Dominican Sisters. Enrolling a diverse community of traditional-age and working adult students, SHU is a coeducational institution accredited by the Higher Learning Commission that was founded in the liberal arts tradition, offering associate's, bachelor's and master's degrees. The university is headquartered in Adrian, Michigan, with degree completion centers in Dearborn, Southfield, Benton Harbor, Monroe, Battle Creek, Kalamazoo, Lansing, Jackson and online. There are 2 undergraduate schools and 1 graduate school. In addition to regional accreditation, SHU has baccalaureate program accreditation with CSWE, NASAD, CCNE, and CAEP. The 140-acre campus is in a small town in Adrian, MI. Including any residence halls, there are 16 buildings.

STUDENT LIFE: 88% of undergraduates are from Michigan. Others are from 39 states, 21 foreign countries, and Canada. 59% are White; 19% race unknown; 11% African American; 5% Hispanic; 2% Foreign; 2% two or more races; 1% Asian American; 1% American Indian/Alaska Native. **Female To Male Ratio:** 1.5:1. The average age of freshmen is 18. 28% do not continue beyond their first year; 51% remain to graduate. **Housing:** 674 students can be accommodated in college housing, which includes dorms and on-campus apartments, and special housing for international students, coed dorms, and floors exclusively for men and women. On-campus housing is available on a first-come, first-served basis, and is available on a lottery system for upperclassmen. 75% of students commute. All students may keep cars.

FACULTY/CLASSROOMS: 48% of faculty are male; 52% are female. No introductory courses are taught by graduate students.

PROGRAMS OF STUDY: SHU confers B.A., B.S., B.A.S., B.S.W., B.B.A., B.S.N., and B.F.A. degrees. Associate and master's degrees are also awarded. Bachelor's degrees are awarded in BIOLOGICAL SCIENCE (biology/biological science), BUSINESS (accounting and business administration and management), COMMUNICATIONS AND THE ARTS (art history and appreciation, communications, English, fine arts, graphic design, music, Spanish, studio art, theatre arts, and visual and performing arts), COMPUTER AND PHYSICAL SCIENCE (chemistry, computer information systems, information sciences and systems, mathematics, and natural sciences), EDUCATION (art education, elementary education, music education, science education, special education, and trade and industrial education), HEALTH PROFESSIONS (pre-health studies and premedicine), SOCIAL SCIENCE (child psychology/development, criminal justice, history, human services, humanities, liberal arts/general studies, philosophy, psychology, public administration, religion, social science, and social work). Business administration, nursing, and biology have the largest enrollments.

ACTIVITIES: 2% of men belong to 1 national fraternity; 2% of women belong to 1 national sorority. There are 30 groups on campus, including art, band, cheerleading, choir, chorus, computers, dance, drama, environmental, ethnic, international, jazz band, LGBT, literary magazine, marching band, musical theater, newspaper, pep band, photography, professional, religious, social, social service, student government, and symphony. Popular campus events include Halo Fest, Alumni/Family Weekend, Homecoming, and Common Dialog Day. **Sports:** There are 10 intercollegiate sports for men and 11 for women. Facilities include football, soccer, track, lacrosse, basketball, volleyball, and practice courts, a 200-meter track, softball field, and track and field. **Graduates:** From July 1, 2016 to June 30, 2017, 814 bachelor's degrees were awarded. The most popular majors were health professions and related programs, business, and law enforcement and related programs. In an average class, 51% graduate in 6 years or less.

SERVICES: Counseling and information services are available, as is tutoring in most subjects. There is remedial math, reading, and writing. **Library/Resources:** The library contains 229,064 volumes, and 1,041 audio/video tapes/CDs/DVDs, and subscribes to 3,893 periodicals including electronic. Computerized library services include interlibrary loans, database searching, Internet access, and Wi-Fi capability. Special learning facilities include an art gallery. **Physically Challenged Students:** 90% of the campus is accessible. Facilities include wheelchair ramps, elevators, special parking, specially equipped restrooms, special class scheduling, and lowered drinking fountains. We have an Office of Accessibility and have long been federal TRIO grant recipients. **Special:** The most unique program is the Bachelors in Applied Science for adult learners looking to complete their degree. SHU also offers Completely Online Programs and many additional distance learning opportunities. There is a Liberal Arts core curriculum that includes traditional general studies groupings of courses as well as liberal arts studies courses that reflect Dominican and university values. SHU also offers dual enrollment credit for high school students and a variety of study abroad opportunities. **Visiting:** There are regularly scheduled orientations for prospective students. There are guides for informal visits, visitors may sit in on classes, and stay overnight. To schedule a visit, contact Trudy Mohre at tmohre@sienaheights.edu. **Campus Safety and Security:** Measures include 24-hour foot and vehicle patrol, emergency notification system, self-defense education, and security escort services. There are lighted pathways/sidewalks, and StormReady Community-National Weather Service.

REQUIREMENTS: SHU began test-optional admissions which focuses on high school coursework and grades as the most important factors, along with a student's writing skills, recommendations, involvement in school and community, and personal qualities and character. Students may be required to submit standardized test scores for admission to specific academic programs, validate athletic eligibility or prove eligibility for some federal and state scholarship programs. AP and CLEP credits are accepted. Degree requirements may vary according to which college you attend and which major you select. Generally, the following requirement applies to at least 120 semester hours with a minimum of a 2.0 GPA. At least 30 semester hours at SHU. At least 12 of the last 30 semester hours at SHU. At least 30 semester hours at the 300/400 level and at least 15 of those at SHU. Demonstration of writing and math proficiency, and the liberal arts core curriculum. **Procedure:** Freshmen are admitted fall and spring. There are deferred admissions and rolling admissions plans. Applications should be filed by August 1 for fall entry. Notifications are sent July 1. Applications are accepted on-line. **Transfer Students:** 539 transfer students enrolled in 2016-2017. 2.5 high school GPA, 2.0 college GPA for College of Arts and Sciences. Please refer to our online catalog or contact a representative from the College for Professional Studies if you are an adult learner looking to complete a degree. 30 of 120 credits required for the bachelor's degree must be completed at SHU. **International Students:** There are 33 international students enrolled. They must take the TOEFL.

ADMISSIONS: 72% of the 2017-2018 applicants were accepted. **Admissions Contact:** Trudy Mohre, Director of Undergraduate Admissions. Email: *admissions@sienaheights.edu* Web: *www.sienaheights.edu*

FINANCIAL AID: SHU is a member of CSS. The FAFSA code is 002316. The deadline for filing freshman financial aid applications for fall entry is August 1.

SPRING ARBOR UNIVERSITY D-5

www.arbor.edu

Spring Arbor, MI 49283	(517) 750-6468 (800) 968-0011
Fax: (517) 750-6620	Email: admissions@arbor.edu
Full-time: 555 men, 815 women	Faculty: IIA
Part-time: 65 men, 120 women	Ph.D.s: 61%
Graduate: 290 men, 950 women	Student/Faculty: n/av
Year: semesters, summer session	Tuition: $27,750
Room & Board: $9640	Freshman Class: n/av
ACT: recommended	CEEB CODE: 1732
Application Deadline: August 1	COMPETITIVE

Spring Arbor University, founded in 1873 by leaders of the Free Methodist Church, offers a Christ-centered, liberal arts education with more than 50 undergraduate programs, 7 degree-completion programs, and 7 graduate programs. The figures given in the above capsule are approximate. There are 3 undergraduate schools and 7 graduate schools. In addition to regional accreditation, SAU has baccalaureate program accreditation with CSWE, and CCNE. The 123-acre campus is in a small town 8 miles southwest of Jackson. Including any residence halls, there are 36 buildings.

STUDENT LIFE: 85% of undergraduates are from Michigan. Others are from 30 states, 6 foreign countries, and Canada. 90% are White; 5% African American; 2% Asian American; 2% Hispanic; 1% Foreign. 67% are Protestant; 20% Unknown denominations; 11% claim no religious affiliation. **Female To Male Ratio:** 2.1:1. 28% do not continue beyond their first year; 59% remain to graduate. **Housing:** 1060 students can be accommodated in college housing, which includes married student dorms and on-campus apartments. On-campus housing is guaranteed for all 4 years. 68% of students live on campus. Alcohol is not permitted. Upperclassmen may keep cars.

FACULTY/CLASSROOMS: 60% of faculty are male; 40% are female. 94% teach undergraduates. No introductory courses are taught by graduate students. The average class size in a regular course is 18.

PROGRAMS OF STUDY: SAU confers B.A., and B.S.W. degrees. Associate and master's degrees are also awarded. Bachelor's degrees are awarded in BIOLOGICAL SCIENCE (biochemistry and biology/biological science), BUSINESS (accounting, business administration and management, and management information systems), COMMUNICATIONS AND THE ARTS (advertising, art, broadcasting, communications, English, film arts, language arts, music, Spanish, video, and visual and performing arts), COMPUTER AND PHYSICAL SCIENCE (chemistry, computer science, mathematics, and physics), EDUCATION (Christian education, music education, and special education), HEALTH PROFESSIONS (exercise science and nursing), SOCIAL SCIENCE (biblical studies, history, missions, philosophy, philosophy and religion, physical fitness/movement, psychology, social science, social studies, social work, sociology, theological studies, and youth ministry). Business, teacher education, and English are the strongest academically. Teacher education, business, and philosophy/religion have the largest enrollments.

ACTIVITIES: There are no fraternities or sororities. There are 41 groups on campus, including art, band, choir, chorale, drama, ethnic, film, honors, international, jazz band, literary magazine, musical theater, newspaper, pep band, radio and TV, religious, social, social service, student government, symphony, and yearbook. Popular campus events include Porchfest, Arbor Games, and Midnight Breakfast. **Sports:** There are 7 intercollegiate sports for men and 7 for women, and 7 intramural sports for men and 6 for women. Facilities include a weight room, basketball courts and volleyball courts, 4-lane indoor track, an Olympic-sized swimming pool, an exercise lab, training room, batting cages, softball, soccer, baseball stadium, softball, a soccer field, an 8-lane outdoor track (with long jump pit, high jump area, steeplechase hurdle, and throwing area), and tennis courts. **Graduates:** From July 1, 2016 to June 30, 2017, 684 bachelor's degrees were awarded. The most popular majors were business (36%), family life (17%), and teacher education (16%). In an average class, 1% graduate in 3 years or less, 38% graduate in 4 years or less, 54% graduate in 5 years or less, and 59% graduate in 6 years or less. Of the 2016 graduating class, 25% were enrolled in graduate school within 6 months of graduation, and 63% were employed.

SERVICES: Counseling and information services are available, as is tutoring in most subjects. There is a reader service for the blind, and remedial math, reading, and writing. Religious counseling and health services are also available. **Library/Resources:** The library contains 112,811 volumes, 576,594 microform items, and 3,943 audio/video tapes/CDs/DVDs, and subscribes to 587 periodicals including electronic. Computerized library services include interlibrary loans, database searching, and Internet access. Special learning facilities include an art gallery, radio station, TV production facilities and equipment. **Physically Challenged Students:** 80% of the campus is accessible. Facilities include wheelchair ramps, elevators, special parking, specially equipped restrooms, lowered drinking fountains, lowered telephones, and special housing. **Special:** Study abroad is available in more than 12 countries. A Washington semester is available through the American Studies Program. The university also offers cross-registration with Jackson Community College, work-study, a dual major in physics/math, student-designed majors, pass/fail options, and nondegree study. Alternative programs for adult learners provide field-based study and assign credit for life experience. An accelerated B.A. program for such students is offered. A 3-2 engineering degree is offered with the University of Michigan, Western Michigan University, and Tri-State University. There are 3 national honor societies and a freshman honors program. **Visiting:** There are regularly scheduled orientations for prospective students, including a tour, class and chapel attendance, lunch, and a student panel discussion. There are guides for informal visits, visitors may sit in on classes, and stay overnight. To schedule a visit, contact the Admissions Office. **Campus Safety and Security:** Measures include 24-hour foot and vehicle patrol, emergency notification system, self-defense education, and security escort services. There are lighted pathways/sidewalks, controlled access to dorms/residences, and key card entry to some dorms.

REQUIREMENTS: Applicants must be graduates of accredited secondary schools or have a GED. ACT or SAT test scores are required. An interview is advised for those who do not meet the requirements. Home-schooled applicants must take the ACT or the SAT, provide transcripts of course work, and submit a 2- to 3-page paper. A GPA of 2.6 is required. AP and CLEP credits are accepted. Important factors in the admissions decision are personality/intangible qualities, parents or siblings attended your school, and leadership record. Students must complete 4 Christian perspective courses plus cross-cultural studies, writing skills, speech, and physical fitness. Liberal arts requirements are in fine arts, humanities, natural science/math, philosophy/religion, and social science. To graduate, at least 124 semester hours, with 40 hours in upper-division courses and including 30 to 60 in the major, are needed. A minimum GPA of 2.0 overall and 2.2 in the major is also required. Students must also complete the University CORE, which includes communication skills, physical fitness, and liberal arts requirements. **Procedure:** Freshmen are admitted to all sessions. Entrance exams should be taken in the spring of the junior year or fall of the senior year. There are deferred admissions and rolling admissions plans. Applications should be filed by August 1 for fall entry. The fall 2017 application fee was $30. Notification is sent on a rolling basis. Applications are accepted on-line. **Transfer Students:** 102 transfer students enrolled in 2016-2017. Applicants should have a minimum GPA of 2.0 and are encouraged to arrange an interview. A release of information form is required from the previous college attended. 30 of 124 credits required for the bachelor's degree must be completed at SAU. **International Students:** There are 20 international students enrolled. They must take the TOEFL with a minimum score of 525 on the paper-based TOEFL (PBT). The SAT or ACT may be required for some students.

ADMISSIONS: 8 freshmen graduated first in their class. **Admissions Contact:** Randy Comfort, Director of Admissions. Email: *admissions@arbor.edu* Web: *www.arbor.edu*

FINANCIAL AID: In 2017-2018, 100% of all full-time freshmen received some form of financial aid. 84% of all full-time freshmen received need-based aid. The average freshman award was $19,168. Need-based scholarships or need-based grants averaged $9,643; need-based self-help aid (loans and jobs) averaged $3,699; and non-need-based athletic scholarships averaged $3,677. 32% of undergraduate students work part-time. The average financial indebtedness of the 2017 graduate was $13,834. The FAFSA code is 002318. Check with the school for current application deadlines.

UNIVERSITY OF DETROIT MERCY — E-5

www.udmercy.edu

Detroit, MI 48221	(313) 993-1245 (800) 635-5020
Fax: (313) 993-3317	Email: admissions@udmercy.edu
Full-time: 870 men, 1459 women	**Faculty:** 334
Part-time: 95 men, 250 women	**Ph.D.s:** 92%
Graduate: 1055 men, 1215 women	**Student/Faculty:** 10 to 1
Year: semesters, summer session	**Tuition:** $28,000
Room & Board: $9736	**Freshman Class:** n/av
SAT CR/M/W: 526/543/517 **ACT:** required	**CEEB CODE:** 1835
Application Deadline: March 1	**COMPETITIVE**

University of Detroit Mercy, founded in 1877, is a private, independent institution affiliated with the Jesuits and Sisters of Mercy. It offers undergraduate programs in liberal arts, education and human services, business administration, engineering and science, architecture, and nursing and health sciences. There are 6 undergraduate schools and 7 graduate schools. In addition to regional accreditation, UDM has baccalaureate program accreditation with AACSB, ABET, ADA, CSWE, NAAB, NLN, CCNE, CAHIIM, and CAHME. The 70-acre campus is in an urban area 7 miles north of downtown Detroit. Including any residence halls, there are 21 buildings.

STUDENT LIFE: 87% of undergraduates are from Michigan. Others are from 34 states, 41 foreign countries, and Canada. 7% are race unknown; 61% White; 8% Foreign; 6% Asian American; 5% Hispanic; 3% two or more races; 13% African American. 37% are Catholic; 19% claim no religious affiliation. **Female To Male Ratio:** 1.5:1. The average age of freshmen is 18; all undergraduates, 22. 17% do not continue beyond their first year; 68% remain to graduate. **Housing:** 955 students can be accommodated in college housing, which includes coed dorms, honors floors, and peace & justice floor. On-campus housing is guaranteed for all 4 years. 49% of students commute. All students may keep cars.

FACULTY/CLASSROOMS: 48% of faculty are male; 51% are female. No introductory courses are taught by graduate students.

PROGRAMS OF STUDY: UDM confers B.A., B.A.E., B.C.E., B.C.I., B.D.H., B.E.E., B.M.E., B.R.M., B.S., B.S.A., B.S.N., B.S.ARCH, B.S.W, B.ENG. and B.F.A. degrees. Master's and doctoral degrees are also awarded. Bachelor's degrees are awarded in BIOLOGICAL SCIENCE (biochemistry, biology/biological science, and industrial/organizational psychology), BUSINESS (accounting, business administration and management, and finance), COMMUNICATIONS AND THE ARTS (communications, digital media, dramatic arts, English, and theatre acting), COMPUTER AND PHYSICAL SCIENCE (chemistry, computer science, information sciences and systems, mathematics, software engineering, and software production & management), EDUCATION (elementary education, middle school education, secondary education, and special education), ENGINEERING AND ENVIRONMENTAL DESIGN (architectural engineering, architecture, civil engineering, electrical/electronics engineering, engineering, mechanical engineering, and robotic & mechatronic systems engineering), HEALTH PROFESSIONS (dental hygiene, health care administration, health services administration, nursing, predentistry, and premedicine), SOCIAL SCIENCE (addiction studies, criminal justice, developmental psychology, economics, history, legal studies, liberal arts/general studies, paralegal studies, philosophy, political science/government, prelaw, psychology, religion, social work, and sociology). Nursing, biology, and engineering are the strongest academically. Nursing, biology (pre-med/pre-dent), and business have the largest enrollments.

ACTIVITIES: 2% of men belong to 6 national fraternities; 4% of women belong to 5 national sororities. There are 50 groups on campus, including cheerleading, chorale, drama, ethnic, film, honors, international, LGBT, literary magazine, musical theater, newspaper, pep band, political, professional, radio and TV, religious, social, social service, and student government. Popular campus events include Homecoming basketball games, Greek Week, Celebrate Spirit!, Ethics Bowl, Halloween Safety Street, Welcome Week Picnic and Alternative Spring Break. **Sports:** There are 8 intercollegiate sports for men and 10 for women, and 4 intramural sports for men and women. Facilities include a fitness center with a gym, basketball courts, an indoor track, racquetball/ handball courts, soccer and softball fields, an outdoor track, and tennis courts. **Graduates:** From July 1, 2016 to June 30, 2017, 668 bachelor's degrees were awarded. The most popular majors were health professions and related programs (52%), biological/life sciences (22%), and business/marketing (9%). In an average class, 53% graduate in 4 years or less, 59% graduate in 5 years or less, and 68% graduate in 6 years or less.

SERVICES: Counseling and information services are available, as is tutoring in most subjects. There is remedial math, reading, and writing. **Library/Resources:** The library contains 741,046 volumes, 1.0 million microform items, and 81,219 audio/video tapes/CDs/DVDs, and subscribes to 4,049 periodicals including electronic. Computerized library services include interlibrary loans, database searching, Internet access, and Wi-Fi capability. Special learning facilities include a radio station. **Physically Challenged Students:** 80% of the campus is accessible. Facilities include wheelchair ramps, elevators, special parking, specially equipped restrooms, and special class scheduling. **Special:** Cooperative education is mandatory for engineering and architecture majors and is optional for others. Internships are available for many programs. Cross-registration is available with a consortium of Catholic colleges in the Detroit area. Many accelerated programs that combine a bachelor and master degree are available. Some programs include BS to DDS, BA to MBA, BEE to MEE. Study abroad experiences are available to students in many different countries; Cuba, Poland, Italy, and many more. Academic exploration courses are provided to help students who are undecided about a future vocation. There are 3 national honor societies and a freshman honors program. **Visiting:** There are regularly scheduled orientations for prospective students, including a look at student life, testing and advising, and registration. There are guides for informal visits; visitors may sit in on classes and stay overnight. To schedule a visit, contact Admissions Office. **Campus Safety and Security:** Measures include 24-hour foot and vehicle patrol, emergency notification system, self-defense education, and security escort services. There are emergency telephones, lighted pathways/sidewalks, and controlled access to dorms/ residences.

REQUIREMENTS: The SAT or ACT is required. Graduation from an accredited secondary school is required; a GED will be accepted. Students must submit 11 academic units, 4 units of English, 3 of math, and 2 each of history, and natural science (with a lab course). Remaining credits are recommended, 1 each in foreign language, social studies, and visual/performing arts. An interview is recommended. AP and CLEP credits are accepted. Students must successfully complete at least 126 credit hours, including a core curriculum, and maintain a minimum GPA of 2.0. Required courses include English composition, religion, philosophy, speech fundamentals, math, and a computer course. **Procedure:** Freshmen are admitted to all sessions. Entrance exams should be taken during the junior or senior year. There are early decision, deferred admissions, and rolling admissions plans. Early decision applications should be filed by November 1; regular application, by March 1 for fall entry. Applications are accepted on-line. **Transfer Students:** 240 transfer students enrolled in 2016-2017. Transfer applicants with fewer than 24 semester hours of credit at an accredited institution must submit SAT or ACT scores and must have maintained a minimum GPA of 2.0. If the student is older than 23 years of age, SAT/ACT scores need not be submitted. Application for transfer admission may enroll in the fall, winter, and summer. Open admission policy does not apply to transfer students. 32 of 126 credits required for the bachelor's degree must be completed at UDM. **International Students:** There are 107 international students enrolled. They must take the college's own test.

ADMISSIONS: The SAT scores for the 2017-2018 freshman class were: Critical Reading-- 39% below 500, 32% between 500 and 599, and 29% between 600 and 699. Math-- 32% below 500, 32% between 500 and 599, 29% between 600 and 699, and 7% between 700 and 800. Writing-- 50% below 500, 21% between 500 and 599, 21% between 600 and 699, and 7% between 700 and 800. The ACT scores were 1% between 12 and 17, 39% between 18 and 23, 46% between 24 and 29, and 14% above 30. 20 freshmen graduated first in their class. **Admissions Contact:** Tyra Rounds, Director of Admissions. Email: *admissions@udmercy.edu* Web: *www.udmercy.edu*

FINANCIAL AID: In 2017-2018, 100% of all full-time freshmen received some form of financial aid and need-based aid. The average freshman award was $37,388. Need-based scholarships or need-based grants averaged $32,183; need-based self-help aid (loans and jobs) averaged $3,969; non-need-based athletic scholarships averaged $25,151; other non-need-based awards and non-need-based scholarships averaged $23,247; and $2,695 from other forms of aid. The average financial indebtedness of the 2017 graduate was $23,247. University of Detroit Mercy is a member of CSS. The FAFSA code is 002323. The priority date for freshman financial aid applications for fall entry is April 1.

UNIVERSITY OF MICHIGAN/ANN ARBOR E-5

www.umich.edu

Ann Arbor, MI 48109 **(734) 764-7433**

Fax: (734) 936-0740	**Email: ua-admissions@umich.edu**
Full-time: 13,891 men, 13,942 women	**Faculty:** 2791; I, +$
Part-time: 539 men, 389 women	**Ph.D.s:** 91%
Graduate: 8378 men, 7357 women	**Student/Faculty:** 15 to 1
Year: trimesters, summer session	**Tuition:** $14,402 ($47,004)
Room & Board: $10,872	**Freshman Class:** 55504 applied, 15871 accepted, 10113 enrolled
SAT CR/M/W: 685/720/695 **ACT:** 31	**CEEB CODE:** 1839
Application Deadline: February 1	**MOST COMPETITIVE**

University of Michigan/Ann Arbor, founded in 1817, is the main campus of the University of Michigan. The public institution offers undergraduate programs in the arts and sciences, architecture, business administration, education, engineering, fine arts, kinesiology, natural resources, nursing, and professional studies, as well as a wide range of graduate and professional programs. There are 12 undergraduate schools and 18 graduate schools. In addition to regional accreditation, UM/Ann Arbor has baccalaureate program accreditation with AACSB, ABET, ACEJMC, ACPE, ADA, ASLA, CSWE, NAAB, NASAD, NASM, NLN, and SAF. The 3177-acre campus is in a suburban area 38 miles west of Detroit. Including any residence halls, there are 538 buildings.

STUDENT LIFE: 62% of undergraduates are from Michigan. Others are from 50 states, 86 foreign countries, and Canada. 7% are Foreign; 61% White; 5% Hispanic; 5% race unknown; 4% African American; 4% two or more races; 14% Asian American. **Male To Female Ratio:** 1.1:1. The average age of freshmen is 18; all undergraduates, 20. 90% remain to graduate. **Housing:** 11664 students can be accommodated in college housing, which includes married student dorms and on-campus apartments. In addition, there are honors houses, language/international houses, special-interest houses, fraternity houses, sorority houses, theme and wellness housing, living learning communities, substance free and gender neutral housing. On-campus housing is guaranteed for the freshman year only, is available on a first-come, first-served basis, and is available on a lottery system for upperclassmen. 98% of students live on campus. All students may keep cars.

FACULTY/CLASSROOMS: All teach undergraduates and all do research. No introductory courses are taught by graduate students. The average class size in an introductory lecture is 70; in a laboratory is 18; and in a regular course is 31.

PROGRAMS OF STUDY: UM/Ann Arbor confers B.A., B.S., A.B.Ed., B.B.A., B.D.A., B.F.A., B.G.S., B.Mus., B.Mus.A., B.S.Chem., B.S.E., B.S.Ed. and B.S.N. degrees. Master's and doctoral degrees are also awarded. Bachelor's degrees are awarded in AGRICULTURE (environmental studies), BIOLOGICAL SCIENCE (biochemistry, biology/biological science, biophysics, botany, cell biology, ecology, evolutionary biology, microbiology, molecular biology, and neurosciences), BUSINESS (business administration and management, organizational behavior, and sports management), COMMUNICATIONS AND THE ARTS (Arabic, art, art history and appreciation, audio technology, ceramic art and design, classical languages, classics, communications, comparative literature, creative writing, dance, design, dramatic arts, drawing, English, English literature, fiber/textiles/weaving, film arts, French, German, Germanic languages and literature, graphic design, Greek, Greek (modern), Hebrew, historic preservation, illustration, industrial design, Italian, jazz, Latin, linguistics, literature, metal/jewelry, music, music history and appreciation, music performance, music technology, music theory and composition, musical theater, painting, performing arts, photography, printmaking, Russian, Russian languages and literature, sculpture, Spanish, speech/debate/rhetoric, theater design, video, and winds), COMPUTER AND PHYSICAL SCIENCE (astronomy, astrophysics, atmospheric sciences and meteorology, chemistry, computer science, earth science, environmental geology, geology, geoscience, mathematics, oceanography, physics, and statistics), EDUCATION (athletic training, elementary education, music education, and physical education), ENGINEERING AND ENVIRONMENTAL DESIGN (aeronautical engineering, aerospace studies, architecture, biomedical engineering, chemical engineering, civil engineering, computer engineering, electrical/electronics engineering, engineering, engineering physics, environmental engineering, geological engineering, geophysical engineering, industrial engineering, materials engineering, materials science, mechanical engineering, naval architecture and marine engineering, and nuclear engineering), HEALTH PROFESSIONS (dental hygiene, exercise science, nursing, pharmaceutical chemistry, pharmaceutical science, pharmacy, and radiological science), SOCIAL SCIENCE (African studies, African American studies, American studies, anthropology, archeology, Asian/Oriental studies, behavioral science, biblical studies, Caribbean studies, classical/ancient civilization, cognitive science, Eastern European studies, economics, European studies, Hispanic American studies, history, humanities, interdisciplinary studies, international studies, Islamic studies, Judaic studies, Latin American studies, liberal arts/general studies, medieval studies, Mexican-American/Chicano studies, Middle Eastern studies, Near Eastern studies, philosophy, physical fitness/movement, political science/government, psychology, public affairs, Puerto Rican studies, religion, Russian and Slavic studies, social science, sociology, Western European studies, and women's studies). Psychology, engineering, and business administration have the largest enrollments.

ACTIVITIES: 17% of men belong to 40 national fraternities; 24% of women belong to 1 local and 27 national sororities. There are 1303 groups on campus, including art, band, cheerleading, chess, choir, chorale, chorus, computers, dance, debate, drama, environmental, ethnic, film, forensics, honors, international, jazz band, LGBT, literary magazine, marching band, musical theater, newspaper, opera, orchestra, pep band, photography, political, professional, radio and TV, religious, social, social service, student government, symphony, and yearbook. Popular campus events include Martin Luther King Day, Native American Powwow, and FestiFall. **Sports:** There are 14 intercollegiate sports for men and 14 for women, and 23 intramural sports for men and 23 for women. Facilities include a stadium, gym, indoor track, tennis complex, a practice center, golf courses, a natatorium with separate swimming pools, an ice arena, soccer and field hockey fields, and athletic arenas. **Graduates:** From July 1, 2016 to June 30, 2017, 7074 bachelor's degrees were awarded. The most popular majors were engineering (16%), social sciences (13%), and psychology (10%). In an average class, 70% graduate in 4 years or less, 86% graduate in 5 years or less, and 88% graduate in 6 years or less.

SERVICES: Counseling and information services are available, as is tutoring in some subjects, such as introductory to English and math. There is a reader service for the blind. **Library/Resources:** The library contains 10.6 million volumes, 10.6 million microform items, and 126,011 audio/video tapes/CDs/DVDs, and subscribes to 83,062 periodicals including electronic. Computerized library services include interlibrary loans, database searching, Internet access, and Wi-Fi capability. Special learning facilities include an art gallery, natural history museum, planetarium, radio station, TV station, archeology museum, botanical gardens, two historical museums, electronics music studio, and digital media commons. **Physically Challenged Students:** 99% of the campus is accessible. Facilities include wheelchair ramps, elevators, special parking, specially equipped restrooms, special class scheduling, lowered drinking fountains, lowered telephones, special housing, para-transit service, specially equipped vans, talking calculators, telecommunication devices for the deaf, an adaptive technology computing site that includes a high-speed scanner, voice input and voice output, braille display and large-print screens, and a braille printer. **Special:** Academic programs that are available are accelerated program, cooperative education program, exchange student program, external degree program, honors, and teachers certification program. There is also cross-registration, distance learning, double major, independent study, internships, student designed major, liberal arts/career combination, and study abroad. Dual and combined baccalaureate degree options in the College of Engineering, dual degree options in the Ross School of Business, College of Literature, Science and Arts, School of Kinesiology, and School of Music, Theater and Dance. There are 22 national honor societies, Phi Beta Kappa, and a freshman honors program. **Visiting:** There are regularly scheduled orientations for prospective students. Students visits include placement testing, academic advising, course registration, social activities, and informational programs on student life, computing resources, campus safety, and career planning. There are guides for informal visits and visitors may sit in on classes. To schedule a visit, contact the Office of Undergraduate Admissions. **Campus Safety and Security:** Measures include 24-hour foot and vehicle patrol, emergency notification system, self-defense education, and security escort services. There are shuttle buses, emergency telephones, lighted pathways/sidewalks, controlled access to dorms/residences, a night-owl bus service, officer bicycle patrols, and a taxi service.

REQUIREMENTS: The SAT or ACT is required. Applicants must be graduates of accredited secondary schools or have earned a GED. The university requires 16 Carnegie units, including 4 in English, 3 each in math (4 for engineering major), history, science (with 1 unit lab), and 1 unit in social studies, and 2 (for LSA) in foreign language. The following are recommended electives: 1 unit of hands-on computer study and 2 units of fine or performing arts. An essay is required for all applicants. Students applying to the School of Art must submit a portfolio; those applying to the School of Music must present an audition. AP and CLEP credits are accepted. Important factors in the admissions decision are advanced placement or honors courses, evidence of special talent, and geographical diversity. Academic requirements vary by program for the College of Literature, Science, and the Arts. Students must complete 7 semester hours each of humanities, social science, and natural science, for a total of 21 credits. Students must also complete 3 additional credits in 3 of the following areas: Natural Science, Social Science, and Humanities, Mathematical and Symbolic Analysis, and Creative Expression for 9 credits. All students must meet the quantitative reasoning requirement, designed to ensure proficiency in using and analyzing quantitative information. To graduate, students must complete a minimum of 120 credits with a cumulative GPA of 2.0. **Procedure:** Freshmen are admitted to all sessions. Entrance exams should be taken by the end of the junior year or the beginning of the senior. There are deferred admissions and rolling admissions plans. Applications should be filed by February 1 for fall entry. The fall 2017 application fee was $75. Notifications are sent April 1. 3970 applicants were on the 2017 waiting list; 36 were admitted. Applications are accepted on-line. **Transfer Students:** 1060 transfer students enrolled in 2016-2017. A minimum college GPA of 3.0 is required for junior-level transfers. Student may enroll in the fall, winter, spring and summer. 60 of 120 credits required for the bachelor's degree must be completed at UM/Ann Arbor. **International Students:** There are 1644 international students enrolled. They must take the TOEFL with a minimum score of 570 on the paper-based TOEFL (PBT) or 88 on the Internet-based version (iBT). Students must take the MELAB. They must also take the SAT or ACT.

ADMISSIONS: 29% of the 2017-2018 applicants were accepted. 95% of the current freshmen were in the top fifth of their class; 99% were in the top two fifths. **Admissions Contact:** Bernadette Lis, Associate Vice Provost. Email: *ua-admissions@umich.edu* Web: *www.umich.edu*

FINANCIAL AID: The average freshman award was $24,025. Need-based scholarships or need-based grants averaged $17,410; need-based self-help aid (loans and jobs) averaged $5,017; non-need-based athletic scholarships averaged $26,931; other non-need-based awards and non-need-based scholarships averaged $5,177; and $1,200 from other forms of aid. The average financial indebtedness of the 2017 graduate was $36,351. UM/Ann Arbor is a member of CSS. The FAFSA code is 002325. The priority date for freshman financial aid applications for fall entry is April 30.

UNIVERSITY OF MICHIGAN/DEARBORN E-5
www.umdearborn.edu

Dearborn, MI 48128 **(313) 593-5170**

Fax: (313) 436-9167	**Email:** umd-admissions@umich.edu
Full-time: 2811 men, 2326 women	**Faculty:** 328; IIA, +$
Part-time: 1006 men, 998 women	**Ph.D.s:** 50%
Graduate: 1481 men, 717 women	**Student/Faculty:** n/av
Year: semesters, summer session	**Tuition:** $12,472 ($24,706)
Room & Board: n/app	**Freshman Class:** 5731 applied, 3684 accepted, 1106 enrolled
SAT or ACT: required	**CEEB CODE:** 1861
Application Deadline: open	**VERY COMPETITIVE**

University of Michigan/Dearborn, founded in 1959, is a public, comprehensive commuter institution that is part of the University of Michigan system. The emphasis of its degree programs is on the liberal arts, management, engineering, and education. There are 4 undergraduate schools and 4 graduate schools. In addition to regional accreditation, UM/Dearborn has baccalaureate program accreditation with AACSB, ABET, CSAB, ACS, MI Dept of Education, and NAEYC. The 202-acre campus is in a suburban area 10 miles from Detroit. Including any residence halls, there are 27 buildings.

STUDENT LIFE: 95% of undergraduates are from Michigan. Others are from 10 states, 52 foreign countries, and Canada. 9% are African American; 8% Asian American; 69% White; 5% Hispanic; 3% two or more races; 3% race unknown; 2% Foreign. **Male To Female Ratio:** 1.3:1. The average age of freshmen is 17; all undergraduates, 22. **Housing:** All students commute. All students may keep cars. Alcohol is not permitted.

FACULTY/CLASSROOMS: 59% of faculty are male; 41% are female. No introductory courses are taught by graduate students.

PROGRAMS OF STUDY: UM/Dearborn confers A.B., B.A., B.S., B.B.A., B.G.S., B.S.A. and B.S.E. (includes BSEBE, BSECE, BSEEE, BSEEM, BSEIE, BSEME, BSEMFE and BSERE depending on Engineering major) degrees. Master's and doctoral degrees are also awarded. Bachelor's degrees are awarded in AGRICULTURE (environmental studies), BIOLOGICAL SCIENCE (biochemistry, biological sciences, and microbiology), BUSINESS (accounting, finance, human resource management, management information systems, marketing, small business management, and supply chain management), COMMUNICATIONS AND THE ARTS (art history, communications, English, French and Francophone studies, and language arts), COMPUTER AND PHYSICAL SCIENCE (chemistry, computer science, cyber intelligence/security studies, data science, geology, information technology management, mathematics, physics, and software engineering), EDUCATION (early childhood education, education, elementary education, general studies, learner designed area of study, mathematics education, reading education, science education, secondary education, social studies education, and special education), ENGINEERING AND ENVIRONMENTAL DESIGN (bioengineering, computer engineering, engineering, environmental science, industrial engineering, manufacturing engineering, and mechanical engineering), HEALTH PROFESSIONS (electrical engineering and public health), SOCIAL SCIENCE (African studies, African American studies, American studies, anthropology, behavioral science, criminal justice, criminology, economics, Hispanic American studies, history, humanities, interdisciplinary studies, international studies, liberal arts/general studies, philosophy, political science/government, psychology, social studies, sociology, urban and regional studies, and women & gender studies). Prebusiness, biological sciences, and mechanical engineering have the largest enrollments.

ACTIVITIES: Groups on campus include art, cheerleading, computers, dance, environmental, ethnic, film, honors, international, LGBT, literary magazine, newspaper, photography, political, professional, radio and TV, religious, social, social service, and student government. Popular campus events include Martin Luther King, Jr. Celebration, Homecoming events, Week of Welcome, Involvement Fairs, Conversations on Race, Greek Week, Panhellenic Recruitment, Alternative Spring Breaks, Wolverine Leadership Cohort, and Annual Student Leadership Awards. **Sports:** There are 5 intercollegiate sports for men and 5 for women, and 5 intramural sports for men and 5 for women. Facilities include a gymnasium, an ice arena, 2 racquetball courts, and a wellness and recreation center. **Graduates:** From July 1, 2016 to June 30, 2017, 1292 bachelor's degrees were awarded. The most popular majors were business/marketing (18%), engineering (12%), and psychology (11%). In an average class, 17% graduate in 4 years or less, 27% graduate in 5 years or less, and 10% graduate in 6 years or less.

SERVICES: Counseling and information services are available, as is tutoring in some subjects. UM/Dearborn will assist visually impaired students with any subject. There is a reader service for the blind, and remedial math. **Library/Resources:** The library contains 647,719 volumes, 537,685 microform items, and 7,448 audio/video tapes/CDs/DVDs, and subscribes to 97,209 periodicals including electronic. Computerized library services include interlibrary loans, database searching, Internet access, and Wi-Fi capability. Special learning facilities include an art gallery, planetarium, and radio station. **Physically Challenged Students:** All of the campus is accessible. Facilities include wheelchair ramps, elevators, special parking, specially equipped restrooms, special class scheduling, lowered drinking fountains, and lowered telephones. **Special:** UM/Dearborn offers a variety of internships, co-op experiences, study abroad opportunities and accelerated degree programs. Students may also dual major (i.e., Marketing and Psychology) or earn dual degrees (i.e., Bioengineering and Mechanical Engineering). Non-degree study and taking classes pass/fail (within established guidelines) are also possible. **Visiting:** There are regularly scheduled orientations for prospective students, consisting of a tour, a student panel, academic unit introduction, and campus life sessions. There are guides for informal visits and visitors may sit in on classes. To schedule a visit, contact the Office of Admissions. **Campus Safety and Security:** Measures include 24-hour foot and vehicle patrol, emergency notification system, and security escort services. There are shuttle buses, emergency telephones, lighted pathways/sidewalks, and AEDs available around campus; response time to call to service is 90 seconds or less.

REQUIREMENTS: The SAT or ACT is required. Other admissions requirements normally include graduation from an accredited secondary school; recommended high school units include 4 years each in math (with at least 2 in college prep math) and English; 3 in science (4 years recommended) and history/social science; a semester in computer science (1 full year recommended), and recommended 2 years of foreign language. Additional work in any subjects offered for high school credit to bring the total for the 4 high school years to the equivalent of at least 15 units is also recommended. The GED is accepted with a minimum score of 600. AP credits are accepted. To graduate, students must complete at least 120 credit hours. **Procedure:** Freshmen are admitted fall, winter, and summer. Entrance exams should be taken in the spring of the junior year or the fall of the senior year. There are deferred admissions and rolling admissions plans. Check with the school for current application deadlines. Notification is sent on a rolling basis. Applications are accepted on-line. **Transfer Students:** 789 transfer students enrolled in 2016-2017. Applicants are required to have 24 transferable semester/credit hours; if they have fewer than 24, the SAT or ACT is mandatory. The required minimum GPA ranges from 2.5 to 3.0, depending on major. 30 of 120 credits required for the bachelor's degree must be completed at UM/Dearborn. **International Students:** There are 165 international students enrolled. They must take the TOEFL with a minimum score of 550 on the paper-based TOEFL (PBT) or 80 on the Internet-based version (iBT) or take the MELAB, or IELTS. They must also take the SAT or ACT.

ADMISSIONS: 64% of the 2017-2018 applicants were accepted. The SAT scores for the 2017-2018 freshman class were: Math-- 13% below 500, 43% between 500 and 599, 35% between 600 and 699, and 9% between 700 and 800. Evidence-Based Reading/Writing-- 11% below 500, 45% between 500 and 599, 38% between 600 and 699, and 6% between 700 and 800. The ACT scores were 2% between 12 and 17, 31% between 18 and 23, 50% between 24 and 29, and 17% above 30. 46% of the current freshmen were in the top fifth of their class; 79% were in the top two fifths. **Admissions Contact:** Deb Peffer, Director of Admissions & Orientation. Email: *umd-admissions@umich.edu* Web: *www.umdearborn.edu*

FINANCIAL AID: The FAFSA code is 002326. The priority date for freshman financial aid applications for fall entry is January 3.

UNIVERSITY OF MICHIGAN/FLINT E-4
www.umflint.edu

Flint, MI 48502 **(810) 762-3300**

Fax: (810) 762-3272
Email: admissions@umflint.edu
Full-time: 1653 men, 2166 women
Part-time: 666 men, 1342 women
Graduate: 534 men, 908 women
Year: semesters, summer session
Room & Board: $8178
Faculty: 316
Ph.D.s: 74%
Student/Faculty: 14 to 1
Tuition: $10,884 ($20,802)
Freshman Class: 3003 applied, 2345 accepted, 724 enrolled
SAT CR/M/W: 534/542/497 **ACT:** 23
CEEB CODE: 1853
Application Deadline: August 20
COMPETITIVE

University of Michigan/Flint, established in 1956, is a public institution offering programs in the liberal arts and sciences, education, health professions, and business. There are 4 undergraduate schools and 6 graduate schools. In addition to regional accreditation, UM/Flint has baccalaureate program accreditation with AACSB, APTA, CSWE, NASM, NLN, AACN, ACS, CCNE, and JRCERT. The 73-acre campus is in an urban area 60 miles northwest of Detroit, 50 miles east of Lansing, and 55 miles north of Ann Arbor. Including any residence halls, there are 9 buildings.

STUDENT LIFE: 98% of undergraduates are from Michigan. Others are from 37 states, 34 foreign countries, and Canada. 97% are from public schools. 68% are White; 14% African American; 5% Foreign; 4% Hispanic; 3% two or more races; 3% race unknown; 2% Asian American; 1% American Indian/Alaska Native. **Female To Male Ratio:** 1.5:1. The average age of freshmen is 18; all undergraduates, 26. 20% do not continue beyond their first year; 40% remain to graduate. **Housing:** 310 students can be accommodated in college housing, which includes dorms and off-campus apartments. On-campus housing is available on a first-come and first-served basis. 77% of students commute. Alcohol is not permitted. All students may keep cars.

FACULTY/CLASSROOMS: All teach undergraduates and all do research. No introductory courses are taught by graduate students. The average class size in an introductory lecture is 24; in a laboratory is 17; and in a regular course is 20.

PROGRAMS OF STUDY: UM/Flint confers B.A., B.S., B.A.S., B.B.A., B.F.A., B.S.E., B.S.N., B.S.W., B.M., B.M.E., and B.I.S. degrees. Master's and doctoral degrees are also awarded. Bachelor's degrees are awarded in BIOLOGICAL SCIENCE (biology/biological science and ecology), BUSINESS (accounting, banking and finance, business administration and management, human resources, and marketing/retailing/merchandising), COMMUNICATIONS AND THE ARTS (art, communications, dramatic arts, English, French, music, and Spanish), COMPUTER AND PHYSICAL SCIENCE (applied science, chemistry, computer science, mathematics, physical sciences, physics, and science), EDUCATION (early childhood education, education, elementary education, foreign languages education, music education, and secondary education), ENGINEERING AND ENVIRONMENTAL DESIGN (engineering), HEALTH PROFESSIONS (environmental health science, health care administration, health science, medical laboratory technology, nursing, physical therapy, and radiation therapy), SOCIAL SCIENCE (anthropology, applied psychology, community psychology, criminal justice, economics, geography, history, philosophy, political science/government, psychology, public administration, social science, social work, sociology, and urban studies). Business, and nursing are the strongest academically. Business, education, and health sciences have the largest enrollments.

ACTIVITIES: 4% of men belong to 6 national fraternities; 4% of women belong to 7 national sororities. There are 103 groups on campus, including art, band, cheerleading, choir, chorale, chorus, computers, dance, debate, drama, ethnic, honors, jazz band, LGBT, literary magazine, musical theater, newspaper, political, professional, radio and TV, religious, social, social service, and student government. Popular campus events include Welcome Back Week, Winter Block Party, and Presidents Ball. **Sports:** There are 13 intramural sports for men and 12 for women. Facilities include a recreation building housing a multipurpose gym, racquetball courts, a weight training area, and a swimming pool. **Graduates:** From July 1, 2016 to June 30, 2017, 1265 bachelor's degrees were awarded. The most popular majors were health professions and related programs (34%), business marketing (18%), and biological/life sciences (7%). In an average class, 11% graduate in 4 years or less, 31% graduate in 5 years or less, and 39% graduate in 6 years or less.

SERVICES: Counseling and information services are available, as is tutoring in every subject. There is a reader service for the blind, and remedial math, reading, and writing. Sign language interpreters, note takers, and testing accomodations are also available. **Library/Resources:** The library contains 353,617 volumes, 600,610 microform items, and 10,581 audio/video tapes/CDs/DVDs, and subscribes to 559 periodicals including electronic. Computerized library services include interlibrary loans, database searching, and Internet access. Special learning facilities include an art gallery and radio station. **Physically Challenged Students:** 97% of the campus is accessible. Facilities include wheelchair ramps, elevators, special parking, specially equipped restrooms, special class scheduling, lowered drinking fountains, and lowered telephones. There are special telephones for the hearing impaired. Reasonable accommodations may be made for students with documented disabilities. **Special:** Special arrangements include co-op programs and dual majors, student-designed majors, cross-registration with Mott Community College, internships, study abroad, work-study, a 3-2 engineering program, an accelerated business degree, a general studies degree, nondegree study, and pass/fail options. There are 5 national honor societies, Phi Beta Kappa, a freshman honors program, and 47 departmental honors programs. **Visiting:** There are regularly scheduled orientations for prospective students. There are guides for informal visits and visitors may sit in on classes. To schedule a visit, contact the Admissions Office. **Campus Safety and Security:** Measures include 24-hour foot and vehicle patrol, emergency notification system, self-defense education, and security escort services. There are shuttle buses, emergency telephones, and lighted pathways/sidewalks.

REQUIREMENTS: The SAT is required, with the ACT preferred. Graduation from secondary school is required, with 4 years of English, 3 each of math and social studies, and 2 years of science. The GED is accepted. SAT: Subject tests and an interview are recommended. Applied music students must audition. AP and CLEP credits are accepted. Important factors in the admissions decision are advanced placement or honors courses, evidence of special talent, and leadership record. To graduate, all students must complete at least 120 credits, including 30 to 70 in the major along with satisfying all major requirements, and maintain a GPA of 2.0. Distribution requirements total 50 credits in English composition, humanities, fine arts, social science, and natural science. **Procedure:** Freshmen are admitted to all sessions. Entrance exams should be taken in the spring of the junior year or fall of the senior year. There are deferred admissions and rolling admissions plans. Applications should be filed by August 20 for fall entry; December 1 for winter entry. The fall 2017 application fee was $30. Notification is sent on a rolling basis. Applications are accepted on-line. **Transfer Students:** 717 transfer students enrolled in 2016-2017. Applicants must have at least 12 college credits and a minimum GPA of 2.0 in transferable courses. An associate degree and an interview are recommended. 45 of 120 credits required for the bachelor's degree must be completed at UM/Flint. **International Students:** There are 425 international students enrolled. They must take the TOEFL with a minimum score of 500 on the paper-based TOEFL (PBT) or 61 on the Internet-based version (iBT) or take the MELAB, or the IELTS. They must also take the SAT or ACT.

ADMISSIONS: 78% of the 2017-2018 applicants were accepted. The SAT scores for the 2017-2018 freshman class were: Critical Reading--30% below 500, 60% between 500 and 599, and 10% between 700 and 800. Math-- 30% below 500, 40% between 500 and 599, and 30% between 600 and 699. Writing-- 60% below 500, 20% between 500 and 599, and 20% between 600 and 699. The ACT scores were 15% between 12 and 17, 41% between 18 and 23, 37% between 24 and 29, and 7% above 30. 34% of the current freshmen were in the top fifth of their class; 63% were in the top two fifths. 7 freshmen graduated first in their class. **Admissions Contact:** Jon Davidson, Director of Admissions. Email: *admissions@umflint.edu* Web: *www.umflint.edu*

FINANCIAL AID: In 2017-2018, 70% of all full-time freshmen received some form of financial aid and need-based aid. The average freshman award was $12,080. Need-based scholarships or need-based grants averaged $6,781; need-based self-help aid (loans and jobs) averaged $3,643;

other non-need-based awards and non-need-based scholarships averaged $3,194; and $2,711 from other forms of aid. The average financial indebtedness of the 2017 graduate was $15,368. The priority date for freshman financial aid applications for fall entry is February 14.

WAYNE STATE UNIVERSITY E-5
www.wayne.edu

Detroit, MI 48202 (313) 577-2100

Email: admissions@wayne.edu

Full-time: 5406 men, 7003 women
Part-time: 2289 men, 2624 women
Graduate: 4321 men, 5446 women
Year: semesters, summer session
Room & Board: $10,106

SAT EBR-W/M: 570/557 **ACT:** 24
Application Deadline: August 1

Faculty: 979; I, -$
Ph.D.s: n/av
Student/Faculty: 13 to 1
Tuition: $12,979 ($27,453)
Freshman Class: 15331 applied, 10334 accepted, 2653 enrolled
CEEB CODE: 1898
COMPETITIVE

Wayne State University, founded in 1868, is a premier public, urban research institution offering more than 350 academic programs through 13 schools and colleges. Wayne State's four satellite campuses offer higher education to students throughout Southeast Michigan. Wayne State is dedicated to preparing students to excel by combining the academic excellence of a major research university with the practical experience of an institution that by its history, location and diversity represents a microcosm of the world we live in. There are 9 undergraduate schools and 11 graduate schools. In addition to regional accreditation, WSU has baccalaureate program accreditation with AACSB, ABET, ABFSE, ACPE, APTA, CSWE, NASM, ACS, CAA, CCNE, IAA, MDE, ABFSE, JRCERT, ACEND, NAACLS, NASD, and NAST. The 195-acre campus is in an urban area 2 miles north of downtown Detroit in the New Center area. Including any residence halls, there are 104 buildings.

STUDENT LIFE: 96% of undergraduates are from Michigan. Others are from 38 states, 41 foreign countries, and Canada. 9% are Asian American; 59% White; 5% Hispanic; 4% two or more races; 4% race unknown; 2% Foreign; 17% African American. **Female To Male Ratio:** 1.3:1. The average age of freshmen is 18; all undergraduates, 24. 81% remain to graduate. **Housing:** College-sponsored housing includes gender neutral, coed, married student dorms, on-campus apartments, and living learning communities. On-campus housing is available on a first-come and first-served basis. 87% of students commute. All students may keep cars.

FACULTY/CLASSROOMS: 51% of faculty are male; 49% are female. Graduate students teach 17% of introductory courses. The average class size in an introductory lecture is 35 and in a laboratory is 21.

PROGRAMS OF STUDY: WSU confers B.S., B.A., B.F.A., B.A.ED., B.S.ED., B.MUS., B.S.RT., B.S.PA., B.S.RDLT., B.S.CLS., B.S.DT., B.H.S., B.S.N., B.S.W., B.S.P., B.S.CHM., B.S.CRJ, B.P.A., B.S.BS., B.S.CT., B.S.CM., B.S.ETME., B.S.MAET., B.S.ETEM., B.S.ETT., B.S.ETEE., B.S.IE., B.S.ME., B.S.E.E., B.S.CIVL, B.S.C.E., B.S.BME., B.S.M.S. and B.S.C.S. degrees. Master's and doctoral degrees are also awarded. Bachelor's degrees are awarded in BIOLOGICAL SCIENCE (biochemistry, biology/biological science, biophysics, and nutrition), BUSINESS (accounting, business administration and management, finance, funeral home services, labor studies, management information systems, marketing/retailing/merchandising, organizational leadership and management, sports management, and supply chain management), COMMUNICATIONS AND THE ARTS (art, art history and appreciation, classics, communications, dance, design, English, film arts, film, television and digital media, German, journalism, linguistics, media arts, music, public relations, romance languages and literature, Slavic languages, and theatre arts), COMPUTER AND PHYSICAL SCIENCE (astronomy, chemistry, computer science, geology, information sciences and systems, mathematics, mathematics – economics, physics, and radiological technology), EDUCATION (Asian studies, educational media, elementary education, global studies, health education, mathematics education, physical education, science education, secondary education, social studies education, and special education), ENGINEERING AND ENVIRONMENTAL DESIGN (biomedical engineering, chemical engineering, civil engineering, computer technology, construction management, electrical and computer engineering, electrical/electronics engineering, electrical/electronics engineering technology, electromechanical technology, environmental science, industrial engineering, manufacturing technology, mechanical engineering, mechanical engineering technology, and textile marketing), HEALTH PROFESSIONS (biology, clinical science, exercise science, health science, kinesiology, nursing, nutrition and dietetics, public health, radiation therapy, and speech pathology/audiology), SOCIAL SCIENCE (African studies, anthropology, communication sciences & disorders, criminal justice, dietetics, economics, history, Near Eastern studies, philosophy, political science/government, psychology, public affairs, social work, sociology, urban studies, and women & gender studies). Medical school, engineering, and social work are the strongest academically. Biology, psychology, and engineering have the largest enrollments.

ACTIVITIES: There are 500 groups on campus, including art, band, cheerleading, chess, choir, chorale, chorus, communications, computers, dance, debate, environmental, ethnic, film, forensics, honors, international, jazz band, LGBT, literary magazine, marching band, musical theater, newspaper, orchestra, pep band, photography, political, professional, radio and TV, religious, social, social service, student government, and symphony. Popular campus events include Student Organization Day, International Fair, Detroit Festival of the Arts, and Alternative Spring Break Detroit. **Sports:** There are 8 intercollegiate sports for men and 9 for women. Facilities include an athletic complex with a full gym, a weight room, racquetball, squash courts, a competition swimming pool, an outdoor track, tennis courts, baseball fields, softball, football fields and a football stadium. The recreation center includes weight rooms, exercise equipment, indoor basketball courts, an indoor track, climbing wall and ropes course, women's only workout area, and indoor putting greens. **Graduates:** From July 1, 2016 to June 30, 2017, 3578 bachelor's degrees were awarded. The most popular majors were business/marketing (17%), psychology (11%), health professions, and related sciences (9%). In an average class, 20% graduate in 4 years or less, 38% graduate in 5 years or less, and 47% graduate in 6 years or less.

SERVICES: Counseling and information services are available, as is tutoring in every subject. There is a reader service for the blind, and remedial math, reading, and writing. Tutorial services are available through centralized counseling or academic departments. **Library/Resources:** The library contains 3.0 million volumes. Computerized library services include interlibrary loans, database searching, Internet access, and Wi-Fi capability. Special learning facilities include an art gallery, natural history museum, planetarium, and radio station. **Physically Challenged Students:** All of the campus is accessible. Facilities include wheelchair ramps, elevators, special parking, specially equipped restrooms, lowered drinking fountains, lowered telephones, and special housing. **Special:** Special academic programs include internships, study abroad, on-campus work-study programs, accelerated degree programs in liberal arts and science, engineering, and nursing, co-op programs, non-degree study, double majors, 3+2 engineering and computer science programs. There is a chapter of Phi Beta Kappa, a freshman honors program, and 49 departmental honors programs. **Visiting:** There are regularly scheduled orientations for prospective students. The agenda includes meeting with advisors, registering for classes, meeting upperclassmen, and touring the campus. There are guides for informal visits, visitors may sit in on classes, and stay overnight. To schedule a visit, contact the Office of Undergraduate Admissions. **Campus Safety and Security:** Measures include 24-hour foot and vehicle patrol, emergency notification system, self-defense education, and security escort services. There are shuttle buses, emergency telephones, lighted pathways/sidewalks, and controlled access to dorms/residences.

REQUIREMENTS: At Wayne State, we know that students come from different backgrounds and experiences, which makes our students so great! That's why we look at each individual applicant as that - an individual. The Office of Undergraduate Admissions will review your high school transcripts, ACT or SAT score and any other supporting documentation you provide us or we request from you. AP and CLEP credits are accepted. To graduate, students must complete at least 120 credit hours and have a minimum GPA of 2.0 for all WSU course work. Students must complete general education requirements, all school/college, departmental and program requirements, and complete at least thirty credits at Wayne State. **Procedure:** Freshmen are admitted to all sessions. Entrance exams should be taken during the junior year. There are deferred admissions and rolling admissions plans. Applications should be filed by August 1 for fall entry; December 1 for winter entry. The fall 2017 application fee was $25. Applications are accepted on-line. **Transfer Students:** 2495 transfer students enrolled in 2016-2017. While we will accept an unlimited number of transfer credits from four-year colleges, a maximum of 90 semester credits can be applied toward your Wayne State degree. We also accept credits from two-year colleges and will apply up to 64 semester credits toward your Wayne State degree. Some academic programs have additional restrictions; contact them individually for details. 30 of 120 credits required for the bachelor's degree must be completed at WSU. **International Students:** There are 367 international students enrolled. They must take the TOEFL with a minimum score of 550 on the paper-based TOEFL (PBT) or 79 on the Internet-based version (iBT) or take the MELAB. They must also take the SAT or ACT.

ADMISSIONS: 67% of the 2017-2018 applicants were accepted. The SAT scores for the 2017-2018 freshman class were: Math-- 19% below 500, 52% between 500 and 599, 23% between 600 and 699, and 5% between 700 and 800. Evidence-Based Reading/Writing-- 16% below 500, 47% between 500 and 599, 33% between 600 and 699, and 4% between 700 and 800. The ACT scores were 5% between 12 and 17, 40% between 18 and 23, 42% between 24 and 29, and 12% above 30. 40% of the current freshmen were in the top fifth of their class; 72% were in the top two fifths. **Admissions Contact:** Ericka M. Jackson, Director of Undergraduate Admissions. Email: *admissions@wayne.edu* Web: *www.wayne.edu*

FINANCIAL AID: In 2017-2018, 92% of all full-time freshmen received some form of financial aid. 68% of all full-time freshmen received need-based aid. WSU is a member of CSS. The FAFSA code is 002329. Check with the school for current application deadlines.

WESTERN MICHIGAN UNIVERSITY D-5

www. wmich.edu

Kalamazoo, MI 49008 | (269) 387-2000 | (800) 400-4968

Fax: (269) 387-2096 | Email: ask-wmu@wmich.edu

Full-time: 7654 men, 7361 women | **Faculty:** 711; I, --$
Part-time: 1304 men, 1385 women | **Ph.D.s:** 77%
Graduate: 1836 men, 2513 women | **Student/Faculty:** 21 to 1
Year: semesters, summer session | **Tuition:** $11,943 ($14,699)
Room & Board: $9848 | **Freshman Class:** 14263 applied, 11741 accepted, 3178 enrolled
SAT EBR-W/M: 548/532 **ACT:** 23 | **CEEB CODE:** 1902
Application Deadline: open | **COMPETITIVE**

Western Michigan University, founded in 1903, is a dynamic, globally engaged institution that combines the resources of a national research university with the support and personal attention often found at a small college. It is a public coeducational institution. Additional WMU locations are in Battle Creek, Benton Harbor, Grand Rapids, Lansing, Metro Detroit, Muskegon and Traverse City. WMU recently began program offerings in the Tampa Bay, Florida region. There are 7 undergraduate schools and 1 graduate school. In addition to regional accreditation, WMU has baccalaureate program accreditation with AACSB, ABET, ADA, CSWE, FIDER, NASAD, NASM, AABI, ACOTE, ACCGC, CAATE, CCNE, NASD, and NAST. The 1289-acre campus is in an urban area 140 miles west of Detroit and 140 miles east of Chicago in Kalamazoo, Michigan. Including any residence halls, there are 171 buildings.

STUDENT LIFE: 87% of undergraduates are from Michigan. Others are from 42 states, 57 foreign countries, and Canada. 71% are White; 6% Hispanic; 4% Foreign; 4% two or more races; 2% Asian American; 12% African American; 1% race unknown. **Female To Male Ratio:** 1.0:1. The average age of freshmen is 18; all undergraduates, 22. 22% do not continue beyond their first year; 51% remain to graduate. **Housing:** 6746 students can be accommodated in college housing, which includes gender neutral, single sex, coed, married student dorms, and on-campus apartments. In addition, there are honors houses, special-interest houses, fraternity houses, sorority houses, second year experience, and transfer student communities. On-campus housing is guaranteed for the freshman year only, is available on a first-come, and first-served basis. 72% of students commute. All students may keep cars.

FACULTY/CLASSROOMS: 49% of faculty are male; 51% are female. Graduate students teach 25% of introductory courses. The average class size in an introductory lecture is 95; in a laboratory is 22; and in a regular course is 31.

PROGRAMS OF STUDY: WMU confers B.A., B.S., B.B.A., B.F.A., B.M., B.M.A., B.S.E., B.S.N. and B.S.W. degrees. Master's and doctoral degrees are also awarded. Bachelor's degrees are awarded in AGRICULTURE (environmental studies), BIOLOGICAL SCIENCE (biochemistry, biology/biological science, and biology/ gen science secondary education), BUSINESS (accounting, apparel and accessories marketing, business economics, business intelligence and analytics, business law, entrepreneurial studies, fashion merchandising, finance, human resources/organizational mgmt, management information systems, management & strategic leadership, marketing/retailing/merchandising, personal financial planning, recreation and leisure services, sports management, supply chain management, and tourism), COMMUNICATIONS AND THE ARTS (advertising, Africana studies, apparel design, art history, art, communication studies, communications, creative writing, dance, English, film, television and digital media, French, German, graphic design, instrumental performance, instrumental music education, Japanese, jazz, journalism, keyboard - piano concentration, Latin, music, music composition, music performance, music theory and composition, musical theater, performing arts, public relations, Spanish, telecommunications, theatre acting, theater design, theatre studies, theater management, vocal performance, and writing & rhetoric), COMPUTER AND PHYSICAL SCIENCE (applied mathematics, chemistry, chemistry secondary education, computer information systems, computer science, earth science, geochemistry, geology, geophysics and seismology, hydrogeology, mathematics, physics secondary education, physics, and statistics), EDUCATION (art education, athletic training, business education, early childhood education, education, education of the emotionally handicapped, education of the mentally handicapped, elementary education, English secondary education, foreign languages education, general studies, health education, health information management, learner designed area of study, middle school education, music education, physical education, secondary education, social studies secondary school education, Spanish education K-12, special education, specific learning disabilities, university studies, and vocational education), ENGINEERING AND ENVIRONMENTAL DESIGN (aerospace engineering, airline piloting and navigation, aviation administration/management, aviation maintenance technology, chemical engineering, city/community/regional planning, civil engineering, computer engineering, construction engineering, drafting and design technology, electrical and computer engineering, engineering graphics & design, engineering management, graphic and printing production, industrial engineering, interior design, manufacturing engineering, manufacturing technology, mechanical engineering, paper engineering, product design engineering technology, textile, and fashion merchandising & design), HEALTH PROFESSIONS (biomedical science, community health work, exercise science, music therapy, nursing, occupational therapy, public health, and speech pathology/audiology), SOCIAL SCIENCE (African studies, African American studies, anthropology, behavioral science, child care/child and family studies, child psychology/development, clothing and textiles management/production/services, criminal justice, dietetics, economics, family/consumer studies, fashion design and technology, food production/management/services, gender studies, geography, history, interdisciplinary studies, international studies, philosophy, political science/government, psychology, public history/archives, religion, social work, sociology, textiles and clothing, and women's studies). Nursing, business, and psychology have the largest enrollments.

ACTIVITIES: 7% of men belong to 19 national fraternities; 8% of women belong to 14 national sororities. There are 385 groups on campus, including art, band, cheerleading, chess, choir, chorale, chorus, communications, computers, dance, drama, environmental, ethnic, film, honors, international, jazz band, LGBT, literary magazine, marching band, musical theater, newspaper, orchestra, pep band, photography, political, professional, radio and TV, religious, social, social service, student government, and symphony. Popular campus events include Bronco Bash, Homecoming, Campus Classic, CommUniversity, Relay for Life, and Family Weekend. **Sports:** There are 6 intercollegiate sports for men and 10 for women, and 16 intramural sports for men and 15 for women. Facilities include a recreational swimming pool, a swirl pool, weight and fitness room with more than 100 stations, basketball, floor hockey, indoor soccer, a climbing wall, an elevated track for jogging, aerobics, indoor cycling, badminton, tennis, and volleyball, a gym, an outdoor track, tennis courts, a football stadium, an ice arena, baseball stadium, and softball stadium. **Graduates:** From July 1, 2016 to June 30, 2017, 3774 bachelor's degrees were awarded. The most popular majors were business/marketing (20%), health professions and related programs (12%), and interdisciplinary studies (8%). In an average class, 22% graduate in 4 years or less, 44% graduate in 5 years or less, and 51% graduate in 6 years or less.

SERVICES: Counseling and information services are available, as is tutoring in most subjects. There is a reader service for the blind, and remedial math, reading, and writing. There is also non-remedial tutoring, placement service, content tutoring, and supplemental instruction. **Library/Resources:** The library contains 1.8 million volumes, 109,111 microform items, and 172,400 audio/video tapes/CDs/DVDs, and subscribes to 81,077 periodicals including electronic. Computerized library services include interlibrary loans, database searching, Internet access, and Wi-Fi capability. Special learning facilities include an art gallery, radio station, archives & regional history library, aviation flight simulators, behavioral research and development center, business incubator for student entrepreneurs and inventors, business technology and research park, center for electron microscopy, historic farm sustainability living/learning community with permaculture landscape, nuclear accelerator, particle accelerator, pilot plant for manufacturing and printing of paper and fiber recovery, and stock trading room with electronic ticker and terminals. **Physically Challenged Students:** 85% of the campus is accessible. Facilities include wheelchair ramps, elevators, special parking, specially equipped restrooms, special class scheduling, lowered drinking fountains, lowered telephones, and special housing. **Special:** Cross-registration is available through the Kalamazoo Consortium. Opportunities are provided for internships in occupational and music therapy, teaching, business, history, and engineering and accelerated degree programs in audiology, engineering, communication, music, social work, Spanish, statistics, orientation & mobility and vision rehabilitation therapy. Also available are work-study programs, student-designed majors, pass/fail options, and credit by exam. WMU offers students study abroad programs in 45 countries, and access to foreign study opportunities in almost every country in the world through linkages with other universities and organizations. There are 20 national honor societies, Phi Beta Kappa, and a freshman honors program. **Visiting:** There are regularly scheduled orientations for prospective students. Visiting students can participate in an admission presentation, departmental advising, lunch, and a campus tour. There are guides for informal visits and visitors may sit in on classes. To schedule a visit, contact the Campus Visit Center at (269) 387-2289. **Campus Safety and Security:** Measures include 24-hour foot and vehicle patrol, emergency notification system, and security escort services. There are shuttle buses, emergency telephones, lighted pathways/sidewalks, and controlled access to dorms/residences. There is also a residence hall security system, engravers for identification of items, free bicycle registration, a select group have been assigned to work with police officers to assist staff with a variety of functions and to develop crime prevention programs, all interior residence hall doors to the living areas are locked 24 hours a day, and all front doors are locked during the night and early morning hours, several resident assistants live on each floor, each residence hall room has a deadbolt door lock, and an effective lock changing procedure is in place.

REQUIREMENTS: Applicants must submit an official high school transcript (or GED test scores). ACT or SAT test scores are required unless the applicant has been out of high school for two or more years. An audition is required for music majors. An interview may be recommended. The College of Fine Arts requires an audition, portfolio, or interview of all applicants. AP and CLEP credits are accepted. Important factors in the admissions decision are advanced placement or honors courses, extracurricular activities record, and recommendations by school officials. Students must complete a minimum of 122 credit hours, including a minimum of 30 hours at WMU. They must complete a major with a minimum of 24 hours and, if required by the curriculum, a minor with a minimum of 15 hours. A minimum GPA of 2.0 is required. Students must complete or qualify for 37 credit hours of general education courses in college-level writing, college-level mathematics, fine arts, humanities, US culture, non-Western world, social science, natural science with lab, science and technology, and health and well-being. Comprehensive exams are required in some departments. All students must demonstrate computer literacy. **Procedure:** Freshmen are admitted to all sessions. Entrance exams should be taken during the junior year or early in the senior year. There is a rolling admissions plan. Application deadlines are open. The fall 2017 application fee was $40. Notification is sent on a rolling basis. Applications are accepted on-line. **Transfer Students:** 2554 transfer students enrolled in 2016-2017. Transfer students must have a minimum 2.0 GPA in transferable courses (as calculated by the Office of Admissions) to be considered for admission. Courses completed and trend of grades will also be taken into account. 30 of 122 credits required for the bachelor's degree must be completed at WMU. **International Students:** There are 708 international students enrolled. They must take the TOEFL with a minimum score of 500 on the paper-based TOEFL (PBT) or 61 on the Internet-based version (iBT), or take the MELAB. Student must take the IELTS.

ADMISSIONS: 82% of the 2017-2018 applicants were accepted. The SAT scores for the 2017-2018 freshman class were: Math-- 33% below 500, 47% between 500 and 599, 17% between 600 and 699, and 3% between 700 and 800. Evidence-Based Reading/Writing-- 26% below 500, 47% between 500 and 599, 24% between 600 and 699, and 3% between 700 and 800. The ACT scores were 10% between 12 and 17, 48% between 18 and 23, 36% between 24 and 29, and 6% above 30. 24% of the current freshmen were in the top fifth of their class; 55% were in the top two fifths. 25 freshmen graduated first in their class. **Admissions Contact:** Terrence Curran, Associate Provost for Enrollment Management. Email: *ask-wmu@wmich.edu* Web: *www. wmich.edu*

FINANCIAL AID: In 2017-2018, 78% of all full-time freshmen received some form of financial aid. 54% of all full-time freshmen received need-based aid. The average freshman award was $17,144. Need-based scholarships or need-based grants averaged $6,154 ($15,000 maximum); need-based self-help aid (loans and jobs) averaged $5,500 ($7,500 maximum); non-need-based athletic scholarships averaged $5,124 ($24,310 maximum); and other non-need-based awards and non-need-based scholarships averaged $2,238 ($17,151 maximum). 17% of undergraduate students work part-time. The average financial indebtedness of the 2017 graduate was $26,633. The FAFSA code is 002330. The priority date for freshman financial aid applications for fall entry is March 1.

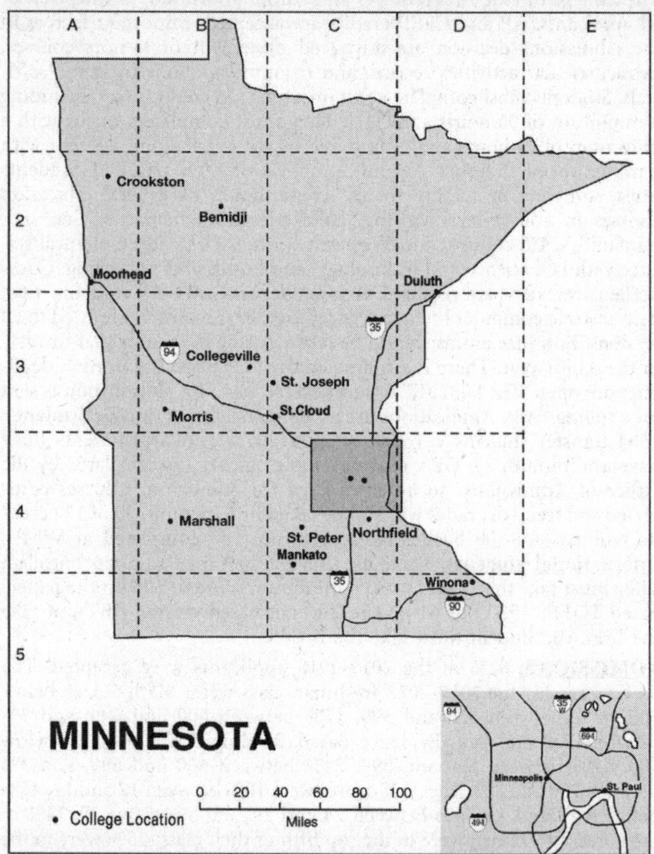

AUGSBURG UNIVERSITY C-4

www.augsburg.edu

Minneapolis, MN 55454	**(612) 330-1001** **(800) 788-5678**
Fax: (612) 330-1581	**Email: admissions@augsburg.edu**
Full-time: 1231 men, 1343 women	**Faculty:** 195; IIB, av$
Part-time: 197 men, 353 women	**Ph.D.s:** 85%
Graduate: 286 men, 606 women	**Student/Faculty:** 15 to 1
Year: varies, summer session	**Tuition:** $37,615
Room & Board: $7514	**Freshman Class:** 2346 applied, 1217 accepted, 449 enrolled
SAT CR/M: 505/565 **ACT:** 22	**CEEB CODE:** 6014
Application Deadline: August 15	**COMPETITIVE**

Augsburg University, established in 1869, is a private liberal arts institution affiliated with the Evangelical Lutheran Church. The figures given in the above capsule and in this profile are approximate. There is 1 undergraduate school and 1 graduate school. In addition to regional accreditation, AU has baccalaureate program accreditation with ACCE, AHEA, CSWE, NASM, CAEP, NLN, ARC-PA, CIC, and AAHE. The 18-acre campus is in an urban area in Minneapolis. Including any residence halls, there are 26 buildings.

STUDENT LIFE: 89% of undergraduates are from Minnesota. Others are from 34 states, 51 foreign countries, and Canada. 8% are African American; 71% White; 6% Asian American; 3% Hispanic; 2% American Indian/Alaska Native; 1% Foreign. 51% are Protestant; 30% claim no religious affiliation; 13% Catholic. **Female To Male Ratio:** 1.3:1. The average age of freshmen is 19; all undergraduates, 26. 19% do not continue beyond their first year; 60% remain to graduate. **Housing:** 1150 students can be accommodated in college housing, which includes married student dorms, on-campus apartments, and special-interest houses. On-campus housing is guaranteed for the freshman year only, and is available on a first-come, first-served basis, and is available on a lottery system for upperclassmen. 54% of students live on campus. All students may keep cars.

FACULTY/CLASSROOMS: 49% of faculty are male; 51% are female. 99% teach undergraduates. No introductory courses are taught by graduate students. The average class size in an introductory lecture is 20; in a laboratory is 16; and in a regular course is 16.

PROGRAMS OF STUDY: AU confers B.A., B.S., B.M., B.S.N., M.A., M.B.A., M.S., M.S.W., and D.N.P. degrees. Master's degrees are also awarded. Bachelor's degrees are awarded in AGRICULTURE (environmental studies), BIOLOGICAL SCIENCE (biology/biological science), BUSINESS (accounting, business administration and management, economics – statistics, international business management, management information systems, and marketing/retailing/merchandising), COMMUNICATIONS AND THE ARTS (art, art history and appreciation, communications, dramatic arts, English, French, German, languages, music, Scandinavian languages, Spanish, speech/debate/rhetoric, and studio art), COMPUTER AND PHYSICAL SCIENCE (chemistry, computer science, mathematics, and physics), EDUCATION (education, elementary education, health education, music education, physical education, and secondary education), HEALTH PROFESSIONS (music therapy and prehealth studies), SOCIAL SCIENCE (East Asian studies, economics, history, international relations, philosophy, political science/government, psychology, religion, Russian and Slavic studies, Scandinavian studies, social work, sociology, urban studies, women's studies, and youth ministry). Physics, chemistry, and English are the strongest academically. Business, communication, and education have the largest enrollments.

ACTIVITIES: There are no fraternities or sororities. There are 40 groups on campus, including art, band, cheerleading, choir, chorus, dance, drama, ethnic, honors, international, jazz band, LGBT, literary magazine, newspaper, orchestra, pep band, political, professional, radio and TV, religious, social, social service, and student government. Popular campus events include Days in May, Spring Affair, Advent Vespers, Peace, Justice and Hunger Concerns, and concerts. **Sports:** There are 9 intercollegiate sports for men and 7 for women, and 4 intramural sports for men and women. Facilities include a sports field, a gym, tennis courts, a double-rink ice arena, and a domed field facility for winter. **Graduates:** From July 1, 2016 to June 30, 2017, 539 bachelor's degrees were awarded. The most popular majors were business management (10%), accounting/public accounting (6%), and elementary education (6%). In an average class, 7% graduate in 3 years or less, 38% graduate in 4 years or less, 53% graduate in 5 years or less, and 55% graduate in 6 years or less. Of the 2016 graduating class, 24% were enrolled in graduate school within 6 months of graduation, and 85% were employed.

SERVICES: Counseling and information services are available, as is tutoring in every subject. There is a reader service for the blind, and remedial math and writing. There is also taped textbooks and adaptive computer technology, a text scanner, speaking software, a touch tablet, and text magnification software. **Library/Resources:** The library contains 190,000 volumes, 21,355 microform items, 3,477 audio/video tapes/CDs/DVDs, and subscribes to 686 periodicals, including electronic. Computerized library services include interlibrary loans, database searching, Internet access, and Wi-Fi capability. Special learning facilities include an art gallery, a planetarium, radio station, the James G. Lindell Family Library, the Gage Family Art Gallery, and the Christensen Center Art Gallery. **Physically Challenged Students:** 95% of the campus is accessible. Facilities include wheelchair ramps, elevators, special parking, specially equipped restrooms, special class scheduling, lowered drinking fountains, lowered telephones, and special housing. **Special:** Special academic programs include internships and co-op programs in business, government, nonprofit and community-based organizations, a Washington semester, and study abroad in Europe, Latin America, and Africa. There are student-designed majors, cross-registration through the Associated Colleges of the Twin Cities (ACTC), dual and 3-2 engineering degrees with Washington University, Michigan Technological University, and the University of Minnesota, and preprofessional programs in dentistry, law, medicine, physical therapy, pharmacy, theology, and veterinary medicine. Credit for previous learning experience may be granted, and pass/fail options are possible. There is 1 national honor society, a freshman honors program, and 1 departmental honors program. **Visiting:** There are regularly scheduled orientations for prospective students, including admissions interviews and campus tours. Students may also arrange to meet with professors and coaches and to attend lectures. There are guides for informal visits; visitors may sit in on classes and stay overnight. To schedule a visit, contact the Admissions Counselor. **Campus Safety and Security:** Measures include 24-hour foot and vehicle patrol, self-defense education, and security escort services. There are emergency telephones, lighted pathways/sidewalks, and controlled access to dorms/residences.

REQUIREMENTS: The ACT is required, with a minimum score of 22. The SAT is recommended. Admissions requirements include graduation from an accredited secondary school with 4 years of English. The GED is also accepted. An essay is required, and an interview is recommended. AP and CLEP credits are accepted. Important factors in the admissions decision are advanced placement or honors courses, leadership record, and recommendations by school officials. To graduate, all students must have a minimum GPA of 2.0 and a total of 32 courses, with 10 to 15 in the major. They must complete 15 courses from 8 perspective areas and a first-year fall orientation and seminar. Students must also satisfy entry-level and graduation skills requirements in writing, critical thinking, math, quantitative reasoning, and speaking and demonstrate proficiency. **Procedure:** Freshmen are admitted in the fall and spring. Entrance exams should be taken during the fall of the senior year in high school. There are deferred admissions and rolling admissions plans. Applications should be filed by August 15 for fall entry; December 1 for spring entry. The fall 2017 application fee was $25. Notification is sent on a rolling basis. Applications are accepted online. **Transfer Students:** 282 transfer students enrolled in 2016-2017. Applicants must have a minimum GPA of 2.2 in college coursework. 9 of 32 credits required for the bachelor's degree must be completed at AU. **International Students:** There are 44 international students enrolled. They must take the TOEFL with a minimum score of 550 on the paper-based TOEFL (PBT) or 80 on the Internet-based version (iBT). They must also take the SAT or ACT, scoring 22.

ADMISSIONS: 52% of the 2017-2018 applicants were accepted. The SAT scores for the 2017-2018 freshman class were: Critical Reading--50% below 500, 25% between 500 and 599, 21% between 600 and 699, and 4% between 700 and 800. Math-- 21% below 500, 33% between 500 and 599, 38% between 600 and 699, and 8% between 700 and 800. The ACT scores were 38% below 12, 27% between 12 and 17, 23% between 18 and 23, 8% between 24 and 29, and 4% above 30. 28% of the current freshmen were in the top fifth of their class; 55% were in the top two fifths. 5 freshmen graduated first in their class. **Admissions Contact:** Carola Thorson, Director of Admissions. Email: *admissions@augsburg.edu* Web: *www.augsburg.edu*

FINANCIAL AID: In 2017-2018, 98% of all full-time freshmen received some form of financial aid and need-based aid. The average freshman award was $12,883. Need-based scholarships or need-based grants averaged $11,308 ($27,892 maximum); and $1,631 from other forms of aid. 44% of undergraduate students work part-time. The average financial indebtedness of the 2017 graduate was $27,000. The college's own financial statement is required. The FAFSA code is 002334. The priority date for freshman financial aid applications for fall entry is April 15.

BEMIDJI STATE UNIVERSITY — B-2

www.bemidjistate.edu

Bemidji, MN 56601 — **(218) 755-2040**, **(877) 236-4354**

Fax: (218) 755-2074 — **Email: admissions@bemidjistate.edu**

Full-time: 1701 men, 1823 women	**Faculty:** n/av
Part-time: 419 men, 801 women	**Ph.D.s:** 79%
Graduate: 79 men, 194 women	**Student/Faculty:** n/av
Year: semesters, summer session	**Tuition:** $8678
Room & Board: $8162	**Freshman Class:** 3343 applied, 2657 accepted, 765 enrolled
ACT: required	**CEEB CODE:** 6676
Application Deadline: open	**COMPETITIVE**

Bemidji State University, founded in 1919, is a public liberal arts university. There are 3 undergraduate schools and 1 graduate school. In addition to regional accreditation, BSU has baccalaureate program accreditation with CSWE, NASM, and NLN. The 89-acre campus is in a small town 220 miles northwest of Minneapolis. Including any residence halls, there are 21 buildings.

STUDENT LIFE: 87% of undergraduates are from Minnesota. Others are from 46 states, 34 foreign countries, and Canada. 95% are from public schools. 89% are White; 5% Foreign; 3% American Indian/Alaska Native; 1% African American; 1% Asian American; 1% Hispanic. **Female To Male Ratio:** 1.3:1. The average age of freshmen is 18; all undergraduates, 24. 28% do not continue beyond their first year; 44% remain to graduate. **Housing:** 1700 students can be accommodated in college housing, which includes dorms and on-campus apartments. In addition, there are special-interest houses, fraternity houses, single-parent apartments. On-campus housing is available on a first-come, first-served basis. 68% of students commute. Alcohol is not permitted. All students may keep cars.

FACULTY/CLASSROOMS: 59% of faculty are male; 41% are female. 99% teach undergraduates, and 15% do research. Graduate students teach 1% of introductory courses. The average class size in an introductory lecture is 35; in a laboratory is 20; and in a regular course is 23.

PROGRAMS OF STUDY: BSU confers B.A., B.S., and B.F.A. degrees. Associate and master's degrees are also awarded. Bachelor's degrees are awarded in AGRICULTURE (environmental studies), BIOLOGICAL SCIENCE (biology/biological science), BUSINESS (accounting and business administration and management), COMMUNICATIONS AND THE ARTS (broadcasting, communications, English, fine arts, German, journalism, languages, music, and Spanish), COMPUTER AND PHYSICAL SCIENCE (chemistry, computer science, earth science, geology, mathematics, and physics), EDUCATION (art education, early childhood education, elementary education, foreign languages education, health education, industrial arts education, middle school education, science education, and secondary education), ENGINEERING AND ENVIRONMENTAL DESIGN (industrial engineering technology), HEALTH PROFESSIONS (medical laboratory technology, nursing, predentistry, and premedicine), SOCIAL SCIENCE (community services, criminal justice, economics, geography, history, parks and recreation management, philosophy, political science/government, prelaw, psychology, social science, social work, and sociology). Nursing, accounting, and engineering are the strongest academically. Business administration, nursing and education have the largest enrollments.

ACTIVITIES: 1% of men belong to 2 national fraternities; 1% of women belong to 1 national sorority. There are 90 groups on campus, including trap shooting clubs, art, band, cheerleading, choir, chorus, computers, dance, drama, environmental, ethnic, fishing, honors, international, jazz band, LGBT, literary magazine, musical theater, newspaper, opera, orchestra, pep band, political, professional, radio and TV, religious, social, social service, and student government. Popular campus events include Funtastic Dance Follies, Madrigal Music, and plays and concerts. **Sports:** There are 5 intercollegiate sports for men and 9 for women, and 8 intramural sports for men and 6 for women. Facilities include a basketball gym, an Olympic-size pool, Rugby, a hockey arena, a football stadium, indoor and outdoor tracks, baseball and softball fields, tennis, racquetball, and handball courts, weight rooms, and a dance studio. **Graduates:** From July 1, 2016 to June 30, 2017, 888 bachelor's degrees were awarded. The most popular majors were business/marketing (18%), education (16%), and health professions and related programs (11%). In an average class, 48% graduate in 6 years or less. Of the 2016 graduating class, 14% were enrolled in graduate school within 6 months of graduation, and 90% were employed.

SERVICES: Counseling and information services are available, as is tutoring in every subject. There is a reader service for the blind, and remedial math, reading, and writing. **Library/Resources:** The library contains 190,000 volumes, 721,255 microform items, 2,500 audio/video tapes/CDs/DVDs, and subscribes to 907 periodicals, including electronic. Computerized library services include interlibrary loans and database searching. Special learning facilities include an art gallery, radio station, and TV station. **Physically Challenged Students:** 95% of the campus is accessible. Facilities include wheelchair ramps, elevators, special parking, specially equipped restrooms, lowered drinking fountains, and lowered telephones. **Special:** Students may attend other schools within the Minnesota State University system and study abroad in 10 countries. Paid internships and work-study programs are available in many fields. Students may receive credit for life, military, and work experience. Student-designed dual majors, nondegree study, and pass/fail options are offered. There are 2 national honor societies and a freshman honors program. **Visiting:** There are regularly scheduled orientations for prospective students, including an interview with an admissions counselor, a tour of the campus, and visits with faculty. There are guides for informal visits; visitors may sit in on classes and stay overnight. To schedule a visit, contact the Admissions Office. **Campus Safety and Security:** Measures include 24-hour foot and vehicle patrol, an an emergency notification system, self-defense education, and security escort services. There are shuttle buses, emergency telephones, lighted pathways/sidewalks, controlled access to dorms/residences, in-room safes, all buildings are locked overnight, controlled sportsman's weapons storage, and 24/7 campus security team.

REQUIREMENTS: Applicants must have a minimum high school rank of 50%, or a composite score of 21 on the ACT. Students should have 4 years of English and 3 years each of math, science, and social studies. BSU requires applicants to be in the upper 50% of their class. AP and CLEP credits are accepted. Important factors in the admissions decision are recommendations by school officials, advanced placement or honors courses, and extracurricular activities record. All students must complete at least 120 semester hours, of which 42 are general education, including courses in freshman English, the humanities, social science, physical science, liberal education activities, and physical education. Students must also maintain a minimum GPA of 2.0, and a 2.3 GPA is required in the major (2.5 for education majors). **Procedure:** Freshmen are admitted to all sessions. Entrance exams should be taken during the junior year. There are deferred admissions and rolling admissions plans. Application deadlines are open. The fall 2017 application fee was $20. Applications are accepted online. **Transfer Students:** 349 transfer students enrolled in 2016-2017. Applicants must have a minimum GPA of 2.0. 32 of 120 credits required for the bachelor's degree must be completed at BSU. **International Students:** There are 150 international students enrolled. They must take the TOEFL.

ADMISSIONS: 79% of the 2017-2018 applicants were accepted. **Admissions Contact:** Paul Muller, Director for Admissions. Email: *admissions@bemidjistate.edu* Web: *www.bemidjistate.edu*

FINANCIAL AID: In 2017-2018, 83% of all full-time freshmen received some form of financial aid. 78% of all full-time freshmen received need-based aid. The average freshman award was $9,457. Need-based scholarships or need-based grants averaged $6,030; need-based self-help aid (loans and jobs) averaged $4,436; non-need-based athletic scholarships averaged $4,080; other non-need-based awards and non-need-based scholarships averaged $3,598; and $9,967 from other forms of aid. 25% of undergraduate students work part-time. The average financial indebtedness of the 2017 graduate was $20,470. The college's own financial statement is required. Check with the school for current application deadlines.

BETHEL UNIVERSITY — C-4

www.bethel.edu

St. Paul, MN 55112 — (651) 638-6242, (800) 255-8706

Fax: (651) 635-1490 — Email: undergrad-admissions@bethel.edu

Full-time: 940 men, 1438 women	**Faculty:** 220; IIA, -$
Part-time: 161 men, 307 women	**Ph.D.s:** 78%
Graduate: 655 men, 992 women	**Student/Faculty:** 15 to 1
Year: 4-1-4, summer session	**Tuition:** $36,210
Room & Board: $10,340	**Freshman Class:** 1798 applied, 1481 accepted, 558 enrolled
SAT: required **ACT:** 25	**CEEB CODE:** 6038
Application Deadline: n/av	**COMPETITIVE+**

Bethel University, established in 1871, is a private liberal arts university affiliated with the Converge Worldwide (Baptist General Conference). The figures given in the above capsule and in this profile are approximate. There are 2 undergraduate schools and 2 graduate schools. In addition to regional accreditation, BU has baccalaureate program accreditation with CSWE, TEAC, CAATE, and CCNE. The 247-acre campus is in a suburban area 10 miles north of Minneapolis/St. Paul. Including any residence halls, there are 39 buildings.

STUDENT LIFE: 79% of undergraduates are from Minnesota. Others are from 43 states, 22 foreign countries, and Canada. 72% are from public schools. 90% are White; 5% Hispanic; 4% African American; 3% Asian American; 3% two or more races; 13% race unknown. 97% are Protestant. **Female To Male Ratio:** 1.6:1. The average age of freshmen is 18; all undergraduates, 20. 15% do not continue beyond their first year; 75% remain to graduate. **Housing:** 2076 students can be accommodated in college housing, which includes dorms, on-campus apartments, and off-campus apartments. In addition, there are honors houses, special-interest houses; united house of justice, mindful living, and ACE housing. On-campus housing is available on a first-come, first-served basis, and is available on a lottery system for upperclassmen. 93% of students live on campus. Upperclassmen may keep cars. Alcohol is not permitted.

FACULTY/CLASSROOMS: 51% of faculty are male; 49% are female. All teach undergraduates. No introductory courses are taught by graduate students. The average class size in a laboratory is 20 and in a regular course is 22.

PROGRAMS OF STUDY: BU confers B.A., B.S., B.Mus., and B.Mus.Ed degrees. Associate, master's, and doctoral degrees are also awarded. Bachelor's degrees are awarded in AGRICULTURE (environmental studies), BIOLOGICAL SCIENCE (biochemistry, biology/biological science, and molecular biology), BUSINESS (accounting, banking and finance, and business administration and management), COMMUNICATIONS AND THE ARTS (art, communications, dramatic arts, English, English literature, French, journalism, multimedia, music, music performance, Spanish, and visual and performing arts), COMPUTER AND PHYSICAL SCIENCE (applied physics, chemistry, computer science, mathematics, and physics), EDUCATION (athletic training, business education, early childhood education, education, elementary education, English education, foreign languages education, health education, mathematics education, middle school education, music education, physical education, science education, secondary education, social studies education, and teaching English as a second/foreign language (TESOL/TEFOL), ENGINEERING AND ENVIRONMENTAL DESIGN (engineering and applied science and environmental science), HEALTH PROFESSIONS (community health work, exercise science, and nursing), SOCIAL SCIENCE (biblical studies, economics, history, international relations, philosophy, political science/government, psychology, religious music, social studies, social work, theological studies, Third World studies, and youth ministry). Physics, chemisty, and nursing are the strongest academically. Business, education, and nursing have the largest enrollments.

ACTIVITIES: There are no fraternities or sororities. There are 74 groups on campus, including art, band, choir, chorale, chorus, dance, debate, drama, drill team, environmental, ethnic, film, forensics, honors, international, jazz band, literary magazine, musical theater, newspaper, orchestra, political, professional, radio station club, religious, social, social service, student government, and symphony. Popular campus events include Nikdg and Gadkin, and Festival of Christmas. **Sports:** There are 9 intercollegiate sports for men and women, and 6 intramural sports for men and women. Facilities include a gym, an indoor recreation center, with 1/8-mile track and multipurpose courts, weight room, and racquetball courts, soccer fields, tennis courts, football, baseball, and softball stadium. **Graduates:** From July 1, 2016 to June 30, 2017, 770 bachelor's degrees were awarded. The most popular majors were business/marketing (100%). In an average class, 63% graduate in 4 years or less, 73% graduate in 5 years or less, and 75% graduate in 6 years or less. Of the 2016 graduating class, 22% were enrolled in graduate school within 6 months of graduation, and 74% were employed.

SERVICES: Counseling and information services are available, as is tutoring in every subject. There is a reader service for the blind. The Academic Enrichment and Support Center offers individual peer tutoring, student-led help sessions, a writing lab, and consultation on a variety of topics. **Library/Resources:** The library contains 194,196 volumes, 195,650 microform items, 15,503 audio/video tapes/CDs/DVDs, and subscribes to 38,080 periodicals including electronic. Computerized library services include interlibrary loans, database searching, Internet access, and Wi-Fi capability. Special learning facilities include an art gallery. **Physically Challenged Students:** 99% of the campus is accessible. Facilities include wheelchair ramps, elevators, special parking, specially equipped restrooms, special class scheduling, lowered drinking fountains, lowered telephones, and special housing. **Special:** Cross-registration is available through the Council for Christian Colleges and Universities. Students may arrange internships and study abroad in various countries. Students may design their own major and earn a 3-2 engineering degree. An adult degree completion program is offered. There are 6 national honor societies, a freshman honors program, and 6 departmental honors programs. **Visiting:** There are regularly scheduled orientations for prospective students, consisting of a campus tour, visits with advisors, faculty, coaches, chapel, and class visits. There are guides for informal visits; visitors may sit in on classes and stay overnight. To schedule a visit, contact the Admissions Office. **Campus Safety and Security:** Measures include 24-hour foot and vehicle patrol, an emergency notification system, self-defense education, and security escort services. There are shuttle buses, emergency telephones, lighted pathways/sidewalks, controlled access to dorms/residences, and camera systems (parking lots and buildings).

REQUIREMENTS: The SAT or ACT is required. The PSAT is accepted. An interview is recommended. Requirements include a personal statement, contact information for an academic or spiritual reference, and an official transcript and class ranking from an accredited secondary school. The GED is accepted. It is required that 14 high school units are completed, 4 each in English, and social studies, 3 each in math and science (with 2 lab), 2 in history, and 1 each in visual arts and computer science. BU requires applicants to be in the upper 50% of their class. AP and CLEP credits are accepted. Important factors in the admissions decision are advanced placement or honors courses, personality/intangible qualities, and recommendations by alumni. Students must complete a minimum of 122 semester credit hours, with 30 to 60 in the major and 51 to 52 in general education. Specific general education courses include Introduction to the Bible, Christianity and Western Culture, College Writing, Creativity in Fine Arts, and Physical Wellness. An overall GPA of 2.0 and a GPA of 2.25 in the major are needed. **Procedure:** Freshmen are admitted in the fall and spring. Entrance exams should be taken spring of junior year. There is a rolling admissions plan. Application deadlines are open. Notifications are sent October 1. 43 applicants were on the 2017 waiting list; 10 were admitted. Applications are accepted on-line. **Transfer Students:** 122 transfer students enrolled in 2016-2017. Applicants must have a minimum GPA of 2.5 and must submit all college transcripts, and a essay or personal statement. 28 of 122 credits required for the bachelor's degree must be completed at BU. **International Students:** There are 8 international students enrolled. They must take the TOEFL with a minimum score of 525 on the paper-based TOEFL (PBT) or 70 on the Internet-based version (iBT).

ADMISSIONS: 82% of the 2017-2018 applicants were accepted. The ACT scores were 4% between 12 and 17, 38% between 18 and 23, 46% between 24 and 29, and 12% above 30. 45% of the current freshmen were in the top fifth of their class; 74% were in the top two fifths. 31 freshmen graduated first in their class. **Admissions Contact:** Jay Fedje, Director of Admissions. Email: *undergrad-admissions@bethel.edu* Web: *www.bethel.edu*

FINANCIAL AID: In 2017-2018, 99% of all full-time freshmen received some form of financial aid. 71% of all full-time freshmen received need-based aid. The average freshman award was $27,448. Need-based scholarships or need-based grants averaged $21,689; need-based self-help aid (loans and jobs) averaged $5,102; other non-need-based awards and non-need-based scholarships averaged $3,151; and $12,687 from other forms of aid. The average financial indebtedness of the 2017 graduate was $34,530. BU is a member of CSS. The college's own financial statement, and International Certification of Finances are required. The FAFSA code is 002338. The priority date for freshman financial aid applications for fall entry is April 15.

CARLETON COLLEGE C-4

www.carleton.edu

Northfield, MN 55057	**(507) 222-4190** **(800) 995-CARL**
Fax: (507) 222-4526	**Email:** admissions@carleton.edu
Full-time: 988 men, 1035 women	**Faculty:** 209; IIB, ++$
Part-time: 8 men, 15 women	**Ph.D.s:** 91%
Graduate: n/av	**Student/Faculty:** 9 to 1
Year: trimesters	**Tuition:** $52,782
Room & Board: $13,632	**Freshman Class:** 6502 applied, 1378 accepted, 521 enrolled
SAT or ACT: required	**CEEB CODE:** 6081
Application Deadline: January 15	**MOST COMPETITIVE**

Carleton College, founded in 1866, is a private liberal arts college. There are 3 undergraduate schools. The 1040-acre campus is in a small town 35 miles south of Minneapolis-St. Paul. Including any residence halls, there are 49 buildings.

STUDENT LIFE: 85% of undergraduates are from out of state, mostly the Midwest. Students are from 50 states, 34 foreign countries, and Canada. 60% are from public schools. 61% are White; 10% Foreign; 8% Asian American; 8% Hispanic; 6% two or more races; 5% African American; 2% race unknown; 1% American Indian/Alaska Native. 49% claim no religious affiliation; 14% Buddhist, Hindu, Muslim, Taoist, and Unitarian Universalist; 13% Protestant. **Female To Male Ratio:** 1.1:1. The average age of freshmen is 18; all undergraduates, 20. 4% do not continue beyond their first year; 96% remain to graduate. **Housing:** 1910 students can be accommodated in college housing, which includes dorms, on-campus apartments, and off-campus apartments. In addition, there are language/international houses and special-interest houses. On-campus housing is guaranteed for all 4 years. 96% of students live on campus. No one may keep cars.

FACULTY/CLASSROOMS: 52% of faculty are male; 48% are female. All teach undergraduates and do research. No introductory courses are taught by graduate students. The average class size in an introductory lecture is 20; in a laboratory is 16; and in a regular course is 17.

PROGRAMS OF STUDY: CC confers B.A. degrees. Bachelor's degrees are awarded in AGRICULTURE (environmental studies), BIOLOGICAL SCIENCE (biology/biological science), COMMUNICATIONS AND THE ARTS (art history and appreciation, classics, English, French, German, Greek, Latin, linguistics, media arts, music, romance languages and literature, Russian, Spanish, and studio art), COMPUTER AND PHYSICAL SCIENCE (chemistry, computer science, geology, mathematics, and physics), SOCIAL SCIENCE (African studies, African American studies, American studies, anthropology, Asian/Oriental studies, classical/ancient civilization, economics, history, international relations, Latin American studies, philosophy, political science/government, psychology, religion, sociology, and women's studies). Sciences, biological, and physical sciences are the strongest academically. Social sciences, compter science, and physical sciences have the largest enrollments.

ACTIVITIES: There are no fraternities or sororities. There are 328 groups on campus, including art, band, chess, choir, chorale, chorus, computers, dance, debate, drama, educational, environmental, ethnic, film, honors, international, jazz band, LGBT, literary magazine, musical theater, newspaper, orchestra, photography, political, professional, radio and TV, religious, social, social service, student government, and symphony. Popular campus events include Mai Fete, Spring Concert, Mid-Winter Ball, Ebony, and Golden Shillers Film Festival. **Sports:** There are 25 intercollegiate sports for men and women, and 14 intramural sports for men and women. Facilities include a gym with arena, a 6-lane swimming pool, a wrestling room, dance studio, indoor tennis court, a stadium complex with handball and racquetball courts, 200-meter indoor track, baseball batting cage, weight room, a 200-meter indoor track, sport courts, dance studio, and a climbing wall, fields for baseball, softball, soccer, ultimate Frisbee, lacrosse, rugby, field hockey, and outdoor tennis courts, and 16 miles of running, biking, hiking, and cross-country skiing trails. **Graduates:** From July 1, 2016 to June 30, 2017, 505 bachelor's degrees were awarded. The most popular majors were biology (11%), computer science (11%), and economics (10%). In an average class, 88% graduate in 4 years or less, 92% graduate in 5 years or less, and 94% graduate in 6 years or less.

SERVICES: Counseling and information services are available, as is tutoring in every subject. There are writing and math skills assistance centers, and a reader service for the blind. **Library/Resources:** The library contains 1.6 million volumes, 356,954 microform items, 63,998 audio/video tapes/CDs/DVDs, and subscribes to 82,879 periodicals, including electronic. Computerized library services include interlibrary loans, database searching, Internet access, and Wi-Fi capability. Special learning facilities include an art gallery, a radio station, an observatory, an 880-acre arboretum, and the Weitz center for creativity. **Physically Challenged Students:** 39% of the campus is accessible. Facilities include wheelchair ramps, elevators, special parking, specially equipped restrooms, special class scheduling, lowered drinking fountains, lowered telephones, and special housing. **Special:** Students may cross-register with St. Olaf College and pursue a variety of internships. The college offers study abroad in over 50 countries, and dual majors in all areas, and student designed majors. Students may earn a 3-2 engineering degree with Washington University. There are 3 national honor societies and a chapter of Phi Beta Kappa. **Visiting:** There are regularly scheduled orientations for prospective students, where they can attend an information sessions, take a tour, interview with admissions, sit in on classes or attend panels on particular topics pertinent to study abroad, financial aid or other topics, and stay overnight. To schedule a visit, contact the Admissions Office. **Campus Safety and Security:** Measures include 24-hour foot and vehicle patrol, an emergency notification system, self-defense education, and security escort services. There are emergency telephones, lighted pathways/sidewalks, controlled access to dorms/residences, and nighttime transport service.

REQUIREMENTS: The SAT or ACT, and the ACT Optional Writing test are required. There are no secondary school requirements, but it is recommended that applicants have completed 4 years of English, 3 years each of math and foreign language, 2 years each of history and science, and 1 year of social studies. An essay and 2 teacher recommendations are required. AP credits are accepted. Important factors in the admissions decision are advanced placement or honors courses, personality/intangible qualities, and evidence of special talent. To graduate, student must complete 210 credits and maintain a 2.0 cumulative GPA. A normal course load is 18 credits per term (there are 3 terms). Students also explore an integrated exercise in their major in the form of a comprehensive exam, an extensive research project, paper or public presentation. Besides a first year seminar, there are six courses required in curricular distribution along with fulfilling coursework in Quantitative Reasoning and Global Understanding. **Procedure:** Freshmen are admitted in the fall. Entrance exams should be taken before February 15. There are early decision and deferred admissions plans. Early decision applications should be filed by November 15; regular applications, by January 15 for fall entry. The fall 2017 application fee was $30. Notification of early decision is sent December 15; regular decision, April 15. 219 early decision candidates were accepted for the 2017-2018 class. 521 applicants were on the 2017 waiting list; 41 were admitted. Applications are accepted online. **Transfer Students:** 10 transfer students enrolled in 2016-2017. Transfers are usually accepted for sophomore and junior classes. A 3.0 GPA is recommended. 108 of 210 credits required for the bachelor's degree must be completed at CC. **International Students:** There are 207 international students enrolled. They must take the TOEFL with a minimum score of 600 on the paper-based TOEFL (PBT) or 100 on the Internet-based version (iBT). They must also take the SAT or ACT.

ADMISSIONS: 21% of the 2017-2018 applicants were accepted. 95% of the current freshmen were in the top fifth of their class; 100% were in the top two fifths. **Admissions Contact:** Paul Thiboutot, Vice President and Dean of Admissions and Financial Aid. Email: *admissions@carleton.edu* Web: *www.carleton.edu*

FINANCIAL AID: In 2017-2018, 77% of all full-time freshmen received some form of financial aid. 52% of all full-time freshmen received need-based aid. The average freshman award was $47,776. Need-based scholarships or need-based grants averaged $42,019; need-based self-help aid (loans and jobs) averaged $5,511; and other non-need-based awards and non-need-based scholarships averaged $2,000. 82% of undergraduate students work part-time. The average financial indebtedness of the 2017 graduate was $21,035. CC is a member of CSS. The CSS/Profile is required. The FAFSA code is 002340. The deadline for filing freshman financial aid applications for fall entry is January 15.

COLLEGE OF SAINT BENEDICT — C-3

www.csbsju.edu

St. Joseph, MN 56374	**(320) 363-5060** **(800) 544-1489**
Fax: (320) 363-3206	**Email: admissions@csbsju.edu**
Full-time: 1916 women	**Faculty:** 143; IIB, +$
Part-time: 21 women	**Ph.D.s:** 92%
Graduate: n/av	**Student/Faculty:** 12 to 1
Year: semesters	**Tuition:** $43,738
Room & Board: $10,742	**Freshman Class:** 1775 applied, 1615 accepted, 519 enrolled
SAT or ACT: required	**CEEB CODE:** 6104
Application Deadline: January 15	**COMPETITIVE**

College of Saint Benedict, and Saint John's University are nationally-leading liberal arts colleges whose unique partnership offers students the educational choices of a large university and the individual attention of a premier small college. In addition to regional accreditation, Saint Ben's has baccalaureate program accreditation with ADA, NASM, ACS, and CCNE. The 600-acre campus is in a small town 70 miles northwest of Minneapolis and 10 miles west of St. Cloud. Including any residence halls, there are 52 buildings.

STUDENT LIFE: 81% of undergraduates are from Minnesota. Others are from 32 states, and 13 foreign countries. 76% are from public schools. 79% are White; 7% Hispanic; 6% Asian American; 4% Foreign; 3% African American; 1% American Indian/Alaska Native. 52% are Catholic; 30% Protestant; 16% claim no religious affiliation. The student base is all female. The average age of freshmen is 18; all undergraduates, 20. 13% do not continue beyond their first year; 82% remain to graduate. **Housing:** 1665 students can be accommodated in college housing, which includes dorms and on-campus apartments. In addition, there are special-interest houses, health and wellness community, 2 Eco houses, and Benedictine Living Community. On-campus housing is guaranteed for the freshman year only, and is available on a first-come, first-served basis, and is available on a lottery system for upperclassmen. 91% of students live on campus. All students may keep cars.

FACULTY/CLASSROOMS: 49% of faculty are male; 51% are female. All teach undergraduates and do research. No introductory courses are taught by graduate students. The average class size in an introductory lecture is 18; in a laboratory is 13; and in a regular course is 19.

PROGRAMS OF STUDY: Saint Ben's confers B.A. and B.S.N. degrees. Bachelor's degrees are awarded in AGRICULTURE (environmental studies), BIOLOGICAL SCIENCE (biochemistry, biology/biological science, and nutrition), BUSINESS (accounting and management science), COMMUNICATIONS AND THE ARTS (art, classics, communications, English, French, German, music, and theatre arts), COMPUTER AND PHYSICAL SCIENCE (chemistry, computer science, mathematics, natural sciences, and physics), EDUCATION (elementary education), ENGINEERING AND ENVIRONMENTAL DESIGN (preengineering), HEALTH PROFESSIONS (nursing, prechiropractic, predentistry, premedicine, preoptometry, pre-occupational therapy, prepharmacy, prephysician assistant, prephysical therapy, and preveterinary science), SOCIAL SCIENCE (Asian/Oriental studies, economics, gender studies, Hispanic American studies, history, humanities, peace studies, philosophy, political science/government, prelaw, psychology, sociology, and theological studies). Nursing, biology and psychology have the largest enrollments.

ACTIVITIES: There are no fraternities or sororities. There are 130 groups on campus, including art, band, choir, chorale, chorus, computers, dance, debate, drama, environmental, ethnic, film, honors, international, jazz band, LGBT, literary magazine, musical theater, newspaper, opera, orchestra, outdoor leadership center and academic clubs, pep band, political, professional, radio and TV, religious, social, social service, student government, and symphony. Popular campus events include Involvement Fair, Festival of Cultures, Family Weekend, Homecoming, weekly Praise in the Pub, Hmong New Year, Asian New Year, Pines Concert, and Martin Luther King Jr. Week. **Sports:** There are 11 intercollegiate sports for women, and 12 intramural sports for women. Facilities include a volleyball and basketball arena, racquetball courts, indoor and outdoor tennis courts, an indoor pool, a field house with an indoor running track, aerobics studio, fitness center, exercise and weight-training equipment, three softball fields (including a stadium field with artificial turf), three soccer/lacrosse fields (including a stadium field with artificial turf), 3 multi-use/intramural fields, and students have access to Saint John's University athletic facilities. **Graduates:** From July 1, 2016 to June 30, 2017, 475 bachelor's degrees were awarded. The most popular majors were biology (11%), communication (11%), and nursing (10%). In an average class, 7% graduate in 3 years or less, 76% graduate in 4 years or less, 81% graduate in 5 years or less, and 82% graduate in 6 years or less. Of the 2016 graduating class, 18% were enrolled in graduate school within 6 months of graduation, and 81% were employed.

SERVICES: Counseling and information services are available, as is tutoring in most subjects, such as math, writing, global languages, and natural sciences. The Disability Services Office has accommodations for students who provide adequate documentation of a disability. Individual tutoring is available as needed, and academic and psychological counseling are available on an unlimited basis. **Library/Resources:** The library contains 729,515 volumes, 21,482 microform items, 27,968 audio/video tapes/CDs/DVDs, and subscribes to 99,409 periodicals, including electronic. Computerized library services include interlibrary loans, database searching, Internet access, and Wi-Fi capability. Special learning facilities include an art gallery, a radio station, TV station, a pottery studio and kiln, a labyrinth, dance studio, a green house and Saint Benedict's Monastery Heritage Museum. At Saint John's University there is an observatory, a greenhouse, a herbarium, a natural history museum, the Sommers Digital Video Studio, a kiln and pottery studio, and the Hill Museum and Manuscript library. **Physically Challenged Students:** 80% of the campus is accessible. Facilities include wheelchair ramps, elevators, special parking, specially equipped restrooms, special class scheduling, lowered drinking fountains, and special housing. Exterior power assist doors, and accessible busing options. **Special:** Students may cross-register with St. Cloud State University. There are study-abroad programs in Australia, Austria, Chile, China, France, Germany, Guatemala, Greece, Ireland (Cork and Galway), Italy, India, Japan, London-England, Northern Ireland, South Africa, and Spain. Many short term study abroad opportunities are also offered. Internships, dual and student-designed majors, preprofessional programs, and liberal studies degrees may be pursued. A 3-1 program in dentistry, nondegree study, and a pass/fail grading option are also available. There are 7 national honor societies, Phi Beta Kappa, and a freshman honors program. **Visiting:** There are regularly scheduled orientations for prospective students, programs include admissions and financial aid presentations, campus tours and student panels. There are guides for informal visits, visitors may sit in on classes, and stay overnight. **Campus Safety and Security:** Measures include 24-hour foot and vehicle patrol, an emergency notification system, self-defense education, and security escort services. There are shuttle buses, emergency telephones, lighted pathways/sidewalks, and controlled access to dorms/residences.

REQUIREMENTS: The SAT or ACT is required. Students should be graduates of an accredited secondary school. Academic preparation should include 17 units, including 4 of English, 3 of math, 2 each of a lab science and social studies, and 4 electives, and a foreign language is recommended. The GED is accepted. Home-schooled applicants are not required to have a high school diploma but are required to provide appropriate documentation of college preparatory curriculum. Saint Ben's requires applicants to be in the upper 50% of their class. A GPA of 3.0 is required. AP and CLEP credits are accepted. Important factors in the admissions decision are advanced placement or honors courses, extracurricular activities record, and parents or siblings attended your school. To graduate students must complete a first-year seminar and a junior-senior ethics seminar intended as a capstone for the liberal arts experience, and fulfill gender, intercultural, experiential learning, and fine arts requirements. Distribution requirements include 4 credits in fine arts, 2 courses each in humanities and theology, and 1 course each in math, natural science, and social science. All students must prove math and foreign language proficiency. A total of 124 credits must be earned, with a minimum GPA of 2.0. Attendance at 8 fine arts experiences is also required. **Procedure:** Freshmen are admitted in the fall and spring. Entrance exams should be taken during the spring of the junior year or fall of the senior year. There are early admissions and deferred admissions plans. Application deadlines are open. Notifications are sent April 1. Applications are accepted online. **Transfer Students:** 15 transfer students enrolled in 2016-2017. Transfer applicants must have a minimum college GPA of 2.75. An essay or personal statement, high school and college transcripts, and a transfer student evaluation form are required. Standardized test scores may be required of some. 76 of 124 credits required for the bachelor's degree must be completed at Saint Ben's. **International Students:** There are 73 international students enrolled. They must take the TOEFL with a minimum score of 550 on the paper-based TOEFL (PBT) or 80 on the Internet-based version (iBT). Students must take the IELTS. In certain cases, the SAT or ACT may replace the TOEFL.

ADMISSIONS: 91% of the 2017-2018 applicants were accepted. The ACT scores were 2% between 12 and 17, 35% between 18 and 23, 47% between 24 and 29, and 16% above 30. 56% of the current freshmen were in the top fifth of their class; 86% were in the top two fifths. **Admissions Contact:** Dr. Calvin Mosley, Vice President for Admission and Financial. Email: *admissions@csbsju.edu* Web: *www.csbsju.edu*

FINANCIAL AID: In 2017-2018, 96% of all full-time freshmen received some form of financial aid. 76% of all full-time freshmen received need-based aid. The average freshman award was $35,942. Need-based scholarships or need-based grants averaged $31,442; need-based self-help aid (loans and jobs) averaged $6,347; and other non-need-based awards and non-need-based scholarships averaged $20,900. 60% of undergraduate students work part-time. The average financial indebtedness of the 2017 graduate was $42,833. Saint Ben's is a member of CSS. The FAFSA code is 002341. The priority date for freshman financial aid applications for fall entry is March 15.

COLLEGE OF ST. SCHOLASTICA D-2

www.css.edu

Duluth, MN 55811 (218) 723-6046 (800) 447-5444

Fax: (218) 723-5991 **Email:** admissions@css.edu

Full-time: 666 men, 1513 women	**Faculty:** 220; IIB, -$
Part-time: 115 men, 425 women	**Ph.D.s:** 61%
Graduate: 412 men, 1194 women	**Student/Faculty:** 14 to 1
Year: semesters, summer session	**Tuition:** $36,212
Room & Board: $9522	**Freshman Class:** 3834 applied, 2617 accepted, 482 enrolled
SAT CR/M/W: 580/540/540 **ACT:** 24	**CEEB CODE:** 6107
Application Deadline: n/av	**COMPETITIVE+**

College of St. Scholastica, founded in 1912, is an independent private college that provides intellectual and moral preparation for responsible living and meaningful work. St. Scholastica has extended campuses in St. Paul, Brainerd, Rochester, and St. Cloud, MN. The college is guided by the Benedictine values of community, hospitality, respect, stewardship, and love of learning. The figures given in the above capsule and in this profile are approximate. There are 6 undergraduate schools and 1 graduate school. In addition to regional accreditation, St. Scholastica has baccalaureate program accreditation with APTA, CSWE, ACOTE, CAHIIM, and CAATE. The 186-acre campus is in a suburban area 150 miles north of Minneapolis and St. Paul, MN. Including any residence halls, there are 18 buildings.

STUDENT LIFE: 89% of undergraduates are from Minnesota. Others are from 49 states, 18 foreign countries, and Canada. 83% are White; 4% Hispanic; 3% African American; 3% Foreign; 3% two or more races; 2% Asian American; 1% American Indian/Alaska Native; 1% race unknown. 11% are Protestant. **Female To Male Ratio:** 2.6:1. The average age of freshmen is 18; all undergraduates, 22. 20% do not continue beyond their first year; 67% remain to graduate. **Housing:** 961 students can be accommodated in college housing, which includes dorms and on-campus apartments. On-campus housing is available on a first-come, first-served basis, and is available on a lottery system for upperclassmen. 52% of students live on campus. All students may keep cars.

FACULTY/CLASSROOMS: 35% of faculty are male; 65% are female. All teach undergraduates. No introductory courses are taught by graduate students. The average class size in an introductory lecture is 21; in a laboratory is 16; and in a regular course is 21.

PROGRAMS OF STUDY: St. Scholastica confers B.A. and B.S. degrees. Master's and doctoral degrees are also awarded. Bachelor's degrees are awarded in BIOLOGICAL SCIENCE (biochemistry and biology/biological science), BUSINESS (accounting, business administration and management, finance, business management, marketing management, organizational behavior, and sustainable management), COMMUNICATIONS AND THE ARTS (advertising, art, communications, English, journalism, languages, and music), COMPUTER AND PHYSICAL SCIENCE (chemistry, computer science, mathematics, and natural sciences), EDUCATION (education, global studies, and social science education), HEALTH PROFESSIONS (exercise science, health care administration, health science, nursing, and physical therapy), SOCIAL SCIENCE (behavioral science, economics, history, humanities, Native American studies, peace studies, philosophy, psychology, religion, and social work). Nursing, management, and biological sciences have the largest enrollments.

ACTIVITIES: There are no fraternities or sororities. There are 68 groups on campus, including band, cheerleading, choir, chorale, chorus, computers, dance, drama, ethnic, honors, international, jazz band, LGBT, literary magazine, newspaper, pep band, photography, political, professional, radio and TV, religious, social, social service, and student government. Popular campus events include Mayfest Week, Fall Fest, and International Week. **Sports:** There are 11 intercollegiate sports for men and women, and 14 intramural sports for men and women. Facilities include a wellness center; 6-lane 200 meter track, aerobic studio, free weight room, complete machine fitness space, athletic trainer's room, and climbing wall. **Graduates:** From July 1, 2016 to June 30, 2017, 836 bachelor's degrees were awarded. The most popular majors were nursing (48%), management (14%), and biological sciences (12%). In an average class, 58% graduate in 4 years or less, 66% graduate in 5 years or less, and 67% graduate in 6 years or less. Of the 2016 graduating class, 29%

were enrolled in graduate school within 6 months of graduation, and 63% were employed.

SERVICES: Counseling and information services are available, as is tutoring in most subjects. There is a reader service for the blind, and remedial writing. There are also Sign language interpreters, a note-taking service, tape recorders, voice input computers, and remedial study skills. **Library/Resources:** The library contains 111,943 volumes, 1,915 microform items, 14,932 audio/video tapes/CDs/DVDs, and subscribes to 55,088 periodicals including electronic. Computerized library services include interlibrary loans, database searching, Internet access, and Wi-Fi capability. Special learning facilities include a radio station, a TV station, and a music library. **Physically Challenged Students:** 95% of the campus is accessible. Facilities include wheelchair ramps, elevators, special parking, specially equipped restrooms, special class scheduling, lowered drinking fountains, lowered telephones, and special housing. **Special:** Students may cross-register with the University of Minnesota of Duluth and the University of Wisconsin of Superior. Self-designed majors, a Washington semester with American University, internships, study abroad in several countries, accelerated degrees, non-degree study, pass/fail options, and credit for life, military, or work experience are available. There are 2 national honor societies. **Visiting:** There are regularly scheduled orientations for prospective students, visting students can participate in a class placement survey, peer and academic advisement, and registration. There are guides for informal visits; visitors may sit in on classes and stay overnight. To schedule a visit, contact the Admissions Office. **Campus Safety and Security:** Measures include 24-hour foot and vehicle patrol, emergency notification system, self-defense education, and security escort services. There are emergency telephones, lighted pathways/sidewalks, controlled access to dorms/residences, electronically operated dorm entrances, and student door monitors in the evening.

REQUIREMENTS: The SAT or ACT, and an official high school transcripts are required. AP and CLEP credits are accepted. To graduate, students must complete 128 semester credits, with a 2.0 GPA. Approximately 52 credits of general education courses are required. The hours required in the major vary, and some majors require an internship for graduation. A senior project may be required for some students. **Procedure:** Freshmen are admitted to all sessions. Entrance exams should be taken by January of the senior year of high school. There are deferred admissions and rolling admissions plans. Application deadlines are open. Notification is sent on a rolling basis. Applications are accepted on-line. **Transfer Students:** 373 transfer students enrolled in 2016-2017. Applicants must have a GPA of 2.0. 32 of 128 credits required for the bachelor's degree must be completed at St. Scholastica. **International Students:** There are 66 international students enrolled. They must take the TOEFL with a minimum score of 550 on the paper-based TOEFL (PBT) or 79 on the Internet-based version (iBT).

ADMISSIONS: 68% of the 2017-2018 applicants were accepted. The SAT scores for the 2017-2018 freshman class were: Math-- 58% below 500, 32% between 500 and 599, and 11% between 600 and 699. Evidence-Based Reading/Writing-- 47% below 500, 42% between 500 and 599, and 11% between 600 and 699. The ACT scores were 5% between 12 and 17, 48% between 18 and 23, 39% between 24 and 29, and 7% above 30. 46% of the current freshmen were in the top fifth of their class; 77% were in the top two fifths. 17 freshmen graduated first in their class. **Admissions Contact:** Ellen Johnson, Vice President for Enrollment Management. Email: *admissions@css.edu* Web: *www.css.edu*

FINANCIAL AID: In 2017-2018, 86% of all full-time freshmen received some form of financial aid. 68% of all full-time freshmen received need-based aid. The average freshman award was $31,038. Need-based scholarships or need-based grants averaged $7,503; need-based self-help aid (loans and jobs) averaged $4,527; and other non-need-based awards and non-need-based scholarships averaged $19,621. 29% of undergraduate students work part-time. The average financial indebtedness of the 2017 graduate was $41,133. The FAFSA code is 002343. The priority date for freshman financial aid applications for fall entry is March 1.

CONCORDIA COLLEGE - MOORHEAD A-2

www.concordiacollege.edu

Moorhead, MN 56562 (218) 299-3004
(800) 699-9897

Fax: (218) 299-4720 **Email: admissions@cord.edu**

Full-time: 952 men, 1536 women
Part-time: 16 men, 27 women
Graduate: 4 men, 23 women
Year: semesters, summer session
Room & Board: $8040

SAT CR/M: 570/550 **ACT:** required
Application Deadline: open

Faculty: 181; IIB, -$
Ph.D.s: 85%
Student/Faculty: 14 to 1
Tuition: $38,378
Freshman Class: 2493 applied, 1944 accepted, 684 enrolled
CEEB CODE: 6113
COMPETITIVE

Concordia College-Moorehead, founded in 1891, is a private, liberal arts institution affiliated with the Evangelical Lutheran Church in America. The figures given in the above capsule and in this profile are approximate. There are 2 undergraduate schools and 1 graduate school. In addition to regional accreditation, CCM has baccalaureate program accreditation with CSWE, NASM, CCNE, ACEND, and MN Board of Examiners for Nursing Home Administrative. The 113-acre campus is in a suburban area 230 miles northwest of Minneapolis and St. Paul. Including any residence halls, there are 42 buildings.

STUDENT LIFE: 67% of undergraduates are from Minnesota. Others are from 33 states, 31 foreign countries, and Canada. 94% are from public schools. 83% are White; 6% race unknown; 4% Foreign; 2% African American; 2% Asian American; 2% Hispanic; 1% American Indian/Alaska Native; 1% two or more races. 43% are Protestant; 36% Unknown religion; 17% Catholic. **Female To Male Ratio:** 1.6:1. The average age of freshmen is 18; all undergraduates, 20. 16% do not continue beyond their first year; 71% remain to graduate. **Housing:** 1792 students can be accommodated in college housing, which includes dorms and on-campus apartments. In addition, there are language/international houses, special-interest houses, and townhouse. On-campus housing is guaranteed for the freshman year only, and is available on a first-come, first-served basis, and is available on a lottery system for upperclassmen. 64% of students live on campus. All students may keep cars. Alcohol is not permitted.

FACULTY/CLASSROOMS: 51% of faculty are male; 49% are female. All teach undergraduates and do research. No introductory courses are taught by graduate students. The average class size in an introductory lecture is 23; in a laboratory is 17; and in a regular course is 19.

PROGRAMS OF STUDY: CCM confers B.A. and B.M. degrees. Master's degrees are also awarded. Bachelor's degrees are awarded in BIOLOGICAL SCIENCE (biology/biological science and nutrition), BUSINESS (accounting, business administration and management, and international business management), COMMUNICATIONS AND THE ARTS (art, Chinese, classical languages, classics, communications, dramatic arts, English, French, German, journalism, Latin, music, music performance, music theory and composition, and Spanish), COMPUTER AND PHYSICAL SCIENCE (applied science, chemistry, mathematics, and physics), EDUCATION (art education, business education, elementary education, foreign languages education, health education, mathematics education, music education, physical education, secondary education, and social studies education), ENGINEERING AND ENVIRONMENTAL DESIGN (environmental science), HEALTH PROFESSIONS (clinical science, exercise science, health, and nursing), SOCIAL SCIENCE (history, humanities, international studies, philosophy, political science/government, psychology, religion, Scandinavian studies, social work, and sociology). Natural sciences is the strongest academically. Education, business, and biology have the largest enrollments.

ACTIVITIES: There are no fraternities or sororities. There are 106 groups on campus, including art, band, cheerleading, choir, chorale, chorus, communications, dance, debate, drama, environmental, ethnic, forensics, honors, international, jazz band, LGBT, literary magazine, musical theater, newspaper, orchestra, pep band, photography, political, professional, radio and TV, religious, social, social service, student government, and symphony. Popular campus events include Christmas Concert, Martin Luther King Jr. Day, and National Book Award Celebration. **Sports:** There are 11 intercollegiate sports for men and women, and 6 intramural sports for men and 5 for women. Facilities include a 200-meter indoor track with multipurpose volleyball/basketball/tennis courts, an indoor swimming pool, a stadium with an all-weather track, a field house with auditorium that features basketball courts, an auxiliary gym, a weight room, outdoor tennis courts, softball and soccer competition fields, a baseball complex, and soccer practice fields. **Graduates:** From July 1, 2016 to June 30, 2017, 540 bachelor's degrees were awarded. The most popular majors were business (17%), education (15%), and biology (12%). In an average class, 65% graduate in 4 years or less, 71% graduate in 5 years or less, and 71% graduate in 6 years or less. Of the 2016 graduating class, 32% were enrolled in graduate school within 6 months of graduation, and 82% were employed.

SERVICES: Counseling and information services are available, as is tutoring in most subjects. There is a reader service for the blind. **Library/Resources:** The library contains 346,744 volumes, 44,055 microform items, 26,572 audio/video tapes/CDs/DVDs, and subscribes to 4,342 periodicals, including electronic. Computerized library services include interlibrary loans, database searching, Internet access, and Wi-Fi capability. Special learning facilities include an art gallery, radio station, TV station, an observatory, a field biology research facility, a laser facility, and a nursing simulation lab. **Physically Challenged Students:** 95% of the campus is accessible. Facilities include wheelchair ramps, elevators, special parking, specially equipped restrooms, special class scheduling, lowered drinking fountains, and special housing. **Special:** Co-op programs and internships are available in most majors, and dual majors are available in all majors. There is a Washington semester and an urban studies semester in Chicago. Study abroad in 26 countries, on- and off-campus work-study, a B.A.-B.M. degree in music, and a 3-2 engineering degree with the University of Minnesota are available. Nondegree study for special students and pass/fail options also are possible. Cross-registration is offered through the Tri-College University Consortium. There are 18 national honor societies, a freshman honors program, and 16 departmental honors programs. **Visiting:** There are regularly scheduled orientations for prospective students, including an extensive campus tour and meetings with admissions counselors and faculty members. There are guides for informal visits; visitors may sit in on classes and stay overnight. To schedule a visit, contact the Office of Admissions. **Campus Safety and Security:** Measures include 24-hour foot and vehicle patrol, an emergency notification system, and security escort services. There are emergency telephones, lighted pathways/sidewalks, and controlled access to dorms/residences.

REQUIREMENTS: The SAT or ACT is required. Two character references are required, and an interview is recommended. The GED is accepted. Academic performance and preparation, as evidenced in a high school transcript, are the most important factors in the admissions decision. AP and CLEP credits are accepted. Important factors in the admissions decision are advanced placement or honors courses, recommendations by school officials, and leadership record. All students must maintain a minimum GPA of 2.0 while taking 126 semester hours, including at least 32 in the major. Required courses include written communication, oral communication, an introduction to liberal arts, and 2 courses each in physical education and religion. Exploration requirements include 7 courses taken from 6 areas: science and math, social science, world language, humanities and arts, plus 2 Perspectives courses to including 1 U.S. Cultural Diversity course and 1 International and Global Perspectives course. The final course in the Core Curriculum is a writing-intensive capstone course. **Procedure:** Freshmen are admitted to all sessions. Entrance exams should be taken by the first semester of the senior year. There are early admissions, deferred admissions, and rolling admissions plans. Application deadlines are open. The fall 2017 application fee was $20. Notification is sent on a rolling basis. Applications are accepted on-line. **Transfer Students:** 42 transfer students enrolled in 2016-2017. Transfer applicants must have a minimum 2.0 GPA and provide official transcripts from previously attended schools. 28 of 126 credits required for the bachelor's degree must be completed at CCM. **International Students:** There are 102 international students enrolled. They must take the TOEFL with a minimum score of 73 on the Internet-based version (iBT).

ADMISSIONS: 78% of the 2017-2018 applicants were accepted. The SAT scores for the 2017-2018 freshman class were: Critical Reading-- 23% below 500, 33% between 500 and 599, 35% between 600 and 699, and 10% between 700 and 800. Math-- 33% below 500, 29% between 500 and 599, 23% between 600 and 699, and 15% between 700 and 800. Writing-- 31% below 500, 37% between 500 and 599, 23% between 600 and 699, and 10% between 700 and 800. The ACT scores were 13% below 12, 22% between 12 and 17, 29% between 18 and 23, 16% between 24 and 29, and 20% above 30. 53% of the current freshmen were in the top fifth of their class; 81% were in the top two fifths. **Admissions Contact:** Peter A Lien, Admissions Director. Email: *admissions@cord.edu* Web: *www.concordiacollege.edu*

FINANCIAL AID: In 2017-2018, 99% of all full-time freshmen received some form of financial aid. 77% of all full-time freshmen received need-based aid. The average freshman award was $27,769. Need-based scholarships or need-based grants averaged $21,188; and need-based self-help aid (loans and jobs) averaged $7,676. 52% of undergraduate students work part-time. Moorhead is a member of CSS. The FAFSA code is 002346. The priority date for freshman financial aid applications for fall entry is July 1.

CONCORDIA UNIVERSITY SAINT PAUL C-4

www.csp.edu

St. Paul, MN 55104	**(651) 641-8230** **(800) 333-4705**
Fax: (651) 603-6320	**Email: admissions@csp.edu**
Full-time: 636 men, 746 women	**Faculty:** 81
Part-time: 434 men, 751 women	**Ph.D.s:** 76%
Graduate: 559 men, 1254 women	**Student/Faculty:** 16 to 1
Year: semesters, summer session	**Tuition:** $20,750
Room & Board: $8300	**Freshman Class:** 1483 applied, 822 accepted, 229 enrolled
ACT: 21	**CEEB CODE:** 6114
Application Deadline: August 1	**COMPETITIVE**

Concordia University Saint Paul, founded in 1893, a member of the Concordia University System and a private institution affiliated with the Lutheran Church Missouri Synod. CUSP offers programs in teacher education, business, church vocations, and the liberal arts, and master's programs and bachelor's degree completion programs for adult learners are also offered. There are 3 undergraduate schools and 1 graduate school. In addition to regional accreditation, CUSP has baccalaureate program accreditation with ACBSP and CAEP. The 37-acre campus is in an urban area in the Midway area of the Twin Cities, between Minneapolis and St. Paul. Including any residence halls, there are 24 buildings.

STUDENT LIFE: 73% of undergraduates are from Minnesota. Others are from 30 states, 17 foreign countries, and Canada. 8% are Asian American; 63% White; 5% Foreign; 4% Hispanic; 4% two or more races; 4% race unknown; 12% African American. 52% are Protestant. **Female To Male Ratio:** 1.7:1. The average age of freshmen is 18; all undergraduates, 26. 30% do not continue beyond their first year; 50% remain to graduate. **Housing:** 514 students can be accommodated in college housing, which includes married student dorms and on-campus apartments. On-campus housing is guaranteed for the freshman year only, and is available on a first-come, first-served basis. 79% of students commute. All students may keep cars.

FACULTY/CLASSROOMS: 48% of faculty are male; 52% are female. 79% teach undergraduates. No introductory courses are taught by graduate students. The average class size in an introductory lecture is 15; in a laboratory is 19; and in a regular course is 15.

PROGRAMS OF STUDY: CUSP confers B.A., B.S., B.B.A., and B.F.A. degrees. Associate, master's, and doctoral degrees are also awarded. Bachelor's degrees are awarded in BIOLOGICAL SCIENCE (biology/biological science), BUSINESS (accounting, banking and finance, business administration and management, marketing management, organizational leadership and management, and sports management), COMMUNICATIONS AND THE ARTS (art, choral music, church music, communications, creative writing, design, dramatic arts, English, English Writing, graphic design, instrumental music education, music, music business management, strategic communication, studio art, theatre arts, and vocal music education), COMPUTER AND PHYSICAL SCIENCE (computer science, information sciences and systems, and mathematics), EDUCATION (art education, Christian education, early childhood education, education of the emotionally handicapped, elementary education, English education, mathematics education, middle school education, music education, physical education, science education, secondary education, social studies education, social studies secondary school education, and special education), HEALTH PROFESSIONS (community health work, nursing, and radiological science), SOCIAL SCIENCE (child care/child and family studies, criminal justice, history, physical fitness/movement, psychology, religion, religious education, religious music, sociology, and theological studies). Business, teacher education, and criminal justice have the largest enrollments.

ACTIVITIES: There are no fraternities or sororities. There are 40 groups on campus, including art, band, cheerleading, choir, chorus, dance, drama, ethnic, honors, international, jazz band, musical theater, newspaper, pep band, political, professional, religious, social, social service, and student government. Popular campus events include Fine Arts Christmas Concert and Spring Honors Convocation. **Sports:** There are 6 intercollegiate sports for men and 7 for women, and 8 intramural sports for men and women. Facilities include a gym, health and wellness center, a stadium for football, soccer, track and field, and baseball and softball playing fields. **Graduates:** From July 1, 2016 to June 30, 2017, 557 bachelor's degrees were awarded. The most popular majors were organizational leadership/business (18%), marketing (8%), and teacher education (7%). In an average class, 1% graduate in 3 years or less, 27% graduate in 4 years or less, 43% graduate in 5 years or less, and 46% graduate in 6 years or less. Of the 2016 graduating class, 15% were enrolled in graduate school within 6 months of graduation, and 79% were employed.

SERVICES: Counseling and information services are available, as is tutoring in every subject. There is a reader service for the blind, and remedial math, reading, and writing. **Library/Resources:** The library contains 161,959 volumes, 11,516 microform items, 3,128 audio/video tapes/CDs/DVDs, and subscribes to 297 periodicals including electronic. Computerized library services include interlibrary loans, database searching, Internet access, and Wi-Fi capability. Special learning facilities include an art gallery. **Physically Challenged Students:** 90% of the campus is accessible. Facilities include wheelchair ramps, elevators, special parking, specially equipped restrooms, special class scheduling, lowered drinking fountains, and lowered telephones. **Special:** CUSP offers cross-registration with other members of the Concordia University System, internships in many programs, and study-abroad opportunities. Accelerated degree programs and interdisciplinary majors are also available. Credit for life experience, nondegree study, and pass/fail options are possible. Degree completion programs designed for working adults are offered in cohort-delivered format via face-to-face or on-line learning. There is 1 national honor society, a freshman honors program, and 1 departmental honors program. **Visiting:** There are regularly scheduled orientations for prospective students, including a campus tour, class visits, and a meeting with professors. There are guides for informal visits; visitors may sit in on classes and stay overnight. To schedule a visit, contact the Office of Undergraduate Admission. **Campus Safety and Security:** Measures include 24-hour foot and vehicle patrol, emergency notification system, self-defense education, and security escort services. There are emergency telephones, lighted pathways/sidewalks, and controlled access to dorms/residences.

REQUIREMENTS: The ACT is required. Applicants are normally expected to have 4 years of English, 2 each of math, science, fine arts, and history/social studies, and 1 of health or phys ed. An interview is recommended, and 2 letters of recommendation are required. The GED is accepted. AP and CLEP credits are accepted. To graduate, students must complete 128 credit hours in the form of 1 major or 2 minors, GPA varies from 2.0 to 2.75, and required hours in the major vary from 32 to 44, depending on the program. The core curriculum consists of 48 hours of liberal arts courses. **Procedure:** Freshmen are admitted in the fall and spring. Entrance exams should be taken during the senior year. There are deferred admissions and rolling admissions plans. Applications should be filed by August 1 for fall entry; December 1 for spring entry. The fall 2017 application fee was $30. Applications are accepted online. **Transfer Students:** 940 transfer students enrolled in 2016-2017. Applicants must have a 2.0 GPA and submit 2 letters of recommendation. Students with fewer than 1 year of college credits must also submit ACT scores and an official high school transcript. 32 of 128 credits required for the bachelor's degree must be completed at CUSP. **International Students:** There are 114 international students enrolled. They must take the TOEFL with a minimum score of 513 on the paper-based TOEFL (PBT) or 65 on the Internet-based version (iBT), or take the MELAB.

ADMISSIONS: 55% of the 2017-2018 applicants were accepted. The ACT scores were 16% between 12 and 17, 54% between 18 and 23, 25% between 24 and 29, and 5% above 30. 22% of the current freshmen were in the top fifth of their class; 45% were in the top two fifths. 3 freshmen graduated first in their class. **Admissions Contact:** Kristin Vogel, Associate Vice President for Traditional Enrollment. Email: *admissions@csp.edu* Web: *www.csp.edu*

FINANCIAL AID: In 2017-2018, 75% of all full-time freshmen received some form of financial aid and need-based aid. The average freshman award was $16,832. Need-based scholarships or need-based grants averaged $12,382; need-based self-help aid (loans and jobs) averaged $4,037; and other non-need-based awards and non-need-based scholarships averaged $4,244. 14% of undergraduate students work part-time. The average financial indebtedness of the 2017 graduate was $25,000. The college's own financial statement, and federal tax return are required. The FAFSA code is 002347. The priority date for freshman financial aid applications for fall entry is March 1.

GUSTAVUS ADOLPHUS COLLEGE C-4

www.gustavus.edu

St. Peter, MN 56082 **(507) 933-7676**

Fax: (507) 933-6270	**Email: admission@gustavus.edu**
Full-time: 1117 men, 1306 women	**Faculty:** 201; IIB, -$
Part-time: 21 men, 11 women	**Ph.D.s:** 85%
Graduate: n/av	**Student/Faculty:** 12 to 1
Year: 4-1-4	**Tuition:** $44,273
Room & Board: $9670	**Freshman Class:** 4804 applied, 3037 accepted, 610 enrolled
ACT: 27	**CEEB CODE:** 6253
Application Deadline: November 1	**HIGHLY COMPETITIVE**

Gustavus Adolphus College, founded in 1862, is a private liberal arts college affiliated with the Evangelical Luteran Church in America. The figures in the above capsule and in this profile are approximate. There are 3 undergraduate schools. In addition to regional accreditation, GAC has baccalaureate program accreditation with NASM, NLN, CCNE, and NASPE. The 340-acre campus is in a small town 65 miles southwest of Minneapolis. Including any residence halls, there are 56 buildings.

STUDENT LIFE: 81% of undergraduates are from Minnesota. Others are from 43 states, 15 foreign countries, and Canada. 94% are from public schools. 85% are White; 4% Asian American; 3% Hispanic; 2% African American; 2% Foreign; 2% two or more races; 1% American Indian/Alaska Native; 1% race unknown. 72% are Protestant; 21% Catholic. **Female To Male Ratio:** 1.2:1. The average age of freshmen is 18; all undergraduates, 20. 9% do not continue beyond their first year; 80% remain to graduate. **Housing:** 2103 students can be accommodated in college housing, which includes dorms and on-campus apartments. In addition, there are language/international houses and special-interest houses. On-campus housing is guaranteed for all 4 years and is available on a lottery system for upperclassmen. 85% of students live on campus. All students may keep cars.

FACULTY/CLASSROOMS: 52% of faculty are male; 48% are female. All teach undergraduates and do research. No introductory courses are taught by graduate students. The average class size in an introductory lecture is 25; in a laboratory is 15; and in a regular course is 15.

PROGRAMS OF STUDY: GAC confers B.A. degrees. Bachelor's degrees are awarded in AGRICULTURE (environmental studies), BIOLOGICAL SCIENCE (biochemistry and biology/biological science), BUSINESS (accounting, business administration and management, business economics, and international business management), COMMUNICATIONS AND THE ARTS (classics, communications, dance, dramatic arts, English, fine arts, French, music, Russian, Scandinavian languages, Spanish, and speech/debate/rhetoric), COMPUTER AND PHYSICAL SCIENCE (chemistry, computer science, geology, mathematics, and physics), EDUCATION (art education, business education, elementary education, foreign languages education, health education, middle school education, music education, science education, and secondary education), HEALTH PROFESSIONS (nursing, physical therapy, predentistry, and premedicine), SOCIAL SCIENCE (anthropology, economics, geography, history, philosophy, political science/government, prelaw, psychology, religion, social science, sociology, and women's studies). Physical science, and social science are the strongest academically. Business, biology, and communication studies have the largest enrollments.

ACTIVITIES: 14% of men belong to 6 local and 1 national fraternities; 14% of women belong to 5 local and 1 national sororities. There are 125 groups on campus, including art, band, cheerleading, choir, chorus, computers, dance, debate, drama, environmental, ethnic, film, forensics, honors, international, jazz band, LGBT, literary magazine, musical theater, newspaper, orchestra, pep band, political, professional, radio and TV, religious, social, social service, student government, symphony, and yearbook. Popular campus events include Christmas in Christ Chapel, Earth Jam All-Day Music Festival, and Building Bridges Diversity Conference. **Sports:** There are 12 intercollegiate sports for men and 13 for women, and 17 intramural sports for men and 10 for women. Facilities include an ice arena, an Olympic-size pool, a gymnastics area, an indoor tennis center, an arena, playing fields, artificial turf football field, racquetball and tennis courts, a weight room, an indoor and an outdoor running track, and varsity and intramural fields for soccer, softball, baseball, lacrosse, rugby, and ultimate Frisbee. **Graduates:** From July 1, 2016 to June 30, 2017, 603 bachelor's degrees were awarded. The most popular majors were biology (9%), economics/management (6%), and psychology (5%). In an average class, 2% graduate in 3 years or less, 80% graduate in 4 years or less, 82% graduate in 5 years or less, and 82% graduate in 6 years or less. Of the 2016 graduating class, 34% were enrolled in graduate school within 6 months of graduation, and 66% were employed.

SERVICES: Counseling and information services are available, as is tutoring in most subjects. There is a writing lab, ESL services, and disability services. **Library/Resources:** The library contains 311,480 volumes, 43,075 microform items, 105,799 audio/video tapes/CDs/DVDs, and subscribes to 32,340 periodicals including electronic. Computerized library services include interlibrary loans, database searching, Internet access, and Wi-Fi capability. Special learning facilities include an art gallery, radio station, an arboretum, observatory, greenhouses, bronze-casting facility, geology museum, and many specialized laboratories. **Physically Challenged Students:** All of the campus is accessible. Facilities include wheelchair ramps, elevators, special parking, specially equipped restrooms, special class scheduling, lowered drinking fountains, lowered telephones, and special housing. **Special:** Co-op programs in nursing with St. Olaf College and cross-registration with Minnesota State University are available. The college offers internships, a Washington semester, study abroad in 22 countries, student-designed majors, nondegree study, work-study, and pass/fail options for some courses. A 3-2 engineering degree program with the University of Minnesota and Minnesota State University, Mankato is offered. The Curriculum II core offers a 12-course interdisciplinary program. There are 16 national honor societies, Phi Beta Kappa, and 12 departmental honors programs. **Visiting:** There are regularly scheduled orientations for prospective students, consisting of an interview, a tour, and meetings with faculty and students. There are guides for informal visits; visitors may sit in on classes and stay overnight. To schedule a visit, contact the Admissions Office. **Campus Safety and Security:** Measures include 24-hour foot and vehicle patrol, an emergency notification system, and security escort services. There are shuttle buses, emergency telephones, lighted pathways/sidewalks, and controlled access to dorms/residences.

REQUIREMENTS: Applicants must have completed 4 years of English, 3 each of math and science, and 2 each of foreign language, history, and social studies. AP credits are accepted. Important factors in the admissions decision are advanced placement or honors courses and evidence of special talent. All students are required to complete 32 courses plus 2 January interim courses and two-half courses in personal fitness and lifetime activity. Nine courses must be in the following areas (1 each): the arts, biblical, and theological studies, literary and rhetorical studies, historical and philosophical studies, mathematical and logical reasoning, natural science perspective, human behavior and social institutions, and non-western cultures. A minimum GPA of 2.0 is necessary for graduation. A total of 7 to 11 courses is required in the major. **Procedure:** Freshmen are admitted in the fall, winter, and spring. Entrance exams should be taken in the fall of the senior year. There are deferred admissions and rolling admissions plans. Applications should be filed by November 1 for fall entry; December 1 for winter entry; and January 1 for spring entry. Notifications are sent in November. Applications are accepted online. **Transfer Students:** 32 transfer students enrolled in 2016-2017. Transfer applicants must have earned a 2.4 GPA at their previous college. 72 of 140 credits required for the bachelor's degree must be completed at GAC. **International Students:** There are 58 international students enrolled. They must take the TOEFL.

ADMISSIONS: 63% of the 2017-2018 applicants were accepted. The ACT scores were 2% below 12, 13% between 12 and 17, 31% between 18 and 23, 20% between 24 and 29, and 34% above 30. 56% of the current freshmen were in the top fifth of their class; 88% were in the top two fifths. 23 freshmen graduated first in their class. **Admissions Contact:** Bob Neuman, Senior Associate Dean. Email: *admission@gustavus.edu* Web: *www.gustavus.edu*

FINANCIAL AID: In 2017-2018, 93% of all full-time freshmen received some form of financial aid. 69% of all full-time freshmen received need-based aid. The average freshman award was $31,279. Need-based scholarships or need-based grants averaged $26,732; and need-based self-help aid (loans and jobs) averaged $9,317. 71% of undergraduate students work part-time. The average financial indebtedness of the 2017 graduate was $33,523. GAC is a member of CSS. The CSS/Profile and the college's own financial statement are required. The FAFSA code is 002353. The priority date for freshman financial aid applications for fall entry is January 1.

HAMLINE UNIVERSITY — C-4

www.hamline.edu

St. Paul, MN 55104 — **(651) 523-2207** / **(800) 753-9753**

Fax: (651) 523-2458 — **Email: admission@hamline.edu**

Full-time: 903 men, 1259 women — **Faculty:** IIA, --$

Part-time: 30 men, 50 women — **Ph.D.s:** 88%

Graduate: 766 men, 1461 women — **Student/Faculty:** 13 to 1

Year: 4-1-4, summer session — **Tuition:** $39,996

Room & Board: $10,156 — **Freshman Class:** 3417 applied, 2378 accepted, 521 enrolled

SAT CR/M/W: 550/540/540 **ACT:** required — **CEEB CODE:** 6265

Application Deadline: open — **COMPETITIVE**

Hamline University, founded in 1854, is a private liberal arts and sciences university affiliated with the United Methodist Church. There are 3 undergraduate schools and 4 graduate schools. In addition to regional accreditation, HU has baccalaureate program accreditation with NASM, ABA, and ACS. The 60-acre campus is in an urban area between the downtowns of Minneapolis and St. Paul.

STUDENT LIFE: 78% of undergraduates are from Minnesota. Others are from 44 states, 34 foreign countries, and Canada. 72% are White; 6% African American; 6% Asian American; 6% Hispanic; 6% two or more races; 2% race unknown; 1% American Indian/Alaska Native; 1% Foreign. 28% are Lutheran, Buddhist, and Unknown; 19% Catholic; 17% claim no religious affiliation. **Female To Male Ratio:** 1.6:1. The average age of freshmen is 18; all undergraduates, 20. 17% do not continue beyond their first year; 65% remain to graduate. **Housing:** 955 students can be accommodated in college housing, which includes married student dorms and on-campus apartments. In addition, there are language/international houses, special-interest houses, fraternity houses, and PRIDE (black student alliance house). On-campus housing is guaranteed for all 4 years. 58% of students commute. All students may keep cars.

FACULTY/CLASSROOMS: 43% of faculty are male; 57% are female. No introductory courses are taught by graduate students.

PROGRAMS OF STUDY: HU confers B.A., B.S., B.B.A. and B.F.A degrees. Master's and doctoral degrees are also awarded. Bachelor's degrees are awarded in AGRICULTURE (environmental studies), BIOLOGICAL SCIENCE (biochemistry and biology/biological science), BUSINESS (accounting, business administration and management, global/general management, and international business management), COMMUNICATIONS AND THE ARTS (art history, art, communications, creative writing, dramatic arts, English, fine arts, French, German, music, music performance, Spanish, and theatre arts), COMPUTER AND PHYSICAL SCIENCE (chemistry, digital arts/technology, mathematics, and physics), EDUCATION (athletic training, education, elementary education, foreign languages education, music education, science education, and secondary education), HEALTH PROFESSIONS (exercise science and premedicine), SOCIAL SCIENCE (anthropology, criminal justice, East Asian studies, economics, forensic studies, history, Latin American studies, paralegal studies, peace studies, philosophy, political science/government, prelaw, psychology, religion, social science, social studies, sociology, urban studies, and women's studies). Social sciences, business, and psychology have the largest enrollments.

ACTIVITIES: There are 60 groups on campus, including art, band,

cheerleading, chess, choir, chorale, chorus, computers, dance, drama, environmental, ethnic, film, forensics, honors, international, jazz band, LGBT, literary magazine, musical theater, newspaper, orchestra, pep band, photography, political, professional, radio and TV, religious, social, social service, student government, and symphony. Popular campus events include World Fest, Fall Organization Fair, and Women's Leadership Retreat. **Sports:** There are 9 intercollegiate sports for men and 10 for women, and 11 intramural sports for men and women. Facilities include a stadium, a field house, a swimming pool, playing field, and an athletic center. **Graduates:** From July 1, 2016 to June 30, 2017, 428 bachelor's degrees were awarded. The most popular majors were social sciences (15%), psychology (13%), and business (5%). In an average class, 56% graduate in 4 years or less, 6% graduate in 5 years or less, and 2% graduate in 6 years or less.

SERVICES: Counseling and information services are available, as is tutoring in every subject. There is a reader service for the blind, and remedial math, reading, and writing. There are also centers for writing and quantitative reasoning. **Library/Resources:** Computerized library services include interlibrary loans, database searching, Internet access, and Wi-Fi capability. Special learning facilities include an art gallery, radio station, centers for global and environmental education, and excellence in urban teaching. **Physically Challenged Students:** Facilities include wheelchair ramps, elevators, special parking, specially equipped restrooms, special class scheduling, lowered drinking fountains, lowered telephones, and special housing. **Special:** Cross-registration with Augsburg, Macalester, Saint Catherine Colleges and the University of Saint Thomas. Students may select cooperative programs, study abroad, a Washington semester with American University, dual majors, student-designed majors, and pass/fail options. Students may earn a 3-2 or 4-2 engineering degree at the University of Minnesota or Washington University. On-campus work-study is available, as are extensive internship opportunities on and off campus. There is a chapter of Phi Beta Kappa and a freshman honors program. **Visiting:** There are guides for informal visits; visitors may sit in on classes and stay overnight. To schedule a visit, contact the Admissions Office at (651) 523-2014. **Campus Safety and Security:** Measures include 24-hour foot and vehicle patrol, emergency notification system, self-defense education, and security escort services. There are emergency telephones, lighted pathways/sidewalks, and controlled access to dorms/residences.

REQUIREMENTS: The SAT or ACT is required. It is recommended that candidates complete 4 years each of English (with 1 year of college preparatory writing), social studies, academic electives, social science, and math, 3 years of lab science, and 2 years of foreign language. The GED is accepted. AP and CLEP credits are accepted. To graduate, students must complete a minimum of 32 course credits within their field of concentration with a minimum overall GPA of 2.0. 63 course credits must be outside the major. All first year students are required to take a freshman seminar and freshman English, and demonstrate computer literacy. All students must also take a variety of general education courses to apply toward the "Hamline Plan." An independent study project and an internship are also required. **Procedure:** Freshmen are admitted to all sessions. There are early decision, early admissions, deferred admissions, and rolling admissions plans. Application deadlines are open. Notification of early decision is sent December 20; regular decision. Applications are accepted on-line. **Transfer Students:** 140 transfer students enrolled in 2016-2017. Transfer applicants must submit the application form, transcript copies, teacher/advisor recommendation, and a secondary school transcript, if fewer than 32 semester hours have been competed. Applicants must submit an essay or personal statement. A minimum college GPA of 2.0 is required. 56 of 128 credits required for the bachelor's degree must be completed at HU. **International Students:** There are 30 international students enrolled. They must take the TOEFL with a minimum score of 550 on the paper-based TOEFL (PBT) or 80 on the Internet-based version (iBT). They must also take the SAT or ACT.

ADMISSIONS: 70% of the 2017-2018 applicants were accepted. The SAT scores for the 2017-2018 freshman class were: Critical Reading-- 36% below 500, 32% between 500 and 599, 22% between 600 and 699, and 10% between 700 and 800. Math-- 27% below 500, 51% between 500 and 599, 19% between 600 and 699, and 3% between 700 and 800. Writing-- 31% below 500, 36% between 500 and 599, 31% between 600 and 699, and 3% between 700 and 800. The ACT scores were 20% below 12, 24% between 12 and 17, 21% between 18 and 23, 11% between 24 and 29, and 19% above 30. **Admissions Contact:** Office of Undergraduate Admission. Email: *admission@hamline.edu* Web: *www.hamline.edu*

FINANCIAL AID: In 2017-2018, 99% of all full-time freshmen received some form of financial aid. 89% of all full-time freshmen received need-based aid. The average freshman award was $31,477. The average financial indebtedness of the 2017 graduate was $36,006. The FAFSA code is 002354. The priority date for freshman financial aid applications for fall entry is March 15.

MACALESTER COLLEGE — C-4
www.macalester.edu/admissions

St. Paul, MN 55105	**(651) 696-6357** **(800) 231-7974**
Fax: (651) 696-6724	**Email: admissions@macalester.edu**
Full-time: 815 men, 1262 women	**Faculty:** 184
Part-time: 20 men, 23 women	**Ph.D.s:** 93%
Graduate: n/av	**Student/Faculty:** 10 to 1
Year: semesters	**Tuition:** $52,464
Room & Board: $11,672	**Freshman Class:** 5900 applied, 2394 accepted, 543 enrolled
SAT EBR-W/M: 710/680 **ACT:** 31	**CEEB CODE:** 6390
Application Deadline: January 15	**MOST COMPETITIVE**

Macalester College, founded in 1874, has been preparing students for world citizenship and providing an integrated international education for over seven decades. The academic program ranks among the top 20 in the nation as a liberal arts and sciences college. Most students study abroad for 15 weeks or more, providing time for substantial experience and study in another country. Graduates reap the benefits of a multicultural student body and global education in the job market and at the nation's top graduate programs. There is 1 undergraduate school. In addition to regional accreditation, MC has baccalaureate program accreditation with NASM. The 53-acre campus is in an urban area midway between downtown St. Paul and Minneapolis. Including any residence halls, there are 43 buildings.

STUDENT LIFE: 86% of undergraduates are from out of state, mostly the Midwest. Students are from 50 states, 90 foreign countries, and Canada. 61% are from public schools. 61% are White; 16% Foreign; 7% Asian American; 7% Hispanic; 6% two or more races; 3% African American; 1% American Indian/Alaska Native; 1% race unknown. **Female To Male Ratio:** 1.5:1. The average age of freshmen is 18; all undergraduates, 20. 7% do not continue beyond their first year; 87% remain to graduate. **Housing:** 1300 students can be accommodated in college housing, which includes dorms and on-campus apartments. In addition, there are language/international houses, special-interest houses, vegetarian Co-op, a cultural house, interfaith house, and a gender neutral section. On-campus housing is available on a lottery system for upperclassmen. 60% of students live on campus. Upperclassmen may keep cars.

FACULTY/CLASSROOMS: 47% of faculty are male; 53% are female. All teach undergraduates and 80% do research. No introductory courses are taught by graduate students. The average class size in an introductory lecture is 20; in a laboratory is 13; and in a regular course is 17.

PROGRAMS OF STUDY: MC confers B.A. degrees. Bachelor's degrees are awarded in AGRICULTURE (environmental studies), BIOLOGICAL SCIENCE (biology/biological science and neurosciences), COMMUNICATIONS AND THE ARTS (art, Chinese, classics, dramatic arts, English, French, Japanese, linguistics, media arts, music, Russian, and Spanish), COMPUTER AND PHYSICAL SCIENCE (chemistry, computer science, geology, mathematics, and physics), EDUCATION (education), SOCIAL SCIENCE (American studies, anthropology, Asian/Oriental studies, economics, geography, German area studies, history, humanities, international studies, Latin American studies, philosophy, political science/government, psychology, religion, sociology, and women's studies). International studies, biology, and political science are the strongest academically. Economics, political science, and mathematics have the largest enrollments.

ACTIVITIES: There are no fraternities or sororities. There are 115 groups on campus, including art, bagpipe, band, chess, choir, chorale, chorus, computers, dance, debate, drama, environmental, ethnic, forensics, honors, international, jazz band, LGBT, literary magazine, multi faith council, newspaper, orchestra, photography, political, professional, radio and TV, religious, social, social service, student government, and symphony. Popular campus events include Midnight Breakfast, Mac Idol, Spring Fest, and Founders Day. **Sports:** There are 10 intercollegiate sports for men and 11 for women, and 12 intramural sports for men and women. Facilities include a field house, a gym, 10-lane swimming pool, a stadium for football, soccer, an outdoor track, racquetball courts, tennis courts, an indoor track and field facility, weight room/fitness center, dance studios, health & wellness center, athletic training room, racquetball/squash courts, and baseball and softball diamonds. **Graduates:** From July 1, 2016 to June 30, 2017, 517 bachelor's degrees were awarded. The most popular majors were biology (14%), economics (13%), and political science (10%). In an average class, 85% graduate in 4 years or less, 87% graduate in 5 years or less, and 87% graduate in 6 years or less. Of the 2016 graduating class, 14% were enrolled in graduate school within 6 months of graduation, and 80% were employed.

SERVICES: Counseling and information services are available, as is tutoring in some subjects, such as math, chemistry, physics, and writing. There is a reader service for the blind. **Library/Resources:** The library contains 348,727 volumes, 87,004 microform items, 16,769 audio/video tapes/CDs/DVDs, and subscribes to 12,151 periodicals, including electronic. Computerized library services include interlibrary loans, database searching, Internet access, and Wi-Fi capability. Special learning facilities include an art gallery, radio station, and academic support center. **Physically Challenged Students:** 90% of the campus is accessible. Facilities include wheelchair ramps, elevators, special parking, specially equipped restrooms, special class scheduling, lowered drinking fountains, lowered telephones, and special housing. **Special:** Cross-registration is offered at Augsburg College, Hamline University, St. Catherine University, the University of St. Thomas and Minneapolis College of Art and Design. There also are cooperative programs in liberal arts and architecture with Washington University in St. Louis, engineering with the same school and the University of Minnesota. Internships are available in government, financial services, law, medicine, research, the arts, and other fields. Students study abroad in more than 68 countries. Student-designed majors and pass/fail options for no more than 1 course per semester also are available. There are 16 national honor societies, Phi Beta Kappa, and 30 departmental honors programs. **Visiting:** There are regularly scheduled orientations for prospective students, including interviews, information sessions, a class visit, and a tour of campus. There are guides for informal visits, visitors may sit in on classes, and stay overnight. To schedule a visit, contact the Admissions Office. **Campus Safety and Security:** Measures include 24-hour foot and vehicle patrol, emergency notification system, self-defense education, and security escort services. There are emergency telephones, lighted pathways/sidewalks, and controlled access to dorms/residences.

REQUIREMENTS: The SAT or ACT is required. Applicants should have earned at least 16 academic credits, including 4 years of English and 3 each in math, laboratory science, foreign language, and social studies/history. The college also expects applicants to have taken honors, AP, or IB courses where available. An essay is required, and an interview is recommended. AP credits are accepted. Important factors in the admissions decision are advanced placement or honors courses, extracurricular activities record, and recommendations by school officials. All students are required to complete 128 semester credits, with 32 to 44 in the major, and an overall minimum GPA of 2.0. Required courses include 12 credits in humanities and fine arts, 8 credits in natural science and/or math, 8 credits in social science, 4 credits each in US identities & differences, internationalism 12 credits on writing, 4 to 12 credits in quantitative reasoning, and a first-year course. Second language proficiency equivalent to 2 years of college-level language must be shown, and every major requires a capstone experience. **Procedure:** Freshmen are admitted in the fall. Entrance exams should be taken fall of the senior year or in their junior year. There are early decision and deferred admissions plans. Early decision applications should be filed by November 15; regular applications, by January 15 for fall entry. The fall 2017 application fee was $40. Notification of early decision is sent December 15; regular decision, March 30. 150 early decision candidates were accepted for the 2017-2018 class. 356 applicants were on the 2017 waiting list; 104 were admitted. Applications are accepted on-line. **Transfer Students:** 16 transfer students enrolled in 2016-2017. Transfer students should follow the application instructions found on the admissions website for U.S. Transfer Students and for International Transfer Students. The application fee for transfer students is $40. Students considering transferring to Macalester may have their transcripts evaluated for the transfer of course credits prior to applying by sending an official transcript and specifically requesting this service from the Registrar's Office. This evaluation is only preliminary, but to be helpful enough in planning for transfer. 64 of 128 credits required for the bachelor's degree must be completed at MC. **International Students:** There are 332 international students enrolled. They must take the TOEFL with a minimum score of 600 on the paper-based TOEFL (PBT) or 100 on the Internet-based version (iBT). Student must take the IELTS, and either the SAT or ACT.

ADMISSIONS: 41% of the 2017-2018 applicants were accepted. The SAT scores for the 2017-2018 freshman class were: Math-- 11% between 500 and 599, 49% between 600 and 699, and 40% between 700 and 800. Evidence-Based Reading/Writing-- 3% between 500 and 599, 35% between 600 and 699, and 62% between 700 and 800. The ACT scores were 1% between 18 and 23, 30% between 24 and 29, and 68% above 30. 88% of the current freshmen were in the top fifth of their class; 99% were in the top two fifths. 50 freshmen graduated first in their class. **Admissions Contact:** Jeffrey Allen, Vice President for Admissions and Financial Aid. Email: *admissions@macalester.edu* Web: *www.macalester.edu/admissions*

FINANCIAL AID: In 2017-2018, 83% of all full-time freshmen received some form of financial aid. 70% of all full-time freshmen received need-based aid. The average freshman award was $43,701. Need-based scholarships or need-based grants averaged $37,960; and need-based self-help aid (loans and jobs) averaged $5,741. 70% of undergraduate students work part-time. The average financial indebtedness of the 2017 graduate was $24,381. Macalester is a member of CSS. The CSS/Profile, and parent's W-2 and tax forms are required. The FAFSA code is 002358. The priority date for freshman financial aid applications for fall entry is February 1.

METROPOLITAN STATE UNIVERSITY C-4

www.metrostate.edu

St. Paul, MN 55106	(651) 793-1302 (651) 793-1300
Fax: (651) 793-1310	**Email:** gateway@metrostate.edu
Full-time: 1232 men, 1787 women	**Faculty:** 115
Part-time: 1383 men, 2572 women	**Ph.D.s:** 81%
Graduate: 340 men, 473 women	**Student/Faculty:** 15 to 1
Year: semesters, summer session	**Tuition:** $7859 ($14,394)
Room & Board: n/app	**Freshman Class:** n/av
SAT or ACT: recommended	**CEEB CODE:** 1245
Application Deadline: June 15	**COMPETITIVE**

Metropolitan State University, founded in 1971, is a public institution primarily serving working adults through a variety of majors and individually designed degree programs. The figures given in the above capsule and in this profile are approximate. There are 6 undergraduate schools and 2 graduate schools. In addition to regional accreditation, MSU has baccalaureate program accreditation with NLN. The campus is in an urban area in the Twin Cities Metro area. Including any residence halls, there are 7 buildings.

STUDENT LIFE: 98% of undergraduates are from Minnesota. Others are from 21 states, 53 foreign countries, and Canada. 95% are from public schools. 69% are White; 2% Hispanic; 2% Foreign; 16% African American; 10% Asian American; 1% American Indian/Alaska Native. **Female To Male Ratio:** 1.6:1. The average age of freshmen is 26; all undergraduates, 31. All students commute.

FACULTY/CLASSROOMS: 55% of faculty are male; 45% are female. All teach undergraduates. No introductory courses are taught by graduate students. The average class size in an introductory lecture is 24; in a laboratory is 24; and in a regular course is 19.

PROGRAMS OF STUDY: MSU confers B.A., B.S., B.A.S. and B.S.N. degrees. Master's and doctoral degrees are also awarded. Bachelor's degrees are awarded in BIOLOGICAL SCIENCE (biology/biological science), BUSINESS (accounting, banking and finance, business administration and management, hospitality management services, human resources, international business management, management information systems, marketing and distribution, marketing management, operations management, and trade and industrial supervision and management), COMMUNICATIONS AND THE ARTS (advertising, communications, dramatic arts, English, playwriting/screenwriting, and technical and business writing), COMPUTER AND PHYSICAL SCIENCE (applied mathematics, computer science, computer security and information assurance, and information sciences and systems), EDUCATION (early childhood education), HEALTH PROFESSIONS (dental hygiene and nursing), SOCIAL SCIENCE (addiction studies, child psychology/development, criminal justice, developmental psychology, early childhood studies, economics, ethnic studies, food production/management/services, history, human services, law enforcement and corrections, liberal arts/general studies, philosophy, psychology, public administration, social science, social work, and women's studies). Nursing is the strongest academically. Accounting, and business administration have the largest enrollments.

ACTIVITIES: There are no fraternities or sororities. There are 26 groups on campus, including drama, ethnic, honors, international, LGBT, literary magazine, newspaper, professional, religious, social, and student government. **Sports:** There is no sports program at Metro State. **Graduates:** From July 1, 2016 to June 30, 2017, 1505 bachelor's degrees were awarded. The most popular majors were business (37%), individualized studies (15%), and law enforcement and criminal justice (9%).

SERVICES: Counseling and information services are available, as is tutoring in some subjects, such as accounting, finance, economics, writing, math, and ESL. **Library/Resources:** The library contains 77,378 volumes, 7,218 audio/video tapes/CDs/DVDs, and subscribes to 242 periodicals, including electronic. Computerized library services include interlibrary loans, database searching, Internet access, and Wi-Fi capability. Special learning facilities include an art gallery. **Physically Challenged Students:** All of the campus is accessible. Facilities include elevators, special parking, specially equipped restrooms, lowered drinking fountains, and lowered telephones. **Special:** Internships, co-op programs in many areas, study abroad, dual majors, and student-designed programs are offered. There is 1 departmental honors program. **Visiting:** There are regularly scheduled orientations for prospective students, including a campus tour, meetings with a financial aid adviser, faculty, and students, and a general information session. To schedule a visit, contact the Admissions Office. **Campus Safety and Security:** Measures include security escort services.

REQUIREMENTS: Metro State requires applicants to be in the upper 50% of their class or have ACT, PSAT, or SAT scores at or above the national median. Applicants not meeting these requirements will be considered in the alternative admissions process. The GED is accepted. AP and CLEP credits are accepted. To graduate, all students must complete 120 to 124 semester credits, with a varying number of hours required in the major, 48 credits in a core curriculum, and a 2.0 GPA. Other requirements include natural/physical science, math/logic, global awareness, humanities, and fine arts. **Procedure:** Freshmen are admitted to all sessions. There is a deferred admissions plan. Applications should be filed by June 15 for fall entry; August 15 for spring entry; and March 15 for summer entry. The fall 2017 application fee was $20. Notification is sent on a rolling basis. Applications are accepted on-line. **Transfer Students:** Applicants must have at least a C average. 30 of 120 credits required for the bachelor's degree must be completed at Metro State. **International Students:** There are 93 international students enrolled. They must take the TOEFL with a minimum score of 500 on the paper-based TOEFL (PBT).

Admissions Contact: the Admissions Office. Email: *gateway@metrostate.edu* Web: *www.metrostate.edu*

FINANCIAL AID: MSU is a member of CSS. The FAFSA code is 010374. Check with the school for current application deadlines.

MINNEAPOLIS COLLEGE OF ART AND DESIGN *(The complete profile is made available exclusively on our website, www.barronspac.com)*

MINNESOTA STATE UNIVERSITY, MANKATO C-4

www.mnsu.edu

Mankato, MN 56001	**(507) 389-1822** **(800) 722-0544**
Fax: (507) 389-1511	**Email: admissions@mnsu.edu**
Full-time: 5324 men, 5786 women	**Faculty:** n/av
Part-time: 871 men, 1321 women	**Ph.D.s:** 85%
Graduate: 746 men, 1235 women	**Student/Faculty:** 20 to 1
Year: semesters, summer session	**Tuition:** $8094 ($16,070)
Room & Board: $9096	**Freshman Class:** 7793 applied, 5198 accepted, 2348 enrolled
ACT: 23	**CEEB CODE:** 6677
Application Deadline: August 22	**COMPETITIVE**

Minnesota State University, Mankato, founded in 1868 and a unit of Minnesota State Colleges and Universities (MN State), offers programs in the liberal arts and sciences, as well as business, education, engineering and technology, and nursing. There are 6 undergraduate schools and 1 graduate school. In addition to regional accreditation, Mankato has baccalaureate program accreditation with AACSB, ABET, ADA, CSWE, NASAD, NASM, NLN, and NRPA. The 354-acre campus is in a rural area 85 miles southwest of Minneapolis-St. Paul. Including any residence halls, there are 28 buildings.

STUDENT LIFE: 83% of undergraduates are from Minnesota. Others are from 49 states, 90 foreign countries, and Canada. 93% are from public schools. 71% are White; 7% African American; 7% Hispanic; 6% Foreign; 4% Asian American; 3% two or more races; 2% race unknown. **Female To Male Ratio:** 1.2:1. The average age of freshmen is 19; all undergraduates, 22. 18% do not continue beyond their first year; 58% remain to graduate. **Housing:** 3300 students can be accommodated in college housing, which includes dorms and on-campus apartments. In addition, there are honors houses, special-interest houses, freshman quiet-study, upperclass, engineering, and computer science floors. There are also various learning communities based on interest and intended academic major. On-campus housing is guaranteed for the freshman year only, and is available on a first-come, first-served basis. 82% of students commute. All students may keep cars. Alcohol is not permitted.

FACULTY/CLASSROOMS: 51% of faculty are male; 49% are female. 96% teach undergraduates, and 54% do research. Graduate students teach 4% of introductory courses. The average class size in an introductory lecture is 43; in a laboratory is 11; and in a regular course is 20.

PROGRAMS OF STUDY: Mankato confers B.A., B.S., B.F.A., B.Mus., B.S.EE., and B.S.ME. degrees. Associate, master's, and doctoral degrees are also awarded. Bachelor's degrees are awarded in BIOLOGICAL SCIENCE (biochemistry, biology/biological science, biotechnology, life science, and life science secondary school education), BUSINESS (accounting, banking and finance, business administration and management, finance, international business, international business management, management science, marketing, recreation and leisure services, and sports management), COMMUNICATIONS AND THE ARTS (art, communication studies, communications, dance, dramatic arts, English, English as a second/foreign language, French, German, journalism, media management, music, music business management, music industry, Spanish, speech/debate/rhetoric, technical communication, and theatre studies), COMPUTER AND PHYSICAL SCIENCE (chemistry, chemistry/adolescence education, computer engineering technology, computer information technology, computer security and information assurance, earth science, information sciences and systems, mathematics, and physics), EDUCATION (art education, dance education, early childhood education, education, elementary education, foreign languages education, general studies, health education, mathematics education, middle school education, music education, physical education, science education, secondary education, social studies education, and special education), ENGINEERING AND ENVIRONMENTAL DESIGN (automotive technology, aviation administration/management, civil engineering, computer engineering, construction management, electrical/electronics engineering, electrical/electronics engineering technology, engineering technology, environmental science, food services technology, manufacturing engineering, manufacturing technology, mechanical engineering, military science, and preengineering), HEALTH PROFESSIONS (allied health, clinical science, community health work, dental hygiene, exercise science, health science, medical laboratory science, nursing, predentistry, premedicine, prepharmacy, preveterinary science, public health, and speech pathology/audiology), SOCIAL SCIENCE (American Indian studies, anthropology, communication sciences and disorders, cognitive science, corrections, criminal justice, dietetics, economics, ethnic studies, family/consumer studies, geography, history, human development, humanities, international relations, law enforcement and corrections, parks and recreation management, philosophy, political science/government, prelaw, psychology, Scandinavian studies, social studies, social work, sociology, urban studies, and women's studies). Nursing, engineering, business, education, and the sciences are the strongest academically. Business, nursing, and education have the largest enrollments.

ACTIVITIES: 6% of men belong to 7 national fraternities; 5% of women belong to 4 national sororities. There are 250 groups on campus, including art, band, cheerleading, choir, chorale, chorus, computers, dance, drama, ethnic, film, forensics, honors, international, jazz band, LGBT, literary magazine, marching band, musical theater, newspaper, opera, orchestra, pep band, photography, political, professional, radio and TV, religious, social, social service, and student government. Popular campus events include Multicultural Activities and Food Festivals, Celebrations, Greek Week, Homecoming and the Big Event. **Sports:** There are 8 intercollegiate sports for men and 10 for women, and 5 intramural sports for men and women. Facilities include a football stadium, indoor field house, recreation center including an indoor swimming pool, racquetball courts, a walking/jogging track, multipurpose rooms, weights, workout machines, gyms, indoor track, tennis courts, and an ice hockey arena. **Graduates:** From July 1, 2016 to June 30, 2017, 2520 bachelor's degrees were awarded. The most popular majors were nursing (9%), management (5%), and engineering (5%). In an average class, 2% graduate in 3 years or less, 22% graduate in 4 years or less, 49% graduate in 5 years or less, and 61% graduate in 6 years or less. Of the 2016 graduating class, 15% were enrolled in graduate school within 6 months of graduation, and 93% were employed.

SERVICES: Counseling and information services are available, as is tutoring in most subjects. There is a reader service for the blind, and remedial math, reading, and writing. Also available are alternative testing accommodations, note taking, sign language interpreting, and taped texts. **Library/Resources:** The library contains 1.2 million volumes, 253,560 microform items, 30,686 audio/video tapes/CDs/DVDs, and subscribes to 3,126 periodicals, including electronic. Computerized library services include interlibrary loans, database searching, Internet access, and Wi-Fi capability. Special learning facilities include an art gallery, radio station, 2 observatories, high ropes course, and experiential education. **Physically Challenged Students:** All of the campus is accessible. Facilities include wheelchair ramps, elevators, special parking, specially equipped restrooms, special class scheduling, lowered drinking fountains, lowered telephones, and special housing. **Special:** The university offers cross-registration within the Minnesota State University System and with Bethany Lutheran College and Gustavus Adolphus College. Students may serve internships, study abroad, or participate in an accelerated degree program. B.A.-B.S. degrees, dual and student-designed majors, nondegree study, and pass/fail options also are available. New 2+2 transfer pathways now exist amongst MSU and all other two-year schools within the MN State system of schools. There are 25 national honor societies and a freshman honors program. **Visiting:** There are regularly scheduled orientations for prospective students, consisting of overview presentations, academic information fairs and course registration. There are guides for informal visits and visitors may sit in on classes. To schedule a visit, contact Office of Admissions. **Campus Safety and Security:** Measures include 24-hour foot and vehicle patrol, emergency notification system, self-defense education, and security escort services. There are shuttle buses, emergency telephones, lighted pathways/sidewalks, controlled access to dorms/residences, closed-circuit parking lot cameras, and motion-sensitive lights.

REQUIREMENTS: Guaranteed Admission to MSU, Mankato if: you rank in the Top 50% of your high school class (with satisfactory ACT score) or have a GPA of at least a 3.0 (on a 4.0 scale) (with satisfactory ACT score) or achieve a 21 or higher composite score on the ACT exam (with satisfactory GPA). If you do not meet the above admission requirements, your application will be reviewed on the basis of strength of college preparation course work, grade point average, probability of success, academic progression, class rank and ACT test scores. Supplemental information may also be requested before an admission decision is made. AP and CLEP credits are accepted. To graduate, students must complete a minimum of 120 semester hours of credit, with a minimum GPA of 2.0 and at least 45 credit hours in the major. Most programs require 44 hours of general education, including courses in English, speech, science, math, social/behavioral science, arts and humanities, cultural diversity, global perspective, ethnic/civic responsibility, and people and the environment. **Procedure:** Freshmen are admitted to all sessions. Entrance exams should be taken in the spring of the junior year or the fall of the senior year. There are deferred admissions and rolling admissions plans. Applications should be filed by August 22 for fall entry; January 8 for spring entry. The fall 2017 application fee was $20. Notification is sent on a rolling basis. Applications are accepted online. **Transfer Students:** 1014 transfer students enrolled in 2016-2017. Transfer applicants must have a minimum GPA of 2.0 and have completed at least 67% of all college-level courses attempted. 30 of 120 credits required for the bachelor's degree must be completed at Mankato. **International Students:** There are 1300 international students enrolled. They must take the TOEFL with a minimum score of 500 on the paper-based TOEFL (PBT) or 61 on the Internet-based version (iBT). Students must also take the IELTS or the SAT Reading Subsection.

ADMISSIONS: 67% of the 2017-2018 applicants were accepted. The SAT scores for the 2017-2018 freshman class were: The ACT scores were 3% below 12, 22% between 12 and 17, 54% between 18 and 23, 18% between 24 and 29, and 3% above 30. 23% of the current freshmen were in the top fifth of their class; 65% were in the top two fifths. 21 freshmen graduated first in their class. **Admissions Contact:** Office of Admissions. Email: *admissions@mnsu.edu* Web: *www.mnsu.edu*

FINANCIAL AID: In 2017-2018, 80% of all full-time freshmen received some form of financial aid. 75% of all full-time freshmen received need-based aid. The average freshman award was $7,134. Need-based scholarships or need-based grants averaged $6,015; need-based self-help aid (loans and jobs) averaged $4,811; non-need-based athletic scholarships averaged $5,827; and other non-need-based awards and non-need-based scholarships averaged $2,271. 24% of undergraduate students work part-time. The FAFSA code is 002360. Check with the school for current application deadlines.

MINNESOTA STATE UNIVERSITY, MOORHEAD — A-2

www.mnstate.edu

Moorhead, MN 56563 — **(218) 477-2161**

Fax: (218) 477-4374 — **Email: admissions@mnstate.edu**

Full-time: 2526 men, 3304 women	**Faculty:** n/av
Part-time: 484 men, 698 women	**Ph.D.s:** n/av
Graduate: 106 men, 379 women	**Student/Faculty:** n/av
Year: semesters, summer session	**Tuition:** $7887 ($15,297)
Room & Board: $13,506	**Freshman Class:** 3393 applied, 2489 accepted, 2238 enrolled
ACT: required	**CEEB CODE:** 6678
Application Deadline: August 1	**COMPETITIVE**

Minnesota State University Moorhead, founded in 1887, is a public comprehensive institution. The figures given in the above capsule and in this profile are approximate. There are 4 undergraduate schools and 1 graduate school. In addition to regional accreditation, Moorhead has baccalaureate program accreditation with AACSB, ACCE, CSWE, NASAD, NASM, ABA, BSN, MS (in nursing), ACS, and ASLH. The 119-acre campus is in a suburban area just 240 miles northwest of Minneapolis-St. Paul and across the river from Fargo, North Dakota. Including any residence halls, there are 28 buildings.

STUDENT LIFE: 83% are White; 6% Foreign; 3% African American; 1% Asian American; 1% Hispanic. **Female To Male Ratio:** 1.4:1. The average age of freshmen is 19; all undergraduates, 23. **Housing:** 1844 students can be accommodated in college housing, which includes dorms, on-campus apartments, sorority houses, and living learning communities. On-campus housing is available on a first-come, first-served basis. 81% of students commute. Alcohol is not permitted. All students may keep cars.

FACULTY/CLASSROOMS: 61% of faculty are male; 39% are female. No introductory courses are taught by graduate students.

PROGRAMS OF STUDY: Moorhead confers B.A., B.S., B.F.A., B.M., B.S.N. and B.S.W. degrees. Associate, master's, and doctoral degrees are also awarded. Bachelor's degrees are awarded in BIOLOGICAL SCIENCE (biology/biological science), BUSINESS (accounting, banking and finance, business administration and management, international business management, management science, marketing/retailing/merchandising, and operations management), COMMUNICATIONS AND THE ARTS (broadcasting, communications, dramatic arts, English, film arts, fine arts, journalism, music, music technology, public relations, Spanish, and speech/debate/rhetoric), COMPUTER AND PHYSICAL SCIENCE (chemistry, computer science, computer security and information assurance, earth science, geoscience, mathematics, and physics), EDUCATION (art education, athletic training, early childhood education, elementary education, English education, foreign languages education, health education, mathematics education, music education, physical education, science education, social studies education, and special education), ENGINEERING AND ENVIRONMENTAL DESIGN (construction management, graphic arts technology, and industrial engineering technology), HEALTH PROFESSIONS (community health work, exercise science, health care administration, medical laboratory technology, nursing, predentistry, premedicine, prepharmacy, preveterinary science, and speech pathology/audiology), SOCIAL SCIENCE (anthropology, criminal justice, East Asian studies, economics, gerontology, history, international studies, law, paralegal studies, philosophy, political science/government, prelaw, psychology, social work, sociology, Spanish studies, and women's studies).

ACTIVITIES: 2% of men belong to 1% of women belong to 2 local and 2 national sororities. There are 150 groups on campus, including art, band, cheerleading, choir, chorus, computers, dance, drama, drill team, ethnic, film, honors, international, jazz band, LGBT, literary magazine, musical theater, newspaper, orchestra, pep band, photography, political, professional, radio and TV, religious, social, social service, and student government. Popular campus events include Celebrations of Nations, Straw Hat Summer Theatre, Dragon Frost, Grass Volleyball Tournament, and Muggle Quidditch. **Sports:** There are 5 intercollegiate sports for men and 9 for women, and 14 intramural sports for men and women. The wellness facility has full basketball/volleyball courts, an exercise room with cardio and strength training equipment, a rock climbing wall and an elevated indoor running track, baseball, fencing, lacrosse, rugby, Tae Kwon Do, soccer, wrestling and martial arts. **Graduates:** From July 1, 2016 to June 30, 2017, 1229 bachelor's degrees were awarded. The most popular majors were mass communication (8%), elementary education (5%), and social work (5%).

SERVICES: Counseling and information services are available, as is tutoring in every subject. There is a reader service for the blind, and remedial math, reading, and writing. **Library/Resources:** The library contains 656,104 volumes, 872,378 microform items, 25,290 audio/video tapes/CDs/DVDs, and subscribes to 2,245 periodicals, including electronic. Computerized library services include interlibrary loans and database searching. Special learning facilities include an art gallery, planetarium, radio station, TV station, and a regional science center. **Physically Challenged Students:** Facilities include wheelchair ramps, elevators, special parking, specially equipped restrooms, lowered drinking fountains, and lowered telephones. **Special:** Internships are available in most disciplines. The university offers cross-registration with North Dakota State University and Concordia College and is a member of the National Student Exchange. Study abroad program allows students to study at any of 125 member universities. Variety of internships are available at local, state & federal government agencies, service organizations and in the private sector. There are 7 national honor societies, a freshman honors program, and 1 departmental honors program. **Visiting:** There are regularly scheduled orientations for prospective students, including a campus tour, and meetings with faculty and an admissions officer. There are guides for informal visits. To schedule a visit, contact the Admissions Office. **Campus Safety and Security:** Measures include 24-hour foot and vehicle patrol, an emergency notification system, self-defense education, and security escort services. There are emergency telephones, lighted pathways/sidewalks, and in-room safes.

REQUIREMENTS: A high school diploma is required, and the GED is accepted. A SAT satisfactory score or ACT score of 21 is required for applicants whose high school rank is below the top half. Moorhead requires applicants to be in the upper 50% of their class. AP and CLEP credits are accepted. To graduate students must have a 2.0 GPA and complete 120 semester hours, including a liberal arts core of 45 credits and 43 semester hours in upper-division courses. Required courses include 2 in English, 6 credits each of natural science, social science, humanities, and communication systems, and 5 credits in cultural diversity. All students must complete an upper-level writing requirement. **Procedure:** Freshmen are admitted in the fall, spring, and summer. Entrance exams should be taken in the junior or senior year of high school. There is a rolling admissions plan. Applications should be filed by August 1 for fall entry; November 15 for spring entry. The fall 2017 application fee was $20. Applications are accepted on-line. **Transfer Students:** 659 transfer students enrolled in 2016-2017. Applicants must submit a high school transcript or GED score and all other transcripts for post-secondary schools attended. A minimum GPA of 2.0 (higher for entry in some departments) is necessary for transfer credit. 30 of 120 credits required for the bachelor's degree must be completed at Moorhead. **International Students:** There are 320 international students enrolled. They must take the TOEFL with a minimum score of 500 on the paper-based TOEFL (PBT) or 61 on the Internet-based version (iBT).

ADMISSIONS: 73% of the 2017-2018 applicants were accepted. **Admissions Contact:** Richard DePaolis-Metz, Director of Undergraduate Admissions. Email: *admissions@mnstate.edu* Web: *www.mnstate.edu*

FINANCIAL AID: The FAFSA code is 002367. The priority date for freshman financial aid applications for fall entry is October 1.

NORTH CENTRAL UNIVERSITY — C-4

www.northcentral.edu

Minneapolis, MN 55404 (612) 343-4406 (800) 289-6222
Fax: (612) 343-4146 **Email:** admissions@northcentral.edu

Full-time: 480 men, 630 women	**Faculty:** 38
Part-time: n/av	**Ph.D.s:** 41%
Graduate: 18 men, 13 women	**Student/Faculty:** 17 to 1
Year: semesters, summer session	**Tuition:** $23,480
Room & Board: $7130	**Freshman Class:** n/av
SAT: required **ACT:** 21	**CEEB CODE:** 0051
Application Deadline: June 1	**COMPETITIVE**

North Central University, founded in 1930 and affiliated with the Assemblies of God, is a Christian University that emphasizes rigorous academic training and spiritual passion. The figures given in the above capsule and in this profile are approximate. There are 3 undergraduate schools and 1 graduate school. In addition to regional accreditation, NCU has baccalaureate program accreditation with CSWE. The 12-acre campus is in an urban area in downtown Minneapolis. Including any residence halls, there are 24 buildings.

STUDENT LIFE: 65% of undergraduates are from Minnesota. Others are from 38 states, 11 foreign countries, and Canada. 88% are from public schools. 70% are White; 6% Hispanic; 5% African American; 4% two or more races; 3% Asian American; 13% race unknown. 99% are Protestant. **Female To Male Ratio:** 1.3:1. The average age of freshmen is 18; all undergraduates, 20. 25% do not continue beyond their first year; 40% remain to graduate. **Housing:** 1031 students can be accommodated in college housing, which includes married student dorms and on-campus apartments. On-campus housing is guaranteed for the freshman year only, and is available on a first-come, first-served basis. 85% of students live on campus. All students may keep cars. Alcohol is not permitted.

FACULTY/CLASSROOMS: 58% of faculty are male; 42% are female. All teach undergraduates. No introductory courses are taught by graduate students. The average class size in an introductory lecture is 40; in a laboratory is 15; and in a regular course is 25.

PROGRAMS OF STUDY: NCU confers B.A. and B.S. degrees. Associate and master's degrees are also awarded. Bachelor's degrees are awarded in BUSINESS (accounting, business administration and management, business administration marketing, entrepreneurial studies, marketing, and sports management), COMMUNICATIONS AND THE ARTS (American Sign Language, communications, English, English literature, English writing, journalism, literature, music, music business management, music ministry, music production/recording technology, music performance, theatre arts, vocal music education, and writing), COMPUTER AND PHYSICAL SCIENCE (computer information systems, computer science, and mathematics), EDUCATION (education, educational studies, elementary education, English secondary education, middle school education, music education, secondary education, and social studies secondary school education), SOCIAL SCIENCE (behavioral science, biblical languages, biblical studies, economics, interdisciplinary studies, ministries, missions, pastoral studies, psychology, religion, religious education, religious music, social work, theological studies, and youth ministry). Pastoral studies, American Sign Language and business administration are the strongest academically. Pastoral studies, business administration and marketing have the largest enrollments.

ACTIVITIES: There are no fraternities or sororities. There are 28 groups on campus, including art, band, choir, chorale, chorus, drama, jazz band, literary magazine, musical theater, newspaper, orchestra, photography, professional, radio and TV, religious, social, and student government. Popular campus events include All-College Picnic, Community Outreach Day, and Spring Banquet. **Sports:** There are 6 intercollegiate sports for men and women, and 4 intramural sports for men and women. Facilities include a gym, and a sports complex. **Graduates:** From July 1, 2016 to June 30, 2017, 215 bachelor's degrees were awarded. The most popular majors were Pastoral studies (9%), youth ministry (8%), and elementary education (7%).

SERVICES: Counseling and information services are available, as is tutoring in every subject. **Library/Resources:** The library contains 89,834 volumes, 29 microform items, and 200 audio/video tapes/CDs/DVDs, and subscribes to 325 periodicals including electronic. Computerized library services include interlibrary loans, database searching, Internet access, and Wi-Fi capability. Special learning facilities include a radio station. **Physically Challenged Students:** All of the campus is accessible. Facilities include wheelchair ramps, elevators, special parking, specially equipped restrooms, special class scheduling, lowered drinking fountains, and lowered telephones. **Special:** Students may pursue co-op programs in nursing or secondary education, study abroad in 6 countries, and nondegree study. Credit for life, military, or work experience is possible. Work-study, dual majors, and student-designed majors are available. There is 1 national honor society and 1 departmental honors program. **Visiting:** There are regularly scheduled orientations for prospective students. There are guides for informal visits, visitors may sit in on classes, and stay overnight. To schedule a visit, contact the Admissions Office. **Campus Safety and Security:** Measures include 24-hour foot and vehicle patrol, emergency notification system, self-defense education, and security escort services. There are shuttle buses, lighted pathways/sidewalks, and controlled access to dorms/residences.

REQUIREMENTS: The college requires a minimum ACT score of 18, high school transcripts, and academic and pastoral references. AP and CLEP credits are accepted. Students must complete a minimum of 124 credits for their particular bachelor's degree. Each program has specific requirements, including general education and Biblical studies core classes. Internships are required for all programs. Students must take 60 or more total hours in their major, with a minimum overall GPA of 2.0 (2.2 for teacher education). **Procedure:** Freshmen are admitted in the fall and spring. Entrance exams should be taken during junior or senior year of high school. There is a rolling admissions plan. Applications should be filed by June 1 for fall entry; December 31 for spring entry. The fall 2017 application fee was $25. Notification is sent on a rolling basis. Applications are accepted on-line. **Transfer Students:** 65 transfer students enrolled in 2016-2017. Transfer applicants must submit a completed application, a pastor's reference, a high school transcript or the GED, and college transcripts. Applicants with less than a year of college credit must also submit ACT or SAT scores and academic references. 27 of 124 credits required for the bachelor's degree must be completed at NCU. **International Students:** They must take the TOEFL, and either the SAT and ACT.

Admissions Contact: Mary Murphy, Registrar/Institutional Reporting. Email: *mlmurphy@northcentral.edu* Web: *www.northcentral.edu*

FINANCIAL AID: In 2017-2018, 99% of all full-time freshmen received some form of financial aid and need-based aid. 100% of undergraduate students work part-time. The FFS and the college's own financial statement are required. The FAFSA code is 002369. Check with the school for current application deadlines.

SAINT JOHN'S UNIVERSITY — B-3

www.csbsju.edu

Collegeville, MN 56321	**(320) 363-5060** **(800) 544-1489**
Fax: (320) 363-3206	**Email: admissions@csbsju.edu**
Full-time: 1703 men	**Faculty:** 132; IIB, +$
Part-time: 17 men	**Ph.D.s:** 92%
Graduate: 54 men, 41 women	**Student/Faculty:** 12 to 1
Year: semesters	**Tuition:** $43,356
Room & Board: $10,116	**Freshman Class:** 1461 applied, 1315 accepted, 465 enrolled
SAT or ACT: required	**CEEB CODE:** 6624
Application Deadline: January 15	**COMPETITIVE**

Saint John's University, and The College of Saint Benedict are nationally-leading liberal arts colleges whose unique partnership offers students the educational choices of a large university and the individual attention of a premier small college. There is 1 undergraduate school and 1 graduate school. In addition to regional accreditation, SJU has baccalaureate program accreditation with ADA, NASM, CAEP, ACS, ATS, and CCNE. The 2500-acre campus is in a rural area 15 miles west of St. Cloud and 75 miles northwest of Minneapolis and St. Paul. Including any residence halls, there are 61 buildings.

STUDENT LIFE: 76% of undergraduates are from Minnesota. Others are from 36 states, and 13 foreign countries. 71% are from public schools. 8% are Hispanic; 78% White; 5% African American; 5% Foreign; 3% Asian American; 1% American Indian/Alaska Native. 51% are Catholic; 30% Protestant; 17% claim no religious affiliation. **Male To Female Ratio:** 43.3:1. The average age of freshmen is 18; all undergraduates, 20. 12% do not continue beyond their first year; 73% remain to graduate. **Housing:** 1529 students can be accommodated in college housing, which includes dorms and on-campus apartments. In addition, there are special-interest houses, Eco houses, and Benedictine Living Community. On-campus housing is guaranteed for the freshman year only, and is available on a first-come, first-served basis, and is available on a lottery system for upperclassmen. 91% of students live on campus. All students may keep cars.

FACULTY/CLASSROOMS: 50% of faculty are male; 50% are female. All teach undergraduates and do research. No introductory courses are taught by graduate students. The average class size in an introductory lecture is 18; in a laboratory is 13; and in a regular course is 19.

PROGRAMS OF STUDY: SJU confers B.A. and B.S.N. degrees. Master's degrees are also awarded. Bachelor's degrees are awarded in AGRICULTURE (environmental studies), BIOLOGICAL SCIENCE (biochemistry, biology/biological science, and nutrition), BUSINESS (accounting and management science), COMMUNICATIONS AND THE ARTS (art, classics, communications, English, French, German, music, and theatre arts), COMPUTER AND PHYSICAL SCIENCE (chemistry, computer science, mathematics, natural sciences, and physics), EDUCATION (elementary education), ENGINEERING AND ENVIRONMENTAL DESIGN (preengineering), HEALTH PROFESSIONS (nursing, predentistry, premedicine, preoptometry, pre-occupational therapy, prepharmacy, pre-physician assistant, prephysical therapy, and preveterinary science), SOCIAL SCIENCE (Asian/Oriental studies, economics, gender studies, Hispanic American studies, history, humanities, peace studies, philosophy, political science/government, prelaw, psychology, social science, and theological studies). Global business leadership, accounting and biology have the largest enrollments.

ACTIVITIES: There are no fraternities or sororities. There are 130 groups on campus, including art, band, choir, chorale, chorus, computers, dance, debate, drama, environmental, ethnic, film, honors, international, jazz band, LGBT, literary magazine, musical theater, newspaper, opera, orchestra, pep band, political, professional, radio and TV, religious, social, social service, student government, and symphony. Popular campus events include Involvement Fair, Festival of Cultures, Family Weekend, Homecoming, weekly Praise in the Pub, Hmong New Year, Asian New Year, Pines Concert and Martin Luther King Jr. Week. **Sports:** There are 12 intercollegiate sports for men, and 13 intramural sports for men. Facilities include an artificial turf football field and stadium with lights, a basketball arena, an artificial turf baseball field, a natural grass soccer field, a seasonal dome with connected indoor golf center, lacrosse and rugby fields, indoor and outdoor tennis courts, indoor and outdoor tracks, a complete fitness center, racquetball courts, swimming pool, climbing wall, wrestling room, training room, an outdoor intramural hockey rink, and students have access to all athletic facilities at the College of Saint Benedict. **Graduates:** From July 1, 2016 to June 30, 2017, 411 bachelor's degrees were awarded. The most popular majors were business management (20%), accounting (12%), and biology (10%). In an average class, 2% graduate in 3 years or less, 66% graduate in 4 years or less, 73% graduate in 5 years or less, and 73% graduate in 6 years or less. Of the 2016 graduating class, 10% were enrolled in graduate school within 6 months of graduation, and 90% were employed.

SERVICES: Counseling and information services are available, as is tutoring in most subjects, such as math, writing, global languages and natural sciences. The College of Saint Benedict and Saint John's University established a Disability Services Office. Accomodations are provided on a case by case basis for enrolled students who provide adequate documentation of a disability. Individual tutoring is available as needed. Academic and psychological counseling are available on an unlimited basis. **Library/Resources:** The library contains 729,515 volumes, 21,482 microform items, 27,968 audio/video tapes/CDs/DVDs, and subscribes to 99,409 periodicals, including electronic. Computerized library services include interlibrary loans, database searching, Internet access, and Wi-Fi capability. Special learning facilities include an art gallery, natural history museum, radio station, TV station, pottery studio, an observatory, greenhouse, herbarium, Sommers digital video studio and the Hill Museum and Manuscript Library, a labyrinth, dance studio and Saint Benedict's Monastery Heritage Museum at the College of Saint Benedict. **Physically Challenged Students:** 90% of the campus is accessible. Facilities include wheelchair ramps, elevators, special parking, specially equipped restrooms, special class scheduling, lowered drinking fountains, and special housing. **Special:** Students may cross-register with St. Cloud State University. There are study-abroad programs in Australia, Austria, Chile, China, France,Germany, Guatemala, Greece, Ireland (Cork and Galway), Italy, India, Japan, London-England, Northern Ireland, South Africa, and Spain. Many short term study abroad opportunities are also offered. Internships, dual and student-designed majors, preprofessional programs, and liberal studies degrees may be pursued. A 3-1 program in dentistry. non-degree study and a pass/fail grading option are also available. There are 6 national honor societies, Phi Beta Kappa, and a freshman honors program. **Visiting:** There are regularly scheduled orientations for prospective students, including programs on admissions, and financial aid as well as campus tours and student panels. There are guides for informal visits, visitors may sit in on classes, and stay overnight. **Campus Safety and Security:** Measures include 24-hour foot and vehicle patrol, emergency notification system, self-defense education, and security escort services. There are shuttle buses, emergency telephones, lighted pathways/sidewalks, and controlled access to dorms/residences.

REQUIREMENTS: The SAT or ACT is required. Students should be graduates of an accredited secondary school. Academic preparation should include 17 units, including 4 of English, 3 of math, 2 each of a lab science and social studies, and 4 electives. A foreign language is recommended. The GED is accepted. Home-schooled applicants are not required to have a high school diploma but are required to provide appropriate documentation of college preparatory curriculum and standardized test scores. St. John's requires applicants to be in the upper 50% of their class. A GPA of 3.0 is required. AP and CLEP credits are accepted. Important factors in the admissions decision are advanced placement or honors courses, extracurricular activities record, and parents or siblings attended your school. To graduate students must complete a first-year seminar and a junior-senior ethics seminar intended as a capstone for the liberal arts experience, and fulfill gender, intercultural, experiential learning, and fine arts requirements. Distribution requirements include 4 credits in fine arts, 2 courses each in humanities and theology, and 1 course each in math, natural science, and social science. All students must prove math and foreign language proficiency. A total of 124 credits must be earned, with a minimum GPA of 2.0. Attendance at 8 fine arts experiences is also required. **Procedure:** Freshmen are admitted in the fall and spring. Entrance exams should be taken during the spring of the junior year or fall of the senior year. There are early admissions and deferred admissions plans. Application deadlines are open. Notifications are sent April 1. Applications are accepted on-line. **Transfer Students:** 18 transfer students enrolled in 2016-2017. Transfer applicants must have a minimum college GPA of 2.75. An essay or personal statement, high school and college transcripts, and a transfer student evaluation form are required. Standardized test scores and an interview may be required of some. 76 of 124 credits required for the bachelor's degree must be completed at SJU. **International Students:** There are 79 international students enrolled. They must take the TOEFL with a minimum score of 550 on the paper-based TOEFL (PBT) or 80 on the Internet-based version (iBT). Students must take the IELTS with minimum score of 6.5. In certain cases, the SAT or ACT may replace TOEFL.

ADMISSIONS: 90% of the 2017-2018 applicants were accepted. The ACT scores were 38% between 18 and 23, 46% between 24 and 29, and 16% above 30. 30% of the current freshmen were in the top fifth of their class; 71% were in the top two fifths. **Admissions Contact:** Dr. Calvin Mosley, Vice President Admission and Financial Aid. Email: *admissions@csbsju.edu* Web: *www.csbsju.edu*

FINANCIAL AID: In 2017-2018, 95% of all full-time freshmen received some form of financial aid. 73% of all full-time freshmen received need-based aid. The average freshman award was $35,367. Need-based scholarships or need-based grants averaged $31,180; need-based self-help aid (loans and jobs) averaged $4,666; and other non-need-based awards and non-need-based scholarships averaged $18,314. 60% of undergraduate students work part-time. The average financial indebtedness of the 2017 graduate was $41,698. SJU is a member of CSS. The FAFSA code is 002379. The priority date for freshman financial aid applications for fall entry is March 15.

SAINT MARY'S UNIVERSITY OF MINNESOTA — D-5

www.smumn.edu

Winona, MN 55987	(507) 457-1700 (800) 635-5987
Fax: (507) 457-1722	**Email:** admission@smumn.edu
Full-time: 553 men, 576 women	**Faculty:** IIA, --$
Part-time: 157 men, 217 women	**Ph.D.s:** 91%
Graduate: 1323 men, 2928 women	**Student/Faculty:** 20 to 1
Year: semesters	**Tuition:** $33,560
Room & Board: $8880	**Freshman Class:** 2417 applied, 1556 accepted, 300 enrolled
SAT EBR-W/M: 545/534 **ACT:** 23	**CEEB CODE:** 6632
Application Deadline: May 1	**COMPETITIVE**

Saint Mary's University of Minnesota, founded in 1912, is a private, Lasallian Catholic, comprehensive institution, guided by the De La Salle Christian Brothers. The Winona campus is the undergraduate college that combines traditional liberal arts and sciences with career preparation in a student-centered environment. The Schools of Graduate and Professional Programs (SGPP) is one of the largest graduate schools in Minnesota offering certificate, bachelor's, master's, and doctoral programs at the university's Twin Cities and Winona campuses, and centers in Rochester, Apple Valley, and Oakdale including courses in Minnesota, Wisconsin, Kenya and Jamaica. There are 4 undergraduate schools and 3 graduate schools. In addition to regional accreditation, SMUM has baccalaureate program accreditation with NASM, IACBE, and JRCNMT. The 350-acre campus is in a small town 110 miles southeast of Twin Cities and 275 miles northwest of Chicago. Including any residence halls, there are 47 buildings.

STUDENT LIFE: 55% of undergraduates are from Minnesota. Others are from 30 states, 15 foreign countries, and Canada. 70% are from public schools. 71% are White; 10% Hispanic; 7% race unknown; 5% Foreign; 4% African American; 2% Asian American; 1% American Indian/Alaska Native; 1% two or more races. 36% are Catholic; 13% Protestant. **Female To Male Ratio:** 1.8:1. The average age of freshmen is 18; all undergraduates, 20. 23% do not continue beyond their first year; 61% remain to graduate. **Housing:** 1046 students can be accommodated in college housing, which includes dorms and on-campus apartments. In addition, there are special-interest houses, living learning communities, first-year residence halls, and substance-free residence halls. On-campus housing is guaranteed for all 4 years. 85% of students live on campus. All students may keep cars.

FACULTY/CLASSROOMS: 61% of faculty are male; 39% are female. No introductory courses are taught by graduate students. The average class size in an introductory lecture is 16; in a laboratory is 14; and in a regular course is 15.

PROGRAMS OF STUDY: SMUM confers B.A. and B.S. degrees. Master's and doctoral degrees are also awarded. Bachelor's degrees are awarded in BIOLOGICAL SCIENCE (biochemistry, biology/biological science, biophysics, environmental biology, and life science secondary school education), BUSINESS (accounting, business administration and management, business intelligence and analytics, entrepreneurial studies, finance, international business, marketing, and sports management), COMMUNICATIONS AND THE ARTS (art, graphic design, journalism, literature, music, music industry, music performance, public relations, Spanish, studio art, and theatre arts), COMPUTER AND PHYSICAL SCIENCE (actuarial science, chemistry, chemistry/adolescence education, computer science, mathematics, and physics), EDUCATION (elementary education, English education, global studies, mathematics education, music education, secondary education, social studies education, and Spanish adolescense education), ENGINEERING AND ENVIRONMENTAL DESIGN (engineering physics and nuclear medicine technology), HEALTH PROFESSIONS (cardiac sonography, cytotechnology, medical laboratory science, and prephysical therapy), SOCIAL SCIENCE (criminal justice, history, human services, pastoral studies, philosophy, political science/government, psychology, social science, sociology, theology, and youth ministry). Biology, biochemistry, and theology are the strongest academically. Marketing, biology, and accounting have the largest enrollments.

ACTIVITIES: 4% of men belong to 2 national fraternities; 3% of women belong to 1 national sorority. There are 85 groups on campus, including art, band, cheerleading, choir, chorale, chorus, dance, drama, environmental, ethnic, honors, international, jazz band, LGBT, literary magazine, musical theater, newspaper, political, professional, radio and TV, religious, social, social service, student government, and yearbook. Popular campus events include Cardinal Days, Taylor Richmond Benefit Dance, and Finals Breakfast. **Sports:** There are 10 intercollegiate sports for men and 11 for women. Facilities include basketball, indoor tennis, and racquetball courts, an indoor ice arena, exercise and weight rooms, baseball, softball, and soccer fields, Nordic ski and running trails, an indoor track, an indoor swimming pool, a dance studio, a Frisbee disc course, an outdoor track, and a high ropes course. **Graduates:** From July 1, 2016 to June 30, 2017, 235 bachelor's degrees were awarded. The most popular majors were business/marketing (36%), health professions (17%), and law enforcement and homeland security (8%). In an average class, 2% graduate in 3 years or less, 51% graduate in 4 years or less, 60% graduate in 5 years or less, and 61% graduate in 6 years or less.

SERVICES: Counseling and information services are available, as is tutoring in most subjects. There is a reader service for the blind, and remedial math, reading, and writing. **Library/Resources:** The library contains 209,807 volumes, 200,692 microform items, 9,789 audio/video tapes/CDs/DVDs, and subscribes to 40,015 periodicals including electronic. Computerized library services include interlibrary loans, database searching, Internet access, and Wi-Fi capability. Special learning facilities include an art gallery, a radio station, and an observatory. **Physically Challenged Students:** 93% of the campus is accessible. Facilities include wheelchair ramps, elevators, special parking, specially equipped restrooms, lowered drinking fountains, lowered telephones, and special housing. **Special:** Students may cross-register with Winona State University. Internships, co-op programs, student teaching and study abroad, work-study programs, and a Washington semester are available. The university also offers dual and student-designed majors, non-degree study, pass/fail options, credit for life, military, and work experience, and an honors program that also serves as an alternative general education program. There are 14 national honor societies and 13 departmental honors programs. **Visiting:** There are regularly scheduled orientations for prospective students, including an interview, a tour, and class visits. Visitors may sit in on classes, and stay overnight. To schedule a visit, contact the Office of Admissions. **Campus Safety and Security:** Measures include 24-hour foot and vehicle patrol, emergency notification system, and security escort services. There are emergency telephones, lighted pathways/sidewalks, and controlled access to dorms/residences.

REQUIREMENTS: The SAT or ACT is required. Candidates for admission should have completed 4 units of English, 3 each of math and natural science, 2 of social studies, and 6 academic electives. Completion of 2 units of foreign language is also recommended. AP and CLEP credits are accepted. Important factors in the admissions decision are advanced placement or honors courses, leadership record, and extracurricular activities record. Students must have a 2.0 cumulative major GPA and complete a minimum of 122 semester credits, including at least 45 at the upper-division level. Students must complete a major program and the general education program. **Procedure:** Freshmen are admitted in the fall and spring. Entrance exams should be taken by the fall of the senior year. There are early admissions, deferred admissions, and rolling admissions plans. Applications should be filed by May 1 for fall entry; December 1 for spring entry. The fall 2017 application fee was $25. Notification is sent on a rolling basis. Applications are accepted on-line. **Transfer Students:** 131 transfer students enrolled in 2016-2017. Applicants must have a 2.0 GPA with at least 12 credits. 60 of 122 credits required for the bachelor's degree must be completed at SMUM. **International Students:** There are 51 international students enrolled. They must take the TOEFL with a minimum score of 550 on the paper-based TOEFL (PBT) or 79 on the Internet-based version (iBT).

ADMISSIONS: 64% of the 2017-2018 applicants were accepted. The SAT scores for the 2017-2018 freshman class were: Math-- 32% below 500, 40% between 500 and 599, and 28% between 600 and 699. Evidence-Based Reading/Writing-- 24% below 500, 48% between 500 and 599, and 28% between 600 and 699. The ACT scores were 10% between 12 and 17, 47% between 18 and 23, 36% between 24 and 29, and 8% above 30. **Admissions Contact:** Dan Meyer, Vice President for Enrollment. Email: *admission@smumn.edu* Web: *www.smumn.edu*

FINANCIAL AID: In 2017-2018, 99% of all full-time freshmen received some form of financial aid. 73% of all full-time freshmen received need-based aid. The average financial indebtedness of the 2017 graduate was $39,196. The college's own financial statement is required. The FAFSA code is 002380. The priority date for freshman financial aid applications for fall entry is March 15.

SOUTHWEST MINNESOTA STATE UNIVERSITY — B-4

www.smsu.edu

Marshall, MN 56258	**(507) 537-6286** **(800) 642-0684**
Fax: (507) 537-7154	**Email: admissions@smsu.edu**
Full-time: 1075 men, 1250 women	**Faculty:** n/av
Part-time: 150 men, 235 women	**Ph.D.s:** 76%
Graduate: 155 men, 370 women	**Student/Faculty:** n/av
Year: semesters, summer session	**Tuition:** $8773 ($18,557)
Room & Board: $9010	**Freshman Class:** n/av
SAT: recommended **ACT:** required	**CEEB CODE:** 6703
Application Deadline: August 1	**COMPETITIVE**

Southwest Minnesota State University, founded in 1963, is a public institution offering programs in liberal arts, technology, and preprofessional training. There are 4 undergraduate schools. In addition to regional accreditation, SWMSU has baccalaureate program accreditation with CSWE and ACS. The 216-acre campus is in a rural area 150 miles southwest of Minneapolis. Including any residence halls, there are 24 buildings.

STUDENT LIFE: 75% of undergraduates are from Minnesota. Others are from 29 states, 33 foreign countries, and Canada. 95% are from public schools. 85% are White; 7% Foreign; 4% African American; 2% Asian American; 1% American Indian/Alaska Native; 1% Hispanic. **Female To Male Ratio:** 1.3:1. The average age of freshmen is 19; all undergraduates, 22. 25% do not continue beyond their first year; 35% remain to graduate. **Housing:** 1182 students can be accommodated in college housing, which includes dorms and on-campus apartments. In addition, there are special-interest houses, a quiet house, and a weekend programming house. On-campus housing is guaranteed for the freshman year only. Alcohol is not permitted. All students may keep cars.

FACULTY/CLASSROOMS: 56% of faculty are male; 44% are female. All teach undergraduates. No introductory courses are taught by graduate students. The average class size in an introductory lecture is 26; in a laboratory is 19; and in a regular course is 21.

PROGRAMS OF STUDY: SWMSU confers B.A., B.S., and B.A.S. degrees. Associate and master's degrees are also awarded. Bachelor's degrees are awarded in AGRICULTURE (agricultural business management), BIOLOGICAL SCIENCE (biology/biological science), BUSINESS (accounting, business administration and management, hotel/motel and restaurant management, and marketing/retailing/merchandising), COMMUNICATIONS AND THE ARTS (art, communications, creative writing, dramatic arts, literature, music, and Spanish), COMPUTER AND PHYSICAL SCIENCE (applied science, chemistry, computer science, and mathematics), EDUCATION (art education, early childhood education, elementary education, foreign languages education, health education, mathematics education, music education, physical education, and science education), ENGINEERING AND ENVIRONMENTAL DESIGN (environmental science), HEALTH PROFESSIONS (dental laboratory technology and medical technology), SOCIAL SCIENCE (history, interdisciplinary studies, law enforcement and corrections, political science/government, psychology, public administration, social work, and sociology). Education, business administration, and psychology have the largest enrollments.

ACTIVITIES: There are no fraternities or sororities. There are 100 groups on campus, including art, band, cheerleading, chess, choir, chorus, computers, dance, debate, drama, ethnic, forensics, honors, international, jazz band, literary magazine, marching band, musical theater, newspaper, orchestra, pep band, political, professional, radio and TV, religious, social, social service, student government, and symphony. Popular campus events include Martin Luther King Celebration, Cinco de Mayo, and Dakota Indigenous Nations Studies Conference. **Sports:** There are 5 intercollegiate sports for men and 6 for women, and 14 intramural sports for men and 13 for women. Facilities include a gym, a baseball complex, softball facilities, racquetball courts, a football stadium, wrestling rooms, a weight room, an Olympic-size pool, a mulitipurpose facility, a soccer field, and a fitness center.

SERVICES: Counseling and information services are available, as is tutoring in most subjects. There is a reader service for the blind, and remedial math, reading, and writing. **Library/Resources:** The library contains 168,000 volumes, 228,000 microform items, 12,000 audio/video tapes/CDs/DVDs, and subscribes to 950 periodicals, including electronic. Computerized library services include interlibrary loans, database searching, Internet access, and Wi-Fi capability. Special learning facilities include an art gallery, natural history museum, planetarium, radio station, and TV station. **Physically Challenged Students:** 98% of the campus is accessible. Facilities include wheelchair ramps, elevators, special parking, specially equipped restrooms, special class scheduling, lowered drinking fountains, lowered telephones, and special housing. **Special:** SWMSU has cooperative programs with various local colleges, cross-registration with several state universities, and an accelerated degree. SWMSU also offers internships in every discipline, work-study programs, student-designed and interdisciplinary majors including speech communication and theater arts, nondegree study, pass/fail options, and credit for life, military, and work experience. There are 2 national honor societies and a freshman honors program. **Visiting:** There are regularly scheduled orientations for prospective students. There are guides for informal visits; visitors may sit in on classes and stay overnight. To schedule a visit, contact the Admissions Office. **Campus Safety and Security:** Measures include 24-hour foot and vehicle patrol, self-defense education, and security escort services. There are emergency telephones and lighted pathways/sidewalks.

REQUIREMENTS: The SAT is recommended. The ACT is preferred. Admission is based on class rank or ACT/SAT composite. Students should be graduates of an accredited secondary school or have a GED certificate. An interview is recommended. SMSU requires applicants to be in the upper 50% of their class. AP and CLEP credits are accepted. Important factors in the admissions decision are recommendations by school officials, leadership record, and personality/intangible qualities. To graduate, students must complete at least 128 semester credit hours, a minimum of 27 of which must be at the 300 or 400 level, and a liberal arts core curriculum, with a minimum GPA of 2.0. **Procedure:** Freshmen are admitted to all sessions. Entrance exams should be taken during the junior or senior year. There are deferred admissions and rolling admissions plans. Applications should be filed by August 1 for fall entry; January 1 for spring entry. The fall 2017 application fee was $20. Notification is sent on a rolling basis. Applications are accepted on-line. **Transfer Students:** Applicants need a minimum GPA of 2.0 in previous college-level work at an accredited institution. High school transcripts are required if students are transferring with fewer than 24 semester credits. 48 of 128 credits required for the bachelor's degree must be completed at SWMSU. **International Students:** They must take the TOEFL.

Admissions Contact: Richard Shearer, Director of Enrollment. Email: *admissions@smsu.edu* Web: *www.smsu.edu*

FINANCIAL AID: The college's own financial statement is required. The FAFSA code is 002375. Check with the school for current application deadlines.

ST. CATHERINE UNIVERSITY — C-4

www.stkate.edu

St. Paul, MN 55105	(651) 690-8850
Fax: (651) 690-8824	**Email:** admissions@stkate.edu
Full-time: 20 men, 2168 women	**Faculty:** 292
Part-time: 103 men, 1268 women	**Ph.D.s:** 55%
Graduate: 150 men, 1308 women	**Student/Faculty:** 12 to 1
Year: 4-1-4, summer session	**Tuition:** $37,628
Room & Board: $8002	**Freshman Class:** 2375 applied, 1473 accepted, 682 enrolled
SAT CR/M: 560/525 **ACT:** 24	**CEEB CODE:** 6105
Application Deadline: open	**COMPETITIVE**

St. Catherine prepares students to make a difference in their professions, their communities and the world. SCU is the largest, most innovative college for women in the nation, offering a range of graduate and associate programs. The figures given in the above capsule and in this profile are approximate. There are 4 undergraduate schools and 1 graduate school. In addition to regional accreditation, SCU has baccalaureate program accreditation with ADA, APTA, CSWE, NASM, NLN, and NAACLS. The 110-acre campus is in an urban area 6 miles southwest of downtown St. Paul, MN. Including any residence halls, there are 22 buildings.

STUDENT LIFE: 89% of undergraduates are from Minnesota. Others are from 30 states, 34 foreign countries, and Canada. 86% are from public schools. 68% are White; 3% Hispanic; 11% African American; 10% Asian American; 1% American Indian/Alaska Native; 1% Foreign. 50% are Catholic; 20% Protestant. **Female To Male Ratio:** 17.4:1. The average age of freshmen is 18; all undergraduates, 22. 16% do not continue beyond their first year; 67% remain to graduate. **Housing:** 900 students can be accommodated in college housing, which includes dorms, on-campus apartments, theme housing, and apartments for student-parents. On-campus housing is available on a first-come, first-served basis, and is available on a lottery system for upperclassmen. 56% of students commute. All students may keep cars.

FACULTY/CLASSROOMS: 21% of faculty are male; 79% are female. All teach undergraduates. No introductory courses are taught by graduate students. The average class size in an introductory lecture is 19; in a laboratory is 14; and in a regular course is 13.

PROGRAMS OF STUDY: SCU confers B.A. and B.S. degrees. Associate, master's, and doctoral degrees are also awarded. Bachelor's degrees are awarded in BIOLOGICAL SCIENCE (biochemistry, biology/biological science, and nutrition), BUSINESS (accounting, business administration and management, fashion merchandising, international business management, international economics, management information systems, and marketing/retailing/merchandising), COMMUNICATIONS AND THE ARTS (American Sign Language, art, classics, communications, dramatic arts, English, fine arts, French, Latin, media arts, music, musical theater, Spanish, and speech/debate/rhetoric), COMPUTER AND PHYSICAL SCIENCE (chemistry, information sciences and systems, and mathematics), EDUCATION (art education, early childhood education, elementary education, home economics education, music education, physical education, and secondary education), ENGINEERING AND ENVIRONMENTAL DESIGN (food services technology), HEALTH PROFESSIONS (exercise science, health care administration, medical records administration/services, nursing, occupational therapy, rehabilitation therapy, and respiratory therapy), SOCIAL SCIENCE (dietetics, economics, ethnic studies, family/consumer studies, fashion design and technology, history, international relations, interpreter for the deaf, philosophy, political science/government, psychology, social studies, social work, sociology, theological studies, and women's studies). Biology, chemistry, and psychology are the strongest academically. Nursing, social work, and accounting have the largest enrollments.

ACTIVITIES: There are no fraternities or sororities. There are 42 groups on campus, including art, band, cheerleading, choir, chorale, chorus, dance, drama, ethnic, honors, international, LGBT, literary magazine, musical theater, newspaper, photography, political, professional, radio and TV, religious, social, social service, and student government. Popular campus events include Winter Charity Ball, Dew Drop Bop, and Kat-Walk Fashion Show. **Sports:** There are 11 intercollegiate sports for women, and 8 intramural sports for women. Facilities include a fitness facility, a gym, a weight room, a swimming pool, an outdoor fitness course, tennis courts, a soccer field, and a softball field. **Graduates:** From July 1, 2016 to June 30, 2017, 534 bachelor's degrees were awarded. The most popular majors were health professions and related programs (32%), business/marketing (14%), and public administration and social service/education (7%). In an average class, 45% graduate in 4 years or less, 63% graduate in 5 years or less, and 67% graduate in 6 years or less. Of the 2016 graduating class, 22% were enrolled in graduate school within 6 months of graduation, and 84% were employed.

SERVICES: Counseling and information services are available, as is tutoring in most subjects. There is a reader service for the blind, and remedial math, reading, and writing. **Library/Resources:** The library contains 250,865 volumes, 180,946 microform items, 7,844 audio/video tapes/CDs/DVDs, and subscribes to 2,763 periodicals including electronic. Computerized library services include interlibrary loans, database searching, Internet access, and Wi-Fi capability. Special learning facilities include an art gallery, radio station, an observatory, and an anatomy lab. **Physically Challenged Students:** 90% of the campus is accessible. Facilities include wheelchair ramps, elevators, special parking, specially equipped restrooms, special class scheduling, lowered drinking fountains, and lowered telephones. **Special:** SCU offers co-op programs with Carondolet College, the University of Minnesota, and George Washington University, and cross-registration with the Associated Colleges of the Twin Cities and other colleges sponsored by the Sisters of St. Joseph. Students may arrange internships, a Washington semester, and study abroad. Dual majors are available in the sciences and engineering programs. Students may receive credit for life, military, or work experience. Student-designed majors, non-degree study, and pass/fail options are also available. The Weekend College offers a B.A. degree. There are 24 national honor societies, Phi Beta Kappa, and a freshman honors program. **Visiting:** There are regularly scheduled orientations for prospective students, including a tour, an admissions interview, and an appointment with a faculty member. There are guides for informal visits; visitors may sit in on classes and stay overnight. To schedule a visit, contact the Admissions Office. **Campus Safety and Security:** Measures include 24-hour foot and vehicle patrol, emergency notification system, self-defense education, and security escort services. There are emergency telephones, lighted pathways/sidewalks, and controlled access to dorms/residences.

REQUIREMENTS: The SAT or ACT is required. Applicants must have completed a college preparatory program including 4 courses in English, 3 in math, and 2 each in a foreign language, science, and social studies. SCU requires applicants to be in the upper 50% of their class. A GPA of 2.5 is required. AP and CLEP credits are accepted. Important factors in the admissions decision are advanced placement or honors courses, recommendations by school officials, and extracurricular activities record. To graduate, students must complete 130 semester credits, including a liberal arts core with courses in history, foreign language, philosophy, math, fine arts, literature, and theology, and 80 credits outside the major. Required courses are the Reflective Woman and the Global Search for Justice. At least 36 hours are required in the major. Students must have a minimum 2.0 GPA and demonstrate proficiency in composition, math, and computer literacy. **Procedure:** Freshmen are admitted in the fall and winter. Entrance exams should be taken during the senior year. There are deferred admissions and rolling admissions plans. Application deadlines are open. Notification is sent on a open basis. Applications are accepted on-line. **Transfer Students:** 354 transfer students enrolled in 2016-2017. Transfer applicants must submit high school and college transcripts. 48 of 130 credits required for the bachelor's degree must be completed at SCU. **International Students:** There are 48 international students enrolled. They must take the TOEFL with a minimum score of 500 on the paper-based TOEFL (PBT) or 61 on the Internet-based version (iBT) or take the MELAB and the college's own test. The SAT is required only if the student attended a U.S. high school.

ADMISSIONS: 62% of the 2017-2018 applicants were accepted. The SAT scores for the 2017-2018 freshman class were: Critical Reading-- 27% below 500, 39% between 500 and 599, 17% between 600 and 699, and 17% between 700 and 800. Math-- 27% below 500, 56% between 500 and 599, and 17% between 600 and 699. The ACT scores were 1% below 12, 48% between 18 and 23, 44% between 24 and 29, and 7% above 30. 53% of the current freshmen were in the top fifth of their class; 85% were in the top two fifths. 11 freshmen graduated first in their class. **Admissions Contact:** Marlene Mohs, Associate Dean of Admissions. Email: *admissions@stkate.edu* Web: *www.stkate.edu*

FINANCIAL AID: In 2017-2018, 99% of all full-time freshmen received some form of financial aid. 63% of all full-time freshmen received need-based aid. The average freshman award was $30,592. Need-based scholarships or need-based grants averaged $10,581; need-based self-help aid (loans and jobs) averaged $5,504; other non-need-based awards and non-need-based scholarships averaged $11,278; and $5,215 from other forms of aid. 100% of undergraduate students work part-time. The average financial indebtedness of the 2017 graduate was $39,607. SCU is a member of CSS. The college's own financial statement is required. The FAFSA code is 002342. The priority date for freshman financial aid applications for fall entry is April 15.

ST. CLOUD STATE UNIVERSITY C-3

www.stcloudstate.edu

St. Cloud, MN 56301 **(320) 308-2244** **(800) 369-4260**

Fax: (320) 308-2243 **Email: scsu4u@stcloudstate.edu**

Full-time: 5400 men, 6250 women	**Faculty:** n/av
Part-time: 1190 men, 1685 women	**Ph.D.s:** n/av
Graduate: 555 men, 925 women	**Student/Faculty:** n/av
Year: semesters, summer session	**Tuition:** $6100 ($12,700)
Room & Board: $4500	**Freshman Class:** n/av
ACT: required	**CEEB CODE:** 6679
Application Deadline: n/av	**COMPETITIVE**

St. Cloud State University, founded in 1869, is a comprehensive university offering programs that include the liberal arts and career preparation with emphasis on diversity, hands-on learning, and service to the community. There are 6 undergraduate schools and 1 graduate school. In addition to regional accreditation, SCSU has baccalaureate program accreditation with AACSB, ABET, ACEJMC, ASLA, CSWE, NASAD, and NASM. The 100-acre campus is in a suburban area 60 miles northwest of Minneapolis. Including any residence halls, there are 50 buildings.

STUDENT LIFE: 92% of undergraduates are from Minnesota. Others are from 50 states, 85 foreign countries, and Canada. 77% are White; 5% Foreign; 2% African American; 2% Asian American; 1% American Indian/Alaska Native; 1% Hispanic. **Female To Male Ratio:** 1.2:1. The average age of freshmen is 19; all undergraduates, 22. 29% do not continue beyond their first year. **Housing:** 3000 students can be accommodated in college housing, which includes dorms, and special housing for international students. 82% of students commute. All students may keep cars. Alcohol is not permitted.

FACULTY/CLASSROOMS: 56% of faculty are male; 44% are female. All teach undergraduates. No introductory courses are taught by graduate students.

PROGRAMS OF STUDY: SCSU confers B.A., B.S., B.E.S., B.F.A., and B.Mus. degrees. Associate, master's, and doctoral degrees are also awarded. Bachelor's degrees are awarded in BIOLOGICAL SCIENCE (biology/biological science), BUSINESS (accounting, banking and finance, business administration and management, business economics, international business management, marketing/retailing/merchandising, and personnel management), COMMUNICATIONS AND THE ARTS (advertising, broadcasting, communications, dramatic arts, English, fine arts, journalism, languages, music, and speech/debate/rhetoric), COMPUTER AND PHYSICAL SCIENCE (atmospheric sciences and meteorology, chemistry, computer science, earth science, geology, mathematics, physics, and statistics), EDUCATION (art education, early childhood education, elementary education, foreign languages education, guidance education, health education, industrial arts education, music education, science education, and secondary education), ENGINEERING AND ENVIRONMENTAL DESIGN (aviation administration/management, electrical/electronics engineering, engineering technology, and manufacturing engineering), HEALTH PROFESSIONS (predentistry, premedicine, public health, and speech pathology/audiology), SOCIAL SCIENCE (anthropology, criminal justice, economics, geography, history, international relations, philosophy, political science/government, prelaw, psychology, public administration, social science, social work, sociology, and urban studies). Mass communication, elementary education, and special education have the largest enrollments.

ACTIVITIES: There are 240 groups on campus, including art, band, cheerleading, chess, choir, chorale, chorus, computers, dance, drama, ethnic, film, honors, international, jazz band, LGBT, literary magazine, marching band, musical theater, opera, orchestra, pep band, photography, political, professional, radio and TV, religious, social, social service, sports, student government, symphony, and yearbook. Popular campus events include Music Festival, Ethnic Awareness Week, and major speakers and workshops.

SERVICES: Counseling and information services are available, as is tutoring in every subject. There is a reader service for the blind, and remedial math, reading, and writing. **Library/Resources:** The library contains 887,462 volumes, 1.8 million microform items, 24,244 audio/video tapes/CDs/DVDs, and subscribes to 1,762 periodicals including electronic. Computerized library services include interlibrary loans, database searching, Internet access, and Wi-Fi capability. Special learning facilities include an art gallery, natural history museum, planetarium, radio station, and TV station. **Physically Challenged Students:** 86% of the campus is accessible. Facilities include wheelchair ramps, elevators, special parking, specially equipped restrooms, special class scheduling, lowered drinking fountains, and lowered telephones. **Special:** The university offers cross-registration, internships in almost all majors, work-study programs, and study abroad in 25 countries. Students may take dual majors, design their own majors for a Bachelor of Elective Studies degree, and earn a general degree or a B.A.-B.S. degree in all majors, including meteorology and photographic technology. The university gives credit for military experience and allows nondegree study and pass/fail options. There are 4 national honor societies and a freshman honors program. **Visiting:** There are regularly scheduled orientations for prospective students. There are guides for informal visits and visitors may sit in on classes. To schedule a visit, contact the Admissions Office. **Campus Safety and Security:** Measures include 24-hour foot and vehicle patrol and security escort services. There are shuttle buses, emergency telephones, lighted pathways/sidewalks, and a safety course.

REQUIREMENTS: The ACT is required. SCSU requires applicants to be in the upper 50% of their class. AP and CLEP credits are accepted. Students must complete a minimum of 120 semester credit hours, including 40 hours of general education requirements and 60 to 180 hours in the major, and maintain at least a 2.0 GPA (higher for many majors). Students must complete English 191, English 192, Speech 192, 2 credits in phys ed, and 24 credits in philosophy, humanities, fine arts, natural science and math, social and behavioral science, and diversity courses. **Procedure:** Freshmen are admitted in the fall, spring, and summer. Entrance exams should be taken in the junior or senior year. Application deadlines are open. The fall 2017 application fee was $20. Notification is sent on a rolling basis. **Transfer Students:** Applicants must have a minimum 2.0 GPA from their previous college if they transfer with 12 or more credits. If they have fewer than 12 credits, they are treated as entering freshmen. 30 of 120 credits required for the bachelor's degree must be completed at SCSU. **International Students:** They must take the TOEFL.

Admissions Contact: Pat Krueger, Associate Director of Admissions. Email: *scsu4u@stcloudstate.edu* Web: *www.stcloudstate.edu*

FINANCIAL AID: The college's own financial statement is required. The FAFSA code is 002377. Check with the school for current application deadlines.

ST. OLAF COLLEGE — C-4

www.stolaf.edu

Northfield, MN 55057 — (507) 786-3025, (800) 800-3025

Fax: (507) 786-3832	**Email:** admissions@stolaf.edu
Full-time: 1264 men, 1739 women	**Faculty:** 209; IIB, ++$
Part-time: 22 men, 10 women	**Ph.D.s:** 76%
Graduate: n/av	**Student/Faculty:** 12 to 1
Year: 4-1-4, summer session	**Tuition:** $46,000
Room & Board: $10,430	**Freshman Class:** 5949 applied, 2571 accepted, 786 enrolled
SAT CR/M: 640/640 **ACT:** 29	**CEEB CODE:** 6638
Application Deadline: January 15	**HIGHLY COMPETITIVE**

St. Olaf College, is one of the nation's leading liberal arts colleges offering a distinctive education grounded in academic rigor, residential learning, global engagement, and a vibrant Lutheran faith tradition. St. Olaf provides an uncommon educational experience that fully prepares students to make a meaningful difference in our changing world. There is 1 undergraduate school. In addition to regional accreditation, St. Olaf has baccalaureate program accreditation with CSWE, NASAD, NASM, CCNE, NASD, and NAST. The 300-acre campus is in a small town 35 miles south of Minneapolis/St. Paul. Including any residence halls, there are 55 buildings.

STUDENT LIFE: 55% of undergraduates are from out of state, mostly the Midwest. Students are from 49 states, 77 foreign countries, and Canada. 71% are White; 7% Asian American; 6% Hispanic; 3% two or more races; 2% African American; 10% Foreign. 43% are Protestant; 22% claim no religious affiliation; 17% Christian, and Unkown religion; 15% Catholic. **Female To Male Ratio:** 1.4:1. The average age of freshmen is 18; all undergraduates, 20. 8% do not continue beyond their first year; 88% remain to graduate. **Housing:** 2970 students can be accommodated in college housing, which includes dorms. In addition, there are honors houses, language/international houses, and special-interest houses. On-campus housing is guaranteed for all 4 years. 94% of students live on campus. Some may keep cars. Alcohol is not permitted.

FACULTY/CLASSROOMS: 51% of faculty are male; 49% are female. All teach undergraduates and do research. No introductory courses are taught by graduate students. The average class size in an introductory lecture is 24; in a laboratory is 18; and in a regular course is 22.

PROGRAMS OF STUDY: St. Olaf confers B.A. and B.Mus. degrees. Bachelor's degrees are awarded in AGRICULTURE (environmental studies), BIOLOGICAL SCIENCE (biology/biological science), COMMUNICATIONS AND THE ARTS (art history and appreciation, classics, dance, English, French, German, Greek, Latin, music, music performance, music theory and composition, Norwegian, Russian, Spanish, studio art, and theatre arts), COMPUTER AND PHYSICAL SCIENCE (chemistry, computer science, mathematics, and physics), EDUCATION (music education and social studies education), HEALTH PROFESSIONS (exercise science and nursing), SOCIAL SCIENCE (American studies, Asian/American studies, classical/ancient civilization, economics, ethnic studies, Hispanic American studies, history, interdisciplinary studies, medieval studies, philosophy, political science/government, psychology, religion, religious music, Russian and Slavic studies, social work, sociology, and women's studies). Biology, economics, and mathematics have the largest enrollments.

ACTIVITIES: There are no fraternities or sororities. There are 214 groups on campus, including art, band, chess, choir, chorus, communications, computers, dance, drama, drill team, environmental, ethnic, film, honors, international, jazz band, LGBT, literary magazine, musical theater, newspaper, opera, orchestra, pep band, photography, political, professional, radio and TV, religious, social, social service, student government, and symphony. Popular campus events include Christmas Festival and President's Ball. **Sports:** There are 22 intercollegiate sports for men and 19 for women, and 36 intramural sports for men and 34 for women. Facilities include weight-training and exercise machines, Nordic and alpine skiing, a 48-foot rock climbing wall, batting cages, an elevated running track, volleyball, basketball, and tennis courts. The gymnasium features basketball and volleyball facilities, a competition pool, and a field house with indoor tennis courts, racquetball courts, a wrestling room, and an indoor running track. Outdoor facilities include an eight-lane all weather track, tennis courts, and fields for football, baseball, softball, soccer, a sand volleyball court, a broomball rink, and disc golf courses. **Graduates:** From July 1, 2016 to June 30, 2017, 681 bachelor's degrees were awarded. The most popular majors were biology (10%), economics (9%), and psychology (7%). In an average class, 85% graduate in 4 years or less, 88% graduate in 5 years or less, and 88% graduate in 6 years or less.

SERVICES: Counseling and information services are available, as is tutoring in every subject, and a reader service for the blind, and study sessions. **Library/Resources:** The library contains 610,051 volumes, 12,285 microform items, and 29,020 audio/video tapes/CDs/DVDs, and subscribes to 119,677 periodicals including electronic. Computerized library services include interlibrary loans, database searching, Internet access, and Wi-Fi capability. Special learning facilities include an art gallery, radio station, 700 acres of land dedicated to natural habitat, sustainable agriculture, and conventional agriculture. **Physically Challenged Students:** 80% of the campus is accessible. Facilities include wheelchair ramps, elevators, special parking, specially equipped restrooms, special class scheduling, lowered drinking fountains, lowered telephones, special housing, electric door openers, curb cuts, and a sling for swimming pool entry. **Special:** St. Olaf offers cross-registration with Carleton College, study abroad in more than 50 countries, 20 domestic off-campus programs, pre-professional programs, internships, and a 3-2 B.A.-B.S.E. degree in engineering with Washington University in St. Louis or the University of Minnesota. There are dual majors, non-degree study, on-campus work study, and pass/fail options. The Center for Integrative Studies allows students to design individual majors with an emphasis on tutorials and seminars. St. Olaf's Conversation programs, focusing on the great books, American studies, Asian studies, environmental studies, scientific inquiry, and public affairs, foster intimate learning communities that engage students in interdisciplinary study, critical thinking, and thoughtful discussion of major issues that transcend disciplinary borders and historical, cultural, and social contexts. There are 22 national honor societies and a chapter of Phi Beta Kappa. **Visiting:** There are regularly scheduled orientations for prospective students, including tours, class visits, information sessions, and interviews. There are guides for informal visits; visitors may sit in on classes and stay overnight. To schedule a visit, contact Abigail DeGezelle at (800) 800-3025. **Campus Safety and Security:** Measures include 24-hour foot and vehicle patrol, emergency notification system, self-defense education, and security escort services. There are emergency telephones, lighted pathways/sidewalks, and controlled access to dorms/residences.

REQUIREMENTS: The SAT or ACT is required. It is recommended that applicants complete 4 years each of English, math, social studies/history, science (with 2 labs), and foreign language. AP credits are accepted. In addition to the distribution requirements, students are required to demonstrate skills at an intermediate level in a foreign language and proficiency in English composition, and to complete the phys ed requirement and to have taken a 1/4-credit oral communication course and a 1-credit mathematical reasoning course. A first-year writing course is also required. Distribution requirements include courses in history, literature, art, science, human behavior, Bible and theology, multicultural studies, and ethical issues. A minimum of 24 full-course credits out of 35 must be graded, and 18 must be upper-division. A minimum of 8 full-credit courses in a disciplinary or interdisciplinary major are required. All majors include writing requirements. Students must complete 35 credits and maintain a minimum GPA of 2.0. **Procedure:** Freshmen are admitted in the fall, winter, and spring. Entrance exams should be taken in the spring of the junior year or the fall of the senior year. There are early decision and deferred admissions plans. Early decision applications should be filed by November 15; regular applications, by January 15 for fall entry. Notification of early decision is sent December 15; regular decision, March 15. 223 early decision candidates were accepted for the 2017-2018 class. 784 applicants were on the 2017 waiting list; 20 were admitted. Applications are accepted on-line. **Transfer Students:** 25 transfer students enrolled in 2016-2017. 17 of 35 credits required for the bachelor's degree must be completed at St. Olaf. **International Students:** There are 294 international students enrolled. They must take the TOEFL with a minimum score of 90 on the Internet-based version (iBT). Students must take the IELTS, and either the SAT or ACT.

ADMISSIONS: 43% of the 2017-2018 applicants were accepted. The SAT scores for the 2017-2018 freshman class were: Critical Reading-- 6% below 500, 24% between 500 and 599, 46% between 600 and 699, and 24% between 700 and 800. Math-- 7% below 500, 29% between 500 and 599, 33% between 600 and 699, and 31% between 700 and 800. The ACT scores were 13% between 18 and 23, 43% between 24 and 29, and 44% above 30. 68% of the current freshmen were in the top fifth of their class; 91% were in the top two fifths. 36 freshmen graduated first in their class. **Admissions Contact:** David Wagner, Director of Admissions. Email: *admissions@stolaf.edu* Web: *www.stolaf.edu*

FINANCIAL AID: In 2017-2018, 97% of all full-time freshmen received some form of financial aid. 80% of all full-time freshmen received need-based aid. The average freshman award was $38,733. Need-based scholarships or need-based grants averaged $32,991 ($54,260 maximum); need-based self-help aid (loans and jobs) averaged $4,503 ($5,800 maximum); and other non-need-based awards and non-need-based scholarships averaged $15,496 ($27,130 maximum). 70% of undergraduate students work part-time. The average financial indebtedness of the 2017 graduate was $29,228. St. Olaf is a member of CSS. The CSS/Profile is required. The FAFSA code is 002382. The deadline for filing freshman financial aid applications for fall entry is January 15.

UNIVERSITY OF MINNESOTA/ CROOKSTON — A-2

www.umcrookston.edu

Crookston, MN 56716	(218) 281-8569 (800) 232-6466
Fax: (218) 281-8575	**Email:** umcinfo@umn.edu
Full-time: 598 men, 545 women	**Faculty:** 71; IIB, -$
Part-time: 316 men, 362 women	**Ph.D.s:** 40%
Graduate: n/av	**Student/Faculty:** 16 to 1
Year: semesters, summer session	**Tuition:** $11,646
Room & Board: $7480	**Freshman Class:** 1288 applied, 878 accepted, 209 enrolled
ACT: 22	**CEEB CODE:** 6893
Application Deadline: August 15	**COMPETITIVE**

University of Minnesota/Crookston, founded in 1965, is a public institution offering applied bachelor degree programs, including on-line opportunities, in agriculture, arts, humanities, and social sciences, business, math, science, technology and natural resourses. There are 4 undergraduate schools. The 108-acre campus is in a small town 290 miles northwest of Minneapolis, and 25 miles southeast of Grand Forks, North Dakota. Including any residence halls, there are 35 buildings.

STUDENT LIFE: 71% of undergraduates are from Minnesota. Others are from 42 states, 16 foreign countries, and Canada. 77% are White; 6% African American; 5% Foreign; 4% Hispanic; 3% Asian American; 3% race unknown; 2% two or more races; 1% American Indian/Alaska Native. **Male To Female Ratio:** 1.0:1. The average age of freshmen is 19; all undergraduates, 26. 27% do not continue beyond their first year; 51% remain to graduate. **Housing:** 563 students can be accommodated in college housing, which includes dorms and on-campus apartments. On-campus housing is available on a first-come, first-served basis. 75% of students live on campus. All students may keep cars. Alcohol is not permitted.

FACULTY/CLASSROOMS: 55% of faculty are male; 45% are female. All teach undergraduates, 40% do research, and 40% do both. No introductory courses are taught by graduate students. The average class size in an introductory lecture is 25; in a laboratory is 18; and in a regular course is 25.

PROGRAMS OF STUDY: UMC confers B.S., B.A.H., and B.M.M. degrees. Bachelor's degrees are awarded in AGRICULTURE (agricultural business management, agronomy, animal science, equine science, horticulture, and natural resource management), BIOLOGICAL SCIENCE (biology/biological science), BUSINESS (accounting, business administration and management, marketing management, organizational behavior, and sports management), COMMUNICATIONS AND THE ARTS (communications), COMPUTER AND PHYSICAL SCIENCE (information sciences and systems and software engineering), EDUCATION (early childhood education and elementary education), ENGINEERING AND ENVIRONMENTAL DESIGN (agricultural engineering technology, airline piloting and navigation, applied aviation, computer technology, environmental science, and industrial administration/ management), HEALTH PROFESSIONS (health, health care administration, and health science), SOCIAL SCIENCE (criminal justice). Business management, natural resources, and equine science have the largest enrollments.

ACTIVITIES: There are 39 groups on campus, including cheerleading, chess, choir, chorale, chorus, computers, drama, environmental, ethnic, honors, international, LGBT, pep band, political, professional, religious, social, social service, and student government. Popular campus events include What's on Wednesday (WOW), Ag-Arama, and Winter Wonderland. **Sports:** There are 4 intercollegiate sports for men and 7 for women, and 10 intramural sports for men and 10 for women. Facilities include a gym, an indoor complex with basketball/volleyball and racquetball courts, a training room, a fitness center, a football field surrounded by an all-weather track, tennis courts, soccer, baseball, and softball fields. **Graduates:** From July 1, 2016 to June 30, 2017, 426 bachelor's degrees were awarded. The most popular majors were natural resources, business marketing, and health professional and related programs. In an average class, 11% graduate in 3 years or less, 36% graduate in 4 years or less, 42% graduate in 5 years or less, and 54% graduate in 6 years or less. Of the 2016 graduating class, 8% were enrolled in graduate school within 6 months of graduation, and 92% were employed.

SERVICES: Counseling and information services are available, as is tutoring in most subjects. There is a reader service for the blind, and remedial math and writing. The Academic Assistance Center also provides help with study strategies and English as a second language, and federally funded student support services are available to those who are eligible. **Library/Resources:** The library contains 244,686 volumes, 26,204 microform items, and 2,222 audio/video tapes/CDs/DVDs. Computerized library services include interlibrary loans, database searching, Internet access, and Wi-Fi capability. **Physically Challenged Students:** 95% of the campus is accessible. Facilities include wheelchair ramps, elevators, special parking, specially equipped restrooms, special class scheduling, lowered drinking fountains, lowered telephones, and special housing. **Special:** UMC offers cross-registration with the University of North Dakota Air Force ROTC. The internship or field experience requirement may be completed through on-the-job experience in the private sector, with a government agency, or through other appropriate work experience; a minimum of 450 hours of employment or volunteer assignments is usually required for satisfactory evaluation of the student's progress. Study abroad in more than 200 locations and student-designed majors are available. There is 1 national honor society, a freshman honors program, and 1 departmental honors program. **Visiting:** There are regularly scheduled orientations for prospective students. There are guides for informal visits, visitors may sit in on classes, and stay overnight. To schedule a visit, contact the Admissions Office. **Campus Safety and Security:** Measures include emergency notification system, self-defense education, and security escort services. There are shuttle buses, emergency telephones, and lighted pathways/sidewalks.

REQUIREMENTS: A minimum score of 21 on the ACT or 980 on the SAT. Applicants must have successfully completed a high school or college preparatory program; the GED is accepted. A minimum 2.0 GPA is required. The strength of the high school curriculum is considered. Students failing to meet minimum requirements of GPA and student should have completed 15 academic units, 4 in English, 3 each in math, social studies, and science (with 2 lab), and 2 in foreign language. AP and CLEP credits are accepted. To graduate, students must complete 120 credit hours, including 40 credits of liberal education and 40 upper-division credits, with a minimum GPA of 2.0. 3 credits of technology are required. **Procedure:** Freshmen are admitted in the fall and spring. Entrance exams should be taken by May 1. There are deferred admissions and rolling admissions plans. Applications should be filed by August 15 for fall entry. The fall 2017 application fee was $30. Notification is sent on a rolling basis. Applications are accepted on-line. **Transfer Students:** 215 transfer students enrolled in 2016-2017. Transfer students with fewer than 24 earned college credits need to submit an official high school transcript, ACT or SAT scores, and official transcripts from previous colleges. Transfer students with 24 or more semester credits need to submit only official transcripts from previous colleges. A minimum 2.0 college GPA is required. 30 of 120 credits required for the bachelor's degree must be completed at UMC. **International Students:** There are 145 international students enrolled. They must take the TOEFL with a minimum score of 520 on the paper-based TOEFL (PBT) or 68 on the Internet-based version (iBT) or take the MELAB, or the IELTS. Native English speaking students are not required to submit TOEFL, but are required to submit ACT, SAT, or other standardized college entrance exams scores.

ADMISSIONS: 68% of the 2017-2018 applicants were accepted. The ACT scores were 7% between 12 and 17, 64% between 18 and 23, 25% between 24 and 29, and 4% above 30. 37% of the current freshmen were in the top fifth of their class; 60% were in the top two fifths. 3 freshmen graduated first in their class. **Admissions Contact:** Peter Phaiah, Admissions Director. Email: *umcinfo@umn.edu* Web: *www.umcrookston.edu*

FINANCIAL AID: In 2017-2018, 74% of all full-time freshmen received some form of financial aid. 72% of all full-time freshmen received need-based aid. The average freshman award was $13,102. Need-based scholarships or need-based grants averaged $10,221; need-based self-help aid (loans and jobs) averaged $4,131; non-need-based athletic scholarships averaged $4,326; other non-need-based awards and non-need-based scholarships averaged $4,326; and $3,450 from other forms of aid. The average financial indebtedness of the 2017 graduate was $18,038. The FAFSA code is 004069. The priority date for freshman financial aid applications for fall entry is March 1.

UNIVERSITY OF MINNESOTA/DULUTH D-2

www.d.umn.edu

Duluth, MN 55812 (218) 726-7171 (800) 232-1339

Fax: (218) 726-6394 **Email:** umdadmis@d.umn.edu

Full-time: 4875 men, 4041 women	**Faculty:** 454; IIA, -$
Part-time: n/av	**Ph.D.s:** 63%
Graduate: 430 men, 576 women	**Student/Faculty:** 20 to 1
Year: semesters, summer session	**Tuition:** $13,082 ($17,032)
Room & Board: $7210	**Freshman Class:** 7456 applied, 5694 accepted, 2105 enrolled
SAT CR/M/W: 510/540/530 **ACT:** 24	**CEEB CODE:** 6873
Application Deadline: August 1	**COMPETITIVE**

University of Minnesota/Duluth, founded in 1895, is a liberal arts institution offering undergraduate and graduate programs. There are 5 undergraduate schools and 1 graduate school. In addition to regional accreditation, UMD has baccalaureate program accreditation with AACSB, ABET, ACPE, ASLA, CSAB, CSWE, NASM, NCATE, ASLHA, CAA, NASM, and NRPA. The 244-acre campus is in an urban area 150 miles north of Minneapolis and St. Paul. Including any residence halls, there are 58 buildings.

STUDENT LIFE: 82% of undergraduates are from Minnesota. Others are from 44 states, 47 foreign countries, and Canada. 95% are from public schools. 81% are White; 5% race unknown; 4% Asian American; 3% African American; 3% Foreign; 2% American Indian/Alaska Native; 2% Hispanic. **Male To Female Ratio:** 1.1:1. The average age of freshmen is 18; all undergraduates, 20. 19% do not continue beyond their first year; 53% remain to graduate. **Housing:** 3171 students can be accommodated in college housing, which includes dorms and on-campus apartments. In addition, there are honors houses, a Global Home Living-Learning Community, GreenHouse Sustainability Community, and Wellness Dwelling Community. On-campus housing is available on a first-come and first-served basis. 72% of students commute. All students may keep cars. Alcohol is not permitted.

FACULTY/CLASSROOMS: 55% of faculty are male; 45% are female. All teach undergraduates, 75% do research, and 75% do both. No introductory courses are taught by graduate students. The average class size in an introductory lecture is 60; in a laboratory is 20; and in a regular course is 30.

PROGRAMS OF STUDY: UMD confers B.A., B.S., B.A.A., B.Acc., B.A.Sc., B.B.A., B.F.A., B.Mus., B.S.Ch.E., B.S.C.E., B.S.E.C.E., and B.S.M.E. degrees. Master's and doctoral degrees are also awarded. Bachelor's degrees are awarded in AGRICULTURE (environmental studies), BIOLOGICAL SCIENCE (biochemistry, biology/biological science, cell biology, and molecular biology), BUSINESS (accounting, business administration and management, management information systems, and organizational leadership and management), COMMUNICATIONS AND THE ARTS (art, art history and appreciation, communications, dramatic arts, English, graphic design, jazz, music, music performance, Spanish, and studio art), COMPUTER AND PHYSICAL SCIENCE (actuarial science, applied physics, chemistry, computer science, geology, information sciences and systems, mathematics, physics, and statistics), EDUCATION (art education, athletic training, elementary education, foreign languages education, health education, mathematics education, middle school education, music education, physical education, recreation education, science education, secondary education, and social studies education), ENGINEERING AND ENVIRONMENTAL DESIGN (chemical engineering, civil engineering, computer engineering, electrical/electronics engineering, environmental science, industrial engineering, and mechanical engineering), HEALTH PROFESSIONS (hospital administration), SOCIAL SCIENCE (anthropology, criminology, early childhood studies, economics, geography, German area studies, history, interdisciplinary studies, international studies, Native American studies, philosophy, political science/government, prelaw, psychology, sociology, urban studies, and women's studies). Business, sciences, and engineering are the strongest academically. Business administration, biology, and psychology have the largest enrollments.

ACTIVITIES: 1% of men belong to 2 local and 3 national fraternities; 1% of women belong to 1 local and 3 national sororities. There are 270 groups on campus, including wind ensemble, jazz choir, art, band, chamber orchestra, cheerleading, chess, choir, chorale, chorus, computers, dance, drama, environmental, ethnic, film, honors, international, jazz band, LGBT, literary magazine, marching band, musical theater, newspaper, opera, orchestra, pep band, photography, political, professional, radio and TV, religious, social, social service, and student government. Popular campus events include Out Cold Winter Festival, Black History Month, Hispanic Heritage Month, and Drag Show. **Sports:** There are 6 intercollegiate sports for men and 8 for women, and 26 intramural sports for men and 26 for women. Facilities include rock-climbing walls, a multipurpose ice center, a football and track-and-field stadium, a baseball park, softball and soccer fields, a field house for track and tennis, and a gym for basketball and volleyball. **Graduates:** From July 1, 2016 to June 30, 2017, 2168 bachelor's degrees were awarded. The most popular majors were psychology (7%), communication (5%), and finance (5%). In an average class, 1% graduate in 3 years or less, 28% graduate in 4 years or less, 49% graduate in 5 years or less, and 54% graduate in 6 years or less. Of the 2016 graduating class, 12% were enrolled in graduate school within 6 months of graduation, and 75% were employed.

SERVICES: Counseling and information services are available, as is tutoring in some subjects, such as math, business, economics, sciences, accounting, computer science, engineering, physics, statistics, biology, American Sign Language, and writing. There is a reader service for the blind, and remedial math and writing. Workshops and seminars are also offered on study skills, note taking, time management, test-taking strategies, and goal setting. **Library/Resources:** The library contains 777,708 volumes, 756,339 microform items, and 13,724 audio/video tapes/CDs/DVDs, and subscribes to 65,686 periodicals including electronic. Computerized library services include interlibrary loans, database searching, Internet access, and Wi-Fi capability. Special learning facilities include an art gallery, planetarium, radio station, historic mansion, child care center, speech and hearing clinic, performing arts centers (theatre and music), a visual imaging lab, and a motion and media across disciplines lab. **Physically Challenged Students:** All of the campus is accessible. Facilities include wheelchair ramps, elevators, special parking, specially equipped restrooms, lowered drinking fountains, lowered telephones, and special housing. **Special:** Students may study abroad in England, Sweden, and Finland, and Australia. UMD also offers cross-registration with the College of St. Scholastica and the University of Wisconsin/Superior, internships, work-study programs, a B.A.-B.S. degree in several fields, student-designed majors, and nondegree study. There are 1 national honor societies, Phi Beta Kappa, a freshman honors program, and 28 departmental honors programs. **Visiting:** There are regularly scheduled orientations for prospective students, including an information session, a campus tour, meeting with admissions counselors, faculty, or coaches, and representatives from the five collegiate units. There are guides for informal visits and visitors may sit in on classes. To schedule a visit, contact the Office of Admissions. **Campus Safety and Security:** Measures include 24-hour foot and vehicle patrol, emergency notification system, self-defense education, and security escort services. There are emergency telephones and lighted pathways/sidewalks.

REQUIREMENTS: The ACT is required. Applicants must have completed 4 years each in English, and math, 3 years each in sciences, and social sciences, and 2 years each in a single second language. Coursework in the visual and performing arts and computer skills is recommended. Students with a GED certificate will be admitted selectively as space permits. AP and CLEP credits are accepted. To graduate, students must complete 120 to 136 semester credits, including 2 courses in college writing, and a liberal education distribution of at least 35 credits in 10 academic areas. At least 4 credits of coursework must emphasize cultural diversity, and 4 should emphasize an international perspective. **Procedure:** Freshmen are admitted in the fall and spring. Entrance exams should be taken at the end of junior year or the beginning of senior year. There is a rolling admissions plan. Applications should be filed by August 1 for fall entry; December 1 for spring entry. The fall 2017 application fee was $40. Notification is sent on a rolling basis. Applications are accepted on-line. **Transfer Students:** 544 transfer students enrolled in 2016-2017. Applicants who have completed 26 or more semester credits must have a minimum 2.0 GPA and a 75% completion ratio; applicants who have attempted fewer than 26 semester credits must have a high school rank at or above the 50th percentile, a 1.8 GPA in their previous college work, and a 75% completion ratio. **International Students:** There are 153 international students enrolled. They must take the TOEFL with a minimum score of 550 on the paper-based TOEFL (PBT) or 80 on the Internet-based version (iBT).

ADMISSIONS: 76% of the 2017-2018 applicants were accepted. The SAT scores for the 2017-2018 freshman class were: Critical Reading-- 40% below 500, 34% between 500 and 599, 23% between 600 and 699, and 3% between 700 and 800. Math-- 28% below 500, 46% between 500 and 599, 21% between 600 and 699, and 5% between 700 and 800. Writing-- 36% below 500, 41% between 500 and 599, 21% between 600 and 699, and 2% between 700 and 800. The ACT scores were 15% below 12, 33% between 12 and 17, 33% between 18 and 23, 11% between 24 and 29, and 8% above 30. 33% of the current freshmen were in the top fifth of their class; 71% were in the top two fifths. **Admissions Contact:** Scott Schulz, Director of Admissions. Email: *umdadmis@d.umn.edu* Web: *www.d.umn.edu*

FINANCIAL AID: In 2017-2018, 63% of all full-time freshmen received some form of financial aid and need-based aid. The average freshman award was $10,478. Need-based scholarships or need-based grants averaged $7,658; need-based self-help aid (loans and jobs) averaged $3,740; and other non-need-based awards and non-need-based scholarships averaged $3,391. 14% of undergraduate students work part-time. The average financial indebtedness of the 2017 graduate was $18,214. The FAFSA code is 002388. The priority date for freshman financial aid applications for fall entry is February 15.

UNIVERSITY OF MINNESOTA/MORRIS B-3
www.morris.umn.edu

Morris, MN 56267 — **(320) 589-6035**, **(888) 866-3382**

Fax: (320) 589-6051 — **Email: admissions@morris.umn.edu**

Full-time: 651 men, 843 women	**Faculty:** 125; IIB, +$
Part-time: 31 men, 29 women	**Ph.D.s:** 93%
Graduate: n/av	**Student/Faculty:** 11 to 1
Year: semesters, summer session	**Tuition:** $13,072 ($15,092)
Room & Board: $8150	**Freshman Class:** 3211 applied, 2048 accepted, 356 enrolled
SAT CR/M/W: 570/610/580 **ACT:** 25	**CEEB CODE:** 6890
Application Deadline: March 15	**VERY COMPETITIVE**

University of Minnesota, Morris, founded in 1959, is a public liberal arts institution within the University of Minnesota system. There is 1 undergraduate school. In addition to regional accreditation, UMM has baccalaureate program accreditation with CAEP. The 130-acre campus is in a small town 150 miles northwest of Minneapolis. Including any residence halls, there are 33 buildings.

STUDENT LIFE: 74% of undergraduates are from Minnesota. Others are from 32 states, and 24 foreign countries. 95% are from public schools. 8% are American Indian/Alaska Native; 58% White; 5% Hispanic; 3% Asian American; 2% African American; 13% two or more races. **Female To Male Ratio:** 1.3:1. The average age of freshmen is 18; all undergraduates, 20. 20% do not continue beyond their first year; 71% remain to graduate. **Housing:** 1032 students can be accommodated in college housing, which includes dorms, on-campus apartments, and housing for disabled students. On-campus housing is guaranteed for all 4 years, and is available on a first-come, first-served basis, and is available on a lottery system for upperclassmen. 60% of students live on campus. All students may keep cars. Alcohol is not permitted.

FACULTY/CLASSROOMS: 54% of faculty are male; 46% are female. All teach undergraduates, 97% do research, and 97% do both. No introductory courses are taught by graduate students. The average class size in an introductory lecture is 27; in a laboratory is 17; and in a regular course is 18.

PROGRAMS OF STUDY: UMM confers B.A. degrees. Bachelor's degrees are awarded in AGRICULTURE (environmental studies), BIOLOGICAL SCIENCE (biology/biological science), BUSINESS (management science), COMMUNICATIONS AND THE ARTS (art history and appreciation, communications, dramatic arts, English, French, German, music, Spanish, speech/debate/rhetoric, and studio art), COMPUTER AND PHYSICAL SCIENCE (chemistry, computer science, geology, mathematics, physics, and statistics), EDUCATION (education, elementary education, secondary education, and sports studies), ENGINEERING AND ENVIRONMENTAL DESIGN (environmental science), HEALTH PROFESSIONS (premedicine), SOCIAL SCIENCE (American Indian studies, anthropology, economics, European studies, history, interdisciplinary studies, Latin American studies, liberal arts/general studies, philosophy, political science/government, prelaw, psychology, social science, sociology, and women's studies). Sciences, education, and performing arts are the strongest academically. Management, psychology, and biology have the largest enrollments.

ACTIVITIES: There are no fraternities or sororities. There are 100 groups on campus, art, band, cheerleading, chess, choir, chorale, chorus, computers, dance, debate, drama, ethnic, forensics, honors, horseback riding (Saddle Club), international, jazz band, LGBT, literary magazine, musical theater, newspaper, orchestra, photography, political, professional, radio and TV, religious, social, social service, student government, and yearbook. Popular campus events include Cultural Heritage Week, Diversity Jam, Jazz Fest, and Performing Arts Series. **Sports:** There are 9 intercollegiate sports for men and 10 for women, and 30 intramural sports for men and 30 for women. Facilities include a stadium, a phys ed center, gyms, wrestling, exercise, and weight rooms, an Olympic-size pool, handball and racquetball courts, an indoor and outdoor track, fields for softball, baseball, soccer, and football, a diving well, a warm-water pool and slide, and a cardiovascular fitness room. **Graduates:** From July 1, 2016 to June 30, 2017, 353 bachelor's degrees were awarded. The most popular majors were psychology (11%), English (8%), and biology (8%). In an average class, 49% graduate in 4 years or less, 61% graduate in 5 years or less, and 63% graduate in 6 years or less. Of the 2016 graduating class, 23% were enrolled in graduate school within 6 months of graduation, and 71% were employed.

SERVICES: Counseling and information services are available, as is tutoring in every subject. There is a reader service for the blind, and remedial math, reading, and writing. **Library/Resources:** The library contains 227,324 volumes, 2,215 microform items, and 8,222 audio/video tapes/CDs/DVDs, and subscribes to 81,792 periodicals including electronic. Computerized library services include interlibrary loans, database searching, Internet access, and Wi-Fi capability. Special learning facilities include an art gallery, radio station, TV station, a language lab, an observatory, and an agricultural experiment station. **Physically Challenged Students:** 70% of the campus is accessible. Facilities include wheelchair ramps, elevators, special parking, specially equipped restrooms, special class scheduling, lowered drinking fountains, and special housing. Special learning equipment and services are available through the academic assistance center and a disability services coordinator is also available. **Special:** UMM offers work-study programs, internships, study abroad, dual majors, student-designed majors, nondegree study, pass/fail options, and credit for life, military, and work experience. There is a 3-2 engineering degree with the University of Minnesota at Twin Cities. A competitive, merit-based program that pairs students and professors to undertake creative projects is available. There is a freshman honors program and 35 departmental honors programs. **Visiting:** There are regularly scheduled orientations for prospective students, consisting of a campus tour, lunch with faculty, a session with admissions staff, and a student panel. There are guides for informal visits, visitors may sit in on classes, and stay overnight. To schedule a visit, contact the Admissions Office. **Campus Safety and Security:** Measures include 24-hour foot and vehicle patrol, emergency notification system, self-defense education, and security escort services. There are shuttle buses, emergency telephones, lighted pathways/sidewalks, and controlled access to dorms/residences.

REQUIREMENTS: The SAT or ACT, and the ACT Optional Writing test are required. Applicants should be graduates of an accredited secondary school or have a GED certificate. They must have completed 4 years of English, 3 each of math and science, 2 of a single foreign language, and 1 each of social studies and American history. AP and CLEP credits are accepted. Important factors in the admissions decision are leadership record, extracurricular activities record, and advanced placement or honors courses. In addition to 40 semester hours in the major, students are required to complete 60 credits of a general education curriculum, including courses in writing, computing, foreign language or equivalent, and advanced study, as well as courses focusing on the arts, the physical and abstract worlds, and the self and others. All first-year students participate in a freshman seminar, and the cumulative of their major work is presented in the senior seminar, which is a requirement for all seniors. **Procedure:** Freshmen are admitted in the fall and spring. Entrance exams should be taken before December 1 of the senior year. There are deferred admissions and rolling admissions plans. Applications should be filed by March 15 for fall entry; September 15 for spring entry. The fall 2017 application fee was $35. Notification is sent on a rolling basis. Applications are accepted on-line. **Transfer Students:** 92 transfer students enrolled in 2016-2017. Applicants must complete the application for admission, submit all college transcripts, and have maintained a minimum GPA of 2.5. 30 of 120 credits required for the bachelor's degree must be completed at UMM. **International Students:** There are 171 international students enrolled. They must take the TOEFL with a minimum score of 79 on the Internet-based version (iBT), and either the SAT, ACT, or IETLS.

ADMISSIONS: 64% of the 2017-2018 applicants were accepted. The SAT scores for the 2017-2018 freshman class were: Critical Reading-- 80% between 500 and 599 and 20% between 600 and 699. Math-- 4% below 500, 36% between 500 and 599, 20% between 600 and 699, and 40% between 700 and 800. Writing-- 40% below 500, 20% between 500 and 599, and 40% between 600 and 699. The ACT scores were 3% between 12 and 17, 36% between 18 and 23, 45% between 24 and 29, and 16% above 30. 11 freshmen graduated first in their class. **Admissions Contact:** Jennifer Zych-Herrmann, Director of Admissions. Email: *admissions@morris.umn.edu* Web: *www.morris.umn.edu*

FINANCIAL AID: In 2017-2018, 74% of all full-time freshmen received some form of financial aid. 72% of all full-time freshmen received need-based aid. The average freshman award was $12,851. Need-based scholarships or need-based grants averaged $10,783; need-based self-help aid (loans and jobs) averaged $4,244; and other non-need-based awards and non-need-based scholarships averaged $4,054. 40% of undergraduate students work part-time. The average financial indebtedness of the 2017 graduate was $24,189. The FAFSA code is 002389. The priority date for freshman financial aid applications for fall entry is April 1.

UNIVERSITY OF MINNESOTA/TWIN CITIES — C-4

www.twin-cities.umn.edu

Minneapolis, MN 55455	(612) 625-2008 (800) 752-1000
Fax: (612) 625-1693	**Email:** admissions@tc.umn.edu.
Full-time: 14,201 men, 15,790 women	**Faculty:** 2599; 1, av$
Part-time: 2613 men, 2829 women	**Ph.D.s:** 80%
Graduate: 7494 men, 8921 women	**Student/Faculty:** 17 to 1
Year: semesters, summer session	**Tuition:** $14,417 ($26,603)
Room & Board: $9852	**Freshman Class:** n/av
SAT or ACT: required	**CEEB CODE:** 6874
Application Deadline: n/av	**MOST COMPETITIVE**

University of Minnesota/Twin Cities, founded in 1851, is a land-grant institution offering programs in liberal and fine arts, physical and biological sciences, health sciences, education, natural resources, human ecology, business, agriculture, and engineering and professional training in law, medicine, dentistry, pharmacy, and veterinary medicine. There are 13 undergraduate schools and 17 graduate schools. In addition to regional accreditation, UMTC has baccalaureate program accreditation with AACSB, ABET, ABFSE, ACEJMC, ADA, APTA, ASLA, CSWE, FIDER, NAAB, NASM, CAEP, NLN, and SAF. The 2000-acre campus is in an urban area within both Minneapolis and St. Paul. Including any residence halls, there are 205 buildings.

STUDENT LIFE: 73% of undergraduates are from Minnesota. Others are from 50 states, 140 foreign countries, and Canada. 85% are from public schools. 8% are Asian American; 64% White; 4% African American; 4% Hispanic; 4% race unknown; 3% two or more races; 12% Foreign. **Female To Male Ratio:** 1.1:1. The average age of freshmen is 18; all undergraduates, 21. 7% do not continue beyond their first year; 80% remain to graduate. **Housing:** 7294 students can be accommodated in college housing, which includes married student dorms, on-campus apartments, and off-campus apartments. In addition, there are honors houses, special-interest houses, fraternity houses, sorority houses, and cooperative housing. On-campus housing is guaranteed for the freshman year only, is available on a first-come, first-served basis, and is available on a lottery system for upperclassmen. 77% of students commute. All students may keep cars. Alcohol is not permitted.

FACULTY/CLASSROOMS: 56% of faculty are male; 44% are female. All teach undergraduates and do research. No introductory courses are taught by graduate students.

PROGRAMS OF STUDY: UMTC confers B.A., B.S., B.S.B, B.F.A., B.A.E.M., B.D.A., B.S.Astrop.,B.I.S., B.Bm.E.,B.B.E.,B.Ch.E., B.S.Chem., B.C.E., B.Comp.E., B.S.CompSc., B.A.Sc., B.S.D.H., B.S. Earth Sciences, B.E.E., B.Env.E., B.GeoE., B.E.D., B.Mat.S.E., B.S.Math., B.M.E., B.Mus., B.S.N., B.S.Phys., and B.S.Stat degrees. Master's and doctoral degrees are also awarded. Bachelor's degrees are awarded in AGRICULTURE (agricultural business management, agricultural communications, animal science, fishing and fisheries, forestry and related sciences, and plant science), BIOLOGICAL SCIENCE (biochemistry, biology/biological science, biology and society, ecology, genetics, microbiology, neurosciences, nutrition, and physiology), BUSINESS (accounting, entreprenurship, finance, human resources, management science, marketing/retailing/merchandising, nonprofit/public organization management, recreation and leisure services, recreational facilities management, retailing, sports management, supply chain management, and sustainable management), COMMUNICATIONS AND THE ARTS (acting, apparel design, art, art history and appreciation, classical languages, communication studies, comparative literature, dance, English, French, German, graphic design, Greek, Hebrew, information technology, Italian, Japanese, journalism, Latin, linguistics, music, Russian, Scandinavian languages, Spanish, speech/debate/rhetoric, technical communication, and theatre arts), COMPUTER AND PHYSICAL SCIENCE (astrophysics, chemistry, computer science, earth science, mathematics, physics, and statistics), EDUCATION (agricultural education, Asian studies, bilingual/bicultural education, business education, classical studies, early childhood education, elementary education, global studies, music education, and special education), ENGINEERING AND ENVIRONMENTAL DESIGN (aerospace engineering, architecture, bioengineering, biomedical engineering, chemical engineering, civil engineering, civil and environmental engineering, computer engineering, construction management, electrical/electronics engineering, geological engineering, industrial engineering, interior design, landscape architecture/design, materials science, mechanical engineering, and product design engineering technology), HEALTH PROFESSIONS (biology, dental hygiene, health services administration, kinesiology, medical laboratory technology, music therapy, nursing, predentistry, premedicine, prepharmacy, preveterinary science, speech pathology/audiology, and veterinary science), SOCIAL SCIENCE (African American studies, American Indian studies, American studies, anthropology, biblical studies, child psychology/development, East Asian studies, economics, food science, gender studies, geography, history, human development & family studies, international relations, Mexican-American/Chicano studies, Middle Eastern studies, modern jewish studies, philosophy, political science/government, prelaw, psychology, religious studies, Russian and Slavic studies, sociology, South Asian studies, and urban studies). Engineering, business, and psychology are the strongest academically. Psychology, biology, and economics have the largest enrollments.

ACTIVITIES: There are 600 groups on campus, including art, band, cheerleading, chess, choir, chorale, chorus, computers, dance, debate, drama, drill team, environmental, ethnic, film, honors, international, jazz band, LGBT, literary magazine, marching band, musical theater, newspaper, orchestra, pep band, photography, political, professional, radio and TV, religious, social, social service, student government, and symphony. Popular campus events include Homecoming. **Sports:** There are 12 intercollegiate sports for men and 11 for women, and 16 intramural sports for men and 16 for women. Facilities include an outdoor stadium, 3 gyms, 2 field houses, a hockey rink, an Olympic-size aquatic center, and a student recreation center. **Graduates:** From July 1, 2016 to June 30, 2017, 7807 bachelor's degrees were awarded. The most popular majors were psychology (4%), journalism (3%), and communication studies (3%). In an average class, 5% graduate in 3 years or less, 64% graduate in 4 years or less, 77% graduate in 5 years or less, and 80% graduate in 6 years or less.

SERVICES: Counseling and information services are available, as is tutoring in every subject. There is a reader service for the blind, and remedial math, reading, and writing, test proctoring, and sign language interpreters. **Library/Resources:** The library contains 6.2 million volumes, 5.4 million microform items, 500,000 audio/video tapes/CDs/DVDs, and subscribes to 48,105 periodicals, including electronic. Computerized library services include interlibrary loans, database searching, and Internet access. Special learning facilities include an art gallery, natural history museum, planetarium, radio station, and TV station. **Physically Challenged Students:** Facilities include wheelchair ramps, elevators, special parking, specially equipped restrooms, special class scheduling, lowered drinking fountains, lowered telephones, special housing, listening devices, TTY and volume-control phones, print enlargers, and adaptive computers. In addition, support groups and counselors provide assistance with all areas of university life and career planning. **Special:** The university offers cooperative programs, cross-registration with the Minnesota Community College system, internships, study abroad in 65 countries, work-study programs both on and off campus, a B.A.-B.S. degree in all majors, a general studies degree, and dual and student-designed majors. Pass/fail options and credit for life, military, or work experience are available. There are 21 national honor societies, Phi Beta Kappa, a freshman honors program, and 8 departmental honors programs. **Visiting:** There are regularly scheduled orientations for prospective students. There are guides for informal visits, visitors may sit in on classes, and stay overnight. **Campus Safety and Security:** Measures include 24-hour foot and vehicle patrol, emergency notification system, self-defense education, and security escort services. There are shuttle buses, emergency telephones, lighted pathways/sidewalks, a 20-member university police force, and blue-light phone centers.

REQUIREMENTS: The university uses a formula index in evaluating high school rank and ACT test scores. A portfolio is required for studio arts and architecture, an audition for music, and an interview for architecture and education. A high school diploma is required; the GED is accepted. AP and CLEP credits are accepted. Important factors in the admissions decision are advanced placement or honors courses, evidence of special talent, and leadership record. To graduate, students must complete 120 to 130 semester credits, including 45 in the major, with a minimum GPA of 2.0. Distribution requirements include course work in the 4 areas of communication, language, and symbolic systems, physical and biological sciences, the individual and society, and artistic expression. Other requirements vary by program. **Procedure:** Freshmen are admitted to all sessions. Entrance exams should be taken by the end of the junior year or October/November/December of the senior year. There are early admissions, deferred admissions, and rolling admissions plans. Application deadlines are open. The fall 2017 application fee was $55. Notification is sent on a rolling basis. Applications are accepted on-line. **Transfer Students:** 2268 transfer students enrolled in 2016-2017. Admission requirements vary by major/program, with a minimum 2.2 GPA needed for consideration. College transcripts are required. 30 of 120 credits required for the bachelor's degree must be completed at UMTC. **International Students:** There are 2691 international students enrolled. They must take the MELAB, and Minnesota Battery and the Institutional TOEFL. They must also take the ACT for residents of Minnesota and neighboring states, and the SAT for residents of other states.

ADMISSIONS: 75% of the current freshmen were in the top fifth of their class; 97% were in the top two fifths. **Admissions Contact:** Heidi Meyer, Executive Director of Admissions. Email: *admissions@tc.umn.edu*. Web: *www.twin-cities.umn.edu*

FINANCIAL AID: In 2017-2018, 49% of all full-time freshmen received some form of financial aid. The average freshman award was $13,686. Need-based scholarships or need-based grants averaged $11,119; and need-based self-help aid (loans and jobs) averaged $5,021. The college's own financial statement is required. The FAFSA code is 003969. Check with the school for current application deadlines.

UNIVERSITY OF NORTHWESTERN - ST. PAUL C-4

www.unwsp.edu

St. Paul, MN 55113 (651) 631-5382

Email: admissions@unwsp.edu

Full-time: 666 men, 947 women	**Faculty:** n/av
Part-time: 123 men, 154 women	**Ph.D.s:** 81%
Graduate: 105 men, 101 women	**Student/Faculty:** 13 to 1
Year: semesters	**Tuition:** $33,960
Room & Board: $5570	**Freshman Class:** n/av
ACT: required	**CEEB CODE:** 6489
Application Deadline: August 1	**COMPETITIVE**

University of Northwestern-St. Paul, founded in 1902, is where students come to learn and develop as leaders through a Christ-centered, liberal arts, academically excellent education. UNW-St. Paul's shared faith brings students, faculty and staff together in a powerful way as we learn and grow together in Christ. There are 4 undergraduate schools and 1 graduate school. In addition to regional accreditation, UNW-St. Paul has baccalaureate program accreditation with NASM. The 107-acre campus is in a suburban area in Roseville, MN, 3 miles from St. Paul and 5 miles from Minneapolis. Including any residence halls, there are 17 buildings.

STUDENT LIFE: 77% of undergraduates are from Minnesota. Others are from 38 states, and 12 foreign countries. 67% are from public schools. 83% are White; 4% Asian American; 4% Hispanic; 3% African American; 3% two or more races; 1% Foreign; 1% race unknown. 99% are Protestant. **Female To Male Ratio:** 1.3:1. The average age of freshmen is 20; all undergraduates, 22. 17% do not continue beyond their first year; 63% remain to graduate. **Housing:** 1280 students can be accommodated in college housing, which includes married student dorms and on-campus apartments. On-campus housing is guaranteed for the freshman year only, and is available on a first-come, first-served basis. 63% of students live on campus. Upperclassmen may keep cars. Alcohol is not permitted.

FACULTY/CLASSROOMS: 56% of faculty are male; 44% are female. All teach undergraduates. No introductory courses are taught by graduate students. The average class size in an introductory lecture is 39; in a laboratory is 17; and in a regular course is 22.

PROGRAMS OF STUDY: UNW-St. Paul confers B.A., B.S., B.M.E., and B.Mus. degrees. Associate and master's degrees are also awarded. Bachelor's degrees are awarded in BIOLOGICAL SCIENCE (biochemistry and biology/biological science), BUSINESS (accounting, banking and finance, business administration and management, business data processing, finance, international business, international business management, management information systems, marketing, and marketing management), COMMUNICATIONS AND THE ARTS (animation, art, art and design, broadcasting, communication studies, communications, computer graphic design, dramatic arts, English, English as a second/foreign language, English literature, English writing, graphic design, illustration, journalism, music, music ministry, music performance, music theory and composition, piano/organ, public relations, Spanish, strings, studio art, video, and voice), COMPUTER AND PHYSICAL SCIENCE (applied mathematics, computer science, and mathematics), EDUCATION (art education, early childhood education, education, elementary education, English secondary education, English education, mathematics education, music education, physical education, physical education/exercise science, social studies education, social studies secondary school education, and Spanish education K-12), ENGINEERING AND ENVIRONMENTAL DESIGN (civil engineering, computer engineering, engineering, engineering management, environmental science, and mechanical engineering), HEALTH PROFESSIONS (biology, electrical engineering, exercise science, health science, and nursing), SOCIAL SCIENCE (biblical studies, criminal justice, crosscultural studies, history, interdisciplinary studies, ministries, pastoral studies, philosophy, psychology, religious education, urban studies, and youth ministry).

Education, business, biology, engineering, music, and communication are the strongest academically. Education, business, and Christian Ministries have the largest enrollments.

ACTIVITIES: There are no fraternities or sororities. There are 30 groups on campus, including band, cheerleading, chess, choir, chorale, chorus, communications, computers, dance, debate, drama, ethnic, film, forensics, honors, international, jazz band, literary magazine, musical theater, newspaper, orchestra, photography, political, professional, radio and TV, religious, social, social service, student government, and yearbook. Popular campus events include Spring Variety Shows, Christmas at Northwestern, Five16 Film Festival, Multicultural Festival, and Day of Prayer and Service. **Sports:** There are 9 intercollegiate sports for men and 9 for women, and 8 intramural sports for men and 8 for women. Facilities include football, soccer, lacrosse, softball, and baseball artificial turf fields, a basketball and volleyball court, racquetball and wallyball courts, a running track, fitness center, athletic training room, and outdoor tennis courts, table tennis, foosball, and a pool table. There are paddleboards and kayaks available for rental in the warmer months and broomball and hockey can be played on the ice during the winter. There are also multiple opportunities to play intramurals.**Graduates:** From July 1, 2016 to June 30, 2017, 433 bachelor's degrees were awarded. The most popular majors were education (19%), Christian ministries/biblical studies (19%), and business (15%). In an average class, 8% graduate in 3 years or less, 45% graduate in 4 years or less, 59% graduate in 5 years or less, and 61% graduate in 6 years or less. Of the 2016 graduating class, 6% were enrolled in graduate school within 6 months of graduation, and 89% were employed.

SERVICES: Counseling and information services are available, as is tutoring in some subjects, such as writing, science, math, accounting, Bible, animation history, Chinese, Spanish, engineering, biology, nursing, psychology, investments, marketing, and music. There is remedial math, reading, and writing. **Library/Resources:** The library contains 93,000 volumes, 70,169 microform items, ,194 audio/video tapes/CDs/DVDs, and subscribes to 24,500 periodicals, including electronic. Computerized library services include interlibrary loans, database searching, Internet access, and Wi-Fi capability. Special learning facilities include an art gallery and a radio station. **Physically Challenged Students:** 70% of the campus is accessible. Facilities include wheelchair ramps, elevators, special parking, specially equipped restrooms, special class scheduling, lowered drinking fountains, and special housing. **Special:** The university offers study-abroad programs in 35+ countries as well as several U.S. off-campus programs through the Council for Christian Colleges and Universities. There is an opportunity for Pastoral Ministry students to pursue a dual B.A./M.Div. degree. International business majors are placed in overseas internships, film students can spend a semester in Los Angeles, and recording arts students can spend a semester in Nashville. There are 6 national honor societies, a freshman honors program, and 11 departmental honors programs. **Visiting:** There are regularly scheduled orientations for prospective students, which includes a campus tour, meetings with a professor/coach, and attend a class. To schedule a visit, contact the Visit Office at visit@unwsp.edu. **Campus Safety and Security:** Measures include 24-hour foot and vehicle patrol, an emergency notification system, self-defense education, and security escort services. There are shuttle buses, emergency telephones, lighted pathways/sidewalks, controlled access to dorms/residences, The campus has limited accessibility due to being surrounded on 3 sides by Lake Johanna, and the main entrance to the campus is gated.

REQUIREMENTS: The ACT is preferred; the SAT is accepted, and a high school diploma is required. The GED is accepted. The minimum high school GPA is 2.0 is required; or a 3.0 or higher is recommended. Applicants are expected to have completed the following Carnegie units: 4 in English, 3 units each in math, science, and social studies, and 2 others, and 2 units in foreign language. A statement of Christian faith and an assent to a lifestyle agreement are required. 2 letters of reference must be submitted, including 1 from the applicant's pastor. A personal interview is required for some students. UNW-St Paul requires applicants to be in the upper 50% of their class. A GPA of 2.0 is required. AP and CLEP credits are accepted. Important factors in the admissions decision are personality/intangible qualities, recommendations by school officials, and leadership record. To graduate, students must complete 125 to 166 semester credits (depends on specific major) with a 2.0 GPA. The number of credits required in the major varies from 36 to 100 (average of 58). A core curriculum of 64 to 68 credits is built around a biblical worldview theme, thoroughly integrating general education and biblical worldview studies. **Procedure:** Freshmen are admitted to all sessions. Entrance exams should be taken during the fall of the senior year of high school. There are deferred admissions and rolling admissions plans. Applications should be filed by August 1 for fall entry; December 15 for spring entry; and May 1 for summer entry. The fall 2017 application fee was $25. Notification is sent on a rolling basis. Applications are accepted on-line. **Transfer Students:** 108 transfer students enrolled in 2016-2017. Applicants must have an average of C or better from an accredited institution. 30 of 125 credits required for the bachelor's degree must be completed at UNW-St. Paul. **International Students:** There are 9 international students enrolled. They must take the TOEFL or MELAB and the SAT or ACT, scoring 18.

Admissions Contact: Micah Stelter, Director of Admissions. Email: *admissions@unwsp.edu* Web: *www.unwsp.edu*

FINANCIAL AID: In 2017-2018, 99% of all full-time freshmen received some form of financial aid and need-based aid. The average freshman award was $24,700. The average financial indebtedness of the 2017 graduate was $25,162. The college's own financial statement is required. The FAFSA code is 002371. The priority date for freshman financial aid applications for fall entry is May 1.

UNIVERSITY OF ST. THOMAS — C-4

www.stthomas.edu

St. Paul, MN 55105 — **(651) 962-6150** **(800) 328-6819**

Fax: (651) 962-6160 — **Email: admissions@stthomas.edu**

Full-time: 3158 men, 2691 women	**Faculty:** 377
Part-time: 150 men, 112 women	**Ph.D.s:** n/av
Graduate: 1768 men, 2104 women	**Student/Faculty:** 14 to 1
Year: 4-1-4, summer session	**Tuition:** $39,594
Room & Board: $9760	**Freshman Class:** 5540 applied, 4774 accepted, 1368 enrolled
SAT CR/M: 580/590 **ACT:** 26	**CEEB CODE:** 6110
Application Deadline: January 15	**VERY COMPETITIVE**

University of St. Thomas, founded in 1885, is a private liberal arts institution affiliated with the Roman Catholic Church. There is 1 undergraduate school and 7 graduate schools. In addition to regional accreditation, UST has baccalaureate program accreditation with AACSB, ABET, CSWE, NASM, and ACS. The 78-acre campus is in an urban area 5 miles west of St. Paul and 5 miles east of Minneapolis. Including any residence halls, there are 60 buildings.

STUDENT LIFE: 79% of undergraduates are from Minnesota. Others are from 43 states, 83 foreign countries, and Canada. 72% are from public schools. 77% are White; 6% Foreign; 5% Asian American; 4% African American; 4% Hispanic; 3% two or more races; 2% race unknown. 38% are Catholic; 29% Protestant; 27% Buddhist, Muslim, and Hindu. **Male To Female Ratio:** 1.0:1. The average age of freshmen is 18; all undergraduates, 20. 12% do not continue beyond their first year; 88% remain to graduate. **Housing:** College-sponsored housing includes dorms, on-campus apartments, and off-campus apartments. In addition, there are special-interest houses, living learning community, chemical-free lifestyle, first-year experience, women in science housing, special housing for disabled students, theme housing, wellness housing, and housing options for Catholic women and Catholic men. On-campus housing is available on a first-come, first-served basis, and is available on a lottery system for upperclassmen. 60% of students commute. All students may keep cars.

FACULTY/CLASSROOMS: 58% of faculty are male; 42% are female. 86% teach undergraduates. No introductory courses are taught by graduate students. The average class size in a laboratory is 15 and in a regular course is 20.

PROGRAMS OF STUDY: UST confers B.A., B.S., B.S.M.E., B.S.E.E. and B.M. degrees. Master's and doctoral degrees are also awarded. Bachelor's degrees are awarded in Engineering, and business are the strongest academically. Business has the largest enrollment.

ACTIVITIES: There are no fraternities or sororities. There are 140 groups on campus, including band, choir, chorus, computers, dance, drama, ethnic, honors, international, jazz band, LGBT, literary magazine, newspaper, pep band, political, professional, radio and TV, religious, social, social service, student government, and yearbook. **Sports:** There are 10 intercollegiate sports for men and 10 for women. Facilities include basketball and volleyball arena, Aquatic center containing an eight-lane swimming pool, diving area, field house with 200-meter, six-lane track, a fitness center, weight room, and aerobics rooms. **Graduates:** From July 1, 2016 to June 30, 2017, 1557 bachelor's degrees were awarded. The most popular majors were marketing (9%), financial management (9%), and accounting (7%). In an average class, 62% graduate in 4 years or less, 75% graduate in 5 years or less, and 76% graduate in 6 years or less. Of the 2016 graduating class, 7% were enrolled in graduate school within 6 months of graduation, and 33% were employed.

SERVICES: Counseling and information services are available, as is tutoring in every subject. There is a reader service for the blind. **Library/Resources:** The library contains 695,137 volumes, 1.1 million microform items, 6,383 audio/video tapes/CDs/DVDs, and subscribes to 193,510 periodicals, including electronic. Computerized library services include interlibrary loans, database searching, and Wi-Fi capability. Special learning facilities include an art gallery, radio station, and TV station. **Physically Challenged Students:** 5% of the campus is accessible. Facilities include wheelchair ramps, elevators, special parking, specially equipped restrooms, lowered drinking fountains, and special housing. **Special:** There is 1 national honor society, a freshman honors program, and 16 departmental honors programs. **Visiting:** There are regularly scheduled orientations for prospective students. There are guides for informal visits; visitors may sit in on classes and stay overnight. To schedule a visit, contact the Visit Coordinator at admvisit@stthomas.edu. **Campus Safety and Security:** Measures include 24-hour foot and vehicle patrol, emergency notification system, and security escort services. There are shuttle buses, emergency telephones, lighted pathways/sidewalks, and controlled access to dorms/residences.

REQUIREMENTS: The ACT is required, the SAT is recommended. An application writing sample and standardized test score are also required. UST recommends 3 years of high school math. The GED is accepted in place of high school transcript (s). AP and CLEP credits are accepted. Important factors in the admissions decision are recommendations by school officials, advanced placement or honors courses, and evidence of special talent. **Procedure:** Freshmen are admitted in the fall and spring. Entrance exams should be taken by the fall of the senior year. There are deferred admissions and rolling admissions plans. Application deadlines are open. Notification of early decision is sent December 15; regular decision, February 15. Applications are accepted on-line. **Transfer Students:** 271 transfer students enrolled in 2016-2017. Transfer applicants must have a minimum GPA of 2.3 in transferable college credits. 32 of 132 credits required for the bachelor's degree must be completed at UST. **International Students:** There are 186 international students enrolled. They must take the TOEFL or MELAB, and either the SAT or ACT.

ADMISSIONS: 86% of the 2017-2018 applicants were accepted. The SAT scores for the 2017-2018 freshman class were: Critical Reading-- 20% below 500, 34% between 500 and 599, 32% between 600 and 699, and 14% between 700 and 800. Math-- 6% below 500, 40% between 500 and 599, 42% between 600 and 699, and 12% between 700 and 800. The ACT scores were 19% between 18 and 23, 62% between 24 and 29, and 19% above 30. 53% of the current freshmen were in the top fifth of their class; 87% were in the top two fifths. 15 freshmen graduated first in their class. **Admissions Contact:** Kristen Hatfield, Director of Admissions. Email: *admissions@stthomas.edu* Web: *www.stthomas.edu*

FINANCIAL AID: In 2017-2018, 61% of all full-time freshmen received some form of financial aid. 47% of all full-time freshmen received need-based aid. The average freshman award was $28,360. The average financial indebtedness of the 2017 graduate was $40,403. The FAFSA code is 002345. The priority date for freshman financial aid applications for fall entry is April 1.

WINONA STATE UNIVERSITY D-5

www.winona.edu

Winona, MN 55987	**(507) 457-5100** **(800) DIAL-WSU**
Fax: (507) 457-5620	**Email: admissions@winona.edu**
Full-time: 2407 men, 4092 women	**Faculty:** 338
Part-time: 322 men, 620 women	**Ph.D.s:** 83%
Graduate: 135 men, 386 women	**Student/Faculty:** 18 to 1
Year: semesters, summer session	**Tuition:** $9379 ($15,302)
Room & Board: $8730	**Freshman Class:** 7476 applied, 4467 accepted, 1586 enrolled
ACT: 23	**CEEB CODE:** 6680
Application Deadline: July 14	**COMPETITIVE**

Winona State University, founded in 1858, is a mid-sized comprehensive regional university and a member of the Minnesota State. There are 5 undergraduate schools and 1 graduate school. In addition to regional accreditation, WSU has baccalaureate program accreditation with AACSB, ABET, CSWE, NASM, CCNE, CAATE, and NAST. The 125-acre campus is in an urban area 120 miles southeast of Minneapolis and St. Paul. Including any residence halls, there are 38 buildings.

STUDENT LIFE: 71% of undergraduates are from Minnesota. Others are from 36 states, 48 foreign countries, and Canada. **Female To Male Ratio:** 1.8:1. 23% do not continue beyond their first year; 60% remain to graduate. **Housing:** 2443 students can be accommodated in college housing, which includes dorms and on-campus apartments, and special-interest houses. On-campus housing is guaranteed for the freshman year only, and is available on a first-come, first-served basis. Alcohol is not permitted. All students may keep cars.

FACULTY/CLASSROOMS: 43% of faculty are male; 57% are female. Graduate students teach 1% of introductory courses. The average class size in a laboratory is 21 and in a regular course is 28.

PROGRAMS OF STUDY: WSU confers B.A.S., B.A., B.S., B.S.Ed., B.S.W., and B.M. degrees. Associate, master's, and doctoral degrees are also awarded. Bachelor's degrees are awarded in BIOLOGICAL SCIENCE (biology/biological science), BUSINESS (accounting, banking and finance, business administration and management, business economics, human resources/organizational management, management information systems, marketing, and recreation and leisure services), COMMUNICATIONS AND THE ARTS (broadcasting, communication studies, dramatic arts, English, fine arts, graphic design, journalism, music, music performance, Spanish, and speech/debate/rhetoric), COMPUTER AND PHYSICAL SCIENCE (applied science, chemistry, computer science, earth science, earth science/adolescence education, geology, mathematics, physics, and statistics), EDUCATION (art education, athletic training, business education, early childhood education, elementary education, foreign languages education, global studies, health education, mathematics education, music education, physical education, science education, secondary education, social studies education, special education, specific learning disabilities, and teaching English as a second/foreign language (TESOL/TEFOL), ENGINEERING AND ENVIRONMENTAL DESIGN (materials engineering and preengineering), HEALTH PROFESSIONS (community health work, cytotechnology, exercise science, health care administration, movement science, nursing, predentistry, premedicine, preoptometry, prepharmacy, prephysical therapy, prepodiatry, preveterinary science, and public health), SOCIAL SCIENCE (criminal justice, economics, history, paralegal studies, physical fitness/movement, political science/government, prelaw, psychology, public administration, social work, sociology, and women and gender studies). Nursing, education, and engineering are the strongest academically. Nursing, elementary education, and business administration have the largest enrollments.

ACTIVITIES: There are 199 groups on campus, including art, band, cheerleading, chess, choir, chorale, chorus, computers, dance, debate, drama, environmental, ethnic, film, forensics, honors, international, jazz band, LGBT, literary magazine, musical theater, newspaper, orchestra, pep band, photography, political, professional, radio and TV, religious, social, social service, student government, and symphony. Popular campus events include Homecoming. **Sports:** There are 5 intercollegiate sports for men and 10 for women, and 16 intramural sports for men and 16 for women. Facilities include a stadium, baseball field, softball field, gyms, weight room, gymnastic practice area, a swimming pool, handball/racquetball courts, cardio-fitness center with machines, and a walking/jogging inside track. **Graduates:** From July 1, 2016 to June 30, 2017, 1790 bachelor's degrees were awarded. The most popular majors were business/marketing (22%), health professions and related programs (19%), and education (10%). In an average class, 57% graduate in 5 years or less and 59% graduate in 6 years or less.

SERVICES: Counseling and information services are available, as is tutoring in most subjects. **Library/Resources:** The library contains 354,326 volumes, 27,501 microform items, 15,899 audio/video tapes/CDs/DVDs, and subscribes to 34,393 periodicals, including electronic. Computerized library services include interlibrary loans, database searching, Internet access, and Wi-Fi capability. Special learning facilities include an art gallery and radio station. **Physically Challenged Students:** 5% of the campus is accessible. Facilities include wheelchair ramps, elevators, special parking, specially equipped restrooms, special class scheduling, lowered drinking fountains, lowered telephones, and special housing. **Special:** WSU offers cross-registration with St. Mary's University, study abroad in 12 countries, internships, work-study programs, student-designed majors, dual majors, pass/fail options, and credit for life, military, and work experience. Students may earn accelerated degrees in all majors and a general studies degree. There are 9 national honor societies and 6 departmental honors programs. **Visiting:** There are regularly scheduled orientations for prospective students, including daily tours and admissions visits from October through January on select Saturday mornings. There are guides for informal visits and visitors may sit in on classes. To schedule a visit, contact the Office of Admissions. **Campus Safety and Security:** Measures include 24-hour foot and vehicle patrol, emergency notification system, self-defense education, and security escort services. There are shuttle buses, emergency telephones, lighted pathways/sidewalks, and controlled access to dorms/residences.

REQUIREMENTS: The ACT is required. Candidates should have completed 4 units of English, 1 of which may be speech, 3 each of math and science, 2 each of foreign language and social studies, 1 of history and elective; preferably in world culture, the arts, or computer science. AP and CLEP credits are accepted. To graduate, students must complete 120 credit hours with a minimum GPA of 2.0. General education requirements include 3 credits in public speaking, 3 credits in English, 7 credits in natural sciences, 3 in math and logical reasoning, 9 in history and social sciences, 9 in humanities and fine arts, and 2 in phys ed. Majors average 46 credits, and some require a capstone experience. **Procedure:** Freshmen are admitted in the fall, spring, and summer. Entrance exams should be taken in the junior year. There is a rolling admissions plan. Applications should be filed by July 14 for fall entry; November 24 for spring entry. The fall 2017 application fee was $20. Applications are accepted on-line. **Transfer Students:** 564 transfer students enrolled in 2016-2017. Applicants must have completed 24 semester hours of credit with a minimum GPA of 2.4. 30 of 120 credits required for the bachelor's degree must be completed at WSU. **International Students:** There are 264 international students enrolled. They must take the TOEFL with a minimum score of 520 on the paper-based TOEFL (PBT) or 68 on the Internet-based version (iBT).

ADMISSIONS: 60% of the 2017-2018 applicants were accepted. **Admissions Contact:** Carl Stange, Director of Admissions. Email: *admissions@winona.edu* Web: *www.winona.edu*

FINANCIAL AID: In 2017-2018, 60% of all full-time freshmen received some form of financial aid. 50% of all full-time freshmen received need-based aid. The average freshman award was $7,135. Need-based scholarships or need-based grants averaged $5,112; need-based self-help aid (loans and jobs) averaged $3,387; non-need-based athletic scholarships averaged $2,417; and other non-need-based awards and non-need-based scholarships averaged $2,485. The average financial indebtedness of the 2017 graduate was $35,221. The FAFSA code is 002394. The priority date for freshman financial aid applications for fall entry is May 15.

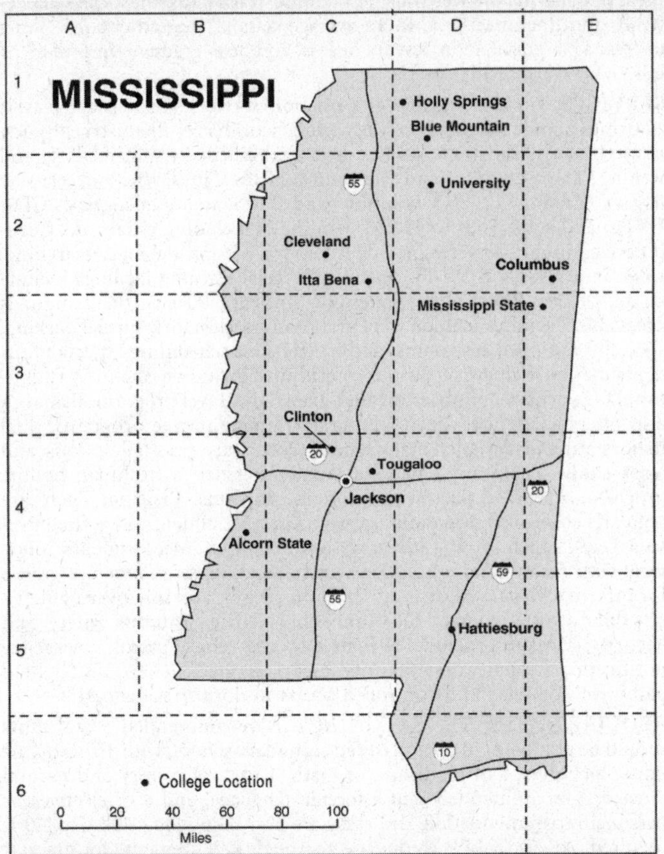

ALCORN STATE UNIVERSITY B-4
www.alcorn.edu

Lorman, MS 39096 (601) 877-6147

Fax: (601) 877-6347	**Email:** ebarnes@alcorn.edu
Full-time: 980 men, 1725 women	**Faculty:** IIB, -$
Part-time: 60 men, 245 women	**Ph.D.s:** 64%
Graduate: 165 men, 505 women	**Student/Faculty:** 17 to 1
Year: semesters, summer session	**Tuition:** $6888
Room & Board: $8996	**Freshman Class:** n/av
SAT: recommended **ACT:** required	**CEEB CODE:** 1008
Application Deadline: open	**COMPETITIVE**

Alcorn State University, founded in 1871, is a public institution offering programs in agriculture, the arts and sciences, business, engineering, and nursing. The figures given in the above capsule and in this profile are approximate. There are 6 undergraduate schools and 1 graduate school. In addition to regional accreditation, ASU has baccalaureate program accreditation with AACSB, ADA, AHEA, NASM, NLN, AAFCS, and NAIT. The 1756-acre campus is in a rural area in Clairborne county, 45 miles south of Vicksburg and 7 miles west of Lorman. Including any residence halls, there are 128 buildings.

STUDENT LIFE: 81% of undergraduates are from Mississippi. Others are from 32 states, 13 foreign countries, and Canada. 95% are from public schools. 91% are African American; 7% White; 2% Foreign. **Female To Male Ratio:** 2.1:1. The average age of freshmen is 24; all undergraduates, 25. 28% do not continue beyond their first year; 45% remain to graduate. **Housing:** 2495 students can be accommodated in college housing, which includes dorms. In addition, there are honors houses. On-campus housing is guaranteed for all 4 years. 56% of students commute. Alcohol is not permitted. All students may keep cars.

FACULTY/CLASSROOMS: 55% of faculty are male; 45% are female. 92% teach undergraduates. No introductory courses are taught by graduate students.

PROGRAMS OF STUDY: ASU confers B.A., B.S., B.M., B.M.E. and B.S.N. degrees. Associate and master's degrees are also awarded. Bachelor's degrees are awarded in AGRICULTURE (agricultural business management and agricultural economics), BIOLOGICAL SCIENCE (biology/biological science and nutrition), BUSINESS (accounting, business administration and management, and recreation and leisure services), COMMUNICATIONS AND THE ARTS (communications, English, and music), COMPUTER AND PHYSICAL SCIENCE (applied science, chemistry, computer science, and mathematics), EDUCATION (elementary education and special education), ENGINEERING AND ENVIRONMENTAL DESIGN (computer technology), HEALTH PROFESSIONS (health science, nursing, and sports medicine), SOCIAL SCIENCE (child psychology/development, criminal justice, economics, history, political science/government, psychology, social work, and sociology). Business administration, biology, and elementary education have the largest enrollments.

ACTIVITIES: 7% of men belong to 4 local and 4 national fraternities; 10% of women belong to 4 local and 4 national sororities. There are 79 groups on campus, including band, cheerleading, choir, chorus, dance, drama, honors, jazz band, marching band, newspaper, photography, radio and TV, religious, student government, and yearbook. Popular campus events include High School Day, and Career Development Day. **Sports:** There are 8 intercollegiate sports for men and 10 for women, and 9 intramural sports for men and 9 for women. Facilities include a stadium and gym. **Graduates:** From July 1, 2016 to June 30, 2017, 399 bachelor's degrees were awarded. The most popular majors were general studies (20%), biology (12%), and nursing (9%). In an average class, 45% graduate in 6 years or less. Of the 2016 graduating class, 38% were enrolled in graduate school within 6 months of graduation, and 99% were employed.

SERVICES: Counseling and information services are available, as is tutoring in most subjects. There is remedial math, reading, and writing. **Library/Resources:** The library contains 225,423 volumes, 581,883 microform items, and 17,200 audio/video tapes/CDs/DVDs, and subscribes to 40,741 periodicals including electronic. Computerized library services include interlibrary loans, database searching, Internet access, and Wi-Fi capability. Special learning facilities include a radio station. **Physically Challenged Students:** 15% of the campus is accessible. Facilities include wheelchair ramps, elevators, special parking, specially equipped restrooms, and lowered drinking fountains. **Special:** The university offers internships, and work-study programs. There is 1 national honor society, Phi Beta Kappa, a freshman honors program, and 5 departmental honors programs. **Visiting:** There are regularly scheduled orientations for prospective students. There are guides for informal visits, visitors may sit in on classes, and stay overnight. To schedule a visit, contact the Admissions Office. **Campus Safety and Security:** Measures include 24-hour foot and vehicle patrol. There are lighted pathways/sidewalks.

REQUIREMENTS: The ACT is required. The SAT is recommended. Students must have graduated from an accredited high school with at least a C average and have completed 15.5 units of a college prep curriculum. AP and CLEP credits are accepted. To graduate, students must complete at least 128 semester hours with a minimum GPA of 2.0. Core requirements include 12 hours of social science, 9 each of natural science and creative arts, 6 of English, 4 of phys ed or military science, and 3 each of math and oral communications, as well as 1 of student adjustment. **Procedure:** Freshmen are admitted to all sessions. Entrance exams should be taken so that scores may be submitted at the time application is made. There are early decision, deferred admissions, and rolling admissions plans. Application deadlines are open. Notification is sent on a rolling basis. **Transfer Students:** 286 transfer students enrolled in 2016-2017. Applicants must have at least 6 hours each of composition and lab sciences, 3 hours of college algebra or above, and 9 other transferable elective hours and must have maintained an overall minimum GPA of 2.0. 104 of 128 credits required for the bachelor's degree must be completed at ASU. **International Students:** There are 30 international students enrolled. They must take the TOEFL with a minimum score of 525 on the paper-based TOEFL (PBT). They must also take the SAT or ACT.

Admissions Contact: Emanuel F. Barnes, Director of Admissions. Email: *ebarnes@alcorn.edu* Web: *www.alcorn.edu*

FINANCIAL AID: In 2017-2018, 42% of all full-time freshmen received some form of financial aid. 31% of all full-time freshmen received need-based aid. The average freshman award was $6,199. Need-based scholarships or need-based grants averaged $3,974 ($4,310 maximum); need-based self-help aid (loans and jobs) averaged $3,308 ($3,500 maximum); non-need-based athletic scholarships averaged $9,192 ($14,696 maximum); and other non-need-based awards and non-need-based scholarships averaged $5,162 ($9,550 maximum). 27% of undergraduate students work part-time. The average financial indebtedness of the 2017 graduate was $22,842. ASU is a member of CSS. The college's own financial statement is required. Check with the school for current application deadlines.

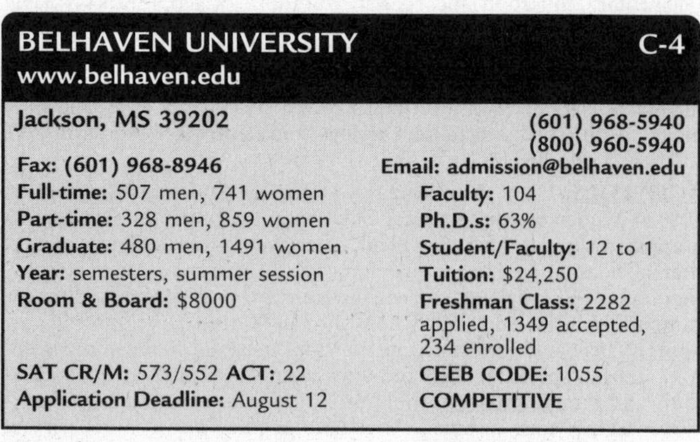

BELHAVEN UNIVERSITY C-4
www.belhaven.edu

Jackson, MS 39202 (601) 968-5940
(800) 960-5940
Fax: (601) 968-8946 Email: admission@belhaven.edu

Full-time: 507 men, 741 women
Part-time: 328 men, 859 women
Graduate: 480 men, 1491 women
Year: semesters, summer session
Room & Board: $8000
SAT CR/M: 573/552 **ACT:** 22
Application Deadline: August 12

Faculty: 104
Ph.D.s: 63%
Student/Faculty: 12 to 1
Tuition: $24,250
Freshman Class: 2282 applied, 1349 accepted, 234 enrolled
CEEB CODE: 1055
COMPETITIVE

Belhaven University, founded in 1883, is a private liberal arts institution with a Presbyterian heritage. There is 1 undergraduate school and 1 graduate school. In addition to regional accreditation, Belhaven has baccalaureate program accreditation with NASAD and NASM. The 42-acre campus is in an urban area in Jackson, MS. Including any residence halls, there are 20 buildings.

STUDENT LIFE: 53% of undergraduates are from Mississippi. Others are from 43 states, and 23 foreign countries. 6% are race unknown; 5% Hispanic; 44% African American; 39% White; 3% two or more races; 2% Foreign; 1% Asian American. 68% are Protestant; 24% Unknown. **Female To Male Ratio:** 2.4:1. The average age of freshmen is 27; all undergraduates, 30. 33% do not continue beyond their first year; 36% remain to graduate. **Housing:** 718 students can be accommodated in college housing, which includes dorms and on-campus apartments. On-campus housing is guaranteed for all 4 years, is available on a first-come, and first-served basis. 78% of students commute. Alcohol is not permitted. All students may keep cars.

FACULTY/CLASSROOMS: 55% of faculty are male; 45% are female. All teach undergraduates. No introductory courses are taught by graduate students. The average class size in a regular course is 15.

PROGRAMS OF STUDY: Belhaven confers B.A., B.S., B.A.A., B.B.A., B.F.A., B.H.A., B.S.M. and B.S.N. degrees. Associate, master's, and doctoral degrees are also awarded. Bachelor's degrees are awarded in BIOLOGICAL SCIENCE (biology/biological science), BUSINESS (accounting and business administration and management), COMMUNICATIONS AND THE ARTS (art, arts administration/management, ballet, broadcasting, communications, creative writing, dance, dramatic arts, English, film arts, and music), COMPUTER AND PHYSICAL SCIENCE (chemistry, computer science, information sciences and systems, and mathematics), EDUCATION (athletic training, education, and elementary education), HEALTH PROFESSIONS (exercise science, nursing, and sports medicine), SOCIAL SCIENCE (applied psychology, biblical studies, history, humanities, interdisciplinary studies, international studies, philosophy, political science/government, psychology, religious music, and social work). Biology, and chemistry are the strongest academically. Business administration, education, and social services have the largest enrollments.

ACTIVITIES: There are no fraternities or sororities. There are 24 groups on campus, including art, band, cheerleading, choir, chorus, dance, drama, ethnic, honors, jazz band, literary magazine, marching band, musical theater, newspaper, orchestra, political, professional, religious, social service, student government, and yearbook. Popular campus events include Singing Christmas Tree, Concert and Lecture Series, and Lake Day. **Sports:** There are 9 intercollegiate sports for men and 8 for women, and 6 intramural sports for men and 6 for women. Facilities include a baseball field, a football/soccer field, an athletic training facility, and an exercise, weight, and conditioning complex. **Graduates:** From July 1, 2016 to June 30, 2017, 559 bachelor's degrees were awarded. The most popular majors were business administration (32%), social sciences (9%), and fine arts (8%). In an average class, 27% graduate in 4 years or less, 35% graduate in 5 years or less, and 36% graduate in 6 years or less.

SERVICES: Counseling and information services are available, as is tutoring in some subjects, such as writing, worldview, chemistry, physics, math, biology, and Bible studies. There is remedial math, reading, and writing. There are also study halls for athletes. **Library/Resources:** The library contains 126,313 volumes, and 2,073 audio/video tapes/CDs/DVDs, and subscribes to 44,795 periodicals including electronic. Computerized library services include interlibrary loans, database searching, Internet access, and Wi-Fi capability. Special learning facilities include an art gallery. **Physically Challenged Students:** 90% of the campus is accessible. Facilities include wheelchair ramps, elevators, special parking, specially equipped restrooms, and special class scheduling. **Special:** Students may participate in various internships, including one in Washington, D.C., or in 6 countries through the study-travel program. Belhaven also offers accelerated degree programs, online degree programs, dual majors, student-designed majors, nondegree study, pass/fail options, and work-study. There are 7 national honor societies, a freshman honors program, and 17 departmental honors programs. **Visiting:** There are regularly scheduled orientations for prospective students, including Preview Days, which allow students to see the campus, meet students, interview with faculty and admissions, and attend classes. There are guides for informal visits, visitors may sit in on classes, and stay overnight. To schedule a visit, contact the Admissions Office. **Campus Safety and Security:** Measures include 24-hour foot and vehicle patrol, emergency notification system, and security escort services. There are lighted pathways/sidewalks and controlled access to dorms/residences.

REQUIREMENTS: The SAT or ACT is recommended. Applicants should be graduates of an accredited secondary school, with 16 academic units, including 4 of English, 2 of math, 1 each of history and natural science, a recommended 2 of a foreign language, and 6 of electives. A personal recommendation and essay are also required. A GPA of 2.0 is required. AP and CLEP credits are accepted. Requirements for graduation vary by degree, but students must complete at least 124 semester hours, including 25 hours of World View Curriculum courses, with a minimum 2.0 GPA. **Procedure:** Freshmen are admitted to all sessions. Entrance exams should be taken in the junior year. There is a rolling admissions plan. Applications should be filed by August 12 for fall entry. The fall 2017 application fee was $25. Applications are accepted on-line. **Transfer Students:** 384 transfer students enrolled in 2016-2017. Transfer applicants must have a minimum 2.0 GPA and submit all college transcripts. 31 of 124 credits required for the bachelor's degree must be completed at Belhaven. **International Students:** There are 48 international students enrolled. They must take the TOEFL. They must also take the SAT or ACT.

ADMISSIONS: 59% of the 2017-2018 applicants were accepted. The SAT scores for the 2017-2018 freshman class were: Critical Reading-- 17% below 500, 45% between 500 and 599, 33% between 600 and 699, and 5% between 700 and 800. Math-- 17% below 500, 60% between 500 and 599, 21% between 600 and 699, and 2% between 700 and 800. The ACT scores were 3% between 12 and 17, 65% between 18 and 23, 28% between 24 and 29, and 4% above 30. **Admissions Contact:** Suzanne Sullivan, Assistant VP for University Advancement. Email: *admission@belhaven.edu* Web: *www.belhaven.edu*

FINANCIAL AID: In 2017-2018, 94% of all full-time freshmen received some form of financial aid. 90% of all full-time freshmen received need-based aid. The average freshman award was $17,514. Need-based scholarships or need-based grants averaged $4,595 ($10,250 maximum); need-based self-help aid (loans and jobs) averaged $2,761 ($3,500 maximum); other non-need-based awards and non-need-based scholarships averaged $4,426 ($11,236 maximum); and $5,632 from other forms of aid. 21% of undergraduate students work part-time. The average financial indebtedness of the 2017 graduate was $23,419. The FAFSA code is 002397. The priority date for freshman financial aid applications for fall entry is March 1.

BLUE MOUNTAIN COLLEGE D-1
www.bmc.edu

Blue Mountain, MS 38610	**(662) 685-4771** **(800) 235-0136**
Fax: (662) 685-4776	**Email: lgibson@bmc.edu**
Full-time: 231 men, 264 women	**Faculty:** 34
Part-time: 13 men, 36 women	**Ph.D.s:** 82%
Graduate: 3 men, 24 women	**Student/Faculty:** 15 to 1
Year: semesters, summer session	**Tuition:** $10,185
Room & Board: $5764	**Freshman Class:** 386 applied, 185 accepted, 111 enrolled
SAT or ACT: required	**CEEB CODE:** 1066
Application Deadline: n/av	**COMPETITIVE**

Blue Mountain College is a Christian liberal arts institution supported by the Mississippi Baptist Convention. Deeply committed to the education of its students since its founding in 1873, the college has continued to attract capable, confident students who desire to pursue knowledge through a Christian worldview in a caring, person-centered environment. There is 1 undergraduate school and 1 graduate school. In addition to regional accreditation, BMC has baccalaureate program accreditation with MCC, Board of Trustees/State Institutions Higher Learning, and MS Commission on Teacher/Admin Licensure/Cert. The 190-acre campus is in a rural area 35 miles from Tupelo, MS, and 65 miles from Memphis, TN. Including any residence halls, there are 23 buildings.

STUDENT LIFE: 78% of undergraduates are from Mississippi. Others are from 15 states, 10 foreign countries, and Canada. 88% are from public schools. 83% are White; 2% Hispanic; 2% Foreign; 2% two or more races; 10% African American; 1% American Indian/Alaska Native. 95% are Protestant. **Female To Male Ratio:** 1.3:1. The average age of freshmen is 19; all undergraduates, 23. 31% do not continue beyond their first year; 55% remain to graduate. **Housing:** 346 students can be accommodated in college housing, which includes dorms. On-campus housing is available on a first-come and first-served basis. 59% of students live on campus. Alcohol is not permitted. All students may keep cars.

FACULTY/CLASSROOMS: 46% of faculty are male; 54% are female. 98% teach undergraduates. No introductory courses are taught by graduate students. The average class size in an introductory lecture is 20; in a laboratory is 18; and in a regular course is 15.

PROGRAMS OF STUDY: BMC confers B.A., B.S., and B.S.Ed. degrees. Master's degrees are also awarded. Bachelor's degrees are awarded in BIOLOGICAL SCIENCE (biology/biological science), BUSINESS (business administration and management), COMMUNICATIONS AND THE ARTS (church music, English, fine arts, and music), COMPUTER AND PHYSICAL SCIENCE (mathematics), EDUCATION (elementary education, English education, mathematics education, music education, physical education, science education, social science education, and Spanish adolescence education), HEALTH PROFESSIONS (exercise science and medical technology), SOCIAL SCIENCE (biblical studies, Christian studies, criminal justice, history, liberal arts/general studies, psychology, and Spanish studies). Elementary education, biology, and business administration are the strongest academically. Elementary education, business administration, and psychology have the largest enrollments.

ACTIVITIES: There are no fraternities or sororities. There are 31 groups on campus, including art, band, cheerleading, choir, chorale, chorus, drama, honors, literary magazine, musical theater, pep band, professional, religious, social, student government, and yearbook. Popular campus events include Society Rush, Founder's Day, Homecoming on the Hill, Ministerial Alumni Day, Homecoming, and Topper Fest. **Sports:** There are 6 intercollegiate sports for men and 6 for women, and 8 intramural sports for men and 9 for women. The athletic and recreation facilities provide a gymnasium, swimming pool, a fitness center, and sportsplex. **Graduates:** From July 1, 2016 to June 30, 2017, 115 bachelor's degrees were awarded. The most popular majors were psychology (18%), business administration (18%), and elementary education (14%). In an average class, 1% graduate in 3 years or less, 37% graduate in 4 years or less, 49% graduate in 5 years or less, and 50% graduate in 6 years or less. Of the 2016 graduating class, 19% were enrolled in graduate school within 6 months of graduation, and 80% were employed.

SERVICES: Counseling and information services are available, as is tutoring in every subject. There is remedial math, reading, and writing. **Library/Resources:** The library contains 80,354 volumes, 1 microform items, and 1,474 audio/video tapes/CDs/DVDs, and subscribes to 146 periodicals including electronic. Computerized library services include interlibrary loans, database searching, Internet access, and Wi-Fi capability. **Physically Challenged Students:** All of the campus is accessible. Facilities include wheelchair ramps, elevators, special parking, specially equipped restrooms, special class scheduling, lowered drinking fountains, and special housing. **Special:** The college offers dual majors and internships (maximum 6 credits); consortial relationship with Union University resulting in dual degrees in Biology/Nursing, Psychology/Nursing; a consortial relationship with Baptist Memorial College of Health Sciences resulting in dual degrees in Biology/Nursing, Biology/Diagnostic Medical Sonography, Biology/Medical Laboratory Technology, Biology/Medical Radiography, Biology/Nuclear Medicine Technology, Biology/Radiation Therapy, Biology/Respiratory Care and a joint program in Business Administration with concentration in Health Care Management; two online degree programs: Business Administration and Psychology. The college offers a Junior-Senior Honors Program. There are 8 national honor societies and 8 departmental honors programs. **Visiting:** There are regularly scheduled orientations for prospective students. There are guides for informal visits, visitors may sit in on classes, and stay overnight. To schedule a visit, contact Nancy McDonald at (662) 685-4771 x.158. **Campus Safety and Security:** Measures include 24-hour foot and vehicle patrol and emergency notification system. There are lighted pathways/sidewalks and controlled access to dorms/residences.

REQUIREMENTS: BMC recommends that applicants for admission have completed 4 units of English, 3 each of math, science, and social studies, and 2 of a foreign language. BMC will accept either the ACT or the SAT; both are not required. A GPA of 2.0 is required. AP and CLEP credits are accepted. Important factors in the admissions decision are recommendations by alumni and recommendations by school officials. All students must take a minimum of 120 semester hours, with a minimum of 40 hours on the junior-senior level; 25% of total degree hours required must be earned at Blue Mountain. No more than 42 hours of course work carrying the same prefix may be credited toward the degree (with few exceptions). Core curriculum requirements include 12 semester hours of English, 6 each of history and biblical studies, 4 of biological science, 3 each of psychology, fine arts, math, physical science, computer applications, and electives, and 2 of phys ed. A 2.0 GPA overall is required (2.5 for teacher education). Most degrees require a minor. **Procedure:** Freshmen are admitted to all sessions. Entrance exams should be taken during junior or senior year. There are deferred admissions and rolling admissions plans. Application deadlines are open. Applications are accepted on-line. **Transfer Students:** 137 transfer students enrolled in 2016-2017. Transfer students who have been enrolled in other colleges must submit official transcripts from each college attended and must be eligible to re-enter the last college attended. A maximum of 70 semester hours of credit may be transferred from a community or junior college. 30 of 120 credits required for the bachelor's degree must be completed at BMC. **International Students:** There are 9 international students enrolled. They must take the TOEFL with a minimum score of 500 on the paper-based TOEFL (PBT) or 61 on the Internet-based version (iBT). They must also take the SAT or ACT.

ADMISSIONS: 48% of the 2017-2018 applicants were accepted. 31% of the current freshmen were in the top fifth of their class; 62% were in the top two fifths. 3 freshmen graduated first in their class. **Admissions Contact:** Lynn Gibson, Vice President for Enrollment Services. Email: *lgibson@bmc.edu* Web: *www.bmc.edu*

FINANCIAL AID: In 2017-2018, 100% of all full-time freshmen received some form of financial aid. 64% of all full-time freshmen received need-based aid. The average freshman award was $13,047. Need-based scholarships or need-based grants averaged $5,011 ($6,215 maximum); need-based self-help aid (loans and jobs) averaged $3,125 ($5,124 maximum); non-need-based athletic scholarships averaged $5,003 ($15,282 maximum); and other non-need-based awards and non-need-based scholarships averaged $6,534 ($19,000 maximum). 17% of undergraduate students work part-time. The average financial indebtedness of the 2017 graduate was $15,256. The FAFSA code is 002398. The priority date for freshman financial aid applications for fall entry is April 1.

DELTA STATE UNIVERSITY *(The complete profile is made available exclusively on our website, www.barronspac.com)*

JACKSON STATE UNIVERSITY *(The complete profile is made available exclusively on our website, www.barronspac.com)*

MILLSAPS COLLEGE C-4
www.millsaps.edu

Jackson, MS 39210 (601) 974-1050
(800) 352-1050
Fax: (601) 974-1059 Email: admissions@millsaps.edu

Full-time: 384 men, 346 women	**Faculty:** 86; IIB, av$
Part-time: 5 men, 9 women	**Ph.D.s:** 95%
Graduate: 41 men, 19 women	**Student/Faculty:** 8 to 1
Year: semesters, summer session	**Tuition:** $37,110
Room & Board: $12,970	**Freshman Class:** 1901 applied, 902 accepted, 171 enrolled
SAT CR/M: 540/560 **ACT:** 26	**CEEB CODE:** 1471
Application Deadline: July 1	**COMPETITIVE+**

Millsaps College, founded in 1890, is an independent liberal arts institution affiliated with the United Methodist Church. Millsaps is known for its academic strength, national-caliber faculty, small class size, and spirit of community service. The figures given in the above capsule and in this profile are approximate. There are 4 undergraduate schools and 1 graduate school. In addition to regional accreditation, Millsaps has baccalaureate program accreditation with AACSB, and ACS. The 100-acre campus is in an urban area in the capital city of Jackson. Including any residence halls, there are 33 buildings.

STUDENT LIFE: 58% of undergraduates are from out of state, mostly the South. Students are from 25 states, 14 foreign countries, and Canada. 61% are from public schools. 76% are White; 5% Asian American; 3% Foreign; 3% race unknown; 2% Hispanic; 10% African American; 1% American Indian/Alaska Native. 51% claim no religious affiliation; 33% Protestant; 14% Catholic. **Male To Female Ratio:** 1.1:1. The average age of freshmen is 18; all undergraduates, 20. 21% do not continue beyond their first year; 67% remain to graduate. **Housing:** 950 students can be accommodated in college housing, which includes dorms. In addition, there are special-interest houses, fraternity houses, designated housing for freshmen, and a service learning residence hall dedicated to community service and leadership. On-campus housing is available on a first-come, first-served basis, and is available on a lottery system for upperclassmen. 88% of students live on campus. All students may keep cars.

FACULTY/CLASSROOMS: 50% of faculty are male; 50% are female. All teach undergraduates, 90% do research, and 90% do both. No introductory courses are taught by graduate students. The average class size in an introductory lecture is 20; in a laboratory is 20; and in a regular course is 13.

PROGRAMS OF STUDY: Millsaps confers B.A., B.S. and B.B.A. degrees. Master's degrees are also awarded. Bachelor's degrees are awarded in BIOLOGICAL SCIENCE (biochemistry, biology/biological science, and neurosciences), BUSINESS (accounting and business administration and management), COMMUNICATIONS AND THE ARTS (art history and appreciation, classics, communications, creative writing, English, music, Spanish, and studio art), COMPUTER AND PHYSICAL SCIENCE (applied mathematics, chemistry, geology, mathematics, and physics), EDUCATION (education), SOCIAL SCIENCE (anthropology, economics, European studies, history, Latin American studies, philosophy, political science/government, psychology, public administration, religion, and sociology). Biology, chemistry, and pre-med are the strongest academically. Business administration, biology and psychology have the largest enrollments.

ACTIVITIES: 60% of men belong to 6 national fraternities; 64% of women belong to 4 national sororities. There are 80 groups on campus, including art, cheerleading, choir, chorale, chorus, computers, dance, debate, drama, environmental, ethnic, honors, international, LGBT, literary magazine, musical theater, newspaper, pep band, photography, political, professional, religious, social, social service, student government, and yearbook. Popular campus events include Major Madness, Project Midtown, and Homecoming. **Sports:** There are 9 intercollegiate sports for men and 9 for women, and 9 intramural sports for men and 9 for women. Facilities include an activities center containing a fitness center with basketball and volleyball courts, a cardio theater, an aerobics room, fitness and weight-training equipment, a free-weight room, an outdoor pool, racquetball and handball courts, and a squash court. Outdoor areas include tennis courts, a sand volleyball court, and softball, baseball, football, soccer, and multipurpose fields. **Graduates:** From July 1, 2016 to June 30, 2017, 202 bachelor's degrees were awarded. The most popular majors were biology (13%), accounting (13%), and business administration (12%). In an average class, 1% graduate in 3 years or less, 62% graduate in 4 years or less, 66% graduate in 5 years or less, and 67% graduate in 6 years or less. Of the 2016 graduating class, 40% were enrolled in graduate school within 6 months of graduation, and 33% were employed.

SERVICES: Counseling and information services are available, as is tutoring in most subjects, by request, as needed. There is also a writing center, a language lab, and a math lab. **Library/Resources:** The library contains 200,396 volumes, 35,525 microform items, and 8,984 audio/video tapes/CDs/DVDs, and subscribes to 38,588 periodicals including electronic. Computerized library services include interlibrary loans, database searching, Internet access, and Wi-Fi capability. Special learning facilities include an art gallery, an observatory, a multi-disciplinary laboratory, and a molecular biology/functional genomics research lab. **Physically Challenged Students:** 90% of the campus is accessible. Facilities include wheelchair ramps, elevators, special parking, specially equipped restrooms, special class scheduling, lowered drinking fountains, lowered telephones, and special housing. Other needs can be addressed through the ADA coordinator on an individual basis. **Special:** Millsaps sponsors international studies programs in Africa, Asia, Europe, and Latin America. Direct exchange options are offered in Japan and Ireland. Students may also participate in a wide variety of field research, honors, internship, fellowships, and service learning programs. There are 28 national honor societies, Phi Beta Kappa, and 19 departmental honors programs. **Visiting:** There are regularly scheduled orientations for prospective students, including meetings with faculty and student services personnel, and tours of the campus. There are guides for informal visits, visitors may sit in on classes, and stay overnight. To schedule a visit, contact the Admissions Office. **Campus Safety and Security:** Measures include 24-hour foot and vehicle patrol, emergency notification system, self-defense education, and security escort services. There are emergency telephones, lighted pathways/sidewalks, controlled access to dorms/residences, controlled access to all buildings during specified hours, and entrances to campus are gated and staffed at night.

REQUIREMENTS: The SAT or ACT is required. Applicants should be graduates of an accredited secondary school or have a GED certificate, and have completed at least 14 academic units, including 4 in English, 3 in math, 2 in social studies, and 2 in history. An essay is required. A GPA of 2.5 is required. AP and CLEP credits are accepted. Important factors in the admissions decision are advanced placement or honors courses, extracurricular activities record, and recommendations by school officials. To graduate, students must complete 128 credit hours with 32 to 48 hours in the major and a minimum GPA of 2.0. The core curriculum includes 4 interdisciplinary courses in humanities and 4 in the sciences and math. Students must also take Introduction to Liberal Studies during the freshman year and Reflections on Liberal Studies during the senior year. Other requirements include satisfactory completion of a 7-paper writing proficiency portfolio and a comprehensive exam in the specific field of study. **Procedure:** Freshmen are admitted fall and spring. Entrance exams should be taken in the spring of the junior year or fall of the senior year. There are early admissions, deferred admissions, and rolling admissions plans. Applications should be filed by July 1 for fall entry. Notification is sent on a rolling basis. Applications are accepted on-line. **Transfer Students:** 36 transfer students enrolled in 2016-2017. Applicants must have a minimum GPA of 2.75 and be in good standing at their previous school. Requirements include high school and college transcripts, an essay or personal statement, and ACT or SAT scores. 32 of 128 credits required for the bachelor's degree must be completed at Millsaps. **International Students:** There are 23 international students enrolled. They must take the TOEFL with a minimum score of 550 on the paper-based TOEFL (PBT) or 80 on the Internet-based version (iBT), or take the IELTS. They must also take the SAT or ACT, scoring 21. The SAT or ACT are accepted in lieu of the TOEFL.

ADMISSIONS: 47% of the 2017-2018 applicants were accepted. The SAT scores for the 2017-2018 freshman class were: Critical Reading-- 25% below 500, 39% between 500 and 599, 28% between 600 and 699, and 8% between 700 and 800. Math-- 17% below 500, 47% between 500 and 599, 33% between 600 and 699, and 3% between 700 and 800. The ACT scores were 9% below 12, 23% between 12 and 17, 27% between 18 and 23, 18% between 24 and 29, and 23% above 30. 48% of the current freshmen were in the top fifth of their class; 79% were in the top two fifths. 6 freshmen graduated first in their class. **Admissions Contact:** Catherine Box, Director of Admissions. Email: *admissions@millsaps.edu* Web: *www.millsaps.edu*

FINANCIAL AID: In 2017-2018, 99% of all full-time freshmen received

some form of financial aid. 67% of all full-time freshmen received need-based aid. The average freshman award was $30,461. Need-based scholarships or need-based grants averaged $24,248 ($44,890 maximum); need-based self-help aid (loans and jobs) averaged $8,358 ($28,790 maximum); and other non-need-based awards and non-need-based scholarships averaged $20,865 ($44,890 maximum). 76% of undergraduate students work part-time. The average financial indebtedness of the 2017 graduate was $27,926. The FAFSA code is 002414. The priority date for freshman financial aid applications for fall entry is March 1.

MISSISSIPPI COLLEGE C-4
www.mc.edu

Clinton, MS 39058 **(601) 925-3800**

Fax: (601) 925-3950	**Email:** kylebrantley@mc.edu
Full-time: n/av	**Faculty:** I, +$
Part-time: n/av	**Ph.D.s:** n/av
Graduate: n/av	**Student/Faculty:** n/av
Year: semesters, summer session	**Tuition:** $16,660
Room & Board: $9190	**Freshman Class:** 3050 applied, 1827 accepted, 585 enrolled
SAT CR/M: 550/520 **ACT:** 24	**CEEB CODE:** 1477
Application Deadline: open	**COMPETITIVE**

Mississippi College, founded in 1826 and affiliated with the Southern Baptist Church, is a private institution offering degrees in liberal arts, business, education, and health sciences. There are 6 undergraduate schools and 8 graduate schools. In addition to regional accreditation, MC has baccalaureate program accreditation with ACBSP, CSWE, and NASM. The 320-acre campus is in a suburban area 15 minutes outside of Jackson, MS. Including any residence halls, there are 30 buildings.

STUDENT LIFE: 60% of undergraduates are from Mississippi. Others are from 42 states, and 34 foreign countries. 94% are Protestant. The average age of freshmen is 18; all undergraduates, 24. **Housing:** 1800 students can be accommodated in college housing, which includes dorms, on-campus apartments, and off-campus apartments. On-campus housing is available on a first-come and first-served basis. 55% of students live on campus. Alcohol is not permitted. All students may keep cars.

FACULTY/CLASSROOMS: No introductory courses are taught by graduate students. The average class size in an introductory lecture is 30; in a laboratory is 25; and in a regular course is 25.

PROGRAMS OF STUDY: MC confers B.A., B.S., B.M., B.M.Ed., B.S.B.A., B.S.Ed., B.S.N. and B.S.W. degrees. Master's and doctoral degrees are also awarded. Bachelor's degrees are awarded in BIOLOGICAL SCIENCE (biochemistry and biology/biological science), BUSINESS (accounting, business administration and management, and marketing/retailing/merchandising), COMMUNICATIONS AND THE ARTS (applied music, art, communications, English, French, graphic design, languages, modern language, music, music theory and composition, piano/organ, Spanish, voice, and winds), COMPUTER AND PHYSICAL SCIENCE (chemistry, computer science, mathematics, and physics), EDUCATION (art education, business education, elementary education, music education, and special education), ENGINEERING AND ENVIRONMENTAL DESIGN (engineering physics and interior design), HEALTH PROFESSIONS (nursing), SOCIAL SCIENCE (American studies, Christian studies, criminal justice, family/consumer studies, history, paralegal studies, political science/government, psychology, religious music, social studies, social work, and sociology). Biology, chemistry, and education are the strongest academically. Business, kinesiology, and education have the largest enrollments.

ACTIVITIES: There are 70 groups on campus, including art, band, cheerleading, chess, choir, chorale, chorus, communications, computers, dance, debate, drama, environmental, ethnic, forensics, honors, international, jazz band, literary magazine, marching band, musical theater, newspaper, opera, pep band, political, professional, radio and TV, religious, social, social service, student government, symphony, and yearbook. Popular campus events include I Love America Day, Derby Day, and Spring Fever Week. **Sports:** There are 9 intercollegiate sports for men and 8 for women, and 8 intramural sports for men and 8 for women. Facilities include a coliseum, a stadium, tennis courts, soccer and softball fields, a swimming pool, a gym, a fitness facility, and a campus weight-training facility.

SERVICES: Counseling and information services are available, as is tutoring in most subjects, such as study skills classes. There is remedial math, reading, and writing. **Library/Resources:** The library contains 370,404 volumes, 540,471 microform items, and 18,348 audio/video tapes/CDs/DVDs, and subscribes to 4,742 periodicals including electronic. Computerized library services include interlibrary loans, database searching, Internet access, and Wi-Fi capability. Special learning facilities include an art gallery, radio station, and TV station. **Physically Challenged Students:** Facilities include wheelchair ramps, elevators, special parking, specially equipped restrooms, special class scheduling, lowered drinking fountains, and lowered telephones. There are also wide doors and special dorm rooms equipped for the physically disabled. **Special:** MC also offers study abroad in up to 10 countries, a 3-3 program with the school of law, work-study programs, internships, B.A.-B.S. degrees, and credit for military experience and by exam. There are 25 national honor societies and a freshman honors program. **Visiting:** There are regularly scheduled orientations for prospective students, including attending classes, touring the campus, and meeting with administrators and departmental advisers. **Campus Safety and Security:** Measures include 24-hour foot and vehicle patrol, emergency notification system, self-defense education, and security escort services. There are shuttle buses, emergency telephones, lighted pathways/sidewalks, and controlled access to dorms/residences.

REQUIREMENTS: An official high school transcript and an official ACT and/or SAT score meeting our standard admission requirement must be submitted in order to be considered for admission. AP and CLEP credits are accepted. To graduate, students must complete 130 credit hours, with an average of C or better in the major. The core curriculum includes English, history, economics, computer science, religion, math, art, social science, phys ed, and chapel. 30 hours are usually required in the major; some majors require 36 to 45. Students must pass a writing proficiency exam. B.A. candidates and English majors must take 12 hours of a foreign language. **Procedure:** Freshmen are admitted fall, spring, and summer. Entrance exams should be taken by June prior to the fall semester. There is a rolling admissions plan. Application deadlines are open. The fall 2017 application fee was $25. Notification is sent on a rolling basis. Applications are accepted on-line. **Transfer Students:** 315 transfer students enrolled in 2016-2017. Applicants must be junior college graduates or students in good academic standing with the college they last attended. They must have a minimum GPA of 2.0. Applicants must submit transcripts from all schools previously attended. 33 of 130 credits required for the bachelor's degree must be completed at MC. **International Students:** There are 350 international students enrolled. They must take the TOEFL.

ADMISSIONS: 60% of the 2017-2018 applicants were accepted. **Admissions Contact:** Kyle Brantley, Director of Admissions. Email: *kylebrantley@mc.edu* Web: *www.mc.edu*

FINANCIAL AID: In 2017-2018, 96% of all full-time freshmen received some form of financial aid. The FAFSA code is 002415. The priority date for freshman financial aid applications for fall entry is October 1.

MISSISSIPPI STATE UNIVERSITY E-3
www.msstate.edu

Mississippi State, MS 39762 **(662) 325-2224**

Fax: (662) 325-7360	**Email:** admit@msstate.edu
Full-time: 8413 men, 8390 women	**Faculty:** 385; I, --$
Part-time: 829 men, 680 women	**Ph.D.s:** 73%
Graduate: 1789 men, 1782 women	**Student/Faculty:** 43 to 1
Year: semesters, summer session	**Tuition:** $8316 ($22,358)
Room & Board: $9750	**Freshman Class:** 13817 applied, 10144 accepted, 3435 enrolled
SAT: required **ACT:** 25	**CEEB CODE:** 1480
Application Deadline: August 1	**COMPETITIVE+**

Mississippi State University is "The People's University." We help students prepare for success with nationally ranked academic programs, transformative leadership experiences, and abundant social opportunities. MSU is big enough to find your place, but small enough to feel like home. MSU has over 80 majors, and is ranked in the Top 100 schools for research. There are 9 undergraduate schools and 1 graduate school.

In addition to regional accreditation, MSU has baccalaureate program accreditation with AACSB, ABET, ASLA, CSAB, FIDER, NAAB, NASAD, NASM, SAF, ACCI, ACEND, AAHA, AAVLD, AAFCS, ACS, APA, AVMA, AAALAC, CACREP, CHEA, ASPA, NALP, NASPAA, NASP, and SWST. The 4200-acre campus is in a small town 125 miles northeast of Jackson, MS.

STUDENT LIFE: 66% of undergraduates are from Mississippi. Others are from 50 states, 78 foreign countries, and Canada. 71% are White; 4% Foreign; 3% Hispanic; 2% two or more races; 19% African American; 1% Asian American. 44% are Jewish; 40% Catholic. **Male To Female Ratio:** 1.0:1. The average age of freshmen is 19; all undergraduates, 22. 18% do not continue beyond their first year; 60% remain to graduate. **Housing:** 5250 students can be accommodated in college housing, which includes dorms. In addition, there are special-interest houses. On-campus housing is guaranteed for the freshman year only, is available on a first-come, and first-served basis. 72% of students commute. Alcohol is not permitted. All students may keep cars.

FACULTY/CLASSROOMS: 59% of faculty are male; 41% are female. 36% teach undergraduates, 29% do research, and 20% do both. Graduate students teach 1% of introductory courses. The average class size in an introductory lecture is 25 and in a laboratory is 33.

PROGRAMS OF STUDY: MSU confers B.A., B.B.A, B.F.A., B.S., B.L.A., B.M.E., B.ARC., BACC and B.S.W. degrees. Master's and doctoral degrees are also awarded. Bachelor's degrees are awarded in AGRICULTURE (agricultural business management, agricultural economics, agriculture, agronomy, animal science, fishing and fisheries, forestry production and processing, horticulture, plant protection (pest management), poultry science, and wildlife management), BIOLOGICAL SCIENCE (biochemistry, biology/biological science, and microbiology), BUSINESS (accounting, banking and finance, business administration and management, insurance, marketing/retailing/merchandising, real estate, and trade and industrial supervision and management), COMMUNICATIONS AND THE ARTS (art, communications, English, and languages), COMPUTER AND PHYSICAL SCIENCE (chemistry, computer science, geoscience, information sciences and systems, mathematics, physics, and science), EDUCATION (agricultural education, business education, education, elementary education, music education, physical education, secondary education, special education, and technical education), ENGINEERING AND ENVIRONMENTAL DESIGN (aerospace studies, agricultural engineering technology, architecture, bioengineering, chemical engineering, civil engineering, computer engineering, electrical/electronics engineering, industrial engineering, industrial engineering technology, landscape architecture/design, and mechanical engineering), HEALTH PROFESSIONS (medical technology), SOCIAL SCIENCE (anthropology, economics, food science, history, interdisciplinary studies, liberal arts/general studies, philosophy, political science/government, psychology, social work, and sociology). Accounting, biochemistry, and physics are the strongest academically. Engineering, business/marketing, and parks & recreation have the largest enrollments.

ACTIVITIES: 18% of men belong to 20 national fraternities; 25% of women belong to 13 national sororities. There are 386 groups on campus, including art, band, chess, choir, communications, computers, dance, debate, drama, environmental, ethnic, Fashion, film, forensics, honors, international, LGBT, literary magazine, marching band, musical theater, newspaper, pep band, photography, political, professional, radio and TV, religious, social, and student government. Popular campus events include Outdoor films, concerts, Salsa in the Streets, Magicians, Comedy Shows, and speakers. **Sports:** There are 7 intercollegiate sports for men and 9 for women, and 40 intramural sports for men and 40 for women. Facilities include a gym, an 1/8 mile jogging track, racquetball courts, a swimming pool, table tennis, strength and aerobic conditioning room, a climbing wall, aerobics/dancing studios, training rooms, soccer and multi-purpose fields.**Graduates:** From July 1, 2016 to June 30, 2017, 3928 bachelor's degrees were awarded. The most popular majors were kinesiology (8%), interdisciplinary studies (8%), and communication (5%). In an average class, 31% graduate in 4 years or less, 53% graduate in 5 years or less, and 60% graduate in 6 years or less.

SERVICES: Counseling and information services are available, as is tutoring in every subject, such as math, English, chemistry, physics and study skills. There is a reader service for the blind, and remedial math, reading, and writing. There is also a writing effectiveness, study assistance, preparation for professional exams and credit courses in reading and study skills. **Library/Resources:** The library contains 2.6 million volumes, 3.5 million microform items, and 107,443 audio/video tapes/CDs/DVDs, and subscribes to 114,771 periodicals including electronic. Computerized library services include interlibrary loans, database searching, Internet access, and Wi-Fi capability. Special learning facilities include an art gallery, natural history museum, planetarium, radio station, TV station, Cullis & Gladys Wade Clock Museum, Dunn-Seiler Museum, Giles Hall Gallery, Lois Dowdle Cobb Museum, and Mississippi Entomological Museum. **Physically Challenged Students:** 90% of the campus is accessible. Facilities include wheelchair ramps, elevators, special parking, specially equipped restrooms, special class scheduling, lowered drinking fountains, lowered telephones, special housing, phones equipped with TTY in the union and library. **Special:** Cooperative education, cross-registration with the Academic Common Market, internships, and study abroad in 15 countries are offered. Work-study programs, a Washington semester, accelerated degree programs, a general studies degree, nondegree study, student-designed majors, B.A.-B.S. degrees, and pass/fail options for some courses are available. There are 27 national honor societies, a freshman honors program, and 2 departmental honors programs. **Visiting:** There are regularly scheduled orientations for prospective students, including 2 day sessions for freshmen, and 1-day session for transfers. There are guides for informal visits, visitors may sit in on classes, and stay overnight. To schedule a visit, contact Lindsey Norman at lcn32@msstate.edu. **Campus Safety and Security:** Measures include 24-hour foot and vehicle patrol, emergency notification system, self-defense education, and security escort services. There are shuttle buses, emergency telephones, lighted pathways/sidewalks, and controlled access to dorms/residences.

REQUIREMENTS: Applicants should have completed 16.5 high school academic credits, including 4 in English, 3 each in math, 2 each in science with lab, and history, 1 each in academic electives, foreign language, social studies, visual/performing arts and 0.5 credit in the computer as a productivity tool (not keyboarding). Student must also have a minimum 3.2 GPA on required high school courses; 2.5 GPA on required high school classes or class standing in top 50% with an ACT score of 16 or higher/SAT I combined score of 750 or higher; 2.0 GPA on required high school classes with ACT score of 18 or higher/SAT I combined 840 or higher; or satisfy National Collegiate Athletic Association standards for student-athletes who are full qualifiers under Division I guidelines. Students with a GED are accepted with the required ACT/SAT I score. A GPA of 2.0 is required. AP and CLEP credits are accepted. To complete a baccalaureate degree, a student must (1) satisfactorily complete the degree curriculum requirements, (2) make an overall C average (2.0 GPA) on all hours scheduled and rescheduled at all institutions attended, including Mississippi State University, (3) make a C average (2.0 GPA) on all hours scheduled and rescheduled at Mississippi State University, (4) complete from Mississippi State University no less than 25 percent of his/her degree program in junior and senior subjects (courses numbered 3000 through 5000) approved by the dean of the college or school in which he or she is enrolled, and (5) complete at least the last 25 percent of semester credit hours of course-work taken to fulfill degree requirements from Mississippi State University. (Any exception to the 25 percent requirement must be approved in writing by the student's dean prior to taking course work at another institution.) Any course in the student's degree program that carries academic credit from Mississippi State University will fulfill these requirements. Hours earned at an approved exchange institution will count toward the 25 percent requirement. (6) Not more than 25 percent of any curriculum may be earned by Advanced Placement (AP) course, advanced standing examinations, College-Level Examination Program (CLEP), International Baccalaureate (IB), Cambridge International, evaluated military service credits, tutorial, and extension courses. Evaluated military training courses granted academic credit are classified as MSU (institutional) academic pass/fail credit with a grade of S and annotated as "ACE Guide Military Credit." Military training courses include all branches of the United States Armed Services, except the United States Air Force. The Air Force provides a Community College of the Air Force transcript and credit is entered as transfer courses. (7) Not more than 20 percent of any curriculum may be earned through correspondence courses. Correspondence courses must be approved by the dean before being taken by students in residence. USAFI credits are classified as correspondence work. (8) No more than 12 hours of Directed Individual Study (DIS) may be used to complete degree requirements. The creation of DIS courses must be approved in advance by the department head. (9) Prior job/ work experience alone can not count as academic credit at MSU. **Procedure:** Freshmen are admitted fall, spring, and summer. Entrance exams should be taken in the spring of junior year or fall semester of senior year. There are deferred admissions and rolling admissions plans. Applications should be filed by August 1 for fall entry; November 15 for spring entry; and May 15 for summer entry. The fall 2017 application fee was $40. Notification is sent on a rolling basis. Applications are accepted on-line. **Transfer Students:** 1832 transfer students enrolled in 2016-2017. Applicants must submit an official college transcript from each college attended, indicating a minimum GPA of 2.0 (some departments require 2.5), and must be in good standing at their previous school. Transfers may enroll in fall, spring and summer. 30 of 124 credits required for the bachelor's degree must be completed at MSU. **International Students:** There are 232 international students enrolled. They must take the TOEFL with a minimum score of 525 on the paper-based TOEFL (PBT) or 71 on the Internet-based version (iBT). They must also take the SAT.

ADMISSIONS: 97% of the 2017-2018 applicants were accepted. The ACT scores were 5% between 12 and 17, 41% between 18 and 23, 39% between 24 and 29, and 15% above 30. 48% of the current freshmen were in the top fifth of their class; 27% were in the top two fifths. 95 freshmen graduated first in their class. **Admissions Contact:** Crystal Sloan, Assistant Director of Admissions. Email: *admit@msstate.edu* Web: *www.msstate.edu*

FINANCIAL AID: In 2017-2018, 91% of all full-time freshmen received some form of financial aid. 55% of all full-time freshmen received need-based aid. The average freshman award was $12,096. Need-based scholarships or need-based grants averaged $4,128 ($15,645 maximum); need-based self-help aid (loans and jobs) averaged $3,571 ($13,494 maximum); non-need-based athletic scholarships averaged $20,010 ($50,881 maximum); and other non-need-based awards and non-need-based scholarships averaged $3,684 ($26,750 maximum). The average financial indebtedness of the 2017 graduate was $34,675. The FAFSA code is 002423. The priority date for freshman financial aid applications for fall entry is April 1. The deadline for filing freshman financial aid applications for fall entry is May 1.

MISSISSIPPI UNIVERSITY FOR WOMEN E-2

www.muw.edu

Columbus, MS 39701	**(662) 329-7106** **(877) 462-8439**
Fax: (662) 241-7481	**Email: admissions@muw.edu**
Full-time: 300 men, 1600 women	**Faculty:** I, --$
Part-time: 300 men, 1000 women	**Ph.D.s:** 68%
Graduate: 20 men, 100 women	**Student/Faculty:** n/av
Year: semesters, summer session	**Tuition:** $7882 ($21,956)
Room & Board: $9183	**Freshman Class:** n/av
SAT or ACT: recommended	**CEEB CODE:** 1481
Application Deadline: open	**COMPETITIVE**

Mississippi University for Women (The W), founded in 1884, is a public institution offering degrees in liberal arts, education, business and communications, nursing, human sciences, science and math, health and kinesiology, and culinary arts. The figures given in the above capsule and in this profile are approximate. There are 4 undergraduate schools and 4 graduate schools. In addition to regional accreditation, Mississippi University for Women has baccalaureate program accreditation with ACBSP, NASAD, NASM, NCATE, and NLN. The 110-acre campus is in a small town 120 miles west of Birmingham, Alabama. Including any residence halls, there are 53 buildings.

STUDENT LIFE: 89% of undergraduates are from Mississippi. Others are from 20 states, 25 foreign countries, and Canada. 84% are from public schools. 70% are White; 27% African American; 2% Foreign; 1% Asian American. **Female To Male Ratio:** 4.4:1. The average age of freshmen is 19; all undergraduates, 29. 30% do not continue beyond their first year; 43% remain to graduate. **Housing:** 1100 students can be accommodated in college housing, which includes married student dorms and on-campus apartments. On-campus housing is available on a first-come and first-served basis. 77% of students commute. Alcohol is not permitted. All students may keep cars.

FACULTY/CLASSROOMS: 39% of faculty are male; 61% are female. 94% teach undergraduates. No introductory courses are taught by graduate students. The average class size in an introductory lecture is 35; in a laboratory is 23; and in a regular course is 25.

PROGRAMS OF STUDY: Mississippi University for Women confers B.A., B.S., B.F.A., B.M. and B.S.N. degrees. Associate, master's, and doctoral degrees are also awarded. Bachelor's degrees are awarded in BIOLOGICAL SCIENCE (biology/biological science and microbiology), BUSINESS (accounting, business administration and management, and sports management), COMMUNICATIONS AND THE ARTS (communications, English, fine arts, music, and Spanish), COMPUTER AND PHYSICAL SCIENCE (chemistry, mathematics, and physical sciences), EDUCATION (art education, elementary education, and music education), HEALTH PROFESSIONS (nursing, public health, and speech pathology/audiology), SOCIAL SCIENCE (culinary arts, food production/management/services, history, paralegal studies, physical fitness/movement, political science/government, psychology, and social science). Biology, chemistry, and English are the strongest academically. Business, nursing, and elementary education have the largest enrollments.

ACTIVITIES: 10% of men belong to 2 local and 1 national fraternities; 20% of women belong to 12 local and 3 national sororities. There are 84 groups on campus, including art, band, choir, chorale, chorus, computers, dance, drama, ethnic, film, honors, international, jazz band, literary magazine, musical theater, newspaper, orchestra, photography, political, professional, radio and TV, religious, social, social service, student government, and yearbook. Popular campus events include Mardi Gras, and Oktoberfest. **Sports:** There are 5 intramural sports for men and 5 for women. Facilities include a gym, tennis and racquetball courts, indoor swimming pool, a gymnastics room, a weight room, a dance studio, a 3-hole pitch-and-putt golf course, a soccer and flag football field. **Graduates:** From July 1, 2016 to June 30, 2017, 617 bachelor's degrees were awarded. The most popular majors were nursing (40%), elementary education (7%), and general studies (7%).

SERVICES: Counseling and information services are available, as is tutoring in most subjects. There is remedial math, reading, and writing. **Library/Resources:** The library contains 232,638 volumes, 569,448 microform items, and 98 audio/video tapes/CDs/DVDs, and subscribes to 1,620 periodicals including electronic. Computerized library services include interlibrary loans and database searching. Special learning facilities include an art gallery, radio station, a distance learning studio. **Physically Challenged Students:** 95% of the campus is accessible. Facilities include wheelchair ramps, elevators, special parking, specially equipped restrooms, special class scheduling, lowered drinking fountains, and lowered telephones. **Special:** Cross-registration and a 3-2 engineering degree are available with Mississippi State University. MUW also offers internships in all colleges, co-op and work-study programs, several combinations of dual majors, study abroad in 5 countries, credit for experience, nondegree study, and a pass/fail option. There are 15 national honor societies, a freshman honors program, and 3 departmental honors programs. **Visiting:** There are regularly scheduled orientations for prospective students, including talks with various student services officers and preregistration. There are guides for informal visits, visitors may sit in on classes, and stay overnight. To schedule a visit, contact the Director of Admissions. **Campus Safety and Security:** Measures include 24-hour foot and vehicle patrol and security escort services. There are lighted pathways/sidewalks, controlled access to dorms/residences, guard gates, and freshman orientation class.

REQUIREMENTS: The SAT or ACT is recommended. In addition, Prospective students should have completed 4 units of English; 3 each of math, science, and social studies courses in U.S. history, world history, government, and economics or geography; 2 of advanced electives, including foreign language or geography; and a course in computer applications. A GPA of 2.0 is required. AP and CLEP credits are accepted. Important factors in the admissions decision are recommendations by school officials, leadership record, and advanced placement or honors courses. To graduate, students must complete 124 credit hours, including 30 to 39 in a major, with a minimum GPA of 2.0. The core curriculum requires 12 hours of English, 8 of lab-based science, 6 each of history and social sciences, 3 each of speech or philosophy, fine arts, and math, 1 each of phys ed, and a freshman seminar. **Procedure:** Freshmen are admitted to all sessions. Entrance exams should be taken as early as possible. There are early decision, early admissions, and rolling admissions plans. Application deadlines are open. The fall 2017 application fee was $25. **Transfer Students:** Applicants must have a GPA of 2.0 in 6 semester hours of both English composition and a lab science, 3 of college algebra or above, and 9 of transferable electives. High school and college transcripts are required. 32 of 128 credits required for the bachelor's degree must be completed at The W. **International Students:** They must take the TOEFL. They must also take the SAT or ACT, scoring 16.

Admissions Contact: Shelley Moss, Director of Admissions. Email: *admissions@muw.edu* Web: *www.muw.edu*

FINANCIAL AID: Mississippi University for Women is a member of

CSS. The FAFSA code is 002422. Check with the school for current application deadlines.

MISSISSIPPI VALLEY STATE UNIVERSITY *(The complete profile is made available exclusively on our website, www.barronspac.com)*

RUST COLLEGE D-1
www.rustcollege.edu

Holly Springs, MS 38635 (662) 252-8000 (888) 886-8492
Fax: (662) 252-8895 **Email:** jmcsonald@rustcollege.edu

Full-time: 300 men, 550 women	**Faculty:** n/av
Part-time: 60 men, 105 women	**Ph.D.s:** 47%
Graduate: n/av	**Student/Faculty:** n/av
Year: semesters, summer session	**Tuition:** $7400
Room & Board: $3200	**Freshman Class:** n/av
SAT or ACT: required	**CEEB CODE:** 1669
Application Deadline: rolling	**COMPETITIVE**

Rust College, founded in 1866, is a private liberal arts college affiliated with the United Methodist Church. The academic year consists of semesters, each divided into two 8-week modules, plus a summer term. The figures given in the above capsule and in this profile are approximate. There are 5 undergraduate schools. The 126-acre campus is in a small town 35 miles southeast of Memphis, Tennessee. Including any residence halls, there are 23 buildings.

STUDENT LIFE: 55% of undergraduates are from Mississippi. Others are from 24 states, and 6 foreign countries. 90% are from public schools. 93% are African American; 6% Foreign; 1% White. 60% are Protestant; 29% claim no religious affiliation. **Female To Male Ratio:** 1.8:1. The average age of freshmen is 19; all undergraduates, 22. 57% do not continue beyond their first year. **Housing:** 856 students can be accommodated in college housing, which includes dorms. In addition, there are honors houses. On-campus housing is guaranteed for all 4 years. 65% of students live on campus. Alcohol is not permitted. All students may keep cars.

FACULTY/CLASSROOMS: 67% of faculty are male; 33% are female. All teach undergraduates. No introductory courses are taught by graduate students. The average class size in an introductory lecture is 10; in a laboratory is 10; and in a regular course is 25.

PROGRAMS OF STUDY: RC confers B.A., B.S. and B.S.W. degrees. Associate degrees are also awarded. Bachelor's degrees are awarded in BIOLOGICAL SCIENCE (biology/biological science), BUSINESS (business administration and management), COMMUNICATIONS AND THE ARTS (communications, English, journalism, and music), COMPUTER AND PHYSICAL SCIENCE (chemistry, computer science, and mathematics), EDUCATION (business education, elementary education, English education, mathematics education, science education, secondary education, and social science education), HEALTH PROFESSIONS (health), SOCIAL SCIENCE (political science/government, social work, and sociology). Business administration, and management are the strongest academically. Biology, computer science, and social work have the largest enrollments.

ACTIVITIES: 2% of men belong to 3 local and 3 national fraternities; 6% of women belong to 4 local and 4 national sororities. There are 32 groups on campus, including band, cheerleading, choir, chorale, computers, drama, ethnic, honors, international, marching band, newspaper, political, radio and TV, religious, social, social service, and student government. Popular campus events include Career Day, Religious Emphasis Week, and African American Student Leadership Conference. **Sports:** There are 7 intercollegiate sports for men and 7 for women. Facilities include a gym, swimming pool, tennis courts, a track, a stadium, a bowling alley, pool tables, and a sports arena.

SERVICES: Counseling and information services are available, as is tutoring in most subjects. There is remedial math, reading, and writing. **Library/Resources:** The library contains 123,055 volumes, and 106 audio/video tapes/CDs/DVDs, and subscribes to 340 periodicals including electronic. Computerized library services include interlibrary loans, database searching, and Internet access. Special learning facilities include a radio station, TV station, the Dr. Ron Trojak collection of African Tribal Art. **Physically Challenged Students:** All of the campus is accessible. Facilities include wheelchair ramps, elevators, special parking, specially equipped restrooms, and lowered drinking fountains. **Special:** Internships are available in all areas and may be required for some majors. On-campus work-study, study abroad, credit by examination, independent study, B.A.-B.S. degrees, and dual majors in a variety of programs are available. There are 3-2 degrees in preprofessional programs and medical technology and a 3-2 engineering degree with the student's school of choice. There are 3 national honor societies, a freshman honors program, and 5 departmental honors programs. **Visiting:** There are regularly scheduled orientations for prospective students, including a campus tour, departmental visits, introduction to the application process, financial aid orientation, and question-and-answer session. There are guides for informal visits, visitors may sit in on classes, and stay overnight. To schedule a visit, contact Enrollment Services. **Campus Safety and Security:** Measures include 24-hour foot and vehicle patrol and security escort services. There are lighted pathways/sidewalks.

REQUIREMENTS: The SAT or ACT is required. Students must submit 19 academic credits, including 4 in English, 3 each in math, science, and social studies, and 6 electives. An audition, an interview, and 2 letters of recommendation are required. The GED is accepted. An essay and portfolio are recommended. A GPA of 2.0 is required. AP and CLEP credits are accepted. Important factors in the admissions decision are evidence of special talent, extracurricular activities record, and recommendations by school officials. All students must earn a minimum of 124 semester hours while maintaining a cumulative GPA of 2.0. Distribution requirements include 59.5 general education credits in the fields of education, humanities, science, and math and a required freshman program. A minimum of 50 credits constitutes a major, and comprehensive exams are given in all programs. Required courses in addition to the freshman program include math, biology, physical science, computer science, English, foreign language, literature, speech, social science, and history. **Procedure:** Freshmen are admitted fall, spring, and summer. Entrance exams should be taken prior to the first semester of the freshman year. There is a rolling admissions plan. Check with the school for current application deadlines. The fall 2017 application fee was $10. Applications are accepted on-line. **Transfer Students:** Transfer applicants with at least 15 semester hours of credit need not take the ACT or SAT. No credits for courses with a grade below C and no credits for any course that are not in keeping with the college's catalog will be accepted. 30 of 124 credits required for the bachelor's degree must be completed at RC. **International Students:** They must take the TOEFL. They must also take the SAT or ACT.

Admissions Contact: Johnny McDonald, Director Enrollment Services. Email: *jmcsonald@rustcollege.edu* Web: *www.rustcollege.edu*

FINANCIAL AID: The FFS and the college's own financial statement are required. The FAFSA code is 002433. Check with the school for current application deadlines.

TOUGALOO COLLEGE *(The complete profile is made available exclusively on our website, www.barronspac.com)*

UNIVERSITY OF MISSISSIPPI D-2
www.olemiss.edu

University, MS 38677 (662) 915-7226
Fax: (662) 915-1831 **Email:** admissions@olemiss.edu

Full-time: 7723 men, 9788 women	**Faculty:** n/av
Part-time: 548 men, 678 women	**Ph.D.s:** n/av
Graduate: 1863 men, 2536 women	**Student/Faculty:** n/av
Year: semesters, summer session	**Tuition:** $8300 ($23,564)
Room & Board: $10,502	**Freshman Class:** n/av
SAT or ACT: required	**CEEB CODE:** 1840
Application Deadline: n/av	**COMPETITIVE**

University of Mississippi, founded in 1848, offering nationally recognized programs across a broad range of undergraduate and graduate studies, from medicine and law to creative writing and accountancy. UM is the state's largest university, and was named as one of the nation's 13th-fastest growing universities. There are 10 undergraduate schools and 7 graduate schools. In addition to regional accreditation, UM has baccalaureate program accreditation with AACSB, ABET, ACEJMC, CSWE, NASAD, NASM, NCATE, NRPA, ACS, ACEND, FEPAC,

CAPRA, and NAST. The 3710-acre campus is in a small town 70 miles southeast of Memphis, TN. Including any residence halls, there are 295 buildings.

STUDENT LIFE: 56% of undergraduates are from Mississippi. Others are from 50 states, 85 foreign countries, and Canada. 76% are White; 4% Foreign; 3% Hispanic; 2% Asian American; 2% two or more races; 13% African American. **Female To Male Ratio:** 1.3:1. The average age of freshmen is 18; all undergraduates, 21. **Housing:** College-sponsored housing includes married student dorms, on-campus apartments, and off-campus apartments. In addition, there are honors houses, special-interest houses, fraternity houses, sorority houses, living learning communities, and freshman interest groups. On-campus housing is guaranteed for the freshman year only, and is available on a first-come, first-served basis, and is available on a lottery system for upperclassmen. 75% of students commute. Alcohol is not permitted. All students may keep cars.

FACULTY/CLASSROOMS: No introductory courses are taught by graduate students.

PROGRAMS OF STUDY: UM confers B.A., B.A.Ed, B.A.J., B.Accy, B.B.A., B.F.A., B.G.S., B.M., B.P.S., B.S., B.S.C.E., B.S.C.J., B.S.Ch.E, B.S.C.S., B.S.E.E., B.S.E.S., B.S.G.E., B.S.J., B.S.M.E., B.S.N., B.E. B.S.G, and B.S.W. degrees. Master's and doctoral degrees are also awarded. Bachelor's degrees are awarded in BIOLOGICAL SCIENCE (biology/biological science), BUSINESS (accounting, banking and finance, business administration and management, business economics, finance, hospitality management services, insurance, management information systems, management science, marketing/retailing/merchandising, and real estate), COMMUNICATIONS AND THE ARTS (Arabic, art, art history and appreciation, Chinese, communication science, English, French, German, journalism, linguistics, music, Spanish, and theatre arts), COMPUTER AND PHYSICAL SCIENCE (chemistry, computer science, geology, mathematics, and physics), EDUCATION (elementary education, English education, health information management, mathematics education, science education, social science education, and special education), ENGINEERING AND ENVIRONMENTAL DESIGN (chemical engineering, civil engineering, electrical/electronics engineering, engineering, geological engineering, and mechanical engineering), HEALTH PROFESSIONS (cytotechnology, dental hygiene, exercise science, health science, medical laboratory science, medical technology, nursing, pharmaceutical science, and radiological science), SOCIAL SCIENCE (African American studies, anthropology, area studies, classical/ancient civilization, criminal justice, dietetics, economics, forensic studies, history, international studies, liberal arts/general studies, paralegal studies, parks and recreation management, philosophy, political science/government, psychology, public administration, religion, social work, and sociology). Accountancy, pharmacy, and creative writing are the strongest academically. Business, accountancy, and integrated marketing communications have the largest enrollments.

ACTIVITIES: Groups on campus include art, band, cheerleading, chess, choir, chorale, chorus, computers, dance, drama, drill team, ethnic, honors, international, jazz band, LGBT, literary magazine, marching band, musical theater, newspaper, orchestra, pep band, political, professional, radio and TV, religious, social, social service, student government, symphony, and yearbook. Popular campus events include Welcome Week, Red and Blue Week, The Big Event, Faulkner and Yoknapatawpha Conference and Oxford Conference for the Book. **Sports:** Facilities include a football stadium, basketball coliseum, baseball stadium, intramural fields, women's soccer complex, softball complex, volleyball courts, an indoor tennis facility, golf course, track and field complex, athletics training center, fitness center with indoor pool, racquetball courts and basketball courts, and equipment rental and guides for high-adventure outdoor activities, including camping, skiing, scuba, canoeing, kayaking and backpacking.

SERVICES: Counseling and information services are available, as is tutoring in most subjects. There is a reader service for the blind, and remedial math and reading. **Library/Resources:** Computerized library services include interlibrary loans, database searching, Internet access, and Wi-Fi capability. Special learning facilities include an art gallery, radio station, TV station, the Mary Buie Museum, the Center for the Study of Southern Culture, the National Center for Physical Acoustics, Rowan Oak, the home of William Faulkner, the National Center for Natural Products Research, the National Food Service Management Institute, the Croft Institute for International Studies, the Sally McDonnell Barksdale Honors College, the Center for Manufacturing Excellence, and the Center for Intelligence and Security Studies. **Physically Challenged Students:** Facilities include wheelchair ramps, elevators, special parking, specially equipped restrooms, special class scheduling, lowered drinking fountains, lowered telephones, and special housing. **Special:** Online programs, dual majors, a general studies degree, credit by exam, special testing in music and languages, credit for military experience, and limited pass/fail options also are available. Co-op programs in the School of Engineering. Study abroad and internships are available in numerous countries. There are 20 national honor societies, including Phi Beta Kappa, and a freshman honors program. **Visiting:** There are regularly scheduled orientations for prospective students. There are guides for informal visits; visitors may sit in on classes and stay overnight. To schedule a visit, contact Martin Barret Fisher at (662) 915-7226. **Campus Safety and Security:** Measures include 24-hour foot and vehicle patrol, emergency notification system, self-defense education, and security escort services. There are shuttle buses, emergency telephones, lighted pathways/sidewalks, and controlled access to dorms/residences.

REQUIREMENTS: Applicants need 15 academic credits, including 4 units in English, 3 each in math (4 recommended), sciences with lab (4 recommended), and social studies, 1 in foreign language, and 0.5 in computer applications. Electives should include 2nd year foreign language or world geography. A portfolio for art majors and an audition for theater and music majors are required. AP and CLEP credits are accepted. The core curriculum is a set of 30 hours of course work taken by students. The core includes the following courses required for all entering freshmen students: 6 hours of English composition (Honors students may satisfy English composition requirements by taking Hon 101 and 102), 3 hours of college algebra or quantitative reasoning or statistics (taken from a department of mathematics) or a more advanced mathematics course, 6 hours of natural science, 9 hours of humanities and fine arts, and 6 hours of social or behavioral science courses. For the award of a bachelor's degree from any school or college of the University of Mississippi, a student must earn a GPA of at least 2.0 on all course work submitted in fulfillment of the course requirements for the degree. In addition, the student must earn a minimum GPA of 2.0 on all course work attempted at the University of Mississippi. Finally, the student must have a minimum 2.0 GPA on all college work attempted at any institution of higher learning. There may be additional grade requirements for the College of Liberal Arts or the professional schools. It is the student's responsibility to check on the requirements applicable to the specific degree for which he or she is a candidate. **Procedure:** Freshmen are admitted to all sessions. There are early admissions, deferred admissions, and rolling admissions plans. Application deadlines are open. The fall 2017 application fee was $40. Applications are accepted on-line. **Transfer Students:** Transfer students must have earned a minimum 2.0 GPA on previous college work. The SAT or ACT may be required depending on credits earned. 30 of 126 credits required for the bachelor's degree must be completed at UM. **International Students:** They must take the TOEFL with a minimum score of 550 on the paper-based TOEFL (PBT) or 79 on the Internet-based version (iBT) and the college's own test, and either the IELTS or Pearson . They must also take the SAT or ACT. if GPA is between 2.75-2.99--SAT of 1150 or above required is required for scholarship consideration.

ADMISSIONS: The SAT scores for the 2017-2018 freshman class were: Critical Reading-- 8% below 500, 44% between 500 and 599, 39% between 600 and 699, and 9% between 700 and 800. Math-- 13% below 500, 47% between 500 and 599, 27% between 600 and 699, and 13% between 700 and 800. The ACT scores were 4% between 12 and 17, 36% between 18 and 23, 40% between 24 and 29, and 20% above 30. **Admissions Contact:** Whitman Smith, Director of Enrollment Services. Email: *admissions@olemiss.edu* Web: *www.olemiss.edu*

FINANCIAL AID: In 2017-2018, 89% of all full-time freshmen received some form of financial aid. 77% of all full-time freshmen received need-based aid. The average freshman award was $16,624. Need-based scholarships or need-based grants averaged $9,987 ($48,022 maximum); need-based self-help aid (loans and jobs) averaged $9,630 ($38,984 maximum); non-need-based athletic scholarships averaged $17,711 ($54,198 maximum); and other non-need-based awards and non-need-based scholarships averaged $9,740 ($54,198 maximum). UM is a member of CSS. The FAFSA code is 002440. The priority date for freshman financial aid applications for fall entry is March 1.

UNIVERSITY OF SOUTHERN MISSISSIPPI D-5

www.usm.edu

Hattiesburg, MS 39406 **(601) 266-5000**

Fax: (601) 266-5148
Full-time: 4250 men, 7143 women
Part-time: 967 men, 1298 women
Graduate: 1039 men, 1771 women
Year: semesters, summer session
Room & Board: $6834

ACT: 22
Application Deadline: June 30

Email: admissions@usm.edu
Faculty: 687; I, --$
Ph.D.s: 76%
Student/Faculty: 18 to 1
Tuition: $6336 ($14,448)
Freshman Class: 4436 applied, 2473 accepted, 1787 enrolled
CEEB CODE: 1479
COMPETITIVE

University of Southern Mississippi, founded in 1910, is a public institution offering comprehensive undergraduate and graduate programs. There are 6 undergraduate schools and 1 graduate school. In addition to regional accreditation, USM has baccalaureate program accreditation with AACSB, ABET, ACEJMC, ADA, AHEA, ASLA, CAHEA, CSAB, CSWE, FIDER, NASAD, NASM, NLN, and NRPA. The 1090-acre campus is in a suburban area 90 miles southeast of Jackson, and 105 miles north of New Orleans. Including any residence halls, there are 176 buildings.

STUDENT LIFE: 88% of undergraduates are from Mississippi. Others are from 50 states, 57 foreign countries, and Canada. 65% are White; 29% African American; 1% Asian American; 1% American Indian/Alaska Native; 1% Hispanic; 1% Foreign; 1% two or more races; 1% race unknown. **Female To Male Ratio:** 1.6:1. The average age of freshmen is 18; all undergraduates, 23. 25% do not continue beyond their first year; 50% remain to graduate. **Housing:** 3400 students can be accommodated in college housing, which includes married student dorms. In addition, there are special-interest houses, fraternity houses, and sorority houses. There is a section in 1 dorm that is reserved for honor students only. Freshmen students are housed together. On-campus housing is available on a first-come and first-served basis. 72% of students commute. Alcohol is not permitted. All students may keep cars.

FACULTY/CLASSROOMS: 49% of faculty are male; 51% are female. 64% teach undergraduates, and 64% do research. No introductory courses are taught by graduate students.

PROGRAMS OF STUDY: USM confers B.A., B.S., B.F.A., B.M., B.M.E. and B.S.B.A degrees. Master's and doctoral degrees are also awarded. Bachelor's degrees are awarded in BIOLOGICAL SCIENCE (biology/biological science), BUSINESS (accounting, banking and finance, business administration and management, business economics, hotel/motel and restaurant management, international business management, marketing/retailing/merchandising, and personnel management), COMMUNICATIONS AND THE ARTS (advertising, communications, dance, design, dramatic arts, English, fine arts, journalism, languages, music, radio/television technology, and speech/debate/rhetoric), COMPUTER AND PHYSICAL SCIENCE (chemistry, computer science, geology, information sciences and systems, mathematics, physics, polymer science, and statistics), EDUCATION (art education, business education, early childhood education, elementary education, foreign languages education, guidance education, health education, home economics education, industrial arts education, middle school education, music education, science education, and secondary education), ENGINEERING AND ENVIRONMENTAL DESIGN (architectural technology, computer technology, construction technology, electrical/electronics engineering technology, engineering technology, and mechanical engineering technology), HEALTH PROFESSIONS (medical laboratory technology, nursing, predentistry, premedicine, and speech pathology/audiology), SOCIAL SCIENCE (anthropology, criminal justice, economics, geography, history, international studies, parks and recreation management, philosophy, political science/government, prelaw, psychology, social science, social work, and sociology). Curriculum instruction special education, human performance, and management international business have the largest enrollments.

ACTIVITIES: 15% of men belong to 14 national fraternities; 17% of women belong to 11 national sororities. There are 239 groups on campus, including art, band, cheerleading, choir, chorale, chorus, computers, dance, drama, drum and bugle corps, ethnic, film, honors, international, jazz band, LGBT, literary magazine, marching band, musical theater, newspaper, opera, orchestra, pep band, photography, political, professional, radio and TV, religious, social, social service, student government, and symphony. **Sports:** There are 6 intercollegiate sports for men and 6 for women, and 36 intramural sports for men and 36 for women. Facilities include a football stadium, a basketball coliseum, baseball park, softball stadium, track and field stadium, fitness institute, a natatorium, volleyball courts, and playing fields for softball, flag football, and soccer. **Graduates:** From July 1, 2016 to June 30, 2017, 2520 bachelor's degrees were awarded. The most popular majors were nursing (9%), elementary education (6%), and psychology (6%). In an average class, 8% graduate in 4 years or less, 43% graduate in 5 years or less, and 49% graduate in 6 years or less.

SERVICES: Counseling and information services are available, as is tutoring in most subjects. There is a reader service for the blind, and remedial math, reading, and writing. **Library/Resources:** The library contains 122,428 volumes, 4.9 million microform items, and 33,189 audio/video tapes/CDs/DVDs, and subscribes to 24,369 periodicals including electronic. Computerized library services include interlibrary loans, database searching, and Internet access. Special learning facilities include an art gallery, natural history museum, radio station, TV production studios, the Museum of Natural Science, and a music resource center. **Physically Challenged Students:** 80% of the campus is accessible. Facilities include wheelchair ramps, elevators, special parking, specially equipped restrooms, special class scheduling, lowered drinking fountains, lowered telephones, and special housing. **Special:** USM offers many cooperative programs, internships, dual majors, nondegree study, limited pass/fail options, credit for life experience, and study abroad in 12 countries. The university also participates in the Title IV College Work-Study Program. Accelerated degrees, distance learning, ESL, independent study, and a teacher certification program are also available. There are 27 national honor societies and a freshman honors program. **Visiting:** There are regularly scheduled orientations for prospective students, including campus tours and general session orientations. There are guides for informal visits and visitors may sit in on classes. To schedule a visit, contact Office of Admissions. **Campus Safety and Security:** Measures include 24-hour foot and vehicle patrol, emergency notification system, self-defense education, and security escort services. There are shuttle buses, emergency telephones, lighted pathways/sidewalks, and controlled access to dorms/residences.

REQUIREMENTS: Full admission will be granted to the following: All students completing the College Preparatory Curriculum (CPC) with a minimum of a 3.2 high school GPA on the CPC and a submitted ACT (composite) or SAT score. All students completing the College Preparatory Curriculum (CPC) with a minimum of a 2.5 high school GPA on the CPC or a class rank in the top 50 percent, as well as a score of 16 or higher on the ACT (composite) or a combined SAT score of 760. All students completing the College Preparatory Curriculum (CPC) with a minimum of 2.0 high school GPA on the CPC and a score of 18 or higher on the ACT (composite) or a combined SAT score of 860. Students who satisfy the National Collegiate Athletic Association (NCAA) standards for student-athletes who are full qualifiers under Division I guidelines. A GPA of 2.0 is required. AP and CLEP credits are accepted. To graduate, students must complete at least 128 semester hours, including 64 at the senior college level, with a minimum GPA of 2.0. Core requirements include courses in reasoning and communication skills, English, composition, history, humanities and fine arts, social and behavioral sciences, human wellness, and natural and applied sciences. **Procedure:** Freshmen are admitted fall, spring, and summer. Entrance exams should be taken in the fall of the senior year. Applications should be filed by June 30 for fall entry; January 1 for spring entry; and May 1 for summer entry. The fall 2017 application fee was $35. Notification is sent on a rolling basis. Applications are accepted on-line. **Transfer Students:** 1787 transfer students enrolled in 2016-2017. Students must have either an associate degree intended for transfer from a regionally accredited institution or have completed the 30 semester hours of designated coursework outlined below with a minimum 2.0 cumulative grade point average for admission. 6 semester hours of English Composition (English Composition I and II), 3 semester hours of mathematics (college algebra, quantitative reasoning, or higher mathematics), 6 semester hours of natural science (courses must be laboratory-based, with the lecture courses accompanied by the respective lab course), 9 semester hours of humanities and fine arts (common examples of acceptable coursework are history, philosophy, religion, world literature, art, music), 6 semester hours of social or behavioral sciences (common examples of acceptable coursework are anthropology, geography, sociology, psychology, and social work). 32 of 128 credits required for the bachelor's degree must be completed at USM. **International Students:** They must take the TOEFL with a minimum score of 525 on the paper-based TOEFL (PBT). They must also take the SAT or ACT, scoring 18.

ADMISSIONS: 56% of the 2017-2018 applicants were accepted. The SAT scores for the 2017-2018 freshman class were: Critical Reading-- 35% below 500, 43% between 500 and 599, 18% between 600 and 699, and 4% between 700 and 800. Math-- 42% below 500, 40% between 500 and 599, and 18% between 600 and 699. The ACT scores were 41% below 12, 24% between 12 and 17, 19% between 18 and 23, 7% between 24 and 29, and 9% above 30. **Admissions Contact:** Amanda King, Admissions Office. Email: *admissions@usm.edu* Web: *www.usm.edu*

FINANCIAL AID: In 2017-2018, 66% of all full-time freshmen received some form of financial aid. 75% of all full-time freshmen received need-based aid. The average freshman award was $10,446. Need-based scholarships or need-based grants averaged $4,505; need-based self-help aid (loans and jobs) averaged $3,552; non-need-based athletic scholarships averaged $7,396; and other non-need-based awards and non-need-based scholarships averaged $5,568. The average financial indebtedness of the 2017 graduate was $29,502. The college's own financial statement is required. The FAFSA code is 002441. Check with the school for current application deadlines.

WILLIAM CAREY UNIVERSITY *(The complete profile is made available exclusively on our website, www.barronspac.com)*

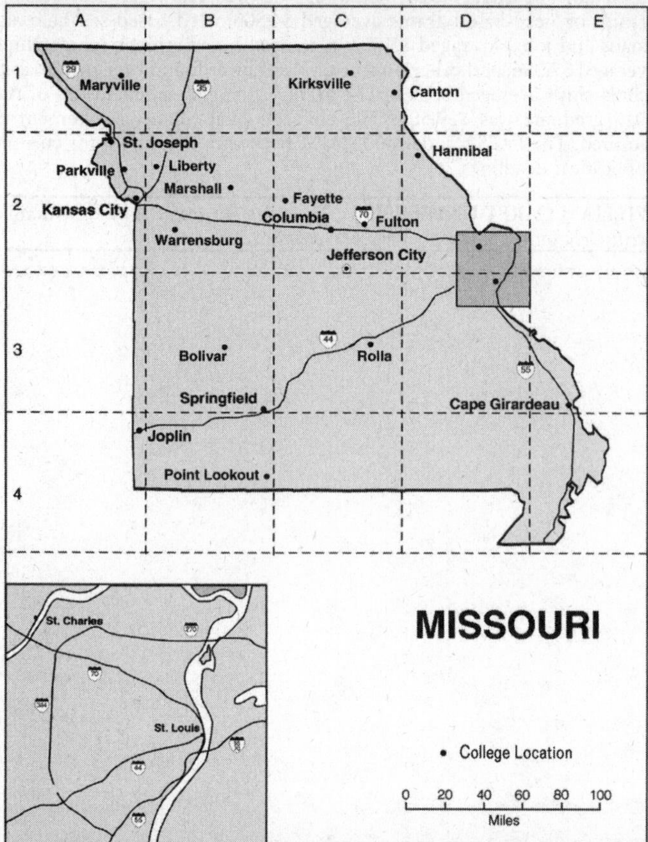

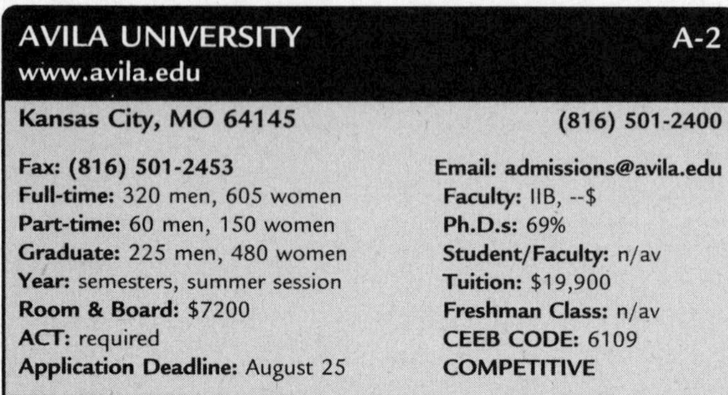

AVILA UNIVERSITY A-2

www.avila.edu

Kansas City, MO 64145 **(816) 501-2400**

Fax: (816) 501-2453 **Email: admissions@avila.edu**

Full-time: 320 men, 605 women	**Faculty:** IIB, --$
Part-time: 60 men, 150 women	**Ph.D.s:** 69%
Graduate: 225 men, 480 women	**Student/Faculty:** n/av
Year: semesters, summer session	**Tuition:** $19,900
Room & Board: $7200	**Freshman Class:** n/av
ACT: required	**CEEB CODE:** 6109
Application Deadline: August 25	**COMPETITIVE**

Avila University, founded in 1916, is a comprehensive liberal arts institution sponsored by the Sisters of St. Joseph of Carondelet. Avila has over 60 undergraduate majors and concentrations and 6 graduate degree programs. The figures given in the above capsule and in this profile are approximate. There are 7 undergraduate schools and 3 graduate schools. In addition to regional accreditation, Avila has baccalaureate program accreditation with CAHEA, CSWE, and CCNE. The 50-acre campus is in a suburban area in Kansas City, MO. Including any residence halls, there are 11 buildings.

STUDENT LIFE: 55% of undergraduates are from Missouri. Others are from 21 states, 34 foreign countries, and Canada. 87% are from public schools. 9% are Foreign; 7% Hispanic; 61% White; 2% two or more races; 19% African American; 1% Asian American; 1% American Indian/Alaska Native. 26% are Catholic. **Female To Male Ratio:** 2.0:1. The average age of freshmen is 18; all undergraduates, 23. 33% do not continue beyond their first year; 51% remain to graduate. **Housing:** 310 students can be accommodated in college housing, which includes dorms and on-campus apartments. On-campus housing is guaranteed for the freshman year only, is available on a first-come, first-served basis, and is available on a lottery system for upperclassmen. 71% of students commute. All students may keep cars.

FACULTY/CLASSROOMS: 33% of faculty are male; 67% are female. All teach undergraduates and all do research. No introductory courses are taught by graduate students. The average class size in an introductory lecture is 22; in a laboratory is 25; and in a regular course is 14.

PROGRAMS OF STUDY: Avila confers B.A., B.S., B.F.A., B.S.B.A., B.S.N. and B.S.W. degrees. Master's degrees are also awarded. Bachelor's degrees are awarded in BIOLOGICAL SCIENCE (biochemistry and biology/biological science), BUSINESS (accounting, banking and finance, business administration and management, international business management, management science, and marketing/retailing/merchandising), COMMUNICATIONS AND THE ARTS (art, communications, dramatic arts, English, and music), COMPUTER AND PHYSICAL SCIENCE (chemistry, computer science, information sciences and systems, mathematics, and radiological technology), EDUCATION (business education, educational studies, elementary education, middle school education, and special education), HEALTH PROFESSIONS (medical laboratory technology, nursing, premedicine, and sports medicine), SOCIAL SCIENCE (history, paralegal studies, political science/government, psychology, religious studies, social work, sociology, and theological studies). Nursing, education, and communications are the strongest academically. Nursing, education, and radiologic technology have the largest enrollments.

ACTIVITIES: There are no fraternities or sororities. There are 37 groups on campus, including art, cheerleading, choir, chorale, chorus, computers, dance, drama, ethnic, film, honors, international, LGBT, literary magazine, musical theater, newspaper, photography, political, professional, radio and TV, religious, social, social service, and student government. Popular campus events include Student Appreciation Day, Organization Fair, and International Festival. **Sports:** There are 4 intercollegiate sports for men and 7 for women. Facilities include a field house with basketball and volleyball courts, a training room, and weight and fitness equipment, baseball, softball, and soccer fields, tennis courts, and practice fields. **Graduates:** From July 1, 2016 to June 30, 2017, 222 bachelor's degrees were awarded. The most popular majors were business (18%), nursing (15%), and radiologic science (12%). In an average class, 32% graduate in 4 years or less, 35% graduate in 5 years or less, and 46% graduate in 6 years or less. Of the 2016 graduating class, 29% were enrolled in graduate school within 6 months of graduation, and 90% were employed.

SERVICES: Counseling and information services are available, as is tutoring in most subjects. There is a reader service for the blind, and remedial math, reading, and writing. **Library/Resources:** The library contains 81,755 volumes, 493,760 microform items, and 2,910 audio/video tapes/CDs/DVDs, and subscribes to 550 periodicals including electronic. Computerized library services include interlibrary loans, database searching, Internet access, and Wi-Fi capability. Special learning facilities include an art gallery, radio station, TV station, a 500-seat theater, an interactive video library, video production facilities, a nursing education and resource center, and dance studio. **Physically Challenged Students:** 95% of the campus is accessible. Facilities include wheelchair ramps, elevators, special parking, specially equipped restrooms, special class scheduling, lowered drinking fountains, and lowered telephones. **Special:** Students may cross-register with the Kansas City Area Student Exchange, the Sisters of Saint Joseph College Consortium, and the Council of Independent Colleges Student Exchange. Avila also offers internships in business, communication, graphic design, paralegal, and other majors, work-study, a Washington center program, dual majors in science, math, and health professions, and accelerated degree programs in business administration and psychology. There are 6 national honor societies and 4 departmental honors programs. **Visiting:** There are regularly scheduled orientations for prospective students, including a visit with admissions and a faculty member a campus tour, and an appointment with the athletics or performance grant manager. There are guides for informal visits, visitors may sit in on classes, and stay overnight. To schedule a visit, contact the Campus Visit Coordinator. **Campus Safety and Security:** Measures include 24-hour foot and vehicle patrol and security escort services. There are emergency telephones, lighted pathways/sidewalks, controlled access to dorms/residences, and 24-hour closed-circuit television in residence hall entryways, computer labs, and the student lounge. Another closed circuit system monitors gym areas. In addition, all university parking lot entrances are monitored by closed circuit system.

REQUIREMENTS: The ACT is required. Applicants must be graduates of an accredited secondary school or have a GED certificate. They should have completed 16 academic units, including 4 in English, 3 in math, 2 to 4 in foreign language, 2 to 3 in natural and social sciences, and 1 to

2 in fine arts. A GPA of 2.5 is required. AP and CLEP credits are accepted. Important factors in the admissions decision are recommendations by school officials, extracurricular activities record, and leadership record. To graduate, students must complete at least 128 semester hours with a minimum 2.0 GPA. The 41 to 46 hour core curriculum consists of courses in composition, communication, math, history, literature, theology, philosophy, the arts, the sciences, and social institutions. The average hours in a major range from 36 to 60. **Procedure:** Freshmen are admitted to all sessions. Entrance exams should be taken in the spring or summer of the junior year. There is a rolling admissions plan. Applications should be filed by August 25 for fall entry. Notification is sent on a rolling basis. Applications are accepted on-line. **Transfer Students:** 194 transfer students enrolled in 2016-2017. Applicants must have a minimum GPA of 2.0. 30 of 128 credits required for the bachelor's degree must be completed at Avila. **International Students:** There are 94 international students enrolled. They must take the TOEFL with a minimum score of 500 on the paper-based TOEFL (PBT) or 61 on the Internet-based version (iBT).

ADMISSIONS: 1 freshman graduated first in the class. **Admissions Contact:** Patti Harper, Director of Admissions. Email: *admissions@avila.edu* Web: *www.avila.edu*

FINANCIAL AID: In 2017-2018, 97% of all full-time freshmen received some form of financial aid. 76% of all full-time freshmen received need-based aid. 92% of undergraduate students work part-time. The FAFSA code is 002449. Check with the school for current application deadlines.

CENTRAL METHODIST UNIVERSITY C-2

www.centralmethodist.edu

Fayette, MO 65248 **(660) 248-6251** **(877) CMU-1854**

Fax: (660) 248-1872 **Email: admissions@centralmethodist.edu**

Full-time: 575 men, 583 women	**Faculty:** 63
Part-time: 5 men, 10 women	**Ph.D.s:** 83%
Graduate: n/av	**Student/Faculty:** 16 to 1
Year: semesters, summer session	**Tuition:** $23,770
Room & Board: $7730	**Freshman Class:** 1344 applied, 897 accepted, 302 enrolled
ACT: required	**CEEB CODE:** 6089
Application Deadline: n/av	**VERY COMPETITIVE**

Central Methodist University, founded in 1854, is a private liberal arts institution affiliated with the Methodist Church. The figures given in the above capsule and in this profile are approximate. There are 4 undergraduate schools. In addition to regional accreditation, CMU has baccalaureate program accreditation with NASM and CCNE. The 83-acre campus is in a small town 30 miles northwest of Columbia. Including any residence halls, there are 16 buildings.

STUDENT LIFE: 90% of undergraduates are from Missouri. Others are from 23 states, 8 foreign countries, and Canada. 96% are from public schools. 85% are White; 8% African American; 2% Hispanic; 1% Asian American; 1% American Indian/Alaska Native; 1% Foreign. 86% are Protestant; 14% Catholic. **Female To Male Ratio:** 1.0:1. The average age of freshmen is 18; all undergraduates, 21. 35% do not continue beyond their first year; 43% remain to graduate. **Housing:** 700 students can be accommodated in college housing, which includes married student dorms and off-campus apartments. On-campus housing is guaranteed for all 4 years. 59% of students live on campus. All students may keep cars. Alcohol is not permitted.

FACULTY/CLASSROOMS: 60% of faculty are male; 63% are female. All teach undergraduates. No introductory courses are taught by graduate students. The average class size in an introductory lecture is 30; in a laboratory is 24; and in a regular course is 12.

PROGRAMS OF STUDY: CMU confers B.A., B.S., B.M., B.M.E., B.S.E. B.S.N., B.G.S., B.A.S.M. and B.ACC. degrees. Associate and master's degrees are also awarded. Bachelor's degrees are awarded in BIOLOGICAL SCIENCE (biology/biological science and marine biology), BUSINESS (accounting, business administration and management, recreational facilities management, and sports management), COMMUNICATIONS AND THE ARTS (broadcasting, communications, dramatic arts, English, music, and Spanish), COMPUTER AND PHYSICAL SCIENCE (chemistry, computer science, mathematics, and physics), EDUCATION (athletic training, early childhood education, elementary education, middle school education, music education, physical education, social science education, and special education), ENGINEERING AND ENVIRONMENTAL DESIGN (environmental science), HEALTH PROFESSIONS (nursing), SOCIAL SCIENCE (criminal justice, history, interdisciplinary studies, philosophy, political science/government, psychology, religion, and sociology). Sciences, music, and preprofessional programs are the strongest academically. Business, education, and nursing have the largest enrollments.

ACTIVITIES: 21% of men belong to 3 local and 2 national fraternities; 24% of women belong to 4 local sororities. There are 37 groups on campus, including premed and criminal justice, band, cheerleading, choir, chorale, chorus, computers, dance, debate, drama, drill team, honors, jazz band, literary magazine, marching band, newspaper, opera, photography, political, prelaw, professional, radio and TV, religious, social, social service, and student government. Popular campus events include Music Festival. **Sports:** There are 5 intercollegiate sports for men and 4 for women, and 10 intramural sports for men and 10 for women. Facilities include a field house with a gym, playing fields, and a recreation center. **Graduates:** From July 1, 2016 to June 30, 2017, 149 bachelor's degrees were awarded. The most popular majors were health professions/related programs (19%), education (19%), and social sciences (15%). In an average class, 30% graduate in 4 years or less, 38% graduate in 5 years or less, and 42% graduate in 6 years or less.

SERVICES: Counseling and information services are available, as is tutoring in some subjects. There is remedial reading. **Library/Resources:** The library contains 102,695 volumes, 140,812 microform items, and 3,736 audio/video tapes/CDs/DVDs, and subscribes to 447 periodicals including electronic. Computerized library services include interlibrary loans, database searching, Internet access, and Wi-Fi capability. Special learning facilities include an art gallery, natural history museum, radio station, TV station, an observatory. **Physically Challenged Students:** 65% of the campus is accessible. Facilities include wheelchair ramps, elevators, special parking, specially equipped restrooms, special class scheduling, and lowered drinking fountains. **Special:** CMU offers cooperative programs in medical technology and physical therapy and 3-2 engineering degrees with the University of Missouri at Rolla, the University of Evansville, Stanford University, and Washington University in St. Louis. Work-study programs, internships, study abroad, dual majors, a general studies degree, and nondegree study are also available. There are 14 national honor societies and a freshman honors program. **Visiting:** There are regularly scheduled orientations for prospective students, including meeting with admissions and financial assistance staff, a campus tour, and visits with faculty members. There are guides for informal visits, visitors may sit in on classes, and stay overnight. To schedule a visit, contact the Admissions Office. **Campus Safety and Security:** Measures include 24-hour foot and vehicle patrol, emergency notification system, and security escort services. There are emergency telephones, lighted pathways/sidewalks, controlled access to dorms/residences, and key-card access to student housing.

REQUIREMENTS: A minimum score of 21 on the ACT is required. Those students with a GPA lower than 2.5 may request conditional admission. Applicants should be graduates of an accredited secondary school or have a GED certificate. Recommended preparatory courses include 4 units of English, 3 of math, and 2 each of science, social studies, and humanities. AP and CLEP credits are accepted. Important factors in the admissions decision are advanced placement or honors courses, evidence of special talent, and extracurricular activities record. To graduate, students must complete 124 to 131 credit hours, including at least 24 in the major, depending on the degree. A minimum GPA of 2.0 is required for all but the athletic training and education programs, which require a 2.5. Students must complete 53 hours of a distribution curriculum, including computer literacy, computer science, phys ed, religion, philosophy, freshman orientation to college life, and a senior capstone. **Procedure:** Freshmen are admitted to all sessions. There is a rolling admissions plan. Application deadlines are open. The fall 2017 application fee was $20. Applications are accepted on-line. **Transfer Students:** 105 transfer students enrolled in 2016-2017. Transfer applicants must be in good academic standing at their previous college and have a 2.0 cumulative GPA. 30 of 124 credits required for the bachelor's degree must be completed at CMU. **International Students:** There are 11 international students enrolled. They must take the TOEFL with a minimum score of 550 on the paper-based TOEFL (PBT).

ADMISSIONS: 67% of the 2017-2018 applicants were accepted. 4 freshmen graduated first in their class. **Admissions Contact:** Adam Jenkins,

Director of Admission. Email: *admissions@centralmethodist.edu* Web: *www.centralmethodist.edu*

FINANCIAL AID: In 2017-2018, 100% of all full-time freshmen received some form of financial aid. 89% of all full-time freshmen received need-based aid. The average freshman award was $17,813. Need-based scholarships or need-based grants averaged $5,030; need-based self-help aid (loans and jobs) averaged $3,187; non-need-based athletic scholarships averaged $4,725; other non-need-based awards and non-need-based scholarships averaged $8,871; and $3,467 from other forms of aid. 27% of undergraduate students work part-time. The average financial indebtedness of the 2017 graduate was $21,828. The FAFSA code is 002453. Check with the school for current application deadlines.

COLLEGE OF THE OZARKS — B-4

www.cofo.edu

Point Lookout, MO 65726	**(417) 334-6411** **(800) 222-0525**
Fax: (417) 335-2618	**Email: admiss4@cofo.edu**
Full-time: 659 men, 818 women	**Faculty:** 91; IIB, -$
Part-time: 18 men, 13 women	**Ph.D.s:** 59%
Graduate: n/av	**Student/Faculty:** 16 to 1
Year: semesters, summer session	**Tuition:** see profile
Room & Board: $7100	**Freshman Class:** 1208 applied, 447 accepted, 368 enrolled
SAT EBR-W/M: 603/580 **ACT:** 23	**CEEB CODE:** 6713
Application Deadline: December 31	**VERY COMPETITIVE**

The cost to attend College of the Ozarks for providing an educational opportunity is approximately $18,700 per year for each student. While most colleges and universities pass along a portion of this cost as tuition, this is not the case at College of the Ozarks. The College guarantees to meet all of this cost for each full-time student by using a combination of earnings from its endowment, operating its own mandatory student Work Education Program, and accepting student aid grants, as well as gifts, and other sources. As a result, each full-time student's Cost of Education is met 100% by participating in the Work Education Program and a combination of private, institutional, and federal/state student aid; without loans of any kind. There is 1 undergraduate school. In addition to regional accreditation, College of the Ozarks has baccalaureate program accreditation with ADA, NCACS, CNE, and Missouri State Board of Nursing. The 1000-acre campus is in a small town 40 miles south of Springfield, adjacent to the resort town of Branson. Including any residence halls, there are 99 buildings.

STUDENT LIFE: 82% of undergraduates are from Missouri. Others are from 24 states, and 14 foreign countries. 78% are from public schools. 93% are White; 2% Hispanic; 2% two or more races; 2% race unknown; 1% Foreign. 68% are Protestant; 29% Morman, and Unknown denomination, non-denominational. **Female To Male Ratio:** 1.2:1. The average age of freshmen is 18; all undergraduates, 20. 26% do not continue beyond their first year; 69% remain to graduate. **Housing:** 1372 students can be accommodated in college housing, which includes dorms. Student members of the volunteer fire department have living facilities at the fire department. On-campus housing is guaranteed for all 4 years. 87% of students live on campus. All students may keep cars. Alcohol is not permitted.

FACULTY/CLASSROOMS: 56% of faculty are male; 44% are female. All teach undergraduates. No introductory courses are taught by graduate students. The average class size in an introductory lecture is 40; in a laboratory is 18; and in a regular course is 30.

PROGRAMS OF STUDY: CO confers B.A. and B.S. degrees. Bachelor's degrees are awarded in AGRICULTURE (agricultural business management, agricultural sciences, agriculture, agronomy, animal science, conservation and regulation, and horticulture), BIOLOGICAL SCIENCE (biology ecology and field biology, biology/adolescence education, and biology/biological science), BUSINESS (accounting, business administration and management, business administration - international, business administration marketing, business economics, hotel/motel and restaurant management, international business management, marketing management, and meeting/special event management), COMMUNICATIONS AND THE ARTS (art, communications, communications technology, dramatic arts, English, journalism, media arts, music, music business management, music ministry, music theatre accompanying, music theory and composition, musical theater, performing arts, public relations, Spanish, communication arts-speech, speech and theatre education, studio art, studio art ceramics, studio art computer art, studio art fibers, studio art graphic design, studio art painting, theater design, theatre studies, and theatre ministry), COMPUTER AND PHYSICAL SCIENCE (chemistry, chemistry/adolescence education, computer science, information sciences and systems, and mathematics), EDUCATION (agricultural education, art education, business education, early childhood education, elementary education, English education, mathematics education, music education, physical education, physical education/exercise science, recreation education, secondary education, social studies education, Spanish education K-12, and vocational education), ENGINEERING AND ENVIRONMENTAL DESIGN (graphic arts technology and preengineering), HEALTH PROFESSIONS (allied health, health, medical technology, nursing, premedicine, prepharmacy, and preveterinary science), SOCIAL SCIENCE (biblical studies, child care/child and family studies, Christian studies, clothing and textiles management/production/services, corrections, criminal justice, criminology, culinary arts, dietetics, family/consumer studies, food science, history, home economics, interdisciplinary studies, law enforcement and corrections, ministries, philosophy, prelaw, psychology, religion, religious music, social science, family studies/social services/marriage family, social work, and sociology). Business, agriculture, education, and health services are the strongest academically. Education, business, and health services have the largest enrollments.

ACTIVITIES: There are no fraternities or sororities. There are 50 groups on campus, including art, band, cheerleading, choir, chorale, computers, dance, drama, honors, international, jazz band, musical theater, newspaper, orchestra, pep band, photography, political, professional, radio and TV, religious, social service, student government, and yearbook. Popular campus events include Honor America, 9/11 Remembrance Ceremony, Convocation Speakers, Spring Fest, Mud Fest, Lip Sync, Homecoming, and NAIA Division II Men's Championship Tournament. **Sports:** There are 5 intercollegiate sports for men and 5 for women, and 5 intramural sports for men and 5 for women. Facilities include a main gym with a training room, swimming pool, dance studio, racquetball courts, weight room, and basketball court. The Athletic Complex, includes a fitness center, indoor running track, and gymnasium, an all-weather track, baseball, intramural fields, tennis courts, and an outdoor track with rubberized tracks, jump pits, and throwing area. **Graduates:** From July 1, 2016 to June 30, 2017, 356 bachelor's degrees were awarded. The most popular majors were business (19%), education (14%), and health services (2%). In an average class, 3% graduate in 3 years or less, 55% graduate in 4 years or less, 71% graduate in 5 years or less, and 72% graduate in 6 years or less. Of the 2016 graduating class, 6% were enrolled in graduate school within 6 months of graduation, and 66% were employed.

SERVICES: Counseling and information services are provided on an individual basis, as is tutoring in some subjects. There is also remedial math and writing. **Library/Resources:** The library contains 461,350 volumes, 30,720 microform items, 2,947 audio/video tapes/CDs/DVDs, and subscribes to 53,095 periodicals, including electronic. Computerized library services include interlibrary loans, database searching, Internet access, and Wi-Fi capability. Special learning facilities include an art gallery, radio station, the Ralph Foster Museum, Edwards Mill (replica of a 1800s working grist mill) and weaving studio, print shop, greenhouses, farm operations, tractor museum and the Ozarkiana room, containing historical periodicals and pictures of the Ozarks, The Missouri Vietnam Veterans Memorial, the Missouri Gold Star Families Memorial, and the Lest We Forget 9/11 Memorial. **Physically Challenged Students:** 80% of the campus is accessible. Facilities include wheelchair ramps, elevators, special parking, specially equipped restrooms, special class scheduling, lowered drinking fountains, and special housing. **Special:** Interdisciplinary programs, Medical Technology through reverse transfer from Cox Health Systems, and pre-professional programs: Pre-Law, Pre-Dentistry, Pre-Medicine, Pre-Pharmacy, Pre-Physician's Assistant, Pre-Veterinary Medicine. Patriotic Education Travel Program, internships and student-designed majors. Bachelor of Science in Nursing, (B.S.N.). There are 9 national honor societies, Phi Beta Kappa, and 9 departmental honors programs. **Visiting:** There are regularly scheduled orientations for prospective students, Monday through Friday. There are guides for informal visits and visitors may sit in on classes. To schedule a visit, contact the Admissions Office. **Campus Safety and Security:** Measures include 24-hour foot and vehicle patrol, emergency notification system, and security escort services. There are emergency telephones, lighted pathways/sidewalks, controlled access to dorms/residences. There is a fire department on campus, and security cameras.

REQUIREMENTS: The ACT as well as the ACT Optional Writing test are required. Students should be in the top half of their graduating class and score at least a 20 on the ACT (950 SAT). Applicants should have a 3.0 GPA, and take the college preparatory curriculum in high school. Current college preparatory courses include 4 units of English, 3 units each of mathematics, social studies, and science. The College is most concerned with the core courses of English, history/social science, mathematics, and science. Because the College's mission focuses on serving students with financial need, students must demonstrate a significant level of financial need. CO requires applicants to be in the upper 50% of their class. A GPA of 3.2 is required. AP and CLEP credits are accepted. Important factors in the admissions decision are recommendations by school officials, leadership record, advanced placement or honors courses, evidence of special talent, personality/intangible qualities, extracurricular activities record, geographical diversity, parents or siblings attended your school, and recommendations by alumni. Graduation Requirements; Completion of a minimum of 125 semester hours of credit with a 2.0 or higher cumulative GPA. Remedial classes, including all College of the Ozarks classes beginning with a zero do not count toward graduation. Completion of at least one major with a minimum of a 2.0 GPA for the major. Some majors have higher GPA requirements. A major must include at least 30 required hours (major/collateral) with at least 15 hours upper division (300-400 level) courses. Completion of all general education courses with a minimum of a 2.0 GPA. Completion of at least 36 credit hours of upper division courses. No more than six of those hours may be in internship. Students with transfer hours must complete a minimum of 45 credit hours at CO. At least 12 credit hours must be in the major field including nine upper division hours. Exceptions may be made with the approval of the Dean of the College. Participation in the College Work Education Program as a full-time student for at least one semester is required for completion of degree. The last 30 hours of credit must be completed at CO unless a waiver is granted in writing from the Dean of the College. The faculty and the Board of Trustees vote on all graduates. To be approved for graduation, all students must have satisfied all current degree and instructional requirements, as well as be in compliance with all College regulations at time of graduation. Students will graduate with either a Bachelor of Arts degree, Bachelor of Science degree, or a Bachelor of Science in Nursing degree. **Procedure:** Freshmen are admitted in the fall and spring. Entrance exams should be taken during junior year, and October of senior year. There is a rolling admissions plan. Applications should be filed by December 31 for fall entry; December 31 for spring entry. Notifications are sent January 15. 646 applicants were on the 2017 waiting list; 24 were admitted. Applications are accepted online. **Transfer Students:** 27 transfer students enrolled in 2016-2017. Students with fewer than 24 transferable college semester hours completed elsewhere should submit the materials listed above plus the transfer student documents that are noted. This includes a college transcript (from all institutions attended) and a transfer student form. The transfer student form attests to the positive character of the student and must be completed by the dean of students at the institution from which the student is transferring. Transfer students with 24 or more transferable college semester hours need not submit ACT scores and high school transcripts, but they are required to submit college transcripts and the transfer student form. Reference forms for transfer students should be submitted by college academic personnel. Transfer applicants with over 60 hours may be ineligible for admission. 45 of 125 credits required for the bachelor's degree must be completed at CO. **International Students:** There are 27 international students enrolled. They must take the TOEFL with a minimum score of 550 on the paper-based TOEFL (PBT) or 79 on the Internet-based version (iBT). Students must take any one of these tests the ACT, SAT, or IELTS.

ADMISSIONS: 37% of the 2017-2018 applicants were accepted. The SAT scores for the 2017-2018 freshman class were: Math-- 1% below 500, 58% between 500 and 599, and 33% between 600 and 699. Evidence-Based Reading/Writing-- 58% between 500 and 599 and 42% between 600 and 699. The ACT scores were 1% between 12 and 17, 50% between 18 and 23, 42% between 24 and 29, and 6% above 30. 51% of the current freshmen were in the top fifth of their class; 86% were in the top two fifths. 22 freshmen graduated first in their class. **Admissions Contact:** Dr. Marci Linson, Dean of Admissions. Email: *admiss4@cofo.edu* Web: *www.cofo.edu*

FINANCIAL AID: In 2017-2018, 100% of all full-time freshmen received some form of financial aid. 90% of all full-time freshmen received need-based aid. The average freshman award was $19,871. Need-based scholarships or need-based grants averaged $4,170 ($5,815 maximum); need-based self-help aid (loans and jobs) averaged $4,312 ($4,312 maximum); and non-need-based athletic scholarships averaged $4,631 ($7,100 maximum). 100% of undergraduate students work part-time. The FAFSA code is 002500. The priority date for freshman financial aid applications for fall entry is November 15.

COLUMBIA COLLEGE - MISSOURI C-2

www.ccis.edu

Columbia, MO 65216	(573) 875-7352 (800) 231-2391
Fax: (573) 875-7506	**Email: admissions@ccis.edu**
Full-time: 378 men, 478 women	**Faculty:** 74; IIB, av$
Part-time: 57 men, 128 women	**Ph.D.s:** 77%
Graduate: 53 men, 102 women	**Student/Faculty:** 11 to 1
Year: semesters, summer session	**Tuition:** $21,936
Room & Board: $6243	**Freshman Class:** 1589 applied, 831 accepted, 174 enrolled
SAT or ACT: recommended	**CEEB CODE:** 6095
Application Deadline: August 12	**COMPETITIVE**

Columbia College-Missouri, founded in 1851, is a private, is a nonprofit institution that helps students change their lives with quality degree programs. Students succeed with small classes, experienced faculty and the choice of day, evening and online classes. There are 3 undergraduate schools and 1 graduate school. In addition to regional accreditation, CCM has baccalaureate program accreditation with CCNE. The 36-acre campus is in an urban area 120 miles east of Kansas City and 120 miles west of St. Louis. Including any residence halls, there are 37 buildings.

STUDENT LIFE: 88% of undergraduates are from Missouri. Others are from 28 states, 14 foreign countries, and Canada. 74% are White; 6% Foreign; 6% two or more races; 5% African American; 4% Hispanic; 3% race unknown; 1% Asian American; 1% American Indian/Alaska Native. 72% claim no religious affiliation; 12% Protestant. **Female To Male Ratio:** 1.5:1. The average age of freshmen is 18; all undergraduates, 22. **Housing:** 395 students can be accommodated in college housing, which includes dorms, on-campus apartments, and off-campus apartments, and living learning communities. On-campus housing is available on a first-come and first-served basis. 63% of students commute. All students may keep cars. Alcohol is not permitted.

FACULTY/CLASSROOMS: 47% of faculty are male; 53% are female. All teach undergraduates. No introductory courses are taught by graduate students. The average class size in an introductory lecture is 15 and in a laboratory is 15.

PROGRAMS OF STUDY: CCM confers B.A., B.S., B.G.S., and B.F.A. degrees. Associate and master's degrees are also awarded. Bachelor's degrees are awarded in AGRICULTURE (environmental studies), BIOLOGICAL SCIENCE (biology/biological science), BUSINESS (business administration and management and international business management), COMMUNICATIONS AND THE ARTS (art, ceramic art and design, communications, English, fine arts, graphic design, painting, photography, and printmaking), COMPUTER AND PHYSICAL SCIENCE (chemistry, computer science, information sciences and systems, and mathematics), EDUCATION (education, education administration, elementary education, middle school education, and secondary education), ENGINEERING AND ENVIRONMENTAL DESIGN (military science), HEALTH PROFESSIONS (nursing), SOCIAL SCIENCE (American studies, criminal justice, fire services administration, forensic studies, history, human services, interdisciplinary studies, liberal arts/general studies, philosophy, political science/government, psychology, social work, and sociology). Psychology, chemisty, and computer science are the strongest academically. Visual arts & music, humanities, and biology have the largest enrollments.

ACTIVITIES: There are no fraternities or sororities. Groups on campus include art, chess, choir, chorale, drama, drum and bugle corps, environmental, ethnic, forensics, honors, international, LGBT, Model UN, photography, political, professional, religious, social, social service, and student government. Popular campus events include Ivy Chain, Holiday Lighting Ceremony, and Schiffman Lecture in Ethics. **Sports:** There are 8 intercollegiate sports for men and 9 for women, and 16 intramural sports for men and 16 for women. Facilities include baseball field, softball field, a gym, exercise/weight room, outdoor recreation field use for soccer and lacrosse, and dance studio. **Graduates:** From July 1, 2016 to June 30, 2017, 158 bachelor's degrees were awarded. The most popular majors were business (26%), general studies (13%), and criminal justice administration (8%). In an average class, 45% graduate in 6 years or less.

SERVICES: Counseling and information services are available, as is tutoring in some subjects, such as American or world history, speech, intro to computer information systems and ethics. **Library/Resources:** The library contains 300,420 volumes, 163,858 audio/video tapes/CDs/DVDs, and subscribes to 161,102 periodicals, including electronic. Computerized library services include interlibrary loans, database searching, Internet access, and Wi-Fi capability. Special learning facilities include an art gallery. **Physically Challenged Students:** All of the campus is accessible. Facilities include wheelchair ramps, elevators, special parking, specially equipped restrooms, special class scheduling, lowered drinking fountains, lowered telephones, and special housing. **Special:** Columbia offers cross-registration with the University of Missouri/Columbia and Stephens College, internships, study abroad in more than 20 countries, B.A.-B.S. degrees in most disciplines, an interdisciplinary studies degree, student-designed and dual majors, nondegree study, and pass/fail options. Select students who complete a special 2-semester project earn a bachelor's degree with distinction (B.A.D.). There are 16 national honor societies, a freshman honors program, and 1 departmental honors program. **Visiting:** There are regularly scheduled orientations for prospective students, including a campus tour, a workshop in financial aid, an academic/organization fair, and a luncheon. To schedule a visit, contact the Admissions Office. **Campus Safety and Security:** Measures include 24-hour foot and vehicle patrol, emergency notification system, self-defense education, and security escort services. There are emergency telephones, lighted pathways/sidewalks, and controlled access to dorms/residences.

REQUIREMENTS: The SAT or ACT and ACT Writing Test are recommended. Applicants must be graduates of an accredited secondary school or have a GED certificate. Students should have completed 4 units of English, 3 units of math including 2 units of algebra and 1 unit of geometry, and 3 units each of natural science and social studies, and 2 units of foreign language AP and CLEP credits are accepted. To graduate, students must complete 60 credit hours for an Associate's degree or 120 credit hours for a Bachelors degree with a minimum GPA of 2.0. Distribution requirements include 12 hours in basic skills (English composition, speech, computer information systems and math), 6 hours in humanities, history, social and behavioral science; 5-6 hours in math/science and 3 hours in ethics. Bachelor of Art degrees require six hours of a foreign language or culture and society courses, ethics course, and 39 hours of upper-level course work. Most majors require students to complete a capstone course with the exception of Bachelors in General Studies and Associates degrees. **Procedure:** Freshmen are admitted to all sessions. Entrance exams should be taken in spring of the junior year or fall of the senior year. There are deferred admissions and rolling admissions plans. Applications should be filed by August 12 for fall entry; January 1 for spring entry. The fall 2017 application fee was $35. Applications are accepted on-line. **Transfer Students:** 146 transfer students enrolled in 2016-2017. Applicants must have a minimum GPA of 2.0 overall and in the last semester attended and must submit a high school transcript and SAT or ACT scores, and a good standing from prior institution. 24 of 120 credits required for the bachelor's degree must be completed at CCM. **International Students:** There are 33 international students enrolled. They must take the TOEFL with a minimum score of 500 on the paper-based TOEFL (PBT) or 61 on the Internet-based version (iBT). They must also take the ACT.

ADMISSIONS: 52% of the 2017-2018 applicants were accepted. The SAT scores for the 2017-2018 freshman class were: Math-- 5% below 500, 47% between 500 and 599, 37% between 600 and 699, and 11% between 700 and 800. Evidence-Based Reading/Writing-- 10% below 500, 53% between 500 and 599, and 37% between 600 and 699. The ACT scores were 5% between 12 and 17, 50% between 18 and 23, 39% between 24 and 29, and 6% above 30. 38% of the current freshmen were in the top fifth of their class; 76% were in the top two fifths. **Admissions Contact:** Stephanie Johnson, Director of Admissions. Email: *admissions@ccis.edu* Web: *www.ccis.edu*

FINANCIAL AID: In 2017-2018, 90% of all full-time freshmen received some form of financial aid. 57% of all full-time freshmen received need-based aid. The average freshman award was $20,499. Need-based scholarships or need-based grants averaged $722 ($2,250 maximum); need-based self-help aid (loans and jobs) averaged $1,870 ($9,687 maximum); non-need-based athletic scholarships averaged $3,614 ($24,876 maximum); and other non-need-based awards and non-need-based scholarships averaged $6,483 ($27,376 maximum). 13% of undergraduate students work part-time. CCM is a member of CSS. The college's own financial statement is required. The FAFSA code is 002456. The priority date for freshman financial aid applications for fall entry is March 1.

COX COLLEGE *(The complete profile is made available exclusively on our website, www.barronspac.com)*

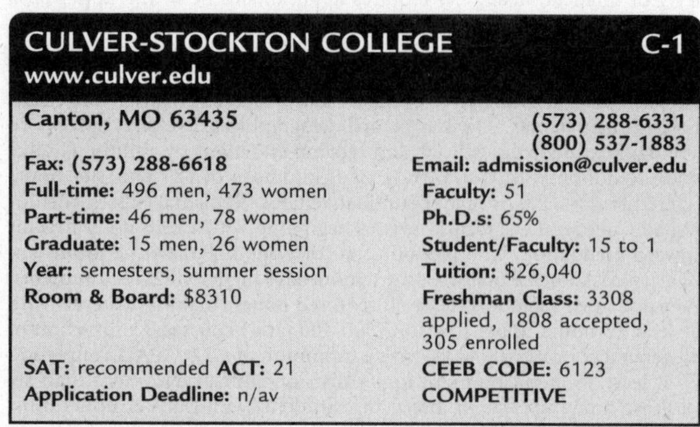

CULVER-STOCKTON COLLEGE — C-1

www.culver.edu

Canton, MO 63435 — (573) 288-6331, (800) 537-1883

Fax: (573) 288-6618 — Email: admission@culver.edu

Full-time: 496 men, 473 women	**Faculty:** 51
Part-time: 46 men, 78 women	**Ph.D.s:** 65%
Graduate: 15 men, 26 women	**Student/Faculty:** 15 to 1
Year: semesters, summer session	**Tuition:** $26,040
Room & Board: $8310	**Freshman Class:** 3308 applied, 1808 accepted, 305 enrolled
SAT: recommended **ACT:** 21	**CEEB CODE:** 6123
Application Deadline: n/av	**COMPETITIVE**

Culver-Stockton College, established in 1853, is a private liberal arts institution affiliated with the Christian Church (Disciples of Christ). There is 1 undergraduate school. In addition to regional accreditation, CSC has baccalaureate program accreditation with NASM, IACBE, CAATE, and CCNE. The 143-acre campus is in a small town 125 miles north of St. Louis. Including any residence halls, there are 23 buildings.

STUDENT LIFE: 57% of undergraduates are from Missouri. Others are from 37 states, 20 foreign countries, and Canada. 95% are from public schools. 73% are White; 6% Foreign; 5% Hispanic; 3% two or more races; 11% African American; 1% Asian American; 1% American Indian/Alaska Native. 56% are Protestant; 27% claim no religious affiliation; 12% Catholic. **Female To Male Ratio:** 1.0:1. The average age of freshmen is 18; all undergraduates, 20. 32% do not continue beyond their first year; 47% remain to graduate. **Housing:** 850 students can be accommodated in college housing, which includes dorms. In addition, there are fraternity houses and sorority houses. On-campus housing is guaranteed for all 4 years. 74% of students live on campus. All students may keep cars.

FACULTY/CLASSROOMS: 47% of faculty are male; 53% are female. All teach undergraduates. No introductory courses are taught by graduate students. The average class size in an introductory lecture is 21; in a laboratory is 17; and in a regular course is 17.

PROGRAMS OF STUDY: CSC confers B.A., B.S., B.F.A., B.M.E., B.A.A.S. and B.S.N. degrees. Master's degrees are also awarded. Bachelor's degrees are awarded in BIOLOGICAL SCIENCE (biochemistry and biology/biological science), BUSINESS (accounting, business administration and management, finance, marketing management, and sports management), COMMUNICATIONS AND THE ARTS (art, arts administration/management, communications, dramatic arts, English, fine arts, graphic design, music, music technology, and musical theater), COMPUTER AND PHYSICAL SCIENCE (chemistry and mathematics), EDUCATION (art education, athletic training, drama education, education, elementary education, music education, and physical education), HEALTH PROFESSIONS (health science and nursing), SOCIAL SCIENCE (criminal justice, history, international studies, legal studies, political science/government, psychology, and religion). Accounting, athletic training, and biological chemistry are the strongest academically. Business, criminal justice, and nursing have the largest enrollments.

ACTIVITIES: 37% of men belong to 7 national fraternities; 38% of women belong to 3 national sororities. There are 45 groups on campus, including art, band, cheerleading, choir, chorus, communications, dance, drama, environmental, ethnic, honors, international, jazz band, LGBT, literary magazine, musical theater, newspaper, photography, political, professional, radio and TV, religious, social, social service, and student government. Popular campus events include Honors Day, Hillstock, Homecoming and Family Weekend, Up 'til Dawn, Wildcat Welcome, and Greek Week. **Sports:** There are 10 intercollegiate sports for men and 9 for women, and 8 intramural sports for men and 8 for women. Facilities include a track, astro turf football and soccer field, baseball field, softball field, intramural fields, a health and fitness center with dance studio, weight room and exercise equipment, and a field house with basketball and volleyball courts. **Graduates:** From July 1, 2016 to June 30, 2017, 190 bachelor's degrees were awarded. The most popular majors were business (19%), criminal justice (11%), and psychology (8%). In an average class, 41% graduate in 4 years or less, 46% graduate in 5 years or less, and 47% graduate in 6 years or less. Of the 2016 graduating class, 15% were enrolled in graduate school within 6 months of graduation, and 99% were employed.

SERVICES: Counseling and information services are available, as is tutoring in most subjects. There is remedial math and writing. **Library/ Resources:** The library contains 288,926 volumes, and 2,517 audio/video tapes/CDs/DVDs, and subscribes to 56,100 periodicals including electronic. Computerized library services include interlibrary loans, database searching, Internet access, and Wi-Fi capability. Special learning facilities include an art gallery, planetarium, radio station, TV station, a phage genomics research facility with DNA sequencer, astronomy observation deck, biological research station, collegiate teaching greenhouse, rare books collection, a performing arts center with a multi-media editing suite and recording studio, a publications lab, a photography studio, a simulated elementary classroom, mock trial courtroom with legal research library, 17 computer labs, and a tutoring center. **Physically Challenged Students:** 40% of the campus is accessible. Facilities include wheelchair ramps, elevators, special parking, specially equipped restrooms, special class scheduling, and lowered drinking fountains. **Special:** Culver-Stockton offers a joint-degree program in nursing in conjunction with Blessing-Rieman College of Nursing and a 3-2 occupational therapy degree with Washington University in St. Louis. Study abroad, internships, and individualized majors are also available. There are 11 national honor societies, a freshman honors program, and 9 departmental honors programs. **Visiting:** There are regularly scheduled orientations for prospective students, includes meetings with professors, students, coaches, financial aid and extracurricular advisers, financial aid information, a student life panel, and campus tours. There are guides for informal visits, visitors may sit in on classes, and stay overnight. To schedule a visit, contact Gaye Redd at (800) 537-1883. **Campus Safety and Security:** Measures include 24-hour foot and vehicle patrol, emergency notification system, self-defense education, and security escort services. There are lighted pathways/sidewalks and controlled access to dorms/residences.

REQUIREMENTS: Requirements include secondary school records with GPA and SAT or ACT (preferred) scores. Recommended is a college preparatory program including 4 years of English, 2 to 4 of science, 3 years of social studies, and 2 of math. The GED is accepted. AP and CLEP credits are accepted. To graduate, students must complete 120 credit hours, including 36 to 60 in the major, with a minimum GPA of 2.0. Distribution requirements include 1 course each in humanities, fine arts, intercultural learning, social science, natural science, and quantitative literacy. English composition I&II, speech, religion, phys ed, 2 courses in experiential learning and Academic and Cultural Events are also required. **Procedure:** Freshmen are admitted in the fall and spring. Entrance exams should be taken by April of the entering school year. There are deferred admissions and rolling admissions plans. Application deadlines are open. Applications are accepted online. **Transfer Students:** 62 transfer students enrolled in 2016-2017. Transfer applicants must submit college transcripts and have a minimum college GPA of 2.0. 30 of 120 credits required for the bachelor's degree must be completed at CSC. **International Students:** There are 68 international students enrolled. They must take the TOEFL with a minimum score of 550 on the paper-based TOEFL (PBT) or 79 on the Internet-based version (iBT). International students are not required to take the TOEFL if they have resided in this country for 1 semester or submit SAT or ACT scores.

ADMISSIONS: 55% of the 2017-2018 applicants were accepted. The SAT scores for the 2017-2018 freshman class were: Critical Reading-- 32% below 500, 62% between 500 and 599, and 6% between 600 and 699. Math-- 44% below 500, 46% between 500 and 599, and 10% between 600 and 699. The ACT scores were 11% between 12 and 17, 69% between 18 and 23, 18% between 24 and 29, and 2% above 30. 16% of the current freshmen were in the top fifth of their class; 38% were in the top two fifths. 7 freshmen graduated first in their class. **Admissions Contact:** Misty McBee, Executive Director of Marketing and Admission. Email: *admission@culver.edu* Web: *www.culver.edu*

FINANCIAL AID: In 2017-2018, 99% of all full-time freshmen received some form of financial aid. 91% of all full-time freshmen received need-based aid. The average freshman award was $21,580. Need-based scholarships or need-based grants averaged $18,544 ($34,560 maximum); need-based self-help aid (loans and jobs) averaged $3,619 ($38,850 maximum); non-need-based athletic scholarships averaged $5,870 ($9,000 maximum); and other non-need-based awards and non-need-based scholarships averaged $10,018 ($34,560 maximum). 47% of undergraduate students work part-time. The average financial indebtedness of the 2017 graduate was $24,837. CSC is a member of CSS. The FAFSA code is 002460. The priority date for freshman financial aid applications for fall entry is January 1.

DRURY UNIVERSITY — B-3

www.drury.edu

Springfield, MO 65802	(417) 873-7205 (800) 922-2274
Fax: (417) 866-3873	**Email: druryad@drury.edu**
Full-time: 617 men, 781 women	**Faculty:** 110; IIB, -$
Part-time: 13 men, 14 women	**Ph.D.s:** 94%
Graduate: 65 men, 169 women	**Student/Faculty:** 13 to 1
Year: semesters, summer session	**Tuition:** $27,350
Room & Board: $9040	**Freshman Class:** 1474 applied, 1067 accepted, 342 enrolled
ACT: 26	**CEEB CODE:** 6169
Application Deadline: August 22	**VERY COMPETITIVE**

Drury is a small, liberal arts university that has held to its core values since its establishment in 1873. Drury values find their origins in Drury's unique church affiliation, and they are responsible for an academic and spiritual environment that provides students with unique opportunities and advantages. There are 3 undergraduate schools and 5 graduate schools. In addition to regional accreditation, DU has baccalaureate program accreditation with AACSB, ACBSP, NAAB, NASM, NCATE, AMTS, and ACS. The 80-acre campus is in an urban area 200 miles southwest of St. Louis and 150 miles southeast of Kansas City Including any residence halls, there are 44 buildings.

STUDENT LIFE: 75% of undergraduates are from Missouri. Others are from 30 states, 55 foreign countries, and Canada. 85% are from public schools. 9% are Foreign; 79% White; 3% African American; 3% Hispanic; 3% two or more races; 2% Asian American; 1% American Indian/ Alaska Native. 70% are Protestant; 16% Catholic. **Female To Male Ratio:** 1.4:1. The average age of freshmen is 19; all undergraduates, 21. 14% do not continue beyond their first year; 86% remain to graduate. **Housing:** 1022 students can be accommodated in college housing, which includes married student dorms, on-campus apartments, and off-campus apartments. In addition, there are honors houses, special-interest houses, fraternity houses, leadership houses, and living learning communities. On-campus housing is guaranteed for all 4 years. 65% of students live on campus. All students may keep cars.

FACULTY/CLASSROOMS: 65% of faculty are male; 45% are female. All teach undergraduates, 40% do research, and 40% do both. No introductory courses are taught by graduate students. The average class size in an introductory lecture is 21; in a laboratory is 21; and in a regular course is 18.

PROGRAMS OF STUDY: DU confers B.A., B.S., M.Arch., B.M.T., B.B.A., A.S., and B.Ed. degrees. Associate and master's degrees are also awarded. Bachelor's degrees are awarded in AGRICULTURE (environmental studies and natural resource management), BIOLOGICAL SCIENCE (biochemistry, biology/biological science, biological sciences, and environmental biology), BUSINESS (accounting, business administration, business administration/aviation, environment and national resource economics, finance, international business management, management, marketing management, and organizational leadership and management), COMMUNICATIONS AND THE ARTS (advertising, animation, arts administration, art history and appreciation, communication studies, English, English literature, English writing, fine arts, French, graphic design, graphic design and media, journalism, multimedia, music, public relations, public relations/advertising, Spanish, Spanish language and literature, theatre arts, and writing), COMPUTER AND PHYSICAL SCIENCE (chemistry, computer game design/development, mathematics, physics, radiological technology, and software engineering), EDUCATION (education, educational media, elementary education, general studies, health information management, mathematics education, music education, psychology education, secondary education, and social science education), ENGINEERING AND ENVIRONMENTAL DESIGN (architectural technology, architecture, computer engineering, energy management technology, instructional technology, and technology), HEALTH PROFESSIONS (community and behavioral health, emergency medical technologies, exercise physiology, health and physical activity, medical technology, music therapy, and radiograph medical technology), SOCIAL SCIENCE (behavioral science, criminal justice, criminology, economics, history, history and political science, human services, law enforcement and corrections, paralegal studies, philosophy, philosophy and religion, political science/government, preministerial studies, psychology, public administration, religion, and sociology). Premedicine, business, and architecture are the strongest academically. Biology, business/marketing, and architecture have the largest enrollments.

ACTIVITIES: 21% of men belong to 4 national fraternities; 26% of women belong to 4 national sororities. There are 100 groups on campus, including academic interests, environment, leadership, student life, art, band, cheerleading, chess, choir, chorale, chorus, computers, dance, debate, drama, environmental, ethnic, film, forensics, honors, international, jazz band, LGBT, literary magazine, minority students, musical theater, newspaper, opera, orchestra, pep band, photography, political, professional, radio and TV, religious, social, social service, student government, and symphony. Popular campus events include Homecoming, Fireworks on Sunderland Field, Fall Festival, Earth Day, and Christmas Vespers. **Sports:** There are 9 intercollegiate sports for men and 10 for women, and 5 intramural sports for men and 5 for women. Facilities include an event center, a gym, tennis court, racquetball courts, a soccer stadium, a baseball training center, baseball field (off-campus), a tennis stadium (off-campus), an Olympic-size pool, a fitness center, a running track, and a wellness program with exercise classes. **Graduates:** From July 1, 2016 to June 30, 2017, 296 bachelor's degrees were awarded. The most popular majors were biological/life sciences (24%), business/marketing (22%), and architecture (7%). In an average class, 1% graduate in 3 years or less, 47% graduate in 4 years or less, 63% graduate in 5 years or less, and 66% graduate in 6 years or less. Of the 2016 graduating class, 39% were enrolled in graduate school within 6 months of graduation.

SERVICES: Counseling and information services are available, as is tutoring in every subject. There is a reader service for the blind, and remedial writing. There is a math and reading learning center, a writing center, and a communications center. **Library/Resources:** The library contains 185,811 volumes, 13,565 microform items, 5,344 audio/video tapes/CDs/DVDs, and subscribes to 469 periodicals, including electronic. Computerized library services include interlibrary loans, database searching, Internet access, and Wi-Fi capability. Special learning facilities include an art gallery, radio station, TV station, an astronomical observatory, a greenhouse, teleconference facility, an art and architecture slide collection, speech communication center, and writing center. **Physically Challenged Students:** 95% of the campus is accessible. Facilities include wheelchair ramps, elevators, special parking, specially equipped restrooms, special class scheduling, lowered drinking fountains, and lowered telephones. **Special:** Drury offers study abroad in Aigina, Greece and 19 other countries as well as cross-registration with colleges in 8 countries; nearly 50% of students study abroad. Premedical early admission arrangements with St. Louis University, the University of Missouri, and Kirksville College of Osteopathic Medicine and a 3-2 engineering dual-degree program in conjunction with the University of Missouri and Washington University are available. Co-op programs include computer information systems and arts administration. 75% of students complete a professional internship; options include public and private sectors and a Washington semester. Work study, credit by exam, non-degree study, dual majors in most majors, and satisfactory/unsatisfactory options are also possible. There are 11 national honor societies, Phi Beta Kappa, a freshman honors program, and 8 departmental honors programs. **Visiting:** There are regularly scheduled orientations for prospective students, as well as visit days specialized for premed, architecture, preengineering, math, physics, computer sciences, arts and sciences, and social sciences students. There are guides for informal visits, visitors may sit in on classes, and stay overnight. To schedule a visit, contact Kim Atkison at (417) 873-7205. **Campus Safety and Security:** Measures include 24-hour foot and vehicle patrol, an emergency notification system, self-defense education, and security escort services. There are shuttle buses, emergency telephones, lighted pathways/sidewalks, controlled access to dorms/residences, and lighted parking lots with security cameras.

REQUIREMENTS: The ACT is required. Applicants must be graduates of an accredited secondary school or have a GED certificate. Recommended high school credits include 4 units of English and at least 3 each of math through algebra II, natural science, and social studies. An essay and a reference from the high school counselor or principal are required. A GPA of 3.0 is required. AP and CLEP credits are accepted. Important factors in the admissions decision are advanced placement or honors courses, recommendations by school officials, and personality/intangible qualities. To graduate, students must complete 124 credit hours (150 for accounting and 170 for B.Arch.). They must also maintain a minimum GPA of 2.0 and complete 26 to 32 credit hours in the major (99 for architecture). Students pursue a broad curriculum which includes requirements in science, math, humanities, fine arts, fitness, foreign language, and social science. **Procedure:** Freshmen are admitted to all sessions. Entrance exams should be taken in the spring of the junior year or fall of the senior year. There are deferred admissions and rolling admissions plans. Applications should be filed by August 22 for fall entry; January 10 for spring entry. Notifications are sent October 1. Applications are accepted online. **Transfer Students:** 74 transfer students enrolled in 2016-2017. Applicants must have a minimum GPA of 2.0 in all college work completed and supply an essay or writing sample. 30 of 124 credits required for the bachelor's degree must be completed at DU. **International Students:** There are 139 international students enrolled. They must take the TOEFL with a minimum score of 530 on the paper-based TOEFL (PBT) or 71 on the Internet-based version (iBT). Students must also take either the IELTS, ACT, or SAT.

ADMISSIONS: 72% of the 2017-2018 applicants were accepted. The ACT scores were 2% between 12 and 17, 26% between 18 and 23, 57% between 24 and 29, and 15% above 30. 66% of the current freshmen were in the top fifth of their class; 87% were in the top two fifths. **Admissions Contact:** Kevin Kropf, Executive Vice President of Enrollment Management. Email: *druryad@drury.edu* Web: *www.drury.edu*

FINANCIAL AID: In 2017-2018, 67% of all full-time freshmen received some form of financial aid and need-based aid. The average freshman award was $21,933. Need-based scholarships or need-based grants averaged $18,391; need-based self-help aid (loans and jobs) averaged $4,531; non-need-based athletic scholarships averaged $12,559; and other non-need-based awards and non-need-based scholarships averaged $10,765. 74% of undergraduate students work part-time. The average financial indebtedness of the 2017 graduate was $31,137. DU is a member of CSS. The college's own financial statement is required. The FAFSA code is 002461. The priority date for freshman financial aid applications for fall entry is December 1.

EVANGEL UNIVERSITY — B-3

www.evangel.edu

Springfield, MO 65802 — **(417) 865-2811**

Fax: (417) 865-9599	**Email:** admissions@evangel.edu
Full-time: 726 men, 978 women	**Faculty:** n/av
Part-time: 90 men, 85 women	**Ph.D.s:** 63%
Graduate: 66 men, 134 women	**Student/Faculty:** n/av
Year: semesters, summer session	**Tuition:** $21,316
Room & Board: $7582	**Freshman Class:** 1163 applied, 857 accepted, 432 enrolled
SAT or ACT: recommended	**CEEB CODE:** 6198
Application Deadline: n/av	**COMPETITIVE**

Evangel University, established in 1955, is a private institution affiliated with the Assemblies of God. As a comprehensive Christian university, Evangel offers more than 100 academic programs, including adult and graduate studies degree programs, and a embedded seminary. There are 2 undergraduate schools and 1 graduate school. In addition to regional accreditation, EU has baccalaureate program accreditation with CSWE, NASM, and NCATE. The 80-acre campus is in an urban area in Springfield, Missouri, just 225 miles west of St. Louis. Including any residence halls, there are 21 buildings.

STUDENT LIFE: 55% of undergraduates are from Missouri. Others are from 50 states, 62 foreign countries, and Canada. 79% are from public schools. 5% are White; 2% Asian American; 1% African American; 1% Hispanic; 1% Foreign. 74% claim no religious affiliation; 12% Protestant. **Female To Male Ratio:** 1.4:1. The average age of freshmen is 18;

all undergraduates, 21. 31% do not continue beyond their first year. **Housing:** 1460 students can be accommodated in college housing, which includes married student dorms. In addition, there are honors houses, and six residents halls. On-campus housing is guaranteed for all 4 years. 75% of students live on campus. All students may keep cars. Alcohol is not permitted.

FACULTY/CLASSROOMS: All teach undergraduates. No introductory courses are taught by graduate students. The average class size in an introductory lecture is 40 and in a regular course is 20.

PROGRAMS OF STUDY: EU confers B.A., B.S., B.B.A., B.F.A., B.M. and B.S.W. degrees. Associate and master's degrees are also awarded. Bachelor's degrees are awarded in BIOLOGICAL SCIENCE (biology/biological science), BUSINESS (accounting, management science, and marketing/retailing/merchandising), COMMUNICATIONS AND THE ARTS (art, broadcasting, communications, design, dramatic arts, English, journalism, music, music performance, Spanish, and speech/debate/rhetoric), COMPUTER AND PHYSICAL SCIENCE (chemistry, computer science, and mathematics), EDUCATION (business education, early childhood education, elementary education, foreign languages education, music education, physical education, science education, secondary education, and special education), HEALTH PROFESSIONS (medical laboratory technology), SOCIAL SCIENCE (biblical studies, criminal justice, history, international studies, missions, parks and recreation management, political science/government, psychology, public administration, religion, religious music, social science, social work, and sociology). Science & technology, and behavioral science are the strongest academically. Business has the largest enrollment.

ACTIVITIES: There are no fraternities or sororities. There are 19 groups on campus, including band, cheerleading, choir, chorale, chorus, drama, forensics, honors, jazz band, marching band, musical theater, newspaper, orchestra, pep band, photography, political, professional, radio and TV, religious, student government, symphony, and yearbook. Popular campus events include College Weekend, Harvest Fest, Homecoming, and Spring Fling. **Sports:** There are 5 intercollegiate sports for men and 6 for women, and 4 intramural sports for men and 4 for women. Facilities include a student activities center and gym. **Graduates:** From July 1, 2016 to June 30, 2017, 322 bachelor's degrees were awarded. The most popular majors were business/marketing (23%), education (13%), and communications/journalism (10%). In an average class, 25% graduate in 4 years or less, 36% graduate in 5 years or less, and 37% graduate in 6 years or less.

SERVICES: Counseling and information services are available, as is tutoring in every subject. There is a reader service for the blind, and remedial math, reading, and writing. **Library/Resources:** The library contains 96,487 volumes, 11,386 microform items, 6,801 audio/video tapes/CDs/DVDs, and subscribes to 748 periodicals, including electronic. Computerized library services include interlibrary loans, database searching, Internet access, and Wi-Fi capability. Special learning facilities include an art gallery, radio station, and TV station. **Physically Challenged Students:** All of the campus is accessible. Facilities include wheelchair ramps, elevators, special parking, specially equipped restrooms, lowered drinking fountains, and lowered telephones. **Special:** There are 3-2 engineering degrees available in conjunction with the University of Missouri at Columbia. Other options include work-study, credit by exam, and a Washington semester. There are 9 national honor societies and 8 departmental honors programs. **Visiting:** There are regularly scheduled orientations for prospective students, consisting of scheduled visits every Friday by appointment. There are guides for informal visits, visitors may sit in on classes, and stay overnight. To schedule a visit, contact the Office of Admissions. **Campus Safety and Security:** Measures include 24-hour foot and vehicle patrol, emergency notification system, and security escort services. There are emergency telephones, lighted pathways/sidewalks, and controlled access to dorms/residences.

REQUIREMENTS: The SAT or ACT is recommended. The recommended preparatory curriculum includes 3 credits in English, 2 each in math and social studies, and 1 in lab science. The GED is accepted. AP and CLEP credits are accepted. All students must complete 50 to 53 general education hours, including courses in phys ed, computer literacy, English composition, English literature, and Bible study. A minimum GPA of 2.0 is required for graduation. Students must complete 124 credit hours, 36 of which are upper division level, with approximately 30 credit hours in the major. **Procedure:** Freshmen are admitted to all sessions. Entrance exams should be taken before high school graduation. There is a rolling admissions plan. Application deadlines are open. The fall 2017 application fee was $25. Applications are accepted online. **Transfer Students:** 134 transfer students enrolled in 2016-2017. Transfer applicants must be in good standing with their previous institutions and have a cumulative GPA of 2.0. 30 of 124 credits required for the bachelor's degree must be completed at EU. **International Students:** There are 9 international students enrolled. They must take the TOEFL, and either the SAT or ACT.

ADMISSIONS: 74% of the 2017-2018 applicants were accepted. **Admissions Contact:** Cheir Meyer, Director of Admissions. Email: *admissions@evangel.edu* Web: *www.evangel.edu*

FINANCIAL AID: In 2017-2018, 84% of all full-time freshmen received some form of financial aid. 47% of all full-time freshmen received need-based aid. The average freshman award was $11,729. 21% of undergraduate students work part-time. The average financial indebtedness of the 2017 graduate was $34,434. The FAFSA code is 002463. Check with the school for current application deadlines.

FONTBONNE UNIVERSITY — D-3

www.fontbonne.edu

St. Louis, MO 63105	(314) 889-1413 (800) 205-5862
Fax: (314) 889-1451	**Email:** fbyou@fontbonne.edu
Full-time: 316 men, 449 women	**Faculty:** n/av
Part-time: 27 men, 101 women	**Ph.D.s:** 69%
Graduate: 122 men, 360 women	**Student/Faculty:** n/av
Year: semesters, summer session	**Tuition:** $25,100
Room & Board: $9506	**Freshman Class:** n/av
SAT or ACT: required	**CEEB CODE:** 6216
Application Deadline: n/av	**COMPETITIVE**

Fontbonne University, a Catholic coeducational institution of higher learning sponsored by the Sisters of St. Joseph of Carondelet, is rooted in the Judeo-Christian tradition. The university is dedicated to the discovery, understanding, preservation and dissemination of truth. Undergraduate and graduate programs are offered in an atmosphere characterized by a commitment to open communication, personal concern, and diversity. Fontbonne seeks to educate students to think critically, to act ethically, and to assume responsibility as citizens and leaders. There are 3 undergraduate schools and 19 graduate schools. In addition to regional accreditation, Fontbonne has baccalaureate program accreditation with ACBSP, ADA, CSWE, CAEP, CAA of ASHA, CED, and ACEND. The 16-acre campus is in a suburban area in Clayton, Missouri, 1 mile west of St. Louis city limits. Including any residence halls, there are 10 buildings.

STUDENT LIFE: 83% of undergraduates are from Missouri. Others are from 26 states, and 25 foreign countries. 55% are from public schools. 9% are Foreign; 70% White; 2% Asian American; 2% Hispanic; 2% two or more races; 2% race unknown; 13% African American. 55% are Catholic; 23% Protestant. **Female To Male Ratio:** 2.0:1. 20% do not continue beyond their first year; 50% remain to graduate. **Housing:** 270 students can be accommodated in college housing, which includes dorms, on-campus apartments, and off-campus apartments. On-campus housing is available on a first-come, first-served basis. 80% of students commute. All students may keep cars.

FACULTY/CLASSROOMS: No introductory courses are taught by graduate students. The average class size in an introductory lecture is 12; in a laboratory is 13; and in a regular course is 12.

PROGRAMS OF STUDY: Fontbonne confers B.A., B.S., B.B.A., and B.F.A. degrees. Master's degrees are also awarded. Bachelor's degrees are awarded in BIOLOGICAL SCIENCE (biology/biological science and nutritional sciences), BUSINESS (accounting, apparel and accessories marketing, business administration and management, fashion merchandising, marketing management, marketing/retailing/merchandising, sports management, and supply chain management), COMMUNICATIONS AND THE ARTS (advertising, art, communications, dramatic arts, English, English literature, English Writing, fine arts, performing arts, theatre acting, theatre arts, theatre production, theater management, and writing), COMPUTER AND PHYSICAL SCIENCE (computer science, computer security and information assurance, information sciences and systems, and mathematics), EDUCATION (drama education, early childhood education, education, education of the deaf and hearing impaired, elementary education, English education, general studies, mathematics education, middle school education, secondary education, and special education), HEALTH PROFESSIONS (predentistry, premedicine, prephysical therapy, and speech pathology/audiology), SOCIAL SCIENCE (behavioral science, child care/child and family studies, communication sciences & disorders, dietetics, family/consumer studies, history, human services, liberal arts/general studies, prelaw, psychology, religion, religious studies, social work, and sociology). Education, computer science, and math are the strongest academically. Business administration, organizational studies, and education have the largest enrollments.

ACTIVITIES: There are no fraternities or sororities. There are 32 groups on campus, including althletic support club, choir, computers, dance, drama, environmental, ethnic, Fontbonne Activities Board, honors, international, LGBT, literary magazine, newspaper, photography, political, professional, religious, social, social service, and student government. Popular campus events include Spring Fest, Art Shows, International Bazaar, Lip Sync Contest, Comedy Nights, and Musical Performances. **Sports:** There are 9 intercollegiate sports for men and 9 for women. Facilities include a student activity center that houses a gym, weight room, track, and aerobics room. **Graduates:** From July 1, 2016 to June 30, 2017, 466 bachelor's degrees were awarded. The most popular majors were business administration (37%), special education (10%), and organizational behavior studies (10%). In an average class, 33% graduate in 4 years or less, 51% graduate in 5 years or less, and 54% graduate in 6 years or less.

SERVICES: Counseling and information services are available, as is tutoring in every subject. There is remedial math, reading, and writing. **Library/Resources:** The library contains 69,574 volumes, 3,797 audio/video tapes/CDs/DVDs, and subscribes to 69,234 periodicals, including electronic. Computerized library services include interlibrary loans, database searching, Internet access, and Wi-Fi capability. Special learning facilities include an art gallery, a biological green house, test and demo kitchens for dietetics, and speech-language and audiology clinics. **Physically Challenged Students:** All of the campus is accessible. Facilities include wheelchair ramps, elevators, special parking, specially equipped restrooms, special class scheduling, lowered drinking fountains, and special housing. **Special:** Fontbonne offers cross-registration with several area colleges and a student exchange program with the Sisters of St. Joseph Consortium. There are also cooperative programs in all majors except education, internships with major companies, study abroad in 2 countries, work-study programs, student-designed and dual majors, credit by exam, nondegree study, pass/fail options, and B.A.-B.S. degrees. In addition, an accelerated degree program in business is available, as are 3-2 degrees in engineering and social work with Washington University. There is 1 national honor society and a freshman honors program. **Visiting:** There are regularly scheduled orientations for prospective students, including a campus tour, a financial aid presentation, and visits with faculty and current students. There are guides for informal visits, visitors may sit in on classes, and stay overnight. To schedule a visit, contact the Admissions Office. **Campus Safety and Security:** Measures include 24-hour foot and vehicle patrol, emergency notification system, and security escort services. There are shuttle buses and controlled access to dorms/residences.

REQUIREMENTS: The SAT or ACT is required, with a satisfactory score. Applicants must be graduates of an accredited secondary school or have a GED certificate. They must have completed 16 academic credits, including 4 in English, 3 in math, 2 each in science and social studies, and 1 in history. An audition or portfolio may be required. Fontbonne requires applicants to be in the upper 50% of their class. A GPA of 2.5 is required. AP and CLEP credits are accepted. Important factors in the admissions decision are advanced placement or honors courses, extracurricular activities record, and leadership record. To graduate, students must complete 128 credit hours, including 44 in general education requirements, with a minimum GPA of 2.0. The number of hours required for the major varies. **Procedure:** Freshmen are admitted to all sessions. Entrance exams should be taken prior to registration. There are deferred admissions and rolling admissions plans. Check with the school for current application deadlines. The fall 2017 application fee was $25. Applications are accepted online. **Transfer Students:** 233 transfer students enrolled in 2016-2017. Applicants must have a minimum GPA of 2.0 and either submit ACT or the SAT scores or take a placement test. Students with fewer than 30 credits must submit a high school transcript. An interview is recommended. 32 of 128 credits required for the bachelor's degree must be completed at Fontbonne. **International Students:** There are 26 international students enrolled. They must take the TOEFL.

ADMISSIONS: 1 freshman graduated first in the class. **Admissions Contact:** Keith Quigley, Director of Freshman Recruitment. Email: *fbyou@fontbonne.edu* Web: *www.fontbonne.edu*

FINANCIAL AID: The CSS/Profile, FFS, and the college's own financial statement are required. The FAFSA code is 002464. Check with the school for current application deadlines.

HANNIBAL-LAGRANGE UNIVERSITY — D-2

www.hlg.edu

Hannibal, MO 63401	**(800) HLG-1119**
Fax: (573) 221-6594	**Email: admissions@hlg.edu**
Full-time: 483 men, 808 women	**Faculty:** n/av
Part-time: n/av	**Ph.D.s:** n/av
Graduate: 30 men, 44 women	**Student/Faculty:** n/av
Year: semesters, summer session	**Tuition:** $21,710
Room & Board: $8105	**Freshman Class:** 696 applied, 448 accepted, 184 enrolled
ACT: required	**CEEB CODE: 6266**
Application Deadline: August	**COMPETITIVE**

Hannibal-LaGrange University, founded in 1858, is a private institution affiliated with the Southern Baptist Church. There are 4 undergraduate schools and 1 graduate school. In addition to regional accreditation, Hannibal-LaGrange has baccalaureate program accreditation with NLN. The 165-acre campus is in a small town 100 miles north of St. Louis. Including any residence halls, there are 22 buildings.

STUDENT LIFE: 80% of undergraduates are from Missouri. Others are from 29 states, and 27 foreign countries. 83% are White; 5% African American; 5% Hispanic; 5% Foreign; 1% Asian American; 1% American Indian/Alaska Native. 80% are Protestant. **Female To Male Ratio:** 1.7:1. 37% do not continue beyond their first year; 54% remain to graduate. **Housing:** 550 students can be accommodated in college housing, which includes dorms and on-campus apartments. On-campus housing is available on a first-come, first-served basis. 53% of students commute. All students may keep cars. Alcohol is not permitted.

FACULTY/CLASSROOMS: 45% of faculty are male; 55% are female. All teach undergraduates. No introductory courses are taught by graduate students. The average class size in an introductory lecture is 25 and in a laboratory is 15.

PROGRAMS OF STUDY: Hannibal-LaGrange confers B.A., B.S., B.A.S., B.S.E., and B.S.N. degrees. Associate and master's degrees are also awarded. Bachelor's degrees are awarded in BIOLOGICAL SCIENCE (biology/biological science), BUSINESS (accounting, business administration and management, organizational behavior, and recreation and leisure services), COMMUNICATIONS AND THE ARTS (art, communications, dramatic arts, English, music, music performance, and speech/debate/rhetoric), COMPUTER AND PHYSICAL SCIENCE (computer programming, information sciences and systems, and mathematics), EDUCATION (Christian education, early childhood education, elementary education, and secondary education), HEALTH PROFESSIONS (exercise science and nursing), SOCIAL SCIENCE (biblical studies, criminal justice, history, liberal arts/general studies, missions, psychology, religious music, social work, and sociology). Nursing, and education are the strongest academically. Education, criminal justice, and nusing have the largest enrollments.

ACTIVITIES: There are no fraternities or sororities. There are 24 groups on campus, including Alpha Tau Beta, and Lambda Alpha Epsilon, Fellowship of Christian Athletes, Gatekeepers, Naturea Investigato Circulus, Phi Beta Lambda (Future Business Leaders), Pi Gamam Mu, Alpha Chi, art, cheerleading, choir, chorus, drama, ethnic, honors, international, musical theater, newspaper, professional, radio and TV, religious, social, social service, student government, and yearbook. Popular campus events include Campus Visitation Days, Experience HLGU Day, Trojan Turkey Trek, Homecoming, and Booster Banquet. **Sports:** There are 8 intercollegiate sports for men and 9 for women, and 7 intramural sports for men and 7 for women. Facilities include baseball, softball, and soccer fields and a sports complex that contains a gym, weight and aerobics rooms, and volleyball, tennis, and racquetball courts. **Graduates:** From July 1, 2016 to June 30, 2017, 167 bachelor's degrees were awarded. The most popular majors were education (50%), nursing (25%), and criminal justice (25%).

SERVICES: Counseling and information services are available, as is

tutoring in some subjects, such as math, English, writing, literature, science, behavioral science, accounting and business, history, and Bible studies. There is also remedial math and writing. **Library/Resources:** The library contains 121,840 volumes, 22,152 microform items, 6,702 audio/video tapes/CDs/DVDs, and subscribes to 266 periodicals, including electronic. Computerized library services include interlibrary loans, database searching, and Internet access. Special learning facilities include an art gallery, radio station, a theatre, mission center, nature trail, and testing lab. **Physically Challenged Students:** 70% of the campus is accessible. Facilities include wheelchair ramps, elevators, special parking, specially equipped restrooms, special class scheduling, and special housing. **Special:** Credit by examination, prior learning assessment, online courses, adult programs, and self-designed liberal arts degree There are 2 national honor societies, a freshman honors program, and 2 departmental honors programs. **Visiting:** There are regularly scheduled orientations for prospective students, consisting of Encounter Days, which are organized tours of the campus covering financial aid, student affairs, and academic areas. There are guides for informal visits, visitors may sit in on classes, and stay overnight. To schedule a visit, contact Ray Carty at rcarty@hlg.edu. **Campus Safety and Security:** Measures include 24-hour foot and vehicle patrol, an emergency notification system, self-defense education, and security escort services. There are emergency telephones, lighted pathways/sidewalks, and controlled access to dorms/residences.

REQUIREMENTS: The ACT is required. Applicants must be graduates of an accredited secondary school or have the GED. AP and CLEP credits are accepted. All students must complete a minimum of 124 credit hours with a 2.0 GPA to graduate. The major usually requires 36 or more credit hours of study. General education requirements include 8 hours in natural science; 6 hours each in Bible, composition, literature, foreign language, history, fine arts, and social science; 3 hours each in speech and algebra; 2 hours in phys ed; and 1 hour in success in education. Different core requirements pertain to education and nursing students. **Procedure:** Freshmen are admitted to all sessions. Entrance exams should be taken before registration. There is a rolling admissions plan. Check with the school for current application deadlines. The fall 2017 application fee was $25. Applications are accepted on-line. **Transfer Students:** 187 transfer students enrolled in 2016-2017. Applicants must submit transcripts from all colleges attended. Students applying with fewer than 30 credit hours must also submit a high school transcript along with ACT or SAT scores. 32 of 124 credits required for the bachelor's degree must be completed at Hannibal-LaGrange. **International Students:** There are 74 international students enrolled. They must take the TOEFL with a minimum score of 520 on the paper-based TOEFL (PBT) or 68 on the Internet-based version (iBT). They must also take the SAT or ACT, scoring 20.

ADMISSIONS: 64% of the 2017-2018 applicants were accepted. 21% of the current freshmen were in the top fifth of their class; 52% were in the top two fifths. **Admissions Contact:** Dr. Ray Carty, Vice President of Enrollment Management. Email: *admissions@hlg.edu* Web: *www.hlg.edu*

FINANCIAL AID: The FAFSA code is 009089. Check with the school for current application deadlines.

HARRIS-STOWE STATE UNIVERSITY *(The complete profile is made available exclusively on our website, www.barronspac.com)*

KANSAS CITY ART INSTITUTE *(The complete profile is made available exclusively on our website, www.barronspac.com)*

LINCOLN UNIVERSITY *(The complete profile is made available exclusively on our website, www.barronspac.com)*

LINDENWOOD UNIVERSITY D-2

www.lindenwood.edu

St. Charles, MO 63301 **(636) 949-4949**

Fax: (636) 949-4989 **Email:** admissions@lindenwood.edu

Full-time: 2460 men, 3185 women	**Faculty:** IIA, -$
Part-time: 100 men, 160 women	**Ph.D.s:** 87%
Graduate: 1065 men, 2680 women	**Student/Faculty:** 29 to 1
Year: 4-1-4, summer session	**Tuition:** $17,260
Room & Board: $8500	**Freshman Class:** n/av
SAT or ACT: required	**CEEB CODE:** 6367
Application Deadline: December 8	**COMPETITIVE**

Lindenwood University, founded in 1827, is a private institution offering undergraduate and graduate degree programs in the arts and sciences, business, education, and preprofessional fields. The figures given in the above capsule and in this profile are approximate. There are 8 undergraduate schools and 5 graduate schools. In addition to regional accreditation, LU has baccalaureate program accreditation with CAEP and CAAHEP. The 500-acre campus is in a suburban area in St. Charles, just 25 miles west of St. Louis. Including any residence halls, there are 37 buildings.

STUDENT LIFE: 73% of undergraduates are from Missouri. Others are from 43 states, 63 foreign countries, and Canada. 9% are Foreign; 76% White; 12% African American; 1% Hispanic. **Female To Male Ratio:** 1.7:1. The average age of freshmen is 19; all undergraduates, 25. 38% do not continue beyond their first year; 40% remain to graduate. **Housing:** 3500 students can be accommodated in college housing, which includes married student dorms and on-campus apartments. In addition, there are sorority houses. On-campus housing is guaranteed for all 4 years. 68% of students live on campus. All students may keep cars. Alcohol is not permitted.

FACULTY/CLASSROOMS: 49% of faculty are male; 51% are female. 99% teach undergraduates. No introductory courses are taught by graduate students. The average class size in an introductory lecture is 30; in a laboratory is 25; and in a regular course is 25.

PROGRAMS OF STUDY: LU confers B.A., B.S., and B.F.A. degrees. Master's and doctoral degrees are also awarded. Bachelor's degrees are awarded in BIOLOGICAL SCIENCE (biology/biological science), BUSINESS (accounting, banking and finance, business administration and management, human resources, management information systems, marketing/retailing/merchandising, and sports management), COMMUNICATIONS AND THE ARTS (art history and appreciation, communications, creative writing, dance, dramatic arts, English, French, music, performing arts, Spanish, and studio art), COMPUTER AND PHYSICAL SCIENCE (chemistry, computer science, and mathematics), EDUCATION (athletic training, business education, early childhood education, elementary education, music education, physical education, science education, and secondary education), ENGINEERING AND ENVIRONMENTAL DESIGN (engineering), HEALTH PROFESSIONS (medical technology), SOCIAL SCIENCE (criminal justice, fashion design and technology, history, human services, international studies, liberal arts/general studies, ministries, political science/government, prelaw, psychology, public administration, religion, social work, and sociology). Biology, education, and mass communications, are the strongest academically and have the largest enrollments.

ACTIVITIES: 1% of men belong to 1 local and 2 national fraternities; 1% of women belong to 1 national sorority. There are 75 groups on campus, including art, band, cheerleading, chess, choir, chorale, chorus, computers, dance, debate, drama, drill team, ethnic, film, forensics, honors, international, jazz band, literary magazine, marching band, musical theater, newspaper, pep band, photography, political, professional, radio and TV, religious, social, social service, and student government. Popular campus events include Spring Fling, Alumni Weekend, and Christmas Walk. **Sports:** There are 20 intercollegiate sports for men and 19 for women, and 9 intramural sports for men and 9 for women. Facilities include an indoor pool, a gym, weight rooms, a stadium, a performance arena, sand volleyball court, tennis courts, softball, baseball, and soccer fields, an all-weather track, and ice rink. Students may use the local golf course and bowling alley for a discounted fee. **Graduates:** From July 1, 2016 to June 30, 2017, 1010 bachelor's degrees were awarded. The most popular majors were business administration (24%), elementary education (7%), and criminology (6%). In an average class,

26% graduate in 4 years or less, 38% graduate in 5 years or less, and 40% graduate in 6 years or less. Of the 2016 graduating class, 14% were enrolled in graduate school within 6 months of graduation, and 94% were employed.

SERVICES: Counseling and information services are available, as is tutoring in every subject. There is a reader service for the blind, and remedial math, reading, and writing. **Library/Resources:** The library contains 171,562 volumes, 26,128 microform items, 2,138 audio/video tapes/CDs/DVDs, and subscribes to 115,000 periodicals including electronic. Computerized library services include interlibrary loans, database searching, Internet access, and Wi-Fi capability. Special learning facilities include an art gallery, radio station, TV station, a greenhouse, wetlands program facility, a success center, and the Boone Home historic site. **Physically Challenged Students:** 50% of the campus is accessible. Facilities include wheelchair ramps, elevators, special parking, specially equipped restrooms, special class scheduling, lowered drinking fountains, and lowered telephones. **Special:** The university offers internships in most majors, a co-op program in computer science, study abroad and a Washington semester for juniors, and cross-registration through a consortium of Greater St. Louis College and Universities. Dual and student-designed majors, accelerated degree programs, 3-2 degrees in engineering with Washington University in St. Louis and the University of Missouri-Columbia, work-study programs, and nondegree study are also available. There are evening and weekend classes for working adults and 5-year bachelor's programs. There are 9 national honor societies, a freshman honors program, and 6 departmental honors programs. **Visiting:** There are regularly scheduled orientations for prospective students, including an admissions interview, a campus tour and advising. There are guides for informal visits; visitors may sit in on classes and stay overnight. To schedule a visit, contact the Office of Undergraduate Admissions. **Campus Safety and Security:** Measures include 24-hour foot and vehicle patrol, an emergency notification system, self-defense education, and security escort services. There are emergency telephones and lighted pathways/sidewalks.

REQUIREMENTS: The SAT or ACT is required. Applicants must be graduates of an accredited secondary school or have a GED. High school preparation should include at least 16 academic units, including 4 years of English, 2 to 3 each of math, science, and social studies, 2 of a foreign language, and some study of fine or performing arts. An essay and an interview are recommended. Lindenwood requires applicants to be in the upper 50% of their class. A GPA of 2.5 is required. AP and CLEP credits are accepted. Important factors in the admissions decision are leadership record, evidence of special talent, and advanced placement or honors courses. In order to graduate, students must complete a minimum of 128 credit hours, including at least 36 in the major and 42 in upper-division courses, with a minimum GPA of 2.0. Core curriculum courses include 10 hours of math and science, 9 each of social sciences, humanities, and civilization, 6 of English, and 3 each of fine arts and communications. They must score at proficiency level on a writing assessment. **Procedure:** Freshmen are admitted to all sessions. There are deferred admissions and rolling admissions plans. Application deadlines are open. The fall 2017 application fee was $30. **Transfer Students:** 803 transfer students enrolled in 2016-2017. Applicants must have a minimum GPA of 2.0 and should submit official college transcripts in order to transfer credits. 38 of 128 credits required for the bachelor's degree must be completed at LU. **International Students:** There are 557 international students enrolled. They must take the TOEFL with a minimum score of 500 on the paper-based TOEFL (PBT) or 61 on the Internet-based version (iBT). They must also take the SAT or ACT.

ADMISSIONS: 3 freshmen graduated first in their class. **Admissions Contact:** Joe Parisi, Associate Dean of Admissions. Email: *admissions@lindenwood.edu* Web: *www.lindenwood.edu*

FINANCIAL AID: In 2017-2018, 98% of all full-time freshmen received some form of financial aid. 66% of all full-time freshmen received need-based aid. 72% of undergraduate students work part-time. The average financial indebtedness of the 2017 graduate was $15,500. The FAFSA code is 002480. Check with the school for current application deadlines.

MARYVILLE UNIVERSITY OF SAINT LOUIS D-3

www.maryville.edu

St. Louis, MO 63141	**(314) 529-9350** **(800) 627-9855**
Fax: (314) 529-9927	**Email: admissions@maryville.edu**
Full-time: 914 men, 1461 women	**Faculty:** I, --$
Part-time: 177 men, 631 women	**Ph.D.s:** 71%
Graduate: 937 men, 3569 women	**Student/Faculty:** 14 to 1
Year: semesters, summer session	**Tuition:** $28,470
Room & Board: $10,088	**Freshman Class:** 2241 applied, 2059 accepted, 604 enrolled
ACT: 24	**CEEB CODE:** 6399
Application Deadline: August 19	**VERY COMPETITIVE**

Maryville University of Saint Louis, founded in 1872, is a selective, comprehensive and nationally ranked private institution, offering more than 90 degrees at the undergraduate, masters and doctoral levels. Maryville's athletics teams compete at the NCAA Division II level in the Great Lakes Valley Conference. There are 5 undergraduate schools and 5 graduate schools. In addition to regional accreditation, MUSL has baccalaureate program accreditation with ACBSP, FIDER, NASAD, NASM, NCATE, AOTA, CAPTE, and CCNE. The 130-acre campus is in a suburban area 20 miles west of downtown St. Louis. Including any residence halls, there are 31 buildings.

STUDENT LIFE: 51% of undergraduates are from Missouri. Others are from 50 states, 60 foreign countries, and Canada. 91% are from public schools. 8% are African American; 73% White; 5% Foreign; 5% race unknown; 4% Hispanic; 3% Asian American; 3% two or more races. 79% claim no religious affiliation. **Female To Male Ratio:** 2.8:1. The average age of freshmen is 18; all undergraduates, 24. 17% do not continue beyond their first year; 72% remain to graduate. **Housing:** 866 students can be accommodated in college housing, which includes dorms and on-campus apartments. On-campus housing is available on a first-come, first-served basis, and is available on a lottery system for upperclassmen. 89% of students commute. All students may keep cars.

FACULTY/CLASSROOMS: 33% of faculty are male; 67% are female. No introductory courses are taught by graduate students. The average class size in an introductory lecture is 16 and in a laboratory is 14.

PROGRAMS OF STUDY: MUSL confers B.A., B.S., B.F.A., B.S.M.T., and B.S.N. degrees. Master's and doctoral degrees are also awarded. Bachelor's degrees are awarded in BIOLOGICAL SCIENCE (biochemistry and biology/biological science), BUSINESS (accounting, business administration and management, international business management, marketing management, organizational leadership and management, and sports management), COMMUNICATIONS AND THE ARTS (communications, English, game design and development, graphic design, and studio art), COMPUTER AND PHYSICAL SCIENCE (actuarial science, chemistry, cyber intelligence/security studies, information sciences and systems, mathematics, and science), EDUCATION (art education, early childhood education, elementary education, middle school education, and secondary education), ENGINEERING AND ENVIRONMENTAL DESIGN (engineering, environmental science, and interior design), HEALTH PROFESSIONS (clinical science, health science, music therapy, nursing, occupational therapy, physical therapy, rehabilitation therapy, and speech pathology/audiology), SOCIAL SCIENCE (criminology, forensic studies, history, international studies, liberal arts/general studies, paralegal studies, psychology, and sociology). Actuarial science, nursing, and physical therapy are the strongest academically. Nursing, business administration, and psychology have the largest enrollments.

ACTIVITIES: There are no fraternities or sororities. There are 100 groups on campus, including art, cheerleading, chorale, dance, environmental, ethnic, forensics, honors, international, LGBT, literary magazine, marching band, newspaper, orchestra, pep band, political, professional, religious, social, social service, and student government. Popular campus events include Saturday Night Live Comedy Series, Fall Festival, and Bingo and Brew. **Sports:** There are 10 intercollegiate sports for men and 11 for women, and 10 intramural sports for men and 10 for women. Facilities include lacrosse and soccer fields, a sport turf field, baseball fields, softball, wrestling facility, a gym, outdoor and indoor basketball arena, an expanded fitness center, table tennis and billiards, and outdoor walking and hiking trails. **Graduates:** From July 1, 2016 to June

30, 2017, 587 bachelor's degrees were awarded. The most popular majors were nursing/health professions (36%), business administration (24%), and psychology (9%). In an average class, 75% graduate in 6 years or less. Of the 2016 graduating class, 15% were enrolled in graduate school within 6 months of graduation, and 76% were employed.

SERVICES: Counseling and information services are available, as is tutoring in every subject. There is a reader service for the blind. There also is a writing center, learning styles inventory, and time management and test-taking skills, study skills materials, workshops, and individual consultations. **Library/Resources:** The library contains 59,580 volumes, 29,773 microform items, 169,059 audio/video tapes/CDs/DVDs, and subscribes to 60,067 periodicals, including electronic. Computerized library services include interlibrary loans, database searching, Internet access, and Wi-Fi capability. Special learning facilities include an art gallery, an observatory, a teaching lab, art and design labs, clinical labs for nursing, occupational therapy, and physical therapy, communications lab, cyber security virtual lab, and multimedia classrooms. **Physically Challenged Students:** All of the campus is accessible. Facilities include wheelchair ramps, elevators, special parking, specially equipped restrooms, special class scheduling, lowered drinking fountains, and lowered telephones. **Special:** There is cross-registration with Missouri Baptist College and Fontbonne, Webster, and Lindenwood Universities. Students may choose internships in various fields, and cooperative programs are available with various employers Other options include dual and student-designed majors,study abroad in England, Italy, Switzerland, a 3-2 engineering degree with Washington University, and a Washington semester. Accelerated degree programs are offered in actuarial science and nursing. A 3+4 B.S/O.D. optometry degree with the University of Missouri-St. Louis and a B.A. criminal justice/criminology degree in association with St. Louis County and Municipal Police Academy are possible. There are 12 national honor societies, a freshman honors program, and 8 departmental honors programs. **Visiting:** There are regularly scheduled orientations for prospective students, including visiting the campus and arranging a personal interview with an admissions counselor. There are guides for informal visits, visitors may sit in on classes, and stay overnight. To schedule a visit, contact the Admissions Office. **Campus Safety and Security:** Measures include 24-hour foot and vehicle patrol, an emergency notification system, self-defense education, and security escort services. There are emergency telephones, lighted pathways/sidewalks, video security systems in residence halls, and security key operated dorm entrances.

REQUIREMENTS: Students must have graduated from an accredited secondary school with 22 academic credits or have the GED. Expected preparatory courses include 4 units of English, 3 of math, and 2 each of science and social studies, plus 3 additional units in any of the preceding areas or in a foreign language. Some majors have additional admission requirements. AP and CLEP credits are accepted. Important factors in the admissions decision are recommendations by school officials, advanced placement or honors courses, and leadership record. To graduate, all students must complete a minimum of 128 credit hours, with a minimum GPA of 2.0. The core curriculum consists of 12 credit hours each of humanities, math and science, and social and behavioral science, and 8 credit hours each of communication skills and fine arts. 48 upper-division credits must be completed. **Procedure:** Freshmen are admitted to all sessions. Entrance exams should be taken during the junior year. There are deferred admissions and rolling admissions plans. Applications should be filed by August 19 for fall entry. Notification is sent on a rolling basis. Applications are accepted on-line. **Transfer Students:** 252 transfer students enrolled in 2016-2017. A minimum GPA of 2.0, or higher for some majors, is required. Some majors may require ACT or SAT. 30 of 128 credits required for the bachelor's degree must be completed at MUSL. **International Students:** There are 136 international students enrolled. They must take the TOEFL with a minimum score of 500 on the paper-based TOEFL (PBT) or 61 on the Internet-based version (iBT).

ADMISSIONS: 92% of the 2017-2018 applicants were accepted. The ACT scores were 6% between 12 and 17, 41% between 18 and 23, 45% between 24 and 29, and 8% above 30. 44% of the current freshmen were in the top fifth of their class; 78% were in the top two fifths. 7 freshmen graduated first in their class. **Admissions Contact:** Shani Lenore-Jenkins, Associate Vice President of Enrollment. Email: *admissions@maryville.edu* Web: *www.maryville.edu*

FINANCIAL AID: In 2017-2018, 79% of all full-time freshmen received some form of financial aid and need-based aid. The average freshman award was $20,091. Need-based scholarships or need-based grants averaged $18,186; need-based self-help aid (loans and jobs) averaged $3,358; non-need-based athletic scholarships averaged $12,608; and other non-need-based awards and non-need-based scholarships averaged $17,829. 11% of undergraduate students work part-time. The FAFSA code is 002482. The priority date for freshman financial aid applications for fall entry is March 1. The deadline for filing freshman financial aid applications for fall entry is April 1.

MISSOURI BAPTIST UNIVERSITY D-3

www.mobap.edu

St. Louis, MO 63141 — **(314) 392-2296**, **(877) 434-1115**

Fax: (314) 434-7596 — **Email: admissions@mobap.edu**

Full-time: 682 men, 837 women	**Faculty:** IIB, --$
Part-time: 1064 men, 1925 women	**Ph.D.s:** 68%
Graduate: 256 men, 724 women	**Student/Faculty:** 20 to 1
Year: semesters, summer session	**Tuition:** $26,020
Room & Board: $10,380	**Freshman Class:** 994 applied, 542 accepted, 279 enrolled
ACT: 22	**CEEB CODE:** 2258
Application Deadline: open	**COMPETITIVE**

Missouri Baptist University, established in 1964, is a private liberal arts institution. There is 1 undergraduate school and 1 graduate school. In addition to regional accreditation, MBU has baccalaureate program accreditation with NASM, CAEP, NACEP, CAAHEP, and CoAES. The 65-acre campus is in a suburban area 15 miles west of St. Louis. Including any residence halls, there are 16 buildings.

STUDENT LIFE: 88% of undergraduates are from Missouri. Others are from 37 states, 16 foreign countries, and Canada. 58% are White; 29% race unknown; 6% African American; 1% Asian American; 1% American Indian/Alaska Native; 1% Hispanic; 1% Foreign; 1% two or more races. 33% are Protestant; 12% Catholic. **Female To Male Ratio:** 1.7:1. The average age of freshmen is 18; all undergraduates, 20. **Housing:** 420 students can be accommodated in college housing, which includes single-sex dorms, on-campus apartments, and off-campus apartments. On-campus housing is available on a first-come and first-served basis. 79% of students commute. All students may keep cars. Alcohol is not permitted.

FACULTY/CLASSROOMS: 49% of faculty are male; 51% are female. No introductory courses are taught by graduate students. The average class size in an introductory lecture is 30; in a laboratory is 20; and in a regular course is 25.

PROGRAMS OF STUDY: MBU confers B.A., B.S., B.M., B.M.E., B.P.S., B.S.E., and B.S.N. degrees. Associate, master's, and doctoral degrees are also awarded. Bachelor's degrees are awarded in BIOLOGICAL SCIENCE (biochemistry, biology/biological science, and biotechnology), BUSINESS (accounting, business administration and management, management, marketing, organizational leadership and management, and sports management), COMMUNICATIONS AND THE ARTS (broadcasting, communications, English, journalism, music, music performance, music technology, musical theater, public relations, speech and theatre education, theatre acting, and theatre arts), COMPUTER AND PHYSICAL SCIENCE (chemistry, chemistry/forensic chemistry, information sciences and systems, mathematics, and radiological technology), EDUCATION (business education, early childhood education, elementary education, health education, middle school education, music education, physical education, secondary education, special education, and special education/early child dual program), HEALTH PROFESSIONS (exercise science, fitness management, health care administration, health science, and nursing), SOCIAL SCIENCE (behavioral science, child psychology/development, Christian studies, criminal justice, gender studies, history, human services, liberal arts/general studies, ministries, psychology, religious music, and social science). Healthcare management, business administration, and elementary education have the largest enrollments.

ACTIVITIES: There are no fraternities or sororities. There are 25 groups on campus, including a business club, band, cheerleading, choir, chorale, chorus, communications, computers, dance, drama, ethnic, film, honors, international, jazz band, literary magazine, musical theater, opera, orchestra, photography, political, professional, radio and TV, religious, social, social service, and student government. Popular campus events include Spring Musical, Christmas Concert, and Hanging of the Green. **Sports:** There are 13 intercollegiate sports for men and 14 for women, and 4 intramural sports for men and 4 for women. Facilities include a sports and recreation complex that consists of a gymnasium, a suspended indoor track, training and fitness centers. The campus also has baseball, softball, and soccer fields. **Graduates:** From July 1, 2016 to June 30, 2017, 422 bachelor's degrees were awarded. The most popular majors were business administration (9%), elementary education (7%), and criminal Justice (6%).

SERVICES: Counseling and information services are available, as is tutoring in some subjects, such as accounting, economics, grammar, Greek, Music Appreciation, Old and New Testament History, Psychology, and Spanish. There is a reader service for the blind, and remedial math and writing, as well as walk-in tutoring in math, biology and chemistry. **Library/Resources:** The library contains 82,337 volumes, 3,708 microform items, 4,615 audio/video tapes/CDs/DVDs, and subscribes to 25,459 periodicals, including electronic. Computerized library services include interlibrary loans, database searching, Internet access, and Wi-Fi capability. Special learning facilities include a radio station, an audiovisual production lab. **Physically Challenged Students:** 80% of the campus is accessible. Facilities include wheelchair ramps, elevators, special parking, specially equipped restrooms, special class scheduling, lowered drinking fountains, and special housing. **Special:** There is cross-registration with Fontbonne, and Maryville, Lindenwood, and Webster Universities. Students may opt for credit by examination, non-degree study, and student-designed majors. A 2-2 engineering degree with the Missouri University of Science and Technology is available. Study abroad is possible at Harlaxton College in England, Hong Kong Baptist University, or through Webster University, Best Semester, Consortium for Global Education, or the Center for Cross Cultural Study. MBU also offers internships in various disciplines and dual majors in some fields. There are 5 national honor societies and a freshman honors program. **Visiting:** There are regularly scheduled orientations for prospective students, including a welcome weekend, open houses, and campus tours. There are guides for informal visits; visitors may sit in on classes and stay overnight. To schedule a visit, contact the Admissions Office. **Campus Safety and Security:** Measures include 24-hour foot and vehicle patrol, an emergency notification system, self-defense education, and security escort services. There are shuttle buses, emergency telephones, lighted pathways/sidewalks, and controlled access to dorms/residences.

REQUIREMENTS: Applicants must have a minimum score of 20 on the ACT or a satisfactory score on the SAT. Applicants must be graduates of an accredited secondary school. GED or HiSET and home-schooled students are accepted. MBU requires applicants to be in the upper 50% of their class. AP and CLEP credits are accepted. Important factors in the admissions decision are advanced placement or honors courses, leadership record, and evidence of special talent. All students must take courses in the humanities/fine arts, social and behavioral sciences, natural sciences, phys ed, computer literacy, and Old and New Testament History. A minimum GPA of 2.0 is required (some majors require a GPA of 2.5 or better). To graduate, students must complete at least 128 credit hours, with a minimum of 30 hours in the major and 45 hours of upper-division courses; pass a general education exam and an exit exam or other assessment in the major; and complete a capstone project. **Procedure:** Freshmen are admitted to all sessions. Entrance exams should be taken during the junior year. There is a rolling admissions plan. Application deadlines are open. The fall 2017 application fee was $35. Applications are accepted on-line. **Transfer Students:** 366 transfer students enrolled in 2016-2017. Applicants must have a 2.0 GPA, with some programs requiring 2.5 or better. Students must submit official transcripts from all previous colleges attended, along with a character reference. 24 of 128 credits required for the bachelor's degree must be completed at MBU. **International Students:** There are 40 international students enrolled. They must take the TOEFL with a minimum score of 550 on the paper-based TOEFL (PBT) or 80 on the Internet-based version (iBT).

ADMISSIONS: 55% of the 2017-2018 applicants were accepted. 19% of the current freshmen were in the top fifth of their class; 49% were in the top two fifths. 2 freshmen graduated first in their class. **Admissions Contact:** Cynthia Sutton, Director of Admissions. Email: *admissions@mobap.edu* Web: *www.mobap.edu*

FINANCIAL AID: In 2017-2018, 99% of all full-time freshmen received some form of financial aid. The college's own financial statement is required. The FAFSA code is 007540. The priority date for freshman financial aid applications for fall entry is February 1.

MISSOURI SOUTHERN STATE UNIVERSITY — A-4

www.mssu.edu

Joplin, MO 64801 — **(417) 625-9379** **(866) 818-6778**

Fax: (417) 659-4429 — **Email: admissions@mssu.edu**

Full-time: 1725 men, 2632 women
Part-time: 656 men, 1008 women
Graduate: 50 men, 103 women
Year: semesters, summer session
Room & Board: $7004
ACT: 22
Application Deadline: September 1

Faculty: 202
Ph.D.s: 66%
Student/Faculty: 20 to 1
Tuition: $6067 ($11,568)
Freshman Class: 2682 applied, 2550 accepted, 1012 enrolled
CEEB CODE: 6322
COMPETITIVE

Missouri Southern State University, founded in 1937, is a public, primarily commuter institution offering undergraduate degree programs in the arts and sciences, health professions, business, education, psychology, and technology. There are 4 undergraduate schools and 3 graduate schools. In addition to regional accreditation, MSSU has baccalaureate program accreditation with ABET, ACBSP, ADA, CAEP, ACEN, CODA, and CoAEMSP. The 365-acre campus is in a small town in the southwest corner of the state, 138 miles south of Kansas City. Including any residence halls, there are 51 buildings.

STUDENT LIFE: 77% of undergraduates are from Missouri. Others are from 40 states, 31 foreign countries, and Canada. 74% are White; 7% Hispanic; 6% African American; 3% American Indian/Alaska Native; 3% Foreign; 3% race unknown; 2% Asian American; 2% two or more races. **Female To Male Ratio:** 1.5:1. The average age of freshmen is 19; all undergraduates, 24. 35% do not continue beyond their first year; 33% remain to graduate. **Housing:** 950 students can be accommodated in college housing, which includes dorms and on-campus apartments, and honors houses. On-campus housing is available on a first-come and first-served basis. 83% of students commute. All students may keep cars. Alcohol is not permitted.

FACULTY/CLASSROOMS: 52% of faculty are male; 48% are female. 99% teach undergraduates. No introductory courses are taught by graduate students.

PROGRAMS OF STUDY: MSSU confers B.A., B.S., B.G.S., B.S.B.A. and B.S.E. degrees. Associate and master's degrees are also awarded. Bachelor's degrees are awarded in AGRICULTURE (conservation and regulation), BIOLOGICAL SCIENCE (biochemistry, bioinformatics, biology/adolescence education, biology/biological science, ecology, forensic science, life science, marine biology, microbiology, and physiology), BUSINESS (accounting, business administration and management, finance, financial services, human resources/organizational management, international business, international business information systems, logistics, management information systems, marketing, and marketing management), COMMUNICATIONS AND THE ARTS (art, art and design, choral music, communications, English, English literature, English writing, fine arts, fine/studio arts, general, French, graphic design, instrumental music education, language arts, literature, music, music industry, piano performance, public relations, speech and theatre education, studio art, studio art painting, theatre arts, theatre studies, and vocal performance), COMPUTER AND PHYSICAL SCIENCE (applied science, chemistry, computer engineering technology, computer information systems, computer science, industrial technology, mathematics, mathematics/computational, physics and mathematics, physics, radiological technology, science, and science technology), EDUCATION (business education, childhood education, computer education, early childhood education, elementary education, English education, general studies, mathematics education, middle school education, physical education, reading education, science education, social science education, social studies education, social studies secondary school education, Spanish education K-12, special education, and teaching English as a second/foreign language (TESOL/TEFOL), ENGINEERING AND ENVIRONMENTAL DESIGN (manufacturing technology and transportation technology), HEALTH PROFESSIONS (biology, dental hygiene, environmental health science, health, health promotion, health science, medical technology, nursing, predentistry, premedicine, preoptometry, pre-occupational therapy, prepharmacy, pre-physician assistant, prephysical therapy, preveterinary science, and respiratory therapy), SOCIAL

SCIENCE (criminal justice, early childhood studies, economics, forensic studies, history, justice and society, law enforcement and corrections, political science/government, psychology, social studies, and sociology). Criminal justice, biology, health professions & related programs, teacher education, and business/marketing are the strongest academically. Teacher education, criminal justice, and biology-environmental health have the largest enrollments.

ACTIVITIES: 3% of men belong to 3 national fraternities; 2% of women belong to 2 national sororities. There are 84 groups on campus, including art, band, cheerleading, chess, choir, chorale, chorus, communications, computers, dance, debate, drama, ethnic, film, forensics, honors, international, jazz band, LGBT, literary magazine, marching band, musical theater, newspaper, orchestra, pep band, photography, political, professional, radio and TV, religious, social, social service, student government, and symphony. Popular campus events include International Themed Semesters. **Sports:** There are 6 intercollegiate sports for men and 6 for women, and 10 intramural sports for men and 10 for women. Facilities include an astroturf football stadium, a natatorium, student life center, a gym with basketball court, a 6-lane 200-meter indoor track, training and weight room, cross-country course, and fields for soccer, softball, and baseball. **Graduates:** From July 1, 2016 to June 30, 2017, 884 bachelor's degrees were awarded. The most popular majors were business/marketing (23%), health professions and related programs (15%), and education (12%). In an average class, 13% graduate in 4 years or less, 28% graduate in 5 years or less, and 33% graduate in 6 years or less. Of the 2016 graduating class, 7% were enrolled in graduate school within 6 months of graduation, and 72% were employed.

SERVICES: Counseling and information services are available, as is tutoring in most subjects. There is a reader service for the blind, and remedial math, reading, and writing. Assistance is also provided for improving time management and test-taking skills. **Library/Resources:** The library contains 1.4 million volumes, 784,368 microform items, and 5,031 audio/video tapes/CDs/DVDs, and subscribes to 236 periodicals including electronic. Computerized library services include interlibrary loans, database searching, Internet access, and Wi-Fi capability. Special learning facilities include an art gallery, radio station, TV station, child development center, a crime lab, small business development center, performing arts center, a greenhouse, an international trade and quality center, and a small business technology and development center. **Physically Challenged Students:** 99% of the campus is accessible. Facilities include wheelchair ramps, elevators, special parking, specially equipped restrooms, special class scheduling, lowered drinking fountains, lowered telephones, and special housing. **Special:** MSSU offers Yours to Lose Advanced Medical School Acceptance Program with Kansas City University's Joplin medical school. In additional, there is a Show me Gold Army National Guard Officer Leadership Program, and Pre-engineering program with Missouri University of Science and Technology and the University of Missouri-Columbia. There are 12 national honor societies, a freshman honors program, and 1 departmental honors program. **Visiting:** There are regularly scheduled orientations for prospective students, tour of campus, and advising with a faculty member in the student's chosen field of study. There are guides for informal visits, visitors may sit in on classes, and stay overnight. To schedule a visit, contact Derek Skaggs at skaggs-d@mssu.edu. **Campus Safety and Security:** Measures include 24-hour foot and vehicle patrol, emergency notification system, self-defense education, and security escort services. There are shuttle buses, emergency telephones, lighted pathways/sidewalks, controlled access to dorms/residences, officers on duty 24/7, and text messages for campus alerts. The RAD self-defense for girls is taught as a regular class in fall/spring. We also teach the ALICE concepts (active shooter response) to students in the University Experience classes.

REQUIREMENTS: The ACT is required. Applicants must be graduates of accredited secondary schools or have earned a GED. The college requires completion of 16 Carnegie units in core courses for high school graduates. AP and CLEP credits are accepted. General education requirements include a total of 42 credit hours. At least 124 semester hours of college credit applicable to a baccalaureate degree are required for graduation. All majors require at least a 2.0 grade point average for graduation (2.75 teacher education). **Procedure:** Freshmen are admitted to all sessions. Entrance exams should be taken during the junior or senior year of high school. There are deferred admissions and rolling admissions plans. Applications should be filed by September 1 for fall entry. The fall 2017 application fee was $25. Notification is sent on a rolling basis. Applications are accepted on-line. **Transfer Students:** 667 transfer students enrolled in 2016-2017. Applicants must have a GPA of 2.0 and must be able to return to their previous college. 30 of 120 credits required for the bachelor's degree must be completed at MSSU. **International Students:** There are 214 international students enrolled. They must take the TOEFL or MELAB. They must also take the SAT or ACT, scoring 18.

ADMISSIONS: 95% of the 2017-2018 applicants were accepted. The ACT scores were 16% between 12 and 17, 55% between 18 and 23, 25% between 24 and 29, and 4% above 30. **Admissions Contact:** Derek S. Skaggs, Director of Admissions. Email: *admissions@mssu.edu* Web: *www.mssu.edu*

FINANCIAL AID: The FAFSA code is 002488. The priority date for freshman financial aid applications for fall entry is April 1.

MISSOURI STATE UNIVERSITY B-3

www.missouristate.edu

Springfield, MO 65897 | **(417) 836-5000**, **(800) 492-7900**

Fax: (417) 836-5137 | **Email: info@MissouriState.edu**

Full-time: 6378 men, 8919 women	**Faculty:** 753; IIA, --$
Part-time: 950 men, 1147 women	**Ph.D.s:** 76%
Graduate: 1238 men, 2115 women	**Student/Faculty:** 21 to 1
Year: semesters, summer session	**Tuition:** $7306 ($14,746)
Room & Board: $8531	**Freshman Class:** 9453 applied, 7944 accepted, 3238 enrolled
SAT EBR-W/M: 568/565 **ACT:** 24	**CEEB CODE:** 6665
Application Deadline: July 20	**COMPETITIVE+**

Missouri State University, founded in 1905, is a public institution offering undergraduate programs in arts and letters, business administration, humanities and social sciences, education and psychology, health and applied sciences, science and math. There are 7 undergraduate schools and 1 graduate school. In addition to regional accreditation, MSU has baccalaureate program accreditation with AACSB, ABET, ACCE, ACPE, APTA, CSWE, NASM, CAEP, ACEND, ACPHA, and ARC-PA. The 304-acre campus is in a suburban area 220 miles southwest of St. Louis. Including any residence halls, there are 61 buildings.

STUDENT LIFE: 87% of undergraduates are from Missouri. Others are from 50 states, 83 foreign countries, and Canada. 81% are White; 5% African American; 4% Hispanic; 4% Foreign; 4% two or more races; 1% Asian American; 1% race unknown. **Female To Male Ratio:** 1.4:1. The average age of freshmen is 18; all undergraduates, 22. 25% do not continue beyond their first year; 55% remain to graduate. **Housing:** 4000 students can be accommodated in college housing, which includes married student dorms and on-campus apartments. In addition, there are honors houses, fraternity houses, sorority houses, apartments for single students, international students, and theme housing. On-campus housing is guaranteed for all 4 years. 85% of students live on campus. All students may keep cars. Alcohol is not permitted.

FACULTY/CLASSROOMS: 50% of faculty are male; 50% are female. No introductory courses are taught by graduate students. The average class size in a regular course is 23.

PROGRAMS OF STUDY: MSU confers B.S.A.T., B.A., B.A.S., B.F.A., B.M.U.S., B.M.E., B.S., B.S.Ed., B.S.N., and B.S.W. degrees. Master's and doctoral degrees are also awarded. Bachelor's degrees are awarded in AGRICULTURE (agriculture, animal science, environmental studies, plant science, and wildlife management), BIOLOGICAL SCIENCE (biology/biological science and cell biology), BUSINESS (accounting, business administration and management, entrepreneurial studies, fashion merchandising, finance, logistics, management science, marketing/retailing/merchandising, and recreation and leisure services), COMMUNICATIONS AND THE ARTS (art history, art, communications, communication science, design, English, French, German, information technology, journalism, Latin, music, musical theater, performing arts, Spanish, speech/debate/rhetoric, and theatre arts), COMPUTER AND PHYSICAL SCIENCE (chemistry, computer science, geology, mathematics, and natural sciences), EDUCATION (agricultural education, athletic training, business education, computer education, early childhood education, education administration, elementary education, global studies, middle school education, physical education, science education, and special education), ENGINEERING AND ENVIRONMENTAL DESIGN (construction management, interior design, and materials science), HEALTH PROFESSIONS (clinical science, exercise science, health care administration, health promotion, hospital administration, nursing, physical therapy, physician's assistant, radiological science, respiratory therapy, and speech pathology/audiology), SOCIAL SCIENCE (anthropology, child psychology/development, counseling/psychology, criminology, dietetics, economics, family/consumer studies, fashion design and technology, geography, gerontology, history, philosophy, political science/government, religion, social work, and sociology). Business, and education have the largest enrollments.

ACTIVITIES: 35% of men belong to 32% of women belong to Groups on campus include art, band, campus ministries, cheerleading, chess, choir, chorale, chorus, communications, computers, dance, drama, drill team, environmental, ethnic, film, honors, international, jazz band, LGBT, literary magazine, marching band, musical theater, newspaper, opera, orchestra, pep band, political, professional, radio and TV, religious, social, social service, student government, and symphony. Popular campus events include Tent Theater, Spring Fling, Community Service Fair, and Leadership Conference. **Sports:** There are 6 intercollegiate sports for men and 10 for women, and 23 intramural sports for men and 22 for women. Facilities include a stadium, an arena, swimming pool, softball and practice fields, tennis courts, bowling, and recreation center. **Graduates:** From July 1, 2016 to June 30, 2017, 3351 bachelor's degrees were awarded. The most popular majors were business/marketing (27%), education (13%), and health professional and related programs (7%). In an average class, 32% graduate in 4 years or less, 50% graduate in 5 years or less, and 52% graduate in 6 years or less. Of the 2016 graduating class, 70% were employed within 6 months of graduation.

SERVICES: Counseling and information services are available, as is tutoring in some subjects. There is a reader service for the blind, and remedial math, reading, and writing. A math center and a writing center are available for student use. Proctors are available for tests given to those with disabilities. **Library/Resources:** The library contains 782,257 volumes, 1.1 million microform items, and 19,708 audio/video tapes/CDs/DVDs, and subscribes to 37,000 periodicals including electronic. Computerized library services include interlibrary loans, database searching, Internet access, and Wi-Fi capability. Special learning facilities include an art gallery, radio station, and TV station. **Physically Challenged Students:** All of the campus is accessible. Facilities include wheelchair ramps, elevators, special parking, specially equipped restrooms, special class scheduling, lowered drinking fountains, lowered telephones, and special housing. **Special:** MSU offers co-op programs, internships, study abroad in 40 countries, and work-study programs. Also available are B.A.-B.S. degrees in 12 majors, preprofessional programs in law and medicine, accelerated degree programs and student-designed and interdisciplinary majors, including antiquities, agriculture business and agriculture education, chemistry/biochemistry, communication management, and finance/real estate. A 3-2 engineering degree is available through the University of Missouri-Rolla. Credit for military experience and pass/not-pass options are offered. There are 27 national honor societies and a freshman honors program. **Visiting:** There are regularly scheduled orientations for prospective students, guests can request an appointment with an admissions advisor, an academic department, or other areas of interest. There are guides for informal visits. To schedule a visit, contact the Admissions Office. **Campus Safety and Security:** Measures include 24-hour foot and vehicle patrol, emergency notification system, self-defense education, and security escort services. There are shuttle buses, emergency telephones, lighted pathways/sidewalks, and controlled access to dorms/residences.

REQUIREMENTS: The SAT or ACT is required for admittance; with the ACT preferred. Admission is based on a sliding scale of rank or GPA and test score. Freshmen must also have a 17-unit high school core curriculum, including 4 in English, 3 each in math, science (with 1 lab), and academic electives, 2 in social studies and 1 each in visual and performing arts, and history. AP and CLEP credits are accepted. Important factors in the admissions decision are leadership record, advanced placement or honors courses, and extracurricular activities record. A total of 125 to 130 semester hours, including 30 to 60 in the major, and a minimum GPA of 2.0 are required. 45 general education semester hours are required, to include 8 in natural sciences, 6 to 9 each in social sciences and humanities, 6 in American studies, 4 in phys ed, 3 to 6 in English composition, 3 each in math and speech, and 1 in freshman orientation. Arts/fine arts and computer literacy classes are also required. **Procedure:** Freshmen are admitted in the fall, spring, and summer. Entrance exams should be taken as early as possible. There is a rolling admissions plan. Applications should be filed by July 20 for fall entry. The fall 2017 application fee was $35. Notification is sent on a rolling basis. Applications are accepted on-line. **Transfer Students:** 1599 transfer students enrolled in 2016-2017. Applicants must present a minimum GPA of 2.0 on transferable courses. College transcripts are required. If they have completed less than 24 semester hours, they are also required to meet freshman admission requirements. Application for Admission is in the fall, spring, and summer. 30 of 125 credits required for the bachelor's degree must be completed at MSU. **International Students:** There are 780 international students enrolled. They must take the TOEFL with a minimum score of 500 on the paper-based TOEFL (PBT) or 61 on the Internet-based version (iBT). They must also take the ACT.

ADMISSIONS: 84% of the 2017-2018 applicants were accepted. The SAT scores for the 2017-2018 freshman class were: Math-- 22% below 500, 47% between 500 and 599, 29% between 600 and 699, and 3% between 700 and 800. Evidence-Based Reading/Writing-- 17% below 500, 49% between 500 and 599, and 35% between 600 and 699. The ACT scores were 2% between 12 and 17, 48% between 18 and 23, 42% between 24 and 29, and 8% above 30. 37% of the current freshmen were in the top fifth of their class; 62% were in the top two fifths. **Admissions Contact:** Michelle Olsen, Ph.D., Director of Institutional Research. Email: *info@MissouriState.edu* Web: *www.missouristate.edu*

FINANCIAL AID: In 2017-2018, 64% of all full-time freshmen received some form of financial aid and need-based aid. The average freshman award was $9,294. Need-based scholarships or need-based grants averaged $6,204; need-based self-help aid (loans and jobs) averaged $5,259; non-need-based athletic scholarships averaged $11,686; other non-need-based awards and non-need-based scholarships averaged $3,314; and $2,881 from other forms of aid. The average financial indebtedness of the 2017 graduate was $18,387. MSU is a member of CSS. The FAFSA code is 002503. The priority date for freshman financial aid applications for fall entry is March 31.

MISSOURI UNIVERSITY OF SCIENCE AND TECHNOLOGY C-3

www.mst.edu

Rolla, MO 65409	(573) 341-4164 (800) 522-0938
Fax: (573) 341-4082	**Email:** admissions@mst.edu
Full-time: 4227 men, 1245 women	**Faculty:** 361
Part-time: 487 men, 187 women	**Ph.D.s:** 89%
Graduate: 1577 men, 407 women	**Student/Faculty:** 15 to 1
Year: semesters, summer session	**Tuition:** $9510 ($24,675)
Room & Board: $9145	**Freshman Class:** n/av
SAT CR/M: 590/640 **ACT:** 28	**CEEB CODE:** 6876
Application Deadline: July 1	**HIGHLY COMPETITIVE**

Missouri University of Science and Technology, founded in 1870, is part of the University of Missouri system. A public research institution, it offers comprehensive undergraduate and graduate programs and confers degrees in arts and sciences, engineering, mines and metallurgy, and management and information systems. There are 4 undergraduate schools. In addition to regional accreditation, MUST has baccalaureate program accreditation with AACSB, ABET, CSAB, EAC, and CAC. The 284-acre campus is in a small town 100 miles southwest of St. Louis, MO and 100 miles northeast of Springfield, MO. Including any residence halls, there are 72 buildings.

STUDENT LIFE: 77% of undergraduates are from Missouri. Others are from 49 states, 60 foreign countries, and Canada. 78% are White; 6% Foreign; 4% African American; 4% race unknown; 2% Asian American; 2% Hispanic; 2% two or more races. **Male To Female Ratio:** 3.4:1. The average age of freshmen is 18; all undergraduates, 21. 17% do not continue beyond their first year; 63% remain to graduate. **Housing:** 2152 students can be accommodated in college housing, which includes married student dorms and on-campus apartments. In addition, there are honors houses, fraternity houses, sorority houses, learning community, and holistic community. On-campus housing is guaranteed for the freshman year only, and is available on a first-come, first-served basis. All students may keep cars. Alcohol is not permitted.

FACULTY/CLASSROOMS: 75% of faculty are male; 25% are female. No introductory courses are taught by graduate students.

PROGRAMS OF STUDY: MUST confers B.A. and B.S. degrees. Master's and doctoral degrees are also awarded. Bachelor's degrees are awarded in BIOLOGICAL SCIENCE (biology/biological science, environmental biology, and life science), BUSINESS (business administration and management and management information systems), COMMUNICATIONS AND THE ARTS (English and technical and business writing), COMPUTER AND PHYSICAL SCIENCE (applied mathematics, chemistry, computer science, geology, geophysics and seismology, information sciences and systems, mathematics, physics, and statistics), EDUCATION (secondary education), ENGINEERING AND ENVIRONMENTAL DESIGN (aeronautical engineering, architectural engineering, ceramic engineering, chemical engineering, civil engineering, computer engineering, electrical/electronics engineering, engineering management, engineering mechanics, environmental engineering, geological engineering, manufacturing engineering, materials engineering, mechanical engineering, metallurgical engineering, mining and mineral engineering, nuclear engineering, petroleum/natural gas engineering, and systems engineering), HEALTH PROFESSIONS (premedicine), SOCIAL SCIENCE (economics, history, philosophy, prelaw, and psychology). Engineering, and science and technology are the strongest academically. Engineering, arts, and science have the largest enrollments.

ACTIVITIES: 21% of men belong to 23 national fraternities; 19% of women belong to 5 national sororities. There are 221 groups on campus, including art, band, cheerleading, chess, choir, chorale, chorus, computers, dance, drama, drill team, ethnic, honors, international, jazz band, LGBT, literary magazine, marching band, musical theater, newspaper, orchestra, pep band, political, professional, radio and TV, religious, social, social service, student government, symphony, and yearbook. Popular campus events include St. Patrick's Day, Homecoming, Campus Block Party, and Celebration of Nations. **Sports:** There are 8 intercollegiate sports for men and 7 for women, and 20 intramural sports for men and 19 for women. Facilities include a gym, weight room, pool, a nine hole golf course, a track, racquetball, tennis, baseball, soccer fields, and stadium. **Graduates:** From July 1, 2016 to June 30, 2017, 1118 bachelor's degrees were awarded. The most popular majors were mechanical engineering (15%), civil engineering (12%), and electrical engineering (8%). In an average class, 63% graduate in 6 years or less. Of the 2016 graduating class, 16% were enrolled in graduate school within 6 months of graduation, and 57% were employed.

SERVICES: Counseling and information services are available, as is tutoring in most subjects. There is a reader service for the blind. **Library/Resources:** The library contains 479,874 volumes, 423,403 microform items, and 4,634 audio/video tapes/CDs/DVDs, subscribes to 3,901 periodicals, including electronic. Computerized library services include interlibrary loans, database searching, Internet access, and Wi-Fi capability. Special learning facilities include a radio station, a writing center, a student design center, nuclear reactor, observatory, explosives testing labs, an underground mine, and a hot glass shop. **Physically Challenged Students:** 95% of the campus is accessible. Facilities include wheelchair ramps, elevators, special parking, specially equipped restrooms, special class scheduling, lowered drinking fountains, lowered telephones, and special housing. **Special:** MS&T offers internships in business and government, co-op programs in which students work and attend school on alternating schedules, and study abroad in more than 40 countries. Accelerated degrees in science and engineering, dual majors, B.A.-B.S. degrees, a 3-2 engineering degree, work-study programs, credit for life/military/work experience, and pass/fail options in certain courses are also available. There are 28 national honor societies, a freshman honors program, and 16 departmental honors programs. **Visiting:** There are regularly scheduled orientations for prospective students, including a tour with a student, admissions and financial aid counseling, special interest contact, and a departmental visit with a faculty member. There are guides for informal visits, visitors may sit in on classes, and stay overnight. To schedule a visit, contact the Admissions Office. **Campus Safety and Security:** Measures include 24-hour foot and vehicle patrol, an emergency notification system, self-defense education, and security escort services. There are shuttle buses, emergency telephones, lighted pathways/sidewalks, crime prevention and rape/sexual assault programs.

REQUIREMENTS: The SAT or ACT is required. The sum of the high school student's class rank percentile and aptitude exam percentile must be 120 or higher. Candidates must be graduates of an accredited secondary school or have the GED. The applicant must have completed 16 academic credit units, including 4 each in English and math, 3 each in science and social studies, and 2 in a foreign language. Students may take the SAT or the ACT, however the ACT is recommended. A GPA of 2.0 is required. AP and CLEP credits are accepted. Important factors in the admissions decision are leadership record, extracurricular activities record, and advanced placement or honors courses. Candidates for graduation must maintain at least a 2.0 GPA. A total of 120 credits is required. A Senior assessment exam is required. **Procedure:** Freshmen are admitted in the fall, winter, and summer. Entrance exams should be taken late in the junior year or early in the senior year. There are deferred admissions and rolling admissions plans. Early decision applications should be filed by December 1; regular applications, by July 1 for fall entry; December 1 for spring entry; and May 1 for summer entry. The fall 2017 application fee was $50. Applications are accepted on-line. **Transfer Students:** 427 transfer students enrolled in 2016-2017. Applicants with fewer than 24 semester hours of college-level work must apply as freshmen; those with 24 or more must have attained at least a 2.0 GPA in all college-level courses. 60 of 120 credits required for the bachelor's degree must be completed at MUST. **International Students:** There are 384 international students enrolled. They must take the TOEFL with a minimum score of 550 on the paper-based TOEFL (PBT) or 79 on the Internet-based version (iBT). They must also take the SAT or ACT.

ADMISSIONS: The SAT scores for the 2017-2018 freshman class were: Critical Reading-- 14% below 500, 35% between 500 and 599, 36% between 600 and 699, and 15% between 700 and 800. Math-- 5% below 500, 21% between 500 and 599, 54% between 600 and 699, and 21% between 700 and 800. The ACT scores were 1% below 12, 8% between 12 and 17, 26% between 18 and 23, 19% between 24 and 29, and 46% above 30. 60% of the current freshmen were in the top fifth of their class; 88% were in the top two fifths. **Admissions Contact:** Lynn Stichnote, Director. Email: *admissions@mst.edu* Web: *www.mst.edu*

FINANCIAL AID: In 2017-2018, 88% of all full-time freshmen received some form of financial aid. 43% of all full-time freshmen received need-based aid. The average freshman award was $11,773. Need-based scholarships or need-based grants averaged $9,131; need-based self-help aid (loans and jobs) averaged $3,755; non-need-based athletic scholarships averaged $5,569; and other non-need-based awards and non-need-based scholarships averaged $6,300. The average financial indebtedness of the 2017 graduate was $6,166. MUST is a member of CSS. The FAFSA code is 002517. The priority date for freshman financial aid applications for fall entry is March 1.

MISSOURI VALLEY COLLEGE B-2

www.moval.edu

Marshall, MO 65340	(660) 831-4157
Fax: (660) 831-4233	**Email:** admissions@moval.edu
Full-time: 840 men, 550 women	**Faculty:** n/av
Part-time: 20 men, 20 women	**Ph.D.s:** 44%
Graduate: n/av	**Student/Faculty:** n/av
Year: semesters, summer session	**Tuition:** $19,750
Room & Board: $8400	**Freshman Class:** n/av
SAT or ACT: required	**CEEB CODE:** 6413
Application Deadline: September 1	**COMPETITIVE**

Missouri Valley College, founded in 1889, is a private liberal arts college, affiliated with the Presbyterian Church, offering 35 majors. There is 1 undergraduate school and 1 graduate school. In addition to regional accreditation, MVC has baccalaureate program accreditation with CAATE and Missouri State Board of Nursing. The 150-acre campus is in a small town 50 miles northwest of Columbia, MO and 80 miles northeast of Kansas City, MO. Including any residence halls, there are 17 buildings.

STUDENT LIFE: 66% of undergraduates are from Missouri. Others are from 43 states, 26 foreign countries, and Canada. 75% are from public schools. 83% are White; 6% Hispanic; 4% Asian American; 17% African American; 10% Foreign; 1% American Indian/Alaska Native. 45% are Protestant; 32% Islamic, Mormon, Orthodox, Agnostic, and unknown; 14% Catholic. **Male To Female Ratio:** 1.5:1. The average age of freshmen is 19; all undergraduates, 21. 48% do not continue beyond their first year; 20% remain to graduate. **Housing:** 1100 students can be accommodated in college housing, which includes dorms, on-campus apartments, and off-campus apartments. In addition, there are honors houses, special-interest houses, fraternity houses, and sorority houses. On-campus housing is guaranteed for all 4 years. 72% of students live on campus. All students may keep cars. Alcohol is not permitted.

FACULTY/CLASSROOMS: 73% of faculty are male; 27% are female. All

teach undergraduates. No introductory courses are taught by graduate students. The average class size in an introductory lecture is 30; in a laboratory is 25; and in a regular course is 18.

PROGRAMS OF STUDY: MVC confers B.A., B.S., B.F.A., and B.S.N degrees. Associate and master's degrees are also awarded. Bachelor's degrees are awarded in BIOLOGICAL SCIENCE (biology/biological science), BUSINESS (accounting, business administration and management, and recreational facilities management), COMMUNICATIONS AND THE ARTS (art, communications, dramatic arts, English, and speech/debate/rhetoric), COMPUTER AND PHYSICAL SCIENCE (information sciences and systems and mathematics), EDUCATION (elementary education, physical education, and social studies education), HEALTH PROFESSIONS (exercise science), SOCIAL SCIENCE (addiction studies, anthropology, criminal justice, economics, history, human services, liberal arts/general studies, philosophy, political science/government, psychology, public administration, religion, and sociology). Education is the strongest academically. Business administration (multiple areas), exercise science, and psychology have the largest enrollments.

ACTIVITIES: 15% of men belong to 4 national fraternities; 8% of women belong to 2 national sororities. There are 40 groups on campus, including art, cheerleading, choir, chorale, chorus, computers, dance, drama, ethnic, film, honors, international, jazz band, literary magazine, musical theater, newspaper, photography, radio and TV, religious, social, social service, student government, and yearbook. Popular campus events include Springfest, Maastricht Institute of Entrepreneurship, and Guerilla Film Festival. **Sports:** There are 13 intercollegiate sports for men and 12 for women, and 7 intramural sports for men and 7 for women. Facilities include a gym, tennis and basketball courts, football and soccer fields, a stadium, and horse stables. **Graduates:** From July 1, 2016 to June 30, 2017, 251 bachelor's degrees were awarded. The most popular majors were exercise science (12%), criminal justice (11%), and management (7%). In an average class, 3% graduate in 3 years or less, 20% graduate in 4 years or less, 27% graduate in 5 years or less, and 22% graduate in 6 years or less.

SERVICES: Counseling and information services are available, as is tutoring in most subjects. There is remedial math, reading, and writing. **Library/Resources:** The library contains 83,000 volumes, 31,000 microform items, and 3,400 audio/video tapes/CDs/DVDs, and subscribes to 250 periodicals including electronic. Computerized library services include interlibrary loans, database searching, Internet access, and Wi-Fi capability. Special learning facilities include an art gallery, a radio station, and TV station. **Physically Challenged Students:** 65% of the campus is accessible. Facilities include wheelchair ramps, elevators, special parking, specially equipped restrooms, and special class scheduling. **Special:** interdisciplinary studies (personalized plan of study), internships, study abroad, work-study, Co-op programs, nondegree study, and pass/fail options are available. There are 3 national honor societies and 3 departmental honors programs. **Visiting:** There are regularly scheduled orientations for prospective students, we have 4 Open Houses a year. There are guides for informal visits; visitors may sit in on classes and stay overnight. To schedule a visit, contact Jessica Green in Admissions. **Campus Safety and Security:** Measures include 24-hour foot and vehicle patrol, an emergency notification system, and security escort services. There are shuttle buses, emergency telephones, lighted pathways/sidewalks, and controlled access to dorms/residences.

REQUIREMENTS: The SAT or ACT is required. Students must have graduated from an accredited secondary school or have the GED. Auditions required for performance-based scholarships MVC requires applicants to be in the upper 50% of their class. AP and CLEP credits are accepted. Important factors in the admissions decision are advanced placement or honors courses, evidence of special talent, and extracurricular activities record. Students must complete 120 credit hours, including the core curriculum (about 47 credits), a major (typically 40-60 credits) and upper division credits (at least 40). A 2.0 GPA is also required for graduation. **Procedure:** Freshmen are admitted to all sessions. Entrance exams should be taken as early as possible. There are early admissions and rolling admissions plans. The fall 2017 application fee was $20. Notification is sent on a rolling basis. Applications are accepted online. **Transfer Students:** A minimum GPA of 2.0 is recommended; D grades do not transfer. Official transcripts are required for all previous colleges attended. Students with fewer than 27 credits transferring must submit high school transcripts as well. 30 of 120 credits required for the bachelor's degree must be completed at MVC. **International Students:** There are 247 international students enrolled. They must take the TOEFL. They must also take the SAT or ACT.

Admissions Contact: Tennille Langdon, Director of Admissions. Email: *admissions@moval.edu* Web: *www.moval.edu*

FINANCIAL AID: In 2017-2018, 99% of all full-time freshmen received some form of financial aid. MVC is a member of CSS. The FAFSA code is 002489. The priority date for freshman financial aid applications for fall entry is March 15.

MISSOURI WESTERN STATE UNIVERSITY *(The complete profile is made available exclusively on our website, www.barronspac.com)*

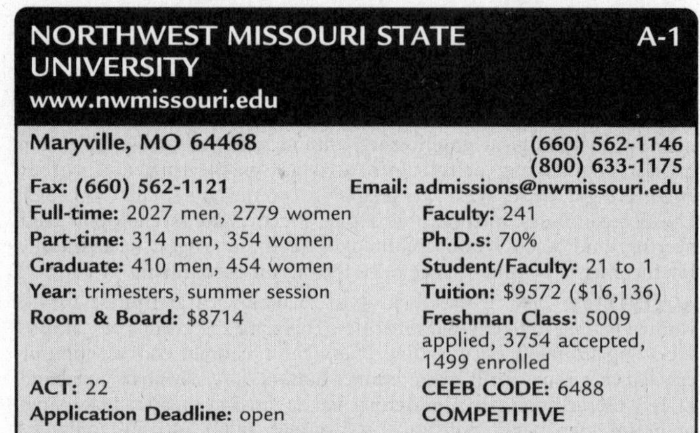

NORTHWEST MISSOURI STATE UNIVERSITY — A-1

www.nwmissouri.edu

Maryville, MO 64468 — **(660) 562-1146**, **(800) 633-1175**

Fax: (660) 562-1121 — **Email: admissions@nwmissouri.edu**

Full-time: 2027 men, 2779 women	**Faculty:** 241
Part-time: 314 men, 354 women	**Ph.D.s:** 70%
Graduate: 410 men, 454 women	**Student/Faculty:** 21 to 1
Year: trimesters, summer session	**Tuition:** $9572 ($16,136)
Room & Board: $8714	**Freshman Class:** 5009 applied, 3754 accepted, 1499 enrolled
ACT: 22	**CEEB CODE:** 6488
Application Deadline: open	**COMPETITIVE**

Northwest Missouri State University, founded in 1905, is a public institution offering undergraduate courses in agriculture, science, arts and humanities, business, communication & mass media, computer science, health and wellness, and education. NWMSU offers several opportunities for profession-based experiences including internships, the university farm for agriculture majors, on-campus radio and television stations, and volunteer work. There are 7 undergraduate schools and 1 graduate school. In addition to regional accreditation, NWMSU has baccalaureate program accreditation with AACSB, ACBSP, ADA, AHEA, NASM, CAEP, AACTE, AAFCS, and ACS. The 370-acre campus is in a small town 90 miles north of Kansas City. Including any residence halls, there are 35 buildings.

STUDENT LIFE: 70% of undergraduates are from Missouri. Others are from 36 states, 30 foreign countries, and Canada. 98% are from public schools. 8% are Foreign; 77% White; 5% African American; 4% Hispanic; 3% two or more races; 2% race unknown; 1% Asian American. **Female To Male Ratio:** 1.3:1. The average age of freshmen is 18; all undergraduates, 20. 33% do not continue beyond their first year; 47% remain to graduate. **Housing:** 2992 students can be accommodated in college housing, which includes gender neutral, coed, and married student dorms and on-campus apartments. In addition, there are special-interest houses, fraternity houses, and sorority houses. Northwest's Living and Academic Learning Communities (LALC) offer students who have similar academic interests the opportunity to connect with one another in a living and learning environment that is tailored towards your academic pursuits. On-campus housing is guaranteed for the freshman year only. 67% of students commute. Alcohol is not permitted. All students may keep cars.

FACULTY/CLASSROOMS: 52% of faculty are male; 48% are female. All teach undergraduates. No introductory courses are taught by graduate students. The average class size in an introductory lecture is 32; in a laboratory is 20; and in a regular course is 25.

PROGRAMS OF STUDY: NWMSU confers B.A., B.S., B.F.A., B.S.ED., B.S.Med.Tech., B.S.N., and B.Tech degrees. Associate and master's degrees are also awarded. Bachelor's degrees are awarded in AGRICULTURE (agricultural business management, agricultural economics, agricultural mechanics, agricultural sciences, agriculture, agronomy, animal science, conservation and regulation, forestry and related sciences, horticulture, and wildlife management), BIOLOGICAL SCIENCE (biology/biological science, botany, ecology, marine biology, and zoology), BUSINESS (accounting, banking and finance, business administration and management, business economics, finance, human resource management, international business, international business management, marketing/retailing/merchandising, and recreation and leisure services), COMMUNICATIONS AND THE ARTS (advertising, art, broadcasting, communications, dramatic arts, English, fine arts, journalism, music, public relations, Spanish, and speech/debate/rhetoric), COMPUTER AND PHYSICAL SCIENCE (chemistry, computer management, computer science, data processing, earth science, geology, information sciences and systems, mathematics, physics, science, and statistics), EDUCATION (agricultural education, art education, business education, early childhood education, education of the mentally handicapped, elementary education, English education, mathematics education, middle school education, music education, physical education, recreation education, science education, secondary education, special education, and specific learning disabilities), ENGINEERING AND ENVIRONMENTAL DESIGN (emergency/disaster science and preengineering), HEALTH PROFESSIONS (biology, predentistry, premedicine, prepharmacy, and preveterinary science), SOCIAL SCIENCE (child care/child and family studies, criminology, dietetics, economics, food science, geography, history, humanities, industrial and organizational psychology, philosophy, political science/government, prelaw, psychology, public administration, social psychology, social science, sociology, and textiles and clothing). Teacher education, business management, psychology, and agriculture are the strongest and have the largest enrollments are the strongest academically. Education, agricultural sciences, and business management have the largest enrollments.

ACTIVITIES: 15% of men belong to 9 national fraternities; 17% of women belong to 6 national sororities. There are 157 groups on campus, including band, cheerleading, choir, chorale, chorus, computers, dance, debate, drama, drill team, drum and bugle corps, ethnic, film, forensics, international, jazz band, LGBT, literary magazine, marching band, newspaper, orchestra, pep band, photography, political, professional, radio and TV, religious, social, social service, student government, symphony, and yearbook. Popular campus events include Fall Music Concert, Homecoming events, Football Games, Up 'Til Dawn Colden Pond Plunge, SAC Late Night events, Greek Life Bid Day, Advantage Week Fireworks, Distinguished Lecture Series, SAC Grocery bingo, and Bearcat Basketball Games. **Sports:** There are 7 intercollegiate sports for men and 9 for women, and 12 intramural sports for men and 13 for women. Facilities include a stadium, a basketball arena, gyms, racquetball courts, a weight-lifting area, baseball and softball fields, volleyball and tennis courts, dance areas, disc golf course, pitch fitness center, and human performance laboratory. **Graduates:** From July 1, 2016 to June 30, 2017, 992 bachelor's degrees were awarded. The most popular majors were business/marketing (20%), education (16%), and agriculture (14%). In an average class, 27% graduate in 4 years or less, 48% graduate in 5 years or less, and 50% graduate in 6 years or less. Of the 2016 graduating class, 20% were enrolled in graduate school within 6 months of graduation, and 76% were employed.

SERVICES: Counseling and information services are available, as is tutoring in most subjects. There is a reader service for the blind, and remedial math, reading, and writing. **Library/Resources:** The library contains 240,370 volumes, 8,421 microform items, 5,234 audio/video tapes/CDs/DVDs, and subscribes to 33,868 periodicals, including electronic. Computerized library services include interlibrary loans, database searching, Internet access, and Wi-Fi capability. Special learning facilities include an art gallery, radio station, TV station, Missouri Arboretum, Mozingo Outdoor Education Recreation Area (observatory, ropes challenge course, trap and archery, canoes and kayaks), Horace Mann Laboratory School, R.T. Wright Farm (dairy operation, swine herd, horticulture complex, experimental farmland), Center for Innovation and Entrepreneurship (business incubator), Studio Theater and Black Box experimental theater, online Northwest History Museum, Science Museum, Agriculture Museum, Jean Jennings Bartik Computing Museum, Warren Stucki Museum of Broadcasting, Student Media Converged Newsroom, Joyce and Harvey White International Plaza. Anita Aldrich Human Performance Lab inside the newly renovated Foster Fitness Center. A state of the art Michael L. Faust student media laboratory. **Physically Challenged Students:** All of the campus is accessible. Facilities include wheelchair ramps, elevators, special parking, specially equipped restrooms, special class scheduling, lowered drinking fountains, and lowered telephones. **Special:** Campus-wide internships, study abroad program (England, Mexico, Spain, Netherlands, Japan and many others). There are also work-study programs, student designed majors, a 3-2 engineering degree with the Missouri University of Science and Technology, credit for military experience, service learning, non degree study, and pass/fail options available. There are 3 national honor societies and a freshman honors program. **Visiting:** There are regularly scheduled orientations for prospective students, consisting of a 90 minute (2 mile) walking tour is guided by Northwest Student Ambassadors who share their individual experiences about Northwest as well as pointers for selecting a university. There are guides for informal visits, visitors may sit in on classes, and stay overnight. To schedule a visit, contact Mabel Cook, Recruitment and Visitors Center at admissions@nwmissouri.edu. **Campus Safety and Security:** Measures include 24-hour foot and vehicle patrol, emergency notification system, self-defense education, and security escort services. There are shuttle buses, lighted pathways/sidewalks, and controlled access to dorms/residences.

REQUIREMENTS: Applicants must have a minimum composite score of 980 or 1060* on the SAT or 21 on the ACT and a minimum 2.00 cumulative GPA or above (on 4.00 scale). If scores are below those levels, a combined percentile index obtained from the SAT or ACT score and high school rank will be used, (*per 2016 SAT redesign). In addtion, if a student has taken the ACT/SAT more than once, they can benefit from the superscore. Northwest will evaluate the ACT and SAT according to the "superscore" which is a composite of the student's best subscores in each subject area, regardless of the test date. The highest subscores will be used for admissions decisions, automatic scholarships and course placement. A GPA of 2.0 is required. AP and CLEP credits are accepted. Important factors in the admissions decision are evidence of special talent and personality/intangible qualities. All students must maintain a minimum GPA of 2.0 while taking at least 124 credit hours. Distribution requirements include 9 hours each in social science and humanities, 8 hours in natural science, 6 hours in composition, 4 hours each in math and phys ed, 3 hours each in oral communications and behavioral sciences, and 1 hour in the freshman seminar. **Procedure:** Freshmen are admitted in the fall, spring, and summer. Entrance exams should be taken in the fall of the senior year. There is a rolling admissions plan. Application deadlines are open. The fall 2017 application fee was $25. Notifications are sent September 1. Applications are accepted on-line. **Transfer Students:** 298 transfer students enrolled in 2016-2017. Applicants must present a minimum GPA of 2.0. 30 of 124 credits required for the bachelor's degree must be completed at NWMSU. **International Students:** There are 159 international students enrolled. They must take the TOEFL with a minimum score of 500 on the paper-based TOEFL (PBT) or 61 on the Internet-based version (iBT).

ADMISSIONS: 75% of the 2017-2018 applicants were accepted. 31% of the current freshmen were in the top fifth of their class; 63% were in the top two fifths. 34 freshmen graduated first in their class. **Admissions Contact:** Tamera Grow, Associate Director of Admissions. Email: *admissions@nwmissouri.edu* Web: *www.nwmissouri.edu*

FINANCIAL AID: In 2017-2018, 71% of all full-time freshmen received some form of financial aid. 65% of all full-time freshmen received need-based aid. The average freshman award was $11,144. Need-based scholarships or need-based grants averaged $6,536; need-based self-help aid (loans and jobs) averaged $3,323; and non-need-based athletic scholarships averaged $7,186. 51% of undergraduate students work part-time. The FAFSA code is 002496. The priority date for freshman financial aid applications for fall entry is April 1.

PARK UNIVERSITY — A-2

www.park.edu

Parkville, MO 64152	**(816) 584-6215** **(800) 745-7275**
Fax: (816) 741-4462	**Email: admissions@park.edu**
Full-time: 547 men, 657 women	**Faculty:** 94
Part-time: 182 men, 288 women	**Ph.D.s:** 54%
Graduate: 336 men, 448 women	**Student/Faculty:** 11 to 1
Year: semesters, summer session	**Tuition:** $13,284
Room & Board: $8850	**Freshman Class:** 778 applied, 539 accepted, 212 enrolled
ACT: 21	**CEEB CODE:** 6574
Application Deadline: n/av	**COMPETITIVE**

Park University, founded in 1875, is a private institution offering degree programs in the humanities, performing arts, natural and life sciences, and social and administrative sciences. The figures given in the above capsule and in this profile are approximate. There are 3 undergraduate schools and 1 graduate school. In addition to regional accreditation, Park has baccalaureate program accreditation with NLN and CAATE. The 700-acre campus is in a suburban area 12 miles north of Kansas City. Including any residence halls, there are 17 buildings.

STUDENT LIFE: 80% of undergraduates are from Missouri. Others are from 50 states, 103 foreign countries, and Canada. 80% are from public schools. 52% are White; 5% Hispanic; 19% Foreign; 10% African American; 1% Asian American; 1% American Indian/Alaska Native. 88% claim no religious affiliation. **Female To Male Ratio:** 1.3:1. The average age of freshmen is 18; all undergraduates, 24. 39% do not continue beyond their first year; 41% remain to graduate. **Housing:** 410 students can be accommodated in college housing, which includes dorms, on-campus apartments, and honors houses. On-campus housing is guaranteed for all 4 years. 80% of students commute. All students may keep cars. Alcohol is not permitted.

FACULTY/CLASSROOMS: 62% of faculty are male; 38% are female. All teach undergraduates, and 80% do research. No introductory courses are taught by graduate students. The average class size in an introductory lecture is 20; in a laboratory is 10; and in a regular course is 15.

PROGRAMS OF STUDY: Park confers B.A., B.S., B.P.A., B.S.W., B.S.N., and B.F.A. degrees. Associate and master's degrees are also awarded. Bachelor's degrees are awarded in BIOLOGICAL SCIENCE (biology/biological science), BUSINESS (accounting, business administration and management, business economics, human resources, management information systems, and marketing management), COMMUNICATIONS AND THE ARTS (communications, dramatic arts, English, fine arts, graphic design, music, public relations, and Spanish), COMPUTER AND PHYSICAL SCIENCE (chemistry, computer science, information sciences and systems, mathematics, and natural sciences), EDUCATION (athletic training, early childhood education, and elementary education), ENGINEERING AND ENVIRONMENTAL DESIGN (aviation administration/management, computational sciences, engineering management, and interior design), HEALTH PROFESSIONS (health care administration), SOCIAL SCIENCE (child care/child and family studies, criminal justice, economics, fire protection, fire services administration, geography, history, human services, law, liberal arts/general studies, political science/government, psychology, public administration, social psychology, social work, and sociology). Management, management/computer information systems, and management/human resources have the largest enrollments.

ACTIVITIES: There are no fraternities or sororities. There are 30 groups on campus, including cheerleading, computers, drama, ethnic, honors, international, literary magazine, newspaper, photography, political, professional, radio and TV, religious, social, social service, and student government. Popular campus events include Fall Harvest Festival, Spring Fling, and International Week. **Sports:** There are 6 intercollegiate sports for men and 7 for women, and 3 intramural sports for men and 3 for women. Facilities include indoor gyms with basketball and volleyball courts, an all-weather outdoor track, soccer and softball fields, a sports medicine room, tennis courts, and outdoor sand volleyball and basketball courts. **Graduates:** From July 1, 2016 to June 30, 2017, 398 bachelor's degrees were awarded. The most popular majors were business/management (24%), education (14%), and computer and information systems (13%). In an average class, 6% graduate in 3 years or less, 53% graduate in 4 years or less, 36% graduate in 5 years or less, and 5% graduate in 6 years or less.

SERVICES: Counseling and information services are available, as is tutoring in most subjects. There is a reader service for the blind, and remedial math, reading, and writing. **Library/Resources:** The library contains 158,422 volumes, 195,530 microform items, 670 audio/video tapes/CDs/DVDs, and subscribes to 775 periodicals, including electronic. Computerized library services include interlibrary loans and database searching. Special learning facilities include an art gallery, radio station, and TV station. **Physically Challenged Students:** 95% of the campus is accessible. Facilities include wheelchair ramps, elevators, special parking, specially equipped restrooms, special class scheduling, and lowered drinking fountains. **Special:** Cross-registration is available through a Kansas City consortium, and study abroad is possible through other schools. The university also offers internships in most majors, work-study programs with local companies, a Washington semester, credit for life and military experience, pass/fail options, and nondegree study. An accelerated degree program is offered in some majors. There are 2 national honor societies and a freshman honors program. **Visiting:** There are regularly scheduled orientations for prospective students, including a campus tour, lunch, an information session with a student panel, sessions on admissions, scholarships, and financial aid, and a chance to attend a class and meet with a faculty member. There are guides for informal visits, visitors may sit in on classes, and stay overnight. To schedule a visit, contact the Admissions and Student Financial Services. **Campus Safety and Security:** Measures include 24-hour foot and vehicle patrol and security escort services. There are emergency telephones and lighted pathways/sidewalks.

REQUIREMENTS: The ACT is required. The GED is accepted with a minimum total score of 225 and no area less than 35. Park requires applicants to be in the upper 50% of their class. A GPA of 2.0 is required. AP and CLEP credits are accepted. Important factors in the admissions decision are advanced placement or honors courses, leadership record, and extracurricular activities record. All students must complete core requirements, including 3 semesters of English composition and 1 of algebra, as well as 1 science course. They must also complete 24 to 27 hours of general education courses and 9 hours of liberal learning courses. Of the 120 credit hours needed for the bachelor's degree, 45 must be completed in upper-division work and 30 to 60 in the major, with a minimum GPA of 2.0. **Procedure:** Freshmen are admitted in the fall, spring, and summer. Entrance exams should be taken during the junior year or early in the senior year. There is a rolling admissions plan. Check with the school for current application deadlines. The fall 2017 application fee was $25. Notification is sent on a rolling basis. Applications are accepted on-line. **Transfer Students:** The college requires a GPA of at least 2.0. A minimum ACT composite score of 20 is recommended but is waived for students age 25 or older. 30 of 120 credits required for the bachelor's degree must be completed at Park. **International Students:** There are 324 international students enrolled. They must take the TOEFL, and the ACT.

ADMISSIONS: 69% of the 2017-2018 applicants were accepted. The ACT scores were 50% below 12, 29% between 12 and 17, 9% between 18 and 23, 5% between 24 and 29, and 7% above 30. 29% of the current freshmen were in the top fifth of their class; 54% were in the top two fifths. **Admissions Contact:** Eric Blair, Director of Undergraduate Admissions. Email: *admissions@park.edu* Web: *www.park.edu*

FINANCIAL AID: In 2017-2018, 62% of all full-time freshmen received some form of financial aid. 49% of all full-time freshmen received need-based aid. The average freshman award was $10,524. The average financial indebtedness of the 2017 graduate was $22,218. The college's own financial statement is required. The FAFSA code is 002498. The priority date for freshman financial aid applications for fall entry is March 15.

RESEARCH COLLEGE OF NURSING *(The complete profile is made available exclusively on our website, www.barronspac.com)*

ROCKHURST UNIVERSITY — A-2

www.rockhurst.edu

Kansas City, MO 64110 — **(816) 501-4100 / (800) 842-6776**

Fax: (816) 501-4241 — **Email: admission@rockhurst.edu**

Full-time: 615 men, 850 women	**Faculty:** n/av
Part-time: 320 men, 540 women	**Ph.D.s:** 84%
Graduate: 335 men, 475 women	**Student/Faculty:** n/av
Year: semesters, summer session	**Tuition:** $17,900
Room & Board: $11,090	**Freshman Class:** n/av
SAT: recommended **ACT:** required	**CEEB CODE:** 6611
Application Deadline: n/av	**COMPETITIVE**

Rockhurst University, founded in 1910, is a private Catholic Jesuit institution that offers undergraduate programs in the arts and sciences, education, nursing, and business. The figures given in the above capsule and in this profile are approximate. There are 4 undergraduate schools and 2 graduate schools. In addition to regional accreditation, RU has baccalaureate program accreditation with APTA, CAHEA, NLN, CAEP, and AACTE. The 55-acre campus is in an urban area in Kansas City. Including any residence halls, there are 19 buildings.

STUDENT LIFE: 58% of undergraduates are from Missouri. Others are from 17 states. 49% are from public schools. 82% are White; 5% African American; 3% Asian American; 3% Hispanic; 1% American Indian/Alaska Native; 1% Foreign. 46% are Catholic; 34% Buddhist, Hindu, Muslim, and Islamic; 20% Protestant. **Female To Male Ratio:** 1.5:1. The average age of freshmen is 18; all undergraduates, 21. 11% do not continue beyond their first year; 66% remain to graduate. **Housing:** 815 students can be accommodated in college housing, which includes dorms and on-campus apartments. In addition, there are honors houses and special-interest houses. On-campus housing is available on a first-come and first-served basis. 61% of students live on campus. All students may keep cars.

FACULTY/CLASSROOMS: 52% of faculty are male; 48% are female.

87% teach undergraduates. No introductory courses are taught by graduate students. The average class size in an introductory lecture is 20; in a laboratory is 14; and in a regular course is 21.

PROGRAMS OF STUDY: RU confers B.A., B.S., B.S.B.A., and B.S.N. degrees. Master's and doctoral degrees are also awarded. Bachelor's degrees are awarded in BIOLOGICAL SCIENCE (biochemistry, bioinformatics, and biology/biological science), BUSINESS (business administration and management, business communications, business economics, and nonprofit/public organization management), COMMUNICATIONS AND THE ARTS (communications, English, French, and Spanish), COMPUTER AND PHYSICAL SCIENCE (chemistry, computer science, mathematics, and physics), EDUCATION (elementary education, foreign languages education, and secondary education), ENGINEERING AND ENVIRONMENTAL DESIGN (computer technology), HEALTH PROFESSIONS (clinical science, nursing, and speech pathology/audiology), SOCIAL SCIENCE (economics, history, international relations, philosophy, political science/government, psychology, and theological studies). Nursing, and business administration are the strongest academically.

ACTIVITIES: 7% of men belong to 4 national fraternities; 7% of women belong to 2 national sororities. There are 55 groups on campus, including art, cheerleading, choir, chorale, chorus, computers, drama, ethnic, honors, international, literary magazine, musical theater, newspaper, photography, political, professional, radio and TV, religious, social, social service, and student government. Popular campus events include Fraternity Socials, Coffee House Events, and Rockstock (live bands). **Sports:** There are 5 intercollegiate sports for men and 5 for women, and 12 intramural sports for men and 12 for women. Facilities include athletic and soccer fields, tennis, handball, racquetball, badminton, basketball, and volleyball courts, a weight and exercise room, gymnastics facilities, and a NCAA baseball field. **Graduates:** From July 1, 2016 to June 30, 2017, 366 bachelor's degrees were awarded. The most popular majors were business (35%), nursing/health professions (21%), and psychology/social science/history (13%). In an average class, 51% graduate in 4 years or less, 63% graduate in 5 years or less, and 66% graduate in 6 years or less.

SERVICES: The Learning Center offers tutoring in many subjects, assistance with any college writing task, and study strategies, SI courses, support for various professional tests, plus a computer bank. **Library/ Resources:** The library contains 314,890 volumes, 596,850 microform items, and 8,078 audio/video tapes/CDs/DVDs, and subscribes to 38,934 periodicals including electronic. Computerized library services include interlibrary loans, database searching, Internet access, and Wi-Fi capability. Special learning facilities include an art gallery, radio station, a multimedia classrooms. **Physically Challenged Students:** 90% of the campus is accessible. Facilities include wheelchair ramps, elevators, special parking, specially equipped restrooms, lowered drinking fountains, and lowered telephones. **Special:** Students may obtain career-related work experience through the Cooperative Education Program. Internships for credit and salary are available. Students are encouraged to study abroad in 1 of 5 countries for a semester, to take a semester in New York at Fordham University, or to participate in a congressional intern/study program in Washington, D.C., through Marquette University. B.A.-B.S. degrees are available in business administration. Work-study and an accelerated degree in nursing are also available. Students may pursue dual majors, a 3-2 engineering degree, and interdisciplinary majors. There are 7 national honor societies, Phi Beta Kappa, a freshman honors program, and 12 departmental honors programs. **Visiting:** There are regularly scheduled orientations for prospective students, including a campus tour, an interview with an admissions counselor, and a classroom visit or meeting with a faculty member. There are guides for informal visits, visitors may sit in on classes, and stay overnight. To schedule a visit, contact the Admissions Office. **Campus Safety and Security:** Measures include 24-hour foot and vehicle patrol, self-defense education, and security escort services. There are shuttle buses, emergency telephones, lighted pathways/sidewalks, formal presentations, and a full in-house security program geared toward integration of security into the overall campus operation.

REQUIREMENTS: The ACT is required. The SAT is recommended. Applicants must be a graduate of an accredited secondary school or have earned a GED. The university requires completion of 15 academic credits, including 4 years of English, 3 to 4 of history/social science, 3 of math, 2 to 4 of a foreign language, and 1 of visual or performing arts. An interview is encouraged, and a recommendation is required. Rockhurst requires applicants to be in the upper 50% of their class. A GPA of 2.0 is required. AP and CLEP credits are accepted. Important factors in the admissions decision are advanced placement or honors courses, recommendations by school officials, and leadership record. Students must complete 128 credit hours with a minimum of 18 in the major, with at least a 2.0 GPA. 52 prescribed semester hours in philosophy, theology, history, literature, science, social studies, and the arts are required. Students must also demonstrate proficiency in oral and written communication and math. **Procedure:** Freshmen are admitted to all sessions. Entrance exams should be taken in April or June of the junior year or October, December, or February of the senior year. There are deferred admissions and rolling admissions plans. Check with the school for current application deadlines. The fall 2017 application fee was $25. Applications are accepted on-line. **Transfer Students:** 95 transfer students enrolled in 2016-2017. Transfer applicants must have a GPA of at least 2.25. An interview is recommended. All college transcripts must be submitted; a high school transcript and test scores are required if the applicant has completed fewer than 24 college semester hours. 30 of 128 credits required for the bachelor's degree must be completed at RU. **International Students:** There are 2 international students enrolled. They must take the TOEFL with a minimum score of 550 on the paper-based TOEFL (PBT) or 79 on the Internet-based version (iBT). They must also take the SAT or ACT.

ADMISSIONS: 5 freshmen graduated first in their class. **Admissions Contact:** Phil Gebauer, Associate Vice President for Enrollment. Email: *admission@rockhurst.edu* Web: *www.rockhurst.edu*

FINANCIAL AID: In 2017-2018, 91% of all full-time freshmen received some form of financial aid. 69% of all full-time freshmen received need-based aid. The average freshman award was $21,879. 22% of undergraduate students work part-time. The average financial indebtedness of the 2017 graduate was $16,579. The FAFSA code is 002499. Check with the school for current application deadlines.

SAINT LOUIS UNIVERSITY — D-2
www.slu.edu

St. Louis, MO 63103	(314) 977-2500
Fax: (314) 977-7136	Email: admission@slu.edu
Full-time: 3156 men, 4332 women	Faculty: 776; I, -$
Part-time: 255 men, 505 women	Ph.D.s: 86%
Graduate: 1898 men, 2768 women	Student/Faculty: 11 to 1
Year: semesters, summer session	Tuition: $39,226
Room & Board: $10,640	Freshman Class: 13216 applied, 8273 accepted, 1618 enrolled
SAT: required ACT: 28	CEEB CODE: 6629
Application Deadline: December 1	HIGHLY COMPETITIVE

Saint Louis University, founded in 1818, is a Catholic, Jesuit institution that values academic excellence, life-changing research, compassionate health care, and a strong commitment to faith and service. SLU is the second oldest Jesuit university in the United States, building on a legacy of nearly 200 years. Offering a complete range of undergraduate, graduate and professional programs, including law and medicine, the University fosters the intellectual and character development of students on campuses in St. Louis and Madrid, Spain. Building on a legacy of nearly 200 years. There are 10 undergraduate schools and 12 graduate schools. In addition to regional accreditation, SLU has baccalaureate program accreditation with AACSB, ABET, CSWE, NASAD, ACS, AABI, CEPH, CAHIIM, ACEND, CAAHEP, CCNE, JRCERT, JRCNMT, NAACLS, and DESE. The 270-acre campus is in an urban area midtown section of St. Louis, approximately 4 miles west of the Gateway Arch. Including any residence halls, there are 134 buildings.

STUDENT LIFE: 63% of undergraduates are from out of state, mostly the Midwest. Students are from 48 states, 52 foreign countries, and Canada. 9% are Asian American; 66% White; 6% African American; 6% Hispanic; 6% Foreign; 4% two or more races; 2% race unknown. 42% claim no religious affiliation; 38% Catholic; 13% Protestant. **Female To Male Ratio:** 1.4:1. The average age of freshmen is 18; all undergraduates, 20. 10% do not continue beyond their first year; 73% remain to graduate. **Housing:** 3865 students can be accommodated in college housing, which includes on-campus apartments, coed dorms, women's dorms, and men's dorm. In addition, there are fraternity houses, sorority houses, and a living learning community. On-campus housing is available on a first-come, first-served basis, and is available on a lottery system for upperclassmen. 51% of students live on campus. All students may keep cars.

FACULTY/CLASSROOMS: 59% of faculty are male; 41% are female. 39% teach undergraduates, 46% do research, and 21% do both. Graduate students teach 7% of introductory courses. The average class size in an introductory lecture is 19; in a laboratory is 17; and in a regular course is 19.

PROGRAMS OF STUDY: SLU confers B.A. and B.S. degrees. Master's and doctoral degrees are also awarded. Bachelor's degrees are awarded in AGRICULTURE (environmental studies), BIOLOGICAL SCIENCE (biochemistry, biology/biological science, forensic science, neurosciences, and nutritional sciences), BUSINESS (accounting, business administration and management, business economics, entrepreneurial studies, finance, international business, international economics, management information systems, marketing, marketing management, organizational behavior, organizational leadership and management, and sustainable management), COMMUNICATIONS AND THE ARTS (art history, classical languages, classics, communications, dramatic arts, English, English literature, English writing, fine/studio arts, general, French, Germanic languages and literature, information technology, Italian, music, Russian languages and literature, Spanish, studio art, theatre arts, and theater management), COMPUTER AND PHYSICAL SCIENCE (applied mathematics, atmospheric sciences and meteorology, chemistry, clinical laboratory science, computer programming, computer information technology, computer information systems, computer science, earth science, geology, mathematics, and physics), EDUCATION (drama education, education, elementary education, English education, general studies, health information management, mathematics education, middle school education, nutrition education, physical science secondary school education, science education, secondary education, and social science education), ENGINEERING AND ENVIRONMENTAL DESIGN (aeronautical engineering, aeronautical technology, aerospace engineering, aerospace studies, airline piloting and navigation, bioengineering, biomedical engineering, civil engineering, civil engineering technology, computer engineering, computer technology, electrical/electronics engineering, electrical technology, electrical/electronics engineering technology, emergency/disaster science, engineering, engineering management, engineering physics, environmental science, and mechanical engineering), HEALTH PROFESSIONS (allied health, biology, biomedical science, clinical science, cytotechnology, exercise science, health, health administration and policy, health care administration, kinesiology, medical laboratory science, medical laboratory technology, medical records administration/services, nuclear medical technology, nursing, nutrition and dietetics, occupational therapy, public health, radiation therapy, radiograph medical technology, radiologic imaging modalities, and speech pathology/audiology), SOCIAL SCIENCE (African American studies, American studies, anthropology, behavioral science, communication sciences and disorders, criminal justice, forensic studies, French studies, history, homeland security/emergency preparedness, international relations, Latin American studies, legal studies, philosophy, political science/government, psychology, safety and security technology, safety management, social work, sociology, theology, theological studies, urban studies, and women's studies). Engineering, public health, and business are the strongest academically. Nursing, physical therapy, and accounting have the largest enrollments.

ACTIVITIES: 18% of men belong to 8 national fraternities; 27% of women belong to 6 national sororities. There are 155 groups on campus, including games/hobbies, improvisational comedy, minority student groups, model UN, singing groups, speakers forum, sports/fitness club, theatre program, wilderness/outdoor programs, art, band, Campus ministry, cheerleading, chess, choir, chorale, chorus, computers, dance, debate, drama, drill team, environmental, ethnic, honors, international, jazz band, LGBT, literary magazine, musical theater, newspaper, pep band, photography, political, professional, radio and TV, religious, social, social service, and student government. Popular campus events include comedians, concerts in fall and spring, Make a Difference Day, Fall Welcome, Winter Welcome, SLU Involvement Fair, Homecoming, Billikens After Dark events, Sunday Night Mass, Relay for Life, Dance Marathon, Atlas Week, and International Banquet. **Sports:** There are 8 intercollegiate sports for men and 10 for women, and 23 intramural sports for men and 23 for women. Facilities include basketball, a practice facility which accommodates volleyball/basketball practices, soccer playing field. The sports center includes a baseball field and softball diamond. The recreation center includes a pool, outdoor/indoor tennis courts and an astroturf field for hockey. **Graduates:** From July 1, 2016 to June 30, 2017, 1988 bachelor's degrees were awarded. The most popular majors were business administration (17%), nursing (8%), and biology (6%). In an average class, 64% graduate in 4 years or less, 73% graduate in 5 years or less, and 74% graduate in 6 years or less. Of the 2016 graduating class, 31% were enrolled in graduate school within 6 months of graduation, and 59% were employed.

SERVICES: Counseling and information services are available, as is tutoring in most subjects. **Library/Resources:** The library contains 1.9 million volumes, 2.8 million microform items, 127,907 audio/video tapes/CDs/DVDs, and subscribes to 11,147 periodicals, including electronic. Computerized library services include interlibrary loans, database searching, Internet access, and Wi-Fi capability. Special learning facilities include an art gallery, radio station, TV station, the Vatican manuscripts microfilm library, LEED Certified Research Facility, Doisy Research Center, biological station, entrepreneurial studies center, earthquake research center, performing arts center, supersonic wind tunnel, water tunnel, shock tube, fabrication labs, flight simulators, airport, sculpture/ceramics studio, physiology/gait research labs, Madrid, Spain Campus, Law School in the heart of the downtown legal community, demonstration clinics (practice with actual clients): counseling and family therapy, child development, speech and hearing, psychology, dental, occupational and physical therapy, organic garden and food service. **Physically Challenged Students:** 95% of the campus is accessible. Facilities include wheelchair ramps, elevators, special parking, specially equipped restrooms, special class scheduling, lowered drinking fountains, lowered telephones, and special housing. **Special:** There are internships available in many departments. We have accelerated degree programs in Nursing (B.S.), Leadership and Organizational Development (M.A.), and Organizational Informatics (M.S.). SLU has dual majors and student-designed majors, and 3-2 Engineering and program degrees with Washington University in St. Louis. In addition there is cross registration with Washington University in St. Louis, University of Missouri at St. Louis, Aquinas Institute of Theology, and Harris-Stowe State College. Students may also participate in the university-sponsored mission trips, as well as study abroad in 30 countries: Argentina, Australia, Austria, Belgium, Chile, China, Denmark, Ecuador, El Salvador, England, France, Germany, Hong Kong, Hungary, India, Ireland, Italy, Mexico, The Netherlands, Nicaragua, Philippines, Russia, South Africa, South Korea, Spain, Sweden, Switzerland, Taiwan, Thailand, and Vietnam. There are 3 national honor societies, Phi Beta Kappa, and a freshman honors program. **Visiting:** There are regularly scheduled orientations for prospective students, and events and visits are available year round. Other options include campus tours, residence hall tours, academic meetings, class visits, and presentations on admission, student development, studying abroad, student life/campus culture, and stays in residence halls. There are guides for informal visits, visitors may sit in on classes, and stay overnight. To schedule a visit, contact Andrea Hitsman at admission@slu.edu. **Campus Safety and Security:** Measures include 24-hour foot and vehicle patrol, emergency notification system, self-defense education, and security escort services. There are shuttle buses, emergency telephones, lighted pathways/sidewalks, controlled access to dorms/residences, video cameras, identification of valuables, smoke detectors in halls, informal safety and security discussions, bike patrols, prevention/awareness programs, mobile security patrols, motorist assistance, security officers, and 24 hour emergency telephone/alarm devices.

REQUIREMENTS: The SAT or ACT is required. A complete application is required for admission consideration, an essay, a high school transcript, and test scores. Auditions and portfolios are required for the music and art programs. AP and CLEP credits are accepted. Important factors in the admissions decision are advanced placement or honors courses, leadership record, and extracurricular activities record. Students must maintain a 2.0 GPA while completing a minimum of 120 credit hours. The core curriculum includes courses in English, Philosophy, Theology, Mathematics, Foreign Language, and Cultural Diversity. **Procedure:** Freshmen are admitted in the fall, spring, and summer. Entrance exams should be taken in the junior or in the senior year. There are deferred admissions and rolling admissions plans. Applications should be filed by December 1 for fall entry; January 1 for spring entry; and June 1 for summer entry. Notification is sent on a rolling basis. 164 applicants were on the 2017 waiting list; 107 were admitted. Applications are accepted on-line. **Transfer Students:** 274 transfer students enrolled in 2016-2017. The university requires original transcripts from each institution even if the student is not planning on transferring credit to SLU.

30 of 120 credits required for the bachelor's degree must be completed at SLU. **International Students:** There are 530 international students enrolled. They must take the TOEFL with a minimum score of 550 on the paper-based TOEFL (PBT) or 80 on the Internet-based version (iBT). Students must also take the college's own test, and the IELTS.

ADMISSIONS: 63% of the 2017-2018 applicants were accepted. The SAT scores for the 2017-2018 freshman class were: Critical Reading-- 13% below 500, 31% between 500 and 599, 44% between 600 and 699, and 12% between 700 and 800. Math-- 7% below 500, 32% between 500 and 599, 45% between 600 and 699, and 16% between 700 and 800. The ACT scores were 13% between 18 and 23, 51% between 24 and 29, and 36% above 30. 65% of the current freshmen were in the top fifth of their class; 87% were in the top two fifths. **Admissions Contact:** Jean M. Gilman, Assistant Vice President, Office of Admissions. Email: *admission@slu.edu* Web: *www.slu.edu*

FINANCIAL AID: In 2017-2018, 95% of all full-time freshmen received some form of financial aid. 52% of all full-time freshmen received need-based aid. 25% of undergraduate students work part-time. The average financial indebtedness of the 2017 graduate was $34,361. SLU is a member of CSS. The FAFSA code is 002506. The priority date for freshman financial aid applications for fall entry is March 1. The deadline for filing freshman financial aid applications for fall entry is May 1.

SOUTHEAST MISSOURI STATE UNIVERSITY — E-3

www.semo.edu

Cape Girardeau, MO 63701 — **(573) 651-2539**

Fax: 573-651-5936	**Email:** admissions@semo.edu
Full-time: 3323 men, 4456 women	**Faculty:** 409; IIA, --$
Part-time: 1055 men, 1624 women	**Ph.D.s:** 75%
Graduate: 353 men, 691 women	**Student/Faculty:** 20 to 1
Year: semesters, summer session	**Tuition:** $7185 ($12,720)
Room & Board: $8963	**Freshman Class:** 4977 applied, 4208 accepted, 1803 enrolled
SAT: required **ACT:** 23	**CEEB CODE:** 6655
Application Deadline: July 1	**COMPETITIVE**

Southeast Missouri State University, founded in 1873, is a public institution offering undergraduate and graduate programs in arts and sciences, agriculture, business, education, health and human services, technology, and the school of visual and performing arts. There are 7 undergraduate schools and 1 graduate school. In addition to regional accreditation, SEMSU has baccalaureate program accreditation with AACSB, ABET, ACEJMC, CSWE, NASM, NRPA, ACEND, ACS, ASHA, ATMAE, AND, CAC, EAC, ETC, CIDA, CAA, CAATE, CACREP, CCNE, CEPR/PRSA, CHRIE, COSMA, CAEP, NAST, NAEYC, NCFR/CFLE, NIBS, and NKBA. The 400-acre campus is in a small town 120 miles south of St. Louis. Including any residence halls, there are 115 buildings.

STUDENT LIFE: 76% of undergraduates are from Missouri. Others are from 42 states, 52 foreign countries, and Canada. 9% are African American; 81% White; 5% Foreign; 2% Hispanic; 1% Asian American; 1% two or more races; 1% race unknown. **Female To Male Ratio:** 1.4:1. The average age of freshmen is 19; all undergraduates, 22. 25% do not continue beyond their first year; 52% remain to graduate. **Housing:** 3112 students can be accommodated in college housing, which includes dorms. In addition, there are special-interest houses, fraternity houses, sorority houses, an honors community, a living and learning community, and theme communities for education, science, transfer students, and health care. On-campus housing is guaranteed for the freshman year only, and is available on a first-come, first-served basis. 71% of students commute. All students may keep cars. Alcohol is not permitted.

FACULTY/CLASSROOMS: 43% of faculty are male; 57% are female. All teach undergraduates and all do research. Graduate students teach 5% of introductory courses. The average class size in an introductory lecture is 21; in a laboratory is 18; and in a regular course is 22.

PROGRAMS OF STUDY: SEMSU confers B.A., B.F.A., B.G.S., B.S., B.S.A.T., B.S.B.A., B.S.Ed., B.F.C.S.E., B.M.E., B.M., and B.S.N. degrees. Associate and master's degrees are also awarded. Bachelor's degrees are awarded in AGRICULTURE (agricultural business management, animal science, and horticulture), BIOLOGICAL SCIENCE (environmental biology, forensic science, and marine biology), BUSINESS (accounting, business administration and management, business communications, business economics, entrepreneurial studies, fashion merchandising, finance, hospitality management services, human resources/organizational management, international business management, management, marketing, and sports management), COMMUNICATIONS AND THE ARTS (advertising, art, communication studies, dance, English, German, historic preservation, information technology, instrumental performance, journalism, music, public relations, recreation administration, and theatre acting), COMPUTER AND PHYSICAL SCIENCE (actuarial science, chemistry, computer information systems, computer science, cyber intelligence/security studies, environmental chemistry, mathematics, and physics), EDUCATION (art education, athletic training, early childhood education, education of the exceptional child, elementary education, English education, foreign languages education, general studies, global studies, industrial arts education, mathematics education, middle school education, music education, physical education/exercise science, science education, and social studies education), ENGINEERING AND ENVIRONMENTAL DESIGN (emergency/disaster science, engineering physics, engineering technology, environmental science, interior design, mechanical design technology, and technological management), HEALTH PROFESSIONS (biology, biomedical science, health, health communication, health care administration, health science, medical laboratory science, and nursing), SOCIAL SCIENCE (criminal justice, economics, history, interdisciplinary studies, philosophy, political science/government, psychology, social science, and social work). Nursing, and general studies have the largest enrollments.

ACTIVITIES: 17% of men belong to 11 national fraternities; 18% of women belong to 8 national sororities. There are 174 groups on campus, including residence hall association, student activities council, art, band, cheerleading, choir, chorus, dance, debate, drama, drill team, environmental, ethnic, forensics, Fraternities and sororities, honors, international, jazz band, LGBT, literary magazine, marching band, musical theater, newspaper, opera, orchestra, pep band, photography, political, professional, radio and TV, religious, social, social service, student government, and symphony. Popular campus events include Family Weekend, Homecoming, Late Night Breakfast, Spring Fling, Ice Cream PigOut, and International Week. **Sports:** There are 5 intercollegiate sports for men and 8 for women, and 16 intramural sports for men and 16 for women. The Student Recreation Center houses an indoor track, a rock climbing wall, racquetball courts, basketball/volleyball/badminton/multi-purpose courts, free-weight room, a dumbbell room, a plyometrics/calisthenics room, cardio areas complete with treadmills/bikes/cross-trainers/steppers/rowers, fitness studios with aerial silks, group exercise bikes, and suspension training. The Student Aquatic Center houses a six lane 25-yd lap pool, a leisure pool, a volleyball court, basketball goal, and a bouldering wall. An outdoor intramural complex with artificial turf softball/soccer/multi-purpose fields, a large flag-football/cricket/multipurpose field, and tennis courts, outdoor sand volleyball courts, and indoor soccer/hockey facility. The athletics facilities include a stadium, field house, tennis, and softball. **Graduates:** From July 1, 2016 to June 30, 2017, 1642 bachelor's degrees were awarded. The most popular majors were general studies (10%), nursing (3%), and psychology (3%). In an average class, 2% graduate in 3 years or less, 30% graduate in 4 years or less, 44% graduate in 5 years or less, and 52% graduate in 6 years or less.

SERVICES: Counseling and information services are available, as is tutoring in most subjects, such a mathematics, chemistry, physics, biology, anatomy and physiology, political science, psychology and Spanish. There is also remedial math. **Library/Resources:** The library contains 424,364 volumes, 1.2 million microform items, 11,240 audio/video tapes/CDs/DVDs, and subscribes to 82,026 periodicals, including electronic. Computerized library services include interlibrary loans, database searching, Internet access, and Wi-Fi capability. Special learning facilities include an art gallery, natural history museum, radio station, center for regional history, school of visual and performing arts, center for innovation and entrepreneurship, agriculture research center, horticulture greenhouse, center for speech and hearing, Southeast Missouri State University Autism Center for Diagnosis and Treatment, Southeast Missouri Music Academy, University School for Young Children, River Campus Art Gallery, center for writing excellence, Academic Support Centers, Rosemary Berkel and Harry L. Crisp II Museum, Center for Scholarship in Teaching and Learning, CATAPULT Creative House (student incubator), The Faulkner Center, the Rust Center for Media, the Douglas C. Greene Center for Innovation and Entrepreneurship, and the Edvolution Center.**Physically Challenged Students:** All of the campus is accessible. Facilities include wheelchair ramps, elevators, special parking, specially equipped restrooms, special class scheduling, lowered drinking fountains, lowered telephones, and special housing. **Special:** Southeast offers a Cooperative Doctorate of Education in Educational Leadership with the University of Missouri and Cooperative Master of Science in Criminal Justice with Missouri Southern State University. Opportunities are provided for individually arranged internships and work-study, study abroad in 40 countries, a general studies degree, dual and student-designed majors (interdisciplinary studies), credit by exam, non-degree study, and pass/fail options. A 3-2 engineering degree is possible in conjunction with the University of Missouri at Rolla or at Columbia. There is cross registration with Three Rivers College to facilitate completion of an AA degree and transfer to a Southeast four-year degree program. There are pre-professional programs in architecture, chiropractic, dentistry, engineering, law, medicine, optometry, pharmacy, physical therapy, occupational therapy, and veterinary medicine. There are 28 national honor societies and a freshman honors program. **Visiting:** There are regularly scheduled orientations for prospective students, including academic advising and other university information. There are guides for informal visits. To schedule a visit, contact the Office of Admissions. **Campus Safety and Security:** Measures include 24-hour foot and vehicle patrol, an emergency notification system, self-defense education, and security escort services. There are shuttle buses, emergency telephones, lighted pathways/sidewalks, and controlled access to dorms/residences.

REQUIREMENTS: The SAT or ACT is required. Graduation from an accredited secondary school is required; the GED is accepted. Applicants should submit an academic record with 4 units in English, 2 units in social studies, 1 unit in history, 3 units in mathematics, 3 units in science (1 unit must be lab course), 1 unit in visual and performing arts, and 3 units of academic electives. A GPA of 2.0 is required. AP and CLEP credits are accepted. Students must complete a minimum of 120 credit hours (24 to 97 hours in the major). The core includes 51 credit hours in the University Studies program, as well as in interdisciplinary studies, English, and math. Minimum GPA of 2.0. Other graduation requirements varies by program. Students must also pass a writing exam and complete 4 career proficiency checks, at the freshman and senior level, including the Measure of Academic Proficiency and Progress (MAPP). **Procedure:** Freshmen are admitted in the fall, spring, and summer. Entrance exams should be taken in the spring of the junior year or fall of the senior year. There is a rolling admissions plan. Applications should be filed by July 1 for fall entry; November 1 for spring entry; and May 1 for summer entry. The fall 2017 application fee was $30. Applications are accepted on-line. **Transfer Students:** 586 transfer students enrolled in 2016-2017. Transcripts from the student's previous college must be submitted, listing at least 24 credits earned and a minimum GPA of 2.0. The ACT is required for those students who have fewer than 24 credit hours. 30 of 120 credits required for the bachelor's degree must be completed at SEMSU. **International Students:** There are 472 international students enrolled. They must take the TOEFL with a minimum score of 500 on the paper-based TOEFL (PBT) or 61 on the Internet-based version (iBT). They must also take the SAT or ACT, scoring 18.

ADMISSIONS: 85% of the 2017-2018 applicants were accepted. The ACT scores were 5% between 12 and 17, 55% between 18 and 23, 33% between 24 and 29, and 7% above 30. 34% of the current freshmen were in the top fifth of their class; 63% were in the top two fifths. 40 freshmen graduated first in their class. **Admissions Contact:** Lenell Hahn, Director of Admissions. Email: *admissions@semo.edu* Web: *www.semo.edu*

FINANCIAL AID: In 2017-2018, 93% of all full-time freshmen received some form of financial aid. 57% of all full-time freshmen received need-based aid. The average freshman award was $11,238. Need-based scholarships or need-based grants averaged $5,135 ($13,915 maximum); need-based self-help aid (loans and jobs) averaged $3,497 ($10,532 maximum); non-need-based athletic scholarships averaged $12,644 ($27,300 maximum); other non-need-based awards and non-need-based scholarships averaged $4,268 ($21,835 maximum); and $4,415 from other forms of aid. 19% of undergraduate students work part-time. The average financial indebtedness of the 2017 graduate was $26,721. The FAFSA code is 002501. The priority date for freshman financial aid applications for fall entry is March 1.

SOUTHWEST BAPTIST UNIVERSITY *(The complete profile is made available exclusively on our website, www.barronspac.com)*

STEPHENS COLLEGE C-2

www.stephens.edu

Columbia, MO 65215 | **(573) 876-2391** | **(800) 876-7207**

Fax: (573)876-7237 | **Email: apply@stephens.edu**

Full-time: 1 men, 556 women	**Faculty:** n/av
Part-time: 6 men, 116 women	**Ph.D.s:** 83%
Graduate: 24 men, 172 women	**Student/Faculty:** n/av
Year: semesters, summer session	**Tuition:** $28,510
Room & Board: $9532	**Freshman Class:** 748 applied, 725 accepted, 259 enrolled
SAT or ACT: required	**CEEB CODE:** 6683
Application Deadline: August 1	**COMPETITIVE**

Stephens College, founded in 1833, is a private college primarily for women, offering undergraduate programs in the arts and sciences, business, education, and fine arts. There are 5 undergraduate schools and 3 graduate schools. The 59-acre campus is in an urban area 120 miles west of St. Louis. Including any residence halls, there are 35 buildings.

STUDENT LIFE: 64% of undergraduates are from Missouri. Others are from 41 states, and 2 foreign countries. 93% are from public schools. 73% are White; 13% African American; 5% two or more races; 4% Hispanic; 3% race unknown; 2% Asian American; 1% American Indian/ Alaska Native; 1% Foreign. **Female To Male Ratio:** 27.2:1. The average age of freshmen is 18; all undergraduates, 24. 33% do not continue beyond their first year; 45% remain to graduate. **Housing:** 724 students can be accommodated in college housing, which includes dorms and on-campus apartments. In addition, there are honors houses, special interest houses for intercultural scholars and fine arts majors, and houses with designated academic floors, nonsmoking floors and pet floors. On-campus housing is guaranteed for all 4 years. 72% of students live on campus. All students may keep cars.

FACULTY/CLASSROOMS: 40% of faculty are male; 60% are female. 92% teach undergraduates and do research. No introductory courses are taught by graduate students. The average class size in an introductory lecture is 30; in a laboratory is 12; and in a regular course is 20.

PROGRAMS OF STUDY: SC confers B.A., B.S., and B.F.A. degrees. Master's degrees are also awarded. Bachelor's degrees are awarded in AGRICULTURE (equine science), BIOLOGICAL SCIENCE (biology/ biological science), BUSINESS (accounting, business administration and management, and fashion merchandising), COMMUNICATIONS AND THE ARTS (creative writing, dance, dramatic arts, English, film arts, graphic design, public relations, and theater design), EDUCATION (early childhood education and elementary education), ENGINEERING AND ENVIRONMENTAL DESIGN (interior design), SOCIAL SCIENCE (fashion design and technology and liberal arts/general studies). Education, and biology are the strongest academically. Performing arts, fashion, and biology have the largest enrollments.

ACTIVITIES: There are no fraternities; 8% of women belong to 2 national sororities. There are 38 groups on campus, including art, choir, chorale, chorus, dance, drama, ethnic, honors, international, LGBT, literary magazine, musical theater, newspaper, photography, political, professional, radio and TV, religious, social, social service, student government, and yearbook. Popular campus events include Opening Convocation, Honors Convocation, and Performing Arts Events. **Sports:** There are 4 intercollegiate sports for women. Facilities include a gym and tennis courts. **Graduates:** From July 1, 2016 to June 30, 2017, 164 bachelor's degrees were awarded. The most popular majors were health information administration (11%), fashion - marketing and management (10%), and counseling (7%). In an average class, 71% graduate in 3 years or less, 96% graduate in 4 years or less, 99% graduate in 5 years or less, and 100% graduate in 6 years or less. Of the 2016 graduating class, 2% were enrolled in graduate school within 6 months of graduation.

SERVICES: Counseling and information services are available, as is tutoring in most subjects, such as English and courses with written expectations, and remedial writing. **Library/Resources:** The library contains 143,229 volumes, 10,792 microform items, and 3,356 audio/video tapes/CDs/DVDs, and subscribes to 45,699 periodicals including electronic. Computerized library services include interlibrary loans, database searching, and Internet access. Special learning facilities include an art gallery, radio station, and TV station. **Physically Challenged Students:** 80% of the campus is accessible. Facilities include wheelchair ramps, elevators, special parking, specially equipped restrooms, special class scheduling, lowered drinking fountains, and special housing. **Special:** Students may study abroad in England, Italy, Mexico, France, Ecuador, South Korea, and Spain. Stephens also offers cross-registration with the Mid-Missouri Association of Colleges and Universities, and offers many internships, a Washington semester, dual and student-designed majors, a 3-2 occupational therapy degree program with Washington University, accelerated degree programs in dance and theater arts, and pass/fail options for electives. There are 8 national honor societies and a freshman honors program. **Visiting:** There are regularly scheduled orientations for prospective students, consisting of attendance at classes, a campus tour, an appointment with instructors, and an interview. There are guides for informal visits, visitors may sit in on classes, and stay overnight. To schedule a visit, contact the Campus Visit Coordinator at apply@stephens.edu. **Campus Safety and Security:** Measures include 24-hour foot and vehicle patrol, emergency notification system, self-defense education, and security escort services. There are emergency telephones, lighted pathways/sidewalks, and controlled access to dorms/residences.

REQUIREMENTS: The SAT or ACT is required. Applicants must be graduates of accredited secondary schools or have earned a GED. An essay is also required and an interview is recommended. AP and CLEP credits are accepted. Important factors in the admissions decision are advanced placement or honors courses, leadership record, and recommendations by school officials. All students must complete 6 hours of English and a distribution of 9 courses in lower-division work, including 6 hours of social sciences and 3 hours each of math, science, literary studies, history, cultural studies, and ethics. The bachelor's degree requires completion of at least 120 semester hours, including 30 to 72 in a major field, with a minimum GPA of 2.0. **Procedure:** Freshmen are admitted in the fall and spring. There are deferred admissions and rolling admissions plans. Applications should be filed by August 1 for fall entry. The fall 2017 application fee was $50. Applications are accepted online. **Transfer Students:** 68 transfer students enrolled in 2016-2017. Applicants must submit official transcripts from all college work attempted or completed as well as a recommendation from an academic college instructor. Transfers must submit an official high school transcript. 36 of 120 credits required for the bachelor's degree must be completed at SC. **International Students:** There are 2 international students enrolled. They must take the TOEFL with a minimum score of 79 on the Internet-based version (iBT).

ADMISSIONS: 97% of the 2017-2018 applicants were accepted. The ACT scores were 29% below 12, 14% between 18 and 23, and 43% between 24 and 29. 27% of the current freshmen were in the top fifth of their class; 60% were in the top two fifths. **Admissions Contact:** Tiffany Goalder, Director of Undergraduate Admissions. Email: *tgoalder@stephens.edu* Web: *www.stephens.edu*

FINANCIAL AID: In 2017-2018, 99% of all full-time freshmen received some form of financial aid. 82% of all full-time freshmen received need-based aid. The average freshman award was $7,025. Need-based scholarships or need-based grants averaged $9,878; need-based self-help aid (loans and jobs) averaged $3,574; non-need-based athletic scholarships averaged $7,656; and other non-need-based awards and non-need-based scholarships averaged $15,398. 10% of undergraduate students work part-time. The average financial indebtedness of the 2017 graduate was $37,467. The FAFSA code is 002512. The priority date for freshman financial aid applications for fall entry is March 1.

TRUMAN STATE UNIVERSITY C-1

www.truman.edu

Kirksville, MO 63501 (660) 785-4114

Fax: (660) 785-7456 Email: admissions@truman.edu

Full-time: 2109 men, 3025 women	**Faculty:** 324; IIA, --$
Part-time: 330 men, 434 women	**Ph.D.s:** 84%
Graduate: 92 men, 282 women	**Student/Faculty:** 16 to 1
Year: semesters, summer session	**Tuition:** $7656 ($14,440)
Room & Board: $8630	**Freshman Class:** 5263 applied, 3552 accepted, 1328 enrolled
SAT EBR-W/M: 680/680 **ACT:** required	**CEEB CODE:** 6483
Application Deadline: March 1	**MOST COMPETITIVE**

Truman State University, founded in 1867, offers 37 undergraduate areas of study and 7 graduate degrees within the liberal arts and sciences and select pre-professional programs. There are 5 undergraduate schools and 5 graduate schools. In addition to regional accreditation, TSU has baccalaureate program accreditation with AACSB, NASM, CAEP, ACS, CCNE, and CAATE ASHA. The 140-acre campus is in a small town in the northeast corner of Missouri. 170 miles from Kansas City, 200 miles from St. Louis, and 90 miles north of Columbia, MO. Including any residence halls, there are 32 buildings.

STUDENT LIFE: 84% of undergraduates are from Missouri. Others are from 42 states, 45 foreign countries, and Canada. 82% are from public schools. 78% are White; 7% Foreign; 4% African American; 3% Asian American; 3% Hispanic; 3% two or more races; 1% race unknown. 41% claim no religious affiliation; 35% Protestant; 20% Catholic. **Female To Male Ratio:** 1.5:1. The average age of freshmen is 18; all undergraduates, 20. 14% do not continue beyond their first year; 75% remain to graduate. **Housing:** 2700 students can be accommodated in college housing, which includes married student dorms and on-campus apartments. In addition, there are language/international houses and special-interest houses. On-campus housing is guaranteed for the freshman year only, and is available on a first-come, first-served basis, and is available on a lottery system for upperclassmen. 58% of students commute. All students may keep cars. Alcohol is not permitted.

FACULTY/CLASSROOMS: 54% of faculty are male; 46% are female. All teach undergraduates. Graduate students teach 2% of introductory courses. The average class size in an introductory lecture is 21; in a laboratory is 22; and in a regular course is 23.

PROGRAMS OF STUDY: TSU confers B.A., B.S., B.F.A., B.M., and B.S.N. degrees. Master's degrees are also awarded. Bachelor's degrees are awarded in AGRICULTURE (agricultural business management, agriculture, agronomy, animal science, equine science, and horticulture), BIOLOGICAL SCIENCE (biology/biological science), BUSINESS (accounting, business administration and management, and international business management), COMMUNICATIONS AND THE ARTS (art, classics, communications, creative writing, dramatic arts, English, fine arts, French, German, journalism, linguistics, music, music performance, romance languages and literature, Spanish, studio art, and visual design), COMPUTER AND PHYSICAL SCIENCE (chemistry, computer science, mathematics, and physics), EDUCATION (physical education), ENGINEERING AND ENVIRONMENTAL DESIGN (preengineering), HEALTH PROFESSIONS (clinical science, exercise science, health science, nursing, physical therapy, predentistry, premedicine, prepharmacy, preveterinary science, public health, and speech pathology/audiology), SOCIAL SCIENCE (anthropology, criminal justice, economics, history, interdisciplinary studies, philosophy, physical fitness/movement, political science/government, prelaw, psychology, religion, and sociology). Chemistry, biology, and accounting are the strongest academically. Business administration, biology, and English have the largest enrollments.

ACTIVITIES: 20% of men belong to 14 national fraternities; 23% of women belong to 7 national sororities. There are 248 groups on campus, including art, band, cheerleading, chess, choir, chorale, chorus, computers, dance, debate, drama, drill team, environmental, ethnic, film, forensics, honors, international, jazz band, LGBT, literary magazine, marching band, musical theater, newspaper, opera, orchestra, pep band, political, professional, radio and TV, religious, social, social service, student government, and symphony. Popular campus events include Final Blowout, Kohlenberg Lyceum Series, and the Big Event. **Sports:** There are 10 intercollegiate sports for men and 10 for women, and 31 intramural sports for men and 31 for women. Facilities include a football stadium, a soccer field, tennis courts, softball and baseball diamond, an arena for basketball, an Olympic-size pool, weight training rooms, indoor and outdoor track facilities, and a student recreation center. **Graduates:** From July 1, 2016 to June 30, 2017, 1180 bachelor's degrees were awarded. The most popular majors were business administration (10%), biology (9%), and psychology (9%). In an average class, 3% graduate in 3 years or less, 59% graduate in 4 years or less, 73% graduate in 5 years or less, and 75% graduate in 6 years or less. Of the 2016 graduating class, 35% were enrolled in graduate school within 6 months of graduation, and 49% were employed.

SERVICES: Counseling and information services are available, as is tutoring in most subjects. There are services for the hearing impaired, a braille scanner and printer, and a reader service. Disability services provides reasonable accommodations to qualified students which include, classroom accommodations such as test or note taking services, housing including placement and bathroom configurations. Client accommodations are based on individualized, qualified guidelines per ADA standards and are determined through a collaborative approach between the student and the Disability Services Coordinator. **Library/Resources:** The library contains 498,227 volumes, 1.5 million microform items, 46,815 audio/video tapes/CDs/DVDs, and subscribes to 3,609 periodicals, including electronic. Computerized library services include interlibrary loans, database searching, Internet access, and Wi-Fi capability. Special learning facilities include an art gallery, planetarium, radio station, nursing simulation lab, an observatory, greenhouse chamber, speech and hearing clinic, a broadcasting studio, language learning center, farm, herpetology lab, writing center, convergent media center, midi music studio, and various labs for science programs. **Physically Challenged Students:** 99% of the campus is accessible. Facilities include wheelchair ramps, elevators, special parking, specially equipped restrooms, special class scheduling, lowered drinking fountains, special housing, and the swimming pool is equipped with a lift to assist physically disabled swimmers. **Special:** Study abroad is offered in over 50 countries through Truman's own programs and those of the College Consortium for International Studies, the Council on International Educational Exchange, and the International Student Exchange Program. The university requires internships in education and health and exercise science. Voluntary legislative internships are offered to all students at the state capitol, and internships through the Washington Center. There is a dual-degree program with Physics and Engineering where Truman provides the Physics and the student transfers to an other institution for Engineering. Upon completion of that work, Truman will award a Physics degree along with earned Engineering degree from the other school. Work-study programs, B.A.-B.S. degrees, dual majors, student-designed interdisciplinary majors, credit for military experience, pass/fail options for internships, and non-degree study are available. There are 21 national honor societies, Phi Beta Kappa, a freshman honors program, and 19 departmental honors programs. **Visiting:** There are regularly scheduled orientations for prospective students, campus visits include a personalized meeting with an admission counselor, a student-led campus tour, and appointments with a faculty member in the student's major or in any areas of special interest upon request. There are guides for informal visits; visitors may sit in on classes and stay overnight. To schedule a visit, contact Elizabeth Gregory at (660) 785-4114. **Campus Safety and Security:** Measures include 24-hour foot and vehicle patrol, emergency notification system, self-defense education, and security escort services. There are emergency telephones, lighted pathways/sidewalks, and controlled access to dorms/residences.

REQUIREMENTS: Truman must have either the SAT or ACT standardized test score on file for admission consideration. Applicants should have completed 4 units of English, 4 units of math are strongly recommended, 3 each of science and social studies, 2 of foreign language, and 1 of art or music. An essay is required and list of activities is strongly recommended. AP and CLEP credits are accepted. Important factors in the admissions decision are advanced placement or honors courses, leadership record, and extracurricular activities record. All students must complete 63 hours of course work in the liberal arts, 16 of which must be in written and oral communication, math and statistics, computer literacy, and personal well-being, and 23 of which must be in history, science, social science, philosophy/religion, math, and aesthetics. Elementary proficiency in a foreign language is required of all majors. The B.A., B.F.A., and B.M. degree require intermediate proficiency in 1 foreign language. The B.S. and B.S.N. require additional coursework in science, math, statistics, computer science, social sciences, or logic. Skills such as writing, quantitative analysis, problem solving, and critical thinking are reinforced throughout the curriculum, and all seniors end their studies with a capstone, or culminating experience, in their majors. Students must also complete a nationally normed exam in their subject areas as part of Truman's assessment program. **Procedure:** Freshmen are admitted in the fall, spring, and summer. Entrance exams should be taken spring of junior year, summer, or fall of senior year. There are deferred admissions and rolling admissions plans. Applications should be filed by March 1 for fall entry; November 15 for spring entry; and March 1 for summer entry. Notification is sent on a rolling basis. Applications are accepted online. **Transfer Students:** 208 transfer students enrolled in 2016-2017. Transfer applicants are considered for admission through a competitive individualized review process that emphasizes preparedness for study based upon a variety of criteria. Cumulative GPA in transferable college credit, strength of college curriculum, and the admission essay are considered for all transfer admission candidates. Cumulative high school record and ACT/SAT scores will also be reviewed for applicants who have completed fewer than 24 hours of transferable post high school college credit at the time of application. 45 of 120 credits required for the bachelor's degree must be completed at TSU. **International Students:** There are 403 international students enrolled. They must take the TOEFL with a minimum score of 550 on the paper-based TOEFL (PBT) or 79 on the Internet-based version (iBT). Student must take the Comprehensive English Language Test. They must also take the SAT or ACT.

ADMISSIONS: 67% of the 2017-2018 applicants were accepted. The SAT scores for the 2017-2018 freshman class were: Math-- 37% between 500 and 599, 21% between 600 and 699, and 42% between 700 and 800. Evidence-Based Reading/Writing-- 21% between 500 and 599, 32% between 600 and 699, and 47% between 700 and 800. The ACT scores were 19% between 18 and 23, 52% between 24 and 29, and 28% above 30. 76% of the current freshmen were in the top fifth of their class; 95% were in the top two fifths. 218 freshmen graduated first in their class. **Admissions Contact:** Melody Chambers, Director of Admission. Email: *admissions@truman.edu* Web: *www.truman.edu*

FINANCIAL AID: In 2017-2018, 99% of all full-time freshmen received some form of financial aid. 44% of all full-time freshmen received need-based aid. The average freshman award was $12,697. Need-based scholarships or need-based grants averaged $5,155 ($17,965 maximum); need-based self-help aid (loans and jobs) averaged $3,967 ($9,050 maximum); non-need-based athletic scholarships averaged $4,690 ($19,611 maximum); and other non-need-based awards and non-need-based scholarships averaged $9,180 ($27,418 maximum). 33% of undergraduate students work part-time. The average financial indebtedness of the 2017 graduate was $24,938. The FAFSA code is 002495. The priority date for freshman financial aid applications for fall entry is February 15.

UNIVERSITY OF CENTRAL MISSOURI B-2

www.ucmo.edu

Warrensburg, MO 64093 **(660) 543-4290**

Fax: (660) 543-8517 **Email: admit@ucmo.edu**

Full-time: 3764 men, 4428 women	**Faculty:** 452; IIA, --$
Part-time: 680 men, 867 women	**Ph.D.s:** 67%
Graduate: 810 men, 1399 women	**Student/Faculty:** 17 to 1
Year: semesters, summer session	**Tuition:** $8610 ($13,435)
Room & Board: $10,372	**Freshman Class:** n/av
ACT: required	**CEEB CODE:** 6090
Application Deadline: August 19	**COMPETITIVE**

University of Central Missouri, founded in 1871, is a public liberal arts institution offering a comprehensive range of degree programs. There are 4 undergraduate schools and 1 graduate school. In addition to regional accreditation, UCM has baccalaureate program accreditation with AACSB, ABET, ACCE, ADA, ASLA, CSWE, CAEP, NASAD, NASM, NLN, ACS, ADDA, ASLHA, CAA, CADE, CCNE, NAIT, NASPE, and and SOA. The 1561-acre campus is in a small town 50 miles southeast of Kansas City. Including any residence halls, there are 107 buildings.

STUDENT LIFE: 89% of undergraduates are from Missouri. Others are from 42 states, 59 foreign countries, and Canada. 92% are from public schools. 9% are African American; 85% White; 6% Foreign; 3% Hispanic; 1% Asian American. 54% are Protestant; 20% Catholic; 12% claim no religious affiliation. **Female To Male Ratio:** 1.3:1. The average age of freshmen is 19; all undergraduates, 22. 32% do not continue beyond their first year; 51% remain to graduate. **Housing:** 3540 students can be accommodated in college housing, which includes married student dorms, on-campus apartments, and off-campus apartments. In addition, there are honors houses, special-interest houses, fraternity houses, sorority houses, and quiet dorms. On-campus housing is guaranteed for the freshman year only, and is available on a first-come, first-served basis. 72% of students commute. All students may keep cars.

FACULTY/CLASSROOMS: 54% of faculty are male; 46% are female. No introductory courses are taught by graduate students. The average class size in an introductory lecture is 30 and in a regular course is 23.

PROGRAMS OF STUDY: UCM confers B.A., B.S., B.F.A., B.M., B.M.E., B.S.B.A., B.S.Ed. and B.S.W. degrees. Associate and master's degrees are also awarded. Bachelor's degrees are awarded in AGRICULTURE (agricultural business management and conservation and regulation), BIOLOGICAL SCIENCE (biology/biological science), BUSINESS (accounting, business administration and management, hotel/motel and restaurant management, human resources, management science, marketing/retailing/merchandising, organizational behavior, recreation and leisure services, and tourism), COMMUNICATIONS AND THE ARTS (broadcasting, communications, English, French, German, journalism, music, photography, public relations, Spanish, speech/debate/rhetoric, studio art, and theater design), COMPUTER AND PHYSICAL SCIENCE (actuarial science, chemistry, computer science, earth science, geology, information sciences and systems, mathematics, and physics), EDUCATION (agricultural education, art education, business education, early childhood education, elementary education, English education, foreign languages education, industrial arts education, mathematics education, middle school education, music education, physical education, science education, secondary education, social studies education, and special education), ENGINEERING AND ENVIRONMENTAL DESIGN (agricultural engineering technology, automotive technology, aviation computer technology, commercial art, construction management, drafting and design technology, electrical/electronics engineering, electrical/electronics engineering technology, engineering, engineering technology, graphic arts technology, industrial engineering technology, interior design, manufacturing technology, and occupational safety and health), HEALTH PROFESSIONS (medical laboratory technology, nursing, predentistry, premedicine, preveterinary science, and speech pathology/audiology), SOCIAL SCIENCE (criminal justice, dietetics, economics, geography, history, political science/government, prelaw, psychology, safety management, social work, sociology, and textiles and clothing). School of technology, elementary education and early childhood, and criminal justice have the largest enrollments.

ACTIVITIES: 6% of men belong to 12 national fraternities; 6% of women belong to 11 national sororities. There are 250 groups on campus, including art, band, cheerleading, chess, choir, chorale, chorus, computers, dance, debate, drama, drill team, ethnic, film, forensics, honors, international, jazz band, LGBT, literary magazine, marching band, musical theater, newspaper, opera, orchestra, pep band, photography, political, professional, radio and TV, religious, social, social service, student government, and symphony. Popular campus events include Performing Arts Series, Technology Fair, and Repertory Theater. **Sports:** There are 7 intercollegiate sports for men and 7 for women, and 32 intramural sports for men and 32 for women. Facilities include a stadium, gyms, baseball, softball, women's soccer, and practice fields, bowling, tennis, and a multipurpose building that contains a swimming pool, weight rooms, courts for basketball, racquetball, and volleyball. The Student Recreation and Wellness Center includes fitness rooms for aerobics, spinning, kickboxing, a free weight room, fitness areas with equipment, a recreation room, inside walking track, and outside climbing wall. **Graduates:** From July 1, 2016 to June 30, 2017, 1805 bachelor's degrees were awarded. The most popular majors were technology (8%), criminal justice (7%), and elementary education and early childhood (6%). In an average class, 28% graduate in 4 years or less, 45% graduate in 5 years or less, and 49% graduate in 6 years or less. Of the 2016 graduating class, 18% were enrolled in graduate school within 6 months of graduation, and 91% were employed.

SERVICES: Counseling and information services are available, as is tutoring in some subjects. There is a fee for tutoring in math, chemistry, physics, biology, accounting, economics, and business. There is a reader service for the blind, and remedial math. The writing and learning labs are available for all students. Tutoring is available through TRIO Student Support Services. **Library/Resources:** The library contains 2.2 million volumes, 815,787 microform items, 20,544 audio/video tapes/CDs/DVDs, and subscribes to 783 periodicals, including electronic. Computerized library services include interlibrary loans, database searching, Internet access, and Wi-Fi capability. Special learning facilities include an art gallery, natural history museum, planetarium, radio station, TV station, an instructional airport, a 200-acre farm, a driving/safety range, a speech and hearing clinic, a child development lab, and an English Language Center. **Physically Challenged Students:** 95% of the campus is accessible. Facilities include wheelchair ramps, elevators, special parking, specially equipped restrooms, special class scheduling, lowered drinking fountains, lowered telephones, and special housing. **Special:** Central offers cross-registration with the Midwest Student Exchange program, credit and non-credit internships, study abroad in more than 15 countries, a B.A. - B.S. degree, dual and student-designed majors, credit for military service, pass/fail options, nondegree study, and a 3-2 engineering degree with the University of Missouri at Columbia and at Rolla and with the University of Indiana. There are 25 national honor societies, a freshman honors program, and 7 departmental honors programs. **Visiting:** There are regularly scheduled orientations for prospective students, including orientation sessions on housing, general education requirements, and enrollment for fall classes. There are guides for informal visits, visitors may sit in on classes, and stay overnight. To schedule a visit, contact the Office of Admissions. **Campus Safety and Security:** Measures include 24-hour foot and vehicle patrol, emergency notification system, self-defense education, and security escort services. There are emergency telephones, lighted pathways/sidewalks, a bike patrol, and canine patrol.

REQUIREMENTS: The ACT is required. Applicants must have completed 16 academic credits, including 4 credits in English with a writing emphasis, 3 credits each in math (algebra and beyond) and social science, 2 credits in natural sciences, and 1 credit in fine or performing arts, as well as 3 credits in academic electives. A foreign language is recommended. The GED is accepted. A GPA of 2.0 is required. AP and CLEP credits are accepted. To graduate, students must complete a minimum of 120 hours, including 35 to 64 in the major, and have a minimum GPA of 2.0; several majors require a higher cumulative GPA. General education requirements include a total of 39 to 45 hours in humanities, social sciences, multicultural studies, technology, English and oral communications, math, science, and individual development. A comprehensive exam may be part of the exit assessment in selected majors. **Procedure:** Freshmen are admitted to all sessions. Entrance exams should be taken in the junior year of high school. There is a rolling admissions plan. Applications should be filed by August 19 for fall entry. The fall 2017 application fee was $30. Notification is sent on a rolling basis. Applications are accepted on-line. **Transfer Students:** 1006 transfer students enrolled in 2016-2017. Applicants must have a minimum GPA of 2.0, as indicated by an official college transcript. 30 of 120 credits required for the bachelor's degree must be completed at UCM. **International Students:** There are 540 international students enrolled. They must take the TOEFL with a minimum score of 500 on the paper-based TOEFL (PBT). They must also take the ACT.

ADMISSIONS: 24% of the current freshmen were in the top fifth of their class; 55% were in the top two fifths. 20 freshmen graduated first in their class. **Admissions Contact:** Dr. Richard Sluder, Assistant Provost of Enrollment Management. Email: *admit@ucmo.edu* Web: *www.ucmo.edu*

FINANCIAL AID: In 2017-2018, 94% of all full-time freshmen received some form of financial aid. 66% of all full-time freshmen received need-based aid. The average freshman award was $9,825. 11% of undergraduate students work part-time. The average financial indebtedness of the 2017 graduate was $23,766. UCM is a member of CSS. The FAFSA code is 002454. The priority date for freshman financial aid applications for fall entry is April 1.

UNIVERSITY OF MISSOURI/ROLLA
(See Missouri University of Science and Technology)

UNIVERSITY OF MISSOURI-COLUMBIA C-2
www.missouri.edu

Columbia, MO 65211	(573) 882-7786
Fax: (573) 882-7887	Email: MU4U@missouri.edu
Full-time: 10,634 men, 11,563 women	**Faculty:** 1686; I, -$
Part-time: 817 men, 803 women	**Ph.D.s:** 91%
Graduate: 2938 men, 4115 women	**Student/Faculty:** 19 to 1
Year: semesters, summer session	**Tuition:** $9787 ($26,506)
Room & Board: $10,676	**Freshman Class:** n/av
ACT: recommended	**CEEB CODE:** 6875
Application Deadline: May 1	**VERY COMPETITIVE**

University of Missouri-Columbia, founded in 1839, offers a comprehensive array of undergraduate and graduate programs, as well as professional training in law, medicine, and veterinary medicine. There are 16 undergraduate schools and 18 graduate schools. In addition to regional accreditation, UM-Columbia has baccalaureate program accreditation with AACSB, ABET, ACEJMC, ADA, APTA, CAHEA, CSWE, FIDER, NASM, CAEP, NRPA, SAF, ACOTE, CAAHEP, and CADE. The 1262-acre campus is in a suburban area 120 miles west of St. Louis and 120 miles east of Kansas City. Including any residence halls, there are 350 buildings.

STUDENT LIFE: 72% of undergraduates are from Missouri. Others are from 50 states, 103 foreign countries, and Canada. 76% are White; 7% African American; 7% Foreign; 4% Hispanic; 3% two or more races; 2% Asian American; 1% race unknown. **Female To Male Ratio:** 1.1:1. The average age of freshmen is 18; all undergraduates, 20. 13% do not continue beyond their first year; 68% remain to graduate. **Housing:** 5348 students can be accommodated in college housing, which includes married student dorms and off-campus apartments. In addition, there are honors houses, language/international houses, special-interest houses, fraternity houses, sorority houses, quiet houses, graduate/professional houses, and learning living communities. 80% of students commute. All students may keep cars. Alcohol is not permitted.

FACULTY/CLASSROOMS: 60% of faculty are male; 40% are female. No introductory courses are taught by graduate students.

PROGRAMS OF STUDY: UM-Columbia confers B.A., B.S., B.E.S., B.F.A., B.G.S., B.H.S., B.J., B.M., B.S.Acc., B.S.B.A., B.S.B.E., B.S.ChE., B.S.CiE., B.O.S., B.S.E.E., B.S.Ed., B.S.F., B.S.F.W., B.S.H.E.S., B.S.I.E., B.S.M.E., B.S.N., and B.S.W. degrees. Master's and doctoral degrees are also awarded. Bachelor's degrees are awarded in AGRICULTURE (agricultural business management, agricultural economics, agriculture, animal science, fishing and fisheries, forestry and related sciences, plant science, and soil science), BIOLOGICAL SCIENCE (biochemistry, biology/biological science, microbiology, and nutrition), BUSINESS (accounting, banking and finance, business administration and management, business economics, hotel/motel and restaurant management, marketing/retailing/merchandising, real estate, and tourism), COMMUNICATIONS AND THE ARTS (advertising, art, art history and appreciation, broadcasting, classics, communications, creative writing, design, dramatic arts, English, English literature, French, German, journalism, linguistics, music, Russian, and Spanish), COMPUTER AND PHYSICAL SCIENCE (atmospheric sciences and meteorology, chemistry, computer science, geology, mathematics, physics, and statistics), EDUCATION (art education, early childhood education, education, education administration, elementary education, English education, mathematics education, middle school education, music education, science education, secondary education, and social studies education), ENGINEERING AND ENVIRONMENTAL DESIGN (biomedical engineering, chemical engineering, civil engineering, computer engineering, electrical/electronics engineering, engineering, industrial engineering, and mechanical engineering), HEALTH PROFESSIONS (nursing, occupational therapy, physical therapy, public health, radiological science, respiratory therapy, and veterinary science), SOCIAL SCIENCE (anthropology, archeology, child care/child and family studies, counseling/psychology, early childhood studies, economics, family/consumer resource management, food science, geography, history, human development, international studies, liberal arts/general studies, parks and recreation management, philosophy, political science/government, psychology, public administration, public affairs, religion, rural sociology, social science, social work, sociology, and textiles and clothing). Biological sciences, accounting, and journalism are the strongest academically. Health sciences, business, and journalism have the largest enrollments.

ACTIVITIES: 23% of men belong to 32 national fraternities; 33% of women belong to 18 national sororities. There are 600 groups on campus, including art, band, cheerleading, chess, choir, chorale, chorus, computers, dance, debate, drama, drill team, drum and bugle corps, environmental, ethnic, film, honors, international, jazz band, LGBT, literary magazine, marching band, musical theater, newspaper, orchestra, pep band, photography, political, professional, radio and TV, religious, social, social service, student government, symphony, and yearbook. Popular campus events include arts/music/cultural events, academic weeks, meet Mizzou day, Homecoming, and SEC athletics. **Sports:** There are 8 intercollegiate sports for men and 10 for women, and 35 intramural sports for men and 37 for women. Facilities include recreation complex with a 50-meter competition pool and diving well, high-tech fitness club, heavy-lifting gym, climbing and bouldering wall, multicourts, racquetball courts, and indoor track. **Graduates:** From July 1, 2016 to June 30, 2017, 6331 bachelor's degrees were awarded. The most popular majors were business (17%), health professions and related sciences (15%), and journalism and communication (11%). In an average class, 48% graduate in 4 years or less, 67% graduate in 5 years or less, and 68% graduate in 6 years or less.

SERVICES: Counseling and information services are available, as is tutoring in some subjects. There is a reader service for the blind. **Library/Resources:** The library contains 2.7 million volumes, 8.1 million microform items, and 35,711 audio/video tapes/CDs/DVDs. Computerized library services include interlibrary loans, database searching, Internet access, and Wi-Fi capability. Special learning facilities include an art gallery, natural history museum, radio station, TV station, astronomy observatory, freedom of information center, herbarium, State Historical Society of Missouri, Western Historical Manuscripts, anthropology, fishery, wildlife collections, Life Sciences Center, research reactor, and Mizzou botanical garden. **Physically Challenged Students:** All of the campus is accessible. Facilities include wheelchair ramps, elevators, special parking, specially equipped restrooms, special class scheduling, lowered drinking fountains, lowered telephones, and special housing. **Special:** Available academic programs include co-op programs and cross-registration with other schools, internships, study abroad, a Washington semester, and work-study programs. Special degrees or studies include an accelerated degree, dual majors, a general studies degree, and student-designed majors. For highly motivated students, there is an honors college and the possibility of early admission to the schools of law and medicine. There are 25 national honor societies, Phi Beta Kappa, a freshman honors program, and 34 departmental honors programs. **Visiting:** There are regularly scheduled orientations for prospective students, consisting of a campus tour, a visit with an admissions representative, and a visit with an academic representative on request. There are guides for informal visits and visitors may sit in on classes. To schedule a visit, contact the Admissions Office. **Campus Safety and Security:** Measures include 24-hour foot and vehicle patrol, emergency notification system, self-defense education, and security escort services. There are shuttle buses, emergency telephones, lighted pathways/sidewalks, and 24-hour bicycle patrol.

REQUIREMENTS: The ACT is recommended. Students may gain probationary admission with sufficient GED scores. The usual requirements are completion of 17 Carnegie units, including 4 each in English and math, 3 each in social studies and science, 2 in a foreign language, and 1 in fine arts. Admission is determined by these units and a combination of class rank and ACT score. AP and CLEP credits are accepted. Important factors in the admissions decision are advanced placement or honors courses and evidence of special talent. To graduate, students must maintain a minimum 2.0 GPA and complete at least 120 credits, of which at least 30 must be in their major, although credit requirements can vary by degree program. All students must take English, plus 2 additional writing-intensive courses, demonstrate competency in college algebra, take 1 additional course in development math and reasoning skills, and complete a course in American history or government. Students must complete 9 hours in social and behavioral sciences, 9 in physical and biological sciences (including 1 lab course), and 9 in humanities and fine arts. A capstone experience is also required. **Procedure:** Freshmen are admitted to all sessions. Entrance exams should be taken late in the junior year or in the senior year. There are deferred admissions and rolling admissions plans. Applications should be filed by May 1 for fall entry. The fall 2017 application fee was $55. Notification is sent on a rolling basis. Applications are accepted on-line. **Transfer Students:** 994 transfer students enrolled in 2016-2017. Transfer students must present 24 hours of completed college-level course work with a minimum 2.5 GPA. Students must also complete college algebra or equivalent as well as freshman English or equivalent with a C- or better. **International Students:** There are 862 international students enrolled. They must take the TOEFL with a minimum score of 500 on the paper-based TOEFL (PBT) or 61 on the Internet-based version (iBT).

ADMISSIONS: 78% of the 2017-2018 applicants were accepted. The ACT scores were 27% between 18 and 23, 52% between 24 and 29, and 19% above 30. **Admissions Contact:** Charles May, Director of Admissions. Email: *MU4U@missouri.edu* Web: *www.missouri.edu*

FINANCIAL AID: In 2017-2018, 51% of all full-time freshmen received some form of financial aid. 45% of all full-time freshmen received need-based aid. The average freshman award was $11,727. Need-based scholarships or need-based grants averaged $10,495; need-based self-help aid (loans and jobs) averaged $4,007; and non-need-based athletic scholarships averaged $18,791. The average financial indebtedness of the 2017 graduate was $26,685. The FAFSA code is 002516. The priority date for freshman financial aid applications for fall entry is February 1.

UNIVERSITY OF MISSOURI-KANSAS CITY A-2
www.umkc.edu

Kansas City, MO 64110	**(816) 235-1111** **(800) 775-8652**
Fax: (816) 235-5544	**Email: admit@umkc.edu**
Full-time: 2851 men, 3818 women	**Faculty:** 1, -$
Part-time: 2119 men, 2920 women	**Ph.D.s:** 68%
Graduate: 2496 men, 2740 women	**Student/Faculty:** 14 to 1
Year: semesters, summer session	**Tuition:** $9553 ($22,714)
Room & Board: $10,010	**Freshman Class:** 5138 applied, 3179 accepted, 1212 enrolled
SAT M/W: 609/578	**CEEB CODE:** 6872
Application Deadline: July 1	**VERY COMPETITIVE**

University of Missouri-Kansas City, founded in 1933, is a public institution offering undergraduate and graduate programs in the arts and sciences, engineering, business, education, health fields, preprofessional, and professional studies. There are 10 undergraduate schools and 12 graduate schools. In addition to regional accreditation, UM-Kansas City has baccalaureate program accreditation with AACSB, ABET, ACPE, ADA, CAEP, NASM, NLN, NASM, NAST, and CCNE. The 149-acre campus is in an urban area in Kansas City. Including any residence halls, there are 68 buildings.

STUDENT LIFE: 81% of undergraduates are from Missouri. Others are from 51 states, 45 foreign countries, and Canada. 60% are White; 11% African American; 8% Foreign; 7% Hispanic; 6% Asian American; 4% race unknown; 3% two or more races; 1% American Indian/Alaska Native. **Female To Male Ratio:** 1.3:1. The average age of freshmen is 18; all undergraduates, 21. 25% do not continue beyond their first year; 75% remain to graduate. **Housing:** 1399 students can be accommodated in college housing, which includes married student dorms and on-campus apartments, fraternity houses and sorority houses. On-campus housing is available on a first-come, first-served basis. 77% of students commute. All students may keep cars. Alcohol is not permitted.

FACULTY/CLASSROOMS: 53% of faculty are male; 47% are female. No introductory courses are taught by graduate students. The average class size in an introductory lecture is 30; in a laboratory is 16; and in a regular course is 24.

PROGRAMS OF STUDY: UM-Kansas City confers B.A., B.S., B.B.A., B.F.A., B.I.T., B.L.A., B.M., B.M.E., B.S.C.I.E., B.S.D.H., B.S.E.E., B.S.M.E., B.H.S. and B.S.N. degrees. Master's and doctoral degrees are also awarded. Bachelor's degrees are awarded in BIOLOGICAL SCIENCE (bioinformatics, biology/biological science, and biotechnology), BUSINESS (accounting and business administration and management), COMMUNICATIONS AND THE ARTS (art history and appreciation, communications, dance, dramatic arts, English, French, German, information technology, music, music performance, music theory and composition, performing arts, Spanish, and studio art), COMPUTER AND PHYSICAL SCIENCE (chemistry, computer science, geology, mathematics, and physics), EDUCATION (early childhood education, elementary education, middle school education, music education, and secondary education), ENGINEERING AND ENVIRONMENTAL DESIGN (civil engineering, electrical/electronics engineering, environmental science, and mechanical engineering), HEALTH PROFESSIONS (dental hygiene, health, health science, music therapy, and nursing), SOCIAL SCIENCE (criminal justice, economics, geography, history, Judaic studies, liberal arts/general studies, philosophy, political science/government, psychology, sociology, and urban studies). Health sciences and performing arts is the strongest academically. Liberal arts, business, and computing/engineering have the largest enrollments.

ACTIVITIES: 4% of men belong to 6 national fraternities; 6% of women belong to 2 local and 7 national sororities. There are 255 groups on campus, including art, band, cheerleading, chess, choir, chorale, chorus, computers, dance, debate, drama, ethnic, honors, international, jazz band, LGBT, literary magazine, newspaper, opera, orchestra, photography, political, professional, radio and TV, religious, social, social service, student government, and yearbook. Popular campus events include International Food and Culture Night, Welcome Back Week, Spring Fling, Homecoming, and Court Warming. **Sports:** There are 6 intercollegiate sports for men and 8 for women, and 13 intramural sports for men and 13 for women. Facilities include a recreation center with gyms, an indoor/outdoor pool, indoor and outdoor tracks, a fitness center, and handball, racquetball, and squash courts. **Graduates:** From July 1, 2016 to June 30, 2017, 1812 bachelor's degrees were awarded. The most popular majors were liberal arts (14%), business administration (11%), and nursing (10%). In an average class, 2% graduate in 3 years or less, 23% graduate in 4 years or less, 40% graduate in 5 years or less, and 53% graduate in 6 years or less.

SERVICES: Counseling and information services are available, as is tutoring in some subjects, such as accounting, biology, chemistry, foreign languages, writing, math, and statistics. There is also a reader service for the blind. **Library/Resources:** The library contains 1.1 million volumes, 1.2 million microform items, 353,243 audio/video tapes/CDs/DVDs, and subscribes to 7,222 periodicals including electronic. Computerized library services include interlibrary loans, database searching, and Internet access. Special learning facilities include a natural history museum, planetarium, and radio station. **Physically Challenged Students:** 95% of the campus is accessible. Facilities include wheelchair ramps, elevators, special parking, specially equipped restrooms, special class scheduling, lowered drinking fountains, lowered telephones, and special housing. **Special:** Special academic programs include co-op programs and internships in several majors, study abroad in 8 countries, an accelerated degree program, and dual majors. Special degrees include a B.A.-B.S. degree in the computer science program and a liberal arts degree offered by the adult program. The pass/fail option is available in some courses. Freshmen may enter 6-year medical and dental programs. There are 4 national honor societies, a freshman honors program, and 1 departmental honors program. **Visiting:** There are regularly scheduled orientations for prospective students, consisting of a 1-day program for new freshmen or a half-day optional program for transfer students. There are guides for informal visits. To schedule a visit, contact the Welcome Center at (816) 235-8652. **Campus Safety and Security:** Measures include 24-hour foot and vehicle patrol, emergency notification system, self-defense education, and security escort services. There are shuttle buses, emergency telephones, lighted pathways/sidewalks, and controlled access to dorms/residences.

REQUIREMENTS: A combination of the student's test score and class rank determines admissibility; if the rank is 47 or below, the ACT score must be 23 or higher. Graduation from an accredited secondary school is a requirement for admission; the GED is also accepted. Required high school subjects include 4 units each of English and math, 3 each of social studies and science, 1 of arts, and 2 of a foreign language. A portfolio is required for art majors, an audition for music majors, and an interview for only those students applying for the pharmacy degree or the 6-year medical and dental programs. AP and CLEP credits are accepted. Most candidates for the B.A. and B.S. degrees must complete a core curriculum that consists of courses in English, a foreign language, math, philosophy, fine arts, history, literature, natural sciences, and social sciences. They must complete 120 credit hours, including 30 in their major, with a 2.0 GPA. **Procedure:** Freshmen are admitted to all sessions. Entrance exams should be taken by March of the senior year. There is a rolling admissions plan. Applications should be filed by July 1 for fall entry; November 1 for spring entry. The fall 2017 application fee was $45. Applications are accepted on-line. **Transfer Students:** 1226 transfer students enrolled in 2016-2017. Transfer Students need to have an overall 2.0 GPA on a 4.0 scale in all coursework, which includes repeated coursework, attempted at previous institutions. Transfer students must send in all official college transcripts from all colleges and universities where coursework was attempted. Transfer students with fewer than 24 hours of transferable college credit must also send in official high school transcripts. Some academic units and departments have specific admission requirements in addition to general university requirements. 30 of 120 credits required for the bachelor's degree must be completed at UM-Kansas City. **International Students:** There are 447 international students enrolled. They must take the TOEFL with a minimum score of 550 on the paper-based TOEFL (PBT) or 80 on the Internet-based version (iBT).

ADMISSIONS: 62% of the 2017-2018 applicants were accepted. The SAT scores for the 2017-2018 freshman class were: Math-- 27% below 500, 37% between 500 and 599, 19% between 600 and 699, and 16% between 700 and 800. Writing-- 23% below 500, 33% between 500 and 599, 30% between 600 and 699, and 14% between 700 and 800. The ACT scores were 5% between 12 and 17, 39% between 18 and 23, 40% between 24 and 29, and 16% above 30. 56% of the current freshmen were in the top fifth of their class; 84% were in the top two fifths. 30 freshmen graduated first in their class. **Admissions Contact:** Tamara Byland, Director of Admissions. Email: *admit@umkc.edu* Web: *www.umkc.edu*

FINANCIAL AID: In 2017-2018, 69% of all full-time freshmen received

some form of financial aid. 66% of all full-time freshmen received need-based aid. The average freshman award was $10,463. Need-based scholarships or need-based grants averaged $7,401; and need-based self-help aid (loans and jobs) averaged $6,935. The FAFSA code is 002518. The priority date for freshman financial aid applications for fall entry is March 1.

UNIVERSITY OF MISSOURI-ST. LOUIS D-2

www.umsl.edu

St. Louis, MO 63121 (314) 516-5451

Fax: (314) 516-5310
Email: admissions@umsl.edu

Full-time: 2456 men, 3036 women
Part-time: 3455 men, 4865 women
Graduate: 958 men, 1970 women
Year: semesters, summer session
Room & Board: $10,140

Faculty: 674; I, --$
Ph.D.s: 75%
Student/Faculty: 16 to 1
Tuition: $9670 ($25,586)
Freshman Class: 1970 applied, 1496 accepted, 482 enrolled

SAT EBR-W/M: 560/595 **ACT:** 24
Application Deadline: August 20

CEEB CODE: 6889
VERY COMPETITIVE

University of Missouri-St. Louis, founded in 1963, is a public institution offering undergraduate and graduate programs and conferring degrees in arts and sciences, business, nursing, education, engineering, and optometry. UM-St. Louis is recognized for its contributions to the social and economic advancement of the St. Louis region. Awards include ranking 14th nationally in "Best College and University Civic Partnerships" for economic, social, and cultural impact on metro regions. UMSL also achieved the Carnegie Foundation's Community Engagement Classification for exceptional collaboration with the community for the mutually beneficial exchange of knowledge and resources. Nationally recognized programs include criminology and criminal justice, biology, and the Harris World Ecology Center, business, and counseling. UM-St. Louis students consistently score high on licensing exams in nursing, optometry, clinical psychology, and education. 2017-18 tuition cost is an estimated figure for 14 credit hours per semester. There are 7 undergraduate schools and 5 graduate schools. In addition to regional accreditation, UM-St.Louis has baccalaureate program accreditation with AACSB, ABET, CSWE, NASM, NCATE, and CCNE. The 450-acre campus is in an urban area 10 miles north of downtown St. Louis, Missouri. Including any residence halls, there are 47 buildings.

STUDENT LIFE: 96% of undergraduates are from Missouri. Others are from 35 states, 46 foreign countries, and Canada. 81% are from public schools. 69% are White; 5% Asian American; 4% race unknown; 3% Hispanic; 2% Foreign; 2% two or more races; 14% African American. **Female To Male Ratio:** 1.4:1. The average age of freshmen is 18; all undergraduates, 25. 26% do not continue beyond their first year; 56% remain to graduate. **Housing:** 1202 students can be accommodated in college housing, which includes married student dorms and on-campus apartments. In addition, there are honors houses, language/international houses, special-interest houses, fraternity houses, sorority houses, including theme house, wellness house, apartments for students over 21, and graduate/professional school housing. On-campus housing is available on a first-come, first-served basis. 94% of students commute. All students may keep cars.

FACULTY/CLASSROOMS: 41% of faculty are male; 59% are female. 46% teach undergraduates, 11% do research, and 21% do both. Graduate students teach 16% of introductory courses. The average class size in an introductory lecture is 26; in a laboratory is 17; and in a regular course is 18.

PROGRAMS OF STUDY: UM-St. Louis confers B.A., B.S., B.F.A., B.L.S., B.M.,B.S.Acc., B.S.B.A., B.S.C.I.E., B.S.Ed., B.S.E.E., B.S.M.E., B.E.S., B.S.N., B.S.P.P.A., B.S.W., B.I.S., and B.S.I.S. degrees. Master's and doctoral degrees are also awarded. Bachelor's degrees are awarded in BIOLOGICAL SCIENCE (biochemistry, biology/biological science, and biotechnology), BUSINESS (accounting, business administration and management, finance, international business management, logistics, management information systems, marketing management, and operations management), COMMUNICATIONS AND THE ARTS (art history and appreciation, communications, dance, dramatic arts, English, French, German, Germanic languages and literature, Japanese, media arts, music, Spanish, and studio art), COMPUTER AND PHYSICAL SCIENCE (chemistry, computer science, information sciences and systems, mathematics, and physics), EDUCATION (early childhood education, education, elementary education, music education, physical education, secondary education, and special education), ENGINEERING AND ENVIRONMENTAL DESIGN (civil engineering, electrical/electronics engineering, and mechanical engineering), HEALTH PROFESSIONS (nursing), SOCIAL SCIENCE (anthropology, criminal justice, economics, history, interdisciplinary studies, liberal arts/general studies, philosophy, political science/government, psychology, public administration, social work, and sociology). International business, criminology, education, nursing, and psychology are the strongest academically. Business, education, and nursing have the largest enrollments.

ACTIVITIES: 2% of men belong to 4 national fraternities; 2% of women belong to 4 national sororities. There are 107 groups on campus, including art, band, cheerleading, choir, chorale, chorus, communications, computers, dance, debate, drama, environmental, ethnic, forensics, honors, international, jazz band, LGBT, literary magazine, newspaper, opera, pep band, photography, political, professional, radio and TV, religious, social, social service, and student government. Popular campus events include Expo, Weeks of Welcome, Family Weekend, MLK Day of Service, Mirthday Week, Homecoming, Lecture Series, History/Heritage months. **Sports:** There are 6 intercollegiate sports for men and 7 for women, and 16 intramural sports for men and 16 for women. Facilities include fitness space, treadmills, ellipticals, strength and functional training equipment, gym courts for basketball, volleyball, badminton, multi-activity court with dasher board system for indoor soccer and floor hockey, indoor track, climbing walls, aquatic facility for classes and therapy, rooms for fitness classes, and dance. **Graduates:** From July 1, 2016 to June 30, 2017, 2246 bachelor's degrees were awarded. The most popular majors were business administration (25%), health professions (12%), and education (11%). In an average class, 3% graduate in 3 years or less, 32% graduate in 4 years or less, 51% graduate in 5 years or less, and 56% graduate in 6 years or less. Of the 2016 graduating class, 15% were enrolled in graduate school within 6 months of graduation, and 70% were employed.

SERVICES: Counseling and information services are available, as is tutoring in most subjects, such as math and writing. There is also remedial math. **Library/Resources:** The library contains 1.3 million volumes, 1.3 million microform items, and 4,127 audio/video tapes/CDs/DVDs, and subscribes to 2,539 periodicals including electronic. Computerized library services include interlibrary loans, database searching, Internet access, and Wi-Fi capability. Special learning facilities include an art gallery, planetarium, radio station, and TV station. Libraries include the Thomas Jefferson library, and the St. Louis Mercantile library that includes a collection of American art and realia, observatory, on-campus pre-school, honors college, nonprofit management/leadership program, women in public life institute, centers for nanoscience, neurodynamics, emerging technologies, entrepreneurship and economic education, international studies, transportation studies, gerontology, and teaching and learning. There are also performing arts, world ecology, technology and learning, math, science education, eye care, ELS language, trauma recovery, student success, and French, German, and Greek cultural centers. **Physically Challenged Students:** All of the campus is accessible. Facilities include wheelchair ramps, elevators, special parking, specially equipped restrooms, special class scheduling, lowered drinking fountains, lowered telephones, and special housing. **Special:** Cross-registration with Washington University, St. Louis University, and St. Louis Community College and cooperative programs in all majors are offered. In addition, study abroad is available in 32 countries, including England, France, and Germany. Most degree programs are offered through the evening courses, and some work-study is available. There is an accelerated nursing degree program and student-designed majors for the B.L.S. There are 24 national honor societies and a freshman honors program. **Visiting:** There are regularly scheduled orientations for prospective students, including a 20-minute information session, special appointments if needed, and a campus walking tour. There are guides for informal visits; visitors may sit in on classes and stay overnight. To schedule a visit, contact Lisa Baker at (314) 516-6877. **Campus Safety and Security:** Measures include 24-hour foot and vehicle patrol, an emergency notification system, self-defense education, and security escort services. There are shuttle buses, emergency telephones, lighted pathways/sidewalks, controlled access to dorms/residences, and criminal investigations.

REQUIREMENTS: The SAT or ACT is required. Applicants are required to have a total of 17 units, such as 4 each in English and math, 3 each in social studies and science, 2 in the same foreign language, and 1 in fine arts. Class rank and test scores are used to determine eligibility for admission. A GPA of 2.3 is required. AP and CLEP credits are accepted. Students must complete 120 hours to graduate including the General Education Plan totaling 42 hours. General Education includes First Year Writing, Communication Proficiency, Mathematics Proficiency, Information Literacy, US History and Government, and additional courses in Humanities and Fine Arts, Social Sciences, and Math and Sciences. Students must also complete a junior-level writing course and a courses that expands cultural awareness. Students must maintain a 2.0 GPA for graduation. The number of hours required for each major varies. **Procedure:** Freshmen are admitted in the fall, spring, and summer. Entrance exams should be taken late in the junior year or early in the senior year. There is a rolling admissions plan. Applications should be filed by August 20 for fall entry; January 2 for winter entry; January 16 for spring entry; and May 7 for summer entry. The fall 2017 application fee was $35. Notification is sent on a rolling basis. Applications are accepted online. **Transfer Students:** 1425 transfer students enrolled in 2016-2017. UM-St. Louis abides by the Coordinating Board of Higher Education articulation agreement between Missouri public institutions. The agreement with CBHE states that students who have earned an associate of arts degree from a Missouri institution that requires, at a minimum, the general education core outlined by the CBHE, and a 2.3 GPA will be admitted in junior standing and considered to have completed the lower division general education requirements. If a student has under a 2.3 GPA, but has earned an AA degree from a Missouri institution, they are admissible. This does not exempt the student from meeting any specialized lower division courses required by particular degree programs. Courses taken at the community or junior college not culminating in an associate degree will be evaluated for applicability to any particular degree program on a course by course basis. If students transfer with an approved General Education Block and a completed associate degree from a Missouri community college, they can transfer in more than 64 hours of credit provided that the credit meets baccalaureate degree requirements or fulfills a lower division prerequisite for an upper division course. 30 of 120 credits required for the bachelor's degree must be completed at UM-St.Louis. **International Students:** There are 259 international students enrolled. They must take the TOEFL with a minimum score of 500 on the paper-based TOEFL (PBT) or 61 on the Internet-based version (iBT). Student must also take the college's own test.

ADMISSIONS: 76% of the 2017-2018 applicants were accepted. The SAT scores for the 2017-2018 freshman class were: Math-- 50% between 500 and 599 and 50% between 600 and 699. Writing-- 64% below 500. Evidence-Based Reading/Writing-- 14% below 500, 50% between 500 and 599, 14% between 600 and 699, and 21% between 700 and 800. The ACT scores were 3% between 12 and 17, 40% between 18 and 23, 47% between 24 and 29, and 10% above 30. 50% of the current freshmen were in the top fifth of their class; 81% were in the top two fifths. 21 freshmen graduated first in their class. **Admissions Contact:** Drew Griffin, Director of Admissions. Email: *admissions@umsl.edu* Web: *www.umsl.edu*

FINANCIAL AID: The FAFSA code is 002519. The priority date for freshman financial aid applications for fall entry is January 1.

WASHINGTON UNIVERSITY IN ST. LOUIS D-3

www.wustl.edu

St. Louis, MO 63130	(314) 935-6000 (800) 638-0700
Fax: (314) 935-4290	**Email:** admissions@wustl.edu
Full-time: 3332 men, 3742 women	**Faculty:** 935; I, +$
Part-time: 210 men, 391 women	**Ph.D.s:** 94%
Graduate: 3734 men, 3894 women	**Student/Faculty:** 8 to 1
Year: semesters, summer session	**Tuition:** $51,533
Room & Board: $16,006	**Freshman Class:** n/av
SAT or ACT: required	**CEEB CODE:** 6929
Application Deadline: January 2	**MOST COMPETITIVE**

Washington University in St. Louis, founded in 1853, is a private institution offering undergraduate and graduate programs in arts and sciences, business, architecture, engineering, art, and professional programs in law, medicine (including physical therapy and occupational therapy), and social work. There are 5 undergraduate schools and 8 graduate schools. In addition to regional accreditation, WUSL has baccalaureate program accreditation with AACSB, ABET, and NASAD. The 169-acre campus is in a suburban area 7 miles west of St. Louis, MO. Including any residence halls, there are 116 buildings.

STUDENT LIFE: 91% of undergraduates are from out of state, mostly the Midwest. Students are from 50 states, 50 foreign countries, and Canada. 56% are from public schools. 8% are African American; 8% Hispanic; 8% Foreign; 52% White; 5% two or more races; 2% race unknown; 17% Asian American. **Female To Male Ratio:** 1.1:1. The average age of freshmen is 18; all undergraduates, 20. 3% do not continue beyond their first year; 94% remain to graduate. **Housing:** 5304 students can be accommodated in college housing, which includes married student dorms, on-campus apartments, and off-campus apartments. In addition, there are special-interest houses, fraternity houses, special-interest suites, upper-class housing, gender-inclusive housing, and small group housing for students who share common interests and goals. On-campus housing is guaranteed for the freshman year only and is available on a lottery system for upperclassmen. 62% of students live on campus. Upperclassmen may keep cars.

FACULTY/CLASSROOMS: 60% of faculty are male; 40% are female. No introductory courses are taught by graduate students. The average class size in an introductory lecture is 31.

PROGRAMS OF STUDY: WUSL confers B.A., B.S., B.F.A., B.M., B.S.B.A., B.S.B.M.E., B.S.C.E., B.S.Ch.E., B.S.C.S., B.S.Co.E., B.S.E.E., B.S.I.M., B.S.M.E., and B.S.S.S.E. degrees. Associate, master's, and doctoral degrees are also awarded. Bachelor's degrees are awarded in AGRICULTURE (environmental studies, natural resource management, and plant science), BIOLOGICAL SCIENCE (biochemistry, bioinformatics, biology/biological science, biomathematics, biophysics, ecology, environmental biology, and neurosciences), BUSINESS (accounting, banking and finance, business administration and management, business economics, entrepreneurial studies, finance, human resources, international business management, international economics, marketing management, marketing/retailing/merchandising, and trade and industrial supervision and management), COMMUNICATIONS AND THE ARTS (advertising, American literature, Arabic, art history and appreciation, ceramic art and design, Chinese, classical languages, classics, communications, comparative literature, creative writing, dance, design, dramatic arts, drawing, East Asian languages and literature, English, English literature, film arts, fine arts, French, German, Germanic languages and literature, graphic design, Greek (classical), Hebrew, illustration, Italian, Japanese, journalism, languages, Latin, linguistics, literature, music, music theory and composition, painting, performing arts, photography, printmaking, romance languages and literature, sculpture, Spanish, studio art, and visual and performing arts), COMPUTER AND PHYSICAL SCIENCE (applied mathematics, chemistry, computer programming, computer science, earth science, geochemistry, geology, geophysics and seismology, information sciences and systems, mathematics, physical sciences, physics, and statistics), EDUCATION (art education, education, elementary education, foreign languages education, mathematics education, middle school education, science education, secondary education, social science education, and social studies education), ENGINEERING AND ENVIRONMENTAL DESIGN (architectural technology, architecture, bioengineering, biomedical engineering, chemical engineering, civil engineering, commercial art, computer engineering, electrical/electronics engineering, engineering, engineering mechanics, environmental science, mechanical engineering, systems engineering, and technology and public affairs), HEALTH PROFESSIONS (allied health, health care administration, health science, pharmacy, predentistry, premedicine, prepharmacy, and preveterinary science), SOCIAL SCIENCE (African studies, African American studies, American studies, anthropology, archeology, area studies, Asian/Oriental studies, biopsychology, East Asian studies, Eastern European studies, economics, ethnic studies, European studies, fashion design and technology, history, humanities, industrial and organizational psychology, interdisciplinary studies, international relations, international studies, Islamic studies, Judaic studies, Latin American studies, Middle Eastern studies, Near Eastern studies, philosophy, political science/government, psychology, religion, social science, South Asian studies, systems science, urban studies, Western European studies, and women's studies). Social sciences, engineering, and business are the strongest academically and have the largest enrollments.

ACTIVITIES: 25% of men belong to 12 national fraternities; 44% of women belong to 9 national sororities. There are 380 groups on campus, including art, band, cheerleading, chess, choir, chorale, chorus, computers, dance, debate, drama, environmental, ethnic, film, forensics, honors, international, jazz band, LGBT, literary magazine, musical theater, newspaper, opera, orchestra, pep band, photography, political, professional, radio and TV, religious, social, social service, student government, symphony, and yearbook. Popular campus events include Multicultural Celebrations, W.I.L.D. (concert festival), and student-run carnival. **Sports:** There are 9 intercollegiate sports for men and 10 for women, and 33 intramural sports for men and 33 for women. The Recreation Center features a full assortment of cardio and strength training equipment, along with a cycling studio and two group exercise studios, and an indoor running track and gymnasium. The Athletics Complex features basketball and volleyball, an eight-lane, 25-yard pool and diving well, racquetball and squash courts, a weight room and practice gym, and field for football and outdoor track. **Graduates:** From July 1, 2016 to June 30, 2017, 1727 bachelor's degrees were awarded. The most popular majors were biology and psychology (18%), business (17%), and engineering (16%). In an average class, 88% graduate in 4 years or less, 93% graduate in 5 years or less, and 94% graduate in 6 years or less. Of the 2016 graduating class, 23% were enrolled in graduate school within 6 months of graduation, and 65% were employed.

SERVICES: Counseling and information services are available, as is tutoring in some subjects. There is a reader service for the blind. **Library/Resources:** The library contains 5.5 million volumes, 3.4 million microform items, and 102,585 audio/video tapes/CDs/DVDs, and subscribes to 147,473 periodicals including electronic. Computerized library services include interlibrary loans, database searching, Internet access, and Wi-Fi capability. Special learning facilities include an art gallery, planetarium, radio station, TV station, a dance studio, a professional theater, observatory, and studio theater. **Physically Challenged Students:** 95% of the campus is accessible. Facilities include wheelchair ramps, elevators, special parking, specially equipped restrooms, special class scheduling, lowered drinking fountains, and lowered telephones. **Special:** Opportunities are provided for cooperative programs with other schools, internships, work-study programs, study abroad, a Washington (D.C.) semester, accelerated degree programs, a B.A.-B.S. engineering degree, credit by examination, nondegree study, pass/fail options, and dual and student-designed majors. There are 19 national honor societies and a chapter of Phi Beta Kappa. **Visiting:** There are regularly scheduled orientations for prospective students, student visits consisting of group presentations followed by a campus tour, as well as class visits and meetings with current students and faculty. There are guides for informal visits, visitors may sit in on classes, and stay overnight. To schedule a visit, contact Office of Undergraduate Admissions. **Campus Safety and Security:** Measures include 24-hour foot and vehicle patrol, emergency notification system, self-defense education, and security escort services. There are shuttle buses, emergency telephones, lighted pathways/sidewalks, controlled access to dorms/residences, and SafeTrek app for reporting emergencies.

REQUIREMENTS: The SAT or ACT is required. An essay is required from all applicants. Portfolios are required for students applying to the College of Art, and the College of Architecture. It is recommended that students have complete 4 years of English, math, science, social studies, foreign language, and history. Recommendations are also required from a teacher and a counselor. AP credits are accepted. Academic requirements for graduation are set by the undergraduate divisions and vary by major. There are no requirements that every student in every degree program must satisfy. **Procedure:** Freshmen are admitted in the fall. Entrance exams should be taken by December of the senior year. There are early decision and deferred admissions plans. Early decision applications should be filed by November 15; regular applications, by January 2 for fall entry. The fall 2017 application fee was $75. Notification of early decision is sent December 15; regular decision, April 1. 692 early decision candidates were accepted for the 2017-2018 class. Applications are accepted on-line. **Transfer Students:** 92 transfer students enrolled in 2016-2017. Academic requirements for graduation are set by the undergraduate divisions and vary by major. There are no requirements that all students in every degree program must satisfy. **International Students:** There are 572 international students enrolled. They must take the TOEFL with a minimum score of 550 on the paper-based TOEFL (PBT) or 100 on the Internet-based version (iBT). They must also take the SAT or ACT.

ADMISSIONS: 16% of the 2017-2018 applicants were accepted. 97% of the current freshmen were in the top fifth of their class; 100% were in the top two fifths. **Admissions Contact:** Office of Undergraduate Admissions. Email: *admissions@wustl.edu* Web: *www.wustl.edu*

FINANCIAL AID: In 2017-2018, 50% of all full-time freshmen received some form of financial aid. 39% of all full-time freshmen received need-based aid. The average freshman award was $48,169. The average financial indebtedness of the 2017 graduate was $22,592. WUSL is a member of CSS. The CSS/Profile or our own institutional financial aid form is required. The FAFSA code is 002519. The deadline for filing freshman financial aid applications for fall entry is February 1.

WEBSTER UNIVERSITY D-2

www.webster.edu

St. Louis, MO 63119 — **(314) 246-7080** / **(800) 753-6765**

Fax: (314) 246-7116 — **Email: admissions@webster.edu**

Full-time: 987 men, 1244 women
Part-time: 210 men, 181 women
Graduate: 536 men, 1065 women
Year: semesters, summer session
Room & Board: $11,190
ACT: 24
Application Deadline: August 1

Faculty: 199; IIA, av$
Ph.D.s: 87%
Student/Faculty: 11 to 1
Tuition: $26,300
Freshman Class: 2630 applied, 1235 accepted, 433 enrolled
CEEB CODE: 6933
COMPETITIVE

Webster University is committed to delivering high-quality learning experiences that transform students for global citizenship and individual excellence. Webster University is the only Tier 1, private, non-profit U.S.-based university providing a network of international residential campuses. Founded in 1915, Webster University's campus network includes traditional, metropolitan, military and corporate locations around the world, and is an independent institution with programs in fine and performing arts, liberal arts and sciences, media communications, education, nursing, and business. There are 5 undergraduate schools and 5 graduate schools. In addition to regional accreditation, WU has baccalaureate program accreditation with ACBSP, NASM, CAEP, NLN, ABA, and COA. The 47-acre campus is in a suburban area 6 miles southwest of St. Louis. Including any residence halls, there are 41 buildings.

STUDENT LIFE: 71% of undergraduates are from Missouri. Others are from 44 states, 80 foreign countries, and Canada. 9% are race unknown; 62% White; 5% Hispanic; 4% Asian American; 3% two or more races; 17% African American. **Female To Male Ratio:** 1.4:1. The average age of freshmen is 18; all undergraduates, 23. 25% do not continue beyond their first year; 59% remain to graduate. **Housing:** 855 students can be accommodated in college housing, which includes dorms, on-campus apartments, and special-interest houses. On-campus housing is available on a first-come, first-served basis, and is available on a lottery system for upperclassmen. 67% of students commute. All students may keep cars.

FACULTY/CLASSROOMS: 54% of faculty are male; 46% are female. All teach undergraduates. No introductory courses are taught by graduate students. The average class size in an introductory lecture is 13; in a laboratory is 10; and in a regular course is 12.

PROGRAMS OF STUDY: WU confers B.A., B.S., B.F.A., B.M., B.M.Ed. and B.S.N. degrees. Master's and doctoral degrees are also awarded. Bachelor's degrees are awarded in AGRICULTURE (environmental studies), BIOLOGICAL SCIENCE (biology/biological science), BUSINESS (accounting, business administration and management, finance, management science, and marketing management), COMMUNICATIONS AND THE ARTS (acting, advertising, animation, art history, art, art history and appreciation, audio technology, ballet, ceramic art and design, choral music, communications, creative writing, dance, digital communications, dramatic arts, English, film arts, French, German, graphic design, information technology, instrumental performance, instrumental music education, jazz, journalism, media arts, music, music performance, music theory and composition, musical theater, painting, photography, piano performance, playwriting/screenwriting, printmaking, public relations, scenic and lighting design, sculpture, Spanish, studio art, theater design, video, vocal performance, voice, and vocal music education), COMPUTER AND PHYSICAL SCIENCE (computer management, computer science, information sciences and systems, and mathematics), EDUCATION (art education, early childhood education, education, elementary education, foreign languages education, journalism education, mathematics education, middle school education, music education, secondary education, social studies education, social studies secondary school education, and special education), HEALTH PROFESSIONS (exercise science and nursing), SOCIAL SCIENCE (American studies, area studies, criminology, cultural anthropology, economics, European studies, history, interdisciplinary studies, international relations, legal studies, philosophy, political science/government, psychology, religion, religious studies, sociology, and women's studies). Fine arts, and communications are the strongest academically. Business, computer science, and education have the largest enrollments.

ACTIVITIES: There are no fraternities; 3% of women belong to 1 local sororities. There are 68 groups on campus, including art, band, cheerleading, chess, choir, chorale, chorus, communications, computers, dance, debate, departmental clubs, drama, environmental, ethnic, film, forensics, international, jazz band, LGBT, literary magazine, musical theater, newspaper, opera, orchestra, photography, political, professional, radio and TV, religious, social, social service, student government, and symphony. Popular campus events include Homecoming, Webster Works Worldwide, and Spring Fest. **Sports:** There are 8 intercollegiate sports for men and 8 for women, and 4 intramural sports for men and 4 for women. Facilities include a gym, an athletic training center, a fitness center, a 25-yard 6-lane indoor swimming pool. **Graduates:** From July 1, 2016 to June 30, 2017, 739 bachelor's degrees were awarded. The most popular majors were management (13%), psychology (5%), and computer science (5%). In an average class, 1% graduate in 3 years or less, 43% graduate in 4 years or less, 56% graduate in 5 years or less, and 59% graduate in 6 years or less.

SERVICES: Counseling and information services are available, as is tutoring in most subjects. There is a reader service for the blind. Peer tutoring and study skills training are also available. **Library/Resources:** The library contains 281,548 volumes, 138,000 microform items, and 30,909 audio/video tapes/CDs/DVDs, and subscribes to 1,175 periodicals including electronic. Computerized library services include interlibrary loans, database searching, Internet access, and Wi-Fi capability. Special learning facilities include an art gallery, radio station, TV station, a media center, a theater, and a community music school. **Physically Challenged Students:** 75% of the campus is accessible. Facilities include wheelchair ramps, elevators, special parking, specially equipped restrooms, special class scheduling, lowered drinking fountains, lowered telephones, special housing. There are also telephones for the hearing impaired, automatic door openers, a reading machine, computer for paraplegic students, reading and writing software, deaf interpreters, note takers, and alternate format textbooks. All TV monitors in classrooms have closed caption capabilities. **Special:** Webster University offers co-op programs, work-study programs, internships, dual majors, student-designed majors, and a 3-2 engineering degree with the University of Missouri/Columbia and Washington University. Study abroad in over 14 countries is also available. **Visiting:** There are regularly scheduled orientations for prospective students. Students visiting campus may participate in a personal tour, meeting with an admissions representative and faculty member, sit in on a class, and attend a campus activity. There are guides for informal visits, visitors may sit in on classes, and stay overnight. To schedule a visit, contact The Office of Admission. **Campus Safety and Security:** Measures include 24-hour foot and vehicle patrol, emergency notification system, self-defense education, and security escort services. There are emergency telephones, lighted pathways/sidewalks, and controlled access to dorms/residences.

REQUIREMENTS: The ACT is required. Applicants must be graduates of an accredited secondary school. The GED is accepted. Webster recommends that students complete 19 high school academic units, including 4 units of English, 3 each of social studies/history, science, math, and electives, 2 units of foreign language, and 1 unit of visual/performing arts. An essay is required of all students, and a portfolio or audition is required for art, dance, music, musical theater, and film. Webster requires applicants to be in the upper 50% of their class. AP and CLEP credits are accepted. To graduate, students must complete at least 128 semester hours, with a minimum GPA of 2.0. They must successfully complete an approved major, which may or may not require more than 128 credit hours, and successfully complete the global citizenship program or general education program requirements. All new degree-seeking freshmen with fewer than 16 college credit hours are required to take a freshman seminar. At least 30 semester credits of a student's final 36 credits must be earned at Webster. **Procedure:** Freshmen are admitted in the fall, spring, and summer. Entrance exams should be taken in the spring of the junior year. There are deferred admissions and rolling admissions plans. Applications should be filed by August 1 for fall entry; December 1 for spring entry. The fall 2017 application fee was $35. Notification is sent on a rolling basis. Applications are accepted on-line. **Transfer Students:** 441 transfer students enrolled in 2016-2017. Applicants for transfer must have a minimum GPA of 2.0 for college credit completed. If they have fewer than 30 transferable hours, they must submit high school transcripts. 30 of 128 credits required for the bachelor's degree must be completed at Webster. **International Students:** There are 100 international students enrolled. They must take the TOEFL with a minimum score of 80 on the Internet-based version (iBT). Students may take either the Comprehensive English Language Test, Equivalent current Cambridge, Oxford, NAEB, TEEP, Academic IELTS, London Certificate, and Pearson tests in lieu of TOEFL. They may also take the SAT or ACT if they are graduates of U.S. high schools or international secondary schools that use English as the language of instruction.

ADMISSIONS: 47% of the 2017-2018 applicants were accepted. The ACT scores were 7% between 12 and 17, 39% between 18 and 23, 44% between 24 and 29, and 10% above 30. 30% of the current freshmen were in the top fifth of their class; 64% were in the top two fifths. 3 freshmen graduated first in their class. **Admissions Contact:** James Myers, Associate VP Undergraduate Admissions. Email: *admissions@webster.edu* Web: *www.webster.edu*

FINANCIAL AID: In 2017-2018, 97% of all full-time freshmen received some form of financial aid. 76% of all full-time freshmen received need-based aid. The average freshman award was $28,334. Need-based scholarships or need-based grants averaged $10,695; need-based self-help aid (loans and jobs) averaged $5,900; other non-need-based awards and non-need-based scholarships averaged $13,461; and $3,738 from other forms of aid. 26% of undergraduate students work part-time. The average financial indebtedness of the 2017 graduate was $26,792. The college's own financial statement is required. The FAFSA code is 002521. The priority date for freshman financial aid applications for fall entry is March 1.

WESTMINSTER COLLEGE — C-2

www.westminister-mo.edu

Fulton, MO 65251 — (573) 592-5251, (800) 475-3361

Fax: (573) 592-5255 — **Email:** admissions@westminster-mo.edu

Full-time: 520 men, 397 women	**Faculty:** 61; IIB, --$
Part-time: 13 men, 3 women	**Ph.D.s:** 89%
Graduate: n/av	**Student/Faculty:** 14 to 1
Year: semesters, summer session	**Tuition:** $23,480
Room & Board: $9340	**Freshman Class:** 1356 applied, 910 accepted, 219 enrolled
SAT: recommended **ACT:** 24	**CEEB CODE:** 6937
Application Deadline: open	**COMPETITIVE**

Westminster College, founded in 1851, is a private liberal arts and sciences college affiliated with the Presbyterian Church. There is 1 undergraduate school. In addition to regional accreditation, WC has baccalaureate program accreditation with ACBSP. The 87-acre campus is in a small town 20 miles east of Columbia and 25 miles north of Jefferson City. Including any residence halls, there are 26 buildings.

STUDENT LIFE: 65% of undergraduates are from Missouri. Others are from 28 states, and 70 foreign countries. 75% are from public schools. 65% are White; 16% Foreign; 9% African American; 3% Hispanic; 2% American Indian/Alaska Native; 2% race unknown; 1% Asian American; 1% two or more races. 56% are Protestant; 20% Catholic; 15% claim no religious affiliation. **Male To Female Ratio:** 1.3:1. The average age of freshmen is 18; all undergraduates, 20. 17% do not continue beyond their first year; 70% remain to graduate. **Housing:** 900 students can be accommodated in college housing, which includes dorms and off-campus apartments. In addition, there are special-interest houses and fraternity houses. On-campus housing is guaranteed for all 4 years. 84% of students live on campus. All students may keep cars.

FACULTY/CLASSROOMS: 59% of faculty are male; 41% are female. All teach undergraduates, 75% do research, and 75% do both. No introductory courses are taught by graduate students. The average class size in an introductory lecture is 19; in a laboratory is 20; and in a regular course is 14.

PROGRAMS OF STUDY: WC confers B.A. degrees. Bachelor's degrees are awarded in BIOLOGICAL SCIENCE (biochemistry and biology/biological science), BUSINESS (accounting, business administration and management, business communications, international business management, management information systems, and sports management), COMMUNICATIONS AND THE ARTS (English, French, and Spanish), COMPUTER AND PHYSICAL SCIENCE (chemistry, computer science, mathematics, and physics), EDUCATION (elementary education, middle school education, physical education, secondary education, and sports and wellness studies), ENGINEERING AND ENVIRONMENTAL DESIGN (environmental science), HEALTH PROFESSIONS (nursing), SOCIAL SCIENCE (anthropology, economics, history, international studies, philosophy, political science/government, psychology, religion, and sociology). English, biology, and psychology are the strongest academically. Business administration, biology, and psychology have the largest enrollments.

ACTIVITIES: 45% of men belong to 5 national fraternities; 34% of women belong to 3 national sororities. There are 65 groups on campus, including multicultural club, international club, art, Blue Blazers investment club, cheerleading, choir, chorale, chorus, computers, dance, drama, environmental, ethnic, honors, international, jazz band, LGBT, literary magazine, musical theater, newspaper, pep band, photography, political, professional, religious, social, social service, and student government. Popular campus events include Alumni Weekend, Westminster Symposium, Undergraduate Scholars Forum, and What if...? Conference and International Week. **Sports:** There are 8 intercollegiate sports for men and 8 for women, and 16 intramural sports for men and 10 for women. Facilities include a gym, aerobic training center, a weight room, a training room, football, baseball, softball, soccer fields, tennis, racquetball, sand volleyball courts, a swimming pool, indoor rifle range, and auditorium/arena. **Graduates:** From July 1, 2016 to June 30, 2017, 205 bachelor's degrees were awarded. The most popular majors were business administration/management (29%), biology and psychology (19%), and education (10%). In an average class, 53% graduate in 4 years or less, 62% graduate in 5 years or less, and 68% graduate in 6 years or less. Of the 2016 graduating class, 24% were enrolled in graduate school within 6 months of graduation, and 90% were employed.

SERVICES: Counseling and information services are available, as is tutoring in most subjects. There is remedial math, reading, and writing. **Library/Resources:** The library contains 100,265 volumes, 6,912 microform items, and 9,691 audio/video tapes/CDs/DVDs, and subscribes to 30,201 periodicals including electronic. Computerized library services include interlibrary loans, database searching, Internet access, and Wi-Fi capability. **Physically Challenged Students:** 80% of the campus is accessible. Facilities include wheelchair ramps, elevators, special parking, specially equipped restrooms, special class scheduling, lowered drinking fountains, and lowered telephones. **Special:** Westminster offers co-op programs with colleges of the Mid-Missouri Associated Colleges and Universities, cross-registration with William Woods University, internships in all areas, study abroad in 15 countries, a Washington semester, a United Nations semester, and an urban studies program in Chicago. Student-designed majors are available as well as a dual degree nursing program with Golfarb School of Nursing at Barnes-Jewish College, dual degree program with Logan University of Chiropractic, and a 3-2 engineering degree with Washington University in St. Louis. The pass/fail option and dual majors are available. There are 16 national honor societies, a freshman honors program, and 8 departmental honors programs. **Visiting:** There are regularly scheduled orientations for prospective students, including 1-day summer programs with a general orientation and class registration. There are guides for informal visits, visitors may sit in on classes, and stay overnight. To schedule a visit, contact Robert Andrews, Vice President & Dean of Enrollment Services at (573) 592-5195. **Campus Safety and Security:** Measures include 24-hour foot and vehicle patrol, emergency notification system, self-defense education, and security escort services. There are emergency telephones and lighted pathways/sidewalks.

REQUIREMENTS: The ACT is required. The SAT is recommended. Applicants must be graduates of an accredited secondary school. The GED is also accepted. Students must have completed 4 years each of social studies and English, 3 years each of math and science, and 2 years each of a foreign language and history. An essay is required and an interview is recommended. Westminster requires applicants to be in the upper 50% of their class. AP and CLEP credits are accepted. Important factors in the admissions decision are advanced placement or honors courses, leadership record, and extracurricular activities record. To graduate, students must complete 122 credit hours, including a maximum of 40 hours in their major, with a minimum GPA of 2.0. All students are required to take Westminster seminar, academic writing, statistics or calculus, 4 hours of foreign language, and 1 hour of phys ed. Students must also take 6 to 10 hours (37 to 42 total) in scientific inquiry, historical awareness, fundamental questions, artistic expression, human behaviors and institutions, cultural diversity, and global interdependence. In addition, an integrative upper-level course, 2 writing intensive courses, and an upper-level course from a non-major academic division are required. **Procedure:** Freshmen are admitted to all sessions. Entrance exams should be taken in the junior year of high school. There are early decision, deferred admissions, and rolling admissions plans. Application deadlines are open. Applications are accepted on-line. **Transfer Students:** 49 transfer students enrolled in 2016-2017. Applicants must have taken either the ACT or the SAT and must complete at least 4 semesters at WC as full-time students. 60 of 122 credits required for the bachelor's degree must be completed at WC. **International Students:** There are 159 international students enrolled. They must take the TOEFL.

ADMISSIONS: 67% of the 2017-2018 applicants were accepted. The ACT scores were 17% below 12, 28% between 12 and 17, 22% between 18 and 23, 17% between 24 and 29, and 18% above 30. 44% of the current freshmen were in the top fifth of their class; 69% were in the top two fifths. 5 freshmen graduated first in their class. **Admissions Contact:** Robert Andrews, Vice President and Dean of Enrollment Services. Email: *admissions@westminster-mo.edu* Web: *www.westminster-mo.edu*

FINANCIAL AID: In 2017-2018, 99% of all full-time freshmen received some form of financial aid. 53% of all full-time freshmen received need-based aid. The average freshman award was $20,155. Need-based scholarships or need-based grants averaged $15,940; and need-based self-help aid (loans and jobs) averaged $4,660. 66% of undergraduate students work part-time. The average financial indebtedness of the 2017 graduate was $26,723. The FAFSA code is 002523. The priority date for freshman financial aid applications for fall entry is February 15.

WILLIAM JEWELL COLLEGE — B-2

www.jewell.edu

Liberty, MO 64068	**(816) 781-7700** **(800) 753-7009**
Fax: (816) 415-5027	**Email: admission@william.jewell.edu**
Full-time: 414 men, 616 women	**Faculty:** 70
Part-time: n/av	**Ph.D.s:** 86%
Graduate: n/av	**Student/Faculty:** 15 to 1
Year: semesters, summer session	**Tuition:** $32,850
Room & Board: $9640	**Freshman Class:** 2497 applied, 1374 accepted, 282 enrolled
SAT: required **ACT:** 26	**CEEB CODE:** 6941
Application Deadline: August 15	**COMPETITIVE+**

William Jewell College, founded in 1849, is an academically selective liberal arts college that offers undergraduate programs in the arts and sciences, business, education, and nursing fields. The figures given in the above capsule and in this profile are approximate. There are 4 undergraduate schools. In addition to regional accreditation, WJC has baccalaureate program accreditation with NASM and CCNE. The 200-acre campus is in a suburban area 15 miles northeast of Kansas City. Including any residence halls, there are 28 buildings.

STUDENT LIFE: 69% of undergraduates are from Missouri. Others are from 30 states, and 11 foreign countries. 91% are from public schools. 82% are White; 4% African American; 3% Hispanic; 2% Asian American; 2% Foreign; 1% American Indian/Alaska Native. 51% are Protestant; 35% claim no religious affiliation; 11% Catholic. **Female To Male Ratio:** 1.5:1. The average age of freshmen is 19; all undergraduates, 20. 22% do not continue beyond their first year; 63% remain to graduate. **Housing:** 1013 students can be accommodated in college housing, which includes dorms. In addition, there are honors houses, language/international houses, fraternity houses, and sorority houses. On-campus housing is guaranteed for all 4 years. 75% of students live on campus. All students may keep cars. Alcohol is not permitted.

FACULTY/CLASSROOMS: 51% of faculty are male; 49% are female. 80% teach undergraduates, 20% do research, and 20% do both. No introductory courses are taught by graduate students. The average class size in an introductory lecture is 20; in a laboratory is 18; and in a regular course is 15.

PROGRAMS OF STUDY: WJC confers B.A. and B.S. degrees. Bachelor's degrees are awarded in BIOLOGICAL SCIENCE (biochemistry and biology/biological science), BUSINESS (accounting, business administration and management, business economics, and international business management), COMMUNICATIONS AND THE ARTS (art, communications, dramatic arts, English, French, music, and Spanish), COMPUTER AND PHYSICAL SCIENCE (chemistry, mathematics, and physics), EDUCATION (elementary education, music education, and secondary education), HEALTH PROFESSIONS (medical laboratory technology and nursing), SOCIAL SCIENCE (history, international relations, Japanese studies, philosophy, political science/government, psychology, and religion). Business has the largest enrollment.

ACTIVITIES: 31% of men belong to 3 national fraternities; 34% of women belong to 4 national sororities. There are 60 groups on campus, including cheerleading, choir, chorale, chorus, computers, dance, debate, drama, drill team, ethnic, honors, international, jazz band, LGBT, musical theater, newspaper, orchestra, pep band, photography, political, professional, radio and TV, religious, social, social service, student government, and symphony. Popular campus events include Hanging of the Green/Lighting of the Quad and Family Weekend. **Sports:** There are 9 intercollegiate sports for men and 9 for women, and 12 intramural sports for men and 12 for women. Facilities include a football and soccer stadium, a complex for baseball and softball, and a phys ed center with an indoor track, a dance room, and facilities for basketball, racquetball, swimming, indoor tennis, volleyball, and weight lifting. **Graduates:** From July 1, 2016 to June 30, 2017, 267 bachelor's degrees were awarded. The most popular majors were business/marketing (22%), health professions and related sciences (17%), and psychology (11%). In an average class, 54% graduate in 4 years or less, 62% graduate in 5 years or less, and 63% graduate in 6 years or less. Of the 2016 graduating class, 25% were enrolled in graduate school within 6 months of graduation, and 75% were employed.

SERVICES: Counseling and information services are available, as is tutoring in most subjects. **Library/Resources:** The library contains 231,031 volumes, 1,050 microform items, 11,232 audio/video tapes/CDs/DVDs, subscribes to 500 periodicals, including electronic. Computerized library services include interlibrary loans, database searching, and Internet access. Special learning facilities include an art gallery, planetarium, and radio station. **Physically Challenged Students:** 85% of the campus is accessible. Facilities include wheelchair ramps, elevators, special parking, specially equipped restrooms, special class scheduling, lowered drinking fountains, lowered telephones, and special housing. **Special:** Internships for juniors or seniors, study abroad in Europe, Japan, Mexico, Australia, and Hong Kong, and a Washington semester are offered. In addition, B.A.-B.S. degrees, dual majors of any combination, internships, an accelerated degree in nursing, student-designed majors, and 3-2 engineering degrees with Washington University and the Universities of Missouri and Kansas are available. The Oxbridge Honors Program for major study is patterned after the teaching methods of Oxford and Cambridge and includes a year at either Oxford or Cambridge. Leadership and service learning programs are offered. There are 13 national honor societies, a freshman honors program, and 13 departmental honors programs. **Visiting:** There are regularly scheduled orientations for prospective students, and personalized visits can be arranged upon request. There are guides for informal visits and visitors may sit in on classes. To schedule a visit, contact the Admission Office. **Campus Safety and Security:** Measures include 24-hour foot and vehicle patrol, emergency notification system, and self-defense education. There are emergency telephones, lighted pathways/sidewalks, and controlled access to dorms/residences.

REQUIREMENTS: The SAT or ACT is required. Students must be graduates of an accredited secondary school; the GED is also accepted. The college requires that applicants have taken 4 English courses and 4 academic electives, 3 courses each in math, social studies, and science; of these, 1 must be a lab, 2 in foreign language. An interview is recommended. An audition is advised for music applicants. AP and CLEP credits are accepted. Important factors in the admissions decision are advanced placement or honors courses, extracurricular activities record, and leadership record. To graduate, students must complete a minimum of 124 credits with a minimum 2.0 GPA, fulfilling the proper core requirements for their major and degree. All students must take The Responsible Self in their first year, and also take courses in oral and written communication, physical education, math, foreign language, interdisciplinary courses in 4 categories, and a core curriculum capstone course. Comprehensive exams in most majors are required. **Procedure:** Freshmen are admitted in the fall, spring, and summer. Entrance exams should be taken in the junior year. There are deferred admissions and rolling admissions plans. Applications should be filed by August 15 for fall entry. The fall 2017 application fee was $25. Notification is sent on a rolling basis. Applications are accepted on-line. **Transfer Students:** 44 transfer students enrolled in 2016-2017. Transfer students must have maintained a 2.5 GPA and be in good academic standing with their former schools and submit all college transcripts. Education majors must take the ACT, achieving a minimum score of 20. An interview is recommended for all students. 30 of 124 credits required for the bachelor's degree must be completed at WJC. **International Students:** There are 22 international students enrolled. They must take the TOEFL with a minimum score of 550 on the paper-based TOEFL (PBT) or 80 on the Internet-based version (iBT) or take the MELAB.

ADMISSIONS: 55% of the 2017-2018 applicants were accepted. The SAT scores for the 2017-2018 freshman class were: Critical Reading--24% below 500, 30% between 500 and 599, 39% between 600 and 699, and 7% between 700 and 800. Math-- 21% below 500, 34% between 500 and 599, 39% between 600 and 699, and 11% between 700 and 800. The ACT scores were 9% below 12, 22% between 12 and 17, 25% between 18 and 23, 18% between 24 and 29, and 26% above 30. 68% of the current freshmen were in the top fifth of their class; 92% were in the top two fifths. 28 freshmen graduated first in their class. **Admissions Contact:** Bridget Gramling, Dean of Admissions. Email: *admission@william.jewell.edu* Web: *www.jewell.edu*

FINANCIAL AID: In 2017-2018, 99% of all full-time freshmen received some form of financial aid. 72% of all full-time freshmen received need-based aid. The average freshman award was $25,316. The average financial indebtedness of the 2017 graduate was $24,102. WJ is a member of CSS. The FAFSA code is 002524. The priority date for freshman financial aid applications for fall entry is March 1.

WILLIAM WOODS UNIVERSITY — C-2

www.williamwoods.edu

Fulton, MO 65251	**(573) 592-1106** **(800) 995-3159**
Fax: (573) 592-1180	**Email: admissions@williamwoods.edu**
Full-time: 220 men, 616 women	**Faculty:** 56; IIA, --$
Part-time: 39 men, 98 women	**Ph.D.s:** 60%
Graduate: 420 men, 683 women	**Student/Faculty:** 11 to 1
Year: semesters, summer session	**Tuition:** $22,740
Room & Board: $9300	**Freshman Class:** 863 applied, 631 accepted, 184 enrolled
SAT CR/M: 490/500 **ACT:** 22	**CEEB CODE:** 6944
Application Deadline: August 15	**COMPETITIVE**

William Woods University, founded in 1870, is an independent professions-oriented, liberal arts institution affiliated with the Christian Church (Disciples of Christ). Unique programs of study include an equestrian studies program and a four-year American Sign Language Interpreting program. There is 1 undergraduate school and 1 graduate school. In addition to regional accreditation, WWU has baccalaureate program accreditation with CSWE, CAATE, and CAAHEP. The 170-acre campus is in a small town 100 miles west of St. Louis. Including any residence halls, there are 35 buildings.

STUDENT LIFE: 60% of undergraduates are from Missouri. Others are from 42 states, 19 foreign countries, and Canada. 80% are White; 5% Hispanic; 4% African American; 4% Foreign; 3% race unknown; 2% two or more races; 1% Asian American; 1% American Indian/Alaska Native. 42% are Baptist, Christian, Methodist, Lutheran, Presbyterian, and Pentecost; 30% claim no religious affiliation; 21% Catholic. **Female To Male Ratio:** 2.1:1. The average age of freshmen is 19; all undergraduates, 21. 26% do not continue beyond their first year; 52% remain to graduate. **Housing:** 760 students can be accommodated in college housing, which includes dorms and on-campus apartments. In addition, there are special-interest houses, fraternity houses, sorority houses, nonsmoking, and independent housing. On-campus housing is guaranteed for all 4 years. 76% of students live on campus. All students may keep cars.

FACULTY/CLASSROOMS: 46% of faculty are male; 54% are female. All teach undergraduates. No introductory courses are taught by graduate students. The average class size in an introductory lecture is 20; in a laboratory is 15; and in a regular course is 15.

PROGRAMS OF STUDY: WWU confers B.A., B.S., B.F.A. and B.S.W. degrees. Associate, master's, and doctoral degrees are also awarded. Bachelor's degrees are awarded in AGRICULTURE (equine science), BIOLOGICAL SCIENCE (biology/biological science), BUSINESS (accounting and business administration and management), COMMUNICATIONS AND THE ARTS (American Sign Language, art, communications, dramatic arts, English, graphic design, journalism, and studio art), COMPUTER AND PHYSICAL SCIENCE (computer science, information sciences and systems, mathematics, and science), EDUCATION (athletic training, early childhood education, elementary education, middle school education, physical education, physical ed teacher education, and special education), SOCIAL SCIENCE (family/juvenile justice, history, interdisciplinary studies, international studies, interpreter for the deaf, paralegal studies, political science/government, psychology, and social work). Business and equestrian studies is the strongest academically.

ACTIVITIES: 43% of men belong to 2 national fraternities; 45% of women belong to 4 national sororities. There are 40 groups on campus, including art, cheerleading, choir, drama, honors, international, musical theater, newspaper, professional, radio and TV, religious, social, social service, and student government. Popular campus events include Salute to the Arts, Campus Involvement and Activities Fair, and Autumn at the Woods. **Sports:** There are 5 intercollegiate sports for men and 6 for women, and 7 intramural sports for men and 7 for women. Facilities include a gym, a fitness center, a sand volleyball court, tennis courts, soccer, baseball, and softball fields, a weight room, table tennis and pool tables, a cross-country trail equipped with FitTrail stations. **Graduates:** From July 1, 2016 to June 30, 2017, 212 bachelor's degrees were awarded. The most popular majors were business (19%), equestrian studies/ equestrian (16%), and education (12%). In an average class, 49% graduate in 4 years or less, 52% graduate in 5 years or less, and 52% graduate in 6 years or less.

SERVICES: Counseling and information services are available, as is tutoring in most subjects. There is a reader service for the blind, and remedial math and writing. Interpreting is provided for the deaf upon request and receipt of supporting documentation. **Library/Resources:** The library contains 134,338 volumes, 11,072 microform items, 28,711 audio/video tapes/CDs/DVDs, and subscribes to 15,796 periodicals, including electronic. Computerized library services include interlibrary loans, database searching, Internet access, and Wi-Fi capability. Special learning facilities include an art gallery, radio station, 12 "smart classrooms" equipped with smartboards and networked computers, labs for photography, foreign languages, art, and American Sign Language interpreting, equestrian studies stables, a model courtroom, and an observatory. **Physically Challenged Students:** 85% of the campus is accessible. Facilities include wheelchair ramps, elevators, special parking, specially equipped restrooms, special class scheduling, and lowered telephones. The campus has access to TTY phones. **Special:** WWU offers cross-registration with schools in the Mid-Missouri Association of Colleges and Universities, internships in various fields, including equestrian studies and computer information systems, study abroad, and work-study. We also offer an accelerated degree program in several majors, and student-designed and dual majors are also possible. Credit for life, and credit for military experience, are available. The LEAD (Leading, Educating, Achieving, and Developing) program provides awards ($5000 to residential students) for incoming students who makes a commitment to attend a minimum number of campus activities and participate within the surrounding community. There are 12 national honor societies and a freshman honors program. **Visiting:** There are regularly scheduled orientations for prospective students, including the opportunity to talk with an academic adviser, and an extensive student development-directed background to campus life. There are guides for informal visits; visitors may sit in on classes and stay overnight. To schedule a visit, contact Ashley Sundin, Admissions Office Coodinator, at Ashley.sundin@williamwoods.edu. **Campus Safety and Security:** Measures include 24-hour foot and vehicle patrol, self-defense education, and security escort services. There are emergency telephones, lighted pathways/sidewalks, and controlled access to dorms/residences.

REQUIREMENTS: A high-school GPA of 2.5 on a 4.0 scale, and a score of 19 on the ACT or 900 on the SAT is generally required for admission. AP and CLEP credits are accepted. Students must complete a minimum of 120 credits to graduate, including at least 30 in the major and 43 in Common Studies. Applicants should have maintained a minimum GPA of 2.0. An internship or other culminating project is required for many majors. **Procedure:** Freshmen are admitted to all sessions. Entrance exams should be taken in the spring of the junior year or the fall of the senior year. There are deferred admissions and rolling admissions plans. Applications should be filed by August 15 for fall entry. Applications are accepted online. **Transfer Students:** 79 transfer students enrolled in 2016-2017. Transfer students are required to have at least 12 college credit hours from an accredited college or university and have at least a 2.0 cumulative GPA. 30 of 120 credits required for the bachelor's degree must be completed at WWU. **International Students:** There are 46 international students enrolled. They must take the TOEFL with a minimum score of 500 on the paper-based TOEFL (PBT) or 61 on the Internet-based version (iBT). They must also take the SAT or ACT, scoring 19.

ADMISSIONS: 73% of the 2017-2018 applicants were accepted. The SAT scores for the 2017-2018 freshman class were: Critical Reading-- 53% below 500, 31% between 500 and 599, and 16% between 600 and 699. Math-- 47% below 500, 27% between 500 and 599, and 16% between 600 and 699. The ACT scores were 14% between 12 and 17, 49% between 18 and 23, 28% between 24 and 29, and 9% above 30. 45% of the current freshmen were in the top fifth of their class; 65% were in the top two fifths. **Admissions Contact:** Kathy Groves, Vice President. Email: *admissions@williamwoods.edu* Web: *www.williamwoods.edu*

FINANCIAL AID: In 2017-2018, 100% of all full-time freshmen received some form of financial aid. 70% of all full-time freshmen received need-based aid. The average freshman award was $12,633. The college's own financial statement is required. The FAFSA code is 002525. The deadline for filing freshman financial aid applications for fall entry is March 1.

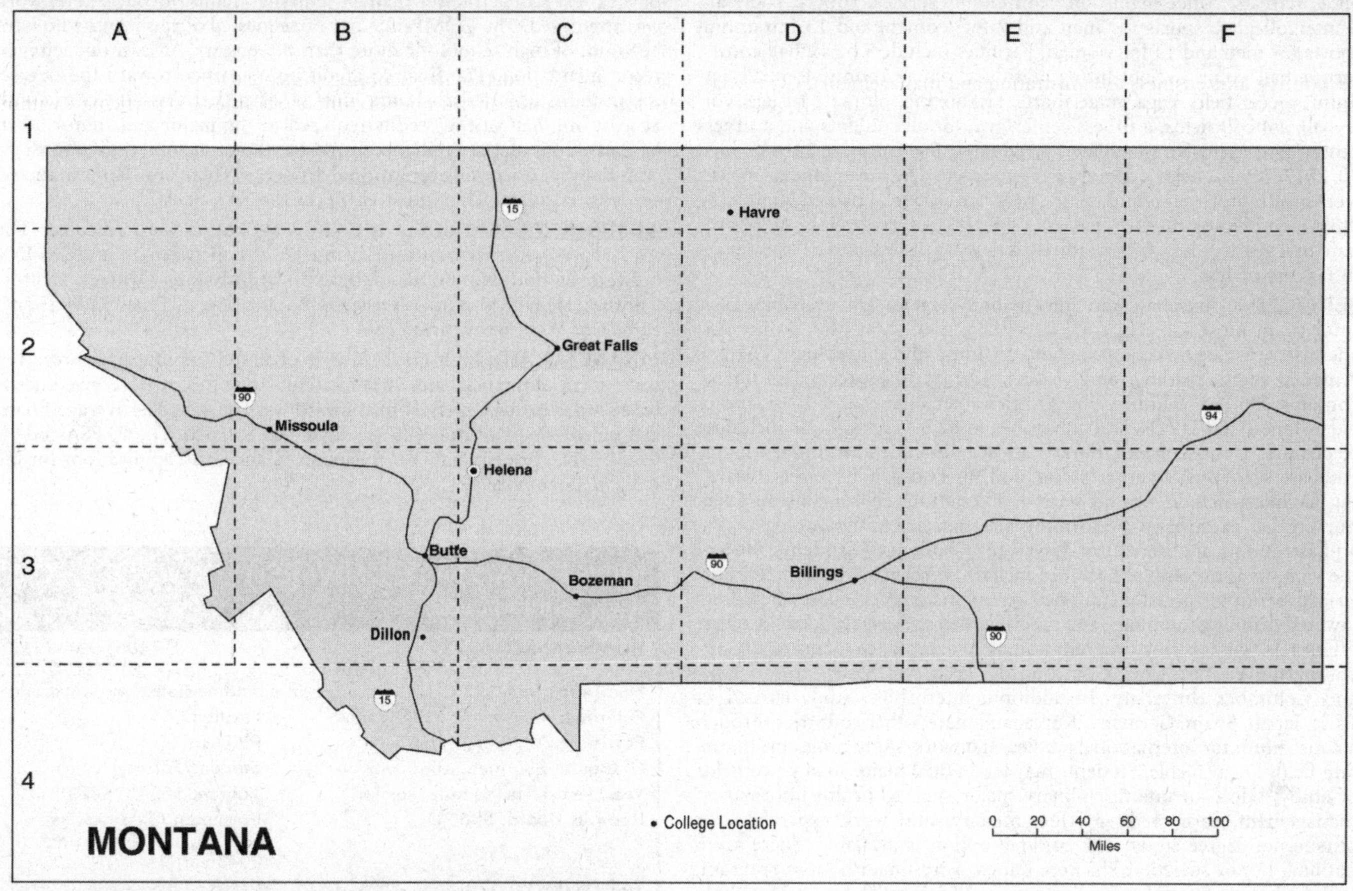

CARROLL COLLEGE C-3

www.carroll.edu

Helena, MT 59625	**(406) 447-4384** **(800) 992-3648**
Fax: (406) 447-4533	**Email: admission@caroll.edu**
Full-time: 521 men, 766 women	**Faculty:** 91
Part-time: 27 men, 38 women	**Ph.D.s:** 77%
Graduate: n/av	**Student/Faculty:** 11 to 1
Year: semesters, summer session	**Tuition:** $34,480
Room & Board: $9824	**Freshman Class:** 2182 applied, 2088 accepted, 298 enrolled
SAT: required **ACT:** 21	**CEEB CODE:** 4041
Application Deadline: February 1	**COMPETITIVE**

Carroll College is a private, Catholic, liberal arts and pre-professional college. Founded in 1909, Carroll has distinguished itself as a preeminent and award-winning leader in academic programs including pre-medical, natural sciences, nursing, engineering, mathematics, the social sciences and the liberal arts. Scientific research, service learning, education abroad and a vibrant campus faith community form cornerstones of the Carroll educational experience. There are 2 undergraduate schools and 1 graduate school. In addition to regional accreditation, Carroll has baccalaureate program accreditation with ABET, CAHEA, CSWE, NASDTEC, NLN, and NRPA. The 64-acre campus is in a small town 110 miles east of Missoula and 100 miles west of Bozeman. Including any residence halls, there are 25 buildings.

STUDENT LIFE: 56% of undergraduates are from out of state, mostly the Northwest. Students are from 33 states, 16 foreign countries, and Canada. 81% are from public schools. 79% are White; 8% race unknown; 5% Hispanic; 3% two or more races; 2% Foreign; 1% African American; 1% Asian American; 1% American Indian/Alaska Native. 41% are Catholic; 29% Protestant. **Female To Male Ratio:** 1.5:1. The average age of freshmen is 18; all undergraduates, 20. 17% do not continue beyond their first year; 71% remain to graduate. **Housing:** 1041 students can be accommodated in college housing, which includes married student dorms, on-campus apartments, and a freshman residence hall. On-campus housing is guaranteed for all 4 years. 66% of students live on campus. All students may keep cars.

FACULTY/CLASSROOMS: 49% of faculty are male; 51% are female. All teach undergraduates. No introductory courses are taught by graduate students. The average class size in an introductory lecture is 22; in a laboratory is 13; and in a regular course is 16.

PROGRAMS OF STUDY: Carroll confers B.A. and B.S. degrees. Associate and master's degrees are also awarded. Bachelor's degrees are awarded in AGRICULTURE (animal science), BIOLOGICAL SCIENCE (biochemistry and biology/biological science), BUSINESS (accounting, business administration and management, and finance), COMMUNICATIONS AND THE ARTS (classical languages, communications, English, English literature, English Writing, French, public relations, Spanish, and theatre arts), COMPUTER AND PHYSICAL SCIENCE (chemistry, computer information systems, computer science, mathematics, and physics), EDUCATION (elementary education, French studies K-12 education, reading education, secondary education, Spanish education K-12, and special education), ENGINEERING AND ENVIRONMENTAL DESIGN (civil engineering, engineering science, and environmental science), HEALTH PROFESSIONS (health science, nursing, predentistry, premedicine, preoptometry, prepharmacy, prephysician assistant, prephysical therapy, preveterinary science, and public health), SOCIAL SCIENCE (history, international relations, philosophy, political science/government, prelaw, psychology, religion, sociology, and theology). Biology, nursing, and health science have the largest enrollments.

ACTIVITIES: There are no fraternities or sororities. Groups on campus include fishing, floating, hiking, skiing, snowshoeing, wilderness training, art, Carroll Adventure and Mountaineering Program, cheerleading, choir, dance, drama, drill team, drum and bugle corps, environmental, ethnic, film, forensics, honors, international, jazz band, LGBT, literary magazine, musical theater, newspaper, pep band, political, professional, radio and TV, religious, social, social service, student government, and yearbook. Popular campus events include Theme Dances, Spring Softball

Tournament, SEARCH, Literary and film festival, Fall Guad Hill Slip n' Slide, retreats, coffee nights, and community service. **Sports:** There are 6 intercollegiate sports for men and 7 for women, and 13 intramural sports for men and 13 for women. Facilities include 3 basketball courts, racquetball court, weight-lifting, aerobics, dance rooms, football stadium, soccer field, yoga, martial arts, kickboxing, ultimate frisbee, volleyball, softball fields, a fitness center/gym for all students and a fitness center/gym exclusive to athletes. **Graduates:** From July 1, 2016 to June 30, 2017, 269 bachelor's degrees were awarded. The most popular majors were health professions and related programs (35%), business/marketing (13%), and biological/life sciences (12%). In an average class, 47% graduate in 4 years or less, 66% graduate in 5 years or less, and 71% graduate in 6 years or less.

SERVICES: Counseling and information services are available, as is tutoring in most subjects, such as writing, math, statistics, economics, chemistry, biology, accounting, and anatomy and physiology. There is remedial math, reading, and writing. **Library/Resources:** The library contains 590,733 volumes, 50,000 microform items, and 1,703 audio/video tapes/CDs/DVDs, and subscribes to 82,997 periodicals including electronic. Computerized library services include interlibrary loans, database searching, Internet access, and Wi-Fi capability. Special learning facilities include a radio station, TV station, civil engineering lab, nursing lab (SimMan), performing arts theater, Anthrozoology barn, and astronomical observatory. **Physically Challenged Students:** 90% of the campus is accessible. Facilities include wheelchair ramps, elevators, special parking, specially equipped restrooms, special class scheduling, lowered drinking fountains, and special housing. **Special:** Carroll College offers a 3-2 engineering program leading to acceptance to any of 6 cooperating universities: USC, Gonzaga, MT Tech, MT State, Notre Dame, and Columbia University. In addition, internships, study abroad in Paris, Japan, Spain, Germany, Korea, and many other countries through a consortium for international studies, and work-study programs in certain fields are available. Students may take a dual major in any two fields of study, select an interdisciplinary major such as health information management, earn credit for life, military, and work experience, or pursue nondegree study. The pass/fail option is available. There are 6 national honor societies, Phi Beta Kappa, a freshman honors program, and 5 departmental honors programs. **Visiting:** There are regularly scheduled orientations for prospective students. There are also personalized events during academic year: Campus tour, meeting with financial aid and admission, meeting with professor and sitting in on a class, lunch with current students, and overnight stay in residence halls if already accepted. Contact the Admission Office at Visit@carroll.edu. **Campus Safety and Security:** Measures include emergency notification system and security escort services. There are emergency telephones, lighted pathways/sidewalks, controlled access to dorms/residences, Private security company: Securitas. 24-hour patrol on Weekdays, 3 PM - 7 AM on Weekends & Holidays.

REQUIREMENTS: Satisfactory scores on the SAT or on the ACT are recommended. Students must be graduates of an accredited secondary school or have a GED. An essay is required. High school recommended units are: 4 in English, 3 in math, 2 each for Science (1 must be a lab), social studies, history, academic electives, and 1 in visual performing arts. A GPA of 2.0 is required. AP and CLEP credits are accepted. Important factors in the admissions decision are advanced placement or honors courses, personality/intangible qualities, leadership record, parents or siblings attended your school, evidence of special talent, extracurricular activities record, recommendations by alumni, recommendations by school officials, and geographical diversity. To graduate, students must complete 122 semester hours and maintain the specific GPA and credit concentration required by their major. The college's general liberal arts requirements include courses in writing, communications, history, math, natural and social sciences, philosophy, theology, and fine arts. **Procedure:** Freshmen are admitted fall and spring. Entrance exams should be taken in the spring of junior year or fall of senior year. There is a rolling admissions plan. Applications should be filed by February 1 for fall entry; December 1 for spring entry. Notification is sent on a rolling basis. Applications are accepted on-line. **Transfer Students:** 78 transfer students enrolled in 2016-2017. Carroll welcomes applications from students whose educational interest will be served by transferring from two-year or four-year colleges. Students are considered transfer candidates if they: Have attempted a minimum of 24 credits from a regionally accredited college or university after high school graduation. 2.50 overall college GPA on a 4.0 scale. Submitted completed application form, including personal statement. Submitted official transcripts from all colleges previously attended and official transcripts from high school if fewer than 24 semester credits of college level work was attempted. ACT or SAT test scores if fewer than 24 semester credits of college level work was attempted. The COMPASS may be requested of applicants who have been out of high school for more than three years. At least one letter of recommendation. The final 45 credit hours earned toward the degree, a minimum of 30 credit hours must be earned at Carroll College with at least one-half of the credits required in the major and minor taken at Carroll. 30 of 122 credits required for the bachelor's degree must be completed at Carroll. **International Students:** There are 18 international students enrolled. They must also take the SAT or ACT.

ADMISSIONS: 96% of the 2017-2018 applicants were accepted. The ACT scores were 4% between 12 and 17, 40% between 18 and 23, 43% between 24 and 29, and 13% above 30. **Admissions Contact:** Cynthia Thornquist, Director of Admissions & Enrollment. Email: *admission@caroll.edu* Web: *www.carroll.edu*

FINANCIAL AID: In 2017-2018, 99% of all full-time freshmen received some form of financial aid. 70% of all full-time freshmen received need-based aid. The average freshman award was $26,421. The average financial indebtedness of the 2017 graduate was $30,640. The FAFSA code is 002526. The priority date for freshman financial aid applications for fall entry is December 1.

MONTANA STATE UNIVERSITY — C-3

www.montana.edu

Bozeman, MT 59717	**(406) 994-2452** **(888) MSU-CATS**
Fax: (406) 994-1923	**Email: admissions@montana.edu**
Full-time: 6466 men, 5205 women	**Faculty:** I, -$
Part-time: 1070 men, 966 women	**Ph.D.s:** 79%
Graduate: 895 men, 1086 women	**Student/Faculty:** 19 to 1
Year: semesters, summer session	**Tuition:** $6850 ($22,081)
Room & Board: $8650	**Freshman Class:** 13799 applied, 11570 accepted, 2943 enrolled
SAT CR/M/W: 570/565/545 **ACT:** 25	**CEEB CODE:** 4488
Application Deadline: n/av	**COMPETITIVE+**

Montana State University, the state's land-grant institution, educates students, creates knowledge and art, and serves communities by integrating learning, discovery and engagement. There are 9 undergraduate schools and 1 graduate school. In addition to regional accreditation, MSU has baccalaureate program accreditation with AACSB, ABET, ADA, CSAB, NAAB, NASAD, NASM, NLN, AAFCS, CACREP, and CCNE. The 1850-acre campus is in a small town 140 miles west of Billings and 90 miles north of Yellowstone National Park. Including any residence halls, there are 90 buildings.

STUDENT LIFE: 69% of undergraduates are from Montana. Others are from 50 states, 65 foreign countries, and Canada. 88% are White; 3% Foreign; 2% Hispanic; 1% Asian American; 1% American Indian/Alaska Native; 1% two or more races; 1% race unknown. **Male To Female Ratio:** 1.2:1. The average age of freshmen is 18; all undergraduates, 22. 29% do not continue beyond their first year; 47% remain to graduate. **Housing:** 5400 students can be accommodated in college housing, which includes married student dorms. In addition, there are honors houses, fraternity houses, sorority houses, floors for older students, nonsmoking floors, and theme and wellness floors. On-campus housing is guaranteed for the freshman year only, is available on a first-come, and first-served basis. 75% of students commute. All students may keep cars.

FACULTY/CLASSROOMS: 62% of faculty are male; 38% are female. All teach undergraduates, and all do research. Graduate students teach 21% of introductory courses. The average class size in an introductory lecture is 66; in a laboratory is 18; and in a regular course is 22.

PROGRAMS OF STUDY: MSU confers B.A., B.S., B.F.A. and B.Mus.Ed. degrees. Associate, master's, and doctoral degrees are also awarded. Bachelor's degrees are awarded in AGRICULTURE (agricultural business management, animal science, horticulture, natural resource management, and plant science), BIOLOGICAL SCIENCE (biology/biological science, biotechnology, cell biology, microbiology, and neurosciences), BUSINESS (business administration and management), COMMUNICATIONS AND THE ARTS (art, English, fine arts, media arts, modern language, and music), COMPUTER AND PHYSICAL SCIENCE (chemistry, computer science, earth science, mathematics, and physics), EDUCATION (agricultural education, elementary education, music education, secondary education, and technical education), ENGINEERING AND ENVIRONMENTAL DESIGN (agricultural engineering technology, chemical engineering, civil engineering, computer engineering, construction engineering, electrical/electronics engineering, environmental design, environmental science, industrial engineering, land use management and reclamation, mechanical engineering, and mechanical engineering technology), HEALTH PROFESSIONS (health and nursing), SOCIAL SCIENCE (anthropology, economics, history, human development, liberal arts/general studies, philosophy, political science/government, psychology, and sociology). Engineering, physical science, and architecture are the strongest academically. Business, education, and nursing have the largest enrollments.

ACTIVITIES: 4% of men belong to 7 national fraternities; 3% of women belong to 4 national sororities. There are 150 groups on campus, including art, band, cheerleading, chess, choir, chorale, chorus, computers, dance, drama, drill team, environmental, ethnic, film, honors, international, jazz band, LGBT, literary magazine, marching band, musical theater, newspaper, opera, orchestra, pep band, photography, political, professional, radio and TV, religious, social, social service, student government, and symphony. Popular campus events include International Food Bazaar, and Native American Pow-Wow. **Sports:** There are 6 intercollegiate sports for men and 7 for women, and 38 intramural sports for men and 40 for women. **Graduates:** From July 1, 2016 to June 30, 2017, 2223 bachelor's degrees were awarded. The most popular majors were engineering (12%), business (12%), and health professions and related sciences (10%). In an average class, 49% graduate in 6 years or less. Of the 2016 graduating class, 15% were enrolled in graduate school within 6 months of graduation, and 95% were employed.

SERVICES: Counseling and information services are available, as is tutoring in most subjects. There is a reader service for the blind, and remedial math, reading, and writing. **Library/Resources:** The library contains 744,989 volumes, 2.2 million microform items, and 13,446 audio/video tapes/CDs/DVDs, and subscribes to 10,131 periodicals including electronic. Computerized library services include interlibrary loans, database searching, and Internet access. Special learning facilities include an art gallery, natural history museum, planetarium, radio station, TV station, Blackstone Business Launchpad, Museum of the Rockies, College of Business and Entrepreneurship Center, nursing simulation lab, Subzero Science/Engineering Research, Optical Technology Center, and a telecommunication Center. **Physically Challenged Students:** 90% of the campus is accessible. Facilities include wheelchair ramps, elevators, special parking, specially equipped restrooms, special class scheduling, lowered drinking fountains, lowered telephones, a resource center, and a taping service for the blind. **Special:** Montana State University offers internships in selected majors, study in 40 countries, cross-registration in selected programs, B.A.-B.S. degrees, dual and interdisciplinary majors, nondegree study, and pass/fail options. There are 23 national honor societies and a freshman honors program. **Visiting:** There are regularly scheduled orientations for prospective students. There are guides for informal visits, visitors may sit in on classes, and stay overnight. To schedule a visit, contact the Office of New Student Services at orientation@montana.edu. **Campus Safety and Security:** Measures include 24-hour foot and vehicle patrol, emergency notification system, self-defense education, and security escort services. There are emergency telephones, lighted pathways/sidewalks, and controlled access to dorms/residences.

REQUIREMENTS: MSU requires applicants to have a minimum GPA of 2.5, rank in the upper 50% of their graduating class or have minimum composite scores of 22 on the ACT or a satisfactory score on the SAT. They must be graduates of an accredited secondary school. The GED is accepted. Students should have completed 4 years of English, 3 years each of social studies and math, 2 years of science with lab, and 2 years of language, computer science, visual and performing arts, or vocational education. A GPA of 2.5 is required. AP and CLEP credits are accepted. To graduate, students must complete a core curriculum of 8 credits of natural sciences, 6 credits each of multicultural studies, humanities, social science, and communications, and 3 credits each of fine arts and math. The total number of credits required varies by program, with 120 being the minimum; at least one third must be in upper-division courses. A minimum 2.0 GPA is needed. Students must be officially registered in their chosen curriculum for at least 2 semesters before graduation. **Procedure:** Freshmen are admitted fall, spring, and summer. Entrance exams should be taken in the fall of the senior year. There are deferred admissions and rolling admissions plans. Application deadlines are open. The fall 2017 application fee was $30. Notification is sent on a rolling basis. Applications are accepted on-line. **Transfer Students:** 848 transfer students enrolled in 2016-2017. Applicants must have a minimum GPA of 2.0, grades of D or better transfer for credit. 30 credits required for the bachelor's degree must be completed at MSU. **International Students:** They must take the TOEFL with a minimum score of 525 on the paper-based TOEFL (PBT). Students must also submit proof of American Cultural Exchange Language Institute Level 6 (available at MSU).

ADMISSIONS: 84% of the 2017-2018 applicants were accepted. The SAT scores for the 2017-2018 freshman class were: Critical Reading-- 22% below 500, 39% between 500 and 599, 32% between 600 and 699, and 7% between 700 and 800. Math-- 22% below 500, 38% between 500 and 599, 33% between 600 and 699, and 7% between 700 and 800. Writing-- 32% below 500, 39% between 500 and 599, 25% between 600 and 699, and 4% between 700 and 800. 114 freshmen graduated first in their class. **Admissions Contact:** Ronda Russell, Director, Admissions. Email: *admissions@montana.edu* Web: *www.montana.edu*

FINANCIAL AID: In 2017-2018, 64% of all full-time freshmen received some form of financial aid. 64% of all full-time freshmen received need-based aid. The average freshman award was $12,022. Need-based scholarships or need-based grants averaged $5,226; need-based self-help aid (loans and jobs) averaged $4,286; non-need-based athletic scholarships averaged $5,925; other non-need-based awards and non-need-based scholarships averaged $1,641; and $4,200 from other forms of aid. 50% of undergraduate students work part-time. The average financial indebtedness of the 2017 graduate was $24,421. Check with the school for current application deadlines.

MONTANA STATE UNIVERSITY BILLINGS *(The complete profile is made available exclusively on our website, www.barronspac.com)*

MONTANA STATE UNIVERSITY-NORTHERN *(The complete profile is made available exclusively on our website, www.barronspac.com)*

MONTANA TECH OF THE UNIVERSITY OF MONTANA — B-3

www.mtech.edu

Butte, MT 59701	**(406) 496-4568** **(800) 445-TECH**
Fax: (406) 496-4710	**Email: enrollment@mtech.edu**
Full-time: 1485 men, 750 women	**Faculty:** n/av
Part-time: 231 men, 304 women	**Ph.D.s:** 60%
Graduate: 134 men, 76 women	**Student/Faculty:** n/av
Year: semesters, summer session	**Tuition:** $6797 ($20,512)
Room & Board: $8650	**Freshman Class:** 969 applied, 857 accepted, 425 enrolled
SAT CR/M/W: 560/600/510 **ACT:** 25	**CEEB CODE:** 4487
Application Deadline: open	**VERY COMPETITIVE**

Montana Tech of the University of Montana possesses an internationally esteemed, century-old tradition of excellence in higher education. The university offers degrees and certificates focused in areas such as nursing, health and safety, responsible development of natural resources, engineering, ecology and restoration, business, information technology, energy, and workforce development. Montana Tech has a long-standing reputation for producing outstanding graduates. There are 3 undergraduate schools and 1 graduate school. In addition to regional accreditation, Montana Tech has baccalaureate program accreditation with ABET, CSAB, ACS, and IACBE. The 56-acre campus is in a small town in Butte, Montana. Including any residence halls, there are 19 buildings.

STUDENT LIFE: 79% of undergraduates are from Montana. Others are from 36 states, 14 foreign countries, and Canada. 9% are Foreign; 79% White; 6% race unknown; 2% American Indian/Alaska Native; 2% Hispanic; 1% African American; 1% Asian American. **Male To Female Ratio:** 1.6:1. 24% do not continue beyond their first year; 45% remain to graduate. **Housing:** College-sponsored housing includes married student dorms and off-campus apartments. On-campus housing is guaranteed for the freshman year only, is available on a first-come, and first-served basis. 89% of students commute. All students may keep cars.

FACULTY/CLASSROOMS: 66% of faculty are male; 34% are female. No introductory courses are taught by graduate students.

PROGRAMS OF STUDY: Montana Tech confers B.S. and B.A.S degrees.

Associate and master's degrees are also awarded. Bachelor's degrees are awarded in BIOLOGICAL SCIENCE (biology/biological science), BUSINESS (business information systems and business systems analysis), COMMUNICATIONS AND THE ARTS (communications and communications technology), COMPUTER AND PHYSICAL SCIENCE (chemistry, computer programming, computer science, mathematics, science, and statistics), EDUCATION (health information management), ENGINEERING AND ENVIRONMENTAL DESIGN (computer engineering, engineering, environmental engineering, geological engineering, geophysical engineering, metallurgical engineering, mining and mineral engineering, occupational safety and health, and petroleum/natural gas engineering), HEALTH PROFESSIONS (nursing), SOCIAL SCIENCE (liberal arts/general studies). Engineering is the strongest academically and has the largest enrollment.

ACTIVITIES: There are no fraternities or sororities. There are 50 groups on campus, including rodeo club, shooting and archery club, band, cheerleading, chess, choir, chorale, computers, dance, environmental, ethnic, honors, international, LGBT, newspaper, pep band, political, professional, radio and TV, religious, ski and snowboard club, social, social service, and student government. Popular campus events include M-Day and Homecoming. **Sports:** There are 3 intercollegiate sports for men and 3 for women. Facilities include a court, and cardio and weight room. **Graduates:** From July 1, 2016 to June 30, 2017, 294 bachelor's degrees were awarded. The most popular majors were petroleum engineering (22%), general engineering (15%), and business (13%). In an average class, 17% graduate in 4 years or less, 38% graduate in 5 years or less, and 43% graduate in 6 years or less.

SERVICES: Counseling and information services are available, as is tutoring in most subjects, such as accounting, algebra, basic math, biology, business, calculus, chemistry, differential equations, dynamics, E-circuits, engineering economics, fluids, nursing, physics, psychology, statics, strengths, survey of metallurgical & materials and engineering. There is a reader service for the blind, and remedial math and writing. There is also a Career exploration program, student/parent mentoring program, financial management workshops and study skills workshops. **Library/Resources:** The library contains 144,204 volumes, 60,704 microform items, and 5,995 audio/video tapes/CDs/DVDs, and subscribes to 73,241 periodicals including electronic. Computerized library services include interlibrary loans, database searching, Internet access, and Wi-Fi capability. Special learning facilities include a radio station, a mineral museum, and METNET 2-way interactive communication studio. **Physically Challenged Students:** 75% of the campus is accessible. Facilities include wheelchair ramps, elevators, special parking, specially equipped restrooms, special class scheduling, lowered drinking fountains, lowered telephones, and special housing. **Special:** 3-2 liberal arts-engineering program with Carroll College, dual enrollment agreement with Flathead Valley Community College, collaborative programs with UM Helena (BAS Business, BS BIT, BAS General Studies), UM Western (Elementary Education Certification and Secondary Education Certification in Biological Sciences, General Sciences, and Mathematical Sciences), and UM-COT (AAS Surgical Technology). Additionally, Tech offers double majors, honors program, independent study, internships, and work study. There are 3 national honor societies, Phi Beta Kappa, and a freshman honors program. **Visiting:** There are regularly scheduled orientations for prospective students, there is an official fall orientation, visits are welcome any time. To schedule a visit, contact the Enrollment Services at (406) 496-4256. **Campus Safety and Security:** Measures include 24-hour foot and vehicle patrol, emergency notification system, self-defense education, and security escort services. There are emergency telephones and lighted pathways/sidewalks.

REQUIREMENTS: The SAT or ACT is required. The ACT Optional Writing test is also required. Applicants must be graduates of an accredited secondary school. The GED is accepted. 14 academic credits are required, including 4 years of English, 3 years each of math and social studies, 2 years each of science, foreign language, computer science, and visual and performing arts, or vocational education. Applicants must have minimum composite scores of 22 on the ACT or satisfactory scores on the SAT or a 2.5 GPA, or be in the top half of their graduating class. Other factors regarding admissions are considered only if the preceding standards are not met. Montana Tech requires applicants to be in the upper 50% of their class. A GPA of 2.5 is required. AP and CLEP credits are accepted. For graduation, students must complete at least 120 semester credits (more for engineering degrees) and maintain a minimum 2.0 GPA. Requirements include 6 hours each of communications, humanities/fine arts, mathematical sciences, and social sciences, and 6 to 7 hours of physical and life sciences with a lab required for 1 course. Engineering students must satisfy specific requirements within the individual curriculum. **Procedure:** Freshmen are admitted to all sessions. Entrance exams should be taken in the senior year. There are deferred admissions and rolling admissions plans. Application deadlines are open. The fall 2017 application fee was $30. Notification is sent on a rolling basis. Applications are accepted on-line. **Transfer Students:** 226 transfer students enrolled in 2016-2017. Transfer applicants must have a minimum GPA of 2.0. Grades of C and above transfer for credit. **International Students:** There are 260 international students enrolled. They must take the TOEFL with a minimum score of 525 on the paper-based TOEFL (PBT) or 71 on the Internet-based version (iBT). They must also take the SAT or ACT, scoring 22.

ADMISSIONS: 88% of the 2017-2018 applicants were accepted. The SAT scores for the 2017-2018 freshman class were: Critical Reading-- 21% below 500, 52% between 500 and 599, 25% between 600 and 699, and 2% between 700 and 800. Math-- 10% below 500, 35% between 500 and 599, 52% between 600 and 699, and 3% between 700 and 800. Writing-- 40% below 500, 54% between 500 and 599, and 6% between 600 and 699. The ACT scores were 33% between 18 and 23, 59% between 24 and 29, and 8% above 30. 28 freshmen graduated first in their class. **Admissions Contact:** Stephanie Crowe, Director of Recruiting. Email: *enrollment@mtech.edu* Web: *www.mtech.edu*

FINANCIAL AID: In 2017-2018, 59% of all full-time freshmen received some form of financial aid. 53% of all full-time freshmen received need-based aid. The average freshman award was $9,477. Need-based scholarships or need-based grants averaged $5,575; need-based self-help aid (loans and jobs) averaged $3,224; non-need-based athletic scholarships averaged $4,026; and other non-need-based awards and non-need-based scholarships averaged $2,054. The average financial indebtedness of the 2017 graduate was $26,198. The college's own financial statement is required. The FAFSA code is 002531. Check with the school for current application deadlines.

ROCKY MOUNTAIN COLLEGE D-3

www.rocky.edu

Billings, MT 59102	**(406) 657-1000** **(800) 877-6259**
Fax: (406) 657-1189	**Email: admissions@rocky.edu**
Full-time: 441 men, 428 women	**Faculty:** 63; IIB, --$
Part-time: 17 men, 13 women	**Ph.D.s:** 83%
Graduate: 43 men, 50 women	**Student/Faculty:** 14 to 1
Year: semesters, summer session	**Tuition:** $27,566
Room & Board: $8210	**Freshman Class:** 1238 applied, 797 accepted, 247 enrolled
SAT EBR-W/M: 530/518 **ACT:** 22	**CEEB CODE:** 4660
Application Deadline: n/av	**COMPETITIVE**

Rocky Mountain College is a private college founded on the unique practice of joining the liberal arts tradition along with practical training for professional development. Established in 1878, RMC functions on a mission of educating students through liberal arts and professional programs that cultivate critical thinking, creative expression, ethical decision-making, informed citizenship, and professional excellence. RMC supports its mission through core themes of academic excellence, transformational learning, and shared responsibility and stewardship. There is 1 undergraduate school and 1 graduate school. In addition to regional accreditation, RMC has baccalaureate program accreditation with ARC-PA and AABI. The 60-acre campus is in a suburban area in a residential section of Billings, Montana. Including any residence halls, there are 17 buildings.

STUDENT LIFE: 53% of undergraduates are from Montana. Others are from 41 states, 16 foreign countries, and Canada. 77% are White; 6% two or more races; 5% Hispanic; 4% Foreign; 3% African American; 2% American Indian/Alaska Native; 2% race unknown; 1% Asian American. **Male To Female Ratio:** 1.0:1. The average age of freshmen is 18; all undergraduates, 21. 31% do not continue beyond their first year; 52% remain to graduate. **Housing:** 570 students can be accommodated in college housing, which includes married student dorms and on-campus apartments. On-campus housing is guaranteed for the freshman year only, is available on a first-come, and first-served basis. 51% of students commute. Alcohol is not permitted. All students may keep cars.

FACULTY/CLASSROOMS: 53% of faculty are male; 47% are female. All teach undergraduates, 5% do research, and 5% do both. No introductory courses are taught by graduate students. The average class size in an introductory lecture is 15; in a laboratory is 11; and in a regular course is 15.

PROGRAMS OF STUDY: RMC confers B.A. and B.S. degrees. Associate and master's degrees are also awarded. Bachelor's degrees are awarded in AGRICULTURE (environmental studies, equestrian studies, and equine science), BUSINESS (accounting, business administration and management, and sports management), COMMUNICATIONS AND THE ARTS (art, communications, creative writing, literature, music performance, and theatre arts), COMPUTER AND PHYSICAL SCIENCE (chemistry, computer science, geology, mathematics, and petroleum systems/ geology), EDUCATION (art education, education, elementary education, English education, health and physical education, mathematics education, music education, psychology education, science education, social science education, and social studies education), ENGINEERING AND ENVIRONMENTAL DESIGN (aeronautical science, aviation administration/management, and environmental science), HEALTH PROFESSIONS (biology and exercise science), SOCIAL SCIENCE (history, philosophy and religion, political science/government, psychology, and sociology). Business, biology, and health and human performance have the largest enrollments.

ACTIVITIES: There are no fraternities or sororities. Groups on campus include art, aviation and equestrian, band, cheerleading, choir, chorale, chorus, computers, debate, drama, environmental, forensics, honors, international, jazz band, LGBT, literary magazine, musical theater, newspaper, pep band, professional, religious, social, social service, student government, and yearbook. Popular campus events include Convocations, Intercollegiate Athletics, Homecoming, Candlelight Dinner, Yule Log Dinner, and International Week. **Sports:** There are 9 intercollegiate sports for men and 9 for women, and 10 intramural sports for men and 10 for women. The athletic and recreational facilities include a football stadium, soccer field, gymnasium, auxiliary exercise areas, weight room, swimming pool, and a climbing wall. **Graduates:** From July 1, 2016 to June 30, 2017, 160 bachelor's degrees were awarded. The most popular majors were business (28%), education (11%), and health and human performance (11%). In an average class, 3% graduate in 3 years or less, 37% graduate in 4 years or less, 11% graduate in 5 years or less, and 1% graduate in 6 years or less. Of the 2016 graduating class, 22% were enrolled in graduate school within 6 months of graduation, and 78% were employed.

SERVICES: Counseling and information services are available, as is tutoring in most subjects, such as accounting, biology, chemistry, economics, mathematics, physics, and writing. There is a reader service for the blind, and remedial math, reading, and writing. Note-taking is available for qualified students. **Library/Resources:** The library contains 140,431 volumes, 11 microform items, and 1,728 audio/video tapes/ CDs/DVDs, and subscribes to 218 periodicals including electronic. Computerized library services include interlibrary loans, database searching, Internet access, and Wi-Fi capability. Special learning facilities include an art gallery, a flight school and equestrian facilities. **Physically Challenged Students:** 75% of the campus is accessible. Facilities include wheelchair ramps, elevators, special parking, specially equipped restrooms, special class scheduling, lowered drinking fountains, and special housing. **Special:** Rocky Mountain College offers internships with local, regional, and national employers. Various study abroad opportunities with formal exchange contracts in the United Kingdom, Finland, Japan, Sweden, and China. There are dual majors, individualized programs of study, credit for life, military, and work experience. Juniors and seniors may elect to take 1 course on a pass/fail basis each semester. Specialized programs offered by Rocky Mountain College include aviation and equestrian studies. There is 1 national honor society and 1 departmental honors program. **Visiting:** There are regularly scheduled orientations for prospective students, students may visit year-round and meet with admission representatives, tour campus, sit in on a class and meet with a faculty member. There are guides for informal visits, visitors may sit in on classes, and stay overnight. To schedule a visit, contact Megan Cabe at (406) 657-1026. **Campus Safety and Security:** Measures include emergency notification system, self-defense education, and security escort services. There are emergency telephones, lighted pathways/ sidewalks, controlled access to dorms/residences, security cameras and electronic access systems.

REQUIREMENTS: The SAT or ACT is required. Applicants must be graduates of an accredited secondary school. The GED is also accepted. Students must have completed 4 units each of English, and math, 3 units each in natural sciences, and social sciences, and 2 units of history. The school recommends a portfolio for admission to the art program, an audition for admission to the music or theatre program, and an interview for academically challenged students. A GPA of 2.5 is required. AP and CLEP credits are accepted. Important factors in the admissions decision are personality/intangible qualities, extracurricular activities record, and advanced placement or honors courses. To graduate, students must complete a minimum of 124 credit hours, complete all major requirements with a minimum overall GPA of 2.00 and 2.25 in the major. If a minor area is chosen, a minimum of 18 hours is required. There are core curriculum requirements in fine arts, humanities, communication, and the natural and social sciences, as well as writing, communication, and math. **Procedure:** Freshmen are admitted fall, spring, and summer. Entrance exams should be taken during the first half of the senior year. There are deferred admissions and rolling admissions plans. Application deadlines are open. The fall 2017 application fee was $35. Applications are accepted on-line. **Transfer Students:** 53 transfer students enrolled in 2016-2017. Transfer students must have a minimum GPA of 2.00 and grades of 2.00 and higher transfer for credit. Transfers are admitted every term. 30 of 124 credits required for the bachelor's degree must be completed at RMC. **International Students:** There are 33 international students enrolled. They must take the TOEFL with a minimum score of 570 on the paper-based TOEFL (PBT) or 72 on the Internet-based version (iBT). Students must take the IELTS, and the SAT or ACT, scoring 940/ SAT (critical reading and math) or 18/ACT.

ADMISSIONS: 64% of the 2017-2018 applicants were accepted. The SAT scores for the 2017-2018 freshman class were: Math-- 36% below 500, 51% between 500 and 599, and 13% between 600 and 699. Evidence-Based Reading/Writing-- 36% below 500, 43% between 500 and 599, 17% between 600 and 699, and 4% between 700 and 800. The ACT scores were 10% between 12 and 17, 56% between 18 and 23, 30% between 24 and 29, and 4% above 30. 23% of the current freshmen were in the top fifth of their class; 42% were in the top two fifths. 7 freshmen graduated first in their class. **Admissions Contact:** Austin Mapston, Dean of Enrollment Services. Email: *admissions@rocky.edu* Web: *www.rocky.edu*

FINANCIAL AID: In 2017-2018, 100% of all full-time freshmen received some form of financial aid. 91% of all full-time freshmen received need-based aid. The average freshman award was $28,263. Need-based scholarships or need-based grants averaged $17,632 ($35,256 maximum); need-based self-help aid (loans and jobs) averaged $6,588 ($24,934 maximum); non-need-based athletic scholarships averaged $4,637 ($14,036 maximum); and other non-need-based awards and non-need-based scholarships averaged $9,370 ($23,820 maximum). 29% of undergraduate students work part-time. The average financial indebtedness of the 2017 graduate was $20,168. The college's own financial statement is required. The FAFSA code is 002534. The priority date for freshman financial aid applications for fall entry is March 1.

THE UNIVERSITY OF MONTANA WESTERN *(The complete profile is made available exclusively on our website, www.barronspac.com)*

UNIVERSITY OF GREAT FALLS — C-2

www.ugf.edu

Great Falls, MT 59405	(406) 791-5210 (800) 856-9544
Fax: (406) 791-5209	**Email:** enroll@ugf.edu
Full-time: 268 men, 309 women	**Faculty:** n/av
Part-time: n/av	**Ph.D.s:** n/av
Graduate: n/av	**Student/Faculty:** n/av
Year: semesters, summer session	**Tuition:** $30,604
Room & Board: $7920	**Freshman Class:** n/av
SAT or ACT: recommended	**CEEB CODE:** 4058
Application Deadline: September 1	**COMPETITIVE**

University of Great Falls, established in 1932, is a private, liberal arts university affiliated with the Roman Catholic Church. Great Falls offers 40 undergraduate, 2 graduate (3 concentrations), and 4 distance learning degrees. There are 3 undergraduate schools and 2 graduate schools. The 44-acre campus is in an urban area in Great Falls Montana. Including any residence halls, there are 14 buildings.

STUDENT LIFE: 56% of undergraduates are from out of state, mostly

the West. Students are from 30 states, 10 foreign countries, and Canada. 70% are White; 7% race unknown; 4% Foreign. 30% claim no religious affiliation; 29% Catholic. **Female To Male Ratio:** 1.2:1. **Housing:** 189 students can be accommodated in college housing, which includes dorms, on-campus apartments, and off-campus apartments. On-campus housing is available on a first-come and first-served basis. Alcohol is not permitted. All students may keep cars.

FACULTY/CLASSROOMS: 59% of faculty are male; 42% are female. All teach undergraduates. No introductory courses are taught by graduate students. The average class size in an introductory lecture is 15; in a laboratory is 10; and in a regular course is 14.

PROGRAMS OF STUDY: UGF confers B.A. and B.S. degrees. Associate and master's degrees are also awarded. Bachelor's degrees are awarded in BIOLOGICAL SCIENCE (biology/biological science, microbiology, molecular biology, and physiology), BUSINESS (accounting, business administration and management, and management science), COMMUNICATIONS AND THE ARTS (art, English, and fine arts), COMPUTER AND PHYSICAL SCIENCE (computer science, mathematics, physical sciences, and science), EDUCATION (education of the exceptional child, elementary education, health and physical education, mathematics education, middle school education, physical education, reading education, science education, secondary education, social studies education, and special education), HEALTH PROFESSIONS (predentistry and premedicine), SOCIAL SCIENCE (addiction studies, counseling/psychology, criminal justice, history, law enforcement and corrections, paralegal studies, political science/government, prelaw, psychology, religion, religious studies, social science, social studies, sociology, and theological studies). Biology, paralegal studies, and computer science are the strongest academically. Biology, education, and business administration have the largest enrollments.

ACTIVITIES: There are no fraternities or sororities. There are 18 groups on campus, including art, cheerleading, chess, choir, chorus, computers, debate, drama, ethnic, forensics, honors, literary magazine, musical theater, orchestra, photography, professional, religious, social, social service, student government, and symphony. Popular campus events include Orientation Barbecue, Spook-a-Roo (Halloween community activity), Alumni Weekend, and Friends and Family Weekend. **Sports:** There are 2 intercollegiate sports for men and 3 for women, and 7 intramural sports for men and 7 for women. Facilities include a gymnasium with training facilities, a game room, and workout room.

SERVICES: Counseling and information services are available, as is tutoring in some subjects, such as 090-level courses, 100-level courses, 200-level courses, and selected 300-level courses. There is a reader service for the blind, and remedial math, reading, and writing. There is also tutoring in basic skills. **Library/Resources:** The library contains 106,135 volumes, 124,608 microform items, and 3,894 audio/video tapes/CDs/DVDs, and subscribes to 587 periodicals including electronic. Computerized library services include interlibrary loans, database searching, Internet access, and Wi-Fi capability. Special learning facilities include an art gallery. **Physically Challenged Students:** All of the campus is accessible. Facilities include wheelchair ramps, special parking, specially equipped restrooms, special class scheduling, and lowered drinking fountains. **Special:** There is 1 national honor society and a freshman honors program. **Visiting:** There are regularly scheduled orientations for prospective students, including meeting with prospective advisers and staff, financial aid presentation, a campus tour, and lunch. To schedule a visit, contact the Admissions Office. **Campus Safety and Security:** Measures include 24-hour foot and vehicle patrol, emergency notification system, self-defense education, and security escort services. There are shuttle buses, emergency telephones, and lighted pathways/sidewalks.

REQUIREMENTS: The SAT or ACT is recommended. Graduation from an accredited secondary school is required; the GED is accepted. Applicants should have 4 years of English, 3 years of math, and 2 years each of social studies, science, electives, foreign language, art, music, and vocational education. A GPA of 2.0 is required. AP and CLEP credits are accepted. Students must complete 128 credit hours, including 30 to 65 in the major, plus 15 to 21 minor credits, maintaining a minimum GPA of 2.0. The 52-credit-hour core curriculum includes math, computer science, art, behavioral science, history, literature, philosophy, science, writing, theology, and religion. Specific disciplines required include human nature, intellectual inquiry, and religious dimension. **Procedure:** Freshmen are admitted fall, spring, and summer. Entrance exams should be taken prior to registration. There are deferred admissions and rolling admissions plans. Applications should be filed by September 1 for fall entry. The fall 2017 application fee was $25. **Transfer Students:** Transfer applicants must be in good academic standing from another accredited college or university, and must submit official transcripts from all colleges or universities attended. Transfer students must also submit an official high school transcript. 30 of 128 credits required for the bachelor's degree must be completed at UGF. **International Students:** There are 27 international students enrolled. They must take the TOEFL with a minimum score of 500 on the paper-based TOEFL (PBT) or 80 on the Internet-based version (iBT).

Admissions Contact: Melanie Houge, Assistant Director of Admission. Email: *enroll@ugf.edu* Web: *www.ugf.edu*

FINANCIAL AID: In 2017-2018, 95% of all full-time freshmen received some form of financial aid. 52% of all full-time freshmen received need-based aid. The average freshman award was $15,002. Non-need-based athletic scholarships averaged $15,527; and other non-need-based awards and non-need-based scholarships averaged $13,971. UGF is a member of CSS. The FAFSA code is 002527. Check with the school for current application deadlines.

UNIVERSITY OF MONTANA — B-2

www.umt.edu

Missoula, MT 59812	**(406) 243-5672** **(800) 462-8636**
Fax: (406) 243-5711	**Email: admiss@umontana.edu**
Full-time: 4303 men, 4978 women	**Faculty:** I, --$
Part-time: 1143 men, 1268 women	**Ph.D.s:** 77%
Graduate: 923 men, 1337 women	**Student/Faculty:** 16 to 1
Year: semesters, summer session	**Tuition:** $6099 ($22,372)
Room & Board: $8006	**Freshman Class:** 5345 applied, 4956 accepted, 2013 enrolled
SAT CR/M/W: 550/542/530 **ACT:** 23	**CEEB CODE:** 4489
Application Deadline: March 1	**COMPETITIVE**

University of Montana, founded in 1893, is a public institution with programs in arts and sciences, business administration, visual and performing arts, education and human sciences, forestry, journalism, and pharmacy and allied health sciences. It is part of the Montana University System. There are 8 undergraduate schools and 2 graduate schools. In addition to regional accreditation, UM has baccalaureate program accreditation with AACSB, ACCE, ACPE, APTA, CAHEA, CSAB, CSWE, NASAD, NASDTEC, NASM, and SAF. The 220-acre campus is in an urban area 200 miles east of Spokane. Including any residence halls, there are 57 buildings.

STUDENT LIFE: 73% of undergraduates are from Montana. Others are from 50 states, 68 foreign countries, and Canada. 80% are from public schools. 76% are White; 7% race unknown; 4% Hispanic; 4% Foreign; 4% two or more races; 3% American Indian/Alaska Native; 1% African American; 1% Asian American. **Female To Male Ratio:** 1.2:1. The average age of freshmen is 19; all undergraduates, 23. 28% do not continue beyond their first year; 50% remain to graduate. **Housing:** 3430 students can be accommodated in college housing, which includes married student dorms and off-campus apartments. In addition, there are honors houses, special-interest houses, an international house, and nontraditional houses. On-campus housing is guaranteed for the freshman year only. 70% of students commute. All students may keep cars.

FACULTY/CLASSROOMS: 56% of faculty are male; 44% are female. All teach undergraduates and all do research. Graduate students teach 2% of introductory courses. The average class size in an introductory lecture is 35; in a laboratory is 25; and in a regular course is 35.

PROGRAMS OF STUDY: UM confers B.A., B.S., B.A.S., B.A.E., B.A.R.TV., B.F.A., B.M., B.M.E., B.S.B.A.D, B.S.F., B.S.M.T. and B.S.W. degrees. Associate, master's, and doctoral degrees are also awarded. Bachelor's degrees are awarded in AGRICULTURE (conservation and regulation, environmental studies, and forestry and related sciences), BIOLOGICAL SCIENCE (biochemistry, biology/biological science, botany, ecology, microbiology, wildlife biology, and zoology), BUSINESS (accounting, banking and finance, business administration and management, international business management, management information systems, marketing/retailing/merchandising, recreational facilities management, and small business management), COMMUNICATIONS AND THE ARTS (classics, communications, dramatic arts, English, fine arts, French, German, Japanese, journalism, linguistics, media arts, music, music performance, radio/television technology, Russian, and Spanish), COMPUTER AND PHYSICAL SCIENCE (applied science, chemistry, combined science, computer science, geology, geoscience, mathematics, and physics), EDUCATION (athletic training, elementary education, music education, physical education/exercise science, science education, and secondary education), HEALTH PROFESSIONS (health promotion, medical technology, and pharmacology), SOCIAL SCIENCE (anthropology, communication sciences & disorders, economics, geography, history, liberal arts/general studies, Native American studies, philosophy, political science/government, psychology, social work, and sociology). Business, forestry, and education have the largest enrollments.

ACTIVITIES: 6% of men belong to 7 national fraternities; 6% of women belong to 4 national sororities. There are 150 groups on campus, including academic, forestry clubs, art, band, cheerleading, chess, choir, chorale, chorus, computers, dance, drill team, ethnic, honors, international, jazz band, LGBT, literary magazine, marching band, newspaper, opera, orchestra, pep band, political, professional, radio and TV, religious, social, social service, student government, symphony, and creative writing. Popular campus events include Foresters Day, Founders Day, International Week, Griz-Cat Football Game, and Kyi-Yo Pow-wow. **Sports:** There are 6 intercollegiate sports for men and 9 for women, and 16 intramural sports for men and 12 for women. Facilities include a field house with an arena, auxiliary gyms, a stadium, fitness center, golf course, soccer and rugby fields, an Olympic-size pool, climbing wall, athlete weight training rooms, and mountain trails. **Graduates:** The most popular majors were business administration and related accounting, MIS (16%), physical sciences (13%), communications, journalism, and natural resources and conservation (8%). In an average class, 25% graduate in 4 years or less, 43% graduate in 5 years or less, and 50% graduate in 6 years or less.

SERVICES: Counseling and information services are available, as is tutoring in every subject. There is a reader service for the blind, and remedial math, reading, and writing. Mentors and note takers are available, as are books on tape for LD students. **Library/Resources:** The library contains 1.4 million volumes, 347,441 microform items, and 73,946 audio/video tapes/CDs/DVDs, and subscribes to 5,000 periodicals including electronic. Computerized library services include interlibrary loans, database searching, Internet access, and Wi-Fi capability. Special learning facilities include an art gallery, radio station, TV station, experimental forest, biological station, ranch, center for people and forests, geology field camp, international language lab, wilderness institute, observatory, and freshwater research center. **Physically Challenged Students:** 75% of the campus is accessible. Facilities include wheelchair ramps, elevators, special parking, specially equipped restrooms, special class scheduling, lowered drinking fountains, lowered telephones, and special housing. **Special:** Students may cross-register with Montana Tech of UM (Butte) and UM-Western (Dillon). Co-op programs exist in business, communications, economics, management, and liberal studies; internships in most majors, work-study programs with nonprofit organizations and on campus, and study abroad in 12 countries are available. The school offers a B.A.-B.S. degree in chemistry, pass/fail options in classes other than major requirements, and dual majors in physics and computer science as well as history and political science. There are 7 national honor societies, Phi Beta Kappa, a freshman honors program, and 5 departmental honors programs. **Visiting:** There are regularly scheduled orientations for prospective students, including placement testing, advising, workshops, and social events. There are guides for informal visits and visitors may sit in on classes. To schedule a visit, contact Enrollment Services at (406) 243-2332. **Campus Safety and Security:** Measures include 24-hour foot and vehicle patrol, emergency notification system, self-defense education, and security escort services. There are shuttle buses, emergency telephones, lighted pathways/sidewalks, and controlled access to dorms/residences. There are also shuttle buses between campus and downtown after hours on weekends.

REQUIREMENTS: The SAT or ACT is required, with a minimum composite ACT score of 22 or a satisfactory SAT verbal-math-writing composite score. Applicants must be graduates of an accredited secondary school. The GED is accepted. Students should have completed 4 years of English, 3 each of math, and social studies, 2 each of lab science, foreign language, computer science, and visual arts, or vocational education. UM requires applicants to be in the upper 50% of their class. A GPA of 2.5 is required. AP and CLEP credits are accepted. Important factors in the admissions decision are advanced placement or honors courses, evidence of special talent, and geographical diversity. A total of 120 credits is required for graduation in most majors. The number of hours in the major varies; some majors require a thesis. There are competency requirements in writing, math, and foreign language or symbolic systems. Distribution requirements include courses in expressive arts, literary and artistic studies, historical and cultural studies, social sciences, ethical and human values, and natural sciences. A minimum GPA of 2.0 must be maintained. **Procedure:** Freshmen are admitted to all sessions. There are deferred admissions and rolling admissions plans. Applications should be filed by March 1 for fall entry; November 15 for spring entry. The fall 2017 application fee was $36. Notification is sent on a rolling basis. Applications are accepted on-line. **Transfer Students:** 1215 transfer students enrolled in 2016-2017. Applicants must have a minimum GPA of 2.0. Grades of 2.0 or better transfer for credit. 30 of 120 credits required for the bachelor's degree must be completed at UM. **International Students:** There are 379 international students enrolled. They must take the TOEFL with a minimum score of 500 on the paper-based TOEFL (PBT). They must also take the ACT with a minimum score 18.

ADMISSIONS: 93% of the 2017-2018 applicants were accepted. The SAT scores for the 2017-2018 freshman class were: Critical Reading-- 26% below 500, 44% between 500 and 599, 25% between 600 and 699, and 5% between 700 and 800. Math-- 26% below 500, 50% between 500 and 599, 20% between 600 and 699, and 3% between 700 and 800. Writing-- 35% below 500, 45% between 500 and 599, 18% between 600 and 699, and 2% between 700 and 800. **Admissions Contact:** Sharon O'Hare, Associate VP for Enrollment. Email: *admiss@umontana.edu* Web: *www.umt.edu*

FINANCIAL AID: In 2017-2018, 62% of all full-time freshmen received some form of financial aid. The average freshman award was $10,836. The average financial indebtedness of the 2017 graduate was $29,918. UM is a member of CSS. The FAFSA code is 002536. The priority date for freshman financial aid applications for fall entry is February 15.

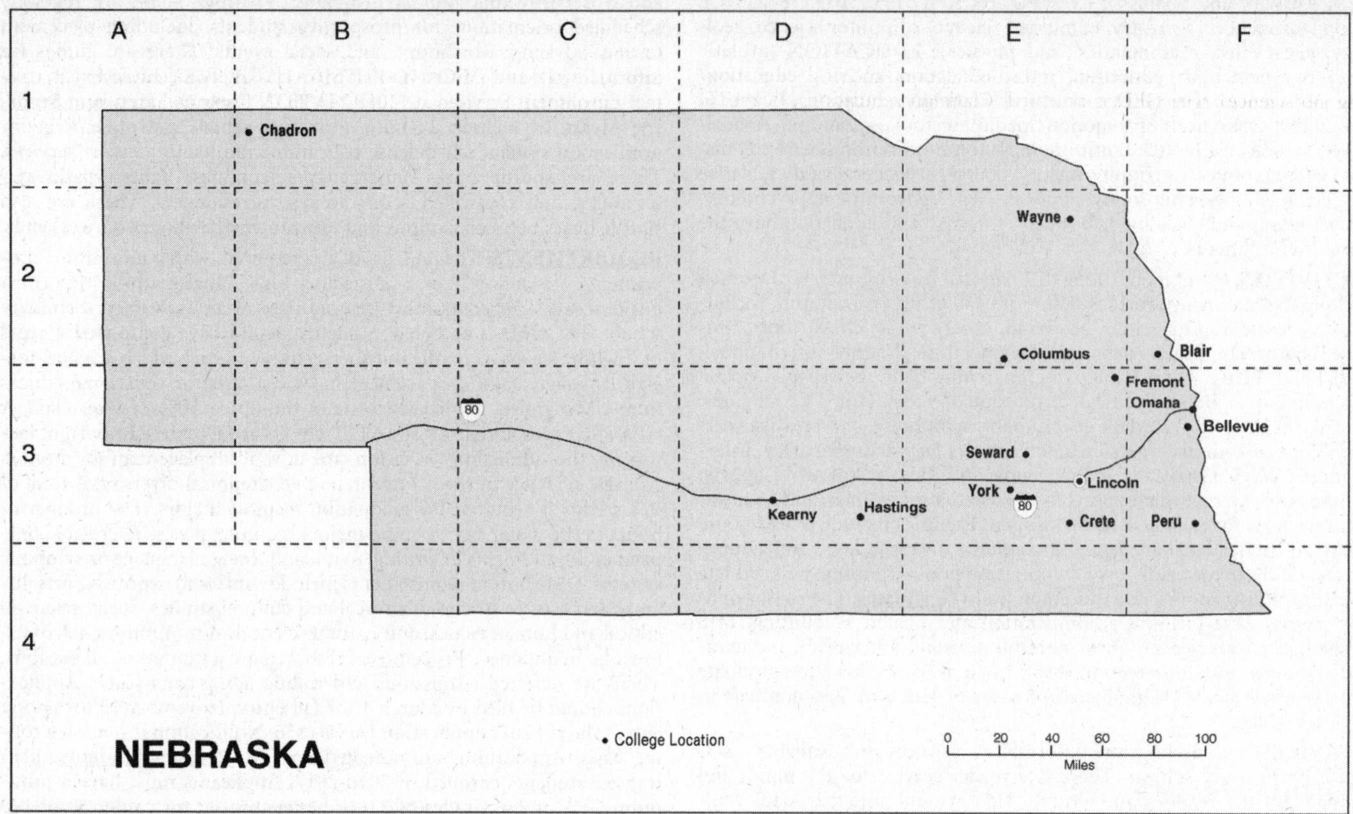

BELLEVUE UNIVERSITY *(The complete profile is made available exclusively on our website, www.barronspac.com)*

CHADRON STATE COLLEGE *(The complete profile is made available exclusively on our website, www.barronspac.com)*

CLARKSON COLLEGE F-3
www.clarksoncollege.edu

Omaha, NE 68131 **(402) 552-3041**
(800) 647-5500
Fax: (402) 552-6057 **Email: admissions@clarksoncollege.edu**

Full-time: 200 men, 350 women	**Faculty:** n/av
Part-time: 100 men, 120 women	**Ph.D.s:** n/av
Graduate: 67 men, 73 women	**Student/Faculty:** n/av
Year: semesters, summer session	**Tuition:** $18,576
Room & Board: $13,904	**Freshman Class:** n/av
SAT or ACT: required	**CEEB CODE:** 2250
Application Deadline: August 16	**COMPETITIVE**

Clarkson College, established in 1888 and affiliated with the Episcopal Church, offers undergraduate and graduate degrees in the health care professions and business. The figures given in the above capsule and in this profile are approximate. The cost for room and board is based on 13 credit hours per semester. There are 3 undergraduate schools and 2 graduate schools. In addition to regional accreditation, Clarkson has baccalaureate program accreditation with NLN. The 3-acre campus is in an urban area in Omaha. Including any residence halls, there are 4 buildings.

STUDENT LIFE: 61% of undergraduates are from Nebraska. Others are from 13 states, and 2 foreign countries. 90% are from public schools. 90% are White; 3% African American; 2% Asian American; 2% Hispanic; 1% American Indian/Alaska Native. 50% are Catholic; 45% Protestant. **Female To Male Ratio:** 1.5:1. The average age of all undergraduates is 22. 87% remain to graduate. **Housing:** 140 students can be accommodated in college housing, which includes on-campus apartments. On-campus housing is available on a first-come and first-served basis. 90% of students commute. Alcohol is not permitted. All students may keep cars.

FACULTY/CLASSROOMS: 16% of faculty are male; 84% are female. All teach undergraduates. No introductory courses are taught by graduate students. The average class size in an introductory lecture is 30; in a laboratory is 20; and in a regular course is 20.

PROGRAMS OF STUDY: Clarkson confers B.S. and B.S.N. degrees. Associate and master's degrees are also awarded. Bachelor's degrees are awarded in BUSINESS (business administration and management), COMPUTER AND PHYSICAL SCIENCE (radiological technology), HEALTH PROFESSIONS (nursing and radiograph medical technology). Radiological technology, and nursing are the strongest academically. Nursing has the largest enrollment.

ACTIVITIES: There are no fraternities or sororities. There are 12 groups on campus, including newspaper, professional, religious, social, social service, and student government. Popular campus events include Talent Show, Game Nights, and Intramural Volleyball. **Sports:** There is no sports program at Clarkson. Facilities include an exercise room available 24 hours, and a small gym area with basketball hoops and volleyball courts.

SERVICES: Counseling and information services are available, as is tutoring in every subject. **Library/Resources:** The library contains 7,613 volumes, and 698 audio/video tapes/CDs/DVDs, and subscribes to 217 periodicals including electronic. Computerized library services include interlibrary loans, database searching, and Internet access. **Physically Challenged Students:** 95% of the campus is accessible. Facilities include wheelchair ramps, elevators, special parking, specially equipped restrooms, special class scheduling, lowered drinking fountains, lowered telephones, and special housing. **Special:** A co-op program in nursing, work-study programs, and dual majors are available. Credit is given for military experience, and nondegree study is possible. The distance education option allows advanced placement students living a distance from the campus to complete their studies at home. There is 1 national honor society. **Visiting:** There are regularly scheduled orientations for prospective students. There are guides for informal visits and visitors may sit in on classes. To schedule a visit, contact the Admissions Office. **Campus Safety and Security:** Measures include 24-hour foot and vehicle patrol, emergency notification system, self-defense education, and security escort services. There are emergency telephones and lighted pathways/sidewalks.

REQUIREMENTS: The SAT or ACT is required, with a minimum composite score of 20 on the ACT or a satisfactory score on the SAT. Tests are not required for applicants more than 2 years out of high school. Applicants must be graduates of an accredited secondary school, with 3 years of English and 2 each of social science, algebra, and science (including lab science). The GED is accepted. Clarkson requires applicants to be in the upper 50% of their class. A GPA of 2.5 is required. AP and CLEP credits are accepted. Important factors in the admissions decision are advanced placement or honors courses, extracurricular activities record, and evidence of special talent. To graduate, students must complete 128 credit hours, including 68 in the major, and maintain a minimum GPA of 2.0. General education requirements include courses in the humanities, English, behavioral and social sciences, science and math, and phys ed. A 9-hour core curriculum is also required. **Procedure:** Freshmen are admitted to all sessions. Entrance exams should be taken during the junior year or first semester of the senior year. There is a deferred admissions plan. Applications should be filed by August 16 for fall entry. The fall 2017 application fee was $35. Notification of early decision is sent April 1; regular decision, June 1. **Transfer Students:** Transfer students must have a minimum GPA of 2.5. Grades of C or better transfer for credit. Transfers are admitted for fall and spring. An interview is sometimes required. 64 of 128 credits required for the bachelor's degree must be completed at Clarkson. **International Students:** They must take the TOEFL, 85 on the MELAB, and 5 on the TWE. They must also take the SAT or ACT.

Admissions Contact: Denise Work, Director of Admissions. Email: *admissions@clarksoncollege.edu* Web: *www.clarksoncollege.edu*

FINANCIAL AID: In 2017-2018, 90% of all full-time freshmen received some form of financial aid. Clarkson is a member of CSS. The college's own financial statement is required. The FAFSA code is 009862. Check with the school for current application deadlines.

COLLEGE OF SAINT MARY — F-3

www.csm.edu

Omaha, NE 68106	**(402) 399-2350** **(800) 926-5534**
Fax: (402) 399-2412	**Email: enroll@csm.edu**
Full-time: 761 women	**Faculty:** 58
Part-time: 8 men, 63 women	**Ph.D.s:** 70%
Graduate: 12 men, 296 women	**Student/Faculty:** 5 to 1
Year: semesters, summer session	**Tuition:** $19,950
Room & Board: $7550	**Freshman Class:** 193 applied, 183 accepted, 71 enrolled
ACT: 21	**CEEB CODE:** 6106
Application Deadline: open	**COMPETITIVE**

College of Saint Mary, founded in 1923, is a women's college committed to the works, values and aspirations of the Sisters of Mercy and dedicated to the education of women in an environment that calls forth potential and fosters leadership. There is 1 undergraduate school and 1 graduate school. In addition to regional accreditation, CSM has baccalaureate program accreditation with NLN, ACOTE, IACBE, and ABA. The 40-acre campus is in an urban area within metro Omaha. Including any residence halls, there are 9 buildings.

STUDENT LIFE: 78% of undergraduates are from Nebraska. Others are from 24 states, 12 foreign countries, and Canada. 80% are from public schools. 8% are African American; 70% White; 3% Asian American; 3% two or more races; 14% Hispanic; 1% American Indian/Alaska Native; 1% Foreign. 38% are Catholic. **Female To Male Ratio:** 56.0:1. The average age of freshmen is 19; all undergraduates, 24. 16% do not continue beyond their first year; 48% remain to graduate. **Housing:** 306 students can be accommodated in college housing, which includes dorms. Residence hall for single student mothers with children. On-campus housing is guaranteed for the freshman year only, is available on a first-come, first-served basis, and is available on a lottery system for upperclassmen. 63% of students commute. All students may keep cars.

FACULTY/CLASSROOMS: 16% of faculty are male; 84% are female. 77% teach undergraduates, and 10% do research. No introductory courses are taught by graduate students. The average class size in an introductory lecture is 25; in a laboratory is 24; and in a regular course is 25.

PROGRAMS OF STUDY: CSM confers B.A., B.S., B.G.S., and B.R.S. degrees. Associate, master's, and doctoral degrees are also awarded. Bachelor's degrees are awarded in BIOLOGICAL SCIENCE (biology/biological science), BUSINESS (business intelligence and analytics), COMMUNICATIONS AND THE ARTS (art, English, language arts, and Spanish), COMPUTER AND PHYSICAL SCIENCE (chemistry, mathematics, and natural sciences), EDUCATION (early childhood education, education, elementary education, special education, and sports and wellness studies), HEALTH PROFESSIONS (medical laboratory technology and nursing), SOCIAL SCIENCE (applied psychology, humanities, liberal arts/general studies, paralegal studies, psychology, social science, and theological studies). Biology, chemistry, and occupational therapy are the strongest academically. Occupational therapy, nursing, and education have the largest enrollments.

ACTIVITIES: There are no fraternities or sororities. There are 18 groups on campus, including campus activities board, business, green team, choir, chorus, drama, environmental, ethnic, forensics, honors, international, multicultural, professional, religious, social, social service, and student government. Popular campus events include Welcome Days, Homecoming Week, Walking Woman Celebration, Casino Night, Improv Night, and Hypnotist. **Sports:** There are 10 intercollegiate sports for women, and 2 intramural sports for women. Facilities include a gym, a swimming pool, weight room, an elevated running track, exercise room, a training room, tennis courts, soccer and softball fields. **Graduates:** From July 1, 2016 to June 30, 2017, 139 bachelor's degrees were awarded. The most popular majors were rehabilitation studies/occupational therapy (33%), biology (17%), and nursing (9%). In an average class, 41% graduate in 4 years or less, 43% graduate in 5 years or less, and 48% graduate in 6 years or less. Of the 2016 graduating class, 37% were enrolled in graduate school within 6 months of graduation, and 39% were employed.

SERVICES: Counseling and information services are available, as is tutoring in most subjects. There is a reader service for the blind, and remedial math, reading, and writing. There are also study groups and learning circles. **Library/Resources:** The library contains 89,613 volumes, and 2,770 audio/video tapes/CDs/DVDs, and subscribes to 375 periodicals including electronic. Computerized library services include interlibrary loans, database searching, Internet access, and Wi-Fi capability. Special learning facilities include an art gallery, cadaver lab, digital piano lab, native fish aquarium, nursing/occupational therapy/physician assistant laboratories, lecture capture system, and online learning platform. **Physically Challenged Students:** All of the campus is accessible. Facilities include wheelchair ramps, elevators, special parking, specially equipped restrooms, special class scheduling, lowered drinking fountains, and special housing. **Special:** Students may pursue internships in any major, including research courses in the sciences. CSM also offers dual majors, study abroad, nondegree study, pass/fail options, an accelerated degree program in business leadership and management, and credit for military and work experience. There are 2 national honor societies, a freshman honors program, and 30 departmental honors programs. **Visiting:** There are regularly scheduled orientations for prospective students, consisting of meeting with Admissions Counselor, tour of the campus, meeting with faculty, meeting with financial aid, student life and lunch. There are guides for informal visits, visitors may sit in on classes, and stay overnight. To schedule a visit, contact Kyra Gause at (402) 399-2355. **Campus Safety and Security:** Measures include 24-hour foot and vehicle patrol, emergency notification system, self-defense education, and security escort services. There are lighted pathways/sidewalks, controlled access to dorms/residences, and camera-monitored entrances to residence halls.

REQUIREMENTS: Students are accepted with a minimum composite score of 18 on the ACT or comparable SAT score. Students must also have a GPA of at least 2.0. Applicants must be graduates of an accredited secondary school. The GED is accepted. Students should have completed 16 academic units, including 4 years of English and 2 each of math, social studies, and science, with biology and chemistry required for the various health profession majors. An interview is recommended. AP and CLEP credits are accepted. To graduate, students must complete 128 semester hours, with a minimum of 30 hours in the major and a 2.0 GPA in the major and overall. Required general education courses total 47 hours, with 10 in quantitative reasoning and science, 6 each in English and theology, 3 each in communications, moral reasoning, fine arts, global cultural diversity, history, philosophy, and social science, and 1 in a first year seminar. Each student prior to graduation completes and presents a research project in her major either individually or with a team. **Procedure:** Freshmen are admitted fall, spring, and summer. Entrance exams should be taken in the junior or senior year. There are deferred admissions and rolling admissions plans. Application deadlines are open. The fall 2017 application fee was $30. Applications are accepted on-line. **Transfer Students:** 149 transfer students enrolled in 2016-2017. Applicants should have a minimum GPA of 2.0 and submit official transcripts from previous colleges attended. Students with fewer than 12 credit hours must also submit ACT or SAT scores. Grades of C or better transfer for credit. Students are admitted every term. 30 of 128 credits required for the bachelor's degree must be completed at CSM. **International Students:** There are 7 international students enrolled. They must take the TOEFL with a minimum score of 550 on the paper-based TOEFL (PBT) or 79 on the Internet-based version (iBT). They must also take the SAT or ACT, scoring 18.

ADMISSIONS: 95% of the 2017-2018 applicants were accepted. The ACT scores were 7% between 12 and 17, 63% between 18 and 23, 29% between 24 and 29, and 1% above 30. 4% of the current freshmen were in the top fifth of their class; 21% were in the top two fifths. **Admissions Contact:** Sara Hanson, VP Enrollment Services. Email: *enroll@csm.edu* Web: *www.csm.edu*

FINANCIAL AID: In 2017-2018, 100% of all full-time freshmen received some form of financial aid. 65% of all full-time freshmen received need-based aid. The average freshman award was $20,824. Need-based scholarships or need-based grants averaged $14,688; need-based self-help aid (loans and jobs) averaged $4,885; non-need-based athletic scholarships averaged $6,121; and other non-need-based awards and non-need-based scholarships averaged $8,440. 38% of undergraduate students work part-time. The average financial indebtedness of the 2017 graduate was $33,598. The FAFSA code is 002540. The priority date for freshman financial aid applications for fall entry is March 15.

CONCORDIA UNIVERSITY NEBRASKA E-3

www.cune.edu

Seward, NE 68434	**(402) 643-7233**
	(800) 535-5494
Fax: (402) 643-4073	**Email: admiss@cune.edu**
Full-time: 500 men, 550 women	**Faculty:** IIB, --$
Part-time: 15 men, 20 women	**Ph.D.s:** n/av
Graduate: 100 men, 105 women	**Student/Faculty:** n/av
Year: semesters, summer session	**Tuition:** $28,480
Room & Board: $7800	**Freshman Class:** n/av
SAT or ACT: required	**CEEB CODE:** 6116
Application Deadline: n/av	**VERY COMPETITIVE**

Concordia University Nebraska, founded in 1894, is a private university owned and operated by the Lutheran Church-Missouri Synod, with degree programs in professional education and liberal arts. Among Concordia's major programs are those for professional work in the Lutheran Church: teacher education, director of Christian education, preseminary pastoral training, and church music. The figures in the above capsule and in this profile are approximate. There is 1 undergraduate school and 1 graduate school. In addition to regional accreditation, Concordia has baccalaureate program accreditation with NCATE. The 120-acre campus is in a small town 25 miles west of Lincoln. Including any residence halls, there are 26 buildings.

STUDENT LIFE: 59% of undergraduates are from out of state, mostly the Midwest. Students are from 37 states, and 9 foreign countries. 95% are White; 2% African American; 2% Asian American; 1% Hispanic. 95% are Protestant. **Female To Male Ratio:** 1.1:1. The average age of freshmen is 18; all undergraduates, 21. 22% do not continue beyond their first year; 48% remain to graduate. **Housing:** 815 students can be accommodated in college housing, which includes single-sex dorms, off-campus apartments, and married student housing. On-campus housing is guaranteed for all 4 years. 85% of students live on campus; of those, 90% remain on campus on weekends. All students may keep cars. Alcohol is not permitted.

FACULTY/CLASSROOMS: 71% of faculty are male; 29% are female. All teach undergraduates. Graduate students teach 1% of introductory courses. The average class size in an introductory lecture is 20; in a laboratory is 15; and in a regular course is 15.

PROGRAMS OF STUDY: Concordia confers B.A., B.S., B.F.A., B.S.Med.Tech., B.Mus., and B.Sacred Music degrees. Master's degrees are also awarded. Bachelor's degrees are awarded in BIOLOGICAL SCIENCE (biology/biological science), BUSINESS (accounting, business administration and management, and sports management), COMMUNICATIONS AND THE ARTS (communications, dramatic arts, English, fine arts, music, speech/debate/rhetoric, and studio art), COMPUTER AND PHYSICAL SCIENCE (chemistry, computer science, mathematics, natural sciences, and physical sciences), EDUCATION (business education, Christian education, early childhood education, elementary education, home economics education, industrial arts education, middle school education, music education, physical education, science education, secondary education, and special education), HEALTH PROFESSIONS (exercise science, health, medical laboratory technology, predentistry, and premedicine), SOCIAL SCIENCE (behavioral science, geography, history, physical fitness/movement, prelaw, psychology, and theological studies). Education, business, and art are the strongest academically. Education has the largest enrollment.

ACTIVITIES: There are no fraternities or sororities. There are 35 groups on campus, including band, cheerleading, choir, chorale, chorus, computers, dance, debate, drama, drill team, ethnic, forensics, honors, international, jazz band, literary magazine, musical theater, newspaper, orchestra, pep band, photography, professional, religious, social, social service, student government, and yearbook. Popular campus events include Spring Weekend and Multicultural Awareness Week. **Sports:** There are 8 intercollegiate sports for men and 8 for women, and 7 intramural sports for men and 7 for women. Facilities include a gym, weight-training room, indoor pool, football, baseball, soccer fields, a track, and field stadium.

SERVICES: Counseling and information services are available, as is tutoring in every subject, and a reader service for the blind. Talking books and tape recorders are also available. **Library/Resources:** The 3 libraries contain 177,683 volumes, 10,719 microform items, and 13,214 audio/video tapes/CDs/DVDs, and subscribe to 545 periodicals including electronic. Computerized library services include database searching. Special learning facilities include an art gallery, natural history museum, and observatory. **Physically Challenged Students:** 35% of the campus is accessible. Facilities include wheelchair ramps, elevators, special parking, specially equipped restrooms, lowered drinking fountains, and lowered telephones. **Special:** Concordia offers cross-registration with the University of Nebraska in Lincoln. Internships are available in education, business, and Christian education. B.A.-B.S. degrees, student-designed majors, dual majors, study abroad in England and China, nondegree studies, and pass/fail options are available. There is an accelerated degree program in organizational management. There is a freshman honors program. **Visiting:** There are regularly scheduled orientations for prospective students, including a campus tour, visits with professors/coaches, and an admission interview. There are guides for informal visits, visitors may sit in on classes, and stay overnight. To schedule a visit, contact the Office of Admission. **Campus Safety and Security:** Measures include 24-hour foot and vehicle patrol, self-defense education, and security escort services, emergency telephones, lighted pathways/sidewalks, vehicle and bicycle registration, and a possession ID engraving program.

REQUIREMENTS: A minimum composite score of 18 is recommended for the ACT. Applicants need not be graduates of an accredited secondary school. The GED is accepted. The school strongly encourages high school courses in art, English, foreign language, history, math, music, phys ed, science, and social studies. An interview is recommended. A GPA of 2.8 is required. AP and CLEP credits are accepted. Important factors in the admissions decision are ability to finance college education, leadership record, and recommendations by alumni. To graduate, students must complete a minimum of 128 credits with a GPA of at least 2.0. Required general education courses include 12 hours of theology, 9 hours each of English/speech, social science, and science, 6 of fine arts, 3 each of math and health and phys ed, 2 to 3 of electives, and 1 hour minimum of computer literacy. **Procedure:** Freshmen are admitted to all sessions. Entrance exams should be taken in the junior or senior year. There is a rolling admissions plan. Application deadlines are open. Applications are accepted on-line. **Transfer Students:** 58 transfer students enrolled in 2015-2016. Applicants should have a minimum GPA of 2.5 and a minimum ACT score of 18. An interview is recommended. Passing grades transfer for credit. Transfers are admitted every term. 30 of 128 credits required for the bachelor's degree must be completed at Concordia. **International Students:** There are 9 international students enrolled. They must take the TOEFL.

Admissions Contact: Aaron Roberts, Director of Undergraduate Admissions. Email: *admiss@cune.edu* Web: *www.cune.edu*

FINANCIAL AID: In 2016-2017, 98% of all full-time freshmen received

some form of financial aid. The college's own financial statement is required. The FAFSA code is 002541. Check with the school for current application deadlines.

CREIGHTON UNIVERSITY F-3

www.creighton.edu

Omaha, NE 68178 (402) 280-2703
(800) 282-5835

Fax: (402) 280-2685 **Email:** admissions@creighton.edu

Full-time: 1772 men, 2239 women	**Faculty:** 349; IIA, +$
Part-time: 92 men, 152 women	**Ph.D.s:** 83%
Graduate: 1725 men, 2674 women	**Student/Faculty:** 11 to 1
Year: semesters, summer session	**Tuition:** $38,750
Room & Board: $10,702	**Freshman Class:** 9727 applied, 7004 accepted, 1120 enrolled
SAT EBR-W/M: 576/603 **ACT:** 27	**CEEB CODE:** 6121
Application Deadline: February 15	**VERY COMPETITIVE**

Creighton University, founded in 1878, is a private Jesuit Catholic institution offering undergraduate programs in arts and sciences, business administration, and nursing as well as graduate, dental, medical, law, pharmacy, physical therapy, and occupational therapy programs. There are 4 undergraduate schools and 5 graduate schools. In addition to regional accreditation, Creighton has baccalaureate program accreditation with AACSB, ACPE, ADA, CSWE, NCATE, ABA, LCME, ACGME, ACCME, ACOTE, CAPTE, CCNE, ANCC, AACN, and CAAHEP. The 139-acre campus is in an urban area near downtown Omaha Nebraska. Including any residence halls, there are 55 buildings.

STUDENT LIFE: 77% of undergraduates are from out of state, mostly the Midwest. Students are from 47 states, and 30 foreign countries. 51% are from public schools. 71% are White; 9% Asian American; 8% Hispanic; 5% two or more races; 3% African American; 3% Foreign; 1% American Indian/Alaska Native; 1% race unknown. 54% are Catholic; 23% Protestant; 17% Jewish, Hinduism, Buddhism, Islam, Sikhism, and Unknown. **Female To Male Ratio:** 1.4:1. The average age of freshmen is 18; all undergraduates, 20. 11% do not continue beyond their first year; 81% remain to graduate. **Housing:** 2522 students can be accommodated in college housing, which includes married student dorms and on-campus apartments. In addition, there are honors houses, special-interest houses, Cortina Community, and Freshman Leadership Program housing. On-campus housing is available on a first-come, first-served basis, and is available on a lottery system for upperclassmen. 57% of students live on campus. All students may keep cars.

FACULTY/CLASSROOMS: 52% of faculty are male; 48% are female. 53% teach undergraduates. No introductory courses are taught by graduate students. The average class size in an introductory lecture is 22 and in a laboratory is 18.

PROGRAMS OF STUDY: Creighton confers B.A., B.F.A., B.S., B.S.B.A., B.S.E.M.S., B.S.N., B.S.Physics, and B.S.W. degrees. Associate, master's, and doctoral degrees are also awarded. Bachelor's degrees are awarded in BIOLOGICAL SCIENCE (neurosciences), BUSINESS (accounting, business intelligence and analytics, finance, international business, leadership, management, and marketing), COMMUNICATIONS AND THE ARTS (art history, classical languages, communication studies, English, French and Francophone studies, German studies, graphic design & media, journalism, music, musical theater, Spanish and Hispanic studies, studio art, and theatre arts), COMPUTER AND PHYSICAL SCIENCE (chemistry, computer science & informatics, mathematics, physics, sustainable energy, and sustainable energy science), EDUCATION (elementary education), ENGINEERING AND ENVIRONMENTAL DESIGN (environmental science), HEALTH PROFESSIONS (biology, dental hygiene, emergency medical services, exercise science, health administration and policy, healthy lifestyle management, and nursing), SOCIAL SCIENCE (American studies, classical and near eastern civilization, cultural anthropology, economics, history, international relations, justice and society, medical anthropology, philosophy, political science/government, psychology, social work, sociology, and theology). Business, science, health science, nursing, biological sciences and psychology are the strongest academically, and have the largest enrollments.

ACTIVITIES: There are 219 groups on campus, including art, cheerleading, chess, choir, chorale, chorus, computers, dance, debate, drama, drill team, environmental, ethnic, forensics, honors, international, LGBT, musical theater, newspaper, orchestra, pep band, photography, political, professional, religious, social, social service, student government, and symphony. Popular campus events include Fallapalooza Concert, Skutt Shutdown, Lip Sync, Christmas at Creighton, Homecoming Week, Paint Party, One Creighton Harvest Fest, Dance Marathon, BINGO and Wellfest. **Sports:** There are 18 intercollegiate sports for men and 16 for women, and 23 intramural sports for men and 23 for women. Facilities include an athletic practice, training and academic support facility that is part of the east campus athletic/fitness/recreation corridor that consists of an intercollegiate soccer facility, an arena for women's basketball and volleyball, a fitness center/athletic practice facility, physical fitness centers with space for basketball, volleyball, badminton, soccer, weight rooms, jogging tracks, playing fields for softball and intramural teams, and indoor batting cages for softball and baseball. **Graduates:** From July 1, 2016 to June 30, 2017, 983 bachelor's degrees were awarded. The most popular majors were health professions and related programs (25%), business/marketing (20%), and biological/life sciences (10%). In an average class, 5% graduate in 3 years or less, 73% graduate in 4 years or less, 80% graduate in 5 years or less, and 81% graduate in 6 years or less. Of the 2016 graduating class, 34% were enrolled in graduate school within 6 months of graduation, and 61% were employed.

SERVICES: Counseling and information services are available, as is tutoring in most subjects. **Library/Resources:** The library contains 658,095 volumes, 663,060 microform items, and 9,799 audio/video tapes/CDs/DVDs, and subscribes to 53,219 periodicals including electronic. Computerized library services include interlibrary loans, database searching, Internet access, and Wi-Fi capability. Special learning facilities include art galleries, a wind energy collection system and the state's largest solar array that acts as an outdoor classroom for students in the energy technology program (iJAY), uniquely blends commercial and educational interests by doubling as a learning center, giving students the opportunity to gain hands-on experience running a retail store as part of a practicum course. The Heider Securities Investment and Analysis Center in the business college is a trading room complete with a real-time stock ticker, interactive market boards and 11 Bloomberg terminals. **Physically Challenged Students:** 87% of the campus is accessible. Facilities include wheelchair ramps, elevators, special parking, specially equipped restrooms, special class scheduling, lowered drinking fountains, and special housing. **Special:** The university offers study abroad, numerous internship, volunteer and service opportunities in countries all over the world. Students may take an accelerated degree program in creative writing, organizational communication, and administration and policy. B.A.-B.S. degrees and dual majors are possible as well as the Art-Engineering degree program with the University of Detroit Mercy and with Marquette University. Army ROTC is offered on campus. Air Force ROTC is available through an arrangement with University of Nebraska Omaha. There are 15 national honor societies, Phi Beta Kappa, and a freshman honors program. **Visiting:** There are regularly scheduled orientations for prospective students, consisting of open house programs with various presentations and campus tours. A daily visit can be scheduled by either calling the Admissions office or completing online request at https:/choose.creighton.edu/portal/campus-visit. **Campus Safety and Security:** Measures include 24-hour foot and vehicle patrol, emergency notification system, self-defense education, and security escort services. There are shuttle buses, emergency telephones, lighted pathways/sidewalks, controlled access to dorms/residences, Bluetooth-enabled personal mobile safety devices, pedestrian escort service, full-time crime prevention officer, violence intervention and prevention center, electronic card access systems, blue light emergency phones, security alarm systems, panic buttons, and surveillance cameras.

REQUIREMENTS: The SAT or ACT is required. Applicants must be graduates of an accredited secondary school. The GED is accepted. Students should have completed 16 credits including 4 credits in English, 3 each in math and electives, and 2 each in foreign language, natural science (with labs), and social sciences. Home-schooled students are welcome. A GPA of 2.5 is required. AP and CLEP credits are accepted. Important factors in the admissions decision are advanced placement or honors courses, extracurricular activities record, and recommendations by school officials. To graduate with a bachelor's degree, students must complete a minimum of 128 credit hours, with at least 48 credit hours in courses numbered 300 or above and maintain a GPA of 2.0. Total number of credit hours required in major and specific disciplines varies by college and major. In addition, a completion of Magis Common Core and College Core Curriculum is required for a bachelor's degree. The Magis Core Curriculum serves as the cornerstone of Creighton University education, laying a shared foundation for all undergraduate students in order to shape responsible citizens of the global community. **Procedure:** Freshmen are admitted fall, spring, and summer. Entrance exams should be taken fall of the senior year. There are early admissions, deferred admissions, and rolling admissions plans. Applications should be filed by February 15 for fall entry; December 15 for spring entry. The fall 2017 application fee was $40. Notification is sent on a rolling basis. Applications are accepted on-line. **Transfer Students:** 45 transfer students enrolled in 2016-2017. Applicants must be in good academic standing at another accredited university, college, or junior college. Both college-level work and high school academic record are considered for admission. An overall college GPA of 2.75 (4.0 scale) or higher is recommended for acceptance. Credit hours earned with grades of "C-" or better at an accredited institution of higher education prior to admission to Creighton University may be transferred at the discretion of the respective college. Transfers are admitted every semester. 48 of 128 credits required for the bachelor's degree must be completed at Creighton. **International Students:** There are 114 international students enrolled. They must take the TOEFL with a minimum score of 570 on the paper-based TOEFL (PBT) or 88 on the Internet-based version (iBT). Student must the IELTS. They must also take the SAT or ACT.

ADMISSIONS: 72% of the 2017-2018 applicants were accepted. The SAT scores for the 2017-2018 freshman class were: Math-- 8% below 500, 35% between 500 and 599, 45% between 600 and 699, and 12% between 700 and 800. Evidence-Based Reading/Writing-- 13% below 500, 54% between 500 and 599, 25% between 600 and 699, and 8% between 700 and 800. The ACT scores were 18% between 18 and 23, 57% between 24 and 29, and 25% above 30. 45 freshmen graduated first in their class. **Admissions Contact:** Sarah Richardson, Director of Admissions and Scholarships. Email: *admissions@creighton.edu* Web: *www.creighton.edu*

FINANCIAL AID: The college's own financial statement is required. The FAFSA code is 002542. The priority date for freshman financial aid applications for fall entry is January 15.

DOANE UNIVERSITY E-3

www.doane.edu

Crete, NE 68333 **(402) 826-8222** **(800) 333-6263**

Fax: (402) 826-8600 **Email: admissions@doane.edu**

Full-time: 560 men, 502 women	**Faculty:** 89
Part-time: 5 men, 1 women	**Ph.D.s:** 82%
Graduate: n/av	**Student/Faculty:** 11 to 1
Year: 4-1-4	**Tuition:** $32,250
Room & Board: $9090	**Freshman Class:** 2392 applied, 1559 accepted, 299 enrolled
SAT: recommended **ACT:** 23	**CEEB CODE:** 6165
Application Deadline: n/av	**VERY COMPETITIVE**

Doane University is known for its leadership in higher education, grounded in the university's commitment to academic excellence, innovation, community and a special sense of place for each individual. These are the values that have made Doane successful for more than 140 years and will help build an even stronger university for the future. There are 3 undergraduate schools and 3 graduate schools. In addition to regional accreditation, Doane University has baccalaureate program accreditation with NCATE. The 300-acre campus is in a small town 25 miles southwest of Lincoln. Including any residence halls, there are 28 buildings.

STUDENT LIFE: 77% of undergraduates are from Nebraska. Others are from 30 states, 7 foreign countries, and Canada. 78% are from public schools. 82% are White; 7% Hispanic; 4% two or more races; 2% African American; 2% Foreign; 1% Asian American; 1% American Indian/Alaska Native; 1% race unknown. 21% are Catholic. **Male To Female Ratio:** 1.1:1. The average age of freshmen is 18; all undergraduates, 20. 22% do not continue beyond their first year; 78% remain to graduate. **Housing:** 815 students can be accommodated in college housing, which includes dorms and on-campus apartments. In addition, there are honors houses and special-interest houses. On-campus housing is guaranteed for all 4 years. 89% of students live on campus. All students may keep cars.

FACULTY/CLASSROOMS: 49% of faculty are male; 51% are female. All teach undergraduates, 5% do research, and 25% do both. No introductory courses are taught by graduate students. The average class size in an introductory lecture is 25; in a laboratory is 10; and in a regular course is 18.

PROGRAMS OF STUDY: Doane confers B.A. and B.S. degrees. Bachelor's degrees are awarded in AGRICULTURE (environmental studies), BIOLOGICAL SCIENCE (biochemistry and biology/biological science), BUSINESS (accounting and business administration and management), COMMUNICATIONS AND THE ARTS (art, art and design, dramatic arts, English, English as a second/foreign language, French, German, journalism, music, and Spanish), COMPUTER AND PHYSICAL SCIENCE (chemistry, computer science, information sciences and systems, mathematics, natural sciences, and physics), EDUCATION (elementary education, physical education, and special education), ENGINEERING AND ENVIRONMENTAL DESIGN (engineering physics and environmental science), SOCIAL SCIENCE (economics, history, international studies, philosophy, political science/government, psychology, public administration, religion, and sociology). Biology, and economics (emphasis business, management) are the strongest academically. Education, biology, and business administration have the largest enrollments.

ACTIVITIES: 26% of men belong to 6 local fraternities; 35% of women belong to 5 local sororities. There are 50 groups on campus, including alternative spring break, and wildlife/conservation, Hanson Leadership program, investment, art, band, cheerleading, choir, chorale, chorus, computers, dance, drama, ethnic, forensics, honors, international, jazz band, LGBT, literary magazine, marching band, musical theater, newspaper, pep band, photography, political, professional, radio and TV, religious, social, social service, speech team, and student government. Popular campus events include Parents Day, Stop Day, Christmas Festival and Concert. **Sports:** There are 6 intercollegiate sports for men and 6 for women, and 4 intramural sports for men and 4 for women. Facilities include a phys ed building, field house, sports field, fitness center, a gym, pool, nature and cross-country trails, challenge course, indoor and outdoor tracks. **Graduates:** From July 1, 2016 to June 30, 2017, 200 bachelor's degrees were awarded. The most popular majors were elementary education (19%), business (14%), and biology (13%). In an average class, 4% graduate in 3 years or less, 55% graduate in 4 years or less, 63% graduate in 5 years or less, and 64% graduate in 6 years or less. Of the 2016 graduating class, 22% were enrolled in graduate school within 6 months of graduation, and 78% were employed.

SERVICES: Counseling and information services are available, as is tutoring in every subject. There is remedial math, reading, and writing. **Library/Resources:** The library contains 107,671 volumes, 54,202 microform items, and 5,360 audio/video tapes/CDs/DVDs, and subscribes to 203 periodicals including electronic. Computerized library services include interlibrary loans, database searching, Internet access, and Wi-Fi capability. Special learning facilities include an art gallery, radio station, TV station, an observatory. **Physically Challenged Students:** 60% of the campus is accessible. Facilities include wheelchair ramps, elevators, special parking, specially equipped restrooms, and special class scheduling. **Special:** Internships for sophomores through seniors, a Washington semester, and study abroad in numerous countries are possible. A 3-2 engineering program in conjunction with Washington at St. Louis and Columbia Universities, work-study, student-designed and interdisciplinary majors, dual majors and accelerated degrees in all areas, credit by exam, nondegree study, and pass/fail options are available. Doane also offers the HELPS program, designed for Doane College graduates who wish to return as full-time students to seek further education in preparation for career advancement. Students may pursue a 3-2 environmental studies/forestry degree in conjunction with Duke University. Doane's Lincoln campus, Grand Island and Omaha designed for adults, offers intensive 8-week classes in the evening and on weekends in both undergraduate and graduate programs. Doane offers an honors program, leadership development program, and the opportunity to conduct summer research projects with faculty. There are 7 national honor societies, a freshman honors program, and 3 departmental honors programs. **Visiting:** There are regularly scheduled orientations for prospective students, including 4 scheduled half-day visits that incorporate a parents program. There are guides for informal visits, visitors may sit in on classes, and stay overnight. To schedule a visit, contact the Admissions Office. **Campus Safety and Security:** Measures include security escort services. There are emergency telephones, lighted pathways/sidewalks, and evening patrols by trained security personnel.

REQUIREMENTS: The ACT is required. The SAT is recommended.

Applicants must be graduates of an accredited secondary school. The GED is accepted. It is recommended that 4 units of English and 3 units each of math, science, and the social sciences be completed. An interview is recommended. Art students must submit a portfolio, and music and drama students must audition. A GPA of 2.0 is required. AP and CLEP credits are accepted. Important factors in the admissions decision are advanced placement or honors courses, leadership record, parents or siblings attended your school, evidence of special talent, personality/intangible qualities, extracurricular activities record, recommendations by alumni, geographical diversity, and recommendations by school officials. The Doane core requires students to complete courses in heritage studies, contemporary issues, international/multicultural perspective, natural science, quantitative reasoning, communication, aesthetic perspective, health and well-being, and community and leadership. Students are also required to complete courses in physical education, demonstrate computer skills in word processing, and in most disciplines, complete a senior seminar. Students must complete 123 credit hours and have a minimum GPA of 2.0 in the major to graduate. **Procedure:** Freshmen are admitted fall, winter, and spring. Entrance exams should be taken by spring of the junior year or early senior year. There are deferred admissions and rolling admissions plans. Application deadlines are open. Notification is sent on a rolling basis. Applications are accepted on-line. **Transfer Students:** 59 transfer students enrolled in 2016-2017. Transfer students must submit a transcript from previously attended colleges and have been in good standing. The SAT or ACT is usually required. Grades of 2.0 or higher generally transfer for credit. 30 of 123 credits required for the bachelor's degree must be completed at Doane. **International Students:** There are 22 international students enrolled. They must take the TOEFL with a minimum score of 525 on the paper-based TOEFL (PBT) or 70 on the Internet-based version (iBT). Students must take the IELTS with a minimum score of 5.5. They must also take the SAT or ACT, scoring 21 or a satisfactory score on the SAT.

ADMISSIONS: 65% of the 2017-2018 applicants were accepted. The ACT scores were 5% between 12 and 17, 53% between 18 and 23, 37% between 24 and 29, and 5% above 30. 30% of the current freshmen were in the top fifth of their class; 91% were in the top two fifths. 9 freshmen graduated first in their class. **Admissions Contact:** Mr. Joal Weyand, Vice President for Enrollment. Email: *admissions@doane.edu* Web: *www.doane.edu*

FINANCIAL AID: In 2017-2018, 100% of all full-time freshmen received some form of financial aid. 80% of all full-time freshmen received need-based aid. The average freshman award was $26,137. Need-based scholarships or need-based grants averaged $23,554 ($31,450 maximum); need-based self-help aid (loans and jobs) averaged $4,141 ($5,150 maximum); non-need-based athletic scholarships averaged $5,748 ($21,450 maximum); and other non-need-based awards and non-need-based scholarships averaged $17,162 ($31,450 maximum). 40% of undergraduate students work part-time. The average financial indebtedness of the 2017 graduate was $25,721. The FAFSA code is 002544. The deadline for filing freshman financial aid applications for fall entry is March 1.

HASTINGS COLLEGE D-3

www.hastings.edu

Hastings, NE 68901	**(402) 461-7403** **(800) 532-7642**
Fax: (402) 461-7490	**Email: hcadmissions@hastings.edu**
Full-time: 564 men, 519 women	**Faculty:** 86; IIB, --$
Part-time: 10 men, 11 women	**Ph.D.s:** 72%
Graduate: 22 men, 28 women	**Student/Faculty:** 13 to 1
Year: 4-1-4, summer session	**Tuition:** $27,300
Room & Board: $8080	**Freshman Class:** 11186 applied, 1126 accepted, 289 enrolled
SAT: required **ACT:** 24	**CEEB CODE:** 6270
Application Deadline: August 1	**COMPETITIVE+**

Hastings College, founded in 1882, and affiliated with the Presbyterian Church, offers programs in the liberal arts and sciences, education, business, and pre-health professions. There is 1 undergraduate school and 1 graduate school. In addition to regional accreditation, Hastings has baccalaureate program accreditation with NASM. The 120-acre campus is in a rural area in south-central, Nebraska, and 2.5 hours west of Omaha. Including any residence halls, there are 40 buildings.

STUDENT LIFE: 69% of undergraduates are from Nebraska. Others are from 23 states, 8 foreign countries, and Canada. 86% are from public schools. 89% are White; 4% Hispanic; 3% African American; 1% Asian American; 1% American Indian/Alaska Native; 1% Foreign. 38% are Protestant; 34% claim no religious affiliation; 21% Catholic. **Male To Female Ratio:** 1.1:1. The average age of freshmen is 19; all undergraduates, 21. 27% do not continue beyond their first year; 63% remain to graduate. **Housing:** 842 students can be accommodated in college housing, which includes dorms and on-campus apartments. In addition, there are honors houses. On-campus housing is guaranteed for the freshman year only, is available on a first-come, and first-served basis. 73% of students live on campus. All students may keep cars.

FACULTY/CLASSROOMS: 56% of faculty are male; 44% are female. All teach undergraduates, 25% do research, and 25% do both. No introductory courses are taught by graduate students. The average class size in an introductory lecture is 25; in a laboratory is 24; and in a regular course is 23.

PROGRAMS OF STUDY: Hastings confers B.A. and B.M. degrees. Master's degrees are also awarded. Bachelor's degrees are awarded in BIOLOGICAL SCIENCE (biology/biological science), BUSINESS (accounting and business administration and management), COMMUNICATIONS AND THE ARTS (broadcasting, communications, dramatic arts, English, fine arts, German, music, Spanish, and speech/debate/rhetoric), COMPUTER AND PHYSICAL SCIENCE (chemistry, computer science, mathematics, and physics), EDUCATION (art education, business education, elementary education, foreign languages education, music education, science education, secondary education, and special education), HEALTH PROFESSIONS (health care administration), SOCIAL SCIENCE (economics, history, human services, philosophy, political science/government, psychology, religion, social science, and sociology). Physics, mathematics, and religion are the strongest academically. Business administration, teacher education, and biology have the largest enrollments.

ACTIVITIES: 30% of men belong to 4 local fraternities; 30% of women belong to 4 local sororities. There are 80 groups on campus, including and public relations, health advisory council, nontraditional students, peer educators, art, band, cheerleading, choir, chorus, computers, dance, debate, drama, environmental, ethnic, flag team, forensics, honors, international, jazz band, LGBT, literary magazine, marching band, musical theater, newspaper, orchestra, pep band, photography, political, professional, radio and TV, religious, social, social service, student government, and symphony. Popular campus events include May Fete, Festival of Lessons and Carols, and Artist Lecture Series. **Sports:** There are 9 intercollegiate sports for men and 10 for women, and 12 intramural sports for men and 12 for women. Facilities include a physical fitness center, a pool, weight room, indoor and outdoor tennis courts, a stadium, basketball, cross country, track and field, golf, soccer, volleyball, softball, rodeo, archery, bowling, a gym, wellness center, and an all-weather track. **Graduates:** From July 1, 2016 to June 30, 2017, 238 bachelor's degrees were awarded. The most popular majors were business administration (9%), psychology (9%), and biology (8%). In an average class, 52% graduate in 4 years or less, 62% graduate in 5 years or less, and 63% graduate in 6 years or less. Of the 2016 graduating class, 27% were enrolled in graduate school within 6 months of graduation, and 71% were employed.

SERVICES: Counseling and information services are available, as is tutoring in most subjects, all core subjects and most lower-division courses. **Library/Resources:** The library contains 135,450 volumes, 87,723 microform items, and 3,802 audio/video tapes/CDs/DVDs, and subscribes to 1,050 periodicals including electronic. Computerized library services include interlibrary loans, database searching, Internet access, and Wi-Fi capability. Special learning facilities include an art gallery, radio station, TV station, an observatory, a glass blowing studio, a greenhouse, and infant study lab. **Physically Challenged Students:** 90% of the campus is accessible. Facilities include wheelchair ramps, elevators, special parking, specially equipped restrooms, special class scheduling, lowered drinking fountains, and lowered telephones. **Special:** There is a co-op nursing program, a 3-2 engineering program with Columbia and Washington Universities and Georgia Institute of Technology, and a 3-2 degree in occupational therapy with Boston and Washington Universities. Internships, study abroad in England, Spain, Russia, Ireland, Holland, and Germany, dual majors in all areas, and student-designed majors are possible. There are 12 national honor societies. **Visiting:** There are regularly scheduled orientations for prospective students, including academic department presentations, a financial aid session, a student panel discussion, a student guided tour, and an activities fair. Visitors may sit in on classes, and stay overnight. To schedule a visit, contact the Admissions Office. **Campus Safety and Security:** Measures include emergency notification system and security escort services. There are emergency telephones, lighted pathways/sidewalks, and a night security patrol.

REQUIREMENTS: The SAT or ACT is required. Applicants should graduate from an accredited secondary school with a minimum of 4 academic credits in English and 2 each in math, science, social studies, and foreign language. Generally, placement in the upper half of the graduating class, a minimum GPA of 2.0, or a composite score of 20 on the enhanced ACT, is a minimal requirement for consideration for admission. Hastings College requires applicants to be in the upper 50% of their class. AP and CLEP credits are accepted. Important factors in the admissions decision are advanced placement or honors courses, leadership record, and personality/intangible qualities. Students are required to take courses in written and oral communication, physical and life science, foreign language, history, social and political science, literature, philosophy, religion, health/wellness, computer science, the fine arts, and phys ed. A minimum 2.0 GPA and 127 credit hours, with 30 to 36 in the major, are required to graduate. **Procedure:** Freshmen are admitted to all sessions. Entrance exams should be taken before November. There is a rolling admissions plan. Applications should be filed by August 1 for fall entry; December 1 for winter entry; January 1 for spring entry; and May 15 for summer entry. The fall 2017 application fee was $20. Applications are accepted on-line. **Transfer Students:** 48 transfer students enrolled in 2016-2017. Transfer students must have completed course work equivalent by description to that of Hastings and have earned grades of C or better. 30 of 127 credits required for the bachelor's degree must be completed at Hastings. **International Students:** There are 16 international students enrolled. They must take the TOEFL. International athletes should take a standardized test for athletic eligibility.

ADMISSIONS: 10% of the 2017-2018 applicants were accepted. The ACT scores were 37% below 12, 23% between 12 and 17, 20% between 18 and 23, 10% between 24 and 29, and 10% above 30. 36% of the current freshmen were in the top fifth of their class; 64% were in the top two fifths. 18 freshmen graduated first in their class. **Admissions Contact:** Chris Schukei, Director of Admissions. Email: *hcadmissions@hastings.edu* Web: *www.hastings.edu*

FINANCIAL AID: In 2017-2018, 100% of all full-time freshmen received some form of financial aid and need-based aid. 40% of undergraduate students work part-time. The average financial indebtedness of the 2017 graduate was $22,882. Hastings is a member of CSS. The FAFSA code is 002548. The deadline for filing freshman financial aid applications for fall entry is May 1.

MIDLAND UNIVERSITY E-3

www.MidlandU.edu

Fremont, NE 68025	**(402) 941-6508** **(800) 642-8382**
Fax: (402)-941-6513	**Email: info@MidlandU.edu**
Full-time: 550 men, 650 women	**Faculty:** n/av
Part-time: n/av	**Ph.D.s:** n/av
Graduate: n/av	**Student/Faculty:** n/av
Year: 4-1-4	**Tuition:** $31,070
Room & Board: $8442	**Freshman Class:** n/av
SAT or ACT: required	**CEEB CODE:** 6406
Application Deadline: n/av	**COMPETITIVE**

Midland University is a private liberal arts institution, and is affiliated with the ELCA, offering more than 40 programs of study, 31 varsity sports, a plethora of performing arts opportunities, and several student organizations. There are 5 undergraduate schools and 4 graduate schools. In addition to regional accreditation, Midland has baccalaureate program accreditation with NLN. The 27-acre campus is in an urban area 30 minutes northwest of Omaha. Including any residence halls, there are 18 buildings.

STUDENT LIFE: 75% of undergraduates are from Nebraska. Others are from 23 states, 10 foreign countries, and Canada. 94% are from public schools. 91% are White; 4% African American; 2% Foreign; 1% Asian American; 1% American Indian/Alaska Native; 1% Hispanic. 57% are Protestant; 32% Catholic. **Female To Male Ratio:** 1.2:1. The average age of freshmen is 18; all undergraduates, 20. 16% do not continue beyond their first year; 56% remain to graduate. **Housing:** 600 students can be accommodated in college housing, which includes both single sex and coed dorms, on-campus apartments, and off-campus apartments. On-campus housing is available on a first-come, first-served basis, and is available on a lottery system for upperclassmen. 30% of students commute. Alcohol is not permitted. All students may keep cars.

FACULTY/CLASSROOMS: 60% of faculty are male; 40% are female. All teach undergraduates. No introductory courses are taught by graduate students. The average class size in a laboratory is 20 and in a regular course is 20.

PROGRAMS OF STUDY: Midland confers B.A., B.S., B.S.B.A. and B.S.N. degrees. Master's degrees are also awarded. Bachelor's degrees are awarded in BIOLOGICAL SCIENCE (biology/biological science), BUSINESS (accounting, business administration and management, business economics, management information systems, and marketing/retailing/merchandising), COMMUNICATIONS AND THE ARTS (advertising, communications, English, fine arts, journalism, and music), COMPUTER AND PHYSICAL SCIENCE (chemistry, computer programming, computer science, and mathematics), EDUCATION (art education, business education, early childhood education, elementary education, middle school education, music education, science education, and secondary education), HEALTH PROFESSIONS (nursing, predentistry, and premedicine), SOCIAL SCIENCE (community services, economics, history, parks and recreation management, prelaw, psychology, religion, social science, and sociology). Business, nursing, and education are the strongest academically and have the largest enrollments.

ACTIVITIES: 20% of men belong to 4 local fraternities; 20% of women belong to 4 local sororities. There are 36 groups on campus, including art, band, cheerleading, choir, chorale, chorus, computers, drama, drill team, drum and bugle corps, ethnic, film, forensics, honors, jazz band, LGBT, literary magazine, musical theater, newspaper, orchestra, pep band, photography, political, professional, radio and TV, religious, social, social service, student government, and yearbook. Popular campus events include Greek Games, Martin Luther King Day, Midland U's Got Talent, and Festival of the ARTS. **Sports:** There are 17 intercollegiate sports for men and 18 for women. Facilities include a phys ed center, an athletic practice field, an indoor pool, indoor track, and weight room. Students also have access to the largest YMCA at no cost to them.

SERVICES: Counseling and information services are available, as is tutoring in every subject. There is remedial reading and writing. **Library/Resources:** The library contains 105,000 volumes, and 1,000 audio/video tapes/CDs/DVDs, and subscribes to 900 periodicals including electronic. Computerized library services include interlibrary loans, database searching, Internet access, and Wi-Fi capability. Special learning facilities include an art gallery, planetarium, and radio station. **Physically Challenged Students:** 90% of the campus is accessible. Facilities include wheelchair ramps, elevators, special parking, specially equipped restrooms, special class scheduling, lowered drinking fountains, and lowered telephones. **Special:** There is cross-registration with Dana College in Blair, internships in business, public relations, journalism, and art, study abroad in 3 countries, student-designed majors, work-study programs, and a 3-2 engineering degree with Washington University. Other options include dual majors, independent study, directed study, and the pass/no credit grading system. There are 2 national honor societies and a freshman honors program. **Visiting:** There are regularly scheduled orientations for prospective students, campus visits are scheduled on an individual basis and as much as possible include visits with faculty, students, and financial aid counselors. Visitors may sit in on classes, and stay overnight. To schedule a visit, contact the Admissions Office at admissions@MidlandU.edu. **Campus Safety and Security:** Measures include 24-hour foot and vehicle patrol, emergency notification system, and security escort services. There are lighted pathways/sidewalks and controlled access to dorms/residences.

REQUIREMENTS: The SAT or ACT is required. Applicants should be graduates of an accredited secondary school. The GED is accepted. Recommended preparation includes 3 units of English, 2 each of math, and foreign language, and 10 of electives. An interview is recommended. AP and CLEP credits are accepted. Important factors in the admissions decision are leadership record, extracurricular activities record, and evidence of special talent. To graduate, students need a total of 120 credit hours, with 33 of these in distribution requirements of the student's selection. 1 year each of English, speech, math courses, and foreign language on the high school or college level. The total number of hours in the major varies from 34 to 48, and students must maintain a GPA of at least 2.0

overall and 2.25 in the major, with some departments requiring a higher minimum GPA. **Procedure:** Freshmen are admitted fall and winter. Entrance exams should be taken during the fall of the senior year. There are deferred admissions and rolling admissions plans. Application deadlines are open. Notification is sent on a rolling basis. Applications are accepted on-line. **Transfer Students:** 125 transfer students enrolled in 2016-2017. Applicants must be in good standing at their previous college and generally have a 2.0 minimum GPA. Grades of C or higher transfer for credit. 30 of 120 credits required for the bachelor's degree must be completed at Midland. **International Students:** They must take the TOEFL, and the SAT or ACT, scoring 20.

ADMISSIONS: **Admissions Contact:** Matt Bojanski, Director of Admissions. Email: *info@MidlandU.edu* Web: *www.MidlandU.edu*

FINANCIAL AID: In 2017-2018, 98% of all full-time freshmen received some form of financial aid. Midland University is a member of CSS. The FFS is required. The FAFSA code is 002553. Check with the school for current application deadlines.

NEBRASKA METHODIST COLLEGE F-3

www.methodistcollege.edu

Omaha, NE 68114	**(402) 354-7200** **(800) 335-5510**
Fax: (402) 354-7020	**Email: admissions@methodistcollege.edu**
Full-time: 52 men, 401 women	**Faculty:** 46
Part-time: 21 men, 273 women	**Ph.D.s:** 31%
Graduate: 29 men, 224 women	**Student/Faculty:** 10 to 1
Year: semesters, summer session	**Tuition:** $16,230
Room & Board: $9084	**Freshman Class:** n/av
ACT: required	**CEEB CODE:** 6510
Application Deadline: March 1	**COMPETITIVE**

Nebraska Methodist College, founded in 1891, is a private non-profit institution offering education opportunities in healthcare careers. The college enrolls students in short term certificate programs, AS and BS degrees, as well as online master's and doctoral degree programs. The tuition cost in the above capsule is approximate, and varies by programs chosen by student. There is 1 undergraduate school. In addition to regional accreditation, NMC has baccalaureate program accreditation with CCNE and CAAHEP. The 9-acre campus is in a suburban area in the center of Omaha, Nebraska. Including any residence halls, there are 20 buildings.

STUDENT LIFE: 95% of undergraduates are from Nebraska. Others are from 32 states, and 2 foreign countries. 95% are from public schools. 87% are White; 4% African American; 3% Hispanic; 2% Asian American; 2% two or more races; 2% race unknown; 1% American Indian/Alaska Native; 1% Foreign. **Female To Male Ratio:** 8.8:1. The average age of freshmen is 24; all undergraduates, 25. 11% do not continue beyond their first year; 68% remain to graduate. **Housing:** 100 students can be accommodated in college housing, which includes married student on-campus apartments. On-campus housing is available on a first-come and first-served basis. 89% of students commute. Alcohol is not permitted. All students may keep cars.

FACULTY/CLASSROOMS: 9% of faculty are male; 91% are female. 89% teach undergraduates. No introductory courses are taught by graduate students. The average class size in a regular course is 19.

PROGRAMS OF STUDY: NMC confers B.S. and B.S.N. degrees. Associate, master's, and doctoral degrees are also awarded. Bachelor's degrees are awarded in COMPUTER AND PHYSICAL SCIENCE (radiological technology), HEALTH PROFESSIONS (allied health, health care administration, health promotion, nursing, physical therapy assistant, and respiratory therapy). Nursing has the largest enrollment.

ACTIVITIES: There are no fraternities; 5% of women belong to 1 local sorority. There are 12 groups on campus, including ethnic, LGBT, professional, religious, social, social service, and student government. Popular campus events include Honors Convocation, Pledging Ceremonies, Fall Carnival and Veteran's Day Activities. **Sports:** There is no sports program at NNC. Facilities include a fitness center. **Graduates:** From July 1, 2016 to June 30, 2017, 172 bachelor's degrees were awarded. The most popular majors were nursing (62%), health promotion management (8%), and radiologic technology (8%). In an average class, 48% graduate in 4 years or less, 68% graduate in 5 years or less, and 68% graduate in 6 years or less. Of the 2016 graduating class, 98% were employed within 6 months of graduation.

SERVICES: Counseling and information services are available, as is tutoring in most subjects. There is remedial math, reading, and writing. A reader service for the blind is available in the metropolitan area. **Library/Resources:** The library contains 13,600 volumes, 1,722 microform items, and 500 audio/video tapes/CDs/DVDs, and subscribes to 640 periodicals including electronic. Computerized library services include interlibrary loans, database searching, Internet access, and Wi-Fi capability. **Physically Challenged Students:** 80% of the campus is accessible. Facilities include elevators, special parking, specially equipped restrooms, and lowered drinking fountains. **Special:** Nebraska Methodist College has a 15-month Accelerated BS in Nursing degree. There is 1 national honor society and 2 departmental honors programs. **Visiting:** There are regularly scheduled orientations for prospective students. There are guides for informal visits and visitors may sit in on classes. To schedule a visit, contact the Admissions Office. **Campus Safety and Security:** Measures include 24-hour foot and vehicle patrol, emergency notification system, self-defense education, and security escort services. There are emergency telephones, lighted pathways/sidewalks, and controlled access to dorms/residences.

REQUIREMENTS: The ACT is required. Students must be graduates of an accredited secondary school with the number of academic credits required under Nebraska state law. The GED is accepted. Students should have completed 4 years of English and 2 years each of math (including algebra) and science (including biology and chemistry) and social science. An essay and an interview are required for admissions consideration. A GPA of 2.5 is required. AP and CLEP credits are accepted. Important factors in the admissions decision are personality/intangible qualities, advanced placement or honors courses, and leadership record. All NMC undergraduate students are required to complete Arts & Science courses in our Educated Citizen Core Curriculum (45 credits for BS degrees; 21 credits for AS degrees). These courses are divided into four categories: communications, humanities, social sciences, natural and applied sciences. An NMC graduate is an educated citizen who is a competent practitioner and engaged citizen who responds productively to the complex dynamics of the world and who utilizes a diversity of disciplines and perspectives. Our goal as an institution is that graduates of NMC will be able to articulate and demonstrate growth in the following areas: as reflective individuals, effective communicators, and change agents in an increasingly educated citizenry. **Procedure:** Freshmen are admitted fall and spring. Entrance exams should be taken as early as possible. There is a rolling admissions plan. Applications should be filed by March 1 for fall entry; October 1 for spring entry. The fall 2017 application fee was $25. Notifications are sent April 15. Applications are accepted on-line. **Transfer Students:** 240 transfer students enrolled in 2016-2017. Applicants must have a GPA above 2.5. Grades of C and above can be transferred for credit. An interview is required. 30 of 127 credits required for the bachelor's degree must be completed at NMC. **International Students:** There are 3 international students enrolled. They must take the TOEFL with a minimum score of 550 on the paper-based TOEFL (PBT) or 80 on the Internet-based version (iBT). They must also take the ACT, scoring 20.

ADMISSIONS: 22% of the current freshmen were in the top fifth of their class; 35% were in the top two fifths. 1 freshman graduated first in the class. **Admissions Contact:** Laurel Zentner, Recruitment and Admissions Coordinator. Email: *admissions@methodistcollege.edu* Web: *www.methodistcollege.edu*

FINANCIAL AID: In 2017-2018, 84% of all full-time freshmen received some form of financial aid. 81% of all full-time freshmen received need-based aid. The average freshman award was $10,113. Need-based scholarships or need-based grants averaged $6,878; need-based self-help aid (loans and jobs) averaged $3,791; and other non-need-based awards and non-need-based scholarships averaged $4,584. 68% of undergraduate students work part-time. The average financial indebtedness of the 2017 graduate was $41,742. The college's own financial statement is required. The priority date for freshman financial aid applications for fall entry is April 1.

NEBRASKA WESLEYAN UNIVERSITY E-3

www.nebrwesleyan.edu

Lincoln, NE 68504 **(402) 465-2544**

Fax: (402) 465-2179 **Email:** admissions@nebrwesleyan.edu

Full-time: 690 men, 980 women	**Faculty:** 105; IIB, --$
Part-time: 78 men, 155 women	**Ph.D.s:** 89%
Graduate: 66 men, 179 women	**Student/Faculty:** 13 to 1
Year: semesters, summer session	**Tuition:** $32,744
Room & Board: $9252	**Freshman Class:** n/av
SAT: required **ACT:** 26	**CEEB CODE:** 6470
Application Deadline: August 15	**COMPETITIVE+**

Nebraska Wesleyan University, founded in 1887, is a private liberal arts institution affiliated with the United Methodist Church. NWU offers 106 majors, minors, and pre-professional programs. The figures given in the above capsule and in this profile are approximate. There are 18 undergraduate schools and 3 graduate schools. In addition to regional accreditation, Nebraska Wesleyan University has baccalaureate program accreditation with ACBSP, CSWE, NASM, NCATE, and NLN. The 50-acre campus is in a suburban area in the city of Lincoln, 50 miles west of Omaha. Including any residence halls, there are 31 buildings.

STUDENT LIFE: 88% of undergraduates are from Nebraska. Others are from 25 states, 14 foreign countries, and Canada. 93% are White; 2% African American; 2% Asian American; 2% Hispanic; 1% American Indian/Alaska Native. 36% are Protestant; 24% Catholic; 14% claim no religious affiliation. **Female To Male Ratio:** 1.6:1. The average age of freshmen is 18; all undergraduates, 20. 18% do not continue beyond their first year; 70% remain to graduate. **Housing:** 1055 students can be accommodated in college housing, which includes dorms, on-campus apartments, and off-campus apartments. In addition, there are fraternity houses and sorority houses. On-campus housing is guaranteed for all 4 years. 65% of students live on campus. All students may keep cars.

FACULTY/CLASSROOMS: 45% of faculty are male; 55% are female. All teach undergraduates. No introductory courses are taught by graduate students. The average class size in an introductory lecture is 22; in a laboratory is 17; and in a regular course is 19.

PROGRAMS OF STUDY: Nebraska Wesleyan University confers B.A., B.S., B.F.A., B.M. and B.S.N. degrees. Master's degrees are also awarded. Bachelor's degrees are awarded in BIOLOGICAL SCIENCE (biochemistry, biology/biological science, and molecular biology), BUSINESS (accounting, business administration and management, international business management, and sports management), COMMUNICATIONS AND THE ARTS (applied music, art, communications, dramatic arts, English, French, German, language arts, music, Spanish, and studio art), COMPUTER AND PHYSICAL SCIENCE (chemistry, computer science, information sciences and systems, mathematics, and physics), EDUCATION (athletic training, elementary education, English education, middle school education, music education, physical education, science education, social science education, and special education), HEALTH PROFESSIONS (exercise science, health, and nursing), SOCIAL SCIENCE (biopsychology, economics, history, international studies, paralegal studies, philosophy, political science/government, psychology, religion, social work, sociology, and women's studies). Business administration, biology, and psychology have the largest enrollments.

ACTIVITIES: 12% of men belong to 1 local and 3 national fraternities; 19% of women belong to 2 local and 2 national sororities. There are 80 groups on campus, including art, band, cheerleading, choir, chorus, computers, debate, drama, drill team, ethnic, forensics, honors, international, jazz band, LGBT, literary magazine, musical theater, newspaper, opera, orchestra, pep band, political, professional, religious, social, social service, student government, and yearbook. Popular campus events include International Dinners, Mosaic Week (week emphasizing multicultural activities), and Visions. **Sports:** There are 8 intercollegiate sports for men and 8 for women, and 8 intramural sports for men and 8 for women. Facilities include a recreation and fitness center, a field house and gym, a football/soccer stadium, a swimming pool, an outdoor track, football and baseball fields, tennis courts, racquetball courts, and volleyball courts. **Graduates:** From July 1, 2016 to June 30, 2017, 403 bachelor's degrees were awarded. The most popular majors were business administration (23%), nursing (13%), and education (9%). In an average class, 1% graduate in 3 years or less, 52% graduate in 4 years or less, 66% graduate in 5 years or less, and 70% graduate in 6 years or less.

SERVICES: Counseling and information services are available, as is tutoring in some subjects, sciences, social sciences, humanities, and math. **Library/Resources:** The library contains 221,084 volumes, 4,897 microform items, and 8,826 audio/video tapes/CDs/DVDs, and subscribes to 832 periodicals including electronic. Computerized library services include interlibrary loans, database searching, Internet access, and Wi-Fi capability. Special learning facilities include an art gallery, planetarium, a laboratory theater, a sleep lab, greenhouse, herbarium, and nuclear magnetic resonance lab. **Physically Challenged Students:** 92% of the campus is accessible. Facilities include wheelchair ramps, elevators, special parking, specially equipped restrooms, special class scheduling, lowered drinking fountains, lowered telephones, special housing. All academic programs can be moved or adapted as needed to accommodate students. **Special:** NWU offers the Capitol Hill Internship Program, study abroad in 38 countries through the International Student Exchange Program and sister schools in Mexico, Japan, and Estonia. A global studies major, and many other interdisciplinary studies majors and minors. Internships are available in most departments and required in many. Natural sciences majors can complete summer research fellowships at labs, universities, and agencies nationwide and internationally. Other options include pass/fail options, dual majors, credit by exam, and a 3-2 engineering degree in conjunction with Washington and Columbia Universities. There are 25 national honor societies. **Visiting:** There are regularly scheduled orientations for prospective students, consisting of a tour, classroom visits, and meetings with faculty, financial aid and admissions personnel, and current students. There are guides for informal visits, visitors may sit in on classes, and stay overnight. To schedule a visit, contact the Admissions Office at (402) 465-2218. **Campus Safety and Security:** Measures include emergency notification system and security escort services. There are emergency telephones, lighted pathways/sidewalks, controlled access to dorms/residences, security service, night time foot patrol, and a uniformed police officer during the day.

REQUIREMENTS: The SAT or ACT is required. In addition, Freshmen must be graduates of an accredited secondary school or submit the GED. A campus visit is recommended. NWU requires applicants to be in the upper 50% of their class. AP and CLEP credits are accepted. To graduate, students must complete approximately 42 to 48 hours of general education requirements, including 9 hours in First-year Experience, 8 in Developing Foundations courses, 7 in Scientific Inquiry, 6 in U.S. Culture and Society, 3 to 11 in Global Perspectives, 3 in Western Intellectual and Religious Traditions, and 3 in Fine Arts. At least 126 credit hours, including 30 in the major, must be completed with a minimum GPA of 2.0. A senior comprehensive is also needed, consisting of a comprehensive exam in the major discipline, a thesis or independent study, or an internship, presentation, or performance. **Procedure:** Freshmen are admitted fall and spring. Entrance exams should be taken no later than December of the senior year. There are early decision and deferred admissions plans. Early decision applications should be filed by November 15; regular applications, by August 15 for fall entry; December 15 for spring entry; and April 15 for summer entry. The fall 2017 application fee was $20. Notification of early decision is sent December 15; regular decision, January 15. 338 early decision candidates were accepted for the 2017-2018 class. Applications are accepted on-line. **Transfer Students:** 61 transfer students enrolled in 2016-2017. Applicants must be in good standing at their previous school and have a 2.0 GPA or higher. Grades of C- or better transfer for credit. 30 of 126 credits required for the bachelor's degree must be completed at NWU. **International Students:** There are 33 international students enrolled. They must take the TOEFL with a minimum score of 525 on the paper-based TOEFL (PBT) or 71 on the Internet-based version (iBT). The SAT or ACT is recommended.

ADMISSIONS: The SAT scores for the 2017-2018 freshman class were: 48% of the current freshmen were in the top fifth of their class; 79% were in the top two fifths. 22 freshmen graduated first in their class. **Admissions Contact:** Gordie Coffin, Director of Admissions. Email: *admissions@nebrwesleyan.edu* Web: *www.nebrwesleyan.edu*

FINANCIAL AID: In 2017-2018, 99% of all full-time freshmen received some form of financial aid. 77% of all full-time freshmen received need-based aid. The average freshman award was $16,769. Need-based scholarships or need-based grants averaged $10,040; need-based self-help aid (loans and jobs) averaged $3,648; and other non-need-based awards and non-need-based scholarships averaged $2,690. 102% of undergraduate students work part-time. The average financial indebtedness of the 2017 graduate was $24,708. The FAFSA code is 002555. The priority date for freshman financial aid applications for fall entry is rolling. The deadline for filing freshman financial aid applications for fall entry is rolling.

PERU STATE COLLEGE *(The complete profile is made available exclusively on our website, www.barronspac.com)*

UNION COLLEGE E-3
www.ucollege.edu

Lincoln, NE 68506 (402) 486-2504 (800) 228-4600

Fax: (402) 486-2566	**Email:** enroll@ucollege.edu
Full-time: 284 men, 380 women	**Faculty:** 53
Part-time: 53 men, 69 women	**Ph.D.s:** 52%
Graduate: 21 men, 49 women	**Student/Faculty:** 15 to 1
Year: semesters, summer session	**Tuition:** $17,430
Room & Board: $5840	**Freshman Class:** n/av
ACT: 22	**CEEB CODE:** 6865
Application Deadline: open	**COMPETITIVE**

Union College, established in 1891, is a private liberal arts institution affiliated with the Seventh-Day Adventist Church. There is 1 undergraduate school. In addition to regional accreditation, UC has baccalaureate program accreditation with CSWE. The 26-acre campus is in a suburban area in southeast Lincoln Nebraska. Including any residence halls, there are 13 buildings.

STUDENT LIFE: 86% of undergraduates are from out of state, mostly the Midwest. Students are from 45 states, 21 foreign countries, and Canada. 30% are from public schools. 8% are Hispanic; 72% White; 6% Foreign; 3% African American; 3% Asian American; 1% American Indian/Alaska Native. **Female To Male Ratio:** 1.4:1. The average age of freshmen is 18; all undergraduates, 22. 35% do not continue beyond their first year; 54% remain to graduate. **Housing:** 642 students can be accommodated in college housing, which includes married student dorms and on-campus apartments. On-campus housing is guaranteed for the freshman year only, and is available on a first-come, first-served basis. 52% of students commute. Alcohol is not permitted. All students may keep cars.

FACULTY/CLASSROOMS: 55% of faculty are male; 45% are female. No introductory courses are taught by graduate students. The average class size in an introductory lecture is 21 and in a regular course is 16.

PROGRAMS OF STUDY: UC confers B.A., B.S., B.A.T., B.Ed., B.M., B.S.W. and B.T. degrees. Associate and master's degrees are also awarded. Bachelor's degrees are awarded in BIOLOGICAL SCIENCE (biology/biological science), BUSINESS (accounting, banking and finance, business administration and management, management science, marketing and distribution, and small business management), COMMUNICATIONS AND THE ARTS (communications, English, French, German, graphic design, journalism, literature, music, music performance, public relations, Spanish, and studio art), COMPUTER AND PHYSICAL SCIENCE (chemistry, computer science, mathematics, physics, and science), EDUCATION (art education, business education, computer education, elementary education, English education, mathematics education, music education, physical education, secondary education, and social science education), HEALTH PROFESSIONS (medical laboratory technology, nursing, and physician's assistant), SOCIAL SCIENCE (history, international public service, international studies, pastoral studies, physical fitness/movement, psychology, religion, religious education, social science, social work, and theological studies). Physician's assistant, and physical science are the strongest academically. Nursing, and international rescue & relief have the largest enrollments.

ACTIVITIES: There are no fraternities or sororities. There are 18 groups on campus, including art, band, choir, chorale, chorus, computers, drama, ethnic, honors, international, literary magazine, newspaper, orchestra, photography, religious, social, student government, and yearbook. **Sports:** There are 2 intercollegiate sports for men and 3 for women, and 8 intramural sports for men and 8 for women. Facilities include an Olympic-size indoor swimming pool, a weight room, tennis courts, and a sandlot volleyball court. **Graduates:** From July 1, 2016 to June 30, 2017, 170 bachelor's degrees were awarded. The most popular majors were nursing (16%), business administration (15%), and elementary education (8%). In an average class, 29% graduate in 4 years or less and 57% graduate in 6 years or less. Of the 2016 graduating class, 15% were enrolled in graduate school within 6 months of graduation, and 80% were employed.

SERVICES: Counseling and information services are available, as is tutoring in most subjects. There is a reader service for the blind, and remedial math, reading, and writing. Tutoring is available upon request. **Library/Resources:** The library contains 161,728 volumes, 1,938 microform items, and 2,066 audio/video tapes/CDs/DVDs, and subscribes to 604 periodicals including electronic. Computerized library services include interlibrary loans, database searching, Internet access, and Wi-Fi capability. Special learning facilities include an art gallery, and a state-run natural arboretum. **Physically Challenged Students:** 75% of the campus is accessible. Facilities include wheelchair ramps, elevators, special parking, specially equipped restrooms, and lowered telephones. **Special:** Special academic programs include study abroad in 7 countries, co-op programs with 9 Adventist institutions abroad, and cross-registration with the University of Nebraska, Nebraska Wesleyan University, and Southeast Community College. Student-designed majors are available through the Personalized Bachelor's Degree Program. There are pass/fail options in electives for upperclassmen with a minimum cumulative GPA of 2.0. Some internships are available. There is a freshman honors program. **Visiting:** There are regularly scheduled orientations for prospective students. There are guides for informal visits, visitors may sit in on classes, and stay overnight. To schedule a visit, contact the Admissions Office Campus Hostess. **Campus Safety and Security:** Measures include 24-hour foot and vehicle patrol and security escort services. There are emergency telephones and lighted pathways/sidewalks.

REQUIREMENTS: The ACT is required. Freshmen with a high school GPA below 2.5 and/or an ACT composite score below the 20th percentile will be enrolled in the freshman development program. Applicants must have graduated from an accredited secondary school with 18 academic credits, including 3 units of English and 1 unit each of math, science, and history. For math and science programs, 2 units of algebra and 1 unit each of geometry and trigonometry are recommended. For majors in nursing, biology, chemistry, physics, or engineering, applicants should complete physics and chemistry courses. The GED is also accepted. An essay and interview are advised, and music students should audition. A GPA of 2.5 is required. AP and CLEP credits are accepted. Students must complete 128 semester hours, with fulfillment of a major, and maintain a minimum GPA of 2.0. There are 56 hours of core classes, including those in art/fine arts, computer science, English, history, math, science, and philosophy/religion. Courses in phy ed are also required. **Procedure:** Freshmen are admitted fall and spring. Entrance exams should be taken by fall of the senior year. There is a rolling admissions plan. Application deadlines are open. **Transfer Students:** Transfer students must have a minimum GPA of 2.0. The ACT is required, and high school and college transcripts must be submitted. 30 of 128 credits required for the bachelor's degree must be completed at UC. **International Students:** There are 109 international students enrolled. They must take the TOEFL with a minimum score of 550 on the paper-based TOEFL (PBT) or 80 on the Internet-based version (iBT). They must also take the ACT, scoring 18.

ADMISSIONS: 32% of the current freshmen were in the top fifth of their class; 69% were in the top two fifths. **Admissions Contact:** Kevin Ericks, Director of Admissions. Email: *enroll@ucollege.edu* Web: *www.ucollege.edu*

FINANCIAL AID: In 2017-2018, 99% of all full-time freshmen received some form of financial aid. 97% of all full-time freshmen received need-based aid. 54% of undergraduate students work part-time. Check with the school for current application deadlines.

UNIVERSITY OF NEBRASKA - KEARNEY *(The complete profile is made available exclusively on our website, www.barronspac.com)*

UNIVERSITY OF NEBRASKA - LINCOLN E-3
www.admissions.unl.edu

Lincoln, NE 68588 (402) 472-2023 (800) 742-8800

Fax: (402) 472-0670	**Email:** admissions@unl.edu
Full-time: 9905 men, 8912 women	**Faculty:** 959; I, av$
Part-time: 796 men, 569 women	**Ph.D.s:** 93%
Graduate: 2410 men, 2668 women	**Student/Faculty:** 18 to 1
Year: semesters, summer session	**Tuition:** $8279 ($22,446)
Room & Board: $10,310	**Freshman Class:** 9724 applied, 7425 accepted, 4628 enrolled
SAT CR/M: 560/580 **ACT:** 25	**CEEB CODE:** 6877
Application Deadline: May 1	**VERY COMPETITIVE**

University of Nebraska at Lincoln, founded in 1869 is an educational institution of international stature, listed by the Carnegie Foundation within the Research Universities. Lincoln is a land-grant university and a member of the Association of Public and Land-grant Universities. Programs are offered through the colleges of agricultural sciences and natural resources, architecture, arts and sciences, business administration, education and human sciences, engineering, fine and performing arts, journalism and mass communications, law, and the exploratory and preprofessonal advising center. There are 8 undergraduate schools and 1 graduate school. In addition to regional accreditation, Lincoln has baccalaureate program accreditation with AACSB, ABET, ACCE, ACEJMC, ADA, ASLA, NAAB, NASAD, NASM, TEAC, NASD, NAST, and CAEP. The 622-acre campus is in an urban area 55 miles southwest of Omaha. Including any residence halls, there are 270 buildings.

STUDENT LIFE: 72% of undergraduates are from Nebraska. Others are from 50 states, 106 foreign countries, and Canada. 8% are Foreign; 77% White; 5% Hispanic; 3% African American; 3% two or more races; 2% Asian American; 2% race unknown. **Male To Female Ratio:** 1.1:1. The average age of freshmen is 18; all undergraduates, 20. 18% do not continue beyond their first year; 67% remain to graduate. **Housing:** 9931 students can be accommodated in college housing, which includes married student dorms, on-campus apartments, and off-campus apartments. In addition, there are honors houses, special-interest houses, fraternity houses, sorority houses, special floors/sections for first-year students in 26 interest groups, and 9 scholar communities. On-campus housing is guaranteed for the freshman year only, is available on a first-come, and first-served basis. 59% of students commute. Alcohol is not permitted. All students may keep cars.

FACULTY/CLASSROOMS: 69% of faculty are male; 31% are female. 89% teach undergraduates and do research, and 86% do both. No introductory courses are taught by graduate students. The average class size in an introductory lecture is 44; in a laboratory is 23; and in a regular course is 27.

PROGRAMS OF STUDY: Lincoln confers B.A., B.S., B.F.A., B.J., B.M., B.M.Ed. and B.L.A. degrees. Master's and doctoral degrees are also awarded. Bachelor's degrees are awarded in AGRICULTURE (agricultural business management, agricultural communications, agricultural economics, agricultural mechanics, agriculture, agronomy, animal science, environmental studies, fish and game management, food technology for companion animals, horticulture, natural resource/environmental economics, natural resource management, plant science, ranch management, range/farm management, turfgrass and landscape management, and wildlife management), BIOLOGICAL SCIENCE (biochemistry, biology/biological science, entomology, forensic science, life science secondary school education, microbiology, and nutrition), BUSINESS (accounting, apparel and accessories marketing, banking and finance, business administration and management, business economics, entrepreneurial studies, fashion merchandising, finance, hospitality management services, human resources, insurance and risk management, international business management, investments and securities, management science, marketing management, marketing/retailing/merchandising, organizational leadership and management, and supply chain management), COMMUNICATIONS AND THE ARTS (advertising, apparel design, art history, art, art history and appreciation, broadcasting, classical languages, classics, communications, communication rhetoric/communication, dance, dramatic arts, English, film arts, film, television and digital media, fine arts, Great Plains studies, French, German, information technology, journalism, language arts, Latin, music, public relations, Russian, Spanish, speech/debate/rhetoric, studio art, theatre arts, and theater design), COMPUTER AND PHYSICAL SCIENCE (actuarial science, applied science, astronomy, atmospheric sciences and meteorology, chemistry, chemistry/adolescence education, computer science, earth science/adolescence education, geology, mathematics, physics, physics with astrophysics option, and science), EDUCATION (agricultural education, athletic training, business education, childhood education, computer education, drama education, early childhood education, education, elementary education, English education, environmental education, foreign languages education, golf enterprise management, home economics education, journalism education, marketing and distribution education, mathematics education, music education, physical science secondary school education, science education, secondary education, social science education, and special education), ENGINEERING AND ENVIRONMENTAL DESIGN (agricultural engineering, architectural engineering, architecture, bioengineering, chemical engineering, civil engineering, computer engineering, construction engineering, construction management, electrical/electronics engineering, environmental science, interior design, landscape architecture, landscape architecture/design, and mechanical engineering), HEALTH PROFESSIONS (exercise science, health science, predentistry, premedicine, prepharmacy, speech pathology/audiology, and veterinary science), SOCIAL SCIENCE (anthropology, architectural studies, child care/child and family studies, classical/ancient civilization, culinary arts, dietetics, early childhood studies, economics, ethnic studies, family/consumer studies, food production/management/services, food science, geography, history, interdisciplinary studies, Latin American studies, liberal arts/general studies, medieval studies, parks and recreation management, philosophy, political science/government, prelaw, psychology, religious studies, sociology, textiles and clothing, water resources, and women & gender studies). Agriculture, biochemistry, and biological sciences are the strongest academically. Business administration, psychology, and pre-health have the largest enrollments.

ACTIVITIES: 19% of men belong to 28 national fraternities; 22% of women belong to 19 national sororities. There are 551 groups on campus, including art, band, cheerleading, choir, chorale, chorus, communications, computers, dance, debate, drama, drill team, environmental, ethnic, film, forensics, honors, international, jazz band, LGBT, literary magazine, marching band, musical theater, newspaper, opera, orchestra, pep band, photography, political, professional, radio and TV, religious, social, social service, student government, and symphony. Popular campus events include Homecoming, Big Red Welcome, The Big Event, Dance Marathon and Football Games. **Sports:** There are 9 intercollegiate sports for men and 13 for women, and 76 intramural sports for men and 76 for women. Facilities include a campus recreation center, multi-sport competition center, soccer and tennis complex, bowling alley, rifle range, athletic conditioning and training center, football stadium, indoor and outdoor practice facilities, soccer fields, track, tennis courts, and swimming pools. **Graduates:** From July 1, 2016 to June 30, 2017, 3855 bachelor's degrees were awarded. The most popular majors were business marketing (23%), engineering (10%), and agriculture (9%). In an average class, 33% graduate in 4 years or less, 62% graduate in 5 years or less, and 67% graduate in 6 years or less. Of the 2016 graduating class, 22% were enrolled in graduate school within 6 months of graduation, and 60% were employed.

SERVICES: There is a reader service for the blind. **Library/Resources:** The library contains 3.8 million volumes, 255,917 microform items, and 429,764 audio/video tapes/CDs/DVDs, and subscribes to 96,522 periodicals including electronic. Computerized library services include interlibrary loans, database searching, Internet access, and Wi-Fi capability. Special learning facilities include an art gallery, natural history museum, planetarium, radio station, TV station, Nebraska State Museum, international quilt study center and museum, museum of art, Diocles Laser/Extreme Light Lab, collection of miniatures, multicultural center, tractor test and power museum, Great Plains Art Museum, an observatory, and Midwest Roadside Safety Facility. **Physically Challenged Students:** All of the campus is accessible. Facilities include wheelchair ramps, elevators, special parking, specially equipped restrooms, special class scheduling, lowered drinking fountains, lowered telephones, special housing. Assistance from Services for Students with Disabilities. **Special:** There is cross-registration with many schools, and co-op programs are available in the Colleges of Engineering and Agriculture. Through membership in the International Student Exchange Program, the university can place students in more than 90 universities around the world. Internship opportunities abound, as do work-study programs and undergraduate research opportunities. Accelerated degree programs, a Washington semester, B.A.-B.S. degrees, dual majors, combined pre-professional programs, student-designed majors, credit by exam, nondegree study, and pass/fail options are also available. There are 35 national honor societies, including Phi Beta Kappa, a freshman honors program, and 39 departmental honors programs. **Visiting:** There are regularly scheduled orientations for prospective students, a campus tour, an information session about academics, scholarships and financial aid, living and dining options, how to get involved, Greek Life and career connections for your future. Visits and visitors may sit in on classes. To schedule a visit, contact the Admissions Office. **Campus Safety and Security:** Measures include 24-hour foot and vehicle patrol, emergency notification system, and self-defense education. There are shuttle buses, emergency telephones, lighted pathways/sidewalks, and controlled access to dorms/residences.

REQUIREMENTS: The SAT or ACT is recommended. Applicants must be graduates of an accredited secondary school. The GED is accepted. Students must have completed 4 years each of English and math, 3 years of science and social studies, and 2 years of a foreign language. Applicants must have a minimum composite ACT score of 20, or a combined SAT score of 950, or rank in the top 50% of their high school class. Lincoln requires applicants to be in the upper 50% of their class. AP and CLEP credits are accepted. Important factors in the admissions decision are advanced placement or honors courses, recommendations by school officials, and evidence of special talent. All students matriculating beginning Fall 2009 must complete the general education requirements for the Achievement-Centered Education (ACE) program. The program is based on a set of four institutional objectives and 10 student learning outcomes. Students complete the equivalent of 3 credit hours for each of the ten student learning outcomes. A minimum GPA of 2.0 is required. Each college and major has its own requirements; few graduation requirements apply to all students. **Procedure:** Freshmen are admitted to all sessions. Entrance exams should be taken in April of the junior year. There is a rolling admissions plan. Applications should be filed by May 1 for fall entry; December 1 for spring entry; and May 1 for summer entry. The fall 2017 application fee was $45. Applications are accepted on-line. **Transfer Students:** 923 transfer students enrolled in 2016-2017. Transfer students must have a 2.0 GPA for both the cumulative average of all post-secondary facilities attended and for the most recent term of attendance. In certain majors, a higher GPA and/or extra course work may be required. **International Students:** There are 1474 international students enrolled. ACT or SAT may be required for admission into some colleges.

ADMISSIONS: 76% of the 2017-2018 applicants were accepted. The SAT scores for the 2017-2018 freshman class were: Critical Reading-- 25% below 500, 37% between 500 and 599, 25% between 600 and 699, and 13% between 700 and 800. Math-- 23% below 500, 33% between 500 and 599, 30% between 600 and 699, and 14% between 700 and 800. The ACT scores were 3% between 12 and 17, 35% between 18 and 23, 43% between 24 and 29, and 19% above 30. 44% of the current freshmen were in the top fifth of their class; 73% were in the top two fifths. 346 freshmen graduated first in their class. **Admissions Contact:** Amber Williams, Associate Dean of Enrollment Management. Email: *admissions@unl.edu* Web: *www.admissions.unl.edu*

FINANCIAL AID: In 2017-2018, 85% of all full-time freshmen received some form of financial aid. 54% of all full-time freshmen received need-based aid. 71% of undergraduate students work part-time. The average financial indebtedness of the 2017 graduate was $20,930. The FAFSA code is 002565. The priority date for freshman financial aid applications for fall entry is April 1.

UNIVERSITY OF NEBRASKA - OMAHA F-3

www.unomaha.edu

Omaha, NE 68182 **(402) 554-2393**

Fax: (402) 554-3472	**Email:** unoadmissions@unomaha.edu
Full-time: 4000 men, 4725 women	**Faculty:** I, av$
Part-time: 1300 men, 1500 women	**Ph.D.s:** n/av
Graduate: 1090 men, 1720 women	**Student/Faculty:** n/av
Year: semesters, summer session	**Tuition:** $7204 ($16,918)
Room & Board: $8916	**Freshman Class:** n/av
SAT or ACT: required	**CEEB CODE:** 6420
Application Deadline: August 1	**COMPETITIVE**

University of Nebraska at Omaha, established in 1908, is a public institution and part of the University of Nebraska system. The figures given in the above capsule and in this profile are approximate. There are 9 undergraduate schools and 1 graduate school. In addition to regional accreditation, Omaha has baccalaureate program accreditation with AACSB, ABET, CSWE, NASAD, NASM, CEAP, CACREP, NASPAA, CAAHEP, CAA, and ACS. The 158-acre campus is in a suburban area within the Omaha city limits. Including any residence halls, there are 46 buildings.

STUDENT LIFE: 93% of undergraduates are from Nebraska. Others are from 34 states, 78 foreign countries, and Canada. 86% are from public schools. 82% are White; 6% African American; 3% Asian American; 3% Hispanic; 2% Foreign; 1% American Indian/Alaska Native. **Female To Male Ratio:** 1.2:1. The average age of freshmen is 18; all undergraduates, 23. 29% do not continue beyond their first year; 39% remain to graduate. **Housing:** 1212 students can be accommodated in college housing, which includes dorms and on-campus apartments. In addition, there are honors houses. On-campus housing is available on a first-come and first-served basis. 91% of students commute. Alcohol is not permitted. All students may keep cars.

FACULTY/CLASSROOMS: 59% of faculty are male; 41% are female. 97% teach undergraduates. Graduate students teach 4% of introductory courses. The average class size in an introductory lecture is 38; in a laboratory is 12; and in a regular course is 21.

PROGRAMS OF STUDY: Omaha confers B.A., B.S., B.A.A.H., B.A.S.A., B.A.T.H., B.F.A., B.I.S., B.G.S., B.M., B.S.B.A., B.S.C.N., B.S.C.S., B.S.E.D., B.S.P.A. and B.S.S.W. degrees. Master's and doctoral degrees are also awarded. Bachelor's degrees are awarded in AGRICULTURE (environmental studies), BIOLOGICAL SCIENCE (bioinformatics, biology/biological science, and biotechnology), BUSINESS (accounting, banking and finance, business communications, management information systems, management science, marketing/retailing/merchandising, real estate, and recreation and leisure services), COMMUNICATIONS AND THE ARTS (art, art history and appreciation, broadcasting, communications, creative writing, dramatic arts, English, fine arts, French, German, journalism, music, Spanish, and speech/debate/rhetoric), COMPUTER AND PHYSICAL SCIENCE (chemistry, computer science, geology, information sciences and systems, mathematics, and physics), EDUCATION (elementary education, library science, physical education, and secondary education), ENGINEERING AND ENVIRONMENTAL DESIGN (aviation administration/management and engineering physics), HEALTH PROFESSIONS (community health work and health care administration), SOCIAL SCIENCE (African American studies, criminal justice, economics, geography, history, interdisciplinary studies, international studies, Latin American studies, liberal arts/general studies, philosophy, political science/government, psychology, public administration, social work, sociology, and women's studies). Elementary education, criminal justice, and marketing management have the largest enrollments.

ACTIVITIES: 2% of men belong to 7 national fraternities; 2% of women belong to 9 national sororities. There are 112 groups on campus, including band, cheerleading, chess, choir, chorale, chorus, dance, drama, drill team, ethnic, film, honors, international, jazz band, LGBT, literary magazine, marching band, musical theater, newspaper, opera, orchestra, pep band, political, professional, radio and TV, religious, social, social service, student government, and symphony. Popular campus events include Celebrate UNO, International Week, and Black History Month. **Sports:** There are 5 intercollegiate sports for men and 8 for women, and 16 intramural sports for men and 16 for women. Facilities include a football field, a field house, a recreation building housing basketball and volleyball courts, weight rooms, and a swimming pool.

SERVICES: Counseling and information services are available, as is tutoring in some subjects, such as math and psychology. There is a reader service for the blind. **Library/Resources:** The library contains 700,000 volumes, 2.0 million microform items, and 7,000 audio/video tapes/CDs/DVDs, and subscribes to 3,000 periodicals including electronic. Computerized library services include interlibrary loans, database searching, and Internet access. Special learning facilities include an art gallery, radio station, and TV station. **Physically Challenged Students:** 99% of the campus is accessible. Facilities include wheelchair ramps, elevators, special parking, specially equipped restrooms, special class scheduling, lowered drinking fountains, and lowered telephones. **Special:** Omaha offers internships for business students, cooperative programs, and credit by examination. Students may study abroad in various European countries. There are 15 national honor societies, a freshman honors program, and 10 departmental honors programs. **Visiting:** There are regularly scheduled orientations for prospective students. There are guides for informal visits and visitors may sit in on classes. To schedule a visit, contact the Office of Orientation at (402) 554-2677. **Campus Safety and Security:** Measures include 24-hour foot and vehicle patrol, self-defense education, and security escort services. There are shuttle buses, emergency telephones, and lighted pathways/sidewalks.

REQUIREMENTS: The SAT or ACT is required. Students must be graduates of an accredited secondary school. The GED is accepted. Students must have completed 4 units of English and 2 each of math, social sciences, and sciences. Omaha requires applicants to be in the upper 50% of their class. A GPA of 2.0 is required. AP and CLEP credits are accepted. Important factors in the admissions decision are recommendations by school officials, evidence of special talent, and personality/intangible qualities. To graduate, students must complete 30 hours of distribution requirements in natural and physical sciences, humanities and fine arts, and social and behavioral sciences; 15 hours in fundamental academic skills in English writing, math, and public speaking; and 6 hours in cultural diversity. **Procedure:** Freshmen are admitted fall, spring, and summer. Entrance exams should be taken by the senior year. There is a rolling admissions plan. Applications should be filed by August 1 for fall entry; December 1 for spring entry; and June 1 for summer entry. The fall 2017 application fee was $45. Applications are accepted on-line. **Transfer Students:** Applicants must present evidence of good standing at the last institution they attended. Grades of C or better transfer for credit. A minimum GPA of 2.0 is required. 30 of 125 credits required for the bachelor's degree must be completed at Omaha. **International Students:** They must take the TOEFL.

ADMISSIONS: 27 freshmen graduated first in their class. **Admissions Contact:** Maureen Pope, Undergraduate Associate Director of Operations. Email: *unoadmissions@unomaha.edu* Web: *www.unomaha.edu*

FINANCIAL AID: The FAFSA code is 002554. Check with the school for current application deadlines.

WAYNE STATE COLLEGE *(The complete profile is made available exclusively on our website, www.barronspac.com)*

YORK COLLEGE — E-3

www.york.edu

York, NE 68467	**(402) 363-5608** **(800) 950-9675**
Fax: (402) 363-5679	**Email: enroll@york.edu**
Full-time: 180 men, 190 women	**Faculty:** n/av
Part-time: 25 men, 20 women	**Ph.D.s:** n/av
Graduate: n/av	**Student/Faculty:** n/av
Year: semesters, summer session	**Tuition:** $19,430
Room & Board: $10,830	**Freshman Class:** n/av
ACT: recommended	**CEEB CODE:** 6984
Application Deadline: August 31	**COMPETITIVE**

York College, founded in 1890, is an independent undergraduate college affiliated with the Churches of Christ. The figures given in the above capsule and in this profile are approximate. There is 1 undergraduate school. In addition to regional accreditation, York has baccalaureate program accreditation with CAEP. The 40-acre campus is in a small town 45 miles west of Lincoln. Including any residence halls, there are 18 buildings.

STUDENT LIFE: 67% of undergraduates are from out of state, mostly the Midwest. Students are from 30 states, 5 foreign countries, and Canada. 90% are from public schools. 87% are White; 5% African American; 4% Foreign; 3% Hispanic; 1% Asian American. 22% are Protestant. **Female To Male Ratio:** 1.0:1. The average age of freshmen is 18; all undergraduates, 21. 15% do not continue beyond their first year; 50% remain to graduate. **Housing:** 472 students can be accommodated in college housing, which includes dorms and on-campus apartments. On-campus housing is guaranteed for all 4 years. 72% of students live on campus. Alcohol is not permitted. All students may keep cars.

FACULTY/CLASSROOMS: 67% of faculty are male; 33% are female. All teach undergraduates. No introductory courses are taught by graduate students. The average class size in an introductory lecture is 30; in a laboratory is 20; and in a regular course is 25.

PROGRAMS OF STUDY: York confers B.A., B.S., B.B.A. and B.Mus. degrees. Associate and master's degrees are also awarded. Bachelor's degrees are awarded in BIOLOGICAL SCIENCE (biology/biological science), BUSINESS (accounting, business administration and management, and human resources), COMMUNICATIONS AND THE ARTS (communications, English, music performance, and voice), COMPUTER AND PHYSICAL SCIENCE (natural sciences), EDUCATION (drama education, education, elementary education, English education, middle school education, music education, psychology education, science education, secondary education, social science education, and special education), SOCIAL SCIENCE (biblical studies, biopsychology, history, human services, liberal arts/general studies, psychology, and youth ministry). Education, natural science, and psychology are the strongest academically. Education, and business have the largest enrollments.

ACTIVITIES: 57% of men belong to 4 local fraternities; 62% of women belong to 4 local sororities. There are 25 groups on campus, including art, choir, chorus, computers, drama, honors, international, literary magazine, musical theater, newspaper, photography, political, professional, religious, social, social service, student government, and yearbook. Popular campus events include High School Days, Fall Musical and an All School Banquet. **Sports:** There are 4 intercollegiate sports for men and 3 for women, and 6 intramural sports for men and 6 for women. Facilities include a gym, basketball and volleyball courts, soccer, baseball, and intramural fields, a weight room and an indoor track. **Graduates:** From July 1, 2016 to June 30, 2017, 57 bachelor's degrees were awarded. The most popular majors were education (29%), business (26%), and psychology (9%). In an average class, 8% graduate in 3 years or less, 35% graduate in 4 years or less, 49% graduate in 5 years or less, and 50% graduate in 6 years or less. Of the 2016 graduating class, 6% were enrolled in graduate school within 6 months of graduation, and 90% were employed.

SERVICES: Counseling and information services are available, as is tutoring in most subjects. There is remedial math, reading, and writing, and a peer tutoring program. **Library/Resources:** The library contains 126,086 volumes, 21,578 microform items, and 7,017 audio/video tapes/CDs/DVDs, and subscribes to 301 periodicals including electronic. Computerized library services include interlibrary loans and database searching. **Physically Challenged Students:** 50% of the campus is accessible. Facilities include wheelchair ramps, elevators, special parking, specially equipped restrooms, lowered drinking fountains, lowered telephones, and special housing. **Special:** Summer internships are required in biblical studies, and psychology, and work-study is available on campus. Honors and independent study are available as adjuncts to a normal course load. There are 2 national honor societies, a freshman honors program, and 2 departmental honors programs. **Visiting:** There are regularly scheduled orientations for prospective students, including a campus tour visit with financial aid and admissions representatives, and a visit with the registrar and possibly with a faculty member within the student's major area of concentration. There are guides for informal visits, visitors may sit in on classes, and stay overnight. **Campus Safety and Security:** Measures include self-defense education. There are emergency telephones, lighted pathways/sidewalks, and evening/night foot patrol.

REQUIREMENTS: For regular acceptance, students must meet 2 of the following 3 requirements: a 2.0 cumulative GPA; graduate in the top half of their graduating class; satisfactory scores on the ACT or SAT. York requires applicants to be in the upper 50% of their class. AP and CLEP credits are accepted. Important factors in the admissions decision are personality/intangible qualities and evidence of special talent. To graduate, students must complete a minimum of 128 credits with a 2.0 GPA. Course work includes a general education requirement of 18 hours of humanities, 16 of Bible, 12 of social science, 6 of science, and 3 of math or computer science. The major requirements vary according to concentration, typically, 40 hours or more are required. Some majors and minors require a 2.5 GPA. **Procedure:** Freshmen are admitted to all sessions. Entrance exams should be taken during March. There is a rolling admissions plan. Applications should be filed by August 31 for fall entry. The fall 2017 application fee was $20. **Transfer Students:** 48 transfer students enrolled in 2016-2017. Transfer students with less than 24 semester hours must have a high school transcript, ACT scores, college transcripts, and 1 reference. Transfers with 24 to 60 hours must have proof of high school graduation (diploma or final), a college transcript, and 1 reference. Transfers with more than 60 hours must have a college transcript and 1 reference letter. 30 of 128 credits required for the bachelor's degree must be completed at York. **International Students:** There are 6 international students enrolled. They must take the TOEFL. They must also take the SAT or ACT.

ADMISSIONS: 7 freshmen graduated first in their class. **Admissions Contact:** Morgan DeBoer, Admissions Recruiter. Email: *enroll@york.edu* Web: *www.york.edu*

FINANCIAL AID: In 2017-2018, 99% of all full-time freshmen received some form of financial aid. 98% of all full-time freshmen received need-based aid. The average freshman award was $14,765. Need-based scholarships or need-based grants averaged $7,182; need-based self-help aid (loans and jobs) averaged $2,762; non-need-based athletic scholarships averaged $1,835; and other non-need-based awards and non-need-based scholarships averaged $2,986. 72% of undergraduate students work part-time. The average financial indebtedness of the 2017 graduate was $19,634. Check with the school for current application deadlines.

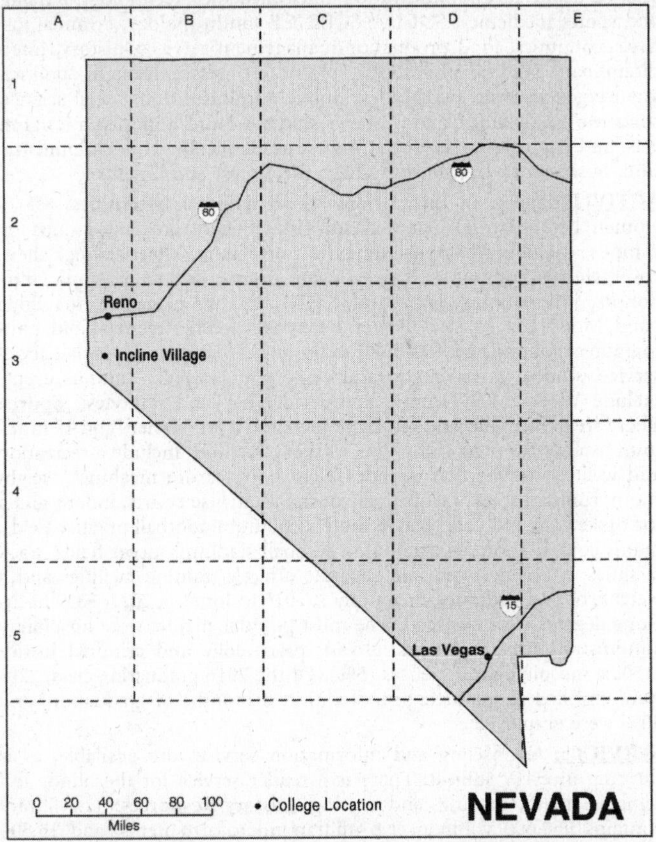

SIERRA NEVADA COLLEGE — A-3

www.sierranevada.edu

Incline Village, NV 89451 (775) 881-7557
(866) 412-4636

Fax: (775) 831-6223 **Email:** admissions@sierranevada.edu

Full-time: 301 men, 185 women
Part-time: 4 men, 8 women
Graduate: 156 men, 381 women
Year: semesters, summer session
Room & Board: $12,764
ACT: 23
Application Deadline: August 22

Faculty: 43
Ph.D.s: n/av
Student/Faculty: 9 to 1
Tuition: $32,639
Freshman Class: 554 applied, 364 accepted, 90 enrolled
CEEB CODE: 4757
COMPETITIVE

Sierra Nevada College, founded in 1969, is a private institution offering programs in liberal arts, fine arts, business, hotel resort management, ski business management, environmental science, interdisciplinary studies, sustainability, and teacher education. There are 7 undergraduate schools. In addition to regional accreditation, SNC has baccalaureate program accreditation with NWCCU. The 19-acre campus is in a rural area 25 miles west of Reno. Including any residence halls, there are 7 buildings.

STUDENT LIFE: 80% of undergraduates are from out of state, mostly the West. Students are from 35 states, 30 foreign countries, and Canada. 60% are from public schools. 93% are White; 3% African American; 2% Foreign. **Female To Male Ratio:** 1.2:1. The average age of freshmen is 19; all undergraduates, 22. 14% do not continue beyond their first year; 62% remain to graduate. **Housing:** 120 students can be accommodated in college housing, which includes dorms and on-campus apartments. On-campus housing is guaranteed for all 4 years. 60% of students commute. Alcohol is not permitted. All students may keep cars.

FACULTY/CLASSROOMS: 60% of faculty are male; 40% are female. All teach undergraduates, 15% do research, and 25% do both. No introductory courses are taught by graduate students. The average class size in an introductory lecture is 12; in a laboratory is 8; and in a regular course is 12.

PROGRAMS OF STUDY: SNC confers B.A., B.S. and B.F.A. degrees. Bachelor's degrees are awarded in BUSINESS (business administration and management and recreational facilities management), COMMUNICATIONS AND THE ARTS (fine arts and music), COMPUTER AND PHYSICAL SCIENCE (science), ENGINEERING AND ENVIRONMENTAL DESIGN (environmental science), SOCIAL SCIENCE (humanities). Environmental and science/ecology are the strongest academically. Business administration has the largest enrollment.

ACTIVITIES: There are no fraternities or sororities. Groups on campus include art, choir, chorale, chorus, computers, dance, environmental, ethnic, honors, international, LGBT, literary magazine, newspaper, photography, political, professional, social, social service, and student government. Popular campus events include Bohemia Night, Nevada Day, and Game Show Take-off. **Sports:** There are 7 intercollegiate sports for men and 6 for women. Facilities include running, hiking and mountain biking trails, volleyball and softball areas, community tennis courts and golf courses, soccer/lacrosse fields, ski and snowboard mountain resorts. **Graduates:** From July 1, 2016 to June 30, 2017, 127 bachelor's degrees were awarded. The most popular majors were business/marketing, visual/performing arts, and biological/life sciences. In an average class, 40% graduate in 6 years or less.

SERVICES: Counseling and information services are available, as is tutoring in every subject. There is remedial math, reading, and writing. **Library/Resources:** The library contains 20,000 volumes, 10,000 microform items, and subscribes to 100 periodicals including electronic. Computerized library services include interlibrary loans, database searching, Internet access, and Wi-Fi capability. Special learning facilities include an art gallery, an environmental science center and a recording studio. **Physically Challenged Students:** All of the campus is accessible. Facilities include wheelchair ramps, elevators, special parking, specially equipped restrooms, special class scheduling, and special housing. **Special:** Business administration concentrations are offered in ski business and resort management and in hotel, restaurant, and resort management. Student-designed majors, work-study programs, internships, credit for life experiences and volunteer community work, and nondegree study are available. **Visiting:** There are regularly scheduled orientations for prospective students, including a student-led campus tour that is available by appointment and 1-night overnight stays. There are guides for informal visits, visitors may sit in on classes, and stay overnight. To schedule a visit, contact the Office of Admissions. **Campus Safety and Security:** Measures include 24-hour foot and vehicle patrol, emergency notification system, and security escort services. There are lighted pathways/sidewalks and controlled access to dorms/residences.

REQUIREMENTS: The ACT is required. The ACT Optional Writing test is also required. In addition, all applicants are reviewed individually. Official transcripts, an essay, and 2 letters of recommendation are required, and an interview is recommended. Required 13 Carnegie units such as 4 in English, 3 in math, 2 each in science with lab, and foreign language. AP and CLEP credits are accepted. Important factors in the admissions decision are advanced placement or honors courses, recommendations by school officials, and personality/intangible qualities. All students must complete at least 120 semester hours, including 40 in upper-division courses with a minimum GPA of 2.0. Students also must pass the writing proficiency exam and meet distribution requirements in 4 interdisciplinary themes: symbols, relationships with nature and humans, memberships in groups and institutions, and ethics, values, and beliefs. **Procedure:** Freshmen are admitted to all sessions. Entrance exams should be taken in the spring of junior year or fall of senior year. There are early decision, early admissions, deferred admissions, and rolling admissions plans. Applications should be filed by August 22 for fall entry. Notifications are sent February 15. Applications are accepted online. **Transfer Students:** 67 transfer students enrolled in 2016-2017. The college accepts applications from students who have completed course work at an accredited post-secondary institution. If fewer than 15 credits have been earned, the high school transcript and standardized test scores are also required. Transfer applicants are expected to be in good academic standing at their college or university. Students may enroll in the fall, spring and summer. 68 of 120 credits required for the bachelor's degree must be completed at SNC. **International Students:** They must take the TOEFL, or take any other English proficiency test.

ADMISSIONS: 66% of the 2017-2018 applicants were accepted. The ACT scores were 21% between 12 and 17, 42% between 18 and 23, 34% between 24 and 29, and 3% above 30. **Admissions Contact:** Stacie Lyans, Director/Undergradute Admission. Email: *admissions@sierranevada.edu* Web: *www.sierranevada.edu*

FINANCIAL AID: In 2017-2018, 80% of all full-time freshmen received some form of financial aid. 80% of all full-time freshmen received need-based aid. The average freshman award was $31,140. Need-based scholarships or need-based grants averaged $26,237; need-based self-help aid (loans and jobs) averaged $4,928; non-need-based athletic scholarships averaged $13,950; other non-need-based awards and non-need-based scholarships averaged $15,639; and $3,299 from other forms of aid. 37% of undergraduate students work part-time. The college's own financial statement is required. The FAFSA code is 009192. The priority date for freshman financial aid applications for fall entry is August.

UNIVERSITY OF NEVADA, LAS VEGAS D-5

www.unlv.edu

Las Vegas, NV 89154 (702) 774-UNLV

Fax: (702) 774-8008
Email: admissions@unlv.edu
Full-time: 12,771 men, 16,931 women
Faculty: 676; I, -$
Part-time: 2785 men, 3211 women
Ph.D.s: 89%
Graduate: 1851 men, 2331 women
Student/Faculty: 22 to 1
Year: semesters, summer session
Tuition: $6823 ($20,732)
Room & Board: $10,730
Freshman Class: 9850 applied, 7970 accepted, 4214 enrolled
SAT CR/M/W: 495/500/475 **ACT:** 22
CEEB CODE: 4861
Application Deadline: November 1
COMPETITIVE

University of Nevada, Las Vegas, established in 1957, is a state-supported institution offering undergraduate and graduate programs in business, education, health science, engineering, science and math, hotel administration, fine arts, liberal arts, urban affairs, and honors. There are 10 undergraduate schools and 1 graduate school. In addition to regional accreditation, UNLV has baccalaureate program accreditation with AACSB, ABET, ACCE, ADA, APTA, ASLA, CSAB, CSWE, FIDER, NAAB, NASAD, NASM, and NLN. The 353-acre campus is in an urban area on the southern tip of Nevada, just east of the Las Vegas strip. Including any residence halls, there are 90 buildings.

STUDENT LIFE: 86% of undergraduates are from Nevada. Others are from 50 states, 57 foreign countries, and Canada. 9% are two or more races; 8% African American; 4% Foreign; 35% White; 26% Hispanic; 15% Asian American; 1% American Indian/Alaska Native. **Female To Male Ratio:** 1.3:1. The average age of freshmen is 18; all undergraduates, 21. 26% do not continue beyond their first year; 39% remain to graduate. **Housing:** 2500 students can be accommodated in college housing, which includes dorms. In addition, there are honors houses, special-interest houses, substance-free, study-intensive recess housing, major-specific houses, a global house, and a leadership focus house. On-campus housing is guaranteed for the freshman year only, is available on a first-come, and first-served basis. 93% of students commute. All students may keep cars.

FACULTY/CLASSROOMS: 60% of faculty are male; 40% are female. 95% teach undergraduates, and 5% do research. No introductory courses are taught by graduate students. The average class size in an introductory lecture is 21 and in a laboratory is 20.

PROGRAMS OF STUDY: UNLV confers B.A., B.S. and B.F.A. degrees. Master's and doctoral degrees are also awarded. Bachelor's degrees are awarded in BIOLOGICAL SCIENCE (biology/biological science), BUSINESS (accounting, banking and finance, hotel/motel and restaurant management, human resources, international business management, management information systems, management science, marketing/retailing/merchandising, real estate, and recreational facilities management), COMMUNICATIONS AND THE ARTS (art history and appreciation, communications, dance, dramatic arts, English, film arts, fine arts, French, German, music, romance languages and literature, and Spanish), COMPUTER AND PHYSICAL SCIENCE (applied physics, chemistry, computer science, earth science, geology, mathematics, physics, and radiological technology), EDUCATION (elementary education, health education, physical education, recreation education, secondary education, special education, and trade and industrial education), ENGINEERING AND ENVIRONMENTAL DESIGN (architectural engineering, civil engineering, computer engineering, construction management, electrical/electronics engineering, environmental science, interior design, landscape architecture/design, mechanical engineering, and urban planning technology), HEALTH PROFESSIONS (clinical science, exercise science, health care administration, nuclear medical technology, nursing, and sports medicine), SOCIAL SCIENCE (anthropology, criminal justice, economics, food production/management/services, history, interdisciplinary studies, philosophy, physical fitness/movement, political science/government, psychology, public administration, social science, social work, sociology, and women's studies). Hotel administration, fine arts, and engineering are the strongest academically. Hotel administration, business, and engineering have the largest enrollments.

ACTIVITIES: 8% of men belong to 18 national fraternities; 8% of women belong to 11 national sororities. There are 330 groups on campus, including campus ministries, art, band, cheerleading, chess, choir, chorus, computers, dance, debate, drama, drill team, ethnic, film, honors, international, jazz band, LGBT, literary magazine, marching band, Model UN, musical theater, newspaper, orchestra, pep band, photography, political, professional, radio and TV, religious, social, social service, student government, and symphony. Popular campus events include Weeks of Welcome, Premier UNLV, and Unityfest. **Sports:** There are 8 intercollegiate sports for men and 9 for women, and 47 intramural sports for men and 47 for women. Facilities include a recreation and wellness center that includes a lap pool, cardio machines, weight room, running track, racquetball courts, multi-use courts, indoor arena for basketball, and volleyball, a football stadium, football practice fields, tennis courts, a softball stadium, a baseball stadium, soccer fields, track facilities, a boxing gym, and separate athletic/training facilities and a weight room. **Graduates:** From July 1, 2016 to June 30, 2017, 3832 bachelor's degrees were awarded. The most popular majors were hospitality administration/management, (16%), psychology and criminal justice (15%), and biological sciences (5%). Of the 2016 graduating class, 22% were enrolled in graduate school within 6 months of graduation, and 30% were employed.

SERVICES: Counseling and information services are available, as is tutoring in every subject. There is a reader service for the blind, and remedial math, reading, and writing. **Library/Resources:** The library contains 950,600 volumes, 1.8 million microform items, and 13,500 audio/video tapes/CDs/DVDs, and subscribes to 1,759 periodicals including electronic. Computerized library services include interlibrary loans, database searching, Internet access, and Wi-Fi capability. Special learning facilities include an art gallery, natural history museum, and radio station. **Physically Challenged Students:** All of the campus is accessible. Facilities include wheelchair ramps, elevators, special parking, specially equipped restrooms, special class scheduling, lowered drinking fountains, lowered telephones, and special housing. **Special:** Opportunities are provided for internships, an accelerated degree program, B.A.-B.S. degrees, dual majors, credit by examination, credit for military service, nondegree study, pass/fail options, and study abroad in 25 countries. There are 16 national honor societies, Phi Beta Kappa, a freshman honors program, and 11 departmental honors programs. **Visiting:** There are regularly scheduled orientations for prospective students, consisting of a complete introduction to the campus, student services, and parent orientation. There are guides for informal visits and visitors may sit in on classes. To schedule a visit, contact Office of Admissions. **Campus Safety and Security:** Measures include 24-hour foot and vehicle patrol, emergency notification system, self-defense education, and security escort services. There are shuttle buses, emergency telephones, and lighted pathways/sidewalks.

REQUIREMENTS: Graduation from an accredited secondary school is required. Applicants must also meet the academic core requirements, which include 4 credits in English and 3 each in history, social studies, math (must include algebra 1 and algebra 2), and science, (of these units 2 must be lab). A GPA of 3.0 is required. AP and CLEP credits are accepted. Important factors in the admissions decision are recommendations by school officials, advanced placement or honors courses, and geographical diversity. Students must complete 124 credits, with 45 in the major, and maintain a minimum GPA of 2.0. All students must meet core requirements that include courses in English, logic and math, the Constitution, social science, fine arts, science, humanities, and international and multicultural diversity. **Procedure:** Freshmen are admitted to all sessions. Entrance exams should be taken by November 1. There is a rolling admissions plan. Applications should be filed by November 1 for fall entry; December 1 for spring entry; and February 1 for summer entry. The fall 2017 application fee was $60. Applications are accepted on-line. **Transfer Students:** 5144 transfer students enrolled in 2016-2017. Applicants should present a minimum GPA of 2.5 and a minimum of 24 credits for transfer. The SAT or the ACT is recommended. Applicants must be in good academic standing and eligible to return to the educational institution last attended. 30 of 124 credits required for the bachelor's degree must be completed at UNLV. **International Students:** There are 919 international students enrolled. They must take the TOEFL with a minimum score of 500 on the paper-based TOEFL (PBT) or 61 on the Internet-based version (iBT) or MELAB. Students must take the IELTS, or the English proficiency test. They must also take the SAT or ACT, scoring 22 ACT or 1120 SAT.

ADMISSIONS: 81% of the 2017-2018 applicants were accepted. The SAT scores for the 2017-2018 freshman class were: Critical Reading-- 49% below 500, 39% between 500 and 599, 11% between 600 and 699, and 1% between 700 and 800. Math-- 48% below 500, 37% between 500 and 599, 13% between 600 and 699, and 2% between 700 and 800. Writing-- 62% below 500, 30% between 500 and 599, 7% between 600 and 699, and 1% between 700 and 800. 52% of the current freshmen were in the top fifth of their class; 82% were in the top two fifths. **Admissions Contact:** Devan Sullivan, Senior Admission Counselor. Email: *admissions@unlv.edu* Web: *www.unlv.edu*

FINANCIAL AID: In 2017-2018, 66% of all full-time freshmen received some form of financial aid. 35% of all full-time freshmen received need-based aid. The average freshman award was $11,374. Need-based scholarships or need-based grants averaged $5,959; need-based self-help aid (loans and jobs) averaged $3,328; non-need-based athletic scholarships averaged $18,533; other non-need-based awards and non-need-based scholarships averaged $3,254; and $3,647 from other forms of aid. 75% of undergraduate students work part-time. UNLV is a member of CSS. The CCS/Profile, FAFSA, FFS, SFS and the college's own financial statement, and a single file form are required. The FAFSA code is 002569. The priority date for freshman financial aid applications for fall entry is November 1.

UNIVERSITY OF NEVADA, RENO — A-3

www.unr.edu

Reno, NV 89557 — **(775) 784-1110**

Fax: (775) 784-4283	**Email:** asknevada@unr.edu
Full-time: 7215 men, 8193 women	**Faculty:** I, -$
Part-time: 1355 men, 1428 women	**Ph.D.s:** 84%
Graduate: 1445 men, 1727 women	**Student/Faculty:** 21 to 1
Year: semesters, summer session	**Tuition:** $7142 ($21,052)
Room & Board: $10,868	**Freshman Class:** 9646 applied, 7988 accepted, 3353 enrolled
SAT CR/M/W: 540/550/520 **ACT:** 24	**CEEB CODE:** 4844
Application Deadline: February 1	**COMPETITIVE**

University of Nevada/Reno, established in 1874, is a land-grant institution and part of the Nevada System of Higher Education. It offers programs in agriculture, arts and science, business administration, education, engineering, human and community sciences, journalism, medicine, and mining, as well as interdisciplinary studies. There are 10 undergraduate schools and 1 graduate school. In addition to regional accreditation, UNR has baccalaureate program accreditation with AACSB, ABET, ACEJMC, AHEA, CSWE, NASM, and NLN. The 268-acre campus is in an urban area 200 miles east of San Francisco, 35 miles from Lake Tahoe. Including any residence halls, there are 128 buildings.

STUDENT LIFE: 70% of undergraduates are from Nevada. Others are from 46 states, 65 foreign countries, and Canada. 59% are White; 19% Hispanic; 7% Asian American; 6% two or more races; 3% African American; 3% Foreign; 2% race unknown; 1% American Indian/Alaska Native. **Female To Male Ratio:** 1.1:1. The average age of freshmen is 18; all undergraduates, 22. 20% do not continue beyond their first year; 54% remain to graduate. **Housing:** 2611 students can be accommodated in college housing, which includes married student dorms, on-campus apartments, and off-campus apartments. In addition, there are honors houses, special-interest houses, fraternity houses, sorority houses, living learning housing. On-campus housing is available on a first-come and first-served basis. 78% of students commute. Alcohol is not permitted. All students may keep cars.

FACULTY/CLASSROOMS: 53% of faculty are male; 47% are female. All teach undergraduates and all do research. Graduate students teach 10% of introductory courses. The average class size in an introductory lecture is 45; in a laboratory is 23; and in a regular course is 34.

PROGRAMS OF STUDY: UNR confers B.A., B.S., B.A.C.J., B.A.Ed., B.F.A., B.G.S., B.M., B.S.Bus.Ad., B.S.C.E., B.S.Chem.E., B.S.Chem., B.S.C.S., B.S.Ed., B.S.E.E., B.S.E.P., B.S.Geog., B.S.Geol., B.S.Geol.E., B.S.Geophys., B.S.M.E., B.S.Met.E., B.S.Min.E., B.S.Nurs. and B.S.Vet.Sc. degrees. Master's and doctoral degrees are also awarded. Bachelor's degrees are awarded in AGRICULTURE (agricultural sciences, natural resource management, and wildlife management), BIOLOGICAL SCIENCE (biochemistry, biology/biological science, biotechnology, neurosciences, nutrition, and nutritional sciences), BUSINESS (accounting, business administration-international, finance, management science, marketing, and marketing/retailing/merchandising), COMMUNICATIONS AND THE ARTS (applied music, art history, art, communications, dramatic arts, English, French, journalism, music, and Spanish), COMPUTER AND PHYSICAL SCIENCE (chemistry, computer science, geology, geophysics and seismology, hydrology, information sciences and systems, mathematics, and physics), EDUCATION (early childhood education, elementary education, general studies, music education, secondary education, and special education), ENGINEERING AND ENVIRONMENTAL DESIGN (chemical engineering, civil engineering, civil and environmental engineering, electrical/electronics engineering, engineering physics, environmental science, geological engineering, mechanical engineering, metallurgical engineering, and mining and mineral engineering), HEALTH PROFESSIONS (kinesiology, nursing, nutrition and dietetics, and speech pathology/audiology), SOCIAL SCIENCE (anthropology, child care/child and family studies, criminal justice, economics, geography, history, international relations, philosophy, political science/government, psychology, social work, sociology, and women's studies). Biology, psychology, and criminal justice have the largest enrollments.

ACTIVITIES: 7% of men belong to 2 local and 7 national fraternities; 7% of women belong to 9 national sororities. There are 240 groups on campus, including art, band, cheerleading, chess, choir, chorale, chorus, computers, dance, debate, drama, drill team, environmental, ethnic, film, forensics, honors, international, jazz band, LGBT, literary magazine, marching band, musical theater, newspaper, orchestra, pep band, photography, political, professional, radio and TV, religious, social, social service, student government, and symphony. Popular campus events include Mackay Week. **Sports:** There are 6 intercollegiate sports for men and 10 for women, and 6 intramural sports for men and 6 for women. Facilities include a recreation center, a stadium, gym, baseball field, a movie theater, and an indoor events center. **Graduates:** From July 1, 2016 to June 30, 2017, 3372 bachelor's degrees were awarded. The most popular majors were business (17%), health sciences (13%), and engineering (11%). In an average class, 23% graduate in 4 years or less, 47% graduate in 5 years or less, and 54% graduate in 6 years or less.

SERVICES: Counseling and information services are available, as is tutoring in most subjects. There is a reader service for the blind, and remedial math, reading, and writing. Students are mainstreamed with special services for the disabled. **Library/Resources:** The library contains 1.2 million volumes, 3.3 million microform items, and 49,433 audio/video tapes/CDs/DVDs, and subscribes to 19,058 periodicals including electronic. Computerized library services include interlibrary loans, database searching, and Internet access. Special learning facilities include an art gallery, planetarium, radio station, TV station, the Nevada Historical Society Museum, and the Keck Mineral Museum. **Physically Challenged Students:** 99% of the campus is accessible. Facilities include wheelchair ramps, elevators, special parking, specially equipped restrooms, special class scheduling, lowered drinking fountains, lowered telephones, special housing, and automatic door openers. **Special:** Students may study abroad in 24 countries, pursue internships, and complete dual majors in many subject areas. There is 1 national honor society and a freshman honors program. **Visiting:** There are regularly scheduled orientations for prospective students, meetings with academic representatives. Campus tours include visiting residence halls. There are guides for informal visits and visitors may sit in on classes. To schedule a visit, contact the Office for Prospective Students. **Campus Safety and Security:** Measures include 24-hour foot and vehicle patrol, emergency notification system, self-defense education, and security escort services. There are shuttle buses, emergency telephones, lighted pathways/sidewalks, and controlled access to dorms/residences.

REQUIREMENTS: The SAT or ACT is required. Test scores are used for placement purposes only. Applicants should have completed 13.5 academic credits, including 4 in English, 3 each in math, science, and social studies/history, and a half credit in computer literacy. The GED is not accepted. A GPA of 3.0 is required. AP and CLEP credits are accepted. To graduate, all students must complete 124 to 138 semester credits and earn a GPA of 2.0. The core curriculum includes 9 credits of Western Traditions, 6 each of capstone courses and natural science, 3 to 6 of writing, 3 each of math, social science, and fine arts, and fulfillment of the diversity requirement. **Procedure:** Freshmen are admitted fall and spring. Entrance exams should be taken in October of the senior year. There are deferred admissions and rolling admissions plans. Applications should be filed by February 1 for fall entry; November 1 for spring entry. The fall 2017 application fee was $60. Notification is sent on a rolling basis. **Transfer Students:** 1324 transfer students enrolled in 2016-2017. Applicants should have a GPA of 2.5 and 24 transferable credits. College transcripts are required. 32 of 120 credits required for the bachelor's degree must be completed at UNR. **International Students:** There are 283 international students enrolled. They must take the TOEFL. The SAT or ACT may also be submitted.

ADMISSIONS: 83% of the 2017-2018 applicants were accepted. The SAT scores for the 2017-2018 freshman class were: Critical Reading-- 29% below 500, 46% between 500 and 599, 22% between 600 and 699, and 3% between 700 and 800. Math-- 27% below 500, 44% between 500 and 599, 26% between 600 and 699, and 3% between 700 and 800. Writing-- 39% below 500, 43% between 500 and 599, 16% between 600 and 699, and 1% between 700 and 800. The ACT scores were 7% between 12 and 17, 47% between 18 and 23, 39% between 24 and 29, and 7% above 30. 45% of the current freshmen were in the top fifth of their class; 76% were in the top two fifths. **Admissions Contact:** Dr. Melisa N. Choroszy, Assistant Vice President, Records/Enrollment Services. Email: *asknevada@unr.edu* Web: *www.unr.edu*

FINANCIAL AID: In 2017-2018, 56% of all full-time freshmen received some form of financial aid. 40% of all full-time freshmen received need-based aid. The average freshman award was $8,293. The average financial indebtedness of the 2017 graduate was $23,110. The FAFSA code is 002568. The priority date for freshman financial aid applications for fall entry is February 1.

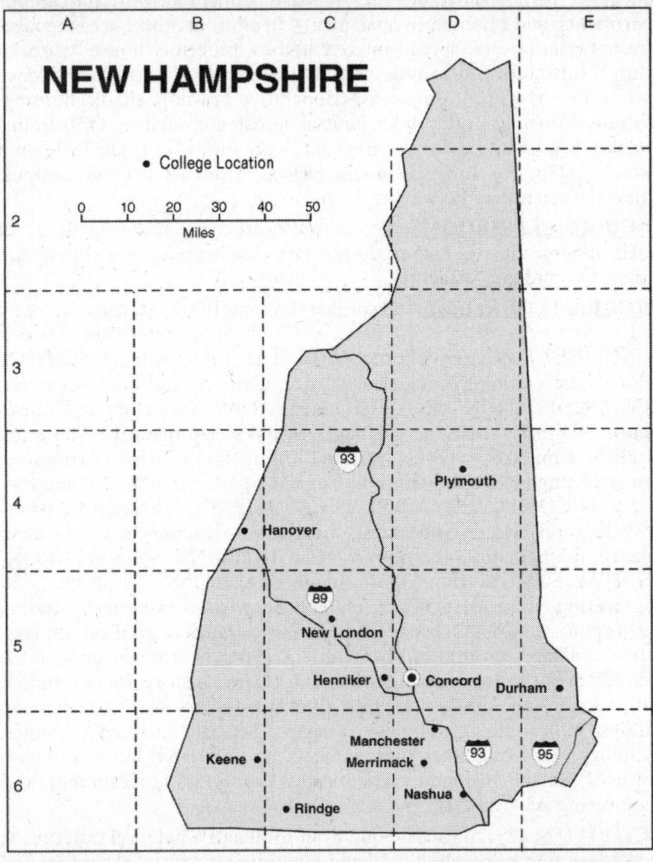

COLBY-SAWYER COLLEGE C-5

www.colby-sawyer.edu

New London, NH 03257 (603) 526-3700 (800) 272-1015

Fax: (603) 526-3452 Email: admissions@colby-sawyer.edu

Full-time: 677 men, 679 women	**Faculty:** n/av
Part-time: 6 men, 12 women	**Ph.D.s:** 79%
Graduate: n/av	**Student/Faculty:** 10 to 1
Year: semesters	**Tuition:** $38,040
Room & Board: $12,750	**Freshman Class:** n/av
SAT or ACT: required	**CEEB CODE:** 3281
Application Deadline: open	**COMPETITIVE**

Colby-Sawyer College, established in 1837, is a private, independent institution offering programs of study that innovatively integrate liberal arts and sciences with professional preparation. Undergraduate majors include environmental studies, graphic design, child development, education, exercise and sport sciences, studio arts, nursing, business, biology, psychology, communications, and history and political studies. There are 2 undergraduate schools. In addition to regional accreditation, Colby-Sawyer has baccalaureate program accreditation with CCNE and CAATE. The 200-acre campus is in a small town 90 minutes north of Boston. Including any residence halls, there are 30 buildings.

STUDENT LIFE: 68% of undergraduates are from out of state, mostly the Northeast. Students are from 28 states, 38 foreign countries, and Canada. 83% are from public schools. 89% are White; 2% Hispanic; 10% Foreign; 1% African American; 1% Asian American. **Female To Male Ratio:** 1.0:1. The average age of freshmen is 18; all undergraduates, 19. 19% do not continue beyond their first year; 64% remain to graduate. **Housing:** 870 students can be accommodated in college housing, which includes dorms, on-campus apartments, off-campus apartments, and substance-free residence hall. On-campus housing is guaranteed for all 4 years. 90% of students live on campus. All students may keep cars.

FACULTY/CLASSROOMS: All teach undergraduates. No introductory courses are taught by graduate students. The average class size in a regular course is 14.

PROGRAMS OF STUDY: Colby-Sawyer confers B.A., B.S. and B.F.A. degrees. Associate degrees are also awarded. Bachelor's degrees are awarded in AGRICULTURE (environmental studies), BIOLOGICAL SCIENCE (biology/biological science), BUSINESS (business administration and management and sports management), COMMUNICATIONS AND THE ARTS (art, communications, creative writing, graphic design, and studio art), COMPUTER AND PHYSICAL SCIENCE (natural sciences), EDUCATION (athletic training), ENGINEERING AND ENVIRONMENTAL DESIGN (environmental science), HEALTH PROFESSIONS (exercise science, nursing, and public health), SOCIAL SCIENCE (child psychology/development, history, humanities, psychology, and sociology). Nursing is the strongest academically. Nursing, exercise & sport sciences, and business administration have the largest enrollments.

ACTIVITIES: There are no fraternities or sororities. There are 40 groups on campus, including art, chorus, dance, drama, environmental, film, honors, international, LGBT, literary magazine, musical theater, newspaper, outing club, photography, political, professional, radio and TV, religious, social, social service, and student government. Popular campus events include Mountain Day, Homecoming, International Festival. **Sports:** There are 11 intercollegiate sports for men and 13 for women, and 15 intramural sports for men and 15 for women. Facilities include outdoor and indoor tennis courts, a fitness center, an NCAA-approved swimming pool, a suspended indoor track, squash and racquetball courts, outdoor competitive fields, and nearby golf courses, ski and biking trails, and an indoor riding arena. **Graduates:** From July 1, 2016 to June 30, 2017, 216 bachelor's degrees were awarded. The most popular majors were business administration (22%), health and physical education (13%), and teacher education (11%). In an average class, 51% graduate in 4 years or less, 59% graduate in 5 years or less, and 60% graduate in 6 years or less. Of the 2016 graduating class, 11% were enrolled in graduate school within 6 months of graduation, and 90% were employed.

SERVICES: Counseling and information services are available, as is tutoring in every subject. There is a reader service for the blind, and remedial math, reading, and writing. **Library/Resources:** The library contains 93,861 volumes, 204,109 microform items, and 2,400 audio/video tapes/CDs/DVDs, and subscribes to 32,019 periodicals including electronic. Computerized library services include interlibrary loans, database searching, and Internet access. Special learning facilities include an art gallery, radio station, Student Learning Collaborative, Windy Hill Laboratory School (K-3), a sustainable classroom built by students, and the Curtis L. Ivey Science Center. **Physically Challenged Students:** 50% of the campus is accessible. Facilities include wheelchair ramps, elevators, special parking, specially equipped restrooms, special class scheduling, and special housing. **Special:** At least one internship is required for every major. Students may study at the Washington Internship Institute. Colby-Sawyer offers study abroad opportunities for students. The college works with the following affiliate programs: Academic Programs International, American Institute of Foreign Study, The School for Field Studies, Center for International Studies, The Education Abroad Network, Council on International Education Exchange, and Harlaxton College in Grantham, England. A Self-Designed Major is also offered such as, Pre-Professional Curriculum, Pre-Medical Curriculum, Pre-Physical Therapy Curriculum, and Pre-Veterinary Curriculum. There are 4 national honor societies and a freshman honors program. **Visiting:** There are regularly scheduled orientations for prospective students, including tours and interviews. Open house programs offer tours as well as academic, athletic, campus life, career development, and academic development presentations; several visiting-day programs offer tours, interviews, and class visits. There are guides for informal visits, visitors may sit in on classes, and stay overnight. To schedule a visit, contact the Admissions Office. **Campus Safety and Security:** Measures include 24-hour foot and vehicle patrol, emergency notification system, self-defense education, and security escort services. There are shuttle buses, emergency telephones, lighted pathways/sidewalks, controlled access to dorms/residences, monthly meetings between students and campus safety personnel.

REQUIREMENTS: The SAT or ACT is required. The ACT Optional Writing test is also required. The GED is accepted. A minimum of 15 college preparatory credits is recommended for admission, including 4 years of English, 3 or more of social studies, 3 of math, 2 of the same foreign language, and 3 or more of lab science. An essay is required, as are 2 letters of recommendation. Interviews are strongly recommended. A GPA of 2.0 is required. AP and CLEP credits are accepted. The Colby-Sawyer academic experience blends the liberal arts and sciences with professional experience to prepare you for a career and graduate studies. By choosing a theme-based, interdisciplinary First-Year Symposium, the foundation of the college's Liberal Education Program, you explore a topic with a faculty member before heading in your chosen academic direction. During your first semester you will choose a First-Year Symposium based on your interest in the theme. At Colby-Sawyer you broaden your knowledge in areas outside of your major by exploring subjects across the curriculum. Some courses may also fulfill requirements in your major. You may choose one course from each of the following areas: Fine and Performing arts, Humanities, Literature, Science, Social Studies, History, Integrative Studies, Internship Experience, Learning Portfolio with the Capstone Experience. Before graduating, you must complete a Capstone research project unique to your major and present the results to faculty, administration, staff and the community at the annual Susan Colby Colgate Scholars' Symposium. **Procedure:** Freshmen are admitted fall and spring. Entrance exams should be taken in the fall of the senior year. There are early decision, deferred admissions, and rolling admissions plans. Early decision applications should be filed by December 1. The fall 2017 application fee was $45. Notification of early decision is sent December 15; regular decision, on a rolling basis. Applications are accepted on-line. **Transfer Students:** 17 transfer students enrolled in 2016-2017. College-level work will be emphasized. College transcripts, course descriptions, and a dean's form are required in addition to the standard requirements. 60 of 120 credits required for the bachelor's degree must be completed at Colby-Sawyer. **International Students:** There are 13 international students enrolled. They must take the TOEFL.

Admissions Contact: Admissions Office Email: *admissions@colby-sawyer.edu* Web: *www.colby-sawyer.edu*

FINANCIAL AID: In 2017-2018, 97% of all full-time freshmen received some form of financial aid. 81% of all full-time freshmen received need-based aid. The average freshman award was $24,043. The average financial indebtedness of the 2017 graduate was $13,578. Colby-Sawyer is a member of CSS. The FAFSA code is 002572. Check with the school for current application deadlines.

DARTMOUTH COLLEGE — B-4
www.dartmouth.edu

Hanover, NH 03755 — **(603) 646-2875**

Fax: (603) 646-1216 — **Email: admissions.office@dartmouth.edu**

Full-time: 2221 men, 2139 women	**Faculty:** 594; I, ++$
Part-time: 25 men, 25 women	**Ph.D.s:** 94%
Graduate: 1119 men, 980 women	**Student/Faculty:** 7 to 1
Year: quarters, summer session	**Tuition:** $52,950
Room & Board: $15,159	**Freshman Class:** 20035 applied, 2093 accepted, 1217 enrolled
SAT or ACT: required	**CEEB CODE:** 3351
Application Deadline: January 1	**MOST COMPETITIVE**

Dartmouth College, founded in 1769, is a member of the Ivy League and consistently ranks among the world's greatest academic institutions. Dartmouth has forged a singular identity for combining its deep commitment to outstanding undergraduate liberal arts and graduate education with distinguished research and scholarship in the arts & sciences and its three leading professional schools the Geisel School of Medicine, Thayer School of Engineering, and the Tuck School of Business. There are 4 undergraduate schools and 4 graduate schools. In addition to regional accreditation, DC has baccalaureate program accreditation with ABET. The 237-acre campus is in a rural area 140 miles northwest of Boston. Including any residence halls, there are 172 buildings.

STUDENT LIFE: 97% of undergraduates are from out of state, mostly the Middle Atlantic. Students are from 50 states, 81 foreign countries, and Canada. 54% are from public schools. 50% are White; 15% Asian American; 10% Hispanic; 9% Foreign; 7% African American; 5% two or more races; 3% race unknown; 2% American Indian/Alaska Native. **Male To Female Ratio:** 1.1:1. The average age of freshmen is 18; all undergraduates, 20. 3% do not continue beyond their first year; 96% remain to graduate. **Housing:** 3801 students can be accommodated in college housing, which includes married student dorms, on-campus apartments, and off-campus apartments. In addition, there are language/international houses, special-interest houses, fraternity houses, sorority houses, substance- and smoke-free residence halls, faculty-in-residence and academic affinity programs, cooperative housing, theme housing, wellness housing, and gender-neutral housing available. On-campus housing is guaranteed for the freshman year only and is available on a lottery system for upperclassmen. 88% of students live on campus. Upperclassmen may keep cars.

FACULTY/CLASSROOMS: 63% of faculty are male; 37% are female. All teach undergraduates, and all do research. No introductory courses are taught by graduate students.

PROGRAMS OF STUDY: DC confers B.A. and B.Eng. degrees. Master's and doctoral degrees are also awarded. Bachelor's degrees are awarded in AGRICULTURE (environmental studies), BIOLOGICAL SCIENCE (biochemistry, biology/biological science, genetics, and neurosciences), COMMUNICATIONS AND THE ARTS (Arabic, art history and appreciation, Chinese, classical languages, classics, comparative literature, English, film arts, French, Italian, linguistics, music, Portuguese, romance languages and literature, Russian, Spanish, studio art, and theatre arts), COMPUTER AND PHYSICAL SCIENCE (astronomy, astronomy and physics, astrophysics, chemistry, computer science, earth science, mathematics, and physics), ENGINEERING AND ENVIRONMENTAL DESIGN (biomedical engineering, engineering physics, and engineering science), SOCIAL SCIENCE (African American studies, anthropology, Asian/Oriental studies, classical/ancient civilization, cognitive science, economics, government, French studies, geography, German area studies, Hispanic American studies, history, Italian studies, Latin American studies, Middle Eastern studies, Native American studies, philosophy, psychology, religion, Russian and Slavic studies, sociology, Spanish studies, and women's studies). Economics, and government are the strongest academically. Economics, government, and engineering sciences have the largest enrollments.

ACTIVITIES: 44% of men belong to 11 local and 6 national fraternities; 46% of women belong to 4 local and 6 national sororities. There are 157 groups on campus, including art, band, cheerleading, chess, choir, chorale, chorus, computers, dance, debate, drama, environmental, ethnic, film, forensics, honors, international, jazz band, LGBT, literary magazine, marching band, musical theater, newspaper, opera, orchestra, pep band, photography, political, professional, radio and TV, religious, social, social service, student government, symphony, and yearbook. Popular campus events include Dartmouth Night/Homecoming Weekend, Winter Carnival and Green Key Service Weekend. **Sports:** There are 16 intercollegiate sports for men and 19 for women, and 12 intramural sports for men and 12 for women. Facilities include an arena, a fitness center, squash and racquetball courts, dance studio, an ice-hockey arena, a gym, football stadium, a boat house, tennis center with indoor and outdoor courts, golf course, skiing, and a riding farm. **Graduates:** From July 1, 2016 to June 30, 2017, 1069 bachelor's degrees were awarded. The most popular majors were economics (17%), government (13%), and computer science (8%). In an average class, 88% graduate in 4 years or less and 96% graduate in 6 years or less.

SERVICES: Counseling and information services are available, as is tutoring in every subject. There is a reader service for the blind. There is an academic skills center for all students. There are also readers, note takers, tape recorders and support for learning-disabled students. **Library/Resources:** The library contains 2.6 million volumes, 490,471 microform items, and 790,868 audio/video tapes/CDs/DVDs, and subscribes to 75,548 periodicals including electronic. Computerized library services include interlibrary loans, database searching, Internet access, and Wi-Fi capability. Special learning facilities include an art gallery, radio station, a creative and performing arts center, life sciences lab, physical and social sciences centers, and observatory. **Physically Challenged Students:** All of the campus is accessible. Facilities include wheelchair ramps, elevators, special parking, specially equipped restrooms, special class scheduling, lowered drinking fountains, lowered telephones, and special housing. **Special:** Students may design programs using the college's unique Dartmouth Plan, which divides the academic calendar into 4 10-week terms, based on the seasons. The plan permits greater flexibility for vacations and for the 45 study-abroad programs in 23 countries in Latin America, Europe, Asia, and Africa. Cross-registration is offered through the Twelve College Exchange Network. Exchange programs also exist with the University of California at San Diego, Stanford, Oxford, and McGill Universities, selected German universities, Keio

University in Tokyo, and Beijing Normal University in China. Students may design their own interdisciplinary majors involving multiple departments, take dual majors in all fields, or create a modified major involving 2 departments, with emphasis in 1. Hands-on computer science education, internships, and work-study programs also are available. A 3-2 engineering degree is offered with Dartmouth's Thayer School of Engineering. There are 3 national honor societies and a chapter of Phi Beta Kappa. **Visiting:** There are regularly scheduled orientations for prospective students, includes a campus tour, group information session, and a student forum. There are guides for informal visits, visitors may sit in on classes, and stay overnight. To schedule a visit, contact the Office of Admissions. **Campus Safety and Security:** Measures include 24-hour foot and vehicle patrol, emergency notification system, self-defense education, and security escort services. There are shuttle buses, emergency telephones, and lighted pathways/sidewalks.

REQUIREMENTS: The SAT or ACT is required. The ACT Optional Writing test is also required. Evidence of intellectual capacity, motivation, and personal integrity are important factors in the highly competitive admissions process, which also considers talent, accomplishment, and involvement in nonacademic areas. Course requirements are flexible, but students are recommended to take 4 units in English, foreign language, math, science, and social studies. The GED is accepted. AP credits are accepted. All students must pass 35 courses, 10 of which must be distributed in the following fields: arts, social analysis, literature, quantitative or deductive science, philosophical, religious, or historical analysis, natural science, technology or applied science, and international or comparative study. 3 world culture courses are required from the U.S., Europe, and at least 1 non-Western society. A multidisciplinary or interdisciplinary course, a freshman seminar, a senior project, and foreign language proficiency are also required. **Procedure:** Freshmen are admitted in the fall. Entrance exams should be taken in November or January of the senior year. There are early decision and deferred admissions plans. Early decision applications should be filed by November 1; regular applications, by January 1 for fall entry. The fall 2017 application fee was $80. Notification of early decision is sent December 15; regular decision, April 10. 565 early decision candidates were accepted for the 2017-2018 class. Applications are accepted on-line. **Transfer Students:** 4 transfer students enrolled in 2016-2017. Applicants must demonstrate high achievement and intellectual motivation through college transcripts as well as standardized test scores and high school transcripts. Fall closing date is March 1. Notification will be May 15, and must reply by June 1. 18 of 35 credits required for the bachelor's degree must be completed at Dartmouth. **International Students:** There are 405 international students enrolled. They must take the TOEFL. They must also take the SAT or ACT.

ADMISSIONS: 10% of the 2017-2018 applicants were accepted. 97% of the current freshmen were in the top fifth of their class; 100% were in the top two fifths. 158 freshmen graduated first in their class. **Admissions Contact:** Paul Sunde, Director of Admissions. Email: *admissions.office@dartmouth.edu* Web: *www.dartmouth.edu*

FINANCIAL AID: In 2017-2018, 48% of all full-time freshmen received some form of financial aid. 48% of all full-time freshmen received need-based aid. The average freshman award was $52,069. Need-based scholarships or need-based grants averaged $51,461; and need-based self-help aid (loans and jobs) averaged $4,288. The average financial indebtedness of the 2017 graduate was $19,571. DC is a member of CSS. The CSS/Profile, parents' and student's federal income tax returns, noncustodial and business/farm supplement are required. The FAFSA code is 002573. The deadline for filing freshman financial aid applications for fall entry is February 1.

FRANKLIN PIERCE UNIVERSITY *(The complete profile is made available exclusively on our website, www.barronspac.com)*

GRANITE STATE COLLEGE *(The complete profile is made available exclusively on our website, www.barronspac.com)*

KEENE STATE COLLEGE — B-6

www.keene.edu

Keene, NH 03435	**(603) 358-2276** **(800) KSC-1909**
Fax: (603) 358-2767	**Email: admissions@keene.edu**
Full-time: 1620 men, 1989 women	**Faculty:** IIA, av$
Part-time: 43 men, 36 women	**Ph.D.s:** n/av
Graduate: 28 men, 34 women	**Student/Faculty:** n/av
Year: semesters, summer session	**Tuition:** $13,868 ($22,614)
Room & Board: $10,736	**Freshman Class:** 5580 applied, 4613 accepted, 1049 enrolled
SAT EBR-W/M: 530/513 **ACT:** 21	**CEEB CODE:** 3472
Application Deadline: April 1	**COMPETITIVE**

Keene State College, founded in 1909, has continuously expanded its mission to offer a broad spectrum of academic programs that are grounded in the values and competencies of the liberal arts tradition. Today, as a preeminent public liberal arts college, Keene State offers more than 40 undergraduate areas of study and three graduate degree programs focused on the enduring qualities that will serve students for a lifetime of professional opportunities defined by innovation and transformation. There are 3 undergraduate schools and 1 graduate school. In addition to regional accreditation, KSC has baccalaureate program accreditation with NASM, CCNE, CAATE, ACEND, ACS, and IACS. The 170-acre campus is in a small town 90 miles northwest of Boston and 100 miles north of Hartford, CT. Including any residence halls, there are 61 buildings.

STUDENT LIFE: 57% of undergraduates are from out of state, mostly the Northeast. Students are from 25 states, and 5 foreign countries. 86% are White; 5% race unknown; 4% Hispanic; 2% African American; 2% Asian American; 2% two or more races. **Female To Male Ratio:** 1.2:1. The average age of freshmen is 18; all undergraduates, 20. 29% do not continue beyond their first year; 64% remain to graduate. **Housing:** 2307 students can be accommodated in college housing, which includes gender neutral, single sex dorms, coed dorms, married student dorms, and on-campus apartments. In addition, there are honors houses, special-interest houses, fraternity houses, sorority houses, and living learning communities. On-campus housing is guaranteed for the freshman year only, is available on a first-come, first-served basis, and is available on a lottery system for upperclassmen. 55% of students live on campus. Upperclassmen may keep cars.

FACULTY/CLASSROOMS: No introductory courses are taught by graduate students.

PROGRAMS OF STUDY: KSC confers B.A., B.S., B.F.A. and B.M. degrees. Master's degrees are also awarded. Bachelor's degrees are awarded in AGRICULTURE (environmental studies), BIOLOGICAL SCIENCE (biology/biological science and nutrition), BUSINESS (human resource management, management, marketing, marketing management, and product design), COMMUNICATIONS AND THE ARTS (art, choral music, communications, dance, English, English literature, English Writing, film arts, French, human performance, instrumental music education, journalism, journalism - news & information, literature, multimedia, music, music composition, music performance, music technology, public relations, Spanish, studio art, studio art graphic design, theatre acting, theater design, theatre production, theatre/dance, and writing), COMPUTER AND PHYSICAL SCIENCE (chemistry, computer mathematics, computer networks & systems, computer information systems, computer science, earth & space science, mathematics, physics and mathematics, physics, science, software engineering, web services, and web technology), EDUCATION (athletic training, dance education, early childhood education, education, elementary education, mathematics education, music education, physical education, physical education/exercise science, science education, and secondary education), ENGINEERING AND ENVIRONMENTAL DESIGN (architecture and occupational safety and health), HEALTH PROFESSIONS (allied health, community and behavioral health, exercise science, health promotion, health science, and nursing), SOCIAL SCIENCE (addiction studies, American studies, anthropology, criminal justice, economics, geography, history, philosophy, political science/government, psychology, sociology, and women & gender studies). Safety & occupational health applied sciences, chemistry, holocaust & genocide studies are the strongest academically. Education, safety & occupational health applied sciences, management, and health science have the largest enrollment.

ACTIVITIES: 6% of men belong to 5 national fraternities; 7% of women belong to 3 national sororities. There are 75 groups on campus, including creative hobbies, Humans vs Zombies, art, band, cheerleading, choir, chorale, chorus, communications, computers, dance, debate, drama, environmental, ethnic, feminist collective, film, honors, international, jazz band, LGBT, literary magazine, musical theater, newspaper, orchestra, photography, political, professional, radio and TV, religious, social, social service, student government, and yearbook. Popular campus events include Spring Concert, Localvore (Local) Day, Global Chef, Student Involvement Fairs, Winter Celebration, Parent-Family Weekend, and SolarFest. **Sports:** There are 8 intercollegiate sports for men and 10 for women, and 27 intramural sports for men and 27 for women. Facilities include indoor basketball court, outdoor basketball court, volleyball court, six-lane swimming pool, racquetball court, gymnastics/multipurpose rooms, multi-purpose courts, basketball, volleyball, floor hockey, indoor soccer, jogging/walking track, fitness center for cardiovascular fitness & free weight areas, aerobics studio, multi-purpose room, tennis courts, and fields for rugby, ultimate frisbee, sand volleyball courts, hockey, lacrosse, baseball, softball, and soccer.**Graduates:** From July 1, 2016 to June 30, 2017, 1058 bachelor's degrees were awarded. The most popular majors were safety and occupational health applied science (14%), psychology (8%), and education (7%). In an average class, 55% graduate in 4 years or less, 59% graduate in 5 years or less, and 62% graduate in 6 years or less. Of the 2016 graduating class, 24% were enrolled in graduate school within 6 months of graduation, and 88% were employed.

SERVICES: Counseling and information services are available, as is tutoring in most subjects. There is a writing process center and a math center. There is also a reader service for the blind, and remedial math, reading, and writing. **Library/Resources:** The library contains 247,720 volumes, and 28,154 audio/video tapes/CDs/DVDs, and subscribes to 73,256 periodicals including electronic. Computerized library services include interlibrary loans, database searching, Internet access, and Wi-Fi capability. Special learning facilities include an art gallery, radio station, TV station, and the Cohen Center for Holocaust Studies/Holocaust Resource Center. **Physically Challenged Students:** 95% of the campus is accessible. Facilities include wheelchair ramps, elevators, special parking, specially equipped restrooms, lowered drinking fountains, and lowered telephones. **Special:** Internships and co-op programs offered in most areas of study, study abroad anywhere in the world, and work-study at the college are available. Student teaching is required for education majors. Students also may pursue dual majors, a general studies degree, individualized majors, accelerated degrees in the psychology honors program, and a 3-2 engineering degree with Clarkson University or the University of New Hampshire. In addition, there are pass/fail options and credit for life experience. There are 25 national honor societies, a freshman honors program, and 3 departmental honors programs. **Visiting:** There are regularly scheduled orientations for prospective students, consisting of an overview with admissions counselor and tour of campus. There are guides for informal visits and visitors may sit in on classes. **Campus Safety and Security:** Measures include 24-hour foot and vehicle patrol, emergency notification system, self-defense education, and security escort services. There are shuttle buses, emergency telephones, lighted pathways/sidewalks, and controlled access to dorms/residences.

REQUIREMENTS: Applicants must complete and submit the Common Application form and KSC supplement at commonapp.org with application fee, official high school transcript including first marking period grades for senior year, SAT test scores or ACT test scores, essay, and a letter of recommendation. Applicants need at least 14 academic credits, including 4 years of English, and 3 years each of math and science, 2 years each of social studies and academic electives or GED. A portfolio or an audition is required for certain programs. A GPA of 2.0 is required. AP and CLEP credits are accepted. Education in the liberal arts and sciences and in several professional fields is provided through bachelor degree programs. These programs include three basic components: Integrative Studies requirements, established by the college, purposefully and intentionally help students engage ethical issues, approach global issues from multiple perspectives, apply diverse perspectives to their thinking and their actions, and analyze key social and environmental issues confronting us all. Major/Option/Specialization or Concentration Requirements, specified by discipline faculty, offer depth of scholarship through specialization in a field of interest. Electives, selected by the student, provide the opportunity to develop a minor, to fulfill teacher certification requirements, or to take courses in other areas for personal and professional growth. All Bachelor's degrees require a minimum of 120 credits with 34 – 110 hours in their major (depending on program). A student must complete a minimum of 40 upper-level credits within the degree program. Students must complete 40 credits in the Integrative Studies Program as follows: 8 credits in two first year foundation courses Thinking & Writing and Quantitative Literacy, 12 credits in arts and humanities, 12 credits in sciences, 4 credits in interdisciplinary studies, 4 additional credits in the Arts, Humanities, Social Sciences, Natural Sciences or Interdisciplinary area. Students must maintain a minimum GPA of 2.0. Students must have a minimum of 30 credits in residence at KSC to graduate. Students with majors in the School of Arts & Humanities must complete one course in a foreign language. **Procedure:** Freshmen are admitted fall and spring. Entrance exams should be taken during the spring of the junior year or fall of the senior year. There are deferred admissions and rolling admissions plans. Applications should be filed by April 1 for fall entry; December 1 for spring entry. The fall 2017 application fee was $50. Notifications are sent December 1. Applications are accepted on-line. **Transfer Students:** 129 transfer students enrolled in 2016-2017. Applicants must complete and submit the Common Application form and KSC supplement at commonapp.org with application fee, official school transcripts from all previous colleges, SAT test scores or ACT test scores, essay, and a letter of reference from a college administrator. A portfolio or an audition is required for certain programs. 30 of 120 credits required for the bachelor's degree must be completed at KSC. **International Students:** There are 15 international students enrolled. They must take the TOEFL with a minimum score of 550 on the paper-based TOEFL (PBT). International students living in the US for 2 or more years attending high school must take SAT.

ADMISSIONS: 83% of the 2017-2018 applicants were accepted. The SAT scores for the 2017-2018 freshman class were: Math-- 40% below 500, 50% between 500 and 599, 10% between 600 and 699, and 1% between 700 and 800. Evidence-Based Reading/Writing-- 31% below 500, 51% between 500 and 599, 17% between 600 and 699, and 1% between 700 and 800. The ACT scores were 20% between 12 and 17, 51% between 18 and 23, 25% between 24 and 29, and 4% above 30. 12% of the current freshmen were in the top fifth of their class; 45% were in the top two fifths. **Admissions Contact:** Peggy Richmond, Director of Admissions. Email: *admissions@keene.edu* Web: *www.keene.edu/*

FINANCIAL AID: In 2017-2018, 97% of all full-time freshmen received some form of financial aid. 68% of all full-time freshmen received need-based aid. The average freshman award was $19,693. Need-based scholarships or need-based grants averaged $3,822 ($22,238 maximum); need-based self-help aid (loans and jobs) averaged $2,932 ($9,000 maximum); and other non-need-based awards and non-need-based scholarships averaged $12,939 ($39,192 maximum). 20% of undergraduate students work part-time. The average financial indebtedness of the 2017 graduate was $40,195. The FAFSA code is 002590. The deadline for filing freshman financial aid applications for fall entry is March 1.

NEW ENGLAND COLLEGE *(The complete profile is made available exclusively on our website, www.barronspac.com)*

PLYMOUTH STATE UNIVERSITY *(The complete profile is made available exclusively on our website, www.barronspac.com)*

RIVIER UNIVERSITY — D-6

www.rivier.edu

Nashua, NH 03060 — **(603) 897-8507**

Fax: (603) 891-1799	**Email: vleclair@rivier.edu**
Full-time: 310 men, 610 women	**Faculty:** n/av
Part-time: 205 men, 505 women	**Ph.D.s:** n/av
Graduate: 255 men, 625 women	**Student/Faculty:** n/av
Year: semesters, summer session	**Tuition:** $29,990
Room & Board: $11,610	**Freshman Class:** n/av
SAT: required	**CEEB CODE:** 3728
Application Deadline: open	**VERY COMPETITIVE**

Rivier University, founded in 1933 by the Sisters of the Presentation of Mary, is a private Roman Catholic college offering a liberal arts and professional curriculum. The figures in the above capsule and in this profile are approximate. There is 1 undergraduate school and 1 graduate school. In addition to regional accreditation, RU has baccalaureate program accreditation with NLN. The 68-acre campus is in a suburban area 45 miles north of Boston. Including any residence halls, there are 44 buildings.

STUDENT LIFE: 68% of undergraduates are from New Hampshire. Others are from 13 states, 13 foreign countries, and Canada. 80% are from public schools. 93% are White; 2% Hispanic; 1% African American; 1% Asian American; 1% Foreign. 80% are Catholic. **Female To Male Ratio:** 2.3:1. The average age of freshmen is 18; all undergraduates, 28. 29% do not continue beyond their first year. **Housing:** 425 students can be accommodated in college housing, which includes dorms, and a substance-free/wellness residence hall. On-campus housing is guaranteed for all 4 years, is available on a first-come, and first-served basis. 56% of students commute. All students may keep cars.

FACULTY/CLASSROOMS: 38% of faculty are male; 62% are female. 88% teach undergraduates. No introductory courses are taught by graduate students. The average class size in an introductory lecture is 25; in a laboratory is 20; and in a regular course is 17.

PROGRAMS OF STUDY: Rivier confers B.A., B.S. and B.F.A. degrees. Associate and master's degrees are also awarded. Bachelor's degrees are awarded in BIOLOGICAL SCIENCE (biology/biological science), BUSINESS (business administration and management, management information systems, and management science), COMMUNICATIONS AND THE ARTS (communications, English, graphic design, illustration, and studio art), COMPUTER AND PHYSICAL SCIENCE (computer science and mathematics), EDUCATION (art education, early childhood education, elementary education, English education, mathematics education, secondary education, and social studies education), HEALTH PROFESSIONS (nursing, predentistry, premedicine, and preveterinary science), SOCIAL SCIENCE (history, human development, liberal arts/general studies, political science/government, prelaw, psychology, and sociology). Art, education, and nursing are the strongest academically. Education, psychology, and business have the largest enrollments.

ACTIVITIES: There are no fraternities or sororities. There are 32 groups on campus, including nursing, behavioral sciences, history, paralegal, art, chorus, computers, debate, drama, ethnic, honors, international, literary magazine, newspaper, political, professional, religious, social, social sciences, social service, student government, and yearbook. Popular campus events include Spirit Week, Black History Month, and Women's History Month. **Sports:** There are 5 intercollegiate sports for men and 5 for women, and 7 intramural sports for men and 7 for women. Facilities include a gym, weight room, soccer and softball fields.

SERVICES: Counseling and information services are available, as is tutoring in some subjects, such as math, English, business, and languages. Tutoring is available in other subjects. There is remedial math and writing. There is a full-service writing center. **Library/Resources:** The library contains 107,200 volumes, 89,572 microform items, and 29,094 audio/video tapes/CDs/DVDs, and subscribes to 480 periodicals including electronic. Computerized library services include interlibrary loans and database searching. Special learning facilities include an art gallery, TV station, education curriculum resources center, legal reference center, early childhood center/laboratory school, and language lab. **Physically Challenged Students:** 75% of the campus is accessible. Facilities include wheelchair ramps, elevators, special parking, specially equipped restrooms, and lowered drinking fountains. **Special:** Rivier offers cross-registration through the New Hampshire College and University Council, internships in most majors, an accelerated master's program in English, dual majors, a liberal studies degree, credit by challenge examination, nondegree study, and pass/fail options. There is 1 national honor society and a freshman honors program. **Visiting:** There are regularly scheduled orientations for prospective students, including an opportunity to interview, a tour, class visits, and opportunities to meet with faculty, coaches, and current students. There are guides for informal visits, visitors may sit in on classes, and stay overnight. To schedule a visit, contact the Office of Undergraduate Admissions. **Campus Safety and Security:** Measures include 24-hour foot and vehicle patrol and security escort services. There are emergency telephones, lighted pathways/sidewalks, 24-hour access by telephone or walkie-talkie, and electronically operated dorm entrances using security cards.

REQUIREMENTS: The SAT is required. Applicants must be high school graduates or hold the GED. The recommended college preparatory curriculum includes 4 years of English, 3 of math, 2 or more each of foreign language and social studies, 1 of lab science, and 4 academic electives. An essay and 1 or 2 letters of recommendation are required, and an interview is highly recommended. Prospective art majors must submit a portfolio. A GPA of 2.5 is required. AP and CLEP credits are accepted. Important factors in the admissions decision are advanced placement or honors courses, recommendations by school officials, and extracurricular activities record. A writing sample is required at entry, and a demonstration of writing proficiency must be shown prior to graduation. Students must complete at least 120 credit hours, ordinarily consisting of 40 3-credit courses with 35 to 60 credits in the student's major, and they must maintain a minimum GPA of 2.0. Distribution requirements include 17 core courses in basic skills of writing and math, the humanities, and the sciences. These courses include religious studies, philosophy, physical and life sciences, fine arts, modern languages, literature, behavioral and social sciences, and Western Civilization. **Procedure:** Freshmen are admitted fall and spring. Entrance exams should be taken in the junior or senior year. There are deferred admissions and rolling admissions plans. Application deadlines are open. The fall 2017 application fee was $25. Notification of early decision is sent December 1; regular decision, on a rolling basis. Applications are accepted on-line. **Transfer Students:** Transfer applicants should have a minimum GPA of 2.5 and submit SAT I or ACT scores if they have earned fewer than 12 credits at the previous institution. Official college transcripts are required and an interview is recommended. 60 of 120 credits required for the bachelor's degree must be completed at RU. **International Students:** They must take the TOEFL and the college's own test.

Admissions Contact: Valerie Leclair, Director of Undergraduate Admissions. Email: *vleclair@rivier.edu* Web: *www.rivier.edu*

FINANCIAL AID: RU is a member of CSS. The FAFSA code is 002586. Check with the school for current application deadlines.

SAINT ANSELM COLLEGE D-6

www.anselm.edu

Manchester, NH 03102	**(603) 641-7500**
Fax: (603) 641-7550	**Email:** admission@anselm.edu
Full-time: 764 men, 1162 women	**Faculty:** 153; IIB, +$
Part-time: 4 men, 34 women	**Ph.D.s:** 92%
Graduate: n/av	**Student/Faculty:** 11 to 1
Year: semesters, summer session	**Tuition:** $39,990
Room & Board: $14,146	**Freshman Class:** 3892 applied, 2960 accepted, 577 enrolled
SAT EBR-W/M: 600/600 **ACT:** 26	**CEEB CODE:** 3748
Application Deadline: February 1	**VERY COMPETITIVE**

Saint Anselm College, founded in 1889, is a private Roman Catholic institution offering a liberal arts education. There is 1 undergraduate school. In addition to regional accreditation, SAC has baccalaureate program accreditation with NLN. The 380-acre campus is in a suburban area in Southern New Hampshire, minutes from downtown Manchester, 50 miles north of Boston. Including any residence halls, there are 64 buildings.

STUDENT LIFE: 81% of undergraduates are from out of state, mostly the Northeast. Students are from 25 states, 4 foreign countries, and Canada. 68% are from public schools. 88% are White; 4% race unknown; 3% Hispanic; 2% African American; 2% two or more races; 1% Asian American; 1% Foreign. 55% are Catholic. **Female To Male Ratio:** 1.6:1. The average age of freshmen is 18; all undergraduates, 20. 10% do not continue beyond their first year; 75% remain to graduate. **Housing:** 1794 students can be accommodated in college housing, which includes dorms and on-campus apartments. In addition, there are special-interest houses, and substance-free housing. On-campus housing is guaranteed for all 4 years. 90% of students live on campus. All students may keep cars.

FACULTY/CLASSROOMS: 44% of faculty are male; 56% are female. All teach undergraduates. No introductory courses are taught by graduate students. The average class size in a laboratory is 18 and in a regular course is 18.

PROGRAMS OF STUDY: SAC confers B.A. and B.S.N. degrees. Bachelor's degrees are awarded in BIOLOGICAL SCIENCE (biochemistry and biology/biological science), BUSINESS (accounting, banking and finance, business administration and management, and marketing), COMMUNICATIONS AND THE ARTS (classics, English, fine arts, French, and Spanish), COMPUTER AND PHYSICAL SCIENCE (chemistry, computer science, mathematics, and natural sciences), EDUCA-

TION (education and secondary education), ENGINEERING AND ENVIRONMENTAL DESIGN (engineering and environmental science), HEALTH PROFESSIONS (nursing, predentistry, and premedicine), SOCIAL SCIENCE (criminal justice, economics, forensic studies, German area studies, history, liberal arts/general studies, philosophy, political science/government, prelaw, psychology, sociology, and theological studies). Nursing is the strongest academically. Nursing, business, and criminal justice have the largest enrollments.

ACTIVITIES: There are no fraternities or sororities. There are 60 groups on campus, including art, band, chess, choir, chorale, chorus, communications, computers, dance, debate, drama, environmental, ethnic, film, forensics, honors, international, jazz band, LGBT, literary magazine, musical theater, newspaper, orchestra, pep band, photography, political, professional, radio and TV, religious, social, social service, student government, and yearbook. Popular campus events include Family Weekend, Road for Hope, Spring Weekend, Running of the Bells, Gingerbread House Competition, and Shakespeare's Birthday. **Sports:** There are 10 intercollegiate sports for men and 10 for women, and 8 intramural sports for men and 8 for women. Facilities include a gym, ice hockey arena, activity center that houses basketball, volleyball, tennis, racquetball courts, weight and training rooms, football stadium, baseball stadium, athletic fields and fitness center. **Graduates:** From July 1, 2016 to June 30, 2017, 417 bachelor's degrees were awarded. The most popular majors were social sciences (20%), business/marketing (19%), and health professions and related programs (19%). In an average class, 71% graduate in 4 years or less, 74% graduate in 5 years or less, and 75% graduate in 6 years or less.

SERVICES: Counseling and information services are available, as is tutoring in most subjects. There is a reader service for the blind. **Library/Resources:** The library contains 219,000 volumes, 65,000 microform items, and 8,000 audio/video tapes/CDs/DVDs, and subscribes to 3,900 periodicals including electronic. Computerized library services include interlibrary loans, database searching, Internet access, and Wi-Fi capability. Special learning facilities include an art gallery, planetarium, radio station, TV station, New Hampshire Institute of Politics and Political Library. **Physically Challenged Students:** 80% of the campus is accessible. Facilities include wheelchair ramps, elevators, special parking, specially equipped restrooms, special class scheduling, lowered drinking fountains, lowered telephones, and special housing. **Special:** Saint Anselm offers a 5-year liberal arts and a 3-2 engineering program in cooperation with Manhattan College, University of Notre Dame, University of Massachusetts Lowell, and Catholic University of America. Cross-registration is possible. In addition, internships, work-study, a Washington semester, a New York City semester, study abroad, and nondegree study are available. There are 11 national honor societies and a freshman honors program. **Visiting:** There are regularly scheduled orientations for prospective students, consisting of daily individual interviews and/or group information sessions followed by a campus tour. There are guides for informal visits and visitors may sit in on classes. To schedule a visit, contact the Office of Admission. **Campus Safety and Security:** Measures include 24-hour foot and vehicle patrol, emergency notification system, and self-defense education. There are emergency telephones, lighted pathways/sidewalks, and controlled access to dorms/residences.

REQUIREMENTS: Applicants must have 16 academic credits and 16 Carnegie units, including 4 years of English, 3 each of math and science, 2 of foreign language, and 1 each of history and social studies. An essay is required, and an interview is recommended. The GED is accepted. AP and CLEP credits are accepted. Important factors in the admissions decision are advanced placement or honors courses, leadership record, extracurricular activities record, recommendations by school officials, parents or siblings attended your school, evidence of special talent, personality/intangible qualities, recommendations by alumni, and geographical diversity. In the spirit of what is best in a liberal arts education, the academic core at Saint Anselm College has been designed to offer students a breadth of experience that will prepare them for life, an education that not only provides professional and career preparation, but also encourages a lifelong pursuit of truth that will sustain and enrich their lives. This education is facilitated through a core curriculum composed of a set of common courses and learning outcomes considered essential for the education of students in all majors. The college has recently revised and reinvigorated its academic core curriculum. The new core is characterized by its balance between common courses that foster a sense of academic community and elective courses that allow for individual student choice. Core Learning Outcomes: Aesthetic & Creative Engagement, Citizenship & Global Engagement, Historical Awareness, Linguistic Awareness, Philosophical Reasoning, Theological Reasoning, Quantitative Reasoning, Scientific Reasoning, Social Scientific Awareness. The new core includes three major elements: Humanities, College Writing, Core Learning Outcomes, and Humanities Program - Conversatio. Each student is welcomed into the academic community at Saint Anselm College through a year-long interdisciplinary course in the humanities program - Conversatio. The course title is taken from the Benedictine vow that encourages faithfulness to a way of life within community, and in this first year course students are provided with an orientation to studies in the Liberal Arts and an introduction to the distinctive value of those studies within the Catholic Benedictine intellectual tradition. College Writing Program: Writing is fundamental to the pursuit of knowledge in the tradition of the liberal arts. The College Writing Program offers students the opportunity to develop written communication skills across and within disciplines. The ability to write well also prepares students for success in professions and graduate study. In order to fulfill the requirements of the College Writing Program, all students must take Freshman English and three additional course offerings designated as Writing Intensive. Core Learning Outcomes: The majority of course requirements in the core curriculum will be taken as elective courses that fulfill core learning outcomes. SAC has identified nine core learning outcomes that are considered essential for the education of each student. Because the core curriculum is based on student learning outcomes, rather than on specific required courses, students are given greater choice in completing their core requirements as they are able to select from among a variety of courses that fulfill each of the different student learning outcomes. Core learning outcomes are specific to the core curriculum and are a subset of a broader list of student learning outcomes that are integrated throughout the entire curriculum. **Procedure:** Freshmen are admitted fall and spring. Entrance exams should be taken during the spring of the junior year or fall of the senior year. There are early admissions and deferred admissions plans. Early decision applications should be filed by November 15; regular applications, by February 1 for fall entry; and November 15 for spring entry. The fall 2017 application fee was $50. Notification of early decision is sent January 15; regular decision, March 15. 196 applicants were on the 2017 waiting list; 38 were admitted. Applications are accepted on-line. **Transfer Students:** 12 transfer students enrolled in 2016-2017. 20 of 40 credits required for the bachelor's degree must be completed at SAC. **International Students:** There are 20 international students enrolled. They must also take the SAT or ACT.

ADMISSIONS: 76% of the 2017-2018 applicants were accepted. The SAT scores for the 2017-2018 freshman class were: Math-- 2% below 500, 38% between 500 and 599, 55% between 600 and 699, and 5% between 700 and 800. Evidence-Based Reading/Writing-- 1% below 500, 36% between 500 and 599, 57% between 600 and 699, and 7% between 700 and 800. The ACT scores were 22% between 18 and 23, 64% between 24 and 29, and 14% above 30. 55% of the current freshmen were in the top fifth of their class; 88% were in the top two fifths. **Admissions Contact:** Eric Nichols, VP for Enrollment and Dean of Admission. Email: *admission@anselm.edu* Web: *www.anselm.edu*

FINANCIAL AID: In 2017-2018, 98% of all full-time freshmen received some form of financial aid. The average freshman award was $28,500. Need-based scholarships or need-based grants averaged $22,800. SAC is a member of CSS. The CSS/Profile is required. The FAFSA code is 002580. The deadline for filing freshman financial aid applications for fall entry is February 15.

SOUTHERN NEW HAMPSHIRE UNIVERSITY — D-6

www.snhu.edu

Manchester, NH 03106	(603) 645-9611 (800) 642-4968
Fax: (603) 645-9693	**Email:** admission@snhu.edu
Full-time: 1447 men, 1470 women	**Faculty:** 146
Part-time: 64 men, 52 women	**Ph.D.s:** 35%
Graduate: 415 men, 465 women	**Student/Faculty:** 14 to 1
Year: semesters, summer session	**Tuition:** $31,136
Room & Board: $13,120	**Freshman Class:** 900 applied, 832 accepted, 414 enrolled
ACT: 23	**CEEB CODE:** 3649
Application Deadline: November 15	**COMPETITIVE**

Southern New Hampshire University, founded in 1932, is a private university offering academic programs in business, education, liberal arts, culinary arts, and community economic development. SNHU also has continuing education and online education programs. There are 5 undergraduate schools and 4 graduate schools. In addition to regional accreditation, SNHU has baccalaureate program accreditation with ACBSP, CIHE, and NEASC. The 338-acre campus is in a suburban area 55 miles north of Boston. Including any residence halls, there are 28 buildings.

STUDENT LIFE: 51% of undergraduates are from out of state, mostly the Northeast. 73% are White; 6% Foreign; 4% Hispanic; 3% African American; 2% Asian American; 2% two or more races; 10% race unknown. **Female To Male Ratio:** 1.0:1. The average age of freshmen is 18; all undergraduates, 21. **Housing:** 1793 students can be accommodated in college housing, which includes dorms and on-campus apartments. On-campus housing is guaranteed for all 4 years, and is available on a first-come, first-served basis. 59% of students live on campus. All students may keep cars.

FACULTY/CLASSROOMS: 52% of faculty are male; 48% are female. No introductory courses are taught by graduate students. The average class size in an introductory lecture is 20; in a laboratory is 15; and in a regular course is 21.

PROGRAMS OF STUDY: SNHU confers B.A., B.S., and B.B.A. degrees. Associate, master's, and doctoral degrees are also awarded. Bachelor's degrees are awarded in AGRICULTURE (environmental studies), BUSINESS (accounting, business administration and management, fashion merchandising, hospitality management services, international business management, marketing management, marketing/retailing/merchandising, retailing, sports management, and tourism), COMMUNICATIONS AND THE ARTS (advertising, communications, creative writing, English, English as a second/foreign language, English literature, and graphic design), COMPUTER AND PHYSICAL SCIENCE (computer science, digital arts/technology, and information sciences and systems), EDUCATION (business education, early childhood education, education, elementary education, English education, secondary education, social studies education, and special education), ENGINEERING AND ENVIRONMENTAL DESIGN (technological management), SOCIAL SCIENCE (child psychology/development, culinary arts, history, liberal arts/general studies, political science/government, psychology, public affairs, and social science). Business administration is the strongest academically. Business, psychology, and education have the largest enrollments.

ACTIVITIES: 3% of men belong to 2 national fraternities; 4% of women belong to 3 local and 1 national sororities. There are 62 groups on campus, including and field hockey, crew club, band, cheerleading, chess, choir, chorus, dance, debate, drama, ethnic, honors, international, jazz band, LGBT, literary magazine, musical theater, newspaper, orchestra, political, professional, radio and TV, religious, social, social service, sports club, student government, and yearbook. Popular campus events include Fall, Winter, and Spring Weekends, International Night, and Trips Abroad to Italy, Greece, and England. **Sports:** Facilities include gyms, an Olympic-sized swimming pool, lighted tennis courts, a lighted artificial surface game field, a fitness room, baseball, softball, and practice fields, a racquetball court, and an aerobic/exercise room. **Graduates:** From July 1, 2016 to June 30, 2017, 836 bachelor's degrees were awarded. The most popular majors were business/marketing (43%), education (10%), and psychology (9%). In an average class, 55% graduate in 4 years or less and 58% graduate in 6 years or less.

SERVICES: Counseling and information services are available, as is tutoring in every subject. There is a reader service for the blind, and remedial math and writing. Peer mentoring and structured learning assistance services are also available. There is also a Jump Start program available for the summer of pre-college. **Library/Resources:** The library contains 94,042 volumes, 378,319 microform items, and 3,170 audio/video tapes/CDs/DVDs, and subscribes to 755 periodicals including electronic. Computerized library services include interlibrary loans, database searching, Internet access, and Wi-Fi capability. Special learning facilities include an art gallery, radio station, a center for financial studies, an advertising agency, an audiovisual studio, a psychology observation lab, a career development center, and an iMAC graphics lab. **Physically Challenged Students:** Facilities include wheelchair ramps, elevators, special parking, specially equipped restrooms, special class scheduling, lowered drinking fountains, lowered telephones, and special housing. **Special:** There are co-ops available, a choice of over 35 study abroad opportunities through the University Studies Abroad Consortium, work-study positions throughout the campus, dual majors, and a 3-year bachelor's degree that is an accelerated degree program in business administration. SNHU also offers cross-registration, distance learning, English as a second language, independent study, internships, and student-design major. There are a freshman honors program. **Visiting:** There are regularly scheduled orientations for prospective students, including a greeting from college administrators, campus tours with students, and informal presentation/discussions with faculty and staff. There are guides for informal visits and visitors may sit in on classes. To schedule a visit, contact the Office of Admission. **Campus Safety and Security:** Measures include 24-hour foot and vehicle patrol, emergency notification system, and security escort services. There are emergency telephones, lighted pathways/sidewalks, controlled access to dorms/residences, winter driving seminars for international students, and public safety officers.

REQUIREMENTS: A general college-preparatory program is required for degree seeking students. Students must have completed 4 years of English, and 3 years each of math, science with 1 unit of lab, and social studies. An essay, a high school transcript, and a letter of recommendation from a guidance counselor or teacher is required. An interview is strongly recommended. SAT or ACT scores are optional. The GED is accepted. AP and CLEP credits are accepted. To graduate, students must complete a minimum of 120 credit hours, including 39 in their majors, with a GPA of 2.0. Distribution requirements total 45 credits from the college core, including 2 to 3 courses in writing, and 2 math, information technology, public speaking, statistics, behavioral, social and natural sciences, courses and electives in fine arts and literature. **Procedure:** Freshmen are admitted in the fall and spring. There are early admissions and rolling admissions plans. Application deadlines are open. The fall 2017 application fee was $40. Notification is sent on a rolling basis. Applications are accepted online. **Transfer Students:** 414 transfer students enrolled in 2016-2017. Transfer applicants must submit a completed application, an attestation form that confirms high school graduation, and official college transcripts from each institution previously attended. Most successful applicants for transfer admission have a cumulative GPA of 2.5 or higher. Students may enroll in the fall and spring semesters on-campus. Military applicants must submit a completed application, an attestation form or final, official high school transcript, Military transcripts and official college transcripts from each institution previously attended (if applicable). Military experience is considered in the admission process and most successful applicants hold a cumulative GPA of 2.5 or higher. Students may enroll in the fall and spring semesters on-campus. 30 of 120 credits required for the bachelor's degree must be completed at SNHU. **International Students:** They must take the TOEFL.

ADMISSIONS: 92% of the 2017-2018 applicants were accepted. The SAT scores for the 2017-2018 freshman class were: The ACT scores were % below 12, 12% between 12 and 17, 51% between 18 and 23, and 37% between 24 and 29. 27% of the current freshmen were in the top fifth of their class; 63% were in the top two fifths. **Admissions Contact:** Tim Whittum, Director of Freshman Admissions. Email: *admission@snhu.edu* Web: *www.snhu.edu*

FINANCIAL AID: The average freshman award was $22,182. Need-based scholarships or need-based grants averaged $5,603; need-based self-help aid (loans and jobs) averaged $5,009; and non-need-based athletic scholarships averaged $12,471. The average financial indebtedness of the 2017 graduate was $40,327. SNHU is a member of CSS. The FAFSA code is 002580. The priority date for freshman financial aid applications for fall entry is March 15.

THOMAS MORE COLLEGE OF LIBERAL ARTS D-6

www.thomasmorecollege.edu

Merrimack, NH 03054 **(603) 880-8308**

Fax: (603) 880-9280 **Email:** admissions@thomasmorecollege.edu

Full-time: 52 men, 44 women	**Faculty:** 5
Part-time: n/av	**Ph.D.s:** 100%
Graduate: n/av	**Student/Faculty:** 14 to 1
Year: semesters	**Tuition:** $20,400
Room & Board: $9700	**Freshman Class:** n/av
SAT or ACT: required	**CEEB CODE:** 3892
Application Deadline: open	**COMPETITIVE**

Thomas More College of Liberal Arts, founded in 1978, by Roman Catholic educators, is an undergraduate institution that combines intensive reading of the Great Books with lectures and seminar discussions placing those works in their historical, cultural, and theological context. Thomas Moore welcomes students of all faiths. The figures in the above capsule and in this profile are approximate. There is 1 undergraduate school. In addition to regional accreditation, TMCLA has baccalaureate program accreditation with AALE. The 14-acre campus is in a small town 40 miles north of Boston. Including any residence halls, there are 5 buildings.

STUDENT LIFE: 81% of undergraduates are from out of state, mostly the Northeast. Students are from 20 states, 2 foreign countries, and Canada. 84% are White; 4% American Indian/Alaska Native; 4% Hispanic; 3% Foreign. **Male To Female Ratio:** 1.2:1. The average age of freshmen is 18; all undergraduates, 20. 9% do not continue beyond their first year. **Housing:** College-sponsored housing includes dorms. On-campus housing is guaranteed for all 4 years. Alcohol is not permitted. All students commute. All students may keep cars.

FACULTY/CLASSROOMS: 80% of faculty are male; 20% are female. All teach undergraduates, 80% do research, and 80% do both. No introductory courses are taught by graduate students.

PROGRAMS OF STUDY: Thomas More confers B.A. degrees. Bachelor's degrees are awarded in SOCIAL SCIENCE (liberal arts/general studies).

ACTIVITIES: There are no fraternities or sororities. Groups on campus include art, choir, chorale, chorus, dance, debate, drama, literary magazine, musical theater, newspaper, photography, radio and TV, and yearbook. Popular campus events include St. Patrick's Day. **Sports:** **Graduates:** From July 1, 2016 to June 30, 2017, 12 bachelor's degrees were awarded. The most popular majors were liberal arts (100%). In an average class, 100% graduate in 4 years or less. Of the 2016 graduating class, 27% were enrolled in graduate school within 6 months of graduation, and 73% were employed.

SERVICES: Counseling and information services are available, as is tutoring in most subjects. Informal tutoring is available by request. **Library/Resources:** The library contains 50,000 volumes, and subscribes to 20 periodicals including electronic. Computerized library services include Internet access. Special learning facilities include a radio station. **Physically Challenged Students:** 70% of the campus is accessible. Facilities include wheelchair ramps, special parking, and specially equipped restrooms. **Special:** A semester in Rome for sophomores is required. Internships are available at Vatican Radio, Zenit News, and the United Nations. **Visiting:** There are regularly scheduled orientations for prospective students. There are guides for informal visits, visitors may sit in on classes, and stay overnight. To schedule a visit, contact the Director of Admissions. **Campus Safety and Security:** Measures include security escort services. There are lighted pathways/sidewalks.

REQUIREMENTS: The SAT or ACT is required. Applicants should be high school graduates with 4 college preparatory units of English, 3 units of math, and 2 units each of foreign language, social science, and lab science. The GED is accepted. An essay and 2 letters of recommendation are required. An interview is strongly recommended. Important factors in the admissions decision are personality/intangible qualities, evidence of special talent, and leadership record. To graduate, students must complete 121 credit hours, including 32 in humanities, 12 each in classical languages, tutorials, philosophy, and Sacred Scripture, 9 in writing/rhetoric/poetics, 7 in fine arts, and 6 each in math, natural science, and theology. In addition, students must complete a junior project of independent study and a senior thesis and seminar. **Procedure:** Freshmen are admitted fall and spring. There is a rolling admissions plan. Application deadlines are open. Applications are accepted on-line. **Transfer Students:** 4 transfer students enrolled in 2016-2017. Applicants must submit a transcript from all higher institutions attended. **International Students:** There are 2 international students enrolled.

Admissions Contact: Mark Schwerdt, Director of Admissions. Email: *admissions@thomasmorecollege.edu* Web: *www.thomasmorecollege.edu*

FINANCIAL AID: In 2017-2018, 80% of all full-time freshmen received some form of financial aid. 65% of all full-time freshmen received need-based aid. The average freshman award was $8,768. 59% of undergraduate students work part-time. The average financial indebtedness of the 2017 graduate was $13,056. Thomas Moore is a member of CSS. The FAFSA code is 030431. Check with the school for current application deadlines.

UNIVERSITY OF NEW HAMPSHIRE E-5

www.unh.edu

Durham, NH 03824 **(603) 862-1360**

Fax: (603) 862-0077
Email: admissions@unh.edu
Full-time: 5663 men, 6983 women
Faculty: 681
Part-time: 207 men, 114 women
Ph.D.s: 88%
Graduate: 1312 men, 1085 women
Student/Faculty: 18 to 1
Year: semesters, summer session
Tuition: $18,067 ($32,637)
Room & Board: $11,266
Freshman Class: 19966 applied, 15275 accepted, 3019 enrolled
SAT CR/M: 590/582 **ACT:** 25
CEEB CODE: 3918
Application Deadline: February 1
VERY COMPETITIVE

University of New Hampshire is the state's flagship public research university, providing comprehensive, high-quality undergraduate programs in liberal arts, engineering, physical sciences, business, life sciences, agriculture, and health and human services, as well as graduate programs (certificate, master's, doctoral). UNH has the feel of a small New England liberal arts college and provides the educational opportunities of a world-class research university, including a distinctive commitment to undergraduate research and one of the nation's largest undergraduate research conferences. There are 6 undergraduate schools and 2 graduate schools. In addition to regional accreditation, UNH has baccalaureate program accreditation with AACSB, ABET, ADA, CSWE, NASM, NRPA, SAF, AACN, ACOTE, AEE, ASHA, AUPHA, CCIE, CEPH, COAMFTE, JRC-AT, NAACLS, and NAEYC. The 2600-acre campus is in a small town 60 miles north of Boston. Including any residence halls, there are 150 buildings.

STUDENT LIFE: 54% of undergraduates are from out of state, mostly the Northeast. Students are from 45 states, 41 foreign countries, and Canada. 81% are from public schools. 82% are White; 5% race unknown; 4% Foreign; 3% Asian American; 3% Hispanic; 2% two or more races; 1% African American. **Female To Male Ratio:** 1.1:1. The average age of freshmen is 18; all undergraduates, 20. 14% do not continue beyond their first year; 77% remain to graduate. **Housing:** 7000 students can be accommodated in college housing, which includes married student dorms and on-campus apartments. In addition, there are honors houses, language/international houses, special-interest houses, and substance-free residence halls. On-campus housing is guaranteed for the freshman year only, is available on a first-come, and first-served basis. 54% of students live on campus. Upperclassmen may keep cars.

FACULTY/CLASSROOMS: 48% of faculty are male; 52% are female. 98% teach undergraduates, 2% do research, and 98% do both. Graduate students teach 2% of introductory courses. The average class size in an introductory lecture is 44; in a laboratory is 19; and in a regular course is 32.

PROGRAMS OF STUDY: UNH confers B.A., B.F.A., B.M., and B.S. degrees. Associate, master's, and doctoral degrees are also awarded. Bachelor's degrees are awarded in AGRICULTURE (animal science, dairy science, EcoGastronomy, environmental studies, and forestry and related sciences), BIOLOGICAL SCIENCE (biochemistry, biology/biological science, genetics, marine biology, microbiology, molecular biology, neurosciences, nutrition, sustainability, wildlife biology, and zoology), BUSINESS (business administration and management, environment & national resource economics, and hospitality management services), COMMUNICATIONS AND THE ARTS (art history, classics, communications, English, fine arts, French, German, information technology, linguistics, music, recreation administration, Russian, Spanish, studio art, and theatre arts), COMPUTER AND PHYSICAL SCIENCE (applied mathematics, chemistry, computer science, earth science, earth science / adolescence education, geology, mathematics, physics, and statistics), EDUCATION (athletic training, mathematics education, and physical education), ENGINEERING AND ENVIRONMENTAL DESIGN (bioengineering, chemical engineering, city/community/regional planning, civil engineering, computer engineering, electrical/electronics engineering, engineering physics, environmental engineering, environmental science, mechanical engineering, and ocean engineering), HEALTH PROFESSIONS (biomedical science, health administration and policy, kinesiology, nursing, occupational therapy, and speech pathology/audiology), SOCIAL SCIENCE (anthropology, economics, European studies, family/consumer studies, French studies, geography, history, human development & family studies, humanities, international studies, Italian studies, justice and society, philosophy, physical fitness/movement, political science/government, psychology, social work, sociology, and women's studies). Business, biology & life sciences, and engineering are the strongest academically. Business administration, psychology, and biomedical science have the largest enrollments.

ACTIVITIES: 14% of men belong to 1 local and 13 national fraternities; 15% of women belong to 8 national sororities. There are 274 groups on campus, including art, band, cheerleading, chess, choir, chorale, chorus, communications, computers, dance, debate, drama, drill team, environmental, ethnic, film, honors, international, jazz band, LGBT, literary magazine, marching band, musical theater, newspaper, opera, orchestra, pep band, photography, political, professional, radio and TV, religious, social, social service, student government, symphony, and yearbook. Popular campus events include Jukebox, Student Activities Fair, Winter Carnival, Homecoming, MUB Lecture Series, May Day, and Kwanzaa Celebration. **Sports:** There are 38 intercollegiate sports for men and 43 for women, and 41 intramural sports for men and 41 for women. Facilities include indoor and outdoor swimming pools, tracks, tennis courts, gyms, wrestling and gymnastics rooms, dance studio, playing fields, indoor ice rink, cross-country ski trails, pond for sailing. A recreation and sports complex, for hockey, basketball and special events, a fitness center, jogging track, weight room, racquetball courts, international squash court, aerobics and martial arts studios, multipurpose courts, and basketball courts. The Northeast Passage center provides recreation equipment and programming for people with disabilities. **Graduates:** From July 1, 2016 to June 30, 2017, 2743 bachelor's degrees were awarded. The most popular majors were business administration (20%), psychology (6%), and communication (6%). In an average class, 68% graduate in 4 years or less, 76% graduate in 5 years or less, and 77% graduate in 6 years or less. Of the 2016 graduating class, 19% were enrolled in graduate school within 6 months of graduation, and 71% were employed.

SERVICES: Counseling and information services are available, as is tutoring in most subjects, such as business, biology, biomedical science, chemistry, economics, foreign languages, math, physics, statistics. Instruction in learning strategies, study skills, time management, and organizational skills. The university writing center offers free assistance by trained consultants. **Library/Resources:** The library contains 1.1 million volumes, 85,727 microform items, and 49,313 audio/video tapes/CDs/DVDs, and subscribes to 108,176 periodicals including electronic. Computerized library services include interlibrary loans, database searching, Internet access, and Wi-Fi capability. Special learning facilities include an art gallery, radio station, optical observatory, marine research labs (coastal, estuarine, island), interoperability lab, experiential learning center with challenge course, electron microscope, child development center, journalism lab, experimental wind tunnel, agricultural and equine facilities including an organic research dairy farm and sustainable agriculture facilities, nursing simulation lab, instructional and recreational climbing wall, exercise physiology lab, sawmill, language labs, performing arts center, and survey center. **Physically Challenged Students:** 88% of the campus is accessible. Facilities include wheelchair ramps, elevators, special parking, specially equipped restrooms, special class scheduling, lowered drinking fountains, lowered telephones, and special housing. **Special:** UNH is committed to providing students with an absorbing and comprehensive educational experience that fosters the development of the whole person. A central mission is to offer students a wide variety of enriching co-curricular programs. There is nationwide study through the National Student Exchange and worldwide study through the Center for International Education. Exciting opportunities for undergraduate research are supported by faculty and the prospect of special funding. Many majors include an internship or service-learning experience. A Washington semester, Semester in the City, work-study, BA/BS degrees, dual majors, student-designed majors and bachelor's/graduate degree plans are also available. Joint programs with Cornell University in marine science are offered. Extensive cross-registration is possible through the New Hampshire College and University Council Consortium. UNH has a vast range of interdisciplinary minors designed to complement a major's focus with intellectual interests and pre-professional experience. There are 25 national honor societies, Phi Beta Kappa, a freshman honors program, and 67 departmental honors programs. **Visiting:** There are regularly scheduled orientations for prospective students, campus tours, group information sessions, and open house programs. There are guides for informal visits and visitors may sit in on classes. To schedule a visit, contact the Admissions Office. **Campus Safety and Security:** Measures include 24-hour foot and vehicle patrol, emergency notification system, self-defense education, and security escort services. There are shuttle buses, emergency telephones, lighted pathways/sidewalks, controlled access to dorms/residences, and prevention awareness programs.

REQUIREMENTS: The SAT or ACT is required. Additional requirements are 15 academic units: 4 English, 3 each in math, science (at least 2 must include lab), and social studies, and 2 foreign language. Recommended: 19 academic units: 4 units each in English, mathematics, and science (3 that include lab), 3 units each in foreign language, social studies, 1 in visual/performing arts. Essay required for all students. Audition is required for music and theatre students. A portfolio is required for students wishing to major in Studio Arts. AP and CLEP credits are accepted. Important factors in the admissions decision are recommendations by school officials and advanced placement or honors courses. To graduate, all students must maintain a GPA of 2.0 and complete at least 128 credits, with a minimum of 36 credits and 10 classes in the major. General education requirements include 4 writing-intensive courses, including Freshman Composition. Students must also take 1 course in each of the following areas: Quantitative Reasoning; Biological Science; Physical Science; Environment, Technology, and Society; Fine and Performing Arts; Historical Perspectives; Humanities; Social Science; World Cultures. All seniors must complete a senior thesis or project. **Procedure:** Freshmen are admitted fall and spring. Entrance exams should be taken before February 1 of the senior year. There are deferred admissions and rolling admissions plans. Early decision applications should be filed by November 15; regular applications, by February 1 for fall entry; and October 15 for spring entry. The fall 2017 application fee was $50. Notification of early decision is sent December 15; regular decision, January 15. Applications are accepted on-line. **Transfer Students:** 544 transfer students enrolled in 2016-2017. Applicants must submit a GPA of 3.0 in a general education curriculum and an overall minimum GPA of 2.8. An essay is recommended. A letter of recommendation is optional. 32 of 128 credits required for the bachelor's degree must be completed at UNH. **International Students:** There are 481 international students enrolled. They must take the TOEFL with a minimum score of 550 on the paper-based TOEFL (PBT) or 80 on the Internet-based version (iBT). They must also take the SAT or ACT.

ADMISSIONS: 77% of the 2017-2018 applicants were accepted. The SAT scores for the 2017-2018 freshman class were: Critical Reading-- 7% below 500, 48% between 500 and 599, 40% between 600 and 699, and 5% between 700 and 800. Math-- 10% below 500, 49% between 500 and 599, 35% between 600 and 699, and 6% between 700 and 800. The ACT scores were 1% between 12 and 17, 31% between 18 and 23, 54% between 24 and 29, and 14% above 30. 41% of the current freshmen were in the top fifth of their class; 73% were in the top two fifths. 14 freshmen graduated first in their class. **Admissions Contact:** Robert McGann, Director of Admissions. Email: *admissions@unh.edu* Web: *www.unh.edu*

FINANCIAL AID: In 2017-2018, 89% of all full-time freshmen received some form of financial aid. 71% of all full-time freshmen received need-based aid. The average freshman award was $23,501. Need-based scholarships or need-based grants averaged $11,120 ($39,276 maximum); need-based self-help aid (loans and jobs) averaged $5,714 ($5,000 maximum); non-need-based athletic scholarships averaged $27,996 ($42,362 maximum); and other non-need-based awards and non-need-based scholarships averaged $11,132 ($45,500 maximum). 13% of undergraduate students work part-time. The average financial indebtedness of the 2017 graduate was $33,013. The FAFSA code is 002589. The deadline for filing freshman financial aid applications for fall entry is March 1.

UNIVERSITY OF NEW HAMPSHIRE - MANCHESTER D6

www.manchester.unh.edu

Manchester, NH 03101 **(603) 641-4150**

Fax: (603) 641-4342 **Email:** manchester.admissions@unh.edu

Full-time: 264 men, 295 women
Part-time: 164 men, 119 women
Graduate: 98 men, 182 women
Year: semesters, summer session
Room & Board: n/app

Faculty: n/av
Ph.D.s: n/av
Student/Faculty: 13 to 1
Tuition: $14,490 ($28,290)
Freshman Class: 205 applied, 149 accepted, 57 enrolled

SAT CR/M/W: 520/517/494 **ACT:** 21
Application Deadline: n/av

CEEB CODE: 002094
COMPETITIVE

University of New Hampshire-Manchester, founded in 1985 is the sixth college under the University of New Hampshire. In addition to regional accreditation, UNHM has baccalaureate program accreditation with ABET and CCIE. The campus is 53 miles from Boston. Including any residence halls, there is 1 building.

STUDENT LIFE: 97% of undergraduates are from New Hampshire. 73% are White; 4% Hispanic; 3% Asian American; 2% two or more races; 16% race unknown; 1% African American. **Female To Male Ratio:** 1.1:1. The average age of freshmen is 18; all undergraduates, 24. 19% do not continue beyond their first year; 67% remain to graduate. **Housing:** College-sponsored housing includes off-campus apartments. All students may keep cars.

FACULTY/CLASSROOMS: No introductory courses are taught by graduate students. The average class size in a regular course is 6.

PROGRAMS OF STUDY: UNHM confers B.A., and B.S. degrees. Associate and master's degrees are also awarded. Bachelor's degrees are awarded in BIOLOGICAL SCIENCE (biological sciences and biotechnology), BUSINESS (business (dual major program)), COMMUNICATIONS AND THE ARTS (communications and English), COMPUTER AND PHYSICAL SCIENCE (computer information technology and computer science), EDUCATION (English education), ENGINEERING AND ENVIRONMENTAL DESIGN (electrical and computer engineering and mechanical engineering technology), SOCIAL SCIENCE (history, homeland security, humanities, and psychology). ASL/English interpreting, engineering technology, and homeland security are the strongest academically. Biological sciences, business, and communication arts have the largest enrollments.

ACTIVITIES: There are no fraternities or sororities. There are 32 groups on campus, including art, band, chorus, communications, computers, dance, drama, environmental, ethnic, film, international, LGBT, literary magazine, musical theater, newspaper, political, professional, and social service. **Sports:** There is no sports program at UNHM. **Graduates:** From July 1, 2016 to June 30, 2017, 177 bachelor's degrees were awarded. The most popular majors were business, biological science, and communication arts. In an average class, 38% graduate in 4 years or less and 67% graduate in 6 years or less.

SERVICES: Counseling and information services are available, as is tutoring in every subject. There is a reader service for the blind. **Library/Resources:** Computerized library services include interlibrary loans, database searching, Internet access, and Wi-Fi capability. **Physically Challenged Students:** Facilities include wheelchair ramps, elevators, special parking, specially equipped restrooms, special class scheduling, lowered drinking fountains, and lowered telephones. **Visiting:** There are regularly scheduled orientations for prospective students, campus tours, open house programs, and information sesssions. There are guides for informal visits. To schedule a visit, contact the Office of Admissions. **Campus Safety and Security:** Measures include emergency notification system, self-defense education, and security escort services. There are lighted pathways/sidewalks.

REQUIREMENTS: AP and CLEP credits are accepted. Important factors in the admissions decision are advanced placement or honors courses, leadership record, and personality/intangible qualities. **Procedure:** Freshmen are admitted fall and spring. There are early admissions and deferred admissions plans. Application deadlines are open. The fall 2017 application fee was $40. Applications are accepted on-line. **Transfer Students:** 157 transfer students enrolled in 2016-2017. 32 of 128 credits required for the bachelor's degree must be completed at UNHM. **International Students:** They must take the TOEFL with a minimum score of 550 on the paper-based TOEFL (PBT) or 79 on the Internet-based version (iBT). They must also take the SAT or ACT.

ADMISSIONS: 73% of the 2017-2018 applicants were accepted. The SAT scores for the 2017-2018 freshman class were: Critical Reading-- 41% below 500, 46% between 500 and 599, 11% between 600 and 699, and 2% between 700 and 800. Math-- 41% below 500, 44% between 500 and 599, and 15% between 600 and 699. Writing-- 50% below 500, 41% between 500 and 599, and 9% between 600 and 699. The ACT scores were 40% below 12, 40% between 12 and 17, 40% between 18 and 23, % between 24 and 29, and 20% above 30. **Admissions Contact:** Erika Couture, Senior Associate Director of Admissions. Email: *manchester.admissions@unh.edu* Web: *www.manchester.unh.edu*

FINANCIAL AID: In 2017-2018, 86% of all full-time freshmen received some form of financial aid. 73% of all full-time freshmen received need-based aid. The priority date for freshman financial aid applications for fall entry is March 1.

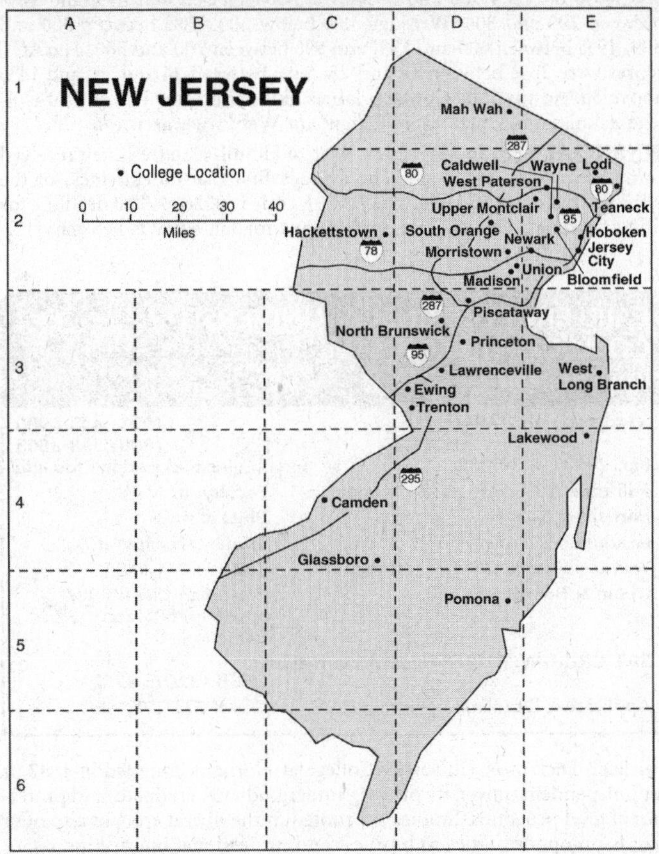

BERKELEY COLLEGE/NEW JERSEY *(The complete profile is made available exclusively on our website, www.barronspac.com)*

BLOOMFIELD COLLEGE *(The complete profile is made available exclusively on our website, www.barronspac.com)*

CALDWELL UNIVERSITY *(The complete profile is made available exclusively on our website, www.barronspac.com)*

CENTENARY COLLEGE *(The complete profile is made available exclusively on our website, www.barronspac.com)*

COLLEGE OF SAINT ELIZABETH *(The complete profile is made available exclusively on our website, www.barronspac.com)*

DREW UNIVERSITY/COLLEGE OF LIBERAL ARTS — D-2

www.drew.edu

Madison, NJ 07940 — **(973) 408-DREW**

Email: cadm@drew.edu

Full-time: 645 men, 862 women
Part-time: 13 men, 17 women
Graduate: 264 men, 316 women
Year: semesters, summer session
Room & Board: $14,108
SAT EBR-W/M: 610/590 **ACT:** 25
Application Deadline: February 1

Faculty: 126; IIB, +$
Ph.D.s: 98%
Student/Faculty: 12 to 1
Tuition: $39,500
Freshman Class: n/av
CEEB CODE: 2193
VERY COMPETITIVE

Drew University/College of Liberal Arts, founded as a Methodist seminary in 1867, is a undergraduate college, a graduate school and a theological school. There is 1 undergraduate school and 2 graduate schools. The 186-acre campus is in a suburban area 30 miles west of New York City in Madison, New Jersey. Including any residence halls, there are 57 buildings.

STUDENT LIFE: 63% of undergraduates are from New Jersey. Others are from 38 states, 49 foreign countries, and Canada. 7% are African American; 55% White; 5% Asian American; 5% two or more races; 5% race unknown; 13% Hispanic; 10% Foreign. **Female To Male Ratio:** 1.3:1. The average age of freshmen is 18; all undergraduates, 20. 15% do not continue beyond their first year; 64% remain to graduate. **Housing:** 1451 students can be accommodated in college housing, which includes married student dorms and on-campus apartments. In addition, there are honors houses, special-interest houses, international house, music appreciation house, spirituality house, Umoja house (Pam-African), WoCo house (Feminist), leadership institute housing, scholars housing, Global Village housing, wellness/substance-free floors, single gender floors, quiet floors, single sex floors, and students can apply for theme houses. On-campus housing is guaranteed for all 4 years. 79% of students live on campus. Upperclassmen may keep cars.

FACULTY/CLASSROOMS: 50% of faculty are male; 50% are female. No introductory courses are taught by graduate students. The average class size in an introductory lecture is 20; in a laboratory is 14; and in a regular course is 17.

PROGRAMS OF STUDY: DU confers B.A. degrees. Master's and doctoral degrees are also awarded. Bachelor's degrees are awarded in AGRICULTURE (environmental studies), BIOLOGICAL SCIENCE (biochemistry, biology/biological science, and neurosciences), BUSINESS (business administration and management), COMMUNICATIONS AND THE ARTS (art, art history and appreciation, Chinese, classics, communications, English, French, German, Italian, music, Spanish, and theatre arts), COMPUTER AND PHYSICAL SCIENCE (chemistry, computer science, mathematics, and physics), SOCIAL SCIENCE (African studies, anthropology, economics, history, international relations, philosophy, political science/government, psychology, religion, sociology, and women's studies). Psychology, business, political science, theatre arts, and natural & physical sciences are the strongest academically. Psychology, business, political science, neuroscience, and biology have the largest enrollments.

ACTIVITIES: There are no fraternities or sororities. There are 90 groups on campus, including art, cheerleading, choir, chorale, chorus, computers, dance, debate, drama, environmental, ethnic, film, honors, international, jazz band, LGBT, literary magazine, musical theater, newspaper, orchestra, pep band, photography, political, professional, radio and TV, religious, social, social service, student government, symphony, and yearbook. Students are encouraged to start new clubs that meet their interests. Popular campus events include Drew Forum Lecture Series, First Annual Picnic, Holiday Ball, JamFest, Chamber Music Society of Lincoln Center Concert Series, Drew Theatre, That Medieval Thing, Bear-B-Que, Boardwalk Night, Hoyt Halloween, 99 Nights, Roast & Roll, First Year Candlelight. **Sports:** There are 9 intercollegiate sports for men and 11 for women, and 12 intramural sports for men and 12 for women. Facilities include an artificial turf athletic field, a gym, indoor track, practice space for athletic teams, an Olympic pool with diving, indoor and outdoor lighted tennis courts, a weight training room, a fitness center, an armory, basketball court, indoor volleyball, racquetball, squash courts, natatorium, dance studio, baseball and softball fields.**Graduates:** From July 1, 2016 to June 30, 2017, 353 bachelor's degrees were awarded. The most popular majors were business/economics (14%), psychology (11%), and English (9%). In an average class, 59% graduate in 4 years or less, 61% graduate in 5 years or less, and 62% graduate in 6 years or less.

SERVICES: Counseling and information services are available, as is tutoring in most subjects. There is a reader service for the blind. The Center for Academic Excellence includes academic coaching, math and science resource center. **Library/Resources:** The library contains 743,441 volumes, 526,964 microform items, 6,170 audio/video tapes/CDs/DVDs, and subscribes to 1,405 periodicals, including electronic. Computerized library services include interlibrary loans, database searching, Internet access, and Wi-Fi capability. Special learning facilities include an art gallery, radio station, mediated classrooms, media and communications lab, an arboretum, a concert hall, the Research Institute of Scientists Emeriti (RISE), an observatory, the United Methodist Archives and History Center, and the Shakespeare Theatre of New Jersey.**Physically Challenged Students:** Facilities include wheelchair ramps, elevators, special parking, specially equipped restrooms, special class scheduling, lowered drinking fountains, lowered telephones, and special housing. The main dining facility, the student center and commons, and the ground floor of every dorm and classroom building are accessible to students with physical disabilities. **Special:** Baldwin Honors Program, Civic Scholars Program, six New York City Semesters (The United Nations, Media & Communications, Theatre, Wall Street, Social Entrepreneurship, Contemporary Art), Washington Semester, Study Abroad opportunities, internships, five-year dual degree program (BA/MA in teaching) program with Drew's Caspersen School of Graduate Studies, seven-year dual degree program (BA/MD) with Rutgers-New Jersey Medical School, five-year dual degree program (BA/BS in engineering) with Columbia University, six-year dual degree (BA/JD) program with Seton Hall Law School, six-year dual degree program (BA/JD) with New York Law School, five-year dual degree program (BA/MEM or MF) in Environmental Management and Forestry with Duke University, five-year dual degree program (BA/MA in Business Management) with Wake Forest University, five-year dual degree program (BA/MS in Software Engineering) with Stevens Institute of Technology, five-year dual degree program (BA/BS) in Nursing) with Drexel University, five-year dual degree program (BA/BS in Nutrition/Dietetics) with Drexel University. There are 15 national honor societies, Phi Beta Kappa, a freshman honors program, and 30 departmental honors programs. **Visiting:** There are regularly scheduled orientations for prospective students, Drew runs regular student-led campus tours, full-day Discover Drew Days, Build-Your-Own Days and Transfer Exploration Days. There are guides for informal visits and visitors may sit in on classes. To schedule a visit, contact the Office of College Admissions. **Campus Safety and Security:** Measures include 24-hour foot and vehicle patrol, emergency notification system, self-defense education, and security escort services. There are emergency telephones, lighted pathways/sidewalks, and controlled access to dorms/residences.

REQUIREMENTS: Standardized test scores are not required for admission, but will be considered along with other academic credentials when submitted. Students without submitting the results from the SAT or ACT must typically have strong high school transcripts in a college-prep or honors program with no grade below a B. Note: some academic scholarships will require standardized test scores. The university strongly recommends 18 academic credits or Carnegie units, including 4 in English, 3 each in math, same foreign language, science with 2 lab courses, and history, with the remaining 2 in other academic courses. An essay is also required, and an interview is strongly recommended, especially for students interested in competing for an academic scholarship. AP and CLEP credits are accepted. To graduate, students must earn at least 128 credits, of which at least 64 must be beyond the introductory level and at least 32 must be at the upper level. All students must fulfill the requirements of a major and those of the general education program. For graduation, the cumulative GPA, both overall and in the major, must be at least 2.0. General education requirements include a first-year seminar, demonstration of writing competency by completion of at least three writing-intensive courses, intermediate proficiency in a foreign language, two quantitative courses, two diversity courses, five breadth courses (one each from the following areas: natural science, social science, humanities, arts, and interdisciplinary) and an off-campus experience. Students have the options to complete a minor. **Procedure:** Freshmen are admitted in the fall and spring. Entrance exams should be taken by fall of the senior year of high school. There are early decision, early admissions, and deferred admissions plans. Early decision applications should be filed by Janurary 15; regular applications, by February 1 for fall entry. The fall 2017 application fee was $40. Notification of early decision is sent February 15; regular decision, March 18. 95 early decision candidates were accepted for the 2017-2018 class. 106 applicants were on the 2017 waiting list; 7 were admitted. Applications are accepted on-line. **Transfer Students:** 85 transfer students enrolled in 2016-2017. Applicants must submit official high school and college transcripts, a personal essay, and a statement of good standing from previous schools attended. An interview also may be required. Drew takes a holistic approach to reviewing the application for admission. Admission decisions are based on the strength of the academic record as well as extra-curricular involvement. We consider college grade-point average, essay and recommendations. If the applicant has earned less than 24 college credits, we may also consider high school grades and course of study. Transfer students are not required to submit the results from standardized tests such as the SAT or ACT, but may choose to do so. 48 of 128 credits required for the bachelor's degree must be completed at DU. **International Students:** There are 244 international students enrolled. They must take the TOEFL with a minimum score of 550 on the paper-based TOEFL (PBT) or 80 on the Internet-based version (iBT).

ADMISSIONS: 63% of the 2017-2018 applicants were accepted. The SAT scores for the 2017-2018 freshman class were: Math-- 7% below 500, 46% between 500 and 599, 37% between 600 and 699, and 10% between 700 and 800. Writing-- 4% below 500, 38% between 500 and 599, 49% between 600 and 699, and 9% between 700 and 800. The ACT scores were 33% between 18 and 23, 53% between 24 and 29, and 14% above 30. **Admissions Contact:** James Skiff, Executive Director of College Admissions. Email: *cadm@drew.edu* Web: *www.drew.edu*

FINANCIAL AID: In 2017-2018, 97% of all full-time freshmen received some form of financial aid. The average financial indebtedness of the 2017 graduate was $24,058. The FAFSA code is 002603. The deadline for filing freshman financial aid applications for fall entry is February 15.

FAIRLEIGH DICKINSON UNIVERSITY/ COLLEGE AT FLORHAM — D-2

www.fdu.edu

Madison, NJ 07940 (973) 443-8900
(800) 338-8803

Fax: (973) 443-8088 **Email:** globaleducation@fdu.edu

Full-time: 1071 men, 1324 women
Part-time: 51 men, 37 women
Graduate: 297 men, 507 women
Year: semesters, summer session
Room & Board: $13,130
Faculty: n/av
Ph.D.s: n/av
Student/Faculty: n/av
Tuition: $41,640
Freshman Class: 3907 applied, 2601 accepted, 646 enrolled
SAT CR/M/W: 510/520/500 **ACT:** required
CEEB CODE: 2262
Application Deadline: open
COMPETITIVE

Fairleigh Dickinson University/College at Florham, founded in 1942, is an independent university offering undergraduate, graduate, and professional level programs. Studies are rooted in the liberal arts but also offer hands-on opportunities in business and professional internships, cooperative education, and global studies abroad. There are 3 undergraduate schools and 2 graduate schools. In addition to regional accreditation, College at Florham has baccalaureate program accreditation with AACSB, NASDTEC, and ACS. The 166-acre campus is in a suburban area 27 miles west of New York City. Including any residence halls, there are 36 buildings.

STUDENT LIFE: 82% of undergraduates are from New Jersey. Others are from 27 states, 12 foreign countries, and Canada. 8% are race unknown; 56% White; 5% Asian American; 17% Hispanic; 11% African American; 1% American Indian/Alaska Native; 1% Foreign. **Female To Male Ratio:** 1.3:1. The average age of freshmen is 18; all undergraduates, 20. 25% do not continue beyond their first year; 52% remain to graduate. **Housing:** 1500 students can be accommodated in college housing, which includes dorms. In addition, there are honors houses, special-interest houses, and theme housing. On-campus housing is available on a first-come, first-served basis. 79% of students live on campus. Upperclassmen may keep cars.

FACULTY/CLASSROOMS: No introductory courses are taught by graduate students.

PROGRAMS OF STUDY: College at Florham confers B.A., B.S., B.S.A.H.T., B.S.C.L.S. and B.S.N. degrees. Master's degrees are also awarded. Bachelor's degrees are awarded in BIOLOGICAL SCIENCE (biochemistry and biology/biological science), BUSINESS (accounting, banking and finance, business administration and management, entrepreneurial studies, hotel/motel and restaurant management, and marketing/retailing/merchandising), COMMUNICATIONS AND THE ARTS (animation, communications, creative writing, dramatic arts, film arts, fine arts, literature, and video), COMPUTER AND PHYSICAL SCIENCE (chemistry, computer science, mathematics, and radiological technology), HEALTH PROFESSIONS (allied health, clinical science, medical laboratory technology, and nursing), SOCIAL SCIENCE (economics, French studies, history, humanities, liberal arts/general studies, philosophy, political science/government, psychology, sociology, and Spanish studies). Psychology, business management, and communications have the largest enrollments.

ACTIVITIES: There are 44 groups on campus, including cheerleading, chorale, computers, dance, environmental, ethnic, honors, international, LGBT, literary magazine, newspaper, political, professional, radio and TV, religious, social, social service, and student government. Popular campus events include Florham Fest and Haunted Mansion. **Sports:** There are 9 intercollegiate sports for men and 9 for women, and 7 intramural sports for men and 5 for women. Facilities include a synthetic turf field for football, field hockey, soccer, and lacrosse. **Graduates:** From July 1, 2016 to June 30, 2017, 463 bachelor's degrees were awarded. The most popular majors were business/marketing (24%), psychology, and visual and performing arts (14%), and communications/journalism (8%). In an average class, 35% graduate in 4 years or less, 48% graduate in 5 years or less, and 52% graduate in 6 years or less.

SERVICES: Counseling and information services are available, as is tutoring in most subjects. There is a reader service for the blind, and remedial math, reading, and writing. There is also oral interpretation for the hearing impaired. Workshops offer assistance with study skills and time management, and support services for basic skills. There is a Regional Center for students with learning disabilities that offers comprehensive support. **Library/Resources:** The library contains 149,850 volumes, 19,236 microform items, and 689 audio/video tapes/CDs/DVDs, and subscribes to 1,182 periodicals including electronic. Computerized library services include interlibrary loans, database searching, Internet access, and Wi-Fi capability. Special learning facilities include an art gallery, radio station, a web-lab, ITV multimedia classrooms, and theaters. **Physically Challenged Students:** 34% of the campus is accessible. Facilities include wheelchair ramps, elevators, special parking, specially equipped restrooms, special class scheduling, lowered drinking fountains, lowered telephones, and special housing. **Special:** The college offers co-op programs in most majors, internships, and study abroad. A Washington semester, work-study, accelerated degrees, and student-designed majors in the humanities and general studies are possible. Pre-pharmacy and joint baccalaureate dental programs are available. There are 10 national honor societies, a freshman honors program, and 11 departmental honors programs. **Visiting:** There are regularly scheduled orientations for prospective students, including standardized placement testing, faculty advisement, class registration, and educational and social activities to prepare students for entrance. There are guides for informal visits, visitors may sit in on classes, and stay overnight. To schedule a visit, contact the Admissions Office. **Campus Safety and Security:** Measures include 24-hour foot and vehicle patrol, emergency notification system, self-defense education, and security escort services. There are shuttle buses, emergency telephones, and lighted pathways/sidewalks.

REQUIREMENTS: The SAT or ACT is required. Applicants should be graduates of an accredited high school or have a GED certificate. They should have completed a minimum of 16 academic units, including 4 in English, 3 in math, 2 each in history, foreign language, and lab science (3 are recommended), and 3 in electives. Those students applying to science and health sciences programs must meet additional requirements. An interview may be requested. AP and CLEP credits are accepted. Important factors in the admissions decision are leadership record, recommendations by school officials, and extracurricular activities record. To graduate, students must complete a 120 to 128 credits, including 30 to 44 in the major, with an overall minimum 2.0 GPA (2.5 in the major). Distribution requirements include courses in English, communications, math, phys ed, foreign language, humanities, social and behavioral sciences, lab and computer science, an integrated, interdisciplinary university core sequence, and a freshman seminar. **Procedure:** Freshmen are admitted to all sessions. Entrance exams should be taken in May of the junior year. There are early admissions, deferred admissions, and rolling admissions plans. Check with the school for current application deadlines. The fall 2017 application fee was $40. Notification is sent on a rolling basis. Applications are accepted on-line. **Transfer Students:** 123 transfer students enrolled in 2016-2017. All transfer applicants must submit official transcripts for all college work taken. Students with fewer than 24 credits must also submit a high school transcript or a copy of their state department of education's equivalency score, and SAT scores. 32 of 120 credits required for the bachelor's degree must be completed at College at Florham. **International Students:** There are 14 international students enrolled. They must take the TOEFL with a minimum score of 550 on the paper-based TOEFL (PBT) or 79 on the Internet-based version (iBT). Students must take the IELTS. The SAT or ACT is also highly recommended.

ADMISSIONS: 67% of the 2017-2018 applicants were accepted. The SAT scores for the 2017-2018 freshman class were: Critical Reading-- 42% below 500, 42% between 500 and 599, 14% between 600 and 699, and 3% between 700 and 800. Math-- 36% below 500, 43% between 500 and 599, 18% between 600 and 699, and 2% between 700 and 800. Writing-- 48% below 500, 40% between 500 and 599, 10% between 600 and 699, and 3% between 700 and 800. 32% of the current freshmen were in the top fifth of their class; 62% were in the top two fifths. 5 freshmen graduated first in their class. **Admissions Contact:** Jonathan Wexler, Associate Vice President of Enrollment Management. Email: *globaleducation@fdu.edu* Web: *www.fdu.edu*

FINANCIAL AID: The FAFSA code is 004738. The priority date for freshman financial aid applications for fall entry is February 15.

FAIRLEIGH DICKINSON UNIVERSITY/ METROPOLITAN CAMPUS — E-2

www.fdu.edu

Teaneck, NJ 07666 — **(201) 692-2553** **(800) 338-8803**

Fax: (201) 692-7319 — **Email: globaleducation@fdu.edu**

Full-time: 995 men, 1334 women
Part-time: 566 men, 555 women
Graduate: 1073 men, 1688 women
Year: semesters, summer session
Room & Board: $13,086
Faculty: n/av
Ph.D.s: n/av
Student/Faculty: n/av
Tuition: $39,306
Freshman Class: 4095 applied, 3146 accepted, 545 enrolled
SAT CR/M/W: 510/530/500 **ACT:** required
CEEB CODE: 2263
Application Deadline: open
COMPETITIVE

Farleigh Dickinson University/Metropolitan Campus, founded in 1942, is an independent university offering undergraduate and graduate degrees in business, arts and sciences, professional studies, public administration, and hotel, restaurant, and tourism management. There are 3 undergraduate schools and 3 graduate schools. In addition to regional accreditation, Metropolitan Campus has baccalaureate program accreditation with AACSB, ABET, JR, and ABA. The 92-acre campus is in a suburban area 13 miles from midtown Manhattan, New York City. Including any residence halls, there are 55 buildings.

STUDENT LIFE: 86% of undergraduates are from New Jersey. Others are from 25 states, 64 foreign countries, and Canada. 7% are Foreign; 5% Asian American; 35% Hispanic; 25% White; 16% race unknown; 11% African American. **Female To Male Ratio:** 1.4:1. The average age of freshmen is 18; all undergraduates, 26. 27% do not continue beyond their first year; 40% remain to graduate. **Housing:** 982 students can be accommodated in college housing, which includes dorms, honors houses, special-interest houses, and theme housing. On-campus housing is available on a first-come, first-served basis, and is available on a lottery system for upperclassmen. 58% of students commute. Alcohol is not permitted. All students may keep cars.

FACULTY/CLASSROOMS: No introductory courses are taught by graduate students.

PROGRAMS OF STUDY: Metropolitan Campus confers B.A., B.S., B.S.Civ.E.T., B.S.C.L.S., B.S.Con.E.T., B.S.E.E., B.S.E.E.T., B.S.M.E.T., and B.S.N. degrees. Associate, master's, and doctoral degrees are also awarded. Bachelor's degrees are awarded in BIOLOGICAL SCIENCE (biochemistry, biology/biological science, and marine biology), BUSINESS (accounting, business administration and management, business economics, entrepreneurial studies, hotel/motel and restaurant management, and marketing/retailing/merchandising), COMMUNICATIONS AND THE ARTS (communications, English literature, and fine arts), COMPUTER AND PHYSICAL SCIENCE (chemistry, computer science, information sciences and systems, mathematics, radiological technology, and science), ENGINEERING AND ENVIRONMENTAL DESIGN (civil engineering technology, construction engineering, electrical/electronics engineering, electrical/electronics engineering technology, and mechanical engineering technology), HEALTH PROFESSIONS (allied health, clinical science, medical laboratory technology, nursing, and physical therapy), SOCIAL SCIENCE (criminal justice, economics, history, humanities, interdisciplinary studies, international studies, liberal arts/general studies, philosophy, political science/government, psychology, and Spanish studies). Nursing, psychology, and business management have the largest enrollments.

ACTIVITIES: 1% of men belong to 5 national fraternities; 1% of women belong to 7 national sororities. There are 72 groups on campus, including cheerleading, chorus, computers, dance, drama, environmental, ethnic, film, honors, international, LGBT, literary magazine, newspaper, pep band, photography, political, professional, radio and TV, religious, social, social service, and student government. Popular campus events include Welcome Back Week, Spring Fest, and Dances. **Sports:** There are 7 intercollegiate sports for men and 10 for women, and 7 intramural sports for men and 7 for women. Facilities include a 6-lane, 200-meter track, basketball courts, volleyball courts, racquetball courts, a weight room, outdoor tennis courts, a baseball field and soccer field, a training room, softball field, fitness center with aerobics room, selectorized weight room, and cardio room. **Graduates:** From July 1, 2016 to June 30, 2017, 940 bachelor's degrees were awarded. The most popular majors were liberal arts/general studies (44%), business/marketing (12%), and psycholgy (8%). In an average class, 21% graduate in 4 years or less, 37% graduate in 5 years or less, and 40% graduate in 6 years or less.

SERVICES: Counseling and information services are available, as is tutoring in every subject. There is a reader service for the blind, and remedial math, reading, and writing. Workshops offer assistance with academic study skills, time management, and advanced reading and writing. Support services for basic skills students and freshmen students are available. There is also a Regional Center for college students with learning disabilities that offers comprehensive support. **Library/Resources:** The library contains 196,703 volumes, 103,808 microform items, and 1,311 audio/video tapes/CDs/DVDs, and subscribes to 1,601 periodicals including electronic. Computerized library services include interlibrary loans, database searching, and Internet access. Special learning facilities include an art gallery, radio station, computer labs, ITV multimedia classrooms, photonics lab, a theater, art galleries, web-lab, and cyber crime lab. **Physically Challenged Students:** 41% of the campus is accessible. Facilities include wheelchair ramps, elevators, special parking, specially equipped restrooms, special class scheduling, lowered drinking fountains, lowered telephones, special housing, and oral interpretation for the hearing impaired. **Special:** FDU offers co-op programs in most majors, cross-registration, internships, and study abroad in England and Vancouver. A Washington semester, work-study, accelerated degrees, and student-designed majors in the humanities and general studies are possible. A 7-year medical program is available with Karol Marcinkowski School of Medicine in Poland, as is an accelerated chiropractic program with New York Chiropractic College and Logan Chiropractic College (B.S., B.A./M.A.T.). There are 12 national honor societies, a freshman honors program, and 16 departmental honors programs. **Visiting:** There are regularly scheduled orientations for prospective students, including standardized placement testing, faculty advisement, class registration, and educational and social activities to prepare students for entrance. There are guides for informal visits, visitors may sit in on classes, and stay overnight. To schedule a visit, contact the Admissions Office. **Campus Safety and Security:** Measures include 24-hour foot and vehicle patrol, emergency notification system, self-defense education, and security escort services. There are emergency telephones and lighted pathways/sidewalks.

REQUIREMENTS: The SAT or ACT is required. Applicants should be graduates of an accredited high school or have a GED certificate. They should have completed a minimum of 16 academic units, (recommended 18 units) including 4 in English, 3 in math, 2 each in history, foreign language, and lab science (3 are recommended), and 3-4 in academic electives. Those students applying to science, engineering, and health sciences programs must meet additional requirements. An interview may be required. AP and CLEP credits are accepted. Important factors in the admissions decision are leadership record, recommendations by school officials, and extracurricular activities record. To graduate, students must complete 120 to 128 credits, including 30 to 44 in the major, with an overall minimum 2.0. GPA. Students must complete a 4-semester interdisciplinary sequence and 1 course in freshman seminar. The core curriculum includes 6 credits in English, 12 in university core, and 3 each in math and computer science. **Procedure:** Freshmen are admitted to all sessions. Entrance exams should be taken by May of the junior year. There are deferred admissions and rolling admissions plans. Check with the school for current application deadlines. The fall 2017 application fee was $40. Notification is sent on a rolling basis. Applications are accepted on-line. **Transfer Students:** 364 transfer students enrolled in 2016-2017. All applicants must submit official transcripts for all college work taken. Those students with fewer than 24 credits must also submit a high school transcript or a copy of their state department of education's equivalency score and SAT scores. 32 of 128 credits required for the bachelor's degree must be completed at Metropolitan Campus. **International Students:** There are 243 international students enrolled. They must take the TOEFL with a minimum score of 550 on the paper-based TOEFL (PBT) or 79 on the Internet-based version (iBT), or take the IELTS. The ACT or SAT is highly recommended.

ADMISSIONS: 77% of the 2017-2018 applicants were accepted. The SAT scores for the 2017-2018 freshman class were: Critical Reading-- 42% below 500, 46% between 500 and 599, and 11% between 600 and 699. Math-- 30% below 500, 52% between 500 and 599, and 16% between 600 and 699. Writing-- 43% below 500, 49% between 500 and 599, and 8% between 600 and 699. 30% of the current freshmen were in the top fifth of their class; 62% were in the top two fifths. 1 freshman graduated first in the class. **Admissions Contact:** Jonathan Wexler, Associate Vice President of Enrollment Management. Email: *globaleducation@fdu.edu* Web: *www.fdu.edu*

FINANCIAL AID: Check with the school for current application deadlines.

FELICIAN UNIVERSITY *(The complete profile is made available exclusively on our website, www.barronspac.com)*

GEORGIAN COURT UNIVERSITY *(The complete profile is made available exclusively on our website, www.barronspac.com)*

KEAN UNIVERSITY — D-2
www.kean.edu

Union, NJ 07083 — **(908) 737-7100**

Fax: (908) 737-7105	**Email: admitme@kean.edu**
Full-time: 3901 men, 5615 women	**Faculty:** IIA, +$
Part-time: 923 men, 1545 women	**Ph.D.s:** 81%
Graduate: 493 men, 1749 women	**Student/Faculty:** n/av
Year: semesters, summer session	**Tuition:** $12,107 ($19,009)
Room & Board: $13,513	**Freshman Class:** 8851 applied, 7277 accepted, 1784 enrolled
SAT CR/M: 526/520 **ACT:** 22	**CEEB CODE:** 2517
Application Deadline: April 30	**COMPETITIVE**

Kean University is a public university serving undergraduate and graduate students in the liberal arts, the sciences, and the professions. There are campuses in Toms River, New Jersey, and Wenzhou China. There are 5 undergraduate schools and 1 graduate school. In addition to regional accreditation, KU has baccalaureate program accreditation with ABET, NASAD, NASM, NLN, NAST, CIDA, CAATE, and CAHIIM. The 185-acre campus is in a suburban area Union, NJ. Including any residence halls, there are 42 buildings.

STUDENT LIFE: 98% of undergraduates are from New Jersey. Others are from 21 states, 43 foreign countries, and Canada. 8% are race unknown; 5% Asian American; 34% White; 3% Foreign; 28% Hispanic; 2% two or more races; 19% African American. **Female To Male Ratio:** 1.7:1. The average age of freshmen is 18; all undergraduates, 23. 24% do not continue beyond their first year; 49% remain to graduate. **Housing:** 1995 students can be accommodated in college housing, which includes gender neutral, coed dorms, and on-campus apartments. In addition, there are special-interest houses, freshman housing, a floor for women-only, transfer and graduate students dorms, living learning communies for SIMS (success in math and science), GREEN (environment, exercise and nutrition) and WELL (women empowered for leadership and learning). On-campus housing is available on a first-come, first-served basis. 84% of students commute. Alcohol is not permitted. Upperclassmen may keep cars.

FACULTY/CLASSROOMS: 45% of faculty are male; 55% are female. No introductory courses are taught by graduate students. The average class size in a regular course is 21.

PROGRAMS OF STUDY: KU confers B.A., B.S., BFA, BID, B.M. and BSN degrees. Master's and doctoral degrees are also awarded. Bachelor's degrees are awarded in BIOLOGICAL SCIENCE (biology/biological science), BUSINESS (accounting, finance, international business management, management science, marketing management, recreational facilities management, and sustainable management), COMMUNICATIONS AND THE ARTS (communications, English, fine arts, fine/studio arts, general, fine arts education, industrial design, information technology, music, music performance, performing arts, Spanish, studio art, theatre arts, theater design, theatre education, and visual and performing arts), COMPUTER AND PHYSICAL SCIENCE (chemistry, computer science, earth science, mathematics, and science and technology studies), EDUCATION (athletic training, early childhood education, elementary education, health information management, middle school education, music education, physical education, secondary education, and special education), ENGINEERING AND ENVIRONMENTAL DESIGN (architecture and interior design), HEALTH PROFESSIONS (medical technology, nursing, and speech pathology/audiology), SOCIAL SCIENCE (Asian/Oriental studies, criminal justice, economics, history, political science/government, psychology, psychology and psychiatric rehabilitation, public administration, and sociology). Speech-language-hearing sciences, design, history, and global business are the strongest academically. Psychology, biology and management science have the largest enrollments.

ACTIVITIES: There are 157 groups on campus, including art, band, choir, chorale, chorus, communications, computers, dance, drama, environmental, ethnic, film, forensics, honors, international, jazz band, LGBT, literary magazine, musical theater, newspaper, orchestra, pep band, photography, political, professional, radio and TV, religious, social, social service, student government, symphony, and yearbook. Popular campus events include Homecoming, Kean Day, Comedy Show, Unity Week, Concerts, Meet the Greeks, Food Bank Luncheon, Student Group Expo, Martin Luther King Jr. Week of Service, Black History Month, Latin Festival Month, Chinese New Year Celebration, and Creolefest. **Sports:** There are 6 intercollegiate sports for men and 8 for women, and 6 intramural sports for men and 6 for women. Facilities include a stadium, 8-lane track, soccer stadium, baseball stadium, softball stadium, practice fields, an arena, indoor basketball courts, outdoor basketball courts, outdoor tennis courts, indoor swimming pool, fitness rooms and pool tables. **Graduates:** From July 1, 2016 to June 30, 2017, 2624 bachelor's degrees were awarded. The most popular majors were psychology (17%), management science (8%), and biology (6%). In an average class, 22% graduate in 4 years or less, 42% graduate in 5 years or less, and 49% graduate in 6 years or less.

SERVICES: Counseling and information services are available, as is tutoring in most subjects. There is remedial math, reading, and writing. **Library/Resources:** The library contains 208,670 volumes, and subscribes to 58,034 periodicals including electronic. Computerized library services include interlibrary loans, database searching, Internet access, and Wi-Fi capability. Special learning facilities include an art gallery, planetarium, radio station, TV station, a center for science, technology, and mathematics, the Holocaust Resource Center, Wynona Moore Lipman Ethnic Studies Center, Liberty Hall Museum, and Human Rights Institute, and New Jersey Highlands. **Physically Challenged Students:** All of the campus is accessible. Facilities include wheelchair ramps, elevators, special parking, specially equipped restrooms, special class scheduling, lowered drinking fountains, and special housing. **Special:** At Kean University, titles of the co-op experience vary; they may be designated as internships, apprenticeships, or co-op education such as criminal justice, design, marketing, management, finance, and recreation and health information management. Dual Majors in English, B.A.: Dual Certification/Teacher of Students with Disabilities, P-12 Option, Mathematical Sciences, and Biology. The Center for International Studies and Programs encourage students to study abroad in over one hundred top universities in over 50 countries, allowing them to grow intellectually, develop intercultural communication skills, and improve foreign language skills. The Federal Work-Study Program (FWS) provides part-time employment to students with financial need (as determined by the FAFSA), their earnings are intended to help meet their costs of education, and all positions are part-time with a maximum of 20 hours per week. There are 28 national honor societies and 2 departmental honors programs. **Visiting:** There are regularly scheduled orientations for prospective students. Kean hosts a variety of events for prospective students, ranging from student for a day and open house includes information sessions and campus tours. To schedule a visit, contact the Center for Academic Success Office. **Campus Safety and Security:** Measures include 24-hour foot and vehicle patrol, emergency notification system, self-defense education, and security escort services. There are shuttle buses, emergency telephones, lighted pathways/sidewalks, controlled access to dorms/residences, all residence halls have surveillance cameras, lounges, elevators and exit doors, and all residence halls have fire sprinkler systems.

REQUIREMENTS: The SAT or ACT is required. Applicants must be graduates of accredited secondary schools or have earned a GED. College preparatory study includes 4 courses in English, 3 in math, 2 each in lab science and history, and 5 in academic electives. An official transcript and SAT/ACT scores are required. An essay and 2 letters of recommendation are recommended, but not required. AP and CLEP credits are accepted. Important factors in the admissions decision are advanced placement or honors courses, recommendations by school officials, and extracurricular activities record. Kean's GE Program has three major components: the Foundation Requirements (13 credits), the Disciplinary/ Interdisciplinary Distribution Requirements (typically 30 – 32 credits for B.A. degree programs and 19 credits for B.S., B.M., B.F.A., and B.I.D. degrees), and the Capstone (3 credits). No course taken to fulfill a GE requirement may be taken on a pass/fail basis. The minimum number of total credits for a bachelor's degree is 120 and the minimum grade point average is 2.0. **Procedure:** Freshmen are admitted in the fall and spring. Entrance exams should be taken April-June of the junior year or October-January of the senior year. There are early admissions, deferred admissions, and rolling admissions plans. Applications should be filed by April 30 for fall entry; December 15 for spring entry; and April 1 for summer entry. The fall 2017 application fee was $75. Notifications are sent November 1. Applications are accepted on-line. **Transfer Students:** 1442 transfer students enrolled in 2016-2017. NACES evaluation of transcripts for any foreign institution attended. The minimum number of credits to transfer with a 2.0 is 30. Between 15-30 credit (semester) hours students must have a 3.0 GPA. 32 of 120 credits required for the bachelor's degree must be completed at Kean. **International Students:** There are 273 international students enrolled. They must take the TOEFL with a minimum score of 550 on the paper-based TOEFL (PBT) or 79 on the Internet-based version (iBT). Students must also take IELTS. The SAT or ACT is required for the majority of applicants.

ADMISSIONS: 82% of the 2017-2018 applicants were accepted. **Admissions Contact:** Director of Admissions. Email: *admitme@kean.edu* Web: *www.kean.edu*

FINANCIAL AID: In 2017-2018, 89% of all full-time freshmen received some form of financial aid. 86% of all full-time freshmen received need-based aid. The average freshman award was $10,551. Need-based scholarships or need-based grants averaged $9,356; need-based self-help aid (loans and jobs) averaged $3,540; and other non-need-based awards and non-need-based scholarships averaged $2,464. 8% of undergraduate students work part-time. The average financial indebtedness of the 2017 graduate was $32,277. The FAFSA code is 002622. The priority date for freshman financial aid applications for fall entry is April 15.

MONMOUTH UNIVERSITY E-3

www.monmouth.edu

West Long Branch, NJ 07764 (732) 571-3456 (800) 543-9671

Fax: (732) 263-5166 **Email:** admission@monmouth.edu

Full-time: 1888 men, 2614 women	**Faculty:** 253; IIA, +$
Part-time: 90 men, 114 women	**Ph.D.s:** 80%
Graduate: 371 men, 1263 women	**Student/Faculty:** 18 to 1
Year: semesters, summer session	**Tuition:** $36,733
Room & Board: $13,451	**Freshman Class:** 9261 applied, 6848 accepted, 1083 enrolled
SAT EBR-W/M: 496/520 **ACT:** 23	**CEEB CODE:** 2416
Application Deadline: March 1	**COMPETITIVE**

Monmouth University, founded in 1933, is a leading private institution that offers a comprehensive array of undergraduate and graduate degree programs. The University provides students with a highly personalized education that builds the knowledge and confidence of tomorrow's leaders. There are 7 undergraduate schools and 1 graduate school. In addition to regional accreditation, MU has baccalaureate program accreditation with AACSB, ABET, CSWE, NCATE, NLN, ACS, CCNE, and CACREP. The 159-acre campus is in a suburban area 55 miles from New York City, and 75 miles from Philadelphia. Including any residence halls, there are 55 buildings.

STUDENT LIFE: 83% of undergraduates are from New Jersey. Others are from 32 states, 22 foreign countries, and Canada. 84% are from public schools. 71% are White; 5% African American; 4% race unknown; 3% Asian American; 2% two or more races; 13% Hispanic; 1% Foreign. **Female To Male Ratio:** 1.7:1. The average age of freshmen is 18.5; all undergraduates, 20.5. 21% do not continue beyond their first year; 79% remain to graduate. **Housing:** 2092 students can be accommodated in college housing, which includes dorms, on-campus apartments, off-campus apartments, and honors houses. On-campus housing is available on a first-come, first-served basis, and is available on a lottery system for upperclassmen. 57% of students commute. All students may keep cars.

FACULTY/CLASSROOMS: 49% of faculty are male; 51% are female. 91% teach undergraduates, 61% do research, and 56% do both. No introductory courses are taught by graduate students. The average class size in an introductory lecture is 22; in a laboratory is 14; and in a regular course is 22.

PROGRAMS OF STUDY: MU confers B.A., B.S., B.F.A., B.S.N., and B.S.W. degrees. Associate, master's, and doctoral degrees are also awarded. Bachelor's degrees are awarded in BIOLOGICAL SCIENCE (biology/biological science and marine biology), BUSINESS (accounting, banking and finance, business administration and management, business administration - international, business administration marketing, business economics, international business management, marketing management, and real estate), COMMUNICATIONS AND THE ARTS (art, art history and appreciation, communications, English, graphic design, modern language, music, music business management, music industry, and Spanish), COMPUTER AND PHYSICAL SCIENCE (chemistry, clinical laboratory science, chemistry education, computer science, mathematics, and software engineering), EDUCATION (art education, early childhood education, education, elementary education, English education, foreign languages education, health education, mathematics education, music education, physical education, science education, secondary education, social studies education, social studies secondary school education, Spanish education K-12, and special education), ENGINEERING AND ENVIRONMENTAL DESIGN (computer graphics), HEALTH PROFESSIONS (medical laboratory science, medical laboratory technology, nursing, and premedicine), SOCIAL SCIENCE (anthropology, criminal justice, history, homeland security, legal studies, political science/government, prelaw, psychology, social work, and sociology). Business, education, and communication have the largest enrollments.

ACTIVITIES: 14% of men belong to 6 national fraternities; 18% of women belong to 10 national sororities. There are 109 groups on campus, including mock trial, veterans club, art, band, cheerleading, choir, chorus, computers, dance, debate, drama, environmental, ethnic, honors, international, jazz band, LGBT, literary magazine, musical theater, newspaper, pep band, photography, political, professional, radio and TV, religious, social, social service, student activities board, student government, and yearbook. Popular campus events include The Big Event, Springfest, Welcome Week, Greek Week, Winter Ball, and Haunted Tours. **Sports:** There are 16 intercollegiate sports for men and 17 for women, and 15 intramural sports for men and 12 for women. Facilities include an arena, 200 meter 6-lane indoor track, an indoor practice facility with basketball courts, a football field, soccer field, outdoor tennis courts, an all-weather track, an indoor pool, exercise and weight facility, a varsity athletics weight room, baseball, softball, and field hockey fields. **Graduates:** From July 1, 2016 to June 30, 2017, 1107 bachelor's degrees were awarded. The most popular majors were business (29%), communication (12%), and health sciences (6%). In an average class, 57% graduate in 4 years or less, 69% graduate in 5 years or less, and 70% graduate in 6 years or less. Of the 2016 graduating class, 42% were enrolled in graduate school within 6 months of graduation, and 65% were employed.

SERVICES: Counseling and information services are available, as is tutoring in every subject. There is a reader service for the blind, and remedial math, reading, and writing. **Library/Resources:** The library contains 363,482 volumes, 985 microform items, and 1,184 audio/video tapes/CDs/DVDs, and subscribes to 80,088 periodicals including electronic. Computerized library services include interlibrary loans, database searching, Internet access, and Wi-Fi capability. Special learning facilities include an art gallery, radio station, TV station, including a theater, financial markets lab, a greenhouse, and a community garden. **Physically Challenged Students:** 95% of the campus is accessible. Facilities include wheelchair ramps, elevators, special parking, specially equipped restrooms, special class scheduling, lowered drinking fountains, special housing. Academic assistance provided within the classroom. **Special:** Students may study abroad in England, Australia, Italy, and Spain. Experiential learning is a graduation requirement. There are cooperative and internship programs and a Washington semester. Five Year Baccalaureate/Mater's Programs in many academice areas. Monmouth also offers student-designed majors, dual major in history/political science, flexible studies programs, and credit for life experience. There are 24 national honor societies and a freshman honors program. **Visiting:** There are regularly scheduled orientations for prospective students, including a tour of the campus. There are guides for informal visits and visitors may sit in on classes. To schedule a visit, contact the Admission Office. **Campus Safety and Security:** Measures include 24-hour foot and vehicle patrol, emergency notification system, self-defense education, and security escort services. There are emergency telephones, lighted pathways/sidewalks, and controlled access to dorms/residences.

REQUIREMENTS: The SAT or ACT and the ACT Optional Writing test are required. Applicants must be graduates of accredited secondary schools or have earned a GED. The university requires 16 Carnegie units, based on 4 years of English, 3 of math, and 2 each of social studies/history, and science, with the remaining 5 units in academic electives. An essay and a letter of recommendation are required. AP and CLEP credits are accepted. Important factors in the admissions decision are advanced placement or honors courses, extracurricular activities record, and leadership record. To graduate, students must earn at least 128 credits, including 30 to 81 in a major, with a minimum GPA of 2.0 overall and 2.1 in the major. Education majors are required to have a cumulative GPA of 3.0. **Procedure:** Freshmen are admitted in the fall and spring. Entrance exams should be taken by December of the senior year. There is a deferred admissions plan. Applications should be filed by March 1 for fall entry; January 1 for spring entry. The fall 2017 application fee was $50. Notifications are sent April 1. 3320 early decision candidates were accepted for the 2017-2018 class. Applications are accepted online. **Transfer Students:** 400 transfer students enrolled in 2016-2017. Transfer applicants with fewer than 24 transferable college credits must provide a high school transcript and SAT or ACT scores. All transfer applicants must submit official college transcripts for all institutions attended. A 2.25 minimum college GPA is required for general admission consideration, does not guarantee acceptance. For education majors, a minimum cumulative GPA of 3.0 is required. 32 of 128 credits required for the bachelor's degree must be completed at MU. **International Students:** There are 42 international students enrolled. They must take the TOEFL with a minimum score of 550 on the paper-based TOEFL (PBT) or 79 on the Internet-based version (iBT) or take the MELAB, and must also take the IELTS, or the Cambridge ESOL (CAE), SAT or ACT, scoring varies by student profile.

ADMISSIONS: 74% of the 2017-2018 applicants were accepted. The SAT scores for the 2017-2018 freshman class were: Math-- 35% below 500, 52% between 500 and 599, and 13% between 600 and 699. Evidence-Based Reading/Writing-- 50% below 500, 42% between 500 and 599, and 8% between 600 and 699. The ACT scores were 1% between 12 and 17, 60% between 18 and 23, 36% between 24 and 29, and 3% above 30. 30% of the current freshmen were in the top fifth of their class; 63% were in the top two fifths. **Admissions Contact:** Victoria Bobik, Director of Undergraduate Admission. Email: *admission@monmouth.edu* Web: *www.monmouth.edu*

FINANCIAL AID: In 2017-2018, 99% of all full-time freshmen received some form of financial aid. 79% of all full-time freshmen received need-based aid. The average freshman award was $28,429. Need-based scholarships or need-based grants averaged $14,099 ($25,706 maximum); need-based self-help aid (loans and jobs) averaged $4,859 ($5,500 maximum); non-need-based athletic scholarships averaged $24,654 ($54,860 maximum); and other non-need-based awards and non-need-based scholarships averaged $11,854 ($17,500 maximum). 25% of undergraduate students work part-time. The average financial indebtedness of the 2017 graduate was $30,985. The state aid form is required. The FAFSA code is 002616. Check with the school for current application deadlines.

MONTCLAIR STATE UNIVERSITY E-2

www.montclair.edu

Montclair, NJ 07042 (973) 655-4444 (800) 331-9205

Fax: (973) 655-7700 **Email: msuadm@mail.montclair.edu**

Full-time: 5790 men, 9154 women	**Faculty:** 636; I, av$
Part-time: 790 men, 1118 women	**Ph.D.s:** 94%
Graduate: 1172 men, 2989 women	**Student/Faculty:** 17 to 1
Year: semesters, summer session	**Tuition:** $12,455 ($20,567)
Room & Board: $14,458	**Freshman Class:** n/av
SAT CR/M: 541/530	**CEEB CODE:** 2520
Application Deadline: March 1	**COMPETITIVE**

Montclair State University, established in 1908, is a public institution offering programs in liberal arts and sciences, business administration, fine and performing arts, and professional studies. There are 5 undergraduate schools and 1 graduate school. In addition to regional accreditation, MSU has baccalaureate program accreditation with AACSB, ABET, ADA, NASAD, NASM, NRPA, NASD, NAST, CAA/ASHA, CAATE, CACREP, and CEPH. The 275-acre campus is in a suburban area 14 miles west of New York City. Including any residence halls, there are 66 buildings.

STUDENT LIFE: 97% of undergraduates are from New Jersey. Others are from 39 states, 66 foreign countries, and Canada. 7% are race unknown; 6% Asian American; 41% White; 3% two or more races; 28% Hispanic; 2% Foreign; 13% African American. **Female To Male Ratio:** 1.7:1. The average age of freshmen is 19; all undergraduates, 22. 18% do not continue beyond their first year; 65% remain to graduate. **Housing:** 5165 students can be accommodated in college housing, which includes married student dorms and on-campus apartments. In addition, there are honors houses, special-interest houses, theme housing, and living learning communities. On-campus housing is available on a first-come and first-served basis. 70% of students commute. Alcohol is not permitted. Upperclassmen may keep cars.

FACULTY/CLASSROOMS: 48% of faculty are male; 52% are female. All teach undergraduates. No introductory courses are taught by graduate students. The average class size in an introductory lecture is 26; in a laboratory is 16; and in a regular course is 25.

PROGRAMS OF STUDY: MSU confers B.A., B.S., B.F.A., B.S./M.S., B.S./M.A.T., and B.Mus. degrees. Master's and doctoral degrees are also awarded. Bachelor's degrees are awarded in BIOLOGICAL SCIENCE (biochemistry, biology/biological science, marine biology, and molecular biology), BUSINESS (accounting, business administration and management, and hospitality management services), COMMUNICATIONS AND THE ARTS (animation, Arabic, classics, communications technology, dance, English, film arts, fine/studio arts, general, French, German, graphic design, industrial design, information technology, Italian, journalism, Latin, linguistics, music, musical theater, public relations, Spanish, theatre acting, television & digital media production, theatre arts, and theatre studies), COMPUTER AND PHYSICAL SCIENCE (chemistry, computer science, mathematics, physics, science and technology studies, and sustainable energy science), EDUCATION (athletic training, dance education, health education, and physical education), ENGINEERING AND ENVIRONMENTAL DESIGN (environmental science), HEALTH PROFESSIONS (music therapy, nursing, nutrition and dietetics, and public health), SOCIAL SCIENCE (anthropology, child care/child and family studies, communication sciences & disorders, criminal justice, economics, family/consumer studies, fashion design and technology, gender studies, geography, history, humanities, justice and society, legal studies, philosophy, political science/government, psychology, religious studies, and sociology). Business administration, psychology, and biology have the largest enrollments.

ACTIVITIES: There are 160 groups on campus, including band, cheerleading, choir, chorus, dance, drama, environmental, ethnic, film, honors, international, jazz band, LGBT, literary magazine, marching band, musical theater, newspaper, orchestra, pep band, political, professional, radio and TV, religious, social, social service, student government, symphony, and yearbook. Popular campus events include Fall Frenzy, Homecoming, Greek Week, and World's Fair. **Sports:** There are 8 intercollegiate sports for men and 10 for women, and 18 intramural sports for men and 18 for women. Facilities include a pool, a competition gymnasium, auxiliary gymnasium, athletic training facility, a stadium, field hockey, football, lacrosse, soccer, baseball stadium, softball stadium, and a 8 lane track.**Graduates:** From July 1, 2016 to June 30, 2017, 3399 bachelor's degrees were awarded. The most popular majors were business administration (16%), psychology (12%), and family and child studies (8%). In an average class, 1% graduate in 3 years or less, 40% graduate in 4 years or less, 61% graduate in 5 years or less, and 65% graduate in 6 years or less.

SERVICES: Counseling and information services are available, as is tutoring in most subjects. There is a reader service for the blind, and remedial math, reading, and writing. **Library/Resources:** The library contains 543,819 volumes, 1.2 million microform items, 25,173 audio/video tapes/CDs/DVDs, and subscribes to 2,613 periodicals, including electronic. Computerized library services include interlibrary loans, database searching, Internet access, and Wi-Fi capability. Special learning facilities include an art gallery, radio station, and TV station. **Physically Challenged Students:** 90% of the campus is accessible. Facilities include wheelchair ramps, elevators, special parking, specially equipped restrooms, special class scheduling, lowered drinking fountains, lowered telephones, special housing, curb cuts, speaker phones, special building signs, TDDs, and priority registration. There is a disability resource center on campus. **Special:** Internships, co-op programs in all majors, credit by exam, pass/fail options, work-study, independent study, and study abroad in 51 countries are offered. Joint-degree programs are offered in practical anthropology and applied economics, and a 5-year B.A.-B.Mus. program in music is available, as is an articulated medical, dental, physical therapy, and physician assistant program with the University of Medicine and Dentistry of New Jersey and an articulated program leading to a Pharm.D. with Rutgers University. There are 28 national honor societies, a freshman honors program, and 3 departmental honors programs. **Visiting:** There are regularly scheduled orientations for prospective students, students engage in activities, registration, policies and procedures, connecting in and out of the classroom, and obtain an MSU. There are guides for informal visits, visitors may sit in on classes, and stay overnight. To schedule a visit, contact Neris Fleming, Coordinator,Special Engagement at flemingne@montclair.edu. **Campus Safety and Security:** Measures include 24-hour foot and vehicle patrol, emergency notification system, self-defense education, and security escort services. There are shuttle buses, emergency telephones, lighted pathways/sidewalks, controlled access to dorms/residences, and a full-time campus police force.

REQUIREMENTS: Applicants must submit 16 Carnegie units, 4 in English, 3 to 4 in math (including algebra I and II and geometry), 2 each in lab science, social studies, and a foreign language, and 3 in academic electives. The GED is accepted. A portfolio, audition, or interview is required for students planning to major in fine arts, music, speech, or theater. Admission to computer science requires 4 years of math, including trigonometry. AP and CLEP credits are accepted. Important factors in the admissions decision are advanced placement or honors courses, recommendations by school officials, and leadership record. Students must successfully complete a minimum of 120 semester hours, with 33 to 82 in the major, while maintaining a minimum GPA of 2.0. General education requirements include courses in communications, contemporary issues, art appreciation, a foreign language, humanities, math, natural/physical science, social sciences, and multicultural awareness, as well as 1 semester hour in phys ed and 3 semester hours in computer science. **Procedure:** Freshmen are admitted in the fall and spring. Entrance exams should be taken during the students senior year. There is a rolling admissions plan. Applications should be filed by March 1 for fall entry; November 1 for spring entry. The fall 2017 application fee was $65. Notification is sent on a rolling basis. Applications are accepted on-line. **Transfer Students:** 1528 transfer students enrolled in 2016-2017. Applicants must have completed a minimum of 15 credits from an accredited college. A cumulative GPA of 2.5 is required for most majors, with higher required in select programs. Applicants must have completed English composition. High school and college transcripts are required. 32 of 128 credits required for the bachelor's degree must be completed at MSU. **International Students:** There are 277 international students enrolled. They must take the TOEFL with a minimum score of 80 on the Internet-based version (iBT). They must also take the SAT.

ADMISSIONS: The SAT scores for the 2017-2018 freshman class were: Critical Reading-- 25% below 500, 55% between 500 and 599, 19% between 600 and 699, and 1% between 700 and 800. Math-- 27% below 500, 56% between 500 and 599, 16% between 600 and 699, and 1% between 700 and 800. 24% of the current freshmen were in the top fifth of their class; 61% were in the top two fifths. **Admissions Contact:** Jeffrey Indivieri-Grant, Director of Admissions. Email: *msuadm@mail.montclair.edu* Web: *www.montclair.edu*

FINANCIAL AID: In 2017-2018, 77% of all full-time freshmen received some form of financial aid. 68% of all full-time freshmen received need-based aid. The average freshman award was $9,164. Need-based scholarships or need-based grants averaged $9,457 ($17,821 maximum); need-based self-help aid (loans and jobs) averaged $5,910 ($7,000 maximum); and other non-need-based awards and non-need-based scholarships averaged $3,175 ($6,000 maximum). 12% of undergraduate students work part-time. The FAFSA code is 002617. The priority date for freshman financial aid applications for fall entry is February 1.

NEW JERSEY CITY UNIVERSITY *(The complete profile is made available exclusively on our website, www.barronspac.com)*

NEW JERSEY INSTITUTE OF TECHNOLOGY E-2

www.njit.edu

Newark, NJ 07102 (973) 596-3300

Fax: (973) 596-3461 Email: admissions@njit.edu

Full-time: 4883 men, 1497 women
Part-time: 1407 men, 696 women
Graduate: 2077 men, 886 women
Year: semesters, summer session
Room & Board: $13,300

SAT EBR-W/M: 627/659 **ACT:** 27
Application Deadline: March 1

Faculty: 439; I, +$
Ph.D.s: 92%
Student/Faculty: 17 to 1
Tuition: $16,898 ($31,918)
Freshman Class: 7254 applied, 4453 accepted, 1114 enrolled
CEEB CODE: 2513
HIGHLY COMPETITIVE

New Jersey Institute of Technology is a public research university providing instruction, research, and public service in engineering, computer science, management, architecture, digital design, industrial design, interior design, engineering technology, applied sciences, and related fields. There are 6 undergraduate schools and 1 graduate school. In addition to regional accreditation, NJIT has baccalaureate program accreditation with AACSB, ABET, NAAB, NASAD, and CIDA. The 45-acre campus is in an urban area 10 miles west of New York City. Including any residence halls, there are 27 buildings.

STUDENT LIFE: 95% of undergraduates are from New Jersey. Others are from 39 states, 78 foreign countries, and Canada. 80% are from public schools. 8% are African American; 5% Foreign; 32% White; 3% two or more races; 21% Asian American; 20% Hispanic; 12% race unknown. 33% are Muslim, Hindu, Buddhist, unknown; 22% Catholic; 20% claim no religious affiliation; 13% Protestant. **Male To Female Ratio:** 2.7:1. The average age of freshmen is 18; all undergraduates, 22. 12% do not continue beyond their first year; 36% remain to graduate. **Housing:** 1663 students can be accommodated in college housing, which includes dorms. On-campus housing is available on a first-come, first-served basis, and is available on a lottery system for upperclassmen. 76% of students commute. All students may keep cars.

FACULTY/CLASSROOMS: 82% of faculty are male; 18% are female. All teach undergraduates. Graduate students teach 10% of introductory courses. The average class size in an introductory lecture is 30; in a laboratory is 27; and in a regular course is 25.

PROGRAMS OF STUDY: NJIT confers B.A., B.S., and B.Arch. degrees. Master's and doctoral degrees are also awarded. Bachelor's degrees are awarded in BIOLOGICAL SCIENCE (biology/biological science), BUSINESS (management science), COMMUNICATIONS AND THE ARTS (communications and technical and business writing), COMPUTER AND PHYSICAL SCIENCE (applied mathematics, applied physics, chemistry, computer management, computer science, information sciences and systems, and mathematics), ENGINEERING AND ENVIRONMENTAL DESIGN (architecture, biomedical engineering, chemical engineering, civil engineering, computer engineering, computer technology, electrical/electronics engineering, engineering and applied science, engineering technology, environmental engineering, environmental science, geophysical engineering, industrial engineering, manufacturing engineering, mechanical engineering, technological management, and technology and public affairs), SOCIAL SCIENCE (history). Engineering, computer science, and architecture are the strongest academically. Computer science, mechanical engineering, and computer engineering have the largest enrollments.

ACTIVITIES: 6% of men belong to 18 local fraternities; 6% of women belong to 6 local sororities. There are 92 groups on campus, including art, band, chess, computers, dance, drama, drum and bugle corps, ethnic, honors, international, LGBT, marching band, musical theater, newspaper, photography, professional, religious, social, social service, student government, and yearbook. Popular campus events include Miniversity, International Students Food Festival, and Leadership Training Weekend. **Sports:** There are 9 intercollegiate sports for men and 6 for women, and 13 intramural sports for men and 7 for women. Facilities include a stadium, a fitness center with an indoor track, swimming pool, tennis courts, racquet sport courts, playing fields, bowling, and gyms. **Graduates:** From July 1, 2016 to June 30, 2017, 1512 bachelor's degrees were awarded. The most popular majors were computer science (26%), mechanical engineering (16%), and computer engineering (15%). In an average class, 1% graduate in 3 years or less, 28% graduate in 4 years or less, 55% graduate in 5 years or less, and 64% graduate in 6 years or less. Of the 2016 graduating class, 7% were enrolled in graduate school within 6 months of graduation, and 54% were employed.

SERVICES: Counseling and information services are available, as is tutoring in most subjects. There is a reader service for the blind, remedial math, reading, and writing. **Library/Resources:** The library contains 391,944 volumes, 703 microform items, and 369 audio/video tapes/CDs/DVDs, and subscribes to 34,374 periodicals including electronic. Computerized library services include interlibrary loans, database searching, Internet access, and Wi-Fi capability. Special learning facilities include an art gallery, TV studios, many government and industry sponsored labs, the EPA Northeast Hazardous Substance Research Center, the National Center for Transportation and Industrial Productivity, the Center for Manufacturing Systems, the Emission Reduction Research Center, the Microelectronics Research Center, the Center for Microwave and Lightwave Engineering, and the Multi-Lifecycle Engineering Center. **Physically Challenged Students:** 95% of the campus is accessible. Facilities include wheelchair ramps, elevators, special parking, specially equipped restrooms, special class scheduling, lowered drinking fountains, and lowered telephones. **Special:** Cross-registration is offered in conjunction with Essex County College, Rutgers University's Newark campus, and the University of Medicine and Dentistry of New Jersey. Cooperative programs, available in all majors, include two 6-month internships. There are 3-2 engineering degree programs with Stockton State College and Lincoln and Seton Hall Universities. NJIT also offers work-study programs, study abroad in 18 countries, dual and interdisciplinary majors, accelerated degree programs, distance learning, and nondegree study. There is 1 national honor society, a freshman honors program, and 17 departmental honors programs. **Visiting:** There are regularly scheduled orientations for prospective students, including tours and meetings with admissions personnel, students, and faculty. There are guides for informal visits and visitors may sit in on classes. To schedule a visit, contact the Director of Admissions. **Campus Safety and Security:** Measures include 24-hour foot and vehicle patrol, self-defense education, and security escort services. There are shuttle buses, emergency telephones, and lighted pathways/sidewalks.

REQUIREMENTS: The SAT and the SAT Subject test in math I or II are required. Applicants should have completed 16 secondary school units, including 4 each in English and math, 2 units in science, of these, 2 units must be laboratory science. Recommended units include, 2 units each in foreign language and academic electives, and 1 unit each in social studies and history. NJIT requires applicants to be in the upper 30% of their class. AP and CLEP credits are accepted. Important factors in the admissions decision are leadership record, advanced placement or honors courses, and recommendations by school officials. General university requirements include 9 credits of humanities and social science electives, 7 of natural sciences, 6 each of math, cultural history, basic social sciences, and engineering technology, 3 each of English and management, and 2 of computer science. Students must also complete 2 courses in phys ed. To graduate, students must earn between 124 and 164 credits, depending on the program, including 50 in the major, with a minimum GPA of 2.0 in upper-level major courses. **Procedure:** Freshmen are admitted fall and spring. Entrance exams should be taken in May of the junior year or November of the senior year. There is a rolling admissions plan. Applications should be filed by March 1 for fall entry. The fall 2017 application fee was $75. Notifications are sent November 15. Applications are accepted on-line. **Transfer Students:** 781 transfer students enrolled in 2016-2017. A minimum college GPA of 2.0 is required, but 2.5 or higher is recommended. Students must submit transcripts of all attempted postsecondary academic work. Applicants with fewer than 30 credits may be asked to provide scores on the SAT and the SAT: Subject test in math, as well as high school transcripts. Engineering technology students must present an associate degree. Admission to the School of Architecture is very competitive for transfer students. 33 credits required for the bachelor's degree must be completed at NJIT. **International Students:** There are 308 international students enrolled. They must take the TOEFL with a minimum score of 550 on the paper-based TOEFL (PBT) or 79 on the Internet-based version (iBT). They must also take the SAT, scoring 1100.

ADMISSIONS: 61% of the 2017-2018 applicants were accepted. The SAT scores for the 2017-2018 freshman class were: Math-- 16% between 500 and 599, 56% between 600 and 699, and 28% between 700 and 800. Evidence-Based Reading/Writing-- 1% below 500, 33% between 500 and 599, 50% between 600 and 699, and 16% between 700 and 800. The ACT scores were 20% between 18 and 23, 48% between 24 and 29, and 32% above 30. 52% of the current freshmen were in the top fifth of their class; 79% were in the top two fifths. **Admissions Contact:** Steve Eck, Director of Admissions. Email: *admissions@njit.edu* Web: *www.njit.edu*

FINANCIAL AID: In 2017-2018, 94% of all full-time freshmen received some form of financial aid. 88% of all full-time freshmen received need-based aid. The average freshman award was $18,364. Need-based scholarships or need-based grants averaged $18,759 ($54,000 maximum); need-based self-help aid (loans and jobs) averaged $3,264 ($5,442 maximum); non-need-based athletic scholarships averaged $24,933 ($54,100 maximum); and other non-need-based awards and non-need-based scholarships averaged $17,918 ($54,000 maximum). 32% of undergraduate students work part-time. The average financial indebtedness of the 2017 graduate was $32,276. The FAFSA code is 002621. The priority date for freshman financial aid applications for fall entry is February 15.

PRINCETON UNIVERSITY D-3
www.princeton.edu

Princeton, NJ 08544 **(609) 258-3060**

Fax: (609) 258-6743	**Email: uaoffice@princeton.edu**
Full-time: 2707 men, 2529 women	**Faculty:** 924; I, ++$
Part-time: n/av	**Ph.D.s:** 93%
Graduate: 1687 men, 1094 women	**Student/Faculty:** 5 to 1
Year: semesters	**Tuition:** $45,320
Room & Board: $14,770	**Freshman Class:** 29303 applied, 1911 accepted, 1306 enrolled
SAT CR/M/W: 740/755/745 **ACT:** 34	**CEEB CODE:** 2672
Application Deadline: January 1	**MOST COMPETITIVE**

Princeton University, established in 1746, is a private institution offering degrees in the liberal arts and sciences, engineering, applied science, architecture, public and international affairs, interdisciplinary and regional studies, and the creative arts. There are 4 undergraduate schools and 4 graduate schools. In addition to regional accreditation, Princeton has baccalaureate program accreditation with ABET and NAAB. The 500-acre campus is in a small town 50 miles south of New York City. Including any residence halls, there are 160 buildings.

STUDENT LIFE: 84% of undergraduates are from out of state, mostly the Middle Atlantic. Students are from 50 states, 88 foreign countries, and Canada. 8% are African American; 4% two or more races; 21% White; 2% race unknown; 10% Hispanic. **Male To Female Ratio:** 1.2:1. The average age of freshmen is 18; all undergraduates, 20. 2% do not continue beyond their first year; 96% remain to graduate. **Housing:** 6729 students can be accommodated in college housing, which includes married student dorms, on-campus apartments, and off-campus apartments. Freshmen and sophomores are assigned to one of 6 residential colleges; most juniors and seniors live in upper-class dorms and can select from dining options as co-ops and private clubs. On-campus housing is guaranteed for all 4 years. 98% of students live on campus. Upperclassmen may keep cars.

FACULTY/CLASSROOMS: 67% of faculty are male; 33% are female. All teach undergraduates and do research. No introductory courses are taught by graduate students.

PROGRAMS OF STUDY: Princeton confers A.B., and B.S.E. degrees. Master's and doctoral degrees are also awarded. Bachelor's degrees are awarded in BIOLOGICAL SCIENCE (ecology, evolutionary biology, and molecular biology), BUSINESS (operations research), COMMUNICATIONS AND THE ARTS (classics, comparative literature, English, French, German, Italian, music, Portuguese, Slavic languages, and Spanish), COMPUTER AND PHYSICAL SCIENCE (astrophysics, chemistry, computer science, geoscience, mathematics, and physics), ENGINEERING AND ENVIRONMENTAL DESIGN (aeronautical engineering, architectural engineering, architecture, chemical engineering, civil engineering, electrical/electronics engineering, and mechanical engineering), SOCIAL SCIENCE (anthropology, archeology, East Asian studies, economics, history, international relations, Near Eastern studies, philosophy, political science/government, psychology, religion, and sociology). Economics, politics, and public policy have the largest enrollments.

ACTIVITIES: There are no fraternities or sororities. There are 250 groups on campus, including art, band, cheerleading, chess, choir, chorale, chorus, communications, computers, dance, debate, drama, environmental, ethnic, forensics, honors, international, jazz band, LGBT, literary magazine, marching band, musical theater, newspaper, opera, orchestra, pep band, photography, political, professional, religious, social, social service, student government, symphony, and yearbook. Popular campus events include Communiversity Day. **Sports:** There are 20 intercollegiate sports for men and 18 for women, and 20 intramural sports for men and 20 for women. Facilities include a gymnasium, a fitness center, an Olympic-size pool with diving facilities, football, track and field, lacrosse and field hockey, a hockey rink, outdoor tennis courts, golf course, baseball, rugby, soccer, and softball. **Graduates:** From July 1, 2016 to June 30, 2017, 1307 bachelor's degrees were awarded. The most popular majors were engineering (25%), social sciences (19%), and public administration and social services (11%).

SERVICES: Counseling and information services are available, as is tutoring in every subject. There is a reader service for the blind. There is also a center for teaching and learning that offers workshops and individual consultations in which students can learn to manage large reading loads, problem-solve, take effective notes and create study tools, prepare for long-term projects and oral presentations; prepare for exams, manage time, and overcome test anxiety. The Princeton's Writing Program works to ensure students' master college-level writing. **Library/Resources:** The library contains 8.2 million volumes, 395,285 microform items, and 120,600 audio/video tapes/CDs/DVDs, and subscribes to 84,283 periodicals including electronic. Computerized library services include interlibrary loans, database searching, Internet access, and Wi-Fi capability. Special learning facilities include an art gallery, natural history museum, a music center, a visual and performing arts center, several theaters, an observatory, a plasma physics lab, and a center for environmental and energy studies. **Physically Challenged Students:** Facilities include wheelchair ramps, elevators, special parking, specially equipped restrooms, lowered drinking fountains, lowered telephones, special housing. Each student's needs are assessed individually. Accommodations may include additional testing time, sign language translators, and dietary accommodations for food allergies. **Special:** Princeton offers independent study, accelerated degree programs, student-proposed courses and majors, field study, community-based learning courses that enrich course work with related service projects, study abroad, freshman seminars, and independent work in the junior and senior year. They also offer a Program in Teacher Preparation. There are 2 national honor societies and a chapter of Phi Beta Kappa. **Visiting:** There are regularly scheduled orientations for prospective students, Including information sessions on Monday to Friday within the Admission Office, and some Saturdays in the fall. Also, Princeton has an open campus, with many free and public events, and students are welcome to attend such events. Visitors may sit in on classes. To schedule a visit, contact the Undergraduate Admission Office. **Campus Safety and Security:** Measures include 24-hour foot and vehicle patrol, emergency notification system, self-defense education, and security escort services. There are shuttle buses, emergency telephones, lighted pathways/sidewalks, and controlled access to dorms/residences.

REQUIREMENTS: The ACT is accepted in lieu of SAT Reasoning test. 3 SAT Subject tests are also required for all applicants. Recommended college preparatory courses include 4 years each of English, math, science, (of those 2 must be lab) and foreign language, 2 each in social studies and history, and 1 in visual/performing arts. Essays are required as part of the application and an interview is recommended. Students with special talent in visual or performing arts may supplement tapes, CDs or DVDs. AP credits are accepted. Important factors in the admissions decision are personality/intangible qualities, recommendations by school officials, and advanced placement or honors courses. To graduate, students must complete 8 semesters, or academic units. Candidates for the A.B. degree must demonstrate proficiency in English composition and foreign language and they must complete distribution requirements in 7 academic areas. Candidates for the B.S.E., must satisfy the English composition requirement and complete a minimum of 7 courses in the humanities and social sciences spread over 4 distribution areas. A junior project and senior thesis are required of virtually all students. **Procedure:** Freshmen are admitted in the fall. Entrance exams should be taken by January of the senior year at the latest. There are early admissions and deferred admissions plans. Applications should be filed by January 1 for fall entry. The fall 2017 application fee was $65. Notifications are sent April 1. 1395 applicants were on the 2017 waiting list; 33 were admitted. Applications are accepted on-line. **Transfer Students:** Princeton does not have a transfer admissions option. **International Students:** There are 569 international students enrolled. The SAT: Writing Test may be substituted for the TOEFL.

ADMISSIONS: 7% of the 2017-2018 applicants were accepted. The SAT scores for the 2017-2018 freshman class were: Critical Reading-- 3% between 500 and 599, 23% between 600 and 699, and 73% between 700 and 800. Math-- 2% between 500 and 599, 18% between 600 and 699, and 81% between 700 and 800. Writing-- 2% between 500 and 599, 22% between 600 and 699, and 76% between 700 and 800. The ACT scores were 8% between 24 and 29, and 92% above 30. 98% of the current freshmen were in the top fifth of their class; 99% were in the top two fifths. 137 freshmen graduated first in their class. **Admissions Contact:** Janet Lavin Rapelye, Dean of Admissions. Email: *uaoffice@princeton.edu* Web: *www.princeton.edu*

FINANCIAL AID: Princeton is a member of CSS. The FAFSA code is 002627. Check with the school for current application deadlines.

RAMAPO COLLEGE OF NEW JERSEY D-1
www.ramapo.edu

Mahwah, NJ 07430	**(201) 684-7300**
Fax: (201) 684-7964	**Email: admissions@ramapo.edu**
Full-time: 2309 men, 2656 women	**Faculty:** 218; IIA, +$
Part-time: 187 men, 293 women	**Ph.D.s:** 94%
Graduate: 127 men, 335 women	**Student/Faculty:** 18 to 1
Year: semesters, summer session	**Tuition:** $14,080 ($23,214)
Room & Board: $11,680	**Freshman Class:** 7172 applied, 3820 accepted, 931 enrolled
SAT EBR-W/M: 615/615 **ACT:** 24	**CEEB CODE:** 2884
Application Deadline: March 1	**VERY COMPETITIVE**

Ramapo College, established in 1969, offers bachelor's degrees in the arts, business, humanities, social sciences and the sciences, and professional studies; business, elementary education, nursing and social work. The college also offers articulated programs; dental, optometry, chiropractic and health professions, visual arts therapy and law, with colleges and institutions in New Jersey and New York. Undergraduate students may choose to concentrate their studies in one of 5 schools with more than 539 course offerings and more than 36 academic programs. In addition to regional accreditation, RCNJ has baccalaureate program accreditation with AACSB, CSWE, MSCHE, NLNAC, and ACS. The 314-acre campus is in a suburban area Mahwah, New Jersey. 25 miles northwest of New York City. Including any residence halls, there are 62 buildings.

STUDENT LIFE: 95% of undergraduates are from New Jersey. Others are from 17 states, and 27 foreign countries. 7% are Asian American; 64% White; 5% African American; 5% race unknown; 43% Hispanic; 2% Foreign. **Female To Male Ratio:** 1.3:1. The average age of freshmen is 18; all undergraduates, 22. 12% do not continue beyond their first year; 72% remain to graduate. **Housing:** 3062 students can be accommodated in college housing, which includes dorms and on-campus apartments. In addition, there are honors houses, special-interest houses, theme housing, and sustainability housing. On-campus housing is guaranteed for all 4 years, and is available on a first-come, first-served basis. 53% of students live on campus. All students may keep cars.

FACULTY/CLASSROOMS: 51% of faculty are male; 49% are female. All teach undergraduates. No introductory courses are taught by graduate students. The average class size in an introductory lecture is 26; in a laboratory is 19; and in a regular course is 23.

PROGRAMS OF STUDY: RCNJ confers B.A., B.S., B.S.N., and B.S.W. degrees. Master's degrees are also awarded. Bachelor's degrees are awarded in AGRICULTURE (environmental studies), BIOLOGICAL SCIENCE (biochemistry, bioinformatics, and biology/biological science), BUSINESS (accounting, business administration and management, and international business management), COMMUNICATIONS AND THE ARTS (art, communications, dramatic arts, literature, music, and visual and performing arts), COMPUTER AND PHYSICAL SCIENCE (chemistry, computer science, information sciences and systems, and mathematics), ENGINEERING AND ENVIRONMENTAL DESIGN (engineering physics and environmental science), HEALTH PROFESSIONS (allied health, clinical science, and nursing), SOCIAL SCIENCE (African studies, American studies, economics, history, international studies, law, liberal arts/general studies, political science/government, psychology, science and society, social science, social work, sociology, and Spanish studies). Physics, nursing, and biology are the strongest academically. Business administration, biology, and nursing have the largest enrollments.

ACTIVITIES: 17% of men belong to 10 national fraternities; 17% of women belong to 12 national sororities. There are 100 groups on campus, including cheerleading, choir, chorale, chorus, computers, dance, debate, drama, environmental, ethnic, honors, international, LGBT, literary magazine, musical theater, newspaper, pep band, photography, political, professional, radio and TV, religious, social, social service, student government, and yearbook. Popular campus events include LollaNoBooza, Octoberfest, and Stress Busters. **Sports:** There are 8 intercollegiate sports for men and 10 for women, and 16 intramural sports for men and 16 for women. Facilities include a stadium, a track, tennis courts, baseball, softball, hockey, soccer fields, an arena for basketball and volleyball, an auxiliary gym for intramurals and recreation, a fitness center with cardio machines, machine weight stations, free weights, training room, and a swimming pool. **Graduates:** From July 1, 2016 to June 30, 2017, 1288 bachelor's degrees were awarded. The most popular majors were business/marketing (23%), psychology (11%), and health professons and related programs (11%). In an average class, 2% graduate in 3 years or less, 60% graduate in 4 years or less, 70% graduate in 5 years or less, and 72% graduate in 6 years or less.

SERVICES: Counseling and information services are available, as is tutoring in every subject. There is a reader service for the blind, and remedial math, reading, and writing. **Library/Resources:** The library contains 191,031 volumes, 2,500 microform items, and 9,373 audio/video tapes/CDs/DVDs, and subscribes to 488 periodicals including electronic. Computerized library services include interlibrary loans, database searching, Internet access, and Wi-Fi capability. Special learning facilities include an art gallery, a radio station, astronomical observatory, international telecommunications satellite center, center for international education and entrepreneurship, a solar greenhouse center, a spirituality center, and a sustainability education center. **Physically Challenged Students:** All of the campus is accessible. Facilities include wheelchair ramps, elevators, special parking, specially equipped restrooms, special class scheduling, lowered drinking fountains, lowered telephones, and special housing. **Special:** Ramapo's curriculum emphasizes the interdependence of global society and includes an international dimension in all academic programs. Students may study abroad in many countries. Cooperative programs are available with various corporations and in foreign countries. Cross-registration is possible with local state colleges. Ramapo offers accelerated degree programs, dual and student-designed majors, credit for life experience, pass/fail options, internships, work-study programs, and certificate programs in gerontology and substance abuse. A teachers education program is offered. There are 23 national honor societies, a freshman honors program, and 5 departmental honors programs. **Visiting:** There are regularly scheduled orientations for prospective students. There are guides for informal visits and visitors may sit in on classes. To schedule a visit, contact the Admissions Office. **Campus Safety and Security:** Measures include 24-hour foot and vehicle patrol, an emergency notification system, and security escort services. There are shuttle buses, emergency telephones, lighted pathways/sidewalks, and controlled access to dorms/residences.

REQUIREMENTS: The SAT or ACT is required. Applicants must be graduates of an accredited secondary schools or have earned a GED. The college requires 18 academic credits, including 4 in English, 3 each in math, science (2 with lab), social studies, and academic electives, and 2 in foreign language. Students must also submit an essay. An interview is recommended. AP and CLEP credits are accepted. Important factors in the admissions decision are advanced placement or honors courses, recommendations by school officials, and evidence of special talent. Students must complete general education requirements of approximately 50 credits in science, social science, humanities, and English composition, as well as core requirements in their school of study and their particular major. A senior seminar is also required. To graduate, students must earn at least 128 credits with a minimum GPA of 2.0. **Procedure:** Freshmen are admitted in the fall and spring. Entrance exams should be taken senior year. There are early decision, early admissions, deferred admissions, and rolling admissions plans. Early decision applications should be filed by November 1; regular applications, by March 1 for fall entry; and December 1 for spring entry. The fall 2017 application fee was $65. Notification of early decision is sent December 5; regular decision, on a rolling basis. Applications are accepted on-line. **Transfer Students:** 559 transfer students enrolled in 2016-2017. Applicants must supply a completed admission application, official transcripts from all previously attended colleges, Transfer Candidate's Form, and an official high school transcript (if fewer than 45 credits from another college). 48 of 128 credits required for the bachelor's degree must be completed at RCNJ. **International Students:** There are 77 international students enrolled. They must take the TOEFL with a minimum score of 550 on the paper-based TOEFL (PBT) or 90 on the Internet-based version (iBT). Student must take the Comprehensive English Language Test. They must also take the SAT or ACT.

ADMISSIONS: 53% of the 2017-2018 applicants were accepted. The ACT scores were 5% between 12 and 17, 50% between 18 and 23, 37% between 24 and 29, and 8% above 30. 57% of the current freshmen were in the top fifth of their class; 89% were in the top two fifths. 2 freshmen graduated first in their class. **Admissions Contact:** Peter Rice, Director of Admissions. Email: *admissions@ramapo.edu* Web: *www.ramapo.edu*

FINANCIAL AID: In 2017-2018, 80% of all full-time freshmen received some form of financial aid. 60% of all full-time freshmen received need-based aid. The average freshman award was $17,874. Need-based scholarships or need-based grants averaged $12,210; need-based self-help aid (loans and jobs) averaged $3,461; non-need-based athletic scholarships averaged $12,149; and $3,305 from other forms of aid. 4% of undergraduate students work part-time. The average financial indebtedness of the 2017 graduate was $27,909. The FAFSA code is 009344. The priority date for freshman financial aid applications for fall entry is March 1.

RIDER UNIVERSITY — D-3

www.rider.edu

Lawrenceville, NJ 08648	**(609) 896-5042** **(800) 257-9026**
Fax: (609) 895-6645	**Email: admissions@rider.edu**
Full-time: 1520 men, 2119 women	**Faculty:** 235; IIA, +$
Part-time: 159 men, 262 women	**Ph.D.s:** 98%
Graduate: 364 men, 682 women	**Student/Faculty:** 16 to 1
Year: semesters, summer session	**Tuition:** $39,820 ($38,360)
Room & Board: $14,230	**Freshman Class:** 9172 applied, 6366 accepted, 871 enrolled
SAT CR/M/W: 490/500/480 **ACT:** 21	**CEEB CODE:** 2758
Application Deadline: rolling	**COMPETITIVE**

Rider University, founded in 1865, is a private institution offering undergraduate programs in the areas of business administration, liberal arts, education, sciences, and continuing studies. Westminster Choir College, located in nearby Princeton, is Rider's fourth college. There are 4 undergraduate schools and 2 graduate schools. In addition to regional accreditation, RU has baccalaureate program accreditation with AACSB, NASM, CACREP, and NASP. The 280-acre campus is in a suburban area 3 miles north of Trenton and 7 miles south of Princeton. Including any residence halls, there are 41 buildings.

STUDENT LIFE: 75% of undergraduates are from New Jersey. Others are from 37 states, 76 foreign countries, and Canada. 60% are White; 5% Asian American; 3% Foreign; 3% two or more races; 3% race unknown; 14% Hispanic; 12% African American. **Female To Male Ratio:** 1.5:1. The average age of freshmen is 18; all undergraduates, 22. 20% do not continue beyond their first year; 64% remain to graduate. **Housing:** 2515 students can be accommodated in college housing, which includes dorms and on-campus apartments. In addition, there are honors houses, language/international houses, special-interest houses, fraternity houses, sorority houses, living learning community, wellness, quiet hall, science area, and first-year experience housing. On-campus housing is available on a lottery system for upperclassmen. 53% of students live on campus. All students may keep cars.

FACULTY/CLASSROOMS: 51% of faculty are male; 49% are female. 98% teach undergraduates, and all do research. No introductory courses are taught by graduate students. The average class size in an introductory lecture is 26; in a laboratory is 14; and in a regular course is 20.

PROGRAMS OF STUDY: RU confers B.A., B.M., B.S., and B.S.B.A. degrees. Associate and master's degrees are also awarded. Bachelor's degrees are awarded in BIOLOGICAL SCIENCE (biochemistry, biology/biological science, and marine science), BUSINESS (accounting, banking and finance, business administration and management, business economics, human resources, international business management, management science, marketing/retailing/merchandising, and office supervision and management), COMMUNICATIONS AND THE ARTS (advertising, communications, dance, dramatic arts, English, English literature, fine arts, French, German, journalism, multimedia, music, piano/organ, public relations, Russian, Spanish, and voice), COMPUTER AND PHYSICAL SCIENCE (actuarial science, chemistry, geoscience, information sciences and systems, mathematics, and physics), EDUCATION (business education, early childhood education, elementary education, English education, foreign languages education, marketing and distribution education, mathematics education, music education, science education, secondary education, and social studies education), ENGINEERING AND ENVIRONMENTAL DESIGN (environmental science), HEALTH PROFESSIONS (premedicine), SOCIAL SCIENCE (American studies, biopsychology, economics, history, liberal arts/general studies, philosophy, political science/government, prelaw, psychology, and sociology). Elementary education, accounting, and business administration have the largest enrollments.

ACTIVITIES: 9% of men belong to 4 national fraternities; 10% of women belong to 7 national sororities. There are 130 groups on campus, including art, band, cheerleading, choir, chorale, chorus, computers, dance, drama, environmental, ethnic, film, honors, international, jazz band, LGBT, literary magazine, musical theater, newspaper, opera, orchestra, pep band, photography, political, professional, radio and TV, religious, social, social service, student government, symphony, and yearbook. Popular campus events include Cranberry Fest, Fall Concert, Family Weekend, and R Factor. **Sports:** There are 10 intercollegiate sports for men and 10 for women, and 10 intramural sports for men and 6 for women. Facilities include a recreation center with basketball, volleyball, and tennis courts, and an elevated jogging/walking track, a fitness center with cardio equipment, and a weight room with machines, and free weights. **Graduates:** From July 1, 2016 to June 30, 2017, 983 bachelor's degrees were awarded. The most popular majors were accounting (11%), psychology (10%), and early childhood education (9%). In an average class, 58% graduate in 4 years or less, 64% graduate in 5 years or less, and 66% graduate in 6 years or less.

SERVICES: Counseling and information services are available, as is tutoring in most subjects. There is remedial math, reading, and writing. **Library/Resources:** The library contains 451,460 volumes, 661,743 microform items, 5,889 audio/video tapes/CDs/DVDs, and subscribes to 45,016 periodicals, including electronic. Computerized library services include interlibrary loans, database searching, Internet access, and Wi-Fi capability. Special learning facilities include an art gallery, radio station, TV station, a journalism and sociology lab, and a holocaust/genocide center. **Physically Challenged Students:** 75% of the campus is accessible. Facilities include wheelchair ramps, elevators, special parking, specially equipped restrooms, special class scheduling, lowered drinking fountains, and lowered telephones. **Special:** Internships in many programs, a co-op program in retail marketing, work-study, study abroad in 14 countries, a B.A.-B.S. degree in all liberal arts and sciences, dual majors in education, a liberal studies degree, and nondegree study are possible. There is a freshman honors program. **Visiting:** There are regularly scheduled orientations for prospective students, including 3 open houses, Saturday information sessions and other programs that consist of a campus tour, and a variety of formal and informal activities to meet faculty, staff, current students, and alumni. To schedule a visit, contact the Office of Admissions. **Campus Safety and Security:** Measures include 24-hour foot and vehicle patrol, emergency notification system, self-defense education, and security escort services. There are shuttle buses, emergency telephones, lighted pathways/sidewalks, a shuttle car, a staffed kiosk at the entrance, video camera surveillance, and a property ID program.

REQUIREMENTS: The SAT or ACT is required. Applicants need 16 Carnegie units, including 4 years of English and 2 of math, 3 units of math are required for prospective math, science, and business majors. An essay is recommended. An audition is required for theater scholarships. The GED is accepted. AP and CLEP credits are accepted. Important factors in the admissions decision are advanced placement or honors courses, extracurricular activities record, and leadership record. To graduate, all students must maintain a minimum GPA of 2.0 while taking 120 semester hours. Students also must fulfill core curriculum requirements, including 9 hours in humanities, 7 to 8 in science, 6 each in English writing and foreign language (may be waived if proficiency is demonstrated), social sciences/communications, and history, and 3 in math. 30 to 76 credits are required in the major. A thesis is required in the honors program and some science majors. **Procedure:** Freshmen are admitted in the fall and spring. Entrance exams should be taken by January of the senior year. There are deferred admissions and rolling admissions plans. Application deadlines are open. The fall 2017 application fee was $50. Notification of early decision is sent December 5; regular decision, on a rolling basis. 62 applicants were on the 2017 waiting list; 28 were admitted. Applications are accepted on-line. **Transfer Students:** 559 transfer students enrolled in 2016-2017. A GPA of 2.5 or better is required for applicants. If students have fewer than 30 credits, they also must submit high school transcripts and SAT scores. An essay or personal statement is required, and an interview is recommended. 30 of 120 credits required for the bachelor's degree must be completed at RU. **International Students:** There are 201 international students enrolled. They must take the TOEFL with a minimum score of 550 on the paper-based TOEFL (PBT) or 80 on the Internet-based version (iBT). They must also take the SAT or ACT.

ADMISSIONS: 69% of the 2017-2018 applicants were accepted. The SAT scores for the 2017-2018 freshman class were: Critical Reading-- 52% below 500, 36% between 500 and 599, 11% between 600 and 699, and 2% between 700 and 800. Math-- 44% below 500, 40% between 500 and 599, 14% between 600 and 699, and 1% between 700 and 800. Writing-- 53% below 500, 34% between 500 and 599, 12% between 600 and 699, and 1% between 700 and 800. The ACT scores were 12% between 12 and 17, 53% between 18 and 23, 30% between 24 and 29, and 5% above 30. **Admissions Contact:** Susan C. Christian, Director of Admissions. Email: *admissions@rider.edu* Web: *www.rider.edu*

FINANCIAL AID: In 2017-2018, 81% of all full-time freshmen received some form of financial aid. 80% of all full-time freshmen received need-based aid. The average freshman award was $31,784. Need-based scholarships or need-based grants averaged $27,328; need-based self-help aid (loans and jobs) averaged $5,490; and $3,147 from other forms of aid. The SFS is required. The FAFSA code is 002628. The priority date for freshman financial aid applications for fall entry is March 1.

ROWAN UNIVERSITY C-4

www.rowan.edu

Glassboro, NJ 08028 (855) 256-4200

Fax: (856) 256-4430	**Email:** admissions@rowan.edu
Full-time: 6405 men, 5300 women	**Faculty:** 362
Part-time: 680 men, 779 women	**Ph.D.s:** 83%
Graduate: 1128 men, 1858 women	**Student/Faculty:** 18 to 1
Year: semesters, summer session	**Tuition:** $12,864 ($20,978)
Room & Board: $11,627	**Freshman Class:** 12158 applied, 6860 accepted, 1770 enrolled
SAT CR/M/W: 582/622/565	**CEEB CODE:** 2515
Application Deadline: March 1	**VERY COMPETITIVE**

Rowan University, a leading state-designated comprehensive public research institution, combines liberal education with professional preparation from the baccalaureate through the doctorate. Rowan provides a collaborative, learning-centered environment in which highly qualified and diverse faculty, staff, and students integrate teaching, research, scholarship, creative activity, and community service. There are 9 undergraduate schools and 1 graduate school. In addition to regional accreditation, RU has baccalaureate program accreditation with AACSB, ABET, CSAB, NASAD, NASDTEC, NASM, LCME, LOCA, COPTI, MUS, CAATE, THEA, NASD, and NAST. The 921-acre campus is in a suburban area 20 miles southeast of Philadelphia. Including any residence halls, there are 85 buildings.

STUDENT LIFE: 95% of undergraduates are from New Jersey. Others are from 33 states, and 19 foreign countries. 90% are from public schools. 66% are White; 4% Asian American; 4% race unknown; 3% two or more races; 12% Hispanic; 10% African American; 1% Foreign. **Male To Female Ratio:** 1.0:1. The average age of freshmen is 18; all undergraduates, 21. 12% do not continue beyond their first year; 66% remain to graduate. **Housing:** 4500 students can be accommodated in college housing, which includes dorms and on-campus apartments. In addition, there are honors houses and special-interest houses. On-campus housing is guaranteed for the freshman year only and is available on a lottery system for upperclassmen. 63% of students commute. Upperclassmen may keep cars.

FACULTY/CLASSROOMS: 53% of faculty are male; 47% are female. 92% teach undergraduates, 8% do research, and 8% do both. No introductory courses are taught by graduate students. The average class size in an introductory lecture is 22; in a laboratory is 16; and in a regular course is 22.

PROGRAMS OF STUDY: RU confers B.A., B.S., B.S.N., B.F.A., B.G.S. and B.M. degrees. Master's and doctoral degrees are also awarded. Bachelor's degrees are awarded in AGRICULTURE (environmental studies), BIOLOGICAL SCIENCE (biochemistry, bioinformatics, and biology/biological science), BUSINESS (accounting, business administration and management, entrepreneurial studies, human resources, marketing/retailing/merchandising, personnel management, and small business management), COMMUNICATIONS AND THE ARTS (advertising, art, broadcasting, communications, dramatic arts, English, fine arts, jazz, journalism, music, public relations, radio/television technology, Spanish, speech/debate/rhetoric, and theatre arts), COMPUTER AND PHYSICAL SCIENCE (chemistry, computer science, mathematics, physical sciences, and physics), EDUCATION (art education, athletic training, collaborative education, early childhood education, education, elementary education, foreign languages education, general studies, music education, and science education), ENGINEERING AND ENVIRONMENTAL DESIGN (biomedical engineering, chemical engineering, civil engineering, engineering, and mechanical engineering), HEALTH PROFESSIONS (health and nursing), SOCIAL SCIENCE (African studies, American studies, criminal justice, economics, geography, history, liberal arts/general studies, philosophy and religion, political science/government, psychology, and sociology). Engineering, biology, and education are the strongest academically. Biological science, psychology, and elementary education have the largest enrollments.

ACTIVITIES: 5% of men belong to 16 national fraternities; 4% of women belong to 10 national sororities. There are 150 groups on campus, including art, band, cheerleading, chess, choir, chorale, chorus, communications, computers, dance, drama, environmental, ethnic, film, honors, international, jazz band, LGBT, literary magazine, musical theater, newspaper, opera, orchestra, pep band, photography, political, professional, radio and TV, religious, social, social service, student government, symphony, and yearbook. Popular campus events include Prof Stock, Back to the Boro, Senior Send Off, Home Coming, and Leadership Conference. **Sports:** There are 8 intercollegiate sports for men and 10 for women, and 15 intramural sports for men and 15 for women. Facilities include football, soccer, cross country, basketball, outdoor track, baseball, volleyball, field hockey, soccer, lacrosse, softball, wiffle-ball, bowling, billiards, racquetball, ping pong, tennis, badminton, dodgeball, battleship, horse stables, golf course, sand volleyball, punt, pass and kick ball, free throw and 3 point competition, and flag football. The student recreation center; 25 yard competition pools, multi-purpose wood courts, indoor jogging track, group fitness studio, cycling studio, racquetball courts, a free weight room, cardiovascular and selectorized equipment areas, and a multi-purpose outdoor recreational field.**Graduates:** From July 1, 2016 to June 30, 2017, 2856 bachelor's degrees were awarded. The most popular majors were psychology (9%), biological science (6%), and law/justice (6%). In an average class, 43% graduate in 4 years or less, 61% graduate in 5 years or less, and 66% graduate in 6 years or less.

SERVICES: Counseling and information services are available, as is tutoring in every subject. There is a reader service for the blind, and remedial math, reading, and writing. **Library/Resources:** The library contains 641,430 volumes, 519,817 microform items, 18,984 audio/video tapes/CDs/DVDs, and subscribes to 77,727 periodicals, including electronic. Computerized library services include interlibrary loans, database searching, Internet access, and Wi-Fi capability. Special learning facilities include an art gallery, planetarium, radio station, TV station, a virtual reality cave, exercise science research laboratory, and assessment and learning center. **Physically Challenged Students:** 95% of the campus is accessible. Facilities include wheelchair ramps, elevators, special parking, specially equipped restrooms, special class scheduling, lowered drinking fountains, lowered telephones, and special housing. **Special:** There is study abroad in 40 countries, internships are available in all majors, accelerated degree programs, 3-2 degrees in optometry, podiatry, pharmacy, and 4-1 degree in business, dual majors, pass/fail options, and credit for military experience, BS/MS accelerated degrees, and joint BS/MS accelerated degrees with Stockton College. There are 12 national honor societies and a freshman honors program. **Visiting:** There are regularly scheduled orientations for prospective students. Visiting students may participate in a 2-day summer program providing schedule confirmation/adjustment, student activities updates, and workshops for students and parents. There are guides for informal visits and visitors may sit in on classes. To schedule a visit, contact Albert Betts at betts@rowan.edu. **Campus Safety and Security:** Measures include 24-hour foot and vehicle patrol, emergency notification system, self-defense education, and security escort services. There are shuttle buses, emergency telephones, lighted pathways/sidewalks, and controlled access to dorms/residences. The Rowan Department of Public Safety has an EMS, and ambulance services.

REQUIREMENTS: The SAT is required. Students are required to score an 1080, or no less than 500 on either part. Students submitting ACT scores should have a minimum composite score of 23. Applicants must be graduates of accredited secondary schools or have earned a GED. Rowan requires 16 academic credits or Carnegie units, including 4 in English, 3 each in math and college preparatory electives, and 2 each in foreign language, history, and lab science. A portfolio or audition is required for specific majors. A GPA of 2.0 is required. AP and CLEP credits are accepted. Important factors in the admissions decision are advanced placement or honors courses, evidence of special talent, and leadership record. General education requirements include 6-12 credits of social and behavior sciences; 6-12 credits of history, humanities and language; 7-15 credits of math and science (one science course must be 4 credits with a lab component), 9 credits of communication, and 6 credits in non-program courses. Students also take requirements in the Rowan Experience, which includes the Rowan Seminar and courses with the following designations: Multicultural/Global, Artistic/Creative Experience, Literature, and Writing Intensive. The Bachelor's degree requires 120-132 semester hours, including 30-42 in a major field, with a minimum GPA of 2.0. **Procedure:** Freshmen are admitted in the fall and spring. Entrance exams should be taken by May or June of the junior year, or by December of the senior year. There is a deferred admissions plan. Applications should be filed by March 1 for fall entry; November 1 for spring entry. The fall 2017 application fee was $65. Notifications are sent April 15. 150 applicants were on the 2017 waiting list; 56 were admitted. Applications are accepted on-line. **Transfer Students:** 1634 transfer students enrolled in 2016-2017. Applicants must have a minimum GPA of 2.0, but should present a GPA of 2.5 to be competitive. An associate degree is recommended. Students who have earned fewer than 24 semester hours must also submit a high school transcript and SAT I results. 30 of 120 credits required for the bachelor's degree must be completed at RU. **International Students:** There are 110 international students enrolled. They must take the TOEFL with a minimum score of 550 on the paper-based TOEFL (PBT) or 79 on the Internet-based version (iBT). Students must take the IELTS. Students whose first language is English and all engineering majors must take the SAT.

ADMISSIONS: 56% of the 2017-2018 applicants were accepted. The SAT scores for the 2017-2018 freshman class were: Critical Reading-- 28% below 500, 46% between 500 and 599, 23% between 600 and 699, and 3% between 700 and 800. Math-- 20% below 500, 43% between 500 and 599, 31% between 600 and 699, and 6% between 700 and 800. Writing-- 35% below 500, 44% between 500 and 599, 19% between 600 and 699, and 2% between 700 and 800. **Admissions Contact:** Albert Betts, Director of Admissions. Email: *admissions@rowan.edu* Web: *www.rowan.edu*

FINANCIAL AID: The average freshman award was $10,662. Need-based scholarships or need-based grants averaged $91,213; need-based self-help aid (loans and jobs) averaged $3,314; and other non-need-based awards and non-need-based scholarships averaged $6,699. 10% of undergraduate students work part-time. The average financial indebtedness of the 2017 graduate was $25,348. The FAFSA code is 002609. The priority date for freshman financial aid applications for fall entry is January 1.

RUTGERS UNIVERSITY - CAMDEN C-4

www.admissions.camden.rutgers.edu

Camden, NJ 08102 **(856) 225-6104**

Email: admissions@camden.rutgers.edu

Full-time: 1840 men, 2653 women	**Faculty:** 202
Part-time: 392 men, 604 women	**Ph.D.s:** 99%
Graduate: 666 men, 698 women	**Student/Faculty:** 20 to 1
Year: semesters, summer session	**Tuition:** $14,501 ($29,924)
Room & Board: $12,094	**Freshman Class:** 11338 applied, 7861 accepted, 758 enrolled
SAT EBR-W/M: 550/540	**CEEB CODE:** 2742
Application Deadline: December 1	**COMPETITIVE**

Rutgers University - Camden Campus, founded in 1926, is comprised of 4 undergraduate, degree-granting schools: College of the Arts and Sciences, University College-Camden, the School of Nursing-Camden and the School of Business-Camden. Each school has individual requirements, policies, and fees. The New Jersey Medical and Health Sciences Education Restructuring Act went into effect, integrating Rutgers, the State University of New Jersey, with all units of the university of Medicine and Dentistry of New Jersey (UMDNJ), except University Hospital in Newark and the School of Osteopathic Medicine in Stratford. The integration of the legacy elements of UMDNJ into Rutgers has created a fourth unit, Rutgers Biomedical and Health Sciences (RBHS), which consists of a number of schools, and units. In addition to regional accreditation, Camden Campus has baccalaureate program accreditation with AACSB, APTA, CSWE, and CCNE. The 29-acre campus is in an urban area 1 mile east of Philadelphia. Including any residence halls, there are 58 buildings.

STUDENT LIFE: 96% of undergraduates are from New Jersey. Others are from 25 states, and 24 foreign countries. 49% are White; 18% African American; 15% Hispanic; 10% Asian American; 4% two or more races; 3% race unknown; 2% Foreign. 30% claim no religious affiliation; 25% Catholic; 21% Protestant. **Female To Male Ratio:** 1.4:1. The average age of freshmen is 18; all undergraduates, 22. 18% do not continue beyond their first year; 59% remain to graduate. **Housing:** 760 students can be accommodated in college housing, which includes gender neutral, coed dorms, and on-campus apartments. In addition, there are special-interest houses, floors dedicated to those interested in health and medical sciences, business, and nursing professions. 82% of students commute. All students may keep cars. Alcohol is not permitted.

FACULTY/CLASSROOMS: 51% of faculty are male; 49% are female. No introductory courses are taught by graduate students. The average class size in an introductory lecture is 26 and in a laboratory is 18.

PROGRAMS OF STUDY: Camden Campus confers B.A., B.S., and B.S.N. degrees. Master's and doctoral degrees are also awarded. Bachelor's degrees are awarded in BIOLOGICAL SCIENCE (biochemistry, bioinformatics, biology/biological science, and biotechnology), BUSINESS (accounting, business administration and management, finance, hospitality management services, human resource management, management science, and marketing management), COMMUNICATIONS AND THE ARTS (art, art history and appreciation, digital communications, dramatic arts, English, French, German, linguistics, music, Spanish, and speech/debate/rhetoric), COMPUTER AND PHYSICAL SCIENCE (chemistry, computer science, mathematics, and physics), EDUCATION (education), HEALTH PROFESSIONS (allied health, medical laboratory technology, nursing, and pharmacy), SOCIAL SCIENCE (African American studies, criminal justice, economics, experimental psychology, history, interdisciplinary studies, liberal arts/general studies, philosophy, political science/government, psychology, religion, social work, sociology, and urban studies). Nursing, psychology, business, and criminal justice are the strongest academically. Nursing, business management, and psychology have the largest enrollments.

ACTIVITIES: There are no fraternities or sororities. There are 75 groups on campus, including art, cheerleading, choir, chorus, computers, drama, ethnic, film, honors, international, LGBT, newspaper, orchestra, political, professional, radio and TV, religious, social, social service, student government, and yearbook. Popular campus events include Raptor Day, Springfest, and Basketball Team Sports. **Sports:** There are 9 intercollegiate sports for men and 10 for women, and 8 intramural sports for men and 8 for women. Facilities include Athletic and Fitness Center with over 40 cardio machines, including treadmills, ellipticals, bikes, steppers, cross trainers and spin bikes, circuit strength training equipment, a free weight area, a resistance pool (natatorium), a training room, basketball, and volleyball programs. **Graduates:** From July 1, 2016 to June 30, 2017, 1309 bachelor's degrees were awarded. The most popular majors were nursing (20%), business administration & management (12%), and psychology (9%). In an average class, 27% graduate in 4 years or less and 59% graduate in 6 years or less.

SERVICES: Counseling and information services are available, as is tutoring in some subjects, such as the introductory classes. There is a reader service for the blind, and remedial math, reading, and writing. **Library/Resources:** The library contains 1.4 million volumes, 43,307 microform items, 40,052 audio/video tapes/CDs/DVDs, and subscribes to 169,698 periodicals, including electronic. Computerized library services include interlibrary loans, database searching, Internet access, and Wi-Fi capability. Special learning facilities include an art gallery, radio station, Center for the Arts, and the Stedman Gallery. **Physically Chal-**

lenged Students: Facilities include wheelchair ramps, elevators, special parking, specially equipped restrooms, special class scheduling, lowered drinking fountains, lowered telephones, special housing. All classes are scheduled in accessible locations for disabled students. **Special:** The University offers a cooperative baccalaureate program in engineering with School of Engineering (New Brunswick Campus). Interdisciplinary programs in African-American studies, general science. Cooperative baccalaureate in medical technology with approved hospital. B.A./M.A. in Childhood Studies, English, history, liberal studies or psychology; B.A./M.S. in biology, chemistry or mathematics (with the Graduate School-Camden). B.A. in economics or political science/Master of Public Administration (with the Graduate School-Camden); BS/Master of Business and Science (MBS). In addition, there is an 8-year B.A./M.D. program and many combined bachelor's and master's programs. There are distance learning, English as a Second Language, honors and independent study programs, and a freshman honors program. There are 11 national honor societies, Phi Beta Kappa, and a freshman honors program. **Visiting:** There are regularly scheduled orientations for prospective students, includes an information session with an admissions officer and a campus tour with a Raptor Ambassador. Visitors may sit in on classes. To schedule a visit, contact the Admissions Office (Camden). **Campus Safety and Security:** Measures include 24-hour foot and vehicle patrol, emergency notification system, self-defense education, and security escort services. There are shuttle buses, emergency telephones, lighted pathways/sidewalks, and controlled access to dorms/residences. The police department is supplemented by security guards.

REQUIREMENTS: The SAT or ACT is required, but not for students who have been out of high school for 2 years or more. SAT: Subject tests are required of students without a high school diploma from an accredited high school and from some GED holders. A high school diploma is required; the GED is accepted. Students must have completed a general college-preparatory program, including 16 academic credits or Carnegie units, with 4 years of English, 3 years of math (4 recommended), and 2 years each of foreign language and science, plus 5 in electives. AP and CLEP credits are accepted. Important factors in the admissions decision are advanced placement or honors courses, evidence of special talent, and leadership record. To graduate, students must complete 120 credits, with 30 to 48 in the major, and maintain a minimum GPA of 2.0. A core curriculum of 60 credits is required, including 3 credits each in literary masterpieces, art, music or theater arts, and foreign language, with an additional 3 credits in English or a foreign language, and 3 credits in math, with an additional 3 credits in math, computer science, or statistics. 1 interdisciplinary course is required, as are 9 credits from social science disciplines, 6 credits in English composition, 6 credits in history, 6 credits in the natural science disciplines, and an additional 9 credits in courses offered outside the major department. **Procedure:** Freshmen are admitted in the fall. Entrance exams should be taken by December of senior year is recommended, but not required. There are early admissions and rolling admissions plans. Early decision applications should be filed by November 1; regular applications, by December 1 for fall entry. The fall 2017 application fee was $70. Notification of early decision is sent January 31; regular decision, February 28. Applications are accepted online. **Transfer Students:** 823 transfer students enrolled in 2016-2017. Applicants must have a minimum of 12 credit hours. Grades of C or better in courses that correspond in content and credit to those offered by the college transfer for credit. Transfer students are admitted in the fall and spring semesters. All high school and previous college transcripts are required. 30 of 120 credits required for the bachelor's degree must be completed at the Camden Campus. **International Students:** There are 88 international students enrolled. They must take the TOEFL with a minimum score of 550 on the paper-based TOEFL (PBT) or 79 on the Internet-based version (iBT). They must take the SAT or ACT, and also the IELTS with a score of 6.

ADMISSIONS: 69% of the 2017-2018 applicants were accepted. The SAT scores for the 2017-2018 freshman class were: Math-- 22% below 500, 56% between 500 and 599, 20% between 600 and 699, and 2% between 700 and 800. Evidence-Based Reading/Writing-- 22% below 500, 53% between 500 and 599, 21% between 600 and 699, and 3% between 700 and 800. 27% of the current freshmen were in the top fifth of their class; 62% were in the top two fifths. 2 freshmen graduated first in their class. **Admissions Contact:** Craig Westman, Camden Office of Admissions. Email: *admissions@camden.rutgers.edu* Web: *www.admissions.camden.rutgers.edu*

FINANCIAL AID: In 2017-2018, 95% of all full-time freshmen received some form of financial aid. 80% of all full-time freshmen received need-based aid. The average freshman award was $13,111. Need-based scholarships or need-based grants averaged $12,068; need-based self-help aid (loans and jobs) averaged $4,246; and other non-need-based awards and non-need-based scholarships averaged $5,806. The average financial indebtedness of the 2017 graduate was $28,816. The FAFSA code is 002629. The priority date for freshman financial aid applications for fall entry is December 1.

RUTGERS UNIVERSITY - NEW BRUNSWICK — D-3

www.newbrunswick.rutgers.edu

Piscataway, NJ 08854 — **(732) 932-4636**

Fax: (732) 445-0237 — **Email:** admissions@rutgers.edu

Full-time: 16,862 men, 16,815 women
Part-time: 866 men, 1098 women
Graduate: 5390 men, 8546 women
Year: semesters, summer session
Room & Board: $12,452

Faculty: 2438
Ph.D.s: 99%
Student/Faculty: 14 to 1
Tuition: $14,638 ($30,579)
Freshman Class: 38384 applied, 22186 accepted, 6268 enrolled

SAT EBR-W/M: 650/660 **ACT:** required
CEEB CODE: 2753
Application Deadline: December 1
HIGHLY COMPETITIVE

Rutgers University - New Brunswick was founded in 1766. Undergraduate students in New Brunswick enroll in the School of Arts and Sciences, the liberal arts college, and/or in one of the professional schools: School of Environmental and Biological Sciences (formerly Cook College); Mason Gross School of the Arts; Rutgers Business School: Undergraduate-New Brunswick; School of Communication, and Information; School of Engineering; Edward J. Bloustein School of Planning and Public Policy; the School of Management and Labor Relations; Ernest Mario School of Pharmacy; College of Nursing; School of Nursing; School of Health Related Professions; or the School of Public Health. Each school has individual requirements, policies, and fees. The New Jersey Medical and Health Sciences Education Restructuring Act went into effect, integrating Rutgers, with all units of the University of Medicine and Dentistry of New Jersey (UMDNJ), except University Hospital in Newark and the School of Osteopathic Medicine in Stratford. The integration of the legacy elements of UMDNJ into Rutgers has created a fourth unit, Rutgers Biomedical and Health Sciences (RBHS), which consists of a number of schools and units. There are 12 undergraduate schools and 17 graduate schools. In addition to regional accreditation, New Brunswick Campus has baccalaureate program accreditation with AACSB, ABET, ACPE, ADA, APTA, ASLA, CSWE, NASAD, NASM, ABOG, ACEND, ACGME, ACME, ACOTE, ANFP, APA, ARC-PA, ARRT, CAAHEP, CACREP, CAHIIM, CCNE, CEPH, COA, COARC, CORE, LCME, NAACLS, and NASD. The 2685-acre campus is in an urban area 33 miles south of New York City. Including any residence halls, there are 664 buildings.

STUDENT LIFE: 86% of undergraduates are from New Jersey. Others are from 48 states, 91 foreign countries, and Canada. 39% are White; 27% Asian American; 13% Hispanic; 9% Foreign; 7% African American; 3% two or more races; 2% race unknown. 33% claim no religious affiliation; 24% Catholic. **Female To Male Ratio:** 1.1:1. The average age of freshmen is 18; all undergraduates, 20. 9% do not continue beyond their first year; 80% remain to graduate. **Housing:** 15917 students can be accommodated in college housing, which includes gender neutral, single-sex, coed, and married student dorms and on-campus apartments. In addition, there are honors houses, language/international houses, special-interest houses, fraternity houses, sorority houses, substance-free house, math/science/engineering house for women, first-year residence, transfer center, and residence for single mothers with children. On-campus housing is available on a lottery system for upperclassmen. 58% of students commute. All students may keep cars. Alcohol is not permitted.

FACULTY/CLASSROOMS: 51% of faculty are male; 49% are female. No introductory courses are taught by graduate students. The average class size in an introductory lecture is 45 and in a laboratory is 36.

PROGRAMS OF STUDY: New Brunswick Campus confers B.A., B.S., B.F.A., B.Mus., and B.S.N. degrees. Associate, master's, and doctoral degrees are also awarded. Bachelor's degrees are awarded in AGRICULTURE (agriculture, animal science, environmental studies, natural resource management, and plant science), BIOLOGICAL SCIENCE (biochemistry, biology/biological science, biometrics and biostatistics, biotechnology, cell biology, entomology, genetics, marine biology, microbiology, molecular biology, and nutritional sciences), BUSINESS (accounting, business administration and management, business administration marketing, finance, human resource management, labor studies, labor studies, logistics, logistics, management science, marketing, supply chain management, and supply chain management), COMMUNICATIONS AND THE ARTS (African languages, art, art history and appreciation, Chinese, classical languages, comparative literature, dance, design, dramatic arts, English literature, film, television and digital media, French language and literature, Germanic languages and literature, Italian, journalism, linguistics, music, music performance, Portuguese, Russian, Spanish language and literature, and speech/debate/rhetoric), COMPUTER AND PHYSICAL SCIENCE (astrophysics, chemistry, computer science, geology, information science, information science, mathematics, physics, and statistics), ENGINEERING AND ENVIRONMENTAL DESIGN (aerospace engineering, agricultural engineering, bioengineering, biomedical engineering, ceramic science, chemical engineering, city/community/regional planning, civil engineering, electrical/electronics engineering, engineering science, environmental science, industry and systems engineering, industry and systems engineering, landscape architecture, landscape architecture, and mechanical engineering), HEALTH PROFESSIONS (allied health, clinical science, cytotechnology, dental hygiene, exercise science, exercise science, health care administration, health science, medical records administration/services, medical technology, nuclear medical technology, nursing, occupational therapy, pharmacy, public health, rehabilitation therapy, respiratory therapy, and ultrasound technology), SOCIAL SCIENCE (African American studies, American studies, anthropology, architectural studies, criminal justice, East Asian studies, economics, experimental psychology, food science, geography, Hispanic American studies, history, interdisciplinary studies, Judaic studies, Judaic studies, Latin American studies, Latin American studies, medieval studies, Middle Eastern studies, philosophy, political science/government, policy studies, psychology, religious studies, Russian and Slavic studies, social science, social work, sociology, urban studies, and women's studies). Agricultural sciences, arts and humanities, mathematics, pharmacology and toxicology are the strongest academically. Business administration and management, nursing, and pharmacy have the largest enrollments.

ACTIVITIES: 12% of men belong to 48 national fraternities; 9% of women belong to 23 national sororities. There are 750 groups on campus, including art, band, cheerleading, chess, choir, chorale, chorus, computers, dance, debate, drama, drill team, environmental, ethnic, film, honors, international, jazz band, LGBT, literary magazine, marching band, musical theater, newspaper, opera, orchestra, pep band, photography, political, professional, radio and TV, religious, social, social service, student government, symphony, and yearbook. Popular campus events include Theater Trips, Rutgers Day, and Football and Basketball games. **Sports:** There are 9 intercollegiate sports for men and 13 for women, and 50 intramural sports for men and 50 for women. Facilities include football and lacrosse stadium, an arena for basketball, gymnastics and wrestling, soccer stadium, volleyball gymnasium, baseball stadium, a softball stadium, an aquatics center, a tennis complex, a golf course, a boat house, and a combined track & field and field hockey complex, facilities for fitness training and indoor/outdoor practice sessions, 4 large recreation centers with 3 swimming pools, a separate freestanding fitness center, and outdoor space for intramural sports and other activities. **Graduates:** From July 1, 2016 to June 30, 2017, 8377 bachelor's degrees were awarded. The most popular majors were psychology (7%), kinesiology and exercise science (5%), and registered nursing (5%). In an average class, 59% graduate in 4 years or less and 80% graduate in 6 years or less.

SERVICES: Counseling and information services are available, as is tutoring in most subjects, such as assistance in difficult first- and second-level courses, and a reading assistance program. There is remedial math, reading, and writing. There is also a computer software with aids, library technology, and assistance. **Library/Resources:** The library contains 3.3 million volumes, 392,284 microform items, 90,247 audio/video tapes/CDs/DVDs, and subscribes to 234,580 periodicals, including electronic. Computerized library services include interlibrary loans, database searching, Internet access, and Wi-Fi capability. Special learning facilities include an art gallery, radio station, TV station, a geology museum, an astronomical observatory, and various research centers. **Physically Challenged Students:** Facilities include wheelchair ramps, elevators, special parking, specially equipped restrooms, special class scheduling, lowered drinking fountains, lowered telephones, and special housing. All classes are scheduled in accessible locations for disabled students. **Special:** 5-year B.A. or B.S./MBA program in Rutgers Business School, BS in Business Discipline/MBA; BA or BS in Science Discipline/MBA; 8-year Bachelor/Medical Dual Degree program with Robert Wood Johnson Medical School, 5-year BS/BS in Bioenvironmental engineering with the School of Engineering, 5-year accelerated baccalaureate-M.B.A with Rutgers Business School, Bureau of Engineering Research, supported by the university, industry, state and federal government, provides research opportunities for students and faculty; Continuing professional education, Exchange program between School of Engineering and the City University of London for qualified students majoring in civil, electrical, or mechanical engineering, 5-year (BA/BS degree) program in liberal arts and engineering, 5-year BA or BS/M.Ed. with the Graduate School of Education, Interdepartmental programs, and certificate programs are also available. There is Study Abroad in England, France, Italy, Ireland, Germany, Greece, Mexico, Israel, Australia, India, Japan, Netherlands, Scotland, South Africa, South Korea, Spain and several others. Alumnae externship program, Language and Cultural House Program, B.A. in Religion/M.A. in Religious Studies, B.A./Master of Communication and Information Studies (with SC&I), B.A./MLER (with School of Management and Labor Relations), Baccalaureate/M.C.R.P. or M.P.P with EJB School of Planning and Public Policy, Baccalaureate in Business major/Master of Human Resource Management (with School of Management and Labor Relations-SMLR), BS/Master of Business and Science (MBS). Pharm.D./MBA program with Rutgers Business School, Pharm.D./M.P.H., Pharm.D./Ph.D.in Pharmaceutical Science, Pharm.D./Ph.D. in Toxicology, and Pharm.D./M.D. There are 2 national honor societies, Phi Beta Kappa, and a freshman honors program. **Visiting:** There are regularly scheduled orientations for prospective students, consisting of residence halls, classroom buildings, and student centers. Student guides will talk about their experiences and admissions counselors will discuss academics and the admissions process. To schedule a visit, contact the Visitor Center at (732) 445-4636. **Campus Safety and Security:** Measures include 24-hour foot and vehicle patrol, emergency notification system, self-defense education, and security escort services. There are shuttle buses, emergency telephones, lighted pathways/sidewalks, and controlled access to dorms/residences. The police department is supplemented by security guards and student safety officers.

REQUIREMENTS: The SAT or ACT is required. A high school diploma is required; the GED is accepted. Students must have completed a general college-preparatory program, including 16 academic credits or Carnegie units, with 4 years of English, 3 years of math (4 recommended), including (algebra I and II, and geometry), 2 years each of foreign language and science, and 5 in electives. Engineering students need 4 years of math and must take chemistry and physics for sciences, and for nursing and pharmacy students they must take biology and chemistry. AP and CLEP credits are accepted. Important factors in the admissions decision are advanced placement or honors courses, evidence of special talent, and geographical diversity. To graduate, students must complete 120 credits, with a minimum GPA of 2.0. A liberal arts core requirement includes 6 credits in Writing, 6 credits in Quantitative Reasoning, 6 credits in Natural Sciences, Social Sciences, 12 credits in Humanities, 3 credits each in Diversity, and Global Awareness. Check with the individual college for specific program requirements. **Procedure:** Freshmen are admitted in the in the fall. Entrance exams should be taken by December of senior year is recommended. There are early admissions and rolling admissions plans. Early decision applications should be filed by November 1; regular applications, by December 1 for fall entry. The fall 2017 application fee was $70. Notification of early decision is sent January 31; regular decision, February 28. Applications are accepted on-line. **Transfer Students:** 2902 transfer students enrolled in 2016-2017. Applicant must have a minimum of 12 credit hours earned. High school and college transcripts are required. Transfers are admitted in the fall or spring. 30 of 120 credits required for the bachelor's degree must be completed at New Brunswick Campus. **International Students:** There are 3119 international students enrolled. They must take the TOEFL with a minimum score of 550 on the paper-based TOEFL (PBT) or 79 on the Internet-based version (iBT). Student's may also take the IELTS, scoring 6.5.

ADMISSIONS: 58% of the 2017-2018 applicants were accepted. The SAT scores for the 2017-2018 freshman class were: Math-- 1% below 500, 20% between 500 and 599, 44% between 600 and 699, and 36% between 700 and 800. Evidence-Based Reading/Writing-- 1% below 500, 20% between 500 and 599, 54% between 600 and 699, and 24% between

700 and 800. 63% of the current freshmen were in the top fifth of their class; 90% were in the top two fifths. 52 freshmen graduated first in their class. **Admissions Contact:** Office of the Undergraduate Admissions. Email: *admissions@rutgers.edu* Web: *www.newbrunswick.rutgers.edu*

FINANCIAL AID: In 2017-2018, 71% of all full-time freshmen received some form of financial aid. 49% of all full-time freshmen received need-based aid. The average freshman award was $13,279. Need-based scholarships or need-based grants averaged $12,590; need-based self-help aid (loans and jobs) averaged $4,706; non-need-based athletic scholarships averaged $29,630; and other non-need-based awards and non-need-based scholarships averaged $9,123. The average financial indebtedness of the 2017 graduate was $24,861. The FAFSA code is 002629. The priority date for freshman financial aid applications for fall entry is December 1.

RUTGERS UNIVERSITY - NEWARK E-2

www.admissions.newark.rutgers.edu

Newark, NJ 07102 **(973) 353-5205**

Fax: (973) 353-3789 **Email: newark@admissions.rutgers.edu**

Full-time: 3220 men, 3942 women	**Faculty:** 383
Part-time: 650 men, 739 women	**Ph.D.s:** 99%
Graduate: 2255 men, 1962 women	**Student/Faculty:** 17 to 1
Year: semesters, summer session	**Tuition:** $14,085 ($30,026)
Room & Board: $13,266	**Freshman Class:** 13435 applied, 8631 accepted, 1325 enrolled
SAT EBR-W/M: 540/540 **ACT:** required	**CEEB CODE:** 2753
Application Deadline: December 1	**COMPETITIVE**

Rutgers University - Newark, founded in 1908, is comprised of 5 undergraduate, degree-granting schools: Newark College of Arts and Sciences, University College-Newark, Rutgers Business School, Undergraduate-Newark, College of Nursing, School of Nursing, School of Criminal Justice and the School of Public Affairs and Administration. Some schools located in Newark and/or New Brunswick are also part of the Rutgers Biomedical and Health Sciences unit and are listed for each campus. Each school has individual requirements, policies, and fees. The New Jersey Medical and Health Sciences Education Restructuring Act went into effect, integrating Rutgers, The State University of New Jersey, with all units of the University of Medicine and Dentistry of New Jersey (UMDNJ), except University Hospital in Newark and the School of Osteopathic Medicine in Stratford. The integration of the legacy elements of UMDNJ into Rutgers has created a fourth unit, Rutgers Biomedical and Health Sciences (RBHS), which consists of a number of schools and units. In addition to regional accreditation, Newark Campus has baccalaureate program accreditation with AACSB, CSWE, and CCNE. The 40-acre campus is in an urban area 7 miles west of New York City. Including any residence halls, there are 70 buildings.

STUDENT LIFE: 93% of undergraduates are from New Jersey. Others are from 22 states, 55 foreign countries, and Canada. 5% are Foreign; 4% race unknown; 3% two or more races; 28% Hispanic; 22% White; 19% African American; 18% Asian American. 30% are Catholic; 26% Protestant; 18% claim no religious affiliation. **Female To Male Ratio:** 1.1:1. The average age of freshmen is 18; all undergraduates, 21. 17% do not continue beyond their first year; 66% remain to graduate. **Housing:** 2050 students can be accommodated in college housing, which includes gender neutral, single-sex, coed, married student dorms, and on-campus apartments. In addition, there are honors houses, language/international houses, special interest housing, language and cultural houses, substance-free house, math/science engineering house for women, first-year residence, transfer center, and residence for single mothers and children. 69% of students commute. All students may keep cars. Alcohol is not permitted.

FACULTY/CLASSROOMS: 63% of faculty are male; 37% are female. No introductory courses are taught by graduate students. The average class size in an introductory lecture is 36 and in a laboratory is 40.

PROGRAMS OF STUDY: Newark Campus confers B.A., B.S. and B.F.A. degrees. Associate, master's, and doctoral degrees are also awarded. Bachelor's degrees are awarded in BIOLOGICAL SCIENCE (biology/biological science and zoology), BUSINESS (accounting, business administration and management, finance, management information systems, management science, marketing, and supply chain management), COMMUNICATIONS AND THE ARTS (art, dramatic arts, English, film arts, journalism, music, Portuguese, Spanish, and visual and performing arts), COMPUTER AND PHYSICAL SCIENCE (applied mathematics, applied physics, chemistry, computer science, geology, geoscience, information sciences and systems, mathematics, and physics), ENGINEERING AND ENVIRONMENTAL DESIGN (environmental science and geological engineering), HEALTH PROFESSIONS (allied health, clinical science, medical laboratory technology, and medical records administration/services), SOCIAL SCIENCE (African American studies, American studies, anthropology, classical/ancient civilization, criminal justice, economics, experimental psychology, history, interdisciplinary studies, philosophy, political science/government, psychology, public administration, social work, sociology, and women's studies). Business and criminal justice is the strongest academically. Accounting, criminal justice, and finance have the largest enrollments.

ACTIVITIES: There are no fraternities or sororities. There are 200 groups on campus, including band, chess, chorus, dance, debate, drama, ethnic, honors, international, jazz band, LGBT, literary magazine, marching band, musical theater, newspaper, opera, orchestra, pep band, professional, radio and TV, religious, social, social service, student government, symphony, and yearbook. Popular campus events include Alpha Sigma Lambda, Black History Month, and Honors Convocation. **Sports:** There are 7 intercollegiate sports for men and 7 for women, and 8 intramural sports for men and 8 for women. Facilities include athletic and recreation facility with a main arena for basketball and volleyball, a fitness center, a 25-yard swimming pool, 2 racquetball courts, a dance/exercise studio, an artificial turf field for outdoor sports including soccer, softball, baseball, and tennis complex. **Graduates:** From July 1, 2016 to June 30, 2017, 1559 bachelor's degrees were awarded. The most popular majors were accounting (16%), psychology (12%), criminal justice, and and safety studies (11%). In an average class, 34% graduate in 4 years or less and 66% graduate in 6 years or less.

SERVICES: Counseling and information services are available, as is tutoring in most subjects. There is a reader service for the blind, and remedial math, reading, and writing. **Library/Resources:** The library contains 1.6 million volumes, 127,095 microform items, 51,384 audio/video tapes/CDs/DVDs, and subscribes to 177,570 periodicals, including electronic. Computerized library services include interlibrary loans, database searching, Internet access, and Wi-Fi capability. Special learning facilities include an art gallery, radio station, a molecular and behavioral neuroscience center, and institutes for jazz, and animal behavior. **Physically Challenged Students:** Facilities include wheelchair ramps, elevators, special parking, specially equipped restrooms, special class scheduling, lowered drinking fountains, lowered telephones, and special housing. Facilities vary from building to building. All classes are scheduled in accessible locations for disabled students. **Special:** Students may cross-register with the New Jersey Institute of Technology. Internships are available. The school offers study abroad in over 30 countries, accelerated degree programs in business administration and criminal justice, co-op programs, independent study, distance learning, English as a Second Language, dual majors, student-designed majors, nondegree study, and pass/fail options. Contact the school for information on the Honors College. 5-year baccalaureate-MBA with Rutgers Business School; BS in Business Discipline/MBA; BA or BS in Science Discipline/MBA; Baccalaureate/M.A. in Criminal Justice with the School of Criminal Justice; Baccalaureate/MPA with the School of Public Affairs and Administration; Cooperative baccalaureate program with School of Engineering (New Brunswick campus); Cooperative baccalaureate in medical technology with affiliated hospitals; Interdisciplinary programs in archaeology, international affairs, legal studies, women's studies; continuing professional education; Baccalaureate in Business Major/Master of Human Resource Management (with School of Management and Labor Relations in New Brunswick); Baccalaureate-master's dual degree programs with the School of Criminal Justice and Rutgers Business School; BA or BS in Biology/MS in Biology; BA in Chemistry/MS in Chemistry; BA in Economics/MA in Economics; BS in Environmental Sciences/MS In Environmental Geology; BS in Environmental Sciences/MS in Environmental Sciences; BA in Political Science, Sociology or Anthropology/MS in Global Affairs; BA in History/MA in History; BA in History, Sociology or Anthropology/MA in Jazz History and Research; BA in Political Science/MA in Political Science; BA/MA in Peace and Conflict Studies; BS in Computer Science or Information Science/Master of Information Technology; BS in Accounting/Master of Accountancy (Governmental Accounting or Financial Accounting); BS in Accounting/

MBA in Professional Accounting; BS in Finance/Master of Quantitative Finance; BS/Master of Business and Science (MBS); BS in Nursing/MS in Nursing; BA in Psychology/MA in Psychology; Master of Public Administration/Master of Accountancy in Governmental Accounting; MS in Global Affairs/Master of Public Policy (with Bloustein School in New Brunswick); Pharm.D./M.B.A. program with Rutgers Business School. There are 12 national honor societies, Phi Beta Kappa, and a freshman honors program. **Visiting:** There are regularly scheduled orientations for prospective students, including an information session with an admissions counselor and a tour of the campus. There are guides for informal visits. To schedule a visit, contact the Office of Undergraduate and Graduate Admissions. **Campus Safety and Security:** Measures include 24-hour foot and vehicle patrol, emergency notification system, self-defense education, and security escort services. There are shuttle buses, emergency telephones, lighted pathways/sidewalks, and controlled access to dorms/residences. There are security guards who assist Rutgers police in providing public safety services.

REQUIREMENTS: A high school diploma is required; the GED is accepted. The ACT and the SAT: Subject tests are required of students without a high school diploma from an accredited high school and from some GED holders. Students should have completed 16 high school academic credits or Carnegie units, with 4 years of English, 3 years of math, (4 recommended) 2 years each of science, a general college-preparatory program, and foreign language, and 5 additional electives. Biology and chemistry are required for nursing students. AP and CLEP credits are accepted. Important factors in the admissions decision are advanced placement or honors courses, evidence of special talent, and leadership record. To graduate, students must complete 124 credits with a minimum GPA of 2.0. Distribution requirements include 8 credits in natural science/math or 3 courses in nonlab science, math, or computer science; 6 credits each in history, literature, social sciences, humanities, and fine arts; 1 course in critical thinking; and 15 credits of electives. All students must take English composition and demonstrate math proficiency either by exam or by successfully completing a college algebra course or any other advanced course in math, a college calculus course, (with a grade of C or better) or a precalculus course (with a grade of B or better). **Procedure:** Freshmen are admitted in the fall. Entrance exams should be taken by December of senior year is recommended, but not required. There are early admissions and rolling admissions plans. Early decision applications should be filed by November 1; regular applications, by December 1 for fall entry. The fall 2017 application fee was $70. Notification of early decision is sent January 31; regular decision, February 28. Applications are accepted on-line. **Transfer Students:** 1088 transfer students enrolled in 2016-2017. Students who have completed at least 12 credit hours at another college with a cumulative GPA of 2.0 are considered for admission as transfer students. Transfers are admitted in the fall and spring. High school and college transcripts are required. 30 of 124 credits required for the bachelor's degree must be completed at the Newark Campus. **International Students:** There are 394 international students enrolled. They must take the TOEFL with a minimum score of 550 on the paper-based TOEFL (PBT) or 79 on the Internet-based version (iBT) and the college's own test. Students may also take the IELTS, scoring 6.

ADMISSIONS: 64% of the 2017-2018 applicants were accepted. The SAT scores for the 2017-2018 freshman class were: Math-- 20% below 500, 57% between 500 and 599, 20% between 600 and 699, and 3% between 700 and 800. Evidence-Based Reading/Writing-- 20% below 500, 58% between 500 and 599, 20% between 600 and 699, and 2% between 700 and 800. 42% of the current freshmen were in the top fifth of their class; 77% were in the top two fifths. 5 freshmen graduated first in their class. **Admissions Contact:** Newark Campus, the Office of Admissions. Email: *newark@admissions.rutgers.edu* Web: *www.admissions.newark.rutgers.edu*

FINANCIAL AID: In 2017-2018, 82% of all full-time freshmen received some form of financial aid. 72% of all full-time freshmen received need-based aid. The average freshman award was $13,988. Need-based scholarships or need-based grants averaged $12,368; need-based self-help aid (loans and jobs) averaged $3,953; and other non-need-based awards and non-need-based scholarships averaged $7,815. The average financial indebtedness of the 2017 graduate was $26,823. The FAFSA code is 002629. The priority date for freshman financial aid applications for fall entry is December 1.

SAINT PETER'S UNIVERSITY — E-2

www.saintpeters.edu

Jersey City, NJ 07306 — (201) 915-9213

Fax: (201) 432-5860	**Email:** admissions@saintpeters.edu
Full-time: 825 men, 1077 women	**Faculty:** IIA, av$
Part-time: 101 men, 314 women	**Ph.D.s:** 80%
Graduate: 282 men, 446 women	**Student/Faculty:** 13 to 1
Year: semesters, summer session	**Tuition:** $34,198
Room & Board: $14,994	**Freshman Class:** 3256 applied, 1973 accepted, 393 enrolled
SAT or ACT: required	**CEEB CODE:** 2806
Application Deadline: open	**COMPETITIVE**

Saint Peter's University, founded in 1872, is a private liberal arts and business college affiliated with the Roman Catholic Church and known as New Jersey's Jesuit College. There are 4 undergraduate schools and 3 graduate schools. In addition to regional accreditation, SPU has baccalaureate program accreditation with CCNE and IACBE. The 30-acre campus is in an urban area in Jersey City, 2 miles west of New York City. Including any residence halls, there are 29 buildings.

STUDENT LIFE: 87% of undergraduates are from New Jersey. Others are from 29 states, and 36 foreign countries. 56% are from public schools. 44% are White; 30% Hispanic; 29% African American; 10% Asian American; 1% American Indian/Alaska Native. 68% are Catholic. **Female To Male Ratio:** 1.5:1. The average age of freshmen is 18; all undergraduates, 24. 23% do not continue beyond their first year; 51% remain to graduate. **Housing:** 863 students can be accommodated in college housing, which includes dorms and on-campus apartments. In addition, there are special-interest houses, and community service houses. On-campus housing is guaranteed for all 4 years. 50% of students commute. Upperclassmen may keep cars.

FACULTY/CLASSROOMS: 50% of faculty are male; 50% are female. All teach undergraduates. No introductory courses are taught by graduate students. The average class size in an introductory lecture is 23; in a laboratory is 14; and in a regular course is 16.

PROGRAMS OF STUDY: SPU confers B.A., B.S., and B.S.N. degrees. Associate, master's, and doctoral degrees are also awarded. Bachelor's degrees are awarded in BIOLOGICAL SCIENCE (biochemistry and biology/biological science), BUSINESS (accounting, business administration and management, international business management, and marketing/retailing/merchandising), COMMUNICATIONS AND THE ARTS (art history and appreciation, classical languages, communications, English, fine arts, graphic design, modern language, Spanish, and visual and performing arts), COMPUTER AND PHYSICAL SCIENCE (chemistry, computer science, mathematics, natural sciences, and physics), EDUCATION (elementary education and secondary education), HEALTH PROFESSIONS (biomedical science, health care administration, medical laboratory technology, nursing, predentistry, and premedicine), SOCIAL SCIENCE (African American studies, American studies, classical/ancient civilization, criminal justice, economics, history, humanities, interdisciplinary studies, international studies, Latin American studies, philosophy, political science/government, prelaw, psychology, social science, sociology, theological studies, and urban studies). Natural sciences, and accounting are the strongest academically. Business management, accounting, and computer sciences have the largest enrollments.

ACTIVITIES: There are no fraternities or sororities. There are 50 groups on campus, including cheerleading, chess, choir, chorus, computers, debate, drama, ethnic, forensics, honors, international, literary magazine, newspaper, pep band, political, professional, radio and TV, religious, social, social service, and student government. Popular campus events include International Day, Career Fairs, and SpringFest. **Sports:** There are 10 intercollegiate sports for men and 8 for women, and 20 intramural sports for men and 18 for women. Facilities include a recreational center, a gym, athletic field, baseball, basketball, cross country, golf, indoor-outdoor track, swimming/diving, tennis, and volleyball. **Graduates:** From July 1, 2016 to June 30, 2017, 489 bachelor's degrees were awarded. The most popular majors were business/marketing (29%), biological/life sciences (10%), and health professions and related programs (9%). In an average class, 53% graduate in 6 years or less.

SERVICES: Counseling and information services are available, as is

tutoring in every subject. There is a reader service for the blind, and remedial math, reading, and writing. **Library/Resources:** The library contains 285,000 volumes, 70,000 microform items, 3,800 audio/video tapes/CDs/DVDs, and subscribes to 1,800 periodicals, including electronic. Computerized library services include interlibrary loans, database searching, Internet access, and Wi-Fi capability. Special learning facilities include an art gallery, radio station, TV station, nursing lab, human perception and performance laboratory. **Physically Challenged Students:** 80% of the campus is accessible. Facilities include wheelchair ramps, elevators, special parking, specially equipped restrooms, special class scheduling, lowered drinking fountains, lowered telephones, and special housing. **Special:** There are co-op programs with local companies, as well as departmental programs, and many internships available in Jersey City and nearby New York City. A Washington semester and study abroad in any of 60 countries are offered. There are preprofessional programs in dentistry, pharmacy, physician assistant, and physical therapy. The college also offers dual majors and student-designed majors, credit for life, military, and work experience, nondegree study, and pass/fail options. There are 9 national honor societies, a freshman honors program, and 1 departmental honors program. **Visiting:** There are regularly scheduled orientations for prospective students, including open houses, weekend and weekday visit days with a tour, class information sessions, and interviews by appointment. To schedule a visit, contact the Admissions Office. **Campus Safety and Security:** Measures include 24-hour foot and vehicle patrol, self-defense education, and security escort services. There are shuttle buses, emergency telephones, and security desk monitoring access to residence halls.

REQUIREMENTS: The SAT or ACT is required. Applicants must be high school graduates or submit the GED certificate. Students should have completed 16 Carnegie units of high school study, including 4 years of English, 3 of math, 2 each of science, history, and a foreign language, and another 3 of additional work in any of these subjects. An essay and 2 letters of recommendation are required, and an interview is recommended. SPU requires applicants to be in the upper 97% of their class. A GPA of 3.1 is required. AP and CLEP credits are accepted. Important factors in the admissions decision are advanced placement or honors courses, extracurricular activities record, and recommendations by school officials. To graduate, students must complete 129 credit hours, including 57 in the core curriculum, 12 in core electives, between 30 and 45 in the major, and the rest in subjects related to the major. The core curriculum requires 9 credits of natural sciences, 6 to 8 of math, and 3 each of social science, philosophy, history, literature, modern language, fine arts, and composition. Students must earn a 2.0 GPA. **Procedure:** Freshmen are admitted in the fall and spring. Entrance exams should be taken by the fall of the senior year. There are early admissions, deferred admissions, and rolling admissions plans. Application deadlines are open. Notification is sent on a rolling basis. 299 applicants were on the 2017 waiting list; 290 were admitted. Applications are accepted on-line. **Transfer Students:** 164 transfer students enrolled in 2016-2017. The school requires a 2.0 college GPA of transfer students, as well as a high school transcript and a satisfactory composite SAT score for students less than 2 years out of high school. An interview is recommended. 30 of 129 credits required for the bachelor's degree must be completed at SPU. **International Students:** They must take the TOEFL.

ADMISSIONS: 61% of the 2017-2018 applicants were accepted. **Admissions Contact:** Joseph Giglio, Director of Admissions. Email: *admissions@saintpeters.edu* Web: *www.saintpeters.edu*

FINANCIAL AID: SPU is a member of CSS. The FAFSA code is 002638. Check with the school for current application deadlines.

SETON HALL UNIVERSITY — D-2

www.shu.edu

South Orange, NJ 07079 — **(973) 313-6146**

Fax: (973) 275-2040	**Email: thehall@shu.edu**
Full-time: 2468 men, 3104 women	**Faculty:** 339
Part-time: 92 men, 154 women	**Ph.D.s:** 88%
Graduate: 1527 men, 1667 women	**Student/Faculty:** 14 to 1
Year: semesters, summer session	**Tuition:** $40,440
Room & Board: $17,568	**Freshman Class:** 6436 applied, 5474 accepted, 993 enrolled
SAT CR/M/W: 530/540/550 **ACT:** 23	**CEEB CODE:** 2811
Application Deadline: March 1	**COMPETITIVE**

Seton Hall University, founded in 1856, is the oldest U.S. diocesan Catholic university, under the Archdiocese of Newark, offering degrees at the baccalaureate, master, and doctoral and professional levels. The figures in the above capsule and in this profile are approximate. There are 8 undergraduate schools and 8 graduate schools. In addition to regional accreditation, SHU has baccalaureate program accreditation with AACSB, CSWE, and CCNE. The 58-acre campus is in a suburban area in south Orange, New Jersey, 14 miles west of New York City. Including any residence halls, there are 35 buildings.

STUDENT LIFE: 76% of undergraduates are from New Jersey. Others are from 43 states, 70 foreign countries, and Canada. 69% are from public schools. 9% are Asian American; 51% White; 5% race unknown; 3% Foreign; 3% two or more races; 19% Hispanic; 10% African American. 69% are Catholic; 14% Protestant. **Female To Male Ratio:** 1.2:1. The average age of freshmen is 18; all undergraduates, 21. 19% do not continue beyond their first year; 65% remain to graduate. **Housing:** 2236 students can be accommodated in college housing, which includes dorms and off-campus apartments. In addition, there are honors houses and special-interest houses. On-campus housing is available on a lottery system for upperclassmen. 80% of students live on campus. Upperclassmen may keep cars.

FACULTY/CLASSROOMS: 53% of faculty are male; 47% are female. No introductory courses are taught by graduate students. The average class size in an introductory lecture is 26; in a laboratory is 17; and in a regular course is 21.

PROGRAMS OF STUDY: SHU confers B.A., B.S., B.A.B.A., B.S.B., B.S.E., B.S.I.R. and B.S.N. degrees. Master's and doctoral degrees are also awarded. Bachelor's degrees are awarded in AGRICULTURE (environmental studies), BIOLOGICAL SCIENCE (biochemistry and biology/biological science), BUSINESS (accounting, business administration and management, business economics, finance, management information systems, marketing management, and sports management), COMMUNICATIONS AND THE ARTS (applied music, art history, broadcasting, classics, communications, creative writing, English, fine arts, French, graphic design, Italian, journalism, modern language, music, Spanish, and theatre arts), COMPUTER AND PHYSICAL SCIENCE (chemistry, computer science, mathematics, and physics), EDUCATION (elementary education, secondary education, and special education), HEALTH PROFESSIONS (nursing), SOCIAL SCIENCE (African American studies, anthropology, Asian/Oriental studies, criminal justice, economics, history, international relations, Latin American studies, liberal arts/general studies, philosophy, political science/government, psychology, religion, social science, social work, sociology, and theological studies). Business, biology, and diplomacy are the strongest academically. Nursing has the largest enrollment.

ACTIVITIES: 7% of men belong to 11 national fraternities; 11% of women belong to 14 national sororities. There are 124 groups on campus, including recreation, student Ambassador Society, art, cheerleading, chess, choir, chorus, commuter council, computers, dance, drama, drill team, environmental, ethnic, film, forensics, honors, international, literary magazine, musical theater, newspaper, pep band, photography, political, professional, radio and TV, religious, social, social service, and student government. Popular campus events include University Day, Theatre-in-the-Round, and Career Day. **Sports:** There are 6 intercollegiate sports for men and 8 for women, and 13 intramural sports for men and 13 for women. Facilities include on-campus arena, recreational field house, indoor track, indoor pool, fitness and aerobics rooms, a soccer and baseball field, a softball field, tennis and racquetball courts, and men's basketball. **Graduates:** From July 1, 2016 to June 30, 2017, 1101 bachelor's degrees were awarded. The most popular majors were health professions and related programs (19%), business/marketing (16%), and social sciences (12%). Of the 2016 graduating class, 29% were enrolled in graduate school within 6 months of graduation, and 77% were employed.

SERVICES: Counseling and information services are available, as is tutoring in most subjects. There is a reader service for the blind, and remedial math, reading, and writing. The Academic Resource Center offers support for students interested in national scholarship opportunities and aids students who are pursuing interdisciplinary and preprofessional majors. **Library/Resources:** The library contains 629,978 volumes, 500,000 microform items, 5,340 audio/video tapes/CDs/DVDs, and subscribes to 29,000 periodicals, including electronic. Computerized library services include interlibrary loans, database searching, Internet access, and Wi-Fi capability. Special learning facilities include an art gallery, radio station, TV station, various institutes, and centers for learning and research. **Physically Challenged Students:** 95% of the campus is accessible. Facilities include wheelchair ramps, elevators, special parking, specially equipped restrooms, special class scheduling, lowered drinking fountains, and special housing. **Special:** Co-op and work-study are possible through the College of Arts and Sciences and the School of Business; internships are available through the College of Arts and Sciences and School of Diplomacy. Education majors go into the field during their sophomore year. Engineering 3+2 degrees are available with the New Jersey Institute of Technology. Study abroad is available in 15 countries. An accelerated B.S.N. degree is offered. There are a total of 17 bachelor/graduate dual degree programs, and non-degree study programs. There are 27 national honor societies, a freshman honors program, and 5 departmental honors programs. **Visiting:** There are regularly scheduled orientations for prospective students, including campus tours weekdays and Saturdays during the academic year and on weekdays during the summer. Open houses for prospective applicants are available each fall. Visitors may sit in on classes. To schedule a visit, contact the Enrollment Services Office at (973) 761-9332. **Campus Safety and Security:** Measures include 24-hour foot and vehicle patrol, emergency notification system, self-defense education, and security escort services. There are shuttle buses, emergency telephones, lighted pathways/sidewalks, controlled access to dorms/residences, and security attendants are posted at residence hall entrances.

REQUIREMENTS: SHU recommends a satisfactory score on the SAT or a minimum composite score on the ACT. Applicants must supply high school transcripts or a GED certificate. Students should have completed 16 Carnegie units of high school study, including 4 years of English, 3 of math, 2 each of foreign language and either history or social studies, 1 of science, and 4 academic electives. An essay is required and an interview is recommended. AP and CLEP credits are accepted. Important factors in the admissions decision are advanced placement or honors courses, leadership record, and parents or siblings attended your school. To graduate, students must complete the University Core Curriculum and complete at least 120 credit hours earning a minimum GPA of 2.0. **Procedure:** Freshmen are admitted in the fall and spring. Entrance exams should be taken by January of the senior year. There are early admissions, deferred admissions, and rolling admissions plans. Application deadlines are open. The fall 2017 application fee was $55. Notification is sent on a rolling basis. Applications are accepted on-line. **Transfer Students:** 315 transfer students enrolled in 2016-2017. Applicants should have earned 30 hours of college credit, with a minimum GPA of 2.5, or 2.8 for the business and science schools. The SAT is required for students with fewer than 30 credits of college-level work at the time of application, and an interview is recommended. 30 of 120 credits required for the bachelor's degree must be completed at SHU. **International Students:** There are 90 international students enrolled. They must take the TOEFL with a minimum score of 550 on the paper-based TOEFL (PBT) or 79 on the Internet-based version (iBT). They must also take the SAT.

ADMISSIONS: 85% of the 2017-2018 applicants were accepted. The SAT scores for the 2017-2018 freshman class were: Critical Reading-- 29% below 500, 49% between 500 and 599, 21% between 600 and 699, and 1% between 700 and 800. Math-- 26% below 500, 49% between 500 and 599, 24% between 600 and 699, and 2% between 700 and 800. Writing-- 24% below 500, 48% between 500 and 599, 26% between 600 and 699, and 2% between 700 and 800. The ACT scores were 20% below 12, 33% between 12 and 17, 27% between 18 and 23, 8% between 24 and 29, and 13% above 30. 48% of the current freshmen were in the top fifth of their class; 72% were in the top two fifths. 1 freshman graduated first in the class. **Admissions Contact:** Wendy Lin-Cook, Assistant Vice President for Admissions. Email: *thehall@shu.edu* Web: *www.shu.edu*

FINANCIAL AID: The FAFSA code is 002632. The priority date for freshman financial aid applications for fall entry is March 1.

STEVENS INSTITUTE OF TECHNOLOGY E-2

www.stevens.edu

Hoboken, NJ 07030	(201) 216-5699 (800) 458-5323 Email: admissions@stevens.edu
Full-time: 2185 men, 928 women	**Faculty:** 257; I, +$
Part-time: 8 men, 2 women	**Ph.D.s:** 95%
Graduate: 2705 men, 1088 women	**Student/Faculty:** 10 to 1
Year: semesters, summer session	**Tuition:** $50,554
Room & Board: $14,400	**Freshman Class:** 8335 applied, 3657 accepted, 762 enrolled
SAT EBR-W/M: 673/712 **ACT:** 31	**CEEB CODE:** 2819
Application Deadline: January 15	**MOST COMPETITIVE**

Stevens Institute of Technology, founded in 1870, is a private institution offering programs of study in science, computer science, engineering, business, and humanities. There are 4 undergraduate schools and 3 graduate schools. In addition to regional accreditation, SIT has baccalaureate program accreditation with ABET, CSAB, MSCHE, ACS, and and AACSB. The 55-acre campus is in an urban area on the banks of the Hudson River. Including any residence halls, there are 25 buildings.

STUDENT LIFE: 59% of undergraduates are from New Jersey. Others are from 37 states, 39 foreign countries, and Canada. 67% are White; 4% Foreign; 4% race unknown; 2% African American; 12% Asian American; 10% Hispanic. **Male To Female Ratio:** 2.4:1. The average age of freshmen is 18; all undergraduates, 20. 6% do not continue beyond their first year; 94% remain to graduate. **Housing:** College-sponsored housing includes single-sex, coed, and off-campus apartments. In addition, there are special-interest houses, fraternity houses, and sorority houses. On-campus housing is guaranteed for all 4 years. 64% of students live on campus. Alcohol is not permitted. Upperclassmen may keep cars.

FACULTY/CLASSROOMS: 73% of faculty are male; 27% are female. 91% teach undergraduates. No introductory courses are taught by graduate students. The average class size in an introductory lecture is 75; in a laboratory is 20; and in a regular course is 25.

PROGRAMS OF STUDY: SIT confers B.A., B.S., B.E., M.S., M.B.A., and M.A. Engineer degrees. Master's and doctoral degrees are also awarded. Bachelor's degrees are awarded in BIOLOGICAL SCIENCE (biochemistry and bioinformatics), BUSINESS (business administration and management), COMMUNICATIONS AND THE ARTS (literature and music technology), COMPUTER AND PHYSICAL SCIENCE (chemistry, computer science, computer security and information assurance, digital arts/technology, information sciences and systems, mathematics, physics, and science technology), ENGINEERING AND ENVIRONMENTAL DESIGN (biomedical engineering, chemical engineering, civil engineering, computational sciences, computer engineering, electrical/electronics engineering, engineering management, engineering physics, environmental engineering, mechanical engineering, naval architecture and marine engineering, and systems engineering), SOCIAL SCIENCE (history and philosophy). Engineering is the strongest academically. Mechanical engineering, civil engineering, and business have the largest enrollments.

ACTIVITIES: 46% of men belong to 12 national fraternities; 34% of women belong to 6 national sororities. There are 120 groups on campus, including anime, paintball, SAE, art, band, chess, choir, chorus, computers, dance, debate, drama, engineers without borders, environmental, ethnic, film, honors, international, jazz band, literary magazine, musical theater, newspaper, orchestra, pep band, photography, political, professional, radio and TV, religious, social, social service, student government, and symphony. Popular campus events include Fall Tech Fest, Spring Boken Festival, and Midnight Breakfast. **Sports:** There are 13 intercollegiate sports for men and 13 for women, and 8 intramural sports for men and 8 for women. Facilities include a complex with swimming pool, a basketball arena, fitness rooms, racquetball/squash courts, playing field, and several outdoor courts. **Graduates:** From July 1, 2016 to June 30, 2017, 638 bachelor's degrees were awarded. The most popular majors were engineering (62%), business/marketing (13%), and computer and information sciences (9%). In an average class, 25% graduate in 4 years or less, 72% graduate in 5 years or less, and 76% graduate in 6 years or less. Of the 2016 graduating class, 20% were enrolled in graduate school within 6 months of graduation, and 75% were employed.

SERVICES: Counseling and information services are available, as is tutoring in every subject. **Library/Resources:** The library contains 66,492 volumes, 497 microform items, and subscribes to 35,353 periodicals including electronic. Computerized library services include interlibrary loans, database searching, Internet access, and Wi-Fi capability. Special learning facilities include a radio station, TV station, a lab for ocean and coastal engineering, an environmental lab, design and manufacturing institute, technology center, telecommunications institute, computer vision lab, an ultrafast laser spectroscopy and high-speed communications lab, and a wireless network security center. **Physically Challenged Students:** All of the campus is accessible. Facilities include wheelchair ramps, elevators, special parking, specially equipped restrooms, lowered drinking fountains, and special housing. **Special:** SIT offers cross-registration and a 3-2 engineering degree with New York University, a work-study program within the school, co-op programs, corporate and research internships through the Undergraduate Projects in Technology and Medicine, study abroad in 7 countries, and pass/fail options for extra courses. Students may undertake dual majors as well as accelerated degree programs in medicine, dentistry, and law and can receive a B.A.-B.E. degree or a B.A.-B.S. degree in all majors. There are 13 national honor societies and a freshman honors program. **Visiting:** There are regularly scheduled orientations for prospective students, including interviews and campus tours. There are guides for informal visits; visitors may sit in on classes and stay overnight. To schedule a visit, contact the Admissions Office. **Campus Safety and Security:** Measures include 24-hour foot and vehicle patrol, an emergency notification system, self-defense education, and security escort services. There are shuttle buses, emergency telephones, lighted pathways/sidewalks, and controlled access to dorms/residences.

REQUIREMENTS: The SAT or ACT is required. Applicants must provide official high school transcripts. Students should have taken 4 years of English, math, 3-4 units of science (with lab), and 2 units each are recommended foreign language, social studies, and history. An interview, essay, and 2 letters of recommendation are required. Applicants to music and technology or visual arts and technology may submit a digital portfolio in place of standardized test scores. International applicants may submit 2 SAT II scores, 2 AP scores, or 2 IB scores in place of standardized test scores. AP credits are accepted. Important factors in the admissions decision are advanced placement or honors courses, evidence of special talent, personality/intangible qualities, extracurricular activities record, leadership record, parents or siblings attended your school, recommendations by alumni, geographical diversity, and recommendations by school officials. To graduate, the student must have earned 122 to 150 credit hours (dependent on program) with a minimum 2.0 GPA; the total hours in the major vary by program. The core curriculum includes courses in engineering, science, computer science, math, liberal arts, and phys ed. **Procedure:** Freshmen are admitted in the fall. Entrance exams should be taken by February 1 of the senior year. There are early decision and deferred admissions plans. Early decision applications should be filed by November 15; regular applications, by January 15 for fall entry. The fall 2017 application fee was $70. Notification of early decision is sent December 15; regular decision, February 15. 388 early decision candidates were accepted for the 2017-2018 class. Applications are accepted on-line. **Transfer Students:** 22 transfer students enrolled in 2016-2017. Applicants should have a minimum GPA of 3.0. They must submit the Common Application, all college transcripts, including course descriptions, final high school transcript with graduation date, and one letter of recommendation from a professor. SAT or ACT scores are required of those students with fewer than 30 hours of college credit. 61 of 122 credits required for the bachelor's degree must be completed at Stevens. **International Students:** There are 129 international students enrolled. They must take the TOEFL, and either the SAT or ACT.

ADMISSIONS: 44% of the 2017-2018 applicants were accepted. The SAT scores for the 2017-2018 freshman class were: Math-- 3% between 500 and 599, 34% between 600 and 699, and 63% between 700 and 800. Evidence-Based Reading/Writing-- 6% between 500 and 599, 61% between 600 and 699, and 33% between 700 and 800. The ACT scores were 27% between 24 and 29, and 73% above 30. 91% of the current freshmen were in the top fifth of their class; 99% were in the top two fifths. 9 freshmen graduated first in their class. **Admissions Contact:** Ken Nilsen, Dean of Students. Email: *admissions@stevens.edu* Web: *www.stevens.edu*

FINANCIAL AID: Stevens Institute of Technology is a member of CSS. The CSS/Profile is required. The FAFSA code is 002639. The priority date for freshman financial aid applications for fall entry is February 15.

STOCKTON UNIVERSITY D-5
www.stockton.edu

Galloway, NJ 08205 **(609) 652-4261**

Fax: (609) 748-5541
Email: admissions@stockton.edu
Full-time: 2460 men, 3420 women
Faculty: IIA, +$
Part-time: 350 men, 560 women
Ph.D.s: n/av
Graduate: 160 men, 440 women
Student/Faculty: n/av
Year: semesters, summer session
Tuition: $13,403 ($20,357)
Room & Board: $12,162
Freshman Class: n/av
SAT or ACT: required
CEEB CODE: 2889
Application Deadline: n/av
COMPETITIVE

Stockton University, founded in 1969, is a public undergraduate and graduate university in the arts, sciences and professional studies with over 40 majors. The figures in the above capsule and in this profile are approximate. There are 7 undergraduate schools and 1 graduate school. In addition to regional accreditation, Stockton has baccalaureate program accreditation with APTA, CSWE, NLN, ACS, ACOTE, and AOTA. The 2000-acre campus is in a suburban area in Galloway Township, NJ, 1 hour west to Philadelphia, and 2 hours north to New York City. Including any residence halls, there are 55 buildings.

STUDENT LIFE: 98% of undergraduates are from New Jersey. Others are from 21 states, 10 foreign countries, and Canada. 74% are from public schools. 8% are African American; 78% White; 6% Hispanic; 5% Asian American. **Female To Male Ratio:** 1.5:1. The average age of freshmen is 18; all undergraduates, 22. 17% do not continue beyond their first year; 67% remain to graduate. **Housing:** 2081 students can be accommodated in college housing, which includes dorms and on-campus apartments. In addition, there are special-interest houses, housing for wellness, substance-free, academic, and smoke-free housing. On-campus housing is guaranteed for the freshman year only, and is available on a first-come, first-served basis, and is available on a lottery system for upperclassmen. 68% of students commute. All students may keep cars.

FACULTY/CLASSROOMS: 54% of faculty are male; 46% are female. No introductory courses are taught by graduate students. The average class size in an introductory lecture is 33; in a laboratory is 18; and in a regular course is 19.

PROGRAMS OF STUDY: Stockton confers B.A., B.S., and B.S.N. degrees. Master's and doctoral degrees are also awarded. Bachelor's degrees are awarded in BIOLOGICAL SCIENCE (biochemistry, biology/biological science, and marine science), BUSINESS (accounting, banking and finance, business administration and management, and management science), COMMUNICATIONS AND THE ARTS (communications, dance, dramatic arts, fine arts, languages, literature, and music), COMPUTER AND PHYSICAL SCIENCE (chemistry, computer science, geology, information sciences and systems, mathematics, and physics), EDUCATION (education), ENGINEERING AND ENVIRONMENTAL DESIGN (computational sciences, environmental science, and preengineering), HEALTH PROFESSIONS (nursing, physical therapy, public health, and speech pathology/audiology), SOCIAL SCIENCE (anthropology, criminal justice, economics, history, liberal arts/general studies, philosophy, political science/government, psychology, and social work). Sciences is the strongest academically. Business, psychology, and criminal justice have the largest enrollments.

ACTIVITIES: 4% of men belong to 11 national fraternities; 5% of women belong to 10 national sororities. There are 94 groups on campus, including art, band, cheerleading, chess, choir, chorale, chorus, computers, dance, drama, ethnic, honors, international, jazz band, LGBT, literary magazine, newspaper, orchestra, pep band, photography, political, professional, radio and TV, religious, social, social service, and student government. Popular campus events include Spring Concert, Spring Fling, and Black History Month. **Sports:** There are 7 intercollegiate sports for men and 10 for women, and 10 intramural sports for men and 10 for women. Facilities include a swimming pool, an outdoor track, a weight-lifting gym, multipurpose gyms, dance studios, playing fields, cross-country courses, bike trails, an all-weather track, tennis, racquetball, and basketball courts. **Graduates:** From July 1, 2016 to June 30, 2017, 1632 bachelor's degrees were awarded. The most popular majors were social science (30%), business and management (19%), and natural sciences (15%). In an average class, 2% graduate in 3 years or less, 43% graduate in 4 years or less, 65% graduate in 5 years or less, and 67% graduate in 6 years or less. Of the 2016 graduating class, 34% were enrolled in graduate school within 6 months of graduation, and 83% were employed.

SERVICES: Counseling and information services are available, as is tutoring in most subjects. There is a reader service for the blind, and remedial math, reading, and writing. There is a skills center and a learning access program for learning-disabled students. **Library/Resources:** The library contains 627,318 volumes, 1.1 million microform items, 15,342 audio/video tapes/CDs/DVDs, and subscribes to 26,375 periodicals, including electronic. Computerized library services include interlibrary loans, database searching, and Internet access. Special learning facilities include an art gallery, radio station, TV station, astronomical observatory, marine science field lab, marina with a fleet of small boats, Holocaust resource center, educational technology, training center, and performing arts center. **Physically Challenged Students:** 99% of the campus is accessible. Facilities include wheelchair ramps, elevators, special parking, specially equipped restrooms, special class scheduling, lowered drinking fountains, and lowered telephones. **Special:** Stockton offers internships in all fields with a wide variety of companies, work-study with various government agencies and corporations, a Washington semester, independent study, and study abroad in 53 countries. Dual majors in all programs, student-designed majors, an accelerated degree in medicine and criminal justice, 3-2 engineering degrees with the New Jersey Institute of Technology and Rutgers University, and general studies degrees are also offered. Nondegree study, pass/fail options, and credit for life, military, and work experience are possible. There are 5 national honor societies and a freshman honors program. **Visiting:** There are regularly scheduled orientations for prospective students, including academic advising and orientation. There are guides for informal visits and visitors may sit in on classes. To schedule a visit, contact Enrollment Management at (609) 652-4251. **Campus Safety and Security:** Measures include 24-hour foot and vehicle patrol, emergency notification system, self-defense education, and security escort services. There are emergency telephones, lighted pathways/sidewalks, and a fully commissioned police department.

REQUIREMENTS: The SAT or ACT is required. Applicants must be high school graduates; the GED is accepted. 16 academic credits are required, including 4 or more each in English, and foreign language, 3 each in math and social studies, and 2 in science. An essay and an interview are recommended, and a portfolio or audition is necessary. AP and CLEP credits are accepted. Important factors in the admissions decision are advanced placement or honors courses, leadership record, and evidence of special talent. To graduate, students must earn 128 credit hours, with 32 in the general studies curriculum and maintain a minimum GPA of 2.0. 3 quantitative reasoning and 4 writing courses as well as freshman seminar are required. **Procedure:** Freshmen are admitted in the fall and spring. Entrance exams should be taken in the junior year and again before January in the senior year. There is a rolling admissions plan. Applications should be filed by December 1 for spring entry. The fall 2017 application fee was $50. Notification is sent on a rolling basis. Applications are accepted on-line. **Transfer Students:** 1088 transfer students enrolled in 2016-2017. Transfer students must have earned at least 16 credits at other colleges, submit college and high school transcripts, and SAT scores. 32 of 128 credits required for the bachelor's degree must be completed at Stockton. **International Students:** There are 25 international students enrolled. They must take the TOEFL, and either the SAT or ACT.

Admissions Contact: Alisa Hogan, Associate Director, Admissions Marketing. Email: *admissions@stockton.edu* Web: *www.stockton.edu*

FINANCIAL AID: In 2017-2018, 77% of all full-time freshmen received some form of financial aid. 40% of all full-time freshmen received need-based aid. The average freshman award was $11,772. Need-based scholarships or need-based grants averaged $8,170 ($15,396 maximum); need-based self-help aid (loans and jobs) averaged $3,702 ($9,900 maximum); and other non-need-based awards and non-need-based scholarships averaged $3,602 ($23,555 maximum). 16% of undergraduate students work part-time. The average financial indebtedness of the 2017 graduate was $15,624. Check with the school for current application deadlines.

THE COLLEGE OF NEW JERSEY D-3

www.tcnj.edu

Ewing, NJ 08628	**(609) 771-2131** **(800) 624-0967**
Fax: (609) 637-5174	**Email: tcnjinfo@tcnj.edu**
Full-time: 2690 men, 3729 women	**Faculty:** 355
Part-time: 86 men, 161 women	**Ph.D.s:** 90%
Graduate: 93 men, 427 women	**Student/Faculty:** 13 to 1
Year: semesters, summer session	**Tuition:** $15,794 ($26,971)
Room & Board: $12,881	**Freshman Class:** 11825 applied, 5778 accepted, 1457 enrolled
SAT CR/M/W: 590/610/595 **ACT:** 28	**CEEB CODE:** 2519
Application Deadline: February 1	**VERY COMPETITIVE+**

The College of New Jersey, founded in 1855, is a public institution offering programs in the liberal arts, sciences, business, engineering, nursing, and education. There are 7 undergraduate schools and 1 graduate school. In addition to regional accreditation, CNJ has baccalaureate program accreditation with AACSB, ABET, NASM, and NLN. The 289-acre campus is in a suburban area between Princeton and Trenton, NJ. Including any residence halls, there are 61 buildings.

STUDENT LIFE: 93% of undergraduates are from New Jersey. Others are from 23 states, 30 foreign countries, and Canada. 70% are from public schools. 66% are White; 6% African American; 3% two or more races; 13% Hispanic; 11% Asian American. 48% are Catholic; 17% Protestant; 15% claim no religious affiliation; 15% Eastern Orthodox, Buddhist, Muslim, Islamic and Quaker. **Female To Male Ratio:** 1.5:1. The average age of freshmen is 18; all undergraduates, 21. 6% do not continue beyond their first year; 86% remain to graduate. **Housing:** 4000 students can be accommodated in college housing, which includes dorms, on-campus apartments, off-campus apartments, and special-interest houses. All freshman participate in the First Seminar Program which are housed in the learning communities, wellness housing, and housing for international students. On-campus housing is guaranteed for the freshman year only and is available on a lottery system for upperclassmen. 90% of students live on campus. Upperclassmen may keep cars.

FACULTY/CLASSROOMS: 47% of faculty are male; 53% are female. All teach undergraduates, 85% do research, and 85% do both. No introductory courses are taught by graduate students. The average class size in an introductory lecture is 25; in a laboratory is 17; and in a regular course is 21.

PROGRAMS OF STUDY: CNJ confers B.A., B.S., B.A.B.M.E., B.F.A., B.M., B.S.C.E., B.S.Co.E., B.S.E.E., B.S.M.E., and B.S.N. degrees. Master's degrees are also awarded. Bachelor's degrees are awarded in BIOLOGICAL SCIENCE (biology/biological science), BUSINESS (accounting and business administration and management), COMMUNICATIONS AND THE ARTS (art, art history and appreciation, communications, English, fine arts, graphic design, multimedia, music, and Spanish), COMPUTER AND PHYSICAL SCIENCE (chemistry, computer science, digital arts/technology, mathematics, and physics), EDUCATION (art education, early childhood education, education of the deaf and hearing impaired, elementary education, English education, health education, mathematics education, music education, physical education, science education, social science education, social studies education, special education, and technical education), ENGINEERING AND ENVIRONMENTAL DESIGN (biomedical engineering, civil engineering, computer engineering, electrical/electronics engineering, engineering and applied science, and mechanical engineering), HEALTH PROFESSIONS (exercise science and nursing), SOCIAL SCIENCE (criminal justice, economics, history, international studies, philosophy, political science/government, psychology, sociology, and women's studies). Biology, education, and engineering are the strongest academically. Psychology, biology, and elementary education have the largest enrollments.

ACTIVITIES: 14% of men belong to 14 national fraternities; 11% of women belong to 13 national sororities. There are 226 groups on campus, including art, band, cheerleading, chess, choir, chorale, chorus, computers, dance, drama, environmental, ethnic, film, forensics, honors, international, jazz band, LGBT, literary magazine, musical theater, newspaper, opera, orchestra, pep band, photography, political, professional, radio and TV, religious, social, social service, student government, symphony, and yearbook. Popular campus events include Lallanobozza, Mystique of the EAST, and TCNJ Later Nighter. **Sports:** There are 9 intercollegiate sports for men and 9 for women, and 14 intramural sports for men and 14 for women. Facilities include a stadium with astroturf field, an aquatic center, baseball and softball diamonds, a soccer/multipurpose field, an all-weather track, a sand volleyball court, playing fields, a gym, a physical enhancement center, a student recreation center, tennis, racquetball, basketball/volleyball courts, and a free weight room. **Graduates:** From July 1, 2016 to June 30, 2017, 1647 bachelor's degrees were awarded. The most popular majors were business/marketing (20%), education (17%), and psychology (9%). In an average class, 1% graduate in 3 years or less, 76% graduate in 4 years or less, 87% graduate in 5 years or less, and 87% graduate in 6 years or less. Of the 2016 graduating class, 33% were enrolled in graduate school within 6 months of graduation, and 95% were employed.

SERVICES: Counseling and information services are available, as is tutoring in most subjects. There is a reader service for the blind, and remedial math, reading, and writing. **Library/Resources:** The library contains 694,144 volumes, 426,253 microform items, 40,127 audio/video tapes/CDs/DVDs, and subscribes to 73,733 periodicals, including electronic. Computerized library services include interlibrary loans, database searching, Internet access, and Wi-Fi capability. Special learning facilities include an art gallery, planetarium, radio station, TV station, electron microscopy lab, nuclear magnetic resonance lab, optical spectroscopy lab, observatory, planetarium, and greenhouse. **Physically Challenged Students:** 90% of the campus is accessible. Facilities include wheelchair ramps, elevators, special parking, specially equipped restrooms, special class scheduling, lowered drinking fountains, lowered telephones, and special housing. **Special:** TCNJ offers cross-registration with the New Jersey Marine Science Consortium, a limited number of overseas internship possibilities, numerous internships in the public and private sectors, a Washington semester, and study abroad in more than a dozen countries. Pass/fail options and some dual majors are possible. Specially designed research courses allow students to participate in collaborative scholarly projects with members of the faculty, and the Bonner Center offers opportunities for community-engaged initiatives. Combined advanced and accelerated degree programs are offered in education of the deaf and hard of hearing, special education, medicine, and optometry. There are 16 national honor societies, including Phi Beta Kappa, a freshman honors program, and 40 departmental honors programs. **Visiting:** There are regularly scheduled orientations for prospective students, consisting of an admissions presentation and a tour of campus. Reservations are required. To schedule a visit, contact the Admissions Office. **Campus Safety and Security:** Measures include 24-hour foot and vehicle patrol, emergency notification system, self-defense education, and security escort services. There are emergency telephones, lighted pathways/sidewalks, and controlled access to dorms/residences.

REQUIREMENTS: The SAT is required. Applicants must have earned 18 academic credits in high school, consisting of 4 each in English, math and science, of those 2 must be lab, 2 each in foreign language, social studies, and 4 recommended academic electives. An essay is required. Art majors must submit a portfolio, and music majors must audition. The GED is accepted. A GPA of 2.0 is required. AP and CLEP credits are accepted. Important factors in the admissions decision are advanced placement or honors courses, extracurricular activities record, evidence of special talent, personality/intangible qualities, geographical diversity, and recommendations by school officials. To graduate, students must complete a liberal learning curriculum of 128 to 136 credit hours that includes at least 1 major, and 3 interdependent structural elements: intellectual and scholarly growth, civic responsibilities, and the broad sectors of human inquiry within the arts and humanities, social sciences, natural sciences, and quantitative reasoning. **Procedure:** Freshmen are admitted in the fall and spring. Entrance exams should be taken by the end of the junior year or early in the senior year. There are early decision and rolling admissions plans. Early decision applications should be filed by November 1; regular applications, by February 1 for fall entry. The fall 2017 application fee was $75. Notification of early decision is sent December 1; regular decision, November 1. 344 early decision candidates were accepted for the 2017-2018 class. 575 applicants were on the 2017 waiting list; 285 were admitted. Applications are accepted on-line. **Transfer Students:** 266 transfer students enrolled in 2016-2017. Transfer students must have a minimum GPA of 2.5, and those with fewer than 33 credits must submit SAT scores. An associate degree is recommended. All transfer students must submit high school transcripts, college transcripts, essay or personal statement, and a statement from prior institutions. 48 of 72 credits required for the bachelor's degree must be completed at TCNJ. **International Students:** There are 23 international students enrolled. They must take the TOEFL with a minimum score of 550 on the paper-based TOEFL (PBT) or 90 on the Internet-based version (iBT). They must also take the SAT or ACT.

ADMISSIONS: 49% of the 2017-2018 applicants were accepted. The SAT scores for the 2017-2018 freshman class were: Critical Reading-- 8% below 500, 46% between 500 and 599, 36% between 600 and 699, and 10% between 700 and 800. Math-- 4% below 500, 35% between 500 and 599, 47% between 600 and 699, and 14% between 700 and 800. Writing-- 9% below 500, 43% between 500 and 599, 38% between 600 and 699, and 11% between 700 and 800. The ACT scores were 11% between 18 and 23, 63% between 24 and 29, and 26% above 30. 87% of the current freshmen were in the top fifth of their class; 98% were in the top two fifths. 13 freshmen graduated first in their class. **Admissions Contact:** Grecia Montero, Director of Admissions. Email: *tcnjinfo@tcnj.edu* Web: *www.tcnj.edu*

FINANCIAL AID: In 2017-2018, 41% of all full-time freshmen received some form of financial aid. 43% of all full-time freshmen received need-based aid. The average freshman award was $11,002. Need-based scholarships or need-based grants averaged $13,272; need-based self-help aid (loans and jobs) averaged $3,594; other non-need-based awards and non-need-based scholarships averaged $5,241; and $3,511 from other forms of aid. The average financial indebtedness of the 2017 graduate was $29,121. CNJ is a member of CSS. The FAFSA code is 002642. The priority date for freshman financial aid applications for fall entry is March 1.

THOMAS EDISON STATE UNIVERSITY *(The complete profile is made available exclusively on our website, www.barronspac.com)*

WESTMINSTER CHOIR COLLEGE *(The complete profile is made available exclusively on our website, www.barronspac.com)*

WILLIAM PATERSON UNIVERSITY OF NEW JERSEY — E-2

www.wpunj.edu

Wayne, NJ 07470 — **(973) 720-2125**

Fax: (973) 720-2910	**Email:** admissions@wpunj.edu
Full-time: 3431 men, 4054 women	**Faculty:** 410
Part-time: 636 men, 841 women	**Ph.D.s:** 92%
Graduate: 323 men, 874 women	**Student/Faculty:** 14 to 1
Year: semesters, summer session	**Tuition:** $12,804 ($20,842)
Room & Board: $11,218	**Freshman Class:** 10784 applied, 8160 accepted, 1376 enrolled
SAT CR/M: 517/526 **ACT:** required	**CEEB CODE:** 2518
Application Deadline: June 1	**COMPETITIVE**

William Paterson University of New Jersey, founded in 1855, and is a public institution comprised of the colleges of arts and communication, education, humanities, social sciences, science and health, and business. There are 5 undergraduate schools and 5 graduate schools. In addition to regional accreditation, WPUNJ has baccalaureate program accreditation with ASLA, NASM, and NLN. The 370-acre campus is in a suburban area 25 miles west of New York City. Including any residence halls, there are 35 buildings.

STUDENT LIFE: 98% of undergraduates are from New Jersey. Others are from 22 states, 58 foreign countries, and Canada. 75% are from public schools. 7% are Asian American; 41% White; 3% two or more races; 29% Hispanic; 2% race unknown; 17% African American. **Female To Male Ratio:** 1.3:1. The average age of freshmen is 18; all undergraduates, 24. **Housing:** College-sponsored housing includes dorms and on-campus apartments. In addition, there are honors houses, as well as apartments for single students 21 or older, or who are 20 with a junior class status. Graduate program students can be assigned to shared apartments or a single room. On-campus housing is guaranteed for all 4 years. 53% of students commute. Upperclassmen may keep cars.

FACULTY/CLASSROOMS: 51% of faculty are male; 49% are female. All teach undergraduates and do research. No introductory courses are taught by graduate students. The average class size in an introductory lecture is 32; in a laboratory is 24; and in a regular course is 19.

PROGRAMS OF STUDY: WPUNJ confers B.A., B.S., B.F.A., and B.M. degrees. Master's and doctoral degrees are also awarded. Bachelor's degrees are awarded in BIOLOGICAL SCIENCE (biology/biological science and biotechnology), BUSINESS (accounting, banking and finance, and business administration and management), COMMUNICATIONS AND THE ARTS (art history and appreciation, communications, dramatic arts, English, fine arts, music, Spanish, and studio art), COMPUTER AND PHYSICAL SCIENCE (chemistry, computer science, and mathematics), EDUCATION (health education, music education, physical education, and special education), ENGINEERING AND ENVIRONMENTAL DESIGN (environmental science), HEALTH PROFESSIONS (community health work, health science, and nursing), SOCIAL SCIENCE (African American studies, anthropology, economics, geography, history, philosophy, political science/government, psychology, and sociology). Biology/biotechnology, computer science, and English are the strongest academically. Management, communications, and education have the largest enrollments.

ACTIVITIES: 2% of men belong to 13 national fraternities; 3% of women belong to 12 national sororities. There are 100 groups on campus, including art, cheerleading, chorus, computers, dance, drama, ethnic, film, honors, international, jazz band, LGBT, literary magazine, musical theater, newspaper, opera, orchestra, photography, political, professional, radio and TV, religious, social, social service, student government, and yearbook. Popular campus events include Pioneer Pride Week, Latin Heritage Celebration, Welcome Week, African Heritage Celebration, WinterFest, Springfest and Meet the Greeks. **Sports:** There are 7 intercollegiate sports for men and 7 for women, and 24 intramural sports for men and 24 for women. Facilities include a recreation center with courts for basketball, tennis, racquetball, volleyball, and badminton, a weight and exercise rooms, Olympic-size pool, tennis courts, and an athletic complex with fields for baseball, field hockey, football, soccer, softball, and track. **Graduates:** From July 1, 2016 to June 30, 2017, 2214 bachelor's degrees were awarded. The most popular majors were business/marketing (21%), psychology (11%), and education (10%). In an average class, 14% graduate in 4 years or less, 40% graduate in 5 years or less, and 47% graduate in 6 years or less.

SERVICES: Counseling and information services are available, as is tutoring in most subjects. There is remedial math, reading, and writing. There is a science enrichment center, a writing center, and a business tutorial lab. **Library/Resources:** The library contains 300,000 volumes, 1,000,000 microform items, 20,000 audio/video tapes/CDs/DVDs, and subscribes to 5,000 periodicals, including electronic. Computerized library services include interlibrary loans and database searching. Special learning facilities include an art gallery, radio station, TV station, a speech and hearing clinic, an academic support center, a computerized writing center, and a teleconference center. **Physically Challenged Students:** Facilities include wheelchair ramps, elevators, special parking, specially equipped restrooms, special class scheduling, lowered drinking fountains, lowered telephones, and special housing. **Special:** Study abroad in 33 countries, cross-registration, internships, work-study programs on campus, accelerated degree programs, dual majors, individual curriculum design, and credit for military experience are available. Nondegree study and some pass/fail options are also possible. In the Learning Clusters Project, students experience how 3 general education courses, taken together, reinforce and better integrate each other. There is a professional program in teacher education leading to certification in early childhood, elementary, middle, and secondary education. There are 19 national honor societies, a freshman honors program, and 11 departmental honors programs. **Visiting:** There are regularly scheduled orientations for prospective students, including a campus tour, guest speakers, and dissemination of printed information. There are guides for informal visits and visitors may sit in on classes. To schedule a visit, contact the Admissions Office. **Campus Safety and Security:** Measures include 24-hour foot and vehicle patrol, emergency notification system, and security escort services. There are shuttle buses, emergency telephones, lighted pathways/sidewalks, and controlled access to dorms/residences.

REQUIREMENTS: The SAT or ACT is required. Applicants must have 16 academic credits or Carnegie units, including 4 in English, 3 in math, 2 each in science lab and social studies, and 5 electives such as foreign language and history. An essay and interview are recommended for some applicants, as are a portfolio and audition. The GED is accepted. AP and CLEP credits are accepted. Important factors in the admissions decision are advanced placement or honors courses, recommendations by school officials, and evidence of special talent. All students must maintain a cumulative GPA of at least 2.0 and take 120 credit hours, typically including 30 to 40 in their major. The University Core Curriculum is the general education program of William Paterson it is a 40 credit program, which constitutes a third of the entire undergraduate curriculum. Students create their Core experience by choosing a sequence of 13 courses from each of the following six areas of study, each area, and sub-area will have a variety of courses to choose from. Also required are 1 course in health or movement science, 1 course dealing with racism or sexism. Courses in areas Four, Five and Six (Diversity and Justice, Community and Civic Engagement, and Global Awareness) may be within student majors. Such courses can thus be used to satisfy both, Core and major requirements. Students at WPU are required to complete four Writing Intensive courses and two Technology Intensive courses. These courses are not additional "stand-alone" courses but any course within the Core, or any major or any minor or any free elective that has been designated as a WI or TI course. **Procedure:** Freshmen are admitted fall and spring. Entrance exams should be taken by January 31. There are early admissions, deferred admissions, and rolling admissions plans. Applications should be filed by June 1 for fall entry; December 1 for spring entry. The fall 2017 application fee was $50. Notification is sent on a rolling basis. 370 applicants were on the 2017 waiting list; 106 were admitted. Applications are accepted on-line. **Transfer Students:** 1133 transfer students enrolled in 2016-2017. Transfer students must present at least 12 college level credits with a minimum 2.0 GPA. Nursing Majors are encouraged to have a minimum of a 3.0 GPA or higher. Communication Disorders must have a minimum GPA of 3.5. Allied Health, Public Health, and Business Majors have specific requirements for admission please check our website, www.wpunj.edu for those requirements. 30 of 120 credits required for the bachelor's degree must be completed at William Patterson. **International Students:** There are 99 international students enrolled. They must take the TOEFL with a minimum score of 550 on the paper-based TOEFL (PBT) or 80 on the Internet-based version (iBT). Students must take the IELTS with a score of 6.0 or higher. TOEFL could be waived based on submission of sufficient SAT/ACT scores.

ADMISSIONS: 76% of the 2017-2018 applicants were accepted. The SAT scores for the 2017-2018 freshman class were: Critical Reading-- 49% below 500, 39% between 500 and 599, 9% between 600 and 699, and 2% between 700 and 800. Math-- 42% below 500, 46% between 500 and 599, and 12% between 600 and 699. **Admissions Contact:** Rohan Howell, Director of Undergraduate Admissions. Email: *admissions@wpunj.edu* Web: *www.wpunj.edu*

FINANCIAL AID: In 2017-2018, 86% of all full-time freshmen received some form of financial aid. 64% of all full-time freshmen received need-based aid. The average freshman award was $10,798. Need-based scholarships or need-based grants averaged $9,222; need-based self-help aid (loans and jobs) averaged $3,441; other non-need-based awards and non-need-based scholarships averaged $7,886; and $3,397 from other forms of aid. The average financial indebtedness of the 2017 graduate was $22,527. WPUNJ is a member of CSS. The FAFSA code is 002625. The priority date for freshman financial aid applications for fall entry is March 1.

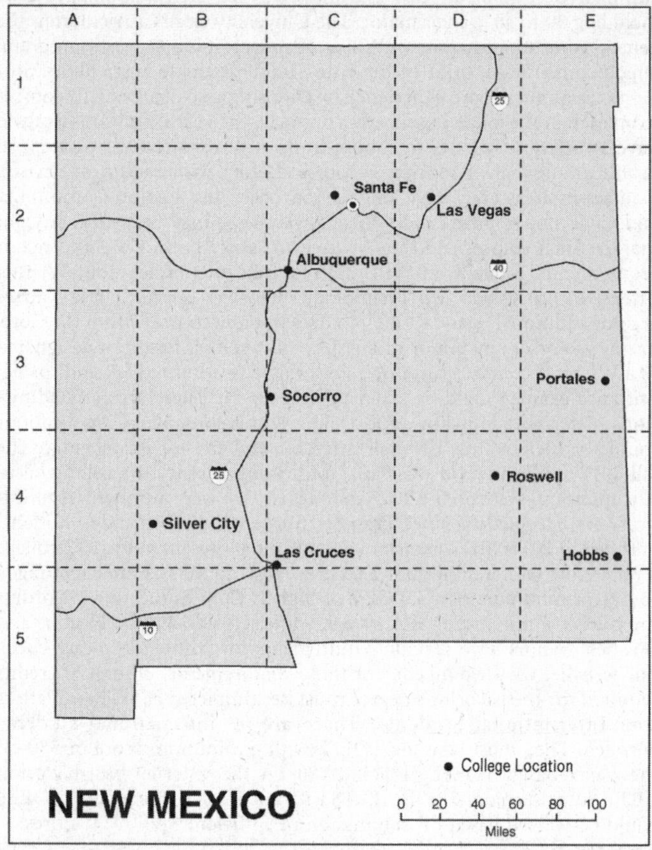

EASTERN NEW MEXICO UNIVERSITY *(The complete profile is made available exclusively on our website, www.barronspac.com)*

NEW MEXICO HIGHLANDS UNIVERSITY *(The complete profile is made available exclusively on our website, www.barronspac.com)*

NEW MEXICO INSTITUTE OF MINING AND TECHNOLOGY C-3
www.nmt.edu

Socorro, NM 87801	**(575) 835-5424** **(800) 428-TECH**
Fax: (575) 835-5989	**Email: admission@nmt.edu**
Full-time: 943 men, 351 women	**Faculty:** 132
Part-time: 85 men, 92 women	**Ph.D.s:** 95%
Graduate: 290 men, 248 women	**Student/Faculty:** 11 to 1
Year: semesters, summer session	**Tuition:** $7183 ($20,991)
Room & Board: $8202	**Freshman Class:** 1513 applied, 328 accepted, 240 enrolled
SAT CR/M: 630/680 **ACT:** 28	**CEEB CODE:** 4533
Application Deadline: August 1	**HIGHLY COMPETITIVE+**

New Mexico Institute of Mining and Technology, founded in 1889 as the New Mexico School of Mines, is a science and engineering university. It has 4 research-associated divisions: the New Mexico Bureau of Geology and Mineral Resources, the Energetic Materials Research and Testing Center, the Petroleum Recovery Research Center, and the Langmuir Laboratory for Atmospheric Research. There is 1 undergraduate school and 1 graduate school. In addition to regional accreditation, NMIMT has baccalaureate program accreditation with ABET. The 320-acre campus is in a small town 75 miles south of Albuquerque. Including any residence halls, there are 28 buildings.

STUDENT LIFE: 88% of undergraduates are from New Mexico. Others are from 30 states, 13 foreign countries, and Canada. 52% are White; 31% Hispanic; 5% two or more races; 4% American Indian/Alaska Native; 3% Asian American; 2% African American; 2% Foreign; 1% race unknown. **Male To Female Ratio:** 1.9:1. The average age of freshmen is 18; all undergraduates, 21. 25% do not continue beyond their first year; 47% remain to graduate. **Housing:** 807 students can be accommodated in college housing, which includes married student dorms, on-campus apartments, and off-campus apartments. On-campus housing is available on a first-come and first-served basis. 55% of students commute. Alcohol is not permitted. All students may keep cars.

FACULTY/CLASSROOMS: 76% of faculty are male; 24% are female. 95% teach undergraduates and 95% do research. No introductory courses are taught by graduate students. The average class size in an introductory lecture is 20; in a laboratory is 14; and in a regular course is 19.

PROGRAMS OF STUDY: NMIMT confers B.S. and B.G.S. degrees. Associate, master's, and doctoral degrees are also awarded. Bachelor's degrees are awarded in BIOLOGICAL SCIENCE (biology/biological science), BUSINESS (business administration and management), COMMUNICATIONS AND THE ARTS (technical and business writing), COMPUTER AND PHYSICAL SCIENCE (chemistry, computer science, earth science, information sciences and systems, mathematics, and physics), ENGINEERING AND ENVIRONMENTAL DESIGN (chemical engineering, civil engineering, electrical/electronics engineering, environmental engineering, environmental science, materials engineering, mechanical engineering, mining and mineral engineering, and petroleum/natural gas engineering), HEALTH PROFESSIONS (biomedical science), SOCIAL SCIENCE (liberal arts/general studies and psychology). Physics, and electrical engineering are the strongest academically. Mechanical engineering, computer science, and computer science have the largest enrollments.

ACTIVITIES: There are no fraternities or sororities. There are 55 groups on campus, including art, band, chess, chorus, computers, drama, ethnic, honors, international, jazz band, LGBT, musical theater, orchestra, political, professional, radio and TV, religious, social, social service, student government, and yearbook. Popular campus events include 49ers, Spring Fling, and International Student Exhibit. **Sports:** There are 9 intramural sports for men and 9 for women. Facilities include a swimming pool, gyms, an 18-hole golf course, athletic field, a climbing wall, weight/fitness room, racquetball/squash, tennis courts, sand volleyball court, a ping-pong area, and a martial arts/combatives room. **Graduates:** From July 1, 2016 to June 30, 2017, 302 bachelor's degrees were awarded. The most popular majors were mechanical engineering (18%), petroleum engineering (15%), and electrical engineering (10%). In an average class, 20% graduate in 4 years or less, 44% graduate in 5 years or less, and 49% graduate in 6 years or less.

SERVICES: Counseling and information services are available, as is tutoring in most subjects. There is a reader service for the blind. **Library/Resources:** The library contains 385,987 volumes, 79,926 microform items, and 2,899 audio/video tapes/CDs/DVDs, and subscribes to 50,000 periodicals including electronic. Computerized library services include interlibrary loans, database searching, Internet access, and Wi-Fi capability. Special learning facilities include a radio station, a mineral museum, a seismic research mine, and a campus astronomical observatory. **Physically Challenged Students:** Facilities include wheelchair ramps, elevators, special parking, specially equipped restrooms, lowered drinking fountains, and lowered telephones. The majority of the campus is wheelchair accessible. **Special:** New Mexico Tech offers co-op programs in computer science and all engineering majors, internships in technical communications, and cross-registration with New Mexico State, University of New Mexico, and Los Alamos National Laboratories in the WERC consortium. Dual majors are offered in engineering, computer science, physics, and math. Work-study, student-designed majors in environmental science, general studies, and basic science, nondegree study, and pass/fail options are also available. There are 4 national honor societies. **Visiting:** There are regularly scheduled orientations for prospective students, including 2 days of get-acquainted social activities, information sessions for parents and students, and transition sessions for parents. There are guides for informal visits, visitors may sit in on classes, and stay overnight. To schedule a visit, contact the Admission Office. **Campus Safety and Security:** Measures include 24-hour foot and vehicle patrol, self-defense education, and security escort services. There are emergency telephones and lighted pathways/sidewalks.

REQUIREMENTS: The SAT is required. The ACT is recommended, with a minimum score of 21. Applicants must be high school graduates or present a GED certificate. Students should have earned 15 academic credits, consisting of 4 units of English, 3 each of social science and math (2 beyond general math), 2 of lab science, and electives. A GPA of 2.5 is required. AP credits are accepted. Important factors in the admissions decision are advanced placement or honors courses, evidence of special talent, and extracurricular activities record. Students must earn at least 130 credit hours to graduate, including 42 hours of basic science, consisting in part of 10 hours of physics and 8 each of chemistry, calculus, biology, geology, and engineering. Further distribution requirements include 9 hours each of written and spoken English, 18 hours of literature, philosophy, the arts, and social science, and a senior seminar or senior design project. The credit hours required in the major vary by program. The student must also maintain a cumulative GPA of 2.0. **Procedure:** Freshmen are admitted to all sessions. Entrance exams should be taken by December of the senior year. There are deferred admissions and rolling admissions plans. Applications should be filed by August 1 for fall entry; December 1 for spring entry. The fall 2017 application fee was $15. Notifications are sent March 1. **Transfer Students:** 67 transfer students enrolled in 2016-2017. Transfer students must have a GPA of 2.0 and have completed 30 semester hours of transferable credit. Those who have fewer than 30 credit hours, or who have not completed freshman English, must present a minimum ACT score of 21, as well as high school transcripts. 30 of 130 credits required for the bachelor's degree must be completed at NMIMT. **International Students:** There are 28 international students enrolled. They must take the TOEFL with a minimum score of 540 on the paper-based TOEFL (PBT) or 76 on the Internet-based version (iBT).

ADMISSIONS: 22% of the 2017-2018 applicants were accepted. The SAT scores for the 2017-2018 freshman class were: Critical Reading-- 14% below 500, 43% between 600 and 699, and 43% between 700 and 800. Math-- 17% below 500, 17% between 500 and 599, 50% between 600 and 699, and 17% between 700 and 800. The ACT scores were 26% between 18 and 23, 51% between 24 and 29, and 23% above 30. 59% of the current freshmen were in the top fifth of their class; 80% were in the top two fifths. 8 freshmen graduated first in their class. **Admissions Contact:** Tony Ortiz, Director of Admission. Email: *admission@nmt.edu* Web: *www.nmt.edu*

FINANCIAL AID: In 2017-2018, 95% of all full-time freshmen received some form of financial aid. 40% of all full-time freshmen received need-based aid. The average freshman award was $2,785. Need-based scholarships or need-based grants averaged $5,739; need-based self-help aid (loans and jobs) averaged $4,230; and other non-need-based awards and non-need-based scholarships averaged $5,601. The average financial indebtedness of the 2017 graduate was $26,817. The FAFSA code is 002654. The priority date for freshman financial aid applications for fall entry is March 1.

NEW MEXICO STATE UNIVERSITY *(The complete profile is made available exclusively on our website, www.barronspac.com)*

ST. JOHN'S COLLEGE, SANTA FE — C-2

www.sjc.edu

Santa Fe, NM 87505	(505) 984-6060 (800) 331-5232
Fax: (505) 984-6162	Email: SantaFe.Admissions@sjcsf.edu
Full-time: 186 men, 139 women	**Faculty:** 45
Part-time: 3 men, 2 women	**Ph.D.s:** 80%
Graduate: 41 men, 26 women	**Student/Faculty:** 8 to 1
Year: semesters, summer session	**Tuition:** $49,219
Room & Board: $10,890	**Freshman Class:** 188 applied, 167 accepted, 94 enrolled
SAT CR/M/W: 695/592/642 **ACT:** 28	**CEEB CODE:** 4737
Application Deadline: February 15	**HIGHLY COMPETITIVE+**

St. John's College, Santa Fe, founded in 1696, offers a curriculum based on the great books of western civilization in which students and faculty learn together in small discussion-based classes. There is 1 undergraduate school and 1 graduate school. The 298-acre campus is in a suburban area in SJC-Santa Fe. Including any residence halls, there are 42 buildings.

STUDENT LIFE: 94% of undergraduates are from out of state, mostly the Southwest. Students are from 41 states, and 18 foreign countries. 68% are from public schools. 60% are White; 20% Foreign; 12% Hispanic; 4% two or more races; 3% Asian American; 1% African American; 1% American Indian/Alaska Native; 1% race unknown. **Male To Female Ratio:** 1.4:1. The average age of freshmen is 20; all undergraduates, 21. 22% do not continue beyond their first year; 60% remain to graduate. **Housing:** 327 students can be accommodated in college housing, which includes married student dorms and on-campus apartments. In addition, there are special-interest houses, substance free residences, and green/sustainable housing. On-campus housing is guaranteed for the freshman year only and is available on a lottery system for upperclassmen. 75% of students live on campus. All students may keep cars.

FACULTY/CLASSROOMS: 75% of faculty are male; 25% are female. All teach undergraduates. No introductory courses are taught by graduate students. The average class size in a laboratory is 15 and in a regular course is 15.

PROGRAMS OF STUDY: SJC-Santa Fe confers B.A. degrees. Master's degrees are also awarded. Bachelor's degrees are awarded in COMPUTER AND PHYSICAL SCIENCE (mathematics and science), SOCIAL SCIENCE (liberal arts/general studies and philosophy). Liberal arts is the strongest academically.

ACTIVITIES: There are no fraternities or sororities. There are 27 groups on campus, including art, chess, chorus, dance, drama, environmental, ethnic, film, international, LGBT, literary magazine, newspaper, orchestra, outdoor leadership programs, political, social service, and student government. Popular campus events include Oktoberfest, Halloween and Christmas parties. **Sports:** There are 7 intramural sports for men and 7 for women. Facilities include soccer field, track, outdoor tennis courts, gym with weight room and cardio equipment, racquetball, squash, and basketball courts. **Graduates:** From July 1, 2016 to June 30, 2017, 84 bachelor's degrees were awarded. The most popular majors were liberal arts and sciences and liberal studies (100%). In an average class, 60% graduate in 4 years or less, 8% graduate in 5 years or less, and 2% graduate in 6 years or less. Of the 2016 graduating class, 13% were enrolled in graduate school within 6 months of graduation, and 51% were employed.

SERVICES: Counseling and information services are available, as is tutoring in every subject. **Library/Resources:** The library contains 68,711 volumes, and 4,707 audio/video tapes/CDs/DVDs, and subscribes to 80 periodicals including electronic. Computerized library services include interlibrary loans, database searching, Internet access, and Wi-Fi capability. Special learning facilities include an art gallery, an art studio, wood working studio, ceramics studio, music practice rooms, Ptolemy stone, and laboratories. **Physically Challenged Students:** 75% of the campus is accessible. Facilities include wheelchair ramps, elevators, special parking, specially equipped restrooms, special class scheduling, lowered drinking fountains, and special housing. **Special:** Internships with alumni in a wide range of fields are available and students may transfer between the Santa Fe and Annapolis campuses. Ariel Internship Program provides stipends to undergraduates for a limited number of summer internship opportunities. Work study programs are available with the state government, museums, galleries, the Santa Fe Institute, businesses, and schools, and pre-medical studies at universities around the country. **Visiting:** There are regularly scheduled orientations for prospective students, a student-led walking tour of the campus, math and language tutorials, spend the night in student housing, and interviews with admission's counselor and faculty member. To schedule a visit, contact Anne Young at ahyoung@sjc.edu. **Campus Safety and Security:** Measures include 24-hour foot and vehicle patrol, emergency notification system, and security escort services. There are shuttle buses, emergency telephones, lighted pathways/sidewalks, controlled access to dorms/residences, informal discussions, and pamphlets/posters/films.

REQUIREMENTS: Applicants must write personal essays and submit 2 references, a secondary school report including a reference from a school official, and transcripts of all academic work in high school and college. A campus visit and interview are recommended. 3 years of math and 2 years of foreign language are required; 4 years each of math, foreign language, and English, and 3 years of science are recommended. The GED is accepted. Important factors in the admissions decision are parents or siblings attended your school, recommendations by alumni, and evidence of special talent. The college has 1 curriculum, based on the great books of western civilization for a total of 136 credits. Students attend seminars, preceptorials on specific works or topics, language, music, and math tutorials, and a 3-year science lab. Students take oral exams each semester and write annual essays. Sophomores take a math exam and seniors write a final essay and take an oral exam. **Procedure:** Freshmen are admitted fall and spring. There are deferred admissions and rolling admissions plans. Early decision applications should be filed by November 15; regular applications, by February 15 for fall entry. Notification of early decision is sent December 15; regular decision. Applications are accepted on-line. **Transfer Students:** 14 transfer students enrolled in 2016-2017. St. John's accepts transfer students only for its freshman class; no previous college credit is recognized. Admission requirements are the same as for freshmen. 136 of 136 credits required for the bachelor's degree must be completed at SJC-Santa Fe. **International Students:** There are 65 international students enrolled. They must take the TOEFL with a minimum score of 550 on the paper-based TOEFL (PBT).

ADMISSIONS: 89% of the 2017-2018 applicants were accepted. The SAT scores for the 2017-2018 freshman class were: Critical Reading-- 11% between 500 and 599, 37% between 600 and 699, and 52% between 700 and 800. Math-- 15% below 500, 41% between 500 and 599, 37% between 600 and 699, and 7% between 700 and 800. Writing-- 4% below 500, 22% between 500 and 599, 52% between 600 and 699, and 19% between 700 and 800. The ACT scores were 14% between 12 and 17, 19% between 18 and 23, 14% between 24 and 29, and 52% above 30. 47% of the current freshmen were in the top fifth of their class; 78% were in the top two fifths. 4 freshmen graduated first in their class. **Admissions Contact:** Yvette Sobky-Shaffer, Director of Admissions. Email: *SantaFe.Admissions@sjcsf.edu* Web: *www.sjc.edu*

FINANCIAL AID: In 2017-2018, 98% of all full-time freshmen received some form of financial aid. 90% of all full-time freshmen received need-based aid. The average freshman award was $45,292. Need-based scholarships or need-based grants averaged $27,729; need-based self-help aid (loans and jobs) averaged $6,763; other non-need-based awards and non-need-based scholarships averaged $15,511; and $35,365 from other forms of aid. 94% of undergraduate students work part-time. The average financial indebtedness of the 2017 graduate was $27,093. SJC-Santa Fe is a member of CSS. The FAFSA code is 002093. The priority date for freshman financial aid applications for fall entry is February 15.

UNIVERSITY OF NEW MEXICO C-2

www.unm.edu

Albuquerque, NM 87131	(505) 277-8900 (800) CALL UNM
Fax: (505) 277-6809	Email: apply@unm.edu
Full-time: 6629 men, 8273 women	**Faculty:** 1033; I, --$
Part-time: 1635 men, 2376 women	**Ph.D.s:** 74%
Graduate: 2646 men, 3221 women	**Student/Faculty:** 20 to 1
Year: semesters, summer session	**Tuition:** $7146 ($22,037)
Room & Board: $9662	**Freshman Class:** 11347 applied, 5604 accepted, 3219 enrolled
SAT CR/M/W: 537/530/513 **ACT:** 22	**CEEB CODE:** 4845
Application Deadline: June 15	**COMPETITIVE**

University of New Mexico, founded in 1889, is a public university offering instruction in liberal and fine arts, business, engineering, health science, teacher preparation, law, and technology. There are 10 undergraduate schools and 5 graduate schools. In addition to regional accreditation, UNM has baccalaureate program accreditation with AACSB, ABET, ACCE, ACEJMC, ACPE, ADA, CAHEA, NAAB, NASM, CDA, CAATE, and NAST/NASD. The 783-acre campus is in an urban area within the city of Albuquerque. Including any residence halls, there are 339 buildings.

STUDENT LIFE: 86% of undergraduates are from New Mexico. Others are from 50 states, 56 foreign countries, and Canada. 49% are Hispanic; 33% White; 6% American Indian/Alaska Native; 4% Asian American; 4% two or more races; 2% African American; 2% Foreign; 1% race unknown. **Female To Male Ratio:** 1.3:1. The average age of freshmen is 19; all undergraduates, 24. 22% do not continue beyond their first year; 49% remain to graduate. **Housing:** 3700 students can be accommodated in college housing, which includes married student dorms and on-campus apartments. In addition, there are honors houses, special-interest houses, fraternity houses, sorority houses, freshman living learning communities, scholar's wing, graduates and senior undergraduate unit, global learning community, and combined BA/MD degree program quarters. 75% of students commute. Alcohol is not permitted. All students may keep cars.

FACULTY/CLASSROOMS: No introductory courses are taught by graduate students.

PROGRAMS OF STUDY: UNM confers B.A., B.S., B.A.A., B.A.E.P.D., B.A.Ed., B.A.F.A., B.B.A., B.F.A., B.I.S., B.L.A., B.M., B.M.E., B.S.C.E., B.S.Ch.E., B.S.Cp.E., B.S.Cn.E., B.S.C.S., B.S.D.H., B.S.E.E., B.S.Ed., B.S.M.E., B.S.M.L., B.S.N., B.S.D.H., and B.S.N.E degrees. Associate, master's, and doctoral degrees are also awarded. Bachelor's degrees are awarded in BIOLOGICAL SCIENCE (biochemistry, biology/biological science, and nutrition), BUSINESS (business administration and management), COMMUNICATIONS AND THE ARTS (Africana studies, American Sign Language, art history, art, classics, communications, comparative literature, dance, English, film, television and digital media, French, German, journalism, languages, linguistics, media arts, music, Portuguese, Russian, Spanish, studio art, theater design, and theatre studies), COMPUTER AND PHYSICAL SCIENCE (astrophysics, chemistry, computer science, earth science, mathematics, physics, and statistics), EDUCATION (art education, athletic training, drama education, early childhood education, elementary education, health education, music education, physical education, secondary education, special education, and technical education), ENGINEERING AND ENVIRONMENTAL DESIGN (architecture, chemical engineering, civil engineering, computer engineering, construction engineering, construction management, electrical/electronics engineering, environmental design, environmental science, mechanical engineering, and nuclear engineering), HEALTH PROFESSIONS (dental hygiene, emergency medical technologies, exercise science, health, medical laboratory technology, nursing, radiological science, and speech pathology/audiology), SOCIAL SCIENCE (American studies, anthropology, Asian/Oriental studies, child care/child and family studies, criminology, economics, European studies, family/consumer studies, geography, history, human development, human services, interdisciplinary studies, international studies, Latin American studies, liberal arts/general studies, Mexican-American/Chicano studies, Native American studies, philosophy, political science/government, psychology, religion, sociology, and women's studies). Business administration, psychology, and biology have the largest enrollments.

ACTIVITIES: 3% of men belong to 15 national fraternities; 3% of women belong to 10 national sororities. There are 400 groups on campus, including art, band, cheerleading, chess, choir, chorale, chorus, communications, dance, drama, drill team, environmental, ethnic, honors, international, jazz band, LGBT, literary magazine, marching band, musical theater, newspaper, opera, orchestra, pep band, political, professional, religious, social, social service, student government, and symphony. Popular campus events include Spring Fiesta, Welcome Back Days, and Hanging of the Greens. **Sports:** There are 8 intercollegiate sports for men and 11 for women, and 5 intramural sports for men and 5 for women. Facilities include a football field, gyms, swimming pools, weight room, racquetball, basketball, and tennis courts, a stadium, and an arena. **Graduates:** From July 1, 2016 to June 30, 2017, 4013 bachelor's degrees were awarded. The most popular majors were psychology (14%), business administration (12%), and biology (8%). In an average class, 1% graduate in 3 years or less, 19% graduate in 4 years or less, 42% graduate in 5 years or less, and 49% graduate in 6 years or less.

SERVICES: Counseling and information services are available, as is tutoring in most subjects. There is remedial math, reading, and writing. **Library/Resources:** The library contains 3.6 million volumes, 713,958 microform items, and 54,238 audio/video tapes/CDs/DVDs, and subscribes to 71,932 periodicals including electronic. Computerized library services include interlibrary loans, database searching, Internet access, and Wi-Fi capability. Special learning facilities include an art gallery, planetarium, TV station, a robotics lab, lithography and meteoritic institutes, observatory, arts lab, and museums of geology, anthropology, biology, and art. **Physically Challenged Students:** All of the campus is accessible. Facilities include wheelchair ramps, elevators, special parking, specially equipped restrooms, lowered drinking fountains, and special housing. **Special:** There is a 3-2 engineering program with the Anderson School of Management. Study abroad is available in 28 countries. The university offers cooperative programs in arts and sciences management, engineering, and fine arts, a Washington semester, work-study, dual and student-designed majors, a general studies degree, credit for military experience, nondegree study, and pass/fail options. There are 20 national honor societies, Phi Beta Kappa, a freshman honors program, and 46 departmental honors programs. **Visiting:** There are regularly scheduled orientations for prospective students, including academic advisement and registration. There are guides for informal visits, visitors may sit in on classes, and stay overnight. To schedule a visit, contact Admissions & Recrutiment Service. **Campus Safety and Security:** Measures include 24-hour foot and vehicle patrol, emergency notification system, self-defense education, and security escort services. There are shuttle buses, emergency telephones, lighted pathways/sidewalks, crime stoppers, jump starts, operation ID, bicycle registration, and a 911 emergency system.

REQUIREMENTS: The SAT or ACT is required. A total of 16 academic credits is required, including 4 units each of English and math, and 3 units of science with 2 units of lab, 2 units each of foreign language and social studies, and 1 unit of history. A GED is accepted. Freshman applicants must be graduates of a high school accredited by a regional accrediting association or by the state department of education or state university of the state in which the high school is located. The minimum GPA requirement for admission to bachelor degree programs is 2.25 (on a 4.00 scale) in all previous academic work from an accredited high school. Grades in all courses allowed toward high school graduation are computed in the average. A GPA of 2.5 is required. AP and CLEP credits are accepted. Important factors in the admissions decision are advanced placement or honors courses. All students must take 2 English courses or pass an English composition competence examination and complete the University Core Curriculum. A minimum of 128 credit hours is required, along with a GPA of 2.0. **Procedure:** Freshmen are admitted fall, spring, and summer. Entrance exams should be taken during the summer following the junior year. There are early admissions, deferred admissions, and rolling admissions plans. June 15 for fall entry; November 15 for spring entry; and May 1 for summer entry. The fall 2017 application fee was $25. Notification is sent on a rolling basis. Applications are accepted on-line. **Transfer Students:** 2504 transfer students enrolled in 2016-2017. Applicants must have at least a 2.0 GPA in all transferable courses. Please note that admission requirements are subject to change. 30 of 128 credits required for the bachelor's degree must be completed at UNM. **International Students:** There are 360 international students enrolled. They must take the TOEFL, University of Cambridge English Examination (CPE or CAE) and IELTS. They must also take the SAT or ACT.

ADMISSIONS: 49% of the 2017-2018 applicants were accepted. The SAT scores for the 2017-2018 freshman class were: Math-- 16% below 500, 47% between 500 and 599, 29% between 600 and 699, and 8% between 700 and 800. Evidence-Based Reading/Writing-- 16% below 500, 39% between 500 and 599, 36% between 600 and 699, and 9% between 700 and 800. The ACT scores were 13% between 12 and 17, 51% between 18 and 23, 30% between 24 and 29, and 6% above 30. **Admissions Contact:** Matthew Hulett, Director of Admissions & Recruitment. Email: *apply@unm.edu* Web: *www.unm.edu*

FINANCIAL AID: The FAFSA code is 002663. Check with the school for current application deadlines.

UNIVERSITY OF THE SOUTHWEST E-4

www.usw.edu

Hobbs, NM 88240	**(575) 392-6563** **(800) 530-4400**
Fax: (575) 392-6006	**Email: admission@usw.edu**
Full-time: 150 men, 200 women	**Faculty:** n/av
Part-time: 20 men, 55 women	**Ph.D.s:** n/av
Graduate: 40 men, 125 women	**Student/Faculty:** 15 to 1
Year: semesters, summer session	**Tuition:** $16,000
Room & Board: $8386	**Freshman Class:** n/av
SAT or ACT: required	**CEEB CODE:** 4116
Application Deadline: open	**COMPETITIVE**

University of the Southwest, founded in 1962, is an independent college offering undergraduate programs in arts and sciences, business, education, psychology, and criminal justice. Graduate programs are offered in education. The figures given in the above capsule and in this profile are approximate. There is 1 undergraduate school and 1 graduate school. The 162-acre campus is in a small town in Hobbs, New Mexico, 110 miles southwest of Lubbock, TX. Including any residence halls, there are 11 buildings.

STUDENT LIFE: 70% of undergraduates are from New Mexico. Others are from 11 states, 5 foreign countries, and Canada. 7% are Foreign; 43% White; 38% Hispanic; 3% African American; 1% Asian American; 1% American Indian/Alaska Native. **Female To Male Ratio:** 1.8:1. The average age of freshmen is 20; all undergraduates, 26. 35% do not continue beyond their first year; 35% remain to graduate. **Housing:** 172 students can be accommodated in college housing, which includes dorms and on-campus apartments. On-campus housing is available on a first-come and first-served basis. 59% of students live on campus. Alcohol is not permitted. All students may keep cars.

FACULTY/CLASSROOMS: 51% of faculty are male; 49% are female. 99% teach undergraduates. No introductory courses are taught by graduate students. The average class size in an introductory lecture is 11; in a laboratory is 7; and in a regular course is 12.

PROGRAMS OF STUDY: USW confers B.S., B.A.S. and B.B.A. degrees. Master's degrees are also awarded. Bachelor's degrees are awarded in BIOLOGICAL SCIENCE (biology/biological science), BUSINESS (accounting and business administration and management), COMMUNICATIONS AND THE ARTS (English and fine arts), COMPUTER AND PHYSICAL SCIENCE (mathematics), EDUCATION (elementary education, secondary education, and special education), SOCIAL SCIENCE (criminal justice, history, humanities, psychology, and sociology). Education, and business are the strongest academically. Education, business, and criminal justice have the largest enrollments.

ACTIVITIES: There are no fraternities or sororities. There are 7 groups on campus, including debate, drama, honors, international, newspaper, professional, religious, and student government. Popular campus events include Annual Students in Free Enterprise Dinner and Award Presentation, Family Week, and Speakers' Presentations. **Sports:** There are 4 intercollegiate sports for men and 6 for women, and 5 intramural sports for men and 5 for women. Facilities include soccer and baseball fields, a game room, and a physical fitness center with a multipurpose gym, racquetball courts, softball, and volleyball. **Graduates:** From July 1, 2016 to June 30, 2017, 98 bachelor's degrees were awarded. The most popular majors were education (29%), psychology (11%), and accounting (10%). In an average class, 19% graduate in 5 years or less. Of the 2016 graduating class, 5% were enrolled in graduate school within 6 months of graduation.

SERVICES: Counseling and information services are available, as is tutoring in most subjects. There is remedial math and writing. **Library/Resources:** The library contains 76,450 volumes, 25,750 microform items, and 1,553 audio/video tapes/CDs/DVDs, and subscribes to 333 periodicals including electronic. Computerized library services include interlibrary loans, database searching, and Internet access. **Physically Challenged Students:** All of the campus is accessible. Facilities include wheelchair ramps, special parking, and specially equipped restrooms. **Special:** The school offers co-op programs in early childhood education. Internships are available for students majoring in business, psychology, and education. CSW also offers nondegree study and credit for military experience. There are 2 national honor societies and 1 departmental honors program. **Visiting:** There are guides for informal visits, visitors may sit in on classes, and stay overnight. To schedule a visit, contact Coordinator of Admissions. **Campus Safety and Security:** Measures include 24-hour foot and vehicle patrol.

REQUIREMENTS: Students must have a minimum composite score of 18 on the ACT or a satisfactory score on the SAT. Applicants must be graduates of an accredited secondary school or have a GED certificate. University of the Southwest requires applicants to be in the upper 50% of their class. A GPA of 2.0 is required. AP and CLEP credits are accepted. Important factors in the admissions decision are advanced placement or honors courses and extracurricular activities record. To graduate, students must complete 128 semester hours with a minimum GPA of 2.0 (2.5 for education majors). General education requirements include 12 semester hours each of social science and math/science, 9 each of humanities/fine arts and communications, 6 of religion, and 3 of economics, as well as a course in free enterprise and a senior seminar in leadership and ethics. **Procedure:** Freshmen are admitted to all sessions. There is a rolling admissions plan. Application deadlines are open. The fall 2017 application fee was $25. Notification is sent on a rolling basis. Applications are accepted on-line. **Transfer Students:** 135 transfer students enrolled in 2016-2017. Applicants must present a minimum GPA of 2.0 and official transcripts from all colleges attended. 30 of 128 credits required for the bachelor's degree must be completed at University of the USW. **International Students:** There are 27 international students enrolled. They must take the TOEFL. They must also take the SAT or ACT.

Admissions Contact: Shelbie Faught, Assistant Admissions, Director New Freshman. Email: *admission@usw.edu* Web: *www.usw.edu*

FINANCIAL AID: In 2017-2018, 97% of all full-time freshmen received

some form of financial aid. 64% of all full-time freshmen received need-based aid. 17% of undergraduate students work part-time. The college's own financial statement is required. The FAFSA code is 013935. Check with the school for current application deadlines.

WESTERN NEW MEXICO UNIVERSITY *(The complete profile is made available exclusively on our website, www.barronspac.com)*

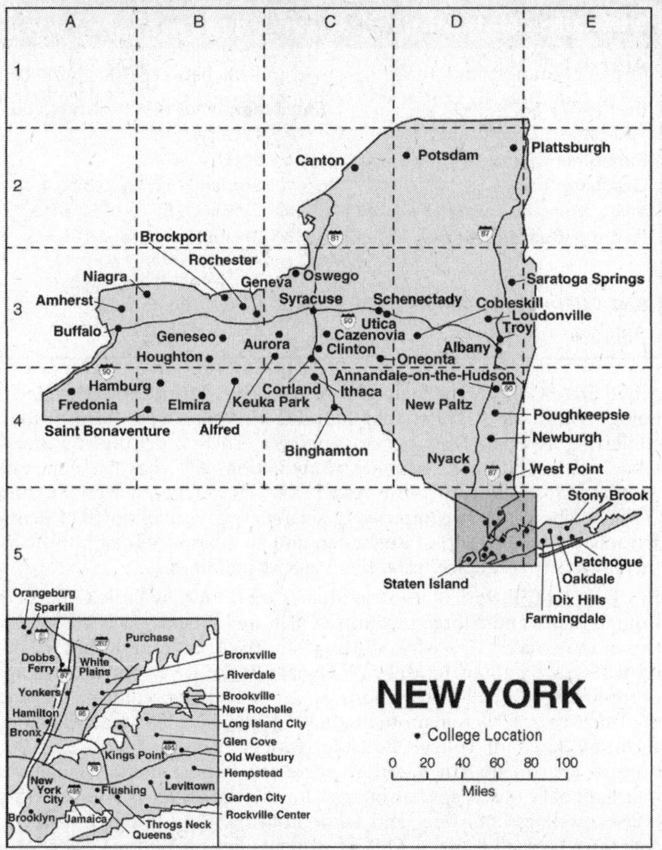

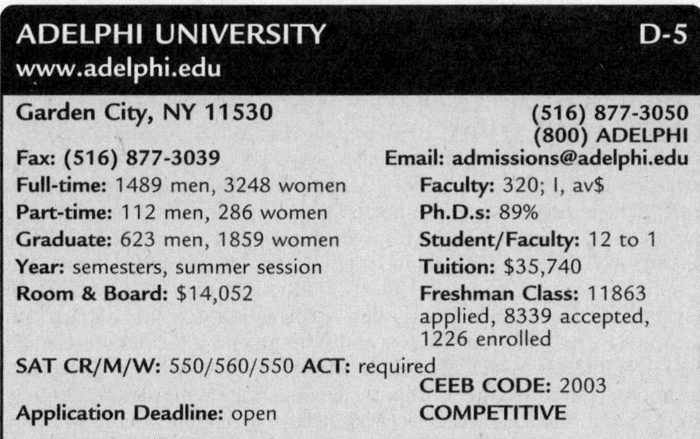

ADELPHI UNIVERSITY D-5

www.adelphi.edu

Garden City, NY 11530 **(516) 877-3050**
(800) ADELPHI

Fax: (516) 877-3039 **Email: admissions@adelphi.edu**

Full-time: 1489 men, 3248 women	**Faculty:** 320; I, av$
Part-time: 112 men, 286 women	**Ph.D.s:** 89%
Graduate: 623 men, 1859 women	**Student/Faculty:** 12 to 1
Year: semesters, summer session	**Tuition:** $35,740
Room & Board: $14,052	**Freshman Class:** 11863 applied, 8339 accepted, 1226 enrolled
SAT CR/M/W: 550/560/550 **ACT:** required	**CEEB CODE:** 2003
Application Deadline: open	**COMPETITIVE**

Adelphi University, founded in 1896, is a private institution. The figure for tuition and fees in the above capsule is for first-year students. Tuition cost varies by programs chosen by student. There are 8 undergraduate schools and 7 graduate schools. In addition to regional accreditation, AU has baccalaureate program accreditation with AACSB, CSWE, NLN, APA, ASHA, and CCNE. The 75-acre campus is in a suburban area 20 miles east of New York City. Including any residence halls, there are 26 buildings.

STUDENT LIFE: 93% of undergraduates are from New York. Others are from 38 states, 40 foreign countries, and Canada. 74% are from public schools. 6% are race unknown; 52% White; 3% Foreign; 2% two or more races; 16% Hispanic; 10% African American; 10% Asian American. 47% are Catholic; 17% Hindu, Buddhist, Muslim, Christian, and Unknown; 16% claim no religious affiliation; 12% Jewish. **Female To Male Ratio:** 2.4:1. The average age of freshmen is 18; all undergraduates, 22. 19% do not continue beyond their first year; 67% remain to graduate. **Housing:** 1282 students can be accommodated in college housing, which includes dorms. In addition, there are honors houses, special-interest houses, theme housing, green living learning community, and gender inclusive housing. On-campus housing is available on a first-come, first-served basis, and is available on a lottery system for upperclassmen. 77% of students commute. Alcohol is not permitted. All students may keep cars.

FACULTY/CLASSROOMS: 46% of faculty are male; 54% are female. All teach undergraduates. No introductory courses are taught by graduate students. The average class size in a regular course is 20.

PROGRAMS OF STUDY: AU confers B.A., B.S., B.B.A., B.F.A., B.S.Ed. and B.S.S.W. degrees. Associate, master's, and doctoral degrees are also awarded. Bachelor's degrees are awarded in AGRICULTURE (environmental studies), BIOLOGICAL SCIENCE (biochemistry and biology/biological science), BUSINESS (accounting, banking and finance, business administration and management, human resources, and management information systems), COMMUNICATIONS AND THE ARTS (art history and appreciation, communications, dance, design, dramatic arts, English, fine arts, French, languages, music, performing arts, Spanish, and theater design), COMPUTER AND PHYSICAL SCIENCE (chemistry, computer science, mathematics, and physics), EDUCATION (art education and physical education), HEALTH PROFESSIONS (nursing and speech pathology/audiology), SOCIAL SCIENCE (anthropology, criminal justice, economics, history, Latin American studies, philosophy, political science/government, psychology, social science, social work, and sociology). Nursing, business, and social work are the strongest academically. Nursing, biology, and psychology have the largest enrollments.

ACTIVITIES: 10% of men belong to 7 national fraternities; 8% of women belong to 10 national sororities. There are 80 groups on campus, including Excel mentoring program, radio station, art, band, cheerleading, chorale, chorus, computers, dance, debate, drama, environmental, ethnic, film, honors, international, jazz band, LGBT, literary magazine, model UN, musical theater, newspaper, opera, orchestra, political, professional, religious, social, social service, student government, and yearbook. Popular campus events include Family Week, Student Holiday Party, Spring-In Festival, Spring Concert, and Commuter Appreciation Week. **Sports:** There are 9 intercollegiate sports for men and 11 for women, and 14 intramural sports for men and 14 for women. Facilities include a stadium, a gym, a swimming pool, a fitness center, racquetball, squash, tennis courts, a dance studio, an indoor track, baseball and softball fields. **Graduates:** From July 1, 2016 to June 30, 2017, 1381 bachelor's degrees were awarded. The most popular majors were health professions (32%), business/marketing (16%), and social science (8%). In an average class, 5% graduate in 3 years or less, 54% graduate in 4 years or less, 61% graduate in 5 years or less, and 64% graduate in 6 years or less. Of the 2016 graduating class, 41% were enrolled in graduate school within 6 months of graduation, and 88% were employed.

SERVICES: Counseling and information services are available, as is tutoring in most subjects. The learning center offers tutoring in writing, quantitative skills and help with class assignments. There is a reader service for the blind. **Library/Resources:** The library contains 632,180 volumes, 789,749 microform items, 26,746 audio/video tapes/CDs/DVDs, and subscribes to 929 periodicals, including electronic. Computerized library services include interlibrary loans, database searching, Internet access, and Wi-Fi capability. Special learning facilities include an art gallery, an observatory, a theater, sculpture and ceramics studios, a bronze casting foundry, and language labs. **Physically Challenged Students:** 95% of the campus is accessible. Facilities include wheelchair ramps, elevators, special parking, specially equipped restrooms, special class scheduling, lowered drinking fountains, lowered telephones, and special housing. **Special:** Cross-registration is possible with New York University College of Dentistry, Tufts University School of Dental Medicine, Columbia University, New York Law School, SUNY State College of Optometry, and New York Medical College. Internships are available in accounting, banking and money management, and communications, among others. Study abroad is available in 65 countries, including Spain, France, Denmark, and England. A 5-year bachelors/masters degree in a number of fields, including biology, social work, and education, is offered. In addition, work-study programs, double majors, the B.A.-B.S. degree, an accelerated degree program, student-designed majors, and a Washington semester are available. A 3-2 engineering degree is offered with Rensselaer Polytechnic, Columbia, Polytechnic, and Stevens Institute of Technology, and joint degree programs are offered in computer science, dentistry, engineering, environmental studies, law, optometry, and physical therapy with other universities and technical institutions. Credit for life experience for adult students, nondegree study in special cases, and pass/fail options are possible. There are 27 national honor societies and a freshman honors program. **Visiting:** There are regularly scheduled orientations for prospective students, including a campus tour, an interview, and information sessions. There are guides for informal visits and visitors may sit in on classes. To schedule a visit, contact the Undergraduate Admissions at undergraduate@adelphi.edu. **Campus Safety and Security:** Measures include 24-hour foot and vehicle patrol, an emergency notification system, self-defense education, and security escort services. There are shuttle buses, emergency telephones, lighted pathways/sidewalks The dorm main entrances are videotaped and locked 24 hours a day.

REQUIREMENTS: Applicants should have 16 academic credits, including recommended 4 units of English, history, and social studies, 3-4 each of math and science, and 2-4 of foreign language. An essay is required and an interview recommended for all applicants. A portfolio for art and technical theater candidates, an audition for music, dance, and theater candidates, and an interview for nursing, social work, and honors candidates are required. The SAT is recommended for the general studies and learning disabilities programs. A GPA of 2.5 is required. AP credits are accepted. Important factors in the admissions decision are leadership record, evidence of special talent, personality/intangible qualities, extracurricular activities record, and recommendations by school officials. To graduate, students need at least a 2.0 cumulative GPA (higher in some programs) and 120 credit hours with a minimum of 27 in the major. 6 credits each are required in the arts, humanities, languages, natural sciences, math, and social sciences. Other course requirements include English composition, freshman seminar (3 credits each), and a 1-credit freshman orientation experience, and a capstone experience for seniors. **Procedure:** Freshmen are admitted in the fall and spring. Entrance exams should be taken in October of the senior year or May of the junior year. There are early admissions, deferred admissions, and rolling admissions plans. Application deadlines are open. The fall 2017 application fee was $40. Applications are accepted online. **Transfer Students:** 596 transfer students enrolled in 2016-2017. A GPA of 2.5 is recommended in addition to an essay, an official high school transcript, and official records of all work completed or in progress from previous colleges and universities. An interview is required for students in social work and nursing, while an audition is needed for music, dance, and theater students and a portfolio for art and technical theater students. 30 of 120 credits required for the bachelor's degree must be completed at Adelphi. **International Students:** There are 203 international students enrolled. They must take the TOEFL with a minimum score of 550 on the paper-based TOEFL (PBT) or 80 on the Internet-based version (iBT). They must also take the SAT or ACT.

ADMISSIONS: 70% of the 2017-2018 applicants were accepted. The SAT scores for the 2017-2018 freshman class were: Critical Reading-- 24% below 500, 49% between 500 and 599, 23% between 600 and 699, and 4% between 700 and 800. Math-- 19% below 500, 50% between 500 and 599, 25% between 600 and 699, and 6% between 700 and 800. Writing-- 23% below 500, 50% between 500 and 599, 23% between 600 and 699, and 4% between 700 and 800. 46% of the current freshmen were in the top fifth of their class; 81% were in the top two fifths. **Admissions Contact:** Christine Murphy, Director of Admissions. Email: *admissions@adelphi.edu* Web: *www.adelphi.edu*

FINANCIAL AID: In 2017-2018, 75% of all full-time freshmen received some form of financial aid. 73% of all full-time freshmen received need-based aid. The average freshman award was $22,500. Need-based scholarships or need-based grants averaged $21,071; need-based self-help aid (loans and jobs) averaged $5,052; non-need-based athletic scholarships averaged $9,132; other non-need-based awards and non-need-based scholarships averaged $18,535; and $3,812 from other forms of aid. The average financial indebtedness of the 2017 graduate was $33,485. AU is a member of CSS. The state aid form is required. The FAFSA code is 002666. The priority date for freshman financial aid applications for fall entry is March 1.

ALBANY COLLEGE OF PHARMACY AND HEALTH SCIENCES *(The complete profile is made available exclusively on our website, www.barronspac.com)*

ALFRED STATE COLLEGE — B-4

www.alfredstate.edu

Alfred, NY 14802 (607) 587-4215 (800) 425-3733

Fax: (607) 587-4299 **Email:** admissions@alfredstate.edu

Full-time: 2276 men, 1171 women
Part-time: 87 men, 201 women
Graduate: n/av
Year: semesters, summer session
Room & Board: $11,820

SAT CR/M/W: 520/540/490 **ACT:** 23
Application Deadline: rolling

Faculty: 168
Ph.D.s: 40%
Student/Faculty: 18 to 1
Tuition: $8075 ($11,345)
Freshman Class: 5073 applied, 3652 accepted, 1176 enrolled
CEEB CODE: 2522
COMPETITIVE

Alfred State College, the State University of New York College of Technology within the SUNY system, founded in 1908, is a public institution conferring associate and bachelors degrees. There are 3 undergraduate schools. In addition to regional accreditation, ASC has baccalaureate program accreditation with ABET, NAAB, ACEN, CAHIIM, and CVTEA. The 150-acre campus is in a rural area 15 miles north of Pennsylvania, 75 miles south of Rochester, and 90 miles southeast of Buffalo. Including any residence halls, there are 50 buildings.

STUDENT LIFE: 96% of undergraduates are from New York. Others are from 32 states and 8 foreign countries. 8% are Hispanic; 73% White; 2% two or more races; 12% African American; 1% Asian American; 1% Foreign; 1% race unknown. **Male To Female Ratio:** 1.7:1. The average age of freshmen is 19; all undergraduates, 21. 28% do not continue beyond their first year; 67% remain to graduate. **Housing:** 2533 students can be accommodated in college housing, which includes dorms and on-campus apartments. In addition, there are honors houses, language/international houses, special-interest houses, fraternity houses, sorority houses, wellness housing, and adult housing. On-campus housing is guaranteed for all 4 years. 71% of students live on campus. Alcohol is not permitted. All students may keep cars.

FACULTY/CLASSROOMS: 61% of faculty are male; 39% are female. All teach undergraduates. No introductory courses are taught by graduate students. The average class size in an introductory lecture is 40; in a laboratory is 20; and in a regular course is 20.

PROGRAMS OF STUDY: ASC confers B.S., B.B.A., B.Arch., and B.T. degrees. Associate degrees are also awarded. Bachelor's degrees are awarded in BUSINESS (banking and finance, business administration and management, finance (financial planning), information and communication technology, and sports management), COMMUNICATIONS AND THE ARTS (digital media, digital media technologies, and graphic design and media), COMPUTER AND PHYSICAL SCIENCE (cyber intelligence/security studies, information science systems and technology, information sciences and systems, and information science), ENGINEERING AND ENVIRONMENTAL DESIGN (architectural technology, architecture, computer engineering, computer technology, construction management, electrical/electronics engineering technology, graphic arts technology, manufacturing technology, mechanical engineering technology, survey and mapping technology, and technological management), HEALTH PROFESSIONS (health care administration and nursing), SOCIAL SCIENCE (criminal justice, forensic studies, and human services). Engineering technology programs are the strongest academically and have the largest enrollments.

ACTIVITIES: 4% of men belong to 5 local fraternities; 3% of women belong to 4 local sororities. There are 120 groups on campus, including rescue and response team, band, cheerleading, chess, choir, chorale, chorus, computers, dance, drama, environmental, ethnic, forensics, honors, international, jazz band, LGBT, literary magazine, musical theater, newspaper, orchestra, peer education network, pep band, professional, radio and TV, social, social service, student government, and yearbook. Popular campus events include Family Weekend and Hot Dog Day. **Sports:** There are 10 intercollegiate sports for men and 9 for women, and 10 intramural sports for men and 10 for women. Facilities include a fitness center/weight room, an indoor swimming pool, a wrestling room, a gym, tennis courts, an outdoor track, baseball and softball fields, and practice fields. **Graduates:** From July 1, 2016 to June 30, 2017, 306 bachelor's degrees were awarded. The most popular majors were business/marketing (48%), engineering technologies (28%), and computer and information science (8%). In an average class, 47% graduate in 4 years or less and 56% graduate in 6 years or less. Of the 2016 graduating class, 99% were enrolled in graduate school within 6 months of graduation, and 99% were employed.

SERVICES: Counseling and information services are available, as is tutoring in most subjects. There is a reader service for the blind, and remedial math, reading, and writing. **Library/Resources:** The library contains 61,500 volumes, 8,148 audio/video tapes/CDs/DVDs, and subscribes to 5,500 periodicals, including electronic. Computerized library services include interlibrary loans, database searching, Internet access, and Wi-Fi capability. Special learning facilities include an art gallery and a radio station. **Physically Challenged Students:** All of the campus is accessible. Facilities include wheelchair ramps, elevators, special parking, specially equipped restrooms, special class scheduling, lowered drinking fountains, lowered telephones, and special housing. **Special:** Cross-registration is offered with Alfred University, Houghton College, Rochester area colleges, and the Western New York Consortium. On-campus work-study programs are available, as are summer internships. There are 2 national honor societies, a freshman honors program, and 52 departmental honors programs. **Visiting:** There are regularly scheduled orientations for prospective students, including open houses during the fall and spring semesters. All aspects of the campus are open for visitation, and accepted students are invited to participate in an overnight visit. There are guides for informal visits; visitors may sit in on classes and stay overnight. To schedule a visit, contact the Admissions Office. **Campus Safety and Security:** Measures include 24-hour foot and vehicle patrol, an emergency notification system, self-defense education, and security escort services. There are shuttle buses, emergency telephones, lighted pathways/sidewalks, and controlled access to dorms/residences.

REQUIREMENTS: The SAT or ACT is required. Applicants must have graduated from an accredited secondary school or earned a GED. Specific course requirements vary by curriculum. A portfolio is required for applicants interested in computer art and design and digital media and animation. AP and CLEP credits are accepted. Important factors in the admissions decision are advanced placement or honors courses, extracurricular activities record, and recommendations by school officials. To graduate, candidates for a bachelor's degree must complete a total of 120 credits. A core sequence, including courses in math, physical sciences, and liberal studies, and a year-long senior technical project, are required. A physical education course is also required. **Procedure:** Freshmen are admitted to all sessions. Entrance exams should be taken November 1 . There is a rolling admissions plan. Application deadlines are open. The fall 2017 application fee was $50. Notifications are sent October 1. 130 applicants were on the 2017 waiting list; 36 were admitted. Applications are accepted online. **Transfer Students:** 309 transfer students enrolled in 2016-2017. Transfer applicants must have a minimum 2.4 GPA. 30 of 120 credits required for the bachelor's degree must be completed at ASC. **International Students:** There are 50 international students enrolled. They must take the TOEFL.

ADMISSIONS: The SAT scores for the 2017-2018 freshman class were: Critical Reading-- 67% below 500, 26% between 500 and 599, 6% between 600 and 699, and 1% between 700 and 800. Math-- 57% below 500, 33% between 500 and 599, 9% between 600 and 699, and 1% between 700 and 800. **Admissions Contact:** Deborah Goodrich, Associate Vice President for Enrollment Management. Email: *admissions@alfredstate.edu* Web: *www.alfredstate.edu*

FINANCIAL AID: In 2017-2018, 82% of all full-time freshmen received some form of financial aid. 70% of all full-time freshmen received need-based aid. The average freshman award was $11,182. Need-based scholarships or need-based grants averaged $7,217; and need-based self-help aid (loans and jobs) averaged $3,380. The average financial indebtedness of the 2017 graduate was $30,796. The FAFSA code is 002854. Check with the school for current application due date.

ALFRED UNIVERSITY B-4

www.alfred.edu

Alfred, NY 14802	**(607) 871-2115** **(800) 541-9229**
Fax: (607) 871-2198	**Email: admissions@alfred.edu**
Full-time: 939 men, 970 women	**Faculty:** 150
Part-time: 24 men, 27 women	**Ph.D.s:** 93%
Graduate: 157 men, 314 women	**Student/Faculty:** 12 to 1
Year: semesters, summer session	**Tuition:** $31,274
Room & Board: $6216	**Freshman Class:** 3417 applied, 2385 accepted, 535 enrolled
SAT CR/M/W: 530/550/510 **ACT:** 24	**CEEB CODE:** 2005
Application Deadline: August 1	**COMPETITIVE**

Alfred University, founded in 1836, is composed of the privately endowed College of Liberal Arts and Sciences, and the College of Ceramics (Inamori School of Engineering and School of Art and Design). AU offers more than 40 undergraduate majors/programs. The figures given in the above capsule and in this profile are approximate. Tuition cost varies by program chosen by student. There are 5 undergraduate schools and 1 graduate school. In addition to regional accreditation, AU has baccalaureate program accreditation with AACSB, ABET, NASAD, CAATE, and ACS. The 232-acre campus is in a rural area in Alfred, NY, about 1 hour west of Corning, 1.5 hours south of Rochester, and 2 hours from Buffalo. Including any residence halls, there are 52 buildings.

STUDENT LIFE: 76% of undergraduates are from New York. Others are from 42 states, 19 foreign countries, and Canada. 8% are African American; 7% Hispanic; 66% White; 3% Foreign; 2% Asian American; 2% two or more races; 12% race unknown. **Female To Male Ratio:** 1.2:1. The average age of freshmen is 18; all undergraduates, 20. 26% do not continue beyond their first year; 62% remain to graduate. **Housing:** 1469 students can be accommodated in college housing, which includes dorms and on-campus apartments. In addition, there are honors houses, language/international houses, special-interest houses, and theme housing. On-campus housing is guaranteed for the freshman year only, and is available on a first-come, first-served basis, and is available on a lottery system for upperclassmen. 76% of students live on campus. All students may keep cars.

FACULTY/CLASSROOMS: 54% of faculty are male; 46% are female. 90% teach undergraduates, and 90% do research. No introductory courses are taught by graduate students. The average class size in an introductory lecture is 30; in a laboratory is 20; and in a regular course is 18.

PROGRAMS OF STUDY: AU confers B.A., B.F.A., and B.S. degrees. Master's and doctoral degrees are also awarded. Bachelor's degrees are awarded in AGRICULTURE (environmental studies), BIOLOGICAL SCIENCE (biology/biological science), BUSINESS (accounting, business administration and management, and marketing/retailing/merchandising), COMMUNICATIONS AND THE ARTS (art history and appreciation, ceramic art and design, communications, dramatic arts, English, fine arts, glass, Spanish, and theatre arts), COMPUTER AND PHYSICAL SCIENCE (chemistry, geology, mathematics, physics, and science), EDUCATION (art education, athletic training, business education, early childhood education, mathematics education, science education, secondary education, and social studies education), ENGINEERING AND ENVIRONMENTAL DESIGN (ceramic engineering, materials engineering, and mechanical engineering), SOCIAL SCIENCE (criminal justice, cross-cultural studies, gerontology, history, interdisciplinary studies, philosophy, political science/government, psychology, and sociology). Engineering is the strongest academically. Art and design, business administration, and mechanical engineering have the largest enrollments.

ACTIVITIES: There are no fraternities or sororities. There are 90 groups on campus, including science, business, communications, diversity and multicultural, engineering, entertainment, art, band, cheerleading, chorale, chorus, computers, cultural, dance, drama, environmental, ethnic, film, honors, international, jazz band, LGBT, literary magazine, musical theater, newspaper, orchestra, pep band, photography, political, professional, radio and TV, religious, social, social service, student government, and yearbook. Popular campus events include Homecoming Weekend, Family Weekend, and Hot Dog Day. **Sports:** There are 10 intercollegiate sports for men and 11 for women, and 14 intramural sports for men and 13 for women. Facilities include a multipurpose field for football, soccer, and lacrosse, an Olympic-size pool, a softball field, tennis courts, racquetball and squash courts, a weight room, dance and exercise studios, an indoor gym, a fitness center, an equestrian center, a four-lane indoor track, and basketball courts. **Graduates:** From July 1, 2016 to June 30, 2017, 356 bachelor's degrees were awarded. The most popular majors were fine arts (31%), engineering (17%), and biology (8%). In an average class, 44% graduate in 4 years or less, 61% graduate in 5 years or less, and 62% graduate in 6 years or less.

SERVICES: Counseling and information services are available, as is tutoring in most subjects. Time management, study skills workshops, and a writing center are available. There are also services for students with learning and physical disabilities. **Library/Resources:** The library contains 286,995 volumes, 79,704 microform items, 179,255 audio/video tapes/CDs/DVDs, and subscribes to 93,502 periodicals, including electronic. Computerized library services include interlibrary loans, database searching, Internet access, and Wi-Fi capability. Special learning facilities include an art gallery, a radio station, an observatory, and a ceramic art museum. **Physically Challenged Students:** 45% of the campus is accessible. Facilities include wheelchair ramps, elevators, special parking, specially equipped restrooms, special class scheduling, and lowered drinking fountains. **Special:** There are cooperative programs in engineering with Duke and Columbia Universities. AU participates in a cross-registration program with more than 15 area colleges and universities through the Rochester Area Colleges consortium. AU also offers study abroad, Washington and Albany semesters, student-designed majors, and a 4+1 M.B.A. program for students majoring in Liberal Arts and Sciences or Engineering. There are 16 national honor societies and a chapter of Phi Beta Kappa. **Visiting:** There are regularly scheduled orientations for prospective students; an agenda is customized per students needs. There are guides for informal visits; visitors may sit in on classes and stay overnight. To schedule a visit, contact the Admissions Office. **Campus Safety and Security:** Measures include 24-hour foot and vehicle patrol, an emergency notification system, and security escort services. There are emergency telephones, lighted pathways/sidewalks, and controlled access to dorms/residences.

REQUIREMENTS: The SAT or ACT is required. A GED is accepted. A minimum of 16 Carnegie units is required, including 4 years of English, and 2 to 3 years each of math, history/social studies, and science. Depending on the school/college applied to, the remaining units may be either in a foreign language, the categories listed above, or business, art, or computer science. Official high school transcripts, 1 letter of recommendation, an essay, and a $50 fee (may be waived by visiting campus or with a NACAC or College Board waiver) are required of all applicants. Applicants to the School of Art and Design must submit a portfolio. Interviews are encouraged. AP credits are accepted. Important factors in the admissions decision are recommendations by school officials, extracurricular activities record, and leadership record. To satisfy the requirements for a bachelors degree a student must: complete all course requirements, including those required for the major, general education, and the minimum number of credits for the degree sought depending on the school or college of enrollment; earn a cumulative GPA of at least 2.0; satisfy the Global Perspective Requirement; satisfy the physical education requirement; request legal conferral of degree and satisfy financial obligations to the University; earn at least 45 semester credit hours at AU; and be in residence at AU at least during the final 30 credit hours earned toward the degree. **Procedure:** Freshmen are admitted in the fall and spring. Entrance exams should be taken by spring of junior year. There are early decision, deferred admissions, and rolling admissions plans. Early decision applications should be filed by December 1; regular applications, by August 1 for fall entry; and December 1 for spring entry. The fall 2017 application fee was $50. Notification of early decision is sent December 15; regular decision, on a rolling basis. 45 early decision candidates were accepted for the 2017-2018 class. 91 applicants were on the 2017 waiting list; 11 were admitted. Applications are accepted online. **Transfer Students:** 49 transfer students enrolled in 2016-2017. Transfer applicants must have a GPA of at least 2.5 on a 4.0 scale. They must submit at least 1 letter of recommendation and official high school and college transcripts. Applicants to the School of Art and Design must also submit a portfolio. 45 of 120 credits required for the bachelor's degree must be completed at AU. **International Students:** There are 51 international students enrolled. They must take the TOEFL with a minimum score of 550 on the paper-based TOEFL (PBT) or 80 on the Internet-based version (iBT). Students must take the TOEFL or IELTS if they do not submit the SAT or ACT.

ADMISSIONS: 70% of the 2017-2018 applicants were accepted. The SAT scores for the 2017-2018 freshman class were: Critical Reading-- 27% below 500, 51% between 500 and 599, 19% between 600 and 699, and 3% between 700 and 800. Math-- 20% below 500, 49% between 500 and 599, 27% between 600 and 699, and 4% between 700 and 800. Writing-- 43% below 500, 40% between 500 and 599, 15% between 600 and 699, and 2% between 700 and 800. The ACT scores were 16% below 12, 28% between 12 and 17, 30% between 18 and 23, 15% between 24 and 29, and 11% above 30. 36% of the current freshmen were in the top fifth of their class; 70% were in the top two fifths. 3 freshmen graduated first in their class. **Admissions Contact:** Earl E. Pierce, Vice President for Enrollment Management. Email: *admissions@alfred.edu* Web: *www.alfred.edu*

FINANCIAL AID: In 2017-2018, 95% of all full-time freshmen received some form of financial aid and need-based aid. The average freshman award was $26,623. Need-based scholarships or need-based grants averaged $20,371; need-based self-help aid (loans and jobs) averaged $6,640; and $4,986 from other forms of aid. 40% of undergraduate students work part-time. The average financial indebtedness of the 2017 graduate was $33,467. Alfred University is a member of CSS. The state aid form and the college's own financial statement, the business/farm supplement, and the noncustodial parent statement are required. The FAFSA code is 002671. The priority date for freshman financial aid applications for fall entry is March 15. The deadline for filing freshman financial aid applications for fall entry is May 1.

BARD COLLEGE — D-4

www.bard.edu

Annandale-on-Hudson, NY 12504 — (845) 758-7472

Fax: (845) 758-5208	**Email:** admission@bard.edu
Full-time: 877 men, 1088 women	**Faculty:** 156; IIB, ++$
Part-time: 39 men, 34 women	**Ph.D.s:** 92%
Graduate: 148 men, 186 women	**Student/Faculty:** 12 to 1
Year: 4-1-4	**Tuition:** $51,384
Room & Board: $14,540	**Freshman Class:** 5181 applied, 2912 accepted, 509 enrolled
SAT CR/M/W: 650/620/650	**CEEB CODE:** 2037
Application Deadline: January 1	**HIGHLY COMPETITIVE**

Bard College, founded in 1860, is an independent liberal arts and sciences institution affiliated historically with the Association of Episcopal Colleges. Discussion-oriented seminars and independent study are encouraged, tutorials are on a one-to-one basis, and most classes are kept small. There is 1 undergraduate school and 12 graduate schools. The 1000-acre campus is in a rural area 100 miles north of New York City. Including any residence halls, there are 70 buildings.

STUDENT LIFE: 66% of undergraduates are from out of state, mostly the Northeast. Students are from 47 states, 57 foreign countries, and Canada. 8% are African American; 61% White; 5% Asian American; 2% Hispanic; 11% Foreign; 11% race unknown; 1% American Indian/Alaska Native. **Female To Male Ratio:** 1.2:1. The average age of freshmen is 18; all undergraduates, 20. 14% do not continue beyond their first year; 78% remain to graduate. **Housing:** 1450 students can be accommodated in college housing, which includes dorms. In addition, there are special-interest houses, suites, and quiet dorms. On-campus housing is guaranteed for the freshman year only and is available on a lottery system for upperclassmen. All students may keep cars.

FACULTY/CLASSROOMS: 57% of faculty are male; 43% are female. All teach undergraduates and do research. No introductory courses are taught by graduate students. The average class size in an introductory lecture is 18; in a laboratory is 13; and in a regular course is 15.

PROGRAMS OF STUDY: BC confers B.A., B.S., B.Music, and B.P.S. (returning to college) degrees, and offers five-year dual-degree programs: B.M./B.A. in music and in another liberal arts field; and B.S. in Economics and Finance/B.A. degree in another liberal arts field. Associate, master's, and doctoral degrees are also awarded. Bachelor's degrees are awarded in AGRICULTURE (environmental studies), BIOLOGICAL SCIENCE (biology/biological science), COMMUNICATIONS AND THE ARTS (Arabic, art history and appreciation, Chinese, classical languages, creative writing, dance, dramatic arts, English literature, film arts, French, Germanic languages and literature, Hebrew, Italian, Japanese, literature, music, photography, Russian, Spanish, studio art, and theatre arts), COMPUTER AND PHYSICAL SCIENCE (chemistry, computer science, mathematics, and physics), SOCIAL SCIENCE (African studies, American studies, anthropology, area studies, Asian/Oriental studies, Celtic studies, classical/ancient civilization, economics, French studies, gender studies, German area studies, history, interdisciplinary studies, international studies, Italian studies, Judaic studies, Latin American studies, medieval studies, Middle Eastern studies, philosophy, political science/government, psychology, religion, Russian and Slavic studies, Sanskrit and Indian studies, science and society, sociology, Spanish studies, theological studies, and Victorian studies). Social studies, visual and performing arts, and languages and literatures have the largest enrollments.

ACTIVITIES: There are no fraternities or sororities. There are 150 groups on campus, including art, band, chamber groups, chess, choir, chorus, computers, dance, debate, drama, environmental, ethnic, film, forensics, international, jazz band, LGBT, literary magazine, musical theater, newspaper, opera, orchestra, photography, political, radio and TV, religious, social, social service, student government, and symphony. Popular campus events include Winter Carnival, Spring Festival, and International Students Cultural Show. **Sports:** There are 10 intercollegiate sports for men and 8 for women, and 9 intramural sports for men and 9 for women. Facilities include a gym with a pool, a baseball field, fitness and weight facilities, rugby, soccer and lacrosse fields, squash and tennis courts, cross-country trails, bike paths, and multipurpose fields for ultimate frisbee and open recreation. **Graduates:** From July 1, 2016 to June 30, 2017, 419 bachelor's degrees were awarded. The most popular majors were social studies (32%), visual and performing arts (28%), and language and literature (21%). In an average class, 68% graduate in 4 years or less, 76% graduate in 5 years or less, and 78% graduate in 6 years or less.

SERVICES: Counseling and information services are available, as is tutoring in every subject. There is a reader service for the blind. **Library/Resources:** The library contains 434,580 volumes, 8,120 microform items, and 5,083 audio/video tapes/CDs/DVDs, and subscribes to 36,900 periodicals, including electronic. Computerized library services include interlibrary loans, database searching, Internet access, and Wi-Fi capability. Special learning facilities include an art gallery, a radio station, an ecology field station, an economics institute, an institute for writing and thinking, institute for advanced theology, a center for curatorial studies and art in contemporary culture, and an archeological station. **Physically Challenged Students:** 70% of the campus is accessible. Facilities include wheelchair ramps, elevators, special parking, specially equipped restrooms, lowered drinking fountains, and lowered telephones. **Special:** Bard offers opportunities for study abroad, internships, Washington and New York semesters, dual majors, student-designed majors, accelerated degree programs, and pass/fail options. A 3-2 engineering degree is available with the Columbia University, Washington University (St. Louis), and Dartmouth College Schools of Engineering. Other 3-2 degrees are available in forestry and environmental studies, social work, architecture, city and regional planning, public health, and business administration. There are also opportunities for independent study, multicultural and ethnic studies, area studies, human rights, and globalization and international affairs. **Visiting:** There are regularly scheduled orientations for prospective students consisting of regularly scheduled daily tours and information sessions. Visitors may sit in on classes. To schedule a visit, contact Mackie Siebens at (845) 758-7472. **Campus Safety and Security:** Measures include 24-hour foot and vehicle patrol, an emergency notification system, self-defense education, and security escort services. There are shuttle buses, emergency telephones, lighted pathways/sidewalks, volunteer emergency medical technicians on call 24 hours a day, and Bard response to Rape and Associated Violence Education (BRAVE).

REQUIREMENTS: Bard places strong emphasis on the academic background and intellectual curiosity of applicants, as well as indications of the students commitment to social and environmental concerns, independent research, volunteer work, and other important extracurricular activities. Students applying for admission are expected to have graduated from an accredited secondary school (the GED is accepted) and must submit written essays with the application. The high school record should include a full complement of college-preparatory courses. Honors and advanced placement courses are also considered. A GPA of 3.0 is required. AP credits are accepted. Important factors in the admissions decision are advanced placement or honors courses, recommendations by school officials, and extracurricular activities record. All students must complete a 3-week workshop in Language and Thinking (August of first year), a two and a half week Citizen Science program (January of first year); a first-year seminar; and a senior project. A conference in the junior year is required, and through a moderation process in the sophomore year, the student chooses a concentration in an academic department. A distribution of at least 1 course in each of the 9 academic areas is required, with 40 credits outside the division of the students major and a total of 128 credit hours needed to graduate. Rethinking Differences, a course fulfilling the diversity requirement, is also required. **Procedure:** Freshmen are admitted in the fall. There are early admissions and deferred admissions plans. Applications should be filed by January 1 for fall entry; November 1 for spring entry. The fall 2017 application fee was $50. Notifications are sent April 1. 33 early decision candidates were accepted for the 2017-2018 class. 675 applicants were on the 2017 waiting list; 154 were admitted. Applications are accepted online. **Transfer Students:** 62 transfer students enrolled in 2016-2017. Admission requirements are the same as for regular applicants. A minimum GPA of 3.0 and an interview are recommended. A high school transcript (when less than 2 years of college-level study completed), a transfer questionnaire, and a deans report are required. 64 of 128 credits required for the bachelor's degree must be completed at BC. **International Students:** There are 229 international students enrolled. They must take the TOEFL with a minimum score of 600 on the paper-based TOEFL (PBT) or 100 on the Internet-based version (iBT).

ADMISSIONS: 56% of the 2017-2018 applicants were accepted. **Admissions Contact:** Mackie Siebens, Deputy Director of Admissions. Email: *admission@bard.edu* Web: *www.bard.edu*

FINANCIAL AID: In 2017-2018, 69% of all full-time freshmen received some form of financial aid. 68% of all full-time freshmen received need-based aid. The average freshman award was $47,604. Need-based scholarships or need-based grants averaged $42,292; need-based self-help aid (loans and jobs) averaged $6,519; and other non-need-based awards and non-need-based scholarships averaged $16,625. 30% of undergraduate students work part-time. The average financial indebtedness of the 2017 graduate was $27,816. BC is a member of CSS. The CSS/Profile and the state aid form, non-custodial profile and/or business/farm supplement if applicable are required. The priority date for freshman financial aid applications for fall entry is February 1.

BARNARD COLLEGE/COLUMBIA UNIVERSITY D-5
www.barnard.edu

New York, NY 10027	(212) 854-2014
Fax: (212) 854-6220	**Email:** admissions@barnard.edu
Full-time: 2536 women	**Faculty:** 215; IIB, ++$
Part-time: 38 women	**Ph.D.s:** 94%
Graduate: n/av	**Student/Faculty:** 10 to 1
Year: semesters	**Tuition:** $52,662
Room & Board: $16,100	**Freshman Class:** 7071 applied, 1184 accepted, 605 enrolled
SAT CR/M/W: 690/680/705 **ACT:** 31	**CEEB CODE:** 2038
Application Deadline: January 1	**MOST COMPETITIVE**

Barnard College, founded in 1889, and is an independent affiliate of Columbia University. It is an undergraduate women's liberal arts college. There is 1 undergraduate school. The 4-acre campus is in an urban area, Manhattans Upper West Side. Including any residence halls, there are 18 buildings.

STUDENT LIFE: 76% of undergraduates are from out of state, mostly the Middle Atlantic. Students are from 48 states, 35 foreign countries, and Canada. 53% are from public schools. 8% are Foreign; 6% African American; 52% White; 5% two or more races; 14% Asian American; 12% Hispanic; 1% race unknown. The average age of freshmen is 18; all undergraduates, 20. 5% do not continue beyond their first year; 89% remain to graduate. **Housing:** 2057 students can be accommodated in college housing, which includes dorms, on-campus apartments, and off-campus apartments. In addition, there are special-interest houses. On-campus housing is guaranteed for all 4 years. 99% of students live on campus. Alcohol is not permitted. All students may keep cars.

FACULTY/CLASSROOMS: All teach undergraduates and all do research. No introductory courses are taught by graduate students. The average class size in an introductory lecture is 30; in a laboratory is 11; and in a regular course is 13.

PROGRAMS OF STUDY: BC confers B.A. degrees. Bachelor's degrees are awarded in BIOLOGICAL SCIENCE (biochemistry and biology/biological science), COMMUNICATIONS AND THE ARTS (art history and appreciation, classics, comparative literature, dance, dramatic arts, English, film arts, French, German, Greek, Italian, Latin, linguistics, music, Russian, and Spanish), COMPUTER AND PHYSICAL SCIENCE (astronomy, chemistry, computer science, mathematics, physics, and statistics), ENGINEERING AND ENVIRONMENTAL DESIGN (architecture and environmental science), SOCIAL SCIENCE (American studies, anthropology, biopsychology, classical/ancient civilization, East Asian studies, economics, European studies, history, international studies, medieval studies, Middle Eastern studies, philosophy, political science/government, psychology, religion, sociology, urban studies, and women's studies). English, psychology, and economics are the strongest academically, and have the largest enrollments.

ACTIVITIES: There are no fraternities or sororities. There are 100

groups on campus, including art, band, cheerleading, choir, chorale, chorus, dance, debate, drama, environmental, ethnic, film, international, jazz band, LGBT, literary magazine, marching band, Model UN, musical theater, newspaper, opera, orchestra, pep band, photography, political, professional, religious, social, social service, student government, symphony, and yearbook. Popular campus events include Spring and Winter Festivals, Founders Day, and Take Back the Night. **Sports:** There are 16 intercollegiate sports for women, and 16 intramural sports for women. Facilities include pools, weight rooms, gyms, tennis courts, and an indoor track. **Graduates:** From July 1, 2016 to June 30, 2017, 632 bachelor's degrees were awarded. The most popular majors were social sciences (27%), psychology (12%), visual and performing arts, and Biological/life sciences (11%).

SERVICES: There is a reader service for the blind. A student-staffed writing room is available for all levels of writing, and a math help room is also available. **Library/Resources:** The library contains 204,906 volumes, 17,705 microform items, and 17,448 audio/video tapes/CDs/DVDs, and subscribes to 543 periodicals, including electronic. Computerized library services include interlibrary loans, database searching, Internet access, and Wi-Fi capability. Special learning facilities include an art gallery, greenhouses, science laboratories, a child development research and study center, dance studios, modern theaters, women's research archives, and multimedia labs and classrooms. **Physically Challenged Students:** 90% of the campus is accessible. Facilities include wheelchair ramps, elevators, special parking, specially equipped restrooms, special class scheduling, lowered drinking fountains, lowered telephones, and special housing. The Office of Disability Services provides a variety of support services to students with permanent and temporary disabilities. **Special:** Barnard offers cross-registration with Columbia University, more than 2500 internships with New York City companies and research centers, and study abroad worldwide. A 3-2 engineering program with the Columbia School of Engineering and double-degree programs with the Columbia University Schools of International and Public Affairs, Law, and Dentistry, and the Jewish Theological Seminary are possible. Cross-registration programs are also possible with the Juilliard School and the Manhattan School of Music. The college offers selective dual and student-designed majors and multidisciplinary majors. There is 1 national honor society and a chapter of Phi Beta Kappa. **Visiting:** There are regularly scheduled orientations for prospective students. Open house programs for prospective students are regularly scheduled throughout the year. There are guides for informal visits; visitors may sit in on classes and stay overnight. To schedule a visit, contact The Office of Admissions. **Campus Safety and Security:** Measures include 24-hour foot and vehicle patrol and security escort services. There are shuttle buses, emergency telephones, lighted pathways/sidewalks, and safety and security education programs.

REQUIREMENTS: Students taking the SAT must also take 2 SAT Subject tests, or take the ACT. The GED is accepted. Applicants should prepare with 4 years of English, and 3 years each of math, science (with lab), foreign language, and history. An interview is recommended. AP credits are accepted. Important factors in the admissions decision are leadership record, advanced placement or honors courses, personality/intangible qualities, recommendations by school officials, evidence of special talent, and extracurricular activities record. A total of 120 credits is required, with a minimum GPA of 2.0. All students must complete a major and may elect a double major or minor as well. Students must take 2 semesters each of a foreign language, and complete a series of other Foundation courses that encompass the humanities, social sciences, and sciences with global, technological, quantitative, and cultural diversity coursework. Students must also complete 1 semester each in first-year seminar and first-year English. **Procedure:** Freshmen are admitted in the fall. Entrance exams should be taken by January of the senior year. There are early decision, early admissions, and deferred admissions plans. Early decision applications should be filed by November 1; regular applications, by January 1 for fall entry. The fall 2017 application fee was $75. Notification of early decision is sent December 15; regular decision, April 1. 280 early decision candidates were accepted for the 2017-2018 class. 787 applicants were on the 2017 waiting list; 277 were admitted. Applications are accepted online. **Transfer Students:** 83 transfer students enrolled in 2016-2017. The SAT or ACT is required. Deadline for transfer applicants is April 1 (fall term) and November 1 (spring term). They must submit the common application, a writing supplement, high school and college transcripts. Applicants must be in good standing from prior institutions attended and will only be considered at sophomore or junior year entry. 60 of 120 credits required for the bachelor's degree must be completed at Barnard College. **International Students:** There are 211 international students enrolled. They must take the TOEFL with a minimum score of 600 on the paper-based TOEFL (PBT) or 100 on the Internet-based version (iBT). The IELTS is also accepted. They must also take the SAT or ACT. Applicants who take the SAT must also take 2 SAT Subject tests.

ADMISSIONS: 17% of the 2017-2018 applicants were accepted. The SAT scores for the 2017-2018 freshman class were: Critical Reading-- 1% below 500, 7% between 500 and 599, 40% between 600 and 699, and 51% between 700 and 800. Math-- 1% below 500, 13% between 500 and 599, 50% between 600 and 699, and 36% between 700 and 800. Writing-- 1% below 500, 5% between 500 and 599, 37% between 600 and 699, and 57% between 700 and 800. The ACT scores were 2% between 18 and 23, 26% between 24 and 29, and 72% above 30. **Admissions Contact:** Jennifer Fondiller, Dean of Enrollment Management. Email: *admissions@barnard.edu* Web: *www.barnard.edu*

FINANCIAL AID: In 2017-2018, 100% of all full-time freshmen received some form of financial aid. The average freshman award was $50,967. Need-based scholarships or need-based grants averaged $46,876; need-based self-help aid (loans and jobs) averaged $4,518; and other non-need-based awards and non-need-based scholarships averaged $3,323. 46% of undergraduate students work part-time. The average financial indebtedness of the 2017 graduate was $41,391. Barnard is a member of CSS. The CSS/Profile, the state aid form, the college's own financial statement, the parents and students federal tax returns, and the business and/or farm supplement are required. The priority date for freshman financial aid applications for fall entry is February 1.

BERKELEY COLLEGE/NEW YORK CITY CAMPUS *(The complete profile is made available exclusively on our website, www.barronspac.com)*

BERKELEY COLLEGE/WHITE PLAINS CAMPUS *(The complete profile is made available exclusively on our website, www.barronspac.com)*

BORICUA COLLEGE — D-5
www.boricuacollege.edu

New York, NY 10032	(212) 694-1000
Fax: (212) 694-1015	**Email:** acruz@boricuacollege.edu
Full-time: 260 men, 910 women	**Faculty:** n/av
Part-time: n/av	**Ph.D.s:** n/av
Graduate: n/av	**Student/Faculty:** n/av
Year: 4-1-4, summer session	**Tuition:** $10,100
Room & Board: n/app	**Freshman Class:** n/av **CEEB CODE:** 2901
Application Deadline: n/av	**COMPETITIVE**

Boricua College, founded in 1974, is a private college for bilingual students, designed to meet the needs of a Spanish-speaking population. The figures given in the above capsule and in this profile are approximate. There are 4 undergraduate schools and 2 graduate schools. In addition to regional accreditation, BC has baccalaureate program accreditation with MSCHE. The campus is in an urban area in Upper Manhattan, New York, in the historic Audubon Terrace complex. Including any residence halls, there are 4 buildings.

STUDENT LIFE: 100% of undergraduates are from New York. 70% are from public schools. 85% are Hispanic; 10% African American; 1% White. 85% are Catholic. **Female To Male Ratio:** 3.5:1. The average age of freshmen is 29; all undergraduates, 32. 12% do not continue beyond their first year; 80% remain to graduate. **Housing:** Alcohol is not permitted. No one may keep cars.

FACULTY/CLASSROOMS: No introductory courses are taught by graduate students.

PROGRAMS OF STUDY: BC confers B.A. degrees. Associate degrees are also awarded. Bachelor's degrees are awarded in BUSINESS (business administration and management), EDUCATION (elementary education), SOCIAL SCIENCE (human services and liberal arts/general studies). Applied science-paralegal studies is the strongest academically. Human services has the largest enrollment.

ACTIVITIES: There are no fraternities or sororities. There are 5 groups on campus, including art, chorus, drama, newspaper, and student government. Popular campus events include Cultural Programs, Puerto

Rican Discovery Day, Christmas, and Spring concerts with Chorus and Orchestra. **Sports:** Facilities include a gymnasium that hosts yoga, dance, martial arts, volleyball, and basketball. **Graduates:** From July 1, 2016 to June 30, 2017, 90 bachelors degrees were awarded. The most popular majors were human services, early childhood education, and business administration. In an average class, 65% graduate in 4 years or less and 35% graduate in 5 years or less.

SERVICES: Counseling and information services are available, as is tutoring in most subjects. **Library/Resources:** The library contains 15,778 volumes,5,000 audio/video tapes/CDs/DVDs, and subscribes to 5,000 periodicals, including electronic. Computerized library services include interlibrary loans, database searching, Internet access, and Wi-Fi capability. Special learning facilities include an art gallery, the Puerto Rican Disapora collection, a map collection, a museum, theatre, a cultural center, natural science laboratories, and lectures on personal health and physical activities. **Physically Challenged Students:** Facilities include elevators and specially equipped restrooms. **Visiting:** There are regularly scheduled orientations for prospective students, letters are sent to prospective students advising them of scheduled orientations. To schedule a visit, contact Abraham Cruzat or Miriam Prefferat at (212) 694-1000. **Campus Safety and Security:** There are shuttle buses, emergency telephones, and lighted pathways/sidewalks.

REQUIREMENTS: Boricua administers its own tests to prospective students, although either the SAT or ACT is accepted. Applicants must be graduates of an accredited secondary school or have a GED. 2 letters of recommendation and an admissions interview are required. Applicants must demonstrate a working knowledge of English and Spanish to a faculty panel. CLEP credits are accepted. Important factors in the admissions decision are leadership record, personality/intangible qualities, and recommendations by school officials. **Procedure:** Freshmen are admitted in the fall, spring, and summer. There are early decision and rolling admissions plans. Application deadlines are open. The fall 2017 application fee was $25. **Transfer Students:** Applicants with associate degrees may transfer up to 60 credits. All college credits passed with grade C and above are accepted. 80 of 124 credits required for the bachelor's degree must be completed at BC.

Admissions Contact: Abraham Cruz, Director of Student Services. Email: *acruz@boricuacollege.edu* Web: *www.boricuacollege.edu*

FINANCIAL AID: In 2017-2018, 100% of all full-time freshmen received some form of financial aid and need-based aid. Boricua is a member of CSS. The FAFSA code is 013029. Check with the school for current application deadlines.

CANISIUS COLLEGE — A-3

www.canisius.edu

Buffalo, NY 14208 — **(716) 888-2200**

Fax: (716) 888-3230	**Email: admissions@canisius.edu**
Full-time: 1148 men, 1155 women	**Faculty:** 172; IIA, av$
Part-time: 57 men, 38 women	**Ph.D.s:** 98%
Graduate: 398 men, 663 women	**Student/Faculty:** 11 to 1
Year: semesters, summer session	**Tuition:** $36,454
Room & Board: $13,218	**Freshman Class:** 4620 applied, 3537 accepted, 600 enrolled
SAT CR/M: 535/545 **ACT:** 25	**CEEB CODE:** 2073
Application Deadline: March 1	**COMPETITIVE**

Canisius College, founded in 1870, is a private Roman Catholic college in the Jesuit tradition. It offers undergraduate programs in the liberal arts and sciences, business, education, and human services. The figures given in the above capsule and in this profile are approximate. There are 3 undergraduate schools and 3 graduate schools. In addition to regional accreditation, CC has baccalaureate program accreditation with AACSB, CAHEA, CACREP, CAATE, CED, and CAEP. The 72-acre campus is in an urban area in Buffalo, NY. Including any residence halls, there are 56 buildings.

STUDENT LIFE: 85% of undergraduates are from New York. Others are from 38 states, 19 foreign countries, and Canada. 70% are from public schools. 8% are African American; 8% race unknown; 70% White; 5% Hispanic; 5% Foreign; 2% Asian American; 2% two or more races. **Female To Male Ratio:** 1.2:1. The average age of freshmen is 18; all undergraduates, 20. 17% do not continue beyond their first year; 71% remain to graduate. **Housing:** 1200 students can be accommodated in college housing, which includes dorms, on-campus apartments, off-campus apartments, and an honors dorm. In addition, there are special-interest houses, an intercultural hall, townhouses, and Bosch or Frisch halls (suite-style rooms) for first-year students. On-campus housing is guaranteed for all 4 years, and is available on a first-come, first-served basis, and is available on a lottery system for upperclassmen. 54% of students commute. All students may keep cars.

FACULTY/CLASSROOMS: 58% of faculty are male; 42% are female. All teach undergraduates and all do research. No introductory courses are taught by graduate students. The average class size in an introductory lecture is 23; in a laboratory is 18; and in a regular course is 20.

PROGRAMS OF STUDY: CC confers B.A., B.S., B.A.Ed., and B.S.Ed. degrees. Master's degrees are also awarded. Bachelor's degrees are awarded in AGRICULTURE (environmental studies), BIOLOGICAL SCIENCE (biochemistry, bioinformatics, biology/biological science, cell biology, neurosciences, and zoology), BUSINESS (accounting, banking and finance, business administration and management, business communications, business economics, entrepreneurial studies, fashion merchandising, finance, international business management, management information systems, management science, marketing management, marketing/retailing/merchandising, operations research, and sports management), COMMUNICATIONS AND THE ARTS (art history, classical languages, communications, creative writing, digital communications, English, fine arts, French, German, journalism, media arts, modern language, music, music performance, Spanish, speech/debate/rhetoric, and theatre arts), COMPUTER AND PHYSICAL SCIENCE (chemistry, computer science, information sciences and systems, mathematics, and physics), EDUCATION (athletic training, business education, childhood education, early childhood education, education, education administration, education of the deaf and hearing impaired, education of the exceptional child, elementary education, English education, foreign languages education, mathematics education, middle school education, physical education, science education, social studies education, special education, and teaching English as a second/foreign language (TESOL/TEFOL), ENGINEERING AND ENVIRONMENTAL DESIGN (computational sciences, environmental science, and preengineering), HEALTH PROFESSIONS (clinical science, exercise science, medical laboratory technology, predentistry, premedicine, prepharmacy, preveterinary science, and sports medicine), SOCIAL SCIENCE (anthropology, biblical studies, cognitive science, criminal justice, European studies, gerontology, history, humanities and social science, international relations, Latin American studies, liberal arts/general studies, philosophy, prelaw, psychology, social science, sociology, urban studies, and womens studies). Accounting, biology, and finance are the strongest academically. Psychology, finance, and biology have the largest enrollments.

ACTIVITIES: 1% of men belong to 1 national fraternity; 1% of women belong to 1 national sorority. There are 140 groups on campus, including art, band, cheerleading, chess, choir, chorale, computers, dance, drama, drill team, environmental, ethnic, honors, international, jazz band, LGBT, literary magazine, musical theater, newspaper, orchestra, pep band, political, professional, radio and TV, religious, social, social service, student government, and yearbook. Popular campus events include Fall Semiformal, International Fest, and Canisius Concert Series. **Sports:** There are 8 intercollegiate sports for men and 9 for women, and 12 intramural sports for men and 12 for women. Facilities include an athletic center with a 25-yard pool, training rooms, a sports complex with playing fields, a rifle range, and a mirrored dance studio. **Graduates:** From July 1, 2016 to June 30, 2017, 648 bachelor's degrees were awarded. The most popular majors were business/marketing (32%), biological/life science (14%), and communications (10%). In an average class, 62% graduate in 4 years or less, 69% graduate in 5 years or less, and 71% graduate in 6 years or less.

SERVICES: Counseling and information services are available, as is tutoring in every subject. There is a reader service for the blind, and remedial math, reading, and writing. **Library/Resources:** The library contains 313,916 volumes, 599,947 microform items, and 14,674 audio/video tapes/CDs/DVDs, and subscribes to 52,472 periodicals, including electronic. Computerized library services include interlibrary loans, database searching, Internet access, and Wi-Fi capability. Special learning facilities include an art gallery, radio and TV stations, a television studio, a foreign language lab, over 85 media-assisted classrooms, a digital media lab, and a musical instrument digital interface classroom. **Physically Challenged Students:** 90% of the campus is accessible. Facilities include wheelchair ramps, elevators, special parking, specially equipped restrooms, special class scheduling, lowered drinking fountains, lowered telephones, automatic doors, TDD, a shuttle service for students with disabilities, distraction-free testing spaces, and adjustable classroom desks. **Special:** CC offers internships, credit by exam, pass/fail options, dual majors, a Washington semester, work-study programs, and study abroad in over a dozen countries. Cooperative programs are available with the Fashion Institute of Technology in New York City. Cross-registration is permitted with the schools in the Western New York Consortium of Higher Education. Canisius also offers early assurance and joint degree programs, with SUNY health professions schools in Buffalo and Syracuse, and a 3-2 MBA. There are 16 national honor societies, a freshman honors program, and 5 departmental honors programs. **Visiting:** There are regularly scheduled orientations for prospective students, including an admissions interview or group session, a campus tour, and financial aid appointment by request. There are also summer visitations for families, on selected Saturdays, Fall Open Houses and an Open House in the Spring, a Financial Aid Workshop in January, and overnight visits for admitted students. There are guides for informal visits and visitors may sit in on classes. To schedule a visit, contact the Admissions Office. **Campus Safety and Security:** Measures include 24-hour foot and vehicle patrol, an emergency notification system, self-defense education, and security escort services. There are shuttle buses, emergency telephones, lighted pathways/sidewalks, controlled access to dorms/residences, crime prevention programs, and officers, bicycle patrols, and blue light emergency stations around campus.

REQUIREMENTS: All students must submit an official high school transcript (or GED) and SAT or ACT results. College preparatory course work should include 4 units each of English and social science, 3 units each of math, science, and foreign language. Students with a B+ average and a satisfactory SAT score are competitive. An essay and an interview are recommended. AP and CLEP credits are accepted. Important factors in the admissions decision are leadership record, recommendations by school officials, and advanced placement or honors courses. Students must take 12 required courses and complete 6 knowledge and skills requirement areas to satisfy their requirements. In addition, students must take ten 3-credit courses in the major. A minimum of 120 credit hours and a GPA of 2.0 are required for graduation. Freshman are admitted in the fall, spring, and summer. Entrance exams should be taken during the junior or senior year. There are deferred admissions and rolling admissions plans. Applications should be filed by March 1 for fall entry. The fall 2017 application fee was $40. Notification is sent on a rolling basis. Applications are accepted online. **Transfer Students:** 117 transfer students enrolled in 2016-2017. Applicants must present a minimum GPA of 2.0 and a Transfer Recommendation Form. Students may enroll during the fall, spring, or summer. 30 of 120 credits required for the bachelor's degree must be completed at Canisius. **International Students:** There are 127 international students enrolled. They must take the TOEFL with a minimum score of 550 on the paper-based TOEFL (PBT) or 79 on the Internet-based version (iBT). Students must also take the IELTS or STEPs, and either the SAT or ACT.

ADMISSIONS: 77% of the 2017-2018 applicants were accepted. The SAT scores for the 2017-2018 freshman class were: Critical Reading-- 33% below 500, 45% between 500 and 599, 20% between 600 and 699, and 2% between 700 and 800. Math-- 27% below 500, 45% between 500 and 599, 24% between 600 and 699, and 4% between 700 and 800. The ACT scores were 2% between 12 and 17, 37% between 18 and 23, 50% between 24 and 29, and 11% above 30. 48% of the current freshmen were in the top fifth of their class; 75% were in the top two fifths. 6 freshmen graduated first in their class. **Admissions Contact:** Justin Rogers, Director of Admissions. Email: *admissions@canisius.edu* Web: *www.canisius.edu*

FINANCIAL AID: In 2017-2018, 98% of all full-time freshmen received some form of financial aid. 86% of all full-time freshmen received need-based aid. The average freshman award was $33,160. Need-based scholarships or need-based grants averaged $10,090 ($45,186 maximum); need-based self-help aid (loans and jobs) averaged $4,735 ($7,900 maximum); non-need-based athletic scholarships averaged $18,922 ($48,426 maximum); other non-need-based awards and non-need-based scholarships averaged $17,337 ($46,003 maximum); and $23,879 from other forms of aid. 22% of undergraduate students work part-time. The average financial indebtedness of the 2017 graduate was $33,973. Canisius is a member of CSS. The FAFSA code is 002681. The priority date for freshman financial aid applications for fall entry is February 15.

CAZENOVIA COLLEGE C-3

www.cazenovia.edu

Cazenovia, NY 13035	**(315) 655-7225** **(800) 654-3210**
Fax: (315) 655-2190	**Email: ssphillips@cazenovia.edu**
Full-time: 208 men, 505 women	**Faculty:** 56; IIB, -$
Part-time: 46 men, 132 women	**Ph.D.s:** 71%
Graduate: n/av	**Student/Faculty:** 12 to 1
Year: semesters, summer session	**Tuition:** $33,656
Room & Board: $14,210	**Freshman Class:** 1802 applied, 1665 accepted, 165 enrolled
SAT or ACT: recommended	**CEEB CODE:** 2078
Application Deadline: open	**COMPETITIVE**

Cazenovia College, founded in 1824, is a private institution offering degree programs in liberal arts and preprofessional studies. There is 1 undergraduate school. In addition to regional accreditation, CC has baccalaureate program accreditation with IACBE and CAEP. The 40-acre campus is in a small town in Madison County, and 18 miles southeast of Syracuse, NY. Including any residence halls, there are 26 buildings.

STUDENT LIFE: 90% of undergraduates are from New York. Others are from 24 states and 3 foreign countries. 66% are White; 13% race unknown; 9% African American; 5% Hispanic; 3% two or more races; 2% Asian American; 1% American Indian/Alaska Native; 1% Foreign. **Female To Male Ratio:** 2.5:1. The average age of freshmen is 18; all undergraduates, 22. 54% remain to graduate. **Housing:** 766 students can be accommodated in college housing, which includes dorms, on-campus apartments, off-campus apartments, international housing, theme housing, and wellness housing. 70% of students live on campus. Upperclassmen may keep cars.

FACULTY/CLASSROOMS: 40% of faculty are male; 60% are female. All teach undergraduates. No introductory courses are taught by graduate students. The average class size in an introductory lecture is 20; in a laboratory is 15; and in a regular course is 16.

PROGRAMS OF STUDY: CC confers B.A., B.S., B.F.A., and B.P.S. degrees. Associate degrees are also awarded. Bachelor's degrees are awarded in AGRICULTURE (environmental studies and equestrian studies), BUSINESS (business administration and management), COMMUNICATIONS AND THE ARTS (communications, English, studio art, and visual design), EDUCATION (early childhood education and elementary education), ENGINEERING AND ENVIRONMENTAL DESIGN (commercial art and interior design), SOCIAL SCIENCE (criminology, fashion design and technology, human services, liberal arts/general studies, psychology, and social science). Interior design and equine management is the strongest academically. Human services, equine management, and visual communications (graphic design) have the largest enrollments.

ACTIVITIES: There are no fraternities or sororities. There are 52 groups on campus, including art, cheerleading, chorale, computers, dance, debate, drama, environmental, ethnic, honors, international, LGBT, literary magazine, musical theater, newspaper, political, professional, religious, social, social service, student government, and yearbook. **Sports:** There are 7 intercollegiate sports for men and 9 for women, and 9 intramural sports for men and 9 for women. Facilities include an athletic center with a pool, gyms, a fitness center, baseball, basketball, cross country, equestrian riding, lacrosse, soccer, softball, and womens volleyball, dodge ball, flag football, floor hockey, ultimate frisbee, cheeringleading, crew, coed golf and tennis. **Graduates:** From July 1, 2016 to June 30, 2017, 282 bachelor's degrees were awarded. The most popular majors were Human Services (14%), interior design (8%), and equine business management (8%). In an average class, 54% graduate in 6 years or less. Of the 2016 graduating class, 11% were enrolled in graduate school within 6 months of graduation, and 76% were employed.

SERVICES: Counseling and information services are available, as is tutoring in most subjects. There is a reader service for the blind, and remedial math, reading, and writing. **Library/Resources:** The library contains 81,677 volumes, 12,284 microform items, and 687 audio/video tapes/CDs/DVDs. Computerized library services include interlibrary loans, database searching, Internet access, and Wi-Fi capability. Special learning facilities include an art gallery. **Physically Challenged Students:** 86% of the campus is accessible. Facilities include wheelchair ramps, elevators, special parking, specially equipped restrooms, special class scheduling, lowered telephones, and special housing. **Special:** CC offers internships, a Washington semester, work-study, and B.A.-B.S. degrees in liberal studies and liberal and professional studies. There is a semester-long study-abroad program at Canterbury Christ Church University in the United Kingdom and other shorter-term study abroad options. There are 3 national honor societies, a freshman honors program, and 2 departmental honors programs. **Visiting:** There are regularly scheduled orientations for prospective students, including a welcome by the president and deans, financial aid sessions, placement testing, academic advising, and registration. There are guides for informal visits; visitors may sit in on classes and stay overnight. To schedule a visit, contact the Admissions Office. **Campus Safety and Security:** Measures include 24-hour foot and vehicle patrol, an emergency notification system, and security escort services. There are emergency telephones, lighted pathways/sidewalks, and controlled access to dorms/residences.

REQUIREMENTS: The SAT or ACT is recommended. Applicants should be graduates of an accredited secondary school or equivalent. Students are advised to complete 16 units, 4 each in English and social studies, and 2 each in math and science. AP and CLEP credits are accepted. Important factors in the admissions decision are advanced placement or honors courses, leadership record, extracurricular activities record, and recommendations by school officials. A total of 120 semester credits and a GPA of 2.0 are required for the bachelors degree. Students must take courses in speech, academic writing, diversity and social consciousness, science or math, visual literacy, communications, ethics, cultural literacy, and research methods. They must also demonstrate math proficiency and complete a senior capstone course. **Procedure:** Freshmen are admitted in the fall and spring. Entrance exams should be taken by the fall of the senior year. There are deferred admissions and rolling admissions plans. Application deadlines are open. Applications are accepted online. **Transfer Students:** 34 transfer students enrolled in 2016-2017. Applicants must present at least 12 college credits, with a minimum GPA of 2.0, and official transcripts from previous colleges attended. Students with fewer than 24 credits must also submit a high school transcript. 30 of 120 credits required for the bachelor's degree must be completed at Cazenovia. **International Students:** There are 5 international students enrolled. They must take the TOEFL.

ADMISSIONS: 92% of the 2017-2018 applicants were accepted. **Admissions Contact:** Sara Phillips, Director of Institutional Research and Assessment. Email: *ssphillips@cazenovia.edu* Web: *www.cazenovia.edu*

FINANCIAL AID: In 2017-2018, 100% of all full-time freshmen received some form of financial aid. 93% of all full-time freshmen received need-based aid. The average freshman award was $36,189. Need-based scholarships or need-based grants averaged $32,666; need-based self-help aid (loans and jobs) averaged $3,523; and other non-need-based awards and non-need-based scholarships averaged $21,011. Cazenovia is a member of CSS. The state aid form and Express TAP are required. The FAFSA code is 002685. The priority date for freshman financial aid applications for fall entry is March 1.

CITY UNIVERSITY OF NEW YORK

The City University of New York, is the public system in New York, established in 1847. It is governed by a board of trustees, whose chief administrator is the chancellor. The primary goal of the system is to maintain and expand its commitment to academic excellence and to provide equal access and opportunity. The main priorities are providing access for all students who seek to enroll, insuring student success, and enhancing instructional and research excellence. The total student enrollment for all 4 campuses is approximately 269,000 with 7313 faculty members. Altogether there are 573 baccalaureate, 451 master's and 65 doctoral programs offered. Profiles of the 4-year campuses are included in this section.

CITY UNIVERSITY OF NEW YORK/ BARUCH COLLEGE — D-5

www.cuny.edu

New York, NY 10010 — **(646) 312-1400**

Fax: (646) 312-1361 — **Email: admissions@baruch.cuny.edu**

Full-time: 5712 men, 5153 women	**Faculty:** IIA, ++$
Part-time: 1884 men, 2108 women	**Ph.D.s:** 59%
Graduate: 1550 men, 1683 women	**Student/Faculty:** 16 to 1
Year: semesters, summer session	**Tuition:** $6561 ($16,581)
Room & Board: $15,048	**Freshman Class:** 19768 applied, 5516 accepted, 1282 enrolled
SAT or ACT: required	**CEEB CODE:** 2034
Application Deadline: February 1	**HIGHLY COMPETITIVE**

Baruch College was founded in 1919 and became a separate unit of the City University of New York. It offers undergraduate programs in business and public administration and liberal arts and sciences. There are 3 undergraduate schools and 3 graduate schools. In addition to regional accreditation, Baruch College has baccalaureate program accreditation with AACSB. The 4-acre campus is in an urban area in New York City. Including any residence halls, there are 6 buildings.

STUDENT LIFE: 85% of undergraduates are from New York. Others are from 2 states and 168 foreign countries. 62% are from public schools. 9% are African American; 30% Asian American; 29% White; 18% Hispanic; 12% Foreign; 1% two or more races. **Male To Female Ratio:** 1.0:1. The average age of freshmen is 18; all undergraduates, 24. 12% do not continue beyond their first year; 66% remain to graduate. **Housing:** 236 students can be accommodated in college housing, which includes dorms. On-campus housing is available on a lottery system for upperclassmen. 98% of students commute. Alcohol is not permitted. No one may keep cars.

FACULTY/CLASSROOMS: 60% of faculty are male; 40% are female. 93% teach undergraduates, and 89% do research. Graduate students teach 8% of introductory courses. The average class size in an introductory lecture is 275; in a laboratory is 20; and in a regular course is 35.

PROGRAMS OF STUDY: Baruch College confers B.A., B.S., and B.B.A. degrees. Master's degrees are also awarded. Bachelor's degrees are awarded in BUSINESS (accounting, investments and securities, management science, marketing management, marketing/retailing/merchandising, operations research, personnel management, and real estate), COMMUNICATIONS AND THE ARTS (advertising, communications, English, journalism, music, and Spanish), COMPUTER AND PHYSICAL SCIENCE (actuarial science, information sciences and systems, mathematics, and statistics), SOCIAL SCIENCE (economics, history, industrial and organizational psychology, philosophy, political science/government, psychology, public affairs, and sociology). Economics, English, and math are the strongest academically. Accounting, finance, and marketing have the largest enrollments.

ACTIVITIES: There are no fraternities or sororities. There are 130 groups on campus, including cheerleading, chess, chorus, computers, dance, debate, drama, ethnic, honors, international, LGBT, literary magazine, newspaper, photography, political, professional, radio and TV, religious, social, social service, student government, and yearbook. Popular campus events include Club Fairs, Relay for Life, and Caribbean Week. **Sports:** There are 7 intercollegiate sports for men and 7 for women, and 5 intramural sports for men and 5 for women. Facilities include a swimming pool, gyms, a weight room, an exercise room, and racquetball courts. **Graduates:** From July 1, 2016 to June 30, 2017, 3082 bachelor's degrees were awarded. The most popular majors were finance and investments (23%), accounting (20%), and marketing (10%). In an average class, 5% graduate in 4 years or less, 63% graduate in 5 years or less, and 67% graduate in 6 years or less.

SERVICES: Counseling and information services are available, as is tutoring in most subjects. There is a reader service for the blind. There are also note takers and large-print computer screens, and interpreters for the deaf. **Library/Resources:** The library contains 655,671 volumes, 2.1 million microform items, 52,880 audio/video tapes/CDs/DVDs, and subscribes to 89,951 periodicals, including electronic. Computerized library services include interlibrary loans, database searching, Internet access, and Wi-Fi capability. Special learning facilities include an art gallery, a radio station, a journalism lab, and a newspaper lab. **Physically**

Challenged Students: All of the campus is accessible. Facilities include wheelchair ramps, elevators, specially equipped restrooms, special class scheduling, lowered drinking fountains, and lowered telephones. **Special:** Students may take courses at all CUNY schools. The college offers internships and study abroad in Great Britain, France, Germany, Mexico, and Israel. Students may design their own liberal arts major. A federal work-study program is available, and pass/fail options are permitted for liberal arts majors. Students may combine any undergraduate major with a masters in accountancy. There are 4 national honor societies, a freshman honors program, and 17 departmental honors programs. **Visiting:** There are regularly scheduled orientations for prospective students, including a meeting with an admissions counselor. There are guides for informal visits. To schedule a visit, contact the Admissions Office. **Campus Safety and Security:** Measures include 24-hour foot and vehicle patrol, self-defense education, and security escort services. There are lighted pathways/sidewalks, and controlled access to dorms/residences. There are fire safety directors and an ID system that uses card swipe in turnstiles for entry.

REQUIREMENTS: The SAT or ACT is required. Applicants must provide a official high school transcript. A GED will be accepted. Students must have a minimum average grade of 81% in academic subjects, with a minimum of 14 academic credits. AP and CLEP credits are accepted. Important factors in the admissions decision are personality/intangible qualities, advanced placement or honors courses, and leadership record. Students must complete a minimum of 120 credits for the B.A. or B.S. and 124 for the B.B.A., with at least 24 hours in the major, and maintain a GPA of 2.0 overall in the major. Students core curriculum should include courses in English, literature, communications, history, philosophy, psychology, microeconomics, and fine and performing arts. **Procedure:** Freshmen are admitted in the fall and spring. Entrance exams should be taken by March 1. There are early decision and rolling admissions plans. Early decision applications should be filed by December 1; regular applications, by February 1 for fall entry; and October 1 for spring entry. The fall 2017 application fee was $65. Notifications are sent February 1. Applications are accepted online. **Transfer Students:** 2085 transfer students enrolled in 2016-2017. Applicants must have a minimum GPA of 2.5 for 12 to 34.9 credits submitted, a minimum GPA of 2.25 for 35 to 59.9 credits, and a minimum GPA of 2.0 for 60 or more credits. Business applicants must have a 2.75 GPA. Students applying for transfer with fewer than 12 credits earned must have a minimum GPA of 2.5 and a minimum high school average of 80%. 32 of 128 credits required for the bachelor's degree must be completed at Baruch College. **International Students:** There are 1281 international students enrolled. They must take the TOEFL with a minimum score of 550 on the paper-based TOEFL (PBT) or 80 on the Internet-based version (iBT). They must also take the SAT or ACT.

ADMISSIONS: 28% of the 2017-2018 applicants were accepted. The SAT scores for the 2017-2018 freshman class were: Critical Reading--14% below 500, 43% between 500 and 599, 35% between 600 and 699, and 8% between 700 and 800. Math-- 3% below 500, 25% between 500 and 599, 51% between 600 and 699, and 22% between 700 and 800. **Admissions Contact:** Marisa Delacruz, Director of Undergraduate Admissions. Email: *admissions@baruch.cuny.edu* Web: *www.cuny.edu*

FINANCIAL AID: The FAFSA code is 007273. The deadline for filing freshman financial aid applications for fall entry is August 12.

CITY UNIVERSITY OF NEW YORK/ BROOKLYN COLLEGE — D-5

www.brooklyn.cuny.edu

Brooklyn, NY 11210 — **(718) 951-5001**

Fax: (718) 951-4506 — **Email: admissions@brooklyn.cuny.edu**

Full-time: 3852 men, 5386 women
Part-time: 1472 men, 2389 women
Graduate: 1169 men, 2256 women
Year: semesters, summer session
Room & Board: n/app

SAT or ACT: required
Application Deadline: October 1

Faculty: 543; IIA, +$
Ph.D.s: 96%
Student/Faculty: 15 to 1
Tuition: $7163
Freshman Class: 19843 applied, 6346 accepted, 1148 enrolled
CEEB CODE: 2046
COMPETITIVE+

Brooklyn College, established in 1930, is a publicly supported college of liberal arts, sciences, humanities, sciences, performing arts, social sciences, education, and preprofessional and professional studies. BC offers 83 undergraduate and 71 graduate programs. It is part of the City University of New York and serves commuter student. There are 5 undergraduate schools and 5 graduate schools. In addition to regional accreditation, Brooklyn College has baccalaureate program accreditation with ADA, ASLHA, AAHE, ACEU, MSCHE, CEPH, and and ADA. The 35-acre campus is in an urban area at Avenue H in the Midwood section of Brooklyn, NY. Including any residence halls, there are 15 buildings.

STUDENT LIFE: 99% of undergraduates are from New York. Others are from 143 foreign countries and Canada. 78% are from public schools. 40% are White; 4% Foreign; 25% African American; 16% Asian American; 14% Hispanic; 1% two or more races. **Female To Male Ratio:** 1.5:1. The average age of freshmen is 18; all undergraduates, 23. 16% do not continue beyond their first year; 84% remain to graduate. Alcohol is not permitted. All students commute. No one may keep cars.

FACULTY/CLASSROOMS: 51% of faculty are male; 49% are female. No introductory courses are taught by graduate students. The average class size in a laboratory is 16 and in a regular course is 32.

PROGRAMS OF STUDY: Brooklyn College confers B.A., B.S., B.F.A., B.B.A. and B.Mus. degrees. Master's degrees are also awarded. Bachelor's degrees are awarded in AGRICULTURE (environmental studies), BIOLOGICAL SCIENCE (biology/biological science), BUSINESS (accounting, banking and finance, business administration and management, business (dual major program), business information systems, and business systems analysis), COMMUNICATIONS AND THE ARTS (art, art history and appreciation, broadcasting, classics, communications, comparative literature, creative writing, English, film arts, French, Italian, journalism, linguistics, multimedia, music, music performance, music theory and composition, radio/television technology, Russian, Spanish, speech/debate/rhetoric, theater management, and visual and performing arts), COMPUTER AND PHYSICAL SCIENCE (chemistry, computer science, earth science, geology, information sciences and systems, mathematics, and physics), EDUCATION (art education, bilingual/bicultural education, childhood education, early childhood education, elementary education, English education, foreign languages education, mathematics education, music education, physical education, science education, secondary education, and social studies education), HEALTH PROFESSIONS (health science and speech pathology/audiology), SOCIAL SCIENCE (African studies, American studies, anthropology, Caribbean studies, child care/child and family studies, economics, Hispanic American studies, history, interdisciplinary studies, Judaic studies, Latin American studies, philosophy, political science/government, psychology, Puerto Rican studies, religion, sociology, and women's studies). Business, accounting, and education have the largest enrollments.

ACTIVITIES: 3% of men belong to 2 local and 6 national fraternities; 3% of women belong to 4 local and 4 national sororities. There are 161 groups on campus, including volunteer and service, health and wellness, academic and professional, art, chess, computers, dance, drama, ethnic, film, forensics, honors, international, LGBT, literary magazine, musical theater, newspaper, political, professional, radio and TV, religious, social, social service, student government, symphony, and yearbook. Popular campus events include Welcome Back Bash, Fall Festival, and Make a Difference Day. **Sports:** There are 6 intercollegiate sports for men and 7 for women, and 3 intramural sports for men and 3 for women. Facilities include a swimming pool, a soccer field, a softball field, volleyball, tennis, and basketball courts, a fitness center, and a jogging track. **Graduates:** From July 1, 2016 to June 30, 2017, 2474 bachelor's degrees were awarded. The most popular majors were business (21%), psychology (13%), and accounting (11%). In an average class, 46% graduate in 5 years or less and 54% graduate in 6 years or less.

SERVICES: Counseling and information services are available, as is tutoring in every subject. There is a reader service for the blind. **Library/Resources:** The library contains 1.7 million volumes, 1.3 million microform items, and 130,093 audio/video tapes/CDs/DVDs, and subscribes to 185,516 periodicals, including electronic. Computerized library services include interlibrary loans, database searching, and Internet access. Special learning facilities include an art gallery, radio and TV stations, and a speech and hearing clinic, the Leonard & Claire Tow Center for the Performing Arts, that serves the Conservatory of Music, and the Department of Theater and related programs. **Physically Challenged Students:** All of the campus is accessible. Facilities include wheelchair ramps, elevators, special parking, specially equipped restrooms, special class scheduling, and lowered drinking fountains. **Special:** There are numerous cross-registration programs with colleges and universities in the area. Many internships and work-study programs are available. Study abroad is possible in more than 29 countries. B.A.-M.D., B.S.-M.P.S., and accelerated B.A.-M.A. programs are available. A number of B.A.-B.S. degrees, dual majors, a 3-2 engineering degree, and student-designed majors are possible. Credit by exam, credit for life experience, nondegree study, and pass/fail options are offered. There is a Latin and Greek Institute offered during the summer through the Graduate Center. There are 9 national honor societies, Phi Beta Kappa, a freshman honors program, and 6 departmental honors programs. **Visiting:** There are regularly scheduled orientations for prospective students, including campus tours, presentations, and meetings with faculty. There are guides for informal visits. To schedule a visit, contact Christopher Milton, Assistant Director for Recruitment, at (718) 951-5001. **Campus Safety and Security:** Measures include 24-hour foot and vehicle patrol, an emergency notification system, and security escort services. There are shuttle buses, emergency telephones, lighted pathways/sidewalks, CCTV cameras, and informational assistants.

REQUIREMENTS: Applicants applying directly from high school must have completed 5 units of math and English with no less than 2 years of either combined (critical reading and math) SAT score or ACT equivalent of 1000 for regular freshmen admissions. Students will be admitted with a GED score of 3000 and have the equivalent of 2 years of high school math. A GPA of 3.0 is required. AP and CLEP credits are accepted. There are 11 required, interrelated courses that cover the following core curriculum areas: classics, art, music, political science, sociology, history, literature, math, computer science, chemistry, physics, biology, geology, philosophy, and comparative cultures. There are basic skills requirements in reading, composition, speech, math, and foreign language. A 2.0 GPA and a minimum of 120 credit hours, with 31 to 36 in the major (67 to 70 for chemistry), are required to graduate. **Procedure:** Freshmen are admitted in the fall and spring. There are early admissions and rolling admissions plans. Applications should be filed by October 1 for fall entry; February 1 for spring entry. The fall 2017 application fee was $65. Notification of early decision is sent December 15; regular decision, on a rolling basis. Applications are accepted online. **Transfer Students:** 2879 transfer students enrolled in 2016-2017. Students with 24 credits or less must have a 2.5 GPA. 30 of 120 credits required for the bachelor's degree must be completed at Brooklyn College. **International Students:** There are 352 international students enrolled. They must take the TOEFL with a minimum score of 500 on the paper-based TOEFL (PBT) or 61 on the Internet-based version (iBT) and the college's own test.

ADMISSIONS: 32% of the 2017-2018 applicants were accepted. **Admissions Contact:** Penelope Terry, Director of Undergraduate Admissions. Email: *admissions@brooklyn.cuny.edu* Web: *www.brooklyn.cuny.edu*

FINANCIAL AID: In 2017-2018, 69% of all full-time freshmen received some form of financial aid. 61% of all full-time freshmen received need-based aid. The average freshman award was $7,500. Need-based scholarships or need-based grants averaged $3,300 ($10,500 maximum); need-based self-help aid (loans and jobs) averaged $3,200 ($3,500 maximum); and other non-need-based awards and non-need-based scholarships averaged $1,500 ($10,500 maximum). 71% of undergraduate students work part-time. The average financial indebtedness of the 2017 graduate was $12,300. The FAFSA code is 002687. The priority date for freshman financial aid applications for fall entry is April 1.

CITY UNIVERSITY OF NEW YORK/CITY COLLEGE D-5

www.ccny.cuny.edu

New York, NY 10031 **(212) 650-6977**

Fax: (212) 650-6417 **Email: admissions@ccny.cuny.edu**

Full-time: 4859 men, 5163 women
Part-time: 1246 men, 1212 women
Graduate: 1060 men, 1552 women
Year: semesters, summer session
Room & Board: $13,424

SAT EBR-W/M: 525/560
Application Deadline: January 15

Faculty: 763; IIA, +$
Ph.D.s: 87%
Student/Faculty: 9 to 1
Tuition: $6939 ($17,650)
Freshman Class: 25373 applied, 10340 accepted, 1417 enrolled
CEEB CODE: 2083
COMPETITIVE

City University of New York/City College, founded in 1847, is a public liberal arts college that is part of the City University of New York. The college offers programs through 4 undergraduate and 4 graduate schools and 2 professional centers. There are 4 undergraduate schools and 6 graduate schools. In addition to regional accreditation, City College has baccalaureate program accreditation with ABET, ABFSE, NAAB, and CAEP. The 35-acre campus is in an urban area in New York City. Including any residence halls, there are 14 buildings.

STUDENT LIFE: 96% of undergraduates are from New York. Others are from 40 states, 158 foreign countries, and Canada. 84% are from public schools. 6% are race unknown; 37% Hispanic; 25% Asian American; 16% White; 16% African American; 10% Foreign; 1% American Indian/Alaska Native. **Female To Male Ratio:** 1.1:1. The average age of freshmen is 19; all undergraduates, 24. 22% do not continue beyond their first year; 42% remain to graduate. **Housing:** 580 students can be accommodated in college housing, which includes married student on-campus apartments, apartments for single students. On-campus housing is available on a first-come, first-served basis. 97% of students commute. Alcohol is not permitted. All students may keep cars.

FACULTY/CLASSROOMS: 40% of faculty are male; 25% are female. 77% teach undergraduates, 65% do research, and 53% do both. No introductory courses are taught by graduate students. The average class size in an introductory lecture is 29; in a laboratory is 15; and in a regular course is 19.

PROGRAMS OF STUDY: City College confers B.A., B.S., B.Arch., B.E., B.F.A., B.M.E., and B.S.Ed. degrees. Master's and doctoral degrees are also awarded. Bachelor's degrees are awarded in BIOLOGICAL SCIENCE (biology/biological science), BUSINESS (business administration and management), COMMUNICATIONS AND THE ARTS (art, communications, comparative literature, dramatic arts, English, film arts, fine arts, French, multimedia, music, performing arts, romance languages and literature, Spanish, and video), COMPUTER AND PHYSICAL SCIENCE (atmospheric sciences and meteorology, chemistry, computer science, earth science, geology, mathematics, physics, and quantitative methods), EDUCATION (art education, bilingual/bicultural education, early childhood education, education of the emotionally handicapped, education of the mentally handicapped, elementary education, English education, foreign languages education, mathematics education, secondary education, social studies education, and special education), ENGINEERING AND ENVIRONMENTAL DESIGN (architecture, biomedical engineering, chemical engineering, civil engineering, computer engineering, electrical/electronics engineering, environmental engineering, environmental science, landscape architecture/design, and mechanical engineering), HEALTH PROFESSIONS (biomedical science, physician's assistant, predentistry, and premedicine), SOCIAL SCIENCE (American studies, anthropology, area studies, Asian/Oriental studies, economics, ethnic studies, history, international studies, Latin American studies, philosophy, political science/government, prelaw, psychology, sociology, and urban studies). Engineering, architecture, and sciences are the strongest academically. Engineering, architecture, and psychology have the largest enrollments.

ACTIVITIES: There are 170 groups on campus, including choral groups, art, band, cheerleading, chess, chorus, computers, dance, debate, drama, ethnic, film, honors, international, jazz band, LGBT, literary magazine, Model UN, newspaper, orchestra, photography, political, professional, radio and TV, religious, social, social service, student government, and yearbook. Popular campus events include Langston Hughes Poetry Contest, Dance Theater of Harlem Performances at Davis Center, and Architecture Lecture Series. **Sports:** There are 9 intercollegiate sports for men and 9 for women, and 9 intramural sports for men and 9 for women. Facilities include a weight room, swimming pools, and gyms. **Graduates:** From July 1, 2016 to June 30, 2017, 2423 bachelor's degrees were awarded. The most popular majors were engineering (16%), social sciences (10%), and biological/life sciences (10%). In an average class, 8% graduate in 4 years or less, 30% graduate in 5 years or less, and 42% graduate in 6 years or less. Of the 2016 graduating class, 18% were enrolled in graduate school within 6 months of graduation.

SERVICES: Counseling and information services are available, as is tutoring in most subjects. There is a reader service for the blind. **Library/Resources:** The library contains 1.8 million volumes, 901,300 microform items, 225,480 audio/video tapes/CDs/DVDs, and subscribes to 56,476 periodicals, including electronic. Computerized library services include interlibrary loans, database searching, Internet access, and Wi-Fi capability. Special learning facilities include an art gallery, a planetarium, radio and TV stations, a weather station, laser labs, microwave labs, and structural biology lab. **Physically Challenged Students:** 94% of the campus is accessible. Facilities include wheelchair ramps, elevators, special parking, specially equipped restrooms, special class scheduling, lowered drinking fountains, and lowered telephones. **Special:** Cross-registration is permitted with other City University colleges. A 7-year biomedical education degree is available. Opportunities are provided for a co-op program in engineering, internships, a Washington semester, work-study programs, a wide variety of accelerated degree programs, dual majors, credit by exam, credit for life experience, study abroad in 12 countries, and B.A.-B.S. degree in biomedical engineering, math, physics, and psychology. There are 2 national honor societies, Phi Beta Kappa, a freshman honors program, and 100 departmental honors programs. **Visiting:** There are regularly scheduled orientations for prospective students. There are guides for informal visits and visitors may sit in on classes. To schedule a visit, contact the Admissions Office. **Campus Safety and Security:** Measures include 24-hour foot and vehicle patrol, an emergency notification system, and security escort services. There are shuttle buses, emergency telephones, lighted pathways/sidewalks, controlled access to dorms/residences, IDs, criminal investigations, and security systems.

REQUIREMENTS: The SAT is required with a satisfactory minimum score. Graduation from an accredited secondary school is generally required, but the GED will be accepted. 19 academic credits should be presented with a minimum grade average of 80%. Students should have completed 4 credits each in English and social studies, 3 units each in math and foreign language, 2 units in science (with lab), and 1 unit in academic electives. AP credits are accepted. Students must successfully complete 120 credits, with 32 to 48 in the major, and maintain a minimum GPA of 2.0. A core curriculum must be met, including courses in anthropology, art, English, psychology, and sociology. Students must complete a college proficiency exam. **Procedure:** Freshmen are admitted to all sessions. Entrance exams should be taken prior to registration. There is a rolling admissions plan. Applications should be filed by January 15 for fall entry. The fall 2017 application fee was $65. Notifications are sent March 1. Applications are accepted online. **Transfer Students:** 1417 transfer students enrolled in 2016-2017. Transfer applicants must have earned a minimum of 24 credit hours and maintained a GPA of 2.0. Requirements need are high school transcript, college transcript(s) and a statement of good standing from prior institution(s). Admission is rolling for transfer students. 32 of 120 credits required for the bachelor's degree must be completed at City College. **International Students:** There are 1758 international students enrolled. They must take the TOEFL with a minimum score of 500 on the paper-based TOEFL (PBT) or 61 on the Internet-based version (iBT). They must also take the CUNY Placement Exam.

ADMISSIONS: 41% of the 2017-2018 applicants were accepted. The SAT scores for the 2017-2018 freshman class were: Math-- 32% below 500, 49% between 500 and 599, 25% between 600 and 699, and 7% between 700 and 800. Evidence-Based Reading/Writing-- 32% below 500, 49% between 500 and 599, 13% between 600 and 699, and 6% between 700 and 800. 60% of the current freshmen were in the top fifth of their class; 87% were in the top two fifths. **Admissions Contact:** Joe Fantozzi, Director of Admissions. Email: *admissions@ccny.cuny.edu* Web: *www.ccny.cuny.edu*

FINANCIAL AID: In 2017-2018, 84% of all full-time freshmen received some form of financial aid. 84% of all full-time freshmen received need-based aid. The average freshman award was $9,212. Need-based scholarships or need-based grants averaged $8,324; need-based self-help aid (loans and jobs) averaged $3,610; other non-need-based awards and non-need-based scholarships averaged $3,279; and $5,530 from other forms of aid. The state aid form is required. The FAFSA code is 002688. The priority date for freshman financial aid applications for fall entry is April 1.

CITY UNIVERSITY OF NEW YORK/ HUNTER COLLEGE D-5

www.hunter.cuny.edu

New York, NY 10065 (212) 772-4490
(800) 772-4000
Email: admissions@hunter.cuny.edu

Full-time: 4185 men, 7611 women	**Faculty:** 750; IIA, +$
Part-time: 1664 men, 3178 women	**Ph.D.s:** 86%
Graduate: 1434 men, 4752 women	**Student/Faculty:** 15 to 1
Year: semesters, summer session	**Tuition:** $17,250
Room & Board: $13,848	**Freshman Class:** n/av
SAT CR/M: 574/598	**CEEB CODE:** 2301
Application Deadline: open	**VERY COMPETITIVE**

Hunter College/City University of New York, founded in 1870, is both city and state-supported. Primarily a commuter college, it emphasizes liberal arts in its undergraduate and graduate programs. There are 3 undergraduate schools and 4 graduate schools. In addition to regional accreditation, Hunter College has baccalaureate program accreditation with ADA, APTA, ASLA, CSWE, and NLN. The 3-acre campus is in an urban area in New York City. Including any residence halls, there are 6 buildings.

STUDENT LIFE: 98% of undergraduates are from New York. Others are from 42 states, 151 foreign countries, and Canada. 71% are from public schools. 6% are Foreign; 44% White; 21% Asian American; 17% Hispanic; 12% African American. **Female To Male Ratio:** 2.1:1. The average age of freshmen is 18; all undergraduates, 24. 17% do not continue beyond their first year. **Housing:** 662 students can be accommodated in college housing, which includes dorms. On-campus housing is available on a first-come, first-served basis, and is available on a lottery system for upperclassmen. 99% of students commute. No one may keep cars.

FACULTY/CLASSROOMS: No introductory courses are taught by graduate students. The average class size in a laboratory is 20 and in a regular course is 30.

PROGRAMS OF STUDY: Hunter College confers B.A., B.S., B.F.A., B.Mus., and B.S.Ed degrees. Master's degrees are also awarded. Bachelor's degrees are awarded in BIOLOGICAL SCIENCE (biology/biological science and nutrition), BUSINESS (accounting), COMMUNICATIONS AND THE ARTS (Chinese, classics, comparative literature, creative writing, dance, dramatic arts, English, English literature, film arts, fine arts, French, German, Greek, Hebrew, Italian, languages, Latin, media arts, music, Russian, and Spanish), COMPUTER AND PHYSICAL SCIENCE (chemistry, computer science, mathematics, physics, and statistics), EDUCATION (art education, early childhood education, elementary education, foreign languages education, health education, middle school education, music education, science education, and secondary education), ENGINEERING AND ENVIRONMENTAL DESIGN (energy management technology, environmental science, and preengineering), HEALTH PROFESSIONS (medical laboratory technology, nursing, physical therapy, predentistry, premedicine, and public health), SOCIAL SCIENCE (African American studies, anthropology, archeology, economics, geography, Hispanic American studies, history, international relations, Judaic studies, Latin American studies, philosophy, political science/government, prelaw, psychology, religion, social science, sociology, urban studies, and women's studies). Nursing is the strongest academically. Psychology has the largest enrollment.

ACTIVITIES: There are 150 groups on campus, including art, band, cheerleading, choir, chorale, chorus, drama, ethnic, film, honors, international, jazz band, LGBT, literary magazine, musical theater, newspaper, orchestra, political, professional, radio and TV, religious, social, social service, student government, and symphony. Popular campus events include Major Day Fair. **Sports:** There are 9 intercollegiate sports for men and 11 for women. Facilities include a gym, fencing, dance, weight rooms, racquetball courts, a pool, and outdoor tennis courts. **Graduates:** From July 1, 2016 to June 30, 2017, 2707 bachelor's degrees were awarded. The most popular majors were psychology (21%), social sciences (18%), and English (14%). In an average class, 46% graduate in 6 years or less.

SERVICES: Counseling and information services are available, as is tutoring in every subject. There is a reader service for the blind, and remedial math, reading, and writing. Review of graduate-level papers through the writing center and a math tutoring center are available. **Library/Resources:** The library contains 865,240 volumes, 651,000 microform items, 75,000 audio/video tapes/CDs/DVDs, and subscribes to 36,000 periodicals, including electronic. Computerized library services include database searching. Special learning facilities include an art gallery, a radio station, a geography/geology lab, on-campus elementary and secondary schools, and a theater. **Physically Challenged Students:** All of the campus is accessible. Facilities include wheelchair ramps, elevators, special parking, specially equipped restrooms, special class scheduling, lowered drinking fountains, lowered telephones. **Special:** Special academic programs include internships, student-designed majors, work-study, study abroad in 24 countries, and dual majors. There is cross-registration with the Brooklyn School of Law, Marymount Manhattan College, and the YIVO Institute. Through the National Student Exchange Program, Hunter students can study for 1 or 2 semesters at any of 150 U.S. campuses. Accelerated degree programs are offered in anthropology, biopharmacology, economics, English, history, math, physics, sociology, and social research. Exchange programs in Paris or

Puerto Rico are possible. There are 2 national honor societies, Phi Beta Kappa, a freshman honors program, and 19 departmental honors programs. **Visiting:** There are regularly scheduled orientations for prospective students, consisting of presentations and tours every Friday. There are guides for informal visits and visitors may sit in on classes. To schedule a visit, contact the Admissions Office. **Campus Safety and Security:** Measures include self-defense education. There are shuttle buses and emergency telephones.

REQUIREMENTS: The SAT is required. Student admission is based on a combination of high school grade average; high school academic credits, including English and math; and SAT scores. AP and CLEP credits are accepted. To graduate, students must complete 120 credits. The total number of hours in a major varies from 24 credits for a liberal arts major to 63 credits for a professional concentration; a minimum GPA of 2.0 is needed overall and in the major. Distribution requirements include 12 credits of social sciences, up to 12 credits of a foreign language, 10 or more of math and science, 9 of humanities and the arts, 6 of literature, and 3 of English composition. **Procedure:** Freshmen are admitted in the fall and spring. Entrance exams should be taken by October of the junior year. There are early admissions, deferred admissions, and rolling admissions plans. Application deadlines are open. The fall 2017 application fee was $65. Notification of early decision is sent December 15; regular decision, January 1. 4 early decision candidates were accepted for the 2017-2018 class. Applications are accepted on-line. **Transfer Students:** 1877 transfer students enrolled in 2016-2017. Applicants must have at least a 2.0 GPA. All students must complete 30 of the 120 to 131 credits required for a bachelor's degree at the college, including half of those needed for both the major and the minor. **International Students:** There are 1352 international students enrolled. They must take the TOEFL with a minimum score of 500 on the paper-based TOEFL (PBT) and the college's own test.

ADMISSIONS: The SAT scores for the 2017-2018 freshman class were: Critical Reading-- 12% below 500, 54% between 500 and 599, 26% between 600 and 699, and 8% between 700 and 800. Math-- 3% below 500, 50% between 500 and 599, 37% between 600 and 699, and 10% between 700 and 800. **Admissions Contact:** Joseph Fantozzie Jr., Associate Director for Undergraduate Admissions. Email: *admissions@hunter.cuny.edu* Web: *www.hunter.cuny.edu*

FINANCIAL AID: The college's own financial statement is required. The FAFSA code is 002689. The deadline for filing freshman financial aid applications for fall entry is May 1.

CITY UNIVERSITY OF NEW YORK/JOHN JAY COLLEGE OF CRIMINAL JUSTICE *(The complete profile is made available exclusively on our website, www.barronspac.com)*

CITY UNIVERSITY OF NEW YORK/LEHMAN COLLEGE *(The complete profile is made available exclusively on our website, www.barronspac.com)*

CITY UNIVERSITY OF NEW YORK/MEDGAR EVERS COLLEGE *(The complete profile is made available exclusively on our website, www.barronspac.com)*

CITY UNIVERSITY OF NEW YORK/ QUEENS COLLEGE D-5

www.qc.cuny.edu

Queens, NY 11367 **(718) 997-5608**

Fax: (718) 997-5617	**Email:** admissions@qc.cuny.edu
Full-time: 5570 men, 6579 women	**Faculty:** 409; IIA, +$
Part-time: 1960 men, 2571 women	**Ph.D.s:** 84%
Graduate: 1000 men, 2186 women	**Student/Faculty:** 21 to 1
Year: semesters, summer session	**Tuition:** $7137 ($14,527)
Room & Board: $14,370	**Freshman Class:** 21923 applied, 10525 accepted, 1672 enrolled
SAT CR/M/W: 526/547/487	**CEEB CODE:** 2750
Application Deadline: February 1	**COMPETITIVE**

Queens College, founded in 1937, and is part of the City University of New York, offers a rigorous education in the liberal arts and sciences under the guidance of a faculty dedicated to both teaching and research. Students graduate with the ability to think critically, address complex problems, explore various cultures, and use modern technologies and information resources. Queens College was cited in a report published by the Education Trust as being one of only five colleges in the U.S. that do a good job serving low-income students. This was based on the colleges graduation rate, low tuition, and the amount of need-based financial aid it awards to students. Queens College participates in CUNYs Macaulay Honors College, a challenging program open to the most academically gifted students, and offers qualified students its own honors programs in the arts and humanities, sciences, and social sciences. There is 1 undergraduate school and 1 graduate school. In addition to regional accreditation, Queens College has baccalaureate program accreditation with ADA, APA, ACEND, ASHA-CAA, CAEP, and New York State Board of Regents. The 80-acre campus is in an urban area 11 miles from Manhattan. Including any residence halls, there are 30 buildings.

STUDENT LIFE: 94% of undergraduates are from New York. Others are from 33 states, 78 foreign countries, and Canada. 70% are from public schools. 9% are African American; 5% Foreign; 30% White; 27% Hispanic; 26% Asian American; 1% two or more races. **Female To Male Ratio:** 1.3:1. The average age of freshmen is 19; all undergraduates, 23. 15% do not continue beyond their first year; 53% remain to graduate. **Housing:** 510 students can be accommodated in college housing, which includes on-campus apartments. On-campus housing is available on a first-come, first-served basis. 98% of students commute. Alcohol is not permitted. All students may keep cars.

FACULTY/CLASSROOMS: 49% of faculty are male; 51% are female. 76% teach undergraduates. No introductory courses are taught by graduate students. The average class size in an introductory lecture is 32; in a laboratory is 21; and in a regular course is 31.

PROGRAMS OF STUDY: Queens College confers B.A., B.S., B.B.A., B.F.A., B.A./M.A. combined, and B.Mus. degrees. Master's degrees are also awarded. Bachelor's degrees are awarded in AGRICULTURE (environmental studies), BIOLOGICAL SCIENCE (neurosciences and nutritional sciences), BUSINESS (accounting, business administration-international, finance, and labor studies), COMMUNICATIONS AND THE ARTS (art history, Chinese, classics, comparative literature, design, English, film, television and digital media, French, German, graphic design, Greek, Hebrew, Italian, Latin, linguistics, film and media studies, music, music performance, Russian, Spanish, communication arts-speech, and studio art), COMPUTER AND PHYSICAL SCIENCE (actuarial science, chemistry, computer science, geology, mathematics, and physics), EDUCATION (art education, early childhood education, elementary education, music education, physical education, physical education/exercise science, secondary education, Spanish education K-12, and teaching English as a second/foreign language (TESOL/TEFOL), HEALTH PROFESSIONS (biology, nutrition and dietetics, and speech pathology/audiology), SOCIAL SCIENCE (African studies, American studies, anthropology, applied social science, East Asian studies, economics, family/consumer studies, history, home economics, Latin American studies, Middle Eastern studies, modern jewish studies, philosophy, political science/government, psychology, religion, sociology, urban studies, and womens studies). Psychology, accounting, and computer science have the largest enrollments.

ACTIVITIES: 1% of men belong to 2 local and 5 national fraternities; 1% of women belong to 6 national sororities. There are 87 groups on campus, including Muslim Students Association, Chabad of QC, La Tertulia, PRISM, art, band, choir, chorus, communications, computers, dance, debate, drama, environmental, ethnic, film, honors, international, jazz band, LGBT, literary magazine, musical theater, newspaper, political, professional, radio and TV, religious, Science Fiction and Animation, social, social service, student government, symphony, and yearbook. Popular campus events include Welcome Day, Orientation Sessions for Freshmen and Transfers, and Career Fair. **Sports:** There are 7 intercollegiate sports for men and 10 for women, and 8 intramural sports for men and 8 for women. Facilities include a gym complex, a swimming pool, dance studios, weight rooms, an outdoor quarter-mile track, fields for soccer, lacrosse, and baseball, and tennis courts. **Graduates:** From July 1, 2016 to June 30, 2017, 2842 bachelor's degrees were awarded. The most popular majors were psychology (20%), accounting (13%), and economics (7%). In an average class, 29% graduate in 4 years or less, 48% graduate in 5 years or less, and 53% graduate in 6 years or less.

SERVICES: Counseling and information services are available, as is tutoring in most subjects. There is a reader service for the blind. **Library/Resources:** The library contains 1.1 million volumes, 988,133 microform items, 49,690 audio/video tapes/CDs/DVDs, and subscribes to 134,400 periodicals, including electronic. Computerized library services include interlibrary loans, database searching, Internet access, and Wi-Fi capability. Special learning facilities include an art gallery, a radio station, a small museum, and a theater. **Physically Challenged Students:** All of the campus is accessible. Facilities include wheelchair ramps, elevators, special parking, specially equipped restrooms, special class scheduling, lowered drinking fountains, lowered telephones, and special housing. **Special:** Queens offers co-op programs; cross-registration with other CUNY campuses; internships in business, liberal arts, journalism, and social sciences and other fields; study abroad; work-study; accelerated degrees; dual majors; pass/fail options; and nondegree study. There are preprofessional programs in engineering, law, and medical/dental/health sciences. The SEEK program provides financial and educational resources for underprepared freshmen. The Macaulay Honors Program is a program for high achieving freshmen, for which eligible students receive a full tuition scholarship, a generous Opportunities Fund study grant and a laptop computer. There are 3 national honor societies, a chapter of Phi Beta Kappa, and a freshman honors program. **Visiting:** There are regularly scheduled orientations for prospective students, including information sessions and a campus tour. Visitors may sit in on classes. To schedule a visit, contact the Admissions Office. **Campus Safety and Security:** Measures include 24-hour foot and vehicle patrol and an emergency notification system. There are shuttle buses, emergency telephones, lighted pathways/sidewalks, and controlled access to dorms/residences.

REQUIREMENTS: The SAT is required. High school preparation should include 4 years each of English, and social studies, 3 each of math and foreign language, and 2 of lab science. A GPA of 3.0 is required. AP and CLEP credits are accepted. To graduate, students must complete 120 credits with a minimum GPA of 2.0. They must fulfill requirements in the major and liberal arts core curriculum. Entering freshmen and transfer students will follow a revised liberal arts curriculum to meet the requirements of the CUNY Pathways Initiative. The Pathways General Education framework is common to all CUNY colleges. This guarantees that the core curriculum requirements fulfilled at one CUNY college will carry over seamlessly if a student transfers to another CUNY college. **Procedure:** Freshmen are admitted in the fall and spring. Entrance exams should be taken in the spring of the junior year or the fall of the senior year. There are deferred admissions and rolling admissions plans. Application deadlines are open. The fall 2017 application fee was $65. Notifications are sent February 1. Applications are accepted on-line. **Transfer Students:** 2660 transfer students enrolled in 2016-2017. Admissions requirements vary depending on the number of credits to be transferred; students should consult with the Admissions Office. 45 of 120 credits required for the bachelor's degree must be completed at Queens. **International Students:** There are 675 international students enrolled. They must take the TOEFL with a minimum score of 500 on the paper-based TOEFL (PBT) or 62 on the Internet-based version (iBT). They must also take the SAT or ACT or the CUNY Skills Assessment Test.

ADMISSIONS: 48% of the 2017-2018 applicants were accepted. The SAT scores for the 2017-2018 freshman class were: Critical Reading-- 33% below 500, 55% between 500 and 599, 9% between 600 and 699, and 3% between 700 and 800. Math-- 22% below 500, 54% between 500 and 599, 21% between 600 and 699, and 2% between 700 and 800. Writing-- 44% below 500, 28% between 500 and 599, 6% between 600 and 699, and 1% between 700 and 800. **Admissions Contact:** Mr. Vincent J. Angrisani, Executive Director of Enrollment. Email: *admissions@qc.cuny.edu* Web: *www.qc.cuny.edu*

FINANCIAL AID: In 2017-2018, 69% of all full-time freshmen received some form of financial aid. 59% of all full-time freshmen received need-based aid. The average freshman award was $5,892. Need-based scholarships or need-based grants averaged $9,104; need-based self-help aid (loans and jobs) averaged $3,177; and non-need-based athletic scholarships averaged $7,591. The average financial indebtedness of the 2017 graduate was $2,610. The state aid form is required. The priority date for freshman financial aid applications for fall entry is February 15.

CITY UNIVERSITY OF NEW YORK/YORK COLLEGE *(The complete profile is made available exclusively on our website, www.barronspac.com)*

CLARKSON UNIVERSITY D-2
www.clarkson.edu

Potsdam, NY 13699 **(315) 268-6480**

Fax: (315) 268-7647 **Email:** admission@clarkson.edu
Full-time: 2249 men, 954 women
Part-time: 39 men, 26 women
Graduate: 686 men, 430 women
Year: semesters, summer session
Room & Board: $14,260
Faculty: 188; I, -$
Ph.D.s: 89%
Student/Faculty: 15 to 1
Tuition: $46,132
Freshman Class: 7066 applied, 4820 accepted, 797 enrolled
SAT CR/M/W: 570/610/540 **ACT:** 26
Application Deadline: January 15
CEEB CODE: 2084
VERY COMPETITIVE

Clarkson University is a nationally recognized research university offering degrees in 60 plus academic programs of study in engineering, business, arts, education, sciences, and the health professions. Clarkson the institution of choice for enterprising, high-ability scholars from diverse backgrounds who embrace challenge and thrive in a rigorous, highly collaborative learning environment. In partnership with leading business and industry, Clarkson is reshaping education to meet the needs of a modern world by connecting knowledge, discipline, nations and cultures. Clarkson encourage its students to push the limits of what is known, and to apply their ingenuity to develop fresh solutions to real-world challenges. For 120 years, our graduates have achieved extraordinary professional success and advanced the global economy ethically and responsibly. There are 4 undergraduate schools and 4 graduate schools. In addition to regional accreditation, Clarkson University has baccalaureate program accreditation with AACSB, ABET, APTA, ARC-PA, CAPTE, CAHME, and CAEP. The 640-acre campus is in a small town in Potsdam, NY, 135 miles northeast of Syracuse, NY. Including any residence halls, there are 84 buildings.

STUDENT LIFE: 73% of undergraduates are from New York. Others are from 39 states, 22 foreign countries, and Canada. 87% are from public schools. 83% are White; 5% Hispanic; 3% Asian American; 3% two or more races; 2% African American; 2% Foreign; 2% race unknown. **Male To Female Ratio:** 2.1:1. The average age of freshmen is 18; all undergraduates, 20. 11% do not continue beyond their first year; 72% remain to graduate. **Housing:** 2509 students can be accommodated in college housing, which includes dorms, on-campus apartments, and off-campus apartments. In addition, there are honors houses, special-interest houses, and fraternity and sorority houses. On-campus housing is guaranteed for all 4 years and is available on a lottery system for upperclassmen. 82% of students live on campus. All students may keep cars.

FACULTY/CLASSROOMS: 70% of faculty are male; 30% are female. 82% teach undergraduates, 82% do research, and 82% do both. No introductory courses are taught by graduate students. The average class size in an introductory lecture is 42; in a laboratory is 20; and in a regular course is 29.

PROGRAMS OF STUDY: Clarkson confers B.S. and B.P.S. degrees. Master's and doctoral degrees are also awarded. Bachelor's degrees are awarded in BIOLOGICAL SCIENCE (biology/biological science and molecular biology), BUSINESS (business intelligence and analytics, entrepreneurial studies, finance, and supply chain management), COMMUNICATIONS AND THE ARTS (communications), COMPUTER AND PHYSICAL SCIENCE (applied mathematics, chemistry, computer science, digital arts/technology, information sciences and systems, mathematics, physics, and software engineering), ENGINEERING AND ENVIRONMENTAL DESIGN (aeronautical engineering, chemical engineering, civil engineering, computer engineering, electrical/electronics engineering, engineering management, environmental engineering, environmental science, and mechanical engineering), HEALTH PROFESSIONS (environmental health science), SOCIAL SCIENCE (history, humanities, interdisciplinary studies, political science/government, and psychology). Engineering, business, and physical/life sciences are the strongest academically and have the largest enrollments.

ACTIVITIES: 13% of men belong to 2 local and 7 national fraternities; 14% of women belong to 4 national sororities. There are 235 groups on campus, including an outing club, cheerleading, chess, chorus, computers, dance, debate, drama, drill team, environmental, ethnic, honors, international, jazz band, LGBT, musical theater, newspaper, orchestra, pep band, photography, political, professional, radio and TV, religious, social, social service, student government, and yearbook. Popular campus events include SpringFest, NCAA Division I Mens and Womens Hockey Games, First Saturday, and Cold Out Gold Out. **Sports:** There are 10 intercollegiate sports for men and 10 for women, and 10 intramural sports for men and 10 for women. Facilities include a multipurpose ice arena, a fitness center, a gym, a swimming pool, a weight room, a field house, tennis courts, all-purpose indoor and outdoor turf fields, baseball and softball fields, and multipurpose grass fields. **Graduates:** From July 1, 2016 to June 30, 2017, 729 bachelor's degrees were awarded. The most popular majors were mechanical engineering (18%), civil engineering (10%), and engineering and management (9%). In an average class, 2% graduate in 3 years or less, 60% graduate in 4 years or less, 73% graduate in 5 years or less, and 72% graduate in 6 years or less. Of the 2016 graduating class, 14% were enrolled in graduate school within 6 months of graduation, and 64% were employed.

SERVICES: Counseling and information services are available, as is tutoring in most subjects. There is a reader service for the blind, and remedial math and writing. **Library/Resources:** The library contains 429,473 volumes, 258,640 microform items, 435 audio/video tapes/CDs/DVDs, and subscribes to 31,596 periodicals, including electronic. Computerized library services include interlibrary loans, database searching, Internet access, and Wi-Fi capability. Special learning facilities include a radio and TV stations, design, prototyping and testing facilities for SPEED team competitions, Institute for a Sustainable Environment, Center for Air Resources Engineering and Science, Center for Advanced Materials Processing, Adirondack Semester study program in Saranac Lake, Trudeau Semester study program in immunology and infectious disease, Beacon Institute for Rivers and Estuaries, Center for Rehabilitation Engineering, Science, and Technology, Shipley Center for Innovation, wind turbine test site, wind turbine blade test facility, wind and water tunnel facilities, a greenhouse, observatory, nature preserve, food digester, 20 kW wood pellet boiler coupled to a 2 kW solar thermal system, and 2MW solar power production facility, and a working laboratory. **Physically Challenged Students:** 85% of the campus is accessible. Facilities include wheelchair ramps, elevators, special parking, specially equipped restrooms, special class scheduling, lowered drinking fountains, lowered telephones, and special housing. **Special:** Students can take advantage of many unique educational experiences at Clarkson. Students can sign up for the Washington Semester or Semester at Sea. Also available is an Adirondack semester in Saranac Lake, and Trudeau Semester in immunology, and the infectious disease. Students can cross-register at St. Lawrence University, SUNY Potsdam, or SUNY Canton, or transfer to Clarkson through one of our many 3-2 engineering degree agreements. Clarkson's 3-2 agreements allow students to take their first 3 years of college at a 4-year liberal arts institution and then transfer with junior standing into one of Clarkson's 4-year engineering programs. Students can choose one of Clarkson's many predesigned interdisciplinary majors, or design their own with a dual major or B.P.S. degree. All Clarkson students are required to complete a professional experience, which usually takes place through a co-op or internship, with one of Clarkson's many industry partners including General Dynamics, General Electric, IBM, GlobalFounrdries, and Proctor & Gamble. Many programs of study also require a study abroad experience, which can take place through instructor-led summer trips or a semester/year abroad in Australia, Austria, China, Croatia, Denmark, England, France, Germany, Hong Kong, Hungary, Ireland, Italy, South Korea, Mexico, Netherlands, New Zealand, Scotland, Singapore, Spain, South Africa, Sweden, and Uruguay. Work-study programs are also available. There are 23 national honor societies, a freshman honors program, and 9 departmental honors programs. **Visiting:** There are regularly scheduled orientations for prospective students. Visits are individually customized to a student's interests, and include a personalized tour with a Clarkson student, and one-on-one meetings with admissions officers, faculty members, and coaches. There are guides for informal visits; visitors may sit in on classes and stay overnight. To schedule a visit, contact the Undergraduate Admission. **Campus Safety and Security:** Measures include 24-hour foot and vehicle patrol, an emergency notification system, self-defense education, and security escort services. There are emergency telephones, lighted pathways/sidewalks, controlled access to dorms/residences, and numerous surveillance cameras in the majority of the academic buildings, laundry rooms, and some parking lots.

REQUIREMENTS: SAT or ACT scores are required. SAT subject tests are recommended. Applicants must have graduated from an accredited secondary school or have a GED. AP and CLEP credits are accepted. Important factors in the admissions decision are advanced placement or honors courses, recommendations by school officials, and extracurricular activities record. An interview is recommended. Students must complete a least 120 credit hours, 30 in a major field of study, with a minimum 2.0 cumulative GPA. Students must meet the requirements of the Clarkson Common Experience, which includes a professional experience such as a co-op or internship, and any additional requirements determined by their major department. A student entering as a first-year freshman must have been in residence for at least four semesters, including the final undergraduate semester or, if entering with advanced standing, have completed at least half of the remaining upper-level undergraduate work in residence at Clarkson. **Procedure:** Freshmen are admitted in the fall and spring. There are early decision, early admissions, and deferred admissions plans. Early decision applications should be filed by December 1; regular applications, by January 15 for fall entry; and October 15 for spring entry. The fall 2017 application fee was $50. Notification of early decision is sent January 1; regular decision, February 1. 131 early decision candidates were accepted for the 2017-2018 class. 65 applicants were on the 2017 waiting list; 11 were admitted. Applications are accepted online. **Transfer Students:** 123 transfer students enrolled in 2016-2017. Must submit 2 letters of recommendation, including one from an academic professor or instructor. Applicants must also submit official secondary school transcripts if not earning an associates degree, and SAT or ACT scores if less than 24 credits at the time of application. Students must submit a Clarkson's Dean of Students recommendation. Transfer applicants into engineering or other majors requiring calculus should have completed at least one college-level calculus course. International students whose first language is not English must submit TOEFL or IELTS scores. 120 of 30 credits required for the bachelors degree must be completed at Clarkson. **International Students:** There are 114 international students enrolled. They must take the TOEFL with a minimum score of 550 on the paper-based TOEFL (PBT) or 80 on the Internet-based version (iBT). They must also take the SAT or ACT.

ADMISSIONS: 68% of the 2017-2018 applicants were accepted. The SAT scores for the 2017-2018 freshman class were: Critical Reading-- 17% below 500, 45% between 500 and 599, 33% between 600 and 699, and 5% between 700 and 800. Math-- 6% below 500, 34% between 500 and 599, 47% between 600 and 699, and 13% between 700 and 800. Writing-- 30% below 500, 47% between 500 and 599, 20% between 600 and 699, and 3% between 700 and 800. The ACT scores were 18% between 18 and 23, 58% between 24 and 29, and 24% above 30. 64% of the current freshmen were in the top fifth of their class; 91% were in the top two fifths. 19 freshmen graduated first in their class. **Admissions Contact:** Brian T. Grant, Vice President for Enrollment and Student Advancement. Email: *admission@clarkson.edu* Web: *www.clarkson.edu*

FINANCIAL AID: In 2017-2018, 99% of all full-time freshmen received some form of financial aid. 81% of all full-time freshmen received need-based aid. The average freshman award was $42,486. Need-based scholarships or need-based grants averaged $30,000 ($63,514 maximum); need-based self-help aid (loans and jobs) averaged $7,700 ($30,000 maximum); non-need-based athletic scholarships averaged $43,993 ($49,161 maximum); and other non-need-based awards and non-need-based scholarships averaged $14,397 ($63,448 maximum). 33% of undergraduate students work part-time. The average financial indebtedness of the 2017 graduate was $23,500. The FAFSA code is 002699. The priority date for freshman financial aid applications for fall entry is February 15.

COLGATE UNIVERSITY D-5

www.colgate.edu

Hamilton, NY 13346 **(315) 228-7401**

Fax: (315) 228-7544
Full-time: 1291 men, 1563 women
Part-time: 12 men, 7 women
Graduate: 1 men, 7 women
Year: semesters
Room & Board: $13,520
SAT EBR-W/M: 680/680 **ACT:** 32
Application Deadline: January 15

Email: admission@colgate.edu
Faculty: 297; IIB, ++$
Ph.D.s: 99%
Student/Faculty: 9 to 1
Tuition: $53,980
Freshman Class: n/av
CEEB CODE: 2086
MOST COMPETITIVE

Colgate University is a highly selective residential liberal arts institution that offers 55 majors and supports 25 Division I athletic teams. Colgate is distinguished by its commitment to global engagement, student-faculty research, off-campus study, sustainable practices, and utilizing technology to enhance learning. There is 1 undergraduate school and 1 graduate school. The 575-acre campus is in a rural area in the geographic center of New York State, about four hours northwest of New York City. Including any residence halls, there are 88 buildings.

STUDENT LIFE: 76% of undergraduates are from out of state, mostly the Northeast. Students are from 48 states, 74 foreign countries, and Canada. 58% are from public schools. 65% are White; 9% Hispanic; 9% Foreign; 5% African American; 4% Asian American; 4% two or more races; 4% race unknown; 1% American Indian/Alaska Native. **Female To Male Ratio:** 1.2:1. The average age of freshmen is 18; all undergraduates, 20. 6% do not continue beyond their first year; 91% remain to graduate. **Housing:** 2680 students can be accommodated in college housing, which includes dorms and on-campus apartments. In addition, there are language/international houses, special-interest houses, fraternity and sorority houses, and living learning community. On-campus housing is guaranteed for all 4 years. All students may keep cars.

FACULTY/CLASSROOMS: 56% of faculty are male; 44% are female. All teach undergraduates and all do research. No introductory courses are taught by graduate students. The average class size in a regular course is 17.

PROGRAMS OF STUDY: Colgate confers B.A. degrees. Master's degrees are also awarded. Bachelor's degrees are awarded in BIOLOGICAL SCIENCE (biochemistry, biology/biological science, environmental biology, molecular biology, and neurosciences), COMMUNICATIONS AND THE ARTS (art history and appreciation, art studies, Chinese, classics, dramatic arts, English, French, German, Greek, Japanese, Latin, music, Russian, Spanish, studio art, and theatre studies), COMPUTER AND PHYSICAL SCIENCE (astronomy, astrophysics, chemistry, computer science, environmental geology, geology, geophysics and seismology, mathematics, natural sciences, physical sciences, and physics), EDUCATION (Asian studies, classical studies, and education), ENGINEERING AND ENVIRONMENTAL DESIGN (environmental science), HEALTH PROFESSIONS (biology), SOCIAL SCIENCE (African studies, anthropology, area studies, economics, geography, history, humanities, international relations, Latin American studies, Middle Eastern studies, Native American studies, peace studies, philosophy, philosophy and religion, political science/government, psychology, religion, Russian and Slavic studies, social science, sociology, and womens studies). Economics, political science, and history have the largest enrollments.

ACTIVITIES: 25% of men belong to 5 national fraternities; 34% of women belong to 3 national sororities. There are 195 groups on campus, including art, band, cheerleading, chess, choir, chorale, chorus, communications, computers, dance, debate, drama, environmental, ethnic, film, forensics, honors, international, jazz band, LGBT, literary magazine, musical theater, newspaper, orchestra, pep band, photography, political, professional, radio and TV, religious, social, social service, student government, symphony, and yearbook. Popular campus events include Colgate/Cornell Hockey Game, Global Leaders Lecture Series, and DanceFest. **Sports:** There are 11 intercollegiate sports for men and 11 for women, and 29 intramural sports for men and 30 for women. Facilities include a stadium, softball complex, a fitness center, golf, a weight room, an outdoor track, gymnasium, a field house, cross country, an athletic center, and a climbing wall. **Graduates:** From July 1, 2016 to June 30, 2017, 724 bachelor's degrees were awarded. In an average class, 87% graduate in 4 years or less and 91% graduate in 6 years or less. Of the 2016 graduating class, 16% were enrolled in graduate school within 6 months of graduation, and 80% were employed.

SERVICES: Counseling and information services are available, as is tutoring in every subject. There is a reader service for the blind, and remedial writing. **Library/Resources:** The library contains 899,850 volumes, 443,423 microform items, 26,768 audio/video tapes/CDs/DVDs, and subscribes to 92,091 periodicals, including electronic. Computerized library services include interlibrary loans, database searching, Internet access, and Wi-Fi capability. Special learning facilities include an art gallery, a planetarium, radio and TV stations, a anthropology museum, an observatory, a visualization lab with planetarium, and a geology museum. **Physically Challenged Students:** Facilities include wheelchair ramps, elevators, special parking, specially equipped restrooms, special class scheduling, lowered drinking fountains, and special housing. **Special:** Colgate offers various internships in addition to semester and summer research opportunities with faculty. Summer funding is available for unpaid and underpaid internships and research. Work-study programs and off-campus study programs in over 20 countries are available (and our financial aid packages inflate for one semester long program and one extended study program.) Students can double majors and design their own majors. A 3-2 engineering degree with Columbia University, Washington University in St. Louis, and Rensselaer Polytechnic Institute is available. An early assurance medical program with George Washington University, University of Rochester, and New York Medical College is available. Credit by exam and pass/fail options are available. There are 11 national honor societies and a chapter of Phi Beta Kappa. **Visiting:** There are regularly scheduled orientations for prospective students, consisting of nonevaluative interviews, information sessions, and student-led tours. There are guides for informal visits; visitors may sit in on classes and stay overnight. To schedule a visit, contact the Office of Admission. **Campus Safety and Security:** Measures include 24-hour foot and vehicle patrol, an emergency notification system, self-defense education, and security escort services. There are shuttle buses, emergency telephones, lighted pathways/sidewalks, and controlled access to dorms/residences.

REQUIREMENTS: Students must submit an application, supplement, standardized test scores (SAT or ACT), and the application fee. Students must also submit the school report, counselor recommendation, 2 teacher recommendations, transcript, and senior grades. AP credits are accepted. Important factors in the admissions decision are recommendations by school officials, advanced placement or honors courses, and extracurricular activities record. To graduate, students must complete a first-year seminar course and the core curriculum, including 4 general education courses and 2 courses each in the natural sciences, social sciences, and humanities. A total of 32 courses is required, with 8 to 12 courses in the major. Study in a foreign language and a physical education credit are also required. **Procedure:** Freshmen are admitted in the fall. Entrance exams should be taken prior to application submission. There are early decision and deferred admissions plans. Early decision applications should be filed by November 15; regular applications, by January 15 for fall entry. The fall 2017 application fee was $60. Notifications are sent in March. 374 early decision candidates were accepted for the 2017-2018 class. 1500 applicants were on the 2017 waiting list; 33 were admitted. Applications are accepted on-line. **Transfer Students:** 24 transfer students enrolled in 2016-2017. The application fee, official high school transcripts, college officials report, midterm report, faculty recommendation, essay on application, and test scores from SAT/ACT. 16 of 32 credits required for the bachelor's degree must be completed at Colgate. **International Students:** There are 271 international students enrolled. International students must submit the TOEFL. The IELTS is also accepted. They must also take the SAT or ACT.

ADMISSIONS: 28% of the 2017-2018 applicants were accepted. 91% of the current freshmen were in the top fifth of their class; 97% were in the top two fifths. **Admissions Contact:** Gary L. Ross, Vice President and Dean of Admission and Financial Aid. Email: *admission@colgate.edu* Web: *www.colgate.edu*

FINANCIAL AID: In 2017-2018, 41% of all full-time freshmen received some form of financial aid. 31% of all full-time freshmen received need-based aid. The average freshman award was $52,075. Need-based scholarships or need-based grants averaged $46,775; and need-based self-help aid (loans and jobs) averaged $5,300. The average financial indebtedness of the 2017 graduate was $15,500. Colgate University is a member of CSS. The CSS/Profile is required. The FAFSA code is 002701. The deadline for filing freshman financial aid applications for fall entry is January 15.

COLLEGE OF MOUNT SAINT VINCENT D-5

www.cmsv.edu

Riverdale, NY 10471 **(718) 405-3267**
(800) 665-2678

Fax: (718) 549-7945 **Email: admissions@mountsaintvincent.edu**

Full-time: 305 men, 1105 women	**Faculty:** IIB, +$
Part-time: 30 men, 155 women	**Ph.D.s:** n/av
Graduate: 105 men, 310 women	**Student/Faculty:** n/av
Year: semesters, summer session	**Tuition:** $35,620
Room & Board: $9500	**Freshman Class:** 2991 applied, 2446 accepted, 450 enrolled
SAT CR/M: 500/500 **ACT:** required	**CEEB CODE:** 2088
Application Deadline: March 1	**COMPETITIVE**

College of Mount Saint Vincent, founded as an academy in 1847 and chartered as a college in 1911, is a private liberal arts institution in the Catholic tradition. The figures given in the above capsule and in this profile are approximate. There is 1 undergraduate school and 1 graduate school. In addition to regional accreditation, CMSV has baccalaureate program accreditation with ACBSP and NLN. The 70-acre campus is in an urban area 12 miles north of New York City. Including any residence halls, there are 11 buildings.

STUDENT LIFE: 89% of undergraduates are from New York. Others are from 28 states and 9 foreign countries. 45% are from public schools. 8% are two or more races; 5% Foreign; 38% Hispanic; 32% White; 14% African American; 10% Asian American. 81% are Catholic. **Female To Male Ratio:** 3.6:1. The average age of freshmen is 18; all undergraduates, 22. 25% do not continue beyond their first year; 62% remain to graduate. **Housing:** 778 students can be accommodated in college housing, which includes dorms. On-campus housing is guaranteed for all 4 years, is available on a first-come, first-served basis, and is available on a lottery system for upperclassmen. 70% of students live on campus. All students may keep cars.

FACULTY/CLASSROOMS: 39% of faculty are male; 61% are female. All teach undergraduates, 80% do research, and 80% do both. No introductory courses are taught by graduate students. The average class size in an introductory lecture is 25; in a laboratory is 15; and in a regular course is 15.

PROGRAMS OF STUDY: CMSV confers B.A. and B.S. degrees. Master's and doctoral degrees are also awarded. Bachelor's degrees are awarded in BIOLOGICAL SCIENCE (biochemistry and biology/biological science), BUSINESS (business administration and management), COMMUNICATIONS AND THE ARTS (communications, English, French, modern language, and Spanish), COMPUTER AND PHYSICAL SCIENCE (chemistry, computer science, mathematics, and physics), EDUCATION (health education, physical education, and special education), HEALTH PROFESSIONS (allied health and nursing), SOCIAL SCIENCE (economics, history, liberal arts/general studies, philosophy, psychology, religion, sociology, and urban studies). Nursing and biology are the strongest academically. Nursing, psychology, and business have the largest enrollments.

ACTIVITIES: There are no fraternities or sororities. There are 30 groups on campus, including art, cheerleading, chess, choir, chorus, computers, dance, debate, drama, ethnic, film, honors, international, LGBT, literary magazine, musical theater, newspaper, photography, professional, radio and TV, religious, social, social service, student government, and yearbook. Popular campus events include Phin Fest, Mount Madness, Brown Bag Bingo, Spring Concert, and Theater Thursdays. **Sports:** There are 7 intercollegiate sports for men and 7 for women, and 5 intramural sports for men and 5 for women. Facilities include gyms, an athletic and recreation center, a weight room, a dance studio, a fitness center with aerobic and Nautilus facilities, basketball, and squash courts.

SERVICES: Counseling and information services are available, as is tutoring in most subjects, such as computer science, math, chemistry, biology, languages, psychology, sociology, writing, and economics. There is a reader service for the blind, and remedial math, reading, and writing. **Library/Resources:** The library contains 129,000 volumes, 7,000 microform items, 6,500 audio/video tapes/CDs/DVDs, and subscribes to 234 periodicals, including electronic. Computerized library services include interlibrary loans, database searching, Internet access, and Wi-Fi capability. Special learning facilities include a radio and TV stations. **Physically Challenged Students:** 90% of the campus is accessible. Facilities include wheelchair ramps, elevators, special parking, specially equipped restrooms, lowered drinking fountains, and lowered telephones. **Special:** Cross-registration with Manhattan College offers cooperative B.A. programs in international studies, philosophy, physical education, physics, religious studies, and urban affairs. Internships, work-study, study abroad in 6 countries, a 3-2 engineering degree with Manhattan College, dual majors, and student-designed majors in liberal arts are available. B.A.-B.S. degrees in computer science, health education, math, and psychology, and teacher dual certification programs with special education and elementary, middle school, and secondary education are possible. There are 15 national honor societies, a freshman honors program, and 5 departmental honors programs. **Visiting:** There are regularly scheduled orientations for prospective students. Upon request, students may have an interview with an admissions counselor, sit in on classes, and tour the campus. All students are invited to an open house. Accepted students may have a one-on-one meeting with a student on campus. There are guides for informal visits and stay overnight. To schedule a visit, contact the Admissions Office. **Campus Safety and Security:** Measures include 24-hour foot and vehicle patrol, an emergency notification system, and security escort services. There are shuttle buses, emergency telephones, lighted pathways/sidewalks, controlled access to dorms/residences, and a college committee on safety and security.

REQUIREMENTS: The SAT or ACT is required. Applicants should have completed 4 high school academic units of English, 3 of science, and 2 each of math, foreign language, and social sciences, as well as electives. An essay is required, and an interview is recommended. One letter of recommendation is required, and additional letters are encouraged. AP and CLEP credits are accepted. Important factors in the admissions decision are advanced placement or honors courses, recommendations by school officials, and extracurricular activities record. All students must complete a 49-credit core curriculum with courses in humanities, social sciences, math and computers, and natural sciences. A total of 120 credits for a B.A. or 126 credits for a B.S., with a minimum of 30 credits in the major, and a minimum GPA of 2.0 are required. **Procedure:** Freshmen are admitted in the fall and spring. Entrance exams should be taken during the junior year and/or fall of the senior year. There are early admissions and rolling admissions plans. Early decision applications should be filed by November 15; regular applications, by March 1 for fall entry. Notification of early decision is sent December 15; regular decision, on a rolling basis. 50 applicants were on the 2017 waiting list; 35 were admitted. Applications are accepted online. **Transfer Students:** 41 transfer students enrolled in 2016-2017. Transfer applicants should have a minimum GPA of 2.0. Those majoring in nursing, the sciences, math, or computer science need at least a 2.5 GPA. An interview is recommended. 45 of 120 credits required for the bachelor's degree must be completed at CMSV. **International Students:** There are 30 international students enrolled. They must take the TOEFL with a minimum score of 80 on the paper-based TOEFL (PBT) or 80 on the Internet-based version (iBT), or complete ELS Level 109, available on campus. They must also take the SAT or ACT, scoring 900.

ADMISSIONS: 82% of the 2017-2018 applicants were accepted. **Admissions Contact:** Curt Dircks, Director for Admission. Email: *admissions@mountsaintvincent.edu* Web: *www.cmsv.edu*

FINANCIAL AID: In 2017-2018, 98% of all full-time freshmen received some form of financial aid. The average freshman award was $17,000. CMSV is a member of CSS. The FAFSA code is 002703. The priority date for freshman financial aid applications for fall entry is February 15.

COLLEGE OF STATEN ISLAND *(The complete profile is made available exclusively on our website, www.barronspac.com)*

COLUMBIA UNIVERSITY/ SCHOOL OF GENERAL STUDIES D-5

www.gs.columbia.edu

New York, NY 10027	**(212) 854-2772**
	(800) 895-1169
Fax: (212) 854-6316	**Email: gs-admit@columbia.edu**
Full-time: 949 men, 586 women	**Faculty:** n/av
Part-time: 224 men, 246 women	**Ph.D.s:** 100%
Graduate: n/av	**Student/Faculty:** 6 to 1
Year: semesters, summer session	**Tuition:** $51,114
Room & Board: $10,356	**Freshman Class:** n/av
SAT or ACT: recommended	**CEEB CODE:** 2095
Application Deadline: June 1	**MOST COMPETITIVE**

Columbia University/School of General Studies, is a liberal arts college created specifically for returning and nontraditional students seeking a rigorous, traditional, Ivy League undergraduate degree full or part time. CUSGS is also home to the oldest and largest Postbaccalaureate Premedical Program in the United States, the Joint Program with Jewish Theological Seminary, the Dual BA Program Between Columbia University and Sciences Po, and the Joint Bachelor's Degree Program between City University of Hong Kong and Columbia University. There are 3 undergraduate schools and 14 graduate schools. The 36-acre campus is in an urban area in the Morningside Heights neighborhood on the Upper West Side of Manhattan in New York City.

STUDENT LIFE: 56% of undergraduates are from out of state. 9% are race unknown; 8% Asian American; 5% African American; 49% White;

10% Hispanic; 1% two or more races. **Male To Female Ratio:** 1.4:1. The average age of freshmen is 20; all undergraduates, 27. **Housing:** College-sponsored housing includes married student off-campus apartments. In addition, there are special-interest houses, fraternity houses, and an international house. On-campus housing is available on a first-come, first-served basis. 72% of students commute. No one may keep cars. Alcohol is not permitted.

FACULTY/CLASSROOMS: 66% of faculty are male; 34% are female. No introductory courses are taught by graduate students.

PROGRAMS OF STUDY: CUSGS confers B.A. degrees. Bachelor's degrees are awarded in BIOLOGICAL SCIENCE (biology/biological science), COMMUNICATIONS AND THE ARTS (art history and appreciation, classics, comparative literature, dance, dramatic arts, English literature, film arts, French, German, Italian, literature, music, Slavic languages, Spanish, and visual and performing arts), COMPUTER AND PHYSICAL SCIENCE (applied mathematics, astronomy, chemistry, computer science, geoscience, mathematics, physics, and statistics), ENGINEERING AND ENVIRONMENTAL DESIGN (architecture and environmental science), SOCIAL SCIENCE (African American studies, anthropology, archeology, classical/ancient civilization, East Asian studies, economics, French studies, German area studies, Hispanic American studies, history, Italian studies, Latin American studies, Middle Eastern studies, philosophy, political science/government, psychology, religion, sociology, urban studies, and women's studies). Political science, economics, and English have the largest enrollments.

ACTIVITIES: There are 541 groups on campus, including art, band, cheerleading, chess, choir, chorale, chorus, computers, dance, debate, drama, environmental, ethnic, film, forensics, honors, international, jazz band, LGBT, literary magazine, marching band, musical theater, newspaper, opera, orchestra, photography, political, professional, radio and TV, religious, social, social service, student government, symphony, and yearbook. **Sports:** There are 14 intercollegiate sports for men and 16 for women, and 11 intramural sports for men and 11 for women. Facilities include gyms, a swimming pool, tennis, squash, and racquetball courts, a training center, dance/martial arts studios, a fencing room, a wrestling room, and an indoor track. **Graduates:** The most popular majors were economics, political science, and history.

SERVICES: Counseling and information services are available, as is tutoring in most subjects, such as English, math, foreign languages, and sciences. **Library/Resources:** The library contains 12.0 million volumes, 6.4 million microform items, 179,457 audio/video tapes/CDs/DVDs, and subscribes to 167,884 periodicals, including electronic. Computerized library services include interlibrary loans, database searching, Internet access, and Wi-Fi capability. Special learning facilities include an art gallery, a radio station, and an observatory. **Physically Challenged Students:** All of the campus is accessible. Facilities include wheelchair ramps, elevators, specially equipped restrooms, lowered drinking fountains, and lowered telephones. **Special:** Preprofessional studies in allied health and medical fields and interdisciplinary majors, minors, and concentrations are offered. Internships in New York City, work-study programs on campus, study abroad, a 3-2 engineering degree at Columbia University School of Engineering and Applied Science, and combined and dual majors are available. There is a chapter of Phi Beta Kappa. **Visiting:** There are regularly scheduled orientations for prospective students, including an information session and campus tour. There are guides for informal visits and visitors may sit in on classes. To schedule a visit, contact Office of Admissions. **Campus Safety and Security:** Measures include 24-hour foot and vehicle patrol, an emergency notification system, self-defense education, and security escort services. There are shuttle buses, emergency telephones, lighted pathways/sidewalks, and controlled access to dorms/residences.

REQUIREMENTS: SAT, ACT, or Columbia's General Studies Admissions Exam (GSAE) scores are required, and must be submitted along with high school and all college transcripts. Students who have not taken the SAT or ACT within the last 8 years may take the GSAE. An autobiographical essay statement is required. Some students are required to complete an interview. GEDs are accepted. AP credits are accepted. Important factors in the admissions decision are extracurricular activities record, personality/intangible qualities, and evidence of special talent. All students must complete 124 credit hours, including 56 distribution requirement credits in literature, humanities, foreign language or literature, social science, science, and global studies, as well as the requirements for a major. At least 64 of the 124 credit hours required to graduate must be completed at CUSGS. Proficiency in English composition and math is required. A GPA of 2.0 is necessary to graduate. **Procedure:** Freshmen are admitted in the fall, spring, and summer. Entrance exams should be taken as early as possible. There are deferred admissions and rolling admissions plans. Early decision applications should be filed by March 1; regular applications, by June 1 for fall entry; November 1 for spring entry; and March 1 for summer entry. The fall 2017 application fee was $80. Notification of early decision is sent May 1; regular decision. Applications are accepted online. **Transfer Students:** 324 transfer students enrolled in 2016-2017. 64 of 124 credits required for the bachelor's degree must be completed at GUSGS. **International Students:** They must take the TOEFL with a minimum score of 600 on the paper-based TOEFL (PBT) or 100 on the Internet-based version (iBT) and the college's own test, International students must take either the TOEFL or an English placement test administered by Columbia's American Language Program. They must also take the SAT or ACT, and the college's own entrance exam. Students with no SAT or ACT scores must take the General Studies Admissions Exam.

Admissions Contact: Matthew Rotstein, Dean of Admissions. Email: *gs-admit@columbia.edu* Web: *www.gs.columbia.edu*

FINANCIAL AID: GUSGS is a member of CSS. The college's own financial statement is required. The priority date for freshman financial aid applications for fall entry is March 1.

COLUMBIA UNIVERSITY/CITY OF NEW YORK — D-5

www.columbia.edu

New York, NY 10027 — **(212) 854-2522**

Fax: (212) 854-1209	**Email: ugrad-ask@columbia.edu**
Full-time: 3174 men, 2910 women	**Faculty:** n/av
Part-time: n/av	**Ph.D.s:** n/av
Graduate: n/av	**Student/Faculty:** 6 to 1
Year: semesters, summer session	**Tuition:** $50,526
Room & Board: $12,432	**Freshman Class:** 33531 applied, 2131 accepted, 1416 enrolled
SAT CR/M/W: 740/750/750 **ACT:** 33	**CEEB CODE:** 2116
Application Deadline: January 1	**MOST COMPETITIVE**

Columbia University/City of New York, founded in 1754, offers undergraduate programs in liberal arts, and science programs in Columbia College and 1,500 majors in The Fu Foundation School of Engineering and Applied Science. Students also have access to more than a dozen graduate and professional schools. The 36-acre campus is in an urban area in New York City. Including any residence halls, there are 50 buildings.

STUDENT LIFE: 77% of undergraduates are from out of state, mostly the Middle Atlantic. Students are from 50 states, 90 foreign countries, and Canada. 36% are White; 3% race unknown; 22% Asian American; 2% American Indian/Alaska Native; 13% Hispanic; 13% Foreign; 11% African American. **Male To Female Ratio:** 1.1:1. The average age of freshmen is 18; all undergraduates, 20. 1% do not continue beyond their first year; 99% remain to graduate. **Housing:** 5606 students can be accommodated in college housing, which includes dorms and on-campus apartments. In addition, there are language/international houses, special-interest houses, and fraternity houses. On-campus housing is guaranteed for all 4 years and is available on a lottery system for upperclassmen. 94% of students live on campus. All students may keep cars.

FACULTY/CLASSROOMS: All teach undergraduates, and do research. No introductory courses are taught by graduate students.

PROGRAMS OF STUDY: Columbia University confers B.A. and B.S. degrees. Master's and doctoral degrees are also awarded. Bachelor's degrees are awarded in BIOLOGICAL SCIENCE (biochemistry, biology/biological science, biophysics, environmental biology, and neurosciences), BUSINESS (operations research), COMMUNICATIONS AND THE ARTS (art history and appreciation, classics, comparative literature, dance, dramatic arts, English, film arts, French, German, Germanic languages and literature, Greek, Latin, linguistics, music, Russian, Spanish, and visual and performing arts), COMPUTER AND PHYSICAL SCIENCE (applied mathematics, applied physics, astronomy, astrophysics, chemistry, computer science, earth science, geochemistry, geology, geophysics and seismology, mathematics, physics, and statistics), EDUCATION (education), ENGINEERING AND ENVIRONMENTAL DESIGN (architecture, biomedical engineering, chemical engineering, civil engineering, computer engineering, electrical/electronics engineering, engineering management, engineering mechanics, environmental science, industrial engineering technology, materials science, mechanical engineering, metallurgical engineering, and mining and mineral engineering), SOCIAL SCIENCE (African American studies, American studies, anthropology, archeology, area studies, Asian/American studies, classical/ancient civilization, East Asian studies, economics, Hispanic American studies, history, Italian studies, Latin American studies, medieval studies, Middle Eastern studies, philosophy, political science/government, psychology, religion, Russian and Slavic studies, sociology, urban studies, and women's studies). Political science, economics, and engineering have the largest enrollments.

ACTIVITIES: 19% of men belong to 22 national fraternities; 9% of women belong to 11 national sororities. There are 500 groups on campus, including art, band, cheerleading, chess, choir, chorale, chorus, communications, computers, dance, debate, drama, environmental, ethnic, film, forensics, honors, international, jazz band, LGBT, literary magazine, marching band, musical theater, newspaper, opera, orchestra, pep band, photography, political, professional, radio and TV, religious, social, social service, student government, symphony, and yearbook. Popular campus events include New Student Orientation Program, Orgo Night, Bacchanal Spring Concert, and Tree Lighting Ceremony/Yule Log. **Sports:** There are 14 intercollegiate sports for men and 15 for women, and 20 intramural sports for men and 20 for women. Facilities include a football stadium, indoor and outdoor track and fields, baseball field, soccer stadium, recreational gym with a swimming pool, basketball/volleyball courts, aerobic, fencing, wrestling, martial arts, weight rooms, boat house, tennis, squash, handball, and racquetball courts. **Graduates:** From July 1, 2016 to June 30, 2017, 1580 bachelor's degrees were awarded. The most popular majors were social sciences (22%), engineering (21%), and biological/life sciences (10%). In an average class, 89% graduate in 4 years or less, 94% graduate in 5 years or less, and 96% graduate in 6 years or less.

SERVICES: Counseling and information services are available, as is tutoring in every subject. There is a reader service for the blind. **Library/Resources:** The library contains 12.0 million volumes. Computerized library services include interlibrary loans, database searching, Internet access, and Wi-Fi capability. Special learning facilities include an art gallery, a planetarium, a radio station, and an observatory. **Physically Challenged Students:** All of the campus is accessible. Facilities include wheelchair ramps, elevators, special parking, specially equipped restrooms, special class scheduling, lowered drinking fountains, lowered telephones, and special housing. **Special:** There are study abroad programs at more than 200 locations, including France, Oxford, Cambridge, Universities in England, the Kyoto Center for Japanese Studies in Japan, and Biosphere 2 (Arizona). Cross-registration is possible with the Juilliard School and Barnard College. Combined B.A.-B.S. degrees are offered via 3-2 or 4-1 engineering programs. A 3-2 engineering degree is offered with Columbia's Fu Foundation School of Engineering and Applied Science. There is also a 5-year B.A./M.I.A. with Columbia's School of International and Public Affairs. The college offers work-study, internships, credit by exam, pass/fail options, dual, student-designed, and interdisciplinary majors, including regional studies and ancient studies. There is a chapter of Phi Beta Kappa. **Visiting:** There are regularly scheduled orientations for prospective students, consisting of group information sessions and student-led tours as well as special science tours and engineering tours. There are guides for informal visits, visitors may sit in on classes, and stay overnight. To schedule a visit, contact the Visitors Center at (212) 854-4900. **Campus Safety and Security:** Measures include 24-hour foot and vehicle patrol, emergency notification system, self-defense education, and security escort services. There are shuttle buses, emergency telephones, lighted pathways/sidewalks, and controlled access to dorms/residences.

REQUIREMENTS: The SAT or ACT and the ACT Optional Writing test are required. The admissions application consists of the Common Application and Columbia Supplement; HS transcript; SAT and 2 SAT Subject Tests or ACT with Writing; 3 letters of reference; and an essay. AP credits are accepted. All students complete a core curriculum consisting of classes in Western and non-Western cultures, literature and philosophy, history, social science, art, sculpture and architecture, and music of the Western tradition and science; 2 courses in non-Western areas are also required. Distribution requirements include 2 years of foreign language (unless competency can be demonstrated), 2 semesters of science, 1 year of phys ed, and 1 semester of writing. A thesis may be required for departmental honors in certain departments. A total of 124 credit hours is required; usually 30 to 40 of these are in the major. The engineering students are required to take Calculus, Physics, Chemistry and Economics and specific introductory engineering design courses in addition to half of the Columbia College core. The minimum required GPA is 2.0. **Procedure:** Freshmen are admitted in the fall. Entrance exams should be taken by Jan. of the senior year (RD) or Nov. (if ED). There are early decision and deferred admissions plans. Early decision applications should be filed by November 1; regular applications, by January 1 for fall entry. The fall 2017 application fee was $85. Notification of early decision is sent December 15; regular decision, April 1. Applications are accepted on-line. **Transfer Students:** 123 transfer students enrolled in 2016-2017. Applicants must have completed 1 full year of college (24 credits). They must submit high school and college transcripts. 60 of 128 credits required for the bachelor's degree must be completed at Columbia. **International Students:** They must take the TOEFL with a minimum score of 100 on the Internet-based version (iBT). Students must take the IELTS, and either the SAT or ACT.

ADMISSIONS: 6% of the 2017-2018 applicants were accepted. The SAT scores for the 2017-2018 freshman class were: Critical Reading-- 3% between 500 and 599, 21% between 600 and 699, and 76% between 700 and 800. Math-- 2% between 500 and 599, 20% between 600 and 699, and 78% between 700 and 800. Writing-- 2% between 500 and 599, 24% between 600 and 699, and 74% between 700 and 800. The ACT scores were 10% between 24 and 29, and 90% above 30. **Admissions Contact:** Admissions Officer, Office of Undergraduate Admissions. Email: *ugrad-ask@columbia.edu* Web: *www.columbia.edu*

FINANCIAL AID: In 2017-2018, 51% of all full-time freshmen received some form of financial aid. 49% of all full-time freshmen received need-based aid. The average freshman award was $43,087. Need-based scholarships or need-based grants averaged $42,785; and need-based self-help aid (loans and jobs) averaged $2,263. Columbia University is a member of CSS. The CSS/Profile and the college's own financial statement, federal tax returns, the business/farm supplement, and/or the divorced/separated parents statement, if applicable, are required. The deadline for filing freshman financial aid applications for fall entry is March 1.

CONCORDIA COLLEGE - NEW YORK *(The complete profile is made available exclusively on our website, www.barronspac.com)*

COOPER UNION FOR THE ADVANCEMENT OF SCIENCE AND ART — D-5

www.cooper.edu

New York, NY 10003 — **(212) 353-4120**

Fax: (212) 353-4342
Full-time: 572 men, 307 women
Part-time: 7 men, 6 women
Graduate: 66 men, 22 women
Year: semesters, summer session
Room & Board: $16,270

Email: admissions@cooper.edu
Faculty: 57
Ph.D.s: 90%
Student/Faculty: 8 to 1
Tuition: $45,100
Freshman Class: 3193 applied, 247 accepted, 186 enrolled

SAT CR/M/W: 660/710/650 **ACT:** 32
Application Deadline: January 9
CEEB CODE: 2097
MOST COMPETITIVE

Cooper Union for the Advancement of Science and Art offers degrees in architecture, art, and engineering. New students will receive a half-tuition scholarship plus additional financial aid to help offset the costs of attendance. There are 3 undergraduate schools and 1 graduate school. In addition to regional accreditation, Cooper Union has baccalaureate program accreditation with ABET, NAAB, and NASAD. The campus is in an urban area in New York City's East Village. Including any residence halls, there are 4 buildings.

STUDENT LIFE: 59% of undergraduates are from out of state, mostly the Northeast. Students are from 39 states, 14 foreign countries, and Canada. 70% are from public schools. 30% are White; 20% Asian American; 18% Foreign; 10% Hispanic; 10% race unknown; 9% two or more races; 3% African American; 1% American Indian/Alaska Native. **Male To Female Ratio:** 1.9:1. The average age of freshmen is 18; all undergraduates, 20. 5% do not continue beyond their first year; 81% remain to graduate. **Housing:** 178 students can be accommodated in college housing, which includes dorms. On-campus housing is available on a first-come, first-served basis, and is available on a lottery system for upperclassmen. 80% of students live on campus. Some may keep cars.

FACULTY/CLASSROOMS: 73% of faculty are male; 27% are female. All teach undergraduates and all do research. No introductory courses are taught by graduate students. The average class size in an introductory lecture is 25; in a laboratory is 16; and in a regular course is 20.

PROGRAMS OF STUDY: Cooper Union confers B.S., B.Arch., B.E., and B.F.A. degrees. Master's degrees are also awarded. Bachelor's degrees are awarded in COMMUNICATIONS AND THE ARTS (fine arts and graphic design), ENGINEERING AND ENVIRONMENTAL DESIGN (architecture, chemical engineering, civil engineering, electrical/electronics engineering, engineering, and mechanical engineering). Architecture, fine art, and engineering are the strongest academically. Engineering has the largest enrollment.

ACTIVITIES: 10% of men belong to 2 national fraternities. There are no sororities. There are 90 groups on campus, including art, band, chess, chorale, computers, dance, drama, environmental, ethnic, film, honors, international, jazz band, LGBT, literary magazine, musical theater, newspaper, orchestra, photography, political, professional, religious, social, social service, student government, and yearbook. Popular campus events include Annual Culture Show, Annual Talent Show, End-of-the-Year Student Art, Architecture and Engineering Exhibit and ongoing events in the Great Hall. **Sports:** There are 5 intercollegiate sports for men and 3 for women, and 12 intramural sports for men and 12 for women. Students have access to local gyms on weekends including access to a nearby swimming pool, and basketball courts. **Graduates:** From July 1, 2016 to June 30, 2017, 185 bachelor's degrees were awarded. The most popular majors were engineering (50%), visual & performing arts (38%), and architecture (12%). In an average class, 1% graduate in 3 years or less, 70% graduate in 4 years or less, 81% graduate in 5 years or less, and 82% graduate in 6 years or less. Of the 2016 graduating class, 42% were enrolled in graduate school within 6 months of graduation, and 42% were employed.

SERVICES: Counseling and information services are available, as is tutoring in some subjects, such as math, physics, speech, writing, and other forms of communication. **Library/Resources:** The library contains 147,552 volumes, 24,217 microform items, 2,228 audio/video tapes/CDs/DVDs, and subscribes to 9,730 periodicals, including electronic. Computerized library services include interlibrary loans, database searching, and Internet access. Special learning facilities include an art gallery, a center for speaking and writing, an electronic resources center, and a visual resources center. **Physically Challenged Students:** 80% of the campus is accessible. Facilities include wheelchair ramps, elevators, specially equipped restrooms, special class scheduling, and special housing. **Special:** Cross-registration with New School University, internships, formal study abroad for art and engineering students. Non-degree study is possible. An accelerated degree in engineering is also available (combined bachelors and masters degree program). Cooper Union also participates in a joint MEng/MD degree program with SUNY Downstate Medical Center. Students are permitted with approval, to take an elective leave to further pursue their interests and long term goals. There are 4 national honor societies and 1 departmental honors program. **Visiting:** There are regularly scheduled orientations for prospective students, consisting of open house and portfolio review days for art, and open house for engineering; architecture tours are by appointment. There are guides for informal visits and visitors may sit in on classes. To schedule a visit, contact the Office of Admissions and Records. **Campus Safety and Security:** Measures include an emergency notification system. There are emergency telephones, lighted pathways/sidewalks, and controlled access to dorms/residences. There are also security guards in all building lobbies and hand-scan technology in the residence hall.

REQUIREMENTS: The SAT or ACT is required. Engineering applicants must take SAT Subject Tests in mathematics I or II and physics or chemistry. Graduation from an approved secondary school is required. Applicants should have completed 16 to 18 high school academic credits, (depending on their major) 4 units in English, 1-4 in math, social studies, and science (with 3 units of lab), 2 units in foreign language, 1 in history, and 8 academic electives. An essay is part of the application process. Art students must submit a portfolio. Art and architecture applicants must complete a project called the home test. AP credits are accepted. Important factors in the admissions decision are leadership record, advanced placement or honors courses, evidence of special talent, personality/intangible qualities, and extracurricular activities record. The 5-year architecture program requires 160 credits, including 30 in liberal arts and electives, for graduation. Art students must complete 128 credits, including 38 in liberal arts and electives. Engineering students are required to complete a minimum of 135 credits, including a computer programming course and approximately 12-28 credits in humanities and social sciences, with a minimum GPA of 2.0. All students must complete a four semester sequence of humanities and social science courses. **Procedure:** Freshmen are admitted in the fall. Entrance exams should be taken before February 1. There are early decision, early admissions, and deferred admissions plans. Early decision applications should be filed by December 1; regular applications, by January 9 for fall entry. The fall 2017 application fee was $75. Notification of early decision is sent February 1; regular decision, April 1. 75 early decision candidates were accepted for the 2017-2018 class. 205 applicants were on the 2017 waiting list; 53 were admitted. Applications are accepted online. **Transfer Students:** 8 transfer students enrolled in 2016-2017. A maximum of 64 semesters hours of credit in the art degree program allows students for the bachelors degree. 80 in architecture, and 67 in engineering program. In general transfer students must complete at least 2 years of full-time coursework at Cooper Union to earn an undergraduate degree. 68 of 128 credits required for the bachelor's degree must be completed at The Cooper Union. **International Students:** There are 86 international students enrolled. They must take the TOEFL with a minimum score of 600 on the paper-based TOEFL (PBT) or 100 on the Internet-based version (iBT). They must also take the SAT or ACT, and the college's own entrance exam. All freshman applicants must take the SAT; art and architecture students must also take the home test.

ADMISSIONS: 8% of the 2017-2018 applicants were accepted. The SAT scores for the 2017-2018 freshman class were: Critical Reading-- 7% below 500, 15% between 500 and 599, 43% between 600 and 699, and 35% between 700 and 800. Math-- 12% below 500, 9% between 500 and 599, 16% between 600 and 699, and 63% between 700 and 800. Writing-- 8% below 500, 19% between 500 and 599, 41% between 600 and 699, and 32% between 700 and 800. The ACT scores were 2% between 18 and 23, 20% between 24 and 29, and 78% above 30. 90% of the current freshmen were in the top fifth of their class; 95% were in the top two fifths. 10 freshmen graduated first in their class. **Admissions Contact:** Mitchell Lipton, Dean of Admissions. Email: *admissions@cooper.edu* Web: *www.cooper.edu*

FINANCIAL AID: In 2017-2018, 100% of all full-time freshmen received some form of financial aid. 36% of all full-time freshmen received need-based aid. The average freshman award was $42,539. Need-based scholarships or need-based grants averaged $19,208; need-based self-help aid (loans and jobs) averaged $3,676; other non-need-based awards and non-need-based scholarships averaged $2,775; and $22,170 from other forms of aid. The average financial indebtedness of the 2017 graduate was $31,545. Cooper Union is a member of CSS. The CSS/Profile is required. The FAFSA code is 002710. The priority date for freshman financial aid applications for fall entry is March 1.

CORNELL UNIVERSITY — C-4

www.cornell.edu

Ithaca, NY 14850 — **(607) 255-5241**

Fax: (607) 255-0659 — **Email: admissions@cornell.edu**

Full-time: 7086 men, 7821 women
Part-time: n/av
Graduate: 4536 men, 3573 women
Year: semesters, summer session
Room & Board: $14,380
SAT or ACT: required
Application Deadline: January 2

Faculty: I, +$
Ph.D.s: n/av
Student/Faculty: n/av
Tuition: $53,211
Freshman Class: 47039 applied, 5962 accepted, 3349 enrolled
CEEB CODE: 2098
MOST COMPETITIVE

Cornell University, founded in 1865, is a private endowed university, a member of the Ivy League/Ancient Eight, and a partner of the State University of New York. It has 7 undergraduate units and 4 graduate and professional units in Ithaca, two medical graduate and professional units in New York City, and 1 in Doha, Qatar. The Cornell NYC Tech Campus in New York City is the latest addition. There are 7 undergraduate schools and 4 graduate schools. In addition to regional accreditation, CU has baccalaureate program accreditation with AACSB, ABET, ASLA,

NAAB, CIDA, ABA, and and PAB. The 745-acre campus is in a rural area 60 miles south of Syracuse, NY. Including any residence halls, there are 651 buildings.

STUDENT LIFE: 65% of undergraduates are from out of state, mostly the Middle Atlantic. Students are from 50 states, 88 foreign countries, and Canada. 8% are race unknown; 7% African American; 5% two or more races; 38% White; 19% Asian American; 13% Hispanic; 10% Foreign. **Male To Female Ratio:** 1.0:1. The average age of freshmen is 18; all undergraduates, 20. 3% do not continue beyond their first year; 97% remain to graduate. **Housing:** 8870 students can be accommodated in college housing, which includes married student dorms and on-campus apartments. In addition, there are language/international houses, special-interest houses, fraternity houses, and sorority houses. On-campus housing is guaranteed for the freshman year only and is available on a lottery system for upperclassmen. 53% of students live on campus. All students may keep cars.

FACULTY/CLASSROOMS: No introductory courses are taught by graduate students.

PROGRAMS OF STUDY: CU confers B.A., B.S., B.Arch., and B.F.A. degrees. Master's and doctoral degrees are also awarded. Bachelor's degrees are awarded in AGRICULTURE (agriculture international, agricultural sciences, animal science, plant science, and viticulture and enology), BIOLOGICAL SCIENCE (biology/biological science, biology and society, biometrics and biostatistics, entomology, human biology, health, and society, and nutritional sciences), BUSINESS (hospitality management services, industrial and labor relations, and policy analysis and management), COMMUNICATIONS AND THE ARTS (Africana studies, art history, China Asia-Pacific studies, classics, communications, comparative literature, design and environmental analysis, English, fiber science and apparel design, fine arts, French, German, Italian, linguistics, media arts, music, performing arts, and Spanish), COMPUTER AND PHYSICAL SCIENCE (astronomy, chemistry/ chemical biology, computer science, inform, science, systems and technology, information science, mathematics, physics, science of earth systems, science of natural and environmental systems, science and technology studies, and statistics), EDUCATION (Asian studies), ENGINEERING AND ENVIRONMENTAL DESIGN (architecture, bioengineering, chemical engineering, civil engineering, electrical and computer engineering, engineering physics, environmental engineering, landscape architecture, materials science and engineering, mechanical engineering, and operations research and engineering), HEALTH PROFESSIONS (global and public health sciences), SOCIAL SCIENCE (American studies, anthropology, archeology, developmental sociology, economics, government, food science, German area studies, history, human development, Near Eastern studies, philosophy, psychology, religious studies, sociology, urban and regional studies, and women and gender studies). Engineering, liberal arts and sciences, and business have the largest enrollments.

ACTIVITIES: 32% of men belong to 1 local and 42 national fraternities; 31% of women belong to 21 national sororities. There are 1004 groups on campus, including art, band, cheerleading, chess, choir, chorale, chorus, communications, computers, dance, debate, drama, drill team, environmental, ethnic, film, forensics, honors, international, jazz band, LGBT, literary magazine, marching band, musical theater, newspaper, orchestra, pep band, photography, political, professional, radio and TV, religious, social, social service, student government, symphony, and yearbook. Popular campus events include Dragon Day, Third World Festival of the Arts, Slope Day, ClubFest, Festival of Black Gospel, Capella Concerts, Fashion Shows, Bhangra Dance Shows, Filthy Gorgeous (LGBTQ Celebration), Mid-Autumn Festival, Yamatai, HOLI, and Israel Day. **Sports:** There are 18 intercollegiate sports for men and 19 for women, and 24 intramural sports for men and 24 for women. Facilities include indoor track and field, squash courts, soccer, strength and conditioning center, a wrestling center, a bowling alley, gymnastics, swimming/diving, a fitness center, and basketball courts; outdoor facilities include baseball, intramural fields, track and field, hockey, a climbing wall, a sailing center, cross country, an arena, field hockey, basketball/volleyball, a softball field, an equestrian center with polo, a golf course, a rowing center, a practice field, football/lacrosse, and fencing. **Graduates:** From July 1, 2016 to June 30, 2017, 3634 bachelor's degrees were awarded. The most popular majors were agriculture, biological/life sciences, and business marketing (40%), engineering (17%), and computer and information sciences (10%). In an average class, 8% graduate in 3 years or less, 86% graduate in 4 years or less, 92% graduate in 5 years or less, and 94% graduate in 6 years or less. Of the 2016 graduating class, 24% were enrolled in graduate school within 6 months of graduation, and 62% were employed.

SERVICES: There is a reader service for the blind. There are biology and math student support centers, and writing workshops. A small, peer-facilitated active-learning study groups are also available for many introductory science classes. **Library/Resources:** The library contains 9.7 million volumes, 184,179 audio/video tapes/CDs/DVDs, and subscribes to 138,978 periodicals, including electronic. Computerized library services include interlibrary loans, database searching, Internet access, and Wi-Fi capability. Special learning facilities include an art gallery, a radio station, a TV station, biotechnology institute, woods sanctuary, 4 designated national resource centers, 2 local optical observatories, Africana studies, a research center, an arboretum, particle accelerator, supercomputers, national research centers, performing arts center, lab of ornithology, a vertebrates museum, campus orchard, dairy pilot plant, mineralogical museum, animal teaching hospital, 2 agricultural experiment stations, a student farm, and a marine laboratory. **Physically Challenged Students:** Facilities include wheelchair ramps, elevators, special parking, specially equipped restrooms, lowered drinking fountains, lowered telephones, and special housing. Testing accommodations, course materials in alternate formats, transportation assistance around campus, assistive listening devices, assistive technology, dining options to address dietary restrictions, classes located in accessible locations. **Special:** Cornell's colleges and schools offer nearly unlimited opportunities for international study internships and exchanges. There are opportunities for dual-majors and minors throughout the university. Refer to information provided by the individual schools, colleges, and programs for details. There are 7 national honor societies and a chapter of Phi Beta Kappa. **Visiting:** There are regularly scheduled orientations for prospective students, which consist of campus tours and information sessions. There are guides for informal visits; visitors may sit in on classes and stay overnight. To schedule a visit, contact the Red Carpet Society at (607) 255-3447. **Campus Safety and Security:** Measures include 24-hour foot and vehicle patrol, an emergency notification system, self-defense education, and security escort services. There are shuttle buses, emergency telephones, lighted pathways/sidewalks, and controlled access to dorms/residences. In addition, there is a University police presence 24/7/365, crime prevention officers, consortiums on hazing, alcohol, sexual and domestic violence, as well as mental health and wellness, which are comprised of students, faculty and staff, and chaired by executive level administrators.

REQUIREMENTS: The SAT or ACT is required. An essay is required as part of the application process. Other requirements vary by division or program, including specific SAT Subject tests and selection of courses within the minimum 16 secondary-school academic units needed. An interview and/or portfolio is required for specific majors. AP credits are accepted. A student's college determines degree requirements such as residency, number of credits, distribution of credits, and grade averages. See the individual requirements listed by each college or school or contact the college registrar's office. **Procedure:** Freshmen are admitted in the fall and spring. There are early decision and deferred admissions plans. Early decision applications should be filed by November 1; regular applications, by January 2 for fall entry. The fall 2017 application fee was $80. Notifications are sent in April. 1393 early decision candidates were accepted for the 2017-2018 class. 5714 applicants were on the 2017 waiting list; 75 were admitted. Applications are accepted online. **Transfer Students:** 614 transfer students enrolled in 2016-2017. All applicants must submit high school and college transcripts, as well as scores from the SAT or ACT if taken previously. Other admission requirements vary by program, including the number of credits that must be completed at CU. 60 of 120 credits required for the bachelor's degree must be completed at CU. **International Students:** There are 1602 international students enrolled. They must take the TOEFL with a minimum score of 600 on the paper-based TOEFL (PBT) or 100 on the Internet-based version (iBT), the IELTS is also accepted. They must also take the SAT or ACT.

ADMISSIONS: 13% of the 2017-2018 applicants were accepted. The SAT scores for the 2017-2018 freshman class were: Critical Reading-- 3% between 500 and 599, 26% between 600 and 699, and 71% between 700 and 800. Math-- 4% between 500 and 599, 20% between 600 and 699, and 76% between 700 and 800. The ACT scores were 1% between 18 and 23, 10% between 24 and 29, and 89% above 30. **Admissions Contact:** Shawn Felton, Director of Undergraduate Admissions. Email: *admissions@cornell.edu* Web: *www.cornell.edu*

FINANCIAL AID: In 2017-2018, 61% of all full-time freshmen received some form of financial aid. 47% of all full-time freshmen received need-based aid. The average freshman award was $47,860. Need-based scholarships or need-based grants averaged $42,053 ($76,997 maximum); and need-based self-help aid (loans and jobs) averaged $5,483 ($16,282 maximum). 40% of undergraduate students work part-time. The average financial indebtedness of the 2017 graduate was $25,542. CU is a member of CSS. The CSS/Profile, and the IRS form are required after enrollment. The FAFSA code is 002711. The priority date for freshman financial aid applications for fall entry is February 15.

DAEMEN COLLEGE A-3
www.daemen.edu

Amherst, NY 14226	(716) 839-8225 (800) 462-7652
Fax: (716) 839-8229	**Email: admissions@daemen.edu**
Full-time: 515 men, 1106 women	**Faculty:** n/av
Part-time: 57 men, 315 women	**Ph.D.s:** n/av
Graduate: 154 men, 614 women	**Student/Faculty:** n/av
Year: semesters, summer session	**Tuition:** $27,990
Room & Board: $12,346	**Freshman Class:** n/av
SAT or ACT: required	**CEEB CODE:** 2762
Application Deadline: open	**COMPETITIVE**

Daemen College, founded in 1947, is a private institution offering undergraduate and graduate programs in the liberal and fine arts, business, education, allied health professions, and natural sciences. There is 1 undergraduate school and 1 graduate school. In addition to regional accreditation, DC has baccalaureate program accreditation with APTA, CSWE, NLN, ARC-PA, IACBE, and ACEN. The 46-acre campus is in a suburban area 9 miles northeast of downtown Buffalo. Including any residence halls, there are 16 buildings.

STUDENT LIFE: 96% of undergraduates are from New York. Others are from 13 states, 20 foreign countries, and Canada. 73% are White; 11% African American; 7% Hispanic; 4% race unknown; 2% Asian American; 1% American Indian/Alaska Native; 1% Foreign; 1% two or more races. **Female To Male Ratio:** 2.8:1. The average age of freshmen is 18; all undergraduates, 23. 79% remain to graduate. **Housing:** 725 students can be accommodated in college housing, which includes dorms, on-campus apartments, off-campus apartments, and quiet dorms. On-campus housing is guaranteed for all 4 years. 64% of students commute. All students may keep cars.

FACULTY/CLASSROOMS: 37% of faculty are male; 63% are female. 64% teach undergraduates, 1% do research, and 1% do both. No introductory courses are taught by graduate students. The average class size in an introductory lecture is 17; in a laboratory is 10; and in a regular course is 14.

PROGRAMS OF STUDY: DC confers B.A., B.S., B.S./M.S., and B.F.A. degrees. Master's and doctoral degrees are also awarded. Bachelor's degrees are awarded in AGRICULTURE (environmental studies), BIOLOGICAL SCIENCE (biochemistry and biology/biological science), BUSINESS (accounting and business administration and management), COMMUNICATIONS AND THE ARTS (animation, applied art, art, arts administration/management, English, fine arts, French, graphic design, and Spanish), COMPUTER AND PHYSICAL SCIENCE (mathematics and natural sciences), EDUCATION (art education, early childhood education, elementary education, English education, foreign languages education, mathematics education, science education, and social studies education), HEALTH PROFESSIONS (health science, nursing, physician's assistant, and preventive/wellness health care), SOCIAL SCIENCE (history, paralegal studies, political science/government, psychology, religion, and social work). Physical therapy, physician assistant, natural science, business administration, and art are the strongest academically. Nursing, physical therapy, and natural science have the largest enrollments.

ACTIVITIES: 2% of men belong to 1 local fraternity; 4% of women belong to 3 local sororities. There are 82 groups on campus, including academic clubs, prelaw association, Student Physical Therapy Association and Physician Assistant Student Society, student without borders, art, cheerleading, choir, dance, drama, environmental, ethnic, honors, international, LGBT, literary magazine, musical theater, newspaper, political, professional, religious, social, social service, student government, wellness club, and yearbook. Popular campus events include Homecoming, Battle of the Bands, Spring Fest and Founders Celebration. **Sports:** There are 7 intercollegiate sports for men and 8 for women, and 7 intramural sports for men and 7 for women. Facilities include basketball, cross country, golf, soccer, tennis, track and field, a gym, weight and exercise rooms, and a volleyball sand court. **Graduates:** From July 1, 2016 to June 30, 2017, 521 bachelor's degrees were awarded. The most popular majors were nursing, natural science, and health promotion. In an average class, 27% graduate in 4 years or less, 51% graduate in 5 years or less, and 47% graduate in 6 years or less. Of the 2016 graduating class, 77% were enrolled in graduate school within 6 months of graduation, and 23% were employed.

SERVICES: Counseling and information services are available, as is tutoring in every subject. There is remedial math, reading, and writing. **Library/Resources:** The library contains 140,576 volumes, 28,055 microform items, 2,354 audio/video tapes/CDs/DVDs, and subscribes to 31,925 periodicals, including electronic. Computerized library services include interlibrary loans, database searching, Internet access, and Wi-Fi capability. Special learning facilities include an art gallery, and a video conference center. **Physically Challenged Students:** 83% of the campus is accessible. Facilities include wheelchair ramps, elevators, special parking, specially equipped restrooms, and lowered drinking fountains. **Special:** DC offers cooperative programs in all majors, internships, cross-registration within the Western New York Consortium of Colleges and Universities, student-designed majors, work-study programs, an accelerated degree program in nursing, dual majors, a Washington semester, and study abroad. There is an International Studies Program that leads to a minor in international studies. There are 2 national honor societies, a freshman honors program, and 20 departmental honors programs. **Visiting:** There are regularly scheduled orientations for prospective students, two 5-day orientations that includes a campus tour, an interview, and placement testing in math and English during July and August. There is also a Fall Open House in October, College Night in September, and Day @ Daemen in September and November. There are guides for informal visits, visitors may sit in on classes, and stay overnight. To schedule a visit, contact the Admissions Office. **Campus Safety and Security:** Measures include 24-hour foot and vehicle patrol, an emergency notification system, and security escort services. There are shuttle buses, emergency telephones, lighted pathways/sidewalks, controlled access to dorms/residences, and video monitors.

REQUIREMENTS: Applicants must be graduates of an accredited secondary school or have the GED equivalent. Some departments have further admissions requirements, such as portfolio reviews, essays and letters of recommendation. A GPA of 86.0 is required. AP and CLEP credits are accepted. Important factors in the admissions decision are advanced placement or honors courses, leadership record, and evidence of special talent. To graduate, students must complete 120 to 203 credit hours (depending on the degree program) with a minimum GPA of 2.0. Students are required to complete a minimum of 30 credit hours of course work in residence. The final semester's course work must be taken in residence. **Procedure:** Freshmen are admitted in the fall, spring, and summer. Entrance exams should be taken by the summer following the senior year. There are deferred admissions and rolling admissions plans. Application deadlines are open. The fall 2017 application fee was $25. Notification is sent on a rolling basis. Applications are accepted on-line. **Transfer Students:** 196 transfer students enrolled in 2016-2017. Applicants must present college transcripts and an indication of good standing from the last institution attended. To be considered for admission, a minimum GPA of 2.0 is required for most programs. Some programs require a minimum 2.8 GPA. 30 of 120 credits required for the bachelor's degree must be completed at DC. **International Students:** There are 15 international students enrolled. They must take the TOEFL with a minimum score of 77 on the Internet-based version (iBT). They must also take the SAT and ACT, scoring 980.

Admissions Contact: Frank Williams, Associate Vice President. Email: *admissions@daemen.edu* Web: *www.daemen.edu*

FINANCIAL AID: In 2017-2018, 96% of all full-time freshmen received some form of financial aid. The average freshman award was $28,882. Need-based scholarships or need-based grants averaged $13,349; need-based self-help aid (loans and jobs) averaged $6,065; and non-need-based athletic scholarships averaged $14,099. 20% of undergraduate students work part-time. The state aid form, and foreign student certification of finances are required. The FAFSA code is 002808. The deadline for filing freshman financial aid applications for fall entry is March 15.

DOMINICAN COLLEGE *(The complete profile is made available exclusively on our website, www.barronspac.com)*

D'YOUVILLE COLLEGE A-3
www.dyc.edu

Buffalo, NY 14201	**(716) 829-7600** **(800) 777-3921**
Fax: (716) 829-7900	**Email: admiss@dyc.edu**
Full-time: 348 men, 947 women	**Faculty:** 179
Part-time: 96 men, 344 women	**Ph.D.s:** 51%
Graduate: 384 men, 902 women	**Student/Faculty:** 10 to 1
Year: semesters, summer session	**Tuition:** $25,870
Room & Board: $11,808	**Freshman Class:** 1343 applied, 1082 accepted, 241 enrolled
SAT CR/M/W: 500/520/470 **ACT:** 23	**CEEB CODE:** 2197
Application Deadline: open	**COMPETITIVE**

D'Youville College, founded in 1908, is a private, nonsectarian liberal arts institution granting degrees at the bachelors, masters, first professional and doctoral levels. There is 1 undergraduate school and 1 graduate school. In addition to regional accreditation, D'Youville has baccalaureate program accreditation with ADA, APTA, CAEP, MSCHE, CCNE, and IACBE. The 10-acre campus is in an urban area 1 mile north of downtown Buffalo. Including any residence halls, there are 12 buildings.

STUDENT LIFE: 81% of undergraduates are from New York. Others are from 24 states, 31 foreign countries, and Canada. 9% are African American; 73% White; 6% Asian American; 5% race unknown; 4% Hispanic; 2% two or more races; 1% Foreign. **Female To Male Ratio:** 2.6:1. The average age of freshmen is 18; all undergraduates, 21. 22% do not continue beyond their first year; 53% remain to graduate. **Housing:** 478 students can be accommodated in college housing, which includes dorms, on-campus apartments, quiet floors, and 21 and older floors. On-campus housing is guaranteed for all 4 years. 82% of students commute. All students may keep cars.

FACULTY/CLASSROOMS: 31% of faculty are male; 69% are female. 68% teach undergraduates. No introductory courses are taught by graduate students.

PROGRAMS OF STUDY: D'Youville confers B.A., B.S., B.S./M.S., and B.S.N. degrees. Master's and doctoral degrees are also awarded. Bachelor's degrees are awarded in BIOLOGICAL SCIENCE (biology/biological science), BUSINESS (accounting and business administration and management), COMMUNICATIONS AND THE ARTS (English), COMPUTER AND PHYSICAL SCIENCE (information sciences and systems and mathematics), HEALTH PROFESSIONS (exercise science, health care administration, nursing, and physician's assistant), SOCIAL SCIENCE (dietetics, history, interdisciplinary studies, international studies, philosophy, psychology, and sociology). Education, and health professions are the strongest academically. Nursing, health professions, and business have the largest enrollments.

ACTIVITIES: There are no fraternities or sororities. There are 42 groups on campus, including cheerleading, chorus, computers, dance, drama, drill team, ethnic, honors, international, LGBT, literary magazine, newspaper, professional, religious, social, social service, and student government. Popular campus events include Moving Up Days, International Fiesta, and Honors Convocation. **Sports:** There are 6 intercollegiate sports for men and 8 for women. Facilities include a gym that houses basketball and volleyball courts, and an indoor batting cage, athletic fields, and a fitness facility with aerobic and free weights, a swimming pool, and dance studio. **Graduates:** From July 1, 2016 to June 30, 2017, 324 bachelor's degrees were awarded. The most popular majors were health professions and related sciences (64%), interdisciplinary studies (11%), and business/marketing (9%). In an average class, 25% graduate in 4 years or less, 39% graduate in 5 years or less, and 53% graduate in 6 years or less.

SERVICES: Counseling and information services are available, as is tutoring in some subjects. There is a reader service for the blind, and remedial math, reading, and writing. **Library/Resources:** The library contains 146,845 volumes, 205,411 microform items, 32,265 audio/video tapes/CDs/DVDs, and subscribes to 150,000 periodicals, including electronic. Computerized library services include interlibrary loans, database searching, Internet access, and Wi-Fi capability. **Physically Challenged Students:** 95% of the campus is accessible. Facilities include wheelchair ramps, elevators, special parking, specially equipped restrooms, lowered drinking fountains, and special housing. **Special:** D'Youville has cross-registration with member colleges of the Western New York Consortium. Internships, work-study programs, dual majors, study abroad in 5 countries, and pass/fail options are available. Accelerated 5-year B.S.-M.S. programs in occupational therapy, international business, elementary education, Physician's Assistant and nursing, and dietetics are offered. For freshmen with undecided majors, the Career Discovery Program offers special courses, internships, and faculty advisers. There are 3 national honor societies and 2 departmental honors programs. **Visiting:** There are regularly scheduled orientations for prospective students. There are guides for informal visits; visitors may sit in on classes and stay overnight. To schedule a visit, contact the Admissions Office. **Campus Safety and Security:** Measures include 24-hour foot and vehicle patrol, emergency notification system, self-defense education, and security escort services. There are emergency telephones, lighted pathways/sidewalks. There is a special focus program, and a security committee.

REQUIREMENTS: The SAT or ACT is required. Applicants should have completed 16 Carnegie units, including 4 years of English, 3 years of social studies, and 1 year each of math and science; some majors require additional years of math and science. The GED is accepted. AP and CLEP credits are accepted. All students must complete general program and core curriculum requirements, including 5 courses in humanities, 2 each in English and natural sciences, and 1 each in ethics, philosophy or religion, history, sociology, psychology, economics or political science, math, and computer science. A minimum of 120 to 144 credit hours, varying by major, with a minimum GPA of 2.0, (higher for some programs), is required to graduate. **Procedure:** Freshmen are admitted in the fall and spring. Entrance exams should be taken by the end of the junior year. There are deferred admissions and rolling admissions plans. Application deadlines are open. Applications are accepted online. **Transfer Students:** 252 transfer students enrolled in 2016-2017. Applicants need a minimum GPA of 2.0, or 2.5 for some programs. 30 of 120 credits required for the bachelor's degree must be completed at D'Youville. **International Students:** There are 31 international students enrolled. They must take the TOEFL with a minimum score of 500 on the paper-based TOEFL (PBT) or 61 on the Internet-based version (iBT). They must also take the SAT or ACT, scoring 900.

ADMISSIONS: 81% of the 2017-2018 applicants were accepted. The SAT scores for the 2017-2018 freshman class were: Critical Reading-- 37% below 500, 50% between 500 and 599, 12% between 600 and 699, and 1% between 700 and 800. Math-- 48% below 500, 44% between 500 and 599, 7% between 600 and 699, and 1% between 700 and 800. Writing-- 60% below 500, 34% between 500 and 599, 5% between 600 and 699, and 1% between 700 and 800. The ACT scores were 4% between 12 and 17, 51% between 18 and 23, 44% between 24 and 29, and 2% above 30. **Admissions Contact:** Meghan Harmond, Interim Director of Undergraduate Admissions. Email: *admiss@dyc.edu* Web: *www.dyc.edu*

FINANCIAL AID: The state aid form is required. The FAFSA code is 002712. The priority date for freshman financial aid applications for fall entry is March 1.

EASTMAN SCHOOL OF MUSIC/UNIVERSITY OF ROCHESTER
(The complete profile is made available exclusively on our website, www.barronspac.com)

ELMIRA COLLEGE B-4
www.elmira.edu

Elmira, NY 14901	**(607) 735-1724** **(800) 935-6472**
Fax: (607) 735-1718	**Email: admissions@elmira.edu**
Full-time: 252 men, 581 women	**Faculty:** 66
Part-time: 18 men, 87 women	**Ph.D.s:** 94%
Graduate: 26 men, 48 women	**Student/Faculty:** 10 to 1
Year: other, summer session	**Tuition:** $41,900
Room & Board: $12,000	**Freshman Class:** 2210 applied, 1886 accepted, 205 enrolled
SAT EBR-W/M: 570/550 **ACT:** 24	**CEEB CODE:** 2226
Application Deadline: rolling	**COMPETITIVE**

Elmira College, founded in 1855, is a private coeducational liberal arts college emphasizing both general and professional education. There is 1 undergraduate school and 1 graduate school. In addition to regional accreditation, EC has baccalaureate program accreditation with ACEN and CAEP. The 55-acre campus is in a suburban area 90 miles southwest of Syracuse and 50 miles west of Binghamton. Including any residence halls, there are 26 buildings.

STUDENT LIFE: 66% of undergraduates are from New York. Others are from 31 states, 12 foreign countries, and Canada. 77% are White; 6% race unknown; 5% African American; 4% Foreign; 3% Hispanic; 2% Asian American; 2% two or more races; 1% American Indian/Alaska Native. **Female To Male Ratio:** 2.4:1. The average age of freshmen is 18; all undergraduates, 21. 35% do not continue beyond their first year; 60% remain to graduate. **Housing:** 1128 students can be accommodated in college housing, which includes gender neutral, single sex dorms, coed dorms, on-campus apartments, quiet floors, alcohol and tobacco free floors, and honors floor. On-campus housing is guaranteed for all 4 years. 85% of students live on campus. All students may keep cars.

FACULTY/CLASSROOMS: 45% of faculty are male; 55% are female. 94% teach undergraduates. No introductory courses are taught by graduate students. The average class size in an introductory lecture is 15; in a laboratory is 13; and in a regular course is 14.

PROGRAMS OF STUDY: EC confers B.A. and B.S. degrees. Associate and master's degrees are also awarded. Bachelor's degrees are awarded in BIOLOGICAL SCIENCE (biochemistry and biology/biological science), BUSINESS (accounting, business administration and management, and business economics), COMMUNICATIONS AND THE ARTS (classics, dramatic arts, English literature, fine arts, languages, music, and theatre arts), COMPUTER AND PHYSICAL SCIENCE (chemistry and mathematics), EDUCATION (art education, early childhood education, education of the deaf and hearing impaired, foreign languages education, science education, secondary education, and special education), HEALTH PROFESSIONS (community health work, nursing, predentistry, premedicine, and speech pathology/audiology), SOCIAL SCIENCE (American studies, criminal justice, history, human services, international studies, liberal arts, sciences, general studies, humanities, philosophy and religion, political science/government, prelaw, psychology, and sociology). Education and nursing is the strongest academically. Nursing, business administration, and psychology have the largest enrollments.

ACTIVITIES: There are no fraternities or sororities. There are 70 groups on campus, including Relay for Life, Enactus, Active Minds, art, cheerleading, chorale, chorus, communications, dance, drama, environmental, ethnic, honors, international, LGBT, literary magazine, musical theater, newspaper, photography, political, professional, religious, social, social service, student government, and yearbook. Popular campus events include Candlelight, Mountain Day, Octagon Fair, Holiday Banquet, and May Days. **Sports:** There are 9 intercollegiate sports for men and 11 for women, and 6 intramural sports for men and 6 for women. On-campus facilities include a soccer field, a gymnasium, a dance studio, racquetball courts, a swimming pool, a hockey arena, a field house with indoor tennis courts, and squash courts. Outdoor facilities include baseball, basketball, cheerleading, cross country, field hockey, golf, ice hockey, lacrosse, soccer, softball, tennis, and volleyball. **Graduates:** From July 1, 2016 to June 30, 2017, 319 bachelor's degrees were awarded. The most popular majors were nursing (24%), business/finance/marketing (13%), and education (12%). In an average class, 57% graduate in 4 years or less, 58% graduate in 5 years or less, and 60% graduate in 6 years or less.

SERVICES: Counseling and information services are available, as is tutoring in most subjects. There is a reader service for the blind. There is also a writing center, tutoring center, math lab, learning and disabilities specialist, and an IT Help Desk. **Library/Resources:** The library contains 117,981 volumes, 26,657 microform items, 3,147 audio/video tapes/CDs/DVDs, and subscribes to 5 periodicals, including electronic. Computerized library services include interlibrary loans, database searching, Internet access, and Wi-Fi capability. Special learning facilities include an art gallery, a finance trading room, speech and hearing clinic, simulation labs for our nursing program, and Mark Twain's study and exhibit. **Physically Challenged Students:** 25% of the campus is accessible. Facilities include wheelchair ramps, elevators, special parking, specially equipped restrooms, special class scheduling, and special housing. **Special:** Term III Travel trips; Honors Program; Student-designed majors; 3-2 chemical engineering degree is offered with Clarkson University; 4+1 MBA with Alfred University, Clarkson University, Rochester Institute of Technology, and Union College. 4+1 MBA with specialization in Accounting or MS in Accounting with Rochester Institute of Technology or University of Buffalo. There are 19 national honor societies, Phi Beta Kappa, a freshman honors program, and 15 departmental honors programs. **Visiting:** There is a tour of the campus, followed by a personalized schedule created by prospective students. There are guides for informal visits; visitors may sit in on classes and stay overnight. To schedule a visit, contact the Office of Admissions. **Campus Safety and Security:** Measures include 24-hour foot and vehicle patrol, an emergency notification system, and security escort services. There are emergency telephones, lighted pathways/sidewalks, controlled access to dorms/residences, and limited shuttles to off-campus activities.

REQUIREMENTS: The SAT or ACT is recommended. Applicants should have completed 4 years of high school English, 3 years of math, and 2 years of science. An essay is part of the application process. An interview is strongly recommended. Test scores are optional. AP and CLEP credits are accepted. Important factors in the admissions decision are recommendations by school officials, advanced placement or honors courses, and extracurricular activities record. A total of 120 credit hours with a minimum GPA of 2.0 overall is required to graduate. All students must complete the following graduation requirements in addition to the requirements of their selected major: Academic Writing Program (3-6 credits; depends on whether entering as a first-time student or transfer); W Course (3 credits) a course in the student's major with an emphasis on written communication; Mathematical Competency and Quantitative Reasoning (3-8 credits); Core Program (3 credits) First-Year Seminar foundation course in the liberal arts and sciences for all entering freshmen; The Pillars and World Engagement (Pillars=27 credits, World Engagement=9 credits) - The Pillars include coursework in the following subject areas: Fine Arts, Humanities and Languages, Social Sciences, Mathematics and Natural Sciences; World Engagement consists of 3 courses designed to help students view the world from multiple perspectives; Physical Education requirement (2 credits) may be waived with participation in sports, ROTC, or other approved campus physical activities; Community Service (60 hours total); and an Internship Requirement (minimum 80 hours in a Career-related internship) or Project submission if completing the Pre-Grad School internship. **Procedure:** Freshmen are admitted in the fall and winter. Entrance exams should be taken by August of the entry year. There are deferred admissions and rolling admissions plans. Application deadlines are open. Notification is sent on a rolling basis. Applications are accepted on-line. **Transfer Students:** 47 transfer students enrolled in 2016-2017. Applicants must have a minimum GPA of 2.0. Transcripts from all schools previously attended are required, along with a letter of recommendation from a Dean, faculty member, college placement, counselor, etc. from your most recently attended institution. If you have earned less than 12 credits, a secondary school transcript is also required. A student conduct form must be completed by the Dean of Students from your most recently attended institution. 30 of 120 credits required for the bachelor's degree must be completed at EC. **International Students:** There are 35 international students enrolled. They must take the TOEFL with a minimum score of 79 on the Internet-based version (iBT). Students must also take either the IELTS or PTE.

ADMISSIONS: 85% of the 2017-2018 applicants were accepted. **Admissions Contact:** Christopher R. Coons, Vice President of Enrollment Management. Email: *admissions@elmira.edu* Web: *www.elmira.edu*

FINANCIAL AID: In 2017-2018, 100% of all full-time freshmen received some form of financial aid. 86% of all full-time freshmen received need-based aid. The average freshman award was $32,600. Need-based scholarships or need-based grants averaged $29,530; need-based self-help aid (loans and jobs) averaged $3,732; and other non-need-based awards and non-need-based scholarships averaged $24,695. 40% of undergraduate students work part-time. The average financial indebtedness of the 2017 graduate was $29,601. The state aid form is required. The FAFSA code is 002718. The priority date for freshman financial aid applications for fall entry is February 1.

EUGENE LANG COLLEGE OF LIBERAL ARTS D-5

www.newschool.edu/lang

New York, NY 10011	**(212) 229-5150** **(800) 292-3040**
Fax: (212) 229-5355	**Email: lang@newschool.edu**
Full-time: 379 men, 1215 women	**Faculty:** 65
Part-time: 23 men, 41 women	**Ph.D.s:** 80%
Graduate: n/av	**Student/Faculty:** 10 to 1
Year: semesters	**Tuition:** $46,340
Room & Board: $18,600	**Freshman Class:** 3067 applied, 2439 accepted, 494 enrolled
SAT CR/M/W: 605/545/595 **ACT:** 26	**CEEB CODE:** 2521
Application Deadline: August 1	**VERY COMPETITIVE**

Eugene Lang College of Liberal Arts, established in 1978, is the liberal arts undergraduate division of the New School. There is 1 undergraduate school. In addition to regional accreditation, ELCLA has baccalaureate program accreditation with MSCHE. The 37-acre campus is in an urban area in Greenwich Village, Manhattan, New York City. Including any residence halls, there are 23 buildings.

STUDENT LIFE: 78% of undergraduates are from out of state, mostly the Middle Atlantic. Students are from 43 states, 46 foreign countries, and Canada. 61% are from public schools. 8% are African American; 8% Foreign; 7% race unknown; 6% Asian American; 6% two or more races; 49% White; 17% Hispanic. **Female To Male Ratio:** 3.1:1. The average age of freshmen is 18; all undergraduates, 20. 20% do not continue beyond their first year; 52% remain to graduate. **Housing:** 1945 students can be accommodated in college housing, which includes dorms, special-interest houses, apartments for single students, and theme and wellness housing. On-campus housing is available on a first-come, first-served basis, and is available on a lottery system for upperclassmen. 73% of students live on campus. All students may keep cars. Alcohol is not permitted.

FACULTY/CLASSROOMS: 43% of faculty are male; 57% are female. All teach undergraduates. No introductory courses are taught by graduate students.

PROGRAMS OF STUDY: ELCLA confers B.A. degrees. Bachelor's degrees are awarded in AGRICULTURE (environmental studies), COMMUNICATIONS AND THE ARTS (dance, dramatic arts, literature, music, theatre acting, theater design, and theatre studies), EDUCATION (education and foreign languages education), SOCIAL SCIENCE (anthropology, Chinese Studies, economics, gender studies, history, interdisciplinary studies, philosophy, political science/government, psychology, religion, sociology, and urban studies). Creative writing, history, and Urban studies are the strongest academically. Writing, and cultural studies have the largest enrollments.

ACTIVITIES: There are no fraternities or sororities. There are 46 groups on campus, including art, band, choir, chorus, communications, computers, dance, debate, drama, environmental, ethnic, film, honors, international, jazz band, LGBT, literary magazine, museum club, musical theater, newspaper, opera, orchestra, photography, political, professional, radio and TV, religious, social, social service, student government, and symphony. Popular campus events include Welcome Back Block party, Seek Relief Week, Midnight Breakfast, 100 Nights Dinner, Leadership Retreat, Service Trips, and a Leadership Awards Banquet. **Sports:** There are 4 intramural sports for men and 4 for women. Facilities include a fitness room for classes and personal training. **Graduates:** From July 1, 2016 to June 30, 2017, 309 bachelor's degrees were awarded. The most popular majors were liberal arts (32%), literary studies (16%), and arts (15%). In an average class, 39% graduate in 4 years or less, 48% graduate in 5 years or less, and 52% graduate in 6 years or less. Of the 2016 graduating class, 10% were enrolled in graduate school within 6 months of graduation, and 6% were employed.

SERVICES: **Library/Resources:** The library contains 15.7 million volumes, 1,184 microform items, 17,426 audio/video tapes/CDs/DVDs, and subscribes to 76,012 periodicals, including electronic. Computerized library services include interlibrary loans, database searching, Internet access, and Wi-Fi capability. Special learning facilities include an art gallery, a radio station, and a writing center. **Physically Challenged Students:** 95% of the campus is accessible. Facilities include wheelchair ramps, elevators, specially equipped restrooms, special class scheduling, lowered drinking fountains, and special housing. **Special:** Lang College offers a concentration rather than a traditional major; there is no core curriculum and students are instructed in small seminars. Students may cross-register with other New School divisions. A large variety of internships for credit, study abroad, B.A./M.A. and B.A./M.S.T. options, a B.A./B.F.A. degree with Parsons The New School for Design and The New School for Jazz and Contemporary Music Program, student-designed majors, and nondegree study are available. **Visiting:** There are regularly scheduled orientations for prospective students, consisting of information sessions every weekday at 2 o'clock; tours every weekday at 3 o'clock. Walk in meetings with counselors are available every weekday between 9 AM and 5 PM. There are guides for informal visits and visitors may sit in on classes. To schedule a visit, contact Denise Rodriguez at rodrigud@newschool.edu. **Campus Safety and Security:** Measures include self-defense education.

REQUIREMENTS: Freshmen: Common App (online); 2 essays; secondary school transcript; counselor recommendation; teacher evaluation; SAT or ACT scores (or a graded academic paper); TOEFL score (for ESL students). 20 academic high school recommended units are 4 units each in math, foreign language, social studies, history and science, and 4 required in English. AP and CLEP credits are accepted. Important factors in the admissions decision are extracurricular activities record, advanced placement or honors courses, personality/intangible qualities, recommendations by school officials, and evidence of special talent. To graduate, students must complete 120 credit hours, with a GPA of 2.0 and a minimum of 36 hours in 1 of 11 paths of study: writing, literature, the arts (includes dance and theater, urban studies, social and historical inquiry, cultural studies, media, philosophy, religious studies, psychology, education studies, and science, technology, and society. Also required are 88 credit hours in Lang College courses and 4 credits of senior work. Required courses include a first-year writing seminar and a freshman workshop program. **Procedure:** Freshmen are admitted in the fall and spring. Entrance exams should be taken in May of the junior year or October of the senior year. There are early decision and deferred admissions plans. Applications should be filed by August 1 for fall entry. The fall 2017 application fee was $50. Notifications are sent April 1. Applications are accepted online. **Transfer Students:** 123 transfer students enrolled in 2016-2017. Applicants must have a minimum college GPA of 2.5 and must submit high school transcripts, or college transcript(s), ACT or SAT scores (if taken in the last 5 years), and 2 recommendations. An interview is recommended. Grades of C or better transfer for credit. 60 of 120 credits required for the bachelor's degree must be completed at ELCLA. **International Students:** There are 96 international students enrolled. They must take the TOEFL with a minimum score of 100 on the paper-based TOEFL (PBT) or 100 on the Internet-based version (iBT). Students must take the IELTS, or the PTE.

ADMISSIONS: 80% of the 2017-2018 applicants were accepted. The SAT scores for the 2017-2018 freshman class were: Critical Reading-- 11% below 500, 32% between 500 and 599, 43% between 600 and 699, and 15% between 700 and 800. Math-- 11% below 500, 42% between 500 and 599, 30% between 600 and 699, and 3% between 700 and 800. Writing-- 11% below 500, 38% between 500 and 599, 42% between 600 and 699, and 9% between 700 and 800. **Admissions Contact:** Candice MacLusky, Director of Admissions. Email: *lang@newschool.edu* Web: *www.newschool.edu/lang*

FINANCIAL AID: In 2017-2018, 47% of all full-time freshmen received some form of financial aid. 41% of all full-time freshmen received need-based aid. The average freshman award was $28,797. Need-based scholarships or need-based grants averaged $19,302; need-based self-help aid (loans and jobs) averaged $3,763; other non-need-based awards and non-need-based scholarships averaged $10,687; and $5,335 from other forms of aid. The average financial indebtedness of the 2017 graduate was $37,693. ELCLA is a member of CSS. The state aid form is required. The priority date for freshman financial aid applications for fall entry is February 1.

EXCELSIOR COLLEGE *(The complete profile is made available exclusively on our website, www.barronspac.com)*

FARMINGDALE STATE COLLEGE E-5
www.farmingdale.edu

Farmingdale, NY 11735 (631) 420-2200

Fax: (631) 420-2633 Email: admissions@farmingdale.edu
Full-time: 4339 men, 3068 women
Part-time: 1089 men, 1056 women
Graduate: 21 men, 1 women
Year: semesters, summer session
Room & Board: $12,892
Faculty: 246; IIB, +$
Ph.D.s: 78%
Student/Faculty: 30 to 1
Tuition: $8076 ($17,726)
Freshman Class: 6053 applied, 3578 accepted, 1325 enrolled
SAT EBR-W/M: 530/530 **ACT:** 21
CEEB CODE: 2526
Application Deadline: June 1
COMPETITIVE

Farmingdale State College, also known as SUNY Farmingdale State College, founded in 1912 is a public institution offering associate, bachelors, and masters degrees in the applied sciences and technology. There are 4 undergraduate schools and one graduate school. In addition to regional accreditation, FSC has baccalaureate program accreditation with ABET, ADA, ATMAE, NAACLS, and CCNE. The 380-acre campus is in a suburban area on Long Island, about 35 miles east of New York City. Including any residence halls, there are 40 buildings.

STUDENT LIFE: 98% of undergraduates are from New York. Others are from 12 states, 74 foreign countries, and Canada. 93% are from public schools. 9% are Asian American; 57% White; 20% Hispanic; 2% two or more races; 10% African American; 1% Foreign; 1% race unknown. **Male To Female Ratio:** 1.3:1. The average age of freshmen is 18; all undergraduates, 23. 19% do not continue beyond their first year; 54% remain to graduate. **Housing:** 600 students can be accommodated in college housing, which includes dorms. On-campus housing is available on a first-come, first-served basis. 94% of students commute. Alcohol is not permitted. All students may keep cars.

FACULTY/CLASSROOMS: 54% of faculty are male; 46% are female. All teach undergraduates. No introductory courses are taught by graduate students. The average class size in an introductory lecture is 28; in a laboratory is 17; and in a regular course is 27.

PROGRAMS OF STUDY: FSC confers B.S. and B.Tech. degrees. Associate and master's degrees are also awarded. Bachelor's degrees are awarded in AGRICULTURE (horticulture), BIOLOGICAL SCIENCE (biology/biological science), BUSINESS (business administration and management, business economics, facilities management, global/general management, and sports management), COMMUNICATIONS AND THE ARTS (English and professional communication, telecommunications engineering technology, and visual design), COMPUTER AND PHYSICAL SCIENCE (applied mathematics, computer engineering technology, computer programming, and information sciences and systems), ENGINEERING AND ENVIRONMENTAL DESIGN (aeronautical science, architectural technology, automotive technology, aviation administration/management, construction technology, electrical/electronics engineering technology, industrial engineering technology, manufacturing technology, and mechanical engineering technology), HEALTH PROFESSIONS (dental hygiene, medical technology, and nursing), SOCIAL SCIENCE (applied psychology, criminal justice, interdisciplinary studies, and safety and security technology). Nursing, dental hygiene, engineering technology, aviation, and business management are the strongest academically. Business management, science, technology and society, and computer programming and infomation systems have the largest enrollments.

ACTIVITIES: 3% of men belong to 4 national fraternities; 4% of women belong to 4 national sororities. There are 66 groups on campus, including art, computers, dance, drama, environmental, ethnic, honors, international, LGBT, musical theater, newspaper, photography, professional, radio and TV, religious, social, social service, student government, and yearbook. Popular campus events include RAMFEST, Club Challenge, Bingo for Books, Casino Night, Spring Concert, and Farewell to Farmingdale. **Sports:** There are 9 intercollegiate sports for men and 9 for women, and 11 intramural sports for men and 11 for women. Facilities include basketball, badminton, volleyball, racquetball, handball, squash, tennis courts, a wrestling room, weight training rooms, indoor and outdoor tracks, a golf driving range and 3-hole golf layout, baseball, softball, soccer/lacrosse, and multipurpose fields. **Graduates:** From July 1, 2016 to June 30, 2017, 1577 bachelor's degrees were awarded. The most popular majors were business management (24%), science, technology, and society (12%), criminal justice and law enforcement technology (9%). In an average class, 54% graduate in 6 years or less. Of the 2016 graduating class, 11% were enrolled in graduate school within 6 months of graduation, and 89% were employed.

SERVICES: Counseling and information services are available, as is tutoring in most subjects. There is a reader service for the blind, and remedial math, reading, and writing. There is also a learning disabilities specialist counselor available on staff. **Library/Resources:** The library contains 120,000 volumes, 5,490 microform items, 250 audio/video tapes/CDs/DVDs, and subscribes to 425 periodicals, including electronic. Computerized library services include interlibrary loans, database searching, Internet access, and Wi-Fi capability. Special learning facilities include an art gallery, a radio station, a dental hygiene clinic, CAD/CAM and CIM labs, a fleet of multi and single engine airplanes, and a greenhouse complex. **Physically Challenged Students:** 90% of the campus is accessible. Facilities include wheelchair ramps, elevators, special parking, specially equipped restrooms, special class scheduling, lowered drinking fountains, and lowered telephones. **Special:** Internships are available, as well as study abroad opportunities. There are 11 national honor societies. **Visiting:** There are regularly scheduled orientations for prospective students, including a tour of the campus and general information about the college, admissions, financial aid, and residence life. There are guides for informal visits. To schedule a visit, contact the Admissions Office. **Campus Safety and Security:** Measures include 24-hour foot and vehicle patrol, an emergency notification system, and security escort services. There are shuttle buses, emergency telephones, lighted pathways/sidewalks, and controlled access to dorms/residences.

REQUIREMENTS: The SAT is required. Applicants must be graduates of an accredited secondary school or have earned a GED. Specific entrance requirements vary by program, but recommended preparation includes 4 units of English and 3 each of math, science, and social science. AP and CLEP credits are accepted. To graduate, students must complete 120 to 130 credits with a minimum GPA of 2.0. The core curriculum includes at least 60 credits of liberal arts and sciences courses in the Bachelor of Science programs and 45 credits in the Bachelor of Technology programs, as well as credits in major coursework. One writing-intensive course and all general education requirements must be satisfactorily completed. **Procedure:** Freshmen are admitted in the fall and spring. There are early admissions, deferred admissions, and rolling admissions plans. Applications should be filed by June 1 for fall entry; November 1 for spring entry. The fall 2017 application fee was $50. Notification is sent on a rolling basis. Applications are accepted on-line. **Transfer Students:** 3403 transfer students enrolled in 2016-2017. Applicants must have a minimum GPA of 2.5. 30 of 120 credits required for the bachelor's degree must be completed at SUNY Farmingdale. **International Students:** There are 102 international students enrolled. They must take the TOEFL with a minimum score of 537 on the paper-based TOEFL (PBT) or 74 on the Internet-based version (iBT), and either the IELTS (6.0) or SAT Critical Reading (400). They must also take the SAT or ACT, scoring 1000. The SAT is not required for international students who attended high school outside of the United States.

ADMISSIONS: 59% of the 2017-2018 applicants were accepted. The SAT scores for the 2017-2018 freshman class were: Math-- 26% below 500, 59% between 500 and 599, 14% between 600 and 699, and 1% between 700 and 800. Evidence-Based Reading/Writing-- 26% below 500, 58% between 500 and 599, 15% between 600 and 699, and 1% between 700 and 800. The ACT scores were 11% between 12 and 17, 66% between 18 and 23, 22% between 24 and 29, and 1% above 30. 24% of the current freshmen were in the top fifth of their class; 54% were in the top two fifths. **Admissions Contact:** Jim Hall, Director of Admissions. Email: *admissions@farmingdale.edu* Web: *www.farmingdale.edu*

FINANCIAL AID: In 2017-2018, 67% of all full-time freshmen received some form of financial aid. 54% of all full-time freshmen received need-based aid. The average freshman award was $9,148. Need-based scholarships or need-based grants averaged $7,250 ($18,710 maximum); need-based self-help aid (loans and jobs) averaged $3,260 ($12,070 maximum); and other non-need-based awards and non-need-based scholarships averaged $3,165 ($28,340 maximum). The state aid form and the college's own financial statement are required. The FAFSA code is 002858. The priority date for freshman financial aid applications for fall entry is April 1. The deadline for filing freshman financial aid applications for fall entry is July 15.

FASHION INSTITUTE OF TECHNOLOGY/STATE UNIVERSITY OF

NEW YORK *(The complete profile is made available exclusively on our website, www.barronspac.com)*

FIVE TOWNS COLLEGE *(The complete profile is made available exclusively on our website, www.barronspac.com)*

FORDHAM UNIVERSITY D-5

www.fordham.edu

Bronx, NY 10458 **(718) 817-4000**

Fax: (718) 367-9404	**Email:** enroll@fordham.edu
Full-time: 3881 men, 5251 women	**Faculty:** 754; I, +$
Part-time: 194 men, 273 women	**Ph.D.s:** 93%
Graduate: 2278 men, 4160 women	**Student/Faculty:** 14 to 1
Year: semesters, summer session	**Tuition:** $50,986
Room & Board: $17,445	**Freshman Class:** 45147 applied, 20966 accepted, 2283 enrolled
SAT EBR-W/M: 659/662 **ACT:** 29	**CEEB CODE:** 2259
Application Deadline: January 1	**MOST COMPETITIVE**

Fordham University, an independent institution offering an education based in the Jesuit tradition, has two major campuses in New York City. With 4 full-time undergraduate colleges and 6 graduate/professional schools. Fordham offers a broad range of studies in liberal arts and sciences, business administration, social service, education, and law. Preprofessional studies in law and medicine are popular programs, as well as the opportunity to study abroad. Fordham also works with more than 2,000 organizations in the New York metropolitan area to arrange internships for students in fields such as business, communications, medicine, law, and education. In addition to regional accreditation, Fordham has baccalaureate program accreditation with AACSB and CAEP. The 93-acre campus is located in an urban area. The Rose Hill campus is located in the Bronx adjacent to the Bronx Zoo and New York Botanical Gardens. The Lincoln Center campus is located in Manhattan at 60th Street and Columbus Avenue, next to Lincoln Center for the Performing Arts. Including any residence halls, there are 42 buildings.

STUDENT LIFE: 57% of undergraduates are from out of state, mostly the Northeast. Students are from 45 states, 73 foreign countries, and Canada. 63% are from public schools. 58% are White; 14% Hispanic; 10% Asian American; 9% Foreign; 4% African American; 3% two or more races; 2% race unknown; 1% American Indian/Alaska Native. 50% are Catholic. **Female To Male Ratio:** 1.5:1. The average age of freshmen is 18; all undergraduates, 20. 90% remain to graduate. **Housing:** 4490 students can be accommodated in college housing, which includes dorms, on-campus apartments, off-campus apartments, and integrated learning communities. On-campus housing is guaranteed for all 4 years, and is available on a first-come, first-served basis, and is available on a lottery system for upperclassmen. 51% of students live on campus. All students may keep cars.

FACULTY/CLASSROOMS: 53% of faculty are male; 47% are female. No introductory courses are taught by graduate students. The average class size in an introductory lecture is 22.

PROGRAMS OF STUDY: Fordham confers B.A., B.S., and B.F.A. degrees. Master's and doctoral degrees are also awarded. Bachelor's degrees are awarded in BIOLOGICAL SCIENCE (biology/biological science and neurosciences), BUSINESS (accounting, business administration and management, business economics, finance, international business management, and marketing management), COMMUNICATIONS AND THE ARTS (art history, classical languages, classics, communication studies, comparative literature, dance, digital media, digital media technologies, dramatic arts, English, English literature, English Writing, film, television and digital media, fine arts, French, German, graphic design, Italian, journalism, Latin, music, music theory and composition, performing arts, Spanish, studio art, theatre acting, theater design, theatre production, and visual and performing arts), COMPUTER AND PHYSICAL SCIENCE (chemistry, computer science, information sciences and systems, mathematics, mathematics – economics, natural sciences, physics, science, and statistics), ENGINEERING AND ENVIRONMENTAL DESIGN (architecture, engineering physics, and environmental science), HEALTH PROFESSIONS (pre-health studies), SOCIAL SCIENCE (African studies, African American studies, American studies, anthropology, classical/ancient civilization, economics, French studies, German area studies, history, international studies, Italian studies, Latin American studies, medieval studies, Middle Eastern studies, philosophy, political science/government, prelaw, psychology, religion, social science, social work, sociology, Spanish studies, theological studies, urban studies, and women's studies). Biology, business, political science, and English are the strongest academically. Business, social sciences, and communications have the largest enrollments.

ACTIVITIES: There are no fraternities or sororities. There are 180 groups on campus, including campus activities board, art, band, cheerleading, chess, choir, chorale, chorus, communications, computers, dance, debate, drama, environmental, ethnic, film, honors, international, jazz band, LGBT, literary magazine, marching band, musical theater, newspaper, orchestra, pep band, photography, political, professional, radio and TV, religious, social, social service, student admission ambassadors, student government, symphony, and yearbook. Popular campus events include Family Weekend, Homecoming, Spring Weekend, Spring Semiformal, and Senior Week. **Sports:** There are 12 intercollegiate sports for men and 10 for women, and 7 intramural sports for men and 7 for women. Facilities include a stadium, an Olympic-size pool with a separate diving area, an indoor track, a gym, and tennis, squash, and racquetball courts. **Graduates:** From July 1, 2016 to June 30, 2017, 2058 bachelor's degrees were awarded. The most popular majors were business administration (28%), social sciences (19%), and communication and media studies (12%). In an average class, 74% graduate in 4 years or less, 79% graduate in 5 years or less, and 80% graduate in 6 years or less.

SERVICES: Counseling and information services are available, as is tutoring in most subjects. **Library/Resources:** The library contains 2.3 million volumes, 3.2 million microform items, 64,833 audio/video tapes/CDs/DVDs, and subscribes to 68,957 periodicals, including electronic. Computerized library services include interlibrary loans, database searching, Internet access, and Wi-Fi capability. Special learning facilities include an art gallery, a radio station, a seismic station, an archeological site, 2 trade rooms, and a biological field station. **Physically Challenged Students:** 80% of the campus is accessible. Facilities include wheelchair ramps, elevators, special parking, specially equipped restrooms, special class scheduling, and lowered drinking fountains. **Special:** Fordham University offers career-oriented internships during the junior or senior year with New York City companies and institutions. A combined 3-2 engineering program is available with Columbia and Case Western Reserve Universities. Accelerated degrees, dual and student-designed majors, and pass/fail options are available. Study abroad programs are available around the globe and include Fordham specific programs in London, England; Grenada, Spain; and Pretoria, South Africa. Fordham additionally offers a B.F.A program in conjunction with the Alvin Ailey School of Dance and a B.A. program in Theatre. There are 6 national honor societies, Phi Beta Kappa, and a freshman honors program. **Visiting:** There are regularly scheduled orientations for prospective students, that include an information session with a tour, a guided tour, or a self-guided tour. During the summer, a partial day visit consists of presentations, Q&A session with current students. There are guides for informal visits and visitors may sit in on classes. To schedule a visit, contact Office of Undergraduate Admission. **Campus Safety and Security:** Measures include 24-hour foot and vehicle patrol, an emergency notification system, and security escort services. There are shuttle buses, emergency telephones, lighted pathways/sidewalks, and controlled access to dorms/residences.

REQUIREMENTS: The SAT or ACT is required. Applicants should complete 4 years of high school English, 3 years of math, science, social studies, and history, and 2 years of foreign language. Applicants should submit the Common Application which includes an essay and questions on the Fordham member screen. A secondary school report and counselor or teacher letter of recommendation is required. SAT II subject tests are not required. Auditions are required for theatre and dance majors. Additionally, Fordham has a no interview policy. AP credits are accepted. Important factors in the admissions decision are advanced placement or honors courses, leadership record, extracurricular activities record, parents or siblings attended your school, evidence of special talent, personality/intangible qualities, geographical diversity, and recommendations by school officials. All students must complete a core curriculum, including courses each in literature, history, philosophy, theology, natural sciences, social sciences, math, English composition, fine arts and foreign language competency. A total of 124 credits and a 2.0 minimum GPA are required for graduation. **Procedure:** Freshmen are admitted in the fall and spring. Entrance exams should be taken by January of the senior year. There are early decision, early admissions, and deferred admissions plans. Early decision applications should be filed by November 1; regular applications, by January 1 for fall entry; and November 1 for spring entry. The fall 2017 application fee was $70. Notification of early decision is sent December 20; regular decision, April 1. 168 early decision candidates were accepted for the 2017-2018 class. 2600 applicants were on the 2017 waiting list; 48 were admitted. Applications are accepted on-line. **Transfer Students:** 344 transfer students enrolled in 2016-2017. A 3.0 minimum GPA is recommended. All applicants are required to submit the Common Application and essay, official high school and college transcripts, and a letter of good standing from the Dean or University Registrar from the institution the student currently attends. Applicants with less than one full year of full-time course work at a post-secondary institution must submit SAT or ACT scores. 64 of 124 credits required for the bachelor's degree must be completed at Fordham. **International Students:** There are 871 international students enrolled. They must take the TOEFL with a minimum score of 90 on the Internet-based version (iBT) and the college's own test. They must also take the SAT or ACT.

ADMISSIONS: 46% of the 2017-2018 applicants were accepted. The SAT scores for the 2017-2018 freshman class were: Math-- 1% below 500, 17% between 500 and 599, 49% between 600 and 699, and 33% between 700 and 800. Evidence-Based Reading/Writing-- 1% below 500, 15% between 500 and 599, 55% between 600 and 699, and 30% between 700 and 800. The ACT scores were 4% between 18 and 23, 47% between 24 and 29, and 49% above 30. 71% of the current freshmen were in the top fifth of their class; 93% were in the top two fifths. 25 freshmen graduated first in their class. **Admissions Contact:** Patricia Peek, Ph.D., Director of Admission. Email: *enroll@fordham.edu* Web: *www.fordham.edu*

FINANCIAL AID: In 2017-2018, 89% of all full-time freshmen received some form of financial aid. Fordham is a member of CSS. The CSS/Profile, and noncustodial profile, business and farm supplement are required. The FAFSA code is 002722. The priority date for freshman financial aid applications for fall entry is November 15.

HAMILTON COLLEGE — C-3

www.hamilton.edu

Clinton, NY 13323	(315) 859-4421 (800) 843-2655
Fax: (315) 859-4457	Email: admission@hamilton.edu
Full-time: 906 men, 960 women	Faculty: 186; IIB, av$
Part-time: 1 men	Ph.D.s: 96%
Graduate: n/av	Student/Faculty: 10 to 1
Year: semesters	Tuition: $51,240
Room & Board: $13,010	Freshman Class: 5230 applied, 1364 accepted, 472 enrolled
SAT CR/M/W: 700/690/700 ACT: 32	CEEB CODE: 2286
Application Deadline: January 1	MOST COMPETITIVE

Hamilton College, chartered in 1812, is a private, nonsectarian, liberal arts school offering undergraduate programs in the arts and sciences. There is 1 undergraduate school. The 1300-acre campus is in a rural area 9 miles southwest of Utica. Including any residence halls, there are 108 buildings.

STUDENT LIFE: 71% of undergraduates are from out of state, mostly the Middle Atlantic. Students are from 48 states, 47 foreign countries, and Canada. 61% are from public schools. 8% are Hispanic; 7% Asian American; 7% Foreign; 7% race unknown; 64% White; 4% African American; 3% two or more races. 31% are Buddhist, Hindu, and Islamic; 26% Protestant; 18% Catholic; 17% claim no religious affiliation. **Female To Male Ratio:** 1.1:1. The average age of freshmen is 18; all undergraduates, 20. 6% do not continue beyond their first year; 92% remain to graduate. **Housing:** 1887 students can be accommodated in college housing, which includes married student dorms and on-campus apartments. In addition, there are special-interest houses, quiet floors, and substance-free areas, cooperative housing, wellness housing, and first year housing. On-campus housing is guaranteed for all 4 years. Upperclassmen may keep cars.

FACULTY/CLASSROOMS: 50% of faculty are male; 48% are female. All teach undergraduates. No introductory courses are taught by graduate students. The average class size in a regular course is 16.

PROGRAMS OF STUDY: HC confers A.B. degrees. Bachelor's degrees are awarded in AGRICULTURE (environmental studies), BIOLOGICAL SCIENCE (biochemistry, biology/biological science, and neurosciences), COMMUNICATIONS AND THE ARTS (art, art history and appreciation, Chinese, classics, comparative literature, creative writing, dance, dramatic arts, English, English literature, film arts, French, languages, music, and studio art), COMPUTER AND PHYSICAL SCIENCE (chemical physics, chemistry, computer science, geoscience, mathematics, and physics), SOCIAL SCIENCE (African studies, American studies, anthropology, archeology, Asian/Oriental studies, economics, German area studies, Hispanic American studies, history, interdisciplinary studies, international relations, philosophy, political science/government, psychobiology, psychology, public affairs, religion, Russian and Slavic studies, sociology, and women's studies). Economics, and government have the largest enrollments.

ACTIVITIES: 26% of men belong to 9 national fraternities; 18% of women belong to 6 local sororities. There are 210 groups on campus, including art, chess, choir, chorale, chorus, communications, computers, dance, debate, drama, environmental, ethnic, film, honors, international, jazz band, LGBT, literary magazine, musical theater, newspaper, orchestra, photography, political, professional, radio and TV, religious, social, social service, student government, and yearbook. Popular campus events include Class and Charter Day and Feb Fest (Winter Carnival). **Sports:** There are 13 intercollegiate sports for men and 14 for women, and 16 intramural sports for men and 16 for women. Facilities include a gym, a field house, a fitness and dance center, squash and racquetball courts, indoor and outdoor tennis courts, an artificial grass football stadium, a swimming pool, indoor and outdoor tracks, baseball and softball fields, an artificial turf field, paddle tennis courts, and an ice rink. **Graduates:** From July 1, 2016 to June 30, 2017, 489 bachelor's degrees were awarded. The most popular majors were economics (15%), mathematics (8%), and psychology (5%). In an average class, 89% graduate in 4 years or less, 91% graduate in 5 years or less, and 92% graduate in 6 years or less.

SERVICES: Counseling and information services are available, as is tutoring in some subjects through the New York State Higher Education Opportunity Program (HEOP). **Library/Resources:** The library contains 627,120 volumes, 293,924 microform items, 38,727 audio/video tapes/CDs/DVDs, and subscribes to 5,263 periodicals, including electronic. Computerized library services include interlibrary loans, database searching, Internet access, and Wi-Fi capability. Special learning facilities include an art gallery, a radio station, an observatory, electron microscope, and the Wellin Museum of Art. **Physically Challenged Students:** Facilities include wheelchair ramps, elevators, special parking, specially equipped restrooms, special class scheduling, and special housing. **Special:** Cross-registration is permitted with Colgate University and Utica College. Opportunities are provided for a Washington semester and a New York City semester. Student-designed majors and study abroad in many countries are available, and 3-2 engineering degrees are offered with Washington University in St. Louis, Rensselaer Polytechnic Institute, and Columbia University. There are 8 national honor societies and a chapter of Phi Beta Kappa. **Visiting:** There are regularly scheduled orientations for prospective students, consisting of an interview, tour, class visit, and open house program. There are guides for informal visits; visitors may sit in on classes and stay overnight. To schedule a visit, contact the Office of Admission. **Campus Safety and Security:** Measures include 24-hour foot and vehicle patrol, an emergency notification system, self-defense education, and security escort services. There are shuttle buses, emergency telephones, lighted pathways/sidewalks, and controlled access to dorms/residences.

REQUIREMENTS: Although graduation from an accredited secondary school or a GED is desirable, and a full complement of college-preparatory courses is recommended, Hamilton will consider all highly recommended candidates who demonstrate an ability and desire to perform at intellectually demanding levels. Students can fulfill test requirements with the SAT, ACT, 3 SAT Subject tests, 3 AP exams, or any combination of these. An essay is required, and an interview is recommended. As of fall 2017 ACT with or without writing will be accepted as well. AP credits are accepted. Important factors in the admissions decision are advanced placement or honors courses, personality/intangible qualities, extracurricular activities record, recommendations by school officials, parents or siblings attended your school, and evidence of special talent. Students must successfully complete 128 credits, with 32 to 40 of these in the student's major, and must maintain at least a 72 average in half the courses taken. **Procedure:** Freshmen are admitted in the fall. Entrance exams should be taken prior to February of the senior year. There are early decision and deferred admissions plans. Early decision applications should be filed by November 15; regular applications, by January 1 for fall entry. The fall 2017 application fee was $50. Notification of early decision is sent December 15; regular decision, February 15. 240 early decision candidates were accepted for the 2017-2018 class. 475 applicants were on the 2017 waiting list; 47 were admitted. Applications are accepted on-line. **Transfer Students:** 23 transfer students enrolled in 2016-2017. Transfer applicants must submit high school and college transcripts, an essay or personal statement, and standardized test scores and must present a minimum GPA of 3.0 in all college-level work. Students may enroll in the fall and spring. 64 of 128 credits required for the bachelor's degree must be completed at HC. **International Students:** There are 122 international students enrolled. They must take the TOEFL, and either the SAT or ACT.

ADMISSIONS: 26% of the 2017-2018 applicants were accepted. The SAT scores for the 2017-2018 freshman class were: Critical Reading-- 10% between 500 and 599, 38% between 600 and 699, and 53% between 700 and 800. Math-- 11% between 500 and 599, 43% between 600 and 699, and 47% between 700 and 800. Writing-- 1% below 500, 9% between 500 and 599, 39% between 600 and 699, and 51% between 700 and 800. The ACT scores were 11% between 24 and 29, and 89% above 30. 88% of the current freshmen were in the top fifth of their class; 96% were in the top two fifths. **Admissions Contact:** Monica Inzer, Vice President and Dean of Admission and Financial Aid. Email: *admission@hamilton.edu* Web: *www.hamilton.edu*

FINANCIAL AID: In 2017-2018, 52% of all full-time freshmen received some form of financial aid and need-based aid. The average freshman award was $48,371. Need-based scholarships or need-based grants averaged $40,802; need-based self-help aid (loans and jobs) averaged $4,380; and other non-need-based awards and non-need-based scholarships averaged $3,291. The average financial indebtedness of the 2017 graduate was $21,491. Hamilton is a member of CSS. The CSS/Profile and the college's own financial statement, and non-custodial profile and/or business/farm supplement if applicable are required. The FAFSA code is 002728. The deadline for filing freshman financial aid applications for fall entry is February 15.

HARTWICK COLLEGE D-3
www.hartwick.edu

Oneonta, NY 13820 (607) 431-4150

Fax: (607) 431-4102	**Email:** admissions@hartwick.edu
Full-time: 540 men, 812 women	**Faculty:** 105; IIB, av$
Part-time: 12 men, 19 women	**Ph.D.s:** 91%
Graduate: n/av	**Student/Faculty:** 13 to 1
Year: 4-1-4, summer session	**Tuition:** $41,840
Room & Board: $11,120	**Freshman Class:** n/av
SAT or ACT: required	**CEEB CODE:** 2288
Application Deadline: rolling	**COMPETITIVE**

Hartwick College, founded in 1797, is a private undergraduate liberal arts and sciences college. There is 1 undergraduate school. In addition to regional accreditation, HC has baccalaureate program accreditation with NASAD, NASM, CCNE, and ACS. The 425-acre campus is in a small town 75 miles southwest of Albany, NY. Including any residence halls, there are 20 buildings.

STUDENT LIFE: 75% of undergraduates are from New York. Others are from 29 states, 20 foreign countries, and Canada. 85% are from public schools. 9% are African American; 7% Hispanic; 67% White; 3% Foreign; 2% Asian American; 12% race unknown. 30% are Protestant; 26% claim no religious affiliation; 24% Catholic. **Female To Male Ratio:** 1.5:1. The average age of freshmen is 18; all undergraduates, 20. 26% do not continue beyond their first year; 51% remain to graduate. **Housing:** 1201 students can be accommodated in college housing, which includes dorms and on-campus apartments. In addition, there are honors houses, fraternity houses, sorority houses, substance-free housing, and community engagement floor. On-campus housing is available on a lottery system for upperclassmen. 77% of students live on campus. All students may keep cars.

FACULTY/CLASSROOMS: 57% of faculty are male; 43% are female. All teach undergraduates. No introductory courses are taught by graduate students. The average class size in an introductory lecture is 20; in a laboratory is 20; and in a regular course is 17.

PROGRAMS OF STUDY: HC confers B.A. and B.S. degrees. Bachelor's degrees are awarded in BIOLOGICAL SCIENCE (biochemistry and biology/biological science), BUSINESS (accounting and business administration and management), COMMUNICATIONS AND THE ARTS (art, art history and appreciation, dramatic arts, English, French, German, languages, music, and Spanish), COMPUTER AND PHYSICAL SCIENCE (chemistry, computer science, geology, information sciences and systems, mathematics, and physics), EDUCATION (music education), ENGINEERING AND ENVIRONMENTAL DESIGN (environmental science), HEALTH PROFESSIONS (medical technology and nursing), SOCIAL SCIENCE (anthropology, economics, history, philosophy, political science/government, psychology, religion, and sociology). Psychology, business administration/accounting, and nursing have the largest enrollments.

ACTIVITIES: 10% of men belong to 2 national fraternities; 8% of women belong to 2 local and 1 national sorority. There are 70 groups on campus, including art, band, cheerleading, choir, chorale, chorus, dance, drama, environmental, ethnic, honors, international, jazz band, LGBT, literary magazine, musical theater, newspaper, pep band, political, professional, radio and TV, religious, social, social service, student government, and yearbook. Popular campus events include Hawk Night Fever (pep rally), Oneonta State and Hartwick Fest (street fair and concert), and Scholar Showcase. **Sports:** There are 7 intercollegiate sports for men and 10 for women, and 5 intramural sports for men and 5 for women. Facilities include gyms, an indoor pool, a dance room, athletic and training facilities, a track, fitness centers, lighted all-weather playing field, lighted soccer field, an equestrian complex (off-campus), courts for handball, racquetball, squash, and tennis. **Graduates:** From July 1, 2016 to June 30, 2017, 333 bachelor's degrees were awarded. The most popular majors were nursing (16%), business administration (15%), and biology (10%). In an average class, 50% graduate in 4 years or less, 54% graduate in 5 years or less, and 56% graduate in 6 years or less. Of the 2016 graduating class, 21% were enrolled in graduate school within 6 months of graduation, and 29% were employed.

SERVICES: Counseling and information services are available, as is tutoring in most subjects. There is a reader service for the blind. **Library/Resources:** The library contains 300,606 volumes, 29,700 microform items, 3,644 audio/video tapes/CDs/DVDs, and subscribes to 13,112 periodicals, including electronic. Computerized library services include interlibrary loans, database searching, Internet access, and Wi-Fi capability. Special learning facilities include an art gallery, a radio station, the museum of art, a culture museum, and an observatory. **Physically Challenged Students:** 50% of the campus is accessible. Facilities include wheelchair ramps, elevators, special parking, and specially equipped restrooms. **Special:** Hartwick's innovative approach emphasizes personalized instruction and practical experiences both inside and outside the classroom with programs such as study abroad, internships, collaborative research, and more. HC offers more than than 30 courses of study leading to a Bachelor of Arts or Bachelor of Science degree, four pre-professional programs, five cooperative programs, and a series of interesting minors and other options, including Certification in Education. Plus, you can design you own major. Within Hartwick's Three-Year Bachelor's Degree Program, there are 24 major areas of study leading to a Bachelor of Arts or Bachelor of Science degree. There is a 3-2 engineering program with Clarkson University or Columbia University, and a 3-3 program with Albany Law School. There are 9 national honor societies and a freshman honors program. **Visiting:** There are regularly scheduled orientations for prospective students, consisting of an interview and tour, departmental open houses, presentations on student life, off-campus programs, and a career planning process. There are guides for informal visits; visitors may sit in on classes and stay overnight. To schedule a visit, contact the Admissions Office. **Campus Safety and Security:** Measures include 24-hour foot and vehicle patrol, emergency notification system, self-defense education, and security escort services. There are emergency telephones, lighted pathways/sidewalks, and controlled access to dorms/residences.

REQUIREMENTS: Reporting of SAT and ACT scores is optional. The recommended secondary course of study includes 4 years of English and 3 years each of math, a foreign language, history, and lab science. Hartwick strongly recommends that applicants plan a campus visit and interview. Prospective art majors should submit a portfolio, and music majors must audition. AP and CLEP credits are accepted. Important factors in the admissions decision are advanced placement or honors courses and recommendations by school officials. Students must complete 120 credit hours with at least a 2.0 GPA. The core curriculum consists of Hartwick's Liberal Arts in Practice. Distribution requirements include a first-year seminar, 9 credits spread through humanities, physical and life sciences, and social and behavioral sciences, 3 credits in quantitative and formal reasoning, foreign language (intermediate-level proficiency), attainment of writing level 4, and a senior capstone. **Procedure:** Freshmen are admitted in the fall and spring. Entrance exams should be taken in the spring of the junior year and/or the fall of the senior year. There are early decision, deferred admissions, and rolling admissions plans. Application deadlines are open. Notification is sent on a rolling basis. 17 early decision candidates were accepted for the 2017-2018 class. 51 applicants were on the 2017 waiting list; 45 were admitted. Applications are accepted online. **Transfer Students:** 34 transfer students enrolled in 2016-2017. Applicants should present a minimum GPA of 2.0. 60 of 120 credits required for the bachelor's degree must be completed at HC. **International Students:** There are 42 international students enrolled. They must take the TOEFL with a minimum score of 550 on the paper-based TOEFL (PBT) or 79 on the Internet-based version (iBT). They must also take the SAT.

Admissions Contact: Lisa Starkey-Wood, Director of Admissions. Email: *admissions@hartwick.edu* Web: *www.hartwick.edu*

FINANCIAL AID: In 2017-2018, 87% of all full-time freshmen received some form of financial aid. 86% of all full-time freshmen received need-based aid. The average freshman award was $27,415. Need-based scholarships or need-based grants averaged $25,788; need-based self-help aid (loans and jobs) averaged $6,942; non-need-based athletic scholarships averaged $19,984; and other non-need-based awards and non-need-based scholarships averaged $23,742. 66% of undergraduate students work part-time. The average financial indebtedness of the 2017 graduate was $27,653. HC is a member of CSS. The college's own financial statement is required. The FAFSA code is 002729. The deadline for filing freshman financial aid applications for fall entry is February 15.

HILBERT COLLEGE *(The complete profile is made available exclusively on our website, www.barronspac.com)*

HOBART AND WILLIAM SMITH COLLEGES B-3
www.hws.edu

Geneva, NY 14456 **(315) 781-3622**

Fax: (315) 781-3471	**Email:** admissions@hws.edu
Full-time: 1190 men, 1121 women	**Faculty:** 221; IIB
Part-time: 11 men, 6 women	**Ph.D.s:** 100%
Graduate: 1 men, 5 women	**Student/Faculty:** 10 to 1
Year: semesters, summer session	**Tuition:** $53,525
Room & Board: $13,525	**Freshman Class:** 4409 applied, 2696 accepted, 636 enrolled
SAT of ACT: required	**CEEB CODE:** 2294
Application Deadline: February 1	**HIGHLY COMPETITIVE+**

Hobart and William Smith Colleges, is defined by a longstanding focus of educating across academic disciplines and the close work of research and creativity that connects faculty and students. The Colleges have a distinguished history of interdisciplinary teaching and scholarship, curricular innovation, and exceptional outcomes. Originally founded as 2 separate colleges (Hobart for men in 1822 and William Smith for women in 1908), students share the same campus, faculty, administration and curriculum. There are 2 undergraduate schools and 1 graduate school. The 320-acre campus is in a small town in Geneva, in the heart of New York State's Finger Lakes region on the north shore of Seneca Lake. Including any residence halls, there are 97 buildings.

STUDENT LIFE: 56% of undergraduates are from out of state, mostly the Northeast. Students are from 40 states, 33 foreign countries, and Canada. 56% are from public schools. 74% are White; 6% African American; 6% Foreign; 5% Hispanic; 5% race unknown; 3% Asian American. **Male To Female Ratio:** 1.1:1. The average age of freshmen is 18; all undergraduates, 20. 14% do not continue beyond their first year; 81% remain to graduate. **Housing:** 1980 students can be accommodated in college housing, which includes gender neutral dorms, single-sex dorms, coed dorms, on-campus apartments, and off-campus apartments. In addition, there are honors houses, language/international houses, special-interest houses, fraternity houses, cooperative, themed houses, and townhouses for upper class years. On-campus housing is guaranteed for all 4 years. 87% of students live on campus. All students may keep cars.

FACULTY/CLASSROOMS: 51% of faculty are male; 49% are female. All teach undergraduates and do research. No introductory courses are taught by graduate students. The average class size in an introductory lecture is 21; in a laboratory is 13; and in a regular course is 20.

PROGRAMS OF STUDY: HWSC confers B.A. and B.S. degrees. Master's degrees are also awarded. Bachelor's degrees are awarded in BIOLOGICAL SCIENCE (biochemistry and biology/biological science), COMMUNICATIONS AND THE ARTS (Africana studies, art history, classics, communication rhetoric, comparative literature, dance, English, film, television and digital media, fine arts, French, Greek, Latin, modern language, music, Russian languages and literature, Spanish and Hispanic studies, studio art, and theatre arts), COMPUTER AND PHYSICAL SCIENCE (chemistry, computer science, geoscience, mathematics, and physics), ENGINEERING AND ENVIRONMENTAL DESIGN (architecture and environmental science), SOCIAL SCIENCE (African studies, American studies, anthropology, architectural studies, Asian/Oriental studies, economics, European studies, history, international relations, Latin American studies, philosophy, political science/government, psychology, religion, Russian and Slavic studies, sociology, Spanish studies, and women's studies). Natural sciences, environmental studies, and economics are the strongest academically. Economics, media and society, and environmental studies have the largest enrollments.

ACTIVITIES: 18% of men belong to 8 national fraternities; 2% of women belong to 1 national sorority. There are 119 groups on campus, including first generation, Latin American Organization, Sankofa, women's collective, art, chess, choir, chorale, chorus, computers, dance, debate, drama, environmental, ethnic, film, honors, HWS Debate Team, international, jazz band, LGBT, literary magazine, musical theater, newspaper, orchestra, photography, political, professional, radio and TV, religious, social, social service, student government, symphony, and yearbook. Popular campus events include Stu Lieblein '90 Pitch Contest (entrepreneurship), Koshare Dance performances, Charter Day and Moving Up Day, Convocation, and Homecoming. **Sports:** There are 11 intercollegiate sports for men and 12 for women, and 18 intramural sports for men and 18 for women. Facilities include a sport and recreation center, gyms, athletic fields, a swimming pool, indoor and outdoor tennis courts, weight rooms, basketball, an indoor track, international squash courts, and boating facilities. **Graduates:** From July 1, 2016 to June 30, 2017, 530 bachelor's degrees were awarded. The most popular majors were economics (12%), environmental studies (9%), and media and society (8%). In an average class, 73% graduate in 4 years or less, 77% graduate in 5 years or less, and 81% graduate in 6 years or less. Of the 2016 graduating class, 14% were enrolled in graduate school within 6 months of graduation, and 82% were employed.

SERVICES: Counseling and information services are available, as is tutoring in most subjects. There is peer learning in anthropology, art history, biology, chemistry, computer science, economics, environmental studies, music, philosophy, physics, sociology and Spanish. There is also a reader service for the blind. Students can get writing and quantitative reasoning support regardless of discipline/course (Writing Fellows and Q Fellows). Study Mentors are available to help with time management, test taking and note taking skills. **Library/Resources:** The library contains 389,139 volumes, 16,670 microform items, 13,255 audio/video tapes/CDs/DVDs, and subscribes to 59,320 periodicals, including electronic. Computerized library services include interlibrary loans, database searching, Internet access, and Wi-Fi capability. Special learning facilities include an art gallery, a radio station, a performing arts center, an observatory, a natural preserve, 35 acres of farmland, the HWSC Finger Lakes Institute, a 65-foot research vessel, HWSC solar farms, and a student entrepreneurship center. **Physically Challenged Students:** 69% of the campus is accessible. Facilities include wheelchair ramps, elevators, special parking, specially equipped restrooms, special class scheduling, and lowered drinking fountains. **Special:** Each HWSC student completes both a major and a minor (or a second major). Students have the option to design, with a faculty adviser, their own major. The Colleges offer special degree programs in business administration (4 + 1 joint degree in conjunction University of Rochester, Syracuse University, Clarkson University and Rochester Institute of Technology), engineering (3 + 2 joint degree in conjunction with Dartmouth College and Columbia University), education (NYS certification for various education levels and disciplines), and Master of Arts in Teaching (HWSC graduates only). Through the Salisbury Center for Career, Professional and Experiential Education, students have numerous opportunities to find credit-bearing internships nationally and internationally. The Colleges guarantee that students of good academic standing who successfully complete the HWSC career development Pathways program are able to participate in at least one internship or research opportunity. Sixty percent of students study abroad in programs available through our nationally ranked Center for Global Education in more than 50 locations. Additionally, the Colleges offer a semester in Washington, D.C. Academic scholarships are available, including The Elizabeth Blackwell Class of 1849 Pioneer in Science Scholarship, which is awarded to applicants who have completed advanced science coursework, relevant research or participated in science related experiences; and Arts Scholarships which are awarded for excellence in the fine and performing arts. There are 10 national honor societies, Phi Beta Kappa, and 100 departmental honors programs. **Visiting:** There are regularly scheduled orientations for prospective students, including daily information sessions and tours offered year round, with admissions interviews strongly recommended. Special Open House events are also held throughout the winter, spring, summer and fall designed for high school juniors and seniors. There are guides for informal visits; visitors may sit in on classes and stay overnight. To schedule a visit, contact the Office of Admissions. **Campus Safety and Security:** Measures include 24-hour foot and vehicle patrol, an emergency notification system, and security escort services. There are shuttle buses, emergency telephones, lighted pathways/sidewalks, controlled access to dorms/residences, and student EMS corps.

REQUIREMENTS: SAT: Subject tests are not required but will be considered if taken. A GED is accepted. A total of 19 academic credits is required, including 4 years of English, 3 years each of math, lab science, foreign language, and history. An essay is required; an interview is highly recommended. AP credits are accepted. Important factors in the admissions decision are advanced placement or honors courses, evidence of special talent, and leadership record. At HWSC a course of study must include: a First-Year Seminar that introduces students to the intellectual community and provides academic mentorship; passing 32 courses (including achieving a minimum grade and GPA standards); completing the requirements for an academic major, including a capstone course or experience, and a minor (or a second major); completing potential faculty-mandated writing requirements through a writing enriched curriculum; and addressing each of the 8 goals of our general curriculum. 2 goals are integrated across the four-year curriculum and 6 are aspirational goals satisfied through the completion of specific coursework that address each goal. Broadly, goals include the integrated goals of critical thinking and communication, and 6 aspirational goals covering: the ability to reason quantitatively, experiential understanding of scientific inquiry, critical and experiential understanding of artistic process, critical understanding of social inequalities, critical understanding of cultural difference, and intellectual foundation for ethical judgment as a basis for socially responsible action. **Procedure:** Freshmen are admitted in the fall and spring. Entrance exams should be taken no later than December of the senior year. There are early decision, early admissions, and deferred admissions plans. Early decision applications should be filed by November 15; regular applications, by February 1 for fall entry. Notification of early decision is sent December 15; regular decision, March 23. 320 early decision candidates were accepted for the 2017-2018 class. 504 applicants were on the 2017 waiting list; 29 were admitted. Applications are accepted online. **Transfer Students:** 13 transfer students enrolled in 2016-2017. Applicants must have a 2.7 GPA and have completed 1 year of college study. They are required to take the SAT or ACT. An interview is highly recommended. 16 of 32 credits required for the bachelor's degree must be completed at HWSC. **International Students:** There are 130 international students enrolled. They must take the TOEFL with a minimum score of 80 on the Internet-based version (iBT), or the iELTS. They must also take the SAT or ACT.

ADMISSIONS: 61% of the 2017-2018 applicants were accepted. 48% of the current freshmen were in the top fifth of their class; 80% were in the top two fifths. 29 freshmen graduated first in their class. **Admissions Contact:** John W. Young, Director of Admissions. Email: *admissions@hws.edu* Web: *www.hws.edu*

FINANCIAL AID: In 2017-2018, 95% of all full-time freshmen received some form of financial aid. 66% of all full-time freshmen received need-based aid. The average freshman award was $42,499. Need-based scholarships or need-based grants averaged $38,710 ($53,525 maximum); need-based self-help aid (loans and jobs) averaged $4,744 ($9,500 maximum); and other non-need-based awards and non-need-based scholarships averaged $19,577 ($53,525 maximum). 32% of undergraduate students work part-time. The average financial indebtedness of the 2017 graduate was $33,725. HWSC is a member of CSS. The CSS/Profile and the state aid form are required. The FAFSA code is 002731. The priority date for freshman financial aid applications for fall entry is February 1.

HOFSTRA UNIVERSITY D-5

www.hofstra.edu

Hempstead, NY 11549 **(516) 463-6700**

Fax: (516) 463-7660
Email: admission@hofstra.edu
Full-time: 2989 men, 3485 women
Faculty: 371; I, +$
Part-time: 219 men, 211 women
Ph.D.s: 92%
Graduate: 1606 men, 2443 women
Student/Faculty: 17 to 1
Year: semesters, summer session
Tuition: $38,900
Room & Board: $12,910
Freshman Class: 26388 applied, 16258 accepted, 1714 enrolled
SAT CR/M: 560/570 **ACT:** 25
CEEB CODE: 2295
Application Deadline: open
COMPETITIVE+

Hofstra University, founded in 1935, is an independent institution offering programs in liberal arts and sciences, business, communications, education, engineering and applied sciences, health and human services, honors studies, law, and medicine. There are 7 undergraduate schools and 8 graduate schools. In addition to regional accreditation, Hofstra has baccalaureate program accreditation with AACSB, ABET, ACEJMC, TEAC, ABA, ACS, APA, MSCHE, ARC-PA, CAATE, CAA, AATA, CORE, LCME, NASP, and TEAC. The 240-acre campus is in a suburban area 25 miles east of New York City. Including any residence halls, there are 115 buildings.

STUDENT LIFE: 63% of undergraduates are from New York. Others are from 46 states, 51 foreign countries, and Canada. 9% are African American; 9% Asian American; 56% White; 4% Foreign; 4% race unknown; 2% two or more races; 14% Hispanic. **Female To Male Ratio:** 1.3:1. The average age of freshmen is 18; all undergraduates, 20. 20% do not continue beyond their first year; 60% remain to graduate. **Housing:** 3600 students can be accommodated in college housing, which includes single-sex and coed dorms and on-campus apartments. In addition, there are honors houses, and special-interest houses. There is a living-learning center, quiet floors, womens floors, themed living communities, and freshman housing. On-campus housing is guaranteed for all 4 years, and is available on a first-come, first-served basis, and is available on a lottery system for upperclassmen. Priority is given to out-of-town students. 50% of students commute. All students may keep cars.

FACULTY/CLASSROOMS: 55% of faculty are male; 45% are female. 81% teach undergraduates, 81% do research, and 81% do both. No introductory courses are taught by graduate students. The average class size in an introductory lecture is 28; in a laboratory is 16; and in a regular course is 21.

PROGRAMS OF STUDY: Hofstra confers B.A., B.S., B.B.A., B.E., B.F.A., and B.S.Ed. degrees. Master's and doctoral degrees are also awarded. Bachelor's degrees are awarded in AGRICULTURE (environmental studies), BIOLOGICAL SCIENCE (biochemistry and biology/biological science), BUSINESS (accounting, banking and finance, business administration and management, business economics, business law, entrepreneurial studies, international business management, labor studies, management information systems, marketing management, and supply chain management), COMMUNICATIONS AND THE ARTS (American literature, art history and appreciation, audio technology, ceramic art and design, China Asia-Pacific studies, Chinese, classics, comparative literature, creative writing, dance, design, dramatic arts, film arts, fine arts, French, German, Hebrew, Italian, Japanese, jazz, journalism, Latin, linguistics, media arts, metal/jewelry, music, music business management, music history and appreciation, music performance, music theory and composition, painting, photography, public relations, publishing, radio/television technology, Russian, Spanish, speech/debate/rhetoric, theater design, theater management, video, and visual and performing arts), COMPUTER AND PHYSICAL SCIENCE (applied mathematics, applied physics, chemistry, computer science, geology, information sciences and systems, mathematics, and physics), EDUCATION (art education, athletic training, business education, childhood education, dance education, elementary education, English education, foreign languages education, global studies, health education, mathematics education, music education, physical education, science education, secondary education, and social studies education), ENGINEERING AND ENVIRONMENTAL DESIGN (biomedical engineering, civil engineering, computer engineering, electrical/electronics engineering, engineering and applied science, industrial engineering, manufacturing engineering, and mechanical engineering), HEALTH PROFESSIONS (allied health, community health work, exercise science, health science, prehealth studies, predentistry, premedicine, preoptometry, preosteopathy, prepodiatry, preveterinary science, and speech pathology/audiology), SOCIAL SCIENCE (African studies, American studies, anthropology, Caribbean studies, Chinese studies, criminology, economics, forensic studies, geography, Hispanic American studies, history, Japanese studies, Judaic studies, Latin American studies, liberal arts/general studies, philosophy, political science/government, psychology, religion, sociology, urban ecology, and women's studies). Engineering, Communication/Radio, Business/marketing, education, humanities, and physician assistant are the strongest academically. Biology, psychology, and accounting have the largest enrollments.

ACTIVITIES: 7% of women belong to 1 local and 11 national sororities. There are 249 groups on campus, including art, band, cheerleading, chess, choir, chorale, chorus, communications, computers, dance, debate, drama, environmental, ethnic, film, forensics, honors, international, jazz band, LGBT, literary magazine, musical theater, newspaper, opera, orchestra, pep band, photography, political, professional, radio and TV, religious, social, social service, student government, symphony, and yearbook. Popular campus events include New Student Convocation, Welcome Week, Hofstra Celebrates the Holidays, Student Leadership Awards, Hofstra Music Fest, Hofstra Fall Festival, Jail and Bail, Alt Spring Break, Greek Week, Relay for Life, Leadership Programs, Senior Week, and Heritage Month. **Sports:** There are 8 intercollegiate sports for men and 9 for women, and 6 intramural sports for men and 6 for women. Facilities include a stadium, an arena, a soccer stadium, a physical education building, a swim center, a softball stadium, intramural fields, a fitness center with a multipurpose gym, indoor track, and a weight room. **Graduates:** From July 1, 2015 to June 30, 2016, 1403 bachelor's degrees were awarded. The most popular majors were psychology (8%), marketing (6%), and management (6%). 239 companies recruited on campus in 2015-2016. In an average class, 50% graduate in 4 years or less, 59% graduate in 5 years or less, and 60% graduate in 6 years or less. Of the 2015 graduating class, 27% were enrolled in graduate school within 6 months of graduation, and 76% were employed.

SERVICES: Counseling and information services are available, as is tutoring in most subjects. There is a reader service for the blind. **Library/Resources:** The 3 libraries contain 1.2 million volumes, 3.4 million microform items, 17,433 audio/video tapes/CDs/DVDs, and subscribe to 14,628 periodicals, including electronic. Computerized library services include interlibrary loans, database searching, Internet access, and Wi-Fi capability. Special learning facilities include an art gallery, science labs and state-of-the-art bio-engineering labs, robotics and big data labs, a rooftop observatory, 6 theaters including a black box teaching theater, a financial trading room, a multimedia converged news room, a comprehensive media production facility including a 24-hour radio station, a multiple 3-D printers, a digital language lab, a state-of-the-art medical school, 100% wireless campus, a child care institute, a cultural center, museum, an arboretum, and a bird sanctuary. **Physically Challenged Students:** All of the campus is accessible. Facilities include wheelchair ramps, elevators, special parking, specially equipped restrooms, special class scheduling, lowered drinking fountains, lowered telephones, and special housing. **Special:** Internships in numerous career fields, Engineering Co-Op Program, SUNY Brockport/Washington Semester, utilization of the Washington Center for internship conferences and programming, an Albany internship with the NY State Assembly, NY State Senate Internship, Study Abroad, and dual and individually designed majors are offered. Credits for prior learning and credit by exam are given with proper credentials. Hofstra offers over 100 dual degree programs. There are 36 national honor societies, Phi Beta Kappa, a freshman honors program, and 35 departmental honors programs. **Visiting:** There are regularly scheduled orientations for prospective students, a group information session, a campus tour, and an optional interview with an admissions counselor. There are guides for informal visits; visitors may sit in on classes and stay overnight. To schedule a visit, contact Andrea Nadler at (516) 463-6798. **Campus Safety and Security:** Measures include 24-hour foot and vehicle patrol, an emergency notification system, self-defense education, and security escort services. There are shuttle buses, emergency telephones, lighted pathways/sidewalks, and controlled access to dorms/residences. Residence halls have security cameras, require card access to enter, and are monitored by resident student safety representatives 24/7, with the help of a CCTV, bike patrol, and a motorist assistance program.

REQUIREMENTS: Applicants should graduate from an accredited secondary school or have a GED. Preparatory work should include 4 years of English, 3 each of history, social studies, math, and science, and 2 of foreign language. Engineering students are required to have 4 years of math and 1 each of chemistry and physics. An essay is required. Interviews are recommended. One counselor or teacher recommendation is helpful. Hofstra is test optional; standardized test scores are not required for most programs with the exception of homeschooled and international applicants. AP and CLEP credits are accepted. Important factors in the admissions decision are advanced placement or honors courses, recommendations by school officials, and leadership record. A total of 124 to 134 credit hours is required for graduation (152 for 5 year accounting) with approximately 30 to 60 in the major depending on the degree program and a minimum GPA of 2.0. Some majors have a higher GPA requirement. Students must pass writing studies and composition 1 and 2, and pass a writing proficiency exam. For the B.A. degree, 33 credits in distribution/general education are required: 9 each in humanities, social science, and natural science/math/computer science, 3 each in cross culture and interdisciplinary. Foreign language study is required for the B.A., the B.B.A. in international business, and some B.S. programs. **Procedure:** Freshmen are admitted in the fall and spring. Entrance exams should be taken in the junior or senior year. There are early admissions, deferred admissions, and rolling admissions plans. Early decision applications should be filed by December 15, along with a $70 fee. Notification of early decision is sent January 15; regular decision, February 1. 47 applicants were on the 2016 waiting list; 10 were admitted. Applications are accepted online. **Transfer Students:** 599 transfer students enrolled in 2015-2016. Admission is based primarily on prior college work. A maximum of 64 credits from a 2-year school or 94 credits from a 4-year school is accepted. There is a 30-credit maximum on AP/CLEP credits. 30 of 124 credits required for the bachelor's degree must be completed at Hofstra. **International Students:** There are 294 international students enrolled. The school actively recruits these students. They must take the TOEFL with a minimum score of 550 on the paper-based TOEFL (PBT) or 80 on the Internet-based version (iBT).

ADMISSIONS: 62% of the 2016-2017 applicants were accepted. The SAT scores for the 2016-2017 freshman class were: Critical Reading-- 12% below 500, 56% between 500 and 599, 27% between 600 and 699, and 5% between 700 and 800. Math-- 9% below 500, 52% between 500 and 599, 33% between 600 and 699, and 6% between 700 and 800. The ACT scores were 3% below 12, 28% between 12 and 17, 32% between 18 and 23, 17% between 24 and 29, and 21% above 30. 50% of the current freshmen were in the top fifth of their class; 78% were in the top two fifths. 8 freshmen graduated first in their class. **Admissions Contact:** Jessica Eads, Vice President of Enrollment Management. Email: *admission@hofstra.edu* Web: *www.hofstra.edu*

FINANCIAL AID: In 2016-2017, 93% of all full-time freshmen and 88% of continuing full-time students received some form of financial aid. 71% of all full-time freshmen and 64% of continuing full-time students received need-based aid. The average freshman award was $27,000. Need-based scholarships or need-based grants averaged $22,000 ($53,000 maximum); need-based self-help aid (loans and jobs) averaged $7,000 ($14,000 maximum); non-need-based athletic scholarships averaged $22,000 ($48,000 maximum); and other non-need-based awards and non-need-based scholarships averaged $18,000 ($40,000 maximum). 41% of undergraduate students work part-time. Average annual earnings from campus work are $3000. The state aid form is required. The FAFSA code is 002732. The priority date for freshman financial aid applications for fall entry is February 15.

HOUGHTON COLLEGE B-3

www.houghton.edu

Houghton, NY 14744 (585) 567-9376 (800) 777-2556

Fax: (585) 567-9522 Email: admission@houghton.edu

Full-time: 373 men, 602 women	**Faculty:** 65
Part-time: 20 men, 41 women	**Ph.D.s:** 91%
Graduate: 6 men, 7 women	**Student/Faculty:** 15 to 1
Year: semesters, summer session	**Tuition:** $31,540
Room & Board: $9018	**Freshman Class:** 821 applied, 750 accepted, 219 enrolled
SAT CR/M: 601/580 **ACT:** 25	**CEEB CODE:** 2299
Application Deadline: March 1	**VERY COMPETITIVE**

Houghton College provides an academically challenging, Christ-centered education in the liberal arts and sciences to students from diverse traditions and economic backgrounds and equips them to lead and labor as scholar-servants in a changing world. There is 1 undergraduate school and 1 graduate school. In addition to regional accreditation, HC has baccalaureate program accreditation with NASM. The 1300-acre campus is in a rural area 65 miles southeast of Buffalo and 70 miles southwest of Rochester. Including any residence halls, there are 20 buildings.

STUDENT LIFE: 64% of undergraduates are from New York. Others are from 34 states, 43 foreign countries, and Canada. 66% are from public schools. 73% are White; 6% Asian American; 5% African American; 5% two or more races; 5% race unknown; 4% Foreign; 2% Hispanic. 85% are Protestant. **Female To Male Ratio:** 1.6:1. The average age of freshmen is 19; all undergraduates, 21. 20% do not continue beyond their first year; 74% remain to graduate. **Housing:** 1066 students can be accommodated in college housing, which includes single-sex and married student dorms and on-campus apartments. In addition, there are special-interest houses. Equestrian students have the opportunity to live on site; cooperative housing. On-campus housing is guaranteed for all 4 years. 90% of students live on campus. All students may keep cars. Alcohol is not permitted.

FACULTY/CLASSROOMS: 60% of faculty are male; 40% are female. All teach undergraduates, and 20% do both. No introductory courses are taught by graduate students. The average class size in an introductory lecture is 26; in a laboratory is 13; and in a regular course is 17.

PROGRAMS OF STUDY: HC confers B.A., B.B.A., B.S., B.F.A., and B.Mus. degrees. Associate and master's degrees are also awarded. Bachelor's degrees are awarded in AGRICULTURE (equine science), BIOLOGICAL SCIENCE (biochemistry, biology/adolescence education, biology/biological science, and environmental biology), BUSINESS (accounting, business administration and management, recreation and leisure services, and recreational facilities management), COMMUNICATIONS AND THE ARTS (art, communications, English, English as a second/foreign language, English literature, English writing, instrumental performance, media arts, music, music performance, music theory and composition, organ performance, printmaking, Spanish, studio art, vocal performance, voice, vocal music education, and writing), COMPUTER AND PHYSICAL SCIENCE (applied physics, chemistry, chemistry/adolescence education, clinical laboratory science, computer science, applied data science analytics, mathematics, physics, and science), EDUCATION (childhood education, Christian education, early childhood education, education of the exceptional child, elementary education, English education, foreign languages education, general studies, health education, mathematics education, music education, physical education, science education, secondary education, special education, and teaching English as a second/foreign language (TESOL/TEFOL), ENGINEERING AND ENVIRONMENTAL DESIGN (environmental science and preengineering), HEALTH PROFESSIONS (medical technology, predentistry, premedicine, preoptometry, prepharmacy, prephysical therapy, preveterinary science, and recreation therapy), SOCIAL SCIENCE (biblical studies, Christian studies, counseling/psychology, crosscultural studies, history, humanities, interdisciplinary studies, international studies, liberal arts/general studies, ministries, parks and recreation management, pastoral studies, philosophy, political science/government, prelaw, psychobiology, psychology, religion, religious education, religious studies, religious music, and sociology). Biology, psychology, physics, music, and art are the strongest academically. Biology, music, and business have the largest enrollments.

ACTIVITIES: There are no fraternities or sororities. There are 50 groups on campus, including art, bagpipe, band, choir, chorale, chorus, communications, drama, drum and bugle corps, environmental, ethnic, honors, international, jazz band, literary magazine, musical theater, newspaper, opera, orchestra, pep band, photography, political, professional, religious, social, social service, student government, symphony, and yearbook. Popular campus events include Christian Life Emphasis Week, Film Festival, SPOT Variety Show, Purple and Gold Week, Faith and Justice Symposium, and Martin Luther King Jr. Service Day. **Sports:** There are 7 intercollegiate sports for men and 9 for women, and 7 intramural sports for men and 7 for women. Facilities include basketball and racquetball courts, a gym, a swimming pool, an indoor track, a downhill ski slope, cross-country ski trails, tennis courts, baseball and softball fields, a climbing wall, an 8-lane all-weather track, a ropes course, and a equestrian center with an indoor riding ring. **Graduates:** From July 1, 2016 to June 30, 2017, 277 bachelor's degrees were awarded. The most popular majors were business administration and management (16%), communication (11%), and education (9%). In an average class, 4% graduate in 3 years or less, 63% graduate in 4 years or less, 72% graduate in 5 years or less, and 76% graduate in 6 years or less. Of the 2016 graduating class, 25% were enrolled in graduate school within 6 months of graduation, and 98% were employed.

SERVICES: Counseling and information services are available, as is tutoring in most subjects. There is a reader service for the blind, and remedial math and writing. There is also support for students with learning-related disabilities. **Library/Resources:** The library contains 596,150 volumes, 38,067 microform items, 21,911 audio/video tapes/CDs/DVDs, and subscribes to 58,919 periodicals, including electronic. Computerized library services include interlibrary loans, database searching, Internet access, and Wi-Fi capability. Special learning facilities include an art gallery, an equestrian center, a ropes course, a digital media lab, a greenhouse, and an outdoor classroom. **Physically Challenged Students:** 85% of the campus is accessible. Facilities include wheelchair ramps, elevators, special parking, specially equipped restrooms, special class scheduling, lowered drinking fountains, lowered telephones, and special housing. **Special:** Students may cross-register with members of the Western New York Consortium, the Christian College Consortium, and the Five College Committee. Internships are available in psychology, social work, business, educational ministries, physical fitness, political science, graphic design, communication, athletic training, recreation, English, and Christian education. Study abroad in 25 countries, a Washington semester, and dual majors. A 3-2 engineering degree with Clarkson and Washington Universities are available as well as a 4-1 BS/MBA degree with Alfred U, Clarkson U, Niagara U and Rochester Institute of Technology. A PharmD 3-4 degree program with University of Buffalo is also available. Students may design their own major as an Interdisciplinary Studies major. Credit for military experience and nondegree study are possible. There are 3 national honor societies, Phi Beta Kappa, a freshman honors program, and 3 departmental honors programs. **Visiting:** There are regularly scheduled orientations for prospective students, including a campus tour, an admissions interview, a financial aid session, a class visit, and an academic information session. There are guides for informal visits; visitors may sit in on classes and stay overnight. To schedule a visit, contact Andrew Oden at (800) 777-2556. **Campus Safety and Security:** Measures include 24-hour foot and vehicle patrol, an emergency notification system, and security escort services. There are emergency telephones, lighted pathways/sidewalks, controlled access to dorms/residences, campus emergency preparedness plan includes agreements with local police departments, American Red Cross, and local schools/businesses for cooperative assistance as needed.

REQUIREMENTS: Applicants must graduate from an accredited secondary school, be home-schooled, or have a GED. A total of 16 academic credits is recommended, including 4 of English, 3 each of social studies, science with 2 units of lab, and history, and 2 of foreign language. An essay is required. Music students must audition. An interview is recommended. AP and CLEP credits are accepted. Important factors in the admissions decision are advanced placement or honors courses, personality/intangible qualities, parents or siblings attended your school, evidence of special talent, extracurricular activities record, and recommendations by school officials. Integrative studies courses are required in the following disciplines: writing, literature, Bible, foreign language, history, math, science, physical education, theology, philosophy, fine arts, social science, and humanities. A minimum GPA of 2.0 is required to graduate. **Procedure:** Freshmen are admitted in the fall and spring. Entrance exams should be taken in the spring of the junior year or fall of the senior year. There are deferred admissions and rolling admissions plans. Application deadlines are open. The fall 2017 application fee was $40. Notification of early decision is sent November 1; regular decision, on a rolling basis. Applications are accepted online. **Transfer Students:** 40 transfer students enrolled in 2016-2017. Applicants should have a 2.75 or better GPA. A character recommendation and high school transcripts must be submitted. The essay, an SAT or ACT and an interview are optional but encouraged. 30 of 124 credits required for the bachelor's degree must be completed at HC. **International Students:** There are 36 international students enrolled. They must take the TOEFL with a minimum score of 550 on the paper-based TOEFL (PBT) or 80 on the Internet-based version (iBT). They must also take the SAT or ACT.

ADMISSIONS: 91% of the 2017-2018 applicants were accepted. The SAT scores for the 2017-2018 freshman class were: Critical Reading-- 11% below 500, 37% between 500 and 599, 36% between 600 and 699, and 17% between 700 and 800. Math-- 17% below 500, 39% between 500 and 599, 33% between 600 and 699, and 11% between 700 and 800. The ACT scores were 6% between 12 and 17, 36% between 18 and 23, 41% between 24 and 29, and 17% above 30. 47% of the current freshmen were in the top fifth of their class; 74% were in the top two fifths. 8 freshmen graduated first in their class. **Admissions Contact:** Ryan Spear, Director of Admission. Email: *admission@houghton.edu* Web: *www.houghton.edu*

FINANCIAL AID: In 2017-2018, 99% of all full-time freshmen received some form of financial aid. 88% of all full-time freshmen received need-based aid. The average freshman award was $28,027. Need-based scholarships or need-based grants averaged $12,334; need-based self-help aid (loans and jobs) averaged $5,668; and other non-need-based awards and non-need-based scholarships averaged $4,067. 43% of undergraduate students work part-time. The average financial indebtedness of the 2017 graduate was $30,845. HC is a member of CSS. The college's own financial statement is required. The FAFSA code is 002734. The priority date for freshman financial aid applications for fall entry is March 1.

IONA COLLEGE — D-5

www.iona.edu

New Rochelle, NY 10801 — **(914) 633-2502**

Fax: (914) 633-2182	**Email:** admissions@iona.edu
Full-time: 1440 men, 1508 women	**Faculty:** 174; IIA, av$
Part-time: 128 men, 102 women	**Ph.D.s:** 90%
Graduate: 235 men, 379 women	**Student/Faculty:** 15 to 1
Year: semesters, summer session	**Tuition:** $37,682
Room & Board: $14,832	**Freshman Class:** 10305 applied, 9502 accepted, 860 enrolled
SAT EBR-W/M: 550/530 **ACT:** 23	**CEEB CODE:** 2324
Application Deadline: February 15	**COMPETITIVE**

Iona College, founded in 1940, is a private college in the tradition of the Christian Brothers and American Catholic higher education, offering programs through schools of arts and science, and business. There are 2 undergraduate schools and 2 graduate schools. In addition to regional accreditation, IC has baccalaureate program accreditation with AACSB, ABET, ACEJMC, CSWE, AAMFT, NASP, and ACS. The 45-acre campus is in a suburban area in New Rochelle (Westchester county) NY, just 2 miles from Long Island Sound and 20 miles north of Midtown Manhattan and 20 miles south of Stamford, CT. Including any residence halls, there are 47 buildings.

STUDENT LIFE: 76% of undergraduates are from New York. Others are from 34 states, 23 foreign countries, and Canada. 9% are African American; 7% race unknown; 54% White; 3% Foreign; 23% Hispanic; 2% Asian American; 2% two or more races. **Female To Male Ratio:** 1.1:1. The average age of freshmen is 18; all undergraduates, 20. 25% do not continue beyond their first year; 64% remain to graduate. **Housing:** 1575 students can be accommodated in college housing, which includes dorms, on-campus apartments, and off-campus apartments. In addition, there are special-interest houses, and living learning community housing. On-campus housing is available on a first-come, first-served basis, and is available on a lottery system for upperclassmen. 54% of students commute. Upperclassmen may keep cars.

FACULTY/CLASSROOMS: 54% of faculty are male; 45% are female. No introductory courses are taught by graduate students.

PROGRAMS OF STUDY: IC confers B.A., B.S., and B.B.A. degrees. Master's degrees are also awarded. Bachelor's degrees are awarded in AGRICULTURE (environmental studies), BIOLOGICAL SCIENCE (biochemistry and biology/biological science), BUSINESS (accounting, business administration and management, finance, international business management, management science, and marketing management), COMMUNICATIONS AND THE ARTS (arts administration/management, communications, English, French, Italian, Spanish, and speech/debate/rhetoric), COMPUTER AND PHYSICAL SCIENCE (applied mathematics, chemistry, computer science, information sciences and systems, mathematics, and physics), EDUCATION (childhood education and early childhood education), HEALTH PROFESSIONS (speech pathology/audiology), SOCIAL SCIENCE (criminal justice, economics, history, interdisciplinary studies, international studies, liberal arts/general studies, philosophy, political science/government, psychology, religion, social work, and sociology). Accounting, biochemistry/chemistry, and mass communications are the strongest academically. Mass communication, marketing, and criminal justice have the largest enrollments.

ACTIVITIES: 3% of men belong to 1 local and 2 national fraternities; 7% of women belong to 4 local and 1 national sororities. There are 80 groups on campus, including academic professional groups - public relations student society of America, and community sevice, black student union, democracy matters, Gaelic society, Hispanic organization of Latin awareness, inter-residence hall council, Italian society, karate club, national student speech and hearing/language association, Rugby, students against destructive, students association, students for veterans students for peace, bagpipe, cheerleading, chorale, communications, computers, dance, debate, drama, environmental, ethnic, film, honors, international, LGBT, literary magazine, musical theater, newspaper, political, professional, radio and TV, religious, social, social service, student government, students Caribbean ancestry, and yearbook. Popular campus events include Spring Weekend/Concert Event, Travel Series, Heritage Week, Fashion Show, Campus Coffee House, Homecoming Carnivel, Week of the Peacemaker and Make a Difference Week, Black History Month, Hispanic Heritage Month, and Alcohol Awareness Week. **Sports:** There are 10 intercollegiate sports for men and 11 for women. Facilities include gymnasiums, weight rooms, a cardio room, a core studio, aerobics studio, rowing tank and a swimming pool/diving/water polo. Outdoor facilities: soccer/lacrosse field and softball field. **Graduates:** From July 1, 2016 to June 30, 2017, 714 bachelor's degrees were awarded. The most popular majors were business (35%), mass communication (18%), and criminal justice (10%). In an average class, 59% graduate in 4 years or less, 64% graduate in 5 years or less, and 64% graduate in 6 years or less.

SERVICES: Counseling and information services are available, as is tutoring in most subjects, such as accounting, biology, chemistry, Columba Cornerstone (freshmen seminar), computer science, computer applications, economics, finance, German, history, Italian, law, math, operations management, philosophy, Spanish, and statistics. There is a reader service for the blind. There is also assistance for students who require electronic versions of texts. **Library/Resources:** The library contains 269,396 volumes, 510,213 microform items, 4,696 audio/video tapes/CDs/DVDs, and subscribes to 742 periodicals, including electronic. Computerized library services include interlibrary loans, database searching, Internet access, and Wi-Fi capability. Special learning facilities include an art gallery, a radio station, TV station, an electron microscope, and a speech and hearing clinic. **Physically Challenged Students:** 70% of the campus is accessible. Facilities include wheelchair ramps, elevators, special parking, specially equipped restrooms, special class scheduling, lowered drinking fountains, and special housing. **Special:** There are internships available for students. Study abroad is available in Ireland, Spain, Italy, England, Greece, Netherlands, and Poland. Work-study positions are available in several locations throughout the College. Iona College offers BA and/or BS degree programs in Arts Leadership, Biochemistry, Biology (including pre-professional prep. track), Chemistry*, Computer Science*, Criminal Justice*, Economics*, Education, English*, Environmental Studies, French, History*, Interdisciplinary Science, International Studies, Italian, Mass Communication, Mathematics*, Philosophy, Physics, Political Science, Psychology*, Religious Studies, Social Work, Sociology, Spanish, Speech Communication Studies, Speech/Language Pathology and Audiology. Iona College offers BBA degree programs in Accounting, Business Administration, Finance, Information Systems, International Business, Management, and Marketing. (* Indicates that this area offers five-year bachelor's/master's degree programs). There are 3 national honor societies, a freshman honors program, and 24 departmental honors programs. **Visiting:** There are regularly scheduled orientations for prospective students, including a meeting with an admissions counselor, a campus tour, and a variety of on-campus programs during the summer and fall. There are guides for informal visits and visitors may sit in on classes. To schedule a visit, contact Raymond Garo at (914) 633-2622. **Campus Safety and Security:** Measures include 24-hour foot and vehicle patrol, an emergency notification system, and security escort services. There are shuttle buses, emergency telephones, lighted pathways/sidewalks, and controlled access to dorms/residences.

REQUIREMENTS: Applicants must complete 16 academic credits, including 4 each units of English and mathematics, 3 units each of natural science (including 2 laboratory sciences) and social studies, 2 units of foreign language (in the same language), 1 unit each of history and academic electives. A GED is accepted. Iona College prefers to see students who have maintained at least a solid B/B+ (85-89) average in high school and earned an SAT or ACT generally in a range above 1000. The type and level of courses taken, is reviewed, and is part of a holistic review, and a complement to the GPA and test scores themselves. Iona does not require the writing section of the SAT or SAT II subject tests. A personal essay and two letters of recommendations are recommended. AP and CLEP credits are accepted. The Iona College Core Curriculum applies to the undergraduate students of both the School of Business as well as the School of Arts and Science who enter as the Class of 2020. The curriculum provides the foundation for a shared Iona College experience that integrates excellent and dynamic academics with meaningful co-curricular engagements through the provision of a common learning experience that prepares students for ethical, engaged citizenship and lifelong learning through the lenses of diversity, sustainability, and a global perspective framed by the values of peace, justice, civic engagement, and service. Students enrolled in BBA programs, BS programs, and the Honors Program take specific core courses that are unique to each program. To be eligible for graduation, students must earn a minimum of 120 credits for a BA, and 126 credits for a BBA. Some BS degrees require more than 120 credits. Credit requirements vary by major. The minimum GPA requirement is 2.0. **Procedure:** Freshmen are admitted in the fall and spring. Entrance exams should be taken in the spring of the junior year. There are early admissions and deferred admissions plans. Applications should be filed by February 15 for fall entry; January 1 for spring entry. The fall 2017 application fee was $50. Applications are accepted on-line. **Transfer Students:** 99 transfer students enrolled in 2016-2017. Transfer applicants must have a GPA of at least 2.0 and must submit high school transcripts if they have earned fewer than 30 college credits. An interview is recommended. 30 of 120 credits required for the bachelor's degree must be completed at IC. **International Students:** There are 85 international students enrolled. They must take the TOEFL with a minimum score of 550 on the paper-based TOEFL (PBT) or 80 on the Internet-based version (iBT). They must also take the SAT or ACT.

ADMISSIONS: 92% of the 2017-2018 applicants were accepted. The SAT scores for the 2017-2018 freshman class were: Math-- 32% below 500, 47% between 500 and 599, 19% between 600 and 699, and 1% between 700 and 800. Evidence-Based Reading/Writing-- 25% below 500, 51% between 500 and 599, 24% between 600 and 699, and 1% between 700 and 800. The ACT scores were 6% between 12 and 17, 51% between 18 and 23, 38% between 24 and 29, and 6% above 30. 16% of the current freshmen were in the top fifth of their class; 41% were in the top two fifths. **Admissions Contact:** Alick Letang, Assistant Vice President of Enrollment. Email: *admissions@iona.edu* Web: *www.iona.edu*

FINANCIAL AID: 15% of undergraduate students work part-time. IC is a member of CSS. The state aid form is required. The FAFSA code is 002737. The deadline for filing freshman financial aid applications for fall entry is April 15.

ITHACA COLLEGE — C-4

www.ithaca.edu

Ithaca, NY 14850	**(607) 274-3124** **(800) 429-4274**
Fax: (607) 274-1900	**Email: admission@ithaca.edu**
Full-time: 2502 men, 3434 women	**Faculty:** 517; IIA, av$
Part-time: 60 men, 63 women	**Ph.D.s:** 88%
Graduate: 152 men, 305 women	**Student/Faculty:** 10 to 1
Year: semesters, summer session	**Tuition:** $42,884
Room & Board: $15,274	**Freshman Class:** 14152 applied, 9980 accepted, 1622 enrolled
SAT EBR-W/M: 620/600 **ACT:** 27	**CEEB CODE:** 2325
Application Deadline: February 1	**VERY COMPETITIVE+**

Ithaca College is home to undergraduates and graduate students and offers more than 100 degree programs in its schools of business, communications, health sciences and human performance, humanities and sciences, and music. IC's integrative core curriculum builds bridges across disciplines and uniquely blends liberal arts with professional study. There are 5 undergraduate schools and 1 graduate school. In addition to regional accreditation, IC has baccalaureate program accreditation with AACSB, APTA, NASM, CAEP, NRPA, AOTA, CAAHEP, CAPTE, CAA ASHA, ACS, NYS Board of Public Accounting, and NAST. The 669-acre campus is in a small town 250 miles northwest of New York City. Including any residence halls, there are 86 buildings.

STUDENT LIFE: 55% of undergraduates are from out of state, mostly the Middle Atlantic. Students are from 43 states, 42 foreign countries, and Canada. 84% are from public schools. 8% are Hispanic; 73% White; 6% African American; 4% Asian American; 4% race unknown; 3% two or more races; 2% Foreign. **Female To Male Ratio:** 1.4:1. The average age of freshmen is 18; all undergraduates, 20. 17% do not continue beyond their first year; 76% remain to graduate. **Housing:** 4512 students can be accommodated in college housing, which includes dorms, coed, and on-campus apartments. In addition, there are honors houses and floors, language/international houses, special-interest houses, first-year students only housing, quiet study hall, smoke-free buildings and a substance-free building. On-campus housing is guaranteed for all 4 years. 70% of students live on campus. All students may keep cars.

FACULTY/CLASSROOMS: 49% of faculty are male; 51% are female. All teach undergraduates. Graduate students teach 6% of introductory courses. The average class size in an introductory lecture is 21.

PROGRAMS OF STUDY: IC confers B.A., B.S., B.F.A., and Mus.B. degrees. Master's and doctoral degrees are also awarded. Bachelor's degrees are awarded in AGRICULTURE (environmental studies), BIOLOGICAL SCIENCE (biochemistry and biology/biological science), BUSINESS (accounting, business administration w/legal studies, business administration and management, business communications, organizational behavior, recreation and leisure services, and sports management), COMMUNICATIONS AND THE ARTS (art history, art, art history and appreciation, audio technology, broadcasting, communications, creative writing, dramatic arts, English, English literature, English writing, film arts, fine arts, French, German, Germanic languages and literature, jazz, journalism, languages, media arts, modern language, music, music performance, music theory and composition, musical theater, performing arts, photography, piano pedagogy, public relations, Spanish, sports media, studio art, telecommunications, theater design, theater management, video, and visual and performing arts), COMPUTER AND PHYSICAL SCIENCE (chemistry, computer mathematics, computer programming, computer science, mathematics, mathematics – economics, physics secondary education, physics and mathematics, and physics), EDUCATION (art education, athletic training, education, education of the deaf and hearing impaired, English secondary education, English education, foreign languages education, health education, mathematics education, middle school education, music education, physical education, secondary education, social science education, social studies education, speech correction, sports and wellness studies, and sports studies), ENGINEERING AND ENVIRONMENTAL DESIGN (engineering chemistry, engineering physics, and environmental science), HEALTH PROFESSIONS (allied health, clinical science, community health work, exercise science, health, health science, occupational therapy, physical therapy, preallied health, pre-health studies, predentistry, premedicine, preoptometry, public health, recreation therapy, rehabilitation therapy, speech pathology/audiology, speech therapy, and sports medicine), SOCIAL SCIENCE (anthropology, applied psychology, architectural studies, area studies, economics, German area studies, gerontology, history, industrial and organizational psychology, interdisciplinary studies, Italian studies, legal studies, liberal arts/general studies, philosophy, philosophy and religion, physical fitness/movement, political science/government, prelaw, psychology, social studies, and sociology). Physical therapy, theater, and music are the strongest academically. Business administration, physical therapy, and music have the largest enrollments.

ACTIVITIES: 1% of men belong to 3 national fraternities.there are no sororities. There are 200 groups on campus, including academic clubs, art, band, cheerleading, chess, choir, chorale, chorus, computers, dance, debate, drama, environmental, ethnic, film, forensics, honors, international, jazz band, LGBT, literary magazine, musical theater, newspaper, opera, orchestra, pep band, photography, political, professional, radio and TV, religious, social, social service, sports, student government, and symphony. Popular campus events include Pep Rallies, Student Involvement Fair, and various multicultural awareness events. **Sports:** There are 11 intercollegiate sports for men and 14 for women, and 16 intramural sports for men and 16 for women. Facilities include gyms, dance studios, a student union, indoor and outdoor pools, a fitness center and wellness clinic, an indoor and outdoor track, rugby pitch, a climbing wall, fields for baseball, football, lacrosse, field hockey, and soccer, tennis courts, an aquatics pavilion and stadium. **Graduates:** From July 1, 2016 to June 30, 2017, 1507 bachelor's degrees were awarded. The most popular majors were business administration (11%), television and radio (9%), and integrated marketing communications (7%). In an average class, 2% graduate in 3 years or less, 69% graduate in 4 years or less, 76% graduate in 5 years or less, and 76% graduate in 6 years or less. Of the 2016 graduating class, 26% were enrolled in graduate school within 6 months of graduation, and 54% were employed.

SERVICES: IC provides content-based tutoring in over 50 courses. **Library/Resources:** The library contains 315,276 volumes, 17,000 microform items, 34,270 audio/video tapes/CDs/DVDs, and subscribes to 72,061 periodicals, including electronic. Computerized library services include interlibrary loans, database searching, Internet access, and Wi-Fi capability. Special learning facilities include an art gallery and studios, a radio station, a TV station, a digital audio/video labs, photography labs, cinematography postproduction studio, a film animation lab, a lighting studio, physical therapy and occupational therapy clinics, speech and hearing clinic, athletic training clinic, wellness clinic, human anatomy lab, movement analysis lab, financial trading room, recording and electroacoustic music studio, music and theatre performance halls, psychology labs, biology, chemistry, and physics labs (including single crystal x-ray diffractometer and 3D printer), an observatory, a greenhouse, organic garden, apiary, emerging media lab, ad lab, robotics lab, dance studios, and sound stage. **Physically Challenged Students:** Facilities include wheelchair ramps, elevators, special parking, specially equipped restrooms, special class scheduling, lowered drinking fountains, lowered telephones, and special housing. **Special:** Cross-registration is available with Cornell University and Wells College. Opportunities are also provided for internships, study abroad (in more than 50 countries), a semester of study/internship in NYC, Los Angeles, and/or London, work-study programs, accelerated degree programs, dual majors, non-degree study, pass/fail options, and student-designed majors. A 3-2 engineering degree with Cornell University, Clarkson University, Rensselaer Polytechnic Institute, and Binghamton University is available. A 4-1 B.S./M.B.A. program, a pre-med and pre-law program, and a one-semester program in marine biology with Duke University and the Sea Education Association are also available. There are 34 national honor societies, a freshman honors program, and 33 departmental honors programs. **Visiting:** There are regularly scheduled orientations for prospective students, including student-led campus tours and information sessions with admission counselors year-round. Open house programs are available in the fall and spring. Faculty appointments, class visits, individual appointments with admission counselors may be available. To schedule a visit, contact the Admission Office. **Campus Safety and Security:** Measures include 24-hour foot and vehicle patrol, an emergency notification system, self-defense education, and security escort services. There are emergency telephones, lighted pathways/sidewalks, controlled access to dorms/residences, and crime prevention programs.

REQUIREMENTS: Applicants should be graduates of an accredited secondary school with a minimum of 16 Carnegie units, including 4 years of English, 3 years each of math, science, and social studies, 2 years of foreign language, and other college-preparatory electives. The GED is accepted. An essay is required, as is an audition for music and theater students. In some majors, a portfolio and an interview are recommended. AP and CLEP credits are accepted. Students must successfully complete a minimum of 120 credits including the course requirements of their specific major. All students participate in Ithaca College's Integrative Core Curriculum (ICC). The centerpiece of the ICC is a "Themes and Perspectives" sequence where students take a minimum of one course each in the natural sciences, creative arts, humanities, and social sciences, all focusing on one of six general themes, such as "Inquiry, Imagination, and Innovation" or "Quest for a Sustainable Future." The Themes and Perspectives sequence kicks off with a first-semester Ithaca Seminar introducing students to the theme and helping them transition to college life and learning. Additional elements of the ICC include coursework in writing, diversity, and quantitative literacy, as well as a capstone experience and learning portfolio. **Procedure:** Freshmen are admitted in the fall and spring. Entrance exams should be taken in spring of the junior year or fall of the senior year. There are early decision, deferred admissions, and rolling admissions plans. Early decision applications should be filed by November 1; regular applications, by February 1 for fall entry; and December 1 for spring entry. The fall 2017 application fee was $60. Notification of early decision is sent December 15; regular decision, April 15. 151 early decision candidates were accepted for the 2017-2018 class. 953 applicants were on the 2017 waiting list; 29 were admitted. Applications are accepted online. **Transfer Students:** 97 transfer students enrolled in 2016-2017. Transfer applicants must submit a high school transcript, transcripts from previously attended colleges, and a personal recommendation from their adviser or Dean of Students. A minimum college GPA of 2.75 is recommended. 30 of 120 credits required for the bachelor's degree must be completed at Ithaca. **International Students:** There are 99 international students enrolled. They must take the TOEFL with a minimum score of 550 on the paper-based TOEFL (PBT) or 80 on the Internet-based version (iBT), and take the IELTS.

ADMISSIONS: 71% of the 2017-2018 applicants were accepted. The SAT scores for the 2017-2018 freshman class were: Math-- 3% below 500, 44% between 500 and 599, 44% between 600 and 699, and 9% between 700 and 800. Evidence-Based Reading/Writing-- 2% below 500, 27% between 500 and 599, 56% between 600 and 699, and 15% between 700 and 800. The ACT scores were 1% between 12 and 17, 14% between 18 and 23, 62% between 24 and 29, and 23% above 30. 46% of the current freshmen were in the top fifth of their class; 80% were in the top two fifths. 6 freshmen graduated first in their class. **Admissions Contact:** Nicole Eversley Bradwell, Director of Admission. Email: *admission@ithaca.edu* Web: *www.ithaca.edu*

FINANCIAL AID: In 2017-2018, 97% of all full-time freshmen received some form of financial aid. 70% of all full-time freshmen received need-based aid. The average freshman award was $39,906. Need-based scholarships or need-based grants averaged $28,655 ($63,504 maximum); need-based self-help aid (loans and jobs) averaged $7,407 ($14,400 maximum); and other non-need-based awards and non-need-based scholarships averaged $12,222 ($61,669 maximum). 34% of undergraduate students work part-time. The average financial indebtedness of the 2017 graduate was $42,000. IC is a member of CSS. The CSS/Profile is required. The FAFSA code is 002739. The priority date for freshman financial aid applications for fall entry is February 1.

KEUKA COLLEGE — B-3

www.keuka.edu

Keuka Park, NY 14478	(315) 279-5254
Fax: (315) 279-5386	**Email:** admissions@keuka.edu
Full-time: 368 men, 945 women	**Faculty:** 91; IIA, --$
Part-time: 69 men, 259 women	**Ph.D.s:** 67%
Graduate: 40 men, 228 women	**Student/Faculty:** n/av
Year: 4-1-4, summer session	**Tuition:** $30,946
Room & Board: $11,452	**Freshman Class:** 2373 applied, 2071 accepted, 365 enrolled
SAT or ACT: required	**CEEB CODE:** 2350
Application Deadline: open	**COMPETITIVE**

Keuka College, founded in 1890, offers undergraduate and graduate, bachelor's and master's degree programs on campus and through its Accelerated Studies for adults program and international programs in China and Vietnam. There is 1 undergraduate school and 6 graduate schools. In addition to regional accreditation, KC has baccalaureate program accreditation with CSWE, IACBE, CCNE, and ACOTE. The 288-acre campus is in a rural area 60 miles south of Rochester. Including any residence halls, there are 35 buildings.

STUDENT LIFE: 92% of undergraduates are from New York. Others are from 26 states, 9 foreign countries, and Canada. 77% are White; 8% African American; 5% Hispanic; 5% race unknown; 2% two or more races; 1% Asian American; 1% American Indian/Alaska Native; 1% Foreign. **Female To Male Ratio:** 3.0:1. The average age of freshmen is 18. 33% do not continue beyond their first year; 52% remain to graduate. **Housing:** 902 students can be accommodated in college housing, which includes gender neutral, single sex dorms, coed dorms, and on-campus apartments. In addition, there are honors houses, special-interest houses, cooperative living, leadership, and wellness housing. On-campus housing is guaranteed for all 4 years. 85% of students live on campus. All students may keep cars. Alcohol is not permitted.

FACULTY/CLASSROOMS: 48% of faculty are male; 55% are female. All teach undergraduates. No introductory courses are taught by graduate students.

PROGRAMS OF STUDY: KC confers B.A. and B.S. degrees. Master's degrees are also awarded. Bachelor's degrees are awarded in BIOLOGICAL SCIENCE (biochemistry and biology/biological science), BUSINESS (accounting, business administration and management, and marketing/retailing/merchandising), COMMUNICATIONS AND THE ARTS (American Sign Language, communications, and English), COMPUTER AND PHYSICAL SCIENCE (mathematics), EDUCATION (elementary education and secondary education), ENGINEERING AND ENVIRONMENTAL DESIGN (environmental science), HEALTH PROFESSIONS (medical laboratory technology, nursing, occupational therapy, predentistry, premedicine, and preveterinary science), SOCIAL SCIENCE (criminal justice, political science/government, prelaw, psychology, social work, and sociology). Occupational therapy, criminal justice, and management are the strongest academically. Occupational therapy, education, and management have the largest enrollments.

ACTIVITIES: There are no fraternities or sororities. There are 40 groups on campus, including leadership, art, cheerleading, choir, chorale, communications, community service, dance, drama, ethnic, honors, international, LGBT, newspaper, political, professional, religious, social, social service, student government, and yearbook. Popular campus events include Spring Weekend, May Day and Family Weekend. **Sports:** There are 7 intercollegiate sports for men and 8 for women, and 5 intramural sports for men and 5 for women. Facilities include a gym, a fitness center, a weight room, and an outdoor athletic facility. **Graduates:** From July 1, 2016 to June 30, 2017, 547 bachelor's degrees were awarded. The most popular majors were nursing (26%), social work (22%), and business (20%). In an average class, 51% graduate in 4 years or less, 5% graduate in 5 years or less, and 1% graduate in 6 years or less. Of the 2016 graduating class, 39% were enrolled in graduate school within 6 months of graduation, and 90% were employed.

SERVICES: Counseling and information services are available, as is tutoring in every subject. There is a reader service for the blind, and remedial math, reading, and writing. Individual and group tutoring is available free through the college's academic support services. **Library/Resources:** The library contains 89,846 volumes, and subscribes to 5,811 periodicals including electronic. Computerized library services include interlibrary loans, database searching, Internet access, and Wi-Fi capability. Special learning facilities include an art gallery. **Physically Challenged Students:** 72% of the campus is accessible. Facilities include wheelchair ramps, elevators, special parking, specially equipped restrooms, special class scheduling, lowered drinking fountains, and special housing. **Special:** There are co-op programs with other members of the Rochester Area Colleges Consortium. The college offers internships, study abroad, a Washington semester, dual majors, and student-designed majors. Credit is also given by exam and for work experience. There are 11 national honor societies. **Visiting:** There are regularly scheduled orientations for prospective students, including a pesentation by a Division Leader, Breakout Sessions based on discipline, and campus tours. There are guides for informal visits; visitors may sit in on classes and stay overnight. **Campus Safety and Security:** Measures include 24-hour foot and vehicle patrol, an emergency notification system, and security escort services. There are shuttle buses, emergency telephones, lighted pathways/sidewalks, and controlled access to dorms/residences.

REQUIREMENTS: The SAT or ACT is recommended. The GED is accepted AP and CLEP credits are accepted. Important factors in the admissions decision are advanced placement or honors courses, extracurricular activities record, and leadership record. Students must complete 1 field period combining academic study and professional experience for each year of enrollment. The core curriculum consists of 43 to 46 credits, including but not limited to required courses in physical education, computer science, and integrative studies. A total of 120 credit hours is required for graduation with a minimum of 30 credits in the major and a major and cumulative GPA of 2.0. **Procedure:** Freshmen are admitted in the fall and spring. There are deferred admissions and rolling admissions plans. Application deadlines are open. Notification is sent on a rolling basis. Applications are accepted online. **Transfer Students:** 373 transfer students enrolled in 2016-2017. Applicants must take the SAT or ACT and submit transcripts. An interview is recommended. A minimum GPA of 2.5 is required in college work. 30 of 120 credits required for the bachelor's degree must be completed at KC. **International Students:** There are 54 international students enrolled. They must take the TOEFL with a minimum score of 59 on the Internet-based version (iBT).

Admissions Contact: Megan Perkins, Director of Admissions. Email: *admissions@keuka.edu* Web: *www.keuka.edu*

FINANCIAL AID: In 2017-2018, 98% of all full-time freshmen received some form of financial aid. 95% of all full-time freshmen received need-based aid. The average freshman award was $26,408. Need-based scholarships or need-based grants averaged $9,280; need-based self-help aid (loans and jobs) averaged $5,092; and other non-need-based awards and non-need-based scholarships averaged $13,303. 65% of undergraduate students work part-time. The average financial indebtedness of the 2017 graduate was $20,156. The college's own financial statement is required. The FAFSA code is 002744. The priority date for freshman financial aid applications for fall entry is March 15.

LE MOYNE COLLEGE C-3
www.lemoyne.edu

Syracuse, NY 13214 (315) 445-4300 (800) 333-4733
Fax: (315) 445-4711 **Email:** admission@lemoyne.edu

Full-time: 1033 men, 1377 women	**Faculty:** 152; IIA, av$
Part-time: 92 men, 286 women	**Ph.D.s:** 89%
Graduate: 182 men, 461 women	**Student/Faculty:** 16 to 1
Year: semesters, summer session	**Tuition:** $33,905
Room & Board: $13,400	**Freshman Class:** 7429 applied, 4751 accepted, 545 enrolled
SAT CR/M: 585/590 **ACT:** 25	**CEEB CODE:** 2366
Application Deadline: February 1	**VERY COMPETITIVE**

Le Moyne College, founded in 1946, is a private liberal arts and sciences institution affiliated with the Roman Catholic Society of Jesus (Jesuit) offering undergraduate and graduate degrees in a variety of disciplines. There is 1 undergraduate school and 3 graduate schools. In addition to regional accreditation, Le Moyne has baccalaureate program accreditation with AACSB, CCNE, and ACS. The 161-acre campus is in a suburban area on the eastern edge of Syracuse. Including any residence halls, there are 49 buildings.

STUDENT LIFE: 94% of undergraduates are from New York. Others are from 22 states, 46 foreign countries, and Canada. 82% are from public schools. 77% are White; 6% African American; 6% race unknown; 5% Hispanic; 3% Asian American; 2% two or more races; 1% Foreign. 41% are Catholic; 38% claim no religious affiliation; 11% Protestant. **Female To Male Ratio:** 1.6:1. The average age of freshmen is 18; all undergraduates, 21. 16% do not continue beyond their first year; 74% remain to graduate.**Housing:** 1609 students can be accommodated in college housing, which includes single-sex dorms, coed dorms, on-campus apartments, and off-campus apartments. In addition, there are special-interest houses, and living learning communities. On-campus housing is guaranteed for all 4 years, and is available on a first-come, first-served basis, and is available on a lottery system for upperclassmen. 58% of students live on campus. All students may keep cars.

FACULTY/CLASSROOMS: 55% of faculty are male; 45% are female. 92% teach undergraduates, and 90% do research. No introductory courses are taught by graduate students. The average class size in an introductory lecture is 23; in a laboratory is 16; and in a regular course is 20.

PROGRAMS OF STUDY: Le Moyne confers B.A. and B.S. degrees. Master's degrees are also awarded. Bachelor's degrees are awarded in BIOLOGICAL SCIENCE (biochemistry, biology/biological science, and ecology), BUSINESS (accounting, banking and finance, finance, human resources, management information systems, marketing, marketing management, operations management, organizational leadership and management, and professional studies), COMMUNICATIONS AND THE ARTS (communications, creative writing, dramatic arts, English, French, literature, Spanish, and theatre arts), COMPUTER AND PHYSICAL SCIENCE (actuarial science, applied mathematics, chemistry, computer programming, computer science, cyber intelligence/security studies, information sciences and systems, mathematics, physical sciences, physics, science, and statistics), EDUCATION (elementary education, English education, foreign languages education, mathematics education, science education, secondary education, social studies education, special education, and teaching English as a second/foreign language (TESOL/TEFOL), ENGINEERING AND ENVIRONMENTAL DESIGN (environmental science and preengineering), HEALTH PROFESSIONS (nursing, predentistry, premedicine, preoptometry, prepharmacy, prepodiatry, and preveterinary science), SOCIAL SCIENCE (anthropology, criminology, economics, history, human services, international relations, international studies, peace studies, philosophy, political science/government, prelaw, psychology, religion, religious studies, and sociology). Biology, psychology, nursing and accounting, are the strongest academically, and have the largest enrollments.

ACTIVITIES: There are no fraternities or sororities. There are 98 groups on campus, including art, band, cheerleading, choir, chorale, chorus, communications, computers, dance, drama, environmental, ethnic, film, honors, international, jazz band, LGBT, literary magazine, musical theater, newspaper, orchestra, photography, political, professional, radio and TV, religious, social, social service, student government, symphony, and yearbook. Popular campus events include Spring Olympics, Halloween Dance, Spring Semi-Formal, Senior Week Activities, Fall Fest, Earth Jam, Welcome Week, Le Moyne's Got Talent, Martin Luther King Celebration, Cultural Banquets and Cultural Extravaganza. **Sports:** There are 10 intercollegiate sports for men and 11 for women, and 12 intramural sports for men and 12 for women. Facilities include a gym, an athletic weight room, a 25-yard lap pool with diving board, a fitness center, an athletic training room, jogging track, racquetball courts, fitness studio, and a recreational gym. Outdoor facilities include fields for intercollegiate baseball, softball, soccer, and lacrosse, a cross-country trail, and several intramural and club sports fields. **Graduates:** From July 1, 2016 to June 30, 2017, 642 bachelor's degrees were awarded. The most popular majors were biology (19%), psychology (14%), and nursing (12%). In an average class, 61% graduate in 4 years or less, 72% graduate in 5 years or less, and 74% graduate in 6 years or less. Of the 2016 graduating class, 30% were enrolled in graduate school within 6 months of graduation, and 28% were employed.

SERVICES: Counseling and information services are available, as is tutoring in some subjects, such as math, biology, chemistry, physics, economics, philosophy, Spanish, French, German, Latin, Arabic, history, Japanese, Italian, Chinese, psychology, finance, statistics, computer science and business analytics. There is a reader service for the blind, and remedial math and writing. Study groups are also available for selected courses, and writing tutor support for all subjects. **Library/Resources:** The library contains 229,569 volumes, 626,471 microform items, 10,771 audio/video tapes/CDs/DVDs, and subscribes to 167,846 periodicals, including electronic. Computerized library services include interlibrary loans, database searching, Internet access, and Wi-Fi capability. Special learning facilities include an art gallery, a radio station, a TV station, the W.Carroll Coyne Performing Arts Center, a media center, Student Success Center, Quantitative Reasoning Center and a Writing Center. **Physically Challenged Students:** 98% of the campus is accessible. Facilities include wheelchair ramps, elevators, special parking, specially equipped restrooms, lowered drinking fountains, lowered telephones, special housing, automatic door openers, strobe fire alarm system, wheelchair tables in classrooms, and braille signage. **Special:** Internships are available to students in all majors. A campus work-study program, study abroad in 16 countries, dual majors, and a Washington semester are offered. Accelerated Bachelor's/Master's Degree Collaborations in engineering, computer science, communication, public administration, information management, library and information sciences, forensic science with Syracuse University; a 3+3 Bachelor's and Law arrangement with Syracuse University; as well as Accelerated Bachelor's/Master's Degree and early assurance collaborative arrangements in medical, dental, podiatry and optometry fields of graduate study with other partner institutions, e.g., a DPT with Upstate Medical University, dental with University of Buffalo and accelerated entry into Physician Assistant Studies. There are 17 national honor societies, a freshman honors program, and 15 departmental honors programs. **Visiting:** There are regularly scheduled orientations for prospective students, including a campus tour and an interview with admissions counselors. Accepted students are invited to attend class, meet with faculty and stay overnight in a residence hall. There are guides for informal visits; visitors may sit in on classes and stay overnight. To schedule a visit, contact the Admission Office. **Campus Safety and Security:** Measures include 24-hour foot and vehicle patrol, an emergency notification system, self-defense education, and security escort services. There are shuttle buses, emergency telephones, lighted pathways/sidewalks, controlled access to dorms/residences, 9 blue light security phones, 200 stationary closed-circuit security cameras, campuswide card access, and 15 pan tilt zoom closed-circuit security cameras.

REQUIREMENTS: Students should graduate from an accredited high school having completed 17 academic units that include 4 in English and social studies, 3 to 4 each in math and science, and 3 in foreign language. A personal statement and letters of recommendation from a teacher and a counselor are required. AP and CLEP credits are accepted. Important factors in the admissions decision are recommendations by school officials, advanced placement or honors courses, and extracurricular activities record. A core curriculum of courses in the humanities, natural sciences, and social sciences is required. Students must earn a GPA of 2.0 overall and in their major, and complete one half of their major in residence and a minimum of 120 total credit hours to graduate. **Procedure:** Freshmen are admitted in the fall and spring. Entrance exams should be taken in the spring of the junior year or fall of the senior year. There are early admissions, deferred admissions, and rolling admissions plans. Applications should be filed by February 1 for fall entry; December 1 for spring entry. Notification is sent on a rolling basis. 142 applicants were on the 2017 waiting list; 50 were admitted. Applications are accepted online. **Transfer Students:** 241 transfer students enrolled in 2016-2017. A 2.6 GPA is required for admission to most programs. A completed application for transfer admission, official college transcripts, and a personal statement must be submitted. Official high school transcripts if fewer than 24 college credits completed. SAT or ACT scores are now optional for students with fewer than 24 college credits. 30 of 120 credits required for the bachelor's degree must be completed at Le Moyne. **International Students:** There are 35 international students enrolled. They must take the TOEFL with a minimum score of 550 on the paper-based TOEFL (PBT) or 79 on the Internet-based version (iBT). They must also take the SAT or ACT.

ADMISSIONS: 64% of the 2017-2018 applicants were accepted. The SAT scores for the 2017-2018 freshman class were: Critical Reading-- 4% below 500, 55% between 500 and 599, 37% between 600 and 699, and 4% between 700 and 800. Math-- 4% below 500, 53% between 500 and 599, 39% between 600 and 699, and 4% between 700 and 800. The ACT scores were 45% between 18 and 23, 50% between 24 and 29, and 5% above 30. 43% of the current freshmen were in the top fifth of their class; 75% were in the top two fifths. 6 freshmen graduated first in their class. **Admissions Contact:** Mary M. Chandler, Senior. Director of Admission. Email: *admission@lemoyne.edu* Web: *www.lemoyne.edu*

FINANCIAL AID: In 2017-2018, 97% of all full-time freshmen received some form of financial aid. 84% of all full-time freshmen received need-based aid. The average freshman award was $27,000. Need-based scholarships or need-based grants averaged $22,747 ($48,205 maximum); need-based self-help aid (loans and jobs) averaged $4,148 ($9,500 maximum); non-need-based athletic scholarships averaged $12,525 ($48,605 maximum); and other non-need-based awards and non-need-based scholarships averaged $16,061 ($25,000 maximum). 40% of undergraduate students work part-time. The average financial indebtedness of the 2017 graduate was $28,440. Le Moyne is a member of CSS. The state aid form is required. The FAFSA code is 002748. The deadline for filing freshman financial aid applications for fall entry is February 15.

LIM COLLEGE *(The complete profile is made available exclusively on our website, www.barronspac.com)*

LIST COLLEGE/THE JEWISH THEOLOGICAL SEMINARY (JTS) *(The complete profile is made available exclusively on our website, www.barronspac.com)*

LIU BROOKLYN — D-5
www.liu.edu/brooklyn

Brooklyn, NY 11201 — **(718) 488-1011**

Fax: (718) 780-6110
Full-time: 1001 men, 2361 women
Part-time: 165 men, 418 women
Graduate: 881 men, 2158 women
Year: semesters, summer session
Room & Board: $13,720

Email: bkln-admissions@liu.edu
Faculty: 166
Ph.D.s: 90%
Student/Faculty: 20 to 1
Tuition: $36,978
Freshman Class: 6830 applied, 5755 accepted, 674 enrolled

SAT EBR-W/M: 560/560 **ACT:** 23
Application Deadline: rolling

CEEB CODE: 2369
COMPETITIVE

LIU Brooklyn, a comprehensive, private university, offers more than 200 academic programs through its school of health professions, school of nursing, college of liberal arts and sciences, school of education, school of arts and communication, school of business, public administration, and information sciences, honors college, college of pharmacy and health sciences, and school of professional and continuing studies. In addition to 19 championship award-winning NCAA Division I athletics teams and a vibrant campus life, the University is home to the internationally acclaimed George Polk Awards, one of the most coveted honors in investigative journalism. There are 8 undergraduate schools and 7 graduate schools. In addition to regional accreditation, LIU Brooklyn has baccalaureate program accreditation with ACPE, CSWE, CAEP, AACN, AOTA, and CAAHEP. The 11-acre campus is in an urban area in Brooklyn, NY. Including any residence halls, there are 11 buildings.

STUDENT LIFE: 85% of undergraduates are from New York. Others are from 37 states, 41 foreign countries, and Canada. 78% are from public schools. 3% are Foreign; 23% African American; 22% White; 2% two or more races; 18% race unknown; 16% Asian American; 16% Hispanic. **Female To Male Ratio:** 2.4:1. The average age of freshmen is 18; all undergraduates, 23. 35% do not continue beyond their first year; 33% remain to graduate. **Housing:** 652 students can be accommodated in college housing, which includes dorms and on-campus apartments. On-campus housing is guaranteed for all 4 years, and is available on a first-come, first-served basis. 86% of students commute. No one may keep cars.

FACULTY/CLASSROOMS: 46% of faculty are male; 54% are female. No introductory courses are taught by graduate students.

PROGRAMS OF STUDY: LIU-Brooklyn confers B.A., B.S., and B.F.A. degrees. Associate, master's, and doctoral degrees are also awarded. Bachelor's degrees are awarded in BIOLOGICAL SCIENCE (biochemistry, biology/adolescence education, and biology/biological science), BUSINESS (accounting, business administration and management, entrepreneurial studies, finance, marketing, and sports management), COMMUNICATIONS AND THE ARTS (communication science, dance, digital communications, English, fine arts, French, journalism, media arts, music performance, Spanish, communication arts-speech, studio art, and visual and performing arts), COMPUTER AND PHYSICAL SCIENCE (chemistry, chemistry/adolescence education, computer information technology, computer science, information sciences and systems, mathematics, and physics), EDUCATION (art education, athletic training, early childhood education, elementary education, English education, mathematics education, middle school education, music education, physical education, science education, secondary education, and social studies education), HEALTH PROFESSIONS (clinical science, diagnostic medical sonography, health care administration, health science, kinesiology, nursing, occupational therapy, pharmacy, public health, and respiratory therapy), SOCIAL SCIENCE (economics, history, humanities, interdisciplinary studies, philosophy, political science/government, psychology, social science, social work, and sociology). Pharmacy, health sciences, and nursing are the strongest academically and have the largest enrollments.

ACTIVITIES: 11% of men belong to 6 national fraternities; 5% of women belong to 5 national sororities. There are 65 groups on campus, including art, band, choir, chorale, chorus, communications, computers, dance, debate, drama, environmental, ethnic, film, honors, international, jazz band, LGBT, literary magazine, newspaper, pep band, political, professional, radio and TV, religious, social, social service, student government, and yearbook. Popular campus events include Homecoming Week, LIU Blackbird Madness, Relay for Life, Holiday Party for Kids, LIU Spring Concert, LIU Spring Week - LIU Pep Rally, LIU Gives Back Month, Last Class Bash, Midnight Breakfast, Welcome Week, and Culture Fest. **Sports:** There are 5 intercollegiate sports for men and 12 for women, and 3 intramural sports for men and 3 for women. Facilities include a Wellness Center which has a swimming pool, therapy pool, an arena, a campus fitness center, workout and track facilities, and health and fitness programs, as well as a multi-sport facility for baseball, softball, soccer, field hockey, and lacrosse programs. **Graduates:** From July 1, 2016 to June 30, 2017, 989 bachelor's degrees were awarded. The most popular majors were health professions (71%), business/marketing (7%), and biological/life sciences (6%). In an average class, 15% graduate in 4 years or less, 22% graduate in 5 years or less, and 31% graduate in 6 years or less.

SERVICES: Counseling and information services are available, as is tutoring in every subject. There is a reader service for the blind, and remedial math, reading, and writing. **Library/Resources:** The library contains 545,709 volumes, 277,866 microform items, 29,019 audio/video tapes/CDs/DVDs, and subscribes to 466,233 periodicals, including electronic. Computerized library services include interlibrary loans, database searching, Internet access, and Wi-Fi capability. Special learning facilities include an art gallery, a radio station, a TV station, Honors College: A school for highly motivated students seeking challenging academics. Kumble Theater for the Performing Arts: a performance venue that welcomes artistic exploration for students and features world-renowned performance artists from the areas of dance, music, and theater. Student-Run Businesses: These fully functional business operations afford students unique experiential learning opportunities as they make executive-level decisions. They include: Browse: A high-tech, Apple-licensed technology store, with "Genius Bar" customer service that employs students; Student Innovation Incubator: A physical and virtual workspace for students to launch startup businesses and collaborate with successful entrepreneurs; Wall Street Trading Floor: Featuring Bloomberg terminals and other business technology, this simulated trading floor empowers students to utilize the latest financial tools and learn in a real-time trading environment. LIU Pharmacy students have access to four state-of-the-art research institutes: The Lachman Institute for Pharmaceutical Analysis provides opportunities for industry-supported research; The Joan B. and Samuel J. Williamson Institute for Pharmacometrics trains students to use computer-based predictive models of drug safety and efficacy; The Natoli Engineering Institute for Industrial Pharmacy Development and Research welcomes industry scientists to partner with academia to research solid dosage forms and instrumentation; and the Cancer Research program, which consists of several laboratories with equipment and core facilities in support of cancer research and anticancer drug discovery and development. **Physically Challenged Students:** 95% of the campus is accessible. Facilities include wheelchair ramps, elevators, special parking, specially equipped restrooms, special class scheduling, lowered drinking fountains, lowered telephones, and special housing. **Special:** Paid internships help students build a resume while still in classes. Study abroad options include Europe, Asia, China, Australia and many other locations. LIU Global offers study options in several locations around the world. Dual majors, accelerated degrees, and a nationally recognized Honors College help motivated students shape a challenging academic schedule. The Arthur O. Eve Higher Education Opportunity Program is specially designed for New York State residents who are economically and educationally disadvantaged. LIU Promise is the University's commitment to assist students with their personal Success Coach who advises them from admission to graduation. A wide range of support services include tutoring, academic advisement, financial aid, career, and personal counseling. There is a freshman honors program. **Visiting:** There are regularly scheduled orientations for prospective students, including a guided campus tour, admissions overview, meet-and-greet with faculty and deans, interacting with student leaders, attending mini classes, becoming a student for a day, and touring our student-run businesses and high tech incubator. **Campus Safety and Security:** Measures include 24-hour foot and vehicle patrol, an emergency notification system, and security escort services. There are emergency telephones, lighted pathways/sidewalks, controlled access to dorms/residences, and in-room safes.

REQUIREMENTS: Average GPA: 87, SAT 1075, and ACT 22. High school students seeking admission to LIU Brooklyn are expected to have completed a college preparatory program includes 4 years of English, 3 years each of math, social studies, and science, and 2 years of foreign language. Students must also submit the following: completed application for admission, official high school transcript or evidence of completion of high school graduation requirements (GED), non-refundable application fee, tests results from the SAT or ACT (school codes: ACT-2687; SAT-2070), personal statement/essay, and letters of recommendation from high school teacher or guidance counselor. Students applying for admission to programs in the performing arts must also schedule an audition through the department AP and CLEP credits are accepted. General Requirements for Graduation: 2.00 cumulative average (higher in some areas) and 120 credits. Core requirements are 33-34 credits including options of English Composition, laboratory sciences, history, philosophy, literature, foreign language, arts, economics, political science, anthropology, geography, psychology, sociology, and mathematics. **Procedure:** Freshmen are admitted in the fall and spring. Entrance exams should be taken by Spring 2018. There are early admissions, deferred admissions, and rolling admissions plans. Application deadlines are open. The fall 2017 application fee was $50. Notification is sent on a rolling basis. Applications are accepted online. **Transfer Students:** 603 transfer students enrolled in 2016-2017. A high school GPA or college

GPA of 2.0 is required. Some programs require a 2.75-3.0 minimum GPA. 32 of 120 credits required for the bachelor's degree must be completed at LIU-Brooklyn. **International Students:** There are 129 international students enrolled. They must take the TOEFL with a minimum score of 527 on the paper-based TOEFL (PBT) or 75 on the Internet-based version (iBT). They must also take the SAT or ACT.

ADMISSIONS: The SAT scores for the 2017-2018 freshman class were: Math-- 23% below 500, 40% between 500 and 599, 28% between 600 and 699, and 9% between 700 and 800. Evidence-Based Reading/Writing-- 21% below 500, 45% between 500 and 599, 30% between 600 and 699, and 4% between 700 and 800. The ACT scores were 12% between 12 and 17, 41% between 18 and 23, 38% between 24 and 29, and 9% above 30. 1 freshman graduated first in the class. **Admissions Contact:** Luis Santiago, Dean of Enrollment. Email: *bkln-admissions@liu.edu* Web: *www.liu.edu/brooklyn*

FINANCIAL AID: In 2017-2018, 91% of all full-time freshmen received some form of financial aid. 67% of all full-time freshmen received need-based aid. The average freshman award was $15,038. Need-based scholarships or need-based grants averaged $3,987 ($7,674 maximum); need-based self-help aid (loans and jobs) averaged $6,409 ($26,270 maximum); non-need-based athletic scholarships averaged $14,672 ($45,676 maximum); and other non-need-based awards and non-need-based scholarships averaged $9,325 ($24,062 maximum). The average financial indebtedness of the 2017 graduate was $66,138. LIU-Brooklyn is a member of CSS. The the state aid form is required. The FAFSA code is 2751. The priority date for freshman financial aid applications for fall entry is February 15.

LIU POST — D-5

www.liu.edu/post

Brookville, NY 11548	**(516) 299-2900**
Fax: (516) 299-2137	**Email: post-enroll@liu.edu**
Full-time: 1140 men, 1683 women	**Faculty:** 180
Part-time: 1434 men, 2059 women	**Ph.D.s:** 90%
Graduate: 533 men, 1650 women	**Student/Faculty:** 16 to 1
Year: semesters, summer session	**Tuition:** $36,978
Room & Board: $13,720	**Freshman Class:** 6951 applied, 5748 accepted, 694 enrolled
SAT EBR-W/M: 570/570 **ACT:** 24	**CEEB CODE:** 2070
Application Deadline: rolling	**COMPETITIVE+**

LIU Post, a comprehensive, private university, offers more than 250 academic programs through its school of computer science, innovation and management engineering, school of business, school of professional accountancy, school of visual arts, communications and digital technologies, school of performing arts, college of education, information and technology, college of liberal arts and sciences, school of health professions and nursing, and honors college. LIU Post students receive all of the resources of a major university, with world-class faculty that includes Fulbright fellows, a vibrant campus life, numerous experiential learning opportunities, and 25 championship award-winning NCAA Division II athletic teams. There are 8 undergraduate schools and 8 graduate schools. In addition to regional accreditation, LIU Post has baccalaureate program accreditation with AACSB, CSWE, CAEP, AACN, JRCERT, and NAACLS. The 308-acre campus is in a suburban area in Nassau County on Long Island, 25 miles east of New York City. Including any residence halls, there are 46 buildings.

STUDENT LIFE: 94% of undergraduates are from New York. Others are from 38 states, 28 foreign countries, and Canada. 89% are from public schools. 6% are African American; 6% Asian American; 53% White; 3% Foreign; 2% two or more races; 18% race unknown; 12% Hispanic. **Female To Male Ratio:** 1.7:1. The average age of freshmen is 18; all undergraduates, 19. 20% do not continue beyond their first year; 49% remain to graduate. **Housing:** 1381 students can be accommodated in college housing, which includes dorms, international student housing, disabled student housing, fraternity/sorority housing, and theme housing. On-campus housing is guaranteed for all 4 years, and is available on a first-come, first-served basis. 70% of students commute. All students may keep cars.

FACULTY/CLASSROOMS: 46% of faculty are male; 54% are female. No introductory courses are taught by graduate students.

PROGRAMS OF STUDY: LIU Post confers B.A., B.F.A., B.S., and B.M. degrees. Associate, master's, and doctoral degrees are also awarded. Bachelor's degrees are awarded in BIOLOGICAL SCIENCE (biology/adolescence education, biology/biological science, and nutrition), BUSINESS (accounting, business administration and management, fashion merchandising, marketing/retailing/merchandising, and sports management), COMMUNICATIONS AND THE ARTS (art, art history and appreciation, arts administration/management, dance, dramatic arts, English, film arts, fine arts, foreign language, French, game design and development, Italian, journalism, music performance, photography, public relations, radio/television technology, Spanish, theatre arts, and vocal performance), COMPUTER AND PHYSICAL SCIENCE (applied mathematics, chemistry, chemistry/adolescence education, computer information technology, computer science, digital arts/technology, earth science / adolescence education, geology, information sciences and systems, mathematics, physics, and radiological technology), EDUCATION (art education, early childhood education, elementary education, English education, foreign languages education, health education, mathematics education, music education, physical education, social studies education, and Spanish adolescense education), HEALTH PROFESSIONS (art therapy, biomedical science, clinical science, health care administration, health science, medical laboratory technology, nursing, and speech pathology/audiology), SOCIAL SCIENCE (American studies, criminal justice, economics, forensic studies, geography, history, international studies, liberal arts, sciences, general studies, humanities, philosophy, political science/government, psychology, public administration, social work, and sociology). Business administration, health sciences, and nursing are the strongest academically. Business administration, health sciences, and nursing have the largest enrollments.

ACTIVITIES: 8% of men belong to 4 national fraternities; 11% of women belong to 4 national sororities. There are 68 groups on campus, including art, band, cheerleading, choir, chorale, chorus, computers, dance, drama, environmental, ethnic, film, forensics, honors, international, LGBT, literary magazine, marching band, musical theater, newspaper, pep band, photography, political, professional, radio and TV, religious, social, social service, student government, and yearbook. Popular campus events include Homecoming and Spirit Week, Midnight Madness, Founder's Day, Move-a-thon, Holidays at Hillwood, Pratt After Dark, Relay for Life, Midnight Breakfast, LIU Gives Back Month, Spring Concert, and Senior Week. **Sports:** There are 8 intercollegiate sports for men and 15 for women, and 11 intramural sports for men and 10 for women. The Pratt Recreation Center is a health and fitness facility featuring an eight-lane swimming pool, basketball courts, racquetball courts, and an elevated jogging track. The University's field hockey and lacrosse teams play at Bethpage Federal Credit Union Stadium, with additional fields for soccer, baseball, and softball, as well as multiple tennis courts.**Graduates:** From July 1, 2016 to June 30, 2017, 771 bachelor's degrees were awarded. The most popular majors were health professions (25%), business/marketing (16%), and education (8%). In an average class, 39% graduate in 4 years or less, 50% graduate in 5 years or less, and 47% graduate in 6 years or less.

SERVICES: Counseling and information services are available, as is tutoring in every subject. There is a reader service for the blind, and remedial math, reading, and writing. **Library/Resources:** The library contains 871,484 volumes, 406,510 microform items, 23,135 audio/video tapes/CDs/DVDs, and subscribes to 466,715 periodicals, including electronic. Computerized library services include interlibrary loans, database searching, Internet access, and Wi-Fi capability. Special learning facilities include an art gallery, a radio station, a TV station, the Tilles Center for the Performing Arts, a concert hall that features a wide range of dance, music, and theater events. Students in the School of Visual and Performing Arts are able to perform alongside world-renowned performers and engage in live stage productions. Student-Run Businesses: These fully functional business operations afford students unique experiential learning opportunities as they make executive-level decisions. They include: Browse: A high-tech, Apple-licensed technology store, with "Genius Bar" customer service that employs students; Post Marketing and PR Agency: A full-service agency managed by students; Student Innovation Incubator: A physical and virtual workspace for students to launch startup businesses and collaborate with successful entrepreneurs; The Student Body Boutique: A trendy clothing boutique that sells the latest fashions at an affordable price; Eateries that include: Hutton and Post, which offers traditional snacks in addition to healthy options; End Zone, a lounge that offers a full menu and HD televisions for watching sports and other entertainment; and Time Out Smoothie Bar, Wall Street Trading Floor: Featuring Bloomberg terminals and other business technology, this simulated trading floor empowers students to utilize the latest financial tools and learn in a real-time trading environment, home to the University's student-run LIU-iF Investment Fund; Student Innovation Incubator: A physical and virtual workspace for students to launch startup businesses and collaborate with successful entrepreneurs; Equestrian Stables: North Shore Equestrian Center houses the LIU Post Equine Studies program, offering a large indoor arena, and two spacious outdoor rings. **Physically Challenged Students:** 80% of the campus is accessible. Facilities include wheelchair ramps, elevators, special parking, specially equipped restrooms, special class scheduling, lowered drinking fountains, lowered telephones, and special housing. **Special:** LIU Post offers a wide range of special academic program to enhance the student's overall experience. Programs across every discipline are focused on experiential learning giving our students opportunities to develop the confidence and real-world experience that will be beneficial to their development and careers. Experiential learning opportunities include our LIU Incubator, LIU-IQ Consulting, Hornstein Center for Policy, Polling and Analysis, LIU's Interprofessional Simulation Center, Post Theatre Company and Student-run Businesses – all cultivating hands-on experience before graduation! LIU Global is a four-year cultural immersion program that allows students to earn their degree while traveling the world, also serving as an arm for study abroad programs for all LIU students across every campus. Our LIU Promise Office ensures that all our students reach their full potential. The LIU Promise is our commitment to ensuring our students have the right tools, guidance and support to achieve their goals. Every incoming student is assigned an LIU Promise Success Coach who will provide individualized mentorship and holistic counseling for all four years of study. Additionally, we offer a distinguished honors program, equestrian center, career readiness workshop, collaborative learning communities and many other opportunities. There are a freshman honors program. **Visiting:** There are regularly scheduled orientations for prospective students, events include a guided campus tour, admissions overview, a meet-and-greet with faculty & deans, interacting with student leaders, attending mini classes, becoming a student for a day, and touring our student-run businesses and high tech incubato. There are guides for informal visits and visitors may sit in on classes. **Campus Safety and Security:** Measures include 24-hour foot and vehicle patrol, emergency notification system, and security escort services. There are shuttle buses, emergency telephones, lighted pathways/sidewalks, and controlled access to dorms/residences.

REQUIREMENTS: All high school students seeking admission to LIU Post must have a solid "B" average (82-85), a minimum math and critical thinking combined SAT score of 1050 or a minimum ACT score of a 20 composite, personal statement/essay, and one letter of recommendation from high school teacher or guidance counselor. Students applying to selected programs in the arts must successfully complete a department audition or portfolio review. Students who have completed the GED and have not attended any other university may apply as a first-time student. LIU accepts and reviews applications on a rolling basis, allowing candidates to apply at any time during the year. However, to ensure consideration for all available scholarships and on-campus housing opportunities, it is strongly recommended that freshman applications be submitted by December 1 for fall admission and by October 1 for spring admission. AP and CLEP credits are accepted. General Requirements for Graduation: 2.00 cumulative average (higher in some areas), 2.00 minor subject average (higher in some areas) if attempted, core and major requirements fulfilled, and minor requirements if attempted, 120 credits (more in some departments), writing across the curriculum courses 3-5 depending on admissions status, and minimum liberal arts requirements (varies depending on degree being earned). **Procedure:** Freshmen are admitted in the fall and spring. Entrance exams should be taken by Spring 2018. There are early admissions, deferred admissions, and rolling admissions plans. Check with the school for current application deadlines. The fall 2017 application fee was $50. Notification is sent on a rolling basis. Applications are accepted on-line. **Transfer Students:** 462 transfer students enrolled in 2016-2017. A high school GPA of 2.5 or college GPA of 2.0 is required. 32 of 120 credits required for the bachelor's degree must be completed at LIU Post. **International Students:** There are 193 international students enrolled. They must take the TOEFL with a minimum score of 550 on the paper-based TOEFL (PBT) or 75 on the Internet-based version (iBT). They must also take the SAT or ACT.

ADMISSIONS: The SAT scores for the 2017-2018 freshman class were: Math-- 12% below 500, 53% between 500 and 599, 31% between 600 and 699, and 4% between 700 and 800. Evidence-Based Reading/ Writing-- 9% below 500, 54% between 500 and 599, 33% between 600 and 699, and 4% between 700 and 800. 1 freshman graduated first in the class. **Admissions Contact:** Anne Marie Caradonna, Director of Admissions Operations. Email: *post-enroll@liu.edu* Web: *www.liu.edu/post*

FINANCIAL AID: In 2017-2018, 95% of all full-time freshmen received some form of financial aid. 51% of all full-time freshmen received need-based aid. The average freshman award was $16,082. Need-based scholarships or need-based grants averaged $4,066 ($17,103 maximum); need-based self-help aid (loans and jobs) averaged $7,361 ($26,321 maximum); non-need-based athletic scholarships averaged $6,621 ($25,749 maximum); and other non-need-based awards and non-need-based scholarships averaged $10,456 ($19,652 maximum). The average financial indebtedness of the 2017 graduate was $43,771. LIU-Post is a member of CSS. The state aid form is required. The FAFSA code is 2751. The priority date for freshman financial aid applications for fall entry is February 15.

MANHATTAN COLLEGE D-5
www.manhattan.edu

Riverdale, NY 10471	(718) 862-7200 (800) 622-9235
Fax: (718) 862-8019	Email: admit@manhattan.edu
Full-time: 1713 men, 1428 women	**Faculty:** n/av
Part-time: 151 men, 59 women	**Ph.D.s:** 93%
Graduate: 196 men, 253 women	**Student/Faculty:** 12 to 1
Year: semesters, summer session	**Tuition:** $40,052
Room & Board: $15,600	**Freshman Class:** 6546 applied, 4555 accepted, 842 enrolled
SAT CR/M/W: 526/535/528 **ACT:** 24	**CEEB CODE:** 2395
Application Deadline: March 1	**COMPETITIVE**

Manhattan College, founded in 1853, offers an exceptional college education enriched by Lasallian Catholic values and access to New York City. MC's faculty and students are committed to the lifelong pursuit of academic excellence, career achievement, and reflection on values, ethics and principles. There are 6 undergraduate schools and 4 graduate schools. In addition to regional accreditation, MC has baccalaureate program accreditation with AACSB, ABET, AHEA, and CAHEA. The 22-acre campus is in an urban area in Riverdale, NY, 10 miles north of midtown Manhattan. Including any residence halls, there are 21 buildings.

STUDENT LIFE: 75% of undergraduates are from New York. Others are from 32 states, 37 foreign countries, and Canada. 60% are from public schools. 60% are White; 4% African American; 3% Asian American; 19% Hispanic; 1% Foreign. 55% are Catholic. **Male To Female Ratio:** 1.2:1. The average age of freshmen is 18; all undergraduates, 23. 12% do not continue beyond their first year; 75% remain to graduate. **Housing:** 2095 students can be accommodated in college housing, which includes dorms, on-campus apartments, and off-campus apartments. In addition, there are special-interest houses, and a living learning environment. On-campus housing is guaranteed for all 4 years. 75% of students live on campus. All students may keep cars.

FACULTY/CLASSROOMS: 60% of faculty are male; 40% are female. All teach undergraduates, 80% do research and teach. No introductory courses are taught by graduate students. The average class size in an introductory lecture is 15 and in a regular course is 22.

PROGRAMS OF STUDY: MC confers B.A., B.S., and B.S.E. degrees. Associate and master's degrees are also awarded. Bachelor's degrees are awarded in BIOLOGICAL SCIENCE (biochemistry and biology/ biological science), BUSINESS (accounting, banking and finance, business economics, international business management, labor studies, and marketing/retailing/merchandising), COMMUNICATIONS AND THE ARTS (broadcasting, communications, English, French, journalism, and Spanish), COMPUTER AND PHYSICAL SCIENCE (chemistry, computer science, information sciences and systems, mathematics, and physics), EDUCATION (early childhood education, education, education of the emotionally handicapped, elementary education, foreign languages education, health education, middle school education, physical education, science education, secondary education, and special education), ENGINEERING AND ENVIRONMENTAL DESIGN (chemical engineering, civil engineering, electrical/electronics engineering, environmental engineering, and mechanical engineering), HEALTH PROFESSIONS (predentistry, premedicine, and radiological science), SOCIAL SCIENCE (economics, history, peace studies, philosophy, political science/government, prelaw, psychology, religion, sociology, and urban studies). Engineering, and business are the strongest academically. Engineering, business, and liberal arts have the largest enrollments.

ACTIVITIES: 3% of men belong to 2 local and 1 national fraternities; 1% of women belong to 2 local sororities. There are 70 groups on campus, including bagpipe, cheerleading, choir, chorus, computers, dance, debate, drama, ethnic, honors, international, jazz band, literary magazine, musical theater, newspaper, orchestra, pep band, political, professional, radio and TV, religious, social, social service, student government, and yearbook. Popular campus events include Annual Springfest, Special Olympics, and Jasper Jingle. **Sports:** There are 8 intercollegiate sports for men and 8 for women, and 7 intramural sports for men and 7 for women. Facilities include a gym with hardwood basketball courts, volleyball, dodge ball, indoor soccer, indoor track, a weight room with free weights and weight lifting machines, a fitness center with cardio machines, a dance studio, turf field for football, soccer, lacrosse, softball and Ultimate Frisbee. **Graduates:** From July 1, 2016 to June 30, 2017, 784 bachelor's degrees were awarded. The most popular majors were civil engineering, communication, management, and childhood education and biology. In an average class, 63% graduate in 4 years or less and 70% graduate in 6 years or less. Of the 2016 graduating class, 18% were enrolled in graduate school within 6 months of graduation, and 65% were employed.

SERVICES: Counseling and information services are available, as is tutoring in every subject. The Center for Academic Success is comprised of three offices with open door policy and extended hours. **Library/Resources:** The library contains 292,438 volumes, 675,489 microform items, 2,676 audio/video tapes/CDs/DVDs, and subscribes to 343 periodicals, including electronic. Computerized library services include interlibrary loans, database searching, Internet access, and Wi-Fi capability. Special learning facilities include a radio station, a research and learning center, 24-hour Internet cafe, Holocaust, Genocide and Interfaith Education Center, and Center for Academic Success. **Physically Challenged Students:** All of the campus is accessible. Facilities include wheelchair ramps, elevators, special parking, specially equipped restrooms, and special housing. **Special:** MC offers credit and noncredit based internships and experiential learning opportunities in for-profit, not-for-profit, social, cultural, educational, religious, government and non-government organizations. Students may enroll in numerous study abroad programs that are offered throughout the world. Five year bachelor's/master's degrees in Business, Education and Engineering are offered and a dual major in international business, credit by exam, and non-degree study are also available. There are 22 national honor societies, Phi Beta Kappa, a freshman honors program, and 28 departmental honors programs. **Visiting:** There are regularly scheduled orientations for prospective students, during 2 days in the summer, which include scheduling, parent workshops, loan seminars, and English and math testing. There are guides for informal visits; visitors may sit in on classes and stay overnight. To schedule a visit, contact the Admission Center. **Campus Safety and Security:** Measures include 24-hour foot and vehicle patrol and an emergency notification system. There are emergency telephones, lighted pathways/sidewalks, and controlled access to dorms/residences.

REQUIREMENTS: The SAT or ACT is required. Applicants must graduate from an accredited secondary school or have earned a GED. 16 academic units are required: 4 of English, 3 each of math and social studies, 2 each of foreign language, lab sciences, and electives. An essay is required and an interview is recommended. AP and CLEP credits are accepted. Important factors in the admissions decision are advanced placement or honors courses, leadership record, and recommendations by school officials. All students must take courses in English composition and literature, religious studies, philosophy, humanities, social science, science, math, and a modern foreign language. About 130 credit hours are required for graduation, with about 36 in the major. The minimum GPA is 2.0. **Procedure:** Freshmen are admitted in the fall and spring. Entrance exams should be taken in the spring of the junior year or the fall of the senior year. There are early decision, deferred admissions, and rolling admissions plans. Early decision applications should be filed by November 15; regular applications, by March 1 for fall entry; and December 1 for spring entry. The fall 2017 application fee was $75. Notification of early decision is sent December 15; regular decision, December 15. 38 early decision candidates were accepted for the 2017-2018 class. 272 applicants were on the 2017 waiting list; 52 were admitted. Applications are accepted online. **Transfer Students:** 143 transfer students enrolled in 2016-2017. Applicants must have a GPA of 2.5 and meet subject course requirements according to their course of study. They must submit transcripts from colleges and high schools attended. An interview is recommended. 66 of 130 credits required for the bachelor's degree must be completed at MC. **International Students:** There are 122 international students enrolled. They must take the TOEFL with a minimum score of 550 on the paper-based TOEFL (PBT) or 80 on the Internet-based version (iBT). Students must take the IELTS, and either the SAT or ACT.

ADMISSIONS: 70% of the 2017-2018 applicants were accepted. The SAT scores for the 2017-2018 freshman class were: Critical Reading-- 38% below 500, 44% between 500 and 599, 16% between 600 and 699, and 2% between 700 and 800. Math-- 29% below 500, 40% between 500 and 599, 27% between 600 and 699, and 4% between 700 and 800. Writing-- 35% below 500, 45% between 500 and 599, 19% between 600 and 699, and 2% between 700 and 800. The ACT scores were 16% below 12, 27% between 12 and 17, 30% between 18 and 23, 12% between 24 and 29, and 15% above 30. **Admissions Contact:** William J. Bisset, Ph.D., Vice President for Enrollment Management. Email: *admit@manhattan.edu* Web: *www.manhattan.edu*

FINANCIAL AID: In 2017-2018, 94% of all full-time freshmen received some form of financial aid and need-based aid. The average freshman award was $22,566. Need-based scholarships or need-based grants averaged $14,551; need-based self-help aid (loans and jobs) averaged $4,900; and non-need-based athletic scholarships averaged $31,336. 26% of undergraduate students work part-time. The average financial indebtedness of the 2017 graduate was $34,375. The college's own financial statement is required. The priority date for freshman financial aid applications for fall entry is February 15.

MANHATTAN SCHOOL OF MUSIC *(The complete profile is made available exclusively on our website, www.barronspac.com)*

MANHATTANVILLE COLLEGE — D-5

www.manhattanville.edu

Purchase, NY 10577 — **(914) 323-5129**

Fax: (914) 694-1732	**Email:** admissions@mville.edu
Full-time: 605 men, 1028 women	**Faculty:** 96
Part-time: 38 men, 55 women	**Ph.D.s:** 86%
Graduate: 286 men, 666 women	**Student/Faculty:** 17 to 1
Year: semesters, summer session	**Tuition:** $37,910
Room & Board: $14,520	**Freshman Class:** 4157 applied, 3325 accepted, 417 enrolled
SAT CR/M/W: 540/528/504 **ACT:** 24	**CEEB CODE:** 2397
Application Deadline: n/av	**COMPETITIVE**

Manhattanville College, founded in 1841, is an independent, coeducational liberal arts institution dedicated to academic excellence, and social and civic action. The college prepares students to be ethical and socially responsible leaders in a global community. The college offers more than 50 undergraduate areas of study that combine in-class learning with on-the-job experiences through access to more than 750 internships ranging from Fortune 500 companies to non-profits, arts and entertainment venues to research opportunities and more. MC also offers graduate programs in education, business, creative writing, as well as continuing and executive education programs. There is 1 undergraduate school and 2 graduate schools. In addition to regional accreditation, MC has baccalaureate program accreditation with IACBE and CAEP. The 100-acre campus is in a suburban area 30 miles north of New York City. Including any residence halls, there are 20 buildings.

STUDENT LIFE: 67% of undergraduates are from New York. Others are from 32 states, 46 foreign countries, and Canada. 9% are race unknown; 7% Foreign; 46% White; 24% Hispanic; 2% Asian American; 2% two or more races; 10% African American. **Female To Male Ratio:** 1.9:1. The average age of freshmen is 18; all undergraduates, 20. 26% do not continue beyond their first year; 55% remain to graduate. **Housing:** 1149 students can be accommodated in college housing, which includes gender neutral and coed dorms. In addition, there are honors houses, wellness and community housing which promotes a substance-free and holistic environment. On-campus housing is guaranteed for all 4 years, and is available on a first-come, first-served basis, and is available on a lottery system for upperclassmen. 58% of students live on campus. All students may keep cars.

FACULTY/CLASSROOMS: 48% of faculty are male; 52% are female. All teach undergraduates. No introductory courses are taught by graduate students. The average class size in a regular course is 18.

PROGRAMS OF STUDY: MC confers B.A., B.S., B.F.A., and B.Mus. degrees. Master's and doctoral degrees are also awarded. Bachelor's degrees are awarded in AGRICULTURE (environmental studies), BIOLOGICAL SCIENCE (biochemistry and biology/biological science), BUSINESS (accounting, banking and finance, business administration and management, finance, and marketing), COMMUNICATIONS AND THE ARTS (art history and appreciation, communications, dance, digital media, dramatic arts, English, French, music, Spanish, and studio art), COMPUTER AND PHYSICAL SCIENCE (chemistry, computer science, and mathematics), EDUCATION (education and sports studies), SOCIAL SCIENCE (American studies, Asian/Oriental studies, criminal justice, economics, history, international studies, legal studies, philosophy, political science/government, psychology, religion, and sociology). Communication studies, business management, dance and theater, and sports studies are the strongest academically. Psychology, communication studies, and business management have the largest enrollments.

ACTIVITIES: There are no fraternities or sororities. There are 50 groups on campus, including art, band, cheerleading, chorale, chorus, computers, dance, drama, environmental, ethnic, film, honors, international, jazz band, LGBT, literary magazine, musical theater, newspaper, opera, orchestra, photography, political, professional, radio and TV, religious, social, social service, and student government. Popular campus events include Fall Fest'ville, Quad Jam, End of semester Brunches, Stress Relief, and Senior Week. **Sports:** There are 8 intercollegiate sports for men and 10 for women, and 2 intramural sports for men and 4 for women. Facilities include athletic and recreation areas with a gym, indoor batting cages, indoor pool, tennis courts, a strength and conditioning center, a turf field for lacrosse, field hockey and soccer, as well as fields for baseball and softball. **Graduates:** From July 1, 2016 to June 30, 2017, 349 bachelor's degrees were awarded. The most popular majors were business administration and management (14%), psychology (13%), and speech communication (9%). In an average class, 1% graduate in 3 years or less, 48% graduate in 4 years or less, 54% graduate in 5 years or less, and 55% graduate in 6 years or less. Of the 2016 graduating class, 19% were enrolled in graduate school within 6 months of graduation, and 77% were employed.

SERVICES: Counseling and information services are available, as is tutoring in every subject. **Library/Resources:** The library contains 209,876 volumes, 259,230 microform items, and 23,100 audio/video tapes/CDs/DVDs, subscribes to 59,881 periodicals, including electronic. Computerized library services include interlibrary loans, database searching, Internet access, and Wi-Fi capability. Special learning facilities include an art gallery, a radio station, Multimedia Production Labs, Environmental Sciences Lab, Performance Theatre, and Dance Studio. **Physically Challenged Students:** 70% of the campus is accessible. Facilities include wheelchair ramps, elevators, special parking, specially equipped restrooms, special class scheduling, and special housing. **Special:** MC offers three types of Study Abroad opportunities for its students: direct exchange; cooperative; and, independent. These academic programs abroad facilitate students successful continuance toward graduation while furthering their education through international institutions for one semester. MC has the unique Duchesne 4th Credit Option whereby students integrate community service and civic engagement projects with academic courses to earn a credit of experiential learning. MC offers cross-registration with SUNY Purchase. Dual, student-designed and interdisciplinary majors are also available at the college. There are 4 national honor societies, a freshman honors program, and 8 departmental honors programs. **Visiting:** There are regularly scheduled orientations for prospective students, consisting of weekday information sessions and tours at 10am, 12pm, and 2pm (except for holiday closures). There are also Saturday and Sunday sessions in the spring and fall. There are guides for informal visits; visitors may sit in on classes and stay overnight. To schedule a visit, contact The Office of Admissions at Joseph.Garzione@mville.edu. **Campus Safety and Security:** Measures include 24-hour foot and vehicle patrol, an emergency notification system, and security escort services. There are shuttle buses, emergency telephones, lighted pathways/sidewalks, and controlled access to dorms/residences.

REQUIREMENTS: The SAT or ACT is recommended. Applicants should graduate in the upper 50% of their class with 4 years of English, 3 each of history, math, and science, including 2 of lab science, and 1 half-year each of art and music. The GED is accepted. Interviews are strongly encouraged. Art applicants must submit a portfolio. Music, dance and theater applicants must audition. AP and CLEP credits are accepted. Important factors in the admissions decision are advanced placement or honors courses, evidence of special talent, and extracurricular activities record. To qualify for a Bachelor's degree and be eligible for participation in the College's commencement ceremony, undergraduate students must complete all of the following degree requirements: General Education requirements for all students regardless of major or program. A minimum of 120 total credits (though some major programs may exceed 120). A minimum cumulative G.P.A. of 2.0. Completion of a Major (normally with final grades of C or better, though some majors accept C- or higher). Minimum number of liberal arts credits for B.A. degree: 90 liberal arts credits, B.S. degree: 60 liberal arts credits, B.F.A. degree: 30 liberal arts credits, B.Mus degree: 30 liberal arts credits. All undergraduate students must complete all of the the following general education credit requirements (Competency and Distribution) to fulfill the College's General Education requirements for degree completion. A minimum letter grade of "C-" must be earned to fulfill a requirement. I: Competency Requirements: Quantitative Reasoning (6 credits), Critical Analysis and Reasoning (6 credits), Scientific Reasoning (6 credits), Oral Communication (3 credits), Written Communication (6 credits), Second Language (minimum of 6 introductory-level credits in one language or demonstration of equivalent competency), and Technological Competency (3 credits). II: Distribution Area Requirements: All Manhattanville undergraduates must complete the indicated credit requirement in all four of the following curricular distribution areas in addition to Competency requirements: Humanities (6 credits), Social Science (6 credits), Mathematical (3 credits) and Scientific (3 credits), Fine Arts (6 credits). A minimum C- letter grade must be earned in any general education competency or distribution course to fulfill a requirement. **Procedure:** Freshmen are admitted fall and spring. Entrance exams should be taken We adhere to Early Action Policy, December 1 deadline. There are early admissions, deferred admissions, and rolling admissions plans. Application deadlines are open. The fall 2017 application fee was $50. Notification of early decision is sent December 20; regular decision, January 3. Applications are accepted on-line. **Transfer Students:** 57 transfer students enrolled in 2016-2017. Student with 30 or more credits, should submit an application, recommendations, and college transcripts. Applicants can adhere to college-wide test-optional policy. An interview is recommended for some. If student has less than 30 credits, they can submit their application, recommendations, and college/high school transcripts. Applicants can adhere to college-wide test-optional policy, and an interview is recommended for some. 30 of 120 credits required for the bachelor's degree must be completed at MC. **International Students:** There are 128 international students enrolled. They must take the TOEFL with a minimum score of 550 on the paper-based TOEFL (PBT) or 80 on the Internet-based version (iBT). Student must take any one of these test: the IELTS, Cambridge English, CEFR B2 or higher, or the IB. They must also take the SAT or ACT.

ADMISSIONS: 80% of the 2017-2018 applicants were accepted. The SAT scores for the 2017-2018 freshman class were: Critical Reading-- 26% below 500, 48% between 500 and 599, 24% between 600 and 699, and 2% between 700 and 800. Math-- 35% below 500, 49% between 500 and 599, 15% between 600 and 699, and 1% between 700 and 800. Writing-- 37% below 500, 42% between 500 and 599, 15% between 600 and 699, and 6% between 700 and 800. The ACT scores were 9% between 12 and 17, 41% between 18 and 23, 40% between 24 and 29, and 10% above 30. 10 freshmen graduated first in their class. **Admissions Contact:** Peter Burns, Vice President, Enrollment Management. Email: *admissions@mville.edu* Web: *www.manhattanville.edu*

FINANCIAL AID: In 2017-2018, 98% of all full-time freshmen received some form of financial aid. 74% of all full-time freshmen received need-based aid. The average freshman award was $30,780. Need-based scholarships or need-based grants averaged $6,813 ($33,835 maximum); need-based self-help aid (loans and jobs) averaged $4,493 ($13,500 maximum); and other non-need-based awards and non-need-based scholarships averaged $19,158 ($36,460 maximum). The average financial indebtedness of the 2017 graduate was $21,569. The state aid form, and international students can apply for need based aid using the International Student Financial Aid Application (ISFAA) are required. The FAFSA code is 002760. The priority date for freshman financial aid applications for fall entry is March 1.

MANNES SCHOOL OF MUSIC *(The complete profile is made available exclusively on our website, www.barronspac.com)*

MARIST COLLEGE D-4

www.marist.edu

Poughkeepsie, NY 12601 (845) 575-3226 (800) 436-5483
Fax: (845) 575-3215 Email: admissions@marist.edu

Full-time: 2046 men, 2920 women
Part-time: 284 men, 366 women
Graduate: 450 men, 503 women
Year: semesters, summer session
Room & Board: $14,650

SAT CR/M/W: 580/600/590 **ACT:** 27
Application Deadline: February 1

Faculty: 232; IIA, av$
Ph.D.s: 75%
Student/Faculty: 22 to 1
Tuition: $35,210
Freshman Class: 11087 applied, 4545 accepted, 1225 enrolled
CEEB CODE: 2400
VERY COMPETITIVE

Marist College, founded in 1929, is a private liberal arts college that overlooks the Hudson River in the heart of the historic Hudson Valley. Marist is dedicated to helping students develop the intellect and character required for enlightened, ethical, and productive lives in the global community of the 21st century. There are 7 undergraduate schools and 5 graduate schools. In addition to regional accreditation, MC has baccalaureate program accreditation with AACSB, CSWE, NAACLS, and CAATE. The 210-acre campus is in a suburban area 75 miles north of New York City on the Hudson River. Including any residence halls, there are 75 buildings.

STUDENT LIFE: 52% of undergraduates are from New York. Others are from 48 states, 52 foreign countries, and Canada. 66% are from public schools. 9% are Hispanic; 73% White; 6% race unknown; 4% African American; 3% Asian American; 2% Foreign; 2% two or more races. **Female To Male Ratio:** 1.4:1. The average age of freshmen is 18; all undergraduates, 21. 10% do not continue beyond their first year; 83% remain to graduate. **Housing:** 3176 students can be accommodated in college housing, which includes dorms, on-campus apartments, and off-campus apartments. In addition, there are special-interest houses, freshman dorms with mentors, and housing for upperclassmen. 61% of students live on campus. Alcohol is not permitted. Upperclassmen may keep cars.

FACULTY/CLASSROOMS: 53% of faculty are male; 47% are female. All teach undergraduates. No introductory courses are taught by graduate students.

PROGRAMS OF STUDY: MC confers B.A., B.S. and B.P.S. degrees. Master's degrees are also awarded. Bachelor's degrees are awarded in AGRICULTURE (conservation and regulation), BIOLOGICAL SCIENCE (biochemistry, biology/adolescence education, and biology/biological science), BUSINESS (accounting, business administration and management, and fashion merchandising), COMMUNICATIONS AND THE ARTS (communications, digital media, English, fashion studies, fine arts, French, game design and development, Italian, film and media studies, Spanish, and studio art), COMPUTER AND PHYSICAL SCIENCE (applied mathematics, chemistry, chemistry/adolescence education, computer game design/development, computer science, information sciences and systems, and mathematics), EDUCATION (athletic training, English education, history education, mathematics education, and special education), ENGINEERING AND ENVIRONMENTAL DESIGN (environmental science and interior design), HEALTH PROFESSIONS (medical technology), SOCIAL SCIENCE (American studies, criminal justice, economics, fashion design and technology, history, liberal arts/general studies, philosophy, political science/government, psychology, religion, and social work). Fashion, computer science/software development, and business administration are the strongest academically. Business administration, communications, and fashion merchandising have the largest enrollments.

ACTIVITIES: 3% of men belong to 3 national fraternities; 3% of women belong to 1 local and 3 national sororities. There are 81 groups on campus, including art, band, cheerleading, chess, choir, chorale, chorus, communications, computers, dance, debate, drama, environmental, ethnic, film, honors, international, jazz band, LGBT, literary magazine, marching band, musical theater, newspaper, orchestra, pep band, photography, political, professional, radio and TV, religious, social, social service, student government, and symphony. Popular campus events include Activities Fair, Foxfest, and Giving Tree Program. **Sports:** There are 11 intercollegiate sports for men and 12 for women, and 11 intramural sports for men and 11 for women. Facilities include a boathouse, a basketball arena, a stadium, playing fields, a field house, a swimming pool, a diving well, racquetball courts, a tennis pavilion, a dance and aerobics studio, a weight room, intramural basketball courts, an all-purpose playing space, and a fitness center. **Graduates:** From July 1, 2016 to June 30, 2017, 1300 bachelor's degrees were awarded. The most popular majors were business (30%), communications (20%), and psychology (13%). In an average class, 1% graduate in 3 years or less, 68% graduate in 4 years or less, 76% graduate in 5 years or less, and 78% graduate in 6 years or less. Of the 2016 graduating class, 10% were enrolled in graduate school within 6 months of graduation, and 74% were employed.

SERVICES: Counseling and information services are available, as is tutoring in every subject. There is a reader service for the blind, and remedial math, reading, and writing. **Library/Resources:** The library contains 196,914 volumes, 10,828 audio/video tapes/CDs/DVDs, and subscribes to 145,583 periodicals, including electronic. Computerized library services include interlibrary loans, database searching, Internet access, and Wi-Fi capability. Special learning facilities include an art gallery, radio station, TV station, a gallery of Lowell Thomas memorabilia, estuarine and environmental studies lab, a public opinion institute, and an economic research center. **Physically Challenged Students:** All of the campus is accessible. Facilities include wheelchair ramps, elevators, special parking, specially equipped restrooms, special class scheduling, lowered drinking fountains, lowered telephones, and special housing. **Special:** Marist offers cross-registration with schools in the Mid-Hudson Career Consortium and study abroad in 38 countries. The school also offers a 3-year degree in social work, co-op programs in computer science and computer information systems, information technology, accounting, and business, work-study programs, and dual and student-designed majors. There are internships available with more than 1100 organizations in the United States and abroad, including New York State Legislature and White House programs. There are 15 national honor societies and a freshman honors program. **Visiting:** There are regularly scheduled orientations for prospective students, including 1-day June visits for freshmen and a 1-week welcome program. There are guides for informal visits; visitors may sit in on classes and stay overnight. To schedule a visit, contact the Admission Office. **Campus Safety and Security:** Measures include 24-hour foot and vehicle patrol, an emergency notification system, and security escort services. There are emergency telephones, lighted pathways/sidewalks, and controlled access to dorms/residences.

REQUIREMENTS: Applicants should have 17 high school units, including at least 4 years in English, 3 each in math and science, 2 each in social studies, foreign language, and an elective, and 1 in American history. An essay and 2 letters of recommendation are also required. AP and CLEP credits are accepted. Important factors in the admissions decision are advanced placement or honors courses, leadership record, and recommendations by school officials. To graduate, students must maintain a GPA of 2.0 in the major while taking 120 credits. A 30-credit core curriculum and 30 to 36 credits in a major are required. Distribution requirements include 6 credits each in natural sciences, social sciences, history, literature, and math and 3 credits each in fine arts and philosophy/religious studies. Specific course requirements include English writing skills and foundation courses in those areas defined by major programs. **Procedure:** Freshmen are admitted in the fall and spring. Entrance exams should be taken during the fall of the senior year. There are early decision and deferred admissions plans. Early decision applications should be filed by November 15; regular applications, by February 1 for fall entry; and November 15 for spring entry. The fall 2017 application fee was $50. Notification of early decision is sent December 15; regular decision, April 1. 270 early decision candidates were accepted for the 2017-2018 class. Applications are accepted on-line. **Transfer Students:** 274 transfer students enrolled in 2016-2017. Applicants must have at least a 2.8 GPA (depending on the college and major program) in at least 30 college credits. Students with fewer than 25 credits will be treated as freshmen. Grades of C or better transfer. 30 of 120 credits required for the bachelor's degree must be completed at Marist. **International Students:** There are 124 international students enrolled. They must take the TOEFL with a minimum score of 550 on the paper-based TOEFL (PBT) or 80 on the Internet-based version (iBT) and the college's own test. The IELTS is accepted if submitted.

ADMISSIONS: 41% of the 2017-2018 applicants were accepted. The SAT scores for the 2017-2018 freshman class were: Critical Reading-- 9% below 500, 47% between 500 and 599, 37% between 600 and 699, and 7% between 700 and 800. Math-- 7% below 500, 41% between 500 and 599, 46% between 600 and 699, and 6% between 700 and 800. Writing--

9% below 500, 44% between 500 and 599, 38% between 600 and 699, and 9% between 700 and 800. The ACT scores were 12% between 18 and 23, 66% between 24 and 29, and 22% above 30. 49% of the current freshmen were in the top fifth of their class; 80% were in the top two fifths. 3 freshmen graduated first in their class. **Admissions Contact:** Kent Rinehart, Dean of Admission. Email: *admissions@marist.edu* Web: *www.marist.edu*

FINANCIAL AID: In 2017-2018, 90% of all full-time freshmen received some form of financial aid. 52% of all full-time freshmen received need-based aid. The average freshman award was $18,946. Need-based scholarships or need-based grants averaged $14,026 ($50,350 maximum); need-based self-help aid (loans and jobs) averaged $6,185 ($9,500 maximum); non-need-based athletic scholarships averaged $15,189 ($56,106 maximum); and other non-need-based awards and non-need-based scholarships averaged $9,435 ($49,860 maximum). 28% of undergraduate students work part-time. The average financial indebtedness of the 2017 graduate was $39,584. MC is a member of CSS. The FAFSA code is 002765. The priority date for freshman financial aid applications for fall entry is February 15.

MARYMOUNT MANHATTAN COLLEGE D-5

www.mmm.edu

New York, NY 10021	**(212) 517-0430** **(800) 627-9668**
Fax: (212) 517-0448	**Email: admissions@mmm.edu**
Full-time: 462 men, 1453 women	**Faculty:** 96; IIB, +$
Part-time: 29 men, 76 women	**Ph.D.s:** 91%
Graduate: n/av	**Student/Faculty:** 11 to 1
Year: semesters, summer session	**Tuition:** $31,950
Room & Board: $16,400	**Freshman Class:** 5407 applied, 4849 accepted, 642 enrolled
SAT EBR-W/M: 570/512 **ACT:** 25	**CEEB CODE:** 2405
Application Deadline: open	**COMPETITIVE**

Marymount Manhattan College offers students the best of both worlds the personal approach of a small college combined with the limitless opportunities of one of the world's greatest cities. MMC provides a college education unlike any other, with notable strengths in the creative and performing arts, communications and media, business, entrepreneurship, and liberal arts and sciences. There is 1 undergraduate school. The 1-acre campus is in an urban area, New York, NY, Upper East Side of Manhattan. Including any residence halls, there are 5 buildings.

STUDENT LIFE: 75% of undergraduates are from out of state, mostly the Middle Atlantic. Students are from 48 states, 50 foreign countries, and Canada. 60% are from public schools. 61% are White; 17% Hispanic; 8% African American; 5% Foreign; 4% Asian American; 2% American Indian/Alaska Native; 2% two or more races; 1% race unknown. **Female To Male Ratio:** 3.1:1. The average age of freshmen is 19; all undergraduates, 21. 24% do not continue beyond their first year; 45% remain to graduate. **Housing:** 780 students can be accommodated in college housing, which includes gender neutral and coed dorms, on-campus apartments, and off-campus apartments. On-campus housing is guaranteed for the freshman year only, is available on a first-come, first-served basis, and is available on a lottery system for upperclassmen. 50% of students commute. Alcohol is not permitted. No one may keep cars.

FACULTY/CLASSROOMS: 49% of faculty are male; 51% are female. 65% teach undergraduates, 35% do research, and 35% do both. No introductory courses are taught by graduate students. The average class size in an introductory lecture is 25; in a laboratory is 12; and in a regular course is 18.

PROGRAMS OF STUDY: MMC confers B.A., B.S. and B.F.A. degrees. Bachelor's degrees are awarded in BIOLOGICAL SCIENCE (biology/biological science), BUSINESS (accounting and business administration and management), COMMUNICATIONS AND THE ARTS (communications, dance, dramatic arts, English, and fine arts), COMPUTER AND PHYSICAL SCIENCE (information sciences and systems), EDUCATION (elementary education), HEALTH PROFESSIONS (premedicine and speech pathology/audiology), SOCIAL SCIENCE (history, international studies, liberal arts/general studies, philosophy and religion, political science/government, psychology, and sociology). English, dance, and art history are the strongest academically. Theatre, communications and media arts, and business have the largest enrollments.

ACTIVITIES: There are no fraternities or sororities. There are 40 groups on campus, including art, choir, computers, dance, drama, ethnic, honors, international, LGBT, literary magazine, musical theater, newspaper, photography, political, professional, radio and TV, religious, social, social service, student government, and yearbook. Popular campus events include Strawberry Festival, Honors Day, and Apple Fest. **Sports:** There is no sports program at MMC. Facilities include an auditorium. **Graduates:** From July 1, 2016 to June 30, 2017, 389 bachelor's degrees were awarded. The most popular majors were visual/performing arts (38%), journalism (27%), and business/marketing (9%). In an average class, 39% graduate in 4 years or less, 48% graduate in 5 years or less, and 49% graduate in 6 years or less. Of the 2016 graduating class, 23% were enrolled in graduate school within 6 months of graduation, and 63% were employed.

SERVICES: Counseling and information services are available, as is tutoring in most subjects. There is remedial math, reading, and writing. **Library/Resources:** The library contains 75,000 volumes, 70 microform items, and 4,000 audio/video tapes/CDs/DVDs, and subscribes to 2,740 periodicals, including electronic. Computerized library services include interlibrary loans, database searching, Internet access, and Wi-Fi capability. Special learning facilities include an art gallery, a radio station, TV station, and a communications arts multimedia suite featuring digital editing technology. **Physically Challenged Students:** All of the campus is accessible. Facilities include wheelchair ramps, elevators, specially equipped restrooms, special class scheduling, and lowered drinking fountains. **Special:** MMC offers study abroad, interdisciplinary courses, pass/fail options, nondegree study, credit for life experience, and some 250 internships in all majors. Cooperative programs in business and finance, dance, music, languages, nursing, and urban education are offered in conjunction with local colleges and institutes. There is a January mini-session, cross-registration with Hunter College and the China Institute, and a 5-year master's in publishing with Pace University. There are 7 national honor societies, a freshman honors program, and 5 departmental honors programs. **Visiting:** There are regularly scheduled orientations for prospective students, including an interview with an admissions counselor, a tour of the school and residence hall, and a meeting with a financial aid adviser. There are guides for informal visits and visitors may sit in on classes. To schedule a visit, contact the Office of Admission. **Campus Safety and Security:** Measures include 24-hour foot and vehicle patrol and an emergency notification system. There are lighted pathways/sidewalks, controlled access to dorms/residences, security cameras, and photo ID check-in.

REQUIREMENTS: The SAT or ACT is required. Applicants should be graduates of an accredited secondary school or have a GED certificate. MMC recommends completion of 16 academic units, including 4 each in English and electives, and 3 each in language, math, social science, and science. Recommendations are required, and an interview is strongly advised. Applicants to the dance and acting programs must audition. A GPA of 2.5 is required. AP and CLEP credits are accepted. Important factors in the admissions decision are evidence of special talent, personality/intangible qualities, and leadership record. To graduate, students must complete 120 credit hours, including 31 to 71 in the major, with a minimum GPA of 2.0. The core plus shared curriculum totals 48 credits in the areas of critical thinking, psychology and philosophy, quantitative reasoning and science, the modern world, communications/language, and the arts. **Procedure:** Freshmen are admitted to all sessions. Entrance exams should be taken as early as possible. There is a rolling admissions plan. Application deadlines are open. The fall 2017 application fee was $60. Notification is sent on a rolling basis. Applications are accepted on-line. **Transfer Students:** 170 transfer students enrolled in 2016-2017. Applicants must submit official transcripts from all colleges attended, proof of high school graduation and a recommendation letter. 30 of 120 credits required for the bachelor's degree must be completed at MMC. **International Students:** There are 100 international students enrolled. They must take the TOEFL with a minimum score of 550 on the paper-based TOEFL (PBT) or 80 on the Internet-based version (iBT). Student must take either the PTE or IELTS. They must also take the SAT or ACT.

ADMISSIONS: 90% of the 2017-2018 applicants were accepted. The SAT scores for the 2017-2018 freshman class were: Math-- 25% below 500, 35% between 500 and 599, 30% between 600 and 699, and 10% between 700 and 800. Evidence-Based Reading/Writing-- 25% below 500, 45% between 500 and 599, 30% between 600 and 699, and 10% between 700 and 800. The ACT scores were 5% between 12 and 17, 50%

between 18 and 23, 40% between 24 and 29, and 5% above 30. **Admissions Contact:** James Rogers, Dean of Admission. Email: *admissions@mmm.edu* Web: *www.mmm.edu*

FINANCIAL AID: In 2017-2018, 90% of all full-time freshmen received some form of financial aid. 75% of all full-time freshmen received need-based aid. The average freshman award was $13,068. Need-based scholarships or need-based grants averaged $10,521; need-based self-help aid (loans and jobs) averaged $3,477; and $5,500 from other forms of aid. 75% of undergraduate students work part-time. The average financial indebtedness of the 2017 graduate was $15,206. The FAFSA code is 002769. The deadline for filing freshman financial aid applications for fall entry is March 15.

MEDAILLE COLLEGE *(The complete profile is made available exclusively on our website, www.barronspac.com)*

MERCY COLLEGE D-5

www.mercy.edu

Dobbs Ferry, NY 10522 **(877) 637-2946**

Fax: 914-674-7382	**Email:** admissions@mercy.edu
Full-time: 1734 men, 3321 women	**Faculty:** 207; IIA, av$
Part-time: 619 men, 1190 women	**Ph.D.s:** 86%
Graduate: 565 men, 2077 women	**Student/Faculty:** 16 to 1
Year: semesters, summer session	**Tuition:** $18,714
Room & Board: $13,900	**Freshman Class:** 6901 applied, 5433 accepted, 910 enrolled
	CEEB CODE: 2409
Application Deadline: open	**COMPETITIVE**

Mercy College, founded in 1950, is a private institution dedicated to offering a curriculum of liberal arts and sciences as well as preprofessional and professional programs. Graduate programs provide advanced preparation in selected disciplines. There are 5 undergraduate schools and 5 graduate schools. In addition to regional accreditation, MC has baccalaureate program accreditation with CSWE, NASAD, CAEP, ACOTE, CCNE, CAPTE, AVMA, and CAEP. The 66-acre campus is in a suburban area 25 miles north of New York City. Including any residence halls, there are 7 buildings.

STUDENT LIFE: 92% of undergraduates are from New York. Others are from 44 states, 47 foreign countries, and Canada. 30% are White; 35% Hispanic; 21% African American; 5% race unknown; 5% Asian American; 1% two or more races; 1% American Indian/Alaska Native; 2% Foreign. **Female To Male Ratio:** 2.3:1. The average age of freshmen is 19; all undergraduates, 24. 27% do not continue beyond their first year; 42% remain to graduate. **Housing:** 744 students can be accommodated in college housing, which includes coed dorms. On-campus housing is available on a first-come, first-served basis. 89% of students commute. Alcohol is not permitted. Upperclassmen may keep cars.

FACULTY/CLASSROOMS: 41% of faculty are male; 38% are female. All teach undergraduates. No introductory courses are taught by graduate students. The average class size in an introductory lecture is 16 and a regular course is 16.

PROGRAMS OF STUDY: MC confers B.A., B.F.A., and B.S. degrees. Associate, master's, and doctoral degrees are also awarded. Bachelor's degrees are awarded in BIOLOGICAL SCIENCE (biology/biological science), BUSINESS (accounting, banking and finance, business administration and management, business (dual major program), entrepreneurial studies, and human resources/organizational management), COMMUNICATIONS AND THE ARTS (broadcasting, communications, English, film, television and digital media, fine arts, journalism, media arts, music, music industry, music technology, and Spanish), COMPUTER AND PHYSICAL SCIENCE (computer science, digital arts/technology, information sciences and systems, and mathematics), EDUCATION (elementary education, special education, sports and wellness studies, and teaching English as a second/foreign language (TESOL/TEFOL), HEALTH PROFESSIONS (exercise science, health science, medical laboratory technology, nursing, speech pathology/audiology, and veterinary science), SOCIAL SCIENCE (behavioral science, communication sciences and disorders, criminal justice, history, interdisciplinary studies, legal studies, liberal arts/general studies, paralegal studies, political science/government, psychology, social work, and sociology). Health profession programs are the strongest academically. Business, education, and psychology have the largest enrollments.

ACTIVITIES: There are no fraternities or sororities. There are 36 groups on campus, including STEM club, veterinary club, art, cheerleading, chorale, communications, computers, dance, environmental, ethnic, film, honors, international, jazz band, LGBT, newspaper, political, professional, religious, social, social service, student government, and student military veteran club. Popular campus events include Veteran's Day Activities, Founders Day/Alumni Weekend, Open Houses, Major League Baseball Events, Broadway Shows, Spring Fling Festival, Poetry Readings and Club Fairs. **Sports:** There are 4 intercollegiate sports for men and 6 for women, and 1 intramural sports for men and 2 for women. Facilities include a gym, a soccer/baseball/softball fields, swimming pools, tennis courts, a track, basketball/volleyball courts and a fitness center. **Graduates:** From July 1, 2016 to June 30, 2017, 1471 bachelor's degrees were awarded. The most popular majors were behavioral science (27%), health professions (22%), and business (18%). In an average class, 42% graduate in 6 years or less.

SERVICES: Counseling and information services are available, as is tutoring in every subject. There is a reader service for the blind. **Library/Resources:** The library contains 85,689 volumes, 1,616 audio/video tapes/CDs/DVDs, and subscribes to 21,126 periodicals, including electronic. Computerized library services include interlibrary loans, database searching, Internet access, and Wi-Fi capability. **Physically Challenged Students:** 75% of the campus is accessible. Facilities include wheelchair ramps, elevators, special parking, specially equipped restrooms, special class scheduling, and lowered drinking fountains. **Special:** Mercy offers internships and cooperative education in each major, an on-campus employment program with a community service component, study abroad, dual majors and degrees, credit for life experience, nondegree study, and pass/fail options. There are 7 national honor societies, including Phi Beta Kappa, a freshman honors program, and 14 departmental honors programs. **Visiting:** There are regularly scheduled orientations for prospective students, including spring and fall open houses and information sessions. There are guides for informal visits and visitors may sit in on classes. To schedule a visit, contact the Admissions Office. **Campus Safety and Security:** Measures include 24-hour foot and vehicle patrol, an emergency notification system, self-defense education, and security escort services. There are shuttle buses, emergency telephones, lighted pathways/sidewalks, and controlled access to dorms/residences.

REQUIREMENTS: Applicants must be graduates of an accredited secondary school or have a GED certificate. They should have completed at least 16 academic units. AP and CLEP credits are accepted. Important factors in the admissions decision are recommendations by school officials, personality/intangible qualities, and leadership record. To graduate, students must complete 120 semester hours with a minimum GPA of 2.0 overall. In total, 30 semester hours must be completed at Mercy. The Mercy College General Education Curriculum includes: 6 English credits, 3 speech credits, 6 history credits, 9 social science credits, 3 philosophy/religion credits, 3 art/music credits, 3 foreign language credits, 3 math credits, 3 computer science credits, and 3 natural science credits. **Procedure:** Freshmen are admitted in the fall, spring, and summer. Entrance exams should be taken between January and August of the senior year. There are deferred admissions and rolling admissions plans. Application deadlines are open. The fall 2017 application fee was $40. Notification is sent on a rolling basis. Applications are accepted online. **Transfer Students:** 687 transfer students enrolled in 2016-2017. Applicants must submit official transcripts from all colleges attended and must also submit their high school transcript. 30 of 120 credits required for the bachelor's degree must be completed at MC. **International Students:** There are 91 international students enrolled. They must take the TOEFL with a minimum score of 550 on the paper-based TOEFL (PBT) or 71 on the Internet-based version (iBT) and the college's own test.

ADMISSIONS: 79% of the 2017-2018 applicants were accepted. **Admissions Contact:** Deirdre Whitman, Vice President for Enrollment Management. Email: *admissions@mercy.edu* Web: *www.mercy.edu*

FINANCIAL AID: In 2017-2018, 81% of all full-time freshmen received some form of financial aid. 55% of all full-time freshmen received need-based aid. The average freshman award was $15,270. Need-based scholarships or need-based grants averaged $12,472; need-based self-help aid (loans and jobs) averaged $3,290; non-need-based athletic scholarships averaged $7,662; and other non-need-based awards and non-need-based scholarships averaged $6,090. 1% of undergraduate students work part-time. The average financial indebtedness of the 2017 graduate was

$26,070. The state aid form is required. The FAFSA code is 002772. The priority date for freshman financial aid applications for fall entry is February 15.

METROPOLITAN COLLEGE OF NEW YORK D-5

www.mcny.edu

New York, NY 10006 (212) 343-1234

Fax: (212) 343-8470	**Email:** admissions@mcny.edu
Full-time: 154 men, 467 women	**Faculty:** n/av
Part-time: 26 men, 50 women	**Ph.D.s:** n/av
Graduate: 106 men, 256 women	**Student/Faculty:** n/av
Year: semesters, summer session	**Tuition:** $19,457
Room & Board: n/app	**Freshman Class:** 257 applied, 104 accepted, 79 enrolled
	CEEB CODE: 4802
Application Deadline: open	**VERY COMPETITIVE**

Metropolitan College of New York, founded in 1964, is a private institution offering programs in business, education, emergency management, human services, healthcare, and public administration. The college operates on a 3-semester calendar, including a complete summer semester. All bachelor degree programs involve a combination of class work and field work and may be completed in 2 years and 8 months. Most Masters degree programs can be completed in 1 year. Tuition cost varies by programs chosen by student. There are 2 undergraduate schools and 3 graduate schools. In addition to regional accreditation, MC of New York has baccalaureate program accreditation with ACBSP. The campus is in an urban area in New York City, NY. Including any residence halls, there is 1 building.

STUDENT LIFE: 99% of undergraduates are from New York. Others are from 4 states, 9 foreign countries, and Canada. **Female To Male Ratio:** 2.7:1.

FACULTY/CLASSROOMS: No introductory courses are taught by graduate students.

PROGRAMS OF STUDY: MCNY confers B.B.A. and B.P.S. degrees. Associate and master's degrees are also awarded. Bachelor's degrees are awarded in BUSINESS (business administration and management), EDUCATION (early childhood education), HEALTH PROFESSIONS (mental health/human services), SOCIAL SCIENCE (child care/child and family studies, community services, gerontology, human services, and social work). Business management is the strongest academically. Human services has the largest enrollment.

ACTIVITIES: There are no fraternities or sororities. There are 10 groups on campus, including computers, ethnic, honors, LGBT, newspaper, professional, social, social service, and student government. Popular campus events include career fairs, and Admissions Open House and Dean's List Ceremonies. **Sports:** There is no sports program at MCNY. **Graduates:** From July 1, 2016 to June 30, 2017, 192 bachelor's degrees were awarded. The most popular majors were human services, business, and healthcare systems management.

SERVICES: Counseling and information services are available, as is tutoring in every subject. There is remedial math, reading, and writing. **Library/Resources:** The library contains 32,000 volumes, 1,800 microform items, and subscribes to 3,300 periodicals, including electronic. Computerized library services include interlibrary loans, database searching, Internet access, and Wi-Fi capability. **Physically Challenged Students:** All of the campus is accessible. Facilities include wheelchair ramps, elevators, specially equipped restrooms, special class scheduling, lowered drinking fountains, and lowered telephones. **Special:** Internships, which include required weekly 14-hour field sites, study abroad in 3 countries, work-study programs, B.A.-B.S. degrees, and accelerated degree programs in human services, business management, and American urban studies are offered, as well as credit by exam, and credit for life experience. **Visiting:** There are regularly scheduled orientations for prospective students. There are guides for informal visits and visitors may sit in on classes. To schedule a visit, contact the Admissions Office. **Campus Safety and Security:** Measures include 24-hour foot and vehicle patrol and an emergency notification system. There are lighted pathways/sidewalks, fire drills, and a fire escape stairwell.

REQUIREMENTS: Students must take the ETS's Accuplacer Test in reading and math. Recent high school graduates who have a satisfactory SAT score may present the SAT instead. Applicants must have graduated from an accredited secondary school. The GED is accepted. An essay and an interview are required. CLEP credits are accepted. Important factors in the admissions decision are evidence of special talent, leadership record, and personality/intangible qualities. To graduate, students must complete 120 credit hours with a minimum GPA of 2.0. The curriculum is prescribed; no electives are featured. A constructive action document based on performance in the field and mastery of coursework is required each semester. **Procedure:** Freshmen are admitted to all sessions. Entrance exams should be taken in the senior year. There are deferred admissions and rolling admissions plans. Applications should be filed by December 1 for spring entry; April 1 for summer entry. The fall 2017 application fee was $30. Applications are accepted online. **Transfer Students:** 45 transfer students enrolled in 2016-2017. Admission is based on current skills and abilities as measured on the entrance exam and essay. 60 of 120 credits required for the bachelor's degree must be completed at MCNY. **International Students:** There are 18 international students enrolled. They must take the TOEFL with a minimum score of 75 on the paper-based TOEFL (PBT) or 75 on the Internet-based version (iBT).

ADMISSIONS: 40% of the 2017-2018 applicants were accepted. **Admissions Contact:** Erica Silbiger, Director of Admissions. Email: *admissions@mcny.edu* Web: *www.mcny.edu*

FINANCIAL AID: In 2017-2018, 96% of all full-time freshmen received some form of financial aid and need-based aid. The average freshman award was $14,593. Need-based scholarships or need-based grants averaged $11,181; and need-based self-help aid (loans and jobs) averaged $3,530. The FAFSA code is 009769. The deadline for filing freshman financial aid applications for fall entry is August 15.

MOLLOY COLLEGE D-5

www.molloy.edu

Rockville Centre, NY 11570 (516) 323-4000

Fax: (516) 256-2247	**Email:** admissions@molloy.edu
Full-time: 713 men, 1966 women	**Faculty:** I, -$
Part-time: 135 men, 522 women	**Ph.D.s:** 75%
Graduate: 211 men, 950 women	**Student/Faculty:** 10 to 1
Year: 4-1-4, summer session	**Tuition:** $29,110
Room & Board: $13,590	**Freshman Class:** 3277 applied, 2471 accepted, 492 enrolled
SAT CR/M/W: 520/530/510 **ACT:** 24	**CEEB CODE:** 2415
Application Deadline: open	**COMPETITIVE**

Molloy College offers students a rich and multidimensional educational experience where they are encouraged to think critically and explore creatively. Combining the strengths of academic excellence and leadership with personal, compassionate mentoring, MC brings out the best in every student, here and around the globe. MC students develop that all-important confidence, that strong, I will attitude that enables them to succeed in their careers, and more importantly, to make a difference in our world. There are 2 undergraduate schools and 6 graduate schools. In addition to regional accreditation, MC has baccalaureate program accreditation with CSWE, NLN, CAAHEP, and CCNE. The 30-acre campus is in a suburban area 20 miles east of New York City. Including any residence halls, there are 6 buildings.

STUDENT LIFE: 98% of undergraduates are from New York. Others are from 20 states, and 9 foreign countries. 7% are Asian American; 63% White; 2% race unknown; 14% Hispanic; 12% African American; 1% two or more races. 61% are Catholic; 13% claim no religious affiliation. **Female To Male Ratio:** 3.2:1. The average age of freshmen is 18; all undergraduates, 24. 10% do not continue beyond their first year; 70% remain to graduate. **Housing:** 258 students can be accommodated in college housing, which includes dorms. 92% of students commute. Alcohol is not permitted. All students may keep cars.

FACULTY/CLASSROOMS: 31% of faculty are male; 69% are female. No introductory courses are taught by graduate students. The average class size in an introductory lecture is 17; in a laboratory is 12; and in a regular course is 17.

PROGRAMS OF STUDY: MC confers B.A., B.S., B.F.A. and B.S.W degrees. Associate, master's, and doctoral degrees are also awarded.

Bachelor's degrees are awarded in AGRICULTURE (environmental studies), BIOLOGICAL SCIENCE (biology/biological science), BUSINESS (accounting, business administration and management, finance, and marketing), COMMUNICATIONS AND THE ARTS (art, communications, English, music, Spanish and Hispanic studies, and theatre arts), COMPUTER AND PHYSICAL SCIENCE (computer information systems, computer science, and mathematics), EDUCATION (early childhood education and music education), ENGINEERING AND ENVIRONMENTAL DESIGN (nuclear medicine technology), HEALTH PROFESSIONS (health, music therapy, nursing, and speech pathology/audiology), SOCIAL SCIENCE (criminal justice, history, interdisciplinary studies, philosophy, political science/government, psychology, social work, sociology, and theology). Nursing, education, and business are the strongest academically and have the largest enrollments.

ACTIVITIES: There are no fraternities or sororities. There are 60 groups on campus, including art, band, cheerleading, chess, chorus, dance, drama, ethnic, honors, international, jazz band, literary magazine, newspaper, professional, religious, social, social service, student government, and yearbook. Popular campus events include Scavenger Hunt, Halloween Party, Relay for Life, Safe Halloween, Hats and Stockings, Stuff a Bear, Maroon Madness, Santa's Workshop, and Bunny Brunch. **Sports:** There are 7 intercollegiate sports for men and 9 for women, and 3 intramural sports for men and 3 for women. Facilities include a gym, a dance studio, a weight room, sports fields, basketball, and tennis courts. **Graduates:** From July 1, 2016 to June 30, 2017, 775 bachelor's degrees were awarded. The most popular majors were nursing (53%), education (10%), and business (7%). In an average class, 40% graduate in 4 years or less, 65% graduate in 5 years or less, and 70% graduate in 6 years or less.

SERVICES: Counseling and information services are available, as is tutoring in every subject. There is a reader service for the blind, and remedial math, reading, and writing. **Library/Resources:** The library contains 72,697 volumes, 427 microform items, and 4,947 audio/video tapes/CDs/DVDs, and subscribes to 52,928 periodicals, including electronic. Computerized library services include interlibrary loans, database searching, and Internet access. Special learning facilities include an art gallery. **Physically Challenged Students:** All of the campus is accessible. Facilities include wheelchair ramps, elevators, special parking, specially equipped restrooms, special class scheduling, lowered drinking fountains, and lowered telephones. **Special:** Molloy offers study abroad programs, dual degree programs, and other unique internship opportunities. There are 18 national honor societies and a freshman honors program. **Visiting:** There are regularly scheduled orientations for prospective students, including the president of the college, department presentations, campus tours, admissions, financial aid, and scholarship information. There are guides for informal visits and visitors may sit in on classes. To schedule a visit, contact the Admissions Office. **Campus Safety and Security:** Measures include 24-hour foot and vehicle patrol, an emergency notification system, and security escort services. There are shuttle buses, emergency telephones, lighted pathways/sidewalks, and campus concerns committee.

REQUIREMENTS: The SAT or ACT is required. The ACT Optional Writing test is also required. Applicants should be graduates of a secondary school or have a GED. Preparation should include 4 units of English and social studies, and 3 units of math, science, foreign language and history. An essay is required and an interview is recommended. Music students must audition and take a theory exam. A GPA of 3.0 is required. AP and CLEP credits are accepted. Important factors in the admissions decision are advanced placement or honors courses, recommendations by school officials, and extracurricular activities record. General Education requirements consist of 45 to 54 credits. A total of 128 to 137 credit hours is required for graduation. **Procedure:** Freshmen are admitted in the fall and spring. Entrance exams should be taken in the fall of the senior year. There are early admissions, deferred admissions, and rolling admissions plans. Application deadlines are open. The fall 2017 application fee was $40. Notifications are sent October 15. Applications are accepted online. **Transfer Students:** 384 transfer students enrolled in 2016-2017. A minimum college GPA of 2.0 is required, with some majors requiring a higher GPA. An interview is recommended. 30 of 128 credits required for the bachelor's degree must be completed at MC. **International Students:** There are 8 international students enrolled. They must take the TOEFL with a minimum score of 500 on the paper-based TOEFL (PBT).

ADMISSIONS: 75% of the 2017-2018 applicants were accepted. The SAT scores for the 2017-2018 freshman class were: Critical Reading-- 29% below 500, 58% between 500 and 599, 11% between 600 and 699, and 2% between 700 and 800. Math-- 26% below 500, 53% between 500 and 599, 19% between 600 and 699, and 2% between 700 and 800. Writing-- 39% below 500, 45% between 500 and 599, 15% between 600 and 699, and 1% between 700 and 800. The ACT scores were 14% below 12, 34% between 12 and 17, 36% between 18 and 23, 10% between 24 and 29, and 6% above 30. **Admissions Contact:** Marguerite Lane, Dean of Admissions. Email: *admissions@molloy.edu* Web: *www.molloy.edu*

FINANCIAL AID: MC is a member of CSS. The FAFSA code is 002775. The priority date for freshman financial aid applications for fall entry is April 15.

MONROE COLLEGE D-5

www.monroecollege.edu

Bronx, NY 10468 **(718) 933-6700**

Fax: (718) 364-3552 **Email: admissions@monroecollege.edu**

Full-time: 1410 men, 3510 women	**Faculty:** III, ++$
Part-time: 155 men, 405 women	**Ph.D.s:** n/av
Graduate: n/av	**Student/Faculty:** n/av
Year: varies, summer session	**Tuition:** $14,796
Room & Board: $9200	**Freshman Class:** n/av
SAT: recommended	**CEEB CODE:** 2462
Application Deadline: August 15	**COMPETITIVE**

Monroe College, founded in 1933, offers bachelors degrees in accounting, business management, computer information systems, criminal justice, hospitality management, and health services administration. The figures given in the above capsule and in this profile are approximate. There is 1 undergraduate school. The campus in the Fordham Road section of the Bronx. Including any residence halls, there are 5 buildings.

STUDENT LIFE: 96% of undergraduates are from New York. 46% are African American; 42% Hispanic; 2% White; 1% Asian American; 1% Foreign. **Female To Male Ratio:** 2.5:1. The average age of freshmen is 23; all undergraduates, 26. **Housing:** 620 students can be accommodated in college housing, which includes dorms, off-campus apartments, and honors houses. On-campus housing is guaranteed for all 4 years. 90% of students commute. All students may keep cars.

FACULTY/CLASSROOMS: All teach undergraduates. No introductory courses are taught by graduate students. The average class size in an introductory lecture is 30.

PROGRAMS OF STUDY: MC confers B.S. and B.B.A. degrees. Associate and master's degrees are also awarded. Bachelor's degrees are awarded in BUSINESS (accounting, business administration and management, and hospitality management services), COMPUTER AND PHYSICAL SCIENCE (information sciences and systems), HEALTH PROFESSIONS (health care administration), SOCIAL SCIENCE (criminal justice). Business management, criminal justuce, and health services administration have the largest enrollments.

ACTIVITIES: There are no fraternities or sororities. Groups on campus include cheerleading, computers, dance, drama, honors, literary magazine, newspaper, professional, and social service. Popular campus events include talent shows, President's and Dean's List Galas, and cultural trips to New York City. **Sports:** There is no sports program at MC.

SERVICES: Counseling and information services are available, as is tutoring in every subject. There is a reader service for the blind, and remedial math, reading, and writing. **Library/Resources:** Computerized library services include interlibrary loans, database searching, Internet access, and Wi-Fi capability. **Physically Challenged Students:** All of the campus is accessible. Facilities include wheelchair ramps, elevators, special parking, specially equipped restrooms, special class scheduling, lowered drinking fountains, lowered telephones, and special housing. **Special:** Co-op programs are available in all degree programs. Study abroad is available for culinary students interested in studying in Italy. There is 1 national honor society, a freshman honors program, and 1 departmental honors program. **Visiting:** There are regularly scheduled orientations for prospective students, including a variety of open houses during the semester in which applicants can tour the campus and talk with faculty and/or chairs of individual departments. There are guides for informal visits; visitors may sit in on classes and stay overnight. **Campus Safety and Security:** Measures include 24-hour foot and vehicle patrol, self-defense education, and security escort services. There are shuttle buses, emergency telephones, and lighted pathways/sidewalks.

REQUIREMENTS: The SAT is recommended. An application, an essay, and an interview are also required. Monroe requires applicants to be in the upper 50% of their class. AP and CLEP credits are accepted. To graduate, students must have 120 credit hours and at least a 2.0 GPA. The core curriculum includes courses in writing/literature, math, liberal arts, and business or technology. **Procedure:** Freshmen are admitted in the fall, winter, and spring. There are early decision and rolling admissions plans. Early decision applications should be filed by February 1; regular applications, by August 15 for fall entry; January 5 for winter entry; and April 15 for spring entry. The fall 2017 application fee was $35. **Transfer Students:** Transfer students must provide an official transcript from any prior institution they have attended in addition to the application and an essay. 30 of 120 credits required for the bachelor's degree must be completed at MC.

Admissions Contact: Evan Jerome, Director of Admissions. Email: *admissions@monroecollege.edu* Web: *www.monroecollege.edu*

FINANCIAL AID: The state aid form and the college's own financial statement are required. The FAFSA code is 004799. Check with the school for current application deadlines.

MOUNT SAINT MARY COLLEGE D-4

www.msmc.edu

Newburgh, NY 12550 **(845) 569-3255**

Fax: (845) 561-0800
Full-time: 530 men, 1207 women
Part-time: 77 men, 222 women
Graduate: 71 men, 258 women
Year: semesters, summer session
Room & Board: $14,528

SAT or ACT: required
Application Deadline: August 15

Email: admissions@msmc.edu
Faculty: 82; IIB, +$
Ph.D.s: 83%
Student/Faculty: 20 to 1
Tuition: $29,920
Freshman Class: 3824 applied, 3571 accepted, 401 enrolled
CEEB CODE: 2423
COMPETITIVE

Mount Saint Mary College, founded in 1959, is a private liberal arts college offering undergraduate programs leading to Bachelor of Arts and Bachelor of Science degrees, and graduate programs leading to the master's in education, nursing, and business administration. An accelerated evening program is offered for nontraditional and adult students. There are 3 undergraduate schools and 3 graduate schools. In addition to regional accreditation, MSMC has baccalaureate program accreditation with CCNE and IACBE. The 86-acre campus is in a suburban area 58 miles north of New York City. Including any residence halls, there are 41 buildings.

STUDENT LIFE: 88% of undergraduates are from New York. Others are from 18 states. 79% are from public schools. 60% are White; 16% Hispanic; 11% race unknown; 8% African American; 2% Asian American; 1% American Indian/Alaska Native; 1% Foreign; 1% two or more races. 54% are Catholic; 45% Baptist, Christian, Episcopalian, Lutheran, and Methodist. **Female To Male Ratio:** 2.5:1. The average age of freshmen is 18; all undergraduates, 22. 22% do not continue beyond their first year; 54% remain to graduate. **Housing:** 1126 students can be accommodated in college housing, which includes dorms and on-campus townhouses. On-campus housing is guaranteed for all 4 years. 52% of students commute. Upperclassmen may keep cars.

FACULTY/CLASSROOMS: 34% of faculty are male; 66% are female. 94% teach undergraduates. No introductory courses are taught by graduate students. The average class size in an introductory lecture is 19; in a laboratory is 10; and in a regular course is 19.

PROGRAMS OF STUDY: MSMC confers B.A., B.S., and B.S.Ed. degrees. Master's degrees are also awarded. Bachelor's degrees are awarded in BIOLOGICAL SCIENCE (biology/biological science), BUSINESS (accounting and business administration and management), COMMUNICATIONS AND THE ARTS (English, information technology, media arts, and public relations), COMPUTER AND PHYSICAL SCIENCE (chemistry, mathematics, and science), EDUCATION (education), HEALTH PROFESSIONS (nursing), SOCIAL SCIENCE (criminology, Hispanic American studies, history, history and political science, human services, interdisciplinary studies, political science/government, psychology, social science, and sociology). Education, nursing, and business are the strongest academically and have the largest enrollments.

ACTIVITIES: There are no fraternities or sororities. There are 39 groups on campus, including art, choir, computers, dance, drama, environmental, ethnic, honors, LGBT, literary magazine, musical theater, newspaper, photography, political, professional, radio and TV, religious, social, student government, and yearbook. Popular campus events include Spring Weekend, Siblings Weekend, and Holiday Formal. **Sports:** There are 10 intercollegiate sports for men and 11 for women, and 10 intramural sports for men and 10 for women. The Physical Recreation Center houses regulation basketball courts, an elevated running track, a cardiovascular room, a fully equipped weight room, an aerobics studio, an indoor swimming pool, a multipurpose room, and the outdoor athletic complex features an all-weather, synthetic turf field, a natural grass field, and tennis courts. **Graduates:** From July 1, 2016 to June 30, 2017, 472 bachelor's degrees were awarded. The most popular majors were nursing (28%), business (14%), and psychology (12%). In an average class, 2% graduate in 3 years or less, 43% graduate in 4 years or less, 52% graduate in 5 years or less, and 54% graduate in 6 years or less. Of the 2016 graduating class, 33% were enrolled in graduate school within 6 months of graduation, and 92% were employed.

SERVICES: Counseling and information services are available, as is tutoring in every subject. There is remedial math, reading, and writing. **Library/Resources:** The library contains 87,924 volumes, and 7,388 audio/video tapes/CDs/DVDs, and subscribes to 70,271 periodicals, including electronic. Computerized library services include interlibrary loans, database searching, Internet access, and Wi-Fi capability. Special learning facilities include a radio station, an elementary school, herbarium field station, and an arboretum. **Physically Challenged Students:** 95% of the campus is accessible. Facilities include wheelchair ramps, elevators, special parking, specially equipped restrooms, and lowered telephones. There is special equipment in the library and computer centers to accommodate students with low vision. **Special:** Co-op programs and internships are available in all majors. There is cross-registration with other mid-Hudson area colleges, as well as accelerated degree programs in business, accounting, and nursing, among others. There are several collaborative programs. The college also offers study abroad in more than 22 countries, a Washington semester, work-study, and dual and student-designed majors. Credit by exam and for life, military, and work experience is available for a maximum of 30 credits. There are 16 national honor societies and a freshman honors program. **Visiting:** There are regularly scheduled orientations for prospective students; student visits include 4 open houses per year, a summer orientation program, and Spend a Day with a Current Student program in the spring. There are guides for informal visits; visitors may sit in on classes and stay overnight. To schedule a visit, contact the Admissions Office. **Campus Safety and Security:** Measures include 24-hour foot and vehicle patrol, an emergency notification system, self-defense education, and security escort services. There are shuttle buses, emergency telephones, lighted pathways/sidewalks, and controlled access to dorms/residences.

REQUIREMENTS: The SAT or ACT is required. Students should be graduates of an accredited secondary school. The GED is accepted. Applicants should prepare with 4 years each of English and history, and at least 3 each of math and science and 2 of foreign language. An essay and an interview are recommended. AP and CLEP credits are accepted. Important factors in the admissions decision are advanced placement or honors courses, evidence of special talent, and personality/intangible qualities. A total of 120 credit hours is required for the B.A. or B.S., with 24 to 40 in the major and a minimum GPA of 2.0. Overall requirements are higher for nursing, medical technology, and education students. All students must achieve computer literacy before graduation. **Procedure:** Freshmen are admitted to all sessions. Entrance exams should be taken by the junior year. There are deferred admissions and rolling admissions plans. Applications should be filed by August 15 for fall entry. The fall 2017 application fee was $45. Notification is sent on a rolling basis. Applications are accepted online. **Transfer Students:** 209 transfer students enrolled in 2016-2017. Applicants must have a GPA of at least 2.0 in all college work. The SAT or ACT, and an interview are recommended. 30 of 120 credits required for the bachelor's degree must be completed at the MSMC. **International Students:** There are 10 international students enrolled. They must take the TOEFL with a minimum score of 550 on the paper-based TOEFL (PBT) or 80 on the Internet-based version (iBT). They must also take the SAT or ACT, and the college's own entrance exam. Freshman students are required to take standard placement test.

ADMISSIONS: 93% of the 2017-2018 applicants were accepted. 22% of the current freshmen were in the top fifth of their class; 57% were in the top two fifths. **Admissions Contact:** Nancy Scaffidi, Director of Admissions. Email: *admissions@msmc.edu* Web: *www.msmc.edu*

FINANCIAL AID: In 2017-2018, 99% of all full-time freshmen received some form of financial aid. 90% of all full-time freshmen received need-based aid. The average freshman award was $27,121. Need-based scholarships or need-based grants averaged $8,183 ($46,313 maximum); need-based self-help aid (loans and jobs) averaged $7,451 ($34,947 maximum); and other non-need-based awards and non-need-based scholarships averaged $14,845 ($33,625 maximum). 13% of undergraduate students work part-time. The average financial indebtedness of the 2017 graduate was $28,313. The FAFSA code is 002778. The priority date for freshman financial aid applications for fall entry is February 15.

NAZARETH COLLEGE B-3

ww.naz.edu

Rochester, NY 14618	**(585) 389-2860** **(800) 462-3944**
Fax: (585) 389-2826	**Email: admissions@naz.edu**
Full-time: 558 men, 1481 women	**Faculty:** 181; IIA, -$
Part-time: 27 men, 59 women	**Ph.D.s:** 82%
Graduate: 141 men, 553 women	**Student/Faculty:** 9 to 1
Year: semesters, summer session	**Tuition:** $33,324
Room & Board: $13,460	**Freshman Class:** 4118 applied, 2969 accepted, 517 enrolled
SAT CR/M/W: 540/545/520 **ACT:** required	**CEEB CODE:** 2511
Application Deadline: February 1	**COMPETITIVE**

Nazareth College, founded in 1924, is an independent institution offering programs in the liberal arts and sciences and preprofessional areas. There are 4 undergraduate schools and 4 graduate schools. In addition to regional accreditation, NC has baccalaureate program accreditation with CSWE, NASM, ACS, CCNE, and IACBE. The 150-acre campus is in a suburban area in Pittsburgh, a suburb of Rochester. Including any residence halls, there are 29 buildings.

STUDENT LIFE: 87% of undergraduates are from New York. Others are from 27 states, 22 foreign countries, and Canada. 88% are from public schools. 78% are White; 7% African American; 5% Hispanic; 4% race unknown; 30% Asian American; 2% two or more races. **Female To Male Ratio:** 2.9:1. The average age of freshmen is 18; all undergraduates, 21. 21% do not continue beyond their first year; 68% remain to graduate. **Housing:** 1232 students can be accommodated in college housing, which includes dorms and on-campus apartments. In addition, there are language/international houses, special-interest houses, substance-free floors, freshman experience floors, and honors floors. On-campus housing is guaranteed for all 4 years. 91% of students live on campus. All students may keep cars.

FACULTY/CLASSROOMS: 37% of faculty are male; 63% are female. 93% teach undergraduates. No introductory courses are taught by graduate students. The average class size in an introductory lecture is 21; in a laboratory is 11; and in a regular course is 19.

PROGRAMS OF STUDY: NC confers B.A., B.S., B.F.A., and B.Mus. degrees. Master's and doctoral degrees are also awarded. Bachelor's degrees are awarded in BIOLOGICAL SCIENCE (biochemistry, biology/adolescence education, biology/biological science, and toxicology), BUSINESS (accounting, business administration and management, finance, international business management, and marketing and distribution), COMMUNICATIONS AND THE ARTS (art history, art, Chinese, communication rhetoric/communication, English, fine arts, French, German, information technology, Italian, literature, music, music business management, music history and appreciation, music performance, music theory and composition, musical theater, Spanish, studio art, theatre arts, and visual design), COMPUTER AND PHYSICAL SCIENCE (chemistry, chemistry/adolescence education, and mathematics), EDUCATION (art education, Asian studies, business education, elementary education, English education, foreign languages education, mathematics education, middle school education, music education, psychology education, social science education, and Spanish adolesense education), ENGINEERING AND ENVIRONMENTAL DESIGN (environmental science), HEALTH PROFESSIONS (health science, music therapy, nursing, and speech pathology/audiology), SOCIAL SCIENCE (American studies, anthropology, communication sciences and disorders, economics, history, international studies, legal studies, peace studies, philosophy, political science/government, psychology, religion, social science, social work, sociology, and women's studies). Physical therapy and history are the strongest academically. Physical therapy, nursing, and business have the largest enrollments.

ACTIVITIES: There are no fraternities or sororities. There are 48 groups on campus, including art, band, choir, chorale, chorus, communications, computers, dance, drama, ethnic, honors, international, jazz band, LGBT, literary magazine, musical theater, newspaper, opera, orchestra, political, professional, radio station, religious, social, student government, and yearbook. Popular campus events include Springfest and Siblings Weekend, Welcome Week, Battle of the Beaks, and Family Weekend. **Sports:** There is no sports program at Nazareth. Facilities include a gym, a 25-meter swimming pool, soccer and lacrosse fields, an outdoor turf field, tennis and racquetball courts, a fitness center, a stadium, and a 400-meter all-weather track. **Graduates:** From July 1, 2016 to June 30, 2017, 476 bachelor's degrees were awarded. The most popular majors were health professions and related programs (23%), education (13%), and business/marketing (11%). In an average class, 69% graduate in 6 years or less. Of the 2016 graduating class, 49% were enrolled in graduate school within 6 months of graduation, and 72% were employed.

SERVICES: Counseling and information services are available, as is tutoring in every subject. **Library/Resources:** The library contains 237,203 volumes, 470,000 microform items, 181,114 audio/video tapes/CDs/DVDs, and subscribes to 86,321 periodicals, including electronic. Computerized library services include interlibrary loans, database searching, Internet access, and Wi-Fi capability. Special learning facilities include an art gallery. **Physically Challenged Students:** 80% of the campus is accessible. Facilities include wheelchair ramps, elevators, special parking, specially equipped restrooms, special class scheduling, lowered drinking fountains, and special housing. **Special:** Nazareth offers cross-registration with members of the Rochester Area College Consortium (about 15 colleges participate in this program). Full-time students can register for courses at any of these institutions. Internships are available in any of our academic programs and are arranged through the students academic adviser and Director of Internships. Nazareth participates in the Washington and Albany internship programs. There is study abroad in France, Spain, Italy, and Germany, and there are exchange programs in Australia, Japan, Italy, France, Peru, United Kingdom, Hungary, and Wales. There are 25 national honor societies, a freshman honors program, and 13 departmental honors programs. **Visiting:** There are regularly scheduled orientations for prospective students, including individual appointments, group sessions, campus tours, open houses, and summer academic orientation. There are guides for informal visits; visitors may sit in on classes and stay overnight. To schedule a visit, contact the Admissions Office. **Campus Safety and Security:** Measures include 24-hour foot and vehicle patrol, an emergency notification system, and security escort services. There are shuttle buses, emergency telephones, lighted pathways/sidewalks, controlled access to dorms/residences, an alarm system, and security beepers free to all students.

REQUIREMENTS: Applicants should graduate from an accredited secondary school or have a GED. A minimum of 16 academic credits is required: 4 years of English and 3-4 each of social studies, foreign language, math, and science. An essay is required, as is an audition for music and theater students and a portfolio for art students. An interview is recommended. Nazareth requires applicants to be in the upper 50% of their class. AP and CLEP credits are accepted. Important factors in the admissions decision are leadership record, advanced placement or honors courses, recommendations by school officials, evidence of special talent, personality/intangible qualities, extracurricular activities record, and geographical diversity. Nazareth's new Core Curriculum is all about integration integrating the various ways that different disciplines explore Enduring Questions, engaging in three Integrative Studies courses that help students explore a question of their own, and participating in an Experiential Learning Pathway that helps students integrate what they have learned in the classroom with what is happening in the world. Additional requirements vary by major program. A total of 120 credit hours are required to graduate, with a minimum GPA of 2.0. **Procedure:** Freshmen are admitted in the fall and spring. Entrance exams should be taken by December of the senior year. There are early decision, early admissions, and deferred admissions plans. Early decision applications should be filed by November 15; regular applications, by February

1 for fall entry. The fall 2017 application fee was $45. Notification of early decision is sent December 15; regular decision, December 1. 59 early decision candidates were accepted for the 2017-2018 class. 21 applicants were on the 2017 waiting list; 5 were admitted. Applications are accepted online. **Transfer Students:** 142 transfer students enrolled in 2016-2017. Applicants must have a college GPA of 2.5 (2.75 for education and physical therapy students). Those with fewer than 30 credits must submit high school transcripts. A interview is also required. 30 of 120 credits required for the bachelor's degree must be completed at NC. **International Students:** There are 62 international students enrolled. They must take the TOEFL with a minimum score of 550 on the paper-based TOEFL (PBT) or 79 on the Internet-based version (iBT).

ADMISSIONS: 72% of the 2017-2018 applicants were accepted. The SAT scores for the 2017-2018 freshman class were: Critical Reading-- 26% below 500, 49% between 500 and 599, 22% between 600 and 699, and 3% between 700 and 800. Math-- 27% below 500, 47% between 500 and 599, 25% between 600 and 699, and 1% between 700 and 800. Writing-- 40% below 500, 41% between 500 and 599, 18% between 600 and 699, and 2% between 700 and 800. The ACT scores were 34% between 18 and 23, 56% between 24 and 29, and 10% above 30. 55% of the current freshmen were in the top fifth of their class; 81% were in the top two fifths. 6 freshmen graduated first in their class. **Admissions Contact:** Ian Mortimer, Vice President of Enrollment Management. Email: *admissions@naz.edu* Web: *ww.naz.edu*

FINANCIAL AID: In 2017-2018, 100% of all full-time freshmen received some form of financial aid. 81% of all full-time freshmen received need-based aid. The average freshman award was $26,585. Need-based scholarships or need-based grants averaged $18,244; need-based self-help aid (loans and jobs) averaged $4,409; non-need-based athletic scholarships averaged $18,512; and $3,389 from other forms of aid. 25% of undergraduate students work part-time. The average financial indebtedness of the 2017 graduate was $43,832. NC is a member of CSS. The FAFSA code is 002779. The priority date for freshman financial aid applications for fall entry is February 15.

NEW YORK CITY COLLEGE OF TECHNOLOGY *(The complete profile is made available exclusively on our website, www.barronspac.com)*

NEW YORK INSTITUTE OF TECHNOLOGY D-5

www.nyit.edu

Old Westbury, NY 11568 **(800) 345-NYIT**

Fax: (516) 686-1000	**Email:** admissions@nyit.edu
Full-time: 2072 men, 1194 women	**Faculty:** IIA, ++$
Part-time: 264 men, 126 women	**Ph.D.s:** 93%
Graduate: 1892 men, 1875 women	**Student/Faculty:** 13 to 1
Year: semesters, summer session	**Tuition:** $35,870
Room & Board: $14,110	**Freshman Class:** 9945 applied, 7651 accepted, 895 enrolled
SAT CR/M: 538/582 **ACT:** 24	**CEEB CODE:** 2561
Application Deadline: rolling	**VERY COMPETITIVE**

New York Institute of Technology (NYIT) offers 90 degree programs, including undergraduate, graduate, and professional degrees in more than 50 fields of study, including architecture and design; arts and sciences; education; engineering and computing sciences; health professions; management; and medicine. It is a nonprofit, independent, private, and nonsectarian institution of higher education. Since 1955, NYIT has pursued its mission to provide career-oriented professional education, give all qualified students access to opportunity, and support applications-oriented research that benefits the larger world. There are 6 undergraduate schools and 7 graduate schools. In addition to regional accreditation, NYIT has baccalaureate program accreditation with AACSB, ABET, NAAB, CCNE, and CIDA. The 215-acre campus is in a suburban area 25 miles east of New York City (Old Westbury); NYIT also operates a campus in Manhattan. Including any residence halls, there are 29 buildings.

STUDENT LIFE: 84% of undergraduates are from New York. Others are from 44 states, 93 foreign countries, and Canada. 7% are African American; 3% two or more races; 29% Foreign; 24% White; 14% Asian American; 12% Hispanic; 11% race unknown. **Male To Female Ratio:** 1.3:1. The average age of freshmen is 18; all undergraduates, 22. **Housing:** 631 students can be accommodated in college housing, which includes dorms. On-campus housing is available on a first-come, first-served basis. 86% of students commute. Alcohol is not permitted. All students may keep cars.

FACULTY/CLASSROOMS: 62% of faculty are male; 38% are female. No introductory courses are taught by graduate students.

PROGRAMS OF STUDY: NYIT confers B.A., B.S., B.Arch., B.F.A. and B.P.S. degrees. Associate, master's, and doctoral degrees are also awarded. Bachelor's degrees are awarded in BIOLOGICAL SCIENCE (biotechnology and life science), BUSINESS (accounting, business administration and management, entrepreneurial studies, finance, hospitality management services, human resources/organizational management international business management, marketing management, and urban administration), COMMUNICATIONS AND THE ARTS (advertising, communications, English, film, television and digital media, graphic design, journalism, and telecommunications), COMPUTER AND PHYSICAL SCIENCE (chemistry, computer information technology, and computer science), ENGINEERING AND ENVIRONMENTAL DESIGN (architectural technology, architecture, computer graphics, construction management, electrical and computer engineering, electrical/electronics engineering technology, engineering management, interior design, and mechanical engineering), HEALTH PROFESSIONS (biology, health, health science, and nursing), SOCIAL SCIENCE (behavioral science, criminal justice, interdisciplinary studies, political science/government, psychology, social work, and sociology). Computer science, electrical and computer engineering, and architectural technology have the largest enrollments.

ACTIVITIES: 1% of men belong to 5 national fraternities; 1% of women belong to 2 national sororities. There are 50 groups on campus, including art, cheerleading, communications, computers, dance, drama, environmental, ethnic, film, honors, international, newspaper, political, professional, radio and TV, religious, social, social service, and student government. Popular campus events include May Fest, Relay for Life, Greek Week, and Welcome Week. **Sports:** There are 6 intercollegiate sports for men and 7 for women. The campus recreation center houses a fitness center, basketball gymnasium, and recreation room with table tennis, outdoor tennis and basketball, and fields for softball, lacrosse, baseball, and soccer. **Graduates:** From July 1, 2016 to June 30, 2017, 718 bachelor's degrees were awarded. The most popular majors were business administration (15%), electrical and computer engineering (12%), and biology (7%). In an average class, 23% graduate in 4 years or less, 40% graduate in 5 years or less, and 44% graduate in 6 years or less. Of the 2016 graduating class, 96% were employed within 6 months of graduation.

SERVICES: Counseling and information services are available, as is tutoring in every subject. There is remedial math, reading, and writing. **Library/Resources:** The library contains 191,165 volumes, and 5,286 audio/video tapes/CDs/DVDs. Computerized library services include interlibrary loans, database searching, Internet access, and Wi-Fi capability. Special learning facilities include an art gallery, a radio station, TV station, Gallery 61; NYIT Auditorium on Broadway; Simulated Trading Floor; NYITCOM Healthcare Center; Center of Excellence in Data Visualization, Entertainment, Engineering; and Entrepreneurship and Technology Innovation Center. **Physically Challenged Students:** All of the campus is accessible. Facilities include wheelchair ramps, elevators, special parking, specially equipped restrooms, and lowered drinking fountains. **Special:** NYIT offers a semester-long study abroad programs at its campuses in China, United Arab Emirates, and Canada. Additionally, NYIT offers semester-long exchange programs at IT University of Copenhagen, Rotterdam University (University of Applied Sciences. Other study abroad programs are available. NYIT offers the following combined programs: B.S. Life Sciences/M.S. Occupational Therapy, B.S. Life Sciences/M.S. Physician Assistant Studies, B.S. Life Sciences/Doctor of Physical Therapy, B.S. Life Sciences/Doctor of Osteopathic Medicine, B.F.A./M.A. Communication Arts, B.S./M.B.A. Accounting – CPA Track, and B.S. Psychology/M.S. School Counseling. There are 14 national honor societies and 1 departmental honors program. **Visiting:** There are regularly scheduled orientations for prospective students. A number of of admissions events are held throughout the year, including Fall Open House, Spring Preview Days, Student for a Day events, and transfer and graduate information sessions. Visit www.nyit.edu/admissions/visit_us_events for upcoming dates. There are guides for informal visits and visitors may sit in on classes. To schedule a visit, contact Office of Admissions. **Campus Safety and Security:** Measures include 24-hour foot and vehicle patrol, an emergency notification system, and security escort services. There are shuttle buses, emergency telephones, lighted pathways/sidewalks, controlled access to dorms/ residences, NYIT Alerts, a mass text and voice messaging notification system for emergency communications, and student outreach.

REQUIREMENTS: The SAT or ACT is required, as well as a completed application for admission and $50 application fee, an essay, transcripts of all high school and previous college work, SAT or ACT scores, and two letters of recommendation. There are additional requirements for admission to the School of Architecture and Design, School of Engineering and Computing Sciences, School of Health Professions, and the B.F.A. program. AP and CLEP credits are accepted. All students must take courses in NYITs Discovery Core Curriculum, which is designed to build core competencies in the following areas: Interdisciplinary Mindset and Skills, Global Perspective/Worldview, Literacy, Ethical and Civic Engagement, Process and Nature of Science and the Arts, Critical/ Analytical Thinking, and Communication. **Procedure:** Freshmen are in the admitted fall, spring, and summer. There are deferred admissions and rolling admissions plans. Application deadlines are open. The fall 2017 application fee was $50. Notification is sent on a rolling basis. Applications are accepted online. **Transfer Students:** 285 transfer students enrolled in 2016-2017. A completed application for admission and $50 application fee; official transcript (s) from all colleges attended (if less than 24 credits of college coursework have been completed, official high school transcript (s) and SAT or ACT exam scores are required); GPA; an essay; and letters of recommendation are recommended and may be required for admission to specific programs. 30 of 120 credits required for the bachelor's degree must be completed at NYIT. **International Students:** There are 521 international students enrolled. They must take the TOEFL with a minimum score of 550 on the paper-based TOEFL (PBT) or 79 on the Internet-based version (iBT). Students must take the IELTS, and either the SAT or ACT.

ADMISSIONS: 77% of the 2017-2018 applicants were accepted. The SAT scores for the 2017-2018 freshman class were: Critical Reading-- 32% below 500, 43% between 500 and 599, 22% between 600 and 699, and 4% between 700 and 800. Math-- 21% below 500, 31% between 500 and 599, 36% between 600 and 699, and 13% between 700 and 800. The ACT scores were 4% between 12 and 17, 42% between 18 and 23, 39% between 24 and 29, and 16% above 30. **Admissions Contact:** Admissions Officer Email: *admissions@nyit.edu* Web: *www.nyit.edu*

FINANCIAL AID: In 2017-2018, 95% of all full-time freshmen received some form of financial aid. 77% of all full-time freshmen received need-based aid. The average freshman award was $30,431. Need-based scholarships or need-based grants averaged $8,879; need-based self-help aid (loans and jobs) averaged $2,802; non-need-based athletic scholarships averaged $13,561; and other non-need-based awards and non-need-based scholarships averaged $15,230. The state aid form, and the New York State Tuition Assistance Program (TAP) form are required. The FAFSA code is 002782. The priority date for freshman financial aid applications for fall entry is March 1.

NEW YORK UNIVERSITY D-5

www.nyu.edu

New York, NY 10011 **(212) 998-4500**

Fax: (212) 995-4902
Email: admission@nyu.edu
Full-time: 10,544 men, 14,158 women
Faculty: 2930
Part-time: 452 men, 562 women
Ph.D.s: n/av
Graduate: 10,637 men, 12,976 women
Student/Faculty: 10 to 1
Year: semesters, summer session
Tuition: $50,474
Room & Board: $17,664
Freshman Class: 60724 applied, 19351 accepted, 6139 enrolled
SAT CR/M/W: 670/695/680 **ACT:** 31
CEEB CODE: 2562
Application Deadline: January 1
MOST COMPETITIVE

New York University, founded in 1831, is the largest private university in the United States. NYU, which is composed of 18 schools, colleges, and divisions, occupies 5 major centers in Manhattan and operates branch campus and research programs in other parts of the United States and abroad. In addition to its Manhattan locations, the University is also formally affiliated with the Polytechnic Institute of NYU in Brooklyn, the second oldest school of engineering and technology in the country, and has research facilities, notably the Nelson Institute of Environmental Medicine, in Sterling Forest, near Tuxedo, New York. There are 5 undergraduate schools and 11 graduate schools. In addition to regional accreditation, NYU has baccalaureate program accreditation with AACSB, ACEJMC, ADA, CSWE, NLN, ACS, and APA. The campus is in an urban area in New York Citys Greenwich Village. Including any residence halls, there are 82 buildings.

STUDENT LIFE: 73% of undergraduates are from out of state, mostly the Northeast. Students are from 50 states, 144 foreign countries, and Canada. 7% are race unknown; 6% African American; 4% two or more races; 32% White; 20% Asian American; 18% Foreign; 13% Hispanic. **Female To Male Ratio:** 1.3:1. The average age of freshmen is 18; all undergraduates, 21. 8% do not continue beyond their first year; 84% remain to graduate. **Housing:** 10,774 students can be accommodated in college housing, which includes dorms and on-campus apartments. In addition, there are special-interest houses, fraternity houses, green house and senior housing, SAFE (Substance and Alcohol-Free Environment), First-Year Residential Experience, Sophomore Residential Experience, and Explorations Learning Communities. On-campus housing is guaranteed for all 4 years. 86% of students live on campus. All students may keep cars.

FACULTY/CLASSROOMS: No introductory courses are taught by graduate students.

PROGRAMS OF STUDY: NYU confers B.A., B.S., B.F.A., B.S.B.E., and Mus.B. degrees. Associate, master's, and doctoral degrees are also awarded. Bachelor's degrees are awarded in AGRICULTURE (environmental studies), BIOLOGICAL SCIENCE (biochemistry, biology/ biological science, cell biology, microbiology, neurosciences, and nutrition), BUSINESS (accounting, banking and finance, business administration and management, business economics, business law, finance, hotel/motel and restaurant management, human resources, industrial and labor relations, international business management, management information systems, management science, marketing management, marketing/retailing/merchandising, operations management, operations research, organizational behavior, property management, real estate, recreation and leisure services, and sports management), COMMUNICATIONS AND THE ARTS (Africana studies, American literature, animation, Arabic, art history, art history and appreciation, arts administration/management, classical languages, classics, communications, communications technology, comparative literature, creative writing, dance, design, digital communications, dramatic arts, English, English literature, film arts, fine arts, French, German, Germanic languages and literature, graphic design, Greek, Greek (classical), Greek (modern), Hebrew, information technology, instrumental performance, Italian, journalism, languages, Latin, linguistics, literature, media arts, music, music business management, music composition, music performance, music technology, music theory and composition, performing arts, photography, piano performance, Portuguese, public relations, publishing, radio/television technology, romance languages and literature, Russian, Slavic languages, Spanish, speech/debate/rhetoric, studio art, technical and business writing, theater management, vocal performance, voice, and writing), COMPUTER AND PHYSICAL SCIENCE (actuarial science, chemistry, computer engineering technology, computer mathematics, computer science, digital arts/technology, earth science, information sciences and systems, mathematics, mathematics – economics, physics, and statistics), EDUCATION (art education, Asian studies, bilingual/bicultural education, childhood education, dance education, early childhood education, education, elementary education, English education, foreign languages education, general studies, global studies, mathematics education, music education, nursing education, school psychology, science education, secondary education, social science education, social studies education, social studies secondary school education, special education, and speech correction), ENGINEERING AND ENVIRONMENTAL DESIGN (biomedical engineering, chemical engineering, civil engineering, computational sciences, computer engineering, construction management, electrical and computer engineering, electrical/electronics engineering, engineering, engineering chemistry, engineering mechanics, engineering physics, graphic arts technology, mechanical engineering, and urban design), HEALTH PROFESSIONS (art therapy, dental hygiene, environmental health science, health care administration, music therapy, nursing, nursing home administration, occupational therapy, pharmacology, physical therapy, prehealth studies, predentistry, premedicine, public health, and speech pathology/ audiology), SOCIAL SCIENCE (African studies, African American studies, American studies, anthropology, applied psychology, architectural studies, area studies, Asian/American studies, Asian/Oriental studies, child care/child and family studies, classical/ancient civilization, counseling/psychology, developmental psychology, early childhood studies, East Asian studies, economics, ethnic studies, European studies, French studies, gender studies, history, humanities, humanities and social science, Iberian studies, international relations, Islamic studies, Italian studies, Japanese studies, Judaic studies, Latin American studies, law, Luso-Brazilian studies, medieval studies, Middle Eastern studies, Pacific area studies, philosophy, philosophy and religion, political science/government, psychology, public administration, religion, religious studies, Russian and Slavic studies, social science, social studies, social work, sociology, and urban studies). Business, individualized majors, and theatre have the largest enrollments.

ACTIVITIES: 5% of men belong to 19 national fraternities; 5% of women belong to 12 national sororities. Groups on campus include art, bagpipe, band, cheerleading, chess, choir, chorale, chorus, computers, dance, debate, drama, environmental, ethnic, film, forensics, honors, international, jazz band, LGBT, literary magazine, marching band, musical theater, newspaper, opera, orchestra, pep band, photography, political, professional, radio and TV, religious, social, social service, student government, and symphony. Popular campus events include Spring Strawberry Festival, Grad Alley, and Career Services Fair. **Sports:** There are 10 intercollegiate sports for men and 9 for women, and 9 intramural sports for men and 9 for women. Facilities include multipurpose courts for basketball, volleyball, tennis, badminton, squash courts, handball and racquetball courts, rooftop tennis courts and a running track, a 25-meter swimming pool, a diving tank, weight-training facilities, an aerobic fitness room, wrestling, judo, fencing, physical fitness, dance, and a rock-climbing wall. The athletic center is equipped with a 25-yard swimming pool, basketball/activities courts, a foot aerobic fitness room with cardio equipment, and a 30-foot indoor climbing wall. **Graduates:** From July 1, 2016 to June 30, 2017, 5914 bachelor's degrees were awarded. The most popular majors were visual and performing arts (19%), social sciences (14%), and business/marketing (12%).

SERVICES: Counseling and information services are available, as is tutoring in every subject. There is a reader service for the blind. There are also Sign Language interpreters, scribes, research aides, and note takers for special needs. **Library/Resources:** Computerized library services include interlibrary loans, database searching, Internet access, and Wi-Fi capability. Special learning facilities include an art gallery, a radio and TV stations, a speech-language-hearing clinic, a center for students with disabilities, and Speaking Freely (free noncredit foreign language classes). **Physically Challenged Students:** 95% of the campus is accessible. Facilities include wheelchair ramps, elevators, specially equipped restrooms, special class scheduling, lowered drinking fountains, lowered telephones, special housing. buses with hydraulic lifts, adaptive computer equipment, CART or C-print services, a CTV enlargement system, a JAWS speech synthesizer, Dragon Dictate Voice Recognition, and Kurzweil Personal Readers. **Special:** A vast array of internships is available, as well as study worldwide at NYUs 10 sites: Berlin, Buenos Aires, Florence, Ghana, London, Madrid, Paris, Prague, Shanghai, and Tel Aviv. B.A.-B.S. degree options, accelerated degrees in more than 230 majors, dual and student-designed majors, credit by exam, and pass/fail options are also available. A Washington semester is available to political science majors. There are exchange programs with several historically black colleges. There is a chapter of Phi Beta Kappa and a freshman honors program. **Visiting:** There are regularly scheduled orientations for prospective students, including campus tours and weekday information sessions by appointment. There are also 2 fall open houses. To schedule a visit, contact the Office of Undergraduate Admissions. **Campus Safety and Security:** Measures include 24-hour foot and vehicle patrol, an emergency notification system, self-defense education, and security escort services. There are shuttle buses, emergency telephones, lighted pathways/sidewalks, 24-hour security in residence halls, and a neighborhood-merchant emergency help service.

REQUIREMENTS: The SAT or ACT is required. The ACT Optional Writing test is also required. Applicants must graduate from an accredited secondary school. The GED is accepted. Students must present at least 16 Carnegie units, including 4 units in English, and 3 units each in math, science with lab, foreign language, social studies, and history. Some majors require an audition or submission of a creative portfolio. All applicants must submit an essay and 2 letters of recommendation. Applicants can submit the SAT and 2 SAT Subject tests; the ACT with Writing; the SAT and 2 Advanced Placement (AP) exam scores; 3 SAT Subject tests (1 in literature or the humanities, 1 in math/science, and 1 in any nonlanguage area); or 3 AP exam scores (1 in literature/humanities, 1 in math/science, and 1 in any nonlanguge area). AP credits are accepted. Important factors in the admissions decision are advanced placement or honors courses, evidence of special talent, personality/intangible qualities, extracurricular activities record, and recommendations by school officials. All students must complete a minimum of 128 credit hours and maintain a minimum GPA of 2.0. A course in expository writing is required. Students must complete a core liberal arts curriculum in addition to major and elective credit. **Procedure:** Freshmen are admitted in the fall and spring. Entrance exams should be taken by November of the senior year. There is a early decision plan. Early decision applications should be filed by November 1; regular applications, by January 1 for fall entry. The fall 2017 application fee was $70. Notification of early decision is sent December 15; regular decision, February 15. 1967 early decision candidates were accepted for the 2017-2018 class. 8060 applicants were on the 2017 waiting list; 2425 were admitted. Applications are accepted online. **Transfer Students:** 807 transfer students enrolled in 2016-2017. Students must submit official college transcripts from all postsecondary institutions attended, a final high school transcript, and SAT scores. 64 of 128 credits required for the bachelor's degree must be completed at NYU. **International Students:** There are 3024 international students enrolled. They must take the TOEFL and the colleges own test, or take the IELTS or have ESL testing. They must also take the SAT or ACT.

ADMISSIONS: 32% of the 2017-2018 applicants were accepted. The SAT scores for the 2017-2018 freshman class were: Critical Reading-- 1% below 500, 13% between 500 and 599, 50% between 600 and 699, and 36% between 700 and 800. Math-- 1% below 500, 12% between 500 and 599, 40% between 600 and 699, and 47% between 700 and 800. Writing-- 1% below 500, 11% between 500 and 599, 45% between 600 and 699, and 43% between 700 and 800. The ACT scores were 1% between 18 and 23, 32% between 24 and 29, and 67% above 30. **Admissions Contact:** Shawn L Abbott, Dean of Admissions. Email: *admission@nyu.edu* Web: *www.nyu.edu*

FINANCIAL AID: The average freshman award was $37,805. Need-based scholarships or need-based grants averaged $34,462; need-based self-help aid (loans and jobs) averaged $5,179; other non-need-based awards and non-need-based scholarships averaged $3,823; and $4,476 from other forms of aid. The average financial indebtedness of the 2017 graduate was $55,949. The CSS/Profile and the state aid form are required. The FAFSA code is 002785. The priority date for freshman financial aid applications for fall entry is February 15.

NIAGARA UNIVERSITY A-3

www.niagara.edu

Niagara University, NY 14109	**(716) 286-8700** **(800) 462-2111**
Fax: (716) 286-8710	**Email: admissions@niagara.edu**
Full-time: 1153 men, 1680 women	**Faculty:** 140
Part-time: 88 men, 255 women	**Ph.D.s:** n/av
Graduate: 293 men, 604 women	**Student/Faculty:** 18 to 1
Year: semesters, summer session	**Tuition:** $29,060
Room & Board: $11,950	**Freshman Class:** 3565 applied, 2348 accepted, 616 enrolled
SAT CR/M/W: 510/530/500 **ACT:** 23	**CEEB CODE:** 2558
Application Deadline: August 1	**COMPETITIVE**

Niagara University, founded in 1856 by the Vincentian Fathers and Brothers, is a private institution rooted in a Roman Catholic tradition. Programs offered include those in liberal arts, business, education, nursing, and travel, hotel, and restaurant administration. There are 4 undergraduate schools and 4 graduate schools. In addition to regional accreditation, NU has baccalaureate program accreditation with AACSB, CSWE, ACPHA, ACS, and CCNE. The 160-acre campus is in a suburban area 4 miles north of Niagara Falls, 20 miles north of Buffalo, and 90 miles from Toronto, Canada. Including any residence halls, there are 32 buildings.

STUDENT LIFE: 78% of undergraduates are from New York. Others are from 32 states, 26 foreign countries, and Canada. 71% are White; 10% Foreign; 6% African American; 6% race unknown; 4% Hispanic; 2%

Asian American; 2% two or more races; 1% American Indian/Alaska Native. 31% are Catholic. **Female To Male Ratio:** 1.7:1. The average age of freshmen is 18; all undergraduates, 21. 16% do not continue beyond their first year; 64% remain to graduate. **Housing:** 1455 students can be accommodated in college housing, which includes dorms and on-campus apartments. In addition, there are special-interest houses. On-campus housing is guaranteed for all 4 years and is available on a lottery system for upperclassmen. 52% of students live on campus. All students may keep cars.

FACULTY/CLASSROOMS: 60% of faculty are male; 40% are female. 89% teach undergraduates. No introductory courses are taught by graduate students. The average class size in an introductory lecture is 23; in a laboratory is 16; and in a regular course is 23.

PROGRAMS OF STUDY: NU confers B.A., B.S., B.B.A., and B.F.A. degrees. Associate, master's, and doctoral degrees are also awarded. Bachelor's degrees are awarded in AGRICULTURE (environmental studies), BIOLOGICAL SCIENCE (biochemistry, bioinformatics, biology/adolescence education, biology/biological science, and life science), BUSINESS (accounting, business administration and management, business administration marketing, business economics, finance, hotel/motel and restaurant management, human resources, international business, marketing/retailing/merchandising, sports management, tourism, and transportation management), COMMUNICATIONS AND THE ARTS (art history, communication studies, communications, dramatic arts, English, foreign language, French, Spanish, theatre arts, and theater design), COMPUTER AND PHYSICAL SCIENCE (chemistry, chemistry/adolescence education, chemistry education, computer information technology, computer information systems, computer science, information sciences and systems, information science, and mathematics), EDUCATION (business education, childhood education, early childhood education, education, education of the exceptional child, elementary education, English education, foreign languages education, mathematics education, middle school education, museum studies, science education, secondary education, social studies education, social studies secondary school education, Spanish education K-12, Spanish adolescense education, special education, and teaching English as a second/foreign language (TESOL/TEFOL), HEALTH PROFESSIONS (biology and nursing), SOCIAL SCIENCE (child psychology/development, criminal justice, criminology, early childhood studies, economics, history, international studies, liberal arts/general studies, philosophy, political science/government, psychology, religion, religious studies, social science, social work, and sociology). Business, social sciences, and biology are the strongest academically. Business and hospitality and tourism management have the largest enrollments.

ACTIVITIES: 4% of men belong to 1 local and 1 national fraternities; 4% of women belong to 2 national sororities. There are 81 groups on campus, including art, cheerleading, choir, dance, drama, drill team, environmental, ethnic, honors, international, literary magazine, musical theater, newspaper, pep band, political, professional, radio and TV, religious, social, social service, student government, and yearbook. Popular campus events include Orientation, CARE, and RidgeFest. **Sports:** There are 8 intercollegiate sports for men and 10 for women, and 25 intramural sports for men and 25 for women. Facilities include a gym, a swimming and diving pool, exercise and weight rooms, dance areas, outdoor tennis and basketball courts, baseball and soccer fields, a rugby pitch, basketball and racquetball courts, a hockey arena, and multipurpose courts with an indoor track, and hiking and biking trails are nearby. **Graduates:** From July 1, 2016 to June 30, 2017, 880 bachelor's degrees were awarded. The most popular majors were education (33%), business (17%), and hospitality and tourism management (14%). In an average class, 3% graduate in 3 years or less, 59% graduate in 4 years or less, 64% graduate in 5 years or less, and 64% graduate in 6 years or less. Of the 2016 graduating class, 26% were enrolled in graduate school within 6 months of graduation, and 80% were employed.

SERVICES: Counseling and information services are available, as is tutoring in most subjects. There is a reader service for the blind, and remedial math and writing. Study skills development, note taking, and escort-assistance services are available, as are educational assistant services for the vision-impaired, educational/classroom assistance and machines for the hearing-impaired, and services for the learning disabled. **Library/Resources:** The library contains 165,444 volumes, 6,450 microform items, 6,603 audio/video tapes/CDs/DVDs, and subscribes to 23,500 periodicals, including electronic. Computerized library services include interlibrary loans, database searching, Internet access, and Wi-Fi capability. Special learning facilities include an art gallery, radio station, an theatre, greenhouse, nursing simulation lab, and a family literacy center. **Physically Challenged Students:** 75% of the campus is accessible. Facilities include wheelchair ramps, elevators, special parking, specially equipped restrooms, special class scheduling, lowered drinking fountains, and special housing. **Special:** NU offers a Washington semester, a semester at the state capitol in Albany, on-campus work-study, internships in most majors with such companies as the Big 6 accounting firms and Walt Disney World, and co-op programs in all areas except nursing, education, and social work. Students may study abroad in 8 countries and cross-register through the Western New York Consortium. An accelerated degree program in business; B.A.-B.S. degrees; dual majors; nondegree study; credit for life, military, and work experience; pass/fail options; and research are also available. There is also an academic exploration program for undeclared majors. There are 19 national honor societies and a freshman honors program. **Visiting:** There are regularly scheduled orientations for prospective students, including individual interviews and campus tours. Other arrangements can be made individually, such as to attend a class, eat in the student cafeteria, and/or speak with a faculty member. There are guides for informal visits; visitors may sit in on classes and stay overnight. To schedule a visit, contact the Admissions Office. **Campus Safety and Security:** Measures include 24-hour foot and vehicle patrol, an emergency notification system, self-defense education, and security escort services. There are emergency telephones, lighted pathways/sidewalks, controlled access to dorms/residences, and a campus security advisory board.

REQUIREMENTS: The SAT or ACT is required. Applicants should be graduates of an accredited high school. The GED is accepted. The high school program should include 16 academic credits, with 4 in English and 2 each in foreign language, history, math, science, and social studies, as well as academic electives. Science, math, and computer majors should have 3 credits each in math and science. AP and CLEP credits are accepted. Important factors in the admissions decision are advanced placement or honors courses, parents or siblings attended your school, and recommendations by school officials. To graduate, students must earn 120 to 126 credit hours and a GPA of at least 2.0; 60 to 66 such hours are required in the major, 20 in specific disciplines, and 20 in liberal arts classes. A comprehensive exam is required in some majors; a thesis is required of honor students and some majors. **Procedure:** Freshmen are admitted to all sessions. Entrance exams should be taken In the junior year or fall of the senior year. There are early decision, early admissions, deferred admissions, and rolling admissions plans. Applications should be filed by August 1 for fall entry. Notification is sent on a rolling basis. Applications are accepted online. **Transfer Students:** 174 transfer students enrolled in 2016-2017. Applicants must have a minimum GPA of 2.0 in travel, hotel, and restaurant administration, arts and sciences, and academic exploration (except for 2.25 in business and 2.5 for nursing and education majors) and submit all high school and college transcripts. The SAT or ACT is recommended. 30 of 120 credits required for the bachelor's degree must be completed at NU. **International Students:** There are 302 international students enrolled. They must take the TOEFL with a minimum score of 550 on the paper-based TOEFL (PBT) or 79 on the Internet-based version (iBT).

ADMISSIONS: 66% of the 2017-2018 applicants were accepted. The SAT scores for the 2017-2018 freshman class were: Critical Reading-- 10% below 500, 48% between 500 and 599, 11% between 600 and 699, and 1% between 700 and 800. Math-- 32% below 500, 51% between 500 and 599, 17% between 600 and 699, and 1% between 700 and 800. Writing-- 49% below 500, 40% between 500 and 599, 10% between 600 and 699, and 1% between 700 and 800. The ACT scores were 27% below 12, 29% between 12 and 17, 26% between 18 and 23, 13% between 24 and 29, and 5% above 30. **Admissions Contact:** Harry Gong, Director of Admissions. Email: *admissions@niagara.edu* Web: *www.niagara.edu*

FINANCIAL AID: NU is a member of CSS. The FAFSA code is 002788. The priority date for freshman financial aid applications for fall entry is February 15.

NYACK COLLEGE *(The complete profile is made available exclusively on our website, www.barronspac.com)*

PACE UNIVERSITY D-5
www.pace.edu

New York, NY 10038 **(212) 346-1323**

Fax: (212) 346-1831 **Email: infoctr@pace.edu**
Full-time: 3003 men, 4875 women
Part-time: 483 men, 639 women
Graduate: 1693 men, 2619 women
Year: semesters, summer session
Room & Board: $16,100

Faculty: 475; I, av$
Ph.D.s: 89%
Student/Faculty: 16 to 1
Tuition: $44,036
Freshman Class: 20944 applied, 16662 accepted, 1999 enrolled

SAT CR/M: 550/540 **ACT:** 25
Application Deadline: February 15

CEEB CODE: 2635
COMPETITIVE

Pace University, founded in 1906, has produced thinking professionals by providing high-quality education for the professions with a firm base in liberal learning amid the advantages of the New York Metropolitan area. A private univerisity, Pace has campuses in New York City and Westchester County, enrolling students in bachelors, masters, and doctoral programs in its College of Health Professions, Dyson College of Arts and Sciences, Lubin School of Business, School of Education, Elizabeth Haub School of Law, and Seidenberg School of Computer Science and Information Systems. There are 5 undergraduate schools and 6 graduate schools. In addition to regional accreditation, Pace has baccalaureate program accreditation with AACSB, ABET, CCNE, ARC-PA, and ACE. The 246-acre campus is in an urban area. Pace University's lower Manhattan campus is in the heart of the Financial District. The Pleasantville campus is in Westchester County. Including any residence halls, there are 65 buildings.

STUDENT LIFE: 59% of undergraduates are from New York. Others are from 48 states, 136 foreign countries, and Canada. 75% are from public schools. 8% are Asian American; 49% White; 4% two or more races; 3% race unknown; 12% Hispanic; 14% Foreign; 10% African American. **Female To Male Ratio:** 1.5:1. The average age of freshmen is 18; all undergraduates, 21. 23% do not continue beyond their first year; 58% remain to graduate. **Housing:** 3642 students can be accommodated in college housing, which includes dorms and on-campus apartments. In addition, there are honors houses, special-interest houses, and a wellness floor. 55% of students commute. There is no student parking in NYC.

FACULTY/CLASSROOMS: 50% of faculty are male; 50% are female. 84% teach undergraduates, and 24% do research. No introductory courses are taught by graduate students. The average class size in an introductory lecture is 35; in a laboratory is 11; and in a regular course is 23.

PROGRAMS OF STUDY: Pace confers B.A., B.S., B.B.A., B.F.A., and B.S.N. degrees. Associate, master's, and doctoral degrees are also awarded. Bachelor's degrees are awarded in AGRICULTURE (environmental studies), BIOLOGICAL SCIENCE (biochemistry, biology/adolescence education, biology/biological science, and forensic science), BUSINESS (accounting, banking and finance, business administration and management, business economics, entrepreneurial studies, finance, hospitality management services, human resources, international business management, international marketing, marketing/retailing/merchandising, and sports marketing), COMMUNICATIONS AND THE ARTS (acting, advertising, art history, art, art history and appreciation, communication studies, communications, dance, English, English literature, film arts, fine arts, information technology, media management, modern language, musical theater, public relations, Spanish, stage management, theatre acting, theatre arts, theater design, theatre production, and theater management), COMPUTER AND PHYSICAL SCIENCE (chemistry, computer science, computer security and information assurance, earth science/adolescence education, information sciences and systems, mathematics, physics, and quantitative methods), EDUCATION (Asian studies, education of the deaf and hearing impaired, and elementary education), ENGINEERING AND ENVIRONMENTAL DESIGN (environmental science), HEALTH PROFESSIONS (health science and nursing), SOCIAL SCIENCE (American studies, applied psychology, biopsychology, communication sciences and disorders, criminal justice, economics, forensic studies, history, Latin American studies, philosophy and religion, political science/government, psychology, social science, sociology, and women and gender studies). Accounting is the strongest academically. Finance, accounting, and nursing have the largest enrollments.

ACTIVITIES: 2% of men belong to 1 local and 11 national fraternities; 3% of women belong to 3 local and 11 national sororities. There are 88 groups on campus, including art, cheerleading, chorus, computers, dance, debate, drama, environmental, ethnic, film, honors, international, LGBT, literary magazine, musical theater, newspaper, photography, political, professional, radio and TV, religious, social, social service, student government, and yearbook. Popular campus events include Homecoming, CariCulture, and Live Love Laugh. **Sports:** There are 6 intercollegiate sports for men and 8 for women, and 9 intramural sports for men and 9 for women. The Civic Center gym in New York City offers football, lacrosse, soccer, softball, baseball fields, and tennis courts. **Graduates:** From July 1, 2016 to June 30, 2017, 1694 bachelor's degrees were awarded. The most popular majors were nursing (9%), accounting (9%), and finance (8%). In an average class, 1% graduate in 3 years or less, 36% graduate in 4 years or less, 52% graduate in 5 years or less, and 55% graduate in 6 years or less. Of the 2016 graduating class, 5% were enrolled in graduate school within 6 months of graduation, and 53% were employed.

SERVICES: Counseling and information services are available, as is tutoring in every subject. There is remedial math, reading, and writing. All services are provided in the University's Center for Academic Excellence. **Library/Resources:** The library contains 766,508 volumes, 53,581 microform items, 5,529 audio/video tapes/CDs/DVDs, and subscribes to 473,330 periodicals, including electronic. Computerized library services include interlibrary loans, database searching, Internet access, and Wi-Fi capability. Special learning facilities include an art gallery, radio station, TV station, 2 art galleries, a performing arts center, biological research labs, an environmental center, a language lab, and computer labs. **Physically Challenged Students:** 90% of the campus is accessible. Facilities include wheelchair ramps, elevators, special parking, special class scheduling, lowered drinking fountains, and lowered telephones. **Special:** Internships, study abroad, and a cooperative education program in all majors are available. Pace also offers accelerated degree programs, B.A.-B.S. degrees, dual majors, general studies degrees, and 3-2 engineering degrees with Manhattan College and Rensselaer Polytechnic Institute. Credit for life, military, and work experience; nondegree study; and pass/fail options are available. There are 25 national honor societies, a freshman honors program, and 19 departmental honors programs. **Visiting:** There are regularly scheduled orientations for prospective students, including student-for-a-day programs and overnight visits by appointment. There are guides for informal visits; visitors may sit in on classes and stay overnight. To schedule a visit, contact the Office of Undergraduate Admission. **Campus Safety and Security:** Measures include 24-hour foot and vehicle patrol, an emergency notification system, land security escort services. Lighted pathways/sidewalks, controlled access to dorms/residences, including closed circuit TV.

REQUIREMENTS: Applicants should be graduates of an accredited secondary school with at least 16 academic credits, including 4 in English, 3-4 each in math, science, and history, and 2-3 in a foreign language. The GED is accepted, as well as the official SAT or ACT scores. An essay is required, two letters of recommendation from a teacher or counselor who can attest to the student's academic potential and personal characteristics. AP and CLEP credits are accepted. Important factors in the admissions decision are advanced placement or honors courses, recommendations by school officials, and leadership record. To graduate, students must complete 128 to 133 credit hours depending on the major, including 32 to 50 in the major, with a minimum GPA of 2.0. A core curriculum with a minimum of 44 credits that includes an introductory computer science course as well as a community-based learning experience and 2 enhanced writing courses is also required. **Procedure:** Freshmen are admitted in the fall and spring. Entrance exams should be taken by December of the senior year. There are early admissions, deferred admissions, and rolling admissions plans. Early decision applications should be filed by November 1; regular applications, by February 15 for fall entry; and December 1 for spring entry. The fall 2017 application fee was $50. Notification of early decision is sent December 1; regular decision, December 15. Applications are accepted on-line. **Transfer Students:** 1086 transfer students enrolled in 2016-2017. Applicants are admitted in the fall or spring. A college GPA of 2.5 is required. Grades of C or better transfer for credit. A maximum of 68 credits will be accepted from a 2-year school. Students who transfer with less than 32 credits also need to submit SAT or ACT scores. 32 of 128 credits required for the bachelor's degree must be completed at Pace. **International Students:** There are 794 international students enrolled. They must take the TOEFL with a minimum score of 570 on the paper-based TOEFL (PBT) or 89 on the Internet-based version (iBT) and the college's own test.

ADMISSIONS: 84% of the 2017-2018 applicants were accepted. The

SAT scores for the 2017-2018 freshman class were: Critical Reading-- 21% below 500, 53% between 500 and 599, 23% between 600 and 699, and 3% between 700 and 800. Math-- 22% below 500, 53% between 500 and 599, 23% between 600 and 699, and 2% between 700 and 800. The ACT scores were 2% between 12 and 17, 44% between 18 and 23, 48% between 24 and 29, and 8% above 30. 36% of the current freshmen were in the top fifth of their class; 70% were in the top two fifths. **Admissions Contact:** Robina C. Schepp, Vice President of Enrollment Management. Email: *infoctr@pace.edu* Web: *www.pace.edu*

FINANCIAL AID: In 2017-2018, 74% of all full-time freshmen received some form of financial aid and need-based aid. The average freshman award was $34,380. Need-based scholarships or need-based grants averaged $29,138; need-based self-help aid (loans and jobs) averaged $8,965; non-need-based athletic scholarships averaged $11,333; and other non-need-based awards and non-need-based scholarships averaged $21,547. The average financial indebtedness of the 2017 graduate was $37,473. The FAFSA code is 002791. The priority date for freshman financial aid applications for fall entry is November 15.

PARSONS THE NEW SCHOOL FOR DESIGN *(The complete profile is made available exclusively on our website, www.barronspac.com)*

PRATT INSTITUTE — D-5
www.pratt.edu

Brooklyn, NY 11205	**(718) 636-3514** **(800) 331-0834**
Fax: (718) 636-3670	**Email: admissions@pratt.edu**
Full-time: 1005 men, 2307 women	**Faculty:** 104; IIA, +$
Part-time: 33 men, 51 women	**Ph.D.s:** 75%
Graduate: 371 men, 1019 women	**Student/Faculty:** 30 to 1
Year: semesters, summer session	**Tuition:** $47,986
Room & Board: $11,496	**Freshman Class:** 4819 applied, 3186 accepted, 703 enrolled
SAT EBR-W/M: 580/620 **ACT:** 27	**CEEB CODE:** 2669
Application Deadline: January 5	**VERY COMPETITIVE+**

Pratt Institute, founded in 1887, is a private institution offering undergraduate and graduate programs in architecture, art and design education, art history, art therapy, critical and visual studies, industrial, interior, and communication design, fine arts, design management, arts and cultural management, writing and library science. There are 4 undergraduate schools and 5 graduate schools. In addition to regional accreditation, PI has baccalaureate program accreditation with FIDER, NAAB, NASAD, and ALA. The 25-acre campus is in an urban area 3 miles east of downtown Manhattan. Including any residence halls, there are 28 buildings.

STUDENT LIFE: 78% of undergraduates are from out of state, mostly the Middle Atlantic. Students are from 47 states, 82 foreign countries, and Canada. 9% are Hispanic; 5% African American; 39% White; 30% Foreign; 3% race unknown; 2% two or more races; 12% Asian American. **Female To Male Ratio:** 2.4:1. The average age of freshmen is 18; all undergraduates, 20. 15% do not continue beyond their first year; 63% remain to graduate. **Housing:** 1700 students can be accommodated in college housing, which includes dorms and on-campus apartments. In addition, there are special-interest houses, special interest communities such as healthy choices, global learning, community service, quiet floor, and gender blind. On-campus housing is guaranteed for the freshman year only, and is available on a first-come, first-served basis, and is available on a lottery system for upperclassmen. 53% of students live on campus. All students may keep cars.

FACULTY/CLASSROOMS: 58% of faculty are male; 42% are female. 76% teach undergraduates. No introductory courses are taught by graduate students. The average class size in an introductory lecture is 22; in a laboratory is 20; and in a regular course is 15.

PROGRAMS OF STUDY: PI confers B.Arch., B.F.A., B.I.D., and B.P.S. degrees. Associate and master's degrees are also awarded. Bachelor's degrees are awarded in COMMUNICATIONS AND THE ARTS (art history and appreciation, communications, creative writing, film arts, fine arts, industrial design, and photography), EDUCATION (art education), ENGINEERING AND ENVIRONMENTAL DESIGN (architecture, computer graphics, construction management, and interior design), SOCIAL SCIENCE (fashion design and technology). Architecture, interior design, and fine arts are the strongest academically. Architecture, communications design, and interior design have the largest enrollments.

ACTIVITIES: There are 50 groups on campus, including art, environmental, ethnic, film, honors, international, LGBT, literary magazine, martial arts, newspaper, photography, professional, radio and TV, religious, social, social service, student government, and yearbook. Popular campus events include Springfest, International Food Fair, and Holiday Ball. **Sports:** There are 6 intercollegiate sports for men and 4 for women, and 3 intramural sports for men and 1 for women. Facilities include an activities resource center containing indoor tennis courts, a 200-meter indoor track, volleyball and basketball courts, a weight room, and dance studios. **Graduates:** From July 1, 2016 to June 30, 2017, 615 bachelor's degrees were awarded. The most popular majors were visual and performing arts (74%), architecture (19%), and liberal arts (5%).

SERVICES: Counseling and information services are available, as is tutoring in some subjects, such as math, English, science, social science, and art history. There is a reader service for the blind. Individual tutoring and testing services are also available. **Library/Resources:** The library contains 212,934 volumes, 6,384 microform items, and 3,500 audio/video tapes/CDs/DVDs, and subscribes to 700 periodicals, including electronic. Computerized library services include interlibrary loans, database searching, Internet access, and Wi-Fi capability. Special learning facilities include an art gallery, a radio station, a foundry, and woodshop. **Physically Challenged Students:** 75% of the campus is accessible. Facilities include wheelchair ramps, elevators, special parking, specially equipped restrooms, lowered drinking fountains, and special housing. **Special:** Internships, study abroad in 4 countries (Denmark, Italy, Japan, and Greece), dual degree programs, work-study programs on campus, credit for work experience, nondegree study, and pass/fail options are available. There are 4 national honor societies. **Visiting:** There are regularly scheduled orientations for prospective students, including a campus tours, schoolwide presentations, departmental presentations, and financial aid workshops. There are guides for informal visits and visitors may sit in on classes. To schedule a visit, contact the Office of Admissions. **Campus Safety and Security:** Measures include 24-hour foot and vehicle patrol, an emergency notification system, and security escort services. There are emergency telephones, lighted pathways/sidewalks, controlled access to dorms/residences, and orientation safety workshops.

REQUIREMENTS: The SAT or ACT is required. The ACT Optional Writing test is also required. SAT Subject tests in writing and mathematics level I or II are recommended for architecture applicants. Applicants must be graduates of an accredited secondary school. The GED is accepted. Students should have completed 4 years each of English and math, and 2 years each of science and history, and 1 of social studies. A portfolio is required. An interview is recommended but not required. AP and CLEP credits are accepted. Important factors in the admissions decision are evidence of special talent, advanced placement or honors courses, and recommendations by school officials. The number of credits needed for graduation varies with the major, but a minimum of 132 is required, one quarter of which must be in liberal arts. Undergraduates must maintain a GPA of 2.0. All students must take 13 credits (15 for architecture majors) of liberal arts electives; 6 credits each of social sciences or philosophy, English, and cultural history; and 3 credits of science. **Procedure:** Freshmen are admitted in the fall and spring. Entrance exams should be taken by November of the senior year. There is a deferred admissions plan. Early decision applications should be filed by November 1; regular applications, by January 5 for fall entry; and October 1 for spring entry. The fall 2017 application fee was $50. Notifications are sent April 1. 930 applicants were on the 2017 waiting list; 10 were admitted. Applications are accepted online. **Transfer Students:** 152 transfer students enrolled in 2016-2017. Applicants should present college transcripts and recommendations. All transfer applicants without an associate degree must submit high school transcripts as well. A portfolio is required for architecture, writing, and art and design students. Applicants must have a statement of good standing from prior institution(s). 48 of 132 credits required for the bachelor's degree must be completed at PI. **International Students:** There are 845 international students enrolled. They must take the TOEFL with a minimum score of 550 on the paper-based TOEFL (PBT) or 79 on the Internet-based version (iBT). Student must take the college's own test.

ADMISSIONS: 66% of the 2017-2018 applicants were accepted. The SAT scores for the 2017-2018 freshman class were: Evidence-Based Reading/Writing-- 9% below 500, 47% between 500 and 599, 37%

between 600 and 699, and 7% between 700 and 800. The ACT scores were 13% between 18 and 23, 62% between 24 and 29, and 25% above 30. **Admissions Contact:** Judith Aaron, Vice President for Enrollment. Email: *admissions@pratt.edu* Web: *www.pratt.edu*

FINANCIAL AID: In 2017-2018, 76% of all full-time freshmen received some form of financial aid. 51% of all full-time freshmen received need-based aid. The average freshman award was $17,267. 45% of undergraduate students work part-time. The average financial indebtedness of the 2017 graduate was $29,471. Pratt is a member of CSS. The state aid form and the college's own financial statement, the parents and students tax returns, are required. The FAFSA code is 002798. The priority date for freshman financial aid applications for fall entry is March 1.

RENSSELAER POLYTECHNIC INSTITUTE D-3

www.rpi.edu

Troy, NY 12180 **(518) 276-6216** **(800) 448-6562**

Fax: (518) 276-4072 **Email: admissions@rpi.edu**

Full-time: 4286 men, 2019 women
Part-time: 8 men, 1 women
Graduate: 868 men, 385 women
Year: semesters, summer session
Room & Board: $14,960
SAT CR/M: 678/722 **ACT:** 30
Application Deadline: January 15

Faculty: 447; I, +$
Ph.D.s: 94%
Student/Faculty: 13 to 1
Tuition: $52,305
Freshman Class: 19505 applied, 8420 accepted, 1663 enrolled
CEEB CODE: 2757
MOST COMPETITIVE

Rensselaer Polytechnic Institute, founded in 1824, is a private institution that offers bachelors, masters, and doctoral degrees in engineering, the sciences, information technology, architecture, management, and the humanities and social sciences. Institute programs serve undergraduates, graduate students, and working professionals around the world. There are 5 undergraduate schools and 5 graduate schools. In addition to regional accreditation, RPI has baccalaureate program accreditation with AACSB, ABET, NAAB, AAAHC, and ACS. The 297-acre campus is in a suburban area 10 miles north of Albany. Including any residence halls, there are 200 buildings.

STUDENT LIFE: 69% of undergraduates are from out of state, mostly the Northeast. Students are from 50 states, 39 foreign countries, and Canada. 68% are from public schools. 9% are Hispanic; 5% two or more races; 48% White; 4% African American; 17% Foreign; 14% Asian American; 1% race unknown. **Male To Female Ratio:** 2.1:1. The average age of freshmen is 18; all undergraduates, 20. 7% do not continue beyond their first year; 93% remain to graduate. **Housing:** 3400 students can be accommodated in college housing, which includes married student dorms and on-campus apartments. In addition, there are fraternity houses, sorority houses, and theme housing. On-campus housing is available on a first-come, first-served basis, and is available on a lottery system for upperclassmen. 57% of students live on campus. Upperclassmen may keep cars.

FACULTY/CLASSROOMS: 75% of faculty are male; 25% are female. No introductory courses are taught by graduate students. The average class size in an introductory lecture is 35; in a laboratory is 18; and in a regular course is 28.

PROGRAMS OF STUDY: RPI confers B.S. and B.Arch. degrees. Master's and doctoral degrees are also awarded. Bachelor's degrees are awarded in BIOLOGICAL SCIENCE (biochemistry, biology/biological science, and biophysics), BUSINESS (management information systems, management science, and recreation and leisure services), COMMUNICATIONS AND THE ARTS (communications and media arts), COMPUTER AND PHYSICAL SCIENCE (applied physics, chemistry, computer science, geology, hydrogeology, mathematics, physics, and science technology), ENGINEERING AND ENVIRONMENTAL DESIGN (aeronautical engineering, architecture, biomedical engineering, chemical engineering, civil engineering, computer engineering, construction engineering, electrical/electronics engineering, engineering, engineering physics, environmental engineering, industrial engineering, materials engineering, mechanical engineering, and nuclear engineering), HEALTH PROFESSIONS (premedicine), SOCIAL SCIENCE (economics, interdisciplinary studies, philosophy, prelaw, and psychology). Engineering, sciences, and architecture are the strongest academically. General engineering, computer science, and management have the largest enrollments.

ACTIVITIES: 30% of men belong to 1 local and 31 national fraternities; 16% of women belong to 1 local and 4 national sororities. There are 229 groups on campus, including Rensselaer Biotechnology Students Association, Biomedical Engineering Society, Entrepreneurship, Finance, art, Astrophysical Society, band, cheerleading, chess, choir, chorale, chorus, computers, dance, drama, drill team, environmental, ethnic, film, honors, international, jazz band, LGBT, literary magazine, musical theater, orchestra, pep band, photography, political, professional, radio and TV, religious, social, social service, student government, and symphony. Popular campus events include Union Program and Activities Committees-Concerts, Comedy, a Cinema, Winter Carnival, and Big Red Freak-out. **Sports:** There are 12 intercollegiate sports for men and 11 for women, and 22 intramural sports for men and 21 for women. Facilities include a field house, a pool, gyms, sports and recreation center, several playing fields, weight rooms, a fitness center, tennis courts, handball/squash courts, artificial turf fields, an indoor track, an ice hockey rink, a stadium, and arena. **Graduates:** From July 1, 2016 to June 30, 2017, 1451 bachelor's degrees were awarded. The most popular majors were engineering (55%), computer science (13%), and business/marketing (5%). In an average class, 61% graduate in 4 years or less, 81% graduate in 5 years or less, and 83% graduate in 6 years or less. Of the 2016 graduating class, 22% were enrolled in graduate school within 6 months of graduation, and 49% were employed.

SERVICES: Counseling and information services are available, as is tutoring in every subject. There is a reader service for the blind, and remedial math, reading, and writing. There is a writing center and an advising and learning assistance center. **Library/Resources:** The library contains 476,510 volumes, 125,616 microform items, 137,094 audio/video tapes/CDs/DVDs, and subscribes to 21,036 periodicals, including electronic. Computerized library services include interlibrary loans, database searching, Internet access, and Wi-Fi capability. Special learning facilities include an art gallery, a radio station, TV station, an observatory. **Physically Challenged Students:** Facilities include wheelchair ramps, elevators, special parking, specially equipped restrooms, special class scheduling, lowered drinking fountains, lowered telephones, and special housing. **Special:** Rensselaer offers co-op programs, internships, study abroad/exchange program, and pass/fail options. Students may pursue dual and student-designed majors, a 3-2 engineering degree with more than 40 universities, 2-2 agreements, and an accelerated degree program in physician-scientist, and law. There are 14 national honor societies and 8 departmental honors programs. **Visiting:** There are regularly scheduled orientations for prospective students, information, and a campus tour. There are guides for informal visits and visitors may sit in on classes. To schedule a visit, contact the Admissions Office. **Campus Safety and Security:** Measures include 24-hour foot and vehicle patrol, self-defense education, and security escort services. There are shuttle buses, emergency telephones, lighted pathways/sidewalks, card-access residence halls, on-campus bicycle patrol, and a student volunteer program.

REQUIREMENTS: SAT subject tests in critical reading, math, and science are required for accelerated-program applicants or the ACT, which must include the optional writing component in lieu of SAT. 15 high school units are required and-or recommended, 4 each in English and math, and 3 each in science (4 recommended), and social studies. AP credits are accepted. Important factors in the admissions decision are leadership record, advanced placement or honors courses, parents or siblings attended the school, evidence of special talent, extracurricular activities record, recommendations by school officials, personality/intangible qualities, recommendations by alumni, and geographical diversity. For graduation, students must earn at least 124 credits in all majors except engineering (128 needed) and the B.Arch. Program (168 needed). The core curriculum includes 48 credits in math, science, humanities, and social sciences. Students must maintain a minimum GPA of 1.8 and must fulfill a writing requirement. **Procedure:** Freshmen are admitted in the fall, spring, and summer. Entrance exams should be taken in the junior or senior year. There are early decision and deferred admissions plans. Early decision applications should be filed by November 1; regular applications, by January 15 for fall entry; and November 1 for spring entry. The fall 2017 application fee was $70. Notification of early decision is sent December 16; regular decision, March 10. 515 early decision candidates were accepted for the 2017-2018 class. 2203 applicants were on the 2017 waiting list; 57 were admitted. Applications are accepted on-line. **Transfer Students:** 109 transfer students enrolled in 2016-2017.

Applicants should have completed 12 or more transferable college credits, and must be in good academic standing at the institutions they are attending or attended. 60 of 120 credits required for the bachelor's degree must be completed at RPI. **International Students:** There are 864 international students enrolled. They must take the TOEFL with a minimum score of 570 on the paper-based TOEFL (PBT) or 88 on the Internet-based version (iBT). They must also take either the SAT or ACT.

ADMISSIONS: 43% of the 2017-2018 applicants were accepted. The SAT scores for the 2017-2018 freshman class were: Critical Reading-- 10% between 500 and 599, 48% between 600 and 699, and 42% between 700 and 800. Math-- 3% between 500 and 599, 28% between 600 and 699, and 69% between 700 and 800. The ACT scores were 4% between 18 and 23, 43% between 24 and 29, and 53% above 30. 82% of the current freshmen were in the top fifth of their class; 95% were in the top two fifths. 43 freshmen graduated first in their class. **Admissions Contact:** Karen S. Long, Director, Undergraduate Admissions. Email: *admissions@rpi.edu* Web: *www.rpi.edu*

FINANCIAL AID: In 2017-2018, 83% of all full-time freshmen received some form of financial aid and need-based aid. The average freshman award was $40,040. Need-based scholarships or need-based grants averaged $36,325; need-based self-help aid (loans and jobs) averaged $4,929; non-need-based athletic scholarships averaged $59,261; other non-need-based awards and non-need-based scholarships averaged $20,910; and $5,741 from other forms of aid. RPI is a member of CSS. The CSS/Profile is required. The FAFSA code is 002803. The priority date for freshman financial aid applications for fall entry is February 1.

ROBERTS WESLEYAN COLLEGE — B-3

www.roberts.edu

Rochester, NY 14624	**(585) 594-6400** **(800) 777-4792**
Fax: (585) 594-6371	**Email: admissions@roberts.edu**
Full-time: 366 men, 841 women	**Faculty:** 95
Part-time: 20 men, 39 women	**Ph.D.s:** 67%
Graduate: 64 men, 318 women	**Student/Faculty:** 11 to 1
Year: semesters, summer session	**Tuition:** $30,686
Room & Board: $10,430	**Freshman Class:** 1270 applied, 822 accepted, 74 enrolled
SAT CR/M/W: 525/535/500 **ACT:** 23	**CEEB CODE:** 2759
Application Deadline: August 20	**COMPETITIVE**

Roberts Wesleyan College, founded in 1866 by leaders of the Free Methodist Church, is an innovative and distinctive Christian college offering excellence in liberal arts and professional programs. There are 2 undergraduate schools and 2 graduate schools. In addition to regional accreditation, RWC has baccalaureate program accreditation with CSWE, NASAD, NASM, IACBE, CCNE, NASP, and RATE. The 75-acre campus is in a suburban area 8 miles southwest of Rochester. Including any residence halls, there are 32 buildings.

STUDENT LIFE: 85% of undergraduates are from New York. Others are from 24 states, 20 foreign countries, and Canada. 73% are White; 5% Hispanic; 4% Foreign; 3% two or more races; 2% Asian American; 2% race unknown; 11% African American. 62% are Protestant; 17% claim no religious affiliation; 16% Catholic. **Female To Male Ratio:** 2.7:1. The average age of freshmen is 18; all undergraduates, 21. 20% do not continue beyond their first year; 60% remain to graduate. **Housing:** 792 students can be accommodated in college housing, which includes dorms, on-campus apartments, and off-campus apartments. On-campus housing is guaranteed for all 4 years. 65% of students live on campus. Alcohol is not permitted. All students may keep cars.

FACULTY/CLASSROOMS: 37% of faculty are male; 63% are female. 85% teach undergraduates. No introductory courses are taught by graduate students. The average class size in an introductory lecture is 30; in a laboratory is 15; and in a regular course is 23.

PROGRAMS OF STUDY: RWC confers B.A. and B.S. degrees. Associate and master's degrees are also awarded. Bachelor's degrees are awarded in BIOLOGICAL SCIENCE (biochemistry, biology/adolescence education, biology/biological science, biotechnology, and forensic science), BUSINESS (accounting, business administration and management, international business management, and marketing), COMMUNICATIONS AND THE ARTS (applied art, applied music, art, communications, English, graphic design, music, music performance, piano performance, Spanish, studio art, and vocal performance), COMPUTER AND PHYSICAL SCIENCE (chemistry, chemistry/adolescence education, digital arts/technology, mathematics, and physics), EDUCATION (early childhood education, elementary education, English education, mathematics education, music education, physical education, secondary education, and special education), ENGINEERING AND ENVIRONMENTAL DESIGN (biomedical equipment technology and preengineering), HEALTH PROFESSIONS (biology, nursing, pharmacy, predentistry, premedicine, prepharmacy, prephysical therapy, and preveterinary science), SOCIAL SCIENCE (biblical studies, Christian studies, criminal justice, history, humanities, interdisciplinary studies, liberal arts/general studies, philosophy, prelaw, psychology, religion, and social work). Music, education, and nursing are the strongest academically. Elementary education, nursing, and music have the largest enrollments.

ACTIVITIES: There are no fraternities or sororities. Groups on campus include band, choir, chorale, chorus, dance, drama, environmental, ethnic, honors, jazz band, musical theater, newspaper, opera, orchestra, pep band, photography, religious, social, social service, student government, symphony, and yearbook. Popular campus events include Winter Weekend, Spring Formal, and Talent and Variety Shows. **Sports:** There are 7 intercollegiate sports for men and 7 for women, and 6 intramural sports for men and 6 for women. Facilities include an athletic center with facilities for basketball, volleyball, tennis, badminton, track, soccer, weight lifting, walleyball, racquetball, flag football, ultimate Frisbee, a swimming pool, and a room for exercise machines. **Graduates:** From July 1, 2016 to June 30, 2017, 416 bachelor's degrees were awarded. The most popular majors were health professions/related programs (40%), business/marketing (18%), and education (9%). In an average class, 49% graduate in 4 years or less, 61% graduate in 5 years or less, and 63% graduate in 6 years or less. Of the 2016 graduating class, 24% were enrolled in graduate school within 6 months of graduation, and 93% were employed.

SERVICES: Counseling and information services are available, as is tutoring in every subject. There are note takers for the hearing impaired, a reader service for the blind, and remedial math, reading, and writing. **Library/Resources:** The library contains 144,199 volumes, 169,823 microform items, and 4,462 audio/video tapes/CDs/DVDs, and subscribes to 35,000 periodicals including electronic. Computerized library services include interlibrary loans, database searching, Internet access, and Wi-Fi capability. Special learning facilities include an art gallery. **Physically Challenged Students:** 85% of the campus is accessible. Facilities include wheelchair ramps, elevators, special parking, specially equipped restrooms, special class scheduling, lowered drinking fountains, lowered telephones, and special housing. **Special:** Students may cross-register with members of the Rochester Area Colleges Consortium. Internships, study abroad in 8 countries, a Washington semester, co-op programs, B.A.-B.S. degrees, dual majors, and 3-2 engineering degrees with Clarkson University, Rensselaer Polytechnic Institute, and Rochester Institute of Technology are available, as well as 3-4 Pharmacy with University at Buffalo. Nondegree study and credit for life, military, and work experience are also offered. The organizational management program, geared to adults, consists of 4-hour weekly sessions, with reliance on out-of-class work. There is a freshman honors program and 100 departmental honors programs. **Visiting:** There are regularly scheduled orientations for prospective students, including a campus tour, class visits, admissions overview, meetings with faculty, and a financial aid presentation. There are guides for informal visits; visitors may sit in on classes and stay overnight. To schedule a visit, contact the Admissions Office. **Campus Safety and Security:** Measures include 24-hour foot and vehicle patrol, emergency notification system, self-defense education, and security escort services. There are emergency telephones, lighted pathways/sidewalks, controlled access to dorms/residences, and personal-safety education programs.

REQUIREMENTS: The SAT or ACT is required. Applicants must be graduates of an accredited secondary school. The GED is accepted. The academic credits required are 4 years of English, and 3 units each in foreign language, social studies, and history (recommended units are 4 each in math, and science with 3 units of lab). A chosen major may modify requirements. An essay is required, and an interview is recommended. Roberts requires applicants to be in the upper 50% of their class. AP and CLEP credits are accepted. Important factors in the admissions decision are leadership record, advanced placement or honors courses, personality/intangible qualities, extracurricular activities record, and recommendations by school officials. To graduate, students must complete a minimum of 124 credit hours, with a minimum of 30 hours in the major. Required courses include first-year experience, phys ed, modern technology, world issues, speech, writing, history, Bible, and philosophy. **Procedure:** Freshmen are admitted in the fall, spring, and summer. There are deferred admissions and rolling admissions plans. Applications should be filed by August 20 for fall entry. Notification is sent on a rolling basis. Applications are accepted on-line. **Transfer Students:** 81 transfer students enrolled in 2016-2017. Applicants must submit transcripts from all previous institutions attended as well as the application and a recommendation. Credit is usually accepted for courses with grade C or better. 30 of 124 credits required for the bachelor's degree must be completed at Roberts. **International Students:** There are 52 international students enrolled. They must take the TOEFL with a minimum score of 540 on the paper-based TOEFL (PBT) or 75 on the Internet-based version (iBT). Student must take the IELTS. Students who take the SAT or ACT and score high enough do not need to take the TOEFL or IELTS.

ADMISSIONS: 65% of the 2017-2018 applicants were accepted. The SAT scores for the 2017-2018 freshman class were: Critical Reading-- 35% below 500, 48% between 500 and 599, 12% between 600 and 699, and 5% between 700 and 800. Math-- 30% below 500, 46% between 500 and 599, 21% between 600 and 699, and 2% between 700 and 800. Writing-- 49% below 500, 35% between 500 and 599, 15% between 600 and 699, and 2% between 700 and 800. The ACT scores were 5% below 12, 22% between 12 and 17, 48% between 18 and 23, 34% between 24 and 29, and 14% above 30. 42% of the current freshmen were in the top fifth of their class; 80% were in the top two fifths. 4 freshmen graduated first in their class. **Admissions Contact:** Randy Comfort, Director of Admissions. Email: *admissions@roberts.edu* Web: *www.roberts.edu*

FINANCIAL AID: In 2017-2018, 98% of all full-time freshmen received some form of financial aid. 90% of all full-time freshmen received need-based aid. The average freshman award was $26,044. Need-based scholarships or need-based grants averaged $21,060; need-based self-help aid (loans and jobs) averaged $6,717; and $4,613 from other forms of aid. 35% of undergraduate students work part-time. The average financial indebtedness of the 2017 graduate was $24,330. RWC is a member of CSS. The FAFSA code is 002805. The priority date for freshman financial aid applications for fall entry is November 1.

ROCHESTER INSTITUTE OF TECHNOLOGY — B-3

www.rit.edu

Rochester, NY 14623	(585) 475-6631
Fax: (585) 475-7424	Email: admissions@rit.edu
Full-time: 8393 men, 4054 women	Faculty: I, -$
Part-time: 758 men, 310 women	Ph.D.s: 70%
Graduate: 1861 men, 1208 women	Student/Faculty: 13 to 1
Year: semesters, summer session	Tuition: $40,068
Room & Board: $12,666	Freshman Class: 20451 applied, 11599 accepted, 2772 enrolled
SAT or ACT: required	CEEB CODE: 2760
Application Deadline: January 15	HIGHLY COMPETITIVE+

Rochester Institute of Technology is one of the world's leading career-oriented technological universities. RIT offers more than 90 undergraduate programs in areas such as engineering, computing, information technology, engineering technology, business, hospitality, science, art, design, photography and film, biomedical sciences, game design and development, and the liberal arts, including psychology, advertising and public relations, and public policy. Students may choose from more than 90 different minors to develop personal and professional interests that complement their academic program. Experiential education is integrated into many programs through cooperative education, internships, study abroad, and undergraduate research. As home to the National Technical Institute for the Deaf (NTID), RIT is a leader in providing access services to deaf and hard-of-hearing students. There are 9 undergraduate schools and 9 graduate schools. In addition to regional accreditation, RIT has baccalaureate program accreditation with AACSB, ABET, ADA, CAHEA, CSAB, CSWE, FIDER, NASAD, and CAAHEP. The 1300-acre campus is in a suburban area 5 miles south of Rochester. Including any residence halls, there are 195 buildings.

STUDENT LIFE: 51% of undergraduates are from New York. Others are from 50 states, 107 foreign countries, and Canada. 85% are from public schools. 9% are Foreign; 70% White; 5% Asian American; 4% African American; 4% Hispanic; 1% American Indian/Alaska Native. **Male To Female Ratio:** 2.0:1. The average age of freshmen is 18; all undergraduates, 21. 8% do not continue beyond their first year; 69% remain to graduate. **Housing:** 7144 students can be accommodated in college housing, which includes married student dorms and on-campus apartments. In addition, there are honors houses, special-interest houses, fraternity houses, and sorority houses. On-campus housing is guaranteed for the freshman year only, and is available on a first-come, first-served basis. 68% of students live on campus. All students may keep cars.

FACULTY/CLASSROOMS: 65% of faculty are male; 35% are female. 97% teach undergraduates, 90% do research, and 90% do both. No introductory courses are taught by graduate students. The average class size in an introductory lecture is 23; in a laboratory is 16; and in a regular course is 20.

PROGRAMS OF STUDY: RIT confers B.S. and B.F.A. degrees. Associate, master's, and doctoral degrees are also awarded. Bachelor's degrees are awarded in BIOLOGICAL SCIENCE (biochemistry, bioinformatics, biology/biological science, biotechnology, nutrition, and nutritional sciences), BUSINESS (accounting, banking and finance, business administration and management, business administration - international, business administration marketing, business information systems, business systems analysis, finance, hospitality management services, hotel/motel and restaurant management, international business, international business management, business management, management information systems, management, management science, marketing, marketing management, and tourism), COMMUNICATIONS AND THE ARTS (advertising, American Sign Language, animation, applied art, art, art and design, ceramic art and design, communication design, communications, communications technology, crafts, design, digital media, film arts, film, television and digital media, fine arts, fine/studio arts, general, glass, graphic design, graphic design and media, illustration, industrial design, information technology, journalism, media arts, metal/jewelry, photography, public relations, publishing, sculpture, studio art, studio art ceramics, studio art-computer art, studio art-graphic design, studio art-painting, telecommunications, video, visual communication, and visual design), COMPUTER AND PHYSICAL SCIENCE (actuarial science, applied mathematics, biomedical art, chemistry, computer engineering technology, computer mathematics, computer networks and systems, computer game design/development, computer information technology, computer information systems, computer security, computer science, computer science and informatics, computer security and information assurance, digital animation and game design, information sciences and systems, information science, mathematics, mathematics-actuarial concentration, physics, polymer science, science, software engineering, statistics, and systems analysis), EDUCATION (education of the deaf and hearing impaired and museum studies), ENGINEERING AND ENVIRONMENTAL DESIGN (aerospace studies, biomedical engineering, chemical engineering, civil engineering technology, computer engineering, computer graphics, computer technology, electrical/electronics engineering, electrical/electronics engineering technology, engineering, engineering technology, environmental engineering technology, environmental science, furniture design, graphic arts technology, graphic and printing production, industrial engineering, interior design, manufacturing engineering, manufacturing technology, materials science, mechanical engineering, mechanical engineering technology, military science, printing technology, and woodworking), HEALTH PROFESSIONS (allied health, applied nutrition, biology, biomedical science, exercise science, medical imaging, nutrition and dietetics, nutrition and wellness, physicians assistant, predentistry, premedicine, preveterinary science, and ultrasound technology), SOCIAL SCIENCE (anthropology, criminal justice, dietetics, economics, food production/management/services, interpreter for the deaf, philosophy, political science/government, prelaw, psychology, public affairs, and sociology). Mechanical engineering, computer science, and film and animation are the strongest academically. Engineering, computing, and photography have the largest enrollments.

ACTIVITIES: 5% of men belong to 17 national fraternities; 5% of women belong to 12 national sororities. There are 307 groups on campus, including gospel choir club, art, band, cheerleading, chess, choir, chorale, chorus, communications, computers, dance, drama, environmental, ethnic, film, honors, international, jazz band, LGBT, literary magazine, newspaper, orchestra, pep band, photography, political, professional, radio and TV, religious, social, social service, and student government. Popular campus events include Brick City Homecoming, Freeze Fest, and Imagine RIT Festival. **Sports:** There are 11 intercollegiate sports for men and 12 for women, and 13 intramural sports for men and 13 for women. Facilities include gyms, ice rinks, swimming pools, tennis courts, a field house, athletic fields, and a student life center with racquetball courts, dance facilities, weight training facilities, and an indoor track. **Graduates:** From July 1, 2016 to June 30, 2017, 2495 bachelor's degrees were awarded. The most popular majors were mechanical engineering (7%), computer science (5%), and electrical engineering (5%). In an average class, 28% graduate in 4 years or less, 56% graduate in 5 years or less, and 70% graduate in 6 years or less. Of the 2016 graduating class, 15% were enrolled in graduate school within 6 months of graduation, and 81% were employed.

SERVICES: Counseling and information services are available, as is tutoring in most subjects. There is a reader service for the blind. There are comprehensive support services for students with physical or learning disabilities and for first-generation college students. **Library/Resources:** The library contains 422,281 volumes, 498,703 microform items, and 54,935 audio/video tapes/CDs/DVDs, and subscribes to 21,208 periodicals, including electronic. Computerized library services include interlibrary loans, database searching, Internet access, and Wi-Fi capability. Special learning facilities include an art gallery, radio and TV stations, a computer chip manufacturing facility, a student-operated restaurant, an electronic prepress lab, an imaging science facility, and an observatory. **Physically Challenged Students:** All of the campus is accessible. Facilities include wheelchair ramps, elevators, special parking, specially equipped restrooms, special class scheduling, lowered drinking fountains, lowered telephones, and special housing. **Special:** Experiential learning is extensive at RIT. Cooperative education is required or recommended in many programs and provides full-time paid work experience. RIT has an employer network of almost 2,200 organizations. Other forms of experiential learning include internships, undergraduate research, and study abroad. There are accelerated dual degrees (B.S./M.S., B.S./M.E., B.S./M.B.A.) offered in many programs. Students may study abroad in 15 countries, and student-designed majors are permitted in applied arts and sciences. There is an Honors Program in general education and home colleges. There are 6 national honor societies, a freshman honors program, and 7 departmental honors programs. **Visiting:** There are regularly scheduled orientations for prospective students, including academic advising and information on housing and student services. There are guides for informal visits; visitors may sit in on classes and stay overnight. To schedule a visit, contact the Admissions Receptionist. **Campus Safety and Security:** Measures include 24-hour foot and vehicle patrol, an emergency notification system, self-defense education, and security escort services. There are shuttle buses, emergency telephones, lighted pathways/sidewalks, and controlled access to dorms/residences.

REQUIREMENTS: The SAT or ACT is required. Applicants must be high school graduates or have a GED certificate. Applicants are required to submit an essay, and an interview is recommended. The School of Art, the School of Design, and the School for American Crafts emphasize a required portfolio of artwork. Required high school math and science credits vary by program, with 3 years in each area generally acceptable. AP and CLEP credits are accepted. Important factors in the admissions decision are advanced placement or honors courses, recommendations by school officials, and extracurricular activities record. Students must have a GPA of 2.0 and have completed a minimum of 120 semester credit hours to graduate. RIT's framework for general education provides students with courses that meet specific university approved general education learning outcomes and New York State Education Department liberal arts and sciences requirements. Students in all Bachelor of Science degree programs are required to complete a minimum of 60 credit hours in General Education; students in all Bachelor of Fine Arts degree programs are required to complete a minimum of 30 credit hours in General Education. The general education framework intentionally moves through three educational phases designed to give students a strong foundation, an introduction to fundamentals of liberal arts and sciences disciplines, and the opportunity for deeper study and integrative learning through immersion in a cluster of related courses. **Procedure:** Freshmen are admitted in the fall, spring, and summer. Entrance exams should be taken during the junior or senior year. There are early decision and deferred admissions plans. Early decision applications should be filed by November 15; regular applications, by January 15 for fall entry. The fall 2017 application fee was $65. Notification of early decision is sent December 15; regular decision, February 15. Applications are accepted online. **Transfer Students:** 768 transfer students enrolled in 2016-2017. Transfer students must have a GPA of 3.0 for admission to most programs; those with fewer than 30 college credits must supply a high school transcript. Other requirements vary by program. 30 of 120 credits required for the bachelor's degree must be completed at RIT. **International Students:** There are 872 international students enrolled. They must take the TOEFL with a minimum score of 550 on the paper-based TOEFL (PBT) or 79 on the Internet-based version (iBT). They must also take the SAT or ACT.

ADMISSIONS: 57% of the 2017-2018 applicants were accepted. 65% of the current freshmen were in the top fifth of their class; 90% were in the top two fifths. **Admissions Contact:** Marian Nicoletti, Interim Director of Admissions. Email: *admissions@rit.edu* Web: *www.rit.edu*

FINANCIAL AID: In 2017-2018, 85% of all full-time freshmen received some form of financial aid. 81% of all full-time freshmen received need-based aid. The average freshman award was $18,900. Need-based scholarships or need-based grants averaged $16,500; and need-based self-help aid (loans and jobs) averaged $5,000. 70% of undergraduate students work part-time. The average financial indebtedness of the 2017 graduate was $23,800. The FAFSA code is 002806. The priority date for freshman financial aid applications for fall entry is March 1.

RUSSELL SAGE COLLEGE — D-3

www.sage.edu

Troy, NY 12180 — **(518) 244-2217**

Fax: (518) 244-6880	**Email:** rscadm@sage.edu
Full-time: 10 men, 772 women	**Faculty:** 61
Part-time: 9 men, 32 women	**Ph.D.s:** 90%
Graduate: n/av	**Student/Faculty:** 10 to 1
Year: semesters, summer session	**Tuition:** $28,000
Room & Board: $11,370	**Freshman Class:** n/av
SAT or ACT: required	**CEEB CODE:** 2764
Application Deadline: rolling	**COMPETITIVE**

Russell Sage College is a comprehensive college for women. RSC offers liberal arts and professional degree programs in an environment aimed at empowering students to become women of influence in their careers and their communities. Figures in the above capsule and in this profile are approximate. There are 2 undergraduate schools and 1 graduate school. In addition to regional accreditation, RSC has baccalaureate program accreditation with ADA, APTA, NASAD, NLN, and AOTA. The 14-acre campus is in an urban area 10 miles from Albany and Schenectady. Including any residence halls, there are 38 buildings.

STUDENT LIFE: 93% of undergraduates are from New York. Others are from 16 states, and 1 foreign country. 8% are African American; 67% White; 6% Hispanic; 4% Asian American; 2% two or more races; 12% race unknown. **Female To Male Ratio:** 42.3:1. The average age of freshmen is 18; all undergraduates, 21. 10% do not continue beyond their first year; 73% remain to graduate. **Housing:** 738 students can be accommodated in college housing, which includes dorms and on-campus apartments. In addition, there are language/international houses and special-interest houses. On-campus housing is guaranteed for all 4 years and is available on a lottery system for upperclassmen. 52% of students commute. Alcohol is not permitted. All students may keep cars.

FACULTY/CLASSROOMS: 28% of faculty are male; 72% are female. All teach undergraduates and all do research. No introductory courses are taught by graduate students. The average class size in an introductory lecture is 19; in a laboratory is 9; and in a regular course is 16.

PROGRAMS OF STUDY: RSC confers B.A. and B.S. degrees. Master's degrees are also awarded. Bachelor's degrees are awarded in BIOLOGICAL SCIENCE (biochemistry, biology/biological science, and nutrition), COMMUNICATIONS AND THE ARTS (English, musical theater, and Spanish), COMPUTER AND PHYSICAL SCIENCE (chemistry and mathematics), EDUCATION (elementary education), ENGINEERING AND ENVIRONMENTAL DESIGN (environmental science), HEALTH PROFESSIONS (art therapy, nursing, occupational therapy, and physical therapy), SOCIAL SCIENCE (applied psychology, criminal justice, forensic studies, history, interdisciplinary studies, international studies, political science/government, psychology, and sociology). Nursing, nutrition, and health sciences are the strongest academically. Health and rehabilitative sciences, education, and psychology have the largest enrollments.

ACTIVITIES: There are no fraternities or sororities. There are 26 groups on campus, including choir, chorus, dance, drama, ethnic, honors, LGBT, literary magazine, musical theater, newspaper, political, religious, social, student government, and yearbook. Popular campus events include Spirit of Sage River Cruise, Rally Day, Sage Fest, and Family Weekend. **Sports:** There are 7 intercollegiate sports for men and 8 for women, and 7 intramural sports for men and 8 for women. Facilities include athletic centers, a weight and fitness center, a swimming pool, tennis courts, a practice field, gyms, and a multipurpose room for indoor recreation. **Graduates:** From July 1, 2016 to June 30, 2017, 212 bachelor's degrees were awarded. The most popular majors were nursing (23%), health sciences (9%), and education (9%). In an average class, 65% graduate in 4 years or less, 71% graduate in 5 years or less, and 73% graduate in 6 years or less. Of the 2016 graduating class, 32% were enrolled in graduate school within 6 months of graduation, and 65% were employed.

SERVICES: Counseling and information services are available, as is tutoring in most subjects. There is remedial math, reading, and writing. **Library/Resources:** The library contains 164,946 volumes, 18,514 microform items, 6,419 audio/video tapes/CDs/DVDs, and subscribes to 65,391 periodicals, including electronic. Computerized library services include interlibrary loans and database searching. **Physically Challenged Students:** 75% of the campus is accessible. Facilities include wheelchair ramps, elevators, and special parking. **Special:** Students may cross-register with the 14 area schools of the Hudson-Mohawk Association of Colleges. A theater major is offered in conjunction with Sage Theater Institute. Study abroad, internships, and work-study programs are available. RSC has several accelerated 5-year programs: a 3 + 2 M.S. in Occupational Therapy, a 3-2 engineering degree with nearby Rensselaer Polytechnic Institute and an accelerated 4+3 D.P.T. program. The college confers credit for life, military, or work experience. Nondegree study, student-designed majors, dual majors, and pass/fail options are also available. There are 14 national honor societies and a freshman honors program. **Visiting:** There are regularly scheduled orientations for prospective students, including meetings with faculty, a campus tour, a financial aid session, and an admissions interview. There are guides for informal visits; visitors may sit in on classes and stay overnight. To schedule a visit, contact Thomas Barresi at rscadm@sage.edu. **Campus Safety and Security:** Measures include 24-hour foot and vehicle patrol, self-defense education, and security escort services. There are emergency telephones, lighted pathways/sidewalks, an evening escort service, and monitored video cameras.

REQUIREMENTS: Applicants must be graduates of an accredited secondary school or have a GED. A minimum of 16 academic units are required. An essay, for applicants still in high school, is required, and an interview is recommended. AP and CLEP credits are accepted. Important factors in the admissions decision are advanced placement or honors courses, recommendations by school officials, leadership record, recommendations by alumni, parents or siblings attended the school, evidence of special talent, extracurricular activities record, and geographical diversity. A minimum of 120 credit hours is required for the baccalaureate degree. Students must complete at least half the major at RSC. Furthermore, 30 of the last 45 credits must be completed in residence (i.e. at Sage or through the Hudson-Mohawk Association). Students must satisfy general education as well as major requirements and must maintain satisfactory standards of scholarship to be eligible for graduation. A Bachelor of Arts degree must include a minimum of 90 credit hours in the liberal arts. A Bachelor of Science degree must include a minimum of 60 credit hours in the liberal arts. Students must achieve a 2.2 grade point average in the major and a 2.0 overall cumulative grade point average. Some majors require a higher grade point average for graduation. The ultimate responsibility for fulfilling graduation requirements rests with the individual student. **Procedure:** Freshmen are admitted in the fall and spring. Entrance exams should be taken during the spring of the junior year or fall of the senior year. There are early admissions, deferred admissions, and rolling admissions plans. Early decision applications should be filed by December 1. The fall 2017 application fee was $30. Notification of early decision is sent December 15; regular decision, on a rolling basis. Applications are accepted online. **Transfer Students:** 84 transfer students enrolled in 2016-2017. Applicants must have a minimum GPA of 2.5. Interviews are strongly encouraged and may be required in some instances. 45 of 120 credits required for the bachelor's degree must be completed at RSC. **International Students:** There are 4 international students enrolled. They must take the TOEFL. For international applicants with English as their native language must also take the SAT or ACT.

Admissions Contact: Elizabeth Robertson, Associate Vice President for Admissions. Email: *rscadm@sage.edu* Web: *www.sage.edu*

FINANCIAL AID: In 2017-2018, 94% of all full-time freshmen received some form of financial aid. 79% of all full-time freshmen received need-based aid. Check with the school for current application deadlines.

SARAH LAWRENCE COLLEGE D-5

www.sarahlawrence.edu

Bronxville, NY 10708	**(914) 395-2510** **(800) 888-2858**
Fax: (914) 395-2515	**Email: slcadmit@slc.edu**
Full-time: 394 men, 990 women	**Faculty:** 108
Part-time: 5 men, 10 women	**Ph.D.s:** 91%
Graduate: 66 men, 231 women	**Student/Faculty:** 10 to 1
Year: semesters	**Tuition:** $54,010
Room & Board: $14,856	**Freshman Class:** 3368 applied, 1842 accepted, 393 enrolled
SAT EBR-W/M: 681/632 **ACT:** 29	**CEEB CODE:** 2810
Application Deadline: January 15	**MOST COMPETITIVE**

Sarah Lawrence College, established in 1926, is an independent institution conferring liberal arts degrees. The academic structure is based on the British don system. Students meet biweekly with professors in tutorials and are enrolled in small seminars. While there are no formal majors, students develop individual concentrations that are usually interdisciplinary. There is 1 undergraduate school and 1 graduate school. The 44-acre campus is in a suburban area 15 miles north of midtown Manhattan, a 25-minute train ride to Grand Central. Including any residence halls, there are 50 buildings.

STUDENT LIFE: 81% of undergraduates are from out of state, mostly the West. Students are from 49 states, 44 foreign countries, and Canada. 65% are from public schools. 54% are White; 13% Foreign; 9% Hispanic; 8% race unknown; 7% two or more races; 4% African American; 4% Asian American; 2% American Indian/Alaska Native. **Female To Male Ratio:** 2.6:1. The average age of freshmen is 18; all undergraduates, 20. 82% remain to graduate. **Housing:** 1134 students can be accommodated in college housing, which includes gender neutral, single sex dorms, and coed dorms. In addition, there are special-interest houses, quiet, sustainable, special housing for people with disabilities, and substance-free housing. On-campus housing is guaranteed for all 4 years. 78% of students live on campus. Upperclassmen may keep cars.

FACULTY/CLASSROOMS: 50% of faculty are male; 50% are female. All teach undergraduates and do research. No introductory courses are taught by graduate students. The average class size in a regular course is 14.

PROGRAMS OF STUDY: SLC confers B.A. degrees. Master's degrees are also awarded. Bachelor's degrees are awarded in AGRICULTURE (environmental studies), BIOLOGICAL SCIENCE (biology/biological science), COMMUNICATIONS AND THE ARTS (Africana studies, art history, Chinese, classics, dance, dramatic arts, English, film arts, fine arts, French, game design and development, German, Greek, Italian, Japanese, Latin, literature, music, Russian, Spanish, visual and performing arts, and writing), COMPUTER AND PHYSICAL SCIENCE (chemistry, computer science, and mathematics), EDUCATION (Asian studies and health education), ENGINEERING AND ENVIRONMENTAL DESIGN (architecture), SOCIAL SCIENCE (anthropology, cognitive science, economics, history, interdisciplinary studies, liberal arts/general studies, Middle Eastern studies, philosophy, political science/government, psychology, religion, sociology, women and gender studies, and women's studies).

ACTIVITIES: There are no fraternities or sororities. There are 152 groups on campus, including art, choir, chorale, chorus, communications, computers, dance, drama, environmental, ethnic, film, international, jazz band, LGBT, literary magazine, musical theater, newspaper, orchestra, photography, political, professional, radio and TV, religious, social, social service, student government, and yearbook. Popular campus events include Fall and Spring Formal, Midnight Breakfast,

Rocky Horror Picture Show Shadow Cast, Mayfair. **Sports:** There are 7 intercollegiate sports for men and 10 for women, and 7 intramural sports for men and 7 for women. Facilities include a sports center with a gym, a jogging track, a swimming pool, a rowing tank, a multipurpose studio, and squash courts, a fitness center and weight room, and tennis. Off-campus, the college has use of a boat house, and stables. **Graduates:** From July 1, 2016 to June 30, 2017, 374 bachelor's degrees were awarded. In an average class, 73% graduate in 4 years or less, 5% graduate in 5 years or less, and 1% graduate in 6 years or less.

SERVICES: Counseling and information services are available, as is tutoring in some subjects. There is a reader service for the blind. **Library/Resources:** The library contains 332,623 volumes, 24,218 microform items, and 9,319 audio/video tapes/CDs/DVDs, subscribes to 916 periodicals, including electronic. Computerized library services include interlibrary loans, database searching, Internet access, and Wi-Fi capability. Special learning facilities include an art gallery, a radio station, Early Childhood Center, an electronic music studio, a concert hall and dance studios, music library, student-run theater and student-run art gallery. **Physically Challenged Students:** 50% of the campus is accessible. Facilities include wheelchair ramps, elevators, special parking, specially equipped restrooms, special class scheduling, lowered drinking fountains, lowered telephones, and special housing. **Special:** Internships are available in a variety of fields, with the school offering proximity to New York City art galleries and agencies. Study abroad in many countries, work-study programs, dual concentrations, a 3-2 engineering degree with Columbia, and a general degree may be pursued. All concentrations are self-designed and can be combined. **Visiting:** There are regularly scheduled orientations for prospective students, information session, a campus tour, and opportunity to schedule an interview. There are guides for informal visits; visitors may sit in on classes and stay overnight. To schedule a visit, contact Students register on line for visits. **Campus Safety and Security:** Measures include 24-hour foot and vehicle patrol, an emergency notification system, and security escort services. There are shuttle buses, emergency telephones, lighted pathways/sidewalks, and controlled access to dorms/residences.

REQUIREMENTS: Students must apply through the Common Application. Secondary school transcripts, counselor recommendation, school report, and 2 teacher evaluations are required. Part of the application requires an essay about their interest in Sarah Lawrence and an optional analytical essay (not creative writing). Other Optional submissions: SAT or ACT scores, Art Supplement, on-campus or off-campus interviews. AP credits are accepted. Important factors in the admissions decision are recommendations by school officials, personality/intangible qualities, and extracurricular activities record. To graduate, students must complete 120 credit hours and meet distribution requirements in 3 of 4 academic areas, including history and social sciences, creative and performing arts, natural science and math, and humanities. Students must fulfill a first-year studies requirement in one of 18 areas and meet a physical education requirement. Students must also take 2 lecture courses, where the average class size is 40. **Procedure:** Freshmen are admitted in the fall. There are early decision, early admissions, and deferred admissions plans. Early decision applications should be filed by November 1; regular applications, by January 15 for fall entry. The fall 2017 application fee was $60. Notification of early decision is sent December 15; regular decision, April 1. 150 early decision candidates were accepted for the 2017-2018 class. 1145 applicants were on the 2017 waiting list; 79 were admitted. Applications are accepted online. **Transfer Students:** 41 transfer students enrolled in 2016-2017. Applicants must complete the Common Application including a required essay about their interest in SLC. An optional analytical essay may be submitted as well. The College Official's report, 2 faculty evaluations, and transcripts from all post-secondary schools as well as the final high school transcript are required. SAT and ACT tests are optional. Other optional supplements are the mid-term report, Art Supplement, and on-campus or off-campus interview. 60 of 120 credits required for the bachelor's degree must be completed at SLC. **International Students:** There are 177 international students enrolled. They must take the TOEFL with a minimum score of 600 on the paper-based TOEFL (PBT) or 100 on the Internet-based version (iBT). Students must take the IELTS.

ADMISSIONS: 55% of the 2017-2018 applicants were accepted. The SAT scores for the 2017-2018 freshman class were: Math-- 4% below 500, 28% between 500 and 599, 47% between 600 and 699, and 21% between 700 and 800. Evidence-Based Reading/Writing-- 1% below 500, 11% between 500 and 599, 43% between 600 and 699, and 45% between 700 and 800. The ACT scores were 0% below 12, 1% between 12 and 17, 4% between 18 and 23, 47% between 24 and 29, and 48% above 30. 56% of the current freshmen were in the top fifth of their class; 77% were in the top two fifths. **Admissions Contact:** Office of Admissions Email: *slcadmit@slc.edu* Web: *www.sarahlawrence.edu*

FINANCIAL AID: In 2017-2018, 66% of all full-time freshmen received some form of financial aid. 65% of all full-time freshmen received need-based aid. The average freshman award was $36,749. Need-based scholarships or need-based grants averaged $34,059; need-based self-help aid (loans and jobs) averaged $4,083; and other non-need-based awards and non-need-based scholarships averaged $17,758. SLC is a member of CSS. The CSS/Profile, and and non-custodial parent statement are required. The FAFSA code is 002813. The priority date for freshman financial aid applications for fall entry is February 1.

SCHOOL OF VISUAL ARTS *(The complete profile is made available exclusively on our website, www.barronspac.com)*

SIENA COLLEGE — D-3
www.siena.edu

Loudonville, NY 12211 — (518) 783-2423

Fax: (518) 783-2436	**Email:** admissions@siena.edu
Full-time: 1470 men, 1591 women	**Faculty:** 224
Part-time: 64 men, 61 women	**Ph.D.s:** 91%
Graduate: 29 men, 32 women	**Student/Faculty:** 14 to 1
Year: semesters, summer session	**Tuition:** $34,811
Room & Board: $14,105	**Freshman Class:** 764 enrolled
SAT CR/M/W: 530/550/520 **ACT:** 25	**CEEB CODE:** 2814
Application Deadline: February 15	**COMPETITIVE**

Siena College is a private, Catholic, liberal arts college. Siena offers 31 majors, over 80 minors, and certificates. Students customize their education based on their interests and career goals. But that's just the beginning. Siena 3,000 students come from all over the world and leave not only with a deeper understanding of it, but also the tools needed to take an active and meaningful part in it. They quickly realize a Siena education isn't something you get, it's something you do. Extensive study abroad programs and immersive service-learning allow for discovery and reflection. A Siena education is strengthened through a robust internship program that includes top startup companies, nonprofits and government organizations that drive this region's growth. High-impact learning centers, caring and engaged faculty who draw out the best in their students, and a Franciscan tradition of service and community define who we are and give students a lifetime advantage. There are 3 undergraduate schools and one graduate school. In addition to regional accreditation, Siena has baccalaureate program accreditation with AACSB, CSWE, and ACS. The 175-acre campus is in a suburban area 2 miles north of Albany in the suburb of Loudonville, NY. Including any residence halls, there are 33 buildings.

STUDENT LIFE: 81% of undergraduates are from New York. Others are from 30 states, 17 foreign countries, and Canada. 8% are Hispanic; 79% White; 4% African American; 4% Asian American; 2% Foreign; 2% two or more races; 1% race unknown. 45% are Catholic; 24% Protestant; 24% claim no religious affiliation. **Female To Male Ratio:** 1.1:1. The average age of freshmen is 18; all undergraduates, 21. 13% do not continue beyond their first year; 77% remain to graduate. **Housing:** 2500 students can be accommodated in college housing, which includes dorms and on-campus apartments. On-campus housing is guaranteed for all 4 years and is available on a lottery system for upperclassmen. 83% of students live on campus. Upperclassmen may keep cars.

FACULTY/CLASSROOMS: 59% of faculty are male; 41% are female. All teach undergraduates. No introductory courses are taught by graduate students. The average class size in an introductory lecture is 21 and in a laboratory is 15.

PROGRAMS OF STUDY: Siena confers B.A. and B.S degrees. Master's degrees are also awarded. Bachelor's degrees are awarded in AGRICULTURE (environmental studies), BIOLOGICAL SCIENCE (biochemistry and biology/biological science), BUSINESS (accounting, banking and finance, business administration and management, and marketing management), COMMUNICATIONS AND THE ARTS (art studies, classics, English, French, Spanish, and visual and performing arts), COMPUTER

AND PHYSICAL SCIENCE (actuarial science, chemistry, computer science, mathematics, and physics), ENGINEERING AND ENVIRONMENTAL DESIGN (environmental science), HEALTH PROFESSIONS (nursing), SOCIAL SCIENCE (American studies, economics, history, philosophy, political science/government, psychology, religion, social work, and sociology). The Biology B.A. - Albany Medical College program is the strongest academically. Accounting, psychology, and biology have the largest enrollments.

ACTIVITIES: There are no fraternities or sororities. There are 80 groups on campus, including art, band, cheerleading, chess, choir, chorale, chorus, communications, computers, dance, debate, drama, environmental, ethnic, film, honors, international, jazz band, LGBT, literary magazine, musical theater, newspaper, orchestra, pep band, photography, political, professional, radio and TV, religious, social, social service, student government, and yearbook. Popular campus events include weekend movies, Charity Week, Mr. Siena, SienaFest and Family Weekend. **Sports:** There are 7 intercollegiate sports for men and 11 for women, and 9 intramural sports for men and 9 for women. Facilities include an athletic complex that offers free weights, a training facility, an indoor track, an 8-lane, 25-meter pool, fitness equipment, life cycles, multipurpose courts, outdoor tennis courts, outdoor fields, squash courts, and racquetball courts. **Graduates:** From July 1, 2016 to June 30, 2017, 769 bachelor's degrees were awarded. The most popular majors were accounting (15%), marketing (11%), and psychology (10%). In an average class, 1% graduate in 3 years or less, 72% graduate in 4 years or less, 76% graduate in 5 years or less, and 78% graduate in 6 years or less.

SERVICES: Counseling and information services are available, as is tutoring in most subjects. There is a reader service for the blind, remedial math and writing, and a writing center that offers free one-to-one assistance. **Library/Resources:** The library contains 369,191 volumes, 27,739 microform items, and 5,922 audio/video tapes/CDs/DVDs, and subscribes to 280 periodicals including electronic. Computerized library services include interlibrary loans, database searching, Internet access, and Wi-Fi capability. Special learning facilities include an art gallery, a radio station, TV station, the Hickey Financial Technology Center, which features real-time capital market trading room with a stock ticker; data screens; workstations; and access to financial information sources and accounting labs. The Center for Undergraduate Research and Creative Activity ensures that undergraduate research and scholarship opportunities are available to as many students as possible, regardless of major. The Stack Center for Innovation and Entrepreneurship is an interdisciplinary program focused on business creation from idea development to commercialization. The Stewart's Advanced Instrumentation and Technology Center is a multidisciplinary instrumentation suite focused on teaching and research across the departments of the School of Science. **Physically Challenged Students:** 90% of the campus is accessible. Facilities include wheelchair ramps, elevators, special parking, specially equipped restrooms, special class scheduling, lowered drinking fountains, special housing, and a center that provides various resources for students with disabilities. **Special:** Siena has opportunities for cross-registration through the Hudson-Mohawk Association. Domestic and international internships, study abroad in over 50 countries, a Washington semester, and work-study programs are available. The College offers dual majors in different divisions and a B.A.-B.S. degree in math, economics, and biology as well as a 3-2 engineering degree with Rensselaer Polytechnic Institute, Catholic University, Clarkson University, Manhattan College, SUNY Binghamton, and Western New England College. Siena also offer a 4-1 degree in engineering with Clarkson Graduate College. A 4-4 medical program with Albany Medical College is also offered. A 4-3 law program is offered with Albany Law, Pace Law, and Western New England. There are 21 national honor societies, a freshman honors program, and 13 departmental honors programs. **Visiting:** There are regularly scheduled orientations for prospective students; students may interview with an admissions counselor, tour campus, or attend a visit on the weekend. There are guides for informal visits and visitors may sit in on classes. To schedule a visit, contact the Admissions Office. **Campus Safety and Security:** Measures include 24-hour foot and vehicle patrol, an emergency notification system, and security escort services. There are shuttle buses, emergency telephones, lighted pathways/sidewalks, controlled access to dorms/residences, as well as a card access system for residence halls, radio dispatch, and a 911 on-campus telephone system.

REQUIREMENTS: In the five core areas of math, English, science, history and language Siena likes to see a B and above. Siena is test optional. To be test optional Siena needs to see 19 academic units. To be test optional for a science major Siena needs to see the student has taken physics and precalculus and to be test optional for a business major and have four years of math. Either the SAT or the ACT is accepted. The essay is optional. An interview is highly recommended, however it is not required. AP and CLEP credits are accepted. Important factors in the admissions decision are advanced placement or honors courses, personality/intangible qualities, and extracurricular activities record. To graduate, students must earn 120 credits, including 30 to 39 depending on major, with at least a 2.0 GPA. At least a C-grade in every major field course used to satisfy the credit hour requirement of the major. The required core curriculum is 42 credits. **Procedure:** Freshmen are admitted in the fall and spring. Entrance exams should be taken during spring of the junior year or fall of the senior year. There are early decision, early admissions, and deferred admissions plans. Early decision applications should be filed by December 1; regular applications, by February 15 for fall entry; January 15 for spring entry; and May 1 for summer entry. The fall 2017 application fee was $50. Notification of early decision is sent December 15; regular decision, March 15. 46 early decision candidates were accepted for the 2017-2018 class. 743 applicants were on the 2017 waiting list. Applications are accepted online. **Transfer Students:** 188 transfer students enrolled in 2016-2017. Applicants must have a minimum 2.5 GPA. An interview is recommended. At least half of the major field requirements must be completed at Siena. 30 of 120 credits required for the bachelor's degree must be completed at Siena. **International Students:** There are 60 international students enrolled. They must take the TOEFL with a minimum score of 530 on the paper-based TOEFL (PBT) or 65 on the Internet-based version (iBT). Student must take the IELTS or the SAT/ACT is optional.

ADMISSIONS: The SAT scores for the 2017-2018 freshman class were: Critical Reading-- 32% below 500, 44% between 500 and 599, 21% between 600 and 699, and 3% between 700 and 800. Math-- 24% below 500, 45% between 500 and 599, 26% between 600 and 699, and 6% between 700 and 800. Writing-- 39% below 500, 44% between 500 and 599, 15% between 600 and 699, and 2% between 700 and 800. The ACT scores were 4% between 12 and 17, 34% between 18 and 23, 50% between 24 and 29, and 13% above 30. 46% of the current freshmen were in the top fifth of their class; 78% were in the top two fifths. **Admissions Contact:** Katie Szalda, Director of Admissions. Email: *admissions@siena.edu* Web: *www.siena.edu*

FINANCIAL AID: In 2017-2018, 99% of all full-time freshmen received some form of financial aid. 71% of all full-time freshmen received need-based aid. The average freshman award was $30,602. Need-based scholarships or need-based grants averaged $23,060 ($20,000 maximum); need-based self-help aid (loans and jobs) averaged $3,989 ($4,500 maximum); non-need-based athletic scholarships averaged $19,883 ($49,000 maximum); and other non-need-based awards and non-need-based scholarships averaged $13,408 ($20,000 maximum). The state aid form is required. The FAFSA code is 002816. The priority date for freshman financial aid applications for fall entry is February 15.

SKIDMORE COLLEGE D-3

www.skidmore.edu

Saratoga Springs, NY 12866 (518) 580-5570 (800) 867-6007

Fax: (518) 580-5584 **Email:** admissions@skidmore.edu

Full-time: 1061 men, 1568 women	**Faculty:** 277
Part-time: 12 men, 18 women	**Ph.D.s:** 87%
Graduate: 1 men, 3 women	**Student/Faculty:** 9 to 1
Year: semesters, summer session	**Tuition:** $52,596
Room & Board: $14,004	**Freshman Class:** 10053 applied, 2465 accepted, 661 enrolled
SAT EBR-W/M: 660/650 **ACT:** 29	**CEEB CODE:** 2815
Application Deadline: January 15	**MOST COMPETITIVE**

Skidmore College, founded in 1903, is an independent, creative, liberal arts college, with nearly 50 majors, preprofessional offerings such as business, education, and exercise science, a popular study-abroad program, and numerous opportunities for student-faculty research and paid internships as early as year one. There is 1 undergraduate school. In addition to regional accreditation, SC has baccalaureate program accreditation with CSWE, NASAD, and CAEP. The 890-acre campus is in a small town in Saratoga Springs, New York, 30 miles north of Albany. Including any residence halls, there are 50 buildings.

STUDENT LIFE: 70% of undergraduates are from out of state, mostly

the Northeast. Students are from 40 states, 61 foreign countries, and Canada. 57% are from public schools. 9% are Hispanic; 63% White; 5% African American; 5% Asian American; 4% two or more races; 3% race unknown; 11% Foreign. **Female To Male Ratio:** 1.5:1. The average age of freshmen is 18; all undergraduates, 20. 7% do not continue beyond their first year; 87% remain to graduate. **Housing:** 2179 students can be accommodated in college housing, which includes single-sex dorms, coed dorms and on-campus apartments. In addition, there are honors houses, language/international houses, special-interest houses, a gender neutral wing, substance free housing, 24 hour quiet floor, women's floors, and global and multicultural communities. On-campus housing is guaranteed for all 4 years and is available on a lottery system for upperclassmen. 89% of students live on campus. All students may keep cars.

FACULTY/CLASSROOMS: 47% of faculty are male; 53% are female. All teach undergraduates and all do research. No introductory courses are taught by graduate students. The average class size in an introductory lecture is 16.

PROGRAMS OF STUDY: SC confers B.A. and B.S. degrees. Bachelor's degrees are awarded in AGRICULTURE (environmental studies), BIOLOGICAL SCIENCE (biology/biological science and neurosciences), BUSINESS (business administration and management and business economics), COMMUNICATIONS AND THE ARTS (art, art history and appreciation, classics, dance, dramatic arts, English, French, German, music, and Spanish), COMPUTER AND PHYSICAL SCIENCE (chemistry, computer science, geology, mathematics, and physics), EDUCATION (elementary education), HEALTH PROFESSIONS (exercise science), SOCIAL SCIENCE (American studies, anthropology, Asian/Oriental studies, economics, French studies, gender studies, history, international relations, liberal arts/general studies, philosophy, political science/government, psychology, religion, social science, social work, and sociology). Social sciences, visual & performing arts, and business/marketing have the largest enrollments.

ACTIVITIES: There are no fraternities or sororities. There are 106 groups on campus, including art, band, chess, choir, chorale, chorus, computers, dance, debate, drama, environmental, ethnic, film, honors, international, jazz band, LGBT, literary magazine, musical theater, newspaper, opera, orchestra, photography, political, professional, radio and TV, religious, social, social service, student government, and symphony. Popular campus events include Oktoberfest, Winter Carnival, and Spring Fling. **Sports:** There are 10 intercollegiate sports for men and 11 for women, and 10 intramural sports for men and 10 for women. Facilities include a sports and recreation center which provides basketball/volleyball courts, intramural and recreation gyms, a swimming pool with diving well, racquetball courts, an athletic training room, human-performance laboratory, aerobics and fitness area, a weight room, tennis courts, an artificial-surface field for field hockey, a softball diamond with field turf outfield, an all-weather track, a field turf playing field for soccer, lacrosse, intramurals, a golf driving range, indoor and outdoor riding rings, a hunter course, and riding trails, a rowing boathouse, and ice hockey rink.**Graduates:** From July 1, 2016 to June 30, 2017, 605 bachelor's degrees were awarded. The most popular majors were social sciences (18%), business (14%), and visual and performing arts (13%). In an average class, 84% graduate in 4 years or less, 87% graduate in 5 years or less, and 87% graduate in 6 years or less.

SERVICES: Counseling and information services are available, as is tutoring in most subjects. Note takers and alternate format texts are also offered. **Library/Resources:** The library contains 350,000 volumes. Computerized library services include interlibrary loans, database searching, Internet access, and Wi-Fi capability. Special learning facilities include an art gallery, a radio station, TV station, an electronic music studio, music and art studios, a theater teaching facility, teaching museum, anthropology lab, and special biological habitats. **Physically Challenged Students:** 98% of the campus is accessible. Facilities include wheelchair ramps, elevators, special parking, specially equipped restrooms, lowered drinking fountains, and special housing. **Special:** Skidmore offers cross-registration with other area colleges, individually designed internships, various study-abroad programs, a Washington semester in conjunction with American University, dual and student-designed majors, credit for life and experience, and pass/fail options, as well as a nondegree study program for senior citizens. There are cooperative programs with other schools in engineering, business administration, and health. There are 11 national honor societies, Phi Beta Kappa, and a freshman honors program. **Visiting:** There are regularly scheduled orientations for prospective students, including full-day open-house programs. There are guides for informal visits; visitors may sit in on classes and stay overnight. To schedule a visit, contact the Admissions Office. **Campus Safety and Security:** Measures include 24-hour foot and vehicle patrol, emergency notification system, and security escort services. There are shuttle buses, emergency telephones, lighted pathways/sidewalks, controlled access to dorms/residences, special security alert system, rigorous fire response procedures, and a lock system on dorm entrances.

REQUIREMENTS: Test-optional applies to all applicants except the following: international students who have not studied in an English-speaking curriculum for at least three years, students who have been homeschooled, and students from schools providing evaluative summaries in lieu of grades. Recommended high school units include 4 units each in English, math, foreign language, social studies, and science (with 3 units in lab). AP and CLEP credits are accepted. Important factors in the admissions decision are advanced placement or honors courses, evidence of special talent, personality/intangible qualities, extracurricular activities record, recommendations by school officials, parents or siblings attended the school, recommendations by alumni, and geographical diversity. To graduate, students must complete 120 credits, including at least 24 at the 300 level, with a minimum GPA of 2.0 overall and in the major. B.A. candidates require 90 credits in the liberal arts to graduate, B.S. candidates require 60 credits. Students must fulfill all core curriculum, distribution, and major requirements. **Procedure:** Freshmen are admitted in the fall. Entrance exams should be taken by December of the senior year. There are early decision, early admissions, and deferred admissions plans. Early decision applications should be filed by November 15; regular applications, by January 15 for fall entry. The fall 2017 application fee was $65. Notification of early decision is sent December 15; regular decision, April 1. 358 early decision candidates were accepted for the 2017-2018 class. 461 applicants were on the 2017 waiting list; 60 were admitted. Applications are accepted online. **Transfer Students:** 31 transfer students enrolled in 2016-2017. Transfer students must submit a high school transcript, all college transcripts, an essay or personal statement, test scores (if no 2-year degree), and a statement of good standing from prior institutions. At least one professor recommendation from the current institution and a mid-term report are also required. 60 of 120 credits required for the bachelor's degree must be completed at SC. **International Students:** There are 298 international students enrolled. They must take the TOEFL with a minimum score of 590 on the paper-based TOEFL (PBT) or 96 on the Internet-based version (iBT). They must also take the SAT or ACT.

ADMISSIONS: 25% of the 2017-2018 applicants were accepted. The SAT scores for the 2017-2018 freshman class were: Math-- 1% below 500, 24% between 500 and 599, 47% between 600 and 699, and 28% between 700 and 800. Evidence-Based Reading/Writing-- 2% below 500, 16% between 500 and 599, 52% between 600 and 699, and 30% between 700 and 800. The ACT scores were 5% between 18 and 23, 51% between 24 and 29, and 45% above 30. **Admissions Contact:** Mary Lou Bates, Director of Admissions. Email: *admissions@skidmore.edu* Web: *www.skidmore.edu*

FINANCIAL AID: In 2017-2018, 41% of all full-time freshmen received some form of financial aid and need-based aid. The average freshman award was $47,700. Need-based scholarships or need-based grants averaged $45,900; need-based self-help aid (loans and jobs) averaged $3,900; and other non-need-based awards and non-need-based scholarships averaged $15,000. The average financial indebtedness of the 2017 graduate was $23,916. SC is a member of CSS. The CSS/Profile is required. The FAFSA code is 002814. The deadline for filing freshman financial aid applications for fall entry is February 1.

ST. BONAVENTURE UNIVERSITY B-4

www.sbu.edu

St. Bonaventure, NY 14778	**(716) 375-2400** **(800) 462-5050**
Fax: (716) 375-4005	**Email: admissions@sbu.edu**
Full-time: 824 men, 767 women	**Faculty:** 127
Part-time: 18 men, 18 women	**Ph.D.s:** 78%
Graduate: 180 men, 282 women	**Student/Faculty:** 12 to 1
Year: semesters, summer session	**Tuition:** $33,331
Room & Board: $12,265	**Freshman Class:** 2986 applied, 2106 accepted, 439 enrolled
SAT EBR-W/M: 560/560 **ACT:** 24	**CEEB CODE:** 2793
Application Deadline: July 1	**COMPETITIVE**

Saint Bonaventure University, founded in 1858, is a private Roman Catholic institution in the Franciscan tradition, offering programs in the arts and sciences, education, business, and journalism and mass communication. There are 4 undergraduate schools and 1 graduate school. In addition to regional accreditation, SBU has baccalaureate program accreditation with AACSB, NCATE, and CACREP. The 500-acre campus is in a small town 75 miles southeast of Buffalo. Including any residence halls, there are 36 buildings.

STUDENT LIFE: 68% of undergraduates are from New York. Others are from 34 states, 18 foreign countries, and Canada. 8% are race unknown; 69% White; 6% African American; 6% Hispanic; 4% Asian American; 3% Foreign; 2% two or more races. 45% are Catholic; 42% Unknown denominations ; 27% claim no religious affiliation; 14% Protestant. **Female To Male Ratio:** 1.0:1. The average age of freshmen is 18; all undergraduates, 19. 16% do not continue beyond their first year; 69% remain to graduate. **Housing:** 1630 students can be accommodated in college housing, which includes dorms and on-campus apartments. In addition, there are special-interest houses, and living and learning communities. On-campus housing is guaranteed for all 4 years. 79% of students live on campus. All students may keep cars.

FACULTY/CLASSROOMS: 47% of faculty are male; 53% are female. 90% teach undergraduates. No introductory courses are taught by graduate students.

PROGRAMS OF STUDY: SBU confers B.A., B.S., B.B.A., and B.S.Ed. degrees. Master's degrees are also awarded. Bachelor's degrees are awarded in AGRICULTURE (environmental studies), BIOLOGICAL SCIENCE (biochemistry, bioinformatics, biology/biological science, and biophysics), BUSINESS (accounting, banking and finance, management information systems, management science, and marketing/retailing/ merchandising), COMMUNICATIONS AND THE ARTS (art history, classical languages, communications, digital communications, dramatic arts, English, journalism, music, and visual and performing arts), COMPUTER AND PHYSICAL SCIENCE (chemistry, computer science, cyber intelligence/security studies, mathematics, and physics), EDUCATION (education, elementary education, physical education, special education, and sports studies), ENGINEERING AND ENVIRONMENTAL DESIGN (engineering physics, environmental science, and industrial administration/management), HEALTH PROFESSIONS (health science), SOCIAL SCIENCE (child care/child and family studies, history, international studies, philosophy, political science/government, psychology, sociology, theological studies, and women's studies). Journalism/ mass communication, biology, and accounting have the largest enrollments.

ACTIVITIES: There are no fraternities or sororities. There are 65 groups on campus, including art, band, cheerleading, choir, chorale, chorus, computers, dance, drama, environmental, ethnic, honors, international, jazz band, LGBT, literary magazine, newspaper, photography, political, professional, radio and TV, religious, social, social service, student government, and yearbook. Popular campus events include Family Weekend, and Spring and Winter Weekends. **Sports:** There are 8 intercollegiate sports for men and 8 for women, and 10 intramural sports for men and 9 for women. Facilities include a basketball arena, indoor swimming pool, 9-hole golf course, weight facilities and free weights, fitness center with strength, aerobics and conditioning areas, an indoor track, multiuse courts, and a rock climbing wall, soccer, baseball, softball, rugby, and intramural fields, and a recreation trail. **Graduates:** From July 1, 2016 to June 30, 2017, 437 bachelor's degrees were awarded. The most popular majors were business (33%), communications/ journalism (16%), and biology (8%). In an average class, 4% graduate in 3 years or less, 59% graduate in 4 years or less, 68% graduate in 5 years or less, and 69% graduate in 6 years or less.

SERVICES: Counseling and information services are available, as is tutoring in most subjects. There is remedial math. **Library/Resources:** The library contains 371,691 volumes, 16,500 microform items, 11,898 audio/video tapes/CDs/DVDs, and subscribes to 32,189 periodicals, including electronic. Computerized library services include interlibrary loans, database searching, Internet access, and Wi-Fi capability. Special learning facilities include an art gallery, a radio station, TV station, and an observatory. **Physically Challenged Students:** 90% of the campus is accessible. Facilities include wheelchair ramps, elevators, special parking, and specially equipped restrooms. **Special:** Internships are available in business, mass communication, political science, psychology, sociology, and other fields. Study abroad in 18 countries, B.A.-B.S. degrees, accelerated degree programs, dual and student-designed majors, a Washington semester with American University, and pass/fail options are offered. Dual admissions with George Washington University School of Medicine, Lake Erie College of Osteopathic Medicine, University at Buffalo School of Dental Medicine, Lake Erie College of Osteopathic Medicine School of Pharmacy, and SUNY-Upstate Medical are also possible. There are 15 national honor societies and a freshman honors program. **Visiting:** There are regularly scheduled orientations for prospective students, including interviews, tours, class visits, and meetings with professors. There are guides for informal visits; visitors may sit in on classes and stay overnight. To schedule a visit, contact Monica Emery at memery@sbu .edu. **Campus Safety and Security:** Measures include 24-hour foot and vehicle patrol, an emergency notification system, and security escort services. There are shuttle buses, emergency telephones, lighted pathways/ sidewalks, and controlled access to dorms/residences.

REQUIREMENTS: The ACT is recommended with a satisfactory score of 24 or a satisfactory score on the SAT. Applicants must be graduates of an accredited secondary school or have a GED. 16 academic credits are required, including 4 years each of English and social studies, 3 each of math and science, and 2 of a foreign language. An essay and an interview are recommended. AP and CLEP credits are accepted. To graduate, students must complete 120 credit hours, at least 30 of them in the major, with a minimum GPA of 2.0. Students must complete general education requirements in addition to major requirements. Students in programs leading to teacher certification must have a minimum GPA of 3.0. **Procedure:** Freshmen are admitted to all sessions. Entrance exams should be taken during the spring of the junior year or the fall of the senior year. There are deferred admissions and rolling admissions plans. Applications should be filed by July 1 for fall entry; October 15 for spring entry. Notification is sent on a rolling basis. Applications are accepted online. **Transfer Students:** 61 transfer students enrolled in 2016-2017. Applicants must have a minimum 2.0 GPA. High school and college transcripts, an essay, and a letter of recommendation are required. 45 of 120 credits required for the bachelor's degree must be completed at SBU. **International Students:** There are 48 international students enrolled. They must take the TOEFL with a minimum score of 550 on the paper-based TOEFL (PBT) or 79 on the Internet-based version (iBT).

ADMISSIONS: 71% of the 2017-2018 applicants were accepted. The SAT scores for the 2017-2018 freshman class were: Math-- 22% below 500, 47% between 500 and 599, 25% between 600 and 699, and 6% between 700 and 800. Evidence-Based Reading/Writing-- 20% below 500, 48% between 500 and 599, 29% between 600 and 699, and 3% between 700 and 800. The ACT scores were 6% between 12 and 17, 38% between 18 and 23, 44% between 24 and 29, and 12% above 30. 19% of the current freshmen were in the top fifth of their class; 32% were in the top two fifths. 2 freshmen graduated first in their class. **Admissions Contact:** Bernard Valento, Vice President for Enrollment. Email: *admissions@sbu.edu* Web: *www.sbu.edu*

FINANCIAL AID: In 2017-2018, 99% of all full-time freshmen received some form of financial aid. 58% of all full-time freshmen received need-based aid. The average freshman award was $33,666. Need-based scholarships or need-based grants averaged $11,095; need-based self-help aid (loans and jobs) averaged $8,262; non-need-based athletic scholarships averaged $13,120; and other non-need-based awards and non-need-based scholarships averaged $18,401. 36% of undergraduate students work part-time. The average financial indebtedness of the 2017 graduate was $27,000. The state aid form is required. The FAFSA code is 002817. The priority date for freshman financial aid applications for fall entry is February 15.

ST. FRANCIS COLLEGE *(The complete profile is made available exclusively on our website, www.barronspac.com)*

ST. JOHN FISHER COLLEGE — B-3

www.sjfc.edu

Rochester, NY 14618	(585) 385-8064 (800) 444-4640
Fax: (585) 385-8386	**Email:** admissions@sjfc.edu
Full-time: 1070 men, 1560 women	**Faculty:** 181; IIA, av$
Part-time: 41 men, 88 women	**Ph.D.s:** 89%
Graduate: 323 men, 700 women	**Student/Faculty:** 12 to 1
Year: semesters, summer session	**Tuition:** $33,120
Room & Board: $12,150	**Freshman Class:** 4432 applied, 2860 accepted, 626 enrolled
SAT EBR-W/M: 569/573 **ACT:** 24	**CEEB CODE:** 2798
Application Deadline: rolling	**VERY COMPETITIVE**

St. John Fisher College is an independent liberal arts institution in the Catholic tradition of American higher education. Guided since its inception in 1948 by the educational philosophy of the Congregation of St. Basil, the college emphasizes liberal learning for students in traditional academic disciplines, as well as for those in more directly career-oriented fields. The college welcomes qualified students, faculty, and staff regardless of religious or cultural background. There are 4 undergraduate schools and 5 graduate schools. In addition to regional accreditation, SJFC has baccalaureate program accreditation with AACSB, ACPE, ACS, CCNE, and CAEP. The 164-acre campus is in a suburban area 6 miles southeast of Rochester. Including any residence halls, there are 27 buildings.

STUDENT LIFE: 97% of undergraduates are from New York. Others are from 24 states, 7 foreign countries, and Canada. 85% are from public schools. 84% are White; 5% Hispanic; 4% African American; 3% Asian American; 2% two or more races; 2% race unknown. **Female To Male Ratio:** 1.6:1. The average age of freshmen is 18; all undergraduates, 21. 15% do not continue beyond their first year; 71% remain to graduate. **Housing:** 1400 students can be accommodated in college housing, which includes dorms. On-campus housing is guaranteed for the freshman year only and is available on a lottery system for upperclassmen. 51% of students live on campus. Upperclassmen may keep cars.

FACULTY/CLASSROOMS: 40% of faculty are male; 60% are female. 86% teach undergraduates. No introductory courses are taught by graduate students. The average class size in an introductory lecture is 22 and in a laboratory is 14.

PROGRAMS OF STUDY: SJFC confers B.A. and B.S. degrees. Master's and doctoral degrees are also awarded. Bachelor's degrees are awarded in BIOLOGICAL SCIENCE (biology/biological science), BUSINESS (accounting, business administration and management, marketing management, and sports management), COMMUNICATIONS AND THE ARTS (communications, digital communications, English, French, and Spanish), COMPUTER AND PHYSICAL SCIENCE (chemistry, computer science, mathematics, physics, and statistics), EDUCATION (elementary education, English education, foreign languages education, mathematics education, middle school education, science education, secondary education, social studies education, and special education), HEALTH PROFESSIONS (nursing), SOCIAL SCIENCE (American studies, anthropology, criminology, economics, history, interdisciplinary studies, international studies, legal studies, philosophy, political science/government, psychology, religion, and sociology). Sciences are the strongest academically. Nursing, biological sciences, and management have the largest enrollments.

ACTIVITIES: There are no fraternities or sororities. There are 70 groups on campus, including Commuter Council, Resident Student Association, Student Senate SGA, art, cheerleading, choir, chorus, computers, dance, drama, environmental, ethnic, honors, international, LGBT, literary magazine, musical theater, newspaper, pep band, photography, political, professional, radio and TV, religious, social, social service, Student Activities Board, student government, and yearbook. Popular campus events include Spring Event, Senior Week, and TEDDI 24-hour Dance Marathon for Charity. **Sports:** There are 10 intercollegiate sports for men and 11 for women, and 4 intramural sports for men and 4 for women. The Student Life Center includes a field house, a varsity gymnasium for basketball, a fitness center/weight room, training facilities, a stadium for football, soccer, and lacrosse, a track and field complex that features an eight-lane, 400-meter competition track with a grass infield, a baseball complex, softball complex, and a regulation-size grass practice field. **Graduates:** From July 1, 2016 to June 30, 2017, 730 bachelor's degrees were awarded. The most popular majors were business (26%), nursing (26%), and biology (10%). In an average class, 3% graduate in 3 years or less, 63% graduate in 4 years or less, 70% graduate in 5 years or less, and 71% graduate in 6 years or less.

SERVICES: Counseling and information services are available, as is tutoring in every subject. There is a reader service for the blind. The math and writing centers provide help to students at all levels. 24 hour online and peer tutoring is available to all students in most undergraduate subject areas. **Library/Resources:** The library contains 156,563 volumes, 1,000 microform items, 25,987 audio/video tapes/CDs/DVDs, and subscribes to 165,284 periodicals, including electronic. Computerized library services include interlibrary loans, database searching, and Internet access. Special learning facilities include an art gallery, a radio station, TV station, a multimedia center, wet and dry multidisciplinary science labs, animal labs, and growth chambers. **Physically Challenged Students:** All of the campus is accessible. Facilities include wheelchair ramps, elevators, special parking, specially equipped restrooms, special class scheduling, lowered drinking fountains, lowered telephones, and accessible dorm rooms. **Special:** The college has cooperative programs and cross-registration with Rochester area colleges. The college offers internships in most majors, independent research in various majors, study abroad, accelerated degree programs in specific majors, Washington semesters, dual and student-designed majors, and degrees in interdisciplinary studies. Navy and Marine ROTC are available at the University of Rochester and Air Force and Army ROTC is available at Rochester Institute of Technology. There are 10 national honor societies, a freshman honors program, and 8 departmental honors programs. **Visiting:** There are regularly scheduled orientations for prospective students, they can schedule a campus tour, an interview with a member of the admissions staff, and a meeting with faculty and coaches. There are guides for informal visits; visitors may sit in on classes and stay overnight. To schedule a visit, contact The Office of Freshman Admissions. **Campus Safety and Security:** Measures include 24-hour foot and vehicle patrol, an emergency notification system, self-defense education, and security escort services. There are shuttle buses, emergency telephones, lighted pathways/sidewalks, controlled access to dorms/residences. Access to the residence halls is controlled by the ID card access system. Residence halls are patrolled and monitored 24 hours a day by security officers or resident advisers. All other campus facilities are locked and unlocked according to established schedules.

REQUIREMENTS: Applicants are required to submit either SAT or ACT standardized test scores for admission to the College. Applicants must be graduates of an accredited secondary school and have completed 16 academic credits including 4 years each in English and history/social studies, 3 years each in math and science, and 2 years in a foreign language. Interviews are recommended. A GPA of 85.0 is required. AP and CLEP credits are accepted. Important factors in the admissions decision are advanced placement or honors courses, extracurricular activities record, and leadership record. To graduate, students must complete at least 120 credit hours, including at least 30 in the major, and maintain a 2.0 minimum GPA. The core curriculum consists of 15 courses that students must successfully complete to graduate. The core is composed of 2 tiers of study: Foundations courses and Perspectives courses. Freshmen must participate in one of the integrative learning communities. **Procedure:** Freshmen are admitted in the fall. There are early decision, deferred admissions, and rolling admissions plans. Application deadlines are open. Notification of early decision is sent January 15; regular decision, on a rolling basis. 65 early decision candidates were accepted for the 2017-2018 class. Applications are accepted online. **Transfer Students:** 201 transfer students enrolled in 2016-2017. Applicants must have a minimum GPA of 2.0 to be considered (mean GPA is 2.8). A high school transcript is required for students with fewer than 24 college credits. Interviews are recommended. 30 of 120 credits required for the bachelor's degree must be completed at SJFC. **International Students:** There are 4 international students enrolled. They must take the TOEFL with a minimum score of 550 on the paper-based TOEFL (PBT) or 80 on the Internet-based version (iBT). International Applicants may submit TOEFL scores or standardized entrance exams such as SAT or ACT.

ADMISSIONS: 65% of the 2017-2018 applicants were accepted. The SAT scores for the 2017-2018 freshman class were: Math-- 9% below 500, 52% between 500 and 599, 36% between 600 and 699, and 3% between 700 and 800. Evidence-Based Reading/Writing-- 10% below 500, 55% between 500 and 599, 32% between 600 and 699, and 2% between 700 and 800. The ACT scores were 4% between 12 and 17, 37% between 18 and 23, 20% between 24 and 29, and 6% above 30. 41% of the current freshmen were in the top fifth of their class; 74% were in the top two fifths. 2 freshmen graduated first in their class. **Admissions Contact:** Stacy Ledermann, Director of Freshman Admissions. Email: *admissions@sjfc.edu* Web: *www.sjfc.edu*

FINANCIAL AID: In 2017-2018, 100% of all full-time freshmen received some form of financial aid. 83% of all full-time freshmen received need-based aid. The average freshman award was $23,070. Need-based scholarships or need-based grants averaged $19,075 ($34,000 maximum); and need-based self-help aid (loans and jobs) averaged $10,524 ($34,000 maximum). 46% of undergraduate students work part-time. The average financial indebtedness of the 2017 graduate was $38,639. The state aid form is required. The FAFSA code is 002821. The priority date for freshman financial aid applications for fall entry is February 15.

ST. JOHN'S UNIVERSITY D-5
www.stjohns.edu

Queens, NY 11439 **(718) 990-2000**

Fax: (718) 990-5686
Email: admission@stjohns.edu
Full-time: 4958 men, 6568 women
Part-time: 2156 men, 3084 women
Graduate: 1764 men, 2816 women
Year: semesters, summer session
Room & Board: $16,640
SAT CR/M: 570/570 **ACT:** 26
Application Deadline: n/av
Faculty: 594
Ph.D.s: 93%
Student/Faculty: 20 to 1
Tuition: $40,520
Freshman Class: 27179 applied, 18408 accepted, 2967 enrolled
CEEB CODE: 2799
COMPETITIVE+

St. John's University, founded in 1870, is a Catholic and Vincentian University that promotes student success through academic excellence, global studies, and a focus on serving those in need. The University prepares students for ethical leadership that brings positive change in their communities, professions, and the world. More than 44 percent of St. John's undergraduates choose to earn credits by participating in the University's varied global studies programs. The Institute of International Education (IIE) has ranked St. John's among doctorate-granting American universities with the greatest proportions of undergraduates studying abroad. In addition, students assist those in need through activities including service "plunges," the Midnight Run program, and Academic Service-Learning, course-related volunteer opportunities. There are 3 New York City campuses in Queens, Manhattan, and Staten Island in addition to a Long Island Graduate Center in Hauppauge, NY. The University also has a campus in Rome, Italy, as well as study abroad locations in Paris, France; Limerick, Ireland; and Seville, Spain. In addition to regional accreditation, SJU has baccalaureate program accreditation with AACSB, ACPE, NASAD, CAEP, ABA, ARC-PA, and NAACLS. The 102-acre campus is in a suburban area. The main campus is in a residential section of Queens. Including any residence halls, there are 53 buildings.

STUDENT LIFE: 79% of undergraduates are from New York. Others are from 46 states, 117 foreign countries, and Canada. 57% are from public schools. 9% are Hispanic; 8% race unknown; 47% White; 4% Foreign; 4% two or more races; 14% Asian American; 13% African American. 45% are Catholic; 20% Muslim, Hindu, Buddhist, Mormon, Jehovah Witness, Pentecostal, Sikh, Greek and Russian Orthodox, Non-Denominational, and Other; 13% Protestant. **Female To Male Ratio:** 1.4:1. The average age of freshmen is 18; all undergraduates, 19. 16% do not continue beyond their first year; 58% remain to graduate. **Housing:** 3537 students can be accommodated in college housing, which includes dorms, on-campus apartments, off-campus apartments, an honors themed floor, an international themed community that focuses on languages, and special interest housing options. On-campus housing is available on a first-come, first-served basis, and is available on a lottery system for upperclassmen. 74% of students commute. Alcohol is not permitted. Upperclassmen may keep cars.

FACULTY/CLASSROOMS: 56% of faculty are male; 44% are female. 91% teach undergraduates. No introductory courses are taught by graduate students.

PROGRAMS OF STUDY: St. John's confers B.A., B.S., B.F.A., and B.S.Ed. degrees. Associate, master's, and doctoral degrees are also awarded. Bachelor's degrees are awarded in AGRICULTURE (environmental studies), BIOLOGICAL SCIENCE (biology/adolescence education, biology/biological science, and toxicology), BUSINESS (accounting, business administration and management, finance, hospitality management services, insurance and risk management, international business management, management science, marketing, and sports management), COMMUNICATIONS AND THE ARTS (advertising, communications, English, film, television and digital media, fine arts, French, graphic design, illustration, information technology, Italian, journalism, photography, public relations, radio/television technology, Spanish, speech/debate/rhetoric, and telecommunications), COMPUTER AND PHYSICAL SCIENCE (actuarial science, chemistry, computer science, computer security and information assurance, mathematics, physical sciences, physics secondary education, physics and mathematics, and physics), EDUCATION (education, elementary education, health information management, secondary education, social studies secondary school education, Spanish adolescense education, and special education/early childhood dual program), HEALTH PROFESSIONS (clinical science, pharmacy, physician's assistant, radiological science, and speech pathology/audiology), SOCIAL SCIENCE (anthropology, Asian/Oriental studies, criminal justice, economics, history, human services, legal studies, liberal arts/general studies, philosophy, political science/government, psychology, public administration, social studies, sociology, and theology). Pharmacy, biology, and psychology are the strongest academically and the largest.

ACTIVITIES: 10% of men belong to 3 local and 17 national fraternities; 9% of women belong to 1 local and 16 national sororities. There are 148 groups on campus, including art, cheerleading, choir, chorus, computers, dance, debate, drama, environmental, ethnic, film, honors, international, jazz band, literary magazine, musical theater, newspaper, pep band, photography, political, professional, radio and TV, religious, social, social service, student government, and yearbook. Popular campus events include Fall Activity Fair, Spring Fling, Founder's Week, Mass of the Holy Spirit, Holy Days of Obligation, Winter Carnival, Relay for Life, Interfaith Dialogue, and Service Plunges. **Sports:** There are 7 intercollegiate sports for men and 10 for women, and 8 intramural sports for men and 4 for women. Facilities include gyms, tennis courts, weight and exercise rooms, baseball and softball diamonds, fields for football/lacrosse and soccer, basketball courts, and an outdoor track. **Graduates:** From July 1, 2016 to June 30, 2017, 1978 bachelor's degrees were awarded. The most popular majors were business/marketing (23%), communications/journalism (11%), and health professions (11%). In an average class, 1% graduate in 3 years or less, 37% graduate in 4 years or less, 46% graduate in 5 years or less, and 58% graduate in 6 years or less. Of the 2016 graduating class, 37% were enrolled in graduate school within 6 months of graduation, and 68% were employed.

SERVICES: Counseling and information services are available, as is tutoring in most subjects. There is a reader service for the blind. **Library/Resources:** The library contains 1.5 million volumes, 484,267 microform items, 20,614 audio/video tapes/CDs/DVDs, and subscribes to 89,557 periodicals, including electronic. Computerized library services include interlibrary loans, database searching, Internet access, and Wi-Fi capability. Special learning facilities include an art gallery, a radio station, TV station, Health Education Resource Center, Model Pharmacy, Speech and Hearing Clinic, Institute of Asian Studies, Global Language and Culture Center, Financial Information Lab, Little Theatre, a Math Learning Center and a Writing Center. **Physically Challenged Students:** 95% of the campus is accessible. Facilities include wheelchair ramps, elevators, special parking, specially equipped restrooms, special class scheduling, and special housing. **Special:** SJU offers internships; cross-registration; study abroad in Europe, Central and South America, Australia, the Caribbean, Africa, and Asia, accelerated degree programs in many majors; B.A.-B.S. degrees, dual majors and dual degree programs, pass/fail options, and some credit for life, military, and work experience. There are accelerated programs in Optometry with SUNY College of Optometry and a D.P.M. from New York College of Podiatric Medicine. St. John's Staten Island campus offers 3-year bachelors degree program opportunities in selected majors. There is a 6-year doctor of pharmacy program for incoming freshmen students. Eligible students may participate in the University Honors Program. There are 20 national honor societies, a freshman honors program, and 16 departmental honors programs. **Visiting:** There are regularly scheduled orientations for prospective students, available Monday-Sunday throughout the year, which includes information session with admission counselor and a student-led campus tour. Open House and Accepted Students events are also available periodically throughout the calendar year. There are guides for informal visits; visitors may sit in on classes and stay overnight. To schedule a visit, contact Corinne Gentile at (888) 9ST-JOHNS. **Campus Safety and Security:** Measures include 24-hour foot and vehicle patrol, emergency notification system, self-defense education, and security escort services. There are shuttle buses, emergency telephones, lighted pathways/sidewalks, controlled access to dorms/residences, and a crime prevention awareness program.

REQUIREMENTS: Admissions decisions are made by committee review and are based upon several criteria presentated at the time of admission. Criteria include high school GPA, academic curriculum, standarized test scores, resume, essay, and letters of recommendation. AP and CLEP credits are accepted. Important factors in the admissions decision are advanced placement or honors courses, leadership record, and extracurricular activities record. To graduate, students must complete at least 126 credit hours, including core courses and distribution requirements, with a minimum GPA of 2.0 overall and in the major. Other requirements vary by program. Core courses include English, theology, philosophy, Discover NY, history, scientific inquiry, and speech. Distribution requirements include a second language, fine arts, language and culture, math, philosophy, theology, and social sciences. **Procedure:** Freshmen are admitted in the fall, spring, and summer. Entrance exams should be taken late in the junior year or early in the senior year. There are early admissions, deferred admissions, and rolling admissions plans. Application deadlines are open. Notifications are sent December 1. Applications are accepted online. **Transfer Students:** 384 transfer students enrolled in 2016-2017. Transfer applicants must present official high school and college transcripts, as well as a list of courses in progress. If the student is not currently enrolled or was out of school for one semester or more in the past, a letter of explanation is also required. 30 of 126 credits required for the bachelor's degree must be completed at SJU. **International Students:** There are 628 international students enrolled. They must take the TOEFL with a minimum score of 500 on the paper-based TOEFL (PBT) or 61 on the Internet-based version (iBT).

ADMISSIONS: 68% of the 2017-2018 applicants were accepted. The SAT scores for the 2017-2018 freshman class were: Critical Reading-- 10% below 500, 54% between 500 and 599, 33% between 600 and 699, and 3% between 700 and 800. Math-- 13% below 500, 50% between 500 and 599, 29% between 600 and 699, and 8% between 700 and 800. The ACT scores were 31% between 18 and 23, 50% between 24 and 29, and 19% above 30. 36% of the current freshmen were in the top fifth of their class; 67% were in the top two fifths. **Admissions Contact:** Samantha Wright, Director of Undergraduate Admission. Email: *admission@stjohns.edu* Web: *www.stjohns.edu*

FINANCIAL AID: In 2017-2018, 99% of all full-time freshmen received some form of financial aid. 79% of all full-time freshmen received need-based aid. The average freshman award was $44,604. Need-based scholarships or need-based grants averaged $8,555 ($23,279 maximum); need-based self-help aid (loans and jobs) averaged $6,432 ($18,000 maximum); non-need-based athletic scholarships averaged $28,142 ($56,688 maximum); other non-need-based awards and non-need-based scholarships averaged $20,914 ($57,434 maximum); and $16,683 from other forms of aid. 9% of undergraduate students work part-time. The average financial indebtedness of the 2017 graduate was $27,816. The FAFSA code is 002823. The priority date for freshman financial aid applications for fall entry is December 15.

ST. JOSEPH'S COLLEGE, NEW YORK/BROOKLYN CAMPUS *(The complete profile is made available exclusively on our website, www.barronspac.com)*

ST. JOSEPH'S COLLEGE, NEW YORK/ LONG ISLAND CAMPUS — E-5

www.sjcny.edu

Patchogue, NY 11772 — **(631) 687-4500**

Fax: (631)447-3601 — **Email:** longislandas@sjcny.edu

Full-time: 903 men, 1688 women	**Faculty:** 110
Part-time: 159 men, 325 women	**Ph.D.s:** 75%
Graduate: 199 men, 640 women	**Student/Faculty:** 24 to 1
Year: semesters, summer session	**Tuition:** $25,124
Room & Board: n/app	**Freshman Class:** 1770 applied, 1272 accepted, 431 enrolled
SAT CR/M/W: 520/530/500 **ACT:** 23	**CEEB CODE:** 2841
Application Deadline: n/av	**COMPETITIVE**

St. Joseph's College, New York/Long Island Campus, founded in 1916, provides an affordable liberal arts education to a diverse group of students at its campuses at SJC Brooklyn, SJC Long Island, and SJC Online. Independent and coeducational, St. Joseph's prepares students for lives of integrity, intellectual and spiritual values, social responsibility and service – lives that are worthy of the College's motto, Esse non videri – "To be and not to seem." There are 2 undergraduate schools and 1 graduate school. In addition to regional accreditation, SJC Long Island has baccalaureate program accreditation with ACEN, COAPRT, and CAEP. The 56-acre campus is in a suburban area 55 miles from midtown Manhattan. Including any residence halls, there are 9 buildings.

STUDENT LIFE: 99% of undergraduates are from New York. Others are from 13 states, 9 foreign countries, and Canada. 68% are White; 5% African American; 2% Asian American; 2% two or more races; 12% race unknown; 11% Hispanic. **Female To Male Ratio:** 2.1:1. The average age of freshmen is 19; all undergraduates, 24. 13% do not continue beyond their first year; 87% remain to graduate. **Housing:** Alcohol is not permitted. All students commute. All students may keep cars.

FACULTY/CLASSROOMS: 45% of faculty are male; 55% are female. All teach undergraduates. No introductory courses are taught by graduate students. The average class size in an introductory lecture is 18; in a laboratory is 15; and in a regular course is 17.

PROGRAMS OF STUDY: SJC Long Island confers B.A., B.S., B.A./M.A., B.S./M.A., B.S./M.S., and B.S./M.B.A. degrees. Master's degrees are also awarded. Bachelor's degrees are awarded in BIOLOGICAL SCIENCE (biology/biological science), BUSINESS (accounting, business administration and management, hospitality management services, marketing management, organizational leadership and management, recreation and leisure services, and tourism), COMMUNICATIONS AND THE ARTS (English, journalism, Spanish, speech/debate/rhetoric, communication arts - speech, and studio art), COMPUTER AND PHYSICAL SCIENCE (chemistry, computer information technology, computer information systems, computer science, and mathematics), EDUCATION (education, secondary education, and special education), HEALTH PROFESSIONS (health care administration, medical technology, nursing, and public health), SOCIAL SCIENCE (child psychology/development, criminal justice, history, human services, liberal arts/general studies, philosophy and religion, political science/government, psychology, social science, and sociology). Education, accounting, biology, and nursing are the strongest academically. Child study, business administration, and organizational management have the largest enrollments.

ACTIVITIES: There are 49 groups on campus, including Campus Activities Board, child study club, LGBTQA, art, chess, chorus, computers, dance, drama, environmental, ethnic, honors, international, musical theater, newspaper, political, professional, radio and TV, religious, social, social service, STARS, student government, and yearbook. Popular campus events include Welcome Back BBQ, Welcome Back Evening Social, Club Fair, Fall Festival, Bowl-a-Thon, Charity BINGO, Spring Fling, Spring Gala, Tom DeLuca (Hypnotist), and Talent Show. **Sports:** There are 9 intercollegiate sports for men and 9 for women. Facilities include multipurpose turf field for soccer and lacrosse, softball and baseball fields, tennis courts, natatorium, and gymnasium. **Graduates:** From July 1, 2016 to June 30, 2017, 774 bachelor's degrees were awarded. The most popular majors were business/marketing (24%), child study/education (23%), and rhetoric and composition (9%). In an average class, 59% graduate in 4 years or less, 73% graduate in 5 years or less, and 76% graduate in 6 years or less.

SERVICES: Counseling and information services are available, as is tutoring in most subjects. There is a reader service for the blind, and remedial math, reading, and writing. **Library/Resources:** The library contains 236,309 volumes, 1,375 microform items, and 2,372 audio/video tapes/CDs/DVDs, and subscribes to 60,421 periodicals including electronic. Computerized library services include interlibrary loans, database searching, Internet access, and Wi-Fi capability. Special learning facilities include an art gallery, a radio station, 3-D Printer, a technology building, computer labs, and the Claire Rose Playhouse. **Physically Challenged Students:** All of the campus is accessible. Facilities include wheelchair ramps, elevators, special parking, specially equipped restrooms, special class scheduling, and lowered drinking fountains. **Special:** SJC offers study abroad in Greece, Costa Rica, France, Romania, England, and Spain, as well as OCICU - Online Consortium of Independent College and Universities. There is a freshman honors program. **Visiting:** There are regularly scheduled orientations for prospective students, including acclimation to the institution, programs, services, and facilities; assistance with developing positive and realistic expectations; the fostering a comfort level at the institution; meet other new students; faculty, and staff. There are guides for informal visits and visitors may sit in on classes. To schedule a visit, contact Elizabeth McGonigle (631) 687-4500 at (631) 687-4500. **Campus Safety and Security:** Measures include 24-hour foot and vehicle patrol, an emergency notification system, and security escort services. There are emergency telephones and lighted pathways/sidewalks.

REQUIREMENTS: The SAT or ACT is required. A high school diploma is required and GED is accepted. An off-campus interview may be arranged with an admissions representative. A GPA of 2.7 is required. AP and CLEP credits are accepted. Important factors in the admissions decision are advanced placement or honors courses, leadership record, and recommendations by school officials. **Procedure:** Freshmen are admitted in the fall, spring, and summer. There are deferred admissions and rolling admissions plans. Application deadlines are open. The fall 2017 application fee was $25. Notifications are sent November 1. Applications are accepted online. **Transfer Students:** 582 transfer students enrolled in 2016-2017. If transferring with less than 24 credits of college level coursework, a high school transcript is required. 30 of 120 credits required for the bachelor's degree must be completed at SJC. **International Students:** There are 11 international students enrolled. The SAT or ACT is recommended.

ADMISSIONS: 72% of the 2017-2018 applicants were accepted. The SAT scores for the 2017-2018 freshman class were: Critical Reading-- 37% below 500, 50% between 500 and 599, 12% between 600 and 699, and 1% between 700 and 800. Math-- 32% below 500, 48% between 500 and 599, 18% between 600 and 699, and 2% between 700 and 800. Writing-- 47% below 500, 44% between 500 and 599, 8% between 600 and 699, and 1% between 700 and 800. The ACT scores were 6% between 12 and 17, 48% between 18 and 23, 43% between 24 and 29, and 3% above 30. **Admissions Contact:** Gigi Lamens, Vice President for Enrollment Management. Email: *longislandas@sjcny.edu* Web: *www.sjcny.edu*

FINANCIAL AID: In 2017-2018, 99% of all full-time freshmen received some form of financial aid. 78% of all full-time freshmen received need-based aid. The average freshman award was $19,746. Need-based scholarships or need-based grants averaged $7,593 ($19,641 maximum); need-based self-help aid (loans and jobs) averaged $3,482 ($8,000 maximum); and other non-need-based awards and non-need-based scholarships averaged $13,281 ($46,180 maximum). 7% of undergraduate students work part-time. The average financial indebtedness of the 2017 graduate was $30,881. The state aid form is required. The FAFSA code is E00505. The priority date for freshman financial aid applications for fall entry is February 25.

ST. LAWRENCE UNIVERSITY C-2

www.stlawu.edu

Canton, NY 13617	**(315) 229-5585** **(800) 285-1856**
Fax: (315) 229-7422	**Email: admissions@stlawu.edu**
Full-time: 1045 men, 1327 women	**Faculty:** 176; IIB, av$
Part-time: 24 men, 18 women	**Ph.D.s:** 99%
Graduate: 30 men, 49 women	**Student/Faculty:** 11 to 1
Year: semesters, summer session	**Tuition:** $52,990
Room & Board: $13,656	**Freshman Class:** 5866 applied, 2835 accepted, 698 enrolled
SAT CR/M: 660/650 **ACT:** 28	**CEEB CODE:** 2805
Application Deadline: February 1	**HIGHLY COMPETITIVE+**

St. Lawrence University, established in 1856, is a private liberal arts institution. There is 1 undergraduate school and 1 graduate school. In addition to regional accreditation, SLU has baccalaureate program accreditation with ACS. The 1100-acre campus is in a small town in Northern New York State, 80 miles south of Ottawa, Canada. Including any residence halls, there are 31 buildings.

STUDENT LIFE: 54% of undergraduates are from out of state, mostly the Northeast. Students are from 43 states, 53 foreign countries, and Canada. 69% are from public schools. 9% are Foreign; 78% White; 5% Hispanic; 3% African American; 2% Asian American; 2% two or more races; 1% race unknown. **Female To Male Ratio:** 1.3:1. The average age of freshmen is 18; all undergraduates, 20. 8% do not continue beyond their first year; 85% remain to graduate. **Housing:** 2272 students can be accommodated in college housing, which includes coed dorms, on-campus apartments, and off-campus apartments. In addition, there are language/international houses, special-interest houses, fraternity houses, sorority houses, theme cottages, wellness housing, and gender-neutral housing. On-campus housing is guaranteed for all 4 years and is available on a lottery system for upperclassmen. 99% of students live on campus. All students may keep cars.

FACULTY/CLASSROOMS: 51% of faculty are male; 49% are female. 99% teach undergraduates, and 99% do research. No introductory courses are taught by graduate students. The average class size in a regular course is 16.

PROGRAMS OF STUDY: SLU confers B.A. and B.S. degrees. Master's degrees are also awarded. Bachelor's degrees are awarded in AGRICULTURE (conservation and regulation and environmental studies), BIOLOGICAL SCIENCE (biochemistry, biology/biological science, biophysics, and neurosciences), BUSINESS (business (dual major program) and international economics), COMMUNICATIONS AND THE ARTS (art history, art, communication rhetoric/communication, creative writing, dramatic arts, English, fine arts, languages, modern language, music, performing arts, studio art, and visual and performing arts), COMPUTER AND PHYSICAL SCIENCE (chemistry, computer science, geology, mathematics, physics, and statistics), EDUCATION (Asian studies), SOCIAL SCIENCE (African studies, anthropology, Canadian studies, economics, French studies, history, interdisciplinary studies, international studies, philosophy, political science/government, psychology, religion, sociology, and Spanish studies). Psychology, economics, and biology have the largest enrollments.

ACTIVITIES: 11% of men belong to 2 national fraternities; 16% of women belong to 1 local and 3 national sororities. There are 100 groups on campus, including art, band, choir, chorus, communications, computers, dance, drama, environmental, ethnic, forensics, honors, international, jazz band, LGBT, literary magazine, musical theater, newspaper, orchestra, photography, political, professional, radio and TV stations, religious, social, social service, student government, and yearbook. Popular campus events include Moving-Up Day, 100th Night, Candlelight Service, and Quadathalon. **Sports:** There are 16 intercollegiate sports for men and 17 for women, and 11 intramural sports for men and 11 for women. Facilities include basketball, squash, and tennis courts, a swimming pool, and a fitness center, field houses, an arena, artificial ice rink, 18-hole golf course, riding stables, jogging and cross-country ski trails, indoor and outdoor competition tracks, soccer, baseball, and softball fields. **Graduates:** From July 1, 2016 to June 30, 2017, 558 bachelor's degrees were awarded. The most popular majors were psychology (10%), business in the liberal arts, and economics. In an average class, 1% graduate in 3 years or less, 79% graduate in 4 years or less, 81% graduate in 5 years or less, and 85% graduate in 6 years or less. Of the 2016 graduating class, 19% were enrolled in graduate school within 6 months of graduation, and 78% were employed.

SERVICES: Counseling and information services are available, as is tutoring in every subject. There is a reader service for the blind. There is also a writing center, Qualitative Resources Center, and science and technology counseling. **Library/Resources:** The library contains 1.0 million volumes, 594,575 microform items, 9,319 audio/video tapes/CDs/DVDs, and subscribes to 124,186 periodicals, including electronic. Computerized library services include interlibrary loans, database searching, Internet access, and Wi-Fi capability. Special learning facilities include an art gallery, a radio station, a science field station, and sustainability program site. **Physically Challenged Students:** 75% of the campus is accessible. Facilities include wheelchair ramps, elevators, special parking, specially equipped restrooms, special class scheduling, and lowered drinking fountains. **Special:** Students may cross-register with the Associated Colleges of the St. Lawrence Valley. Internships are available through the sociology, psychology, and English departments; Career Services; and a service learning program. International and domestic study-abroad programs (28) in 18 countries plus Adirondack, Washington (D.C.) and New York semesters are offered as well as participation in the International Student Exchange Program (ISEP). Students may earn 3-2 engineering degrees in conjunction with 7 engineering schools, a 3+4 doctor of pharmacy with SUNY Buffalo, 3+2 B.S. in nursing with New York University, 4+2 M.S. physician assistant studies and 4+4, doctor of physical therapy at Clarkson University. Nondegree study and pass/fail options are available. Students may transfer in up to 17.5 courses with grades of C (2.0) or higher. There are 20 national honor societies, Phi Beta Kappa, and 17 departmental honors programs. **Visiting:** There are regularly scheduled orientations for prospective students, including interviews and tours. There are guides for informal visits; visitors may sit in on classes and stay overnight. To schedule a visit, contact the Admissions Office. **Campus Safety and Security:** Measures include 24-hour foot and vehicle patrol, an emergency notification system, self-defense education, and security escort services. There are emergency telephones, lighted pathways/sidewalks, and student patrols.

REQUIREMENTS: Applicants must be graduates of an accredited high school. 20 academic credits are recommended, including 4 years each of English, math, science, and foreign language, and 2 years each of social studies, and history. Essays are required and interviews are recommended for all applicants. Submission of standardized test scores is optional. AP credits are accepted. Important factors in the admissions decision are advanced placement or honors courses, extracurricular activities record, and recommendations by school officials. To graduate, students must maintain a minimum GPA of 2.0 and complete 120 course hours, with 29 to 43 in the major. Freshmen must take a first-year program, a 2-semester team-taught course. Requirements also include 1 course each in arts/expression, humanities, social science, math, or a foreign language, and 2 in natural science/science studies and diversity. **Procedure:** Freshmen are admitted in the fall and spring. Entrance exams should be taken during the spring of the junior year or the fall of the senior year. There are early decision and deferred admissions plans. Early decision applications should be filed by November 1; regular applications, by February 1 for fall entry; and December 1 for spring entry. The fall 2017 application fee was $60. Notification of early decision is sent November 1; regular decision, March 15. 240 early decision candidates were accepted for the 2017-2018 class. 85 applicants were on the 2017 waiting list. Applications are accepted online. **Transfer Students:** 30 transfer students enrolled in 2016-2017. The high school transcript and SAT scores will be evaluated, but college work is more important. High school and college recommendations are required. 58 of 120 credits required for the bachelor's degree must be completed at SLU. **International Students:** There are 214 international students enrolled. They must take the SAT.

ADMISSIONS: 48% of the 2017-2018 applicants were accepted. The SAT scores for the 2017-2018 freshman class were: Math-- 2% below 500, 20% between 500 and 599, 56% between 600 and 699, and 23% between 700 and 800. Evidence-Based Reading/Writing-- 2% below 500, 15% between 500 and 599, 60% between 600 and 699, and 23% between 700 and 800. The ACT scores were 9% between 18 and 23, 58% between 24 and 29, and 32% above 30. 70% of the current freshmen were in the top fifth of their class; 90% were in the top two fifths. 15 freshmen graduated first in their class. **Admissions Contact:** Jeremy Freeman, Executive Director for Admissions. Email: *admissions@stlawu.edu* Web: *www.stlawu.edu*

FINANCIAL AID: In 2017-2018, 100% of all full-time freshmen received some form of financial aid. 67% of all full-time freshmen received need-based aid. The average freshman award was $45,406. Need-based scholarships or need-based grants averaged $26,791 ($68,296 maximum); need-based self-help aid (loans and jobs) averaged $7,600 ($45,150 maximum); and non-need-based athletic scholarships averaged $48,757 ($66,646 maximum). 33% of undergraduate students work part-time. The average financial indebtedness of the 2017 graduate was $33,653. SLU is a member of CSS. The FAFSA code is 002829. The deadline for filing freshman financial aid applications for fall entry is February 1.

ST. THOMAS AQUINAS COLLEGE D-5

www.stac.edu

Sparkill, NY 10976	(914) 398-4100 (800) 999-STAC
Fax: (914) 398-4114	**Email:** admissions@stac.edu
Full-time: 700 men, 710 women	**Faculty:** IIB, +$
Part-time: 350 men, 360 women	**Ph.D.s:** n/av
Graduate: 75 men, 125 women	**Student/Faculty:** n/av
Year: 4-1-4, summer session	**Tuition:** $24,500
Room & Board: $7950	**Freshman Class:** n/av
SAT or ACT: required	**CEEB CODE:** 0807
Application Deadline: rolling	**COMPETITIVE**

St. Thomas Aquinas College, founded in 1952, is an independent liberal arts institution. Figures in above capsule and in this profile are approximate. There is 1 undergraduate school and 2 graduate schools. The 43-acre campus is in a suburban area 15 miles north of New York City. Including any residence halls, there are 12 buildings.

STUDENT LIFE: 75% of undergraduates are from New York. Others are from 6 states, 8 foreign countries, and Canada. 80% are from public schools. 9% are race unknown; 52% White; 3% Asian American; 3% Foreign; 22% Hispanic; 10% African American; 1% two or more races. 62% are Catholic; 23% Protestant. **Female To Male Ratio:** 1.1:1. The average age of freshmen is 18; all undergraduates, 23. 16% do not continue beyond their first year; 62% remain to graduate. **Housing:** 450 students can be accommodated in college housing, which includes dorms and on-campus apartments. On-campus housing is guaranteed for all 4 years. 65% of students commute. Alcohol is not permitted. All students may keep cars.

FACULTY/CLASSROOMS: 55% of faculty are male; 45% are female. 99% teach undergraduates, 50% do research, and 50% do both. No introductory courses are taught by graduate students. The average class size in an introductory lecture is 35; in a laboratory is 15; and in a regular course is 20.

PROGRAMS OF STUDY: STAC confers B.A., B.S., and B.S.E. degrees. Associate and master's degrees are also awarded. Bachelor's degrees are awarded in BUSINESS (accounting, banking and finance, business administration and management, marketing/retailing/merchandising, and recreation and leisure services), COMMUNICATIONS AND THE ARTS (communications, English, English literature, fine arts, romance languages and literature, Spanish, and visual and performing arts), COMPUTER AND PHYSICAL SCIENCE (computer information systems and mathematics), EDUCATION (art education, bilingual/bicultural education, elementary education, foreign languages education, science education, secondary education, and special education), ENGINEERING AND ENVIRONMENTAL DESIGN (commercial art), HEALTH PROFESSIONS (medical laboratory technology and premedicine), SOCIAL SCIENCE (criminal justice, history, liberal arts, sciences, general studies, humanities, parks and recreation management, philosophy, prelaw, psychology, religion, and social science). Education, business administration, and natural sciences are the strongest academically. Business administration has the largest enrollment.

ACTIVITIES: There are no fraternities or sororities. There are 15 groups on campus, including band, cheerleading, chorus, computers, dance, drama, honors, international, literary magazine, musical theater, newspaper, professional, religious, social service, student government, and yearbook. Popular campus events include Trips to Broadway shows, and Halloween and Christmas mixers. **Sports:** There are 5 intercollegiate sports for men and 4 for women, and 6 intramural sports for men and 5 for women. Facilities include an auditorium, gym, weight room, baseball, basketball, bowling, cross-country, field hockey, football, golf, handball, ice hockey, lacrosse, soccer, softball, track and field, and tennis courts.

SERVICES: Counseling and information services are available, as is tutoring in most subjects. There is remedial math and writing. **Library/Resources:** The library contains 102,943 volumes, 45,900 microform items, and subscribes to 108 periodicals, including electronic. Computerized library services include interlibrary loans and database searching. **Physically Challenged Students:** 90% of the campus is accessible. Facilities include wheelchair ramps, elevators, special parking, specially equipped restrooms, special class scheduling, and lowered telephones. **Special:** The college offers cross-registration with Barry University and Aquinas College and internships in business, criminal justice, commercial design, recreation and leisure, and communications. Study abroad in Europe and Asia, a 3-2 engineering degree with George Washington University and Manhattan College and in physical therapy with New York Medical College, and work-study programs are available. Nondegree study and pass/fail options are possible. There are 7 national honor societies, Phi Beta Kappa, and a freshman honors program. **Visiting:** There are guides for informal visits; visitors may sit in on classes and stay overnight. To schedule a visit, contact the Admissions Office. **Campus Safety and Security:** Measures include 24-hour foot and vehicle patrol and security escort services. There are emergency telephones and lighted pathways/sidewalks.

REQUIREMENTS: The SAT or ACT is required. Applicants must be graduates of an accredited secondary school or have a GED certificate. 16 Carnegie units are recommended, including 4 years of English and social science, 2 years each of math, foreign language, and science, including 2 years of lab science. AP and CLEP credits are accepted. Important factors in the admissions decision are leadership record, extracurricular activities record, and advanced placement or honors courses. To graduate, all students must complete a total of 120 credit hours, with 36 to 54 in the major and a minimum GPA of 2.0. A core curriculum of 51 credits in liberal arts courses is required. **Procedure:** Freshmen are admitted in the fall and spring. Entrance exams should be taken by the spring of the junior year. There are early decision, early admissions, deferred admissions, and rolling admissions plans. Early decision applications should be filed by October 1. The fall 2017 application fee was $30. Notification is sent on a rolling basis. Applications are accepted online. **Transfer Students:** 175 transfer students enrolled in 2016-2017. Applicants must have a 2.0 GPA from the previous school. Students may enroll in the fall and spring. 30 of 120 credits required for the bachelor's degree must be completed at STAC. **International Students:** They must take the TOEFL.

Admissions Contact: Samantha Bazile, Director of Admissions. Email: *admissions@stac.edu* Web: *www.stac.edu*

FINANCIAL AID: STAC is a member of CSS. The FAFSA code is 002832. The deadline for filing freshman financial aid applications for fall entry is June 30.

STATE UNIVERSITY OF NEW YORK

State University of New York - System, established in 1948, is a public organization in New York. It is governed by a board of trustees, whose chief administrator is the chancellor. The primary goal of the system is teaching, research, and public service. The main priorities are to educate the largest number of people possible at the highest level, including educationally disadvantaged groups, and to provide students with enhanced educational skills and techniques. The total student enrollment is approximately 465,000 with 88,000 faculty members. Altogether there are approximately 7,660 degrees and certificates offered for baccalaureate, master's, and doctoral programs. Profiles of the 4-year campuses are included in this section.

STATE UNIVERSITY OF NEW YORK /COLLEGE OF AGRICULTURE AND TECH AT COBLESKILL *(The complete profile is made available exclusively on our website, www.barronspac.com)*

STATE UNIVERSITY OF NEW YORK ALBANY — D-3

www.albany.edu

Albany, NY 12222 — **(518) 956-8220**

Fax: (518) 442-5383	**Email: ugadmissions@albany.edu**
Full-time: 6271 men, 6150 women	**Faculty:** 634; I, -$
Part-time: 368 men, 350 women	**Ph.D.s:** 91%
Graduate: 1651 men, 2583 women	**Student/Faculty:** 18 to 1
Year: semesters, summer session	**Tuition:** $9223 ($24,303)
Room & Board: $12,942	**Freshman Class:** 23799 applied, 12944 accepted, 2729 enrolled
SAT or ACT: required	**CEEB CODE:** 2532
Application Deadline: August 1	**COMPETITIVE**

State University of New York at Albany offers students the expansive opportunities of a major research university and an environment designed to foster academic and career success. UAlbany students choose from 120 undergraduate majors and minors and more than 125 graduate programs. Students can take advantage of more than 600 study abroad opportunities in more than 50 countries through UAlbany and SUNY's networks. There are 9 undergraduate schools and 9 graduate schools. In addition to regional accreditation, SUNY Albany has baccalaureate program accreditation with AACSB, CSWE, CAEP, ACS, ALA, APA, CEPH, NASPAA, and PAB. The 560-acre campus is in a suburban area 5 miles west of downtown Albany. Including any residence halls, there are 187 buildings.

STUDENT LIFE: 95% of undergraduates are from New York. Others are from 42 states, 53 foreign countries, and Canada. 8% are Asian American; 6% Foreign; 47% White; 3% two or more races; 3% race unknown; 17% African American; 16% Hispanic. **Female To Male Ratio:** 1.1:1. The average age of freshmen is 18.5; all undergraduates, 20.5. 16% do not continue beyond their first year; 66% remain to graduate. **Housing:** 7980 students can be accommodated in college housing, which includes married student dorms and on-campus apartments. In addition, there are honors houses, language/international houses, and special-interest houses. On-campus housing is available on a first-come, first-served basis, and is available on a lottery system for upperclassmen. 57% of students live on campus. Alcohol is not permitted. Upperclassmen may keep cars.

FACULTY/CLASSROOMS: 61% of faculty are male; 39% are female. 93% teach undergraduates, and 75% do research. Graduate students teach 11% of introductory courses. The average class size in an introductory lecture is 65; in a laboratory is 13; and in a regular course is 35.

PROGRAMS OF STUDY: SUNY Albany confers B.A. and B.S. degrees. Master's and doctoral degrees are also awarded. Bachelor's degrees are awarded in AGRICULTURE (environmental studies), BIOLOGICAL SCIENCE (biochemistry, biology/biological science, and molecular biology), BUSINESS (accounting and business administration and management), COMMUNICATIONS AND THE ARTS (art history and appreciation, Chinese, communications, English, fine arts, information technology, linguistics, music, romance languages and literature, sculpture, Spanish, studio art, studio art graphic design, and studio art painting), COMPUTER AND PHYSICAL SCIENCE (actuarial science, applied mathematics, atmospheric sciences and meteorology, chemistry, computer science, computer security and information assurance, earth science, information sciences and systems, mathematics, and physics), ENGINEERING AND ENVIRONMENTAL DESIGN (computer engineering, materials engineering, materials science, and urban design), HEALTH PROFESSIONS (predentistry and premedicine), SOCIAL SCIENCE (African American studies, anthropology, Asian/Oriental studies, Caribbean studies, criminal justice, East Asian studies, economics, geography, Hispanic American studies, history, homeland security, homeland security/emergency preparedness, interdisciplinary studies, Latin American studies, medieval studies, philosophy, political science/government, prelaw, psychology, social work, sociology, Spanish studies, women and gender studies, and women's studies). Criminal justice, accounting, and public administration and policy are the strongest academically. Business, psychology, and communication and rhetoric have the largest enrollments.

ACTIVITIES: 1% of men belong to 21 national fraternities; 2% of women belong to 1 local and 17 national sororities. There are 226 groups on campus, including chamber singers, percussion ensemble, art, band, cheerleading, chess, chorale, chorus, computers, dance, debate, drama, electronic music ensemble, environmental, ethnic, film, honors, international, jazz band, LGBT, literary magazine, marching band, musical theater, newspaper, orchestra, pep band, photography, political, professional, radio and TV, religious, social, social service, student government, symphony, and yearbook. Popular campus events include Great Danes sports, Relay for Life, and New York State Writer's Series. **Sports:** There are 8 intercollegiate sports for men and 11 for women, and 9 intramural sports for men and 8 for women. Facilities include a gym with a pool, ancillary gym with a quarter-mile track, football stadium, baseball, softball, soccer, field hockey and practice fields, an all-weather lacrosse field, and a recreation and convocation center. **Graduates:** From July 1, 2016 to June 30, 2017, 2944 bachelor's degrees were awarded. The most popular majors were English (14%), business (12%), and psychology (11%). In an average class, 56% graduate in 4 years or less, 64% graduate in 5 years or less, and 66% graduate in 6 years or less.

SERVICES: Counseling and information services are available, as is tutoring in most subjects. There is a reader service for the blind. The Excel program provides low-income and first-generation college students with a variety of mentoring, tutorial, and counseling services. **Library/Resources:** The library contains 2.3 million volumes, 2.9 million microform items, and 13,928 audio/video tapes/CDs/DVDs, and subscribes to 97,614 periodicals, including electronic. Computerized library services include interlibrary loans, database searching, Internet access, and Wi-Fi capability. Special learning facilities include an art gallery, a radio station, an Linear accelerator, a sophisticated weather data system, a national lightning detection system, interactive media center, extensive art studios, state-of-the-art electronic library, and the Northeast Regional Forensic Institute (NERFI). **Physically Challenged Students:** 99% of the campus is accessible. Facilities include wheelchair ramps, elevators, special parking, specially equipped restrooms, lowered drinking fountains, lowered telephones. Disabled Student Services provides a broad range of personalized services to people with disabilities, including preadmission information and accessible housing information. **Special:** Cross-registration is available with Rensselaer Polytechnic Institute, Albany Law School, and Union, Siena, and Russell Sage colleges. Internships may be arranged with state government agencies and private organizations. Study abroad in many countries, a Washington semester, B.A.-B.S. degrees, and work-study programs are offered. Dual and student-designed majors, nondegree study, and pass/fail grading options are available. There are accelerated 5-year bachelor's/master's programs in 40 fields; most arts and sciences fields may be combined with an accelerated M.B.A. A 3-2 engineering degree with 1 of 4 institutions is also possible. There are 15 national honor societies, Phi Beta Kappa, a freshman honors program, and 30 departmental honors programs. **Visiting:** There are regularly scheduled orientations for prospective students, including a 2-day summer orientation session. There are guides for informal visits and visitors may sit in on classes. To schedule a visit, contact the Undergraduate Admissions Office. **Campus Safety and Security:** Measures include 24-hour foot and vehicle patrol, an emergency notification system, self-defense education, and security escort services. There are shuttle buses, emergency telephones, lighted pathways/sidewalks, controlled access to dorms/residences, and 5-Quad ambulance service.

REQUIREMENTS: The SAT or ACT is required. Applicants must be graduates of an accredited secondary school or have a GED. 18 academic credits are required, including 2 to 3 units of math, 2 units of lab sciences, and 1 unit of foreign language. AP and CLEP credits are accepted. Important factors in the admissions decision are advanced placement or honors courses, personality/intangible qualities, and leadership record. To graduate, students must complete a total of 120 credits with a 2.0 GPA in their major and minor, including 30 to 36 credits required in the major for a B.A. degree and 30 to 42 credits for a B.S. degree. B.A. degree candidates must complete 90 credits in liberal arts courses and B.S. candidates must complete 60. The general education program at the University at Albany consists of a minimum of 30 credits of coursework in the following areas: disciplinary perspectives, cultural and historical perspectives, and communication and reasoning competencies. **Procedure:** Freshmen are admitted in the fall, spring, and summer. Entrance exams should be taken by November of the senior year. There are early decision, deferred admissions, and rolling admissions plans. Early decision applications should be filed by November 15; regular applications, by August 1 for fall entry; December 1 for spring entry; and April 1 for summer entry. The fall 2017 application fee was $50. Notification of early decision is sent January 1. Applications are accepted on-line. **Transfer Students:** 1371 transfer students enrolled in 2016-2017. Admission to certain programs is competitive and based not only on a required GPA but also on completion of a certain set of prerequisite core courses. A grade average of B or better is required for applicants to the accounting, business administration, criminal justice, and social welfare programs. 30 of 120 credits required for the bachelor's degree must be completed at SUNY Albany. **International Students:** There are 735 international students enrolled. They must also take the SAT or ACT.

ADMISSIONS: 54% of the 2017-2018 applicants were accepted. **Admissions Contact:** Timothy Lee, Director of Undergraduate Admissions. Email: *ugadmissions@albany.edu* Web: *www.albany.edu*

FINANCIAL AID: In 2017-2018, 64% of all full-time freshmen received some form of financial aid. 55% of all full-time freshmen received need-based aid. The average freshman award was $10,933. Need-based scholarships or need-based grants averaged $7,679; need-based self-help aid (loans and jobs) averaged $4,847; non-need-based athletic scholarships averaged $19,384; and other non-need-based awards and non-need-based scholarships averaged $3,882. 9% of undergraduate students work part-time. The average financial indebtedness of the 2017 graduate was $25,729. The FAFSA code is 002835. The priority date for freshman financial aid applications for fall entry is March 15.

STATE UNIVERSITY OF NEW YORK AT BINGHAMTON C-4

www.binghamton.edu

Binghamton, NY 13902	**(607) 777-2171**
Fax: (607) 777-4445	**Email: admit@binghamton.edu**
Full-time: 6770 men, 6415 women	**Faculty:** 724; I, -$
Part-time: 249 men, 198 women	**Ph.D.s:** 92%
Graduate: 1910 men, 1750 women	**Student/Faculty:** 20 to 1
Year: semesters, summer session	**Tuition:** $9271 ($24,351)
Room & Board: $13,590	**Freshman Class:** 32106 applied, 13023 accepted, 2747 enrolled
SAT CR/M/W: 650/670/620 **ACT:** 29	**CEEB CODE:** 2335
Application Deadline: January 15	**MOST COMPETITIVE**

State University of New York at Binghamton, founded in 1946, became a part of the State University of New York system in 1950 and a University Center in 1965. The university offers programs in arts and sciences, education, nursing, business, engineering and applied science, and community and public affairs. Its new pharmacy school is expected to begin enrolling students in fall 2017. There are 5 undergraduate schools and 2 graduate schools. In addition to regional accreditation, SUNY Binghamton has baccalaureate program accreditation with AACSB, ABET, CSWE, NASM, CAEP, APA, NASPAA, and CCNE. The 930-acre campus is in a suburban area 1 mile west of Binghamton. Including any residence halls, there are 102 buildings.

STUDENT LIFE: 84% of undergraduates are from New York. Others are from 48 states, 120 foreign countries, and Canada. 90% are from public schools. 9% are Foreign; 57% White; 5% African American; 2% two or more races; 2% race unknown; 14% Asian American; 11% Hispanic. **Male To Female Ratio:** 1.1:1. The average age of freshmen is 18; all undergraduates, 20. 9% do not continue beyond their first year; 81% remain to graduate. **Housing:** 7362 students can be accommodated in college housing, which includes coed dorms, on-campus apartments, and off-campus apartments. In addition, there are special-interest houses, chemical and smoke-free housing, living learning communities, quiet living, gender inclusive housing, and family housing. On-campus housing is guaranteed for the freshman year only, and is available on a first-come, first-served basis. 52% of students live on campus; of those, 95% remain on campus on weekends. Upperclassmen may keep cars.

FACULTY/CLASSROOMS: 58% of faculty are male; 42% are female. All teach undergraduates and all do research. Graduate students teach 5% of introductory courses. The average class size in an introductory lecture is 55; in a laboratory is 20; and in a regular course is 33.

PROGRAMS OF STUDY: SUNY Binghamton confers B.A., B.S., and Mus.B. degrees. Master's and doctoral degrees are also awarded. Bachelor's degrees are awarded in AGRICULTURE (environmental studies), BIOLOGICAL SCIENCE (biochemistry, biology/biological science, cell biology, environmental earth resources, evolutionary biology, molecular biology, and neurosciences), BUSINESS (accounting, business administration and management, entrepreneurial studies, finance, management information systems, management science, marketing management, and supply chain management), COMMUNICATIONS AND THE ARTS (Africana studies, Arabic, art history, art, classics, comparative literature, creative writing, dance, dramatic arts, drawing, English, English literature, film arts, French, German, Germanic languages and literature, Hebrew, Italian, Korean, Latin, linguistics, literature, music, music performance, painting, printmaking, sculpture, Spanish, speech/debate/rhetoric, studio art, theatre arts, theater design, and visual and performing arts), COMPUTER AND PHYSICAL SCIENCE (actuarial mathematics, chemistry, computer science, environmental chemistry, environmental geology, geology, information sciences and systems, mathematics, and physics), ENGINEERING AND ENVIRONMENTAL DESIGN (bioengineering, biomedical engineering, computer engineering, electrical/electronics engineering, engineering, environmental design, environmental science, industrial engineering, mechanical engineering, and systems engineering), HEALTH PROFESSIONS (nursing and prehealth studies), SOCIAL SCIENCE (anthropology, Asian/American studies, Caribbean studies, Chinese studies, classical/ancient civilization, East Asian studies, economics, geography, history, human development, interdisciplinary studies, international studies, Japanese studies, Judaic studies, Latin American studies, medieval studies, philosophy, political science/government, psychobiology, psychology, sociology, and South Asian studies). Business administration, political science, and biology are the strongest academically. Engineering, business administration, and psychology have the largest enrollments.

ACTIVITIES: 11% of women belong to 17 national sororities. There are 373 groups on campus, including special interest groups, club sports/intramurals, art, band, cheerleading, chess, choir, chorale, chorus, communications, computers, cultural, dance, debate, drama, environmental, ethnic, film, honors, international, jazz band, LGBT, literary magazine, musical theater, newspaper, opera, orchestra, pep band, photography, political, professional, radio and TV, religious, social, social service, student government, symphony, and yearbook. Popular campus events include Spring Fling, University Fest, Shindig at the Fountain, Student Cultural Festival, university sporting events, Basketball Showcase, concerts, and comedic shows. **Sports:** There are 11 intercollegiate sports for men and 10 for women, and 11 intramural sports for men and 11 for women. Facilities include a events center with basketball and tennis courts, a track, gyms equipped with swimming pools, a fitness center, basketball, volleyball, racquetball and squash courts, dance and karate studios, a soccer and lacrosse complex and separate facilities for baseball, softball, track and field, tennis, and cross-country. **Graduates:** From July 1, 2015 to June 30, 2016, 3463 bachelor's degrees were awarded. The most popular majors were management (16%), psychology (12%), and engineering (10%). 239 companies recruited on campus in 2015-2016. In an average class, 5% graduate in 3 years or less, 71% graduate in 4 years or less, 81% graduate in 5 years or less, and 81% graduate in 6 years or less. Of the 2015 graduating class, 30% were enrolled in graduate school within 6 months of graduation.

SERVICES: Counseling and information services are available, as is tutoring in most subjects. There are alternate format reading materials for those with visual/reading disabilities, and academic success consultation/instruction sessions provided for SSD-registered students. There is a reader service for the blind, and walk-in and by appointment tutoring 7 days a week. **Library/Resources:** The 4 libraries contain 2.5 million volumes, 1.9 million microform items, 120,055 audio/video tapes/CDs/DVDs, and subscribe to 140,509 periodicals, including electronic. Computerized library services include interlibrary loans, database searching, Internet access, and Wi-Fi capability. Special learning facilities include an art gallery, radio and TV stations, theaters, art/dance studios, sculpture foundry, art museum, teaching greenhouse, information commons/workstations, public archaeology facility, child development institute, GIS core facility, biotechnology start-up suites, an innovative technologies complex, analytical diagnostics laboratory, electron microscopy laboratory, an innovative practice center simulation lab, a collaboratory, a learning studio, a public speaking lab, and centers for performing arts, learning and teaching, organized research, integrated electronics engineering, advanced microelectronics manufacturing and autonomous solar power. **Physically Challenged Students:** 95% of the campus is accessible. Facilities include wheelchair ramps, elevators, special parking, specially equipped restrooms, lowered drinking fountains, lowered telephones, and special housing. Comprehensive array of services for students with physical, learning, or other disabilities. **Special:** The university offers a number of accelerated programs (3+2 and 4+1) to earn combined bachelor's and master's degrees, access to nearly 900 study-abroad opportunities in over 100 countries, internship opportunities in New York City and other major cities, dual and interdisciplinary majors such as philosophy, politics, and law, an individualized major program in Harpur College of Arts and Sciences, prehealth programs in medicine, dentistry, optometry, veterinary medicine, podiatry, nutrition, physical and occupational therapy, and chiropractic. Early assurance programs guarantee graduate admission at partner SUNY schools (Buffalo, Upstate Medical-Syracuse, and College of Optometry). Also offered is the three-semester Freshman Research Immersion Program for first-year STEM students to combine academics with real research in one of eight research streams that can yield publishable results. There are 28 national honor societies, Phi Beta Kappa, a freshman honors program, and 34 departmental honors programs. **Visiting:** There are regularly scheduled orientations for prospective students, including an information session and a student-led tour of campus. To schedule a visit, contact the Office of Undergraduate Admissions. **Campus Safety and Security:** Measures include 24-hour foot and vehicle patrol, an emergency notification system, self-defense education, and security escort services. There are shuttle buses, emergency telephones, lighted pathways/sidewalks, controlled access to dorms/residences, bike and car patrols, monitored entrance to campus with proper identification, LED vehicle speed monitoring signs, emergency text messaging/communications, and formal personal safety programs.

REQUIREMENTS: The SAT or ACT, the ACT Optional Writing test are required. In addition, applicants must be graduates of an accredited secondary school or have a GED certificate and complete 16 academic credits. These include 4 units of English, 3 units of 1 foreign language or 2 units each of 2 foreign languages, 3 units of math, and 2 units each of science and social studies. Students may submit slides of artwork, request an audition for music, prepare a videotape for dance or theater, or share athletic achievements. An essay is required. Binghamton University requires that each enrolling student fulfills the graduation requirements at their high school. AP and CLEP credits are accepted. To graduate, all students must complete 124 to 128 credit hours, with 36 to 72 in the major and a minimum GPA of 2.0. General education requirements include courses in language and communication, global vision, science, aesthetic perspective, foreign language, humanities, math, social science, physical activity/wellness, and pluralism. Other requirements vary by school. **Procedure:** Freshmen are admitted in the fall and spring. Entrance exams should be taken in the spring of the junior year or the fall of the senior year. There are early admissions, deferred admissions, and rolling admissions plans. Application deadlines are open. Application fee is $50. Notification is sent on a rolling basis. 4106 applicants were on the 2016 waiting list; 276 were admitted. Applications are accepted online. **Transfer Students:** 1057 transfer students enrolled in 2015-2016. Applicants must submit college transcripts; students who wish to transfer after their first year of college must also submit their high school transcripts. 44 of 126 credits required for the bachelor's degree must be completed at Binghamton University. **International Students:** There are 998 international students enrolled. The school actively recruits these students. They must take the TOEFL with a minimum score of 560 on the paper-based TOEFL (PBT) or 83 on the Internet-based version (iBT). If the student attends a high school in the US or a high school where the primary language of instruction is English, the SAT/ACT is required.

ADMISSIONS: 41% of the 2016-2017 applicants were accepted. The SAT scores for the 2016-2017 freshman class were: Critical Reading-- 4% below 500, 17% between 500 and 599, 58% between 600 and 699, and 21% between 700 and 800. Math-- 1% below 500, 12% between 500 and 599, 57% between 600 and 699, and 30% between 700 and 800. Writing-- 3% below 500, 17% between 500 and 599, 58% between 600 and 699, and 22% between 700 and 800. The ACT scores were 3% between 18 and 23, 50% between 24 and 29, and 48% above 30. **Admissions Contact:** Randall Edouard, Assistant Provost for Undergraduate Admission. Email: *admit@binghamton.edu* Web: *www.binghamton.edu*

FINANCIAL AID: In 2016-2017, 84% of all full-time freshmen and 68% of continuing full-time students received some form of financial aid. 63% of all full-time freshmen and 57% of continuing full-time students received need-based aid. The average freshman award was $11,426. Need-based scholarships or need-based grants averaged $4,943; need-based self-help aid (loans and jobs) averaged $2,524; non-need-based athletic scholarships averaged $507; and other non-need-based awards and non-need-based scholarships averaged $7,220. 17% of undergraduate students work part-time. Average annual earnings from campus work are $1507. The average financial indebtedness of the 2016 graduate was $20,671. The state aid form is required. The FAFSA code is 002836. The priority date for freshman financial aid applications for fall entry is February 1.

STATE UNIVERSITY OF NEW YORK AT GENESEO B-3

www.geneseo.edu

Geneseo, NY 14454 **(585) 245-5571**

Fax: (585) 245-5550	**Email: admissions@geneseo.edu**
Full-time: 2129 men, 3262 women	**Faculty:** IIA, -$
Part-time: 54 men, 50 women	**Ph.D.s:** n/av
Graduate: 26 men, 70 women	**Student/Faculty:** n/av
Year: semesters, summer session	**Tuition:** $8408 ($18,058)
Room & Board: $13,214	**Freshman Class:** 8789 applied, 6360 accepted, 1340 enrolled
SAT CR/M: 618/612 **ACT:** 26	**CEEB CODE:** 2540
Application Deadline: January 1	**VERY COMPETITIVE**

State University of New York at Geneseo, founded in 1871, is a public institution offering liberal arts, business, and accounting programs, and teaching certification. There are 2 undergraduate schools and 1 graduate school. In addition to regional accreditation, SUNY Geneseo has baccalaureate program accreditation with AACSB, NCATE, and ACS. The 220-acre campus is in a small town 30 miles south of Rochester, NY. Including any residence halls, there are 46 buildings.

STUDENT LIFE: 98% of undergraduates are from New York. Others are from 26 states, 24 foreign countries, and Canada. 8% are Hispanic; 75% White; 6% Asian American; 3% African American; 3% two or more races; 3% race unknown; 2% Foreign. 57% claim no religious affiliation; 32% Baptist, Buddhist, Episcopal, Hindu, Lutheran, Methodist, Mormon, Muslim, Presbyterian, Unitarian Universal, and others. **Female To Male Ratio:** 1.5:1. The average age of freshmen is 18; all undergraduates, 20. 14% do not continue beyond their first year; 77% remain to graduate. **Housing:** 3255 students can be accommodated in college housing, which includes coed dorms and on-campus apartments. In addition, there are honors houses, special-interest houses, town houses, theme housing, and housing for international students. On-campus housing is guaranteed for all 4 years, and is available on a first-come, first-served basis. 54% of students live on campus. All students may keep cars.

FACULTY/CLASSROOMS: All teach undergraduates. No introductory courses are taught by graduate students. The average class size in an introductory lecture is 45; in a laboratory is 21; and in a regular course is 30.

PROGRAMS OF STUDY: SUNY Geneseo confers B.A., B.S., and B.S.Ed. degrees. Master's degrees are also awarded. Bachelor's degrees are awarded in BIOLOGICAL SCIENCE (biochemistry, biology/biological science, biophysics, and neurosciences), BUSINESS (accounting and business administration and management), COMMUNICATIONS AND THE ARTS (art history and appreciation, communications, comparative literature, English, French, music, musical theater, performing arts, Spanish, and theater design), COMPUTER AND PHYSICAL SCIENCE (applied physics, chemistry, geochemistry, geology, geophysics and seismology, mathematics, natural sciences, and physics), EDUCATION (early childhood education, elementary education, and special education), SOCIAL SCIENCE (African American studies, American studies, anthropology, economics, geography, history, international relations, philosophy, political science/government, psychology, and sociology). Biology, psychology, and English are the strongest academically. Biology, psychology, and business administration have the largest enrollments.

ACTIVITIES: 23% of men belong to 8 local and 5 national fraternities; 33% of women belong to 8 local and 5 national sororities. There are 190 groups on campus, including art, band, cheerleading, chess, choir, chorale, chorus, computers, dance, debate, drama, environmental, ethnic, honors, international, jazz band, LGBT, literary magazine, musical theater, newspaper, orchestra, pep band, political, professional, radio and TV, religious, social, social service, student government, and symphony. Popular campus events include Siblings Weekend, Blue and White Day, Student Organization Expo, Geneseo Recognizing Excellence, Achievement and Talent Day (Great Day), Relay for Life, and Weeks of Welcome. **Sports:** There are 8 intercollegiate sports for men and 12 for women, and 20 intramural sports for men and 20 for women. Facilities include an ice arena, a swimming pool, gyms, squash, tennis courts, racquetball courts, an indoor jogging area, nautilus and weight rooms, an outdoor track, several playing fields, artificial turf fields, soccer, lacrosse and field hockey. **Graduates:** From July 1, 2016 to June 30, 2017, 1222 bachelor's degrees were awarded. The most popular majors were social sciences (19%), psychology (14%), and business/marketing (14%). In an average class, 68% graduate in 4 years or less, 77% graduate in 5 years or less, and 77% graduate in 6 years or less. Of the 2016 graduating class, 40% were enrolled in graduate school within 6 months of graduation, and 56% were employed.

SERVICES: Counseling and information services are available, as is tutoring in some subjects, such as foreign languages. There is a reader service for the blind. There is also a writing center and a math center for all students. **Library/Resources:** Computerized library services include interlibrary loans, database searching, Internet access, and Wi-Fi capability. Special learning facilities include an art gallery, a planetarium, radio and TV stations, a trading room, four theaters, Integrated Science Center (including a particle accelerator lab in physics and wave tank/flume in geological sciences), and eGarden (energy garden). **Physically Challenged Students:** 95% of the campus is accessible. Facilities include wheelchair ramps, elevators, special parking, specially equipped restrooms, special class scheduling, lowered drinking fountains, lowered telephones, and special housing. **Special:** Geneseo offers 3-2 Engineering: Case Western Reserve, Clarkson, Columbia, and SUNY University at Buffalo, 3-4 Dentistry: SUNY University at Buffalo, 3+3 Doctorate of Physical Therapy Degree: SUNY Upstate Medical University, 4+1 MBA: Alfred University, SUNY Binghamton, Clarkson, RIT, and Union College, 3+4 Optometry: SUNY Optometry, 3+4 Osteopathic Medicine: New York Institute of Technology College of Osteopathic Medicine. Cross-registration is available with the Rochester Area Colleges Consortium and all other SUNY Campuses. Geneseo offers internships, a vast study abroad program, a Washington semester, dual majors, and work-study programs. There is a chapter of Phi Beta Kappa and a freshman honors program. **Visiting:** There are regularly scheduled orientations for prospective students, generally including a 90-minute campus tour and a 45-minute information session. Students may also elect to sit in on classes, visit faculty and coaches, or stay overnight. To schedule a visit, contact the Office of Admissions. **Campus Safety and Security:** Measures include 24-hour foot and vehicle patrol, an emergency notification system, self-defense education, and security escort services. There are shuttle buses, emergency telephones, lighted pathways/sidewalks, controlled access to dorms/residences.

REQUIREMENTS: SAT or ACT is required. Applicants must be graduates of an accredited secondary school or have a GED certificate. Total 20 academic units recommended: 4 years each of English, math, science, social studies, and foreign language. An essay is required. A portfolio or audition for certain programs and an interview are recommended. Rigor of secondary school programs is reviewed. AP and CLEP credits are accepted. Important factors in the admissions decision are advanced placement or honors courses, leadership record, evidence of special talent, extracurricular activities record, and recommendations by school officials. To graduate, students must complete 120 credit hours with a minimum 2.0 GPA. The required core curriculum includes 2 courses each in fine arts, social sciences, and natural sciences and 1 course each in humanities, non-Western traditions, critical writing/reading, numeric and symbolic reasoning, U.S. history, and foreign language proficiency. Of the 120 total credits required to graduate, students may apply no more than 20 credits combined from Directed Studies, undergraduate teaching assistantships, EMT/EMS training, ROTC, and H&PE. The limits for each individual program are: Directed Studies 12 credits, teaching assistantships 6 credits, EMT/EMS 6 credits, ROTC 8 credits, and H&PE 10 credits of which no more than 4 credits can be from 100-level activity courses. Teaching assistantships, H&PE activity courses, and some internships and EMT/EMS courses have the S/U grading option only and, therefore, will not be counted toward students' cumulative GPA. **Procedure:** Freshmen are admitted in the fall and spring. Entrance exams should be taken during the spring of the junior year. There are early decision and deferred admissions plans. Early decision applications should be filed by November 15; regular applications, by January 1 for fall entry; and December 1 for spring entry. The fall 2017 application fee was $50. Notification of early decision is sent December 15; regular decision, March 1. 189 early decision candidates were accepted for the 2017-2018 class. 1172 applicants were on the 2017 waiting list; 350 were admitted. Applications are accepted online. **Transfer Students:** 258 transfer students enrolled in 2016-2017. Applicants must provide transcripts from all previously attended colleges. A minimum 3.0 GPA is required. Students with fewer than 24 credit hours must submit SAT or ACT scores. Application for transfers admission may enroll in the fall (May 1, rolling), and spring (December 15, rolling) 30 of 120 credits required for the bachelor's degree must be completed at Geneseo. **International Students:** There are 98 international students enrolled. They must take the TOEFL with a minimum score of 525 on the paper-based TOEFL (PBT) or 71 on the Internet-based version (iBT), and the IELTS with a minimum score of 6.5. They must also take the SAT or ACT.

ADMISSIONS: 72% of the 2017-2018 applicants were accepted. The SAT scores for the 2017-2018 freshman class were: Math-- 6% below 500, 40% between 500 and 599, 45% between 600 and 699, and 9% between 700 and 800. Evidence-Based Reading/Writing-- 4% below 500, 38% between 500 and 599, 48% between 600 and 699, and 10% between 700 and 800. The ACT scores were 17% between 18 and 23, 66% between 24 and 29, and 17% above 30. 69% of the current freshmen were in the top fifth of their class; 85% were in the top two fifths. 23 freshmen graduated first in their class. **Admissions Contact:** Kimberly Harvey, Director Of Admissions. Email: *admissions@geneseo.edu* Web: *www.geneseo.edu*

FINANCIAL AID: In 2017-2018, 58% of all full-time freshmen received some form of financial aid. 44% of all full-time freshmen received need-based aid. The average freshman award was $9,567. Need-based scholarships or need-based grants averaged $2,181; and need-based self-help aid (loans and jobs) averaged $3,913. 42% of undergraduate students work part-time. The average financial indebtedness of the 2017 graduate was $24,784. SUNY Geneseo is a member of CSS. The FAFSA code is 002845. The priority date for freshman financial aid applications for fall entry is March 15.

STATE UNIVERSITY OF NEW YORK AT NEW PALTZ D-4

www.newpaltz.edu

New Paltz, NY 12561 **(845) 257-3200**

Fax: (845) 257-3209	**Email:** admissions@newpaltz.edu
Full-time: 1690 men, 3585 women	**Faculty:** n/av
Part-time: 295 men, 560 women	**Ph.D.s:** n/av
Graduate: 490 men, 940 women	**Student/Faculty:** n/av
Year: semesters, summer session	**Tuition:** $7960 ($17,610)
Room & Board: $12,880	**Freshman Class:** n/av
SAT or ACT: required	**CEEB CODE:** 2541
Application Deadline: April 1	**COMPETITIVE**

State University of New York/at New Paltz, founded in 1828, is a public institution offering undergraduate and graduate programs in the liberal arts and sciences, business, education, engineering, fine and performing arts, and the health professions. The figures in the above capsule and in this profile are approximate. There are 5 undergraduate schools and 1 graduate school. In addition to regional accreditation, SUNY at New Paltz has baccalaureate program accreditation with ABET, CSAB, NASAD, and NASM. The 216-acre campus is in a small town 100 miles north of New York City and 65 miles south of Albany. Including any residence halls, there are 53 buildings.

STUDENT LIFE: 92% of undergraduates are from New York. Others are from 28 states, 48 foreign countries, and Canada. 90% are from public schools. 8% are Hispanic; 6% African American; 58% White; 4% Foreign; 3% Asian American. **Female To Male Ratio:** 2.1:1. The average age of freshmen is 18; all undergraduates, 20. 16% do not continue beyond their first year; 59% remain to graduate. **Housing:** 2800 students can be accommodated in college housing, which includes dorms, and special-interest houses. On-campus housing is guaranteed for the freshman year only, and is available on a first-come, first-served basis. 51% of students live on campus. Upperclassmen may keep cars.

FACULTY/CLASSROOMS: 45% of faculty are male; 55% are female. 97% teach undergraduates and do research. Graduate students teach 1% of introductory courses. The average class size in an introductory lecture is 19; in a laboratory is 10; and in a regular course is 19.

PROGRAMS OF STUDY: SUNY at New Paltz confers B.A., B.S., and B.F.A. degrees. Master's degrees are also awarded. Bachelor's degrees are awarded in BIOLOGICAL SCIENCE (biology/biological science), BUSINESS (accounting, banking and finance, business administration and management, international business management, and marketing/retailing/merchandising), COMMUNICATIONS AND THE ARTS (art history and appreciation, communications, dramatic arts, English, French, German, graphic design, journalism, metal/jewelry, music, painting, photography, sculpture, Spanish, speech/debate/rhetoric, studio art, theater design, and visual and performing arts), COMPUTER AND PHYSICAL SCIENCE (chemistry, computer science, environmental geology, geology, mathematics, and physics), EDUCATION (art education, early childhood education, elementary education, English education, foreign languages education, mathematics education, middle school education, science education, secondary education, and social studies education), ENGINEERING AND ENVIRONMENTAL DESIGN (computer engineering, electrical/electronics engineering, and woodworking), HEALTH PROFESSIONS (music therapy, nursing, and speech pathology/audiology), SOCIAL SCIENCE (African American studies, anthropology, Asian/Oriental studies, economics, geography, history, international relations, Latin American studies, liberal arts/general studies, philosophy, political science/government, psychology, social science, sociology, and women's studies). Business, computer science, and math are the strongest academically. Business, visual arts, and elementary education have the largest enrollments.

ACTIVITIES: 3% of men belong to 5 local and 5 national fraternities; 2% of women belong to 5 local and 8 national sororities. There are 136 groups on campus, including art, band, cheerleading, chess, choir, chorale, chorus, computers, dance, drama, ethnic, honors, international, jazz band, LGBT, literary magazine, musical theater, newspaper, orchestra, photography, political, professional, radio and TV, religious, social, social service, student government, and yearbook. Popular campus events include Spirit Weekend, New Paltz Summer Repertory Theater, and Rainbow Month. **Sports:** There are 9 intercollegiate sports for men and 11 for women, and 12 intramural sports for men and 9 for women. Facilities include a gym, swimming and diving, playing fields, jogging, volleyball, basketball, and softball, crew teams, riding teams, outdoor tennis courts, golf, lacrosse, and ice hockey. **Graduates:** From July 1, 2016 to June 30, 2017, 1592 bachelor's degrees were awarded. The most popular majors were education (21%), business and marketing (14%), and social science (11%). In an average class, 36% graduate in 4 years or less, 59% graduate in 5 years or less, and 61% graduate in 6 years or less.

SERVICES: Counseling and information services are available, as is tutoring in most subjects. There is a reader service for the blind, and remedial math, reading, and writing. **Library/Resources:** The library contains 499,048 volumes, 1.2 million microform items, and 4,030 audio/video tapes/CDs/DVDs, and subscribes to 32,361 periodicals, including electronic. Computerized library services include interlibrary loans, database searching, Internet access, and Wi-Fi capability. Special learning facilities include a planetarium, a radio station, TV station, a greenhouse, a robotics lab, electron microscope facility, a speech and hearing clinic, an art museum, music therapy training facility, an observatory, Fournier transform mass spectrometer, an honors center, an electronic media center, electronic classroom, and an IBM e-business virtual lab. **Physically Challenged Students:** 90% of the campus is accessible. Facilities include wheelchair ramps, elevators, special parking, specially equipped restrooms, special class scheduling, lowered drinking fountains, lowered telephones, and special housing. **Special:** There is cross-registration with the Mid-Hudson Consortium of Colleges. The university offers co-op programs and internships in most majors, work-study programs on campus and at the Children's Center of New Paltz, and opportunities for student-designed or dual majors. Students may study abroad in 18 countries. A 3-2 advanced degree in environmental biology is offered with SUNY Environmental Science and Forestry. There are 7-year medical and optometry accelerated degree programs. B.A.-B.S. degrees are offered in liberal arts and science, education, business, science and, engineering, and fine and performing arts. There are 4 national honor societies, a freshman honors program, and 6 departmental honors programs. **Visiting:** There are regularly scheduled orientations for prospective students, including daily information sessions and campus tours. Visitors may sit in on classes. To schedule a visit, contact the Admissions Office. **Campus Safety and Security:** Measures include 24-hour foot and vehicle patrol, self-defense education, and security escort services. There are emergency telephones, lighted pathways/sidewalks, bicycle patrol, locked residence halls, and a campus 911 system.

REQUIREMENTS: The SAT or ACT is required. Additional requirements are 4 units each of English and social studies, 3 to 4 units each of mathematics and science (including 2 units of lab science), and 2 to 4 units of foreign language are required. The GED is accepted but must be accompanied by a high school transcript and SAT or ACT scores. SUNY New Paltz requires applicants to be in the upper 50% of their class. A GPA of 3.0 is required. AP and CLEP credits are accepted. Important factors in the admissions decision are advanced placement or honors courses, recommendations by school officials, and evidence of special talent. To graduate, students must complete a minimum of 120 credits with a 2.0 GPA. The core curriculum of 16 to 17 credits includes courses in English composition, math and analytical skills, and modern world studies. The number of credits required in the major varies. Distribution requirements include courses in cultures and civilizations, American experience, social sciences, physical and biological sciences, foreign languages, and aesthetic expression; 1 writing-intensive course in the major; and 60 credits in upper-division courses. New York State Teacher Competency Exams are required of education majors. Engineering students must complete a senior project, and art majors must show their work in a senior exhibition. **Procedure:** Freshmen are admitted in the fall. Entrance exams should be taken before December 31. There are early admissions, deferred admissions, and rolling admissions plans. Applications should be filed by April 1 for fall entry. The fall 2017 application fee was $40. Notification is sent on a rolling basis. Applications are accepted online. **Transfer Students:** 1011 transfer students enrolled in 2016-2017. To be considered, applicants must have maintained a minimum GPA of 2.75 in all previous college work at accredited institutions. Some programs require a higher GPA for consideration. 30 of 120 credits required for the bachelor's degree must be completed at SUNY New Paltz. **International Students:** There are 219 international students enrolled. They must take the TOEFL with a minimum score of 550 on the paper-based TOEFL (PBT) or 80 on the Internet-based version (iBT). Students must take the SAT or demonstrate English proficiency. Conditional acceptance is available to both graduate and undergraduate programs. Accepted students must take a placement test upon arrival at SUNY New Paltz. If the student is not yet proficient, he or she must take ESL courses until required proficiency is achieved.

Admissions Contact: Kimberly Lavoie, Director of Freshman/International Admissions. Email: *admissions@newpaltz.edu* Web: *www.newpaltz.edu*

FINANCIAL AID: In 2017-2018, 70% of all full-time freshmen received some form of financial aid. 55% of all full-time freshmen received need-based aid. The average freshman award was $5,500. Need-based scholarships or need-based grants averaged $2,400; need-based self-help aid (loans and jobs) averaged $2,600; and other non-need-based awards and non-need-based scholarships averaged $500. 45% of undergraduate students work part-time. The average financial indebtedness of the 2017 graduate was $19,000. The FAFSA code is 002846. The deadline for filing freshman financial aid applications for fall entry is March 15.

STATE UNIVERSITY OF NEW YORK AT OSWEGO C-3

www.oswego.edu

Oswego, NY 13126 **(315) 312-2250**

Fax: (315) 312-3260
Email: admiss@oswego.edu
Full-time: 3456 men, 3380 women
Faculty: 375
Part-time: 149 men, 140 women
Ph.D.s: 88%
Graduate: 346 men, 852 women
Student/Faculty: 17 to 1
Year: semesters, summer session
Tuition: $8191 ($17,841)
Room & Board: $13,740
Freshman Class: 11727 applied, 6300 accepted, 1464 enrolled
SAT EBR-W/M: 579/575 **ACT:** 24
CEEB CODE: 2543
Application Deadline: January 15
VERY COMPETITIVE

State University of New York at Oswego, founded in 1861, is a comprehensive institution offering more than 110 cooperative, preprofessional, and graduate programs through the College of Liberal Arts and Sciences, School of Business, School of Communication, Media, and the Arts, and School of Education. There are 4 undergraduate schools and 1 graduate school. In addition to regional accreditation, SUNY at Oswego has baccalaureate program accreditation with AACSB, NASAD, NASM, ACS, and NASP. The 696-acre campus is in a small town on the southeast shore of Lake Ontario, 35 miles northwest of Syracuse. Including any residence halls, there are 40 buildings.

STUDENT LIFE: 95% of undergraduates are from New York. Others are from 28 states, 35 foreign countries, and Canada. 90% are from public schools. 9% are African American; 71% White; 3% Asian American; 3% two or more races; 2% Foreign; 12% Hispanic. **Female To Male Ratio:** 1.1:1. The average age of freshmen is 18; all undergraduates, 21. 18% do not continue beyond their first year; 62% remain to graduate. **Housing:** 4600 students can be accommodated in college housing, which includes gender neutral and coed dorms and on-campus apartments. In addition, there are special-interest houses, resident hall living and learning communities, a freshmen-only building, upperclassmen suites, and upperclassmen townhouses. On-campus housing is guaranteed for all 4 years. 65% of students live on campus. All students may keep cars.

FACULTY/CLASSROOMS: 49% of faculty are male; 51% are female. 96% teach undergraduates. No introductory courses are taught by graduate students. The average class size in an introductory lecture is 40; in a laboratory is 15; and in a regular course is 24.

PROGRAMS OF STUDY: SUNY at Oswego confers B.A., B.S. and B.F.A. degrees. Master's degrees are also awarded. Bachelor's degrees are awarded in BIOLOGICAL SCIENCE (biochemistry, biology/adolescence education, biology/biological science, and zoology), BUSINESS (accounting, business administration and management, finance, human resources, insurance and risk management, management science, marketing/retailing/merchandising, operations management, and recreational facilities management), COMMUNICATIONS AND THE ARTS (art, broadcasting, communications, creative writing, dramatic arts, English, English as a second/foreign language, English writing, film arts, French, German, graphic design, journalism, linguistics, music, musical theater, public relations, Spanish, theatre acting, theatre arts, and theatre production), COMPUTER AND PHYSICAL SCIENCE (applied mathematics, atmospheric sciences and meteorology, chemistry, computer science, earth science, earth science/adolescence education, environmental geology, geochemistry, geology, information sciences and systems, mathematics, physics, and software engineering), EDUCATION (agricultural education, business education, childhood education, elementary education, English education, foreign languages education, mathematics education, secondary education, social studies education, Spanish adolescense education, teaching English as a second/foreign language (TESOL/TEFOL), technical education, trade and industrial education, and vocational education), ENGINEERING AND ENVIRONMENTAL DESIGN (electrical and computer engineering, preengineering, and technological management), HEALTH PROFESSIONS (prehealth studies, prehealth biological studies, predentistry, premedicine, preoptometry, prephysical therapy, and preveterinary science), SOCIAL SCIENCE (American studies, anthropology, cognitive science, criminal justice, economics, family/consumer studies, French studies, history, human development, international studies, philosophy, political science/government, prelaw, psychology, sociology, women and gender studies, and women's studies). Biological sciences, chemistry, accounting, computer science, and software engineering are the strongest academically. Childhood/adolescence education, business administration, biological sciences, and psychology have the largest enrollments.

ACTIVITIES: 7% of men belong to 6 local and 10 national fraternities; 6% of women belong to 4 local and 7 national sororities. There are 200 groups on campus, including equestrian teams, art, band, cheerleading, choir, chorale, chorus, communications, computers, crew, dance, debate, drama, environmental, ethnic, film, honors, international, jazz band, LGBT, literary magazine, musical theater, newspaper, opera, orchestra, pep band, photography, political, professional, radio and TV, religious, social, social service, student government, symphony, and yearbook. Popular campus events include Honors Convocations, Quest, May Day, Fall and Spring Concerts, Family and Friends Weekend, and Hockey Nights in Oswego. **Sports:** There are 12 intercollegiate sports for men and 12 for women, and 21 intramural sports for men and 21 for women. Facilities include an outdoor turf stadium for field sports, an ice hockey rink, a field house with an artificial-grass practice area, tennis courts, an outdoor track, soccer and lacrosse fields, baseball and softball fields, basketball courts, racquetball and squash courts, indoor pools, a diving well, and a gym. There are also membership fitness centers and weight rooms, a cross-country ski lodge, and a martial arts/dance studio. **Graduates:** From July 1, 2016 to June 30, 2017, 1639 bachelor's degrees were awarded. The most popular majors were education (23%), business (23%), and communications (11%). In an average class, 49% graduate in 4 years or less, 64% graduate in 5 years or less, and 66% graduate in 6 years or less. Of the 2016 graduating class, 25% were enrolled in graduate school within 6 months of graduation, and 79% were employed.

SERVICES: Counseling and information services are available, as is tutoring in every subject. The Office of Learning Services provides individual and small-group tutoring. There is no cost for tutoring services. There is a reader service for the blind, and remedial math, reading, and writing. In addition, the Office of Disability Services provides general foundation support. **Library/Resources:** The library contains 554,986 volumes, 1.6 million microform items, 31,384 audio/video tapes/CDs/DVDs, and subscribes to 52,600 periodicals, including electronic. Computerized library services include interlibrary loans, database searching, Internet access, and Wi-Fi capability. Special learning facilities include an art gallery, a planetarium, a radio station, TV station, and the 330-acre biological Rice Creek Field Station. **Physically Challenged Students:** 85% of the campus is accessible. Facilities include wheelchair ramps, elevators, special parking, specially equipped restrooms, special class scheduling, lowered drinking fountains, lowered telephones, and special housing. **Special:** Oswego offers cross-registration with ACUSNY-Visiting Student Program. More than 1000 internships are available with business, social, cultural, and government agencies. In addition 12 departments offer co-op opportunities as well. The university also offers a Washington semester, study abroad in more than 80 programs, a 5-year accounting B.S./M.B.A. program, dual majors, B.A.-B.S. degrees in several sciences and a B.A.-B.F.A. in art, credit for military experience, nondegree study, and pass/fail options. A preengineering option is available. A 3-4 degree in optometry with SUNY College of Optometry, and 2+2 medical imaging/3+3 physical therapy with SUNY Upstate Medical Center are also possible. There are 21 national honor societies, a freshman honors program, and 9 departmental honors programs. **Visiting:** There are regularly scheduled orientations for prospective students, usually including a campus tour and a meeting/presentation with a counselor. There are guides for informal visits and visitors may sit in on classes. To schedule a visit, contact the Office of Admissions. **Campus Safety and Security:** Measures include 24-hour foot and vehicle patrol, an emergency notification system, self-defense education, and security escort services. There are shuttle buses, emergency telephones, lighted pathways/sidewalks, controlled access to dorms/residences, and an electronic device that locates students and alerts the police when pressed.

REQUIREMENTS: The SAT or ACT is required. Applicants must be graduates of an accredited secondary school or have a GED/TASC certificate. 18 academic units are required, preferring 4 years each of English and social studies, 7 years combined of math and science, and 2 years of foreign language. An essay and interview are strongly recommended. AP and CLEP credits are accepted. Important factors in the admissions decision are advanced placement or honors courses, extracurricular activities record, and personality/intangible qualities. To graduate, all students must complete 30 to 33 general education credits, including 9-12 in writing, mathematics, foreign language, natural science and 15 student selected credits from areas of natural sciences, social and behavior sciences, American history, Western civilization, humanities, fine and performing arts and world awareness. Students must have a minimum 2.0 GPA and complete 120 total credit hours (127 hours for technology and vocational education students). The total number of hours in the major varies from 33 to 95. **Procedure:** Freshmen are admitted in the fall and spring. Entrance exams should be taken during the spring of the junior year and fall of the senior year. There are early admissions, deferred admissions, and rolling admissions plans. Applications should be filed by January 15 for fall entry. The fall 2017 application fee was $50. Notifications are sent January 15. Applications are accepted online. **Transfer Students:** 690 transfer students enrolled in 2016-2017. Applicants must submit official transcripts from previously attended colleges. Students with a minimum GPA of 2.3 are encouraged to apply. SUNY associate degree holders are given preference. Secondary school records may be required for 1-year transfers. 30 of 122 credits required for the bachelor's degree must be completed at SUNY at Oswego. **International Students:** There are 147 international students enrolled. They must take the TOEFL with a minimum score of 550 on the paper-based TOEFL (PBT) or 80 on the Internet-based version (iBT).

ADMISSIONS: 54% of the 2017-2018 applicants were accepted. The SAT scores for the 2017-2018 freshman class were: Math-- 7% below 500, 60% between 500 and 599, 30% between 600 and 699, and 3% between 700 and 800. Evidence-Based Reading/Writing-- 5% below 500, 58% between 500 and 599, 34% between 600 and 699, and 3% between 700 and 800. The ACT scores were 2% between 12 and 17, 48% between 18 and 23, 46% between 24 and 29, and 4% above 30. 28% of the current freshmen were in the top fifth of their class; 63% were in the top two fifths. **Admissions Contact:** Daniel B. Griffin, Director of Admissions. Email: *admiss@oswego.edu* Web: *www.oswego.edu*

FINANCIAL AID: In 2017-2018, 70% of all full-time freshmen received some form of financial aid. 65% of all full-time freshmen received need-based aid. The average freshman award was $7,044. Need-based scholarships or need-based grants averaged $6,391; need-based self-help aid (loans and jobs) averaged $3,843; other non-need-based awards and non-need-based scholarships averaged $3,728; and $3,204 from other forms of aid. 65% of undergraduate students work part-time. The average financial indebtedness of the 2017 graduate was $26,611. SUNY at Oswego is a member of CSS. The state aid form is required. The FAFSA code is 002848. The priority date for freshman financial aid applications for fall entry is March 1.

STATE UNIVERSITY OF NEW YORK AT PURCHASE COLLEGE — D-5

www.purchase.edu

Purchase, NY 10577 — **(914) 251-6300**

Fax: (914) 251-6314
Email: admissions@purchase.edu

Full-time: 1584 men, 2178 women	**Faculty:** 167; IIB, av$
Part-time: 172 men, 168 women	**Ph.D.s:** n/av
Graduate: 46 men, 58 women	**Student/Faculty:** 14 to 1
Year: semesters, summer session	**Tuition:** $8498 ($18,148)
Room & Board: $13,334	**Freshman Class:** 6762 applied, 2942 accepted, 732 enrolled
SAT CR/M: 555/520 **ACT:** 24	**CEEB CODE:** 2878
Application Deadline: March 15	**COMPETITIVE**

State University of New York at Purchase College, founded in 1967, is a public institution that offers programs in visual arts, music, acting, dance, film, theater/stage design technology, natural science, social science, and humanities. There is 1 undergraduate school and 1 graduate school. In addition to regional accreditation, SUNY at Purchase College has baccalaureate program accreditation with NASAD. The 500-acre campus is in a suburban area 35 miles north of midtown Manhattan. Including any residence halls, there are 52 buildings.

STUDENT LIFE: 81% of undergraduates are from New York. Others are from 42 states, 27 foreign countries, and Canada. 53% are White; 5% two or more races; 4% Asian American; 3% Foreign; 22% Hispanic; 12% African American; 1% race unknown. **Female To Male Ratio:** 1.3:1. The average age of freshmen is 17.9; all undergraduates, 21. 17% do not continue beyond their first year; 68% remain to graduate. **Housing:** 2700 students can be accommodated in college housing, which includes dorms and on-campus apartments. In addition, there are special-interest houses, transfer student units, nontraditional-aged student units, wellness halls, presidential scholars halls, sophmore communities, conservatory halls, and learning community halls. On-campus housing is guaranteed for the freshman year only, and is available on a first-come, first-served basis. 90% of students live on campus. All students may keep cars.

FACULTY/CLASSROOMS: All teach undergraduates. No introductory courses are taught by graduate students. The average class size in an introductory lecture is 27; in a laboratory is 12; and in a regular course is 14.

PROGRAMS OF STUDY: SUNY at Purchase College confers B.A., B.S., B.A.L.A., B.F.A., and Mus.B. degrees. Master's degrees are also awarded. Bachelor's degrees are awarded in BIOLOGICAL SCIENCE (biology/biological science), COMMUNICATIONS AND THE ARTS (art history and appreciation, communications, creative writing, dance, dramatic arts, film arts, journalism, literature, music, theater design, and visual and performing arts), COMPUTER AND PHYSICAL SCIENCE (chemistry and mathematics), ENGINEERING AND ENVIRONMENTAL DESIGN (environmental science), SOCIAL SCIENCE (anthropology, economics, ethnic studies, history, liberal arts/general studies, philosophy, political science/government, psychology, sociology, and women's studies). Dance, psychology, and film are the strongest academically. Psychology, liberal studies, and arts management have the largest enrollments.

ACTIVITIES: There are no fraternities or sororities. There are 60 groups on campus, including art, band, cheerleading, choir, chorale, computers, dance, drama, environmental, ethnic, film, jazz band, literary magazine, newspaper, opera, orchestra, photography, political, professional, radio and TV, religious, social, social service, student government, and symphony. Popular campus events include Spring Concert, Alcohol Awareness Week, and Film Programs. **Sports:** There are 17 intercollegiate sports for men and 8 for women, and 10 intramural sports for men and 10 for women. Facilities include a fitness center, a pool, aerobics studio, basketball courts, raquetball courts, squash courts, tennis courts, an outdoor climbing wall, soccer fields, baseball and softball fields, and a bowling alley. **Graduates:** From July 1, 2016 to June 30, 2017, 968 bachelor's degrees were awarded. The most popular majors were liberal studies (12%), psychology (6%), and arts management (6%). In an average class, 53% graduate in 4 years or less, 61% graduate in 5 years or less, and 68% graduate in 6 years or less.

SERVICES: Counseling and information services are available, as is tutoring in most subjects, The Learning Center offers subject-specific tutoring in writing, journalism, cinema studies, theater and performance, sociology, psychology, creative writing, literature, and music history and theory. There is a reader service for the blind. Students may also submit papers electronically and get written feedback through SUNY Purchase's Online Writing Lab (OWL). The Einstein Corner offers tutoring for math and science courses. **Library/Resources:** The library contains 235,698 volumes, 237,715 microform items, 26,976 audio/video tapes/CDs/DVDs, and subscribes to 64,633 periodicals, including electronic. Computerized library services include interlibrary loans, database searching, Internet access, and Wi-Fi capability. Special learning facilities include a radio station, a TV station, a listening and viewing center, science and photography labs, music practice rooms and instruments, multitrack synthesizers, music composition labs, digital video editing labs, typesetting and computer graphics labs, an experimental stage, a performing arts complex, an electron microscope, and a children's center. **Physically Challenged Students:** All of the campus is accessible. Facilities include wheelchair ramps, elevators, special parking, specially equipped restrooms, special housing. note takers, extended test times, quiet rooms for tests, interpreters for the hearing impaired, readers for the visually impaired, a reading machine in the library, and special note-taking paper. **Special:** Purchase College offers cross-registration with Empire State College; internships with corporations newspapers, and local agencies; and student-designed majors, dual majors, study abroad, work-study, nondegree study, and pass/fail options. There is also an arts conservatory program. **Visiting:** There are regularly scheduled orientations for prospective students, including group question and answer sessions followed by a tour of the campus. To schedule a visit, contact the Admissions Office. **Campus Safety and Security:** Measures include 24-hour foot and vehicle patrol, an emergency notification system, self-defense education, and security escort services. There are shuttle buses, emergency telephones, lighted pathways/sidewalks, and controlled access to dorms/residences.

REQUIREMENTS: Applicants must be graduates of an accredited secondary school and have completed 16 academic units: 4 each in English, social studies and math, 3 in science and foreign language, and 2 in academic electives. In addition Visual Arts, Design Technology, Dance, Film, Creative Writing, Music, and Acting applicants must submit talent assessment requirements (portfolios, auditions, or interviews). The GED is accepted. All students must also submit a "Think Wide Open" Essay, and at least 1 teacher recommendation. AP and CLEP credits are accepted. Important factors in the admissions decision are evidence of special talent and leadership record. A minimum 2.0 GPA is required with a minimum of 120 credits. Students majoring in the arts must complete a minimum of 90 professional credits and the SUNY general education curriculum. Students majoring in the liberal arts and sciences complete the general education curriculum and major requirements and must complete a senior thesis. **Procedure:** Freshmen are admitted fall and spring. Entrance exams should be taken by the fall of the senior year. There are early admissions and rolling admissions plans. Applications should be filed by March 15 for fall entry. The fall 2017 application fee was $50. Notifications are sent May 1. Applications are accepted online. **Transfer Students:** 403 transfer students enrolled in 2016-2017. Students transferring to the School of Arts (visual or performing arts) must pass an audition or portfolio review. Transfer credit is limited; students can contact the Office of Admissions to get a preliminary credit evaluation. Students transferring to programs in liberal arts and sciences must have a minimum 2.0 G.P.A. if they have completed 30 or more semester hours; if they have fewer than 30 semester hours, the high school transcript is also reviewed. Liberal arts and science transfers can transfer a maximum of 90 semester hours from 4-year colleges and 75 semester hours from 2-year colleges. 30 of 120 credits required for the bachelor's degree must be completed at SUNY at Purchase College. **International Students:** There are 88 international students enrolled. They must take the TOEFL with a minimum score of 550 on the paper-based TOEFL (PBT) or 80 on the Internet-based version (iBT). Students must take the IELTS or score 430 on the SAT: Verbal test.

ADMISSIONS: 44% of the 2017-2018 applicants were accepted. The SAT scores for the 2017-2018 freshman class were: Critical Reading-- 23% below 500, 44% between 500 and 599, 26% between 600 and 699, and 6% between 700 and 800. Math-- 4% below 500, 35% between 500 and 599, 13% between 600 and 699, and 2% between 700 and 800. The ACT scores were 6% between 12 and 17, 40% between 18 and 23, 42% between 24 and 29, and 12% above 30. **Admissions Contact:** Dennis Craig, Vice President of Admissions. Email: *admissions@purchase.edu* Web: *www.purchase.edu*

FINANCIAL AID: In 2017-2018, 85% of all full-time freshmen received some form of financial aid. 64% of all full-time freshmen received need-based aid. The average freshman award was $9,087. Need-based scholarships or need-based grants averaged $8,807; need-based self-help aid (loans and jobs) averaged $3,597; other non-need-based awards and non-need-based scholarships averaged $2,465 ($17,625 maximum); and $3,468 from other forms of aid. The average financial indebtedness of the 2017 graduate was $22,825. SUNY at Purchase College is a member of CSS. The FAFSA code is 006791. The priority date for freshman financial aid applications for fall entry is February 1.

STATE UNIVERSITY OF NEW YORK POLYTECHNIC INSTITUTE — C-3

www.sunypoly.edu

Utica, NY 13502	(315) 792-7500
Fax: (315) 792-7837	**Email:** admissions@sunypoly.edu
Full-time: 1339 men, 521 women	**Faculty:** n/av
Part-time: 98 men, 226 women	**Ph.D.s:** 81%
Graduate: 315 men, 434 women	**Student/Faculty:** 14 to 1
Year: semesters, summer session	**Tuition:** $7998 ($17,648)
Room & Board: $12,440	**Freshman Class:** 2984 applied, 1863 accepted, 463 enrolled
SAT CR/M: 570/590 **ACT:** required	**CEEB CODE:** 0755
Application Deadline: July 1	**VERY COMPETITIVE**

State University of New York Polytechnic Institute, formerly SUNY Institute of Technology at Utica-Rome, is New York's globally recognized, high-tech educational ecosystem, formed from the merger of the SUNY College of Nanoscale Science and Engineering and SUNY Institute of Technology. SUNY Polytechnic Institute offers undergraduate and graduate degrees in the emerging disciplines of nanoscience and nanoengineering, as well as cutting-edge nanobioscience and nanoeconomics programs at its Albany campus, and degrees in technology, professional studies, and the arts and sciences at its Utica/Rome campus. There are 6 undergraduate schools and 6 graduate schools. In addition to regional accreditation, SUNY Polytechnic Institute has baccalaureate program accreditation with AACSB, ABET, CAHIIM, and CCNE. The 800-acre campus is in a suburban area at the western end of the Mohawk Valley. Including any residence halls, there are 21 buildings.

STUDENT LIFE: 98% of undergraduates are from New York. Others are from 15 states and 16 foreign countries. 9% are Hispanic; 74% White; 7% Asian American; 6% African American; 3% two or more races; 1% Foreign. **Male To Female Ratio:** 1.5:1. The average age of freshmen is 18; all undergraduates, 25. 20% do not continue beyond their first year; 80% remain to graduate. **Housing:** 984 students can be accommodated in college housing, which includes gender neutral, single-sex, and coed dorms, and housing for international students. On-campus housing is available on a first-come, first-served basis, and is available on a lottery system for upperclassmen. 56% of students commute. All students may keep cars.

FACULTY/CLASSROOMS: 60% of faculty are male; 40% are female. No introductory courses are taught by graduate students.

PROGRAMS OF STUDY: SUNY Polytechnic Institute confers B.A., B.S., B.B.A. and B.P.S. degrees. Master's and doctoral degrees are also awarded. Bachelor's degrees are awarded in BIOLOGICAL SCIENCE (biology/biological science), BUSINESS (accounting and business administration and management), COMMUNICATIONS AND THE ARTS (game design and development and interactive media), COMPUTER AND PHYSICAL SCIENCE (applied mathematics, communication information design, computer information systems, computer science, and network & computer security), EDUCATION (health information management), ENGINEERING AND ENVIRONMENTAL DESIGN (civil engineering, civil engineering technology, computer technology, electrical/electronics engineering, electrical/electronics engineering technology, mechanical engineering, mechanical engineering technology, nanoscale engineering, nanoscale science, and nanotechnology), HEALTH PROFESSIONS (community and behavioral health, health care administration, and nursing), SOCIAL SCIENCE (interdisciplinary studies, liberal arts/general studies, psychology, and sociology). Engineering, computer science, and business have the largest enrollments.

ACTIVITIES: There are no fraternities or sororities. There are 30 groups on campus, including Black Latino African Student Union, West Indian African Club, cheerleading, chess, computers, dance, drama, environmental, ethnic, international, LGBT, literary magazine, newspaper, professional, radio and TV, religious, social, social service, student government, Veteran's, and yearbook. Popular campus events include Wildcat Weekend, Diwali and Holi Festivals, and Apocalypse Week. **Sports:** There are 6 intercollegiate sports for men and 6 for women, and 10 intramural sports for men and 10 for women. Facilities include an indoor and outdoor facilities, a fitness center, a fitness trail, a gym with indoor track, a field house, a turf field, and baseball, softball and soccer fields. **Graduates:** From July 1, 2016 to June 30, 2017, 502 bachelor's degrees were awarded. The most popular majors were business administration (17%), computer science (8%), and mechanical engineering technology (7%).

SERVICES: Counseling and information services are available, as is tutoring in some subjects, such as accounting, biology, chemistry, computer science, electrical engineering, economics, engineering science, math, mechanical engineering technology, and physics. There is a reader service for the blind, and remedial math and writing. **Library/Resources:** The library contains 141,800 volumes, 1,315 audio/video tapes/CDs/DVDs, and subscribes to 25,100 periodicals, including electronic. Computerized library services include interlibrary loans, database searching, Internet access, and Wi-Fi capability. Special learning facilities include an art gallery, radio station, and TV station. **Physically Challenged Students:** 99% of the campus is accessible. Facilities include wheelchair ramps, elevators, special parking, specially equipped restrooms, lowered drinking fountains, and special housing. **Special:** SUNY Polytechnic Institute participates in the SUNY wide cross-registration program; internships; co-ops in computer and information science, civil engineering technology, electrical engineering technology, and network and computer security; and work study. An accelerated degree program in nursing, communications and information design, and computer information science are also offered. There is a joint partnership with St. Elizabeth's College of Nursing. There are 2 national honor societies. **Visiting:** There are regularly scheduled orientations for prospective students, during registration and orientation to campus. There are guides for informal visits; visitors may sit in on classes and stay overnight. To schedule a visit, contact the Admissions Office. **Campus Safety and Security:** Measures include 24-hour foot and vehicle patrol, an emergency notification system, self-defense education, and security escort services. There are emergency telephones, lighted pathways/sidewalks, controlled access to dorms/residences, and emergency call boxes.

REQUIREMENTS: The SAT or ACT is required. Official transcripts, test scores, an essay, and a supplemental application are required. A GPA of 3.0 is required. AP and CLEP credits are accepted. Important factors in the admissions decision are advanced placement or honors courses, evidence of special talent, and recommendations by school officials. Students must meet general education requirements and complete 124 to 128 credit hours to graduate. **Procedure:** Freshmen are admitted in the fall and spring. Entrance exams should be taken by April of the year the applicant intends to enroll. There are early admissions, deferred admissions, and rolling admissions plans. Early decision applications should be filed by November 15; regular applications, by July 1 for fall entry; and December 1 for spring entry. The fall 2017 application fee was $50. Notification of early decision is sent December 15; regular decision, January 15. 529 early decision candidates were accepted for the 2017-2018 class. Applications are accepted online. **Transfer Students:** 297 transfer students enrolled in 2016-2017. Transfer students generally must present a minimum cumulative GPA of 2.7 or better. Applicants presenting a GPA below 2.5 will be considered on an individual basis. 30 of 124 credits required for the bachelor's degree must be completed at SUNY Polytechnic Institute. **International Students:** There are 31 international students enrolled. They must take the TOEFL with a minimum score of 550 on the paper-based TOEFL (PBT) or 79 on the Internet-based version (iBT), and take the IELTS. First-time, full-time students must take the SAT or ACT.

ADMISSIONS: 62% of the 2017-2018 applicants were accepted. The SAT scores for the 2017-2018 freshman class were: Critical Reading--16% below 500, 54% between 500 and 599, 27% between 600 and 699, and 3% between 700 and 800. Math-- 12% below 500, 50% between 500 and 599, 31% between 600 and 699, and 7% between 700 and 800. The ACT scores were 6% between 12 and 17, 53% between 18 and 23, 32% between 24 and 29, and 9% above 30. **Admissions Contact:** Gina Liscio, Director of Admissions. Email: *admissions@sunypoly.edu* Web: *www.sunypoly.edu*

FINANCIAL AID: In 2017-2018, 75% of all full-time freshmen received some form of financial aid. 72% of all full-time freshmen received need-based aid. The average freshman award was $12,153. Need-based scholarships or need-based grants averaged $9,458; and need-based self-help aid (loans and jobs) averaged $3,918. 23% of undergraduate students work part-time. The state aid form is required. The priority date for freshman financial aid applications for fall entry is March 1.

STATE UNIVERSITY OF NEW YORK/BUFFALO STATE *(The complete profile is made available exclusively on our website, www.barronspac.com)*

STATE UNIVERSITY OF NEW YORK/ COLLEGE AT OLD WESTBURY — D-5

www.oldwestbury.edu

Old Westbury, NY 11568	(516) 876-3014
Fax: (516) 876-3307	**Email:** enroll@oldwestbury.edu
Full-time: 1486 men, 2070 women	**Faculty:** 145; IIA, av$
Part-time: 277 men, 325 women	**Ph.D.s:** 85%
Graduate: 86 men, 570 women	**Student/Faculty:** 25 to 1
Year: semesters, summer session	**Tuition:** $6470 ($16,320)
Room & Board: $10,390	**Freshman Class:** 3341 applied, 1939 accepted, 416 enrolled
	CEEB CODE: 2866
Application Deadline: rolling	**COMPETITIVE**

State University of New York/College at Old Westbury, founded in 1965, is a public institution offering degree programs in the arts and sciences, business, education, fine arts, and health science. Figures in the above capsule and in this profile are approximate. There are 3 undergraduate schools and 3 graduate schools. In addition to regional accreditation, SUNY Old Westbury has baccalaureate program accreditation with ACS. The 604-acre campus is in a suburban area 20 miles east of New York City. Including any residence halls, there are 23 buildings.

STUDENT LIFE: 97% of undergraduates are from New York. Others are from 13 states and 9 foreign countries. 85% are from public schools. 33% are White; 30% African American; 21% Hispanic; 10% Asian American; 3% two or more races; 2% race unknown; 1% American Indian/Alaska Native; 1% Foreign. **Female To Male Ratio:** 1.6:1. The average age of freshmen is 19; all undergraduates, 24. 20% do not continue beyond their first year; 35% remain to graduate. **Housing:** 1500 students can be accommodated in college housing, which includes dorms and honors houses. On-campus housing is available on a first-come, first-served basis, and is available on a lottery system for upperclassmen. 77% of students commute. Alcohol is not permitted. All students may keep cars.

FACULTY/CLASSROOMS: 47% of faculty are male; 53% are female. 98% teach undergraduates, 11% do research, and 11% do both. No introductory courses are taught by graduate students. The average class size in an introductory lecture is 25; in a laboratory is 20; and in a regular course is 25.

PROGRAMS OF STUDY: SUNY Old Westbury confers B.A., B.S., B.F.A., and B.P.S. degrees. Master's degrees are also awarded. Bachelor's degrees are awarded in BIOLOGICAL SCIENCE (biochemistry and biology/biological science), BUSINESS (accounting, banking and finance, business administration and management, labor studies, management information systems, and marketing/retailing/merchandising), COMMUNICATIONS AND THE ARTS (communications, media arts, Spanish, and visual and performing arts), COMPUTER AND PHYSICAL SCIENCE (chemistry, computer science, information sciences and systems, and mathematics), EDUCATION (bilingual/bicultural education, early childhood education, elementary education, foreign languages education, mathematics education, middle school education, science education, secondary education, social studies education, and special education), HEALTH PROFESSIONS (community health work and health), SOCIAL SCIENCE (American studies, criminology, history, humanities, philosophy, political science/government, psychology, religion, and sociology). Education, business, and biological sciences are the strongest academically. Psychology, accounting, and biological sciences have the largest enrollments.

ACTIVITIES: 1% of men belong to 6 national fraternities; 2% of women belong to 8 national sororities. There are 60 groups on campus, including art, cheerleading, choir, chorale, computers, dance, drama, ethnic, film, honors, international, LGBT, newspaper, photography, political, professional, radio and TV, religious, social, social service, student government, and yearbook. Popular campus events include Welcome Back Festival, Wellness at Old Westbury, and Panther Pride Week. **Sports:** There are 7 intercollegiate sports for men and 7 for women, and 7 intramural sports for men and 7 for women. Facilities include a gym, an auxiliary gym, a cross-country course, playing fields, a swimming pool, a fitness center, a weight room, jogging trails, a student union building, and courts for tennis, paddleball, handball, racquetball, and squash. **Graduates:** From July 1, 2016 to June 30, 2017, 864 bachelor's degrees were awarded. The most popular majors were psychology (16%), accounting (12%), and media and communications (9%). In an average class, 1% graduate in 3 years or less, 21% graduate in 4 years or less, 31% graduate in 5 years or less, and 35% graduate in 6 years or less.

SERVICES: Counseling and information services are available, as is tutoring in most subjects, such as mathematics, and writing. There is a reader service for the blind, and remedial math, reading, and writing. **Library/Resources:** The library contains 251,930 volumes, 18,864 microform items, and 1,634 audio/video tapes/CDs/DVDs, and subscribes to 2,532 periodicals including electronic. Computerized library services include interlibrary loans, database searching, Internet access, and Wi-Fi capability. Special learning facilities include an art gallery, a radio station, and TV studio. **Physically Challenged Students:** 90% of the campus is accessible. Facilities include wheelchair ramps, elevators, special parking, specially equipped restrooms, special class scheduling, lowered drinking fountains, lowered telephones, and limited volunteer transportation. **Special:** SUNY Old Westbury offers cross-registration with SUNY Empire State, Lirache, and colleges in Nassau and Suffolk counties, internships in teacher education, extensive study-abroad programs, a

B.A.-B.S. in psychology, chemistry, industrial labor and relations, and sociology, dual majors, and a 3-2 engineering degree with SUNY at Stony Brook and SUNY Maritime College; an accelerated B.S. in Biological Sciences/D.O. in Osteopathic Medicine (offered in collaboration with the New York College of Osteopathic Medicine). Credit for military and life experience, nondegree study, and pass/fail options are available. There are 5 national honor societies, a freshman honors program, and 6 departmental honors programs. **Visiting:** There are regularly scheduled orientations for prospective students. There are guides for informal visits. To schedule a visit, contact Enrollment Services at (516) 876-3073. **Campus Safety and Security:** Measures include 24-hour foot and vehicle patrol, an emergency notification system, and security escort services. There are shuttle buses, emergency telephones, lighted pathways/sidewalks, and officer patrols the dormitories.

REQUIREMENTS: The SAT is required. Applicants must be graduates of an accredited secondary school or have a GED. An essay, portfolio, and interview are also recommended. Students are evaluated according to qualifying categories of academic achievement, special knowledge and creative ability, paid work experience, and social or personal experience. AP and CLEP credits are accepted. Important factors in the admissions decision are leadership record, recommendations by school officials, and evidence of special talent. General education requirements include courses in writing and reasoning skills, creative arts, ideas and ideology, cross-cultural perspectives, U.S. society and history, physical or life science, and foreign language. A senior project or capstone course is required, based on the major. To be eligible for graduation, all candidates must satisfy all College and departmental requirements for the specific degree. Students must complete a minimum of 120 credits of satisfactory work. Some departmental requirements exceed this number. 45 of these credits must be earned in course work above the survey and the introductory levels (at or above the 300 level). To fulfill graduation requirements, School of Education majors must have a 3.0 cumulative GPA, School of Business majors must have a 2.5 cumulative GPA as well as for all School of Business courses, all other students must have at least a 2.0 cumulative GPA for all work completed at SUNY Old Westbury. **Procedure:** Freshmen are admitted fall and spring. There are early decision, deferred admissions, and rolling admissions plans. Application deadlines are open. The fall 2017 application fee was $50. Notification is sent on a rolling basis. Applications are accepted on-line. **Transfer Students:** 1280 transfer students enrolled in 2016-2017. Applicants must submit official transcripts from all colleges attended. Those students with fewer than 24 college credits must also submit a high school transcript. The college requires a minimum overall GPA of 2.0. Specific academic majors may require a higher GPA. 48 of 120 credits required for the bachelor's degree must be completed at Old Westbury. **International Students:** There are 34 international students enrolled. They must take the TOEFL with a minimum score of 513 on the paper-based TOEFL (PBT) or 80 on the Internet-based version (iBT), and take the college's own test.

Admissions Contact: Andrea Klaff, Director of Admissions. Email: *enroll@oldwestbury.edu* Web: *www.oldwestbury.edu*

FINANCIAL AID: In 2017-2018, 69% of all full-time freshmen received some form of financial aid. 65% of all full-time freshmen received need-based aid. The average freshman award was $7,207. Need-based scholarships or need-based grants averaged $7,016; need-based self-help aid (loans and jobs) averaged $7,351; and other non-need-based awards and non-need-based scholarships averaged $1,971. The average financial indebtedness of the 2017 graduate was $17,340. The college's own financial statement, and the IFAA (Institutional Application), and previous year's household income are required. The FAFSA code is 007109. The deadline for filing freshman financial aid applications for fall entry is April 19.

STATE UNIVERSITY OF NEW YORK/ CORTLAND C-4

www2.cortland.edu

Cortland, NY 13045	(607) 753-4711
Fax: (607) 753-5598	Email: admissions@cortland.edu
Full-time: 2716 men, 3480 women	Faculty: 303; IIA, --$
Part-time: 65 men, 85 women	Ph.D.s: n/av
Graduate: 212 men, 355 women	Student/Faculty: 16 to 1
Year: semesters, summer session	Tuition: $8106 ($17,950)
Room & Board: $12,810	Freshman Class: 10875 applied, 5673 accepted, 1238 enrolled
SAT M: 567 ACT: 24	CEEB CODE: 2538
Application Deadline: rolling	COMPETITIVE

State University of New York/Cortland, founded in 1868, is a public institution offering academic programs leading to baccalaureate and master's degrees in liberal arts and professional studies. There are 3 undergraduate schools and 3 graduate schools. In addition to regional accreditation, SUNY Cortland has baccalaureate program accreditation with CAHEA, and NRPA. The 191-acre campus is in a small town 18 miles north of Ithaca and 29 miles south of Syracuse.

STUDENT LIFE: 94% of undergraduates are from New York. 73% are White; 6% African American; 4% race unknown; 2% two or more races; 12% Hispanic; 1% Asian American. **Female To Male Ratio:** 2.6:1. **Housing:** 3224 students can be accommodated in college housing, which includes dorms and off-campus apartments. In addition, there are special-interest houses, fraternity houses, sorority houses, apartments for single students, cooperative housing, wellness housing, leadership house, transfer floor, 21 + floors, and quiet floor. All students may keep cars.

FACULTY/CLASSROOMS: All teach undergraduates, 15% do research, and 15% do both. No introductory courses are taught by graduate students.

PROGRAMS OF STUDY: SUNY Cortland confers B.A., B.S., B.S.Ed., and B.F.A. degrees. Master's degrees are also awarded. Bachelor's degrees are awarded in BIOLOGICAL SCIENCE (biology/biological science), BUSINESS (management science and sports management), COMMUNICATIONS AND THE ARTS (art, communications, English, film arts, and musical theater), COMPUTER AND PHYSICAL SCIENCE (chemistry, geochemistry, geology, geophysics and seismology, mathematics, and physics), EDUCATION (athletic training, foreign languages education, health education, middle school education, physical education, recreation education, and secondary education), ENGINEERING AND ENVIRONMENTAL DESIGN (environmental science), HEALTH PROFESSIONS (health science and speech pathology/audiology), SOCIAL SCIENCE (African American studies, anthropology, economics, geography, history, human services, international studies, philosophy, political science/government, psychology, and sociology).

ACTIVITIES: There are 100 groups on campus, including art, band, cheerleading, chess, choir, chorale, chorus, computers, dance, drama, ethnic, film, honors, international, LGBT, literary magazine, Model UN, musical theater, newspaper, orchestra, political, professional, radio and TV, religious, social, social service, student government, symphony, and yearbook. Popular campus events include Cortland-Ithaca College Football Game, Winterfest, and Multicultural Festival. **Sports:** There are 11 intercollegiate sports for men and 14 for women, and 55 intramural sports for men and 55 for women. Facilities include a student life center, an outdoor multipurpose stadium complex, an Olympic-size pool, gym, an ice arena, gymnastics arena, wrestling and weight rooms, dance studio, handball/racquetball courts, squash courts, an athletic training facility, fitness centers, swimming pool, track, baseball field, football/lacrosse/track field, a lighted soccer field, a field house and athletic fields. **Graduates:** From July 1, 2016 to June 30, 2017, 1541 bachelor's degrees were awarded. The most popular majors were education (24%), parks and recreation (21%), and social sciences (11%).

SERVICES: Counseling and information services are available, as is tutoring in some subjects. There is a reader service for the blind. There is also a fully staffed Academic Support and Achievement Program for writing, math, study skills, and learning strategies. Specific course tutoring is available with peer tutors. **Library/Resources:** The library contains 464,422 volumes, 8,808 microform items, and 2,378 audio/video tapes/CDs/DVDs, and subscribes to 231 periodicals including electronic. Computerized library services include interlibrary loans, database searching, Internet access, and Wi-Fi capability. Special learning facilities include an art gallery, a planetarium, a radio station, TV station, a greenhouse, a center for speech and hearing disorders, classrooms equipped with integrated technologies, multimedia enhanced instruction, and many specialized labs to support various program offerings. **Physically Challenged Students:** 75% of the campus is accessible. Facilities include wheelchair ramps, elevators, special parking, specially equipped restrooms, special class scheduling, lowered drinking fountains, lowered telephones, and special housing. **Special:** Cortland offers cross-registration with Tompkins Cortland Communinty College and has cooperative programs with the State University of New York College of Environmental Science and Forestry, Centers at Binghamton and Buffalo, and Cornell and Case Western Reserve Universities. Students may study abroad in over 30 countries, and they may enroll in a Washington semester. Work-study programs are available. The college confers an individualized studies degree and allows dual majors. Students may pursue a 3-2 engineering degree in conjunction with Alfred, Case Western Reserve, and Clarkson Universities, and the State University of New York Centers at Binghamton, Buffalo, and Stony Brook. Cortland offers nondegree study opportunities. There are 19 national honor societies, Phi Beta Kappa, a freshman honors program, and 5 departmental honors programs. **Visiting:** There are regularly scheduled orientations for prospective students consisting of Autumn Preview Days as well as Spring Open House for accepted students. There are guides for informal visits and visitors may sit in on classes. To schedule a visit, contact the Admissions Office. **Campus Safety and Security:** Measures include 24-hour foot and vehicle patrol, an emergency notification system, self-defense education, and security escort services. There are shuttle buses, emergency telephones, lighted pathways/sidewalks, university police maintain a Web site with safety information and links, and a silent witness program for reporting crimes anonymously.

REQUIREMENTS: The SAT is required. Applicants must graduate from an accredited secondary school or have a GED. They must have earned 16 Carnegie units and 20 academic credits, 4 units each in English, history and social studies, 3-4 each in math, and science (with lab), and 3 units in foreign language. Essays and recommendations are required, and in some cases auditions are required. Interviews are strongly recommended. AP and CLEP credits are accepted. Important factors in the admissions decision are advanced placement or honors courses, evidence of special talent, extracurricular activities record, recommendations by alumni, and recommendations by school officials. To graduate, undergraduates must complete 6 hours in English composition, and at least 6 hours of writing-intensive courses, with 3 of those in the major. One course meeting the Quantitative Skills criteria must be passed; 30 hours of courses in the General Education program must also be completed, with no more than 2 courses taken in any one of the 8 disciplines in the program. A major of 30 to 36 hours, with no more than 45 credits in discipline-specific courses must be completed. Completion of 90 credits of Liberal Arts and Science courses toward a B.A., 60 credits toward a B.S.Ed or a B.S. is required. A 2.0 GPA, both overall and in all minors and concentrations, must be maintained. Special requirements may be designated by each school of the college. **Procedure:** Freshmen are admitted in the fall and spring. Entrance exams should be taken during the spring of the junior year or fall of the senior year. There are early decision, early admissions, deferred admissions, and rolling admissions plans. The fall 2017 application fee was $50. Notification is sent on a rolling basis. Applications are accepted on-line. **Transfer Students:** 654 transfer students enrolled in 2016-2017. Applicants must have a minimum GPA of 2.5. Some programs are more competitive. Interviews are encouraged. 45 of 124 credits required for the bachelor's degree must be completed at SUNY Cortland. **International Students:** They must also take the SAT or ACT.

ADMISSIONS: 52% of the 2017-2018 applicants were accepted. The SAT scores for the 2017-2018 freshman class were: Math-- 6% below 500, 66% between 500 and 599, 27% between 600 and 699 and 1% between 700-800. **Admissions Contact:** Mark Yacavone, Assistant Vice President of Enrollment. Email: *admissions@cortland.edu* Web: *www2.cortland.edu*

FINANCIAL AID: The average freshman award was $14,839. Need-based scholarships or need-based grants averaged $5,369; need-based self-help aid (loans and jobs) averaged $3,689; other non-need-based awards and non-need-based scholarships averaged $3,542; and $3,674 from other forms of aid. The average financial indebtedness of the 2017 graduate was $25,533. The FAFSA code is 002843. The priority date for freshman financial aid applications for fall entry is March 15.

STATE UNIVERSITY OF NEW YORK/EMPIRE STATE COLLEGE
(The complete profile is made available exclusively on our website, www.barronspac.com)

STATE UNIVERSITY OF NEW YORK/ FREDONIA — A-4
www.fredonia.edu

Fredonia, NY 14063	**(716) 673-3251** **(800) 252-1212**
Fax: (716) 673-3249	**Email: admissions@fredonia.edu**
Full-time: 1805 men, 2472 women	**Faculty:** 252; IIA, -$
Part-time: 54 men, 35 women	**Ph.D.s:** 87%
Graduate: 61 men, 178 women	**Student/Faculty:** 14 to 1
Year: semesters, summer session	**Tuition:** $8288 ($17,938)
Room & Board: $12,490	**Freshman Class:** 5474 applied, 3553 accepted, 1129 enrolled
SAT CR/M: 550/530 **ACT:** 24	**CEEB CODE:** 2539
Application Deadline: rolling	**COMPETITIVE**

State University of New York at Fredonia, established in 1826, is a public institution offering undergraduate programs in the arts and sciences, business and professional curricula, teacher preparation, and the fine and performing arts. There are 5 undergraduate schools and 1 graduate school. In addition to regional accreditation, SUNY at Fredonia has baccalaureate program accreditation with AACSB, CSWE, NASAD, NASM, NAST, ASHA, and CAEP. The 256-acre campus is in a small town 50 miles south of Buffalo and 45 miles north of Erie, Pennsylvania. Including any residence halls, there are 63 buildings.

STUDENT LIFE: 95% of undergraduates are from New York. Others are from 24 states, 14 foreign countries, and Canada. 91% are from public schools. 74% are White; 9% Hispanic; 8% African American; 3% Foreign; 2% Asian American; 2% two or more races; 1% American Indian/Alaska Native; 1% race unknown. **Female To Male Ratio:** 1.4:1. The average age of freshmen is 18; all undergraduates, 20. 18% do not continue beyond their first year; 63% remain to graduate. **Housing:** 2900 students can be accommodated in college housing, which includes dorms and on-campus apartments. In addition, there are honors houses, special-interest houses, and living space for fraternities and sororities available in residence halls. In addition, there are special interest houses for computer and athletics students and quiet-hour centers. On-campus housing is guaranteed for the freshman year only, and is available on a first-come, first-served basis, and is available on a lottery system for upperclassmen. 7% of students commute. All students may keep cars.

FACULTY/CLASSROOMS: 55% of faculty are male; 45% are female. All teach undergraduates and all do research. No introductory courses are taught by graduate students. The average class size in an introductory lecture is 35; in a laboratory is 16; and in a regular course is 20.

PROGRAMS OF STUDY: SUNY at Fredonia confers B.A., B.F.A., B.S., B.S.Ed., and Mus.B. degrees. Master's degrees are also awarded. Bachelor's degrees are awarded in AGRICULTURE (environmental studies), BIOLOGICAL SCIENCE (biochemistry, biology/adolescence education, biology/biological science, and genetics), BUSINESS (accounting, business administration and management, business economics, finance, institutional management, and sports management), COMMUNICATIONS AND THE ARTS (acting, animation, arts administration/management, audio technology, communication studies, communications, dance, dramatic arts, drawing, English, film, television and digital media, fine arts, French, graphic design, illustration, journalism, media arts, music, music performance, music theory and composition, musical theater, painting, photography, public relations, Spanish, theatre arts, theater design, theatre production, theatre studies, and video), COMPUTER AND PHYSICAL SCIENCE (applied mathematics, chemistry, chemistry/adolescence education, computer information systems, computer science, earth science, geochemistry, geology, geoscience, mathematics, and physics), EDUCATION (early childhood education, education, elementary education, English education, foreign languages education, mathematics education, middle school education, music education, science education, secondary education, social studies education, and social studies secondary school education), ENGINEERING AND ENVIRONMENTAL DESIGN (environmental science), HEALTH PROFESSIONS (health care administration, medical laboratory technology, music therapy, predentistry, premedicine, preoptometry, and speech pathology/audiology), SOCIAL SCIENCE (American studies, early childhood studies, economics, history, interdisciplinary studies, liberal arts/general studies, philosophy, political science/government, prelaw, psychology, social work, sociology, and women's studies). Music, theatre, and visual arts are the strongest academically. STEM, arts, and business have the largest enrollments.

ACTIVITIES: 3% of men belong to 2 national fraternities; 5% of women belong to 3 national sororities. There are 170 groups on campus, including Spectrum Entertainment Board, art, band, cheerleading, chess, choir, chorale, chorus, communications, computers, dance, debate, drama, drill team, environmental, ethnic, film, honors, international, jazz band, LGBT, literary magazine, musical theater, newspaper, opera, orchestra, pep band, photography, political, professional, radio and TV, religious, ski club, social, social service, student government, and symphony. **Sports:** There are 8 intercollegiate sports for men and 9 for women, and 15 intramural sports for men and 15 for women. Facilities include a basketball arena, an ice rink, a swimming pool, gyms, weight rooms, dance studios, soccer fields, indoor and outdoor tracks, racquetball, tennis, volleyball courts, and soccer/lacrosse stadium. **Graduates:** From July 1, 2016 to June 30, 2017, 1043 bachelor's degrees were awarded. The most popular majors were business administration (18%), education (14%), and visual and performing arts (13%). In an average class, 48% graduate in 4 years or less, 61% graduate in 5 years or less, and 63% graduate in 6 years or less.

SERVICES: Counseling and information services are available, as is tutoring in every subject. There is a reader service for the blind. **Library/Resources:** The library contains 391,121 volumes, 1.1 million microform items, and 26,574 audio/video tapes/CDs/DVDs, and subscribes to 1,983 periodicals, including electronic. Computerized library services include interlibrary loans, database searching, Internet access, and Wi-Fi capability. Special learning facilities include an art gallery, a natural history museum, a planetarium, radio station, TV station, a greenhouse, child-care center, speech and audiology clinic, and Rockefeller Arts Center. **Physically Challenged Students:** 85% of the campus is accessible. Facilities include wheelchair ramps, elevators, special parking, specially equipped restrooms, special class scheduling, lowered drinking fountains, lowered telephones, and special housing. **Special:** Cooperative programs are available with many other institutions. Students may cross-register with colleges in the Western New York Consortium. Fredonia offers a variety of internships, study-abroad programs in more than 60 countries, and a Washington semester. Accelerated degrees, a general studies degree, dual and student-designed majors, a 3-2 engineering degree program with 14 universities, nondegree study, and pass/fail grading options are available. There are 19 national honor societies, a freshman honors program, and 19 departmental honors programs. **Visiting:** There are regularly scheduled orientations for prospective students, including various open house programs and information sessions and tours Monday through Friday, morning and afternoon, and varied Saturday tours. Visitors may sit in on classes and stay overnight. To schedule a visit, contact the Office of Admissions. **Campus Safety and Security:** Measures include 24-hour foot and vehicle patrol, an emergency notification system, self-defense education, and security escort services. There are shuttle buses, emergency telephones, lighted pathways/sidewalks, controlled access to dorms/residences, and card swipe access to residence halls.

REQUIREMENTS: The SAT or ACT is required, with a satisfactory score. Applicants must possess a high school diploma or have a GED. 16 academic credits are recommended, including 4 credits each in English and social studies and 3 each in math, science, and a foreign language. 4 years of math and science are encouraged. Essays are required. Where applicable, an audition or portfolio is required. AP and CLEP credits are accepted. Important factors in the admissions decision are advanced placement or honors courses, leadership record, parents or siblings attended your school, evidence of special talent, personality/intangible qualities, extracurricular activities record, recommendations by alumni, geographical diversity, and recommendations by school officials. To graduate, students must complete 120 hours, including 36 to 90 or more in the major, with a 2.0 GPA. Students must take specific courses in English and math and complete 50 hours of general education courses, including writing, statistical/quantitative abilities, oral communication, natural and social sciences, humanities, and arts. **Procedure:** Freshmen are admitted fall and spring. Entrance exams should be taken Spring of the junior year or fall of the senior year. There are deferred admissions and rolling admissions plans. Application deadlines are open. The fall 2017 application fee was $50. Notifications are sent October 14. Applications are accepted online. **Transfer Students:** 309 transfer students enrolled in 2016-2017. Applicants should have a minimum GPA of 2.0 and appropriate academic course work to be considered. 45 of 120 credits required for the bachelor's degree must be completed at SUNY at Fredonia. **International Students:** There are 170 international students enrolled. They must take the TOEFL with a minimum score of 78 on the Internet-based version (iBT), and take the IELTS.

ADMISSIONS: 65% of the 2017-2018 applicants were accepted. The SAT scores for the 2017-2018 freshman class were: Critical Reading-- 24% below 500, 48% between 500 and 599, 24% between 600 and 699, and 4% between 700 and 800. Math-- 31% below 500, 48% between 500 and 599, 20% between 600 and 699, and 1% between 700 and 800. The ACT scores were 18% between 12 and 17, 43% between 18 and 23, 33% between 24 and 29, and 6% above 30. 30% of the current freshmen were in the top fifth of their class; 62% were in the top two fifths. 13 freshmen graduated first in their class. **Admissions Contact:** Cory Bezek, Director of Admissions. Email: *admissions@fredonia.edu* Web: *www.fredonia.edu*

FINANCIAL AID: In 2017-2018, 80% of all full-time freshmen received some form of financial aid. 86% of all full-time freshmen received need-based aid. The average freshman award was $13,113. Need-based scholarships or need-based grants averaged $7,425; need-based self-help aid (loans and jobs) averaged $6,028; and other non-need-based awards and non-need-based scholarships averaged $3,813. The average financial indebtedness of the 2017 graduate was $27,586. The state aid form and Express TAP Application (ETA) are required. The FAFSA code is 002844. The priority date for freshman financial aid applications for fall entry is February 1.

STATE UNIVERSITY OF NEW YORK/ MARITIME COLLEGE — D-5

www.sunymaritime.edu

Throgs Neck, NY 10465 — (718) 409-7221, (800) 642-1874

Fax: (718) 409-7465 — **Email:** admissions@sunymaritime.edu

Full-time: 1326 men, 137 women	**Faculty:** 69; IIA, -$
Part-time: 97 men, 15 women	**Ph.D.s:** 49%
Graduate: 151 men, 31 women	**Student/Faculty:** 21 to 1
Year: semesters, summer session	**Tuition:** $6090 ($13,990)
Room & Board: $9930	**Freshman Class:** 1397 applied, 888 accepted, 356 enrolled
SAT CR/M: 510/550 **ACT:** 22	**CEEB CODE:** 2536
Application Deadline: January 31	**COMPETITIVE**

State University of New York/Maritime College, founded in 1874, is a public institution that prepares students for the U.S. Merchant Marine officer's license and for bachelor's degrees in engineering, naval architecture, marine environmental science, and marine transportation/business administration. The figures in the above capsule and in this profile are approximate. There is 1 undergraduate school and 1 graduate school. In addition to regional accreditation, SUNY Maritime College has baccalaureate program accreditation with ABET. The 52-acre campus is in a suburban area on the Throgs Neck peninsula where Long Island Sound meets the East River. Including any residence halls, there are 31 buildings.

STUDENT LIFE: 65% of undergraduates are from New York. Others are from 28 states and 20 foreign countries. 70% are from public schools. 9% are Hispanic; 71% White; 7% Foreign; 6% African American; 4% Asian American. **Male To Female Ratio:** 8.6:1. The average age of freshmen is 19; all undergraduates, 21. 23% do not continue beyond their first year; 77% remain to graduate. **Housing:** 1281 students can be accommodated in college housing, which includes dorms. On-campus housing is guaranteed for all 4 years, and is available on a first-come, first-served basis. 82% of students live on campus. Alcohol is not permitted. Upperclassmen may keep cars.

FACULTY/CLASSROOMS: 89% of faculty are male; 11% are female. 96% teach undergraduates, 20% do research, and 20% do both. No introductory courses are taught by graduate students. The average class size in an introductory lecture is 28; in a laboratory is 16; and in a regular course is 30.

PROGRAMS OF STUDY: SUNY Maritime College confers B.E. and B.S. degrees. Associate and master's degrees are also awarded. Bachelor's degrees are awarded in BIOLOGICAL SCIENCE (marine science), BUSINESS (business administration and management and transportation management), COMPUTER AND PHYSICAL SCIENCE (atmospheric sciences and meteorology), ENGINEERING AND ENVIRONMENTAL DESIGN (electrical/electronics engineering, engineering, environmental science, marine engineering, maritime science, and naval architecture and marine engineering), SOCIAL SCIENCE (humanities). Marine operations, marine environmental science, and electrical engineering are the strongest academically. Marine transportation, marine engineering, and international transportation and trade have the largest enrollments.

ACTIVITIES: There are no fraternities or sororities. There are 30 groups on campus, including art, bagpipe, band, chorus, computers, drill team, ethnic, honors, international, jazz band, marching band, newspaper, pep band, photography, political, professional, religious, social, social service, and student government. Popular campus events include Thursdays in the TIV, Ring Dance, and Super Bowl Party. **Sports:** There are 9 intercollegiate sports for men and 9 for women, and 6 intramural sports for men and 6 for women. Facilities include an athletic center with a gym, a swimming pool, exercise and weight rooms, a rifle and pistol range, and handball/racquetball and squash courts, a sailing center, and football, baseball, lacrosse, and soccer fields. **Graduates:** From July 1, 2016 to June 30, 2017, 306 bachelor's degrees were awarded. The most popular majors were marine transportation (30%), international transportation and trade (18%), and naval architecture (9%). In an average class, 31% graduate in 4 years or less, 47% graduate in 5 years or less, and 49% graduate in 6 years or less. Of the 2016 graduating class, 4% were enrolled in graduate school within 6 months of graduation, and 100% were employed.

SERVICES: Counseling and information services are available, as is tutoring in every subject. **Library/Resources:** The library contains 85,984 volumes, 28,400 microform items, and 774 audio/video tapes/CDs/DVDs, and subscribes to 38,735 periodicals including electronic. Computerized library services include interlibrary loans, database searching, and Internet access. **Physically Challenged Students:** 81% of the campus is accessible. Facilities include wheelchair ramps, elevators, special parking, and specially equipped restrooms. **Special:** The college offers co-op programs in engineering, an accelerated degree program in marine transportation/transportation management, and internships as cadet observers aboard commercial ships. There are 2 national honor societies, a freshman honors program, and 2 departmental honors programs. **Visiting:** There are regularly scheduled orientations for prospective students, including a tour of the campus and facilities and meetings with faculty and students. There are guides for informal visits; visitors may sit in on classes and stay overnight. To schedule a visit, contact the Admissions Office. **Campus Safety and Security:** Measures include 24-hour foot and vehicle patrol, an emergency notification system, self-defense education, and security escort services. There are emergency telephones, lighted pathways/sidewalks, and controlled access to dorms/residences.

REQUIREMENTS: The SAT is required. Applicants must be high school graduates or hold a GED. 16 Carnegie units are required, including 4 of English and social studies, and 3 years of math (pre-calculus is required for engineering) and science (chemistry and physics are strongly recommended). An essay is required and an interview is recommended. AP and CLEP credits are accepted. Important factors in the admissions decision are advanced placement or honors courses, extracurricular activities record, and leadership record. Bachelor's degree candidates must earn 126 to 181 credit hours, with a GPA of 2.0, and distribution requirements vary by the major. If pursuing the U.S. Merchant Marine officer's license, all students must spend 3 summer semesters at sea acquiring hands-on experience aboard the college's training vessel. **Procedure:** Freshmen are admitted in the fall and spring. Entrance exams should be taken during the junior or senior year. There are early decision, early admissions, deferred admissions, and rolling admissions plans. Early decision applications should be filed by November 1; regular applications, by January 31 for fall entry. The fall 2017 application fee was $40. Applications are accepted online. **Transfer Students:** 77 transfer students enrolled in 2016-2017. Transfer students must have a 2.5 GPA. **International Students:** There are 94 international students enrolled. They must take the TOEFL, and the SAT or ACT.

ADMISSIONS: 64% of the 2017-2018 applicants were accepted. The SAT scores for the 2017-2018 freshman class were: Critical Reading-- 42% below 500, 45% between 500 and 599, 11% between 600 and 699, and 2% between 700 and 800. Math-- 20% below 500, 52% between 500 and 599, 26% between 600 and 699, and 2% between 700 and 800. The ACT scores were 35% below 12, 40% between 12 and 17, 16% between 18 and 23, 4% between 24 and 29, and 5% above 30. 19% of the current freshmen were in the top fifth of their class; 52% were in the top two fifths. **Admissions Contact:** Jonathan White, Dean of Admissions. Email: *admissions@sunymaritime.edu* Web: *www.sunymaritime.edu*

FINANCIAL AID: In 2017-2018, 77% of all full-time freshmen received some form of financial aid. 44% of all full-time freshmen received need-based aid. The average financial indebtedness of the 2017 graduate was $17,345. The college's own financial statement and student and parent federal income tax returns are required. The FAFSA code is 002853. The priority date for freshman financial aid applications for fall entry is March 1.

STATE UNIVERSITY OF NEW YORK/ONEONTA D-3

www.oneonta.edu

Oneonta, NY 13820 (607) 436-2524 (800) 786-9123

Fax: (607) 436-3074 **Email:** admissions@oneonta.edu

Full-time: 2119 men, 3936 women	**Faculty:** 284; IIA, --$
Part-time: 54 men, 51 women	**Ph.D.s:** 85%
Graduate: 72 men, 242 women	**Student/Faculty:** 18 to 1
Year: semesters, summer session	**Tuition:** $8136 ($17,786)
Room & Board: $12,658	**Freshman Class:** 10606 applied, 5604 accepted, 1123 enrolled
SAT CR/M: 565/565 **ACT:** 23	**CEEB CODE:** 2542
Application Deadline: open	**COMPETITIVE**

State University of New York/Oneonta, founded in 1889, offers undergraduate and graduate programs in the arts and sciences with a campus-wide emphasis on student engagement, diversity, and community service. There is 1 undergraduate school and 1 graduate school. In addition to regional accreditation, SUNY Oneonta has baccalaureate program accreditation with AACSB, ADA, NASM, ACS, and AAFCS. The 250-acre campus is in a rural area 75 miles southwest of Albany and 55 miles northeast of Binghamton. Including any residence halls, there are 36 buildings.

STUDENT LIFE: 99% of undergraduates are from New York. Others are from 25 states and 18 foreign countries. 83% are Hispanic; 77% White; 4% African American; 21% two or more races; 2% Asian American; 2% Foreign; 1% race unknown. **Female To Male Ratio:** 1.9:1. The average age of freshmen is 18; all undergraduates, 20. 16% do not continue beyond their first year; 67% remain to graduate. **Housing:** 3557 students can be accommodated in college housing, which includes gender neutral dorms and on-campus apartments, freshman housing and special-interest groupings within residence halls, and theme housing. On-campus housing is guaranteed for all 4 years, is guaranteed for the freshman year only, is available on a first-come, first-served basis, and is available on a lottery system for upperclassmen. 98% of students live on campus. Alcohol is not permitted. Upperclassmen may keep cars.

FACULTY/CLASSROOMS: 52% of faculty are male; 48% are female. 96% teach undergraduates. No introductory courses are taught by graduate students. The average class size in an introductory lecture is 28; in a laboratory is 18; and in a regular course is 23.

PROGRAMS OF STUDY: SUNY Oneonta confers B.A. and B.S. degrees. Master's degrees are also awarded. Bachelor's degrees are awarded in BIOLOGICAL SCIENCE (biology/biological science), BUSINESS (accounting, business economics, and fashion merchandising), COMMUNICATIONS AND THE ARTS (art, communications, dramatic arts, English, fine arts, French, music, music business management, and Spanish), COMPUTER AND PHYSICAL SCIENCE (atmospheric sciences and meteorology, chemistry, computer science, earth science, geology, mathematics, physics, and statistics), EDUCATION (business education, elementary education, English education, foreign languages education, home economics education, mathematics education, science education, secondary education, and social science education), ENGINEERING AND ENVIRONMENTAL DESIGN (environmental science), HEALTH PROFESSIONS (predentistry and premedicine), SOCIAL SCIENCE (African studies, anthropology, child care/child and family studies, criminal justice, dietetics, economics, geography, gerontology, Hispanic American studies, history, home economics, international studies, philosophy, political science/government, prelaw, psychology, sociology, and water resources). Physical and natural sciences, business economics, and education are the strongest academically. Elementary education, adolescent education, and business have the largest enrollments.

ACTIVITIES: 1% of men belong to 11 national fraternities; 1% of women belong to 9 national sororities. There are 157 groups on campus, including academic, cultural and special-interest organizations, art, band, cheerleading, choir, chorale, chorus, communications, computers, dance, debate, drama, environmental, ethnic, film, honors, international, jazz band, LGBT, literary magazine, marching band, musical theater, newspaper, opera, orchestra, pep band, photography, political, professional, radio and TV, religious, social, social service, student government, symphony, volunteer, and yearbook. Popular campus events include Into the Streets Day of Service, OH-Fest, Battle of the Red Dragons, Red Day, and Passing through the Pillars. **Sports:** There are 10 intercollegiate sports for men and 11 for women, and 13 intramural sports for men and 13 for women. Facilities include a gym, a field house, dance studios, weight rooms, a pool, indoor racquetball courts, tennis courts, indoor and outdoor tracks, athletic fields, and a lighted all-weather field. **Graduates:** From July 1, 2016 to June 30, 2017, 1501 bachelor's degrees were awarded. The most popular majors were communications, and education (12%), business/marketing (11%), psychology, and family and consumer sciences (10%). In an average class, 72% graduate in 6 years or less.

SERVICES: Counseling and information services are available, as is tutoring in most subjects. There is a reader service for the blind, and remedial math, reading, and writing. Tutoring is also available in all introductory-level courses and most upper-level courses. **Library/Resources:** The library contains 482,408 volumes, 1.2 million microform items, and 19,174 audio/video tapes/CDs/DVDs, and subscribes to 50,000 periodicals, including electronic. Computerized library services include interlibrary loans, database searching, Internet access, and Wi-Fi capability. Special learning facilities include an art gallery, a planetarium, radio station, TV station, a digital planetarium, science discovery center, community service center, a college camp, a children's center, and off-campus biological field station. **Physically Challenged Students:** 90% of the campus is accessible. Facilities include wheelchair ramps, elevators, special parking, specially equipped restrooms, special class scheduling, and lowered drinking fountains. All academic buildings and most residence halls are accessible. **Special:** Oneonta offers limited cross-registration with Hartwick College, internships in most fields, and dual majors. Students can study abroad through 8 exchange programs in Ghana, Finland, Germany, Sweden, Japan, and South Korea, as well as more than 500 study abroad programs around the world through the SUNY network. A 3-1 fashion program with the Fashion Institute of Technology, a 3-2 engineering degree, and other cooperative programs are offered. There are 20 national honor societies. **Visiting:** There are regularly scheduled orientations for prospective students, open houses, Friday and Saturday information sessions and individual appointments for prospective students; also available are Academic Exploration Day and summer orientation sessions for admitted students. There are guides for informal visits and visitors may sit in on classes. To schedule a visit, contact the Admissions Office. **Campus Safety and Security:** Measures include 24-hour foot and vehicle patrol, an emergency notification system, self-defense education, and security escort services. There are shuttle buses, emergency telephones, lighted pathways/sidewalks, and controlled access to dorms/residences.

REQUIREMENTS: The SAT or ACT is required. Applicants should be graduates of an accredited secondary school and have 19 academic credits, 4 years each of English, social studies, mathematics, and science with lab, and 3-4 years of foreign language. The GED is accepted. AP and CLEP credits are accepted. Important factors in the admissions decision are advanced placement or honors courses, evidence of special talent, and personality/intangible qualities. Students must complete 122 semester hours, with 30 to 36 hours in the major. A minimum GPA of 2.0 (2.5 for education majors) must be maintained. In addition, students must complete a 36-hour general education requirement including courses in math, natural sciences, social sciences, American history, Western civilization, humanities, the arts, foreign language, and basic communications. Students must also pass a writing exam. **Procedure:** Freshmen are admitted in the fall and spring. Entrance exams should be taken in the spring of the junior year or the fall of the senior year. There are deferred admissions and rolling admissions plans. Application deadlines are open. The fall 2017 application fee was $40. Applications are accepted on-line. **Transfer Students:** 585 transfer students enrolled in 2016-2017. Official transcripts of all previous college work must be submitted. A minimum of 15 semester hours of transferable credit and a GPA of 2.0 (2.5 for education majors) are required. 45 of 122 credits required for the bachelor's degree must be completed at SUNY Oneonta. **International Students:** There are 111 international students enrolled. They must take the TOEFL with a minimum score of 500 on the paper-based TOEFL (PBT) or 61 on the Internet-based version (iBT).

ADMISSIONS: 53% of the 2017-2018 applicants were accepted. The SAT scores for the 2017-2018 freshman class were: Critical Reading-- 29% below 500, 55% between 500 and 599, 15% between 600 and 699, and 1% between 700 and 800. Math-- 25% below 500, 56% between 500 and 599, 18% between 600 and 699, and 1% between 700 and 800. The ACT scores were 3% between 12 and 17, 43% between 18 and 23, 50% between 24 and 29, and 4% above 30. **Admissions Contact:** Rebecca Lynch, Director of Admissions. Email: *admissions@oneonta.edu* Web: *www.oneonta.edu*

FINANCIAL AID: In 2017-2018, 83% of all full-time freshmen received some form of financial aid. 61% of all full-time freshmen received need-based aid. The average freshman award was $8,839. Need-based scholarships or need-based grants averaged $8,934; need-based self-help aid (loans and jobs) averaged $9,004; other non-need-based awards and non-need-based scholarships averaged $3,837; and $3,945 from other forms of aid. The average financial indebtedness of the 2017 graduate was $24,716. The state aid form is required. The FAFSA code is 002847. The priority date for freshman financial aid applications for fall entry is March 15.

STATE UNIVERSITY OF NEW YORK/ PLATTSBURGH D-2

www.plattsburgh.edu

Plattsburgh, NY 12901 **(518) 564-2040** **(888) 673-0012**

Fax: (518) 564-2045 **Email: admissions@plattsburgh.edu**

Full-time: 2311 men, 2875 women	**Faculty:** IIA, -$
Part-time: 159 men, 294 women	**Ph.D.s:** 81%
Graduate: 107 men, 305 women	**Student/Faculty:** 16 to 1
Year: semesters, summer session	**Tuition:** $8010 ($17,660)
Room & Board: $11,304	**Freshman Class:** 8139 applied, 3739 accepted, 954 enrolled
SAT CR/M: 525/535 **ACT:** required	**CEEB CODE:** 2844
Application Deadline: August 1	**COMPETITIVE**

State University of New York/Plattsburgh, founded in 1889, is a public institution offering degree programs in the liberal arts and professional programs. There are 3 undergraduate schools and 2 graduate schools. In addition to regional accreditation, SUNY Plattsburgh has baccalaureate program accreditation with AACSB, ADA, CSWE, and NLN. The 300-acre campus is in a suburban area 150 miles north of Albany, 25 miles west of Burlington, Vermont, and 65 miles south of Montreal, Canada. Including any residence halls, there are 36 buildings.

STUDENT LIFE: 90% of undergraduates are from New York. Others are from 27 states, 67 foreign countries, and Canada. 95% are from public schools. 8% are Hispanic; 71% White; 6% African American; 6% Foreign; 4% race unknown; 2% Asian American; 2% two or more races. **Female To Male Ratio:** 1.3:1. The average age of freshmen is 18; all undergraduates, 21. 22% do not continue beyond their first year; 61% remain to graduate. **Housing:** 2682 students can be accommodated in college housing, which includes dorms and on-campus apartments. In addition, there are special-interest houses, adult student halls/floors, wellness floors, and substance-free buildings. On-campus housing is available on a first-come, first-served basis, and is available on a lottery system for upperclassmen. 56% of students commute. All students may keep cars.

FACULTY/CLASSROOMS: 48% of faculty are male; 52% are female. All teach undergraduates and all do research. No introductory courses are taught by graduate students. The average class size in an introductory lecture is 27; in a laboratory is 17; and in a regular course is 24.

PROGRAMS OF STUDY: SUNY Plattsburgh confers B.A., B.S., B.F.A., and B.S.Ed. degrees. Master's degrees are also awarded. Bachelor's degrees are awarded in BIOLOGICAL SCIENCE (biochemistry, biology/adolescence education, biology/biological science, ecology, and nutrition), BUSINESS (accounting, business administration and management, entrepreneurial studies, finance, hotel/motel and restaurant management, international business management, management information systems, marketing/retailing/merchandising, and supply chain management), COMMUNICATIONS AND THE ARTS (art, communications, English, English literature, English writing, French, journalism, music, public relations, and Spanish), COMPUTER AND PHYSICAL SCIENCE (chemistry, chemistry/adolescence education, computer science, geology, mathematics, and physics), EDUCATION (English education, mathematics education, Spanish adolescense education, special education, and sports and wellness studies), ENGINEERING AND ENVIRONMENTAL DESIGN (environmental science), HEALTH PROFESSIONS (cytotechnology, medical laboratory technology, medical technology, and nursing), SOCIAL SCIENCE (anthropology, Canadian studies, child care/child and family studies, communication sciences and disorders, criminal justice, economics, French studies, gender studies, geography, history, home economics, human development, interdisciplinary studies, Latin American studies, philosophy, political science/government, psychology, social work, sociology, and women's studies). Adolescence education (physics), multimedia journalism, and global supply and chain management are the strongest academically. Psychology, education, and business have the largest enrollments.

ACTIVITIES: 6% of men belong to 1 local and 11 national fraternities; 5% of women belong to 1 local and 8 national sororities. There are 120 groups on campus, including art, band, cheerleading, choir, chorale, chorus, computers, dance, debate, drama, ethnic, film, honors, international, jazz band, LGBT, literary magazine, musical theater, newspaper, orchestra, pep band, photography, political, professional, radio and TV, religious, social, social service, student government, and yearbook. Popular campus events include volunteer opportunities (Relay for Life, Up 'til Dawn), Family Weekend, Night of Nations, Presidents Gala, Plattsburghs Best Dance Crew. and Plattsburgh's Got Talent Competitions. **Sports:** There are 7 intercollegiate sports for men and 8 for women, and 9 intramural sports for men and 9 for women. Facilities include an ice arena, a gym, an indoor track, soccer and volleyball areas, an indoor swimming pool, exercise and weight rooms, an aerobics studio, racquetball courts, lighted tennis courts, fields for softball, lacrosse, and rugby, and a fitness center. **Graduates:** From July 1, 2016 to June 30, 2017, 1417 bachelor's degrees were awarded. The most popular majors were business/marketing (22%), communication/journalism (10%), and education (10%). In an average class, 1% graduate in 3 years or less, 40% graduate in 4 years or less, 17% graduate in 5 years or less, and 1% graduate in 6 years or less. Of the 2016 graduating class, 12% were enrolled in graduate school within 6 months of graduation, and 79% were employed.

SERVICES: Counseling and information services are available, as is tutoring in every subject. There is a reader service for the blind, and remedial math, reading, and writing. **Library/Resources:** The library contains 541,609 volumes, 723,474 microform items, and 25,698 audio/video tapes/CDs/DVDs, and subscribes to 114,144 periodicals, including electronic. Computerized library services include interlibrary loans, database searching, Internet access, and Wi-Fi capability. Special learning facilities include an art gallery, a planetarium, radio and TV stations, an environmental science institute, a child care center, a research institute, a teacher resource center, a speech and hearing clinic, the Alzheimer's Disease Assistance Center, auditory research labs, a virtual reality simulator, and distance learning facilities. **Physically Challenged Students:** 95% of the campus is accessible. Facilities include wheelchair ramps, elevators, special parking, specially equipped restrooms, special class scheduling, lowered drinking fountains, lowered telephones, special housing, curb cuts, and electronic doors. **Special:** The college offers cross-registration with Clinton Community College and Empire State College, internships, study abroad in 10 countries, cooperative programs in all majors, B.A.-B.S. degrees, dual and student-designed majors, an accelerated degree program in any major except nursing, and B.A./M.S.T. and B.S./M.S.E.D. combined undergraduate and graduate programs. A 3-2 engineering degree is offered with SUNY Stony Brook and Binghamton, Clarkson, Syracuse, and McGill Universities, and the University of Vermont. There are 31 national honor societies and a freshman honors program. **Visiting:** There are regularly scheduled orientations for prospective students, including a group, student-led tour, and either a group or individual interview. Special overnight events for accepted freshmen include meals with students and faculty, classroom visits, discussions with faculty, and special workshops. There are guides for informal visits; visitors may sit in on classes and stay overnight. To schedule a visit, contact the Admissions Office. **Campus Safety and Security:** Measures include 24-hour foot and vehicle patrol, an emergency notification system, self-defense education, and security escort services. There are shuttle buses, emergency telephones, lighted pathways/sidewalks, controlled access to dorms/residences, bicycle patrols, combination locks on students room, a computerized keyless entry system for residence hall access, door viewers, and basement and ground-level security windows in residence halls.

REQUIREMENTS: The SAT or ACT is required. Applicants must have at least 12 academic credits, including 4 years of English, 5 combined years of math and science, and 3 years of social studies. An essay, portfolio, audition, and interview may be recommended in some programs. The GED is accepted. SUNY Plattsburgh requires applicants to be in the upper 50% of their class. AP and CLEP credits are accepted. Important factors in the admissions decision are advanced placement or honors courses, recommendations by school officials, and leadership record. To graduate, students must have a 2.0 GPA and complete at least 120 semester hours. Core curriculum courses total 41 to 46 credits. In addition, all students must demonstrate proficiency in writing by completion of English composition and an advanced writing requirement. Specific courses such as library research skills and computer science are offered. A comprehensive exam in some majors and a thesis in the upper-division honors program are required. Many majors require practicum and/or internship experience to complete a degree. **Procedure:** Freshmen are admitted in the fall and spring. Entrance exams should be taken during the second half of the junior year or the beginning of the senior year. There is a rolling admissions plan. Early decision applications should be filed by November 15; regular applications, by August 1 for fall entry; and November 1 for spring entry. The fall 2017 application fee was $50. Notification of early decision is sent December 15; regular decision, January 15. 310 applicants were on the 2017 waiting list; 26 were admitted. Applications are accepted online. **Transfer Students:** 612 transfer students enrolled in 2016-2017. Applicants must have a minimum 2.0 GPA. Most academic programs require a 2.5 GPA or better. 36 of 120 credits required for the bachelor's degree must be completed at Plattsburgh. **International Students:** There are 308 international students enrolled. They must take the TOEFL with a minimum score of 450 on the paper-based TOEFL (PBT) or 45 on the Internet-based version (iBT).

ADMISSIONS: 34% of the current freshmen were in the top fifth of their class; 75% were in the top two fifths. **Admissions Contact:** Jessica Fish, Director of Admissions. Email: *admissions@plattsburgh.edu* Web: *www.plattsburgh.edu*

FINANCIAL AID: In 2017-2018, 65% of all full-time freshmen received some form of financial aid. 58% of all full-time freshmen received need-based aid. The average freshman award was $11,845. Need-based scholarships or need-based grants averaged $7,093; need-based self-help aid (loans and jobs) averaged $6,510; and other non-need-based awards and non-need-based scholarships averaged $6,227. 34% of undergraduate students work part-time. The average financial indebtedness of the 2017 graduate was $26,894. The FAFSA code is 002849. The priority date for freshman financial aid applications for fall entry is February 15.

STATE UNIVERSITY OF NEW YORK/POTSDAM — D-2

www.potsdam.edu

Potsdam, NY 13676 — **(315) 267-2180**

Fax: (315) 267-2163	**Email:** admissions@potsdam.edu
Full-time: 1316 men, 1880 women	**Faculty:** 261; IIA, --$
Part-time: 68 men, 57 women	**Ph.D.s:** 84%
Graduate: 74 men, 186 women	**Student/Faculty:** 11 to 1
Year: semesters, summer session	**Tuition:** $8221 ($17,871)
Room & Board: $12,830	**Freshman Class:** 5581 applied, 3717 accepted, 783 enrolled
SAT CR/M: 600/590 **ACT:** 26	**CEEB CODE:** 2545
Application Deadline: rolling	**VERY COMPETITIVE**

State University of New York/Potsdam, founded in 1816, joined the State University System in 1948. SUNY Potsdam offers over 55 programs in Arts and Sciences, 6 in the Crane School of Music, and over 20 in the School of Education and Professional Studies as well as programs in Interdisciplinary Studies. Bachelor degrees are offered in Arts, Science, and Fine Arts and Music and master's degrees in Arts, Education, Science, and Music. There are 3 undergraduate schools and 1 graduate school. In addition to regional accreditation, SUNY/Potsdam has baccalaureate program accreditation with NASM, NAST, ICABE, and AAAHC. The 240-acre campus is in a rural area 30 miles from Massena and Ogdensburg, and 140 miles northeast of Syracuse and 80 miles from Montreal, Canada. Including any residence halls, there are 56 buildings.

STUDENT LIFE: 95% of undergraduates are from New York. Others are from 30 states, 6 foreign countries, and Canada. 85% are from public schools. 61% are White; 15% Hispanic; 13% African American; 4% race unknown; 3% two or more races; 2% Asian American; 2% American Indian/Alaska Native; 1% Foreign. **Female To Male Ratio:** 1.5:1. The average age of freshmen is 18; all undergraduates, 20. 25% do not continue beyond their first year; 54% remain to graduate. **Housing:** 2713 students can be accommodated in college housing, which includes coed dorms, on-campus apartments, and off-campus apartments. In addition, there are special-interest houses, study intensive housing, transfer student housing, gender neutral housing, and academic year housing. On-campus housing is guaranteed for all 4 years. 58% of students live on campus. All students may keep cars.

FACULTY/CLASSROOMS: 48% of faculty are male; 52% are female. All teach undergraduates. No introductory courses are taught by graduate students.

PROGRAMS OF STUDY: SUNY Potsdam confers B.A., B.F.A., B.M., and B.S. degrees. Master's degrees are also awarded. Bachelor's degrees are awarded in AGRICULTURE (environmental studies), BIOLOGICAL SCIENCE (biochemistry and biology/biological science), BUSINESS (business administration and management and business economics), COMMUNICATIONS AND THE ARTS (art history, art, art history and appreciation, communications, creative writing, dance, English, French, graphic design, music, music business management, music composition, music performance, Spanish, communication arts-speech, studio art, theatre arts, and visual and performing arts), COMPUTER AND PHYSICAL SCIENCE (chemistry, computer science, earth science/adolescence education, geology, mathematics, and physics), EDUCATION (art education, early childhood education, education, English education, mathematics education, music education, science education, social studies education, and Spanish adolescense education), HEALTH PROFESSIONS (community health work and exercise science), SOCIAL SCIENCE (anthropology, archeology, criminal justice, early childhood studies, economics, French studies, history, interdisciplinary studies, philosophy, political science/government, psychology, sociology, and women's studies). Psychology, education, and visual/performing arts have the largest enrollments.

ACTIVITIES: 4% of men belong to 1 local and 2 national fraternities; 9% of women belong to 5 local and 2 national sororities. There are 87 groups on campus, including art, band, cheerleading, choir, chorale, chorus, communications, computers, dance, drama, environmental, environmental awareness, ethnic, honors, international, jazz band, LGBT, literary magazine, musical theater, newspaper, opera, orchestra, photography, political, professional, radio and TV, religious, social, social service, student government, and symphony. Popular campus events include Welcome Weekend Carnival, Spring Fest, and Crane Candlelight Concert. **Sports:** There are 9 intercollegiate sports for men and 10 for women, and 10 intramural sports for men and 9 for women. Facilities include a 50-foot rock climbing wall, a full high ropes course and bouldering cave, a fitness center with treadmills, spin cycles, ellipticals, strength equipment, free weights, a gymnasium, hockey rink, an Olympic-size swimming pool with a diving well, a field house with an indoor track, basketball, volleyball, indoor lacrosse courts, racquetball courts, squash courts, a dance studio, a physical therapy/training room, tennis, basketball, a quarter-mile track plus, and fields for softball, soccer, lacrosse, and intramural competition. **Graduates:** From July 1, 2016 to June 30, 2017, 757 bachelor's degrees were awarded. The most popular majors were visual and performing arts (15%), education (12%), and psychology (10%). In an average class, 34% graduate in 4 years or less, 50% graduate in 5 years or less, and 53% graduate in 6 years or less. Of the 2016 graduating class, 55% were enrolled in graduate school within 6 months of graduation, and 41% were employed.

SERVICES: Counseling and information services are available, as is tutoring in every subject. There is a reader service for the blind. There are math labs and a writing center available. **Library/Resources:** The library contains 510,359 volumes, and 6,920 audio/video tapes/CDs/DVDs, and subscribes to 166 periodicals, including electronic. Computerized library services include interlibrary loans, database searching, Internet access, and Wi-Fi capability. Special learning facilities include a natural history museum, a planetarium, a radio station, electronic music and recording studios, a seismographic laboratory, an anthropology museum, a biology museum, Learning and Teaching Excellence Center located in Crumb Library, six fine arts studios, an art museum that includes the Gibson Gallery, and the Hosmer Hall Gallery. Also included is the Performing Arts Center which includes an education lab, digital/audio lab, design/drafting lab, CAD lab, lighting lab, movement studios, recording studio, scene/costume/craft shop key performance spaces-proscenium theater, black box theater, and a dance performance hall. **Physically Challenged Students:** 95% of the campus is accessible. Facilities include wheelchair ramps, elevators, special parking, specially equipped restrooms, special class scheduling, lowered drinking fountains, lowered telephones, special housing, and electric doors. **Special:** Cross-registration is offered with Clarkson University, St. Lawrence University, and SUNY Canton. 600 internships are available in over 50 countries. SUNY Postdam also offers work-study opportunities, a 3-2 engineering degree with Clarkson University, study abroad, 3-2 management and accounting degrees, student-designed majors, dual majors in interdisciplinary natural science, nondegree study, and pass/fail options, as well as handcrafted education for students who enroll in the Honors Program or engage in Research through the UG Research and Presidential Scholars programs. There are 21 national honor societies and 6 departmental honors programs. **Visiting:** There are regularly scheduled orientations for prospective students consisting of individual campus visit Monday through Friday; high school juniors and seniors, and transfer students will all benefit from our Open House Programs. There are guides for informal visits and visitors may sit in on classes. To schedule a visit, contact the Admissions Office, Lisa Martin, at visit@potsdam.edu. **Campus Safety and Security:** Measures include 24-hour foot and vehicle patrol, emergency notification system, self-defense education, and security escort services. There are emergency telephones, lighted pathways/sidewalks, controlled access to dorms/residences, and a safety app: Rave Guardian video surveillance system.

REQUIREMENTS: Applicants must be high school graduates in a college preparatory program or hold a GED. 4 years each of English and social studies, 3 years each of math, foreign language, and science, and 1 year of art or music are recommended. An interview is important; an audition when appropriate is required. The majority of our applicants will not have to submit an SAT or ACT score. If students would like to have their scores submitted as part of their application, they must request their scores be sent directly from the testing agency. Also, students must submit an SAT or ACT score to be considered for Potsdam's Mount Emmons Scholarship. Minimum scores for scholarship consideration are a 1300 on the SAT or a 29 on the ACT. AP and CLEP credits are accepted. Important factors in the admissions decision are recommendations by school officials, extracurricular activities record, and parents or siblings attended the school. To graduate, students must complete a major and earn at least a 2.0 in 30 hours of their major coursework (some majors have higher standards). 15 of those 30 hours must be upper division (U.D.)--level 300 or higher--and for transfer students at least 15 U.D. hours must be taken at SUNY Potsdam. 120 credits + 4 P.E. credits (for the B.A., B.F.A., and B.S.), 120-130 credits + 4 P.E. credits (for B.M.), Thus, in order to graduate in 4 years (8 semesters) students need to take at least 16 credit hours per semester. The college allows students to take 12 credit hours and still maintain full-time student status. This may work well for some students, however, unless classes are taken during the summer or winterim sessions, a student taking less than 15 credits per semester cannot graduate in 4 years. A certain number of your 120 credits must be designated as liberal arts credits. Student must complete the general education requirements, and graduate with an overall GPA of 2.0. Out of the total 120 credits, 45 of those must be designated as upper division courses (level 300 or higher). **Procedure:** Freshmen are admitted in the fall and spring. Entrance exams should be taken in the junior year or early senior year. There are early admissions, deferred admissions, and rolling admissions plans. Application deadlines are open. The fall 2017 application fee was $50. Notifications are sent October 1. Applications are accepted online. **Transfer Students:** 259 transfer students enrolled in 2016-2017. Applicants must have earned 12 hours of college credit. Transfers with fewer than 24 credit hours must submit a high school transcript. A college transcript, an essay (required of some) or a personal statement are required. 30 of 124 credits required for the bachelor's degree must be completed at SUNY Potsdam. **International Students:** There are 23 international students enrolled. They must take the TOEFL with a minimum score of 550 on the paper-based TOEFL (PBT) or 79 on the Internet-based version (iBT), and take the IELTS.

ADMISSIONS: 67% of the 2017-2018 applicants were accepted. The SAT scores for the 2017-2018 freshman class were: Math-- 24% below 500, 56% between 500 and 599, 19% between 600 and 699, and 2% between 700 and 800. Evidence-Based Reading/Writing-- 23% below 500, 50% between 500 and 599, 23% between 600 and 699, and 3% between 700 and 800. The ACT scores were 10% between 12 and 17, 45% between 18 and 23, 37% between 24 and 29, and 9% above 30. **Admissions Contact:** Thomas Nesbitt, Director of Admissions. Email: *admissions@potsdam.edu* Web: *www.potsdam.edu*

FINANCIAL AID: In 2017-2018, 95% of all full-time freshmen received

some form of financial aid. 83% of all full-time freshmen received need-based aid. The average freshman award was $16,880. Need-based scholarships or need-based grants averaged $8,553 ($23,681 maximum); need-based self-help aid (loans and jobs) averaged $4,080 ($10,800 maximum); and other non-need-based awards and non-need-based scholarships averaged $2,647 ($13,000 maximum). The average financial indebtedness of the 2017 graduate was $26,438. The state aid form is required. The FAFSA code is 002850. The priority date for freshman financial aid applications for fall entry is March 1.

STATE UNIVERSITY OF NEW YORK/THE COLLEGE OF ENVIRONMENTAL SCIENCE AND FORESTRY C-3

www.esf.edu

Syracuse, NY 13210 **(315) 470-6600**

Fax: (315) 470-6933 **Email: esfinfo@esf.edu**

Full-time: 919 men, 825 women
Part-time: 95 men, 105 women
Graduate: 209 men, 221 women
Year: semesters
Room & Board: $15,160

Faculty: 128; I, -$
Ph.D.s: 77%
Student/Faculty: 13 to 1
Tuition: $8568 ($18,218)
Freshman Class: 1818 applied, 955 accepted, 329 enrolled

SAT CR/M/W: 622/615/555 **ACT:** 26
Application Deadline: February 1

CEEB CODE: 2530
VERY COMPETITIVE

State University of New York/The College of Environmental Science and Forestry, founded in 1911, is the nation's oldest and largest college focused exclusively on the science, design, engineering, and management of our environment and natural resources. The college offers 21 undergraduate and 28 graduate degree programs, including 8 Ph.D. programs. Students also benefit from a special partnership with Syracuse University (SU) that provides access to courses, housing, and student organizations. There is 1 undergraduate school and 1 graduate school. In addition to regional accreditation, SUNY/The College of Environmental Science and Forestry has baccalaureate program accreditation with ABET, ASLA, SAF, and EHAC. The 12-acre campus is in an urban area in Syracuse, NY. Including any residence halls, there are 7 buildings.

STUDENT LIFE: 77% of undergraduates are from New York. Others are from 25 states and 3 foreign countries. 79% are White; 7% Hispanic; 5% race unknown; 4% Asian American; 3% two or more races; 2% African American; 1% Foreign. **Male To Female Ratio:** 1.1:1. The average age of freshmen is 18; all undergraduates, 21. 18% do not continue beyond their first year; 82% remain to graduate. **Housing:** 620 students can be accommodated in college housing, which includes dorms, on-campus apartments, and off-campus apartments. In addition, there are special-interest houses, fraternity houses, sorority houses, substance-free floors, quiet floors, and learning communities. On-campus housing is guaranteed for all 4 years and is available on a lottery system for upperclassmen. 65% of students commute. Alcohol is not permitted. Upperclassmen may keep cars.

FACULTY/CLASSROOMS: 70% of faculty are male; 30% are female. All teach undergraduates and all do research. No introductory courses are taught by graduate students. The average class size in an introductory lecture is 32; in a laboratory is 23; and in a regular course is 7.

PROGRAMS OF STUDY: SUNY/The College of Environmental Science and Forestry confers B.S. and B.L.A. degrees. Associate, master's, and doctoral degrees are also awarded. Bachelor's degrees are awarded in AGRICULTURE (animal science, environmental studies, fishing and fisheries, forest engineering, forestry and related sciences, natural resource management, plant science, soil science, and wood science), BIOLOGICAL SCIENCE (biology/biological science, biotechnology, botany, ecology, entomology, environmental biology, microbiology, molecular biology, plant genetics, plant pathology, plant physiology, and wildlife biology), COMPUTER AND PHYSICAL SCIENCE (chemistry and polymer science), EDUCATION (environmental education), ENGINEERING AND ENVIRONMENTAL DESIGN (chemical engineering, construction management, environmental design, environmental engineering, environmental science, landscape architecture/design, paper and pulp science, paper engineering, and survey and mapping technology), HEALTH PROFESSIONS (predentistry, premedicine, and pharmacy), SOCIAL SCIENCE (prelaw). Engineering, chemistry, and biology are the strongest academically. Biology, forest resource management, and environmental science have the largest enrollments.

ACTIVITIES: 2% of men belong to 20 national fraternities; 2% of women belong to 20 national sororities. There are 350 groups on campus, including art, bagpipe, band, cheerleading, choir, chorale, chorus, computers, dance, debate, drama, environmental, ethnic, film, honors, international, jazz band, LGBT, literary magazine, marching band, musical theater, newspaper, orchestra, pep band, photography, political, professional, radio and TV, religious, social, social service, student government, symphony, and yearbook. Popular campus events include Earth Week, Awards Banquet, and December Soiree. **Sports:** There are 6 intercollegiate sports for men and 5 for women, and 15 intramural sports for men and 15 for women. Facilities include soccer, golf, cross-country, and woodsmans teams. Students can participate in all Syracuse University club teams, intramural sports, and recreational activities. **Graduates:** From July 1, 2016 to June 30, 2017, 400 bachelor's degrees were awarded. The most popular majors were environmental/conservation biology (23%), natural resources management (11%), and environmental resources engineering (9%). In an average class, 1% graduate in 3 years or less, 57% graduate in 4 years or less, 74% graduate in 5 years or less, and 74% graduate in 6 years or less.

SERVICES: Counseling and information services are available, as is tutoring in most subjects. There is a reader service for the blind. **Library/Resources:** The library contains 137,381 volumes, 644 audio/video tapes/CDs/DVDs, and subscribes to 1,741 periodicals, including electronic. Computerized library services include interlibrary loans, database searching, Internet access, and Wi-Fi capability. Special learning facilities include an art gallery, a natural history museum, a radio station, and a TV station. Regarding microform items in the library collection: As this is no longer disaggregated from media for ACRL/IPEDS reporting purposes, it is not available as a distinct metric for our institutional library. **Physically Challenged Students:** 95% of the campus is accessible. Facilities include wheelchair ramps, elevators, special parking, specially equipped restrooms, lowered drinking fountains, lowered telephones, and special housing. **Special:** Cross-registration is offered with Syracuse University. Co-op programs, internships, and dual options in forest ecosystem science are available. Study abroad is available in landscape architecture and through Syracuse University. There is an Honors Program for outstanding students. There is 1 national honor society, a freshman honors program, and 8 departmental honors programs. **Visiting:** There are regularly scheduled orientations for prospective students, including a fall open house, which provides campus tours, faculty sessions, an activities fair, and student affairs presentations. There are guides for informal visits and visitors may sit in on classes. To schedule a visit, contact the Admissions Office at esfinfo@esf.edu. **Campus Safety and Security:** Measures include 24-hour foot and vehicle patrol, an emergency notification system, self-defense education, and security escort services. There are shuttle buses, emergency telephones, lighted pathways/sidewalks, and controlled access to dorms/residences.

REQUIREMENTS: The SAT or ACT is required. Applicants are required to have a minimum of 3 years of math and science, including chemistry, in a college preparatory curriculum. A supplemental application form, an essay, and results from SAT or ACT exams are required. A campus visit, letters of recommendation, and a personal portfolio or resume are also recommended. AP and CLEP credits are accepted. Important factors in the admissions decision are advanced placement or honors courses, leadership record, and extracurricular activities record. Students must complete 125 to 130 credit hours for the B.S. (160 for the B.L.A.), including 60 in the major, with a minimum 2.0 GPA. Courses in chemistry, English, math, and biology or physics are required. **Procedure:** Freshmen are admitted in the fall and spring. Entrance exams should be taken by October of the senior year. There are early decision, deferred admissions, and rolling admissions plans. Early decision applications should be filed by December 1; regular applications, by February 1 for fall entry; and November 1 for spring entry. The fall 2017 application fee was $50. Notification of early decision is sent December 15; regular decision, March 1. 148 early decision candidates were accepted for the 2017-2018 class. 203 applicants were on the 2017 waiting list; 32 were admitted. Applications are accepted online. **Transfer Students:** 241 transfer students enrolled in 2016-2017. Transfer requirements vary by major. Students must successfully complete prerequisite coursework and must have a 2.5 or higher GPA to be considered. 24 of 125 credits required for the bachelor's degree must be completed at SUNY/The College of Environmental Science and Forestry. **International Students:** There are 25 international students enrolled. They must take the TOEFL with a minimum score of 550 on the paper-based TOEFL (PBT) or 79 on the Internet-based version (iBT). They must also take the SAT or ACT.

ADMISSIONS: 62% of the current freshmen were in the top fifth of their class; 94% were in the top two fifths. **Admissions Contact:** Thomas Fletcher, Associate Director of Admissions. Email: *esfinfo@esf.edu* Web: *www.esf.edu*

FINANCIAL AID: The state aid form is required. The FAFSA code is 002851. The priority date for freshman financial aid applications for fall entry is February 1.

STATE UNIVERSITY OF NEW YORK/ UNIVERSITY AT BUFFALO — A-3

www.buffalo.edu

Buffalo, NY 14214 — **(716) 645-6900**

Fax: (716) 645-6411 — **Email:** ubadmissions@buffalo.edu

Full-time: 10,878 men, 7998 women	**Faculty:** n/av
Part-time: 719 men, 816 women	**Ph.D.s:** 100%
Graduate: 4773 men, 4999 women	**Student/Faculty:** 13 to 1
Year: semesters, summer session	**Tuition:** $9574 ($26,814)
Room & Board: $13,548	**Freshman Class:** n/av
SAT or ACT: required	**CEEB CODE:** 2533
Application Deadline: rolling	**COMPETITIVE**

State University of New York/University at Buffalo, established in 1846, is a public institution offering more than 300 bachelor's, master's, and doctoral degree programs. UB is a comprehensive research-extensive university and the largest campus in the State University of New York system. There are 8 undergraduate schools and 12 graduate schools. In addition to regional accreditation, SUNY University at Buffalo has baccalaureate program accreditation with AACSB, ABET, ACPE, ADA, APTA, CSWE, NAAB, NASAD, ABA, ACCNE, ACOTE, CCNE, COA, LCME, APA, ASHA, JRCNM, ACS, ACEND, CORE, ASHP, NAACLS, CEPH, PAB, ACGME, and ALA. The 1350-acre campus is in a suburban area 3 miles north of Buffalo. Including any residence halls, there are 195 buildings.

STUDENT LIFE: 97% of undergraduates are from New York. Others are from 50 states, 87 foreign countries, and Canada. 48% are White; 16% Foreign; 14% Asian American; 7% African American; 7% Hispanic; 5% race unknown; 2% two or more races; 1% American Indian/Alaska Native. **Male To Female Ratio:** 1.2:1. The average age of freshmen is 18; all undergraduates, 21. 14% do not continue beyond their first year. **Housing:** 7328 students can be accommodated in college housing, which includes married student dorms and on-campus apartments. In addition, there are honors houses, special-interest houses, freshmen-only housing, and cultural interest housing. On-campus housing is guaranteed for all 4 years, is guaranteed for the freshman year only, is available on a first-come, first-served basis, and is available on a lottery system for upperclassmen. 62% of students commute. All students may keep cars.

FACULTY/CLASSROOMS: 60% of faculty are male; 40% are female. No introductory courses are taught by graduate students.

PROGRAMS OF STUDY: SUNY University at Buffalo confers B.A., B.S., B.F.A., and Mus.B. degrees. Master's and doctoral degrees are also awarded. Bachelor's degrees are awarded in AGRICULTURE (environmental studies), BIOLOGICAL SCIENCE (biochemistry, bioinformatics, biology/biological science, biophysics, and biotechnology), BUSINESS (accounting and business administration and management), COMMUNICATIONS AND THE ARTS (art history and appreciation, classics, communications, dance, English, film arts, fine arts, French, German, Italian, linguistics, media arts, music, music performance, musical theater, Spanish, studio art, and theatre arts), COMPUTER AND PHYSICAL SCIENCE (chemistry, computer science, environmental geology, geology, informatics and computer science, mathematics, mathematics-economics, physics, and statistics), EDUCATION (global studies), ENGINEERING AND ENVIRONMENTAL DESIGN (aerospace studies, architecture, biomedical engineering, chemical engineering, civil engineering, computational sciences, computer engineering, electrical/electronics engineering, engineering physics, environmental design, environmental engineering, industrial engineering, and mechanical engineering), HEALTH PROFESSIONS (biomedical science, exercise science, medical technology, nuclear medical technology, nursing, occupational therapy, pharmaceutical science, pharmacology, pharmacy, and speech pathology/audiology), SOCIAL SCIENCE (African American studies, American studies, anthropology, Asian/Oriental studies, economics, geography, geography information science, history, philosophy, political science/government, psychology, social science, and sociology). Engineering, business administration, and psychology have the largest enrollments.

ACTIVITIES: 2% of men belong to 1 local and 20 national fraternities; 2% of women belong to 14 national sororities. There are 651 groups on campus, including art, band, cheerleading, chess, choir, chorale, chorus, computers, dance, debate, drama, drill team, environmental, ethnic, film, honors, international, jazz band, LGBT, literary magazine, marching band, musical theater, newspaper, opera, orchestra, pep band, photography, political, professional, radio and TV, religious, social, social service, student government, and symphony. Popular campus events include Homecoming, Family Weekend, and Fallfest. **Sports:** There are 9 intercollegiate sports for men and 9 for women, and 8 intramural sports for men and 8 for women. Facilities include badminton, baseball, basketball, boxing, crew, cricket, cross-country, gymnastics, ice hockey, lacrosse, roller hockey, rugby, skiing, soccer, Tae Kwon Do, volleyball, an indoor jogging track, an Olympic-size pool and diving well, tennis, weight training and wrestling rooms, dance studios, a spinning room, and ultimate frisbee. **Graduates:** From July 1, 2016 to June 30, 2017, 5379 bachelor's degrees were awarded. The most popular majors were business marketing (19%), social sciences (16%), and engineering (14%). In an average class, 55% graduate in 4 years or less, 70% graduate in 5 years or less, and 74% graduate in 6 years or less. Of the 2016 graduating class, 36% were enrolled in graduate school within 6 months of graduation, and 47% were employed.

SERVICES: Counseling and information services are available, as is tutoring in most subjects, such as note-taking services, readers, tutors, text on tape, tape recorders, and extended time for tests. There is a reader service for the blind, and remedial math, reading, and writing. Peer tutoring and some computer-assisted instruction are also available. **Library/Resources:** The library contains 4.2 million volumes, 6.2 million microform items, and 285,659 audio/video tapes/CDs/DVDs, and subscribes to 162,556 periodicals, including electronic. Computerized library services include interlibrary loans, database searching, Internet access, and Wi-Fi capability. Special learning facilities include an art gallery, radio station, TV station, UB Art Gallery at the Center for the Arts, Slee Concert Hall, Marian E. White Anthropology Research Museum, the School of Pharmacy and Pharmaceutical Sciences Apothecary and Historical Exhibits, the Museum of Radiology and Medical Physics, the Museum of Neuroanatomy, Anderson Gallery, New York State Center of Excellence in Bioinformatics & Life Sciences (CBLS), Center for Computational Research (CCR), Center of Excellence for Document Analysis and Recognition (CEDAR), Center of Excellence in Materials Informatics, Buffalo Clinical and Translational Research Center (CTRC), New York State Center for Engineering Design and Industrial Innovation (NYSCEDII), Electronic Poetry Center, the Archaeological Survey, and numerous research centers. **Physically Challenged Students:** 90% of the campus is accessible. Facilities include wheelchair ramps, elevators, special parking, specially equipped restrooms, special class scheduling, lowered drinking fountains, lowered telephones, and special housing. **Special:** Students may cross-register with the Western New York Consortium. Internships are available, and students may study abroad in 29 countries. UB offers a Washington semester, work-study programs, accelerated degree programs, B.A.-B.S. degrees, dual, student-designed, and interdisciplinary majors, and credit for military experience. A 3-2 engineering degree can be pursued. Students may choose a successful/unsuccessful (S/U) grading option for selected courses. There is an early assurance of admission program to medical school for undergraduate sophomore students who possess a minimum approximate overall and science GPA of 3.75 and complete particular science courses. There are 34 national honor societies, Phi Beta Kappa, and a freshman honors program. **Visiting:** There are regularly scheduled orientations for prospective students, including the Visit UB program, in which visitors tour the campus and attend an information session to learn about application procedures, admissions criteria, housing, financial aid, and scholarship programs. The program is offered, with some exceptions, Monday through Friday year-round and on selected Saturdays during the academic year. Reservations are required. Visitors may sit in on classes. To schedule a visit, contact the Office of Admissions. **Campus Safety and Security:** Measures include 24-hour foot and vehicle patrol, emergency notification system, self-defense education, and security escort services. There are shuttle buses, emergency telephones, lighted pathways/sidewalks, controlled access to dorms/residences, an alarm system, routine patrols, student aides in residence halls, some security cameras, blue-light phones, and a university-wide safety committee.

REQUIREMENTS: The SAT is required. Freshmen are evaluated based on secondary school performance, strength of curriculum, standardized test scores, and, in some cases, a supplemental application. A high school diploma is required and the GED is accepted. Dance, and music theatre applicants must audition. Architecture requires a portfolio. Recommended 17 academic units include: 4 each of English and social studies, and 3 each of math, science, and foreign language. AP and CLEP credits are accepted. Important factors in the admissions decision are advanced placement or honors courses, leadership record, recommendations by school officials, parents or siblings attended your school, evidence of special talent, personality/intangible qualities, extracurricular activities record, recommendations by alumni, and geographical diversity. To graduate, students must complete 120 semester hours with a minimum GPA of 2.0. General education requirements include writing skills, mathematical sciences, library skills, world civilizations, American pluralism, natural sciences, language, humanities, arts, social and behavioral sciences, and depth requirement. The total number of hours in the major varies. **Procedure:** Freshmen are admitted in the fall and spring. Entrance exams should be taken during the spring of the junior year or the fall of the senior year. There are early admissions and rolling admissions plans. Early decision applications should be filed by November 1. The fall 2017 application fee was $50. Notifications are sent in February. Applications are accepted online. **Transfer Students:** 1862 transfer students enrolled in 2016-2017. Transfer applicants with fewer than 24 credit hours must supply high school transcripts, SAT and/or ACT test scores, and the previous college academic record. It is recommended that students present a strong record of college study, with a 2.5 GPA. Entry at the junior level requires a higher GPA for some programs. Credit may be awarded for military experience and other nontraditional sources. 30 of 120 credits required for the bachelor's degree must be completed at SUNY University at Buffalo. **International Students:** There are 2683 international students enrolled. They must take the TOEFL with a minimum score of 550 on the paper-based TOEFL (PBT) or 79 on the Internet-based version (iBT). The SAT or ACT is strongly recommended.

Admissions Contact: Jose Aviles, Director of Admissions. Email: *ubadmissions@buffalo.edu* Web: *www.buffalo.edu*

FINANCIAL AID: In 2017-2018, 60% of all full-time freshmen received some form of financial aid. 46% of all full-time freshmen received need-based aid. The average freshman award was $10,577. Need-based scholarships or need-based grants averaged $7,952; need-based self-help aid (loans and jobs) averaged $3,320; non-need-based athletic scholarships averaged $16,984; and other non-need-based awards and non-need-based scholarships averaged $4,075. SUNY at Buffalo is a member of CSS. The FAFSA code is 002837. The priority date for freshman financial aid applications for fall entry is March 1.

STONY BROOK UNIVERSITY/THE STATE UNIVERSITY OF NEW YORK — E-5

www.stonybrook.edu

Stony Brook, NY 11794 — (631) 632-6868

Fax: 631) 632-9898	**Email:** enroll@stonybrook.edu
Full-time: 8630 men, 7582 women	**Faculty:** 1075; I, av$
Part-time: 628 men, 524 women	**Ph.D.s:** 91%
Graduate: 3655 men, 4970 women	**Student/Faculty:** 18 to 1
Year: semesters, summer session	**Tuition:** $9257 ($26,767)
Room & Board: $13,446	**Freshman Class:** 35313 applied, 14899 accepted, 3167 enrolled
SAT EBR-W/M: 650/680 **ACT:** 29	**CEEB CODE:** 2548
Application Deadline: January 15	**MOST COMPETITIVE**

Stony Brook University, founded in 1957, and part of the State University of New York, is a public institution offering degree programs in arts and sciences, engineering and applied sciences, business, journalism, atmospheric and marine sciences, sustainability studies, public health, nursing, health technology and management, and social work. A number of accelerated bachelor's/master's degree programs also are offered, as well as professional programs in medicine and dental medicine at the graduate level. There are 8 undergraduate schools and 12 graduate schools. In addition to regional accreditation, SBU has baccalaureate program accreditation with ABET, ADA, APTA, CSWE, CAEP, ACS, APA, PCAS, CAATE, AAMC, ACOTE, ASPT, ACME, CAPTE, ARC-PA, CAAHEP, CoARC, LCME, CEPH, NAACLS, ACGME, ACEND, CCNE, ACNM, APTA, CODA, ACEJMC, and JRCERT. The 1454-acre campus is in a suburban area on Long Island, 55 miles from New York City. Including any residence halls, there are 215 buildings.

STUDENT LIFE: 80% of undergraduates are from New York. Others are from 41 states, 131 foreign countries, and Canada. 89% are from public schools. 7% are African American; 6% race unknown; 33% White; 3% two or more races; 24% Asian American; 15% Foreign; 12% Hispanic. **Female To Male Ratio:** 1.0:1. The average age of freshmen is 18; all undergraduates, 21. 10% do not continue beyond their first year; 72% remain to graduate. **Housing:** 10,301 students can be accommodated in college housing, which includes married student dorms and on-campus apartments. In addition, there are honors houses, and special-interest houses, and a choice of undergraduate colleges that integrate academic experience with living environments. On-campus housing is guaranteed for all 4 years. 53% of students live on campus. Alcohol is not permitted. Upperclassmen may keep cars.

FACULTY/CLASSROOMS: 59% of faculty are male; 41% are female. No introductory courses are taught by graduate students. The average class size in an introductory lecture is 38; in a laboratory is 21; and in a regular course is 33.

PROGRAMS OF STUDY: SBU confers B.A., B.S., and B.E. degrees. Master's and doctoral degrees are also awarded. Bachelor's degrees are awarded in AGRICULTURE (environmental studies), BIOLOGICAL SCIENCE (biochemistry, biology/biological science, human evolutionary biology, marine vertebrate biology, and marine science), BUSINESS (business administration and management), COMMUNICATIONS AND THE ARTS (Africana studies, art history, comparative literature, English, French language and literature, Germanic languages and literature, journalism, linguistics, music, Russian languages and literature, Spanish language and literature, studio art, and theatre arts), COMPUTER AND PHYSICAL SCIENCE (applied mathematics, astronomy, chemistry, clinical laboratory science, computer science, earth and space science, geology, information sciences and systems, mathematics, and physics), EDUCATION (athletic training), ENGINEERING AND ENVIRONMENTAL DESIGN (biomedical engineering, chemical engineering, civil engineering, computer engineering, electrical/electronics engineering, engineering chemistry, engineering science, environmental design, environmental science, mechanical engineering, and technological management), HEALTH PROFESSIONS (health science, multidisciplinary studies, polysomnographic technology, nursing, pharmacology, respiratory therapy, and respiratory care), SOCIAL SCIENCE (American studies, anthropology, Asian/American studies, economics, European studies, French studies, history, interdisciplinary studies, Italian studies, liberal arts/general studies, philosophy, political science/government, psychology, religious studies, social work, sociology, Spanish studies, and women and gender studies). Biology, business management, and economics are the strongest academically. Biology, health science, and psychology have the largest enrollments.

ACTIVITIES: 2% of men belong to 1 local and 21 national fraternities; 2% of women belong to 2 local and 13 national sororities. There are 353 groups on campus, including band, cheerleading, chess, choir, chorale, computers, dance, debate, drama, environmental, ethnic, film, forensics, honors, international, jazz band, LGBT, literary magazine, marching band, musical theater, newspaper, opera, orchestra, pep band, photography, political, professional, radio and TV, religious, social, social service, student government, and symphony. Popular campus events include Fall Fest, Opening Week Activities, and Caribbean Weekend. **Sports:** There are 7 intercollegiate sports for men and 9 for women, and 12 intramural sports for men and 12 for women. Facilities include a sports complex that houses an arena, a gym, a swimming pool, squash and racquetball courts, a dance studio, and exercise and universal gym rooms. Outdoor facilities include softball, baseball, tennis, multi-sport practice facilities, basketball and handball courts, softball fields, and a multi-sport recreational area. **Graduates:** From July 1, 2016 to June 30, 2017, 4289 bachelor's degrees were awarded. The most popular majors were health sciences (11%), biology (10%), and psychology (10%). In an average class, 2% graduate in 3 years or less, 53% graduate in 4 years or less, 69% graduate in 5 years or less, and 71% graduate in 6 years or less.

SERVICES: There is a reader service for the blind, and remedial math and writing. **Library/Resources:** The library contains 2.3 million volumes, 3.5 million microform items, and 35,371 audio/video tapes/CDs/DVDs, and subscribes to 103,035 periodicals, including electronic. Computerized library services include interlibrary loans, database searching, Internet access, and Wi-Fi capability. Special learning facilities include an art gallery, radio station, TV station, the Centers for Molecular Medicine and Biology Learning Laboratories, the Institute for Advanced Computational Science, the Louis and Beatrice Laufer Center for Physical and Quantitative Biology, the Marine Sciences Center at Southampton, the Center for Planetary Exploration, Stony Brook University Hospital, the Staller Center for the Arts, and the School of Journalism's newsroom, affording students the opportunity to work across multiple multimedia platforms. **Physically Challenged Students:** All of the campus is accessible. Facilities include wheelchair ramps, elevators, special parking, specially equipped restrooms, special class scheduling, lowered drinking fountains, lowered telephones, and special housing. **Special:** The university offers a variety of internships, including internships in the arts, business and government, with hospitals and clinics, and in legal and social agencies. The URECA Program promotes undergraduate research and creative projects both on and off campus including nearby Brookhaven National Laboratory, which Stony Brook University has a role in running. A fast-track MBA program and more than thirty additional combined degree programs are available to undergraduates. Scholars for Medicine and Scholars for Dental Medicine are highly selective programs in which a small number of freshmen are admitted to 8-year combined-degree programs in medicine and dental medicine. Women in Science and Engineering, the Honors College, and University Scholars programs provide additional experiences to challenge, inspire, and sustain SBU's most academically talented students. Students may declare double majors or pursue dual degrees. The multidisciplinary studies major is student-designed. Students have the opportunity to study at another college or university through the national student exchange program or SBU's study-abroad programs in more than 30 countries, including China, New Zealand, France, Sweden, Taiwan, Denmark, England, Korea, Madagascar, Australia, Costa Rica, Jamaica, Tanzania, Kenya, Spain, Norway, Russia, Japan, Italy, Greece, and Germany. Cross-registration may be arranged through the Long Island Regional Advisory Council for Higher Education. There are 16 national honor societies, Phi Beta Kappa, a freshman honors program, and 35 departmental honors programs. **Visiting:** There are regularly scheduled orientations for prospective students, including informative sessions about campus life. There are guides for informal visits and visitors may sit in on classes. To schedule a visit, contact the Admissions Office. **Campus Safety and Security:** Measures include 24-hour foot and vehicle patrol, emergency notification system, self-defense education, and security escort services. There are shuttle buses, emergency telephones, lighted pathways/sidewalks, controlled access to dorms/residences, a campus crime stoppers program, building access through use of cards, and controlled campus access after midnight.

REQUIREMENTS: The SAT is required. Applicants must be graduates of an accredited secondary school or have a GED certificate. 16 or 17 academic credits are required, including 4 years each of English and social studies, 3 or 4 years of math (4 for STEM majors, 3 years of science (4 for STEM majors), and 2 or 3 years of foreign language. One letter of recommendation and supplemental application, including an essay, are required AP and CLEP credits are accepted. Important factors in the admissions decision are advanced placement or honors courses, extracurricular activities record, and evidence of special talent. To graduate, students must have a minimum 2.0 GPA in 120 credit hours (B.A. and B.S.) or 128 (B.E.). The required number of hours in the major varies. At least 39 credits must be earned in upper-division courses. Students must complete the SBU's general education requirements, through which they are expected to demonstrate versatility, explore interconnectedness, pursue deeper understanding, and prepare for life-long learning. Arts and sciences majors must fulfill a foreign language requirement, unless completed through advanced high-school study. Other requirements vary by school. **Procedure:** Freshmen are admitted in the fall and spring. Entrance exams should be taken during the junior year or in the fall of the senior year. There is a deferred admissions plan. Applications should be filed by January 15 for fall entry; November 1 for spring entry. The fall 2017 application fee was $50. Notifications are sent April 1. 3778 applicants were on the 2017 waiting list; 68 were admitted. Applications are accepted online. **Transfer Students:** 2423 transfer students enrolled in 2016-2017. Applicants must have a minimum 3.0 GPA. Applicants who have earned fewer than 24 college credits must submit a high school transcript and standardized test scores. 36 of 120 credits required for the bachelor's degree must be completed at SBU. **International Students:** There are 2504 international students enrolled. They must take the TOEFL with a minimum score of 550 on the paper-based TOEFL (PBT) or 80 on the Internet-based version (iBT). Student must take either the IELTS, or the SAT Critical Reading.

ADMISSIONS: 42% of the 2017-2018 applicants were accepted. The SAT scores for the 2017-2018 freshman class were: Math-- 10% between 500 and 599, 46% between 600 and 699, and 44% between 700 and 800. Evidence-Based Reading/Writing-- 15% between 500 and 599, 63% between 600 and 699, and 22% between 700 and 800. The ACT scores were 3% between 18 and 23, 51% between 24 and 29, and 46% above 30. 78% of the current freshmen were in the top fifth of their class; 96% were in the top two fifths. **Admissions Contact:** Judith Burke-Berhanan, Dean of Admissions. Email: *enroll@stonybrook.edu* Web: *www.stonybrook.edu*

FINANCIAL AID: In 2017-2018, 78% of all full-time freshmen received some form of financial aid. 52% of all full-time freshmen received need-based aid. The average freshman award was $13,800. Need-based scholarships or need-based grants averaged $8,800 ($24,100 maximum); need-based self-help aid (loans and jobs) averaged $3,700 ($7,500 maximum); non-need-based athletic scholarships averaged $23,700 ($45,600 maximum); and other non-need-based awards and non-need-based scholarships averaged $7,600 ($45,700 maximum). 13% of undergraduate students work part-time. The average financial indebtedness of the 2017 graduate was $26,200. SBU is a member of CSS. The state aid form is required. The priority date for freshman financial aid applications for fall entry is March 1.

SYRACUSE UNIVERSITY — C-3

www.syracuse.edu

Syracuse, NY 13244	**(315) 443-3611**
Fax: (315) 443-4226	**Email: orange@syr.edu**
Full-time: 6749 men, 7926 women	**Faculty:** n/av
Part-time: 277 men, 300 women	**Ph.D.s:** 90%
Graduate: 3651 men, 3581 women	**Student/Faculty:** 15 to 1
Year: semesters, summer session	**Tuition:** $46,755
Room & Board: $15,558	**Freshman Class:** 33099 applied, 15517 accepted, 3649 enrolled
SAT EBR-W/M: 621/633 **ACT:** 27	**CEEB CODE:** 2823
Application Deadline: January 1	**HIGHLY COMPETITIVE**

Syracuse University is a private, international research university dedicated to advancing knowledge and fostering student success through teaching excellence, rigorous scholarship, and interdisciplinary research. The University has a long legacy of excellence in the liberal arts, sciences, and professional disciplines that prepares students for the complex challenges and emerging opportunities of a rapidly changing world. Syracuse also has a long legacy of supporting veterans and is home to the nationally recognized Institute for Veterans and Military families, the first university-based institute in the U.S. There are 11 undergraduate schools and 12 graduate schools. In addition to regional accreditation, Syracuse University has baccalaureate program accreditation with AACSB, ABET, ACEJMC, CSWE, NAAB, NASAD, NASM, ACEI, ACTFL, ACS, CAEP, CEC, CIDA, CAEP, ACEND, NAEYC, NCSS, NCTE, NCTM, NSTA, SHAPE-Health, SHAPE-Phys. Ed., and CEPH. The 270-acre campus is in an urban area in the city of Syracuse, it is approximately 280 miles northwest of New York City and located at the intersection of the New York State Thruway (I-90) and Interstate 81. Including any residence halls, there are 261 buildings.

STUDENT LIFE: 59% of undergraduates are from out of state, mostly the Northeast. Students are from 50 states, 86 foreign countries, and Canada. 65% are from public schools. 57% are White; 13% Foreign; 9% Hispanic; 7% African American; 7% Asian American; 3% two or more races; 3% race unknown; 1% American Indian/Alaska Native. 44% claim no religious affiliation; 25% Catholic; 12% Jewish. **Female To Male Ratio:** 1.1:1. The average age of freshmen is 18; all undergraduates, 20.

9% do not continue beyond their first year; 82% remain to graduate. **Housing:** 8000 students can be accommodated in college housing, which includes coed dorms and on-campus apartments. In addition, there are special-interest houses, fraternity houses, sorority houses, and theme/wellness housing. On-campus housing is available on a lottery system for upperclassmen. 75% of students live on campus. Upperclassmen may keep cars.

FACULTY/CLASSROOMS: 56% of faculty are male; 44% are female. No introductory courses are taught by graduate students. The average class size in an introductory lecture is 225; in a laboratory is 19; and in a regular course is 25.

PROGRAMS OF STUDY: SU confers B.A., B.S., B.Arch., B.F.A., B.I.D., B.Mus., and B.P.S. degrees. Associate, master's, and doctoral degrees are also awarded. Bachelor's degrees are awarded in BIOLOGICAL SCIENCE (biochemistry, biology/general science secondary education, biophysics, biotechnology, forensic science, neurosciences, and nutrition), BUSINESS (accounting, entrepreneurial studies, finance, knowledge management, leadership, management, marketing, real estate, retailing, sports management, and supply chain management), COMMUNICATIONS AND THE ARTS (acting, advertising, art history, art, art history and appreciation, art studies, broadcasting, ceramic art and design, classics, communication design, communication rhetoric/communication, dramatic arts, English, film arts, fine arts, French and Francophone studies, German studies, graphic design, illustration, industrial design, journalism and technical communications, journalism-magazine journalism, journalism-news and information, linguistics, metal/jewelry, modern language, music, music composition, music history and appreciation, music industry, music production/recording technology, musical theater, painting, percussion, photography, piano/organ, printmaking, public relations, Russian languages and literature, sculpture, stage management, strings, television and digital media production, theater design, video, voice, winds, and writing and rhetoric), COMPUTER AND PHYSICAL SCIENCE (applied mathematics, chemistry, chemistry/general science second education, chemistry secondary education, computer science, earth science, earth science/adolescence education, energy science, inform, science, systems and technology, information sciences and systems, mathematics, physics/general science secondary education, and physics), EDUCATION (art education, early childhood education, educational studies, elementary education, English education, health and physical education, mathematics education, music education, physical education, social studies education, Spanish education K-12, and special education/early child dual program), ENGINEERING AND ENVIRONMENTAL DESIGN (aerospace engineering, architecture, bioengineering, chemical engineering, civil engineering, computer engineering, computer graphics, environmental engineering, interior architecture, and mechanical engineering), HEALTH PROFESSIONS (biology, electrical engineering, health science, predentistry, premedicine, and public health), SOCIAL SCIENCE (African American studies, anthropology, child care/child and family studies, classical/ancient civilization, communication sciences and disorders, economics, ethics, politics, and social policy, fashion design and technology, food science, geography, history, international relations, Italian studies, Latin American studies, legal studies, liberal arts/general studies, Middle Eastern studies, modern jewish studies, philosophy, philosophy (political thought), political science/government, prelaw, psychology, religion, religious studies, Russian and Slavic studies, social work, sociology, Spanish studies, and women and gender studies). Architecture, public communications, management, and life sciences (biology, biochemistry, biophysical science, physics) are the strongest academically. Information management and technology, psychology, and management have the largest enrollments.

ACTIVITIES: 27% of men belong to 36 national fraternities; 40% of women belong to 22 national sororities. There are 254 groups on campus, including art, band, cheerleading, chess, choir, chorale, chorus, communications, computers, dance, debate, drama, environmental, ethnic, film, forensics, honors, international, jazz band, LGBT, literary magazine, marching band, musical theater, newspaper, opera, orchestra, pep band, photography, political, professional, radio and TV, religious, social, social service, special interest clubs, student government, symphony, and yearbook. Popular campus events include Syracuse Welcome, Winter Carnival, Senior Celebration, Dance Works, First Year Players, Block Party, University lectures, athletic events, Veterans Day, Martin Luther King Jr. Dinner, Latino/Hispanic Heritage Month, Asian/Pacific Heritage Month. **Sports:** There are 8 intercollegiate sports for men and 12 for women, and 9 intramural sports for men and 9 for women. Facilities include Recreation Services offering 48 sport clubs, 30 outdoor adventure trips, 10 multi-function indoor facilities, outdoor playing fields, outdoor ropes challenge course, an ice rink, golf course, rowing facilities, intramural sports and fitness programs, basketball, outdoor soccer, flag football, indoor soccer, and volleyball. **Graduates:** From July 1, 2016 to June 30, 2017, 3563 bachelor's degrees were awarded. The most popular majors were communications/journalism (14%), social sciences (13%), and business and marketing (12%). In an average class, 70% graduate in 4 years or less, 81% graduate in 5 years or less, and 83% graduate in 6 years or less. Of the 2016 graduating class, 24% were enrolled in graduate school within 6 months of graduation, and 64% were employed.

SERVICES: Counseling and information services are available, as is tutoring in most subjects. There is a reader service for the blind. A variety of services are offered by the Syracuse University Student Success Center, including subject specific help, tutoring by academic program, and study resources. Additional services such as the Writing Center, the Math Clinic, and the Physics Clinic are offered by individual schools/colleges, departments, and/or honor societies. The Office of Disability Services provides additional services for those with documented disabilities. **Library/Resources:** The library contains 2.2 million volumes, 65,843 microform items, and 89,185 audio/video tapes/CDs/DVDs, and subscribes to 146,459 periodicals, including electronic. Computerized library services include interlibrary loans, database searching, Internet access, and Wi-Fi capability. Special learning facilities include an art gallery, a radio station, TV station, the Syracuse University Library Special Collections Research Center; the Blackstone Launchpad; the Global Collaboratory; the Syracuse Center of Excellence in Environmental and Energy Systems; Center for Science and Technology; Life Sciences Complex; Fidelity MODUS 622i flight simulator; the Dick Clark Studios; the Alan Gerry Center for Media Innovation; the Diane and Bob Miron Digital News Center; Falcone Center for Entreprenuership; Ballentine Investment Institute; architecture studios; the Dorothea Ilgen Shaffer Art Building; the JP Morgan Chase Technology Center; Syracuse Stage; the Bernice M. Wright Child Development Laboratory; the Belfer Audio Laboratory and Archive; the Gebbie Speech, Language, and Hearing Clinic; and Syracuse University Humanities Center. **Physically Challenged Students:** 95% of the campus is accessible. Facilities include wheelchair ramps, elevators, special parking, specially equipped restrooms, special class scheduling, lowered drinking fountains, lowered telephones, and special housing. **Special:** Co-op programs exist for aerospace engineering, bioengineering, chemical engineering, civil engineering, computer engineering, computer science, electric engineering, environmental engineering, mechanical engineering, and systems and information science majors. Syracuse University students are encouraged to undertake internships during both the academic year and summers in the Syracuse community, across the nation, and internationally. Internships can be for credit or paid, depending upon the field and degree requirements of the students college of enrollment. The Syracuse University Career Services Office aids students in finding internships, as do individual school/college career services units. Syracuse currently operates 8 overseas centers, in Beijing, Florence, Hong Kong, Istanbul, London, Madrid, Santiago (Chile), and Strasbourg (France). Through SU's World Partners, summer, and short-term programs, SU Abroad students have study abroad options in over 30 additional countries. SU also enrolls small cohorts of entering freshmen students in the College of Arts and Sciences to First-Semester Liberal Arts Study Abroad Programs: Discovery Florence and Discovery Strasbourg. These students begin their collegiate careers at the SU Centers in Florence or Strasbourg in the fall semester. There are dozens of short term study abroad trips ranging from 1 to 3 weeks in duration, generally including travel to multiple countries. The Maxwell School of Citizenship and Public Affairs (within the College of Arts and Sciences) offers the Maxwell-Washington semester. Hundreds of Syracuse University undergraduate students work on campus through the Federal Work-Study (FWS) program. FWS employers include student affairs, career services, advising, residence life, dining and catering services, university and libraries, and academic and administrative offices across campus. There are 10 dual and combined enrollment options through which a variety of major combinations may be undertaken. The College of Arts and Sciences at Syracuse University offers customized programs of study with advisor consultation and approval. There are 34 national honor societies, Phi Beta Kappa, and a freshman honors program. **Visiting:** There are regularly scheduled orientations for prospective students. Prospective students can visit Syracuse University nearly year-round. Options include daily visits which offer an information session and campus tour. There are guides for informal visits; visitors may sit in on classes and stay overnight. To schedule a visit, contact the Office of Admissions. **Campus Safety and Security:** Measures include 24-hour foot and vehicle patrol, an emergency notification system, self-defense education, and security escort services. There are shuttle buses, emergency telephones, lighted pathways/sidewalks, controlled access to dorms/residences, campus wide video security system with central monitoring, and a crisis alert notification system.

REQUIREMENTS: Applicants must submit the Common Application; scores for either the SAT or ACT with or without essay component/writing; secondary school transcript; counselor evaluation; 2 academic recommendations; and an essay and short written answers to questions. Applicants should have a strong college preparatory record from an accredited secondary school or have a GED equivalent. A portfolio is required for art and architecture majors, and an audition is required for music and drama majors. AP and CLEP credits are accepted. All undergraduates must complete a minimum of 120 credit hours through a combination of course work, experiential learning (e.g., internships), and transfer credit. Arts and Sciences and Education students must all take a liberal arts core. To avoid probation, students must maintain a minimum GPA of 2.0. Academic requirements for majors and minors are provided in the Syracuse University course catalog. **Procedure:** Freshmen are admitted in the fall and spring. Entrance exams should be taken prior to January of the senior year for regular decision. There are early decision and deferred admissions plans. Early decision applications should be filed by November 15; regular applications, by January 1 for fall entry; and November 15 for spring entry. The fall 2017 application fee was $75. Notification of early decision is sent January 1; regular decision, March 15. 1314 early decision candidates were accepted for the 2017-2018 class. 2601 applicants were on the 2017 waiting list; 1202 were admitted. Applications are accepted online. **Transfer Students:** 321 transfer students enrolled in 2016-2017. Students must submit an online Common Application form; $75 application fee; one academic letter of recommendation; most recent official college transcript, in addition to any transcripts from colleges previously attended or enrolled in classes. If transfer applicant has completed fewer than 30 college credits at the time of application, the following must be provided: standardized test scores; an official copy of your final high school transcript; a college report/statement of good standing. A portfolio is required for art and architecture applicants, and an audition for music and drama applicants. TOEFL or IELTS scores are required for students whose native language is not English. Additional requirements may apply to international students. **International Students:** There are 1940 international students enrolled. They must take the TOEFL, or IELTS. The SAT and ACT are not required for international applicants studying outside the U.S. who are not prospective student-athletes and are not attending an American-system school.

ADMISSIONS: 47% of the 2017-2018 applicants were accepted. 60% of the current freshmen were in the top fifth of their class; 86% were in the top two fifths. **Admissions Contact:** Office of Admissions Email: *orange@syr.edu* Web: *www.syracuse.edu/admissions/*

FINANCIAL AID: In 2017-2018, 83% of all full-time freshmen received some form of financial aid. 44% of all full-time freshmen received need-based aid. The average freshman award was $38,450. Need-based scholarships or need-based grants averaged $31,030; and need-based self-help aid (loans and jobs) averaged $7,140. 45% of undergraduate students work part-time. The average financial indebtedness of the 2017 graduate was $38,918. SU is a member of CSS. The CSS/Profile, and noncustodial profile are required. The FAFSA code is 002882. The deadline for filing freshman financial aid applications for fall entry is January 1.

THE COLLEGE AT BROCKPORT - STATE UNIVERSITY OF NEW YORK B-3

www.brockport.edu

Brockport, NY 14420	(585) 395-2751
Fax: (585) 395-5452	**Email:** admit@brockport.edu
Full-time: 2806 men, 3613 women	**Faculty:** 205; IIA
Part-time: 288 men, 473 women	**Ph.D.s:** 69%
Graduate: 362 men, 771 women	**Student/Faculty:** 18 to 1
Year: semesters, summer session	**Tuition:** $8154 ($17,804)
Room & Board: $12,904	**Freshman Class:** 9628 applied, 5120 accepted, 1262 enrolled
SAT EBR-W/M: 550/540 **ACT:** 22	**CEEB CODE:** 2537
Application Deadline: rolling	**COMPETITIVE**

The College at Brockport, State University of New York, established in 1835, is a comprehensive public liberal arts college with offerings including 50 undergraduate majors, more than 50 masters programs, 13 nationally accredited programs, and 31 teacher certification areas. There are 5 undergraduate schools and 1 graduate school. In addition to regional accreditation, the College at Brockport has baccalaureate program accreditation with AACSB, ABET, CSWE, NASD, CCNE, ACS, NAST, CAEP, COAPRT, NAADAC, and CAATE. The 464-acre campus is in a small town 16 miles west of Rochester. Including any residence halls, there are 80 buildings.

STUDENT LIFE: 98% of undergraduates are from New York. Others are from 26 states, 24 foreign countries, and Canada. 70% are White; 11% African American; 7% Hispanic; 5% race unknown; 4% two or more races; 2% Asian American; 1% Foreign. **Female To Male Ratio:** 1.4:1. The average age of freshmen is 18; all undergraduates, 21. 18% do not continue beyond their first year; 68% remain to graduate. **Housing:** 2770 students can be accommodated in college housing, which includes coed dorms and on-campus apartments. In addition, there are special-interest houses, special residence hall communities for first-year students, and academic excellence floors. On-campus housing is available on a first-come, first-served basis. 72% of students commute. All students may keep cars.

FACULTY/CLASSROOMS: 47% of faculty are male; 53% are female. 90% teach undergraduates. No introductory courses are taught by graduate students.

PROGRAMS OF STUDY: The College at Brockport confers B.A., B.S., B.F.A., and B.S.N. degrees. Master's degrees are also awarded. Bachelor's degrees are awarded in BIOLOGICAL SCIENCE (biochemistry and biology/biological science), BUSINESS (accounting, business administration and management, finance, international business management, marketing management, recreation and leisure services, and sports management), COMMUNICATIONS AND THE ARTS (communications, dance, English, French, journalism, Spanish, studio art, and theatre acting), COMPUTER AND PHYSICAL SCIENCE (atmospheric sciences and meteorology, chemistry, computer science, earth science, geology, mathematics, and physics), EDUCATION (athletic training and physical education), ENGINEERING AND ENVIRONMENTAL DESIGN (computational sciences and environmental science), HEALTH PROFESSIONS (exercise science, health science, kinesiology, medical technology, and nursing), SOCIAL SCIENCE (African studies, African American studies, anthropology, criminal justice, history, international studies, liberal arts/general studies, philosophy, political science/government, psychology, social work, sociology, water resources, and womens studies). Nursing, business administration, and psychology have the largest enrollments.

ACTIVITIES: 1% of men belong to 2 national fraternities; 1% of women belong to 2 national sororities. There are 130 groups on campus, including art, band, cheerleading, choir, chorus, communications, computers, dance, drama, environmental, ethnic, honors, international, jazz band, LGBT, literary magazine, many academic clubs, newspaper, orchestra, photography, political, professional, radio and TV, religious, social, social service, and student government. Popular campus events include Scholar's Day, Honors and Awards Ceremony, Diversity Conference, and International Student Festival. **Sports:** There are 12 intercollegiate sports for men and 13 for women, and 12 intramural sports for men and 12 for women. Facilities include field hockey, baseball, softball fields, a soccer pitch, a swimming pool, gyms, a wrestling room, weight rooms, handball, squash, tennis, and racquetball courts, an ice arena, and a special Olympics stadium with turf fields, a recreation facility with a fitness center, shot put and discus center, and a running track. **Graduates:** From July 1, 2016 to June 30, 2017, 1865 bachelor's degrees were awarded. The most popular majors were nursing (12%), health services (10%), and kinesiology and excercise science (8%). In an average class, 3% graduate in 3 years or less, 48% graduate in 4 years or less, 65% graduate in 5 years or less, and 68% graduate in 6 years or less. Of the 2016 graduating class, 35% were enrolled in graduate school within 6 months of graduation, and 54% were employed.

SERVICES: Counseling and information services are available, as is tutoring in most subjects. Tutoring for specific classes may vary by semester, depending upon the demand for tutoring and the availability of qualified tutors. Study skills support is available to all students. **Library/Resources:** The library contains 770,000 volumes, 30,000 microform items, and 10,900 audio/video tapes/CDs/DVDs, and subscribes to 115,000 periodicals, including electronic. Computerized library services include interlibrary loans, database searching, Internet access, and Wi-Fi capability. Special learning facilities include an art gallery, a planetarium, radio station, TV station, Proscenium Theatre and Black Box performance space, modern dance facilities, art galleries, ceramic and painting, photography and sculpture studios, a greenhouse, a planetarium, electron microscope, nuclear magnetic resonance spectrometer, Faraday Cage, Geographic Information Systems (GIS) lab with Dopplar radar station, aquaculture ponds, environmental science deciduous woodlot, 25-foot research boat, 20 computer labs, smart classrooms, and a student learning center. **Physically Challenged Students:** 95% of the campus is accessible. Facilities include wheelchair ramps, elevators, special parking, specially equipped restrooms, special class scheduling, lowered drinking fountains, lowered telephones, and special housing. **Special:** Co-op programs, internships in most majors, and work-study programs in education are available, as well as Honors College with full tuition scholarship. Brockport offers cross-registration with Rochester area colleges, a Washington semester, study abroad in over 35 countries, accelerated degree programs, and an interdisciplinary major in arts for children, emphasizing art, dance, music, and theater. Credit for military and work experience, nondegree study, and pass/fail grading options are available. An alternative general education program, Delta College, is an interdisciplinary program that emphasizes global issues and provides opportunities for work or study in other countries, as well as locally, regionally, and nationally. There are 15 national honor societies, a freshman honors program, and 5 departmental honors programs. **Visiting:** There are regularly scheduled orientations for prospective students, admissions information presentations, campus tours, and class observations. There are guides for informal visits; visitors may sit in on classes and stay overnight. To schedule a visit, contact the Undergraduate Admissions Office. **Campus Safety and Security:** Measures include 24-hour foot and vehicle patrol, emergency notification system, and security escort services. There are shuttle buses, emergency telephones, lighted pathways/sidewalks, controlled access to dorms/residences, a community policing program, bicycle patrols, and 24-hour locked residence halls.

REQUIREMENTS: The College at Brockport will consider many factors when reviewing admissions applications: strength of the academic program, course grades and high school average, standardized test scores (SAT and/or ACT), class rank, supplemental application information, letters of recommendation, a resume, and a portfolio (required by some students). Most students who enter Brockport today have: the equivalent of an Advanced Regents Diploma, 4 years of English, 3 years or more of math, sciences and social studies, 3 years or more of a foreign language, additional electives as appropriate, some college-level course work, including Advanced Placement (AP), International Baccalaureate (IB), and college-affiliated programs such as Syracuse University Project Advance (SUPA). AP and CLEP credits are accepted. Important factors in the admissions decision are advanced placement or honors courses, recommendations by school officials, and personality/intangible qualities. To graduate, students must complete a minimum of 120 credits, including 30 or more credits in the major, with a 2.0 GPA. The core curriculum includes the SUNY-wide general education requirements (1 course each in math, natural sciences, social sciences, American history, Western civilization, world (non-Western) civilization, humanities, the arts, foreign language, and basic communication). All students must take courses in contemporary issues, diversity, and perspectives on women and pass the appropriate competency exams. An academic planning seminar is required of entering freshmen and recommended for incoming transfer students. **Procedure:** Freshmen are admitted in the fall and spring. Entrance exams should be taken in the spring of the junior year and fall of the senior year. There are deferred admissions and rolling admissions plans. Application deadlines are open. The fall 2017 application fee was $50. Notification is sent on a rolling basis. Applications are accepted online. **Transfer Students:** 935 transfer students enrolled in 2016-2017. Applicants must have a minimum GPA of 2.00 to be considered. Many departments specify prerequisite courses and a higher GPA (nursing, social work, education). 30 of 120 credits required for the bachelor's degree must be completed at The College at Brockport. **International Students:** There are 66 international students enrolled. They must take the TOEFL with a minimum score of 530 on the paper-based TOEFL (PBT) or 76 on the Internet-based version (iBT). Students must take the IELTS, or complete ELS level 112. They must also take the SAT or ACT.

ADMISSIONS: 53% of the 2017-2018 applicants were accepted. The SAT scores for the 2017-2018 freshman class were: Critical Reading-- 20% below 500, 57% between 500 and 599, 21% between 600 and 699, and 2% between 700 and 800. Math-- 22% below 500, 57% between 500 and 599, 20% between 600 and 699, and 1% between 700 and 800. The ACT scores were 6% between 12 and 17, 57% between 18 and 23, 32% between 24 and 29, and 4% above 30. 13% of the current freshmen were in the top fifth of their class; 32% were in the top two fifths. **Admissions Contact:** Megan Sarkis, Assistant Director of Admissions. Email: *admit@brockport.edu* Web: *www.brockport.edu*

FINANCIAL AID: In 2017-2018, 74% of all full-time freshmen received some form of financial aid. 66% of all full-time freshmen received need-based aid. The average freshman award was $16,032. Need-based scholarships or need-based grants averaged $7,563 ($17,478 maximum); need-based self-help aid (loans and jobs) averaged $4,766 ($9,500 maximum); and other non-need-based awards and non-need-based scholarships averaged $7,998 ($30,500 maximum). 70% of undergraduate students work part-time. The average financial indebtedness of the 2017 graduate was $30,416. The state aid form is required. The FAFSA code is 002841. The priority date for freshman financial aid applications for fall entry is March 15.

THE COLLEGE OF NEW ROCHELLE *(The complete profile is made available exclusively on our website, www.barronspac.com)*

THE COLLEGE OF SAINT ROSE D-3

www.strose.edu

Albany, NY 12203	**(518) 454-5154** **(800) 637-8556**
Fax: (518) 454-2013	**Email: admit@strose.edu**
Full-time: 790 men, 1636 women	**Faculty:** 170
Part-time: 44 men, 53 women	**Ph.D.s:** 91%
Graduate: 350 men, 1077 women	**Student/Faculty:** 14 to 1
Year: semesters, summer session	**Tuition:** $31,654
Room & Board: $12,356	**Freshman Class:** 6727 applied, 5565 accepted, 577 enrolled
SAT CR/M: 538/522 **ACT:** 23	**CEEB CODE:** 2091
Application Deadline: February 1	**COMPETITIVE**

The College of Saint Rose offers students the benefits of an urban environment as well as a close-knit campus community. Saint Rose has 45 Undergraduate Degree Programs, 6 Post-Secondary Certificate Programs, 29 Master's Degree Programs, 19 Certificate of Advanced Study, and 13 dual-degree programs through its four schools: School of Arts and Humanities, School of Business, School of Education, and School of Mathematics and Sciences. There are 4 undergraduate schools and 3 graduate schools. In addition to regional accreditation, Saint Rose has baccalaureate program accreditation with ACBSP, CSWE, NASAD, NASM, CAEP, NASP, and ASHA. The 49-acre campus is in an urban area in the Capital Region of New York state. Including any residence halls, there are 90 buildings.

STUDENT LIFE: 86% of undergraduates are from New York. Others are from 30 states, 33 foreign countries, and Canada. 8% are Hispanic; 8% two or more races; 8% race unknown; 57% White; 3% Foreign; 2% Asian American; 14% African American. **Female To Male Ratio:** 2.3:1. The average age of freshmen is 18; all undergraduates, 20. 25% do not continue beyond their first year; 59% remain to graduate. **Housing:** 1363 students can be accommodated in college housing, which includes single sex dorms, coed dorms, on-campus apartments, apartments for single students, and special-interest houses. On-campus housing is guaranteed for all 4 years, and is available on a first-come, first-served basis, and is available on a lottery system for upperclassmen. 52% of students commute. Upperclassmen may keep cars.

FACULTY/CLASSROOMS: 46% of faculty are male; 54% are female. All teach undergraduates and do research. No introductory courses are taught by graduate students. The average class size in an introductory lecture is 18; in a laboratory is 14; and in a regular course is 16.

PROGRAMS OF STUDY: Saint Rose confers B.A., B.S., B.M., and B.F.A. degrees. Master's degrees are also awarded. Bachelor's degrees are awarded in BIOLOGICAL SCIENCE (biochemistry, biology/adolescence education, biology/biological science, forensic psychology, and forensic science), BUSINESS (accounting, business administration and management, management, and marketing), COMMUNICATIONS AND THE ARTS (communications, English, graphic design, information technology, music, music industry, music performance, and studio art), COMPUTER AND PHYSICAL SCIENCE (chemistry, computer science, and mathematics), EDUCATION (early childhood education, English education, mathematics education, music education, science education, social studies secondary school education, and special education), HEALTH PROFESSIONS (cytotechnology, medical technology, and public health), SOCIAL SCIENCE (communication sciences and disorders, criminal justice, history, interdisciplinary studies, law, political science/government, psychology, and social work). Communication sciences and disorders, art, and music are the strongest academically. Criminal justice behavior and law, communications, and psychology have the largest enrollments.

ACTIVITIES: There are no fraternities or sororities. There are 40 groups on campus, including geology club, psychology club, Student Events Board, Acapella Performance Groups, adventure club, band, cheerleading, chorale, dance, debate, drama, environmental, ethnic, international, jazz band, LGBT, literary magazine, musical theater, newspaper, orchestra, pep band, political, professional, radio and TV, religious, social, social service, student government, and symphony. Popular campus events include Harvest Fest, Rose Rock Music Festival, Midnight Madnes, and Dodgeball Madness. **Sports:** There are 9 intercollegiate sports for men and 10 for women, and 6 intramural sports for men and 6 for women. Facilities include basketball courts, volleyball courts, indoor pool, a fitness center, synthetic turf field for lacrosse and soccer, and fields for baseball, softball, and a practice field. **Graduates:** From July 1, 2016 to June 30, 2017, 558 bachelor's degrees were awarded. The most popular majors were business administration (10%), communications (9%), and criminal justice behavior and law (7%). In an average class, 48% graduate in 4 years or less, 59% graduate in 5 years or less, and 59% graduate in 6 years or less. Of the 2016 graduating class, 37% were enrolled in graduate school within 6 months of graduation, and 82% were employed.

SERVICES: Counseling and information services are available, as is tutoring in most subjects. There is a reader service for the blind. There is also a full-time director of disabled student services. **Library/Resources:** The library contains 205,426 volumes, 31,339 microform items, 5,567 audio/video tapes/CDs/DVDs, and subscribes to 46,301 periodicals, including electronic. Computerized library services include interlibrary loans, database searching, Internet access, and Wi-Fi capability. Special learning facilities include an art gallery, Internship office, entrepreneurship center, TV and radio stations, music recording studios, performance venue, art galleries, 3-D printing and photography studios, screenprinting facility music/video editing computer labs, recital hall, theater, vocal and instrument rehearsal rooms, speech-hearing/special education clinic, on-site pre-school and labs for, biology, chemistry, computer science, graphic design, journalism and neuro-psychology. **Physically Challenged Students:** 71% of the campus is accessible. Facilities include wheelchair ramps, elevators, special parking, specially equipped restrooms, lowered drinking fountains, lowered telephones, and special housing. **Special:** Saint Rose offers cross-registration with several local colleges, internships, work-study programs, study abroad in several countries, dual and student-designed majors, non-degree study, and pass/fail options. There are 3-2 engineering degree programs with Rensselaer Polytechnic University, a 6-year law program with Albany Law School, Pace University Law School, and Western New England School of Law, as well as Medical Technology programs in conjunction with Albany College of Pharmacy and Health Sciences, Methodist Hospital and Rochester General Hospital. There are 16 national honor societies. **Visiting:** There are regularly scheduled orientations for prospective students, (visits vary by month, day and time). There are guides for informal visits and visitors may sit in on classes. To schedule a visit, contact the Undergraduate Admissions Office. **Campus Safety and Security:** Measures include 24-hour foot and vehicle patrol, an emergency notification system, and security escort services. There are shuttle buses, emergency telephones, lighted pathways/sidewalks, and controlled access to dorms/residences.

REQUIREMENTS: Applicants must be graduates of an accredited secondary school or have a GED certificate. They should have completed college preparatory programs, including 4 years of English and history, 3 years of math, and science, as well as 2 years of foreign language. All students must submit a letter of recommendation and a high school transcript. Supporting materials such as an essay, personal statement, resume and SAT/ACT scores are recommended but not required. Art students must submit portfolios, and music students must audition. AP and CLEP credits are accepted. Important factors in the admissions decision are advanced placement or honors courses, extracurricular activities record, and leadership record. To graduate, students must complete 122 credits with a minimum GPA of 2.0 overall and in the major. These requirements are higher for certain majors. At least 32 of the required 122 credits must be completed in residence. 41 credits of Liberal Education required. **Procedure:** Freshmen are admitted in the fall and spring. Entrance exams should be taken during junior year or the fall of senior year. There are early admissions, deferred admissions, and rolling admissions plans. Early decision applications should be filed by December 1; regular applications, by February 1 for fall entry; and December 1 for spring entry. Notification is sent on a rolling basis. Applications are accepted on-line. **Transfer Students:** 250 transfer students enrolled in 2016-2017. Applicants must submit official transcripts from all colleges attended, a letter of recommendation, and a personal statement. Art majors must submit a portfolio, and music majors must audition. The minimum overall college GPA is 2.5. Students may transfer 70 credits from a two-year college and 90 credits from a four-year college. 32 of 122 credits required for the bachelor's degree must be completed at College of Saint Rose. **International Students:** There are 55 international students enrolled. They must take the TOEFL with a minimum score of 550 on the paper-based TOEFL (PBT) or 80 on the Internet-based version (iBT). Students must IELTS (min. 5.5) or PTE (min. 56) also accepted. They must also take the SAT or ACT. Students can be test-optional if they have alternate English proficiency (IB, A-levels, for example).

ADMISSIONS: 83% of the 2017-2018 applicants were accepted. The SAT scores for the 2017-2018 freshman class were: Critical Reading--25% below 500, 54% between 500 and 599, 20% between 600 and 699, and 1% between 700 and 800. Math-- 31% below 500, 55% between 500 and 599, 13% between 600 and 699, and 1% between 700 and 800. The ACT scores were 7% between 12 and 17, 55% between 18 and 23, 31% between 24 and 29, and 7% above 30. 17% of the current freshmen were in the top fifth of their class; 48% were in the top two fifths. 1 freshman graduated first in the class. **Admissions Contact:** Kathleen Lesko, Assistant Vice President of Undergraduate Admissions. Email: *admit@strose.edu* Web: *www.strose.edu*

FINANCIAL AID: In 2017-2018, 99% of all full-time freshmen received some form of financial aid. 85% of all full-time freshmen received need-based aid. The average freshman award was $27,008. Need-based scholarships or need-based grants averaged $7,221; need-based self-help aid (loans and jobs) averaged $6,219; non-need-based athletic scholarships averaged $10,888; and other non-need-based awards and non-need-based scholarships averaged $19,137. 67% of undergraduate students work part-time. The average financial indebtedness of the 2017 graduate was $36,432. Saint Rose is a member of CSS. The state aid form is required. The FAFSA code is 002705. The priority date for freshman financial aid applications for fall entry is December 1.

THE JUILLIARD SCHOOL *(The complete profile is made available exclusively on our website, www.barronspac.com)*

TOURO COLLEGE — D-5

www.touro.edu

New York, NY 10018 — **(646) 565-6000**

Fax: (718) 253-9455 — **Email:** registrarinfo@touro.edu

Full-time: 1510 men, 3460 women	**Faculty:** 482
Part-time: 409 men, 990 women	**Ph.D.s:** n/av
Graduate: 1846 men, 4592 women	**Student/Faculty:** 17 to 1
Year: semesters, summer session	**Tuition:** $19,870
Room & Board: $11,170	**Freshman Class:** 1578 applied, 817 accepted, 609 enrolled

SAT CR/M/W: 565/540/535 **ACT:** recommended

CEEB CODE: 2902

Application Deadline: April 15 — **COMPETITIVE**

Touro College, founded in 1971, is a private institution offering undergraduate programs primarily through the Lander College of Liberal Arts and Sciences, the School of General Studies, and the School of Health Sciences. Campuses are in midtown Manhattan, Brooklyn, and Queens. There are 6 undergraduate schools and 8 graduate schools. In addition to regional accreditation, Touro has baccalaureate program accreditation with APTA, CAHEA, AOTA, and ASHA. The campus is in an urban area on 7th Avenue, New York, N.Y. Including any residence halls, there are 12 buildings.

STUDENT LIFE: 88% of undergraduates are from New York. Others are from 25 states, 30 foreign countries, and Canada. 9% are race unknown; 60% White; 3% Asian American; 3% Foreign; 14% African American; 10% Hispanic. **Female To Male Ratio:** 2.4:1. The average age of freshmen is 20; all undergraduates, 25. 27% do not continue beyond their first year; 47% remain to graduate. **Housing:** 200 students can be accommodated in college housing, which includes on-campus apartments and off-campus apartments. On-campus housing is available on a first-come, first-served basis. Alcohol is not permitted. All students may keep cars.

FACULTY/CLASSROOMS: 49% of faculty are male; 51% are female. No introductory courses are taught by graduate students. The average class size in an introductory lecture is 16; in a laboratory is 12; and in a regular course is 15.

PROGRAMS OF STUDY: Touro confers B.A., B.S., B.S.N., and B.P.S. degrees. Associate, master's, and doctoral degrees are also awarded. Bachelor's degrees are awarded in BIOLOGICAL SCIENCE (biology/biological science), BUSINESS (accounting, banking and finance, business administration and management, management science, and marketing/retailing/merchandising), COMMUNICATIONS AND THE ARTS (English, Hebrew, literature, and speech/debate/rhetoric), COMPUTER AND PHYSICAL SCIENCE (chemistry, computer science, mathematics, and physics), EDUCATION (elementary education and special education), HEALTH PROFESSIONS (nursing, occupational therapy, physical therapy, predentistry, and premedicine), SOCIAL SCIENCE (economics, history, human services, interdisciplinary studies, Judaic studies, liberal arts/general studies, philosophy, political science/government, prelaw, psychology, social science, and sociology). Business/accounting, education, and health sciences are the strongest academically. Psychology, education, and business have the largest enrollments.

ACTIVITIES: There are no fraternities or sororities. There are 8 groups on campus, including dance, literary magazine, newspaper, political, religious, and student government. Popular campus events include Student-sponsored Lecture Series and Student-Faculty Social Events. **Sports:** There is no sports program at Touro. Facilities include a baseball field, tennis courts, and basketball courts. **Graduates:** From July 1, 2016 to June 30, 2017, 1432 bachelor's degrees were awarded. The most popular majors were psychology (20%), health professions and related programs (19%), and business/marketing (14%). In an average class, 55% graduate in 6 years or less.

SERVICES: Counseling and information services are available, as is tutoring in some subjects, such as accounting, math, English, and natural sciences. There is remedial math, reading, and writing. **Library/Resources:** The library contains 271,509 volumes, 14,100 microform items, 4,054 audio/video tapes/CDs/DVDs, and subscribes to 3,163 periodicals, including electronic. Computerized library services include interlibrary loans, database searching, Internet access, and Wi-Fi capability. **Physically Challenged Students:** All of the campus is accessible. Facilities include wheelchair ramps, elevators, specially equipped restrooms, lowered drinking fountains, and lowered telephones. **Special:** The college offers cross-registration with the Fashion Institute of Technology; internships for juniors and seniors; study abroad in Israel; work-study programs; interdisciplinary majors; an accelerated degree program; credit for life military, and work experience; pass/fail options; and dual majors. Early and/or preferential admission to professional programs is also possible. There are 2 national honor societies, a freshman honors program, and 5 departmental honors programs. **Visiting:** There are guides for informal visits; visitors may sit in on classes and stay overnight. **Campus Safety and Security:** Measures include 24-hour foot and vehicle patrol and an emergency notification system. There are shuttle buses, lighted pathways/sidewalks, and controlled access to dorms/residences.

REQUIREMENTS: The SAT or ACT is recommended. Applicants must be graduates of an accredited secondary school with a satisfactory high school average. A high school diploma is required or a GED is accepted. A satisfactory SAT score is recommended. 16 required academic units includes 4 in English and academic electives and 2 units each in math, science, foreign language, and history. AP and CLEP credits are accepted. Important factors in the admissions decision are advanced placement or honors courses. To graduate, all students must complete at least 120 credit hours (varies by major), with 30 to 70 in the major; 45 of the 120 credits must be from Touro and 1/2 of the student's major has to be completed at Touro. A minimum 2.0 GPA is required, with 2.3 in the major. Specific disciplines include Judaic studies or ethnic studies. Required courses include English composition, history, literature, math, and social and natural sciences. **Procedure:** Freshmen are admitted in the fall, spring, and summer. Entrance exams should be taken in May of the junior year or fall of the senior year. There are early admissions, deferred admissions, and rolling admissions plans. Applications should be filed by April 15 for fall entry; December 15 for spring entry; and June 1 for summer entry. Notification of early decision is sent December 1; regular decision, on a rolling basis. Applications are accepted online. **Transfer Students:** 1334 transfer students enrolled in 2016-2017. A 2.5 GPA is required. If the student has less than 60 credits, high school documentation is also required. Transfer students may enroll in the fall, spring, and summer. 45 of 120 credits required for the bachelor's degree must be completed at Touro. **International Students:** There are 159 international students enrolled. They must take the TOEFL with a minimum score of 550 on the paper-based TOEFL (PBT) or 83 on the Internet-based version (iBT). Students must take the college's own test, or take the IELTS. They must also take the SAT or ACT, and in-house math and English proficiency examinations.

ADMISSIONS: 52% of the 2017-2018 applicants were accepted. The SAT scores for the 2017-2018 freshman class were: Critical Reading-- 3% below 500, 32% between 500 and 599, 26% between 600 and 699, and 18% between 700 and 800. Math-- 6% below 500, 26% between 500 and 599, 27% between 600 and 699, and 7% between 700 and 800. Writing-- 50% below 500, 27% between 500 and 599, 18% between 600 and 699, and 5% between 700 and 800. **Admissions Contact:** Erica Kaplan, Institutional Research Analyst. Email: *registrarinfo@touro.edu* Web: *www.touro.edu*

FINANCIAL AID: In 2017-2018, 95% of all full-time freshmen received some form of financial aid. 95% of all full-time freshmen received need-based aid. The average freshman award was $8,231. Need-based scholarships or need-based grants averaged $8,642; need-based self-help aid (loans and jobs) averaged $3,256; other non-need-based awards and non-need-based scholarships averaged $2,428; and $1,702 from other forms of aid. Touro College is a member of CSS. The CSS/Profile is required. The FAFSA code is 010142. The priority date for freshman financial aid applications for fall entry is May 15.

UNION COLLEGE — C-3
www.union.edu

Schenectady, NY 12308 — **(518) 388-6112**

Fax: (518) 388-6986	**Email:** admissions@union.edu
Full-time: 1151 men, 981 women	**Faculty:** n/av
Part-time: 5 men	**Ph.D.s:** 98%
Graduate: n/av	**Student/Faculty:** 10 to 1
Year: trimesters	**Tuition:** $51,642
Room & Board: $12,678	**Freshman Class:** 6648 applied, 2453 accepted, 560 enrolled
	CEEB CODE: 2920
Application Deadline: January 15	**MOST COMPETITIVE**

Union College, founded in 1795, is an independent liberal arts and engineering college. There is 1 undergraduate school. In addition to regional accreditation, UC has baccalaureate program accreditation with ABET. The 100-acre campus is in a small town 15 miles west of Albany. Including any residence halls, there are 100 buildings.

STUDENT LIFE: 67% of undergraduates are from out of state, mostly the Northeast. Students are from 40 states, 35 foreign countries, and Canada. 65% are from public schools. 8% are Foreign; 72% White; 7% Hispanic; 6% Asian American; 4% African American; 3% two or more races. **Male To Female Ratio:** 1.2:1. The average age of freshmen is 19; all undergraduates, 20. 9% do not continue beyond their first year; 91% remain to graduate. **Housing:** 1978 students can be accommodated in college housing, which includes dorms and on-campus apartments. In addition, there are language/international houses, special-interest houses, fraternity houses, and sorority houses; in the Minerva Houses, up to 45 students live in each of seven distinct houses. On-campus housing is available on a lottery system for upperclassmen. 90% of students live on campus. Upperclassmen may keep cars.

FACULTY/CLASSROOMS: No introductory courses are taught by graduate students.

PROGRAMS OF STUDY: UC confers B.A. and B.S degrees. Bachelor's degrees are awarded in AGRICULTURE (environmental studies), BIOLOGICAL SCIENCE (biochemistry, biology/biological science, and neurosciences), COMMUNICATIONS AND THE ARTS (classics, English, fine arts, modern language, and studio art), COMPUTER AND PHYSICAL SCIENCE (astronomy, chemistry, computer science, geology, mathematics, physics, and science), ENGINEERING AND ENVIRONMENTAL DESIGN (bioengineering, computer engineering, electrical/electronics engineering, environmental science, and mechanical engineering), SOCIAL SCIENCE (American studies, anthropology, Asian/Oriental studies, Caribbean studies, economics, French studies, German area studies, history, humanities, interdisciplinary studies, liberal arts/general studies, philosophy, political science/government, psychology, religion, social science, sociology, Spanish studies, and women's studies). Chemistry, geology, and classics are the strongest academically. Economics, mechanical engineering, and psychology have the largest enrollments.

ACTIVITIES: 35% of men belong to 11 national fraternities; 42% of women belong to 1 local and 6 national sororities. There are 101 groups on campus, including art, band, cheerleading, chess, choir, computers, dance, debate, drama, environmental, ethnic, honors, international, jazz band, LGBT, literary magazine, newspaper, orchestra, pep band, photography, political, professional, radio and TV, religious, social, social service, and student government. Popular campus events include Spring Fest, Lectures, and Concerts. **Sports:** Facilities include a field house for volleyball, recreational basketball, indoor track, and intramural activities, synthetic grass fields for soccer, football, field hockey, lacrosse, intramurals, and recreation, basketball/volleyball courts, an ice rink, a gym that includes a weight room, a fitness center, racquetball/squash courts, an aerobics room, and swimming pool, outdoor tennis courts, outdoor basketball/street hockey court, and a boathouse with docks. **Graduates:** From July 1, 2016 to June 30, 2017, 572 bachelor's degrees were awarded. The most popular majors were economics (16%), political science (10%), and psychology (10%). In an average class, 80% graduate in 4 years or less, 86% graduate in 5 years or less, and 86% graduate in 6 years or less. Of the 2016 graduating class, 20% were enrolled in graduate school within 6 months of graduation, and 71% were employed.

SERVICES: Counseling and information services are available, as is tutoring in most subjects, such as science and math. A writing center, and a language center are also available. **Library/Resources:** Computerized library services include interlibrary loans, database searching, Internet access, and Wi-Fi capability. Special learning facilities include a radio station, a theater, high-tech classroom, a lab center, multimedia auditorium, a music center, art, science, and a history gallery. **Physically Challenged Students:** 80% of the campus is accessible. Facilities include wheelchair ramps, elevators, special parking, specially equipped restrooms, special class scheduling, lowered drinking fountains, lowered telephones, and special housing. **Special:** Cross-registration is permitted with the Hudson Mohawk Consortium. Opportunities are provided for legislative internships in Albany and Washington, D.C., as well as pass/fail options, B.A.-B.S. degrees, dual and student-designed majors, accelerated degree programs in law and medicine, and study abroad in 38 countries. There are 15 national honor societies, Phi Beta Kappa, a freshman honors program, and 19 departmental honors programs. **Visiting:** There are regularly scheduled orientations for prospective students, including interviews and a tour of the campus. There are guides for informal visits and visitors may sit in on classes. To schedule a visit, contact the Admissions Office. **Campus Safety and Security:** Measures include 24-hour foot and vehicle patrol, emergency notification system, self-defense education, and security escort services. There are shuttle buses, an emergency telephones, lighted pathways/sidewalks, controlled access to dorms/residences, 24-hour locked residence halls, emergency medical assistance, awareness programs, a bicycle patrol, a trolley escort service, a shuttle van, and a security measures sheet.

REQUIREMENTS: Testing is optional except for combined programs. Leadership in Medicine program applicants must submit the SAT I and SAT II or the ACT; Law and Public Policy program applicants must submit the SAT I or the ACT. Applicants to these programs must complete the necessary tests no later than December of the senior year. Applicants must submit a minimum of 16 full-year credits, distributed as follows: 4 years of English, 2 of a foreign language, 2 1/2 to 3 1/2 years of math, 2 years each of science and social studies, and the remainder in college-preparatory courses. Engineering and math majors are expected to have completed additional math and science courses beyond the minimum requirements. An essay is also required and an interview is recommended. AP credits are accepted. Important factors in the admissions decision are advanced placement or honors courses, extracurricular activities record, and recommendations by school officials. Students must complete a minimum of 36 term courses (engineering may require up to 40), requirements in the major field, degree program, or interdepartmental major, including the major field examination and/or thesis, as applicable, and attain a minimum GPA of 1.8 or 2.0 in the major (2.0 in the minor if a minor has been declared). **Procedure:** Freshmen are admitted fall, winter, and spring. Entrance exams should be taken by January of the senior year. There are early decision, early admissions, and deferred admissions plans. Early decision applications should be filed by November 15; regular applications, by January 15 for fall entry. Notification of early decision is sent December 15; regular decision, April 1. 227 early decision candidates were accepted for the 2017-2018 class. Applications are accepted on-line. **Transfer Students:** 22 transfer students enrolled in 2016-2017. A 3.0 GPA and 1 full year of college academic work is recommended. Transfer students must study at Union for at least 2 years. 18 of 36 credits required for the bachelor's degree must be completed at Union. **International Students:** There are 163 international students enrolled. They must take the TOEFL. Testing is optional except for combined programs. International students are required to submit the SAT or ACT.

ADMISSIONS: 37% of the 2017-2018 applicants were accepted. The SAT scores for the 2017-2018 freshman class were: Critical Reading-- 3% below 500, 25% between 500 and 599, 53% between 600 and 699, and 19% between 700 and 800. Math-- 2% below 500, 17% between 500 and 599, 52% between 600 and 699, and 29% between 700 and 800. Writing-- 4% below 500, 31% between 500 and 599, 48% between 600 and 699, and 17% between 700 and 800. **Admissions Contact:** Ann Fleming Brown, Director of Admission. Email: *admissions@union.edu* Web: *www.union.edu*

FINANCIAL AID: 75% of all full-time freshmen received need-based aid. UC is a member of CSS. The CSS/Profile, the state aid form, and noncustodial profile are required. The deadline for filing freshman financial aid applications for fall entry is February 1.

UNITED STATES MERCHANT MARINE ACADEMY D-5

www.usmma.edu

Kings Point, NY 11024 **(516) 726-5641**
(866) 546-4778
Fax: (516) 773-5390 **Email: admissions@usmma.edu**

Full-time: 851 men, 136 women	**Faculty:** 120
Part-time: n/av	**Ph.D.s:** 34%
Graduate: 23 men, 2 women	**Student/Faculty:** 11 to 1
Year: trimesters	**Tuition:** see profile
Room & Board: see profile	**Freshman Class:** 758 applied, 279 accepted
SAT CR/M: 630/638 **ACT:** required	**CEEB CODE:** 2923
Application Deadline: March 1	**HIGHLY COMPETITIVE**

United States Merchant Marine Academy, founded in 1943, is a publicly supported institution offering maritime, military, and engineering programs for the purpose of training officers for the U.S. Merchant Marine, the Maritime industry, and the Armed Forces. Students make no conventional tuition and room/board payments. Required fees for freshmen are approximately $1,020; costs in subsequent years are less. There is 1 undergraduate school. In addition to regional accreditation, USMMA has baccalaureate program accreditation with ABET. The 82-acre campus is in a suburban area 19 miles east of midtown New York City. Including any residence halls, there are 28 buildings.

STUDENT LIFE: 88% of undergraduates are from out of state, mostly the Middle Atlantic. Students are from 46 states, and 3 foreign countries. 72% are from public schools. 9% are Asian American; 74% White; 2% African American; 2% American Indian/Alaska Native; 2% Foreign; 11% Hispanic. 48% are Catholic; 42% Protestant. **Male To Female Ratio:** 6.3:1. The average age of freshmen is 19; all undergraduates, 21. 8% [illegible] not continue beyond their first year; 92% remain to graduate. **Housi[illegible]:** 930 students can be accommodated in college housing, which inclu[illegible] dorms. On-campus housing is guaranteed for all 4 years. Alc[illegible] permitted. Upperclassmen may keep cars.

FACULTY/CLASSROOMS: 87% of faculty are male; 13% are female. All

teach undergraduates, 25% do research, and 25% do both. No introductory courses are taught by graduate students. The average class size in an introductory lecture is 28; in a laboratory is 16; and in a regular course is 28.

PROGRAMS OF STUDY: USMMA confers B.S. degrees. Master's degrees are also awarded. Bachelor's degrees are awarded in ENGINEERING AND ENVIRONMENTAL DESIGN (marine engineering, marine engineering/shipyard management, marine engineering systems, marine transportation, and maritime logistics and security). Marine engineering systems is the strongest academically. Logistics and intermodal transportation, marine engineering systems, and marine engineering have the largest enrollments.

ACTIVITIES: There are no fraternities or sororities. There are 51 groups on campus, including band, chess, choir, chorus, communications, computers, dance, debate, drill team, drum and bugle corps, ethnic, marching band, newspaper, pep band, photography, professional, religious, and student government. Popular campus events include Regimental Thanksgiving and Holiday Dinners, Battle Standard Dinner, Lanier Lecture Dinners, Ring Dance, Festival of Lights, Holiday Dance, Valentine's Dance, and Midshipman Appreciation Day. **Sports:** There are 14 intercollegiate sports for men and 9 for women, and 10 intramural sports for men and 10 for women. Facilities include a gymnasium with a swimming pool, basketball and racquetball courts, an outdoor track, a football field, and a waterfront and sailing facility. **Graduates:** From July 1, 2016 to June 30, 2017, 201 bachelor's degrees were awarded. The most popular majors were marine engineering (23%), marine transportation (22%), and logistics and intermodal transportation (21%). In an average class, 77% graduate in 4 years or less and 83% graduate in 5 years or less. Of the 2016 graduating class, 100% were employed within 6 months of graduation.

SERVICES: Counseling and information services are available, as is tutoring in most subjects. **Library/Resources:** The library contains 209,217 volumes, 21,306 microform items, and 4,750 audio/video tapes/CDs/DVDs, and subscribes to 573 periodicals, including electronic. Computerized library services include interlibrary loans, database searching, Internet access, and Wi-Fi capability. Special learning facilities include a planetarium and the American Merchant Marine Museum. **Physically Challenged Students:** 5% of the campus is accessible. Facilities include wheelchair ramps, elevators, special parking, and specially equipped restrooms. **Special:** The college offers internships in the maritime industry and work-study programs with U.S. shipping companies. **Visiting:** There are regularly scheduled orientations for prospective students, including Spring Open House for accepted students; and Summer Open House for prospective students. There are guides for informal visits; visitors may sit in on classes and stay overnight. To schedule a visit, contact the Admissions Office. **Campus Safety and Security:** Measures include 24-hour foot and vehicle patrol. There are lighted pathways/sidewalks.

REQUIREMENTS: The SAT or ACT is required. Candidates for admission to the academy must be nominated by a member of the U.S. Congress. They must be between the ages of 17 and 25, U.S. citizens (except by special arrangement), and in excellent physical condition. Applicants should be graduates of an accredited secondary school or have a GED equivalent. 18 academic credits are required, including 4 credits in English, 3 credits in math, 1 credit in physics or chemistry with a lab, and 10 credits in electives. An essay is required. AP credits are accepted. Important factors in the admissions decision are advanced placement or honors courses, leadership record, and extracurricular activities record. To graduate, students must complete a minimum of 163 credit hours according to the new curriculum with a minimum cumulative and major GPA of 2.0. The required curriculum includes courses in math, science, computer science, English, humanities, history, naval science, physical education, and ship's medicine. Students must complete 1 year of sea service on U.S flag merchant ships. All students must pass resident and sea project courses, the U.S. Coast Guard licensing exam and all required certificates, and the academy physical fitness test. Students must apply for and accept, if offered, a commission in the U.S. uniformed services. **Procedure:** Freshmen are admitted in the summer. Entrance exams should be taken by January for the SAT and February for the ACT. There is a rolling admissions plan. Applications should be filed by March 1 for fall entry. Notifications are sent April 1. 204 applicants were on the 2017 waiting list. Applications are accepted online. **Transfer Students:** The requirements are the same as for high school students, except college-level applicants must submit college transcipts (and must have at least a 2.5 cumulative GPA in college level work), and 2 letters of recommendation from college instructors/professors. 172 credits required for the bachelor's degree must be completed at USMMA. **International Students:** There are 15 international students enrolled. They must take the TOEFL with a minimum score of 540 on the paper-based TOEFL (PBT) or 83 on the Internet-based version (iBT). They must also take the SAT or ACT.

ADMISSIONS: 37% of the 2017-2018 applicants were accepted. The SAT scores for the 2017-2018 freshman class were: Critical Reading-- 1% below 500, 40% between 500 and 599, 40% between 600 and 699, and 19% between 700 and 800. Math-- 17% between 500 and 599, 70% between 600 and 699, and 13% between 700 and 800. 55% of the current freshmen were in the top fifth of their class; 92% were in the top two fifths. 3 freshmen graduated first in their class. **Admissions Contact:** Mike Bedryk, Director of Admissions. Email: *admissions@usmma.edu* Web: *www.usmma.edu*

FINANCIAL AID: In 2017-2018, 34% of all full-time freshmen received some form of financial aid. 13% of all full-time freshmen received need-based aid. The average freshman award was $4,340. Need-based scholarships or need-based grants averaged $4,256 ($5,920 maximum); need-based self-help aid (loans and jobs) averaged $4,370 ($5,500 maximum); and other non-need-based awards and non-need-based scholarships averaged $4,433 ($6,500 maximum). The average financial indebtedness of the 2017 graduate was $5,500. The FAFSA code is 002892. The deadline for filing freshman financial aid applications for fall entry is June 1.

UNITED STATES MILITARY ACADEMY AT WEST POINT D-4

www.usma.edu

West Point, NY 10996 **(845) 938-4041**

Fax: (845) 938-8121
Email: admissions@usma.edu

Full-time: 3507 men, 984 women	**Faculty:** 611
Part-time: n/av	**Ph.D.s:** 52%
Graduate: n/av	**Student/Faculty:** 7 to 1
Year: semesters	**Tuition:** see profile
Room & Board: see profile	**Freshman Class:** 12973 applied, 1240 accepted, 1210 enrolled
SAT EBR-W/M: 650/650 **ACT:** 25	**CEEB CODE:** 2924
Application Deadline: February 28	**HIGHLY COMPETITIVE+**

The United States Military Academy at West Point, founded in 1802, is specifically charged with educating, training, and inspiring young men and women for service as commissioned officers in the United States Army. West Point is an internationally recognized institution for academic, military and physical excellence. Career development starts on the first day; everything cadets' experience is focused on developing them as leaders committed to the values of Duty, Honor, and Country. The cadets who graduate as commissioned officers and serve the nation are USMA's lasting legacy and are what makes West Point great. There is 1 undergraduate school. In addition to regional accreditation, USMA at West Point has baccalaureate program accreditation with ABET and MSCHE. The 16080-acre campus is in a small town West Point is a picturesque campus along the lovely Hudson River, and is approximately 50 miles north of New York City. Including any residence halls, there are 906 buildings.

STUDENT LIFE: 94% of undergraduates are from out of state, mostly the Northeast. Students are from 50 states, and 33 foreign countries. 81% are from public schools. 64% are White; 12% Hispanic; 11% African American; 6% Asian American; 4% two or more races; 1% American Indian/Alaska Native; 1% Foreign; 1% race unknown. 51% are Protestant; 35% Catholic. **Male To Female Ratio:** 4.0:1. The average age of freshmen is 18; all undergraduates, 20. 8% do not continue beyond their first year; 93% remain to graduate. **Housing:** 4500 students can be accommodated in college housing. All cadets live in cadet barracks. On-campus housing is guaranteed for all 4 years. 100% of students live on campus. Upperclassmen may keep cars.

FACULTY/CLASSROOMS: 83% of faculty are male; 17% are female. All teach undergraduates and 40% do research. No introductory courses are taught by graduate students. The average class size in an introductory lecture is 15; in a laboratory is 15; and in a regular course is 15.

PROGRAMS OF STUDY: USMA at West Point confers B.S. degrees.

Bachelor's degrees are awarded in AGRICULTURE (environmental studies), BIOLOGICAL SCIENCE (life science), BUSINESS (management science, operations research, and organizational behavior), COMMUNICATIONS AND THE ARTS (English, foreign language, and literature), COMPUTER AND PHYSICAL SCIENCE (chemistry, computer science, mathematics, and physics), ENGINEERING AND ENVIRONMENTAL DESIGN (civil engineering, electrical/electronics engineering, engineering management, engineering physics, environmental engineering, environmental science, mechanical engineering, military science, nuclear engineering, and systems engineering), HEALTH PROFESSIONS (kinesiology), SOCIAL SCIENCE (economics, geography, history, humanities, international studies, legal studies, philosophy, political science/government, sociology, and systems science). Engineering is the strongest academically. Engineering, foreign languages, and social sciences have the largest enrollments.

ACTIVITIES: There are no fraternities or sororities. There are 86 groups on campus, including diversity, hobby, military, academic, art, bagpipe, band, cheerleading, chess, choir, chorus, debate, drama, drill team, drum and bugle corps, environmental, ethnic, film, honors, international, jazz band, LGBT, literary magazine, marching band, opera, pep band, photography, professional, radio and TV, social, social service, student government, and yearbook. Popular campus events include Ring Weekend, 100th Night for Seniors, 500th Night for Juniors, Yearling Winter Weekend for Sophomores, and Branch Week. **Sports:** There are 16 intercollegiate sports for men and 11 for women, and 11 intramural sports for men and 11 for women. The athletic facility include football, basketball, hockey, gymnasiums, swimming pools, squash, handball, racquetball, rock climbing walls, and wrestling and weight training. The field house has an indoor track, volleyball, a tartan surface, indoor pitching mounds, pitching machines, batting cages, and a fully-equipped weight room. The Athletic Center provides climate-controlled indoor practice facility, an all-weather outdoor oval track and a football field, a lacrosse center, sports medicine areas, a weight room, tennis, a gym, and ranges for pistols, rifles, and air rifle. The recreation facilities is used for field exercises. **Graduates:** From July 1, 2016 to June 30, 2017, 991 bachelor's degrees were awarded. The most popular majors were engineering (27%), social sciences (19%), and foreign languages (7%). In an average class, 82% graduate in 4 years or less, 85% graduate in 5 years or less, and 85% graduate in 6 years or less. Of the 2016 graduating class, 2% were enrolled in graduate school within 6 months of graduation, and 100% were employed.

SERVICES: There is remedial reading and writing. **Library/Resources:** The library contains 368,258 volumes, 38,818 microform items, 15,786 audio/video tapes/CDs/DVDs, and subscribes to 110,650 periodicals, including electronic. Computerized library services include interlibrary loans, database searching, Internet access, and Wi-Fi capability. Special learning facilities include a radio station, TV station, Combating Terrorism Center, Center for Environmental and Geographical Science, Center for Advancement of Leader Development and Organizational Learning, Center for Nation Reconstruction and Capacity Development, Cyber Research Center, Photonics Research Center, Operations Research Center, West Point Simulation Center, Center for Leadership and Diversity in STEM, US Army Space and Missile Defense Command Research and Analysis Center, and Nuclear Science and Engineering Research Center. **Physically Challenged Students:** 30% of the campus is accessible. Facilities include wheelchair ramps, elevators, special parking, specially equipped restrooms. Disability services are only available for faculty, staff, and visitors at West Point. **Special:** During the summers before the junior and senior years, cadets participate in Advanced Individual Academic Development (AIAD) academic, military, or physical-development programs to enrich their individual development. Cadets may choose from more than 100 academic-enrichment opportunities that normally involve 3 weeks of active summer participation and that might include Operation Crossroads Africa, research work in technical laboratories throughout the United States, immersion language training in foreign countries, study at other civilian and military institutions, and numerous work-fellow positions with federal and Department of Defense agencies. If a cadet is an exceptional student, he or she may enroll in advanced individual study in many of the disciplines taught at West Point. These programs emphasize independent or tutorial work and are excellent preparation for graduate study. There are 17 national honor societies and 5 departmental honors programs. **Visiting:** There are regularly scheduled orientations for prospective students, candidates are escorted by a cadet, attend class, have lunch with the Corps of Cadets, and talk with cadets about all phases of West Point life. There are guides for informal visits; visitors may sit in on classes and stay overnight. To schedule a visit, contact the General Admission Information and Visits at admission-info@usma.edu. **Campus Safety and Security:** Measures include 24-hour foot and vehicle patrol, emergency notification system, and self-defense education. There are shuttle buses, lighted pathways/sidewalks, and controlled access to dorms/residences.

REQUIREMENTS: The SAT or ACT is required. The ACT Optional Writing test is also required. Applicants must be qualified academically, physically, and medically. Candidates must be nominated for admission by members of the U.S. Congress or executive sources. West Point recommends that applicants have 4 years each of English and math, 2 years each of foreign language and lab science, such as chemistry and physics, and 1 year of U.S. history. Courses in geography, government, and economics are also suggested. An essay is required, and an interview is recommended. The GED is accepted. Applicants must be 17 to 22 years old, a U.S. citizen at the time of enrollment (except by agreement with another country), unmarried, and not pregnant or legally obligated to support children. AP credits are accepted. Important factors in the admissions decision are leadership record, extracurricular activities record, and recommendations by school officials. To graduate from West Point with a Bachelor of science degree, every First Class cadets must successfully completed the course of instruction in academic, military, and physical education: Successfully complete or validate each course in the core curriculum, including the common core courses and a core engineering sequence equivalent. Satisfy the requirements of at least one major. Successfully complete 40 academic courses of at least 3.0 credit hours each. Achieve a 2.00 Cumulative Quality Point Average (CQPA) in the curses above. (The CQPA is an index of cumulative performance in the academic, military science and physical education courses). Successfully complete the Military and Physical Program at West Point. Meet the height/weight standards of Army Regulation 600-9. Meet the physical fitness standards in Army Regulation 350-1. Cadets who are deficient in one or more of the three developmental programs for failure to maintain minimum program performance standards may be considered by the Academic Board for separation. **Procedure:** Freshmen are admitted in the fall. Entrance exams should be taken in the spring of the junior year and not later than the fall of the senior year. Applications should be filed by February 28 for fall entry. Applications are accepted online. **Transfer Students:** Students in college or with previous college credit may apply to West Point if they meet the basic requirements. However, those students still enter West Point as plebes (freshmen) and must complete the four-year program. **International Students:** There are 57 international students enrolled. They must take the TOEFL with a minimum score of 580 on the paper-based TOEFL (PBT) or 88 on the Internet-based version (iBT). They must also take the SAT or ACT, scoring SAT Math - 530, or ACT Math - 23.

ADMISSIONS: 10% of the 2017-2018 applicants were accepted. The SAT scores for the 2017-2018 freshman class were: Math-- 25% between 500 and 599, 46% between 600 and 699, and 29% between 700 and 800. Evidence-Based Reading/Writing-- 2% below 500, 29% between 500 and 599, 47% between 600 and 699, and 22% between 700 and 800. The ACT scores were 29% between 18 and 23, 55% between 24 and 29, and 16% above 30. 46% of the current freshmen were in the top fifth of their class; 80% were in the top two fifths. 84 freshmen graduated first in their class. **Admissions Contact:** COL Deborah McDonald, Director of Admissions. Email: *admissions@usma.edu* Web: *www.usma.edu*

FINANCIAL AID: Check with the school for current application deadlines.

UNIVERSITY OF ROCHESTER — B-3

www.rochester.edu

Rochester, NY 14627 — **(585) 275-3221**, **(888) 822-2256**

Fax: (585) 461-4595 — **Email: admit@admissions.rochester.edu**

Full-time: 3133 men, 3043 women	**Faculty:** I, +$
Part-time: 60 men, 154 women	**Ph.D.s:** 94%
Graduate: 2114 men, 2273 women	**Student/Faculty:** 10 to 1
Year: semesters, summer session	**Tuition:** $50,142
Room & Board: $14,890	**Freshman Class:** 16503 applied, 5845 accepted, 1338 enrolled
SAT or ACT: recommended	**CEEB CODE:** 2928
Application Deadline: January 5	**MOST COMPETITIVE**

University of Rochester, founded in 1850, is a private research institution offering programs in the arts and sciences, engineering and applied science, nursing, medicine and dentistry, business administration, music, and education. There are 3 undergraduate schools and 6 graduate schools. In addition to regional accreditation, University of Rochester has baccalaureate program accreditation with AACSB, ABET, ACPE, ADA, NASM, and NLNAC. The 707-acre campus is in a suburban area 2 miles south of downtown Rochester, NY. Including any residence halls, there are 192 buildings.

STUDENT LIFE: 70% of undergraduates are from out of state, mostly the Middle Atlantic. Students are from 50 states, 100 foreign countries, and Canada. 75% are from public schools. 7% are Hispanic; 7% race unknown; 5% African American; 48% White; 3% two or more races; 18% Foreign; 11% Asian American. 37% claim no religious affiliation; 19% Catholic; 13% Jewish. **Female To Male Ratio:** 1.0:1. The average age of freshmen is 18; all undergraduates, 20. 4% do not continue beyond their first year; 88% remain to graduate. **Housing:** 4112 students can be accommodated in college housing, which includes married student dorms and on-campus apartments. In addition, there are language/international houses, special-interest houses, and fraternity houses. On-campus housing is guaranteed for all 4 years, is guaranteed for the freshman year only, and is available on a lottery system for upperclassmen. 93% of students live on campus. Upperclassmen may keep cars.

FACULTY/CLASSROOMS: No introductory courses are taught by graduate students. The average class size in an introductory lecture is 75; in a laboratory is 20; and in a regular course is 20.

PROGRAMS OF STUDY: University of Rochester confers B.A., B.S., and B.M. degrees. Master's and doctoral degrees are also awarded. Bachelor's degrees are awarded in AGRICULTURE (environmental studies), BIOLOGICAL SCIENCE (biochemistry, biology/biological science, cell biology, ecology, microbiology, molecular biology, and neurosciences), BUSINESS (business administration and management and marketing), COMMUNICATIONS AND THE ARTS (American Sign Language, art history and appreciation, audio technology, classics, comparative literature, digital communications, English, English literature, film arts, French, German, Japanese, jazz, linguistics, media arts, music, music performance, music theory and composition, Russian, Spanish, studio art, and theatre arts), COMPUTER AND PHYSICAL SCIENCE (applied mathematics, astronomy, chemistry, computer science, geology, mathematics, optics, physics, and statistics), EDUCATION (music education), ENGINEERING AND ENVIRONMENTAL DESIGN (biomedical engineering, chemical engineering, electrical/electronics engineering, engineering and applied science, environmental science, geological engineering, mechanical engineering, and optical engineering), HEALTH PROFESSIONS (health, nursing, and public health), SOCIAL SCIENCE (African American studies, American studies, anthropology, archeology, cognitive science, East Asian studies, economics, history, interdisciplinary studies, international relations, Latin American studies, philosophy, political science/government, psychology, religion, Russian and Slavic studies, and women's studies). Biomedical engineering, optics, and political science are the strongest academically. Biology, economics, and engineering have the largest enrollments.

ACTIVITIES: 20% of men belong to 18 national fraternities; 20% of women belong to 15 national sororities. There are 279 groups on campus, including art, band, campus activities board, cheerleading, chess, choir, chorale, chorus, communications, computers, dance, debate, drama, drill team, environmental, ethnic, film, forensics, honors, international, jazz band, LGBT, literary magazine, marching band, musical theater, newspaper, opera, orchestra, pep band, photography, political, professional, radio and TV, religious, social, social service, student government, symphony, and yearbook. Popular campus events include Meliora Weekend, Yellowjacket Day, and Boar's Head Dinner. **Sports:** There are 10 intercollegiate sports for men and 11 for women, and 7 intramural sports for men and 7 for women. Facilities include an athletic center, a stadium, field house, an ice rink, courts for handball, racquetball, squash, and tennis, an indoor track, a fitness center and weight room, a jogging path, and an aquatic center. **Graduates:** From July 1, 2016 to June 30, 2017, 1658 bachelor's degrees were awarded. The most popular majors were psychology, economics, and business. In an average class, 76% graduate in 4 years or less and 86% graduate in 6 years or less.

SERVICES: Counseling and information services are available, as is tutoring in most subjects. There is access to screen reading and adaptive software. **Library/Resources:** The library contains 4.2 million volumes. Computerized library services include interlibrary loans, database searching, Internet access, and Wi-Fi capability. Special learning facilities include an art gallery, a radio station, labs for nuclear structure research and laser energetics, a center for visual science, the Strong Memorial Hospital, CEK Mees Observatory, Eastman School of Music, and Institute of Optics. **Physically Challenged Students:** 90% of the campus is accessible. Facilities include wheelchair ramps, elevators, special parking, specially equipped restrooms, special class scheduling, lowered drinking fountains, lowered telephones, and special housing. **Special:** Cross-registration is offered with Rochester Area Colleges. Selective programs for exceptional undergraduates in medicine (REMS), engineering (GEAR), and education (GRADE) guarantee admission to professional or graduate school upon completion of the bachelor's degree. The Take Five Scholars Program allows students to stay tuition-free for a fifth year of study. Rochester offers 3-2 programs in business, human development, neuroscience, physics and astronomy, and public health. Study abroad is possible in more than 40 countries. Internships, a Washington semester, B.A.-B.S. degrees, accelerated degree programs, dual and student-designed majors, nondegree study, and pass/fail options are available. There are 8 national honor societies, Phi Beta Kappa, a freshman honors program, and 13 departmental honors programs. **Visiting:** There are regularly scheduled orientations for prospective students, including a group information session, campus tour, and interview (optional for seniors). There are guides for informal visits; visitors may sit in on classes and stay overnight. To schedule a visit, contact the Office of Admissions. **Campus Safety and Security:** Measures include 24-hour foot and vehicle patrol, an emergency notification system, self-defense education, and security escort services. There are shuttle buses, emergency telephones, lighted pathways/sidewalks, and controlled access to dorms/residences.

REQUIREMENTS: The SAT or ACT is recommended. Applicants should be graduates of an accredited secondary school or have a GED equivalent. An essay or personal statement and recommendations are required. An interview is recommended. An audition is required for music majors. Applicants should complete the Common Application, Coalition Application, or the Universal College Application. Admission to the College of Arts, Sciences, and Engineering is based on a holistic review process that includes a "test-flexible" philosophy. As Rochester seeks to enroll a diverse and talented class each year, review procedures incorporate a variety of factors, including many kinds of academic records. In addition to submitting a record of courses and grades during secondary school, applicants must show evidence of preparation through examination results. A wide variety of test results can fulfill this requirement, including SAT Reasoning exams, the ACT, two or more results from SAT Subject exams, Advanced Placement, International Baccalaureate, AS- and A-level exams (in UK and Commonwealth countries), Gao Kao (China), and results from many other national secondary exams. AP credits are accepted. Important factors in the admissions decision are advanced placement or honors courses, personality/intangible qualities, and recommendations by school officials. Students focus on the humanities, social sciences, and natural sciences; 1 of the 3 areas will be their major, and they select a 3-course cluster in each of the other 2. A total of 128 credit hours with a minimum GPA of 2.0 is required to graduate. Additionally, all students must satisfy a freshman writing requirement and take 2 upper-level courses in their major that are writing intensive. **Procedure:** Freshmen are admitted in the fall. Entrance exams should be taken by December of the senior year. There are early decision and deferred admissions plans. Early decision applications should be filed by November 1; regular applications, by January 5 for fall entry. The fall 2017 application fee was $50. Notification of early decision is sent December 15; regular decision, April 1. Applications are accepted online. **Transfer Students:** 196 transfer students enrolled in 2016-2017. The most important criterion is an applicant's college record. 64 of 128 credits required for the bachelor's degree must be completed at University of Rochester. **International Students:** There are 1100 international students enrolled. They must take the TOEFL with a minimum score of 600 on the paper-based TOEFL (PBT) or 100 on the Internet-based version (iBT). They must also take the SAT or ACT.

ADMISSIONS: 35% of the 2017-2018 applicants were accepted. **Admissions Contact:** Jonathan Burdick, Dean of College Admissions. Email: *admit@admissions.rochester.edu* Web: *www.rochester.edu*

FINANCIAL AID: In 2017-2018, 86% of all full-time freshmen received some form of financial aid. 72% of all full-time freshmen received need-based aid. 20% of undergraduate students work part-time. University of Rochester is a member of CSS. The CSS/Profile and the state aid form are required. The FAFSA code is 002894. The priority date for freshman financial aid applications for fall entry is February 1.

UTICA COLLEGE C-3
www.utica.edu

Utica, NY 13502	**(315) 792-3006** **(800) 782-8884**
Fax: (315) 792-3003	**Email: admiss@utica.edu**
Full-time: 1234 men, 1667 women	**Faculty:** 143; IIB, av$
Part-time: 242 men, 542 women	**Ph.D.s:** 85%
Graduate: 677 men, 896 women	**Student/Faculty:** 11 to 1
Year: semesters, summer session	**Tuition:** $20,676
Room & Board: $10,834	**Freshman Class:** n/av
SAT or ACT: recommended	**CEEB CODE:** 2931
Application Deadline: open	**COMPETITIVE**

Utica College is a private, comprehensive institution founded by Syracuse University in 1946. There are 4 undergraduate schools and 1 graduate school. In addition to regional accreditation, UC has baccalaureate program accreditation with APTA, NLN, AOTA, and AACN. The 128-acre campus is in a suburban area 50 miles east of Syracuse. Including any residence halls, there are 18 buildings.

STUDENT LIFE: 82% of undergraduates are from New York. Others are from 47 states, 32 foreign countries, and Canada. 80% are from public schools. 66% are White; 11% African American; 8% Hispanic; 5% race unknown; 3% Asian American; 3% Foreign; 3% two or more races; 1% American Indian/Alaska Native. **Female To Male Ratio:** 1.4:1. The average age of freshmen is 18; all undergraduates, 21. 24% do not continue beyond their first year; 46% remain to graduate. **Housing:** 1034 students can be accommodated in college housing, which includes dorms. In addition, there are special-interest houses. On-campus housing is guaranteed for all 4 years and is available on a lottery system for upperclassmen. 65% of students commute. All students may keep cars.

FACULTY/CLASSROOMS: 49% of faculty are male; 51% are female. All teach undergraduates and do research. No introductory courses are taught by graduate students. The average class size in an introductory lecture is 23; in a laboratory is 11; and in a regular course is 17.

PROGRAMS OF STUDY: UC confers B.A., B.B.A., and B.S. degrees. Master's and doctoral degrees are also awarded. Bachelor's degrees are awarded in AGRICULTURE (animal science), BIOLOGICAL SCIENCE (biochemistry, biology/biological science, and neurosciences), BUSINESS (accounting, business administration and management, business economics, and insurance and risk management), COMMUNICATIONS AND THE ARTS (communications, English, journalism, and public relations), COMPUTER AND PHYSICAL SCIENCE (chemistry, computer science, computer security and information assurance, cyber intelligence/security studies, geoscience, mathematics, and physics), EDUCATION (education and foreign languages education), ENGINEERING AND ENVIRONMENTAL DESIGN (construction management), HEALTH PROFESSIONS (nursing, occupational therapy, physical therapy, and recreation therapy), SOCIAL SCIENCE (child psychology/development, criminal justice, economics, gerontology, history, liberal arts/general studies, philosophy, political science/government, psychobiology, psychology, social studies, and sociology). Occupational therapy, psychology, and biology are the strongest academically. Health studies, nursing, and criminal justice have the largest enrollments.

ACTIVITIES: 2% of men belong to 2 local and 3 national fraternities; 2% of women belong to 2 local and 3 national sororities. There are 86 groups on campus, including art, band, cheerleading, chess, choir, chorus, communications, computers, dance, drama, environmental, ethnic, film, honors, international, jazz band, LGBT, literary magazine, musical theater, newspaper, orchestra, pep band, photography, political, professional, radio and TV, religious, social, social service, student government, symphony, and yearbook. Popular campus events include outdoor concerts, Mock Elections, and Winter Weekend. **Sports:** There are 10 intercollegiate sports for men and 11 for women, and 28 intramural sports for men and 28 for women. Facilities include a gym, a swimming pool, tennis, racquetball, handball, and squash courts, Nautilus and weight rooms, dance and aerobic rooms, playing fields, a stadium, and hockey facilities. **Graduates:** From July 1, 2016 to June 30, 2017, 724 bachelor's degrees were awarded. The most popular majors were health studies (47%), criminal justice (20%), and business and marketing (9%). In an average class, 30% graduate in 4 years or less, 42% graduate in 5 years or less, and 44% graduate in 6 years or less.

SERVICES: Counseling and information services are available, as is tutoring in most subjects. There is a reader service for the blind, and remedial math, reading, and writing. **Library/Resources:** The library contains 307,523 volumes, 24,458 microform items, and 2,861 audio/video tapes/CDs/DVDs, and subscribes to 413 periodicals, including electronic. Computerized library services include interlibrary loans, database searching, Internet access, and Wi-Fi capability. Special learning facilities include an art gallery, radio and TV stations, an early childhood education lab, a math and writing center, a stock trading room, and occupational therapy, physical therapy, nursing, and physical science labs. **Physically Challenged Students:** 85% of the campus is accessible. Facilities include wheelchair ramps, elevators, special parking, specially equipped restrooms, and lowered drinking fountains. **Special:** UC offers co-op programs, internships, work-study programs in all majors, accelerated degrees, dual majors, and cross-registration with Hamilton College and the Mohawk Valley Consortium. Study abroad may be arranged in 9 countries. There is a 3-2 engineering degree with Syracuse University. There are 5 national honor societies and a freshman honors program. **Visiting:** There are regularly scheduled orientations for prospective students, including an interview, financial aid information, and a tour of the campus. There are guides for informal visits; visitors may sit in on classes and stay overnight. To schedule a visit, contact the Admissions Office. **Campus Safety and Security:** Measures include 24-hour foot and vehicle patrol, an emergency notification system, and security escort services. There are shuttle buses, emergency telephones, lighted pathways/sidewalks, and controlled access to dorms/residences.

REQUIREMENTS: The SAT or ACT and ACT Writing Test are recommended. Graduation from an accredited secondary school or satisfactory scores on the GED are required. Recommended high school courses include 4 years of English, 3 years each of math and social studies, and 2 years each of foreign language and science. An essay and an interview are also recommended. AP and CLEP credits are accepted. Important factors in the admissions decision are advanced placement or honors courses, extracurricular activities record, and leadership record. To graduate, students must complete a total of 120 to 128 hours with a minimum 2.0 GPA. They must complete a general education requirement including basic skills and distribution requirements. **Procedure:** Freshmen are admitted in the fall and spring. Entrance exams should be taken during the junior year. There are early decision, early admissions, deferred admissions, and rolling admissions plans. Application deadlines are open. The fall 2017 application fee was $40. Notification of early decision is sent December 15; regular decision, on a rolling basis. 834 early decision candidates were accepted for the 2017-2018 class. Applications are accepted online. **Transfer Students:** 136 transfer students enrolled in 2016-2017. Applicants must have a minimum GPA of 2.0. 30 of 128 credits required for the bachelor's degree must be completed at UC. **International Students:** There are 109 international students enrolled. They must take the TOEFL with a minimum score of 525 on the paper-based TOEFL (PBT) or 69 on the Internet-based version (iBT) and the Comprehensive English Language Test, and any one of the following tests: IELTS, APIEL, or MELAB. The SAT is recommended if the student's primary language is English.

Admissions Contact: Jeffery Gates, Vice President for Enrollment Management. Email: *admiss@utica.edu* Web: *www.utica.edu*

FINANCIAL AID: In 2017-2018, 90% of all full-time freshmen received some form of financial aid. 90% of all full-time freshmen received need-based aid. The average freshman award was $14,292. Need-based scholarships or need-based grants averaged $5,486; and need-based self-help aid (loans and jobs) averaged $3,751. UC is a member of CSS. The priority date for freshman financial aid applications for fall entry is February 15.

VASSAR COLLEGE D-4
www.vassar.edu

Poughkeepsie, NY 12604	**(845) 437-7300** **(800) 827-7270**
Fax: (845) 437-7063	**Email: admissions@vassar.edu**
Full-time: 956 men, 1378 women	**Faculty:** 281; IIB, ++$
Part-time: 4 men, 15 women	**Ph.D.s:** 85%
Graduate: n/av	**Student/Faculty:** 8 to 1
Year: semesters	**Tuition:** $55,210
Room & Board: $12,900	**Freshman Class:** 7746 applied, 1842 accepted, 626 enrolled
SAT EBR-W/M: 720/713 **ACT:** 32	**CEEB CODE:** 2956
Application Deadline: January 1	**MOST COMPETITIVE**

Vassar College, founded in 1861, is a highly selective, residential, private college of liberal arts and sciences. There is 1 undergraduate school. The 1000-acre campus is in a suburban area 75 miles north of New York City in the Mid-Hudson River Valley. Including any residence halls, there are 100 buildings.

STUDENT LIFE: 75% of undergraduates are from out of state, mostly the West. Students are from 49 states, 52 foreign countries, and Canada. 68% are from public schools. 8% are Foreign; 7% two or more races; 57% White; 4% African American; 13% Asian American; 11% Hispanic. **Female To Male Ratio:** 1.5:1. The average age of freshmen is 18; all undergraduates, 20. 4% do not continue beyond their first year; 91% remain to graduate. **Housing:** 2380 students can be accommodated in college housing, which includes gender neutral, single sex dorms, coed dorms, on-campus apartments, and off-campus apartments, an all-female residence hall, and cooperative living unit. On-campus housing is guaranteed for all 4 years. 97% of students live on campus. All students may keep cars.

FACULTY/CLASSROOMS: 53% of faculty are male; 47% are female. All teach undergraduates and all do research. No introductory courses are taught by graduate students. The average class size in an introductory lecture is 21; in a laboratory is 15; and in a regular course is 19.

PROGRAMS OF STUDY: VC confers B.A. degrees. Master's degrees are also awarded. Bachelor's degrees are awarded in AGRICULTURE (environmental studies), BIOLOGICAL SCIENCE (biochemistry and neurosciences), COMMUNICATIONS AND THE ARTS (art history, art, Chinese, dramatic arts, English, film arts, French and Francophone studies, German studies, Italian, Japanese, media arts, music, Russian, Spanish and Hispanic studies, and studio art), COMPUTER AND PHYSICAL SCIENCE (astronomy, chemistry, computer science, earth science, geology, mathematics, and physics), EDUCATION (educational studies), HEALTH PROFESSIONS (biology and premedicine), SOCIAL SCIENCE (African studies, American studies, anthropology, Asian/Oriental studies, classical/ancient civilization, cognitive science, economics, geography, Hispanic American studies, history, international studies, Judaic studies, Latin American studies, medieval studies, philosophy, political science/government, prelaw, psychology, religion, science and society, sociology, urban studies, Victorian studies, and women's studies). Economics, political science, English, and biology have the largest enrollments.

ACTIVITIES: There are no fraternities or sororities. There are 130 groups on campus, including art, band, chess, choir, chorale, chorus, communications, computers, dance, debate, drama, environmental, ethnic, film, honors, international, jazz band, LGBT, literary magazine, musical theater, newspaper, opera, orchestra, outdoors club, photography, political, professional, radio and TV, religious, social, social service, student government, symphony, and yearbook. Popular campus events include Founders Day, Spring and Fall Formals, and Family Weekend. **Sports:** There are 12 intercollegiate sports for men and 13 for women, and 18 intramural sports for men and 18 for women. Facilities include a field house with a swimming pool, indoor tennis courts, weight and conditioning room, gyms with squash and basketball facilities, a 9-hole golf course, outdoor tennis courts, an all-weather track, soccer fields, turf field for field hockey and lacrosse, a baseball diamond, rugby field, club and intramural fields, running track, and an exercise and fitness center. **Graduates:** From July 1, 2016 to June 30, 2017, 616 bachelor's degrees were awarded. The most popular majors were economics (12%), political science (8%), and psychological sciences (7%). In an average class, 1% graduate in 3 years or less, 86% graduate in 4 years or less, 90% graduate in 5 years or less, and 91% graduate in 6 years or less. Of the 2016 graduating class, 19% were enrolled in graduate school within 6 months of graduation, and 67% were employed.

SERVICES: Counseling and information services are available, as is tutoring in most subjects. There is a reader service for the blind. **Library/Resources:** The library contains 1.1 million volumes, 107,525 microform items, and 25,000 audio/video tapes/CDs/DVDs, and subscribes to 98,608 periodicals including electronic. Computerized library services include interlibrary loans, database searching, Internet access, and Wi-Fi capability. Special learning facilities include an art gallery, a natural history museum, a radio station, studio art buildings with studios, a large astronomical observatory, 3 theaters, a dance theater and studios, concert halls and music practice rooms, an environmental field station and ecological preserve, an intercultural center, and many teaching and research-oriented lab facilities for the sciences. **Physically Challenged Students:** 70% of the campus is accessible. Facilities include wheelchair ramps, elevators, special parking, specially equipped restrooms, special class scheduling, and lowered drinking fountains. There is an Office for Accessibility and Educational Opportunity, signage in braille, and assisted listening devices. **Special:** The school offers community-engaged learning/internships in all academic areas, as well as dual majors, independent/self-designed majors, and nonrecorded grade options. Vassar runs study-abroad programs in 7 countries and students have access to study in over 250 other approved programs around the world, as well as domestic exchange options. A 3-2 engineering degree with Dartmouth College is offered. There is a chapter of Phi Beta Kappa. **Visiting:** There are regularly scheduled orientations for prospective students, including a campus tour, an information session, and a class visit or overnight when possible. To schedule a visit, contact the Office of Admission. **Campus Safety and Security:** Measures include 24-hour foot and vehicle patrol, an emergency notification system, self-defense education, and security escort services. There are shuttle buses, emergency telephones, lighted pathways/sidewalks, and controlled access to dorms/residences.

REQUIREMENTS: The SAT or ACT is required; optional writing tests are not required. A high school diploma or an approved alternative is required for admission. The high school program should typically include advanced level work with 4 years each of English, social studies, math, foreign language, and science. An essay and 2 letters of recommendation are also required. AP credits are accepted. Important factors in the admissions decision are recommendations by school officials, advanced placement or honors courses, and extracurricular activities record. To graduate, students must have a total of 34 units equivalent to 120 credit hours, with a minimum GPA of 2.0. Of this total, no more than 17 units may be in a single field of concentration and 8 1/2 units must be outside the major field. Entering freshmen must take the freshman writing course. All students must meet the foreign language proficiency requirement and must take a quantitative skills course before their third year. A thesis is required in most departments. **Procedure:** Freshmen are admitted in the fall. Entrance exams should be taken as early as possible but no later than December of the senior year. There are early decision and deferred admissions plans. Early decision applications should be filed by November 15; regular applications, by January 1 for fall entry. The fall 2017 application fee was $70. Notification of early decision is sent December 15; regular decision, March 30. 274 early decision candidates were accepted for the 2017-2018 class. 985 applicants were on the 2017 waiting list; 74 were admitted. Applications are accepted online. **Transfer Students:** 10 transfer students enrolled in 2016-2017. Applicants must have a high level of achievement in both high school and college work. SAT or ACT is required along with 2 recommendations. 17 of 34 credits required for the bachelor's degree must be completed at VC. **International Students:** There are 192 international students enrolled. They must take the TOEFL with a minimum score of 600 on the paper-based TOEFL (PBT) or 100 on the Internet-based version (iBT). They must take the IELTS, and either the SAT or ACT.

ADMISSIONS: 24% of the 2017-2018 applicants were accepted. The SAT scores for the 2017-2018 freshman class were: Math-- 1% below 500, 2% between 500 and 599, 34% between 600 and 699, and 63% between 700 and 800. Evidence-Based Reading/Writing-- 2% between 500 and 599, 26% between 600 and 699, and 72% between 700 and 800. The ACT scores were 11% between 24 and 29, and 89% above 30. 88% of the current freshmen were in the top fifth of their class; 99% were in the top two fifths. **Admissions Contact:** J.C. Tesone, Director of Admission. Email: *admissions@vassar.edu* Web: *www.vassar.edu*

FINANCIAL AID: In 2017-2018, 71% of all full-time freshmen received some form of financial aid. 64% of all full-time freshmen received need-based aid. The average freshman award was $52,284. Need-based scholarships or need-based grants averaged $46,709 ($66,324 maximum); need-based self-help aid (loans and jobs) averaged $4,504 ($5,900 maximum); and $967 from other forms of aid. 65% of undergraduate students work part-time. The average financial indebtedness of the 2017 graduate was $15,465. Vassar is a member of CSS. The CSS/Profile and the college's own financial statement are required. The FAFSA code is 002895. The priority date for freshman financial aid applications for fall entry is November 15.

VAUGHN COLLEGE OF AERONAUTICS AND TECHNOLOGY *(The complete profile is made available exclusively on our website, www.barronspac.com)*

WAGNER COLLEGE D-5
www.wagner.edu

Staten Island, NY 10301 (718) 390-3411 (800) 221-1010
Fax: (718) 390-3105 **Email:** admissions@wagner.edu
Full-time: 629 men, 1078 women
Part-time: 12 men, 22 women
Graduate: 149 men, 303 women
Year: semesters, summer session
Room & Board: $13,260
Faculty: 96
Ph.D.s: 90%
Student/Faculty: 15 to 1
Tuition: $43,980
Freshman Class: 2803 applied, 1920 accepted, 421 enrolled
SAT CR/M/W: 575/550/550 **ACT:** 25
CEEB CODE: 2966
Application Deadline: February 15
COMPETITIVE+

Wagner College, founded in 1883, is a private liberal arts institution. There is 1 undergraduate school and 1 graduate school. In addition to regional accreditation, WC has baccalaureate program accreditation with AACSB, ACBSP, NLN, ARC-PA, and ACS. The 105-acre campus is in a suburban area 10 miles from Manhattan. Including any residence halls, there are 19 buildings.

STUDENT LIFE: 54% of undergraduates are from out of state, mostly the Middle Atlantic. Students are from 48 states, 19 foreign countries, and Canada. 62% are from public schools. 77% are White; 6% African American; 3% Asian American; 2% Foreign; 2% two or more races; 11% race unknown; 10% Hispanic. **Female To Male Ratio:** 1.8:1. The average age of freshmen is 18; all undergraduates, 22. 17% do not continue beyond their first year; 70% remain to graduate. **Housing:** 1600 students can be accommodated in college housing, which includes dorms and off-campus apartments. In addition, there are honors houses, language/international houses, special-interest houses, fraternity and sorority houses, quiet floors, medical floors, themed and wellness housing, and senior year housing. On-campus housing is guaranteed for all 4 years and is available on a lottery system for upperclassmen. 67% of students live on campus. All students may keep cars.

FACULTY/CLASSROOMS: 45% of faculty are male; 55% are female. All teach undergraduates. No introductory courses are taught by graduate students. The average class size in an introductory lecture is 21; in a laboratory is 13; and in a regular course is 19.

PROGRAMS OF STUDY: WC confers B.A. and B.S. degrees. Master's degrees are also awarded. Bachelor's degrees are awarded in BIOLOGICAL SCIENCE (biology/biological science and microbiology), BUSINESS (accounting and business administration and management), COMMUNICATIONS AND THE ARTS (arts administration/management, dramatic arts, English, fine arts, music, theater design, and visual and performing arts), COMPUTER AND PHYSICAL SCIENCE (chemistry, computer science, mathematics, and physics), EDUCATION (elementary education, middle school education, and secondary education), HEALTH PROFESSIONS (nursing and physician's assistant), SOCIAL SCIENCE (anthropology, history, philosophy, political science/government, psychology, public administration, and sociology). Natural sciences and health professions are the strongest academically. Business, nursing, and psychology have the largest enrollments.

ACTIVITIES: 5% of men belong to 2 local and 2 national fraternities; 12% of women belong to 1 local and 3 national sororities. There are 65 groups on campus, including art, band, cheerleading, chess, choir, chorale, chorus, communications, computers, dance, debate, drama, environmental, ethnic, honors, international, jazz band, LGBT, literary magazine, marching band, musical theater, newspaper, pep band, political, professional, religious, social, social service, student government, symphony, and yearbook. Popular campus events include Songfest, WagnerStock, Homecoming, Spring Fling Week, Fall Fest, and Family Weekend. **Sports:** There are 8 intercollegiate sports for men and 10 for women, and 5 intramural sports for men and 4 for women. Facilities include a football stadium, a gym, a regulation-sized pool, a fitness center, track and field, a basketball arena, golf, lacrosse, tennis courts, soccer/softball/baseball field, rugby, and ice hockey. **Graduates:** From July 1, 2016 to June 30, 2017, 445 bachelor's degrees were awarded. The most popular majors were health professions/related programs (31%), business and marketing (15%), and visual and preforming arts (14%). In an average class, 60% graduate in 4 years or less, 64% graduate in 5 years or less, and 66% graduate in 6 years or less. Of the 2016 graduating class, 20% were enrolled in graduate school within 6 months of graduation, and 79% were employed.

SERVICES: Counseling and information services are available, as is tutoring in every subject. There is a reader service for the blind, and remedial math, reading, and writing. **Library/Resources:** The library contains 158,160 volumes, 218 microform items, and 2,453 audio/video tapes/CDs/DVDs, and subscribes to 56,399 periodicals, including electronic. Computerized library services include interlibrary loans, database searching, Internet access, and Wi-Fi capability. Special learning facilities include an art gallery, a planetarium, and a nursing resource center. **Physically Challenged Students:** 25% of the campus is accessible. Facilities include wheelchair ramps, elevators, special parking, specially equipped restrooms, special class scheduling, and lowered drinking fountains. **Special:** Internships or field-based research is required of all majors. Students may earn B.A.-B.S. degrees in psychology. Student-designed and dual majors, credit for life experience, a Washington semester, nondegree study, and pass/fail options are available. Study abroad in most countries is possible. Learning Communities are available for freshmen, sophomores/juniors, and seniors. There are 11 national honor societies and a freshman honors program. **Visiting:** There are regularly scheduled orientations for prospective students, including a presentation by the Admissions Office. There are guides for informal visits; visitors may sit in on classes and stay overnight. To schedule a visit, contact the Admissions Office. **Campus Safety and Security:** Measures include 24-hour foot and vehicle patrol, an emergency notification system, and security escort services. There are shuttle buses, emergency telephones, lighted pathways/sidewalks, controlled access to dorms/residences, and ID card access into residence halls.

REQUIREMENTS: Graduation from an accredited secondary school is required, with 21 academic credits or Carnegie units, including 4 years of English, 3 years each of history and math, 2 years each of foreign language, and science with 1 unit of lab, and 7 units of academic electives. An essay is required, and an interview is strongly recommended. Auditions are required for music and theater applicants. An interview is required for the Physician Assistant Program. A GPA of 3.0 is required. AP and CLEP credits are accepted. Important factors in the admissions decision are advanced placement or honors courses, recommendations by school officials, and extracurricular activities record. To graduate, students must complete 36 units with 12 to 18 in the major and a minimum GPA of 2.0. All students must take courses in English, math, and multidisciplinary studies. In addition, students must fulfill distribution requirements in physical science, life science, math and computers, history, literature, philosophy and religion, foreign culture, aesthetics, and human behavior. All students are required to enroll in Learning Communities. **Procedure:** Freshmen are admitted in the fall and spring. Entrance exams should be taken by December of the senior year. There are early decision and deferred admissions plans. Early decision applications should be filed by December 1; regular applications, by February 15 for fall entry; and November 1 for spring entry. Notification of early decision is sent December 1; regular decision, March 1. 76 early decision candidates were accepted for the 2017-2018 class. 95 applicants were on the 2017 waiting list; 20 were admitted. Applications are accepted online. **Transfer Students:** 130 transfer students enrolled in 2016-2017. Transfer students should have a minimum of 30 credit hours earned with a GPA of 2.5. Applicants must submit all college and high school transcripts, a letter of recommendation, and a personal statement. An interview is recommended. SAT or ACT scores taken within the past 5 years may be submitted. 9 of 36 credits required for the bachelor's degree must be completed at WC. **International Students:** There are 36 international students enrolled. They must take the TOEFL with a minimum score of 550 on the paper-based TOEFL (PBT) or 79 on the Internet-based version (iBT).

ADMISSIONS: 68% of the 2017-2018 applicants were accepted. The SAT scores for the 2017-2018 freshman class were: Critical Reading-- 26% below 500, 44% between 500 and 599, 25% between 600 and 699, and 5% between 700 and 800. Math-- 23% below 500, 50% between 500 and 599, 26% between 600 and 699, and 1% between 700 and 800. Writing-- 28% below 500, 40% between 500 and 599, 29% between 600 and 699, and 3% between 700 and 800. The ACT scores were 2% between 12 and 17, 39% between 18 and 23, 53% between 24 and 29, and 6% above 30. 38% of the current freshmen were in the top fifth of their class; 86% were in the top two fifths. **Admissions Contact:** James Gibbons, Director of Admissions. Email: *admissions@wagner.edu* Web: *www.wagner.edu*

FINANCIAL AID: In 2017-2018, 94% of all full-time freshmen received some form of financial aid. The average freshman award was $31,362. Need-based scholarships or need-based grants averaged $17,324; need-based self-help aid (loans and jobs) averaged $4,368; non-need-based athletic scholarships averaged $31,875; other non-need-based awards and non-need-based scholarships averaged $2,361; and $22,530 from other forms of aid. 19% of undergraduate students work part-time. The average financial indebtedness of the 2017 graduate was $31,850. WC is a member of CSS. The state aid form is required. The FAFSA code is 002899. The priority date for freshman financial aid applications for fall entry is January 15.

WEBB INSTITUTE D-5
www.webb-institute.edu

Glen Cove, NY 11542	**(516) 671-2213**
Fax: (516) 674-9838	**Email: admissions@webb-institute.edu**
Full-time: 75 men, 17 women	**Faculty:** 7
Part-time: n/av	**Ph.D.s:** 60%
Graduate: n/av	**Student/Faculty:** 9 to 1
Year: semesters	**Tuition:** see profile
Room & Board: $14,400	**Freshman Class:** n/av
SAT CR/M: 700/740 **ACT:** 34	**CEEB CODE:** 2970
Application Deadline: August 16	**MOST COMPETITIVE**

Webb Institute, founded in 1889 by William Webb, is a unique, top-ranked undergraduate institution offering 1 academic option: a double major in Naval Architecture and Marine Engineering. It is also the only full-tuition scholarship, private undergraduate program of its kind in the country. There is 1 undergraduate school. In addition to regional accreditation, Webb has baccalaureate program accreditation with ABET. The 26-acre campus is in a suburban area 30 miles from New York City on the north shore of Long Island. Including any residence halls, there are 11 buildings.

STUDENT LIFE: 79% of undergraduates are from out of state, mostly the Northeast. Students are from 26 states, and 2 foreign countries. **Male To Female Ratio:** 4.4:1. The average age of freshmen is 18; all undergraduates, 20. 18% do not continue beyond their first year; 71% remain to graduate. **Housing:** 110 students can be accommodated in college housing, which includes dorms. On-campus housing is guaranteed for all 4 years. All students may keep cars.

FACULTY/CLASSROOMS: 90% of faculty are male; 10% are female. All teach undergraduates, 50% do research, and 50% do both. No introductory courses are taught by graduate students. The average class size in an introductory lecture is 23; in a laboratory is 12; and in a regular course is 51.

PROGRAMS OF STUDY: Webb confers B.S. degrees. Bachelor's degrees are awarded in ENGINEERING AND ENVIRONMENTAL DESIGN (naval architecture and marine engineering). Naval architecture and marine engineering are the strongest academically and have the largest enrollments.

ACTIVITIES: There are no fraternities or sororities. Students can participate in the North Shore Symphony Orchestra or the North Shore Community Chorus. There are athletic clubs, sailing, rowing, chorale, jazz band, orchestra, professional, social, student government, and yearbook. Popular campus events include Parents Weekend, Webbstock, and Great Gatsby. **Sports:** There are 5 intercollegiate sports for men and 5 for women, and 4 intramural sports for men and 4 for women. Facilities include a gymnasium, tennis courts, basketball and vollyball courts, and athletic fields. **Graduates:** The most popular majors were naval architecture and marine engineering (100%). Of the 2016 graduating class, 100% were employed within 6 months of graduation.

SERVICES: Counseling and information services are available, as is tutoring in most subjects. **Library/Resources:** The library contains 55,000 volumes, 1,633 microform items, and 1,851 audio/video tapes/CDs/DVDs, and subscribes to 267 periodicals, including electronic. Computerized library services include interlibrary loans, database searching, Internet access, and Wi-Fi capability. **Physically Challenged Students:** 90% of the campus is accessible. Facilities include elevators and special parking. **Special:** All students are employed 2 months each year through co-op programs. **Visiting:** There are regularly scheduled orientations for prospective students, and Weekend Open House in October. There are guides for informal visits; visitors may sit in on classes and stay overnight. To schedule a visit, contact Lauren Carballo at lcarballo@webb.edu. **Campus Safety and Security:** Measures include 24-hour foot and vehicle patrol. There are emergency telephones, lighted pathways/sidewalks, and student and professional security services.

REQUIREMENTS: Applicants should be graduates of an accredited secondary school with 16 academic credits completed, including 4 each in English and math, 2 each in history and science, 1 in foreign language, and 3 in electives. 3 SAT Subject tests in writing, math level I or II, and physics or chemistry are required, as is an interview. Candidates must be U.S. citizens. Important factors in the admissions decision are advanced placement or honors courses, evidence of special talent, and personality/intangible qualities. The curriculum is prescribed, with all students taking the same courses in each of the 4 years. The Webb program has 4 practical 8-week paid work periods: freshman year, a mechanic in a shipyard; sophomore year, a cadet in the engine room of a ship; and junior and senior years, a junior engineer in a design office. All students must complete a senior seminar, thesis, and technical reports, as well as make engineering inspection visits. A total of 146 credits with a minimum passing grade of 70% is required to graduate. **Procedure:** Freshmen are admitted in the fall. Entrance exams should be taken by January of the senior year. There is a early decision plan. Applications should be filed by August 16 for fall entry. The fall 2017 application fee was $25. **Transfer Students:** Transfers must enter as freshmen. SAT/ACT scores and an interview are required. 146 credits required for the bachelor's degree must be completed at Webb. **International Students:** There are 2 international students enrolled. They must also take the SAT or ACT, and the college's own entrance exam.

Admissions Contact: Steven P Ostendorff, Director of Admissions. Email: *admissions@webb-institute.edu* Web: *www.webb-institute.edu*

FINANCIAL AID: The CSS/Profile and the college's own financial statement are required. The FAFSA code is 002900. Check with the school for current application deadlines.

WELLS COLLEGE C-3
www.wells.edu

Aurora, NY 13026	**(315) 364-3266** **(800) 952-9355**
	Email: admissions@wells.edu
Full-time: 181 men, 377 women	**Faculty:** 34
Part-time: 7 men, 7 women	**Ph.D.s:** 91%
Graduate: n/av	**Student/Faculty:** 16 to 1
Year: semesters	**Tuition:** $37,500
Room & Board: $13,000	**Freshman Class:** 2217 applied, 1388 accepted, 168 enrolled
SAT CR/M/W: 510/500/480 **ACT:** 24	**CEEB CODE:** 2971
Application Deadline: March 1	**COMPETITIVE**

Wells College, founded in 1868, is a private liberal arts institution. The figures in the above capsule and in this profile are approximate. There is 1 undergraduate school. The 365-acre campus is in a small town in the heart of New Yorks Finger Lakes, in the village of Aurora, 30 miles north of Ithaca, 1 hour from Rochester and Syracuse, and 4 hours from New York City. Including any residence halls, there are 22 buildings.

STUDENT LIFE: 74% of undergraduates are from New York. Others are from 23 states, 5 foreign countries, and Canada. 93% are from public schools. 62% are White; 15% African American; 9% race unknown; 8% Hispanic; 4% two or more races; 2% Asian American; 1% American Indian/Alaska Native; 1% Foreign. **Female To Male Ratio:** 2.0:1. The average age of freshmen is 18; all undergraduates, 20. 30% do not continue beyond their first year; 55% remain to graduate. **Housing:** 450 students can be accommodated in college housing, which includes dorms and off-campus apartments. In addition, there are special-interest houses, and housing for nontraditional-age students. On-campus housing is guaranteed for all 4 years. 85% of students live on campus. All students may keep cars.

FACULTY/CLASSROOMS: 44% of faculty are male; 56% are female. All teach undergraduates, and 10% do research. No introductory courses are taught by graduate students. The average class size in an introductory lecture is 25; in a laboratory is 16; and in a regular course is 14.

PROGRAMS OF STUDY: WC confers B.A. and B.S. degrees. Bachelor's degrees are awarded in BIOLOGICAL SCIENCE (biochemistry, biology/biological science, and molecular biology), BUSINESS (business administration and management), COMMUNICATIONS AND THE ARTS (creative writing, dance, dramatic arts, English, literature, film and media studies, Spanish, theatre studies, and visual and performing arts), COMPUTER AND PHYSICAL SCIENCE (chemistry, computer science, mathematics, and physics), EDUCATION (early childhood education and elementary education), ENGINEERING AND ENVIRONMENTAL DESIGN (environmental science), SOCIAL SCIENCE (anthropology, economics, history, international studies, philosophy, political science/ government, psychology, sociology, and women and gender studies). Psychology, and biology are the strongest academically. Psychology, English, and biological and chemical sciences have the largest enrollments.

ACTIVITIES: There are no fraternities or sororities. There are 50 groups on campus, including campus greens, Japanese cultural club, Model UN, Spanish club, WILL (Women in Lifelong Learning), art, band, bell ringers, choir, chorale, chorus, computers, dance, drama, environmental, ethnic, forensics, international, jazz band, LGBT, literary magazine, newspaper, orchestra, photography, political, professional, religious, social, social service, and student government. Popular campus events include Odd-Even Weekends, Spring Weekend, and Senior Day. **Sports:** There are 7 intercollegiate sports for men and 9 for women, and 2 intramural sports for men and 2 for women. Facilities include artificial turf complex for baseball, softball, field hockey, soccer, lacross, grass fields, softball fields, 5-lane competition pool, gymnasium, basketball, and volleyball. The sports medicine facility has tennis courts. **Graduates:** From July 1, 2016 to June 30, 2017, 82 bachelor's degrees were awarded. The most popular majors were psychology (17%), English (10%), and sociology/anthropology (6%). In an average class, 2% graduate in 3 years or less, 60% graduate in 4 years or less, 61% graduate in 5 years or less, and 62% graduate in 6 years or less. Of the 2016 graduating class, 15% were enrolled in graduate school within 6 months of graduation, and 37% were employed.

SERVICES: Counseling and information services are available, as is tutoring in most subjects, such as math, biology, chemistry, political science, women and gender studies, Shakespeare, Spanish, Statistics, Calculus 1, Calculus 2, psychology, history, and international studies. There is remedial reading. Assistance is provided as needed on an individual basis. Extended-time testing options are also available. **Library/ Resources:** The library contains 218,000 volumes, 14,882 microform items, and 1,154 audio/video tapes/CDs/DVDs, and subscribes to 371 periodicals, including electronic. Computerized library services include interlibrary loans, database searching, Internet access, and Wi-Fi capability. Special learning facilities include an art gallery, the Wells College archives, an education curriculum center, and a walk-through art gallery. Database training is available as part of the library's information literacy program. There is also a Book Arts Center containing facilities for bookbinding, letter-press, and calligraphy. **Physically Challenged Students:** 43% of the campus is accessible. Facilities include wheelchair ramps, elevators, special parking, special class scheduling, and lowered telephones. **Special:** Wells offers cross-registration with Cornell University, Cayuga Community College, and Ithaca College; internships; and accelerated degree programs in all majors. Study abroad in 20 countries is permitted. A 3-2 engineering degree is available with Columbia, Clarkson, and Cornell Universities. Students may also earn a 4+1 MBA through the University of Clarkson, and a 4+1 MEd through the University of Rochester (30% tuition reduction agreement). Student-designed majors and pass/ fail options are available. Work-study, B.A.-B.S. degrees, and dual majors are also available. There are 2 national honor societies and a chapter of Phi Beta Kappa. **Visiting:** There are regularly scheduled orientations for prospective students, including tours, interviews, class attendance, presentations, open houses, an overnight host program, and meetings with faculty and coaches. There are guides for informal visits; visitors may sit in on classes and stay overnight. To schedule a visit, contact the Admissions Office. **Campus Safety and Security:** Measures include 24-hour foot and vehicle patrol, emergency notification system, self-defense education, and security escort services. There are shuttle buses, emergency telephones, and lighted pathways/sidewalks. The campus safety officers are N.Y.S. licensed security guards.

REQUIREMENTS: The SAT or ACT is required. Graduation from an accredited secondary school should include 20 academic credits or Carnegie units. High school courses must include 4 years of English, 3 years each of a foreign language and math, and 2 years each of history and lab science. 1 teacher recommendation, an essay/personal statement are required, and an interview is strongly recommended. AP and CLEP credits are accepted. Important factors in the admissions decision are recommendations by school officials, extracurricular activities record, and advanced placement or honors courses. To graduate, students must complete a total of 120 credit hours, including 33 to 63 in the major, with a minimum GPA of 2.0 overall and in the major. All students must complete 2 first-year experience courses, a comprehensive exam, 3 January intersession internships/courses, and a senior project/thesis. Distribution requirements include 4 courses in physical education and wellness, 3 each in natural and social sciences and arts and humanities, 2 in foreign language, and 1 in formal reasoning. **Procedure:** Freshmen are admitted in the fall. Entrance exams should be taken prior to application. There are early decision, early admissions, and deferred admissions plans. Early decision applications should be filed by December 15; regular applications, by March 1 for fall entry. The fall 2017 application fee was $40. Notification of early decision is sent January 15. Applications are accepted online. **Transfer Students:** 56 transfer students enrolled in 2016-2017. Applicants must be in good standing at the institution last attended. A minimum GPA of 2.0 is required. Wells requires official college and high school transcripts, a personal statement, standardized test scores, and a recommendation from a professor. An interview is strongly recommended. 60 of 120 credits required for the bachelor's degree must be completed at Wells. **International Students:** There are 14 international students enrolled. They must take the TOEFL with a minimum score of 550 on the paper-based TOEFL (PBT) or 80 on the Internet-based version (iBT). They must also take the SAT or ACT.

ADMISSIONS: 63% of the 2017-2018 applicants were accepted. The SAT scores for the 2017-2018 freshman class were: Critical Reading-- 49% below 500, 37% between 500 and 599, 12% between 600 and 699, and 2% between 700 and 800. Math-- 56% below 500, 35% between 500 and 599, 7% between 600 and 699, and 2% between 700 and 800. Writing-- 59% below 500, 32% between 500 and 599, and 9% between 600 and 699. The ACT scores were 54% between 18 and 23, 41% between 24 and 29, and 5% above 30. 3 freshmen graduated first in their class. **Admissions Contact:** Kishan Zuber, Vice President for Enrollment Services. Email: *admissions@wells.edu* Web: *www.wells.edu*

FINANCIAL AID: In 2017-2018, 99% of all full-time freshmen received some form of financial aid. 78% of all full-time freshmen received need-based aid. The average freshman award was $18,505. Need-based scholarships or need-based grants averaged $13,645 ($21,320 maximum); need-based self-help aid (loans and jobs) averaged $4,900 ($6,600 maximum); and other non-need-based awards and non-need-based scholarships averaged $6,850 ($10,500 maximum). 82% of undergraduate students work part-time. The average financial indebtedness of the 2017 graduate was $20,355. WC is a member of CSS. The FAFSA code is 002901. The priority date for freshman financial aid applications for fall entry is March 15.

YESHIVA UNIVERSITY — D-5

www.yu.edu

New York, NY 10033 — **(212) 960-5277**

Fax: (212) 960-0086	**Email:** yuadmit@ymail.yu.edu
Full-time: 1438 men, 1379 women	**Faculty:** I, av$
Part-time: 36 men, 16 women	**Ph.D.s:** 79%
Graduate: 1701 men, 2183 women	**Student/Faculty:** n/av
Year: semesters, summer session	**Tuition:** $42,000
Room & Board: $10,750	**Freshman Class:** 1898 applied, 1319 accepted, 911 enrolled
SAT CR/M/W: 619/622/610 **ACT:** 26	**CEEB CODE:** 2990
Application Deadline: December 1	**VERY COMPETITIVE**

Yeshiva University, founded in 1886, is an independent liberal arts institution offering undergraduate programs through its undergraduate college for men, Stern College for women, and the Sy Syms School of Business. The figures in the above capsule and in this profile are approximate. There are 3 undergraduate schools and 9 graduate schools. In addition to regional accreditation, Yeshiva has baccalaureate program accreditation with CSWE. The 26-acre campus is in an urban area in New York City.

STUDENT LIFE: 44% of undergraduates are from out of state. Students are from 31 states, 16 foreign countries, and Canada. 14% are from public schools. **Female To Male Ratio:** 1.1:1. The average age of freshmen is 17; all undergraduates, 19. 8% do not continue beyond their first year; 92% remain to graduate. **Housing:** 1600 students can be accommodated in college housing, which includes dorms and off-campus apartments. On-campus housing is guaranteed for all 4 years. 85% of students live on campus. Alcohol is not permitted. All students may keep cars.

FACULTY/CLASSROOMS: 73% of faculty are male; 27% are female. 58% teach undergraduates. No introductory courses are taught by graduate students. The average class size in an introductory lecture is 38; in a laboratory is 15; and in a regular course is 18.

PROGRAMS OF STUDY: Yeshiva confers B.A. and B.S. degrees. Associate degrees are also awarded. Bachelor's degrees are awarded in BIOLOGICAL SCIENCE (biology/biological science), BUSINESS (accounting, business administration and management, and marketing/retailing/merchandising), COMMUNICATIONS AND THE ARTS (classical languages, communications, English, French, Hebrew, music, and speech/debate/rhetoric), COMPUTER AND PHYSICAL SCIENCE (chemistry, computer science, and mathematics), ENGINEERING AND ENVIRONMENTAL DESIGN (preengineering), HEALTH PROFESSIONS (health science), SOCIAL SCIENCE (economics, history, philosophy, political science/government, psychology, religion, and sociology). Liberal arts, and Jewish studies are the strongest academically. Accounting, psychology, and economics have the largest enrollments.

ACTIVITIES: There are no fraternities or sororities. There are 70 groups on campus, including art, choir, computers, drama, honors, international, jazz band, literary magazine, musical theater, newspaper, political, professional, religious, social service, student government, and yearbook. Popular campus events include a holiday and dramatic presentations, and parents day. **Sports:** There are 8 intercollegiate sports for men and 2 for women, and 5 intramural sports for men and 4 for women. Facilities include variety of facilities, and a gym. **Graduates:** From July 1, 2016 to June 30, 2017, 631 bachelor's degrees were awarded. The most popular majors were business (27%), psychology (17%), and biology (14%).

SERVICES: There is remedial reading and writing. There is also a writing center, which helps students with composition and verbal skills. There is also a peer tutoring program, a career center, writing centers, and academic support. **Library/Resources:** The library contains 900,000 volumes, 759,000 microform items, 980 audio/video tapes/CDs/DVDs, and subscribes to 7,790 periodicals, including electronic. Computerized library services include interlibrary loans and database searching. Special learning facilities include an art gallery. **Physically Challenged Students:** 95% of the campus is accessible. Facilities include wheelchair ramps and elevators. **Special:** YU offers a 3-2 degree in occupational therapy with Columbia and New York Universities; a 3-4 degree in podiatry with the New York College of Podiatric Medicine; and a 3-2 or 4-2 degree in engineering with Columbia University. Stern College students may take courses in advertising, photography, and design at the Fashion Institute of Technology. Study-abroad programs may be arranged in Israel. The school offers independent study options and an optional pass/no credit system. There are 9 national honor societies and 20 departmental honors programs. **Visiting:** There are regularly scheduled orientations for prospective students. YU holds open houses for high school students. There are guides for informal visits; visitors may sit in on classes and stay overnight. To schedule a visit, contact the Office of Admissions. **Campus Safety and Security:** Measures include 24-hour foot and vehicle patrol and security escort services. There are shuttle buses, emergency telephones, lighted pathways/sidewalks, ID cards, vulnerability surveys, fire drills, alarm systems, and transportation for routine and special events.

REQUIREMENTS: The SAT or ACT is required. Graduation from an accredited secondary school with 16 academic credits is required for admission. The GED is accepted under limited and specific circumstances. The SAT Subject test in Hebrew is recommended for placement purposes. An interview and an essay are required. A GPA of 3.3 is required. AP and CLEP credits are accepted. Important factors in the admissions decision are extracurricular activities record, personality/intangible qualities, and evidence of special talent. To graduate, students must complete a total of 128 credit hours. Under the dual program, students pursue a liberal arts or business curriculum together with courses in Hebrew language, literature, and culture. Courses in Jewish learning are geared to the student's level of preparation. **Procedure:** Freshmen are admitted to all sessions. There are early admissions, deferred admissions, and rolling admissions plans. Applications should be filed by December 1 for fall entry. Notifications are sent February 1. **Transfer Students:** 95 of 128 credits required for the bachelor's degree must be completed at YU. **International Students:** They must take the TOEFL. They must also take the SAT or ACT.

ADMISSIONS: 69% of the 2017-2018 applicants were accepted. **Admissions Contact:** Michael Kranzler, Director of Undergraduate Admissions. Email: *yuadmit@ymail.yu.edu* Web: *www.yu.edu*

FINANCIAL AID: Yeshiva University is a member of CSS. The CSS/Profile and the college's own financial statement are required. The FAFSA code is 002903. The priority date for freshman financial aid applications for fall entry is February 1.

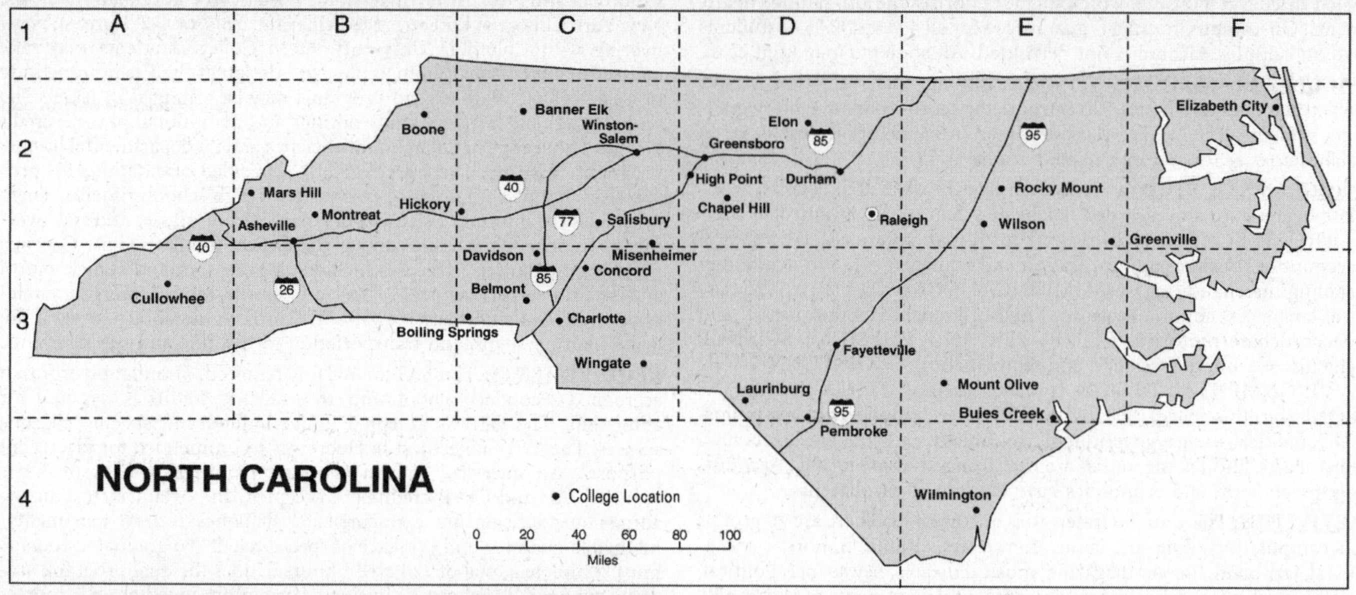

APPALACHIAN STATE UNIVERSITY B-2

www.appstate.edu

Boone, NC 28608 **(828) 262-2120**

Fax: (828) 262-3296 **Email:** admissions@appstate.edu

Full-time: 6978 men, 8477 women

Part-time: 399 men, 588 women

Graduate: 532 men, 536 women

Year: semesters, summer session

Room & Board: $8174

SAT CR/M/W: 572/581/548 **ACT:** 26

Application Deadline: February 1

Faculty: 814; IIA, -$

Ph.D.s: 99%

Student/Faculty: 16 to 1

Tuition: $7220 ($21,736)

Freshman Class: 12248 applied, 7744 accepted, 3028 enrolled

CEEB CODE: 5010

VERY COMPETITIVE

Appalachian State University, founded in 1899 and a member of the University of North Carolina system, is a comprehensive university offering undergraduate and graduate programs in the arts and sciences, business, teacher education, fine and applied arts, music, and health sciences. The figures given in the above capsule and in this profile are approximate. There are 8 undergraduate schools and 1 graduate school. In addition to regional accreditation, App State has baccalaureate program accreditation with AACSB, CSAB, CSWE, NASAD, NASM, and NRPA. The 1300-acre campus is in a small town in northwestern North Carolina. Including any residence halls, there are 90 buildings.

STUDENT LIFE: 92% of undergraduates are from North Carolina. Others are from 46 states, 61 foreign countries, and Canada. 84% are from public schools. 87% are White; 5% Hispanic; 4% African American; 3% two or more races; 2% Asian American; 1% race unknown. **Female To Male Ratio:** The average age of freshmen is 18; all undergraduates, 21. 12% do not continue beyond their first year; 66% remain to graduate. **Housing:** 5775 students can be accommodated in college housing, which includes dorms. In addition, there are sorority houses and living learning communities. On-campus housing is guaranteed for the freshman year only and is available on a lottery system for upperclassmen. 67% of students commute. All students may keep cars.

FACULTY/CLASSROOMS: 53% of faculty are male; 47% are female. 88% teach undergraduates. Graduate students teach 6% of introductory courses. The average class size in a laboratory is 22 and in a regular course is 33.

PROGRAMS OF STUDY: App State confers B.A., B.S., B.F.A., B.M., B.S.B.A., B.S.C.J., B.S.N., and B.S.W. degrees. Master's and doctoral degrees are also awarded. Bachelor's degrees are awarded in AGRICULTURE (agricultural business management and environmental studies), BIOLOGICAL SCIENCE (biology/biological science, ecology, molecular biology, and nutrition), BUSINESS (accounting, banking and finance, hospitality management services, insurance and risk management, international business management, management engineering, marketing/retailing/merchandising, and recreational facilities management), COMMUNICATIONS AND THE ARTS (advertising, apparel design, art, art and design, arts administration/management, communications, dance, dramatic arts, English, French, graphic design, industrial design, journalism, languages, music business management, music performance, performing arts, photography, public relations, Spanish, and studio art), COMPUTER AND PHYSICAL SCIENCE (actuarial science, chemistry, computer science, geology, mathematics, physics, and statistics), EDUCATION (art education, athletic training, business education, computer education, drama education, education, elementary education, English education, foreign languages education, global studies, health education, mathematics education, middle school education, music education, physical education, science education, secondary education, social science education, social studies education, and special education), ENGINEERING AND ENVIRONMENTAL DESIGN (architecture, computer technology, construction management, construction technology, electrical/electronics engineering technology, engineering technology, environmental science, graphic arts technology, industrial engineering technology, and interior design), HEALTH PROFESSIONS (exercise science, health care administration, health science, music therapy, nursing, preventive/wellness health care, and speech pathology/audiology), SOCIAL SCIENCE (anthropology, area studies, child psychology/development, criminal justice, East Asian studies, economics, family/consumer studies, French studies, geography, geography information science, German area studies, history, interdisciplinary studies, Latin American studies, Middle Eastern studies, philosophy, political science/government, psychology, religion, social work, sociology, South Asian studies, Third World studies, and women's studies). Business/marketing, elementary education, and social sciences have the largest enrollments.

ACTIVITIES: 7% of men belong to 13 national fraternities; 11% of women belong to 9 national sororities. There are 289 groups on campus, including art, band, cheerleading, chess, choir, chorale, chorus, communications, computers, dance, debate, drama, drill team, environmental, ethnic, film, forensics, honors, international, jazz band, LGBT, literary magazine, marching band, musical theater, newspaper, opera, orchestra, pep band, photography, political, professional, radio and TV, religious, social, social service, student government, and symphony. Popular campus events include football and basketball games, Annual Diversity Celebration, Legends Concerts, and Greek Week. **Sports:** There are 10 intercollegiate sports for men and 10 for women, and 20 intramural sports for men and 20 for women. Facilities include a convocation center with a varsity gym, a stadium, fitness and recreation centers, football, soccer, field hockey, basketball, volleyball, wrestling, indoor and outdoor track, a golf course, a baseball field, tennis courts, a swimming pool, a climbing wall, racquetball courts, aerobics studio, weight room, and cardio equipment. **Graduates:** From July 1, 2016 to June 30, 2017, 3922 bachelor's degrees were awarded. The most popular majors were business/marketing (19%), education, and health professions (17%), and communication/journalism (8%). In an average class, 2% graduate in 3 years or less, 44% graduate in 4 years or less, 65% graduate in 5 years or less, and 66% graduate in 6 years or less.

SERVICES: Counseling and information services are available, as is tutoring in most subjects. There is a reader service for the blind, and remedial math, reading, and writing. **Library/Resources:** The library contains 937,956 volumes, 1.5 million microform items, 72,813 audio/video tapes/CDs/DVDs, and subscribes to 23,861 periodicals, including electronic. Computerized library services include interlibrary loans, database searching, and Internet access. Special learning facilities include an art gallery, a radio station, and an observatory. **Physically Challenged Students:** All of the campus is accessible. Facilities include wheelchair ramps, elevators, special parking, specially equipped restrooms, special class scheduling, lowered drinking fountains, lowered telephones, and special housing. **Special:** App State offers dual degrees in Communications with Universidad de las Americas Puebla, a private university in Mexico; a 3-2 engineering degree with Clemson and Auburn Universities; internships; work-study programs; B.A.-B.S. degrees, dual majors; and study abroad. There are 16 national honor societies, a freshman honors program, and 25 departmental honors programs. **Visiting:** There are regularly scheduled orientations for prospective students, starting at the end of May for all new students. There are guides for informal visits and visitors may sit in on classes. **Campus Safety and Security:** Measures include 24-hour foot and vehicle patrol, an emergency notification system, self-defense education, and security escort services. There are shuttle buses, emergency telephones, lighted pathways/sidewalks, and controlled access to dorms/residences.

REQUIREMENTS: The SAT or ACT is required. The ACT Optional Writing test is also required. Applicants must be graduates of an accredited secondary school, Applicants must have completed 4 course units in high school English and math, 3 in science, and 2 in foreign languages and social studies. AP and CLEP credits are accepted. Important factors in the admissions decision are advanced placement or honors courses, extracurricular activities record, and evidence of special talent. To graduate, students must complete 122 credit hours for most programs, including 60 in the major, with a minimum 2.0 GPA. General education requirements include courses in math, science, history, physical education, English, social sciences, and humanities. **Procedure:** Freshmen are admitted in the fall, spring, and summer. Entrance exams should be taken prior to senior year. There are deferred admissions and rolling admissions plans. Early decision applications should be filed by November 15; regular applications, by February 1 for fall entry; and March 15 for spring entry. The fall 2017 application fee was $55. 630 applicants were on the 2017 waiting list; 200 were admitted. Applications are accepted online. **Transfer Students:** 1153 transfer students enrolled in 2016-2017. Transfer students must have earned a minimum 2.0 GPA on collegiate work. They must have a minimum of 30 semester credits or else apply as a freshman. Transfer admissions operates on a rolling basis. 30 of 128 credits required for the bachelor's degree must be completed at App State. **International Students:** There are 145 international students enrolled. The SAT or ACT may be accepted in lieu of the TOEFL.

ADMISSIONS: 63% of the 2017-2018 applicants were accepted. The SAT scores for the 2017-2018 freshman class were: Critical Reading-- 11% below 500, 55% between 500 and 599, 30% between 600 and 699, and 4% between 700 and 800. Math-- 6% below 500, 52% between 500 and 599, 38% between 600 and 699, and 4% between 700 and 800. Writing-- 22% below 500, 55% between 500 and 599, 21% between 600 and 699, and 2% between 700 and 800. The ACT scores were 3% below 12, 14% between 12 and 17, 47% between 18 and 23, 19% between 24 and 29, and 17% above 30. 45% of the current freshmen were in the top fifth of their class; 80% were in the top two fifths. **Admissions Contact:** Alexis Pope, Director of Admissions. Email: *admissions@appstate.edu* Web: *www.appstate.edu*

FINANCIAL AID: In 2017-2018, 68% of all full-time freshmen received some form of financial aid and need-based aid. The average freshman award was $9,886. Need-based scholarships or need-based grants averaged $9,777 ($30,679 maximum); need-based self-help aid (loans and jobs) averaged $3,345 ($6,577 maximum); non-need-based athletic scholarships averaged $14,554 ($25,727 maximum); other non-need-based awards and non-need-based scholarships averaged $3,382 ($12,929 maximum); and $5,313 from other forms of aid. The average financial indebtedness of the 2017 graduate was $17,889. The FAFSA code is 002906. The priority date for freshman financial aid applications for fall entry is rolling.

BARTON COLLEGE — E-2

www.barton.edu

Wilson, NC 27893	**(252) 399-6315** **(800) 345-4973**
Fax: (252) 399-6572	**Email: enroll@barton.edu**
Full-time: 265 men, 565 women	**Faculty:** 72; IIA
Part-time: 13 men, 44 women	**Ph.D.s:** 73%
Graduate: 15 men, 58 women	**Student/Faculty:** 12 to 1
Year: semesters, summer session	**Tuition:** $29,998
Room & Board: $9856	**Freshman Class:** 2632 applied, 1024 accepted, 198 enrolled
SAT CR/M: 540/520 **ACT:** 20	**CEEB CODE:** 5016
Application Deadline: August 1	**COMPETITIVE**

Barton College, founded in 1902, is a private baccalaureate college affiliated with the Christian Church (Disciples of Christ) offering professional and liberal arts degrees. There are 8 undergraduate schools and 3 graduate schools. In addition to regional accreditation, BC has baccalaureate program accreditation with CSWE, CAEP, and CCNE. The 65-acre campus is in a suburban area 45 miles east of Raleigh, NC. Including any residence halls, there are 24 buildings.

STUDENT LIFE: 78% of undergraduates are from North Carolina. Others are from 20 states, 17 foreign countries, and Canada. 55% are White; 23% African American; 8% Hispanic; 5% race unknown; 4% Foreign; 3% two or more races; 1% Asian American; 1% American Indian/Alaska Native. **Female To Male Ratio:** 2.3:1. The average age of freshmen is 18.75; all undergraduates, 22.7. 33% do not continue beyond their first year; 40% remain to graduate. **Housing:** 612 students can be accommodated in college housing, which includes single-sex and coed dorms. In addition, there are fraternity houses, sorority houses, and womens dorm. On-campus housing is guaranteed for the freshman year only, and is available on a first-come, first-served basis. 56% of students commute. All students may keep cars.

FACULTY/CLASSROOMS: 49% of faculty are male; 51% are female. All teach undergraduates. No introductory courses are taught by graduate students. The average class size in an introductory lecture is 18 and in a laboratory is 13.

PROGRAMS OF STUDY: BC confers B.A., B.S., B.F.A., B.L.S., B.S.N., and B.S.W. degrees. Master's degrees are also awarded. Bachelor's degrees are awarded in BIOLOGICAL SCIENCE (biology/biological science), BUSINESS (business administration and management and sports management), COMMUNICATIONS AND THE ARTS (art and design, communications, dramatic arts, English, graphic design, painting, sports administration, studio art, and theatre studies), COMPUTER AND PHYSICAL SCIENCE (chemistry and mathematics), EDUCATION (education of the deaf and hearing impaired, elementary education, middle school education, physical education, special education, and specific learning disabilities), ENGINEERING AND ENVIRONMENTAL DESIGN (environmental science), HEALTH PROFESSIONS (exercise science, health care administration, health promotion, and nursing), SOCIAL SCIENCE (criminal justice, economics, gerontology, history, interdisciplinary studies, political science/government, psychology, religion, social studies, social work, and Spanish studies). Nursing and education are the strongest academically. Business, nursing, and education have the largest enrollments.

ACTIVITIES: There are 50 groups on campus, including academic clubs, art, choir, chorus, dance, drama, environmental, ethnic, honors, international, LGBT, literary magazine, musical theater, newspaper, orchestra, photography, political, professional, radio and TV, religious, social, social service, student government, and symphony. Popular campus events include Pre-exam Jam, Lighting of the Luminaries Christmas Celebration, and Welcome Back Barton Day. **Sports:** There are 10 intercollegiate sports for men and 10 for women. Facilities include a recreation gym, a workout room, indoor pool, a track, basketball, a tennis complex, baseball, softball and soccer fields. **Graduates:** From July 1, 2016 to June 30, 2017, 243 bachelor's degrees were awarded. The most popular majors were nursing (19%), business (15%), and social work (9%). In an average class, 29% graduate in 4 years or less, 30% graduate in 5 years or less, and 44% graduate in 6 years or less.

SERVICES: Counseling and information services are available, as is tutoring in most subjects, such as the core courses for freshman and sophomores. There is remedial math, reading, and writing. In-class interpreting for hearing-impaired students is available upon request, as are in-class note takers for certain circumstances. **Library/Resources:** The library contains 145,626 volumes, 1,726 microform items, and 2,952 audio/video tapes/CDs/DVDs, and subscribes to 79,748 periodicals, including electronic. Computerized library services include interlibrary loans, database searching, Internet access, and Wi-Fi capability. Special learning facilities include an art gallery, radio station, TV station, a writing center, a rare book room, a greenhouse, and theater. **Physically Challenged Students:** 95% of the campus is accessible. Facilities include wheelchair ramps, elevators, special parking, specially equipped restrooms, special class scheduling, lowered drinking fountains, and special housing. **Special:** Barton offers an honors program, a 3+2 Strategic Leadership Program (resulting in a BS/BA and MBA degree), internships, a Washington semester, a general studies degree, an Interdisciplinary studies major (allowing students to design their own course of study), dual majors, work study, study abroad (through Central College in Iowa and Charles University in Prague, Czech Republic), and credit by exam in entry-level courses. Preprofessional programs are offered in law and a variety of health-related fields. There are 9 national honor societies, a freshman honors program, and 1 departmental honors program. **Visiting:** There are regularly scheduled orientations for prospective students, including visiting classes, financial aid and freshman advising workshops, tours of the campus, and meetings with administrators, faculty, and students. There are guides for informal visits; visitors may sit in on classes and stay overnight. To schedule a visit, contact the Admissions Office. **Campus Safety and Security:** Measures include 24-hour foot and vehicle patrol, emergency notification system, self-defense education, and security escort services. There are emergency telephones, lighted pathways/sidewalks, controlled access to dorms/residences, campus-wide surveillance cameras, peephole doors to residence rooms, and a city police substation on campus.

REQUIREMENTS: The SAT or ACT is required. Applicants must be high school graduates with at least 13 college preparatory credits. Barton recommends 4 units of English, 3 units of math (including algebra), social sciences, and 2 units of natural science (including 1 lab science). A foreign language is encouraged. Admission criteria vary for the Graduate and Professional Studies programs. A GPA of 2.0 is required. AP and CLEP credits are accepted. Important factors in the admissions decision are parents or siblings attended the school, evidence of special talent, personality/intangible qualities, and extracurricular activities record. All students must complete a minimum of 126 credit hours, including 36 in the major and 48 in the General College Core, with a minimum GPA of 2.0. Core requirements include 14 semester hours in sufficiency Foundations courses (to develop communication skills, quantitative reasoning, and self-sufficiency), 28 semester hours in Perspectives courses (to explore, understand, and appreciate the world in which we live), and 6 semester hours in Applications courses (to develop and refine skills, explore ideas and apply these skills to address problems in today's world). **Procedure:** Freshmen are admitted to all sessions. There is a rolling admissions plan. Notification is sent on a rolling basis. Applications are accepted on-line. **Transfer Students:** 81 transfer students enrolled in 2016-2017. Applicants must have a college GPA of 2.0 and be eligible to return to the school they last attended. 32 of 126 credits required for the bachelor's degree must be completed at BC. **International Students:** There are 41 international students enrolled. They must take the TOEFL with a minimum score of 525 on the paper-based TOEFL (PBT) or 71 on the Internet-based version (iBT).

ADMISSIONS: 39% of the 2017-2018 applicants were accepted. The SAT scores for the 2017-2018 freshman class were: Critical Reading-- 31% below 500, 57% between 500 and 599, and 12% between 600 and 699. Math-- 33% below 500, 52% between 500 and 599, 13% between 600 and 699, and 1% between 700 and 800. The ACT scores were 18% between 12 and 17, 63% between 18 and 23, 19% between 24 and 29, and % above 30. 24% of the current freshmen were in the top fifth of their class; 51% were in the top two fifths. 2 freshmen graduated first in their class. **Admissions Contact:** Amanda Metts, Assistant Vice President for Admissions. Email: *enroll@barton.edu* Web: *www.barton.edu*

FINANCIAL AID: In 2017-2018, 98% of all full-time freshmen received some form of financial aid and need-based aid. The average freshman award was $31,462. Need-based scholarships or need-based grants averaged $5,299; need-based self-help aid (loans and jobs) averaged $929; and non-need-based athletic scholarships averaged $3,133. 25% of undergraduate students work part-time. The average financial indebtedness of the 2017 graduate was $30,987. The FAFSA code is 002908. The priority date for freshman financial aid applications for fall entry is August 19.

BELMONT ABBEY COLLEGE — C-3

www.belmontabbeycollege.edu

Belmont, NC 28012	(704) 461-6214
Fax: (704) 461-6220	Email: admissions@BAC.edu
Full-time: 726 men, 801 women	Faculty: 74; IIB, +$
Part-time: 40 men, 80 women	Ph.D.s: 70%
Graduate: n/av	Student/Faculty: 12 to 1
Year: semesters, summer session	Tuition: $18,500
Room & Board: $10,294	Freshman Class: 1843 applied, 1185 accepted, 303 enrolled
SAT CR/M: 510/510 ACT: 23	CEEB CODE: 5055
Application Deadline: August 15	COMPETITIVE

Belmont Abbey College, founded by the Benedictine Monks in 1876, is a private, liberal arts college affiliated with the Roman Catholic Church. There is 1 undergraduate school. The 50-acre campus is in a small town 10 miles west of Charlotte, North Carolina. Including any residence halls, there are 23 buildings.

STUDENT LIFE: 62% of undergraduates are from North Carolina. Others are from 39 states, 6 foreign countries, and Canada. 66% are from public schools. 56% are White; 21% race unknown; 2% Asian American; 2% Hispanic; 2% Foreign; 19% African American; 1% American Indian/Alaska Native. 69% claim no religious affiliation; 31% Catholic. **Female To Male Ratio:** 1.2:1. The average age of freshmen is 20; all undergraduates, 28. 49% do not continue beyond their first year; 44% remain to graduate. **Housing:** 870 students can be accommodated in college housing, which includes dorms, on-campus apartments, and off-campus apartments. In addition, there are special-interest houses, quiet residence halls, and single housing. On-campus housing is guaranteed for all 4 years, and is available on a first-come, first-served basis. 82% of students live on campus. All students may keep cars.

FACULTY/CLASSROOMS: 57% of faculty are male; 43% are female. All teach undergraduates, 60% do research, and 60% do both. No introductory courses are taught by graduate students. The average class size in an introductory lecture is 16; in a laboratory is 15; and in a regular course is 4.

PROGRAMS OF STUDY: BAC confers B.A. and B.S. degrees. Bachelor's degrees are awarded in BIOLOGICAL SCIENCE (biology/biological science), BUSINESS (accounting, business administration and management, and sports management), COMMUNICATIONS AND THE ARTS (English), COMPUTER AND PHYSICAL SCIENCE (mathematics), EDUCATION (education and elementary education), SOCIAL SCIENCE (applied psychology, criminal justice, history, liberal arts/general studies, parks and recreation management, philosophy, political science/government, psychology, and theological studies). Business, theology, psychology, elementary education, and English are the strongest academically. Business administration, education, and elementary education have the largest enrollments.

ACTIVITIES: 6% of men belong to 1 local and 2 national fraternities; 5% of women belong to 4 local sororities. There are 21 groups on campus, including Abbey volunteers, campus activities board club, mens household club, motorsports club, womens household, art, cheerleading, chess, chess club, choir, chorus, computers, dance, drama, honors, international, literary magazine, newspaper, political, professional, religious, social, social service, and student government. Popular campus events include The Abbey Players, Crusader Welcome Week, Presidents Ball, Homecoming Festivities, Giveaway Novelties, Halloween Festival, and Crawfish Boil on the Quad. **Sports:** There are 14 intercollegiate sports for men and 14 for women. Facilities include a physical education center with a gym, baseball, basketball, cross country, golf, lacrosse, soccer, track and field, wrestling and volleyball, lacrosse, soccer, softball, tennis, and strength and conditioning. **Graduates:** From July 1, 2016 to June 30, 2017, 379 bachelor's degrees were awarded. The most popular majors were business management (39%), education (15%), and elementary education (13%). In an average class, 40% graduate in 4 years or less, 45% graduate in 5 years or less, and 46% graduate in 6 years or less. Of the 2016 graduating class, 16% were enrolled in graduate school within 6 months of graduation, and 88% were employed.

SERVICES: Counseling and information services are available, as is tutoring in most subjects, such as English/writing, math, business, accounting, economics, computer science, science, biology, chemistry, physics, criminal justice, history, political science, statistics, psychology and theology There is also a reader service for the blind. **Library/Resources:** The library contains 118,827 volumes, 116,173 microform items, 7,418 audio/video tapes/CDs/DVDs, and subscribes to 275 periodicals, including electronic. Computerized library services include interlibrary loans, database searching, Internet access, and Wi-Fi capability. **Physically Challenged Students:** 60% of the campus is accessible. Facilities include wheelchair ramps, elevators, special parking, specially equipped restrooms, special class scheduling, and lowered drinking fountains. **Special:** Cross-registration is offered through the Charlotte Area Educational Consortium. There are internships in many majors, including required internships in educational studies, as well as on-campus work-study, accelerated degree programs, nondegree study, dual majors, and study abroad in Guatemala, Germany, and France. There are 5 national honor societies and a freshman honors program. **Visiting:** There are regularly scheduled orientations for prospective students, consisting of a campus tour and meetings with a financial aid adviser, faculty, and students. There are guides for informal visits; visitors may sit in on classes and stay overnight. To schedule a visit, contact the Admissions Office. **Campus Safety and Security:** Measures include 24-hour foot and vehicle patrol, an emergency notification system, self-defense education, and security escort services. There are emergency telephones and lighted pathways/sidewalks.

REQUIREMENTS: The SAT or ACT and ACT Writing Test are recommended. Candidates must be graduates of an accredited secondary school and have a 2.0 GPA. A minimum of 16 academic credits must be completed, including 4 in English, 3 each in math and electives, and 2 each in foreign language, history, and science. AP and CLEP credits are accepted. Important factors in the admissions decision are advanced placement or honors courses, extracurricular activities record, and leadership record. To graduate, all students must complete a minimum of 120 credits, including 60 credits of core curriculum and 30 upper-level credits in the major. Among the core requirements are history, math, natural sciences, theology, philosophy, English, fine arts, and rhetoric. A minimum 2.0 GPA must be maintained. Honors students must submit a thesis. **Procedure:** Freshmen are admitted in the fall and spring. Entrance exams should be taken by October of the senior year. There are deferred admissions and rolling admissions plans. Applications should be filed by August 15 for fall entry. The fall 2017 application fee was $35. Applications are accepted online. **Transfer Students:** 185 transfer students enrolled in 2016-2017. Students with 24 or more credit hours must submit all college transcripts, and those with fewer than 24 credit hours must also submit a high school transcript and SAT scores. All candidates must have a minimum 2.0 GPA and be eligible to return to the last college attended. An interview is recommended. 30 of 120 credits required for the bachelor's degree must be completed at BAC. **International Students:** There are 33 international students enrolled. They must take the TOEFL with a minimum score of 550 on the paper-based TOEFL (PBT) or 79 on the Internet-based version (iBT). They must also take the SAT or ACT, scoring 900.

ADMISSIONS: 64% of the 2017-2018 applicants were accepted. The SAT scores for the 2017-2018 freshman class were: Critical Reading-- 54% below 500, 29% between 500 and 599, 13% between 600 and 699, and 3% between 700 and 800. Math-- 42% below 500, 39% between 500 and 599, 17% between 600 and 699, and 2% between 700 and 800. The ACT scores were 27% below 12, 33% between 12 and 17, 28% between 18 and 23, 4% between 24 and 29, and 7% above 30. 20% of the current freshmen were in the top fifth of their class; 46% were in the top two fifths. 3 freshmen graduated first in their class. **Admissions Contact:** Nicole Focareto, Director of Admissions. Email: *admissions@BAC.edu* Web: *www.belmontabbeycollege.edu*

FINANCIAL AID: In 2017-2018, 97% of all full-time freshmen received some form of financial aid. 61% of all full-time freshmen received need-based aid. The average freshman award was $7,931. Need-based scholarships or need-based grants averaged $6,229 ($8,721 maximum); need-based self-help aid (loans and jobs) averaged $3,500 ($5,500 maximum); non-need-based athletic scholarships averaged $2,000 ($18,000 maximum); and other non-need-based awards and non-need-based scholarships averaged $2,500 ($9,000 maximum). 12% of undergraduate students work part-time. The average financial indebtedness of the 2017 graduate was $27,000. BAC is a member of CSS. The state aid form is required. The FAFSA code is 002910. The priority date for freshman financial aid applications for fall entry is February 1.

BENNETT COLLEGE *(The complete profile is made available exclusively on our website, www.barronspac.com)*

CABARRUS COLLEGE OF HEALTH SCIENCES *(The complete profile is made available exclusively on our website, www.barronspac.com)*

CAMPBELL UNIVERSITY — E-3

www.campbell.edu

Buies Creek, NC 27506 — **(800) 334-4111**

Fax: (910) 893-1288	**Email:** admissions@campbell.edu
Full-time: 1500 men, 1500 women	**Faculty:** n/av
Part-time: 750 men, 750 women	**Ph.D.s:** 92%
Graduate: n/av	**Student/Faculty:** n/av
Year: semesters, summer session	**Tuition:** $27,670
Room & Board: $9860	**Freshman Class:** n/av
SAT or ACT: required	**CEEB CODE:** 5100
Application Deadline: n/av	**VERY COMPETITIVE**

Campbell University, founded in 1887, is a private, nonsectarian institution offering degree programs in liberal arts and sciences, law, medicine, business, engineering, and education. There are 8 undergraduate schools and 6 graduate schools. In addition to regional accreditation, CU has baccalaureate program accreditation with CAEP. The 1300-acre campus is in a rural area 28 miles south of Raleigh and 30 miles north of Fayetteville. Including any residence halls, there are 84 buildings.

STUDENT LIFE: Students are from 50 states, 42 foreign countries, and Canada. 90% are from public schools. **Male To Female Ratio:** 1:1. The average age of freshmen is 18; all undergraduates, 20. **Housing:** 2000 students can be accommodated in college housing, which includes dorms, on-campus apartments, and fraternity houses. On-campus housing is guaranteed for all 4 years. Alcohol is not permitted. All students may keep cars.

FACULTY/CLASSROOMS: No introductory courses are taught by graduate students.

PROGRAMS OF STUDY: CU confers B.A., B.S., B.Applied Science., B.B.A., B.H.S., and B.S.W. degrees. Associate, master's, and doctoral degrees are also awarded. Bachelor's degrees are awarded in BIOLOGICAL SCIENCE (biochemistry and biology/biological science), BUSINESS (accounting, banking and finance, business administration and management, business administration - international, business administration marketing, business economics, international business, international business management, investments and securities, and sports management), COMMUNICATIONS AND THE ARTS (advertising, art, choral music, church music, communications, English, fine arts, French, graphic design, information technology, journalism, music, Spanish, studio art, studio art graphic design, and theatre arts), COMPUTER AND PHYSICAL SCIENCE (chemistry, computer information technology, computer information systems, computer science, information sciences and systems, and mathematics), EDUCATION (athletic training, childhood education, early childhood education, education, elementary education, English education, and middle school education), ENGINEERING AND ENVIRONMENTAL DESIGN (military science), HEALTH PROFESSIONS (biology, clinical science, exercise science, health communication, health care administration, nursing, predentistry, premedicine, preoptometry, and prepharmacy), SOCIAL SCIENCE (counseling/psychology, criminal justice, economics, history, homeland security, physical fitness/movement, political science/government, prelaw, psychology, religion, and social work). Health science, trust management (business), and education, are the strongest academically. Education, pharmacy and biology have the largest enrollments.

ACTIVITIES: There are 50 groups on campus, including art, band, cheerleading, choir, chorale, chorus, computers, debate, drama, ethnic, honors, international, jazz band, literary magazine, musical theater, newspaper, orchestra, pep band, photography, political, professional, religious, social, social service, student government, and yearbook. Popular campus events include Staley Lecture Series, Spring Fling, Christmas Formals, Homecoming, Parents Weekend, concerts and plays. **Sports:** Facilities include a gym, a football field, athletic complex, golf facilities, a nature trail, a track, workout facilities for tennis, and baseball, softball, and soccer fields, and an indoor pool. **Graduates:** From July 1, 2016 to June 30, 2017, 932 bachelor's degrees were awarded. The most popular majors were history (4%) and business administration (17%). In an average class, 31% graduate in 4 years or less, 49% graduate in 5 years or less, and 51% graduate in 6 years or less. Of the 2016 graduating class, 16% were enrolled in graduate school within 6 months of graduation, and 67% were employed.

SERVICES: Counseling and information services are available, as is tutoring in most subjects. There is remedial math and writing. **Library/ Resources:** The library contains 319,561 volumes, 180,914 microform items, 17,350 audio/video tapes/CDs/DVDs, and subscribes to 83,898 periodicals, including electronic. Computerized library services include interlibrary loans, database searching, Internet access, and Wi-Fi capability. Special learning facilities include an art gallery, TV station, computer labs, computerized music lab, an athletic learning resources center, drug information center for the school of pharmacy, a pharmacy research facility, and an animal museum. **Physically Challenged Students:** 95% of the campus is accessible. Facilities include wheelchair ramps, elevators, special parking, specially equipped restrooms, special class scheduling, lowered drinking fountains, lowered telephones, and special housing. **Special:** Campbell offers co-op programs, internships, study abroad in 7 countries, a Washington semester, numerous apprenticeships, accelerated degrees, dual majors, and a general studies degree. There is credit for military and work experience. Cross-registration with the North Carolina Model Teacher Education Consortium is possible. There are 14 national honor societies, Phi Beta Kappa, and a freshman honors program. **Visiting:** There are regularly scheduled orientations for prospective students, including a campus tour, student panel, and department visits. There are guides for informal visits, visitors may sit in on classes, and stay overnight. To schedule a visit, contact the Admissions Office. **Campus Safety and Security:** Measures include 24-hour foot and vehicle patrol, an emergency notification system, self-defense education, and security escort services. There are emergency telephones, lighted pathways/sidewalks, and controlled access to dorms/residences.

REQUIREMENTS: The SAT or ACT is required. Applicants should have completed 12 high school academic credits, including 4 credits of English, 3 of math, and 2 each of history or social studies, science, and foreign language. An essay, an interview, and a portfolio are recommended. An audition is required for some majors. A GPA of 2.7 is required. AP and CLEP credits are accepted. Important factors in the admissions decision are advanced placement or honors courses, leadership record, and personality/intangible qualities. To graduate, students must complete 124 credit hours with a minimum GPA of 2.0 overall and in the major. All students must take a core curriculum of 45 to 65 hours including English, math, science, social science, religion, fine arts, physical education, and the Cultural Enrichment Program. **Procedure:** Freshmen are admitted to all sessions. Entrance exams should be taken during the junior year or the fall of the senior year. There are deferred admissions and rolling admissions plans. Application deadlines are open. Applications are accepted online. **Transfer Students:** Applicants should have a minimum GPA of 2.5 and supply transcripts from previously attended colleges. 36 of 124 credits required for the bachelor's degree must be completed at CU. **International Students:** There are 153 international students enrolled. They must take the TOEFL with a minimum score of 500 on the paper-based TOEFL (PBT) or 63 on the Internet-based version (iBT). They must also take the SAT or ACT.

ADMISSIONS: 30 freshmen graduated first in their class. **Admissions Contact:** Jason Hall, Assistant Vice President for Admissions. Email: *admissions@campbell.edu* Web: *www.campbell.edu*

FINANCIAL AID: The FAFSA code is 002913. Check with the school for current application deadlines.

CATAWBA COLLEGE *(The complete profile is made available exclusively on our website, www.barronspac.com)*

DAVIDSON COLLEGE C-3
www.davidson.edu

Davidson, NC 28035 (704) 894-2230 (800) 768-0380

Fax: (704) 894-2016	**Email:** admission@davidson.edu
Full-time: 911 men, 885 women	**Faculty:** 185; IIB, ++$
Part-time: n/av	**Ph.D.s:** 97%
Graduate: n/av	**Student/Faculty:** 10 to 1
Year: semesters	**Tuition:** $46,966
Room & Board: $13,153	**Freshman Class:** 5673 applied, 1148 accepted, 519 enrolled
SAT CR/M/W: 670/680/670 **ACT:** 31	**CEEB CODE:** 5150
Application Deadline: January 2	**MOST COMPETITIVE**

Davidson College, founded in 1837, is a private liberal arts institution affiliated with the Presbyterian Church. There is 1 undergraduate school. In addition to regional accreditation, DC has baccalaureate program accreditation with ACS. The 665-acre campus is in a small town 19 miles north of Charlotte, NC. Including any residence halls, there are 124 buildings.

STUDENT LIFE: 77% of undergraduates are from out of state, mostly the South. Students are from 49 states, 49 foreign countries, and Canada. 50% are from public schools. 67% are White; 7% African American; 7% Hispanic; 7% Foreign; 5% Asian American; 4% two or more races; 2% race unknown; 1% American Indian/Alaska Native. **Male To Female Ratio:** 1.0:1. The average age of freshmen is 18; all undergraduates, 20. 6% do not continue beyond their first year; 93% remain to graduate. **Housing:** 1758 students can be accommodated in college housing, which includes dorms, on-campus apartments, and off-campus apartments. In addition, there are special-interest houses, substance-free housing. On-campus housing is guaranteed for the freshman year only and is available on a lottery system for upperclassmen. 95% of students live on campus. All students may keep cars.

FACULTY/CLASSROOMS: 57% of faculty are male; 43% are female. All teach undergraduates and all do research. No introductory courses are taught by graduate students. The average class size in an introductory lecture is 15; in a laboratory is 12; and in a regular course is 15.

PROGRAMS OF STUDY: DC confers A.B. and B.S. degrees. Bachelor's degrees are awarded in AGRICULTURE (environmental studies), BIOLOGICAL SCIENCE (biology/biological science), COMMUNICATIONS AND THE ARTS (Africana studies, art, Chinese, classics, dramatic arts, English, French, German, music, and Spanish), COMPUTER AND PHYSICAL SCIENCE (chemistry, mathematics, and physics), SOCIAL SCIENCE (anthropology, East Asian studies, economics, gender studies, history, interdisciplinary studies, Latin American studies, philosophy, political science/government, psychology, religion, and sociology). Biology, economics, and political science have the largest enrollments.

ACTIVITIES: 39% of men belong to 6 national fraternities; 70% of women belong to 4 local and 2 national sororities. There are 200 groups on campus, including an outing club, art, cheerleading, choir, chorale, chorus, computers, dance, drama, ethnic, honors, international, jazz band, LGBT, literary magazine, musical theater, newspaper, opera, orchestra, pep band, political, professional, radio and TV, religious, social, social service, student government, symphony, and yearbook. Popular campus events include Fall Concert, Spring Concert, and Convocations. **Sports:** There are 11 intercollegiate sports for men and 10 for women. Facilities include basketball arena, baseball field, indoor and outdoor tennis courts, racquetball courts, a squash court, natatorium with a diving well, nautilus rooms, a gym, a wrestling room, a dance studio, golf facilities, a cross-country course and trail, a football and soccer stadium, and facilities for sailing, swimming, water skiing, and canoeing. **Graduates:** From July 1, 2016 to June 30, 2017, 468 bachelor's degrees were awarded. The most popular majors were biology (14%), political science (12%), and economics (12%). In an average class, 90% graduate in 4 years or less, 93% graduate in 5 years or less, and 93% graduate in 6 years or less. Of the 2016 graduating class, 13% were enrolled in graduate school within 6 months of graduation, and 72% were employed.

SERVICES: Counseling and information services are available, as is tutoring in some subjects. Tutoring is available as needed through the Student Affairs Office. There is a reader service for the blind. The Center for Teaching and Learning also provides student support. **Library/ Resources:** The library contains 561,427 volumes, 601,821 microform items, 17,878 audio/video tapes/CDs/DVDs, and subscribes to 108,090 periodicals, including electronic. Computerized library services include interlibrary loans, database searching, Internet access, and Wi-Fi capability. Special learning facilities include an art gallery, a radio station, and an arboretum. **Physically Challenged Students:** 90% of the campus is accessible. Facilities include wheelchair ramps, elevators, special parking, specially equipped restrooms, special class scheduling, lowered drinking fountains, and lowered telephones. **Special:** DC offers interdisciplinary studies programs and study abroad in 12 countries as well as through other schools' study-abroad programs. A 3-2 engineering program may be arranged with Columbia and Washington (St. Louis) Universities. Students may design their own majors and cross-register with any college in the Charlotte Area Educational Consortium. There are 15 national honor societies, Phi Beta Kappa, and 20 departmental honors programs. **Visiting:** There are guides for informal visits; visitors may sit in on classes and stay overnight. To schedule a visit, contact the Office of Admission. **Campus Safety and Security:** Measures include 24-hour foot and vehicle patrol, an emergency notification system, self-defense education, and security escort services. There are shuttle buses, emergency telephones, lighted pathways/sidewalks, and controlled access to dorms/residences.

REQUIREMENTS: The SAT or ACT is required. The SAT Subject Tests are strongly recommended. At least 16 high school units are required, although 20 units are recommended. These should include 4 units of English, 3 units of math, and 2 units each of the same foreign language, science, and history/social studies. It is strongly recommended that high school students continue for the third and fourth years in science and in the same foreign language, continue math through calculus, and take additional courses in history. AP credits are accepted. Important factors in the admissions decision are advanced placement or honors courses, recommendations by school officials, and leadership record. Students must complete 32 courses, including 10 to 12 in the major, with a 2.0 GPA in order to graduate. Core curriculum requirements include courses in literature, fine arts, history, religion and philosophy, natural science, math, and social sciences. In addition, students must meet foreign language, composition, cultural diversity, and physical education requirements. Comprehensive exams and a thesis are required in some majors. **Procedure:** Freshmen are admitted in the fall. Entrance exams should be taken by the end of the junior year. There are early decision and deferred admissions plans. Early decision applications should be filed by November 15; regular applications, by January 2 for fall entry. The fall 2017 application fee was $50. Notification of early decision is sent December 15; regular decision, April 1. 297 early decision candidates were accepted for the 2017-2018 class. Applications are accepted on-line. **Transfer Students:** 9 transfer students enrolled in 2016-2017. Applicants must have at least 1 full year of college work, generally with a 3.0 GPA. They must submit official college and high school transcripts, as well as required letters of recommendation, and be in good standing at their previous college. 16 of 32 credits required for the bachelor's degree must be completed at DC. **International Students:** There are 125 international students enrolled. They must take the TOEFL with a minimum score of 600 on the paper-based TOEFL (PBT) or 100 on the Internet-based version (iBT). They must also take the SAT or ACT.

ADMISSIONS: 20% of the 2017-2018 applicants were accepted. The SAT scores for the 2017-2018 freshman class were: Critical Reading-- 2% below 500, 13% between 500 and 599, 46% between 600 and 699, and 40% between 700 and 800. Math-- 12% between 500 and 599, 50% between 600 and 699, and 38% between 700 and 800. Writing-- 3% below 500, 13% between 500 and 599, 44% between 600 and 699, and 40% between 700 and 800. The ACT scores were 1% between 18 and 23, 35% between 24 and 29, and 64% above 30. 89% of the current freshmen were in the top fifth of their class; 98% were in the top two fifths. **Admissions Contact:** Christopher J. Gruber, Dean of Admission and Financial Aid. Email: *admission@davidson.edu* Web: *www.davidson.edu*

FINANCIAL AID: In 2017-2018, 51% of all full-time freshmen received some form of financial aid and received need-based aid. The average freshman award was $46,079. Need-based scholarships or need-based grants averaged $42,011; need-based self-help aid (loans and jobs) averaged $2,688; non-need-based athletic scholarships averaged $18,394; and other non-need-based awards and non-need-based scholarships averaged $31,207. 45% of undergraduate students work part-time. The CSS/Profile and the colleges own financial statement, and noncustodial (divorced/separated) parents statement, corporate tax return are required. The FAFSA code is 002918. The deadline for filing freshman financial aid applications for fall entry is February 15.

DUKE UNIVERSITY — D-2

www.duke.edu

Durham, NC 27708 — **(919) 684-3214**

Fax: (919) 681-8941 — **Email: undergrad-admissions@duke.edu**

Full-time: 3259 men, 3190 women	**Faculty:** 1670; I, ++$
Part-time: 17 men, 15 women	**Ph.D.s:** 92%
Graduate: 4647 men, 4672 women	**Student/Faculty:** 8 to 1
Year: semesters, summer session	**Tuition:** $53,500
Room & Board: $14,798	**Freshman Class:** 34488 applied, 3287 accepted, 1751 enrolled
SAT CR/M/W: 725/750/730 **ACT:** 33	**CEEB CODE:** 5156
Application Deadline: January 2	**MOST COMPETITIVE**

Duke University, founded in 1838, is a private research institution that offers undergraduate programs in arts and sciences and engineering. There are 2 undergraduate schools and 8 graduate schools. In addition to regional accreditation, DU has baccalaureate program accreditation with AACSB, ABET, ACPE, AHEA, APTA, CAEP, NLN, and SAF. The 9000-acre campus is in a suburban area in Durham, N.C., about 285 miles southwest of Washington, D.C. Including any residence halls, there are 208 buildings.

STUDENT LIFE: 85% of undergraduates are from out of state, mostly the South. Students are from 50 states, 80 foreign countries, and Canada. 60% are from public schools. 9% are Hispanic; 5% race unknown; 44% White; 21% Asian American; 10% African American; 10% Foreign; 1% American Indian/Alaska Native. 37% are Protestant; 23% Catholic; 16% claim no religious affiliation. **Male To Female Ratio:** 1.0:1. The average age of freshmen is 18; all undergraduates, 20. 3% do not continue beyond their first year; 97% remain to graduate. **Housing:** 5481 students can be accommodated in college housing, which includes gender neutral, single sex, coed, married student dorms, and on-campus apartments. In addition, there are language/international houses, special-interest houses, fraternity houses, sorority houses, theme houses in womens studies, the arts, and community service (APO), and wellness housing. On-campus housing is guaranteed for all 4 years. All students may keep cars.

FACULTY/CLASSROOMS: All teach undergraduates and do research. No introductory courses are taught by graduate students. The average class size in an introductory lecture is 39; in a laboratory is 246; and in a regular course is 21.

PROGRAMS OF STUDY: DU confers B.S., B.A., and B.S.E. degrees. Master's and doctoral degrees are also awarded. Bachelor's degrees are awarded in BIOLOGICAL SCIENCE (anatomy and biology/biological science), COMMUNICATIONS AND THE ARTS (African languages, art history and appreciation, classical languages, dramatic arts, English, Germanic languages and literature, linguistics, literature, music, Slavic languages, Spanish, and visual and performing arts), COMPUTER AND PHYSICAL SCIENCE (chemistry, computer science, geology, mathematics, and physics), ENGINEERING AND ENVIRONMENTAL DESIGN (biomedical engineering, civil engineering, electrical/electronics engineering, environmental science, materials science, and mechanical engineering), SOCIAL SCIENCE (African studies, African American studies, anthropology, area studies, Asian/Oriental studies, Canadian studies, classical/ancient civilization, economics, French studies, history, Italian studies, medieval studies, philosophy, political science/government, psychology, public affairs, religion, sociology, and women's studies). Public policy studies, political science, and economics are the strongest academically. Biology, psychology, and history have the largest enrollments.

ACTIVITIES: 30% of men belong to 22 national fraternities; 40% of women belong to 17 national sororities. There are 400 groups on campus, including art, band, cheerleading, chess, choir, chorale, chorus, computers, dance, debate, drama, drill team, environmental, ethnic, film, honors, international, jazz band, LGBT, literary magazine, marching band, musical theater, newspaper, opera, orchestra, pep band, photography, political, professional, radio and TV, religious, social, social service, student government, and symphony. Popular campus events include K-Ville and Cameron Crazies, Springternational, Froshlife, Bricks to Stone, and Midnight Breakfast. **Sports:** There are 13 intercollegiate sports for men and 13 for women, and 21 intramural sports for men and 19 for women. Facilities include stadiums for baseball, softball, basketball/volleyball, football, soccer/lacrosse, squash, racquetball, and tennis courts, an aquatic center, training and weight rooms, a golf course, cross-country and jogging trails, and practice and intramural sport club fields. **Graduates:** From July 1, 2016 to June 30, 2017, 1810 bachelor's degrees were awarded. The most popular majors were social sciences (16%), biological life sciences (16%), and engineering (13%).

SERVICES: Counseling and information services are available, as is tutoring in every subject. There is a reader service for the blind. **Library/Resources:** The library contains 5.5 million volumes, 4.2 million microform items, and 61,281 audio/video tapes/CDs/DVDs, and subscribes to 33,934 periodicals including electronic. Computerized library services include interlibrary loans, database searching, Internet access, and Wi-Fi capability. Special learning facilities include an art gallery, a radio station, a TV station, a marine lab at Beaufort, a primate center, a center for international studies, a nuclear lab, a free electron laser, a science research center, institutes of the arts, statistics and decision sciences, policy sciences and public affairs, and centers for teaching and learning, community service, geometric computing, and culture and women. **Physically Challenged Students:** Facilities include wheelchair ramps, elevators, special parking, specially equipped restrooms, special class scheduling, lowered drinking fountains, lowered telephones, and special housing. Activities such as concerts can be moved to accessible facilities upon request. **Special:** Duke offers cross-registration with the University of North Carolina/Chapel Hill and North Carolina State and North Carolina Central Universities. Also available are internships through the Career Development Center, and study away/abroad in 5 US cities and 36 international locations. Dual majors of any combination, student-designed majors, nondegree study, and pass/fail options are possible. There are 3 national honor societies, Phi Beta Kappa, and 38 departmental honors programs. **Visiting:** There are regularly scheduled orientations for prospective students, including student-led tours, counselor-led group information sessions, class visits, and lunch with students. There are guides for informal visits; visitors may sit in on classes and stay overnight. To schedule a visit, contact the Undergraduate Admissions. **Campus Safety and Security:** Measures include 24-hour foot and vehicle patrol, self-defense education, and security escort services. There are shuttle buses, emergency telephones, lighted pathways/sidewalks, and a crime prevention program.

REQUIREMENTS: The SAT or ACT is required. The ACT Optional Writing test, 3 SAT: Subject tests, and writing, are also required. Applicants must be graduates of an accredited secondary school and have completed 15 academic credits, with 4 in English, 3 each in math, science, foreign language, and social studies. Engineering students must have 4 credit units in math and 1 in physics or chemistry. An essay is required and an interview is recommended. A portfolio or audition is advised in appropriate instances. AP credits are accepted. Important factors in the admissions decision are advanced placement or honors courses, evidence of special talent, personality/intangible qualities, extracurricular activities record, and recommendations by school officials. A minimum of 34 course credits is required for graduation including natural sciences, quantitative reasoning, and social sciences. No more than 17 course credits are allowed in a major for the B.A. and no more than 19 for the B.S. At least 12 courses must be at or above the 100 level. At least 3 courses designated as seminars, tutorials, independent study, or thesis completion are required. Computer proficiency must be demonstrated by engineering students. **Procedure:** Freshmen are admitted fall and spring. Entrance exams should be taken in October of the junior year for early decision applicants and by January of the senior year for regular decision. There are early decision, early admissions, and deferred admissions plans. Early decision applications should be filed by November 1; regular applications, by January 2 for fall entry. The fall 2017 application fee was $85. Notification of early decision is sent December 15; regular decision, 3455 applicants were on the 2017 waiting list; 816 were admitted. Applications are accepted online. **Transfer Students:** 16 transfer students enrolled in 2016-2017. A minimum 3.6 GPA is recommended. The SAT and 3 SAT: Subject tests or the ACT are required. 17 of 34 credits required for the bachelor's degree must be completed at DU. **International Students:** They must also take the SAT or ACT.

ADMISSIONS: 10% of the 2017-2018 applicants were accepted. The SAT scores for the 2017-2018 freshman class were: Critical Reading-- 1% below 500, 5% between 500 and 599, 27% between 600 and 699, and 67% between 700 and 800. Math-- 1% below 500, 4% between 500 and 599, 18% between 600 and 699, and 77% between 700 and 800. Writing-- 2% below 500, 6% between 500 and 599, 21% between 600 and 699, and 71% between 700 and 800. The ACT scores were 1% between 18 and 23, 14% between 24 and 29, and 85% above 30. 97% of the current freshmen were in the top fifth of their class; 99% were in the top two fifths. **Admissions Contact:** Christoph Guttentag, Director of Undergraduate Admissions. Email: *undergrad-admissions@duke.edu* Web: *www.duke.edu*

FINANCIAL AID: In 2017-2018, 100% of all full-time freshmen received some form of financial aid. The average freshman award was $46,370. Need-based scholarships or need-based grants averaged $45,074; need-based self-help aid (loans and jobs) averaged $4,662; non-need-based athletic scholarships averaged $57,336; other non-need-based awards and non-need-based scholarships averaged $3,608; and $65,459 from other forms of aid. The average financial indebtedness of the 2017 graduate was $58,171. The CSS/Profile is required. The priority date for freshman financial aid applications for fall entry is February 1.

EAST CAROLINA UNIVERSITY E-2

www.ecu.edu

Greenville, NC 27858 **(252) 328-6640**

Fax: (252) 328-6945 **Email: admis@ecu.edu**

Full-time: 7637 men, 10,680 women
Part-time: 1114 men, 1867 women
Graduate: 1981 men, 3668 women
Year: semesters, summer session
Room & Board: $9396

SAT CR/M/W: 510/540/490 **ACT:** 22
Application Deadline: March 15

Faculty: I, --$
Ph.D.s: 81%
Student/Faculty: 18 to 1
Tuition: $7143 ($23,420)
Freshman Class: 15535 applied, 9658 accepted, 4015 enrolled
CEEB CODE: 5180
COMPETITIVE

East Carolina University, founded in 1907, is a state-supported institution offering degree programs in the arts and sciences, business, education, fine arts and communication, health and human performance, human ecology, technology and computer science, medicine, allied health sciences, and nursing. The figures given in the above capsule and in this profile are approximate. There are 11 undergraduate schools and 1 graduate school. In addition to regional accreditation, ECU has baccalaureate program accreditation with CAEP. The 400-acre campus is in an urban area in the area of Greenville, 90 miles east of Raleigh. Including any residence halls, there are 239 buildings.

STUDENT LIFE: 88% of undergraduates are from North Carolina. Others are from 42 states, 54 foreign countries, and Canada. 80% are White; 2% Asian American; 2% Hispanic; 16% African American; 1% American Indian/Alaska Native; 1% Foreign. **Female To Male Ratio:** 1.5:1. The average age of freshmen is 18; all undergraduates, 23. 22% do not continue beyond their first year; 58% remain to graduate. **Housing:** 5497 students can be accommodated in college housing, which includes dorms. In addition, there are honors houses, fraternity houses, sorority houses, first-year students' floor, a leadership hall, an extended-quiet-hours floor, a substance-free hall, a nonsmoking floor, and an academic-year hall. On-campus housing is guaranteed for the freshman year only, and is available on a first-come, first-served basis. 76% of students commute. Alcohol is not permitted. All students may keep cars.

FACULTY/CLASSROOMS: 48% of faculty are male; 52% are female. No introductory courses are taught by graduate students. The average class size in an introductory lecture is 42; in a laboratory is 26; and in a regular course is 35.

PROGRAMS OF STUDY: ECU confers B.A., B.S., B.F.A., B.M., B.S.A., B.S.A.P., B.S.B.A., B.S.B.E., B.S.N. and B.S.W. degrees. Master's and doctoral degrees are also awarded. Bachelor's degrees are awarded in BIOLOGICAL SCIENCE (biochemistry, biology/biological science, and nutrition), BUSINESS (accounting, banking and finance, business administration and management, hospitality management services, management information systems, marketing management, marketing/retailing/merchandising, and recreational facilities management), COMMUNICATIONS AND THE ARTS (art, art history and appreciation, communications, dance, design, dramatic arts, English, French, German, music performance, music theory and composition, speech/debate/rhetoric, and studio art), COMPUTER AND PHYSICAL SCIENCE (applied physics, atmospheric sciences and meteorology, chemistry, computer science, geology, information sciences and systems, mathematics, and physics), EDUCATION (art education, athletic training, business education, dance education, drama education, early childhood education, education of the emotionally handicapped, education of the mentally handicapped, elementary education, English education, foreign languages education, health education, home economics education, marketing and distribution education, mathematics education, middle school education, music education, physical education, science education, social studies education, and special education), ENGINEERING AND ENVIRONMENTAL DESIGN (city/community/regional planning, construction management, electrical/electronics engineering technology, engineering, environmental engineering technology, industrial engineering technology, and interior design), HEALTH PROFESSIONS (environmental health science, exercise science, health care administration, medical records administration/services, medical technology, music therapy, nursing, occupational therapy, public health, recreation therapy, rehabilitation therapy, and speech pathology/audiology), SOCIAL SCIENCE (African American studies, anthropology, applied social science, child care/child and family studies, clothing and textiles management/production/services, criminal justice, dietetics, economics, family and community services, geography, Hispanic American studies, history, liberal arts/general studies, parks and recreation management, philosophy, physical fitness/movement, political science/government, psychology, public history/archives, social work, sociology, and women's studies). Allied health, art, and music are the strongest academically. Elementary education, management, and communication have the largest enrollments.

ACTIVITIES: 9% of men belong to 24 national fraternities; 8% of women belong to 14 national sororities. There are 399 groups on campus, including and mind body dance, and team training, campus wellness, military, academic, art, band, cheerleading, choir, chorale, chorus, communications, computers, dance, drama, drill team, environmental, ethnic, honors, international, jazz band, LGBT, literary magazine, marching band, musical theater, newspaper, opera, orchestra, pep band, photography, political, professional, radio and TV, religious, social, social service, student government, symphony, and yearbook. Popular campus events include Barefoot on the Mall, Midnight Madness, and Pirate Palooza. **Sports:** There are 9 intercollegiate sports for men and 9 for women, and 14 intramural sports for men and 14 for women. Facilities include a stadium, a coliseum, baseball, basketball, cross-country, football, golf, swimming and diving, tennis, indoor and outdoor track and field, basketball, cross-country, golf, soccer, fast-pitch softball, swimming and diving, tennis, indoor and outdoor track and field, and volleyball. **Graduates:** From July 1, 2016 to June 30, 2017, 4315 bachelor's degrees were awarded. The most popular majors were nursing (7%), communication (7%), and elementary education (6%). In an average class, 33% graduate in 4 years or less, 53% graduate in 5 years or less, and 58% graduate in 6 years or less.

SERVICES: Counseling and information services are available, as is tutoring in most subjects. There is a reader service for the blind, and remedial math and reading. Tutoring is established on a department by department basis. **Library/Resources:** The library contains 2.4 million volumes, 200,000 microform items, 439,000 audio/video tapes/CDs/DVDs, and subscribes to 73,498 periodicals, including electronic. Computerized library services include interlibrary loans, database searching, and Wi-Fi capability. Special learning facilities include an art gallery, a radio station, special collections, manuscripts, rare books, a music library, the Walker center, and the William E. Laupus Health Science Library, laboratories such as biomechanics, biofeedback, human performance, activity promotion, developmental motor, and visual motor. **Physically Challenged Students:** 95% of the campus is accessible. Facilities include wheelchair ramps, elevators, special parking, specially equipped restrooms, special class scheduling, lowered drinking fountains, lowered telephones, and automatic doors. **Special:** ECU offers cooperative programs in most majors, internships, study abroad in 42 countries, a Washington semester, accelerated degrees, a B.A.-B.S. in accounting, dual majors, work-study, and a student-designed major in multidisciplinary studies. There are 18 national honor societies, Phi Beta Kappa, a freshman honors program, and 39 departmental honors programs. **Visiting:** There are regularly scheduled orientations for prospective students, including information sessions and campus tours. There are guides for informal visits. To schedule a visit, contact the Admissions Office. **Campus Safety and Security:** Measures include 24-hour foot and vehicle patrol, an emergency notification system, self-defense education, and security escort services. There are shuttle buses, emergency telephones, lighted pathways/sidewalks, controlled access to dorms/residences, and locked residence hall doors, bicycle patrols and registration, motorist assistance lost and found, operation ID, the residence hall liason officer program, on-and off campus crime prevention safety tips, staff and faculty eyes (SAFE), campus community watch program, and alcohol awareness.

REQUIREMENTS: The SAT or ACT is required. The ACT Optional Writing test is also required. Applicants must be graduates of an accredited secondary school. All degree-seeking students are required to complete 20 academic units, including 4 in English, and math, 3 in science with 1 lab course, 2 in social studies with 1 in U.S. history, and 2 units in foreign language, 1 unit in fine arts is recommended, and 1 unit each in foreign language, natural science, and math should be taken in the senior year. Special circumstances exist for applicants with a GED. AP and CLEP credits are accepted. To graduate, students must complete 120 to 128 semester hours with a minimum GPA of 2.0 overall and in the major. General education requirements include 12 hours of social science, 10 of humanities and fine arts, 8 of science, 6 of English, 3 of math, and 3 of health and exercise and sport science. The total must include 12 hours of writing-intensive courses and a course in cultural diversity. **Procedure:** Freshmen are admitted to all sessions. Entrance exams should be taken in the spring of the junior year or the fall of the senior year. There are deferred admissions and rolling admissions plans. Applications should be filed by March 15 for fall entry; November 1 for spring entry; and March 15 for summer entry. The fall 2017 application fee was $70. Notifications are sent April 15. Applications are accepted online. **Transfer Students:** 1427 transfer students enrolled in 2016-2017. Applicants must submit official transcripts from high school and all colleges attended and have a satisfactory GPA in courses attempted. Applicants who will have completed less than 30 semester hours will also be required to meet the freshmen requirements. **International Students:** There are 200 international students enrolled. They must take the TOEFL with a minimum score of 80 on the Internet-based version (iBT). Students must take the IELTS. SAT or ACT scores are required if a student will receive an athletic scholarship or if a student will graduate from a U.S. high school.

ADMISSIONS: 62% of the 2017-2018 applicants were accepted. The SAT scores for the 2017-2018 freshman class were: Critical Reading-- 49% below 500, 43% between 500 and 599, 7% between 600 and 699, and 1% between 700 and 800. Math-- 32% below 500, 55% between 500 and 599, 12% between 600 and 699, and 1% between 700 and 800. Writing-- 57% below 500, 37% between 500 and 599, and 6% between 600 and 699. The ACT scores were 18% below 12, 55% between 12 and 17, 19% between 18 and 23, 6% between 24 and 29, and 3% above 30. 35% of the current freshmen were in the top fifth of their class; 68% were in the top two fifths. **Admissions Contact:** James Coker, Associate Director of Undergraduate Admissions. Email: *admis@ecu.edu* Web: *www.ecu.edu*

FINANCIAL AID: In 2017-2018, 60% of all full-time freshmen received some form of financial aid. 55% of all full-time freshmen received need-based aid. The average freshman award was $9,614. Need-based scholarships or need-based grants averaged $8,031; need-based self-help aid (loans and jobs) averaged $3,834; non-need-based athletic scholarships averaged $11,120; and other non-need-based awards and non-need-based scholarships averaged $4,532. The average financial indebtedness of the 2017 graduate was $25,983. ECU is a member of CSS. The priority date for freshman financial aid applications for fall entry is March 1.

ELIZABETH CITY STATE UNIVERSITY F-2

www.ecsu.edu

Elizabeth City, NC 27909	(252) 335-3400
Fax: (252) 335-3537	**Email:** admissions@ecsu.edu
Full-time: 1035 men, 1474 women	**Faculty:** 113; IIA, -$
Part-time: 68 men, 183 women	**Ph.D.s:** 68%
Graduate: 29 men, 89 women	**Student/Faculty:** 16 to 1
Year: semesters, summer session	**Tuition:** $6821 ($19,175)
Room & Board: $7924	**Freshman Class:** 3925 applied, 2243 accepted, 527 enrolled
SAT or ACT: required	**CEEB CODE:** 5629
Application Deadline: August 1	**COMPETITIVE**

Elizabeth City State University, founded in 1891 as part of the University of North Carolina System, is a public institution offering undergraduate programs in liberal arts and sciences, education, and business. The figures given in the above capsule and in this profile are approximate. There is 1 undergraduate school. The 829-acre campus is in a small town 55 miles from Norfolk, Virginia.

STUDENT LIFE: 90% of undergraduates are from North Carolina. Others are from 25 states. 73% are African American; 12% White. 12% are ethnicity unknown. **Female To Male Ratio:** 1.5:1. 25% do not continue beyond their first year; 50% remain to graduate. **Housing:** 1019 students can be accommodated in college housing, which includes dorms and on-campus apartments. In addition, there are honors houses and wellness housing. On-campus housing is guaranteed for all 4 years. 52% of students commute. Alcohol is not permitted. All students may keep cars.

FACULTY/CLASSROOMS: 50% of faculty are male; 50% are female. All teach undergraduates. No introductory courses are taught by graduate students.

PROGRAMS OF STUDY: ECSU confers B.A., B.S., and B.S.Ed. degrees.

Master's degrees are also awarded. Bachelor's degrees are awarded in BIOLOGICAL SCIENCE (biology/biological science), BUSINESS (accounting and business administration and management), COMMUNICATIONS AND THE ARTS (art, English, and music), COMPUTER AND PHYSICAL SCIENCE (chemistry, computer science, geology, mathematics, and physics), EDUCATION (business education, elementary education, industrial arts education, middle school education, physical education, special education, and technical education), ENGINEERING AND ENVIRONMENTAL DESIGN (industrial engineering technology), SOCIAL SCIENCE (criminal justice, history, political science/government, psychology, social science, social work, and sociology).

ACTIVITIES: Groups on campus include band, cheerleading, choir, chorus, dance, drama, honors, international, jazz band, literary magazine, marching band, musical theater, newspaper, pep band, radio and TV, religious, social, student government, symphony, and yearbook. **Sports:** Facilities include a gym, a stadium, an all-weather track, a golf range, an Olympic pool, a weight room, tennis courts, dance and exercise studios, handball and racquetball courts, and playing fields. **Graduates:** From July 1, 2016 to June 30, 2017, 379 bachelor's degrees were awarded. The most popular majors were business/marketing (21%), education (15%), and homeland security (13%). In an average class, 33% graduate in 4 years or less, 46% graduate in 5 years or less, and 49% graduate in 6 years or less. Of the 2016 graduating class, 79% were enrolled in graduate school within 6 months of graduation.

SERVICES: **Library/Resources:** The library contains 174,566 volumes, 486,884 microform items, 1,220 audio/video tapes/CDs/DVDs, and subscribes to 1,698 periodicals, including electronic. Computerized library services include interlibrary loans. Special learning facilities include an art gallery, planetarium, a radio station, a TV station, a farm, and a 639-acre educational research tract. **Physically Challenged Students:** Facilities include wheelchair ramps, elevators, special parking, specially equipped restrooms, and lowered drinking fountains. **Special:** Opportunities are provided for internships, dual majors, weekend/evening degree completion programs, work-study, credit by exam, and for military service. There are 5 national honor societies and a freshman honors program. **Visiting:** There are regularly scheduled orientations for prospective students. There are guides for informal visits. To schedule a visit, contact the Admissions Office. **Campus Safety and Security:** There are emergency telephones, and ECSU has its own police department on campus.

REQUIREMENTS: The SAT or ACT is required. Graduation from an accredited secondary school is required; the GED is accepted. Applicants should submit an academic record with 4 courses in English, 3 in math and 2 each in science, and social studies; it is recommended that applicants have at least 2 course units in foreign languages. Students must also pass the NC Competency Examination or its equivalent. AP and CLEP credits are accepted. Students must have maintained a minimum GPA of 2.0, fulfilled a major, and completed the requirements of general education courses in the fields of grammar, composition, and literature. **Procedure:** Freshmen are admitted in the fall, spring, and summer. Entrance exams should be taken as early as possible. There are early admissions and deferred admissions plans. Early decision applications should be filed by May 1; regular applications, by August 1 for fall entry; and November 1 for spring entry. The fall 2017 application fee was $30. **Transfer Students:** 201 transfer students enrolled in 2016-2017. Applicants must have a minimum college GPA of 2.0 and submit high school and college transcripts. Those with fewer than 30 credit hours must meet both freshman and transfer admission requirements. 30 credits required for the bachelor's degree must be completed at ECSU. **International Students:** There are 6 international students enrolled. They must take the TOEFL or MELAB. They must also take the SAT or ACT.

ADMISSIONS: 57% of the 2017-2018 applicants were accepted. The SAT scores for the 2017-2018 freshman class were: Critical Reading-- 89% below 500, 10% between 500 and 599, and 1% between 600 and 699. Math-- 83% below 500, 16% between 500 and 599, and 1% between 600 and 699. Writing-- 92% below 500 and 8% between 500 and 599. **Admissions Contact:** Bridgett Golham, Director of Admissions and Recruitment. Email: *admissions@ecsu.edu* Web: *www.ecsu.edu*

FINANCIAL AID: The college's own financial statement, and income tax forms are required. The FAFSA code is 002926. Check with the school for current application deadlines.

ELON UNIVERSITY — D-2

www.elon.edu

Elon, NC 27244 — (336) 278-3566, (800) 334-8448

Fax: (336) 278-7699 — **Email:** admissions@elon.edu

Full-time: 2371 men, 3514 women	**Faculty:** 392; IIA, av$
Part-time: 70 men, 90 women	**Ph.D.s:** 86%
Graduate: 284 men, 462 women	**Student/Faculty:** 12 to 1
Year: 4-1-4, summer session	**Tuition:** $34,273
Room & Board: $11,869	**Freshman Class:** 9623 applied, 6402 accepted, 1573 enrolled
SAT EBR-W/M: 618/605 **ACT:** 27	**CEEB CODE:** 5183
Application Deadline: January 10	**HIGHLY COMPETITIVE**

Elon University, founded in 1889 as Elon College, was established in 2001 as a private liberal arts university. Elons student-centered learning environment prepares students to be ethical leaders in the world. There are 4 undergraduate schools and 5 graduate schools. In addition to regional accreditation, EU has baccalaureate program accreditation with AACSB, ACEJMC, CAEP, CAPTE, ARC-PA, ABS, and ACS. The 646-acre campus is in a suburban area adjacent to Burlington and 17 miles east of Greensboro. Including any residence halls, there are 215 buildings.

STUDENT LIFE: 82% of undergraduates are from out of state, mostly the Middle Atlantic. Students are from 49 states, 58 foreign countries, and Canada. 60% are from public schools. 80% are White; 6% Hispanic; 5% African American; 3% two or more races; 2% Asian American; 2% Foreign. 38% are Protestant; 35% Catholic. **Female To Male Ratio:** 1.5:1. The average age of freshmen is 18; all undergraduates, 20. 11% do not continue beyond their first year; 81% remain to graduate. **Housing:** 3893 students can be accommodated in college housing, which includes dorms, on-campus apartments, off-campus apartments, and honors houses, language/international houses, special-interest houses, fraternity houses, and sorority houses. Elon's high-tech campus encompasses seven distinct residential neighborhoods for students at various stages of their college careers. On-campus housing is guaranteed for the freshman year only and is available on a lottery system for upperclassmen. 64% of students live on campus. All students may keep cars.

FACULTY/CLASSROOMS: 50% of faculty are male; 50% are female. 91% teach undergraduates, 65% do research, and 65% do both. No introductory courses are taught by graduate students. The average class size in an introductory lecture is 23; in a laboratory is 19; and in a regular course is 20.

PROGRAMS OF STUDY: EU confers B.A., B.S., B.F.A., and B.S.B.A. degrees. Master's and doctoral degrees are also awarded. Bachelor's degrees are awarded in AGRICULTURE (environmental studies), BIOLOGICAL SCIENCE (biochemistry, biophysics, and neurosciences), BUSINESS (accounting, business administration and management, entrepreneurial studies, finance, international business management, international economics, leadership, management, marketing, marketing management, and sports management), COMMUNICATIONS AND THE ARTS (acting, art history, art, arts administration/management, communication design , communications, creative writing, dance, dramatic arts, English, film arts, fine arts, French, German studies, human performance, journalism, literature, media arts, media management, music, music performance, music technology, musical theater, Spanish, strategic communication, theatre acting, theatre arts, theater design, theatre production, theatre studies, and writing), COMPUTER AND PHYSICAL SCIENCE (applied mathematics, chemistry, computer science, digital arts/technology, information sciences and systems, mathematics, physics, and statistics), EDUCATION (Asian studies, early childhood education, education, elementary education, foreign languages education, health education, history education, mathematics education, middle school education, music education, physical education, science education, secondary education, and special education), ENGINEERING AND ENVIRONMENTAL DESIGN (biomedical engineering, chemical engineering, computer engineering, engineering, engineering physics, environmental engineering, and environmental science), HEALTH PROFESSIONS (biology, exercise science, and public health), SOCIAL SCIENCE (African American studies, American studies, anthropology, criminal justice, economics, geography, geography information science, history, human services, international studies,

Italian studies, Judaic studies, justice and society, Latin American studies, Middle Eastern studies, peace studies, philosophy, political science/government, psychology, public administration, religious studies, sociology, and women and gender studies). Business, music theater, and biology are the strongest academically. Business, strategic communications, and psychology have the largest enrollments.

ACTIVITIES: 20% of men belong to 12 national fraternities; 39% of women belong to 13 national sororities. There are 241 groups on campus, including art, band, cheerleading, chess, choir, chorale, chorus, communications, computers, dance, debate, drama, drill team, environmental, ethnic, film, honors, international, jazz band, LGBT, literary magazine, marching band, musical theater, newspaper, orchestra, pep band, photography, political, professional, radio and TV, religious, social, social service, student government, symphony, and yearbook. Popular campus events include Family Weekend, Homecoming, Greek Week, Spring Undergraduate Research Forum (SURF Day), College Coffee and CELEBRATE!, a week-long celebration of Student Achievements in Academics and the Arts, and Festival of Holiday Lights. **Sports:** There are 7 intercollegiate sports for men and 9 for women, and 21 intramural sports for men and 21 for women. Facilities include tennis courts, a softball field, a baseball stadium, a field house, and athletic fields. The athletic center has racquetball courts, aerobic rooms, a human performance lab, a weight room, a fitness center, gyms, a driving range, and an indoor swimming pool. **Graduates:** From July 1, 2016 to June 30, 2017, 1391 bachelor's degrees were awarded. The most popular majors were busines/marketing (31%), communications (17%), and psychology (5%). In an average class, 78% graduate in 4 years or less, 83% graduate in 5 years or less, and 84% graduate in 6 years or less. Of the 2016 graduating class, 21% were enrolled in graduate school within 6 months of graduation, and 77% were employed.

SERVICES: Counseling and information services are available, as is tutoring in most subjects, such as lower-level courses. Preparatory courses are offered, which count as elective credit toward graduation. We offer texts in alternative formats for students with print disabilities (both learning and visual disabilities). **Library/Resources:** The library contains 1.7 million volumes, 460,600 microform items, 24,809 audio/video tapes/CDs/DVDs, and subscribes to 64,848 periodicals, including electronic. Computerized library services include interlibrary loans, database searching, Internet access, and Wi-Fi capability. Special learning facilities include a radio station, a TV station, a writing center, a botanical preserve, a protected Elon Forest, an art collection walk, and an observatory. **Physically Challenged Students:** 85% of the campus is accessible. Facilities include wheelchair ramps, elevators, special parking, specially equipped restrooms, special class scheduling, lowered drinking fountains, lowered telephones, and special housing. **Special:** EU offers co-op programs in most majors, dual majors, student-designed majors, cross-registration with 6 other colleges and universities in North Carolina, paid and unpaid internships, more than 100 study abroad programs, study USA programs, Washington semester, Los Angeles semester, New York semester, work-study programs, pass/fail options, and 3-2 dual engineering degree programs. The month-long January term includes extensive international study opportunities as well as courses focused on domestic travel. There are 31 national honor societies, Phi Beta Kappa, a freshman honors program, and 25 departmental honors programs. **Visiting:** There are regularly scheduled orientations for prospective students, consisting of 2 weekends in spring for deposited freshmen or a spring open house for nondeposited students. There are guides for informal visits and visitors may sit in on classes. To schedule a visit, contact the Admissions Office. **Campus Safety and Security:** Measures include 24-hour foot and vehicle patrol, an emergency notification system, and security escort services. There are shuttle buses, emergency telephones, lighted pathways/sidewalks, controlled access to dorms/residences, over 200 cameras on campus, annual fire inspections through the County Fire Marshall's Office, campus safety and police operating 24 hours/day 7 days/week, and Operation ID, blue light phones, panic alarms in certain buildings that call campus police, LiveSafe Application, and safety walks conducted periodically with Residence Life, SGA, and Physical Plant.

REQUIREMENTS: The SAT or ACT is required. Students must be graduates of an accredited secondary school or have a GED certificate. They should have completed 4 credits of English, 3 credits or more in math (must include algebra 1 and 2, and geometry), 2 credits or more in foreign language, and science, including at least 1 lab science, social studies, and U.S. history. AP and CLEP credits are accepted. To graduate, students must complete 132 semester hours, including 32 to 68 in the major, with a minimum GPA of 2.0. All students must fulfill the requirements of the Core Curriculum, which includes a first-year core, experiential learning, liberal studies, and advanced studies, for a total of 59 semester hours, and must satisfactorily complete a comprehensive exam in the major. **Procedure:** Freshmen are admitted in the fall and spring. Entrance exams should be taken in the spring of the junior year and the fall of the senior year. There are early decision, early admissions, and deferred admissions plans. Early decision applications should be filed by November 1; regular applications, by January 10 for fall entry; and December 1 for spring entry. The fall 2017 application fee was $50. Notification of early decision is sent December 1; regular decision, March 20. 378 early decision candidates were accepted for the 2017-2018 class. 2117 applicants were on the 2017 waiting list; 153 were admitted. Applications are accepted online. **Transfer Students:** 71 transfer students enrolled in 2016-2017. Applicants must present a high school transcript, 12 credit hours of college transferable classes in the liberal arts and sciences, and a minimum GPA of 2.7 from a two-year or four-year accredited institution. An interview is recommended. A deans evaluation form is required from all colleges or universities attended, and the applicant must be eligible to return to the former institution. 60 of 132 credits required for the bachelor's degree must be completed at EU. **International Students:** There are 137 international students enrolled. They must take the TOEFL with a minimum score of 550 on the paper-based TOEFL (PBT) or 79 on the Internet-based version (iBT). They must also take the SAT or ACT, scoring 1330.

ADMISSIONS: 67% of the 2017-2018 applicants were accepted. The SAT scores for the 2017-2018 freshman class were: Math-- 4% below 500, 40% between 500 and 599, 47% between 600 and 699, and 9% between 700 and 800. Evidence-Based Reading/Writing-- 2% below 500, 31% between 500 and 599, 53% between 600 and 699, and 13% between 700 and 800. The ACT scores were 1% between 12 and 17, 14% between 18 and 23, 63% between 24 and 29, and 23% above 30. 8 freshmen graduated first in their class. **Admissions Contact:** Lisa Keegan, Dean of Admissions. Email: *admissions@elon.edu* Web: *www.elon.edu*

FINANCIAL AID: In 2017-2018, 73% of all full-time freshmen received some form of financial aid. 35% of all full-time freshmen received need-based aid. The average freshman award was $21,984. Need-based scholarships or need-based grants averaged $13,012 ($47,142 maximum); need-based self-help aid (loans and jobs) averaged $4,761 ($10,000 maximum); non-need-based athletic scholarships averaged $30,138 ($48,099 maximum); and other non-need-based awards and non-need-based scholarships averaged $8,808 ($42,829 maximum). 37% of undergraduate students work part-time. The average financial indebtedness of the 2017 graduate was $30,475. EU is a member of CSS. The CSS/Profile and the college's own financial statement are required. The priority date for freshman financial aid applications for fall entry is February 15.

FAYETTEVILLE STATE UNIVERSITY D-3

www.uncfsu.edu

Fayetteville, NC 28301	**(910) 672-1371** **(800) 222-2594**
Fax: (910) 672-1414	**Email: admissions@uncfsu.edu**
Full-time: 1297 men, 2619 women	**Faculty:** 276; IIA, av$
Part-time: 323 men, 1048 women	**Ph.D.s:** n/av
Graduate: 186 men, 587 women	**Student/Faculty:** 16 to 1
Year: semesters, summer session	**Tuition:** $9686 ($18,600)
Room & Board: $8070	**Freshman Class:** n/av
SAT or ACT: required	**CEEB CODE:** 5212
Application Deadline: August 25	**COMPETITIVE**

Fayetteville State University, founded in 1867 and today part of the University of North Carolina system, is a public institution offering degree programs in the arts and sciences, business, and teacher preparation. The figures given in the above capsule and in this profile are approximate. There are 3 undergraduate schools and 1 graduate school. In addition to regional accreditation, FSU has baccalaureate program accreditation with CAEP. The 156-acre campus is in an urban area 60 miles south of Raleigh. Including any residence halls, there are 43 buildings.

STUDENT LIFE: 95% of undergraduates are from North Carolina. 76% are African American; 7% Hispanic; 20% White; 1% Asian American; 1% American Indian/Alaska Native. **Female To Male Ratio:** 2.4:1. The average age of freshmen is 19; all undergraduates, 27. 24% do not continue beyond their first year; 31% remain to graduate. **Housing:** 1298 students can be accommodated in college housing, which includes dorms, on-campus apartments and honors dorm. On-campus housing is available on a first-come, first-served basis. 71% of students commute. Alcohol is not permitted. All students may keep cars.

FACULTY/CLASSROOMS: 54% of faculty are male; 46% are female. All teach undergraduates and all do research. No introductory courses are taught by graduate students. The average class size in an introductory lecture is 30; in a laboratory is 20; and in a regular course is 30.

PROGRAMS OF STUDY: FSU confers B.A. and B.S. degrees. Master's and doctoral degrees are also awarded. Bachelor's degrees are awarded in BIOLOGICAL SCIENCE (biology/biological science), BUSINESS (accounting, banking and finance, business administration and management, business economics, management information systems, and office supervision and management), COMMUNICATIONS AND THE ARTS (dramatic arts, English, Spanish, speech/debate/rhetoric, and visual and performing arts), COMPUTER AND PHYSICAL SCIENCE (chemistry, computer science, and mathematics), EDUCATION (business education, early childhood education, elementary education, health education, marketing and distribution education, middle school education, music education, secondary education, and social science education), HEALTH PROFESSIONS (medical laboratory technology and nursing), SOCIAL SCIENCE (criminal justice, economics, geography, history, political science/government, psychology, public administration, social science, social work, and sociology).

ACTIVITIES: 1% of men belong to 4 local and 4 national fraternities; 1% of women belong to 3 national sororities. There are 30 groups on campus, including band, cheerleading, choir, chorus, dance, drama, film, honors, international, jazz band, literary magazine, marching band, newspaper, pep band, political, radio and TV, religious, social service, student government, and yearbook. Popular campus events include The Lyceum, Martin Luther King Day, and Black History Month. **Sports:** There are 8 intercollegiate sports for men and 8 for women, and 7 intramural sports for men and 5 for women. Facilities include gyms, a stadium, tennis courts, a bowling alley, a dance studio, a swimming pool, and playing fields. **Graduates:** From July 1, 2016 to June 30, 2017, 991 bachelor's degrees were awarded. The most popular majors were criminal justice (16%), psychology (16%), and business administration (14%).

SERVICES: Counseling and information services are available, as is tutoring in some subjects. There is remedial math, reading, and writing. **Library/Resources:** The library contains 335,922 volumes, 1.0 million microform items, and 20,676 audio/video tapes/CDs/DVDs. Computerized library services include interlibrary loans and database searching. Special learning facilities include a planetarium and radio station. **Physically Challenged Students:** 75% of the campus is accessible. Facilities include wheelchair ramps, elevators, special parking, specially equipped restrooms, and lowered drinking fountains. **Special:** FSU offers cooperative programs in business, math, and biological and physical sciences with North Carolina State University, internships, B.A.-B.S. degrees, dual majors, 3-2 engineering degree programs, credit for military experience, and nondegree study. There are 17 national honor societies, a freshman honors program, and 7 departmental honors programs. **Visiting:** There are regularly scheduled orientations for prospective students, including a campus tour, recreational activity, placement tests, preregistration, and orientation to FSU services. There are guides for informal visits; visitors may sit in on classes and stay overnight. To schedule a visit, contact the Director of Enrollment Management at (910) 672-1784. **Campus Safety and Security:** Measures include 24-hour foot and vehicle patrol and security escort services. There are lighted pathways/sidewalks.

REQUIREMENTS: The SAT or ACT is required. Successful scores are also required on the North Carolina Competency Exam. Applicants must be graduates of an accredited secondary school or have the GED. They should have completed 4 academic units of English, 3 each of math and science with 1 lab course, and 2 of social studies; also recommended are 2 units of a foreign language and completion of 1 unit each of foreign language and math in the senior year. AP and CLEP credits are accepted. Important factors in the admissions decision are advanced placement or honors courses, recommendations by school officials, and leadership record. To graduate, students must complete 120 credit hours with a minimum GPA of 2.0 overall and in the major. The core curriculum includes 8 to 11 credits in natural science, 6 to 15 in humanities, 6 to 7 in math, 3 to 9 in social science, 3 each in critical thinking and speech, and 2 each in physical education/health and university seminar. **Procedure:** Freshmen are admitted to all sessions. Entrance exams should be taken in November. There are early decision, early admissions, deferred admissions, and rolling admissions plans. Applications should be filed by August 25 for fall entry. The fall 2017 application fee was $35. Notification is sent on a rolling basis. **Transfer Students:** 670 transfer students enrolled in 2016-2017. Applicants must submit official transcripts from all colleges attended, have a minimum GPA of 2.0, and be eligible to return to their previous institution. 33 of 120 credits required for the bachelor's degree must be completed at FSU. **International Students:** They must take the TOEFL or other English proficiency exams administered in their country. They must also take the SAT or ACT.

Admissions Contact: Ulisa E. Bowles, Director of Admissions. Email: *admissions@uncfsu.edu* Web: *www.uncfsu.edu*

FINANCIAL AID: FSU is a member of CSS. The FAFSA code is 002928. Check with the school for current application deadlines.

GARDNER-WEBB UNIVERSITY — C-3

www.gardner-webb.edu

Boiling Springs, NC 28017 — (704) 406-4495, (800) 253-6472

Fax: (704) 406-4488 — **Email:** admissions@gardner-webb.edu

Full-time: 779 men, 1309 women	**Faculty:** 122; I, +$
Part-time: 118 men, 366 women	**Ph.D.s:** 79%
Graduate: 594 men, 1470 women	**Student/Faculty:** 13 to 1
Year: semesters, summer session	**Tuition:** $15,155
Room & Board: $9780	**Freshman Class:** 5456 applied, 2640 accepted, 434 enrolled
	CEEB CODE: 5242
Application Deadline: open	**COMPETITIVE+**

Gardner-Webb University, founded in 1905, is an independent institution affiliated with the Baptist Convention of North Carolina and offering undergraduate programs in the arts and sciences, business, education, nursing, and professional studies. The figures given in the above capsule and in this profile are approximate. There are 5 undergraduate schools and 2 graduate schools. In addition to regional accreditation, Gardner-Webb has baccalaureate program accreditation with ACBSP, NASM, NLN, ATS, CHEA, CAATE, and NLNAC. The 200-acre campus is in a small town 50 miles west of Charlotte, in the Piedmont area of Western North Carolina. Including any residence halls, there are 46 buildings.

STUDENT LIFE: 78% of undergraduates are from North Carolina. Others are from 37 states, 21 foreign countries, and Canada. 70% are from public schools. 69% are White; 20% African American; 2% Hispanic; 1% Asian American. 64% are Protestant. **Female To Male Ratio:** 2.1:1. The average age of freshmen is 18; all undergraduates, 21. 26% do not continue beyond their first year; 48% remain to graduate. **Housing:** 1368 students can be accommodated in college housing, which includes dorms, on-campus apartments, and honors houses. On-campus housing is guaranteed for all 4 years. 77% of students live on campus. Alcohol is not permitted. All students may keep cars.

FACULTY/CLASSROOMS: 51% of faculty are male; 49% are female. All teach undergraduates. No introductory courses are taught by graduate students. The average class size in an introductory lecture is 25; in a laboratory is 9; and in a regular course is 18.

PROGRAMS OF STUDY: Gardner-Webb confers B.A., B.S., B.F.A., B.M., and B.S.N. degrees. Associate, master's, and doctoral degrees are also awarded. Bachelor's degrees are awarded in BIOLOGICAL SCIENCE (biology/biological science), BUSINESS (accounting, business administration and management, international business management, and sports management), COMMUNICATIONS AND THE ARTS (American Sign Language, art, communications, English, French, music, and Spanish), COMPUTER AND PHYSICAL SCIENCE (chemistry, computer science, information sciences and systems, and mathematics), EDUCATION (athletic training, elementary education, foreign languages education, health education, middle school education, music education, physical education, and secondary education), ENGINEERING AND ENVIRONMENTAL DESIGN (industrial administration/management), HEALTH PROFESSIONS (health care administration, medical technology, nursing, and physician's assistant), SOCIAL SCIENCE (history, interpreter for the deaf, psychology, religion, religious music, social science, and sociology). Nursing, music, and biology are the strongest academically. Business, social science, and education have the largest enrollments.

ACTIVITIES: There are no fraternities or sororities. There are 65 groups on campus, including art, band, cheerleading, choir, chorale, chorus, debate, drama, drill team, film, honors, international, jazz band, literary magazine, marching band, musical theater, newspaper, opera, orchestra, pep band, photography, political, professional, radio and TV, religious, social, social service, student government, symphony, and yearbook. Popular campus events include Festival of Lights, Bulldog Madness, and Spring's Alive. **Sports:** There are 11 intercollegiate sports for men and 10 for women, and 28 intramural sports for men and 28 for women. Facilities include an athletic and recreation facility; include a stadium, gyms, tennis and racquetball courts, a weight room, swimming pool, playing fields for softball, soccer, football, and baseball, an arena, aerobics room, and a ropes course. **Graduates:** From July 1, 2016 to June 30, 2017, 645 bachelor's degrees were awarded. The most popular majors were business administration (27%), social sciences (21%), and nursing and other health related majors (12%). In an average class, 9% graduate in 3 years or less, 37% graduate in 4 years or less, 47% graduate in 5 years or less, and 48% graduate in 6 years or less.

SERVICES: Counseling and information services are available, as is tutoring in every subject. There is a reader service for the blind, and remedial math, reading, and writing. **Library/Resources:** The library contains 244,133 volumes, 653,778 microform items, 12,494 audio/video tapes/CDs/DVDs, and subscribes to 108,251 periodicals, including electronic. Computerized library services include interlibrary loans, database searching, Internet access, and Wi-Fi capability. Special learning facilities include an art gallery, radio station, and observatory. **Physically Challenged Students:** All of the campus is accessible. Facilities include wheelchair ramps, elevators, special parking, specially equipped restrooms, special class scheduling, lowered drinking fountains, and special housing. **Special:** The university offers work-study programs, internships, and study abroad in 11 countries. There are 11 national honor societies, a freshman honors program, and 3 departmental honors programs. **Visiting:** There are regularly scheduled orientations for prospective students, including a campus tour and a meeting with an admissions counselor. There are guides for informal visits; visitors may sit in on classe and stay overnight. To schedule a visit, contact the Visit Coordinator. **Campus Safety and Security:** Measures include 24-hour foot and vehicle patrol, an emergency notification system, self-defense education, and security escort services. There are emergency telephones, lighted pathways/sidewalks, controlled access to dorms/residences, and police foot patrol inside of dorms.

REQUIREMENTS: Candidates should be graduates of an accredited secondary school or have a GED certificate. The recommended preparatory curriculum includes 4 units of English, 3 of math, and 2 each of social science, natural science, foreign language, and electives. One standardized test, either the SAT or the ACT, is required. Gardner-Webb requires applicants to be in the upper 50% of their class. AP and CLEP credits are accepted. Important factors in the admissions decision are leadership record, extracurricular activities record, and recommendations by school officials. To graduate, students must complete 128 credit hours, including 24 to 36 in the major, with a minimum GPA of 2.0. The required core curriculum consists of 44 hours of general education, liberal arts courses. Students also receive 1 credit hour per year of Dimensions. **Procedure:** Freshmen are admitted to all sessions. Entrance exams should be taken During the junior or senior year of high school. There are deferred admissions and rolling admissions plans. Application deadlines are open. The fall 2017 application fee was $40. Applications are accepted online. **Transfer Students:** 114 transfer students enrolled in 2016-2017. Applicants must submit the standard application and fee, official high school and college transcripts, and SAT or ACT scores. High school transcripts and test scores are waived for applicants with 15 or more semester credits and a GPA of 2.25 and submission of a college tanscript. 32 of 128 credits required for the bachelor's degree must be completed at Gardner-Webb. **International Students:** There are 67 international students enrolled. They must take the TOEFL with a minimum score of 500 on the paper-based TOEFL (PBT) or 61 on the Internet-based version (iBT). They must also take the SAT or ACT.

ADMISSIONS: 48% of the 2017-2018 applicants were accepted. 42% of the current freshmen were in the top fifth of their class; 66% were in the top two fifths. 3 freshmen graduated first in their class. **Admissions Contact:** Angela Sundell, Assistant Vice President of Admissions. Email: *admissions@gardner-webb.edu* Web: *www.gardner-webb.edu*

FINANCIAL AID: In 2017-2018, 100% of all full-time freshmen received some form of financial aid. The average freshman award was $18,540. Need-based scholarships or need-based grants averaged $7,336; need-based self-help aid (loans and jobs) averaged $4,283; non-need-based athletic scholarships averaged $15,287; and other non-need-based awards and non-need-based scholarships averaged $11,745. The average financial indebtedness of the 2017 graduate was $19,725. Gardner-Webb is a member of CSS. The state aid form and federal tax returns are required. The FAFSA code is 002929. The priority date for freshman financial aid applications for fall entry is March 1.

GREENSBORO COLLEGE *(The complete profile is made available exclusively on our website, www.barronspac.com)*

GUILFORD COLLEGE — D-2

www.guilford.edu

Greensboro, NC 27410	(336) 316-2124 (800) 992-7759
Fax: (336) 316-2954	Email: admission@guilford.edu
Full-time: 670 men, 759 women	**Faculty:** 90; IIB, --$
Part-time: 113 men, 132 women	**Ph.D.s:** 90%
Graduate: 3 men, 3 women	**Student/Faculty:** 16 to 1
Year: semesters, summer session	**Tuition:** $35,373
Room & Board: $10,600	**Freshman Class:** 342 enrolled
SAT CR/M/W: 508/505/484 **ACT:** 22	**CEEB CODE:** 5261
Application Deadline: December 1	**COMPETITIVE**

Guilford's purpose is to provide a transformative, practical, and excellent liberal arts education that produces critical thinkers in an inclusive, diverse environment, guided by Quaker testimonies of community, equality, integrity, peace, and simplicity and emphasizing the creative problem-solving skills, experiences, enthusiasm, and international perspectives necessary to promote positive change in the world. There is 1 undergraduate school and 1 graduate school. In addition to regional accreditation, GC has baccalaureate program accreditation with ACBSP. The 351-acre campus is in a suburban area in the residential area of Greensboro, NC. Including any residence halls, there are 31 buildings.

STUDENT LIFE: 73% of undergraduates are from North Carolina. Others are from 38 states and 12 foreign countries. 75% are from public schools. 53% are White; 25% African American; 8% Hispanic; 5% Asian American; 4% two or more races; 2% race unknown; 1% American Indian/Alaska Native; 1% Foreign. 53% claim no religious affiliation; 33% Protestant. **Female To Male Ratio:** 1.1:1. The average age of freshmen is 19; all undergraduates, 24. 34% do not continue beyond their first year; 61% remain to graduate. **Housing:** 997 students can be accommodated in college housing, which includes gender neutral and both single sex and coed dorms and on-campus apartments. In addition, there are special-interest houses. On-campus housing is guaranteed for all 4 years and is available on a lottery system for upperclassmen. 74% of students live on campus. All students may keep cars.

FACULTY/CLASSROOMS: 50% of faculty are male; 50% are female. All teach undergraduates. No introductory courses are taught by graduate students. The average class size in an introductory lecture is 15; in a laboratory is 10; and in a regular course is 15.

PROGRAMS OF STUDY: GC confers A.B., B.S., and B.F.A. degrees. Master's degrees are also awarded. Bachelor's degrees are awarded in AGRICULTURE (environmental studies), BIOLOGICAL SCIENCE (biology/biological science), BUSINESS (accounting, business administration and management, and sports management), COMMUNICATIONS AND THE ARTS (art, creative writing, design and environmental analysis, English, French, German, music, Spanish, and theatre arts), COMPUTER AND PHYSICAL SCIENCE (chemistry, computer security and information assurance, geology, mathematics, and physics), EDUCATION (education), ENGINEERING AND ENVIRONMENTAL DESIGN (computer technology), HEALTH PROFESSIONS (exercise science, health science, and public health), SOCIAL SCIENCE (African American studies, criminal justice, economics, food production/management/services, forensic studies, history, interdisciplinary studies, international studies, justice and society, peace studies, philosophy, political science/government, psychology, religion, sociology, and womens studies). Biology, health science, and psychology are the strongest academically. Business administration, psychology, and health science have the largest enrollments.

ACTIVITIES: There are no fraternities or sororities. There are 45 groups

on campus, including the Bayard Rustin Center for LGBTQA Activism, Community Aids Awareness Project, Guilford Peace Society, Inter–Club Council, poetry club, archery club, art, cheerleading, chess, choir, chorale, chorus, computers, dance, debate, drama, environmental, ethnic, film, honors, international, jazz band, LGBT, literary magazine, musical theater, newspaper, pep band, photography, political, professional, radio and TV, religious, social, social service, and student government. Popular campus events include Serendipity Spring Festival, Bryan Lecture Series in the Arts, Guilford Undergraduate Symposium, Eastern Music Festival, and Holiday Choir Concerts. **Sports:** There are 9 intercollegiate sports for men and 9 for women, and 7 intramural sports for men and 7 for women. Facilities include a football and track stadium, lacrosse, soccer, a field house gymnasium with multiple courts for basketball and volleyball, a baseball field, cross–country course, a swimming pool, an intramural field, playing fields, tennis courts, and weight and cardio room. **Graduates:** From July 1, 2016 to June 30, 2017, 411 bachelor's degrees were awarded. The most popular majors were psychology (10%), business administration (9%), and criminal justice (8%). In an average class, 50% graduate in 4 years or less and 61% graduate in 6 years or less. Of the 2016 graduating class, 12% were enrolled in graduate school within 6 months of graduation, and 72% were employed.

SERVICES: Counseling and information services are available, as is tutoring in most subjects. There is a reader service for the blind, and remedial math, reading, and writing as well as faculty tutoring for skills development, student tutoring for course-specific help, non–remedial writing, and the Learning Commons center devoted to student support. **Library/Resources:** The library contains 170,134 volumes, 21,550 microform items, 1,994 audio/video tapes/CDs/DVDs, and subscribes to 28,673 periodicals, including electronic. Computerized library services include interlibrary loans, database searching, Internet access, and Wi-Fi capability. Special learning facilities include an art gallery, a planetarium, a radio station, the Cline Observatory (physics and astronomy), a photography studio, an outdoor sculpture studio, Guilford college farm, a community garden, and the Friends Historical collection. **Physically Challenged Students:** 95% of the campus is accessible. Facilities include wheelchair ramps, elevators, special parking, specially equipped restrooms, special class scheduling, lowered drinking fountains, and lowered telephones. **Special:** Guilford offers many internships, a Washington semester, work-study programs, dual majors, student-designed majors, study abroad in 13 countries, B.A.-B.S. degrees, and cross-registration with members of the Greater Greensboro Consortium; Preprofessional programs that are designed specifically as preparation for graduate study; integrated lab chemistry research, sports management internships with national or major sports leagues, internships with senators, and mayors, ACLU, Greenpeace, geology fieldwork, archaeology labs, internships, and Domestic Off–campus Semester–away; formal internship agreements or partnerships: Center for Principled Problem Solving, semester abroad, Quaker Leadership Program, Bonner Center for Community Service and Learning, and the Bryan Series (brings world–class experts in their fields to address the community and meet with students); and Consortia that allow open registration in seven area colleges and universities without additional fees. There are 2 national honor societies and a freshman honors program. **Visiting:** There are regularly scheduled orientations for prospective students; visits can be scheduled throughout the year. A typical visit includes an information session led by an admission counselor followed by a student–led tour. Class visits, professor meetings, and lunch buddies are available when classes are in session. There are guides for informal visits; visitors may sit in on classes and stay overnight. To schedule a visit, contact Kyle Wooden at (800) 992-7759. **Campus Safety and Security:** Measures include 24-hour foot and vehicle patrol, emergency notification system, self-defense education, and security escort services. There are emergency telephones, lighted pathways/sidewalks, and controlled access to dorms/residences.

REQUIREMENTS: The admission committee reviews each applicant to determine academic preparedness as well as to evaluate other qualities such as leadership, creativity and school and community involvement. Coursework and grades are considered and at least four college prep courses for each school year are expected. Test scores are optional, with the alternative being a portfolio of work plus a personal essay and school recommendations from a counselor and a teacher. A GPA of 2.0 is required. AP and CLEP credits are accepted. Important factors in the admissions decision are advanced placement or honors courses, leadership record, and evidence of special talent. Students must fulfill requirements in fine arts, English, humanities, sciences, social sciences, and foreign language. They must take a first-year experience and an interdisciplinary capstone course, and courses in historical perspectives, intercultural studies, social justice and environmental responsibility, and diversity. 128 credit hours must be completed with at least 32 in residence. **Procedure:** Freshmen are admitted in the fall, spring, and summer. Entrance exams should be taken spring of the junior year or fall of the senior year. There are early decision, early admissions, deferred admissions, and rolling admissions plans. Early decision applications should be filed by November 1; regular applications, by December 1 for fall entry; and December 1 for spring entry. Notification of early decision is sent November 15; regular decision, December 15. Applications are accepted on-line. **Transfer Students:** 123 transfer students enrolled in 2016-2017. Applicants for transfer must have a minimum GPA of 2.5 and must be in satisfactory academic and social standing at their current instituion. If students have earned less than 30 semester hours, students must also supply high school transcripts and either SAT/ACT scores or an academic portfolio with two writing samples. 32 of 128 credits required for the bachelor's degree must be completed at GC. **International Students:** There are 25 international students enrolled. They must take the TOEFL with a minimum score of 550 on the paper-based TOEFL (PBT) or 80 on the Internet-based version (iBT).

ADMISSIONS: 25% of the current freshmen were in the top fifth of their class; 55% were in the top two fifths. 2 freshmen graduated first in their class. **Admissions Contact:** Kyle Wooden, Interim Director of Admission. Email: *admission@guilford.edu* Web: *www.guilford.edu*

FINANCIAL AID: In 2017-2018, 98% of all full-time freshmen received some form of financial aid and need-based aid. The average freshman award was $15,776. The FAFSA code is 002931. The priority date for freshman financial aid applications for fall entry is February 1.

HIGH POINT UNIVERSITY — D-2

www.highpoint.edu

High Point, NC 27268	**(336) 841-9216** **(800) 345-6993**
Fax: (336) 888-6382	**Email: admiss@highpoint.edu**
Full-time: 1818 men, 2600 women	**Faculty:** 264
Part-time: 17 men, 32 women	**Ph.D.s:** 80%
Graduate: 159 men, 325 women	**Student/Faculty:** 17 to 1
Year: semesters, summer session	**Tuition:** $34,005
Room & Board: $13,350	**Freshman Class:** 8936 applied, 7208 accepted, 1111 enrolled
SAT EBR-W/M: 576/573 **ACT:** 24	**CEEB CODE:** 5293
Application Deadline: March 15	**VERY COMPETITIVE**

High Point University combines the warmth and intimacy of a small liberal arts college with the academic offerings and amenities of a large state university. The HPU student body is both diverse and dynamic, allowing students to interact with instructors who are well-trained career teachers, not graduate assistants. Students may earn academic credit by participating in internships or by studying abroad. HPU also offers 16 NCAA Division I athletic programs and numerous extracurricular opportunities. There are 6 undergraduate schools and 5 graduate schools. In addition to regional accreditation, HPU has baccalaureate program accreditation with CAEP, CAATE, and CIDA. The 430-acre campus is in a suburban area 15 miles southeast of Winston-Salem and 15 miles southwest of Greensboro. Including any residence halls, there are 112 buildings.

STUDENT LIFE: 79% of undergraduates are from out of state, mostly the Middle Atlantic. Students are from 46 states, 36 foreign countries, and Canada. 64% are from public schools. 75% are White; 6% African American; 6% two or more races; 5% Hispanic; 3% Foreign; 2% Asian American; 2% race unknown. 35% are Protestant; 35% other or unknown affiliations; 28% Catholic; 11% claim no religious affiliation. **Female To Male Ratio:** 1.5:1. The average age of freshmen is 18; all undergraduates, 20. 21% do not continue beyond their first year; 63% remain to graduate. **Housing:** 4684 students can be accommodated in college housing, which includes dorms, on-campus apartments, off-campus apartments. In addition, there are honors houses, special-interest houses, fraternity houses, sorority houses, wellness halls, honors housing, and discipline-specific housing. On-campus housing is guaranteed for all 4 years. 94% of students live on campus. All students may keep cars.

FACULTY/CLASSROOMS: 50% of faculty are male; 50% are female. All teach undergraduates. No introductory courses are taught by graduate

students. The average class size in an introductory lecture is 32; in a laboratory is 16; and in a regular course is 21.

PROGRAMS OF STUDY: HPU confers B.A., B.S., and B.S.B.A. degrees. Master's and doctoral degrees are also awarded. Bachelor's degrees are awarded in BIOLOGICAL SCIENCE (biochemistry, biology/biological science, and neurosciences), BUSINESS (business administration and management, entrepreneurial studies, international business management, marketing, nonprofit/public organization management, and sales management and leadership), COMMUNICATIONS AND THE ARTS (communications, English literature, English Writing, French, graphic design, music, Spanish, studio art, theatre arts, and visual design), COMPUTER AND PHYSICAL SCIENCE (actuarial science, chemistry, computer science, mathematics, mathematics – economics, and physics), EDUCATION (educational studies, elementary education, middle school education, physical education, and special education), ENGINEERING AND ENVIRONMENTAL DESIGN (interior design), HEALTH PROFESSIONS (exercise science, human relations, predentistry, premedicine, preoccupational therapy, prepharmacy, prephysical therapy, and preveterinary science), SOCIAL SCIENCE (anthropology, criminal justice, history, international relations, philosophy, political science/government, prelaw, psychology, religion, and sociology). Business administration, communication, and exercise science have the largest enrollments.

ACTIVITIES: 7% of men belong to 7 national fraternities; 22% of women belong to 9 national sororities. There are 90 groups on campus, including art, band, cheerleading, choir, chorale, chorus, communications, computers, dance, debate, drama, environmental, ethnic, film, honors, international, LGBT, literary magazine, musical theater, newspaper, orchestra, pep band, political, professional, radio and TV, religious, social, social service, and student government. Popular campus events include Derby Day, Family Weekends, Earth Day, and Campus Activities Team monthly events. **Sports:** There are 8 intercollegiate sports for men and 8 for women, and 9 intramural sports for men and 9 for women. Facilities include intramural fields, tennis courts, an intramural gym, an indoor heated pool, 5 outdoor heated pools, racquetball courts, a student activities center, a soccer stadium and track, a sand volleyball court, indoor and outdoor basketball courts, challenge ropes course, and sports center. **Graduates:** From July 1, 2016 to June 30, 2017, 902 bachelor's degrees were awarded. The most popular majors were business (25%), communication (15%), and biology (7%). In an average class, 59% graduate in 4 years or less, 63% graduate in 5 years or less, and 63% graduate in 6 years or less. Of the 2016 graduating class, 18% were enrolled in graduate school within 6 months of graduation, and 69% were employed.

SERVICES: Counseling and information services are available, as is tutoring in most subjects. There is a reader service for the blind, and remedial math, reading, and writing. **Library/Resources:** The library contains 649,000 volumes, 66,000 microform items, 11,000 audio/video tapes/CDs/DVDs, and subscribes to 32,300 periodicals, including electronic. Computerized library services include interlibrary loans, database searching, Internet access, and Wi-Fi capability. Special learning facilities include an art gallery, a radio station, and TV station. **Physically Challenged Students:** 98% of the campus is accessible. Facilities include wheelchair ramps, elevators, special parking, specially equipped restrooms, special class scheduling, and lowered drinking fountains. **Special:** There is cross-registration with the University of North Carolina at Greensboro, North Carolina Agricultural and Technical State University, and Greensboro, Elon, Guilford, and Bennett Colleges. HPU also offers study abroad in many countries, the Student Career Internship Program, accelerated degree programs, work-study programs, student-designed majors, and a 3-2 engineering program with Vanderbilt and Virginia Tech. There are 14 national honor societies, a freshman honors program, and 17 departmental honors programs. **Visiting:** There are regularly scheduled orientations for prospective students, including a welcome session for parents and students, orientation to major sessions, a meeting with a success coach about course scheduling, campus tours, and peer interactions. There are guides for informal visits and visitors may sit in on classes. To schedule a visit, contact Undergraduate Admissions Office. **Campus Safety and Security:** Measures include 24-hour foot and vehicle patrol, an emergency notification system, self-defense education, and security escort services. There are shuttle buses, emergency telephones, lighted pathways/sidewalks, controlled access to dorms/residences, and 24-hour secured residence halls.

REQUIREMENTS: HPU is test optional. If applicants would like to be considered for our Presidential Scholarship Program or Honors Scholar Program, the SAT or ACT test score is required. Applicants should be graduates of an accredited secondary school or have a GED certificate. They should have completed 15 academic units, including 4 in English, 3 units each in math, science, and social studies/history, 1 unit in science lab, and at least 2 units of the same spoken foreign language. A GPA of 2.0 is required. AP and CLEP credits are accepted. To graduate, students must complete a minimum of 128 credit hours with a minimum GPA of 2.0. The core curriculum consists of 1 course in each of the following subject areas: English, foreign language, mathematics, and ethical reasoning, First Year Seminar course, President's Seminar, and a physical education activity course. Distribution requirements include 2 courses in the social sciences and 1 course in each of the following areas: performing or visual arts, literature, history, religion, and natural science with laboratory. **Procedure:** Freshmen are admitted in the fall, spring, and summer. Entrance exams should be taken prior to high school graduation. There are early decision, early admissions, deferred admissions, and rolling admissions plans. Early decision applications should be filed by November 1; regular applications, by March 15 for fall entry. The fall 2017 application fee was $50. Notification of early decision is sent November 27; regular decision, on a rolling basis. 375 early decision candidates were accepted for the 2017-2018 class. 287 applicants were on the 2017 waiting list; 149 were admitted. Applications are accepted online. **Transfer Students:** 56 transfer students enrolled in 2016-2017. Applicants must submit official transcripts from colleges and high schools previously attended, as well as SAT or ACT scores, if available. Generally, a minimum GPA of 2.5 is required. 32 of 128 credits required for the bachelor's degree must be completed at HPU. **International Students:** There are 143 international students enrolled. They must take the TOEFL with a minimum score of 79 on the Internet-based version (iBT). Students must take the IELTS, with a minimum score of 6.0. For academic scholarship consideration, in addition to superior grades, a qualifying score on the SAT or ACT must be submitted.

ADMISSIONS: 81% of the 2017-2018 applicants were accepted. The SAT scores for the 2017-2018 freshman class were: Math-- 12% below 500, 51% between 500 and 599, 32% between 600 and 699, and 5% between 700 and 800. Evidence-Based Reading/Writing-- 11% below 500, 53% between 500 and 599, 33% between 600 and 699, and 3% between 700 and 800. The ACT scores were 3% between 12 and 17, 46% between 18 and 23, 42% between 24 and 29, and 8% above 30. 40% of the current freshmen were in the top fifth of their class; 66% were in the top two fifths. 6 freshmen graduated first in their class. **Admissions Contact:** Dr. Kerr Ramsay, Associate VP of Admissions Recruitment. Email: *admiss@highpoint.edu* Web: *www.highpoint.edu*

FINANCIAL AID: In 2017-2018, 82% of all full-time freshmen received some form of financial aid. 35% of all full-time freshmen received need-based aid. The average freshman award was $15,612. Need-based scholarships or need-based grants averaged $6,438 ($45,298 maximum); need-based self-help aid (loans and jobs) averaged $3,427 ($9,960 maximum); non-need-based athletic scholarships averaged $17,380 ($53,834 maximum); and other non-need-based awards and non-need-based scholarships averaged $8,467 ($41,070 maximum). 30% of undergraduate students work part-time. The average financial indebtedness of the 2017 graduate was $35,897. HPU is a member of CSS. The FAFSA code is 002933. The priority date for freshman financial aid applications for fall entry is October 1.

JOHNSON & WALES UNIVERSITY/ CHARLOTTE CAMPUS C-3

www1.jwu.edu/charlotte

Charlotte, NC 28202 **(866) 598-2427**

Fax: (950) 598-1111
Full-time: 679 men, 1384 women
Part-time: 15 men, 23 women
Graduate: n/av
Year: quarters, summer session
Room & Board: $13,260

Application Deadline: November 1

Email: clt@admissions.jwu.edu
Faculty: 86
Ph.D.s: n/av
Student/Faculty: 22 to 1
Tuition: $31,508
Freshman Class: 4537 applied, 3287 accepted, 641 enrolled
CEEB CODE: 4360
COMPETITIVE

Johnson & Wales University/Charlotte Campus, founded in 2004, offers degree programs in business, culinary arts, and hospitality. There are 3 undergraduate schools. The campus is in an urban area in the center of the New South, Charlotte. Including any residence halls, there are 6 buildings.

STUDENT LIFE: 62% of undergraduates are from out of state, mostly the South. Students are from 47 states, 22 foreign countries, and Canada. 6% are Hispanic; 6% two or more races; 5% race unknown; 43% African American; 38% White; 2% Foreign. **Female To Male Ratio:** 2.0:1. The average age of freshmen is 18; all undergraduates, 21. 75% remain to graduate. **Housing:** College-sponsored housing includes dorms, on-campus apartments, and wellness housing. On-campus housing is available on a lottery system for upperclassmen. 59% of students live on campus. Alcohol is not permitted. All students may keep cars.

FACULTY/CLASSROOMS: All teach undergraduates. No introductory courses are taught by graduate students.

PROGRAMS OF STUDY: JWU/Charlotte confers B.S. degrees. Associate degrees are also awarded. Bachelor's degrees are awarded in BUSINESS (accounting, business administration and management, entrepreneurial studies, hospitality management services, hotel/motel and restaurant management, marketing and distribution, marketing management, marketing/retailing/merchandising, sports management, and tourism), ENGINEERING AND ENVIRONMENTAL DESIGN (food services technology), SOCIAL SCIENCE (clothing and textiles management/production/services, food production/management/services, and parks and recreation management).

ACTIVITIES: There are no fraternities or sororities. There are 36 groups on campus, including cheerleading, dance, honors, international, LGBT, newspaper, photography, religious, social, student government, and yearbook. Popular campus events include Welcome Week, Western Day, and Spring Week. **Sports:** Facilities include basketball, soccer, and volleyball for women. **Graduates:** From July 1, 2016 to June 30, 2017, 322 bachelor's degrees were awarded. The most popular majors were family and consumer sciences (55%), business/marketing (34%), and parks and recreation (11%).

SERVICES: Counseling and information services are available, as is tutoring in every subject. **Library/Resources:** The library contains 28,690 volumes, 8,474 audio/video tapes/CDs/DVDs, and subscribes to 196 periodicals, including electronic. Computerized library services include interlibrary loans, database searching, Internet access, and Wi-Fi capability. **Physically Challenged Students:** All of the campus is accessible. Facilities include wheelchair ramps, elevators, special parking, specially equipped restrooms, special class scheduling, lowered drinking fountains, lowered telephones, and special housing. **Special:** The university offers co-op programs, accelerated degree programs, dual majors, study abroad, and worldwide work-study opportunities in business, hospitality, technology, and culinary arts. Most majors require 11-week internships. There is a freshman honors program. **Visiting:** There are regularly scheduled orientations for prospective students, an introduction to the academic and social aspects of the campus experience through interactive sessions. There are guides for informal visits; visitors may sit in on classes and stay overnight. To schedule a visit, contact the Admissions Office. **Campus Safety and Security:** Measures include 24-hour foot and vehicle patrol, self-defense education, and security escort services. There are shuttle buses, emergency telephones, and lighted pathways/sidewalks.

REQUIREMENTS: Although SAT and ACT scores are required only for students applying for honors admissions, students who have taken these tests are encouraged to submit their scores. Requirements are 4 years of English, 3 years each of mathematics and science, and 2 years of social studies. A high school diploma is required and the GED is accepted. AP and CLEP credits are accepted. Important factors in the admissions decision are advanced placement or honors courses, extracurricular activities record, parents or siblings attended the school, evidence of special talent, personality/intangible qualities, and recommendations by school officials. To graduate, students must complete 180 quarter credit hours, including at least 36 in the major, with a minimum GPA of 2.0. Required courses include English, math, history, economics, science, psychology, sociology, and professional development. **Procedure:** Freshmen are admitted to all sessions. There are deferred admissions and rolling admissions plans. Application deadlines are open. Applications are accepted online. **Transfer Students:** 98 transfer students enrolled in 2016-2017. Applicants are required to submit official high school and college transcripts and must have earned a minimum college GPA of 2.0. Students may enroll in the fall, winter, spring and summer. 45 of 180 credits required for the bachelor's degree must be completed at JWU. **International Students:** There are 46 international students enrolled. They must take the TOEFL with a minimum score of 550 on the paper-based TOEFL (PBT) or 80 on the Internet-based version (iBT).

ADMISSIONS: 72% of the 2017-2018 applicants were accepted. **Admissions Contact:** Joseph Campos, Director of Admissions. Email: *clt@admissions.jwu.edu* Web: *www1.jwu.edu/charlotte*

FINANCIAL AID: The average freshman award was $24,485. Need-based scholarships or need-based grants averaged $9,159; need-based self-help aid (loans and jobs) averaged $3,781; other non-need-based awards and non-need-based scholarships averaged $3,381; and $9,679 from other forms of aid. JWU-Charlotte is a member of CSS. The priority date for freshman financial aid applications for fall entry is March 1.

JOHNSON C. SMITH UNIVERSITY *(The complete profile is made available exclusively on our website, www.barronspac.com)*

LEES-MCRAE COLLEGE *(The complete profile is made available exclusively on our website, www.barronspac.com)*

LENOIR-RHYNE UNIVERSITY *(The complete profile is made available exclusively on our website, www.barronspac.com)*

LIVINGSTONE COLLEGE *(The complete profile is made available exclusively on our website, www.barronspac.com)*

MARS HILL UNIVERSITY — B-2

www.mhu.edu

Mars Hill, NC 28754	(828) 642-4968 (800) 543-1514
Fax: (828) 689-1473	Email: admissions@mhu.edu
Full-time: 505 men, 605 women	Faculty: 80; IIB, --$
Part-time: 40 men, 100 women	Ph.D.s: 70%
Graduate: n/av	Student/Faculty: 13 to 1
Year: semesters, summer session	Tuition: $31,804
Room & Board: $9300	Freshman Class: n/av
SAT or ACT: required	CEEB CODE: 5395
Application Deadline: open	COMPETITIVE

Mars Hill University, founded in 1856, is a private institution affiliated with the Baptist Church and offers undergraduate programs in the arts and sciences, business, education, and preprofessional studies. The figures given in the above capsule and in this profile are approximate. There is 1 undergraduate school. In addition to regional accreditation, MHU has baccalaureate program accreditation with CSWE, NASM, and CAEP. The 180-acre campus is in a rural area 18 miles north of Asheville. Including any residence halls, there are 47 buildings.

STUDENT LIFE: 60% of undergraduates are from North Carolina. Others are from 19 states, 20 foreign countries, and Canada. 2% are Foreign; 14% African American; 1% American Indian/Alaska Native; 1% Hispanic. 81% are Protestant; 13% claim no religious affiliation. **Female To Male Ratio:** 1.3:1. The average age of freshmen is 18; all undergraduates, 21. 20% do not continue beyond their first year; 49% remain to graduate. **Housing:** College-sponsored housing includes married student dorms, on-campus apartments, and honors houses. On-campus housing is guaranteed for all 4 years. 80% of students live on campus. Alcohol is not permitted. All students may keep cars.

FACULTY/CLASSROOMS: 58% of faculty are male; 42% are female. All teach undergraduates. No introductory courses are taught by graduate students. The average class size in an introductory lecture is 20; in a laboratory is 15; and in a regular course is 15.

PROGRAMS OF STUDY: MHU confers B.A., B.S., B.F.A., B.M., and B.S.W. degrees. Bachelor's degrees are awarded in BIOLOGICAL SCIENCE (biology/biological science, botany, and zoology), BUSINESS (accounting, business administration and management, fashion merchandising, and recreation and leisure services), COMMUNICATIONS AND THE ARTS (art history and appreciation, communications, dramatic arts, English, music, music performance, musical theater, performing arts, and Spanish), COMPUTER AND PHYSICAL SCIENCE (chemistry, computer science, and mathematics), EDUCATION (art education, athletic training, drama education, elementary education, mathematics education, middle school education, music education, physical education, science education, and social studies education), HEALTH PROFESSIONS (allied health, physician's assistant, predentistry, premedicine, prepharmacy, and preveterinary science), SOCIAL SCIENCE (history, international studies, political science/government, prelaw, psychology, religion, social work, and sociology). Music, education, and science are the strongest academically. Education has the largest enrollment.

ACTIVITIES: 30% of men belong to 4 local and 2 national fraternities; 12% of women belong to 4 local and 1 national sororities. There are 80 groups on campus, including art, band, cheerleading, choir, chorale, chorus, dance, drama, ethnic, honors, international, jazz band, literary magazine, marching band, musical theater, newspaper, orchestra, photography, political, professional, radio and TV, religious, social, social service, student government, and yearbook. Popular campus events include Culturefest, Spring Fling, and the Bascom Lamar Lunsford Festival. **Sports:** There are 7 intercollegiate sports for men and 6 for women, and 5 intramural sports for men and 5 for women. Facilities include a stadium, a gym, an indoor Olympic-size swimming pool, a complex with a track, a baseball diamond, a soccer field, an all-purpose playing field, and tennis courts.

SERVICES: Counseling and information services are available, as is tutoring in every subject. There is remedial math, reading, and writing. **Library/Resources:** The library contains 98,150 volumes, 1,050 microform items, 6,180 audio/video tapes/CDs/DVDs, and subscribes to 650 periodicals, including electronic. Computerized library services include interlibrary loans and database searching. Special learning facilities include an art gallery, a radio station, the Southern Appalachian Center of Regional History and Culture, and the Rural Life Museum. **Physically Challenged Students:** 41% of the campus is accessible. Facilities include wheelchair ramps, elevators, special parking, and specially equipped restrooms. **Special:** MHU offers cooperative programs with the Bowman Gray School of Medicine at Wake Forest, internships, study abroad, B.A.-B.S. degrees, dual majors, student-designed majors, and credit for life experience. The Community Life program promotes student involvement in culture and community activities. There are 4 national honor societies and a freshman honors program. **Visiting:** There are regularly scheduled orientations for prospective students consisting of 2 days, during which a variety of special programs are offered. Individual students and their families may visit anytime throughout the year. There are guides for informal visits; visitors may sit in on classes and stay overnight. To schedule a visit, contact the Admissions Office. **Campus Safety and Security:** Measures include 24-hour foot and vehicle patrol, self-defense education, and security escort services. There are emergency telephones and lighted pathways/sidewalks.

REQUIREMENTS: The SAT or ACT is required. Applicants need at least 18 academic credits, including 4 in English, 3 in math, and 2 each in history, science, and foreign language. The GED is accepted. A GPA of 2.0 is required. AP and CLEP credits are accepted. Important factors in the admissions decision are advanced placement or honors courses, leadership record, and extracurricular activities record. To graduate, students must complete at least 128 semester hours with a minimum GPA of 2.0. Distribution requirements include courses in fine arts, literature, American culture, foreign culture, math, natural science, social/behavioral science, ethics, and physical education. **Procedure:** Freshmen are admitted to all sessions. There are early decision, early admissions, and rolling admissions plans. Application deadlines are open. The fall 2017 application fee was $25. 3 early decision candidates were accepted for the 2017-2018 class. **Transfer Students:** 66 transfer students enrolled in 2016-2017. Transfer applicants must be eligible to return to their previous college or have been out of school for at least 1 semester. They must have a minimum GPA of 2.0 for at least 30 semester credit hours. Remedial and developmental hours do not apply. 32 of 128 credits required for the bachelor's degree must be completed at MHU. **International Students:** They must take the TOEFL.

Admissions Contact: Kristie Vance, Director of Admissisons. Email: *admissions@mhu.edu* Web: *www.mhu.edu*

FINANCIAL AID: In 2017-2018, 96% of all full-time freshmen received some form of financial aid. 35% of undergraduate students work part-time. MHU is a member of CSS. The FAFSA code is 002944. The deadline for filing freshman financial aid applications for fall entry is May 1.

MEREDITH COLLEGE — D-2

www.meredith.edu

Raleigh, NC 27607 — (919) 760-8581

Fax: (919) 760-2348 — **Email:** admissions@meredith.edu
Full-time: 1600 women
Part-time: 2 men, 79 women
Graduate: 37 men, 262 women
Year: semesters, summer session
Room & Board: $10,718
SAT CR/M: 559/536 **ACT:** 22
Application Deadline: February 15
Faculty: 131; IIA, --$
Ph.D.s: 88%
Student/Faculty: 12 to 1
Tuition: $35,916
Freshman Class: 1737 applied, 1197 accepted, 395 enrolled
CEEB CODE: 5410
COMPETITIVE

Meredith College, founded in 1891, is a private, independent women's college at the undergraduate level, with co-educational graduate programs. MC is accredited by the Commission on Colleges of the Southern Association of Colleges and Schools to award baccalaureate and masters degrees. One of only two women's colleges in the world accredited by AACSB International, MC also holds program accreditation in education, social work, nutrition, music, and interior design. Strong Points an academic and personal coaching program, ensures each student that will create a plan to make the most of her college experience. The program ensures that students graduate with a clear plan for their career and strong financial literacy, including knowing how to develop and adhere to a budget and how to negotiate their first job offers. There are 6 undergraduate schools and 1 graduate school. The 225-acre campus is in an urban area in Raleigh, NC. Including any residence halls, there are 30 buildings.

STUDENT LIFE: 88% of undergraduates are from North Carolina. Others are from 31 states, 32 foreign countries, and Canada. 71% are White; 8% African American; 8% Hispanic; 4% two or more races; 4% race unknown; 3% Asian American; 2% Foreign; 1% American Indian/Alaska Native. **Female To Male Ratio:** 49.8:1. The average age of freshmen is 18; all undergraduates, 21. 20% do not continue beyond their first year; 80% remain to graduate. **Housing:** 1150 students can be accommodated in college housing, which includes dorms, on-campus apartments, womens only nonsmoking halls, and apartments for single students. On-campus housing is guaranteed for all 4 years. 54% of students live on campus. Alcohol is not permitted. All students may keep cars.

FACULTY/CLASSROOMS: 31% of faculty are male; 69% are female. All teach undergraduates. No introductory courses are taught by graduate students. The average class size in an introductory lecture is 16; in a laboratory is 13; and in a regular course is 17.

PROGRAMS OF STUDY: MC confers B.A., B.S., B.M., and B.S.W. degrees. Master's degrees are also awarded. Bachelor's degrees are awarded in AGRICULTURE (environmental studies), BIOLOGICAL SCIENCE (biology/biological science and nutrition), BUSINESS (accounting, business administration and management, and fashion merchandising), COMMUNICATIONS AND THE ARTS (applied music, art, communications, dance, dramatic arts, English, fine arts, music, and Spanish), COMPUTER AND PHYSICAL SCIENCE (chemistry, computer science, information sciences and systems, and mathematics), EDUCATION (music education), ENGINEERING AND ENVIRONMENTAL DESIGN (interior design), HEALTH PROFESSIONS (exercise science), SOCIAL SCIENCE (child psychology/development, criminology, economics, family/consumer studies, history, international studies, political science/government, psychology, public affairs, religion, social work, and sociology). Business, psychology, and biology have the largest enrollments.

ACTIVITIES: There are no fraternities or sororities. There are 100 groups on campus, including nutrition and wellness, foreign language, art, chorale, chorus, commuter, computers, dance, drama, environmental, ethnic, honors, international, LGBT, literary magazine, musical theater, newspaper, orchestra, photography, political, professional, religious, social, social service, student government, symphony, and yearbook. Popular campus events include Academics and Leadership Awards Day, White Iris Ball, and Undergraduate Research Conference. **Sports:** There are 7 intercollegiate sports for women. Facilities include a dance studio, a fitness center, a putting green and driving range, softball diamond, tennis courts, soccer field, gymnasium, and a track. **Graduates:** From July 1, 2016 to June 30, 2017, 424 bachelor's degrees were awarded. The most popular majors were Biology (11%), Psychology (10%), and Business Administration (7%). In an average class, 61% graduate in 6 years or less.

SERVICES: Counseling and information services are available, as is tutoring in some subjects, such as math, writing, computer lab, French, Spanish, biology, chemistry, study skills, German, GRE prep, Praxis prep, and grammar. There is a reader service for the blind. **Library/Resources:** The library contains 155,165 volumes, 16,116 microform items, 14,671 audio/video tapes/CDs/DVDs, and subscribes to 2,867 periodicals, including electronic. Computerized library services include interlibrary loans, database searching, and Internet access. Special learning facilities include an art gallery, experimental and clinical psychology labs including one on autism, child-care lab, a greenhouse, an electron microscope suite, an astronomy observation deck, a student/faculty research labs, and a language lab. **Physically Challenged Students:** 81% of the campus is accessible. Facilities include wheelchair ramps, elevators, special parking, specially equipped restrooms, special class scheduling, lowered drinking fountains, and special housing. **Special:** Meredith offers cooperative programs, cross-registration with Cooperating Raleigh Colleges, internships, study abroad in Europe and Asia, a Washington semester at American University, a U.N. semester at Drew University, and work-study programs on campus. Dual majors, interdisciplinary and student-designed majors, preprofessional programs, and pass/fail options are available. Certification in social work and licensure for teaching are possible. Business administration, management, and social work majors can be completed through evening classes. There are 19 national honor societies and a freshman honors program. **Visiting:** There are regularly scheduled orientations for prospective students, including student participation in information sessions for students and parents, class visitation, informal conversations with students and faculty/staff, and campus tours. There are guides for informal visits; visitors may sit in on classes and stay overnight. To schedule a visit, contact the Admissions Office. **Campus Safety and Security:** Measures include 24-hour foot and vehicle patrol, self-defense education, and security escort services. There are emergency telephones, lighted pathways/sidewalks, controlled campus access at night, and 24- hour locked residence halls.

REQUIREMENTS: The SAT or ACT is required. Applicants must also have a minimum of 16 units of credit, including 4 units in English, 3 units each in math, social studies, history and science, 2 in foreign language, and 1 elective. A student is expected to rank in the top half of her class, and grades in academic subjects are very important. A campus visit and an interview are strongly encouraged. AP and CLEP credits are accepted. Important factors in the admissions decision are personality/intangible qualities, recommendations by school officials, advanced placement or honors courses, evidence of special talent, and extracurricular activities record. To graduate, students must complete a total of 124 credit hours, including general education requirements, a major field, and electives, with a minimum GPA of 2.0. General Education is comprised of a core curriculum focusing on understanding diverse cultures, fields of knowledge that ensure breadth in the liberal arts, and across-the-curriculum threads and independent learning experiences that build competencies. Some major fields offer or require a concentration, and contract majors are possible. Electives may be used to complete a second major, a minor, a teacher licensure, or to explore areas of personal, career, or preprofessional interest. **Procedure:** Freshmen are admitted in the fall and spring. Entrance exams should be taken by December of the senior year. There are early decision, deferred admissions, and rolling admissions plans. Early decision applications should be filed by October 15; regular applications, by February 15 for fall entry. The fall 2017 application fee was $40. Notification of early decision is sent November 15; regular decision, on a rolling basis. Applications are accepted on-line. **Transfer Students:** 80 transfer students enrolled in 2016-2017. Applicants must have a minimum GPA of 2.0, college transcript (s), an essay, and be recommended by college officials. An interview is also required. Those students with fewer than 30 hours of credit must also meet freshman admission requirements. 31 of 124 credits required for the bachelor's degree must be completed at MC. **International Students:** There are 29 international students enrolled. They must take the TOEFL. If English is the student's native language or primary language of instruction, the SAT should be taken instead of the TOEFL.

ADMISSIONS: 69% of the 2017-2018 applicants were accepted. The SAT scores for the 2017-2018 freshman class were: Critical Reading-- 19% below 500, 49% between 500 and 599, 30% between 600 and 699, and 2% between 700 and 800. Math-- 28% below 500, 52% between 500 and 599, 17% between 600 and 699, and 2% between 700 and 800. The ACT scores were 12% between 12 and 17, 49% between 18 and 23, 35% between 24 and 29, and 4% above 30. 36% of the current freshmen were in the top fifth of their class; 68% were in the top two fifths. **Admissions Contact:** Shery Boyles, Director of Admissions. Email: *admissions@meredith.edu* Web: *www.meredith.edu*

FINANCIAL AID: MC is a member of CSS. The FAFSA code is 002945. The priority date for freshman financial aid applications for fall entry is February 15.

METHODIST UNIVERSITY — D-3

www.methodist.edu

Fayetteville, NC 28311 — (910) 630-7027, (800) 488-7110

Fax: (910) 630-7285 — **Email:** admissions@methodist.edu

Full-time: 1059 men, 960 women	**Faculty:** 142
Part-time: 109 men, 152 women	**Ph.D.s:** 79%
Graduate: 83 men, 113 women	**Student/Faculty:** 13 to 1
Year: semesters, summer session	**Tuition:** $33,540
Room & Board: $12,295	**Freshman Class:** 3823 applied, 2315 accepted, 488 enrolled
SAT CR/M/W: 484/510/466 **ACT:** 21	**CEEB CODE:** 5426
Application Deadline: n/av	**COMPETITIVE**

Methodist University, founded in 1956, is a private institution affiliated with the United Methodist Church. The university offers programs in the arts and sciences, education, business, and professional training. The figures given in the above capsule and in this profile are approximate. There are 4 undergraduate schools and 3 graduate schools. In addition to regional accreditation, MU has baccalaureate program accreditation with ACBSP, CSWE, CAEP, and CAAHEP. The 620-acre campus is in a suburban area 5 miles north of Fayetteville. Including any residence halls, there are 38 buildings.

STUDENT LIFE: 56% of undergraduates are from North Carolina. Others are from 44 states, 31 foreign countries, and Canada. 86% are from public schools. 65% are White; 6% Hispanic; 4% Foreign; 20% African American; 2% Asian American; 2% American Indian/Alaska Native. 41% are Protestant; 16% Catholic. **Male To Female Ratio:** 1.0:1. The average age of freshmen is 19; all undergraduates, 24. 33% do not continue beyond their first year; 44% remain to graduate. **Housing:** 1095 students can be accommodated in college housing, which includes dorms and on-campus apartments. In addition, there are honors houses, fraternity houses, sorority houses, first year experience housing, and a health and wellness hall. On-campus housing is guaranteed for all 4 years. 57% of students live on campus. Alcohol is not permitted. All students may keep cars.

FACULTY/CLASSROOMS: 52% of faculty are male; 48% are female. All teach undergraduates. No introductory courses are taught by graduate students. The average class size in an introductory lecture is 23; in a laboratory is 20; and in a regular course is 20.

PROGRAMS OF STUDY: MU confers B.A., B.S., B.F.A, B.M., and B.S.W. degrees. Associate and master's degrees are also awarded. Bachelor's degrees are awarded in BIOLOGICAL SCIENCE (biology/biological science), BUSINESS (accounting, business administration and management, marketing/retailing/merchandising, organizational behavior, and sports management), COMMUNICATIONS AND THE ARTS (art, communications, creative writing, dramatic arts, English, French, music, music performance, and Spanish), COMPUTER AND PHYSICAL SCIENCE (chemistry, computer science, and mathematics), EDUCATION (art education, athletic training, elementary education, middle school education, music education, physical education, secondary education, and special education), ENGINEERING AND ENVIRONMENTAL DESIGN (computer technology), HEALTH PROFESSIONS (nursing, physicians assistant, and predentistry), SOCIAL SCIENCE (criminal justice, economics, history, international studies, political science/government, prelaw, psychology, religion, social studies, social work, and sociology). Business administration, biology, and education are the strongest academically, and have the largest enrollments.

ACTIVITIES: 6% of men belong to 1 local and 1 national fraternities; 6% of women belong to 2 local and 1 national sororities. There are 104 groups on campus, including art, band, cheerleading, choir, chorale, chorus, computers, dance, debate, drama, environmental, ethnic, forensics, honors, international, jazz band, literary magazine, marching band, musical theater, newspaper, orchestra, pep band, photography, political, professional, radio and TV, religious, social, social service, student government, and symphony. Popular campus events include Show You Care Day, Annual Woodcutting, and Spring Fest. **Sports:** There are 9 intercollegiate sports for men and 10 for women, and 7 intramural sports for men and 4 for women. Facilities include a fitness center, a stadium, a gym, a golf course, a track and field area, tennis courts, and fields for baseball, softball, and soccer. **Graduates:** From July 1, 2016 to June 30, 2017, 290 bachelor's degrees were awarded. The most popular majors were business (46%), social sciences (11%), and education (7%). In an average class, 1% graduate in 3 years or less, 33% graduate in 4 years or less, 38% graduate in 5 years or less, and 40% graduate in 6 years or less. Of the 2016 graduating class, 24% were enrolled in graduate school within 6 months of graduation, and 70% were employed.

SERVICES: Counseling and information services are available, as is tutoring in most subjects. There is a reader service for the blind, and remedial math and writing. **Library/Resources:** The library contains 181,833 volumes, 57,759 microform items, 13,412 audio/video tapes/CDs/DVDs, and subscribes to 587 periodicals, including electronic. Computerized library services include interlibrary loans, database searching, Internet access, and Wi-Fi capability. Special learning facilities include an art gallery and a radio station. **Physically Challenged Students:** 90% of the campus is accessible. Facilities include wheelchair ramps, elevators, special parking, specially equipped restrooms, and lowered drinking fountains. **Special:** MU offers internships in political science and social work, study abroad in 4 countries, a Washington semester, a general studies degree, a 3-2 engineering degree with North Carolina State University, pass/fail options, dual majors, and nondegree study. The business administration major offers concentrations in professional golf, tennis, and resort management with specialized facilities and co-op programs. There are 7 national honor societies, a freshman honors program, and 5 departmental honors programs. **Visiting:** There are regularly scheduled orientations for prospective students 3 days prior to the first day of fall semester. There are guides for informal visits; visitors may sit in on classes and stay overnight. To schedule a visit, contact the Admissions Office. **Campus Safety and Security:** Measures include 24-hour foot and vehicle patrol, emergency notification system, self-defense education, and security escort services. There are shuttle buses, emergency telephones, lighted pathways/sidewalks, and controlled access to dorms/residences.

REQUIREMENTS: The SAT or ACT is required. Applicants should be graduates of an accredited secondary school or have a GED certificate. They must have 16 academic credits, including 4 in English and 3 each in history, math, and science. 2 years of foreign language are recommended. An essay and interview are also recommended. AP and CLEP credits are accepted. Important factors in the admissions decision are recommendations by school officials, evidence of special talent, and advanced placement or honors courses. To graduate, students must complete at least 124 semester hours, including core requirements, with a minimum GPA of 2.0. A liberal arts core, ranging from 36 to 62 hours, is required in all majors. **Procedure:** Freshmen are admitted in the fall, spring, and summer. There are deferred admissions and rolling admissions plans. Application deadlines are open. The fall 2017 application fee was $25. Applications are accepted online. **Transfer Students:** 292 transfer students enrolled in 2016-2017. Applicants must have a minimum GPA of 2.0. They must also submit a high school transcript, college transcripts, and the SAT or ACT scores. 30 of 124 credits required for the bachelor's degree must be completed at MU. **International Students:** There are 70 international students enrolled. They must take the TOEFL with a minimum score of 500 on the paper-based TOEFL (PBT) or 60 on the Internet-based version (iBT). Students may take the SAT or ACT in place of the TOEFL if English proficiency is demonstrated.

ADMISSIONS: 61% of the 2017-2018 applicants were accepted. The SAT scores for the 2017-2018 freshman class were: Critical Reading-- 59% below 500, 34% between 500 and 599, 6% between 600 and 699, and 1% between 700 and 800. Math-- 45% below 500, 40% between 500 and 599, 14% between 600 and 699, and 1% between 700 and 800. Writing-- 60% below 500, 33% between 500 and 599, 6% between 600 and 699, and 1% between 700 and 800. The ACT scores were 50% below 12, 30% between 12 and 17, 10% between 18 and 23, 6% between 24 and 29, and 4% above 30. 27% of the current freshmen were in the top fifth of their class; 54% were in the top two fifths. 4 freshmen graduated first in their class. **Admissions Contact:** Jamie Legg, Director of Admissions. Email: *admissions@methodist.edu* Web: *www.methodist.edu*

FINANCIAL AID: In 2017-2018, 92% of all full-time freshmen received some form of financial aid and need-based aid. The average freshman award was $9,780. 60% of undergraduate students work part-time. The average financial indebtedness of the 2017 graduate was $20,026. The FAFSA code is 002946. The priority date for freshman financial aid applications for fall entry is March 15.

MONTREAT COLLEGE *(The complete profile is made available exclusively on our website, www.barronspac.com)*

NORTH CAROLINA A&T STATE UNIVERSITY — D-2
www.ncat.edu

Greensboro, NC 27411	**(336) 334-7946** **(800) 443-8964**
Fax: (336) 256-2145	**Email: uadmit@ncat.edu**
Full-time: 4028 men, 5319 women	**Faculty:** 513; I, --$
Part-time: 488 men, 506 women	**Ph.D.s:** 77%
Graduate: 653 men, 883 women	**Student/Faculty:** 18 to 1
Year: semesters, summer session	**Tuition:** $6526 ($19,416)
Room & Board: $7260	**Freshman Class:** 10745 applied, 6699 accepted, 2309 enrolled
SAT EBR-W/M: 516/506 **ACT:** 20	**CEEB CODE:** 5003
Application Deadline: June 30	**COMPETITIVE**

North Carolina A&T State University, founded in 1891, is a public institution within the University of North Carolina System. NCA&T offers programs in arts and sciences, education, business and economics, agriculture, nursing, engineering, and technology. There are 9 undergraduate schools and 1 graduate school. In addition to regional accreditation, NCA&T has baccalaureate program accreditation with AACSB, ABET, ACCE, CSWE, CAEP, and NLN. The 191-acre campus is in an urban area 90 miles northeast of Charlotte. Including any residence halls, there are 107 buildings.

STUDENT LIFE: 77% of undergraduates are from North Carolina. Others are from 46 states, and 38 foreign countries. 78% are African American; 7% White; 4% Hispanic; 4% two or more races; 3% Foreign; 3% race unknown; 1% Asian American. **Female To Male Ratio:** 1.3:1. The average age of freshmen is 18; all undergraduates, 21. **Housing:** 4451 students can be accommodated in college housing, which includes dorms. In addition, there are honors houses, and theme and wellness housing. On-campus housing is available on a first-come, first-served basis and is available on a lottery system for upperclassmen. 58% of students commute. Alcohol is not permitted. All students may keep cars.

FACULTY/CLASSROOMS: 53% of faculty are male; 47% are female. No introductory courses are taught by graduate students. The average class size in an introductory lecture is 29; in a laboratory is 20; and in a regular course is 27.

PROGRAMS OF STUDY: NCA&T confers B.A., B.S., B.F.A., B.S.I.E., B.S.M.E., B.S.N., and B.S.W. degrees. Master's and doctoral degrees are also awarded. Bachelor's degrees are awarded in AGRICULTURE (agricultural business management, agricultural economics, and animal science), BIOLOGICAL SCIENCE (biology/biological science), BUSINESS (accounting and business administration and management), COMMUNICATIONS AND THE ARTS (communications, dramatic arts, English, French, music, and speech/debate/rhetoric), COMPUTER AND PHYSICAL SCIENCE (chemistry, computer science, mathematics, and physics), EDUCATION (agricultural education, art education, business education, early childhood education, English education, home economics education, industrial arts education, mathematics education, music education, physical education, social science education, and special education), ENGINEERING AND ENVIRONMENTAL DESIGN (architectural engineering, chemical engineering, civil engineering, electrical/electronics engineering, engineering physics, industrial engineering, landscape architecture/design, mechanical engineering, and occupational safety and health), HEALTH PROFESSIONS (nursing), SOCIAL SCIENCE (child psychology/development, clothing and textiles management/production/services, economics, history, political science/government, psychology, social work, and sociology). Business, accounting, electronics, and computer technology are the strongest academically. Psychology, sports recreation, and biology have the largest enrollments.

ACTIVITIES: Groups on campus include art, band, cheerleading, choir, chorus, computers, dance, drama, drill team, ethnic, film, honors, international, jazz band, marching band, newspaper, orchestra, pep band, photography, political, professional, radio and TV, religious, social, social service, student government, symphony, and yearbook. Popular campus events include Graduation, Martin Luther Kings Birthday, and Ron McNair Commemoration. **Sports:** Facilities include a gym, sports center, a stadium, tennis courts, a student union, a field house, and softball/baseball facilities. **Graduates:** From July 1, 2016 to June 30, 2017, 1513 bachelor's degrees were awarded. The most popular majors were engineering (13%), business/marketing (10%), and communications/journalism (10%).

SERVICES: Counseling and information services are available, as is tutoring in every subject. There is a reader service for the blind, and remedial math, reading, and writing. **Library/Resources:** The library contains 1.1 million volumes. Computerized library services include interlibrary loans and database searching. Special learning facilities include an art gallery, a planetarium, a radio station, TV station, and an African Heritage Center. **Physically Challenged Students:** 85% of the campus is accessible. Facilities include wheelchair ramps, elevators, special parking, specially equipped restrooms, special class scheduling, lowered drinking fountains, and lowered telephones. **Special:** NCA&T offers cross-registration with the Greensboro Regional Consortium, internships, B.A.-B.S. degrees, cooperative programs in most majors, study-abroad programs, work-study programs, and dual majors. There is a freshman honors program. **Visiting:** There are regularly scheduled orientations for prospective students. There are guides for informal visits and visitors may sit in on classes. To schedule a visit, contact the Admissions Office. **Campus Safety and Security:** Measures include 24-hour foot and vehicle patrol, self-defense education, and security escort services. There are shuttle buses, emergency telephones, and lighted pathways/sidewalks.

REQUIREMENTS: The SAT or ACT is required. Applicants must be graduates of an accredited secondary school or have a GED certificate. All students must satisfy the University of North Carolina (UNC) minimum admissions requirements to be eligible for admissions. They must have completed at least 16 academic credits: 4 in English and math, 3 in science with 1 lab, and 2 in social sciences and foreign language. An interview is suggested for all applicants. AP and CLEP credits are accepted. To graduate, students must complete a minimum of 120 credit hours, with an overall GPA of 2.0 or better. Specific coursework is required in English, math, natural science, social science, humanities, and health or physical education. **Procedure:** Freshmen are admitted to all sessions. Entrance exams should be taken before April 1. There are deferred admissions and rolling admissions plans. Applications should be filed by June 30 for fall entry. The fall 2017 application fee was $55. Notifications are sent February 15. **Transfer Students:** 908 transfer students enrolled in 2016-2017. There are multiple requirements for different types of transfers: please visit http:/www.ncat.edu/admissions/transfer-students/transfer-requirements/ for more information. **International Students:** There are 184 international students enrolled. They must take the TOEFL with a minimum score of 550 on the paper-based TOEFL (PBT) or 79 on the Internet-based version (iBT). They must also take the SAT or ACT.

ADMISSIONS: The SAT scores for the 2017-2018 freshman class were: Math-- 45% below 500, 48% between 500 and 599, 7% between 600 and 699, and 1% between 700 and 800. Evidence-Based Reading/Writing-- 40% below 500, 50% between 500 and 599, and 10% between 600 and 699. The ACT scores were 28% between 12 and 17, 60% between 18 and 23, 11% between 24 and 29, and 1% above 30. **Admissions Contact:** Erin Hart, Associate Vice Provost for SEM. Email: *uadmit@ncat.edu* Web: *www.ncat.edu*

FINANCIAL AID: In 2017-2018, 86% of all full-time freshmen received some form of financial aid. 74% of all full-time freshmen received need-based aid. The average freshman award was $11,487. Need-based scholarships or need-based grants averaged $7,656 ($22,420 maximum); need-based self-help aid (loans and jobs) averaged $3,407 ($7,500 maximum); non-need-based athletic scholarships averaged $9,000 ($18,000 maximum); and other non-need-based awards and non-need-based scholarships averaged $5,186 ($20,643 maximum). NCA&T is a member of CSS. The FAFSA code is 002905. The priority date for freshman financial aid applications for fall entry is March 15.

NORTH CAROLINA CENTRAL UNIVERSITY D-2

www.nccu.edu

Durham, NC 27707 **(919) 560-6298**

Fax: (919) 530-7625	**Email:** admissions@nccu.edu
Full-time: 1500 men, 2700 women	**Faculty:** 257; IIA, -$
Part-time: 300 men, 800 women	**Ph.D.s:** 75%
Graduate: 500 men, 1300 women	**Student/Faculty:** 16 to 1
Year: semesters, summer session	**Tuition:** $5000 ($14,000)
Room & Board: $5000	**Freshman Class:** n/av
SAT or ACT: required	**CEEB CODE:** 5495
Application Deadline: August 1	**COMPETITIVE**

North Carolina Central University, founded in 1910, is a publicly funded liberal arts institution in the University of North Carolina system. There are 3 undergraduate schools and 2 graduate schools. In addition to regional accreditation, NCCU has baccalaureate program accreditation with CAEP and NLN. The 103-acre campus is in an urban area 2 miles from the center of Durham. Including any residence halls, there are 57 buildings.

STUDENT LIFE: 89% of undergraduates are from North Carolina. Others are from 39 states and 17 foreign countries. 80% are African American; 3% Foreign; 14% White; 1% Asian American; 1% American Indian/Alaska Native; 1% Hispanic. **Female To Male Ratio:** 2.1:1. The average age of freshmen is 19; all undergraduates, 24. **Housing:** 2377 students can be accommodated in college housing, which includes dorms, on-campus housing, and honors houses. On-campus housing is available on a first-come, first-served basis, and is available on a lottery system for upperclassmen. 63% of students commute. Alcohol is not permitted. All students may keep cars.

FACULTY/CLASSROOMS: 53% of faculty are male; 47% are female. All teach undergraduates. No introductory courses are taught by graduate students.

PROGRAMS OF STUDY: NCCU confers B.A., B.S., B.B.A., B.M., B.S.N., and B.S.W. degrees. Master's degrees are also awarded. Bachelor's degrees are awarded in BIOLOGICAL SCIENCE (biology/biological science and nutrition), BUSINESS (accounting and business administration and management), COMMUNICATIONS AND THE ARTS (art, dramatic arts, English, French, jazz, music, and Spanish), COMPUTER AND PHYSICAL SCIENCE (chemistry, computer science, mathematics, and physics), EDUCATION (elementary education, health education, middle school education, and physical education), ENGINEERING AND ENVIRONMENTAL DESIGN (environmental science), HEALTH PROFESSIONS (nursing), SOCIAL SCIENCE (child care/child and family studies, child psychology/development, criminal justice, geography, history, human services, political science/government, psychology, social work, and sociology). Criminal justice, and business are the strongest academically. Business, biology, and political science have the largest enrollments.

ACTIVITIES: There are 45 groups on campus, including art, band, cheerleading, chess, choir, computers, dance, drama, drill team, ethnic, honors, international, jazz band, literary magazine, marching band, newspaper, political, professional, radio and TV, religious, social, social service, student government, symphony, and yearbook. **Sports:** There are 6 intercollegiate sports for men and 5 for women. Facilities include a stadium, a gym, a swimming pool, handball and tennis courts, a track, a bowling alley, dance studios, and a weight room. **Graduates:** From July 1, 2016 to June 30, 2017, 604 bachelor's degrees were awarded. The most popular majors were business administration (21%), education (11%), and criminal justice (9%).

SERVICES: There is a reader service for the blind, and remedial math, reading, and writing. There is assistance for students in obtaining needed documentations, registration, and appropriate individual accommodations. **Library/Resources:** The library contains 663,913 volumes, 1.2 million microform items, and 10,991 audio/video tapes/CDs/DVDs, and subscribes to 6,688 periodicals including electronic. Computerized library services include database searching. Special learning facilities include an art gallery and radio station. **Physically Challenged Students:** 90% of the campus is accessible. Facilities include wheelchair ramps, elevators, special parking, specially equipped restrooms, special class scheduling, lowered drinking fountains, and lowered telephones. **Special:**

NCCU offers internships, study abroad, a Washington semester, work-study programs, dual majors, and nondegree study. There are 10 national honor societies, a freshman honors program, and 10 departmental honors programs. **Visiting:** There are regularly scheduled orientations for prospective students. There are guides for informal visits; visitors may sit in on classes and stay overnight. **Campus Safety and Security:** Measures include 24-hour foot and vehicle patrol and security escort services. There are emergency telephones and lighted pathways/sidewalks.

REQUIREMENTS: The SAT or ACT is required. Applicants must be graduates of an accredited secondary school or have a GED certificate. They must have completed 11 academic credits based on 4 years of English, 3 each of math and science, and 2 each of foreign language and social studies. Music applicants must audition. AP and CLEP credits are accepted. Important factors in the admissions decision are advanced placement or honors courses, leadership record, and evidence of special talent. To graduate, students must complete 124 semester hours, including 30 in the major, with a minimum GPA of 2.0. Core requirements include courses in communications, math and natural science, social science, humanities, and health and physical education. **Procedure:** Entrance exams should be taken in the spring of the junior year. There is a rolling admissions plan. Applications should be filed by August 1 for fall entry; November 1 for spring entry. The fall 2017 application fee was $30. Applications are accepted online. **Transfer Students:** 373 transfer students enrolled in 2016-2017. Applicants must have a minimum GPA of 2.0 in all college-level courses. 30 of 124 credits required for the bachelor's degree must be completed at NCCU. **International Students:** They must take the TOEFL. They must also take the SAT or ACT unless these tests are not administered in their country.

Admissions Contact: Nicole Gibbs, Director of Admissions. Email: *admissions@nccu.edu* Web: *www.nccu.edu*

FINANCIAL AID: In 2017-2018, 85% of all full-time freshmen received some form of financial aid. 70% of all full-time freshmen received need-based aid. The FAFSA code is 002950. The deadline for filing freshman financial aid applications for fall entry is August 1.

NORTH CAROLINA STATE UNIVERSITY D-2

www.ncsu.edu

Raleigh, NC 27695 **(919) 515-2434**

Fax: (919) 515-5039 **Email: undergrad-admissions@ncsu.edu**

Full-time: 11,554 men, 9805 women	**Faculty:** 1091; I, av$
Part-time: 1646 men, 1172 women	**Ph.D.s:** 90%
Graduate: 5491 men, 4764 women	**Student/Faculty:** 20 to 1
Year: semesters, summer session	**Tuition:** $11,581 ($29,929)
Room & Board: $10,854	**Freshman Class:** 26859 applied, 13690 accepted, 4659 enrolled
SAT EBR-W/M: 647/662 **ACT:** 29	**CEEB CODE:** 5496
Application Deadline: January 15	**HIGHLY COMPETITIVE+**

North Carolina State University, founded in 1887, is a member of the University of North Carolina System. Its degree programs emphasize the arts and sciences, agriculture, business, education, engineering, and preprofessional training. There are 10 undergraduate schools and 10 graduate schools. In addition to regional accreditation, NCSU has baccalaureate program accreditation with AACSB, ABET, CSAB, CSWE, NAAB, NASAD, CAEP, NRPA, and SAF. The 2110-acre campus is in an urban area in Raleigh, NC. Including any residence halls, there are 197 buildings.

STUDENT LIFE: 87% of undergraduates are from North Carolina. Others are from 50 states, 109 foreign countries, and Canada. 81% are from public schools. 70% are White; 7% Asian American; 6% African American; 6% Hispanic; 4% Foreign; 4% two or more races; 3% race unknown; 1% American Indian/Alaska Native. **Male To Female Ratio:** 1.2:1. The average age of freshmen is 18; all undergraduates, 21. 6% do not continue beyond their first year; 78% remain to graduate. **Housing:** 10108 students can be accommodated in college housing, which includes single sex dorms, coed dorms, married student dorms, on-campus apartments, and off-campus apartments. In addition, there are honors houses, special-interest houses, fraternity houses, sorority houses, arts and creative living dorms, computer theme housing, leadership village, and entrepreneurs village. On-campus housing is guaranteed for the freshman year only, is available on a first-come, and first-served basis. 58% of students commute. Alcohol is not permitted. All students may keep cars.

FACULTY/CLASSROOMS: 63% of faculty are male; 37% are female. 54% teach undergraduates, all do research, and 54% do both. Graduate students teach 23% of introductory courses. The average class size in an introductory lecture is 50; in a laboratory is 25; and in a regular course is 50.

PROGRAMS OF STUDY: NCSU confers B.A., B.S., B.Arch., B.E.D.A., B.L.A., and B.S.W. degrees. Associate, master's, and doctoral degrees are also awarded. Bachelor's degrees are awarded in AGRICULTURE (agricultural business management, agricultural economics, agriculture, agronomy, animal science, conservation and regulation, fishing and fisheries, forestry and related sciences, horticulture, natural resource management, poultry science, soil science, and wood science), BIOLOGICAL SCIENCE (biochemistry, biology/biological science, botany, microbiology, and zoology), BUSINESS (accounting, business administration and management, business economics, and recreation and leisure services), COMMUNICATIONS AND THE ARTS (communications, design, English, French, graphic design, industrial design, and Spanish), COMPUTER AND PHYSICAL SCIENCE (atmospheric sciences and meteorology, chemistry, computer science, earth science, geology, mathematics, physics, and statistics), EDUCATION (agricultural education, education, foreign languages education, industrial arts education, marketing and distribution education, mathematics education, middle school education, science education, secondary education, social studies education, technical education, and vocational education), ENGINEERING AND ENVIRONMENTAL DESIGN (aeronautical engineering, agricultural engineering, architecture, chemical engineering, civil engineering, computer engineering, construction management, electrical/electronics engineering, engineering, environmental design, environmental engineering, environmental science, furniture design, industrial engineering, landscape architecture/design, materials science, mechanical engineering, nuclear engineering, paper and pulp science, and textile engineering), HEALTH PROFESSIONS (medical laboratory technology, predentistry, premedicine, preveterinary science, and speech pathology/audiology), SOCIAL SCIENCE (clothing and textiles management/production/services, criminal justice, economics, food science, history, interdisciplinary studies, parks and recreation management, philosophy, political science/government, prelaw, psychology, religion, social science, social work, sociology, and textiles and clothing). Electrical engineering, chemical engineering, and architecture are the strongest academically. Business management, mechanical engineering, and electrical engineering have the largest enrollments.

ACTIVITIES: 12% of men belong to 26 national fraternities; 17% of women belong to 20 national sororities. There are 725 groups on campus, including art, bagpipe, band, cheerleading, chess, choir, chorale, chorus, communications, computers, dance, debate, drama, drill team, drum and bugle corps, environmental, ethnic, film, honors, international, jazz band, LGBT, literary magazine, marching band, musical theater, newspaper, orchestra, pep band, photography, political, professional, radio and TV, religious, social, social service, student government, symphony, and yearbook. Popular campus events include Pan African Festival, Wolfstock, and Greek Week. **Sports:** There are 48 intercollegiate sports for men and 50 for women, and 39 intramural sports for men and 39 for women. Facilities include a football stadium, a sports arena, a soccer stadium, a baseball stadium, a gym, a tennis complex, a track, indoor pools, and an indoor rock-climbing wall. **Graduates:** The most popular majors were engineering (27%), business/marketing (15%), and biological/life sciences (9%). In an average class, 54% graduate in 4 years or less, 76% graduate in 5 years or less, and 78% graduate in 6 years or less. Of the 2016 graduating class, 24% were enrolled in graduate school within 6 months of graduation, and 64% were employed.

SERVICES: Counseling and information services are available, as is tutoring in some subjects, such as math, physics, and chemistry. There is a reader service for the blind. **Library/Resources:** The library contains 5.2 million volumes, 5.5 million microform items, 324,456 audio/video tapes/CDs/DVDs, and subscribes to 103,673 periodicals, including electronic. Computerized library services include interlibrary loans, database searching, Internet access, and Wi-Fi capability. Special learning facilities include an art gallery, a radio station, TV station, a Nuclear reactor, a phytotron, electron microscope facilities, Materials Research Center, Integrated Manufacturing Systems Engineering Institute, Japan Center, Confucius Institute, Textile Protection and Comfort Center, and Precision Engineering Center. **Physically Challenged Students:** 88% of the campus is accessible. Facilities include wheelchair ramps, elevators, special parking, specially equipped restrooms, special class scheduling, lowered drinking fountains, lowered telephones, and special housing. **Special:** NCSU offers cross-registration within the Cooperating Raleigh Colleges network, study abroad in more than 90 countries, internships, work-study programs, an accelerated degree plan, dual majors within any program, a general studies degree in education, a 3-2 engineering degree with the University of North Carolina at Asheville, student-designed multidisciplinary studies majors, credit by examination, nondegree study, and pass/fail options. There are 18 national honor societies, including Phi Beta Kappa, a freshman honors program, and 27 departmental honors programs. **Visiting:** There are regularly scheduled orientations for prospective students consisting of admissions information sessions. There are guides for informal visits and visitors may sit in on classes. To schedule a visit, contact the Admissions Office. **Campus Safety and Security:** Measures include 24-hour foot and vehicle patrol, an emergency notification system, self-defense education, and security escort services. There are shuttle buses, emergency telephones, lighted pathways/sidewalks, controlled access to dorms/residences, bicycle patrol, and mounted police.

REQUIREMENTS: The SAT or ACT and ACT Writing Test are recommended. Applicants must be graduates of an accredited secondary school or have a GED certificate. They must have completed 20 academic credits, including 4 units of English, 3 units each of science and math (4 of math is recommended), 2 units each of social studies and foreign language, and 1 unit of history. An essay is recommended for all applicants. A portfolio and an interview are required for studio-based majors. The SAT Math Subject Test is recommended for class placement for new students. AP and CLEP credits are accepted. Important factors in the admissions decision are advanced placement or honors courses, leadership record, and evidence of special talent. To graduate, students must complete 120 to 142 semester hours, including 60 to 70 in the major, with a minimum GPA of 2.0. Distribution requirements include 12 to 18 hours in humanities and social sciences, 6 to 8 each in math and science, 6 in English composition, and 4 in physical education. **Procedure:** Freshmen are admitted to all sessions. Entrance exams should be taken in the spring of the junior year and the fall of the senior year. There is a deferred admissions plan. Early decision applications should be filed by October 15; regular applications, by January 15 for fall entry; October 1 for spring entry; and January 15 for summer entry. The fall 2017 application fee was $85. Notification of early decision is sent January 30; regular decision, March 30. 2479 applicants were on the 2017 waiting list; 7 were admitted. Applications are accepted online. **Transfer Students:** 1697 transfer students enrolled in 2016-2017. Applicants must have completed 30 semester hours of college-level work with a minimum GPA of 2.0. Priority is given to students who have completed 60 hours of relevant coursework. An associate degree and an interview are recommended. Applicants must have math, English, and foreign language proficiency. 30 of 120 credits required for the bachelor's degree must be completed at NCSU. **International Students:** There are 957 international students enrolled. They must take the TOEFL with a minimum score of 85 on the Internet-based version (iBT). Students must take either the IELTS or PTE Academic. They must also take the SAT or ACT if it is available to students in their country.

ADMISSIONS: 51% of the 2017-2018 applicants were accepted. The SAT scores for the 2017-2018 freshman class were: Math-- 0% below 500, 15% between 500 and 599, 54% between 600 and 699, and 31% between 700 and 800. Evidence-Based Reading/Writing-- 1% below 500, 15% between 500 and 599, 64% between 600 and 699, and 20% between 700 and 800. The ACT scores were 4% between 18 and 23, 57% between 24 and 29, and 39% above 30. 74% of the current freshmen were in the top fifth of their class; 96% were in the top two fifths. 106 freshmen graduated first in their class. **Admissions Contact:** Thomas Griffin, Director of Admissions. Email: *undergrad-admissions@ncsu.edu* Web: *www.ncsu.edu*

FINANCIAL AID: In 2017-2018, 66% of all full-time freshmen received some form of financial aid. 47% of all full-time freshmen received need-based aid. The average freshman award was $13,225. Need-based scholarships or need-based grants averaged $10,165 ($29,320 maximum); need-based self-help aid (loans and jobs) averaged $5,903 ($7,500 maximum); non-need-based athletic scholarships averaged $21,574 ($45,456 maximum); and other non-need-based awards and non-need-based scholarships averaged $5,903 ($43,747 maximum). 19% of undergraduate students work part-time. The average financial indebtedness of the 2017 graduate was $21,507. The college's own financial statement is required. The FAFSA code is 002972. The priority date for freshman financial aid applications for fall entry is March 1.

NORTH CAROLINA WESLEYAN COLLEGE E-2

www.ncwc.edu

Rocky Mount, NC 27804 **(252) 985-5200**

Fax: (252) 985-5295	**Email: adm@ncwc.edu**
Full-time: 615 men, 515 women	**Faculty:** IIB, --$
Part-time: 289 men, 337 women	**Ph.D.s:** 45%
Graduate: n/av	**Student/Faculty:** n/av
Year: semesters, summer session	**Tuition:** $29,350
Room & Board: $9850	**Freshman Class:** 1169 applied, 951 accepted, 288 enrolled
SAT or ACT: required	**CEEB CODE:** 5501
Application Deadline: n/av	**COMPETITIVE**

North Carolina Wesleyan College, founded in 1956, is a private liberal arts institution affiliated with the United Methodist Church. There is 1 undergraduate school. In addition to regional accreditation, NCWC has baccalaureate program accreditation with CAEP. The 200-acre campus is in a suburban area 57 miles east of Raleigh. Including any residence halls, there are 18 buildings.

STUDENT LIFE: 85% of undergraduates are from North Carolina. Others are from 24 states, and 9 foreign countries. 70% are from public schools. 45% are African American; 43% White; 3% Hispanic; 1% Asian American; 1% American Indian/Alaska Native; 1% Foreign. 70% are Protestant; 16% Catholic; 14% claim no religious affiliation. **Male To Female Ratio:** 1.1:1. The average age of freshmen is 19; all undergraduates, 26. 36% do not continue beyond their first year; 26% remain to graduate. **Housing:** 504 students can be accommodated in college housing, which includes dorms and off-campus apartments. There are also single-occupancy residence halls with kitchens on each floor and smoke/substance free housing. On-campus housing is guaranteed for all 4 years. 68% of students commute. All students may keep cars.

FACULTY/CLASSROOMS: 62% of faculty are male; 38% are female. All teach undergraduates. No introductory courses are taught by graduate students. The average class size in an introductory lecture is 23; in a laboratory is 15; and in a regular course is 18.

PROGRAMS OF STUDY: NCWC confers B.A. and B.S. degrees. Bachelor's degrees are awarded in BIOLOGICAL SCIENCE (biology/biological science), BUSINESS (accounting, business administration and management, and hotel/motel and restaurant management), COMMUNICATIONS AND THE ARTS (dramatic arts and English), COMPUTER AND PHYSICAL SCIENCE (chemistry, information sciences and systems, and mathematics), EDUCATION (elementary education and middle school education), ENGINEERING AND ENVIRONMENTAL DESIGN (environmental science), HEALTH PROFESSIONS (exercise science and premedicine), SOCIAL SCIENCE (criminal justice, history, political science/government, psychology, religion, and sociology). Business administration, justice studies, and computer information systems have the largest enrollments.

ACTIVITIES: 1% of men belong to 3 national fraternities; 1% of women belong to 3 national sororities. There are 23 groups on campus, including cheerleading, chess, choir, chorus, computers, drama, ethnic, honors, international, LGBT, literary magazine, musical theater, newspaper, political, professional, religious, social, social service, and student government. Popular campus events include Spring Fling, Parents Weekend, and Alumni Homecoming. **Sports:** There are 5 intercollegiate sports for men and 5 for women, and 13 intramural sports for men and 13 for women. Facilities include a gym with areas for basketball, volleyball, and indoor soccer, tennis courts, a skeet range, fields for intramurals and for varsity baseball, softball, and soccer. **Graduates:** From July 1, 2016 to June 30, 2017, 391 bachelor's degrees were awarded. The most popular majors were business/marketing (48%), computer and information sciences (24%), and law/legal studies (10%). In an average class, 15% graduate in 4 years or less, 23% graduate in 5 years or less, and 10% graduate in 6 years or less.

SERVICES: Counseling and information services are available, as is tutoring in most subjects. There is remedial math, reading, and writing. **Library/Resources:** The library contains 65,721 volumes, 2,830 microform items, 4,200 audio/video tapes/CDs/DVDs, and subscribes to 4,645 periodicals, including electronic. Computerized library services include interlibrary loans and database searching. Special learning facilities include an art gallery, and performing arts center. **Physically Challenged Students:** 90% of the campus is accessible. Facilities include wheelchair ramps, elevators, special parking, specially equipped restrooms, special class scheduling, lowered drinking fountains, lowered telephones, and special housing. **Special:** NCWC offers cooperative programs in all majors, internships, work-study programs through the college offices, credit for military experience, nondegree study, and pass/fail options. The B.A.-B.S. degree may be earned in all majors. There are 2 national honor societies and a freshman honors program. **Visiting:** There are regularly scheduled orientations for prospective students, including an individual campus tour, an interview, a financial aid session, and meetings with faculty and coaches. There are guides for informal visits; visitors may sit in on classes and stay overnight. To schedule a visit, contact the Admissions Office. **Campus Safety and Security:** Measures include 24-hour foot and vehicle patrol and security escort services. There are emergency telephones and lighted pathways/sidewalks.

REQUIREMENTS: The SAT or ACT is required, with a satisfactory SAT composite score or ACT score of 19 recommended. Applicants should be graduates of an accredited secondary school or have a GED. They should have completed at least 13 academic courses, including 4 in English, 3 in math, and 2 each in foreign language, social studies, and lab sciences. An essay and an interview are advised. AP and CLEP credits are accepted. Important factors in the admissions decision are advanced placement or honors courses, extracurricular activities record, and leadership record. To graduate, students must complete 124 semester hours, including 30 to 54 in the major, with a minimum GPA of 2.0. Distribution requirements consist of 6 semester hours of English composition or demonstrated proficiency; 4 each of biological and physical science; 3 each of ethics, non-Western culture, math, history, social science, psychology or sociology, religion, literature, and fine arts; 2 of physical education; and 2 of introduction to college life. Some majors require a thesis. **Procedure:** Freshmen are admitted in the fall and spring. Entrance exams should be taken in spring of the junior year or fall or winter of the senior year. There are deferred admissions and rolling admissions plans. Application deadlines are open. The fall 2017 application fee was $25. Applications are accepted on-line. **Transfer Students:** Applicants must have a minimum GPA of 2.0 in their college courses. They must submit transcripts of all high school and college work, along with proof of high school graduation. 31 of 124 credits required for the bachelor's degree must be completed at NCWC. **International Students:** They must take the TOEFL and the SAT.

ADMISSIONS: 81% of the 2017-2018 applicants were accepted. **Admissions Contact:** Cecelia Summers, Director of Admissions. Email: *adm@ncwc.edu* Web: *www.ncwc.edu*

FINANCIAL AID: 93% of all full-time freshmen received need-based aid. The average freshman award was $8,480. Need-based scholarships or need-based grants averaged $2,917; and need-based self-help aid (loans and jobs) averaged $9,193. NCWC is a member of CSS. The FAFSA code is 002951. The priority date for freshman financial aid applications for fall entry is March 15.

PFEIFFER UNIVERSITY *(The complete profile is made available exclusively on our website, www.barronspac.com)*

QUEENS UNIVERSITY OF CHARLOTTE C-3

www.queens.edu

Charlotte, NC 28274	**(704) 337-2212** **(800) 849-0202**
Fax: (704) 337-2403	**Email: admissions@queens.edu**
Full-time: 408 men, 997 women	**Faculty:** n/av
Part-time: 66 men, 232 women	**Ph.D.s:** 79%
Graduate: 183 men, 368 women	**Student/Faculty:** 12 to 1
Year: semesters, summer session	**Tuition:** $29,045
Room & Board: $10,498	**Freshman Class:** 1949 applied, 1498 accepted, 316 enrolled
SAT CR/M/W: 520/520/510 **ACT:** 24	**CEEB CODE:** 5560
Application Deadline: rolling	**COMPETITIVE**

Queens University of Charlotte is a private, co-ed, comprehensive university with a commitment to liberal arts and professional studies. Queens serves undergraduate and graduate students through the College of Arts and Sciences, School of Business, School of Education, School of Communication, College of Graduate and Continuing Studies, and the College of Health, which features the Presbyterian School of Nursing. The university today offers 39 undergraduate majors and 19 graduate programs. There are 5 undergraduate schools and one graduate school. In addition to regional accreditation, Queens has baccalaureate program accreditation with AACSB, ACBSP, NASM, CAEP, NLN, AMTA, CCNE, NASM, and SACS-COC. The 30-acre campus is in a suburban area 2 miles south of uptown Charlotte. Including any residence halls, there are 38 buildings.

STUDENT LIFE: 59% of undergraduates are from North Carolina. Others are from 36 states, 21 foreign countries, and Canada. 80% are from public schools. 59% are White; 13% African American; 12% race unknown; 6% Foreign; 4% Hispanic; 3% Asian American; 2% two or more races; 1% American Indian/Alaska Native. 17% are Protestant; 13% Catholic. **Female To Male Ratio:** 2.4:1. The average age of freshmen is 18; all undergraduates, 20. 30% do not continue beyond their first year; 52% remain to graduate. **Housing:** 916 students can be accommodated in college housing, which includes dorms and off-campus apartments. On-campus housing is guaranteed for all 4 years, and is available on a first-come, first-served basis, and is available on a lottery system for upperclassmen. 83% of students live on campus. All students may keep cars.

FACULTY/CLASSROOMS: 33% of faculty are male; 67% are female. All teach undergraduates. No introductory courses are taught by graduate students. The average class size in an introductory lecture is 15; in a laboratory is 10; and in a regular course is 15.

PROGRAMS OF STUDY: Queens confers B.A., B.B.A., B.S., B.Mus., and B.S.N. degrees. Master's degrees are also awarded. Bachelor's degrees are awarded in AGRICULTURE (environmental studies), BIOLOGICAL SCIENCE (biochemistry and biology/biological science), BUSINESS (accounting, business administration and management, finance, and sports management), COMMUNICATIONS AND THE ARTS (art, communications, creative writing, digital communications, dramatic arts, English literature, French, graphic design, music, romance languages and literature, and Spanish), COMPUTER AND PHYSICAL SCIENCE (chemistry and mathematics), EDUCATION (elementary education), ENGINEERING AND ENVIRONMENTAL DESIGN (environmental science and interior design), HEALTH PROFESSIONS (exercise science, music therapy, and nursing), SOCIAL SCIENCE (community services, history, human services, philosophy, political science/government, psychology, religion, and sociology). Liberal arts and sciences, business, and nursing are the strongest academically. Business, nursing, and communications have the largest enrollments.

ACTIVITIES: 13% of men belong to 2 national fraternities; 21% of women belong to 5 national sororities. There are 72 groups on campus, including art, cheerleading, choir, chorale, chorus, dance, drama, environmental, ethnic, honors, international, jazz band, LGBT, literary magazine, musical theater, newspaper, political, professional, religious, social, social service, student government, Triatholon club, and yearbook. Popular campus events include Casino Night, Midnight on Ice, Spring Carnival, Exam Break Breakfast, Homecoming Week, Welcome Back Week, Moravian Love Feast, Boar's Head, International Week, and Queens After Dark. **Sports:** There are 9 intercollegiate sports for men and 11 for women, and 6 intramural sports for men and 6 for women. Facilities include lacrosse and soccer teams. The Queens Sports Complex offers multisport champion, cross country, and a grass practice field. The Levine Center for Wellness and Recreation is home to basketball, and volleyball teams, a fitness center, 1/10th mile indoor walking/jogging track, a swimming pool, and dance/yoga studio. **Graduates:** From July 1, 2016 to June 30, 2017, 414 bachelor's degrees were awarded. The most popular majors were health professions and related programs (30%), business (12%), and communications (11%). In an average class, 44% graduate in 4 years or less, 51% graduate in 5 years or less, and 52% graduate in 6 years or less.

SERVICES: Counseling and information services are available, as is tutoring in most subjects, such as math, science, social sciences, foreign languages, nursing, and core classes. The Center for Student Success offers free individual peer tutoring, review sessions, knowledge workshops, academic success strategies, individual academic assistance and guidance, access to the writing center, and referrals to the Office of Disability Services. **Library/Resources:** The library contains 42,081 volumes, 97,670 audio/video tapes/CDs/DVDs, and subscribes to 74 periodicals, including electronic. Computerized library services include interlibrary loans, database searching, Internet access, and Wi-Fi capability. Special learning facilities include an art gallery, Platinum LEED Science Building "living" wallrare books and archival collection, a photographic lab, a ceramics studio, and a recital hall. **Physically Challenged Students:** 70% of the campus is accessible. Facilities include wheelchair ramps, special parking, specially equipped restrooms, special class scheduling, and lowered drinking fountains. **Special:** Required internships in all majors, cross-registration with colleges of the Charlotte Area Educational Consortium, dual majors, nondegree study, and pass/fail options are available. The school offers a Washington semester. Study tours in over 14 countries (included in the cost of tuition) may be arranged through the schools John Belk International Program. There are 5 national honor societies and a freshman honors program. **Visiting:** There are regularly scheduled orientations for prospective students, including a sampling of classes, campus tours, a college overview, a question/answer segment, a meet-the-faculty session, and a scholarship/ financial aid session. There are guides for informal visits and visitors may sit in on classes. To schedule a visit, contact the Undergraduate Admissions Office. **Campus Safety and Security:** Measures include 24-hour foot and vehicle patrol, emergency notification system, self-defense education, and security escort services. There are shuttle buses, emergency telephones, lighted pathways/sidewalks, and controlled access to dorms/ residences.

REQUIREMENTS: The SAT or ACT is required. The ACT Optional Writing test is also required. Applicants should have a college preparatory background in an accredited secondary school. The GED is accepted. High school courses should include 4 years of English, 3 of math, 2 each of history or social studies and a foreign language, and 2 years of science, including 1 of lab science. An interview is recommended. An audition or portfolio is recommended for art and music students. AP and CLEP credits are accepted. Important factors in the admissions decision are recommendations by school officials, advanced placement or honors courses, and leadership record. To graduate, students must complete a total of 122 credit hours with a minimum GPA of 2.0. For the B.A., between 30 and 40 hours are required in the students major; for the B.S., 32 are required. 2 courses in English composition, 2 in physical education, and 1 in lab science are required. If entering freshmen do not pass the placement exams given in math and a foreign language, additional courses will be required. Some majors require a thesis or research project. **Procedure:** Freshmen are admitted in the fall, spring, and summer. Entrance exams should be taken in the junior year or as early as possible in the senior year. There are early admissions, deferred admissions, and rolling admissions plans. Application deadlines are open. The fall 2017 application fee was $40. Notifications are sent September 15. Applications are accepted on-line. **Transfer Students:** 163 transfer students enrolled in 2016-2017. Transfer students are accepted in all but the senior class. A GPA of 2.0 is required for all previous college-level work. 45 of 122 credits required for the bachelor's degree must be completed at Queens. **International Students:** They must take the TOEFL with a minimum score of 550 on the paper-based TOEFL (PBT). Students must also take the SAT or ACT.

ADMISSIONS: 77% of the 2017-2018 applicants were accepted. The SAT scores for the 2017-2018 freshman class were: Critical Reading-- 41% below 500, 44% between 500 and 599, 11% between 600 and 699, and 3% between 700 and 800. Math-- 39% below 500, 43% between 500 and 599, 17% between 600 and 699, and 1% between 700 and 800. Writing-- 45% below 500, 37% between 500 and 599, 15% between 600 and 699, and 3% between 700 and 800. The ACT scores were 22% below 12, 26% between 12 and 17, 29% between 18 and 23, 13% between 24 and 29, and 10% above 30. 32% of the current freshmen were in the top fifth of their class; 64% were in the top two fifths. **Admissions Contact:** Woody O'Cain, Assoc. Vice President, Dean of Admission. Email: *admissions@queens.edu* Web: *www.queens.edu*

FINANCIAL AID: In 2017-2018, 97% of all full-time freshmen received some form of financial aid. 58% of all full-time freshmen received need-based aid. The average freshman award was $26,550. Need-based scholarships or need-based grants averaged $9,074 ($24,446 maximum); need-based self-help aid (loans and jobs) averaged $4,763 ($8,732 maximum); non-need-based athletic scholarships averaged $9,839 ($33,800 maximum); and other non-need-based awards and non-need-based scholarships averaged $12,377 ($28,800 maximum). 15% of undergraduate students work part-time. The average financial indebtedness of the 2017 graduate was $28,507. Queens is a member of CSS. The FAFSA code is 002957. The priority date for freshman financial aid applications for fall entry is March 1.

SAINT AUGUSTINE'S UNIVERSITY D-2

www.st-aug.edu

Raleigh, NC 27610	**(919) 516-4000** **(800) 948-1126**
Fax: (919) 516-5805	**Email: admissions@st.aug.edu**
Full-time: 505 men, 705 women	**Faculty:** 87
Part-time: 50 men, 100 women	**Ph.D.s:** 59%
Graduate: n/av	**Student/Faculty:** 16 to 1
Year: semesters, summer session	**Tuition:** $17,890
Room & Board: $7692	**Freshman Class:** n/av
SAT or ACT: required	**CEEB CODE:** 5596
Application Deadline: n/av	**COMPETITIVE**

Saint Augustine's University, founded in 1867, is a historically black liberal arts institution affiliated with the Episcopal Church. The figures given in the above capsule and in this profile are approximate. There is 1 undergraduate school. The 110-acre campus is in an urban area 1 mile northeast of downtown Raleigh. Including any residence halls, there are 37 buildings.

STUDENT LIFE: 51% of undergraduates are from North Carolina. Others are from 34 states, 16 foreign countries, and Canada. 99% are from public schools. 90% are African American; 9% Foreign; 1% White. 58% are Protestant; 39% claim no religious affiliation. **Female To Male Ratio:** 1.5:1. The average age of freshmen is 18; all undergraduates, 22. 38% do not continue beyond their first year; 27% remain to graduate. **Housing:** 1143 students can be accommodated in college housing, which includes dorms and honors houses. On-campus housing is guaranteed for all 4 years. 62% of students live on campus. Alcohol is not permitted. All students may keep cars.

FACULTY/CLASSROOMS: 60% of faculty are male; 40% are female. All teach undergraduates. No introductory courses are taught by graduate students. The average class size in an introductory lecture is 22; in a laboratory is 13; and in a regular course is 14.

PROGRAMS OF STUDY: SAU confers B.A. and B.S. degrees. Bachelor's degrees are awarded in BIOLOGICAL SCIENCE (biology/biological science), BUSINESS (accounting, business administration and management, and international business management), COMMUNICATIONS AND THE ARTS (communications, English, fine arts, French, music, music business management, Spanish, and visual and performing arts), COMPUTER AND PHYSICAL SCIENCE (applied mathematics, chemistry, computer science, information sciences and systems, and mathematics), EDUCATION (business education, education of the exceptional child, elementary education, English education, mathematics education, music education, physical education, science education, and social studies education), ENGINEERING AND ENVIRONMENTAL DESIGN (industrial administration/management and industrial engineering), HEALTH PROFESSIONS (industrial hygiene, medical laboratory technology, and premedicine), SOCIAL SCIENCE (African American studies, criminal justice, history, physical fitness/movement, political science/government, prelaw, psychology, sociology, and urban studies). Engineering, math, and premedicine are the strongest academically. Computer science, business administration, and communications have the largest enrollments.

ACTIVITIES: 6% of men belong to 5 national fraternities; 12% of women belong to 4 national sororities. There are 20 groups on campus, including band, cheerleading, chorale, dance, drama, ethnic, honors, international, newspaper, photography, professional, radio and TV, religious, social service, student government, and yearbook. Popular campus events include Opening Convocation each semester, CIAA tournament, and career/job fairs. **Sports:** There are 5 intercollegiate sports for men and 4 for women, and 4 intramural sports for men and 3 for women. Facilities include a gym, a track, baseball fields, and tennis and basketball courts. **Graduates:** From July 1, 2016 to June 30, 2017, 242 bachelor's degrees were awarded. The most popular majors were business (28%), psychology (12%), and criminal justice (8%). In an average class, 1% graduate in 3 years or less, 12% graduate in 4 years or less, 25% graduate in 5 years or less, and 27% graduate in 6 years or less. Of the 2016 graduating class, 23% were enrolled in graduate school within 6 months of graduation, and 60% were employed.

SERVICES: There is remedial math, reading, and writing. Help with writing and test-taking skills is available. **Library/Resources:** Computerized library services include database searching. Special learning facilities include a radio station. **Physically Challenged Students:** 64% of the campus is accessible. Facilities include wheelchair ramps, elevators, special parking, and specially equipped restrooms. **Special:** Students may cross-register at any of 5 area colleges, study abroad, or pursue a 3-2 engineering program with North Carolina State University. There is an accelerated degree program in organizational management for adult learners. Field experience programs, nondegree study, internships, work-study, cooperative programs, and credit for military service are offered. There is 1 national honor society and a freshman honors program. **Visiting:** There are guides for informal visits and visitors may sit in on classes. To schedule a visit, contact the Admissions Office. **Campus Safety and Security:** Measures include 24-hour foot and vehicle patrol. There are emergency telephones and lighted pathways/sidewalks.

REQUIREMENTS: The SAT or ACT is required. Applicants must be graduates of an accredited secondary school with a C+ average in at least 18 academic units, including 4 in English, 3 in math, and 2 each in social studies and science. AP credits are accepted. Important factors in the admissions decision are geographical diversity, evidence of special talent, and leadership record. Students must complete at least 120 hours with a minimum 2.0 GPA for graduation. All students must complete a 50 to 55 credit core curriculum that includes courses in reading and communication, foreign language, science, math, philosophy, ethics, humanities, world civilization, psychology, and physical education. Seniors must pass written and oral examinations in their major fields. Total credit hours required for a degree in offered majors range from 124 to 154. **Procedure:** Freshmen are admitted to all sessions. There are deferred admissions and rolling admissions plans. Check with the school for current application deadlines. The fall 2017 application fee was $25. **Transfer Students:** 43 transfer students enrolled in 2016-2017. Transfers must submit high school and college transcripts and must be eligible to reenter the last institution attended. 30 of 124 credits required for the bachelor's degree must be completed at SAU. **International Students:** There are 133 international students enrolled. They must take the TOEFL. They must also take the SAT or ACT.

Admissions Contact: Tim Chapman, Interim Director of Admissions. Email: *admissions@st.aug.edu* Web: *www.st-aug.edu*

FINANCIAL AID: In 2017-2018, 95% of all full-time freshmen received some form of financial aid. 87% of all full-time freshmen received need-based aid. The average freshman award was $10,474. 69% of undergraduate students work part-time. The average financial indebtedness of the 2017 graduate was $12,850. SAU is a member of CSS. The deadline for filing freshman financial aid applications for fall entry is April 15.

SALEM COLLEGE — C-2
www.salem.edu

Winston-Salem, NC 27101 — (336) 721-2621, (800) 327-2536

Fax: (336) 917-5572	**Email:** admissions@salem.edu
Full-time: 625 women	**Faculty:** 58; IIB, --$
Part-time: n/av	**Ph.D.s:** 86%
Graduate: 160 women	**Student/Faculty:** 12 to 1
Year: 4-1-4, summer session	**Tuition:** $28,566
Room & Board: $11,640	**Freshman Class:** 692 applied, 580 accepted, 162 enrolled
SAT CR/M: 550/540 **ACT:** 24	**CEEB CODE:** 5607
Application Deadline: open	**COMPETITIVE**

Salem College, founded in 1772 as a school for girls by the Moravians, an early Protestant denomination. Today the private college, which retains a historical relationship with the church, offers a liberal arts education for women. There is 1 undergraduate school and 1 graduate school. In addition to regional accreditation, Salem has baccalaureate program accreditation with NASM and CAEP. The 64-acre campus is in an urban area in the center of Old Salem, a restored 18th-century village, near downtown Winston-Salem, NC. Including any residence halls, there are 20 buildings.

STUDENT LIFE: 60% of undergraduates are from North Carolina. Others are from 23 states and 6 foreign countries. 80% are from public schools. 55% are White; 5% Foreign; 20% African American; 18% Hispanic; 1% Asian American; 1% American Indian/Alaska Native. The student base is all female. The average age of freshmen is 18; all undergraduates, 20. 25% do not continue beyond their first year; 63% remain to graduate. **Housing:** 488 students can be accommodated in college housing, which includes single-sex dorms, on-campus apartments, off-campus apartments, and honors houses. On-campus housing is guaranteed for all 4 years. 90% of students live on campus. All students may keep cars.

FACULTY/CLASSROOMS: 40% of faculty are male; 60% are female. All teach undergraduates and do research. No introductory courses are taught by graduate students. The average class size in an introductory lecture is 18; in a laboratory is 15; and in a regular course is 15.

PROGRAMS OF STUDY: Salem onfers B.A., B.S., B.M., and B.S.B.A. degrees. Master's degrees are also awarded. Bachelor's degrees are awarded in AGRICULTURE (environmental studies), BIOLOGICAL SCIENCE (biology/biological science), BUSINESS (accounting, business administration and management, international business management, and nonprofit/public organization management), COMMUNICATIONS AND THE ARTS (art history and appreciation, arts administration/management, communications, creative writing, dance, design, English, French, music, Spanish, and studio art), COMPUTER AND PHYSICAL SCIENCE (chemistry and mathematics), HEALTH PROFESSIONS (exercise and movement science), SOCIAL SCIENCE (economics, history, philosophy, political science/government, psychology, religion, sociology, and womens studies). Biology, psychology, and business have the largest enrollments.

ACTIVITIES: There are no sororities. There are 41 groups on campus, including band, chorale, chorus, dance, drama, ethnic, honors, international, LGBT, literary magazine, marching band at Wake Forest University, musical theater, newspaper, political, professional, radio and TV, religious, social, social service, student government, and yearbook. Popular campus events include Fall Fest, Spring Fling, and Celebration of Academic Excellence. **Sports:** There are 7 intercollegiate sports for women. Facilities include multiple athletic fields, a swimming pool, 2 gyms, tennis courts, a dance studio, a softball field, and a universal weight room. **Graduates:** The most popular majors were biology, business, and communication. In an average class, 1% graduate in 3 years or less, 52% graduate in 4 years or less, 55% graduate in 5 years or less, and 63% graduate in 6 years or less.

SERVICES: Counseling and information services are available, as is tutoring in every subject. There is a writing center available when needed. **Library/Resources:** The library contains 135,000 volumes, 302,534 microform items, and 13,553 audio/video tapes/CDs/DVDs, and subscribes to 15,000 periodicals, including electronic. Computerized library services include interlibrary loans, database searching, Internet access, and Wi-Fi capability. Special learning facilities include an art gallery, a radio station, and a learning lab (computer lab with multimedia capability). **Physically Challenged Students:** 75% of the campus is accessible. Facilities include special parking, specially equipped restrooms, special class scheduling, and lowered drinking fountains. Many buildings are historic, so disability access is limited to individual areas that have had recent renovations or were already accessible. **Special:** Salem offers an extensive internship program in all majors, cross-registration with Wake Forest University, and study abroad at various locations, including a summer program in Oxford, England. A Washington semester, student-designed and interdisciplinary majors, B.A.-B.S. degrees, nondegree study, and pass/fail options during the January term are available. There are 9 national honor societies and a freshman honors program. **Visiting:** There are regularly scheduled orientations for prospective students. There are guides for informal visits; visitors may sit in on classes and stay overnight. To schedule a visit, contact the Office of Admissions. **Campus Safety and Security:** Measures include 24-hour foot and vehicle patrol and security escort services. There are emergency telephones, lighted pathways/sidewalks, and controlled access to dorms/residences.

REQUIREMENTS: The SAT or ACT is required. Graduation from an accredited secondary school or the GED is needed. Students must have 12 academic credits plus electives, including 4 years of high school English, 3 each of math and science, and 2 each of foreign language and history. An essay is required for all students. Music students must audition. A GPA of 2.8 is required. AP and CLEP credits are accepted. Important factors in the admissions decision are advanced placement or honors courses, leadership record, and evidence of special talent. To graduate, students must complete a total of 36 courses, or 144 semester hours, with a minimum GPA of 2.0 both cumulative and in the major.

All traditional students must complete 4 January-term courses and 2 terms of physical education. Bachelor of Arts degree students must complete the following general education courses: 3 in a modern foreign language, 3 in math/science (including at least 1 math and 1 lab science), 2 each in English, social science, and history, and 1 each in fine arts and philosophy/religion. **Procedure:** Freshmen are admitted in the fall and spring. Entrance exams should be taken by January of the senior year. There are early admissions, deferred admissions, and rolling admissions plans. Application deadlines are open. Applications are accepted online. **Transfer Students:** 20 transfer students enrolled in 2016-2017. Applicants must have a minimum GPA of 2.0 in all previous college work and must submit a statement of good standing from the Dean of Students of the college previously attended, 2 letters of recommendation from teachers, a high school transcript, and a transcript and catalog from each college attended. SAT or ACT scores may be required on an individual basis. An interview is recommended. 36 of 144 credits required for the bachelor's degree must be completed at Salem. **International Students:** There are 15 international students enrolled. They must take the TOEFL with a minimum score of 79 on the Internet-based version (iBT). They must also take the SAT or ACT.

ADMISSIONS: 84% of the 2017-2018 applicants were accepted. 2 freshmen graduated first in their class. **Admissions Contact:** Katherine Knapp Watts, Vice President for Enrollment and Financial Aid. Email: *admissions@salem.edu* Web: *www.salem.edu*

FINANCIAL AID: In 2017-2018, 90% of all full-time freshmen received some form of financial aid. 80% of all full-time freshmen received need-based aid. The average freshman award was $32,763. 70% of undergraduate students work part-time. The average financial indebtedness of the 2017 graduate was $25,000. The FAFSA code is 002960. The priority date for freshman financial aid applications for fall entry is February 1.

SHAW UNIVERSITY D-2

www.shawu.edu

Raleigh, NC 27601	(919) 719-1996 (800) 214-6683
Fax: (919) 546-8271	Email: admissions@shawu.edu
Full-time: 700 men, 904 women	Faculty: 68
Part-time: 45 men, 64 women	Ph.D.s: 75%
Graduate: 51 men, 80 women	Student/Faculty: 19 to 1
Year: semesters, summer session	Tuition: $16,480
Room & Board: $8158	Freshman Class: 9608 applied, 4695 accepted, 643 enrolled
SAT or ACT: required	CEEB CODE: 5612
Application Deadline: July 30	COMPETITIVE

Shaw University, founded in 1865, is a private liberal arts university affiliated with the Baptist Church. There is 1 undergraduate school and 2 graduate schools. In addition to regional accreditation, Shaw has baccalaureate program accreditation with CSWE, CAEP, and CAAHEP. The 30-acre campus is in an urban area in downtown Raleigh.

STUDENT LIFE: 68% of undergraduates are from North Carolina. Others are from 31 states and 15 foreign countries. 67% are African American; 27% race unknown; 2% Foreign; 2% two or more races; 1% White. **Female To Male Ratio:** 1.3:1. The average age of freshmen is 19; all undergraduates, 22. **Housing:** 1049 students can be accommodated in college housing, which includes dorms. On-campus housing is available on a first-come, first-served basis. 58% of students live on campus. Alcohol is not permitted. Some may keep cars.

FACULTY/CLASSROOMS: 54% of faculty are male; 46% are female. 87% teach undergraduates. No introductory courses are taught by graduate students. The average class size in a laboratory is 14 and in a regular course is 20.

PROGRAMS OF STUDY: Shaw confers B.A., B.S., and B.S.W. degrees. Master's degrees are also awarded. Bachelor's degrees are awarded in BIOLOGICAL SCIENCE (biology/biological science), BUSINESS (accounting, business administration and management, and recreation and leisure services), COMMUNICATIONS AND THE ARTS (broadcasting, English, and visual and performing arts), COMPUTER AND PHYSICAL SCIENCE (chemistry, computer science, mathematics, and physics), EDUCATION (athletic training, elementary education, English education, mathematics education, physical education, science education, secondary education, social studies education, and special education), ENGINEERING AND ENVIRONMENTAL DESIGN (environmental science and preengineering), HEALTH PROFESSIONS (recreation therapy, rehabilitation therapy, and speech pathology/audiology), SOCIAL SCIENCE (African studies, criminal justice, gerontology, international relations, international studies, liberal arts/general studies, political science/government, psychology, public administration, religion, social work, and sociology). Business administration/management, criminal justice, and sociology have the largest enrollments.

ACTIVITIES: 4% of men belong to 4 national fraternities; 5% of women belong to 4 national sororities. Groups on campus include band, cheerleading, choir, chorus, criminal justice club, business club, dance, drama, ethnic, honors, international, jazz band, marching band, musical theater, newspaper, pep band, professional, radio and TV, religious, social, social service, student government, and yearbook. Popular campus events include Career Day, Awards Day, and Religious Emphasis Week. **Sports:** There are 6 intercollegiate sports for men and 7 for women, and 5 intramural sports for men and 4 for women. **Graduates:** From July 1, 2016 to June 30, 2017, 203 bachelor's degrees were awarded. The most popular majors were business administration/management (22%), social work (14%), and mass communications (10%). In an average class, 13% graduate in 4 years or less, 22% graduate in 5 years or less, and 26% graduate in 6 years or less. Of the 2016 graduating class, 19% were enrolled in graduate school within 6 months of graduation.

SERVICES: Counseling and information services are available, as is tutoring in some subjects, such as English, math, biology, chemistry, physical science, statistics, and social science. There is remedial math, reading, and writing. **Library/Resources:** The library contains 193,780 volumes, 138,950 microform items, 1,306 audio/video tapes/CDs/DVDs, and subscribes to 15,357 periodicals, including electronic. Computerized library services include interlibrary loans, database searching, and Internet access. Special learning facilities include a radio station, a writing center, math labs, a tutorial center, Praxis Lab, Kinesiotherapy Clinic, academic success, and supplemental instruction. **Physically Challenged Students:** Facilities include wheelchair ramps, elevators, special parking, specially equipped restrooms, and lowered drinking fountains. **Special:** There are 4 national honor societies and a freshman honors program. **Visiting:** There are regularly scheduled orientations for prospective students, including an introduction to campus services, resources and the expectations of collegiate life at Shaw University, information sessions, social activities, academic advising, and registration. There are guides for informal visits and visitors may sit in on classes. To schedule a visit, contact Ashley Conner at ashley.conner@shawu.edu. **Campus Safety and Security:** Measures include 24-hour foot and vehicle patrol, an emergency notification system, self-defense education, and security escort services. There are lighted pathways/sidewalks, controlled access to dorms/residences, and 24-hour electronic surveillance.

REQUIREMENTS: The SAT or ACT is required. Applicants must be graduates of an accredited secondary school or have a GED certificate. They should have completed 3 units of English, 2 each of math, natural science, and social science; and 9 of academic electives. Electives should be in English, foreign languages, mathematics, natural sciences, or social sciences. Admission to the Teacher Education Program follows separate guidelines. AP and CLEP credits are accepted. To graduate (in most majors), students must earn 120 credits and maintain a minimum GPA of 2.0. The general core curriculum includes a total of 37-50 credits in college orientation, English, math, ethics, humanities, natural sciences, and social sciences. **Procedure:** Freshmen are admitted to all sessions. Entrance exams should be taken prior to enrollment. There are deferred admissions and rolling admissions plans. Applications should be filed by July 30 for fall entry; November 30 for spring entry. The fall 2017 application fee was $25. Applications are accepted online. **Transfer Students:** 89 transfer students enrolled in 2016-2017. Applicants must submit official transcripts from all colleges attended. Transfer credit is given only for coursework of grade C or better completed at an accredited degree-granting institution. 30 of 120 credits required for the bachelor's degree must be completed at Shaw. **International Students:** There are 38 international students enrolled. They must also take the SAT or ACT.

ADMISSIONS: 49% of the 2017-2018 applicants were accepted. The ACT scores were 6% below 12, 82% between 12 and 17, 11% between 18 and 23, and 1% between 24 and 29. 5% of the current freshmen were in the top fifth of their class; 11% were in the top two fifths. **Admissions Contact:** Stacey Sowell, Director of Admissions and Recruitment. Email: *admissions@shawu.edu* Web: *www.shawu.edu*

FINANCIAL AID: The FAFSA code is 002962. The deadline for filing freshman financial aid applications for fall entry is open.

ST. ANDREWS UNIVERSITY *(The complete profile is made available exclusively on our website, www.barronspac.com)*

UNIVERSITY OF MOUNT OLIVE E-3

www.umo.edu

Mount Olive, NC 28365	**(919) 658-2502** **(800) 653-0854**
Fax: (919) 658-7180	**Email: admissions@umo.edu**
Full-time: 816 men, 1660 women	**Faculty:** 85
Part-time: 227 men, 413 women	**Ph.D.s:** 39%
Graduate: n/av	**Student/Faculty:** 29 to 1
Year: semesters, summer session	**Tuition:** $13,126
Room & Board: $5300	**Freshman Class:** 975 applied, 654 accepted, 404 enrolled
SAT or ACT: required	**CEEB CODE:** 5435
Application Deadline: n/av	**COMPETITIVE**

University of Mount Olive, founded in 1951, is a private liberal arts institution affiliated with the Original Free Will Baptist Church. There is 1 undergraduate school. The 123-acre campus is in a small town 65 miles southeast of Raleigh. Including any residence halls, there are 16 buildings.

STUDENT LIFE: 92% of undergraduates are from North Carolina. Others are from 21 states, 7 foreign countries, and Canada. 93% are from public schools. 55% are White; 32% African American; 1% Asian American. **Female To Male Ratio:** 2.0:1. The average age of freshmen is 22; all undergraduates, 33. 36% do not continue beyond their first year. **Housing:** 306 students can be accommodated in college housing, which includes dorms and on-campus apartments. On-campus housing is guaranteed for the freshman year only. 90% of students commute. Alcohol is not permitted. All students may keep cars.

FACULTY/CLASSROOMS: 58% of faculty are male; 42% are female. All teach undergraduates, 14% do research, and 86% do both. No introductory courses are taught by graduate students.

PROGRAMS OF STUDY: Mount Olive confers B.A., B.S., and B.Applied Science. degrees. Associate degrees are also awarded. Bachelor's degrees are awarded in BIOLOGICAL SCIENCE (biology/biological science), BUSINESS (accounting, business administration and management, human resources, and recreation and leisure services), COMMUNICATIONS AND THE ARTS (art, communications, English, fine arts, and music), COMPUTER AND PHYSICAL SCIENCE (computer management, information sciences and systems, and mathematics), EDUCATION (middle school education and secondary education), ENGINEERING AND ENVIRONMENTAL DESIGN (environmental science), SOCIAL SCIENCE (criminal justice, history, human services, liberal arts/general studies, ministries, psychology, and religion). Business, accounting, and psychology are the strongest academically. Business, psychology, and recreation have the largest enrollments.

ACTIVITIES: There are no fraternities or sororities. There are 20 groups on campus, including art, cheerleading, choir, chorale, chorus, drama, honors, international, literary magazine, newspaper, orchestra, pep band, photography, political, professional, religious, and student government. Popular campus events include Founders Day, Pickle Classic Weekend, and the North Carolina Pickle Festival. **Sports:** There are 6 intercollegiate sports for men and 6 for women, and 10 intramural sports for men and 8 for women. Facilities include a gym, racquetball and tennis courts, a track, wrestling/gymnastics and weight rooms, an athletic field, outdoor basketball areas, a student center, and baseball, softball, and soccer fields. **Graduates:** From July 1, 2016 to June 30, 2017, 629 bachelor's degrees were awarded. The most popular majors were business (52%), criminal justice administration (15%), and education (12%).

SERVICES: Counseling and information services are available, as is tutoring in most subjects, such as math, English, and science. There is remedial math and reading. **Library/Resources:** The library contains 77,545 volumes, 48,735 microform items, 2,005 audio/video tapes/CDs/DVDs, and subscribes to 5,979 periodicals, including electronic. Computerized library services include interlibrary loans and database searching. Special learning facilities include an art gallery, and a church archives collection. **Physically Challenged Students:** 90% of the campus is accessible. Facilities include wheelchair ramps, elevators, special parking, specially equipped restrooms, and special class scheduling. **Special:** Mount Olive offers co-op programs and internships in all majors, work-study, B.A.-B.S. degrees, dual majors, and accelerated degree programs in business, accounting, and criminal justice administration. Cross-registration with James Sprunt Community College and Wayne Community College, study abroad, and credit for life, military, and work experience are also possible. Professional degree completion programs run continuously for 55 to 57 weeks. There is 1 national honor society and a freshman honors program. **Visiting:** There are regularly scheduled orientations for prospective students, consisting of 2 days of advising, sports, and entertainment. There are guides for informal visits and visitors may sit in on classes. To schedule a visit, contact the Admissions Office. **Campus Safety and Security:** There are lighted pathways/sidewalks and evening and weekend patrols.

REQUIREMENTS: A satisfactory minimum SAT composite score or ACT score of 16 is recommended. Applicants must be graduates of an accredited secondary school or have a GED certificate. They must have completed 4 units of English, 3 units each of math and science, and 2 units of history. An essay and interview are suggested. AP and CLEP credits are accepted. To graduate, students must have completed a total of 126 credit hours, with a minimum 2.0 overall GPA in 63 credit hours for the B.A. or B.S. or in 53 hours for the B.Applied Science. Distribution requirements include 30 to 36 hours in humanities, 18 in science/math/ and 12 in social science. Specific coursework includes 6 hours of religion, 4 of physical education, and 3 hours of computer competency. **Procedure:** Freshmen are admitted to all sessions. Entrance exams should be taken in the junior or senior year. There are deferred admissions and rolling admissions plans. Application deadlines are open. The fall 2017 application fee was $20. Notification is sent on a rolling basis. Applications are accepted online. **Transfer Students:** 548 transfer students enrolled in 2016-2017. Applicants must have a minimum GPA of 2.0 and submit an official transcript from the previous institution. An interview may be required. 32 of 126 credits required for the bachelor's degree must be completed at Mount Olive. **International Students:** They must take the TOEFL with a minimum score of 513 on the paper-based TOEFL (PBT) or 65 on the Internet-based version (iBT). They must also take the SAT or ACT.

ADMISSIONS: 67% of the 2017-2018 applicants were accepted. **Admissions Contact:** Tim Woodard, Director of Admissions. Email: *admissions@umo.edu* Web: *www.umo.edu*

FINANCIAL AID: In 2017-2018, 83% of all full-time freshmen received some form of financial aid. 89% of all full-time freshmen received need-based aid. The average freshman award was $8,679. Need-based scholarships or need-based grants averaged $7,351; need-based self-help aid (loans and jobs) averaged $2,210; non-need-based athletic scholarships averaged $3,689; and other non-need-based awards and non-need-based scholarships averaged $4,976. The average financial indebtedness of the 2017 graduate was $12,450. The college's own financial statement is required. The FAFSA code is 002949. The priority date for freshman financial aid applications for fall entry is March 15.

UNIVERSITY OF NORTH CAROLINA AT ASHEVILLE B-2

www.unca.edu

Asheville, NC 28804	**(828) 251-6481** **(800) 531-9842**
Fax: (828) 251-6482	**Email: admissions@unca.edu**
Full-time: 1401 men, 1884 women	**Faculty:** 326; IIB, +$
Part-time: 252 men, 289 women	**Ph.D.s:** 89%
Graduate: 14 men, 12 women	**Student/Faculty:** 15 to 1
Year: semesters, summer session	**Tuition:** $7145 ($23,868)
Room & Board: $9106	**Freshman Class:** 3358 applied, 2730 accepted, 648 enrolled
SAT CR/M/W: 580/558/544 **ACT:** 26	**CEEB CODE:** 5013
Application Deadline: February 15	**VERY COMPETITIVE+**

University of North Carolina at Asheville is a designated public liberal arts university in the University of North Carolina system. There is 1 undergraduate school and 1 graduate school. In addition to regional accreditation, UNC-Asheville has baccalaureate program accreditation with AACSB and CAEP. The 365-acre campus is in an urban area approximately 1 mile north of downtown Asheville. Including any residence halls, there are 34 buildings.

STUDENT LIFE: 89% of undergraduates are from North Carolina. Others are from 42 states and 20 foreign countries. 88% are from public schools. 78% are White; 6% Hispanic; 5% African American; 3% two or more races; 3% race unknown; 2% Asian American; 1% American Indian/Alaska Native; 1% Foreign. **Female To Male Ratio:** 1.4:1. The average age of freshmen is 18; all undergraduates, 21. 25% do not continue beyond their first year; 62% remain to graduate. **Housing:** 1347 students can be accommodated in college housing, which includes dorms, quiet dorms, and wellness housing. On-campus housing is guaranteed for the freshman year only, and is available on a first-come, first-served basis. 62% of students commute. Some may keep cars.

FACULTY/CLASSROOMS: 51% of faculty are male; 49% are female. All teach undergraduates and all do research. No introductory courses are taught by graduate students. The average class size in an introductory lecture is 21; in a laboratory is 18; and in a regular course is 18.

PROGRAMS OF STUDY: UNC-Asheville confers B.A., B.S., and B.F.A. degrees. Master's degrees are also awarded. Bachelor's degrees are awarded in BIOLOGICAL SCIENCE (biology/biological science), BUSINESS (accounting and business administration and management), COMMUNICATIONS AND THE ARTS (art, classics, communications, dramatic arts, English, fine arts, French, German, jazz, literature, multimedia, music, music technology, and Spanish), COMPUTER AND PHYSICAL SCIENCE (atmospheric sciences and meteorology, chemistry, computer science, mathematics, and physics), ENGINEERING AND ENVIRONMENTAL DESIGN (engineering, engineering management, environmental science, and industrial administration/management), HEALTH PROFESSIONS (health promotion), SOCIAL SCIENCE (anthropology, economics, history, history and political science, liberal arts/general studies, philosophy, political science/government, psychology, religion, sociology, and women's studies). Psychology, biology, and management have the largest enrollments.

ACTIVITIES: 3% of men belong to 2 national fraternities; 3% of women belong to 2 national sororities. There are 85 groups on campus, including art, band, cheerleading, choir, chorus, communications, computers, dance, departmental clubs, drama, environmental, ethnic, honors, international, jazz band, LGBT, literary magazine, newspaper, pep band, political, professional, religious, social, social service, and student government. Popular campus events include Undergraduate Research Symposium, Arts Festival, and Rockypalooza. **Sports:** There are 7 intercollegiate sports for men and 8 for women, and 14 intramural sports for men and 14 for women. Facilities include a sports and health complex with weight/cardio room, basketball courts, volleyball and racquetball courts, dance and group exercise studios, an indoor swimming pool, basketball arena, indoor and outdoor tracks, soccer and baseball fields, disc golf course, mountain biking, paddling, and hiking/walking trails. **Graduates:** From July 1, 2016 to June 30, 2017, 767 bachelor's degrees were awarded. The most popular majors were psychology (11%), environmental Studies (7%), and English (6%). In an average class, 2% graduate in 3 years or less, 45% graduate in 4 years or less, 60% graduate in 5 years or less, and 62% graduate in 6 years or less. Of the 2016 graduating class, 14% were enrolled in graduate school within 6 months of graduation.

SERVICES: Counseling and information services are available, as is tutoring in most subjects. There is a reader service for the blind. **Library/Resources:** The library contains 821,290 volumes, 759 microform items, and 29,379 audio/video tapes/CDs/DVDs, and subscribes to 48,935 periodicals including electronic. Computerized library services include interlibrary loans, database searching, Internet access, and Wi-Fi capability. Special learning facilities include an art gallery, Bob Moog Electric Music Studio, Center for Health and Wellness, including BodPod, Balance Lab, Biofeedback Lab, Meditation Space, Lookout Observatory for astronomical research, and Botanical Gardens. **Physically Challenged Students:** 95% of the campus is accessible. Facilities include wheelchair ramps, elevators, special parking, specially equipped restrooms, special class scheduling, lowered drinking fountains, lowered telephones, and special housing. **Special:** UNC Asheville participates in a consortium with Warren Wilson College and Mars Hill University, and there is cross-registration with a number of North Carolina universities and colleges. Study-abroad programs are available in over 50 countries. The school offers internships, dual majors, student-designed interdisciplinary majors, and a 2-2 engineering degree and 3-1 joint engineering degree with North Carolina State University. Nondegree study is available. There are 4 national honor societies, a freshman honors program, and 1 departmental honors program. **Visiting:** There are regularly scheduled orientations for prospective students, including meetings with admissions counselors, faculty, or other departments, information session for students and families, and a campus tour. Preregistration is prior to fall enrollment during the summer months. There are guides for informal visits; visitors may sit in on classes and stay overnight. To schedule a visit, contact Nate Corbitt at (828) 350-4553. **Campus Safety and Security:** Measures include 24-hour foot and vehicle patrol, an emergency notification system, self-defense education, and security escort services. There are shuttle buses, emergency telephones, lighted pathways/sidewalks, controlled access to dorms/residences, and security cameras.

REQUIREMENTS: The SAT or ACT is required. Graduation from an accredited secondary school is required. UNC-Asheville requires a minimum of 16 high school academic units, including 4 units each of English, and math (algebra I, geometry, algebra II, and a class beyond algebra II), 3 units in science (biology, physical science, and a lab course), and 2 units of social studies/history, and foreign language which needs to be a sequence (Spanish I and II, French I and II, etc.). Applicants are evaluated primarily on their academic achievement record, extracurricular activities that support academic achievement, and SAT or ACT scores. A GPA of 2.5 is required. AP and CLEP credits are accepted. Important factors in the admissions decision are advanced placement or honors courses, leadership record, parents or siblings attended the school, evidence of special talent, personality/intangible qualities, extracurricular activities record, recommendations by alumni, geographical diversity, and recommendations by school officials. To graduate, students must complete a minimum of 120 credit hours, including at least 27 hours in the major and a senior capstone experience. The core curriculum requires a 3-4 hour liberal studies introductory colloquium; 12 hours of humanities; 3-4 hours of interdisciplinary arts; a minimum of 7 hours of natural science including lab; 3-4 hours of social science; up to 8 hours of foreign language; 4 hours of math; 4 hours of academic writing; and a 4-hour liberal studies senior colloquium. In addition, students are required to do intensive coursework in diversity and demonstrate competency in writing and information literacy. These courses can be taken in the major, in general education, or as electives, and need not add credit hours to a student's program. **Procedure:** Freshmen are admitted in the fall and spring. Entrance exams should be taken at the end of the junior year or the beginning of the senior year. There are early admissions, deferred admissions, and rolling admissions plans. Early decision applications should be filed by November 15; regular applications, by February 15 for fall entry; and October 15 for spring entry. The fall 2017 application fee was $60. Notification of early decision is sent December 15; regular decision, on a rolling basis. Applications are accepted online. **Transfer Students:** 355 transfer students enrolled in 2016-2017. Applicants under 24 years of age or with fewer than 24 semester or 36 quarter credit hours must submit high school transcripts and SAT or ACT scores. UNC-Ashville does not need SAT scores if transferring in unless a student has not received grades from present institutions (a student's first semester at school and submission of an application in October for the spring semester). If there are no grades to submit UNC-Ashville looks at high school record and test scores. 30 of 120 credits required for the bachelor's degree must be completed at UNC-Asheville. **International Students:** There are 46 international students enrolled. They must take the TOEFL with a minimum score of 550 on the paper-based TOEFL (PBT) or 79 on the Internet-based version (iBT). They must also take the SAT or ACT.

ADMISSIONS: 78% of the 2017-2018 applicants were accepted. The SAT scores for the 2017-2018 freshman class were: Critical Reading-- 16% below 500, 41% between 500 and 599, 34% between 600 and 699, and 8% between 700 and 800. Math-- 20% below 500, 48% between 500 and 599, 29% between 600 and 699, and 3% between 700 and 800. Writing-- 29% below 500, 47% between 500 and 599, 21% between 600 and 699, and 4% between 700 and 800. The ACT scores were 31% between 18 and 23, 54% between 24 and 29, and 14% above 30. 45% of the current freshmen were in the top fifth of their class; 80% were in the top two fifths. **Admissions Contact:** Pat McClellan, Director of Admissions and Financial Aid. Email: *admissions@unca.edu* Web: *www.unca.edu*

FINANCIAL AID: In 2017-2018, 77% of all full-time freshmen received some form of financial aid. 60% of all full-time freshmen received need-based aid. The average freshman award was $11,146. Need-based scholarships or need-based grants averaged $7,295 ($32,981 maximum); need-based self-help aid (loans and jobs) averaged $4,668 ($18,500 maximum); non-need-based athletic scholarships averaged $12,449 ($33,060 maximum); and other non-need-based awards and non-need-based scholarships averaged $3,817 ($17,500 maximum). 27% of undergraduate students work part-time. The average financial indebtedness of the 2017 graduate was $22,026. The FAFSA code is 002907. The priority date for freshman financial aid applications for fall entry is March 1.

UNIVERSITY OF NORTH CAROLINA AT CHAPEL HILL D-2

www.unc.edu

Chapel Hill, NC 27599 (919) 962-3621

Fax: (919) 962-3045 Email: unchelp@admissions.unc.edu

Full-time: 7467 men, 10,811 women	**Faculty:** 1667; I, +$
Part-time: 297 men, 262 women	**Ph.D.s:** 85%
Graduate: 4973 men, 6076 women	**Student/Faculty:** 13 to 1
Year: semesters, summer session	**Tuition:** $9005 ($34,588)
Room & Board: $11,556	**Freshman Class:** 39754 applied, 9709 accepted, 4356 enrolled
SAT EBR-W/M: 680/670 **ACT:** 30	**CEEB CODE:** 5816
Application Deadline: January 15	**MOST COMPETITIVE**

University of North Carolina at Chapel Hill offers 77 bachelors, 110 masters, 65 doctorate, and 7 professional degree programs through 14 schools and the college of arts and sciences. In addition to regional accreditation, UNC-Chapel Hill has baccalaureate program accreditation with AACSB, ACEJMC, ACPE, ADA, APTA, CSWE, CAEP, NLN, CCNE, CEPA, and URTA. The 729-acre campus is in a suburban area 25 miles west of Raleigh. Including any residence halls, there are 683 buildings.

STUDENT LIFE: 84% of undergraduates are from North Carolina. Others are from 48 states, 93 foreign countries, and Canada. 82% are from public schools. 8% are African American; 8% Hispanic; 62% White; 4% two or more races; 4% race unknown; 3% Foreign; 11% Asian American. **Female To Male Ratio:** 1.3:1. The average age of freshmen is 18; all undergraduates, 20. 3% do not continue beyond their first year; 91% remain to graduate. **Housing:** 10113 students can be accommodated in college housing, which includes single sex dorms, coed dorms, married student dorms, on-campus apartments, and off-campus apartments. In addition, there are honors houses, language/international houses, special-interest houses, fraternity houses, sorority houses, and substance-free housing. On-campus housing is guaranteed for the freshman year only and is available on a lottery system for upperclassmen. 51% of students live on campus. Upperclassmen may keep cars.

FACULTY/CLASSROOMS: 55% of faculty are male; 45% are female. 56% teach undergraduates, 6% do research, and 2% do both. Graduate students teach 39% of introductory courses. The average class size in an introductory lecture is 44; in a laboratory is 20; and in a regular course is 35.

PROGRAMS OF STUDY: UNC-Chapel Hill confers B.A.Ed., B.A., B.S., B.F.A., B.S.B.A., B.S.N., B.S.Ph., B.Mus., and B.S.I.S. degrees. Master's and doctoral degrees are also awarded. Bachelor's degrees are awarded in AGRICULTURE (environmental studies), BIOLOGICAL SCIENCE (biology/biological science, biometrics and biostatistics, and nutrition), BUSINESS (business administration and management and management science), COMMUNICATIONS AND THE ARTS (art history and appreciation, classics, communications, comparative literature, dramatic arts, English, German, journalism, linguistics, music, music performance, romance languages and literature, and studio art), COMPUTER AND PHYSICAL SCIENCE (applied mathematics, applied science, chemistry, computer science, geology, information sciences and systems, mathematics, and physics), EDUCATION (elementary education and middle school education), ENGINEERING AND ENVIRONMENTAL DESIGN (biomedical engineering and environmental science), HEALTH PROFESSIONS (clinical science, dental hygiene, environmental health science, exercise science, health care administration, nursing, and radiological science), SOCIAL SCIENCE (African American studies, American studies, anthropology, archeology, Asian/Oriental studies, child care/child and family studies, economics, European studies, geography, history, interdisciplinary studies, international studies, Latin American studies, peace studies, philosophy, political science/government, psychology, public affairs, religion, Russian and Slavic studies, sociology, and women and gender studies). Business, chemistry, and media/journalism are the strongest academically. Biology, psychology, and economics have the largest enrollments.

ACTIVITIES: 18% of men belong to 34 national fraternities; 18% of women belong to 24 national sororities. There are 796 groups on campus, including public/community service, panhellenic council, academic, art, band, cheerleading, chess, choir, chorale, chorus, computers, dance, debate, drama, drill team, environmental, ethnic, film, forensics, honors, international, jazz band, LGBT, literary magazine, marching band, musical theater, newspaper, opera, orchestra, pep band, photography, political, professional, radio and TV, religious, social, social service, student government, symphony, and yearbook. Popular campus events include FallFest, Late Night with Roy, and Homecoming. **Sports:** There are 11 intercollegiate sports for men and 17 for women, and 21 intramural sports for men and 21 for women. Facilities include a football stadium, swimming pools, a sports and student activities center, tennis courts, lacrosse and soccer fields, a golf course, a boathouse, gym facilities, softball fields, and a student recreation center with aerobics, weights, and wellness programs. **Graduates:** From July 1, 2016 to June 30, 2017, 4557 bachelor's degrees were awarded. The most popular majors were journalism and mass communication (11%), biology (9%), and psychology (8%). In an average class, 2% graduate in 3 years or less, 84% graduate in 4 years or less, 90% graduate in 5 years or less, and 91% graduate in 6 years or less. Of the 2016 graduating class, 22% were enrolled in graduate school within 6 months of graduation, and 72% were employed.

SERVICES: Counseling and information services are available, as is tutoring in most subjects. There is a reader service for the blind. **Library/Resources:** The library contains 9.3 million volumes, 5.3 million microform items, 588,085 audio/video tapes/CDs/DVDs, and subscribes to 180,757 periodicals, including electronic. Computerized library services include interlibrary loans, database searching, Internet access, and Wi-Fi capability. Special learning facilities include an art gallery, planetarium, radio station, TV station, a theater, and Botanical Garden. **Physically Challenged Students:** 97% of the campus is accessible. Facilities include wheelchair ramps, elevators, special parking, specially equipped restrooms, special class scheduling, lowered drinking fountains, and special housing. **Special:** Students may participate in joint programs with Duke University, North Carolina State University, and the National University of Singapore (NUS). UNC-Chapel Hill also has undergraduate programs in business, journalism/mass communications, information science, and nursing through its professional schools. UNC-Chapel Hill has a strong Creative Writing Program and an innovative entrepreneurship minor that is open to all students regardless of major. Chapel Hill's Program in Philosophy, Politics and Economics is internationally recognized. The University offers 12 dual bachelor-graduate degree programs in areas such as computer science, statistics and analytics, linguistics, environmental science and information science, and environmental studies and public administration. Students also have the opportunity to develop an interdisciplinary major. Chapel Hills new course-based undergraduate research programs gives students research experience in departments of the College of Arts and Sciences. In addition, Chapel Hill offers special opportunities for undergraduates to work with top scholars in First Year Seminars, Honors Carolina Seminars, and Undergraduate Research, which are ranked among the best programs of their kind in the nation. There are 30 national honor societies, Phi Beta Kappa, a freshman honors program, and 48 departmental honors programs. **Visiting:** There are regularly scheduled orientations for prospective students, including campus tours and information sessions, offered twice each weekday. Visitors may sit in on classes. To schedule a visit, contact the Office of Undergraduate Admissions. **Campus Safety and Security:** Measures include 24-hour foot and vehicle patrol, an emergency notification system, self-defense education, and security escort services. There are shuttle buses, emergency telephones, lighted pathways/sidewalks, controlled access to dorms/residences, crime prevention (e.g. a classes/initiatives addressing date rape, violence, larceny reduction), a campus-wide emergency alert system, and cellphone app/GPS-based security options.

REQUIREMENTS: The SAT or ACT is required. Applicants should present a minimum of 16 units of high school coursework within the 5 traditional academic areas (literature, math, physical and biological sciences, social sciences, and foreign languages), including 4 units each of English, college preparatory mathematics (2 algebra, 1 geometry, and a higher level math course for which algebra II is a prerequisite), 3 units in science, (including at least 1 unit in life or biological science and at least 1 in a physical science, and at least 1 lab course) and 2 units each of social science, (including United States history), and a single foreign language. AP credits are accepted. To graduate, students must complete 120 credits (more for some B.S. degrees) with a 2.0 GPA. The general education requirements fall under 3 categories: Foundations, Approaches, and Connections. B.A. degree candidates must satisfy a supplemental education requirement by completing a second major or a minor, in addition to a student's major requirements-9 credit hours outside the home department of the major, or by completing a concentration outside a professional school as part of the degree requirements for graduating from that school. **Procedure:** Freshmen are admitted in the fall. Entrance exams should be taken in the junior or senior year. There are early admissions and deferred admissions plans. Early decision applications should be filed by October 15; regular applications, by January 15 for fall entry. The fall 2017 application fee was $80. Notification of early decision is sent January 31; regular decision, March 31. 2339 applicants were on the 2017 waiting list; 35 were admitted. Applications are accepted on-line. **Transfer Students:** 789 transfer students enrolled in 2016-2017. Sophomore transfers need at least 30 credit hours and a minimum GPA of 2.0; junior transfers need at least 60 credit hours and a minimum GPA of 2.0. High school diploma or equivalent, meeting minimum course requirements, also required. 45 of 120 credits required for the bachelor's degree must be completed at UNC-Chapel Hill. **International Students:** There are 509 international students enrolled. They must take the TOEFL with a minimum score of 100 on the Internet-based version (iBT). Students must take the IELTS. They must also take the SAT or ACT.

ADMISSIONS: 24% of the 2017-2018 applicants were accepted. The SAT scores for the 2017-2018 freshman class were: Math-- 1% below 500, 14% between 500 and 599, 50% between 600 and 699, and 35% between 700 and 800. Evidence-Based Reading/Writing-- 1% below 500, 9% between 500 and 599, 51% between 600 and 699, and 39% between 700 and 800. The ACT scores were 6% between 18 and 23, 39% between 24 and 29, and 55% above 30. 94% of the current freshmen were in the top fifth of their class; 99% were in the top two fifths. 256 freshmen graduated first in their class. **Admissions Contact:** Leslie Guier, Director for Admissions. Email: *unchelp@admissions.unc.edu* Web: *www.unc.edu*

FINANCIAL AID: In 2017-2018, 67% of all full-time freshmen received some form of financial aid. 39% of all full-time freshmen received need-based aid. The average freshman award was $16,234. Need-based scholarships or need-based grants averaged $16,184 ($58,386 maximum); need-based self-help aid (loans and jobs) averaged $3,902 ($13,229 maximum); non-need-based athletic scholarships averaged $29,803 ($66,693 maximum); other non-need-based awards and non-need-based scholarships averaged $6,102 ($51,222 maximum); and $6,052 from other forms of aid. 12% of undergraduate students work part-time. The average financial indebtedness of the 2017 graduate was $22,214. UNC-Chapel Hill is a member of CSS. The CSS/Profile is required. The FAFSA code is 002974. The priority date for freshman financial aid applications for fall entry is March 1.

UNIVERSITY OF NORTH CAROLINA AT CHARLOTTE — C-3

www.uncc.edu

Charlotte, NC 28223	**(704) 687-5507**
Fax: (704) 687-6483	**Email:** admissions@uncc.edu
Full-time: 11060 men, 9537 women	**Faculty:** 891
Part-time: 1672 men, 1645 women	**Ph.D.s:** 84%
Graduate: 2371 men, 3032 women	**Student/Faculty:** 19 to 1
Year: semesters, summer session	**Tuition:** $7023 ($20,457)
Room & Board: $10,780	**Freshman Class:** 16743 applied, 11061 accepted, 3373 enrolled
SAT EBR-W/M: 595/597 **ACT:** 24	**CEEB CODE:** 5105
Application Deadline: June 1	**VERY COMPETITIVE**

University of North Carolina at Charlotte, founded in 1946, is the largest institution of higher education in the Charlotte region and the fourth largest of the 16 institutions within the University of North Carolina system. UNC-Charlotte offers 7 colleges with 79 programs leading to Bachelor's degrees, 65 programs leading to Master's degrees and 21 programs leading to Doctoral degrees. As an urban research university, we are frequently recognized for our contributions to higher education and to the region. In addition to regional accreditation, UNC-Charlotte has baccalaureate program accreditation with AACSB, ABET, CSWE, NAAB, NASM, CAEP, NASD, CACREP, CAAHEP, CCNE, CEPH, CAHME, COA, CAATE, PRSA, NASPAA, and APA. The 1000-acre campus is in a suburban area 8 miles north of uptown Charlotte, North Carolina.

STUDENT LIFE: 96% of undergraduates are from North Carolina. Others are from 44 states, 106 foreign countries, and Canada. 9% are Hispanic; 7% Foreign; 6% Asian American; 56% White; 4% two or more races; 2% race unknown; 16% African American. **Male To Female Ratio:** 1.1:1. The average age of freshmen is 18; all undergraduates, 22. 17% do not continue beyond their first year; 83% remain to graduate. **Housing:** 6127 students can be accommodated in college housing, which includes coed dorms and on-campus apartments. In addition, there are honors houses, language/international houses, special-interest houses, fraternity houses, sorority houses, freshman experience housing, learning communities, nontraditional students, transfer students, and graduate student housing. On-campus housing is available on a first-come, first-served basis, and is available on a lottery system for upperclassmen. 76% of students commute. All students may keep cars.

FACULTY/CLASSROOMS: 49% of faculty are male; 51% are female. 98% teach undergraduates. Graduate students teach 5% of introductory courses. The average class size in an introductory lecture is 44 and in a laboratory is 27.

PROGRAMS OF STUDY: UNC-Charlotte confers B.A., B.S., B.Arch., B.F.A., B.M., B.S.B.A, B.S.C.E., B.S.Cp.E., B.S.C.M., B.S.E.E., B.S.S.E., B.S.E.T., B.S.P.H. B.S.R.T., B.S.M.E., B.S.N. and B.S.W. degrees. Master's and doctoral degrees are also awarded. Bachelor's degrees are awarded in BIOLOGICAL SCIENCE (biology/biological science), BUSINESS (accounting, banking and finance, business administration and management, business economics, finance, international business management, management information systems, marketing, marketing/retailing/merchandising, real estate, and supply chain management), COMMUNICATIONS AND THE ARTS (Africana studies, art, art history and appreciation, communications, dance, English, fine arts, French, German, music, music performance, Spanish, and theatre arts), COMPUTER AND PHYSICAL SCIENCE (atmospheric sciences and meteorology, chemistry, computer science, earth science, geology, mathematics, physics, and software engineering), EDUCATION (athletic training, elementary education, English education, foreign languages education, mathematics education, middle school education, social studies education, and special education), ENGINEERING AND ENVIRONMENTAL DESIGN (architecture, civil engineering, civil engineering technology, computer engineering, construction management, electrical/electronics engineering, electrical/electronics engineering technology, engineering technology, industrial administration/management, mechanical engineering, mechanical engineering technology, and systems engineering), HEALTH PROFESSIONS (exercise science, medical technology, nursing, public health, and respiratory therapy), SOCIAL SCIENCE (anthropology, child care/child and family studies, child psychology/development, criminal justice, economics, fire control and safety technology, geography, history, international studies, Japanese studies, Latin American studies, liberal arts/general studies, philosophy, physical fitness/movement, political science/government, psychology, religious studies, social work, and sociology). Computer science, psychology, and mechanical engineering have the largest enrollments.

ACTIVITIES: 7% of men belong to 22 national fraternities; 11% of women belong to 16 national sororities. Groups on campus include art, cheerleading, chess, choir, chorale, chorus, communications, computers, dance, debate, drama, environmental, ethnic, film, honors, international, jazz band, LGBT, literary magazine, marching band, musical theater, newspaper, opera, pep band, photography, political, professional, radio and TV, religious, social, social service, and student government. Popular campus events include Week of Welcome, Greek Week, International Festival, and Homecoming. **Sports:** There are 8 intercollegiate sports for men and women, and 8 intramural sports for men and women. Facilities include a gym for basketball, racquetball, squash courts, and a Olympic-size swimming pool. The Student Activity Center contains a jogging track, recreational courts, a climbing wall, a weight room, a group fitness room, a training center and an event arena. There are outdoor recreational fields along with tennis, sand volleyball, basketball courts, fitness/biking trails, and ropes courses. **Graduates:** From July 1, 2016 to June 30, 2017, 5086 bachelor's degrees were awarded. The most popular majors were business/marketing (19%), engineering (9%), and health professions and related programs (8%). In an average class, 29% graduate in 4 years or less, 21% graduate in 5 years or less, and 54% graduate in 6 years or less.

SERVICES: Counseling and information services are available, as is tutoring in some subjects. There is a reader service for the blind. **Library/Resources:** The library contains 18,000 audio/video tapes/CDs/DVDs, and subscribes to 113,800 periodicals, including electronic. Computerized library services include interlibrary loans, database searching, Internet access, and Wi-Fi capability. Special learning facilities include an art gallery, a radio station, TV station, Motorsports and Automotive Research Center, Charlotte Visualization Center, eBusiness Technology Institute, Center for Applied Geographic Information Science, Center for Precision Metrology, Center for Optoelectronics and Optical Communications, Bioinformatics Research Center, IDEAS Center, Center for Biomedical Engineering Systems, Center for Global Public Relations, Center for Professional and Applied Ethics, Multicultural Resource Center, UNC-Charlotte Botanical Gardens and McMillan Greenhouse, which includes a tropical rain forest. **Physically Challenged Students:** 90% of the campus is accessible. Facilities include wheelchair ramps, elevators, special parking, specially equipped restrooms, special class scheduling, lowered drinking fountains, lowered telephones, and special housing. The Disability Services Office assists students with all academic and physical accommodations. **Special:** Cross-registration is available through the Charlotte Area Educational Consortium. Also available are cooperative programs in numerous majors and internships of 1 semester arranged with public and private community organizations. There are 27 national honor societies, a freshman honors program, and 20 departmental honors programs. **Visiting:** There are regularly scheduled orientations for prospective students, including tours. There are guides for informal visits; visitors may sit in on classes and stay overnight. To schedule a visit, contact the Undergraduate Admissions Office. **Campus Safety and Security:** Measures include 24-hour foot and vehicle patrol, emergency notification system, self-defense education, and security escort services. There are shuttle buses, emergency telephones, lighted pathways/sidewalks, and controlled access to dorms/residences.

REQUIREMENTS: The SAT or ACT is required. Graduation from an accredited secondary school or the GED is required. The school requires 14 academic credits: 4 years each of English and math, 3 years of science (including 1 of physical science), 2-3 years of foreign language, and 1 year each of social studies, and U.S. history. Seniors should select a challenging academic schedule that includes English, math, science, social studies or history, and foreign language. A portfolio and an interview are required for art and architecture students only. AP and CLEP credits are accepted. Students must complete a minimum of 120 credit hours with an overall minimum GPA of 2.0. Between 30 and 42 hours are required in the major with a minimum GPA of 2.0 in major and minor courses. All students must complete the general education requirements. **Procedure:** Freshmen are admitted in the fall, spring, and summer. Entrance exams should be taken at the end of the junior year or by December of the senior year. There are early admissions and rolling admissions plans. Applications should be filed by June 1 for fall entry. The fall 2017 application fee was $60. Applications are accepted on-line. **Transfer Students:** 2942 transfer students enrolled in 2016-2017. Transfer students must have a minimum GPA of 2.0 on all college courses attempted. Certain majors have limited space and require a higher GPA and/or prerequisites. Applicants with fewer than 24 hours of transferable credit must meet both transfer and freshman admissions requirements. An interview is required only for architecture students. 30 of 120 credits required for the bachelor's degree must be completed at UNC-Charlotte. **International Students:** There are 600 international students enrolled. They must take the TOEFL with a minimum score of 523 on the paper-based TOEFL (PBT) or 70 on the Internet-based version (iBT), or take the MELAB. They must also take the SAT or ACT. Students with a score of 500 or higher on the Evidence Based Reading and Writing section do not have to take TOEFL Exam.

ADMISSIONS: 66% of the 2017-2018 applicants were accepted. The SAT scores for the 2017-2018 freshman class were: Math-- 2% below 500, 50% between 500 and 599, 42% between 600 and 699, and 6% between 700 and 800. Evidence-Based Reading/Writing-- 2% below 500, 52% between 500 and 599, 42% between 600 and 699, and 4% between 700 and 800. The ACT scores were 1% between 12 and 17, 51% between 18 and 23, 43% between 24 and 29, and 5% above 30. **Admissions Contact:** Claire Kirby, Director of Admissions. Email: *admissions@uncc.edu* Web: *www.uncc.edu*

FINANCIAL AID: In 2017-2018, 76% of all full-time freshmen received some form of financial aid. The average freshman award was $13,675. Need-based scholarships or need-based grants averaged $7,026; need-based self-help aid (loans and jobs) averaged $3,729; non-need-based athletic scholarships averaged $19,224; and other non-need-based awards and non-need-based scholarships averaged $8,051. UNC-Charlotte is a member of CSS. The FAFSA code is 002975. The priority date for freshman financial aid applications for fall entry is March 1.

UNIVERSITY OF NORTH CAROLINA AT GREENSBORO D-2

www.uncg.edu

Greensboro, NC 27412 **(336) 334-5243**

Fax: (336) 334-5051
Full-time: 4864 men, 9272 women
Part-time: 728 men, 1575 women
Graduate: 1028 men, 2455 women
Year: semesters, summer session
Room & Board: $8834
SAT or ACT: required
Application Deadline: March 1

Email: admissions@uncg.edu
Faculty: 760; I, --$
Ph.D.s: 79%
Student/Faculty: 18 to 1
Tuition: $7164 ($22,410)
Freshman Class: n/av
CEEB CODE: 5913
COMPETITIVE

University of North Carolina at Greensboro, founded in 1891, is a publicly funded liberal arts institution in the University of North Carolina system. There are 7 undergraduate schools and 8 graduate schools. In addition to regional accreditation, UNC-Greensboro has baccalaureate program accreditation with AACSB, ABET, ADA, CSWE, NASAD, NASM, CAEP, NRPA, NLNAC, NAEYC, and NASD. The 210-acre campus is in an urban area located 1 mile from the center of Greensboro. Including any residence halls, there are 141 buildings.

STUDENT LIFE: 95% of undergraduates are from North Carolina. Others are from 44 states, 38 foreign countries, and Canada. 51% are White; 26% African American; 8% Hispanic; 5% Asian American; 4% two or more races; 3% Foreign; 2% race unknown; 1% American Indian/Alaska Native. **Female To Male Ratio:** 2.0:1. The average age of freshmen is 18; all undergraduates, 23. 24% do not continue beyond their first year; 76% remain to graduate. **Housing:** 5732 students can be accommodated in college housing, which includes gender neutral dorms, on-campus apartments, and off-campus apartments. In addition, there are language/international houses, special-interest houses, and ADA mobility, ADA deaf, and residential college program. On-campus housing is available on a first-come, first-served basis. 68% of students commute. All students may keep cars.

FACULTY/CLASSROOMS: 44% of faculty are male; 56% are female. 94% teach undergraduates, and 26% do both. Graduate students teach 20% of introductory courses. The average class size in an introductory lecture is 35; in a laboratory is 19; and in a regular course is 42.

PROGRAMS OF STUDY: UNC-Greensboro confers B.A., B.F.A., B.M., B.S., B.S.B.T., B.S.M.T., B.S.N., and B.S.W. degrees. Master's and doctoral degrees are also awarded. Bachelor's degrees are awarded in AGRICULTURE (environmental studies), BIOLOGICAL SCIENCE (biochemistry, biotechnology, environmental biology, nutrition, nutritional sciences, and sustainability), BUSINESS (accounting, business administration, entreprenurship, finance, human resources, international business, integrative studies, international business management, management, marketing, marketing/retailing/merchandising, recreational facilities management, retailing, supply chain management, sustainable management, and tourism), COMMUNICATIONS AND THE ARTS (acting, American Sign Language, apparel design, art history, art, arts administration/management, Chinese, classical languages, communication studies, composition, dance, design, dramatic arts, drawing, English, French, German, graphic design and media, information technology, jazz, keyboard - piano concentration, language arts, languages, Latin, film and media studies, music, musical theater, percussion, performing arts, photography, piano performance, printmaking, radio/television technology, Russian, sculpture, Spanish, Spanish language and literature, studio art, studio art ceramics, studio art painting, theatre education, and vocal performance), COMPUTER AND PHYSICAL SCIENCE (chemistry, chemistry secondary education, computer science, earth science, information science, systems and techology, mathematics, physics secondary education, physics, and statistics), EDUCATION (art education, Asian studies, business education, childhood education, classical studies, dance education, drama education, early childhood education, education, education administration, education of the deaf and hearing impaired, elementary education, English secondary education, mathematics education, middle school education, music education, physical ed teacher education, psychology education, science education, and special education), ENGINEERING AND ENVIRONMENTAL DESIGN (interior architecture, interior design, preengineering, and urban planning technology), HEALTH PROFESSIONS (biology, community health work, dental education, human biology, kinesiology, nursing, nutrition and dietetics, pre-health studies, predentistry, premedicine, prenursing, preoccupational therapy, prepharmacy, prephysical therapy, preveterinary science, public health, recreation therapy, and speech pathology/audiology), SOCIAL SCIENCE (African studies, African American studies, anthropology, archeology, Caribbean studies, child care/child and family studies, child psychology/development, classical/ancient civilization, clothing and textiles management/production/services, criminology, early childhood studies, economics, ethics, politics, and social policy, family/consumer resource management, family/consumer studies, geography, geography information science, gerontology, history, human development and family studies, international studies, interpreter for the deaf, Latin American studies, liberal arts/general studies, peace studies, philosophy, philosophy of law, political science/government, prelaw, psychology, public affairs, religious studies, Russian and Slavic studies, social science, social work, sociology, and women and gender studies). Business, nursing, and education are the strongest academically. Business administration, biology, and psychology have the largest enrollments.

ACTIVITIES: 4% of men belong to 12 national fraternities; 4% of women belong to 8 national sororities. There are 295 groups on campus, including art, band, chess, choir, chorale, chorus, communications, dance, drama, environmental, ethnic, film, honors, international, jazz band, LGBT, literary magazine, musical theater, newspaper, opera, orchestra, pep band, photography, political, professional, radio and TV, religious, social, social service, student government, and symphony. Popular campus events include Rawkin' Welcome Week, Homecoming, SpartanFest, WinterFest. Spring Fling, and International Festival. **Sports:** There are 7 intercollegiate sports for men and 8 for women, and 15 intramural sports for men and 15 for women. Facilities include 2 and 3 court multipurpose gyms, group fitness studios, weight/cardio space, a 54 foot climbing wall, a bouldering wall, pools, 2 racquetball courts, a mat room, an indoor running track, a recreation field, an outdoor basketball and volleyball courts, an outdoor recreation track, tennis courts, golf greens, softball, soccer, and baseball. **Graduates:** From July 1, 2016 to June 30, 2017, 3116 bachelor's degrees were awarded. The most popular majors were business administration (7%), psychology (4%), and nursing (4%). In an average class, 28% graduate in 4 years or less, 48% graduate in 5 years or less, and 52% graduate in 6 years or less.

SERVICES: Counseling and information services are available, as is tutoring in most subjects. There is a reader service for the blind. There is also tutoring services that are provided by the Tutoring and Academic Skills Program. **Library/Resources:** The library contains 1.3 million volumes, 324,773 microform items, 355,625 audio/video tapes/CDs/DVDs, and subscribes to 137,858 periodicals, including electronic. Computerized library services include interlibrary loans, database searching, Internet access, and Wi-Fi capability. Special learning facilities include an art gallery and radio station. **Physically Challenged Students:** 98% of the campus is accessible. Facilities include wheelchair ramps, elevators, special parking, specially equipped restrooms, special class scheduling, and special housing. **Special:** Internships and accelerated degree programs can be arranged in all majors. Cross-registration is offered with the Greater Greensboro Consortium. Students may study abroad in more than 40 countries. Dual and student-designed majors are also available. The Residential College, a 2-year program for freshmen and sophomores, offers an interdisciplinary curriculum. Students in this program participate in independent study, community work, and workshops. Students with AP or other preadmission college credit can complete their degree early with Greensboro in 3 accelerated degree program. There are 27 national honor societies, Phi Beta Kappa, a freshman honors program, and 49 departmental honors programs. **Visiting:** There are regularly scheduled orientations for prospective students, Spartan Orientation, and advising and registration programs offered by Student Affairs for new freshmen and new transfer students. There are guides for informal visits. To schedule a visit, contact the Office of Undergraduate Admissions. **Campus Safety and Security:** Measures include 24-hour foot and vehicle patrol, an emergency notification system, self-defense education, and security escort services. There are shuttle buses, emergency telephones, lighted pathways/sidewalks, and controlled access to dorms/residences.

REQUIREMENTS: The SAT is required. The ACT is recommended. Graduation from an accredited secondary school or the GED is required. High school courses must include 4 credits each of English and math, 3 credits of science, 2 of foreign language, 1 each of U.S. history and social studies, and an elective. A portfolio or audition is required of art and music students. AP and CLEP credits are accepted. Important factors in the admissions decision are advanced placement or honors courses, leadership record, and evidence of special talent. In order to graduate, students must complete a minimum of 122 credit hours with a GPA of at least 2.0. Major requirements vary from a minimum of 12 credit hours. The general education curriculum for all students requires at least 36 to 37 credit hours chosen from specified courses in the humanities, math and physical sciences, social and behavioral sciences, and foreign language. Students must take 36 hours at the upper-division level and earn 31 hours of resident credit. **Procedure:** Freshmen are admitted to all sessions. Entrance exams should be taken in June of the junior year or in the fall of the senior year. There is a rolling admissions plan. Applications should be filed by March 1 for fall entry; December 1 for spring entry. The fall 2017 application fee was $65. Notification is sent on a rolling basis. Applications are accepted online. **Transfer Students:** 1870 transfer students enrolled in 2016-2017. Transfer students must have a minimum GPA of 2.0. Students having fewer than 30 semester hours from a regionally accredited institution must meet requirements under both transfer and freshman admissions programs. 31 of 122 credits required for the bachelor's degree must be completed at UNC-Greensboro. **International Students:** There are 565 international students enrolled. They must take the TOEFL with a minimum score of 550 on the paper-based TOEFL (PBT) or 79 on the Internet-based version (iBT), or take either the MELAB, or the IELTS. They must also take the SAT or ACT.

ADMISSIONS: 31% of the current freshmen were in the top fifth of their class; 63% were in the top two fifths. 3 freshmen graduated first in their class. **Admissions Contact:** Christopher Keller, Director, Undergraduate Admissions. Email: *admissions@uncg.edu* Web: *www.uncg.edu*

FINANCIAL AID: In 2017-2018, 99% of all full-time freshmen received some form of financial aid. 92% of all full-time freshmen received need-based aid. The average freshman award was $12,287. Need-based scholarships or need-based grants averaged $7,149 ($19,420 maximum); need-based self-help aid (loans and jobs) averaged $3,494 ($11,800 maximum); non-need-based athletic scholarships averaged $12,637 ($34,564 maximum); and other non-need-based awards and non-need-based scholarships averaged $3,757 ($21,000 maximum). The average financial indebtedness of the 2017 graduate was $26,841. The FAFSA code is 002976. The priority date for freshman financial aid applications for fall entry is March 1.

UNIVERSITY OF NORTH CAROLINA AT PEMBROKE *(The complete profile is made available exclusively on our website, www.barronspac.com)*

UNIVERSITY OF NORTH CAROLINA SCHOOL OF THE ARTS *(The complete profile is made available exclusively on our website, www.barronspac.com)*

UNIVERSITY OF NORTH CAROLINA WILMINGTON — E-4

www.uncw.edu

Wilmington, NC 28403 — (910) 962-3243

Fax: (910) 962-3038	**Email:** admissions@uncw.edu
Full-time: 4943 men, 7403 women	**Faculty:** IIA, -$
Part-time: 542 men, 1614 women	**Ph.D.s:** 89%
Graduate: 545 men, 1440 women	**Student/Faculty:** 18 to 1
Year: semesters, summer session	**Tuition:** $7048 ($21,064)
Room & Board: $9736	**Freshman Class:** 2145 enrolled
SAT CR/M/W: 595/600/565 **ACT:** 24	**CEEB CODE:** 5907
Application Deadline: February 1	**VERY COMPETITIVE**

University of North Carolina Wilmington, founded in 1947, is a publicly funded institution offering programs in the liberal arts and sciences, education, and business. It is a part of the University of North Carolina

System. There are 4 undergraduate schools and 1 graduate school. In addition to regional accreditation, UNC-Wilmington has baccalaureate program accreditation with AACSB, NASM, CAEP, CCNE, CAATE, and CARPRLS. The 661-acre campus is in a suburban area 128 miles southeast of Raleigh. Including any residence halls, there are 162 buildings.

STUDENT LIFE: 88% of undergraduates are from North Carolina. Others are from 48 states, 45 foreign countries, and Canada. 78% are White; 7% Hispanic; 5% African American; 3% two or more races; 3% race unknown; 2% Asian American; 2% Foreign; 1% American Indian/Alaska Native. **Female To Male Ratio:** 1.7:1. The average age of freshmen is 18; all undergraduates, 23. 13% do not continue beyond their first year; 72% remain to graduate. **Housing:** 4190 students can be accommodated in college housing, which includes single sex dorms, coed dorms, and on-campus apartments. In addition, there are honors houses, special-interest houses, and sorority houses. On-campus housing is guaranteed for the freshman year only, and is available on a first-come, first-served basis. 70% of students commute. All students may keep cars.

FACULTY/CLASSROOMS: 46% of faculty are male; 54% are female. No introductory courses are taught by graduate students.

PROGRAMS OF STUDY: UNC-Wilmington confers B.A., B.S., B.F.A., B.S.W., and B.M. degrees. Master's and doctoral degrees are also awarded. Bachelor's degrees are awarded in BIOLOGICAL SCIENCE (biology/biological science and marine biology), BUSINESS (business administration and recreation and leisure services), COMMUNICATIONS AND THE ARTS (art history, communication rhetoric/communications, creative writing, English, film arts, French, German, information technology, music, Spanish, studio art, and theatre arts), COMPUTER AND PHYSICAL SCIENCE (chemistry, computer science, digital arts/technology, geology, mathematics, oceanography, physics, and statistics), EDUCATION (athletic training, early childhood education, elementary education, middle school education, music education, physical education, and special education), ENGINEERING AND ENVIRONMENTAL DESIGN (environmental science), HEALTH PROFESSIONS (clinical science, nursing, public health, and recreation therapy), SOCIAL SCIENCE (anthropology, criminology, economics, geography, history, international studies, philosophy and religion, political science/government, psychology, social work, and sociology). Professional nursing, psychology, and business administration have the largest enrollments.

ACTIVITIES: 5% of men belong to 15 national fraternities; 8% of women belong to 13 national sororities. There are 262 groups on campus, including art, band, choir, chorale, chorus, computers, dance, debate, drama, environmental, ethnic, film, honors, international, LGBT, literary magazine, newspaper, orchestra, pep band, photography, political, professional, radio and TV, religious, social, social service, and student government. Popular campus events include Involvement Carnival, Festapalooza, and Beach Blast. **Sports:** There are 8 intercollegiate sports for men and 10 for women, and 12 intramural sports for men and 12 for women. Facilities include a coliseum, swimming pool and separate diving tank, a track and field complex, softball and baseball fields, and basketball, tennis, and volleyball courts. The Student Recreation Center contains basketball courts, exercise equipment and exercise classes, an indoor track, and a rock climbing wall. **Graduates:** From July 1, 2016 to June 30, 2017, 3484 bachelor's degrees were awarded. The most popular majors were business administration (20%), professional nursing (13%), and psychology (7%). In an average class, 53% graduate in 4 years or less and 72% graduate in 6 years or less.

SERVICES: Counseling and information services are available, as is tutoring in most subjects. **Library/Resources:** The library contains 2.0 million volumes, 450,000 microform items, 45,000 audio/video tapes/CDs/DVDs, and subscribes to 20,000 periodicals, including electronic. Computerized library services include interlibrary loans, database searching, Internet access, and Wi-Fi capability. Special learning facilities include an art gallery, a radio station, TV station, wildflower preserve, a nature preserve, museum of world cultures, a center for marine science, and an electronic trading room. **Physically Challenged Students:** 96% of the campus is accessible. Facilities include wheelchair ramps, elevators, special parking, specially equipped restrooms, special class scheduling, lowered drinking fountains, lowered telephones, and special housing. **Special:** UNC-Wilmington offer internships, over 800 study abroad opportunities, mentored research, and work-study programs. Dual majors may be pursued if requirements are met. There are 16 national honor societies and a freshman honors program. **Visiting:** There are regularly scheduled orientations for prospective students. There are guides for informal visits. To schedule a visit, contact the Admissions Office. **Campus Safety and Security:** Measures include 24-hour foot and vehicle patrol, emergency notification system, and self-defense education. There are shuttle buses, emergency telephones, lighted pathways/sidewalks, controlled access to dorms/residences, rape awareness defense (RAD) training, and counseling services; university police.

REQUIREMENTS: The SAT or ACT is required. Graduation from an accredited secondary school or the GED is required for admission. High school courses must include 4 units of English and math, 3 units of science with 1 unit of lab, 2 units of foreign language, and 1 unit each of history and social studies. AP and CLEP credits are accepted. To graduate in 4 years, a student must successfully complete all graduation requirements and an average annual course load of 31 semester hours. This course load requires the student to take approximately 15-16 hours per semester or earn hours through summer enrollment. Among the factors responsible for extending the time necessary to complete degree requirements beyond 4 years are a student's late decision to change majors, requiring additional coursework; part-time employment while enrolled; family responsibilities; and unilateral decisions to take fewer than the recommended average of 15.5 hours per semester. **Procedure:** Freshmen are admitted in the fall and summer. Entrance exams should be taken during the junior or senior year. There are early admissions and deferred admissions plans. Early decision applications should be filed by November 1; regular applications, by February 1 for fall entry. The fall 2017 application fee was $80. Notification of early decision is sent January 20; regular decision, April 1. Applications are accepted on-line. **Transfer Students:** 1987 transfer students enrolled in 2016-2017. Of the 24 credit hours of transferable college-level coursework, at least 6 hours is needed of college-level English and at least 3 hours of college-level mathematics. An applicant should be eligible to return to the last institution attended. If under the age of 21, applicants must have met the Minimum Course Requirements in high school unless they have already completed 24 hours of college-level coursework. Grades below a C, including C-, are not transferable but are included in the GPA calculation. 31 of 124 credits required for the bachelor's degree must be completed at UNC-Wilmington. **International Students:** There are 311 international students enrolled. They must take the TOEFL with a minimum score of 527 on the paper-based TOEFL (PBT) or 71 on the Internet-based version (iBT), and either the IELTS (minimum score 6.0), or DET (minimum score 54). They must also take the SAT or ACT.

ADMISSIONS: The SAT scores for the 2017-2018 freshman class were: Critical Reading-- 2% below 500, 49% between 500 and 599, 42% between 600 and 699, and 6% between 700 and 800. Math-- 3% below 500, 47% between 500 and 599, 47% between 600 and 699, and 3% between 700 and 800. Writing-- 12% below 500, 57% between 500 and 599, 29% between 600 and 699, and 1% between 700 and 800. The ACT scores were 42% between 18 and 23, 52% between 24 and 29, and 6% above 30. **Admissions Contact:** Marcio Moreno, Director of Admissions. Email: *admissions@uncw.edu* Web: *www.uncw.edu*

FINANCIAL AID: The college's own financial statement is required. The FAFSA code is 002984. The priority date for freshman financial aid applications for fall entry is March 1.

WAKE FOREST UNIVERSITY — C-2

www.wfu.edu

Winston-Salem, NC 27109	(336) 758-5201
	Email: admissions@wfu.edu
Full-time: 2346 men, 2700 women	**Faculty:** 579; IIA, --$
Part-time: 20 men, 35 women	**Ph.D.s:** 93%
Graduate: 1304 men, 1710 women	**Student/Faculty:** 10 to 1
Year: semesters, summer session	**Tuition:** $53,322
Room & Board: $16,032	**Freshman Class:** 14006 applied, 4249 accepted, 1306 enrolled
SAT EBR-W/M: 670/680 **ACT:** 30	**CEEB CODE:** 5885
Application Deadline: January 1	**MOST COMPETITIVE**

Wake Forest University, established in 1834, is a private institution offering undergraduate programs in the liberal arts and sciences, education, and preprofessional fields. There are 2 undergraduate schools and 6 graduate schools. In addition to regional accreditation, WFU has baccalaureate program accreditation with AACSB and NCATE. The 340-acre campus is in a suburban area 4 miles northwest of Winston-Salem. Including any residence halls, there are 47 buildings.

STUDENT LIFE: 79% of undergraduates are from out of state, mostly the South. Students are from 48 states, 28 foreign countries, and Canada. 60% are from public schools. 8% are African American; 70% White; 7% Hispanic; 4% Asian American; 3% two or more races; 10% Foreign. 48% are Muslim, Hindu, Buddhist, Mormon, and Greek Orthodox.; 40% Protestant; 25% Catholic. **Female To Male Ratio:** 1.2:1. The average age of freshmen is 19; all undergraduates, 20. 6% do not continue beyond their first year; 86% remain to graduate. **Housing:** 3380 students can be accommodated in college housing, which includes coed dorms, and on-campus apartments. In addition, there are special-interest houses, fraternity houses, sorority houses, theme and wellness housing, and single student housing. On-campus housing is guaranteed for all 4 years. 98% of students live on campus. Upperclassmen may keep cars.

FACULTY/CLASSROOMS: 86% teach undergraduates, and 73% do research. No introductory courses are taught by graduate students. The average class size in a regular course is 21.

PROGRAMS OF STUDY: WFU confers B.A. and B.S. degrees. Master's and doctoral degrees are also awarded. Bachelor's degrees are awarded in BIOLOGICAL SCIENCE (biology/biological science), BUSINESS (accounting, banking and finance, and business administration and management), COMMUNICATIONS AND THE ARTS (art history, art, Chinese, classics, communications, English, French, German, Greek, Japanese, Latin, music, Russian, Spanish, studio art, and theatre studies), COMPUTER AND PHYSICAL SCIENCE (chemistry, computer science, mathematics, mathematics – economics, and physics), EDUCATION (education), HEALTH PROFESSIONS (exercise science), SOCIAL SCIENCE (anthropology, economics, history, philosophy, political science/government, psychology, religion, and sociology). Business and enterprise management, psychology, and political science have the largest enrollments.

ACTIVITIES: 35% of men belong to 16 national fraternities; 60% of women belong to 11 national sororities. There are 160 groups on campus, including art, band, cheerleading, choir, chorale, chorus, computers, dance, debate, drama, drill team, environmental, ethnic, film, honors, international, jazz band, LGBT, literary magazine, marching band, newspaper, orchestra, pep band, photography, political, professional, radio and TV, religious, social, social service, student government, symphony, women's club, and yearbook. Popular campus events include Project Pumpkin, Springfest, and President's Ball. **Sports:** There are 8 intercollegiate sports for men and 8 for women, and 18 intramural sports for men and 15 for women. Facilities include the Reynolds Gym for indoor sports and outdoor sports are played at the Water Tower field and courts, and tennis. **Graduates:** From July 1, 2016 to June 30, 2017, 1137 bachelor's degrees were awarded. The most popular majors were social sciences, and business/marketing (21%), communication/journalism (10%), and psychology (9%). Of the 2016 graduating class, 26% were enrolled in graduate school within 6 months of graduation, and 68% were employed.

SERVICES: Counseling and information services are available, as is tutoring in some subjects, such as all sciences, math, and foreign languages. There is a reader service for the blind. The Learning Assistance Center offers instructional support and skill development in writing, reading, and study strategies. **Library/Resources:** The library contains 2.1 million volumes, 2.2 million microform items, 38,265 audio/video tapes/CDs/DVDs, and subscribes to 51,262 periodicals, including electronic. Computerized library services include interlibrary loans, database searching, Internet access, and Wi-Fi capability. Special learning facilities include an art gallery, a radio station, a fine arts center, an anthropology museum, and a laser research facility. **Physically Challenged Students:** 85% of the campus is accessible. Facilities include wheelchair ramps, elevators, special parking, specially equipped restrooms, special class scheduling, lowered drinking fountains, and lowered telephones. **Special:** WFU offers cooperative programs in engineering with other schools of engineering accredited by ABET; political science majors who minor in Latin American studies have the opportunity to pursue a 5-year cooperative B.A./M.A. program with Georgetown University. Cross-registration with Salem College is available for full-time students. WFU sponsors study-abroad semester programs in 13 countries. Other special opportunities include internships, work-study programs, dual majors, and a minor in entrepreneurship and social enterprise. Students can also be certified in Spanish language translation and interpreting. An accelerated degree program may be arranged in medical technology. Interdisciplinary honors courses and the Open Curriculum program are available for selected students. WFU owns residences in London, Venice, and Vienna where students and professors attend semester-long courses in a variety of disciplines, and a semester-long program in Washington, D.C., is also offered. There are 11 national honor societies, Phi Beta Kappa, a freshman honors program, and 23 departmental honors programs. **Visiting:** There are regularly scheduled orientations for prospective students, including group information sessions and tours by appointment. There are guides for informal visits; visitors may sit in on classes and stay overnight. To schedule a visit, contact the Admissions Office. **Campus Safety and Security:** Measures include 24-hour foot and vehicle patrol, an emergency notification system, self-defense education, and security escort services. There are shuttle buses, emergency telephones, and lighted pathways/sidewalks. The gatehouses at 2 of the university's 3 entrances operate from 6 p.m. to 6 a.m.; during those hours the third entrance is closed.

REQUIREMENTS: SAT Subject Tests are considered if submitted. Graduation from an accredited secondary school or the GED is required. The school requires 16 academic credits, including 4 credits of English, 3 of math, 2 each of foreign language and social studies, and 1 of science, including 1 credit each of art and music. All students must submit an essay. AP and CLEP credits are accepted. Important factors in the admissions decision are personality/intangible qualities, recommendations by school officials, leadership record, evidence of special talent, and extracurricular activities record. To graduate, students must complete a total of 120 credits with a minimum GPA of 2.0. The number of hours required in the major varies. All students must take 1 semester of a writing seminar, a first-year seminar, and 1 course in foreign language literature. In addition, students must complete 2 courses each in natural sciences and math, social and behavioral sciences, history, religion, and philosophy, and 1 course each in literature and fine arts. **Procedure:** Freshmen are admitted in the fall and spring. There are early decision and deferred admissions plans. Early decision applications should be filed by November 15; regular applications, by January 1 for fall entry; and November 15 for spring entry. The fall 2017 application fee was $65. Notifications are sent April 1. 815 early decision candidates were accepted for the 2017-2018 class. Applications are accepted online. **Transfer Students:** 43 transfer students enrolled in 2016-2017. Transfer students must have a minimum GPA of 2.0 on all college work attempted. An essay is required, as well as an interview, and a statement of good standing from prior institution (s). Admissions is rolling, beginning November 1. 60 of 120 credits required for the bachelor's degree must be completed at WFU. **International Students:** There are 143 international students enrolled. They must take the TOEFL. They must also take the SAT or ACT.

ADMISSIONS: 30% of the 2017-2018 applicants were accepted. The SAT scores for the 2017-2018 freshman class were: Math-- 3% below 500, 14% between 500 and 599, 37% between 600 and 699, and 47% between 700 and 800. Evidence-Based Reading/Writing-- 2% below 500, 10% between 500 and 599, 55% between 600 and 699, and 34% between 700 and 800. The ACT scores were % below 12, % between 12 and 17, 6% between 18 and 23, 33% between 24 and 29, and 61% above 30. 94% of the current freshmen were in the top fifth of their class; 98% were in the top two fifths. 35 freshmen graduated first in their class. **Admissions Contact:** Martha B. Allman, Director of Admissions. Email: *admissions@wfu.edu* Web: *www.wfu.edu*

FINANCIAL AID: In 2017-2018, 100% of all full-time freshmen received some form of financial aid. 100% of all full-time freshmen received need-based aid. The average freshman award was $49,145. Need-based scholarships or need-based grants averaged $45,652; need-based self-help aid (loans and jobs) averaged $10,383; non-need-based athletic scholarships averaged $57,537; other non-need-based awards and non-need-based scholarships averaged $20,377; and $9,056 from other forms of aid. The average financial indebtedness of the 2017 graduate was $38,988. WFU is a member of CSS. The CSS/Profile, state aid form, and noncustodial profile are required. The FAFSA code is 002978. The priority date for freshman financial aid applications for fall entry is January 1.

WARREN WILSON COLLEGE B-2

www.warren-wilson.edu

Asheville, NC 28815 **(828) 771-2073**

Email: admit@warren-wilson.edu

Full-time: 247 men, 397 women
Part-time: 2 men, 4 women
Graduate: 20 men, 46 women
Year: semesters, summer session
Room & Board: $10,250

Faculty: 68
Ph.D.s: 92%
Student/Faculty: 10 to 1
Tuition: $33,970
Freshman Class: 809 applied, 678 accepted, 195 enrolled

SAT CR/M: 580/540 **ACT:** 26
Application Deadline: n/av

CEEB CODE: 5886
VERY COMPETITIVE

Warren Wilson College, founded in 1894, is the country's only liberal arts college with a national student body and integrated work and service programs. Through a blend of strong academics, work, and service, called the Triad, WWC's students graduate not only with a rigorous liberal arts education, but also with skills such as problem-solving and team leadership that equip them for life. It's an innovative approach to a well-rounded education that has stood the test of time. There is 1 undergraduate school and 1 graduate school. In addition to regional accreditation, WWC has baccalaureate program accreditation with CSWE. The 1135-acre campus is in a suburban area 5 miles east of Asheville, NC and in the Swannanoa Valley of the Blue Ridge Mountains. Including any residence halls, there are 110 buildings.

STUDENT LIFE: 74% of undergraduates are from out of state, mostly the Middle Atlantic. Students are from 40 states and 9 foreign countries. 74% are from public schools. 74% are White; 9% Hispanic; 5% African American; 5% race unknown; 2% American Indian/Alaska Native; 2% Foreign; 2% two or more races; 1% Asian American. **Female To Male Ratio:** 1.7:1. The average age of freshmen is 18; all undergraduates, 20. 34% do not continue beyond their first year; 52% remain to graduate. **Housing:** 820 students can be accommodated in college housing, which includes dorms. In addition, there are special-interest houses, a wellness/substance-free dorm, and an eco-dorm. On-campus housing is guaranteed for the freshman year only, is available on a first-come, first-served basis, and is available on a lottery system for upperclassmen. 90% of students live on campus. Upperclassmen may keep cars.

FACULTY/CLASSROOMS: 51% of faculty are male; 49% are female. All teach undergraduates and all do research. No introductory courses are taught by graduate students. The average class size in an introductory lecture is 16; in a laboratory is 15; and in a regular course is 11.

PROGRAMS OF STUDY: WWC confers B.A. and B.S. degrees. Master's degrees are also awarded. Bachelor's degrees are awarded in AGRICULTURE (environmental studies), BIOLOGICAL SCIENCE (biochemistry and biology/biological science), COMMUNICATIONS AND THE ARTS (art, creative writing, English, English literature, English writing, music, and theatre arts), COMPUTER AND PHYSICAL SCIENCE (chemistry and mathematics), EDUCATION (global studies), HEALTH PROFESSIONS (biology), SOCIAL SCIENCE (anthropology, history, interdisciplinary studies, philosophy, political science/government, psychology, social work, and sociology). Biology is the strongest academically. Environmental studies, biology, and art have the largest enrollments.

ACTIVITIES: There are no fraternities or sororities. Groups on campus include peace and social justice, art, band, choir, chorale, chorus, computers, dance, debate, drama, environmental, ethnic, film, honors, international, jazz band, LGBT, literary magazine, musical theater, newspaper, outdoor activities, photography, political, professional, religious, social, and student government. Popular campus events include Homecoming, Family Weekend, Work Day, Service Day, and Circus. **Sports:** There are 7 intercollegiate sports for men and 7 for women, and 5 intramural sports for men and 5 for women. Facilities include gyms, weight and fitness rooms, tennis courts, playing fields, hiking/biking trails, kayak slalom gates, an alpine climbing/challenge tower, a mountain bike skills area, and outdoor basketball court. **Graduates:** From July 1, 2016 to June 30, 2017, 196 bachelor's degrees were awarded. The most popular majors were environmental studies (20%), psychology (9%), and history (9%). In an average class, 40% graduate in 4 years or less, 51% graduate in 5 years or less, and 52% graduate in 6 years or less.

SERVICES: Counseling and information services are available, as is tutoring in most subjects. Tutoring is available through the Academic Support Center and the writing center. ESL tutoring is also available. **Library/Resources:** The library contains 403,500 volumes, 4,400 audio/video tapes/CDs/DVDs, and subscribes to 42,000 periodicals, including electronic. Computerized library services include interlibrary loans, database searching, Internet access, and Wi-Fi capability. Special learning facilities include an art gallery, an outdoor adventure learning lab, digital sound lab, a GIS lab, a working farm, a 5-acre garden, and a 776-acre managed forest. **Physically Challenged Students:** 90% of the campus is accessible. Facilities include wheelchair ramps, elevators, special parking, specially equipped restrooms, and special housing. **Special:** Cross-registration is offered with Mars Hill College and the University of North Carolina at Asheville via the Asheville Area Educational Consortium. Students may apply for one of many internship experiences in various disciplines. Students may participate in a semester or year of study abroad in Asia, Latin America, Africa, or Europe, or in one of the College's short-term Study Abroad Courses with on-campus study and travel to places such as Chile, Costa Rica, England, Ghana, Greece, Ireland, Italy, Micronesia, New Zealand, Thailand, China, and Nicaragua. Students may choose to double-major by completing the requirements for more than one major program at a time. WWC participates in the Cooperative College Program with the Nicolas School of the Environment at Duke University in a combined program of liberal arts and professional education in environmental resource management. There are 4 departmental honors programs. **Visiting:** There are regularly scheduled orientations for prospective students. There are guides for informal visits; visitors may sit in on classes and stay overnight. To schedule a visit, contact Monique Cote at mcote@warren-wilson.edu. **Campus Safety and Security:** Measures include 24-hour foot and vehicle patrol, an emergency notification system, and security escort services. There are emergency telephones, lighted pathways/sidewalks, and controlled access to dorms/residences.

REQUIREMENTS: The SAT or ACT is required. A high school diploma and completion of a college preparatory curriculum, including the following classes are required: 4 years of English, Algebra I, Algebra II, Geometry, 3 years of social sciences, and 2 years of laboratory sciences. A foreign language and AP courses are strongly recommended. Applicants must submit the Common Application and official high school transcripts. Standardized test scores and the WWC writing supplement are optional. In order to graduate, baccalaureate students must complete all the requirements of the Triad Educational Program, which includes components in academics, work, and service. All students must complete a total of 128 credit hours with a minimum GPA of 2.0. The Aims Curriculum (general education) honors a traditional Liberal Arts curriculum while embedding that curriculum in the College's distinctive mission. The curriculum includes a breadth of perspectives (Liberal Arts Disciplines), continuous writing instruction (Writing Across the Curriculum), pedagogies (Work-Learning and Service-Learning), and ethical (Values) Aims. Students work individually with an academic advisor to select courses that meet program requirements and align with their interests. Between 32 and 40 credit hours are required in the student's major, and most majors require a culminating or capstone experience. Students must have worked a minimum of 300 hours in WWC's Work Program in order to graduate. All students must also complete a community engagement commitment, demonstrating learning in four different Points of Engagement and Growth (PEGs). Finally, each candidate for a baccalaureate degree must write a Senior Letter addressed to the faculty and staff of the college, which includes an evaluation of his/her experiences at the college and reflections on the college career. **Procedure:** Freshmen are admitted in the fall and winter. There are early decision, early admissions, deferred admissions, and rolling admissions plans. Early decision applications should be filed by November 15. Notification of early decision is sent December 1. Applications are accepted online. **Transfer Students:** 50 transfer students enrolled in 2016-2017. Transfer applicants must have a minimum college GPA of 2.5. Applicants must have left their previous institutions in good standing, and be eligible to return. Transfer applicants must submit the Common Application, high school transcript, all college transcripts, and the Common Application's Registrar Report Form from the most recent institution. Standardized test scores and the WWC writing supplement are optional. 32 of 128 credits required for the bachelor's degree must be completed at WWC. **International Students:** There are 13 international students enrolled. They must take the TOEFL. They must also take the SAT or ACT. Test scores are considered if submitted.

ADMISSIONS: 46% of the current freshmen were in the top fifth of their class; 64% were in the top two fifths. 1 freshman graduated first in the class. **Admissions Contact:** Janelle Holmboe, Vice President for

Enrollment and Marketing. Email: *admit@warren-wilson.edu* Web: *www.warren-wilson.edu*

FINANCIAL AID: 90% of undergraduate students work part-time. The FAFSA code is 002979. Check with the school for current application deadlines.

WESTERN CAROLINA UNIVERSITY A-3

www.wcu.edu

Cullowhee, NC 28723	**(828) 227-7211**
Fax: (828) 227-7319	**Email: admiss@wcu.edu**
Full-time: 3216 men, 3579 women	**Faculty:** 420; IIA, -$
Part-time: 504 men, 680 women	**Ph.D.s:** 70%
Graduate: 543 men, 1086 women	**Student/Faculty:** 16 to 1
Year: semesters, summer session	**Tuition:** $6479 ($16,076)
Room & Board: $7477	**Freshman Class:** 15234 applied, 5739 accepted, 1560 enrolled
SAT CR/M/W: 515/526/486 **ACT:** 22	**CEEB CODE:** 5897
Application Deadline: March 1	**COMPETITIVE**

Western Carolina University, founded in 1889 and part of the University of North Carolina system, is a public-funded institution offering undergraduate programs in the arts, sciences, technology, business, and humanities. There are 6 undergraduate schools and 1 graduate school. In addition to regional accreditation, WCU has baccalaureate program accreditation with AACSB, ABET, ACCE, ADA, APTA, CSWE, FIDER, NASM, CAEP, NLN, ACS, AANA, CAATE, CAAHEP, CCNE, EHAC, NAACLS, NCTE, and NASSM. The 682-acre campus is in a rural area 150 miles northeast of Atlanta, Georgia, and 50 miles west of Asheville. Including any residence halls, there are 91 buildings.

STUDENT LIFE: 93% of undergraduates are from North Carolina. Others are from 40 states, 13 foreign countries, and Canada. 95% are from public schools. 83% are White; 7% African American; 3% Hispanic; 3% two or more races; 1% Asian American; 1% American Indian/Alaska Native; 1% Foreign; 1% race unknown. **Female To Male Ratio:** 1.3:1. The average age of freshmen is 18; all undergraduates, 23. 16% do not continue beyond their first year; 48% remain to graduate. **Housing:** 4023 students can be accommodated in college housing, which includes married student dorms and on-campus apartments. In addition, there are honors houses, language/international houses, fraternity houses, and sorority houses. On-campus housing is guaranteed for all 4 years. 51% of students commute. All students may keep cars.

FACULTY/CLASSROOMS: 51% of faculty are male; 49% are female. 81% teach undergraduates. Graduate students teach 5% of introductory courses.

PROGRAMS OF STUDY: WCU confers B.A., B.S., B.F.A., B.M., B.S.B.A., B.S.Ed., B.S.E.E., B.S.N., and B.S.W. degrees. Master's and doctoral degrees are also awarded. Bachelor's degrees are awarded in AGRICULTURE (natural resource management), BIOLOGICAL SCIENCE (biology/biological science), BUSINESS (accounting, banking and finance, business law, entrepreneurial studies, hospitality management services, international business management, management science, marketing and distribution, and sports management), COMMUNICATIONS AND THE ARTS (art, communications, dramatic arts, English, French, German, music, Spanish, and speech/debate/rhetoric), COMPUTER AND PHYSICAL SCIENCE (chemistry, computer science, geology, and mathematics), EDUCATION (art education, early childhood education, elementary education, English education, foreign languages education, mathematics education, middle school education, music education, physical education, science education, secondary education, social science education, special education, speech correction, and teaching English as a second/foreign language (TESOL/TEFOL), ENGINEERING AND ENVIRONMENTAL DESIGN (construction management, electrical/electronics engineering, electrical/electronics engineering technology, emergency/disaster science, engineering technology, interior design, manufacturing technology, and preengineering), HEALTH PROFESSIONS (emergency medical technologies, environmental health science, health care administration, medical laboratory science, medical records administration/services, nursing, predentistry, premedicine, preoptometry, prepharmacy, prephysical therapy, preveterinary science, recreation therapy, and sports medicine), SOCIAL SCIENCE (anthropology, criminal justice, dietetics, forensic studies, geography, history, liberal arts/general studies, parks and recreation management, philosophy, political science/government, prelaw, psychology, social science, social work, and sociology). Elementary and middle school education, criminal justice, and nursing have the largest enrollments.

ACTIVITIES: 9% of men belong to 13 national fraternities; 7% of women belong to 9 national sororities. There are 150 groups on campus, including art, band, cheerleading, choir, chorale, chorus, computers, dance, debate, drama, drill team, environmental, ethnic, film, honors, international, jazz band, LGBT, literary magazine, marching band, musical theater, newspaper, pep band, photography, political, professional, radio and TV, religious, social, social service, and student government. Popular campus events include Mountain Heritage Day, Greek Week, and the Fine and Performing Arts Season. **Sports:** There are 6 intercollegiate sports for men and 8 for women, and 33 intramural sports for men and 34 for women. Facilities include a football stadium, a baseball diamond, track/tennis complex, softball fields, flag football fields, a disc golf course, a soccer field, gyms, a field house, jogging trails, a weight training room, a swimming pool, a golf driving range and golf putting green, strength training, cardiovascular equipment, and indoor track, and a group exercise studio. **Graduates:** From July 1, 2016 to June 30, 2017, 1783 bachelor's degrees were awarded. The most popular majors were criminal justice (10%), nursing (7%), and elementary and middle school education (7%). In an average class, 1% graduate in 3 years or less, 28% graduate in 4 years or less, 44% graduate in 5 years or less, and 48% graduate in 6 years or less.

SERVICES: Counseling and information services are available, as is tutoring in most subjects. There is a reader service for the blind, and remedial math, reading, and writing. **Library/Resources:** Computerized library services include interlibrary loans, database searching, Internet access, and Wi-Fi capability. Special learning facilities include an art gallery, natural history museum, a radio station, TV station, the Mountain Heritage Center, the Fine and Performing Arts Center, and the Center for Applied Technology. **Physically Challenged Students:** 90% of the campus is accessible. Facilities include wheelchair ramps, elevators, special parking, specially equipped restrooms, special class scheduling, lowered drinking fountains, lowered telephones, and special housing. **Special:** WCU offers cooperative education programs in most majors, extensive internship opportunities, an accelerated degree in nursing, B.A.-B.S. degrees, dual and student designed majors, nondegree study, pass/fail options in designated courses, and credit for life experience. Study-abroad programs may be arranged in 14 countries and a Washington internship is available to a select few junior- or senior-level students each semester. A joint degree program in electrical engineering with the University of North Carolina-Charlotte is offered. There are 12 national honor societies and a freshman honors program. **Visiting:** There are regularly scheduled orientations for prospective students consisting of 6 open houses and 8 regional tour events annually and twice-daily campus tours every Monday, Tuesday, Thursday, and Friday. There are guides for informal visits; visitors may sit in on classes and stay overnight. To schedule a visit, contact the Admissions Office at (877) 928-4968. **Campus Safety and Security:** Measures include 24-hour foot and vehicle patrol, an emergency notification system. There are shuttle buses, emergency telephones, lighted pathways/sidewalks, controlled access to dorms/residences, and crime-prevention education programs.

REQUIREMENTS: The SAT is required. Graduation from an accredited secondary school or the GED is required. High school courses must include 4 units of English, 4 units of math, 3 units of lab science, 2 units each of social studies (including 1 of U.S. history), and foreign language, and 5 units of academic electives. AP and CLEP credits are accepted. Important factors in the admissions decision are advanced placement or honors courses, recommendations by school officials, and evidence of special talent. In order to graduate, students must complete a total of 120 to 128 credit hours with a minimum GPA of 2.0. Between 27 and 64 hours are required in the major. All students must fulfill liberal studies requirements in writing, oral communication, wellness, social sciences, physical and biological sciences, math, humanities, history, fine and performing arts, world cultures, the freshman seminar, and 1 course in upper-level perspectives outside the major. Most degree plans include a minimum of 12 hours of free electives. **Procedure:** Freshmen are admitted in the fall, spring, and summer. Entrance exams should be taken during the spring of the junior year or the fall of the senior year. There are early decision, early admissions, and rolling admissions plans. Early decision applications should be filed by November 15; regular applications, by March 1 for fall entry; November 15 for spring entry; and April

15 for summer entry. The fall 2017 application fee was $50. Notification of early decision is sent December 15; regular decision, on a rolling basis. Applications are accepted online. **Transfer Students:** 784 transfer students enrolled in 2016-2017. Transfer students must have a minimum GPA of 2.0 and meet freshman admissions requirements 32 of 128 credits required for the bachelor's degree must be completed at WCU. **International Students:** There are 81 international students enrolled. They must take the TOEFL with a minimum score of 550 on the paper-based TOEFL (PBT) or 79 on the Internet-based version (iBT). They must also take the SAT.

ADMISSIONS: 38% of the 2017-2018 applicants were accepted. The SAT scores for the 2017-2018 freshman class were: Critical Reading-- 43% below 500, 43% between 500 and 599, 13% between 600 and 699, and 1% between 700 and 800. Math-- 36% below 500, 47% between 500 and 599, 16% between 600 and 699, and 1% between 700 and 800. Writing-- 60% below 500, 32% between 500 and 599, 7% between 600 and 699, and 1% between 700 and 800. The ACT scores were 34% below 12, 38% between 12 and 17, 16% between 18 and 23, 6% between 24 and 29, and 6% above 30. 28% of the current freshmen were in the top fifth of their class; 62% were in the top two fifths. **Admissions Contact:** Undergraduate Admissions Email: *admiss@wcu.edu* Web: *www.wcu.edu*

FINANCIAL AID: In 2017-2018, 66% of all full-time freshmen received some form of financial aid. 65% of all full-time freshmen received need-based aid. The average freshman award was $8,551. Need-based scholarships or need-based grants averaged $6,214; need-based self-help aid (loans and jobs) averaged $3,386; non-need-based athletic scholarships averaged $9,802; and other non-need-based awards and non-need-based scholarships averaged $3,071. 15% of undergraduate students work part-time. The average financial indebtedness of the 2017 graduate was $22,608. The college's own financial statement is required. The FAFSA code is 002981. The priority date for freshman financial aid applications for fall entry is March 15.

WILLIAM PEACE UNIVERSITY *(The complete profile is made available exclusively on our website, www.barronspac.com)*

WINGATE UNIVERSITY C-3

www.wingate.edu

Wingate, NC 28174

(704) 233-8200
(800) 755-5550
Email: admit@wingate.edu

Full-time: 984 men, 1553 women
Part-time: 26 men, 29 women
Graduate: 396 men, 632 women
Year: semesters, summer session
Room & Board: $10,780

SAT: 520/510 **ACT:** 20
Application Deadline: rolling

Faculty: 121
Ph.D.s: 85%
Student/Faculty: 16 to 1
Tuition: $31,120
Freshman Class: 15198 applied, 14170 accepted, 1073 enrolled
CEEB CODE: 5908
COMPETITIVE

Wingate University, founded in 1896, is a private liberal arts institution. There are 5 undergraduate schools and 5 graduate schools. In addition to regional accreditation, WU has baccalaureate program accreditation with ACBSP, ACPE, NASM, ARCEPA, ACEN, and CAPTE. The 330-acre campus is in a small town 25 miles east of Charlotte. Including any residence halls, there are 44 buildings.

STUDENT LIFE: 73% of undergraduates are from North Carolina. Others are from 36 states, 53 foreign countries, and Canada. 9% are two or more races; 58% White; 4% Foreign; 4% race unknown; 3% Hispanic; 17% African American; 1% Asian American. **Female To Male Ratio:** 1.6:1. The average age of freshmen is 18; all undergraduates, 20. 27% do not continue beyond their first year; 52% remain to graduate. **Housing:** 1901 students can be accommodated in college housing, which includes single sex dorms, coed dorms, and on-campus apartments. In addition, there are special-interest houses, fraternity houses, and sorority houses. On-campus housing is guaranteed for all 4 years. 73% of students live on campus. All students may keep cars.

FACULTY/CLASSROOMS: 45% of faculty are male; 55% are female. 72% teach undergraduates, 1% do research, and 2% do both. No introductory courses are taught by graduate students. The average class size in an introductory lecture is 22; in a laboratory is 20; and in a regular course is 21.

PROGRAMS OF STUDY: WU confers B.A., B.S., B.S.N., B.L.S., and B.M.E. degrees. Master's and doctoral degrees are also awarded. Bachelor's degrees are awarded in BIOLOGICAL SCIENCE (biology/biological science, biology/general science secondary education, and environmental biology), BUSINESS (accounting, finance, management, marketing, sports management, and project management), COMMUNICATIONS AND THE ARTS (church music, communication studies, communication rhetoric/communication, English, instrumental performance, journalism, music, public relations, and vocal performance), COMPUTER AND PHYSICAL SCIENCE (chemistry and mathematics), EDUCATION (athletic training, education administration, elementary education, English education, mathematics education, middle school education, music education, and reading education), ENGINEERING AND ENVIRONMENTAL DESIGN (preengineering), HEALTH PROFESSIONS (biology, exercise science, nursing, pharmacy, physical therapy, physician's assistant, predentistry, premedicine, prepharmacy, prephysician assistant, prephysical therapy, and preveterinary science), SOCIAL SCIENCE (criminal justice, history, human services, liberal arts/general studies, parks and recreation management, political science/government, prelaw, psychology, religious studies, and sociology). Pharmacy, biology, business, and education are the strongest academically. Biology, nursing, and psychology have the largest enrollments.

ACTIVITIES: 6% of men belong to 4 national fraternities; 19% of women belong to 4 national sororities. There are 50 groups on campus, including art, band, cheerleading, choir, chorale, chorus, communications, computers, drama, environmental, ethnic, honors, international, jazz band, LGBT, literary magazine, newspaper, opera, pep band, photography, political, professional, religious, social, social service, student government, and yearbook. Popular campus events include Spring Fling and Fall Festival at Campus Lake, and concerts. **Sports:** There are 10 intercollegiate sports for men and 10 for women, and 13 intramural sports for men and 13 for women. Facilities include an athletic complex with an indoor track, gyms, swimming pool, racquetball courts, exercise and weight rooms, tennis courts, pool tables, tennis, a football stadium, and baseball, soccer, and softball fields. **Graduates:** From July 1, 2016 to June 30, 2017, 338 bachelor's degrees were awarded. The most popular majors were business/marketing (10%), human services (10%), and psychology (8%). In an average class, 41% graduate in 4 years or less, 47% graduate in 5 years or less, and 52% graduate in 6 years or less. Of the 2016 graduating class, 40% were enrolled in graduate school within 6 months of graduation, and 53% were employed.

SERVICES: Counseling and information services are available, as is tutoring in every subject. There is also additional academic support available for students with learning disabilities. **Library/Resources:** The library contains 96,597 volumes, 6,856 microform items, 6,779 audio/video tapes/CDs/DVDs, and subscribes to 84 periodicals, including electronic. Computerized library services include interlibrary loans, database searching, Internet access, and Wi-Fi capability. Special learning facilities include an art gallery, a fine arts center, exercise science labs, and cadaver lab. **Physically Challenged Students:** 95% of the campus is accessible. Facilities include wheelchair ramps, elevators, special parking, specially equipped restrooms, special class scheduling, and lowered drinking fountains. **Special:** Cross-registration through the Greater Charlotte Area Consortium, Army and Air Force ROTC programs, internships, a liberal studies degree for adult completion, B.A.-B.S. degrees, and non-degree study are available. Wingate conducts foreign study semesters in London, Denmark, and China. The school also sponsors Winternational, a semester seminar with a 10-day trip to a foreign country for which students earn academic credits. A community engagement program, W-Engage, is designed for sophomores to contribute to surrounding communities and travel for 5-7 days to a U.S. destination in order to promote positive social change. Dual majors are offered in biology and education, history and education, English and education, math and education, and chemistry and business. Students can earn a B.S. in biology and Pharm.D. through a 3 + 1 program. There are 11 national honor societies and a freshman honors program. **Visiting:** There are regularly scheduled orientations for prospective students. There are guides for informal visits; visitors may sit in on classes and stay overnight. To schedule a visit, contact the Admissions Office. **Campus Safety and Security:** Measures include 24-hour foot and vehicle patrol, an emergency notification system, self-defense education, and security escort services. There are shuttle buses, emergency telephones, lighted pathways/sidewalks, and controlled access to dorms/residences.

REQUIREMENTS: The SAT or ACT is required. Graduation from an accredited secondary school or the GED is also required. The high school curriculum should include 4 courses in English, 3 in math, 2 each in social and natural science (1 with a lab), and foreign language. An essay and an interview are recommended in some cases. AP and CLEP credits are accepted. Important factors in the admissions decision are advanced placement or honors courses, leadership record, and recommendations by school officials. To graduate, students must complete a minimum of 125 credit hours with a GPA of 2.0. At least 30 hours must be completed in the students major. All students must complete the Core Curriculum, which includes 18 hours of Global Perspectives. **Procedure:** Freshmen are admitted in the fall, spring, and summer. Entrance exams should be taken in spring of the junior year or fall of the senior year. There is a rolling admissions plan. Application deadlines are open. Applications are accepted online. **Transfer Students:** 108 transfer students enrolled in 2016-2017. Applicants must have a minimum GPA of 2.0 and must be eligible to return to the institution last attended. The SAT or ACT is required if a student has been out of high school for less than 5 years or has fewer than 24 transferable hours. An interview may be recommended in some cases. 30 of 125 credits required for the bachelor's degree must be completed at WU. **International Students:** There are 114 international students enrolled. They must take the TOEFL with a minimum score of 550 on the paper-based TOEFL (PBT) or 80 on the Internet-based version (iBT), and either the IELTS, ITEP, SAT or ACT.

ADMISSIONS: 93% of the 2017-2018 applicants were accepted. The SAT scores for the 2017-2018 freshman class were: Critical Reading-- 35% below 500, 49% between 500 and 599, 14% between 600 and 699, and 2% between 700 and 800. Math-- 39% below 500, 46% between 500 and 599, 14% between 600 and 699, and 1% between 700 and 800. The ACT scores were 22% between 12 and 17, 59% between 18 and 23, 16% between 24 and 29, and 3% above 30. 28% of the current freshmen were in the top fifth of their class; 58% were in the top two fifths. 5 freshmen graduated first in their class. **Admissions Contact:** Gabe Hollingsworth, Director of Admissions. Email: *admit@wingate.edu* Web: *www.wingate.edu*

FINANCIAL AID: In 2017-2018, 99% of all full-time freshmen received some form of financial aid. 75% of all full-time freshmen received need-based aid. The average freshman award was $28,432. Need-based scholarships or need-based grants averaged $7,784; need-based self-help aid (loans and jobs) averaged $4,063; non-need-based athletic scholarships averaged $9,617; and other non-need-based awards and non-need-based scholarships averaged $19,408. 20% of undergraduate students work part-time. The average financial indebtedness of the 2017 graduate was $27,689. The state aid form is required. The FAFSA code is 002985. The priority date for freshman financial aid applications for fall entry is March 1.

WINSTON-SALEM STATE UNIVERSITY *(The complete profile is made available exclusively on our website, www.barronspac.com)*

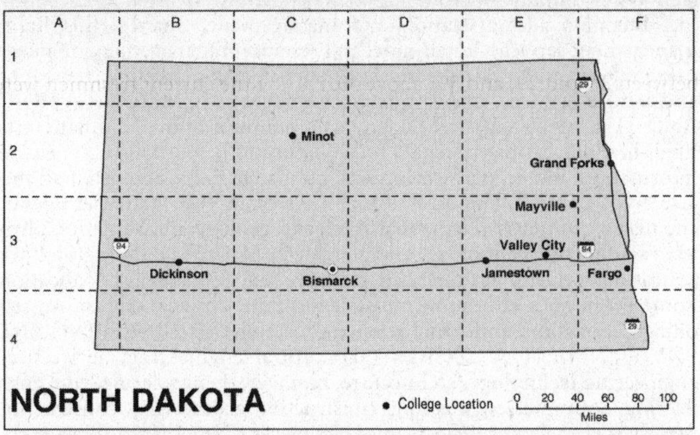

DICKINSON STATE UNIVERSITY *(The complete profile is made available exclusively on our website, www.barronspac.com)*

MAYVILLE STATE UNIVERSITY *(The complete profile is made available exclusively on our website, www.barronspac.com)*

MINOT STATE UNIVERSITY — C-2

www.minotstateu.edu

Minot, ND 58707 (701) 858-4347
(800) 777-0750

Fax: (701) 839-6933
Email: askmsu@minotstateu.edu

Full-time: 676 men, 1027 women
Part-time: 154 men, 273 women
Graduate: 90 men, 170 women
Year: semesters, summer session
Room & Board: $6476
SAT M: 520 **ACT:** 22
Application Deadline: April 1

Faculty: 151
Ph.D.s: 60%
Student/Faculty: 12 to 1
Tuition: $6809
Freshman Class: 708 applied, 489 accepted, 373 enrolled
CEEB CODE: 6479
COMPETITIVE

Minot State University, founded in 1913, is a public institution offering undergraduate and graduate programs in arts and sciences, education, business, nursing, and human services. There are 3 undergraduate schools and 1 graduate school. In addition to regional accreditation, MSU has baccalaureate program accreditation with CAEP and NLN. The 103-acre campus is in a small town in the northwest region of North Dakota. Including any residence halls, there are 21 buildings.

STUDENT LIFE: 81% of undergraduates are from North Dakota. Others are from 44 states, 18 foreign countries, and Canada. 95% are from public schools. 9% are Foreign; 7% Hispanic; 69% White; 5% African American; 4% two or more races; 2% Asian American; 2% American Indian/Alaska Native. **Female To Male Ratio:** 1.6:1. The average age of freshmen is 19; all undergraduates, 24. 36% do not continue beyond their first year; 32% remain to graduate. **Housing:** 643 students can be accommodated in college housing, which includes married student dorms and on-campus apartments. In addition, there are language/international houses and special-interest houses. On-campus housing is guaranteed for the freshman year only, is available on a first-come, first-served basis, and is available on a lottery system for upperclassmen. 54% of students live on campus. Alcohol is not permitted. All students may keep cars.

FACULTY/CLASSROOMS: 49% of faculty are male; 51% are female. All teach undergraduates, and 20% do research. No introductory courses are taught by graduate students. The average class size in an introductory lecture is 60; in a laboratory is 20; and in a regular course is 16.

PROGRAMS OF STUDY: MSU confers B.A., B.S., B.A.S., B.G.S., B.S. Ed., B.S.N., and B.S.W. degrees. Associate and master's degrees are also awarded. Bachelor's degrees are awarded in BIOLOGICAL SCIENCE (biology/biological science), BUSINESS (accounting, banking and finance, international business management, management information systems, management science, and marketing/retailing/merchandising), COMMUNICATIONS AND THE ARTS (art, broadcasting, communications, English, French, German, multimedia, music, and Spanish), COMPUTER AND PHYSICAL SCIENCE (chemistry, computer science, earth science, geology, mathematics, physical sciences, physics, and radiological technology), EDUCATION (business education, drama education, education of the deaf and hearing impaired, education of the exceptional child, education of the mentally handicapped, elementary education, English education, foreign languages education, health and education science, mathematics education, music education, physical education, and science education), HEALTH PROFESSIONS (dental laboratory technology, nursing, and speech pathology/audiology), SOCIAL SCIENCE (addiction studies, criminal justice, economics, history, liberal arts/general studies, physical fitness/movement, psychology, social science, social work, and sociology). Communication disorders, special education, and elementary education are the strongest academically. Business, criminal justice, and education have the largest enrollments.

ACTIVITIES: There are no fraternities or sororities. There are 60 groups on campus, including art, band, choir, chorale, chorus, drama, ethnic, honors, international, marching band, musical theater, newspaper, orchestra, pep band, political, professional, radio and TV, religious, social service, student government, and symphony. Popular campus events include Welcome Week, Final Frenzy, and Native American Awareness Week. **Sports:** There are 6 intercollegiate sports for men and 6 for women, and 4 intramural sports for men and 4 for women. Facilities include baseball, basketball, cross country, golf, track & field, wrestling, club hockey, a field house, football stadium, and a gym. **Graduates:** From July 1, 2016 to June 30, 2017, 604 bachelor's degrees were awarded. The most popular majors were business/marketing (22%), personal and culinary services (21%), and health professions & related programs (16%). In an average class, 37% graduate in 6 years or less. Of the 2016 graduating class, 11% were enrolled in graduate school within 6 months of graduation, and 89% were employed.

SERVICES: Counseling and information services are available, as is tutoring in most subjects. Special services are offered for disabled students on request. **Library/Resources:** The library contains 411,678 volumes, 687,708 microform items, and 12,722 audio/video tapes/CDs/DVDs, and subscribes to 802 periodicals including electronic. Computerized library services include interlibrary loans and database searching. Special learning facilities include an art gallery, natural history museum, radio station, and TV station. **Physically Challenged Students:** 99% of the campus is accessible. Facilities include wheelchair ramps, elevators, special parking, specially equipped restrooms, special class scheduling, lowered drinking fountains, lowered telephones, and special housing. **Special:** A general studies degree, independent research, internships, work-study, and unique programs of study, including student-designed majors, are available. Cross-registration through the North Dakota University System, co-op programs in all majors, and study abroad in 3 countries also are offered. Preliminary programs are available in dental hygiene, dentistry, engineering, law, medicine, and many other areas. There are a freshman honors program. **Visiting:** There are regularly scheduled orientations for prospective students, prior to the beginning of the fall term. There are guides for informal visits and visitors may sit in on classes. To schedule a visit, contact the Enrollment Services. **Campus Safety and Security:** Measures include self-defense education. There are emergency telephones and lighted pathways/sidewalks.

REQUIREMENTS: 13 academic units are required, 4 in English, and 3 units each in math (must be Algebra 1 of above), science (should include biology, chemistry, physics or physical science), and social studies. SAT or ACT scores are also required. ACT scores must be no less than 18 composite. New freshman and transfer students are required to complete a new student orientation. Applicants must submit a high school diploma or GED certificate. Core course requirements include 4 years of English and 3 each of math, social studies, and science. AP and CLEP credits are accepted. Important factors in the admissions decision are leadership record and advanced placement or honors courses. Students must take a number of general education courses in humanities, history, communication, math, natural sciences, social and behavorial sciences, and leisure-time education. They must complete at least 128 semester hours, with 30 to 37 in the major and a minimum GPA of 2.0. **Procedure:** Freshmen are admitted to all sessions. Entrance exams should be taken any time. There are deferred admissions and rolling admissions plans. Application deadlines are open. The fall 2017 application fee was

$35. Applications are accepted on-line. **Transfer Students:** 338 transfer students enrolled in 2016-2017. Transfers must submit transcripts from each college attended. 30 of 128 credits required for the bachelor's degree must be completed at MSU. **International Students:** There are 41 international students enrolled. They must take the TOEFL.

ADMISSIONS: 69% of the 2017-2018 applicants were accepted. The ACT scores were 8% between 12 and 17, 51% between 18 and 23, 21% between 24 and 29, and 3% above 30. **Admissions Contact:** Alexis Hendricks, Enrollment Services Representative. Email: *askmsu@minotstateu.edu* Web: *www.minotstateu.edu*

FINANCIAL AID: In 2017-2018, 67% of all full-time freshmen received some form of financial aid. 64% of all full-time freshmen received need-based aid. The average freshman award was $9,976. Need-based scholarships or need-based grants averaged $6,284; need-based self-help aid (loans and jobs) averaged $4,334; non-need-based athletic scholarships averaged $2,826; other non-need-based awards and non-need-based scholarships averaged $4,401; and $1,115 from other forms of aid. The average financial indebtedness of the 2017 graduate was $11,390. The FAFSA code is 002994. The priority date for freshman financial aid applications for fall entry is February 15.

NORTH DAKOTA STATE UNIVERSITY F-3

www.ndsu.edu

Fargo, ND 58108	**(701) 231-8643** **(800) 488-NDSU**
Fax: (701) 231-8802	**Email: ndsu.admission@ndsu.edu**
Full-time: 5966 men, 4713 women	**Faculty:** n/av
Part-time: 575 men, 755 women	**Ph.D.s:** n/av
Graduate: 1046 men, 1036 women	**Student/Faculty:** n/av
Year: semesters, summer session	**Tuition:** $8327 ($19,891)
Room & Board: $7918	**Freshman Class:** 5980 applied, 4759 accepted, 2503 enrolled
SAT: required **ACT:** 24	**CEEB CODE:** 6474
Application Deadline: August 1	**VERY COMPETITIVE**

North Dakota is a student-focused, land grant, research university an economic engine that educates students, conducts primary research, creates new knowledge, and advances technology. We provide affordable access to an excellent education at a top-ranked research institution that combines teaching and research in a rich learning environment, educating future leaders who will create solutions to national and global challenges that will shape a better world. There are 8 undergraduate schools and 1 graduate school. In addition to regional accreditation, NDSU has baccalaureate program accreditation with AACSB, ABET, ACCE, ACPE, ADA, AHEA, CAHEA, CSAB, FIDER, NAAB, NASAD, NASM, CAEP, and ACS. The 258-acre campus is in an urban area 229 miles northwest of Minneapolis-St. Paul. Including any residence halls, there are 97 buildings.

STUDENT LIFE: 57% of undergraduates are from out of state, mostly the Midwest. Students are from 48 states, 69 foreign countries, and Canada. 82% are White; 3% African American; 3% two or more races; 2% Asian American; 2% Hispanic; 2% race unknown; 1% American Indian/Alaska Native. **Male To Female Ratio:** 1.2:1. The average age of freshmen is 18; all undergraduates, 21. 20% do not continue beyond their first year; 50% remain to graduate. **Housing:** 4996 students can be accommodated in college housing, which includes married student dorms, on-campus apartments, learning communities and first-year student halls. On-campus housing is guaranteed for the freshman year only. 67% of students commute. Alcohol is not permitted. All students may keep cars.

FACULTY/CLASSROOMS: No introductory courses are taught by graduate students.

PROGRAMS OF STUDY: NDSU confers B.A., B.F.A., B.L.A., B.Mus., B.S., B.S.A.B.En., B.S.Arch., B.S.C.E., B.S.Cpr.E., B.S.Con.E., B.S.Cons.M., B.S.E.E., B.S.I.E.Mgt., B.S.Mfg.E., B.S.M.E., B.S.N. and B.U.S. degrees. Master's and doctoral degrees are also awarded. Bachelor's degrees are awarded in AGRICULTURE (agricultural business management, agricultural communications, agricultural economics, agricultural mechanics, agriculture, animal science, equine science, horticulture, natural resource management, plant protection (pest management), plant science, range/farm management, and soil science), BIOLOGICAL SCIENCE (biochemistry, biology/biological science, biotechnology, botany, microbiology, and nutrition), BUSINESS (accounting, business administration and management, finance, hospitality management services, hotel/motel and restaurant management, management information systems, management science, marketing, recreation and leisure services, and sports management), COMMUNICATIONS AND THE ARTS (apparel design, art, communications, dramatic arts, English, French, instrumental music education, journalism - news & information, music, performing arts, public relations, Spanish, and theatre arts), COMPUTER AND PHYSICAL SCIENCE (actuarial science, chemistry, computer science, earth science, geology, mathematics, physics, radiological technology, and statistics), EDUCATION (agricultural education, athletic training, elementary education, health education, home economics education, music education, physical education, secondary education, and social science education), ENGINEERING AND ENVIRONMENTAL DESIGN (agricultural engineering, agricultural engineering technology, architecture, biomedical engineering, civil engineering, computer engineering, construction engineering, construction management, electrical/electronics engineering, emergency/disaster science, engineering management, environmental design, industrial engineering, interior design, landscape architecture/design, manufacturing engineering, and mechanical engineering), HEALTH PROFESSIONS (clinical science, health communication, nursing, pharmacy, preveterinary science, respiratory therapy, and veterinary science), SOCIAL SCIENCE (anthropology, child care/child and family studies, criminal justice, dietetics, economics, food science, history, human development, humanities, international studies, philosophy and religion, physical fitness/movement, political science/government, psychology, social science, sociology, textiles and clothing, and women & gender studies). Engineering, pharmacy, and nursing are the strongest academically. Sciences, engineering, and human development have the largest enrollments.

ACTIVITIES: 5% of men belong to 12 national fraternities; 2% of women belong to 3 national sororities. There are 300 groups on campus, including academic, leisure learning, art, band, cheerleading, choir, chorus, computers, dance, debate, drama, drill team, ethnic, forensics, honors, international, jazz band, LGBT, marching band, musical theater, newspaper, orchestra, pep band, political, professional, radio and TV, recreational, religious, social, social service, student government, and symphony. Popular campus events include International Students' Week, and Multicultural Activities. **Sports:** There are 8 intercollegiate sports for men and 8 for women, and 11 intramural sports for men and 10 for women. Facilities include a sports arena, indoor and outdoor tracks, baseball and softball fields, wrestling and weight rooms, a multipurpose fitness room, volleyball, tennis, basketball, racquetball courts, and a wellness center including aquatics facility. **Graduates:** From July 1, 2016 to June 30, 2017, 2308 bachelor's degrees were awarded. The most popular majors were business (15%), engineering (13%), health professions, and related sciences (11%). In an average class, 25% graduate in 4 years or less, 49% graduate in 5 years or less, and 56% graduate in 6 years or less.

SERVICES: Counseling and information services are available, as is tutoring in most subjects. There is a reader service for the blind, and remedial math, reading, and writing, and note takers. **Library/Resources:** The library contains 784,978 volumes, 444,951 microform items, and 2,873 audio/video tapes/CDs/DVDs, and subscribes to 5,090 periodicals including electronic. Computerized library services include interlibrary loans, database searching, Internet access, and Wi-Fi capability. Special learning facilities include an art gallery, radio station, and TV station. **Physically Challenged Students:** All of the campus is accessible. Facilities include wheelchair ramps, elevators, special parking, specially equipped restrooms, special class scheduling, lowered drinking fountains, and lowered telephones. **Special:** Special academic programs include cooperative work programs and internships. There is cross-registration with the Tri-college Consortium and all North Dakota State institutions. Student-designed and dual majors, study abroad, a B.A.-B.S. degree, nondegree study, and pass/fail options are possible. There are 22 national honor societies and a freshman honors program. **Visiting:** There are regularly scheduled orientations for prospective students, including tours of the campus, academic appointments, and meetings with admissions counselors and financial aid counselors. There are guides for informal visits and visitors may sit in on classes. To schedule a visit, contact Office of Admission. **Campus Safety and Security:** Measures include 24-hour foot and vehicle patrol, emergency notification system, self-defense education, and security escort services. There are shuttle buses, emergency telephones, lighted pathways/sidewalks, and controlled access to dorms/residences.

REQUIREMENTS: The SAT or ACT is required. Applicants must have completed 4 units of English, and 3 each of math (algebra I or above), lab science, and social science. An additional unit from one of the core areas (English, math, lab science, social science) OR from a world language (including foreign languages, Native American languages or American Sign Language) is also required. The GED is accepted, with a minimum score of 45 and no subject score lower than 40. A GPA of 2.5 is required. AP and CLEP credits are accepted. Students must complete at least 122 semester credits, with at least 24 in the major, and maintain at least a 2.0 GPA. General education requirements include 10 credits in science and technology, including a 1-credit lab course, 12 credits in communication, which includes freshman English and public speaking, 6 credits each in humanities, fine arts and social and behavioral science, 3 credits in quantitative reasoning, at least 2 credits in a wellness course, and a first-year experience course. Included in these courses must be 1 course designated as a cultural diversity course and 1 designated as a global perspectives course. **Procedure:** Freshmen are admitted to all sessions. Entrance exams should be taken in the spring of the junior year or in the fall of the senior year. There are deferred admissions and rolling admissions plans. Applications should be filed by August 1 for fall entry; December 1 for spring entry; and May 1 for summer entry. The fall 2017 application fee was $35. Applications are accepted on-line. **Transfer Students:** Transfer students must have a minimum GPA of 2.0; ACT or SAT scores are required if the applicant has fewer than 24 semester credits. 36 of 122 credits required for the bachelor's degree must be completed at NDSU. **International Students:** There are 1059 international students enrolled. They must take the TOEFL with a minimum score of 525 on the paper-based TOEFL (PBT) or 71 on the Internet-based version (iBT).

ADMISSIONS: 80% of the 2017-2018 applicants were accepted. The SAT scores for the 2017-2018 freshman class were: Critical Reading-- 26% below 500, 36% between 500 and 599, 32% between 600 and 699, and 6% between 700 and 800. Math-- 23% below 500, 26% between 500 and 599, 36% between 600 and 699, and 15% between 700 and 800. Writing-- 34% below 500, 38% between 500 and 599, 26% between 600 and 699, and 2% between 700 and 800. The ACT scores were 45% between 18 and 23, 44% between 24 and 29, and 8% above 30. **Admissions Contact:** Merideth Sherlin, Director of Admission. Email: *ndsu.admission@ndsu.edu* Web: *www.ndsu.edu*

FINANCIAL AID: The FAFSA code is 002997. The priority date for freshman financial aid applications for fall entry is February 1.

THE UNIVERSITY OF MARY — C-3

www.umary.edu

Bismarck, ND 58504	**(701) 355-8190** **(800) 288-6279**
Fax: (701) 255-7687	**Email: enroll@umary.edu**
Full-time: 647 men, 998 women	**Faculty:** 95
Part-time: 187 men, 228 women	**Ph.D.s:** 36%
Graduate: 272 men, 451 women	**Student/Faculty:** 18 to 1
Year: semesters, summer session	**Tuition:** $16,310
Room & Board: $6870	**Freshman Class:** 1010 applied, 855 accepted, 367 enrolled
SAT: recommended **ACT:** 23	**CEEB CODE:** 6428
Application Deadline: August 15	**COMPETITIVE**

University of Mary, founded in 1959, is a private institution affiliated with the Roman Catholic Church. Undergraduate and graduate programs emphasize liberal arts, humanities, social sciences, business, health science, music, professional training, philosophy and religious studies, and teacher preparation. There are 8 undergraduate schools and 4 graduate schools. In addition to regional accreditation, University of Mary has baccalaureate program accreditation with CAHEA, CSWE, CCNE, ACOTE, CAPTE, and CAATE. The 107-acre campus is in a suburban area 7 miles south of Bismarck. Including any residence halls, there are 13 buildings.

STUDENT LIFE: 70% of undergraduates are from North Dakota. Others are from 33 states, 23 foreign countries, and Canada. 95% are from public schools. 87% are White; 5% American Indian/Alaska Native; 3% African American; 2% Hispanic; 1% Asian American; 1% Foreign. 60% are Catholic; 30% Protestant. **Female To Male Ratio:** 1.5:1. The average age of freshmen is 18; all undergraduates, 25. 26% do not continue beyond their first year; 51% remain to graduate. **Housing:** 791 students can be accommodated in college housing, which includes dorms and on-campus apartments. On-campus housing is guaranteed for all 4 years. 61% of students commute. Alcohol is not permitted. All students may keep cars.

FACULTY/CLASSROOMS: 48% of faculty are male; 52% are female. 95% teach undergraduates, 15% do research, and 15% do both. No introductory courses are taught by graduate students. The average class size in an introductory lecture is 15; in a laboratory is 20; and in a regular course is 20.

PROGRAMS OF STUDY: University of Mary confers B.A., B.S., and B.Univ.Studies degrees. Master's degrees are also awarded. Bachelor's degrees are awarded in BIOLOGICAL SCIENCE (biology/biological science), BUSINESS (accounting, business administration and management, business communications, and management information systems), COMMUNICATIONS AND THE ARTS (communications, English, and music), COMPUTER AND PHYSICAL SCIENCE (information sciences and systems, mathematics, and radiological technology), EDUCATION (athletic training, early childhood education, elementary education, English education, mathematics education, music education, physical education, social science education, and special education), ENGINEERING AND ENVIRONMENTAL DESIGN (engineering and applied science), HEALTH PROFESSIONS (exercise science, nursing, occupational therapy, physical therapy, premedicine, and respiratory therapy), SOCIAL SCIENCE (addiction studies, behavioral science, criminal justice, liberal arts/general studies, ministries, pastoral studies, prelaw, psychology, social science, social work, and theological studies). Business administration, education, and nursing are the strongest academically. Business, nursing, and elementary education have the largest enrollments.

ACTIVITIES: There are no fraternities or sororities. There are 22 groups on campus, including band, cheerleading, choir, chorale, chorus, computers, drama, drill team, environmental, ethnic, forensics, jazz band, musical theater, newspaper, orchestra, pep band, photography, political, professional, radio and TV, religious, social, social service, student government, and symphony. Popular campus events include Intramural Sports, and the Convocation Series. **Sports:** There are 8 intercollegiate sports for men and 7 for women, and 10 intramural sports for men and 10 for women. Facilities include an activity center housing a gym, basketball and racquetball courts, wrestling and weight rooms, a swimming pool, indoor track, basketball/volleyball/tennis courts, a climbing wall, track/football, intramural, and softball fields, tennis courts, a fitness center, and a stadium. **Graduates:** From July 1, 2016 to June 30, 2017, 502 bachelor's degrees were awarded. The most popular majors were business (40%), nursing (19%), and education (10%). In an average class, 5% graduate in 3 years or less, 39% graduate in 4 years or less, 50% graduate in 5 years or less, and 1% graduate in 6 years or less. Of the 2016 graduating class, 17% were enrolled in graduate school within 6 months of graduation, and 80% were employed.

SERVICES: Counseling and information services are available, as is tutoring in every subject. There is a reader service for the blind, and remedial math, reading, and writing. **Library/Resources:** The library contains 78,137 volumes, 2 microform items, and 7,866 audio/video tapes/CDs/DVDs, and subscribes to 6,997 periodicals including electronic. Computerized library services include interlibrary loans, database searching, Internet access, and Wi-Fi capability. Special learning facilities include an art gallery and radio station. **Physically Challenged Students:** All of the campus is accessible. Facilities include wheelchair ramps, elevators, special parking, specially equipped restrooms, special class scheduling, lowered drinking fountains, lowered telephones, and special housing. **Special:** A co-op program in engineering is available as is cross-registration with the University of Minnesota. Special academic programs include internships in all fields and all programs, study abroad in France, Germany, and Spain, on-campus work-study, and a general studies degree. Dual majors include elementary education/early childhood, elementary education/special education, athletic training/biology, athletic training/phys ed, business/accounting, and business/computer information systems. There are accelerated degree programs in several majors, and a 3-2 engineering program with the University of Minnesota. There are 3 national honor societies, a freshman honors program, and 2 departmental honors programs. **Visiting:** There are regularly scheduled orientations for prospective students, including a campus tour and meetings with individual professors, coaches, students, and music instructors. There are guides for informal visits, visitors may sit in on classes, and stay overnight. To schedule a visit, contact the Admissions Office. **Campus Safety and Security:** Measures include emergency notification system and security escort services. There are emergency telephones, lighted pathways/sidewalks, and controlled access to dorms/residences.

REQUIREMENTS: The SAT or ACT and ACT Writing Test are recommended. Applicants should be graduates of an accredited secondary school; the GED is accepted. For automatic acceptance, 3 requirements must be met: a minimum 2.5 GPA; an 18 or higher score on the ACT; and rank in the upper half of the graduating class. The school's own testing can also be used to determine acceptance. A recommendation from a school counselor, teacher, or employer is requested. A GPA of 2.5 is required. AP and CLEP credits are accepted. Important factors in the admissions decision are evidence of special talent, leadership record, and advanced placement or honors courses. To graduate, students must complete 128 semester hours, with 32 to 56 in the major and 44 at the 300-400 level, and have a minimum GPA of 2.0. At least 56 semester hours must be in liberal arts courses. In addition, a B.A. degree requires 16 semester hours of a foreign language or 20 semester hours of philosophy/theology, with 12 such hours at the 300-400 level. All students must take 3 courses each in humanities, math/science, philosophy/theology, and social sciences. **Procedure:** Freshmen are admitted fall and spring. Entrance exams should be taken in the fall of the senior year. There are early admissions, deferred admissions, and rolling admissions plans. Applications should be filed by August 15 for fall entry; December 15 for spring entry. The fall 2017 application fee was $15. Applications are accepted on-line. **Transfer Students:** 259 transfer students enrolled in 2016-2017. Transfer students should have a 2.0 minimum GPA and should present a recommendation from a school counselor, instructor, or employer. 32 of 128 credits required for the bachelor's degree must be completed at the University of Mary. **International Students:** There are 25 international students enrolled. They must take the TOEFL with a minimum score of 500 on the paper-based TOEFL (PBT).

ADMISSIONS: 85% of the 2017-2018 applicants were accepted. The ACT scores were 27% below 12, 33% between 12 and 17, 27% between 18 and 23, 8% between 24 and 29, and 5% above 30. 37% of the current freshmen were in the top fifth of their class; 69% were in the top two fifths. 20 freshmen graduated first in their class. **Admissions Contact:** Dave Heringer, Vice President For Enrollment. Email: *enroll@umary.edu* Web: *www.umary.edu*

FINANCIAL AID: In 2017-2018, 100% of all full-time freshmen received some form of financial aid. 85% of all full-time freshmen received need-based aid. 70% of undergraduate students work part-time. The average financial indebtedness of the 2017 graduate was $15,500. The FAFSA code is 002992. The priority date for freshman financial aid applications for fall entry is March 15.

UNIVERSITY OF JAMESTOWN E-3

www.uj.edu

Jamestown, ND 58405 **(701) 252-3467** **(800) 336-2554**

Fax: (701) 253-4318 **Email: admission@uj.edu**

Full-time: 480 men, 475 women	**Faculty:** 57
Part-time: n/av	**Ph.D.s:** 54%
Graduate: 71 men, 108 women	**Student/Faculty:** 13 to 1
Year: semesters, summer session	**Tuition:** $21,158
Room & Board: $7350	**Freshman Class:** 1560 applied, 894 accepted, 267 enrolled
SAT CR/M: required **ACT:** 22	**CEEB CODE:** 6318
Application Deadline: open	**COMPETITIVE**

University of Jamestown, founded in 1883, is a private institution founded by the Presbyterian Church. Its emphases are on the liberal arts, business, arts, health science, music, religious studies, and teacher preparation. There is 1 undergraduate school and 4 graduate schools. In addition to regional accreditation, University of Jamestown has baccalaureate program accreditation with NLN and IACBE. The 110-acre campus is in a small town in central North Dakota, 100 miles west of Fargo, and 350 miles west of Minneapolis. Including any residence halls, there are 27 buildings.

STUDENT LIFE: 55% of undergraduates are from out of state, mostly the Midwest. Students are from 31 states, 13 foreign countries, and Canada. 83% are White; 6% Foreign; 5% Hispanic; 4% African American; 1% Asian American; 1% American Indian/Alaska Native. 50% are Protestant; 27% claim no religious affiliation; 19% Catholic. **Female To Male Ratio:** 1.1:1. The average age of freshmen is 18; all undergraduates, 21. 22% do not continue beyond their first year; 52% remain to graduate. **Housing:** 744 students can be accommodated in college housing, which includes married student dorms, on-campus apartments, and off-campus apartments. On-campus housing is guaranteed for the freshman year only, is available on a first-come, first-served basis, and is available on a lottery system for upperclassmen. 65% of students live on campus. Alcohol is not permitted. All students may keep cars.

FACULTY/CLASSROOMS: 54% of faculty are male; 46% are female. All teach undergraduates. No introductory courses are taught by graduate students. The average class size in an introductory lecture is 26; in a laboratory is 15; and in a regular course is 20.

PROGRAMS OF STUDY: University of Jamestown confers B.A., B.S., and B.S.N. degrees. Master's and doctoral degrees are also awarded. Bachelor's degrees are awarded in BIOLOGICAL SCIENCE (biochemistry and biology/biological science), BUSINESS (accounting, business administration and management, and management information systems), COMMUNICATIONS AND THE ARTS (communications, English, fine arts, French, German, music, and Spanish), COMPUTER AND PHYSICAL SCIENCE (chemistry, computer science, information sciences and systems, mathematics, and radiological technology), EDUCATION (elementary education and physical education), ENGINEERING AND ENVIRONMENTAL DESIGN (graphic arts technology), HEALTH PROFESSIONS (clinical science, exercise science, and nursing), SOCIAL SCIENCE (criminal justice, history, history of science, psychology, religion, and religious education). Physical therapy, business, and nursing are the strongest academically. Business, nursing, and exercise science have the largest enrollments.

ACTIVITIES: There are no fraternities or sororities. There are 35 groups on campus, including art, band, cheerleading, choir, chorale, chorus, computers, dance, drama, environmental, film, honors, international, jazz band, literary magazine, musical theater, newspaper, orchestra, pep band, political, professional, radio and TV, religious, social, social service, and student government. Popular campus events include Jimmie Jive Week, Homecoming, and Character in Leadership Fall Conference. **Sports:** There are 10 intercollegiate sports for men and 11 for women, and 6 intramural sports for men and 6 for women. Facilities include an athletic center with a basketball court, wrestling and volleyball practice and composition area, a football stadium with an all-weather track, a soccer field, and a sports center with a swimming pool, weight room, running track, basketball, handball, and racquetball courts. **Graduates:** From July 1, 2016 to June 30, 2017, 142 bachelor's degrees were awarded. The most popular majors were nursing (22%), business (13%), and elementary education and exercise science (7%). In an average class, 1% graduate in 3 years or less, 30% graduate in 4 years or less, 47% graduate in 5 years or less, and 49% graduate in 6 years or less. Of the 2016 graduating class, 15% were enrolled in graduate school within 6 months of graduation, and 91% were employed.

SERVICES: Counseling and information services are available, as is tutoring in most subjects. There is remedial math, reading, and writing. **Library/Resources:** The library contains 112,169 volumes, 9,000 microform items, and 5,518 audio/video tapes/CDs/DVDs, and subscribes to 18,610 periodicals including electronic. Computerized library services include interlibrary loans, database searching, and Internet access. Special learning facilities include an art gallery, radio station, and TV station. **Physically Challenged Students:** 90% of the campus is accessible. Facilities include wheelchair ramps, elevators, special parking, specially equipped restrooms, special class scheduling, lowered drinking fountains, lowered telephones, and special housing. **Special:** Special academic options include co-op programs in business, nursing, computer science, and criminal justice, on-campus work-study, internships, study abroad, dual majors within any of the concentrations, and student-designed majors. There is a 3-2 engineering program with North Dakota State University. There are 5 national honor societies and 10 departmental honors programs. **Visiting:** There are regularly scheduled orientations for prospective students, including a campus tour and faculty visits. There are guides for informal visits, visitors may sit in on classes, and stay overnight. To schedule a visit, contact Admissions Office. **Campus Safety and Security:** Measures include emergency notification system, self-defense education, and security escort services. There are lighted pathways/sidewalks, controlled access to dorms/residences, and shuttle services.

REQUIREMENTS: The SAT or ACT is required. Requirements include graduation from an accredited secondary school. The GED is accepted. A GPA of 2.5 is required. AP and CLEP credits are accepted. Important factors in the admissions decision are evidence of special talent, leadership record, and personality/intangible qualities. To graduate, students must have a minimum of 128 semester credits, at least 48 of which must be at the upper-division level, with an average of 48 semester credits in the major, and maintain at least a 2.0 GPA. **Procedure:** Freshmen are admitted to all sessions. Entrance exams should be taken before or during the fall of the senior year. There is a rolling admissions plan. Application deadlines are open. Applications are accepted on-line. **Transfer Students:** 60 transfer students enrolled in 2016-2017. Applicants must have at least a 2.0 GPA and be in good standing with their previous college; Applicants are required to submit official high school and college transcripts. 35 of 128 credits required for the bachelor's degree must be completed at University of Jamestown. **International Students:** There are 90 international students enrolled. They must take the TOEFL with a minimum score of 525 on the paper-based TOEFL (PBT) or 70 on the Internet-based version (iBT) or take the MELAB.

ADMISSIONS: 57% of the 2017-2018 applicants were accepted. The SAT scores for the 2017-2018 freshman class were: Critical Reading--55% below 500, 28% between 500 and 599, 13% between 600 and 699, and 2% between 700 and 800. Math-- 57% below 500, 28% between 500 and 599, 11% between 600 and 699, and 2% between 700 and 800. The ACT scores were 6% between 12 and 17, 61% between 18 and 23, 28% between 24 and 29, and 4% above 30. **Admissions Contact:** Mike Heitkamp, Vice President of Enrollment. Email: *admission@uj.edu* Web: *www.uj.edu*

FINANCIAL AID: In 2017-2018, 100% of all full-time freshmen received some form of financial aid and need-based aid. The average freshman award was $14,135. Need-based scholarships or need-based grants averaged $4,981 ($10,315 maximum); need-based self-help aid (loans and jobs) averaged $3,770 ($8,500 maximum); non-need-based athletic scholarships averaged $4,129 ($12,930 maximum); and other non-need-based awards and non-need-based scholarships averaged $9,875 ($19,930 maximum). 33% of undergraduate students work part-time. The average financial indebtedness of the 2017 graduate was $22,925. The FAFSA code is 002990. The priority date for freshman financial aid applications for fall entry is March 15.

UNIVERSITY OF NORTH DAKOTA E-2

www.und.edu

Grand Forks, ND 58202 **(701) 777-3000**

Fax: (701) 777-2721	**Email:** und.admissions@und.edu
Full-time: 4626 men, 3999 women	**Faculty:** 488; I, -$
Part-time: 1634 men, 841 women	**Ph.D.s:** 94%
Graduate: 1284 men, 2122 women	**Student/Faculty:** 18 to 1
Year: semesters, summer session	**Tuition:** $8447 ($20,047)
Room & Board: $8226	**Freshman Class:** 5145 applied, 4306 accepted, 1928 enrolled
SAT: required **ACT:** 24	**CEEB CODE:** 6878
Application Deadline: July 1	**COMPETITIVE**

University of North Dakota, founded in 1883. UND offers baccalaureate through doctoral and professional degrees, law, medicine, and more than 40 degree and graduate certificate programs through distance education. The university offers students online academic courses, and other non-academic activities, including workforce development, conferences, professional certificates, teacher workshops, and lifelong learning courses. There are 8 undergraduate schools and 3 graduate schools. In addition to regional accreditation, UND has baccalaureate program accreditation with CAHEA, CSWE, NASM, and CADE. The 521-acre campus is in an urban area 4 hours from Minneapolis, St. Paul and 2 hours from Winnipeg, Manitoba. Including any residence halls, there are 244 buildings.

STUDENT LIFE: 64% of undergraduates are from out of state, mostly the Midwest. Students are from 50 states, 72 foreign countries, and Canada. 95% are from public schools. 80% are White; 4% Hispanic; 4% two or more races; 2% Foreign; 3% African American; 2% Asian American; 1% American Indian/Alaska Native; 1% race unknown. **Male To Female Ratio:** 1.1:1. The average age of freshmen is 19; all undergraduates, 23. 20% do not continue beyond their first year; 80% remain to graduate. **Housing:** 4135 students can be accommodated in college housing, which includes married student dorms and on-campus apartments. In addition, there are special-interest houses. On-campus housing is guaranteed for all 4 years. 72% of students commute. Alcohol is not permitted. All students may keep cars.

FACULTY/CLASSROOMS: 56% of faculty are male; 44% are female. 70% teach undergraduates. No introductory courses are taught by graduate students. The average class size in an introductory lecture is 28; in a laboratory is 16; and in a regular course is 24.

PROGRAMS OF STUDY: UND confers B.A., B.Acc., B.B.A., B.F.A., B.G.S., B.M., B.S., B.S.A., B.S.A.T., B.S.AtSc, B.S.C.E., B.S.C.H.E., B.S.Chem., B.S.C.J.S., B.S.C.N., B.S.C.S.C.I., B.S.Cyto., B.S.D., B.S.E.E., B.S.E.D., B.S.E.G., B.S.F.W.B., B.S.G.D.T., B.S.G.E., B.S.Geol., B.S.I.T., B.S.M.E., B.S.M.L.S., B.S.N., B.S.O.S.E.H., B.S.P.A., B.S.PTE., B.S.R.T.S., B.S.R.H.S., B.S.S.W., and B.S.KIN degrees. Master's and doctoral degrees are also awarded. Bachelor's degrees are awarded in AGRICULTURE (environmental studies and fishing and fisheries), BIOLOGICAL SCIENCE (biology/biological science), BUSINESS (accounting, banking and finance, business economics, human resources, investments and securities, marketing management, and operations management), COMMUNICATIONS AND THE ARTS (Chinese, classical languages, communications, English, French, German, graphic design, music, music performance, musical theater, Norwegian, Spanish, and visual and performing arts), COMPUTER AND PHYSICAL SCIENCE (atmospheric sciences and meteorology, chemistry, computer science, geology, information sciences and systems, mathematics, natural sciences, physics, and science), EDUCATION (athletic training, business education, early childhood education, elementary education, middle school education, music education, and physical education), ENGINEERING AND ENVIRONMENTAL DESIGN (air traffic control, aviation maintenance management, chemical engineering, civil engineering, electrical/electronics engineering, geological engineering, industrial engineering technology, mechanical engineering, occupational safety and health, and petroleum/natural gas engineering), HEALTH PROFESSIONS (clinical science, cytotechnology, medical laboratory science, music therapy, nursing, and physical therapy), SOCIAL SCIENCE (American Indian studies, anthropology, criminal justice, dietetics, early childhood studies, economics, forensic studies, geography, history, interdisciplinary studies, international studies, philosophy, political science/government, psychology, public administration, religion, social science, social work, and sociology). Science technologies, education, and foreign languages are the strongest academically. Engineering, health professions, and business have the largest enrollments.

ACTIVITIES: 10% of men belong to 12 national fraternities; 11% of women belong to 7 national sororities. There are 275 groups on campus, including art, band, cheerleading, chess, choir, chorale, chorus, computers, dance, debate, departmental club, drama, drill team, ethnic, film, honors, international, jazz band, LGBT, literary magazine, marching band, musical theater, newspaper, opera, orchestra, pep band, photography, political, professional, radio and TV, religious, social, social service, special interest club, student government, and symphony. Popular campus events include The Big Event-a City Wide Community Event, Athletic Events, Potato Bowl, Homecoming, Time Out and Wacipi. **Sports:** There are 8 intercollegiate sports for men and 9 for women, and 14 intramural sports for men and 14 for women. Facilities include a stadium, hockey arena, basketball center, sports/field house with racquetball and basketball courts, weight rooms and a dance studio. The wellness center houses a three-court gymnasium, multi-activity court, cardiovascular, weight rooms, a running track, and a rock-climbing wall. **Graduates:** From July 1, 2016 to June 30, 2017, 1948 bachelor's degrees were awarded. The most popular majors were psychology (6%), nursing (6%), and commercial aviation (5%). In an average class, 1% graduate in 3 years or less, 23% graduate in 4 years or less, 46% graduate in 5 years or less, and 55% graduate in 6 years or less. Of the 2016 graduating class, 16% were enrolled in graduate school within 6 months of graduation, and 81% were employed.

SERVICES: Counseling and information services are available, as is tutoring in every subject. There is a reader service for the blind. **Library/Resources:** The library contains 1.7 million volumes, 856,469 microform items, and 22,034 audio/video tapes/CDs/DVDs, and subscribes to 62,508 periodicals including electronic. Computerized library services include interlibrary loans, database searching, Internet access, and Wi-Fi capability. Special learning facilities include a natural history museum, planetarium, radio station, TV station, an entrepreneur center, atmospherium, art museum, gallery, and one stop student services. **Physically Challenged Students:** 99% of the campus is accessible. Facilities include wheelchair ramps, elevators, special parking, specially equipped restrooms, special class scheduling, lowered drinking fountains, lowered telephones, and special housing. There is also accessible transportation, and academic and personal support services. **Special:** Special academic programs include cooperative programs, accelerated degree programs in most majors, internships in many majors, study abroad in at least 20 countries, work-study, and dual majors in all areas. Also offered are a general studies degree, honors programs, student-designed majors, B.A.-B.S. degrees, nondegree study, and pass/fail options. Alternative academic programs include the Division of Continuing Education's correspondence study, the Integrated Studies Program, which offers a means of fulfilling general education requirements by a semester of related course work, and study via telecommunications. Cross-registration with all North Dakota 2- and 4-year public institutions is possible. There are 20 national honor societies, Phi Beta Kappa, a freshman honors program, and 1 departmental honors program. **Visiting:** There are regularly scheduled orientations for prospective students, including a visit with an admissions counselor, a campus tour, an academic appointment, and an athletic appointment (if applicable). There are guides for informal visits, visitors may sit in on classes, and stay overnight. To schedule a visit, contact the Office of Admissions. **Campus Safety and Security:** Measures include 24-hour foot and vehicle patrol, emergency notification system, self-defense education, and security escort services. There are shuttle buses, emergency telephones, lighted pathways/sidewalks, and emergency phones throughout the campus.

REQUIREMENTS: The SAT is required; the ACT is preferred. Applicants must be graduates of an accredited secondary school or have passed the GED with an average of 50. A GPA of 2.5 is required. AP and CLEP credits are accepted. To graduate, students must complete at least 125 credit hours, 30 in the major, with a minimum GPA of 2.0. At least 36 credits must be numbered 300 or above, and at least 60 credits must be from a 4-year institution. Distribution requirements include 12 credits of math, science, and technology, 9 each of social sciences and arts, and humanities, and 6 of English composition. One course in social science or arts and humanities must meet the world cultures designation. **Procedure:** Freshmen are admitted to all sessions. Entrance exams should be taken in spring of the junior year or fall of the senior year. There are early decision and rolling admissions plans. Applications should be filed by July 1 for fall entry. The fall 2017 application fee was $35. Notification is sent on a rolling basis. **Transfer Students:** 706 transfer students enrolled in 2016-2017. Transfer students must have a minimum GPA of 2.0 and be in good academic standing. A higher GPA may be required in specific programs. 30 of 125 credits required for the bachelor's degree must be completed at UND. **International Students:** There are 353 international students enrolled. They must take the TOEFL. They must also take the SAT or ACT.

ADMISSIONS: 84% of the 2017-2018 applicants were accepted. The ACT scores were 4% between 12 and 17, 48% between 18 and 23, 41% between 24 and 29, and 7% above 30. 35% of the current freshmen were in the top fifth of their class; 66% were in the top two fifths. 80 freshmen graduated first in their class. **Admissions Contact:** Jason Trainer, Director of Admissions. Email: *und.admissions@und.edu* Web: *www.und.edu*

FINANCIAL AID: In 2017-2018, 90% of all full-time freshmen received some form of financial aid. 42% of all full-time freshmen received need-based aid. The average freshman award was $3,065. Need-based scholarships or need-based grants averaged $2,244 ($5,920 maximum); need-based self-help aid (loans and jobs) averaged $2,871 ($5,500 maximum); non-need-based athletic scholarships averaged $7,664 ($18,546 maximum); and other non-need-based awards and non-need-based scholarships averaged $3,296 ($43,190 maximum). The FAFSA code is 003005. The priority date for freshman financial aid applications for fall entry is February 1.

VALLEY CITY STATE UNIVERSITY — E-3

www.vcsu.edu

Valley City, ND 58072	**(701) 845-7101** **(800) 532-8641**
Fax: (701) 845-7299	**Email: enrollment.services@vcsu.edu**
Full-time: 379 men, 419 women	**Faculty:** 70; IIB, --$
Part-time: 167 men, 330 women	**Ph.D.s:** 51%
Graduate: 46 men, 111 women	**Student/Faculty:** 11 to 1
Year: semesters, summer session	**Tuition:** $7195 ($16,016)
Room & Board: $6072	**Freshman Class:** 372 applied, 285 accepted, 190 enrolled
ACT: 21	**CEEB CODE:** 6480
Application Deadline: open	**COMPETITIVE**

Valley City State University, founded in 1890 as a teachers college. VCSU prepares people for life through visionary leadership and exemplary practices in teaching, learning and service, and has built on that rich tradition with a student-focused, learning-centered approach, offering more than 80 degree programs. One of the first "laptop universities" in the nation (each full-time student receives a laptop computer), VCSU continues its innovative use of technology with many online offerings, including several undergraduate majors and a master of education degree program. There is 1 undergraduate school and 1 graduate school. In addition to regional accreditation, VCSU has baccalaureate program accreditation with NASM, and CAATE. The 64-acre campus is in a small town on the banks of the Sheyenne River, Valley City, and 58 miles west of Fargo, ND. Including any residence halls, there are 29 buildings.

STUDENT LIFE: 66% of undergraduates are from North Dakota. Others are from 46 states, 7 foreign countries, and Canada. 84% are White; 4% Hispanic; 3% African American; 3% two or more races; 2% Foreign; 2% race unknown; 1% Asian American; 1% American Indian/Alaska Native. **Female To Male Ratio:** 1.5:1. The average age of freshmen is 19; all undergraduates, 23. 29% do not continue beyond their first year. **Housing:** 465 students can be accommodated in college housing, which includes married student dorms. On-campus housing is guaranteed for all 4 years. 75% of students commute. Alcohol is not permitted. All students may keep cars.

FACULTY/CLASSROOMS: 45% of faculty are male; 55% are female. All teach undergraduates, 25% do research, and 25% do both. No introductory courses are taught by graduate students. The average class size in an introductory lecture is 40; in a laboratory is 20; and in a regular course is 25.

PROGRAMS OF STUDY: VCSU confers B.A., B.S., B.S.Ed., and B.University Studies. degrees. Master's degrees are also awarded. Bachelor's degrees are awarded in BIOLOGICAL SCIENCE (biology/biological science), BUSINESS (business administration and management, human resources, and office supervision and management), COMMUNICATIONS AND THE ARTS (art, English, music, and Spanish), COMPUTER AND PHYSICAL SCIENCE (chemistry, information sciences and systems, mathematics, and science), EDUCATION (business education, elementary education, health education, physical education, technical education, and vocational education), SOCIAL SCIENCE (history and social science). Education, business, and fisheries & wildlife science are the strongest academically. Elementary education, business, and fisheries & wildlife science have the largest enrollments.

ACTIVITIES: 1% of men belong to 1 local fraternity; 1% of women belong to 1 local sorority. There are 30 groups on campus, including art, band, cheerleading, choir, chorale, chorus, computers, drama, honors, international, jazz band, musical theater, newspaper, pep band, photography, political, professional, religious, social, student government, and yearbook. Popular campus events include Sno-Daze, and Medicine Wheel Seasonal Celebrations. **Sports:** There are 6 intercollegiate sports for men and 6 for women. Facilities include a football stadium with an all-weather track, an arena, indoor pool, a field house, tennis and racquetball courts, a cross-country course, softball and baseball fields, a golf course, weight rooms, and a fitness room. **Graduates:** From July 1, 2016 to June 30, 2017, 260 bachelor's degrees were awarded. The most popular majors were elementary education (53%), business administration (8%), and fisheries & wildlife science (5%). In an average class, 21% graduate in 4 years or less, 37% graduate in 5 years or less, and 45% graduate in 6 years or less.

SERVICES: Counseling and information services are available, as is tutoring in most subjects. There is a reader service for the blind, and remedial math and writing. **Library/Resources:** The library contains 110,000 volumes, 250 microform items, and 4,500 audio/video tapes/CDs/DVDs, and subscribes to 27,700 periodicals including electronic. Computerized library services include interlibrary loans, database searching, Internet access, and Wi-Fi capability. Special learning facilities include an art gallery and planetarium. **Physically Challenged Students:** 97% of the campus is accessible. Facilities include wheelchair ramps, elevators, special parking, specially equipped restrooms, special class scheduling, lowered drinking fountains, lowered telephones, and special housing. **Special:** VCSU offers internships, dual majors, on-campus work-study, study abroad in 2 countries, pass/fail options for some courses, and credit for life, military, and work experience. There are 6 national honor societies and 4 departmental honors programs. **Visiting:** There are regularly scheduled orientations for prospective students. There are guides for informal visits, visitors may sit in on classes, and stay overnight. To schedule a visit, contact the Office of Enrollment Services at enrollment.services@vcsu.edu. **Campus Safety and Security:** Measures include 24-hour foot and vehicle patrol, emergency notification system, and self-defense education. There are lighted pathways/sidewalks, a night patrol, and surveillance cameras.

REQUIREMENTS: The ACT is required. Applicants must be graduates of an accredited secondary school or have a GED certificate. Core curriculum requirements include 4 units of English and 3 units each of math, lab science, and social science. AP and CLEP credits are accepted. To graduate, students must complete at least 120 semester hours with a minimum GPA of 2.0, or 2.5 for a B.S.Ed. degree. Except for those pursuing the Bachelor of University Studies degree, all students must complete the foundation studies curriculum, which includes 9 hours in communication, 6 in aesthetic engagement, 5 in global perspective, 12 in problem solving, 6 in wellness, 3 in technology, and 15 to 16 in foreign language. Students must complete 48 hours in their major if they do not have a minor, or 36 hours in their major if they have a minor. All students must complete a digital portfolio specific to their major. **Procedure:** Freshmen are admitted to all sessions. There are deferred admissions and rolling admissions plans. Application deadlines are open. The fall 2017 application fee was $35. Notification is sent on a rolling basis. Applications are accepted on-line. **Transfer Students:** Applicants must be in good academic standing, have a minimum GPA of 2.0, and be eligible to return to their previous institution. Official transcripts from all colleges attended are required. Some students may be required to submit high school transcripts and standardized test scores. 30 of 120 credits required for the bachelor's degree must be completed at VCSU. **International Students:** There are 19 international students enrolled.

ADMISSIONS: 77% of the 2017-2018 applicants were accepted. The ACT scores were 17% between 12 and 17, 57% between 18 and 23, 19% between 24 and 29, and 3% above 30. **Admissions Contact:** Charlene Stenson, Director of Enrollment Services. Email: *enrollment.services@vcsu.edu* Web: *www.vcsu.edu*

FINANCIAL AID: VCSU is a member of CSS. The FAFSA code is 003008. The priority date for freshman financial aid applications for fall entry is March 15.

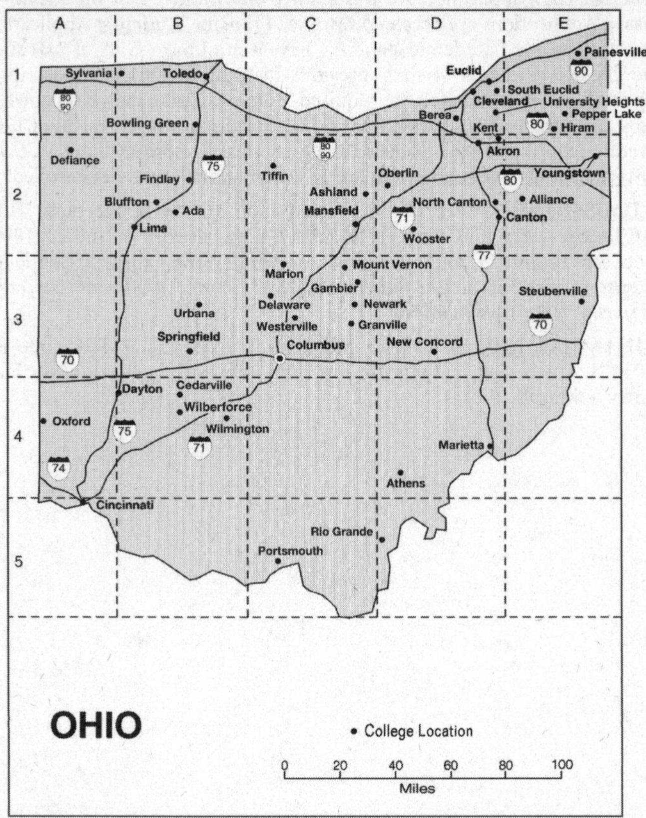

ART ACADEMY OF CINCINNATI *(The complete profile is made available exclusively on our website, www.barronspac.com)*

ASHLAND UNIVERSITY C-2
www.ashland.edu

Ashland, OH 44805 (419) 289-5052
(800) 882-1548
Fax: (419) 289-5333 **Email:** enrollme@ashland.edu
Full-time: 995 men, 1425 women
Part-time: 95 men, 270 women
Graduate: 1470 men, 2475 women
Year: semesters, summer session
Room & Board: $9746
SAT or ACT: required
Application Deadline: open
Faculty: 215; IIA, --$
Ph.D.s: 79%
Student/Faculty: 11 to 1
Tuition: $20,700
Freshman Class: n/av
CEEB CODE: 1021
COMPETITIVE

Ashland University, founded in 1878, is a private liberal arts and sciences institution affiliated with the Brethren Church. The figures given in the above capsule and in this profile are approximate. There are 6 undergraduate schools and 3 graduate schools. In addition to regional accreditation, Ashland has baccalaureate program accreditation with AACSB, AHEA, CSWE, NASM, CAEP, and NLN. The 150-acre campus is in a small town midway between Cleveland and Columbus. Including any residence halls, there are 38 buildings.

STUDENT LIFE: 94% of undergraduates are from Ohio. Others are from 29 states, 13 foreign countries, and Canada. 86% are White; 8% African American; 2% Foreign; 1% Asian American; 1% American Indian/Alaska Native; 1% Hispanic. 46% claim no religious affiliation; 34% Protestant; 14% Catholic. **Female To Male Ratio:** 1.6:1. The average age of freshmen is 18; all undergraduates, 23. 42% do not continue beyond their first year; 58% remain to graduate. **Housing:** 1620 students can be accommodated in college housing, which includes dorms and on-campus apartments. In addition, there are honors houses, fraternity houses, honors floors, and sorority suites. On-campus housing is guaranteed for all 4 years. 72% of students live on campus. Alcohol is not permitted. All students may keep cars.

FACULTY/CLASSROOMS: 61% of faculty are male; 39% are female. 81% teach undergraduates. No introductory courses are taught by graduate students. The average class size in an introductory lecture is 20; in a laboratory is 11; and in a regular course is 18.

PROGRAMS OF STUDY: Ashland confers B.A., B.S., B.M., B.S.B.A., B.S.Ed., B.S.N., and B.S.W. degrees. Associate, master's, and doctoral degrees are also awarded. Bachelor's degrees are awarded in BIOLOGICAL SCIENCE (biology/biological science, biotechnology, and toxicology), BUSINESS (accounting, banking and finance, business administration and management, business economics, entrepreneurial studies, fashion merchandising, hotel/motel and restaurant management, management information systems, marketing/retailing/merchandising, recreational facilities management, and sports management), COMMUNICATIONS AND THE ARTS (art, broadcasting, communications, creative writing, dramatic arts, English, fine arts, French, journalism, media arts, music, musical theater, Spanish, and speech/debate/rhetoric), COMPUTER AND PHYSICAL SCIENCE (actuarial science, chemistry, chemistry education, computer science, environmental chemistry, geology, mathematics, and physics), EDUCATION (art education, athletic training, early childhood education, education administration, education of the exceptional child, elementary education, English education, foreign languages education, health education, home economics education, music education, physical education, science education, and secondary education), ENGINEERING AND ENVIRONMENTAL DESIGN (commercial art and environmental science), HEALTH PROFESSIONS (nursing, predentistry, premedicine, preoptometry, preveterinary science, and recreation therapy), SOCIAL SCIENCE (American studies, child care/child and family studies, criminal justice, economics, food science, forensic studies, history, international studies, philosophy, physical fitness/movement, political science/government, prelaw, psychology, religion, religious studies, social science, social work, sociology, and Spanish studies). Preprofessional science is the strongest academically. Business, and teacher education have the largest enrollments.

ACTIVITIES: 14% of men belong to 4 national fraternities; 22% of women belong to 5 national sororities. There are 100 groups on campus, including art, band, cheerleading, choir, chorus, dance, drama, drill team, ethnic, health club and environmental club, honors, international, jazz band, literary magazine, marching band, musical theater, newspaper, orchestra, pep band, photography, political, professional, radio and TV, religious, social, social service, student government, symphony, and yearbook. Popular campus events include Spectrum Series, Plays, and Little Sibs Weekend. **Sports:** There are 10 intercollegiate sports for men and 9 for women, and 20 intramural sports for men and 20 for women. Facilities include a stadium, gym, all-weather track, field house, weight-training center, swimming pool with diving board, exercise rooms, basketball courts, handball/racquetball courts, playing fields, slow-pitch softball, a fitness center, and a soccer complex with 2 full-size fields, golf, quidditch, running, and snow sports. **Graduates:** Of the 2016 graduating class, 8% were enrolled in graduate school within 6 months of graduation, and 34% were employed.

SERVICES: Counseling and information services are available, as is tutoring in every subject. There is a reader service for the blind. **Library/Resources:** The library contains 270,000 volumes, 250,000 microform items, and 8,800 audio/video tapes/CDs/DVDs, and subscribes to 700 periodicals including electronic. Computerized library services include interlibrary loans and database searching. Special learning facilities include an art gallery, radio station, TV station, a writing center, a media center, and theater. **Physically Challenged Students:** 5% of the campus is accessible. Facilities include wheelchair ramps, elevators, special parking, specially equipped restrooms, special class scheduling, lowered drinking fountains, lowered telephones, and special housing. **Special:** Opportunities are provided for internships, co-op programs in all business majors, work-study programs, dual majors, credit by exam, study abroad in 27 countries, a Washington semester, and pass/fail options. There are 17 national honor societies, a freshman honors program, and 10 departmental honors programs. **Visiting:** There are regularly scheduled orientations for prospective students. There are guides for informal visits, visitors may sit in on classes, and stay overnight. To schedule a visit, contact the Office of Admissions. **Campus Safety and Security:** Measures include 24-hour foot and vehicle patrol, self-defense education, and security escort services. There are emergency telephones, lighted pathways/sidewalks, controlled access to dorms/residences, encoded student identification cards, and response to reports of crime and criminal behavior.

REQUIREMENTS: The SAT or ACT is required. Applicants must be graduates of an accredited secondary school. The GED is accepted. The recommended preparatory program includes 4 units of English, 3 each of science, social studies, and math, and 2 of foreign language. An interview is recommended. AP and CLEP credits are accepted. Important factors in the admissions decision are advanced placement or honors courses, evidence of special talent, and leadership record. To graduate, students must complete at least 128 semester hours with a minimum GPA of 2.0 overall and 2.25 in the major. All students must complete 3 semester hours of freshman studies and 44 semester hours of interdisciplinary studies, including courses in English, phys ed, religion, speech, business or economics, fine arts, humanities, science, and social science. **Procedure:** Freshmen are admitted to all sessions. Entrance exams should be taken in the spring of the junior year. There are deferred admissions and rolling admissions plans. Application deadlines are open. The fall 2017 application fee was $25. Applications are accepted on-line. **Transfer Students:** Official transcripts from all previous colleges, showing course credits and a minimum GPA of 2.25, must be submitted when applying for transfer. Generally, if the student has successfully completed a minimum of 1 year of college, the SAT I or ACT will not be required. 32 of 128 credits required for the bachelor's degree must be completed at Ashland. **International Students:** They must take the TOEFL.

ADMISSIONS: 13 freshmen graduated first in their class. **Admissions Contact:** Jeffery S Steele, Director for Admissions. Email: *enrollme@ashland.edu* Web: *www.ashland.edu*

FINANCIAL AID: In 2017-2018, 99% of all full-time freshmen received some form of financial aid. 82% of all full-time freshmen received need-based aid. The average freshman award was $17,408. Need-based scholarships or need-based grants averaged $10,382 ($18,687 maximum); need-based self-help aid (loans and jobs) averaged $4,785 ($6,625 maximum); non-need-based athletic scholarships averaged $434 ($24,464 maximum); other non-need-based awards and non-need-based scholarships averaged $843 ($17,974 maximum); and $964 from other forms of aid. 30% of undergraduate students work part-time. The average financial indebtedness of the 2017 graduate was $18,250. The college's own financial statement, and federal tax returns are required. The FAFSA code is 003012. The priority date for freshman financial aid applications for fall entry is March 15.

BALDWIN WALLACE UNIVERSITY D-1

www.bw.edu

Berea, OH 44017	(440) 826-6970
Fax: (440) 826-3830	**Email:** admission@bw.edu
Full-time: 1360 men, 1619 women	**Faculty:** 196; IIB, av$
Part-time: 92 men, 133 women	**Ph.D.s:** 75%
Graduate: 215 men, 393 women	**Student/Faculty:** 15 to 1
Year: semesters, summer session	**Tuition:** $31,668
Room & Board: $10,796	**Freshman Class:** 3576 applied, 2791 accepted, 685 enrolled
SAT EBR-W/M: 600/580 **ACT:** 24	**CEEB CODE:** 1050
Application Deadline: n/av	**VERY COMPETITIVE**

Baldwin Wallace University, established in 1845, is an independent liberal arts institution that blends the hallmarks of the liberal arts with an emphasis on professional and career preparation through undergraduate and graduate degree programs. There are 8 undergraduate schools and 3 graduate schools. In addition to regional accreditation, BWU has baccalaureate program accreditation with NASM, CAEP, CAATE, CCNE, and ARC-PA (Provisional). The 153-acre campus is in a suburban area 14 miles southwest of Cleveland, OH. Including any residence halls, there are 82 buildings.

STUDENT LIFE: 78% of undergraduates are from Ohio. Others are from 41 states, 37 foreign countries, and Canada. 86% are from public schools. 9% are African American; 77% White; 5% Hispanic; 5% two or more races; 2% Asian American; 1% Foreign. 46% are Protestant; 32% Catholic; 14% Buddhist, Hindu, Mormon, Muslim, Orthodox, and Unitarian. **Female To Male Ratio:** 1.3:1. The average age of freshmen is 18; all undergraduates, 20. 22% do not continue beyond their first year; 92% remain to graduate. **Housing:** 1847 students can be accommodated in college housing, which includes dorms and on-campus apartments. In addition, there are honors houses, language/international houses, special-interest houses, fraternity houses, sorority houses, student-directed learning community, and themed housing. On-campus housing is available on a first-come, first-served basis, and is available on a lottery system for upperclassmen. 61% of students live on campus. All students may keep cars.

FACULTY/CLASSROOMS: 51% of faculty are male; 49% are female. 86% teach undergraduates. No introductory courses are taught by graduate students. The average class size in an introductory lecture is 19; in a laboratory is 15; and in a regular course is 17.

PROGRAMS OF STUDY: BWU confers B.A., B.F.A., B.S., B.M., B.M.E, B.S.Ed., and B.S.N degrees. Master's degrees are also awarded. Bachelor's degrees are awarded in BIOLOGICAL SCIENCE (biology/biological science and neurosciences), BUSINESS (accounting, business administration and management, entrepreneurial studies, finance, human resources, international business, international security/conflict resolution mgmt, marketing, organizational leadership and management, sports management, and sustainable management), COMMUNICATIONS AND THE ARTS (acting, applied music, arts administration/management, broadcasting, communication studies, creative writing, dance, English, film, television and digital media, French, German, graphic design & media, instrumental performance, keyboard - piano concentration, music, music composition, music history and appreciation, music performance, music theory and composition, musical theater, public relations, Spanish, studio art, theatre acting, theater design, theater management, and voice), COMPUTER AND PHYSICAL SCIENCE (applied mathematics, chemistry, computer science, computer security and information assurance, digital arts/technology, mathematics, mathematics – economics, physics, software engineering, and systems analysis), EDUCATION (art education, athletic training, early childhood education, health and physical education, middle school education, music education, physical education, science education, and specific learning disabilities), ENGINEERING AND ENVIRONMENTAL DESIGN (engineering and preengineering), HEALTH PROFESSIONS (exercise science, health care administration, health promotion, music therapy, nursing, predentistry, premedicine, prepharmacy, prephysical therapy, preveterinary science, and public health), SOCIAL SCIENCE (communication sciences & disorders, criminal justice, economics, history, industrial and organizational psychology, interdisciplinary studies, international studies, philosophy, political science/government, psychology, public administration, public history/archives, religion, and sociology). Biology, psychology, and sport management have the largest enrollments.

ACTIVITIES: 12% of men belong to 7 national fraternities; 17% of women belong to 5 national sororities. There are 128 groups on campus, including art, band, cheerleading, choir, chorale, chorus, computers, dance, drama, drill team, environmental, ethnic, film, forensics, honors, international, jazz band, LGBT, literary magazine, marching band, musical theater, newspaper, opera, orchestra, pep band, political, professional, radio and TV, religious, social, social service, student government, and symphony. Popular campus events include Culture Night, Dance Marathon, and April Reign. **Sports:** There are 12 intercollegiate sports for men and 11 for women, and 28 intramural sports for men and 28 for women. Facilities include a stadium with polyturf and all-weather track, a gym, athletic field, baseball fields, a 6-court tennis complex, a 200-meter track, swimming pool, dance studio, athletic training/rehab facility, wrestling/gymnastics/weight rooms, basketball, racquetball, tennis,volleyball, and a fitness and wellness programs/activities. **Graduates:** From July 1, 2016 to June 30, 2017, 769 bachelor's degrees were awarded. The most popular majors were biology (6%), psychology (6%), and business administration (5%). In an average class, 2% graduate in 3 years or less, 50% graduate in 4 years or less, 66% graduate in 5 years or less, and 67% graduate in 6 years or less. Of the 2016 graduating class, 16% were enrolled in graduate school within 6 months of graduation, and 65% were employed.

SERVICES: Counseling and information services are available, as is tutoring in most subjects. There is a reader service for the blind, and remedial math, reading, and writing. Software for students who have difficulty reading or with visual impairments is available as well as access to Learning Ally & Bookshare which both come with a downloadable reader. **Library/Resources:** The library contains 515,449 volumes, 3,000 microform items, and 108,258 audio/video tapes/CDs/DVDs, and subscribes to 74,129 periodicals including electronic. Computerized library services include interlibrary loans, database searching, Internet access, and Wi-Fi capability. Special learning facilities include an art gallery, radio station, a neuroscience lab, and an observatory. **Physically Challenged Students:** 80% of the campus is accessible. Facilities include wheelchair ramps, elevators, special parking, specially equipped restrooms, special class scheduling, lowered telephones, and special housing. **Special:** Special academic programs include internships that can qualify for credit, work-study programs and study abroad. There is cross-registration with 7 participating institutions within the Greater Cleveland area, as well as a 3-2 program in social work with Case Western Reserve University, 3-2 master's program in accounting, human resources, computer science/information systems, 3-2 program in engineering with Case Western Reserve University. BWU also offers the Consortium for Music Therapy, accelerated Bachelor of Science in Nursing degree, a Bachelor of Fine Arts in Acting, Associate to Bachelor (A2BW) accelerated transfer programs, interdisciplinary/student designed majors & minors, credit for life, military, work experience, and pass/fail options. The Adult, Transfer and Military Services Program offers degrees in evening and weekend formats. Pre-professional programs are available in dentistry, law, medicine, pharmacy, and veterinary. Study abroad in Argentina, Australia, Austria, China, Ecuador, England, France, Germany, Ghana, Guatemala, India, Ireland, Italy, Japan, Mexico, Morocco, Scotland, South Korea, Spain, Sweden, Switzerland and Zambia. There are 26 national honor societies and a freshman honors program. **Visiting:** There are regularly scheduled orientations for prospective students, student visits include an interview, a tour, and classroom visits. There are guides for informal visits, visitors may sit in on classes, and stay overnight. To schedule a visit, contact Michele Sepesy at (440) 826-2222. **Campus Safety and Security:** Measures include 24-hour foot and vehicle patrol, emergency notification system, self-defense education, and security escort services. There are emergency telephones, lighted pathways/sidewalks, controlled access to dorms/residences, and more than 100 exterior/interior security cameras.

REQUIREMENTS: The SAT or ACT is recommended. Applicants must be graduates of an accredited secondary school or have earned a GED. Applicants must have completed 16 academic credits, including 4 in English, 3 each in math, natural science, and social science, 2 in a foreign language; however, alternative distributions are considered. Students who apply to any program within the Conservatory of Music or the BFA in Acting program must audition as part of their evaluation process. BW requires applicants to be in the upper 50% of their class. A GPA of 2.8 is required. AP and CLEP credits are accepted. Important factors in the admissions decision are leadership record, advanced placement or honors courses, and extracurricular activities record. Traditional undergraduate baccalaureate programs at BWU require at least 124 semester hours (conservatory programs may require additional hours) and at least a 2.0 GPA. The Bachelor of Arts and Sciences core requirements include coursework in the following areas: foundation courses in Mathematics, English Composition, and First-Year Experience (FYE 100), perspectives courses in Humanities, Interdisciplinary, Social Sciences and Natural Sciences, wellness courses in Health and Physical Education, extension courses in writing and quantitative reasoning, International coursework or experiences, and coursework in Diversity Studies. Completion of a minor adds depth in a particular area of study, to balance the breadth provided by distribution requirements across the Liberal Arts and Sciences. Comprehensive exams are required in some majors. **Procedure:** Freshmen are admitted fall and spring. Entrance exams should be taken during junior year or early in senior year. There are deferred admissions and rolling admissions plans. Application deadlines are open. Applications are accepted on-line. **Transfer Students:** 233 transfer students enrolled in 2016-2017. Students must be in good academic and social standing at prior institution(s). 45 of 124 credits required for the bachelor's degree must be completed at BWU. **International Students:** There are 46 international students enrolled. They must take the TOEFL with a minimum score of 550 on the paper-based TOEFL (PBT) or 79 on the Internet-based version (iBT). Students must take the college's own test, and take either one of these tests, IELTS, LADO ESL Level 10 Completion. The SAT or ACT, scoring SAT EBRW = 590; ACT English = 23, which can be used to replace the TOEFL or IELTS if score is strong.

ADMISSIONS: 81% of the 2017-2018 applicants were accepted. The SAT scores for the 2017-2018 freshman class were: Math-- 14% below 500, 44% between 500 and 599, 33% between 600 and 699, and 8% between 700 and 800. Evidence-Based Reading/Writing-- 14% below 500, 35% between 500 and 599, 42% between 600 and 699, and 10% between 700 and 800. The ACT scores were 6% between 12 and 17, 41% between 18 and 23, 46% between 24 and 29, and 8% above 30. 39% of the current freshmen were in the top fifth of their class; 70% were in the top two fifths. 9 freshmen graduated first in their class. **Admissions Contact:** Scott Schulz, VP for Enrollment Management. Email: *admission@bw.edu* Web: *www.bw.edu*

FINANCIAL AID: In 2017-2018, 100% of all full-time freshmen received some form of financial aid. 84% of all full-time freshmen received need-based aid. The average freshman award was $28,019. Need-based scholarships or need-based grants averaged $22,838 ($31,668 maximum); need-based self-help aid (loans and jobs) averaged $5,744 ($10,150 maximum); and other non-need-based awards and non-need-based scholarships averaged $14,894 ($31,668 maximum). 32% of undergraduate students work part-time. The average financial indebtedness of the 2017 graduate was $28,862. The FAFSA code is 003014. The priority date for freshman financial aid applications for fall entry is January 4.

BLUFFTON UNIVERSITY — B-2

www.bluffton.edu

Blufton, OH 45817	**(419) 358-3257** **(800) 488-3257**
Fax: (419) 358-3232	**Email: admissions@bluffton.edu**
Full-time: 377 men, 351 women	**Faculty:** 56; IIB, --$
Part-time: 57 men, 80 women	**Ph.D.s:** 78%
Graduate: 23 men, 64 women	**Student/Faculty:** 13 to 1
Year: semesters, summer session	**Tuition:** $30,762
Room & Board: $10,188	**Freshman Class:** 1480 applied, 733 accepted, 208 enrolled
SAT: required **ACT:** 22	**CEEB CODE:** 1067
Application Deadline: August 15	**COMPETITIVE+**

Bluffton University is a small liberal arts university, with more than 40 undergraduate programs, adult degree-completion programs and master's degrees. We bring together academic quality with deep personal caring for each of our students. We bring together academic preparation with essential career/interpersonal skill training for life-success for our graduates. We bring together modest tuition with outstanding financial aid for a truly affordable private education. There is 1 undergraduate school and 1 graduate school. In addition to regional accreditation, Bluffton has baccalaureate program accreditation with ADA, CSWE, NASM, and CAEP. The 65-acre campus is in a small town off I-75 60 miles south of Toledo, Ohio and 75 miles north of Dayton, Ohio. Including any residence halls, there are 28 buildings.

STUDENT LIFE: 87% of undergraduates are from Ohio. Others are from 18 states, 10 foreign countries, and Canada. 91% are from public schools. 83% are White; 6% African American; 4% Hispanic; 4% two or more races; 1% Asian American; 1% Foreign; 1% race unknown. 47% are Protestant; 41% unknown religion; 12% Catholic. **Female To Male Ratio:** 1.1:1. The average age of freshmen is 19; all undergraduates, 22. 31% do not continue beyond their first year; 54% remain to graduate. **Housing:** 758 students can be accommodated in college housing, which includes dorms, on-campus apartments, and special-interest houses. All full-time students must live in residence halls unless commuting from the home of their parents. On-campus housing is guaranteed for all 4 years. 85% of students live on campus. Alcohol is not permitted. All students may keep cars.

FACULTY/CLASSROOMS: 56% of faculty are male; 44% are female. 97% teach undergraduates. No introductory courses are taught by graduate students. The average class size in an introductory lecture is 23; in a laboratory is 9; and in a regular course is 16.

PROGRAMS OF STUDY: Bluffton confers B.A. degrees. Master's degrees are also awarded. Bachelor's degrees are awarded in BIOLOGICAL SCIENCE (biology/biological science), BUSINESS (accounting, business administration and management, human resources, information & communication technology, marketing/retailing/merchandising, organizational leadership and management, recreational facilities management, and sports management), COMMUNICATIONS AND THE ARTS (art, broadcasting, communications, creative writing, English, graphic design & media, music, public relations, and Spanish), COMPUTER AND PHYSICAL SCIENCE (chemistry, computer science, mathematics, physical sciences, and physics), EDUCATION (early childhood education, health information management, home economics education, middle school education, music education, physical education, and special education), HEALTH PROFESSIONS (nursing, premedicine, public health, and speech pathology/audiology), SOCIAL SCIENCE (biblical studies, child psychology/development, criminal justice, early childhood studies, economics, family/consumer studies, food science, history, ministries, psychology, social science, social studies, social work, sociology, and youth ministry). Social work, education, and business have the largest enrollments.

ACTIVITIES: There are no fraternities or sororities. There are 40 groups on campus, including youth ministries, student senate, art, band, cheerleading, choir, chorale, chorus, dance, drama, ethnic, honors, international, jazz band, LGBT, literary magazine, multicultural student organization, musical theater, newspaper, pep band, political, professional, radio and TV, religious, social, social service, and student government. Popular campus events include International Week, Spiritual Emphasis Weeks, and Artist Series. **Sports:** There are 7 intercollegiate sports for men and 7 for women, and 6 intramural sports for men and 6 for women. Facilities include a recreation and fitness center, basketball/volleyball, an athletic complex with baseball, softball, soccer and football stadium, and indoor sports and intramurals. **Graduates:** From July 1, 2016 to June 30, 2017, 240 bachelor's degrees were awarded. The most popular majors were business/marketing (30%), education (15%), and social work (10%). In an average class, 2% graduate in 3 years or less, 48% graduate in 4 years or less, 53% graduate in 5 years or less, and 54% graduate in 6 years or less. Of the 2016 graduating class, 16% were enrolled in graduate school within 6 months of graduation, and 79% were employed.

SERVICES: Counseling and information services are available, as is tutoring in every subject. There is a reader service for the blind, and remedial math, reading, and writing. Tutoring is available for most students, as are classes at the student's request and/or faculty designation. **Library/Resources:** The library contains 381,832 volumes, 83,822 microform items, and 12,567 audio/video tapes/CDs/DVDs, and subscribes to 89,472 periodicals including electronic. Computerized library services include interlibrary loans, database searching, Internet access, and Wi-Fi capability. Special learning facilities include an art gallery, radio station, the Lion and Lamb Peace Arts Center, and a Nature Preserve. **Physically Challenged Students:** 75% of the campus is accessible. Facilities include wheelchair ramps, elevators, special parking, specially equipped restrooms, special class scheduling, lowered drinking fountains, lowered telephones, and special computers for visually impaired students. **Special:** Special arrangements include internships in business, recreation, social work, and education, a Washington semester through the Council for Christian Colleges and Universities, and study abroad. Student-designed majors and independent study are possible, as is credit for prior learning and for learning in voluntary service. There is an accelerated degree program in organizational management. Nondegree study and pass/fail options are offered. There are 2 national honor societies, a freshman honors program, and 14 departmental honors programs. **Visiting:** There are regularly scheduled orientations for prospective students. Personal visits are scheduled according to students' specific interests and may include observing a class, visit with faculty and a tour of campus. Group visits are scheduled regularly throughout the year, and are listed on website with online registration. There are guides for informal visits, visitors may sit in on classes, and stay overnight. To schedule a visit, contact Deanna Haan at (800) 488-3257. **Campus Safety and Security:** Measures include emergency notification system and self-defense education. There are emergency telephones, lighted pathways/sidewalks, controlled access to dorms/residences, and village police who cruisers regularly patrol the campus during night hours. There are also 2 night security officers who communicate directly with village police and routinely patrol campus at night.

REQUIREMENTS: The SAT or ACT is required. To be considered for regular admission to Bluffton as an undergraduate student, you need to have earned a score of 920 on the SAT (critical reading plus math) OR 19 on the ACT. Other admissions requirements include graduation from an accredited secondary school with a 2.3 GPA or class rank above 50%. Recommended courses include 4 units of English and 3 units each of math, science, social studies, and a foreign language. The GED is accepted. A personal campus visit and an interview are strongly recommended. Music students must audition and art students submit a portfolio. Bluffton requires applicants to be in the upper 50% of their class. AP and CLEP credits are accepted. Important factors in the admissions decision are leadership record, recommendations by school officials, and extracurricular activities record. To graduate, students must complete 124 semester hours with 40 to 60 in the major and have a minimum GPA of 2.0. The general education requirements must be met, and satisfactory achievement in departmental senior comprehensives demonstrated. Distribution requirements are approximately one third for general education requirements, including 6 hours of religion, and one third to one half for the major. **Procedure:** Freshmen are admitted fall and spring. Entrance exams should be taken in the spring of the junior year or fall of the senior year. There are deferred admissions and rolling admissions plans. Applications should be filed by August 15 for fall entry. Applications are accepted on-line. **Transfer Students:** 29 transfer students enrolled in 2016-2017. Transfer students must have a minimum college GPA of 2.0, meet eligibility criteria from previous institutions, and have met their financial obligations at the former institution. A signed transfer recommendation must be submitted from each college attended. 30 of 124 credits required for the bachelor's degree must be completed at Bluffton. **International Students:** There are 11 international students enrolled. They must take the TOEFL with a minimum score of 500 on the paper-based TOEFL (PBT) or 64 on the Internet-based version (iBT). They must also take the SAT, scoring 920, and the college's own entrance exam. The SAT can substitute for the TOEFL.

ADMISSIONS: 50% of the 2017-2018 applicants were accepted. The ACT scores were 17% between 12 and 17, 57% between 18 and 23, 24% between 24 and 29, and 2% above 30. 30% of the current freshmen were in the top fifth of their class; 50% were in the top two fifths. 7 freshmen graduated first in their class. **Admissions Contact:** Robin Hopkins, Director of Undergraduate Admissions. Email: *admissions@bluffton.edu* Web: *www.bluffton.edu*

FINANCIAL AID: In 2017-2018, 88% of all full-time freshmen received some form of financial aid. 80% of all full-time freshmen received need-based aid. The average freshman award was $27,236. Need-based scholarships or need-based grants averaged $221,909 ($29,575 maximum); need-based self-help aid (loans and jobs) averaged $5,859 ($6,590 maximum); and other non-need-based awards and non-need-based scholarships averaged $15,631 ($30,312 maximum). 65% of undergraduate students work part-time. The average financial indebtedness of the 2017 graduate was $38,701. The FAFSA code is 003016. The priority date for freshman financial aid applications for fall entry is May 1.

BOWLING GREEN STATE UNIVERSITY — B-1

www.bgsu.edu

Bowling Green, OH 43403	**(419) 372-2478** **(866) 246-6732**
Fax: (419) 372-6955	**Email: choosebgsu@bgsu.edu**
Full-time: 5665 men, 7439 women	**Faculty:** 659; I, --$
Part-time: 802 men, 774 women	**Ph.D.s:** 78%
Graduate: 1041 men, 1636 women	**Student/Faculty:** 20 to 1
Year: semesters, summer session	**Tuition:** $11,057 ($18,593)
Room & Board: $8918	**Freshman Class:** 16739 applied, 11438 accepted, 3344 enrolled
SAT EBR-W/M: 560/540 **ACT:** 22	**CEEB CODE:** 1069
Application Deadline: July 15	**COMPETITIVE**

Bowling Green State University, founded in 1910, is a public institution with 7 undergraduate schools and 1 graduate school. In addition to regional accreditation, BGSU has baccalaureate program accreditation with AACSB, ACCE, ACEJMC, ADA, CSWE, NASAD, NASM, CAEP, NRPA, ACS, and NAST. The 1338-acre campus is in a small town 23 miles south of Toledo, adjacent to Interstate 75. Including any residence halls, there are 119 buildings.

STUDENT LIFE: 86% of undergraduates are from Ohio. Others are from 51 states, 81 foreign countries, and Canada. 8% are African American; 76% White; 5% Foreign; 4% Hispanic; 3% two or more races; 2% race unknown; 1% Asian American. **Female To Male Ratio:** 1.3:1. The average age of freshmen is 19; all undergraduates, 21. 23% do not continue beyond their first year; 54% remain to graduate. **Housing:** 6705 students can be accommodated in college housing, which includes dorms and on-campus apartments. In addition, there are honors houses, language/international houses, special-interest houses, fraternity houses, sorority houses, no-alcohol wings, residential/theme communities, and gender-neutral housing. 61% of students commute. All students may keep cars.

FACULTY/CLASSROOMS: 49% of faculty are male; 51% are female. No introductory courses are taught by graduate students. The average class size in an introductory lecture is 27; in a laboratory is 17; and in a regular course is 26.

PROGRAMS OF STUDY: BGSU confers B.A., B.A.C., B.F.A., B.L.S., B.S., B.S.J., B.S.F.A., B.S.BA., B.S.Econ., B.S.AMPD., B.S.Diet., B.S.Ed., B.S.HDFS, B.S.ID., B.S.NS., B.A.HS., B.S.Comm., B.S.CJ., B.S.Gero., B.S.MLS., B.S.Nur., B.S.SW., B.Mus., B.M.Art., B.S.Tech., B.S.Arch., B.S.C.M., B.S.ECET. and B.S.ET. degrees. Master's and doctoral degrees are also awarded. Bachelor's degrees are awarded in AGRICULTURE (environmental studies), BIOLOGICAL SCIENCE (avian sciences, life science, neurosciences, and nutrition), BUSINESS (accounting, business administration and management, management information systems, marketing, sports management, and tourism), COMMUNICATIONS AND THE ARTS (apparel design, art history, art, classics, communications, creative writing, dance, design, English, English literature, film arts, fine arts, foreign language, French, German, graphic design, instrumental performance, jazz, journalism, Latin, music, music history and appreciation, music performance, music theory and composition, performing arts, romance languages and literature, Russian, Spanish, technical communication, telecommunications, theatre studies, and visual and performing arts), COMPUTER AND PHYSICAL SCIENCE (chemistry, computer science, digital arts/technology, earth science, geology, mathematics, physics, science, and statistics), EDUCATION (art education, athletic training, business education, early childhood education, education, education of the deaf and hearing impaired, education of the multiply handicapped, elementary education, foreign languages education, learner designed area of study, mathematics education, middle school education, music education, physical education, science education, secondary education, social science education, special education, and technical education), ENGINEERING AND ENVIRONMENTAL DESIGN (construction management, electrical and computer engineering, electrical/electronics engineering technology, engineering technology, environmental science, and interior design), HEALTH PROFESSIONS (biology, exercise science, health science, nursing, and public health), SOCIAL SCIENCE (African studies, American studies, architectural studies, Asian/Oriental studies, criminal justice, dietetics, economics, ethnic studies, family/consumer studies, fire services administration, geography, gerontology, history, human development, interdisciplinary studies, international studies, liberal arts/general studies, philosophy, political science/government, psychology, social science, social work, sociology, and women's studies). Inclusive early childhood, biology, and criminal justice have the largest enrollments.

ACTIVITIES: 13% of men belong to 22 national fraternities; 12% of women belong to 17 national sororities. There are 369 groups on campus, including art, band, cheerleading, chess, choir, chorale, chorus, communications, computers, dance, debate, drama, drill team, environmental, ethnic, film, honors, international, jazz band, LGBT, literary magazine, marching band, musical theater, newspaper, opera, pep band, photography, political, professional, radio and TV, religious, social, social service, student government, symphony, and yearbook. Popular campus events include Homecoming, Campus Fest, Move-in Weekend, and Week of Welcome. **Sports:** There are 7 intercollegiate sports for men and 11 for women, and 9 intramural sports for men and 8 for women. **Graduates:** From July 1, 2016 to June 30, 2017, 3091 bachelor's degrees were awarded. The most popular majors were inclusive early childhood (4%), individualized studies (4%), and psychology (4%). In an average class, 3% graduate in 3 years or less, 35% graduate in 4 years or less, 49% graduate in 5 years or less, and 52% graduate in 6 years or less.

SERVICES: Counseling and information services are available, as is tutoring in some subjects, such as writing, math and stats, and other subjects requested by student. There is a reader service for the blind, and remedial math, reading, and writing. **Library/Resources:** The library contains 2.6 million volumes, 316,556 microform items, and 437,668 audio/video tapes/CDs/DVDs, and subscribes to 12,520 periodicals including electronic. Computerized library services include interlibrary loans, database searching, Internet access, and Wi-Fi capability. Special learning facilities include an art gallery, planetarium, radio station, and TV station. **Physically Challenged Students:** 92% of the campus is accessible. Facilities include wheelchair ramps, elevators, special parking, specially equipped restrooms, special class scheduling, lowered drinking fountains, lowered telephones, and special housing. **Special:** Special academic programs include co-op programs in all majors with the National Student Exchange, internships, a Washington semester, work-study, and study abroad. Dual majors are available in all programs, and a B.A.-B.S. degree is offered in computer science, geology, math, psychology, statistics, scientific and technical communication, and individualized planned program. Student-designed majors, independent study, credit for experience, nondegree study, and pass/fail options are possible. There is a chapter of Phi Beta Kappa and a freshman honors program. **Visiting:** There are regularly scheduled orientations for prospective students. There are guides for informal visits and visitors may sit in on classes. To schedule a visit, contact the Office of Admissions. **Campus Safety and Security:** Measures include 24-hour foot and vehicle patrol, emergency notification system, self-defense education, and security escort services. There are shuttle buses, emergency telephones, lighted pathways/sidewalks, controlled access to dorms/residences, in-room safes, and campus 911.

REQUIREMENTS: The ACT is required. The SAT is recommended. AP and CLEP credits are accepted. Students must earn a minimum of 122 semester hours of credit and at least 30 credit hours must be BGSU courses, earn an accumulative GPA of at least 2.0 ("C" average) for all coursework attempted, complete the BG Perspective requirements, have at least 40 hours of credit in courses numbered 3000 and above, satisfy all college requirements for a degree, and file an application for graduation. **Procedure:** Freshmen are admitted fall, spring, and summer. Entrance exams should be taken in the junior year. There are deferred admissions and rolling admissions plans. Applications should be filed by July 15 for fall entry; December 15 for spring entry; and May 15 for summer entry. The fall 2017 application fee was $45. Notifications are sent August 1. Applications are accepted on-line. **Transfer Students:** 834 transfer students enrolled in 2016-2017. 30 of 122 credits required for the bachelor's degree must be completed at BGSU. **International Students:** There are 292 international students enrolled. They must take the TOEFL with a minimum score of 500 on the paper-based TOEFL (PBT) or 71 on the Internet-based version (iBT) or take the MELAB. SAT and ACT scores are considered if submitted.

ADMISSIONS: 68% of the 2017-2018 applicants were accepted. The SAT scores for the 2017-2018 freshman class were: Math-- 19% below 500, 51% between 500 and 599, 34% between 600 and 699, and 6% between 700 and 800. Evidence-Based Reading/Writing-- 17% below 500, 49% between 500 and 599, 28% between 600 and 699, and 6% between 700 and 800. The ACT scores were 5% between 12 and 17, 55% between 18 and 23, 35% between 24 and 29, and 5% above 30. 28% of the current freshmen were in the top fifth of their class; 58% were in the top two fifths. 41 freshmen graduated first in their class. **Admissions Contact:** Adrea Nicole Spoon, Director of Admissions. Email: *choosebgsu@bgsu.edu* Web: *www.bgsu.edu*

FINANCIAL AID: In 2017-2018, 94% of all full-time freshmen received some form of financial aid. 56% of all full-time freshmen received need-based aid. The average freshman award was $15,282. Need-based scholarships or need-based grants averaged $5,057 ($13,731 maximum); need-based self-help aid (loans and jobs) averaged $3,370 ($7,565 maximum); non-need-based athletic scholarships averaged $20,668 ($37,924 maximum); other non-need-based awards and non-need-based scholarships averaged $7,578 ($35,712 maximum); and $13,574 from other forms of aid. 15% of undergraduate students work part-time. The average financial indebtedness of the 2017 graduate was $30,002. BGSU is a member of CSS. The FAFSA code is 003018. Check with the school for current application deadlines.

CAPITAL UNIVERSITY — C-3

www.capital.edu

Columbus, OH 43209	(614) 236-6232 (866) 544-6175
Fax: (614) 236-6926	**Email:** ghudson@capital.edu
Full-time: 987 men, 1506 women	**Faculty:** 142; IIA, av$
Part-time: 62 men, 144 women	**Ph.D.s:** 76%
Graduate: 328 men, 357 women	**Student/Faculty:** 18 to 1
Year: semesters, summer session	**Tuition:** $34,600
Room & Board: $10,178	**Freshman Class:** 4208 applied, 2889 accepted, 595 enrolled
SAT EBR-W/M: 588/573 **ACT:** 24	**CEEB CODE:** 1099
Application Deadline: May 1	**VERY COMPETITIVE**

Capital University, established in 1830, is a private institution affiliated with the Evangelical Lutheran Church in America. Its undergraduate and graduate programs emphasize the liberal arts and sciences, music, and nursing along with professional studies such as business. There are 5 undergraduate schools and 3 graduate schools. In addition to regional accreditation, CU has baccalaureate program accreditation with ACBSP, CSWE, NASM, ABA, ACS, and CAEP. The 48-acre campus is in a suburban area 5 miles east of downtown Columbus. Including any residence halls, there are 24 buildings.

STUDENT LIFE: 90% of undergraduates are from Ohio. Others are from 34 states, 14 foreign countries, and Canada. 74% are White; 10% African American; 5% two or more races; 4% Hispanic; 3% race unknown; 2% Foreign; 1% Asian American; 1% American Indian/Alaska Native. 30% are Protestant; 20% Catholic; 14% claim no religious affiliation. **Female To Male Ratio:** 1.5:1. The average age of freshmen is 18; all undergraduates, 21. 22% do not continue beyond their first year; 59% remain to graduate. **Housing:** 1629 students can be accommodated in college housing, which includes gender neutral dorms, on-campus apartments, and off-campus apartments. In addition, there are honors houses, special-interest floors, substance-free floors, Greek organization floors, and a self-governing unit. On-campus housing is guaranteed for all 4 years and is available on a lottery system for upperclassmen. 58% of students live on campus. All students may keep cars.

FACULTY/CLASSROOMS: 45% of faculty are male; 55% are female. 87% teach undergraduates. No introductory courses are taught by graduate students. The average class size in an introductory lecture is 20; in a laboratory is 12; and in a regular course is 17.

PROGRAMS OF STUDY: CU confers B.A., B.M., B.S.N., and B.S.W. degrees. Master's and doctoral degrees are also awarded. Bachelor's degrees are awarded in BIOLOGICAL SCIENCE (biochemistry and biology/biological science), BUSINESS (accounting and business administration and management), COMMUNICATIONS AND THE ARTS (art, communications, creative writing, dramatic arts, English, French, music, public relations, Spanish, speech/debate/rhetoric, and theatre studies), COMPUTER AND PHYSICAL SCIENCE (chemistry, computer science, and mathematics), EDUCATION (art education, athletic training, elementary education, middle school education, physical education, and secondary education), ENGINEERING AND ENVIRONMENTAL DESIGN (environmental science), HEALTH PROFESSIONS (art therapy, exercise science, nursing, predentistry, premedicine, and sports medicine), SOCIAL SCIENCE (behavioral science, criminal justice, economics, history, international relations, philosophy, physical fitness/movement, political science/government, prelaw, psychology, religion, social work, and sociology). Nursing, business, and education have the largest enrollments.

ACTIVITIES: 2% of men belong to 5 local and 5 national fraternities; 3% of women belong to 6 local and 6 national sororities. There are 63 groups on campus, including art, band, cheerleading, choir, chorale, chorus, communications, dance, debate, drama, environmental, ethnic, film, honors, international, jazz band, LGBT, literary magazine, musical theater, newspaper, opera, orchestra, photography, political, professional, radio and TV, religious, social, social service, student government, and symphony. Popular campus events include Symposium on Undergraduate Scholarship, Honors Convocation, Greek Week, Martin Luther King Jr. Day of Learning, and Kids and Sibs Weekend. **Sports:** There are 10 intercollegiate sports for men and 10 for women, and 9 intramural sports for men and 9 for women. Facilities include a football stadium, a gym, tennis courts, and weight and game rooms. The recreation center offers bowling, billiards, and other game facilities. **Graduates:** From July 1, 2016 to June 30, 2017, 582 bachelor's degrees were awarded. The most popular majors were nursing (20%), business (13%), and education (11%). In an average class, 54% graduate in 4 years or less, 58% graduate in 5 years or less, and 59% graduate in 6 years or less. Of the 2016 graduating class, 20% were enrolled in graduate school within 6 months of graduation, and 69% were employed.

SERVICES: Counseling and information services are available, as is tutoring in most subjects. There is remedial math and writing. **Library/Resources:** The library contains 225,644 volumes, 148,096 microform items, and 103,078 audio/video tapes/CDs/DVDs, and subscribes to 156,739 periodicals including electronic. Computerized library services include interlibrary loans, database searching, Internet access, and Wi-Fi capability. Special learning facilities include an art gallery, radio station, and TV station. **Physically Challenged Students:** All of the campus is accessible. Facilities include wheelchair ramps, elevators, special parking, specially equipped restrooms, and special housing. **Special:** Special academic programs include cross-registration with the Higher Education Council of Columbus, semester internships in most majors, and a Washington semester. Study abroad in 21 countries on 5 continents includes opportunities in Jamaica and at the Kodaly Institute of Music in Hungary. Also possible are a general studies degree and student-designed majors. A dual degree in engineering is offered with Case Western Reserve University and Washington University in St. Louis. Credit for life, military, and work experience may be granted, and nondegree study and pass/fail options are offered. There are 17 national honor societies and a freshman honors program. **Visiting:** There are regularly scheduled orientations for prospective students, including an interview with a counselor and a campus tour. There are guides for informal visits, visitors may sit in on classes, and stay overnight. To schedule a visit, contact Nathan Bell at (614) 236-6101. **Campus Safety and Security:** Measures include 24-hour foot and vehicle patrol, emergency notification system, self-defense education, and security escort services. There are shuttle buses, emergency telephones, lighted pathways/sidewalks, and controlled access to dorms/residences.

REQUIREMENTS: The SAT or ACT is required. Admissions requirements include graduation from an accredited secondary school with 16 academic credits, including 4 units of English, 3 each of math, science, and social science, 2 units of a foreign language, and 1 of electives; nursing applicants need chemistry. The GED is accepted. High school students must submit recommendations from their guidance counselor. An interview is recommended. Students must audition for entry to the Conservatory of Music. A GPA of 2.6 is required. AP and CLEP credits are accepted. Important factors in the admissions decision are advanced placement or honors courses, recommendations by school officials, and evidence of special talent. To graduate, all students must complete at least 124 semester hours, with a varying number of hours in the major, and maintain a minimum 2.0 GPA. The university core, 36 semester hours, must be followed in an ordered sequence throughout the 4 years: considered an assessment program, which includes specific courses in reading and writing, communication, health, art, science, social science, the humanities, ethics, and religion. **Procedure:** Freshmen are admitted fall, spring, and summer. Entrance exams should be taken by December of the senior year. There are deferred admissions and rolling admissions plans. Applications should be filed by May 1 for fall entry. The fall 2017 application fee was $25. Notifications are sent September 30. Applications are accepted on-line. **Transfer Students:** 85 transfer students enrolled in 2016-2017. Transfer students must have a minimum college GPA of 2.25. The SAT or ACT is recommended, as is an interview. 30 of 124 credits required for the bachelor's degree must be completed at CU. **International Students:** There are 42 international students enrolled. They must take the TOEFL with a minimum score of 500 on the paper-based TOEFL (PBT) or 61 on the Internet-based version (iBT).

ADMISSIONS: 69% of the 2017-2018 applicants were accepted. The SAT scores for the 2017-2018 freshman class were: Math-- 14% below 500, 53% between 500 and 599, 30% between 600 and 699, and 3% between 700 and 800. Evidence-Based Reading/Writing-- 7% below 500, 44% between 500 and 599, 45% between 600 and 699, and 4% between 700 and 800. The ACT scores were 3% between 12 and 17, 38% between 18 and 23, 50% between 24 and 29, and 9% above 30. 37% of the current freshmen were in the top fifth of their class; 67% were in the top two fifths. 13 freshmen graduated first in their class. **Admissions Contact:** Garien Hudson, Director of Admission. Email: *ghudson@capital.edu* Web: *www.capital.edu*

FINANCIAL AID: In 2017-2018, 99% of all full-time freshmen received some form of financial aid. 76% of all full-time freshmen received need-based aid. The average freshman award was $25,304. 33% of undergraduate students work part-time. The average financial indebtedness of the 2017 graduate was $32,515. The FAFSA code is 003023. The priority date for freshman financial aid applications for fall entry is February 28.

CASE WESTERN RESERVE UNIVERSITY D-1

www.case.edu

Cleveland, OH 44106	**(216) 368-4450**
Fax: (216) 368-5111	**Email:** admission@case.edu
Full-time: 2763 men, 2215 women	**Faculty:** 621
Part-time: 80 men, 92 women	**Ph.D.s:** 91%
Graduate: 2960 men, 3714 women	**Student/Faculty:** 11 to 1
Year: semesters, summer session	**Tuition:** $47,500
Room & Board: $14,784	**Freshman Class:** 25380 applied, 8405 accepted, 1309 enrolled
SAT EBR-W/M: 700/750 **ACT:** 32	**CEEB CODE:** 1105
Application Deadline: January 15	**MOST COMPETITIVE**

Case Western Reserve University, founded in 1826, is a private institution offering undergraduate, graduate, and professional programs in arts and sciences, dentistry, engineering, law, management, medicine, nursing, and social work. There are 4 undergraduate schools and 8 graduate schools. In addition to regional accreditation, CWRU has baccalaureate program accreditation with AACSB, ABET, ADA, CSAB, NASM, CAEP, and CCNE. The 267-acre campus is in an urban area 4 miles east of downtown Cleveland, OH. Including any residence halls, there are 186 buildings.

STUDENT LIFE: 60% of undergraduates are from out of state, mostly the Middle Atlantic. Students are from 47 states, 46 foreign countries, and Canada. 70% are from public schools. 6% are Hispanic; 5% two or more races; 49% White; 4% African American; 20% Asian American; 2% race unknown; 13% Foreign. **Female To Male Ratio:** 1.0:1. The average age of freshmen is 18; all undergraduates, 20. 7% do not continue beyond their first year; 83% remain to graduate. **Housing:** 4265 students can be accommodated in college housing, which includes dorms and on-campus apartments. In addition, there are special-interest houses, fraternity houses, sorority houses, a recovery house, and residential colleges for first year students only. On-campus housing is guaranteed for the freshman year only, is available on a first-come, first-served basis, and is available on a lottery system for upperclassmen. 80% of students live on campus. All students may keep cars.

FACULTY/CLASSROOMS: 56% of faculty are male; 44% are female. 75% teach undergraduates, 75% do research, and 75% do both. Graduate students teach 5% of introductory courses. The average class size in an introductory lecture is 35; in a laboratory is 23; and in a regular course is 29.

PROGRAMS OF STUDY: CWRU confers B.A., B.S., B.S.E., B.S. Management, and B.S.N. degrees. Master's and doctoral degrees are also awarded. Bachelor's degrees are awarded in BIOLOGICAL SCIENCE (biochemistry, biology/biological science, evolutionary biology, and nutrition), BUSINESS (accounting, business administration and management, finance, and marketing management), COMMUNICATIONS AND THE ARTS (art history, classics, comparative literature, dance, dramatic arts, English, French, German, music, Spanish, and theatre arts), COMPUTER AND PHYSICAL SCIENCE (applied mathematics, astronomy, chemistry, chemistry / chemical biology, computer science, environmental geology, geology, mathematics, natural sciences, physics, polymer science, and statistics), EDUCATION (art education, Asian studies, education, and music education), ENGINEERING AND ENVIRONMENTAL DESIGN (aerospace engineering, biomedical engineering, chemical engineering, civil engineering, computer engineering, electrical/electronics engineering, engineering, engineering physics, environmental science, materials science, mechanical engineering, and systems engineering), HEALTH PROFESSIONS (nursing and speech pathology/audiology), SOCIAL SCIENCE (anthropology, cognitive science, dietetics, economics, French studies, German area studies, gerontology, history, history of science, international studies, Japanese studies, philosophy, political science/government, psychology, religion, sociology, systems science, and women & gender studies). Engineering, biology, and management are the strongest academically. Engineering, management, and nursing have the largest enrollments.

ACTIVITIES: 27% of men belong to 17 national fraternities; 26% of women belong to 9 national sororities. There are 249 groups on campus, including percussion ensemble, symphonic winds ensemble, art, band, cheerleading, chess, choir, chorale, chorus, communications, computers, dance, debate, drama, environmental, ethnic, film, honors, international, jazz band, LGBT, literary magazine, marching band, musical theater, newspaper, orchestra, pep band, photography, political, professional, radio, religious, social, social service, student government, symphony, and yearbook. Popular campus events include Hudson Relays, Relay-for-Life, Thwing Study Over, Snow Ball Semi-Formal, and Springfest. **Sports:** There are 9 intercollegiate sports for men and 8 for women, and 27 intramural sports for men and 27 for women. Facilities include a facility with multipurpose courts for tennis, badminton, basketball and volleyball, an indoor running track, basketball and volleyball, a gym, swimming pools, cardio room and weight rooms, racquetball and squash courts, rock climbing wall, a multipurpose aerobics room, an auxiliary gym, an archery range, football and soccer field/stadium, outdoor track, baseball/softball ballparks, and a throwing field. **Graduates:** From July 1, 2016 to June 30, 2017, 1249 bachelor's degrees were awarded. The most popular majors were biomedical engineering (10%), mechanical engineering (8%), and psychology (7%). In an average class, 2% graduate in 3 years or less, 68% graduate in 4 years or less, 83% graduate in 5 years or less, and 83% graduate in 6 years or less. Of the 2016 graduating class, 41% were enrolled in graduate school within 6 months of graduation, and 86% were employed.

SERVICES: Counseling and information services are available, as is tutoring in most subjects, such as biology, chemistry, and physics. There is a reader service for the blind. There is also supplemental instruction available in the writing resource center. **Library/Resources:** The library contains 3.4 million volumes, 35,876 microform items, and 33,736 audio/video tapes/CDs/DVDs, and subscribes to 196,361 periodicals including electronic. Computerized library services include interlibrary loans, database searching, Internet access, and Wi-Fi capability. Special learning facilities include an art gallery, natural history museum, planetarium, and a biology field station. **Physically Challenged Students:** 90% of the campus is accessible. Facilities include wheelchair ramps, elevators, special parking, specially equipped restrooms, special class scheduling, lowered drinking fountains, lowered telephones. TDD, special testing arrangements, note-taking assistance, individualized academic counseling and planning, adaptive equipment, interpreters, and access to audiotaped text materials are available. **Special:** CWRU offers co-op programs with nearly 200 employers, and students may alternate classroom study with full-time employment. Cross-registration with four institutions in the Cleveland area is available, as well as internships in government, corporations, and nonprofit agencies. Students may participate in study abroad, a Washington semester, work-study programs, and accelerated-degree programs. B.A.-B.S. degrees, dual and student-designed majors, 3-2 engineering degrees, non-degree study, independent study, and pass/fail options are possible. There are extensive opportunities for undergraduates to work with faculty on research projects. Pre-professional Scholars Programs in medicine, dental medicine, social work, and law are available. Interdisciplinary majors, such as environmental geology, and intradisciplinary majors, such as nutritional biochemistry and metabolism, are available. There are 3 national honor societies, Phi Beta Kappa, and 16 departmental honors programs. **Visiting:** There are regularly scheduled orientations for prospective students. There are guides for informal visits, visitors may sit in on classes, and stay overnight. To schedule a visit, contact the Office of Undergraduate Admission at (216) 368-4450. **Campus Safety and Security:** Measures include 24-hour foot and vehicle patrol, emergency notification system, self-defense education, and security escort services. There are shuttle buses, emergency telephones, lighted pathways/sidewalks, controlled access to dorms/residences, property crime prevention programs, bicycle lock rental, vehicle ID etching, and equipment bolting.

REQUIREMENTS: For students who take the ACT, the writing test is recommended. For those who take the SAT, the essay is recommended. SAT subject tests are also recommended. Applicants must be graduates of an accredited secondary school. The GED is accepted. 16 high academic credits are required, including 4 years of English, 3 years of math (4 years for science, math, and engineering majors), 2 years of lab science (3 years for science and math majors and premedical students), 3 years of social studies (4 recommended for liberal arts students), and 2 years of foreign language (3 recommended for liberal arts students). Engineering, math, and science students should take the SAT Subject tests in math I/IC of IIC and physics and/or chemistry. An interview for is recommended for prospective students across all disciplines. AP credits are accepted. Important factors in the admissions decision are advanced placement or honors courses, extracurricular activities record, and recommendations by school officials. To graduate, students must complete a minimum of 120 semester hours, with at least 30 hours in the major, and maintain a minimum GPA of 2.0. Students must complete the SAGES (Seminar Approach to General Education and Scholarship) core curriculum and two semesters of physical education. **Procedure:** Freshmen are admitted fall, spring, and summer. Entrance exams should be taken by the fall of the senior year. There are early decision and deferred admissions plans. Early decision applications should be filed by November 1; regular applications, by January 15 for fall entry. The fall 2017 application fee was $70. Notification of early decision is sent December 15; regular decision, March 20. 182 early decision candidates were accepted for the 2017-2018 class. 7178 applicants were on the 2017 waiting list; 586 were admitted. Applications are accepted on-line. **Transfer Students:** 34 transfer students enrolled in 2016-2017. Transfer students should meet all high school requirements. Grades of C or better transfer for credit. 60 of 120 credits required for the bachelor's degree must be completed at CWRU. **International Students:** There are 675 international students enrolled. They must take the TOEFL with a minimum score of 577 on the paper-based TOEFL (PBT) or 90 on the Internet-based version (iBT). Student must take the International English Language Testing System. They must also take the SAT or ACT.

ADMISSIONS: 33% of the 2017-2018 applicants were accepted. The SAT scores for the 2017-2018 freshman class were: Critical Reading-- 1% below 500, 14% between 500 and 599, 35% between 600 and 699, and 50% between 700 and 800. Math-- 3% between 500 and 599, 22% between 600 and 699, and 75% between 700 and 800. Writing-- 2% below 500, 14% between 500 and 599, 37% between 600 and 699, and 47% between 700 and 800. Evidence-Based Reading/Writing-- 4% between 500 and 599, 44% between 600 and 699, and 52% between 700 and 800. The ACT scores were 1% between 18 and 23, 23% between 24 and 29, and 76% above 30. 91% of the current freshmen were in the top fifth of their class; 99% were in the top two fifths. 47 freshmen graduated first in their class. **Admissions Contact:** Robert McCullough, Director of Undergraduate Admissions. Email: *admission@case.edu* Web: *www.case.edu*

FINANCIAL AID: In 2017-2018, 87% of all full-time freshmen received some form of financial aid. 55% of all full-time freshmen received need-based aid. The average freshman award was $46,967. Need-based scholarships or need-based grants averaged $36,474; and need-based self-help aid (loans and jobs) averaged $6,659. 30% of undergraduate students work part-time. The average financial indebtedness of the 2017 graduate was $32,377. CWRU is a member of CSS. The CSS/profile and the college's own financial statement are required. The FAFSA code is 003137. The priority date for freshman financial aid applications for fall entry is February 15.

CEDARVILLE UNIVERSITY B-4
www.cedarville.edu

Cedarville, OH 45314 **(937) 766-7700**

Fax: (937) 766-2760	**Email: admiss@cedarville.edu**
Full-time: 1467 men, 1642 women	**Faculty:** 209
Part-time: 187 men, 250 women	**Ph.D.s:** 75%
Graduate: 129 men, 222 women	**Student/Faculty:** 14 to 1
Year: semesters, summer session	**Tuition:** $29,156
Room & Board: $7088	**Freshman Class:** 4039 applied, 2886 accepted, 872 enrolled
SAT CR/M: 630/610 **ACT:** 26	**CEEB CODE:** 1151
Application Deadline: open	**VERY COMPETITIVE**

Cedarville University, founded in 1887, for the Word of God and the Testimony of Jesus Christ, is recognized nationally as a baptist college with caring, authentic community, and rigorous and Christ-centered academic programs. The school has strong graduation and retention rates, with an intentional focus on the Gospel, accredited professional and health science majors, and leading student satisfaction ratings. Cedarville has been honored as the top-ranked Christian university granting bachelor's degrees and a best college for studying the Bible, with academic teams that regularly win or rank in the top tier of national and international competitions. There are 15 undergraduate schools and 4 graduate schools. In addition to regional accreditation, Cedarville has baccalaureate program accreditation with ABET, ACBSP, ACPE, CSWE, NASM, CAEP, CAATE, and CCNE. The 441-acre campus is in a small town 12 miles south of Springfield. Including any residence halls, there are 49 buildings.

STUDENT LIFE: 57% of undergraduates are from out of state, mostly the Midwest. Students are from 48 states, 39 foreign countries, and Canada. 52% are from public schools. 84% are White; 6% race unknown; 3% two or more races; 2% Asian American; 2% Hispanic; 1% African American; 1% American Indian/Alaska Native; 1% Foreign. 99% are Protestant. **Female To Male Ratio:** 1.2:1. The average age of freshmen is 18; all undergraduates, 20. 16% do not continue beyond their first year; 72% remain to graduate. **Housing:** 2668 students can be accommodated in college housing, which includes married student dorms and on-campus apartments. On-campus housing is guaranteed for all 4 years. 73% of students live on campus. Alcohol is not permitted. All students may keep cars.

FACULTY/CLASSROOMS: 64% of faculty are male; 36% are female. 88% teach undergraduates. No introductory courses are taught by graduate students. The average class size in an introductory lecture is 30; in a laboratory is 18; and in a regular course is 21.

PROGRAMS OF STUDY: Cedarville confers B.A., B.S., B.M., B.M.E., B.S.E.E., B.S.M.E., B.S.N., and B.S.Cp.E. degrees. Master's and doctoral degrees are also awarded. Bachelor's degrees are awarded in BIOLOGICAL SCIENCE (biology/biological science, life science secondary school education, and molecular biology), BUSINESS (accounting, business administration and management, finance, international business, marketing/retailing/merchandising, and sports management), COMMUNICATIONS AND THE ARTS (broadcasting, communication rhetoric/communication, digital media, English, graphic design, industrial design, information technology, journalism, keyboard - piano concentration, linguistics, music, music composition, music performance, Spanish, studio art, technical and business writing, theatre arts, and visual design), COMPUTER AND PHYSICAL SCIENCE (chemistry, chemistry education, computer science, geology, geoscience, mathematics, physics secondary education, and physics), EDUCATION (athletic training, Christian education, early childhood education, English education, mathematics education, middle school education, music education, physical education, physical science secondary school education, science education, social studies education, Spanish education K-12, and special education), ENGINEERING AND ENVIRONMENTAL DESIGN (computer engineering, electrical/electronics engineering, environmental science, and mechanical engineering), HEALTH PROFESSIONS (allied health, exercise science, nursing, and pharmaceutical science), SOCIAL SCIENCE (biblical studies, criminal justice, economics, forensic studies, history, international studies, liberal arts/general studies, missions, political science/government, prelaw, psychology, public administration, religious education, social work, theological studies, and youth ministry). Engineering & computer science, business administration, and nursing are the strongest academically. Nursing, mechanical engineering, and early childhood education have the largest enrollments.

ACTIVITIES: There are no fraternities or sororities. There are 85 groups on campus, including art, band, cheerleading, chess, choir, chorale, chorus, dance, debate, drama, environmental, ethnic, forensics, honors, international, jazz band, musical theater, newspaper, orchestra, pep band, photography, political, professional, radio and TV, religious, social, social service, student government, and yearbook. Popular campus events include Junior and Senior Banquet, Lil' Sibs Weekend, and Campus Christmas. **Sports:** There are 8 intercollegiate sports for men and 8 for women, and 31 intramural sports for men and 31 for women. Facilities include a gym, volleyball and badminton courts, a fitness center with 3 racquetball courts, a climbing wall, exercise studio, free weight room, Nautilus strength training areas and cardiovascular areas, a field house with a 200-meter track, basketball, volleyball, tennis, indoor soccer courts, indoor batting cages and a training room, outdoor facilities includes tennis, sand volleyball courts, a track, soccer, baseball, softball fields, golf driving range, and intramural sports playing fields. **Graduates:** From July 1, 2016 to June 30, 2017, 681 bachelor's degrees were awarded. The most popular majors were nursing (13%), mechanical engineering (7%), and pharmaceutical sciences (4%). In an average class, 3% graduate in 3 years or less, 62% graduate in 4 years or less, 71% graduate in 5 years or less, and 72% graduate in 6 years or less. Of the 2016 graduating class, 19% were enrolled in graduate school within 6 months of graduation, and 78% were employed.

SERVICES: Counseling and information services are available, as is tutoring in every subject. There is a reader service for the blind, and remedial math, reading, and writing. There are also tutoring and academic peer coaches, tutoring labs, and mentors. **Library/Resources:** The library contains 321,682 volumes, 10,791 microform items, and 12,033 audio/video tapes/CDs/DVDs, and subscribes to 26,936 periodicals including electronic. Computerized library services include interlibrary loans, database searching, Internet access, and Wi-Fi capability. Special learning facilities include a radio station, a media resource center, observatory, and simulation labs for nursing and pharmacy students. **Physically Challenged Students:** 90% of the campus is accessible. Facilities include wheelchair ramps, elevators, special parking, specially equipped restrooms, special class scheduling, lowered drinking fountains, lowered telephones, and special housing. We provide academic accommodations for students with disabilities as per ADAA, which includes private room, extended time, scribe, reader, CART services, alternative texts, and more. **Special:** Internships, study abroad programs, a Washington semester, dual majors, student-designed majors, B.A.-B.S. degrees in biology, chemistry, and math, and work-study programs with the university are available. Cross-registration with the Southwest Ohio Consortium for Higher Education is possible. Cooperative Learning Agreement with the International Center for Creativity for the Industrial and Innovative Design major. There are 5 national honor societies, a freshman honors program, and 1 departmental honors program. **Visiting:** There are regularly scheduled orientations for prospective students, including campus tours, chapel services, class visits, and meetings with faculty, coaches, and admissions counselors. There are guides for informal visits, visitors may sit in on classes, and stay overnight. To schedule a visit, contact the Admissions Office at (937) 766-7700. **Campus Safety and Security:** Measures include 24-hour foot and vehicle patrol, emergency notification system, self-defense education, and security escort services. There are emergency telephones, lighted pathways/sidewalks, and controlled access to dorms/residences.

REQUIREMENTS: The SAT or ACT is required, with scores above the national average preferred. The university recommends that applicants have 4 years of English, 3 to 4 of math, and 3 each of social studies/history, math, science, and a foreign language. The GED is accepted. Recommendation from a local pastor is required. Cedarville requires applicants to be in the upper 50% of their class. A GPA of 3.0 is required. AP and CLEP credits are accepted. Important factors in the admissions decision are personality/intangible qualities, recommendations by school officials, and advanced placement or honors courses. To graduate, all students must maintain a minimum GPA of 2.0 while taking 128 semester hours, with a minimum of 32 in specific disciplines, 52 in core curriculum, and 36 in major. Specific courses required include English Composition, Fundamentals of Speech, Politics and American Culture, Introduction to Humanities, and Physical Activity and the Christian life. **Procedure:** Freshmen are admitted fall, spring, and summer. Entrance exams should be taken by late junior year or early senior year. There are early admissions, deferred admissions, and rolling admissions plans. Application deadlines are open. The fall 2017 application fee was $30. Applications are accepted on-line. **Transfer Students:** 108 transfer students enrolled in 2016-2017. Applicants must have a minimum college GPA of 3.0. The SAT or ACT is strongly recommended. 32 of 128 credits required for the bachelor's degree must be completed at Cedarville. **International Students:** There are 51 international students enrolled. They must take the TOEFL with a minimum score of 80 on the Internet-based version (iBT). They must also take the SAT or ACT, scoring 1020 SAT 22 ACT.

ADMISSIONS: 71% of the 2017-2018 applicants were accepted. The SAT scores for the 2017-2018 freshman class were: Critical Reading-- 4% below 500, 25% between 500 and 599, 52% between 600 and 699, and 19% between 700 and 800. Math-- 6% below 500, 40% between 500 and 599, 39% between 600 and 699, and 15% between 700 and 800. The ACT scores were 26% between 18 and 23, 55% between 24 and 29, and 19% above 30. 59% of the current freshmen were in the top fifth of their class; 95% were in the top two fifths. 32 freshmen graduated first in their class. **Admissions Contact:** Scott Van Loo, Vice President for Enrollment Management. Email: *admiss@cedarville.edu* Web: *www.cedarville.edu*

FINANCIAL AID: In 2017-2018, 100% of all full-time freshmen received some form of financial aid. 71% of all full-time freshmen received need-based aid. The average freshman award was $28,639. Need-based scholarships or need-based grants averaged $7,697 ($28,456 maximum); need-based self-help aid (loans and jobs) averaged $5,490 ($12,500 maximum); non-need-based athletic scholarships averaged $7,160 ($33,345 maximum); and other non-need-based awards and non-need-based scholarships averaged $22,723 ($64,978 maximum). 44% of undergraduate students work part-time. The average financial indebtedness of the 2017 graduate was $29,475. The college's own financial statement is required. The FAFSA code is 003025. Check with the school for current application deadlines.

CENTRAL STATE UNIVERSITY B-4

www.centralstate.edu

Wilberforce, OH 45384	(937) 376-6348 (800) 388-CSU1
Fax: (937) 376-6648	**Email:** admissions@csu.ces.edu
Full-time: 560 men, 650 women	**Faculty:** 77
Part-time: 55 men, 70 women	**Ph.D.s:** 62%
Graduate: 30 men, 55 women	**Student/Faculty:** 16 to 1
Year: trimesters, summer session	**Tuition:** $9246 ($13,928)
Room & Board: $9318	**Freshman Class:** n/av
ACT: required	**CEEB CODE:** 1107
Application Deadline: August 1	**COMPETITIVE**

Central State University, founded in 1887, is a public institution offering programs in liberal arts, business, engineering, teacher preparation, and professional training. The figures given in the above capsule and in this profile are approximate. There are 3 undergraduate schools and 1 graduate school. In addition to regional accreditation, CSU has baccalaureate program accreditation with ABET and NASM. The 60-acre campus is in a rural area 18 miles east of Dayton. Including any residence halls, there are 34 buildings.

STUDENT LIFE: 77% of undergraduates are from Ohio. Others are from 24 states, and 2 foreign countries. 96% are African American; 2% White; 1% Foreign. **Female To Male Ratio:** 1.2:1. The average age of freshmen is 18; all undergraduates, 22. 42% do not continue beyond their first year; 23% remain to graduate. **Housing:** 745 students can be accommodated in college housing, which includes dorms. On-campus housing is guaranteed for the freshman year only, is available on a first-come, and first-served basis. 57% of students live on campus. Alcohol is not permitted. All students may keep cars.

FACULTY/CLASSROOMS: 77% of faculty are male; 23% are female. All teach undergraduates, and 75% do research. No introductory courses are taught by graduate students. The average class size in an introductory lecture is 25; in a laboratory is 20; and in a regular course is 15.

PROGRAMS OF STUDY: CSU confers B.A., B.S., B.M., B.S.Ed., and B.S.M.E. degrees. Master's degrees are also awarded. Bachelor's degrees are awarded in BIOLOGICAL SCIENCE (biology/biological science), BUSINESS (accounting, banking and finance, business administration and management, and marketing/retailing/merchandising), COMMUNICATIONS AND THE ARTS (advertising, broadcasting, English, journalism, and music), COMPUTER AND PHYSICAL SCIENCE (chemistry, computer science, and mathematics), EDUCATION (art education, elementary education, health education, music education, physical education, secondary education, and special education), ENGINEERING AND ENVIRONMENTAL DESIGN (graphic arts technology and manufacturing engineering), SOCIAL SCIENCE (economics, history, political science/government, psychology, public administration, social work, sociology, and water resources). Communication, music, and education are the strongest academically. Business administration has the largest enrollment.

ACTIVITIES: 1% of men belong to 2 national fraternities; 1% of women belong to 2 national sororities. There are 30 groups on campus, including the entrepreneurship club, finance club, optimist club, art, band, cheerleading, choir, chorale, chorus, communications, computers, dance, drama, drill team, ethnic, honors, J'adore fashion, jazz band, marching band, pep band, political, professional, radio and TV, religious, social, and student government. Popular campus events include Career Day, and May Week. **Sports:** There are 3 intercollegiate sports for men and 4 for women, and 8 intramural sports for men and 7 for women. Facilities include 2 gyms, a stadium, swimming pool, a pool room, baseball diamond, tennis courts, and a weight room. **Graduates:** From July 1, 2016 to June 30, 2017, 81 bachelor's degrees were awarded. The most popular majors were education (25%), business (21%), and social sciences and history (17%). In an average class, 1% graduate in 3 years or less, 9% graduate in 4 years or less, 20% graduate in 5 years or less, and 22% graduate in 6 years or less. Of the 2016 graduating class, 37% were enrolled in graduate school within 6 months of graduation, and 96% were employed.

SERVICES: Counseling and information services are available, as is tutoring in most subjects. There are Student Support Services. **Library/Resources:** The library contains 179,241 volumes, 622,727 microform items, and 500 audio/video tapes/CDs/DVDs, and subscribes to 26,316 periodicals including electronic. Computerized library services include interlibrary loans and database searching. Special learning facilities include an art gallery, radio station, and the National Afro-American Museum and Cultural Center. **Physically Challenged Students:** All of the campus is accessible. Facilities include wheelchair ramps, elevators, special parking, specially equipped restrooms, lowered drinking fountains, and lowered telephones. **Special:** CSU offers co-op programs in all majors, cross-registration with 15 area colleges, study abroad in 3 countries, internships, on-campus work-study programs, and B.A.-B.S. degrees. There is a freshman honors program. **Visiting:** There are regularly scheduled orientations for prospective students, SOAR is a full-day event, begining at 8:00 a.m., with registration to 3:00 p.m. There are guides for informal visits and visitors may sit in on classes. To schedule a visit, contact the Admissions Office. **Campus Safety and Security:** Measures include 24-hour foot and vehicle patrol. There are lighted pathways/sidewalks.

REQUIREMENTS: The ACT is required. The SAT I is accepted. Applicants must be graduates of an accredited secondary school. The GED is accepted. Students should have completed 4 years of high school English, 3 years each of math, science, and social studies, and 2 years of the same foreign language. Ohio applicants should have a GPA of 2.0 and a minimum ACT composite score of 15 or SAT I score of 720. Criteria are higher for out-of-state applicants. AP and CLEP credits are accepted. To graduate, students must complete 186 quarter credits, with a minimum GPA of 2.0 (2.5 in education). Required university core courses include 64 credits in English composition, math, computer skills, humanities, natural sciences, social sciences, health and phys ed, and African American history. **Procedure:** Freshmen are admitted to all sessions. There are early admissions, deferred admissions, and rolling admissions plans. Applications should be filed by August 1 for fall entry; October 15 for winter entry; February 15 for spring entry; and April 15 for summer entry. The fall 2017 application fee was $15. Applications are accepted on-line. **Transfer Students:** 127 transfer students enrolled in 2016-2017. Applicants should have a minimum college GPA of 2.0. Grades of C or better transfer for credit. Transfer students with fewer than 47 quarter hours must submit high school transcripts and test scores. Transfers are admitted every term. 45 of 186 credits required for the bachelor's degree must be completed at CSU. **International Students:** There are 8 international students enrolled. They must take the TOEFL. They must also take the SAT or ACT, scoring 19.

Admissions Contact: Curtis Pettis, Executive Director of Administration. Email: *admissions@csu.ces.edu* Web: *www.centralstate.edu*

FINANCIAL AID: The average freshman award was $10,765. 48% of undergraduate students work part-time. The college's own financial statement is required. The FAFSA code is 003026. The deadline for filing freshman financial aid applications for fall entry is March 31.

CLEVELAND INSTITUTE OF ART *(The complete profile is made available exclusively on our website, www.barronspac.com)*

CLEVELAND INSTITUTE OF MUSIC *(The complete profile is made available exclusively on our website, www.barronspac.com)*

CLEVELAND STATE UNIVERSITY D-1

www.engagecsu.com

Cleveland, OH 44115 **(216) 523-7417**

Email: admissions@csuohio.edu

Full-time: 4363 men, 4907 women	**Faculty:** 540
Part-time: 1338 men, 1698 women	**Ph.D.s:** 87%
Graduate: 1728 men, 2573 women	**Student/Faculty:** 16 to 1
Year: semesters, summer session	**Tuition:** $9790 ($13,841)
Room & Board: $12,500	**Freshman Class:** 7533 applied, 6784 accepted, 1949 enrolled
SAT CR/M: 510/510 **ACT:** 22	**CEEB CODE:** 1221
Application Deadline: August 15	**COMPETITIVE**

Cleveland State University, founded in 1964, is primarily a commuter public institution offering undergraduate and graduate programs through the colleges of arts and sciences, business administration, education, engineering, law, urban affairs, and the school of nursing. There are 8 undergraduate schools and 8 graduate schools. In addition to regional accreditation, CSU has baccalaureate program accreditation with AACSB, ABET, CSWE, NASM, CAEP, NLN, CCNE, APA, and ASHA. The 85-acre campus is in an urban area in downtown Cleveland, Ohio. Including any residence halls, there are 45 buildings.

STUDENT LIFE: 98% of undergraduates are from Ohio. Others are from 38 states, 84 foreign countries, and Canada. 63% are White; 6% Hispanic; 5% Foreign; 4% Asian American; 4% two or more races; 2% race unknown; 17% African American. **Female To Male Ratio:** 1.2:1. The average age of freshmen is 22; all undergraduates, 24. 31% do not continue beyond their first year; 42% remain to graduate. **Housing:** 1010 students can be accommodated in college housing, which includes dorms and on-campus apartments. In addition there are law, quiet study, and first-year experience floors. On-campus housing is available on a first-come and first-served basis. 92% of students commute. All students may keep cars.

FACULTY/CLASSROOMS: 46% of faculty are male; 54% are female. No introductory courses are taught by graduate students.

PROGRAMS OF STUDY: CSU confers B.A., B.S., B.B.A., B.C.E., B.Ch.E., B.E.E., B.M., B.M.E., B.S.C.I.S., B.S.Ed., B.S.I.E., B.S.N. and B.S.T. degrees. Master's and doctoral degrees are also awarded. Bachelor's degrees are awarded in BIOLOGICAL SCIENCE (biology/biological science), BUSINESS (accounting, business economics, finance, labor studies, management information systems, management science, and marketing/retailing/merchandising), COMMUNICATIONS AND THE ARTS (art, communications, dramatic arts, English, film, television and digital media, French, linguistics, music, and Spanish), COMPUTER AND PHYSICAL SCIENCE (chemistry, computer science, geology, information sciences and systems, mathematics, and physics), EDUCATION (early childhood education, elementary education, health education, physical education, secondary education, and special education), ENGINEERING AND ENVIRONMENTAL DESIGN (chemical engineering, civil engineering, electrical/electronics engineering, electrical/electronics engineering technology, environmental science, mechanical engineering, and mechanical engineering technology), HEALTH PROFESSIONS (exercise science, health science, medical technology, nursing, occupational therapy, pharmaceutical science, physical therapy, premedicine, speech pathology/audiology, and speech therapy), SOCIAL SCIENCE (anthropology, classical/ancient civilization, criminology, economics, history, international relations, liberal arts/general studies, philosophy, political science/government, psychology, religion, social science, social studies, social work, sociology, urban studies, and women's studies). Psychology, biology, and business have the largest enrollments.

ACTIVITIES: 1% of men belong to 5 national fraternities; 1% of women belong to 5 national sororities. There are 234 groups on campus, including art, cheerleading, chess, choir, chorale, chorus, computers, dance, drama, environmental, ethnic, film, honors, international, jazz band, LGBT, literary magazine, musical theater, newspaper, opera, orchestra, pep band, photography, political, professional, radio and TV, religious, social, social service, student government, and symphony. Popular campus events include Weeks of Welcome, Homecoming, and Springfest. **Sports:** There are 8 intercollegiate sports for men and 10 for women, and 12 intramural sports for men and 8 for women. Facilities include a recreation center with a gym and weight rooms, a dance studio, a swimming pool, fitness trail, an indoor track, handball and squash courts, a soccer stadium, and a convocation center. **Graduates:** From July 1, 2016 to June 30, 2017, 2506 bachelor's degrees were awarded. The most popular majors were health sciences (12%), psychology (9%), and nursing (6%). In an average class, 22% graduate in 4 years or less, 38% graduate in 5 years or less, and 42% graduate in 6 years or less.

SERVICES: Counseling and information services are available, as is tutoring in most subjects. There is remedial math, reading, and writing. **Library/Resources:** The library contains 1.8 million volumes, 258,371 microform items, and 148,242 audio/video tapes/CDs/DVDs, and subscribes to 49,433 periodicals including electronic. Computerized library services include interlibrary loans, database searching, Internet access, and Wi-Fi capability. Special learning facilities include an art gallery and radio station. **Physically Challenged Students:** All of the campus is accessible. Facilities include wheelchair ramps, elevators, special parking, specially equipped restrooms, lowered drinking fountains, and special housing. **Special:** CSU offers a developmental program for Ohio students not qualified for regular freshman admission. There are also cooperative education programs, nondegree study, work-study programs, accelerated degree programs, internships, pass/fail options, and cross-registration at other Cleveland area colleges. Student-designed and dual majors, study abroad in 10 countries, and volunteer opportunities are available, as well as a combined liberal arts and engineering degree and a 3-2 engineering degree. There are 6 national honor societies, a freshman honors program, and 38 departmental honors programs. **Visiting:** There are regularly scheduled orientations for prospective students, including general visitation days for the university (in the fall) and each of the colleges (in the spring). There are guides for informal visits, visitors may sit in on classes, and stay overnight. To schedule a visit, contact the Office of Undergraduate Admissions. **Campus Safety and Security:** Measures include 24-hour foot and vehicle patrol, emergency notification system, self-defense education, and security escort services. There are emergency telephones, lighted pathways/sidewalks, controlled access to dorms/residences, and a campus watch organization for faculty and staff.

REQUIREMENTS: The SAT or ACT is required. A high school diploma is required or the GED is accepted. Students should have completed the following academic credits: 4 years of English, 3 of math, social studies, and science (1 must be a lab), and 2 of a foreign language. A general college-preparatory program is recommended. AP and CLEP credits are accepted. Students must complete at least 120 semester hours with a minimum 2.0 GPA for graduation. Requirements include a core curriculum containing courses in English composition, arts and humanities, social science, natural sciences, math and logic, non-Western culture and civilization, Western culture and civilization, and human diversity and the African American experience. **Procedure:** Freshmen are admitted to all sessions. Entrance exams should be taken prior to application. There are deferred admissions and rolling admissions plans. Applications should be filed by August 15 for fall entry. The fall 2017 application fee was $30. Notification is sent on a rolling basis. Applications are accepted on-line. **Transfer Students:** 1265 transfer students enrolled in 2016-2017. Applicants must have a minimum GPA of 2.0 and submit previous college transcripts. Transfer students entering with fewer than 24 semester hours must submit official high school transcripts and test scores if they have been out of high school less than 5 years. 30 of 120 credits required for the bachelor's degree must be completed at CSU. **International Students:** There are 649 international students enrolled. They must take the TOEFL with a minimum score of 550 on the paper-based TOEFL (PBT) or 78 on the Internet-based version (iBT).

ADMISSIONS: 90% of the 2017-2018 applicants were accepted. The SAT scores for the 2017-2018 freshman class were: Critical Reading-- 45% below 500, 37% between 500 and 599, 14% between 600 and 699, and 3% between 700 and 800. Math-- 42% below 500, 41% between 500 and 599, 14% between 600 and 699, and 3% between 700 and 800. The ACT scores were 14% between 12 and 17, 50% between 18 and 23, 32% between 24 and 29, and 4% above 30. **Admissions Contact:** Lee Furbeck, Director, Undergraduate Admissions. Email: *admissions@csuohio.edu* Web: *www.engagecsu.com*

FINANCIAL AID: In 2017-2018, 74% of all full-time freshmen received some form of financial aid. 61% of all full-time freshmen received need-based aid. The average freshman award was $8,902. Need-based scholarships or need-based grants averaged $6,986; need-based self-help aid (loans and jobs) averaged $3,876; non-need-based athletic scholarships averaged $10,929; and other non-need-based awards and non-need-based scholarships averaged $5,560. The FAFSA code is 003032. The priority date for freshman financial aid applications for fall entry is February 15.

COLUMBUS COLLEGE OF ART AND DESIGN *(The complete profile is made available exclusively on our website, www.barronspac.com)*

DEFIANCE COLLEGE *(The complete profile is made available exclusively on our website, www.barronspac.com)*

DENISON UNIVERSITY — C-3

www.denison.edu

Granville, OH 43023 — **(740) 587-6276**

Fax: (740) 587-6306	**Email:** admission@denison.edu
Full-time: 1032 men, 1287 women	**Faculty:** 218; IIB, +$
Part-time: 2 men	**Ph.D.s:** 100%
Graduate: n/av	**Student/Faculty:** 9 to 1
Year: semesters	**Tuition:** $50,440
Room & Board: $12,330	**Freshman Class:** 7540 applied, 2808 accepted, 617 enrolled
SAT CR/M: 644/640 **ACT:** 29	**CEEB CODE:** 1164
Application Deadline: January 15	**HIGHLY COMPETITIVE+**

Denison University, founded in 1831, is a private residential institution of liberal arts and sciences. There is 1 undergraduate school. The 931-acre campus is in a suburban area in Granville, Ohio, and 25 miles east of Columbus. Including any residence halls, there are 62 buildings.

STUDENT LIFE: 68% of undergraduates are from out of state, mostly the Midwest. Students are from 50 states, 34 foreign countries, and Canada. 70% are from public schools. 9% are Hispanic; 7% African American; 64% White; 4% Asian American; 3% two or more races; 2% race unknown; 10% Foreign. 36% are Protestant; 30% Catholic; 28% Muslim, Hindu, Buddhist, and Nondenominational. **Female To Male Ratio:** 1.2:1. The average age of freshmen is 19; all undergraduates, 21. 8% do not continue beyond their first year; 82% remain to graduate. **Housing:** 2250 students can be accommodated in college housing, which includes single sex, coed dorms and on-campus apartments. In addition, there are honors houses, special-interest houses, first-year center, substance-free dorms, quiet dorms, all-women dorms, suite-style dorms, and apartments for juniors and seniors with high GPAs. On-campus housing is guaranteed for all 4 years and is available on a lottery system for upperclassmen. 99% of students live on campus. All students may keep cars.

FACULTY/CLASSROOMS: 53% of faculty are male; 47% are female. All teach undergraduates, and all do research. No introductory courses are taught by graduate students. The average class size in an introductory lecture is 20; in a laboratory is 21; and in a regular course is 19.

PROGRAMS OF STUDY: Denison confers B.A., B.F.A., and B.S. degrees. Bachelor's degrees are awarded in AGRICULTURE (environmental studies), BIOLOGICAL SCIENCE (biochemistry and biology/biological science), COMMUNICATIONS AND THE ARTS (art history and appreciation, communications, dance, dramatic arts, English, film arts, fine arts, French, German, languages, Latin, media arts, music, Spanish, speech/debate/rhetoric, and studio art), COMPUTER AND PHYSICAL SCIENCE (chemistry, computer science, geology, mathematics, and physics), EDUCATION (education and physical education), SOCIAL SCIENCE (African American studies, anthropology, classical/ancient civilization, East Asian studies, economics, history, international studies, Latin American studies, philosophy, political science/government, psychology, religion, sociology, Western European studies, and women's studies). Psychology, biology, English, data analytics, and global commerce are the strongest academically. Psychology, biology, and economics have the largest enrollments.

ACTIVITIES: 28% of men belong to 10 national fraternities; 45% of women belong to 8 national sororities. There are 180 groups on campus, including art, cheerleading, choir, chorale, chorus, communications, computers, dance, debate, drama, environmental, ethnic, film, honors, international, jazz band, LGBT, literary magazine, musical theater, newspaper, orchestra, pep band, photography, political, professional, radio and TV, religious, social, social service, student government, and symphony. Popular campus events include Community Picnics and Fairs, Homecoming Gala, Academic Awards Convocation, D-Day, Diwali Festival of Lights, and Vail Arts Series. **Sports:** There are 11 intercollegiate sports for men and 12 for women, and 17 intramural sports for men and 14 for women. Facilities include a stadium, aquatic center, a gym, outdoor tennis courts, squash courts, 8-lane quarter-mile track, field house with a 200-meter track and tennis courts, baseball/softball fields, recreation gym with volleyball/basketball courts, and weight, aerobic, and fitness rooms, soccer, lacrosse stadium, field hockey, and multiple practice fields. **Graduates:** From July 1, 2016 to June 30, 2017, 491 bachelor's degrees were awarded. The most popular majors were economics (14%), communications (12%), and biology (9%). In an average class, 77% graduate in 4 years or less, 84% graduate in 5 years or less, and 85% graduate in 6 years or less. Of the 2016 graduating class, 16% were enrolled in graduate school within 6 months of graduation, and 67% were employed.

SERVICES: Counseling and information services are available, as is tutoring in most subjects. There is a reader service for the blind. A writing center is available, as are study sessions for math, chemistry, and some languages, reduced course loads, special counselor services, note-taking services, oral tests, extended time for tests, untimed tests, talking books, tape recorders, and readers. **Library/Resources:** The library contains 1.3 million volumes, 128,175 microform items, and 37,365 audio/video tapes/CDs/DVDs, and subscribes to 21,805 periodicals including electronic. Computerized library services include interlibrary loans, database searching, Internet access, and Wi-Fi capability. Special learning facilities include an art gallery, planetarium, radio station, TV station, an observatory, a multimedia MIX lab, a field research station in a 350-acre biological reserve, a high-resolution spectrometer, economics computer labs, a museum, studio arts facilities for painting, printmaking, photography, ceramics, metal and wood, 3-D and laser printing, filmmaking studio and equipment, and a modern languages lab. **Physically Challenged Students:** 80% of the campus is accessible. Facilities include wheelchair ramps, elevators, special parking, specially equipped restrooms, special class scheduling, lowered drinking fountains, and lowered telephones. **Special:** Denison offers internships, study abroad, and interdisciplinary team-taught seminars with an off-campus study component, summer research programs, and an advising/mentoring program for first-year students. There are 15 national honor societies and a chapter of Phi Beta Kappa. **Visiting:** There are regularly scheduled orientations for prospective students, including orientation programs, class visits, tours, and interviews. There are guides for informal visits, visitors may sit in on classes, and stay overnight. To schedule a visit, contact the Admissions Office. **Campus Safety and Security:** Measures include 24-hour foot and vehicle patrol, emergency notification system, self-defense education, and security escort services. There are emergency telephones, lighted pathways/sidewalks, and controlled access to dorms/residences.

REQUIREMENTS: The SAT or ACT is recommended. Denison operates under a test optional admissions policy. Applicants should have completed 19 Carnegie units, including 4 units each in English, math, and science, 3 units in foreign language, 2 units in social studies, and 1 unit each in history and academic electives. An essay is part of the application process. An interview is advised, and a portfolio or an audition is recommended for art and music majors, respectively. AP and CLEP credits are accepted. Important factors in the admissions decision are personality/ intangible qualities, evidence of special talent, and advanced placement or honors courses. The General Education requirements ensure that students develop core liberal arts competencies and encounter a broad range of liberal arts inquiries social, scientific, humanistic, and artistic-embraced by the faculty of Denison. In addition, the requirements expose students to a diversity of perspectives that enable them to interact more effectively in an increasingly interdependent world. Thus, the General Education program seeks to accomplish three goals: Development of competencies, exposure to a broad variety of disciplines, and development of a global perspective. Summary of requirements: Two courses each of fine arts, sciences (one fulfilling a lab requirement), social sciences, and humanities. One interdivisional course from one of the following areas: Black Studies, East Asian Studies, Environmental Studies, International Studies, Latin American and Caribbean Studies, Queer Studies, and Women Studies. One W101 Writing Workshop, two "W" Writing Competency courses. At a minimum, all students must complete an elementary year of Foreign Language 111-112 at the college level. Students who have studied a language in high school and who wish to continue study of that language at Denison in order to fulfill this requirement will, however, be expected to complete three semesters of that language (i.e., to pass or demonstrate proficiency in the language at the 211 level). All entering students who have studied a foreign language in high school must take the appropriate placement test during the orientation period. Language courses 111, 112, and 211 will not count toward the divisional distribution requirements, except for Latin and Greek 211 which may count toward the Humanities requirement unless used to satisfy the Foreign Language requirement. Three of these general education courses (or other courses) must fulfill one power and justice, one quantitative, and one oral communication requirement. Only one course from a single department may be used to fulfill the divisional requirements. **Procedure:** Freshmen are admitted fall and spring. Entrance exams should be taken by December of the senior year. There are early decision, early admissions, and deferred admissions plans. Early decision applications should be filed by December 1; regular applications, by January 15 for fall entry. Notification of early decision is sent January 1; regular decision, April 1. 245 early decision candidates were accepted for the 2017-2018 class. 1502 applicants were on the 2017 waiting list; 55 were admitted. Applications are accepted on-line. **Transfer Students:** 27 transfer students enrolled in 2016-2017. SAT or ACT scores should be submitted, as well as high school and college transcripts, an essay, and a statement of good standing from previous institutions. An interview is recommended. 64 of 127 credits required for the bachelor's degree must be completed at Denison. **International Students:** There are 233 international students enrolled. They must take the TOEFL with a minimum score of 550 on the paper-based TOEFL (PBT) or 80 on the Internet-based version (iBT).

ADMISSIONS: 37% of the 2017-2018 applicants were accepted. The SAT scores for the 2017-2018 freshman class were: Critical Reading-- 22% between 500 and 599, 58% between 600 and 699, and 20% between 700 and 800. Math-- 24% between 500 and 599, 52% between 600 and 699, and 24% between 700 and 800. The ACT scores were 57% between 24 and 29, and 43% above 30. 87% of the current freshmen were in the top fifth of their class; 98% were in the top two fifths. 22 freshmen graduated first in their class. **Admissions Contact:** Greg Sneed, Vice President of Enrollment Management. Email: *admission@denison.edu* Web: *www.denison.edu*

FINANCIAL AID: In 2017-2018, 96% of all full-time freshmen received some form of financial aid and need-based aid. The average freshman award was $48,404. Need-based scholarships or need-based grants averaged $40,588; and need-based self-help aid (loans and jobs) averaged $7,750. 51% of undergraduate students work part-time. The average financial indebtedness of the 2017 graduate was $27,823. Denison University is a member of CSS. The CSS/Profile and the college's own financial statement are required. The FAFSA code is 003042. The priority date for freshman financial aid applications for fall entry is January 15. The deadline for filing freshman financial aid applications for fall entry is February 15.

FRANCISCAN UNIVERSITY OF STEUBENVILLE — E-3

www.franciscan.edu

Steubenville, OH 43952	(740) 283-6860 (800) 783-6220
Fax: (740) 284-5456	**Email:** admissions@franciscan.edu
Full-time: 779 men, 1216 women	**Faculty:** 120; IIA, --$
Part-time: 53 men, 42 women	**Ph.D.s:** 82%
Graduate: 292 men, 377 women	**Student/Faculty:** 14 to 1
Year: semesters, summer session	**Tuition:** $25,680
Room & Board: $8300	**Freshman Class:** 1760 applied, 1386 accepted, 456 enrolled
SAT CR/M/W: 590/560/570 **ACT:** 25	**CEEB CODE:** 1133
Application Deadline: n/av	**VERY COMPETITIVE**

Franciscan University of Steubenville, founded in 1946 by the Franciscan Friars, is a private liberal arts institution which embraces the call to dynamic orthodoxy and whose mission is "to educate, to evangelize, and to send forth joyful disciples," thereby restoring all things in Christ. There is 1 undergraduate school and 7 graduate schools. In addition to regional accreditation, FUS has baccalaureate program accreditation with CSWE, CAEP, and CCNE. The 235-acre campus is in a small town 40 miles west of Pittsburgh. Including any residence halls, there are 25 buildings.

STUDENT LIFE: 80% of undergraduates are from out of state, mostly the Midwest. Students are from 50 states, 10 foreign countries, and Canada. 37% are from public schools. 82% are White; 2% Asian American; 2% two or more races; 2% race unknown; 11% Hispanic; 1% African American; 1% Foreign. 97% are Catholic. **Female To Male Ratio:** 1.5:1. The average age of freshmen is 18; all undergraduates, 20. 16% do not continue beyond their first year; 76% remain to graduate. **Housing:** 1394 students can be accommodated in college housing, which includes dorms, on-campus apartments, and Christian faith households in residence halls. On-campus housing is available on a first-come and first-served basis. 80% of students live on campus. Upperclassmen may keep cars.

FACULTY/CLASSROOMS: 63% of faculty are male; 37% are female. 96% teach undergraduates. No introductory courses are taught by graduate students. The average class size in an introductory lecture is 28; in a laboratory is 15; and in a regular course is 21.

PROGRAMS OF STUDY: FUS confers B.A., B.S., and B.S.N. degrees. Associate and master's degrees are also awarded. Bachelor's degrees are awarded in BIOLOGICAL SCIENCE (biology/biological science), BUSINESS (accounting, business administration and management, international business management, management, and marketing management), COMMUNICATIONS AND THE ARTS (classics, communications, dramatic arts, English, French, German, and Spanish), COMPUTER AND PHYSICAL SCIENCE (chemistry, computer science, information sciences and systems, and mathematics), EDUCATION (elementary education), HEALTH PROFESSIONS (nursing), SOCIAL SCIENCE (anthropology, economics, history, humanities and social science, philosophy, political science/government, psychology, religious education, religious music, social work, sociology, and theological studies). Theology, catechetics, and biology are the strongest academically. Theology, business, and nursing education have the largest enrollments.

ACTIVITIES: There are no fraternities or sororities. There are 35 groups on campus, including choir, chorale, chorus, computers, drama, ethnic, honors, international, literary magazine, newspaper, orchestra, political, pro-life club, professional, radio and TV, religious, social, social service, student government, and yearbook. Popular campus events include Feast of St. Francis, Pro-Life Rally, and All-school Evangelism Events. **Sports:**

There are 7 intercollegiate sports for men and 9 for women, and 8 intramural sports for men and 8 for women. Facilities include a campus athletic center, which houses basketball courts, and racquetball courts. Outdoor athletic facilities include a sand volleyball court, baseball, softball, flag football, and soccer fields. **Graduates:** From July 1, 2016 to June 30, 2017, 474 bachelor's degrees were awarded. The most popular majors were theology (20%), nursing (8%), and education (8%). In an average class, 7% graduate in 3 years or less, 67% graduate in 4 years or less, 74% graduate in 5 years or less, and 76% graduate in 6 years or less. Of the 2016 graduating class, 20% were enrolled in graduate school within 6 months of graduation, and 67% were employed.

SERVICES: Counseling and information services are available, as is tutoring in most subjects. There is a reader service for the blind, and remedial reading and writing. Tutoring and counseling are available for learning-disabled students. Tutoring is also available for students on academic probation. **Library/Resources:** The library contains 224,280 volumes, 269 microform items, and 892 audio/video tapes/CDs/DVDs, and subscribes to 399 periodicals including electronic. Computerized library services include interlibrary loans, database searching, Internet access, and Wi-Fi capability. Special learning facilities include an art gallery and radio station. **Physically Challenged Students:** 80% of the campus is accessible. Facilities include wheelchair ramps, elevators, special parking, specially equipped restrooms, special class scheduling, lowered drinking fountains, and lowered telephones. **Special:** Dual majors and internships for up to 6 credit hours are available in most majors. A humanities and Catholic culture major in Western tradition and minors in human life studies, film studies, Franciscan studies, and music are offered. Study abroad is offered through our highly ranked program in Gaming, Austria, where students spend a semester studying humanities as well as traveling through Europe. There are 5 national honor societies, a freshman honors program, and 25 departmental honors programs. **Visiting:** There are regularly scheduled orientations for prospective students, including tours, interviews with professors, admissions, and financial aid officers, and class scheduling. There are guides for informal visits, visitors may sit in on classes, and stay overnight. To schedule a visit, contact Bernardo Gonzalez at bgonzalez@franciscan.edu. **Campus Safety and Security:** Measures include 24-hour foot and vehicle patrol, emergency notification system, self-defense education, and security escort services. There are shuttle buses, emergency telephones, lighted pathways/sidewalks, and controlled access to dorms/residences.

REQUIREMENTS: Applicants should have completed 15 academic high school units, including 10 in 4 of the 5 following areas: English, foreign language, social science, math, and natural sciences. The GED is accepted. The ACT or SAT is required and an interview is recommended. A GPA of 2.4 is required. AP and CLEP credits are accepted. All students must complete core curriculum courses. Bachelor of Arts students must complete 9 credits each in theology and philosophy, 6 credits each in literature and natural science, and 3 credits each in American founding principles, Catholic traditions in fine arts, history, social science and math or economics for a total of 45 credits. In addition, they must complete a foreign language at the intermediate level. Bachelor of Science students must complete 15 credits in theology and/or philosophy, 6 credits in natural science, and 3 credits each in American founding principles, Catholic traditions in fine arts, economics, history, literature, math and social science **Procedure:** Freshmen are admitted fall, spring, and summer. Entrance exams should be taken in the spring of the junior year or the fall of the senior year. There is a rolling admissions plan. Application deadlines are open. Notification is sent on a rolling basis. Applications are accepted on-line. **Transfer Students:** 122 transfer students enrolled in 2016-2017. A minimum 2.0 college GPA is required. High school and college transcripts must be submitted. An interview is recommended. 30 of 124 credits required for the bachelor's degree must be completed at FUS. **International Students:** There are 17 international students enrolled. They must take the TOEFL with a minimum score of 550 on the paper-based TOEFL (PBT) or 80 on the Internet-based version (iBT).

ADMISSIONS: 79% of the 2017-2018 applicants were accepted. The SAT scores for the 2017-2018 freshman class were: Critical Reading-- 9% below 500, 42% between 500 and 599, 32% between 600 and 699, and 17% between 700 and 800. Math-- 21% below 500, 44% between 500 and 599, 28% between 600 and 699, and 7% between 700 and 800. Writing-- 18% below 500, 45% between 500 and 599, 30% between 600 and 699, and 7% between 700 and 800. The ACT scores were 32% between 18 and 23, 52% between 24 and 29, and 16% above 30. 44% of the current freshmen were in the top fifth of their class; 72% were in the top two fifths. 4 freshmen graduated first in their class. **Admissions Contact:** Christopher Krivoniak, Director of Admissions. Email: *admissions@franciscan.edu* Web: *www.franciscan.edu*

FINANCIAL AID: Check with the school for current application deadlines.

FRANKLIN UNIVERSITY *(The complete profile is made available exclusively on our website, www.barronspac.com)*

HEIDELBERG UNIVERSITY *(The complete profile is made available exclusively on our website, www.barronspac.com)*

HIRAM COLLEGE — E-1

www.hiram.edu

Hiram, OH 44234	**(330) 569-5169** **(800) 362-5280**
Fax: (330) 569-5944	**Email: admission@hiram.edu**
Full-time: 400 men, 453 women	**Faculty:** 79
Part-time: 155 men, 202 women	**Ph.D.s:** 95%
Graduate: 5 men, 6 women	**Student/Faculty:** 10 to 1
Year: other, summer session	**Tuition:** $34,300
Room & Board: $10,290	**Freshman Class:** 2761 applied, 1754 accepted, 258 enrolled
SAT CR/M: 550/530 **ACT:** 22	**CEEB CODE:** 1297
Application Deadline: n/av	**COMPETITIVE**

Hiram College is a 168-year-old liberal arts college known for changing students' lives. Hiram's academic calendar, known as the Hiram Plan, is unique to the nation. The college provides students one of the country's oldest and most respected study-abroad programs and is one of 10 percent of colleges and universities to be awarded a chapter of the prestigious honor society Phi Beta Kappa. Hiram offers 33 majors and 39 minors, many of which are interdisciplinary, as well as more than 20 three-year undergraduate degrees, an M.A. in interdisciplinary studies and a Weekend College program. There is 1 undergraduate school. In addition to regional accreditation, Hiram College has baccalaureate program accreditation with NASM, CAEP, and CCNE. The 110-acre campus is in a rural area 35 miles southeast of Cleveland. Including any residence halls, there are 39 buildings.

STUDENT LIFE: 84% of undergraduates are from Ohio. Others are from 33 states, 12 foreign countries, and Canada. 53% are White; 3% Hispanic; 3% two or more races; 25% race unknown; 2% Foreign; 13% African American; 1% Asian American. **Female To Male Ratio:** 1.2:1. The average age of freshmen is 18; all undergraduates, 21. 30% do not continue beyond their first year; 56% remain to graduate. **Housing:** 785 students can be accommodated in college housing, which includes gender neutral, single sex and coed dorms, and on-campus apartments. In addition, there are honors houses, and special-interest houses includes entrepreneurship. On-campus housing is guaranteed for all 4 years and is available on a lottery system for upperclassmen. 80% of students live on campus. All students may keep cars.

FACULTY/CLASSROOMS: 42% of faculty are male; 58% are female. No introductory courses are taught by graduate students. The average class size in an introductory lecture is 13; in a laboratory is 11; and in a regular course is 12.

PROGRAMS OF STUDY: Hiram confers B.A., and B.S.N. degrees. Master's degrees are also awarded. Bachelor's degrees are awarded in BIOLOGICAL SCIENCE (biochemistry, biology/biological science, and neurosciences), BUSINESS (accounting and management), COMMUNICATIONS AND THE ARTS (art history, art, communications, creative writing, English, French, music, Spanish, and theatre acting), COMPUTER AND PHYSICAL SCIENCE (chemistry, computer science, mathematics, and physics), EDUCATION (education), ENGINEERING AND ENVIRONMENTAL DESIGN (environmental science), HEALTH PROFESSIONS (biomedical science, exercise science, nursing, and public health), SOCIAL SCIENCE (economics, history, philosophy, political science/government, psychology, religion, and sociology). Biomedical humanities and entrepreneurship are the strongest academically. Accounting and financial management, business management, and nursing have the largest enrollments.

ACTIVITIES: There are no fraternities; 2% of women belong to 3 local sororities. There are 50 groups on campus, including art, cheerleading, choir, chorale, chorus, computers, dance, drama, drill team, environmental, ethnic, honors, international, LGBT, literary magazine, musical theater, photography, political, professional, radio and TV, religious, social, student government, and yearbook. Popular campus events include Campus Days, Springfest, Homecoming, Parents Weekend, Alumni Weekend. **Sports:** There are 8 intercollegiate sports for men and 8 for women, and 10 intramural sports for men and 10 for women. Facilities include a sports center with a gym, courts for tennis, volleyball, basketball, and baseball, an elevated 3-lane track, a multipurpose activity court, a 25-meter swimming pool, a fitness center, a weight room, an aerobics studio, racquetball courts, and a training room. Outdoor facilities include football, baseball, soccer, and softball fields, practice fields, and tennis courts. **Graduates:** From July 1, 2016 to June 30, 2017, 236 bachelor's degrees were awarded. The most popular majors were accounting and financial management (18%), accounting/financial management (17%), and nursing (10%). In an average class, 50% graduate in 4 years or less, 55% graduate in 5 years or less, and 56% graduate in 6 years or less. Of the 2016 graduating class, 16% were enrolled in graduate school within 6 months of graduation, and 82% were employed.

SERVICES: Counseling and information services are available, as is tutoring in most subjects, such as accounting, biology, chemistry, communication, computer science, economics, French, history, Latin, math, marketing, music, philosophy, physics, psychology, religious studies, sociology, and Spanish. Note takers are available for most classes. **Library/Resources:** The library contains 519,594 volumes, 131 microform items, and 25,714 audio/video tapes/CDs/DVDs, and subscribes to 10,886 periodicals including electronic. Computerized library services include interlibrary loans, database searching, Internet access, and Wi-Fi capability. Special learning facilities include an art gallery, planetarium, and radio station. The James H. Barrow Field Station offers over 550 acres of land to support hands-on research and education. **Physically Challenged Students:** 55% of the campus is accessible. Facilities include wheelchair ramps, elevators, special parking, specially equipped restrooms, and special housing. **Special:** Hiram is known for its distinctive Hiram Plan. Under this plan, students complete 12 weeks of traditional coursework, take a weeklong break and finish their academic semester with three weeks of intensive study in a single class. Unique to the nation, this plan has been described as a near-perfect approach to fostering student learning and engagement. Hiram takes yet another thoughtful approach to higher education through Hiram Connect, which links coursework, internships, study-away explorations and hands-on learning opportunities. This process, which encourages students to reflect upon their academic experiences, not only helps them determine what they want to do professionally, but who they want to be personally. Other college offerings, such as Hiram Health, which prepares health professionals as compassionate caregivers, and offers pathways to graduate programs at such schools as Case Western Reserve University, Washington University in St. Louis and Northeast Ohio Medical University, serve Hiram students who come from throughout the United States and 20 foreign countries. The college offers 32 majors and 38 minors, many of which are interdisciplinary, as well as 20 three-year undergraduate degrees, an M.A. in interdisciplinary studies and a Weekend College program for nontraditional students. There are 6 national honor societies, Phi Beta Kappa, and a freshman honors program. **Visiting:** There are regularly scheduled orientations for prospective students, campus visits for prospective students consist of tours and overnights while school is in session, if requested. There are guides for informal visits, visitors may sit in on classes, and stay overnight. To schedule a visit, contact Kelly Adams at AdamsKL@hiram.edu. **Campus Safety and Security:** Measures include emergency notification system, self-defense education, and security escort services. There are emergency telephones, lighted pathways/sidewalks, and controlled access to dorms/residences.

REQUIREMENTS: Applicants should have completed 16 academic units or the GED equivalent. An essay, portfolio, audition, and interview are recommended. AP and CLEP credits are accepted. Important factors in the admissions decision are advanced placement or honors courses, personality/intangible qualities, and extracurricular activities record. All students must complete courses in a core curriculum across a minimum of 6 disciplines; complete at least 120 semester hours (133 for Bachelor of Science in Nursing); and a GPA of at least 2.0 overall, and in each major and minor. A capstone project is required in all undergraduate majors. Additionally, all Hiram students complete an internship, study away exploration or research experience as part of Hiram Connect. **Procedure:** Freshmen are admitted fall and spring. Entrance exams should be taken no later than the fall of the senior year of high school. There are deferred admissions and rolling admissions plans. Application deadlines are open. The fall 2017 application fee was $25. Notification is sent on a rolling basis. Applications are accepted on-line. **Transfer Students:** 22 transfer students enrolled in 2016-2017. Applicants should have at least a 2.5 GPA and be in good academic and social standing with the previous institution. An interview is recommended. 45 of 120 credits required for the bachelor's degree must be completed at Hiram. **International Students:** There are 18 international students enrolled. They must take the TOEFL with a minimum score of 550 on the paper-based TOEFL (PBT) or 79 on the Internet-based version (iBT). Students must take the International English Language Testing System.

ADMISSIONS: 64% of the 2017-2018 applicants were accepted. The SAT scores for the 2017-2018 freshman class were: Critical Reading-- 33% below 500, 37% between 500 and 599, 18% between 600 and 699, and 12% between 700 and 800. Math-- 41% below 500, 35% between 500 and 599, 20% between 600 and 699, and 4% between 700 and 800. The ACT scores were 19% between 12 and 17, 51% between 18 and 23, 23% between 24 and 29, and 7% above 30. **Admissions Contact:** Sherman C. Dean, Director of Admission. Email: *admission@hiram.edu* Web: *www.hiram.edu*

FINANCIAL AID: Hiram College is a member of CSS. The FAFSA code is 003049. The priority date for freshman financial aid applications for fall entry is February 15.

JOHN CARROLL UNIVERSITY — D-1

www.sites.jcu.edu

University Heights, OH 44118	**(216) 397-4294** **(888) 335-6800**
Fax: (216) 397-4981	**Email: enrollment@jcu.edu**
Full-time: 1491 men, 1446 women	**Faculty:** 185; IIA, av$
Part-time: 46 men, 45 women	**Ph.D.s:** 97%
Graduate: 179 men, 318 women	**Student/Faculty:** 14 to 1
Year: semesters, summer session	**Tuition:** $39,900
Room & Board: $11,580	**Freshman Class:** 3873 applied, 3211 accepted, 799 enrolled
SAT CR/M/W: 544/549/532 **ACT:** required	**CEEB CODE:** 1342
Application Deadline: February 1	**COMPETITIVE**

John Carroll University is a private, coeducational, Jesuit Catholic university providing programs in the liberal arts, sciences, and business at the undergraduate and master's levels. As a Jesuit Catholic university, JCU inspires its students to excel in learning, leadership, and service in the region and in the world. Our unique size, structure, culture, and environment make us very successful at providing an outstanding education for our students. There are 2 undergraduate schools and 2 graduate schools. In addition to regional accreditation, JCU has baccalaureate program accreditation with AACSB, CAEP, HLC, CACREP, and NASP. The 62-acre campus is in a suburban area in University Heights, Ohio, 10 miles east of Cleveland with easy access to the city. Including any residence halls, there are 21 buildings.

STUDENT LIFE: 65% of undergraduates are from Ohio. Others are from 34 states, 34 foreign countries, and Canada. 49% are from public schools. 86% are White; 4% African American; 4% Hispanic; 2% Asian American; 2% Foreign; 2% two or more races; 1% race unknown. 64% are Catholic; 15% Buddhist, Hindu, Muslim, Orthodox Christian, and Unitarian; 11% Protestant. **Female To Male Ratio:** 1.1:1. The average age of freshmen is 18; all undergraduates, 20. 14% do not continue beyond their first year; 77% remain to graduate. **Housing:** 1810 students can be accommodated in college housing, which includes dorms and off-campus apartments. In addition, there are special-interest houses, wellness, and fraternity/sorority floors in residence halls. On-campus housing is available on a lottery system for upperclassmen. 57% of students live on campus. All students may keep cars.

FACULTY/CLASSROOMS: 49% of faculty are male; 51% are female. 92% teach undergraduates, 40% do research, and 38% do both. Graduate students teach 1% of introductory courses. The average class size in an introductory lecture is 17; in a laboratory is 15; and in a regular course is 19.

PROGRAMS OF STUDY: JCU confers B.A., B.S., B.A.Classics, B.S.B.A., and B.S.Econ. degrees. Master's degrees are also awarded. Bachelor's degrees are awarded in BIOLOGICAL SCIENCE (biochemistry, biology/biological science, cell biology, and molecular biology), BUSINESS (accounting, banking and finance, business administration and management, business (dual major program), entrepreneurial studies, finance, human resources, international business management, logistics, management information systems, and marketing/retailing/merchandising), COMMUNICATIONS AND THE ARTS (art history, art history and appreciation, classical languages, classics, communications, English, French, German, Greek, Latin, literature, modern language, Spanish, theatre arts, and theatre studies), COMPUTER AND PHYSICAL SCIENCE (chemistry, computer science, mathematics, natural sciences, and physics), EDUCATION (early childhood education, education, health information management, mathematics education, middle school education, physical education, secondary education, and sports studies), ENGINEERING AND ENVIRONMENTAL DESIGN (engineering physics and environmental science), HEALTH PROFESSIONS (exercise science, health services technology, and pre-health biological studies), SOCIAL SCIENCE (Asian/Oriental studies, criminal justice, criminology, East Asian studies, economics, European studies, gender studies, history, humanities, liberal arts/general studies, peace studies, philosophy, political science/government, psychology, religion, sociology, theological studies, and women's studies). Accounting, biology, health and healthcare IT, and education are the strongest academically. Communication & theatre arts, biology, and accountancy have the largest enrollments.

ACTIVITIES: 11% of men belong to 4 national fraternities; 23% of women belong to 5 national sororities. There are 110 groups on campus, including band, cheerleading, chess, choir, chorale, chorus, communications, computers, dance, debate, drama, drill team, environmental, ethnic, film, forensics, honors, international, jazz band, LGBT, literary magazine, musical theater, newspaper, pep band, photography, political, professional, radio and TV, religious, social, social service, student government, and yearbook. Popular campus events include Celebration of Scholarship, Winter Formal, Christmas Carroll Eve, Relay for Life, Carroll Fest (concert), Homecoming, Senior Week, Greek Week, Grad Fair, and Spring Concert. **Sports:** There are 12 intercollegiate sports for men and 11 for women, and 7 intramural sports for men and 6 for women. Facilities include a swimming pool and diving well, football stadium and track, a baseball stadium, soccer and softball fields, an indoor track, tennis, volleyball, racquetball, and basketball courts, wrestling room, weight room, a fitness center, hockey, rugby, lacrosse, field hockey, crew, women's basketball, Ultimate Frisbee, volleyball, and sailing. **Graduates:** From July 1, 2016 to June 30, 2017, 620 bachelor's degrees were awarded. The most popular majors were communications (11%), accountancy (8%), and biology (8%). In an average class, 1% graduate in 3 years or less, 66% graduate in 4 years or less, 74% graduate in 5 years or less, and 77% graduate in 6 years or less. Of the 2016 graduating class, 68% were enrolled in graduate school within 6 months of graduation.

SERVICES: Counseling and information services are available, as is tutoring in some subjects, such as accounting, biology, chemistry, economics, finance, physics, psychology, Chinese, French, German, Spanish, and Theology/Religion. There is a reader service for the blind, and remedial writing. **Library/Resources:** The library contains 456260 volumes, 3288 microform items, and 12,337 audio/video tapes/CDs/DVDs, and subscribes to 11,378 periodicals including electronic. Computerized library services include interlibrary loans, database searching, Internet access, and Wi-Fi capability. Special learning facilities include a radio station, TV station, a learning commons/academic resource center, various computer commons, a digital media center, modern language labs, and group study rooms. **Physically Challenged Students:** 96% of the campus is accessible. Facilities include wheelchair ramps, elevators, special parking, specially equipped restrooms, special class scheduling, lowered drinking fountains, lowered telephones, and special housing. **Special:** Cross-registration is offered with 9 area colleges, universities, and institutes. Study abroad is possible in 16 countries. Joint engineering degrees are offered with Case Western Reserve University or the University of Detroit Mercy. Other dual-degree options: after two years of study at JCU students can enter the University of Toledo College of Medicine MEDStart program, and after 3 years at JCU biology majors can enroll in the Bolton School of Nursing at Case Western Reserve University towards a Doctor of Nursing Practice. Work-study programs with local corporations, internships, a Washington semester, student-designed majors, dual majors, and some pass/fail options are available. We offer 32 Study Abroad programs in the following countries: Australia, China, Costa Rica, Denmark, El Salvador, France, Germany, Ghana, Ireland, Italy, Japan, South Africa, South Korea, Spain, Turkey, and United Kingdom. There are 15 national honor societies and a freshman honors program. **Visiting:** There are regularly scheduled orientations for prospective students, consisting of open houses, admission and financial aid presentations, campus and Cleveland tours, and opportunities to meet faculty, coaches, and other campus officials. There are guides for informal visits and visitors may sit in on classes. To schedule a visit, contact the Office of Admission. **Campus Safety and Security:** Measures include 24-hour foot and vehicle patrol, emergency notification system, self-defense education, and security escort services. There are shuttle buses, emergency telephones, lighted pathways/sidewalks, and controlled access to dorms/residences.

REQUIREMENTS: The SAT or ACT is required. Applicants should be graduates of an accredited secondary school with a minimum of 16 academic credits, including 4 in English, 3 each in math and academic electives, 2 each in foreign language, science with lab, social studies, and history. An essay is part of the application process, and an interview is highly encouraged for students concerned about admissions standards. AP and CLEP credits are accepted. Important factors in the admissions decision are advanced placement or honors courses, extracurricular activities record, and personality/intangible qualities. In addition to courses in oral and written expression, quantitative analysis, and foreign language, students will choose 5 courses that will include at least 1 science, and 1 social science and humanities, and 4 of which will be linked with another course, offering multiple cross-disciplinary experiences. The core also includes student selection of: 2 philosophy courses, and 2 theology and religious studies courses, 1 social justice course, and 1 arts course. A capstone course in the major, and 120 credit hours with a minimum GPA of 2.0, are required for graduation. **Procedure:** Freshmen are admitted fall, spring, and summer. Entrance exams should be taken in the spring of the junior year or the fall of the senior year. There are deferred admissions and rolling admissions plans. Applications should be filed by February 1 for fall entry. Notification is sent on a rolling basis. Applications are accepted on-line. **Transfer Students:** 76 transfer students enrolled in 2016-2017. Students must be in good standing at the time of application. The most recent term average and the cumulative average at the home school must be 2.0 or better to be considered for admission, and the cumulative average for all schools attended must be 2.0 or better. 30 of 120 credits required for the bachelor's degree must be completed at JCU. **International Students:** There are 62 international students enrolled. They must take the TOEFL with a minimum score of 550 on the paper-based TOEFL (PBT) or 79 on the Internet-based version (iBT). Student must take the Comprehensive English Language Test. The IELTS is accepted in place of TOEFL.

ADMISSIONS: 83% of the 2017-2018 applicants were accepted. The SAT scores for the 2017-2018 freshman class were: Critical Reading-- 25% below 500, 53% between 500 and 599, 19% between 600 and 699, and 3% between 700 and 800. Math-- 22% below 500, 49% between 500 and 599, 28% between 600 and 699, and 3% between 700 and 800. Writing-- 31% below 500, 51% between 500 and 599, 15% between 600 and 699, and 3% between 700 and 800. The ACT scores were 1% between 12 and 17, 36% between 18 and 23, 51% between 24 and 29, and 12% above 30. 56% of the current freshmen were in the top fifth of their class; 32% were in the top two fifths. 35 freshmen graduated first in their class. **Admissions Contact:** Steven P. Vitatoe, Assistant Vice President for Admission. Email: *enrollment@jcu.edu* Web: *www.sites.jcu.edu*

FINANCIAL AID: In 2017-2018, 98% of all full-time freshmen received some form of financial aid. 82% of all full-time freshmen received need-based aid. The average freshman award was $30,761. Need-based scholarships or need-based grants averaged $24,834; need-based self-help aid (loans and jobs) averaged $4,964; and other non-need-based awards and non-need-based scholarships averaged $2,613. 31% of undergraduate students work part-time. The average financial indebtedness of the 2017 graduate was $29,137. The FAFSA code is 003050. The priority date for freshman financial aid applications for fall entry is March 15.

KENT STATE UNIVERSITY D-2
www.kent.edu

Kent, OH 44242	**(330) 672-2444** **(800) 988-KENT**
Fax: (330) 672-2499	**Email: kentadm@kent.edu**
Full-time: 8257 men, 12,403 women	**Faculty:** I, --$
Part-time: 1179 men, 1768 women	**Ph.D.s:** n/av
Graduate: 2279 men, 3876 women	**Student/Faculty:** n/av
Year: semesters, summer session	**Tuition:** $10,012 ($18,376)
Room & Board: $10,916	**Freshman Class:** 15772 applied, 13369 accepted, 4334 enrolled
SAT CR/M/W: 530/530/510 **ACT:** 23	**CEEB CODE:** 1367
Application Deadline: n/av	**COMPETITIVE**

Kent State University, founded in 1910, is a public university offering degree programs in liberal and fine arts, business, health science, public health, teacher and professional training, and aviation. The figures in the above capsule and in this profile are approximate. There are 11 undergraduate schools and 11 graduate schools. In addition to regional accreditation, KSU has baccalaureate program accreditation with AACSB, ABET, ACEJMC, CAHEA, FIDER, NAAB, NASAD, NASM, CAEP, NLN, NRPA, CPME, FAA, and CACREP. The 950-acre campus is in a suburban area 45 miles southeast of Cleveland, 15 miles east of Akron. Including any residence halls, there are 128 buildings.

STUDENT LIFE: 87% of undergraduates are from Ohio. Others are from 49 states, 75 foreign countries, and Canada. 9% are African American; 74% White; 7% Foreign; 3% Hispanic; 3% two or more races; 3% race unknown; 1% Asian American. **Female To Male Ratio:** 1.5:1. The average age of freshmen is 18; all undergraduates, 21. 19% do not continue beyond their first year; 56% remain to graduate. **Housing:** 6622 students can be accommodated in college housing, which includes coed dorms and on-campus apartments. In addition, there are honors houses, and special-interest houses. A number of living-learning communities are available for incoming students based on major or interest. On-campus housing is available on a first-come and first-served basis. 72% of students commute. Alcohol is not permitted. All students may keep cars.

FACULTY/CLASSROOMS: 45% of faculty are male; 55% are female. No introductory courses are taught by graduate students. The average class size in an introductory lecture is 35 and in a laboratory is 20.

PROGRAMS OF STUDY: KSU confers B.A., B.S., B.B.A., B.F.A, B.S.E., B.S.P.H., B.S.N., B.M., and B.I.S. degrees. Associate, master's, and doctoral degrees are also awarded. Bachelor's degrees are awarded in BIOLOGICAL SCIENCE (biology/biological science, biotechnology, botany, environmental biology, life science secondary school education, nutrition, and zoology), BUSINESS (accounting, business administration and management, business information systems, entrepreneurial studies, fashion merchandising, finance, hospitality management services, management, marketing, marketing management, sports management, and tourism), COMMUNICATIONS AND THE ARTS (advertising, American Sign Language, art history and appreciation, classics, communication studies, crafts, dance, English, French and Francophone studies, Germanic languages and literature, journalism, language arts, languages, music, photography, public relations, recreation administration, Russian languages and literature, telecommunications systems management, television & digital media production, theatre arts, visual and performing arts, and visual design), COMPUTER AND PHYSICAL SCIENCE (applied mathematics, applied science, chemistry, computer science, earth science, geology, mathematics, mathematics - actuarial concentration, and physics), EDUCATION (art education, athletic training, early childhood education, education, general studies, health education, mathematics education, middle school education, music education, physical education, physical science secondary school education, science education, social studies secondary school education, special education, and teaching English as a second/foreign language (TESOL/TEFOL), ENGINEERING AND ENVIRONMENTAL DESIGN (aeronautical science, aerospace engineering, architecture, engineering technology, interior design, and technology and public affairs), HEALTH PROFESSIONS (community health work, exercise science, health science, medical laboratory technology, nursing, predentistry, premedicine, preosteopathy, preveterinary science, public health, and speech pathology/audiology), SOCIAL SCIENCE (African studies, American studies, anthropology, architectural studies, criminology, economics, fashion design and technology, geography, history, human development, international relations, paralegal studies, parks and recreation management, philosophy, political science/government, psychology, sociology, and Spanish studies). Nursing, psychology, and business management have the largest enrollments.

ACTIVITIES: There are 400 groups on campus, including academic club, art, band, cheerleading, chess, choir, chorale, chorus, communications, computers, dance, drama, drill team, environmental, ethnic, film, honors, international, jazz band, LGBT, literary magazine, marching band, musical theater, newspaper, opera, orchestra, pep band, photography, political, professional, radio and TV, religious, social, social service, and student government. Popular campus events include Black Squirrel Festival, Folk Festival, FlashFest, and Back to School Blast-Off. **Sports:** There are 8 intercollegiate sports for men and 10 for women, and 13 intramural sports for men and 13 for women. Facilities include a gym, recreation and wellness center, football stadium, field house, fitness circuits, a golf course, bowling alley, tennis courts, lighted basketball courts, an ice arena, a pool, weight room, soccer, lacrosse, rugby, baseball, softball, and field hockey fields, an indoor track, and outdoor track, and a wrestling room. **Graduates:** From July 1, 2016 to June 30, 2017, 4747 bachelor's degrees were awarded. The most popular majors were nursing (11%), psychology (6%), and business management (6%). In an average class, 32% graduate in 4 years or less, 51% graduate in 5 years or less, and 56% graduate in 6 years or less.

SERVICES: Counseling and information services are available, as is tutoring in some subjects, such as math, writing, foreign languages, chemistry, biology, academic coaching, and study skills. There is a reader service for the blind, and remedial math, reading, and writing. **Library/Resources:** The library contains 2.5 million volumes, and 46,019 audio/video tapes/CDs/DVDs, and subscribes to 334 periodicals including electronic. Computerized library services include interlibrary loans, database searching, Internet access, and Wi-Fi capability. Special learning facilities include an art gallery, planetarium, radio station, TV station, a fashion museum, art galleries and the Liquid Crystal Institute. **Physically Challenged Students:** 95% of the campus is accessible. Facilities include wheelchair ramps, elevators, special parking, specially equipped restrooms, special class scheduling, lowered drinking fountains, lowered telephones, special housing. **Special:** Cross-registration is available with the University of Akron, Cleveland State University, Youngstown State University, and Northeastern Ohio Medical University (NEOMED) for graduate students. Work-study programs and internships are offered, and co-op programs are available in several programs. Study abroad in 58 countries, semester away programs in Washington, Columbus, and New York Fashion District, an accelerated medical degree program, B.A.-B.S. degrees, dual majors, a general studies degree, an integrative studies degree, student-designed majors, credit for military education, nondegree study, and pass/fail options are also possible. The Honors College provides honors coursework in all majors. KSU is a member of the National Student Exchange program. There are 37 national honor societies, Phi Beta Kappa, and a freshman honors program. **Visiting:** There are regularly scheduled orientations for prospective students, including information sessions (financial aid, residence halls, student panel), a campus tour, and meetings with academic representatives. There are guides for informal visits. To schedule a visit, contact the Admissions Office. **Campus Safety and Security:** Measures include 24-hour foot and vehicle patrol, emergency notification system, self-defense education, and security escort services. There are shuttle buses, emergency telephones, lighted pathways/sidewalks, controlled access to dorms/residences, 24-hour campus police department, overnight security guards, and a 2-key system for entrance into residence halls and rooms.

REQUIREMENTS: Admission decisions are based on the following: cumulative GPA, ACT and/or SAT scores, strength of high school college preparatory curriculum and grade trends. A GPA of 2.5 is required. AP and CLEP credits are accepted. Students are required to complete 120 credit hours, of which 39 must be upper division. Distribution requirements are encompassed in the Kent Core general education requirements, a minimum of 36 credit hours, including 9 credit hours in humanities/fine arts, 6 credit hours each in basic sciences (including one laboratory course), composition, and social sciences, 3 hours in mathematics/critical reasoning, and an additional 6 credit hours. Students must also satisfy an experiential learning requirement, a writing-intensive course requirement, and a diversity course requirement. Students must maintain an overall GPA of 2.0. **Procedure:** Freshmen are admitted fall, spring, and summer. Entrance exams should be taken in the spring of the junior year or the fall of the senior year. There is a rolling admissions plan. Application deadlines are open. The fall 2017 application fee was $40. Notification is sent on a rolling basis. Applications are accepted on-line. **Transfer Students:** 1077 transfer students enrolled in 2016-2017. Applicants must present a minimum GPA of 2.0 on completed college coursework. For students with fewer than 12 semester hours in college-level coursework, a high school transcript and ACT or SAT scores are also required. 30 of 120 credits required for the bachelor's degree must be completed at KSU. **International Students:** There are 1456 international students enrolled. They must take the TOEFL with a minimum score of 525 on the paper-based TOEFL (PBT) or 71 on the Internet-based version (iBT), and either the MELAB or IELTS.

ADMISSIONS: 85% of the 2017-2018 applicants were accepted. The SAT scores for the 2017-2018 freshman class were: Critical Reading-- 63% below 500, 35% between 500 and 599, and 2% between 600 and 699. Math-- 65% below 500, 32% between 500 and 599, and 3% between 600 and 699. Writing-- 54% below 500, 41% between 500 and 599, and 5% between 600 and 699. The ACT scores were 2% between 12 and 17, 57% between 18 and 23, 35% between 24 and 29, and 6% above 30. 91 freshmen graduated first in their class. **Admissions Contact:** Nancy J. Dellavecchia, Executive Director of Admissions. Email: *kentadm@kent.edu* Web: *www.kent.edu*

FINANCIAL AID: In 2017-2018, 93% of all full-time freshmen received some form of financial aid. The average freshman award was $10,556. Need-based scholarships or need-based grants averaged $5,813; need-based self-help aid (loans and jobs) averaged $4,301; non-need-based athletic scholarships averaged $18,159; and other non-need-based awards and non-need-based scholarships averaged $5,398. 16% of undergraduate students work part-time. The average financial indebtedness of the 2017 graduate was $36,538. The FAFSA code is 003051. The priority date for freshman financial aid applications for fall entry is March 1.

KENYON COLLEGE — C-3
www.kenyon.edu

Gambier, OH 43022	**(740) 427-5776** **(800) 848-2468**
Fax: (740) 427-5770	**Email: admissions@kenyon.edu**
Full-time: 734 men, 927 women	**Faculty:** 167; IIB, ++$
Part-time: 7 men, 9 women	**Ph.D.s:** 91%
Graduate: n/av	**Student/Faculty:** 9 to 1
Year: semesters	**Tuition:** $53,560
Room & Board: $12,280	**Freshman Class:** 5603 applied, 1896 accepted, 453 enrolled
SAT EBR-W/M: 687/650 **ACT:** 30	**CEEB CODE:** 1370
Application Deadline: January 15	**MOST COMPETITIVE**

Kenyon College, among the nation's finest liberal arts institutions, takes pride in its exceptionally strong academic programs, especially in English (Kenyon is the home of the internationally known Kenyon Review), the sciences, and fine arts. There is 1 undergraduate school. The 1000-acre campus is in a rural area 50 miles northeast of Columbus, OH. Including any residence halls, there are 155 buildings.

STUDENT LIFE: 85% of undergraduates are from out of state, mostly the Middle Atlantic. Students are from 47 states, 47 foreign countries, and Canada. 50% are from public schools. 72% are White; 7% two or more races; 6% Hispanic; 6% Foreign; 3% African American; 3% Asian American; 3% race unknown. **Female To Male Ratio:** 1.3:1. The average age of freshmen is 19; all undergraduates, 20. 7% do not continue beyond their first year; 91% remain to graduate. **Housing:** 1778 students can be accommodated in college housing, which includes dorms and on-campus apartments. In addition, there are special-interest houses, special interest floors, community service or social group halls, a substance-free hall, a wellness hall, and an international wing. On-campus housing is guaranteed for all 4 years. All students may keep cars.

FACULTY/CLASSROOMS: 54% of faculty are male; 46% are female. All teach undergraduates and all do research. No introductory courses are taught by graduate students. The average class size in an introductory lecture is 16 and in a regular course is 16.

PROGRAMS OF STUDY: Kenyon confers A.B. degrees. Bachelor's degrees are awarded in BIOLOGICAL SCIENCE (biochemistry, biology/biological science, molecular biology, and neurosciences), COMMUNICATIONS AND THE ARTS (art history, art, classics, dance, dramatic arts, English, film arts, French, German, Greek (classical), Latin, modern language, music, and Spanish), COMPUTER AND PHYSICAL SCIENCE (chemistry, mathematics, and physics), EDUCATION (Asian studies), SOCIAL SCIENCE (American studies, anthropology, economics, history, international studies, philosophy, political science/government, psychology, religious studies, sociology, and women and gender studies). English, economics, and psychology have the largest enrollments.

ACTIVITIES: 27% of men belong to 7 national fraternities; 32% of women belong to 4 local sororities. There are 144 groups on campus, including sports clubs, student lectureships, art, band, chess, choir, chorale, chorus, computers, dance, debate, drama, environmental, environmental/conservation, ethnic, film, honors, international, jazz band, LGBT, literary magazine, musical theater, newspaper, opera, orchestra, pep band, photography, political, professional, radio and TV, religious, social, social service, student government, and symphony. Popular campus events include Founder's Day/Matriculation, Convocation, Summer Send-Off, Fandango, Honors Day, Family Weekend, and Martin Luther King, Jr. Day. **Sports:** There are 11 intercollegiate sports for men and 11 for women, and 9 intramural sports for men and 9 for women. Facilities include an athletic/recreation/fitness center, 70 acres of playing field, football, softball, and soccer fields, a 50-yard pool, field house, Nautilus center and weight rooms, basketball, tennis, squash, and racquetball courts. **Graduates:** From July 1, 2016 to June 30, 2017, 538 bachelor's degrees were awarded. The most popular majors were English (14%), economics (10%), and political science (9%). In an average class, 1% graduate in 3 years or less, 86% graduate in 4 years or less, 90% graduate in 5 years or less, and 91% graduate in 6 years or less.

SERVICES: Counseling and information services are available, as is tutoring in some subjects. There is a reader service for the blind, and remedial writing. There is also peer note-taking services, oral test option, extended time on tests, use of computer for essay based tests or notes, advance syllabus access, priority registration, priority seating, permission to use digital audio recordings, digital text format and content specific tutors. **Library/Resources:** The library contains 495,501 volumes, 12,167 microform items, and 30,798 audio/video tapes/CDs/DVDs, and subscribes to 8,685 periodicals including electronic. Computerized library services include interlibrary loans, database searching, Internet access, and Wi-Fi capability. Special learning facilities include an art gallery, radio station, an observatory, and an environmental center. **Physically Challenged Students:** Facilities include wheelchair ramps, elevators, special parking, specially equipped restrooms, special class scheduling, lowered drinking fountains, lowered telephones, and special housing. **Special:** Kenyon offers more than 200 off-campus study programs. The college also offers dual and student-designed majors, pass/fail options, internships, winter and/or spring break externship programs, a Washington semester consisting of apprenticeships in any of several U.S. programs, and a 3-2 engineering degree with Case Western Reserve, Washington University in St. Louis, and Rensselaer Polytechnic Institute, as well as a 3-2 environmental studies program with Duke University. 3-2 or 4-1 master's (certification) programs with The Bank Street College of Education are also possible. There is a chapter of Phi Beta Kappa and 24 departmental honors programs. **Visiting:** There are regularly scheduled orientations for prospective students, consisting of interviews with staff, a campus tour, and a class visit. Students may also request to meet with faculty and coaches. Kenyon students are also available to host a prospective student overnight in their dorm. There are guides for informal visits, visitors may sit in on classes, and stay overnight. To schedule a visit, contact the Admissions Office. **Campus Safety and Security:** Measures include 24-hour foot and vehicle patrol, emergency notification system, self-defense education, and security escort services. There are emergency telephones, lighted pathways/sidewalks, controlled access to dorms/residences, formal safety awareness events, and student patrols.

REQUIREMENTS: The SAT or ACT is required. Applicants should be graduates of an accredited secondary school. Kenyon recommends 4 units each of English, math, foreign language, and science, and 3 units of social studies, and to take advance placement or honors work in at least 2 subjects. Talent in music, theater, art, writing, and athletics is given extra consideration. AP credits are accepted. Important factors in the admissions decision are an interview, advanced placement or honors courses, evidence of special talent, and leadership record. Students are required to complete a total of 16 units, including 4 to 7 units in the major, 1 unit in each of 4 divisions representing the arts, humanities, natural sciences, and social sciences, 1 unit of foreign language, and 1/2 units of quantitative reasoning. Students must maintain a minimum GPA of 2.0 and complete the senior exercise in their major. A thesis is required for honor students. **Procedure:** Freshmen are admitted in the fall. Entrance exams should be taken in the fall of the senior year. There are early decision, early admissions, and deferred admissions plans. Early decision applications should be filed by November 15; regular applications, by January 15 for fall entry. Notification of early decision is sent February 1; regular decision, April 1. 229 early decision candidates were accepted for the 2017-2018 class. 766 applicants were on the 2017 waiting list; 38 were admitted. Applications are accepted on-line. **Transfer Students:** 13 transfer students enrolled in 2016-2017. Transfer applicants must have a minimum college GPA of 3.0 and a high school record suggesting ability and potential. Kenyon requires a letter of recommendation from a professor, the Transfer Common Application, and the Transfer Supplement. 8 of 16 credits required for the bachelor's degree must be completed at Kenyon. **International Students:** There are 94 international students enrolled. They must take the TOEFL with a minimum score of 600 on the paper-based TOEFL (PBT) or 100 on the Internet-based version (iBT). They must also take the SAT or ACT.

ADMISSIONS: 34% of the 2017-2018 applicants were accepted. The SAT scores for the 2017-2018 freshman class were: Math-- 1% below 500, 14% between 500 and 599, 46% between 600 and 699, and 39% between 700 and 800. Evidence-Based Reading/Writing-- 7% between 500 and 599, 46% between 600 and 699, and 47% between 700 and 800. The ACT scores were 3% between 18 and 23, 29% between 24 and 29, and 68% above 30. 78% of the current freshmen were in the top fifth of their class; 96% were in the top two fifths. 13 freshmen graduated first in their class. **Admissions Contact:** Diane Anci, Interim Dean of Admissions and Financial Aid. Email: *admissions@kenyon.edu* Web: *www.kenyon.edu*

FINANCIAL AID: In 2017-2018, 40% of all full-time freshmen received some form of financial aid and need-based aid. The average freshman award was $45,461. Need-based scholarships or need-based grants averaged $43,736; need-based self-help aid (loans and jobs) averaged $3,985; other non-need-based awards and non-need-based scholarships averaged $14,855; and $2,686 from other forms of aid. 30% of undergraduate students work part-time. The average financial indebtedness of the 2017 graduate was $22,025. Kenyon is a member of CSS. The CSS/Profile, tax return, and non-custodial parent income are required. The FAFSA code is 003065. The deadline for filing freshman financial aid applications for fall entry is February 15.

LAKE ERIE COLLEGE *(The complete profile is made available exclusively on our website, www.barronspac.com)*

LOURDES UNIVERSITY *(The complete profile is made available exclusively on our website, www.barronspac.com)*

MALONE UNIVERSITY — D-2

www.malone.edu

Canton, OH 44709	**(330) 471-8145** **(800) 521-1146**
Fax: (330) 471-8149	**Email: admissions@malone.edu**
Full-time: 477 men, 622 women	**Faculty:** 76
Part-time: 79 men, 155 women	**Ph.D.s:** 86%
Graduate: 105 men, 291 women	**Student/Faculty:** 14 to 1
Year: semesters, summer session	**Tuition:** $29,900
Room & Board: $9300	**Freshman Class:** 1864 applied, 1230 accepted, 338 enrolled
SAT CR/M: 530/528 **ACT:** 22	**CEEB CODE:** 1439
Application Deadline: n/av	**COMPETITIVE**

Malone University, founded in 1892, is a private Christian university for the arts, sciences, and professions in the liberal arts tradition. The mission of Malone is to provide students with an education based on biblical faith in order to develop men and women in intellectual maturity, wisdom, and Christian faith who are committed to serving the church, community, and world. There are 4 undergraduate schools and 3 graduate schools. In addition to regional accreditation, Malone has baccalaureate program accreditation with ACBSP, CSWE, NASM, CCNE, CACREP, and CAEP. The 96-acre campus is in a suburban area 56 miles southeast of Cleveland. Including any residence halls, there are 22 buildings.

STUDENT LIFE: 88% of undergraduates are from Ohio. Others are from 25 states, 11 foreign countries, and Canada. 83% are from public schools. 80% are White; 3% two or more races; 2% Hispanic; 2% race unknown; 11% African American; 1% Asian American; 1% Foreign. 74% are Protestant; 16% claim no religious affiliation. **Female To Male Ratio:** 1.6:1. The average age of freshmen is 18; all undergraduates, 22. 29% do not continue beyond their first year; 57% remain to graduate. **Housing:** 1197 students can be accommodated in college housing, which includes single-sex dorms, and one theme floor for mentoring Freshman women by upperclass women. On-campus housing is guaranteed for the freshman year only, is available on a first-come, first-served basis, and is available on a lottery system for upperclassmen. 63% of students live on campus. Alcohol is not permitted. All students may keep cars.

FACULTY/CLASSROOMS: 50% of faculty are male; 50% are female. 90% teach undergraduates. No introductory courses are taught by graduate students. The average class size in an introductory lecture is 26; in a laboratory is 15; and in a regular course is 18.

PROGRAMS OF STUDY: Malone confers B.A., B.S.Ed., and B.S.N. degrees. Master's degrees are also awarded. Bachelor's degrees are awarded in AGRICULTURE (environmental studies), BIOLOGICAL SCIENCE (biochemistry, biology/biological science, life science, and zoology), BUSINESS (accounting, business administration and management, finance, marketing and distribution, and sports management), COMMUNICATIONS AND THE ARTS (art, art history and appreciation, broadcasting, communications, crafts, creative writing, English, graphic design, language arts, music, music technology, public relations, and theatre studies), COMPUTER AND PHYSICAL SCIENCE (chemistry, computer science, and mathematics), EDUCATION (Christian education, early childhood education, middle school education, music education, science education, secondary education, social studies education, and special education), ENGINEERING AND ENVIRONMENTAL DESIGN (engineering/mechanical emp/energy sys focus and environmental science), HEALTH PROFESSIONS (community health work, exercise science, medical laboratory technology, nursing, and public health), SOCIAL SCIENCE (biblical studies, criminal justice, crosscultural studies, history, international studies, liberal arts/general studies, ministries, philosophy, political science/government, psychology, religious music, social work, theological studies, and youth ministry). Nursing, social work, and exercise science are the strongest academically. Nursing, business administration, and zoo and wildlife biology have the largest enrollments.

ACTIVITIES: There are no fraternities or sororities. There are 50 groups on campus, including art, band, cheerleading, chess, choir, chorale, communications, computers, drama, drill team, environmental, ethnic, film, honors, international, jazz band, literary magazine, marching band, musical theater, newspaper, opera, photography, political, professional, radio and TV, religious, social, social service, and student government. Popular campus events include Little Sibs Weekend, Christmas Celebration, and Worldview Forums. **Sports:** There are 9 intercollegiate sports for men and 9 for women, and 6 intramural sports for men and 6 for women. Facilities include a gym, a wellness center with a strength room and a cardio room, an outdoor track, baseball, softball, and soccer fields, practice soccer and football fields, intramural fields, a cross-country course, and outdoor volleyball and basketball courts.**Graduates:** From July 1, 2016 to June 30, 2017, 319 bachelor's degrees were awarded. The most popular majors were business administration/management (27%), nursing and other health professions and related programs (20%), and education (9%). In an average class, 2% graduate in 3 years or less, 45% graduate in 4 years or less, 56% graduate in 5 years or less, and 57% graduate in 6 years or less.

SERVICES: Counseling and information services are available, as is tutoring in most subjects. There is a reader service for the blind, and remedial math and writing. There are also disability support services such as a distraction-reduced testing room. **Library/Resources:** The library contains 169,479 volumes, 472,213 microform items, and 7,675 audio/video tapes/CDs/DVDs, and subscribes to 41,889 periodicals including electronic. Computerized library services include interlibrary loans, database searching, Internet access, and Wi-Fi capability. Special learning facilities include an art gallery, radio station, a writing lab, subject area tutoring, a broadcast production studio with green screen and virtual set technology available for student and classroom use. **Physically**

Challenged Students: Facilities include wheelchair ramps, elevators, special parking, specially equipped restrooms, special class scheduling, lowered drinking fountains, lowered telephones, and special housing. **Special:** Students may participate in co-op programs and internships in many majors and may cross-register within the Christian College Consortium. Malone offers study abroad in England, Costa Rica, Jordan, Northern Ireland, Australia, and Uganda, as well as Hollywood (Film Studies), Nashville (Contemporary Music), or Washington semesters through the Council for Christian Colleges and Universities. Approximately 20 other study abroad opportunities are available through Brethren Colleges Abroad (BCA). A liberal arts degree, dual and student-designed majors, and credit for life, military, or work experience are also available. The Malone Management Program (MGMT) offers accelerated degree- completion for students with 5 years of work experience and 40 to 88 transfer hours. MGMT offers 4 majors: Organizational Management, Environmental Management, Marketing Management, and Project Management. The School of Nursing and Health Sciences offers a traditional BSN program and a degree-completion BSN program for RNs. There are 10 national honor societies and a freshman honors program. **Visiting:** There are regularly scheduled orientations for prospective students, including a tour of campus, attending a Spiritual Formation Opportunity and a class, meeting with faculty from chosen major, a financial aid session, a student panel, an activity fair, a meeting with an athletic coach, and buffet lunch on us. There are guides for informal visits, visitors may sit in on classes, and stay overnight. To schedule a visit, contact Jody Dimit at (330) 471-8147. **Campus Safety and Security:** Measures include 24-hour foot and vehicle patrol, emergency notification system, and security escort services. There are emergency telephones, lighted pathways/sidewalks, and controlled access to dorms/residences.

REQUIREMENTS: The ACT is preferred; the SAT is accepted. Applicants should be graduates of an accredited secondary school with a minimum GPA of 2.5. The GED is accepted. AP and CLEP credits are accepted. Important factors in the admissions decision are advanced placement or honors courses, personality/intangible qualities, and extracurricular activities record. Students must maintain a GPA of 2.0 overall and 2.25 to 2.75 in the major, depending upon the major. At least 30 hours in the major and 39 hours at the 300 or 400 level are required. To graduate, all students must complete at least 124 credit hours. The 41- to 43-credit-hour general education curriculum includes 10 hours of Faith Learning courses, 9 hours of Foundational Skills courses, 9 hours of Engaging in Human Experience courses, 7-9 hours in Engaging Cultures and Institutions courses, 3 hours in Engaging the Created Order (one course) and 3 hours in Faith in the World (one course). **Procedure:** Freshmen are admitted fall, spring, and summer. Entrance exams should be taken in the junior year. There are early admissions, deferred admissions, and rolling admissions plans. Application deadlines are open. The fall 2017 application fee was $20. Notifications are sent September 1. Applications are accepted on-line. **Transfer Students:** 70 transfer students enrolled in 2016-2017. Applicants must submit official transcripts from any previously attended institution(s). Average grade in courses allowed for transfer must be 2.0 or higher (on a 4.0 scale). 30 of 124 credits required for the bachelor's degree must be completed at Malone. **International Students:** There are 11 international students enrolled. They must take the TOEFL with a minimum score of 550 on the paper-based TOEFL (PBT) or 79 on the Internet-based version (iBT). They must also take the SAT or ACT, scoring 860-SAT or 18-ACT not required of all international students, but definitely athletes due to NCAA requirements.

ADMISSIONS: 66% of the 2017-2018 applicants were accepted. The SAT scores for the 2017-2018 freshman class were: Critical Reading-- 38% below 500, 42% between 500 and 599, 14% between 600 and 699, and 6% between 700 and 800. Math-- 33% below 500, 47% between 500 and 599, 14% between 600 and 699, and 6% between 700 and 800. The ACT scores were 9% between 12 and 17, 63% between 18 and 23, 25% between 24 and 29, and 3% above 30. 25% of the current freshmen were in the top fifth of their class; 55% were in the top two fifths. 6 freshmen graduated first in their class. **Admissions Contact:** Linda Kurtz Hoffman, Director of Admissions. Email: *admissions@malone.edu* Web: *www.malone.edu*

FINANCIAL AID: In 2017-2018, 100% of all full-time freshmen received some form of financial aid. 78% of all full-time freshmen received need-based aid. The average freshman award was $33,810. Need-based scholarships or need-based grants averaged $13,623 ($25,752 maximum); need-based self-help aid (loans and jobs) averaged $4,845 ($7,500 maximum); non-need-based athletic scholarships averaged $11,318 ($23,900 maximum); other non-need-based awards and non-need-based scholarships averaged $15,161 ($41,430 maximum); and $11,403 from other forms of aid. 37% of undergraduate students work part-time. The average financial indebtedness of the 2017 graduate was $33,330. The FAFSA code is 003072. The priority date for freshman financial aid applications for fall entry is March 1.

MARIETTA COLLEGE — D-5

www.marietta.edu

Marietta, OH 45750	(740) 376-4600 (800) 331-7896
Fax: (740) 376-8888	**Email:** admit@mcnet.marietta.edu
Full-time: 816 men, 602 women	**Faculty:** 87; IIB, -$
Part-time: 27 men, 42 women	**Ph.D.s:** 82%
Graduate: 26 men, 109 women	**Student/Faculty:** 12 to 1
Year: semesters, summer session	**Tuition:** $35,090
Room & Board: $11,100	**Freshman Class:** 4157 applied, 2811 accepted, 395 enrolled
SAT CR/M/W: 539/555/517 **ACT:** 24	**CEEB CODE:** 1444
Application Deadline: rolling	**COMPETITIVE**

Marietta College, founded in 1835, is a private liberal arts college. There is 1 undergraduate school and 4 graduate schools. In addition to regional accreditation, Marietta has baccalaureate program accreditation with ABET, NASM, CAEP, CAAHEP, ACS, and ARC-PA. The 90-acre campus is in a small town 115 miles southeast of Columbus. Including any residence halls, there are 40 buildings.

STUDENT LIFE: 64% of undergraduates are from Ohio. Others are from 40 states, 15 foreign countries, and Canada. 89% are from public schools. 71% are White; 6% African American; 6% Foreign; 6% race unknown; 3% Hispanic; 1% Asian American; 1% two or more races. **Male To Female Ratio:** 1.2:1. The average age of freshmen is 18; all undergraduates, 20. 22% do not continue beyond their first year; 56% remain to graduate. **Housing:** 1175 students can be accommodated in college housing, which includes dorms and on-campus apartments. In addition, there are honors houses, special-interest houses, fraternity houses, and sorority houses. On-campus housing is guaranteed for all 4 years. 71% of students live on campus. All students may keep cars.

FACULTY/CLASSROOMS: 51% of faculty are male; 49% are female. 95% teach undergraduates, 80% do research, and 80% do both. No introductory courses are taught by graduate students. The average class size in an introductory lecture is 16; in a laboratory is 13; and in a regular course is 16.

PROGRAMS OF STUDY: Marietta confers B.A., B.S., B.M., B.S.P.E., and B.F.A. degrees. Associate and master's degrees are also awarded. Bachelor's degrees are awarded in AGRICULTURE (environmental studies), BIOLOGICAL SCIENCE (biochemistry and biology/biological science), BUSINESS (accounting, banking and finance, business administration and management, human resources, international business management, management information systems, marketing/retailing/merchandising, and sports management), COMMUNICATIONS AND THE ARTS (advertising, broadcasting, communications, dramatic arts, English, graphic design, journalism, music, public relations, Spanish, speech/debate/rhetoric, and studio art), COMPUTER AND PHYSICAL SCIENCE (applied physics, chemistry, computer science, geology, information sciences and systems, mathematics, and physics), EDUCATION (athletic training, early childhood education, and music education), ENGINEERING AND ENVIRONMENTAL DESIGN (environmental science and petroleum/natural gas engineering), HEALTH PROFESSIONS (health science and physician's assistant), SOCIAL SCIENCE (Asian/Oriental studies, economics, history, interdisciplinary studies, political science/government, and psychology). Petroleum engineering is the strongest academically. Petroleum engineering, advertising public relations, and psychology have the largest enrollments.

ACTIVITIES: 23% of men belong to 4 national fraternities; 41% of women belong to 3 national sororities. There are 80 groups on campus, including art, athletic training, band, cheerleading, choir, chorale, chorus, computers, dance, debate, drama, drill team, environmental, ethnic, film, forensics, honors, international, jazz band, LGBT, literary magazine, marching band, musical theater, newspaper, orchestra, pep band, photography, political, professional, radio and TV, religious, social, social service, student government, and yearbook. Popular campus events include DooDah Day, Little Sibs Weekend, and Welcome Back Bash. **Sports:** There are 9 intercollegiate sports for men and 9 for women, and 12 intramural sports for men and 12 for women. Facilities include a stadium, performance gym, field house, baseball, softball, soccer fields, a boat house, cross-country course, tennis courts, and a recreational center housing a track, multipurpose and racquetball courts, an ergometer training room, cardio equipment, and a climbing wall. **Graduates:** From July 1, 2016 to June 30, 2017, 222 bachelor's degrees were awarded. The most popular majors were petroleum engineering (7%), advertising/public relations (7%), and psychology (6%). In an average class, 3% graduate in 3 years or less, 46% graduate in 4 years or less, 55% graduate in 5 years or less, and 56% graduate in 6 years or less. Of the 2016 graduating class, 24% were enrolled in graduate school within 6 months of graduation, and 95% were employed.

SERVICES: Counseling and information services are available, as is tutoring in most subjects. There is a reader service for the blind, and remedial math and writing. There is also a peer tutoring program. **Library/Resources:** The library contains 449,123 volumes, 146,583 microform items, and 5,031 audio/video tapes/CDs/DVDs, and subscribes to 13,557 periodicals including electronic. Computerized library services include interlibrary loans, database searching, and Internet access. Special learning facilities include an art gallery, planetarium, radio station, TV station, an observatory, a greenhouse, and a geology annex. **Physically Challenged Students:** 90% of the campus is accessible. Facilities include wheelchair ramps, elevators, special parking, specially equipped restrooms, special class scheduling, lowered drinking fountains, lowered telephones, and special housing. **Special:** There are 3-2 binary engineering programs with Case Western Reserve, Columbia, and Ohio Universities. Internships are available in many majors, and students may study abroad in numerous countries and participate in a Washington semester through American University. Work-study programs, B.A.-B.S. degrees in all majors, and student-designed majors are also available. There are 23 national honor societies, Phi Beta Kappa, a freshman honors program, and 17 departmental honors programs. **Visiting:** There are regularly scheduled orientations for prospective students, including fall and spring open houses, tours, and meetings with faculty, coaches, and financial aid representatives. There are guides for informal visits, visitors may sit in on classes, and stay overnight. To schedule a visit, contact The Office of Admissions at admit@marietta.edu. **Campus Safety and Security:** Measures include 24-hour foot and vehicle patrol, emergency notification system, self-defense education, and security escort services. There are shuttle buses, emergency telephones, lighted pathways/sidewalks, and controlled access to dorms/residences.

REQUIREMENTS: The SAT or ACT is required. Students seeking admission should have completed 4 years of English and 3 of history, math, and science; 2 years of a foreign language is also recommended. An interview is strongly recommended. AP and CLEP credits are accepted. Important factors in the admissions decision are advanced placement or honors courses, parents or siblings attended your school, personality/intangible qualities, evidence of special talent, extracurricular activities record, recommendations by alumni, geographical diversity, recommendations by school officials, and leadership record. To graduate, students must complete at least 120 total credit hours, with general education requirements. The minimum number of hours required for a major is 36. A minimum GPA of 2.0 must be maintained. Seniors must complete a capstone project in their major. **Procedure:** Freshmen are admitted fall and spring. Entrance exams should be taken no later than February 1 of the senior year. There are deferred admissions and rolling admissions plans. Check with the school for current application deadlines. Notification is sent on a rolling basis. Applications are accepted online. **Transfer Students:** 40 transfer students enrolled in 2016-2017. A minimum GPA of 2.5, a recommendation, and an essay are recommended. 36 of 120 credits required for the bachelor's degree must be completed at Marietta. **International Students:** There are 155 international students enrolled. They must take the TOEFL with a minimum score of 550 on the paper-based TOEFL (PBT) or 79 on the Internet-based version (iBT). Student must take the college's own test, or the IELTS.

ADMISSIONS: 68% of the 2017-2018 applicants were accepted. The SAT scores for the 2017-2018 freshman class were: Critical Reading-- 33% below 500, 40% between 500 and 599, 25% between 600 and 699, and 2% between 700 and 800. Math-- 27% below 500, 36% between 500 and 599, 34% between 600 and 699, and 3% between 700 and 800. Writing-- 40% below 500, 42% between 500 and 599, 17% between 600 and 699, and 1% between 700 and 800. The ACT scores were 23% below 12, 27% between 12 and 17, 23% between 18 and 23, 13% between 24 and 29, and 15% above 30. 49% of the current freshmen were in the top fifth of their class; 79% were in the top two fifths. 19 freshmen graduated first in their class. **Admissions Contact:** Stephen Lazowski, Vice President for Enrollment Management. Email: *admit@mcnet.marietta.edu* Web: *www.marietta.edu*

FINANCIAL AID: In 2017-2018, 97% of all full-time freshmen received some form of financial aid. 87% of all full-time freshmen received need-based aid. The average freshman award was $30,481. Need-based scholarships or need-based grants averaged $16,589 ($25,598 maximum); need-based self-help aid (loans and jobs) averaged $5,246 ($7,500 maximum); and other non-need-based awards and non-need-based scholarships averaged $19,903 ($46,430 maximum). 35% of undergraduate students work part-time. The average financial indebtedness of the 2017 graduate was $20,911. The FAFSA code is 003073. The priority date for freshman financial aid applications for fall entry is December 15. The deadline for filing freshman financial aid applications for fall entry is February 15.

MIAMI UNIVERSITY — A-4

www.MiamiOH.edu

Oxford, OH 45056 — **(513) 529-2531**

Fax: (513) 529-1550	**Email: admission@MiamiOH.edu**
Full-time: 8281 men, 8338 women	**Faculty:** I, --$
Part-time: 268 men, 260 women	**Ph.D.s:** n/av
Graduate: 801 men, 1752 women	**Student/Faculty:** n/av
Year: semesters, summer session	**Tuition:** $14,736 ($32,555)
Room & Board: $12,454	**Freshman Class:** 30255 applied, 20635 accepted, 3817 enrolled
ACT: 29	**CEEB CODE:** 1463
Application Deadline: February 1	**HIGHLY COMPETITIVE+**

Miami University, founded in 1809, is an original Public Ivy that consistently ranks among the top public universities in the nation for the quality of academic programs, faculty commitment to students, for experiences that lead to student success, and as a "Best Value." Undergraduates benefit from a well-rounded liberal arts foundation, developing skills for life and careers. More than 42% of students study abroad, and more than two-thirds participate in internships or field work. Undergraduate students participate with faculty and graduate students in significant research and scholarship activities. Retention and graduation rates are among the highest of NCAA Division I schools. There are 6 undergraduate schools and 1 graduate school. In addition to regional accreditation, Miami has baccalaureate program accreditation with AACSB, ABET, CSAB, CSWE, FIDER, NAAB, NASAD, CAEP, and NLN. The 2138-acre campus is in a small town in Oxford, Ohio, 35 miles north of Cincinnati, OH. Including any residence halls, there are 119 buildings.

STUDENT LIFE: 64% of undergraduates are from Ohio. Others are from 50 states, 79 foreign countries, and Canada. 68% are from public schools. 71% are White; 15% Foreign; 5% Hispanic; 3% African American; 3% two or more races; 2% Asian American; 1% American Indian/Alaska Native; 1% race unknown. **Female To Male Ratio:** 1.1:1. The average age of freshmen is 18; all undergraduates, 20. 9% do not continue beyond their first year; 79% remain to graduate. **Housing:** 7786 students can be accommodated in college housing, which includes married student dorms, on-campus apartments, and off-campus apartments. In addition, there are honors houses, language/international houses, special-interest houses, sorority houses, international housing, and first-year only housing. On-campus housing is guaranteed for the freshman year only and is available on a lottery system for upperclassmen. 55% of students commute. All students may keep cars.

FACULTY/CLASSROOMS: All teach undergraduates. No introductory courses are taught by graduate students. The average class size in a regular course is 30.

PROGRAMS OF STUDY: Miami confers A.B., B.S., B.F.A., B.Mus., A.B.Arc., A.B.Art., A.B.The., B.I.S., B.S.Aps., B.S.Art., B.S.AT., B.S.Bus., B.S.Cj., B.S.Cs., B.S.Ed., B.S.Egr., B.S.Ff., B.S.IT., B.S.Knh., B.W.Se., and

B.S.Swk degrees. Associate, master's, and doctoral degrees are also awarded. Bachelor's degrees are awarded in BIOLOGICAL SCIENCE (biochemistry, biological sciences, botany, microbiology, neurosciences, nutrition, and zoology), BUSINESS (accounting, business economics, business leadership, finance, management information systems, management science, marketing/retailing/merchandising, sports management, supply chain management, and sustainable management), COMMUNICATIONS AND THE ARTS (art, art history and appreciation, classical languages, classics, communications, dramatic arts, East Asian languages and literature, English, film arts, French, German, graphic design, journalism, linguistics, media arts, music, music performance, Russian, Spanish, speech/debate/rhetoric, and theatre arts), COMPUTER AND PHYSICAL SCIENCE (chemistry, computer science, earth science, energy science, geology, information sciences and systems, mathematics, physics, software engineering, and statistics), EDUCATION (art education, athletic training, early childhood education, elementary education, English education, foreign languages education, mathematics education, middle school education, music education, science education, secondary education, and special education), ENGINEERING AND ENVIRONMENTAL DESIGN (architectural history, architecture, bioengineering, chemical engineering, computer engineering, electrical/electronics engineering, engineering, engineering management, engineering physics, environmental science, interior design, manufacturing engineering, and mechanical engineering), HEALTH PROFESSIONS (nursing, public health, and speech pathology/audiology), SOCIAL SCIENCE (African American studies, American studies, anthropology, criminal justice, economics, family/consumer studies, geography, gerontology, history, interdisciplinary studies, international relations, international studies, Italian studies, justice and society, Latin American studies, philosophy, physical fitness/movement, political science/government, psychology, public administration, religion, social work, sociology, urban studies, and women's studies). Finance, marketing, and biology have the largest enrollments.

ACTIVITIES: 19% of men belong to 29 national fraternities; 31% of women belong to 20 national sororities. There are 548 groups on campus, including art, bagpipe, band, cheerleading, chess, choir, chorale, chorus, communications, computers, dance, debate, drama, drill team, environmental, ethnic, film, forensics, honors, international, jazz band, LGBT, literary magazine, marching band, musical theater, newspaper, opera, orchestra, pep band, photography, political, professional, radio and TV, religious, social, social service, student government, symphony, and yearbook. Popular campus events include Parents Weekend, Kidsfest Weekend, and Unity Fest. **Sports:** There are 8 intercollegiate sports for men and 10 for women, and 17 intramural sports for men and 16 for women. Facilities include a football stadium, indoor sports center for Miami student-athlete training, an ice arena, playing fields, outdoor tennis courts, a recreational sports center, indoor basketball/volleyball courts, racquetball, handball, and squash courts, a floor hockey/indoor soccer court, a climbing wall, equestrian stables and dressage course, indoor swimming pools, jogging paths, a par course, sand volleyball courts, aerobics and weight rooms, and a frisbee golf course. **Graduates:** From July 1, 2016 to June 30, 2017, 4517 bachelor's degrees were awarded. The most popular majors were marketing (7%), finance (7%), and strategic communications (5%). In an average class, 1% graduate in 3 years or less, 67% graduate in 4 years or less, 77% graduate in 5 years or less, and 79% graduate in 6 years or less.

SERVICES: Counseling and information services are available, as is tutoring in most subjects. Assistance in study skills is available. **Library/Resources:** The library contains 2.0 million volumes, 16,536 microform items, and 219,310 audio/video tapes/CDs/DVDs, and subscribes to 27,418 periodicals including electronic. Computerized library services include interlibrary loans, database searching, Internet access, and Wi-Fi capability. Special learning facilities include an art gallery, natural history museum, radio station, and TV station. **Physically Challenged Students:** All of the campus is accessible. Facilities include wheelchair ramps, elevators, special parking, specially equipped restrooms, special class scheduling, lowered drinking fountains, lowered telephones, and special housing. **Special:** The university offers cross-registration with Cincinnati area colleges, study abroad in multiple countries, co-op programs in the School of Applied Science, internships in health and sport studies and applied science, a 3-2 engineering degree with Case Western Reserve and Columbia Universities, and a 3-2 forestry degree with Duke University. Students may pursue student-designed majors through the Western Program or interdisciplinary majors. There is a chapter of Phi Beta Kappa and a freshman honors program. **Visiting:** There are regularly scheduled orientations for prospective students, information sessions and guided tours are available throughout the year. There are guides for informal visits and visitors may sit in on classes. To schedule a visit, contact the Office of Admissions. **Campus Safety and Security:** Measures include 24-hour foot and vehicle patrol, emergency notification system, self-defense education, and security escort services. There are shuttle buses, emergency telephones, lighted pathways/sidewalks, and controlled access to dorms/residences.

REQUIREMENTS: Applicants must complete either the ACT or the SAT. Candidates for admission must ordinarily be graduates of accredited secondary schools or hold the GED. Students should have completed 4 units each of English and math, 3 units of science, 2 units each of social studies and foreign language, 1 unit each of history and fine arts. An audition, a portfolio, or an interview are required for direct admission to majors in the School of Fine Arts. AP and CLEP credits are accepted. To graduate students must complete 128 semester hours, with a minimum 2.0 GPA. At least 32 semester hours must be from Miami. Students must fulfill all requirements for the Global Miami Plan which includes 27 semester hours of foundation courses, 9 semester hours in a thematic sequence, a 3 hour capstone experience, 3 hours of Advanced Writing, and 3 hours in Intercultural Perspectives. **Procedure:** Freshmen are admitted to all sessions. There are early decision and deferred admissions plans. Early decision applications should be filed by November 15; regular applications, by February 1 for fall entry; and December 1 for spring entry. The fall 2017 application fee was $50. Notification of early decision is sent December 15; regular decision, March 15. 668 early decision candidates were accepted for the 2017-2018 class. 954 applicants were on the 2017 waiting list; 16 were admitted. Applications are accepted on-line. **Transfer Students:** 239 transfer students enrolled in 2016-2017. A limited number of transfer students will be accepted. A GPA of 2.0 or higher is necessary. 32 of 128 credits required for the bachelor's degree must be completed at Miami. **International Students:** There are 2543 international students enrolled. They must take the TOEFL with a minimum score of 550 on the paper-based TOEFL (PBT) or 80 on the Internet-based version (iBT) or take either the MELAB, IELTS or alternative proof of English language proficiency. They must also take the SAT or ACT. Standardized tests are generally not required but are recommended for international students.

ADMISSIONS: 68% of the 2017-2018 applicants were accepted. The SAT scores for the 2017-2018 freshman class were: Math-- 1% below 500, 19% between 500 and 599, 50% between 600 and 699, and 30% between 700 and 800. Evidence-Based Reading/Writing-- 4% below 500, 28% between 500 and 599, 54% between 600 and 699, and 14% between 700 and 800. The ACT scores were 5% between 18 and 23, 57% between 24 and 29, and 38% above 30. 22% of the current freshmen were in the top fifth of their class; 34% were in the top two fifths. 95 freshmen graduated first in their class. **Admissions Contact:** Susan Schaurer, Asst. VP and Dir. of Admission. Email: *admission@MiamiOH.edu* Web: *www.MiamiOH.edu*

FINANCIAL AID: In 2017-2018, 38% of all full-time freshmen received some form of financial aid. 34% of all full-time freshmen received need-based aid. The average freshman award was $14,415. Need-based scholarships or need-based grants averaged $11,417 ($29,658 maximum); need-based self-help aid (loans and jobs) averaged $3,640 ($5,500 maximum); non-need-based athletic scholarships averaged $29,746 ($22,500 maximum); and other non-need-based awards and non-need-based scholarships averaged $9,531 ($32,000 maximum). The average financial indebtedness of the 2017 graduate was $29,956. The FAFSA code is 003077. The priority date for freshman financial aid applications for fall entry is February 15.

MOUNT ST. JOSEPH UNIVERSITY *(The complete profile is made available exclusively on our website, www.barronspac.com)*

MOUNT VERNON NAZARENE UNIVERSITY — C-3

www.mvnu.edu

Mount Vernon, OH 43050 — **(740) 392-6868**

Fax: (740) 393-0511	**Email:** admissions@mvnu.edu
Full-time: 540 men, 899 women	**Faculty:** 61
Part-time: 128 men, 261 women	**Ph.D.s:** 72%
Graduate: 137 men, 257 women	**Student/Faculty:** 18 to 1
Year: semesters, summer session	**Tuition:** $28,090
Room & Board: $7550	**Freshman Class:** 1187 applied, 910 accepted, 330 enrolled
ACT: 23	**CEEB CODE:** 1531
Application Deadline: May 1	**COMPETITIVE**

Mount Vernon Nazarene University, founded in 1968, is a private liberal arts college affiliated with the Church of the Nazarene. There are 6 undergraduate schools and 1 graduate school. In addition to regional accreditation, MVNU has baccalaureate program accreditation with ACBSP, CSWE, NASM, CAEP, and CCNE. The 332-acre campus is in a small town 45 miles northeast of Columbus. Including any residence halls, there are 57 buildings.

STUDENT LIFE: 92% of undergraduates are from Ohio. Others are from 30 states, and 19 foreign countries. 85% are White; 3% Hispanic; 3% two or more races; 3% race unknown; 2% African American; 1% Asian American; 1% American Indian/Alaska Native; 1% Foreign. 55% are Protestant; 17% Unknown religious affiliation. **Female To Male Ratio:** 1.8:1. The average age of freshmen is 18; all undergraduates, 19. 21% do not continue beyond their first year; 59% remain to graduate. **Housing:** 1116 students can be accommodated in college housing, which includes dorms and on-campus apartments. On-campus housing is guaranteed for the freshman year only, is available on a first-come, and first-served basis. 72% of students live on campus. Alcohol is not permitted. All students may keep cars.

FACULTY/CLASSROOMS: 50% of faculty are male; 50% are female. 86% teach undergraduates. No introductory courses are taught by graduate students. The average class size in an introductory lecture is 20; in a laboratory is 18; and in a regular course is 16.

PROGRAMS OF STUDY: MVNU confers B.A., B.S., B.S.N., B.S.W., and B.B.A. degrees. Associate and master's degrees are also awarded. Bachelor's degrees are awarded in BIOLOGICAL SCIENCE (life science), BUSINESS (accounting, business administration and management, business data processing, finance, international business management, management information systems, management, marketing, and sports management), COMMUNICATIONS AND THE ARTS (art, church music, communication studies, communications, dramatic arts, English, graphic design, information technology, journalism, language arts, music, public relations, and Spanish), COMPUTER AND PHYSICAL SCIENCE (chemistry, computer networks & systems, computer science, and mathematics), EDUCATION (business education, early childhood education, English education, mathematics education, middle school education, music education, physical education, science education, social studies education, and special education), ENGINEERING AND ENVIRONMENTAL DESIGN (engineering), HEALTH PROFESSIONS (biology, exercise science, nursing, premedicine, prepharmacy, and prephysical therapy), SOCIAL SCIENCE (biblical studies, communication sciences & disorders, criminal justice, history, ministries, missions, pastoral studies, philosophy, political science/government, prelaw, psychology, religion, religious education, religious music, social work, sociology, theological studies, and youth ministry). Biology, nursing, and education are the strongest academically. Nursing, business, and education have the largest enrollments.

ACTIVITIES: There are no fraternities or sororities. There are 25 groups on campus, including art, band, cheerleading, choir, chorale, chorus, communications, computers, drama, environmental, ethnic, honors, international, jazz band, literary magazine, musical theater, newspaper, orchestra, pep band, photography, political, professional, radio and TV, religious, social, social service, student government, symphony, and yearbook. Popular campus events include Friday Night Live, Block Party, Sonfest, Annual Luau, and all Cougars Sporting Events. **Sports:** There are 7 intercollegiate sports for men and 8 for women, and 9 intramural sports for men and 9 for women. Facilities include a main gym, intramural/practice gym, weight room, game room, fitness/exercise facility, tennis courts, soccer fields, and a baseball/softball batting facility. **Graduates:** From July 1, 2016 to June 30, 2017, 400 bachelor's degrees were awarded. The most popular majors were business administration (18%), nursing (10%), and education (9%). In an average class, 54% graduate in 4 years or less, 59% graduate in 5 years or less, and 60% graduate in 6 years or less. Of the 2016 graduating class, 15% were enrolled in graduate school within 6 months of graduation, and 93% were employed.

SERVICES: Counseling and information services are available, as is tutoring in most subjects. There is a reader service for the blind, and remedial math, reading, and writing. Students in the at-risk program are required to take College Success Strategies. **Library/Resources:** The library contains 160,658 volumes, 23 microform items, and 3,267 audio/video tapes/CDs/DVDs, and subscribes to 926 periodicals including electronic. Computerized library services include interlibrary loans, database searching, Internet access, and Wi-Fi capability. Special learning facilities include an art gallery, radio station, Center for Student Success. **Physically Challenged Students:** 95% of the campus is accessible. Facilities include wheelchair ramps, elevators, special parking, specially equipped restrooms, special class scheduling, lowered drinking fountains, lowered telephones, and special housing. **Special:** MVNU offers internships with local businesses and organizations, on-campus work-study programs, study abroad in 20 countries, dual majors, a general studies degree, and nondegree study. Cross-registration is available with Nazarene Universities, and the Council for Christian College and Universities program. There are 5 national honor societies, a freshman honors program, and 21 departmental honors programs. **Visiting:** There are regularly scheduled orientations for prospective students, campus tour, professor visit, admissions presentation, financial aid information, coach visit. There are guides for informal visits, visitors may sit in on classes, and stay overnight. To schedule a visit, contact Bonnie Van Winkle at (866) 462-6868. **Campus Safety and Security:** Measures include 24-hour foot and vehicle patrol, emergency notification system, self-defense education, and security escort services. There are shuttle buses, emergency telephones, lighted pathways/sidewalks, controlled access to dorms/residences, fire safety training with student leadership, and blood-borne pathogen seminars. Campus-wide sexual harassment training is required of all faculty, staff, and students. There is also a Campus Safety and Security Review Committee.

REQUIREMENTS: Applicants should be graduates of an accredited high school or home-school program and have ACT composite and subscores of 19 or above, or comparable SAT scores. Recommended preparatory courses include 4 units each in English, math (algebra I and II,geometry, other), social studies, science, lab science, and 3 units in foreign language. An essay is required. Applicants not meeting minimum academic standards may be granted conditional admission with additional course requirements. AP and CLEP credits are accepted. Important factors in the admissions decision are recommendations by school officials, personality/intangible qualities, and leadership record. Students must complete 120 semester hours, at least 39 in upper-division courses, and maintain a minimum GPA of 2.0. Students must also complete the 44- to 57-hour B.A. general education core requirements and the general education and major assessment programs. Additional preparatory courses may be required up to 12 hours. Students who desire two or more majors are required to complete the assessment in each major. **Procedure:** Freshmen are admitted fall and spring. Entrance exams should be taken in early fall. There are deferred admissions and rolling admissions plans. Applications should be filed by May 1 for fall entry; December 1 for spring entry. The fall 2017 application fee was $25. Applications are accepted on-line. **Transfer Students:** 26 transfer students enrolled in 2016-2017. Transfer students must be in good standing academically and financially. Official transcripts from all colleges attended must be submitted. 30 of 120 credits required for the bachelor's degree must be completed at MVNU. **International Students:** There are 23 international students enrolled. They must take the TOEFL with a minimum score of 525 on the paper-based TOEFL (PBT) or 70 on the Internet-based version (iBT). Students must take the Comprehensive English Language Test. They must also take the SAT or ACT.

ADMISSIONS: 77% of the 2017-2018 applicants were accepted. The ACT scores were 8% between 12 and 17, 53% between 18 and 23, 36% between 24 and 29, and 3% above 30. **Admissions Contact:** Tracy Waal, Director of Admissions. Email: *admissions@mvnu.edu* Web: *www.mvnu.edu*

FINANCIAL AID: In 2017-2018, 100% of all full-time freshmen received some form of financial aid. The average freshman award was $21,135. 44% of undergraduate students work part-time. The FAFSA code is 007085. The priority date for freshman financial aid applications for fall entry is November 15.

MUSKINGUM UNIVERSITY — D-3

www.muskingum.edu

New Concord, OH 43762	**(740) 826-8137** **(800) 752-6082**
Fax: (740) 826-8100	**Email: adminfo@muskingum.edu**
Full-time: 802 men, 771 women	**Faculty:** 99; IIB, av$
Part-time: 44 men, 132 women	**Ph.D.s:** 87%
Graduate: 146 men, 395 women	**Student/Faculty:** 14 to 1
Year: semesters, summer session	**Tuition:** $25,779
Room & Board: $10,190	**Freshman Class:** 2134 applied, 1656 accepted, 438 enrolled
SAT CR/M: 491/513 **ACT:** 22	**CEEB CODE:** 1496
Application Deadline: August 1	**COMPETITIVE**

Muskingum University, founded in 1837, is a private liberal arts and sciences institution affiliated with the Presbyterian Church. The figures in the above capsule and in this profile are approximate. There is 1 undergraduate school and 1 graduate school. In addition to regional accreditation, Muskingum has baccalaureate program accreditation with NASM and CAEP. The 245-acre campus is in a small town 9 miles west of Cambridge and 50 miles east of Columbus. Including any residence halls, there are 35 buildings.

STUDENT LIFE: 86% of undergraduates are from Ohio. Others are from 28 states, and 10 foreign countries. 85% are from public schools. 87% are White; 7% African American; 3% Foreign; 2% Hispanic; 1% Asian American. 42% are Protestant; 30% claim no religious affiliation; 16% Catholic. **Female To Male Ratio:** 1.3:1. The average age of freshmen is 18; all undergraduates, 20. 33% do not continue beyond their first year; 55% remain to graduate. **Housing:** 1200 students can be accommodated in college housing, which includes dorms and on-campus apartments. In addition, there are language/international houses, special-interest houses, fraternity houses, and upperclassmen apartments and townhouses. On-campus housing is guaranteed for all 4 years. 87% of students live on campus. All students may keep cars.

FACULTY/CLASSROOMS: 56% of faculty are male; 44% are female. 85% teach undergraduates and 85% do research. No introductory courses are taught by graduate students. The average class size in an introductory lecture is 25; in a laboratory is 16; and in a regular course is 22.

PROGRAMS OF STUDY: Muskingum confers B.A. and B.S. degrees. Master's degrees are also awarded. Bachelor's degrees are awarded in AGRICULTURE (conservation and regulation), BIOLOGICAL SCIENCE (biology/biological science, molecular biology, and neurosciences), BUSINESS (accounting, business administration and management, and international business management), COMMUNICATIONS AND THE ARTS (art, communications, digital communications, dramatic arts, English, French, German, journalism, music, Spanish, and speech/debate/rhetoric), COMPUTER AND PHYSICAL SCIENCE (chemistry, computer science, earth science, geology, mathematics, and physics), EDUCATION (Christian education, early childhood education, elementary education, foreign languages education, music education, physical education, reading education, science education, secondary education, and special education), ENGINEERING AND ENVIRONMENTAL DESIGN (engineering and environmental science), HEALTH PROFESSIONS (nursing), SOCIAL SCIENCE (American studies, criminal justice, economics, history, international relations, philosophy, political science/government, psychology, public affairs, religion, religious education, social science, and sociology). Sciences, and education are the strongest academically. Education, business, and psychology have the largest enrollments.

ACTIVITIES: 24% of men belong to 3 local and 2 national fraternities; 37% of women belong to 4 local and 2 national sororities. There are 90 groups on campus, including art, band, cheerleading, choir, chorus, computers, dance, debate, drama, environmental, ethnic, forensics, honors, international, jazz band, LGBT, literary magazine, marching band, musical theater, newspaper, orchestra, pep band, political, professional, radio and TV, religious, social, social service, student government, symphony, and yearbook. Popular campus events include Li'l Sibs Weekend, and Muskiepalooza. **Sports:** There are 9 intercollegiate sports for men and 8 for women, and 8 intramural sports for men and 8 for women. Facilities include gyms, weight lifting/training rooms, an aerobics room, a baseball batting cage, swimming pool, walking/jogging trail, an all-weather track, football, baseball, soccer fields, tennis, basketball, and racquetball courts. **Graduates:** From July 1, 2016 to June 30, 2017, 268 bachelor's degrees were awarded. The most popular majors were business (23%), education (21%), and biology (8%). In an average class, 1% graduate in 3 years or less, 38% graduate in 4 years or less, 54% graduate in 5 years or less, and 55% graduate in 6 years or less. Of the 2016 graduating class, 15% were enrolled in graduate school within 6 months of graduation, and 93% were employed.

SERVICES: Counseling and information services are available, as is tutoring in every subject. There is a reader service for the blind. The PLUS program is available for learning-disabled and disabled students. **Library/Resources:** The library contains 209,220 volumes, 171,964 microform items, and 3,471 audio/video tapes/CDs/DVDs, and subscribes to 14,127 periodicals including electronic. Computerized library services include interlibrary loans, database searching, and Internet access. Special learning facilities include an art gallery, radio station, TV station, and a greenhouse. **Physically Challenged Students:** 40% of the campus is accessible. Facilities include wheelchair ramps, elevators, special parking, specially equipped restrooms, and lowered drinking fountains. **Special:** Internships, both national and regional, work-study programs, study abroad in 13 countries, and a Washington semester are possible. Dual and student-designed majors, nondegree study, pass/fail options, and credit for life, military, or work experience are also available. There are 18 national honor societies. **Visiting:** There are regularly scheduled orientations for prospective students, consisting of an admission presentation, faculty panel, student panel, and class attendance. There are guides for informal visits, visitors may sit in on classes, and stay overnight. To schedule a visit, contact the Admission Office. **Campus Safety and Security:** Measures include 24-hour foot and vehicle patrol, emergency notification system, and security escort services. There are emergency telephones, lighted pathways/sidewalks, and controlled access to dorms/residences.

REQUIREMENTS: The SAT or ACT is required. Candidates for admission must have a high school diploma or its equivalent and should have 4 years of English, 3 years of college preparatory math, and 2 years each of science, social science, and foreign language. AP and CLEP credits are accepted. Important factors in the admissions decision are advanced placement or honors courses, extracurricular activities record, and leadership record. To graduate, students must complete a minimum of 124 credit hours, including at least 30 in a major and 40 in upper-level courses. Students must maintain a GPA of at least 2.0 and must also complete the 50 to 55 credit hours of Liberal Arts Essentials, with courses in writing, speech, math, arts and humanities, religion and ethics, science, social science, American studies, and phys ed. A senior capstone experience is required in all areas. **Procedure:** Freshmen are admitted fall and spring. Entrance exams should be taken in the junior year or the fall of the senior year. There are deferred admissions and rolling admissions plans. Applications should be filed by August 1 for fall entry. Applications are accepted on-line. **Transfer Students:** 61 transfer students enrolled in 2016-2017. Applicants must submit an official college transcript and be in good academic standing at their previous institution. 32 of 124 credits required for the bachelor's degree must be completed at Muskingum. **International Students:** There are 41 international students enrolled. They must take the TOEFL with a minimum score of 550 on the paper-based TOEFL (PBT) or 79 on the Internet-based version (iBT). Either the SAT or the ACT is recommended.

ADMISSIONS: 78% of the 2017-2018 applicants were accepted. The SAT scores for the 2017-2018 freshman class were: Critical Reading-- 50% below 500, 43% between 500 and 599, 5% between 600 and 699, and 2% between 700 and 800. Math-- 45% below 500, 36% between 500 and 599, 14% between 600 and 699, and 5% between 700 and 800. The ACT scores were 40% below 12, 28% between 12 and 17, 19% between 18 and 23, 6% between 24 and 29, and 6% above 30. 39% of the current freshmen were in the top fifth of their class; 59% were in the top two fifths. 11 freshmen graduated first in their class. **Admissions Contact:** Beth DaLonzo, Senior Director of Admission and Student Financial Services. Email: *adminfo@muskingum.edu* Web: *www.muskingum.edu*

FINANCIAL AID: In 2017-2018, 99% of all full-time freshmen received some form of financial aid. 84% of all full-time freshmen received need-based aid. The average freshman award was $19,518. Need-based scholarships or need-based grants averaged $15,314 ($30,500 maximum); and need-based self-help aid (loans and jobs) averaged $4,204 ($8,500 maximum). 45% of undergraduate students work part-time. The average financial indebtedness of the 2017 graduate was $34,207. Muskingum is a member of CSS. The FAFSA code is 003084. The priority date for freshman financial aid applications for fall entry is March 1.

NOTRE DAME COLLEGE — D-1

www.notredamecollege.edu

South Euclid, OH 44121 — **(216) 373-5351**

Fax: (216) 937-0357	**Email:** admissions@ndc.edu
Full-time: 600 men, 764 women	**Faculty:** n/av
Part-time: n/av	**Ph.D.s:** n/av
Graduate: n/av	**Student/Faculty:** n/av
Year: semesters, summer session	**Tuition:** $29,300
Room & Board: $9850	**Freshman Class:** n/av
SAT or ACT: required	**CEEB CODE:** 1566
Application Deadline: August 1	**VERY COMPETITIVE**

Notre Dame College, founded in 1922, is a private liberal arts and sciences college affiliated with the Roman Catholic Church. The figures given in the above capsule and in this profile are approximate. There is 1 undergraduate school and 1 graduate school. In addition to regional accreditation, NDC has baccalaureate program accreditation with ADA, CAEP, CCNE, and AACN. The 53-acre campus is in a suburban area 13 miles east of Cleveland. Including any residence halls, there are 10 buildings.

STUDENT LIFE: Students are from 20 states, 12 foreign countries, and Canada. 65% are from public schools. 65% are White; 3% Hispanic; 23% African American; 1% Asian American; 1% Foreign. 55% are Catholic; 20% Baptist, and Muslim; 15% Protestant. **Female To Male Ratio:** 1.3:1. The average age of freshmen is 18; all undergraduates, 26. 34% do not continue beyond their first year; 52% remain to graduate. **Housing:** 650 students can be accommodated in college housing, which includes dorms and on-campus apartments, nonsmoking floors, quiet floors, and gender specific for underclassman dorms. On-campus housing is guaranteed for the freshman year only, and is available on a lottery system for upperclassmen. 60% of students live on campus. Alcohol is not permitted. All students may keep cars.

FACULTY/CLASSROOMS: All teach undergraduates. No introductory courses are taught by graduate students. The average class size in an introductory lecture is 16.

PROGRAMS OF STUDY: NDC confers B.A. and B.S. degrees. Associate and master's degrees are also awarded. Bachelor's degrees are awarded in BIOLOGICAL SCIENCE (biology/biological science), BUSINESS (accounting, business economics, human resources, management science, and marketing/retailing/merchandising), COMMUNICATIONS AND THE ARTS (art, communications, English, graphic design, public relations, studio art, and visual and performing arts), COMPUTER AND PHYSICAL SCIENCE (chemistry, information sciences and systems, and mathematics), EDUCATION (early childhood education, elementary education, middle school education, secondary education, and special education), ENGINEERING AND ENVIRONMENTAL DESIGN (environmental science), HEALTH PROFESSIONS (nursing and physical therapy), SOCIAL SCIENCE (economics, history, ministries, political science/government, psychology, and theological studies). Business, education, and science are the strongest academically. Business administration, education, and sciences have the largest enrollments.

ACTIVITIES: There are no fraternities or sororities. There are 32 groups on campus, including indoor colorguard, indoor percussions ensemble, art, band, cheerleading, choir, chorus, computers, dance, drama, ethnic, honors, international, jazz band, LGBT, literary magazine, marching band, newspaper, pep band, political, professional, religious, social, social service, and student government. Popular campus events include Founders Weekend, Welcome Weekend, and Spring Fest Week. **Sports:** There are 11 intercollegiate sports for men and 11 for women. Facilities include a gym, a swimming pool, and a fitness center.

SERVICES: Counseling and information services are available, as is tutoring in every subject. Notre Dame offers free peer tutoring within our Dwyer Learning Center. We also have an Academic Support Center for students with learning differences. There is remedial math, reading, and writing. **Library/Resources:** The library contains 89,292 volumes, 14,200 microform items, and 1,768 audio/video tapes/CDs/DVDs, and subscribes to 300 periodicals including electronic. Computerized library services include interlibrary loans and database searching. Special learning facilities include an art gallery, and Tolerance Resource Center. **Physically Challenged Students:** 75% of the campus is accessible. Facilities include wheelchair ramps, elevators, special parking, specially equipped restrooms, lowered drinking fountains, and lowered telephones. **Special:** There are a freshman honors program. **Visiting:** There are regularly scheduled orientations for prospective students, students and their families will meet with an admissions counselor individually to discuss admissions, financial aid, and any other questions they may have. They also have the options of taking a tour of campus or meeting with a professor. There are guides for informal visits, visitors may sit in on classes, and stay overnight. To schedule a visit, contact the Admissions Office. **Campus Safety and Security:** Measures include emergency notification system, self-defense education, and security escort services. There are emergency telephones, lighted pathways/sidewalks, controlled access to dorms/residences, and 24/7 campus security that work hand in hand with the South Euclid Police Department.

REQUIREMENTS: The SAT or ACT is required. Applicants should be graduates of an accredited secondary school with 15 academic credits, including 4 of English, 2 of foreign language, 1 each of math, social studies, and science, plus 5 electives. The GED is accepted. An interview is recommended. AP and CLEP credits are accepted. To graduate, students must complete 128 semester hours with a minimum GPA of 2.0. Students must have successfully completed courses fulfilling the General Education Requirements and those pertaining to their field of study. The following must be completed at NDC: 50% of major coursework, at least 45 upper-biennium courses, at least 1 semester and have completed a minimum of 32 semester credits. **Procedure:** Freshmen are admitted fall and spring. There are deferred admissions and rolling admissions plans. Application deadlines are open. Notification is sent on a rolling basis. Applications are accepted on-line. **Transfer Students:** Applicants must have a college GPA of at least 2.5. Perspective students must submit all college transcripts as well as high school. 32 of 128 credits required for the bachelor's degree must be completed at NDC. **International Students:** They must take the TOEFL, or take the ELS Proficiency Test 109.

Admissions Contact: Beth Ford, Director of Admissions/Financial Aid. Email: *admissions@ndc.edu* Web: *www.notredamecollege.edu*

FINANCIAL AID: In 2017-2018, 99% of all full-time freshmen received some form of financial aid. The FAFSA code is 003085. Check with the school for current application deadlines.

OBERLIN COLLEGE — D-2

www.oberlin.edu

Oberlin, OH 44074 — (440) 775-8411, (800) 622-6243

Fax: (440) 775-6905 — **Email:** college.admissions@oberlin.edu

Full-time: 1184 men, 1609 women	**Faculty:** 331; IIB, ++$
Part-time: 17 men, 17 women	**Ph.D.s:** 96%
Graduate: 5 men, 2 women	**Student/Faculty:** 10 to 1
Year: 4-1-4	**Tuition:** $53,470
Room & Board: $15,472	**Freshman Class:** 7762 applied, 2617 accepted, 728 enrolled
SAT CR/M/W: 687/680/682 **ACT:** 31	**CEEB CODE:** 1587
Application Deadline: January 15	**MOST COMPETITIVE**

Oberlin College is a liberal arts college of intense energy and creativity, built on a foundation of academic, artistic, and musical excellence. The only institution in the United States where a top-ranked liberal arts college and a world-renowned conservatory of music share a seamless student culture and campus, Oberlin also boasts an art museum that is known as one of the best in the country. Noted for its sustainability initiatives and achievements, Oberlin has been recognized as one of the "greenest" institutions in the US and continues to challenge itself and its students to find better and more efficient ways to be environmentally responsible. Oberlin provides a world-class education to its students, the majority of whom continue on to prestigious fellowships and PhD programs. There are 2 undergraduate schools and 1 graduate school. In addition to regional accreditation, Oberlin has baccalaureate program accreditation with HLC. The 442-acre campus is in a small town 35 miles southwest of Cleveland, OH. Including any residence halls, there are 68 buildings.

STUDENT LIFE: 94% of undergraduates are from out of state, mostly the Middle Atlantic. Students are from 50 states, 45 foreign countries, and Canada. 66% are from public schools. 8% are Hispanic; 8% two or more races; 64% White; 5% African American; 4% Asian American; 10% Foreign; 1% race unknown. **Female To Male Ratio:** 1.3:1. The average age of freshmen is 18; all undergraduates, 20. 8% do not continue beyond their first year; 86% remain to graduate. **Housing:** 2700 students can be accommodated in college housing, which includes gender neutral and coed dorms, on-campus apartments, and off-campus apartments. In addition, there are language/international houses, special-interest houses, and co-op housing. On-campus housing is guaranteed for all 4 years. 93% of students live on campus. All students may keep cars.

FACULTY/CLASSROOMS: All teach undergraduates, and all do research. No introductory courses are taught by graduate students. The average class size in a laboratory is 14 and in a regular course is 20.

PROGRAMS OF STUDY: Oberlin confers B.A. and B.Mus. degrees. Master's degrees are also awarded. Bachelor's degrees are awarded in AGRICULTURE (environmental studies), BIOLOGICAL SCIENCE (biochemistry, biology/biological science, and neurosciences), COMMUNICATIONS AND THE ARTS (acting, Africana studies, art history, art, classics, composition, comparative literature, conducting, creative writing, dance, dramatic arts, English, film arts, fine arts, French, German, Germanic languages and literature, music, music composition, music history and appreciation, music performance, music theory and composition, painting, performing arts, photography, piano/organ, romance languages and literature, Russian, Russian languages and literature, Spanish, Spanish and Hispanic studies, strings, studio art, studio art painting, theatre acting, theater design, theatre studies, and winds), COMPUTER AND PHYSICAL SCIENCE (applied mathematics, astronomy, astronomy and physics, chemistry, computer science, geology, mathematics, and physics), EDUCATION (music education), HEALTH PROFESSIONS (biology and premedicine), SOCIAL SCIENCE (African American studies, American studies, anthropology, archeology, East Asian studies, Eastern European studies, economics, gender studies, history, humanities, international studies, Judaic studies, Latin American studies, law, Near Eastern studies, philosophy, political science/government, prelaw, psychology, religion, Russian and Slavic studies, sociology, women & gender studies, and women's studies). Sciences, the arts, economics, and environmental studies are the strongest academically. Biology, politics, and economics have the largest enrollments.

ACTIVITIES: There are no fraternities or sororities. There are 175 groups on campus, including art, band, chess, choir, chorale, chorus, communications, computers, dance, debate, drama, environmental, ethnic, film, forensics, honors, international, jazz band, LGBT, literary magazine, musical theater, newspaper, opera, orchestra, photography, political, professional, radio and TV, religious, social, social service, student government, and symphony. Popular campus events include Big Parade, Earth Day, Art Rental. **Sports:** There are 10 intercollegiate sports for men and 11 for women, and 10 intramural sports for men and 10 for women. Facilities include an all-weather multi-purpose field, field house, indoor track, outdoor track, outdoor and indoor tennis courts, cross-country course, a fitness trail, swimming pool, Nautilus center, free-weight room, 22 practice/play fields, indoor space for football, soccer, lacrosse practice, a climbing wall, 6 racquetball courts, 8 squash courts, indoor batting cage. **Graduates:** From July 1, 2016 to June 30, 2017, 676 bachelor's degrees were awarded. The most popular majors were biology (7%), politics (7%), and environmental studies (6%). In an average class, 75% graduate in 4 years or less, 85% graduate in 5 years or less, and 86% graduate in 6 years or less. Of the 2016 graduating class, 19% were enrolled in graduate school within 6 months of graduation, and 63% were employed.

SERVICES: Counseling and information services are available, as is tutoring in every subject. There is a reader service for the blind, and remedial math, reading, and writing. There is also a computer-assisted services for hearing and visually impaired students. **Library/Resources:** The library contains 1.4 million volumes, 362,082 microform items, and 115,097 audio/video tapes/CDs/DVDs, and subscribes to 181,044 periodicals including electronic. Computerized library services include interlibrary loans, database searching, Internet access, and Wi-Fi capability. Special learning facilities include an art gallery, radio station, an observatory, art museum, art library, arboretum, conservatory of music, music library, science library, and a learning center specializing in foreign language education. **Physically Challenged Students:** 90% of the campus is accessible. Facilities include wheelchair ramps, elevators, special parking, specially equipped restrooms, special class scheduling, lowered drinking fountains, lowered telephones, special housing, and indoor/outdoor lift. **Special:** Internships are available through the Business Initiatives Program. Students may study abroad in 38 countries. Three-quarters of Oberlin students spend time abroad for study or service. More than 50 majors are available. The college offers independent and dual majors, 3-2 engineering programs with other institutions, non-degree study for special and visiting students, and a 5-year B.A.-B.Mus. double degree. There are 4 national honor societies, Phi Beta Kappa, and 35 departmental honors programs. **Visiting:** There are regularly scheduled orientations for prospective students, consisting of campus tour, information session, class visits, interview, and an overnight stay in the dorm. There are guides for informal visits, visitors may sit in on classes, and stay overnight. To schedule a visit, contact the Campus Visit Office at (800) 622-6243. **Campus Safety and Security:** Measures include 24-hour foot and vehicle patrol, emergency notification system, self-defense education, and security escort services. There are emergency telephones, lighted pathways/sidewalks, controlled access to dorms/residences, full-time crime prevention officer, a 24-hour headquarters facility staffed by professional dispatchers, and an electronic card-access system in all dorms.

REQUIREMENTS: Candidates for admission should have completed 4 years each of English and math, and 3 each of lab science, social studies, and the same foreign language. Either the SAT or ACT is required. An audition is required for students applying to the Conservatory of Music. AP credits are accepted. Important factors in the admissions decision are advanced placement or honors courses, personality/intangible qualities, and recommendations by school officials. Students are required to complete 32 full courses, including 2 in each of the 3 academic divisions (arts/humanities, social/behavioral sciences, natural science/math), 3 courses dealing with cultural diversity, plus 3 winter term projects. In addition, they must earn a writing and quantitative proficiency certification. **Procedure:** Freshmen are admitted fall. Entrance exams should be taken in the junior year or early in the senior year. There are early decision, early admissions, and deferred admissions plans. Early decision applications should be filed by November 15; regular applications, by January 15 for fall entry; and November 15 for spring entry. Notification of early decision is sent December 15; regular decision, April 1. 246 early decision candidates were accepted for the 2017-2018 class. 1125 applicants were on the 2017 waiting list; 124 were admitted. Applications are accepted on-line. **Transfer Students:** 14 transfer students enrolled in 2016-2017. Applicants should submit official transcripts of all college work completed, plus a list of current courses and midterm grades. An average of B or better should be presented. A high school transcript, recommendations, and standardized test scores are also required. 16 of 32 credits required for the bachelor's degree must be completed at Oberlin. **International Students:** There are 289 international students enrolled. They must take the TOEFL with a minimum score of 600 on the paper-based TOEFL (PBT) or 100 on the Internet-based version (iBT). Students must take the IELTS. They must also take the SAT or ACT.

ADMISSIONS: 34% of the 2017-2018 applicants were accepted. The SAT scores for the 2017-2018 freshman class were: Critical Reading-- 6% between 500 and 599, 50% between 600 and 699, and 44% between 700 and 800. Math-- 1% below 500, 14% between 500 and 599, 45% between 600 and 699, and 40% between 700 and 800. The ACT scores were 3% between 18 and 23, 33% between 24 and 29, and 64% above 30. 79% of the current freshmen were in the top fifth of their class; 97% were in the top two fifths. **Admissions Contact:** Manuel Carballo, VP/Dean of Admissions & Financial Aid. Email: *college.admissions@oberlin.edu* Web: *www.oberlin.edu*

FINANCIAL AID: In 2017-2018, 56% of all full-time freshmen received some form of financial aid and need-based aid. The average freshman award was $42,825. Need-based scholarships or need-based grants averaged $37,998; need-based self-help aid (loans and jobs) averaged $5,413; and other non-need-based awards and non-need-based scholarships averaged $16,847. 59% of undergraduate students work part-time. The average financial indebtedness of the 2017 graduate was $25,760. Oberlin is a member of CSS. The CSS/Profile and the college's own financial statement are required. The FAFSA code is 003086. The priority date for freshman financial aid applications for fall entry is February 1.

OHIO DOMINICAN UNIVERSITY C-3

www.ohiodominican.edu

Columbus, OH 43219	(614) 251-4500
Fax: (614) 252-0776	Email: admissions@ohiodominican.edu
Full-time: 611 men, 780 women	Faculty: n/av
Part-time: 239 men, 375 women	Ph.D.s: 91%
Graduate: 178 men, 390 women	Student/Faculty: 12 to 1
Year: semesters, summer session	Tuition: $32,960
Room & Board: $8380	Freshman Class: 2652 applied, 1310 accepted
ACT: required	CEEB CODE: 1131
Application Deadline: open	COMPETITIVE+

Ohio Dominican University, founded in 1911 by the Dominican Sisters of St. Mary of the Springs, is a private liberal arts university affiliated with the Roman Catholic Church. The figures given in the above capsule and in this profile are approximate. There are 2 undergraduate schools and 1 graduate school. In addition to regional accreditation, ODU has baccalaureate program accreditation with ACBSP, CSWE, and CAEP. The 98-acre campus is in an urban area 5 miles from downtown Columbus. Including any residence halls, there are 16 buildings.

STUDENT LIFE: 96% of undergraduates are from Ohio. Others are from 16 states, 12 foreign countries, and Canada. 82% are from public schools. 67% are White; 23% African American; 3% Hispanic; 3% two or more races; 2% race unknown; 1% Asian American; 1% American Indian/Alaska Native; 1% Foreign. 37% are Catholic; 34% Protestant. **Female To Male Ratio:** 1.5:1. The average age of freshmen is 18; all undergraduates, 24. 34% do not continue beyond their first year; 66% remain to graduate. **Housing:** 620 students can be accommodated in college housing, which includes dorms. In addition, there are honors houses. On-campus housing is available on a first-come and first-served basis. 73% of students commute. Alcohol is not permitted. All students may keep cars.

FACULTY/CLASSROOMS: 54% of faculty are male; 46% are female. All teach undergraduates. No introductory courses are taught by graduate students. The average class size in an introductory lecture is 20 and in a regular course is 20.

PROGRAMS OF STUDY: ODU confers B.A., B.S., and B.S.Ed. degrees. Associate and master's degrees are also awarded. Bachelor's degrees are awarded in AGRICULTURE (environmental studies), BIOLOGICAL SCIENCE (biology/biological science), BUSINESS (accounting, banking and finance, business administration and management, international business management, management information systems, and sports management), COMMUNICATIONS AND THE ARTS (art, communications, English, graphic design, and public relations), COMPUTER AND PHYSICAL SCIENCE (chemistry, computer science, and mathematics), EDUCATION (early childhood education, middle school education, and special education), HEALTH PROFESSIONS (exercise science), SOCIAL SCIENCE (criminal justice, economics, history, interdisciplinary studies, liberal arts/general studies, peace studies, philosophy, political science/government, psychology, social work, sociology, and theological studies). Business, education, and psychology have the largest enrollments.

ACTIVITIES: There are no fraternities or sororities. There are 40 groups on campus, including academic, commuter, art, association of resident students, band, cheerleading, choir, dance, drama, drill team, environmental, ethnic, honors, international, literary magazine, newspaper, pep band, political, professional, radio and TV, religious, social, social service, and student government. Popular campus events include Black History Week, International Student Week, and ODU Day in the Spring. **Sports:** There are 8 intercollegiate sports for men and 8 for women, and 5 intramural sports for men and 5 for women. Facilities include an athletic center, a gym, football stadium, a baseball and softball field, soccer field, outdoor basketball courts, and outdoor tennis courts. **Graduates:** From July 1, 2016 to June 30, 2017, 338 bachelor's degrees were awarded. The most popular majors were business (41%), early childhood education (14%), and criminal justice (5%). In an average class, 1% graduate in 3 years or less, 29% graduate in 4 years or less, 40% graduate in 5 years or less, and 42% graduate in 6 years or less.

SERVICES: Counseling and information services are available, as is tutoring in most subjects. There is remedial math, reading, and writing. The Academic Center is a support unit designed to help all students meet their academic commitment and improve their learning skills. The staff offers workshops in study-related topics, and provides professional and peer tutoring. **Library/Resources:** The library contains 161,704 volumes, 10,878 microform items, and 4,422 audio/video tapes/CDs/DVDs, and subscribes to 13,282 periodicals including electronic. Computerized library services include interlibrary loans, database searching, Internet access, and Wi-Fi capability. Special learning facilities include an art gallery and radio station. **Physically Challenged Students:** 90% of the campus is accessible. Facilities include wheelchair ramps, elevators, special parking, specially equipped restrooms, special class scheduling, and lowered drinking fountains. **Special:** Students may cross-register with members of the Higher Education Council of Columbus Consortium, study abroad in various countries, and participate in a Washington semester. Internships are required in some majors. ODU offers dual majors and pass/fail options in some courses. Nondegree study and credit for life, military, and work experience are available. There is an accelerated degree program in business administration. There are 2 national honor societies and a freshman honors program. **Visiting:** There are regularly scheduled orientations for prospective students, including an August orientation for fall entry and a January orientation for the second semester. Individual appointments can be arranged. There are guides for informal visits, visitors may sit in on classes, and stay overnight. To schedule a visit, contact the Director of Admissions. **Campus Safety and Security:** Measures include 24-hour foot and vehicle patrol, emergency notification system, and security escort services. There are shuttle buses, emergency telephones, and lighted pathways/sidewalks.

REQUIREMENTS: The ACT is required. Candidates for admission should have completed 4 units of English and 3 units each of a foreign language, math, science, and social studies. The freshman applicant is required to submit a completed application and transcripts of secondary courses and grades. An essay and an interview (in-state applicants) are required. AP and CLEP credits are accepted. Core curriculum requirements include 9 semester hours in arts and ideas, 6 each in English, behavioral science, philosophy and theology, 3 each in literature, math, and science, 3 or 6 in language, 3 addressing diversity, and 4 core curriculum seminars. All students beyond the freshman year must maintain a GPA of 2.0. Students must complete 120 semester credits. Individual departments set the total hours in the major. **Procedure:** Freshmen are admitted to all sessions. There are deferred admissions and rolling admissions plans. Application deadlines are open. The fall 2017 application fee was $25. Applications are accepted on-line. **Transfer Students:** 114 transfer students enrolled in 2016-2017. A completed application, an interview, and transcripts of all college work are required of transfer applicants. 32 of 124 credits required for the bachelor's degree must be completed at ODU. **International Students:** There are 17 international students enrolled. They must take the TOEFL with a minimum score of 550 on the paper-based TOEFL (PBT) or 79 on the Internet-based version (iBT). They must also take the ACT.

ADMISSIONS: 49% of the 2017-2018 applicants were accepted. The SAT scores for the 2017-2018 freshman class were: Critical Reading-- 53% below 500, 28% between 500 and 599, 14% between 600 and 699, and 5% between 700 and 800. Math-- 35% below 500, 42% between 500 and 599, and 23% between 600 and 699. The ACT scores were 33% below 12, 33% between 12 and 17, 22% between 18 and 23, 7% between 24 and 29, and 4% above 30. 36% of the current freshmen were in the top fifth of their class; 68% were in the top two fifths. 7 freshmen graduated first in their class. **Admissions Contact:** Nicole Evans, Director of Admissions. Email: *admissions@ohiodominican.edu* Web: *www.ohiodominican.edu*

FINANCIAL AID: In 2017-2018, 100% of all full-time freshmen received some form of financial aid. 88% of all full-time freshmen received need-based aid. The average freshman award was $23,000. Need-based scholarships or need-based grants averaged $4,200 ($6,000 maximum); need-based self-help aid (loans and jobs) averaged $5,200 ($8,000 maximum); and other non-need-based awards and non-need-based scholarships averaged $7,000 ($13,000 maximum). 35% of undergraduate students work part-time. The FAFSA code is 003035. Check with the school for current application deadlines.

OHIO NORTHERN UNIVERSITY — B-2

www.onu.edu

Ada, OH 45810	**(419) 772-2529** **(800) 408-4668**
Fax: (419) 772-1932	**Email: admissions-ug@onu.edu**
Full-time: 1139 men, 1046 women	**Faculty:** IIB, +$
Part-time: 35 men, 14 women	**Ph.D.s:** 82%
Graduate: 326 men, 511 women	**Student/Faculty:** 12 to 1
Year: trimesters, summer session	**Tuition:** $33,000
Room & Board: $11,050	**Freshman Class:** 3337 applied, 2289 accepted, 628 enrolled
SAT CR/M/W: 570/590/555 **ACT:** 26	**CEEB CODE:** 1591
Application Deadline: August 15	**VERY COMPETITIVE**

Ohio Northern University, founded in 1871, is a private institution affiliated with the United Methodist Church. Undergraduate programs are offered in arts and sciences, business administration, engineering, and pharmacy. The figures given in the above capsule and in this profile are approximate. The tuition cost varies by programs chosen by student. There are 4 undergraduate schools and 1 graduate school. In addition to regional accreditation, ONU has baccalaureate program accreditation with ABET, ACPE, NASM, CAEP, ACS, and CAAHEP. The 342-acre campus is in a small town about 75 miles south of Toledo. Including any residence halls, there are 60 buildings.

STUDENT LIFE: 86% of undergraduates are from Ohio. Others are from 42 states, 17 foreign countries, and Canada. 82% are from public schools. 95% are White; 2% African American; 1% Asian American; 1% Hispanic; 1% Foreign. 43% are Baptist, Muslim, Lutheran, and Presbyterian; 26% Catholic; 12% claim no religious affiliation. **Female To Male Ratio:** 1.0:1. The average age of freshmen is 18; all undergraduates, 20. 18% do not continue beyond their first year; 66% remain to graduate. **Housing:** 1915 students can be accommodated in college housing, which includes dorms, on-campus apartments, and off-campus apartments. In addition, there are honors houses, special-interest houses, fraternity houses, sorority houses, and theme housing. On-campus housing is guaranteed for all 4 years. 63% of students live on campus. All students may keep cars.

FACULTY/CLASSROOMS: 49% of faculty are male; 48% are female. 90% teach undergraduates. No introductory courses are taught by graduate students. The average class size in an introductory lecture is 29; in a laboratory is 14; and in a regular course is 25.

PROGRAMS OF STUDY: ONU confers B.A., B.S., B.F.A., B.M., B.S.B.A., B.S.C.E., B.S.C.P.E., B.S.E.E., B.S.M.E., B.S.M.T., and B.S.Ph. degrees. Doctoral degrees are also awarded. Bachelor's degrees are awarded in AGRICULTURE (environmental studies), BIOLOGICAL SCIENCE (biochemistry, biology/biological science, and molecular biology), BUSINESS (accounting, business administration and management, business economics, international business management, management science, and sports management), COMMUNICATIONS AND THE ARTS (broadcasting, ceramic art and design, communications, creative writing, dramatic arts, English, fine arts, French, graphic design, journalism, language arts, literature, music, music business management, music performance, music theory and composition, public relations, and Spanish), COMPUTER AND PHYSICAL SCIENCE (chemistry, computer science, mathematics, physics, and statistics), EDUCATION (athletic training, early childhood education, health education, middle school education, music education, and physical education), ENGINEERING AND ENVIRONMENTAL DESIGN (civil engineering, computer engineering, electrical/electronics engineering, mechanical engineering, and technological management), HEALTH PROFESSIONS (health, medical technology, and pharmacy), SOCIAL SCIENCE (criminal justice, history, international studies, philosophy, political science/government, psychology, religion, social studies, sociology, and youth ministry). Chemistry, engineering, and pharmacy are the strongest academically. Pharmacy, engineering, and biology have the largest enrollments.

ACTIVITIES: 14% of men belong to 8 national fraternities; 21% of women belong to 4 national sororities. There are 170 groups on campus, including art, band, cheerleading, chess, choir, chorale, chorus, computers, dance, debate, drama, drill team, ethnic, honors, international, jazz band, literary magazine, marching band, musical theater, newspaper, orchestra, pep band, political, professional, radio and TV, religious, social, social service, student government, symphony, and yearbook. Popular campus events include Tunes on the Tundra, International Week, and Little Sibs Weekend. **Sports:** There are 11 intercollegiate sports for men and 10 for women, and 12 intramural sports for men and 11 for women. Facilities include a pool, wrestling room, weight rooms, indoor/outdoor tennis courts, basketball courts, football stadium, training room, bowling lanes, billiards room, dance room, fitness lab, an indoor track, outdoor track, racquetball courts, a Nautilus room, and a jogging/walking path. **Graduates:** From July 1, 2016 to June 30, 2017, 434 bachelor's degrees were awarded. The most popular majors were business marketing (9%), education and visual and performing arts (14%), and public administration and social services and biology science (14%). In an average class, 65% graduate in 6 years or less.

SERVICES: Counseling and information services are available, as is tutoring in most subjects. There is a reader service for the blind, and remedial math and writing. **Library/Resources:** The library contains 250,518 volumes, 72,067 microform items, and 10,815 audio/video tapes/CDs/DVDs, and subscribes to 1,038 periodicals including electronic. Computerized library services include interlibrary loans and database searching. Special learning facilities include an art gallery, radio station, TV station, and a pharmacy museum. **Physically Challenged Students:** 95% of the campus is accessible. Facilities include wheelchair ramps, elevators, special parking, specially equipped restrooms, special class scheduling, lowered drinking fountains, and lowered telephones. **Special:** Co-op programs are available in civil, electrical, computer, and mechanical engineering and technology, computer science, and math. Students may take internships in pharmacy, engineering, and business and may study abroad in 15 countries. B.A.-B.S. degrees and dual majors are available in arts/engineering, arts/pharmacy, and arts/business. The university also offers pass/fail options and work-study programs. There are 38 national honor societies, a freshman honors program, and 21 departmental honors programs. **Visiting:** There are regularly scheduled orientations for prospective students, including a tour, lunch, and appointments in academics, admissions, and financial aid. A meeting with a coach can also be arranged. There are guides for informal visits, visitors may sit in on classes, and stay overnight. To schedule a visit, contact the Admissions Office. **Campus Safety and Security:** Measures include 24-hour foot and vehicle patrol, self-defense education, and security escort services. There are emergency telephones and lighted pathways/sidewalks.

REQUIREMENTS: The SAT or ACT is required. The preparatory program should include 4 years of English, and 2 each of math, science, and social. Recommended units are computer science, and visual/performing arts. ONU requires applicants to be in the upper 50% of their class. AP and CLEP credits are accepted. Important factors in the admissions decision are advanced placement or honors courses, leadership record, evidence of special talent, extracurricular activities record, and recommendations by alumni. To graduate, students must complete a minimum of 182 quarter hours, maintain a cumulative GPA of 2.0, and fulfill all departmental/college core requirements. Also, students must submit a formal application for graduation. **Procedure:** Freshmen are admitted to all sessions. Entrance exams should be taken in the spring of the junior year or the fall of the senior year. There are deferred admissions and rolling admissions plans. Applications should be filed by August 15 for fall entry. The fall 2017 application fee was $30. Notification of early decision is sent September 1; regular decision, on a rolling basis. Applications are accepted on-line. **Transfer Students:** 59 transfer students enrolled in 2016-2017. Applicants should have a minimum college GPA of 2.0 and submit official transcripts from all the schools they have attended. 45 of 182 credits required for the bachelor's degree must be completed at ONU. **International Students:** They must take the TOEFL or MELAB.

Admissions Contact: Omer Minhas, Director of Institutional Research. Email: *admissions-ug@onu.edu* Web: *www.onu.edu*

FINANCIAL AID: ONU is a member of CSS. The college's own financial statement is required. The FAFSA code is 003089. Check with the school for current application deadlines.

OHIO STATE UNIVERSITY AT COLUMBUS C-3

www.osu.edu

Columbus, OH 43210 **(614) 292-3980**

Fax: (614) 292-4818	**Email:** askabuckeye@osu.edu
Full-time: 21,719 men, 20,284 women	**Faculty:** 1963; I, +$
Part-time: 2117 men, 1826 women	**Ph.D.s:** n/av
Graduate: 6307 men, 7584 women	**Student/Faculty:** n/av
Year: semesters, summer session	**Tuition:** $10,591 ($29,141)
Room & Board: $12,252	**Freshman Class:** 47782 applied, 22964 accepted, 7209 enrolled
SAT EBR-W/M: 670/680 **ACT:** 30	**CEEB CODE:** 1152
Application Deadline: February 1	**MOST COMPETITIVE**

The Ohio State University at Columbus, founded in 1870, is one of America's largest and most comprehensive institutions. There are 200 undergraduate majors, and 250 master's, doctoral, and professional degree programs. Ohio State is further recognized by a top-rated academic medical center and a premier cancer hospital and research center. The university's innovative prowess attains world-class status, particularly in critical areas such as cancer, infectious disease, advanced materials, and ag-bio products that feed and fuel the world. Ohio State's regional campuses are located in Lima, Mansfield, Marion, and Newark, and the Agricultural Technical Institute is in Wooster. There are 15 undergraduate schools and 1 graduate school. In addition to regional accreditation, OSU-Columbus has baccalaureate program accreditation with AACSB, ABET, ACCE, ACPE, ADA, APTA, ASLA, CAHEA, CSWE, FIDER, NAAB, NASAD, NASM, and CAEP. The 1665-acre campus is in an urban area 2 miles north of downtown Columbus, OH. Including any residence halls, there are 593 buildings.

STUDENT LIFE: 80% of undergraduates are from Ohio. Others are from 50 states, 65 foreign countries, and Canada. 86% are from public schools. 8% are Foreign; 7% Asian American; 68% White; 6% African American; 4% Hispanic; 4% race unknown; 3% two or more races. **Male To Female Ratio:** 1.0:1. The average age of freshmen is 18; all undergraduates, 21. 6% do not continue beyond their first year; 94% remain to graduate. **Housing:** 14313 students can be accommodated in college housing, which includes gender neutral, single sex and coed, married student dorms, and on-campus apartments. In addition, there are honors houses, language/international houses, and special-interest houses. On-campus housing is guaranteed for the freshman year only, is available on a first-come, first-served basis, and is available on a lottery system for upperclassmen. 78% of students commute. Upperclassmen may keep cars.

FACULTY/CLASSROOMS: 55% of faculty are male; 45% are female. No introductory courses are taught by graduate students. The average class size in an introductory lecture is 48; in a laboratory is 22; and in a regular course is 28.

PROGRAMS OF STUDY: OSU-Columbus Campus confers B.A., B.S., B.F.A., B.Mus., and B.Mus.Ed., and B.S. Design degrees. Associate, master's, and doctoral degrees are also awarded. Bachelor's degrees are awarded in AGRICULTURE (agricultural business management, agricultural economics, animal science, fishing and fisheries, forestry and related sciences, natural resource management, and plant science), BIOLOGICAL SCIENCE (avian sciences, biochemistry, biology/biological science, ecology, entomology, evolutionary biology, microbiology, molecular biology, neurosciences, nutrition, plant pathology, plant physiology, and zoology), BUSINESS (accounting, banking and finance, business administration and management, fashion merchandising, finance, hospitality management services, human resources, insurance and risk management, international business management, logistics, management information systems, marketing and distribution, operations management, real estate, and transportation management), COMMUNICATIONS AND THE ARTS (Arabic, art, art history and appreciation, Chinese, classics, communications, dance, English, film arts, fine arts, French, German, Germanic languages and literature, Greek, Hebrew, industrial design, Italian, Japanese, jazz, journalism, Korean, linguistics, music, music history and appreciation, music performance, music theory and composition, musicology/ethnomusicology, piano/organ, Portuguese, Russian, Spanish, sport & lifestyle studies, studio art, theatre arts, theater design, and visual design), COMPUTER AND PHYSICAL SCIENCE (actuarial science, astronomy, astrophysics, atmospheric sciences and meteorology, chemistry, computer science, data analytics, earth science, geology, information sciences and systems, mathematics, and physics), EDUCATION (agricultural education, art education, athletic training, dance education, education, environmental education, health information management, middle school education, music education, physical education, teaching English as a second/foreign language (TESOL/TEFOL), and technical education), ENGINEERING AND ENVIRONMENTAL DESIGN (aeronautical engineering, architecture, aviation administration/management, biomedical engineering, chemical engineering, city/community/regional planning, civil engineering, computer engineering, construction management, electrical/electronics engineering, engineering physics, environmental engineering, environmental science, industrial engineering, interior design, landscape architecture/design, materials engineering, materials science, mechanical engineering, and welding engineering), HEALTH PROFESSIONS (biomedical science, dental hygiene, exercise science, health promotion, health science, medical laboratory science, medical technology, nursing, occupational therapy, pharmaceutical science, physical therapy, public health, radiograph medical technology, radiological science, respiratory therapy, speech pathology/audiology, and speech therapy), SOCIAL SCIENCE (African American studies, anthropology, community services, criminal justice, criminology, culinary arts, dietetics, early childhood studies, economics, family/consumer resource management, family/consumer studies, food production/management/services, food science, French studies, geography, geography information science, history, human development, human ecology, industrial and organizational psychology, international studies, Islamic studies, Judaic studies, medieval studies, philosophy, physical fitness/movement, political science/government, psychology, public affairs, public policy, religious studies, social work, sociology, and women's studies). Finance, biology, and psychology have the largest enrollments.

ACTIVITIES: 13% of men belong to 45 national fraternities; 14% of women belong to 25 national sororities. There are 1356 groups on campus, including art, band, cheerleading, chess, choir, chorale, chorus, communications, computers, dance, debate, drama, drill team, environmental, ethnic, film, forensics, honors, international, jazz band, LGBT, literary magazine, marching band, musical theater, newspaper, opera, orchestra, pep band, photography, political, professional, radio and TV, religious, social, social service, student government, and symphony. Popular campus events include Welcome Week, Student Involvement Fairs, Homecoming Parade, BuckeyeThon (philanthropy/dance marathon), Thanksgiving Dinner, Taste of OSU, African American Heritage Festival, Asian and Pacific American Heritage Month, HackOHI/O, Greek Week. **Sports:** There are 18 intercollegiate sports for men and 19 for women, and 28 intramural sports for men and 28 for women. Facilities include a football stadium, a multipurpose event center, an arena, archery range, running track, cricket field, in-line hockey rink, weight rooms, swimming pools, basketball, volleyball, squash courts and racquetball courts. There are field houses for tennis, volleyball, basketball, soccer, and baseball and softball fields. **Graduates:** From July 1, 2016 to June 30, 2017, 11244 bachelor's degrees were awarded. The most popular majors were psychology (5%), communication (5%), and finance (4%). In an average class, 3% graduate in 3 years or less, 59% graduate in 4 years or less, 79% graduate in 5 years or less, and 83% graduate in 6 years or less.

SERVICES: Counseling and information services are available, as is tutoring in most subjects. There is a reader service for the blind, and remedial math, reading, and writing. **Library/Resources:** The library contains 5.1 million volumes. Computerized library services include interlibrary loans, database searching, Internet access, and Wi-Fi capability. Special learning facilities include an art gallery, planetarium, radio station, TV station, the Museum of Biological Diversity, the John Glenn Institute for Public Service and Public Policy, and the Cartoon Research Library. **Physically Challenged Students:** All of the campus is accessible. Facilities include wheelchair ramps, elevators, special parking, special class scheduling, lowered drinking fountains, and lowered telephones. **Special:** Students may cross-register with all central Ohio colleges. OSU-Columbus offers internships, co-op programs, extensive study abroad in about 40 countries, work-study programs, dual and student-designed majors, a general degree, an accelerated degree, credit by exam, nondegree study, and pass/fail options. There are 60 national honor societies, including Phi Beta Kappa, a freshman honors program, and 15 departmental honors programs. **Visiting:** There are regularly scheduled orientations for prospective students, including campus tours, placement tests, course scheduling, and special sessions designed for parents. There are guides for informal visits, visitors may sit in on classes, and stay overnight. To schedule a visit, contact the Student Visitor Center at campusvisit.osu.edu. **Campus Safety and Security:** Measures include 24-hour foot and vehicle patrol, emergency notification system, self-defense education, and security escort services. There are shuttle buses, emergency telephones, lighted pathways/sidewalks, controlled access to dorms/residences, crisis action teams, and off-campus patrols in cooperation with the city police.

REQUIREMENTS: The SAT or ACT is required. Applicants must complete high school with at least 19 academic credits, including 4 in English, 3 each in math and science, 2 each in foreign language and history or social studies, and 1 in art or music. The GED is accepted. AP and CLEP credits are accepted. Important factors in the admissions decision are advanced placement or honors courses, evidence of special talent, and extracurricular activities record. To graduate, students must complete 120 or more semester hours, depending on major, including 30 to 40 in the major, with a minimum GPA of 2.0. The core curriculum consists of courses in writing skills, quantitative and logical skills, foreign language, the sciences, math, and the arts. **Procedure:** Freshmen are admitted fall and spring. Entrance exams should be taken by October of the senior year. There are deferred admissions and rolling admissions plans. Applications should be filed by February 1 for fall entry; October 1 for spring entry. The fall 2017 application fee was $60. Notifications are sent March 31. 5051 applicants were on the 2017 waiting list; 852 were admitted. Applications are accepted on-line. **Transfer Students:** 3373 transfer students enrolled in 2016-2017. High school graduates with 30 semester hours of college credit and a minimum GPA of 2.0 are considered for admission. Admission standards to selected majors vary and can be higher than the 2.0 minimum. Admission of transfer students is competitive based on the applicant pool. 30 of 120 credits required for the bachelor's degree must be completed at OSU-Columbus. **International Students:** There are 3554 international students enrolled. They must take the TOEFL with a minimum score of 550 on the paper-based TOEFL (PBT) or 79 on the Internet-based version (iBT). They must also take the SAT or ACT.

ADMISSIONS: 48% of the 2017-2018 applicants were accepted. The SAT scores for the 2017-2018 freshman class were: Math-- 1% below 500, 14% between 500 and 599, 44% between 600 and 699, and 41% between 700 and 800. Evidence-Based Reading/Writing-- 2% below 500,

11% between 500 and 599, 55% between 600 and 699, and 32% between 700 and 800. The ACT scores were 1% between 12 and 17, 6% between 18 and 23, 41% between 24 and 29, and 52% above 30. 90% of the current freshmen were in the top fifth of their class; 98% were in the top two fifths. 361 freshmen graduated first in their class. **Admissions Contact:** Undergraduate Admissions Email: *askabuckeye@osu.edu* Web: *www.osu.edu*

FINANCIAL AID: In 2017-2018, 86% of all full-time freshmen received some form of financial aid. 40% of all full-time freshmen received need-based aid. The average freshman award was $16,078. Need-based scholarships or need-based grants averaged $7,754 ($26,625 maximum); need-based self-help aid (loans and jobs) averaged $4,215 ($8,500 maximum); non-need-based athletic scholarships averaged $24,455 ($57,600 maximum); and other non-need-based awards and non-need-based scholarships averaged $11,402 ($52,500 maximum). The average financial indebtedness of the 2017 graduate was $28,158. The CCS/Profile, FAFSA, or FFS, or SFS are required. The FAFSA code is 003090. The priority date for freshman financial aid applications for fall entry is February 1.

OHIO STATE UNIVERSITY AT LIMA B-2
www.lima.osu.edu

Lima, OH 45804 (419) 995-8391

Email: lima-askabuckeye@osu.edu

Full-time: 369 men, 475 women
Part-time: 64 men, 99 women
Graduate: 1 men, 10 women
Year: semesters, summer session
Room & Board: n/app
SAT EBR-W/M: 550/590 **ACT:** 23
Application Deadline: June 1

Faculty: 32; IIB, +$
Ph.D.s: n/av
Student/Faculty: n/av
Tuition: $7553 ($26,657)
Freshman Class: 1294 applied, 1282 accepted, 325 enrolled
CEEB CODE: 1541
COMPETITIVE

Ohio State University at Lima develops leaders and provides access to the resources and strength of the state's top university. OSU-Lima students earn their degrees from the No. 1 public university in the state, leveraging a Big 10 quality education with the affordability of a regional campus. Offering 11 bachelors degree programs, 4 degree completion programs and access to the 200 plus Ohio State majors, our students find a unique campus spirit with a truly personalized academic experience. There is 1 undergraduate school. In addition to regional accreditation, OSU-Lima has baccalaureate program accreditation with AACSB, ABET, ACCE, ACPE, ADA, APTA, ASLA, CAHEA, CSAB, CSWE, FIDER, NAAB, NASAD, NASM, and CAEP. The 562-acre campus is in a suburban area 3 miles east of Lima, OH. Including any residence halls, there are 13 buildings.

STUDENT LIFE: 99% of undergraduates are from Ohio. Others are from 7 states, and 1 foreign country. 94% are from public schools. 83% are White; 4% African American; 4% Hispanic; 4% two or more races; 3% race unknown; 2% Asian American. **Female To Male Ratio:** 1.3:1. The average age of freshmen is 18; all undergraduates, 21. 36% do not continue beyond their first year; 65% remain to graduate. Alcohol is not permitted. All students may keep cars.

FACULTY/CLASSROOMS: 43% of faculty are male; 57% are female. No introductory courses are taught by graduate students. The average class size in an introductory lecture is 19; in a laboratory is 18; and in a regular course is 24.

PROGRAMS OF STUDY: OSU-Lima confers B.A., B.S., and B.S.Ed. degrees. Associate and master's degrees are also awarded. Bachelor's degrees are awarded in BIOLOGICAL SCIENCE (biology/biological science), BUSINESS (business administration and management), COMMUNICATIONS AND THE ARTS (English and theatre arts), EDUCATION (education), HEALTH PROFESSIONS (dental hygiene, health science, and nursing), SOCIAL SCIENCE (history, psychology, and social work). Biology, psychology, and social work have the largest enrollments.

ACTIVITIES: There are no fraternities or sororities. There are 29 groups on campus, including choir, chorale, chorus, dance, drama, environmental, honors, international, LGBT, literary magazine, musical theater, political, professional, religious, social, social service, and student government. **Sports:** There are 3 intercollegiate sports for men and 3 for women, and 9 intramural sports for men and 9 for women. Facilities include a gymnasium, sand volleyball court, and intramural field. **Graduates:** In an average class, 1% graduate in 3 years or less, 18% graduate in 4 years or less, 36% graduate in 5 years or less, and 38% graduate in 6 years or less.

SERVICES: Counseling and information services are available, as is tutoring in some subjects. **Library/Resources:** The library contains 5.1 million volumes. Computerized library services include interlibrary loans, database searching, Internet access, and Wi-Fi capability. Special learning facilities include an art gallery, a greenhouse, geology museum, nature preserve, and observatory. **Physically Challenged Students:** 98% of the campus is accessible. Facilities include wheelchair ramps, elevators, special parking, specially equipped restrooms, and lowered drinking fountains. **Special:** Students may cross-register with all central Ohio colleges. OSU-Lima offers internships, co-op programs, extensive study abroad in about 40 countries, work-study programs, dual and student-designed majors, a general degree, an accelerated degree, credit by exam, nondegree study, and pass/fail options. There is a freshman honors program and 6 departmental honors programs. **Visiting:** There are regularly scheduled orientations for prospective students, including meetings with Admissions and Financial Aid counselors, campus tour, and special programs. There are guides for informal visits and visitors may sit in on classes. To schedule a visit, contact the Office of Admissions. **Campus Safety and Security:** Measures include emergency notification system. There are lighted pathways/sidewalks.

REQUIREMENTS: There is an open admission policy for in-state students. Applicants must complete high school and should have 4 credits in English, 3 each in math and science, 2 each in foreign language and history or social studies, and 1 in art or music. The GED is accepted. AP and CLEP credits are accepted. To graduate, all students must complete an average of 120 semester hours, with a minimum GPA of 2.0, and fulfill the general education curriculum requirements. **Procedure:** Freshmen are admitted fall, spring, and summer. Entrance exams should be taken October of Senior Year. There is a rolling admissions plan. Application deadlines are open. The fall 2017 application fee was $60. Applications are accepted on-line. **Transfer Students:** 101 transfer students enrolled in 2016-2017. Students must be a high school graduate with a minimum college GPA of 2.0. 30 of 120 credits required for the bachelor's degree must be completed at OSU-Lima. **International Students:** There are 2 international students enrolled. They must take the TOEFL. They must also take the SAT or ACT.

ADMISSIONS: 99% of the 2017-2018 applicants were accepted. The SAT scores for the 2017-2018 freshman class were: Math-- 22% below 500, 45% between 500 and 599, and 33% between 600 and 699. Evidence-Based Reading/Writing-- 22% below 500, 56% between 500 and 599, and 22% between 600 and 699. The ACT scores were 9% between 12 and 17, 49% between 18 and 23, 39% between 24 and 29, and 3% above 30. 25% of the current freshmen were in the top fifth of their class; 57% were in the top two fifths. 3 freshmen graduated first in their class. **Admissions Contact:** Undergraduate Admissions and First Year Experience. Email: *lima-askabuckeye@osu.edu* Web: *www.lima.osu.edu*

FINANCIAL AID: In 2017-2018, 96% of all full-time freshmen received some form of financial aid. 74% of all full-time freshmen received need-based aid. The average freshman award was $9,668. Need-based scholarships or need-based grants averaged $3,956 ($8,241 maximum); need-based self-help aid (loans and jobs) averaged $4,083 ($9,500 maximum); and $4,442 from other forms of aid. The CCS/Profile, FAFSA, FFS, or SFS are required. The FAFSA code is 003090. The priority date for freshman financial aid applications for fall entry is February 1.

OHIO STATE UNIVERSITY AT MANSFIELD C-2
www.mansfield.osu.edu

Mansfield, OH 44906 (419) 755-4317

Email: askabuckeye@osu.edu

Full-time: 423 men, 449 women
Part-time: 95 men, 89 women
Graduate: 1 men, 4 women
Year: semesters, summer session
Room & Board: $7976
SAT EBR-W/M: 570/560 **ACT:** 23
Application Deadline: June 1

Faculty: 37; IIB, av$
Ph.D.s: n/av
Student/Faculty: n/av
Tuition: $7553 ($26,657)
Freshman Class: 1770 applied, 1758 accepted, 444 enrolled
CEEB CODE: 0744
COMPETITIVE

Ohio State University at Mansfield, founded in 1958, is a regional campus of the Ohio State University system. There is 1 undergraduate school. In addition to regional accreditation, OSU- Mansfield has baccalaureate program accreditation with AACSB, ABET, ACCE, ACPE, ADA, APTA, ASLA, CAHEA, CSAB, CSWE, FIDER, NAAB, NASAD, NASM, and CAEP. The 620-acre campus is in a suburban area 2 miles from Mansfield, OH. Including any residence halls, there are 32 buildings.

STUDENT LIFE: 99% of undergraduates are from Ohio. Others are from 6 states, 1 foreign country, and Canada. 93% are from public schools. 9% are African American; 78% White; 4% Hispanic; 3% two or more races; 3% race unknown; 2% Asian American. **Female To Male Ratio:** 1.0:1. The average age of freshmen is 18; all undergraduates, 21. 32% do not continue beyond their first year; 68% remain to graduate. **Housing:** 197 students can be accommodated in college housing, which includes single-sex on-campus apartments. On-campus housing is available on a first-come and first-served basis. 70% of students commute. All students may keep cars.

FACULTY/CLASSROOMS: 43% of faculty are male; 57% are female. No introductory courses are taught by graduate students. The average class size in an introductory lecture is 21; in a laboratory is 16; and in a regular course is 15.

PROGRAMS OF STUDY: OSU-Mansfield confers B.A., B.S., B.S.Ed., B.S.N., and B.S.S.W. degrees. Associate and master's degrees are also awarded. Bachelor's degrees are awarded in BUSINESS (business administration and management), COMMUNICATIONS AND THE ARTS (English), EDUCATION (early childhood education, elementary education, and middle level education), HEALTH PROFESSIONS (nursing), SOCIAL SCIENCE (criminal justice, criminology, history, psychology, social work, and sociology). Psychology, social work, and criminology & criminal justice have the largest enrollments.

ACTIVITIES: There are no fraternities or sororities. There are 17 groups on campus, including cheerleading, choir, computers, drama, ethnic, forensics, honors, LGBT, musical theater, political, professional, religious, and social service. Popular campus events include Tuesday Afternoon Get Togethers, Trunk or Treat, Thanksgiving Dinner, and Dances. **Sports:** There are 2 intercollegiate sports for men and 2 for women, and 8 intramural sports for men and 8 for women. Facilities include a single building which houses a gym, weight room, cardio area, multi purpose field for intramural sports and a tennis court.**Graduates:** In an average class, 1% graduate in 3 years or less, 21% graduate in 4 years or less, 38% graduate in 5 years or less, and 44% graduate in 6 years or less.

SERVICES: Counseling and information services are available, as is tutoring in most subjects. There is remedial math, reading, and writing. **Library/Resources:** The library contains 5.1 million volumes. Computerized library services include interlibrary loans, database searching, Internet access, and Wi-Fi capability. Special learning facilities include a TV station. **Physically Challenged Students:** All of the campus is accessible. Facilities include wheelchair ramps, elevators, special parking, specially equipped restrooms, and lowered drinking fountains. **Special:** Students may cross-register with all central Ohio colleges. OSU-Mansfield offers internships, co-op programs, extensive study abroad in about 40 countries, work-study programs, dual and student-designed majors, a general degree, an accelerated degree, credit by exam, nondegree study, and pass/fail options. **Visiting:** There are regularly scheduled orientations for prospective students. There are guides for informal visits, visitors may sit in on classes, and stay overnight. To schedule a visit, contact The Student Visitor Center at (419) 755-4317. **Campus Safety and Security:** Measures include 24-hour foot and vehicle patrol, emergency notification system, and security escort services. There are lighted pathways/sidewalks and controlled access to dorms/residences.

REQUIREMENTS: There is an open admission policy for in-state students. Applicants must complete high school and should have 4 credits in English, 3 each in math and science, 2 each in foreign language and history or social studies, and 1 in art or music. The GED is accepted. AP and CLEP credits are accepted. To graduate, students must complete 120 or more semester hours, including 30 or more in the major, with a minimum GPA of 2.0. The core curriculum consists of courses in writing skills, quantitative and logical skills, foreign language, the sciences, math, and the arts. **Procedure:** Freshmen are admitted fall, spring, and summer. Entrance exams should be taken By October of senior year. There is a rolling admissions plan. Application deadlines are open. The fall 2017 application fee was $60. Applications are accepted on-line. **Transfer Students:** 113 transfer students enrolled in 2016-2017. Student must be a high school graduate with a minimum college GPA of 2.0. 30 of 120 credits required for the bachelor's degree must be completed at OSU-Mansfield. **International Students:** There is 1 international student enrolled. They must also take the SAT or ACT.

ADMISSIONS: 99% of the 2017-2018 applicants were accepted. The SAT scores for the 2017-2018 freshman class were: Math-- 30% below 500, 30% between 500 and 599, 38% between 600 and 699, and 2% between 700 and 800. Evidence-Based Reading/Writing-- 16% below 500, 46% between 500 and 599, and 38% between 600 and 699. The ACT scores were 10% between 12 and 17, 48% between 18 and 23, 39% between 24 and 29, and 3% above 30. 22% of the current freshmen were in the top fifth of their class; 53% were in the top two fifths. 2 freshmen graduated first in their class. **Admissions Contact:** Undergraduate Admissions and First Year Experience. Email: *askabuckeye@osu.edu* Web: *www.mansfield.osu.edu*

FINANCIAL AID: In 2017-2018, 94% of all full-time freshmen received some form of financial aid. 71% of all full-time freshmen received need-based aid. The average freshman award was $11,776. Need-based scholarships or need-based grants averaged $4,910 ($8,241 maximum); need-based self-help aid (loans and jobs) averaged $4,333 ($7,500 maximum); and other non-need-based awards and non-need-based scholarships averaged $5,577 ($22,716 maximum). OSU-Mansfield is a member of CSS. The CCS/Profile, FAFSA, FFS, or SFS are required. The FAFSA code is 003090. The priority date for freshman financial aid applications for fall entry is February 1.

OHIO STATE UNIVERSITY AT MARION C-3
www.osu.edu

Marion, OH 43302 (740) 389-6786

Email: askabuckeye@osu.edu

Full-time: 481 men, 497 women
Part-time: 88 men, 128 women
Graduate: 4 women
Year: semesters, summer session
Room & Board: n/app

Faculty: 36; IIB, +$
Ph.D.s: n/av
Student/Faculty: n/av
Tuition: $7553 ($26,657)
Freshman Class: 1025 applied, 1012 accepted, 437 enrolled

SAT EBR-W/M: 590/575 **ACT:** required

CEEB CODE: 0751

Application Deadline: June 1

VERY COMPETITIVE

Ohio State University at Marion, founded in 1957, is a commuter campus of the Ohio State University system. Students may earn a bachelor's degree in elementary education, English, history, business management, and psychology as well as 1 to 3 years of credit applicable to any other degree, including more than 170 academic programs, conferred by OSU, provided the program is completed at the main campus in Columbus. There is 1 undergraduate school. In addition to regional accreditation, OSU-Marion has baccalaureate program accreditation with AACSB, ABET, ACCE, ACPE, ADA, APTA, ASLA, CAHEA, CSAB, CSWE, FIDER, NAAB, NASAD, NASM, and CAEP. The 188-acre campus is in a rural area 45 miles north of Columbus, OH. Including any residence halls, there are 16 buildings.

STUDENT LIFE: 99% of undergraduates are from Ohio. Others are from 4 states, 2 foreign countries, and Canada. 98% are from public schools. 81% are White; 4% Asian American; 4% Hispanic; 4% two or more races; 4% race unknown; 3% African American; 1% American Indian/Alaska Native. **Female To Male Ratio:** 1.1:1. The average age of freshmen is 19; all undergraduates, 21. 30% do not continue beyond their first year; 70% remain to graduate. **Housing:** On-campus housing is available on a first-come and first-served basis. Alcohol is not permitted. All students commute. All students may keep cars.

FACULTY/CLASSROOMS: 47% of faculty are male; 53% are female. No introductory courses are taught by graduate students. The average class size in an introductory lecture is 19; in a laboratory is 18; and in a regular course is 24.

PROGRAMS OF STUDY: OSU-Marion confers B.A., B.S., and B.S.Ed. degrees. Associate degrees are also awarded. Bachelor's degrees are awarded in BIOLOGICAL SCIENCE (biology/biological science), BUSINESS (business administration and management), COMMUNICATIONS AND THE ARTS (English), EDUCATION (education and elementary education), HEALTH PROFESSIONS (nursing), SOCIAL SCIENCE (history, psychology, and social work). Biology, psychology, and social work have the largest enrollments.

ACTIVITIES: There are no fraternities or sororities. There are 31 groups on campus, including art, choir, computers, debate, environmental, ethnic, honors, international, LGBT, literary magazine, musical theater, newspaper, political, religious, social, social service, and student government. **Sports:** There are 2 intramural sports for men and 1 for women. Facilities include a gym, weight room, indoor rock climbing wall, aerobic room, pool tables, ping pong table, air hockey, and outdoor volleyball. **Graduates:** In an average class, 1% graduate in 3 years or less, 16% graduate in 4 years or less, 35% graduate in 5 years or less, and 42% graduate in 6 years or less.

SERVICES: Counseling and information services are available, as is tutoring in most subjects. There is remedial math, reading, and writing. **Library/Resources:** The library contains 5.1 million volumes. Computerized library services include interlibrary loans, database searching, Internet access, and Wi-Fi capability. Special learning facilities include an art gallery, planetarium, TV station, natural prairie site, greenhouse, psychology lab, and early childhood education center. **Physically Challenged Students:** All of the campus is accessible. Facilities include wheelchair ramps, elevators, special parking, specially equipped restrooms, and lowered drinking fountains. **Special:** OSU-Marion offers cross-registration with Ohio State University Columbus, various co-op and work-study programs, nondegree study in continuing education, and pass/fail options. There is a freshman honors program and 4 departmental honors programs. **Visiting:** There are regularly scheduled orientations for prospective students. There are guides for informal visits and visitors may sit in on classes. To schedule a visit, contact the Student Visitor Center at (740) 725-6242. **Campus Safety and Security:** Measures include emergency notification system and security escort services. There are emergency telephones and lighted pathways/sidewalks.

REQUIREMENTS: There is an open admission policy for in-state students. Applicants must complete high school and should have 4 credits in English, 3 each in math and science, 2 each in foreign language and history or social studies, and 1 in art or music. The GED is accepted. AP and CLEP credits are accepted. To graduate, students must complete 120 or more semester hours, including 30 or more in the major, with a minimum GPA of 2.0. The core curriculum consists of courses in writing skills, quantitative and logical skills, foreign language, the sciences, math, and the arts. **Procedure:** Freshmen are admitted fall and summer. Entrance exams should be taken October of senior year. There is a rolling admissions plan. Application deadlines are open. The fall 2017 application fee was $60. Applications are accepted on-line. **Transfer Students:** 122 transfer students enrolled in 2016-2017. Student must be a high school graduate with a minimum college GPA of 2.0. 30 of 120 credits required for the bachelor's degree must be completed at OSU-Marion. **International Students:** There are 3 international students enrolled. They must take the TOEFL. They must also take the SAT or ACT.

ADMISSIONS: 99% of the 2017-2018 applicants were accepted. The SAT scores for the 2017-2018 freshman class were: Math-- 12% below 500, 42% between 500 and 599, 38% between 600 and 699, and 8% between 700 and 800. Evidence-Based Reading/Writing-- 8% below 500, 42% between 500 and 599, 46% between 600 and 699, and 4% between 700 and 800. The ACT scores were 12% between 12 and 17, 49% between 18 and 23, 37% between 24 and 29, and 2% above 30. 23% of the current freshmen were in the top fifth of their class; 57% were in the top two fifths. 3 freshmen graduated first in their class. **Admissions Contact:** Undergraduate Admissions and First Year Experience. Email: *askabuckeye@osu.edu* Web: *www.osu.edu*

FINANCIAL AID: In 2017-2018, 94% of all full-time freshmen received some form of financial aid. 62% of all full-time freshmen received need-based aid. The average freshman award was $9,842. Need-based scholarships or need-based grants averaged $4,228 ($8,241 maximum); need-based self-help aid (loans and jobs) averaged $4,079 ($7,500 maximum); and other non-need-based awards and non-need-based scholarships averaged $5,070 ($22,716 maximum). The CCS/Profile, FAFSA, FFS, or SFS are required. The FAFSA code is 003090. The priority date for freshman financial aid applications for fall entry is February 1.

OHIO STATE UNIVERSITY AT NEWARK C-3

www.newark.osu.edu

Newark, OH 43055 **(740) 366-3321**

Email: askabuckeye@osu.edu

Full-time: 1105 men, 1113 women
Part-time: 188 men, 201 women
Graduate: 2 men, 14 women
Year: semesters, summer session
Room & Board: $9132

SAT EBR-W/M: 550/550 **ACT:** 22
Application Deadline: June 1

Faculty: 47; IIB, +$
Ph.D.s: n/av
Student/Faculty: n/av
Tuition: $7553 ($26,657)
Freshman Class: 3665 applied, 3632 accepted, 1369 enrolled
CEEB CODE: 0824
COMPETITIVE

Ohio State University at Newark, founded in 1957, is a regional public commuter campus of the Ohio State University system. Students may earn a bachelor's degree in elementary education, psychology, history, or English as well as 1 to 3 years of credit applicable to any other degree, including 219 academic programs, conferred by OSU, provided the program is completed at the main campus in Columbus. In addition to regional accreditation, OSU-Newark has baccalaureate program accreditation with AACSB, ABET, ACCE, ACPE, ADA, APTA, ASLA, CAHEA, CSAB, CSWE, FIDER, NAAB, NASAD, NASM, and CAEP. The 111-acre campus is in a suburban area 40 miles east of Columbus, OH. Including any residence halls, there are 21 buildings.

STUDENT LIFE: 100% of undergraduates are from Ohio. Others are from 9 states, and 1 foreign country. 93% are from public schools. 69% are White; 4% Asian American; 4% two or more races; 4% race unknown; 3% Hispanic; 15% African American. **Female To Male Ratio:** 1.0:1. The average age of freshmen is 18; all undergraduates, 20. 32% do not continue beyond their first year; 68% remain to graduate. **Housing:** 310 students can be accommodated in college housing, which includes gender neutral, single sex and coed dorms, and on-campus apartments. On-campus housing is available on a lottery system for upperclassmen. 88% of students commute. All students may keep cars.

FACULTY/CLASSROOMS: 48% of faculty are male; 52% are female. No introductory courses are taught by graduate students. The average class size in an introductory lecture is 27; in a laboratory is 18; and in a regular course is 21.

PROGRAMS OF STUDY: OSU-Newark confers B.A., B.S., B.S.N., and B.S.Ed. degrees. Associate and master's degrees are also awarded. Bachelor's degrees are awarded in BUSINESS (business administration and management), COMMUNICATIONS AND THE ARTS (English), EDUCATION (early childhood education and elementary education), HEALTH PROFESSIONS (nursing), SOCIAL SCIENCE (history, psychology, and social work). Psychology, biology, and social work have the largest enrollments.

ACTIVITIES: There are no fraternities or sororities. There are 34 groups on campus, including art, band, choir, chorus, computers, drama, environmental, ethnic, honors, international, LGBT, musical theater, pep band, political, professional, religious, social, social service, and student government. Popular campus events include Welcome Week, Convocation, Fall Festival, Family & Friends Day, Black Heritage Dinner, and Career Fair. **Sports:** There is no sports program at OSU-Newark. Facilities include a cardio room, weight room, a gym, a baseball field and other outdoor areas. **Graduates:** In an average class, 1% graduate in 3 years or less, 15% graduate in 4 years or less, 32% graduate in 5 years or less, and 37% graduate in 6 years or less.

SERVICES: Counseling and information services are available, as is tutoring in most subjects. There is remedial math and writing. **Library/Resources:** The library contains 5.1 million volumes. Computerized library services include interlibrary loans, database searching, Internet access, and Wi-Fi capability. Special learning facilities include an art gallery. **Physically Challenged Students:** All of the campus is accessible. Facilities include wheelchair ramps, elevators, special parking, specially equipped restrooms, and lowered drinking fountains. **Special:** Co-op programs and internships are available in some majors, and study abroad is available in some departments. Cross-registration is possible with Central Ohio Technical College and HECC member schools, and there is work-study with Ohio State. B.A.-B.S. degrees are offered in early childhood and middle childhood education, child and youth studies, business management, English, history, psychology, social work, and nursing.

Dual and student-designed majors and nondegree study are possible, and pass/fail options are available. There are 2 national honor societies, a freshman honors program, and 4 departmental honors programs. **Visiting:** There are regularly scheduled orientations for prospective students, campus tours, placement tests, course scheduling, and special sessions. There are guides for informal visits, visitors may sit in on classes, and stay overnight. To schedule a visit, contact the Student Visitor Center at (740) 366-9333. **Campus Safety and Security:** Measures include 24-hour foot and vehicle patrol, emergency notification system, self-defense education, and security escort services. There are emergency telephones and lighted pathways/sidewalks.

REQUIREMENTS: There is an open admission policy for in-state students. Applicants must complete high school and should have 4 credits in English, 3 each in math and science, 2 each in foreign language and history or social studies, and 1 in art or music. The GED is accepted. AP and CLEP credits are accepted. To graduate, students must complete 120 or more semester hours, including 30 or more in the major, with a minimum GPA of 2.0. The core curriculum consists of courses in writing skills, quantitative and logical skills, foreign language, the sciences, math, and the arts. **Procedure:** Freshmen are admitted fall and spring. Entrance exams should be taken October of Senior Year. There is a rolling admissions plan. Applications should be filed by June 1 for fall entry; November 1 for winter entry; and March 1 for spring entry. The fall 2017 application fee was $60. Notifications are sent in November. Applications are accepted on-line. **Transfer Students:** 247 transfer students enrolled in 2016-2017. Student must be a high school graduate with a minimum college GPA of 2.0. 30 of 120 credits required for the bachelor's degree must be completed at OSU Newark. **International Students:** There are 3 international students enrolled. They must take the TOEFL.

ADMISSIONS: 99% of the 2017-2018 applicants were accepted. The SAT scores for the 2017-2018 freshman class were: Math-- 18% below 500, 55% between 500 and 599, 26% between 600 and 699, and 1% between 700 and 800. Evidence-Based Reading/Writing-- 20% below 500, 51% between 500 and 599, 27% between 600 and 699, and 2% between 700 and 800. The ACT scores were 13% between 12 and 17, 50% between 18 and 23, 35% between 24 and 29, and 2% above 30. 17% of the current freshmen were in the top fifth of their class; 49% were in the top two fifths. 1 freshman graduated first in the class. **Admissions Contact:** Undergraduate Admissions and First Year Experience. Email: *askabuckeye@osu.edu* Web: *www.newark.osu.edu*

FINANCIAL AID: In 2017-2018, 90% of all full-time freshmen received some form of financial aid. 65% of all full-time freshmen received need-based aid. The average freshman award was $10,598. Need-based scholarships or need-based grants averaged $4,800 ($8,241 maximum); need-based self-help aid (loans and jobs) averaged $4,303 ($7,500 maximum); and other non-need-based awards and non-need-based scholarships averaged $5,032 ($25,000 maximum). The CCS/Profile, FAFSA, FFS, SFS or required. The FAFSA code is 003090. The priority date for freshman financial aid applications for fall entry is February 1.

OHIO UNIVERSITY — D-4

www.ohio.edu

Athens, OH 45701 — **(740) 593-4100**

Fax: (740) 593-0560	**Email: admissions@ohio.edu**
Full-time: 8324 men, 9478 women	**Faculty:** 994; I, -$
Part-time: 1061 men, 4460 women	**Ph.D.s:** 81%
Graduate: 3079 men, 3123 women	**Student/Faculty:** 18 to 1
Year: semesters, summer session	**Tuition:** $11,896 ($21,360)
Room & Board: $11,498	**Freshman Class:** 26263 applied, 19416 accepted, 4045 enrolled
SAT EBR-W/M: 590/580 **ACT:** 24	**CEEB CODE:** 1593
Application Deadline: December 1	**VERY COMPETITIVE**

Ohio University, founded in 1804, is a public university offering approximately 250 areas of undergraduate study. On the graduate level, the university grants master's degrees in nearly all of its major academic divisions and doctoral degrees in selected departments. The university strives to be a "home away from home" for its students, with a welcoming atmosphere and supportive professors who are both teachers and mentors. There are 9 undergraduate schools and 11 graduate schools. In addition to regional accreditation, Ohio University has baccalaureate program accreditation with AACSB, ABET, ACEJMC, CSWE, NASM, NRPA, AAFCS, ACEN, ACEND, ACS, APA, ARC-PA, ATMAE, CAAHEP, CAATE, CACREP, CAPTE, CCA, CCNE, CEPH, COAPRT, COCA, CORE, COSMA, FEPAC, NAB, NASD, NAST, NEHA, OBN, PATH, and UCIEP. The 1800-acre campus is in a small town 75 miles southeast of Columbus. Including any residence halls, there are 209 buildings.

STUDENT LIFE: 83% of undergraduates are from Ohio. Others are from 44 states, 72 foreign countries, and Canada. 83% are from public schools. 83% are White; 6% African American; 3% Hispanic; 3% two or more races; 2% Foreign; 2% race unknown; 1% Asian American. 43% are Protestant; 30% Catholic; 19% claim no religious affiliation. **Female To Male Ratio:** 1.4:1. The average age of freshmen is 19; all undergraduates, 21. 20% do not continue beyond their first year; 63% remain to graduate. **Housing:** 8100 students can be accommodated in college housing, which includes gender neutral and single sex and coed dorms. In addition, there are honors houses, special-interest houses, fraternity houses, and sorority houses. On-campus housing is guaranteed for the freshman year only and is available on a lottery system for upperclassmen. 10% of students commute. Upperclassmen may keep cars.

FACULTY/CLASSROOMS: 54% of faculty are male; 46% are female. All teach undergraduates, 79% do research, and 79% do both. Graduate students teach 11% of introductory courses. The average class size in an introductory lecture is 51; in a laboratory is 20; and in a regular course is 33.

PROGRAMS OF STUDY: Ohio University confers A.B., B.A., B.A.H.C.S., B.B.A., B.C.J., B.F.A., B.Mus., B.S., B.S.A., B.S.A.M., B.S.A.T., B.S.C., B.S.C.E., B.S.C.F.S., B.S.Ch.E., B.S.C.S., B.S.C.S.D., B.S.Ed., B.S.E.E., B.S.E.H., B.S.E.N.E.N.G., B.S.E.T.M, B.S.F.N.S., B.S.G.S., B.S.H., B.S.H.C.S., B.S.I.H.S., B.S.I.S.E., B.S.J., B.S.M., B.S.M.E., B.S.N., B.S.O.H.S., B.S.T.O.M., B.S.P.E., B.S.P.E.X., B.S.R.S., B.S.S., B.S.S.L.S., B.S.V.C., B.S.W., B.T.A.S., B.S.T.R.A.N.H. and B.F.A.-DA. degrees. Associate, master's, and doctoral degrees are also awarded. Bachelor's degrees are awarded in BIOLOGICAL SCIENCE (biochemistry, biology/biological science, biotechnology, botany, cell biology, ecology, environmental biology, life science, marine biology, microbiology, molecular biology, neurosciences, nutrition, wildlife biology, and zoology), BUSINESS (accounting, banking and finance, business administration and management, business economics, business law, entrepreneurial studies, fashion merchandising, finance, hotel/motel and restaurant management, international business management, management information systems, management science, management & strategic leadership, marketing management, recreation and leisure services, recreational facilities management, retailing, sports management, and tourism), COMMUNICATIONS AND THE ARTS (acting, art history, art, audio technology, broadcasting, ceramic art and design, choral music, classics, communications, communications technology, creative writing, dance, design, digital communications, digital media, dramatic arts, English, film arts, French, German, graphic design, Greek, Greek (classical), illustration, instrumental music education, journalism, journalism-magazine journalism, journalism-news & information, journalism-newswriting/edit, language arts, Latin, linguistics, literature, media arts, media management, modern language, multimedia, music, music composition, music history and appreciation, music performance, music theory and composition, painting, performing arts, photography, piano/organ, piano pedagogy, playwriting/screenwriting, printmaking, public relations, radio/television technology, Russian, sculpture, Spanish, speech/debate/rhetoric, stage management, sports administration, sport & lifestyle studies, studio art, telecommunications, theater design, theater management, video, visual and performing arts, vocal performance, and voice), COMPUTER AND PHYSICAL SCIENCE (actuarial science, applied mathematics, applied physics, astrophysics, atmospheric sciences and meteorology, chemistry, computer science, digital arts/technology, earth science, environmental chemistry, environmental geology, geology, geoscience, mathematics, physics, and statistics), EDUCATION (athletic training, business education, early childhood education, global studies, mathematics education, music education, nutrition education, physical education, recreation education, science education, social studies education, special education, and technical & applied studies), ENGINEERING AND ENVIRONMENTAL DESIGN (airline piloting and navigation, aviation administration/management, bioengineering, chemical engineering, civil engineering, computer engineering, electrical and computer engineering, electrical/electronics engineering, energy management technology, engineering physics, engineering technology, environmental engineering, industrial engineering, interior design, materials engineering, mechanical engineering, and technical operations management), HEALTH PROFESSIONS (applied nutrition, community health work, environmental health science, exercise science, health care administration, human biology, industrial hygiene, music therapy, nursing, nursing home administration, occupational hygiene & safety, predentistry, premedicine, prepharmacy, prephysical therapy, public health, and sports medicine), SOCIAL SCIENCE (African American studies, anthropology, Asian/American studies, child care/child and family studies, classical/ancient civilization, communication sciences & disorders, community services, criminal justice, criminology, Eastern European studies, economics, European studies, family and community services, family/consumer resource management, family/consumer studies, forensic studies, gender studies, geography, geography information science, history, human development, international studies, Latin American studies, parks and recreation management, philosophy, political science/government, prelaw, psychology, public administration, religion, social work, sociology, urban and regional studies, urban studies, women & gender studies, and women's studies). Nursing, biological sciences, and journalism have the largest enrollments.

ACTIVITIES: 12% of men belong to 21 national fraternities; 17% of women belong to 14 national sororities. There are 524 groups on campus, including art, band, cheerleading, chess, choir, chorale, chorus, computers, dance, debate, drama, environmental, ethnic, film, forensics, honors, international, jazz band, LGBT, literary magazine, marching band, musical theater, newspaper, opera, orchestra, pep band, photography, political, professional, radio and TV, religious, social, social service, student government, symphony, and yearbook. Popular campus events include Performing Arts Series, Kennedy Lecture Series, University Program Council (UPC) and Black Student Cultural Programming Board. **Sports:** There are 6 intercollegiate sports for men and 10 for women, and 27 intramural sports for men and 27 for women. Facilities include a recreation center, a football stadium, a fieldhouse, a convocation center for basketball, volleyball, and wrestling, an aquatic center, ice rink, tennis courts, golf course, intramural gym, running track, fitness and aerobic center, baseball and softball stadiums, soccer field, field hockey, and outdoor recreation facilities. **Graduates:** From July 1, 2016 to June 30, 2017, 6720 bachelor's degrees were awarded. The most popular majors were nursing (40%), health administration (5%), and communication studies (4%). In an average class, 1% graduate in 3 years or less, 39% graduate in 4 years or less, 59% graduate in 5 years or less, and 63% graduate in 6 years or less. Of the 2016 graduating class, 29% were enrolled in graduate school within 6 months of graduation, and 86% were employed.

SERVICES: Counseling and information services are available, as is tutoring in most subjects. There is remedial math, reading, and writing. **Library/Resources:** The library contains 3.4 million volumes, 1.4 million microform items, and 87,762 audio/video tapes/CDs/DVDs, and subscribes to 82,599 periodicals including electronic. Computerized library services include interlibrary loans, database searching, Internet access, and Wi-Fi capability. Special learning facilities include an art gallery, radio station, TV station, a quarterly magazine, an accelerator lab, a hearing and speech and other wellness (physical & mental) clinics, integrated technology labs, specialized academic labs within buildings, land labs, recreational facilities and fields, maker space, 3D printer and observatory. **Physically Challenged Students:** 89% of the campus is accessible. Facilities include wheelchair ramps, elevators, special parking, specially equipped restrooms, special class scheduling, lowered drinking fountains, lowered telephones, and special housing. **Special:** The university offers co-op programs in engineering and computer science, internships, study abroad, work-study programs, and an accelerated degree program for students in the Honors Tutorial College. Students may earn a B.A. - B.S. degree in most arts and sciences majors, or a general studies degree. Dual and student-designed majors, non-degree study, limited pass/fail options, and credit for life, military, or work experience are also available. There are 10 national honor societies and a freshman honors program. **Visiting:** There are regularly scheduled orientations for prospective students, includes information session & campus tours daily and most Saturdays as well as special visit programs throughout the year. Visitors may sit in on classes. To schedule a visit, contact the Office of Undergraduate Admissions. **Campus Safety and Security:** Measures include 24-hour foot and vehicle patrol, emergency notification system, self-defense education, and security escort services. There are shuttle buses, emergency telephones, lighted pathways/sidewalks, and controlled access to dorms/residences.

REQUIREMENTS: The SAT or ACT is required. Applicants should graduate with 4 units each of English and math, 3 each of science and social studies, 2 of foreign language, and 5 academic electives (which includes 1 unit of visual/performing arts). Ohio University operates on holistic review and rolling admissions. Application, application fee, test scores and official transcripts are required for admission. AP and CLEP credits are accepted. Important factors in the admissions decision are advanced placement or honors courses, recommendations by school officials, and extracurricular activities record. Ohio University has two sets of graduation requirements: University-wide requirements, which all students must complete, and college-level requirements, which include the requirements for completing a major or minor. In general, you must have a minimum of 120 semester hours of credit for a bachelor's degree, with all other requirements met. All baccalaureate students (except Honors Tutorial College students) also must complete Ohio University's General Education requirements. Ohio University believes that, as an educated person, you need certain intellectual skills in order to participate effectively in society. These include the following: the ability to communicate effectively through the written word and the ability to use quantitative or symbolic reasoning, broad knowledge of the major fields of learning, and a capacity for evaluation and synthesis. **Procedure:** Freshmen are admitted fall, spring, and summer. Entrance exams should be taken in spring of the junior year or fall of the senior year. There are early admissions, deferred admissions, and rolling admissions plans. Check with the school for current application deadlines. The fall 2017 application fee was $50. Notifications are sent September 15. Applications are accepted on-line. **Transfer Students:** 461 transfer students enrolled in 2016-2017. Transfer students are evaluated individually, but must have a GPA of at least 2.0 and 20 semester hours of transferable college credit. Business and journalism majors usually require a GPA of 3.0 or higher. 30 of 120 credits required for the bachelor's degree must be completed at Ohio. **International Students:** There are 409 international students enrolled. They must take the TOEFL with a minimum score of 525 on the paper-based TOEFL (PBT) or 71 on the Internet-based version (iBT). Students must also take the IELTS.

ADMISSIONS: 74% of the 2017-2018 applicants were accepted. The SAT scores for the 2017-2018 freshman class were: Math-- 10% below 500, 52% between 500 and 599, 33% between 600 and 699, and 5% between 700 and 800. Evidence-Based Reading/Writing-- 9% below 500, 43% between 500 and 599, 42% between 600 and 699, and 6% between 700 and 800. The ACT scores were 1% between 12 and 17, 45% between 18 and 23, 46% between 24 and 29, and 8% above 30. 38% of the current freshmen were in the top fifth of their class; 70% were in the top two fifths. 66 freshmen graduated first in their class. **Admissions Contact:** Candace Boeninger, A.V. Provost for Enroll Management & Director of Admissions. Email: *admissions@ohio.edu* Web: *www.ohio.edu*

FINANCIAL AID: In 2017-2018, 91% of all full-time freshmen received some form of financial aid. 56% of all full-time freshmen received need-based aid. The average freshman award was $15,644. Need-based scholarships or need-based grants averaged $4,772 ($12,156 maximum); need-based self-help aid (loans and jobs) averaged $3,925 ($8,031 maximum); non-need-based athletic scholarships averaged $25,647 ($46,907 maximum); and other non-need-based awards and non-need-based scholarships averaged $10,975 ($31,878 maximum). 35% of undergraduate students work part-time. The average financial indebtedness of the 2017 graduate was $27,993. The FAFSA code is 003100. The priority date for freshman financial aid applications for fall entry is January 15.

OHIO WESLEYAN UNIVERSITY C-3

www.choose.owu.edu

Delaware, OH 43015 — **(740) 368-3020** / **(800) 922-8953**

Fax: (740) 368-3314 — **Email: owuadmit@owu.edu**

Full-time: 778 men, 846 women	**Faculty:** 134; IIB, +$
Part-time: 5 men, 10 women	**Ph.D.s:** 100%
Graduate: n/av	**Student/Faculty:** 10 to 1
Year: semesters, summer session	**Tuition:** $44,090
Room & Board: $11,770	**Freshman Class:** 3030 applied, 2823 accepted, 541 enrolled
SAT CR/M: 569/581 **ACT:** 26	**CEEB CODE:** 1594
Application Deadline: March 1	**VERY COMPETITIVE**

Ohio Wesleyan University, founded in 1842, is an independent liberal arts institution affiliated with the United Methodist Church. There is 1 undergraduate school. In addition to regional accreditation, OWU has baccalaureate program accreditation with NASM, CAEP, and ACS. The 200-acre campus is in a small town 20 miles north of Columbus. Including any residence halls, there are 55 buildings.

STUDENT LIFE: 53% of undergraduates are from Ohio. Others are from 41 states, 45 foreign countries, and Canada. 9% are African American; 69% White; 6% Foreign; 5% Hispanic; 5% two or more races; 3% Asian American; 3% race unknown. **Female To Male Ratio:** 1.1:1. The average age of freshmen is 18; all undergraduates, 20. 16% do not continue beyond their first year; 68% remain to graduate. **Housing:** 1720 students can be accommodated in college housing, which includes dorms and on-campus apartments. In addition, there are honors houses, language/international houses, special-interest houses, and fraternity houses. Students are invited to submit theme proposals to run a residential house for 10 to 15 students. On-campus housing is guaranteed for all 4 years. 90% of students live on campus. All students may keep cars.

FACULTY/CLASSROOMS: 56% of faculty are male; 44% are female. All teach undergraduates and all do research. No introductory courses are taught by graduate students. The average class size in an introductory lecture is 30; in a laboratory is 19; and in a regular course is 16.

PROGRAMS OF STUDY: OWU confers B.A., B.F.A., and B.M. degrees. Bachelor's degrees are awarded in BIOLOGICAL SCIENCE (biochemistry, biology/biological science, biological sciences, botany, genetics, microbiology, neurosciences, nutrition, and zoology), BUSINESS (accounting, business administration and management, business economics, international business, and international business management), COMMUNICATIONS AND THE ARTS (art history, art, art studies, classics, communications, creative writing, dance, dramatic arts, English, fine arts, French, German, German studies, journalism, music, music composition, music performance, Spanish, and theatre arts), COMPUTER AND PHYSICAL SCIENCE (chemistry, computer science, earth science, geology, mathematics, and physics), EDUCATION (art education, early childhood education, education, elementary education, foreign languages education, middle school education, music education, physical education, and science education), ENGINEERING AND ENVIRONMENTAL DESIGN (environmental science), HEALTH PROFESSIONS (biology, kinesiology, predentistry, premedicine, preoccupational therapy, and preveterinary science), SOCIAL SCIENCE (African American studies, anthropology, East Asian studies, economics, geography, history, international relations, philosophy, political science/government, prelaw, psychology, public administration, religion, social science, sociology, urban studies, and women's studies). Economics & business, biological sciences, and psychology have the largest enrollments.

ACTIVITIES: 40% of men belong to 8 national fraternities; 32% of women belong to 5 national sororities. There are 100 groups on campus, including art, cheerleading, chess, choir, chorale, chorus, communications, computers, dance, drama, ethnic, honors, international, jazz band, LGBT, literary magazine, musical theater, newspaper, opera, orchestra, pep band, political, professional, radio and TV, religious, social, social service, student government, symphony, and yearbook. Popular campus events include Sagan National Colloquium Fallfest, Black Family, and Alumni Weekend Celebration. **Sports:** There are 11 intercollegiate sports for men and 11 for women, and 17 intramural sports for men and 17 for women. Facilities include a gym, football and lacrosse stadium, field hockey, soccer, practice fields, a weight room, indoor and outdoor tracks, handball and squash courts, indoor pool, an exercise facility, and weight resistance equipment. **Graduates:** From July 1, 2016 to June 30, 2017, 471 bachelor's degrees were awarded. The most popular majors were biological science (12%), psychology (10%), and economics management (9%). In an average class, 1% graduate in 3 years or less, 61% graduate in 4 years or less, 67% graduate in 5 years or less, and 68% graduate in 6 years or less.

SERVICES: Counseling and information services are available, as is tutoring in most subjects. Students with learning disabilities may receive special help in writing, organization, and in quantitive areas. **Library/Resources:** The library contains 498,717 volumes, 98,574 microform items, and 4,789 audio/video tapes/CDs/DVDs, and subscribes to 18,478 periodicals including electronic. Computerized library services include interlibrary loans, database searching, Internet access, and Wi-Fi capability. Special learning facilities include an art gallery, radio station, an astronomical observatory. **Physically Challenged Students:** 60% of the campus is accessible. Facilities include wheelchair ramps, elevators, special parking, specially equipped restrooms, special class scheduling, lowered drinking fountains, lowered telephones, and special housing. **Special:** Cross-registration is available with members of the Great Lakes Colleges Association. Students may study abroad in 20 countries or participate in a Washington semester or a departmental internship. Students may also take dual majors in any combination, design their own majors, or pursue a 3-2 engineering degree in conjunction with 4 major universities. Nondegree study and pass/fail options are available. There are 27 national honor societies, Phi Beta Kappa, a freshman honors program, and 22 departmental honors programs. **Visiting:** There are regularly scheduled orientations for prospective students, the visit is approximately two hours and 15 minutes and includes a short presentation, a walking/riding tour of campus, and a conversation with an admission counselor. Optional class visit, meeting with a professor or coach, and/or lunch on campus available. To schedule a visit, contact the Office of Admission. **Campus Safety and Security:** Measures include 24-hour foot and vehicle patrol, emergency notification system, self-defense education, and security escort services. There are emergency telephones and lighted pathways/sidewalks.

REQUIREMENTS: The SAT or ACT is required. Candidates for admission should complete a recommended 4 units of English and 3 each of math, foreign language, social studies, and science. AP credits are accepted. Important factors in the admissions decision are advanced placement or honors courses, extracurricular activities record, and recommendations by school officials. Students are required to complete at least 34 units, including 3 units each of humanities/English, social sciences, and science, 2 units of foreign languages, and 1 unit of fine or performing arts. Each unit equals a full course and 3.75 semester hours. All students must also take 8 to 12 units in the major, maintain a minimum GPA of 2.0, and satisfy the university writing skills requirements. **Procedure:** Freshmen are admitted fall and spring. Entrance exams should be taken in the spring of the junior year or fall of the senior year. There are early decision, early admissions, deferred admissions, and rolling admissions plans. Early decision applications should be filed by November 15; regular applications, by March 1 for fall entry. Notification of early decision is sent November 30; regular decision, on a rolling basis. 182 applicants were on the 2017 waiting list; 77 were admitted. Applications are accepted on-line. **Transfer Students:** 29 transfer students enrolled in 2016-2017. Applicants should have better than a 2.5 college GPA. High school and college transcripts and an essay are required, along with a statement of good standing from the previous institution. An interview is recommended. 16 of 34 credits required for the bachelor's degree must be completed at OWU. **International Students:** There are 142 international students enrolled. They must take the TOEFL with a minimum score of 550 on the paper-based TOEFL (PBT) or 80 on the Internet-based version (iBT). Student must take the IELTS. They must also take the SAT or ACT.

ADMISSIONS: 93% of the 2017-2018 applicants were accepted. The SAT scores for the 2017-2018 freshman class were: Critical Reading-- 20% below 500, 44% between 500 and 599, 26% between 600 and 699, and 10% between 700 and 800. Math-- 13% below 500, 41% between 500 and 599, 36% between 600 and 699, and 10% between 700 and 800. The ACT scores were 11% below 12, 23% between 12 and 17, 26% between 18 and 23, 19% between 24 and 29, and 25% above 30. 29% of the current freshmen were in the top fifth of their class; 42% were in the top two fifths. 20 freshmen graduated first in their class. **Admissions Contact:** Alisha Couch, Director of Admission. Email: *owuadmit@owu.edu* Web: *www.choose.owu.edu*

FINANCIAL AID: In 2017-2018, 97% of all full-time freshmen received some form of financial aid. 63% of all full-time freshmen received need-based aid. The average freshman award was $34,662. Need-based scholarships or need-based grants averaged $29,200; and need-based self-help aid (loans and jobs) averaged $6,422. 50% of undergraduate students work part-time. The average financial indebtedness of the 2017 graduate was $34,666. OWU is a member of CSS. The FAFSA code is 003109. The priority date for freshman financial aid applications for fall entry is December 1.

OTTERBEIN UNIVERSITY C-3

www.otterbein.edu

Westerville, OH 43081	**(614) 823-1500** **(800) 488-8144**
Fax: (614) 823-1200	**Email: uotterb@otterbein.edu**
Full-time: 825 men, 1297 women	**Faculty:** 178; IIB, av$
Part-time: 79 men, 140 women	**Ph.D.s:** 94%
Graduate: 126 men, 338 women	**Student/Faculty:** 10 to 1
Year: trimesters, summer session	**Tuition:** $31,624
Room & Board: $10,006	**Freshman Class:** 2917 applied, 2197 accepted, 569 enrolled
SAT CR/M/W: 530/531/527 **ACT:** 23	**CEEB CODE:** 1597
Application Deadline: August 15	**COMPETITIVE**

Otterbein University, founded in 1847, is an independent institution affiliated with the United Methodist Church. The university provides a solid liberal arts education combined with professional/career preparation. Figures in the above capsule and in this profile are approximate. There is 1 undergraduate school and 3 graduate schools. In addition to regional accreditation, Otterbein has baccalaureate program accreditation with NASM, CAEP, NLN, and CAAHEP. The 140-acre campus is in a suburban area 12 miles northeast of Columbus. Including any residence halls, there are 69 buildings.

STUDENT LIFE: 91% of undergraduates are from Ohio. Others are from 29 states, 28 foreign countries, and Canada. 75% are White; 6% African American; 4% two or more races; 2% Hispanic; 10% race unknown; 1% Asian American; 1% Foreign. 26% claim no religious affiliation; 22% Catholic. **Female To Male Ratio:** 1.7:1. The average age of freshmen is 18; all undergraduates, 24. 19% do not continue beyond their first year; 61% remain to graduate. **Housing:** 1183 students can be accommodated in college housing, which includes dorms and on-campus apartments. In addition, there are honors houses, special-interest houses, fraternity houses, and sorority houses. On-campus housing is guaranteed for the freshman year only, is available on a first-come, first-served basis, and is available on a lottery system for upperclassmen. 53% of students live on campus. Alcohol is not permitted. All students may keep cars.

FACULTY/CLASSROOMS: 40% of faculty are male; 60% are female. All teach undergraduates. No introductory courses are taught by graduate students. The average class size in an introductory lecture is 10; in a laboratory is 10; and in a regular course is 10.

PROGRAMS OF STUDY: Otterbein confers B.A., B.S., B.F.A., B.M., B.Mus.Ed., B.S.E., and B.S.N. degrees. Master's and doctoral degrees are also awarded. Bachelor's degrees are awarded in AGRICULTURE (equine science), BIOLOGICAL SCIENCE (biochemistry, life science, molecular biology, and zoology), BUSINESS (accounting and business administration and management), COMMUNICATIONS AND THE ARTS (acting, art, broadcasting, communications, dance, dramatic arts, English, English literature, French, journalism, music, music performance, musical theater, public relations, Spanish, speech/debate/rhetoric, and visual and performing arts), COMPUTER AND PHYSICAL SCIENCE (actuarial science, chemistry, computer science, earth science, mathematics, and physics), EDUCATION (athletic training, early childhood education, elementary education, global studies, health education, middle school education, music education, and physical education), ENGINEERING AND ENVIRONMENTAL DESIGN (environmental science), HEALTH PROFESSIONS (biology and nursing), SOCIAL SCIENCE (economics, French studies, history, international studies, liberal arts/general studies, philosophy, political science/government, psychology, public administration, religion, sociology, and women & gender studies). Life science, chemistry, and athletic training are the strongest academically. Business, education, and communications have the largest enrollments.

ACTIVITIES: 29% of men belong to 8 local and 1 national fraternities; 30% of women belong to 6 local sororities. There are 82 groups on campus, including art, band, cheerleading, choir, chorale, chorus, communications, dance, debate, drama, drill team, equestrian, ethnic, forensics, honors, international, jazz band, LGBT, literary magazine, marching band, musical theater, newspaper, opera, orchestra, pep band, photography, political, professional, radio and TV, religious, social, social service, student government, symphony, and yearbook. Popular campus events include Athletics, Music and Theater Events, Shakespearean dramas, and British comedies, and students perform with the Westerville Symphony. **Sports:** There are 10 intercollegiate sports for men and 9 for women, and 11 intramural sports for men and 11 for women. Facilities include a basketball and volleyball center, a football stadium, soccer field, weight room, tennis courts, a cross-country course, track & field, golf, softball, lacrosse, a student recreation center, and a men's wrestling program team. **Graduates:** From July 1, 2016 to June 30, 2017, 527 bachelor's degrees were awarded. The most popular majors were health professions and related programs (18%), business/marketing (12%), and education (11%). In an average class, 50% graduate in 4 years or less, 53% graduate in 5 years or less, and 61% graduate in 6 years or less. Of the 2016 graduating class, 95% were employed within 6 months of graduation.

SERVICES: Counseling and information services are available, as is tutoring in every subject. There is a reader service for the blind, and remedial math, reading, and writing. **Library/Resources:** The library contains 284,241 volumes, and 11,978 audio/video tapes/CDs/DVDs, and subscribes to 296,219 periodicals including electronic. Computerized library services include interlibrary loans, database searching, Internet access, and Wi-Fi capability. Special learning facilities include an art gallery, planetarium, radio station, TV station, an equine facility, 2 theaters, radio station (WOBN), and a recital hall, and the Austin E Knowlton Center for Equine Sciences and the Science Center. **Physically Challenged Students:** All of the campus is accessible. Facilities include wheelchair ramps, elevators, special parking, specially equipped restrooms, special class scheduling, lowered drinking fountains, lowered telephones, and special housing. The Disability Services Coordinator will assist with accomodation's, also consult with the Academic Support Center. **Special:** Students may cross-register with members of the Higher Education Council of Columbus, study abroad in 9 countries, have an internship in most majors, or participate in a Washington semester. B.A.-B.S. degrees, 3-2 engineering degrees with Case Western Reserve and Washington Universities, credit for military experience, student-designed majors, nondegree study, and limited pass/fail options are also available. There are 12 national honor societies and a freshman honors program. **Visiting:** There are regularly scheduled orientations for prospective students, includes a conference with an admissions counselor and a campus tour. There are guides for informal visits, visitors may sit in on classes, and stay overnight. To schedule a visit, contact Mark Moffitt at mmoffitt@otterbein.edu. **Campus Safety and Security:** Measures include 24-hour foot and vehicle patrol, self-defense education, and security escort services. There are emergency telephones, lighted pathways/sidewalks, controlled access to dorms/residences, and 24-hour locked dorm facilities.

REQUIREMENTS: The SAT or ACT is required. Applicants should be graduates of an accredited secondary school. The recommended preparatory program includes 4 units of English, 3 to 4 units each of math, science, and social studies, 2 to 3 units of foreign language, and 1 to 2 units of performing arts. A high school GPA of 2.5 or better is recommended. Students who were home-schooled are considered for enrollment. The university requires applicants to be in the upper 50% of their class. AP and CLEP credits are accepted. Important factors in the admissions decision are advanced placement or honors courses, evidence of special talent, and recommendations by school officials. All students must complete 126 semester hours, including 27 to 97 in the major, with a minimum GPA of 2.0. The liberal arts core includes 8 hours in English composition and literature, 8 hours each in natural and social sciences, 5 hours each in religion/philosophy, fine arts, and non-Western cultures, and 3 in phys ed. **Procedure:** Freshmen are admitted to all sessions. Entrance exams should be taken in the spring of the junior year. There are deferred admissions and rolling admissions plans. Applications should be filed by August 15 for fall entry. The fall 2017 application fee was $25. Notification is sent on a rolling basis. Applications are accepted on-line. **Transfer Students:** 99 transfer students enrolled in 2016-2017. Applicants should present a college GPA of 2.5, and a minimum of 9 semester credits transferred. 48 of 126 credits required for the bachelor's degree must be completed at Otterbein. **International Students:** There are 70 international students enrolled. They must take the TOEFL with a minimum score of 523 on the paper-based TOEFL (PBT) or 69 on the Internet-based version (iBT). They must also take the SAT or ACT.

ADMISSIONS: 75% of the 2017-2018 applicants were accepted. The SAT scores for the 2017-2018 freshman class were: Critical Reading-- 35% below 500, 41% between 500 and 599, 22% between 600 and 699, and 2% between 700 and 800. Math-- 33% below 500, 43% between 500 and 599, 22% between 600 and 699, and 2% between 700 and 800. Writing-- 36% below 500, 39% between 500 and 599, 20% between 600 and

699, and 4% between 700 and 800. The ACT scores were 31% below 12, 29% between 12 and 17, 24% between 18 and 23, 9% between 24 and 29, and 7% above 30. 36% of the current freshmen were in the top fifth of their class; 59% were in the top two fifths. 16 freshmen graduated first in their class. **Admissions Contact:** Mark Moffitt, Exec. Director of Admissions. Email: *uotterb@otterbein.edu* Web: *www.otterbein.edu*

FINANCIAL AID: In 2017-2018, 94% of all full-time freshmen received some form of financial aid and need-based aid. The average freshman award was $23,489. Need-based scholarships or need-based grants averaged $18,819; need-based self-help aid (loans and jobs) averaged $5,669; and other non-need-based awards and non-need-based scholarships averaged $19,045. 28% of undergraduate students work part-time. The average financial indebtedness of the 2017 graduate was $26,583. The FAFSA code is 003110. The deadline for filing freshman financial aid applications for fall entry is April 1.

SHAWNEE STATE UNIVERSITY — C-5

www.shawnee.edu

Portsmouth, OH 45662 — **(740) 351-3450**

Fax: (740) 351-3111	**Email:** to_ssu@shawnee.edu
Full-time: 1355 men, 1477 women	**Faculty:** 151
Part-time: 199 men, 375 women	**Ph.D.s:** 56%
Graduate: 43 men, 133 women	**Student/Faculty:** 16 to 1
Year: semesters, summer session	**Tuition:** $7439 ($13,247)
Room & Board: $9558	**Freshman Class:** 2913 applied, 2038 accepted, 700 enrolled
ACT: 22	**CEEB CODE:** 1790
Application Deadline: n/av	**COMPETITIVE**

Shawnee State University is a small, student-focused public university offering over 80 academic programs, both associate's and bachelor's degrees, and a nationally ranked Game Design program. A highly personalized, affordable, and accessible education makes the institution a best academic value. Other features include successful pre-professional preparatory programs, an undergraduate cadaver lab, unique plastics engineering technology degrees, and hands on clinical experiences. University athletics include 17 intercollegiate NAIA teams with plans to grow annually. There are 3 undergraduate schools and 1 graduate school. In addition to regional accreditation, SSU has baccalaureate program accreditation with ADA, CAEP, NLN, AOTA, CoARC, OBN, OBR, ODE-DVE, CAATE, CAPTE, ODPS-DEMS, OBENHA, JRCERT, NAACLS, ODE, and USDE. The 62-acre campus is in a small town located along the Ohio River in historic Portsmouth, Ohio. Including any residence halls, there are 42 buildings.

STUDENT LIFE: 88% of undergraduates are from Ohio. Others are from 26 states, 18 foreign countries, and Canada. 96% are from public schools. 85% are White; 5% African American; 4% race unknown; 2% two or more races; 1% Asian American; 1% American Indian/Alaska Native; 1% Hispanic; 1% Foreign. **Female To Male Ratio:** 1.2:1. The average age of freshmen is 20; all undergraduates, 22. 37% do not continue beyond their first year; 31% remain to graduate. **Housing:** 934 students can be accommodated in college housing, which includes on-campus apartments. In addition, there are honors houses, and special-interest houses. We offer specific housing for the Game and Simulation Arts Program. On-campus housing is available on a first-come and first-served basis. 77% of students commute. Alcohol is not permitted. All students may keep cars.

FACULTY/CLASSROOMS: 46% of faculty are male; 54% are female. All teach undergraduates. No introductory courses are taught by graduate students. The average class size in an introductory lecture is 17; in a laboratory is 16; and in a regular course is 16.

PROGRAMS OF STUDY: SSU confers B.A., B.A.T., B.F.A., B.I.S., B.S., B.S.B., B.S.E., and B.S.N. degrees. Associate and master's degrees are also awarded. Bachelor's degrees are awarded in BIOLOGICAL SCIENCE (biology/biological science), BUSINESS (accounting, management, marketing, and sports management), COMMUNICATIONS AND THE ARTS (ceramic art and design, drawing, English, language arts, musical theater, and studio art), COMPUTER AND PHYSICAL SCIENCE (chemistry, computer engineering technology, computer game design/development, geology, inform, science, systms & tech, mathematics, natural sciences, and physics), EDUCATION (art education, athletic training, early childhood education, education, elementary education, music education, social science education, and special education), ENGINEERING AND ENVIRONMENTAL DESIGN (engineering technology, environmental engineering technology, and plastics technology), HEALTH PROFESSIONS (health administration and policy, nursing, occupational therapy, and premedicine), SOCIAL SCIENCE (history, humanities, interdisciplinary studies, international relations, legal studies, paralegal studies, philosophy and religion, political science/government, prelaw, psychology, social science, and sociology). Nursing is the strongest academically. General studies, fine arts, and natural studies have the largest enrollments.

ACTIVITIES: 1% of men belong to 2 national fraternities. There are 48 groups on campus, including art, cheerleading, choir, computers, drama, ethnic, honors, international, LGBT, literary magazine, marching band, musical theater, newspaper, pep band, photography, political, professional, religious, social, social service, and student government. Popular campus events include Weekend of Welcome, Family Weekend, Bear Runs, Fall Fest, Spring Fest, and Scare Week. **Sports:** There are 10 intercollegiate sports for men and 11 for women, and 9 intramural sports for men and 9 for women. Facilities include a cardio room, weight room, racquet courts, gymnasium with basketball and volleyball courts, swimming pool, tennis, and soccer field. **Graduates:** From July 1, 2016 to June 30, 2017, 422 bachelor's degrees were awarded. The most popular majors were nursing (10%), psychology (6%), and fine arts (5%). In an average class, 9% graduate in 4 years or less and 20% graduate in 6 years or less.

SERVICES: Counseling and information services are available, as is tutoring in most subjects. Free tutoring is provided for the majority of introductory courses except English or Writing. There is a reader service for the blind, and remedial math, reading, and writing. Tutoring can usually be arranged for other courses that are not introductory courses provided that the Student Success Center can secure a qualified tutor for that subject. **Library/Resources:** The library contains 136,334 volumes, 93,438 microform items, and 4,460 audio/video tapes/CDs/DVDs, and subscribes to 146 periodicals including electronic. Computerized library services include interlibrary loans, database searching, Internet access, and Wi-Fi capability. Special learning facilities include an art gallery, planetarium, and a student success center. **Physically Challenged Students:** All of the campus is accessible. Facilities include wheelchair ramps, elevators, special parking, specially equipped restrooms, lowered drinking fountains, and lowered telephones. **Special:** Study abroad available in several countries, internships in sports studies, business, psychology, and health management, and student-designed programs are available. Cross-registration with Miami University, a Washington semester, and 2+2 programs are also possible as well as a 3+2 program in psychology and occupational therapy. There are 3 national honor societies, a freshman honors program, and 3 departmental honors programs. **Visiting:** There are regularly scheduled orientations for prospective students, including fall and spring visitation days, which consist of small sessions with deans and faculty, orientation by student affairs offices, and tours with current college students. There are guides for informal visits and visitors may sit in on classes. To schedule a visit, contact the Office of Admissions. **Campus Safety and Security:** Measures include 24-hour foot and vehicle patrol, emergency notification system, self-defense education, and security escort services. There are emergency telephones, lighted pathways/sidewalks, safety awareness programs such as I.C.E. and Operation Identification. The department also puts on a Safety Week to help educate students on a variety of safety topics.

REQUIREMENTS: Applicants must graduate from an accredited high school or have a GED. AP and CLEP credits are accepted. To graduate, students must complete a general education program of at least 34 semester hours and a senior seminar. A total of 120 to 135 semester hours including 40 hours in the major is required along with a 2.0 GPA in all course work and in the major. **Procedure:** Freshmen are admitted to all sessions. Entrance exams should be taken in late spring or early summer. There is a rolling admissions plan. Application deadlines are open. Notification is sent on a rolling basis. Applications are accepted on-line. **Transfer Students:** 175 transfer students enrolled in 2016-2017. A completed application and college and high school transcripts sent directly to SSU from previous institutions are required. 45 of 120 credits required for the bachelor's degree must be completed at SSU. **International Students:** There are 31 international students enrolled. They must take the TOEFL with a minimum score of 500 on the paper-based TOEFL (PBT) or 60 on the Internet-based version (iBT) or take either the MELAB, TIBT, or IELTS.

ADMISSIONS: 70% of the 2017-2018 applicants were accepted. The

ACT scores were 12% between 12 and 17, 57% between 18 and 23, 28% between 24 and 29, and 3% above 30. 15 freshmen graduated first in their class. **Admissions Contact:** Amanda Means, Director of Admissions. Email: *to_ssu@shawnee.edu* Web: *www.shawnee.edu*

FINANCIAL AID: In 2017-2018, 91% of all full-time freshmen received some form of financial aid. 71% of all full-time freshmen received need-based aid. The average freshman award was $11,903. Need-based scholarships or need-based grants averaged $6,024 ($10,831 maximum); need-based self-help aid (loans and jobs) averaged $3,342 ($6,092 maximum); non-need-based athletic scholarships averaged $3,953 ($23,884 maximum); other non-need-based awards and non-need-based scholarships averaged $6,537 ($27,076 maximum); and $5,444 from other forms of aid. 9% of undergraduate students work part-time. The average financial indebtedness of the 2017 graduate was $24,054. SSU is a member of CSS. The FAFSA code is 009942. The priority date for freshman financial aid applications for fall entry is December 1.

THE COLLEGE OF WOOSTER — D-2

www.wooster.edu

Wooster, OH 44691	**(330) 263-2322** **(800) 877-9905**
Fax: (330) 263-2621	**Email: admissions@wooster.edu**
Full-time: 892 men, 1067 women	**Faculty:** 169
Part-time: 5 men, 6 women	**Ph.D.s:** 96%
Graduate: n/av	**Student/Faculty:** 11 to 1
Year: semesters, summer session	**Tuition:** $48,600
Room & Board: $11,400	**Freshman Class:** 5615 applied, 3169 accepted, 568 enrolled
SAT CR/M/W: 628/636 **ACT:** 27	**CEEB CODE:** 1134
Application Deadline: n/av	**HIGHLY COMPETITIVE**

The College of Wooster, founded in 1866, is a private liberal arts college, and America's premier college for mentored undergraduate research. There is 1 undergraduate school. In addition to regional accreditation, Wooster has baccalaureate program accreditation with NASM, CAEP, and ACS. The 240-acre campus is in a suburban area 55 miles southwest of Cleveland. Including any residence halls, there are 50 buildings.

STUDENT LIFE: 63% of undergraduates are from out of state, mostly the Midwest. Students are from 42 states, and 42 foreign countries. 58% are from public schools. 9% are African American; 66% White; 5% Asian American; 5% Hispanic; 13% Foreign; 1% American Indian/Alaska Native; 1% race unknown. 36% claim no religious affiliation; 21% Protestant; 17% Catholic. **Female To Male Ratio:** 1.2:1. The average age of freshmen is 18; all undergraduates, 20. 13% do not continue beyond their first year; 87% remain to graduate. **Housing:** 2051 students can be accommodated in college housing, which includes dorms and on-campus apartments. In addition, there are special-interest houses, fraternity houses, sorority houses, and theme housing which includes program housing, language suites, and gender neutral housing. On-campus housing is guaranteed for all 4 years. 99% of students live on campus. All students may keep cars.

FACULTY/CLASSROOMS: 54% of faculty are male; 46% are female. All teach undergraduates, and all do research. No introductory courses are taught by graduate students. The average class size in an introductory lecture is 15 and in a regular course is 20.

PROGRAMS OF STUDY: Wooster confers B.A., B.Mus., and B.Mus.Ed. degrees. Bachelor's degrees are awarded in BIOLOGICAL SCIENCE (biochemistry and biology/biological science), BUSINESS (business economics), COMMUNICATIONS AND THE ARTS (communications, communications technology, comparative literature, dance, dramatic arts, English, fine arts, French, German, Greek (classical), Latin, music, music theory and composition, Russian languages and literature, and Spanish), COMPUTER AND PHYSICAL SCIENCE (chemistry, computer science, geology, mathematics, and physics), ENGINEERING AND ENVIRONMENTAL DESIGN (architecture), SOCIAL SCIENCE (African American studies, anthropology, archeology, area studies, economics, history, interdisciplinary studies, international relations, Latin American studies, Middle Eastern studies, Near Eastern studies, philosophy, political science/government, psychology, religion, Russian and Slavic studies, sociology, urban studies, Western European studies, and women's studies). History, chemistry, and political science are the strongest academically. English, psychology, and political science have the largest enrollments.

ACTIVITIES: 14% of men belong to 4 local fraternities; 17% of women belong to 7 local sororities. There are 125 groups on campus, including art, bagpipe, band, cheerleading, chess, choir, chorus, dance, drama, ethnic, film, honors, international, jazz band, LGBT, literary magazine, marching band, musical theater, newspaper, orchestra, pep band, photography, political, radio and TV, religious, social, social service, student government, symphony, and yearbook. Popular campus events include Gala, Springfest, Skotoberfest, International Education Week Culture Show, WVN Carnival, Rake a Difference, Greek Week: Lip Sync, I.S. Week activities, and Scot Spirit Day. **Sports:** There are 10 intercollegiate sports for men and 11 for women, and 11 intramural sports for men and 11 for women. Facilities include an athletic and recreation center, a track, multi-purpose courts, and a fitness center with Cybex machines. **Graduates:** From July 1, 2016 to June 30, 2017, 472 bachelor's degrees were awarded. The most popular majors were social sciences (24%), biology & life sciences (15%), and physical sciences (11%). In an average class, 70% graduate in 4 years or less, 76% graduate in 5 years or less, and 77% graduate in 6 years or less. Of the 2016 graduating class, 27% were enrolled in graduate school within 6 months of graduation, and 67% were employed.

SERVICES: Counseling and information services are available, as is tutoring in every subject. There is a reader service for the blind, and remedial math, reading, and writing. **Library/Resources:** The library contains 465,382 volumes, and subscribes to 2,007,864 periodicals including electronic. Computerized library services include interlibrary loans, database searching, Internet access, and Wi-Fi capability. Special learning facilities include an art gallery and radio station. **Physically Challenged Students:** 95% of the campus is accessible. Facilities include wheelchair ramps, elevators, special parking, specially equipped restrooms, special class scheduling, and lowered drinking fountains. **Special:** A 3-2 engineering degree is offered in conjunction with Case Western Reserve and Washington Universities. A B.A.-B.S. degree is offered in music/music education. Cross-registration is possible with off-campus programs of the Great Lakes Colleges Association. Internships are available in American politics in Washington, D.C., the Ohio State Legislature, and the U.S. State Department, as well as in professional theater and economics. Student-designed majors, dual majors, study abroad in 50 countries, a Washington semester, accelerated degree programs, nondegree study, and pass/fail options for a limited number of courses are available. All seniors participate in a 2-term independent-study project in the major. The student chooses the topic and works on a one-to-one basis with a faculty mentor. A sophomore research program is available by application. There are 12 national honor societies and a chapter of Phi Beta Kappa. **Visiting:** There are regularly scheduled orientations for prospective students, including an interview, tour, class visits, and meetings with faculty and coaches. There are guides for informal visits, visitors may sit in on classes, and stay overnight. To schedule a visit, contact Melanie Schultz at melaschultz@wooster.edu. **Campus Safety and Security:** Measures include 24-hour foot and vehicle patrol, emergency notification system, and security escort services. There are emergency telephones, lighted pathways/sidewalks, and controlled access to dorms/residences.

REQUIREMENTS: Applicants should be a graduate of an accredited secondary school. The GED is accepted. Completion of a minimum of 16 high school academic credits including 4 years of English, 3 years each of math, history, social science, and natural science (with 2 units of lab), 2 in foreign language, and 1 in academic electives. In addition to completion of the application, including an essay, either SAT or ACT test scores are required. A campus visit and interview are highly recommended. AP credits are accepted. Important factors in the admissions decision are advanced placement or honors courses, leadership record, personality/intangible qualities, extracurricular activities record, recommendations by school officials, parents or siblings attended your school, evidence of special talent, recommendations by alumni, and geographical diversity. 32 course credits are required for graduation with 9 to 13 in the major and a minimum GPA of 2.0. All students must take 1 course each in critical inquiry, studies in cultural differences, religious perspectives, and quantitative reasoning, and demonstrate basic writing and foreign language proficiency. 2 courses each in English, foreign languages, social science/history, natural science/math, and arts/humanities are required. **Procedure:** Freshmen are admitted fall and winter. Entrance exams should be taken in the fall of the senior year. There are early decision, early admissions, and deferred admissions plans. Early decision applications should be filed by November 1. Notification of early decision is sent November 15. 109 early decision candidates were accepted for the 2017-2018 class. 130 applicants were on the 2017 waiting list; 12 were admitted. Applications are accepted on-line. **Transfer Students:** 12 transfer students enrolled in 2016-2017. Applicants for transfer must have a minimum GPA of 2.5 and must submit either the SAT or ACT scores as well as a dean's reference, a high school transcript, and an essay or personal statement. An interview is recommended. Grades of C or better transfer for credit. Transfers are admitted every semester. 16 of 64 credits required for the bachelor's degree must be completed at Wooster. **International Students:** There are 254 international students enrolled. They must take the TOEFL with a minimum score of 81 on the Internet-based version (iBT). Students must take the American Language Institute test, and either the the SAT or ACT.

ADMISSIONS: 56% of the 2017-2018 applicants were accepted. The SAT scores for the 2017-2018 freshman class were: Critical Reading-- 19% below 500, 35% between 500 and 599, 37% between 600 and 699, and 9% between 700 and 800. Math-- 9% below 500, 42% between 500 and 599, 40% between 600 and 699, and 9% between 700 and 800. Writing-- 13% below 500, 35% between 500 and 599, 39% between 600 and 699, and 13% between 700 and 800. The ACT scores were 1% between 12 and 17, 21% between 18 and 23, 52% between 24 and 29, and 26% above 30. **Admissions Contact:** Jennifer Winge, Dean of Admissions. Email: *admissions@wooster.edu* Web: *www.wooster.edu*

FINANCIAL AID: In 2017-2018, 100% of all full-time freshmen received some form of financial aid. 61% of all full-time freshmen received need-based aid. The average freshman award was $42,174. Need-based scholarships or need-based grants averaged $34,309; need-based self-help aid (loans and jobs) averaged $7,722; and $5,559 from other forms of aid. 42% of undergraduate students work part-time. The average financial indebtedness of the 2017 graduate was $30,053. The College of Wooster is a member of CSS. The CSS/Profile and the college's own financial statement are required. The FAFSA code is 003037. The priority date for freshman financial aid applications for fall entry is February 15.

THE UNIVERSITY OF AKRON — D-2

www.uakron.edu

Akron, OH 44325 — (330) 972-6345, (800) 655-4884

Fax: (330) 972-7022
Email: admissions@uakron.edu
Full-time: 7346 men, 6216 women
Faculty: 642
Part-time: 1631 men, 1678 women
Ph.D.s: 80%
Graduate: 1538 men, 1760 women
Student/Faculty: 18 to 1
Year: semesters, summer session
Tuition: $10,270 ($18,801)
Room & Board: $12,296
Freshman Class: 15109 applied, 13983 accepted, 3440 enrolled
SAT CR/M: 563/571 **ACT:** 22
CEEB CODE: 1829
Application Deadline: August 11
COMPETITIVE

The University of Akron, known for an innovative approach to higher education, is the region's most influential public research university, contributing to the resurgence of the local economy, and providing a workforce highly trained in diverse disciplines. With more than 300 associate, bachelor's, master's, doctorate and law degree programs, UA offers career-focused and experiential learning that helps students get ahead in the job market. The university welcomes a diverse groups of learners, including full-time, part-time and online students, veterans, and adults returning to the classroom. There are 8 undergraduate schools and 8 graduate schools. In addition to regional accreditation, The UA has baccalaureate program accreditation with AACSB, ABET, ADA, CSWE, NASAD, NASM, CAEP, APA, ABA, and AAFCS. The 223-acre campus is in an urban area in downtown Akron, 40 miles south of Cleveland. Including any residence halls, there are 89 buildings.

STUDENT LIFE: 92% of undergraduates are from Ohio. Others are from 38 states, 60 foreign countries, and Canada. 73% are White; 5% two or more races; 3% Asian American; 3% Hispanic; 2% Foreign; 2% race unknown; 12% African American. **Male To Female Ratio:** 1.1:1. The average age of freshmen is 17; all undergraduates, 22. 26% do not continue beyond their first year; 40% remain to graduate. **Housing:** 2891 students can be accommodated in college housing, which includes dorms and on-campus apartments. In addition, there are honors houses, special-interest houses, fraternity houses, sorority houses, private apartment-type halls, and private residence halls. On-campus housing is available on a first-come and first-served basis. 81% of students commute. Alcohol is not permitted. All students may keep cars.

FACULTY/CLASSROOMS: 50% of faculty are male; 50% are female. 94% teach undergraduates. Graduate students teach 8% of introductory courses. The average class size in an introductory lecture is 25; in a laboratory is 24; and in a regular course is 25.

PROGRAMS OF STUDY: UA confers B.A., B.A.E., B.A.S.W., B.B.A., B.F.A., B.M., B.S., B.S.A., B.S.A.T., B.S.B.A, B.S.C.S., B.S.E., B.S.N. and B.S.T. degrees. Associate, master's, and doctoral degrees are also awarded. Bachelor's degrees are awarded in BIOLOGICAL SCIENCE (biology/biological science), BUSINESS (accounting, banking and finance, business administration and management, business communications, fashion merchandising, international business management, labor studies, management science, and marketing/retailing/merchandising), COMMUNICATIONS AND THE ARTS (art, classics, dance, English, French, media arts, music, music history and appreciation, music performance, music theory and composition, musical theater, public relations, Spanish, studio art, and theater management), COMPUTER AND PHYSICAL SCIENCE (applied mathematics, chemistry, computer science, computer security and information assurance, environmental geology, geology, geophysics and seismology, mathematics, natural sciences, physics, and statistics), EDUCATION (art education, athletic training, early childhood education, education, home economics education, middle school education, music education, physical education, special education, and technical education), ENGINEERING AND ENVIRONMENTAL DESIGN (automotive technology, biomedical engineering, chemical engineering, civil engineering, computer engineering, construction technology, electrical/electronics engineering, electrical/electronics engineering technology, emergency/disaster science, engineering, geological engineering, interior design, mechanical engineering, mechanical engineering technology, and survey and mapping technology), HEALTH PROFESSIONS (exercise science, nursing, physical therapy, respiratory therapy, and speech pathology/audiology), SOCIAL SCIENCE (anthropology, child psychology/development, criminal justice, criminology, dietetics, economics, family/consumer studies, family/juvenile justice, geography, history, interdisciplinary studies, philosophy, political science/government, psychology, social science, social work, and sociology). Business, health professions, and engineering are the strongest academically and have the largest enrollments.

ACTIVITIES: 4% of men belong to 1 local and 13 national fraternities; 4% of women belong to 9 national sororities. There are 300 groups on campus, including art, band, cheerleading, chess, choir, chorale, chorus, computers, dance, drama, ethnic, honors, international, jazz band, LGBT, marching band, musical theater, newspaper, opera, orchestra, pep band, photography, political, professional, radio and TV, religious, social, social service, student government, and symphony. Popular campus events include Celebrating Akron Traditions, and Zips Fest. **Sports:** There are 7 intercollegiate sports for men and 10 for women, and 19 intramural sports for men and 19 for women. Facilities include a recreation and wellness center with a rock climbing wall, aerobics/dance studio, a natatorium with an Olympic-sized pool, an athletic fieldhouse, indoor varsity golf, football, a track, basketball/volleyball, an arena, weight room, athletic training room, outdoor practice field, soccer field, and baseball field. **Graduates:** From July 1, 2016 to June 30, 2017, 3111 bachelor's degrees were awarded. The most popular majors were nursing (8%), business (6%), and mechanical engineering (5%). In an average class, 19% graduate in 4 years or less, 34% graduate in 5 years or less, and 38% graduate in 6 years or less. Of the 2016 graduating class, 20% were enrolled in graduate school within 6 months of graduation, and 81% were employed.

SERVICES: Counseling and information services are available, as is tutoring in most subjects. There is a reader service for the blind, and remedial math, reading, and writing. TDDs are available. **Library/Resources:** The library contains 1.1 million volumes, and 25,089 audio/video tapes/CDs/DVDs. Computerized library services include interlibrary loans, database searching, Internet access, and Wi-Fi capability. Special learning facilities include an art gallery, radio station, TV station, speech and hearing center, dance institute, educational media lab, and synchro hours learning classrooms. **Physically Challenged Students:** 90% of the campus is accessible. Facilities include wheelchair ramps, elevators, special parking, specially equipped restrooms, special class scheduling, lowered drinking fountains, lowered telephones, special housing, city/campus bus service, residence hall accommodations, and priority registration for disabled students. **Special:** UA offers co-op programs with local and out-of-state employers, study abroad in 22 countries, internships and work-study opportunities with community employers, a 6-year accelerated B.S.-M.D. program, B.A.-B.S. degrees in 10 majors, credit for military experience, nondegree study, and pass/fail options. There are 15 national honor societies, a freshman honors program, and 46 departmental honors programs. **Visiting:** There are regularly scheduled orientations for prospective students, including small groups for information on financial aid, student organizations, campus tours, and meetings with college faculty. There are guides for informal visits, visitors may sit in on classes, and stay overnight. To schedule a visit, contact the Office of Undergraduate Admissions. **Campus Safety and Security:** Measures include 24-hour foot and vehicle patrol, emergency notification system, self-defense education, and security escort services. There are shuttle buses, emergency telephones, lighted pathways/sidewalks, controlled access to dorms/residences, in-room safes, and security cameras.

REQUIREMENTS: The SAT or ACT is required. Students who demonstrate outstanding college preparation through completion of a college prep curriculum may be directly admitted to a specific academic program. Criteria considered include high school GPA, test scores, and class rank. For some majors/programs additional information is reviewed, such as activities, leadership, recommendations, essays, portfolios, and auditions. AP and CLEP credits are accepted. Important factors in the admissions decision are advanced placement or honors courses, leadership record, and evidence of special talent. To graduate, all students must complete at least 120 credits, with a varying number of hours in the major, and maintain a GPA of 2.0. Specific course requirements include English composition, oral communications, Western cultural traditions, math, natural science, social science, humanities, speech, cultural diversity, and phys ed. **Procedure:** Freshmen are admitted to all sessions. Entrance exams should be taken received by November 1 for scholarship consideration. There are deferred admissions and rolling admissions plans. Applications should be filed by August 11 for fall entry. The fall 2017 application fee was $50. Notification is sent on a rolling basis. Applications are accepted on-line. **Transfer Students:** 756 transfer students enrolled in 2016-2017. Applicants should present a minimum college GPA of 2.0. There are other requirements for direct admission to specific academic programs. 32 of 120 credits required for the bachelor's degree must be completed at UA. **International Students:** There are 331 international students enrolled. They must take the TOEFL with a minimum score of 71 on the Internet-based version (iBT). Students must take the IELTS. The English proficiency tests are in lieu of the SAT or ACT unless students are interested in scholarships and the scholarships require it.

ADMISSIONS: 93% of the 2017-2018 applicants were accepted. The SAT scores for the 2017-2018 freshman class were: Critical Reading-- 21% below 500, 40% between 500 and 599, 30% between 600 and 699, and 9% between 700 and 800. Math-- 27% below 500, 34% between 500 and 599, 24% between 600 and 699, and 15% between 700 and 800. The ACT scores were 17% between 12 and 17, 42% between 18 and 23, 33% between 24 and 29, and 9% above 30. 41% of the current freshmen were in the top fifth of their class; 69% were in the top two fifths. **Admissions Contact:** Kim Gentile, Senior Associate Director Admission Outreach. Email: *admissions@uakron.edu* Web: *www.uakron.edu*

FINANCIAL AID: In 2017-2018, 77% of all full-time freshmen received some form of financial aid. 53% of all full-time freshmen received need-based aid. The average freshman award was $7,696. Need-based scholarships or need-based grants averaged $5,240; need-based self-help aid (loans and jobs) averaged $3,241; non-need-based athletic scholarships averaged $4,531; and other non-need-based awards and non-need-based scholarships averaged $6,153. 11% of undergraduate students work part-time. The average financial indebtedness of the 2017 graduate was $25,474. The FAFSA code is 003123. The priority date for freshman financial aid applications for fall entry is February 1.

TIFFIN UNIVERSITY *(The complete profile is made available exclusively on our website, www.barronspac.com)*

UNION INSTITUTE & UNIVERSITY *(The complete profile is made available exclusively on our website, www.barronspac.com)*

UNIVERSITY OF CINCINNATI — A-5

www.uc.edu

Cincinnati, OH 45221 **(513) 556-1100**

Fax: (513) 556-1105 **Email:** admissions@uc.edu
Full-time: 14,010 men, 13,217 women
Part-time: 2551 men, 4365 women
Graduate: 4197 men, 6263 women
Year: semesters, summer session
Room & Board: $11,118
Faculty: 1264
Ph.D.s: n/av
Student/Faculty: 17 to 1
Tuition: $11,000 ($26,234)
Freshman Class: 21161 applied, 16517 accepted, 5400 enrolled
SAT EBR-W/M: 610/610 **ACT:** 25
Application Deadline: March 1
CEEB CODE: 1833
VERY COMPETITIVE

University of Cincinnati, founded in 1819, is a state-supported institution offering undergraduate programs in art and architecture, business, engineering, health science, liberal arts and sciences, music, and technical training. There are 11 undergraduate schools and 11 graduate schools. In addition to regional accreditation, UC has baccalaureate program accreditation with AACSB, ABET, ACCE, ADA, APTA, CAHEA, CSWE, NAAB, NASAD, NASM, CAEP, and NLN. The 473-acre campus is in an urban area in uptown Cincinnati. Including any residence halls, there are 117 buildings.

STUDENT LIFE: 75% of undergraduates are from Ohio. Others are from 50 states, 138 foreign countries, and Canada. 8% are African American; 8% Foreign; 69% White; 4% Asian American; 4% Hispanic; 4% race unknown; 3% two or more races. **Female To Male Ratio:** 1.1:1. The average age of freshmen is 18; all undergraduates, 22. 14% do not continue beyond their first year. **Housing:** 6500 students can be accommodated in college housing, which includes dorms, on-campus apartments, off-campus apartments, and honors houses. On-campus housing is guaranteed for the freshman year only. 82% of students commute. Alcohol is not permitted. All students may keep cars.

FACULTY/CLASSROOMS: 57% of faculty are male; 43% are female. No introductory courses are taught by graduate students.

PROGRAMS OF STUDY: UC confers B.A., B.S., B.F.A., B.M., B.S.Des., B.U.P., B.S.M.E., B.S.N., B.S.I.M., B.S.Ed., B.A.ArtHis., B.S.Ch.E., B.S.C.E., B.S.E.E., B.S.Comp.E., B.S.Aero.E., B.S.Arch., B.S.Int.Des., B.S.H.S., B.I.S., B.S.Bm.E., B.R.S.T., B.S.Mat.E., B.B.A., B.S.C.S., B.S.A.E.T., B.S.C.E.T., B.S.C.M., B.S.E.E.T., B.S.M.E.T., B.S.W., B.S.F.S.E.T., B.S.A.E., B.S.E.V.E., B.S.I.T. and B.T.A.S. degrees. Associate, master's, and doctoral degrees are also awarded. Bachelor's degrees are awarded in AGRICULTURE (environmental studies and horticulture), BIOLOGICAL SCIENCE (biochemistry, biology/biological science, and neurosciences), BUSINESS (accounting, banking and finance, business administration and management, finance, insurance, international business, management science, marketing/retailing/merchandising, operations management, organizational behavior, real estate, and sports management), COMMUNICATIONS AND THE ARTS (Arabic, art history, broadcasting, communications, communication science, comparative literature, creative writing, dance, design, digital communications, dramatic arts, English, fine arts, French, German, graphic design, Hebrew, information technology, jazz, journalism, keyboard - piano concentration, linguistics, music, music history and appreciation, music performance, music theory and composition, piano/organ, radio/television technology, Spanish, speech/debate/rhetoric, theater design, visual and performing arts, and voice), COMPUTER AND PHYSICAL SCIENCE (astrophysics, chemical technology, chemistry, computer engineering technology, computer information technology, computer science, geology, information sciences and systems, mathematics, physics, and quantitative methods), EDUCATION (art education, athletic training, business education, early childhood education, elementary education, foreign languages education, guidance education, health education, health information management, industrial arts education, middle school education, music education, nutrition education, science education, secondary education, and special education), ENGINEERING AND ENVIRONMENTAL DESIGN (aeronautical engineering, architectural engineering, architectural technology, bioengineering, biomedical engineering, chemical engineering, city/community/regional planning, civil engineering, computer engineering, construction management, electrical/electronics engineering, electrical/electronics engineering technology, engineering, engineering mechanics, engineering technology, industrial administration/management, industrial engineering technology, interior design, materials engineering, mechanical engineering, mechanical engineering technology, metallurgical engineering, and nuclear engineering), HEALTH PROFESSIONS (medical laboratory technology, nuclear medical technology, nursing, predentistry, premedicine, prepharmacy, respiratory therapy, and speech pathology/audiology), SOCIAL SCIENCE (addiction studies, African American studies, anthropology, archeology, Asian/Oriental studies, classical/ancient civilization, criminal justice, dietetics, economics, fashion design and technology, geography, history, international studies, Judaic studies, Latin American studies, liberal arts/general studies, philosophy, political science/government, prelaw, psychology, social science, social work, sociology, urban studies, and women's studies). Architecture, music, and engineering are the strongest academically. Marketing, biological sciences, and nursing have the largest enrollments.

ACTIVITIES: There are 567 groups on campus, including art, band, cheerleading, chess, choir, chorale, chorus, computers, dance, drama, environmental, ethnic, honors, international, jazz band, LGBT, literary magazine, marching band, musical theater, newspaper, opera, orchestra, pep band, photography, political, professional, radio and TV, religious, social, social service, student government, and symphony. Popular campus events include College Conservatory of Music Productions. **Sports:** There are 8 intercollegiate sports for men and 9 for women, and 14 intramural sports for men and 14 for women. Facilities include a stadium, a field house, a gym, indoor and outdoor tracks, a climbing wall, recreation center with cardiovascular and weight equipment, swimming pools, tennis courts, and athletic fields. **Graduates:** From July 1, 2016 to June 30, 2017, 5744 bachelor's degrees were awarded. The most popular majors were health professions and related programs (20%), business/marketing (17%), and engineering (9%). In an average class, 2% graduate in 3 years or less, 33% graduate in 4 years or less, 63% graduate in 5 years or less, and 68% graduate in 6 years or less.

SERVICES: Counseling and information services are available, as is tutoring in most subjects. There is a reader service for the blind, and remedial math, reading, and writing. Other services include interpreting services for the hearing impaired and note taking and reading services for the blind. **Library/Resources:** The library contains 2.7 million volumes, 2.5 million microform items, and 123,671 audio/video tapes/CDs/DVDs, and subscribes to 167,738 periodicals including electronic. Computerized library services include interlibrary loans, database searching, Internet access, and Wi-Fi capability. Special learning facilities include an art gallery and radio station. **Physically Challenged Students:** All of the campus is accessible. Facilities include wheelchair ramps, elevators, special parking, specially equipped restrooms, special class scheduling, lowered drinking fountains, and lowered telephones. **Special:** The Professional Practice Program, a 5-year cooperative plan offering alternate work in academic subjects and industry, is available for students in engineering, business, arts and sciences, design, architecture, and art. Study abroad is available in 29 countries. Nondegree study is possible. There is a chapter of Phi Beta Kappa and a freshman honors program. **Visiting:** There are regularly scheduled orientations for prospective students. There are guides for informal visits, visitors may sit in on classes, and stay overnight. To schedule a visit, contact the Admissions Office. **Campus Safety and Security:** Measures include emergency notification system, self-defense education, and security escort services. There are shuttle buses, emergency telephones, and lighted pathways/sidewalks.

REQUIREMENTS: The SAT is accepted, with the ACT preferred. Applicants should be graduates of an accredited secondary school with 4 units of high school English, 3 of math, 2 each of science, social science, foreign language, and electives, and 1 of fine arts. A GPA of 2.0 is required. AP and CLEP credits are accepted. Important factors in the admissions decision are evidence of special talent, personality/intangible qualities, and extracurricular activities record. The General Education Core has a firm foundation in UC's Academic Plan, and reaffirms our institutional commitment to the idea that a liberal education is central to preparing students as life-long learners. Undergraduate courses at the University of Cincinnati promote development of four Baccalaureate Competencies: Critical Thinking, Knowledge Integration, Effective Communication, Social Responsibility, and Information Literacy. Students must complete coursework in English Composition and Quantitative Reasoning. Students must complete at least 120 semester credit hours in order to earn a baccalaureate degree. **Procedure:** Freshmen are admitted to all sessions. Entrance exams should be taken in May of the junior year or January or March of the senior. There are deferred admissions and rolling admissions plans. Applications should be filed by March 1 for fall entry. The fall 2017 application fee was $50. Notifications are sent November 1. Applications are accepted on-line. **Transfer Students:** 1889 transfer students enrolled in 2016-2017. A minimum college GPA of 2.0 is required. Specific programs may have higher GPA, requirements, and prerequisite courses. 30 of 120 credits required for the bachelor's degree must be completed at UC. **International Students:** There are 1045 international students enrolled. They must take the TOEFL with a minimum score of 66 on the Internet-based version (iBT). Students must take either the IELTS or PET.

ADMISSIONS: 78% of the 2017-2018 applicants were accepted. The SAT scores for the 2017-2018 freshman class were: Math-- 4% below 500, 36% between 500 and 599, 41% between 600 and 699, and 19% between 700 and 800. Evidence-Based Reading/Writing-- 6% below 500, 35% between 500 and 599, 44% between 600 and 699, and 15% between 700 and 800. The ACT scores were 30% between 18 and 23, 52% between 24 and 29, and 18% above 30. 40% of the current freshmen were in the top fifth of their class; 70% were in the top two fifths. 55 freshmen graduated first in their class. **Admissions Contact:** Caroline Miller, Vice Provost for Enrollment Management. Email: *admissions@uc.edu* Web: *www.uc.edu*

FINANCIAL AID: In 2017-2018, 82% of all full-time freshmen received some form of financial aid. 50% of all full-time freshmen received need-based aid. The average freshman award was $7,444. Need-based scholarships or need-based grants averaged $6,689 ($26,859 maximum); need-based self-help aid (loans and jobs) averaged $4,401 ($13,000 maximum); non-need-based athletic scholarships averaged $17,806 ($32,574 maximum); and other non-need-based awards and non-need-based scholarships averaged $11,654 ($54,483 maximum). The average financial indebtedness of the 2017 graduate was $34,581. The FAFSA code is 003125. The priority date for freshman financial aid applications for fall entry is December 1.

UNIVERSITY OF DAYTON — B-4

www.udayton.edu

Dayton, OH 45469	**(937) 229-4411 (800) 837-7433**
Fax: (937) 229-4729	**Email: admission@udayton.edu**
Full-time: 4210 men, 3869 women	**Faculty:** 509; I, --$
Part-time: 249 men, 171 women	**Ph.D.s:** 88%
Graduate: 1141 men, 1242 women	**Student/Faculty:** 15 to 1
Year: semesters, summer session	**Tuition:** $41,750
Room & Board: $13,180	**Freshman Class:** 15944 applied, 11427 accepted, 2256 enrolled
SAT EBR-W/M: 602/604 **ACT:** 27	**CEEB CODE:** 1834
Application Deadline: February 1	**VERY COMPETITIVE**

The University of Dayton is a top-tier Catholic research university with academic offerings from the undergraduate to the doctoral levels. We are a diverse community committed, in the Marianist tradition, to educating the whole person and linking learning and scholarship with leadership and service. There are 4 undergraduate schools and 5 graduate schools. In addition to regional accreditation, UD has baccalaureate program accreditation with AACSB, ABET, NASAD, NASM, ACEND, and CAEP. The 398-acre campus is in a suburban area 2 miles south of downtown Dayton. Including any residence halls, there are 59 buildings.

STUDENT LIFE: 55% of undergraduates are from out of state, mostly the Midwest. Students are from 47 states, 42 foreign countries, and Canada. 52% are from public schools. 79% are White; 7% Foreign; 5% Hispanic; 3% African American; 3% two or more races; 1% Asian American; 1% race unknown. 55% are Catholic; 12% Protestant. **Male To Female Ratio:** 1.1:1. The average age of freshmen is 18; all undergraduates, 20. 10% do not continue beyond their first year; 77% remain to graduate. **Housing:** 6600 students can be accommodated in college housing, which includes dorms and on-campus apartments. In addition, there are honors houses, special-interest houses, fraternity houses, and sorority houses. On-campus housing is available on a first-come, first-served basis, and is available on a lottery system for upperclassmen. 74% of students live on campus. Upperclassmen may keep cars.

FACULTY/CLASSROOMS: 56% of faculty are male; 44% are female. 90% teach undergraduates. No introductory courses are taught by graduate students. The average class size in an introductory lecture is 27; in a laboratory is 16; and in a regular course is 27.

PROGRAMS OF STUDY: UD confers B.A., B.S., B.C.E., B.Ch.E., B.E.E., B.F.A., B.G.S., B.M.E., and B.Mus. degrees. Master's and doctoral degrees are also awarded. Bachelor's degrees are awarded in BIOLOGICAL SCIENCE (biochemistry, biology/biological science, and environmental biology), BUSINESS (accounting, banking and finance, business administration and management, business economics, entrepreneurial studies, international business management, management information systems, marketing, marketing/retailing/merchandising, operations management, and sports management), COMMUNICATIONS AND THE ARTS (art history, art, art and design, art history and appreciation, communications, English, fine arts, French, German, graphic design, music, music performance, music theory and composition, musicology/ethnomusicology, performing arts, photography, Spanish, theatre studies, theatre/dance, and visual design), COMPUTER AND PHYSICAL SCIENCE (chemistry, computer engineering technology, computer information systems, computer science, environmental geology, geology, mathematics, mathematics – economics, physical sciences, physics/computer, and physics), EDUCATION (art education, early childhood education, education, elementary education, general studies, middle school education, music education, secondary education, and special education), ENGINEERING AND ENVIRONMENTAL DESIGN (chemical engineering, civil engineering, computer engineering, computer technology, electrical and computer engineering, electrical/electronics engineering, electrical/electronics engineering technology, engineering technology, industrial engineering technology, manufacturing technology, mechanical engineering, and mechanical engineering technology), HEALTH PROFESSIONS (biology, exercise science, exercise and movement science, music therapy, pharmaceutical chemistry, predentistry, premedicine, and prephysical therapy), SOCIAL SCIENCE (criminal justice, dietetics, early childhood studies, economics, ethics, politics, and social policy, gender studies, history, international studies, philosophy, political science/government, psychology, religion, religious education, sociology, and women's studies). Engineering, business, and education are the strongest academically. Business/marketing, and engineering/engineering technologies have the largest enrollments.

ACTIVITIES: 16% of men belong to 1 local and 9 national fraternities; 30% of women belong to 11 national sororities. There are 270 groups on campus, including art, band, cheerleading, chess, choir, chorale, chorus, computers, dance, debate, drama, drill team, environmental, ethnic, film, honors, international, jazz band, LGBT, literary magazine, marching band, musical theater, newspaper, orchestra, pep band, photography, political, professional, radio and TV, students supporting Dayton Flyer Athletics, religious, social, social service, student government, symphony, and yearbook. Popular campus events include Christmas on Campus, Culture Fest, Office of Multicultural Affairs Days, International Festival, Campus Activities Board and #UDLateNight events. **Sports:** There are 7 intercollegiate sports for men and 9 for women, and 38 intramural sports for men and 38 for women. Facilities include an arena, football stadium with a track, soccer field, volleyball, baseball, softball stadium, a recreational sports facility containing a main gym, an aquatic center, a climbing wall, a gym, racquetball courts, fitness studios, a fitness center, and an indoor track. Outdoor recreational facilities include outdoor basketball and sand volleyball courts, turf field, and a walking/running track. **Graduates:** From July 1, 2016 to June 30, 2017, 2036 bachelor's degrees were awarded. The most popular majors were mechanical engineering (10%), finance (9%), and marketing (7%). In an average class, 65% graduate in 4 years or less, 78% graduate in 5 years or less, and 79% graduate in 6 years or less. Of the 2016 graduating class, 20% were enrolled in graduate school within 6 months of graduation, and 74% were employed.

SERVICES: Counseling and information services are available, as is tutoring in some subjects. Walk-in tutoring and/or Supplemental Instruction (SI) are available for many entry-level courses and some high-attrition upper level courses. Support is available for writing at all levels. **Library/Resources:** The library contains 1.7 million volumes, 747,497 microform items, and 4,743 audio/video tapes/CDs/DVDs, and subscribes to 96,661 periodicals including electronic. Computerized library services include interlibrary loans, database searching, Internet access, and Wi-Fi capability. Special learning facilities include an art gallery, radio station, TV station, UD Research Institute, Bombeck Family Learning Center, a learning teaching center, Davis Center for Portfolio Management, Hanley Sustainability Institute, Flyer Enterprises (student run businesses), Institute of Applied Creativity for Transformation. **Physically Challenged Students:** Facilities include wheelchair ramps, elevators, special parking, specially equipped restrooms, special class scheduling, lowered drinking fountains, and special housing. The university provides access to programs and services through the Office of Learning Resources. **Special:** Traditional co-op programs are available in the School of Engineering; however, any student in any discipline may co-op, and qualification is determined on a case-by-case basis. Internships are available in all majors. Cross-registration is available with the Southwestern Ohio Council for Higher Education. Study abroad, work-study programs, a Washington semester, accelerated degree programs, and B.A.-B.S. degrees in chemistry, math, economics, and psychology are available. For students who wish to have a dual major, almost all programs may be combined. Student-designed majors include general studies and interdisciplinary studies. An engineering curriculum agreement exists with Sinclair Community College. There is a freshman honors program. **Visiting:** There are regularly scheduled orientations for prospective students, including an admission interview, financial aid consultation, campus tour, residence hall tour, and faculty or class visit. High school seniors who have been accepted to the university may participate in an overnight visit during the spring semester. There are guides for informal visits, visitors may sit in on classes, and stay overnight. To schedule a visit, contact the Office of Admission. **Campus Safety and Security:** Measures include 24-hour foot and vehicle patrol, emergency notification system, and security escort services. There are shuttle buses, emergency telephones, lighted pathways/sidewalks, controlled access to dorms/residences, a bike patrol, electronic access control for residence hall access, about 1000 video cameras, on-campus ambulance service, automated external debrillators in residence halls and key facilities, centrally monitored fire alarm systems in all residential facilities, and fire suppression in high-density residential facilities.

REQUIREMENTS: The SAT or ACT is required. Applicants should be graduates of an accredited secondary school with 16 units in English, math, science, social studies, and academic electives. In addition, 2 units of foreign language are required for admission to the College of Arts and Sciences. The GED is accepted. High school transcripts must be submitted. An essay or personal statement, a recommendation from the high school guidance counselor, and an interview are recommended. Music students must audition. AP and CLEP credits are accepted. To graduate, all students must complete a minimum of 120 semester hours with at least 30 hours of residence, and maintain a minimum GPA of 2.0. All students following four-year programs are required to complete successfully the University requirements in the Common Academic Program. Other specific requirements may vary according to major. **Procedure:** Freshmen are admitted fall, spring, and summer. Entrance exams should be taken by December of the senior year. There is a deferred admissions plan. Early decision applications should be filed by November 1; regular applications, by February 1 for fall entry. Notifications are sent November 15. Applications are accepted on-line. **Transfer Students:** 115 transfer students enrolled in 2016-2017. Attention is directed to college and high school GPA and course selection. The minimum GPA is 2.0. The School of Education and Allied Professions requires a minimum 2.5 GPA in previous college work. Achievement of the minimum GPA does not guarantee admission. For students under 21 years of age, results of the SAT or ACT are required. All students applying to the School of Education and Allied Professions must submit SAT or ACT and Praxis I scores. 30 of 120 credits required for the bachelor's degree must be completed at UD. **International Students:** There are 573 international students enrolled.

ADMISSIONS: 72% of the 2017-2018 applicants were accepted. The SAT scores for the 2017-2018 freshman class were: Math-- 6% below 500, 42% between 500 and 599, 41% between 600 and 699, and 11% between 700 and 800. Evidence-Based Reading/Writing-- 6% below 500, 41% between 500 and 599, 44% between 600 and 699, and 9% between 700 and 800. The ACT scores were 21% between 18 and 23, 54% between 24 and 29, and 25% above 30. **Admissions Contact:** Robert F. Durkle, Associate VP Dean of Admission. Email: *admission@udayton.edu* Web: *www.udayton.edu*

FINANCIAL AID: In 2017-2018, 98% of all full-time freshmen received some form of financial aid. 68% of all full-time freshmen received need-based aid. The average freshman award was $31,283. Need-based scholarships or need-based grants averaged $24,438; need-based self-help aid (loans and jobs) averaged $4,396; non-need-based athletic scholarships averaged $22,905; and other non-need-based awards and non-need-based scholarships averaged $13,572. 35% of undergraduate students work part-time. The average financial indebtedness of the 2017 graduate was $21,096. University of Dayton is a member of CSS. The FAFSA code is 003127. The priority date for freshman financial aid applications for fall entry is February 1.

UNIVERSITY OF FINDLAY B-2

www.findlay.edu

Findlay, OH 45840	**(419) 424-4732** **(800) 548-0932**
Fax: (419) 424-4822	**Email: admissions@findlay.edu**
Full-time: 1077 men, 1798 women	**Faculty:** 176; I, --$
Part-time: 474 men, 655 women	**Ph.D.s:** 53%
Graduate: 679 men, 705 women	**Student/Faculty:** 16 to 1
Year: semesters, summer session	**Tuition:** $33,320
Room & Board: $9720	**Freshman Class:** 3605 applied, 2347 accepted, 820 enrolled
SAT CR/M/W: 510/530/515 **ACT:** 23	**CEEB CODE:** 1223
Application Deadline: August 1	**COMPETITIVE**

University of Findlay, founded in 1882, is a private, independent institution affiliated with the Churches of God, General Conference, offering liberal arts and sciences and career preparation programs. The figures given in the above capsule and in this profile are approximate. Tuition varies by programs chosen by student. There are 4 undergraduate schools and 1 graduate school. In addition to regional accreditation, Findlay has baccalaureate program accreditation with CAEP. The 250-acre campus is in a small town 45 miles south of Toledo and 100 miles northwest of Columbus. Including any residence halls, there are 55 buildings.

STUDENT LIFE: 80% of undergraduates are from Ohio. Others are from 45 states, 30 foreign countries, and Canada. 80% are from public schools. 85% are White; 6% African American; 5% Asian American; 3% Hispanic; 1% American Indian/Alaska Native. 60% are Protestant; 35% Catholic. **Female To Male Ratio:** 1.4:1. The average age of freshmen is 18; all undergraduates, 22. 25% do not continue beyond their first year; 55% remain to graduate. **Housing:** 1350 students can be accommodated in college housing, which includes dorms and on-campus apartments. In addition, there are honors houses, language/international houses, special-interest houses, fraternity houses, and sorority houses. On-campus housing is guaranteed for all 4 years. 65% of students commute. Alcohol is not permitted. All students may keep cars.

FACULTY/CLASSROOMS: 53% of faculty are male; 47% are female. All teach undergraduates. No introductory courses are taught by graduate students. The average class size in an introductory lecture is 23; in a laboratory is 15; and in a regular course is 22.

PROGRAMS OF STUDY: Findlay confers B.A.,B.S., B.S.B.M., B.S.C.J., and B.S.E.M. degrees. Associate, master's, and doctoral degrees are also awarded. Bachelor's degrees are awarded in AGRICULTURE (animal science and equine science), BIOLOGICAL SCIENCE (biology/biological science), BUSINESS (accounting, banking and finance, business administration and management, business economics, business systems analysis, hospitality management services, human resources, international business management, and marketing/retailing/merchandising), COMMUNICATIONS AND THE ARTS (art, arts administration/management, broadcasting, communications, dramatic arts, English, English as a second/foreign language, graphic design, illustration, Japanese, journalism - news & information, Spanish, studio art, and technical and business writing), COMPUTER AND PHYSICAL SCIENCE (chemistry, computer science, mathematics, and science), EDUCATION (art education, bilingual/bicultural education, elementary education, foreign languages education, middle school education, physical education, and secondary education), ENGINEERING AND ENVIRONMENTAL DESIGN (environmental science, occupational safety and health, and technological management), HEALTH PROFESSIONS (health care administration, health science, nuclear medical technology, nursing, occupational therapy, physician's assistant, premedicine, and preveterinary science), SOCIAL SCIENCE (criminal justice, economics, forensic studies, history, international studies, philosophy, political science/government, prelaw, psychology, religion, religious studies, social work, and sociology). Business administration, preveterinary medicine, and education are the strongest academically. Business administration, equestrian studies, and education have the largest enrollments.

ACTIVITIES: 4% of men belong to 3 national fraternities; 1% of women belong to 2 national sororities. There are 40 groups on campus, including preveterinary club, art, band, cheerleading, choir, chorale, chorus, computers, drama, drum and bugle corps, equestrian, ethnic, honors, international, jazz band, literary magazine, marching band, musical theater, newspaper, pep band, political, professional, radio and TV, religious, social, social service, and student government. Popular campus events include Family Weekend, International Night, Box, City event, and Spring Bash. **Sports:** There are 12 intercollegiate sports for men and 11 for women, and 18 intramural sports for men and 15 for women. Facilities include a fitness center, stadium, swimming pool, aerobics area, racquetball courts, phys ed center with gym, an ice arena, indoor track, and an athletic building, basketball court, billards, bowling, cricket, dodgeball, Euchre Tournament, flag football, frisbee golf, floor hockey, golf, kickball, ping pong, kickball, sand-vollyball, soccer, tennis court, volleyball courts, wallyball, and wiffleball.

SERVICES: Counseling and information services are available, as is tutoring in most subjects. There is a reader service for the blind, and remedial math, reading, and writing. Other services include assistance with note taking, test taking, and study skills, and assistive technology. **Library/Resources:** The library contains 135,000 volumes, 90,000 microform items, and 1,200 audio/video tapes/CDs/DVDs, and subscribes to 2,500 periodicals including electronic. Computerized library services include interlibrary loans, database searching, Internet access, and Wi-Fi capability. Special learning facilities include an art gallery, planetarium, radio station, TV station, university-owned farm, equine facility, and emergency response training center. **Physically Challenged Students:** 90% of the campus is accessible. Facilities include wheelchair ramps, elevators, special parking, specially equipped restrooms, special class scheduling, and lowered drinking fountains. **Special:** Co-op programs are available in accounting and occupational health and safety. There is cross-registration with Mount Carmel College of Nursing and Lourdes College. The field experience program provides up to 20 semester hours in field placement. Internships are available for many majors, including business, business education, communication, hazardous materials management, and theater majors. Through the College Consortium for International Studies, study abroad is possible in 16 countries. Work-study, a Washington semester, dual and student-designed majors, a general studies degree, pass/fail options, and credit for life experience are offered. Nondegree study is possible. There is a freshman honors program. **Visiting:** There are regularly scheduled orientations for prospective students, including a tour, interview, and coach/faculty visits. There are guides for informal visits, visitors may sit in on classes, and stay overnight. To schedule a visit, contact the Admissions Office. **Campus Safety and Security:** Measures include 24-hour foot and vehicle patrol, emergency notification system, self-defense education, and security escort services. There are emergency telephones, lighted pathways/sidewalks, and on-campus sexual assault/domestic violence advocate.

REQUIREMENTS: The SAT or ACT is required. The ACT Optional Writing test is also required. Applicants should have completed 16 high school credits or GED equivalents, including 4 years of English, 2 years of social studies/history, 3 to 4 math courses, and 2 to 3 science courses. A letter of recommendation and an essay are required for all applicants. AP and CLEP credits are accepted. Important factors in the admissions decision are advanced placement or honors courses, evidence of special talent, and extracurricular activities record. All students must complete 36 semester hours of general education requirements, including fine arts, humanities, natural science, math, social science, and religion or philosophy, and must take courses in wellness, computer science, and statistics. There are competency requirements in English composition and reading, and a wellness course. A total of 124 semester hours with a minimum GPA of 2.0 is required to graduate. **Procedure:** Freshmen are admitted to all sessions. Entrance exams should be taken during fall of the senior year or the spring of the junior year. There are deferred admissions and rolling admissions plans. Applications should be filed by August 1 for fall entry; December 1 for spring entry. Notification is sent on a rolling basis. Applications are accepted on-line. **Transfer Students:** 105 transfer students enrolled in 2016-2017. A minimum 2.25 GPA and eligibility to return to the current institution are required. An interview is recommended. 30 of 124 credits required for the bachelor's degree must be completed at Findlay. **International Students:** There are 800 international students enrolled. They must take the TOEFL.

ADMISSIONS: 65% of the 2017-2018 applicants were accepted. The SAT scores for the 2017-2018 freshman class were: Critical Reading-- 37% below 500, 45% between 500 and 599, 16% between 600 and 699, and 2% between 700 and 800. Math-- 31% below 500, 46% between 500 and 599, 21% between 600 and 699, and 2% between 700 and 800. Writing-- 36% below 500, 41% between 500 and 599, 19% between 600 and 699, and 4% between 700 and 800. The ACT scores were 16% below 12, 31% between 12 and 17, 27% between 18 and 23, 15% between 24 and

29, and 11% above 30. 54% of the current freshmen were in the top fifth of their class; 81% were in the top two fifths. **Admissions Contact:** Robin Hopkins, Director of Undergraduate Admissions. Email: *admissions@findlay.edu* Web: *www.findlay.edu*

FINANCIAL AID: In 2017-2018, 91% of all full-time freshmen received some form of financial aid. 15% of undergraduate students work part-time. The average financial indebtedness of the 2017 graduate was $31,000. University of Findlay is a member of CSS. The FAFSA code is 003045. The priority date for freshman financial aid applications for fall entry is April 15.

UNIVERSITY OF MOUNT UNION E-2

www.mountunion.edu

Alliance, OH 44601	(330) 821-5320 (800) 992-6682
Fax: (330) 823-3457	Email: admission@mountunion.edu
Full-time: 1063 men, 983 women	**Faculty:** 124; IIB, av$
Part-time: 21 men, 28 women	**Ph.D.s:** 90%
Graduate: 54 men, 108 women	**Student/Faculty:** 14 to 1
Year: semesters, summer session	**Tuition:** $29,890
Room & Board: $10,100	**Freshman Class:** 2271 applied, 1782 accepted, 591 enrolled
ACT: 23	**CEEB CODE:** 1492
Application Deadline: open	**COMPETITIVE**

University of Mount Union, founded in 1846, is a private, liberal arts college affiliated with the United Methodist Church. There is 1 undergraduate school and 1 graduate school. In addition to regional accreditation, UMU has baccalaureate program accreditation with ABET, NASM, CAEP, CCNE, NASPE, and COSMA. The 123-acre campus is in a suburban area 20 miles east of Canton. Including any residence halls, there are 38 buildings.

STUDENT LIFE: 83% of undergraduates are from Ohio. Others are from 32 states, 12 foreign countries, and Canada. 88% are from public schools. 80% are White; 6% African American; 5% race unknown; 3% Hispanic; 3% two or more races; 1% Asian American; 1% American Indian/Alaska Native; 1% Foreign. 38% are Protestant; 35% claim no religious affiliation; 24% Catholic. **Male To Female Ratio:** 1.0:1. The average age of freshmen is 18; all undergraduates, 20. 25% do not continue beyond their first year; 62% remain to graduate. **Housing:** 1585 students can be accommodated in college housing, which includes gender neutral, single sex and coed dorms, and on-campus apartments. In addition, there are honors houses, fraternity houses, sorority houses, and substance-free (tobacco/alcohol) houses. On-campus housing is guaranteed for the freshman year only, is available on a first-come, first-served basis, and is available on a lottery system for upperclassmen. 67% of students live on campus. All students may keep cars.

FACULTY/CLASSROOMS: 56% of faculty are male; 44% are female. 95% teach undergraduates. No introductory courses are taught by graduate students. The average class size in an introductory lecture is 20; in a laboratory is 15; and in a regular course is 18.

PROGRAMS OF STUDY: UMU confers B.A., B.S., B.Mus., and B.S.N. degrees. Master's and doctoral degrees are also awarded. Bachelor's degrees are awarded in BIOLOGICAL SCIENCE (biochemistry and neurosciences), BUSINESS (accounting, finance, human resource management, management, marketing, and sports management), COMMUNICATIONS AND THE ARTS (art, communications, English, French, German, intermedia/multimedia, Japanese, media arts, music, public relations, Spanish, theatre arts, and writing), COMPUTER AND PHYSICAL SCIENCE (chemistry, computer science, geology, mathematics, and physics), EDUCATION (early childhood education, middle school education, music education, physical education, and special education), ENGINEERING AND ENVIRONMENTAL DESIGN (biomedical engineering, civil engineering, computer engineering, environmental science, and mechanical engineering), HEALTH PROFESSIONS (biology, electrical engineering, exercise science, health, medical laboratory science, and nursing), SOCIAL SCIENCE (criminal justice, economics, history, international political science, international studies, philosophy, political science/government, psychology, religion, and sociology). Engineering, nursing, and exercise science are the strongest academically. Business, early childhood education, and sports management have the largest enrollments.

ACTIVITIES: 25% of men belong to 4 national fraternities; 52% of women belong to 1 local and 3 national sororities. There are 80 groups on campus, including art, band, cheerleading, chess, choir, chorale, chorus, computers, dance, debate, drama, drill team, environmental, ethnic, forensics, honors, international, jazz band, LGBT, literary magazine, marching band, musical theater, newspaper, orchestra, pep band, political, professional, radio and TV, religious, social, social service, student government, and symphony. Popular campus events include Spring Fest, Greek Week, and Schooler Lecture series. **Sports:** There are 11 intercollegiate sports for men and 10 for women, and 8 intramural sports for men and 8 for women. Facilities include a gym, field house, stadium, tennis courts, wellness center, exercise and aerobics rooms, swimming pool, and the campus center. **Graduates:** From July 1, 2016 to June 30, 2017, 452 bachelor's degrees were awarded. The most popular majors were exercise science (9%), psychology (7%), and biology (7%). In an average class, 1% graduate in 3 years or less, 54% graduate in 4 years or less, 60% graduate in 5 years or less, and 62% graduate in 6 years or less. Of the 2016 graduating class, 27% were enrolled in graduate school within 6 months of graduation, and 66% were employed.

SERVICES: Counseling and information services are available, as is tutoring in most subjects, such as general education courses and most introductory courses. Facilitated study groups for most general education courses meet once a week. **Library/Resources:** The library contains 302,000 volumes, 45,000 microform items, and 51,000 audio/video tapes/CDs/DVDs, and subscribes to 950 periodicals including electronic. Computerized library services include interlibrary loans, database searching, Internet access, and Wi-Fi capability. Special learning facilities include an art gallery, radio station, an astronomical observatory, university theater, playhouse, nature center, and the DWOC studio (digital, written and oral communication studio). **Physically Challenged Students:** 98% of the campus is accessible. Facilities include wheelchair ramps, elevators, special parking, specially equipped restrooms, special class scheduling, lowered drinking fountains, and special housing. **Special:** UMU offers internships for credit in many majors, study abroad in 29 countries, co-op programs in business, work-study programs with various employers, student-designed majors, pass/fail options. 3+3 BA JD degree with University of Akron School of Law. Adults in the nontraditional study program may receive credit for military. There are 18 national honor societies, a freshman honors program, and 19 departmental honors programs. **Visiting:** There are regularly scheduled orientations for prospective students, including interviews, a campus tour, meetings with faculty, and classroom visits. There are guides for informal visits, visitors may sit in on classes, and stay overnight. To schedule a visit, contact the Office of Admissions. **Campus Safety and Security:** Measures include 24-hour foot and vehicle patrol, emergency notification system, self-defense education, and security escort services. There are emergency telephones, lighted pathways/sidewalks, and controlled access to dorms/residences.

REQUIREMENTS: The ACT is recommended. Preference is given to high school graduates who have completed a minimum of 15 academic units, including 4 in English, 3 each in math, social science, and lab science, and 2 in foreign language. A GPA of 2.0 is required. AP and CLEP credits are accepted. Important factors in the admissions decision are advanced placement or honors courses, recommendations by school officials, and personality/intangible qualities. A minimum of 128 semester hours is required for all degrees. At least 48 semester hours must be completed at the University of Mount Union. The last 32 semester hours of a degree program must be pursued in residence at the University – cooperative and other special programs may be excepted from this requirement. A minimum GPA of 2.0 on a 4.0 scale must be achieved for all Mount Union and transient work attempted. Completion of a major with at least a 2.0 GPA, and a completion of a minor with at least a 2.0 GPA. If required by the major, completion of a concentration with at least a 2.0 GPA, Completion of the Integrative Core requirements for the degree to be earned; Demonstration of proficiency in foreign language and math, General Education/Integrative Core Requirements, First Year Seminar (4 semester hours), Foundations (16 semester hours), Themes (8 semester hours), and Senior Capstone (4 semester hours). **Procedure:** Freshmen are admitted fall, spring, and summer. Entrance exams should be taken in the spring of the junior year. There are deferred admissions and rolling admissions plans. Application deadlines are open. Notification is sent on a rolling basis. Applications are accepted on-line. **Transfer Students:** 70 transfer students enrolled in 2016-2017. Applicants must have a college GPA of 2.0 for consideration and must submit a statement of honorable dismissal and an official transcript from the last college attended. A personal statement must accompany the transfer application. 48 of 128 credits required for the bachelor's degree must be completed at UMU. **International Students:** There are 50 international students enrolled. They must take the TOEFL with a minimum score of 450 on the paper-based TOEFL (PBT) or 79 on the Internet-based version (iBT). Students must take the IELTS, or provide a certification of completion of ELS. They must also take the SAT or ACT.

ADMISSIONS: 78% of the 2017-2018 applicants were accepted. The ACT scores were 8% between 12 and 17, 53% between 18 and 23, 34% between 24 and 29, and 5% above 30. 35% of the current freshmen were in the top fifth of their class; 66% were in the top two fifths. 12 freshmen graduated first in their class. **Admissions Contact:** Michelle Sundstrom, Vice President of Enrollment Services. Email: *admission@mountunion.edu* Web: *www.mountunion.edu*

FINANCIAL AID: In 2017-2018, 99% of all full-time freshmen received some form of financial aid. 84% of all full-time freshmen received need-based aid. The average freshman award was $26,647. Need-based scholarships or need-based grants averaged $19,274 ($38,552 maximum); need-based self-help aid (loans and jobs) averaged $5,280 ($9,300 maximum); and other non-need-based awards and non-need-based scholarships averaged $12,169 ($29,560 maximum). 30% of undergraduate students work part-time. The average financial indebtedness of the 2017 graduate was $27,652. The FAFSA code is 003083. The priority date for freshman financial aid applications for fall entry is March 1.

UNIVERSITY OF RIO GRANDE & RIO GRANDE COMMUNITY COLLEGE *(The complete profile is made available exclusively on our website, www.barronspac.com)*

UNIVERSITY OF TOLEDO — B-1
www.utoledo.edu

Toledo, OH 43606 — **(419) 530-5445**

Fax: (419) 530-1202	**Email: enroll@utoledo.edu**
Full-time: 6927 men, 6611 women	**Faculty:** I, -$
Part-time: 1622 men, 1717 women	**Ph.D.s:** n/av
Graduate: 2105 men, 2519 women	**Student/Faculty:** n/av
Year: semesters, summer session	**Tuition:** $9242 ($18,580)
Room & Board: $10,094	**Freshman Class:** 11040 applied, 10465 accepted, 3431 enrolled
SAT: recommended **ACT:** 22	**CEEB CODE:** 1845
Application Deadline: open	**COMPETITIVE**

University of Toledo, founded in 1872, is a public comprehensive institution emphasizing undergraduate degree programs in the liberal arts and sciences, business, engineering, teacher preparation, and health professions. Many graduate and professional degree programs, including medicine, are also offered. There are 11 undergraduate schools and 10 graduate schools. In addition to regional accreditation, Toledo has baccalaureate program accreditation with AACSB, ABET, ACPE, APTA, NASAD, NASM, and CAEP. The 813-acre campus is in an urban area 6 miles northwest of downtown Toledo. Including any residence halls, there are 107 buildings.

STUDENT LIFE: 85% of undergraduates are from Ohio. Others are from 47 states, 92 foreign countries, and Canada. 8% are Foreign; 68% White; 15% African American; 1% Asian American; 1% Hispanic. **Female To Male Ratio:** 1.0:1. The average age of freshmen is 19; all undergraduates, 23. 32% do not continue beyond their first year; 45% remain to graduate. **Housing:** 4001 students can be accommodated in college housing, which includes dorms. In addition, there are honors houses, special-interest houses, fraternity houses, sorority houses, and international housing. On-campus housing is available on a first-come and first-served basis. 69% of students commute. All students may keep cars.

FACULTY/CLASSROOMS: 56% of faculty are male; 44% are female. No introductory courses are taught by graduate students. The average class size in an introductory lecture is 38; in a laboratory is 18; and in a regular course is 31.

PROGRAMS OF STUDY: Toledo confers B.A., B.A.Env.Studies, B.A. in Africana Studies, B.B.A., B.Ed., B.E.T., B.F.A., B.M., B.S.Admin.Svcs., B.S.C.E., B.S.Chem.Eng., B.S.Comp.Sci. and Eng., B.S.Const.Eng., B.S.Crim.Just., B.S.C.S.E., B.S.E., B.S.E.E., B.S.El.Eng.Tech., B.S.Eng.Phys., B.S.Env.Sci., B.S.Exer.Sci., B.S.Health Care Spvsn., B.S.I.E., B.S. in Bioeng., B.S.Comp.Sci./Eng.Tech., B.S.M.E., B.S.Med.Tech., B.S.N., B.S.Pharm., B.S.P.T., B.S.Rad.Sci., B.S.Resp.Care, B.S.W. and B.Voc.Ed. degrees. Associate, master's, and doctoral degrees are also awarded. Bachelor's degrees are awarded in BIOLOGICAL SCIENCE (biology/biological science), BUSINESS (accounting, banking and finance, business administration and management, marketing/retailing/merchandising, and recreation and leisure services), COMMUNICATIONS AND THE ARTS (art history and appreciation, communications, dramatic arts, English, film arts, fine arts, French, German, linguistics, music, and Spanish), COMPUTER AND PHYSICAL SCIENCE (chemistry, computer science, geology, information sciences and systems, mathematics, and physics), EDUCATION (art education, business education, early childhood education, elementary education, foreign languages education, health education, music education, physical education, science education, secondary education, special education, and vocational education), ENGINEERING AND ENVIRONMENTAL DESIGN (bioengineering, chemical engineering, civil engineering, computer engineering, electrical/electronics engineering, electromechanical technology, engineering, engineering technology, environmental science, industrial engineering, and mechanical engineering), HEALTH PROFESSIONS (nursing, pharmacy, physical therapy, and speech pathology/audiology), SOCIAL SCIENCE (anthropology, community services, criminal justice, economics, geography, history, humanities, international relations, philosophy, physical fitness/movement, political science/government, psychology, social work, sociology, and women's studies). Engineering, pharmacy, and business are the strongest academically. Pharmacy, nursing, and business have the largest enrollments.

ACTIVITIES: 5% of men belong to 17 local and 7 national fraternities; 4% of women belong to 13 local and 7 national sororities. There are 200 groups on campus, including art, band, cheerleading, chess, choir, chorale, chorus, computers, dance, drama, drill team, ethnic, film, honors, international, jazz band, LGBT, literary magazine, marching band, musical theater, newspaper, orchestra, pep band, photography, political, professional, radio and TV, religious, social, social service, student government, and symphony. Popular campus events include Songfest, and Greek Week. **Sports:** There are 6 intercollegiate sports for men and 9 for women, and 48 intramural sports for men and 48 for women. Facilities include a recreation center, a stadium, an arena, field house, pools, tennis courts, an indoor/outdoor track, a recreational softball complex, and recreational/sport club fields. **Graduates:** From July 1, 2016 to June 30, 2017, 2684 bachelor's degrees were awarded. The most popular majors were interdisciplinary studies (7%), marketing (6%), and criminal justice (6%). In an average class, 24% graduate in 4 years or less, 42% graduate in 5 years or less, and 46% graduate in 6 years or less.

SERVICES: Counseling and information services are available, as is tutoring in most subjects. There is a reader service for the blind, and remedial math, reading, and writing. **Library/Resources:** The library contains 2.1 million volumes, 1.8 million microform items, and 42,941 audio/video tapes/CDs/DVDs. Computerized library services include interlibrary loans, database searching, Internet access, and Wi-Fi capability. Special learning facilities include an art gallery, planetarium, and radio station. **Physically Challenged Students:** 96% of the campus is accessible. Facilities include wheelchair ramps, elevators, special parking, specially equipped restrooms, special class scheduling, lowered drinking fountains, and lowered telephones. **Special:** Special academic programs include internships in most majors, study abroad in 25 countries, and on-campus employment through the Financial Aid Office. There is a Co-op program with the College of Engineering and cross-registration with Bowling Green State University. The B.A.-B.S. degree and dual majors are available in many areas of study. A general studies degree, student-designed majors, an accelerated degree, credit for life, military, and work experience, non-degree study, and pass/fail options are also offered. There are 56 national honor societies, a freshman honors program, and 21 departmental honors programs. **Visiting:** There are regularly scheduled orientations for prospective students, including an interview with an admissions representative and a student-guided campus tour. Academic appointments are available by request. There are guides for informal visits, visitors may sit in on classes, and stay overnight. To schedule a visit, contact the Office of Undergraduate Admissions. **Campus Safety and Security:** Measures include 24-hour foot and vehicle patrol, emergency notification system, self-defense education, and security escort services. There are shuttle buses, emergency telephones, lighted pathways/sidewalks, and controlled access to dorms/residences.

REQUIREMENTS: The SAT or ACT and ACT Writing Test are recommended. The university follows an open admissions policy for Ohio applicants. Students should be graduates of an accredited secondary school or hold the GED. The preparatory program should include 4 years of English, 3 each of math, natural science, and social studies, and 2 of a foreign language. A GPA of 2.0 is required. AP and CLEP credits are accepted. To graduate, all students must complete a minimum of 124 hours of credit, with a minimum of 60 in the major. To maintain good academic standing students must maintain a minimum GPA of 2.0. A core curriculum is required of all students. A thesis is required in the honors program. The number of hours required in the major varies. **Procedure:** Freshmen are admitted to all sessions. Entrance exams should be taken by the junior year or early in the senior year. There are deferred admissions and rolling admissions plans. Application deadlines are open. The fall 2017 application fee was $40. Applications are accepted on-line. **Transfer Students:** 1045 transfer students enrolled in 2016-2017. Applicants must have earned college credit at another regionally accredited college or university and a GPA of 2.0. An interview is recommended. **International Students:** There are 602 international students enrolled. They must take the TOEFL with a minimum score of 61 on the Internet-based version (iBT).

ADMISSIONS: 95% of the 2017-2018 applicants were accepted. The ACT scores were 41% below 12, 25% between 12 and 17, 19% between 18 and 23, 8% between 24 and 29, and 6% above 30. **Admissions Contact:** William Pierce, Director of Undergraduate Admissions. Email: *enroll@utoledo.edu* Web: *www.utoledo.edu*

FINANCIAL AID: In 2017-2018, 99% of all full-time freshmen received some form of financial aid. 77% of all full-time freshmen received need-based aid. The average freshman award was $10,732. Need-based scholarships or need-based grants averaged $8,179 ($40,890 maximum); need-based self-help aid (loans and jobs) averaged $3,547 ($6,345 maximum); non-need-based athletic scholarships averaged $16,078 ($35,385 maximum); other non-need-based awards and non-need-based scholarships averaged $5,770 ($22,494 maximum); and $9,070 from other forms of aid. The average financial indebtedness of the 2017 graduate was $28,438. University of Toledo is a member of CSS. The FAFSA code is 003131. The priority date for freshman financial aid applications for fall entry is April 1.

URBANA UNIVERSITY B-3

www.urbana.edu

Urbana, OH 43078	(937) 484-1356
Fax: (937) 484-1322	Email: admissions@urbana.edu
Full-time: 500 men, 420 women	**Faculty:** 55
Part-time: 191 men, 346 women	**Ph.D.s:** 74%
Graduate: 32 men, 58 women	**Student/Faculty:** 17 to 1
Year: semesters, summer session	**Tuition:** $22,012
Room & Board: $8808	**Freshman Class:** n/av
SAT or ACT: required	**CEEB CODE:** 1847
Application Deadline: open	**COMPETITIVE**

Urbana University, founded in 1850, serves students from around the world. Known for innovative academic programs that feature personal attention from faculty, the university offers more than 30 undergraduate programs and several graduate degrees, delivering coursework in class, online, or a combination of both. Urbana was the first college in the state to offer a nontraditional degree completion program and the second institution of higher education in Ohio to admit women. There are 3 undergraduate schools and 1 graduate school. In addition to regional accreditation, Urbana has baccalaureate program accreditation with CAEP, CCNE, and IACBE. The 128-acre campus is in a small town 40 miles west of Columbus and 50 miles north of Dayton. Including any residence halls, there are 30 buildings.

STUDENT LIFE: 90% of undergraduates are from Ohio. Others are from 5 states, and 5 foreign countries. 95% are from public schools. 79% are White; 17% African American; 1% Hispanic. **Female To Male Ratio:** 1.1:1. The average age of freshmen is 20; all undergraduates, 24. 23% do not continue beyond their first year; 35% remain to graduate. **Housing:** 500 students can be accommodated in college housing, which includes dorms. In addition, there are honors houses. On-campus housing is guaranteed for the freshman year only, and is available on a lottery system for upperclassmen. 54% of students commute. All students may keep cars.

FACULTY/CLASSROOMS: 60% of faculty are male; 40% are female. All teach undergraduates. No introductory courses are taught by graduate students. The average class size in an introductory lecture is 18; in a laboratory is 7; and in a regular course is 19.

PROGRAMS OF STUDY: Urbana confers B.A., B.S., and B.S.N. degrees. Associate and master's degrees are also awarded. Bachelor's degrees are awarded in AGRICULTURE (agricultural business management), BUSINESS (business administration and management, business administration marketing, and sports management), COMMUNICATIONS AND THE ARTS (communications and English), COMPUTER AND PHYSICAL SCIENCE (mathematics and science), EDUCATION (early childhood education, education of the mentally handicapped, elementary education, English education, middle school education, and secondary education), HEALTH PROFESSIONS (exercise science, nursing, prehealth biological studies, and premedicine), SOCIAL SCIENCE (criminal justice, family/consumer studies, history, liberal arts/general studies, philosophy and religion, prelaw, psychology, and sociology). Business, education, and exercise science are the strongest academically. Business, education, and sport studies have the largest enrollments.

ACTIVITIES: There are no fraternities or sororities. There are 30 groups on campus, including art, band, cheerleading, choir, chorus, dance, drama, environmental, ethnic, honor societies, honors, international, LGBT, literary magazine, marching band, musical theater, newspaper, pep band, political, professional, religious, social, social service, and student government. Popular campus events include Spring Week, Founders Day, and Activities Fair. **Sports:** There are 11 intercollegiate sports for men and 12 for women, and 6 intramural sports for men and 6 for women. Facilities include a community center with a gym, a pool, handball and racquetball courts, a weight room, outdoor sand volleyball court, and outdoor tennis courts.

SERVICES: Counseling and information services are available, as is tutoring in most subjects. There is remedial math, reading, and writing. There are taped textbooks, reading and writing labs, and study skills seminars. **Library/Resources:** The library contains 316,000 volumes, and 1,000 audio/video tapes/CDs/DVDs, and subscribes to 6,000 periodicals including electronic. Computerized library services include interlibrary loans, database searching, Internet access, and Wi-Fi capability. **Physically Challenged Students:** 70% of the campus is accessible. Facilities include wheelchair ramps, elevators, special parking, and special class scheduling. **Special:** Special academic programs include internships, cross-registration with the Southwestern Ohio Council for Higher Education, study abroad, and accelerated degree programs in teacher certification. B.A.-B.S. degrees, dual and student-designed majors, credit for life, military, and work experience, and nondegree study are also available. There are 5 national honor societies, a freshman honors program, and 3 departmental honors programs. **Visiting:** There are regularly scheduled orientations for prospective students, consisting of a campus tour, admissions, financial aid, student life, meetings with coaches, attending classes. There are guides for informal visits, visitors may sit in on classes, and stay overnight. To schedule a visit, contact the Admissions Office at admissions@urbana.edu. **Campus Safety and Security:** Measures include 24-hour foot and vehicle patrol, emergency notification system, self-defense education, and security escort services. There are emergency telephones, lighted pathways/sidewalks, and controlled access to dorms/residences.

REQUIREMENTS: The SAT is required. ACT scores are preferred. An applicant must present evidence of high school completion in the form of a high school diploma or GED Certificate. The recommended high school curriculum includes 4 units of English, 3 units of mathematics, 2 units each of science and social science, 1 additional unit in English, mathematics, or science, and 4 additional units from English, mathematics, science, social science, foreign language or philosophy. AP and CLEP credits are accepted. Important factors in the admissions decision are advanced placement or honors courses, evidence of special talent, and extracurricular activities record. To graduate, all students must complete 126 semester credits, with a minimum overall GPA of 2.0 and 2.5 in the major. Distribution requirements in a 47-49 credit core curriculum include 12 to 13 credit hours in math and science, 12 credits social sciences, 13 credits in humanities, 9 in communications, and 2-3 in health and physical education. The number of credits required per major varies. **Procedure:** Freshmen are admitted to all sessions. Entrance exams should be taken during the junior or senior year. There are deferred admissions and rolling admissions plans. Application deadlines are open. The fall 2017 application fee was $25. Applications are accepted on-line. **Transfer Students:** 50 transfer students enrolled in 2016-2017. Applicants must have a cumulative GPA of 2.0. 30 of 126 credits required for the bachelor's degree must be completed at Urbana. **International Students:** There are 4 international students enrolled. They must take the TOEFL.

Admissions Contact: Melissa Tolle, Director of Admissions. Email: *admissions@urbana.edu* Web: *www.urbana.edu*

FINANCIAL AID: The state aid form and the college's own financial statement are required. Check with the school for current application deadlines.

URSULINE COLLEGE *(The complete profile is made available exclusively on our website, www.barronspac.com)*

WALSH UNIVERSITY D-2

www.walsh.edu

North Canton, OH 44720	(330) 490-7172 (800) 362-9846
Fax: (330) 490-7165	Email: admissions@walsh.edu
Full-time: 731 men, 1050 women	Faculty: 118; IIB, -$
Part-time: 124 men, 231 women	Ph.D.s: 65%
Graduate: 192 men, 444 women	Student/Faculty: 13 to 1
Year: semesters, summer session	Tuition: $28,770
Room & Board: $10,240	Freshman Class: 1693 applied, 1315 accepted, 439 enrolled
SAT CR/M: 520/520 ACT: 23	CEEB CODE: 1926
Application Deadline: August 15	COMPETITIVE

Walsh University was established in 1958 by the Brothers of Christian Instruction, a religious order of the Roman Catholic Church. The private institution offers undergraduate programs in liberal arts, business, communication, education, professional training, and nursing. There are 5 undergraduate schools and 5 graduate schools. In addition to regional accreditation, Walsh has baccalaureate program accreditation with CCNE and and CAEP. The 143-acre campus is in a small town 20 miles south of Akron. Including any residence halls, there are 24 buildings.

STUDENT LIFE: 87% of undergraduates are from Ohio. Others are from 30 states, 31 foreign countries, and Canada. 74% are from public schools. 74% are White; 6% African American; 3% Hispanic; 2% Foreign; 2% two or more races; 12% race unknown; 1% Asian American. 42% are Catholic; 30% claim no religious affiliation; 26% Protestant. **Female To Male Ratio:** 1.6:1. The average age of freshmen is 18; all undergraduates, 24. 15% do not continue beyond their first year; 64% remain to graduate. **Housing:** 1050 students can be accommodated in college housing, which includes dorms and on-campus apartments. In addition, there are honors houses, special-interest houses, study floors, and substance-free floors. On-campus housing is guaranteed for all 4 years. 56% of students commute. All students may keep cars.

FACULTY/CLASSROOMS: 45% of faculty are male; 55% are female. 90% teach undergraduates, 37% do research, and 20% do both. No introductory courses are taught by graduate students. The average class size in an introductory lecture is 15; in a laboratory is 14; and in a regular course is 16.

PROGRAMS OF STUDY: Walsh confers B.A., B.S., B.S.Ed., and B.S.N. degrees. Associate, master's, and doctoral degrees are also awarded. Bachelor's degrees are awarded in BIOLOGICAL SCIENCE (biochemistry, bioinformatics, and biology/biological science), BUSINESS (accounting, business administration and management, business communications, finance, international business management, and marketing management), COMMUNICATIONS AND THE ARTS (art history, communications, digital media, English, French, graphic design, music, and Spanish), COMPUTER AND PHYSICAL SCIENCE (chemistry, computer science, mathematics, and science), EDUCATION (early childhood education, education of the emotionally handicapped, education of the exceptional child, education of the mentally handicapped, education of the physically handicapped, elementary education, middle school education, museum studies, physical education, secondary education, and special education), ENGINEERING AND ENVIRONMENTAL DESIGN (environmental science), HEALTH PROFESSIONS (clinical science, exercise science, nursing, physical therapy, predentistry, premedicine, preoptometry, pre-occupational therapy, prepharmacy, prephysical therapy, and preveterinary science), SOCIAL SCIENCE (criminal justice, history, international relations, liberal arts/general studies, philosophy, political science/government, prelaw, psychology, sociology, and theological studies). Biology, nursing, and business are the strongest academically. Biology, nursing, and management have the largest enrollments.

ACTIVITIES: There are no fraternities or sororities. There are 40 groups on campus, including art, band, cheerleading, choir, chorale, chorus, dance, debate, drama, environmental, ethnic, honors, international, leadership honor societies, literary magazine, marching band, newspaper, pep band, political, professional, radio and TV, religious, social, social service, special interest, student government, and yearbook. Popular campus events include Walshfest, Spring Formal, Coffee House, and Improv. **Sports:** There are 9 intercollegiate sports for men and 9 for women, and 10 intramural sports for men and 9 for women. Facilities include gymnasiums, outdoor basketball and tennis courts, a track, softball and baseball fields, practice and intramural fields, a lighted soccer field, a game room, student exercise and weight rooms, and an all-purpose artifical practice field. **Graduates:** From July 1, 2016 to June 30, 2017, 541 bachelor's degrees were awarded. The most popular majors were nursing (19%), management (18%), and biology (11%). In an average class, 52% graduate in 4 years or less, 62% graduate in 5 years or less, and 64% graduate in 6 years or less. Of the 2016 graduating class, 13% were enrolled in graduate school within 6 months of graduation, and 78% were employed.

SERVICES: Counseling and information services are available, as is tutoring in every subject. There is remedial math, reading, and writing. One-on-one and group tutoring and a study skills course are available. **Library/Resources:** The library contains 131,614 volumes, and 27,051 audio/video tapes/CDs/DVDs, and subscribes to 32,206 periodicals including electronic. Computerized library services include interlibrary loans, database searching, Internet access, and Wi-Fi capability. Special learning facilities include an art gallery, radio station, a child development center, a corporate museum, bioinformatics lab, and a community clinic with counseling and wellness programs. **Physically Challenged Students:** All of the campus is accessible. Facilities include wheelchair ramps, elevators, special parking, specially equipped restrooms, special class scheduling, lowered drinking fountains, lowered telephones, and special housing. **Special:** Work-study programs are available to students having financial need. Walsh offers internships for all majors; study abroad in 14 countries, with a campus outside Rome, Italy and a partner school in Kisubi, Uganda; accelerated degree programs in nursing, business and management; pre-medical, pre-dental, pre-pharmacy, pre-veterinary, pre-physical therapy, graduate programs in business, physical therapy, education, counseling, theology, and nursing; evening and continuing education programs, and credit for life experience. Reduced core for transfer students. There are 12 national honor societies, a freshman honors program, and 12 departmental honors programs. **Visiting:** There are regularly scheduled orientations for prospective students, consisting of a campus tour, a session with financial aid and admissions staff, and an opportunity to meet with faculty, coaches, and other personnel. There are guides for informal visits, visitors may sit in on classes, and stay overnight. To schedule a visit, contact the Admissions Office. **Campus Safety and Security:** Measures include 24-hour foot and vehicle patrol, emergency notification system, self-defense education, and security escort services. There are emergency telephones, lighted pathways/sidewalks, and controlled access to dorms/residences.

REQUIREMENTS: ACT or SAT scores are not required if the applicant has a high school GPA of 3.0 or better. Test scores are required for student athletes to comply with NCAA regulations. The applicant must be a graduate of an accredited secondary school; the GED is accepted. Walsh recommends completion of 4 units of English, 3 units each of math, science, and social studies, 2 units of foreign language, and 1 unit of fine or performing arts. An essay and an interview are recommended. AP and CLEP credits are accepted. Important factors in the admissions decision are recommendations by school officials, leadership record, and extracurricular activities record. To graduate, students must complete 125 semester hours with a minimum 2.0 GPA. The number of hours required in the major varies. A core curriculum of 37 hours is required, including courses in English, art or music, science, social science, math, humanities, theology, philosophy, service learning, diversity, and a foreign language. **Procedure:** Freshmen are admitted to all sessions. Entrance exams should be taken during the junior year. There are deferred admissions and rolling admissions plans. Applications should be filed by August 15 for fall entry; January 1 for spring entry; and April 29 for summer entry. The fall 2017 application fee was $25. Notification is sent on a rolling basis. Applications are accepted on-line. **Transfer Students:** 103 transfer students enrolled in 2016-2017. Applicants must have a minimum GPA of 2.0 from previous colleges attended. 32 of 125 credits required for the bachelor's degree must be completed at Walsh. **International Students:** There are 93 international students enrolled. They must take the TOEFL with a minimum score of 500 on the paper-based TOEFL (PBT) or 61 on the Internet-based version (iBT). Students must take the STEP.

ADMISSIONS: 78% of the 2017-2018 applicants were accepted. The ACT scores were 8% between 12 and 17, 57% between 18 and 23, 30% between 24 and 29, and 5% above 30. 34% of the current freshmen were in the top fifth of their class; 60% were in the top two fifths. 9 freshmen graduated first in their class. **Admissions Contact:** Dr. Ute S. Lahaie, Dean of Admissions. Email: *admissions@walsh.edu* Web: *www.walsh.edu*

FINANCIAL AID: In 2017-2018, 99% of all full-time freshmen received some form of financial aid. 78% of all full-time freshmen received need-based aid. The average freshman award was $27,073. Need-based scholarships or need-based grants averaged $7,746 ($19,230 maximum); need-based self-help aid (loans and jobs) averaged $4,729 ($8,500 maximum); non-need-based athletic scholarships averaged $10,764 ($38,960 maximum); and other non-need-based awards and non-need-based scholarships averaged $11,961 ($27,220 maximum). 95% of undergraduate students work part-time. The average financial indebtedness of the 2017 graduate was $27,598. Walsh University is a member of CSS. The college's own financial statement is required. The FAFSA code is 003135. The priority date for freshman financial aid applications for fall entry is February 14.

WILBERFORCE UNIVERSITY B-4

www.wilberforce.edu

Wilberforce, OH 45384 (937) 376-2911 (800) 367-8568

Fax: (937) 376-4751 **Email: admissions@wilberforce.edu**

Full-time: 300 men, 480 women	**Faculty:** 46
Part-time: 10 men, 10 women	**Ph.D.s:** 53%
Graduate: n/av	**Student/Faculty:** 17 to 1
Year: semesters	**Tuition:** $13,250
Room & Board: $6650	**Freshman Class:** n/av
SAT or ACT: recommended	**CEEB CODE:** 1906
Application Deadline: n/av	**COMPETITIVE**

Wilberforce University, founded in 1856, is a private institution operated under the auspices of the African Methodist Episcopal Church; it was the first black college in America. It's programs emphasize the liberal arts, business, art and fine arts, engineering, and music. The figures given in the above capsule and in this profile are approximate. There is 1 undergraduate school. The 125-acre campus is in a rural area 20 miles east of Dayton. Including any residence halls, there are 21 buildings.

STUDENT LIFE: 64% of undergraduates are from out of state, mostly the Midwest. Students are from 32 states, and 2 foreign countries. 97% are African American. **Female To Male Ratio:** 1.6:1. The average age of freshmen is 18; all undergraduates, 20. **Housing:** 775 students can be accommodated in college housing, which includes married student dorms. In addition, there are honors houses. On-campus housing is guaranteed for all 4 years. Alcohol is not permitted. All students may keep cars.

FACULTY/CLASSROOMS: 50% of faculty are male; 50% are female. No introductory courses are taught by graduate students. The average class size in an introductory lecture is 12 and in a regular course is 18.

PROGRAMS OF STUDY: Wilberforce confers B.A. and B.S. degrees. Master's degrees are also awarded. Bachelor's degrees are awarded in BIOLOGICAL SCIENCE (biology/biological science), BUSINESS (accounting, banking and finance, business administration and management, business economics, management science, and marketing/retailing/merchandising), COMMUNICATIONS AND THE ARTS (communications, fine arts, literature, and music), COMPUTER AND PHYSICAL SCIENCE (chemistry, computer science, information sciences and systems, mathematics, and science), ENGINEERING AND ENVIRONMENTAL DESIGN (preengineering), HEALTH PROFESSIONS (health care administration and rehabilitation therapy), SOCIAL SCIENCE (economics, liberal arts/general studies, political science/government, prelaw, psychology, social science, social work, and sociology). Business administration, accounting, and banking & finance are the strongest academically.

ACTIVITIES: 10% of men belong to 5 national fraternities; 10% of women belong to 4 national sororities. There are 30 groups on campus, including choir, computers, dance, ethnic, honors, international, literary magazine, newspaper, political, religious, social, student government, and yearbook. Popular campus events include Fall Festival, and Dawn Dance. **Sports:** There are 5 intercollegiate sports for men and 4 for women, and 4 intramural sports for men and 4 for women. Facilities include a gym, outdoor and cross-country track, a softball field, basketball, volleyball, and tennis courts.

SERVICES: Counseling and information services are available, as is tutoring in most subjects. There is a reader service for the blind, and remedial math, reading, and writing. **Library/Resources:** The library contains 60,000 volumes, 12,000 microform items, and 200 audio/video tapes/CDs/DVDs, and subscribes to 350 periodicals including electronic. **Physically Challenged Students:** 50% of the campus is accessible. Facilities include wheelchair ramps, special parking, specially equipped restrooms, and limited elevator service in classroom only. **Special:** Wilberforce offers a co-op arrangement with St. John's University School of Law and cross-registration through the Southwestern Ohio Council for Higher Education. B.A.-B.S. degrees are available in all majors, and there are dual majors in engineering along with a 3-2 engineering degree with the University of Dayton. Credit is given for the mandatory co-op education program, in which students participate in paid work experience in their chosen field. Nondegree study is possible in military science. There is 1 national honor society, Phi Beta Kappa, a freshman honors program, and 4 departmental honors programs. **Visiting:** There are regularly scheduled orientations for prospective students. There are guides for informal visits. To schedule a visit, contact the Office of Admissions. **Campus Safety and Security:** Measures include 24-hour foot and vehicle patrol, and controlled access to dorms/residences.

REQUIREMENTS: The SAT or ACT is recommended. Students should be graduates of an accredited secondary school and have 15 Carnegie units, including 4 units of English, 2 to 3 of math, including algebra, 2 to 3 of science, including a lab course, and 2 of social studies, including U.S. history. The GED is accepted with a score of 45 or better. SAT II: Subject tests are recommended. A GPA of 2.0 is required. AP and CLEP credits are accepted. Important factors in the admissions decision are recommendations by school officials, advanced placement or honors courses, and evidence of special talent. To graduate, students must complete 126 credit hours with a minimum GPA of 2.0 and no grade in the major below a C. To fulfill the general studies requirements, all students must complete a first-year program, which includes composition and computer literacy courses, and they must also take at least 1 course from each of the following areas: humanistic traditions, music, art, religion, communication arts, literature and language, non-Western studies, behavioral sciences, economics and political science, physical sciences, and life science. 2 credits in health and phys ed and completion of 2 cooperative education experiences are also required. **Procedure:** Freshmen are admitted fall and spring. Entrance exams should be taken by the fall of the senior year. There are early decision, early admissions, and rolling admissions plans. Application deadlines are open. **Transfer Students:** A minimum college GPA of 2.0 is required. 30 of 126 credits required for the bachelor's degree must be completed at Wilberforce. **International Students:** They must take the TOEFL. They must also take the SAT or ACT.

Admissions Contact: Kenneth C. Christmon, Director of Admissions. Email: *admissions@wilberforce.edu* Web: *www.wilberforce.edu*

FINANCIAL AID: Wilberforce University is a member of CSS. The college's own financial statement, and parent and student federal income tax returns are required. The FAFSA code is 003141. Check with the school for current application deadlines.

WILMINGTON COLLEGE B-4

www.wilmington.edu

Wilmington, OH 45177 (937) 382-6661 (800) 341-9318

Fax: (937) 382-7077 **Email: admissions@wilmington.edu**

Full-time: 528 men, 631 women	**Faculty:** n/av
Part-time: 88 men, 148 women	**Ph.D.s:** 69%
Graduate: n/av	**Student/Faculty:** n/av
Year: semesters, summer session	**Tuition:** $25,500
Room & Board: $9600	**Freshman Class:** 1922 applied, 1603 accepted, 380 enrolled
SAT CR/M: 510/550 **ACT:** 21	**CEEB CODE:** 0909
Application Deadline: August 1	**COMPETITIVE**

Wilmington College, established in 1870, is a private institution sponsored by the Society of Friends. The college offers programs in the liberal arts, business, health science, teacher preparation, agricultural studies, religious studies, and athletic training. The figures given in the above capsule and in this profile are approximate. There is 1 undergraduate school and 1 graduate school. In addition to regional accreditation, Wilmington has baccalaureate program accreditation with CAEP and CAAHEP. The 65-acre campus is in a small town 50 miles from Cincinnati and from Columbus. Including any residence halls, there are 21 buildings.

STUDENT LIFE: 98% of undergraduates are from Ohio. Others are from 13 states, and 4 foreign countries. 67% are White; 11% African American; 1% Hispanic. 40% claim no religious affiliation; 17% Catholic. **Female To Male Ratio:** 1.3:1. The average age of freshmen is 18; all undergraduates, 21. 31% do not continue beyond their first year. **Housing:** 842 students can be accommodated in college housing, which includes dorms and on-campus apartments. In addition, there are fraternity houses. On-campus housing is guaranteed for all 4 years. 65% of students live on campus. All students may keep cars.

FACULTY/CLASSROOMS: 65% of faculty are male; 57% are female. All teach undergraduates. No introductory courses are taught by graduate students. The average class size in an introductory lecture is 25 and in a regular course is 19.

PROGRAMS OF STUDY: Wilmington confers B.A. and B.S. degrees. Master's degrees are also awarded. Bachelor's degrees are awarded in AGRICULTURE (agricultural business management, agronomy, animal science, equine science, and range/farm management), BIOLOGICAL SCIENCE (bacteriology, biochemistry, biology/biological science, and environmental biology), BUSINESS (accounting, business administration and management, management science, marketing and distribution, marketing management, and sports management), COMMUNICATIONS AND THE ARTS (advertising, art, communications, dramatic arts, English, journalism, music, public relations, Spanish, and speech/debate/rhetoric), COMPUTER AND PHYSICAL SCIENCE (astronomy, chemistry, computer science, geology, information sciences and systems, mathematics, and planetary and space science), EDUCATION (agricultural education, athletic training, early childhood education, education, elementary education, English education, health education, mathematics education, middle school education, physical education, science education, secondary education, social science education, and social studies education), HEALTH PROFESSIONS (premedicine and preveterinary science), SOCIAL SCIENCE (criminal justice, economics, history, liberal arts/general studies, philosophy, political science/government, prelaw, psychology, religion, social science, social work, and sociology). Chemistry, biology, and athletic training are the strongest academically. Business, agriculture, and athletic training have the largest enrollments.

ACTIVITIES: 8% of men belong to 4 local and 1 national fraternities; 8% of women belong to 4 local sororities. There are 63 groups on campus, including band, cheerleading, choir, chorale, drama, ethnic, honors, international, LGBT, literary magazine, musical theater, newspaper, orchestra, photography, political, professional, religious, social, social service, student government, and yearbook. Popular campus events include Community Day, Westheimer Peace Symposium, and Fall Fest. **Sports:** There are 11 intercollegiate sports for men and 10 for women, and 8 intramural sports for men and 8 for women. Facilities include an Olympic-size pool, a Nautilus weight-training room, an exercise room, racquetball courts, a gym, and a stadium. **Graduates:** From July 1, 2016 to June 30, 2017, 340 bachelor's degrees were awarded. The most popular majors were education (25%), business/marketing (24%), and psychology (10%).

SERVICES: Counseling and information services are available, as is tutoring in every subject. There is remedial math, reading, and writing. **Library/Resources:** The library contains 110,000 volumes, 42,000 microform items, and 1,400 audio/video tapes/CDs/DVDs, and subscribes to 400 periodicals including electronic. Computerized library services include interlibrary loans, database searching, Internet access, and Wi-Fi capability. Special learning facilities include an art gallery, a Peace Resource Center, Quaker museum, a greenhouse, and academic farm. **Physically Challenged Students:** 20% of the campus is accessible. Facilities include wheelchair ramps, elevators, special parking, specially equipped restrooms, and special class scheduling. **Special:** Special academic programs include work-study, internships, a Washington semester, and cross-registration with the Southwest Ohio Consortium. Study abroad may be arranged in Mexico, Austria, France, and other countries. Dual majors in any subject and student-designed majors are offered. Credit for experience, nondegree study, and pass/fail options are possible. There are 5 national honor societies, a freshman honors program, and 3 departmental honors programs. **Visiting:** There are regularly scheduled orientations for prospective students, including meetings with faculty and a tour of the campus. There are guides for informal visits, visitors may sit in on classes, and stay overnight. To schedule a visit, contact the Admissions Office. **Campus Safety and Security:** Measures include 24-hour foot and vehicle patrol and security escort services. There are emergency telephones and lighted pathways/sidewalks.

REQUIREMENTS: The SAT or ACT is required. Applicants must be graduates of an accredited secondary school, with 4 units of English, 2 units each of math, science, and social studies, and a recommended 2 units of foreign language. An additional 6 units is required in other areas. The GED is accepted. An interview is recommended. An essay may be required. AP and CLEP credits are accepted. Important factors in the admissions decision are recommendations by school officials, parents or siblings attended your school, and recommendations by alumni. To graduate, students must complete 124 semester hours, with no more than 60 hours in the major, with a minimum GPA of 2.0. At least 40 hours must be in upper-division work. General education requirements include courses in English and math competence, international knowledge, basic areas of thought and expression, and personal fitness. **Procedure:** Freshmen are admitted fall and spring. Entrance exams should be taken as early as possible. There are deferred admissions and rolling admissions plans. Applications should be filed by August 1 for fall entry. The fall 2017 application fee was $25. Notification is sent on a rolling basis. **Transfer Students:** 63 transfer students enrolled in 2016-2017. Applicants' college and high school transcripts are evaluated on an individual basis. They must have a 2.0 GPA and a completed transfer recommendation form. 30 of 124 credits required for the bachelor's degree must be completed at Wilmington. **International Students:** They must take the TOEFL with a minimum score of 500 on the paper-based TOEFL (PBT). Students who have been previously enrolled in a U.S. high school must also take the SAT or ACT.

ADMISSIONS: 83% of the 2017-2018 applicants were accepted. The SAT scores for the 2017-2018 freshman class were: Critical Reading-- 61% below 500, 28% between 500 and 599, 9% between 600 and 699, and 1% between 700 and 800. Math-- 49% below 500, 35% between 500 and 599, and 16% between 600 and 699. The ACT scores were 20% below 12, 59% between 12 and 17, 10% between 18 and 23, 10% between 24 and 29, and 1% above 30. 39% of the current freshmen were in the top fifth of their class; 70% were in the top two fifths. **Admissions Contact:** Adam Lohrey, Interim Director of Admissions. Email: *admissions@wilmington.edu* Web: *www.wilmington.edu*

FINANCIAL AID: In 2017-2018, 99% of all full-time freshmen received some form of financial aid. The average freshman award was $15,604. Need-based scholarships or need-based grants averaged $10,016; need-based self-help aid (loans and jobs) averaged $4,380; and other non-need-based awards and non-need-based scholarships averaged $6,614. The FAFSA code is 003142. The priority date for freshman financial aid applications for fall entry is March 31. The deadline for filing freshman financial aid applications for fall entry is June 1.

WITTENBERG UNIVERSITY B-3

www.wittenberg.edu

Springfield, OH 45501 (937) 327-6377
(877) 206-0332

Fax: (937) 327-6379 **Email:** admission@wittenberg.edu

Full-time: 829 men, 946 women	**Faculty:** n/av
Part-time: 29 men, 53 women	**Ph.D.s:** n/av
Graduate: 13 men, 14 women	**Student/Faculty:** n/av
Year: semesters, summer session	**Tuition:** $39,480
Room & Board: $10,356	**Freshman Class:** 7249 applied, 5232 accepted, 539 enrolled
SAT EBR-W/M: 590/570 **ACT:** 25	**CEEB CODE:** 1922
Application Deadline: March 15	**VERY COMPETITIVE**

Wittenberg University, founded in 1845, is a private liberal arts and sciences institution affiliated with the Evangelical Lutheran Church of America. There is 1 undergraduate school. In addition to regional accreditation, Wittenberg has baccalaureate program accreditation with

NASM, CAEP, and CCNE. The 114-acre campus is in a suburban area in Springfield, Ohio off of I-70, 25 miles east of Dayton, 40 miles west of Columbus, and 75 miles north of Cincinnati. Including any residence halls, there are 43 buildings.

STUDENT LIFE: 77% of undergraduates are from Ohio. Others are from 37 states, 12 foreign countries, and Canada. 80% are from public schools. 77% are White; 6% two or more races; 4% Hispanic; 10% African American; 1% Asian American; 1% Foreign; 1% race unknown. 34% are Protestant; 33% claim no religious affiliation; 17% Catholic. **Female To Male Ratio:** 1.2:1. The average age of freshmen is 18; all undergraduates, 20. 28% do not continue beyond their first year; 72% remain to graduate. **Housing:** 1606 students can be accommodated in college housing, which includes married student dorms, on-campus apartments, and off-campus apartments. In addition, there are honors houses, language/international houses, special-interest houses, fraternity houses, sorority houses, a substance-free residence hall, and an international awareness house. On-campus housing is guaranteed for the freshman year only and is available on a lottery system for upperclassmen. 85% of students live on campus. All students may keep cars.

FACULTY/CLASSROOMS: All teach undergraduates. No introductory courses are taught by graduate students. The average class size in an introductory lecture is 25; in a laboratory is 20; and in a regular course is 20.

PROGRAMS OF STUDY: Wittenberg confers B.A., B.F.A., B.M.E., and B.S. degrees. Master's degrees are also awarded. Bachelor's degrees are awarded in BIOLOGICAL SCIENCE (biochemistry and biology/biological science), BUSINESS (accounting, business administration and management, finance, management, marketing, and sports management), COMMUNICATIONS AND THE ARTS (art, communications, dance, dramatic arts, English, fine arts, French, German, music, and Spanish), COMPUTER AND PHYSICAL SCIENCE (chemistry, computer science, geology, geology & geology oceanography, mathematics, and physics), EDUCATION (education, elementary education, foreign languages education, middle school education, music education, science education, secondary education, and special education), ENGINEERING AND ENVIRONMENTAL DESIGN (environmental science), HEALTH PROFESSIONS (exercise science), SOCIAL SCIENCE (East Asian studies, economics, history, international relations, philosophy, political science/government, psychology, religion, and sociology). Biology, business, and education have the largest enrollments.

ACTIVITIES: 2% of men belong to 6 national fraternities; 32% of women belong to 5 national sororities. There are 100 groups on campus, including mock trail association, caving club, fishing club, outdoor club, anime club, art, band, cheerleading, choir, chorale, communications, computers, dance, debate, drama, environmental, ethnic, film, honors, international, jazz band, LGBT, literary magazine, musical theater, newspaper, opera, orchestra, pep band, photography, political, professional, radio and TV, religious, social, social service, and student government. Popular campus events include Wittenberg Series, International Festival, Wittfest, and Martin Luther King Jr. Convocation. **Sports:** There are 11 intercollegiate sports for men and 11 for women. Facilities include a multipurpose field house, a swimming pool, racquetball/handball courts, a cardio fitness center, a strength center, sports medicine rooms, a gym, playing fields, baseball stadium, softball field, rugby playing field, a track, and tennis courts. **Graduates:** From July 1, 2016 to June 30, 2017, 423 bachelor's degrees were awarded. The most popular majors were business (18%), social sciences (15%), and biology (14%). In an average class, 61% graduate in 4 years or less and 67% graduate in 6 years or less.

SERVICES: Counseling and information services are available, as is tutoring in most subjects. There is a math workshop, a writing center, an oral communication center, and a language laboratory. **Library/Resources:** The library contains 436,385 volumes, 83,166 microform items, and 7,381 audio/video tapes/CDs/DVDs, and subscribes to 11,933 periodicals including electronic. Computerized library services include interlibrary loans, database searching, Internet access, and Wi-Fi capability. Special learning facilities include an art gallery, radio station, a geology museum, an observatory, a GIS lab with supercomputer, and a parallel processing lab. **Physically Challenged Students:** 81% of the campus is accessible. Facilities include wheelchair ramps, elevators, special parking, specially equipped restrooms, special class scheduling, lowered drinking fountains, and lowered telephones. **Special:** Special academic programs include internships, cross-registration through the Southwest Ohio Consortium, a Washington semester, work-study programs, study-abroad opportunities in many countries, accelerated degree programs, dual and student-designed majors, nondegree study, and pass/fail options. A 3-2 engineering degree is offered through Washington, Columbia, and Case Western Reserve Universities and Georgia Institute of Technology. There is also a 3-2 nursing program with Johns Hopkins University and an occupational therapy program with Washington University. There are 11 national honor societies, Phi Beta Kappa, a freshman honors program, and 19 departmental honors programs. **Visiting:** There are regularly scheduled orientations for prospective students, including a tour and interview. There are guides for informal visits, visitors may sit in on classes, and stay overnight. To schedule a visit, contact Karen Hunt at (877) 206-0332. **Campus Safety and Security:** Measures include 24-hour foot and vehicle patrol, emergency notification system, self-defense education, and security escort services. There are emergency telephones, lighted pathways/sidewalks, a bicycle patrol, and various prevention programs. City police support campus police during the evening. There is also a student Eyes and Ears program and a campus security committee made up of students and faculty.

REQUIREMENTS: Students should have graduated from an accredited secondary school with 16 academic credits, including 4 units of English and 3 units each of foreign language, math, science, and social studies, which includes history. An essay is required and an interview advised. Art students must present a portfolio, and music students must audition. Wittenberg is test score optional. AP credits are accepted. Important factors in the admissions decision are advanced placement or honors courses, evidence of special talent, and extracurricular activities record. To graduate, students must complete at least 126 credits and have a minimum GPA of 2.0. The required minimum GPA and number of hours in the major vary by department. All Wittenberg students complete a program of general education built on 16 learning goals. These include acquisition of foundations skills in writing, math, foreign language, speaking, research, and computing, the understanding of the different arts and sciences disciplines and their distinct methodological approaches to knowledge, and an introduction to non-Western culture, the diversity of human experience, and inter and transdisciplinary knowledge. Students achieve each general education learning goal by completing 1 to 2 courses. As part of general education, students perform 30 hours of community service. **Procedure:** Freshmen are admitted to all sessions. Entrance exams should be taken by the fall of the senior year, but as early as possible. There are early decision, early admissions, deferred admissions, and rolling admissions plans. Early decision applications should be filed by November 15; regular applications, by March 15 for fall entry; and December 1 for spring entry. The fall 2017 application fee was $40. Notification of early decision is sent January 1; regular decision, on a rolling basis. 773 early decision candidates were accepted for the 2017-2018 class. Applications are accepted on-line. **Transfer Students:** 31 transfer students enrolled in 2016-2017. Applicants should have a minimum GPA of 2.0 at an accredited college and be in good academic and social standing. High school transcripts are required in some cases. An interview is recommended. 32 of 126 credits required for the bachelor's degree must be completed at Wittenberg. **International Students:** There are 26 international students enrolled. They must take the TOEFL with a minimum score of 550 on the paper-based TOEFL (PBT) or 79 on the Internet-based version (iBT). Student must take the SAT or ACT. Wittenberg has math and language placement tests.

ADMISSIONS: 72% of the 2017-2018 applicants were accepted. The SAT scores for the 2017-2018 freshman class were: Math-- 20% below 500, 35% between 500 and 599, 35% between 600 and 699, and 10% between 700 and 800. Evidence-Based Reading/Writing-- 12% below 500, 38% between 500 and 599, 36% between 600 and 699, and 14% between 700 and 800. The ACT scores were 3% between 12 and 17, 36% between 18 and 23, 47% between 24 and 29, and 14% above 30. 21% of the current freshmen were in the top fifth of their class; 41% were in the top two fifths. **Admissions Contact:** Karen Hunt, Executive Director of Admissions. Email: *admission@wittenberg.edu* Web: *www.wittenberg.edu*

FINANCIAL AID: The FAFSA code is 003143. The priority date for freshman financial aid applications for fall entry is March 1.

WRIGHT STATE UNIVERSITY B-4
www.wright.edu

Dayton, OH 45435 **(937) 775-5700**

Fax: (937) 775-4410
Email: admissions@wright.edu
Full-time: 4882 men, 5055 women
Faculty: I, -$
Part-time: 1304 men, 1441 women
Ph.D.s: n/av
Graduate: 1969 men, 2191 women
Student/Faculty: n/av
Year: semesters, summer session
Tuition: $8354 ($16,182)
Room & Board: $8629
Freshman Class: 5237 applied, 5067 accepted, 2359 enrolled
SAT CR/M/W: 520/520/490 **ACT:** 22
CEEB CODE: 1179
Application Deadline: open
COMPETITIVE

Wright State University, founded in 1964, is a state-supported institution offering undergraduate programs in business and administration, education and human services, engineering and computer science, liberal arts, math, science, nursing, and health. There are 6 undergraduate schools and 8 graduate schools. In addition to regional accreditation, WSU has baccalaureate program accreditation with AACSB, ABET, CAHEA, CSWE, NASM, CAEP, and NLN. The 557-acre campus is in a suburban area 10 miles northeast of Dayton. Including any residence halls, there are 60 buildings.

STUDENT LIFE: 90% of undergraduates are from Ohio. Others are from 49 states, 69 foreign countries, and Canada. 85% are from public schools. 68% are White; 3% Asian American; 3% Hispanic; 3% two or more races; 12% African American; 11% Foreign. **Female To Male Ratio:** 1.1:1. The average age of freshmen is 18; all undergraduates, 23. 44% do not continue beyond their first year; 40% remain to graduate. **Housing:** 3000 students can be accommodated in college housing, which includes married student dorms and on-campus apartments. In addition, there are honors houses and special-interest houses. On-campus housing is available on a first-come, first-served basis, and is available on a lottery system for upperclassmen. 81% of students commute. Alcohol is not permitted. All students may keep cars.

FACULTY/CLASSROOMS: No introductory courses are taught by graduate students.

PROGRAMS OF STUDY: WSU confers B.A., B.A.C.S., B.A.Mus., B.F.A., B.S., B.S.B., B.S.B.E., B.S.C.E., B.S.C.L.S., B.S.C.S., B.S.Ed., B.S.E.E., B.S.E.P., B.S.I.S.E., B.S.M.E., B.S.M.S.E., B.S.N., and B.T.A.S. degrees. Associate, master's, and doctoral degrees are also awarded. Bachelor's degrees are awarded in BIOLOGICAL SCIENCE (biology/biological science and life science), BUSINESS (accounting, banking and finance, business economics, management information systems, management science, marketing/retailing/merchandising, nonprofit/public organization management, organizational leadership and management, real estate finance, and supply chain management), COMMUNICATIONS AND THE ARTS (American Sign Language, art history, art, art history and appreciation, arts administration/management, classical languages, communications, creative writing, dance, dramatic arts, English, film arts, fine arts, French, German, Greek, guitar, instrumental performance, language arts, Latin, literature, modern language, music, music history and appreciation, music theory and composition, musical theater, organ performance, percussion, Spanish, strings, studio art, theatre acting, theater design, theatre studies, theater management, vocal performance, and winds), COMPUTER AND PHYSICAL SCIENCE (applied mathematics, chemistry, computer science, geology, geophysics and seismology, mathematics, physics, and statistics), EDUCATION (art education, athletic training, business education, childhood education, career, technical education & training, early childhood education, education, elementary education, foreign languages education, mathematics education, middle school education, music education, physical education, science education, secondary education, social science education, and special education), ENGINEERING AND ENVIRONMENTAL DESIGN (biomedical engineering, computer engineering, electrical/electronics engineering, engineering physics, environmental science, industrial engineering, materials engineering, mechanical engineering, systems engineering, and water and wastewater technology), HEALTH PROFESSIONS (clinical science, community health work, environmental health science, exercise science, medical laboratory technology, nursing, predentistry, premedicine, and rehabilitation therapy), SOCIAL SCIENCE (African American studies, anthropology, applied psychology, cognitive science, criminal justice, economics, geography, history, humanities, international relations, liberal arts/general studies, philosophy, political science/government, prelaw, psychology, religion, social work, sociology, and urban studies). Business education, theater arts, and engineering are the strongest academically. Nursing, mechanical engineering, and biological sciences have the largest enrollments.

ACTIVITIES: 3% of men belong to 11 local fraternities; 4% of women belong to 11 local sororities. There are 200 groups on campus, including band, cheerleading, chess, choir, chorale, chorus, computers, dance, drill team, ethnic, film, honors, international, jazz band, LGBT, literary magazine, newspaper, orchestra, pep band, political, professional, radio and TV, religious, social, social service, and student government. Popular campus events include Fall Fest, April Craze, Lunar New Year Celebration, and Madrigal Dinner. **Sports:** There are 7 intercollegiate sports for men and 8 for women, and 26 intramural sports for men and 23 for women. Facilities include an athletic and entertainment center with an arena, an auxiliary gym, baseball and practice fields. The student union houses a natatorium, climbing wall, weight rooms, workout center, game rooms, and playing courts. **Graduates:** From July 1, 2016 to June 30, 2017, 2374 bachelor's degrees were awarded. The most popular majors were nursing (10%), organizational leadership (8%), and psychology (7%). In an average class, 1% graduate in 3 years or less, 21% graduate in 4 years or less, 33% graduate in 5 years or less, and 38% graduate in 6 years or less.

SERVICES: Counseling and information services are available, as is tutoring in most subjects. There is a reader service for the blind, and remedial math, reading, and writing. **Library/Resources:** The library contains 842,026 volumes, 1.4 million microform items, and 20,738 audio/video tapes/CDs/DVDs, and subscribes to 5,700 periodicals including electronic. Computerized library services include interlibrary loans, database searching, Internet access, and Wi-Fi capability. Special learning facilities include an art gallery, radio station, a TV production studio. The Department of Archives and Special Collections houses one of the most complete depositories of information on the Wright Brothers in the world. **Physically Challenged Students:** All of the campus is accessible. Facilities include wheelchair ramps, elevators, special parking, specially equipped restrooms, lowered drinking fountains, lowered telephones, special housing, an underground tunnel system connects all academic buildings. **Special:** B.A.-B.S. degrees are offered in computer science, geography, urban affairs, biological sciences, chemistry, geological sciences, math, and psychology. Cross-registration with other area colleges is available through the Southwestern Ohio Council for Higher Education. Dual majors, co-op programs, internships, study abroad, work-study programs, student-designed majors, nondegree study, and credit for military experience are available. There are 3 national honor societies, a freshman honors program, and 32 departmental honors programs. **Visiting:** There are regularly scheduled orientations for prospective students, including a campus tour and information on academic and student services. There are guides for informal visits and visitors may sit in on classes. To schedule a visit, contact the Office of Undergraduate Admissions. **Campus Safety and Security:** Measures include 24-hour foot and vehicle patrol, emergency notification system, self-defense education, and security escort services. There are shuttle buses, emergency telephones, and lighted pathways/sidewalks.

REQUIREMENTS: The SAT or ACT is required. Applicants should be graduates of an accredited secondary school and have 4 units in English, 3 units each in math, science, and social studies, 2 units in a foreign language, and 1 unit in the arts. A portfolio is required for art majors, an audition for theater and music majors. The GED is accepted. AP and CLEP credits are accepted. To graduate, students must complete 183 quarter hours, with a minimum GPA of 2.0. All students are required to take 56 credit hours of general education courses in 4 areas: communication and math skills, the Western experience, the non-Western world, and understanding the contemporary world. **Procedure:** Freshmen are admitted to all sessions. Entrance exams should be taken in the spring of the junior year. There are deferred admissions and rolling admissions plans. Application deadlines are open. The fall 2017 application fee was $30. Applications are accepted on-line. **Transfer Students:** 2031 transfer students enrolled in 2016-2017. Applicants must have a 2.0 GPA. 45 of 183 credits required for the bachelor's degree must be completed at WSU. **International Students:** There are 671 international students enrolled. They must take the TOEFL with a minimum score of 500 on the paper-based TOEFL (PBT) or 61 on the Internet-based version (iBT).

ADMISSIONS: 97% of the 2017-2018 applicants were accepted. The

SAT scores for the 2017-2018 freshman class were: Critical Reading-- 40% below 500, 36% between 500 and 599, 21% between 600 and 699, and 3% between 700 and 800. Math-- 40% below 500, 39% between 500 and 599, 18% between 600 and 699, and 3% between 700 and 800. Writing-- 54% below 500, 33% between 500 and 599, 11% between 600 and 699, and 1% between 700 and 800. The ACT scores were 40% below 12, 25% between 12 and 17, 18% between 18 and 23, 9% between 24 and 29, and 8% above 30. 31% of the current freshmen were in the top fifth of their class; 57% were in the top two fifths. **Admissions Contact:** Cathy Davis, Assistant VP for Undergraduate Admission. Email: *admissions@wright.edu* Web: *www.wright.edu*

FINANCIAL AID: In 2017-2018, 83% of all full-time freshmen received some form of financial aid. 71% of all full-time freshmen received need-based aid. The average freshman award was $8,912. Need-based scholarships or need-based grants averaged $5,937; need-based self-help aid (loans and jobs) averaged $4,370; non-need-based athletic scholarships averaged $10,010; and other non-need-based awards and non-need-based scholarships averaged $3,132. 14% of undergraduate students work part-time. The average financial indebtedness of the 2017 graduate was $28,349. WSU is a member of CSS. The FAFSA code is 003078. The priority date for freshman financial aid applications for fall entry is March 1.

XAVIER UNIVERSITY — A-5

www.xavier.edu

Cincinnati, OH 45207 — (513) 745-1014, (877) 982-3648

Fax: (513) 745-4319	**Email:** xuadmit@xavier.edu
Full-time: 2022 men, 2348 women	**Faculty:** 352
Part-time: 136 men, 139 women	**Ph.D.s:** 79%
Graduate: 821 men, 1332 women	**Student/Faculty:** 12 to 1
Year: semesters, summer session	**Tuition:** $37,230
Room & Board: $12,150	**Freshman Class:** 13006 applied, 9613 accepted, 1239 enrolled
SAT EBR-W/M: 580/570 **ACT:** 25	**CEEB CODE:** 1965
Application Deadline: February 1	**VERY COMPETITIVE**

Xavier University, founded in 1831, is a comprehensive Jesuit institution affiliated with the Roman Catholic Church. There are 3 undergraduate schools and 3 graduate schools. In addition to regional accreditation, Xavier has baccalaureate program accreditation with AACSB, CSWE, NASM, CAEP, ACS, CEA, ACOTE, CAHME, CACREP, CCNE, JRCERT, MACTE, APA, CAATE, and COSMA. The 175-acre campus is in an urban area 5 miles northeast of the center of Cincinnati. Including any residence halls, there are 55 buildings.

STUDENT LIFE: 55% of undergraduates are from out of state, mostly the Midwest. Students are from 48 states, 47 foreign countries, and Canada. 52% are from public schools. 9% are African American; 74% White; 6% Hispanic; 4% two or more races; 3% Asian American; 2% Foreign; 2% race unknown. 54% are Catholic; 15% Protestant. **Female To Male Ratio:** 1.3:1. The average age of freshmen is 18; all undergraduates, 21. 16% do not continue beyond their first year; 69% remain to graduate. **Housing:** 2301 students can be accommodated in college housing, which includes dorms, on-campus apartments, and off-campus apartments. In addition, there are honors houses, and living learning communities. On-campus housing is guaranteed for the freshman year only, is available on a first-come, first-served basis, and is available on a lottery system for upperclassmen. 51% of students live on campus. All students may keep cars.

FACULTY/CLASSROOMS: 44% of faculty are male; 56% are female. 96% teach undergraduates. No introductory courses are taught by graduate students. The average class size in an introductory lecture is 20; in a laboratory is 16; and in a regular course is 20.

PROGRAMS OF STUDY: Xavier confers B.A., B.S., Honors A.B., B.F.A., B.L.A., B.D.U., B.S.B.A., B.S.N., and B.S.W. degrees. Associate, master's, and doctoral degrees are also awarded. Bachelor's degrees are awarded in AGRICULTURE (agriculture), BIOLOGICAL SCIENCE (biology/biological science, biophysics, and life science), BUSINESS (accounting, banking and finance, business administration and management, business economics, business intelligence and analytics, entrepreneurial studies, human resources, international business management, management science, marketing/retailing/merchandising, purchasing/inventory management, sports management, sports marketing, and sustainable management), COMMUNICATIONS AND THE ARTS (advertising, art, classics, communication rhetoric/communication, design, digital media, English, fine arts, French, German, media arts, modern language, music, public relations, Spanish, theatre arts, and theatre studies), COMPUTER AND PHYSICAL SCIENCE (actuarial science, applied physics, chemistry, computer science, information sciences and systems, mathematics, natural sciences, physics, and radiological technology), EDUCATION (early childhood education, education, health information management, middle school education, music education, science education, and special education), ENGINEERING AND ENVIRONMENTAL DESIGN (engineering physics and environmental science), HEALTH PROFESSIONS (biomedical science, health administration and policy, health care administration, nursing, preallied health, and prepharmacy), SOCIAL SCIENCE (counseling/psychology, criminal justice, economics, gender studies, history, humanities, international studies, liberal arts/general studies, philosophy, political science/government, psychology, social work, sociology, theological studies, and urban ecology). Natural sciences & philosophy, politics, and public honors program are the strongest academically. Nursing, liberal arts, and biology have the largest enrollments.

ACTIVITIES: There are no fraternities or sororities. There are 163 groups on campus, including art, band, cheerleading, choir, chorale, chorus, communications, computers, dance, debate, drama, drill team, environmental, ethnic, honors, international, jazz band, LGBT, literary magazine, musical theater, newspaper, orchestra, pep band, political, professional, radio and TV, religious, social, social service, student government, and symphony. Popular campus events include Club Day, Week of Welcome, Community Action Day, Family Weekend, Spirit Celebration, Winter Week of Welcome, Winter Club Day, and Community Action Day. **Sports:** There are 8 intercollegiate sports for men and 8 for women, and 12 intramural sports for men and 12 for women. Facilities include a field house, sports center, six-lane, 25-meter pool, basketball and volleyball courts, baseball and soccer fields, rifle range, tennis courts, golf center, student-athlete lounge, strength and conditioning facility, and an athletic training facility. **Graduates:** From July 1, 2016 to June 30, 2017, 1161 bachelor's degrees were awarded. The most popular majors were nursing (8%), finance (7%), and Liberal arts (6%). In an average class, 61% graduate in 4 years or less, 68% graduate in 5 years or less, and 69% graduate in 6 years or less. Of the 2016 graduating class, 68% were employed within 6 months of graduation.

SERVICES: Counseling and information services are available, as is tutoring in every subject. There is a reader service for the blind, and remedial math, reading, and writing. Xavier has a Learning Assistance Center which provides individual and small group tutoring in almost all subjects and study skills assistance, a math lab, and a writing center. There is also an efficient reading and study skills course. **Library/Resources:** The library contains 915,154 volumes, 19,402 microform items, and 30,797 audio/video tapes/CDs/DVDs, and subscribes to 208,232 periodicals including electronic. Computerized library services include interlibrary loans, database searching, Internet access, and Wi-Fi capability. Special learning facilities include an art gallery, radio station, TV station, an observatory and a financial trading room. **Physically Challenged Students:** 99% of the campus is accessible. Facilities include wheelchair ramps, elevators, special parking, specially equipped restrooms, special class scheduling, lowered drinking fountains, lowered telephones, and special housing. **Special:** Xavier offers internships related to some majors, cross-registration through the Greater Cincinnati Consortium, and co-op programs in business and computer science. Students may study abroad in over 100 countries through Xavier's network of program providers. A Washington semester and nondegree study are available. A 4-2 engineering degree is offered with the University of Cincinnati, and a 3-2 applied biology degree is offered with Duke University. There are 11 national honor societies, Phi Beta Kappa, a freshman honors program, and 2 departmental honors programs. **Visiting:** There are regularly scheduled orientations for prospective students, including an interview and a tour of the campus. There are guides for informal visits and visitors may sit in on classes. To schedule a visit, contact Office of Undergraduate Admission. **Campus Safety and Security:** Measures include 24-hour foot and vehicle patrol, emergency notification system, self-defense education, and security escort services. There are shuttle buses, emergency telephones, lighted pathways/sidewalks, controlled access to dorms/residences, alcohol awareness, drug awareness, sexual assault programs, security camera system for certain areas on campus, a Title IX Coordinator, a Bias Advisory Response Team (BART), and an Xavier Action and Care Team (X-ACT).

REQUIREMENTS: Graduation from an accredited secondary school or satisfactory scores on the GED are required for admission. The school requires 21 academic credits, including 4 years of English, 3 each of math, social studies, and science, 2 of foreign language, and 1 of health/phys ed, plus 5 electives, one essay no fewer than 250 words, at least one recommendation from a high school counselor (preferred) or teacher, satisfactory results on the ACT or the SAT, and a resume or list of activities. AP and CLEP credits are accepted. Important factors in the admissions decision are advanced placement or honors courses, leadership record, and extracurricular activities record. To graduate, students must complete a minimum of 120 credit hours with a minimum GPA of 2.0. The total number of hours required in the major varies. All students must take core curriculum courses in English composition, cultural diversity, math, science, social science, history, theology, philosophy, a foreign language, literature, fine arts, and an ethics/religion and society focus, as well as a zero-credit first-year journey course ("GOA") that meets six times each semester for the first year, and an additional first-year seminar course. **Procedure:** Freshmen are admitted fall, spring, and summer. Entrance exams should be taken by fall of the senior year. There are deferred admissions and rolling admissions plans. Applications should be filed by February 1 for fall entry; December 1 for spring entry; and May 10 for summer entry. The fall 2017 application fee was $35. Notifications are sent April 15. Applications are accepted on-line. **Transfer Students:** 61 transfer students enrolled in 2016-2017. Transfer students must have a minimum GPA of 2.0 in all college-level work. Students who transfer to Xavier with 30 or more semester hours are not required to submit results of the ACT or SAT tests or a counselor recommendation. 30 of 120 credits required for the bachelor's degree must be completed at Xavier. **International Students:** There are 118 international students enrolled. They must take the TOEFL with a minimum score of 550 on the paper-based TOEFL (PBT) or 79 on the Internet-based version (iBT). They must also take the SAT or ACT.

ADMISSIONS: 74% of the 2017-2018 applicants were accepted. The SAT scores for the 2017-2018 freshman class were: Math-- 15% below 500, 49% between 500 and 599, 31% between 600 and 699, and 5% between 700 and 800. Evidence-Based Reading/Writing-- 11% below 500, 47% between 500 and 599, 37% between 600 and 699, and 5% between 700 and 800. The ACT scores were 2% between 12 and 17, 34% between 18 and 23, 50% between 24 and 29, and 14% above 30. 45% of the current freshmen were in the top fifth of their class; 80% were in the top two fifths. 11 freshmen graduated first in their class. **Admissions Contact:** Lauren Parcell, Dean of Undergraduate Admissions. Email: *xuadmit@xavier.edu* Web: *www.xavier.edu*

FINANCIAL AID: In 2017-2018, 99% of all full-time freshmen received some form of financial aid. 67% of all full-time freshmen received need-based aid. The average freshman award was $24,999. Need-based scholarships or need-based grants averaged $22,459 ($40,365 maximum); need-based self-help aid (loans and jobs) averaged $3,723 ($5,900 maximum); non-need-based athletic scholarships averaged $9,830 ($40,384 maximum); and other non-need-based awards and non-need-based scholarships averaged $17,937 ($37,920 maximum). 33% of undergraduate students work part-time. The average financial indebtedness of the 2017 graduate was $32,687. Xavier is a member of CSS. The FAFSA code is 003144. The priority date for freshman financial aid applications for fall entry is February 15.

YOUNGSTOWN STATE UNIVERSITY E-2

www.ysu.edu

Youngstown, OH 44555	**(330) 941-2000** **(877) 468-6978**
Fax: (330) 941-3674	**Email: enroll@ysu.edu**
Full-time: 4365 men, 4515 women	**Faculty:** 399; IIA, -$
Part-time: 1142 men, 1363 women	**Ph.D.s:** 87%
Graduate: 496 men, 761 women	**Student/Faculty:** 22 to 1
Year: semesters, summer session	**Tuition:** $8397 ($14,397)
Room & Board: $9090	**Freshman Class:** 6446 accepted, 2278 enrolled
SAT CR/M/W: 490/500/465 **ACT:** 21	**CEEB CODE:** 1975
Application Deadline: August 1	**COMPETITIVE**

Youngstown State University, founded in 1908, is a publicly funded, primarily commuter institution offering undergraduate, graduate and doctoral programs in education, business, creative arts and communication, health and human services, liberal arts and social sciences, science, technology, engineering, and mathematics. There are 6 undergraduate schools and 1 graduate school. In addition to regional accreditation, YSU has baccalaureate program accreditation with AACSB, ABET, ADA, CSWE, NASAD, NASM, NCATE, NLN, ACS, ACEND, AAFS, AAFCS, CoARC, NAACLS, NAST, ETAC-ABET, and ACTFL. The 160-acre campus is in an urban area 65 miles southeast of Cleveland. Including any residence halls, there are 57 buildings.

STUDENT LIFE: 85% of undergraduates are from Ohio. Others are from 36 states, 72 foreign countries, and Canada. 74% are White; 10% African American; 4% Hispanic; 4% race unknown; 3% Foreign; 3% two or more races; 1% Asian American; 1% American Indian/Alaska Native. **Female To Male Ratio:** 1.1:1. The average age of freshmen is 18.5; all undergraduates, 22.1. 23% do not continue beyond their first year; 36% remain to graduate. **Housing:** 1400 students can be accommodated in college housing, which includes gender neutral, single sex, coed, married student dorms, and on-campus apartments. In addition, there are honors houses, academic learning communities. On-campus housing is available on a first-come and first-served basis. 87% of students commute. All students may keep cars.

FACULTY/CLASSROOMS: 50% of faculty are male; 50% are female. All teach undergraduates. No introductory courses are taught by graduate students.

PROGRAMS OF STUDY: YSU confers B.A., B.S., B.E., B.F.A., B.G.S., B.M., B.S., B.S.A.S., B.S.B.A., B.S.Ed., B.S.N., B.S.R.C., B.S.W and B.S.D.H degrees. Associate, master's, and doctoral degrees are also awarded. Bachelor's degrees are awarded in AGRICULTURE (environmental studies), BIOLOGICAL SCIENCE (biochemistry, biology/biological science, and nutrition), BUSINESS (accounting, apparel and accessories marketing, banking and finance, business administration and management, business economics, fashion merchandising, hospitality management services, hotel/motel and restaurant management, human resources, management information systems, marketing management, marketing/retailing/merchandising, retailing, and supply chain management), COMMUNICATIONS AND THE ARTS (advertising, applied music, art history, art, art history and appreciation, broadcasting, communications, dance, design, digital media, dramatic arts, English, English literature, film, television and digital media, graphic design, information technology, Italian, jazz, journalism, keyboard - piano concentration, literature, media arts, music, music composition, music history and appreciation, music performance, music theory and composition, musical theater, painting, percussion, performing arts, photography, piano/organ, piano performance, printmaking, public relations, Spanish, sports media, strings, studio art, technical and business writing, telecommunications, theatre acting, theatre arts, theatre production, theatre studies, vocal performance, voice, vocal music education, and winds), COMPUTER AND PHYSICAL SCIENCE (actuarial mathematics, applied mathematics, astronomy and physics, chemistry, computer programming, computer science, digital arts/technology, geology, information sciences and systems, mathematics, physical sciences, physics, and statistics), EDUCATION (art education, childhood education, early childhood education, education, English education, general studies, health education, mathematics education, middle school education, music education, physical education, physical science secondary school education, science education, secondary education, social science education, social studies education, social studies secondary school education, Spanish adolescence education, special education, and vocational education), ENGINEERING AND ENVIRONMENTAL DESIGN (chemical engineering, civil engineering, civil engineering technology, computer technology, electrical/electronics engineering, electrical/electronics engineering technology, engineering, graphic and printing production, industrial engineering, manufacturing engineering, mechanical engineering, and mechanical engineering technology), HEALTH PROFESSIONS (allied health, clinical science, dental hygiene, exercise science, nursing, nursing home administration, predentistry, premedicine, preoptometry, preosteopathy, preveterinary science, public health, and respiratory therapy), SOCIAL SCIENCE (anthropology, child care/child and family studies, criminal justice, dietetics, early childhood studies, economics, family/consumer studies, food science, forensic studies, geography, gerontology, history, Italian studies, law enforcement and corrections, philosophy, philosophy and religion, political science/government, prelaw, psychology, religion, social studies, social work, sociology, and Spanish studies). Teacher education, criminal justice, and biological sciences have the largest enrollments.

ACTIVITIES: 2% of men belong to 6 national fraternities; 3% of women

belong to 5 national sororities. There are 206 groups on campus, including art, band, cheerleading, choir, chorale, chorus, clubs for engineering and education, computers, dance, debate, drama, environmental, ethnic, film, forensics, honors, international, jazz band, LGBT, literary magazine, marching band, musical theater, newspaper, opera, orchestra, pep band, photography, political, professional, radio and TV, religious, social, social service, student government, symphony, and yearbook. Popular campus events include Organizational Fair, Greek Sing, Homecoming and Welcome Week, Martin Luther King Jr. Breakfast, and Cinco de Mayo. **Sports:** There are 8 intercollegiate sports for men and 10 for women, and 9 intramural sports for men and 8 for women. Facilities include a recreation and wellness center which contains strength and conditioning equipment, a rock wall, a multi-purpose sports forum with courts for volleyball, basketball, and an 1/8-mile track, a tranquil meditation studio, an outdoor complex, indoor athletic facility containing a 300-meter competition track, a full-length football field, batting cages, a putting green, track and field, softball, soccer, baseball, and football. **Graduates:** From July 1, 2016 to June 30, 2017, 1632 bachelor's degrees were awarded. The most popular majors were criminal justice (7%), social work (6%), and nursing (6%). In an average class, 2% graduate in 3 years or less, 14% graduate in 4 years or less, 28% graduate in 5 years or less, and 36% graduate in 6 years or less. Of the 2016 graduating class, 17% were enrolled in graduate school within 6 months of graduation, and 55% were employed.

SERVICES: Counseling and information services are available, as is tutoring in most subjects. There is a reader service for the blind, and remedial math, reading, and writing. **Library/Resources:** The library contains 773,051 volumes, 997,833 microform items, and 17,382 audio/video tapes/CDs/DVDs, and subscribes to 70,584 periodicals including electronic. Computerized library services include interlibrary loans, database searching, Internet access, and Wi-Fi capability. Special learning facilities include an art gallery, natural history museum, planetarium, radio station, a center for historic preservation, university archives and special collections, and the Rose Melnick medical museum, McDonough Museum of Art, planetarium. **Physically Challenged Students:** 98% of the campus is accessible. Facilities include wheelchair ramps, elevators, special parking, specially equipped restrooms, special class scheduling, lowered drinking fountains, and special housing. **Special:** YSU offers co-op programs in a variety of majors, as well as internships, work study, dual majors, credit for military experience, nondegree study, honors degree programs, distance learning, accelerated degrees, and pass/fail options. Student-designed majors are available through the Individualized Curriculum Program, Washington Semester, study abroad in a variety of countries and cross registration opportunities and accelerated degree program, partnerships with community colleges, The English Language Institute, off-site degree programs, University honors program, 4+1 program Economics and Mathematics, combined BS/MS program in chemistry, and online programs. There are 18 national honor societies and a freshman honors program. **Visiting:** There are regularly scheduled orientations for prospective students, including an official academic advising session, registration for classes, and complete overview of the university resources and services. There are guides for informal visits and visitors may sit in on classes. To schedule a visit, contact the Office of Admissions. **Campus Safety and Security:** Measures include 24-hour foot and vehicle patrol, emergency notification system, self-defense education, and security escort services. There are shuttle buses, emergency telephones, lighted pathways/sidewalks, controlled access to dorms/residences, night security posts in dorms, and concentrated security in parking and other critical areas.

REQUIREMENTS: Students who have a 2.0 H.S. GPA and a 17 or higher ACT composite, or a SAT combined Math and Evidence-based Reading and Writing score of 910 or higher will be admitted to the university. Students not meeting these requirements may be admitted conditionally. Students who have been out of school for 2 or more years and who are not pursuing a restricted program of study are exempt from test requirements. Graduation from an accredited secondary school or satisfactory scores on the GED are required for all applicants. High school courses recommended are 4 units each of English and math, 3 each of science and social studies, 2 of foreign language, and 1 of fine or performing arts. AP and CLEP credits are accepted. A minimum of 120 semester hours must be successfully completed to earn a bachelor's degree, with a minimum GPA of 2.0. At least 60 semester hours must be completed in courses numbered 2600 or higher; at least 48 of these 60 hours must be in courses numbered 3700 or higher. All students must fulfill core requirements including requirements in English, speech, and math. **Procedure:** Freshmen are admitted fall, spring, and summer. Entrance exams should be taken during spring of the junior year or fall of the senior year. There are deferred admissions and rolling admissions plans. Applications should be filed by August 1 for fall entry; December 1 for spring entry; and April 15 for summer entry. The fall 2017 application fee was $45. Notification is sent on a rolling basis. Applications are accepted on-line. **Transfer Students:** 927 transfer students enrolled in 2016-2017. Transfer applicants in good standing at the last institution attended with an aggregate cumulative point average of 2.0 or higher for all courses taken at other colleges or universities are admitted in good standing. Those on probation or with an aggregate cumulative point average of less than 2.0 may be considered for probationary transfer if their overall academic record, including high school grades and test scores, indicates potential success. Applicants suspended or dismissed from other institutions are not eligible for consideration (without appeal to the Office of Undergraduate Admission) until at least 1 semester has passed following the term in which the suspension occurred. 30 of 120 credits required for the bachelor's degree must be completed at YSU. **International Students:** There are 196 international students enrolled. They must take the TOEFL with a minimum score of 500 on the paper-based TOEFL (PBT) or 61 on the Internet-based version (iBT). Students must take the MELAB with a minimum score of 80.

ADMISSIONS: The SAT scores for the 2017-2018 freshman class were: Critical Reading-- 52% below 500, 30% between 500 and 599, 12% between 600 and 699, and 6% between 700 and 800. Math-- 45% below 500, 27% between 500 and 599, 17% between 600 and 699, and 11% between 700 and 800. Writing-- 61% below 500, 19% between 500 and 599, 15% between 600 and 699, and 5% between 700 and 800. The ACT scores were 16% between 12 and 17, 53% between 18 and 23, 26% between 24 and 29, and 5% above 30. 27% of the current freshmen were in the top fifth of their class; 55% were in the top two fifths. 91 freshmen graduated first in their class. **Admissions Contact:** Sue Davis, Director, Admissions. Email: *enroll@ysu.edu* Web: *www.ysu.edu*

FINANCIAL AID: In 2017-2018, 95% of all full-time freshmen received some form of financial aid. 70% of all full-time freshmen received need-based aid. The average freshman award was $10,287. 18% of undergraduate students work part-time. The average financial indebtedness of the 2017 graduate was $21,297. YSU is a member of CSS. The college's own financial statement is required. The FAFSA code is 003145. The deadline for filing freshman financial aid applications for fall entry is December 1.

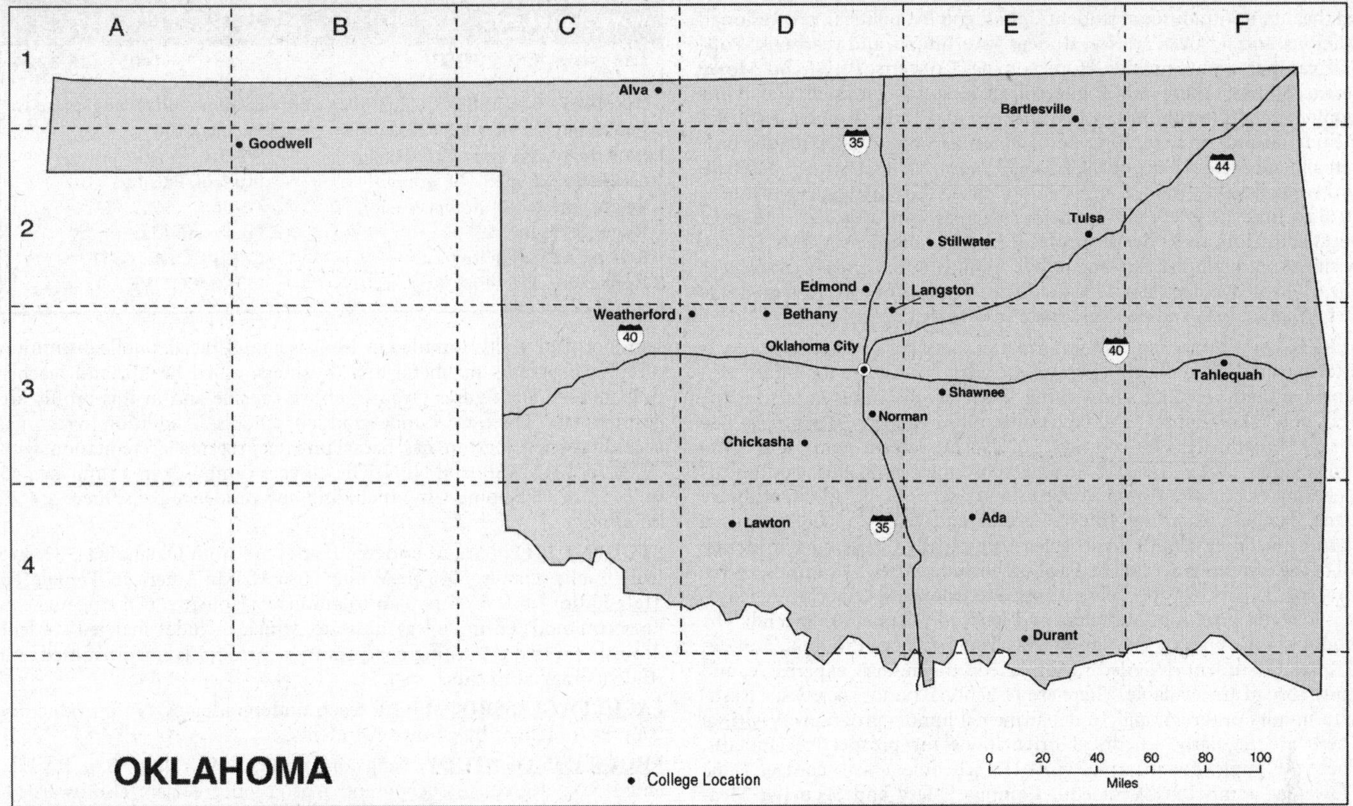

CAMERON UNIVERSITY *(The complete profile is made available exclusively on our website, www.barronspac.com)*

EAST CENTRAL UNIVERSITY E-4

www.ecok.edu

Ada, OK 74820

(580) 559-5628
(877) 310-5628
Email: admissions@ecok.edu

Full-time: 985 men, 1384 women
Part-time: 230 men, 427 women
Graduate: 175 men, 434 women
Year: semesters, summer session
Room & Board: $6730

SAT M/W: 540/400
Application Deadline: open

Faculty: n/av
Ph.D.s: 50%
Student/Faculty: 19 to 1
Tuition: $6600 ($15,720)
Freshman Class: 1423 applied, 822 accepted, 597 enrolled
CEEB CODE: 6186
COMPETITIVE

East Central University, founded in 1909, is a publicly funded institution offering undergraduate programs in liberal arts and sciences, education, business, and health-related fields, and graduate programs in accounting, education, human resources, psychology, and water management. There are 4 undergraduate schools and 4 graduate schools. In addition to regional accreditation, ECU has baccalaureate program accreditation with ACBSP, CSWE, NASM, CAEP, ACEN, CACR, and NEHS. The 144-acre campus is in a small town 90 miles south of Oklahoma City. Including any residence halls, there are 40 buildings.

STUDENT LIFE: 87% of undergraduates are from Oklahoma. Others are from 22 states, 32 foreign countries, and Canada. 98% are from public schools. 60% are White; 14% American Indian/Alaska Native; 8% Foreign; 8% two or more races; 5% African American; 5% Asian American; 4% Hispanic; 3% race unknown. **Female To Male Ratio:** 1.6:1. The average age of freshmen is 19; all undergraduates, 25. 35% do not continue beyond their first year; 36% remain to graduate. **Housing:** 1275 students can be accommodated in college housing, which includes dorms. In addition, there are special-interest houses, fraternity houses, and sorority houses. On-campus housing is available on a first-come and first-served basis. 65% of students commute. Alcohol is not permitted. All students may keep cars.

FACULTY/CLASSROOMS: 48% of faculty are male; 52% are female. 97% teach undergraduates, 50% do research, and 50% do both. Graduate students teach 3% of introductory courses.

PROGRAMS OF STUDY: ECU confers B.A., B.S., B.Gen.Studies., B.S.Ed., and B.S.W. degrees. Master's degrees are also awarded. Bachelor's degrees are awarded in BIOLOGICAL SCIENCE (biology/biological science), BUSINESS (accounting, banking and finance, business administration w/legal studies, business administration and management, business administration marketing, business information systems, entrepreneurial studies, fashion merchandising, management, marketing, recreation and leisure services, and retailing), COMMUNICATIONS AND THE ARTS (advertising, art, communications, dramatic arts, English, fine/studio arts, general, keyboard - piano concentration, music, piano/organ, speech/debate/rhetoric, communication arts-speech, sports administration, studio art, theatre arts, vocal performance, voice, and vocal music education), COMPUTER AND PHYSICAL SCIENCE (applied mathematics, chemistry, computer science, mathematics, mathematics-actuarial concentration, and physics), EDUCATION (art education, athletic training, business education, early childhood education, elementary education, English education, general studies, mathematics education, music education, physical education, and special education), ENGINEERING AND ENVIRONMENTAL DESIGN (cartography, textile, and fashion merchandising & design), HEALTH PROFESSIONS (dental hygiene, environmental health science, exercise science, kinesiology, medical technology, nursing, premedicine, preoptometry, prepharmacy, and pre-physician assistant), SOCIAL SCIENCE (child care/child and family studies, counseling/psychology, criminal justice, family/consumer resource management, family/consumer studies, family/juvenile justice, geography, history, human services, law enforcement and corrections, legal studies, liberal arts/general studies, Native American studies, political science/government, prelaw, psychology, social work, and sociology). Nursing, accounting, and biology have the largest enrollments.

ACTIVITIES: 3% of men belong to 3 national fraternities; 2% of women belong to 2 national sororities. There are 63 groups on campus, including art, band, cheerleading, choir, chorale, chorus, computers, dance, debate, drama, drill team, environmental, ethnic, forensics, honors, international, jazz band, LGBT, literary magazine, marching band, musical theater, nontraditional students, photography, political, professional, religious, social, social service, student government, and yearbook. Popular campus events include Homecoming, Concerts, Plays, and Movie Series. **Sports:** There are 4 intercollegiate sports for men and 5 for women, and 10 intramural sports for men and 10 for women. Facilities include an indoor swimming pool, fitness/aerobics center, tennis, basketball, and racquetball courts, a weight room, football, soccer, baseball, and softball fields, indoor and outdoor tracks. **Graduates:** From July 1, 2016 to June 30, 2017, 688 bachelor's degrees were awarded. The most popular majors were health professions and related programs (20%), business/marketing (12%), and public administration and social sciences (10%). In an average class, 17% graduate in 4 years or less, 30% graduate in 5 years or less, and 36% graduate in 6 years or less.

SERVICES: Counseling and information services are available, as is tutoring in every subject. There is a reader service for the blind, and remedial math, reading, and writing. There are also interpreters for the deaf, note taking/typing, and tape transcription. **Library/Resources:** The library contains 615,700 volumes, 337,298 microform items, and 3,106 audio/video tapes/CDs/DVDs, and subscribes to 87,965 periodicals including electronic. Computerized library services include interlibrary loans, database searching, Internet access, and Wi-Fi capability. Special learning facilities include an art gallery. **Physically Challenged Students:** All of the campus is accessible. Facilities include wheelchair ramps, elevators, special parking, specially equipped restrooms, special class scheduling, lowered drinking fountains, and lowered telephones. **Special:** The school is a member of the National Student Exchange Program. Nondegree study, student designed majors, credit for military experience, and study abroad are available. There are 11 national honor societies, a freshman honors program, and 16 departmental honors programs. **Visiting:** There are regularly scheduled orientations for prospective students. There are guides for informal visits. To schedule a visit, contact Dana Clower at admissions@ecok.edu. **Campus Safety and Security:** Measures include 24-hour foot and vehicle patrol, emergency notification system, self-defense education, and security escort services. There are emergency telephones, lighted pathways/sidewalks, and controlled access to dorms/residences.

REQUIREMENTS: The ACT is required, with a minimum composite score of 20, but the SAT will be accepted in place of the ACT. Applicants must be graduates of an accredited secondary school or have the GED. High school courses must include 4 years of English, 3 years each of math, science (1 year must be a lab), history and citizenship skills, and 2 years of subjects previously listed or selected from computer science, foreign language, or any Advanced Placement course except courses in the fine arts. ECU requires applicants to be in the upper 50% of their class. A GPA of 2.7 is required. AP and CLEP credits are accepted. To graduate, students must complete a minimum of 124 credit hours with a minimum GPA of 2.0. 60 hours must be from a 4-year college/university. At least 15 hours of his/her last semester before graduation or at least 50 percent of the hours required by the major must be earned from ECU. All students must take 40 hours of upper-level courses, as well as 45 hours in general studies, and must meet computer proficiency requirements. **Procedure:** Freshmen are admitted to all sessions. Entrance exams should be taken during the junior or senior year of high school. Application deadlines are open. The fall 2017 application fee was $20. Applications are accepted on-line. **Transfer Students:** 235 transfer students enrolled in 2016-2017. Applicants having fewer than 24 credit hours must meet the criteria for entering freshmen. The required minimum GPA for transfer students is 2.7. 30 of 124 credits required for the bachelor's degree must be completed at ECU. **International Students:** There are 225 international students enrolled. They must take the TOEFL with a minimum score of 500 on the paper-based TOEFL (PBT) or 61 on the Internet-based version (iBT). They must also take the SAT or ACT, scoring 20.

ADMISSIONS: 58% of the 2017-2018 applicants were accepted. The SAT scores for the 2017-2018 freshman class were: Critical Reading-- 95% below 500 and 5% between 500 and 599. Math-- 30% below 500, 48% between 500 and 599, 18% between 600 and 699, and 4% between 700 and 800. The ACT scores were 26% between 12 and 17, 53% between 18 and 23, 18% between 24 and 29, and 3% above 30. **Admissions Contact:** Sheppard McConnell, Director of Admissions. Email: *admissions@ecok.edu* Web: *www.ecok.edu*

FINANCIAL AID: The FAFSA code is 003154. The priority date for freshman financial aid applications for fall entry is March 1.

LANGSTON UNIVERSITY — D-3

www.lunet.edu

Langston, OK 73050 — **(405) 466-3224**

Fax: (405) 466-3381	**Email:** admissions@langston.edu
Full-time: 1290 men, 1920 women	**Faculty:** 105
Part-time: 290 men, 520 women	**Ph.D.s:** 50%
Graduate: 20 men, 40 women	**Student/Faculty:** 31 to 1
Year: semesters, summer session	**Tuition:** $6059 ($13,459)
Room & Board: $9600	**Freshman Class:** n/av
SAT or ACT: required	**CEEB CODE:** 6361
Application Deadline: August 10	**COMPETITIVE**

Langston University, founded in 1897, is a multiracial, public institution offering programs in liberal arts, business, allied health, and teacher preparation. The figures given in above capsule and in this profile are approximate. There are 9 undergraduate schools. In addition to regional accreditation, Langston has baccalaureate program accreditation with ADA, APTA, CAEP, and NLN. The 40-acre campus is in a rural area 45 miles from Oklahoma City. Including any residence halls, there are 20 buildings.

STUDENT LIFE: 66% of undergraduates are from Oklahoma. 98% are from public schools. 50% are White; 50% African American. **Female To Male Ratio:** 1.6:1. 65% remain to graduate. **Housing:** 676 students can be accommodated in college housing, which includes married student dorms, and living learning communities. Alcohol is not permitted. All students may keep cars.

FACULTY/CLASSROOMS: All teach undergraduates. No introductory courses are taught by graduate students.

PROGRAMS OF STUDY: Langston confers B.A., B.B.A., B.S., B.S.Ed., and B.S.N. degrees. Associate and master's degrees are also awarded. Bachelor's degrees are awarded in AGRICULTURE (agricultural economics and animal science), BIOLOGICAL SCIENCE (biology/biological science and nutrition), BUSINESS (accounting, business administration and management, and management science), COMMUNICATIONS AND THE ARTS (dramatic arts, English, music, and speech/debate/rhetoric), COMPUTER AND PHYSICAL SCIENCE (chemistry, computer science, and mathematics), EDUCATION (business education, elementary education, home economics education, industrial arts education, mathematics education, physical education, and science education), ENGINEERING AND ENVIRONMENTAL DESIGN (industrial engineering technology), HEALTH PROFESSIONS (health care administration, medical laboratory technology, nursing, and physical therapy), SOCIAL SCIENCE (criminal justice, early childhood studies, economics, gerontology, history, home economics, psychology, social science, sociology, and urban studies).

ACTIVITIES: 25% of men belong to 4 national fraternities; 30% of women belong to 4 national sororities. There are 30 groups on campus, including band, cheerleading, choir, drama, ethnic, international, jazz band, marching band, newspaper, professional, religious, social service, student government, and yearbook. Popular campus events include Student Theater Productions, Holiday Concerts, and a Performing Arts Series. **Sports:** There are 4 intercollegiate sports for men and 2 for women, and 6 intramural sports for men and 5 for women. Facilities include basketball, football, volleyball, track and field, cross country, softball, and a recreation and wellness center.

SERVICES: Counseling and information services are available, as is tutoring in some subjects. There is remedial math, reading, and writing. **Library/Resources:** The library contains 110,248 volumes, 465,319 microform items, and subscribes to 80 periodicals including electronic. Computerized library services include interlibrary loans. **Physically Challenged Students:** 70% of the campus is accessible. Facilities include wheelchair ramps, elevators, special parking, specially equipped restrooms, and special class scheduling. **Special:** Work-study programs, internships, and nondegree and noncredit study are available. There are 6 national honor societies and a freshman honors program. **Visiting:** There are regularly scheduled orientations for prospective students. There are guides for informal visits, visitors may sit in on classes, and stay overnight.

REQUIREMENTS: The SAT or ACT is required. In general, test scores should place students in the upper 60% of Oklahoma high school seniors. Applicants should be graduates of accredited high schools with at least a C average (2.7 on a 4.0 scale). Required secondary preparation includes 4 years of English, 3 years of math, and 2 years each of lab science and history, including 1 year of American history. 4 additional academic units, including a foreign language, are strongly recommended. There are alternative admission programs for students with varying backgrounds. AP and CLEP credits are accepted. To graduate, students must complete a total of 124 semester hours, with a GPA of 2.0. The required general education core consists of 50 credits in English, math, computer science, biological and physical sciences, social science, and health and phys ed. 6 credits are required in American history and government, and all students must complete an internship or field experience. **Procedure:** Freshmen are admitted to all sessions. There is a rolling admissions plan. Applications should be filed by August 10 for fall entry. The fall 2017 application fee was $15. **Transfer Students:** Applicants should be in good standing and have earned at least a C average in previous college work. 30 of 124 credits required for the bachelor's degree must be completed at Langston.

Admissions Contact: Gayle T. Robertson, Director of Admissions and Enrollment Management. Email: *admissions@langston.edu* Web: *www.lunet.edu*

FINANCIAL AID: In 2017-2018, 70% of all full-time freshmen received some form of financial aid. 65% of all full-time freshmen received need-based aid. The average freshman award was $2,800. The CSS/Profile, FFS, SFS, FAFSA, are required. The FAFSA code is 003157. The deadline for filing freshman financial aid applications for fall entry is March 1.

NORTHEASTERN STATE UNIVERSITY F-3

www.nsuok.edu

Tahlequah, OK 74464	(918) 456-5511
Fax: (918) 458-2342	Email: nsuinfo@nsuok.edu
Full-time: 2700 men, 3850 women	Faculty: 314
Part-time: 716 men, 1393 women	Ph.D.s: 72%
Graduate: 334 men, 743 women	Student/Faculty: 21 to 1
Year: semesters, summer session	Tuition: $5335 ($11,210)
Room & Board: $3280	Freshman Class: 1651 accepted, 1102 enrolled
ACT: 24	CEEB CODE: 6485
Application Deadline: open	VERY COMPETITIVE

Northeastern State University, founded in 1846, is a public institution offering programs in arts and sciences, professional training, teacher preparation, and business. The figures given in the above capsule and in this profile are approximate. There are 4 undergraduate schools and 5 graduate schools. In addition to regional accreditation, NESU has baccalaureate program accreditation with ACBSP, ADA, ASLA, CSWE, NASM, CAEP, and NLN. The 200-acre campus is in a small town 70 miles from Tulsa. Including any residence halls, there are 51 buildings.

STUDENT LIFE: 94% of undergraduates are from Oklahoma. Others are from 34 states, 47 foreign countries, and Canada. 61% are White; 6% African American; 3% Foreign; 28% American Indian/Alaska Native; 1% Asian American; 1% Hispanic. **Female To Male Ratio:** 1.6:1. The average age of freshmen is 19; all undergraduates, 26. 30% do not continue beyond their first year. **Housing:** 1653 students can be accommodated in college housing, which includes married student dorms and on-campus apartments. In addition, there are special-interest houses. On-campus housing is available on a first-come and first-served basis. 80% of students commute. Alcohol is not permitted. All students may keep cars.

FACULTY/CLASSROOMS: 56% of faculty are male; 44% are female. 90% teach undergraduates. Graduate students teach 5% of introductory courses. The average class size in an introductory lecture is 60; in a laboratory is 24; and in a regular course is 20.

PROGRAMS OF STUDY: NESU confers B.A., B.S., B.A.Ed., B.B.A., B.S.Ed., B.S.Sci.Ed., B.S.N., and B.S.W. degrees. Master's and doctoral degrees are also awarded. Bachelor's degrees are awarded in BIOLOGICAL SCIENCE (biology/biological science), BUSINESS (accounting, banking and finance, business administration and management, and marketing/retailing/merchandising), COMMUNICATIONS AND THE ARTS (advertising, communications, English, fine arts, journalism, music, Spanish, and speech/debate/rhetoric), COMPUTER AND PHYSICAL SCIENCE (chemistry, computer science, information sciences and systems, and mathematics), EDUCATION (art education, early childhood education, elementary education, health education, industrial arts education, music education, science education, secondary education, and special education), HEALTH PROFESSIONS (medical laboratory technology and nursing), SOCIAL SCIENCE (criminal justice, geography, history, political science/government, social science, social work, and sociology). Elementary education, early childhood education, and business are the strongest academically. Administration, psychology, and criminal justice have the largest enrollments.

ACTIVITIES: 5% of men belong to 7 national fraternities; 2% of women belong to 5 national sororities. There are 80 groups on campus, including art, band, cheerleading, choir, chorus, dance, drama, drill team, ethnic, film, honors, international, jazz band, LGBT, literary magazine, marching band, musical theater, newspaper, orchestra, pep band, photography, political, professional, radio and TV, religious, social service, student government, and symphony. Popular campus events include Cherokee Seminaries, Symposium on the American Indian, and Sequoyah Institute Shows. **Sports:** There are 5 intercollegiate sports for men and 5 for women, and 16 intramural sports for men and 16 for women. Facilities include a football stadium, indoor practice facility, exercise/fitness track, baseball field, softball field, tennis courts, soccer fields, baseball field house, soccer/softball field house, basketball gymnasium, and basketball court. **Graduates:** From July 1, 2016 to June 30, 2017, 1404 bachelor's degrees were awarded.

SERVICES: Counseling and information services are available, as is tutoring in most subjects. There is remedial math, reading, and writing. **Library/Resources:** The library contains 400,000 volumes, 766,300 microform items, and 8,659 audio/video tapes/CDs/DVDs, and subscribes to 15,000 periodicals including electronic. Computerized library services include interlibrary loans, database searching, Internet access, and Wi-Fi capability. Special learning facilities include a radio station. **Physically Challenged Students:** 70% of the campus is accessible. Facilities include wheelchair ramps, elevators, special parking, specially equipped restrooms, special class scheduling, lowered drinking fountains, lowered telephones, and special housing. **Special:** Internships are offered in business, mass communications, and education. There are 10 national honor societies, a freshman honors program, and 5 departmental honors programs. **Visiting:** There are regularly scheduled orientations for prospective students, including a general campus visit with highlights presented by trained tour guides. Visitors may sit in on classes and stay overnight. To schedule a visit, contact High School and College Relations. **Campus Safety and Security:** Measures include 24-hour foot and vehicle patrol, self-defense education, and security escort services. There are shuttle buses, emergency telephones, lighted pathways/sidewalks, and a campus security police department.

REQUIREMENTS: The ACT is required, with a minimum composite score on the ACT of 20. Applicants should be high school graduates or have a GED. Students should have completed 4 years of English, 3 of math, and 2 each of history and science. NSU requires applicants to be in the upper 50% of their class. A GPA of 2.7 is required. AP and CLEP credits are accepted. To graduate, students must complete at least 124 credit hours, with 24 to 50 in the major. General education requirements include 40 hours in language arts, social science, natural science, humanities, and phys ed. Freshman orientation and English proficiency are required. **Procedure:** Freshmen are admitted to all sessions. There is a rolling admissions plan. Application deadlines are open. Notification is sent on a rolling basis. **Transfer Students:** 1404 transfer students enrolled in 2016-2017. Transfer applicants must have a minimum GPA of 2.0, with 24 transfer hours completed, and be in good standing at the last institution attended. 30 of 124 credits required for the bachelor's degree must be completed at NESU. **International Students:** There are 252 international students enrolled. They must take the TOEFL.

Admissions Contact: Dawn Cain, Director of Admissions. Email: *nsuinfo@nsuok.edu* Web: *www.nsuok.edu*

FINANCIAL AID: In 2017-2018, 86% of all full-time freshmen received some form of financial aid. 67% of all full-time freshmen received need-based aid. 7% of undergraduate students work part-time. The average financial indebtedness of the 2017 graduate was $17,824. The college's own financial statement is required. The FAFSA code is 003161. The priority date for freshman financial aid applications for fall entry is March 1.

NORTHWESTERN OKLAHOMA STATE UNIVERSITY *(The complete profile is made available exclusively on our website, www.barronspac.com)*

OKLAHOMA BAPTIST UNIVERSITY E-3
www.okbu.edu

Shawnee, OK 74804	**(405) 585-5120** **(800) 654-3285**
Fax: (405) 585-5105	**Email: admissions@okbu.edu**
Full-time: 760 men, 1121 women	**Faculty:** 127
Part-time: 31 men, 18 women	**Ph.D.s:** 68%
Graduate: 47 men, 57 women	**Student/Faculty:** 15 to 1
Year: 4-1-4, summer session	**Tuition:** $26,840
Room & Board: $7150	**Freshman Class:** 4070 applied, 2634 accepted, 555 enrolled
SAT CR/M: 538/520 **ACT:** 24	**CEEB CODE:** 6541
Application Deadline: August 1	**COMPETITIVE**

Oklahoma Baptist University, founded in 1910, is a liberal arts institution affiliated with the Southern Baptist Convention. OBU offers degrees in Christian service, business, nursing, fine arts, telecommunications, teacher education, and the traditional liberal arts areas. There are 6 undergraduate schools and 1 graduate school. In addition to regional accreditation, OBU has baccalaureate program accreditation with ACBSP, NASM, CAEP, and CCNE. The 226-acre campus is in a small town 35 miles east of Oklahoma City, 90 miles southwest of Tulsa, and 200 miles from Dallas/Forth Worth. Including any residence halls, there are 36 buildings.

STUDENT LIFE: 66% of undergraduates are from Oklahoma. Others are from 40 states, 35 foreign countries, and Canada. 79% are from public schools. 67% are White; 12% two or more races; 5% African American; 5% American Indian/Alaska Native; 4% Foreign; 4% race unknown; 2% Hispanic; 1% Asian American. 72% are Protestant; 26% claim no religious affiliation. **Female To Male Ratio:** 1.5:1. The average age of freshmen is 18; all undergraduates, 20. 21% do not continue beyond their first year; 53% remain to graduate. **Housing:** 1634 students can be accommodated in college housing, which includes married student dorms and on-campus apartments. On-campus housing is guaranteed for all 4 years. 94% of students live on campus. Alcohol is not permitted. All students may keep cars.

FACULTY/CLASSROOMS: 62% of faculty are male; 39% are female. All teach undergraduates. No introductory courses are taught by graduate students. The average class size in an introductory lecture is 25; in a laboratory is 19; and in a regular course is 15.

PROGRAMS OF STUDY: OBU confers B.A., B.S., B.B.A., B.F.A., B.M., B.M.A., B.Mus.Ed., and B.S.E. degrees. Associate and master's degrees are also awarded. Bachelor's degrees are awarded in BIOLOGICAL SCIENCE (biology/biological science, forensic science, and physiology), BUSINESS (accounting, banking and finance, business administration and management, business information systems, international business, management, marketing, recreational facilities management, and sports management), COMMUNICATIONS AND THE ARTS (art, broadcasting, church music, communication studies, communications, conducting, congregational and youth ministries, creative writing, digital media, dramatic arts, English, fine arts, graphic design, information technology, instrumental performance, instrumental music education, journalism, journalism - news & information, English and Professional Communication, modern language, music, piano pedagogy, piano performance, recreation administration, Spanish, speech/debate/rhetoric, telecommunications, and vocal music education), COMPUTER AND PHYSICAL SCIENCE (chemistry, chemistry/forensic chemistry, computer information systems, computer science, information sciences and systems, mathematics, natural sciences, and physics), EDUCATION (early childhood education, education, elementary education, English secondary education, English education, global studies, health and physical education, music education, physical education, science education, secondary education, social studies education, special education, and special education/early child dual program), HEALTH PROFESSIONS (allied health, kinesiology, nursing, physical therapy, and premedicine), SOCIAL SCIENCE (anthropology, biblical languages, biblical studies, child care/child and family studies, child psychology/development, Christian studies, community psychology, counseling/psychology, criminal justice, crosscultural studies, history, interdisciplinary studies, international relations, pastoral studies, philosophy, philosophy and religion, political science/government, prelaw, psychology, religion, religious studies, social science, family studies/social service/marriage family, social work, sociology, and youth ministry). Elementary education, and pre-allied health and nursing have the largest enrollments.

ACTIVITIES: There are 85 groups on campus, including art, band, cheerleading, choir, chorale, chorus, computers, debate, drama, environmental, ethnic, film, honors, international, jazz band, literary magazine, marching band, musical theater, newspaper, opera, orchestra, pep band, photography, political, professional, radio and TV, religious, social, social service, student government, and yearbook. Popular campus events include Be a Bison Day, Night on the Hill, and Fall, Winter, or Spring Preview Day. **Sports:** There are 10 intercollegiate sports for men and 12 for women, and 18 intramural sports for men and 18 for women. Facilities include an arena, recreation and wellness center, which includes 3 basketball/volleyball courts, a climbing wall, exercise and fitness equipment, weight rooms, a swimming pool, and a walking track on the top floor, an all-weather track, and football, baseball, softball, soccer, lacrosse and sand volleyball facilities. **Graduates:** From July 1, 2016 to June 30, 2017, 339 bachelor's degrees were awarded. The most popular majors were health profession & related programs (20%), education (19%), and theology/religion (6%). In an average class, 44% graduate in 4 years or less and 52% graduate in 6 years or less. Of the 2016 graduating class, 19% were enrolled in graduate school within 6 months of graduation, and 77% were employed.

SERVICES: Counseling and information services are available, as is tutoring in most subjects. There is a reader service for the blind, and remedial math, reading, and writing. **Library/Resources:** The library contains 162,334 volumes, 31,070 microform items, and 11,392 audio/video tapes/CDs/DVDs. Computerized library services include interlibrary loans, database searching, Internet access, and Wi-Fi capability. Special learning facilities include an art gallery, planetarium, radio station, TV station, a language lab, and a biblical research library. **Physically Challenged Students:** 95% of the campus is accessible. Facilities include wheelchair ramps, elevators, special parking, specially equipped restrooms, lowered drinking fountains, lowered telephones, and special housing. **Special:** OBU offers co-op programs in business, and a 3-2 engineering degree with Oklahoma State University. Students may study abroad in 15 countries in Europe, Central and South America, Asia, and Africa. Internships in several fields, student-designed majors, including an interdisciplinary program in humanities, and pass/fail options are available. There are 2 national honor societies and a freshman honors program. **Visiting:** There are regularly scheduled orientations for prospective students, including tours, faculty visits, and general information sessions. There are guides for informal visits, visitors may sit in on classes, and stay overnight. To schedule a visit, contact the Admissions Office. **Campus Safety and Security:** Measures include 24-hour foot and vehicle patrol, emergency notification system, self-defense education, and security escort services. There are emergency telephones, lighted pathways/sidewalks, and controlled access to dorms/residences.

REQUIREMENTS: Admission is granted to students with composite scores of 950 on the SAT or 20 on the ACT, and a 3.0 GPA. Graduation from an accredited secondary school or satisfactory scores on the GED are required for admission. The recommended high school courses should include 4 units of English, 3 units of math, and 2 units each of social studies, lab science, and a foreign language. OBU requires applicants to be in the upper 50% of their class. AP and CLEP credits are accepted. Important factors in the admissions decision are advanced placement or honors courses, recommendations by school officials, and leadership record. To graduate, students must complete a total of 128 credit hours, including 30 to 48 hours in the major, with a 2.0 GPA. Students are also required to complete 6 credits each of English, literature, history, science, Bible, social sciences, and language; 3 each in math, fine arts, and comparative civilization; 2 each in speech, philosophy, and phys ed; and 1 in computer literacy. **Procedure:** Freshmen are admitted to all sessions. Entrance exams should be taken during the spring of the junior year. There are deferred admissions and rolling admissions plans. Applications should be filed by August 1 for fall entry; December 15 for winter entry; January 15 for spring entry; and May 15 for summer entry. Applications are accepted on-line. **Transfer Students:** 74 transfer students enrolled in 2016-2017. Transfer students must have a GPA of 2.5 for all college work attempted. 32 of 128 credits required for the bachelor's degree must be completed at OBU. **International Students:** There are 60 international students enrolled. They must take the TOEFL with a minimum score of 550 on the paper-based TOEFL (PBT) or 61 on the Internet-based version (iBT) or take the MELAB. They must also take the SAT or ACT, scoring 20.

ADMISSIONS: 65% of the 2017-2018 applicants were accepted. The

SAT scores for the 2017-2018 freshman class were: Critical Reading-- 29% below 500, 47% between 500 and 599, 21% between 600 and 699, and 3% between 700 and 800. Math-- 35% below 500, 51% between 500 and 599, 11% between 600 and 699, and 3% between 700 and 800. The ACT scores were 6% between 12 and 17, 51% between 18 and 23, 36% between 24 and 29, and 8% above 30. 56% of the current freshmen were in the top fifth of their class; 81% were in the top two fifths. **Admissions Contact:** Bruce Perkins, AVP of Enrollment Management. Email: *admissions@okbu.edu* Web: *www.okbu.edu*

FINANCIAL AID: In 2017-2018, 100% of all full-time freshmen received some form of financial aid. 64% of all full-time freshmen received need-based aid. The average freshman award was $24,504. Need-based scholarships or need-based grants averaged $7,710. 61% of undergraduate students work part-time. The average financial indebtedness of the 2017 graduate was $26,006. The FAFSA code is 003164. The priority date for freshman financial aid applications for fall entry is April 1.

OKLAHOMA CHRISTIAN UNIVERSITY D-3

www.oc.edu

Oklahoma City, OK 73136	**(405) 425-5050** **(800) 877-5010**
Fax: (405) 425-5069	**Email: admissions@oc.edu**
Full-time: 944 men, 926 women	**Faculty:** 92
Part-time: 62 men, 54 women	**Ph.D.s:** 77%
Graduate: 329 men, 156 women	**Student/Faculty:** 14 to 1
Year: semesters, summer session	**Tuition:** $21,670
Room & Board: $7590	**Freshman Class:** 2530 applied, 1589 accepted, 517 enrolled
SAT CR/M/W: 538/553/499 **ACT:** 24	**CEEB CODE:** 6086
Application Deadline: September 1	**COMPETITIVE**

Oklahoma Christian University, founded in 1950, is a private, liberal arts institution affiliated with Churches of Christ. Ranked as one of the best universities in the western region of the United States, OCU offers undergraduate programs in more than 60 fields of study, an undergraduate Honors Program, ABET accredited programs in mechanical, electrical and computer engineering, and graduate programs in accountancy, business administration, computer science, engineering, Christian ministry, divinity and theological studies. There are 5 undergraduate schools and 3 graduate schools. In addition to regional accreditation, OCU has baccalaureate program accreditation with ABET, ACBSP, NASM, CAEP, CIDA, and CCNE. The 200-acre campus is in a suburban area in north Oklahoma City, just south of the city of Edmond. Including any residence halls, there are 33 buildings.

STUDENT LIFE: 55% of undergraduates are from out of state, mostly the Midwest. Students are from 43 states, 36 foreign countries, and Canada. 9% are African American; 71% White; 7% Hispanic; 7% Foreign; 6% American Indian/Alaska Native; 5% Asian American. 31% are Protestant. **Male To Female Ratio:** 1.2:1. The average age of freshmen is 18; all undergraduates, 20. 21% do not continue beyond their first year; 47% remain to graduate. **Housing:** 1756 students can be accommodated in college housing, which includes single-sex and married student dorms and on-campus apartments. In addition, there are honors houses. On-campus housing is guaranteed for all 4 years, is available on a first-come, and first-served basis. 80% of students live on campus. Alcohol is not permitted. All students may keep cars.

FACULTY/CLASSROOMS: 70% of faculty are male; 30% are female. All teach undergraduates, 10% do research, and 10% do both. No introductory courses are taught by graduate students. The average class size in an introductory lecture is 19; in a laboratory is 15; and in a regular course is 21.

PROGRAMS OF STUDY: OCU confers B.A., B.S., B.B.A., B.F.A., B.M.E., B.S.C.E., B.S.E., B.S.E.E., B.S.N. and B.S.M.E. degrees. Master's degrees are also awarded. Bachelor's degrees are awarded in BIOLOGICAL SCIENCE (biochemistry, biology/biological science, forensic science, and nutritional sciences), BUSINESS (accounting, banking and finance, business administration and management, business administration - international, business administration marketing, finance, international business management, marketing management, and marketing/retailing/merchandising), COMMUNICATIONS AND THE ARTS (advertising, art, broadcasting, communications, creative writing, design, English, English Writing, game design and development, instrumental performance, journalism, music, photography, public relations, Spanish, visual design, vocal performance, and writing), COMPUTER AND PHYSICAL SCIENCE (chemistry, computer game design/development, computer science, information sciences and systems, and mathematics), EDUCATION (early childhood education, elementary education, English education, mathematics education, middle school education, music education, physical education, science education, social science education, social studies education, sports and wellness studies, sports studies, and teaching English as a second/foreign language (TESOL/TEFOL)), ENGINEERING AND ENVIRONMENTAL DESIGN (computer engineering, electrical and computer engineering, electrical/electronics engineering, interior design, and mechanical engineering), HEALTH PROFESSIONS (biology, exercise and movement science, medical laboratory technology, and nursing), SOCIAL SCIENCE (biblical studies, child care/child and family studies, criminal justice, history, history and political science, interdisciplinary studies, liberal arts/general studies, ministries, missions, prelaw, psychology, religious education, social studies, and youth ministry). Engineering programs, gaming & animation, accounting, and pre-med programs are the strongest academically. Business/marketing, engineering, and health professionals have the largest enrollments.

ACTIVITIES: 30% of men belong to 5 local fraternities; 36% of women belong to 6 local sororities. There are 56 groups on campus, including art, band, cheerleading, choir, chorale, chorus, communications, computers, debate, drama, ethnic, film, honors, international, jazz band, literary magazine, musical theater, newspaper, opera, orchestra, pep band, photography, political, professional, radio and TV, religious, social, social service, student government, symphony, and yearbook. Popular campus events include History Speaks, Spring Sing, Homecoming, Winter Wonderland Week, Earn Your Wings, and McGaw Lecture Series. **Sports:** There are 7 intercollegiate sports for men and 7 for women, and 10 intramural sports for men and 10 for women. Facilities include basketball courts, a 25-meter six-lane swimming pool, baseball, softball, intramural football, soccer fields, a track and field facility, tennis courts, a fitness center, and auxiliary gym. **Graduates:** From July 1, 2016 to June 30, 2017, 389 bachelor's degrees were awarded. The most popular majors were business (18%), engineering (14%), and health professions and related programs (11%). In an average class, 39% graduate in 4 years or less, 53% graduate in 5 years or less, and 52% graduate in 6 years or less.

SERVICES: Counseling and information services are available, as is tutoring in some subjects, such as English, math, speech, chemistry, physics, business, education, and computer science. There is remedial math, reading, and writing. **Library/Resources:** The library contains 195,754 volumes, 682,861 microform items, and 6,775 audio/video tapes/CDs/DVDs, and subscribes to 42,000 periodicals including electronic. Computerized library services include interlibrary loans, database searching, Internet access, and Wi-Fi capability. Special learning facilities include an art gallery, radio station, TV station, journalism, media lab, audio visualization lab, and finance lab. **Physically Challenged Students:** 98% of the campus is accessible. Facilities include wheelchair ramps, elevators, special parking, specially equipped restrooms, special class scheduling, lowered drinking fountains, lowered telephones, and special housing. **Special:** OCU offers a wide range of undergraduate degrees and graduate programs in Accounting, Business, Computer Science, Theology, Ministry, and Engineering. Our ABET accredited undergraduate engineering programs complement a full spectrum of majors across the arts, sciences, and humanities. Internships and practice are commonly required or offered in the nearby city. Students may study abroad in Austria, Japan, China, and Honduras. Major-minor combinations and interdisciplinary studies options help students combine fields such as business, mass communications, family life, pre-law, advertising design, speech communication, education, English, music, and math. An interdisciplinary Honors program serves students with high ACT/SAT scores. Many chapters of disciplinary societies, such as Sigma Tau Delta or Phil Alpha Theta achieve national awards for excellence. Cross-registration can be offered with the University of Central Oklahoma. Students can apply to participate in the Best Semester programs offered by the Council for Christian Colleges and Universities. There are 8 national honor societies, a freshman honors program, and 18 departmental honors programs. **Visiting:** There are regularly scheduled orientations for prospective students, consisting of comprehensive campus overview including academic conversations. There are guides for informal visits, visitors may sit in on classes, and stay overnight. To schedule a visit, contact Dawn Eckhart at dawn.eckhart@oc.edu. **Campus Safety and Security:** Measures include 24-hour foot and vehicle patrol, emergency notification system, and security escort services. There are emergency telephones, lighted pathways/sidewalks, controlled access to dorms/residences, and campus police.

REQUIREMENTS: The SAT or ACT is required. High school graduation with college prep courses or satisfactory scores on the GED are required for admission. An interview is required for some students not meeting minimum test score thresholds. AP and CLEP credits are accepted. To graduate, students must have a minimum of 126 credit hours, including 30 to 104 in the major, with a GPA of 2.0. All students must complete 55 hours in our general education area, which includes courses in American history, behavioral science, Bible, communication, English, fine arts, foreign language, liberal arts, literature, mathematics, music, non-western civilization, political science, science, social science, and western civilization. **Procedure:** Freshmen are admitted to all sessions. Entrance exams should be taken by August 20. There are deferred admissions and rolling admissions plans. Applications should be filed by September 1 for fall entry; January 5 for spring entry. The fall 2017 application fee was $25. Notification is sent on a rolling basis. Applications are accepted on-line. **Transfer Students:** 88 transfer students enrolled in 2016-2017. Applicants must be eligible to return to the school from which they are transferring. 30 of 126 credits required for the bachelor's degree must be completed at OCU. **International Students:** There are 128 international students enrolled. They must take the TOEFL with a minimum score of 500 on the paper-based TOEFL (PBT) or 61 on the Internet-based version (iBT).

ADMISSIONS: 63% of the 2017-2018 applicants were accepted. The SAT scores for the 2017-2018 freshman class were: Critical Reading-- 18% below 500, 46% between 500 and 599, 27% between 600 and 699, and 9% between 700 and 800. Math-- 25% below 500, 41% between 500 and 599, 28% between 600 and 699, and 6% between 700 and 800. Writing-- 49% below 500, 33% between 500 and 599, 14% between 600 and 699, and 4% between 700 and 800. The ACT scores were 8% between 12 and 17, 41% between 18 and 23, 38% between 24 and 29, and 14% above 30. **Admissions Contact:** Jancy Scott, Director of Admissions. Email: *admissions@oc.edu* Web: *www.oc.edu*

FINANCIAL AID: In 2017-2018, 99% of all full-time freshmen received some form of financial aid. 75% of all full-time freshmen received need-based aid. The average freshman award was $19,184. Need-based scholarships or need-based grants averaged $7,121; need-based self-help aid (loans and jobs) averaged $3,970; non-need-based athletic scholarships averaged $7,062; other non-need-based awards and non-need-based scholarships averaged $6,944; and $1,760 from other forms of aid. 39% of undergraduate students work part-time. The average financial indebtedness of the 2017 graduate was $26,282. The FAFSA code is 003165. The priority date for freshman financial aid applications for fall entry is December 1.

OKLAHOMA CITY UNIVERSITY — D-3

www.okcu.edu

Oklahoma City, OK 73106 — (405) 208-5055, (800) 633-7242

Fax: (405) 208-5916 — **Email:** uadmissions@okcu.edu

Full-time: 553 men, 1056 women
Part-time: 76 men, 119 women
Graduate: 554 men, 629 women
Year: semesters, summer session
Room & Board: $9750
SAT CR/M/W: 560/540/550 **ACT:** 25
Application Deadline: rolling
Faculty: n/av
Ph.D.s: 66%
Student/Faculty: 11 to 1
Tuition: $30,726
Freshman Class: 1562 applied, 1096 accepted, 320 enrolled
CEEB CODE: 6543
COMPETITIVE

Oklahoma City University, founded in 1904, is a private, comprehensive university affiliated with the United Methodist Church, offering undergraduate and graduate programs in arts and sciences, business, music and performing arts, religion and church vocations, nursing, and law. There are 7 undergraduate schools and 6 graduate schools. In addition to regional accreditation, Oklahoma City University has baccalaureate program accreditation with AACSB, NASM, NCATE, NLN, AAPL, ACEN, and Oklahoma Commission for Teacher Preparation. The 104-acre campus is in an urban area within Oklahoma City. Including any residence halls, there are 37 buildings.

STUDENT LIFE: 44% of undergraduates are from out of state, mostly the Southwest. Students are from 47 states, 36 foreign countries, and Canada. 88% are from public schools. 9% are Hispanic; 8% two or more races; 60% White; 5% African American; 3% Asian American; 2% American Indian/Alaska Native; 13% Foreign. 55% are Protestant; 27% claim no religious affiliation; 12% Catholic. **Female To Male Ratio:** 1.5:1. The average age of freshmen is 18; all undergraduates, 22. 14% do not continue beyond their first year; 70% remain to graduate. **Housing:** 1270 students can be accommodated in college housing, which includes married student dorms and on-campus apartments. In addition, there are honors houses, special-interest houses, fraternity houses, Including learning communities. On-campus housing is guaranteed for all 4 years. 50% of students commute. Alcohol is not permitted. All students may keep cars.

FACULTY/CLASSROOMS: 51% of faculty are male; 49% are female. 80% teach undergraduates. No introductory courses are taught by graduate students. The average class size in an introductory lecture is 16 and in a laboratory is 13.

PROGRAMS OF STUDY: Oklahoma City University confers B.A., B.S., B.F.A., B.M., B.Perf.Arts, B.S.B., B.B.A., B.M., B.M.E. and B.S.N. degrees. Master's and doctoral degrees are also awarded. Bachelor's degrees are awarded in AGRICULTURE (environmental studies), BIOLOGICAL SCIENCE (biochemistry and cell biology), BUSINESS (accounting, banking and finance, business administration and management, management science, and marketing), COMMUNICATIONS AND THE ARTS (acting, advertising, art, broadcasting, church music, communications, dance, English, film arts, French, guitar, instrumental performance, instrumental music education, instrumental music education, music, music composition, photography, piano/organ, piano pedagogy, piano performance, public relations, Spanish, studio art, theatre acting, theatre arts, theater design, theatre production, and vocal performance), COMPUTER AND PHYSICAL SCIENCE (chemistry, mathematics, physics, science, and software engineering), EDUCATION (early childhood education, education, elementary education, music education, and secondary education), HEALTH PROFESSIONS (biology, biomedical science, exercise science, health care administration, nursing, pre-health studies, and premedicine), SOCIAL SCIENCE (addiction studies, behavioral science, economics, history, humanities, liberal arts/general studies, philosophy, philosophy and religion, political science/government, prelaw, psychology, religion, religious education, and sociology). Nursing, business, and performing arts are the strongest academically. Sciences, performing arts, and liberal arts have the largest enrollments.

ACTIVITIES: 25% of men belong to 3 national fraternities; 14% of women belong to 4 national sororities. There are 87 groups on campus, including art, band, cheerleading, choir, chorus, computers, dance, debate, drama, environmental, ethnic, film, honors, international, jazz band, LGBT, literary magazine, musical theater, newspaper, opera, orchestra, pep band, photography, political, professional, radio and TV, religious, social, social service, student government, symphony, and yearbook. Popular campus events include Midnight Breakfast, Movie Night, Oozeball, Homecoming, and Relay for Life. **Sports:** There are 9 intercollegiate sports for men and 11 for women, and 7 intramural sports for men and 7 for women. Facilities include a baseball, softball, and soccer fields, a wellness and activity center which houses basketball, volleyball, and wrestling. **Graduates:** From July 1, 2016 to June 30, 2017, 594 bachelor's degrees were awarded. The most popular majors were nursing (26%), liberal arts and sciences (23%), and performing arts (16%). In an average class, 49% graduate in 4 years or less, 59% graduate in 5 years or less, and 60% graduate in 6 years or less.

SERVICES: Counseling and information services are available, as is tutoring in most subjects. There is a reader service for the blind, and remedial math, reading, and writing. There are writing and learning enhancement centers and a math lab. **Library/Resources:** The library contains 327,229 volumes, 635,725 microform items, and 16,618 audio/video tapes/CDs/DVDs, and subscribes to 10,976 periodicals including electronic. Computerized library services include interlibrary loans, database searching, Internet access, and Wi-Fi capability. Special learning facilities include an art gallery, radio station, and TV station. **Physically Challenged Students:** 98% of the campus is accessible. Facilities include wheelchair ramps, elevators, special parking, specially equipped restrooms, lowered drinking fountains, and lowered telephones. **Special:** OCU offers internships, a Washington semester, work-study programs, a general studies degree, dual and student-designed majors, credit for life experience, and study-abroad programs in many countries. B.A.-B.S. degrees and an accelerated degree program in nursing and law are also available. There are 8 national honor societies, a freshman honors program, and 10 departmental honors programs. **Visiting:** There are regularly scheduled orientations for prospective students, consisting of 9 am and 1 pm informational presentation, and a campus tour. There are guides for informal visits and visitors may sit in on classes. To schedule a visit, contact Tasha Casey-Loveless. **Campus Safety and Security:** Measures include 24-hour foot and vehicle patrol, emergency notification system, and security escort services. There are emergency telephones, lighted pathways/sidewalks, and controlled access to dorms/residences.

REQUIREMENTS: The SAT or ACT is required. In addition, Graduation from an accredited secondary school or satisfactory scores on the GED is required for admission. High school courses must include 4 units of English, 2-3 units of science (at least one should be lab), 1 unit each of world history, state history and civics, and US History, 2 units each of math, and foreign language. We look for a 3.0 unweighted GPA and 22 on the ACT or 1020 on the SAT. Additionally, we review the essay, letter of recommendation, and application materials. Dance and arts management, music, and theatre all require an audition. Studio art and photography require portfolio review. A GPA of 3.0 is required. AP and CLEP credits are accepted. Important factors in the admissions decision are evidence of special talent, advanced placement or honors courses, and leadership record. To graduate, students must complete a total of 124 credit hours, including 30 to 80 in the major, with a minimum GPA of 2.0. Students must complete their last 15 hours, including the last 6 in the major, at OCU with a minimum GPA of 2.0. All students must take 43 hours in the core curriculum as specified by their college or department. **Procedure:** Freshmen are admitted to all sessions. Entrance exams should be taken by February of the senior year. There are deferred admissions and rolling admissions plans. Application deadlines are open. The fall 2017 application fee was $55. Notification is sent on a rolling basis. Applications are accepted on-line. **Transfer Students:** 265 transfer students enrolled in 2016-2017. Applicants must submit a transcript from each college attended and must have a minimum cumulative GPA of 2.0 from an accredited institution. Applicants having fewer than 29 credit hours must submit a high school transcript and ACT or SAT scores. The application also requires an essay and recommendation from their Dean of Students. 30 of 124 credits required for the bachelor's degree must be completed at OCU. **International Students:** There are 158 international students enrolled. They must take the TOEFL with a minimum score of 550 on the paper-based TOEFL (PBT) or 80 on the Internet-based version (iBT), or take the IELTS.

ADMISSIONS: 70% of the 2017-2018 applicants were accepted. The SAT scores for the 2017-2018 freshman class were: Critical Reading-- 28% below 500, 42% between 500 and 599, 23% between 600 and 699, and 7% between 700 and 800. Math-- 29% below 500, 42% between 500 and 599, 24% between 600 and 699, and 3% between 700 and 800. Writing-- 35% below 500, 46% between 500 and 599, 14% between 600 and 699, and 5% between 700 and 800. The ACT scores were % below 12, 1% between 12 and 17, 31% between 18 and 23, 55% between 24 and 29, and 12% above 30. 56% of the current freshmen were in the top fifth of their class; 82% were in the top two fifths. 5 freshmen graduated first in their class. **Admissions Contact:** Michelle Cook, Director of Admissions Operations. Email: *uadmissions@okcu.edu* Web: *www.okcu.edu*

FINANCIAL AID: In 2017-2018, 97% of all full-time freshmen received some form of financial aid. 82% of all full-time freshmen received need-based aid. The average freshman award was $19,902. Need-based scholarships or need-based grants averaged $16,612 ($38,836 maximum); need-based self-help aid (loans and jobs) averaged $2,348 ($12,000 maximum); non-need-based athletic scholarships averaged $7,398 ($20,000 maximum); and other non-need-based awards and non-need-based scholarships averaged $19,120 ($44,851 maximum). 31% of undergraduate students work part-time. The average financial indebtedness of the 2017 graduate was $24,864. Oklahoma City University is a member of CSS. The FAFSA code is 003166. The priority date for freshman financial aid applications for fall entry is March 1. The deadline for filing freshman financial aid applications for fall entry is June 30.

OKLAHOMA PANHANDLE STATE UNIVERSITY — B-2

www.opsu.edu

Goodwell, OK 73939	**(580) 349-1376** **(800) 664-6778**
Fax: (580) 349-1371	**Email: opus.admissions@opsu.edu**
Full-time: 615 men, 501 women	**Faculty:** 65; IIB
Part-time: 82 men, 189 women	**Ph.D.s:** 32%
Graduate: n/av	**Student/Faculty:** 15 to 1
Year: semesters, summer session	**Tuition:** $3568 ($4269)
Room & Board: $2584	**Freshman Class:** 316 applied, 316 accepted, 286 enrolled
SAT CR/M: 525/520 **ACT:** 22	**CEEB CODE:** 6571
Application Deadline: open	**COMPETITIVE**

Oklahoma Panhandle State University, founded in 1909, is a publicly funded institution offering undergraduate programs in the liberal arts, business and technology, education, agriculture, mathematics, sciences, and nursing. There are 5 undergraduate schools. In addition to regional accreditation, OPSU has baccalaureate program accreditation with CAEP and NLN. The 120-acre campus is in a rural area 100 miles north of Amarillo, Texas. Including any residence halls, there are 29 buildings.

STUDENT LIFE: 50% of undergraduates are from out of state, mostly the Midwest. Students are from 35 states, 15 foreign countries, and Canada. 98% are from public schools. 65% are White; 6% African American; 3% American Indian/Alaska Native; 3% Foreign; 18% Hispanic; 1% Asian American. **Male To Female Ratio:** 1.0:1. The average age of freshmen is 20; all undergraduates, 24. 42% do not continue beyond their first year; 38% remain to graduate. **Housing:** 613 students can be accommodated in college housing, which includes married student on-campus apartments. On-campus housing is guaranteed for the freshman year only, is available on a first-come, and first-served basis. 60% of students commute. Alcohol is not permitted. All students may keep cars.

FACULTY/CLASSROOMS: 58% of faculty are male; 42% are female. All teach undergraduates. No introductory courses are taught by graduate students. The average class size in an introductory lecture is 30; in a laboratory is 20; and in a regular course is 20.

PROGRAMS OF STUDY: OPSU confers B.A., B.S., B.B.A., B.F.A., B.I.T., B.M., B.S.N. and B.T. degrees. Associate degrees are also awarded. Bachelor's degrees are awarded in AGRICULTURE (agricultural business management, agronomy, animal science, and equine science), BIOLOGICAL SCIENCE (biology/biological science), BUSINESS (accounting and business administration and management), COMMUNICATIONS AND THE ARTS (English, fine arts, and music), COMPUTER AND PHYSICAL SCIENCE (chemistry, information sciences and systems, mathematics, and physical sciences), EDUCATION (agricultural education, business education, and physical education), ENGINEERING AND ENVIRONMENTAL DESIGN (industrial engineering technology and technological management), HEALTH PROFESSIONS (nursing), SOCIAL SCIENCE (history, psychology, and social studies). Agruiculture is the strongest academically. Biology, business administration, and nursing have the largest enrollments.

ACTIVITIES: 5% of men belong to 1 local fraternity. There are 40 groups on campus, including art, band, cheerleading, choir, chorale, computers, dance, drama, drill team, ethnic, honors, international, jazz band, marching band, musical theater, newspaper, pep band, photography, professional, radio and TV, religious, Rodeo Club, student government, and yearbook. Popular campus events include Mardi Gras, Talent Show, and Holiday Dinner. **Sports:** There are 10 intercollegiate sports for men and 8 for women. Facilities include a field house, athletic field, golf course, tennis courts, a gym, and activity center. **Graduates:** From July 1, 2016 to June 30, 2017, 198 bachelor's degrees were awarded. The most popular majors were business administration (16%), registered nursing (12%), and biology (12%). In an average class, 38% graduate in 6 years or less.

SERVICES: There is remedial math, reading, and writing. Free tutoring is provided through the peer counseling center. **Library/Resources:** The library contains 123,026 volumes, 12,764 microform items, and 7,159 audio/video tapes/CDs/DVDs, and subscribes to 275 periodicals including electronic. Computerized library services include interlibrary loans, database searching, Internet access, and Wi-Fi capability. Special learning facilities include a radio station, a writing lab, academic support lab, farm lab, children's collection library, and 2 instructional ITV facilities. **Physically Challenged Students:** 97% of the campus is accessible. Facilities include wheelchair ramps, elevators, special parking, specially equipped restrooms, and special class scheduling. **Special:** The university offers dual majors and B.A.-B.S. degrees in several majors. There are 2 national honor societies and 1 departmental honors program. **Visiting:** There are regularly scheduled orientations for prospective students. There are guides for informal visits, visitors may sit in on classes, and stay overnight. To schedule a visit, contact High School and Community Relations. **Campus Safety and Security:** Measures include emergency notification system. There are lighted pathways/sidewalks.

REQUIREMENTS: The ACT is recommended, with a minimum composite score of 19. Graduation from an accredited secondary school or satisfactory scores on the GED are required. High school courses must include 4 units of English, 3 units of math (beginning with Algebra I), 3 units of other courses such as foreign language or computer application courses, 2 units each of history (including 1 unit of American history) and lab science, and 1 unit of citizenship (for example, government, civics). AP and CLEP credits are accepted. To graduate, students must complete a total of 124 semester hours with a minimum GPA of 2.0. The number of hours required in the major varies. All students must complete 45 hours of general education courses, with at least 1 course at the upper-division level. Students must complete 40 upper-level hours and must have completed 60 hours at a 4-year institution. **Procedure:** Freshmen are admitted to all sessions. There is a rolling admissions plan. Application deadlines are open. **Transfer Students:** An application for admission, a medical history form, college transcripts, high school transcripts, and ACT scores are required. If students are transferring in with a GPA below 2.0, they come in on academic probation. 30 of 124 credits required for the bachelor's degree must be completed at OPSU. **International Students:** There are 42 international students enrolled. They must take the TOEFL with a minimum score of 500 on the paper-based TOEFL (PBT). They must also take the SAT or ACT, scoring 19.

ADMISSIONS: 100% of the 2017-2018 applicants were accepted. The SAT scores for the 2017-2018 freshman class were: Critical Reading--16% below 500, 67% between 500 and 599, and 17% between 600 and 699. Math-- 33% below 500, 50% between 500 and 599, and 17% between 600 and 699. The ACT scores were 25% below 12, 35% between 12 and 17, 28% between 18 and 23, 11% between 24 and 29, and 1% above 30. **Admissions Contact:** Bobby Jenkins, Registrar and Director of Admissions. Email: *opus.admissions@opsu.edu* Web: *www.opsu.edu*

FINANCIAL AID: The college's own financial statement is required. The FAFSA code is 003174. Check with the school for current application deadlines.

OKLAHOMA STATE UNIVERSITY E-2

www.okstate.edu

Stillwater, OK 74078 | **(405) 744-5000** **(800) 223-5019**

Fax: (405) 744-7092 | **Email: admissions@okstate.edu**

Full-time: 9171 men, 8903 women | **Faculty:** 808; I, -$

Part-time: 1330 men, 1177 women | **Ph.D.s:** 91%

Graduate: 2651 men, 2186 women | **Student/Faculty:** 20 to 1

Year: semesters, summer session | **Tuition:** $8320 ($22,442)

Room & Board: $8860 | **Freshman Class:** 12259 applied, 9188 accepted, 4057 enrolled

SAT CR/M: 540/565 **ACT:** 25 | **CEEB CODE:** 6546

Application Deadline: n/av | **COMPETITIVE+**

Oklahoma State University, founded in 1890, is a publicly funded land-grant institution, offering undergraduate programs in agricultural sciences and natural resources, arts and sciences, business, education, engineering, architecture, technology, and human environmental resources. There are 6 undergraduate schools and 1 graduate school. In addition to regional accreditation, OSU has baccalaureate program accreditation with AACSB, ABET, ACEJMC, ADA, AHEA, ASLA, FIDER, NAAB, NASM, CAEP, NRPA, SAF, ACS, APA, ASLHA, and NAACLS. The 840-acre campus is in a small town 65 miles north of Oklahoma City.

STUDENT LIFE: 74% of undergraduates are from Oklahoma. Others are from 48 states, 128 foreign countries, and Canada. 70% are White; 7% Foreign; 6% two or more races; 5% American Indian/Alaska Native; 4% African American; 4% Hispanic; 2% Asian American; 1% race unknown. **Male To Female Ratio:** 1.1:1. The average age of freshmen is 18; all undergraduates, 22. 21% do not continue beyond their first year; 79% remain to graduate. **Housing:** College-sponsored housing includes married student dorms, on-campus apartments, and off-campus apartments. In addition, there are honors houses, language/international houses, special-interest houses, fraternity houses, sorority houses, theme and wellness housing. On-campus housing is guaranteed for the freshman year only, is available on a first-come, and first-served basis. 55% of students commute. Alcohol is not permitted. All students may keep cars.

FACULTY/CLASSROOMS: 63% of faculty are male; 37% are female. Graduate students teach 19% of introductory courses. The average class size in an introductory lecture is 30 and in a laboratory is 21.

PROGRAMS OF STUDY: OSU confers B.A., B.S., B.Arch.,B.E.N., B.F.A., B.Land.Arch., B.M., B.S.A.E, B.S.A.G., B.S.B.A., B.S.B.E., B.S.C.H., B.S.C.P., B.S.C.V., B.S.E.E., B.S.E.T., B.S.I.E., B.S.M.E. and B.U.S. degrees. Master's and doctoral degrees are also awarded. Bachelor's degrees are awarded in AGRICULTURE (agricultural business management, agricultural communications, agricultural economics, animal science, horticulture, natural resource management, plant science, and soil science), BIOLOGICAL SCIENCE (biochemistry, biology/biological science, botany, cell biology, entomology, microbiology, molecular biology, nutrition, physiology, and zoology), BUSINESS (accounting, banking and finance, business administration and management, entrepreneurial studies, hotel/motel and restaurant management, international business management, management information systems, marketing/retailing/merchandising, and recreation and leisure services), COMMUNICATIONS AND THE ARTS (art, broadcasting, design, dramatic arts, English, French, German, journalism, music, Russian languages and literature, and Spanish), COMPUTER AND PHYSICAL SCIENCE (chemistry, computer science, geology, mathematics, physics, and statistics), EDUCATION (agricultural education, athletic training, education, elementary education, health education, music education, physical education, secondary education, and vocational education), ENGINEERING AND ENVIRONMENTAL DESIGN (aerospace studies, architectural engineering, architecture, bioengineering, chemical engineering, civil engineering, computer engineering, construction management, construction technology, electrical/electronics engineering, electrical/electronics engineering technology, environmental science, industrial administration/management, industrial engineering, landscape architecture/design, mechanical engineering, and mechanical engineering technology), HEALTH PROFESSIONS (speech pathology/audiology), SOCIAL SCIENCE (American studies, child care/child and family studies, economics, fire control and safety technology, food science, geography, history, human development, liberal arts/general studies, philosophy, political science/government, psychology, and sociology).

ACTIVITIES: There are 400 groups on campus, including art, band, cheerleading, choir, chorale, chorus, computers, dance, drama, environmental, ethnic, honors, international, jazz band, LGBT, literary magazine, marching band, musical theater, newspaper, opera, orchestra, pep band, political, professional, radio and TV, religious, social, social service, student government, and symphony. Popular campus events include Freshmen Follies, Salsa Ball, and African Night. **Sports:** There are 8 intercollegiate sports for men and 8 for women. Facilities include a recreation center, with basketball-volleyball courts, a large multipurpose court, weight and fitness equipment, cardio-theater, indoor climbing wall, golf practice area, golf simulators, a jogging track, indoor and outdoor swimming pools, and racquetball-handball courts. **Graduates:** From July 1, 2016 to June 30, 2017, 4102 bachelor's degrees were awarded. The most popular majors were business/marketing (26%), engineering (10%), and agriculture (8%). In an average class, 2% graduate in 3 years or less, 32% graduate in 4 years or less, 55% graduate in 5 years or less, and 61% graduate in 6 years or less.

SERVICES: Counseling and information services are available, as is tutoring in most subjects. There is a reader service for the blind, and remedial math, reading, and writing. Academic assessment and minority programs are also available. **Library/Resources:** The library contains 3.5 million volumes, 4.6 million microform items, and 445,551 audio/video tapes/CDs/DVDs. Computerized library services include interlibrary loans, database searching, Internet access, and Wi-Fi capability. Special learning facilities include an art gallery and radio station. **Physically Challenged Students:** 99% of the campus is accessible. Facilities include wheelchair ramps, elevators, special parking, specially equipped restrooms, special class scheduling, lowered drinking fountains, lowered telephones, and special housing. **Special:** OSU offers cross-registration with Northern Oklahoma College and Tulsa Community College, a Washington semester, and an internship program. A B.A.-B.S. degree, dual majors, an individualized university studies degree, multidisciplinary majors in biosystems engineering and in cell and molecular biology, nondegree study, and pass/fail options are available. Students may study abroad in several countries. The school also sponsors Semester at Sea, a 1-semester program of study on a ship traveling to ports throughout the world. There is a freshman honors program. **Visiting:** There are regularly scheduled orientations for prospective students, including personal meetings and tours. Appointments are scheduled with other campus departments, as needed, to assist prospective students. There are guides for informal visits, visitors may sit in on classes, and stay overnight. To schedule a visit, contact the Undergraduate Admissions Office. **Campus Safety and Security:** Measures include 24-hour foot and vehicle patrol, emergency notification system, self-defense education, and security escort services. There are shuttle buses, emergency telephones, lighted pathways/sidewalks, and controlled access to dorms/residences.

REQUIREMENTS: The SAT or ACT is required. Freshman applicants must have a cumulative high school GPA of 3.0 and rank in the upper third of their graduating class; or achieve at least a 24 composite score on the ACT or 1090 on the SAT; or have a 3.0 GPA in the required 15 curricular units, which include 4 years of English, 3 of math (algebra I and above), 2 each of history and lab science, 1 of citizenship skills, and 3 more from any of the above or computer science or foreign language, along with an ACT score of 21 or SAT 980. Important factors in the admissions decision are advanced placement or honors courses, evidence of special talent, and recommendations by school officials. To graduate, students must have a minimum GPA of 2.0 and at least 120 hours, including a minimum of 30 hours in the major for most programs. A higher GPA may be required in some majors. All students must take a minimum of 40 credit hours of core courses, including 6 each of English, humanities, analytical and quantitative thought, natural sciences, and social and behavioral sciences, 3 each of American history and government, and 1 each of scientific investigation and international studies. **Procedure:** Freshmen are admitted fall, spring, and summer. Entrance exams should be taken during the junior or senior year. There is a rolling admissions plan. Application deadlines are open. The fall 2017 application fee was $40. Applications are accepted on-line. **Transfer Students:** 1655 transfer students enrolled in 2016-2017. Applicants must submit official transcripts from all colleges attended. Students having fewer than 24 credit hours must also meet the requirements for entering freshmen and have a 2.25 GPA. Students that have earned 24-59 hours of college credit must achieve a minimum transfer GPA of 2.25 or higher in all college-level course work attempted. Students that have earned 60 or more hours of college credit must achieve a minimum transfer GPA of 2.0 or higher in all college-level coursework attempted. 30 of 120 credits required for the bachelor's degree must be completed at OSU. **International Students:** There are 757 international students enrolled. They must take the TOEFL with a minimum score of 500 on the paper-based TOEFL (PBT) or 61 on the Internet-based version (iBT). They must also take the SAT or ACT, scoring 24.

ADMISSIONS: 75% of the 2017-2018 applicants were accepted. The SAT scores for the 2017-2018 freshman class were: Critical Reading--28% below 500, 45% between 500 and 599, 23% between 600 and 699, and 4% between 700 and 800. Math-- 21% below 500, 45% between 500 and 599, 29% between 600 and 699, and 6% between 700 and 800. 48% of the current freshmen were in the top fifth of their class; 78% were in the top two fifths. **Admissions Contact:** Christine Crenshaw, Director Undergraduate Admissions. Email: *admissions@okstate.edu* Web: *www.okstate.edu*

FINANCIAL AID: In 2017-2018, 51% of all full-time freshmen received some form of financial aid. 51% of all full-time freshmen received need-based aid. The average freshman award was $13,284. Need-based scholarships or need-based grants averaged $7,006; need-based self-help aid (loans and jobs) averaged $3,324; non-need-based athletic scholarships averaged $12,820; other non-need-based awards and non-need-based scholarships averaged $3,237; and $6,461 from other forms of aid. The average financial indebtedness of the 2017 graduate was $22,591. The college's own financial statement is required. The FAFSA code is 003170. The priority date for freshman financial aid applications for fall entry is February 1.

OKLAHOMA WESLEYAN UNIVERSITY E-1

www.okwu.edu

Bartlesville, OK 74006 (918) 335-6219 (866) 222-8226

Fax: (918) 335-6229 **Email:** admissions@okwu.edu

Full-time: 278 men, 290 women	**Faculty:** 31
Part-time: 163 men, 328 women	**Ph.D.s:** 48%
Graduate: n/av	**Student/Faculty:** 18 to 1
Year: semesters, summer session	**Tuition:** $26,090
Room & Board: $8344	**Freshman Class:** n/av
SAT or ACT: recommended	**CEEB CODE:** 6135
Application Deadline: n/av	**COMPETITIVE**

Oklahoma Wesleyan University, founded in 1909, is a private liberal arts institution affiliated with the Wesleyan Church. The figures given in the above capsule and in this profile are approximate. OWU has received national recognition for its excellent academic as well as missional integrity. There are 5 undergraduate schools and 1 graduate school. In addition to regional accreditation, OWU has baccalaureate program accreditation with CAEP, CCNE, and IACBE. The 101-acre campus is in a suburban area 40 miles north of Tulsa. Including any residence halls, there are 15 buildings.

STUDENT LIFE: 73% of undergraduates are from Oklahoma. Others are from 33 states, and 9 foreign countries. 80% are from public schools. 83% are White; 2% African American; 2% Hispanic; 2% Foreign; 1% Asian American. 74% are Protestant; 23% claim no religious affiliation. **Female To Male Ratio:** 1.4:1. The average age of freshmen is 18; all undergraduates, 26. 20% do not continue beyond their first year; 60% remain to graduate. **Housing:** 315 students can be accommodated in college housing, which includes dorms. In addition, there are honors houses. On-campus housing is guaranteed for all 4 years. 69% of students commute. Alcohol is not permitted. All students may keep cars.

FACULTY/CLASSROOMS: 65% of faculty are male; 35% are female. All teach undergraduates. No introductory courses are taught by graduate students. The average class size in an introductory lecture is 20; in a laboratory is 20; and in a regular course is 20.

PROGRAMS OF STUDY: OWU confers B.A. and B.S. degrees. Associate and master's degrees are also awarded. Bachelor's degrees are awarded in BIOLOGICAL SCIENCE (biology/biological science), BUSINESS (accounting, business administration and management, and human resources), COMMUNICATIONS AND THE ARTS (communications, English, music, and visual communication), COMPUTER AND PHYSICAL SCIENCE (chemistry, mathematics, and science), EDUCATION (business education, elementary education, English education, mathematics education, middle school education, music education, physical education, science education, secondary education, social studies education, and sports studies), HEALTH PROFESSIONS (predentistry and premedicine), SOCIAL SCIENCE (behavioral science, criminal justice, history, liberal arts/general studies, ministries, pastoral studies, philosophy, political science/government, prelaw, religion, religious music, social studies, sociology, and youth ministry). Business, and education are the strongest academically, and have the largest enrollments.

ACTIVITIES: There are no fraternities or sororities. There are 10 groups on campus, including band, cheerleading, choir, chorale, chorus, computers, drama, ethnic, honors, international, musical theater, photography, political, professional, religious, social service, and student government. Popular campus events include Spiritual Emphasis Week, and Youth Conference. **Sports:** There are 7 intercollegiate sports for men and 7 for women, and 10 intramural sports for men and 10 for women. Facilities include a gym and an 8-acre athletic field. **Graduates:** The most popular majors were business/marketing (99%), biological/life science (18%), and parks/recreation (10%).

SERVICES: Counseling and information services are available, as is tutoring in most subjects. There is remedial math, reading, and writing. **Library/Resources:** The library contains 120,000 volumes, 20,000 microform items, and 500 audio/video tapes/CDs/DVDs, and subscribes to 18,000 periodicals including electronic. Computerized library services include interlibrary loans and database searching. **Physically Challenged Students:** 73% of the campus is accessible. Facilities include wheelchair ramps, elevators, special parking, and specially equipped restrooms. **Special:** OWU offers cross-registration with Tri-County Tech, a Washington semester, a co-op program, internships, a general studies degree, credit for life experience, and an accelerated degree program in business and the B.S.N. **Visiting:** There are regularly scheduled orientations for prospective students. There are guides for informal visits, visitors may sit in on classes, and stay overnight. To schedule a visit, contact the Enrollment Services Office. **Campus Safety and Security:** There are lighted pathways/sidewalks, an evening patrol by a security guard.

REQUIREMENTS: The SAT or ACT is recommended. Graduation from an accredited secondary school or satisfactory scores on the GED are required for admission. 18 academic credits must be completed, including 4 credits of English and 2 credits each of history, math, science, and social studies. AP and CLEP credits are accepted. To graduate, students must complete a total of 126 credit hours with a minimum GPA of 2.0. About 40 hours are required in the major. All students must take 9 hours of religion and a writing proficiency exam. **Procedure:** Freshmen are admitted to all sessions. Entrance exams should be taken during the senior year. There is a rolling admissions plan. Application deadlines are open. The fall 2017 application fee was $25. Applications are accepted on-line. **Transfer Students:** 54 transfer students enrolled in 2016-2017. Applicants must have a minimum GPA of 2.0. 24 of 126 credits required for the bachelor's degree must be completed at OWU. **International Students:** There are 16 international students enrolled. They must take the TOEFL or MELAB.

Admissions Contact: Audrey Kelleher, Associate Vice President for Enrollment. Email: *admissions@okwu.edu* Web: *www.okwu.edu*

FINANCIAL AID: In 2017-2018, 98% of all full-time freshmen received some form of financial aid. 90% of all full-time freshmen received need-based aid. 60% of undergraduate students work part-time. The average financial indebtedness of the 2017 graduate was $20,000. The college's own financial statement is required. The FAFSA code is 003151. The deadline for filing freshman financial aid applications for fall entry is open.

ORAL ROBERTS UNIVERSITY E-2

www.oru.edu

Tulsa, OK 74171	(918) 495-6161 (800) 678-8876
Fax: (918) 495-6166	Email: admissions@oru.edu
Full-time: 1078 men, 1435 women	Faculty: 135
Part-time: 211 men, 333 women	Ph.D.s: 3%
Graduate: 278 men, 279 women	Student/Faculty: 14 to 1
Year: semesters, summer session	Tuition: $25,676
Room & Board: $8640	Freshman Class: 2378 applied, 522 accepted, 437 enrolled
SAT CR/M: 503/505 ACT: 22	CEEB CODE: 6552
Application Deadline: rolling	COMPETITIVE

Oral Roberts University, founded in 1963, is a private, Christian university offering more than 60 undergraduate degree programs, 13 master's degree programs and 2 doctoral degree programs. The figures given in the above capsule and in this profile are approximate. There are 6 undergraduate schools and 3 graduate schools. In addition to regional accreditation, ORU has baccalaureate program accreditation with ABET, ACBSP, CSWE, NASM, CAEP, CCNE, ATS, and OCTP. The 263-acre campus is in an urban area in Tulsa, Oklahoma. Including any residence halls, there are 29 buildings.

STUDENT LIFE: 51% of undergraduates are from out of state, mostly the Midwest. Students are from 50 states, 83 foreign countries, and Canada. 75% are from public schools. 5% are Hispanic; 5% Foreign; 42% White; 2% American Indian/Alaska Native; 2% two or more races; 11% African American; 1% Asian American. 98% are Protestant. **Female To Male Ratio:** 1.3:1. The average age of freshmen is 19; all undergraduates, 21. 8% do not continue beyond their first year; 54% remain to graduate. **Housing:** 2218 students can be accommodated in college housing, which includes honors wings of several dorms, men's dorms, and women's dorms. On-campus housing is available on a first-come and first-served basis. 66% of students live on campus. Alcohol is not permitted. All students may keep cars.

FACULTY/CLASSROOMS: 56% of faculty are male; 44% are female. And 84% do research. No introductory courses are taught by graduate students. The average class size in an introductory lecture is 30; in a laboratory is 20; and in a regular course is 20.

PROGRAMS OF STUDY: ORU confers B.A., B.S., B.M., B.Mus.Ed., B.S.E., B.S.N. and B.S.W. degrees. Master's and doctoral degrees are also awarded. Bachelor's degrees are awarded in BIOLOGICAL SCIENCE (biology/biological science), BUSINESS (accounting, banking and finance, business administration and management, international business management, management information systems, management science, marketing/retailing/merchandising, organizational behavior, and recreation and leisure services), COMMUNICATIONS AND THE ARTS (applied art, broadcasting, communications, dance, dramatic arts, English, English literature, film arts, French, German, literature, music, music performance, music theory and composition, Spanish, speech/debate/rhetoric, and studio art), COMPUTER AND PHYSICAL SCIENCE (chemistry, computer science, mathematics, and physics), EDUCATION (art education, business education, drama education, early childhood education, elementary education, English education, foreign languages education, health education, mathematics education, music education, physical education, recreation education, science education, social studies education, and special education), ENGINEERING AND ENVIRONMENTAL DESIGN (bioengineering, commercial art, computer engineering, electrical/electronics engineering, engineering, engineering management, mechanical engineering, and preengineering), HEALTH PROFESSIONS (biomedical science, health science, medical laboratory technology, nursing, optometry, predentistry, and premedicine), SOCIAL SCIENCE (biblical studies, history, international relations, international studies, liberal arts/general studies, ministries, philosophy, political science/government, prelaw, psychology, religion, religious education, religious music, and social work). All science programs, and music & theology are the strongest academically. Nursing, media, and business have the largest enrollments.

ACTIVITIES: There are no fraternities or sororities. There are 40 groups on campus, including art, band, cheerleading, choir, chorale, chorus, Community Outreach and Summer Mission, computers, dance, debate, drama, environmental, ethnic, honors, international, jazz band, musical theater, newspaper, opera, pep band, photography, political, professional, radio and TV, religious, social, social service, student government, symphony, and yearbook. **Sports:** There are 8 intercollegiate sports for men and 8 for women, and 20 intramural sports for men and 20 for women. Facilities include an physical fitness center, track, tennis, racquetball, squash, volleyball, and basketball courts, and baseball and soccer fields. **Graduates:** From July 1, 2016 to June 30, 2017, 592 bachelor's degrees were awarded. The most popular majors were business marketing (22%), theology and religious vocations (13%), and communication/journalism (11%). In an average class, 55% graduate in 6 years or less.

SERVICES: Counseling and information services are available, as is tutoring in most subjects. There is a reader service for the blind, and remedial math, reading, and writing. **Library/Resources:** The library contains 487,000 volumes, 50,000 microform items, and 18,000 audio/video tapes/CDs/DVDs, and subscribes to 65 periodicals including electronic. Computerized library services include interlibrary loans, database searching, Internet access, and Wi-Fi capability. Special learning facilities include a natural history museum, radio station, and TV production studio. **Physically Challenged Students:** 90% of the campus is accessible. Facilities include wheelchair ramps, elevators, special parking, specially equipped restrooms, special class scheduling, lowered drinking fountains, lowered telephones, and special housing. **Special:** ORU offers combined B.A.-B.S. degrees, internships, 3-2 programs, a Washington semester, work-study programs, dual and student-designed majors, study abroad in 5 countries, independent study, nondegree study, an accelerated degree in business and education, and a liberal arts degree. An honors program/leadership academy is also offered. There are 4 national honor societies, a freshman honors program, and 12 departmental honors programs. **Visiting:** There are regularly scheduled orientations for prospective students, College Weekend, which consists of visiting classes, meeting with faculty and staff, attending chapel services, and attending student life events. Visitors may sit in on classes and stay overnight. To schedule a visit, contact the Admissions Office at campusvisits@oru.edu. **Campus Safety and Security:** Measures include 24-hour foot and vehicle patrol, emergency notification system, self-defense education, and security escort services. There are shuttle buses, lighted pathways/sidewalks, and controlled access to dorms/residences.

REQUIREMENTS: The SAT or ACT is required. Students should be graduates of an accredited secondary school or hold a GED. High school preparation should include 4 years of English, 2 years each of math, (including algebra and geometry), or only 2 years algebra, foreign language, social studies, and science (with lab), and 4 of academic electives.

A recommendation from the student's minister is required. An academic recommendation and an interview are recommended. A GPA of 2.6 is required. AP and CLEP credits are accepted. A minimum of 128 credit hours, with a minimum of 30 hours in the major, and a 2.0 GPA are required to graduate. All students must complete specific courses in the Bible, theology, and English, plus 12 hours in social sciences, 11 in biological or physical and mathematical sciences, 6 to 7 in modern foreign language, 3 in communication arts, 2 in fine arts, and 1 physical activity course is required per semester, along with regular, semiweekly chapel attendance. A senior paper must be completed in most majors. Some other courses may be required such as history, humanities, philosophy, and government. **Procedure:** Freshmen are admitted to all sessions. Entrance exams should be taken the last semester of the junior year or during senior year. There are deferred admissions and rolling admissions plans. Application deadlines are open. The fall 2017 application fee was $35. Applications are accepted on-line. **Transfer Students:** 209 transfer students enrolled in 2016-2017. An official transcript showing honorable dismissal from each previous institution is required. 30 of 128 credits required for the bachelor's degree must be completed at ORU. **International Students:** There are 167 international students enrolled. They must take the TOEFL with a minimum score of 500 on the paper-based TOEFL (PBT) or 61 on the Internet-based version (iBT). They must also take the SAT or ACT.

ADMISSIONS: 22% of the 2017-2018 applicants were accepted. The SAT scores for the 2017-2018 freshman class were: Critical Reading-- 47% below 500, 40% between 500 and 599, 10% between 600 and 699, and 3% between 700 and 800. Math-- 49% below 500, 35% between 500 and 599, 15% between 600 and 699, and 1% between 700 and 800. The ACT scores were 16% between 12 and 17, 54% between 18 and 23, 24% between 24 and 29, and 6% above 30. 21 freshmen graduated first in their class. **Admissions Contact:** Cal Easterling, Ph. D., Dean of Institutional Effectiveness. Email: *admissions@oru.edu* Web: *www.oru.edu*

FINANCIAL AID: In 2017-2018, 75% of all full-time freshmen received some form of financial aid. 74% of all full-time freshmen received need-based aid. The average freshman award was $24,735. Need-based scholarships or need-based grants averaged $17,314; need-based self-help aid (loans and jobs) averaged $7,927; non-need-based athletic scholarships averaged $21,104; other non-need-based awards and non-need-based scholarships averaged $7,077; and $12,154 from other forms of aid. 8% of undergraduate students work part-time. The average financial indebtedness of the 2017 graduate was $32,799. The FAFSA code is 003985. The priority date for freshman financial aid applications for fall entry is March 15.

SOUTHEASTERN OKLAHOMA STATE UNIVERSITY E-4

www.se.edu

Durant, OK 74701 **(580) 745-2060**

Fax: (580) 745-7502
Full-time: 1163 men, 1248 women
Part-time: 270 men, 449 women
Graduate: 275 men, 257 women
Year: semesters, summer session
Room & Board: $6030

SAT: required **ACT:** 21
Application Deadline: open

Email: admissions@sosu.edu
Faculty: 111; IIA, --$
Ph.D.s: 72%
Student/Faculty: 20 to 1
Tuition: $5845 ($12,019)
Freshman Class: 1107 applied, 856 accepted, 519 enrolled
CEEB CODE: 6657
COMPETITIVE

Southeastern Oklahoma State University, founded in 1909, is a public institution offering programs in the arts and sciences, business, education, music, and technology to a primarily commuter student body. There are 3 undergraduate schools and 1 graduate school. In addition to regional accreditation, SEOSU has baccalaureate program accreditation with AACSB, ACBSP, NASM, and CAEP. The 268-acre campus is in a rural area 90 miles north of Dallas. Including any residence halls, there are 46 buildings.

STUDENT LIFE: 69% of undergraduates are from Oklahoma. Others are from 39 states, 25 foreign countries, and Canada. 99% are from public schools. 60% are White; 54% African American; 30% American Indian/Alaska Native; 3% Hispanic; 1% Asian American; 1% Foreign. **Female To Male Ratio:** 1.1:1. The average age of freshmen is 19; all undergraduates, 24. 42% do not continue beyond their first year; 40% remain to graduate. **Housing:** 648 students can be accommodated in college housing, which includes dorms and on-campus apartments. On-campus housing is guaranteed for all 4 years. 57% of students live on campus. Alcohol is not permitted. All students may keep cars.

FACULTY/CLASSROOMS: All teach undergraduates, and 10% do research. No introductory courses are taught by graduate students. The average class size in an introductory lecture is 28; in a laboratory is 18; and in a regular course is 23.

PROGRAMS OF STUDY: SEOSU confers B.A., B.S., B.A.A.S., B.B.A., B.G.S., B.M., and B.M.Ed. degrees. Master's degrees are also awarded. Bachelor's degrees are awarded in AGRICULTURE (conservation and regulation and environmental studies), BIOLOGICAL SCIENCE (biology/biological science and biotechnology), BUSINESS (accounting, business administration and management, recreation and leisure services, and secretarial studies/office management), COMMUNICATIONS AND THE ARTS (art, communications, dramatic arts, English, fine arts, music, and speech/debate/rhetoric), COMPUTER AND PHYSICAL SCIENCE (chemistry, computer science, information sciences and systems, mathematics, and physics), EDUCATION (art education, business education, early childhood education, education of the mentally handicapped, elementary education, mathematics education, music education, physical education, science education, secondary education, and social studies education), ENGINEERING AND ENVIRONMENTAL DESIGN (aviation administration/management and occupational safety and health), HEALTH PROFESSIONS (medical laboratory technology), SOCIAL SCIENCE (criminal justice, economics, gerontology, history, political science/government, psychology, social science, and sociology). Chemistry, history, and music are the strongest academically. Occupational safety & health, elementary education, and criminal justice have the largest enrollments.

ACTIVITIES: 12% of men belong to 2 national fraternities; 29% of women belong to 2 national sororities. There are 70 groups on campus, including art, band, cheerleading, chess, choir, chorale, chorus, communications, computers, dance, debate, drama, drill team, environmental, ethnic, forensics, honors, international, jazz band, literary magazine, marching band, musical theater, newspaper, opera, pep band, photography, political, professional, religious, social, social service, student government, and yearbook. Popular campus events include Parents Day, Candlelighting, and Springfest. **Sports:** There are 6 intercollegiate sports for men and 6 for women, and 2 intramural sports for men and 1 for women. Facilities include a football stadium, a gym, baseball and softball fields, a track, tennis courts, playing fields, and swimming pool. **Graduates:** From July 1, 2016 to June 30, 2017, 664 bachelor's degrees were awarded. The most popular majors were engineering technologies (19%), liberal arts and general studies (12%), and business/marketing (11%). In an average class, 77% graduate in 4 years or less and 81% graduate in 5 years or less.

SERVICES: Counseling and information services are available, as is tutoring in every subject. There is a reader service for the blind, and remedial math, reading, and writing. Tutoring in study skills is also available. **Library/Resources:** The library contains 306,071 volumes, 591,277 microform items, and 9,254 audio/video tapes/CDs/DVDs, and subscribes to 841 periodicals including electronic. Computerized library services include interlibrary loans, database searching, and Internet access. **Physically Challenged Students:** 90% of the campus is accessible. Facilities include wheelchair ramps, elevators, special parking, specially equipped restrooms, special class scheduling, lowered drinking fountains, lowered telephones, and special housing. **Special:** Internships, study abroad, credit for military experience, pass/fail options in some courses, and nondegree study are available. There are 15 national honor societies and 9 departmental honors programs. **Visiting:** There are guides for informal visits and visitors may sit in on classes. To schedule a visit, contact the Admissions and Recruitment Services. **Campus Safety and Security:** Measures include 24-hour foot and vehicle patrol, emergency notification system, self-defense education, and security escort services. There are lighted pathways/sidewalks, in-room safes, and safety training.

REQUIREMENTS: The SAT or ACT is required. Applicants should be graduates of an accredited secondary school or have earned a GED. High school courses must include 4 units of English, 3 units each of math, science with lab, and history, 1 unit recommended foreign language, 2 units in academic electives, and 1 unit in computer science. SOSU requires applicants to be in the upper 50% of their class. AP and CLEP credits are accepted. Important factors in the admissions decision are advanced placement or honors courses. A total of 124 credit hours with a minimum GPA of 2.0 (2.5 for teacher education majors) is required for graduation. All students must complete 41 semester hours of general education requirements, including English, American history, government, humanities, arts, social and lab sciences, math, communications, and health education, and 3 hours of computer science. **Procedure:** Freshmen are admitted to all sessions. Entrance exams should be taken by the fall of the senior year. There is a rolling admissions plan. Application deadlines are open. The fall 2017 application fee was $20. Notification is sent on a rolling basis. Applications are accepted on-line. **Transfer Students:** 347 transfer students enrolled in 2016-2017. Out-of-state applicants must have a 2.0 GPA. In-state applicants must have a 1.7 GPA with 24 to 36 credit hours earned, 1.8 with 37 to 72 hours, and 2.0 with 73 or more hours. 30 of 124 credits required for the bachelor's degree must be completed at SEOSU. **International Students:** There are 39 international students enrolled. They must take the TOEFL with a minimum score of 500 on the paper-based TOEFL (PBT) or 61 on the Internet-based version (iBT). They must also take the SAT or ACT.

ADMISSIONS: 77% of the 2017-2018 applicants were accepted. The ACT scores were 19% between 12 and 17, 64% between 18 and 23, 16% between 24 and 29, and 2% above 30. 30% of the current freshmen were in the top fifth of their class; 59% were in the top two fifths. 28 freshmen graduated first in their class. **Admissions Contact:** Kristie Luke, Associate Dean of Admissions and Records/Registrar. Email: *admissions@sosu.edu* Web: *www.se.edu*

FINANCIAL AID: In 2017-2018, 78% of all full-time freshmen received some form of financial aid. 56% of all full-time freshmen received need-based aid. The average freshman award was $11,434. Need-based scholarships or need-based grants averaged $1,899; need-based self-help aid (loans and jobs) averaged $1,233; non-need-based athletic scholarships averaged $2,385; other non-need-based awards and non-need-based scholarships averaged $1,369; and $1,008 from other forms of aid. 45% of undergraduate students work part-time. The average financial indebtedness of the 2017 graduate was $20,983. SEOSU is a member of CSS. The college's own financial statement is required. The FAFSA code is 003179. The priority date for freshman financial aid applications for fall entry is March 1.

SOUTHERN NAZARENE UNIVERSITY D-3

www.snu.edu

Bethany, OK 73008 | **(405) 491-6324**
(800) 648-9899
Fax: (405) 491-6320 | **Email: SNU-jamie@snu.edu**
Full-time: 759 men, 843 women | **Faculty:** 74
Part-time: 23 men, 28 women | **Ph.D.s:** 74%
Graduate: 178 men, 279 women | **Student/Faculty:** 15 to 1
Year: semesters, summer session | **Tuition:** $25,188
Room & Board: $8496 | **Freshman Class:** 852 applied, 852 accepted, 284 enrolled
SAT: required **ACT:** 23 | **CEEB CODE:** 6036
Application Deadline: August 6 | **COMPETITIVE**

Southern Nazarene University, founded in 1899 is a private, Christian, liberal arts institution affiliated with the Church of the Nazarene. SNU is committed to the service of God and their fellow man. The figures given in the above capsule and in this profile are approximate. There are 3 undergraduate schools and 1 graduate school. In addition to regional accreditation, SNU has baccalaureate program accreditation with NASM, CAEP, and NLN. The 40-acre campus is in a suburban area just west of Oklahoma City. Including any residence halls, there are 20 buildings.

STUDENT LIFE: 70% of undergraduates are from Oklahoma. Others are from 36 states, 34 foreign countries, and Canada. 73% are White; 6% American Indian/Alaska Native; 5% Hispanic; 2% Asian American; 2% Foreign; 11% African American. 45% are Protestant; 19% claim no religious affiliation. **Female To Male Ratio:** 1.2:1. The average age of freshmen is 18; all undergraduates, 22. 12% do not continue beyond their first year; 49% remain to graduate. **Housing:** 800 students can be accommodated in college housing, which includes dorms and on-campus apartments. On-campus housing is guaranteed for all 4 years. 68% of students live on campus. Alcohol is not permitted. All students may keep cars.

FACULTY/CLASSROOMS: 50% of faculty are male; 50% are female. All teach undergraduates. No introductory courses are taught by graduate students. The average class size in an introductory lecture is 20 and in a laboratory is 15.

PROGRAMS OF STUDY: SNU confers A.B., B.Mus.Ed., and B.S. degrees. Associate and master's degrees are also awarded. Bachelor's degrees are awarded in AGRICULTURE (environmental studies), BIOLOGICAL SCIENCE (biochemistry, biology/biological science, and biophysics), BUSINESS (accounting, banking and finance, business administration and management, management information systems, management science, marketing/retailing/merchandising, sports management, and sports marketing), COMMUNICATIONS AND THE ARTS (communications, English, graphic design, journalism, music, music business management, music performance, Spanish, speech/debate/rhetoric, and sports media), COMPUTER AND PHYSICAL SCIENCE (chemistry, computer science, mathematics, physics, and science), EDUCATION (athletic training, Christian education, early childhood education, education, elementary education, English education, mathematics education, music education, physical education, science education, social studies education, and sports studies), ENGINEERING AND ENVIRONMENTAL DESIGN (aviation administration/management and systems engineering), HEALTH PROFESSIONS (exercise science and nursing), SOCIAL SCIENCE (American studies, history, human development, international studies, Latin American studies, missions, philosophy, physical fitness/movement, political science/government, psychology, religious music, sociology, Spanish studies, theological studies, urban studies, and youth ministry). Premedicine, physics, and theology are the strongest academically. Business, and education have the largest enrollments.

ACTIVITIES: There are no fraternities or sororities. There are 40 groups on campus, including band, cheerleading, choir, chorale, chorus, computers, drama, drum and bugle corps, honors, international, jazz band, literary magazine, musical theater, newspaper, opera, orchestra, pep band, photography, political, professional, religious, social, social service, student government, symphony, and yearbook. Popular campus events include Valentine Banquet, Fall Fest, and Yule Feast. **Sports:** There are 7 intercollegiate sports for men and 7 for women, and 3 intramural sports for men and 3 for women. Facilities include baseball, basketball, cross country, volleyball, equestrian, football, golf, soccer, track and field, softball, and tennis. **Graduates:** From July 1, 2016 to June 30, 2017, 540 bachelor's degrees were awarded. The most popular majors were organizational leadership (36%), business administration (11%), and nursing (10%). In an average class, 2% graduate in 3 years or less, 31% graduate in 4 years or less, 42% graduate in 5 years or less, and 49% graduate in 6 years or less.

SERVICES: Counseling and information services are available, as is tutoring in most subjects. There is remedial math, reading, and writing. Services may be arranged for deaf or learning-disabled students. **Library/Resources:** The library contains 101,901 volumes, 332,461 microform items, and 4,360 audio/video tapes/CDs/DVDs. Computerized library services include interlibrary loans, database searching, Internet access, and Wi-Fi capability. **Physically Challenged Students:** All of the campus is accessible. Facilities include wheelchair ramps, elevators, special parking, specially equipped restrooms, special class scheduling, lowered drinking fountains, lowered telephones, and special housing. **Special:** Cross-registration and co-op programs are available through the Southwestern Colleges of Christian Ministry. Internships may be arranged in the major. A Washington semester, accelerated degree programs, study abroad in England, Russia, Costa Rica, Australia, China, and Egypt through the Council of Christian Colleges and Universities, work-study programs in sociology, and dual and student-designed majors are available. SNU offers nondegree study for life/military/work experience. There are 6 national honor societies, Phi Beta Kappa, and a freshman honors program. **Visiting:** There are regularly scheduled orientations for prospective students, including visits with faculty and students and seminars on financial aid and admissions. There are campus tours, group social activities, and small group mentoring throughout the fall semester. There are guides for informal visits, visitors may sit in on classes, and stay overnight. To schedule a visit, contact the Office of Admissions. **Campus Safety and Security:** Measures include 24-hour foot and vehicle patrol, emergency notification system, self-defense education, and security escort services. There are lighted pathways/sidewalks, controlled access to dorms/residences, and each residence hall is equipped with a controlled access security system.

REQUIREMENTS: The SAT or ACT is required. Applicants must be graduates of an accredited secondary school or have a GED. AP and CLEP credits are accepted. Important factors in the admissions decision are advanced placement or honors courses, extracurricular activities record, and leadership record. A total of 124 semester hours, including at least 32 hours in the major, with a minimum GPA of 2.0, is required to graduate. All students must complete 53 hours of general education requirements covering core areas of self and identity, faith and tradition, and service and society. Skills courses must be taken in computer science, composition, speech communication, math, natural science, citizenship, foreign language, and phys ed. **Procedure:** Freshmen are admitted fall and spring. Entrance exams should be taken by April of the senior year or at orientation. There are early admissions, deferred admissions, and rolling admissions plans. Applications should be filed by August 6 for fall entry. **Transfer Students:** 92 transfer students enrolled in 2016-2017. Transfer applicants must have a 2.0 GPA and be in good standing at their previous college. 30 of 124 credits required for the bachelor's degree must be completed at SNU. **International Students:** There are 52 international students enrolled. They must take the TOEFL with a minimum score of 500 on the paper-based TOEFL (PBT) or 61 on the Internet-based version (iBT).

ADMISSIONS: 100% of the 2017-2018 applicants were accepted. The ACT scores were 36% below 12, 26% between 12 and 17, 18% between 18 and 23, 8% between 24 and 29, and 12% above 30. 32% of the current freshmen were in the top fifth of their class; 53% were in the top two fifths. **Admissions Contact:** Todd Brant, Director of Recruitment. Email: *SNU-jamie@snu.edu* Web: *www.snu.edu*

FINANCIAL AID: In 2017-2018, 90% of all full-time freshmen received some form of financial aid. The FAFSA code is 003149. Check with the school for current application deadlines.

SOUTHWESTERN OKLAHOMA STATE UNIVERSITY — D-3

www.swosu.edu

Weatherford, OK 73096 — **(580) 774-3782**

Fax: (580) 774-7131	**Email:** admissions@swosu.edu
Full-time: 1576 men, 2139 women	**Faculty:** 177; IIA, --$
Part-time: 314 men, 607 women	**Ph.D.s:** 65%
Graduate: 287 men, 535 women	**Student/Faculty:** 21 to 1
Year: semesters, summer session	**Tuition:** $6705 ($13,605)
Room & Board: $5500	**Freshman Class:** 2602 applied, 2515 accepted, 1022 enrolled
ACT: 21	**CEEB CODE:** 6673
Application Deadline: n/av	**COMPETITIVE**

Southwestern Oklahoma State University is known for its quality academic programs and its friendly service to students, and alumni. Students may take classes on the main campus located in Weatherford and on the branch campus located in Sayre. Students may complete associate, bachelor's, master's, and doctoral degrees and post-master's certificates while attending either the traditional on-campus classes or participating in distance-learning opportunities provided through state-of-the-art technology. There are 3 undergraduate schools and 2 graduate schools. In addition to regional accreditation, SWOSU has baccalaureate program accreditation with ABET, ABHES, ACPE, NASM, ACS, ACOTE, AMTA, CAEP, IACBE, JRCERT, ACEN, ATMAE, CAAHIM, and CAPTE. The 292-acre campus is in a small town 70 miles west of Oklahoma City. Including any residence halls, there are 69 buildings.

STUDENT LIFE: 86% of undergraduates are from Oklahoma. Others are from 38 states, 33 foreign countries, and Canada. 63% are White; 10% Hispanic; 8% two or more races; 5% Foreign; 4% African American; 4% American Indian/Alaska Native; 3% Asian American; 3% race unknown. **Female To Male Ratio:** 1.5:1. The average age of freshmen is 19; all undergraduates, 23. 31% do not continue beyond their first year; 35% remain to graduate. **Housing:** 1133 students can be accommodated in college housing, which includes married student dorms. On-campus housing is available on a first-come and first-served basis. 79% of students commute. Alcohol is not permitted. All students may keep cars.

FACULTY/CLASSROOMS: 43% of faculty are male; 57% are female. 93% teach undergraduates. No introductory courses are taught by graduate students. The average class size in a regular course is 24.

PROGRAMS OF STUDY: SWOSU confers B.A., B.A.E., B.S., B.S.E., B.S.N., B.A.S., B.B.A., B.F.A., B.M., and B.M.E. degrees. Associate, master's, and doctoral degrees are also awarded. Bachelor's degrees are awarded in BIOLOGICAL SCIENCE (biology/biological science, environmental biology, and microbiology), BUSINESS (accounting, business administration and management, entrepreneurial studies, finance, management, marketing/retailing/merchandising, organizational leadership and management, and sports management), COMMUNICATIONS AND THE ARTS (art, communications, English, graphic design, and music), COMPUTER AND PHYSICAL SCIENCE (chemistry, computer science, industrial technology, mathematics, and natural sciences), EDUCATION (art education, early childhood education, elementary education, English education, health information management, health and physical education, history education, mathematics education, music education, science education, social science education, and special education), ENGINEERING AND ENVIRONMENTAL DESIGN (engineering physics, engineering technology, and fire protection science), HEALTH PROFESSIONS (biomedical science, exercise science, health care administration, health science, medical laboratory technology, medical records administration/services, music therapy, nursing, and pharmacy), SOCIAL SCIENCE (criminal justice, history, interdisciplinary studies, law enforcement and corrections, parks and recreation management, political science/government, and psychology). Pharmacy, chemistry, and biological sciences are the strongest academically. Health sciences, nursing, and pharmacy have the largest enrollments.

ACTIVITIES: 4% of men belong to 2 local and 2 national fraternities; 5% of women belong to 3 local sororities. There are 104 groups on campus, including art, band, cheerleading, choir, chorale, chorus, computers, drama, drill team, ethnic, honors, international, jazz band, LGBT, literary magazine, marching band, musical theater, newspaper, opera, orchestra, pep band, political, professional, religious, social, social service, student government, symphony, and yearbook. Popular campus events include Fall Homecoming, Bull Dog Blitz Talent Show, and Organization Fair. **Sports:** There are 5 intercollegiate sports for men and 8 for women, and 5 intramural sports for men and 4 for women. Facilities include a football field, event center for basketball and volleyball, fieldhouse, athletic complex for baseball, softball, soccer, golf training facility, strength and conditioning center, wellness center rock wall, basketball courts, indoor running track, exercise room, weight room, indoor pool, outdoor track, rodeo arena and horse barn, ropes course, soccer practice field, sand volleyball courts, and outdoor basketball courts. **Graduates:** From July 1, 2016 to June 30, 2017, 745 bachelor's degrees were awarded. The most popular majors were nursing (24%), business (13%), and parks and recreation (7%). In an average class, 17% graduate in 4 years or less, 29% graduate in 5 years or less, and 35% graduate in 6 years or less.

SERVICES: Counseling and information services are available, as is tutoring in some subjects, such as mathematics, writing, psychology, physics, biological sciences, chemistry, language, and social sciences. There is remedial math, reading, and writing. A student development center offers counseling and tutoring on an individual basis. **Library/Resources:** The library contains 303,978 volumes, 422,418 microform items, and 4,604 audio/video tapes/CDs/DVDs, and subscribes to 128 periodicals including electronic. Computerized library services include interlibrary loans, database searching, Internet access, and Wi-Fi capability. **Physically Challenged Students:** 98% of the campus is accessible. Facilities include wheelchair ramps, elevators, special parking, specially equipped restrooms, special class scheduling, lowered drinking fountains, and lowered telephones. **Special:** More than 40% of SWOSU students participate in some form of practicum, internship, field experience, co-op, service learning, or clinical assignment by the spring of the senior year. Assignments include a variety of local and state businesses, manufacturers, schools, health care entities, and government agencies, as well as national placements such as NASA. Recent study abroad opportunities include England, Spain, Italy, France, Jordan, South Korea, Taiwan, Costa Rica. There are 3 national honor societies and a freshman honors program. **Visiting:** There are regularly scheduled orientations for prospective students. New Student Orientation includes an Orientation Session prior to the beginning of the fall semester, Mass Orientation, a one-hour freshman orientation, and planned activities during the first few weeks of the fall semester. There are guides for informal visits, visitors may sit in on classes, and stay overnight. To schedule a visit, contact Todd Boyd, Director at (580) 774-3782. **Campus Safety and Security:** Measures include 24-hour foot and vehicle patrol, emergency notification system, self-defense education, and security escort services. There are lighted pathways/sidewalks and controlled access to dorms/residences.

REQUIREMENTS: Applicants must meet one of the following requirements: have a minimum of have a 20 on the ACT; rank in the top 50 percent of high school class with a 2.7 GPA; or have a 2.7 GPA in a 15-unit core high school curriculum that includes 4 credits in English, 3 each in mathematics, history, and lab science, and 2 additional units in one of the previously listed subjects, computer science, or foreign language. Open admission is available at the Sayre campus. AP and CLEP credits are accepted. To graduate, students must complete a minimum of 120 semester hours with a minimum GPA of 2.0. (Some degree programs may require more semester hours and/or higher GPA.) Each student must complete 40 semester hours in general education courses, including 6 hours in written communication, 3 each in mathematics, U.S. history and American government, 7-8 in science, 6 in humanities, 3-4 in human, cultural and social diversity, and elective hours to bring the total to 40. Additionally, each student must demonstrate computer proficiency with through a course at high school or SWOSU or through a SWOSU computer proficiency exam. **Procedure:** Freshmen are admitted to all sessions. Entrance exams should be taken during the senior year. There is a rolling admissions plan. Application deadlines are open. The fall 2017 application fee was $15. Notification is sent on a rolling basis. Applications are accepted on-line. **Transfer Students:** 550 transfer students enrolled in 2016-2017. Applicants must have a minimum college GPA of 1.7 for 30 hours or less, and 2.0 GPA for 31 or more hours. 30 of 120 credits required for the bachelor's degree must be completed at SWOSU. **International Students:** There are 241 international students enrolled. They must take the TOEFL with a minimum score of 500 on the paper-based TOEFL (PBT) or 61 on the Internet-based version (iBT). They must also take the SAT or ACT, scoring 19.

ADMISSIONS: 97% of the 2017-2018 applicants were accepted. The ACT scores were 20% between 12 and 17, 50% between 18 and 23, 24% between 24 and 29, and 6% above 30. 40% of the current freshmen were in the top fifth of their class; 66% were in the top two fifths. 106 freshmen graduated first in their class. **Admissions Contact:** Todd Boyd, Director of Enrollment Management. Email: *admissions@swosu.edu* Web: *www.swosu.edu*

FINANCIAL AID: In 2017-2018, 80% of all full-time freshmen received some form of financial aid. 40% of all full-time freshmen received need-based aid. The college's own financial statement is required. The FAFSA code is 003181. The priority date for freshman financial aid applications for fall entry is March 1.

ST. GREGORY'S UNIVERSITY *(The complete profile is made available exclusively on our website, www.barronspac.com)*

UNIVERSITY OF CENTRAL OKLAHOMA D-2

www.uco.edu

Edmond, OK 73034 **(405) 974-2450** **(800) 254-4215**

Fax: 405-974-3930 **Email: onestop@uco.edu**

Full-time: 4274 men, 6173 women	**Faculty:** 548
Part-time: 1613 men, 2282 women	**Ph.D.s:** 77%
Graduate: 486 men, 1151 women	**Student/Faculty:** 19 to 1
Year: semesters, summer session	**Tuition:** $7100 ($17,447)
Room & Board: $8050	**Freshman Class:** 4718 applied, 3830 accepted, 2180 enrolled
ACT: 21	**CEEB CODE:** 6091
Application Deadline: n/av	**COMPETITIVE**

University of Central Oklahoma, founded in 1890. The university's goal is to help students learn by providing transformative education experiences so that they may become productive, creative, ethical and engaged citizens and leaders serving our global community. UCO contributes to the intellectual, cultural, economic and social advancement of the communities and individuals it serves. There are 5 undergraduate schools and 1 graduate school. In addition to regional accreditation, UCO has baccalaureate program accreditation with AACSB, ABET, ABFSE, ADA, NASAD, NASM, CAEP, PGA, CIDA, and ASHA. The 210-acre campus is in a suburban area North of Oklahoma City. Including any residence halls, there are 58 buildings.

STUDENT LIFE: 90% of undergraduates are from Oklahoma. Others are from 43 states, 88 foreign countries, and Canada. 56% are White; 10% Hispanic; 10% two or more races; 9% African American; 7% Foreign; 4% American Indian/Alaska Native; 3% Asian American; 1% race unknown. **Female To Male Ratio:** 1.5:1. The average age of freshmen is 19; all undergraduates, 23. 36% do not continue beyond their first year; 33% remain to graduate. **Housing:** 1910 students can be accommodated in college housing, which includes single sex, coed, married student dorms and on-campus apartments. In addition, there are fraternity houses and sorority houses. On-campus housing is available on a first-come, first-served basis, and is available on a lottery system for upperclassmen. 89% of students commute. Alcohol is not permitted. All students may keep cars.

FACULTY/CLASSROOMS: 44% of faculty are male; 55% are female. No introductory courses are taught by graduate students.

PROGRAMS OF STUDY: UCO confers B.A., B.S., B.A.Ed., B.B.A., B.F.A., B.F.A.Ed., B.M.Ed., B.M., B.A.T., and B.S.Ed. degrees. Associate and master's degrees are also awarded. Bachelor's degrees are awarded in BIOLOGICAL SCIENCE (biology/biological science, forensic psychology, forensic science, and nutrition), BUSINESS (accounting, banking and finance, business administration w/legal studies, business administration and management, fashion merchandising, finance, funeral home services, human resources, insurance, management information systems, marketing, marketing/retailing/merchandising, and professional golf management), COMMUNICATIONS AND THE ARTS (advertising, art history, art, broadcasting, communications, creative writing, dance, design, English, English as a second/foreign language, French, German, graphic design, journalism, music, photography, piano performance, public relations, Spanish, studio art, theatre acting, theatre arts, theater design, and theatre studies), COMPUTER AND PHYSICAL SCIENCE (actuarial science, applied mathematics, chemistry, computer science, and mathematics), EDUCATION (art education, athletic training, bilingual/bicultural education, dance education, early childhood education, elementary education, English education, foreign languages education, general studies, mathematics education, museum studies, music education, physical education, science education, secondary education, social studies education, and special education), ENGINEERING AND ENVIRONMENTAL DESIGN (biomedical engineering, electrical/electronics engineering, engineering, engineering physics, and interior design), HEALTH PROFESSIONS (allied health, community health work, exercise science, industrial hygiene, nursing, predentistry, premedicine, preoptometry, and speech pathology/audiology), SOCIAL SCIENCE (addiction studies, child psychology/development, criminal justice, economics, family/consumer studies, forensic studies, geography, gerontology, history, humanities, legal studies, liberal arts/general studies, philosophy, physical fitness/movement, political science/government, psychology, public administration, and sociology). Forensic science, accounting, business, nursing, and funeral service are the strongest academically. Nursing, biology, psychology, and forensic science have the largest enrollments.

ACTIVITIES: 2% of men belong to 12 national fraternities; 4% of women belong to 11 national sororities. There are 236 groups on campus, including art, band, cheerleading, chess, choir, chorus, communications, computers, dance, debate, drama, drum and bugle corps, environmental, ethnic, film, forensics, honors, international, jazz band, LGBT, marching band, musical theater, newspaper, orchestra, pep band, photography, political, professional, radio and TV, religious, social, social service, student government, symphony, and yearbook. Popular campus events include Homecoming, Earth Day, May Day, The Big Event, Winterglow, International Festival, Big Pink Volleyball, and Miss UCO. **Sports:** There are 5 intercollegiate sports for men and 9 for women, and 17 intramural sports for men and 17 for women. Facilities include a field house with a gym, a track, weight room, a stadium with a track and a softball field, a wellness center with basketball courts, aerobic classes, cardiovascular equipment, weights, and various classes. **Graduates:** From July 1, 2016 to June 30, 2017, 2624 bachelor's degrees were awarded. The most popular majors were general studies (10%), psychology (4%), and nursing (4%). In an average class, 2% graduate in 3 years or less, 35% graduate in 4 years or less, 41% graduate in 5 years or less, and 14% graduate in 6 years or less.

SERVICES: Counseling and information services are available, as is tutoring in some subjects, such as English, math, reading, writing, biology, and chemistry. There is a reader service for the blind, and remedial math and writing. **Library/Resources:** The library contains 676,768 volumes, 162,562 microform items, and 35,112 audio/video tapes/CDs/DVDs, and subscribes to 29,681 periodicals including electronic. Computerized library services include interlibrary loans, database searching, Internet access, and Wi-Fi capability. Special learning facilities include an art gallery, radio station, and TV station. **Physically Challenged Students:** All of the campus is accessible. Facilities include wheelchair ramps, elevators, special parking, specially equipped restrooms, special class scheduling, and lowered drinking fountains. **Special:** Opportunities are provided for internships, dual majors, a general studies degree, credit by exam, nondegree study, and credit for military experience. Work-study programs may be arranged through the Federal College Work-Study Program. There are 15 national honor societies and 10 departmental honors programs. **Visiting:** There are regularly scheduled orientations for prospective students, including a brief tour, a question-and-answer period, and access to an information booth. There are guides for informal visits. To schedule a visit, contact Amity Smith at asmith213@uco.edu. **Campus Safety and Security:** Measures include 24-hour foot and vehicle patrol, emergency notification system, and security escort services. There are emergency telephones, lighted pathways/sidewalks, controlled access to dorms/residences, and a crime and terrorism tip line.

REQUIREMENTS: A minimum composite ACT of 20 or a 2.7 non-weighted, cumulative GPA are required. Student must also have a class ranking in the upper 50% of graduating class. Graduation from an accredited secondary school is required and a GED is accepted. The applicant's academic record should include 4 units of English, 3 units each of math (first-year algebra and beyond), lab science, and history, of which 1 year must be in American history, and 2 additional units. AP and CLEP credits are accepted. Important factors in the admissions decision are evidence of special talent, extracurricular activities record, and leadership record. Students must complete 124 semester hours with a 2.0 GPA. Up to 4 of the 124 semester hours required for graduation may be physical education activity courses. Students must take 40 hours of upper division courses with at least 15 hours from the major. 10 hours of major course work must be earned from UCO. 60 hours must be earned from a bachelor's granting university, exclusive of physical education activity courses. 30 semester hours at UCO, exclusive of extra-institutional credit. 15 of the last 30 semester hours applying toward a degree must be completed at UCO. **Procedure:** Freshmen are admitted to all sessions. Entrance exams should be taken within 30 days of submitting the application. There is a rolling admissions plan. Application deadlines are open. The fall 2017 application fee was $50. Applications are accepted on-line. **Transfer Students:** 1460 transfer students enrolled in 2016-2017. Applicants must submit official transcripts from all previously attended colleges and have a minimum GPA of 1.7 if the student has 29 or less credit hours or a 2.0 GPA for students with 30 or more credit hours. Students who have completed fewer than 24 hours of transferable credit must meet the requirements for entering freshmen. Out of state students must have a minimum 2.0 GPA. 30 of 124 credits required for the bachelor's degree must be completed at UCO. **International Students:** There are 781 international students enrolled. They must take the TOEFL with a minimum score of 500 on the paper-based TOEFL (PBT) or 61 on the Internet-based version (iBT).

ADMISSIONS: 81% of the 2017-2018 applicants were accepted. The ACT scores were 14% between 12 and 17, 58% between 18 and 23, 25% between 24 and 29, and 3% above 30. 25% of the current freshmen were in the top fifth of their class; 50% were in the top two fifths. 51 freshmen graduated first in their class. **Admissions Contact:** John Stephens, Director of Undergraduate Admissions. Email: *onestop@uco.edu* Web: *www.uco.edu*

FINANCIAL AID: In 2017-2018, 84% of all full-time freshmen received some form of financial aid. 56% of all full-time freshmen received need-based aid. The average freshman award was $8,800. Need-based scholarships or need-based grants averaged $3,091 ($16,038 maximum); need-based self-help aid (loans and jobs) averaged $2,032 ($8,964 maximum); non-need-based athletic scholarships averaged $211 ($24,623 maximum); and other non-need-based awards and non-need-based scholarships averaged $1,527 ($23,000 maximum). 6% of undergraduate students work part-time. The average financial indebtedness of the 2017 graduate was $13,339. The CSS/Profile, FFS, and the college's own financial statement are required. The FAFSA code is 003152. The deadline for filing freshman financial aid applications for fall entry is May 31.

UNIVERSITY OF OKLAHOMA — D-3

www.ou.edu

Norman, OK 73019 — (405) 325-2252, (800) 234-6868

Fax: (405) 325-7124 — **Email:** admrec@ou.edu

Full-time: 9532 men, 9522 women
Part-time: 1580 men, 1398 women
Graduate: 3121 men, 3374 women
Year: semesters, summer session
Room & Board: $10,588

SAT CR/M: 630/620 **ACT:** 26
Application Deadline: February 1

Faculty: 1206
Ph.D.s: 89%
Student/Faculty: 18 to 1
Tuition: $9063 ($24,444)
Freshman Class: 15744 applied, 11552 accepted, 4473 enrolled
CEEB CODE: 6879
HIGHLY COMPETITIVE

University of Oklahoma, founded in 1890, is a comprehensive research university offering 158 majors for undergraduate study. There are 13 undergraduate schools and 13 graduate schools. In addition to regional accreditation, University of Oklahoma has baccalaureate program accreditation with AACSB, ABET, ACCE, ACEJMC, CSWE, NAAB, NASM, CAEP, NAST, EAC, and AAM. The 3337-acre campus is in a suburban area 20 miles south of Oklahoma City. Including any residence halls, there are 347 buildings.

STUDENT LIFE: 64% of undergraduates are from Oklahoma. Others are from 50 states, 128 foreign countries, and Canada. 60% are White; 10% Hispanic; 8% two or more races; 6% Asian American; 5% African American; 5% Foreign; 4% American Indian/Alaska Native; 2% race unknown. **Female To Male Ratio:** 1.0:1. The average age of freshmen is 18; all undergraduates, 21. 8% do not continue beyond their first year; 68% remain to graduate. **Housing:** 6417 students can be accommodated in college housing, which includes married student dorms and on-campus apartments. In addition, there are honors houses, international floors, cultural housing, national merit, scholastic, and quiet lifestyle floor. On-campus housing is guaranteed for the freshman year only, is available on a first-come, and first-served basis. 68% of students commute. Alcohol is not permitted. All students may keep cars.

FACULTY/CLASSROOMS: 61% of faculty are male; 39% are female. Graduate students teach 28% of introductory courses. The average class size in an introductory lecture is 43; in a laboratory is 20; and in a regular course is 39.

PROGRAMS OF STUDY: University of Oklahoma confers B.A., B.S., B.Arch., B.B.A., B.F.A., B.Int.Des., B.Mus.Arts, B.Mus.Ed., and B.Mus. degrees. Master's and doctoral degrees are also awarded. Bachelor's degrees are awarded in AGRICULTURE (environmental studies and plant science), BIOLOGICAL SCIENCE (biochemistry, botany, microbiology, and zoology), BUSINESS (accounting, business administration, entreprenurship, environment & natural resource economics, finance, international business, international business management, leadership, management information systems, management, marketing, supply chain management, and professional studies), COMMUNICATIONS AND THE ARTS (advertising, Arabic, art history, art, communications, dance, dramatic arts, English, film arts, film, television and digital media, French language and literature, German, Italian, Japanese, journalism, language arts, linguistics, music, music composition, music performance, musical theater, new media production, public relations, Russian, Spanish, studio art, technical and business writing, and visual communication), COMPUTER AND PHYSICAL SCIENCE (astronomy, astrophysics, atmospheric sciences and meteorology, chemistry, chemistry/chemical biology, combined science, environmental geology, geology, geophysics and seismology, information science, information security & risk management, mathematics, paleontology, and physics), EDUCATION (Asian studies, classical studies, dance education, early childhood education, elementary education, mathematics education, music education, science education, social studies education, and special education), ENGINEERING AND ENVIRONMENTAL DESIGN (aerospace engineering, applied aviation, architectural engineering, architecture, bioengineering, chemical engineering, civil engineering, computer engineering, construction technology, energy management technology, engineering physics, environmental design, environmental engineering, environmental science, industrial engineering, interior design, mechanical engineering, and petroleum/natural gas engineering), HEALTH PROFESSIONS (biology, electrical engineering, exercise science, human biology, human relations, and multidisciplinary studies), SOCIAL SCI-

ENCE (African American studies, anthropology, Chinese Studies, criminal justice, criminology, economics, ethics, politics, and social policy, European studies, geography, geography information science, history, history of science, international studies, Latin American studies, liberal arts, sciences, general studies, humanities, Middle Eastern studies, Native American studies, philosophy, political science/government, psychology, public administration, religious studies, social work, sociology, women & gender studies, and world cultural studies). Chemistry, finance & accounting, and meteorology are the strongest academically. Biology, psychology, and health & exercise science have the largest enrollments.

ACTIVITIES: 26% of men belong to 31 national fraternities; 33% of women belong to 26 national sororities. There are 528 groups on campus, including art, band, cheerleading, chess, choir, chorale, chorus, computers, dance, debate, drama, drill team, environmental, ethnic, film, forensics, honors, international, jazz band, LGBT, literary magazine, marching band, musical theater, newspaper, opera, orchestra, pep band, photography, political, professional, radio and TV, religious, social, social service, student government, symphony, and yearbook. Popular campus events include Homecoming, Eve of Nations, Pink and Black Ball, CAC Soonerthon, Stompdown, Spring Pow Wow, Asian New Year, and Day of the Dead Street Festival. **Sports:** There are 10 intercollegiate sports for men and 11 for women, and 13 intramural sports for men and 13 for women. Facilities include a golf course, a field house with arena, a gymnastics center, tennis courts, swimming pool, a fitness center, football stadium, track and field facilities, baseball, soccer, softball fields and an indoor rowing facility. **Graduates:** From July 1, 2016 to June 30, 2017, 4347 bachelor's degrees were awarded. The most popular majors were finance (4%), petroleum engineering (4%), and psychology (4%). In an average class, 2% graduate in 3 years or less, 42% graduate in 4 years or less, 63% graduate in 5 years or less, and 68% graduate in 6 years or less.

SERVICES: Counseling and information services are available, as is tutoring in some subjects. There is a reader service for the blind, and remedial math, reading, and writing. There are also volunteer note takers, interpreters and real-time reporting services for the deaf or hearing impaired, and alternative testing services. **Library/Resources:** The library contains 5.5 million volumes, 3.6 million microform items, and 13,460 audio/video tapes/CDs/DVDs, and subscribes to 201,151 periodicals including electronic. Computerized library services include interlibrary loans, database searching, Internet access, and Wi-Fi capability. Special learning facilities include an art gallery, natural history museum, radio station, TV station, and observatory. **Physically Challenged Students:** 95% of the campus is accessible. Facilities include wheelchair ramps, elevators, special parking, specially equipped restrooms, special class scheduling, lowered drinking fountains, lowered telephones, and special housing. **Special:** Co-op programs are available in Arts and Sciences, Business, and Engineering. A variety of voluntary and required internships are available in more than 50 fields of study. OU offers study abroad in over 100 countries, work-study programs, a Washington, D.C. fellowship, a general studies degree, dual and student-designed majors, non-degree study, pass/fail options, credit for life experience, award-winning online programs, practicum opportunities, unique Presidential Dream Courses, and undergraduate health programs in conjunction with the OU Health Sciences Center in Oklahoma City. BA/BS degrees and accelerated degrees are offered in many subjects. The interdisciplinary major in Letters combines the classics, history, philosophy, and languages. There are 18 national honor societies, Phi Beta Kappa, and a freshman honors program. **Visiting:** There are regularly scheduled orientations for prospective students, consisting of sessions tailored to individual needs and interests. There are guides for informal visits and visitors may sit in on classes. To schedule a visit, contact Admissions & Recruitment Office. **Campus Safety and Security:** Measures include 24-hour foot and vehicle patrol, emergency notification system, self-defense education, and security escort services. There are shuttle buses, emergency telephones, lighted pathways/sidewalks, controlled access to dorms/residences, a bicycle patrol, and safe ride program.

REQUIREMENTS: The SAT or ACT is required. Applicants will be considered for admission using a holistic review and selection process which considers several factors that predict academic success (i.e. GPA point average, high school course rigor, academic engagement, writing ability, leadership and ACT/SAT scores). Students must have a total of 15 curricular units, including 4 units of English, 3 units each of math, lab science, history and citizenship, and 2 elective units from areas previously mentioned or computer science or foreign language. Some alternative admission opportunities are available, but limited. AP and CLEP credits are accepted. A minimum of 40 credit hours of general education courses is required for graduation. Freshmen are admitted to all sessions. Entrance exams should be taken during the junior year or the first part of the senior year. There is a rolling admissions plan. Applications should be filed by February 1 for fall entry; November 1 for spring entry; and March 1 for summer entry. The fall 2017 application fee was $40. Notification is sent on a rolling basis. 1929 applicants were on the 2017 waiting list; 163 were admitted. Applications are accepted on-line. **Transfer Students:** 1077 transfer students enrolled in 2016-2017. Applicants with 60 or more semester hours attempted must have a minimum GPA of 2.0. The College of Architecture, College of Atmospheric and Geographic Sciences, College of Arts & Sciences, College of International Studies, College of Professional and Continuing Studies, College of Engineering, College of Earth and Energy, and College of Fine Arts require a 2.5. The College of Business, College of Education, and College of Journalism and Mass Communication require a 2.75. Nonresident Engineering applicants must have a minimum GPA of 3.0. The Applicants with fewer than 24 semester hours of college-level work must also meet freshman admission requirements. Applicants must be in good standing at the last institution attended. 30 of 120 credits required for the bachelor's degree must be completed at University of Oklahoma. **International Students:** There are 837 international students enrolled. They must take the TOEFL with a minimum score of 79 on the Internet-based version (iBT).

ADMISSIONS: 73% of the 2017-2018 applicants were accepted. The SAT scores for the 2017-2018 freshman class were: Math-- 4% below 500, 33% between 500 and 599, 38% between 600 and 699, and 25% between 700 and 800. Evidence-Based Reading/Writing-- 4% below 500, 30% between 500 and 599, 41% between 600 and 699, and 25% between 700 and 800. The ACT scores were 27% between 18 and 23, 50% between 24 and 29, and 23% above 30. 57% of the current freshmen were in the top fifth of their class; 83% were in the top two fifths. 258 freshmen graduated first in their class. **Admissions Contact:** Jeffrey Blahnik, Director of Admissions and Recruitment. Email: *admrec@ou.edu* Web: *www.ou.edu*

FINANCIAL AID: The average financial indebtedness of the 2017 graduate was $29,283. University of Oklahoma is a member of CSS. The FAFSA code is 003184. The priority date for freshman financial aid applications for fall entry is December 15.

UNIVERSITY OF SCIENCE AND ARTS OF OKLAHOMA — D-3

www.usao.edu

Chickasha, OK 73018 — (405) 574-1350, (800) 933-8726

Fax: (405) 574-1220	**Email:** usao-admissions@usao.edu
Full-time: 271 men, 515 women	**Faculty:** 53; IIB, --$
Part-time: 41 men, 56 women	**Ph.D.s:** 85%
Graduate: n/av	**Student/Faculty:** 13 to 1
Year: trimesters, summer session	**Tuition:** $5670 ($15,210)
Room & Board: $5470	**Freshman Class:** 567 applied, 383 accepted, 170 enrolled
ACT: 24	**CEEB CODE:** 6544
Application Deadline: September 1	**VERY COMPETITIVE**

University of Science and Arts of Oklahoma, founded in 1908, is Oklahoma's only publicly funded liberal arts college, providing interdisciplinary learning opportunities. There is 1 undergraduate school and 5 graduate schools. In addition to regional accreditation, USAO has baccalaureate program accreditation with NASM, CAEP, and CED. The 75-acre campus is in a small town 40 miles southwest of Oklahoma City. Including any residence halls, there are 14 buildings.

STUDENT LIFE: 85% of undergraduates are from Oklahoma. Others are from 23 states, 19 foreign countries, and Canada. 96% are from public schools. 9% are Foreign; 72% White; 7% African American; 2% Asian American; 16% American Indian/Alaska Native; 11% Hispanic. **Female To Male Ratio:** 1.8:1. The average age of freshmen is 18; all undergraduates, 23. **Housing:** College-sponsored housing includes dorms and on-campus apartments. On-campus housing is guaranteed for the freshman year only, is available on a first-come, and first-served basis. 54% of students live on campus. All students may keep cars.

FACULTY/CLASSROOMS: 49% of faculty are male; 51% are female. All

teach undergraduates, 55% do research, and 55% do both. No introductory courses are taught by graduate students. The average class size in an introductory lecture is 20; in a laboratory is 20; and in a regular course is 17.

PROGRAMS OF STUDY: USAO confers B.A., B.S., and B.F.A. degrees. Bachelor's degrees are awarded in BIOLOGICAL SCIENCE (biology/biological science), BUSINESS (business administration and management), COMMUNICATIONS AND THE ARTS (art, communications, dramatic arts, English, fine arts, and music), COMPUTER AND PHYSICAL SCIENCE (chemistry, mathematics, natural sciences, and physics), EDUCATION (early childhood education, education of the deaf and hearing impaired, elementary education, and physical education), HEALTH PROFESSIONS (speech pathology/audiology), SOCIAL SCIENCE (American Indian studies, economics, history, political science/government, psychology, and sociology). Humanities, and physical science are the strongest academically. Business administration, psychology, and art have the largest enrollments.

ACTIVITIES: 2% of men belong to 1 national fraternity; 12% of women belong to 1 national sorority. There are 45 groups on campus, including art, band, cheerleading, choir, chorale, computers, dance, drama, drill team, ethnic, honors, jazz band, LGBT, musical theater, pep band, political, professional, religious, social, social service, and student government. Popular campus events include Montmartre Art Festival/Droverstock, Festival of Arts and Ideas, and Drover Difference Day. **Sports:** There are 5 intercollegiate sports for men and 5 for women, and 5 intramural sports for men and 5 for women. Facilities include a field house, a gym, an auditorium, baseball and softball fields, a soccer field, tennis courts, a weight room, a fitness center, an indoor pool, an outdoor pool, and volleyball courts. **Graduates:** From July 1, 2016 to June 30, 2017, 183 bachelor's degrees were awarded. The most popular majors were business marketing, education, and history. In an average class, 6% graduate in 3 years or less, 28% graduate in 4 years or less, 38% graduate in 5 years or less, and 41% graduate in 6 years or less. Of the 2016 graduating class, 46% were enrolled in graduate school within 6 months of graduation.

SERVICES: Counseling and information services are available, as is tutoring in some subjects, such as math, writing, and reading. Tutors and interpreters are available for hearing-impaired students. **Library/Resources:** The library contains 69,605 volumes, 214 microform items, and 3,562 audio/video tapes/CDs/DVDs, and subscribes to 55,000 periodicals including electronic. Computerized library services include interlibrary loans, database searching, and Internet access. Special learning facilities include an art gallery, TV station, a commercial art computer lab, a child development center, a herbarium, art gallery and a speech pathology clinic. **Physically Challenged Students:** 95% of the campus is accessible. Facilities include wheelchair ramps, elevators, special parking, specially equipped restrooms, special class scheduling, lowered drinking fountains, lowered telephones, and special housing. **Special:** USAO offers dual majors, accelerated degree programs in all majors through year-round study, work-study programs, internship placement in community institutions, a Tutorial Scholars Program for student-designed majors, an interdisciplinary studies program, and a limited number of pass/fail options. There are 7 national honor societies, a freshman honors program, and 1 departmental honors program. **Visiting:** There are guides for informal visits, visitors may sit in on classes, and stay overnight. To schedule a visit, contact the Admissions Office. **Campus Safety and Security:** Measures include 24-hour foot and vehicle patrol, emergency notification system, and security escort services. There are lighted pathways/sidewalks, and security cameras near housing and parking lots.

REQUIREMENTS: Applicants must meet one of the following 3 options: (1) have a minimum score of 24 on the ACT or 1090 on the SAT and (3.0 GPA or top 50% of their high school class); (2) have a high school GPA of 3.0 and be in the top 25% of their high school class; or (3) have a minimum GPA of 3.0 in their high school core courses and a minimum score of 22 on the ACT or 1020 on the SAT. USAO requires applicants to be in the upper 50% of their class. AP and CLEP credits are accepted. Important factors in the admissions decision are evidence of special talent, leadership record, and personality/intangible qualities. To graduate, students must complete a total of 124 credit hours with a minimum GPA of 2.0. **Procedure:** Freshmen are admitted to all sessions. Entrance exams should be taken by May of the preceding spring. There is a rolling admissions plan. Applications should be filed by September 1 for fall entry. The fall 2017 application fee was $40. Notification is sent on a rolling basis. Applications are accepted on-line. **Transfer Students:** 103 transfer students enrolled in 2016-2017. Applicants must have a minimum GPA of 2.0. Those students with fewer than 30 college-level credit hours must submit a high school transcript or GED and ACT scores. 30 of 124 credits required for the bachelor's degree must be completed at USAO. **International Students:** There are 63 international students enrolled. They must take the TOEFL with a minimum score of 500 on the paper-based TOEFL (PBT) or 61 on the Internet-based version (iBT). They must also take the SAT or ACT, scoring 22.

ADMISSIONS: 68% of the 2017-2018 applicants were accepted. The ACT scores were 18% below 12, 29% between 12 and 17, 28% between 18 and 23, 16% between 24 and 29, and 9% above 30. 57% of the current freshmen were in the top fifth of their class; 85% were in the top two fifths. **Admissions Contact:** Laura Coponiti, Dean of Admissions and Financial Aid. Email: *usao-admissions@usao.edu* Web: *www.usao.edu*

FINANCIAL AID: In 2017-2018, 74% of all full-time freshmen received some form of financial aid and need-based aid. The average freshman award was $10,779. Need-based scholarships or need-based grants averaged $8,911; need-based self-help aid (loans and jobs) averaged $3,321; non-need-based athletic scholarships averaged $10,463; other non-need-based awards and non-need-based scholarships averaged $2,727; and $3,132 from other forms of aid. The average financial indebtedness of the 2017 graduate was $20,074. The college's own financial statement, and International Student's Certification of Finances are required. The FAFSA code is 003167. The priority date for freshman financial aid applications for fall entry is March 1.

UNIVERSITY OF TULSA — E-2

www.utulsa.edu

Tulsa, OK 74104 — (918) 631-2307, (800) 331-3050

Fax: (918) 631-5003 — **Email:** admission@utulsa.edu

Full-time: 1787 men, 1416 women
Part-time: 83 men, 57 women
Graduate: 627 men, 463 women
Year: semesters, summer session
Room & Board: $11,116
SAT CR/M/W: 640/640/600 **ACT:** required
Application Deadline: n/av

Faculty: 316; IIA, +$
Ph.D.s: 94%
Student/Faculty: 11 to 1
Tuition: $41,509
Freshman Class: 7869 applied, 3065 accepted, 743 enrolled
CEEB CODE: 6883
HIGHLY COMPETITIVE

University of Tulsa, founded in 1894, is a private comprehensive institution offering over 60 undergraduate major areas of study through its programs in liberal arts and social sciences, engineering and natural sciences, business and finance, and health sciences. A number of interdisciplinary programs are also available and students are encouraged to participate in individual research, scholarship, and creative endeavors beginning in their freshman year. The university also offers a number of combined undergraduate/graduate degree programs which allow interested and qualified students to earn an undergraduate and graduate degree in less time than would normally be required to earn both degrees separately. There are 4 undergraduate schools and 2 graduate schools. In addition to regional accreditation, University of Tulsa has baccalaureate program accreditation with AACSB, ABET, CSAB, NASM, CED, NLNAC, and CAATE. The 209-acre campus is in an urban area in the city of Tulsa. Including any residence halls, there are 95 buildings.

STUDENT LIFE: 59% of undergraduates are from Oklahoma. Others are from 48 states, 68 foreign countries, and Canada. 66% are from public schools. 57% are White; 19% Foreign; 6% Hispanic; 5% African American; 5% Asian American; 3% American Indian/Alaska Native; 3% two or more races; 2% race unknown. 44% are Protestant; 28% claim no religious affiliation; 15% Catholic. **Male To Female Ratio:** 1.3:1. The average age of freshmen is 18; all undergraduates, 21. 12% do not continue beyond their first year; 69% remain to graduate. **Housing:** 2809 students can be accommodated in college housing, which includes single sex, coed, married student dorms, on-campus apartments, and off-campus apartments. In addition, there are honors houses, special-interest houses, fraternity houses, and sorority houses. On-campus housing is guaranteed for the freshman year only, is available on a first-come, first-served basis, and is available on a lottery system for upperclassmen. 67% of students live on campus. All students may keep cars.

FACULTY/CLASSROOMS: 66% of faculty are male; 34% are female.

92% teach undergraduates, 98% do research, and 92% do both. Graduate students teach 6% of introductory courses. The average class size in an introductory lecture is 20; in a laboratory is 19; and in a regular course is 20.

PROGRAMS OF STUDY: University of Tulsa confers B.A., B.F.A., B.A.D.E., B.M., B.M.E., B.S., B.S.A.M., B.S.A.T., B.S.B., B.S.B.A., B.S.Ch.E., B.S.C., B.S.C.S., B.S.D.E., B.S.S.P., B.S.E.C.E., B.S.I.T., B.S.E.E., B.S.E.P., B.S.E.S.S., B.S.G.S., B.S.I.B.L., B.S.M.E., B.S.N., B.S.P.E., B.S.E.P., B.S.B.G., and B.S.G.P. degrees. Master's and doctoral degrees are also awarded. Bachelor's degrees are awarded in AGRICULTURE (environmental studies), BIOLOGICAL SCIENCE (biology ecology and field biology, biochemistry, and biology/biological science), BUSINESS (accounting, banking and finance, business administration and management, business (dual major program), business administration - international, business administration marketing, international business management, management information systems, management science, marketing/retailing/merchandising, organizational behavior, and sports management), COMMUNICATIONS AND THE ARTS (American literature, art history, art, arts administration/management, communications, creative writing, English, film arts, French, game design and development, game programming, German, music, music performance, musical theater, piano/organ, Spanish, studio art, theatre arts, visual and performing arts, and voice), COMPUTER AND PHYSICAL SCIENCE (applied mathematics, chemistry, computer game design/development, computer science, geology, geophysics and seismology, geoscience, information sciences and systems, mathematics, and physics), EDUCATION (athletic training, education, education of the deaf and hearing impaired, elementary education, and music education), ENGINEERING AND ENVIRONMENTAL DESIGN (chemical engineering, computer engineering, electrical/electronics engineering, energy management technology, engineering physics, mechanical engineering, and petroleum/natural gas engineering), HEALTH PROFESSIONS (allied health, biology, exercise science, nursing, premedicine, speech pathology/audiology, and speech therapy), SOCIAL SCIENCE (anthropology, archeology, Chinese Studies, communication sciences & disorders, economics, history, philosophy, political science/government, prelaw, psychology, religion, Russian and Slavic studies, sociology, women & gender studies, and women's studies). Computer science, psychology, English, and finance are the strongest academically. Mechanical engineering, psychology, and finance have the largest enrollments.

ACTIVITIES: 18% of men belong to 7 national fraternities; 20% of women belong to 9 national sororities. There are 172 groups on campus, including art, band, cheerleading, choir, chorale, chorus, communications, computers, dance, drama, drill team, environmental, ethnic, film, forensics, honors, international, jazz band, LGBT, literary magazine, marching band, musical theater, newspaper, orchestra, pep band, photography, political, professional, radio and TV, religious, social, social service, student government, symphony, and yearbook. Popular campus events include Homecoming, Springfest, Hurricane Thursdays, and International Education Week. **Sports:** There are 7 intercollegiate sports for men and 10 for women, and 22 intramural sports for men and 22 for women. Facilities include a stadium, basketball arena, a gym, athletic field, indoor racquetball courts, basketball and tennis courts, handball court, weight room, dance studio, student fitness center, soccer fields, softball field, track, multi-purpose recreational field, and outdoor track. **Graduates:** From July 1, 2016 to June 30, 2017, 807 bachelor's degrees were awarded. The most popular majors were mechanical engineering (9%), finance (9%), and psychology (5%). In an average class, 50% graduate in 4 years or less, 66% graduate in 5 years or less, and 69% graduate in 6 years or less. Of the 2016 graduating class, 29% were enrolled in graduate school within 6 months of graduation, and 61% were employed.

SERVICES: Counseling and information services are available, as is tutoring in most subjects. There is a reader service for the blind. Special labs are available to students in need of assistance in math and writing. **Library/Resources:** The library contains 1.5 million volumes, 255,422 microform items, and 159,781 audio/video tapes/CDs/DVDs, and subscribes to 64,177 periodicals including electronic. Computerized library services include interlibrary loans, database searching, Internet access, and Wi-Fi capability. Special learning facilities include an art gallery, natural history museum, radio station, and TV station. **Physically Challenged Students:** 97% of the campus is accessible. Facilities include wheelchair ramps, elevators, special parking, specially equipped restrooms, special class scheduling, lowered drinking fountains, lowered telephones, and special housing. **Special:** Internships are available in the Tulsa area during the school year and in cities throughout the world during the summer. Students are encouraged to participate in study abroad, with more than 60 study-abroad programs in countries across the entire globe available. The university offers B.A.-B.S. degrees, combined bachelors/master's degree programs in a variety majors, dual and student-designed majors, accelerated degree programs, non-degree study, work-study programs, and pass/fail options. There are 34 national honor societies, Phi Beta Kappa, and a freshman honors program. **Visiting:** There are regularly scheduled orientations for prospective students, one hour walking tour of campus, an admission presentation and interview, appointments with relevant faculty members, classroom visits, and lunch with current students. To schedule a visit, contact the Office of Admission. **Campus Safety and Security:** Measures include 24-hour foot and vehicle patrol, emergency notification system, self-defense education, and security escort services. There are shuttle buses, emergency telephones, lighted pathways/sidewalks, and controlled access to dorms/residences.

REQUIREMENTS: The SAT or ACT is required. Graduation from an accredited secondary school or satisfactory scores on the GED are also required for admission. The school recommends a minimum of 18 academic credits, including 4 years each of English, math, 3 years of science and social studies (including history), 2 years of a single foreign language and 1 year of fine arts and humanities. Computer competency is also expected. An essay and an interview are highly recommended. An audition or a portfolio is required for students applying for music, theater, or art scholarships. AP credits are accepted. Important factors in the admissions decision are advanced placement or honors courses, leadership record, and extracurricular activities record. To graduate, students must complete 124 to 134 credit hours, including 24 to 51 in the major, with a minimum GPA determined by the major. Freshmen in liberal arts and business administration must complete a First Seminar. All students must complete the core curriculum, which includes 2 writing courses and at least 1 course in math. All students must also complete the general curriculum, which requires 25 credit hours in 3 categories (aesthetic inquiry and creative expression; historical and social interpretation; and scientific investigation). A foreign language requirement of 2 years for liberal arts and sciences students and 1 year for business majors must be completed. **Procedure:** Freshmen are admitted fall and spring. Entrance exams should be taken during spring of the junior year or fall of the senior year. There are early admissions, deferred admissions, and rolling admissions plans. Application deadlines are open. The fall 2017 application fee was $50. Notification is sent on a rolling basis. Applications are accepted on-line. **Transfer Students:** 135 transfer students enrolled in 2016-2017. Transfer students must submit official transcripts from all colleges attended and should have a minimum GPA of 2.75 for all college and high school work. Applicants with fewer than 30 credit hours must submit ACT or SAT scores. Those with fewer than 60 credit hours must submit an official high school transcript. Applicants 25 years of age or older are exempt from submitting ACT or SAT scores unless requested to do so by the Admission Office. 45 of 124 credits required for the bachelor's degree must be completed at University of Tulsa. **International Students:** There are 656 international students enrolled. They must take the TOEFL with a minimum score of 525 on the paper-based TOEFL (PBT) or 70 on the Internet-based version (iBT). Students must also take the IELTS with a minimum score of 6.0.

ADMISSIONS: 39% of the 2017-2018 applicants were accepted. The SAT scores for the 2017-2018 freshman class were: Critical Reading-- 7% below 500, 19% between 500 and 599, 42% between 600 and 699, and 32% between 700 and 800. Math-- 9% below 500, 25% between 500 and 599, 32% between 600 and 699, and 34% between 700 and 800. Writing-- 10% below 500, 29% between 500 and 599, 33% between 600 and 699, and 28% between 700 and 800. 79% of the current freshmen were in the top fifth of their class; 94% were in the top two fifths. 31 freshmen graduated first in their class. **Admissions Contact:** Casey Reed, Dean of Admission. Email: *admission@utulsa.edu* Web: *www.utulsa.edu*

FINANCIAL AID: In 2017-2018, 95% of all full-time freshmen received some form of financial aid. 38% of all full-time freshmen received need-based aid. The average freshman award was $28,991. Need-based scholarships or need-based grants averaged $6,780 ($14,400 maximum); need-based self-help aid (loans and jobs) averaged $4,920 ($7,800 maximum); non-need-based athletic scholarships averaged $37,778 ($58,566 maximum); and other non-need-based awards and non-need-based scholarships averaged $24,225 ($52,625 maximum). 28% of undergraduate students work part-time. The average financial indebtedness of the 2017 graduate was $34,869. The FAFSA code is 003185. The priority date for freshman financial aid applications for fall entry is January 15.

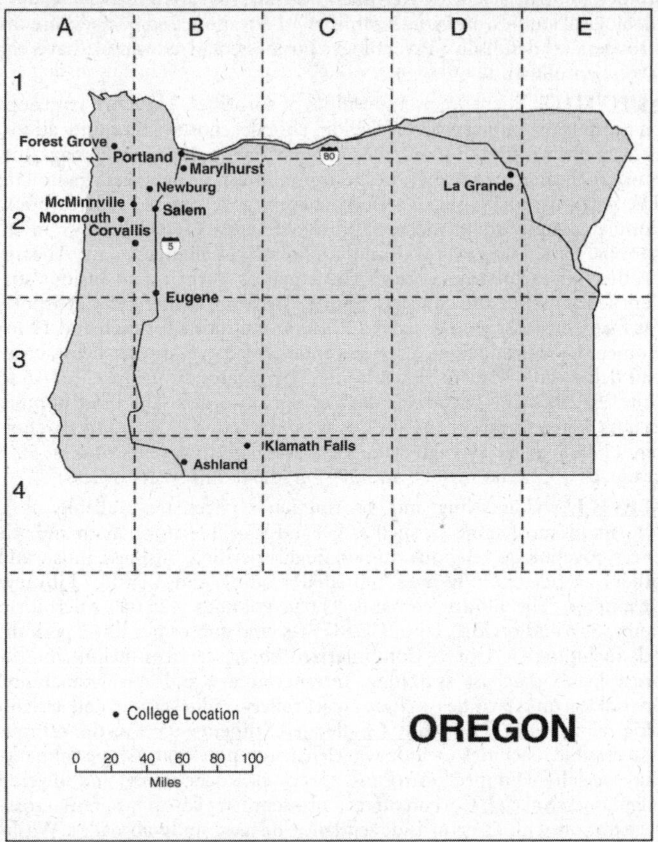

ART INSTITUTE OF PORTLAND *(The complete profile is made available exclusively on our website, www.barronspac.com)*

CONCORDIA UNIVERSITY B-1

www.cu-portland.edu

Portland, OR 97211 **(503) 280-8501** **(800) 321-9371**
Fax: (503) 280-8531 **Email: admission@cu-portland.edu**

Full-time: 369 men, 706 women	**Faculty:** 40
Part-time: 44 men, 138 women	**Ph.D.s:** 57%
Graduate: 1271 men, 4907 women	**Student/Faculty:** 20 to 1
Year: semesters, summer session	**Tuition:** $28,510
Room & Board: $8010	**Freshman Class:** 804 applied, 532 accepted, 201 enrolled
SAT CR/M: 500/500 **ACT:** 20	**CEEB CODE:** 4079
Application Deadline: open	**COMPETITIVE**

Concordia University, founded in 1905, is a private liberal arts institution affiliated with the Lutheran Church Missouri Synod and is 1 of 10 institutions of the Concordia University System. There are 4 undergraduate schools and 3 graduate schools. In addition to regional accreditation, CU has baccalaureate program accreditation with NWCCU. The 24-acre campus is in an urban area in Portland. Including any residence halls, there are 20 buildings.

STUDENT LIFE: 65% of undergraduates are from Oregon. Others are from 14 states, 18 foreign countries, and Canada. 75% are White; 4% African American; 4% Hispanic; 3% Asian American; 2% American Indian/Alaska Native; 1% Foreign. 59% are Protestant; 30% claim no religious affiliation. **Female To Male Ratio:** 3.4:1. The average age of freshmen is 19; all undergraduates, 25. 25% do not continue beyond their first year; 45% remain to graduate. **Housing:** 500 students can be accommodated in college housing, which includes married student dorms and on-campus apartments. On-campus housing is guaranteed for the freshman year only, and is available on a first-come, first-served basis, and is available on a lottery system for upperclassmen. 59% of students live on campus. Alcohol is not permitted. All students may keep cars.

FACULTY/CLASSROOMS: 67% of faculty are male; 33% are female. All teach undergraduates and 5% do research. No introductory courses are taught by graduate students. The average class size in an introductory lecture is 19; in a laboratory is 19; and in a regular course is 17.

PROGRAMS OF STUDY: CU confers B.A. and B.S. degrees. Associate, master's, and doctoral degrees are also awarded. Bachelor's degrees are awarded in BIOLOGICAL SCIENCE (biology/biological science), BUSINESS (business administration and management), COMMUNICATIONS AND THE ARTS (English), COMPUTER AND PHYSICAL SCIENCE (chemistry), EDUCATION (early childhood education, elementary education, and secondary education), ENGINEERING AND ENVIRONMENTAL DESIGN (environmental science), HEALTH PROFESSIONS (health care administration, nursing, and premedicine), SOCIAL SCIENCE (humanities, psychology, social work, theological studies, and youth ministry). Nursing, biology, and business administration are the strongest academically. Nursing, business, and education have the largest enrollments.

ACTIVITIES: There are no fraternities or sororities. There are 14 groups on campus, including handbell choir, brass ensemble, cheerleading, choir, chorus, communications, drama, environmental, honors, international, literary magazine, newspaper, orchestra, professional, religious, social, social service, and student government. **Sports:** There are 6 intercollegiate sports for men and 7 for women, and 10 intramural sports for men and 10 for women. Facilities include a weight room, a gym, and baseball/soccer stadium. **Graduates:** From July 1, 2016 to June 30, 2017, 219 bachelor's degrees were awarded. The most popular majors were business administration (36%), education (34%), and nursing . In an average class, 30% graduate in 4 years or less, 39% graduate in 5 years or less, and 43% graduate in 6 years or less.

SERVICES: Counseling and information services are available, as is tutoring in most subjects. There is remedial math, reading, and writing. There are also student-supported individual help and media resources. **Library/Resources:** The library contains 70,000 volumes, 56,706 microform items, 2,888 audio/video tapes/CDs/DVDs, and subscribes to 424 periodicals including electronic. Computerized library services include interlibrary loans, database searching, and Internet access. **Physically Challenged Students:** 80% of the campus is accessible. Facilities include wheelchair ramps, elevators, special parking, specially equipped restrooms, special class scheduling, and lowered telephones. **Special:** Cross-registration may be arranged through the Concordia University System and with Oregon Independent. There is a dual enrollement program with Portland Community College. There are also internships, study abroad in more than 20 countries, and an accelerated degree program in business, health care administration, and social work. There is 1 national honor society, a freshman honors program, and 1 departmental honors program. **Visiting:** There are regularly scheduled orientations for prospective students, including class visitations and meetings with program deans and faculty. There are guides for informal visits, visitors may sit in on classes, and stay overnight. To schedule a visit, contact the Office of Admission. **Campus Safety and Security:** Measures include 24-hour foot and vehicle patrol, self-defense education, and security escort services. There are emergency telephones, lighted pathways/sidewalks, controlled access to dorms/residences, and emergency cell phone available 24 hours.

REQUIREMENTS: The SAT or ACT is required, with satisfactory SAT verbal scores recommended. Graduation from an accredited secondary school or satisfactory scores on the GED are required. The school recommends that high school courses include 4 units of English, 3 units each of social studies, math, and science, 2 units of foreign language, and 1 unit of art and music. An interview is recommended. A GPA of 2.5 is required. AP and CLEP credits are accepted. Important factors in the admissions decision are recommendations by school officials, leadership record, and personality/intangible qualities. To graduate, students must complete a total of 124 semester hours, with a minimum GPA of 2.0. General education requirements total 48 semester hours. All students must take freshman composition and courses in math, phys ed, humanities, religion, science, writing, fine arts, and social sciences. In the major, 45 hours of 300-400 level courses must be taken. **Procedure:** Freshmen are admitted in the fall, spring, and summer. Entrance exams should be taken during the junior year or early in the senior year. There is a rolling admissions plan. Early decision applications should be filed by March 1. Notification is sent on a rolling basis. Applications are accepted on-line. **Transfer Students:** 141 transfer students enrolled in 2016-2017. Transfer students must have a minimum GPA of 2.0. 45 of 124 credits required for the bachelor's degree must be completed at CU. **International Students:** There are 15 international students enrolled. They must take the TOEFL. They must also take the SAT or ACT.

ADMISSIONS: 66% of the 2017-2018 applicants were accepted. The ACT scores were 40% below 12, 35% between 12 and 17, 16% between 18 and 23, 9% between 24 and 29, and 2% above 30. 42% of the current freshmen were in the top fifth of their class; 69% were in the top two fifths. **Admissions Contact:** Andrew Wright, Director of Undergraduate Admission. Email: *admission@cu-portland.edu* Web: *www.cu-portland.edu*

FINANCIAL AID: The average freshman award was $13,000. The FAFSA code is 003191. Check with the school for current application deadlines.

CORBAN UNIVERSITY — B-2
www.corban.edu

Salem, OR 97317 — (503) 375-8180, (800) 845-3005

Fax: (503) 375-7042 — **Email:** admissions@corban.edu

Full-time: 363 men, 564 women	**Faculty:** n/av
Part-time: 11 men, 25 women	**Ph.D.s:** n/av
Graduate: 69 men, 97 women	**Student/Faculty:** n/av
Year: semesters, summer session	**Tuition:** $31,640
Room & Board: $10,060	**Freshman Class:** 1943 applied, 641 accepted, 197 enrolled
SAT or ACT: required	**CEEB CODE:** 4956
Application Deadline: August 1	**COMPETITIVE**

Corban University, is a Christian college offering degrees in biblical-theological studies, business administration, education, humanities, math, phys ed, social sciences, psychology, intercultural studies, and youth work. There are 4 undergraduate schools and 3 graduate schools. In addition to regional accreditation, CU has baccalaureate program accreditation with Association of Christian Schools International, Teacher Standards and Practices Commission, and CACREP. The 142-acre campus is in a suburban area in Salem, Oregon. Including any residence halls, there are 28 buildings.

STUDENT LIFE: 54% of undergraduates are from Oregon. Others are from 32 states, 13 foreign countries, and Canada. 60% are from public schools. 75% are White; 8% two or more races; 6% Foreign; 5% race unknown; 2% Asian American; 2% Hispanic; 1% African American; 1% American Indian/Alaska Native. **Female To Male Ratio:** 1.5:1. The average age of freshmen is 18; all undergraduates, 20. 20% do not continue beyond their first year; 59% remain to graduate. **Housing:** 547 students can be accommodated in college housing, which includes on-campus apartments, men's dorms, women's dorms, and apartments for single students. On-campus housing is guaranteed for the freshman year only, and is available on a first-come, first-served basis. 51% of students commute. Alcohol is not permitted. All students may keep cars.

FACULTY/CLASSROOMS: No introductory courses are taught by graduate students.

PROGRAMS OF STUDY: CU confers B.A. and B.S. degrees. Associate, master's, and doctoral degrees are also awarded. Bachelor's degrees are awarded in BIOLOGICAL SCIENCE (forensic psychology), BUSINESS (accounting, business administration and management, business administration marketing, and sports management), COMMUNICATIONS AND THE ARTS (communications, creative writing, English, journalism, linguistics, media arts, music, and music performance), COMPUTER AND PHYSICAL SCIENCE (mathematics), EDUCATION (Christian education, early childhood education, education, elementary education, mathematics education, music education, physical education, science education, social studies education, and sports and wellness studies), HEALTH PROFESSIONS (exercise science, health science, kinesiology, predentistry, premedicine, preoptometry, prepharmacy, prephysical therapy, and preveterinary science), SOCIAL SCIENCE (behavioral science, biblical studies, counseling/psychology, criminal justice, criminology, crosscultural studies, history, history and political science, humanities, interdisciplinary studies, ministries, pastoral studies, political science/government, prelaw, psychology, social science, theological studies, and youth ministry). Education, and business are the strongest academically. Psychology, business, and education have the largest enrollments.

ACTIVITIES: There are no fraternities or sororities. There are 16 groups on campus, including art, band, choir, chorale, chorus, communications, debate, drama, film, honors, international, jazz band, literary magazine, musical theater, newspaper, orchestra, political, professional, radio and TV, religious, social, social service, student government, and yearbook. Popular campus events include Sports Weekends, Chapel Services, International Fair, Turkey Trot, Pumpkin Smash, Lumberjack days, Theatre Productions, Corban Weekend, Christmas at Corban, and various student-led activities and concerts. **Sports:** There are 6 intercollegiate sports for men and 7 for women, and 12 intramural sports for men and 12 for women. Facilities include a sports center with a gym, soccer fields, baseball fields and a student fitness center. **Graduates:** From July 1, 2016 to June 30, 2017, 212 bachelor's degrees were awarded. The most popular majors were education (24%), business/marketing (19%), and psychology (19%). In an average class, 44% graduate in 4 years or less, 50% graduate in 5 years or less, and 59% graduate in 6 years or less.

SERVICES: Counseling and information services are available, as is tutoring in most subjects, such as US and World History, math and sciences, psychology, religious studies, English/writing, business, music and others as needed. There is remedial reading and writing. **Library/Resources:** The library contains 84,054 volumes, 125,000 microform items, 547 audio/video tapes/CDs/DVDs, and subscribes to 62 periodicals including electronic. Computerized library services include interlibrary loans, database searching, Internet access, and Wi-Fi capability. Special learning facilities include an art gallery, radio station, and archaeological museum. **Physically Challenged Students:** 95% of the campus is accessible. Facilities include wheelchair ramps, elevators, special parking, specially equipped restrooms, special class scheduling, and lowered telephones. **Special:** Corban offers a pre-seminary co-op program, cross-registration with Oregon Independent Colleges, study abroad, a Washington semester, internships with the approval of a program adviser, accelerated programs in business and psychology and in family studies, and student-designed majors with adviser approval. Also, Corban offers at Fast-Track B.S./M.Div. degree, and AMBEX Study Abroad in Germany. There is a freshman honors program. **Visiting:** There are regularly scheduled orientations for prospective students, including a campus tour, classroom visit, and activities with the student body. There are guides for informal visits, visitors may sit in on classes, and stay overnight. To schedule a visit, contact the Admissions Office. **Campus Safety and Security:** Measures include 24-hour foot and vehicle patrol, emergency notification system, self-defense education, and security escort services. There are emergency telephones, lighted pathways/sidewalks, controlled access to dorms/residences, 24 hour emergency response not patrol, threat assessment, safety planning, emergency planning, self defense education mentoring, events and mass gatherings, travel security planning, crisis management, executive protection, bomb threats, intellectual property protection, personal protection best practices, loss prevention, security risk assessment, access management, crime prevention through environmental design, Clery compliance and reporting, media relations, money transport, armed and unarmed security, environmental security, business continuity, counter-terrorism, intelligence gathering, security management, and internal investigations.

REQUIREMENTS: The SAT or ACT is required. Recommended requirements for admission consist of 14 units of 4 in English, 3 each in math and social studies, and 2 each in social studies and science. Corban University requires a Statement of Faith Essay. A GPA of 2.7 is required. AP and CLEP credits are accepted. Important factors in the admissions decision are parents or siblings attended your school, extracurricular activities record, recommendations by alumni, personality/intangible qualities, and advanced placement or honors courses. To graduate, students must complete 129 credits with 36 to 74 in the major. The minimum required GPA is 2.0 for most programs; the education major requires a 3.0 GPA. The general education core consists of 69credits. Courses must be taken in Bible, humanities, social sciences, math, science, and phys ed. **Procedure:** Freshmen are admitted in the fall and spring. There is a rolling admissions plan. Applications should be filed by August 1 for fall entry; December 1 for spring entry. The fall 2017 application fee was $40. Notification is sent on a rolling basis. Applications are accepted on-line. **Transfer Students:** 65 transfer students enrolled in 2016-2017. Transfer applicants are required to have a minimum 2.0 cumulative college GPA and submit the college transcript and 3 references. Transfer students may enroll in the fall, and spring. 30 of 129 credits required for the bachelor's degree must be completed at Corban. **International Students:** There are 56 international students enrolled. They must take the TOEFL with a minimum score of 500 on the paper-based TOEFL (PBT) or 61 on the Internet-based version (iBT). They must also take the SAT or ACT, scoring 1000 SAT, and the CLT.

ADMISSIONS: 33% of the 2017-2018 applicants were accepted. 60% of the current freshmen were in the top fifth of their class; 91% were in the top two fifths. 15 freshmen graduated first in their class. **Admissions Contact:** Chris Vetter, Associate Provost of Enrollment Services. Email: *admissions@corban.edu* Web: *www.corban.edu*

FINANCIAL AID: In 2017-2018, 100% of all full-time freshmen received some form of financial aid. 86% of all full-time freshmen received need-based aid. The average freshman award was $22,280. Need-based scholarships or need-based grants averaged $19,400; need-based self-help aid (loans and jobs) averaged $3,728; non-need-based athletic scholarships averaged $14,650; other non-need-based awards and non-need-based scholarships averaged $7,800; and $11,200 from other forms of aid. The FAFSA code is 001339. The priority date for freshman financial aid applications for fall entry is February 1.

EASTERN OREGON UNIVERSITY D-2

www.eou.edu

La Grande, OR 97850	**(541) 962-3672** **(800) 452-8639**
Fax: (541) 962-3418	**Email: admissions@eou.edu**
Full-time: 671 men, 993 women	**Faculty:** 96
Part-time: 336 men, 526 women	**Ph.D.s:** 88%
Graduate: 85 men, 194 women	**Student/Faculty:** 18 to 1
Year: n/app	**Tuition:** $8362 ($19,682)
Room & Board: $9250	**Freshman Class:** 994 applied, 967 accepted, 325 enrolled
SAT: required **ACT:** 21	**CEEB CODE:** 4300
Application Deadline: September 1	**COMPETITIVE**

Eastern Oregon University, founded in 1929, prepares students for the world beyond college with high-quality liberal arts and professional programs. As one of the best values in higher education today, EOU offers small classes, flexible programs, and low tuition, to help graduates get ahead with an education personalized to meet their goals. Classes are available when and where students need them at the university's main campus in La Grande, online from almost anywhere in the world and onsite at centers across the state of Oregon. There are 4 undergraduate schools and 2 graduate schools. In addition to regional accreditation, EOU has baccalaureate program accreditation with CAEP, IACBE, and TSPC. The 121-acre campus is in a rural area 260 miles east of Portland. Including any residence halls, there are 15 buildings.

STUDENT LIFE: 69% of undergraduates are from Oregon. Others are from 15 states, and 6 foreign countries. 73% are White; 10% Hispanic; 5% two or more races; 3% race unknown; 2% African American; 2% Asian American; 2% American Indian/Alaska Native; 1% Foreign. **Female To Male Ratio:** 1.6:1. The average age of freshmen is 19; all undergraduates, 27. **Housing:** 436 students can be accommodated in college housing, which includes married student dorms, on-campus apartments, and off-campus apartments. a wellness floor, and academic focus floor. On-campus housing is available on a first-come and first-served basis. All students may keep cars.

FACULTY/CLASSROOMS: 57% of faculty are male; 43% are female. All teach undergraduates and do research. No introductory courses are taught by graduate students. The average class size in an introductory lecture is 60; in a laboratory is 20; and in a regular course is 35.

PROGRAMS OF STUDY: EOU confers B.A. and B.S degrees. Master's degrees are also awarded. Bachelor's degrees are awarded in AGRICULTURE (agricultural business management, agricultural economics, forestry and related sciences, range/farm management, and soil science), BIOLOGICAL SCIENCE (biology/biological science), BUSINESS (accounting and business administration and management), COMMUNICATIONS AND THE ARTS (art, dramatic arts, English, and music), COMPUTER AND PHYSICAL SCIENCE (chemistry, computer science, mathematics, and physics), EDUCATION (education and physical education), HEALTH PROFESSIONS (health and nursing), SOCIAL SCIENCE (anthropology, history, liberal arts/general studies, psychology, and sociology). Sciences is the strongest academically. Business, and education have the largest enrollments.

ACTIVITIES: There are no fraternities or sororities. Groups on campus include art, band, cheerleading, choir, chorale, chorus, communications, computers, dance, drama, environmental, ethnic, international, jazz band, LGBT, literary magazine, musical theater, newspaper, orchestra, photography, political, professional, radio and TV, religious, social, student government, and symphony. Popular campus events include Casino Night, Spring Fling, and Spring Symposium. **Sports:** Facilities include football field, soccer fields, a weight room, gyms, aerobics facilities, a track, and outdoor tennis courts, and sand volleyball court. **Graduates:** From July 1, 2016 to June 30, 2017, 703 bachelor's degrees were awarded. The most popular majors were business/marketing (31%), liberal arts and general studies (24%), and social science (7%). In an average class, 20% graduate in 4 years or less, 45% graduate in 5 years or less, and 37% graduate in 6 years or less.

SERVICES: Counseling and information services are available, as is tutoring in most subjects. There is a reader service for the blind, and remedial math, reading, and writing. **Library/Resources:** The library contains 340,132 volumes, and 396,568 audio/video tapes/CDs/DVDs. Computerized library services include interlibrary loans, database searching, Internet access, and Wi-Fi capability. Special learning facilities include an art gallery, natural history museum, radio station, EOU features a learning center which provides one-on-one tutoring in math and writing for all students. Computer lab facilities are available to students in multiple locations across campus. **Physically Challenged Students:** All of the campus is accessible. Facilities include wheelchair ramps, elevators, special parking, and specially equipped restrooms. **Special:** There are cooperative and 3-2 engineering degree programs with Oregon State University. The university offers internships, work-study with federal agencies, accelerated degree program, student-designed and dual majors, study abroad in 8 countries, a general studies degree, B.A.-B.S. degrees, a multidisciplinary degree, numerous preprofessional programs, credit by exam, and for life/military/work experience, external degrees, and pass/fail options. The university also serves students with course work via telecommunications and video, and with a weekend University. There are 6 national honor societies, Phi Beta Kappa, and 6 departmental honors programs. **Visiting:** There are regularly scheduled orientations for prospective students, including a campus tour, academic advising, and information sessions on financial aid and residence life. There are guides for informal visits, visitors may sit in on classes, and stay overnight. To schedule a visit, contact the Admissions Office/New Student Programs. **Campus Safety and Security:** Measures include 24-hour foot and vehicle patrol, emergency notification system, and security escort services. There are shuttle buses, emergency telephones, lighted pathways/sidewalks, and controlled access to dorms/residences.

REQUIREMENTS: The SAT or ACT is required. A GED is accepted. Applicants must complete 15-16 academic credit units, 4 units of English, 3 each of math, social studies, science with 1 unit must be lab, and 2 of foreign language. AP and CLEP credits are accepted. Important factors in the admissions decision are extracurricular activities record and geographical diversity. Students must complete 180 credit hours, including 60 hours of general education courses that include 15 hours each of social science, natural science, humanities, art-language, and logic, with a GPA of at least 2.0. They must demonstrate computer competency and pass a writing proficiency exam. A senior capstone experience is required. **Procedure:** Freshmen are admitted to all sessions. Entrance exams should be taken in the senior year. There are deferred admissions and rolling admissions plans. Applications should be filed by September 1 for fall entry. The fall 2017 application fee was $50. Notifications are sent February 1. **Transfer Students:** 378 transfer students enrolled in 2016-2017. Applicants must have 30 credits of transferable academic work with a GPA of 2.25. Transfer Student may enroll in the fall, winter, spring, and summer. 45 of 180 credits required for the bachelor's degree must be completed at Eastern. **International Students:** There are 92 international students enrolled. They must take the TOEFL or MELAB, and the University of Michigan Language Test for placement.

ADMISSIONS: 97% of the 2017-2018 applicants were accepted. The SAT scores for the 2017-2018 freshman class were: Critical Reading-- 61% below 500, 31% between 500 and 599, and 7% between 600 and 699. Math-- 65% below 500, 27% between 500 and 599, and 7% between

600 and 699. Writing-- 77% below 500, 19% between 500 and 599, and 4% between 600 and 699. The ACT scores were 25% between 12 and 17, 58% between 18 and 23, and 17% between 24 and 29. **Admissions Contact:** Gina Galaviz Yap, Director of Admissions. Email: *admissions@eou.edu* Web: *www.eou.edu*

FINANCIAL AID: The average freshman award was $9,287. Need-based scholarships or need-based grants averaged $6,609; need-based self-help aid (loans and jobs) averaged $3,198; non-need-based athletic scholarships averaged $3,213; other non-need-based awards and non-need-based scholarships averaged $3,033; and $1,759 from other forms of aid. EOU is a member of CSS. The FAFSA code is 003193. The priority date for freshman financial aid applications for fall entry is January 1.

GEORGE FOX UNIVERSITY B-2

www.georgefox.edu

Newberg, OR 97132	**(503) 554-2240** **(800) 765-4369**
Fax: (503) 554-3110	**Email: admissions@georgefox.edu**
Full-time: 1003 men, 1247 women	**Faculty:** 110; IIA, -$
Part-time: 87 men, 159 women	**Ph.D.s:** 75%
Graduate: 514 men, 615 women	**Student/Faculty:** 14 to 1
Year: semesters, summer session	**Tuition:** $32,786
Room & Board: $10,152	**Freshman Class:** 2777 applied, 2122 accepted, 608 enrolled
SAT CR/M/W: 540/545/528 **ACT:** 23	**CEEB CODE:** 4325
Application Deadline: February 1	**COMPETITIVE**

George Fox University, founded in 1891, is a Christian university of the humanities, sciences and professional studies. It offers bachelor's degrees in more than 40 majors, adult degree programs, 6 seminary degrees, and 13 master's and doctoral degrees at its main campus, and at teaching centers in Portland and Salem, Oregon. There are 6 undergraduate schools and 4 graduate schools. In addition to regional accreditation, GFU has baccalaureate program accreditation with ABET, ACBSP, CSWE, NASM, CAEP, CAATE, and CCNE. The 85-acre campus is in a small town in Newberg, Oregon and 23 miles southwest of Portland. Including any residence halls, there are 80 buildings.

STUDENT LIFE: 65% of undergraduates are from Oregon. Others are from 27 states, 17 foreign countries, and Canada. 72% are from public schools. 71% are White; 8% race unknown; 5% Hispanic; 5% Foreign; 4% Asian American; 4% two or more races; 2% African American; 1% American Indian/Alaska Native. 82% are Protestant; 14% claim no religious affiliation. **Female To Male Ratio:** 1.3:1. The average age of freshmen is 18; all undergraduates, 21. 18% do not continue beyond their first year; 62% remain to graduate. **Housing:** 1211 students can be accommodated in college housing, which includes on-campus apartments. In addition, there are special-interest houses, smoke-free and drug-free housing, and theme housing. On-campus housing is available on a first-come, first-served basis, and is available on a lottery system for upperclassmen. 54% of students live on campus. Alcohol is not permitted. All students may keep cars.

FACULTY/CLASSROOMS: 55% of faculty are male; 45% are female. 64% teach undergraduates. No introductory courses are taught by graduate students. The average class size in an introductory lecture is 36; in a laboratory is 17; and in a regular course is 20.

PROGRAMS OF STUDY: GFU confers B.A., B.S., B.S.A.T., and B.S.W. degrees. Master's and doctoral degrees are also awarded. Bachelor's degrees are awarded in BIOLOGICAL SCIENCE (biology/biological science), BUSINESS (accounting, business administration and management, business communications, management information systems, management science, and organizational leadership and management), COMMUNICATIONS AND THE ARTS (art, communications, creative writing, dramatic arts, film arts, literature, multimedia, music, and Spanish), COMPUTER AND PHYSICAL SCIENCE (chemistry, computer science, information sciences and systems, and mathematics), EDUCATION (athletic training, elementary education, and music education), ENGINEERING AND ENVIRONMENTAL DESIGN (engineering and applied science), HEALTH PROFESSIONS (allied health, exercise science, health, health care administration, nursing, predentistry, premedicine, and preveterinary science), SOCIAL SCIENCE (behavioral science, biblical studies, cognitive science, economics, family/consumer studies, history, international studies, ministries, philosophy, political science/government, prelaw, psychology, religion, social science, social work, and sociology). Nursing, and engineering are the strongest academically. Business, engineering, and nursing have the largest enrollments.

ACTIVITIES: There are no fraternities or sororities. There are 20 groups on campus, including art, band, choir, chorale, chorus, computers, debate, drama, ethnic, film, forensics, honors, international, jazz band, literary magazine, musical theater, newspaper, orchestra, outdoor club, pep band, political, professional, radio and TV, religious, social, social service, student government, symphony, and yearbook. Popular campus events include Serve Day, Juniors Abroad, and Cultural Celebration Week. **Sports:** There are 7 intercollegiate sports for men and 8 for women, and 7 intramural sports for men and 7 for women. Facilities include an all-weather track, a fitness center, tennis and handball/racquetball courts, a climbing wall, a gym, and fields for baseball, softball, and soccer. **Graduates:** From July 1, 2016 to June 30, 2017, 589 bachelor's degrees were awarded. The most popular majors were interdisciplinary studies (9%), visual and performing arts/healh professions and related programs/engineering (7%), psychology/area, ethnic, and and gender studies (6%). In an average class, 2% graduate in 3 years or less, 50% graduate in 4 years or less, 62% graduate in 5 years or less, and 64% graduate in 6 years or less.

SERVICES: Counseling and information services are available, as is tutoring in most subjects. There is a reader service for the blind, and remedial math, reading, and writing. **Library/Resources:** The library contains 174,988 volumes, 210,708 microform items, 5,372 audio/video tapes/CDs/DVDs, and subscribes to 60,000 periodicals including electronic. Computerized library services include interlibrary loans, database searching, Internet access, and Wi-Fi capability. Special learning facilities include an art gallery, radio station, a television production studio, a pottery kiln, physical therapy, nursing, and engineering labs. **Physically Challenged Students:** All of the campus is accessible. Facilities include wheelchair ramps, elevators, special parking, specially equipped restrooms, special class scheduling, lowered drinking fountains, lowered telephones, and special housing. **Special:** Half of George Fox students participate in study abroad programs, which include a three-week faculty-led, subsidized trip in the spring of a student's junior year. The university offers a dual-degree 3/2 program through its applied science major, enabling students to pursue engineering in a discipline such as chemical, environmental or aerospace engineering. Students can complete a semester at the Contemporary Music Center in Martha's Vineyard or the Los Angeles Film Studies Center. George Fox offers internships with area companies, study abroad, and a Washington semester through the Council of Christian Colleges and Universities. Work-study programs, accelerated degrees, dual and student-designed interdisciplinary majors, and pass/fail options in upper-division courses outside of the major are also offered. There are 3 national honor societies, a freshman honors program, and 1 departmental honors program. **Visiting:** There are regularly scheduled orientations for prospective students, including observation of classes and talking with professors. There are guides for informal visits, visitors may sit in on classes, and stay overnight. To schedule a visit, contact the Office of Admissions. **Campus Safety and Security:** Measures include 24-hour foot and vehicle patrol, emergency notification system, self-defense education, and security escort services. There are emergency telephones, lighted pathways/sidewalks, controlled access to dorms/residences, parking lot cameras, and video surveillance of buildings.

REQUIREMENTS: The SAT or ACT is required. Applicants need 16 academic credits or 14 Carnegie units, 4 units of English, 3 units of social studies, 2 units each of a foreign language, math, history, and science with lab, and 1 unit of health and physical education. An essay and 2 personal recommendations are required; a portfolio, audition, and interview are recommended in certain majors. AP and CLEP credits are accepted. Important factors in the admissions decision are advanced placement or honors courses, extracurricular activities record, and leadership record. To graduate, students must have a minimum 2.0 GPA and complete 126 semester hours, including 15 hours of sciences, 11 hours of humanities, 10 hours of Bible and religion, 6 hours each of communication and global and cultural understanding, 3 hours of health and human performance, and a 3 hour senior capstone. Majors require a minimum of 36 hours. A thesis is required in biology, chemistry, and social and behavioral sciences. **Procedure:** Freshmen are admitted fall and spring. Entrance exams should be taken in fall or winter. There are early admissions, deferred admissions, and rolling admissions plans. Applications should be filed by February 1 for fall entry; December 1 for spring entry. The fall 2017 application fee was $40. Notification is sent on a rolling basis. Applications are accepted on-line. **Transfer Students:** 107 transfer students enrolled in 2016-2017. Transfers must have a minimum 2.6 GPA and 16 semester hours from their previous college. An essay and two personal recommendations are required. 30 of 126 credits required for the bachelor's degree must be completed at GFU. **International Students:** There are 150 international students enrolled. They must take the TOEFL with a minimum score of 550 on the paper-based TOEFL (PBT) or 80 on the Internet-based version (iBT) and the college's own test.

ADMISSIONS: 76% of the 2017-2018 applicants were accepted. The SAT scores for the 2017-2018 freshman class were: Critical Reading-- 30% below 500, 42% between 500 and 599, 22% between 600 and 699, and 6% between 700 and 800. Math-- 29% below 500, 42% between 500 and 599, 22% between 600 and 699, and 6% between 700 and 800. Writing-- 38% below 500, 41% between 500 and 599, 19% between 600 and 699, and 3% between 700 and 800. 36 freshmen graduated first in their class. **Admissions Contact:** Lindsay Knox, Director of Undergraduate Admissions. Email: *admissions@georgefox.edu* Web: *www.georgefox.edu*

FINANCIAL AID: In 2017-2018, 100% of all full-time freshmen received some form of financial aid. 84% of all full-time freshmen received need-based aid. The average freshman award was $27,919. Need-based scholarships or need-based grants averaged $7,896; need-based self-help aid (loans and jobs) averaged $4,685; other non-need-based awards and non-need-based scholarships averaged $11,561; and $2,872 from other forms of aid. The average financial indebtedness of the 2017 graduate was $25,143. GFU is a member of CSS. The state aid form is required. The FAFSA code is 003194. The priority date for freshman financial aid applications for fall entry is February 1.

LEWIS & CLARK COLLEGE — B-1
www.lclark.edu

Portland, OR 97219	(503) 768-7040 (800) 444-4111
Fax: (503) 768-7055	Email: admissions@lclark.edu
Full-time: 863 men, 1205 women	Faculty: 212
Part-time: 20 men, 18 women	Ph.D.s: 92%
Graduate: 386 men, 847 women	Student/Faculty: 12 to 1
Year: semesters, summer session	Tuition: $48,988
Room & Board: $11,996	Freshman Class: 6309 applied, 4503 accepted, 526 enrolled
SAT or ACT: required	CEEB CODE: 4384
Application Deadline: January 15	MOST COMPETITIVE

Lewis & Clark College, founded in 1867, is a private, independent liberal arts and sciences institution with a global reach. There is 1 undergraduate school and 2 graduate schools. In addition to regional accreditation, LCC has baccalaureate program accreditation with CAEP, ABA, CACREP, and COAMFTE. The 137-acre campus is in a suburban area 6 miles south of downtown Portland. Including any residence halls, there are 58 buildings.

STUDENT LIFE: 89% of undergraduates are from out of state, mostly the West. Students are from 46 states, 81 foreign countries, and Canada. 77% are from public schools. 65% are White; 10% Hispanic; 6% Foreign; 5% Asian American; 5% race unknown; 4% two or more races; 3% African American; 1% American Indian/Alaska Native. **Female To Male Ratio:** 1.6:1. The average age of freshmen is 18; all undergraduates, 20. 17% do not continue beyond their first year; 77% remain to graduate. **Housing:** 1394 students can be accommodated in college housing, which includes dorms and on-campus apartments. In addition, there are special-interest houses, and theme communities. On-campus housing is available on a lottery system for upperclassmen. 66% of students live on campus. Upperclassmen may keep cars.

FACULTY/CLASSROOMS: 46% of faculty are male; 54% are female. All teach undergraduates and do research. No introductory courses are taught by graduate students. The average class size in a regular course is 20.

PROGRAMS OF STUDY: LCC confers B.A. degrees. Master's and doctoral degrees are also awarded. Bachelor's degrees are awarded in AGRICULTURE (environmental studies), BIOLOGICAL SCIENCE (biochemistry and biology/biological science), COMMUNICATIONS AND THE ARTS (art history and appreciation, classics, communications, dramatic arts, English, fine arts, languages, music, and studio art), COMPUTER AND PHYSICAL SCIENCE (chemistry, computer mathematics, computer science, mathematics, and physics), SOCIAL SCIENCE (anthropology, East Asian studies, economics, French studies, German area studies, Hispanic American studies, history, interdisciplinary studies, international relations, philosophy, political science/government, psychology, religion, and sociology). Psychology, biology, and sociology/anthropology have the largest enrollments.

ACTIVITIES: There are no fraternities or sororities. There are 111 groups on campus, including art, band, choir, chorale, chorus, computers, dance, debate, drama, environmental, ethnic, forensics, honors, international, jazz band, LGBT, literary magazine, newspaper, orchestra, outdoors club, photography, political, professional, radio and TV, religious, social, social service, student government, and symphony. Popular campus events include Gender Studies Symposium, International Affairs Symposium, and Environmental Studies Symposium, Day of Service, and Alternative Breaks. **Sports:** There are 9 intercollegiate sports for men and 10 for women, and 19 intramural sports for men and 19 for women. Facilities include a gym, courts for basketball, volleyball, indoor practice facilities for several intercollegiate teams, a weight room, and a swimming pavilion, with diving boards. **Graduates:** From July 1, 2016 to June 30, 2017, 464 bachelor's degrees were awarded. The most popular majors were social sciences (23%), psychology (13%), and biological/life science (13%). In an average class, 74% graduate in 4 years or less, 78% graduate in 5 years or less, and 79% graduate in 6 years or less.

SERVICES: Counseling and information services are available, as is tutoring in most subjects. There is a reader service for the blind. There are also mentors, note takers, books on tape, math and a writing skills center. **Library/Resources:** The library contains 586,144 volumes, 1.5 million microform items, and 23,851 audio/video tapes/CDs/DVDs, and subscribes to 42,560 periodicals including electronic. Computerized library services include interlibrary loans, database searching, Internet access, and Wi-Fi capability. Special learning facilities include an art gallery, radio station, a telescope, research astronomical observatory, a language lab, greenhouse, and adaptive technology lab. **Physically Challenged Students:** 80% of the campus is accessible. Facilities include wheelchair ramps, elevators, special parking, specially equipped restrooms, lowered drinking fountains, and lowered telephones. **Special:** LCC offers internships; study-abroad programs in 60 countries; semesters in Washington and New York City; dual and student-designed majors; and cross-registration with schools that are a part of the Oregon Independent College Association; A 3-2 engineering program is available with Columbia University, Washington University, and the University of Southern California. There are 5 national honor societies and a chapter of Phi Beta Kappa. **Visiting:** There are regularly scheduled orientations for prospective students, information sessions and daily campus tours; class visits, interviews, special-interest appointments, and 4 open house events. Visitors may sit in on classes and stay overnight. To schedule a visit, contact the Office of Admissions. **Campus Safety and Security:** Measures include 24-hour foot and vehicle patrol, an emergency notification system, self-defense education, and security escort services. There are shuttle buses, emergency telephones, lighted pathways/sidewalks, controlled access to dorms/residences, and card key locks in all residence halls.

REQUIREMENTS: When admitting new students, our admissions staff look for individuals from diverse backgrounds, with unusual talents and interests, and who will not only meet the rigorous academic challenges of a Lewis & Clark education, but will also take full advantage of the opportunities for individual achievement and growth offered. Academic Preparation: your high school course load (grades 9-12) should include a minimum of: 4 years each of English and math, 3-4 years of history and social sciences, 2-3 years of a foreign language, 3 years of lab sciences, 1 year of creative arts. Advanced Placement, International Baccalaureate, or honors courses are viewed as further evidence of serious preparation for college-level studies. Successful candidates have taken some of these advanced courses if they are offered at their schools. We look not only at your performance in a challenging curriculum, but at the following criteria as well: SAT or ACT scores (unless applying through the Portfolio Path), counselor report (first-year students only), teacher recommendation, personal essay, leadership, community service and work experience, and extracurricular involvements, expressed interest in the college or personal interview (interviews are optional, not required). The committee weighs all of these factors to make a prediction about an applicant's potential for academic success at Lewis & Clark. We want to make sure that any student enrolls at the college will have the tools they need to flourish in and enjoy our academic program. The committee also looks for students who will contribute to our community as musicians, leaders, athletes, or community service participants, while they are succeeding academically. AP credits are accepted. To graduate, students must complete a total of 128 semester hours with a GPA of at least 2.0. A third of the student's credits generally falls in the major program, a third in electives, and a third in general requirements, which include a required first-year course, 12 hours in scientific and quantitative reasoning, 8 hours in international studies, 3 semesters of a foreign language, 2 semesters of phys ed, and 1 course in creative arts. Certain majors require a thesis or a senior project/recital. **Procedure:** Freshmen are admitted in the fall and spring. Entrance exams should be taken during spring of the junior year or fall of the senior year. There are early decision and deferred admissions plans. Early decision applications should be filed by November 1; regular applications, by January 15 for fall entry. Notification of early decision is sent December 15; regular decision, April 1. 51 early decision candidates were accepted for the 2017-2018 class. 181 applicants were on the 2017 waiting list; 24 were admitted. Applications are accepted on-line. **Transfer Students:** 51 transfer students enrolled in 2016-2017. Applicants must submit high school and college transcripts, and 2 essays. SAT or ACT scores are required for transfers with fewer than 2 years of transferable credit (60 semester units) 60 of 128 credits required for the bachelor's degree must be completed at Lewis & Clark. **International Students:** There are 160 international students enrolled. They must take the TOEFL with a minimum score of 575 on the paper-based TOEFL (PBT) or 91 on the Internet-based version (iBT) or take the MELAB. Student must also take either one of these tests the ELPT, IB English, SAT or ACT, ECPE, FCE, CAE, CPE or IELTS.

ADMISSIONS: 71% of the 2017-2018 applicants were accepted. **Admissions Contact:** Erica Johnson, Director of Admissions. Email: *admissions@lclark.edu* Web: *www.lclark.edu*

FINANCIAL AID: In 2017-2018, 94% of all full-time freshmen received some form of financial aid. 65% of all full-time freshmen received need-based aid. The average freshman award was $39,084. Need-based scholarships or need-based grants averaged $32,156; need-based self-help aid (loans and jobs) averaged $5,283; and other non-need-based awards and non-need-based scholarships averaged $18,713. The average financial indebtedness of the 2017 graduate was $27,591. The CSS/Profile is required. The FAFSA code is 003197. The priority date for freshman financial aid applications for fall entry is February 15.

LINFIELD COLLEGE — B-2

www.linfield.edu

McMinnville, OR 97128 — (503) 883-2213, (800) 640-2287

Fax: (503) 883-2472 — **Email:** admission@linfield.edu

Full-time: 590 men, 891 women	**Faculty:** 123; IIB, av$
Part-time: 10 men, 12 women	**Ph.D.s:** 95%
Graduate: n/av	**Student/Faculty:** 10 to 1
Year: 4-1-4, summer session	**Tuition:** $41,576
Room & Board: $12,380	**Freshman Class:** 2325 applied, 1878 accepted, 400 enrolled
SAT EBR-W/M: 510/540 **ACT:** 23	**CEEB CODE:** 4387
Application Deadline: February 1	**COMPETITIVE**

Linfield College is dedicated exclusively to undergraduate education and is home to a vibrant community of engaged students. There are 3 undergraduate schools. In addition to regional accreditation, LC has baccalaureate program accreditation with NASM, CCNE, CAATE, NAEYC, and ACS. The 189-acre campus is in a small town 40 miles southwest of Portland, Oregon. Including any residence halls, there are 79 buildings.

STUDENT LIFE: 56% of undergraduates are from Oregon. Others are from 21 states, 23 foreign countries, and Canada. 81% are from public schools. 58% are White; 16% Hispanic; 10% two or more races; 5% Asian American; 4% Foreign; 3% race unknown; 2% African American; 1% American Indian/Alaska Native. **Female To Male Ratio:** 1.5:1. The average age of freshmen is 18; all undergraduates, 20. 19% do not continue beyond their first year; 78% remain to graduate. **Housing:** 1273 students can be accommodated in college housing, which includes coed dorms and on-campus apartments. In addition, there are special-interest houses, fraternity houses, sorority houses, and wellness housing. On-campus housing is guaranteed for all 4 years. 74% of students live on campus. All students may keep cars.

FACULTY/CLASSROOMS: 48% of faculty are male; 52% are female. All teach undergraduates and do research. No introductory courses are taught by graduate students. The average class size in an introductory lecture is 18; in a laboratory is 13; and in a regular course is 14.

PROGRAMS OF STUDY: LC confers B.A., B.S., and B.S.N. degrees. Bachelor's degrees are awarded in AGRICULTURE (environmental studies), BIOLOGICAL SCIENCE (biochemistry and biology/biological science), BUSINESS (accounting, banking and finance, business administration and management, international business management, and marketing management), COMMUNICATIONS AND THE ARTS (art, communications, creative writing, dramatic arts, English, fine/studio arts, general, French, French and Francophone studies, German, Japanese, journalism, literature, music, Spanish, studio art, and theatre arts), COMPUTER AND PHYSICAL SCIENCE (applied physics, chemistry, computer science, mathematics, and physics), EDUCATION (athletic training, elementary education, health education, and physical education), ENGINEERING AND ENVIRONMENTAL DESIGN (engineering physics), HEALTH PROFESSIONS (exercise science and nursing), SOCIAL SCIENCE (African studies, anthropology, crosscultural studies, economics, German area studies, history, international relations, Japanese studies, Latin American studies, philosophy, political science/government, psychology, religion, and sociology). Nursing, accounting, and exercise science are the strongest academically. Nursing, psychology, and exercise science have the largest enrollments.

ACTIVITIES: 23% of men belong to 2 local and 2 national fraternities; 24% of women belong to 1 local and 3 national sororities. There are 85 groups on campus, including ultimate frisbee, the Hawaiian club, art, band, cheerleading, choir, chorale, chorus, communications, computers, dance, debate, drama, environmental, ethnic, forensics, honors, international, jazz band, LGBT, literary magazine, marching band, musical theater, newspaper, opera, orchestra, pep band, photography, political, professional, radio and TV, religious, social, social service, student government, and symphony. Popular campus events include Wildstock (outdoor fair, including music and activities booths), Luau, Hispanic Heritage Day, and Homecoming. **Sports:** There are 9 intercollegiate sports for men and 10 for women, and 6 intramural sports for men and 6 for women. Facilities include a football stadium with turf field, all-weather track, soccer field, indoor complex with a gym, basketball courts, swimming pool, racquetball courts, weight room, baseball stadium, softball stadium, field house with tennis courts and hitting cages. **Graduates:** From July 1, 2016 to June 30, 2017, 329 bachelor's degrees were awarded. The most popular majors were business/marketing (22%), education (12%), and social sciences (11%). In an average class, 1% graduate in 3 years or less, 65% graduate in 4 years or less, 75% graduate in 5 years or less, and 78% graduate in 6 years or less. Of the 2016 graduating class, 10% were enrolled in graduate school within 6 months of graduation.

SERVICES: Counseling and information services are available, as is tutoring in every subject. There is a reader service for the blind. There are also learning support services, a speaking center, and a writing center. **Library/Resources:** The library contains 153,191 volumes, 17,491 microform items, 5,039 audio/video tapes/CDs/DVDs, and subscribes to 30,997 periodicals including electronic. Computerized library services include interlibrary loans, database searching, Internet access, and Wi-Fi capability. Special learning facilities include an art gallery, radio station, center for the Northwest, Delkin Recital Hall, Ford Theatre, Anthropology Museum, Career Development Center, multimedia studio, science and computer labs, and the Linfield Research Institute. **Physically Challenged Students:** 85% of the campus is accessible. Facilities include wheelchair ramps, elevators, special parking, specially equipped restrooms, special class scheduling, lowered drinking fountains, lowered telephones, and special housing. **Special:** Linfield is highly ranked among U.S. undergraduate schools for participation in study abroad. Through Linfield's January Term and Semester Abroad programs, students study in 30 locations around the globe in China, Africa, Europe and Southeast Asia. During the past five years, almost 700 students completed internships off campus, many in the industry of their choice. Some students intern abroad through the IE3 Global Internships program, and others take advantage of off-campus work-study programs that target literacy and disadvantaged youth. Education is personalized, and student-designed majors are available. Last year more than 50 students collaborated on research projects with their professors, and many presented papers at professional conferences. In addition to Linfield's campus-based programs, online degrees and certificates are available, including accelerated degrees. Students may also choose a 3-2 engineering degree as part of a collaboration with the University of Southern California and Oregon and Washington State Universities. Students partner with more than 100 community-based organizations for service learning, sponsored through Linfield's Community Engagement and Service Office. Many outreach projects lead to job opportunities. New students are introduced to college with rich immersion experiences that include First CLAS (Community, Leadership, Action, and Service); iFocus (for those interested in the sciences); SOIL (sustainability); and AHA (arts & humanities). In addition, all new students participate in a Colloquium and Inquiry Seminars. Many also choose to get to know their faculty through the "Take a Professor to Lunch" program. There are 19 national honor societies and 15 departmental honors programs. **Visiting:** There are regularly scheduled orientations for prospective students, tours and interviews. There are guides for informal visits and visitors may sit in on classes. To schedule a visit, contact the Office of Admission. **Campus Safety and Security:** Measures include 24-hour foot and vehicle patrol, emergency notification system, self-defense education, and security escort services. There are emergency telephones, lighted pathways/sidewalks, and controlled access to dorms/residences.

REQUIREMENTS: The SAT or ACT is required. Linfield recommends that applicants have 4 years each of English and math, 3 to 4 years each of natural science and social studies, and 2 to 4 years of a foreign language. An essay is required, and an interview is recommended. The GED is accepted. AP and CLEP credits are accepted. Important factors in the admissions decision are advanced placement or honors courses, evidence of special talent, and recommendations by school officials. Core requirements include courses from the sciences, literature, fine arts, religion or philosophy, the social sciences, history, and quantitative reasoning. An inquiry seminar in critical thinking and writing is also required. Students also take courses in American pluralism and global diversity. 3 credits of activity courses in phys ed, music, or community service are required. Students must maintain 2.0 cumulative GPA and complete 125 semester credit hours, including 35 to 45 in the major. **Procedure:** Freshmen are admitted in the fall and spring. Entrance exams should be taken during the fall of their senior year. There are early admissions and deferred admissions plans. Early decision applications should be filed by November 1; by February 1 for fall entry; and December 1 for spring entry. Notification of early decision is sent January 15; regular decision, April 1. Applications are accepted on-line. **Transfer Students:** 69 transfer students enrolled in 2016-2017. Transfer students from regionally accredited colleges and universities with at least a B average/3.0 GPA at their previous institution (s) are most likely to succeed. Consistent academic progress, leadership and likelihood of contribution to the Linfield community are also considered. 30 of 125 credits required for the bachelor's degree must be completed at Linfield. **International Students:** There are 66 international students enrolled. They must take the TOEFL with a minimum score of 550 on the paper-based TOEFL (PBT) or 80 on the Internet-based version (iBT), or take the MELAB. One or more of these exams are required: EIKEN, IELTS, SAT Critical Reading, ACT English, or TOEIC. The SAT or ACT is required for international students whose first language is English.

ADMISSIONS: 81% of the 2017-2018 applicants were accepted. The SAT scores for the 2017-2018 freshman class were: Math-- 18% below 500, 48% between 500 and 599, 31% between 600 and 699, and 3% between 700 and 800. Evidence-Based Reading/Writing-- 19% below 500, 47% between 500 and 599, 30% between 600 and 699, and 4% between 700 and 800. The ACT scores were 7% between 12 and 17, 50% between 18 and 23, 37% between 24 and 29, and 7% above 30. 53% of the current freshmen were in the top fifth of their class; 87% were in the top two fifths. 17 freshmen graduated first in their class. **Admissions Contact:** Lisa Knodle-Bragiel, Director of Admission. Email: *admission@linfield.edu* Web: *www.linfield.edu*

FINANCIAL AID: In 2017-2018, 83% of all full-time freshmen received some form of financial aid. 67% of all full-time freshmen received need-based aid. The average freshman award was $36,595. Need-based scholarships or need-based grants averaged $31,393; need-based self-help aid (loans and jobs) averaged $6,009; and other non-need-based awards and non-need-based scholarships averaged $21,043. 110% of undergraduate students work part-time. The average financial indebtedness of the 2017 graduate was $24,529. LC is a member of CSS. The FAFSA code is 003198. The priority date for freshman financial aid applications for fall entry is February 1.

MARYLHURST UNIVERSITY *(The complete profile is made available exclusively on our website, www.barronspac.com)*

NORTHWEST CHRISTIAN UNIVERSITY B-2

www.nwcu.edu

Eugene, OR 97401	**(541) 684-7201** **(877) 463-6622**
Fax: (541) 684-7317	**Email: admissions@nwcu.edu**
Full-time: 505 men, 200 women	**Faculty:** 19
Part-time: n/av	**Ph.D.s:** 47%
Graduate: n/av	**Student/Faculty:** 12 to 1
Year: trimesters, summer session	**Tuition:** $27,930
Room & Board: $8650	**Freshman Class:** 179 applied, 114 accepted, 50 enrolled
SAT or ACT: required	**CEEB CODE:** 4543
Application Deadline: n/av	**COMPETITIVE**

Northwest Christian University, founded in 1895, is a private institution affiliated with the Christian Church, offering programs in the arts and sciences, business, education, and ministries. The figures given in the above capsule and in this profile are approximate. There is 1 undergraduate school. In addition to regional accreditation, NCU has baccalaureate program accreditation with IACBE, NCCU, Board of Licensed Professional Counselors and Therapy, and Teachers Standards and Practices Commission. The 8-acre campus is in an urban area at the south end of the Willamette Valley, near McKenzie and Willamette rivers, about 50 miles east of the Oregon Coast. Including any residence halls, there are 14 buildings.

STUDENT LIFE: 92% of undergraduates are from Oregon. Others are from 8 states. 94% are from public schools. 70% are White; 1% African American; 1% Asian American; 1% Hispanic. 64% claim no religious affiliation; 35% Protestant. **Male To Female Ratio:** 2.5:1. The average age of freshmen is 18; all undergraduates, 30. 38% do not continue beyond their first year; 38% remain to graduate. **Housing:** 213 students can be accommodated in college housing, which includes dorms and off-campus apartments. On-campus housing is guaranteed for the freshman year only. 73% of students commute. All students may keep cars. Alcohol is not permitted.

FACULTY/CLASSROOMS: 40% of faculty are male; 60% are female. All teach undergraduates. No introductory courses are taught by graduate students. The average class size in an introductory lecture is 40 and in a regular course is 25.

PROGRAMS OF STUDY: NCU confers B.A. and B.S. degrees. Associate and master's degrees are also awarded. Bachelor's degrees are awarded in BUSINESS (accounting, business administration and management, and management information systems), COMMUNICATIONS AND THE ARTS (communications and music), COMPUTER AND PHYSICAL SCIENCE (computer science), EDUCATION (education and elementary education), HEALTH PROFESSIONS (exercise science and health care administration), SOCIAL SCIENCE (human services, humanities, interdisciplinary studies, international studies, ministries, psychology, and social science). Business administration, and elementary education are the strongest academically. Accounting, business administration, and exercise science have the largest enrollments.

ACTIVITIES: There are no fraternities or sororities. There are 15 groups on campus, including cheerleading, choir, chorale, debate, drama, forensics, literary magazine, musical theater, newspaper, religious, social service, student government, and yearbook. Popular campus events include Annual Musical, Spirit Week, and Wellness Week. **Sports:** There are 1 intercollegiate sports for men and 2 for women, and 4 intramural sports for men and 4 for women. Facilities include an event center with a basketball court, fitness rooms, and softball practice area. **Graduates:** From July 1, 2016 to June 30, 2017, 103 bachelor's degrees were awarded. The most popular majors were management (51%), teacher education (27%), and psychology (6%). In an average class, 30% graduate in 4 years or less, 38% graduate in 5 years or less, and 38% graduate in 6 years or less. Of the 2016 graduating class, 13% were enrolled in graduate school within 6 months of graduation, and 72% were employed.

SERVICES: Counseling and information services are available, as is tutoring in most subjects. There is remedial math, reading, and writing. **Library/Resources:** The library contains 60,250 volumes, 766 microform items, 10,367 audio/video tapes/CDs/DVDs, and subscribes to 261 periodicals including electronic. Computerized library services include interlibrary loans, database searching, and Internet access. **Physically Challenged Students:** 60% of the campus is accessible. Facilities include wheelchair ramps, elevators, special parking, specially equipped restrooms, special class scheduling, lowered drinking fountains, and lowered telephones. **Special:** NCC offers internships, study abroad in 4 countries, a Washington semester, work study, accelerated degree programs, and student-designed majors. **Visiting:** There are regularly scheduled orientations for prospective students. There are guides for informal visits, visitors may sit in on classes, and stay overnight. To schedule a visit, contact the Admissions Office at (541) 684-7209. **Campus Safety and Security:** Measures include 24-hour foot and vehicle patrol and security escort services. There are emergency telephones and lighted pathways/sidewalks.

REQUIREMENTS: The SAT or ACT is required. Students are required to submit a completed admission application, high school transcripts, and 2 references. An interview is recommended. A GPA of 2.5 is required. AP and CLEP credits are accepted. Important factors in the admissions decision are advanced placement or honors courses, recommendations by school officials, and extracurricular activities record. To graduate, students must complete 124-186 quarter credits with at least 40 in the major and a minimum GPA of 2.0. The core curriculum consists of 55-86 credit hours in humanities, social sciences, math and science, and Bible; a 1-credit-hour chapel for every term enrolled is also required as are 3 service credits. **Procedure:** Freshmen are admitted in the fall and spring. There are early admissions, deferred admissions, and rolling admissions plans. Check with the school for current application deadlines. Notification is sent on a rolling basis. Applications are accepted on-line. **Transfer Students:** 55 transfer students enrolled in 2016-2017. Students are required to submit a completed application, official transcripts from each college or university attended, an academic reference, and official high school transcripts if they have fewer than 36 transferable credits. 30 of 124 credits required for the bachelor's degree must be completed at NCU. **International Students:** They must take the TOEFL.

ADMISSIONS: 64% of the 2017-2018 applicants were accepted. 36% of the current freshmen were in the top fifth of their class; 67% were in the top two fifths. **Admissions Contact:** Randy Jones, Dean of Admissions. Email: *admissions@nwcu.edu* Web: *www.nwcu.edu*

FINANCIAL AID: In 2017-2018, 100% of all full-time freshmen received some form of financial aid. NCU is a member of CSS. The college's own financial statement is required. The FAFSA code is 003208. Check with the school for current application deadlines.

OREGON INSTITUTE OF TECHNOLOGY B-4

www.oit.edu

Klamath Falls, OR 97601	(541) 885-1150
Fax: (541) 885-1115	Email: oit@oit.edu
Full-time: 1115 men, 840 women	**Faculty:** 107
Part-time: 560 men, 555 women	**Ph.D.s:** 31%
Graduate: 15 men	**Student/Faculty:** 18 to 1
Year: trimesters, summer session	**Tuition:** $9625 ($27,326)
Room & Board: $9602	**Freshman Class:** n/av CEEB CODE: 4587
Application Deadline: June 1	COMPETITIVE

Oregon Institute of Technology, the only public institute of technology in the Pacific Northwest, provides degree programs in engineering, health technologies, management, communications and applied sciences and prepares students to be effective participants in their professional, public and international communities. There are 3 undergraduate schools and 1 graduate school. In addition to regional accreditation, OIT has baccalaureate program accreditation with ABET and NLN. The 173-acre campus is in a small town 60 miles east of Medford in south central Oregon. Including any residence halls, there are 19 buildings.

STUDENT LIFE: 85% of undergraduates are from Oregon. Others are from 35 states, and 17 foreign countries. 95% are from public schools. 80% are White; 5% Asian American; 4% Hispanic; 2% American Indian/Alaska Native; 1% African American; 1% Foreign. **Male To Female Ratio:** 1.2:1. The average age of freshmen is 23; all undergraduates, 26. 26% do not continue beyond their first year; 29% remain to graduate. **Housing:** 500 students can be accommodated in college housing, and dorms. On-campus housing is guaranteed for all 4 years. 82% of students commute. All students may keep cars.

FACULTY/CLASSROOMS: 77% of faculty are male; 23% are female. All teach undergraduates. No introductory courses are taught by graduate students. The average class size in an introductory lecture is 30; in a laboratory is 18; and in a regular course is 30.

PROGRAMS OF STUDY: OIT confers B.S. degrees. Associate and master's degrees are also awarded. Bachelor's degrees are awarded in BUSINESS (management information systems), ENGINEERING AND ENVIRONMENTAL DESIGN (civil engineering, computer technology, electrical/electronics engineering technology, engineering technology, environmental science, industrial administration/management, laser electro-optics technology, manufacturing technology, mechanical engineering technology, and surveying engineering), HEALTH PROFESSIONS (dental hygiene, health science, radiograph medical technology, and ultrasound technology), SOCIAL SCIENCE (industrial and organizational psychology). Engineering technology programs has the largest enrollment.

ACTIVITIES: 3% of men belong to 1 local and 1 national fraternities; 3% of women belong to 1 local and 1 national sororities. There are 37 groups on campus, including cheerleading, communications, computers, ethnic, honors, international, newspaper, outdoor club, pep band, professional, radio and TV, religious, social, and student government. Popular campus events include Tech Challenge, Family Weekend Tech Fest, and a Skills Contest for Business and Math Students. **Sports:** There are 4 intercollegiate sports for men and 6 for women. Facilities include a stadium, gym, football, baseball, softball fields, free weights and aerobics areas, indoor swimming pool, a track, tennis, volleyball, basketball, and badminton courts. **Graduates:** Of the 2016 graduating class, 11% were enrolled in graduate school within 6 months of graduation, and 86% were employed.

SERVICES: Counseling and information services are available, as is tutoring in some subjects, such as math, sciences, and computers. There is a reader service for the blind, and remedial math, reading, and writing. **Library/Resources:** The library contains 145,988 volumes, 158,278 microform items, 2,069 audio/video tapes/CDs/DVDs, and subscribes to 1,815 periodicals including electronic. Computerized library services include interlibrary loans, database searching, Internet access, and Wi-Fi capability. Special learning facilities include an art gallery and radio station. **Physically Challenged Students:** 90% of the campus is accessible. Facilities include wheelchair ramps, elevators, special parking, specially equipped restrooms, and special class scheduling. **Special:** Cross-registration with Klamath Community College, internships in all majors, and co-op programs in all engineering technologies are available. OIT also offers advanced degree programs in software engineering technology and vascular imaging. There are 2 national honor societies. **Visiting:** There are regularly scheduled orientations for prospective students, including tours and meetings with admissions counselors, faculty, and students. There are guides for informal visits, visitors may sit in on classes, and stay overnight. To schedule a visit, contact the Admissions Office. **Campus Safety and Security:** Measures include 24-hour foot and vehicle patrol and security escort services. There are lighted pathways/sidewalks.

REQUIREMENTS: A composite score of 1000 on the SAT I or 21 on the ACT is required for applicants who do not meet the minimum GPA requirement. Applicants must have 14 academic units, including 4 years of English, 3 each of math and social sciences, and 2 each of science and a foreign language. The GED is accepted. Applications are accepted on disk. AP and CLEP credits are accepted. General education requirements include 12 hours in social science and 9 hours each in communication, business, and humanities. Students also must take 9 hours in English composition and technical report writing. Completion of about 200 quarter hours, with a minimum GPA of 2.0, is required to graduate. **Procedure:** Freshmen are admitted to all sessions. Entrance exams should be taken. The SAT I or ACT should be taken during the senior year, and placement tests just prior to registration. There are early admissions and rolling admissions plans. Applications should be filed by June 1 for fall entry; December 1 for winter entry; March 1 for spring entry; and June 1 for summer entry. The fall 2017 application fee was $50. Notification is sent on a rolling basis. **Transfer Students:** 168 transfer students enrolled in 2016-2017. Applicants must have a minimum GPA of 2.0 and at least 24 quarter credit hours; students with fewer credit hours must submit high school transcripts or GED scores. An associate degree is recommended. 45 of 190 credits required for the bachelor's degree must be completed at OIT. **International Students:** There are 29 international students enrolled. They must take the TOEFL.

Admissions Contact: Palmer Muntz, Director of Admissions. Email: *oit@oit.edu* Web: *www.oit.edu*

FINANCIAL AID: In 2017-2018, 85% of all full-time freshmen received some form of financial aid. 80% of all full-time freshmen received need-based aid. The average freshman award was $9,700. 40% of undergraduate students work part-time. The average financial indebtedness of the 2017 graduate was $22,629. The FAFSA code is 003211. The deadline for filing freshman financial aid applications for fall entry is May 1.

OREGON STATE UNIVERSITY B-2
www.oregonstate.edu

Corvallis, OR 97331 **(541) 737-4411**
(800) 291-4192
Email: osuadmit@oregonstate.edu

Full-time: 10,256 men, 8573 women	**Faculty:** 1183; I, -$
Part-time: 3702 men, 3307 women	**Ph.D.s:** 86%
Graduate: 2518 men, 2540 women	**Student/Faculty:** 16 to 1
Year: quarters, summer session	**Tuition:** $10,797 ($29,457)
Room & Board: $12,540	**Freshman Class:** 14890 applied, 11740 accepted, 3824 enrolled
SAT EBR-W/M: 594/592 **ACT:** 25	**CEEB CODE:** 4586
Application Deadline: September 1	**VERY COMPETITIVE**

Oregon State University is 1 of only 2 American universities that are designated a land, sea, sun and space grant institution. Since the 1860s, states have selected a university for the unique role of land-grant institution. This role entails providing students of all economic backgrounds access to instruction and research in agriculture, science, and engineering, as well as the traditional liberal arts. The sea, sun, and space grants reflect national recognition of expertise and research leadership in marine, environmental, and space sciences and technologies. The university has an intense focus on science and technology; the majority of students major in a STEM field. Among the most popular undergraduate majors are Computer Science, Business Administration, Mechanical Engineering, Kinesiology, and Human Development and Family Sciences. There are 12 undergraduate schools and 12 graduate schools. In addition to regional accreditation, OSU has baccalaureate program accreditation with AACSB, ABET, ACCE, ACPE, AHEA, CSAB, NASM, CAEP, and SAF. The 400-acre campus is in a small town 90 miles south of Portland. Including any residence halls, there are 203 buildings.

STUDENT LIFE: 70% of undergraduates are from Oregon. Others are from 50 states, 80 foreign countries, and Canada. 64% are White; 10% Hispanic; 8% Asian American; 7% Foreign; 7% two or more races; 2% race unknown; 1% African American; 1% American Indian/Alaska Native. **Male To Female Ratio:** 1.1:1. The average age of freshmen is 19; all undergraduates, 23. 15% do not continue beyond their first year; 65% remain to graduate. **Housing:** 5134 students can be accommodated in college housing, which includes married student dorms. In addition, there are honors houses, language/international houses, special-interest houses, fraternity houses, sorority houses, and housing for entrepreneurship majors. On-campus housing is guaranteed for the freshman year only, and is available on a first-come, first-served basis. 83% of students commute. Alcohol is not permitted. All students may keep cars.

FACULTY/CLASSROOMS: 56% of faculty are male; 44% are female. Graduate students teach 11% of introductory courses. The average class size in an introductory lecture is 57; in a laboratory is 26; and in a regular course is 38.

PROGRAMS OF STUDY: OSU confers B.A., B.S., and B.F.A. degrees. Master's and doctoral degrees are also awarded. Bachelor's degrees are awarded in AGRICULTURE (agricultural business management, agriculture, agronomy, animal science, fishing and fisheries, forest engineering, forestry and related sciences, horticulture, natural resource management, range/farm management, and soil science), BIOLOGICAL SCIENCE (biochemistry, biology/biological science, botany, ecology, microbiology, nutrition, wildlife biology, and zoology), BUSINESS (accounting, business administration and management, business systems analysis, environment & national resource economics, finance, hospitality management services, management science, marketing, marketing/retailing/merchandising, recreation and leisure services, and tourism), COMMUNICATIONS AND THE ARTS (apparel design, applied art, art, digital communications, English, French, German, graphic design, music, Spanish, and speech/debate/rhetoric), COMPUTER AND PHYSICAL SCIENCE (chemistry, computer science, earth science, mathematics, medical physics, and physics), EDUCATION (education), ENGINEERING AND ENVIRONMENTAL DESIGN (agricultural engineering, bioengineering, bioresource engineering, chemical engineering, civil engineering, computer engineering, construction management, electrical/electronics engineering, engineering/mechanical energy system focus, environmental engineering, environmental science, industrial engineering, interior design, manufacturing engineering, mechanical engineering, and nuclear engineering), HEALTH PROFESSIONS (biomedical science, kinesiology, predentistry, premedicine, preoptometry, prepharmacy, prephysical therapy, prepodiatry, and public health), SOCIAL SCIENCE (American studies, anthropology, economics, ethnic studies, food science, history, human development, international studies, liberal arts/general studies, parks and recreation management, philosophy, political science/government, psychology, religious studies, social science, sociology, and women's studies). Engineering, agricultural sciences, and forestry are the strongest academically. Computer science, business administration, and mechanical engineering have the largest enrollments.

ACTIVITIES: 11% of men belong to 24 national fraternities; 16% of women belong to 20 national sororities. There are 360 groups on campus, including adventure club, art, band, cheerleading, chess, choir, chorale, chorus, communications, computers, dance, debate, drama, drill team, drum and bugle corps, environmental, ethnic, film, forensics, honors, international, jazz band, LGBT, literary magazine, marching band, musical theater, newspaper, orchestra, pep band, photography, political, professional, radio and TV, religious, social, social service, student government, student sustainability initiative, symphony, and yearbook. Popular campus events include Connect Week, Dads Weekend, Civil War, Moms Weekend, Battle of the Bands, and Bard in the Quad. **Sports:** There are 7 intercollegiate sports for men and 10 for women, and 19 intramural sports for men and 17 for women. Facilities include a recreation center that houses cardio rooms, weight rooms, gyms, racquetball courts, squash courts, multipurpose rooms, a climbing wall, indoor track, a pool and dive well, sand volleyball courts, and the Adventure Leadership Institute. A field house has indoor multipurpose courts, turf field, a rock climbing wall, and fields for tennis, and basketball. **Graduates:** From July 1, 2016 to June 30, 2017, 5416 bachelor's degrees were awarded. The most popular majors were computer science (9%), human development and family sciences (6%), and kinesiology (5%). In an average class, 33% graduate in 4 years or less, 59% graduate in 5 years or less, and 65% graduate in 6 years or less. Of the 2016 graduating class, 19% were enrolled in graduate school within 6 months of graduation, and 42% were employed.

SERVICES: Counseling and information services are available, as is tutoring in most subjects. There is a reader service for the blind, and remedial math, reading, and writing. There is also a communication skills center and a math sciences learning center. **Library/Resources:** The library contains 2.0 million volumes, 2.2 million microform items, 27,256 audio/video tapes/CDs/DVDs, and subscribes to 107,975 periodicals including electronic. Computerized library services include interlibrary loans, database searching, Internet access, and Wi-Fi capability. Special learning facilities include an art gallery, natural history museum, radio station, TV station, arboretum, a wave research lab, research farm, research vessel, and the Linus Pauling Collection. **Physically Challenged Students:** 92% of the campus is accessible. Facilities include wheelchair ramps, elevators, special parking, specially equipped restrooms, special class scheduling, lowered drinking fountains, and lowered telephones. **Special:** Oregon State University offers a double degree in Education, where a student has a primary degree in any field and then also earns an Education degree. With the Education degree the student also earns an Oregon teaching license. There is also a double degree, in sustainability, where students take an additional 36 credits beyond their primary degree. The Sustainability degree is interdisciplinary drawing on courses from many disciplines in the university. OSU has a list of over 200 approved study abroad programs in 77 different countries. There are 14 national honor societies and a freshman honors program. **Visiting:** There are regularly scheduled orientations for prospective students. There are guides for informal visits, visitors may sit in on classes, and stay overnight. To schedule a visit, contact the Visitor Center at (541) 737-2626. **Campus Safety and Security:** Measures include 24-hour foot and vehicle patrol, emergency notification system, and security escort services. There are shuttle buses, emergency telephones, lighted pathways/sidewalks, and controlled access to dorms/residences.

REQUIREMENTS: The SAT or ACT is required. Applicants should be high school graduates or hold the GED. Required high school preparation includes 4 years of English; 3 years each of math, including algebra II, science, social science; and 2 years of foreign language. Some subject requirements may be fulfilled by test scores. AP and CLEP credits are accepted. To graduate, students must complete at least 180 quarter credits with a GPA of 2.0. The required core curriculum includes writing, mathematics, speech, physical science, biological science, culture, difference and power, technology and society, global issues, fitness. Students must also take a writing-intensive course in their major field and meet additional distribution requirements. **Procedure:** Freshmen are admitted to all sessions. Entrance exams should be taken during the junior or senior year. There are early admissions, deferred admissions, and rolling admissions plans. Early decision applications should be filed by February 1; regular applications, by September 1 for fall entry; December 12 for winter entry; March 6 for spring entry; and June 26 for summer entry. The fall 2017 application fee was $60. Notification of early decision is sent March 15; regular decision, Applications are accepted on-line. **Transfer Students:** 1947 transfer students enrolled in 2016-2017. Applicants must present a GPA of at least 2.25 in previous college work. Students should have completed at least 36 hours of college credit. Must have a C- or better on English Composition and College Algebra. Transfer students must show two years of foreign language in high school or two semesters of foreign language. Either SAT I or ACT scores must be submitted. 45 of 180 credits required for the bachelor's degree must be completed at Oregon State. **International Students:** There are 1149 international students enrolled. They must take the TOEFL with a minimum score of 80 on the Internet-based version (iBT).

ADMISSIONS: 79% of the 2017-2018 applicants were accepted. The SAT scores for the 2017-2018 freshman class were: Math-- 11% below 500, 41% between 500 and 599, 36% between 600 and 699, and 12% between 700 and 800. Evidence-Based Reading/Writing-- 11% below 500, 38% between 500 and 599, 40% between 600 and 699, and 11% between 700 and 800. The ACT scores were 4% between 12 and 17, 35% between 18 and 23, 44% between 24 and 29, and 17% above 30. 46% of the current freshmen were in the top fifth of their class; 79% were in the top two fifths. 57 freshmen graduated first in their class. **Admissions Contact:** Noah Buckley, Director of Admissions. Email: *osuadmit@oregonstate.edu* Web: *www.oregonstate.edu*

FINANCIAL AID: In 2017-2018, 56% of all full-time freshmen received some form of financial aid. 48% of all full-time freshmen received need-based aid. The average freshman award was $13,018. Need-based scholarships or need-based grants averaged $8,612; need-based self-help aid (loans and jobs) averaged $4,466; non-need-based athletic scholarships averaged $23,940; and other non-need-based awards and non-need-based scholarships averaged $5,403. 22% of undergraduate students work part-time. The average financial indebtedness of the 2017 graduate was $26,400. OSU is a member of CSS. The FAFSA code is 003210. The priority date for freshman financial aid applications for fall entry is February 28.

PACIFIC NORTHWEST COLLEGE OF ART *(The complete profile is made available exclusively on our website, www.barronspac.com)*

PACIFIC UNIVERSITY — A-1

www.pacificu.edu

Forest Grove, OR 97116	**(503) 359-2218** **(800) 677-6712**
Fax: (503) 359-2975	**Email: admissions@pacificu.edu**
Full-time: 752 men, 1112 women	**Faculty:** 284
Part-time: 10 men, 10 women	**Ph.D.s:** 78%
Graduate: 601 men, 1285 women	**Student/Faculty:** 11 to 1
Year: 4-1-4, summer session	**Tuition:** $29,469
Room & Board: $8148	**Freshman Class:** 3004 applied, 2374 accepted, 479 enrolled
SAT CR/M: 540/550 **ACT:** 24	**CEEB CODE:** 4601
Application Deadline: February 15	**COMPETITIVE**

Pacific University, founded in 1849, is an independent educational institution affiliated with the Congregational Church (United Church of Christ), and offering degree programs in liberal arts, science, business, education, and health professions. The figures given in the above capsule and in this profile are approximate. There are 4 undergraduate schools. In addition to regional accreditation, Pacific has baccalaureate program accreditation with NASM. The 55-acre campus is in a small town 25 miles west of Portland. Including any residence halls, there are 18 buildings.

STUDENT LIFE: 50% of undergraduates are from out of state, mostly the West. Students are from 31 states, 7 foreign countries, and Canada. 91% are from public schools. 64% are White; 2% Hispanic; 2% Foreign; 18% Asian American; 1% African American; 1% American Indian/Alaska Native. **Female To Male Ratio:** 1.8:1. The average age of freshmen is 18; all undergraduates, 21. 22% do not continue beyond their first year; 54% remain to graduate. **Housing:** 680 students can be accommodated in college housing, which includes dorms and off-campus apartments. In addition, there are special-interest houses, women's floor, and apartments for singles. On-campus housing is guaranteed for the freshman year only, is available on a first-come, first-served basis, and is available on a lottery system for upperclassmen. 50% of students commute. All students may keep cars.

FACULTY/CLASSROOMS: 52% of faculty are male; 48% are female. All teach undergraduates and do research. No introductory courses are taught by graduate students. The average class size in an introductory lecture is 35; in a laboratory is 20; and in a regular course is 19.

PROGRAMS OF STUDY: Pacific confers B.A., B.S., and B.M. degrees. Master's and doctoral degrees are also awarded. Bachelor's degrees are awarded in BIOLOGICAL SCIENCE (biology/biological science), BUSINESS (business administration and management), COMMUNICATIONS AND THE ARTS (creative writing, dramatic arts, Japanese, literature, music, and Spanish), COMPUTER AND PHYSICAL SCIENCE (chemistry, computer science, mathematics, and physics), SOCIAL SCIENCE (economics, history, humanities, philosophy, political science/government, psychology, social work, and sociology). Natural sciences, literature, and creative writing are the strongest academically. Business administration, English, and psychology have the largest enrollments.

ACTIVITIES: 6% of men belong to 3 local fraternities; 9% of women belong to 3 local sororities. There are 35 groups on campus, including art, band, cheerleading, choir, chorale, chorus, computers, dance, debate, drama, ethnic, film, forensics, honors, international, jazz band, LGBT, literary magazine, newspaper, orchestra, pep band, photography, political, professional, radio and TV, religious, social, social service, student government, and symphony. Popular campus events include Hawaiian Club Luau, International Club Banquet, and Japan Day. **Sports:** There are 8 intercollegiate sports for men and 8 for women, and 10 intramural sports for men and 10 for women. Facilities include a gym, various courts, weight and wrestling rooms, a dance studio, outdoor playing fields, a field house, and racquetball courts. **Graduates:** From July 1, 2016 to June 30, 2017, 379 bachelor's degrees were awarded. The most popular majors were health professions and related programs (41%), psychology (15%), and engineering (8%). In an average class, 44% graduate in 4 years or less, 57% graduate in 5 years or less, and 63% graduate in 6 years or less. Of the 2016 graduating class, 82% were employed within 6 months of graduation.

SERVICES: Counseling and information services are available, as is tutoring in most subjects. There is a reader service for the blind. **Library/Resources:** The library contains 152,060 volumes, 76,609 microform items, 3,708 audio/video tapes/CDs/DVDs, and subscribes to 945 periodicals including electronic. Computerized library services include interlibrary loans and database searching. Special learning facilities include an art gallery, radio station, and a Pacific University museum. **Physically Challenged Students:** 80% of the campus is accessible. Facilities include wheelchair ramps, elevators, special parking, specially equipped restrooms, lowered drinking fountains, and special housing. **Special:** Cross-registration is available with Oregon Independent Colleges and Oregon Graduate Institute of Science and Technology (OGIST). The university also offers cooperative programs with Washington University in St. Louis, OGIST, and Oregon School of Arts and Crafts, as well as study abroad in 13 countries. Full-time, semester-long internships, including one in Washington D.C., are possible. Dual majors, a general studies degree in humanities, nondegree study, 3-2 engineering programs with Washington University in St. Louis and OGIST, and an interdisciplinary program in peace and conflict studies are available. There are 2 national honor societies, a freshman honors program, and 1 departmental honors program. **Visiting:** There are regularly scheduled orientations for prospective students, a campus tour, classroom visitations, and meetings with faculty and coaches. There are guides for informal visits, visitors may sit in on classes, and stay overnight. To schedule a visit, contact the Admissions Office. **Campus Safety and Security:** Measures include 24-hour foot and vehicle patrol, emergency notification system, and security escort services. There are emergency telephones, lighted pathways/sidewalks, and controlled access to dorms/residences.

REQUIREMENTS: The SAT or ACT is required. Applicants are expected to be high school graduates or hold the GED. A personal essay is required, and an interview is recommended. On-line applications are available on Pacific's Web pages. 21 high school units are recommended: 4 each in English, and academic electives, 3 each in math, science, of these units, 1 must be with lab, and social studies, 2 in foreign language, and 1 in history. A GPA of 3.0 is required. AP and CLEP credits are accepted. Important factors in the admissions decision are advanced placement or honors courses, recommendations by school officials, and extracurricular activities record. All students take a core curriculum that includes a first-year seminar and courses in writing, foreign language, social and natural sciences, art, and cross-cultural studies. A cumulative GPA of 2.0 in 124 semester hours is required for graduation. 34 to 64 hours are required in the major, depending on the discipline. **Procedure:** Freshmen are admitted in the fall and spring. There are deferred admissions and rolling admissions plans. Applications should be filed by February 15 for fall entry. The fall 2017 application fee was $40. Applications are accepted on-line. **Transfer Students:** 118 transfer students enrolled in 2016-2017. Transfer applicants must present at least a 2.75 GPA in previous college work; those with fewer than 30 semester hours or 45 quarter hours must also submit SAT I or ACT test scores and high school transcripts. A personal interview is strongly recommended. Application for admission is in the fall, August 15, and spring January 15. 30 of 124 credits required for the bachelor's degree must be completed at Pacific. **International Students:** There are 48 international students enrolled.

ADMISSIONS: 79% of the 2017-2018 applicants were accepted. The SAT scores for the 2017-2018 freshman class were: Critical Reading-- 28% below 500, 48% between 500 and 599, 20% between 600 and 699, and 3% between 700 and 800. Math-- 21% below 500, 52% between 500 and 599, 25% between 600 and 699, and 2% between 700 and 800. The ACT scores were 5% between 12 and 17, 42% between 18 and 23, 46% between 24 and 29, and 7% above 30. 18 freshmen graduated first in their class. **Admissions Contact:** Beth Woodward, Director of Admissions. Email: *admissions@pacificu.edu* Web: *www.pacificu.edu*

FINANCIAL AID: In 2017-2018, 87% of all full-time freshmen received some form of financial aid. 84% of all full-time freshmen received need-based aid. The average freshman award was $33,920. Need-based scholarships or need-based grants averaged $11,440; need-based self-help aid (loans and jobs) averaged $6,195; non-need-based athletic scholarships averaged $19,599; and other non-need-based awards and non-need-based scholarships averaged $4,341. 54% of undergraduate students work part-time. The average financial indebtedness of the 2017 graduate was $22,163. Pacific is a member of CSS. The FAFSA code is 003212. The priority date for freshman financial aid applications for fall entry is March 1.

PORTLAND STATE UNIVERSITY — B-1

www.pdx.edu

Portland, OR 97207	503-725-5504 (800) 547-8887
Fax: 503-725-5525	**Email:** mtrifi@pdx.edu
Full-time: 6935 men, 7582 women	**Faculty:** I, --$
Part-time: 4074 men, 4579 women	**Ph.D.s:** n/av
Graduate: 2237 men, 3324 women	**Student/Faculty:** 18 to 1
Year: quarters, summer session	**Tuition:** $8730 ($24,012)
Room & Board: $11,019	**Freshman Class:** n/av
SAT CR/M: 520/510 **ACT:** 22	**CEEB CODE:** 4610
Application Deadline: open	**COMPETITIVE**

Portland State University, founded in 1946 as a public research university, is a nationally acclaimed leader in sustainability and community-based learning, offering more than 220 undergraduate, master's, and doctoral degree options, as well as graduate certificates and continuing education programs. The figures given in the above capsule and in this profile are approximate. The tuition varies by programs chosen by student. There are 8 undergraduate schools. In addition to regional accreditation, PSU has baccalaureate program accreditation with AACSB, ABET, ASLA, CSWE, NASAD, NASM, CAEP, CACREP, ABE, and ASLHA. The 50-acre campus is in an urban area in the center of Portland. Including any residence halls, there are 56 buildings.

STUDENT LIFE: 89% of undergraduates are from Oregon. 65% are White; 8% Hispanic; 7% Asian American; 7% Foreign; 4% two or more races; 4% race unknown; 3% African American; 2% American Indian/Alaska Native. **Female To Male Ratio:** 1.2:1. The average age of all undergraduates is 27. 26% do not continue beyond their first year; 74% remain to graduate. **Housing:** 1729 students can be accommodated in college housing, which includes dorms, on-campus apartments, off-campus apartments, and first year experience housing. On-campus housing is available on a first-come, first-served basis. 93% of students commute. All students may keep cars.

FACULTY/CLASSROOMS: 50% of faculty are male; 50% are female. No introductory courses are taught by graduate students.

PROGRAMS OF STUDY: PSU confers B.A., B.S., and B.M. degrees. Master's and doctoral degrees are also awarded. Bachelor's degrees are awarded in BIOLOGICAL SCIENCE (biochemistry and biology/biological science), BUSINESS (accounting, business administration and management, management science, marketing/retailing/merchandising, and personnel management), COMMUNICATIONS AND THE ARTS (advertising, art history and appreciation, Chinese, dramatic arts, English, fine arts, French, German, Japanese, languages, music, Russian, Spanish, and speech/debate/rhetoric), COMPUTER AND PHYSICAL SCIENCE (chemistry, computer science, geology, information sciences and systems, mathematics, and physics), EDUCATION (health education), ENGINEERING AND ENVIRONMENTAL DESIGN (architecture, civil engineering, computer engineering, electrical/electronics engineering, and environmental science), SOCIAL SCIENCE (anthropology, child care/child and family studies, community services, economics, geography, history, international studies, law enforcement and corrections, liberal arts/general studies, philosophy, political science/government, psychology, social work, sociology, and women's studies). Electrical engineering, environmental science, and physics are the strongest academically. Psychology, business administration, and art have the largest enrollments.

ACTIVITIES: There are 246 groups on campus, including art, band, cheerleading, chess, choir, chorale, chorus, communications, computers, dance, debate, drama, drill team, environmental, ethnic, film, forensics, honors, international, jazz band, LGBT, literary magazine, musical theater, newspaper, opera, orchestra, outdoor, pep band, photography, political, professional, a radio and TV station, religious, social, social service, student government, and symphony. Popular campus events include Portland State of Mind, International Student Cultural Night, Friends of Chamber Music, and the Lunch Box Theater. **Sports:** There are 6 intercollegiate sports for men and 9 for women, and 6 intramural sports for men and 6 for women. Facilities include a practice field, an all-weather tennis facility, gyms, circuit training and weight rooms, a golf putting green, running track, racquetball, handball, and squash courts. Students have access to the nearby Civic Stadium and Duniway Park that provides football, baseball, and track and field. **Graduates:** From July 1, 2016 to June 30, 2017, 4320 bachelor's degrees were awarded. The most popular majors were social sciences/general (7%), business administration/management (6%), and psychology/general (6%). In an average class, 11% graduate in 4 years or less, 30% graduate in 5 years or less, and 40% graduate in 6 years or less.

SERVICES: Counseling and information services are available, as is tutoring in most subjects. There is a reader service for the blind, and remedial math and writing. The Student Support Services, provides assistance to students who are low-income, have a physical disability, or whose parents did not graduate from college. **Library/Resources:** Computerized library services include interlibrary loans, database searching, and Internet access. Special learning facilities include an art gallery, radio station, a multicultural center and a Native American center. **Physically Challenged Students:** 95% of the campus is accessible. Facilities include wheelchair ramps, elevators, special parking, specially equipped restrooms, special class scheduling, lowered drinking fountains, lowered telephones, and special housing. **Special:** Students may study abroad in 59 countries. There are numerous internships, co-op programs, a Washington semester, and work-study programs available. Most undergraduate programs may be taken on an accelerated basis, and students in all programs may undertake dual majors or design their own majors. A general studies program is available in arts and letters, science, or social science. Nondegree study and pass/fail grading options are possible.

Students may enroll for 7 or fewer credits per term without formal admission. There are 8 national honor societies and a freshman honors program. **Visiting:** There are regularly scheduled orientations for prospective students, including daily campus tours led by student guides and opportunities for prospective students to meet with faculty, staff, and advisers. There are guides for informal visits; visitors may sit in on classes, and stay overnight. To schedule a visit, contact the Campus Tour Coordinator at (503) 725-5555. **Campus Safety and Security:** Measures include 24-hour foot and vehicle patrol, emergency notification system, self-defense education, and security escort services. There are emergency telephones, lighted pathways/sidewalks, a campus watch newsletter, information lectures, and community liaison.

REQUIREMENTS: The SAT or ACT is required. A minimum GPA of 3.0 is required. Various combination of test scores and the GPA score may qualify students for admissions under the Special Action by the admissions commitee. Applicants should be high school graduates or have earned the GED. Secondary preparation should include 4 years of English, 3 years of math, and 2 years each of science, foreign language and social studies and 1 year of history including 1 unit of laboratory science. AP and CLEP credits are accepted. All students must complete at least 180 quarter credits with a 2.0 GPA in all courses in the major, and in all residence work. Other requirements and the number of hours that must be completed in the major vary by degree program. Freshmen must complete three 5-credit freshman inquiry courses, sophomores; must complete three 4-credit courses from different interdisciplinary programs or general education clusters, juniors and seniors; must complete 1 interdisciplinary program or general education cluster (4 3-credit courses), and seniors must also complete a Senior Capstone. A thesis is required in the honors program only. **Procedure:** Freshmen are admitted to all sessions. Entrance exams should be taken as early as possible. There are deferred admissions and rolling admissions plans. Application deadlines are open. The fall 2017 application fee was $50. Notification is sent on a rolling basis. Applications are accepted on-line. **Transfer Students:** 2827 transfer students enrolled in 2016-2017. Applicants who are Oregon residents must have earned at least a 2.0 GPA in 30 college credits; those with 12 to 30 credits must meet freshman admission requirements and have a 2.0 GPA in all college work attempted. Nonresident applicants must have at least a 2.25 GPA in 30 hours of college work; those with 12 to 30 hours must meet freshman requirements and have a 2.5 GPA in all college work attempted. 45 of 180 credits required for the bachelor's degree must be completed at PSU. **International Students:** There are 880 international students enrolled. They must take the international TOEFL or the PSU institutional TOEFL.

ADMISSIONS: The SAT scores for the 2017-2018 freshman class were: Critical Reading-- 39% below 500, 39% between 500 and 599, 19% between 600 and 699, and 3% between 700 and 800. Math-- 42% below 500, 4% between 500 and 599, 16% between 600 and 699, and 1% between 700 and 800. Writing-- 50% below 500, 36% between 500 and 599, 13% between 600 and 699, and 1% between 700 and 800. The ACT scores were 38% below 12, 26% between 12 and 17, 20% between 18 and 23, 10% between 24 and 29, and 6% above 30. **Admissions Contact:** Dana Tasson, Executive Director of Student Affairs. Email: *mtrifi@pdx.edu* Web: *www.pdx.edu*

FINANCIAL AID: In 2017-2018, 73% of all full-time freshmen received some form of financial aid. 58% of all full-time freshmen received need-based aid. The average freshman award was $11,540. Need-based scholarships or need-based grants averaged $5,350 ($18,500 maximum); need-based self-help aid (loans and jobs) averaged $6,916 ($27,661 maximum); non-need-based athletic scholarships averaged $14,168 ($28,610 maximum); and other non-need-based awards and non-need-based scholarships averaged $3,589 ($33,152 maximum). 80% of undergraduate students work part-time. The college's own financial statement is required. The FAFSA code is 003216. Check with the school for current application deadlines.

REED COLLEGE B-1

www.reed.edu

Portland, OR 97202

(503) 777-7511
(800) 547-4750

Fax: (503) 777-7553	**Email:** admission@reed.edu
Full-time: 620 men, 750 women	**Faculty:** 153; IIB, ++$
Part-time: 1 men, 5 women	**Ph.D.s:** 96%
Graduate: 8 men, 9 women	**Student/Faculty:** 9 to 1
Year: semesters	**Tuition:** $52,150
Room & Board: $13,150	**Freshman Class:** 3956 applied, 1532 accepted, 347 enrolled
SAT CR/M/W: 715/670/685 **ACT:** 31	**CEEB CODE:** 4654
Application Deadline: January 15	**MOST COMPETITIVE**

Reed College, founded in 1908, is a private, nonsectarian institution offering programs in liberal arts and sciences, and emphasizing instruction through small conference-style classes. There is 1 undergraduate school and 1 graduate school. In addition to regional accreditation, Reed has baccalaureate program accreditation with ACS. The 116-acre campus is in an urban area in Portland, Oregon. Including any residence halls, there are 43 buildings.

STUDENT LIFE: 92% of undergraduates are from out of state, mostly the Southwest. Students are from 47 states, 45 foreign countries, and Canada. 56% are from public schools. 59% are White; 11% Hispanic; 8% Asian American; 8% race unknown; 7% Foreign; 3% African American; 3% two or more races; 1% American Indian/Alaska Native. **Female To Male Ratio:** 1.2:1. The average age of freshmen is 18; all undergraduates, 20. **Housing:** 946 students can be accommodated in college housing, which includes dorms, on-campus apartments, and off-campus apartments. In addition, there are language/international houses, special-interest houses, quiet hall, substance-free, cooperative housing, theme and wellness housing, and no-smoking dorms. On-campus housing is guaranteed for the freshman year only, is available on a first-come, first-served basis, and is available on a lottery system for upperclassmen. 67% of students live on campus. Alcohol is not permitted. All students may keep cars.

FACULTY/CLASSROOMS: 56% of faculty are male; 44% are female. All teach undergraduates, and do research. No introductory courses are taught by graduate students.

PROGRAMS OF STUDY: Reed confers B.A. degrees. Master's degrees are also awarded. Bachelor's degrees are awarded in AGRICULTURE (environmental studies), BIOLOGICAL SCIENCE (biochemistry and biology/biological science), COMMUNICATIONS AND THE ARTS (art, Chinese, classics, dramatic arts, English literature, Germanic languages and literature, linguistics, literature, music, and Russian languages and literature), COMPUTER AND PHYSICAL SCIENCE (chemical physics, chemistry, mathematics, mathematics-economics, and physics), SOCIAL SCIENCE (American studies, anthropology, economics, French studies, history, international political science, philosophy, political science/government, psychology, religion, sociology, and Spanish studies). English, biology, and psychology have the largest enrollments.

ACTIVITIES: There are no fraternities or sororities. There are 104 groups on campus, including art, chess, choir, chorus, computers, dance, debate, drama, environmental, ethnic, international, jazz band, LGBT, literary magazine, musical theater, newspaper, orchestra, photography, radio club, religious, social service, student government, and symphony. Popular campus events include Performing Arts Festival, Campus Clean Up Day (Canyon Day), and Reed Arts Week (RAW). **Sports:** There are 7 intramural sports for men and 6 for women. Facilities include a sports center that houses gyms, an indoor pool, squash and racquetball courts, a weight room, an exercise room, and a dance studio. Outdoor facilities include tennis courts, a track, and areas for soccer, rugby, volleyball, and baseball. **Graduates:** From July 1, 2016 to June 30, 2017, 314 bachelor's degrees were awarded. The most popular majors were social sciences (15%), biological/life sciences, and physical sciences (13%), and visual and performing arts (10%). In an average class, 70% graduate in 4 years or less, 80% graduate in 5 years or less, and 82% graduate in 6 years or less.

SERVICES: Counseling and information services are available, as is tutoring in every subject. There is a reader service for the blind, and remedial math, reading, and writing. **Library/Resources:** The library contains 629,871 volumes, 180,996 microform items, 31,456 audio/video tapes/CDs/DVDs, and subscribes to 17,169 periodicals including electronic. Computerized library services include interlibrary loans, database searching, Internet access, and Wi-Fi capability. Special learning facilities include an art gallery, a research reactor, and centers for bio science, math, quantitative skills, science, and writing. **Physically Challenged Students:** Facilities include wheelchair ramps, elevators, special parking, specially equipped restrooms, special class scheduling, lowered drinking fountains, lowered telephones, and special housing. **Special:** Cross-registration is available through the Oregon Independent Colleges organization and Pacific Northwest College of Art. 3-2 programs are available for computer science with University of Washington and for engineering with CalTech, Columbia University, and Rensselaer Polytechnic Institute. Also available are combined programs with the Pacific Northwest College of Art for Visual Arts. Study abroad in 18 countries, a domestic exchange program with Howard University in Washington, D.C., Sarah Lawrence College, and Sea Education Association (SEA), accelerated degree programs, dual majors, student-designed majors, numerous interdisciplinary majors, nondegree study, and pass/fail options are also offered. There is a chapter of Phi Beta Kappa. **Visiting:** There are regularly scheduled orientations for prospective students, including an information session, campus tour, and an admission interview. Visitors may sit in on classes and stay overnight. To schedule a visit, contact the Office of Admission. **Campus Safety and Security:** Measures include 24-hour foot and vehicle patrol, emergency notification system, self-defense education, and security escort services. There are shuttle buses, emergency telephones, lighted pathways/sidewalks, and controlled access to dorms/residences.

REQUIREMENTS: The results of either the SAT or ACT are required, and SAT Subject tests are recommended. Reed strongly recommends that applicants have 4 years of English, 3-4 of math 3 each of science, and foreign language, 3-4 of social studies. An essay is required, and an interview is recommended. The GED is accepted. AP credits are accepted. Important factors in the admissions decision are advanced placement or honors courses, personality/intangible qualities, and evidence of special talent. All students are required to maintain a C average while fulfilling 120 semester hours of credit. The liberal arts program also requires a year-long humanities course and year-long senior research project, in addition to distribution requirements in literature, philosophy, religion, and the arts, history, social sciences, and psychology, natural sciences, mathematics, logic, or foreign language or linguistics. Students are also required to take 6 quarters of phys ed. **Procedure:** Freshmen are admitted in the fall. Entrance exams should be taken No later than December of application year. There are early decision and deferred admissions plans. Early decision applications should be filed by November 15; regular applications, by January 15 for fall entry. The fall 2017 application fee was $50. Notification of early decision is sent February 1; regular decision, April 1. 114 early decision candidates were accepted for the 2017-2018 class. 437 applicants were on the 2017 waiting list. Applications are accepted on-line. **Transfer Students:** 32 transfer students enrolled in 2016-2017. Transfer students must submit their high school transcripts, college transcripts, an essay or personal statement, all standardized test scores, and a statement of good standing from prior institution (s). An interview is also recommended. Students may enroll in the fall March 1; notification is sent May 15, and must reply by June 1. 60 of 120 credits required for the bachelor's degree must be completed at Reed. **International Students:** There are 92 international students enrolled. They must take the TOEFL with a minimum score of 600 on the paper-based TOEFL (PBT) or 100 on the Internet-based version (iBT). They must also take the SAT or ACT.

ADMISSIONS: 39% of the 2017-2018 applicants were accepted. The SAT scores for the 2017-2018 freshman class were: Critical Reading-- 5% between 500 and 599, 36% between 600 and 699, and 59% between 700 and 800. Math-- 1% below 500, 12% between 500 and 599, 50% between 600 and 699, and 37% between 700 and 800. Writing-- 1% below 500, 8% between 500 and 599, 50% between 600 and 699, and 41% between 700 and 800. The ACT scores were 1% between 18 and 23, 25% between 24 and 29, and 74% above 30. 84% of the current freshmen were in the top fifth of their class; 94% were in the top two fifths. 13 freshmen graduated first in their class. **Admissions Contact:** Keith Todd, Dean of Admission. Email: *admission@reed.edu* Web: *www.reed.edu*

FINANCIAL AID: In 2017-2018, 53% of all full-time freshmen received some form of financial aid. 50% of all full-time freshmen received need-based aid. The average freshman award was $40,911. Need-based scholarships or need-based grants averaged $38,279; need-based self-help aid (loans and jobs) averaged $4,168; and other non-need-based awards and non-need-based scholarships averaged $3,449. 39% of undergraduate students work part-time. The average financial indebtedness of the 2017 graduate was $19,010. Reed is a member of CSS. The CSS/Profile and the college's own financial statement, and parent and student federal tax forms are required. The FAFSA code is 003217. The deadline for filing freshman financial aid applications for fall entry is February 1.

SOUTHERN OREGON UNIVERSITY B-4

www.sou.edu

Ashland, OR 97520 **(541) 552-6411**

Fax: (541) 552-8403
Full-time: 1551 men, 2086 women
Part-time: 759 men, 1048 women
Graduate: 234 men, 508 women
Year: quarters, summer session
Room & Board: $11,397
SAT CR/M/W: 525/505/490 **ACT:** 23
Application Deadline: September 9

Email: admissions@sou.edu
Faculty: 199
Ph.D.s: 93%
Student/Faculty: 21 to 1
Tuition: $7720 ($21,296)
Freshman Class: 2209 applied, 2064 accepted, 629 enrolled
CEEB CODE: 4702
COMPETITIVE

Southern Oregon University, founded in 1926, is a public comprehensive university providing undergraduate and graduate programs in humanities, science, business, fine and performing arts, social sciences, and teacher education. There are 3 undergraduate schools and 1 graduate school. In addition to regional accreditation, SOU has baccalaureate program accreditation with ACBSP, NASM, CAEP, ACS, and CACREP. The 175-acre campus is in a small town 10 miles southeast of Medford Oregon. Including any residence halls, there are 40 buildings.

STUDENT LIFE: 71% of undergraduates are from Oregon. Others are from 44 states, 17 foreign countries, and Canada. 85% are from public schools. 64% are White; 15% race unknown; 10% Hispanic; 4% two or more races; 2% African American; 2% Asian American; 2% Foreign; 1% American Indian/Alaska Native. **Female To Male Ratio:** 1.4:1. The average age of freshmen is 19; all undergraduates, 24. 30% do not continue beyond their first year; 40% remain to graduate. **Housing:** 1300 students can be accommodated in college housing, which includes married student dorms, on-campus apartments, and off-campus apartments. In addition, there are special-interest houses, 24-hour and 12-hour quiet halls, a wellness hall, a freshman hall, a smoke and incense-free hall, and age 21-plus hall. On-campus housing is guaranteed for the freshman year only, and is available on a first-come, first-served basis. 74% of students commute. All students may keep cars.

FACULTY/CLASSROOMS: 55% of faculty are male; 45% are female. All teach undergraduates. No introductory courses are taught by graduate students. The average class size in a regular course is 25.

PROGRAMS OF STUDY: SOU confers B.A., B.S., and B.F.A. degrees. Master's degrees are also awarded. Bachelor's degrees are awarded in AGRICULTURE (environmental studies and natural resource management), BIOLOGICAL SCIENCE (biology/biological science), BUSINESS (accounting, business administration and management, business (dual major program), hospitality management services, marketing, and marketing/retailing/merchandising), COMMUNICATIONS AND THE ARTS (art history, art, communications, digital media, dramatic arts, English, English Writing, film, television and digital media, fine arts, foreign language, graphic design, graphic design & media, languages, music, music business management, music composition, music performance, Spanish, studio art, theatre arts, theatre production, theatre studies, visual and performing arts, and writing), COMPUTER AND PHYSICAL SCIENCE (chemistry, computer mathematics, computer programming, computer information systems, computer science, digital arts/technology, mathematics, mathematics-economics, and science), EDUCATION (early childhood education, education, elementary education, English education, environmental education, physical education, and recreation education), ENGINEERING AND ENVIRONMENTAL DESIGN (environmental science and preengineering), HEALTH PROFESSIONS (biology, biomedical science, health, mental health/human services, nursing, premedicine, prepharmacy, prephysical therapy, and sports medicine), SOCIAL SCIENCE (American Indian studies, anthropology, criminal justice, criminology, economics, gender studies, geography, history, human services, interdisciplinary studies, international studies, liberal arts/general studies, Native American studies, philosophy, political science/government, prelaw, psychology, social science, sociology, and women & gender studies). Fine & performing arts, psychology, and criminology/criminal justice are the strongest academically. Business, psychology, and communication have the largest enrollments.

ACTIVITIES: There are no fraternities or sororities. There are 125 groups on campus, including art, band, cheerleading, chess, choir, chorale, chorus, communications, computers, dance, drama, environmental, ethnic, film, forensics, honors, international, jazz band, LGBT, literary magazine, musical theater, newspaper, pep band, photography, political, professional, radio and TV, religious, social, social service, student government, and symphony. Popular campus events include Raider Orientation, Convocation, Southern Oregon Arts and Research Symposium, Commencement Weekend, International Week, and One World Series. **Sports:** There are 6 intercollegiate sports for men and 7 for women, and 11 intramural sports for men and 7 for women. Facilities include an indoor swimming pool, racquetball courts, tennis courts, gyms, a climbing-wall gym, a dance studio, wrestling and weight rooms, football stadium, an all-weather track, and a student fitness and recreations center. **Graduates:** From July 1, 2016 to June 30, 2017, 838 bachelor's degrees were awarded. The most popular majors were business/marketing (17%), visual and performing arts (13%), and psychology (10%). In an average class, 2% graduate in 3 years or less, 16% graduate in 4 years or less, 28% graduate in 5 years or less, and 32% graduate in 6 years or less.

SERVICES: Counseling and information services are available, as is tutoring in some subjects, such as all levels of math and writing. There is a reader service for the blind, and remedial math and writing. **Library/Resources:** The library contains 336,000 volumes, 807,000 microform items, 90,000 audio/video tapes/CDs/DVDs, and subscribes to 4,300 periodicals including electronic. Computerized library services include interlibrary loans, database searching, Internet access, and Wi-Fi capability. Special learning facilities include a radio station, TV station, a center for the visual arts, an art museum, art galleries, a wildlife forensics lab, a music recital hall, 2 theaters, a greenhouse, and an ecology center. **Physically Challenged Students:** 95% of the campus is accessible. Facilities include wheelchair ramps, elevators, special parking, specially equipped restrooms, special class scheduling, lowered drinking fountains, lowered telephones, and special housing. **Special:** Cross-registration through the National Student and Western Student Exchanges, study abroad in 23 countries, internships, and federal work-study are all available. Accelerated degrees in business, communication, computer science, economics, geography, math, political science, foreign languages and literature, and sociology, dual majors in business and chemistry, physics, math, or music, and in math and computer science, and interdisciplinary majors in environmental or international studies are all offered. There are 13 national honor societies, a freshman honors program, and 10 departmental honors programs. **Visiting:** There are regularly scheduled orientations for prospective students, including tours of the campus, residence halls, and a meeting with an admissions representative. Appointments with faculty and class visits can be arranged. There are guides for informal visits; visitors may sit in on classes, and stay overnight. To schedule a visit, contact the Admissions Office. **Campus Safety and Security:** Measures include 24-hour foot and vehicle patrol, emergency notification system, self-defense education, and security escort services. There are emergency telephones, lighted pathways/sidewalks, and controlled access to dorms/residences.

REQUIREMENTS: The SAT or ACT is required. A satisfactory score on the SAT is needed if the high school GPA is less than 2.75. Applicants need 14 academic credits, including 4 years of English, 3 each of math and social studies, 2 of science with 1 unit of lab, and 2 years of 1 foreign language. The GED is accepted. AP and CLEP credits are accepted. Students need a minimum GPA of 2.0 earned over 180 quarter hours, with 50 to 100 in the major and at least 60 in upper-division course work. Competency must be demonstrated through course work in writing and research. General education requirements include a yearlong course in speaking, writing, and critical thinking and both lower- and upper-division courses in arts and letters, natural sciences, social sciences, and quantitative reasoning. There is a required senior capstone experience. **Procedure:** Freshmen are admitted to all sessions. Entrance exams should be taken during the junior or senior year. There are early admissions, deferred admissions, and rolling admissions plans. Application deadlines are open. The fall 2017 application fee was $50. Notification of early decision is sent March 15; regular decision, October 9. Applications are accepted on-line. **Transfer Students:** 540 transfer students enrolled in 2016-2017. Transfer students need a minimum GPA of 2.25 and at least 36 quarter credits. 45 of 180 credits required for the bachelor's degree must be completed at SOU. **International Students:** There are 166 international students enrolled. They must take the TOEFL with a minimum score of 520 on the paper-based TOEFL (PBT) or 68 on the Internet-based version (iBT).

ADMISSIONS: 93% of the 2017-2018 applicants were accepted. The SAT scores for the 2017-2018 freshman class were: Critical Reading-- 39% below 500, 38% between 500 and 599, 19% between 600 and 699, and 3% between 700 and 800. Math-- 47% below 500, 40% between 500 and 599, and 12% between 600 and 699. Writing-- 52% below 500, 38% between 500 and 599, and 9% between 600 and 699. **Admissions Contact:** Kelly Moutsatson, Director of Admissions. Email: *admissions@sou.edu* Web: *www.sou.edu*

FINANCIAL AID: In 2017-2018, 88% of all full-time freshmen received some form of financial aid. 88% of all full-time freshmen received need-based aid. The average freshman award was $8,560. Need-based scholarships or need-based grants averaged $6,728; need-based self-help aid (loans and jobs) averaged $3,260; non-need-based athletic scholarships averaged $2,869; other non-need-based awards and non-need-based scholarships averaged $3,047; and $3,560 from other forms of aid. 50% of undergraduate students work part-time. The average financial indebtedness of the 2017 graduate was $30,936. The FAFSA code is 003219. The priority date for freshman financial aid applications for fall entry is March 1.

UNIVERSITY OF OREGON — B-2

www.uoregon.edu

Eugene, OR 97403	**(541) 346-3201** **(800) 232-3825**
Fax: (541) 346-5815	**Email: uoadmit@uoregon.edu**
Full-time: 8229 men, 9572 women	**Faculty:** 1099; I, -$
Part-time: 760 men, 779 women	**Ph.D.s:** 98%
Graduate: 1695 men, 1852 women	**Student/Faculty:** 16 to 1
Year: quarters, summer session	**Tuition:** $11,571 ($34,611)
Room & Board: $12,450	**Freshman Class:** 20317 applied, 16824 accepted, 3938 enrolled
SAT EBR-W/M: 600/580 **ACT:** 25	**CEEB CODE:** 4846
Application Deadline: January 15	**VERY COMPETITIVE**

University of Oregon, founded in 1876, is a comprehensive public research university, encompassing the humanities & arts, natural & social sciences, and the professions. The college strives for excellence in teaching, artistic expression, and the generation, dissemination, preservation, and application of knowledge. There are 7 undergraduate schools and 8 graduate schools. In addition to regional accreditation, University of Oregon has baccalaureate program accreditation with AACSB, ACEJMC, ASLA, FIDER, NAAB, NASM, ACS, APA, and ASLA. The 295-acre campus is in a suburban area 110 miles south of Portland. Including any residence halls, there are 80 buildings.

STUDENT LIFE: 51% of undergraduates are from Oregon. Others are from 49 states, 69 foreign countries, and Canada. 58% are White; 12% Hispanic; 12% Foreign; 8% two or more races; 6% Asian American; 2% African American; 1% American Indian/Alaska Native; 1% race unknown. **Female To Male Ratio:** 1.1:1. The average age of freshmen is 19; all undergraduates, 21. 14% do not continue beyond their first year; 72% remain to graduate. **Housing:** 4793 students can be accommodated in college housing, which includes married student dorms, on-campus apartments, and off-campus apartments. In addition, there are special-interest houses, gender inclusive hall, a quiet hall, a wellness hall, academic residence communities, and global scholars hall. On-campus housing is available on a first-come, first-served basis. 79% of students commute. All students may keep cars.

FACULTY/CLASSROOMS: 54% of faculty are male; 46% are female. 96% teach undergraduates. Graduate students teach 27% of introductory courses. The average class size in an introductory lecture is 41; in a laboratory is 20; and in a regular course is 43.

PROGRAMS OF STUDY: University of Oregon confers B.A., B.S., B.Arch., B.Ed., B.F.A., B.I.Arch., B.L.A., B.Mus., and B.Mme degrees. Master's and doctoral degrees are also awarded. Bachelor's degrees are awarded in AGRICULTURE (environmental studies), BIOLOGICAL SCIENCE (biochemistry, biology/biological science, marine biology, and physiology), BUSINESS (accounting and business administration and management), COMMUNICATIONS AND THE ARTS (advertising, art, arts administration, art history and appreciation, ceramic art and design, Chinese, classics, communications, communication science, comparative literature, dance, design, digital communications, dramatic arts, English, fiber/textiles/weaving, film arts, fine arts, folklore and mythology, French, German, Greek, Italian, Japanese, jazz, journalism, linguistics, metal/jewelry, music, music performance, music theory and composition, painting, photography, printmaking, public relations, romance languages and literature, Russian languages and literature, sculpture, Spanish, and theatre arts), COMPUTER AND PHYSICAL SCIENCE (chemistry, computer science, data science, earth science, mathematics, physics, and science), EDUCATION (education and music education), ENGINEERING AND ENVIRONMENTAL DESIGN (architecture, environmental science, interior architecture, and landscape architecture/design), HEALTH PROFESSIONS (speech pathology/audiology), SOCIAL SCIENCE (anthropology, Asian/Oriental studies, classical/ancient civilization, economics, ethnic studies, family and community services, geography, history, human services, humanities, international studies, Judaic studies, Latin American studies, medieval studies, philosophy, political science/government, psychology, public administration, religion, social science, sociology, and women's studies). Pre-business administration, psychology, and human physiology have the largest enrollments.

ACTIVITIES: 16% of men belong to 20 national fraternities; 21% of women belong to 1 local and 16 national sororities. There are 250 groups on campus, including art, band, cheerleading, chess, choir, chorale, chorus, communications, computers, dance, debate, drama, drill team, environmental, ethnic, film, forensics, honors, international, jazz band, LGBT, literary magazine, marching band, musical theater, newspaper, pep band, photography, political, professional, radio and TV, religious, social, social service, and student government. Popular campus events include University Day, Family Weekends, and Convocation. **Sports:** There are 7 intercollegiate sports for men and 11 for women, and 15 intramural sports for men and 15 for women. Facilities include a football stadium, basketball arena, track and field complex, a softball field and softball complex, a baseball stadium that includes a player development area, tennis courts, soccer, lacrosse, and an indoor practice facility for athletic teams. The student recreation center contains a fitness space, exercise and yoga studios, a cycling studio, a gym for basketball, volleyball, and badminton, a pool, water polo, water aerobics, and instructional classes, water volleyball, and basketball. **Graduates:** From July 1, 2016 to June 30, 2017, 5168 bachelor's degrees were awarded. The most popular majors were business administration (16%), journalism & communication (11%), and general social science (9%). In an average class, 3% graduate in 3 years or less, 52% graduate in 4 years or less, 69% graduate in 5 years or less, and 72% graduate in 6 years or less. Of the 2016 graduating class, 8% were enrolled in graduate school within 6 months of graduation, and 57% were employed.

SERVICES: Counseling and information services are available, as is tutoring in some subjects. There is a reader service for the blind, and remedial math, reading, and writing. There is also private tutoring available for many courses plus small group tutoring for some courses, and math and writing labs that offer free drop in support. **Library/Resources:** The library contains 3.2 million volumes, 2.6 million microform items, and 101,898 audio/video tapes/CDs/DVDs, and subscribes to 230,050 periodicals including electronic. Computerized library services include interlibrary loans, database searching, Internet access, and Wi-Fi capability. Special learning facilities include an art gallery, radio station, TV station, an art museum, a natural and cultural history museum, centers for sports marketing and entrepreneurship, a green chemistry lab, and a longhouse. **Physically Challenged Students:** 95% of the campus is accessible. Facilities include wheelchair ramps, elevators, special parking, specially equipped restrooms, and lowered drinking fountains. There is an adviser is available for students with disabilities. Other accommodations are made upon request. **Special:** Matriculation agreements with more than 30 Oregon and Washington community colleges, dual enrollment with Lane and Southwestern Oregon Community Colleges, study abroad in more than 90 countries, pre-engineering in conjunction with Lane Community College, and a 3-2 engineering degree with Oregon State University. In addition, numerous internship opportunities, dual majors, and pass/fail options are available. There are 21 national honor societies, Phi Beta Kappa, and 48 departmental honors programs. **Visiting:** There are regularly scheduled orientations for prospective students, including IntroDUCKtion, a 2-day program scheduled for late July that includes both advising and Web-based registration. There are guides for informal visits and visitors may sit in on classes. **Campus Safety and Security:** Measures include 24-hour foot and vehicle patrol, emergency notification system, self-defense education, and security escort services. There are shuttle buses, emergency telephones, lighted pathways/sidewalks, controlled access to dorms/residences, a campuswide emergency management program, campus emergency operations, and mitigation plans.

REQUIREMENTS: The SAT or ACT is required. Standard freshman admission requirements include graduation from a standard or regionally accredited high school, and C- or higher in 15 college preparatory courses. Applications are evaluated based on strength of academic course work, grades earned, grade trends, senior year course load, standardized test scores, academic motivation as demonstrated in the application essay, academic potential, special talents, extracurricular activities, including community service or the need to work to assist your family, and ability to enhance the diversity of the university. AP and CLEP credits are accepted. For graduation, at least 180 quarter credits are required of all students, with a minimum GPA of 2.0 and a minimum of 62 credits upper division. A minimum of 36 credits must be in the major, including 24 in upper-division work. Basic courses vary by major, but all students must complete 12 to 16 credits each in the areas of arts and letters, social science, and science, as well as 2 courses in written English and 2 courses in multicultural studies. A bachelor of science degree requires one year college level or equivalent mathematics or computer science or combination of the two. A bachelor of arts requires two years college level or equivalent of a second language. **Procedure:** Freshmen are admitted to all sessions. Entrance exams should be taken by February 15, is latest date scores accepted for fall term admission. There are deferred admissions and rolling admissions plans. Applications should be filed by January 15 for fall entry; October 15 for winter entry; February 1 for spring entry; and March 1 for summer entry. The fall 2017 application fee was $65. Notifications are sent April 1. 79 applicants were on the 2017 waiting list; 73 were admitted. Applications are accepted on-line. **Transfer Students:** 1196 transfer students enrolled in 2016-2017. If transfer students have completed 35 or fewer transferable quarter credits (23 semester credits), they must meet admission requirements for both freshmen and transfer students. Admission will be based on both high school and college work. If transfer students have completed 36 or more quarter credits (24 of which must be graded), admission will be based on college-level coursework only. Transfer students must be eligible to return to their most recent institution and have completed 1 college-level composition course and 1 college-level mathematics course with grades of C- or better, P (pass), or S (satisfactory); earned a minimum GPA of 2.25 if they are Oregon residents or 2.5 if they are nonresidents; and demonstrate second-language proficiency. 45 of 180 credits required for the bachelor's degree must be completed at University of Oregon. **International Students:** There are 2136 international students enrolled. They must take the TOEFL with a minimum score of 500 on the paper-based TOEFL (PBT) or 61 on the Internet-based version (iBT). The SAT or ACT is required only for students applying to architecture programs or honors college.

ADMISSIONS: 83% of the 2017-2018 applicants were accepted. The SAT scores for the 2017-2018 freshman class were: Math-- 13% below 500, 46% between 500 and 599, 34% between 600 and 699, and 7% between 700 and 800. Evidence-Based Reading/Writing-- 10% below 500, 39% between 500 and 599, 42% between 600 and 699, and 9% between 700 and 800. The ACT scores were 5% between 12 and 17, 32% between 18 and 23, 51% between 24 and 29, and 12% above 30. 49% of the current freshmen were in the top fifth of their class; 77% were in the top two fifths. **Admissions Contact:** Admissions Department. Email: *uoadmit@uoregon.edu* Web: *www.uoregon.edu*

FINANCIAL AID: 15% of undergraduate students work part-time. The average financial indebtedness of the 2017 graduate was $26,164. The FAFSA code is 003223. The priority date for freshman financial aid applications for fall entry is March 1.

UNIVERSITY OF PORTLAND B-1

www.up.edu

Portland, OR 97203	**(503) 943-7147** **(888) 627-5601**
Fax: (503) 943-7315	**Email: admissio@up.edu**
Full-time: 1522 men, 2176 women	**Faculty:** 214
Part-time: 20 men, 23 women	**Ph.D.s:** 92%
Graduate: 197 men, 312 women	**Student/Faculty:** 14 to 1
Year: semesters, summer session	**Tuition:** $40,250
Room & Board: $11,902	**Freshman Class:** 11202 applied, 6939 accepted, 941 enrolled
SAT CR/M: 590/600 **ACT:** required	**CEEB CODE:** 4847
Application Deadline: February 1	**VERY COMPETITIVE**

University of Portland, founded in 1901, is an independent institution affiliated with the Roman Catholic Church, offering degree programs in the arts and sciences, business administration, education, engineering, and nursing. There are 5 undergraduate schools and 1 graduate school. In addition to regional accreditation, University of Portland has baccalaureate program accreditation with AACSB, ABET, CSWE, NASM, CAEP, CCNE, and NAST. The 155-acre campus is in an urban area 4 miles north of downtown Portland. Including any residence halls, there are 30 buildings.

STUDENT LIFE: 71% of undergraduates are from out of state, mostly the Northwest. Students are from 44 states, 37 foreign countries, and Canada. 67% are from public schools. 62% are White; 12% Asian American; 12% Hispanic; 8% two or more races; 3% Foreign; 2% race unknown; 1% African American; 1% American Indian/Alaska Native. 45% are Catholic; 18% claim no religious affiliation. **Female To Male Ratio:** 1.4:1. The average age of freshmen is 19; all undergraduates, 20. 10% do not continue beyond their first year; 79% remain to graduate. **Housing:** 2100 students can be accommodated in college housing, which includes dorms and on-campus apartments. In addition, there are honors houses, language/international houses, special-interest houses, university-owned rental houses, women's dorms, and theme housing. On-campus housing is guaranteed for the freshman year only, and is available on a lottery system for upperclassmen. 57% of students live on campus. Upperclassmen may keep cars.

FACULTY/CLASSROOMS: 56% of faculty are male; 44% are female. All teach undergraduates. No introductory courses are taught by graduate students. The average class size in an introductory lecture is 25; in a laboratory is 20; and in a regular course is 20.

PROGRAMS OF STUDY: University of Portland confers B.A., B.S., B.A.Ed., B.B.A., B.M.Ed., B.S.C.E., B.S.E.E., B.S.E.M., B.S.E.S., B.S.M.E., and B.S.N. degrees. Master's and doctoral degrees are also awarded. Bachelor's degrees are awarded in BIOLOGICAL SCIENCE (biology/biological science), BUSINESS (accounting, banking and finance, entrepreneurial studies, international business management, marketing/retailing/merchandising, and operations management), COMMUNICATIONS AND THE ARTS (communications, dramatic arts, English, music, and Spanish), COMPUTER AND PHYSICAL SCIENCE (chemistry, computer science, mathematics, and physics), EDUCATION (elementary education and secondary education), ENGINEERING AND ENVIRONMENTAL DESIGN (civil engineering, electrical/electronics engineering, engineering, environmental science, and mechanical engineering), HEALTH PROFESSIONS (nursing), SOCIAL SCIENCE (economics, French studies, German area studies, history, interdisciplinary studies, philosophy, political science/government, psychology, social work, sociology, and theological studies). Engineering, nursing, and biology are the strongest academically. Nursing, biology, and mechanical engineering have the largest enrollments.

ACTIVITIES: There are no fraternities or sororities. There are 62 groups on campus, including art, band, cheerleading, choir, chorale, chorus, computers, dance, debate, drama, environmental, ethnic, film, honors, international, jazz band, LGBT, literary magazine, musical theater, newspaper, orchestra, pep band, photography, political, professional, radio station, religious, social, social service, student government, symphony, and yearbook. Popular campus events include Dance of the Decade, International Night, Pilotpalooza and Luau. **Sports:** There are 6 intercollegiate sports for men and 6 for women, and 20 intramural sports for men and 20 for women. Facilities include a cardio machine loft, weight training area, studios for exercise/spin classes, gymnasiums, a rock wall, and a suspended track. Rental equipment is available for biking and camping activities. **Graduates:** From July 1, 2016 to June 30, 2017, 854 bachelor's degrees were awarded. The most popular majors were health professions and related programs (20%), business/marketing (15%), and engineering (14%). In an average class, 75% graduate in 4 years or less, 81% graduate in 5 years or less, and 80% graduate in 6 years or less. Of the 2016 graduating class, 12% were enrolled in graduate school within 6 months of graduation.

SERVICES: Counseling and information services are available, as is tutoring in most subjects, such as English and math. The faculty is also available for individual assistance. **Library/Resources:** The library contains 220,340 volumes, 41,624 microform items, and 15,002 audio/video tapes/CDs/DVDs, and subscribes to 6,830 periodicals including electronic. Computerized library services include interlibrary loans, database searching, Internet access, and Wi-Fi capability. Special learning facilities include an art gallery. **Physically Challenged Students:** All of the campus is accessible. Facilities include wheelchair ramps, elevators, special parking, specially equipped restrooms, special class scheduling, lowered drinking fountains, and lowered telephones. **Special:** UP offers internships through individual departments, cross-registration with members of the Oregon Independent College Association, dual and interdisciplinary majors, including engineering chemistry and organizational communications, work-study programs, and pass/fail options. Study abroad may be arranged in Japan, Mexico, Australia, Chile, and several European countries. There are 9 national honor societies and a freshman honors program. **Visiting:** There are regularly scheduled orientations for prospective students, including a campus tour, class attendance, and a meeting with an admissions counselor. There are guides for informal visits, visitors may sit in on classes, and stay overnight. To schedule a visit, contact the Office of Admissions. **Campus Safety and Security:** Measures include 24-hour foot and vehicle patrol, emergency notification system, self-defense education, and security escort services. There are shuttle buses, emergency telephones, lighted pathways/sidewalks, and controlled access to dorms/residences.

REQUIREMENTS: The SAT or ACT is required, with a minimum score of 550 on each section of the SAT or a composite of 19 on the ACT. Graduation from an accredited secondary school or satisfactory scores on the GED are required. The high school curriculum should include 3-4 units in English composition, 2-3 units in math, 2 each in social studies, science, and history, and 7 in academic electives. 2 essays are required, as is a letter of recommendation from the high school counselor or principal. For new applicants, the ACT with or without writing is accepted. UP requires applicants to be in the upper 50% of their class. AP and CLEP credits are accepted. Important factors in the admissions decision are advanced placement or honors courses, leadership record, recommendations by school officials, parents or siblings attended your school, evidence of special talent, personality/intangible qualities, extracurricular activities record, and geographical diversity. To graduate, students must complete 120 credit hours, including at least 24 upper-division classes in the major, with a minimum GPA of 2.0. Required courses include 9 hours each of philosophy and theology, 6 each of science, social sciences, and electives, and 3 each of fine arts, history, math, and literature. Some majors may require a comprehensive exam and/or thesis. **Procedure:** Freshmen are admitted to all sessions. Entrance exams should be taken preferably before February 1 but no later than June 1 of the senior year. There are deferred admissions and rolling admissions plans. Applications should be filed by February 1 for fall entry. The fall 2017 application fee was $50. Notification is sent on a rolling basis. 3031 applicants were on the 2017 waiting list. Applications are accepted on-line. **Transfer Students:** 81 transfer students enrolled in 2016-2017. Applicants with 26 or more credits must have a minimum GPA of 2.5 and be in good standing at their previous school. Students with fewer credits may need to meet freshman requirements. 30 of 120 credits required for the bachelor's degree must be completed at UP. **International Students:** There are 115 international students enrolled. They must take the TOEFL with a minimum score of 71 on the Internet-based version (iBT).

ADMISSIONS: 62% of the 2017-2018 applicants were accepted. The SAT scores for the 2017-2018 freshman class were: Critical Reading-- 10% below 500, 43% between 500 and 599, 32% between 600 and 699, and 15% between 700 and 800. Math-- 8% below 500, 35% between 500 and 599, 47% between 600 and 699, and 9% between 700 and 800. **Admissions Contact:** Jason McDonald, Dean of Admissions. Email: *admissio@up.edu* Web: *www.up.edu*

FINANCIAL AID: In 2017-2018, 97% of all full-time freshmen received some form of financial aid. 67% of all full-time freshmen received need-based aid. The average freshman award was $29,487. Need-based scholarships or need-based grants averaged $23,025; need-based self-help aid (loans and jobs) averaged $4,382; non-need-based athletic scholarships averaged $23,189; other non-need-based awards and non-need-based scholarships averaged $17,079; and $3,632 from other forms of aid. The average financial indebtedness of the 2017 graduate was $36,221. The FAFSA code is 003224. The priority date for freshman financial aid applications for fall entry is February 1.

WARNER PACIFIC COLLEGE B-1
www.warnerpacific.edu

Portland, OR 97215 (503) 517-1024
(800) 804-1510
Fax: (503) 517-1540 **Email: admissions@warnerpacific.edu**
Full-time: 532 men, 956 women
Part-time: 19 men, 43 women
Graduate: 49 men, 80 women
Year: semesters, summer session
Room & Board: $8900
SAT or ACT: required
Application Deadline: open
Faculty: 34
Ph.D.s: 50%
Student/Faculty: 14 to 1
Tuition: $22,710
Freshman Class: 476 accepted, 299 enrolled
CEEB CODE: 4595
COMPETITIVE

Warner Pacific College, founded in 1937, is a private Christian liberal arts college affiliated with the Church of God. Since tuition cost varies by programs chosen by the student, the above figures in the capsule and in this profile are approximate. There is 1 undergraduate school and 1 graduate school. The 15-acre campus is in an urban area 5 miles east of downtown Portland. Including any residence halls, there are 10 buildings.

STUDENT LIFE: 71% of undergraduates are from Oregon. Others are from 18 states, 3 foreign countries, and Canada. 78% are from public schools. 78% are White; 13% Hispanic; 10% African American; 8% race unknown; 7% Foreign; 4% Asian American; 4% two or more races; 1% American Indian/Alaska Native. 51% claim no religious affiliation; 42% Protestant. **Female To Male Ratio:** 1.8:1. The average age of freshmen is 27; all undergraduates, 31. 25% do not continue beyond their first year; 45% remain to graduate. **Housing:** 288 students can be accommodated in college housing, which includes married student dorms and on-campus apartments. Freshman are given priority consideration for housing. On-campus housing is guaranteed for all 4 years, is available on a first-come, first-served basis, and is available on a lottery system for upperclassmen. 55% of students commute. Alcohol is not permitted. All students may keep cars.

FACULTY/CLASSROOMS: 62% of faculty are male; 38% are female. All teach undergraduates and 40% do research. No introductory courses are taught by graduate students. The average class size in an introductory lecture is 15; in a laboratory is 10; and in a regular course is 15.

PROGRAMS OF STUDY: WPC confers B.A. and B.S degrees. Associate degrees are also awarded. Bachelor's degrees are awarded in BIOLOGICAL SCIENCE (biology/biological science), BUSINESS (business administration and management), COMMUNICATIONS AND THE ARTS (English and music), EDUCATION (music education and physical education), SOCIAL SCIENCE (American studies, history, human development, liberal arts/general studies, ministries, religious music, social science, and sociology). Biological science, and business administration are the strongest academically. Business administration, human development, and education have the largest enrollments.

ACTIVITIES: There are no fraternities or sororities. There are 11 groups on campus, including art, band, Bible study, choir, chorale, chorus, dance, debate, drama, environmental, ethnic, international, jazz band, literary magazine, newspaper, orchestra, professional, religious, social, social service, student government, and yearbook. Popular campus events include Winter Banquet, and Spring Banquet. **Sports:** There are 5 intercollegiate sports for men and 6 for women, and 2 intramural sports for men and 2 for women. Facilities include a gym, basketball, cross country, soccer, outdoor track and field, volley ball, golf, wrestling, and a weight-training room. **Graduates:** From July 1, 2016 to June 30, 2017, 149 bachelor's degrees were awarded. The most popular majors were business (35%), human development (30%), and education (10%). In an average class, 2% graduate in 3 years or less, 29% graduate in 4 years or less, 8% graduate in 5 years or less, and 2% graduate in 6 years or less.

SERVICES: Counseling and information services are available, as is tutoring in most subjects. There is remedial math, reading, and writing. There is also a testing and study skills workshops. **Library/Resources:** The library contains 67,948 volumes, 2,093 microform items, and 2,899 audio/video tapes/CDs/DVDs, and subscribes to 27,038 periodicals including electronic. Computerized library services include interlibrary loans, database searching, and Internet access. **Physically Challenged Students:** 75% of the campus is accessible. Facilities include wheelchair ramps, elevators, special parking, specially equipped restrooms, special class scheduling, lowered drinking fountains, and special housing. **Special:** Warner Pacific offers cross-registration through OICA, a Washington semester, a co-op nursing program, 27 majors, accelerated degree programs in human development and business administration, and study abroad in Latin America, the Middle East, and Russia. Internships, work-study programs, double majors, individualized majors, independent study credit for life and military experience, and pass/fail options are available. **Visiting:** There are regularly scheduled orientations for prospective students, including 2 campus preview days, 2 Knight Life visit weekends, academic fairs, and scholarship days. To schedule a visit, contact the Office of Enrollment. **Campus Safety and Security:** Measures include 24-hour foot and vehicle patrol, emergency notification system, self-defense education, and security escort services. There are emergency telephones, lighted pathways/sidewalks, and controlled access to dorms/residences.

REQUIREMENTS: The SAT or ACT is required. Applicants must be graduates of an accredited secondary school. The GED is accepted. High school preparation should include 4 years of English, 3 of social studies, and 2 each of math and science lab. AP and CLEP credits are accepted. Important factors in the admissions decision are evidence of special talent, leadership record, and advanced placement or honors courses. To graduate, students must complete 124 credits with a minimum GPA of 2.0. All students must take a core curriculum of 42 credits, consisting of 15 hours in humanities, 9 in communication, 7 to 9 in religion, 6 in social science, 4 in fine arts, and 3 each in science and health and phys ed. **Procedure:** Freshmen are admitted to all sessions. Entrance exams should be taken no later than the early fall of the senior year. There is a rolling admissions plan. Application deadlines are open. The fall 2017 application fee was $50. Applications are accepted on-line. **Transfer Students:** 170 transfer students enrolled in 2016-2017. Applicants must provide transcripts from their previous college. A minimum GPA of 2.0 is required. 30 of 124 credits required for the bachelor's degree must be completed at Warner Pacific. **International Students:** There are 12 international students enrolled. They must take the TOEFL and the college's own test.

ADMISSIONS: The SAT scores for the 2017-2018 freshman class were: Critical Reading-- 65% below 500, 26% between 500 and 599, and 9% between 600 and 699. Math-- 64% below 500, 31% between 500 and 599, 4% between 600 and 699, and 1% between 700 and 800. Writing-- 53% below 500, 44% between 500 and 599, and 3% between 600 and 699. **Admissions Contact:** Shannon Mackey, Executive Director of Enrollment Management. Email: *admissions@warnerpacific.edu* Web: *www.warnerpacific.edu*

FINANCIAL AID: In 2017-2018, 93% of all full-time freshmen received some form of financial aid. 89% of all full-time freshmen received need-based aid. The average freshman award was $16,182. Need-based scholarships or need-based grants averaged $6,461; and need-based self-help aid (loans and jobs) averaged $5,274. WPC is a member of CSS. The FAFSA code is 003225. The priority date for freshman financial aid applications for fall entry is March 1.

WESTERN OREGON UNIVERSITY *(The complete profile is made available exclusively on our website, www.barronspac.com)*

WILLAMETTE UNIVERSITY B-2
www.willamette.edu

Salem, OR 97301 (503) 370-6928
(503) 370-6300
Fax: (503) 375-5363 **Email: bearcat@willamette.edu**
Full-time: 737 men, 1015 women
Part-time: 11 men, 9 women
Graduate: 278 men, 272 women
Year: semesters
Room & Board: $12,440
SAT CR/M/W: 624/597/572 **ACT:** 26
Application Deadline: January 15
Faculty: 214; IIB
Ph.D.s: 94%
Student/Faculty: 10 to 1
Tuition: $50,074
Freshman Class: 6181 applied, 4825 accepted, 474 enrolled
CEEB CODE: 4954
VERY COMPETITIVE+

Willamette University, founded in 1842, is an independent liberal arts institution affiliated with the Methodist Church. There is 1 undergraduate school and 2 graduate schools. In addition to regional accreditation,

Willamette has baccalaureate program accreditation with NASM. The 72-acre campus is in an urban area 50 minutes south of Portland. Including any residence halls, there are 45 buildings.

STUDENT LIFE: 77% of undergraduates are from out of state, mostly the West. Students are from 45 states, 20 foreign countries, and Canada. 69% are from public schools. 62% are White; 13% Hispanic; 9% Asian American; 9% two or more races; 3% race unknown; 2% African American; 1% American Indian/Alaska Native; 1% Foreign. 50% claim no religious affiliation; 27% Protestant; 12% Catholic. **Female To Male Ratio:** 1.3:1. The average age of freshmen is 18; all undergraduates, 20. 14% do not continue beyond their first year; 77% remain to graduate. **Housing:** 1493 students can be accommodated in college housing, which includes dorms and on-campus apartments. In addition, there are special-interest houses, fraternity houses, sorority houses, 24-hour quiet-hour dorm (intensive study), substance-free options, and apartments for single students. On-campus housing is guaranteed for the freshman year only and is available on a lottery system for upperclassmen. 64% of students live on campus. All students may keep cars.

FACULTY/CLASSROOMS: All teach undergraduates and do research. No introductory courses are taught by graduate students. The average class size in an introductory lecture is 30; in a laboratory is 14; and in a regular course is 16.

PROGRAMS OF STUDY: Willamette confers B.A. and B.M. degrees. Master's and doctoral degrees are also awarded. Bachelor's degrees are awarded in BIOLOGICAL SCIENCE (biology/biological science), COMMUNICATIONS AND THE ARTS (art history and appreciation, comparative literature, dramatic arts, English, French, German, music, music performance, music theory and composition, Spanish, speech/debate/rhetoric, and studio art), COMPUTER AND PHYSICAL SCIENCE (chemistry, computer science, mathematics, physics, and science), EDUCATION (music education), ENGINEERING AND ENVIRONMENTAL DESIGN (environmental science), HEALTH PROFESSIONS (exercise science), SOCIAL SCIENCE (American studies, anthropology, Asian/Oriental studies, classical/ancient civilization, economics, history, humanities, international studies, Japanese studies, Latin American studies, philosophy, political science/government, psychology, religion, sociology, and women's studies). Politics, biology, and economics have the largest enrollments.

ACTIVITIES: 18% of men belong to 5 national fraternities; 12% of women belong to 3 national sororities. There are 105 groups on campus, including art, band, cheerleading, choir, chorale, chorus, computers, dance, debate, drama, ethnic, film, forensics, honors, international, jazz band, LGBT, literary magazine, musical theater, newspaper, orchestra, pep band, photography, political, professional, religious, social, social service, student government, symphony, and yearbook. Popular campus events include Lu'au, Black Tie Affair, and Wulapalooza. **Sports:** There are 10 intercollegiate sports for men and 10 for women, and 10 intramural sports for men and 10 for women. Facilities include a phys ed and recreation center, a football stadium, indoor gym, an auditorium, a baseball stadium, soccer field, an all-weather track, indoor and outdoor swimming pool, and indoor and outdoor tennis courts, handball/racquetball courts, and weight training facilities. **Graduates:** From July 1, 2016 to June 30, 2017, 389 bachelor's degrees were awarded. The most popular majors were social sciences (24%), biological/life sciences (9%), physical sciences, pyschology, and and visual and performing arts (7%). In an average class, 67% graduate in 4 years or less, 74% graduate in 5 years or less, and 78% graduate in 6 years or less. Of the 2016 graduating class, 20% were enrolled in graduate school within 6 months of graduation, and 70% were employed.

SERVICES: Counseling and information services are available, as is tutoring in most subjects. There is a reader service for the blind. There are also therapists for students on an individual need basis, including braille services and readers. **Library/Resources:** The library contains 403,135 volumes, 290,140 microform items, and 13,425 audio/video tapes/CDs/DVDs, and subscribes to 26,430 periodicals including electronic. Computerized library services include interlibrary loans, database searching, and Internet access. Special learning facilities include an art gallery, natural history museum, Botanical and Japanese gardens, a multimedia center, and "smart" classrooms. **Physically Challenged Students:** 90% of the campus is accessible. Facilities include wheelchair ramps, elevators, special parking, specially equipped restrooms, special class scheduling, lowered drinking fountains, and lowered telephones. **Special:** Willamette offers internships with the state and city governments, a Chicago semester, a Washington semester, and a 3-2 engineering degree with Washington University, University of Southern California, and Columbia University. Nondegree study, B.A.-B.S. degrees, dual majors, work-study programs with numerous employers in the Salem area and at the university, and credit/no-credit options are also available. Study abroad programs are available in 14 countries. There are 3-2 degrees in management, forestry, and computer science. There are 7 national honor societies and a chapter of Phi Beta Kappa. **Visiting:** There are regularly scheduled orientations for prospective students, consisting of fall and spring campus preview days, tours, and faculty and student presentations. There are guides for informal visits, visitors may sit in on classes, and stay overnight. To schedule a visit, contact Associate Director of Admissions. **Campus Safety and Security:** Measures include 24-hour foot and vehicle patrol, emergency notification system, self-defense education, and security escort services. There are emergency telephones, lighted pathways/sidewalks, formal programs and education, and a weekly published campus safety report.

REQUIREMENTS: The SAT or ACT and ACT Writing Test are recommended. Graduation from an accredited secondary school or satisfactory scores on the GED are required. Institutional preferences recommend 4 units each in English, math, science, foreign language, social studies, academic electives, and visual/performing arts. 2 essays are required and an interview is recommended. Portfolios or auditions are recommended for art and music students. AP credits are accepted. Important factors in the admissions decision are advanced placement or honors courses and recommendations by school officials. To graduate, students must complete a total of 124 semester hours, including a minimum of 32 in the major, with a minimum GPA of 2.0. All students must complete general education requirements in fine arts, humanities, literature, foreign language, interdisciplinary courses, natural sciences, and social sciences, and meet math and English proficiency levels. Freshmen are required to take a World Views seminar. Seniors are required to complete a senior thesis or other project in their major. **Procedure:** Freshmen are admitted in the fall and spring. Entrance exams should be taken December 1. There are early decision, early admissions, and deferred admissions plans. Early decision applications should be filed by November 15; regular applications, by January 15 for fall entry. The fall 2017 application fee was $50. Notification of early decision is sent December 30; regular decision, October 1. 17 early decision candidates were accepted for the 2017-2018 class. 27 applicants were on the 2017 waiting list; 3 were admitted. Applications are accepted on-line. **Transfer Students:** 28 transfer students enrolled in 2016-2017. Transfer students must submit transcripts for all college and high school courses. A Transfer Reference (recommendation form) and essay are required. SAT/ACT required for applicants with less than 2 years transferable course work. Students may enroll in the fall, February 1, and spring, November 1. 60 of 124 credits required for the bachelor's degree must be completed at Willamette. **International Students:** There are 18 international students enrolled. They must take the TOEFL with a minimum score of 560 on the paper-based TOEFL (PBT) or 83 on the Internet-based version (iBT), also take the ELPT (English Language Placement Test). They must also take the SAT or ACT.

ADMISSIONS: 78% of the 2017-2018 applicants were accepted. The SAT scores for the 2017-2018 freshman class were: Critical Reading-- 5% below 500, 29% between 500 and 599, 50% between 600 and 699, and 16% between 700 and 800. Math-- 8% below 500, 41% between 500 and 599, 44% between 600 and 699, and 7% between 700 and 800. The ACT scores were 14% between 18 and 23, 59% between 24 and 29, and 28% above 30. 16 freshmen graduated first in their class. **Admissions Contact:** Jeremy Bogan, Vice President and Dean. Email: *bearcat@willamette.edu* Web: *www.willamette.edu*

FINANCIAL AID: In 2017-2018, 100% of all full-time freshmen received some form of financial aid. 98% of all full-time freshmen received need-based aid. The average freshman award was $35,088. Need-based scholarships or need-based grants averaged $30,353; need-based self-help aid (loans and jobs) averaged $5,548; other non-need-based awards and non-need-based scholarships averaged $3,420; and $22,792 from other forms of aid. The average financial indebtedness of the 2017 graduate was $32,117. Willamette is a member of CSS. The FAFSA code is 003227. The priority date for freshman financial aid applications for fall entry is February 1.

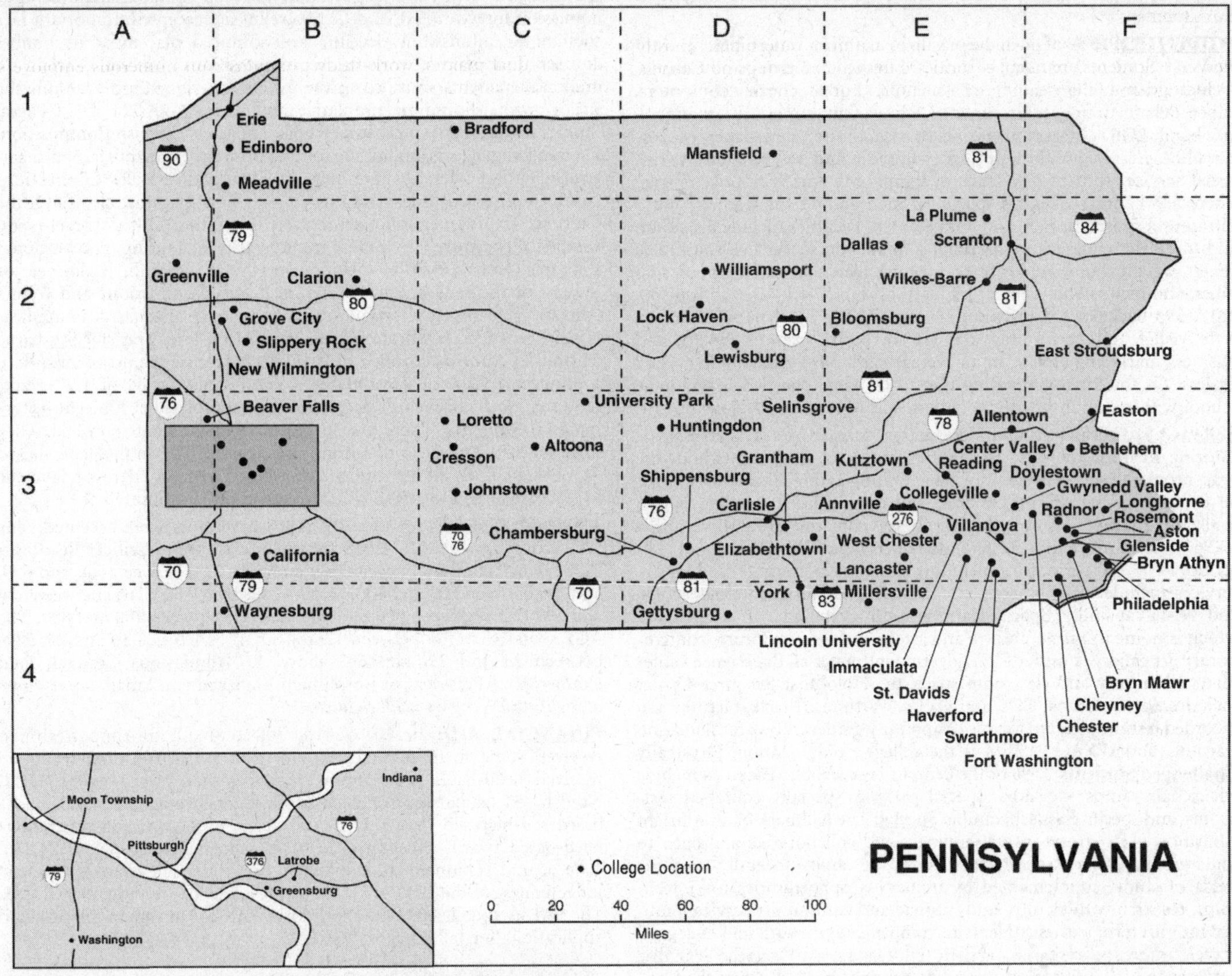

ALBRIGHT COLLEGE E-3

www.albright.edu

Reading, PA 19612 (610) 921-7260
(800) 252-1856

Fax: (610) 921-7294
Email: admission@albright.edu
Full-time: 808 men, 1185 women
Part-time: 12 men, 10 women
Graduate: 4 men, 17 women
Year: 4-1-4, summer session
Room & Board: $12,070
Faculty: 113; IIB
Ph.D.s: 61%
Student/Faculty: 14 to 1
Tuition: $45,256
Freshman Class: 8332 applied, 4169 accepted, 464 enrolled
SAT CR/M: 529/525 **ACT:** 22
CEEB CODE: 2004
Application Deadline: open
COMPETITIVE

Albright College, founded in 1856, educates creative, curious students to become adaptable, global citizens who discover and reach their full potential. The college's flexible interdisciplinary curriculum encourages students to combine majors and disciplines to create individualized academic programs. Close faculty mentorship, numerous experiential learning options, and a diverse, supportive and nurturing community of scholars and learners help students exceed their own expectations and graduate with a commitment to a lifetime of service and learning. There are 2 undergraduate schools and 1 graduate school. In addition to regional accreditation, AC has baccalaureate program accreditation with CPTA. The 118-acre campus is in a suburban area 55 miles west of Philadelphia. Including any residence halls, there are 47 buildings.

STUDENT LIFE: 60% of undergraduates are from Pennsylvania. Others are from 27 states, and 14 foreign countries. 84% are from public schools. 51% are White; 21% African American; 12% Hispanic; 3% Asian American; 2% Foreign; 2% two or more races; 8% race unknown; 1% American Indian/Alaska Native. **Female To Male Ratio:** 1.4:1. The average age of freshmen is 18; all undergraduates, 20. 31% do not continue beyond their first year; 54% remain to graduate. **Housing:** 1527 students can be accommodated in college housing, which includes gender neutral, single sex, coed, on-campus apartments, and off-campus apartments. In addition, there are honors houses, special-interest houses, and affinity housing. On-campus housing is guaranteed for all 4 years. 67% of students live on campus. All students may keep cars.

FACULTY/CLASSROOMS: 47% of faculty are male; 52% are female. All teach undergraduates. No introductory courses are taught by graduate students. The average class size in an introductory lecture is 25; in a laboratory is 15; and in a regular course is 18.

PROGRAMS OF STUDY: AC confers B.A. and B.S. degrees. Master's degrees are also awarded. Bachelor's degrees are awarded in BIOLOGICAL SCIENCE (biochemistry and biology/biological science), BUSINESS (accounting, business administration and management, and fashion merchandising), COMMUNICATIONS AND THE ARTS (art, communications, digital communications, dramatic arts, English, French, music business management, and Spanish), COMPUTER AND PHYSICAL SCIENCE (chemistry, computer science, information sciences and systems, mathematics, and physics), EDUCATION (elementary education, secondary education, and special education), ENGINEERING AND ENVIRONMENTAL DESIGN (environmental science), SOCIAL SCIENCE (American studies, child care/child and family studies, criminal justice, economics, history, Latin American studies, philosophy, political science/government, psychobiology, psychology, religion, sociology, textiles and clothing, and women's studies). Visual & performing arts, business, and social sciences have the largest enrollments.

ACTIVITIES: 16% of men belong to 4 national fraternities; 21% of women belong to 3 national sororities. There are 72 groups on campus, including band, cheerleading, chess, choir, chorale, chorus, computers, dance, debate, drama, environmental, ethnic, film, honors, international, jazz band, LGBT, literary magazine, musical theater, newspaper, orchestra, photography, political, professional, radio and TV, religious, social, social service, student government, symphony, and yearbook. **Sports:** There are 11 intercollegiate sports for men and 12 for women, and 5 intramural sports for men and 3 for women. Facilities include a stadium and turf field, gymnasium, baseball, softball, and soccer fields, a fitness center, weight room, indoor track, bowling alley, a swimming pool, spin bikes, and racquetball courts. **Graduates:** From July 1, 2016 to June 30, 2017, 395 bachelor's degrees were awarded. The most popular majors were visual and performing arts (18%), social sciences (16%), and business/marketing (16%). In an average class, 54% graduate in 6 years or less. Of the 2016 graduating class, 18% were enrolled in graduate school within 6 months of graduation, and 61% were employed.

SERVICES: Counseling and information services are available, as is tutoring in most subjects. The writing center is open throughout the year, providing one-on-one tutoring in writing and reading strategies for all courses. In-person, online chat, and e-mail based tutoring is also available. **Library/Resources:** The library contains 210,904 volumes, 13,967 microform items, 5,730 audio/video tapes/CDs/DVDs, and subscribes to 37,520 periodicals including electronic. Computerized library services include interlibrary loans, database searching, Internet access, and Wi-Fi capability. Special learning facilities include: an Arts Center which is home to music, theatre and art, an outdoor sculpture, contemporary art gallery, a center local government material, the science center offers laboratory and classroom space, the Holocaust Resource Center includes books, videos, CDs, and DVDs, wartime artifacts, pictures and recorded testimonies, an organic community garden allows for hands-on learning, and WXAC 91.3FM is the college's radio station. **Physically Challenged Students:** 75% of the campus is accessible. Facilities include wheelchair ramps, elevators, special parking, specially equipped restrooms, and special class scheduling. **Special:** The hallmark of an Albright education is its strong interdisciplinary and collaborative approach to undergraduate learning, which includes the ability to easily combine fields of study, supplemented by numerous opportunities for internships, research with faculty, study abroad and community service. January Interim term allows students to complete coursework and engage in travel, intensive research, artistic endeavors, and service learning between the fall and spring semesters. Albright has a distinguished history of leadership in undergraduate science education, premedical study, and preparation for careers in health services, and has been recognized as one of the 25 best colleges in the nation for artistic students. The college has also been named one of the nation's top private fashion merchandising schools. For those unsure of what to major in, Albright's Alpha program helps students explore career fields through academic guidance, peer support, special events and career counseling. AC also offers accelerated programs for adult learners and a graduate program in education through its School of Professional Studies. There are 11 national honor societies and a freshman honors program. **Visiting:** There are regularly scheduled orientations for prospective students, including an interview with a counselor and a tour of the campus with a currently enrolled student. There are guides for informal visits, visitors may sit in on classes, and stay overnight. To schedule a visit, contact the Admissions Office. **Campus Safety and Security:** Measures include 24-hour foot and vehicle patrol, emergency notification system, self-defense education, and security escort services. There are shuttle buses, emergency telephones, lighted pathways/sidewalks, controlled access to dorms/residences, bicycle patrol, and several college officers who are sworn in as police officers. All officers are CPR/First Aid, and AED certified. There is also a monitoring system with numerous cameras in the campus area, operations manual in place for response to common incidents, and a comprehensive action plan. Officers who investigate incidents of sexual misconduct, domestic violence, dating violence and stalking are certified as investigators as required by the VAWA act.

REQUIREMENTS: Graduation from an accredited secondary school or satisfactory scores on the GED are required for admission. Students must have a total of 16 Carnegie units, including 4 years of English, 3 each in math and science (with 1 lab), 2 years each of foreign language and social studies, and 1 year each of history and visual/performing arts. An essay is required, an interview is recommended, and submission of test scores is optional. Students applying test optional must complete an on-campus admission interview. AP and CLEP credits are accepted. Important factors in the admissions decision are advanced placement or honors courses, leadership record, and recommendations by school officials. To graduate, students must complete 32 courses, including 13-14 in the major, with minimum cumulative and major GPAs of 2.0. General Studies requirements include a First Year Seminar, English Composition, Foreign Language, Foundations courses from the Humanities, Social Sciences, Natural Sciences, Fine Arts and Quantitative Skills, Connections courses and a capstone Synthesis course. Students must also fulfill the Cultural Experience requirement by attending cultural events on campus. **Procedure:** Freshmen are admitted fall, spring, and summer. Entrance exams should be taken during the spring of the junior year or the fall of the senior year. There are deferred admissions and rolling admissions plans. Application deadlines are open. The fall 2017 application fee was $35. Applications are accepted on-line. **Transfer Students:** 34 transfer students enrolled in 2016-2017. Transfer students must have a minimum GPA of 2.5 and be in good standing. 64 of 128 credits required for the bachelor's degree must be completed at Albright. **International Students:** There are 36 international students enrolled. They must take the TOEFL with a minimum score of 520 on the paper-based TOEFL (PBT) or 68 on the Internet-based version (iBT) or take the MELAB. The SAT or ACT will be considered if submitted.

ADMISSIONS: 50% of the 2017-2018 applicants were accepted. The SAT scores for the 2017-2018 freshman class were: Critical Reading-- 22% below 500, 54% between 500 and 599, 23% between 600 and 699, and 1% between 700 and 800. Math-- 24% below 500, 56% between 500 and 599, 17% between 600 and 699, and 1% between 700 and 800. The ACT scores were 9% between 12 and 17, 47% between 18 and 23, 38% between 24 and 29, and 6% above 30. **Admissions Contact:** Paul Cramer, Vice President of Enrollment Management. Email: *admission@albright.edu* Web: *www.albright.edu*

FINANCIAL AID: In 2017-2018, 100% of all full-time freshmen received some form of financial aid. 91% of all full-time freshmen received need-based aid. The average freshman award was $36,013. Need-based scholarships or need-based grants averaged $36,013; need-based self-help aid (loans and jobs) averaged $6,178; and other non-need-based awards and non-need-based scholarships averaged $24,885. 40% of undergraduate students work part-time. The average financial indebtedness of the 2017 graduate was $38,599. AC is a member of CSS. The FAFSA code is 003229. The priority date for freshman financial aid applications for fall entry is March 1.

ALLEGHENY COLLEGE — B-1

www.allegheny.edu

Meadville, PA 16335	**(814) 332-4351** **(800) 521-5293**
Fax: (814) 337-0431	**Email: admissions@allegheny.edu**
Full-time: 801 men, 951 women	**Faculty:** 167; IIB, +$
Part-time: 19 men, 31 women	**Ph.D.s:** 92%
Graduate: n/av	**Student/Faculty:** 11 to 1
Year: semesters	**Tuition:** $45,970
Room & Board: $11,650	**Freshman Class:** 5114 applied, 3472 accepted, 481 enrolled
SAT EBR-W/M: 625/605 **ACT:** 26	**CEEB CODE:** 2006
Application Deadline: February 15	**VERY COMPETITIVE**

Allegheny College is the premier college for students with "Unusual Combinations" of interests, skills, and talents. It is one of the nation's oldest and most innovative liberal arts institutions. For more than 200 years, Allegheny has prepared graduates for extraordinary outcomes through its academic rigor and commitment to experiential learning, including undergraduate research. The 566-acre campus is in a suburban area 90 miles north of Pittsburgh, 35 miles south of Erie. Including any residence halls, there are 41 buildings.

STUDENT LIFE: 52% of undergraduates are from out of state, mostly the Middle Atlantic. Students are from 47 states, 50 foreign countries, and Canada. 86% are from public schools. 9% are African American; 9% Hispanic; 70% White; 4% two or more races; 3% Asian American; 3% Foreign; 2% race unknown. 44% claim no religious affiliation; 23%

Catholic; 19% Protestant; 11% Buddhist, Hindu, Muslim and other Christian. **Female To Male Ratio:** 1.2:1. The average age of freshmen is 19; all undergraduates, 20. 19% do not continue beyond their first year; 81% remain to graduate. **Housing:** 1860 students can be accommodated in college housing, which includes single sex, coed dorms, and on-campus apartments. In addition, there are language/international houses, special-interest houses, fraternity houses, a wellness community, quiet study floors, townhouses, ADA accessible, gender inclusive, and living and learning residential communities. On-campus housing is guaranteed for all 4 years and is available on a lottery system for upperclassmen. 94% of students live on campus. All students may keep cars.

FACULTY/CLASSROOMS: 50% of faculty are male; 50% are female. All teach undergraduates, and 81% do research and teach. No introductory courses are taught by graduate students. The average class size in an introductory lecture is 17; in a laboratory is 17; and in a regular course is 15.

PROGRAMS OF STUDY: Allegheny confers B.A. and B.S. degrees. Bachelor's degrees are awarded in AGRICULTURE (environmental studies), BIOLOGICAL SCIENCE (biochemistry, biology/biological science, and neurosciences), COMMUNICATIONS AND THE ARTS (art, art history and appreciation, communications, dramatic arts, English, French, German, music, Spanish, and studio art), COMPUTER AND PHYSICAL SCIENCE (chemistry, computer science, environmental geology, geology, mathematics, physics, and software engineering), ENGINEERING AND ENVIRONMENTAL DESIGN (environmental science), HEALTH PROFESSIONS (public health), SOCIAL SCIENCE (economics, history, international studies, justice and society, philosophy, political science/government, psychology, religion, and women & gender studies). Physical & biological sciences, economics, environmental science, international studies, psychology are the strongest academically. Biology, economics, and psychology have the largest enrollments.

ACTIVITIES: 26% of men belong to 6 national fraternities; 24% of women belong to 5 national sororities. There are 134 groups on campus, including art, band, cheerleading, chess, choir, chorale, chorus, computers, dance, debate, drama, environmental, ethnic, honors, international, jazz band, LGBT, literary magazine, musical theater, newspaper, opera, orchestra, political, professional, radio and TV, religious, social, social service, student government, symphony, and yearbook. Popular campus events include Homecoming, Orchesis Dance Performance, Make A Difference Day, Springfest, Black Heritage Month, Wingfest, Relay For Life, Coming Out Week, Athletic Talent Show, Hispanic Heritage Month, and International Dinner. **Sports:** There are 10 intercollegiate sports for men and 11 for women, and 3 intramural sports for men and 3 for women. Facilities include a comprehensive sports and fitness center that includes a training track, natatorium, weight rooms, cardio machines, multipurpose indoor courts for volleyball, basketball, tennis, badminton, putting green and batting cage, dance studio, and racquetball courts. Outdoor sports complex has a lighted stadium, a FieldTurf playing surface, cross-country course, lighted tennis courts, baseball, softball, soccer, rugby grass fields, field for shot put, discus and hammer throw and a 400 meter double bend 8-lane competition track. **Graduates:** From July 1, 2016 to June 30, 2017, 465 bachelor's degrees were awarded. The most popular majors were biology (12%), economics (11%), and psychology (8%). In an average class, 67% graduate in 4 years or less, 74% graduate in 5 years or less, and 75% graduate in 6 years or less. Of the 2016 graduating class, 31% were enrolled in graduate school within 6 months of graduation, and 42% were employed.

SERVICES: Counseling and information services are available, as is tutoring in some subjects, such as biology, chemistry, economics, geology, mathematics, modern languages, physics, psychology. Other support services available for students include study strategies, test taking strategies, time management, speaking consultations, writing consultations, academic advising, note-taking scribe services, recorders, audio books, peer mentoring, and non-department specific-study skills, reading, speaking, and writing. **Library/Resources:** The library contains 855,874 volumes, 133,500 microform items, and 147,273 audio/video tapes/CDs/DVDs, and subscribes to 56,578 periodicals including electronic. Computerized library services include interlibrary loans, database searching, Internet access, and Wi-Fi capability. Special learning facilities include an art gallery, planetarium, radio station, TV station, an observatory, 283-acre experimental research reserve, 17-acre sustainable forest, 80-acre protected forest, geographic information systems learning laboratory, language learning center, science complex and greenhouse, seismographic network station, center for political participation, theater and communication arts center, environmental roof garden, center for environmental science, sustainable luminescent solar concentrator roof greenhouse, neuroscience and psychology research facility, center for business and economics, Creek Connections, and an augmented reality sandbox. **Physically Challenged Students:** 50% of the campus is accessible. Facilities include wheelchair ramps, elevators, special parking, specially equipped restrooms, special class scheduling, and lowered drinking fountains. Reasonable accommodations are made for special needs. **Special:** Allegheny offers domestic off campus semesters in 7 programs such as New York Arts, Oak Ridge Science Center, Philadelphia Center, Washington semester, Duke Marine Lab NC, Ecosystems Center MA, Newberry Seminar Research in the Humanities IL. Internships, double majors, independent study, student-designed majors, study abroad in 16 countries, and a work study program. A 3-2 engineering degree is available with Case Western Reserve, Columbia, Duke, University of Pittsburgh, and Washington University. Accelerated masters in public policy & management, occupational therapy, and physician assistant. Accelerated doctorates in nursing, medicine, pharmacy, and dental. Preprofessional programs, graduate school partnerships, and an experiential learning term are also available. There are 14 national honor societies, Phi Beta Kappa, a freshman honors program, and 12 departmental honors programs. **Visiting:** There are regularly scheduled orientations for prospective students, consisting of tours, panels, presentations on academic programs, student life, admissions, and financial aid. There are guides for informal visits, visitors may sit in on classes, and stay overnight. To schedule a visit, contact the Office of Admissions. **Campus Safety and Security:** Measures include 24-hour foot and vehicle patrol, emergency notification system, and security escort services. There are shuttle buses, emergency telephones, lighted pathways/sidewalks, controlled access to dorms/residences, property engraving, on-campus sworn police officers, CCTV cameras, and 1st aid/CPR/A.E.D certified officers.

REQUIREMENTS: The SAT or ACT is optional but will be considered if submitted. Graduation from an accredited secondary school is required for admission. The GED is accepted. Students must have 16 Carnegie units, including 4 years of English, 3 years each of math, science, and social studies, and 2 years of a foreign language. An essay is required, and an interview is recommended. A college prep program and 2 letters of recommendation (1 from guidance counselor, 1 from teacher) are required. AP and CLEP credits are accepted. Important factors in the admissions decision are advanced placement or honors courses, extracurricular activities record, and leadership record. To graduate, students must complete 128 credit hours with a minimum GPA of 2.0 in both the major and a minor. Between 40 and 64 hours are required in the major, including the junior seminar and senior research thesis. The major and minor must be from different division or interdivisional areas of study. All students must fulfill liberal arts studies requirements of 4 credit hours in each of 8 specified areas of inquiry. Additional required courses include first-year first seminar, first-year second seminar, a sophomore writing and speaking seminar. All graduating seniors complete an independent research thesis and an oral defense of the thesis. **Procedure:** Freshmen are admitted in the fall and spring. Entrance exams should be taken by January of the senior year. There are early decision, early admissions, and deferred admissions plans. Early decision applications should be filed by February 1; regular applications, by February 15 for fall entry; and November 1 for spring entry. Notification of early decision is sent February 15; regular decision, March 15. 82 early decision candidates were accepted for the 2017-2018 class. 223 applicants were on the 2017 waiting list; 14 were admitted. Applications are accepted on-line. **Transfer Students:** 15 transfer students enrolled in 2016-2017. Transfer applicants must submit a transcript of all college courses, a high school transcript, college official's report from prior institutions, essay/personal statement, a letter describing reasons for transfer, and one recommendation from college official. A minimum GPA of 2.5 from college and high school is required, with 3.0 from college recommended. An interview is also recommended. 64 of 128 credits required for the bachelor's degree must be completed at Allegheny. **International Students:** There are 128 international students enrolled. SAT or ACT can be submitted in place of TOEFL if applicant is native English speaking.

ADMISSIONS: 68% of the 2017-2018 applicants were accepted. The SAT scores for the 2017-2018 freshman class were: Math-- 5% below 500, 38% between 500 and 599, 51% between 600 and 699, and 6% between 700 and 800. Evidence-Based Reading/Writing-- 5% below 500, 27% between 500 and 599, 53% between 600 and 699, and 15% between 700 and 800. The ACT scores were 4% between 12 and 17, 25% between 18 and 23, 50% between 24 and 29, and 21% above 30. 56% of the current freshmen were in the top fifth of their class; 80% were in the top two fifths. 14 freshmen graduated first in their class. **Admissions Contact:** Cornell B. LeSane, II, V.P. of Enrollment & Dean of Admissions. Email: *admissions@allegheny.edu* Web: *www.allegheny.edu/admissions*

FINANCIAL AID: In 2017-2018, 100% of all full-time freshmen received some form of financial aid. 81% of all full-time freshmen received need-based aid. The average freshman award was $41,975. Need-based scholarships or need-based grants averaged $36,480 ($57,620 maximum); need-based self-help aid (loans and jobs) averaged $5,464 ($10,000 maximum); other non-need-based awards and non-need-based scholarships averaged $25,905 ($42,000 maximum); and $41,592 from other forms of aid. 82% of undergraduate students work part-time. The FAFSA code is 003230. The priority date for freshman financial aid applications for fall entry is February 15.

ALVERNIA UNIVERSITY E-3
www.alvernia.edu

Reading, PA 19607 **(610) 796-3005**

Fax: (610) 796-8336
Email: admissions@alvernia.edu
Full-time: 502 men, 1168 women
Part-time: 110 men, 471 women
Graduate: 189 men, 398 women
Year: semesters, summer session
Room & Board: $11,690
Faculty: IIB, -$
Ph.D.s: 70%
Student/Faculty: 13 to 1
Tuition: $33,640
Freshman Class: 2179 applied, 1543 accepted, 371 enrolled
SAT EBR-W/M: 530/520 **ACT:** 21
Application Deadline: October 1
CEEB CODE: 2431
COMPETITIVE

Alvernia University is a thriving small university that combines all of the best features of a small college with the range of opportunities typically found only at large universities. Alvernia empowers students through real world learning to discover their passion for life while providing the training and education to turn what they love into lifetimes of career success and personal fulfillment. Our students follow their hearts into productive careers and vibrant lives where they help make the world a better place. There are 3 undergraduate schools and 1 graduate school. In addition to regional accreditation, Alvernia has baccalaureate program accreditation with ACBSP, CSWE, ACOTE, CCNE, and CAPTE. The 121-acre campus is in a suburban area 3 miles southwest of Reading. Including any residence halls, there are 22 buildings.

STUDENT LIFE: 75% of undergraduates are from Pennsylvania. Others are from 23 states, and 10 foreign countries. 9% are Hispanic; 66% White; 2% Asian American; 2% two or more races; 11% race unknown; 10% African American. **Female To Male Ratio:** 2.5:1. The average age of freshmen is 18; all undergraduates, 25. 53% remain to graduate. **Housing:** 1019 students can be accommodated in college housing, which includes dorms, on-campus apartments, honors houses, theme, and townhouses. On-campus housing is guaranteed for the freshman year only, and is available on a first-come, first-served basis. 62% of students live on campus. All students may keep cars.

FACULTY/CLASSROOMS: 46% of faculty are male; 54% are female. No introductory courses are taught by graduate students. The average class size in an introductory lecture is 20; in a laboratory is 23; and in a regular course is 18.

PROGRAMS OF STUDY: Alvernia confers B.A., B.S., B.S.N., and B.S.W. degrees. Associate, master's, and doctoral degrees are also awarded. Bachelor's degrees are awarded in BIOLOGICAL SCIENCE (biochemistry, biology/biological science, environmental biology, and forensic science), BUSINESS (accounting, business administration and management, finance, human resources, marketing and distribution, and sports management), COMMUNICATIONS AND THE ARTS (communications, English, and theatre arts), COMPUTER AND PHYSICAL SCIENCE (chemistry, mathematics, and science), EDUCATION (athletic training, elementary education, pre K-4 education, middle school education, secondary education, and special education/early child dual program), ENGINEERING AND ENVIRONMENTAL DESIGN (biomedical equipment technology), HEALTH PROFESSIONS (health care administration, health science, and nursing), SOCIAL SCIENCE (behavioral science, criminal justice, history, liberal arts/general studies, philosophy, political science/government, psychology, social work, and theological studies). Occupational therapy, nursing, and business have the largest enrollments.

ACTIVITIES: There are no fraternities or sororities. There are 36 groups on campus, including art, cheerleading, chorus, computers, dance, drama, environmental, ethnic, honors, international, literary magazine, musical theater, newspaper, political, professional, religious, social, social service, and student government. Popular campus events include Christmas on Campus, Spring Fling, and Club Fair. **Sports:** There are 11 intercollegiate sports for men and 12 for women, and 5 intramural sports for men and 5 for women. Facilities include a gym, physical fitness and recreation center, playing fields, outdoor tennis, basketball, and volleyball courts. **Graduates:** From July 1, 2016 to June 30, 2017, 487 bachelor's degrees were awarded. The most popular majors were health professions and related programs (44%), business/marketing (16%), and homeland security (10%).

SERVICES: Counseling and information services are available, as is tutoring in every subject. There is remedial math, reading, and writing. There is also a writing center and a math/science tutorial lab. **Library/Resources:** The library contains 91,653 volumes, and 3,211 audio/video tapes/CDs/DVDs, and subscribes to 64,154 periodicals including electronic. Computerized library services include interlibrary loans, database searching, Internet access, and Wi-Fi capability. Special learning facilities include an art gallery. **Physically Challenged Students:** 95% of the campus is accessible. Facilities include wheelchair ramps, elevators, special parking, specially equipped restrooms, special class scheduling, lowered drinking fountains, lowered telephones, and special housing. **Special:** The university offers co-op programs in business and sports management, internships, cross-registration with Kutztown University, Pennsylvania State University, Albright College, and Reading area community colleges, a Washington semester, dual and student-designed majors, and practicums in psychology, criminal justice, education, addiction studies, social work, athletic training, and occupational therapy. There are 14 national honor societies, a freshman honors program, and 10 departmental honors programs. **Visiting:** There are regularly scheduled orientations for prospective students, including faculty displays, lunch, tours of the campus, and the opportunity to interact with current students. There are guides for informal visits, visitors may sit in on classes, and stay overnight. To schedule a visit, contact the Admissions Office. **Campus Safety and Security:** Measures include 24-hour foot and vehicle patrol, emergency notification system, and security escort services. There are shuttle buses, emergency telephones, lighted pathways/sidewalks, controlled access to dorms/residences, and photo ID cards which must be carried by students.

REQUIREMENTS: The SAT or ACT is required. All applicants must be graduates of an accredited secondary school or have a GED certificate. They should have completed at least 16 academic units, including 4 each in English and math, 3 in social studies, 2 in science and foreign language, and 1 in academic electives. An interview is required for nursing applicants and strongly recommended for all others. AP and CLEP credits are accepted. To graduate, all students must complete at least 123 credit hours with a minimum GPA of 2.0 overall and in the major (2.5 for elementary education and nursing majors). Requirements include 54 to 55 credits in a liberal arts core, consisting of theology and philosophy, social science, communications, literature, fine arts, math, and science. All students also must perform 40 clock hours of service to others before graduation, complete coursework in college success skills and in human diversity, and demonstrate computer proficiency. **Procedure:** Freshmen are admitted in the fall, spring, and summer. Entrance exams should be taken in the spring of the junior year or fall of the senior year. There are deferred admissions and rolling admissions plans. Application deadlines are open. Notification is sent on a rolling basis. Applications are accepted online. **Transfer Students:** 61 transfer students enrolled in 2016-2017. Applicants must have a college GPA of 2.0 or better. Student may enroll in the fall, spring, and summer. High school and college transcript (s), and an essay are required. 45 of 123 credits required for the bachelor's degree must be completed at Alvernia. **International Students:** There are 16 international students enrolled. They must take the TOEFL with a minimum score of 550 on the paper-based TOEFL (PBT) or 75 on the Internet-based version (iBT). They must also take the SAT or ACT.

ADMISSIONS: 71% of the 2017-2018 applicants were accepted. The SAT scores for the 2017-2018 freshman class were: Math-- 36% below 500, 48% between 500 and 599, and 15% between 600 and 699. Evidence-Based Reading/Writing-- 32% below 500, 52% between 500 and 599, 16% between 600 and 699, and 1% between 700 and 800. The ACT scores were 17% between 12 and 17, 57% between 18 and 23, 24% between 24 and 29, and 1% above 30. **Admissions Contact:** Dan Hartman, Director of Undergraduate Admsissions. Email: *admissions@alvernia.edu* Web: *www.alvernia.edu*

FINANCIAL AID: In 2017-2018, 88% of all full-time freshmen received some form of financial aid. 87% of all full-time freshmen received need-based aid. The average freshman award was $25,553. Need-based scholarships or need-based grants averaged $21,767; need-based self-help aid (loans and jobs) averaged $4,377; other non-need-based awards and non-need-based scholarships averaged $3,209; and $15,322 from other forms of aid. The average financial indebtedness of the 2017 graduate was $44,300. Alvernia University is a member of CSS. The state aid form, and the noncustodial parent's statement, if applicable are required. The FAFSA code is 003233. The priority date for freshman financial aid applications for fall entry is May 1.

ARCADIA UNIVERSITY F-3

www.arcadia.edu

Glenside, PA 19038	(215) 572-2910
Fax: (215) 572-4049	Email: admiss@arcadia.edu
Full-time: 678 men, 1499 women	Faculty: 141
Part-time: 74 men, 139 women	Ph.D.s: 91%
Graduate: 352 men, 1069 women	Student/Faculty: 15 to 1
Year: semesters, summer session	Tuition: $42,330
Room & Board: $13,660	Freshman Class: 8931 applied, 5564 accepted, 569 enrolled
SAT EBR-W/M: 584/564 ACT: 24	CEEB CODE: 2039
Application Deadline: open	COMPETITIVE+

Arcadia University, founded in 1853, is a private institution offering undergraduate and graduate degrees in the fine arts, sciences, business, education, and pre-professional fields. There is 1 undergraduate school and 1 graduate school. In addition to regional accreditation, Arcadia University has baccalaureate program accreditation with ACBSP, APTA, CAHEA, and NASAD. The 76-acre campus is in a suburban area 10 miles north of Philadelphia.

STUDENT LIFE: 60% of undergraduates are from Pennsylvania. Others are from 41 states, and 13 foreign countries. 9% are African American; 7% Asian American; 7% Hispanic; 7% race unknown; 63% White; 4% Foreign; 3% two or more races. **Female To Male Ratio:** 2.5:1. The average age of freshmen is 18; all undergraduates, 22. 22% do not continue beyond their first year; 66% remain to graduate. **Housing:** College-sponsored housing includes dorms, on-campus apartments, and off-campus apartments. There is also a living and learning community. On-campus housing is guaranteed for all 4 years. 51% of students commute. Upperclassmen may keep cars.

FACULTY/CLASSROOMS: No introductory courses are taught by graduate students.

PROGRAMS OF STUDY: Arcadia confers B.A., B.S. and B.F.A. degrees. Master's and doctoral degrees are also awarded. Bachelor's degrees are awarded in BIOLOGICAL SCIENCE (biology/biological science and molecular biology), BUSINESS (accounting, banking and finance, business administration and management, international business management, marketing/retailing/merchandising, and sports management), COMMUNICATIONS AND THE ARTS (acting, art, art history and appreciation, ceramic art and design, communications, dramatic arts, English, fine arts, graphic design, illustration, metal/jewelry, musical theater, photography, printmaking, Spanish, and theater design), COMPUTER AND PHYSICAL SCIENCE (actuarial science, chemistry, computer science, mathematics, and science), EDUCATION (early childhood education, elementary education, music education, secondary education, and special education), ENGINEERING AND ENVIRONMENTAL DESIGN (engineering and interior design), HEALTH PROFESSIONS (art therapy, biomedical science, health care administration, predentistry, premedicine, preoptometry, preveterinary science, public health, and sports psychology), SOCIAL SCIENCE (criminal justice, history, international studies, liberal arts/general studies, philosophy, political science/government, prelaw, psychobiology, psychology, and sociology). Biology, psychology, and math are the strongest academically. Biology, psychology, and business have the largest enrollments.

ACTIVITIES: There are no fraternities or sororities. There are 57 groups on campus, including art, cheerleading, choir, chorale, chorus, communications, computers, dance, debate, drama, environmental, ethnic, forensics, honors, international, LGBT, literary magazine, musical theater, newspaper, pep band, photography, political, professional, radio and TV, religious, social, social service, student government, and yearbook. Popular campus events include Mr. Beaver Contest, Woodstock Weekend, and International Festival. **Sports:** There are 9 intercollegiate sports for men and 10 for women, and 5 intramural sports for men and 5 for women. Facilities include a softball field, outdoor tennis and basketball courts, field hockey and soccer/lacrosse fields, an athletic and recreation center with a gym for basketball and volleyball, an indoor track, swimming pool, aerobics and dance studio, and fitness and training rooms. **Graduates:** From July 1, 2016 to June 30, 2017, 540 bachelor's degrees were awarded. The most popular majors were biology (14%), psychology (11%), and business administration (9%). In an average class, 63% graduate in 4 years or less, 66% graduate in 5 years or less, and 66% graduate in 6 years or less.

SERVICES: Counseling and information services are available, as is tutoring in every subject. There is a reader service for the blind, and remedial math, reading, and writing. **Library/Resources:** Computerized library services include interlibrary loans, database searching, Internet access, and Wi-Fi capability. Special learning facilities include an art gallery, radio station, an observatory, a theater, computer graphics and communication labs, and multimedia classrooms. **Physically Challenged Students:** Facilities include wheelchair ramps, elevators, special parking, specially equipped restrooms, special class scheduling, lowered drinking fountains, and lowered telephones. **Special:** Internships are encouraged in all majors. There are study-abroad programs in 13 countries and co-op programs in business, computer science, chemistry, actuarial science, and accounting. There is a 3+2 engineering program with Columbia University or Washington University in St. Louis, as well as a 3+4 optometry program with Salus University. Arcadia also offers work study, student-designed majors, and credit by exam. There are 11 national honor societies and a freshman honors program. **Visiting:** There are regularly scheduled orientations for prospective students, including personal interviews Monday through Saturday, open houses, and opportunities to dine on campus and meet with faculty, financial aid officers, and current students. There are guides for informal visits, visitors may sit in on classes, and stay overnight. To schedule a visit, contact the Office of Enrollment Management. **Campus Safety and Security:** Measures include 24-hour foot and vehicle patrol, self-defense education, and security escort services. There are shuttle buses, emergency telephones, lighted pathways/sidewalks, alarmed doors, night receptionists, and card access to residence halls.

REQUIREMENTS: The SAT is required. The ACT and ACT Writing Test are recommended. Applicants must be graduates of an accredited secondary school or have a GED. A total of 16 academic credits is required, including 4 years of English, 3 each of math and social studies, and 2 each of a foreign language and science. An essay is required. All art and illustration majors (except art education) must submit a portfolio. AP and CLEP credits are accepted. Important factors in the admissions decision are advanced placement or honors courses, recommendations by school officials, and extracurricular activities record. Students must take English composition, math, and 2 semesters each of a lab science and a foreign language. They must also fulfill 24 credits of distribution requirements in the arts, humanities, and social sciences; core courses in American pluralism and non-Western cultures; and a final project or thesis. 128 credit hours are required to graduate, including 40 to 52 in the major, with a minimum GPA of 2.0. **Procedure:** Freshmen are admitted in the fall and spring. Entrance exams should be taken during orientation. There are early decision, early admissions, deferred admissions, and rolling admissions plans. Application deadlines are open. The fall 2017 application fee was $30. Notification of early decision is sent December 1; regular decision, on a rolling basis. Applications are accepted on-line. **Transfer Students:** 118 transfer students enrolled in 2016-2017. Applicants must have a GPA of 2.5. Art majors must submit a portfolio. The SAT or the ACT is required if the student has earned less than 1 year of college credit. An interview is encouraged. 32 of 128 credits required for the bachelor's degree must be completed at Arcadia. **International Students:** There are 61 international students enrolled. They must take the TOEFL or the IELTS.

ADMISSIONS: 62% of the 2017-2018 applicants were accepted. The SAT scores for the 2017-2018 freshman class were: Math-- 15% below 500, 51% between 500 and 599, 29% between 600 and 699, and 5% between 700 and 800. Evidence-Based Reading/Writing-- 11% below 500, 46% between 500 and 599, 38% between 600 and 699, and 5% between 700 and 800. The ACT scores were 4% between 12 and 17, 36% between 18 and 23, 49% between 24 and 29, and 11% above 30. 45%

of the current freshmen were in the top fifth of their class; 76% were in the top two fifths. 2 freshmen graduated first in their class. **Admissions Contact:** Office of Enrollment Management Email: *admiss@arcadia.edu* Web: *www.arcadia.edu*

FINANCIAL AID: The college's own financial statement, PHEAA, and parent and student tax returns are required. The FAFSA code is 003235. The priority date for freshman financial aid applications for fall entry is March 1.

BLOOMSBURG UNIVERSITY OF PENNSYLVANIA E-2

www.bloomu.edu

Bloomsburg, PA 17815 **(570) 389-4316**

Fax: (570) 389-4741
Email: buadmiss@bloomu.edu
Full-time: 3416 men, 4447 women
Faculty: 419
Part-time: 316 men, 427 women
Ph.D.s: 84%
Graduate: 195 men, 486 women
Student/Faculty: 19 to 1
Year: semesters, summer session
Tuition: $10,500 ($21,980)
Room & Board: $9430
Freshman Class: 9683 applied, 7093 accepted, 1860 enrolled
SAT EBR-W/M: 534/524 **ACT:** 20
CEEB CODE: 2646
Application Deadline: open
COMPETITIVE

Bloomsburg University of Pennsylvania, founded in 1839, is a public institution offering undergraduate programs in the liberal arts, sciences, business, teacher education, technology, and health professions. There are 4 undergraduate schools and 1 graduate school. In addition to regional accreditation, Bloomsburg has baccalaureate program accreditation with AACSB, ABET, CSWE, NASAD, NASM, CAEP, CCNE, CAAHEP, and NAST. The 366-acre campus is in a small town 80 miles northeast of Harrisburg. Including any residence halls, there are 73 buildings.

STUDENT LIFE: 91% of undergraduates are from Pennsylvania. Others are from 22 states, and 30 foreign countries. 87% are from public schools. 8% are African American; 79% White; 7% Hispanic; 3% two or more races; 1% Asian American; 1% Foreign; 1% race unknown. **Female To Male Ratio:** 1.4:1. The average age of freshmen is 18; all undergraduates, 21. 26% do not continue beyond their first year; 58% remain to graduate. **Housing:** 3857 students can be accommodated in college housing, which includes dorms, on-campus apartments, and off-campus apartments. In addition, there are honors houses, special-interest houses, suite style residence hall, and living & learning communities. On-campus housing is guaranteed for the freshman year only, and is available on a first-come, first-served basis. 58% of students commute. Alcohol is not permitted. All students may keep cars.

FACULTY/CLASSROOMS: 54% of faculty are male; 46% are female. No introductory courses are taught by graduate students. The average class size in an introductory lecture is 29; in a laboratory is 16; and in a regular course is 29.

PROGRAMS OF STUDY: Bloomsburg confers B.A., B.A.S., B.S., B.S.B.A., B.S.Ed., B.S.N., and B.S.W. degrees. Master's and doctoral degrees are also awarded. Bachelor's degrees are awarded in BIOLOGICAL SCIENCE (biology/biological science), BUSINESS (accounting, business administration and management, business economics, international business management, and supply chain management), COMMUNICATIONS AND THE ARTS (American Sign Language, art history, communication studies, communications, English, foreign language, journalism, music, speech/debate/rhetoric, studio art, and theatre arts), COMPUTER AND PHYSICAL SCIENCE (chemistry, computer science, cyber intelligence/security studies, geoscience, mathematics, physics, and radiological technology), EDUCATION (business education, early childhood education, mathematics education, middle school education, music education, secondary education, social studies education, special education, and technical & applied studies), ENGINEERING AND ENVIRONMENTAL DESIGN (electrical/electronics engineering), HEALTH PROFESSIONS (exercise science, health science, medical laboratory technology, nursing, and speech pathology/audiology), SOCIAL SCIENCE (anthropology, criminal justice, economics, history, philosophy, political science/government, psychology, social work, and sociology). Digital forensics, supply chain management and nursing are the strongest academically. Business administration, nursing, and psychology have the largest enrollments.

ACTIVITIES: There are 250 groups on campus, including art, band, cheerleading, chess, choir, chorale, chorus, computers, dance, drama, drill team, ethnic, forensics, honors, international, jazz band, LGBT, literary magazine, marching band, newspaper, orchestra, pep band, political, professional, radio and TV, religious, social, social service, student government, and yearbook. Popular campus events include Renaissance Jamboree, The Big Event, and Siblings & Children Weekend. **Sports:** There are 9 intercollegiate sports for men and 10 for women, and 6 intramural sports for men and 6 for women. Facilities include a stadium, gym, an athletic field, indoor track, a swimming pool, practice field, tennis courts, racquetball/handball courts, and a recreation facility. **Graduates:** From July 1, 2016 to June 30, 2017, 1838 bachelor's degrees were awarded. The most popular majors were business administration (19%), communication studies (6%), and nursing (6%). In an average class, 37% graduate in 4 years or less, 56% graduate in 5 years or less, and 58% graduate in 6 years or less. Of the 2016 graduating class, 20% were enrolled in graduate school within 6 months of graduation.

SERVICES: Counseling and information services are available, as is tutoring in some subjects. There is a reader service for the blind, and remedial math, reading, and writing. **Library/Resources:** The library contains 372,812 volumes, 2.1 million microform items, and 11,681 audio/video tapes/CDs/DVDs. Computerized library services include interlibrary loans, database searching, Internet access, and Wi-Fi capability. Special learning facilities include an art gallery, radio station, and TV station. **Physically Challenged Students:** All of the campus is accessible. Facilities include wheelchair ramps, elevators, special parking, specially equipped restrooms, special class scheduling, lowered drinking fountains, and lowered telephones. **Special:** Internships for upperclassmen, study abroad in more than 11 countries, work-study programs, and dual majors are available. Bloomsburg has partnered with several Pennsylvania community colleges to offer a BS degree in Technical Leadership for associate degree graduates of community college partners. A campus-wide initiative called Professional U combines Alumni and Professional Engagement in collaboration with Global Education, Undergraduate Research and professional institutes in the Zeigler College of Business and the College of Education to complement classroom learning by providing students with professional development and career experiences each year until graduation. There are 6 national honor societies, a freshman honors program, and 14 departmental honors programs. **Visiting:** There are regularly scheduled orientations for prospective students, consisting of a general meeting with admissions staff, a question-and-answer session, a campus tour, and meetings with academic faculty. To schedule a visit, contact the Admissions Office. **Campus Safety and Security:** Measures include 24-hour foot and vehicle patrol, emergency notification system, self-defense education, and security escort services. There are shuttle buses, emergency telephones, lighted pathways/sidewalks, controlled access to dorms/residences, monitored surveillance cameras, and strict residence hall security.

REQUIREMENTS: The SAT is required. The ACT is recommended. Applicants must be graduates of an accredited secondary school. To be competitive, a student should also rank in the top 30% of the high school class with a B average. The GED is accepted. Applicants should complete 4 years each of English, 3-4 each of math and science, and 2 each of a foreign language, and history, and 1 of computer science or visual/performing arts. AP and CLEP credits are accepted. To graduate, students must complete 120 credit hours with a minimum GPA of 2.0. The General Education Program Requirements are based on the achievement of the ten goals for general education student learning outcomes. Students meet the requirements of the general education program by earning General Education Points (GEPs). These GEP's are aligned with the general education goals. GEP's are earned through successful completion of approved coursework and Co-curricular learning Experiences (CLEs). Any approved course or CLE at the university can contribute its full or partial content toward one or more goals of general education, but it is not necessary that any given course/CLE participate in the general education program. **Procedure:** Freshmen are admitted to all sessions. Entrance exams should be taken during the junior year. There are early admissions, deferred admissions, and rolling admissions plans. Application deadlines are open. The fall 2017 application fee was $35. Notification is sent on a rolling basis. Applications are accepted on-line. **Transfer Students:** 442 transfer students enrolled in 2016-2017. Either the SAT or ACT is required from applicants who have completed fewer than 24 semester hours of college credits. An official secondary school transcript or a GED and official transcripts from any postsecondary schools attended are also required. Applicants must have a minimum GPA of 2.0 (2.5 or 2.8 for some majors) and be in good standing at the college they last attended. Those who have completed 30 semester hours must select a major upon entering BU. 30 of 120 credits required for the bachelor's degree must be completed at Bloomsburg. **International Students:** There are 57 international students enrolled. They must take the TOEFL with a minimum score of 500 on the paper-based TOEFL (PBT) or 65 on the Internet-based version (iBT), and take the IELTS.

ADMISSIONS: 73% of the 2017-2018 applicants were accepted. 29% of the current freshmen were in the top fifth of their class; 63% were in the top two fifths. **Admissions Contact:** Christopher Lapos, Director of Admissions. Email: *buadmiss@bloomu.edu* Web: *www.bloomu.edu*

FINANCIAL AID: The FAFSA code is 003315. The priority date for freshman financial aid applications for fall entry is March 15. The deadline for filing freshman financial aid applications for fall entry is rolling.

BRYN ATHYN COLLEGE F-3

www.brynathyn.edu

Bryn Athyn, PA 19009 **(267) 502-6021**

Fax: (267) 502-2593	**Email:** admissions@brynathyn.edu
Full-time: 153 men, 160 women	**Faculty:** 32; IIB, ++$
Part-time: 10 men, 8 women	**Ph.D.s:** 56%
Graduate: 4 men	**Student/Faculty:** 8 to 1
Year: trimesters	**Tuition:** $21,126
Room & Board: $11,538	**Freshman Class:** 241 applied, 211 accepted, 108 enrolled
SAT EBR-W/M: 530/510 **ACT:** 22	**CEEB CODE:** 2002
Application Deadline: February 1	**COMPETITIVE**

Bryn Athyn College of the New Church, founded in 1877, is a small private, coeducational, independent, liberal arts institution affiliated with the General Church of the New Jerusalem. There is 1 undergraduate school and 1 graduate school. The 130-acre campus is in a suburban area in Bryn Athyn, PA, 14 miles north of center city Philadelphia. Including any residence halls, there are 21 buildings.

STUDENT LIFE: 71% of undergraduates are from Pennsylvania. Others are from 16 states, 11 foreign countries, and Canada. 39% are from public schools. 8% are African American; 67% White; 3% Asian American; 2% Hispanic; 19% Foreign. **Female To Male Ratio:** 1.3:1. The average age of freshmen is 18; all undergraduates, 21. 9% do not continue beyond their first year; 91% remain to graduate. **Housing:** 210 students can be accommodated in college housing, which includes dorms, on-campus apartments, and off-campus apartments. Upperclassmen can choose to live in one of our apartment-style residences, and cottages or suites. On-campus housing is guaranteed for all 4 years. 60% of students live on campus. Alcohol is not permitted. All students may keep cars.

FACULTY/CLASSROOMS: 50% of faculty are male; 50% are female. All teach undergraduates, 24% do research, and 24% do both. No introductory courses are taught by graduate students. The average class size in a regular course is 12.

PROGRAMS OF STUDY: BAC confers B.A. and B.S. degrees. Associate and master's degrees are also awarded. Bachelor's degrees are awarded in BIOLOGICAL SCIENCE (biology/biological science), COMMUNICATIONS AND THE ARTS (dance, English, and fine arts), EDUCATION (education), HEALTH PROFESSIONS (nursing), SOCIAL SCIENCE (anthropology, history, interdisciplinary studies, philosophy, political science/government, psychology, religion, religious studies, and sociology). Interdisciplinary studies, history, and education have the largest enrollments.

ACTIVITIES: There are no fraternities or sororities. There are 18 groups on campus, including business, psychology, chorale, chorus, dance, drama, international, newspaper, social, social service, student government, and outing clubs. Popular campus events include Charter Day, Service Day, and Alumni Weekend. **Sports:** There are 6 intercollegiate sports for men and 5 for women. Facilities include a gym, an open air ice hockey/skating rink, tennis courts, athletic fields, a fitness center, cross country, soccer, lacrosse, volleyball, basketball, golf, and a dance studio. **Graduates:** From July 1, 2016 to June 30, 2017, 29 bachelor's degrees were awarded. The most popular majors were interdisciplinary studies (28%), elementary education (24%), and religion and history (14%). Of the 2016 graduating class, 17% were enrolled in graduate school within 6 months of graduation, and 57% were employed.

SERVICES: Counseling and information services are available, as is tutoring in most subjects. **Library/Resources:** The library contains 144,475 volumes, 3,593 microform items, and 2,017 audio/video tapes/CDs/DVDs, and subscribes to 8,497 periodicals including electronic. Computerized library services include interlibrary loans, database searching, Internet access, and Wi-Fi capability. **Physically Challenged Students:** 90% of the campus is accessible. Facilities include wheelchair ramps, elevators, special parking, specially equipped restrooms, lowered drinking fountains, and special housing. **Special:** Cross-registration is available with Holy Family University, Co-op programs, internships, B.A.-B.S. degrees, student-designed majors, non-degree study, and study-abroad opportunities are also available. **Visiting:** There are regularly scheduled orientations for prospective students, consisting of touring the campus, attending chapel, and visiting classes. There are guides for informal visits, visitors may sit in on classes, and stay overnight. To schedule a visit, contact Angella Irwin at (267) 502-6044. **Campus Safety and Security:** Measures include 24-hour foot and vehicle patrol. There are emergency telephones, lighted pathways/sidewalks, and controlled access to dorms/residences.

REQUIREMENTS: SAT or ACT scores must reflect promise of success in college work. Applicants must complete and essay, and be graduates of an accredited secondary school or achieve satisfactory scores on the GED. An interview is recommended. A GPA of 2.2 is required. AP and CLEP credits are accepted. Important factors in the admissions decision are recommendations by school officials, personality/intangible qualities, and advanced placement or honors courses. To graduate, students must complete a total of 130 credit hours with a minimum GPA of 2.0 and must satisfy the Core Program. All students must take required courses in religion, writing, philosophy, and physical education. Some majors require a comprehensive project, exam, or thesis. **Procedure:** Freshmen are admitted in the fall, winter, and spring. Entrance exams should be taken by fall of senior year. There are deferred admissions and rolling admissions plans. Application deadlines are open. Notification is sent on a rolling basis. Applications are accepted on-line. **Transfer Students:** 20 transfer students enrolled in 2016-2017. Transfer students with less than 30 credits must supply SAT or ACT scores, a high school transcript, transcripts from all colleges attended, and a letter of recommendation. An interview is also recommended. Transfers with 30+ credits need not supply SAT/ACT and high school transcript. 60 of 130 credits required for the bachelor's degree must be completed at BAC. **International Students:** There are 38 international students enrolled. They must take the TOEFL with a minimum score of 520 on the paper-based TOEFL (PBT) or 70 on the Internet-based version (iBT). They must also take the SAT or ACT.

ADMISSIONS: 88% of the 2017-2018 applicants were accepted. The SAT scores for the 2017-2018 freshman class were: Math-- 42% below 500, 42% between 500 and 599, 14% between 600 and 699, and 2% between 700 and 800. Evidence-Based Reading/Writing-- 33% below 500, 45% between 500 and 599, 18% between 600 and 699, and 4% between 700 and 800. The ACT scores were 44% between 12 and 17, 12% between 18 and 23, 44% between 24 and 29. **Admissions Contact:** Jose Sandino, Senior Admissions Counselor. Email: *admissions@brynathyn.edu* Web: *www.brynathyn.edu*

FINANCIAL AID: In 2017-2018, 96% of all full-time freshmen received some form of financial aid. 64% of all full-time freshmen received need-based aid. The average freshman award was $7,800. Need-based scholarships or need-based grants averaged $10,106 ($14,000 maximum); need-based self-help aid (loans and jobs) averaged $5,789 ($7,000 maximum); and other non-need-based awards and non-need-based scholarships averaged $6,124 ($12,500 maximum). 40% of undergraduate students work part-time. The average financial indebtedness of the 2017 graduate was $21,822. The FAFSA code is 003228. The priority date for freshman financial aid applications for fall entry is February 15.

BRYN MAWR COLLEGE F-3
www.brynmawr.edu

Bryn Mawr, PA 19010 (610) 526-5152
(800) 262-1885
Fax: (610) 526-7471 **Email:** admissions@brynmawr.edu
Full-time: 1291 women
Part-time: 17 women
Graduate: 80 men, 321 women
Year: semesters, summer session
Room & Board: $15,910
Faculty: 152; IIB
Ph.D.s: 97%
Student/Faculty: 8 to 1
Tuition: $49,310
Freshman Class: 3012 applied, 1203 accepted, 407 enrolled
SAT CR/M/W: 670/665/675 **ACT:** 30
Application Deadline: January 15
CEEB CODE: 2049
MOST COMPETITIVE

Bryn Mawr College, founded in 1885, is an independent liberal arts institution, primarily for women. The Graduate School of Social Work and Research, Arts and Sciences, and the postbaccalaureate premedical programs are coed. There is 1 undergraduate school and 2 graduate schools. The 135-acre campus is in a suburban area 11 miles west of Philadelphia. Including any residence halls, there are 40 buildings.

STUDENT LIFE: 81% of undergraduates are from out of state, mostly the Middle Atlantic. Students are from 44 states, 57 foreign countries, and Canada. 64% are from public schools. 9% are Hispanic; 9% race unknown; 5% African American; 5% two or more races; 36% White; 25% Foreign; 12% Asian American. **Female To Male Ratio:** 20.4:1. The average age of freshmen is 18; all undergraduates, 20. 9% do not continue beyond their first year; 82% remain to graduate. **Housing:** 1247 students can be accommodated in college housing, which includes dorms and off-campus apartments. In addition, there are language/international houses, special-interest houses, Co-ops, and a Vegan house. Foreign language houses are available to students studying Chinese, French, German, Hebrew, Italian, Russian or Spanish. Special housing is also available for non-traditional-aged students. On-campus housing is guaranteed for all 4 years. 91% of students live on campus. Upperclassmen may keep cars.

FACULTY/CLASSROOMS: All teach undergraduates, and all do research. No introductory courses are taught by graduate students. The average class size in an introductory lecture is 25; in a laboratory is 15; and in a regular course is 16.

PROGRAMS OF STUDY: Bryn Mawr confers A.B. degrees. Master's and doctoral degrees are also awarded. Bachelor's degrees are awarded in BIOLOGICAL SCIENCE (biology/biological science), COMMUNICATIONS AND THE ARTS (art history and appreciation, classical languages, classics, comparative literature, English, fine arts, French, German, Greek, Italian, Latin, linguistics, music, romance languages and literature, Russian, and Spanish), COMPUTER AND PHYSICAL SCIENCE (astronomy, chemistry, computer science, geology, mathematics, and physics), SOCIAL SCIENCE (anthropology, archeology, East Asian studies, economics, history, international studies, philosophy, political science/government, psychology, religion, sociology, and urban studies). English, psychology, and math have the largest enrollments.

ACTIVITIES: There are no fraternities or sororities. There are 100 groups on campus, including art, business, chess, choir, chorale, chorus, computers, dance, drama, environmental, ethnic, forensics, Girl Scouts, honors, international, investing, LGBT, literary magazine, media, Model UN, musical theater, orchestra, photography, political, professional, religious, social, social service, and student government. Popular campus events include May Day, Lantern Night, and Fall Frolic. **Sports:** There are 12 intercollegiate sports and 10 intramural sports for women. Facilities include playing fields, indoor track, a gym with an 8-lane pool and diving well, basketball, badminton, and volleyball courts, a gymnastics room and dance studio, a weight-training and fitness room, an auditorium, and a student center. **Graduates:** From July 1, 2016 to June 30, 2017, 333 bachelor's degrees were awarded. The most popular majors were social science (26%), biological/life sciences (11%), psychology, and foreign languages, literatures, and linguistics (11%). In an average class, 2% graduate in 3 years or less, 78% graduate in 4 years or less, 84% graduate in 5 years or less, and 84% graduate in 6 years or less. Of the 2016 graduating class, 19% were enrolled in graduate school within 6 months of graduation, and 35% were employed.

SERVICES: Counseling and information services are available, as is tutoring in every subject. There is also a reader service for the blind. **Library/Resources:** The library contains 951,791 volumes, 18,726 microform items, and 10,352 audio/video tapes/CDs/DVDs, and subscribes to 102,519 periodicals including electronic. Computerized library services include interlibrary loans, database searching, Internet access, and Wi-Fi capability. Special learning facilities include an art gallery, an archeological museum, and a language learning center with audio, video, and computer technology. **Physically Challenged Students:** Facilities include wheelchair ramps, elevators, special parking, specially equipped restrooms, special class scheduling, lowered drinking fountains, lowered telephones, and special housing. **Special:** Students may cross-register with Haverford and Swarthmore Colleges and the University of Pennsylvania. Bryn Mawr sponsors more than 100 grants and internships for summer study in a wide range of disciplines and sponsors/co-sponsors study abroad in 27 countries. Student-designed and dual majors are possible. Pass/fail options, work-study programs, a 3-2 degree in engineering with the California Institute of Technology, and a 3-2 degree in city and regional planning with the University of Pennsylvania are also offered. **Visiting:** There are regularly scheduled orientations for prospective students, including student-guided campus tours and interviews can be arranged. There are guides for informal visits, visitors may sit in on classes, and stay overnight. To schedule a visit, contact the Office of Admissions. **Campus Safety and Security:** Measures include 24-hour foot and vehicle patrol, emergency notification system, self-defense education, and security escort services. There are shuttle buses, emergency telephones, lighted pathways/sidewalks, controlled access to dorms/residences, bicycle registration, and personal safety education (road safety and car maintenance).

REQUIREMENTS: Requirements for admission are 4 years of English, 3 years each of math (2 of algebra and 1 of geometry), and foreign language (or 2 years of 2 languages), and 1 year each of science and history. Most applicants have taken at least 3 lab science courses and trigonometry. An essay is required. An interview is strongly recommended. Submission of the SAT or ACT test scores is optional for US citizens and permanent residents. Non-US citizens and nonpermanent residents are required to submit the SAT I or ACT test scores as well as either the TOEFL or IELTS if their primary language is not English and/or their language of instruction over the past four years has not been English. AP credits are accepted. Important factors in the admissions decision are advanced placement or honors courses, evidence of special talent, and extracurricular activities record. To graduate, students must complete 128 semester hours, with 40 to 60 in the major and a minimum GPA of 2.0. All students must complete 2 courses each in the social sciences, humanities, and natural sciences or math, including 1 lab science. Additional required courses include 1 college seminar and 1 quantitative skills course. Students must also be able to demonstrate proficiency in 1 foreign language. **Procedure:** Freshmen are admitted in the fall. Entrance exams should be taken in the spring of the junior year or the fall of the senior year. There are early decision and deferred admissions plans. Early decision applications should be filed by November 15; regular applications, by January 15 for fall entry. The fall 2017 application fee was $50. Notification of early decision is sent December 15; regular decision, February 1. 150 early decision candidates were accepted for the 2017-2018 class. Applications are accepted on-line. **Transfer Students:** 46 transfer students enrolled in 2016-2017. Applicants for transfer must be in good academic standing at their current institutions. An official SAT or ACT scores for transfer international students, 2 professor recommendations, a school official's report, high school transcripts, college transcripts, and the Bryn Mawr Supplement to the College Application for Transfers must be submitted. 96 of 128 credits required for the bachelor's degree must be completed at Bryn Mawr. **International Students:** There are 377 international students enrolled. They must take the TOEFL with a minimum score of 600 on the paper-based TOEFL (PBT) or 90 on the Internet-based version (iBT). Students must score a 7 or above on the IELTS. They must also take the SAT or ACT.

ADMISSIONS: 40% of the 2017-2018 applicants were accepted. The SAT scores for the 2017-2018 freshman class were: Critical Reading-- 2% below 500, 19% between 500 and 599, 42% between 600 and 699, and 40% between 700 and 800. Math-- 1% below 500, 20% between 500 and 599, 45% between 600 and 699, and 34% between 700 and 800. Writing-- 2% below 500, 14% between 500 and 599, 47% between 600 and 699, and 37% between 700 and 800. The ACT scores were 1% between 18 and 23, 34% between 24 and 29, and 65% above 30. 83% of the current freshmen were in the top fifth of their class; 96% were in the top two fifths. 5 freshmen graduated first in their class. **Admissions Contact:** Peaches Valdes, Director of Admissions. Email: *admissions@brynmawr.edu* Web: *www.brynmawr.edu*

FINANCIAL AID: In 2017-2018, 100% of all full-time freshmen

received some form of financial aid. The average freshman award was $46,357. Need-based scholarships or need-based grants averaged $41,321; need-based self-help aid (loans and jobs) averaged $4,845; other non-need-based awards and non-need-based scholarships averaged $19,833; and $3,675 from other forms of aid. The average financial indebtedness of the 2017 graduate was $16,106. Bryn Mawr is a member of CSS. The CSS/Profile, prior year's tax returns, noncustodial parent statement, and the business/farm supplement are required. The FAFSA code is 003237. The priority date for freshman financial aid applications for fall entry is January 15.

BUCKNELL UNIVERSITY — D-2

www.bucknell.edu

Lewisburg, PA 17837 — **(570) 577-3000**

Fax: (570) 577-3538 — **Email: admissions@bucknell.edu**

Full-time: 1772 men, 1813 women	**Faculty:** 384; IIA, +$
Part-time: 12 men, 14 women	**Ph.D.s:** 97%
Graduate: 27 men, 40 women	**Student/Faculty:** 9 to 1
Year: semesters, summer session	**Tuition:** $53,986
Room & Board: $13,150	**Freshman Class:** 10253 applied, 3187 accepted, 973 enrolled
SAT EBR-W/M: 660/680 **ACT:** 30	**CEEB CODE:** 2050
Application Deadline: January 15	**MOST COMPETITIVE**

Bucknell University, established in 1846, is a private independent institution offering undergraduate and graduate programs in arts, music, education, humanities, management, engineering, sciences, and social sciences. There are 3 undergraduate schools and 1 graduate school. In addition to regional accreditation, Bucknell has baccalaureate program accreditation with AACSB, ABET, NASM, CAC, and ACS. The 450-acre campus is in a small town 75 miles north of Harrisburg. Including any residence halls, there are 135 buildings.

STUDENT LIFE: 80% of undergraduates are from out of state, mostly the Middle Atlantic. Students are from 43 states, 45 foreign countries, and Canada. 61% are from public schools. 74% are White; 7% Hispanic; 6% Foreign; 5% Asian American; 4% African American; 4% two or more races. 38% are Catholic; 24% Protestant; 17% claim no religious affiliation; 12% Muslims, Buddhists, Hindu, Mormon, and unknown. **Female To Male Ratio:** 1.0:1. The average age of freshmen is 18; all undergraduates, 20. 6% do not continue beyond their first year; 90% remain to graduate. **Housing:** 3361 students can be accommodated in college housing, which includes dorms and on-campus apartments. In addition, there are special-interest houses, fraternity houses, sustainable living, and substance-free housing. There are also 7 residential colleges for first year student in arts, discovery, environmental, humanities, global, science and technology, languages and cultures and social justice. On-campus housing is guaranteed for all 4 years and is available on a lottery system for upperclassmen. 91% of students live on campus. Upperclassmen may keep cars.

FACULTY/CLASSROOMS: 59% of faculty are male; 41% are female. All teach undergraduates and do research. No introductory courses are taught by graduate students. The average class size in an introductory lecture is 22; in a laboratory is 14; and in a regular course is 18.

PROGRAMS OF STUDY: Bucknell confers B.A., B.S., B.S.B.A., B.E.V.E., B.S.B.E., B.S.C.E., B.S.C.M., B.S.C.S., B.S.E.D., B.S.E.E., B.S.M.E., B.C.E.N., and B.M.U.S. degrees. Master's degrees are also awarded. Bachelor's degrees are awarded in AGRICULTURE (animal science), BIOLOGICAL SCIENCE (biochemistry, biology/biological science, cell biology, and neurosciences), BUSINESS (accounting, business administration and management, international finance, and marketing), COMMUNICATIONS AND THE ARTS (art, art history and appreciation, classics, dramatic arts, English, fine arts, French, German, linguistics, music, music history and appreciation, music performance, music theory and composition, Russian, Spanish, visual and performing arts, and voice), COMPUTER AND PHYSICAL SCIENCE (applied mathematics, chemistry, computer science, geology, mathematics, physics, and quantitative methods), EDUCATION (early childhood education, education, and music education), ENGINEERING AND ENVIRONMENTAL DESIGN (biomedical engineering, chemical engineering, civil engineering, computer engineering, electrical/electronics engineering, engineering, environmental engineering, environmental science, and mechanical engineering), SOCIAL SCIENCE (anthropology, East Asian studies, economics, geography, history, humanities, interdisciplinary studies, international relations, Latin American studies, philosophy, political science/government, psychology, religion, sociology, and women's studies). Humanities, biology, and engineering are the strongest academically. Biology, economics, and mechanical engineering have the largest enrollments.

ACTIVITIES: 36% of men belong to 8 national fraternities; 45% of women belong to 9 national sororities. There are 150 groups on campus, including art, band, cheerleading, chess, choir, chorale, chorus, communications, computers, dance, debate, drama, environmental, ethnic, film, forensics, honors, international, jazz band, LGBT, literary magazine, musical theater, newspaper, opera, orchestra, pep band, photography, political, professional, radio station club, religious, social, social service, student government, symphony, and yearbook. Popular campus events include Celebration for the Arts, Chrysalis Ball, Family Weekend, Christy's (a capella concert) and Christmas Candlelight Service. **Sports:** There are 13 intercollegiate sports for men and 14 for women, and 16 intramural sports for men and 16 for women. Facilities include an athletic and recreation center with an Olympic-size pool, a fitness center, basketball arena, a stadium with track, hockey and lacrosse fields, baseball fields, and recreational fields for soccer, softball, a field house with a 4-lane track, tennis, squash, and racquetball courts, climbing wall, dance studio, golf course with a training facility, tennis courts and high-ropes course. **Graduates:** From July 1, 2016 to June 30, 2017, 867 bachelor's degrees were awarded. The most popular majors were economics (11%), psychology (7%), and accounting and finance (7%). In an average class, 86% graduate in 4 years or less, 90% graduate in 5 years or less, and 90% graduate in 6 years or less. Of the 2016 graduating class, 17% were enrolled in graduate school within 6 months of graduation, and 74% were employed.

SERVICES: Counseling and information services are available, as is tutoring in some subjects, such as biology, chemistry, physics, math, and writing across the curriculum. **Library/Resources:** The library contains 1.4 million volumes, 19,158 microform items, and 39,854 audio/video tapes/CDs/DVDs, and subscribes to 47,190 periodicals including electronic. Computerized library services include interlibrary loans, database searching, Internet access, and Wi-Fi capability. Special learning facilities include an art gallery, an outdoor natural area, greenhouse, primate facility, observatory, photography lab, race and gender resource center, library resources training lab, electronic classroom, multimedia lab, performing arts center, and multicultural, writing, craft, environmental, public policy and poetry centers, herbarium, and engineering structural test lab. **Physically Challenged Students:** 80% of the campus is accessible. Facilities include wheelchair ramps, elevators, special parking, specially equipped restrooms, special class scheduling, lowered drinking fountains, lowered telephones, and special housing. **Special:** Bucknell offers internships, service learning, study abroad in more than 60 countries, a Washington semester, 5-year dual degree programs in arts & sciences and engineering and business management and engineering as well as dual and student-designed majors. Interdisciplinary majors include Africana studies, animal behavior, cell biology & biochemistry, interdisciplinary studies in economics & mathematics, Italian studies, neuroscience and women's and gender studies. Academic centers include the Bucknell Center for the Study of Sustainability and the Environment, the Bucknell Institute for Public Policy, the Center for the Study of Race, Ethnicity and Gender, the Griot Institute for Africana Studies, the Institute for Leadership in Technology and Management and the Stadler Center for Poetry. The Residential College program offers an academically focused, residential experience for first year students. Undergraduate research opportunities are available across the College of Arts & Sciences, College of Management and College of Engineering. There are 26 national honor societies, Phi Beta Kappa, a freshman honors program, and 55 departmental honors programs. **Visiting:** There are regularly scheduled orientations for prospective students, and several activities available. There are guides for informal visits and visitors may sit in on classes. To schedule a visit, contact the Admissions Office. **Campus Safety and Security:** Measures include 24-hour foot and vehicle patrol, emergency notification system, self-defense education, and security escort services. There are shuttle buses, emergency telephones, lighted pathways/sidewalks, controlled access to dorms/residences, campus safety alerts, and intrusion alarms in residence halls.

REQUIREMENTS: The SAT or ACT is required, and the ACT Optional Writing test are required. Applicants must graduate from an accredited secondary school or have a GED. 16 units must be earned, including 4 in English, 3 in math, and 2 each in history, science, social studies, and foreign language, and 1 additional elective. An essay is required, and a campus visit is recommended. Music applicants are required to audition. A portfolio is recommended for art applicants. AP and CLEP credits are accepted. Important factors in the admissions decision are advanced placement or honors courses, evidence of special talent, and extracurricular activities record. **Procedure:** Freshmen are admitted in the fall. Entrance exams should be taken before January 1. There are early decision and deferred admissions plans. Early decision applications should be filed by November 15; regular applications, by January 15 for fall entry. The fall 2017 application fee was $40. Notification of early decision is sent December 15; regular decision, April 1. 420 early decision candidates were accepted for the 2017-2018 class. 2883 applicants were on the 2017 waiting list; 55 were admitted. Applications are accepted online. **Transfer Students:** 25 transfer students enrolled in 2016-2017. Transfer students must have a minimum GPA of 2.5 in courses comparable to those offered at Bucknell. The SAT or ACT is required. A minimum of 16 credit hours must have been earned; 32 are recommended. Students are accepted on a space-available basis. 48 of 128 credits required for the bachelor's degree must be completed at Bucknell. **International Students:** There are 228 international students enrolled. They must take the TOEFL with a minimum score of 600 on the paper-based TOEFL (PBT) or 100 on the Internet-based version (iBT). They must also take the SAT or ACT.

ADMISSIONS: 31% of the 2017-2018 applicants were accepted. The SAT scores for the 2017-2018 freshman class were: Math-- 14% between 500 and 599, 49% between 600 and 699, and 37% between 700 and 800. Evidence-Based Reading/Writing-- 1% below 500, 14% between 500 and 599, 56% between 600 and 699, and 29% between 700 and 800. The ACT scores were 3% between 18 and 23, 42% between 24 and 29, and 55% above 30. 83% of the current freshmen were in the top fifth of their class; 97% were in the top two fifths. 11 freshmen graduated first in their class. **Admissions Contact:** Kevin Mathes, Dean of Admissions. Email: *admissions@bucknell.edu* Web: *www.bucknell.edu*

FINANCIAL AID: In 2017-2018, 54% of all full-time freshmen received some form of financial aid. 34% of all full-time freshmen received need-based aid. The average freshman award was $37,500. Need-based scholarships or need-based grants averaged $32,700 ($67,136 maximum); need-based self-help aid (loans and jobs) averaged $4,200 ($7,300 maximum); non-need-based athletic scholarships averaged $30,871 ($67,136 maximum); and other non-need-based awards and non-need-based scholarships averaged $11,958 ($53,986 maximum). 35% of undergraduate students work part-time. The average financial indebtedness of the 2017 graduate was $22,600. Bucknell is a member of CSS. The CSS/Profile, and noncustodial parent's statement are required. The FAFSA code is 003238. The deadline for filing freshman financial aid applications for fall entry is January 15.

CABRINI UNIVERSITY *(The complete profile is made available exclusively on our website, www.barronspac.com)*

CAIRN UNIVERSITY — F-3

www.cairn.edu

Langhorne, PA 19047	**(215) 752-5800** **(800) 366-0049**
Fax: (215) 702-4248	**Email: admissions@cairn.edu**
Full-time: 321 men, 407 women	**Faculty:** 40
Part-time: 18 men, 25 women	**Ph.D.s:** 69%
Graduate: 139 men, 151 women	**Student/Faculty:** 12 to 1
Year: semesters, summer session	**Tuition:** $27,279
Room & Board: $10,294	**Freshman Class:** 514 applied, 501 accepted, 255 enrolled
SAT EBR-W/M: 540/520 **ACT:** 20	**CEEB CODE:** 2661
Application Deadline: open	**COMPETITIVE**

Cairn University, founded in 1913, is a Christian Liberal Arts institution. There are 6 undergraduate schools and 4 graduate schools. In addition to regional accreditation, CU has baccalaureate program accreditation with CSWE, NASM, ABHE, IACBE, and ACSI. The 113-acre campus is in a suburban area 30 miles north of Philadelphia. Including any residence halls, there are 20 buildings.

STUDENT LIFE: 54% of undergraduates are from Pennsylvania. Others are from 27 states, 20 foreign countries, and Canada. 45% are from public schools. 72% are White; 6% Hispanic; 4% Asian American; 3% Foreign; 2% two or more races; 13% African American. 100% are Protestant. **Female To Male Ratio:** 1.2:1. The average age of freshmen is 18; all undergraduates, 22. 27% do not continue beyond their first year; 63% remain to graduate. **Housing:** 510 students can be accommodated in college dorms. On-campus housing is guaranteed for all 4 years. 62% of students live on campus. Alcohol is not permitted. All students may keep cars.

FACULTY/CLASSROOMS: 59% of faculty are male; 41% are female. 82% teach undergraduates. No introductory courses are taught by graduate students. The average class size in an introductory lecture is 18 and in a regular course is 15.

PROGRAMS OF STUDY: CU confers B.A., B.S., B.S.Bible, B.Mus., B.S.BusAdmin, B.S.Ed. B.S.W., and B.S.Youth & Family degrees. Master's degrees are also awarded. Bachelor's degrees are awarded in BUSINESS (accounting and business administration), COMMUNICATIONS AND THE ARTS (art studies, English, graphic design, music, music composition, music ministry, and music performance), COMPUTER AND PHYSICAL SCIENCE (computer science and information science), EDUCATION (education, education administration, elementary education, English secondary education, health and physical education, pre K-4 education, mathematics education, music education, secondary education, and social studies secondary school education), SOCIAL SCIENCE (biblical studies, Christian studies, criminal justice, history, liberal arts/general studies, pastoral studies, psychology, social work, and youth ministry). Biblical studies is the strongest academically. Teacher education, and social work have the largest enrollments.

ACTIVITIES: There are no fraternities or sororities. There are 18 groups on campus, including art, band, choir, chorale, chorus, drama, honors, international, musical theater, newspaper, opera, orchestra, professional, religious, social, social service, student government, symphony, and yearbook. Popular campus events include Homecoming, Luau, Hoedown, and Christmas Celebration. **Sports:** There are 6 intercollegiate sports for men and 6 for women, and 18 intramural sports for men and 18 for women. Facilities include a gym, baseball diamond, soccer, hockey, softball fields, lighted tennis courts, fitness circuit, and weight room. **Graduates:** From July 1, 2016 to June 30, 2017, 142 bachelor's degrees were awarded. The most popular majors were Bible (42%), teacher education (23%), and social work (12%). In an average class, 26% graduate in 4 years or less, 54% graduate in 5 years or less, and 57% graduate in 6 years or less. Of the 2016 graduating class, 38% were enrolled in graduate school within 6 months of graduation, and 86% were employed.

SERVICES: Counseling and information services are available, as is tutoring in most subjects. **Library/Resources:** The library contains 116,328 volumes, 63,817 microform items, and 9,201 audio/video tapes/CDs/DVDs, and subscribes to 54,240 periodicals including electronic. Computerized library services include interlibrary loans, database searching, Internet access, and Wi-Fi capability. **Physically Challenged Students:** 99% of the campus is accessible. Facilities include wheelchair ramps, elevators, special parking, specially equipped restrooms, lowered drinking fountains, and special housing. **Special:** Cairn University offers an accelerated degree program in Biblical Studies, along with multiple internship and study abroad opportunities in the traditional undergraduate programs. There are double degree programs in social work, music, education, and business administration. There is 1 national honor society and a freshman honors program. **Visiting:** There are regularly scheduled orientations for prospective students, class and chapel visits, and an interview with a counselor. There are guides for informal visits, visitors may sit in on classes, and stay overnight. To schedule a visit, contact Kristina O'Connell at (215) 702-4235. **Campus Safety and Security:** Measures include 24-hour foot and vehicle patrol, emergency notification system, and security escort services. There are emergency telephones, lighted pathways/sidewalks, and controlled access to dorms/residences.

REQUIREMENTS: The SAT or ACT is required. AP and CLEP credits are accepted. Students must complete 30 credits in Biblical Studies. At least 121 credits, with a minimum GPA of 2.0, is required. Approximately 30% of the students are enrolled in dual degree programs and receive the BS in Bible degree plus a baccalaureate or masters in their professional area. **Procedure:** Freshmen are admitted in the fall and spring. Entrance exams should be taken in the junior or senior year of high school. There are deferred admissions and rolling admissions plans.

Application deadlines are open. The fall 2017 application fee was $25. Notification is sent on a rolling basis. Applications are accepted on-line. **Transfer Students:** 91 transfer students enrolled in 2016-2017. Transfers must submit an application, a pastor's reference, college transcripts, and a health form. SAT scores and high school transcripts are also required if the student has fewer than 30 college credit hours. 60 of 121 credits required for the bachelor's degree must be completed at CU. **International Students:** There are 23 international students enrolled. They must take the TOEFL with a minimum score of 520 on the paper-based TOEFL (PBT) or 68 on the Internet-based version (iBT).

ADMISSIONS: 97% of the 2017-2018 applicants were accepted. The SAT scores for the 2017-2018 freshman class were: Math-- 37% below 500, 45% between 500 and 599, 16% between 600 and 699, and 2% between 700 and 800. Evidence-Based Reading/Writing-- 35% below 500, 40% between 500 and 599, 21% between 600 and 699, and 4% between 700 and 800. The ACT scores were 27% between 12 and 17, 55% between 18 and 23, 15% between 24 and 29, and 3% above 30. 25% of the current freshmen were in the top fifth of their class; 51% were in the top two fifths. **Admissions Contact:** Thomas Sherf, Director of Undergraduate Admissions. Email: *admissions@cairn.edu* Web: *www.cairn.edu*

FINANCIAL AID: In 2017-2018, 85% of all full-time freshmen received some form of financial aid and need-based aid. The average freshman award was $23,175. Need-based scholarships or need-based grants averaged $18,778; need-based self-help aid (loans and jobs) averaged $4,871; and other non-need-based awards and non-need-based scholarships averaged $13,011. 55% of undergraduate students work part-time. The average financial indebtedness of the 2017 graduate was $31,166. The FAFSA code is 003351. Check with the school for current application deadlines.

CALIFORNIA UNIVERSITY OF PENNSYLVANIA *(The complete profile is made available exclusively on our website, www.barronspac.com)*

CARLOW UNIVERSITY *(The complete profile is made available exclusively on our website, www.barronspac.com)*

CARNEGIE MELLON UNIVERSITY — B-3

www.cmu.edu

Pittsburgh, PA 15213 — **(412) 268-2000**

Fax: (412) 268-7838	**Email:** admissions@andrew.cmu.edu
Full-time: 3404 men, 3035 women	**Faculty:** I, +$
Part-time: 133 men, 101 women	**Ph.D.s:** 90%
Graduate: 4689 men, 2599 women	**Student/Faculty:** 13 to 1
Year: semesters, summer session	**Tuition:** $52,310
Room & Board: $13,270	**Freshman Class:** n/av
SAT or ACT: required	**CEEB CODE:** 2074
Application Deadline: n/av	**MOST COMPETITIVE**

Carnegie Mellon University, established in 1900, is a private institution offering undergraduate programs in liberal arts and science and technology. There are 6 undergraduate schools and 7 graduate schools. In addition to regional accreditation, CMU has baccalaureate program accreditation with AACSB, ABET, NAAB, NASM, and NASPAA. The 148-acre campus is in an urban area 4 miles from downtown Pittsburgh. Including any residence halls, there are 158 buildings.

STUDENT LIFE: 85% of undergraduates are from out of state, mostly the Middle Atlantic. Students are from 50 states, 69 foreign countries, and Canada. 8% are Hispanic; 5% race unknown; 4% African American; 4% two or more races; 29% White; 26% Asian American; 23% Foreign. **Male To Female Ratio:** 1.4:1. The average age of freshmen is 18; all undergraduates, 20. 2% do not continue beyond their first year; 88% remain to graduate. **Housing:** 4058 students can be accommodated in college housing, which includes dorms, on-campus apartments, and off-campus apartments. In addition, there are special-interest houses, fraternity houses, sorority houses, wellness housing, theme housing, and block housing. On-campus housing is guaranteed for all 4 years. 61% of students live on campus. Alcohol is not permitted. All students may keep cars.

FACULTY/CLASSROOMS: 72% of faculty are male; 28% are female. No introductory courses are taught by graduate students.

PROGRAMS OF STUDY: CMU confers B.A., B.S., B.H.A., B.Arch., B.C.S.A., B.Design, B.F.A., and B.S.A. degrees. Master's and doctoral degrees are also awarded. Bachelor's degrees are awarded in BIOLOGICAL SCIENCE (biochemistry, biology/biological science, and neurosciences), BUSINESS (business administration and management, business economics, marketing/retailing/merchandising, and policy analysis and management), COMMUNICATIONS AND THE ARTS (acting, art, communications, creative writing, design, dramatic arts, English, fine arts, French, German, journalism, languages, linguistics, music, music composition, music performance, Spanish, and technical communication), COMPUTER AND PHYSICAL SCIENCE (chemistry, computer programming, computer science, information sciences and systems, mathematics, physics, and statistics), EDUCATION (music education), ENGINEERING AND ENVIRONMENTAL DESIGN (architecture, chemical engineering, civil engineering, computer engineering, electrical/electronics engineering, engineering, materials engineering, and mechanical engineering), SOCIAL SCIENCE (Chinese Studies, economics, Hispanic American studies, history, international political science, Japanese studies, philosophy, political science/government, psychology, public administration, Russian and Slavic studies, social science, and urban studies). Engineering, and computer science have the largest enrollments.

ACTIVITIES: 17% of men belong to 16 national fraternities; 14% of women belong to 11 national sororities. There are 357 groups on campus, including art, bagpipe, band, cheerleading, chess, choir, chorale, chorus, computers, dance, debate, drama, ethnic, film, honors, international, LGBT, literary magazine, marching band, musical theater, newspaper, orchestra, pep band, photography, political, professional, radio station, religious, social, social service, student government, symphony, and yearbook. Popular campus events include Spring Carnival, International Festival, and Jill Watson Festival Across the Arts. **Sports:** There are 9 intercollegiate sports for men and 9 for women, and 38 intramural sports for men and 38 for women. Facilities include a gym, a football stadium with track, athletic fields, tennis and racquetball courts, and a pool. **Graduates:** From July 1, 2016 to June 30, 2017, 1483 bachelor's degrees were awarded. The most popular majors were computer science (12%), electrical and computer engineering (9%), and mechanical engineering (8%). In an average class, 85% graduate in 5 years or less and 88% graduate in 6 years or less. Of the 2016 graduating class, 22% were enrolled in graduate school within 6 months of graduation, and 59% were employed.

SERVICES: Counseling and information services are available, as is tutoring in most subjects. There is a reader service for the blind. **Library/Resources:** The library contains 1.1 million volumes, 1.2 million microform items, and 43,936 audio/video tapes/CDs/DVDs, and subscribes to 140,006 periodicals including electronic. Computerized library services include interlibrary loans, database searching, Internet access, and Wi-Fi capability. Special learning facilities include an art gallery. **Physically Challenged Students:** 95% of the campus is accessible. Facilities include wheelchair ramps, elevators, special parking, specially equipped restrooms, special class scheduling, lowered drinking fountains, lowered telephones, and special housing. **Special:** Students may cross-register with other Pittsburgh Council of Higher Education institutions. Also available are internships, work-study programs, study abroad in 45+ countries, a Washington semester, accelerated degrees, B.A.-B.S. degrees, co-op programs, dual majors, independent study, double major, distance learning, liberal arts/career combination and limited student-designed majors. There are 18 national honor societies, Phi Beta Kappa, and a freshman honors program. **Visiting:** There are regularly scheduled orientations for prospective students, consisting of Saturday group sessions in September, October, November, and January. There are guides for informal visits, visitors may sit in on classes, and stay overnight. To schedule a visit, contact the Admissions Office. **Campus Safety and Security:** Measures include 24-hour foot and vehicle patrol, emergency notification system, self-defense education, and security escort services. There are shuttle buses, emergency telephones, lighted pathways/sidewalks, controlled access to dorms/residences, and safewalk program.

REQUIREMENTS: The SAT or ACT is required. SAT Subject tests are not required for drama, design, art, or music applicants. All other applicants must take appropriate tests, preferably by November but no later than December. Applicants must graduate from an accredited secondary school or have a GED and must have completed 4 years of English. All other preferred Carnegie credits vary by college and program. Essays are required and interviews are recommended. Art and design applicants must submit a portfolio. Drama and music applicants must audition. AP credits are accepted. Requirements vary considerably across colleges and programs. **Procedure:** Freshmen are admitted in the fall. Entrance exams should be received by Jan 1 (Dec 1 for college of fine arts). There are early decision, early admissions, and deferred admissions plans. Early decision applications should be filed by November 1. The fall 2017 application fee was $75. Notification of early decision is sent December 15; regular decision, April 15. 326 early decision candidates were accepted for the 2017-2018 class. 2835 applicants were on the 2017 waiting list; 4 were admitted. Applications are accepted on-line. **Transfer Students:** 20 transfer students enrolled in 2016-2017. Applicants must submit secondary school and college transcripts (including school catalogs with course descriptions so that Carnegie Mellon can evaluate transferable credits). **International Students:** There are 1449 international students enrolled. They must take the TOEFL with a minimum score of 600 on the paper-based TOEFL (PBT) or 100 on the Internet-based version (iBT), and take the International English Language Testing System (IELTS). They must also take the SAT or ACT.

ADMISSIONS: 24% of the 2017-2018 applicants were accepted. 92% of the current freshmen were in the top fifth of their class; 99% were in the top two fifths. **Admissions Contact:** Michael Steidel, Director of Admissions. Email: *admissions@andrew.cmu.edu* Web: *www.cmu.edu*

FINANCIAL AID: In 2017-2018, 46% of all full-time freshmen received some form of financial aid. 45% of all full-time freshmen received need-based aid. The average freshman award was $36,002. Need-based scholarships or need-based grants averaged $31,926; need-based self-help aid (loans and jobs) averaged $6,334; and other non-need-based awards and non-need-based scholarships averaged $13,140. CMU is a member of CSS. The CSS/Profile and the college's own financial statement, noncustodial profile, parent and student federal tax returns, and W-2 forms are required. The FAFSA code is 003242. The deadline for filing freshman financial aid applications for fall entry is February 15.

CEDAR CREST COLLEGE — E-3

www.cedarcrest.edu

Allentown, PA 18104 — (610) 740-3780, (800) 360-1222

Fax: (610) 606-4647 — **Email:** admissions@cedarcrest.edu

Full-time: 116 men, 815 women	**Faculty:** 77; IIB, av$
Part-time: 60 men, 442 women	**Ph.D.s:** 71%
Graduate: 35 men, 196 women	**Student/Faculty:** 10 to 1
Year: semesters, summer session	**Tuition:** $39,566
Room & Board: $11,544	**Freshman Class:** 1208 applied, 765 accepted, 213 enrolled
SAT CR/M: 537/516 **ACT:** 22	**CEEB CODE:** 2079
Application Deadline: open	**COMPETITIVE**

Cedar Crest College, founded in 1867, was one of the first women's colleges in the nation. Today it remains an independent, comprehensive liberal arts college for women that combines excellence in scholarship and undergraduate education with an extensive School of Adult and Graduate Education (SAGE) program and growing graduate programs that serve women and men in the surrounding region. There is 1 undergraduate school and 1 graduate school. In addition to regional accreditation, Cedar Crest College has baccalaureate program accreditation with ACBSP, CSWE, NLNAC, and FEPAC. The 84-acre campus is in a suburban area 55 miles north of Philadelphia and 90 miles west of New York City. Including any residence halls, there are 20 buildings.

STUDENT LIFE: 67% of undergraduates are from Pennsylvania. Others are from 21 states, and 28 foreign countries. 95% are from public schools. 9% are African American; 9% Foreign; 58% White; 4% race unknown; 3% Asian American; 15% Hispanic; 1% two or more races. **Female To Male Ratio:** 6.9:1. The average age of freshmen is 18; all undergraduates, 28. 18% do not continue beyond their first year; 50% remain to graduate. **Housing:** 550 students can be accommodated in college housing, which includes dorms. smoke-free floors, and living learning communities. On-campus housing is guaranteed for all 4 years. 78% of students commute. All students may keep cars.

FACULTY/CLASSROOMS: 32% of faculty are male; 68% are female. All teach undergraduates. No introductory courses are taught by graduate students. The average class size in an introductory lecture is 20; in a laboratory is 13; and in a regular course is 14.

PROGRAMS OF STUDY: CCC confers B.A. and B.S degrees. Master's degrees are also awarded. Bachelor's degrees are awarded in BIOLOGICAL SCIENCE (biochemistry, biology/biological science, environmental biology, forensic science, genetics, neurosciences, and nutrition), BUSINESS (accounting and business administration and management), COMMUNICATIONS AND THE ARTS (art, communications, dance, dramatic arts, English, media arts, new media production, theatre acting, and writing), COMPUTER AND PHYSICAL SCIENCE (chemistry and mathematics), EDUCATION (early childhood education, education, and educational studies), HEALTH PROFESSIONS (art therapy, global & public health sciences, health promotion, health science, nuclear medical technology, nursing, and public health), SOCIAL SCIENCE (applied psychology, criminal justice, history, political science/government, psychology, social work, and Spanish studies). Sciences, and nursing are the strongest academically. Nursing, social work, and business have the largest enrollments.

ACTIVITIES: There are no fraternities or sororities. There are 51 groups on campus, including art, band, cheerleading, choir, chorus, computers, dance, drama, ethnic, forensics, honors, international, LGBT, literary magazine, musical theater, newspaper, political, professional, radio and TV, religious, social, social service, student government, and yearbook. Popular campus events include Student Faculty Frolic, Midnight Breakfast, and Ring Ceremony. **Sports:** There are 8 intercollegiate sports, and 4 intramural sports for women. Facilities include tennis courts, softball, field hockey, soccer, and lacrosse fields, a cross-country course, a gym for basketball, volleyball, badminton, dance and aerobics studios, weight training, a swimming pool, and fitness center. **Graduates:** From July 1, 2016 to June 30, 2017, 292 bachelor's degrees were awarded. The most popular majors were nursing (35%), psychology (15%), and business administration (6%). In an average class, 51% graduate in 4 years or less, 57% graduate in 5 years or less, and 60% graduate in 6 years or less. Of the 2016 graduating class, 7% were enrolled in graduate school within 6 months of graduation, and 70% were employed.

SERVICES: Counseling and information services are available, as is tutoring in most subjects. There is remedial math and writing. There is also a computer software skills program for underprepared students. **Library/Resources:** Computerized library services include interlibrary loans, database searching, Internet access, and Wi-Fi capability. Special learning facilities include an art gallery, radio station, theaters, an arboretum and a sculpture garden. **Physically Challenged Students:** 35% of the campus is accessible. Facilities include wheelchair ramps, elevators, special parking, specially equipped restrooms, special class scheduling, lowered drinking fountains, and lowered telephones. **Special:** Cross-registration is available through the Lehigh Valley Association of Independent Colleges and Online Consortium. Also available are internships, work-study programs, an accelerated degree program in business, and B.A.-B.S. degrees in math, biology, and psychology. Dual majors, student-designed majors, pass/fail options, and credit for life, military, and work experience are also offered. There are 15 national honor societies, a freshman honors program, and 1 departmental honors program. **Visiting:** There are regularly scheduled orientations for prospective students. There are guides for informal visits, visitors may sit in on classes, and stay overnight. To schedule a visit, contact the Admissions Office. **Campus Safety and Security:** Measures include 24-hour foot and vehicle patrol, emergency notification system, self-defense education, and security escort services. There are emergency telephones, lighted pathways/sidewalks, residence halls are equipped with fire/intrusion alarms, and monitored 24 hours a day. A keyless access system, and exterior doors are locked.

REQUIREMENTS: The SAT is required. Applicants must be graduates of an accredited secondary school. The GED is accepted. Students should have completed 16 high school academic credits, including 4 years of English, 3 of math, 2 each of science, history, and foreign language, and 1 each of art, music, and social studies. An essay is required. Cedar Crest requires applicants to be in the upper 50% of their class. A GPA of 2.0 is required. AP and CLEP credits are accepted. Important factors in the admissions decision are advanced placement or honors courses, leadership record, and evidence of special talent. To graduate, students must complete 120 credit hours (122 for nursing) with a minimum GPA of 2.0 (some majors have higher requirements). Distribution requirements include 7 credits in natural sciences, 6 each in writing, mathematics and logic, humanities, the arts, and social sciences, and 3 each in global studies and ethics. A major capstone experience is required. **Procedure:** Freshmen are admitted fall and spring. Entrance exams should be taken in the junior year or early in the senior year. There are deferred admissions and rolling admissions plans. Application deadlines are open.

Applications are accepted on-line. **Transfer Students:** 49 transfer students enrolled in 2016-2017. Applicants should have a minimum college GPA of 2.0. An interview is recommended. 30 of 120 credits required for the bachelor's degree must be completed at CCC. **International Students:** There are 140 international students enrolled. They must take the TOEFL with a minimum score of 550 on the paper-based TOEFL (PBT) or 61 on the Internet-based version (iBT).

ADMISSIONS: 63% of the 2017-2018 applicants were accepted. The SAT scores for the 2017-2018 freshman class were: Critical Reading-- 64% below 500, 30% between 500 and 599, and 6% between 600 and 699. Math-- 57% below 500, 38% between 500 and 599, and 5% between 600 and 699. Writing-- 70% below 500, 23% between 500 and 599, and 7% between 600 and 699. 55% of the current freshmen were in the top fifth of their class; 92% were in the top two fifths. **Admissions Contact:** Mary Alice Ozechoski, VP of Student Affairs and Enrollment. Email: *admissions@cedarcrest.edu* Web: *www.cedarcrest.edu*

FINANCIAL AID: In 2017-2018, 98% of all full-time freshmen received some form of financial aid. 94% of all full-time freshmen received need-based aid. The average freshman award was $31,302. Need-based scholarships or need-based grants averaged $27,930; need-based self-help aid (loans and jobs) averaged $3,761; and other non-need-based awards and non-need-based scholarships averaged $3,364. 53% of undergraduate students work part-time. The average financial indebtedness of the 2017 graduate was $27,200. CCC is a member of CSS. The FAFSA code is 003243. The deadline for filing freshman financial aid applications for fall entry is May 1.

CHATHAM UNIVERSITY B-3

www.chatham.edu

Pittsburgh, PA 15232	**(412) 365-1139** **(800) 837-1290**
Fax: (412) 365-1609	**Email: admission@chatham.edu**
Full-time: 240 men, 711 women	**Faculty:** 70; IIA, --$
Part-time: 48 men, 209 women	**Ph.D.s:** 92%
Graduate: 231 men, 830 women	**Student/Faculty:** 14 to 1
Year: semesters, summer session	**Tuition:** $36,510
Room & Board: $11,373	**Freshman Class:** 2231 applied, 1217 accepted, 284 enrolled
SAT EBR-W/M: 610/570 **ACT:** 24	**CEEB CODE:** 2081
Application Deadline: August 1	**VERY COMPETITIVE**

Chatham University, founded in 1869, is a private university composed of the Falk School of Sustainability, the School of Health Sciences, the School of Arts, Science and Business, and the College for Continuing and Professional Studies. Chatham offers undergraduate and graduate degrees in more than 60 programs, on campus and online. There are 4 undergraduate schools and 3 graduate schools. In addition to regional accreditation, Chatham has baccalaureate program accreditation with ACS. The 427-acre campus is in an urban area 5 miles east of downtown Pittsburgh. Including any residence halls, there are 62 buildings.

STUDENT LIFE: 78% of undergraduates are from Pennsylvania. Others are from 47 states, 24 foreign countries, and Canada. 96% are from public schools. 64% are White; 17% race unknown; 6% African American; 6% Foreign; 3% Hispanic; 2% Asian American; 1% American Indian/Alaska Native; 1% two or more races. **Female To Male Ratio:** 3.4:1. The average age of freshmen is 19; all undergraduates, 23. 15% do not continue beyond their first year; 85% remain to graduate. **Housing:** 739 students can be accommodated in college housing, which includes dorms, on-campus apartments, off-campus apartments, special-interest houses, and intercultural residence hall. On-campus housing is available on a lottery system for upperclassmen. 51% of students live on campus. Upperclassmen may keep cars.

FACULTY/CLASSROOMS: 32% of faculty are male; 68% are female. All teach undergraduates. No introductory courses are taught by graduate students. The average class size in an introductory lecture is 14; in a laboratory is 14; and in a regular course is 14.

PROGRAMS OF STUDY: Chatham confers B.A., B.S., B.S.N., B.F.A., B.I.A., and B.S.W. degrees. Master's and doctoral degrees are also awarded. Bachelor's degrees are awarded in AGRICULTURE (environmental studies), BIOLOGICAL SCIENCE (biochemistry and biology/biological science), BUSINESS (accounting, business administration and management, business economics, international business management, management information systems, management, marketing, marketing management, sustainable management, and women's entrepreneurship & institutional culture), COMMUNICATIONS AND THE ARTS (art history and appreciation, arts administration/management, communications, creative writing, English, English literature, film, television and digital media, media arts, music, Spanish, theatre studies, and visual and performing arts), COMPUTER AND PHYSICAL SCIENCE (chemistry, applied data science analytics, mathematics, and physics), EDUCATION (early childhood education, education, elementary education, and pre K-4 education), ENGINEERING AND ENVIRONMENTAL DESIGN (environmental science, interior architecture, and interior design), HEALTH PROFESSIONS (exercise science, health care administration, health science biology interdisciplinary, health science exercise science interdisciplinary, integrative health studies, nursing, and physical therapy), SOCIAL SCIENCE (criminology, crosscultural studies, cultural studies/critical theory & analysis, economics, forensic studies, history, interdisciplinary studies, international relations, international studies, political science/government, policy studies, psychology, public affairs, social work, and women's studies). Biology, sustainability, and business are the strongest academically. Biology, psychology, and exercise science have the largest enrollments.

ACTIVITIES: There are no fraternities or sororities. There are 43 groups on campus, including cheerleading, choir, computers, dance, drama, environmental, ethnic, film, forensics, honors, international, LGBT, newspaper, pep band, photography, political, professional, religious, social, social service, and student government. Popular campus events include University Day, Harvest Dinner, and Mocktails. **Sports:** There are 9 intercollegiate sports for men and 11 for women, and 7 intramural sports for men and 7 for women. Facilities include athletic and fitness center which provides a competition swimming pool, regulation squash courts, a rock-climbing wall, a varsity athletic training room, weight room, treadmills, elliptical machines, bikes, free weights, and circuit strength machines. The dance and aerobics studio houses Pilates, Martial Arts, aerobic classes, and dance courses. There is also a gymnasium, a walking track, and an out-door turf field for soccer. **Graduates:** From July 1, 2016 to June 30, 2017, 188 bachelor's degrees were awarded. The most popular majors were nursing (29%), biology (13%), and psychology (7%). In an average class, 2% graduate in 3 years or less, 52% graduate in 4 years or less, 62% graduate in 5 years or less, and 63% graduate in 6 years or less. Of the 2016 graduating class, 17% were enrolled in graduate school within 6 months of graduation, and 48% were employed.

SERVICES: Counseling and information services are available, as is tutoring in every subject. There is a reader service for the blind, and remedial math, reading, and writing. There is also one-on-one, group tutoring by students and professional specialists, a computer-aid tutor, and an organized study group. **Library/Resources:** The library contains 144,499 volumes, 22,434 microform items, and 1,923 audio/video tapes/CDs/DVDs, and subscribes to 326,403 periodicals including electronic. Computerized library services include interlibrary loans, database searching, Internet access, and Wi-Fi capability. Special learning facilities include an art gallery, theaters, a media center, and an arboretum. **Physically Challenged Students:** 40% of the campus is accessible. Facilities include wheelchair ramps, elevators, special parking, specially equipped restrooms, special class scheduling, lowered drinking fountains, lowered telephones, and special housing. **Special:** Chatham offers a study-abroad program in 12 countries, cross-registration with other Pittsburgh Council on Higher Education institutions, co-op programs in all majors, internships in the public and private sectors, and a Washington semester in conjunction with American University and the Public Leadership Education Network. Accelerated degree programs, work-study, combined B.A.-B.S. degrees, multidisciplinary majors, and dual and student-designed majors are available. There are 3-2 engineering degrees with Carnegie Mellon and Penn State Universities and the University of Pittsburgh, dual degree programs, and an accelerated Master's program with Carnegie Mellon's Heinz School. There are 8 national honor societies, Phi Beta Kappa, and a freshman honors program. **Visiting:** There are regularly scheduled orientations for prospective students, including campus tours, student and faculty panels, financial aid presentations, and athletic coach meetings. There are guides for informal visits, visitors may sit in on classes, and stay overnight. To schedule a visit, contact Gabrielle Matich at (800)837-1290. **Campus Safety and Security:** Measures include 24-hour foot and vehicle patrol, emergency notification system, self-defense education, and security escort services. There are shuttle buses, emergency telephones, lighted pathways/sidewalks, and controlled access to dorms/residences.

REQUIREMENTS: Applicants who choose not to submit the SAT or ACT will be required to submit a graded writing sample, a resume or list of curricular and cocurricular activities. Applicants will also have the option to submit a portfolio or special project or activity. These materials may also be applied toward Chatham's scholarship review process upon acceptance. AP and CLEP credits are accepted. Important factors in the admissions decision are recommendations by school officials, leadership record, and extracurricular activities record. To graduate, students must complete 120 credit hours, including a general education curriculum of 7 courses and a senior tutorial, with a minimum GPA of 2.0. Students must also demonstrate proficiencies in writing, math, and computer literacy. **Procedure:** Freshmen are admitted in the fall and spring. Entrance exams should be taken by fall of the senior year. There are deferred admissions and rolling admissions plans. Applications should be filed by August 1 for fall entry. The fall 2017 application fee was $35. Notification is sent on a rolling basis. Applications are accepted on-line. **Transfer Students:** 116 transfer students enrolled in 2016-2017. Applicants must present college transcripts 45 of 120 credits required for the bachelor's degree must be completed at Chatham. **International Students:** There are 64 international students enrolled. They must take the TOEFL with a minimum score of 550 on the paper-based TOEFL (PBT) or 79 on the Internet-based version (iBT), or take either the MELAB or IELTS. The SAT is required if student doesn't submit the TOEFL.

ADMISSIONS: 55% of the 2017-2018 applicants were accepted. The SAT scores for the 2017-2018 freshman class were: Math-- 9% below 500, 53% between 500 and 599, 36% between 600 and 699, and 2% between 700 and 800. Evidence-Based Reading/Writing-- 11% below 500, 31% between 500 and 599, 49% between 600 and 699, and 9% between 700 and 800. The ACT scores were 1% between 12 and 17, 41% between 18 and 23, 48% between 24 and 29, and 10% above 30. 41% of the current freshmen were in the top fifth of their class; 69% were in the top two fifths. 1 freshman graduated first in the class. **Admissions Contact:** Amy Becher, Vice President for Enrollment Management. Email: *admission@chatham.edu* Web: *www.chatham.edu*

FINANCIAL AID: In 2017-2018, 100% of all full-time freshmen received some form of financial aid. 77% of all full-time freshmen received need-based aid. The average freshman award was $37,356. Need-based scholarships or need-based grants averaged $9,515 ($10,169 maximum); need-based self-help aid (loans and jobs) averaged $4,392 ($5,500 maximum); and other non-need-based awards and non-need-based scholarships averaged $16,394 ($23,000 maximum). The average financial indebtedness of the 2017 graduate was $26,075. The FAFSA code is 003244. The priority date for freshman financial aid applications for fall entry is March 1.

CHESTNUT HILL COLLEGE

F-3

www.chc.edu

Philadelphia, PA 19118	(215) 242-7134 (800) 248-0052
Fax: (215) 248-7082	**Email: chcapply@chc.edu**
Full-time: 419 men, 684 women	**Faculty:** 71
Part-time: 65 men, 205 women	**Ph.D.s:** 85%
Graduate: 100 men, 369 women	**Student/Faculty:** 12 to 1
Year: semesters, summer session	**Tuition:** $34,140
Room & Board: $9270	**Freshman Class:** 1242 applied, 1165 accepted, 245 enrolled
SAT EBR-W/M: 530/520 **ACT:** 22	**CEEB CODE:** 2082
Application Deadline: open	**COMPETITIVE**

Chestnut Hill College, founded in 1924, is a private, liberal arts institution affiliated with the Roman Catholic Church. In addition to the traditional program including more than 30 majors, CHC also offers an accelerated evening and weekend program for working adults and several graduate programs. Courses in the accelerated program are offered in 6 8-week sessions per year, with 10 career-oriented majors. Graduate programs lead to master's degrees in early level education, middle level education, secondary education, educational leadership, instructional technology, administration of human services, psychology, and the PsyD in clinical psychology. There are 2 undergraduate schools and 1 graduate school. In addition to regional accreditation, CHC has baccalaureate program accreditation with APA and AMS. The 75-acre campus is in a suburban area 25 miles northwest of downtown Philadelphia, at the very edge of the city. Including any residence halls, there are 17 buildings.

STUDENT LIFE: 75% of undergraduates are from Pennsylvania. Others are from 22 states, 37 foreign countries, and Canada. 49% are from public schools. 8% are Asian American; 7% race unknown; 6% Hispanic; 4% two or more races; 37% White; 35% African American; 3% Foreign. 31% are Protestant; 27% claim no religious affiliation; 26% Catholic. **Female To Male Ratio:** 2.2:1. The average age of freshmen is 17; all undergraduates, 27. 31% do not continue beyond their first year; 48% remain to graduate. **Housing:** 537 students can be accommodated in college housing, which includes dorms, off-campus apartments, honors houses and special-interest houses. On-campus housing is available on a first-come, first-served basis. 52% of students live on campus. Alcohol is not permitted. Upperclassmen may keep cars.

FACULTY/CLASSROOMS: 39% of faculty are male; 61% are female. 75% teach undergraduates, 65% do research, and 50% do both. No introductory courses are taught by graduate students. The average class size in an introductory lecture is 25; in a laboratory is 15; and in a regular course is 20.

PROGRAMS OF STUDY: CHC confers B.A., B.S., and B.Mus. degrees. Associate, master's, and doctoral degrees are also awarded. Bachelor's degrees are awarded in BIOLOGICAL SCIENCE (biochemistry, biology/biological science, and molecular biology), BUSINESS (accounting, business administration and management, business communications, human resources, and marketing/retailing/merchandising), COMMUNICATIONS AND THE ARTS (art, communications, communications technology, digital media technologies, English literature, French, music, and Spanish), COMPUTER AND PHYSICAL SCIENCE (chemistry, computer management, computer science, information sciences and systems, and mathematics), EDUCATION (early childhood education, elementary education, and music education), ENGINEERING AND ENVIRONMENTAL DESIGN (computer technology and environmental science), HEALTH PROFESSIONS (health care administration), SOCIAL SCIENCE (child care/child and family studies, criminal justice, forensic studies, German area studies, gerontology, history, human services, international studies, liberal arts/general studies, political science/government, psychology, and sociology). Biological, computer, physical sciences, and humanities are the strongest academically. Business, human services, and education have the largest enrollments.

ACTIVITIES: There are no fraternities or sororities. There are 31 groups on campus, including cheerleading, chorale, chorus, communications, computers, drama, environmental, ethnic, honors, instrumental ensemble, international, LGBT, literary magazine, musical theater, newspaper, orchestra, political, professional, radio and TV, religious, social, social service, student government, and yearbook. Popular campus events include Drama Club performances, Musical performances, Empty Bowl Night, Intramural One-Act Play Night, Christmas Decorations and Dance. **Sports:** There are 9 intercollegiate sports for men and 9 for women. Facilities include 2 gyms, an athletic training room, a fitness room, indoor swimming pool, tennis courts, hockey, lacrosse, softball, and soccer. **Graduates:** From July 1, 2016 to June 30, 2017, 391 bachelor's degrees were awarded. The most popular majors were human services (18%), criminal justice (9%), and pyschology (7%). In an average class, 45% graduate in 4 years or less, 37% graduate in 5 years or less, and 47% graduate in 6 years or less. Of the 2016 graduating class, 32% were enrolled in graduate school within 6 months of graduation, and 75% were employed.

SERVICES: Counseling and information services are available, as is tutoring in most subjects. There is a reader service for the blind, and remedial math and writing. **Library/Resources:** The library contains 130,880 volumes, 11,204 microform items, and 1,047 audio/video tapes/CDs/DVDs, and subscribes to 1,296 periodicals including electronic. Computerized library services include interlibrary loans, database searching, Internet access, and Wi-Fi capability. Special learning facilities include an art gallery, planetarium, radio station, TV station, a rotating observatory and technology center. **Physically Challenged Students:** 90% of the campus is accessible. Facilities include wheelchair ramps, elevators, special parking, specially equipped restrooms, and a shower area in residence halls. **Special:** Cross-registration is available among the seven local members of the Southeasern Pennslvania Consortium of Higher Education. Semesters may be taken at the 10 colleges in the Sisters of St. Joseph College Consortium Student Exchange Program, which are located in various states from Massachusetts to California. The college offers internships, study abroad in England, Spain, Italy, Austria, and France. There are also work-study programs, interdisciplinary majors, and dual and student-designed majors. Nondegree study and pass/fail options are available. The college offers unique career preparation programs in communications, international studies, environmental science, and international business. There are 16 national honor societies, a freshman honors program, and 14 departmental honors programs. **Visiting:** There are regularly scheduled orientations for prospective students, faculty/staff presentations and workshops on specific issues related to admissions (financial aid, curriculum, student life). Opportunities to speak with faculty/staff/students. There are guides for informal visits, visitors may sit in on classes, and stay overnight. To schedule a visit, contact the Admissions Office. **Campus Safety and Security:** Measures include 24-hour foot and vehicle patrol, emergency notification system, and security escort services. There are escorted shuttle cars and buses, emergency telephones, lighted pathways/sidewalks, and controlled access to dorms/residences. Doors are locked after 6 p.m. on weekends and monitored by cameras.

REQUIREMENTS: SAT or ACT test scores are required. Applicants must be graduates of an accredited secondary school. 16 Carnegie units are required, with a recommended 4 units each of English, math, science, and social studies and 3 of foreign language. An interview is recommended for all students. An essay is required. GED is accepted. A GPA of 2.0 is required. AP and CLEP credits are accepted. Important factors in the admissions decision are leadership record, extracurricular activities record, and advanced placement or honors courses. To graduate, students must complete at least 120 credit hours with a general average of 2.0 overall and in the major. Coursework must include 12 to 15 courses in the major; the Core reading/writing course, a writing course, 1 or 2 courses in a foreign language, Interdisciplinary Global Awareness Seminar, 1 math course (most students test out of this requirement), 1 ethics course, 2 courses in religious studies, the First-Year Initiative, 2 1-credit courses in phys ed or two semesters of a sport, 1 course each in art/music, history, literature, natural sciences, social sciences, a senior seminar and senior thesis. Students may choose from a wide variety of minors. **Procedure:** Freshmen are admitted in the fall, spring, and summer. Entrance exams should be taken early in the senior year. There are deferred admissions and rolling admissions plans. Application deadlines are open. The fall 2017 application fee was $35. Notification is sent on a rolling basis. Applications are accepted on-line. **Transfer Students:** 74 transfer students enrolled in 2016-2017. Applicants must have a minimum GPA of 2.0; a 2.5 is recommended. 45 of 120 credits required for the bachelor's degree must be completed at CHC. **International Students:** There are 42 international students enrolled. They must take the TOEFL with a minimum score of 550 on the paper-based TOEFL (PBT) or 79 on the Internet-based version (iBT). They must also take the SAT or ACT. The college also requires a complete set of academic credentials with English translations.

ADMISSIONS: 94% of the 2017-2018 applicants were accepted. The SAT scores for the 2017-2018 freshman class were: Evidence-based Reading/Writing-- 32% below 500, 46% between 500 and 599, 20% between 600 and 699, and 2% between 700 and 800. Math-- 30% below 500, 59% between 500 and 599, and 11% between 600 and 699. The ACT scores were 6% between 12 and 17, 75% between 18 and 23, 16% between 24 and 29, and 3% above 30. 14% of the current freshmen were in the top fifth of their class; 52% were in the top two fifths. **Admissions Contact:** Alaina Costa, Director of Admissions. Email: *chcapply@chc.edu* Web: *www.chc.edu*

FINANCIAL AID: In 2017-2018, 87% of all full-time freshmen received some form of financial aid, need-based aid. The average freshman award was $29,275. Need-based scholarships or need-based grants averaged $25,185; need-based self-help aid (loans and jobs) averaged $4,689; and non-need-based athletic scholarships averaged $7,664. The average financial indebtedness of the 2017 graduate was $42,058. CHC is a member of CSS. The FAFSA code is 003245. The priority date for freshman financial aid applications for fall entry is February 15.

CHEYNEY UNIVERSITY OF PENNSYLVANIA *(The complete profile is made available exclusively on our website, www.barronspac.com)*

CLARION UNIVERSITY OF PENNSYLVANIA *(The complete profile is made available exclusively on our website, www.barronspac.com)*

CURTIS INSTITUTE OF MUSIC *(The complete profile is made available exclusively on our website, www.barronspac.com)*

DELAWARE VALLEY UNIVERSITY F-3

www.devalcol.edu

Doylestown, PA 18901 **(215) 489-2372**

Fax: (215) 230-2968	**Email:** admitme@devalcol.edu
Full-time: 700 men, 900 women	**Faculty:** 79; IIA, -$
Part-time: 209 men, 191 women	**Ph.D.s:** 62%
Graduate: 27 men, 43 women	**Student/Faculty:** 20 to 1
Year: semesters, summer session	**Tuition:** $36,805
Room & Board: $14,466	**Freshman Class:** 1476 applied, 1164 accepted, 451 enrolled
SAT: required **ACT:** 22	**CEEB CODE:** 2510
Application Deadline: open	**COMPETITIVE**

Delaware Valley University, founded in 1896, is a private institution offering undergraduate programs in specialized fields of agriculture, business administration, English, the sciences, math, criminal justice administration, and secondary education. The college also offers graduate programs in educational leadership, and in food and agribusiness. The figures given in the above capsule and in this profile are approximate. There is 1 undergraduate school. The 550-acre campus is in a suburban area 20 miles north of Philadelphia. Including any residence halls, there are 36 buildings.

STUDENT LIFE: 67% of undergraduates are from Pennsylvania. Others are from 22 states, 1 foreign country, and Canada. 85% are from public schools. 80% are White; 4% African American; 1% Hispanic. 35% are Catholic; 32% Protestant; 16% claim no religious affiliation; 14% Buddhist, and Seventh-day Adventist. **Female To Male Ratio:** 1.2:1. The average age of freshmen is 18; all undergraduates, 21. 26% do not continue beyond their first year; 75% remain to graduate. **Housing:** 960 students can be accommodated in college housing, which includes dorms, honors houses, and 9 housing halls. On-campus housing is available on a first-come, first-served basis, and is available on a lottery system for upperclassmen. 63% of students live on campus. Upperclassmen may keep cars.

FACULTY/CLASSROOMS: 66% of faculty are male; 34% are female. All teach undergraduates. No introductory courses are taught by graduate students. The average class size in an introductory lecture is 24; in a laboratory is 21; and in a regular course is 20.

PROGRAMS OF STUDY: DVU confers B.A. and B.S. degrees. Associate and master's degrees are also awarded. Bachelor's degrees are awarded in AGRICULTURE (agronomy, animal science, dairy science, equine science, horticulture, and wildlife management), BIOLOGICAL SCIENCE (biology/biological science and zoology), BUSINESS (accounting, business administration and management, marketing/retailing/merchandising, and sports management), COMMUNICATIONS AND THE ARTS (English), COMPUTER AND PHYSICAL SCIENCE (chemistry and computer science), EDUCATION (secondary education), ENGINEERING AND ENVIRONMENTAL DESIGN (environmental science and food services technology), SOCIAL SCIENCE (criminal justice, food production/management/services, and food science). Physical & biological science, and animal science are the strongest academically. Business administration, and animal science have the largest enrollments.

ACTIVITIES: 4% of men belong to 5 national fraternities; 5% of women belong to 3 national sororities. There are 40 groups on campus, including habitat for humanity, block and bridle, bowling, colleges against cancer club, landscape nursery club, rock climbing club, ski and outdoor club, animal service club, art, band, cheerleading, chess, choir, chorale, chorus, computers, dance, drama, ethnic, honors, international, jazz band, literary magazine, newspaper, pep band, photography, professional, radio and TV, religious, social, social service, student government, symphony, and yearbook. Popular campus events include A-Day, Parents Day, and Family Weekend. **Sports:** There are 8 intercollegiate sports for men and 7 for women, and 9 intramural sports for men and 9 for women. Facilities include gyms, tennis courts, outdoor playing courts and fields, a football stadium, a running track, lacrosse, ultimate frisbee, wrestling, riding trails, and indoor and outdoor equine facilities. **Graduates:** From July 1, 2016 to June 30, 2017, 281 bachelor's degrees were awarded. The most popular majors were business administration (30%), animal science (22%), and ornamental horticulture (10%). In an average class, 44% graduate in 4 years or less, 54% graduate in 5 years or less, and 57% graduate in 6 years or less. Of the 2016 graduating class, 24% were enrolled in graduate school within 6 months of graduation, and 80% were employed.

SERVICES: Counseling and information services are available, as is tutoring in most subjects. There is a reader service for the blind, and remedial math, reading, and writing. **Library/Resources:** The library contains 70,000 volumes, 162,914 microform items, and subscribes to 728 periodicals including electronic. Computerized library services include interlibrary loans, database searching, Internet access, and Wi-Fi capability. Special learning facilities include a radio station, TV station, a dairy science center, a livestock farm, horse facilities, an apiary, a small animal lab, a tissue culture lab, an arboretum, and greenhouses. **Physically Challenged Students:** 85% of the campus is accessible. Facilities include wheelchair ramps, elevators, special parking, specially equipped restrooms, special class scheduling, and lowered drinking fountains. **Special:** DelVal offers a specialized methods and techniques program that enables students to learn lab techniques and gain experience in the practical aspects of their majors. There is a zoo science major that prepares students for careers in zoo management and animal conservation. There are co-op programs in all majors, dual majors, study abroad in England, internships, and work-study programs in a wide variety of employment and research settings. Cross-registration is available with Rutgers University and Middle Bucks Technical Institute. Nondegree study and pass/fail options are also available. There are 3 national honor societies, a freshman honors program, and 2 departmental honors programs. **Visiting:** There are regularly scheduled orientations for prospective students, consisting of a student panel, meetings with department chairs, and general information sessions. There are guides for informal visits, visitors may sit in on classes, and stay overnight. To schedule a visit, contact the Admissions Department. **Campus Safety and Security:** Measures include 24-hour foot and vehicle patrol, self-defense education, and security escort services. There are shuttle buses, emergency telephones, and lighted pathways/sidewalks.

REQUIREMENTS: The SAT or ACT is required. Applicants must be graduates of accredited secondary schools or have earned a GED. The college requires 15 academic units, including 6 in electives, 3 in English, and 2 each in math, science, and social studies. An interview is recommended. DelVal requires applicants to be in the upper 50% of their class. AP and CLEP credits are accepted. Important factors in the admissions decision are leadership record, personality/intangible qualities, and extracurricular activities record. The bachelor's degree requires completion of at least 128 credits, including 48 in the major, with a minimum GPA of 2.0. The core curriculum consists of 48 credits of liberal arts courses, including cultural enrichment, phys ed, and an introduction to computers. Students must also fulfill employment program requirements. **Procedure:** Freshmen are admitted in the fall and spring. Entrance exams should be taken in the junior or senior year. There are deferred admissions and rolling admissions plans. Application deadlines are open. The fall 2017 application fee was $35. Applications are accepted on-line. **Transfer Students:** 109 transfer students enrolled in 2016-2017. Applicants must have a minimum GPA of 2.0 and must submit SAT scores. An interview is recommended. 60 of 130 credits required for the bachelor's degree must be completed at DelVal. **International Students:** There was 1 international student enrolled. They must take the TOEFL, and either the SAT or ACT.

ADMISSIONS: 79% of the 2017-2018 applicants were accepted. The ACT scores were 38% below 12, 25% between 12 and 17, 25% between 18 and 23, 13% between 24 and 29, and % above 30. 25% of the current freshmen were in the top fifth of their class; 49% were in the top two fifths. 1 freshman graduated first in the class. **Admissions Contact:** Thomas O'Connor, Director of Admissions. Email: *admitme@devalcol.edu* Web: *www.devalcol.edu*

FINANCIAL AID: In 2017-2018, 97% of all full-time freshmen received some form of financial aid, and full-time freshmen received need-based aid. 20% of undergraduate students work part-time. The FAFSA code is 003252. The deadline for filing freshman financial aid applications for fall entry is April 1.

DESALES UNIVERSITY — F-3
www.desales.edu

Center Valley, PA 18034 — **(610) 282-1100**

Fax: (610) 282-0131	**Email:** admiss@desales.edu
Full-time: 760 men, 1024 women	**Faculty:** 125; IIA, -$
Part-time: 189 men, 408 women	**Ph.D.s:** 84%
Graduate: 309 men, 498 women	**Student/Faculty:** 16 to 1
Year: semesters, summer session	**Tuition:** $35,900
Room & Board: $11,620	**Freshman Class:** 2658 applied, 2117 accepted, 406 enrolled
SAT: required	**CEEB CODE:** 2021
Application Deadline: August 1	**COMPETITIVE**

DeSales University, is a private, four-year Catholic university with a Salesian mission administered by the Oblates of St. Francis DeSales. Our priority is to give our students a quality, broad-based liberal arts and career-centered education. Students are exposed to Catholic teachings but are also afforded the luxury of exploring in an atmosphere of intellectual freedom. There is 1 undergraduate school. In addition to regional accreditation, DeSales has baccalaureate program accreditation with MSCHE. The 480-acre campus is in a suburban area in Lehigh County, PA, 50 miles north of Philadelphia. Including any residence halls, there are 33 buildings.

STUDENT LIFE: 68% of undergraduates are from Pennsylvania. Others are from 28 states, and 5 foreign countries. 93% are White; 6% race unknown; 3% African American; 3% Asian American; 12% Hispanic; 1% American Indian/Alaska Native. **Female To Male Ratio:** 1.5:1. The average age of freshmen is 18. 15% do not continue beyond their first year; 70% remain to graduate. **Housing:** 1192 students can be accommodated in college housing, which includes dorms and on-campus apartments, and special-interest houses. On-campus housing is guaranteed for all 4 years, is available on a first-come, first-served basis, and is available on a lottery system for upperclassmen. 64% of students live on campus. All students may keep cars.

FACULTY/CLASSROOMS: 42% of faculty are male; 58% are female. 85% teach undergraduates, and 85% do research. No introductory courses are taught by graduate students.

PROGRAMS OF STUDY: DeSales confers B.A., B.S., and B.S.N. degrees. Master's and doctoral degrees are also awarded. Bachelor's degrees are awarded in BIOLOGICAL SCIENCE (biochemistry and biology/biological science), BUSINESS (accounting, business administration and management, finance, human resources, management information systems, marketing/retailing/merchandising, and sports management), COMMUNICATIONS AND THE ARTS (communications, dance, dramatic arts, English, film arts, media arts, performing arts, radio/television technology, Spanish, theatre acting, theater design, theatre production, and theater management), COMPUTER AND PHYSICAL SCIENCE (chemistry, computer game design/development, computer science, and mathematics), EDUCATION (early childhood education and elementary education), HEALTH PROFESSIONS (exercise science, nursing, pharmaceutical science, physical therapy, and physician's assistant), SOCIAL SCIENCE (criminal justice, history, liberal arts/general studies, philosophy, political science/government, psychology, and theological studies). Physician assistant, physical therapy, and theatre are the strongest academically. Biology, physician assistant, and nursing have the largest enrollments.

ACTIVITIES: There are no fraternities or sororities. There are 50 groups on campus, including band, cheerleading, choir, chorale, chorus, communications, computers, dance, debate, drama, ethnic, film, honors, international, literary magazine, marching band, musical theater, newspaper, pep band, political, professional, radio and TV, religious, social, social service, student government, and yearbook. **Sports:** There are 7 intercollegiate sports for men and 7 for women, and 9 intramural sports for men and 9 for women. Facilities include soccer, baseball, softball, tennis, basketball, lacrosse, cross country, volleyball, field hockey, tennis, golf, and indoor and outdoor track and field. The sports and recreation facility features a fitness center, and multipurpose athletic courts. **Graduates:** From July 1, 2016 to June 30, 2017, 557 bachelor's degrees were awarded. The most popular majors were business (23%), health professions and related fields (23%), and visual and performing arts (11%). In an average class, 64% graduate in 4 years or less, 69% graduate in 5 years or less, and 70% graduate in 6 years or less.

SERVICES: Counseling and information services are available, as is tutoring in most subjects. There is a reader service for the blind, and remedial math, reading, and writing. The Academic Resource Center (ARC) provides services (including tutoring) for students. **Library/ Resources:** The library contains 388,812 volumes, 373,050 microform items, and 4,464 audio/video tapes/CDs/DVDs, and subscribes to 23,000 periodicals including electronic. Computerized library services include interlibrary loans, database searching, Internet access, and Wi-Fi capability. Special learning facilities include a radio station. The Gambet Building for Business and Healthcare includes science simulation laboratories to replicate clinical scenarios specific to adult, pediatric and birthing care, as well as globally integrated classrooms and administrative operations for undergraduate and graduate health care and business degree programs. The Priscilla Payne Hurd Science Center provides teaching and research laboratories in chemistry, biology, biotechnology, environmental, and human performance. The Labuda Center for the Performing Arts is home to most Act 1 events. The Trexler Library collection includes a diverse range of American and international films as well as a current collection of reference materials related to film, television, and media studies. **Physically Challenged Students:** 99% of the campus is accessible. Facilities include wheelchair ramps, elevators, special parking, specially equipped restrooms, special class scheduling, lowered drinking fountains, lowered telephones, and special housing. **Special:** Students may cross-register with schools in the Lehigh Valley Association of Independent Colleges, with Cedar Crest, Lafayette, Moravian, and Muhlenberg Colleges. Internships are strongly encouraged in all majors, and study abroad in seven countries is possible. Dual majors, a Washington semester, pass/fail options, accelerated degree programs, and credit for life, military, and work experience are offered. 5 Year BA/MACJ, 4 1/2 Year BS/MBA, and 5 Year Medical Studies/Physician Assistant Programs are also available. There are 11 national honor societies and a freshman honors program. **Visiting:** There are regularly scheduled orientations for prospective students, including meetings with faculty advisers and social activities. There are guides for informal visits, visitors may sit in on classes, and stay overnight. To schedule a visit, contact Mr. Derrick Wetzel at (610) 282-4443. **Campus Safety and Security:** Measures include 24-hour foot and vehicle patrol, emergency notification system, self-defense education, and security escort services. There are emergency telephones, lighted pathways/sidewalks, and controlled access to dorms/ residences.

REQUIREMENTS: The SAT is required. Applicants must be graduates of an accredited secondary school. The GED is accepted. Applicants should have completed 17 college preparatory courses including 4 years each of English, history, and math, 3 years of science, and 2 years of foreign language. The school will accept an essay but strongly recommends an interview. For theater students, a performance appraisal is required. For dance students an audition is required. AP and CLEP credits are accepted. Important factors in the admissions decision are advanced placement or honors courses, leadership record, recommendations by school officials, and evidence of special talent. For graduation, students must complete a minimum of 120 credit hours including a maximum of 48 in the major with a minimum GPA of 2.0 overall and in the major. Liberal arts distribution requirements consist of 12 to 16 courses including cultural literacy, modes of thinking, and Christian values and theology, as well as 3 courses in phys ed (one-credit courses). Internships are strongly encouraged for most majors. **Procedure:** Freshmen are admitted fall and spring. Entrance exams should be taken during the junior or senior year. There are deferred admissions and rolling admissions plans. Applications should be filed by August 1 for fall entry. The fall 2017 application fee was $30. Notification is sent on a rolling basis. Applications are accepted on-line. **Transfer Students:** 72 transfer students enrolled in 2016-2017. Applicants for transfer should have completed a minimum of 24 college credit hours with a GPA of 2.5. An interview is recommended. 45 of 120 credits required for the bachelor's degree must be completed at DeSales. **International Students:** They must take the TOEFL with a minimum score of 550 on the paper-based TOEFL (PBT) or 100 on the Internet-based version (iBT). They must also take the SAT or ACT.

ADMISSIONS: 80% of the 2017-2018 applicants were accepted. The SAT scores for the 2017-2018 freshman class were: Critical Reading-- 44% below 500, 37% between 500 and 599, 15% between 600 and 699, and 5% between 700 and 800. Math-- 46% below 500, 36% between 500 and 599, 15% between 600 and 699, and 3% between 700 and 800. Writing-- 48% below 500, 34% between 500 and 599, 15% between 600 and 699, and 3% between 700 and 800. **Admissions Contact:** Mary Birkhead, Dean of Enrollment Management. Email: *admiss@desales.edu* Web: *www.desales.edu*

FINANCIAL AID: In 2017-2018, 86% of all full-time freshmen received some form of financial aid, and need-based aid. The average freshman award was $25,787. Need-based scholarships or need-based grants averaged $20,398; need-based self-help aid (loans and jobs) averaged $5,097; and other non-need-based awards and non-need-based scholarships averaged $13,014. The average financial indebtedness of the 2017 graduate was $25,875. DeSales is a member of CSS. The state aid form and the college's own financial statement are required. The FAFSA code is 003986. The deadline for filing freshman financial aid applications for fall entry is February 1.

DICKINSON COLLEGE D-3

www.dickinson.edu

Carlisle, PA 17013	(717) 245-5121 (800) 644-1773
Fax: (717) 245-1442	Email: admissions@dickinson.edu
Full-time: 970 men, 1355 women	Faculty: 225; IIB, +$
Part-time: 8 men, 6 women	Ph.D.s: 93%
Graduate: n/av	Student/Faculty: 9 to 1
Year: semesters	Tuition: $52,930
Room & Board: $13,236	Freshman Class: 5941 applied, 2894 accepted, 607 enrolled
SAT EBR-W/M: 650/660 ACT: 30	CEEB CODE: 2186
Application Deadline: January 15	MOST COMPETITIVE

Dickinson is a premier four-year residential liberal-arts institution chartered in 1783 and widely recognized as a leader in global and sustainability education. We prepare our graduates to face the world's challenges so they are always equipped and eager to collaborate with others to make an impact. There is 1 undergraduate school. In addition to regional accreditation, Dickinson has baccalaureate program accreditation with ACS, PA Department of Education, and University Senate of the United Methodist Church. The 144-acre campus is in a suburban area about 20 miles west of Harrisburg, PA and 2 hours from Washington, D.C. Including any residence halls, there are 134 buildings.

STUDENT LIFE: 79% of undergraduates are from out of state, mostly the Middle Atlantic. Students are from 38 states, 44 foreign countries, and Canada. 55% are from public schools. 8% are Hispanic; 66% White; 5% African American; 4% Asian American; 4% two or more races; 13% Foreign; 1% race unknown. 26% are Protestant; 24% claim no religious affiliation; 21% Catholic; 11% Jewish. **Female To Male Ratio:** 1.4:1. The average age of freshmen is 18; all undergraduates, 20. 10% do not continue beyond their first year; 83% remain to graduate. **Housing:** 2071 students can be accommodated in college housing, which includes coed dorms and on-campus apartments. In addition, there are language/ international houses, special-interest houses, fraternity houses, sorority houses, arts, environmental, living/learning communities, multicultural and wellness housing. On-campus housing is guaranteed for all 4 years and is available on a lottery system for upperclassmen. 95% of students live on campus. Upperclassmen may keep cars.

FACULTY/CLASSROOMS: 51% of faculty are male; 49% are female. All teach undergraduates, and all do research. No introductory courses are taught by graduate students. The average class size in an introductory lecture is 35 and in a laboratory is 21.

PROGRAMS OF STUDY: Dickinson confers B.A. and B.S. degrees. Bachelor's degrees are awarded in AGRICULTURE (environmental studies), BIOLOGICAL SCIENCE (biochemistry, biology/biological science, and neurosciences), BUSINESS (international business management), COMMUNICATIONS AND THE ARTS (art history, classical languages, dance, English, French, German, Greek, Latin, music, Russian, Spanish, and theatre arts), COMPUTER AND PHYSICAL SCIENCE (chemistry, computer science, earth science, mathematics, and physics), EDUCATION (educational studies), ENGINEERING AND ENVIRONMENTAL DESIGN (environmental science), SOCIAL SCIENCE (African studies, American studies, anthropology, archeology, classical/ancient civilization, East Asian studies, economics, history, international studies, Italian studies, Judaic studies, Latin American studies, law, Medieval studies, Middle Eastern studies, philosophy, political science/government, psychology, public affairs, religion, sociology, and women's studies). International education/foreign languages, sciences, and sustainability education & preprofessional programs are the strongest academically. Economics, international business & management, and biology have the largest enrollments.

ACTIVITIES: 16% of men belong to 4 national fraternities; 27% of women belong to 1 local and 5 national sororities. There are 135 groups on campus, including art, band, cheerleading, chess, choir, chorale, chorus, computers, dance, debate, drama, environmental, ethnic, film, honors, international, jazz band, LGBT, literary magazine, musical theater, newspaper, orchestra, photography, political, professional, radio station, religious, social, social service, student government, symphony, and yearbook. Popular campus events include All-College Formal, Spring Fest, and Relay For Life. **Sports:** There are 12 intercollegiate sports for men and 13 for women, and 6 intramural sports for men and 6 for women. Facilities include a fitness center with strength training equipment, cardio machines and five international squash courts, basketball and volleyball, racquetball courts. The gymnasium features 200-meter, four-lane track with a hidden jump pit, indoor rock-climbing wall, swimming pool with diving well, a dance studio, multi-purpose indoor training areas, fitness classes, tennis courts, synthetic turf fields for varsity football, field hockey, lacrosse, softball, baseball, soccer complex, a golf simulator, jogging, and bicycle trails. **Graduates:** From July 1, 2016 to June 30, 2017, 530 bachelor's degrees were awarded. The most popular majors were economics (9%), international business & management (8%), and biology (7%). In an average class, 80% graduate in 4 years or less, 84% graduate in 5 years or less, and 83% graduate in 6 years or less. Of the 2016 graduating class, 37% were enrolled in graduate school within 6 months of graduation, and 82% were employed.

SERVICES: Counseling and information services are available, as is tutoring in every subject. Services are provided as necessary on case-by-case basis. There is a reader service for the blind. **Library/Resources:** The library contains 1.1 million volumes, 168,703 microform items, and 168,487 audio/video tapes/CDs/DVDs, and subscribes to 70,927 periodicals including electronic. Computerized library services include interlibrary loans, database searching, Internet access, and Wi-Fi capability. Special learning facilities include an art gallery, planetarium, fiber-optic and satellite telecommunications networks, a telescope observatory, scanning electron microscope, research-quality greenhouse, archival collection, Dog House (service dog-training program), Center for Sustainable Living (aka treehouse), Landis House (center for service, spirituality, and social justice), the Makery (community center with tools and supplies that combine equipment, community, and educational resources to empower members to design, prototype and create manufactured works), media center, biogas facility, college farm, and the Hive (apiary). **Physically Challenged Students:** 70% of the campus is accessible. Facilities include wheelchair ramps, elevators, special parking, specially equipped restrooms, special class scheduling, lowered drinking fountains, lowered telephones, and special housing. **Special:** Students may cross-register with Central Pennsylvania Consortium Colleges. Instruction in 13 languages is available. Internships are available on and off campus. Dickinson now sponsors more than 39 programs on six continents in 24 countries. These options include academic year programs, semester programs, summer programs, globally-integrated courses that include a January international field experience and specialized programs which combine domestic study with international study. A Washington semester, work-study, and accelerated degree programs are available, as are dual majors, student-designed majors, non-degree study, pass/fail options, and a 3-3 law degree with the Dickinson School of Law of Pennsylvania State University. There are 3-2 engineering degrees offered with Case Western Reserve University, Rensselaer Polytechnic Institute, and with Columbia University. There is also a 3-1-1 dual-degree program with Johns Hopkins School of Advanced International Studies (SAIS). Graduate school agreements are currently in place for: Medicine/Health programs with Jefferson School of Population Health at the Jefferson Medical College; Business with American University's Kogod School of Business; The Thunderbird School of Global Management; Simon School of Business at The University of Rochester; International Graduate Education with The Network of Autonomous Schools of the Lombardy Region (Italy); University of Bremen (Bremen, Germany); University of East Anglia (Norwich, England); University of Maine; University of Malaga (Malaga, Spain), and the University of Queensland (Queensland, Australia). There are 16 national honor societies, Phi Beta Kappa, and 36 departmental honors programs. **Visiting:** There are regularly scheduled orientations for prospective students, including campus tours, individual interviews, group information sessions, class visits, overnight stays in residence halls, and open houses. To schedule a visit, contact the Admissions Office. **Campus Safety and Security:** Measures include 24-hour foot and vehicle patrol, emergency notification system, self-defense education, and security escort services. There are shuttle buses, emergency telephones, lighted pathways/sidewalks, controlled access to dorms/residences, electronic access to residence halls, and required electronic access for on-campus administrative and academic buildings.

REQUIREMENTS: The SAT or ACT and the ACT Writing Test are recommended. The GED is accepted. Applicants should have completed 16 academic credits, including 4 years of English, 3 each of math and science, of those, 2 must be lab, 2-3 of foreign language, 2 each of social studies, and academic electives. An essay is required, and an interview is recommended. AP credits are accepted. Important factors in the admissions decision are advanced placement or honors courses, evidence of special talent, personality/intangible qualities, extracurricular activities record, leadership record, and geographical diversity. To graduate, students must complete 32 courses with a minimum GPA of 2.0. The school requires 1 course each in the arts, humanities, social sciences, sustainability, and lab sciences. Also required are 3 courses of cross-cultural studies (including foreign language, comparative civilizations, and U.S. diversity), a first-year seminar, phys ed, and the completion of a major averaging 9 to 15 courses. Writing in the discipline and quantitative reasoning courses are also required. **Procedure:** Freshmen are admitted in the fall. Entrance exams should be taken in the spring of the junior year or the fall of the senior year. There are early decision, early admissions, and deferred admissions plans. Early decision applications should be filed by November 15; regular applications, by January 15 for fall entry. The fall 2017 application fee was $65. Notification of early decision is sent December 15; regular decision, March 20. 257 early decision candidates were accepted for the 2017-2018 class. 252 applicants were on the 2017 waiting list; 35 were admitted. Applications are accepted on-line. **Transfer Students:** 8 transfer students enrolled in 2016-2017. Applicants for transfer must have at least a 2.0 cumulative GPA and submit secondary school and college transcripts and 1 professor recommendation in addition to the standard application for admission. 16 of 32 credits required for the bachelor's degree must be completed at Dickinson. **International Students:** There are 295 international students enrolled. They must take the TOEFL with a minimum score of 90 on the Internet-based version (iBT). Students must also take the IELTS.

ADMISSIONS: 49% of the 2017-2018 applicants were accepted. The SAT scores for the 2017-2018 freshman class were: Math-- 1% below 500, 17% between 500 and 599, 49% between 600 and 699, and 33% between 700 and 800. Evidence-Based Reading/Writing-- 12% between 500 and 599, 61% between 600 and 699, and 27% between 700 and 800. The ACT scores were 4% between 18 and 23, 45% between 24 and 29, and 51% above 30. **Admissions Contact:** Dr. Jason Rivera, Director of Institutional Research. Email: *admissions@dickinson.edu* Web: *www.dickinson.edu*

FINANCIAL AID: In 2017-2018, 78% of all full-time freshmen received some form of financial aid. 62% of all full-time freshmen received need-based aid. The average freshman award was $40,880. Need-based scholarships or need-based grants averaged $38,793 ($64,490 maximum); need-based self-help aid (loans and jobs) averaged $6,107 ($8,000 maximum); other non-need-based awards and non-need-based scholarships averaged $12,342 ($60,430 maximum); and $9,597 from other forms of aid. 48% of undergraduate students work part-time. The average financial indebtedness of the 2017 graduate was $25,881. Dickinson is a member of CSS. The CSS/Profile and the state aid form, and noncustodial parent statement are required. The FAFSA code is 003253. The priority date for freshman financial aid applications for fall entry is November 15.

DREXEL UNIVERSITY — F-3

www.drexel.edu

Philadelphia, PA 19104 — **(215) 895-2000**

Fax: (215) 895-5939	**Email:** enroll@drexel.edu
Full-time: 7425 men, 6144 women	**Faculty:** 1536; I, av$
Part-time: 593 men, 1336 women	**Ph.D.s:** 86%
Graduate: 3209 men, 5483 women	**Student/Faculty:** 12 to 1
Year: quarters, summer session	**Tuition:** $52,037
Room & Board: $13,890	**Freshman Class:** 28454 applied, 22489 accepted, 3268 enrolled
SAT CR/M: 619/633 **ACT:** 28	**CEEB CODE:** 2149
Application Deadline: January 15	**HIGHLY COMPETITIVE**

Drexel University, founded in 1891, is a comprehensive national research university ranked among the top 100 in the United States. The University has built its global reputation on core achievements that include: leadership in experiential learning through its cooperative education program; a history of academic technology firsts; and recognition as a model of best practices in translational research initiatives. Drexel engages with students and communities around the world via three Philadelphia campuses and other regional sites, Drexel University Sacramento, The Academy of Natural Sciences of Drexel University and international research partnerships in several countries around the globe. Drexel Online is one of the oldest and most successful providers of online degree programs. There are 15 undergraduate schools and 12 graduate schools. In addition to regional accreditation, Drexel has baccalaureate program accreditation with AACSB, ABET, ACCE, ADA, NAAB, and NASAD. The 96-acre campus is in an urban area in the University City neighborhood of Philadelphia. Including any residence halls, there are 111 buildings.

STUDENT LIFE: 56% of undergraduates are from out of state, mostly the Middle Atlantic. Students are from 48 states, 117 foreign countries, and Canada. 7% are African American; 6% Hispanic; 52% White; 4% two or more races; 3% race unknown; 16% Asian American; 11% Foreign. **Female To Male Ratio:** 1.2:1. The average age of freshmen is 18; all undergraduates, 22. 11% do not continue beyond their first year; 71% remain to graduate. **Housing:** College-sponsored housing includes dorms, on-campus apartments, and off-campus apartments. In addition, there are fraternity houses, sorority houses, honors floors in residence halls, and international student housing. On-campus housing is guaranteed for the freshman year only, is available on a first-come, first-served basis, and is available on a lottery system for upperclassmen. 78% of students commute. All students may keep cars.

FACULTY/CLASSROOMS: 50% of faculty are male; 50% are female. No introductory courses are taught by graduate students.

PROGRAMS OF STUDY: Drexel confers B.S.B.A., B.A.C.S., B.S.S.M., B.S.I.S., B.S.A.E., B.S.I., B.S.E.T., B.S.C.S., BSc.MGT., B.Arch., B.S.M.E., B.S.I.T., B.S.ClSc., B.S., B.S.C.A., B.S.Civ., B.S.S.E., B.S.Ch.E., B.A., B.S.B.E., B.S.Ee.E., B.S.C.A.E., B.S.N., B.S.ECON, B.S.Ma.E., B.S.C.E., B.S.E., B.S.E.E., B.S.B.A.E., B.A.Econ., B.S.Pr.Mt., B.S.M.S.E., and B.S.H.M. degrees. Master's and doctoral degrees are also awarded. Bachelor's degrees are awarded in AGRICULTURE (environmental studies), BIOLOGICAL SCIENCE (biology/biological science and nutrition), BUSINESS (accounting, business administration and management, business economics, business intelligence and analytics, entrepreneurial studies, fashion merchandising, hotel/motel and restaurant management, international business, management information systems, marketing/retailing/merchandising, organizational leadership and management, and sports management), COMMUNICATIONS AND THE ARTS (animation, art history, communications, dance, design, English, film arts, graphic design, media arts, music industry, photography, television & digital media production, and video), COMPUTER AND PHYSICAL SCIENCE (chemistry, computer engineering technology, computer game design/development, computer science, computer security and information assurance, digital arts/technology, geoscience, information sciences and systems, mathematics, physics, science, software engineering, and web technology), EDUCATION (education and elementary education), ENGINEERING AND ENVIRONMENTAL DESIGN (architectural engineering, architecture, biomedical engineering, chemical engineering, civil engineering, computer engineering, construction management, electrical/electronics engineering, engineering, engineering technology, environmental engineering, environmental science, interior design, materials engineering, materials science and engineering, and mechanical engineering), HEALTH PROFESSIONS (health services administration, health science, nursing, premedicine, and public health), SOCIAL SCIENCE (anthropology, criminal justice, criminology, culinary arts, economics, fashion design and technology, history, international studies, legal studies, philosophy, political science/government, psychology, and sociology). Engineering, business, and design arts are the strongest academically. Nursing, mechanical engineering, and finance have the largest enrollments.

ACTIVITIES: 9% of men belong to 21 national fraternities; 8% of women belong to 14 national sororities. There are 250 groups on campus, including art, band, cheerleading, chess, choir, chorus, communications, computers, dance, drama, environmental, ethnic, film, forensics, honors, international, jazz band, LGBT, literary magazine, musical theater, newspaper, orchestra, pep band, photography, political, professional, radio and TV, religious, social, social service, student government, and yearbook. Popular campus events include Musical, Cultural, and Art Events. **Sports:** There are 10 intercollegiate sports for men and 10 for women, and 11 intramural sports for men and 11 for women. Facilities include an athletic center with gyms, squash courts, a 25-yard swimming pool with a diving well, exercise rooms, wrestling room, a recreation center with gyms, fitness and exercise studios, squash courts, a climbing wall, indoor track, and armory with multipurpose courts. **Graduates:** From July 1, 2016 to June 30, 2017, 4270 bachelor's degrees were awarded. The most popular majors were nursing (4%), mechanical engineering (3%), and finance (3%). In an average class, 71% graduate in 6 years or less. Of the 2016 graduating class, 12% were enrolled in graduate school within 6 months of graduation, and 83% were employed.

SERVICES: Counseling and information services are available, as is tutoring in most subjects. There is remedial math, reading, and writing. **Library/Resources:** The library contains 772,895 volumes, 18,121 microform items, and 45,465 audio/video tapes/CDs/DVDs, and subscribes to 54,877 periodicals including electronic. Computerized library services include interlibrary loans, database searching, Internet access, and Wi-Fi capability. Special learning facilities include an art gallery, natural history museum, radio station, and TV station. **Physically Challenged Students:** 98% of the campus is accessible. Facilities include wheelchair ramps, elevators, special parking, specially equipped restrooms, special class scheduling, lowered drinking fountains, and special housing. **Special:** Cooperative education enables students to alternate full-time classroom study and 6-month full-time employment periods with university-approved employers. As part of its global initiatives, Drexel offers study abroad and co-op abroad experiences as well as global classrooms and a global engagement certificate. As part of its commitment to community engagement, all freshmen enroll in an introductory civic engagement course that combines classroom study with community service. Undergraduate research and research co-ops allow students to work with faculty, post-docs, and graduate students on state-of-the art projects that contribute to academic research, scholarship, and creative work. Drexel offers several disciplinary or interdisciplinary bachelor's-master's accelerated degree programs as well as minors, and concentrations. Drexel offers a custom-designed major that enables students to pursue an individualized course of study not readily available through an existing major. The program of study incorporates an early intensive research experience and cooperative education as part of its degree requirements and culminates in an original, and interdisciplinary senior-year project. There is 1 national honor society and a freshman honors program. **Visiting:** There are regularly scheduled orientations for prospective students, consisting of a 2-day program for new freshmen and their parents in late July. There are guides for informal visits, visitors may sit in on classes, and stay overnight. To schedule a visit, contact the Admissions Office. **Campus Safety and Security:** Measures include 24-hour foot and vehicle patrol, emergency notification system, self-defense education, and security escort services. There are shuttle buses, emergency telephones, lighted pathways/sidewalks, controlled access to dorms/residences, and residential and commuter safety and security programs.

REQUIREMENTS: The SAT is required. Applicants must be graduates of an accredited secondary school. The GED is accepted. AP and CLEP credits are accepted. The graduation requirements for undergraduate programs require the completion of between 180 and 192 quarter credits depending on the major with a 2.0 cumulative GPA. The successful completion of co-op terms is required of students with programs of study that include cooperative education experience (s). **Procedure:** Freshmen are admitted in the fall. There are early decision, early admissions, and deferred admissions plans. Early decision applications should be filed by November 1; regular applications, by January 15 for fall entry. The fall 2017 application fee was $50. Notification of early decision is sent December 15; regular decision, April 1. Applications are accepted online. **Transfer Students:** 767 transfer students enrolled in 2016-2017. Applicants must have a minimum GPA of 2.5. Other requirements vary among the individual colleges within the university. 45 of 180 credits required for the bachelor's degree must be completed at Drexel. **International Students:** There are 1985 international students enrolled. They must take the TOEFL with a minimum score of 79 on the Internet-based version (iBT). Students must also take the IELTS.

ADMISSIONS: 79% of the 2017-2018 applicants were accepted. The SAT scores for the 2017-2018 freshman class were: Critical Reading-- 2% below 500, 33% between 500 and 599, 51% between 600 and 699, and 13% between 700 and 800. Math-- 2% below 500, 35% between 500 and 599, 44% between 600 and 699, and 19% between 700 and 800. The ACT scores were 1% between 12 and 17, 20% between 18 and 23, 52%

between 24 and 29, and 28% above 30. 56% of the current freshmen were in the top fifth of their class; 84% were in the top two fifths. **Admissions Contact:** Evelyn Thimba, AVP, Freshman & International Admissions. Email: *enroll@drexel.edu* Web: *www.drexel.edu*

FINANCIAL AID: In 2017-2018, 99% of all full-time freshmen received some form of financial aid. 69% of all full-time freshmen received need-based aid. The average freshman award was $42,995. Need-based scholarships or need-based grants averaged $33,006; need-based self-help aid (loans and jobs) averaged $9,096; non-need-based athletic scholarships averaged $32,568; and other non-need-based awards and non-need-based scholarships averaged $14,619. 71% of undergraduate students work part-time. Drexel is a member of CSS. The CSS/Profile is required. The FAFSA code is 003256. The priority date for freshman financial aid applications for fall entry is February 15.

DUQUESNE UNIVERSITY B-3

www.duq.edu

Pittsburgh, PA 15282	**(412) 396-6222** **(800) 456-0590**
Fax: (412) 396-5644	**Email: admissions@duq.edu**
Full-time: 2117 men, 3709 women	**Faculty:** 477; I, -$
Part-time: 45 men, 71 women	**Ph.D.s:** 94%
Graduate: 1240 men, 1835 women	**Student/Faculty:** 14 to 1
Year: semesters, summer session	**Tuition:** $36,394
Room & Board: $12,114	**Freshman Class:** 7336 applied, 5260 accepted, 1562 enrolled
SAT EBR-W/M: 606/597 **ACT:** 26	**CEEB CODE:** 2196
Application Deadline: July 1	**VERY COMPETITIVE**

Duquesne University is a private, Catholic institution, consistently ranked among the nation's top-tier universities for its award-winning faculty and tradition of academic excellence. Duquesne offers more than 80 undergraduate and 85 graduate programs in liberal arts, sciences, music, business, nursing, pharmacy, health sciences, education, law and biomedical engineering. Several online programs are available, ranging from bachelor's degree completion to masters and doctoral degrees. Duquesne is a Yellow Ribbon Program participant, and is ranked as a Military Friendly School by GI Jobs. Founded in 1878 by Spiritans, Duquesne is guided by a core set of values: promoting high academic standards, building community, having a global vision, and fostering a commitment to service. There are 9 undergraduate schools and 9 graduate schools. In addition to regional accreditation, Duquesne has baccalaureate program accreditation with AACSB, NASM, AMTA, APA, and CAATE. The 50-acre campus is in an urban area on a private, self-contained campus in the center of Pittsburgh. Including any residence halls, there are 46 buildings.

STUDENT LIFE: 72% of undergraduates are from Pennsylvania. Others are from 44 states, 48 foreign countries, and Canada. 79% are White; 6% Foreign; 5% African American; 3% Asian American; 3% Hispanic; 2% two or more races; 2% race unknown. 47% are Catholic; 27% claim no religious affiliation; 16% Protestant. **Female To Male Ratio:** 1.7:1. The average age of freshmen is 18; all undergraduates, 20. 13% do not continue beyond their first year; 72% remain to graduate. **Housing:** 3728 students can be accommodated in college housing, which includes gender neutral, single sex, coed dorms and on-campus apartments. In addition, there are honors houses, special-interest houses, fraternity and sorority wings, international wings, and club wings. On-campus housing is available on a first-come, first-served basis, and is available on a lottery system for upperclassmen. 59% of students live on campus. All students may keep cars.

FACULTY/CLASSROOMS: 49% of faculty are male; 51% are female. 95% teach undergraduates. No introductory courses are taught by graduate students. The average class size in an introductory lecture is 25; in a laboratory is 20; and in a regular course is 27.

PROGRAMS OF STUDY: Duquesne confers B.A., B.S., B.M., B.S.A.T., B.S.B.A., B.S.Ed., B.S.H.M.S., B.S.H.S., and B.S.N. degrees. Master's and doctoral degrees are also awarded. Bachelor's degrees are awarded in BIOLOGICAL SCIENCE (biochemistry, biology/adolescence education, and biology/biological science), BUSINESS (accounting, banking and finance, business administration and management, business communications, business economics, entrepreneurial studies, international business management, management information systems, management science, marketing/retailing/merchandising, nonprofit/public organization management, sports management, sports marketing, and supply chain management), COMMUNICATIONS AND THE ARTS (advertising, art history and appreciation, classical languages, communications, dramatic arts, English, Greek (classical), journalism, Latin, modern language, multimedia, music business management, music performance, music technology, public relations, Spanish, and speech/debate/rhetoric), COMPUTER AND PHYSICAL SCIENCE (chemistry, chemistry/adolescence education, computer science, mathematics, and physics), EDUCATION (athletic training, early childhood education, education, English education, foreign languages education, health information management, mathematics education, middle school education, music education, physical science secondary school education, social studies education, and special education), ENGINEERING AND ENVIRONMENTAL DESIGN (biomedical engineering, computer technology, and environmental science), HEALTH PROFESSIONS (health care administration, health science, music therapy, nursing, occupational therapy, pharmaceutical science, pharmacy, physical therapy, physician's assistant, and speech pathology/audiology), SOCIAL SCIENCE (behavioral science, classical/ancient civilization, economics, history, humanities, international relations, liberal arts/general studies, philosophy, political science/government, psychology, sociology, theological studies, and women & gender studies). Pharmacy, nursing science, and law have the largest enrollments.

ACTIVITIES: 17% of men belong to 1 local and 9 national fraternities; 24% of women belong to 10 national sororities. There are 258 groups on campus, including social programming, art, band, cheerleading, chess, choir, chorale, chorus, communications, computers, dance, debate, drama, drill team, environmental, ethnic, film, forensics, honors, international, jazz band, LGBT, literary magazine, marching band, musical theater, newspaper, opera, orchestra, pep band, photography, political, professional, radio and TV, religious, social, social service, student government, symphony, and yearbook. Popular campus events include Orientation, Carnival, International Student Organization Week, Christmas Ball, Family Weekend, Greek Week, Trivia Nights, Spotlight Musical Theater Shows, and Night of Lights. **Sports:** There are 6 intercollegiate sports for men and 11 for women, and 6 intramural sports for men and 6 for women. Facilities include a multipurpose building with aerobics space, cardio machines, multipurpose courts, walking/running track, free weight rooms, racquetball courts, an arena, regulation-sized basketball courts, athletic training room, weight training, cardiovascular areas, a center for outdoor intramural activity, a four-lane all-weather track, football, soccer, lacrosse, a swimming pool, tennis court and an outdoor basketball/deck hockey court. **Graduates:** From July 1, 2016 to June 30, 2017, 1578 bachelor's degrees were awarded. The most popular majors were nursing (17%), biology (7%), and psychology (5%). In an average class, 68% graduate in 4 years or less, 76% graduate in 5 years or less, and 77% graduate in 6 years or less. Of the 2016 graduating class, 27% were enrolled in graduate school within 6 months of graduation, and 57% were employed.

SERVICES: Counseling and information services are available, as is tutoring in every subject. There is developmental tutoring in preparation for upcoming subjects. There is a reader service for the blind, and remedial math, reading, and writing. Also available are tutorials in prep for Praxis test and various grad school entrance exams. **Library/Resources:** The library contains 749,772 volumes, 56,762 microform items, and 87,151 audio/video tapes/CDs/DVDs, and subscribes to 84,137 periodicals including electronic. Computerized library services include interlibrary loans, database searching, Internet access, and Wi-Fi capability. Special learning facilities include an art gallery, radio station, TV station, The University has nine FlexTech collaborative learning classrooms, one collaborative lecture hall, an anatomy lab wired with large flat screen monitors tied into a 3D software based system, a nursing simulation learning lab, a LightBoard room for recording lectures and interviews, a moc pharmacy, and a Sales Center floor in the School of Business that is wired for video capture and role play simulations. **Physically Challenged Students:** 95% of the campus is accessible. Facilities include wheelchair ramps, elevators, special parking, specially equipped restrooms, special class scheduling, lowered drinking fountains, and special housing. **Special:** The university offers cross-registration through the Pittsburgh Council on Higher Education, internships, study abroad in 23 countries, and a Washington semester. Also available are B.A.-B.S. degrees, accelerated degree programs, dual and student-designed majors, a 3-2 engineering program with Case Western Reserve University and University of Pittsburgh, the nation's first dual degree in biomedical engineering and nursing (BME-BSN), a 3-3 law degree and a 3-2 business degree, pass/fail options, and credit evaluation for life, military, and work experience. There are 26 national honor societies, a freshman honors program, and 60 departmental honors programs. **Visiting:** There are regularly scheduled orientations for prospective students, consisting of a campus tour and individual interviews with counselors and professors. There are guides for informal visits and visitors may sit in on classes. To schedule a visit, contact Robbyn Snyder at (412) 396-6222. **Campus Safety and Security:** Measures include 24-hour foot and vehicle patrol, emergency notification system, self-defense education, and security escort services. There are shuttle buses, emergency telephones, lighted pathways/sidewalks, controlled access to dorms/residences. There are also security cameras throughout campus that monitor exterior areas 24 hours a day.

REQUIREMENTS: Business, Liberal Arts, and Music applicants meeting select criteria can choose to apply as standardized test-optional candidates. Students should have either a high school diploma or the GED. Applicants are required to have 16 academic credits, including 4 each in English and academic electives, and 8 combined in social studies, language, math, and science. An essay, letter of recommendation, and interview are recommended. An audition is required for music majors. 40 hours shadowing for physical therapy (prior to enrollment). A GPA of 3.0 is required. AP and CLEP credits are accepted. Important factors in the admissions decision are advanced placement or honors courses, recommendations by school officials, and extracurricular activities record. To graduate, students are required to complete at least 120 credit hours, including a specified number in the major (varies by program), with a minimum 2.0 GPA. General requirements vary by department, but there is a 33 credit liberal arts core curriculum. **Procedure:** Freshmen are admitted fall, spring, and summer. Entrance exams should be taken during the spring of the junior year or the fall of the senior year. There are early decision, early admissions, deferred admissions, and rolling admissions plans. Early decision applications should be filed by November 1; regular applications, by July 1 for fall entry; December 1 for spring entry; and April 1 for summer entry. The fall 2017 application fee was $50. Notification of early decision is sent December 15; regular decision, on a rolling basis. 55 early decision candidates were accepted for the 2017-2018 class. Applications are accepted on-line. **Transfer Students:** 217 transfer students enrolled in 2016-2017. Applicants must submit complete high school and college transcripts. Students should have a minimum GPA of 2.5. A minimum of 12 credits earned is required, and an interview is recommended. 30 of 120 credits required for the bachelor's degree must be completed at Duquesne. **International Students:** There are 201 international students enrolled. They must take the college's own test, and the ILETS. Students are required to sit for ENG language placement tests as part of their arrival program.

ADMISSIONS: 72% of the 2017-2018 applicants were accepted. The SAT scores for the 2017-2018 freshman class were: Math-- 2% below 500, 51% between 500 and 599, 42% between 600 and 699, and 5% between 700 and 800. Evidence-Based Reading/Writing-- 1% below 500, 42% between 500 and 599, 51% between 600 and 699, and 6% between 700 and 800. The ACT scores were 21% between 18 and 23, 59% between 24 and 29, and 20% above 30. 45% of the current freshmen were in the top fifth of their class; 77% were in the top two fifths. 22 freshmen graduated first in their class. **Admissions Contact:** Debra Zugates, Director, Admissions. Email: *admissions@duq.edu* Web: *www.duq.edu*

FINANCIAL AID: In 2017-2018, 99% of all full-time freshmen received some form of financial aid. 72% of all full-time freshmen received need-based aid. The average freshman award was $27,704. Need-based scholarships or need-based grants averaged $21,794 ($52,531 maximum); need-based self-help aid (loans and jobs) averaged $5,191 ($8,800 maximum); non-need-based athletic scholarships averaged $21,868 ($54,163 maximum); and other non-need-based awards and non-need-based scholarships averaged $17,683 ($53,714 maximum). 15% of undergraduate students work part-time. The average financial indebtedness of the 2017 graduate was $24,689. The college's own financial statement is required. The FAFSA code is 003258. The priority date for freshman financial aid applications for fall entry is May 1.

EAST STROUDSBURG UNIVERSITY *(The complete profile is made available exclusively on our website, www.barronspac.com)*

EASTERN UNIVERSITY E-3

www.eastern.edu

St. Davids, PA 19087 **(800) 452-0996**

Fax: (610) 341-1723	**Email: ugadm@eastern.edu**
Full-time: 590 men, 1402 women	**Faculty:** IIA, --$
Part-time: 99 men, 311 women	**Ph.D.s:** 77%
Graduate: 479 men, 881 women	**Student/Faculty:** 11 to 1
Year: semesters, summer session	**Tuition:** $29,600
Room & Board: $9940	**Freshman Class:** n/av
SAT or ACT: required	**CEEB CODE:** 2220
Application Deadline: n/av	**COMPETITIVE**

Eastern University, founded in 1932, is a private liberal arts institution affiliated with the American Baptist Church, offering undergraduate and graduate programs. There are 4 undergraduate schools and 2 graduate schools. In addition to regional accreditation, EU has baccalaureate program accreditation with CSWE, CCNE, CAATE, and CAAHEP. The 114-acre campus is in a suburban area 20 miles northwest of Philadelphia. Including any residence halls, there are 23 buildings.

STUDENT LIFE: 56% of undergraduates are from Pennsylvania. Others are from 41 states, 41 foreign countries, and Canada. 6% are race unknown; 51% White; 22% African American; 2% Asian American; 2% Foreign; 16% Hispanic. 59% are Unknown denominations; 32% Protestant. **Female To Male Ratio:** 2.2:1. The average age of freshmen is 18; all undergraduates, 21. 22% do not continue beyond their first year; 62% remain to graduate. **Housing:** 1242 students can be accommodated in college housing, which includes dorms and on-campus apartments. On-campus housing is guaranteed for all 4 years. 75% of students live on campus. Alcohol is not permitted. Upperclassmen may keep cars.

FACULTY/CLASSROOMS: 54% of faculty are male; 46% are female. No introductory courses are taught by graduate students.

PROGRAMS OF STUDY: EU confers B.A., B.S., B.S.N., and B.S.W. degrees. Associate, master's, and doctoral degrees are also awarded. Bachelor's degrees are awarded in BIOLOGICAL SCIENCE (biochemistry and biology/biological science), BUSINESS (accounting, business administration and management, entrepreneurial studies, marketing/retailing/merchandising, and organizational leadership and management), COMMUNICATIONS AND THE ARTS (communications, dance, English, music, and Spanish), COMPUTER AND PHYSICAL SCIENCE (chemistry and mathematics), EDUCATION (athletic training, early childhood education, and middle school education), ENGINEERING AND ENVIRONMENTAL DESIGN (environmental science), HEALTH PROFESSIONS (exercise science and nursing), SOCIAL SCIENCE (biblical studies, criminal justice, history, missions, philosophy, political science/government, psychology, social work, sociology, theological studies, and youth ministry). Youth Ministry, education, and social work are the strongest academically. Social work, early childhood education, and psychology have the largest enrollments.

ACTIVITIES: There are no fraternities or sororities. There are 53 groups on campus, including cheerleading, choir, chorale, chorus, communications, computers, dance, drama, ethnic, honors, international, literary magazine, musical theater, newspaper, political, professional, radio and TV, religious, social, social service, student government, and yearbook. Popular campus events include Welcome Back Bash/Club Fair, Homecoming, and Concert. **Sports:** There are 7 intercollegiate sports for men and 9 for women, and 4 intramural sports for men and 4 for women. Facilities include a gym, soccer, baseball, field hockey, softball field, a weight room, an outdoor track, tennis courts, a health fitness trail, an outdoor pool, basketball and volleyball courts. **Graduates:** From July 1, 2016 to June 30, 2017, 497 bachelor's degrees were awarded. The most popular majors were early childhood education (18%), business administration (8%), and psychology (7%). In an average class, 53% graduate in 4 years or less and 9% graduate in 5 years or less. Of the 2016 graduating class, 21% were enrolled in graduate school within 6 months of graduation, and 71% were employed.

SERVICES: Counseling and information services are available, as is tutoring in every subject. There is a reader service for the blind, and remedial math, reading, and writing. **Library/Resources:** The library contains 277,660 volumes, 868,506 microform items, and 19,366 audio/video tapes/CDs/DVDs, and subscribes to 108,376 periodicals including electronic. Computerized library services include interlibrary loans, database searching, Internet access, and Wi-Fi capability. Special learning facilities include a planetarium, radio station, and observatory. **Physically Challenged Students:** 75% of the campus is accessible. Facilities include wheelchair ramps, elevators, special parking, specially equipped restrooms, special class scheduling, lowered drinking fountains, lowered telephones, and special housing. **Special:** The college offers cross-registration with Cabrini and Rosemont Colleges, Valley Forge Military Academy, and Villanova University, internships, a Washington semester in the American studies program, and student-designed majors. Also available are accelerated degree programs in organizational management and management of information systems, credit for experience, nondegree study, and pass/fail options. There is a different calendar for the organizational management program. There are 10 national honor societies, a freshman honors program, and 1 departmental honors program. **Visiting:** There are regularly scheduled orientations for prospective students. There are guides for informal visits, visitors may sit in on classes, and stay overnight. To schedule a visit, contact Admissions Office. **Campus Safety and Security:** Measures include 24-hour foot and vehicle patrol, emergency notification system, self-defense education, and security escort services. There are shuttle buses, emergency telephones, lighted pathways/sidewalks, and controlled access to dorms/residences.

REQUIREMENTS: The SAT or ACT is required. AP and CLEP credits are accepted. Important factors in the admissions decision are advanced placement or honors courses, recommendations by school officials, and geographical diversity. To graduate, all students must complete at least 127 credit hours with a minimum 2.0 GPA. The required hours in the major vary. Students must take courses in the Old and New Testament, humanities, social sciences, non-Western heritage, natural sciences, and college writing. There are Living and Learning in Communities, Heritage of Western Thought and Civilization, Science Technology and Values, Justice in a Pluralistic Society and complete a capstone. **Procedure:** Freshmen are admitted in the fall and spring. Entrance exams should be taken as early as possible. There are early admissions, deferred admissions, and rolling admissions plans. Application deadlines are open. The fall 2017 application fee was $25. Notification is sent on a rolling basis. Applications are accepted on-line. **Transfer Students:** 86 transfer students enrolled in 2016-2017. Applicants should have a 2.0 GPA with more than 24 credits, and a 2.5 GPA with fewer than 24 credits. Candidates must be in good standing at their previous institution. 32 of 127 credits required for the bachelor's degree must be completed at EU. **International Students:** There are 55 international students enrolled. They must take the TOEFL with a minimum score of 79 on the Internet-based version (iBT).

ADMISSIONS: 44% of the current freshmen were in the top fifth of their class; 69% were in the top two fifths. 2 freshmen graduated first in their class. **Admissions Contact:** Michael Dziedziak, Executive Director of Enrollment Management. Email: *ugadm@eastern.edu* Web: *www.eastern.edu*

FINANCIAL AID: In 2017-2018, 86% of all full-time freshmen received some form of financial aid. 67% of all full-time freshmen received need-based aid. The average freshman award was $30,641. Need-based scholarships or need-based grants averaged $6,969 ($22,396 maximum); need-based self-help aid (loans and jobs) averaged $4,324 ($5,948 maximum); other non-need-based awards and non-need-based scholarships averaged $13,506 ($33,000 maximum); and $10,929 from other forms of aid. 63% of undergraduate students work part-time. The average financial indebtedness of the 2017 graduate was $32,284. EU is a member of CSS. The FAFSA code is 003259. Check with the school for current application deadlines.

EDINBORO UNIVERSITY *(The complete profile is made available exclusively on our website, www.barronspac.com)*

ELIZABETHTOWN COLLEGE — D-3

www.etown.edu

Elizabethtown, PA 17022 — **(717) 361-1400**

Fax: (717) 361-1365
Full-time: 617 men, 1019 women
Part-time: 19 men, 16 women
Graduate: 3 men, 61 women
Year: semesters, summer session
Room & Board: $10,990
SAT or ACT: required
Application Deadline: n/av

Email: admissions@etown.edu
Faculty: 128; IIB, +$
Ph.D.s: 95%
Student/Faculty: 13 to 1
Tuition: $45,350
Freshman Class: n/av
CEEB CODE: 2225
VERY COMPETITIVE

Elizabethtown College offering more than four dozen degrees in liberal arts, fine and performing arts, science and engineering, business, communications and education. Elizabethtown links classroom instruction with experiential learning through five Signature Learning Experiences (SLEs) including internships, community-based learning, cross-cultural experiences, supervised research and a capstone course/project/portfolio. Every student at E-town is guaranteed the opportunity to experience at least two of five SLEs, which supplement classroom learning. Students are encouraged to develop and challenge their own values, while seeking to understand and appreciate alternative perspectives. There are 2 undergraduate schools. In addition to regional accreditation, E-town has baccalaureate program accreditation with ABET, ACBSP, CSWE, NASM, ACOTE, ACS, and ACBSP. The 203-acre campus is in a small town in Lancaster County, PA. It is 10 minutes from Hershey and 25 minutes from Lancaster and Harrisburg. Including any residence halls, there are 60 buildings.

STUDENT LIFE: 68% of undergraduates are from Pennsylvania. Others are from 28 states, 23 foreign countries, and Canada. 84% are from public schools. 85% are White; 4% Hispanic; 3% African American; 3% Asian American; 3% Foreign; 2% two or more races. 35% are Protestant; 26% Catholic. **Female To Male Ratio:** 1.7:1. The average age of freshmen is 18; all undergraduates, 20. 13% do not continue beyond their first year; 75% remain to graduate. **Housing:** 1490 students can be accommodated in college housing, which includes dorms, on-campus apartments, and off-campus apartments. In addition, there are honors houses, special-interest houses, substance free and quiet study. On-campus housing is guaranteed for all 4 years. 84% of students live on campus. All students may keep cars.

FACULTY/CLASSROOMS: 53% of faculty are male; 48% are female. All teach and do research. No introductory courses are taught by graduate students. The average class size in an introductory lecture is 20 and in a laboratory is 17.

PROGRAMS OF STUDY: E-town confers B.A., B.S., B.S.W., and B.Mus. degrees. Master's degrees are also awarded. Bachelor's degrees are awarded in AGRICULTURE (forestry and related sciences), BIOLOGICAL SCIENCE (biochemistry, biology/adolescence education, biology/biological science, and biotechnology), BUSINESS (accounting, business administration and management, business economics, business systems analysis, international business management, and marketing management), COMMUNICATIONS AND THE ARTS (art history and appreciation, communications, dramatic arts, English, English literature, English writing, fine arts, French, German, Japanese, modern language, music, performing arts, Spanish, studio art, and theatre acting), COMPUTER AND PHYSICAL SCIENCE (actuarial science, chemistry, chemistry/adolescence education, computer science, earth science/adolescence education, information sciences and systems, mathematics, and physics), EDUCATION (art education, early childhood education, education, elementary education, English education, mathematics education, music education, science education, secondary education, social studies education, social studies secondary school education, and Spanish adolescense education), ENGINEERING AND ENVIRONMENTAL DESIGN (computer engineering, electrical/electronics engineering, engineering, environmental science, industrial engineering, mechanical engineering, and preengineering), HEALTH PROFESSIONS (music therapy, occupational therapy, predentistry, premedicine, and prephysical therapy), SOCIAL SCIENCE (criminal justice, economics, history, legal studies, philosophy, political science/government, psychology, public administration, religion, social work, and sociology). Business administration, occupational therapy, and engineering/physics have the largest enrollments.

ACTIVITIES: There are no fraternities or sororities. There are 84 groups on campus, including art, band, choir, chorale, chorus, computers, dance, drama, environmental, ethnic, film, forensics, honors, international, jazz band, LGBT, literary magazine, musical theater, newspaper, orchestra, photography, political, professional, radio and TV, religious, social, social service, student government, and yearbook. Popular campus events include Scholarship and Creative Arts Day, Martin Luther King Celebration Week, Hispanic Heritage Month, and Into the Streets. **Sports:** There are 11 intercollegiate sports for men and 12 for women, and 10 intramural sports for men and 10 for women. Facilities include a soccer stadium, a gymnasium, swimming pool, track and field complex, fitness center, racquetball and tennis courts, sand volleyball courts, and baseball, softball, lacrosse, and hockey fields. **Graduates:** From July 1, 2016 to June 30, 2017, 503 bachelor's degrees were awarded. The most popular majors were business administration (15%), occupational therapy (13%), and engineering and physics (9%). In an average class, 65% graduate in 4 years or less, 72% graduate in 5 years or less, and 75% graduate in 6 years or less. Of the 2016 graduating class, 25% were enrolled in graduate school within 6 months of graduation, and 60% were employed.

SERVICES: Counseling and information services are available, as is tutoring in most subjects. There are also Workshops and individual help with study skills as well as assistive technology. **Library/Resources:** The library contains 243,909 volumes, 22,856 microform items, 4,752 audio/video tapes/CDs/DVDs, and subscribes to 421,968 periodicals, including electronic. Computerized library services include interlibrary loans, database searching, Internet access, and Wi-Fi capability. Special learning facilities include an art gallery, radio station, TV station, the Young Center for Anabaptist and Pietist Studies, a nationally unique academic research facility, and a mineral gallery. **Physically Challenged Students:** 75% of the campus is accessible. Facilities include wheelchair ramps, elevators, special parking, specially equipped restrooms, special class scheduling, lowered drinking fountains, lowered telephones, and special housing. **Special:** Students can participate in short-term, semester-long, and year-long study-abroad experiences in 26 different locations worldwide. Also available are work-study programs, internships, a Washington semester, and dual majors. There are two 5-year cooperative programs where the student will participate in two 7-month co-op rotations, one in engineering and one in business; a 3-3 allied health degree and a 3-3 physical therapy degree with Thomas Jefferson University and Widener University; a Premedical Primary Care Program with Penn State University College of Medicine; Biotechnology (B.S.) and Molecular Medicine (M.S.) with Drexel University College of Medicine; a 3-4 B.S. in biology/D.M.D. program with Temple University; a Cardiovascular Invasive Specialty program with Lancaster General College of Nursing and Health Sciences; a D.O program with Philadelphia College of Osteopathic Medicine; a 3-3 and 3-4 D.O. with Lake Erie College of Osteopathic Medicine; a 3-3 and 3-4 Doctor of Pharmaceutical with Lake Erie College of Osteopathic Medicine; and a 4+4 DDS program with West Virginia University School of Dentistry. There are 20 national honor societies, a freshman honors program, and 19 departmental honors programs. **Visiting:** There are regularly scheduled orientations for prospective students, including 5 open houses and weekday appointments throughout the year. Special academic department days are also hosted. There are guides for informal visits, visitors may sit in on classes, and stay overnight. To schedule a visit, contact the Admissions Office. **Campus Safety and Security:** Measures include 24-hour foot and vehicle patrol, an emergency notification system, self-defense education, and security escort services. There are shuttle buses, emergency telephones, lighted pathways/sidewalks, controlled access to dorms/residences, and crime prevention program.

REQUIREMENTS: Recommended SAT scores range from 1030 to 1230; for the ACT, 20 to 26. Applicants must be graduates of an accredited secondary school or have earned a GED. The college encourages completion of 18 academic credits, based on 4 years of English, 3 years of math, 2 years each of lab science, social studies, and consecutive foreign language, and 5 additional college preparatory units. An audition is required for music majors and an interview is required for occupational therapy majors. AP credits are accepted. Important factors in the admissions decision are advanced placement or honors courses, recommendations by school officials, and extracurricular activities record. The core curriculum includes a first-year seminar and courses in math, language, creative expression, western cultural heritage, non-western cultural heritage, natural and social sciences, and humanities. Distribution requirements include 40 hours in 8 areas of understanding. Students must complete a minimum of 125 credit hours and maintain a GPA of 2.0 overall and in their major. Additional requirements depend on the enrolled major. **Procedure:** Freshmen are admitted to all sessions. Entrance exams should be taken in spring of the junior year or fall of the senior year. There are deferred admissions and rolling admissions plans. Application deadlines are open. The fall 2017 application fee was $30. Applications are accepted on-line. **Transfer Students:** 23 transfer students enrolled in 2016-2017. Applicants should present a minimum GPA of 3.0 in at least 15 credit hours earned from a community college, or 2.5 from a 4-year institution. 30 of 125 credits required for the bachelor's degree must be completed at E-town. **International Students:** There are 45 international students enrolled. They must take the TOEFL with a minimum score of 500 on the paper-based TOEFL (PBT) or 61 on the Internet-based version (iBT). They must also take the SAT or ACT.

ADMISSIONS: 52% of the current freshmen were in the top fifth of their class; 28% were in the top two fifths. 3 freshmen graduated first in their class. **Admissions Contact:** George Walter, Interim Vice President for Enrollment. Email: *admissions@etown.edu* Web: *www.etown.edu*

FINANCIAL AID: In 2017-2018, 84% of all full-time freshmen received some form of financial aid and received need-based aid. The average freshman award was $34,258. Need-based scholarships or need-based grants averaged $30,472 ($34,173 maximum); and need-based self-help aid (loans and jobs) averaged $4,752 ($6,500 maximum). 59% of undergraduate students work part-time. E-town is a member of CSS. The college's own financial statement, and family federal tax returns are required. The FAFSA code is 003262. The priority date for freshman financial aid applications for fall entry is March 15.

ELIZABETHTOWN COLLEGE SCHOOL OF CONTINUING AND PROFESSIONAL STUDIES

www.etowndegrees.com

Elizabethtown, PA 17022	**(717) 361-3750**
Fax: (717) 361-1466	**Email: randazzob@etown.edu**
Full-time: n/av	**Faculty:** n/av
Part-time: 106 men, 240 women	**Ph.D.s:** n/av
Graduate: 33 men, 43 women	**Student/Faculty:** n/av
Year: other, summer session	**Tuition:** $18,900
Room & Board: n/app	**Freshman Class:** n/av **CEEB CODE:** 2225
Application Deadline: n/av	**COMPETITIVE**

Elizabethtown College School of Continuing and Professional Studies, offers more than four dozen degrees in liberal arts, fine and performing arts, science and engineering, business,communications and education. Through personal attention, creative inspiration and academic challenge, Elizabethtown students are encouraged to expand their intellectual curiosity. The figures given in the above capsule and in this profile are approximate. There is 1 undergraduate school. The 201-acre campus is in a small town 10 minutes from Hershey and 25 minutes from Lancaster and Harrisburg. Including any residence halls, there are 52 buildings.

STUDENT LIFE: 98% of undergraduates are from Pennsylvania. Others are from 3 states, and 2 foreign countries. 9% are African American; 85% White; 5% Hispanic; 1% Asian American. **Female To Male Ratio:** 2.0:1. The average age of all undergraduates is 37. All students commute. All students may keep cars.

FACULTY/CLASSROOMS: 63% of faculty are male; 37% are female. All teach undergraduates. No introductory courses are taught by graduate students. The average class size in an introductory lecture is 20.

PROGRAMS OF STUDY: Elizabethtown confers B.A., B.S., and B.P.S. degrees. Associate and master's degrees are also awarded. Bachelor's degrees are awarded in BUSINESS (accounting, business administration and management, human resources, and marketing/retailing/merchandising), COMMUNICATIONS AND THE ARTS (communications and information technology), SOCIAL SCIENCE (addiction studies, behavioral science, criminal justice, human services, public administration, and religion). Business administration, accounting, and human services have the largest enrollments.

ACTIVITIES: There are no fraternities or sororities. **Sports:** There is no sports program at Elizabethtown. **Graduates:** From July 1, 2016 to June 30, 2017, 128 bachelor's degrees were awarded. The most popular majors were business administration (38%), accounting (17%), and corporate communications (12%).

SERVICES: Library/Resources: The library contains 262,101 volumes, 24,078 microform items, and 9,750 audio/video tapes/CDs/DVDs, and subscribes to 96,260 periodicals including electronic. Computerized library services include interlibrary loans, database searching, Internet access, and Wi-Fi capability. Special learning facilities include an art gallery, TV station, the Young Center for Anabaptist and Pietist Studies, a nationally unique academic research facility, and a mineral gallery. **Physically Challenged Students:** 75% of the campus is accessible. Facilities include wheelchair ramps, elevators, special parking, specially equipped restrooms, special class scheduling, lowered drinking fountains, and lowered telephones. **Campus Safety and Security:** Measures include 24-hour foot and vehicle patrol, emergency notification system, self-defense education, and security escort services. There are shuttle buses, emergency telephones, lighted pathways/sidewalks, controlled access to dorms/residences, and crime prevention programs.

Procedure: Freshmen are admitted to all sessions. There is a rolling admissions plan. Application deadlines are open. Applications are accepted on-line. **Transfer Students:** 65 transfer students enrolled in 2016-2017.

Admissions Contact: Barbara Randazzo, Assistant Dean of Enrollment Management. Email: *randazzob@etown.edu* Web: *www.etowndegrees.com*

FINANCIAL AID: Check with the school for current application deadlines.

FRANKLIN AND MARSHALL COLLEGE E-3
www.fandm.edu

Lancaster, PA 17604	**(717) 358-3953** **(877) 678-9111**
Fax: (717) 358-4389	**Email: admission@fandm.edu**
Full-time: 1037 men, 1226 women	**Faculty:** 245; IIB, +$
Part-time: 8 men, 12 women	**Ph.D.s:** 95%
Graduate: n/av	**Student/Faculty:** 9 to 1
Year: semesters, summer session	**Tuition:** $54,380
Room & Board: $13,580	**Freshman Class:** 6720 applied, 2292 accepted, 645 enrolled
SAT CR/M: 655/680 **ACT:** 30	**CEEB CODE:** 2261
Application Deadline: January 15	**MOST COMPETITIVE**

Franklin and Marshall College, founded in 1787, is a private liberal arts institution. There is 1 undergraduate school. The 209-acre campus is in a suburban area 60 miles west of Philadelphia. Including any residence halls, there are 45 buildings.

STUDENT LIFE: 73% of undergraduates are from out of state, mostly the Middle Atlantic. Students are from 43 states, 54 foreign countries, and Canada. 62% are from public schools. 8% are Hispanic; 6% African American; 6% race unknown; 59% White; 5% Asian American; 2% two or more races; 14% Foreign. **Female To Male Ratio:** 1.1:1. The average age of freshmen is 18; all undergraduates, 20. 9% do not continue beyond their first year; 87% remain to graduate. **Housing:** 2367 students can be accommodated in college housing, which includes dorms, on-campus apartments, and off-campus apartments. In addition, there are language/international houses, special-interest houses, an arts house, and a community outreach house. On-campus housing is guaranteed is guaranteed for the freshman year only, and is available on a lottery system for upperclassmen. 99% of students live on campus. Upperclassmen may keep cars.

FACULTY/CLASSROOMS: 53% of faculty are male; 47% are female. All teach undergraduates and all do research. No introductory courses are taught by graduate students. The average class size in an introductory lecture is 23; in a laboratory is 19; and in a regular course is 17.

PROGRAMS OF STUDY: F&M confers B.A. degrees. Bachelor's degrees are awarded in AGRICULTURE (environmental studies), BIOLOGICAL SCIENCE (biochemistry, biology/biological science, and neurosciences), BUSINESS (business administration and management), COMMUNICATIONS AND THE ARTS (art history and appreciation, classics, dramatic arts, English, fine arts, French, German, Greek, Latin, music, Spanish, and studio art), COMPUTER AND PHYSICAL SCIENCE (astronomy, astrophysics, chemistry, geology, mathematics, and physics), ENGINEERING AND ENVIRONMENTAL DESIGN (environmental science), SOCIAL SCIENCE (African studies, American studies, anthropology, economics, history, interdisciplinary studies, philosophy, political science/government, psychology, religion, and sociology). Chemistry, geosciences, and psychology are the strongest academically. Government, business, and organizations & society have the largest enrollments.

ACTIVITIES: 20% of men belong to 7 national fraternities; 30% of women belong to 3 national sororities. There are 120 groups on campus, including a student-run club/restaurant, art, band, cheerleading, chess, choir, chorale, chorus, communications, computers, dance, debate, drama, environmental, ethnic, film, forensics, honors, international, jazz band, LGBT, literary magazine, musical theater, newspaper, opera, orchestra, photography, political, professional, radio and TV, religious, social, social service, student government, symphony, and yearbook. Popular campus events include Spring Arts Weekend. **Sports:** There are 13 intercollegiate sports for men and 13 for women, and 12 intramural sports for men and 12 for women. Facilities include a gym, squash courts, a wrestling room, playing fields, 400-meter all-weather track, wellness/aerobic center, strength training center, tennis courts, a fitness center, multipurpose courts, jogging tracks, and an Olympic-size pool. **Graduates:** From July 1, 2016 to June 30, 2017, 553 bachelor's degrees were awarded. The most popular majors were business, organizations, and society (12%), government (11%), and English (7%). In an average class, 83% graduate in 4 years or less, 86% graduate in 5 years or less, and 87% graduate in 6 years or less.

SERVICES: Counseling and information services are available, as is tutoring in every subject. **Library/Resources:** The library contains 588,333 volumes, 22,924 microform items, and 8,722 audio/video tapes/CDs/DVDs, and subscribes to 2,366 periodicals including electronic. Computerized library services include interlibrary loans, database searching, Internet access, and Wi-Fi capability. Special learning facilities include an art gallery, natural history museum, planetarium, radio station, academic technology services, a writing center, and student newspaper. **Physically Challenged Students:** 80% of the campus is accessible. Facilities include wheelchair ramps, elevators, special parking, specially equipped restrooms, special class scheduling, lowered drinking fountains, lowered telephones, and special housing. **Special:** There is a 3-2 degree program in forestry and environmental studies with Duke University as well as 3-2 degree programs in engineering with the Pennsylvania State University College of Engineering, Columbia University, Rensselaer Polytechnic Institute, Case Western Reserve, and Washington University at St. Louis. Cross-registration is possible with the Lancaster Theological Seminary, the Central Pennsylvania Consortium, and Millersville University allows students to study at nearby Dickinson College or Gettysburg College. Students may also study architecture and urban planning at Columbia University, studio art at the School of Visual Arts in New York City, theater in Connecticut, oceanography in Massachusetts, and American studies at American University. There are study-abroad programs in England, France, Germany, Greece, Italy, Denmark, India, Japan, and other countries. There are internships for credit, joint majors, many minors, dual majors, student-designed majors, independent study, interdisciplinary studies, optional first-year seminars, collaborative projects, pass/fail options, and nondegree study. There are 12 national honor societies and a chapter of Phi Beta Kappa. **Visiting:** There are regularly scheduled orientations for prospective students, including a campus tour, an interview, and a class visit. To schedule a visit, contact the Admission Office. **Campus Safety and Security:** Measures include 24-hour foot and vehicle patrol, emergency notification system, self-defense education, and security escort services. There are shuttle buses, emergency telephones, lighted pathways/sidewalks, controlled access to dorms/residences, and regular fire safety drills held in residence halls and academic buildings.

REQUIREMENTS: Standardized tests are optional for students; if this option is selected, 2 recent graded writing samples are required. Applicants must be graduates of accredited secondary schools. Recommended college preparatory study includes 4 years each of English and math, 3 or 4 of foreign language, 3 each of lab science and history/social studies, and 1 or 2 courses in art or music. All students must also submit their high school transcripts, recommendations from a teacher and a counselor, and a personal essay. An interview is recommended. AP and CLEP credits are accepted. Important factors in the admissions decision are advanced placement or honors courses, recommendations by school officials, and extracurricular activities record. General education requirements proceed from 2 connections courses and a distribution requirement to a major. Students must take at least 1 course in arts, humanities, social science, non-Western cultures, and 1 natural science (including a lab) and a second lab course or natural science in perspective course. 3 semesters of language study are required. The bachelor's degree requires completion of 32 courses, including a minimum of 8 in the major, with a minimum GPA of 2.0. **Procedure:** Freshmen are admitted in the fall and spring. Entrance exams should be taken by December of the senior year. There are early decision and deferred admissions plans. Early decision applications should be filed by November 15; regular applications, by January 15 for fall entry. The fall 2017 application fee was $60. Notification of early decision is sent December 15; regular decision, April 1. 338 early decision candidates were accepted for the 2017-2018 class. 2600 applicants were on the 2017 waiting list; 16 were admitted. Applications are accepted on-line. **Transfer Students:** 22 transfer students enrolled in 2016-2017. An interview, SAT or ACT scores, college and secondary school transcripts, a dean's form, recommendations from 2 professors, and a letter explaining the reason for transfer are also required. 16 of 32 credits required for the bachelor's degree must be completed at F&M. **International Students:** There are 340 international students enrolled. They must take the TOEFL, and either the SAT or ACT.

ADMISSIONS: 34% of the 2017-2018 applicants were accepted. The SAT scores for the 2017-2018 freshman class were: Critical Reading-- 11% between 500 and 599, 65% between 600 and 699, and 24% between 700 and 800. Math-- 8% between 500 and 599, 54% between 600 and 699, and 38% between 700 and 800. The ACT scores were 41% between 24 and 29, and 59% above 30. **Admissions Contact:** Eric Maguire, Vice President for Enrollment Management and Dean of Admissions. Email: *admission@fandm.edu* Web: *www.fandm.edu*

FINANCIAL AID: In 2017-2018, 56% of all full-time freshmen received some form of financial aid, and need-based aid. The average freshman award was $47,895. Need-based scholarships or need-based grants averaged $44,761; and need-based self-help aid (loans and jobs) averaged $4,600. The average financial indebtedness of the 2017 graduate was $27,133. F&M is a member of CSS. The CSS/Profile and the college's own financial statement, and if applicable, the business/farm supplement and noncustodial parents statement are required. The FAFSA code is 003265. The deadline for filing freshman financial aid applications for fall entry is February 15.

GANNON UNIVERSITY — B-1

www.gannon.edu

Erie, PA 16541	(814) 871-7408 (800) 426-6668 Email: admissions@gannon.edu
Full-time: 1106 men, 1425 women	**Faculty:** 183; IIA, -$
Part-time: 232 men, 313 women	**Ph.D.s:** 78%
Graduate: 436 men, 637 women	**Student/Faculty:** 14 to 1
Year: semesters, summer session	**Tuition:** $30,932
Room & Board: $11,990	**Freshman Class:** 4642 applied, 3709 accepted, 645 enrolled
SAT CR/M: 550/550 **ACT:** 23	**CEEB CODE:** 2270
Application Deadline: open	**COMPETITIVE**

Gannon University is a Catholic, Diocesan university dedicated to excellence in teaching, scholarship and service. Our faculty and staff prepare students to be global citizens through programs grounded in the liberal arts and sciences and professional specializations. Inspired by the Catholic Intellectual Tradition, we offer a comprehensive, values-centered learning experience that emphasizes faith, leadership, inclusiveness, and social responsibility. There are 3 undergraduate schools and 3 graduate schools. In addition to regional accreditation, GU has baccalaureate program accreditation with ABET, ACBSP, APTA, CSWE, ACOTE, ARC-PA, CoARC, CAAHEP, CCNE, PDE, FLDOE, and JRCERT. The 63-acre campus is in an urban area in downtown Erie, Pennsylvania, 128 miles north of Pittsburgh, 99 miles east of Cleveland, and 106 miles southwest of Buffalo. Including any residence halls, there are 52 buildings.

STUDENT LIFE: 69% of undergraduates are from Pennsylvania. Others are from 34 states, 42 foreign countries, and Canada. 8% are Foreign; 69% White; 5% African American; 3% Hispanic; 3% two or more races; 2% Asian American; 11% race unknown. 53% claim no religious affiliation; 27% Catholic; 11% Protestant. **Female To Male Ratio:** 1.3:1. The average age of freshmen is 18; all undergraduates, 20. 15% do not continue beyond their first year; 85% remain to graduate. **Housing:** 1410 students can be accommodated in college housing, which includes dorms, on-campus apartments, and off-campus apartments. In addition, there are honors houses, special-interest houses, fraternity houses, and sorority houses. On-campus housing is guaranteed for the freshman year only. 60% of students commute. Upperclassmen may keep cars.

FACULTY/CLASSROOMS: 48% of faculty are male; 52% are female. 78% teach undergraduates. No introductory courses are taught by graduate students. The average class size in an introductory lecture is 22 and in a laboratory is 21.

PROGRAMS OF STUDY: GU confers B.A., B.S., B.S.E., B.S.M., B.S.B.A., and B.S.N. degrees. Associate, master's, and doctoral degrees are also awarded. Bachelor's degrees are awarded in BIOLOGICAL SCIENCE (biochemistry, bioinformatics, biology/biological science, and nutrition), BUSINESS (accounting, banking and finance, business administration and management, entrepreneurial studies, finance, funeral home services, insurance and risk management, international business management, management science, marketing/retailing/merchandising, sports management, and supply chain management), COMMUNICATIONS AND THE ARTS (advertising, communications, dramatic arts, English, foreign language, journalism, radio/TV broadcasting, sports administration, and visual and performing arts), COMPUTER AND PHYSICAL SCIENCE (chemistry, computer programming, computer science, information sciences and systems, mathematics, science, and software engineering), EDUCATION (early childhood education, elementary education, English education, health information management, mathematics education, middle school education, middle level education, secondary education, social studies education, and special education), ENGINEERING AND ENVIRONMENTAL DESIGN (biomedical engineering, chemical engineering, computer engineering, electrical/electronics engineering, environmental engineering, environmental science, and mechanical engineering), HEALTH PROFESSIONS (health science, kinesiology, medical technology, multidisciplinary studies, nursing, nutrition and wellness, occupational therapy, physical therapy, physician's assistant, predentistry, premedicine, preoptometry, prepodiatry, preveterinary science, and respiratory therapy), SOCIAL SCIENCE (area studies, criminal justice, forensic studies, history, interdisciplinary studies, international studies, legal studies, liberal arts, sciences, general studies, humanities, philosophy, political science/government, psychology, social work, and theological studies). Health Professions is the strongest academically. Nursing, physician's assistant, and sport and exercise science have the largest enrollments.

ACTIVITIES: 13% of men belong to 7 national fraternities; 13% of women belong to 5 national sororities. There are 95 groups on campus, including art, band, cheerleading, choir, chorus, computers, dance, drama, environmental, ethnic, honors, international, LGBT, literary magazine, musical theater, newspaper, pep band, professional, radio and TV, religious, social, social service, and student government. Popular campus events include Active Minds, Black Student Union, Dance Marathon, Day of Caring, Family Weekend, GIVE Day (annual volunteer event), Greek Week, Home Coming Weekend, LIFE (LGBTQ group), Preview GU (welcome events), Relay for Life, Springtopia, & Take Back the Night. **Sports:** There are 11 intercollegiate sports for men and 10 for women, and 24 intramural sports for men and 24 for women. Facilities include a large multi-purpose stadium for basketball and volleyball. Our recreation and wellness center comprises a large swimming pool, indoor turf field, basketball courts, racquetball courts, an indoor running track, a human performance laboratory, weight machines, cardio equipment, and group fitness classes from yoga to kick boxing. **Graduates:** From July 1, 2016 to June 30, 2017, 536 bachelor's degrees were awarded. The most popular majors were health sciences (20%), sport and exercise science (9%), and nursing (9%). In an average class, 47% graduate in 4 years or less, 62% graduate in 5 years or less, and 64% graduate in 6 years or less.

SERVICES: Counseling and information services are available, as is tutoring in most subjects. There is a reader service for the blind, and remedial math, reading, and writing. STEM Center, writing and research center, speech communication center, and academic advising center. **Library/Resources:** The library contains 193,601 volumes, 79 microform items, and 4,216 audio/video tapes/CDs/DVDs, and subscribes to 53,341 periodicals including electronic. Computerized library services include interlibrary loans, database searching, Internet access, and Wi-Fi capability. Special learning facilities include an art gallery, radio station, a floating laboratory, that provides hands-on environmental study on Lake Erie and Presque Isle Bay, a Patient Simulation Center in the Morosky College of Health Professions and Sciences, a Human Performance Center, and an Archaeology Museum. **Physically Challenged Students:** 70% of the campus is accessible. Facilities include wheelchair ramps, elevators, special parking, specially equipped restrooms, lowered drinking fountains, and special housing. **Special:** We offer co-op programs, dual majors, summer internships, pass/fail options, work-study programs, a general studies program, pre-health programs in medicine, optometry, podiatry, dentistry, veterinary, and pharmacy, and pre-law. We also partner with other colleges and universities such as Charleston School of Pharmacy, LECOM (Lake Erie College of Osteopathic Medicine), PCOM (Philadelphia College of Osteopathic Medicine), Ross University School of Medicine, and the law school at Duquesne University. In addition, our institution also offers study abroad, including semester exchange, summer programs, ABST (Alternative Break Service Trip), and short-term faculty led courses in over 18 countries. Gannon University provides students with numerous service and experiential learning opportunities, such as the Washington Center Internship where students spend a semester in Washington D.C., and a dual-degree program in software engineering with one of our German partner universities, in which students will be able to spend a year in Germany (and German students a year here) and earn degrees from both Gannon as well as our partner university. There are 15 national honor societies, a freshman honors program, and 11 departmental honors programs. **Visiting:** There are regularly scheduled orientations for prospective students, The visits consist of open houses for prospective students in the fall and spring. Students may meet with faculty, tour the campus, meet with financial aid advisors, and sit in on a variety of presentations. There are guides for informal visits, visitors may sit in on classes, and stay overnight. To schedule a visit, contact Stacie Pecar at (814) 871-7407. **Campus Safety and Security:** Measures include 24-hour foot and vehicle patrol, emergency notification system, and security escort services. There are shuttle buses, emergency telephones, lighted pathways/sidewalks, controlled access to dorms/residences, security cameras in buildings and outside of campus facilities, including streets and sidewalks, card access systems to all residential halls, fire alarm systems in all building, fire suppression systems in all residential halls, card access for after hour access in educational buildings.

REQUIREMENTS: The SAT or ACT is required. Candidates should have completed 16 academic units, including 4 in English, and 3 each in social sciences, foreign languages, math, and science, depending on the degree sought. Specific courses in math and science are required for some majors in health sciences and engineering. Essays are required for some programs and encouraged for all applicants. The same is true for letters of recommendation. Credits may be earned for those who complete AP exams and IB exams. Gannon accepts the GED in replacement of a high school diploma with appropriate scores earned overall and in each subject matter. AP and CLEP credits are accepted. Important factors in the admissions decision are advanced placement or honors courses, leadership record, recommendations by school officials, parents or siblings attended your school, personality/intangible qualities, and extracurricular activities record. Students must complete at least 128 hours of academic work. Each academic program has specific course requirements. Students must have a cumulative GPA of at least 2.0 overall and in the area of concentration. **Procedure:** Freshmen are admitted fall, spring, and summer. Entrance exams should be taken either at the end of junior year or beginning of senior year. There are deferred admissions and rolling admissions plans. Application deadlines are open. The fall 2017 application fee was $25. Notification is sent on a rolling basis. Applications are accepted on-line. **Transfer Students:** 174 transfer students enrolled in 2016-2017. Transfer students should be in good standing at their previous institution with at least a 2.0 GPA. They must submit transcripts from the college most recently attended and transcripts from all institutions attended. A high school transcript is required for students with fewer than 30 credits or for those pursuing a health related field. 40 of 128 credits required for the bachelor's degree must be completed at Gannon. **International Students:** There are 250 international students enrolled. They must take the TOEFL with a minimum score of 550 on the paper-based TOEFL (PBT) or 79 on the Internet-based version (iBT).

ADMISSIONS: 80% of the 2017-2018 applicants were accepted. The SAT scores for the 2017-2018 freshman class were: Critical Reading--22% below 500, 46% between 500 and 599, 29% between 600 and 699, and 3% between 700 and 800. Math-- 25% below 500, 46% between 500 and 599, 25% between 600 and 699, and 4% between 700 and 800. The ACT scores were 9% between 12 and 17, 42% between 18 and 23, 40% between 24 and 29, and 8% above 30. 44% of the current freshmen were in the top fifth of their class; 69% were in the top two fifths. 6 freshmen graduated first in their class. **Admissions Contact:** Patricia Maughn, Coordinator, Admissions Inquiries. Email: *admissions@gannon.edu* Web: *www.gannon.edu*

FINANCIAL AID: In 2017-2018, 99% of all full-time freshmen received some form of financial aid. 83% of all full-time freshmen received need-based aid. The average freshman award was $25,699. Need-based scholarships or need-based grants averaged $22,430; need-based self-help aid (loans and jobs) averaged $3,934; non-need-based athletic scholarships averaged $10,423; and other non-need-based awards and non-need-based scholarships averaged $16,559. 18% of undergraduate students work part-time. The average financial indebtedness of the 2017 graduate was $27,092. GU is a member of CSS. The FAFSA code is 003266. The priority date for freshman financial aid applications for fall entry is March 15.

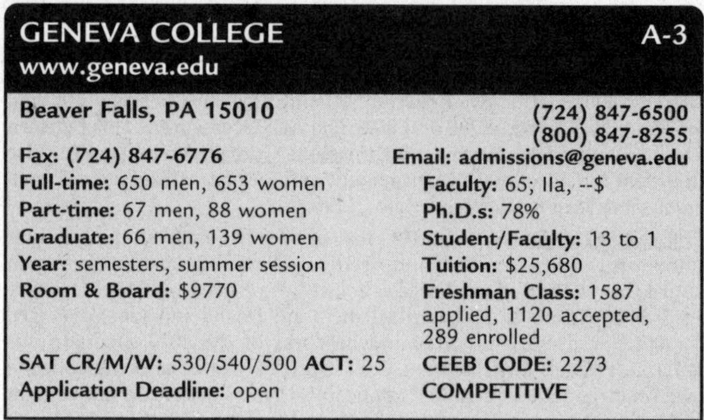

GENEVA COLLEGE — A-3

www.geneva.edu

Beaver Falls, PA 15010	**(724) 847-6500** **(800) 847-8255**
Fax: (724) 847-6776	**Email: admissions@geneva.edu**
Full-time: 650 men, 653 women	**Faculty:** 65; IIa, --$
Part-time: 67 men, 88 women	**Ph.D.s:** 78%
Graduate: 66 men, 139 women	**Student/Faculty:** 13 to 1
Year: semesters, summer session	**Tuition:** $25,680
Room & Board: $9770	**Freshman Class:** 1587 applied, 1120 accepted, 289 enrolled
SAT CR/M/W: 530/540/500 **ACT:** 25	**CEEB CODE:** 2273
Application Deadline: open	**COMPETITIVE**

Geneva College, founded in 1848, is a private institution affiliated with the Reformed Presbyterian Church of North America. The college offers undergraduate programs in the arts and sciences, business, education, health science, biblical and religious studies, engineering, and preprofessional training. There are also 440 nontraditional undergraduates. There is 1 undergraduate school. In addition to regional accreditation, Geneva has baccalaureate program accreditation with ABET and ACBSP. The 50-acre campus is in a small town 35 miles northwest of Pittsburgh. Including any residence halls, there are 30 buildings.

STUDENT LIFE: 75% of undergraduates are from Pennsylvania. Others are from 36 states, 11 foreign countries, and Canada. 87% are from public schools. 9% are African American; 82% White; 3% two or more races; 3% race unknown; 2% Hispanic; 1% Asian American; 1% Foreign. 79% are Protestant; 13% Unknown denomination. **Female To Male Ratio:** 1.1:1. The average age of freshmen is 18; all undergraduates, 23. 19% do not continue beyond their first year; 57% remain to graduate. **Housing:** 942 students can be accommodated in college housing, which includes dorms, on-campus apartments, off-campus apartments, and a discipleship house for those interested in structural growth opportunities. On-campus housing is guaranteed for all 4 years. 60% of students live on campus. Alcohol is not permitted. All students may keep cars.

FACULTY/CLASSROOMS: 64% of faculty are male; 36% are female. 76% teach undergraduates. No introductory courses are taught by graduate students. The average class size in an introductory lecture is 128; in a laboratory is 14; and in a regular course is 20.

PROGRAMS OF STUDY: Geneva confers B.A., B.S., B.S.B.A., B.S.E., B.S.Ed., and B.P.S. degrees. Associate and master's degrees are also awarded. Bachelor's degrees are awarded in BIOLOGICAL SCIENCE (biology/biological science), BUSINESS (accounting and business administration and management), COMMUNICATIONS AND THE ARTS (applied music, broadcasting, communications, creative writing, English, languages, music, music business management, Spanish, and speech/debate/rhetoric), COMPUTER AND PHYSICAL SCIENCE (applied mathematics, chemistry, computer science, and physics), EDUCATION (early childhood education, education, elementary education, mathematics education, and music education), ENGINEERING AND ENVIRONMENTAL DESIGN (aviation administration/management, chemical engineering, and engineering), HEALTH PROFESSIONS (speech pathology/audiology), SOCIAL SCIENCE (biblical studies, counseling/psychology, history, human services, interdisciplinary studies, ministries, philosophy, political science/government, psychology, and sociology). Engineering, business administration, and education are the strongest academically. Engineering, business, and elementary education have the largest enrollments.

ACTIVITIES: There are no fraternities or sororities. There are 50 groups on campus, including band, cheerleading, chess, choir, chorale, chorus, computers, drama, ethnic, forensics, honors, international, literary magazine, marching band, newspaper, photography, political, professional, radio club, religious, social, social service, student government, and yearbook. Popular campus events include International Day, Fall Fest, The Big Event, and Homecoming. **Sports:** There are 7 intercollegiate sports for men and 7 for women, and 6 intramural sports for men and 5 for women. Facilities include a stadium, a field house, a gym, a practice gym, a track, athletic fields, racquetball and tennis courts, weight training rooms, and a soccer/track complex. **Graduates:** From July 1, 2016 to June 30, 2017, 407 bachelor's degrees were awarded. The most popular majors were engineering, general (14%), human services, general (11%), business administration and management, and general (10%). In an average class, 39% graduate in 3 years or less, 50% graduate in 4 years or less, 52% graduate in 5 years or less, and 52% graduate in 6 years or less.

SERVICES: Counseling and information services are available, as is tutoring in most subjects. There is remedial math, reading, and writing. **Library/Resources:** The library contains 167,206 volumes, 198,624 microform items, and 12,901 audio/video tapes/CDs/DVDs, and subscribes to 879 periodicals including electronic. Computerized library services include interlibrary loans, database searching, and Internet access. Special learning facilities include a TV station, and an observatory. **Physically Challenged Students:** 90% of the campus is accessible. Facilities include wheelchair ramps, elevators, special parking, specially equipped restrooms, special class scheduling, lowered drinking fountains, and lowered telephones. **Special:** Cross-registration is offered in conjunction with Pennsylvania State University/Beaver Campus and Community College of Beaver County. There are accelerated degree programs in human resources and community ministry. Off-campus study includes programs at the Philadelphia Center for Urban Theological Studies, a Washington semester, a summer program at AuSable, Institute of Environmental Studies in Michigan, art studies in Pittsburgh, CCCU music program in Martha's Vineyard, film studies in Los Angeles, and study abroad in Costa Rica, Egypt, China, England, Russia, and Israel. Geneva also offers internships, independent study, and credit by proficiency exam. Nondegree study is available through adult education programs. There are 7 national honor societies, a freshman honors program, and 1 departmental honors program. **Visiting:** There are regularly scheduled orientations for prospective students, including class visits, a campus tour, meetings with faculty, admissions, and financial aid counselors, and meetings with coaches. There are guides for informal visits, visitors may sit in on classes, and stay overnight. To schedule a visit, contact the Campus Visit Coordinator. **Campus Safety and Security:** Measures include 24-hour foot and vehicle patrol and security escort services. There are emergency telephones, lighted pathways/sidewalks, and an off-duty city policemen on campus.

REQUIREMENTS: The SAT or ACT is required. Applicants must be graduates of an accredited secondary school or have earned a GED. Geneva requires 16 academic units, based on 4 each of English and electives, 3 of social studies, 2 each of math and foreign language, and 1 of science. An essay is required and an interview is recommended. A GPA of 2.5 is required. AP and CLEP credits are accepted. Important factors in the admissions decision are recommendations by school officials, advanced placement or honors courses, and leadership record. The core curriculum includes 12 hours of humanities, 9 each of biblical studies and social science, 8 to 10 of natural science, 6 of communications, 2 of phys ed, and the 1-hour Freshman Experience course. Students must also fulfill a chapel requirement per semester. To graduate, students must complete 120 to 138 semester hours, including those required for a major, with a minimum GPA of 2.0 in the major. **Procedure:** Freshmen are admitted to all sessions. Entrance exams should be taken during the junior or senior year. There are deferred admissions and rolling admissions plans. Application deadlines are open. The fall 2017 application fee was $25. Notification is sent on a rolling basis. Applications are accepted on-line. **Transfer Students:** 52 transfer students enrolled in 2016-2017. Applicants must have a GPA of 2.0 from college, and complete 48 semester hours at Geneva, including 15 in a chosen major, have a high school diploma or GED, and take the SAT I/ACT if less than 3 years out of high school. Letters of recommendation are required. 48 of 120 credits required for the bachelor's degree must be completed at Geneva. **International Students:** There are 21 international students enrolled. They must take the TOEFL with a minimum score of 550 on the paper-based TOEFL (PBT) or 80 on the Internet-based version (iBT). Students must take the college's own test, and either the SAT or ACT.

ADMISSIONS: 71% of the 2017-2018 applicants were accepted. The SAT scores for the 2017-2018 freshman class were: Critical Reading-- 32% below 500, 43% between 500 and 599, 21% between 600 and 699, and 4% between 700 and 800. Math-- 36% below 500, 34% between 500 and 599, 24% between 600 and 699, and 6% between 700 and 800. Writing-- 47% below 500, 34% between 500 and 599, 15% between 600 and 699, and 3% between 700 and 800. The ACT scores were 9% between 12 and 17, 34% between 18 and 23, 41% between 24 and 29, and 16% above 30. 3 freshmen graduated first in their class. **Admissions Contact:** Roger Blevins, Assistant Director of Admissions. Email: *admissions@geneva.edu* Web: *www.geneva.edu*

FINANCIAL AID: In 2017-2018, 93% of all full-time freshmen received some form of financial aid. 80% of all full-time freshmen received need-based aid. The average freshman award was $21,573. Need-based scholarships or need-based grants averaged $16,892 ($25,680 maximum); need-based self-help aid (loans and jobs) averaged $5,593 ($7,500 maximum); and other non-need-based awards and non-need-based scholarships averaged $11,299 ($15,000 maximum). 68% of undergraduate students work part-time. The average financial indebtedness of the 2017 graduate was $32,900. Geneva is a member of CSS. The state aid form is required. The FAFSA code is 003267. The priority date for freshman financial aid applications for fall entry is March 15. The deadline for filing freshman financial aid applications for fall entry is April 15.

GETTYSBURG COLLEGE — D-4

www.gettysburg.edu

Gettysburg, PA 17325	**(717) 337-6100** **(800) 431-0803**
Fax: (717) 337-6145	**Email: admiss@gettysburg.edu**
Full-time: 1136 men, 1264 women	**Faculty:** 227; IIB, ++$
Part-time: 2 men, 7 women	**Ph.D.s:** 98%
Graduate: n/av	**Student/Faculty:** 9 to 1
Year: semesters	**Tuition:** $52,640
Room & Board: $12,570	**Freshman Class:** 6384 applied, 2924 accepted, 721 enrolled
SAT EBR-W/M: 673/673 **ACT:** 28	**CEEB CODE:** 2275
Application Deadline: January 15	**MOST COMPETITIVE**

Gettysburg College, founded in 1832, is a nationally ranked college offering programs in the liberal arts and sciences. There is 1 undergraduate school. The 200-acre campus is in a suburban area 45 minutes from Harrisburg, 60 minutes from Baltimore, and 80 minutes from Washington, D.C. Including any residence halls, there are 81 buildings.

STUDENT LIFE: 74% of undergraduates are from out of state, mostly the Middle Atlantic. Students are from 38 states, 38 foreign countries, and Canada. 8% are Hispanic; 75% White; 7% Foreign; 4% African American; 3% two or more races; 2% Asian American; 2% race unknown. 32% are Catholic. **Female To Male Ratio:** 1.1:1. The average age of freshmen is 18; all undergraduates, 20. 10% do not continue beyond their first year; 84% remain to graduate. **Housing:** 2340 students can be accommodated in college housing, which includes gender neutral dorms, on-campus apartments. language/international houses, special-interest houses, and fraternity houses. The College House Program, fosters intellectual and social communities around common interests. On-campus housing is guaranteed for all 4 years and is available on a lottery system for upperclassmen. Upperclassmen may keep cars.

FACULTY/CLASSROOMS: 57% of faculty are male; 43% are female. All teach undergraduates and do research. No introductory courses are taught by graduate students. The average class size in an introductory lecture is 17 and in a regular course is 17.

PROGRAMS OF STUDY: GC confers B.A., B.S., B.Mus., and B.M.E. degrees. Bachelor's degrees are awarded in BIOLOGICAL SCIENCE (biochemistry and biology/biological science), BUSINESS (business administration and management), COMMUNICATIONS AND THE ARTS (Africana studies, art history and appreciation, classics, dramatic arts, English, French, German, Greek, Latin, film and media studies, music, music performance, Spanish, studio art, and writing), COMPUTER AND PHYSICAL SCIENCE (chemistry, computer science, mathematics, mathematics – economics, and physics), EDUCATION (elementary education, foreign languages education, music education, science education, and secondary education), ENGINEERING AND ENVIRONMENTAL DESIGN (environmental science), HEALTH PROFESSIONS (health science, predentistry, and premedicine), SOCIAL SCIENCE (anthropology, Caribbean studies, Chinese Studies, East Asian studies, economics, gender studies, German area studies, history, interdisciplinary studies, international relations, international studies, Islamic studies, Italian studies, Japanese studies, Judaic studies, Latin American studies, Middle Eastern studies, philosophy, political science/government, prelaw, psychology, public policy, religion, religious studies, sociology, women & gender studies, and women's studies). Natural sciences, psychology, political science, management, and history are the strongest academically. Political science, management, and psychology have the largest enrollments.

ACTIVITIES: 32% of men belong to 9 national fraternities; 35% of women belong to 7 national sororities. There are 120 groups on campus, including dance ensemble, campus activities board, art, band, cheerleading, choir, chorale, chorus, communications, computers, dance, debate, drama, environmental, ethnic, film, honors, international, jazz band, LGBT, literary magazine, marching band, musical theater, newspaper, opera, orchestra, outdoor recreation program, pep band, photography, political, professional, radio and TV, religious, social, social service, student government, symphony, and yearbook. Popular campus events include Thanksgiving Dinner, First-Year Walk, International Food Festival, Snowball, and Springfest. **Sports:** There are 12 intercollegiate sports for men and 12 for women, and 10 intramural sports for men and 10 for women. Facilities include a recreation center, fitness area, natatorium, rock climbing walls, basketball courts, indoor and outdoor tennis courts, several tracks and fields, outdoor turf fields, and a field house. **Graduates:** From July 1, 2016 to June 30, 2017, 667 bachelor's degrees were awarded. The most popular majors were political science (11%), organization & management studies (10%), and psychology (7%). In an average class, 80% graduate in 4 years or less, 83% graduate in 5 years or less, and 84% graduate in 6 years or less. Of the 2016 graduating class, 21% were enrolled in graduate school within 6 months of graduation, and 77% were employed.

SERVICES: Counseling and information services are available, as is tutoring in most subjects. **Library/Resources:** The library contains 370,584 volumes, 71,289 microform items, and 27,785 audio/video tapes/CDs/DVDs, and subscribes to 102,805 periodicals including electronic. Computerized library services include interlibrary loans, database searching, Internet access, and Wi-Fi capability. Special learning facilities include an art gallery, planetarium, radio station, TV station, electron microscopes, spectrometers, an optics lab, plasma physics lab, a greenhouse, a geographic information systems lab, an observatory, child study lab, and fine and performing arts. **Physically Challenged Students:** 90% of the campus is accessible. Facilities include wheelchair ramps, elevators, special parking, specially equipped restrooms, special class scheduling, lowered drinking fountains, and special housing. **Special:** The college offers an extensive global education (study abroad) program. There are summer internships and a Washington semester with American University or Lutheran College. Cross-registration is possible with members of the Central Pennsylvania Consortium. There is a United Nations semester at Drew University, and a 3-2 engineering program with Columbia University, Rensselaer Polytechnic, University of Pittsburgh, and Washington University in St. Louis. There are also joint programs in optometry with the Pennsylvania College of Optometry, forestry and environmental studies with Duke University, nursing with Johns Hopkins University, and human resource management with Rutgers University. The college offers double majors, student-designed majors, and B.A.-B.S. degrees in biology, chemistry, physics, biochemistry, and molecular biology, environmental studies and health and exercise sciences. Secondary education certification is also available. There are 15 national honor societies and a chapter of Phi Beta Kappa. **Visiting:** There are regularly scheduled orientations for prospective students, including interviews, tours, day visits, open houses, and group information sessions. There are guides for informal visits and visitors may sit in on classes. To schedule a visit, contact the Admissions Office. **Campus Safety and Security:** Measures include 24-hour foot and vehicle patrol, emergency notification system, self-defense education, and security escort services. There are emergency telephones, lighted pathways/sidewalks, and controlled access to dorms/residences.

REQUIREMENTS: An essay is required. Students planning to major in music must audition and art students can submit a portfolio. An interview is recommended. AP credits are accepted. Important factors in the admissions decision are advanced placement or honors courses, recommendations by school officials, and evidence of special talent. All students must complete 32 courses including a concentration in a major field of study culminating with a capstone experience, 1 course each in the arts, humanities, social sciences, quantitative reasoning, interdisciplinary, and science, technology and society, first-year writing, 2 courses in natural sciences, cultural diversity, and in foreign language. The minimum GPA is 2.0. **Procedure:** Freshmen are admitted in the fall and spring. Entrance exams should be taken by January of senior year. There are early decision and deferred admissions plans. Early decision applications should be filed by November 15; regular applications, by January 15 for fall entry. The fall 2017 application fee was $60. Notification of early decision is sent December 15; regular decision, April 1. 286 early decision candidates were accepted for the 2017-2018 class. 917 applicants were on the 2017 waiting list. Applications are accepted on-line. **Transfer Students:** 22 transfer students enrolled in 2016-2017. Transfer applicants must have a GPA of at least 2.5. An interview is recommended. The high school record, test scores, college official's report and transcript from college (s) attended are also required. 16 of 32 credits required for the bachelor's degree must be completed at GC. **International Students:** There are 179 international students enrolled. They must take the TOEFL, and either the SAT or ACT.

ADMISSIONS: 46% of the 2017-2018 applicants were accepted. The SAT scores for the 2017-2018 freshman class were: Math-- 4% between 500 and 599, 63% between 600 and 699, and 33% between 700 and 800. Evidence-Based Reading/Writing-- 3% between 500 and 599, 66% between 600 and 699, and 31% between 700 and 800. 84% of the current freshmen were in the top fifth of their class; 98% were in the top two fifths. **Admissions Contact:** Gail Sweezey, Director of Admissions. Email: *admiss@gettysburg.edu* Web: *www.gettysburg.edu*

FINANCIAL AID: In 2017-2018, 65% of all full-time freshmen received some form of financial aid. 64% of all full-time freshmen received need-based aid. The average freshman award was $40,147. 46% of undergraduate students work part-time. The average financial indebtedness of the 2017 graduate was $31,323. GC is a member of CSS. The CSS/Profile is required. The FAFSA code is 003268. The priority date for freshman financial aid applications for fall entry is January 15. The deadline for filing freshman financial aid applications for fall entry is February 1.

GROVE CITY COLLEGE — B-2
www.gcc.edu

Grove City, PA 16127	(724) 458-2100
Fax: (724) 458-3395	Email: admissions@gcc.edu
Full-time: 1180 men, 1135 women	**Faculty:** 155
Part-time: 36 men, 22 women	**Ph.D.s:** 84%
Graduate: n/av	**Student/Faculty:** 15 to 1
Year: semesters, summer session	**Tuition:** $17,254
Room & Board: $9400	**Freshman Class:** 1783 applied, 1424 accepted, 636 enrolled
SAT CR/M: 625/607 **ACT:** 27	**CEEB CODE:** 2277
Application Deadline: January 20	**VERY COMPETITIVE**

Grove City College, founded in 1876, is a private, Christian college committed to providing the best liberal arts and sciences education in the country. Our mission is to promote Christian values worldview, the foundations of free society, faithfulness, excellence, community, stewardship, and independence. There are 2 undergraduate schools. In addition to regional accreditation, GCC has baccalaureate program accreditation with ABET, ACBSP, CAAHEP, and ACS. The 180-acre campus is in a small town 60 miles north of Pittsburgh, PA. Including any residence halls, there are 30 buildings.

STUDENT LIFE: 55% of undergraduates are from Pennsylvania. Others are from 44 states, and 13 foreign countries. 61% are from public schools. 92% are White; 3% two or more races; 2% Asian American; 1% African American; 1% Hispanic; 1% Foreign. 51% claim no religious affiliation; 35% Protestant. **Male To Female Ratio:** 1.1:1. The average age of freshmen is 18; all undergraduates, 20. 11% do not continue beyond their first year; 83% remain to graduate. **Housing:** 2309 students can be accommodated in college housing, which includes dorms and on-campus apartments. On-campus housing is guaranteed for all 4 years and is available on a lottery system for upperclassmen. 95% of students live on campus. Alcohol is not permitted. Upperclassmen may keep cars.

FACULTY/CLASSROOMS: 60% of faculty are male; 40% are female. All teach undergraduates, 30% do research, and 30% do both. No introductory courses are taught by graduate students. The average class size in an introductory lecture is 21; in a laboratory is 20; and in a regular course is 21.

PROGRAMS OF STUDY: GCC confers B.A., B.S., B.Mus., B.S.E.E., and B.S.M.E. degrees. Bachelor's degrees are awarded in AGRICULTURE (conservation and regulation), BIOLOGICAL SCIENCE (biochemistry, biology/biological science, biology/general science secondary education, molecular biology, and neurosciences), BUSINESS (accounting, business administration and management, business economics, entrepreneurial studies, finance, international business, and marketing management), COMMUNICATIONS AND THE ARTS (communication studies, English, French, music, music business management, music performance, and Spanish), COMPUTER AND PHYSICAL SCIENCE (chemistry, chemistry/gen science second education, chemistry secondary education, computer information systems, computer science, mathematics, physics/general science secondary education, physics secondary education, physics/computer, and physics), EDUCATION (early childhood education, English secondary education, French studies K-12 education, mathematics education, middle school education, music education, social studies secondary school education, Spanish education K-12, and special education), ENGINEERING AND ENVIRONMENTAL DESIGN (electrical and computer engineering, industrial administration/ management, and mechanical engineering), HEALTH PROFESSIONS (exercise science and health science), SOCIAL SCIENCE (biblical studies, economics, history, ministries, philosophy, political science/ government, psychology, religious music, social work, and sociology). Engineering, computer science, and biology are the strongest academically. Mechanical engineering, accounting, and communication studies have the largest enrollments.

ACTIVITIES: 14% of men belong to 10 local fraternities; 20% of women belong to 8 local sororities. There are 173 groups on campus, including art, band, cheerleading, chess, choir, chorale, chorus, communications, computers, dance, debate, drama, drill team, environmental, ethnic, film, forensics, honors, international, jazz band, literary magazine, marching band, musical theater, newspaper, opera, orchestra, pep band, photography, political, professional, radio and TV, religious, social, social service, student government, symphony, and yearbook. Popular campus events include Family Weekend, Christmas Candlelight Service, Homecoming, and President's Gala. **Sports:** There are 11 intercollegiate sports for men and 11 for women, and 14 intramural sports for men and 11 for women. Facilities include a field house, indoor pools, indoor running track, an intramural room with basketball courts, volleyball, tennis courts, racquetball courts, a bowling alley, fitness rooms, outdoor tennis courts, turf football stadium with an all-weather track, baseball, soccer, and softball fields, and intramural fields. **Graduates:** From July 1, 2016 to June 30, 2017, 609 bachelor's degrees were awarded. The most popular majors were biology (8%), communication studies (8%), and mechanical engineering (7%). In an average class, 2% graduate in 3 years or less, 78% graduate in 4 years or less, 83% graduate in 5 years or less, and 83% graduate in 6 years or less. Of the 2016 graduating class, 13% were enrolled in graduate school within 6 months of graduation, and 81% were employed.

SERVICES: Counseling and information services are available, as is tutoring in most subjects. A free, drop-in peer tutoring program is available during various hours throughout the week. A one-on-one peer tutoring program is available for a small fee. **Library/Resources:** The library contains 166,600 volumes, 4,000 microform items, and 3,910 audio/video tapes/CDs/DVDs, and subscribes to 32,720 periodicals including electronic. Computerized library services include interlibrary loans, database searching, Internet access, and Wi-Fi capability. Special learning facilities include an art gallery, radio station, TV station, and an off-site research grade observatory. **Physically Challenged Students:** 10% of the campus is accessible. Facilities include wheelchair ramps, elevators, special parking, specially equipped restrooms, special class scheduling, lowered drinking fountains, and special housing. **Special:** The college offers domestic and international travel courses, study abroad, accelerated and double major degrees, semester and summer internships, and a Washington, DC semester. There are 17 national honor societies and 14 departmental honors programs. **Visiting:** There are regularly scheduled orientations for prospective students, daily interviews and tours; high school visitation days: 5 in the fall and 2 in the spring. There are various department-specific open houses throughout the year. There are guides for informal visits, visitors may sit in on classes, and stay overnight. To schedule a visit, contact the Admissions Office. **Campus Safety and Security:** Measures include 24-hour foot and vehicle patrol, emergency notification system, and security escort services. There are emergency telephones, lighted pathways/sidewalks, controlled access to dorms/residences. There is also an emergency response program is in place, which includes a public warning siren and cell phone call/text message system.

REQUIREMENTS: The SAT or ACT is required. An academic or college preparatory curriculum is highly recommended, including 4 units of English, 3 units each of math, science, and a foreign language, and 2 units of history. One essay is required of all applicants, and an audition is required of music students. An interview is highly recommended. AP and CLEP credits are accepted. Important factors in the admissions decision are extracurricular activities record, personality/intangible qualities, and parents or siblings attended your school. Students are required to complete a minimum of 128 credit hours. All students must complete the 40-46 semester-hour general education curriculum, which includes 15 hours of humanities; a 3 hour writing course; 8 hours of natural science; 3 hours of science, faith, and technology; 3 hours of social science; and 6 hours of quantitative and logical reasoning. Specific courses required include 2 hours of physical/wellness education and 2 years demonstrated proficiency in a foreign language. A minimum GPA of 2.0 is required. **Procedure:** Freshmen are admitted in the fall and spring. Entrance exams should be taken during the spring of the junior year or the fall of the senior. There are early decision, early admissions, and deferred admissions plans. Early decision applications should be filed by November 1; regular applications, by January 20 for fall entry; and December 15 for spring entry. The fall 2017 application fee was $50. Notification of early decision is sent December 15; regular decision, February 20. 295 early decision candidates were accepted for the 2017-2018 class. 114 applicants were on the 2017 waiting list; 15 were admitted. Applications are accepted on-line. **Transfer Students:** 32 transfer students enrolled in 2016-2017. Either the SAT or the ACT is required as well as two letters of recommendation, official high school and college transcripts, and an essay. An interview is highly recommended. 64 of 128 credits required for the bachelor's degree must be completed at GCC. **International Students:** There are 23 international students enrolled. They must take the TOEFL with a minimum score of 550 on the paper-based TOEFL (PBT) or 79 on the Internet-based version (iBT). If the TOEFL is not available, either the SAT or the ACT is required.

ADMISSIONS: 80% of the 2017-2018 applicants were accepted. The SAT scores for the 2017-2018 freshman class were: Critical Reading-- 3% below 500, 33% between 500 and 599, 45% between 600 and 699, and 19% between 700 and 800. Math-- 6% below 500, 40% between 500 and 599, 41% between 600 and 699, and 13% between 700 and 800. The ACT scores were 1% between 12 and 17, 23% between 18 and 23, 49% between 24 and 29, and 27% above 30. 58% of the current freshmen were in the top fifth of their class; 85% were in the top two fifths. 38 freshmen graduated first in their class. **Admissions Contact:** Sarah E. Gibbs, Director of Admissions. Email: *admissions@gcc.edu* Web: *www.gcc.edu*

FINANCIAL AID: In 2017-2018, 75% of all full-time freshmen received some form of financial aid. 51% of all full-time freshmen received need-based aid. The average freshman award was $14,784. Need-based scholarships or need-based grants averaged $6,098; need-based self-help aid (loans and jobs) averaged $13,535; and other non-need-based awards and non-need-based scholarships averaged $5,887. 43% of undergraduate students work part-time. The average financial indebtedness of the 2017 graduate was $40,747. The college's own financial statement is required. The FAFSA code is G03269. The deadline for filing freshman financial aid applications for fall entry is April 15.

GWYNEDD MERCY UNIVERSITY *(The complete profile is made available exclusively on our website, www.barronspac.com)*

HAVERFORD COLLEGE — E-4
www.haverford.edu

Haverford, PA 19041 — **(610) 896-1350**

Fax: (610) 896-1338	**Email:** admission@haverford.edu
Full-time: 613 men, 655 women	**Faculty:** 131; IIB, ++$
Part-time: n/av	**Ph.D.s:** 96%
Graduate: n/av	**Student/Faculty:** 9 to 1
Year: semesters	**Tuition:** $51,024
Room & Board: $15,466	**Freshman Class:** 4066 applied, 870 accepted, 349 enrolled
SAT CR/M/W: 710/710/710 **ACT:** 33	**CEEB CODE:** 2289
Application Deadline: January 15	**MOST COMPETITIVE**

Haverford College, founded in 1833, is a private liberal arts college. There is 1 undergraduate school. The 200-acre campus is in a suburban area 8 miles west of Philadelphia, PA. Including any residence halls, there are 87 buildings.

STUDENT LIFE: 89% of undergraduates are from out of state, mostly the Middle Atlantic. Students are from 41 states, 37 foreign countries, and Canada. 54% are from public schools. 9% are Foreign; 8% Hispanic; 7% African American; 60% White; 4% two or more races; 3% race unknown; 17% Asian American. **Female To Male Ratio:** 1.1:1. The average age of freshmen is 18; all undergraduates, 20. 3% do not continue beyond their first year; 90% remain to graduate. **Housing:** 1236 students can be accommodated in college housing, which includes dorms, on-campus apartments, language/international houses, and special-interest houses. Haverford students may also live at Bryn Mawr College through a dorm exchange program. On-campus housing is guaranteed for all 4 years and is available on a lottery system for upperclassmen. 99% of students live on campus. Upperclassmen may keep cars.

FACULTY/CLASSROOMS: 52% of faculty are male; 48% are female. All teach undergraduates, 80% do research, and 80% do both. No introductory courses are taught by graduate students. The average class size in a regular course is 20.

PROGRAMS OF STUDY: Haverford confers B.A. and B.S. degrees. Bachelor's degrees are awarded in BIOLOGICAL SCIENCE (biology/biological science), COMMUNICATIONS AND THE ARTS (art history and appreciation, classics, comparative literature, English, fine arts, French, German, Greek, Italian, Latin, linguistics, music, romance languages and literature, Russian, Spanish, and visual and performing arts), COMPUTER AND PHYSICAL SCIENCE (astronomy, astrophysics, chemistry, computer science, geology, information sciences and systems, mathematics, and physics), SOCIAL SCIENCE (anthropology, archeology, East Asian studies, economics, history, interdisciplinary studies, liberal arts/general studies, philosophy, political science/government, psychology, religion, sociology, and urban studies). Natural Sciences is the strongest academically. Biology, psychology, and English have the largest enrollments.

ACTIVITIES: There are no fraternities or sororities. There are 145 groups on campus, including art, chess, choir, chorale, communications, computers, dance, debate, drama, environmental, ethnic, film, international, LGBT, literary magazine, musical theater, newspaper, photography, political, religious, social, social service, student government, and yearbook. Popular campus events include Haverfest, Snowball, and Haverford vs Swarthmore Athletic Events. **Sports:** There are 11 intercollegiate sports for men and 13 for women, and 3 intramural sports for men and 3 for women. The Integrated Athletic Center is for basketball, and volleyball, a fitness center, cybex exercise equipment, multipurpose room for dance, martial arts, 5 international squash courts, and sports medicine. **Graduates:** From July 1, 2016 to June 30, 2017, 304 bachelor's degrees were awarded. The most popular majors were biology (12%), psychology (9%), and English (7%). In an average class, 86% graduate in 4 years or less, 89% graduate in 5 years or less, and 90% graduate in 6 years or less. Of the 2016 graduating class, 18% were enrolled in graduate school within 6 months of graduation, and 60% were employed.

SERVICES: Counseling and information services are available, as is tutoring in every subject. There is a reader service for the blind. **Library/Resources:** The library contains 592,984 volumes, 8,039 microform items, and 16,280 audio/video tapes/CDs/DVDs, and subscribes to 14,775 periodicals including electronic. Computerized library services include interlibrary loans, database searching, Internet access, and Wi-Fi capability. Special learning facilities include an art gallery, planetarium, an observatory, and arboretum. **Physically Challenged Students:** 60% of the campus is accessible. Facilities include wheelchair ramps, elevators, special parking, specially equipped restrooms, special class scheduling, lowered drinking fountains, lowered telephones, and reasonable accommodations are made for special needs. **Special:** Haverford offers internship programs, cross-registration with Bryn Mawr and Swarthmore Colleges, study abroad in 38 countries, dual majors, and student-designed majors. Pass/fail options are limited to 4 in 4 years. Haverford offers a 3-2 program in engineering with the California Institute of Technology; a 3-2 program in City Planning with the University of Pennsylvania; a 4-1 program in Engineering with the University of Pennsylvania; a 4-1 program in Bioethics with UPENN; a 5 year program with Georgetown University; a 1 year Master's program in Finance at Claremont McKenna; and a 2 year Master's program in China Studies at Zhejiang University **Visiting:** There are guides for informal visits, visitors may sit in on classes, and stay overnight. To schedule a visit, contact the Admissions Office. **Campus Safety and Security:** Measures include 24-hour foot and vehicle patrol, emergency notification system, self-defense education, and security escort services. There are shuttle buses, emergency telephones, lighted pathways/sidewalks, controlled access to dorms/residences, and a fire safety program.

REQUIREMENTS: First-year applicants must take the SAT or the ACT before the deadline for the decision plan chosen. Candidates for admission must be graduates of an accredited secondary school and have taken 4 courses in English, 3 each in foreign language and math, 2 in social studies, and 1 in science. The GED is accepted. An essay is required, and an interview is recommended. AP credits are accepted. Important factors in the admissions decision are advanced placement or honors courses, leadership record, and recommendations by school officials. All students must take a minimum of 32 course credits, including freshman writing and 3 courses each in social science, natural science, and the humanities. Students must also take 3 semesters of phys ed and demonstrate proficiency in foreign language. Students must take a minimum of 6 courses in the major and 6 in related fields. Each major includes a capstone experience. **Procedure:** Freshmen are admitted in the fall. Entrance exams should be taken by February 1. There are early decision, early admissions, and deferred admissions plans. Early decision applications should be filed by November 15; regular applications, by January 15 for fall entry. The fall 2017 application fee was $65. Notification of early decision is sent December 15; regular decision, April 1. 173 early decision candidates were accepted for the 2017-2018 class. 412 applicants were on the 2017 waiting list; 26 were admitted. Applications are accepted on-line. **Transfer Students:** 9 transfer students enrolled in 2016-2017. Transfer students must be able to enter the sophomore or junior class. Admission depends mainly on the strength of college grades. A minimum GPA of 3.0 is necessary and the SAT is recommended. The equivalent of 1 year of courses must have been earned. A liberal arts curriculum is also recommended. 64 of 128 credits required for the bachelor's degree must be completed at Haverford. **International Students:** There are 115 international students enrolled. They must take the TOEFL with a minimum score of 600 on the paper-based TOEFL (PBT) or 100 on the Internet-based version (iBT). They must also take the SAT or ACT.

ADMISSIONS: 21% of the 2017-2018 applicants were accepted. The SAT scores for the 2017-2018 freshman class were: Critical Reading-- 6% between 500 and 599, 34% between 600 and 699, and 60% between 700 and 800. Math-- 7% between 500 and 599, 32% between 600 and 699, and 61% between 700 and 800. Writing-- 3% between 500 and 599, 38% between 600 and 699, and 59% between 700 and 800. The ACT scores were 12% between 24 and 29, and 88% above 30. 98% of the current freshmen were in the top fifth of their class; 100% were in the top two fifths. **Admissions Contact:** Jess Lord, Dean of Admission & Financial Aid. Email: *admission@haverford.edu* Web: *www.haverford.edu*

FINANCIAL AID: In 2017-2018, 46% of all full-time freshmen received some form of financial aid. 45% of all full-time freshmen received need-based aid. The average freshman award was $49,928. Need-based scholarships or need-based grants averaged $46,398; and need-based self-help aid (loans and jobs) averaged $2,931. 64% of undergraduate students work part-time. The average financial indebtedness of the 2017 graduate was $18,932. Haverford is a member of CSS. The CSS/Profile is required. The FAFSA code is 003274. The deadline for filing freshman financial aid applications for fall entry is February 1.

HOLY FAMILY UNIVERSITY *(The complete profile is made available exclusively on our website, www.barronspac.com)*

IMMACULATA UNIVERSITY — E-4

www.immaculata.edu

Immaculata, PA 19345 — **(610) 647-4400**

Fax: (610) 640-0836
Full-time: 283 men, 660 women
Part-time: 109 men, 503 women
Graduate: 236 men, 819 women
Year: semesters, summer session
Room & Board: $12,500

Application Deadline: n/av

Email: admiss@immaculata.edu
Faculty: 96; I
Ph.D.s: 85%
Student/Faculty: 10 to 1
Tuition: $26,500
Freshman Class: 1584 applied, 1304 accepted, 217 enrolled
CEEB CODE: 2320
COMPETITIVE

Immaculata University, founded in 1920, is a private, Catholic, comprehensive, coeducational university that offers associate, bachelor's, master's and doctoral degrees. Immaculata offers more than 60 majors, minors, and pre-professional certifications, including accelerated and online career-oriented programs. There are 2 undergraduate schools and 1 graduate school. In addition to regional accreditation, Immaculata has baccalaureate program accreditation with ACBSP, AHEA, NASM, NLN, CCNE, and CAATE. The 400-acre campus is in a suburban area 20 miles west of Philadelphia. Including any residence halls, there are 22 buildings.

STUDENT LIFE: 74% of undergraduates are from Pennsylvania. Others are from states. 57% are from public schools. 76% are White; 6% Hispanic; 2% Asian American; 2% two or more races; 13% African American; 1% Foreign; 1% race unknown. 59% are Catholic; 19% Protestant; 15% Islamic. **Female To Male Ratio:** 3.2:1. The average age of freshmen is 18. 20% do not continue beyond their first year; 63% remain to graduate. **Housing:** 568 students can be accommodated in college housing, which includes dorms and on-campus apartments. On-campus housing is guaranteed for all 4 years. 53% of students live on campus. Alcohol is not permitted. All students may keep cars.

FACULTY/CLASSROOMS: 21% of faculty are male; 79% are female. No introductory courses are taught by graduate students.

PROGRAMS OF STUDY: Immaculata confers B.A., B.S., B.Mus., and B.S.N. degrees. Associate, master's, and doctoral degrees are also awarded. Bachelor's degrees are awarded in BIOLOGICAL SCIENCE (biology/biological science), BUSINESS (accounting, business administration and management, fashion merchandising, finance, human resources/organizational management, and marketing management), COMMUNICATIONS AND THE ARTS (communications, digital media, English, music, and Spanish), COMPUTER AND PHYSICAL SCIENCE (chemistry, chemistry secondary education, information sciences and systems, and mathematics), EDUCATION (athletic training, early childhood education, elementary education, English secondary education, foreign languages education, mathematics education, middle school education, music education, science education, secondary education, and social studies secondary school education), HEALTH PROFESSIONS (allied health, exercise science, music therapy, nursing, premedicine, pre-occupational therapy, and prephysical therapy), SOCIAL SCIENCE (biopsychology, criminology, dietetics, economics, history, international relations, political science/government, prelaw, psychology, social science, social work, sociology, and theological studies). Healthcare professions, education, and business are the strongest academically. Nursing, exercise science, and business management have the largest enrollments.

ACTIVITIES: There are 40 groups on campus, including fashion group, sign language, art, band, cheerleading, choir, chorale, chorus, computers, dance, debate, drama, environmental, ethnic, honors, international, jazz band, literary magazine, newspaper, orchestra, photography, political, professional, religious, social, social service, student government, and wellness. Popular campus events include Rose Arbor Dinner, Senior Ball, Carol Night, Amethyst Day, Family Week, Block Party, and Beyond the Campus. **Sports:** There are 9 intercollegiate sports for men and 10 for women. Facilities include a baseball stadium, outdoor basketball courts, full indoor gymnasium, indoor multi-sport training facility with turf surface, athletic training facility, tennis courts, indoor swimming pool, and a fitness center (weights, exercise equipment). **Graduates:** From July 1, 2016 to June 30, 2017, 613 bachelor's degrees were awarded. The most popular majors were health professions (51%), exercise science (6%), and psychology (4%). In an average class, 55% graduate in 4 years or less, 60% graduate in 5 years or less, and 62% graduate in 6 years or less.

SERVICES: Counseling and information services are available, as is tutoring in most subjects. There is remedial math and writing, and other ADA-related services provided.**Library/Resources:** The library contains 120,000 volumes, and 10,000 audio/video tapes/CDs/DVDs, and subscribes to 250 periodicals including electronic. Computerized library services include interlibrary loans, database searching, Internet access, and Wi-Fi capability. **Physically Challenged Students:** All of the campus is accessible. Facilities include wheelchair ramps, elevators, special parking, specially equipped restrooms, special class scheduling, lowered drinking fountains, lowered telephones, and special housing. **Special:** All academic departments offer opportunities for internships, and some majors require internships. Students may also study abroad. Immaculata offers accelerated degree programs in 10 areas: Cybersecurity; Emergency Planning and Management; Organizational Behavior; Health Care Management, Nursing (RN to BSN), Marketing Management; Human Resource Management; Finance; Business Management; and Business Administration. Immaculata also offers dual-majors, non-degree study, and pass/fail options for students. There are 21 national honor societies, Phi Beta Kappa, and a freshman honors program. **Visiting:** There are regularly scheduled orientations for prospective students, campus tour, information session, class visit, and visitors may stay overnight. To schedule a visit, contact the Office of Admissions. **Campus Safety and Security:** Measures include 24-hour foot and vehicle patrol, emergency notification system, self-defense education, and security escort services. There are emergency telephones, lighted pathways/sidewalks, controlled access to dorms/residences, and security cameras.

REQUIREMENTS: Candidates for admission should be graduates of an accredited secondary school with a minimum of 16 academic courses including 4 in English, 2 each in social studies, foreign language, math, and science, and 4 more in college preparatory courses. The GED is accepted. An essay and letter of recommendation are required for all applicants. An audition is required for music students. A GPA of 2.0 is required. AP and CLEP credits are accepted. Important factors in the admissions decision are advanced placement or honors courses, recommendations by school officials, and extracurricular activities record. To graduate, all students must complete the Liberal Arts Core requirements for the university which include 42-54 credits in humanities, social sciences, sciences, foreign language, and theology. Students in the College of Undergraduate Studies must take a minimum of 128 credits, including 36 to 52 in the major. 2 credits of phys ed are also required. Immaculata requires a minimum GPA of 2.0 to graduate. Undergraduates requires the completion a capstone project or culminating learning experience. Internships are required for several majors, including dietetics, music therapy, communications, and education. **Procedure:** Freshmen are admitted in the fall and spring. Entrance exams should be taken in the junior year or fall of the senior year. There are deferred admissions and rolling admissions plans. Application deadlines are open. The fall 2017 application fee was $35. Applications are accepted on-line. **Transfer Students:** 54 transfer students enrolled in 2016-2017. In addition, to high school credentials, transfer applicants must present college transcripts. Courses in which the student has achieved a C or better are accepted if they are comparable to Immaculata's courses up to a maximum of 64 credits for the college of undergraduate studies or 72 credits for the college of lifelong learning. Students must have a minimum GPA of 2.0. **International Students:** They must take the TOEFL with a minimum score of 513 on the paper-based TOEFL (PBT) or 65 on the Internet-based version (iBT). They must also take the SAT or ACT.

ADMISSIONS: 82% of the 2017-2018 applicants were accepted. **Admissions Contact:** Nicola Di Fronzo-Heitzer, Director of Admissions. Email: *admiss@immaculata.edu* Web: *www.immaculata.edu*

FINANCIAL AID: In 2017-2018, 100% of all full-time freshmen received some form of financial aid. 75% of all full-time freshmen received need-based aid. The average freshman award was $28,463. Need-based scholarships or need-based grants averaged $8,835; need-based self-help aid (loans and jobs) averaged $5,888; and other non-need-based awards and non-need-based scholarships averaged $16,136. 35% of undergraduate students work part-time. Immaculata is a member of CSS. The FAFSA code is 003276. The deadline for filing freshman financial aid applications for fall entry is April 15.

INDIANA UNIVERSITY OF PENNSYLVANIA B-3

www.iup.edu

Indiana, PA 15705 (724) 357-2230
(800) 442-6830

Fax: (724) 357-6281 **Email:** admissions-inquiry@iup.edu

Full-time: 3921 men, 5429 women	**Faculty:** 548
Part-time: 424 men, 369 women	**Ph.D.s:** 95%
Graduate: 851 men, 1322 women	**Student/Faculty:** 16 to 1
Year: semesters, summer session	**Tuition:** $12,146 ($17,271)
Room & Board: $12,328	**Freshman Class:** 9880 applied, 8973 accepted, 2400 enrolled
SAT EBR-W/M: 513/500	**CEEB CODE:** 2652
Application Deadline: open	**COMPETITIVE**

Indiana University of Pennsylvania was established in 1875 and was the first doctoral/research university in Pennsylvania's State System of

Higher Education. Academic offerings include more than 140 undergraduate programs with a variety of options for internships and study abroad, more than 60 master's degree programs, and 14 doctoral programs. There are unusual opportunities for research at all levels, plus the Cook Honors College, which provide special challenges for academic growth. The variety and quality of instruction are characteristic of a big university, yet at IUP, close, one-to-one relationships develop within the teaching framework, and a strong sense of community prevails. There are 7 undergraduate schools and 1 graduate school. In addition to regional accreditation, Indiana University of Pennsylvania has baccalaureate program accreditation with AACSB, ABET, ADA, NASAD, NASM, ASHA, ACPHA, ACEND, APA, ACFEF, CACREP, CCNE, CAAHEP, CAATE, CoARC, NAST, and PAB. The 374-acre campus is in a small town 50 miles northeast of Pittsburgh. Including any residence halls, there are 75 buildings.

STUDENT LIFE: 95% of undergraduates are from Pennsylvania. Others are from 46 states, 56 foreign countries, and Canada. 72% are White; 7% Foreign; 4% Hispanic; 4% two or more races; 11% African American; 1% Asian American; 1% race unknown. **Female To Male Ratio:** 1.4:1. The average age of freshmen is 18; all undergraduates, 21. 26% do not continue beyond their first year; 46% remain to graduate. **Housing:** 3528 students can be accommodated in college housing, which includes dorms and on-campus apartments. In addition, there are honors houses, 24-hour intensified study floors, substance-free housing, academic specialty housing, and residence hall suggested for international students (available during breaks). On-campus housing is guaranteed for the freshman year only and is available on a lottery system for upperclassmen. 68% of students commute. Alcohol is not permitted. All students may keep cars.

FACULTY/CLASSROOMS: 49% of faculty are male; 51% are female. No introductory courses are taught by graduate students.

PROGRAMS OF STUDY: IUP confers B.A., B.S., B.F.A. and B.S.Ed. degrees. Associate, master's, and doctoral degrees are also awarded. Bachelor's degrees are awarded in BIOLOGICAL SCIENCE (biochemistry, biology/biological science, cell & molecular biology, and nutrition), BUSINESS (accounting, fashion merchandising, finance, hospitality management services, human resources, international business management, management information systems, and marketing management), COMMUNICATIONS AND THE ARTS (art, communications technology, English, fine arts, journalism, music, music performance, Spanish, studio art, and theatre arts), COMPUTER AND PHYSICAL SCIENCE (applied physics, chemistry, clinical laboratory science, chemistry education, computer science, earth science, geology, mathematics, mathematics - actuarial concentration, natural sciences, physics secondary education, and physics), EDUCATION (art education, Asian studies, business education, early childhood education, English education, general studies, health education, music education, physical education, social studies education, Spanish adolescense education, and vocational education), ENGINEERING AND ENVIRONMENTAL DESIGN (city/community/regional planning, environmental engineering, and interior design), HEALTH PROFESSIONS (disabilities studies, nuclear medical technology, nursing, nutrition and dietetics, public health, respiratory therapy, and speech pathology/audiology), SOCIAL SCIENCE (anthropology, child care/child and family studies, criminology, economics, family/consumer resource management, geography, history, international studies, philosophy, political science/government, psychology, religious studies, safety science, social science, and sociology). Nursing, criminology, and psychology have the largest enrollments.

ACTIVITIES: 8% of men belong to 18 national fraternities; 8% of women belong to 15 national sororities. There are 300 groups on campus, including art, band, cheerleading, chess, choir, chorale, chorus, computers, dance, debate, drama, drill team, environmental, ethnic, film, honors, international, jazz band, LGBT, marching band, musical theater, newspaper, orchestra, pep band, photography, political, professional, radio and TV, religious, social, social service, student government, and symphony. Popular campus events include Welcome Weekend, Homecoming, IUP Day, Winter Warm Up, International Day. **Sports:** There are 7 intercollegiate sports for men and 10 for women, and 7 intramural sports for men and 7 for women. Facilities include the athletic complex, a stadium, swimming pools, a fitness/bike trail, softball fields, baseball fields and courts for tennis, badminton, handball/racquetball courts, basketball courts, rugby field, outdoor track, soccer fields, grass practice fields, volleyball courts, sailing base, frisbee course, fishing ponds, archery range, simulated golf range, and fitness centers. **Graduates:** From July 1, 2016 to June 30, 2017, 2270 bachelor's degrees were awarded. The most popular majors were criminology (9%), nursing (7%), and marketing (6%). In an average class, 53% graduate in 5 years or less and 54% graduate in 6 years or less.

SERVICES: Counseling and information services are available, as is tutoring in some subjects, such as high risk sciences, PSYC, math, and selected other subjects varying by semester. There is a reader service for the blind, and remedial math and reading, and other mandated services, tied to student documentation: adapted testing, note taker services, some equipment loans, letters to professors, and weekly meetings with assigned DSS adviser. **Library/Resources:** The library contains 516,096 volumes, 146,806 microform items, and 26,886 audio/video tapes/CDs/DVDs, and subscribes to 77,350 periodicals including electronic. Computerized library services include interlibrary loans, database searching, Internet access, and Wi-Fi capability. Special learning facilities include an art gallery, planetarium, radio station, and TV station. **Physically Challenged Students:** 99% of the campus is accessible. Facilities include wheelchair ramps, elevators, special parking, specially equipped restrooms, special class scheduling, and special housing. **Special:** IUP offers co-op programs, cross-registration through the National Student Exchange Consortium, a 3-2 engineering degree with the University of Pittsburgh and Drexel University, and a B.A.-B.S. degree. Internships and dual and student-designed majors are available. Students may study abroad in over 60 countries. Also available are work-study programs, a Washington semester, an accelerated degree program, credit for military experience. We have an Honors College and AA and BS program in General Studies which students design their major with help from a faculty advisor. There are 23 national honor societies and a freshman honors program. **Visiting:** There are regularly scheduled orientations for prospective students. There are guides for informal visits and visitors may sit in on classes. To schedule a visit, contact the Admissions Office. **Campus Safety and Security:** Measures include 24-hour foot and vehicle patrol, emergency notification system, self-defense education, and security escort services. There are shuttle buses, emergency telephones, lighted pathways/sidewalks, controlled access to dorms/residences, bicycle registration, operation ID, and a crime tip hotline.

REQUIREMENTS: The SAT is required. Candidates for admission should be graduates of an accredited secondary school. There are no specific course requirements. Art majors must have a portfolio and music majors must audition. AP and CLEP credits are accepted. Important factors in the admissions decision are advanced placement or honors courses, extracurricular activities record, and evidence of special talent. All candidates for graduation must complete approximately 120 credits, including 48 credits in the liberal studies core. The total number of hours and the minimum GPA vary with the major. **Procedure:** Freshmen are admitted in the fall and spring. Entrance exams should be taken by December of the preceding year. There are deferred admissions and rolling admissions plans. Application deadlines are open. The fall 2017 application fee was $25. Notification is sent on a rolling basis. Applications are accepted on-line. **Transfer Students:** 518 transfer students enrolled in 2016-2017. Transfer students must have a minimum GPA of 2.0 for all subjects. Education students transferring 36 or more credits must have a minimum GPA of 3.0 & those with 35 or less credits must have a minimum GPA of 2.75. Nursing and Speech-Language Pathology students must have a cumulative GPA of 3.0 or higher. 30 of 120 credits required for the bachelor's degree must be completed at IUP. **International Students:** There are 315 international students enrolled. They must take the TOEFL with a minimum score of 500 on the paper-based TOEFL (PBT) or 61 on the Internet-based version (iBT), and take the IELTS.

ADMISSIONS: 91% of the 2017-2018 applicants were accepted. The SAT scores for the 2017-2018 freshman class were: Math-- 48% below 500, 43% between 500 and 599, and 8% between 600 and 699. Evidence-Based Reading/Writing-- 41% below 500, 45% between 500 and 599, and 14% between 600 and 699. 20% of the current freshmen were in the top fifth of their class; 40% were in the top two fifths. 9 freshmen graduated first in their class. **Admissions Contact:** Stacy Hopkins, Executive. Direct of Undergraduate Admissions. Email: *admissions-inquiry@iup.edu* Web: *www.iup.edu*

FINANCIAL AID: In 2017-2018, 78% of all full-time freshmen received some form of financial aid. 55% of all full-time freshmen received need-based aid. The average freshman award was $11,469. Need-based scholarships or need-based grants averaged $6,747; need-based self-help aid (loans and jobs) averaged $4,743; and non-need-based athletic scholarships averaged $6,055. 20% of undergraduate students work part-time. The average financial indebtedness of the 2017 graduate was $39,833.

The FAFSA code is 003277. The priority date for freshman financial aid applications for fall entry is October 1.

JEFFERSON (PHILADELPHIA UNIVERSITY + THOMAS JEFFERSON UNIVERSITY) F-3

www.philau.edu

Philadelphia, PA 19144	(215) 951-2700 (800) 951-7287
Fax: (215) 951-2907	**Email:** admissions@philau.edu
Full-time: 765 men, 1506 women	**Faculty:** 123
Part-time: 99 men, 299 women	**Ph.D.s:** 83%
Graduate: 367 men, 694 women	**Student/Faculty:** 13 to 1
Year: semesters, summer session	**Tuition:** $40,501
Room & Board: $13,465	**Freshman Class:** 3746 applied, 2235 accepted, 498 enrolled
SAT CR/M/W: 535/545/520 **ACT:** 24	**CEEB CODE:** 2666
Application Deadline: July 1	**COMPETITIVE**

Jefferson University (Philadelphia University + Thomas Jefferson University), founded in 1884, is a private institution offering preprofessional programs in architecture, design, business, sciences, textiles, fashion, and health. Tuition cost varies by programs chosen by student. There are 6 undergraduate schools and 1 graduate school. In addition to regional accreditation, Philadelphia University has baccalaureate program accreditation with ABET, FIDER, NAAB, NASAD, and ACS. The 100-acre campus is in a suburban area in the section of East Falls, 15 minutes from Center City Philadelphia. Including any residence halls, there are 56 buildings.

STUDENT LIFE: 59% of undergraduates are from Pennsylvania. Others are from 37 states, 24 foreign countries, and Canada. 65% are from public schools. 72% are White; 6% Hispanic; 3% Asian American; 10% African American. 18% claim no religious affiliation **Female To Male Ratio:** 2.0:1. The average age of freshmen is 18; all undergraduates, 23. 20% do not continue beyond their first year; 56% remain to graduate. **Housing:** 1265 students can be accommodated in college housing, which includes dorms, on-campus apartments, and off-campus apartments, and town houses. On-campus housing is guaranteed for the freshman year only, is available on a first-come, first-served basis, and is available on a lottery system for upperclassmen. 50% of students commute. Upperclassmen may keep cars.

FACULTY/CLASSROOMS: 58% of faculty are male; 42% are female. All teach undergraduates, 50% do research, and 50% do both. No introductory courses are taught by graduate students. The average class size in an introductory lecture is 25; in a laboratory is 14; and in a regular course is 17.

PROGRAMS OF STUDY: Philadelphia University confers B.S. and B.Arch. degrees. Associate, master's, and doctoral degrees are also awarded. Bachelor's degrees are awarded in BIOLOGICAL SCIENCE (biochemistry and biology/biological science), BUSINESS (accounting, banking and finance, fashion merchandising, international business management, management information systems, management science, and marketing/retailing/merchandising), COMMUNICATIONS AND THE ARTS (graphic design and industrial design), COMPUTER AND PHYSICAL SCIENCE (chemistry, digital arts/technology, and science and management), ENGINEERING AND ENVIRONMENTAL DESIGN (architecture, engineering, environmental science, industrial engineering, interior design, landscape architecture/design, textile engineering, and textile technology), HEALTH PROFESSIONS (physician's assistant and premedicine), SOCIAL SCIENCE (biopsychology, fashion design and technology, and psychology). Physician's assistant, architecture, and engineering are the strongest academically. Architecture, fashion merchandising, and fashion design have the largest enrollments.

ACTIVITIES: 1% of men belong to 1 national fraternity; 1% of women belong to 1 national sorority. There are 30 groups on campus, including cheerleading, choir, dance, drama, ethnic, honors, international, LGBT, newspaper, professional, religious, social, social service, and student government. Popular campus events include Annual Fashion Show and Design Competition, Welcome Week, and Spring Weekend. **Sports:** There are 6 intercollegiate sports for men and 8 for women, and 13 intramural sports for men and 13 for women. Facilities include 2 gyms, basketball, a fitness center, 6 tennis courts, 3 athletic fields, soccer, softball, track, rowing, cross country, golf, volleyball, lacrosse, cheerleading, group exercise, and a student center recreation and wellness room. **Graduates:** From July 1, 2016 to June 30, 2017, 648 bachelor's degrees were awarded. The most popular majors were business/marketing (28%), architecture (18%), and health professions & related programs (17%). In an average class, 43% graduate in 4 years or less, 58% graduate in 5 years or less, and 65% graduate in 6 years or less. Of the 2016 graduating class, 19% were enrolled in graduate school within 6 months of graduation, and 71% were employed.

SERVICES: Counseling and information services are available, as is tutoring in every subject. There is a reader service for the blind, and remedial math, reading, and writing. Study skills workshops, course-related workshops, math review sessions, writing review sessions, time management and stress reduction workshops. **Library/Resources:** The library contains 109,235 volumes, 125,000 microform items, and 50,630 audio/video tapes/CDs/DVDs, and subscribes to 1,011 periodicals including electronic. Computerized library services include interlibrary loans and database searching. Special learning facilities include an art gallery, TV station, the Design Center at Philadelphia University, and the Kanbar campus center for sustainability, energy efficiency, and design. **Physically Challenged Students:** 85% of the campus is accessible. Facilities include wheelchair ramps, elevators, special parking, specially equipped restrooms, special class scheduling, lowered drinking fountains, and lowered telephones. **Special:** Internships in all academic majors, study abroad, a dual major in international business, an accelerated business administration degree program, and an integrated major in business and science are available. There are a freshman honors program. **Visiting:** There are regularly scheduled orientations for prospective students, including an interview and a campus tour. There are guides for informal visits, visitors may sit in on classes, and stay overnight. To schedule a visit, contact the Admissions Office at colemanp@philau.edu. **Campus Safety and Security:** Measures include 24-hour foot and vehicle patrol, self-defense education, and security escort services. There are shuttle buses, emergency telephones, and lighted pathways/sidewalks.

REQUIREMENTS: The SAT or ACT is required. In addition, Applicants should be high school graduates or have earned the GED. Recommended secondary preparation includes 4 years each of English and history, 3 years of math which must include algebra II and geometry, and 3 years of science and 2 years of social studies, and 1 year of history. Potential science majors are strongly urged to take 4 years of math and science. A GPA of 2.5 is required. AP and CLEP credits are accepted. Important factors in the admissions decision are evidence of special talent and extracurricular activities record. All students are required to complete 60-credit residency with courses in math, science, social science, computer literacy, English, history, and the humanities. A total of 121 to 146 credits is required with an overall GPA of 2.0 **Procedure:** Freshmen are admitted fall and spring. There are deferred admissions and rolling admissions plans. Application deadlines are open. The fall 2017 application fee was $40. Notifications are sent November 1. Applications are accepted on-line. **Transfer Students:** 207 transfer students enrolled in 2016-2017. A 2.5 GPA is usually required, and previously attended college transcripts. An interview is recommended. 60 of 121 credits required for the bachelor's degree must be completed at PhilaU. **International Students:** There are 14 international students enrolled. They must take the TOEFL with a minimum score of 500 on the paper-based TOEFL (PBT). an English placement test.

ADMISSIONS: 64% of the 2017-2018 applicants were accepted. The SAT scores for the 2017-2018 freshman class were: Critical Reading-- 31% below 500, 51% between 500 and 599, and 17% between 600 and 699. Math-- 28% below 500, 46% between 500 and 599, 23% between 600 and 699, and 3% between 700 and 800. Writing-- 34% below 500, 47% between 500 and 599, 15% between 600 and 699, and 1% between 700 and 800. The ACT scores were % below 12, 3% between 12 and 17, 51% between 18 and 23, 40% between 24 and 29, and 6% above 30. 31% of the current freshmen were in the top fifth of their class; 65% were in the top two fifths. **Admissions Contact:** Greg Potts, Director of Admissions. Email: *admissions@philau.edu* Web: *www.philau.edu*

FINANCIAL AID: In 2017-2018, 78% of all full-time freshmen received some form of financial aid. 78% of all full-time freshmen received need-based aid. The average freshman award was $32,021. Need-based scholarships or need-based grants averaged $27,568; need-based self-help aid (loans and jobs) averaged $5,430; non-need-based athletic scholarships averaged $9,750; other non-need-based awards and non-need-based scholarships averaged $12,760; and $3,741 from other forms of aid. 28% of undergraduate students work part-time. The average financial indebtedness of the 2017 graduate was $39,938. The FAFSA code is 003354. The priority date for freshman financial aid applications for fall entry is March 1.

JUNIATA COLLEGE D-3
www.juniata.edu

Huntingdon, PA 16652 **(814) 641-3420**

Fax: (814) 641-3100
Email: admissions@juniata.edu
Full-time: 622 men, 778 women
Faculty: 99; IIB, +$
Part-time: 38 men, 47 women
Ph.D.s: 95%
Graduate: 7 men, 3 women
Student/Faculty: 13 to 1
Year: semesters, summer session
Tuition: $45,597
Room & Board: $12,521
Freshman Class: 2289 applied, 1620 accepted, 341 enrolled
SAT CR/M: 590/590 **ACT:** recommended
CEEB CODE: 2341
Application Deadline: February 15
VERY COMPETITIVE

Juniata College, founded in 1876, is an independent liberal arts college. There are no undergraduate schools. In addition to regional accreditation, JC has baccalaureate program accreditation with CSWE and ACS. The 110-acre campus is in a small town 31 miles south of State College, in the heart of rural Pennsylvania. Including any residence halls, there are 50 buildings.

STUDENT LIFE: 63% of undergraduates are from Pennsylvania. Others are from 35 states, and 35 foreign countries. 70% are from public schools. 72% are White; 10% Foreign; 5% race unknown; 4% Asian American; 4% Hispanic; 3% African American; 3% two or more races. 62% are Protestant; 30% Catholic. **Female To Male Ratio:** 1.2:1. The average age of freshmen is 18; all undergraduates, 20. 19% do not continue beyond their first year; 81% remain to graduate. **Housing:** 1277 students can be accommodated in college housing, which includes dorms, on-campus apartments, off-campus apartments, and special-interest houses, and international housing. On-campus housing is guaranteed for all 4 years. 82% of students live on campus. All students may keep cars.

FACULTY/CLASSROOMS: 59% of faculty are male; 41% are female. All teach undergraduates. No introductory courses are taught by graduate students. The average class size in an introductory lecture is 19.

PROGRAMS OF STUDY: JC confers B.A. and B.S. degrees. Master's degrees are also awarded. Bachelor's degrees are awarded in AGRICULTURE (environmental studies), BIOLOGICAL SCIENCE (biochemistry and biology/biological science), BUSINESS (accounting, banking and finance, business administration and management, entrepreneurial studies, human resources, international business management, marketing/retailing/merchandising, and nonprofit/public organization management), COMMUNICATIONS AND THE ARTS (art history and appreciation, communications, digital communications, dramatic arts, English, French, German, information technology, Russian, Spanish, and studio art), COMPUTER AND PHYSICAL SCIENCE (chemistry, computer science, environmental geology, geology, information sciences and systems, mathematics, and physics), EDUCATION (early childhood education, elementary education, English education, foreign languages education, mathematics education, museum studies, science education, secondary education, social studies education, and special education), ENGINEERING AND ENVIRONMENTAL DESIGN (engineering physics and environmental science), HEALTH PROFESSIONS (health communication), SOCIAL SCIENCE (anthropology, economics, history, humanities, international studies, peace studies, philosophy, philosophy and religion, political science/government, psychology, public administration, social science, social work, sociology, and theological studies). Biology, psychology, and business are the strongest academically. Biology, business, and environmental studies/science have the largest enrollments.

ACTIVITIES: There are no fraternities or sororities. There are 97 groups on campus, including art, band, cheerleading, chess, choir, chorale, chorus, computers, dance, drama, environmental, ethnic, honors, international, jazz band, LGBT, literary magazine, musical theater, newspaper, orchestra, photography, political, professional, radio and TV, religious, social, social service, student government, and symphony. Popular campus events include Mountain Day, Madrigal Dinner and Dance, Spring Fest, and Relay for Life. **Sports:** There are 10 intercollegiate sports for men and 12 for women, and 5 intramural sports for men and 5 for women. Facilities include 2 gyms, a swimming pool, a fitness center, racquetball courts, a multipurpose fitness/dance room, a varsity football field and stadium, baseball, soccer, softball, and hockey fields, an outdoor running track, tennis courts, and outdoor basketball court. **Graduates:** From July 1, 2016 to June 30, 2017, 354 bachelor's degrees were awarded. The most popular majors were biology/prehealth (17%), business/accounting (15%), and natural resources and conservation (10%). In an average class, 80% graduate in 4 years or less, 83% graduate in 5 years or less, and 84% graduate in 6 years or less. Of the 2016 graduating class, 28% were enrolled in graduate school within 6 months of graduation, and 73% were employed.

SERVICES: Counseling and information services are available, as is tutoring in most subjects, wide doors, temporary assistance provided to those with mobility challanges as a result of accident, injury or surgery. There is a reader service for the blind, and Juniata also offers courses and workshops in studying, reading, and writing skills. **Library/Resources:** The library contains 170,000 volumes, 400 microform items, and 4,000 audio/video tapes/CDs/DVDs, and subscribes to 241 periodicals including electronic. Computerized library services include interlibrary loans, database searching, Internet access, and Wi-Fi capability. Special learning facilities include an art gallery, radio station, an observatory, environmental studies field station, a nature preserve, an early childhood education center, and a ceramics studio. **Physically Challenged Students:** 75% of the campus is accessible. Facilities include wheelchair ramps, elevators, special parking, specially equipped restrooms, and lowered drinking fountains. **Special:** JC offers cooperative programs in marine science, cytogenetics, cytotechnology, marine biology, biotechnology, nursing, medical technology, diagnostic imaging, occupational and physical therapy, dentistry, medicine, optometry, and podiatry. Internships, study abroad in 26 countries, Washington and Philadelphia semesters, and nondegree study are also offered. There are 3-2 engineering degrees with Columbia, Washington, and Pennsylvania State Universities, a 3-3 law program with Duquesne University, and various preprofessional programs, including optometry, chiropractic, medicine, dentistry, pharmacy, physician assistant, and podiatry. With the assistance of faculty advisers, most students design their own majors to meet their individual goals. There are 16 national honor societies, a freshman honors program, and 15 departmental honors programs. **Visiting:** There are regularly scheduled orientations for prospective students, including a campus tour, interviews, attend classes, meet with faculty, coaches, and members of the financial planning staff, and stay overnight. To schedule a visit, contact Pam Zilch, Campus Visit Coordinator at (814) 641-3428. **Campus Safety and Security:** Measures include 24-hour foot and vehicle patrol, an emergency notification system, self-defense education, and security escort services. There are also emergency telephones, awareness programs, fire safety training, weather alerts, terror alerts, an emergency operation plan, a firearms storage vault, vehicle lockout service, identification processing, and evacuation mapping.

REQUIREMENTS: The SAT or ACT is recommended. Candidates for admission should be graduates of an accredited secondary school and have completed 16 academic credits, including 4 in English, 2 in a foreign language, and a combination of 10 in math, social studies, and lab science. The GED is accepted, and homeschoolers are encouraged to apply. An essay is required, and an interview is recommended. A GPA of 3.0 is required. AP credits are accepted. Important factors in the admissions decision are advanced placement or honors courses, leadership record, and recommendations by school officials. Students are required to complete a minimum of 120 credit hours, including courses in fine arts, international studies, social sciences, humanities, and natural sciences, as well as 4 communications-based courses, 2 cultural analysis courses, a math and statistics course, and the college writing seminar. The total number of hours required for the program of emphasis varies from 45 to 60; majors do not exist as such, and students must develop a program of emphasis and complete it to obtain their degree. Students must have a minimum GPA of 2.0. **Procedure:** Freshmen are admitted in the fall and spring. Entrance exams should be taken by the January test date of the year of admission for fall entry. There are early decision, early admissions, deferred admissions, and rolling admissions plans. Early decision applications should be filed by November 15; regular applications, by February 15 for fall entry; and December 1 for spring entry. Notification of early decision is sent December 23; regular decision, on a rolling basis. 65 early decision candidates were accepted for the 2017-2018 class. Applications are accepted on-line. **Transfer Stu-**

dents: 27 transfer students enrolled in 2016-2017. A GPA of 2.5 is required. Applicants must submit a high school transcript, a college transcript, and an essay. SAT scores are required of some students. 30 of 120 credits required for the bachelor's degree must be completed at JC. **International Students:** There are 153 international students enrolled. They must take the TOEFL with a minimum score of 550 on the paper-based TOEFL (PBT) or 79 on the Internet-based version (iBT).

ADMISSIONS: 71% of the 2017-2018 applicants were accepted. The SAT scores for the 2017-2018 freshman class were: Critical Reading-- 7% below 500, 44% between 500 and 599, 39% between 600 and 699, and 9% between 700 and 800. Math-- 6% below 500, 45% between 500 and 599, 41% between 600 and 699, and 8% between 700 and 800. The ACT scores were 3% between 12 and 17, 31% between 18 and 23, 48% between 24 and 29, and 19% above 30. 55% of the current freshmen were in the top fifth of their class; 84% were in the top two fifths. 6 freshmen graduated first in their class. **Admissions Contact:** Michelle Bartol, Office of Enrollment. Email: *admissions@juniata.edu* Web: *www.juniata.edu*

FINANCIAL AID: In 2017-2018, 99% of all full-time freshmen received some form of financial aid. 84% of all full-time freshmen received need-based aid. The average freshman award was $37,720. Need-based scholarships or need-based grants averaged $32,238 ($58,938 maximum); and need-based self-help aid (loans and jobs) averaged $6,221 ($13,500 maximum). 53% of undergraduate students work part-time. The average financial indebtedness of the 2017 graduate was $38,478. The FAFSA code is 003279. The priority date for freshman financial aid applications for fall entry is February 15.

KEYSTONE COLLEGE *(The complete profile is made available exclusively on our website, www.barronspac.com)*

KING'S COLLEGE — E-2

www.kings.edu

Wilkes Barre, PA 18711	**(570) 208-5858** **(888) 546-4772**
Fax: (570) 208-5971	**Email: admissions@kings.edu**
Full-time: 1111 men, 914 women	**Faculty:** 131; IIB, -$
Part-time: 65 men, 107 women	**Ph.D.s:** 89%
Graduate: 70 men, 201 women	**Student/Faculty:** 15 to 1
Year: semesters, summer session	**Tuition:** $35,830
Room & Board: $12,410	**Freshman Class:** 4354 applied, 3080 accepted, 624 enrolled
SAT CR/M: 546/543 **ACT:** 24	**CEEB CODE:** 2353
Application Deadline: n/av	**COMPETITIVE**

King's College, founded in 1946, is a private institution affiliated with the Roman Catholic Church. The college offers 38 undergraduate majors plus master's degree programs in health care administration, education with a concentration in reading, curriculum and instruction, special education, and a 5-year physician assistant program. In addition to our on campus degrees in civil and mechanical engineering, King's offers a 3-2 engineering degree with the University of Notre Dame. There is 1 undergraduate school and 1 graduate school. In addition to regional accreditation, King's College has baccalaureate program accreditation with AACSB, CAEP, ACS, ARC-PA, and CAATE. The 48-acre campus is in an urban area in northeastern Pennsylvania 19 miles south of Scranton. Including any residence halls, there are 30 buildings.

STUDENT LIFE: 70% of undergraduates are from Pennsylvania. Others are from 25 states, 6 foreign countries, and Canada. 77% are from public schools. 8% are Foreign; 72% White; 7% Hispanic; 4% African American; 4% race unknown; 3% two or more races; 2% Asian American. 39% are Catholic. **Male To Female Ratio:** 1.0:1. The average age of freshmen is 18; all undergraduates, 20. 26% do not continue beyond their first year; 65% remain to graduate. **Housing:** 1075 students can be accommodated in college housing, which includes dorms and on-campus apartments. On-campus housing is guaranteed for all 4 years. 53% of students live on campus. All students may keep cars.

FACULTY/CLASSROOMS: 50% of faculty are male; 50% are female. 97% teach undergraduates. No introductory courses are taught by graduate students. The average class size in an introductory lecture is 20; in a laboratory is 14; and in a regular course is 17.

PROGRAMS OF STUDY: King's confers B.A., B.S., and B.S.B.A degrees. Master's degrees are also awarded. Bachelor's degrees are awarded in AGRICULTURE (environmental studies), BIOLOGICAL SCIENCE (biology/biological science and neurosciences), BUSINESS (accounting, banking and finance, business administration and management, international business management, marketing/retailing/merchandising, and personnel management), COMMUNICATIONS AND THE ARTS (communications, dramatic arts, English, French, and Spanish), COMPUTER AND PHYSICAL SCIENCE (chemistry, computer science, information sciences and systems, mathematics, physics, and science), EDUCATION (early childhood education, elementary education, foreign languages education, middle school education, science education, secondary education, and special education), ENGINEERING AND ENVIRONMENTAL DESIGN (civil engineering and mechanical engineering), HEALTH PROFESSIONS (exercise science, medical laboratory technology, nursing, physician's assistant, predentistry, premedicine, and sports medicine), SOCIAL SCIENCE (criminal justice, economics, history, philosophy, political science/government, prelaw, psychology, sociology, and theological studies). Physician assistant,,accounting, and engineering are the strongest academically. Physician assistant, accounting, business management have the largest enrollments.

ACTIVITIES: There are no fraternities or sororities. There are 50 groups on campus, including art, cheerleading, choir, chorale, chorus, communications, computers, dance, drama, environmental, ethnic, film, honors, international, literary magazine, musical theater, newspaper, photography, political, professional, radio and TV, religious, social, social service, student government, and yearbook. Popular campus events include All College Ball, Student Activities Fair, and Spring Fling. **Sports:** There are 12 intercollegiate sports for men and 11 for women, and 6 intramural sports for men and 6 for women. Facilities include a phys ed center, multipurpose courts, a fitness center, wrestling room, racquetball courts, a swimming pool, multipurpose area, gym, free weight area, an outdoor athletic complex with a field house, a multipurpose turf for football, lacrosse, soccer, field hockey fields, baseball and softball field, and an 8-lane NCAA standard track. **Graduates:** From July 1, 2016 to June 30, 2017, 393 bachelor's degrees were awarded. The most popular majors were medical studies (14%), accounting (14%), and neuroscience (7%). In an average class, 60% graduate in 4 years or less, 64% graduate in 5 years or less, and 65% graduate in 6 years or less. Of the 2016 graduating class, 30% were enrolled in graduate school within 6 months of graduation, and 66% were employed.

SERVICES: Counseling and information services are available, as is tutoring in every subject. The academic skills center provides a writing center, learning skills workshops, a tutoring program, and learning disability services. **Library/Resources:** The library contains 182,499 volumes, 13,985 microform items, and 3,071 audio/video tapes/CDs/DVDs, and subscribes to 15,165 periodicals including electronic. Computerized library services include interlibrary loans, database searching, Internet access, and Wi-Fi capability. Special learning facilities include an art gallery, radio station, a TV studio. **Physically Challenged Students:** 99% of the campus is accessible. Facilities include wheelchair ramps, elevators, special parking, specially equipped restrooms, special class scheduling, lowered drinking fountains, lowered telephones, and special housing. **Special:** In addition to our bachelor's degrees in civil and mechanical engineering, King's College offers a 3-2 engineering degree with the University of Notre Dame. The Experiential Learning Program provides internship opportunities in all majors with a variety of employers. King's also offers an accelerated degree program in Healthcare Administration, dual majors, and credit for life experience. Student-designed majors are available through the King's honors program. Cross-registrations with Wilkes University and College Misericordia are also offered. In addition, King's offers study-abroad through affiliation agreements with 20 overseas institutions of higher education as well as numerous summer study abroad opportunities, including short-term faculty-led study abroad programs. There are 11 national honor societies and a freshman honors program. **Visiting:** There are regularly scheduled orientations for prospective students, consisting of interviews, financial aid presentations, faculty one-on-one meetings, and campus tours. There are guides for informal visits, visitors may sit in on classes, and stay overnight. To schedule a visit, contact the Admissions Office. **Campus Safety and Security:** Measures include 24-hour foot and vehicle patrol, emergency notification system, self-defense education, and security escort services. There are shuttle buses, emergency telephones, lighted pathways/sidewalks, and controlled access to dorms/residences.

REQUIREMENTS: The SAT is recommended. King's requires 16 academic credits, although 24 are recommended, including 4 in English, 3 each in science, math, and social studies, and 2 in foreign language. AP and CLEP credits are accepted. Important factors in the admissions decision are extracurricular activities record, recommendations by school officials, and leadership record. All students must earn a minimum of 120 credits and maintain a GPA of 2.0. The core requirements represent between 52 and 59 credits. The major comprises a maximum of 60 credits, of which up to 40 can be specified in the major department, with the balance designated for related fields. **Procedure:** Freshmen are admitted in the fall, spring, and summer. Entrance exams should be taken so that scores are received by April 1. There are deferred admissions and rolling admissions plans. Application deadlines are open. The fall 2017 application fee was $30. Notification is sent on a rolling basis. Applications are accepted on-line. **Transfer Students:** 110 transfer students enrolled in 2016-2017. Applicants must present a minimum GPA of 2.0 to 3.0. Students must have earned at least 12 credit hours at another college. An interview is recommended. 60 of 120 credits required for the bachelor's degree must be completed at King's. **International Students:** There are 159 international students enrolled. They must take the TOEFL with a minimum score of 530 on the paper-based TOEFL (PBT) or 71 on the Internet-based version (iBT). They must also take the SAT or ACT.

ADMISSIONS: 71% of the 2017-2018 applicants were accepted. The SAT scores for the 2017-2018 freshman class were: Critical Reading-- 26% below 500, 47% between 500 and 599, 25% between 600 and 699, and 2% between 700 and 800. Math-- 26% below 500, 49% between 500 and 599, 23% between 600 and 699, and 2% between 700 and 800. The ACT scores were 7% between 12 and 17, 38% between 18 and 23, 47% between 24 and 29, and 8% above 30. 35% of the current freshmen were in the top fifth of their class; 62% were in the top two fifths. **Admissions Contact:** Corry Unis, Vice President Enrollment Management. Email: *admissions@kings.edu* Web: *www.kings.edu*

FINANCIAL AID: In 2017-2018, 94% of all full-time freshmen received some form of financial aid. 81% of all full-time freshmen received need-based aid. The average freshman award was $24,312. Need-based scholarships or need-based grants averaged $21,701 ($34,630 maximum); need-based self-help aid (loans and jobs) averaged $4,262 ($7,500 maximum); and other non-need-based awards and non-need-based scholarships averaged $13,791 ($34,630 maximum). 53% of undergraduate students work part-time. The average financial indebtedness of the 2017 graduate was $34,468. King's is a member of CSS. The FAFSA code is 003282. The priority date for freshman financial aid applications for fall entry is February 15.

KUTZTOWN UNIVERSITY OF PENNSYLVANIA — E-3

www.kutztown.edu

Kutztown, PA 19530	**(484) 646-4144** **(877) 628-1915**
Fax: (610) 683-1375	**Email: admissions@kutztown.edu**
Full-time: 3278 men, 3775 women	**Faculty:** 379
Part-time: 230 men, 206 women	**Ph.D.s:** 93%
Graduate: 201 men, 639 women	**Student/Faculty:** 18 to 1
Year: semesters, summer session	**Tuition:** $9987 ($13,975)
Room & Board: $9490	**Freshman Class:** 8073 applied, 5965 accepted, 1605 enrolled
SAT EBR-W/M: 538/525 **ACT:** 21	**CEEB CODE:** 2653
Application Deadline: open	**COMPETITIVE**

Kutztown University of Pennsylvania, founded in 1866, is a four-year public institution that has undergraduate and graduate programs in more than 100 areas of study, and 200 student organizations. There are 4 undergraduate schools and 1 graduate school. In addition to regional accreditation, KUP has baccalaureate program accreditation with AACSB, CSWE, NASAD, NASM, CACREP, CAEP, and COSMA. The 289-acre campus is in a small town 90 miles north of Philadelphia, midway between Reading and Allentown. Including any residence halls, there are 65 buildings.

STUDENT LIFE: 88% of undergraduates are from Pennsylvania. Others are from 27 states, 33 foreign countries, and Canada. 91% are from public schools. 9% are Hispanic; 76% White; 7% African American; 3% two or more races; 1% Asian American; 1% Foreign; 1% race unknown. **Female To Male Ratio:** 1.2:1. The average age of freshmen is 18; all undergraduates, 21. 26% do not continue beyond their first year; 53% remain to graduate. **Housing:** 4500 students can be accommodated in college housing, which includes coed dorms, on-campus apartments, and off-campus apartments. In addition, there are honors houses, women's dorms and cooperative housing. On-campus housing is guaranteed for the freshman year only, and is available on a first-come, first-served basis. 55% of students commute. Alcohol is not permitted. All students may keep cars.

FACULTY/CLASSROOMS: 50% of faculty are male; 50% are female. 98% teach undergraduates. No introductory courses are taught by graduate students. The average class size in an introductory lecture is 43; in a laboratory is 20; and in a regular course is 22.

PROGRAMS OF STUDY: KUP confers B.A., B.S., B.F.A., B.S.B.A, B.S.Ed., and B.S.W. degrees. Master's and doctoral degrees are also awarded. Bachelor's degrees are awarded in AGRICULTURE (environmental studies), BIOLOGICAL SCIENCE (biochemistry, biology/biological science, biological sciences, biology/general science secondary education, cell & molecular biology, ecology, environmental biology, marine biology, marine science, microbiology, and molecular biology), BUSINESS (accounting, business administration and management, business administration marketing, business economics, finance, international business, international business management, management, marketing management, marketing/retailing/merchandising, recreation and leisure services, and sports management), COMMUNICATIONS AND THE ARTS (applied art, art history, ceramic art and design, communication design, communication studies, communications, crafts, digital communications, dramatic arts, drawing, English, English as a second/foreign language, English writing, fiber/textiles/weaving, film, television and digital media, fine arts, fine/studio arts, general, foreign language, French, German, German studies, graphic design, illustration, information technology, literature, film and media studies, modern language, music, music history and appreciation, music production/recording technology, music performance, musical theater, new media production, painting, photography, printmaking, sculpture, social media marketing, Spanish, speech/debate/rhetoric, communication arts-speech, studio art, studio art painting, telecommunications, and visual and performing arts), COMPUTER AND PHYSICAL SCIENCE (chemistry, computer information technology, computer science, earth & space science, environmental chemistry, environmental geology, geology, geology & geology oceanography, information sciences and systems, mathematics, physical sciences, physics, software engineering, and software production & management), EDUCATION (art education, childhood education, early childhood education, education of the deaf and hearing impaired, education of the emotionally handicapped, education of the exceptional child, education of the mentally handicapped, education of the multiply handicapped, education of the physically handicapped, education of the visually handicapped, elementary education, English secondary education, English education, foreign languages education, general studies, library science, mathematics education, music education, psychology education, science education, secondary education, social science education, social studies education, social studies secondary school education, Spanish education K-12, special education, and speech correction), ENGINEERING AND ENVIRONMENTAL DESIGN (engineering physics, environmental science, and preengineering), HEALTH PROFESSIONS (biology, medical laboratory technology, medical technology, nursing, predentistry, premedicine, and speech pathology/audiology), SOCIAL SCIENCE (anthropology, child psychology/development, clinical psychology, counseling/psychology, criminal justice, economics, gender studies, geography, history, industrial and organizational psychology, liberal arts/general studies, paralegal studies, philosophy, philosophy and religion, political science/government, psychology, public administration, social work, sociology, women & gender studies, and women's studies). Secondary education, elementary education, special education, art education, communication design, studio arts are the strongest academically. Business administration, criminal justice, and communication studies have the largest enrollments.

ACTIVITIES: 5% of men belong to 8 national fraternities; 11% of women belong to 10 national sororities. There are 168 groups on campus, including programming board club, art, band, cheerleading, chess, choir, chorale, chorus, communications, computers, dance, debate, drama, environmental, ethnic, film, honors, international, jazz band, LGBT, literary magazine, marching band, musical theater, newspaper, orchestra, photography, political, professional, radio and TV, recreational sports, religious, social, social service, student government, symphony, and yearbook. Popular campus events include Bearfest, Homecoming, and Family Day. **Sports:** There are 8 intercollegiate sports for men and 12 for women, and 11 intramural sports for men and 11 for women. Facilities include a stadium, outdoor track, field house, indoor track, swimming pool, outdoor tennis courts, an arena, athletic fields, street hockey rink, basketball courts, rifle range, fitness center, free-weight room, and a student recreation center with fitness center/weight room, fitness studios, racquetball courts, indoor rock climbing wall, and a suspended jogging track. **Graduates:** From July 1, 2016 to June 30, 2017, 1775 bachelor's degrees were awarded. The most popular majors were business administration/management (7%), criminal justice (7%), and communication studies (7%). In an average class, 38% graduate in 4 years or less, 52% graduate in 5 years or less, and 53% graduate in 6 years or less. Of the 2016 graduating class, 14% were enrolled in graduate school within 6 months of graduation, and 63% were employed.

SERVICES: Counseling and information services are available, as is tutoring in most subjects. There is a reader service for the blind. **Library/Resources:** The library contains 317,044 volumes, 1.3 million microform items, and 44,513 audio/video tapes/CDs/DVDs, and subscribes to 88,613 periodicals including electronic. Computerized library services include interlibrary loans, database searching, Internet access, and Wi-Fi capability. Special learning facilities include an art gallery, planetarium, radio station, TV station, a women's center, cartography lab, and German Cultural Heritage Center. **Physically Challenged Students:** 90% of the campus is accessible. Facilities include wheelchair ramps, elevators, special parking, specially equipped restrooms, special class scheduling, lowered drinking fountains, and special housing. All programs are accessible to students with disabilities. **Special:** KUP offers internships, student-designed majors, dual majors, and a general studies degree. Non degree study is possible. Students may choose from more than 70 study abroad opportunities. KUP offers undergraduate research opportunities, where students conduct original research with members of our esteemed faculty, have the chance to present their findings at professional conferences, and may publish their findings in scholarly journals. KUP is the only Pennsylvania state university to offer five-year BS/MS programs in Computer Science and a BSW/MSW program in Social Work. KUP boasts one of the few Library Science and Special Education-Visually Impaired programs in the country. There are 11 national honor societies, a freshman honors program, and 25 departmental honors programs. **Visiting:** There are regularly scheduled orientations for prospective students, consisting of daily visits, including group tours. There is a comprehensive summer orientation program for enrolling students. There are guides for informal visits and visitors may sit in on classes. To schedule a visit, contact the Admissions Office. **Campus Safety and Security:** Measures include 24-hour foot and vehicle patrol, emergency notification system, self-defense education, and security escort services. There are shuttle buses, emergency telephones, lighted pathways/sidewalks, controlled access to dorms/residences, bike patrol, crime prevention programs, automatic fire protection systems, door alarms, safety screens, and student monitors in the dorms.

REQUIREMENTS: The SAT or ACT is required. Applicants must be graduates of accredited secondary schools or have earned a GED. Recommended Carnegie units include 4 English, 3 units each in mathematics, social studies, and science, of which at least 2 must be labs. SAT Subject tests in biology/chemistry are required for medical technology. Portfolios or auditions are required for art or music majors. AP and CLEP credits are accepted. General education requirements vary by program, but all students must take phys ed, speech, and English composition. Distribution requirements also include courses in humanities, social sciences, natural sciences, and math. To graduate, students must complete at least 120 semester hours, including 33 to 80 in a major field, with a minimum GPA of 2.0. Students in the College of Liberal Arts and Sciences must take a comprehensive exam. **Procedure:** Freshmen are admitted in the fall, spring, and summer. Entrance exams should be taken no later than fall of the senior year. There are early admissions, deferred admissions, and rolling admissions plans. Application deadlines are open. The fall 2017 application fee was $35. Notification is sent on a rolling basis. Applications are accepted on-line. **Transfer Students:** 603 transfer students enrolled in 2016-2017. Applicants must present a GPA of 2.0 (3.0 for education) and official transcripts from all colleges and secondary schools previously attended. Students transferring fewer than 12 credit hours must also submit the SAT or ACT scores. Students may enroll in the fall and spring. 30 of 120 credits required for the bachelor's degree must be completed at KUP. **International Students:** There are 64 international students enrolled. They must take the TOEFL with a minimum score of 550 on the paper-based TOEFL (PBT) or 79 on the Internet-based version (iBT). Students must take either the IELTS, PTE, SAT, or ACT.

ADMISSIONS: 74% of the 2017-2018 applicants were accepted. The SAT scores for the 2017-2018 freshman class were: Math-- 32% below 500, 55% between 500 and 599, 12% between 600 and 699, and 1% between 700 and 800. Evidence-Based Reading/Writing-- 28% below 500, 52% between 500 and 599, 18% between 600 and 699, and 2% between 700 and 800. The ACT scores were 17% between 12 and 17, 57% between 18 and 23, 22% between 24 and 29, and 4% above 30. 19% of the current freshmen were in the top fifth of their class; 43% were in the top two fifths. **Admissions Contact:** Jeffery Jones, Director of Admissions. Email: *admissions@kutztown.edu* Web: *www.kutztown.edu*

FINANCIAL AID: In 2017-2018, 83% of all full-time freshmen received some form of financial aid. 63% of all full-time freshmen received need-based aid. The average freshman award was $8,384. Need-based scholarships or need-based grants averaged $5,888; need-based self-help aid (loans and jobs) averaged $3,456; non-need-based athletic scholarships averaged $1,787; other non-need-based awards and non-need-based scholarships averaged $919; and $3,356 from other forms of aid. 18% of undergraduate students work part-time. The average financial indebtedness of the 2017 graduate was $40,084. The FAFSA code is 003322. The priority date for freshman financial aid applications for fall entry is March 1.

LA ROCHE COLLEGE — B-3

www.laroche.edu

Pittsburgh, PA 15237 — (412) 536-1266, (800) 838-4LRC

Fax: (412) 847-1820 — **Email: admissions@laroche.edu**

Full-time: 552 men, 611 women	**Faculty:** 65; IIA, --$
Part-time: 74 men, 141 women	**Ph.D.s:** 84%
Graduate: 47 men, 110 women	**Student/Faculty:** 17 to 1
Year: semesters, summer session	**Tuition:** $27,720
Room & Board: $11,220	**Freshman Class:** 1197 applied, 1156 accepted, 226 enrolled
SAT EBR-W/M: 520/510 **ACT:** 21	**CEEB CODE:** 2379
Application Deadline: open	**COMPETITIVE**

La Roche College is a private liberal arts college offering more than 50 undergraduate majors, 6 graduate degree programs, and 1 doctoral program, with particular strengths in education, business, criminal justice, psychology, and health and medical sciences, interior design and graphic design. Founded by the Sisters of Divine Providence in 1963, La Roche embraces its Catholic heritage while welcoming people of all faiths and backgrounds. There is 1 undergraduate school and 7 graduate schools. In addition to regional accreditation, La Roche has baccalaureate program accreditation with ACBSP, FIDER, NASAD, NLN, JCERT, and COA. The 43-acre campus is in a suburban area 10 miles north of Pittsburgh. Including any residence halls, there are 11 buildings.

STUDENT LIFE: 90% of undergraduates are from Pennsylvania. Others are from 18 states, 29 foreign countries, and Canada. 88% are from public schools. 63% are White; 15% Foreign; 10% African American; 4% race unknown; 3% Hispanic; 2% Asian American; 2% two or more races; 1% American Indian/Alaska Native. 75% claim no religious affiliation; 18% Catholic. **Female To Male Ratio:** 1.3:1. The average age of freshmen is 18; all undergraduates, 23. 32% do not continue beyond their first year; 51% remain to graduate. **Housing:** 569 students can be accommodated in college dorms. On-campus housing is guaranteed for all 4 years. 56% of students commute. Alcohol is not permitted. All students may keep cars.

FACULTY/CLASSROOMS: 43% of faculty are male; 57% are female. 88% teach undergraduates. No introductory courses are taught by graduate students. The average class size in an introductory lecture is 25; in a laboratory is 10; and in a regular course is 16.

PROGRAMS OF STUDY: La Roche confers B.A., B.S., B.S.I.D., and B.S.N. degrees. Associate, master's, and doctoral degrees are also awarded. Bachelor's degrees are awarded in BIOLOGICAL SCIENCE (biochemistry and biology/biological science), BUSINESS (accounting, banking and finance, business administration and management, international business management, and marketing management), COMMU-

NICATIONS AND THE ARTS (communications, creative writing, dance, English, graphic design, and information technology), COMPUTER AND PHYSICAL SCIENCE (chemistry, computer science, and mathematics), EDUCATION (elementary education), ENGINEERING AND ENVIRONMENTAL DESIGN (interior design), HEALTH PROFESSIONS (exercise science, health science, nursing, and radiograph medical technology), SOCIAL SCIENCE (child care/child and family studies, criminal justice, history, homeland security/emergency preparedness, international studies, liberal arts/general studies, political science/government, psychology, religion, and sociology). Graphic design, interior design, and health sciences are the strongest academically. Criminal justice, accounting, and psychology have the largest enrollments.

ACTIVITIES: There are no fraternities or sororities. There are 51 groups on campus, including art, cheerleading, computers, dance, environmental, ethnic, film, honors, international, literary magazine, newspaper, photography, political, professional, radio and TV, religious, social, social service, and student government. Popular campus events include Gateway Clipper Cruise, Festival of Lights, Global Problems Global Solutions Conferende, and Globe Fashion Show. **Sports:** There are 6 intercollegiate sports for men and 7 for women, and 10 intramural sports for men and 9 for women. Facilities include a soccer and lacrosse field, softball and baseball fields, fitness/sports center with gym, an indoor track, aerobics room, and weight room. **Graduates:** From July 1, 2016 to June 30, 2017, 310 bachelor's degrees were awarded. The most popular majors were business (25%), health professions (22%), and computer and information sciences (9%). In an average class, 2% graduate in 3 years or less, 35% graduate in 4 years or less, 50% graduate in 5 years or less, and 51% graduate in 6 years or less.

SERVICES: Counseling and information services are available, as is tutoring in every subject. There is a reader service for the blind, and remedial math and writing. **Library/Resources:** The library contains 77,471 volumes, 89,000 microform items, and 1,359 audio/video tapes/CDs/DVDs, and subscribes to 87,299 periodicals including electronic. Computerized library services include interlibrary loans, database searching, Internet access, and Wi-Fi capability. Special learning facilities include an art gallery, radio station, interior and graphic design studios, and a CSI lab. **Physically Challenged Students:** All of the campus is accessible. Facilities include wheelchair ramps, elevators, special parking, specially equipped restrooms, special class scheduling, lowered drinking fountains, lowered telephones, and special housing. **Special:** There is cross-registration with members of the Pittsburgh Council of Higher Education. Internships, for which students may receive up to 6 credits, are available for juniors and seniors with numerous employers in the Pittsburgh area. La Roche also offers study abroad experiences at no cost after 60 credits, dual majors, credit for life experience, directed research, honors programs, self-designed majors, independent study, and pass/fail options. 3+2 engineering degree with the University of Pittsburgh is possible, as well as software engineering with Gannon University and medicine, pharmacy and dental medicine with LECOM. There is a freshman honors program. **Visiting:** There are regularly scheduled orientations for prospective students, information and interactive sessions, class attendance, and meeting with faculty. There are guides for informal visits, visitors may sit in on classes, and stay overnight. To schedule a visit, contact the Admissions Office. **Campus Safety and Security:** Measures include 24-hour foot and vehicle patrol, emergency notification system, self-defense education, and security escort services. There are shuttle buses, emergency telephones, lighted pathways/sidewalks, controlled access to dorms/residences, an intercom security system, and residence halls that are locked 24 hours a day.

REQUIREMENTS: The SAT or ACT is required. Applicants must be graduates of accredited secondary schools or have earned a GED. An interview is recommended for all applicants. At least 2 letters of recommendation are required. A GPA of 2.0 is required. AP and CLEP credits are accepted. Important factors in the admissions decision are advanced placement or honors courses, personality/intangible qualities, and recommendations by school officials. The La Roche Experience is composed of four 1-credit courses taken over four semesters. The course emphasizes the history of La Roche College and introduces students to issues in Diversity and Discrimination, Regions of Conflict, and Economic Justice. 12 credits in basic skills areas, including English, math and computer applications. 12 to 15 credits in liberal arts areas, including history, science, religion or philosophy, aesthetics, literature, and social and cultural systems are required. A 6-credit sequence of 2 interdisciplinary courses. These courses emphasize the integration of knowledge and the interconnections between the local and the global. Students are required to take 1 Community course and 1 Global course. **Procedure:** Freshmen are admitted in the fall, spring, and summer. Entrance exams should be taken by the fall of the senior year. There are deferred admissions and rolling admissions plans. Application deadlines are open. The fall 2017 application fee was $50. Applications are accepted on-line. **Transfer Students:** 168 transfer students enrolled in 2016-2017. Transfer design students must submit all post-secondary trancripts, have a 2.0 GPA, and may be required to submit a portfolio. 30 of 120 credits required for the bachelor's degree must be completed at La Roche. **International Students:** There are 200 international students enrolled. They must take the college's own test, or if their native language is English, they must take the SAT or ACT.

ADMISSIONS: 97% of the 2017-2018 applicants were accepted. The SAT scores for the 2017-2018 freshman class were: Math-- 42% below 500, 48% between 500 and 599, and 10% between 600 and 699. Evidence-Based Reading/Writing-- 34% below 500, 46% between 500 and 599, 19% between 600 and 699, and 1% between 700 and 800. The ACT scores were 23% between 12 and 17, 53% between 18 and 23, 20% between 24 and 29, and 4% above 30. 25% of the current freshmen were in the top fifth of their class; 60% were in the top two fifths. 1 freshman graduated first in the class. **Admissions Contact:** Hope Schiffgens, Director of Admissions. Email: *admissions@laroche.edu* Web: *www.laroche.edu*

FINANCIAL AID: In 2017-2018, 96% of all full-time freshmen received some form of financial aid. 62% of all full-time freshmen received need-based aid. The average freshman award was $32,879. Need-based scholarships or need-based grants averaged $8,712 ($10,543 maximum); need-based self-help aid (loans and jobs) averaged $5,415 ($5,500 maximum); and other non-need-based awards and non-need-based scholarships averaged $21,189 ($38,728 maximum). 23% of undergraduate students work part-time. The average financial indebtedness of the 2017 graduate was $26,478. The FAFSA code is 003987. The priority date for freshman financial aid applications for fall entry is May 1.

LA SALLE UNIVERSITY F-3

www.lasalle.edu

Philadelphia, PA 19141	**(215) 951-1500** **(800) 328-1910**
Fax: (215) 951-1656	**Email: admiss@lasalle.edu**
Full-time: 1335 men, 1987 women	**Faculty:** 217; IIA, av$
Part-time: 139 men, 360 women	**Ph.D.s:** 85%
Graduate: 404 men, 972 women	**Student/Faculty:** 11 to 1
Year: semesters, summer session	**Tuition:** $29,500
Room & Board: $13,976	**Freshman Class:** 6267 applied, 5060 accepted, 932 enrolled
SAT EBR-W/M: 546/533 **ACT:** 23	**CEEB CODE:** 2363
Application Deadline: April 1	**COMPETITIVE**

La Salle University, is inspired by St. John Baptist de La Salle, the patron saint of teachers, and shaped by Lasallian and Catholic values. La Salle provides excellence in teaching and learning, personal attention, a sense of community and a global perspective. La Salle puts theory into practice by guiding each student's intellectual and spiritual development. There are 3 undergraduate schools and 22 graduate schools. In addition to regional accreditation, La Salle has baccalaureate program accreditation with AACSB, CSWE, NLN, CCNE, CAA-ASHA, APA, COA, CACREP, CADE, ACEND, AACTE, PDE, ACS, COAMFTE, and AAMFT. The 133-acre campus is in an urban area 8 miles northwest of Center City, Philadelphia. Including any residence halls, there are 58 buildings.

STUDENT LIFE: 68% of undergraduates are from Pennsylvania. Others are from 33 states, 34 foreign countries, and Canada. 59% are from public schools. 54% are White; 18% African American; 14% Hispanic; 5% Asian American; 3% Foreign; 3% race unknown; 2% two or more races; 1% American Indian/Alaska Native. 58% are Catholic; 26% Protestant. **Female To Male Ratio:** 1.8:1. The average age of freshmen is 18; all undergraduates, 22. 24% do not continue beyond their first year; 67% remain to graduate. **Housing:** 1868 students can be accommodated in college housing, which includes dorms and on-campus apartments. In addition, there are honors houses, special-interest houses, and townhouses that are owned and operated by La Salle University. On-campus housing is guaranteed for all 4 years, is available on a first-come, first-served basis, and is available on a lottery system for upperclassmen. 53% of students live on campus. Upperclassmen may keep cars.

FACULTY/CLASSROOMS: 43% of faculty are male; 57% are female. No introductory courses are taught by graduate students. The average class size in an introductory lecture is 13; in a laboratory is 11; and in a regular course is 21.

PROGRAMS OF STUDY: La Salle confers B.A., B.S., B.S.N., B.S.P.H., and B.S.W. degrees. Associate, master's, and doctoral degrees are also awarded. Bachelor's degrees are awarded in BIOLOGICAL SCIENCE (biochemistry, biology/biological science, and nutrition), BUSINESS (accounting, banking and finance, business administration and management, business intelligence and analytics, international business, international economics, management information systems, marketing/retailing/merchandising, and organizational behavior), COMMUNICATIONS AND THE ARTS (communications, English, fine arts, information technology, multimedia, and Spanish), COMPUTER AND PHYSICAL SCIENCE (chemistry, computer science, information sciences and systems, mathematics, and science), EDUCATION (elementary education, foreign languages education, science education, secondary education, social studies education, and special education), ENGINEERING AND ENVIRONMENTAL DESIGN (computer graphics and environmental science), HEALTH PROFESSIONS (nursing, preallied health, and speech pathology/audiology), SOCIAL SCIENCE (criminal justice, economics, history, international political science, philosophy, political science/government, psychology, religion, social work, and sociology). Accounting, education, and communication sciences & disorders are the strongest academically. Nursing, communication, biology, and psychology have the largest enrollments.

ACTIVITIES: 12% of men belong to 1 local and 4 national fraternities; 11% of women belong to 1 local and 3 national sororities. There are 121 groups on campus, including art, band, cheerleading, choir, chorus, computers, dance, drama, drill team, environmental, ethnic, film, forensics, honors, international, jazz band, LGBT, literary magazine, musical theater, newspaper, orchestra, pep band, photography, political, professional, radio and TV, religious, social, social service, student government, and yearbook. **Sports:** There are 9 intercollegiate sports for men and 13 for women, and 5 intramural sports for men and 5 for women. Facilities include a fitness center, an arena, a stadium and track, swimming pool, wrestling rooms, basketball, volleyball, tennis, and squash courts. **Graduates:** From July 1, 2016 to June 30, 2017, 769 bachelor's degrees were awarded. The most popular majors were nursing (15%), accounting (10%), and psychology (7%). In an average class, 59% graduate in 4 years or less, 66% graduate in 5 years or less, and 67% graduate in 6 years or less. Of the 2016 graduating class, 18% were enrolled in graduate school within 6 months of graduation, and 69% were employed.

SERVICES: Counseling and information services are available, as is tutoring in most subjects. There is a reader service for the blind, and remedial writing, and a writing center. **Library/Resources:** The library contains 404,452 volumes, 7,154 microform items, and 14,466 audio/video tapes/CDs/DVDs, and subscribes to 125,913 periodicals including electronic. Computerized library services include interlibrary loans, database searching, Internet access, and Wi-Fi capability. Special learning facilities include an art gallery, radio station, and La Salle 56 is a cable television station housed in the university's communication center. The La Salle University Art Museum: is a collection of European and American artifacts since the Middle Ages, illustrated rare bibles, Old Master prints and drawings from the 19th and 20th centuries, Japanese prints, Indian miniatures, African tribal art, pre-Columbian pottery, and ancient Greek cotta pottery. **Physically Challenged Students:** 95% of the campus is accessible. Facilities include wheelchair ramps, elevators, special parking, specially equipped restrooms, special class scheduling, lowered drinking fountains, and special housing. **Special:** La Salle also offers travel study courses, study abroad programs in many countries. There are many experiential learning programs in most majors, dual majors, a honors program, a Business Scholars CoŸ Op Program, and three interdisciplinary majors, four different five-year Education programs a 4-year BS/MBA in Accounting, a 5-year BA/BS/MS in Computer Science, a 5-year BA/MA in History, and a 5-year BS/MA in Communication Sciences and Disorders. Cross-registration is also offered in conjunction with Chestnut Hill College. The university also has dual admission agreements with the following community colleges: Bucks County Community College, Camden County College, Community College of Philadelphia, Delaware County Community College, Harcum College, Manor College, Mercer County Community College, and Montgomery County Community College. There are 16 national honor societies, Phi Beta Kappa, a freshman honors program, and 2 departmental honors programs. **Visiting:** There are regularly scheduled orientations for prospective students, as well as group information sessions and tours scheduled 5 days a week. There are also two Open Houses in the fall. In addition, we have opportunities for prospective student to sit in on classes for the day. To schedule a visit, contact Office of Undergraduate Admissions. **Campus Safety and Security:** Measures include 24-hour foot and vehicle patrol, emergency notification system, and security escort services. There are shuttle buses, emergency telephones, lighted pathways/sidewalks, controlled access to dorms/residences, and magnetic card access to residence facilities.

REQUIREMENTS: The SAT is required. The ACT is recommended. In addition, the SAT: Subject Test in math is also recommended. Applicants must be graduates of accredited secondary schools or have earned a GED. La Salle requires 16 academic units, 4 years of English, 3 of math, 2 of foreign language, and 1 of history, with the remaining 5 units in academic electives; science and math majors must have an additional one-half unit of math. An essay is required, and an interview is recommended. AP and CLEP credits are accepted. Important factors in the admissions decision are advanced placement or honors courses, leadership record, and recommendations by school officials. All courses in the core may be counted towards any minor or major barring exclusions by the academic departments sponsoring the minor or major. To complete the core requirements, most School of Arts and Sciences majors must complete a maximum of 19 courses, School of Business Administration majors, a maximum of 17 courses, and School of Nursing majors, a maximum of 20 courses. **Procedure:** Freshmen are admitted in the fall and spring. Entrance exams should be taken before January of the senior year. There are early admissions, deferred admissions, and rolling admissions plans. Applications should be filed by April 1 for fall entry; December 15 for spring entry. Notifications are sent December 15. Applications are accepted on-line. **Transfer Students:** 139 transfer students enrolled in 2016-2017. Minimum cumulative GPA of 2.5 (2.75 preferred) required for consideration. Individual programs may have higher GPA requirements. Nursing program applicants must have minimum GPA of 3.0 as well as science and education. Communication Science Disorders program applicants should have minimum cumulative GPA of 3.2 (3.4 preferred) for consideration. 50 of 120 credits required for the bachelor's degree must be completed at La Salle. **International Students:** There are 89 international students enrolled. They must take the TOEFL with a minimum score of 540 on the paper-based TOEFL (PBT) or 80 on the Internet-based version (iBT). Students must also take the IELTS.

ADMISSIONS: 81% of the 2017-2018 applicants were accepted. The SAT scores for the 2017-2018 freshman class were: Math-- 31% below 500, 50% between 500 and 599, 16% between 600 and 699, and 2% between 700 and 800. Evidence-Based Reading/Writing-- 24% below 500, 51% between 500 and 599, 22% between 600 and 699, and 2% between 700 and 800. The ACT scores were 13% between 12 and 17, 47% between 18 and 23, 31% between 24 and 29, and 9% above 30. 30% of the current freshmen were in the top fifth of their class; 52% were in the top two fifths. 6 freshmen graduated first in their class. **Admissions Contact:** James Plunkett, Executive Director of Admission. Email: *admiss@lasalle.edu* Web: *www.lasalle.edu*

FINANCIAL AID: In 2017-2018, 99% of all full-time freshmen received some form of financial aid. 80% of all full-time freshmen received need-based aid. The average freshman award was $24,013. Need-based scholarships or need-based grants averaged $18,531 ($41,462 maximum); need-based self-help aid (loans and jobs) averaged $3,911 ($9,300 maximum); non-need-based athletic scholarships averaged $9,208 ($26,108 maximum); and other non-need-based awards and non-need-based scholarships averaged $8,457 ($24,539 maximum). 18% of undergraduate students work part-time. The average financial indebtedness of the 2017 graduate was $36,484. The FAFSA code is 003287. The priority date for freshman financial aid applications for fall entry is February 15.

LAFAYETTE COLLEGE F-3
www.lafayette.edu

Easton, PA 18042 **(610) 330-5100**

Fax: (610) 330-5355 **Email:** admissions@lafayette.edu
Full-time: 1227 men, 1324 women
Part-time: 22 men, 21 women
Graduate: n/av
Year: semesters, summer session
Room & Board: $15,640
Faculty: 237; IIB, ++$
Ph.D.s: 98%
Student/Faculty: 10 to 1
Tuition: $52,880
Freshman Class: 8469 applied, 2609 accepted, 680 enrolled
SAT EBR-W/M: 664/678 **ACT:** 29
CEEB CODE: 2361
Application Deadline: January 15
MOST COMPETITIVE

Lafayette College, founded in 1826, is a highly selective private, exclusively undergraduate college, emphasizing the liberal arts, sciences, and engineering. There is 1 undergraduate school. In addition to regional accreditation, Lafayette has baccalaureate program accreditation with ABET and ACS. The 342-acre campus is in a suburban area 70 miles west of New York City, off Interstate 78 and US 22. Including any residence halls, there are 81 buildings.

STUDENT LIFE: 81% of undergraduates are from out of state, mostly the Middle Atlantic. Students are from 44 states, 61 foreign countries, and Canada. 61% are from public schools. 7% are Hispanic; 66% White; 6% race unknown; 5% African American; 4% Asian American; 3% two or more races; 10% Foreign. 26% are Catholic; 22% claim no religious affiliation; 18% Protestant. **Female To Male Ratio:** 1.1:1. The average age of freshmen is 18; all undergraduates, 20. 5% do not continue beyond their first year; 90% remain to graduate. **Housing:** 2308 students can be accommodated in college housing, which includes dorms, on-campus apartments, and off-campus apartments. In addition, there are honors houses, special-interest houses, fraternity houses, sorority houses, diversity-oriented houses, arts housing, a black cultural center, and language and special-interest floors. On-campus housing is guaranteed for all 4 years. 93% of students live on campus. Upperclassmen may keep cars.

FACULTY/CLASSROOMS: 58% of faculty are male; 42% are female. All teach undergraduates, and all do research. No introductory courses are taught by graduate students. The average class size in a laboratory is 12 and in a regular course is 17.

PROGRAMS OF STUDY: Lafayette confers A.B. and B.S. degrees. Bachelor's degrees are awarded in BIOLOGICAL SCIENCE (biochemistry, biology/biological science, and neurosciences), BUSINESS (business economics and international economics), COMMUNICATIONS AND THE ARTS (art, English, French, German, music, and Spanish), COMPUTER AND PHYSICAL SCIENCE (chemistry, computer science, geology, mathematics, and physics), ENGINEERING AND ENVIRONMENTAL DESIGN (chemical engineering, civil engineering, electrical/electronics engineering, engineering, and mechanical engineering), SOCIAL SCIENCE (African studies, American studies, anthropology, Asian/Oriental studies, economics, history, interdisciplinary studies, international relations, philosophy, political science/government, prelaw, psychology, religion, Russian and Slavic studies, and sociology). Social sciences, engineering, and biological life sciences are the strongest academically. mechanical engineering, economics and biology have the largest enrollments.

ACTIVITIES: 22% of men belong to 3 national fraternities; 34% of women belong to 6 national sororities. There are 250 groups on campus, including art, band, cheerleading, chess, choir, chorale, chorus, computers, dance, debate, drama, environmental, ethnic, film, forensics, honors, international, jazz band, LGBT, literary magazine, musical theater, newspaper, orchestra, pep band, photography, political, professional, radio and TV, religious, social, social service, and student government. Popular campus events include 1,000 Nights, Block pARTy, Rivalry Week, Earth Day, International Extravaganza, and Presidential Ball. **Sports:** There are 11 intercollegiate sports for men and 11 for women, and 18 intramural sports for men and 18 for women. Facilities include a stadium, sports center with an arena, a field house, varsity house, a natatorium, fitness center, exercise rooms, weight training room, outdoor track, indoor track, climbing wall, racquet courts, multipurpose courts, and an athletic complex for outdoor track lacrosse, field hockey, soccer, and baseball. **Graduates:** From July 1, 2016 to June 30, 2017, 606 bachelor's degrees were awarded. The most popular majors were social sciences (34%), engineering (22%), and biological life sciences (11%). In an average class, 86% graduate in 4 years or less, 89% graduate in 5 years or less, and 90% graduate in 6 years or less.

SERVICES: Counseling and information services are available, as is tutoring in most subjects, such as most 100-level and many 200-level classes. **Library/Resources:** The library contains 510,000 volumes, 120,000 microform items, and subscribes to 2,600 periodicals including electronic. Computerized library services include interlibrary loans, database searching, Internet access, and Wi-Fi capability. Special learning facilities include an art gallery, radio station, a geological museum, foreign languages lab, and calculus lab. **Physically Challenged Students:** 95% of the campus is accessible. Facilities include wheelchair ramps, elevators, special parking, specially equipped restrooms, special class scheduling, lowered drinking fountains, and lowered telephones. **Special:** Cross-registration is available through the Lehigh Valley Association of Independent Colleges, internships in all academic departments, study abroad in 3 countries as well as through other individually arranged plans, a Washington semester at American University, and work-study programs with area employers are possible. An accelerated degree plan in all majors, dual and student-designed majors, 5-year dual-degree programs, and pass/fail options in any non major subject also are available. There are 12 national honor societies, Phi Beta Kappa, and 24 departmental honors programs. **Visiting:** There are regularly scheduled orientations for prospective students, student visits include student/faculty panel discussions, tours, and departmental open houses. There are guides for informal visits, visitors may sit in on classes, and stay overnight. To schedule a visit, contact Ed Bianchi at (610) 330-5100. **Campus Safety and Security:** Measures include 24-hour foot and vehicle patrol, emergency notification system, self-defense education, and security escort services. There are shuttle buses, emergency telephones, lighted pathways/sidewalks, controlled access to dorms/residences. There are advisors in all residence halls and lock down from 8 p.m. to 7 a.m.

REQUIREMENTS: The SAT or ACT is required. The ACT Optional Writing test is also required. Applicants should have taken 4 years of English, 3 of math (4 for science or engineering majors), 2 each of foreign language and lab science (with physics and chemistry for science or engineering students), and at least 5 additional units in academic subjects. An essay is required and an interview recommended. Evaluations from the secondary school counselor and a teacher are required. The GED is accepted. AP credits are accepted. Important factors in the admissions decision are advanced placement or honors courses, leadership record, evidence of special talent, extracurricular activities record, parents or siblings attended your school, personality/intangible qualities, and geographical diversity. To graduate, students must maintain a GPA of 2.0, and take a minimum of 32 to 36 courses (36 for engineering). The common course of study, designed to build a background in the liberal arts and sciences includes interdisciplinary seminars, a course in humanities, social science, natural science with a lab,and quantitative reasoning. Students must take 2 courses dealing with global and multicultural issues, and must demonstrate elementary proficiency in a foreign language (typically 2 courses). A Science and Technology in a Social Context requirement can be met by taking two classes designated as STSC outside of the student's home division. Finally, students must take 1 course that explores values in society and 4 writing intensive courses. **Procedure:** Freshmen are admitted in the fall. Entrance exams should be taken by January of the senior year. There are early decision, early admissions, and deferred admissions plans. Early decision applications should be filed by November 15; regular applications, by January 15 for fall entry. The fall 2017 application fee was $65. Notification of early decision is sent December 15; regular decision, April 1. 335 early decision candidates were accepted for the 2017-2018 class. 412 applicants were on the 2017 waiting list; 111 were admitted. Applications are accepted on-line. **Transfer Students:** Acceptance usually depends on college-level performance and achievements. An interview is required if the student lives within 200 miles of the college. No minimum GPA is required, and neither the SAT nor the ACT is needed. The number of credit hours required varies with the program, but usually enough for freshman status with advanced standing is needed. Typically, Lafayette will enroll about 15 transfers in the fall and about 5 in the spring of each year. 16 of 32 credits required for the bachelor's degree must be completed at Lafayette. **International Students:** There are 260 international students enrolled. They must take the TOEFL with a minimum score of 513 on the paper-based TOEFL (PBT) or 80 on the Internet-based version (iBT) and the Comprehensive English Language Test. They must also take the SAT or ACT.

ADMISSIONS: 31% of the 2017-2018 applicants were accepted. The

SAT scores for the 2017-2018 freshman class were: Math-- 1% below 500, 12% between 500 and 599, 46% between 600 and 699, and 41% between 700 and 800. Evidence-Based Reading/Writing-- 13% between 500 and 599, 53% between 600 and 699, and 33% between 700 and 800. The ACT scores were 4% between 18 and 23, 43% between 24 and 29, and 53% above 30. 82% of the current freshmen were in the top fifth of their class; 95% were in the top two fifths. 12 freshmen graduated first in their class. **Admissions Contact:** Matthew Hyde, Director of Admissions. Email: *admissions@lafayette.edu* Web: *www.lafayette.edu*

FINANCIAL AID: In 2017-2018, 58% of all full-time freshmen received some form of financial aid. 41% of all full-time freshmen received need-based aid. The average freshman award was $45,100. Need-based scholarships or need-based grants averaged $42,548 ($69,040 maximum); need-based self-help aid (loans and jobs) averaged $3,929 ($5,500 maximum); non-need-based athletic scholarships averaged $36,803 ($67,682 maximum); other non-need-based awards and non-need-based scholarships averaged $13,676 ($52,800 maximum); and $19,810 from other forms of aid. 45% of undergraduate students work part-time. The average financial indebtedness of the 2017 graduate was $32,974. Lafayette is a member of CSS. The CSS/Profile and the college's own financial statement, and the business/farm supplement, and divorce/separation parent statement (if applicable) are required. The FAFSA code is 003284. The priority date for freshman financial aid applications for fall entry is January 15. The deadline for filing freshman financial aid applications for fall entry is March 1.

LEBANON VALLEY COLLEGE E-3

www.lvc.edu

Annville, PA 17003	(717) 867-6181
Fax: (717) 867-6026	**Email:** admission@lvc.edu
Full-time: 735 men, 889 women	**Faculty:** 118; IIB, av$
Part-time: 61 men, 71 women	**Ph.D.s:** 90%
Graduate: 59 men, 95 women	**Student/Faculty:** 13 to 1
Year: semesters, summer session	**Tuition:** $43,650
Room & Board: $11,860	**Freshman Class:** 2832 applied, 2068 accepted, 466 enrolled
SAT EBR-W/M: 579/584 **ACT:** 26	**CEEB CODE:** 2364
Application Deadline: February 15	**VERY COMPETITIVE**

Lebanon Valley College, founded in 1866 is a private, coeducational institution, dedicated to the liberal arts. The college offers 41 undergraduate majors plus self-designed majors and a range of minors, concentrations, and pre-professional options. In addition, there are graduate degree programs in athletic training, business administration, music education, physical therapy, science in STEM education, and speech-language pathology. There is 1 undergraduate school and 1 graduate school. In addition to regional accreditation, LVC has baccalaureate program accreditation with ACBSP, NASM, and CAPTE. The 357-acre campus is in a small town 15 minutes east of Hershey and 35 minutes east of Harrisburg; Philadelphia, Washington, D.C., and Baltimore. Including any residence halls, there are 53 buildings.

STUDENT LIFE: 80% of undergraduates are from Pennsylvania. Others are from 22 states, 11 foreign countries, and Canada. 83% are White; 6% Hispanic; 3% African American; 3% two or more races; 2% Asian American; 2% race unknown; 1% Foreign. **Female To Male Ratio:** 1.2:1. The average age of freshmen is 18; all undergraduates, 20. 19% do not continue beyond their first year; 73% remain to graduate. **Housing:** 1310 students can be accommodated in college housing, which includes coed dorms and on-campus apartments. In addition, there are special-interest houses, theme and wellness housing, STEM house, Stonewall LGBTQIA, and a community house. On-campus housing is guaranteed for all 4 years and is available on a lottery system for upperclassmen. 80% of students live on campus. All students may keep cars.

FACULTY/CLASSROOMS: 58% of faculty are male; 42% are female. 95% teach undergraduates, and 95% do both. No introductory courses are taught by graduate students. The average class size in an introductory lecture is 20; in a laboratory is 14; and in a regular course is 20.

PROGRAMS OF STUDY: LVC confers B.A., B.S., B.M., B.S.Ch., and B.S.Med.Tech. degrees. Master's and doctoral degrees are also awarded. Bachelor's degrees are awarded in BIOLOGICAL SCIENCE (biochemistry, biology/biological science, and neurosciences), BUSINESS (accounting, business administration and management, finance, and international business), COMMUNICATIONS AND THE ARTS (art, audio technology, communication science, communications technology, digital communications, English, French, German, music, music business management, and Spanish), COMPUTER AND PHYSICAL SCIENCE (actuarial science, chemistry, computer science, computer science & informatics, mathematics, and physics), EDUCATION (athletic training, early childhood education, education, elementary education, music education, and special education), ENGINEERING AND ENVIRONMENTAL DESIGN (environmental science), HEALTH PROFESSIONS (biology, communicative disorders, exercise science, health, health care administration, medical laboratory technology, and physical therapy), SOCIAL SCIENCE (American studies, criminal justice, economics, French studies, history, philosophy, political science/government, psychobiology, psychology, religion, religious studies, sociology, and Spanish studies). Actuarial science, STEM, physical therapy, health sciences, and education are the strongest academically. Education, health sciences, business, and STEM have the largest enrollments.

ACTIVITIES: 6% of men belong to 1 local and 3 national fraternities; 9% of women belong to 4 national sororities. There are 90 groups on campus, including art, band, cheerleading, choir, chorus, concert band, dance, drama, environmental, ethnic, honors, international, jazz band, LGBT, literary magazine, marching band, musical theater, newspaper, orchestra, political, professional, radio and TV, religious, social, social service, student government, and symphony. Popular campus events include Christmas at the Valley, ValleyPalooza, Symposium on Inclusive Excellence, VALE Media Industries Conference. **Sports:** There are 12 intercollegiate sports for men and 11 for women, and 12 intramural sports for men and 12 for women. Facilities include a stadium, a sports center, athletic fields, indoor and outdoor tracks, a gym, playing courts for basketball, handball, squash, and tennis, baseball, several intramural fields, stadium, softball field, football field, golf, swimming, men's and women's ice hockey, lacrosse, track and field, and volleyball. **Graduates:** From July 1, 2016 to June 30, 2017, 394 bachelor's degrees were awarded. The most popular majors were education (19%), business and marketing (17%), and health professions and related programs (9%). In an average class, 69% graduate in 4 years or less, 72% graduate in 5 years or less, and 73% graduate in 6 years or less. Of the 2016 graduating class, 36% were enrolled in graduate school within 6 months of graduation, and 63% were employed.

SERVICES: Counseling and information services are available, as is tutoring in every subject. There is a reader service for the blind. **Library/Resources:** The library contains 152,349 volumes, 6,777 microform items, and 18,084 audio/video tapes/CDs/DVDs, and subscribes to 59,331 periodicals including electronic. Computerized library services include interlibrary loans, database searching, Internet access, and Wi-Fi capability. Special learning facilities include an art gallery, radio station, audio and music production technology center, a physical therapy and sports rehabilitation center, a learning resource center, an arboretum, keyboard lab, mathematical sciences center, rehabilitation experience clinic, volunteer income tax assistance center, global studies, career development, learning commons, disability resources, writing and tutoring resources, two greenhouses, green roof initiative, theater acting lab, biology wetlands, and a pond. **Physically Challenged Students:** 80% of the campus is accessible. Facilities include wheelchair ramps, elevators, special parking, specially equipped restrooms, special class scheduling, lowered drinking fountains, lowered telephones, and special housing. **Special:** Full-semester study abroad programs are offered each year in Argentina, China, Dominican Republic, England, France, Germany, Italy, New Zealand, Northern Ireland, and Spain, and several short-term, faculty-led programs. There are also domestic-based programs in Philadelphia and Washington, D.C. LVC has a 3+2 engineering program with Penn State University and Case Western Reserve University, and a medical technology program in collaboration with various hospitals. The College also offers internships in many majors. There are 6 national honor societies and 11 departmental honors programs. **Visiting:** There are regularly scheduled orientations for prospective students, visiting students can take tours, and schedule interviews and meetings with professors. There are guides for informal visits, visitors may sit in on classes, and stay overnight. To schedule a visit, contact Tami Morgan at tmorgan@lvc.edu. **Campus Safety and Security:** Measures include 24-hour foot and vehicle patrol, emergency notification system, self-defense education, and security escort services. There are emergency telephones, lighted pathways/sidewalks, and controlled access to dorms/residences.

REQUIREMENTS: Applicants must be graduates of an accredited secondary school or have earned a GED. LVC requires 16 academic units or 16 Carnegie units, including 4 units in English, 3 units each in math, social studies, and science (with 2 lab units recommended), 2-3 units of foreign language, and 2 units recommended in history. An interview is also recommended. Students applying as music majors must audition. A GPA of 2.0 is required. AP and CLEP credits are accepted. Important factors in the admissions decision are advanced placement or honors courses, leadership record, evidence of special talent, personality/intangible qualities, and extracurricular activities record. **Procedure:** Freshmen are admitted in the fall and spring. There are early decision and rolling admissions plans. Application deadlines are open. Notification of early decision is sent December 1; regular decision, November 15. 124 early decision candidates were accepted for the 2017-2018 class. Applications are accepted on-line. **Transfer Students:** 47 transfer students enrolled in 2016-2017. Requirements for transfer applicants include a minimum GPA of 2.0, SAT scores, and an interview. 30 of 120 credits required for the bachelor's degree must be completed at LVC. **International Students:** There are 20 international students enrolled. They must take the TOEFL with a minimum score of 550 on the paper-based TOEFL (PBT) or 80 on the Internet-based version (iBT).

ADMISSIONS: 73% of the 2017-2018 applicants were accepted. The SAT scores for the 2017-2018 freshman class were: Math-- 7% below 500, 56% between 500 and 599, 30% between 600 and 699, and 7% between 700 and 800. Evidence-Based Reading/Writing-- 10% below 500, 8% between 500 and 599, 37% between 600 and 699, and 4% between 700 and 800. The ACT scores were 5% between 12 and 17, 34% between 18 and 23, 47% between 24 and 29, and 10% above 30. 35% of the current freshmen were in the top fifth of their class; 59% were in the top two fifths. 1 freshman graduated first in the class. **Admissions Contact:** Edwin Wright, Vice President for Enrollment Management. Email: *admission@lvc.edu* Web: *www.lvc.edu*

FINANCIAL AID: In 2017-2018, 99% of all full-time freshmen received some form of financial aid. 85% of all full-time freshmen received need-based aid. The average freshman award was $33,822. Need-based scholarships or need-based grants averaged $28,114; need-based self-help aid (loans and jobs) averaged $5,341; and $21,402 from other forms of aid. 55% of undergraduate students work part-time. The average financial indebtedness of the 2017 graduate was $43,588. The FAFSA code is 003288. The priority date for freshman financial aid applications for fall entry is February 15.

LEHIGH UNIVERSITY — F-3

www.lehigh.edu

Bethlehem, PA 18015 (610) 758-3100

Fax: (610) 758-4361	**Email:** admissions@lehigh.edu
Full-time: 2738 men, 2275 women	**Faculty:** 509; I, +$
Part-time: 37 men, 25 women	**Ph.D.s:** 96%
Graduate: 1071 men, 871 women	**Student/Faculty:** 9 to 1
Year: semesters, summer session	**Tuition:** $50,740
Room & Board: $13,120	**Freshman Class:** 13871 applied, 3489 accepted, 1234 enrolled
SAT CR/M: 660/690 **ACT:** 31	**CEEB CODE:** 2365
Application Deadline: January 1	**MOST COMPETITIVE**

Lehigh University, founded in 1865, is a private research university offering both undergraduate and graduate programs in liberal arts, sciences, business, education, and engineering. Our students experience interesting, independent research, and work closely with faculty who offer their time and attention to hands-on projects, internships, and innovative studies. There are 3 undergraduate schools and 4 graduate schools. In addition to regional accreditation, Lehigh has baccalaureate program accreditation with AACSB, and ABET. The 2355-acre campus is in a suburban area 50 miles north of Philadelphia and 75 miles southwest of New York City. Including any residence halls, there are 164 buildings.

STUDENT LIFE: 73% of undergraduates are from out of state, mostly the Middle Atlantic. Students are from 50 states, 62 foreign countries, and Canada. 9% are Hispanic; 8% Asian American; 8% Foreign; 64% White; 4% African American; 4% race unknown; 3% two or more races. **Male To Female Ratio:** 1.2:1. The average age of freshmen is 18; all undergraduates, 20. 4% do not continue beyond their first year; 86% remain to graduate. **Housing:** 3345 students can be accommodated in college housing, which includes married student dorms and on-campus apartments. In addition, there are special-interest houses, fraternity houses, sorority houses, substance free housing, UMOJA house, and ROTC housing. On-campus housing is guaranteed for the freshman year only, and is available on a first-come, first-served basis, and is available on a lottery system for upperclassmen. 65% of students live on campus. Upperclassmen may keep cars.

FACULTY/CLASSROOMS: 62% of faculty are male; 38% are female. All teach undergraduates and all do research. No introductory courses are taught by graduate students. The average class size in a regular course is 28.

PROGRAMS OF STUDY: Lehigh confers B.A. and B.S. degrees. Master's and doctoral degrees are also awarded. Bachelor's degrees are awarded in AGRICULTURE (environmental studies), BIOLOGICAL SCIENCE (biochemistry, biology/biological science, and molecular biology), BUSINESS (accounting, business economics, business information systems, finance, marketing, management & strategic leadership, and supply chain management), COMMUNICATIONS AND THE ARTS (art, art history and appreciation, Chinese, classics, design, English, French, German, journalism, music, music theory and composition, Spanish, and theater design), COMPUTER AND PHYSICAL SCIENCE (applied mathematics, applied science, astronomy, astrophysics, chemistry, computer science, earth science, mathematics, physics, science technology, and statistics), EDUCATION (global studies), ENGINEERING AND ENVIRONMENTAL DESIGN (architecture, bioengineering, chemical engineering, civil engineering, computer engineering, electrical/electronics engineering, engineering mechanics, engineering physics, environmental engineering, environmental science, industrial engineering, materials science and engineering, and mechanical engineering), HEALTH PROFESSIONS (pharmaceutical chemistry, predentistry, premedicine, and preoptometry), SOCIAL SCIENCE (African studies, anthropology, Asian/Oriental studies, behavioral science, classical/ancient civilization, cognitive science, economics, history, interdisciplinary studies, international relations, philosophy, political science/government, psychology, religion, sociology, and women's studies). Finance, mechanical engineering, and accounting have the largest enrollments.

ACTIVITIES: 38% of men belong to 17 national fraternities; 45% of women belong to 11 national sororities. There are 150 groups on campus, including art, band, cheerleading, chess, choir, chorale, chorus, computers, dance, debate, drama, environmental, ethnic, honors, international, jazz band, LGBT, literary magazine, marching band, musical theater, newspaper, orchestra, pep band, photography, political, professional, radio and TV, religious, social, social service, student government, symphony, and yearbook. Popular campus events include Spirit Week, Spring Fling, International Week, Move Out Collection Drive, and Great South Side Sale. **Sports:** There are 12 intercollegiate sports for men and 13 for women, and 8 intramural sports for men and 8 for women. Facilities include a stadium, an arena, a gym, cross-country course, a field house with basketball and tennis courts, swimming pools, a track, indoor squash and racquetball courts, playing fields, astro-turf for field hockey, football, lacrosse, soccer, softball and baseball complexes, weight rooms, a fitness center, climbing wall, indoor tennis center, and golf range (driving/chipping/putting). **Graduates:** From July 1, 2016 to June 30, 2017, 1225 bachelor's degrees were awarded. The most popular majors were finance (13%), mechanical engineering (10%), and accounting (6%). In an average class, 1% graduate in 3 years or less, 76% graduate in 4 years or less, 83% graduate in 5 years or less, and 86% graduate in 6 years or less. Of the 2016 graduating class, 25% were enrolled in graduate school within 6 months of graduation, and 68% were employed.

SERVICES: Counseling and information services are available, as is tutoring in most subjects, such as calculus, physics, English, accounting, finance, and economics. There is a reader service for the blind. Tutoring is available upon request, and there are special programs for students with learning disabilities, and English as a Second Language. **Library/Resources:** The library contains 882,975 volumes, 148,134 microform items, and 2,681 audio/video tapes/CDs/DVDs, and subscribes to 53,678 periodicals including electronic. Computerized library services include interlibrary loans, database searching, Internet access, and Wi-Fi capability. Special learning facilities include an art gallery, radio station, TV station, special collections/rare book reading room, digital media studio, financial services lab, center for teaching and learning (CITL), data visualization lab and international multimedia resource center. **Physically**

Challenged Students: Facilities include wheelchair ramps, elevators, special parking, specially equipped restrooms, special class scheduling, lowered drinking fountains, lowered telephones, and special housing. **Special:** Lehigh offers many interdisciplinary programs including Integrated Product Development, Computer Science and Business, Integrated Business and Engineering, Integrated Degree in Engineering, Arts and Sciences, Global Citizenship, Lehigh Earth Observatory, and South Mountain College, Lehigh's residential academic program. The university offers co-op programs, cross-registration with the Lehigh Valley Association of Independent Colleges, many combinations of dual majors, study abroad programs in 40 countries, internships, a Washington semester, work-study, a 7-year BA/MD program with Drexel University College of Medicine, a 7-year BA/OD program with SUNY Optometry and a 7-year BA/DMD program with the School of Dental Medicine at the University of Pennsylvania. There are 18 national honor societies, Phi Beta Kappa, and a freshman honors program. **Visiting:** There are regularly scheduled orientations for prospective students. There are group information sessions and tours which are scheduled Monday through Friday, and some Saturdays, special events, and open houses. There are guides for informal visits, visitors may sit in on classes, and stay overnight. To schedule a visit, contact the Office of Admissions. **Campus Safety and Security:** Measures include 24-hour foot and vehicle patrol, emergency notification system, self-defense education, and security escort services. There are shuttle buses, emergency telephones, lighted pathways/sidewalks, controlled access to dorms/residences, LU-alert text messaging system, and emergency preparedness presentations.

REQUIREMENTS: The SAT or ACT is required. In addition, Candidates for admission should have completed 4 years of English, 3 years of math and electives, and 2 years each of foreign language, science, and social science. Most students present 4 years each of science, math, and English. Opportunities for an on-campus interview are made available to prospective students but are not required. Interviews are by appointment only. AP credits are accepted. Important factors in the admissions decision are advanced placement or honors courses, recommendations by school officials, evidence of special talent, and extracurricular activities record. Graduation requirements vary by degree sought, but all students must complete 2 semesters of English, at least 30 credits in the chosen major, and a minimum of 121 credit hours. Students must also maintain a minimum GPA of 2.0. **Procedure:** Freshmen are admitted in the fall and spring. Entrance exams should be taken by the January test date. There are early decision, early admissions, and deferred admissions plans. Early decision applications should be filed by November 15; regular applications, by January 1 for fall entry; and November 1 for spring entry. The fall 2017 application fee was $70. Notification of early decision is sent December 15; regular decision, April 1. 669 early decision candidates were accepted for the 2017-2018 class. 2799 applicants were on the 2017 waiting list; 53 were admitted. Applications are accepted on-line. **Transfer Students:** 30 transfer students enrolled in 2016-2017. Transfer candidates should have a minimum GPA of 3.25 and submit high school and college transcripts, an essay, and a statement of good standing from previous institutions. 30 of 121 credits required for the bachelor's degree must be completed at Lehigh. **International Students:** There are 434 international students enrolled. They must take the TOEFL with a minimum score of 570 on the paper-based TOEFL (PBT) or 90 on the Internet-based version (iBT). Students whose first language is not English must take the IELTS. They must also take the SAT or ACT.

ADMISSIONS: 25% of the 2017-2018 applicants were accepted. The SAT scores for the 2017-2018 freshman class were: Critical Reading-- 14% between 500 and 599, 57% between 600 and 699, and 29% between 700 and 800. Math-- 9% between 500 and 599, 43% between 600 and 699, and 48% between 700 and 800. The ACT scores were 3% between 18 and 23, 31% between 24 and 29, and 66% above 30. 83% of the current freshmen were in the top fifth of their class; 97% were in the top two fifths. 23 freshmen graduated first in their class. **Admissions Contact:** Bruce Bunnick, Director of Admissions. Email: *admissions@lehigh.edu* Web: *www.lehigh.edu*

FINANCIAL AID: In 2017-2018, 47% of all full-time freshmen received some form of financial aid. 42% of all full-time freshmen received need-based aid. The average freshman award was $46,421. Need-based scholarships or need-based grants averaged $41,234; need-based self-help aid (loans and jobs) averaged $4,940; non-need-based athletic scholarships averaged $37,698; and other non-need-based awards and non-need-based scholarships averaged $13,964. 31% of undergraduate students work part-time. The average financial indebtedness of the 2017 graduate was $35,440. Lehigh is a member of CSS. The CSS/Profile, and noncustodial profile, and business/farm supplement are requied. The FAFSA code is 003289. The deadline for filing freshman financial aid applications for fall entry is February 15.

LINCOLN UNIVERSITY *(The complete profile is made available exclusively on our website, www.barronspac.com)*

LOCK HAVEN UNIVERSITY OF PENNSYLVANIA *(The complete profile is made available exclusively on our website, www.barronspac.com)*

LYCOMING COLLEGE D-2
www.lycoming.edu

Williamsport, PA 17701	(570) 321-4026 (800) 345-3920
Fax: (570) 321-4317	**Email:** admissions@lycoming.edu
Full-time: 599 men, 600 women	**Faculty:** 89; IIB, av$
Part-time: 10 men, 14 women	**Ph.D.s:** 94%
Graduate: n/av	**Student/Faculty:** 12 to 1
Year: semesters, summer session	**Tuition:** $28,618
Room & Board: $11,980	**Freshman Class:** 1924 applied, 1232 accepted, 282 enrolled
SAT EBR-W/M: 560/540 **ACT:** 23	**CEEB CODE:** 2372
Application Deadline: August 1	**COMPETITIVE**

Lycoming College, established in 1812, is a selective, private, residential, liberal arts and sciences institution. There is 1 undergraduate school. In addition to regional accreditation, Lycoming has baccalaureate program accreditation with ACS. The 35-acre campus is in an urban area in the city of Williamsport in north central Pennsylvania, 90 miles from Harrisburg and 170 miles from Philadelphia and New York City. Including any residence halls, there are 25 buildings.

STUDENT LIFE: 59% of undergraduates are from Pennsylvania. Others are from 28 states, 21 foreign countries, and Canada. 62% are White; 6% race unknown; 5% Foreign; 3% two or more races; 12% African American; 10% Hispanic; 1% Asian American. 62% claim no religious affiliation; 17% Protestant; 15% Catholic. **Female To Male Ratio:** 1.0:1. The average age of freshmen is 18; all undergraduates, 20. 20% do not continue beyond their first year; 67% remain to graduate. **Housing:** 1163 students can be accommodated in college housing, which includes single-sex dorms, coed dorms, on-campus apartments, and off-campus apartments. In addition, there are special-interest houses, nonsmoking, Greek floors, wellness housing, and living learning communities. On-campus housing is guaranteed for all 4 years. 87% of students live on campus. All students may keep cars.

FACULTY/CLASSROOMS: 54% of faculty are male; 46% are female. All teach undergraduates. No introductory courses are taught by graduate students. The average class size in an introductory lecture is 18 and in a laboratory is 18.

PROGRAMS OF STUDY: Lycoming confers B.A. and B.S. degrees. Bachelor's degrees are awarded in BIOLOGICAL SCIENCE (biology/biological science, neurosciences, and biochemistry), BUSINESS (accounting and business administration and management), COMMUNICATIONS AND THE ARTS (art, art history and appreciation, comparative literature, creative writing, digital communications, dramatic arts, English, French, German, literature, media arts, film and media studies, music, Spanish, studio art, theatre acting, and theater management), COMPUTER AND PHYSICAL SCIENCE (actuarial science, actuarial mathematics, astronomy, astrophysics, chemistry, mathematics, and physics), EDUCATION (education), SOCIAL SCIENCE (American studies, anthropology, archeology, criminal justice, criminology, economics, history, international studies, medieval studies, medical anthropology, philosophy, political science/government, psychology, religion, and sociology). Archaeology, creative writing, astrophysics, actuarial math, biology, chemistry, physics, criminal justice and criminology are the strongest academically. Business, psychology, biology, criminal justice & criminology have the largest enrollments.

ACTIVITIES: 11% of men belong to 3 national fraternities; 23% of women belong to 3 local and 3 national sororities. There are 72 groups on campus, including art, band, cheerleading, choir, chorus, communications, computers, dance, drama, environmental, ethnic, film, honors, international, jazz band, LGBT, literary magazine, musical theater, newspaper, orchestra, pep band, photography, political, professional, radio and TV, religious, social, social service, student government, and yearbook. Popular campus events include Outdoor Leadership and Education, Christmas Candlelight, Leadership and Service Awards, choir and concert band performances, student theatre productions, Honors Convocation, and distinguished lectureship/speaker series. **Sports:** There are 9 intercollegiate sports for men and 8 for women, and 7 intramural sports for men and 5 for women. Facilities include softball, football, soccer, and lacrosse complex, a field house, indoor court area for basketball, tennis & volleyball, indoor track, weight and exercise rooms, a fitness center, indoor pool, and multipurpose room for dancing and karate, and intramural fields. **Graduates:** From July 1, 2016 to June 30, 2017, 256 bachelor's degrees were awarded. The most popular majors were business/marketing (21%), social sciences (15%), and psychology (12%). In an average class, 59% graduate in 4 years or less, 66% graduate in 5 years or less, and 67% graduate in 6 years or less.

SERVICES: Counseling and information services are available, as is tutoring in every subject. There is remedial math and writing. **Library/Resources:** The library contains 348,214 volumes, 201,005 microform items, and 1,431 audio/video tapes/CDs/DVDs, and subscribes to 23,796 periodicals including electronic. Computerized library services include interlibrary loans, database searching, Internet access, and Wi-Fi capability. Special learning facilities include an art gallery, planetarium, radio station, and science center. **Physically Challenged Students:** 90% of the campus is accessible. Facilities include wheelchair ramps, elevators, special parking, specially equipped restrooms, special class scheduling, lowered drinking fountains, lowered telephones, and special housing. **Special:** Lycoming delivers a 21st century education that combines the traditional strength of the liberal arts and sciences with experiential learning. Internships, study abroad, and research with faculty opportunities across all disciplines are coordinated through the Center for Enhanced Academic Experiences. The highly regarded Clean Water Institute provides ongoing opportunities for field work. May term travel courses led by Lycoming faculty to Europe, Asia, Latin America and Africa. The Dominican Republic provides applied learning as part of the 4-4-1 academic year. Semester study abroad agreements in more than 20 different countries include institutions in China, England, France, Mexico and Spain. The archaeology program is affiliated with expeditions in Cyprus, Israel and Guatemala. Special academic programs include a 3-2 engineering program with the Watson School at Binghamton University, a 4-1 MBA program with Rochester Institute of Technology, and a 3-2 master's program with Duke University's Environmental Science and Forestry program. Distinctive academic programs include the Washington Semester at American University, interdisciplinary scholars program, an Institute for Management Studies, Center for Energy and the Future, entrepreneurship maker's space, and a 150-hour Accounting program. There are 22 national honor societies, a freshman honors program, and 35 departmental honors programs. **Visiting:** There are regularly scheduled orientations for prospective students, consisting of a student-guided tour of campus and an interview with an admissions counselor. Meetings with professors and coaches and attending a class are possible upon request. To schedule a visit, contact Barb Carlin in Admissions. **Campus Safety and Security:** Measures include 24-hour foot and vehicle patrol, emergency notification system, self-defense education, and security escort services. There are emergency telephones, lighted pathways/sidewalks, and controlled access to dorms/residences.

REQUIREMENTS: The SAT or ACT is recommended. Applicants must graduate from an accredited secondary school or have a GED. Students must have earned 16 academic units including a minimum of 4 years of English, 3 each of math and social studies, and 2 each of natural or physical science, modern language, and academic electives. 2 personal letters of recommendation, and an interview are also recommended. Portfolios and auditions may be required for students seeking scholarships in the arts. AP and CLEP credits are accepted. Important factors in the admissions decision are advanced placement or honors courses, leadership record, and evidence of special talent. To graduate, students must complete 128 credits with a minimum overall GPA of 2.0 and a minimum GPA of 2.0 within the major (with an exception of one accounting major that requires 150 credits). Distribution requirements include 4 courses in humanities and 2 each in math (unless exempted on the basis of placement), fine arts, natural science, and social science, 1 in English composition, global diversity, and domestic diversity. Foreign language requirements include a course numbered 101 (unless exempted on the basis of placement) and a course numbered above 101 in the same language. (if English is a second language, another writing intensive course or an English course above 107 would meet the foreign language requirement.) Students must also complete 3 writing intensive courses (1 in major, 1 outside the major, and 1 additional). Regardless of major, students must complete the first-year seminar and an enhanced academic experience (such as a faculty-supervised independent research, study abroad, an internship for academic credit). The Enhanced Academic Experience (EAE) provides students with the opportunity to reach their greatest potential by fulfilling an in-depth academic experience outside of the requirements of their major. This added-value experience ensures academic excellence by requiring that students expand their horizons beyond the distribution and major requirements. **Procedure:** Freshmen are admitted in the fall and spring. Entrance exams should be taken during the junior year or by January of the senior year. There are early decision, early admissions, deferred admissions, and rolling admissions plans. Early decision applications should be filed by November 15; regular applications, by August 1 for fall entry; and December 1 for spring entry. Notification of early decision is sent December 1; regular decision, on a rolling basis. 17 early decision candidates were accepted for the 2017-2018 class. 285 applicants were on the 2017 waiting list; 44 were admitted. Applications are accepted on-line. **Transfer Students:** 49 transfer students enrolled in 2016-2017. Applicants must submit appropriate transcripts and have a minimum GPA of 2.0 in transferable courses. Students who have completed 24 transferable semester hours are not required to submit SAT I or ACT results. 32 of 128 credits required for the bachelor's degree must be completed at Lycoming. **International Students:** There are 55 international students enrolled. They must take the TOEFL with a minimum score of 525 on the paper-based TOEFL (PBT) or 70 on the Internet-based version (iBT), and take the IELTS.

ADMISSIONS: 64% of the 2017-2018 applicants were accepted. The SAT scores for the 2017-2018 freshman class were: Math-- 25% below 500, 50% between 500 and 599, 23% between 600 and 699, and 1% between 700 and 800. Evidence-Based Reading/Writing-- 26% below 500, 45% between 500 and 599, 27% between 600 and 699, and 2% between 700 and 800. The ACT scores were 4% between 12 and 17, 54% between 18 and 23, 39% between 24 and 29, and 3% above 30. 26% of the current freshmen were in the top fifth of their class; 57% were in the top two fifths. 1 freshman graduated first in the class. **Admissions Contact:** Mike Konopski, VP for Enrollment Management. Email: *admissions@lycoming.edu* Web: *www.lycoming.edu*

FINANCIAL AID: In 2017-2018, 100% of all full-time freshmen received some form of financial aid. 89% of all full-time freshmen received need-based aid. The average freshman award was $43,152. Need-based scholarships or need-based grants averaged $15,893 ($43,773 maximum); need-based self-help aid (loans and jobs) averaged $3,886 ($6,600 maximum); and other non-need-based awards and non-need-based scholarships averaged $27,843 ($54,095 maximum). 51% of undergraduate students work part-time. Lycoming is a member of CSS. The FAFSA code is 003293. The deadline for filing freshman financial aid applications for fall entry is May 1.

MANSFIELD UNIVERSITY OF PENNSYLVANIA *(The complete profile is made available exclusively on our website, www.barronspac.com)*

MARYWOOD UNIVERSITY — E-2

www.marywood.edu

Scranton, PA 18509 — **(570) 348-6234** **(866) 279-9663**

Fax: (570) 961-4763 — **Email: yourfuture@marywood.edu**

Full-time: 556 men, 1200 women — **Faculty:** IIA, -$

Part-time: 59 men, 149 women — **Ph.D.s:** 87%

Graduate: 224 men, 762 women — **Student/Faculty:** 11 to 1

Year: semesters, summer session — **Tuition:** $33,940

Room & Board: $13,900 — **Freshman Class:** 2246 applied, 1694 accepted, 454 enrolled

SAT EBR-W/M: 554/544 **ACT:** recommended — **CEEB CODE:** 2407

Application Deadline: open — **COMPETITIVE**

Marywood University, founded in 1915, is a comprehensive, Catholic university with 99 undergraduate, graduate and doctoral degree programs. Established by the Sisters, Servants of the Immaculate Heart of Mary, Marywood offered the region's first doctoral degree program and is a leading provider of graduate education in the region, with 36 master's degree programs and 37 certificate offerings. Marywood has 8 divisions and includes 4 colleges and 4 schools: The Insalaco College of Creative and Performing Arts, the Reap College of Education and Human Development, the College of Health and Human Services, the Munley College of Liberal Arts and Sciences, school of architecture, school of business and global innovation, school of social work, and the center for interdisciplinary studies. Committed to enriching human lives through ethical and religious values and a tradition of service, and motivated by a pioneering, progressive spirit, Marywood provides a framework for educational excellence that enables students to develop fully and to master professional and leadership skills necessary for meeting human needs. In addition to regional accreditation, MU has baccalaureate program accreditation with ACBSP, ADA, CSWE, NASAD, NASM, AATA, AMTA, APA, ACEN, ARC-PA, ASHA, CAATE, and CACREP. The 123-acre campus is in a suburban area 120 miles west of New York City and 115 miles north of Philadelphia. Including any residence halls, there are 33 buildings.

STUDENT LIFE: 70% of undergraduates are from Pennsylvania. Others are from 30 states, and 16 foreign countries. 73% are White; 6% Hispanic; 3% African American; 3% Foreign; 2% Asian American; 2% two or more races; 11% race unknown. **Female To Male Ratio:** 2.5:1. The average age of freshmen is 19; all undergraduates, 21. 14% do not continue beyond their first year; 70% remain to graduate. **Housing:** 934 students can be accommodated in college housing, which includes dorms, on-campus apartments, themed, and special interest housing. On-campus housing is guaranteed for all 4 years. 63% of students commute. Alcohol is not permitted. All students may keep cars.

FACULTY/CLASSROOMS: 43% of faculty are male; 57% are female. No introductory courses are taught by graduate students.

PROGRAMS OF STUDY: Marywood confers B.A., B.Arch., B.E.D.A., B.S., B.B.A., B.F.A., B.M., B.S.N., and B.S.W. degrees. Master's and doctoral degrees are also awarded. Bachelor's degrees are awarded in BIOLOGICAL SCIENCE (biology/biological science and biotechnology), BUSINESS (accounting, banking and finance, business administration and management, hospitality management services, information & communication technology, international business management, marketing/retailing/merchandising, and retailing), COMMUNICATIONS AND THE ARTS (advertising, arts administration/management, broadcasting, ceramic art and design, communications, digital communications, dramatic arts, English, French, graphic design, illustration, music business management, music performance, musical theater, painting, photography, sculpture, Spanish, studio art, and theater management), COMPUTER AND PHYSICAL SCIENCE (information sciences and systems, mathematics, and science), EDUCATION (art education, athletic training, dance education, early childhood education, education of the deaf and hearing impaired, elementary education, English education, foreign languages education, mathematics education, music education, physical education, science education, secondary education, social science education, and special education), ENGINEERING AND ENVIRONMENTAL DESIGN (architecture, aviation administration/management, environmental design, environmental science, and interior design), HEALTH PROFESSIONS (art therapy, health care administration, health science, medical technology, music therapy, nursing, physician's assistant, premedicine, preosteopathy, and speech pathology/audiology), SOCIAL SCIENCE (clinical psychology, communication sciences & disorders, criminal justice, dietetics, family/consumer studies, gerontology, history, industrial and organizational psychology, philosophy, physical fitness/movement, political science/government, prelaw, psychology, religion, social science, and social work). Architecture, pre-physician assistant, and communication sciences & disorders are the strongest academically. Pre-physician assistant, nursing, and communication sciences & disorders have the largest enrollments.

ACTIVITIES: There are no fraternities; 31% of women belong to 2 local sororities. There are 60 groups on campus, including art, band, cheerleading, choir, chorus, dance, drama, environmental, ethnic, film, honors, international, jazz band, LGBT, literary magazine, musical theater, newspaper, orchestra, photography, political, professional, radio and TV, religious, social, social service, student government, symphony, and volunteers in action. Popular campus events include Spring Fling, Homecoming formal, Flapjack Fest, and Midnight Madness. **Sports:** There are 9 intercollegiate sports for men and 11 for women. The center for athletics and wellness provides fitness classes, a climbing wall, an elevated running track, a dance/aerobics studio, an arena, and high tech athletic training areas. The aquatics center features eight lanes, onemeter and three meter diving boards, a multipurpose turf field, tennis courts, sand volleyball court, basketball courts, and grass fields. **Graduates:** From July 1, 2016 to June 30, 2017, 446 bachelor's degrees were awarded. The most popular majors were health professions and related programs (30%), business, management, marketing & related support services (14%), architecture, and interior architecture (10%). In an average class, 4% graduate in 3 years or less, 47% graduate in 4 years or less, 66% graduate in 5 years or less, and 67% graduate in 6 years or less.

SERVICES: Counseling and information services are available, as is tutoring in most subjects. There is a reader service for the blind and a writing center. **Library/Resources:** The library contains 220,273 volumes, and 25,040 audio/video tapes/CDs/DVDs, and subscribes to 31,928 periodicals including electronic. Computerized library services include interlibrary loans, database searching, Internet access, and Wi-Fi capability. Special learning facilities include an art gallery, radio station, an academic excellence center, a student counseling center, a human physiology lab, human development (counseling, psychology) laboratories, biotechnology lab, a communication sciences and disorders clinic, a nutrition and dietetics lab, an assistive technology center, an outpatient mental health clinic, multiple "smart" classrooms, multiple computer labs, a center for architectural studies studios, a television studio and editing suites, an art center (including ceramic, painting, drawing/foundation, sculpture, glass, metal, clay, wood, photography, fabric, jewelry, and printmaking studios), a visual arts center (including graphic design and interior architecture computer labs), 2 art exhibit galleries, the Maslow collection of contemporary art and study gallery, a theater, and a black box theater. **Physically Challenged Students:** 95% of the campus is accessible. Facilities include wheelchair ramps, elevators, special parking, specially equipped restrooms, special class scheduling, and lowered drinking fountains. **Special:** Marywood offers cross-registration with the University of Scranton, internships, and study abroad (Argentina, Austria, Brazil, China, England, France, Greece Ireland, Italy, Japan, New Zealand, Portugal, South Africa, South Korea, Spain, Taiwan, Turkey, Wales). Also offered are accelerated degree programs in dietetics and social work, dual majors, and student-designed majors. Students may earn credit for life, military and work experience. There are 20 national honor societies, a freshman honors program, and 18 departmental honors programs. **Visiting:** There are regularly scheduled orientations for prospective students, including a presentation/overview of Marywood University, talking with academic department faculty members and meeting and talking with current students. There are guides for informal visits, visitors may sit in on classes, and stay overnight. To schedule a visit, contact the Office of Admissions. **Campus Safety and Security:** Measures include 24-hour foot and vehicle patrol, emergency notification system, self-defense education, and security escort services. There are emergency telephones, lighted pathways/sidewalks, controlled access to dorms/residences, night security in dorms, card access to dorm floors, and transportation on request.

REQUIREMENTS: The SAT is required. The ACT is recommended. Applicants are expected to be graduates of an accredited secondary school or have the GED. A minimum of 17 academic credits is required, including 4 in English, 3 each in social studies and science (1 as lab), 2 in math and 6 academic electives. A letter of support is required in selected majors, as is a portfolio or an audition where appropriate. A personal interview is strongly recommended. AP and CLEP credits are accepted. Important factors in the admissions decision are advanced placement or honors courses, leadership record, and recommendations by school officials. To graduate, students must complete a liberal arts core consisting of religious studies, philosophy, math, science, history, social science, literature, writing, foreign language and fine arts. Additional course requirements include a first-year experience course for new undergraduate students who have not transferred from another post-secondary institution and one course with a global studies perspective. **Procedure:** Freshmen are admitted in the fall and spring. Entrance exams should be taken in the junior and senior year before graduation. There are deferred admissions and rolling admissions plans. Application deadlines are open. The fall 2017 application fee was $35. Notification of early decision is sent September 1; regular decision, Applications are accepted on-line. **Transfer Students:** 114 transfer students enrolled in 2016-2017. SAT or ACT scores are required of transfer applicants who have earned fewer then 12 college credits; both secondary school and college transcripts are required. Transfer students are required to have earned a minimum GPA of 2.25 at the college most recently attended (3.0 minimum for some majors). A grade of C is the minimum requirement for transfer of academic credit. The SAT is required for nursing transfer students. 42 of 120 credits required for the bachelor's degree must be completed at Marywood. **International Students:** There are 57 international students enrolled. They must take the TOEFL with a minimum score of 71 on the Internet-based version (iBT). Students must take the IELTS with a score of 5.5 minimum. They must also take the SAT or ACT.

ADMISSIONS: 75% of the 2017-2018 applicants were accepted. The SAT scores for the 2017-2018 freshman class were: Critical Reading-- 39% below 500, 49% between 500 and 599, and 12% between 600 and 699. Math-- 24% below 500, 54% between 500 and 599, 20% between 600 and 699, and 2% between 700 and 800. Writing-- 43% below 500, 47% between 500 and 599, and 10% between 600 and 699. Evidence-Based Reading/Writing-- 19% below 500, 51% between 500 and 599, 27% between 600 and 699, and 3% between 700 and 800. 2 freshmen graduated first in their class. **Admissions Contact:** Christian DiGregorio, Director of University Admissions. Email: *yourfuture@marywood.edu* Web: *www.marywood.edu*

FINANCIAL AID: In 2017-2018, 90% of all full-time freshmen received some form of financial aid, and need-based aid. The average freshman award was $32,452. Need-based scholarships or need-based grants averaged $23,381; need-based self-help aid (loans and jobs) averaged $3,445; other non-need-based awards and non-need-based scholarships averaged $1,361; and $4,265 from other forms of aid. The average financial indebtedness of the 2017 graduate was $36,446. The state aid form is required. The FAFSA code is 003296. The priority date for freshman financial aid applications for fall entry is February 15.

MERCYHURST UNIVERSITY — B-1

www.mercyhurst.edu

Erie, PA 16546	(814) 824-2202 (800) 825-1926
Fax: (814) 824-3634	**Email:** admissions@mercyhurst.edu
Full-time: 1390 men, 1988 women	**Faculty:** IIB, -$
Part-time: 129 men, 333 women	**Ph.D.s:** 60%
Graduate: 140 men, 140 women	**Student/Faculty:** n/av
Year: semesters, summer session	**Tuition:** $34,420
Room & Board: $13,000	**Freshman Class:** 3000 applied, 1900 accepted, 650 enrolled
SAT CR/M/W: 550/530/510 **ACT:** 23	**CEEB CODE:** 2410
Application Deadline: September 1	**COMPETITIVE**

Mercyhurst University, established in 1926, is a private, nonprofit institution affiliated with the Roman Catholic Church. The university offers undergraduate degrees in the arts, business, health science, liberal arts, religious studies, and teacher preparation as well as a degree-directed program for the learning disabled. There is 1 undergraduate school and 1 graduate school. In addition to regional accreditation, Mercyhurst University has baccalaureate program accreditation with ADA and CSWE. The 88-acre campus is in a suburban area within Erie, PA. Including any residence halls, there are 44 buildings.

STUDENT LIFE: 60% of undergraduates are from Pennsylvania. Others are from 37 states, 14 foreign countries, and Canada. 76% are from public schools. 91% are White; 4% African American; 3% Foreign; 1% Asian American; 1% Hispanic. 53% are Catholic; 21% Protestant; 18% claim no religious affiliation. **Female To Male Ratio:** 1.5:1. The average age of freshmen is 18; all undergraduates, 26. 20% do not continue beyond their first year; 62% remain to graduate. **Housing:** 1718 students can be accommodated in college housing, which includes married student dorms and on-campus apartments. On-campus housing is guaranteed for all 4 years. 65% of students live on campus. Upperclassmen may keep cars.

FACULTY/CLASSROOMS: 57% of faculty are male; 43% are female. All teach undergraduates and 30% do research. No introductory courses are taught by graduate students. The average class size in an introductory lecture is 35; in a laboratory is 12; and in a regular course is 25.

PROGRAMS OF STUDY: Mercyhurst confers B.A., B.S., B.F.A., and B.M. degrees. Associate, master's, and doctoral degrees are also awarded. Bachelor's degrees are awarded in BIOLOGICAL SCIENCE (biochemistry and biology/biological science), BUSINESS (accounting, banking and finance, business administration and management, fashion merchandising, hotel/motel and restaurant management, insurance and risk management, management information systems, and marketing/retailing/merchandising), COMMUNICATIONS AND THE ARTS (advertising, broadcasting, communications, dance, English, graphic design, journalism, languages, music, musical theater, public relations, and studio art), COMPUTER AND PHYSICAL SCIENCE (chemistry, earth science, geology, mathematics, web services, and web technology), EDUCATION (art education, athletic training, business education, early childhood education, elementary education, home economics education, mathematics education, music education, science education, secondary education, social science education, and special education), ENGINEERING AND ENVIRONMENTAL DESIGN (environmental science and interior design), HEALTH PROFESSIONS (art therapy, medical laboratory technology, predentistry, premedicine, preosteopathy, prepharmacy, preveterinary science, and sports medicine), SOCIAL SCIENCE (anthropology, archeology, criminal justice, family/consumer studies, forensic studies, history, philosophy, political science/government, prelaw, psychology, religion, religious education, social work, and sociology). Applied forensic science, intelligence studies, and sports medicine are the strongest academically. Business, education, and sports medicine have the largest enrollments.

ACTIVITIES: There are no fraternities or sororities. There are 93 groups on campus, including art, band, cheerleading, choir, chorus, communications, computers, dance, debate, drama, ethnic, film, honors, international, jazz band, LGBT, literary magazine, musical theater, newspaper, opera, orchestra, pep band, photography, political, professional, radio and TV, religious, social, social service, and student government. Popular campus events include Activities Day, Parents Weekend, and Winter and Spring Formals. **Sports:** There are 13 intercollegiate sports for men and 12 for women, and 9 intramural sports for men and 9 for women. Facilities include indoor crew tanks, football, field hockey, lacrosse, soccer fields, an ice hockey rink/arena, Nautilus facilities, free-weight room, baseball/softball complex, training room, and a basketball arena. **Graduates:** From July 1, 2016 to June 30, 2017, 800 bachelor's degrees were awarded.

SERVICES: Counseling and information services are available, as is tutoring in every subject. There is remedial math, reading, and writing. **Library/Resources:** The library contains 165,644 volumes, 50,631 microform items, and 9,309 audio/video tapes/CDs/DVDs, and subscribes to 848 periodicals including electronic. Computerized library services include interlibrary loans and database searching. Special learning facilities include an art gallery, planetarium, radio station, TV station, Northwestern Pennsylvania historical archives, and archeological institute. **Physically Challenged Students:** 90% of the campus is accessible. Facilities include wheelchair ramps, elevators, special parking, specially equipped restrooms, and lowered drinking fountains. **Special:** There are 7 national honor societies, a freshman honors program, and 4 departmental honors programs. **Visiting:** There are regularly scheduled orientations for prospective students, including tours, class visits, faculty meetings, and interviews with financial aid and admissions counselors. There are guides for informal visits, visitors may sit in on classes, and stay overnight. To schedule a visit, contact the Admissions Office. **Campus Safety and Security:** Measures include 24-hour foot and vehicle patrol, emergency notification system, and self-defense education. There are shuttle buses, emergency telephones, lighted pathways/sidewalks, controlled access to dorms/residences, 24-hour security camera surveillance system.

REQUIREMENTS: The SAT or ACT is required. Applicants must graduate from an accredited secondary school or have a GED. 16 academic credits are required, including 4 years of English, 3 each of math and social studies, and 2 each of history, science, and a foreign language. Interviews are recommended. Art applicants must submit portfolios; auditions are required of music and dance applicants. Mercyhurst requires applicants to be in the upper 50% of their class. A GPA of 2.8 is required. AP and CLEP credits are accepted. Important factors in the admissions decision are recommendations by alumni, evidence of special talent, and personality/intangible qualities. To graduate, students must complete the core curriculum, which includes English, math, science, religion, philosophy, history, and a computer course. Distribution requirements include American history, cultural appreciation, human behavior, and ethics. A minimum GPA of 2.0 is required, with a 2.5 in the major, and a minimum total of 123 credit hours. The number of credit hours in the major varies, with a minimum of 30. A thesis is necessary for history and English majors. **Procedure:** Freshmen are admitted to all sessions. Entrance exams should be taken during the spring of the junior year. There are deferred admissions and rolling admissions plans. Applications should be filed by September 1 for fall entry. Notification is sent on a rolling basis. Applications are accepted on-line. **Transfer Stu-**

dents: 90 transfer students enrolled in 2016-2017. A minimum GPA of 2.5 on previous college work is required 45 of 121 credits required for the bachelor's degree must be completed at Mercyhurst. **International Students:** There are 250 international students enrolled. They must take the TOEFL. They must also take the SAT or ACT.

ADMISSIONS: 63% of the 2017-2018 applicants were accepted. The ACT scores were 21% below 12, 46% between 12 and 17, and 33% between 18 and 23. 79% were in the top two fifths. 20 freshmen graduated first in their class. **Admissions Contact:** Christian Beyer, Director of Admissions. Email: *admissions@mercyhurst.edu* Web: *www.mercyhurst.edu*

FINANCIAL AID: In 2017-2018, 95% of all full-time freshmen received some form of financial aid. 76% of all full-time freshmen received need-based aid. The average freshman award was $18,000. Need-based scholarships or need-based grants averaged $12,000. 60% of undergraduate students work part-time. The average financial indebtedness of the 2017 graduate was $27,000. Mercyhurst is a member of CSS. The FAFSA code is 003297. The priority date for freshman financial aid applications for fall entry is May 1.

MESSIAH COLLEGE D-3

www.messiah.edu

Mechanicsburg, PA 17055	(717) 691-6000 (800) 233-4220
Fax: (717) 796-5374	Email: admiss@messiah.edu
Full-time: 1061 men, 1576 women	Faculty: 174; IIB, +$
Part-time: 45 men, 77 women	Ph.D.s: 85%
Graduate: 140 men, 432 women	Student/Faculty: 12 to 1
Year: semesters, summer session	Tuition: $34,160
Room & Board: $10,220	Freshman Class: 2558 applied, 1970 accepted, 665 enrolled
SAT EBR-W/M: 611/595 ACT: 26	CEEB CODE: 2411
Application Deadline: open	VERY COMPETITIVE

Messiah College, founded in 1909, is a private Christian college of the liberal and applied arts and sciences. The college is committed to the evangelical spirit rooted in the Anabaptist, Pietist, and Wesleyan traditions. There are 4 undergraduate schools and 1 graduate school. In addition to regional accreditation, Messiah has baccalaureate program accreditation with ABET, ACBSP, CSWE, NASAD, NASM, CACREP, CCNE, and ACEND. The 471-acre campus is in a small town 12 miles southwest of Harrisburg. Including any residence halls, there are 53 buildings.

STUDENT LIFE: 63% of undergraduates are from Pennsylvania. Others are from 37 states, and 32 foreign countries. 74% are from public schools. 81% are White; 5% Hispanic; 5% Foreign; 3% two or more races; 2% African American; 2% Asian American; 1% race unknown. 85% are Protestant. **Female To Male Ratio:** 1.7:1. The average age of freshmen is 18; all undergraduates, 20. 12% do not continue beyond their first year; 80% remain to graduate. **Housing:** 2383 students can be accommodated in college housing, which includes dorms, on-campus apartments, and off-campus apartments. In addition, there are special-interest houses. On-campus housing is guaranteed for all 4 years. 87% of students live on campus. Alcohol is not permitted. Upperclassmen may keep cars.

FACULTY/CLASSROOMS: 49% of faculty are male; 51% are female. 88% teach undergraduates. No introductory courses are taught by graduate students. The average class size in an introductory lecture is 27; in a laboratory is 18; and in a regular course is 24.

PROGRAMS OF STUDY: Messiah confers B.A., B.S., B.M., B.S.E., B.S.N., B.S.W. and B.F.A. degrees. Master's and doctoral degrees are also awarded. Bachelor's degrees are awarded in BIOLOGICAL SCIENCE (biochemistry, biology/adolescence education, biology/biological science, and molecular biology), BUSINESS (accounting, business administration and management, finance, international business, marketing/retailing/merchandising, sports management, and sustainable management), COMMUNICATIONS AND THE ARTS (art history and appreciation, arts administration/management, communications, dance, digital media, dramatic arts, English, film arts, film, television and digital media, French language and literature, Germanic languages and literature, journalism, music, music business management, music ministry, music performance, musical theater, public relations, Spanish language and literature, studio art, and theater management), COMPUTER AND PHYSICAL SCIENCE (actuarial science, applied science, chemistry, chemistry/adolescence education, computer science, mathematics, physics/gen science secondary education, and physics), EDUCATION (art education, athletic training, early childhood education, elementary education, English education, foreign languages education, mathematics education, music education, outdoor leadership/education, physical education, science education, secondary education, social studies education, and Spanish adolescense education), ENGINEERING AND ENVIRONMENTAL DESIGN (engineering and environmental science), HEALTH PROFESSIONS (nursing), SOCIAL SCIENCE (biblical studies, biopsychology, child care/child and family studies, Chinese Studies, criminal justice, dietetics, economics, ethnic studies, family/consumer studies, history, interdisciplinary studies, ministries, peace studies, philosophy, political science/government, psychology, social work, sociology, Spanish studies, and theological studies). Engineering, nursing, and business administration have the largest enrollments.

ACTIVITIES: There are no fraternities or sororities. There are 79 groups on campus, including art, band, choir, chorale, chorus, dance, drama, environmental, ethnic, film, honors, international, jazz band, literary magazine, musical theater, newspaper, orchestra, political, professional, radio and TV, religious, social, social service, student government, symphony, and yearbook. Popular campus events include Cultural Series, Traveling Music Ensembles, and Theater Productions. **Sports:** There are 12 intercollegiate sports for men and 11 for women, and 5 intramural sports for men and 5 for women. Facilities include indoor and outdoor tracks, a pool, a wrestling area, weight room, numerous playing fields, and courts for racquetball, basketball, and tennis. **Graduates:** From July 1, 2016 to June 30, 2017, 606 bachelor's degrees were awarded. The most popular majors were engineering (11%), applied health science (6%), and business administration (6%). In an average class, 75% graduate in 4 years or less, 78% graduate in 5 years or less, and 78% graduate in 6 years or less. Of the 2016 graduating class, 14% were enrolled in graduate school within 6 months of graduation, and 84% were employed.

SERVICES: Counseling and information services are available, as is tutoring in most subjects. There is a reader service for the blind, and remedial math, reading, and writing. **Library/Resources:** The library contains 249,852 volumes, 7 microform items, and 22,030 audio/video tapes/CDs/DVDs, and subscribes to 116,041 periodicals including electronic. Computerized library services include interlibrary loans, database searching, Internet access, and Wi-Fi capability. Special learning facilities include an art gallery, natural history museum, and radio station. **Physically Challenged Students:** 80% of the campus is accessible. Facilities include wheelchair ramps, elevators, special parking, specially equipped restrooms, special class scheduling, lowered drinking fountains, and special housing. **Special:** Off-campus study is available through over 30 carefully selected programs on every continent (except Antarctica) and in a variety of major metropolitan cities around the world, including Paris and London, and in such diverse counties as Chile, China, India, and Lithuania. Off-campus options within the United States include the Contemporary Music Center in Nashville, the American Studies Program in Washington DC, the AuSable Institute of Environmental Studies, Los Angeles Film Studies, Oregon Extension, and others. Students may also spend a semester or year at any of 12 other Christian Consortium Colleges in a student exchange program. Numerous internships, practicum, and service opportunities are also available both domestically and around the globe, with an average of over 400 students traveling around the world each year through Messiah College. There are 5 national honor societies, a freshman honors program, and 26 departmental honors programs. **Visiting:** There are regularly scheduled orientations for prospective students, including a campus tour, academic and career advising, and a financial aid information session. There are guides for informal visits, visitors may sit in on classes, and stay overnight. To schedule a visit, contact the Admissions Office. **Campus Safety and Security:** Measures include 24-hour foot and vehicle patrol, emergency notification system, self-defense education, and security escort services. There are emergency telephones, lighted pathways/sidewalks, controlled access to dorms/residences, and text messaging alert system.

REQUIREMENTS: The SAT or ACT is required. Applicants must have graduated from an accredited high school or the equivalent. Course units from grades nine through twelve should include 4 units in academic English, 2 units (preferably 3 or more) in academic mathematics, 2 units (preferably 3 or more) in academic natural science, 2 or more units in academic social studies and foreign language and 4 units in additional electives. Most students who apply exceed the minimum requirements. The average high school GPA is 3.78, the average SAT total is 1206, and the average ACT composite is 26. An audition is required of all students who wish to major in dance, music, musical theatre or theatre. Admission to the Bachelor of Fine Arts requires a portfolio review. A campus visit with an information session is recommended. AP and CLEP credits are accepted. All students must complete at least 123 credits with a minimum GPA of 2.0. The last 30 credits must be taken at Messiah College and a minimum of 12 credits must be in the major. **Procedure:** Freshmen are admitted fall and spring. Entrance exams should be taken in the spring of the junior year. There are early admissions and rolling admissions plans. Application deadlines are open. The fall 2017 application fee was $50. Notification is sent on a rolling basis. Applications are accepted on-line. **Transfer Students:** 93 transfer students enrolled in 2016-2017. Transfer applicants should have earned a 2.5 GPA in at least 12 college credits. The college prefers that applicants seek a campus visit. Students with fewer than 24 credits in college should submit a high school transcript as well. 30 of 123 credits required for the bachelor's degree must be completed at Messiah. **International Students:** There are 131 international students enrolled. They must take the TOEFL with a minimum score of 550 on the paper-based TOEFL (PBT) or 80 on the Internet-based version (iBT). They must also take the SAT or ACT.

ADMISSIONS: 77% of the 2017-2018 applicants were accepted. The SAT scores for the 2017-2018 freshman class were: Math-- 8% below 500, 43% between 500 and 599, 37% between 600 and 699, and 11% between 700 and 800. Evidence-Based Reading/Writing-- 5% below 500, 39% between 500 and 599, 41% between 600 and 699, and 14% between 700 and 800. The ACT scores were 1% between 12 and 17, 31% between 18 and 23, 51% between 24 and 29, and 17% above 30. 56% of the current freshmen were in the top fifth of their class; 82% were in the top two fifths. 18 freshmen graduated first in their class. **Admissions Contact:** John Chopka, Vice President for Enrollment Management. Email: *admiss@messiah.edu* Web: *www.messiah.edu*

FINANCIAL AID: In 2017-2018, 100% of all full-time freshmen received some form of financial aid. 75% of all full-time freshmen received need-based aid. The average freshman award was $16,934.. 56% of undergraduate students work part-time. The average financial indebtedness of the 2017 graduate was $37,399. The FAFSA code is 003298. The priority date for freshman financial aid applications for fall entry is April 1.

MILLERSVILLE UNIVERSITY OF PENNSYLVANIA — E-4

www.millersville.edu

Millersville, PA 17551	**(717) 871-4625**
Fax: (717) 871-2147	**Email:** admissions@millersville.edu
Full-time: 2469 men, 3202 women	**Faculty:** 287
Part-time: 462 men, 645 women	**Ph.D.s:** 98%
Graduate: 249 men, 721 women	**Student/Faculty:** 20 to 1
Year: 4-1-4, summer session	**Tuition:** $11,858 ($21,560)
Room & Board: $13,440	**Freshman Class:** 5890 applied, 5329 accepted, 1351 enrolled
SAT EBR-W/M: 540/520 **ACT:** 22	**CEEB CODE:** 2656
Application Deadline: rolling	**COMPETITIVE**

Millersville University of Pennsylvania, founded in 1855, is one of the most highly regarded universities in the northeast region of the United States. MSU's mission is to provide diverse, dynamic, meaningful experiences to inspire learners to grow both intellectually and personally, and to enable them to contribute positively to local and global communities. Millersville is one of 14 universities within the PA State System of Higher Education with more than 100 programs to choose from. Students select Millersville for its academic reputation and array of academic programs that are supported by state-of-the-art science and industrial technology laboratories, art studios, writing and language laboratories. There are 3 undergraduate schools and 1 graduate school. In addition to regional accreditation, MUP has baccalaureate program accreditation with ABET, ACBSP, CSWE, NASAD, NASM, AACTE, ACEN, ACS, ATMAE, CAEP, CoARC, ITEEA, and NASP. The 250-acre campus is in a small town 5 miles southwest of Lancaster. Including any residence halls, there are 88 buildings.

STUDENT LIFE: 93% of undergraduates are from Pennsylvania. Others are from 34 states, 64 foreign countries, and Canada. 8% are African American; 74% White; 3% Asian American; 2% two or more races; 11% Hispanic; 1% Foreign; 1% race unknown. **Female To Male Ratio:** 1.4:1. The average age of freshmen is 18; all undergraduates, 22. 23% do not continue beyond their first year; 77% remain to graduate. **Housing:** 2233 students can be accommodated in college housing, which includes coed dorms, on-campus apartments, and off-campus apartments. In addition, there are honors houses, special-interest houses, apartments for single students, housing for international students, theme housing, wellness housing, and academic interest housing for several subject areas. University-affiliated apartments and dormitories for single students are adjacent to the campus. On-campus housing is available on a first-come, first-served basis, and is available on a lottery system for upperclassmen. 69% of students commute. Alcohol is not permitted. All students may keep cars.

FACULTY/CLASSROOMS: 48% of faculty are male; 52% are female. 87% teach undergraduates. No introductory courses are taught by graduate students. The average class size in an introductory lecture is 28; in a laboratory is 20; and in a regular course is 27.

PROGRAMS OF STUDY: MUP confers B.A., B.Des., B.S., B.F.A., B.S.Ed. and B.S.N. degrees. Associate, master's, and doctoral degrees are also awarded. Bachelor's degrees are awarded in AGRICULTURE (animal science and environmental studies), BIOLOGICAL SCIENCE (biochemistry, biology/biological science, biotechnology, botany, environmental biology, and marine biology), BUSINESS (accounting, business administration and management, business administration - international, business administration marketing, finance, and international business), COMMUNICATIONS AND THE ARTS (art, broadcasting, communication studies, English, English as a second/foreign language, English literature, English Writing, film, television and digital media, French, German, graphic communications, graphic design, journalism, linguistics, music, music technology, public relations, Spanish, communication arts-speech, and theatre acting), COMPUTER AND PHYSICAL SCIENCE (actuarial science, applied mathematics, atmospheric sciences and meteorology, chemistry, chemistry secondary education, computer science, earth science, environmental chemistry, environmental geology, geology, mathematics, oceanography, physics secondary education, physics, polymer science, quantitative methods, and statistics), EDUCATION (art education, athletic training, early childhood education, elementary education, English education, general studies, global studies, mathematics education, middle school education, music education, science education, social studies education, special education, special education/early child dual program, and technical education), ENGINEERING AND ENVIRONMENTAL DESIGN (construction management, drafting and design technology, engineering, industrial engineering technology, manufacturing technology, nuclear medicine technology, occupational safety and health, and robotic & mechatronic systems engineering), HEALTH PROFESSIONS (allied health, biology, medical technology, nursing, preoptometry, prepharmacy, prepodiatry, respiratory therapy, and sports medicine), SOCIAL SCIENCE (anthropology, archeology, criminology, economics, geography, history, interdisciplinary studies, international studies, philosophy, political science/government, psychology, social studies, social work, and sociology). Applied engineering technology is the strongest academically. Business administration, biology, and special education preK-8/early childhood preK-4 dual major have the largest enrollments.

ACTIVITIES: 4% of men belong to 8 national fraternities; 4% of women belong to 6 national sororities. There are 198 groups on campus, including art, band, cheerleading, choir, chorale, chorus, communications, computers, dance, drama, environmental, ethnic, film, honors, international, jazz band, LGBT, literary magazine, marching band, musical theater, newspaper, orchestra, political, professional, radio and TV, religious, social, social service, student government, and symphony. Popular campus events include Organization Outbreak, Homecoming, Superfest, Spring Concert, PrideFest, Wellness Fair/Breast-A-Ville, Greek Week, MultiCultural Showcase, Marauder Malooza, and Marauder's Lead sessions. **Sports:** There are 7 intercollegiate sports for men and 12 for women, and 20 intramural sports for men and 20 for women. Facilities include football a stadium, soccer field, softball and baseball fields, 2 pools, 2 gymnasiums, 2 fitness centers, dance studio, ropes course, wrestling and weight rooms, basketball, volleyball, tennis, and badminton courts, indoor & outdoor running track, and golf course. **Graduates:** From July 1, 2016 to June 30, 2017, 1493 bachelor's degrees were awarded. The most popular majors were business administration

(12%), speech communication (9%), and psychology (8%). In an average class, 37% graduate in 4 years or less, 57% graduate in 5 years or less, and 62% graduate in 6 years or less.

SERVICES: Counseling and information services are available, as is tutoring in most subjects. There is a reader service for the blind, and remedial math and writing. Every effort is made to tailor tutoring services to individual needs. **Library/Resources:** The library contains 324,236 volumes, 81,132 microform items, and 4,604 audio/video tapes/CDs/DVDs, and subscribes to 396,189 periodicals including electronic. Computerized library services include interlibrary loans, database searching, Internet access, and Wi-Fi capability. Special learning facilities include an art gallery, radio station, TV station, recording studio, teleconferencing center, weather information center, foreign language lab, 2 performing arts centers - Winter and Ware, Atmospheric Research and Aerostat Facility, Center for Disaster Research & Education, Foucault Pendulum, Chincoteague Bay Field Station at the Marine Science Consortium, Servicemembers Opportunity Colleges Consortium (SOCC), aircraft flight simulators, and safety engineering and training modules. **Physically Challenged Students:** 85% of the campus is accessible. Facilities include wheelchair ramps, elevators, special parking, specially equipped restrooms, special class scheduling, lowered drinking fountains, lowered telephones, and special housing. **Special:** Numerous co-ops and internship programs, including student teaching opportunities, are available. Millersville has formal agreements, e.g. cross-registration, with the following institutions: West Chester University, Shippensburg University, Kutztown University, Franklin and Marshall College, Harrisburg Area Commuity College, Reading Area Community College, Lancaster Theological Seminary, Chincoteague Bay Field Station at the Marine Science Consortium, and Servicemembers Opportunity Colleges Consortium (SOCC). There are also 3-2 and 4-2 programs with Penn State University, the University of Southern California, and the University of Delaware. Study abroad is offered in Australia, Chile, China, France, Germany, Japan, South Africa, Spain, and United Kingdom. Dual majors, student-designed majors, and accelerated degrees are possible in most disciplines. There are 17 national honor societies, a freshman honors program, and 17 departmental honors programs. **Visiting:** There are regularly scheduled orientations for prospective students, campus information sessions, and tours are offered on a daily basis, open houses, off-campus decision days, department sessions, and virtual tours. There are also special group visits and info sessions in Spanish throughout the year. There are guides for informal visits and visitors may sit in on classes. To schedule a visit, contact the Office of Admissions. **Campus Safety and Security:** Measures include 24-hour foot and vehicle patrol, emergency notification system, self-defense education, and security escort services. There are shuttle buses, emergency telephones, lighted pathways/sidewalks, controlled access to dorms/residences, emergency notification system, crime awareness programs & timely warning alerts, self-defense education, shuttle buses, lighted pathways/sidewalks, threat assessment team (online incident report), and LiveSafe.

REQUIREMENTS: To be considered for admission one must be a graduate of an approved secondary school or hold a GED high school equivalency diploma. Traditional students applying directly from high school must have completed a college preparatory curriculum. Generally, the student's academic program should include 4 units of English, 3 units or more of mathematics, science, and social science. Also required are satisfactory scores on the SAT or ACT. Auditions are required for music majors, portfolios are required for art majors, and an associate degree in Nursing or Diploma and RN license is required for the nursing program. MUP requires applicants to be in the upper 40% of their class. A GPA of 2.0 is required. AP and CLEP credits are accepted. Important factors in the admissions decision are advanced placement or honors courses, recommendations by alumni, and leadership record. All students must complete at least 120 hours, demonstrating proficiency in mathematics and English and maintaining a minimum of 2.0 GPA. Students must complete the general education program and complete specific courses in physical education, fundamentals of speech, writing, and cultural diversity and community. **Procedure:** Freshmen are admitted to all sessions. Entrance exams should be taken during spring of the junior year. There are early admissions, deferred admissions, and rolling admissions plans. Application deadlines are open. The fall 2017 application fee was $50. Notification is sent on a rolling basis. 275 applicants were on the 2017 waiting list; 95 were admitted. Applications are accepted on-line. **Transfer Students:** 862 transfer students enrolled in 2016-2017. All transfer applicants must submit a college transcript, essay or personal statement, and a statement of good standing. Some are required to submit a high school transcript and standardized test scores. The students review is based on course selection and performance at previous college. Preference is given to students with 2.5 GPA or higher, and to graduates of in-state community colleges and students transferring from other PA State System of Higher Education Schools. 30 of 120 credits required for the bachelor's degree must be completed at MUP. **International Students:** There are 47 international students enrolled. They must take the TOEFL with a minimum score of 550 on the paper-based TOEFL (PBT) or 70 on the Internet-based version (iBT). MUP will accept the IELTS with a minimum score of 6. Students must also take the SAT or ACT.

ADMISSIONS: 90% of the 2017-2018 applicants were accepted. The SAT scores for the 2017-2018 freshman class were: Math-- 31% below 500, 52% between 500 and 599, 15% between 600 and 699, and 2% between 700 and 800. Evidence-Based Reading/Writing-- 26% below 500, 51% between 500 and 599, 20% between 600 and 699, and 3% between 700 and 800. The ACT scores were 17% between 12 and 17, 49% between 18 and 23, 28% between 24 and 29, and 6% above 30. 15% of the current freshmen were in the top fifth of their class; 36% were in the top two fifths. 1 freshman graduated first in the class. **Admissions Contact:** Katy Ferrier, Director of Admissions. Email: *admissions@millersville.edu* Web: *www.millersville.edu*

FINANCIAL AID: In 2017-2018, 88% of all full-time freshmen received some form of financial aid. 65% of all full-time freshmen received need-based aid. The average freshman award was $15,719. Need-based scholarships or need-based grants averaged $5,250 ($14,541 maximum); need-based self-help aid (loans and jobs) averaged $3,307 ($7,464 maximum); non-need-based athletic scholarships averaged $3,298 ($16,367 maximum); and other non-need-based awards and non-need-based scholarships averaged $8,122 ($32,210 maximum). The average financial indebtedness of the 2017 graduate was $31,476. The FAFSA code is 003325. The priority date for freshman financial aid applications for fall entry is March 15.

MISERICORDIA UNIVERSITY — E-2

www.misericordia.edu

Dallas, PA 18612	**(570) 674-6400** **(866) 262-6363**
Fax: (570) 675-2441	**Email: admiss@misericordia.edu**
Full-time: 594 men, 1066 women	**Faculty:** 111; IIA, -$
Part-time: 109 men, 377 women	**Ph.D.s:** 78%
Graduate: 158 men, 460 women	**Student/Faculty:** 15 to 1
Year: semesters, summer session	**Tuition:** $31,660
Room & Board: $13,550	**Freshman Class:** 1740 applied, 1371 accepted, 435 enrolled
SAT CR/M: 560/550 **ACT:** 23	**CEEB CODE:** 2087
Application Deadline: n/av	**COMPETITIVE**

Misericordia University, founded in 1924, by the Sisters of Mercy, is a private liberal arts institution affiliated with the Roman Catholic Church that offers professional programs in health-related fields. There are 3 undergraduate schools. In addition to regional accreditation, MU has baccalaureate program accreditation with APTA, ASLA, CAHEA, CSWE, ACOTE, CCNE, JRCERT, and IACBE. The 120-acre campus is in a suburban area 9 miles north of Wilkes-Barre, PA. Including any residence halls, there are 22 buildings.

STUDENT LIFE: 74% of undergraduates are from Pennsylvania. Others are from 29 states, and 1 foreign country. 88% are from public schools. 87% are White; 4% race unknown; 3% African American; 3% Hispanic; 2% two or more races; 1% Asian American. 47% are Catholic; 20% Protestant; 17% claim no religious affiliation; 14% Christian, Buddhist, and Hindu. **Female To Male Ratio:** 2.2:1. The average age of freshmen is 18; all undergraduates, 24. 15% do not continue beyond their first year; 74% remain to graduate. **Housing:** 993 students can be accommodated in college housing, which includes dorms, and special-interest houses. On-campus housing is guaranteed for the freshman year only, is available on a first-come, first-served basis, and is available on a lottery system for upperclassmen. 57% of students live on campus. Upperclassmen may keep cars.

FACULTY/CLASSROOMS: 41% of faculty are male; 59% are female. 80% teach undergraduates, 10% do research, and 10% do both. No introductory courses are taught by graduate students. The average class size in an introductory lecture is 19; in a laboratory is 14; and in a regular course is 19.

PROGRAMS OF STUDY: MU confers B.A., B.S., B.S.N., and B.S.W. degrees. Master's and doctoral degrees are also awarded. Bachelor's degrees are awarded in BIOLOGICAL SCIENCE (biochemistry and biology/biological science), BUSINESS (accounting, business administration and management, and sports management), COMMUNICATIONS AND THE ARTS (communications and English), COMPUTER AND PHYSICAL SCIENCE (chemistry, computer science, information sciences and systems, and mathematics), EDUCATION (early childhood education and middle school education), HEALTH PROFESSIONS (health care administration, medical laboratory technology, nursing, occupational therapy, physical therapy, radiograph medical technology, and speech therapy), SOCIAL SCIENCE (history, liberal arts/general studies, philosophy, psychology, and social work). Occupational therapy, physical therapy, and speech language pathology are the strongest academically. Nursing, business, and occupational therapy have the largest enrollments.

ACTIVITIES: There are no fraternities or sororities. There are 41 groups on campus, including art, cheerleading, choir, chorale, chorus, drama, environmental, ethnic, honors, international, literary magazine, musical theater, newspaper, political, professional, radio and TV, religious, social service, and student government. Popular campus events include Winter Snowball Dance, Homecoming, and Spring Fest. **Sports:** There are 11 intercollegiate sports for men and 11 for women, and 14 intramural sports for men and 14 for women. Facilities include an outdoor athletics complex, a field house, softball, 6 tennis courts, basketball, volleyball, a six-lane swimming pool, indoor track, racquetball courts, fitness center and an aerobic/dance studio, football, soccer, field hockey, lacrosse, and track & field. **Graduates:** From July 1, 2016 to June 30, 2017, 514 bachelor's degrees were awarded. The most popular majors were nursing (18%), business (14%), and medical imaging (5%). In an average class, 68% graduate in 4 years or less, 74% graduate in 5 years or less, and 74% graduate in 6 years or less. Of the 2016 graduating class, 21% were enrolled in graduate school within 6 months of graduation, and 85% were employed.

SERVICES: Counseling and information services are available, as is tutoring in every subject. There is a reader service for the blind. Services for students with disabilities are provided through the Alternative Learners Program. **Library/Resources:** The library contains 80,125 volumes, 4,219 microform items, and 8,153 audio/video tapes/CDs/DVDs, and subscribes to 178 periodicals including electronic. Computerized library services include interlibrary loans, database searching, Internet access, and Wi-Fi capability. Special learning facilities include an art gallery and radio station. **Physically Challenged Students:** 95% of the campus is accessible. Facilities include wheelchair ramps, elevators, special parking, specially equipped restrooms, special class scheduling, and lowered drinking fountains. **Special:** Students may cross-register with King's College and Wilkes University. The college offers internships, work-study programs, study abroad, an accelerated degree program in Business, Government Law and National Security, Applied Behavioral Science, and Nursing for adult students, and a student-designed major. Credit may be granted for life, military, and work experience through prior learning assessment. Nondegree study is also available. The college offers an alternative learner's project, which accepts a limited number of learning disabled students each year. There are 10 national honor societies, a freshman honors program, and 3 departmental honors programs. **Visiting:** There are regularly scheduled orientations for prospective students, meetings with admissions and financial aid counselors, a tour of the campus, and optional meetings with faculty and coaches. There are guides for informal visits, visitors may sit in on classes, and stay overnight. To schedule a visit, contact Donna Cerza at (570) 675-6264. **Campus Safety and Security:** Measures include 24-hour foot and vehicle patrol, emergency notification system, and security escort services. There are shuttle buses, emergency telephones, lighted pathways/sidewalks, and controlled access to dorms/residences.

REQUIREMENTS: The SAT is required. Applicants must graduate from an accredited secondary school or have a GED. 16 Carnegie units must be earned, and students must complete 3 years each in English, math, history, and science, and 2 to 3 years in social studies. Applicants are required to be in the upper 50% of their class. A GPA of 2.0 is required. AP and CLEP credits are accepted. Important factors in the admissions decision are extracurricular activities record, advanced placement or honors courses, and leadership record. To graduate, students must earn a minimum of 120 credits. The required core curriculum includes courses in behavioral science, English literature, fine arts, history, math, philosophy, religious studies, and natural science. Within the core curriculum, students must complete 1 university writing seminar, and 2 additional courses that are writing intensive. **Procedure:** Freshmen are admitted in the fall and spring. Entrance exams should be taken during the junior year. There are deferred admissions and rolling admissions plans. Application deadlines are open. The fall 2017 application fee was $35. Applications are accepted online. **Transfer Students:** 67 transfer students enrolled in 2016-2017. Applicants must have a minimum GPA of 2.0. Requirements may be higher for selected majors. 30 of 120 credits required for the bachelor's degree must be completed at Misericordia. **International Students:** There are 3 international students enrolled. They must take the TOEFL with a minimum score of 500 on the paper-based TOEFL (PBT) or 75 on the Internet-based version (iBT).

ADMISSIONS: 79% of the 2017-2018 applicants were accepted. The SAT scores for the 2017-2018 freshman class were: Critical Reading-- 17% below 500, 53% between 500 and 599, 27% between 600 and 699, and 3% between 700 and 800. Math-- 16% below 500, 59% between 500 and 599, 23% between 600 and 699, and 2% between 700 and 800. The ACT scores were 7% between 12 and 17, 45% between 18 and 23, 48% between 24 and 29, and 0% above 30. 41% of the current freshmen were in the top fifth of their class; 71% were in the top two fifths. 2 freshmen graduated first in their class. **Admissions Contact:** Donna Cerza, Director of Admissions. Email: *admiss@misericordia.edu* Web: *www.misericordia.edu*

FINANCIAL AID: In 2017-2018, 100% of all full-time freshmen received some form of financial aid. 70% of all full-time freshmen received need-based aid. The average freshman award was $32,706. Need-based scholarships or need-based grants averaged $6,242 ($37,890 maximum); need-based self-help aid (loans and jobs) averaged $3,630 ($7,500 maximum); other non-need-based awards and non-need-based scholarships averaged $18,070 ($31,030 maximum); and $10,670 from other forms of aid. The average financial indebtedness of the 2017 graduate was $35,140. MU is a member of CSS. The college's own financial statement is required. The FAFSA code is 003247. The priority date for freshman financial aid applications for fall entry is March 1.

MOORE COLLEGE OF ART AND DESIGN *(The complete profile is made available exclusively on our website, www.barronspac.com)*

MORAVIAN COLLEGE — F-3

www.moravian.edu

Bethlehem, PA 18018	**(610) 625-7115** **(800) 441-3191**
Fax: (610) 625-7930	**Email: admissions@moravian.edu**
Full-time: 761 men, 1076 women	**Faculty:** 137; IIB, av$
Part-time: 67 men, 126 women	**Ph.D.s:** 87%
Graduate: 118 men, 312 women	**Student/Faculty:** 12 to 1
Year: semesters, summer session	**Tuition:** $42,164
Room & Board: $13,324	**Freshman Class:** 3059 applied, 2324 accepted, 484 enrolled
SAT CR/M: 554/546 **ACT:** 24	**CEEB CODE:** 2418
Application Deadline: March 1	**COMPETITIVE**

As America's sixth-oldest college, Moravian College has been a little revolutionary from the start. MC believes in the power of the liberal arts, which means students have the freedom to own their education, and choose from more than 50 academic programs. Students get hands-on, in-the field opportunities, like helping elephants in Thailand and interning with NASA. They work one-on-one with professors on SOAR (Student Opportunities for Academic Research) projects, and study abroad in nearly 20 countries. There are 2 undergraduate schools and 3 graduate schools. In addition to regional accreditation, MC has baccalaureate program accreditation with ACBSP, CAHEA, NASM, ACS, and CCNE. The 85-acre campus is in a suburban area in historic Bethlehem, 60 miles north of Philadelphia and 90 miles west of New York City. Including any residence halls, there are 73 buildings.

STUDENT LIFE: 69% of undergraduates are from Pennsylvania. Others are from 22 states, and 16 foreign countries. 90% are from public schools. 70% are White; 6% Foreign; 5% African American; 4% race unknown; 2% Asian American; 2% two or more races; 11% Hispanic. **Female To Male Ratio:** 1.6:1. The average age of freshmen is 18; all undergraduates, 20. 18% do not continue beyond their first year; 63% remain to graduate. **Housing:** 1093 students can be accommodated in college housing, which includes gender neutral, single-sex, coed dorms, and on-campus apartments. In addition, there are special-interest houses, fraternity houses, sorority houses, and townhouses. On-campus housing is guaranteed for all 4 years. 65% of students live on campus. Upperclassmen may keep cars.

FACULTY/CLASSROOMS: 45% of faculty are male; 55% are female. All teach undergraduates and all do research. No introductory courses are taught by graduate students. The average class size in an introductory lecture is 19; in a laboratory is 15; and in a regular course is 17.

PROGRAMS OF STUDY: MC confers B.A., B.S. and B.Mus. degrees. Master's and doctoral degrees are also awarded. Bachelor's degrees are awarded in AGRICULTURE (environmental studies and natural resource/environmental economics), BIOLOGICAL SCIENCE (biochemistry, biology/biological science, and neurosciences), BUSINESS (accounting, business administration and management, business economics, international business management, management, and nonprofit/public organization management), COMMUNICATIONS AND THE ARTS (art, art history and appreciation, English, French, French and Francophone studies, German, German studies, music, and Spanish), COMPUTER AND PHYSICAL SCIENCE (chemistry, computer science, geology, mathematics, physics/general science secondary education, and physics), EDUCATION (art education, early childhood education, elementary education, middle level education, music education, and secondary education), ENGINEERING AND ENVIRONMENTAL DESIGN (environmental science), HEALTH PROFESSIONS (global & public health sciences, health science, nursing, and public health), SOCIAL SCIENCE (economics, history, philosophy, political science/government, psychology, religion, and sociology). Nursing, biochemistry, neuroscience, and computer science are the strongest academically. Management, nursing, and sociology have the largest enrollments.

ACTIVITIES: 10% of men belong to 1 local and 3 national fraternities; 22% of women belong to 4 national sororities. There are 85 groups on campus, including art, band, cheerleading, choir, chorale, chorus, communications, computers, dance, debate, drama, environmental, ethnic, honors, international, jazz band, LGBT, literary magazine, marching band, newspaper, orchestra, outdoor recreation, pep band, photography, political, professional, religious, radio, social, social service, student government, symphony, and yearbook. Popular campus events include Arts and Lectures series, InFocus, Christmas Vespers Services, Heritage Day, and Spring Fest. **Sports:** There are 10 intercollegiate sports for men and 10 for women, and 9 intramural sports for men and 9 for women. Facilities include a gym, football, soccer, field hockey, lacrosse fields, baseball and softball diamonds, indoor and all-weather tracks, indoor and outdoor tennis courts, a field house, a fitness room center, a performance center, basketball, cross country, golf, cheerleading, volleyball, an aerobics and dance studio, and multipurpose courts. **Graduates:** From July 1, 2016 to June 30, 2017, 421 bachelor's degrees were awarded. The most popular majors were nursing (22%), management (12%), and sociology (7%). In an average class, 1% graduate in 3 years or less, 59% graduate in 4 years or less, 63% graduate in 5 years or less, and 63% graduate in 6 years or less. Of the 2016 graduating class, 20% were enrolled in graduate school within 6 months of graduation, and 76% were employed.

SERVICES: Counseling and information services are available, as is tutoring in most subjects. There is a reader service for the blind. The Academic & Accessibility Support Center coordinates services and support for students with documented learning disabilities. **Library/Resources:** The library contains 220,954 volumes, 1,361 microform items, and 5,558 audio/video tapes/CDs/DVDs, and subscribes to 2,682 periodicals including electronic. Computerized library services include interlibrary loans, database searching, Internet access, and Wi-Fi capability. Special learning facilities include an art gallery, and SOAR (student opportunities for academic research). **Physically Challenged Students:** Facilities include wheelchair ramps, elevators, special parking, specially equipped restrooms, special class scheduling, lowered drinking fountains, lowered telephones, and special housing. **Special:** The college offers 3-2 engineering degrees in conjunction with Washington University and a 4-1 engineering program with Lehigh University. MC also offers cooperative programs in allied health, natural resource management, and geology with Lehigh, Duke, and Thomas Jefferson Universities. Cross-registration is available with Lehigh and DeSales Universities and Lafayette, Muhlenberg, and Cedar Crest Colleges. There is an accelerated BS Nursing program. There are also internships, co-ops for computer science and business students, study abroad in many countries, a Washington semester, and student-designed majors. There are 21 national honor societies and 30 departmental honors programs. **Visiting:** There are regularly scheduled orientations for prospective students, including information sessions, tours and interviews with admissions staff. There are guides for informal visits, visitors may sit in on classes, and stay overnight. To schedule a visit, contact Kim Shank at shankk@moravian.edu. **Campus Safety and Security:** Measures include 24-hour foot and vehicle patrol, emergency notification system, self-defense education, and security escort services. There are shuttle buses, emergency telephones, lighted pathways/sidewalks, controlled access to dorms/residences, and an ongoing crime prevention program supervised by a crime prevention officer.

REQUIREMENTS: The SAT or ACT is required. Applicants must graduate from an accredited secondary school or have a GED. Moravian requires 16 Carnegie units, based on 4 years each of English and social science, 3 year of math, (4 if majoring in economics and business) 3 years of natural science, (2 must include a lab), and 2 of same foreign language, and electives (for liberal arts program). Essays are required and interviews are recommended. For music students, auditions are required; for art students, portfolios and a completed application form. AP and CLEP credits are accepted. Important factors in the admissions decision are advanced placement or honors courses, extracurricular activities record, recommendations by school officials, and leadership record. To graduate, students must complete a Learning in Common curriculum, which includes courses in writing, quantitative reasoning, historical studies, ultimate questions, cultural values and global issues, natural sciences, a foreign language, social sciences, aesthetic expression, literature, moral life, and phys ed. They must maintain a minimum GPA of 2.0 and complete 32 courses equivalent to 128 credits. The number of hours required in the major varies. **Procedure:** Freshmen are admitted in the fall and spring. Entrance exams should be taken and received by March 1. There are deferred admissions and rolling admissions plans. Applications should be filed by March 1 for fall entry; November 15 for spring entry. Notifications are sent November 15. Applications are accepted on-line. **Transfer Students:** 83 transfer students enrolled in 2016-2017. Applicants must have a minimum GPA of 3.0 and are required to submit recommendations, secondary and postsecondary transcripts, and standardized test scores. 48 of 128 credits required for the bachelor's degree must be completed at MC. **International Students:** There are 111 international students enrolled. They must take the TOEFL, and the IELTS. The SAT or ACT is preferred for all students and required if the student's first language is English.

ADMISSIONS: 76% of the 2017-2018 applicants were accepted. The SAT scores for the 2017-2018 freshman class were: Critical Reading--18% below 500, 56% between 500 and 599, 23% between 600 and 699, and 3% between 700 and 800. Math-- 21% below 500, 53% between 500 and 599, 24% between 600 and 699, and 2% between 700 and 800. **Admissions Contact:** Scott Myers, Director of Undergraduate Admission. Email: *myersj02@moravian.edu* Web: *www.moravian.edu*

FINANCIAL AID: In 2017-2018, 99% of all full-time freshmen received some form of financial aid. 82% of all full-time freshmen received need-based aid. The average freshman award was $27,056. 43% of undergraduate students work part-time. The average financial indebtedness of the 2017 graduate was $33,096. The FAFSA code is 003301. The priority date for freshman financial aid applications for fall entry is February 14.

MOUNT ALOYSIUS COLLEGE C-3

www.mtaloy.edu

Cresson, PA 16630	**(814) 886-6383** **(888) 823-2220**
Fax: (814) 886-6441	**Email: admissions@mtaloy.edu**
Full-time: 385 men, 881 women	**Faculty:** 68
Part-time: 78 men, 267 women	**Ph.D.s:** 44%
Graduate: 11 men, 27 women	**Student/Faculty:** 18 to 1
Year: semesters, summer session	**Tuition:** $20,790
Room & Board: $9186	**Freshman Class:** 1189 applied, 850 accepted, 338 enrolled
SAT or ACT: required	**CEEB CODE:** 2420
Application Deadline: August 3	**COMPETITIVE**

Mount Aloysius College is a comprehensive private, Catholic, coeducational, liberal arts and sciences institution offering undergraduate and graduate education with an emphasis on career preparation and Mercy values. There are 3 undergraduate schools and 1 graduate school. In addition to regional accreditation, MAC has baccalaureate program accreditation with APTA, NLN, CAPTE, CAAHEP, and NAACLS. The 220-acre campus is in a small town in the southern Allegheny Mountains between Altoona and Johnstown. Including any residence halls, there are 14 buildings.

STUDENT LIFE: 90% of undergraduates are from Pennsylvania. Others are from 20 states, 15 foreign countries, and Canada. 80% are from public schools. 94% are White; 3% African American; 1% Asian American; 1% Hispanic; 1% Foreign. 40% are Catholic; 35% Protestant. **Female To Male Ratio:** 2.5:1. The average age of freshmen is 19; all undergraduates, 25. 30% do not continue beyond their first year; 60% remain to graduate. **Housing:** 545 students can be accommodated in college housing, which includes dorms, on-campus apartments, and off-campus apartments. In addition, there are special-interest houses, and Christian Living Community. On-campus housing is guaranteed for all 4 years, is available on a first-come, and first-served basis. 60% of students commute. Alcohol is not permitted. All students may keep cars.

FACULTY/CLASSROOMS: 39% of faculty are male; 61% are female. All teach undergraduates, and all do research. No introductory courses are taught by graduate students. The average class size in an introductory lecture is 17; in a laboratory is 12; and in a regular course is 17.

PROGRAMS OF STUDY: MAC confers B.A. and B.S. degrees. Associate and master's degrees are also awarded. Bachelor's degrees are awarded in BIOLOGICAL SCIENCE (biology/biological science, biotechnology, and environmental biology), BUSINESS (accounting, business administration and management, business economics, entrepreneurial studies, human resources, management information systems, management science, marketing management, nonprofit/public organization management, organizational leadership and management, and small business management), COMMUNICATIONS AND THE ARTS (American Sign Language, choral music, English, and voice), COMPUTER AND PHYSICAL SCIENCE (computer security and information assurance, information sciences and systems, radiological technology, science, and web technology), EDUCATION (childhood education, early childhood education, education, elementary education, English education, middle school education, science education, secondary education, and social studies education), ENGINEERING AND ENVIRONMENTAL DESIGN (computational sciences and environmental science), HEALTH PROFESSIONS (allied health, chiropractic, health care administration, medical laboratory technology, medical technology, nuclear medical technology, nursing, nursing home administration, occupational therapy, physical therapy, physical therapy assistant, physician's assistant, preallied health, predentistry, premedicine, preoptometry, preosteopathy, prepharmacy, prephysical therapy, prepodiatry, preventive/wellness health care, preveterinary science, radiation therapy, radiograph medical technology, radiological science, and ultrasound technology), SOCIAL SCIENCE (behavioral science, child care/child and family studies, community psychology, criminal justice, criminology, history, humanities, humanities and social science, interpreter for the deaf, law, law enforcement and corrections, liberal arts/general studies, paralegal studies, political science/government, prelaw, psychology, public administration, religion, social studies, and women's studies). Nursing, medical imaging, and allied health sciences are the strongest academically. Nursing, medical imaging, and business have the largest enrollments.

ACTIVITIES: There are no fraternities or sororities. There are 100 groups on campus, including art, band, campus ministry (community service organization) and all academic majors have a club, cheerleading, choir, chorale, chorus, computers, dance, drama, environmental, ethnic, forensics, honors, international, musical theater, newspaper, photography, political, professional, religious, social, social service, student government, and yearbook. Popular campus events include Madrigal Dinner, Heritage days, Mountie Madness, and Christmas at MAC. **Sports:** There are 6 intercollegiate sports for men and 8 for women, and 13 intramural sports for men and 12 for women. Facilities include an athletic convocation and wellness center with floating gym floor, an auxillary gym, and weight-and-exercise rooms. **Graduates:** From July 1, 2016 to June 30, 2017, 176 bachelor's degrees were awarded. The most popular majors were nursing (28%), business administration (14%), and criminology (10%). In an average class, 27% graduate in 3 years or less, 45% graduate in 4 years or less, 50% graduate in 5 years or less, and 51% graduate in 6 years or less. Of the 2016 graduating class, 22% were enrolled in graduate school within 6 months of graduation, and 97% were employed.

SERVICES: Counseling and information services are available, as is tutoring in every subject. There is remedial math, reading, and writing. **Library/Resources:** The library contains 77,186 volumes, 4,680 microform items, and 2,431 audio/video tapes/CDs/DVDs, and subscribes to 275 periodicals including electronic. Computerized library services include interlibrary loans, database searching, Internet access, and Wi-Fi capability. Special learning facilities include an art gallery. **Physically Challenged Students:** All of the campus is accessible. Facilities include wheelchair ramps, elevators, special parking, specially equipped restrooms, special class scheduling, lowered drinking fountains, lowered telephones, and special housing. **Special:** The Professional Studies curriculum provides a student-designed course of study, with an emphasis in behavior and social science, humanities, math/science/computer science, or prelaw. B.A.-B.S. degrees are offered, as are internships in nursing, business, criminology, and student teaching. Our education department offers early level pre K-4/middle level 4-8, and secondary education. There are 3 national honor societies, a freshman honors program, and 1 departmental honors program. **Visiting:** There are regularly scheduled orientations for prospective students, on the hour and select Saturdays. There are guides for informal visits, visitors may sit in on classes, and stay overnight. To schedule a visit, contact the Admissions Office. **Campus Safety and Security:** Measures include 24-hour foot and vehicle patrol, emergency notification system, self-defense education, and security escort services. There are shuttle buses, emergency telephones, lighted pathways/sidewalks, and controlled access to dorms/residences.

REQUIREMENTS: The SAT or ACT is required. Applicants must graduate from an accredited high school or have the GED. A placement test and any necessary developmental studies classes may need to be taken. Science classes and an interview are required of some allied health programs. AP and CLEP credits are accepted. Important factors in the admissions decision are recommendations by school officials, advanced placement or honors courses, and leadership record. Baccalaureate-level students are required during their final semester of study to complete 2 3-credit courses designed to integrate and synthesize scientific, behavioral, and moral concepts. Students in allied health programs must complete an approved clinical experience. Courses in research writing and speech are required. A total of 120 credits is required with an overall 2.0 GPA, including a C average in all core courses. **Procedure:** Freshmen are admitted in the fall and spring. Entrance exams should be taken as early as possible. There is a rolling admissions plan. Applications should be filed by August 3 for fall entry. The fall 2017 application fee was $30. Notifications are sent in weekly. Applications are accepted on-line. **Transfer Students:** 250 transfer students enrolled in 2016-2017. Transfer students must have a 2.0 GPA. Only courses with a C or better will be considered for transfer; all other requirements are the same as for freshmen. 30 of 120 credits required for the bachelor's degree must be completed at MAC. **International Students:** There are 23 international students enrolled. They must take the TOEFL with a minimum score of 500 on the paper-based TOEFL (PBT) or 61 on the Internet-based version (iBT). Students must take the Comprehensive English Language Test. They must also take the SAT or ACT, and the New Jersey Basic Skills Test.

ADMISSIONS: 71% of the 2017-2018 applicants were accepted. 5 freshmen graduated first in their class. **Admissions Contact:** Francis Crouse, Vice President for Enrollment Management. Email: *admissions@mtaloy.edu* Web: *www.mtaloy.edu*

FINANCIAL AID: In 2017-2018, 94% of all full-time freshmen received some form of financial aid. 85% of all full-time freshmen received need-based aid. The average freshman award was $11,000. Need-based scholarships or need-based grants averaged $3,000 ($5,000 maximum); need-based self-help aid (loans and jobs) averaged $3,000 ($5,000 maximum); and other non-need-based awards and non-need-based scholarships averaged $3,000 ($7,000 maximum). 65% of undergraduate students work part-time. The average financial indebtedness of the 2017 graduate was $17,125. MAC is a member of CSS. The FAFSA code is 003302. The priority date for freshman financial aid applications for fall entry is April 1. The deadline for filing freshman financial aid applications for fall entry is May 1.

MUHLENBERG COLLEGE E-3
www.muhlenberg.edu

Allentown, PA 18104 **(484) 664-3200**

Fax: (484) 664-3234 **Email:** admissions@muhlenberg.edu
Full-time: 924 men, 1383 women
Part-time: 37 men, 53 women
Graduate: n/av
Year: semesters, summer session
Room & Board: $10,770
Faculty: 177
Ph.D.s: 85%
Student/Faculty: 11 to 1
Tuition: $45,875
Freshman Class: 5015 applied, 2426 accepted, 582 enrolled
SAT CR/M/W: 605/613/604 **ACT:** required
CEEB CODE: 2424
Application Deadline: February 15
VERY COMPETITIVE

Muhlenberg College, founded in 1848, is an independent, undergraduate, coeducational institution related to the Evangelical Lutheran Church in America. Muhlenberg's mission is to provide a liberal arts education in the Judeo-Christian humanistic tradition, and is committed to the highest standards of academic integrity and excellence. As a liberal arts college, Muhlenberg offers programs in the humanities, the natural and social sciences, and in professional areas such as business, education, pre-medical, pre-theological, and pre-law studies. Flexibility is provided through course options and opportunities for independent study, research and internships, and through a plan for self-designed majors. There is 1 undergraduate school. The 82-acre campus is in a suburban area 50 miles north of Philadelphia and 90 miles west of New York City. Including any residence halls, there are 102 buildings.

STUDENT LIFE: 73% of undergraduates are from out of state, mostly the Middle Atlantic. Students are from 31 states, 18 foreign countries, and Canada. 74% are from public schools. 75% are White; 7% Hispanic; 7% race unknown; 3% African American; 3% Asian American; 3% Foreign; 2% two or more races. 30% are Catholic; 29% Jewish; 13% claim no religious affiliation. **Female To Male Ratio:** 1.5:1. The average age of freshmen is 18; all undergraduates, 21. 7% do not continue beyond their first year; 85% remain to graduate. **Housing:** 2006 students can be accommodated in college housing, which includes dorms, on-campus apartments, and off-campus apartments. In addition, there are language/international houses, special-interest houses, and fraternity houses. There are also college-owned houses in the surrounding community. On-campus housing is guaranteed for all 4 years. 92% of students live on campus. Upperclassmen may keep cars.

FACULTY/CLASSROOMS: 50% of faculty are male; 50% are female. All teach undergraduates, 84% do research, and 84% do both. No introductory courses are taught by graduate students. The average class size in an introductory lecture is 26; in a laboratory is 16; and in a regular course is 19.

PROGRAMS OF STUDY: Muhlenberg confers B.A. and B.S. degrees. Associate degrees are also awarded. Bachelor's degrees are awarded in BIOLOGICAL SCIENCE (biochemistry, biology/biological science, and neurosciences), BUSINESS (accounting, banking and finance, and business administration and management), COMMUNICATIONS AND THE ARTS (art, communications, dance, dramatic arts, English, film arts, French, German, music, and Spanish), COMPUTER AND PHYSICAL SCIENCE (chemistry, computer science, mathematics, natural sciences, physical sciences, and physics), ENGINEERING AND ENVIRONMENTAL DESIGN (environmental science), SOCIAL SCIENCE (American studies, anthropology, economics, German area studies, history, international studies, philosophy, political science/government, psychology, religion, Russian and Slavic studies, and sociology). Biology, theatre, and psychology are the strongest academically. Biology, business administration, and psychology have the largest enrollments.

ACTIVITIES: 14% of men belong to 4 national fraternities; 17% of women belong to 1 local and 4 national sororities. There are 126 groups on campus, including and step team, art, band, cheerleading, chess, choir, chorale, chorus, computers, dance, drama, environmental, ethnic, film, honors, human rights, international, jazz band, LGBT, literary magazine, musical theater, newspaper, opera, orchestra, pep band, photography, political, professional, radio and TV, religious, social, social service, student government, and yearbook. Popular campus events include Spring Fling Weekend, Candlelight Carols, and Jefferson Field Day. **Sports:** There are 11 intercollegiate sports for men and 11 for women, and 13 intramural sports for men and 13 for women. Facilities include a sports center, which contains a 6-lane swimming pool, racquetball and squash courts, wrestling and weight training rooms, a multipurpose field house with indoor tennis courts, a running track, basketball and tennis courts, an aerobic fitness center and weight room, outdoor volleyball, and football/lacrosse/field hockey stadium. **Graduates:** From July 1, 2016 to June 30, 2017, 614 bachelor's degrees were awarded. The most popular majors were psychology (12%), business administration (10%), and theatre (9%). In an average class, 2% graduate in 3 years or less, 83% graduate in 4 years or less, 85% graduate in 5 years or less, and 85% graduate in 6 years or less. Of the 2016 graduating class, 35% were enrolled in graduate school within 6 months of graduation, and 62% were employed.

SERVICES: Counseling and information services are available, as is tutoring in every subject. There is a reader service for the blind. There is also a writing center. **Library/Resources:** Computerized library services include interlibrary loans, database searching, Internet access, and Wi-Fi capability. Special learning facilities include an art gallery, natural history museum, radio station, TV station, a wildlife preserve and arboretum. **Physically Challenged Students:** 95% of the campus is accessible. Facilities include wheelchair ramps, elevators, special parking, specially equipped restrooms, special class scheduling, lowered drinking fountains, lowered telephones, and special housing. **Special:** Students may cross-register with Lehigh, Lafayette, Cedar Crest, Moravian, and Allentown Colleges. Internships, work-study programs, B.A-B.S. degrees, study abroad in Asia, Australia, Latin America, Russia, and Europe, and a Washington semester are available. Dual majors and student-designed majors may be pursued. A 3-2 engineering degree is available in cooperation with Columbia and Washington Universities, a 4-4 assured admission medical program is offered with Drexel University College of Medicine, a 3-4 dental program is offered with University of Pennsylvania, and a 3-2 forestry degree is offered in cooperation with Duke University. An army ROTC program is also available. Nondegree study and a pass/fail grading option are also offered. There are 14 national honor societies, Phi Beta Kappa, a freshman honors program, and 8 departmental honors programs. **Visiting:** There are regularly scheduled orientations for prospective students, consisting of a tour of the campus and a personal interview. There are 2 open houses in the fall and 1 in the spring. There are guides for informal visits, visitors may sit in on classes, and stay overnight. **Campus Safety and Security:** Measures include 24-hour foot and vehicle patrol, self-defense education, and security escort services. There are shuttle buses, emergency telephones, and lighted pathways/sidewalks.

REQUIREMENTS: Applicants must graduate from an accredited secondary school or have a GED. 16 Carnegie units are required, and students must complete 4 courses in English, 3 in math, and 2 each in history, science, and a foreign language. All students must submit essays. Interviews are recommended and are required for those who do not submit SAT scores. AP and CLEP credits are accepted. Important factors in the admissions decision are geographical diversity, evidence of special talent, personality/intangible qualities, parents or siblings attended your school, extracurricular activities record, recommendations by alumni, recommendations by school officials, leadership record, and advanced placement or honors courses. The Muhlenberg curriculum is designed to engage students in thoughtful deliberation, critical analysis, and creative thinking. Students will complete a diverse set of general academic requirements and a major in their chosen field of specialization. They will earn no fewer than 34 course units with a cumulative grade point average of not less than 2.0. Skills are acquired through courses emphasizing writing, critical thinking, and language proficiency. Required courses include a First Year Seminar, writing-intensive courses, two semesters of foreign language, and a course in logic or mathematical reasoning. A breadth of knowledge is achieved through study in each of the four academic divisions are required 1 in arts, 2 each in social sciences and natural sciences, and 3 in Humanities. Required courses include a two-course cluster focused on related subject matter approached from different disciplinary angles or points of view, two courses in human difference and global engagement, and a culminating undergraduate experience specified by the major. Students may choose from a wide variety of majors, from accounting to sociology (40 majors in all, plus a self-designed major option). The major provides an in-depth study in the selected field and preparation for work, graduate, or professional school. Majors vary in the number of units required from nine to fifteen, but all students must earn a grade point average of not less than 2.0. A significant percentage of MC seniors graduate with double majors, and many majors offer departmental honors programs, senior portfolios, recitals, and mentored research opportunities. **Procedure:** Freshmen are admitted in the fall and spring. Entrance exams should be taken during the spring of the junior year or the fall of the senior year. There are early decision and deferred admissions plans. Early decision applications should be filed by February 1; regular applications, by February 15 for fall entry. The fall 2017 application fee was $50. Notifications are sent March 15. 354 early decision candidates were accepted for the 2017-2018 class. 314 applicants were on the 2017 waiting list; 41 were admitted. Applications are accepted on-line. **Transfer Students:** 12 transfer students enrolled in 2016-2017. A minimum college GPA of 2.5 and an interview are required. 17 of 34 credits required for the bachelor's degree must be completed at MC. **International Students:** There are 62 international students enrolled. They must take the TOEFL with a minimum score of 550 on the paper-based TOEFL (PBT).

ADMISSIONS: 48% of the 2017-2018 applicants were accepted. The SAT scores for the 2017-2018 freshman class were: Critical Reading-- 7% below 500, 39% between 500 and 599, 40% between 600 and 699, and 13% between 700 and 800. Math-- 10% below 500, 32% between 500 and 599, 52% between 600 and 699, and 10% between 700 and 800. Writing-- 13% below 500, 42% between 500 and 599, 36% between 600 and 699, and 8% between 700 and 800. The ACT scores were 9% between 18 and 23, 60% between 24 and 29, and 31% above 30. **Admissions Contact:** Christopher Hooker-Haring, Dean of Admissions. Email: *admissions@muhlenberg.edu* Web: *www.muhlenberg.edu*

FINANCIAL AID: In 2017-2018, 89% of all full-time freshmen received some form of financial aid. 52% of all full-time freshmen received need-based aid. The average freshman award was $28,883. Need-based scholarships or need-based grants averaged $26,247 ($56,646 maximum); need-based self-help aid (loans and jobs) averaged $5,150 ($9,300 maximum); and other non-need-based awards and non-need-based scholarships averaged $16,134 ($44,000 maximum). 20% of undergraduate students work part-time. The average financial indebtedness of the 2017 graduate was $23,279. MC is a member of CSS. The CSS/Profile and the college's own financial statement, parent and student tax returns, and W-2 forms are required. The FAFSA code is 003304. The deadline for filing freshman financial aid applications for fall entry is February 15.

NEUMANN UNIVERSITY *(The complete profile is made available exclusively on our website, www.barronspac.com)*

PEIRCE COLLEGE *(The complete profile is made available exclusively on our website, www.barronspac.com)*

PENN STATE ALTOONA — C-3
www.altoona.psu.edu

Altoona, PA 16601
(814) 949-5466
(800) 848-9843
Email: aaadmit@psu.edu

Full-time: 1818 men, 1503 women	**Faculty:** 194
Part-time: 58 men, 52 women	**Ph.D.s:** n/av
Graduate: n/av	**Student/Faculty:** 16 to 1
Year: semesters, summer session	**Tuition:** $14,826 ($22,834)
Room & Board: $11,860	**Freshman Class:** 5120 applied, 4582 accepted, 1203 enrolled
SAT CR/M: 490/515 **ACT:** 22	**CEEB CODE:** 2660
Application Deadline: rolling	**COMPETITIVE**

Penn State Altoona, founded in 1939, offers 18 baccalaureate degree programs, 8 associate degrees, and 19 minors. There are 17 undergraduate schools and 1 graduate school. In addition to regional accreditation, Altoona has baccalaureate program accreditation with ABET, NASAD, and NRPA. The 150-acre campus is in an urban area in Logan Township, PA, just outside of Altoona. Including any residence halls, there are 33 buildings.

STUDENT LIFE: 79% of undergraduates are from Pennsylvania. Others are from 28 states, 20 foreign countries, and Canada. 75% are White; 7% African American; 6% Hispanic; 5% Foreign; 3% Asian American; 3% two or more races. **Male To Female Ratio:** 1.2:1. The average age of freshmen is 18; all undergraduates, 22. 12% do not continue beyond their first year; 65% remain to graduate. **Housing:** 900 students can be accommodated in college housing, which includes dorms. In addition, there are honors houses, alcohol-free and substance-free housing, suites, and special interest housing. On-campus housing is available on a first-come, first-served basis, and is available on a lottery system for upperclassmen. 78% of students commute. Alcohol is not permitted. All students may keep cars.

FACULTY/CLASSROOMS: No introductory courses are taught by graduate students. The average class size in an introductory lecture is 50; in a laboratory is 24; and in a regular course is 28.

PROGRAMS OF STUDY: Altoona confers B.A. and B.S. degrees. Associate and master's degrees are also awarded. Bachelor's degrees are awarded in AGRICULTURE (environmental studies), BIOLOGICAL SCIENCE (biology/biological science), BUSINESS (business administration and management), COMMUNICATIONS AND THE ARTS (communications, English, and visual and performing arts), COMPUTER AND PHYSICAL SCIENCE (mathematics and science), EDUCATION (elementary education), ENGINEERING AND ENVIRONMENTAL DESIGN (electromechanical technology), HEALTH PROFESSIONS (nursing), SOCIAL SCIENCE (criminal justice, history, human development, and liberal arts/general studies). Engineering, and education are the strongest academically. Business, criminal justice, and elementary education have the largest enrollments.

ACTIVITIES: There are 70 groups on campus, including cheerleading, choir, communications, dance, drama, ethnic, honors, international, jazz band, LGBT, literary magazine, martial arts, newspaper, pep band, political, professional, religious, social, social service, student government, and yearbook. Popular campus events include Distinguished Speaker Series, Hoops Hysteria, Black History, and Women's History Month events. **Sports:** There are 6 intercollegiate sports for men and 6 for women. Facilities include a gym, indoor pool, racquetball courts, a weight room, a fitness loft, tennis courts, an outdoor track, sand volleyball courts, and baseball, softball, and soccer fields. **Graduates:** From July 1, 2016 to June 30, 2017, 350 bachelor's degrees were awarded. The most popular majors were engineering, homeland security, law enforcement, firefighting, and busiess/marketing.

SERVICES: Counseling and information services are available, as is tutoring in most subjects. There is remedial math, reading, and writing. **Library/Resources:** The library contains 90,000 audio/video tapes/CDs/DVDs, and subscribes to 500 periodicals including electronic. Computerized library services include interlibrary loans, database searching, Internet access, and Wi-Fi capability. Special learning facilities include an art gallery, Pic-Tel teleconferencing, engineering labs, and CAD/CAM computer lab facilities. **Physically Challenged Students:** 95% of the campus is accessible. Facilities include wheelchair ramps, elevators, special parking, specially equipped restrooms, special class scheduling, lowered drinking fountains, and lowered telephones. **Special:** Internships, study abroad in 5 countries, work-study programs, B.A.-B.S. degrees, accelerated degree programs, and dual and student-designed majors are available. There is an integrative arts major, which allows students to pursue interest across artistic boundaries. There is a chapter of Phi Beta Kappa and a freshman honors program. **Visiting:** There are regularly scheduled orientations for prospective students, campus tours and meetings with academic counselors and faculty. There are guides for informal visits, visitors may sit in on classes, and stay overnight. To schedule a visit, contact the Admissions Office at the Altoona campus. **Campus Safety and Security:** Measures include 24-hour foot and vehicle patrol, emergency notification system, self-defense education, and security escort services. There are shuttle buses, emergency telephones, and lighted pathways/sidewalks.

REQUIREMENTS: The SAT or ACT is required. Applicants should have 15 Carnegie units, 4 in English, 3 each in math, science, and social studies, and 2 in foreign language (required for some majors). The GED is accepted. AP and CLEP credits are accepted. To graduate, students must complete a minimum of 120 credit hours with a minimum GPA of 2.0. They must complete 46 general education credits, including 27 in arts, humanities, natural science, and social and behavioral sciences and 15 in quantification and communication skills. **Procedure:** Freshmen are admitted to all sessions. Entrance exams should be taken during the junior year. There are deferred admissions and rolling admissions plans. Application deadlines are open. The fall 2017 application fee was $65. Notification is sent on a rolling basis. Applications are accepted on-line. **Transfer Students:** 103 transfer students enrolled in 2016-2017. High school and college transcripts are required, as is good academic standing. The minimum GPA varies by major. 36 of 120 credits required for the bachelor's degree must be completed at Altoona. **International**

Students: There are 8 international students enrolled. They must take the TOEFL. They must also take the SAT or ACT.

ADMISSIONS: 89% of the 2017-2018 applicants were accepted. The SAT scores for the 2017-2018 freshman class were: Critical Reading-- 55% below 500, 35% between 500 and 599, and 9% between 600 and 699. Math-- 42% below 500, 38% between 500 and 599, 16% between 600 and 699, and 4% between 700 and 800. The ACT scores were 8% between 12 and 17, 60% between 18 and 23, 31% between 24 and 29, and 2% above 30. **Admissions Contact:** Richard Shaffer, Director of Admissions. Email: *aaadmit@psu.edu* Web: *www.altoona.psu.edu*

FINANCIAL AID: The average freshman award was $9,690. Need-based scholarships or need-based grants averaged $6,906; need-based self-help aid (loans and jobs) averaged $3,558; other non-need-based awards and non-need-based scholarships averaged $3,251; and $3,403 from other forms of aid. The average financial indebtedness of the 2017 graduate was $40,626. The priority date for freshman financial aid applications for fall entry is February 15. The deadline for filing freshman financial aid applications for fall entry is rolling.

PENN STATE ERIE,THE BEHREND COLLEGE B-1

www.psbehrend.psu.edu

Erie, PA 16563 **(814) 898-6000** **(866) 374-3378**

Fax: (814) 898-6044 **Email: behrend.admissions@psu.edu**

Full-time: 2739 men, 1408 women	**Faculty:** 270
Part-time: 108 men, 83 women	**Ph.D.s:** 54%
Graduate: 96 men, 40 women	**Student/Faculty:** 15 to 1
Year: semesters, summer session	**Tuition:** $4828 ($22,834)
Room & Board: $11,860	**Freshman Class:** 3853 applied, 3385 accepted, 1166 enrolled
SAT CR/M: 523/575 **ACT:** 24	**CEEB CODE:** 2660
Application Deadline: rolling	**VERY COMPETITIVE**

Penn State Erie, The Behrend College, founded in 1948, offers 34 baccalaureate programs as well as the first 2 years of most Penn State University Park baccalaureate programs. It offers courses in business, humanities, social sciences, science, engineering technology, and engineering. There are 5 undergraduate schools and 1 graduate school. In addition to regional accreditation, Penn State Erie, The Behrend College has baccalaureate program accreditation with AACSB, ABET, and NLN. The 840-acre campus is in a suburban area 5 miles east of Erie. Including any residence halls, there are 45 buildings.

STUDENT LIFE: 89% of undergraduates are from Pennsylvania. Others are from 28 states, 23 foreign countries, and Canada. 9% are Foreign; 89% White; 4% Asian American; 3% African American; 3% Hispanic. **Male To Female Ratio:** 1.9:1. The average age of freshmen is 18; all undergraduates, 22. 9% do not continue beyond their first year; 61% remain to graduate. **Housing:** 1650 students can be accommodated in college housing, which includes dorms and on-campus apartments. In addition, there are honors houses, suites, and special interest housing. On-campus housing is guaranteed for the freshman year only, is available on a first-come, first-served basis, and is available on a lottery system for upperclassmen. 53% of students commute. Alcohol is not permitted. All students may keep cars.

FACULTY/CLASSROOMS: All teach undergraduates, and all do research. No introductory courses are taught by graduate students. The average class size in an introductory lecture is 35; in a laboratory is 18; and in a regular course is 29.

PROGRAMS OF STUDY: Penn State Erie, The Behrend College confers B.A., B.S., and B.F.A. degrees. Associate and master's degrees are also awarded. Bachelor's degrees are awarded in AGRICULTURE (agriculture), BIOLOGICAL SCIENCE (biology/biological science), BUSINESS (accounting, banking and finance, business administration and management, business economics, management information systems, and marketing management), COMMUNICATIONS AND THE ARTS (communications, English, and foreign language), COMPUTER AND PHYSICAL SCIENCE (chemistry, computer science, mathematics, physics, and science), ENGINEERING AND ENVIRONMENTAL DESIGN (computer engineering, engineering, engineering technology, mechanical engineering technology, and plastics technology), SOCIAL SCIENCE (area studies, economics, history, political science/government, and psychology). Management information systems, psychology, and math are the strongest academically. Engineering, business, and psychology have the largest enrollments.

ACTIVITIES: 5% of men belong to 3 national fraternities; 16% of women belong to 3 national sororities. There are 80 groups on campus, including band, cheerleading, chess, choir, computers, dance, drama, ethnic, honors, international, jazz band, LGBT, literary magazine, newspaper, pep band, political, professional, radio and TV, religious, ROTC Army; Gannon University, social, social service, student government, and yearbook. Popular campus events include Speaker Series, Parents Events, and Black Cultural Awareness Month. **Sports:** There are 10 intercollegiate sports for men and 11 for women, and 18 intramural sports for men and 18 for women. Facilities include an athletic center with an indoor track, 8-lane pool, tennis courts, weight room, fitness trail, basketball courts, baseball, softball, and soccer fields. **Graduates:** From July 1, 2016 to June 30, 2017, 676 bachelor's degrees were awarded. The most popular majors were engineering, health professions, and psychology.

SERVICES: Counseling and information services are available, as is tutoring in every subject. There is a reader service for the blind, and remedial math, reading, and writing. **Library/Resources:** Computerized library services include interlibrary loans, database searching, Internet access, and Wi-Fi capability. Special learning facilities include a radio station, engineering workstation labs, media labs, and an observatory. **Physically Challenged Students:** 90% of the campus is accessible. Facilities include wheelchair ramps, elevators, special parking, specially equipped restrooms, special class scheduling, lowered drinking fountains, and lowered telephones. **Special:** Internships, study abroad in 14 countries, work-study programs, and accelerated degree programs are available. In addition, a B.A.-B.S. degree in psychology, a 3-2 engineering degree with Edinboro University, dual majors, a general studies degree, and student-designed majors in business and general arts and sciences are offered. Nondegree study and up to 12 credits of pass/fail options are possible. There are 4 national honor societies and a freshman honors program. **Visiting:** There are regularly scheduled orientations for prospective students, meetings with a counselor and faculty, a campus tour, and a class visit. There are guides for informal visits, visitors may sit in on classes, and stay overnight. To schedule a visit, contact the Admissions Office. **Campus Safety and Security:** Measures include 24-hour foot and vehicle patrol, self-defense education, and security escort services. There are emergency telephones and lighted pathways/sidewalks.

REQUIREMENTS: The SAT or ACT is required. Candidates for admission must have 15 Carnegie units, 4 units in English, 3 units each in math, science, and social studies, 2-3 units in foreign language. The GED is accepted. AP and CLEP credits are accepted. Important factors in the admissions decision are advanced placement or honors courses and leadership record. All baccalaureate degree candidates must take 46 general education credits, including 27 in arts, humanities, natural science, and social and behavioral sciences including a cultural diversity course, 15 in quantification and communication skills including a writing intensive course, and 3 in health, phys ed, and a freshman seminar. All students must complete a minimum of 120 credit hours with a minimum GPA of 2.0. Further requirements vary by degree program. **Procedure:** Freshmen are admitted to all sessions. Entrance exams should be taken during the junior year. There are deferred admissions and rolling admissions plans. Application deadlines are open. The fall 2017 application fee was $65. Notifications are sent October 15. Applications are accepted online. **Transfer Students:** 110 transfer students enrolled in 2016-2017. Transfer candidates need a minimum GPA of 2.4, good academic standing, and 18 or more credits from a regionally accredited institution at the college level. 36 of 120 credits required for the bachelor's degree must be completed at Penn State Erie, The Behrend College. **International Students:** There are 32 international students enrolled. They must take the TOEFL.

ADMISSIONS: 88% of the 2017-2018 applicants were accepted. The SAT scores for the 2017-2018 freshman class were: Critical Reading-- 39% below 500, 45% between 500 and 599, 14% between 600 and 699, and 2% between 700 and 800. Math-- 20% below 500, 40% between 500 and 599, 28% between 600 and 699, and 12% between 700 and 800. The ACT scores were 7% between 12 and 17, 39% between 18 and 23, 48% between 24 and 29, and 7% above 30. 25% of the current freshmen were in the top fifth of their class; 40% were in the top two fifths. 12 freshmen graduated first in their class. **Admissions Contact:** Andrea Konkol, Associate Director of Admissions. Email: *behrend.admissions@psu.edu* Web: *www.psbehrend.psu.edu*

FINANCIAL AID: The average freshman award was $10,712. Need-based scholarships or need-based grants averaged $7,493; need-based self-help aid (loans and jobs) averaged $3,629; other non-need-based awards and non-need-based scholarships averaged $3,408; and $3,518 from other forms of aid. The average financial indebtedness of the 2017 graduate was $39,209. The priority date for freshman financial aid applications for fall entry is February 15.

PENNSYLVANIA COLLEGE OF TECHNOLOGY *(The complete profile is made available exclusively on our website, www.barronspac.com)*

PENNSYLVANIA STATE UNIVERSITY - UNIVERSITY PARK C-3

www.psu.edu

University Park, PA 16802	(814) 865-5471
Fax: (814) 863-7590	**Email:** admissions@psu.edu
Full-time: 21,053 men, 18,630 women	**Faculty:** 3350
Part-time: 527 men, 342 women	**Ph.D.s:** 82%
Graduate: 3411 men, 2771 women	**Student/Faculty:** 16 to 1
Year: semesters, summer session	**Tuition:** $18,436 ($33,664)
Room & Board: $11,280	**Freshman Class:** 54271 applied, 27388 accepted, 7863 enrolled
SAT EBR-W/M: 620/630 **ACT:** 27	**CEEB CODE:** 2660
Application Deadline: November 30	**HIGHLY COMPETITIVE**

Pennsylvania State University-University Park, founded in 1855, is a public institution that is the oldest and largest of 24 campuses in the Penn State system. The university offers undergraduate and graduate degrees in agricultural sciences, arts and architecture, business, earth and mineral sciences, education, engineering, health and human development, liberal arts, science, communications, information sciences and technology, and nursing. University Park also offers graduate and first professional degrees in medicine and law. There are 14 undergraduate schools and 1 graduate school. In addition to regional accreditation, University Park has baccalaureate program accreditation with AACSB, ABET, ACEJMC, APTA, NAAB, NASAD, NASM, SAF, LAAB, NAST, and CAEP. The 7958-acre campus is in a suburban area 90 miles west of Harrisburg, PA. Including any residence halls, there are 965 buildings.

STUDENT LIFE: 58% of undergraduates are from Pennsylvania. Others are from 50 states, 145 foreign countries, and Canada. 63% are White; 16% Foreign; 6% Asian American; 6% Hispanic; 4% African American; 3% two or more races; 2% race unknown. **Male To Female Ratio:** 1.1:1. The average age of freshmen is 18; all undergraduates, 20. 7% do not continue beyond their first year; 85% remain to graduate. **Housing:** 13721 students can be accommodated in college housing, which includes gender neutral, single-sex, coed, married student dorms and on-campus apartments. In addition, there are honors houses, language/international houses, special-interest houses, fraternity houses, and sorority houses. On-campus housing is guaranteed for the freshman year only and is available on a lottery system for upperclassmen. 65% of students commute. Upperclassmen may keep cars.

FACULTY/CLASSROOMS: 59% of faculty are male; 41% are female. No introductory courses are taught by graduate students.

PROGRAMS OF STUDY: University Park confers B.A., B.S., B.A.E., B.Arch., B.Des., B.Eled., B.F.A., B.Hum., B.L.A., B.M., B.M.A., B.M.E., B.Ph. and B.Sosc. degrees. Associate, master's, and doctoral degrees are also awarded. Bachelor's degrees are awarded in AGRICULTURE (agricultural business management, agricultural sciences, animal science, forestry and related sciences, plant science, and turfgrass and landscape management), BIOLOGICAL SCIENCE (biochemistry, biology/biological science, biotechnology, forensic science, microbiology, nutrition, and toxicology), BUSINESS (accounting, entrepreneurial studies, finance, hospitality management services, management information systems, marketing management, and supply chain management), COMMUNICATIONS AND THE ARTS (acting, advertising, art, communication science, comparative literature, English literature, French, Germanic languages and literature, graphic design, journalism, film and media studies, music, Russian languages and literature, and theater design), COMPUTER AND PHYSICAL SCIENCE (astronomy, atmospheric sciences and meteorology, chemistry, information science, mathematics, physics, science technology, and statistics), EDUCATION (agricultural education, art education, Asian studies, athletic training, early childhood education, elementary education, foreign languages education, music education, secondary education, and special education), ENGINEERING AND ENVIRONMENTAL DESIGN (aerospace engineering, architectural engineering, architecture, biomedical engineering, chemical engineering, civil engineering, computer engineering, electrical/electronics engineering, engineering science, industrial engineering, landscape architecture, materials science, mechanical engineering, mining and mineral engineering, nuclear engineering, and petroleum/natural gas engineering), HEALTH PROFESSIONS (health care administration, kinesiology, nursing, premedicine, rehabilitation therapy, and veterinary science), SOCIAL SCIENCE (African American studies, anthropology, archeology, Chinese Studies, economics, food science, geography information science, human development & family studies, Italian studies, Japanese studies, Judaic studies, Latin American studies, liberal arts, sciences, general studies, humanities, medieval studies, parks and recreation management, philosophy, political science/government, psychology, sociology, Spanish studies, and women's studies). Engineering, business and marketing, and computer and information sciences have the largest enrollments.

ACTIVITIES: 17% of men belong to 2 local and 45 national fraternities; 20% of women belong to 30 national sororities. There are 986 groups on campus, including art, band, cheerleading, chess, choir, chorale, chorus, computers, dance, debate, drama, drill team, environmental, ethnic, film, forensics, honors, international, jazz band, LGBT, literary magazine, marching band, musical theater, newspaper, opera, orchestra, pep band, photography, political, professional, radio and TV, religious, social, social service, student government, symphony, and yearbook. Popular campus events include Late Night Penn State, Dance Marathon, Penn State football, and Distinguished Speaker Series. **Sports:** There are 15 intercollegiate sports for men and 14 for women, and 25 intramural sports for men and 25 for women. Facilities include a football stadium, baseball field, basketball center, golf courses, an ice skating pavilion, an indoor track/multipurpose field, an outdoor track, a soccer field, indoor and outdoor swimming pools, a bowling alley, and a tennis center. The Stone Valley Recreation Center offers fishing, swimming, canoeing, sailing, and kayaking, in addition to a rifle range, gymnastics, volleyball, field hockey, lacrosse, fencing, wrestling, a softball field, ice arena, and fitness facilities. **Graduates:** From July 1, 2016 to June 30, 2017, 11174 bachelor's degrees were awarded. The most popular majors were engineering (17%), business/marketing (17%), and computer and information sciences (9%). In an average class, 67% graduate in 4 years or less, 83% graduate in 5 years or less, and 85% graduate in 6 years or less. Of the 2016 graduating class, 18% were enrolled in graduate school within 6 months of graduation, and 53% were employed.

SERVICES: Counseling and information services are available, as is tutoring in most subjects. There is a reader service for the blind. **Library/Resources:** The library contains 8.0 million volumes, 2.8 million microform items, and 100,700 audio/video tapes/CDs/DVDs, and subscribes to 200,713 periodicals including electronic. Computerized library services include interlibrary loans, database searching, Internet access, and Wi-Fi capability. Special learning facilities include an art gallery, planetarium, radio station, and TV station. There are also six major museums at University Park house significant research and educational collections in the fields of agriculture, anthropology, entomology, earth and mineral sciences, and the fine arts. **Physically Challenged Students:** 95% of the campus is accessible. Facilities include wheelchair ramps, elevators, special parking, specially equipped restrooms, special class scheduling, lowered drinking fountains, lowered telephones, and special housing. Reasonable accommodations are available to provide access to all campus services, programs, and activities. **Special:** Co-op programs, internships, study-abroad in more than 50 countries, and work-study programs are available. Dual majors and student-designed majors are possible. Accelerated degree programs and a 3-2 engineering degree are also offered. Also offered are Integrated Bachelors/Masters degrees in several areas such as Engineering, Accounting, Computer Science, Meteorology, and Labor Studies and Employment Relations. There are 41 national honor societies and a freshman honors program. **Visiting:** There are regularly scheduled orientations for prospective students. These sessions include an information session with admissions, a campus walking tour, and lunch in a dining commons. Visitors may sit in on classes and stay overnight. To schedule a visit, contact the Undergraduate Admissions Office. **Campus Safety and Security:** Measures include 24-hour foot and vehicle patrol, emergency notification system, self-defense education, and security escort services. There are shuttle buses, emergency telephones, lighted pathways/sidewalks, and controlled access to dorms/residences.

REQUIREMENTS: Applicants are required to submit SAT or ACT scores. Admissions decisions for first-year students are made on the basis of several combined factors. Approximately two thirds of the decision for each student is based upon the high school GPA. The remaining one third of the decision is based on factors, which may include standardized critical reading and math test scores, class rank, personal statement, and activities list. AP and CLEP credits are accepted. The typical baccalaureate Penn State academic program requires the completion of between 120 and 130 credits. The General Education requirements are common to all degree programs and compose about one third of the course work (45 credits). All students must also complete a Writing-Across-The-Curriculum course (3 credits), a first-year seminar (1 credit), United States Culture (3 credits), and International Cultures (3 credits) as part of their degree program. **Procedure:** Freshmen are admitted in the fall, spring, and summer. Entrance exams should be taken in the junior year. There are early admissions, deferred admissions, and rolling admissions plans. Applications should be filed by November 30 for fall entry. The fall 2017 application fee was $65. Notification is sent on a rolling basis. 2168 applicants were on the 2017 waiting list. Applications are accepted on-line. **Transfer Students:** 286 transfer students enrolled in 2016-2017. Transfer applicants need a minimum GPA of 2.5 and good academic standing at University Park and 2.0 at other Penn State campuses. 36 of 120 credits required for the bachelor's degree must be completed at University Park. **International Students:** There are 4758 international students enrolled. They must take the TOEFL with a minimum score of 550 on the paper-based TOEFL (PBT) or 80 on the Internet-based version (iBT). Students must take the IELTS. They must also take the SAT or ACT.

ADMISSIONS: 50% of the 2017-2018 applicants were accepted. The SAT scores for the 2017-2018 freshman class were: Math-- 3% below 500, 31% between 500 and 599, 47% between 600 and 699, and 19% between 700 and 800. Evidence-Based Reading/Writing-- 3% below 500, 31% between 500 and 599, 55% between 600 and 699, and 11% between 700 and 800. The ACT scores were 10% between 18 and 23, 61% between 24 and 29, and 29% above 30. **Admissions Contact:** Clark Brigger, Executive Director Undergraduate Admissions. Email: *admissions@psu.edu* Web: *www.psu.edu*

FINANCIAL AID: The average financial indebtedness of the 2017 graduate was $37,307. University Park is a member of CSS. The FAFSA code is 003329. The priority date for freshman financial aid applications for fall entry is February 15.

POINT PARK UNIVERSITY B-3

www.pointpark.edu

Pittsburgh, PA 15222 **(412) 392-3430**

Fax: (412) 392-3902	**Email:** enroll@pointpark.edu
Full-time: 1070 men, 1481 women	**Faculty:** n/av
Part-time: 313 men, 362 women	**Ph.D.s:** 75%
Graduate: 273 men, 342 women	**Student/Faculty:** 19 to 1
Year: semesters, summer session	**Tuition:** $28,250
Room & Board: $13,020	**Freshman Class:** 3237 applied, 2393 accepted, 548 enrolled
SAT or ACT: required	**CEEB CODE:** 2676
Application Deadline: open	**COMPETITIVE**

Point Park University, is a comprehensive, master's-level institute with a strong liberal arts tradition. The university offers 82 undergraduate programs and 17 graduate programs through its School of Arts and Sciences, Rowland School of Business, School of Communication, and Conservatory of Performing Arts. There are 4 undergraduate schools and 4 graduate schools. In addition to regional accreditation, Point Park has baccalaureate program accreditation with ABET, IACBE, and NASD. The campus is in an urban area in Downtown Pittsburgh. Including any residence halls, there are 15 buildings.

STUDENT LIFE: 79% of undergraduates are from Pennsylvania. Others are from 49 states, 25 foreign countries, and Canada. 72% are White; 4% two or more races; 3% Hispanic; 3% Foreign; 16% African American; 1% Asian American; 1% race unknown. **Female To Male Ratio:** 1.3:1. The average age of freshmen is 18; all undergraduates, 24. 26% do not continue beyond their first year; 50% remain to graduate. **Housing:** 1022 students can be accommodated in college housing, which includes dorms and on-campus apartments, and living and learning communities. On-campus housing is available on a first-come, first-served basis. 70% of students commute. Some may keep cars.

FACULTY/CLASSROOMS: No introductory courses are taught by graduate students.

PROGRAMS OF STUDY: Point Park confers B.A., B.S., and B.F.A. degrees. Associate and master's degrees are also awarded. Bachelor's degrees are awarded in AGRICULTURE (environmental studies), BIOLOGICAL SCIENCE (biology/biological science, biotechnology, and forensic science), BUSINESS (accounting, business administration and management, finance, funeral home services, human resources, management science, organizational leadership and management, and sports management), COMMUNICATIONS AND THE ARTS (advertising, applied art, arts administration/management, broadcasting, communications, dance, dramatic arts, English, film arts, journalism, media arts, performing arts, photography, public relations, theatre arts, and video), COMPUTER AND PHYSICAL SCIENCE (computer science, digital arts/technology, earth science, and information sciences and systems), EDUCATION (childhood education, dance education, drama education, early childhood education, education, elementary education, secondary education, and special education), ENGINEERING AND ENVIRONMENTAL DESIGN (civil engineering, civil engineering technology, electrical/electronics engineering, electrical/electronics engineering technology, engineering management, engineering technology, environmental science, mechanical engineering, mechanical engineering technology, and systems engineering), HEALTH PROFESSIONS (environmental health science, health care administration, pre-health studies, premedicine, and respiratory therapy), SOCIAL SCIENCE (behavioral science, criminal justice, early childhood studies, history, international studies, law enforcement and corrections, legal studies, liberal arts/general studies, paralegal studies, political science/government, psychology, and public administration). Business, dance, and theater have the largest enrollments.

ACTIVITIES: There are no fraternities or sororities. There are 34 groups on campus, including choir, chorale, computers, dance, drama, ethnic, film, honors, international, LGBT, literary magazine, musical theater, newspaper, photography, political, professional, radio and TV, religious, social, social service, and student government. **Sports:** There are 5 intercollegiate sports for men and 6 for women, and 8 intramural sports for men and 8 for women. Facilities include an auditorium and a student center which includes a gymnasium, racquetball court, fitness and a training facility. **Graduates:** From July 1, 2016 to June 30, 2017, 719 bachelor's degrees were awarded. The most popular majors were business management (12%), theatre arts (9%), and dance (9%). In an average class, 50% graduate in 6 years or less.

SERVICES: Counseling and information services are available, as is tutoring in some subjects. Learning-disabled services are available on a case-by-case basis. There is a reader service for the blind, and remedial math, reading, and writing. **Library/Resources:** The library contains 82,565 volumes, 16,275 microform items, and 6,831 audio/video tapes/CDs/DVDs, and subscribes to 77,064 periodicals including electronic. Computerized library services include interlibrary loans, database searching, Internet access, and Wi-Fi capability. Special learning facilities include an art gallery, radio station, TV station, natural sciences labs, engineering technology labs, forensic crime scene house, computer newsrooms, MAC and PC multimedia labs, black/white and color photography darkrooms, digital photography lab, radio station, TV studio/newsroom, cinema production and editing suites, performance and dance studios, performing arts center/theaters, and art galleries. **Physically Challenged Students:** 95% of the campus is accessible. Facilities include wheelchair ramps, elevators, specially equipped restrooms, special class scheduling, lowered drinking fountains, lowered telephones, and special housing. **Special:** Cross-registration is available through the Pittsburgh Council on Higher Education. The university offers internships, work study, dual and student-designed majors, credit by exam and for life/military/work experience, and nondegree study. Capstone programs are available for students with associate degrees. Accelerated degree programs are available. There are 2 national honor societies and a freshman honors program. **Visiting:** There are regularly scheduled orientations for prospective students. There are guides for informal visits and visitors may sit in on classes. To schedule a visit, contact the Office of Admissions. **Campus Safety and Security:** Measures include 24-hour foot and vehicle patrol, emergency notification system, self-defense education, and security escort services. There are shuttle buses, emergency telephones, and lighted pathways/sidewalks.

REQUIREMENTS: The SAT or ACT is required. Students should have completed 12 academic credits or 16 Carnegie units consisting of 4 in English, 3 in history, science, and math, and 2 years of foreign language. The GED is accepted. Theater and dance students must audition, and an interview is requested for all candidates. A GPA of 2.0 is required. AP and CLEP credits are accepted. All majors leading to a baccalaureate degree require a minimum of 120 credits. Most programs require 42 core curriculum credits, with at least 30 completed in residence. **Procedure:** Freshmen are admitted to all sessions. Entrance exams should be taken in the junior or senior year. There are deferred admissions and rolling admissions plans. Application deadlines are open. The fall 2017 application fee was $40. Notification is sent on a rolling basis. Applications are accepted on-line. **Transfer Students:** 446 transfer students enrolled in 2016-2017. Applicants must have completed 12 credit hours with at least a 2.0 GPA. The SAT or ACT and an interview are recommended. 30 of 120 credits required for the bachelor's degree must be completed at Point Park. **International Students:** There are 101 international students enrolled. They must take the TOEFL with a minimum score of 500 on the paper-based TOEFL (PBT) or 61 on the Internet-based version (iBT). Students whose native language is English may submit SAT scores.

ADMISSIONS: 74% of the 2017-2018 applicants were accepted. The SAT scores for the 2017-2018 freshman class were: Critical Reading-- 45% below 500, 39% between 500 and 599, 14% between 600 and 699, and 2% between 700 and 800. Math-- 57% below 500, 34% between 500 and 599, 8% between 600 and 699, and 1% between 700 and 800. Writing-- 52% below 500, 35% between 500 and 599, 12% between 600 and 699, and 2% between 700 and 800. The ACT scores were 34% below 12, 22% between 12 and 17, 25% between 18 and 23, 20% between 24 and 29, and 6% above 30. **Admissions Contact:** Joell Minford. Email: *enroll@pointpark.edu* Web: *www.pointpark.edu*

FINANCIAL AID: In 2017-2018, 99% of all full-time freshmen received some form of financial aid. 75% of all full-time freshmen received need-based aid. The average freshman award was $29,218. Need-based scholarships or need-based grants averaged $5,664 ($16,000 maximum); need-based self-help aid (loans and jobs) averaged $5,788 ($7,000 maximum); non-need-based athletic scholarships averaged $5,335 ($14,000 maximum); and other non-need-based awards and non-need-based scholarships averaged $11,086 ($31,540 maximum). 16% of undergraduate students work part-time. The average financial indebtedness of the 2017 graduate was $21,838. The FAFSA code is 003357. The priority date for freshman financial aid applications for fall entry is March 15.

ROBERT MORRIS UNIVERSITY A-3

www.rmu.edu

Moon Township, PA 15108 **(800) 762-0097**

Fax: (412) 397-2425	**Email: admissionsoffice@rmu.edu**
Full-time: 2210 men, 1630 women	**Faculty:** 202; I, av$
Part-time: 198 men, 205 women	**Ph.D.s:** 90%
Graduate: 374 men, 459 women	**Student/Faculty:** 21 to 1
Year: semesters, summer session	**Tuition:** $29,420
Room & Board: $11,180	**Freshman Class:** 6407 applied, 5338 accepted, 868 enrolled
SAT EBR-W/M: 558/559 **ACT:** 24	**CEEB CODE:** 2769
Application Deadline: May 1	**COMPETITIVE**

Robert Morris University, founded in 1921, is a private institution offering more than 80 bachelor's, master's, and doctoral degree programs, many of which are available fully online. There are 5 undergraduate schools and 5 graduate schools. In addition to regional accreditation, RMU has baccalaureate program accreditation with AACSB, ABET, CCNE, Society of Actuaries, and JRC on Educational Programs in Nuclear Medicine. The 230-acre campus is in a suburban area 17 miles southwest of downtown Pittsburgh. Including any residence halls, there are 32 buildings.

STUDENT LIFE: 83% of undergraduates are from Pennsylvania. Others are from 43 states, 37 foreign countries, and Canada. 90% are from public schools. 73% are White; 6% African American; 3% two or more races; 2% Hispanic; 2% race unknown; 12% Foreign; 1% Asian American. 41% are Catholic; 35% Protestant. **Male To Female Ratio:** 1.2:1. The average age of freshmen is 18.6; all undergraduates, 22.1. 19% do not continue beyond their first year; 81% remain to graduate. **Housing:** 2015 students can be accommodated in college housing, which includes dorms and on-campus apartments. On-campus housing is guaranteed for the freshman year only, and is available on a first-come, first-served basis. 54% of students commute. Alcohol is not permitted. All students may keep cars.

FACULTY/CLASSROOMS: 46% of faculty are male; 54% are female. 99% teach undergraduates, 80% do research, and 80% do both. No introductory courses are taught by graduate students. The average class size in an introductory lecture is 22; in a laboratory is 12; and in a regular course is 22.

PROGRAMS OF STUDY: RMU confers B.A., B.S., B.F.A., B.S.B.A., and B.S.N. degrees. Master's and doctoral degrees are also awarded. Bachelor's degrees are awarded in BIOLOGICAL SCIENCE (biology/biological science), BUSINESS (accounting, banking and finance, business administration and management, hospitality management services, marketing/retailing/merchandising, organizational behavior, and sports management), COMMUNICATIONS AND THE ARTS (communications, English, media arts, and television & digital media production), COMPUTER AND PHYSICAL SCIENCE (actuarial science, applied mathematics, and information sciences and systems), EDUCATION (business education and elementary education), ENGINEERING AND ENVIRONMENTAL DESIGN (engineering, environmental science, and manufacturing engineering), HEALTH PROFESSIONS (health care administration, nuclear medical technology, and nursing), SOCIAL SCIENCE (economics, history, psychology, social science, and sociology). Actuarial science, and engineering are the strongest academically. Accounting, nursing, and engineering have the largest enrollments.

ACTIVITIES: 10% of men belong to 8 national fraternities; 13% of women belong to 6 national sororities. There are 131 groups on campus, including band, cheerleading, chess, choir, chorale, chorus, computers, dance, drama, environmental, ethnic, film, honors, international, jazz band, LGBT, literary magazine, marching band, musical theater, newspaper, orchestra, pep band, photography, political, professional, radio and TV, religious, social, social service, student government, and yearbook. Popular campus events include Homecoming, and Prom and Dances. **Sports:** There are 6 intercollegiate sports for men and 9 for women, and 11 intramural sports for men and 11 for women. Facilities include a field house, a gym, health club, and athletic fields. **Graduates:** From July 1, 2016 to June 30, 2017, 974 bachelor's degrees were awarded. The most popular majors were business/marketing (38%), nursing (16%), and engineering (16%). In an average class, 44% graduate in 4 years or less, 60% graduate in 5 years or less, and 61% graduate in 6 years or less. Of the 2016 graduating class, 7% were enrolled in graduate school within 6 months of graduation, and 85% were employed.

SERVICES: Counseling and information services are available, as is tutoring in most subjects. There is a reader service for the blind, and remedial math, reading, and writing. **Library/Resources:** The library contains 260,164 volumes, and 48,215 audio/video tapes/CDs/DVDs, and subscribes to 244 periodicals including electronic. Computerized library services include interlibrary loans, database searching, Internet access, and Wi-Fi capability. Special learning facilities include an art gallery, radio station, TV station, manufacturing and 3D printing labs for engineering, and a nursing laboratory where bedside computers and patient simulators assist in developing clinical decision-making skills. **Physically Challenged Students:** 75% of the campus is accessible. Facilities include wheelchair ramps, elevators, special parking, specially equipped restrooms, special class scheduling, lowered drinking fountains, lowered telephones, and special housing. **Special:** The university offers internship programs in most majors, cross-registration with the 9 colleges of the Pittsburgh Council of Higher Education, work-study programs, study abroad in 12 countries, and non-degree study. Credit by exam and pass/fail options are also available. There are 9 national honor societies, a freshman honors program, and 1 departmental honors program. **Visiting:** There are regularly scheduled orientations for prospective students, consisting of placement testing, orientation, and academic advising. There are guides for informal visits, visitors may sit in on classes, and stay overnight. To schedule a visit, contact the Admissions Office. **Campus Safety and Security:** Measures include 24-hour foot and vehicle patrol, emergency notification system, and security escort services. There are shuttle buses, emergency telephones, lighted pathways/sidewalks, and controlled access to dorms/residences.

REQUIREMENTS: The SAT is required. Applicants should be graduates of an accredited secondary school or hold a GED diploma. They must have completed 16 Carnegie units, including 4 in English and social studies, 3 in math and 2 in science. An interview is required for some and recommended for all others. A GPA of 2.0 is required. AP and CLEP credits are accepted. Important factors in the admissions decision are advanced placement or honors courses, leadership record, and personality/intangible qualities. All candidates must complete 120 to 135 credit hours, including 24 to 31 in the major, with a 2.0 GPA overall and a 2.5 in the major. A core curriculum varies with each major and consists of humanities, communication skills, social sciences, computing, and math. All students must demonstrate competency in computer software applications. **Procedure:** Freshmen are admitted in the fall, spring, and summer. Entrance exams should be taken by fall or late winter of the senior year. There are deferred admissions and rolling admissions plans. Applications should be filed by May 1 for fall entry; December 1 for spring entry. The fall 2017 application fee was $30. Notification is sent on a rolling basis. 191 applicants were on the 2017 waiting list; 38 were admitted. Applications are accepted on-line. **Transfer Students:** 266 transfer students enrolled in 2016-2017. Students must have a minimum 2.0 GPA in nondevelopmental academic courses. Those with fewer than 30 earned credits must also submit an official high school transcript and test results of the SAT or ACT. An interview is recommended. 30 of 120 credits required for the bachelor's degree must be completed at RMU. **International Students:** There are 503 international students enrolled. They must take the TOEFL with a minimum score of 500 on the paper-based TOEFL (PBT) or 61 on the Internet-based version (iBT).

ADMISSIONS: 83% of the 2017-2018 applicants were accepted. The SAT scores for the 2017-2018 freshman class were: Math-- 18% below 500, 55% between 500 and 599, 24% between 600 and 699, and 4% between 700 and 800. Evidence-Based Reading/Writing-- 18% below 500, 55% between 500 and 599, 24% between 600 and 699, and 3% between 700 and 800. The ACT scores were 2% between 12 and 17, 48% between 18 and 23, 39% between 24 and 29, and 12% above 30. 11% of the current freshmen were in the top fifth of their class; 23% were in the top two fifths. 7 freshmen graduated first in their class. **Admissions Contact:** Kellie Laurenzi, Associate Vice President of Admissions. Email: *admissionsoffice@rmu.edu* Web: *www.rmu.edu*

FINANCIAL AID: In 2017-2018, 81% of all full-time freshmen received some form of financial aid. 80% of all full-time freshmen received need-based aid. The average freshman award was $25,418. Need-based scholarships or need-based grants averaged $19,385; need-based self-help aid (loans and jobs) averaged $6,864; and non-need-based athletic scholarships averaged $20,453. 100% of undergraduate students work part-time. The average financial indebtedness of the 2017 graduate was $39,856. RMU is a member of CSS. The FAFSA code is 003359. The deadline for filing freshman financial aid applications for fall entry is May 1.

ROSEMONT COLLEGE *(The complete profile is made available exclusively on our website, www.barronspac.com)*

SAINT FRANCIS UNIVERSITY *(The complete profile is made available exclusively on our website, www.barronspac.com)*

SAINT JOSEPH'S UNIVERSITY — F-3

www.sju.edu

Philadelphia, PA 19131 — **(610) 660-1300**

Fax: (610) 660-1314 — **Email: admit@sju.edu**

Full-time: 2079 men, 2403 women	**Faculty:** 287; IIA, +$
Part-time: 266 men, 397 women	**Ph.D.s:** 91%
Graduate: 1113 men, 1828 women	**Student/Faculty:** 16 to 1
Year: semesters, summer session	**Tuition:** $43,700
Room & Board: $14,840	**Freshman Class:** 8972 applied, 6925 accepted, 1075 enrolled
SAT CR/M: 604/597 **ACT:** 26	**CEEB CODE:** 2801
Application Deadline: February 1	**VERY COMPETITIVE**

Saint Joseph's University, founded by the Society of Jesus in 1851, advances the professional and personal ambitions of men and women by providing a demanding, yet supportive, educational experience. Saint Joseph's has two principal academic colleges: the College of Arts and Sciences, and the Erivan K. Haub School of Business. SJU offers over 55 undergraduate day majors and 50 minors and over 30 degree completion and certificate programs including online options. Graduate programs include over 40 areas of study with many programs offering both campus-based and online delivery options. Special programs include Study Abroad, Honors program, Cooperative Education Program, Summer Scholars, Service-Learning, and Faith-Justice Studies. There are 2 undergraduate schools and 2 graduate schools. In addition to regional accreditation, SJU has baccalaureate program accreditation with AACSB. The 113-acre campus is in a suburban area on the western edge of Philadelphia and eastern Montgomery County. Including any residence halls, there are 81 buildings.

STUDENT LIFE: 53% of undergraduates are from out of state, mostly the Middle Atlantic. Students are from 40 states, 37 foreign countries, and Canada. 78% are White; 7% Hispanic; 6% African American; 3% Asian American; 2% Foreign; 2% two or more races; 2% race unknown. 73% are Catholic; 17% Protestant. **Female To Male Ratio:** 1.3:1. The average age of freshmen is 18; all undergraduates, 21. 9% do not continue beyond their first year; 82% remain to graduate. **Housing:** 2938 students can be accommodated in college housing, which includes single sex, coed dorms, on-campus apartments, and off-campus apartments. In addition, there are honors houses, special-interest houses, and special interest floors. On-campus housing is available on a lottery system for upperclassmen. 54% of students live on campus. Some may keep cars.

FACULTY/CLASSROOMS: 55% of faculty are male; 45% are female. No introductory courses are taught by graduate students. The average class size in an introductory lecture is 28; in a laboratory is 16; and in a regular course is 25.

PROGRAMS OF STUDY: SJU confers B.A. and B.S. degrees. Associate, master's, and doctoral degrees are also awarded. Bachelor's degrees are awarded in BIOLOGICAL SCIENCE (biochemistry and biology/biological science), BUSINESS (accounting, business administration and management, entrepreneurial studies, finance, human resources, insurance and risk management, international business management, investments and securities, management information systems, marketing management, marketing/retailing/merchandising, organizational leadership and management, and sports marketing), COMMUNICATIONS AND THE ARTS (art, art studies, communications, English, French, German, Italian, Latin, music, Spanish, and theatre arts), COMPUTER AND PHYSICAL SCIENCE (actuarial science, chemistry, computer science, information sciences and systems, mathematics, and physics), EDUCATION (art education, Asian studies, early childhood education, elementary education, and special education), ENGINEERING AND ENVIRONMENTAL DESIGN (environmental science), HEALTH PROFESSIONS (health care administration and health science), SOCIAL SCIENCE (criminal justice, economics, European studies, French studies, history, international relations, liberal arts/general studies, philosophy, political science/government, psychology, public administration, religious studies, sociology, and theological studies). Risk management and insurance, biology, and accounting are the strongest academically. Marketing, accounting, and biology have the largest enrollments.

ACTIVITIES: 11% of men belong to 4 national fraternities; 25% of women belong to 5 national sororities. There are 90 groups on campus, including band, cheerleading, choir, chorale, dance, debate, drama, environmental, ethnic, film, forensics, honors, international, jazz band, LGBT, literary magazine, musical theater, newspaper, orchestra, pep band, political, professional, radio and TV, religious, social, social service, and student government. Popular campus events include Community Day, Spring Concert, and Hawk-A-Palooza. **Sports:** There are 10 intercollegiate sports for men and 10 for women, and 16 intramural sports for men and 16 for women. Facilities include an athletic center and recreation center, indoor and outdoor athletic and recreational events. **Graduates:** From July 1, 2016 to June 30, 2017, 1230 bachelor's degrees were awarded. The most popular majors were food marketing (11%), marketing (9%), and accounting (8%). In an average class, 76% graduate in 4 years or less, 81% graduate in 5 years or less, and 82% graduate in 6 years or less. Of the 2016 graduating class, 14% were enrolled in graduate school within 6 months of graduation, and 82% were employed.

SERVICES: Counseling and information services are available, as is tutoring in most subjects. There is a reader service for the blind. In addition to tutoring, there are study and life skills workshops, supplemental instruction, a writing center, and other educational support services to help students. **Library/Resources:** The library contains 280,000 volumes, 870,519 microform items, and 2,882 audio/video tapes/CDs/DVDs, and subscribes to 76,837 periodicals including electronic. Computerized library services include interlibrary loans, database searching, Internet access, and Wi-Fi capability. Special learning facilities include an art gallery, radio station, an instructional media center, foreign language labs, Wall Street Trading Room, Honors House, and Post Learning Commons. **Physically Challenged Students:** 85% of the campus is accessible. Facilities include wheelchair ramps, elevators, special parking, specially equipped restrooms, special class scheduling, lowered drinking fountains, lowered telephones, and special housing. There is also automatic eye doors, curb cuts, a specially equipped van for wheelchairs, a pool lift, and a bell system at major road crossings. **Special:** The University offers internships, a Washington semester, 5-year combined Bachelors/Masters degree programs, dual majors, minor concentrations, and study abroad. There are co-op programs for business majors. There are 23 national honor societies, Phi Beta Kappa, a freshman honors program, and 16 departmental honors programs. **Visiting:** There are regularly scheduled orientations for prospective students, consisting of open houses, tours, and information sessions. There are guides for informal visits and visitors may sit in on classes. To schedule a visit, contact the Office of Admission. **Campus Safety and Security:** Measures include 24-hour foot and vehicle patrol, emergency notification system, and security escort services. There are shuttle buses, emergency telephones, lighted pathways/sidewalks, controlled access to dorms/residences, a bicycle patrol, public safety orientation/education, emergency preparedness awareness training, active shooter training, building evacuation drills, fire extinguisher use training, close circuit television cameras and monitoring. Additional measures includes CPR/AED/First Aid certification of Public Safety personnel, defensive driver's training, public safety presentations, traffic and parking lot access controls, crime and safety bulletins, and local law enforcement to patrol communities around campus where students live.

REQUIREMENTS: The SAT and ACT standardized test scores is optional for admission. Academic information, recommendations, and the record of extracurricular involvement and evidence of special talent, leadership and service will be reviewed. A variety of factors are considered during the application process including, but not limited to strength of high school, rigor of academic curriculum, and overall academic achievement and community involvement. AP and CLEP credits are accepted. Important factors in the admissions decision are advanced placement or honors courses, recommendations by school officials, and extracurricular activities record. The General Education Program (GEP) consists of 6 signature core courses; up to 10 variable courses(AP and transfer credits may be accepted); 3 integrative learning courses; and 3 overlay courses focusing on the areas of diversity/globalization, ethics,and writing-intensive. **Procedure:** Freshmen are admitted in the fall and spring. Entrance exams should be taken in the spring of the junior year and/or the fall of the senior year. There are early decision, early admissions, and deferred admissions plans. Early decision applications should be filed by November 1; regular applications, by February 1 for fall entry; and December 15 for spring entry. The fall 2017 application fee was $50. Notification of early decision is sent December 20; regular decision, March 15. Applications are accepted on-line. **Transfer Students:** 88 transfer students enrolled in 2016-2017. Transfer students requirements include a minimum of 12 transferable credits. Typically, students with a 2.5 cumulative GPA or higher are considered for admission. Transfer applicants must submit high school and college transcripts. 60 of 120 credits required for the bachelor's degree must be completed at SJU. **International Students:** There are 99 international students enrolled. They must take the TOEFL with a minimum score of 550 on the paper-based TOEFL (PBT) or 80 on the Internet-based version (iBT). They must also take the SAT or ACT, scoring 450. or the TOEFL.

ADMISSIONS: 77% of the 2017-2018 applicants were accepted. The SAT scores for the 2017-2018 freshman class were: Critical Reading-- 3% below 500, 42% between 500 and 599, 49% between 600 and 699, and 6% between 700 and 800. Math-- 4% below 500, 47% between 500 and 599, 44% between 600 and 699, and 6% between 700 and 800. The ACT scores were 25% between 18 and 23, 59% between 24 and 29, and 16% above 30. 43% of the current freshmen were in the top fifth of their class; 75% were in the top two fifths. 5 freshmen graduated first in their class. **Admissions Contact:** Maureen Mathis, Assistant Provost. Email: *admit@sju.edu* Web: *www.sju.edu*

FINANCIAL AID: In 2017-2018, 98% of all full-time freshmen received some form of financial aid. 70% of all full-time freshmen received need-based aid. The average freshman award was $34,505. SJU is a member of CSS. The FAFSA code is 003367. The priority date for freshman financial aid applications for fall entry is December 1.

SAINT VINCENT COLLEGE — B-3

www.stvincent.edu

Latrobe, PA 15650	**(724) 532-6600** **(800) 782-5549**
Fax: (724) 805-2953	**Email: admission@stvincent.edu**
Full-time: 886 men, 730 women	**Faculty:** 105; IIB, av$
Part-time: 26 men, 24 women	**Ph.D.s:** 90%
Graduate: 91 men, 107 women	**Student/Faculty:** 16 to 1
Year: semesters, summer session	**Tuition:** $34,830
Room & Board: $11,399	**Freshman Class:** 2490 applied, 1542 accepted, 456 enrolled
SAT CR/M: 565/554 **ACT:** 23	**CEEB CODE:** 2808
Application Deadline: May 1	**COMPETITIVE**

Saint Vincent College, founded in 1846, is a private Catholic college of liberal arts and sciences sponsored by Benedictine Monks. There are 4 undergraduate schools and 3 graduate schools. In addition to regional accreditation, SVC has baccalaureate program accreditation with ACBSP. The 200-acre campus is in a suburban area 35 miles east of Pittsburgh. Including any residence halls, there are 27 buildings.

STUDENT LIFE: 78% of undergraduates are from Pennsylvania. Others are from 28 states, and 6 foreign countries. 83% are White; 6% African American; 4% Hispanic; 3% race unknown; 2% two or more races; 1% Asian American; 1% Foreign. 55% are Catholic; 23% Unknown denominations; 19% Protestant. **Male To Female Ratio:** 1.2:1. The average age of freshmen is 18; all undergraduates, 20. 14% do not continue beyond their first year; 70% remain to graduate. **Housing:** 1283 students can be accommodated in college housing, which includes dorms and on-campus apartments. On-campus housing is guaranteed for the freshman year only, is available on a first-come, first-served basis, and on a lottery system for upperclassmen. 73% of students live on campus. All students may keep cars.

FACULTY/CLASSROOMS: 62% of faculty are male; 38% are female. All teach undergraduates, and do research. No introductory courses are taught by graduate students. The average class size in an introductory lecture is 20; in a laboratory is 20; and in a regular course is 25.

PROGRAMS OF STUDY: SVC confers B.A. and B.S. degrees. Master's and doctoral degrees are also awarded. Bachelor's degrees are awarded in BIOLOGICAL SCIENCE (biochemistry, bioinformatics, and biology/biological science), BUSINESS (accounting, banking and finance, business administration and management, international business management, and marketing/retailing/merchandising), COMMUNICATIONS AND THE ARTS (art, art history and appreciation, arts administration/management, communications, English, fine arts, French, music, music performance, Spanish, studio art, and visual and performing arts), COMPUTER AND PHYSICAL SCIENCE (chemistry, computer science, mathematics, and physics), EDUCATION (art education, business education, early childhood education, middle school education, psychology education, and science education), ENGINEERING AND ENVIRONMENTAL DESIGN (engineering and environmental science), HEALTH PROFESSIONS (occupational therapy, physical therapy, physician's assistant, predentistry, premedicine, prepharmacy, and preveterinary science), SOCIAL SCIENCE (anthropology, economics, history, liberal arts/general studies, philosophy, political science/government, prelaw, psychology, public affairs, sociology, and theological studies). Biology, economics, and psychology are the strongest academically. Biology, business, and criminology have the largest enrollments.

ACTIVITIES: There are no fraternities or sororities. There are 58 groups on campus, including art, band, cheerleading, choir, chorus, dance, drama, environmental, ethnic, honors, international, literary magazine, marching band, musical theater, newspaper, pep band, political, professional, radio and TV, religious, social, social service, and student government. Popular campus events include Founders' Day, Threshold Lecture Series, and Pittsburgh Steelers Training Camp. **Sports:** There are 10 intercollegiate sports for men and 11 for women, and 6 intramural sports for men and 6 for women. Facilities include a gym, basketball and volleyball facilities, a weight and exercise room, an indoor pool, tennis courts, baseball, soccer, football fields, a student union, and game room area.

Graduates: From July 1, 2016 to June 30, 2017, 396 bachelor's degrees were awarded. The most popular majors were business (24%), biology (16%), and psychology (9%). In an average class, 2% graduate in 3 years or less, 65% graduate in 4 years or less, 71% graduate in 5 years or less, and 73% graduate in 6 years or less.

SERVICES: Counseling and information services are available, as is tutoring in most subjects. The Opportunity Office provides individual counseling and a study skills class for students. **Library/Resources:** The library contains 288,601 volumes, 99,262 microform items, and 8,019 audio/video tapes/CDs/DVDs, and subscribes to 249 periodicals including electronic. Computerized library services include interlibrary loans, database searching, Internet access, and Wi-Fi capability. Special learning facilities include an art gallery, planetarium, radio station, TV station, an observatory, radio telescope, a small-business development center, nature reserve, and the Fred Rogers archives. **Physically Challenged Students:** 95% of the campus is accessible. Facilities include wheelchair ramps, elevators, special parking, specially equipped restrooms, lowered drinking fountains, special housing, and lowered computer desks. **Special:** There is cross-registration with Seton Hill University, co-op programs, internships, study abroad in Europe and Asia, a work-study program, double majors, a general studies degree, credit by exam and for life/military/work experience, nondegree study, and pass/fail options. There is a 3-2 engineering option with Pennsylvania State University, the University of Pittsburgh, and the Catholic University of America. The college offers teacher certificate courses in early childhood (K-12) and secondary education. There are 18 national honor societies, a freshman honors program, and 15 departmental honors programs. **Visiting:** There are regularly scheduled orientations for prospective students, consisting of a general information session, an informal meeting with faculty, and campus tours. To schedule a visit, contact the Admission Office. **Campus Safety and Security:** Measures include 24-hour foot and vehicle patrol, emergency notification system, and security escort services. There are emergency telephones, lighted pathways/sidewalks, and controlled access to dorms/residences.

REQUIREMENTS: The SAT or ACT is required. Applicants must complete 16 academic credits (20 recommended), including 4 of English, 3 each of social studies and math, and 1 science with lab (3 science and lab recommended). Also recommended are two credits of foreign language. Art students must submit a portfolio, and music must audition. An essay is required. A GED is accepted. AP and CLEP credits are accepted. To graduate, students must complete 124 credit hours with a minimum GPA of 2.0. All students are required to take Language and Rhetoric, First Theology, and First Philosophy. The core curriculum includes 9 hours each of social science, theology, and English, 8 of natural sciences, 6 hours each of history, philosophy, and foreign language, and 3/4 of math. All students complete a first-year seminar experience. Total number of hours in major varies depending on the program. The majority of majors require a culminating activity, such as a thesis, research project, or capstone course/seminar. **Procedure:** Freshmen are admitted in the fall and spring. Entrance exams should be taken at the end of the junior year or the beginning of the senior year. There are deferred admissions and rolling admissions plans. Applications should be filed by May 1 for fall entry; January 1 for spring entry. The fall 2017 application fee was $25. Applications are accepted on-line. **Transfer Students:** 38 transfer students enrolled in 2016-2017. Transfer applicants must submit transcripts from postsecondary schools attended and a catalog describing courses taken, plus secondary school transcript (s). 34 of 124 credits required for the bachelor's degree must be completed at SVC. **International Students:** There are 9 international students enrolled. They must take the TOEFL with a minimum score of 550 on the paper-based TOEFL (PBT). They must also take the SAT or ACT.

ADMISSIONS: 62% of the 2017-2018 applicants were accepted. The SAT scores for the 2017-2018 freshman class were: Critical Reading-- 17% below 500, 50% between 500 and 599, 26% between 600 and 699, and 7% between 700 and 800. Math-- 21% below 500, 51% between 500 and 599, 24% between 600 and 699, and 4% between 700 and 800. The ACT scores were 7% between 12 and 17, 48% between 18 and 23, 36% between 24 and 29, and 9% above 30. 31% of the current freshmen were in the top fifth of their class; 60% were in the top two fifths. **Admissions Contact:** Admission and Financial Aid Office. Email: *admission@stvincent.edu* Web: *www.stvincent.edu*

FINANCIAL AID: In 2017-2018, 100% of all full-time freshmen received some form of financial aid. 76% of all full-time freshmen received need-based aid. The average freshman award was $37,877. Need-based scholarships or need-based grants averaged $5,872 ($17,048 maximum); need-based self-help aid (loans and jobs) averaged $3,517 ($7,716 maximum); and other non-need-based awards and non-need-based scholarships averaged $28,487 ($50,485 maximum). 29% of undergraduate students work part-time. The average financial indebtedness of the 2017 graduate was $38,240. The FAFSA code is 003368. The priority date for freshman financial aid applications for fall entry is May 1.

SETON HILL UNIVERSITY B-4

www.setonhill.edu

Greensburg, PA 15601	(724) 838-4255 (800) 826-6234
Fax: (724) 830-1294	**Email:** admit@setonhill.edu
Full-time: 519 men, 964 women	**Faculty:** 101; IIB, +$
Part-time: 41 men, 82 women	**Ph.D.s:** 43%
Graduate: 100 men, 229 women	**Student/Faculty:** 12 to 1
Year: 4-1-4, summer session	**Tuition:** $33,362
Room & Board: $13,610	**Freshman Class:** 2206 applied, 1612 accepted, 363 enrolled
SAT or ACT: recommended	**CEEB CODE:** 2812
Application Deadline: August 15	**VERY COMPETITIVE**

Seton Hill University, founded in 1885, is a private university affiliated with the Roman Catholic Church offering programs in liberal arts and career preparation. There is 1 undergraduate school and 1 graduate school. In addition to regional accreditation, SHU has baccalaureate program accreditation with ADA, CSWE, NASM, ARC-PA, AAMFT, ACEND, CODA, IACBE, NAEYC, AATA, and AMTA. The 200-acre campus is in a small town in Greenburg, PA, just 35 miles east of Pittsburgh, PA. Including any residence halls, there are 19 buildings.

STUDENT LIFE: 74% of undergraduates are from Pennsylvania. Others are from 36 states, 15 foreign countries, and Canada. 80% are White; 8% African American; 3% Hispanic; 3% Foreign; 3% two or more races; 2% race unknown; 1% Asian American. **Female To Male Ratio:** 1.9:1. The average age of freshmen is 18; all undergraduates, 21. 21% do not continue beyond their first year; 57% remain to graduate. **Housing:** 750 students can be accommodated in college housing, which includes dorms and honors houses. On-campus housing is guaranteed for all 4 years. 54% of students commute. Alcohol is not permitted. All students may keep cars.

FACULTY/CLASSROOMS: 47% of faculty are male; 53% are female. 87% teach undergraduates, and 60% do research. No introductory courses are taught by graduate students. The average class size in an introductory lecture is 25; in a laboratory is 16; and in a regular course is 17.

PROGRAMS OF STUDY: SHU confers B.A., B.S., B.F.A., B.Mus., B.S.Med.Tech. and B.S.W. degrees. Master's degrees are also awarded. Bachelor's degrees are awarded in BIOLOGICAL SCIENCE (biochemistry and biology/biological science), BUSINESS (accounting, business administration and management, business economics, entrepreneurial studies, human resources, international business management, management information systems, marketing/retailing/merchandising, personnel management, sports management, and tourism), COMMUNICATIONS AND THE ARTS (art and design, art history and appreciation, arts administration/management, communications, creative writing, dance, dramatic arts, English, English Writing, fine arts, graphic design, journalism, music, music theory and composition, musical theater, performing arts, Spanish, studio art, theatre arts, theater design, and theater management), COMPUTER AND PHYSICAL SCIENCE (actuarial science, chemistry, computer science, mathematics, and physics), EDUCATION (art education, early childhood education, elementary education, English education, foreign languages education, home economics education, mathematics education, music education, science education, secondary education, social science education, and special education), ENGINEERING AND ENVIRONMENTAL DESIGN (engineering), HEALTH PROFESSIONS (art therapy, biology, dental education, medical laboratory technology, music therapy, pharmacy, physician's assistant, predentistry, premedicine, preosteopathy, and preveterinary science), SOCIAL SCIENCE (child care/child and family studies, criminal justice, dietetics, economics, family/consumer resource management, family/consumer studies, food production/management/

services, forensic studies, gender studies, history, human services, international studies, liberal arts/general studies, philosophy, political science/government, prelaw, psychology, religion, religious music, social work, sociology, and women & gender studies). Sciences, education, and fine arts are the strongest academically. Psychology, art, and business have the largest enrollments.

ACTIVITIES: There are no fraternities or sororities. There are 40 groups on campus, including make-a-wish club, best buddies club, entrepreneur's, respect life club, animal service club, art, bagpipe, band, cheerleading, choir, chorale, chorus, dance, drama, environmental, ethnic, honors, international, jazz band, LGBT, literary magazine, marching band, musical theater, newspaper, orchestra, pep band, political, professional, religious, social, social service, student government, and symphony. Popular campus events include Christmas on the Hill, Family Weekend, President's Reception, Battle of the Building, and Midnight Breakfast. **Sports:** There are 10 intercollegiate sports for men and 12 for women. Facilities include gyms, a fitness center, an aerobics room, a swimming pool, a field house with weight and training rooms, playing fields, and a football stadium. **Graduates:** From July 1, 2016 to June 30, 2017, 324 bachelor's degrees were awarded. The most popular majors were business/marketing (20%), visual/performing arts (11%), and health Professions and related programs (10%). In an average class, 43% graduate in 4 years or less, 55% graduate in 5 years or less, and 57% graduate in 6 years or less.

SERVICES: Counseling and information services are available, as is tutoring in most subjects. There is a reader service for the blind, and remedial math and writing. **Library/Resources:** The library contains 123,538 volumes, 5,403 microform items, and 6,684 audio/video tapes/CDs/DVDs, and subscribes to 423 periodicals including electronic. Computerized library services include interlibrary loans, database searching, and Internet access. Special learning facilities include an art gallery, TV station, a nursery school that functions as a laboratory school for education students, performing arts center, visual arts center, and a technology wing. **Physically Challenged Students:** 95% of the campus is accessible. Facilities include wheelchair ramps, elevators, special parking, specially equipped restrooms, special class scheduling, lowered drinking fountains, and lowered telephones. **Special:** There are cooperative programs in all majors and cross-registration with St. Vincent College, the University of Pittsburgh at Greensburg, and Westmoreland County Community College. Internships are encouraged. Seton Hill offers study abroad, a Washington semester, work-study, dual and student-designed majors, accelerated degree programs, a 3-2 engineering program with Pennsylvania State University and Georgia Institute of Technology, a 2-2 nursing program with Catholic University of America, a 3-2 or 3-1 medical technology program with area hospitals, credit by exam and for life/military/work experience, nondegree study, and pass/fail options. There are 5 national honor societies and a freshman honors program. **Visiting:** There are regularly scheduled orientations for prospective students, consisting of an introduction, an address by the president or dean, an open reception with faculty, a financial aid session, a student panel, and a campus tour. There are guides for informal visits, visitors may sit in on classes, and stay overnight. To schedule a visit, contact the Campus Visit Coordinator. **Campus Safety and Security:** Measures include 24-hour foot and vehicle patrol, emergency notification system, self-defense education, and security escort services. There are shuttle buses, emergency telephones, and lighted pathways/sidewalks.

REQUIREMENTS: The SAT or ACT is recommended. Two graded writing samples are accepted in place of SAT or ACT scores. A total of 15 Carnegie units is required, including 4 each of English and electives, 2 each of math, social studies, and foreign language, and 1 of a lab science, and 4 academic electives. Art students must submit a portfolio; music and theater students must audition. An interview is recommended. The GED is accepted with supporting recommendations. A GPA of 2.5 is required. AP and CLEP credits are accepted. Important factors in the admissions decision are advanced placement or honors courses, evidence of special talent, personality/intangible qualities, extracurricular activities record, leadership record, and recommendations by alumni. The core curriculum requires 6 credits in Western cultures, 6 credits in writing, and 3 each in theology, philosophy/senior seminar, math, computer science, science, college-level foreign language, U.S. cultures, non-Western cultures, and artistic expression. A total of 120 credit hours with a minimum GPA of 2.0 is required for graduation. **Procedure:** Freshmen are admitted in the fall and spring. Entrance exams should be taken in spring of the junior year or fall of the senior year. There are deferred admissions and rolling admissions plans. Applications should be filed by August 15 for fall entry. The fall 2017 application fee was $35. Notification is sent on a rolling basis. Applications are accepted on-line. **Transfer Students:** 58 transfer students enrolled in 2016-2017. Applicants must submit college transcripts and have a GPA of at least 2.0. An interview is recommended, as are supporting letters. 48 of 120 credits required for the bachelor's degree must be completed at Seton Hill. **International Students:** There are 39 international students enrolled. They must take the TOEFL with a minimum score of 550 on the paper-based TOEFL (PBT) or 79 on the Internet-based version (iBT).

ADMISSIONS: 73% of the 2017-2018 applicants were accepted. The SAT scores for the 2017-2018 freshman class were: Critical Reading-- 37% below 500, 42% between 500 and 599, 16% between 600 and 699, and 5% between 700 and 800. Math-- 36% below 500, 45% between 500 and 599, 17% between 600 and 699, and 2% between 700 and 800. Writing-- 43% below 500, 39% between 500 and 599, 15% between 600 and 699, and 3% between 700 and 800. The ACT scores were 7% between 12 and 17, 42% between 18 and 23, 41% between 24 and 29, and 10% above 30. 56% of the current freshmen were in the top fifth of their class; 81% were in the top two fifths. **Admissions Contact:** Ashley Zullo, Director of Admissions. Email: *admit@setonhill.edu* Web: *www.setonhill.edu*

FINANCIAL AID: In 2017-2018, 86% of all full-time freshmen received some form of financial aid and need-based aid. The average freshman award was $25,298. Need-based scholarships or need-based grants averaged $20,878; need-based self-help aid (loans and jobs) averaged $5,777; non-need-based athletic scholarships averaged $12,088; and other non-need-based awards and non-need-based scholarships averaged $15,028. 30% of undergraduate students work part-time. The average financial indebtedness of the 2017 graduate was $38,414. The college's own financial statement is required. The FAFSA code is 003362. The priority date for freshman financial aid applications for fall entry is April 30.

SHIPPENSBURG UNIVERSITY OF PENNSYLVANIA — D-3

www.ship.edu

Shippensburg, PA 17257 — **(717) 477-1231**

Fax: (717) 477-4016
Email: admiss@ship.edu
Full-time: 2552 men, 2608 women
Part-time: 222 men, 203 women
Graduate: 405 men, 591 women
Year: semesters, summer session
Room & Board: $12,010
SAT EBR-W/M: 530/530 **ACT:** 21
Application Deadline: n/av
Faculty: n/av
Ph.D.s: n/av
Student/Faculty: 20 to 1
Tuition: $12,086 ($20,186)
Freshman Class: 5248 applied, 4385 accepted, 1219 enrolled
CEEB CODE: 2657
COMPETITIVE

Shippensburg University, founded in 1871, is a public university that is part of the Pennsylvania State System of Higher Education offering undergraduate, graduate, and doctoral degree programs in the college of arts and sciences, college of business, and college of education and human services. There are 4 undergraduate schools and 1 graduate school. In addition to regional accreditation, SUP has baccalaureate program accreditation with AACSB, ABET, ACEJMC, CSWE, ACS, ACJS, CACREP, CAEP, CEC, and IACS. The 200-acre campus is in a rural area 40 miles southwest of Harrisburg. Including any residence halls, there are 51 buildings.

STUDENT LIFE: 93% of undergraduates are from Pennsylvania. Others are from 23 states, 19 foreign countries, and Canada. 87% are from public schools. 77% are White; 5% Hispanic; 3% two or more races; 2% Asian American; 2% Foreign; 10% African American; 1% race unknown. **Female To Male Ratio:** 1.1:1. The average age of freshmen is 18; all undergraduates, 21. 29% do not continue beyond their first year; 52% remain to graduate. **Housing:** 1986 students can be accommodated in college housing, which includes dorms, on-campus apartments, and off-campus apartments. Living Learning Communities provide the opportunity to live together with those who have similar academic, personal, or social interests. Academic Communities include: Biology First-year Interest Group, Computer Science & Engineering Deck, Future Educators, Grove StartUp for Business majors, Student Media for Communication/Jouralism majors,Get Psyched for Psychology majors,

Hall of Justice for Criminal Justice majors, Honors Program, and Discover SU for first-year exploratory majors. Interest Communities include the following: ROTC/Vets, Healthy Living Community, Shippensburg Leadership Academy and Transformations for incoming transfer students. On-campus housing is guaranteed for the freshman year only and is available on a lottery system for upperclassmen. 70% of students commute. Alcohol is not permitted. All students may keep cars.

FACULTY/CLASSROOMS: No introductory courses are taught by graduate students.

PROGRAMS OF STUDY: SUP confers B.A., B.S., B.S.B.A., B.S.Ed. and B.S.W. degrees. Master's and doctoral degrees are also awarded. Bachelor's degrees are awarded in BIOLOGICAL SCIENCE (biology/biological science), BUSINESS (accounting, business administration and management, entrepreneurial studies, finance, management information systems, marketing management, supply chain management, and professional studies), COMMUNICATIONS AND THE ARTS (art, communications, English, French, journalism, Spanish, and speech/debate/rhetoric), COMPUTER AND PHYSICAL SCIENCE (applied physics, chemistry, computer science, earth science, geoenvironmental studies, mathematics, physics, software engineering, and sustainable energy science), EDUCATION (art education, early childhood education, elementary education, English education, foreign languages education, mathematics education, middle school education, secondary education, social studies education, and special education), ENGINEERING AND ENVIRONMENTAL DESIGN (computer engineering, electrical/electronics engineering, and environmental science), HEALTH PROFESSIONS (exercise science, health care administration, and pre-health biological studies), SOCIAL SCIENCE (criminal justice, economics, geography, history, interdisciplinary studies, international studies, political science/government, psychology, public administration, social work, and sociology). Psychology, criminal justice, and biology have the largest enrollments.

ACTIVITIES: There are 101 groups on campus, including BigBrother/Big Sister, ROTC Ranger Challenge Team, art, band, cheerleading, choir, chorale, chorus, computers, dance, debate, drama, environmental, ethnic, honors, international, jazz band, LGBT, literary magazine, marching band, musical theater, newspaper, orchestra, pep band, photography, political, professional, radio and TV, religious, social, social service, student government, Vet's club, and yearbook. Popular campus events include Planetarium Shows, Senior Olympics, and Summer Music Festival. **Sports:** There are 8 intercollegiate sports for men and 10 for women, and 7 intramural sports for men and 7 for women. Facilities include a stadium with artificial turf for football, track and field, a field for baseball, a field for softball, a nine-court tennis facility, a stadium with artificial turf for soccer, field hockey, and lacrosse, an indoor arena for basketball, volleyball, wrestling, and a swimming pool. Intramurals are conducted on a multi-field outdoor complex and a multi-court indoor recreation center. **Graduates:** From July 1, 2016 to June 30, 2017, 1292 bachelor's degrees were awarded. The most popular majors were psychology (9%), criminal justice (8%), and management (7%). In an average class, 34% graduate in 4 years or less, 49% graduate in 5 years or less, and 52% graduate in 6 years or less.

SERVICES: Counseling and information services are available, as is tutoring in most general courses. There is remedial math, reading, and writing. There are JAWS and Zoom Text for the blind and visually impaired, including enlarged printing, extended time for tests, alternative testing sites, classroom accessibility, note taking, reader and scribe services for exams, books in alternate format, and priority scheduling. There are also individual meetings with Learning Specialists who are available to help students interested in developing individual strategies and group study. **Library/Resources:** The library contains 359,138 volumes, 1.2 million microform items, and 69,322 audio/video tapes/CDs/DVDs, and subscribes to 57,662 periodicals including electronic. Computerized library services include interlibrary loans, database searching, Internet access, and Wi-Fi capability. Special learning facilities include an art gallery, planetarium, radio station, TV station, a closed-circuit television, fashion archives center, vertebrate museum, women's center, on-campus elementary school, electron microscope, greenhouse, and herbarium. **Physically Challenged Students:** 92% of the campus is accessible. Facilities include wheelchair ramps, elevators, special parking, special class scheduling, lowered drinking fountains, and lowered telephones. **Special:** There are 20 national honor societies, a freshman honors program, and 1 departmental honors program. **Visiting:** There are regularly scheduled orientations for prospective students, including daily academic group meetings, campus tours, and 5 weekend open house programs per year. There are guides for informal visits and visitors may sit in on classes. To schedule a visit, contact the Admissions Office. **Campus Safety and Security:** Measures include 24-hour foot and vehicle patrol, emergency notification system, self-defense education, and security escort services. There are shuttle buses, emergency telephones, lighted pathways/sidewalks, and controlled access to dorms/residences. The residence halls are equipped with an automatic heat/smoke detection sprinkler system monitored 24 hours a day by police. The system also includes strobe lights to notify students who are hearing impaired. All exterior doors to residence hall doors are locked 24 hours a day and require card access for entry. There are security cameras at the main entrance to residence halls, computer labs, and academic buildings, and many exterior cameras covering the parking lots. A text emergency message system has also been implemented to notify students, faculty, and staff of impending or active emergency situations.

REQUIREMENTS: The SAT is required. Applicants are urged to pursue a typical college preparatory program, which should include 4 units of English, 3 units each of social sciences, math, lab science, and foreign language. A GED is accepted. AP and CLEP credits are accepted. Important factors in the admissions decision are advanced placement or honors courses, recommendations by school officials, and evidence of special talent. General education courses include English composition, oral communications, math, and history, logic and numbers for rational thinking, linguistic, literary, artistic, and cultural traditions, lab science, biological and physical science, political, economic, and geographic sciences, and social and behavioral sciences. The core curriculum varies for degree programs. Most degree programs require 120 credit hours, with 22 to 30 hours in the major, and a 2.0 minimum GPA for graduation. **Procedure:** Freshmen are admitted to all sessions. Entrance exams should be taken in the junior year and senior year. There are early admissions, deferred admissions, and rolling admissions plans. Application deadlines are open. The fall 2017 application fee was $45. Notification is sent on a rolling basis. Applications are accepted on-line. **Transfer Students:** 440 transfer students enrolled in 2016-2017. Applicants must provide high school and college transcripts and SAT or ACT scores if they have fewer than 30 college credits. 30 of 120 credits required for the bachelor's degree must be completed at Ship. **International Students:** There are 43 international students enrolled. They must take the TOEFL with a minimum score of 550 on the paper-based TOEFL (PBT) or 66 on the Internet-based version (iBT). Students whose native language is English must submit SAT scores instead of TOEFL.

ADMISSIONS: 84% of the 2017-2018 applicants were accepted. The SAT scores for the 2017-2018 freshman class were: Math-- 28% below 500, 55% between 500 and 599, 16% between 600 and 699, and 1% between 700 and 800. Evidence-Based Reading/Writing-- 29% below 500, 51% between 500 and 599, 19% between 600 and 699, and 1% between 700 and 800. The ACT scores were 17% between 12 and 17, 59% between 18 and 23, 21% between 24 and 29, and 3% above 30. 19% of the current freshmen were in the top fifth of their class; 45% were in the top two fifths. 2 freshmen graduated first in their class. **Admissions Contact:** Dr. Jennifer A. Haughie, Assistant VP for Enrollment Management and Dean of Admission. Email: *admiss@ship.edu* Web: *www.ship.edu*

FINANCIAL AID: SUP is a member of CSS. The FAFSA code is 003326. The deadline for filing freshman financial aid applications for fall entry is May 1.

SLIPPERY ROCK UNIVERSITY OF PENNSYLVANIA — B-2

www.sru.edu

Slippery Rock, PA 16057 — (724) 738-2015, (800) 929-4778

Fax: (724) 738-2913	**Email:** asktherock@sru.edu
Full-time: 2860 men, 3565 women	**Faculty:** 366
Part-time: 225 men, 415 women	**Ph.D.s:** 78%
Graduate: 235 men, 510 women	**Student/Faculty:** 18 to 1
Year: semesters, summer session	**Tuition:** $10,110 ($14,070)
Room & Board: $10,340	**Freshman Class:** 4310 applied, 3481 accepted, 1491 enrolled
SAT: required	**CEEB CODE:** 2658
Application Deadline: n/av	**COMPETITIVE**

Slippery Rock University of Pennsylvania, founded in 1889, is a public institution that is part of the Pennsylvania State System of Higher Education. It offers programs in business, information, social sciences, education, health, environment, science, humanities, and fine and performing arts. The figures given in the above capsule and in his profile are approximate. There are 4 undergraduate schools and 1 graduate school. In addition to regional accreditation, SRUP has baccalaureate program accreditation with ACBSP, APTA, CSWE, NASAD, NASM, NLN, NRPA, and CAAHEP. The 600-acre campus is in a small town 50 miles north of Pittsburgh. Including any residence halls, there are 60 buildings.

STUDENT LIFE: 96% of undergraduates are from Pennsylvania. Others are from 35 states, 47 foreign countries, and Canada. 70% are from public schools. 87% are White; 4% African American; 2% Foreign; 1% Asian American; 1% Hispanic. **Female To Male Ratio:** 1.4:1. The average age of freshmen is 18; all undergraduates, 22. 22% do not continue beyond their first year; 49% remain to graduate. **Housing:** 2810 students can be accommodated in college housing, which includes married student dorms, on-campus apartments, and off-campus apartments. In addition, there are honors houses, language/international houses, special-interest houses, fraternity houses, and sorority houses. On-campus housing is guaranteed for the freshman year only, and is available on a first-come, first-served basis. 62% of students commute. Alcohol is not permitted. All students may keep cars.

FACULTY/CLASSROOMS: 53% of faculty are male; 47% are female. All teach undergraduates. No introductory courses are taught by graduate students. The average class size in an introductory lecture is 33; in a laboratory is 20; and in a regular course is 25.

PROGRAMS OF STUDY: SRUP confers B.A., B.S., B.F.A., B.Mus., B.Mus.Ed., B.S.B.A., B.S.Ed. and B.S.N. degrees. Master's and doctoral degrees are also awarded. Bachelor's degrees are awarded in BIOLOGICAL SCIENCE (biology/biological science), BUSINESS (accounting, business administration and management, international business management, and marketing/retailing/merchandising), COMMUNICATIONS AND THE ARTS (communications, dance, English, fine arts, French, German, music, and Spanish), COMPUTER AND PHYSICAL SCIENCE (chemistry, computer science, earth science, geology, information sciences and systems, mathematics, and physics), EDUCATION (early childhood education, elementary education, foreign languages education, health education, music education, science education, secondary education, and special education), HEALTH PROFESSIONS (community health work, medical laboratory technology, and nursing), SOCIAL SCIENCE (anthropology, economics, geography, history, parks and recreation management, philosophy, political science/government, psychology, public administration, social science, social work, and sociology). Business, education, and health science areas have the largest enrollments.

ACTIVITIES: 7% of men belong to 11 national fraternities; 6% of women belong to 9 national sororities. There are 100 groups on campus, including art, band, cheerleading, chess, choir, chorale, chorus, communications, computers, dance, drama, ethnic, film, honors, international, jazz band, LGBT, literary magazine, marching band, musical theater, newspaper, orchestra, pep band, photography, political, professional, radio and TV, religious, social, social service, student government, symphony, and yearbook. Popular campus events include Spring Weekend event. **Sports:** There are 12 intercollegiate sports for men and 12 for women, and 7 intramural sports for men and 7 for women. Facilities include a field house, a gym, and a fitness center. **Graduates:** From July 1, 2016 to June 30, 2017, 1190 bachelor's degrees were awarded. The most popular majors were education (23%), marketing (15%), and parks and recreation (13%). In an average class, 24% graduate in 4 years or less, 46% graduate in 5 years or less, and 49% graduate in 6 years or less. Of the 2016 graduating class, 12% were enrolled in graduate school within 6 months of graduation, and 81% were employed.

SERVICES: Counseling and information services are available, as is tutoring in some subjects, such as 60 introductory-level general liberal studies courses. There is a reader service for the blind, and remedial math and writing. **Library/Resources:** The library contains 502,974 volumes, 1.5 million microform items, 22,707 audio/video tapes/CDs/DVDs, and subscribes to 1,300 periodicals including electronic. Computerized library services include interlibrary loans, database searching, and Internet access. Special learning facilities include an art gallery, natural history museum, planetarium, radio station, TV station, and a wellness center. **Physically Challenged Students:** 80% of the campus is accessible. Facilities include wheelchair ramps, elevators, special parking, specially equipped restrooms, special class scheduling, lowered drinking fountains, lowered telephones, and special housing. **Special:** Study abroad is available in 16 countries. Internships are offered in most majors, and international internships are available in Scotland and England. There is a 3-2 engineering program with Pennsylvania State University. The dual major is an option, and credit is given for military experience. Pass/fail options also are available. There are 26 national honor societies, a freshman honors program, and 33 departmental honors programs. **Visiting:** There are regularly scheduled orientations for prospective students, including a meeting with faculty, an information fair, and a campus tour. There are guides for informal visits, visitors may sit in on classes, and stay overnight. To schedule a visit, contact the Admissions Office. **Campus Safety and Security:** Measures include 24-hour foot and vehicle patrol, self-defense education, and security escort services. There are shuttle buses, emergency telephones, lighted pathways/sidewalks, The university maintains its own police department, with officers having the same powers as municipal police.

REQUIREMENTS: The SAT is required. The ACT is recommended. Students should graduate from an accredited secondary school or have a GED. A total of 16 academic credits is required. The recommended college preparatory program includes 4 years of English and social studies, 3 each of science and math, and 2 of a foreign language. An interview is recommended. AP and CLEP credits are accepted. Important factors in the admissions decision are advanced placement or honors courses, extracurricular activities record, and evidence of special talent. B.A. students must demonstrate proficiency in a foreign language, and all must complete 42 to 53 credits in a 7-part liberal studies program, including basic competencies, arts, cultural diversity/global perspective, human institutions, science and math, natural experience, and modern age. Specific requirements include public speaking, college writing, algebra, and phys ed. A minimum of 120 credit hours, with at least 30 in the major, is required for graduation. **Procedure:** Freshmen are admitted in the fall, spring, and summer. Entrance exams should be taken in the junior year or fall of the senior year. There are deferred admissions and rolling admissions plans. The fall 2017 application fee was $25. Notification is sent on a rolling basis. Applications are accepted on-line. **Transfer Students:** 559 transfer students enrolled in 2016-2017. Applicants should have completed at least 24 credit hours with a GPA of 2.5. The SAT I or ACT, as well as an interview, are recommended. 36 of 120 credits required for the bachelor's degree must be completed at SRUP. **International Students:** There are 130 international students enrolled. They must take the TOEFL.

ADMISSIONS: 81% of the 2017-2018 applicants were accepted. 10 freshmen graduated first in their class. **Admissions Contact:** Jim Barrett, Director of Admissions. Email: *asktherock@sru.edu* Web: *www.sru.edu*

FINANCIAL AID: In 2017-2018, 64% of all full-time freshmen received some form of financial aid. 51% of all full-time freshmen received need-based aid. The average freshman award was $6,074. Need-based scholarships or need-based grants averaged $2,907; need-based self-help aid (loans and jobs) averaged $2,437; non-need-based athletic scholarships averaged $2,507; and other non-need-based awards and non-need-based scholarships averaged $3,590. 30% of undergraduate students work part-time. The average financial indebtedness of the 2017 graduate was $19,195. SRUP is a member of CSS. The FAFSA code is 003327. The priority date for freshman financial aid applications for fall entry is May 1.

SUSQUEHANNA UNIVERSITY D-3

www.susqu.edu

Selinsgrove, PA 17870	**(570) 372-4260** **(800) 326-9672**
Fax: (570) 372-2722	**Email: suadmiss@susqu.edu**
Full-time: 965 men, 1225 women	**Faculty:** 142; IIB, av$
Part-time: 9 men, 7 women	**Ph.D.s:** 90%
Graduate: n/av	**Student/Faculty:** 13 to 1
Year: semesters, summer session	**Tuition:** $45,470
Room & Board: $12,090	**Freshman Class:** 4896 applied, 4159 accepted, 634 enrolled
SAT or ACT: recommended	**CEEB CODE:** 2820
Application Deadline: February 1	**VERY COMPETITIVE**

Susquehanna University is a selective, residential liberal arts college that provides a solid foundation in the liberal arts and sciences, as well as professional experiences. Students develop critical thinking, writing, teamwork and communication skills which, combined with internships and research opportunities, prepare them for a lifetime of personal and professional success. There are 2 undergraduate schools. In addition to regional accreditation, SU has baccalaureate program accreditation with AACSB, NASM, and ACS. The 325-acre campus is in a small town 50 miles north of Harrisburg. Including any residence halls, there are 95 buildings.

STUDENT LIFE: 55% of undergraduates are from Pennsylvania. Others are from 33 states, and 5 foreign countries. 83% are from public schools. 78% are White; 7% African American; 6% Hispanic; 3% two or more races; 2% Asian American; 2% Foreign; 2% race unknown. 33% are Protestant; 26% Catholic; 20% Buddhist, Muslim, Hindu, Mormon, and Eastern Orthodox, and unknown; 17% claim no religious affiliation. **Female To Male Ratio:** 1.3:1. The average age of freshmen is 18; all undergraduates, 20. 13% do not continue beyond their first year; 70% remain to graduate. **Housing:** 2056 students can be accommodated in college housing, which includes gender neutral and coed dorms and on-campus apartments. In addition, there are honors houses, language/international houses, special-interest houses, fraternity houses, and sorority houses. On-campus housing is guaranteed for all 4 years and is available on a lottery system for upperclassmen. 91% of students live on campus. All students may keep cars.

FACULTY/CLASSROOMS: 54% of faculty are male; 46% are female. All teach undergraduates, and all do research. No introductory courses are taught by graduate students. The average class size in a laboratory is 19 and in a regular course is 19.

PROGRAMS OF STUDY: SU confers B.A., B.S. and B.M. degrees. Bachelor's degrees are awarded in BIOLOGICAL SCIENCE (biochemistry, biology/biological science, and ecology), BUSINESS (accounting, business administration and management, finance, and marketing), COMMUNICATIONS AND THE ARTS (art history and appreciation, communications, English, French, German, graphic design, Italian, music, music performance, Spanish, studio art, theatre arts, and visual and performing arts), COMPUTER AND PHYSICAL SCIENCE (chemistry, computer science, earth science, mathematics, and physics), EDUCATION (early childhood education and music education), ENGINEERING AND ENVIRONMENTAL DESIGN (environmental science), HEALTH PROFESSIONS (biomedical science), SOCIAL SCIENCE (anthropology, economics, history, international studies, liberal arts/general studies, philosophy, political science/government, psychology, religion, and sociology). Business, communications, and biology have the largest enrollments.

ACTIVITIES: 21% of men belong to 6 national fraternities; 19% of women belong to 5 national sororities. There are 157 groups on campus, including academic clubs, Asian Student Coalition, Big Brothers/Big Sisters, Black Student Union, Habitat for Humanity, Hispanic Organization for Student Awareness, National Organization of Women, Student Awareness of the Value of the Environment, art, band, cheerleading, chess, choir, chorale, chorus, communications, computers, dance, drama, environmental, ethnic, film, honors, international, jazz band, LGBT, literary magazine, musical theater, newspaper, opera, orchestra, outdoors club, pep band, photography, political, professional, radio and TV, religious, social, social service, sports club, student government, and yearbook. Popular campus events include Thanksgiving Dinner, Spring Weekend, Candlelight Christmas Service, Homecoming Semi-Formal Ball, Annual Concert, and Fall Frenzy. **Sports:** There are 11 intercollegiate sports for men and 12 for women, and 6 intramural sports for men and 6 for women. Facilities include a field house with indoor track, tennis courts, basketball courts, football stadium and track, soccer, baseball, equestrian, lacrosse, rugby, hockey fields, ice hockey, ultimate frisbee, basketball, tennis courts, swimming pool, racquetball courts, weight training room, and a fitness center. **Graduates:** From July 1, 2016 to June 30, 2017, 519 bachelor's degrees were awarded. The most popular majors were business/administration (24%), communications (15%), and biological/life sciences (8%). In an average class, 69% graduate in 4 years or less, 70% graduate in 5 years or less, and 71% graduate in 6 years or less.

SERVICES: Counseling and information services are available, as is tutoring in some subjects, such as writing, math, foreign languages, and study skills. The academic departments also provides tutoring. **Library/Resources:** The library contains 532,071 volumes, 693 microform items, and 1.0 million audio/video tapes/CDs/DVDs, and subscribes to 76,567 periodicals including electronic. Computerized library services include interlibrary loans, database searching, Internet access, and Wi-Fi capability. Special learning facilities include an art gallery, radio station, multimedia classrooms, video studios, a campus wide telecommunications network, satellite dishes and distribution system for foreign-language broadcasts, video conferencing facility, an ecological field station, an observatory, a child development center, and an electronic music lab. **Physically Challenged Students:** 95% of the campus is accessible. Facilities include wheelchair ramps, elevators, special parking, specially equipped restrooms, special class scheduling, lowered drinking fountains, lowered telephones, and special housing. **Special:** 78% of Susquehanna students get professional experience before graduation in the form of internships and research opportunities. The Global Opportunities program places students in short-term or semester-long study with programs in 75 countries on 6 continents. The School of Business offers a semester in London specifically for junior business majors. The university offers dual and student-designed majors, work-study programs, credit by examination, non-degree study, and pass/fail options. The B.A., B.S. and B.M. degree is available in 42 majors. In addition, the university offers a 2-2 program in allied health with Thomas Jefferson University, and a 3-2 program in dentistry with Temple University. Highly motivated students have the option of earning their baccalaureate degree in three years. There are 23 national honor societies and a freshman honors program. **Visiting:** There are regularly scheduled orientations for prospective students, and special visiting days for these students and their parents held in the spring, fall, and summer. Events include sessions with faculty, admissions, financial aid, and placement staff and tours of the campus. There are guides for informal visits; visitors may sit in on classes, and stay overnight. To schedule a visit, contact Taylor Clark at (570) 372-4260. **Campus Safety and Security:** Measures include 24-hour foot and vehicle patrol, emergency notification system, self-defense education, and security escort services. There are shuttle buses, emergency telephones, lighted pathways/sidewalks, controlled access to dorms/residences, and closed circuit TV cameras in common exterior areas on campus.

REQUIREMENTS: The SAT or ACT is recommended. Either the Susquehanna Application or Common Application, along with an official high school transcript, school report, and SAT/ACT scores or a writing sample under our Test Score Optional plan. Students should be graduates of an accredited high school. Academic preparation should include 4 years of English and math, 3 to 4 years of science, and 2 to 3 years each of social studies and foreign language, 1 unit of art or music is recommended. An essay is required, as are, for relevant fields, a music audition or writing or graphic design portfolio. An interview is recommended. AP and CLEP credits are accepted. Important factors in the admissions decision are advanced placement or honors courses, evidence of special talent, and recommendations by school officials. The Central Curriculum is at the heart of a Susquehanna education. The diverse courses in the Central Curriculum comprise 40 percent of the graduation requirement, and are divided into five complementary sections: Richness of Thought, Natural World, Human Interactions, Intellectual Skills, and Connections. All students at Susquehanna are required to participate in a unique, nationally recognized cross-cultural program, Global Opportunities. Students study in the U.S. or abroad, for at least two weeks or as long as a semester, a reflection course is required after their return. **Procedure:** Freshmen are admitted in the fall and spring. Entrance exams should be taken by January of the senior year. There are early decision, early admissions, deferred admissions, and rolling admissions plans. Early decision applications should be filed by November 15; regular applications, by February 1 for fall entry; and January 1 for spring entry. Notification of early decision is sent December 1; regular decision, March 1. 55 early decision candidates were accepted for the 2017-2018 class. Applications are accepted on-line. **Transfer Students:** 32 transfer students enrolled in 2016-2017. Applicants must submit high school and college transcripts, test scores, and a recommendation from a dean. An interview is strongly recommended. A music audition or writing portfolio is required for relevant fields. 65 of 130 credits required for the bachelor's degree must be completed at Susquehanna. **International Students:** They must take the TOEFL with a minimum score of 550 on the paper-based TOEFL (PBT) or 80 on the Internet-based version (iBT), and take the IELTS.

ADMISSIONS: 46% of the current freshmen were in the top fifth of their class; 77% were in the top two fifths. **Admissions Contact:** Philip M. Betz, Director of Admissions. Email: *suadmiss@susqu.edu* Web: *www.susqu.edu*

FINANCIAL AID: The average financial indebtedness of the 2017 graduate was $33,757. Susquehanna is a member of CSS. The CSS/Profile, and prior year federal tax return for parents and students are required. The FAFSA code is 003369. The priority date for freshman financial aid applications for fall entry is March 1. The deadline for filing freshman financial aid applications for fall entry is May 1.

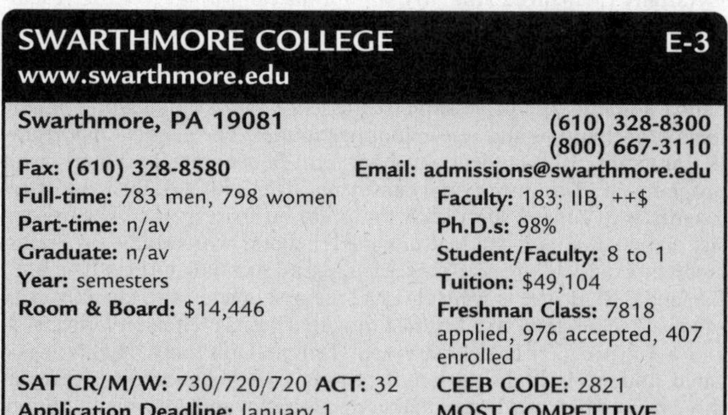

SWARTHMORE COLLEGE E-3
www.swarthmore.edu

Swarthmore, PA 19081 (610) 328-8300
(800) 667-3110
Fax: (610) 328-8580 **Email: admissions@swarthmore.edu**

Full-time: 783 men, 798 women	**Faculty:** 183; IIB, ++$
Part-time: n/av	**Ph.D.s:** 98%
Graduate: n/av	**Student/Faculty:** 8 to 1
Year: semesters	**Tuition:** $49,104
Room & Board: $14,446	**Freshman Class:** 7818 applied, 976 accepted, 407 enrolled
SAT CR/M/W: 730/720/720 **ACT:** 32	**CEEB CODE:** 2821
Application Deadline: January 1	**MOST COMPETITIVE**

Swarthmore College, a highly selective college of liberal arts and engineering, has empowered students to pursue their academic curiosity with purpose for over 150 years. Swarthmore's students collaborate with world-class faculty on joint research projects, call on their diverse backgrounds to engage in the free and critical exchange of ideas, and are just as passionate about life outside the classroom as they are about academic pursuits. There is 1 undergraduate school. In addition to regional accreditation, Swarthmore has baccalaureate program accreditation with ABET. The 425-acre campus is in a suburban area Swarthmore, PA, 11 miles southwest of Philadelphia. Including any residence halls, there are 56 buildings.

STUDENT LIFE: 87% of undergraduates are from out of state, mostly the Middle Atlantic. Students are from 50 states, 70 foreign countries, and Canada. 59% are from public schools. 42% are White; 17% Asian American; 13% Hispanic; 11% Foreign; 8% two or more races; 6% African American; 3% race unknown; 1% American Indian/Alaska Native. **Female To Male Ratio:** 1.0:1. The average age of freshmen is 18; all undergraduates, 20. 4% do not continue beyond their first year; 93% remain to graduate. **Housing:** 1429 students can be accommodated in college housing, which includes dorms and gender neutral housing (students of any gender may share rooms and/or bathrooms). On-campus housing is guaranteed for all 4 years. 95% of students live on campus. Upperclassmen may keep cars.

FACULTY/CLASSROOMS: 57% of faculty are male; 43% are female. All teach undergraduates and do research. No introductory courses are taught by graduate students. The average class size in a laboratory is 12 and in a regular course is 16.

PROGRAMS OF STUDY: Swarthmore confers B.A. and B.S. degrees. Bachelor's degrees are awarded in BIOLOGICAL SCIENCE (biochemistry, biology/biological science, and neurosciences), COMMUNICATIONS AND THE ARTS (art, art history and appreciation, Chinese, classics, comparative literature, dance, dramatic arts, English literature, film arts, French, German, Greek, Latin, linguistics, literature, media arts, music, Russian, Spanish, and theatre arts), COMPUTER AND PHYSICAL SCIENCE (astronomy, astrophysics, chemical physics, chemistry, computer science, mathematics, and physics), EDUCATION (education), ENGINEERING AND ENVIRONMENTAL DESIGN (engineering), SOCIAL SCIENCE (anthropology, Asian/Oriental studies, Chinese Studies, classical/ancient civilization, economics, gender studies, German area studies, history, Japanese studies, medieval studies, peace studies, philosophy, political science/government, psychobiology, psychology, religion, and sociology). Economics, biology, and computer science have the largest enrollments.

ACTIVITIES: 11% of men belong to 1 local and 1 national fraternities; 6% of women belong to 1 national sorority. There are 150 groups on campus, including a cappella groups, drama board activities, art, band, chess, choir, chorus, club sports, computers, dance, debate, drama, environmental, ethnic, film, honors, international, jazz band, LGBT, literary magazine, musical theater, newspaper, orchestra, photography, political, radio and TV, religious, social, social service, student government, and yearbook. Popular campus events include Large Scale Event, Worthstock, and the Crum Regatta. **Sports:** There are 10 intercollegiate sports for men and 12 for women, and 7 intramural sports for men and 7 for women. Facilities include a wellness and fitness space, weights and cardio training, sport-specific training, yoga, and pilates, a field house with indoor courts for basketball, tennis, badminton, volleyball, baseball, softball batting cage, and a 215-meter banked tartan track. There are also outdoor fields for lacrosse, field hockey, soccer, Rugby, ultimate frisbee, tennis, softball, baseball, natural grass multipurpose fields, lacrosse, soccer, hockey, a 400-meter track, tennis, and a pool. The gymnasium, is used for basketball, volleyball and badminton, a fully equipped for athletic training. **Graduates:** From July 1, 2016 to June 30, 2017, 397 bachelor's degrees were awarded. The most popular majors were social sciences (24%), biology/life sciences, political science (13%), computer and informatin sciences, and and visual & performing arts (13%). In an average class, 89% graduate in 4 years or less, 83% graduate in 5 years or less, and 94% graduate in 6 years or less. Of the 2016 graduating class, 17% were enrolled in graduate school within 6 months of graduation, and 67% were employed.

SERVICES: Counseling and information services are available, as is tutoring in most subjects. There is a reader service for the blind, and the campus writing center, Student Academic Mentors, Science Associates, and Math Associates provide academic support to students. **Library/Resources:** The library contains 100,000 volumes, 40,000 microform items, 50,000 audio/video tapes/CDs/DVDs, and subscribes to 75,000 periodicals including electronic. Computerized library services include interlibrary loans, database searching, Internet access, and Wi-Fi capability. Special learning facilities include a radio station, LEED-certified integrated science center includes an observatory, robotics and solar energy labs, two galleries, one of which is curated by students, dance studios, cinema, and theater, a music and dance library, a science library, the Friends Historical Library, and the Swarthmore Peace Collection. Students interested in community-based learning are supported by the Lang Center for Civic and Social Responsibility. **Physically Challenged Students:** 85% of the campus is accessible. Facilities include wheelchair ramps, elevators, special parking, specially equipped restrooms, special class scheduling, lowered drinking fountains, lowered telephones, and special housing. **Special:** Special educational opportunities include the Honors Program, which features small groups of students working closely with faculty and peers; an emphasis on independent learning, and a final examination by outside scholars. Swarthmore also offers an engineering major and a program leading toward Teacher Certification. Students may cross-register courses at Bryn Mawr, Haverford Colleges and the University of Pennsylvania. Cooperative exchange programs are available with Tufts University and Harvey Mudd, Pomona, Mills, and Middlebury colleges. The off-campus study office supports students who wish to study abroad, opportunities are widely available and off campus study is encouraged. There are 3 national honor societies, Phi Beta Kappa, and 31 departmental honors programs. **Visiting:** There are regularly scheduled orientations for prospective students, tours, information sessions, and interviews are offered throughout the year. There are guides for informal visits, visitors may sit in on classes, and stay overnight. To schedule a visit, contact the Admissions Office. **Campus Safety and Security:** Measures include 24-hour foot and vehicle patrol, emergency notification system, self-defense education, and security escort services. There are shuttle buses, emergency telephones, lighted pathways/sidewalks, and controlled access to dorms/residences.

REQUIREMENTS: Swarthmore does not require a specific high school curriculum. We do, however, recommend the inclusion of 4 years of English, 3 years each of mathematics, the sciences, history, and social studies, 1 or 2 foreign languages, and coursework in art and music. Applicants are required to submit scores for either the SAT or the ACT. We do not require the optional essay section of the SAT or the optional writing section of the ACT, or the SAT Subject Tests, but we will consider these scores if you submit them. If you have indicated an interest in our engineering program, you are encouraged to submit the Math 2 Subject Test. Two essays are required. Interviews are recommended, though not required for first-year applicants. AP credits are accepted. Important factors in the admissions decision are parents or siblings attended your school, evidence of special talent, recommendations by alumni, geographical diversity, extracurricular activities record, leadership record, advanced placement or honors courses, personality/intangible qualities, and recommendations by school officials. In order to graduate, students must complete 3 courses in each of 3 divisions consisting of humanities, natural sciences and engineering, and social sciences. Concurrent with distribution and/or major requirements, there is a requirement of 3 writing courses and a science laboratory. Students must demonstrate foreign language competency, and fulfill a physical education requirement including a swimming test. Each major has a culminating experience, which may be a thesis, project, or comprehensive exam. **Procedure:** Freshmen are admitted in the fall. Entrance exams should be taken in spring of the junior year or fall of the senior year. There are early decision and deferred admissions plans. Early decision applications should be filed by November 15; regular applications, by January 1 for fall entry. The fall 2017 application fee was $60. Notification of early decision is sent December 15; regular decision, April 1. 202 early decision candidates were accepted for the 2017-2018 class. Applications are accepted on-line. **Transfer Students:** 7 transfer students enrolled in 2016-2017. Applicants for transfer must present both secondary and college transcripts, an essay or personal statement, and an official statement of good standing from the tertiary institution. Application closing date is fall, April 1, and notification date is May 15. 16 of 32 credits required for the bachelor's degree must be completed at Swarthmore. **International Students:** There are 130 international students enrolled. They must also take the SAT or ACT.

ADMISSIONS: 12% of the 2017-2018 applicants were accepted. The SAT scores for the 2017-2018 freshman class were: Critical Reading-- 4% between 500 and 599, 33% between 600 and 699, and 62% between 700 and 800. Math-- 3% between 500 and 599, 34% between 600 and 699, and 62% between 700 and 800. Writing-- 4% between 500 and 599, 29% between 600 and 699, and 67% between 700 and 800. The ACT scores were 22% between 24 and 29, and 78% above 30. 88% of the current freshmen were in the top fifth of their class; 99% were in the top two fifths. 30 freshmen graduated first in their class. **Admissions Contact:** Joseph J.T. Duck, Director of Admissions. Email: *admissions@swarthmore.edu* Web: *www.swarthmore.edu*

FINANCIAL AID: In 2017-2018, 60% of all full-time freshmen received some form of financial aid, and need-based aid. The average freshman award was $47,676. Need-based scholarships or need-based grants averaged $46,053; and need-based self-help aid (loans and jobs) averaged $1,623. 81% of undergraduate students work part-time. Swarthmore is a member of CSS. The CSS/Profile, the state aid form, the college's own financial statement, federal tax returns, W-2 statements, and noncustodial are required. The FAFSA code is 003370. The priority date for freshman financial aid applications for fall entry is February 15.

TEMPLE UNIVERSITY

F-3

www.temple.edu

Philadelphia, PA 19122

(215) 204-8556
(888) 340-2222
Email: tuadm@temple.edu

Full-time: 12,116 men, 12,800 women	**Faculty:** 2205; I, av$
Part-time: 1749 men, 1578 women	**Ph.D.s:** 76%
Graduate: 4204 men, 5174 women	**Student/Faculty:** 18 to 1
Year: semesters, summer session	**Tuition:** $14,096 ($24,122)
Room & Board: $10,296	**Freshman Class:** 18813 applied, 12016 accepted, 4390 enrolled
SAT CR/M/W: 558/571/553 **ACT:** 24	**CEEB CODE:** 2906
Application Deadline: February 1	**COMPETITIVE+**

Temple University, founded in 1888, is part of the Commonwealth System of Higher Education in Pennsylvania, offering more than 140 undergraduate programs. Temple has 8 campuses, including 1 in Rome and 1 in Tokyo. Temple also offers programs in London, Beijing, China, Greece, Korea, Israel, and other locations. In addition to regional accreditation, Temple has baccalaureate program accreditation with AACSB, ABET, ACEJMC, ACPE, ADA, APTA, ASLA, CSWE, NAAB, NASAD, NASM, NRPA, ACS, APA-COA, AOTA, NATA, CAAHEP, COAPRT, ABA, ASHA, NASP, CAHIIM, CAATE, AMTA, U/RTA, PDE, UCEA, NAST, CAHME, CCNE, CEPH, NASD, APMA, and LCME. The 384-acre campus is in an urban area approximately 1.5 miles from downtown Philadelphia. Including any residence halls, there are 166 buildings.

STUDENT LIFE: 79% of undergraduates are from Pennsylvania. Others are from 50 states, 96 foreign countries, and Canada. 9% are race unknown; 6% Foreign; 6% two or more races; 56% White; 22% Asian American; 17% African American; 12% Hispanic. **Female To Male Ratio:** 1.1:1. The average age of freshmen is 18; all undergraduates, 22. 11% do not continue beyond their first year; 66% remain to graduate. **Housing:** 5506 students can be accommodated in college housing, which includes dorms, on-campus apartments, and off-campus apartments. In addition, there are honors houses, special-interest houses, and living learning communities. On-campus housing is guaranteed for the freshman year only. 78% of students live on campus. Alcohol is not permitted. All students may keep cars.

FACULTY/CLASSROOMS: 61% of faculty are male; 39% are female. No introductory courses are taught by graduate students.

PROGRAMS OF STUDY: Temple confers B.A., B.F.A., B.B.A., B.MUS, B.S., B.S.BioE, B.S. Arch, B.S.A.T., B.S.C.E., B.S.Ed., B.S.E.E., B.S.E.T., B.S.M.E., B.S.N., and B.S.W. degrees. Associate, master's, and doctoral degrees are also awarded. Bachelor's degrees are awarded in AGRICULTURE (environmental studies and horticulture), BIOLOGICAL SCIENCE (biochemistry, biology/adolescence education, biology/biological science, and biophysics), BUSINESS (accounting, banking and finance, business administration and management, entrepreneurial studies, finance, international business management, management information systems, marketing/retailing/merchandising, real estate, sports management, and tourism), COMMUNICATIONS AND THE ARTS (advertising, art, art history and appreciation, broadcasting, ceramic art and design, classics, communications, dance, English, fiber/textiles/weaving, film arts, French, German, glass, graphic design, Italian, jazz, journalism, linguistics, media arts, metal/jewelry, music, music composition, music history and appreciation, music performance, music theory and composition, painting, performing arts, photography, piano/organ, printmaking, public relations, sculpture, Spanish, speech/debate/rhetoric, telecommunications, theater design, theater management, and visual and performing arts), COMPUTER AND PHYSICAL SCIENCE (actuarial science, applied mathematics, chemistry, chemistry/adolescence education, computer science, earth science / adolescence education, geology, information sciences and systems, mathematics, mathematics/computational, mathematics – economics, and physics), EDUCATION (art education, athletic training, career, technical education & training, early childhood education, elementary education, health information management, mathematics education, music education, physical education, secondary education, and technical education), ENGINEERING AND ENVIRONMENTAL DESIGN (architecture, city/community/regional planning, civil engineering, construction management, electrical/electronics engineering, engineering, engineering technology, environmental science, landscape architecture/design, and mechanical engineering), HEALTH PROFESSIONS (music therapy, nursing, predentistry, premedicine, public health, recreation therapy, and speech therapy), SOCIAL SCIENCE (African American studies, American studies, anthropology, Asian/Oriental studies, criminal justice, economics, geography, history, Latin American studies, legal studies, philosophy, physical fitness/movement, political science/government, prelaw, psychology, religion, social science, social work, sociology, and women's studies). Art, journalism, and business are the strongest academically. Biology, psychology, and accounting have the largest enrollments.

ACTIVITIES: 4% of men belong to 19 national fraternities; 4% of women belong to 15 national sororities. There are 329 groups on campus, including art, band, cheerleading, chess, choir, chorale, chorus, communications, computers, dance, debate, drama, drill team, environmental, ethnic, film, forensics, honors, international, jazz band, LGBT, literary magazine, marching band, musical theater, newspaper, opera, orchestra, pep band, photography, political, professional, radio and TV, religious, social, social service, student government, symphony, and yearbook. Popular campus events include Homecoming, and Cherry and White Day. **Sports:** There are 12 intercollegiate sports for men and 13 for women, and 14 intramural sports for men and 14 for women. Several campus recreation facilities include a climbing wall, a fitness mezzanine, cardio machines, selectorized machines, and areas designated for circuit training, light weights, basketball, football, volleyball, gymnastics, fencing, field hockey, women's lacrosse, tennis, baseball, softball stadium, and soccer. **Graduates:** From July 1, 2016 to June 30, 2017, 6080 bachelor's degrees were awarded. The most popular majors were business/marketing (20%), visual and performing arts (11%), and communication/journalism (11%). In an average class, 38% graduate in 4 years or less, 61% graduate in 5 years or less, and 66% graduate in 6 years or less.

SERVICES: Counseling and information services are available, as is tutoring in most subjects. There is a reader service for the blind, and remedial math, reading, and writing. **Library/Resources:** The library contains 4.8 million volumes, 3.4 million microform items, 45,385 audio/video tapes/CDs/DVDs, and subscribes to 67,942 periodicals including electronic. Computerized library services include interlibrary loans, database searching, Internet access, and Wi-Fi capability. Special learning facilities include an art gallery, planetarium, radio station, TV station, online learning programs for undergraduate and graduate levels, and to continuing education students, workstations, smart classrooms, and computer labs. **Physically Challenged Students:** All of the campus is accessible. Facilities include wheelchair ramps, elevators, special parking, specially equipped restrooms, special class scheduling, lowered drinking fountains, lowered telephones, and special housing. Additional services may be arranged through the Disabled Student Services Office. **Special:** Temple offers co-op programs in business/marketing, computer/information sciences, and engineering, internships, study abroad in 15 countries, an extern program in which participating students receive 2 or 3 academic credits, dual majors, distance learning, dual enrollment, ESL, domestic exchange, independent study, and a teacher certification program. There are 3 national honor societies, Phi Beta Kappa, and a freshman honors program. **Visiting:** There are regularly scheduled orientations for prospective students. There are guides for informal visits and visitors may sit in on classes. To schedule a visit, contact the Office of Undergraduate Admissions. **Campus Safety and Security:** Measures include 24-hour foot and vehicle patrol, emergency notification system, self-defense education, and security escort services. There are shuttle buses, emergency telephones, lighted pathways/sidewalks, controlled access to dorms/residences24-hour security in residence halls.

REQUIREMENTS: The SAT or ACT is required. Applicants should complete 16 academic units, 4 years of English and math, 3 units each of history, social studies, science, (with 2 units of lab), and academic electives, 2 units of foreign language (same language/culture), and 1 unit in art. A GED is accepted. A portfolio and audition are required in relevant fields. An essay is also required. AP and CLEP credits are accepted. Important factors in the admissions decision are advanced placement or honors courses, parents or siblings attended your school, evidence of special talent, and recommendations by school officials. The required core curriculum includes 9 areas of learning and a total of 11 courses. Areas include: Analytical Reading & Writing, Quantitative Literacy, Mosaic I and Mosaic II, Arts, Human Behavior, Race & Diversity, World Society, Science & Technology, and U.S. Society. All GenEd courses must be completed with a grade of C- or higher to satisfy a GenEd requirement. **Procedure:** Freshmen are admitted in the fall and spring. Entrance exams should be taken by fall junior year or spring senior year. There is a rolling admissions plan. Applications should be filed by February 1 for fall entry; November 15 for spring entry. The fall 2017 application fee was $55. Notification is sent on a rolling basis. Applications are accepted on-line. **Transfer Students:** 3847 transfer students enrolled in 2016-2017. Applicants must have earned at least 15 college credit hours with at least a 2.5 GPA and must submit official high school and college transcripts. 30 of 124 credits required for the bachelor's degree must be completed at Temple. **International Students:** There are 1022 international students enrolled. They must take the TOEFL with a minimum score of 550 on the paper-based TOEFL (PBT) or 79 on the Internet-based version (iBT). They must also take the SAT or ACT.

ADMISSIONS: 64% of the 2017-2018 applicants were accepted. The SAT scores for the 2017-2018 freshman class were: Critical Reading-- 22% below 500, 48% between 500 and 599, 25% between 600 and 699, and 5% between 700 and 800. Math-- 17% below 500, 46% between 500 and 599, 30% between 600 and 699, and 7% between 700 and 800. Writing-- 24% below 500, 46% between 500 and 599, 25% between 600 and 699, and 5% between 700 and 800. The ACT scores were 16% below 12, 27% between 12 and 17, 28% between 18 and 23, 12% between 24 and 29, and 17% above 30. 42% of the current freshmen were in the top fifth of their class; 77% were in the top two fifths. 13 freshmen graduated first in their class. **Admissions Contact:** Karin Mormando, Director of Undergraduate Admissions. Email: *tuadm@temple.edu* Web: *www.temple.edu*

FINANCIAL AID: The average freshman award was $15,200. Need-based scholarships or need-based grants averaged $6,193; need-based self-help aid (loans and jobs) averaged $3,518; non-need-based athletic scholarships averaged $17,929; and other non-need-based awards and non-need-based scholarships averaged $5,192. The average financial indebtedness of the 2017 graduate was $34,382. The college's own financial statement, and the PHEAA (Pennsylvania residents) are required. The FAFSA code is 003371. The priority date for freshman financial aid applications for fall entry is March 1.

THIEL COLLEGE *(The complete profile is made available exclusively on our website, www.barronspac.com)*

UNIVERSITY OF PENNSYLVANIA F-3

www.upenn.edu

Philadelphia, PA 19104 **(215) 898-7507**

Fax: (215) 898-9670	**Email:** info@admissions.upenn.edu
Full-time: 4703 men, 4704 women	**Faculty:** 1456; I, ++$
Part-time: 169 men, 136 women	**Ph.D.s:** 100%
Graduate: 5455 men, 6191 women	**Student/Faculty:** 6 to 1
Year: semesters, summer session	**Tuition:** $49,536
Room & Board: $13,990	**Freshman Class:** 35866 applied, 3718 accepted, 2425 enrolled
SAT or ACT: required	**CEEB CODE:** 2926
Application Deadline: January 1	**MOST COMPETITIVE**

University of Pennsylvania, founded in 1740, is a member of the Ivy League. There are 4 undergraduate schools: College of Arts & Sciences, School of Engineering & Applied Science, School of Nursing, and the Wharton school. Students can pursue interdisciplinary study within the schools, and the university's 12 graduate schools, engaging in learning within our 165 research centers. In addition to regional accreditation, University of Pennsylvania has baccalaureate program accreditation with AACSB, ABET, CCNE, and ACNM. The 302-acre campus is in an urban area in Philadelphia. Including any residence halls, there are 187 buildings.

STUDENT LIFE: 82% of undergraduates are from out of state, mostly the Middle Atlantic. Students are from 50 states, 103 foreign countries, and Canada. 59% are from public schools. 46% are White; 19% Asian American; 11% Foreign; 10% Hispanic; 7% African American; 4% two or more races; 4% race unknown. 29% claim no religious affiliation; 26% Protestant; 19% Catholic; 19% Jewish. **Female To Male Ratio:** 1.1:1. The average age of freshmen is 18; all undergraduates, 20. 2% do not continue beyond their first year; 96% remain to graduate. **Housing:** 6850 students can be accommodated in college housing, which includes married student dorms, on-campus apartments, and off-campus apartments. In addition, there are language/international houses, special-interest houses, fraternity houses. There are over 40 academic residence programs, including the areas of: arts, entrepreneurship, politics, law & society, international studies, media, visual arts, and women in science. On-campus housing is guaranteed for the freshman year only, is available on a first-come, first-served basis, and is available on a lottery system for upperclassmen. All students may keep cars.

FACULTY/CLASSROOMS: 63% of faculty are male; 37% are female. All teach undergraduates, and all do research. No introductory courses are taught by graduate students.

PROGRAMS OF STUDY: University of Pennsylvania confers B.A., B.S., B.Applied Sc., B.B.A., B.F.A., B.S.E. and B.S.N. degrees. Associate, master's, and doctoral degrees are also awarded. Bachelor's degrees are awarded in AGRICULTURE (environmental studies), BIOLOGICAL SCIENCE (biochemistry, biology/biological science, and biophysics), BUSINESS (accounting, business administration and management, entrepreneurial studies, human resources, insurance and risk management, logistics, management information systems, marketing/retailing/merchandising, operations management, real estate, retailing, and transportation management), COMMUNICATIONS AND THE ARTS (art history and appreciation, classics, communications, comparative literature, design, dramatic arts, English, fine arts, folklore and mythology, French, German, linguistics, music, Russian, and visual and performing arts), COMPUTER AND PHYSICAL SCIENCE (actuarial science, applied science, chemistry, computer science, digital arts/technology, geology, information sciences and systems, mathematics, physics, science technology, and statistics), EDUCATION (elementary education), ENGINEERING AND ENVIRONMENTAL DESIGN (architecture, bioengineering, chemical engineering, civil engineering, computer engineering, electrical/electronics engineering, and materials engineering), HEALTH PROFESSIONS (health, health care administration, and nursing), SOCIAL SCIENCE (African studies, African American studies, American studies, anthropology, Asian/Oriental studies, cognitive science, economics, gender studies, Hispanic American studies, history, history of science, international relations, international studies, Italian studies, Judaic studies, Latin American studies, law, Middle Eastern studies, Near Eastern studies, philosophy, political science/government, psychology, public administration, religion, sociology, South Asian studies, urban studies, and women's studies). Finance, economics, and nursing have the largest enrollments.

ACTIVITIES: 30% of men belong to 36 national fraternities; 17% of women belong to 13 national sororities. There are 450 groups on campus, including art, band, cheerleading, chess, choir, chorale, chorus, computers, dance, debate, drama, environmental, ethnic, film, forensics, honors, international, jazz band, LGBT, literary magazine, marching band, musical theater, newspaper, opera, orchestra, pep band, photography, political, professional, radio and TV, religious, social, social service, student government, and symphony. **Sports:** There are 17 intercollegiate sports for men and 16 for women, and 11 intramural sports for men and 11 for women. Facilities include gyms, a swimming pool, squash courts, indoor and outdoor tennis courts, playing fields, an indoor ice rink, rowing tanks, weight rooms, exercise facilities, a boathouse, and a stadium. **Graduates:** From July 1, 2016 to June 30, 2017, 2848 bachelor's degrees were awarded. The most popular majors were finance (14%), nursing (6%), and economics (5%). In an average class, 88% graduate in 4 years or less and 96% graduate in 6 years or less. Of the 2016 graduating class, 20% were enrolled in graduate school within 6 months of graduation, and 60% were employed.

SERVICES: Counseling and information services are available, as is tutoring in most subjects. There is a reader service for the blind. The WHEEL academic support program is available in all residences. **Library/Resources:** The library contains 5.9 million volumes, 4.2 million microform items, and 121,233 audio/video tapes/CDs/DVDs, and subscribes to 98,145 periodicals including electronic. Computerized library services include interlibrary loans, database searching, Internet access, and Wi-Fi capability. Special learning facilities include a natural history museum, planetarium, radio station, TV station, Museum of Archaeology and Anthropology, Institute of Contemporary Art, an arboretum, a theater, astronomical observatory, animal research center, Equine Sports Medicine and Imaging Rehabilitation Center, Women's Center, Center for Undergraduate Research, a wind tunnel, The Cyclotron Facility, many galleries, Kelly Writer's House, Center for Advanced Judaic Studies, and LRSM (is the center for materials research laboratories). **Physically Challenged Students:** 93% of the campus is accessible. Facilities include wheelchair ramps, elevators, special parking, specially equipped restrooms, special class scheduling, lowered drinking fountains, lowered telephones, and special housing. **Special:** Cross-registration is permitted with Haverford, Swarthmore, and Bryn Mawr Colleges and through the Quaker Consortium. Opportunities are provided for internships, a Washington semester, accelerated degree programs, joint degree programs, preprofessional programs, B.A.-B.S. degrees, dual and student-designed majors, credit by exam, limited pass/fail options, and study abroad in 39 countries. Through the "one university" concept, students in one undergraduate school may study in any of the other three. There are 11 national honor societies, a freshman honors program, and 27 departmental honors programs. **Visiting:** There are regularly scheduled orientations for prospective students, including an information session by the admissions office and a tour of the campus led by current students. There are guides for informal visits, visitors may sit in on classes, and stay overnight. To schedule a visit, contact the Admissions Office. **Campus Safety and Security:** Measures include 24-hour foot and vehicle patrol, emergency notification system, self-defense education, and security escort services. There are shuttle buses, emergency telephones, lighted pathways/sidewalks, controlled access to dorms/residences, a bicycle patrol, police officers, victim support and special services, Students Together Against Acquaintance Rape, Penn Watch, student walking escort, and security guard personnel.

REQUIREMENTS: The SAT or ACT is required. Graduation from an accredited secondary school is not required. Recommended preparation includes 4 years of high school English, 3 or 4 each of a foreign language and math, and 3 each of history and social science. An essay is required. A portfolio is recommended for prospective art majors. AP credits are accepted. The bachelor's degree requires completion of 32 to 40 course units, depending on the student's major, with 12 to 18 of these units in the major and a GPA of 2.0. **Procedure:** Freshmen are admitted in the fall. Entrance exams should be taken by December of the senior year. There are early decision and deferred admissions plans. Early decision applications should be filed by November 1; regular applications, by January 1 for fall entry. The fall 2017 application fee was $75. Notification of early decision is sent December 15; regular decision, April 1. 1299 early decision candidates were accepted for the 2017-2018 class. 1600 applicants were on the 2017 waiting list; 136 were admitted. Applications are accepted on-line. **Transfer Students:** 170 transfer students enrolled in 2016-2017. Applicants must provide college and high school transcripts, essays, and 2 recommendations. SAT or ACT scores are required for transfer students. 16 of 32 credits required for the bachelor's degree must be completed at Penn. **International Students:** There are 1077 international students enrolled. They must take the TOEFL, SAT Subject tests or the ACT with writing.

ADMISSIONS: 10% of the 2017-2018 applicants were accepted. The SAT scores for the 2017-2018 freshman class were: Critical Reading-- 5% between 500 and 599, 31% between 600 and 699, and 64% between 700 and 800. Math-- 2% between 500 and 599, 24% between 600 and 699, and 74% between 700 and 800. Writing-- 3% between 500 and 599, 22% between 600 and 699, and 75% between 700 and 800.; 100% were in the top two fifths. **Admissions Contact:** Email: *info@admissions.upenn.edu* Web: *www.upenn.edu*

FINANCIAL AID: In 2017-2018, 50% of all full-time freshmen received some form of financial aid and need-based aid. The average freshman award was $41,713. Need-based scholarships or need-based grants averaged $39,459; and need-based self-help aid (loans and jobs) averaged $2,890. 44% of undergraduate students work part-time. The average financial indebtedness of the 2017 graduate was $19,798. University of Pennsylvania is a member of CSS. The CSS/Profile and the college's own financial statement, and parents' and student's most recently completed income tax returns are required. The FAFSA code is 003378. The priority date for freshman financial aid applications for fall entry is February 15.

UNIVERSITY OF PITTSBURGH — B-3

www.pitt.edu

Pittsburgh, PA 15260 — **(412) 624-PITT**

Fax: (412) 648-4138 — **Email:** oafa@pitt.edu

Full-time: 8885 men, 9505 women	**Faculty:** n/av
Part-time: 496 men, 440 women	**Ph.D.s:** 94%
Graduate: 4101 men, 5215 women	**Student/Faculty:** 15 to 1
Year: semesters, summer session	**Tuition:** $19,080 (30,642)
Room & Board: $10,950	**Freshman Class:** 27679 applied, 16528 accepted, 4026 enrolled
SAT CR/M: 660/670 **ACT:** 30	**CEEB CODE:** 2927
Application Deadline: open	**MOST COMPETITIVE**

The University of Pittsburgh, founded in 1787, is a state-related, public research university with programs in arts and sciences, business, computing and information, dental medicine, education, engineering, health and rehabilitation sciences, law, public and international affairs, social work, nursing, pharmacy, dental medicine, medicine, and public health. There are 9 undergraduate schools and 8 graduate schools. In addition to regional accreditation, University of Pittsburgh has baccalaureate program accreditation with AACSB, ABET, ADA, and CSWE. The 145-acre campus is in a suburban area 3 miles east of downtown Pittsburgh. Including any residence halls, there are 131 buildings.

STUDENT LIFE: 69% of undergraduates are from Pennsylvania. Others are from 50 states, 56 foreign countries, and Canada. 72% are White; 5% African American; 4% Hispanic; 4% Foreign; 4% two or more races; 10% Asian American; 1% race unknown. **Female To Male Ratio:** 1.1:1. The average age of all undergraduates is 20. 7% do not continue beyond their first year; 83% remain to graduate. **Housing:** 7831 students can be accommodated in college housing, which includes gender neutral, single-sex, coed, on-campus apartments, and off-campus apartments. In addition, there are honors houses, language/international houses, special-interest houses, fraternity houses, sorority houses, emerging leaders, engineering, nursing, business, international living, health sciences, healthyU, service to others, and appreciation of the arts. On-campus housing is guaranteed for the freshman year only, is available on a first-come, first-served basis, and is available on a lottery system for upperclassmen. 57% of students commute. All students may keep cars.

FACULTY/CLASSROOMS: 55% of faculty are male; 45% are female. No introductory courses are taught by graduate students.

PROGRAMS OF STUDY: University of Pittsburgh confers B.A., B.S., B.A.S.W., B.Phil., B.S.B.A., B.S.E., B.S.N., and B.S.P.S. degrees. Master's and doctoral degrees are also awarded. Bachelor's degrees are awarded in AGRICULTURE (environmental studies), BIOLOGICAL SCIENCE (bioinformatics, biology/biological science, ecology, microbiology, molecular biology, and neurosciences), BUSINESS (accounting, business (dual major program), business information systems, economics – statistics, finance, global/general management, human resources, international business management, marketing/retailing/merchandising, and supply chain management), COMMUNICATIONS AND THE ARTS (Africana studies, Chinese, classics, communication rhetoric/communication, communication science, creative writing, English literature, film arts, French, German studies, Germanic languages and literature, Italian, Japanese, linguistics, media arts, music, Polish, Russian, Slavic languages, Spanish, studio art, and theatre arts), COMPUTER AND PHYSICAL SCIENCE (actuarial mathematics, applied mathematics, astronomy, chemistry, computer science, geology, information sciences and systems, mathematics, mathematics – economics, natural sciences, physics, and statistics), EDUCATION (athletic training, health information management, and health and physical education), ENGINEERING AND ENVIRONMENTAL DESIGN (bioengineering, chemical engineering, civil engineering, computer engineering, electrical/electronics engineering, engineering physics, engineering science, environmental science, industrial engineering, materials engineering, materials science, and mechanical engineering), HEALTH PROFESSIONS (dental hygiene, emergency medical technologies, health services technology, nursing, pharmaceutical science, and rehabilitation therapy), SOCIAL SCIENCE (anthropology, applied psychology, architectural studies, economics, history, history of philosophy, humanities, interdisciplinary studies, international studies, legal studies, liberal arts/general studies, philosophy, political science/government, psychology, public administration, public affairs, religion, social science, social work, sociology, urban studies, and women's studies). Psychology, mechanical engineering, and biological sciences have the largest enrollments.

ACTIVITIES: 10% of men belong to 24 national fraternities; 12% of women belong to 18 national sororities. There are 595 groups on campus, including art, band, cheerleading, chess, choir, chorale, chorus, communications, dance, debate, drama, ethnic, film, honors, international, jazz band, LGBT, literary magazine, marching band, musical theater, newspaper, pep band, political, professional, radio and TV, religious, social, social service, student government, and symphony. Popular campus events include Lantern Night, Fall Fest, Homecoming, and Bigelow Bash. **Sports:** There are 8 intercollegiate sports for men and 9 for women, and 15 intramural sports for men and 14 for women. Facilities include a field house for basketball, volleyball, gymnastics, wrestling, indoor track and field, a pool, and a gymnastics training center. The sports complex has a baseball stadium, soccer, and softball. **Graduates:** From July 1, 2016 to June 30, 2017, 4453 bachelor's degrees were awarded. The most popular majors were psychology (7%), finance (6%), and biological sciences (5%). In an average class, 83% graduate in 6 years or less.

SERVICES: Counseling and information services are available, as is tutoring in some subjects, many lower-level undergraduate science and humanities courses. There is remedial math and writing. **Library/Resources:** The library contains 7.5 million volumes, 454,503 audio/video tapes/CDs/DVDs, and subscribes to 337,491 periodicals including electronic. Computerized library services include interlibrary loans, database searching, Internet access, and Wi-Fi capability. Special learning facilities include an art gallery, radio station, TV station, international classrooms, an observatory, and a music hall. **Physically Challenged Students:** 90% of the campus is accessible. Facilities include wheelchair ramps, elevators, special parking, specially equipped restrooms, lowered drinking fountains, lowered telephones, and special housing. **Special:** Students may cross-register with 9 neighboring colleges and universities. Internships, unlimited study abroad, work-study programs, a dual major in business and any other subject in arts and sciences, and student-designed majors are available. There is a 5-year joint degree in arts and sciences/engineering. There are co-op programs in engineering, computer science, and chemistry. An accelerated second degree B.S.N. program is available as well as a 3-2 engineering degree. There are 32 national honor societies, Phi Beta Kappa, and a freshman honors program. **Visiting:** There are regularly scheduled orientations for prospective students, including information sessions, student-guided tours, and class attendance. There are guides for informal visits and visitors may sit in on classes. To schedule a visit, contact the Office of Admissions and Financial Aid at (877) SEE-PITT. **Campus Safety and Security:** Measures include 24-hour foot and vehicle patrol, emergency notification system, self-defense education, and security escort services. There are shuttle buses, emergency telephones, lighted pathways/sidewalks, and controlled access to dorms/residences.

REQUIREMENTS: The SAT or ACT and the ACT Optional Writing test is also required. Applicants for admission to the Kenneth P. Dietrich School of Arts and Sciences must be graduates of an accredited secondary school. Students must have 17 high school academic credits, including 4 units of English, 3 to 4 each of math and lab science, 2-3 of social studies, plus 3 to 5 units in academic electives. Pitt recommends that the student have 3 or more years of a single foreign language. An essay is recommended if the student is seeking scholarship consideration. AP and CLEP credits are accepted. Important factors in the admissions decision are advanced placement or honors courses, leadership record, and evidence of special talent. All students in the Kenneth P. Dietrich School of Arts and Sciences must take a minimum of 120 credits. Skills and general education requirements vary but include course work in the humanities, social and natural sciences, and foreign culture. A 2.0 GPA is required. Students must earn their last 30 credits while enrolled in Arts and Sciences and earn at least half of the credits for their majors while enrolled in Arts and Sciences. **Procedure:** Freshmen are admitted to all sessions. Entrance exams should be taken preferably by January for September admission. There are deferred admissions and rolling admissions plans. Application deadlines are open. The fall 2017 application fee was $45. Notification is sent on a rolling basis. 2382 applicants were on the 2017 waiting list; 170 were admitted. Applications are accepted on-line. **Transfer Students:** 753 transfer students enrolled in 2016-2017. Applicants for transfer to the Kenneth P. Dietrich School of Arts and Sciences must supply transcripts of all secondary school and college course work and have a minimum GPA of 3.0. An interview is recommended. Grades of C or better transfer for credit. Application deadlines vary by school. 30 of 120 credits required for the bachelor's degree must be completed at University of Pittsburgh. **International Students:** There are 776 international students enrolled. They must take the TOEFL with a minimum score of 600 on the paper-based TOEFL (PBT) or 100 on the Internet-based version (iBT). Students must take the IELTS, and the SAT or ACT.

ADMISSIONS: 60% of the 2017-2018 applicants were accepted. The SAT scores for the 2017-2018 freshman class were: Critical Reading-- 2% below 500, 28% between 500 and 599, 50% between 600 and 699, and 20% between 700 and 800. Math-- 1% below 500, 11% between 500 and 599, 53% between 600 and 699, and 35% between 700 and 800. Writing-- 11% below 500, 35% between 500 and 599, 37% between 600 and 699, and 17% between 700 and 800. The ACT scores were 1% below 12, 1% between 12 and 17, 14% between 18 and 23, 22% between 24 and 29, and 62% above 30. 79% of the current freshmen were in the top fifth of their class; 97% were in the top two fifths. **Admissions Contact:** Marc L. Harding, Chief Enrollment Officer. Email: *oafa@pitt.edu* Web: *www.pitt.edu*

FINANCIAL AID: In 2017-2018, 52% of all full-time freshmen received some form of financial aid. 82% of all full-time freshmen received need-based aid. The average freshman award was $12,459. Need-based scholarships or need-based grants averaged $9,960; need-based self-help aid (loans and jobs) averaged $4,180; and non-need-based athletic scholarships averaged $10,734. The average financial indebtedness of the 2017 graduate was $38,612. University of Pittsburgh is a member of CSS. The FAFSA code is 008815. The priority date for freshman financial aid applications for fall entry is March 1.

UNIVERSITY OF PITTSBURGH AT BRADFORD C-1

www.upb.pitt.edu

Bradford, PA 16701	**(814) 362-7555** **(800) 872-1787**
Fax: (814) 362-7578	**Email: admissions@upb.pitt.edu**
Full-time: 564 men, 669 women	**Faculty:** 75; IIB, av$
Part-time: 40 men, 67 women	**Ph.D.s:** 71%
Graduate: n/av	**Student/Faculty:** 17 to 1
Year: semesters, summer session	**Tuition:** $13,900 ($25,144)
Room & Board: $9058	**Freshman Class:** 2293 applied, 416 accepted, 348 enrolled
SAT EBR-W/M: 540/530 **ACT:** 22	**CEEB CODE:** 2935
Application Deadline: n/av	**COMPETITIVE**

University of Pittsburgh at Bradford, established in 1963, is a public, state-related institution for students who want to earn a world-renowned education in a personalized environment. There is 1 undergraduate school. In addition to regional accreditation, Pitt-Brad has baccalaureate program accreditation with CAATE and ACEN. The 317-acre campus is in a small town 160 miles northeast of Pittsburgh and 80 miles south of Buffalo. Including any residence halls, there are 32 buildings.

STUDENT LIFE: 77% of undergraduates are from Pennsylvania. Others are from 27 states, 16 foreign countries, and Canada. 91% are from public schools. 69% are White; 5% Hispanic; 5% race unknown; 3% Foreign; 3% two or more races; 2% Asian American; 12% African American. **Female To Male Ratio:** 1.2:1. The average age of freshmen is 18; all undergraduates, 21. 33% do not continue beyond their first year; 50% remain to graduate. **Housing:** 1000 students can be accommodated in college housing, which includes on-campus apartments. On-campus housing is available on a first-come, first-served basis. 74% of students live on campus. All students may keep cars.

FACULTY/CLASSROOMS: 51% of faculty are male; 49% are female. All teach undergraduates. No introductory courses are taught by graduate students. The average class size in an introductory lecture is 19; in a laboratory is 12; and in a regular course is 16.

PROGRAMS OF STUDY: Pitt-Brad confers B.A., B.S. and B.S.N. degrees. Associate degrees are also awarded. Bachelor's degrees are awarded in AGRICULTURE (environmental studies), BIOLOGICAL SCIENCE (biology/biological science), BUSINESS (accounting, business administration and management, hospitality management services, and sports management), COMMUNICATIONS AND THE ARTS (communications, English, and public relations), COMPUTER AND PHYSICAL SCIENCE (applied mathematics, chemistry, mathematics, and physical sciences), EDUCATION (athletic training, business education, elementary education, English education, environmental education, health education, mathematics education, science education, and social studies education), ENGINEERING AND ENVIRONMENTAL DESIGN (engineering), HEALTH PROFESSIONS (nursing, radiological science, and sports medicine), SOCIAL SCIENCE (criminal justice, economics, history, human development, interdisciplinary studies, liberal arts/general studies, psychology, social science, and sociology). Engineering, nursing, and biology are the strongest academically. Biology, business management, and computer information systems have the largest enrollments.

ACTIVITIES: 4% of men belong to 4 local fraternities; 1% of women belong to 2 local sororities. There are 60 groups on campus, including art, cheerleading, choir, chorale, computers, dance, drama, environmental, ethnic, honors, international, LGBT, literary magazine, newspaper, pep band, political, professional, radio and TV, religious, social, social service, and student government. Popular campus events include Winter Weekend, Spring Fling, and Alumni Weekend. **Sports:** There are 6 intercollegiate sports for men and 7 for women, and 15 intramural sports for men and 15 for women. Facilities include a sport and fitness center that has a performance arena for basketball, volleyball, and general recreation, a fitness center with physical conditioning equipment, an exercise arts studio for dance, martial arts, and aerobics, and an auxiliary gym for recreated and intramurals, phys ed classes, and a swimming pool. Outdoor facilities include a lighted softball field, a baseball field, tennis courts, handball courts, basketball courts, football/softball fields, and a sand volleyball court. **Graduates:** From July 1, 2016 to June 30, 2017, 225 bachelor's degrees were awarded. The most popular majors were criminal justice (11%), business management (10%), and biology (7%). In an average class, 36% graduate in 4 years or less, 49% graduate in 5 years or less, and 50% graduate in 6 years or less. Of the 2016 graduating class, 30% were enrolled in graduate school within 6 months of graduation, and 80% were employed.

SERVICES: Counseling and information services are available, as is tutoring in most subjects. There is remedial math, reading, and writing. **Library/Resources:** The library contains 105,844 volumes, 14,125 microform items, and 4,705 audio/video tapes/CDs/DVDs, and subscribes to 75 periodicals including electronic. Computerized library services include interlibrary loans, database searching, and Internet access. Special learning facilities include an art gallery, radio station, a crime scene investigation house, a nursing suite with computerized mannequins, a psychology lab, a human performance lab, and athletic training facilities. Systems network advanced projects lab and a virtual computing lab. **Physically Challenged Students:** 99% of the campus is accessible. Facilities include elevators, special parking, specially equipped restrooms, lowered drinking fountains, lowered telephones, and special housing. **Special:** Students may cross-register with colleges in the University of Pittsburgh system. Internships are required or strongly recommended for all majors. The school offers study abroad, dual majors, nondegree study, and a 3-2 engineering degree with the University of Pittsburgh (Oakland campus). Interdisciplinary majors are offered in human relations combining anthropology, psychology, and sociology; social sciences, combining anthropology, economics, history, political science, and sociology; and in interdisciplinary arts, combining art, music, and theater. Professional preparation is available in many areas including premedicine, prelaw, preveterinary science, prepharmacy, and predentistry. Teacher certification is also offered. There are 7 national honor societies. **Visiting:** There are regularly scheduled orientations for prospective students, and programs throughout the year, offering a workshop with admissions representatives on academics, admissions, guidance, standardized tests, the application process, and financial aid. Tours led by students, a financial aid presentation, and a special campus event are also offered. To schedule a visit, contact Alexander Nazemetz at (800) 872-1787. **Campus Safety and Security:** Measures include 24-hour foot and vehicle patrol, emergency notification system, and security escort services. There are shuttle buses, emergency telephones, and lighted pathways/sidewalks.

REQUIREMENTS: The SAT or ACT is required. Students must be graduates of an accredited secondary school with 16 Carnegie units, including 4 in English, 3 each in history or social studies, science and math. The GED is accepted. Also used in the admissions decision are standardized test scores, rank in class, extracurricular activities, and recommendations. An essay is strongly recommended, as is an interview. AP and CLEP credits are accepted. Important factors in the admissions decision are advanced placement or honors courses, extracurricular activities record, and leadership record. To graduate, students must complete a minimum of 120 credits with 30 to 76 in the major, and maintan a minimum GPA of 2.0. At least 30 should be upper-level courses. The core curriculum varies from 12 to 30 credits and distribution requirements from 56 to 59. English, math competency, and phys ed courses are required. **Procedure:** Freshmen are admitted in the fall, spring, and summer. Entrance exams should be taken during the junior year or the fall of the senior year. There are deferred admissions and rolling admissions plans. Application deadlines are open. Notifications are sent October 14. Applications are accepted on-line. **Transfer Students:** 67 transfer students enrolled in 2016-2017. A GPA of 2.0 or higher is required. 30 of 120 credits required for the bachelor's degree must be completed at Pitt-Bradford. **International Students:** There are 38 international students enrolled. They must take the TOEFL with a minimum score of 550 on the paper-based TOEFL (PBT) or 80 on the Internet-based version (iBT). Students must also take the IELTS, scoring 6.5.

ADMISSIONS: 18% of the 2017-2018 applicants were accepted. The SAT scores for the 2017-2018 freshman class were: Math-- 28% below 500, 56% between 500 and 599, 13% between 600 and 699, and 3% between 700 and 800. Writing-- 63% below 500, 30% between 500 and 599, 5% between 600 and 699, and 2% between 700 and 800. Evidence-Based Reading/Writing-- 28% below 500, 49% between 500 and 599, 22% between 600 and 699, and 1% between 700 and 800. The ACT scores were 9% between 12 and 17, 61% between 18 and 23, 23% between 24 and 29, and 7% above 30. 27% of the current freshmen were in the top fifth of their class; 57% were in the top two fifths. 10 freshmen graduated first in their class. **Admissions Contact:** Alexander P. Nazemetz, Associate Vice President for Enrollment and Director of Admissions. Email: *admissions@upb.pitt.edu* Web: *www.upb.pitt.edu*

FINANCIAL AID: In 2017-2018, 98% of all full-time freshmen received some form of financial aid. 76% of all full-time freshmen received need-based aid. The average freshman award was $17,996. Need-based scholarships or need-based grants averaged $9,770 ($13,900 maximum); need-based self-help aid (loans and jobs) averaged $6,280 ($7,190 maximum); and other non-need-based awards and non-need-based scholarships averaged $5,730 ($25,296 maximum). 17% of undergraduate students work part-time. The average financial indebtedness of the 2017 graduate was $36,721. The FAFSA code is 008816. The priority date for freshman financial aid applications for fall entry is March 1.

UNIVERSITY OF PITTSBURGH AT GREENSBURG B-3

www.greensburg.pitt.edu

Greensburg, PA 15632	(724) 837-7040
Fax: (724) 836-7471	Email: upgadmit@pitt.edu
Full-time: 687 men, 748 women	Faculty: 76; IIB, -$
Part-time: 47 men, 35 women	Ph.D.s: 78%
Graduate: n/av	Student/Faculty: 18 to 1
Year: semesters, summer session	Tuition: $13,870 ($25,114)
Room & Board: $10,270	Freshman Class: 2505 applied, 1877 accepted, 467 enrolled
SAT CR/M/W: 510/508/480 ACT: 23	CEEB CODE: 2936
Application Deadline: open	COMPETITIVE

University of Pittsburgh at Greensburg, established in 1963, is a public state-related institution, offering students the option to begin their undergraduate majors at Pitt-Greensburg, and complete their program at any other Pitt campuses. There is 1 undergraduate school. The 219-acre campus is in a suburban area 33 miles southeast of Pittsburgh. Including any residence halls, there are 26 buildings.

STUDENT LIFE: 92% of undergraduates are from Pennsylvania. Others are from 5 states, 1 foreign country, and Canada. 76% are White; 6% African American; 6% Hispanic; 4% Asian American; 4% two or more races; 3% race unknown; 1% Foreign. **Female To Male Ratio:** 1.1:1. The average age of freshmen is 18; all undergraduates, 21. 25% do not continue beyond their first year; 55% remain to graduate. **Housing:** 585 students can be accommodated in college housing, which includes dorms and on-campus apartments. In addition, there are special-interest houses, theme housing, and single student apartments. On-campus housing is available on a first-come, first-served basis. 71% of students live on campus. Alcohol is not permitted. All students may keep cars.

FACULTY/CLASSROOMS: All teach undergraduates, and 50% do research. No introductory courses are taught by graduate students. The average class size in an introductory lecture is 30; in a laboratory is 15; and in a regular course is 25.

PROGRAMS OF STUDY: Pitt-Greensburg confers B.A. and B.S. degrees. Bachelor's degrees are awarded in BIOLOGICAL SCIENCE (biology/biological science), BUSINESS (accounting and management science), COMMUNICATIONS AND THE ARTS (communications, creative writing, and English literature), COMPUTER AND PHYSICAL SCIENCE (applied mathematics and natural sciences), SOCIAL SCIENCE (American studies, anthropology, humanities, political science/government, psychology, and social science). Management, and psychology are the strongest academically. Management, and administration of justice have the largest enrollments.

ACTIVITIES: There are no fraternities or sororities. There are 44 groups on campus, including academic club, band, cheerleading, chess, choir, chorale, chorus, computers, dance, debate, drama, ethnic, honors, literary magazine, newspaper, pep band, political, religious, social, social service, and student government. Popular campus events include La Cultura Study, St. Clair History Lecture, and Westmoreland Forum. **Sports:** There are 6 intercollegiate sports for men and 6 for women, and 8 intramural sports for men and 8 for women. Facilities include baseball, golf, basketball, cross country, soccer, softball, volleyball, and tennis. **Graduates:** From July 1, 2016 to June 30, 2017, 212 bachelor's degrees were awarded. The most popular majors were buisness/marketing (21%), psychology, and biological sciences (18%), and English (14%). Of the 2016 graduating class, 23% were enrolled in graduate school within 6 months of graduation, and 56% were employed.

SERVICES: Counseling and information services are available, as is tutoring in most subjects, such as math, computer science, and English. There is remedial math, reading, and writing. **Library/Resources:** The library contains 78,000 volumes, 9,458 microform items, and 1,280 audio/video tapes/CDs/DVDs. Computerized library services include interlibrary loans, database searching, Internet access, and Wi-Fi capability. **Physically Challenged Students:** 95% of the campus is accessible. Facilities include wheelchair ramps, elevators, special parking, specially equipped restrooms, special class scheduling, lowered drinking fountains, lowered telephones, and special housing. **Special:** Pitt-Greensburg offers cross-registration with the Pittsburgh and Johnstown campuses of the university system and with Seton Hill College and Westmoreland County Community College. Internships are also available in all majors and required for English writing and criminology. Double majors, student-designed majors, a Washington semester, nondegree study, and pass/fail options also offered. There are 2 national honor societies and a chapter of Phi Beta Kappa. **Visiting:** There are regularly scheduled orientations for prospective students, there are Open House, Preview Day, and Junior Jump Start days, weekday visits that include campus tours and information sessions. There are guides for informal visits and visitors may sit in on classes. To schedule a visit, contact the Admissions Office. **Campus Safety and Security:** Measures include 24-hour foot and vehicle patrol and security escort services. There are emergency telephones and lighted pathways/sidewalks.

REQUIREMENTS: The SAT is required. Students must be graduates of an accredited secondary school. The GED is also accepted. Students must complete 15 college-preparatory high school units, including 4 each of English and foreign language, 2 each in math (recommended 4 for specific programs), social studies, and history (3 recommended), 1 each of science with lab (2-4 recommended) and 1 each in academic electives, and computer science for engineering. An essay is optional; an interview is recommended. Students must also submit scores from the SAT or ACT (including the Writing test). GPA and class rank are also considered heavily. Pitt-Greensburg requires applicants to be in the upper 60% of their class. AP and CLEP credits are accepted. Important factors in the admissions decision are leadership record and advanced placement or honors courses. To graduate, students must complete 120 to 126 hours, with 24 to 36 in the major, and maintain a minimum GPA of 2.0. General education requirements include 15 credits each in humanities, social sciences, and natural sciences, 6 to 15 in writing courses, 3 each in speech and critical reasoning, and 2 to 3 in math. **Procedure:** Freshmen are admitted in the fall and spring. Entrance exams should be taken by November of the senior year. There are deferred admissions and rolling admissions plans. Application deadlines are open. The fall 2017 application fee was $45. Applications are accepted on-line. **Transfer Students:** 84 transfer students enrolled in 2016-2017. Applicants must have a minimum GPA of 2.0 and at least 12 college credits. 30 of 120 credits required for the bachelor's degree must be completed at Pitt-Greensburg. **International Students:** They must take the TOEFL.

ADMISSIONS: 75% of the 2017-2018 applicants were accepted. The SAT scores for the 2017-2018 freshman class were: Critical Reading-- 43% below 500, 44% between 500 and 599, 12% between 600 and 699, and 1% between 700 and 800. Math-- 43% below 500, 43% between 500 and 599, 13% between 600 and 699, and 1% between 700 and 800. Writing-- 53% below 500, 39% between 500 and 599, and 8% between 600 and 699. The ACT scores were 11% between 12 and 17, 49% between 18 and 23, 39% between 24 and 29, and 1% above 30. 22% of the current freshmen were in the top fifth of their class; 60% were in the top two fifths. **Admissions Contact:** Brandi S. Darr, Director of Admissions and Financial Aid. Email: *upgadmit@pitt.edu* Web: *www.greensburg.pitt.edu*

FINANCIAL AID: In 2017-2018, 70% of all full-time freshmen received some form of financial aid and need-based aid. The average freshman award was $11,436. Need-based scholarships or need-based grants averaged $9,033; need-based self-help aid (loans and jobs) averaged $3,809; other non-need-based awards and non-need-based scholarships averaged $3,681; and $3,973 from other forms of aid. The average financial indebtedness of the 2017 graduate was $25,651. The college's own financial statement is required. The priority date for freshman financial aid applications for fall entry is February 1.

UNIVERSITY OF PITTSBURGH AT JOHNSTOWN C-3

www.upj.pitt.edu

Johnstown, PA 15904	(814) 269-7050 (800) 765-4875
Fax: (814) 269-7044	Email: upjadmit@pitt.edu
Full-time: 1521 men, 1185 women	Faculty: 143; IIB, -$
Part-time: 29 men, 30 women	Ph.D.s: 68%
Graduate: n/av	Student/Faculty: 19 to 1
Year: semesters, summer session	Tuition: $12,892 ($23,288)
Room & Board: $9200	Freshman Class: 4352 applied, 3232 accepted, 714 enrolled
SAT CR/M/W: 500/520/470 ACT: 23	CEEB CODE: 2934
Application Deadline: n/av	COMPETITIVE

University of Pittsburgh at Johnstown is a public institution offering programs in arts and sciences, education, engineering technology, and nursing. There is 1 undergraduate school. In addition to regional accreditation, Pitt-Johnstown has baccalaureate program accreditation with ABET. The 650-acre campus is in a suburban area 70 miles east of Pittsburgh. Including any residence halls, there are 35 buildings.

STUDENT LIFE: 98% of undergraduates are from Pennsylvania. Others are from 14 states, and 12 foreign countries. 85% are White; 4% African American; 3% race unknown; 2% Asian American; 2% Hispanic; 2% two or more races. **Male To Female Ratio:** 1.3:1. The average age of freshmen is 18; all undergraduates, 20. 27% do not continue beyond their first year; 55% remain to graduate. **Housing:** 1700 students can be accommodated in college housing, which includes married student dorms. In addition, there are special-interest houses, fraternity houses, sorority houses, and apartments for single students. On-campus housing is guaranteed for all 4 years. 76% of students live on campus. All students may keep cars.

FACULTY/CLASSROOMS: 63% of faculty are male; 37% are female. All teach undergraduates. No introductory courses are taught by graduate students. The average class size in an introductory lecture is 25; in a laboratory is 18; and in a regular course is 25.

PROGRAMS OF STUDY: Pitt-Johnstown confers B.A. and B.S. degrees. Associate degrees are also awarded. Bachelor's degrees are awarded in AGRICULTURE (environmental studies), BIOLOGICAL SCIENCE (biology/biological science), BUSINESS (accounting, banking and finance, business administration and management, and business economics), COMMUNICATIONS AND THE ARTS (communications, creative writing, dramatic arts, English, and journalism), COMPUTER AND PHYSICAL SCIENCE (chemistry, computer science, geology, and mathematics), EDUCATION (elementary education, English education, mathematics education, science education, secondary education, and social science education), ENGINEERING AND ENVIRONMENTAL DESIGN (civil engineering technology, computer engineering, electrical/electronics engineering technology, and mechanical engineering technology), HEALTH PROFESSIONS (medical laboratory technology and nursing), SOCIAL SCIENCE (American studies, criminal justice, economics, geography, history, humanities, political science/government, psychology, social science, and sociology). Business, education, and biology have the largest enrollments.

ACTIVITIES: 7% of men belong to 5 national fraternities; 7% of women belong to 3 national sororities. There are 85 groups on campus, including band, cheerleading, choir, chorus, computers, dance, drama, environmental, ethnic, honors, LGBT, literary magazine, musical theater, newspaper, political, professional, radio and TV, religious, social, social service, student government, symphony, and yearbook. Popular campus events include Spring Concert, Pitt Fest, and Sephia Fashion Show. **Sports:** There are 7 intercollegiate sports for men and 7 for women, and 11 intramural sports for men and 11 for women. Facilities include a gym, a swimming pool, dance studio, weight room, cross-country track, and basketball courts. **Graduates:** From July 1, 2016 to June 30, 2017, 494 bachelor's degrees were awarded. The most popular majors were business marketing (20%), engineering technologies (16%), English, and and psychology (8%). In an average class, 63% graduate in 6 years or less.

SERVICES: Counseling and information services are available, as is tutoring in most subjects. There is a reader service for the blind, and remedial math. **Library/Resources:** Computerized library services include interlibrary loans, database searching, and Internet access. Special learning facilities include an art gallery, radio station, and TV station. **Physically Challenged Students:** 80% of the campus is accessible. Facilities include elevators, special parking, specially equipped restrooms, special class scheduling, lowered drinking fountains, lowered telephones, and special housing. **Special:** Students may cross-register with schools in the Pittsburgh Council for Higher Education. Internships are available on and off campus, including study abroad, work-study programs, accelerated degree programs, dual majors, student-designed majors, nondegree study, and pass/fail options. There are 10 national honor societies. **Visiting:** There are regularly scheduled orientations for prospective students, including 5 programs held on Saturdays in the fall, 2 Saturdays in the spring, 3 Fridays in the spring, and 4 Fridays in the summer. There are guides for informal visits, visitors may sit in on classes, and stay overnight. To schedule a visit, contact the Admissions Office. **Campus Safety and Security:** Measures include 24-hour foot and vehicle patrol, emergency notification system, self-defense education, and security escort services. There are shuttle buses, emergency telephones, and lighted pathways/sidewalks.

REQUIREMENTS: The SAT or ACT is required. Applicants must be graduates of an accredited secondary school. The GED is accepted. For admission to freshman standing, 15 academic credits are required, including 4 units each of English and social studies, 2-4 of math, 2 each of foreign language, and science (with 1 unit of lab. Engineering students must have completed chemistry, physics, and trigonometry. An interview is recommended, and an essay is highly recommended. AP credits are accepted. Important factors in the admissions decision are advanced placement or honors courses, leadership record, evidence of special talent, and extracurricular activities record. To graduate, students must complete 120 to 139 credits, with 30 to 36 credits in the major and a minimum GPA of 2.0. The school requires a core set of general education courses to include 12 credits each in humanities, natural sciences, and social sciences. **Procedure:** Freshmen are admitted to all sessions. Entrance exams should be taken between April and June of the junior year or by November of the senior year. There are early admissions, deferred admissions, and rolling admissions plans. Application deadlines are open. The fall 2017 application fee was $45. Notification is sent on a rolling basis. **Transfer Students:** 100 transfer students enrolled in 2016-2017. Students wishing to transfer must have a minimum GPA of 2.5 and at least 15 credit hours earned. The SAT or ACT is required. Grades of C or better transfer for credit. 30 of 120 credits required for the bachelor's degree must be completed at UPJ. **International Students:** They must take the TOEFL with a minimum score of 550 on the paper-based TOEFL (PBT) or 80 on the Internet-based version (iBT). The SAT may be required for some students.

ADMISSIONS: 74% of the 2017-2018 applicants were accepted. The SAT scores for the 2017-2018 freshman class were: Critical Reading-- 48% below 500, 41% between 500 and 599, 8% between 600 and 699, and 1% between 700 and 800. Math-- 36% below 500, 45% between 500 and 599, 17% between 600 and 699, and 2% between 700 and 800. Writing-- 63% below 500, 33% between 500 and 599, and 4% between 600 and 699. The ACT scores were 10% between 12 and 17, 53% between 18 and 23, 35% between 24 and 29, and 2% above 30. 35% of the current freshmen were in the top fifth of their class; 73% were in the top two fifths. **Admissions Contact:** Therese Grimes, Director of Admissions. Email: *upjadmit@pitt.edu* Web: *www.upj.pitt.edu*

FINANCIAL AID: In 2017-2018, 85% of all full-time freshmen received some form of financial aid. 54% of all full-time freshmen received need-based aid. The average freshman award was $10,712. Need-based scholarships or need-based grants averaged $8,367; need-based self-help aid (loans and jobs) averaged $3,365; other non-need-based awards and non-need-based scholarships averaged $3,053; and $5,674 from other forms of aid. The average financial indebtedness of the 2017 graduate was $33,692. The deadline for filing freshman financial aid applications for fall entry is April 1.

UNIVERSITY OF SCRANTON E-2

www.scranton.edu

Scranton, PA 18510	(570) 941-7540
Fax: (570) 941-5928	**Email: admissions@scranton.edu**
Full-time: 1735 men, 2112 women	**Faculty:** IIA, +$
Part-time: 88 men, 106 women	**Ph.D.s:** 85%
Graduate: 755 men, 1102 women	**Student/Faculty:** n/av
Year: semesters, summer session	**Tuition:** $41,044
Room & Board: $13,918	**Freshman Class:** 9672 applied, 6655 accepted, 971 enrolled
SAT or ACT: required	**CEEB CODE:** 2929
Application Deadline: March 1	**VERY COMPETITIVE**

University of Scranton, founded in 1888, is a private institution operated by the Jesuit order of the Roman Catholic Church. It offers programs in business, behavioral sciences, education, health science, humanities, math, science, and social science. There are 4 undergraduate schools and 1 graduate school. In addition to regional accreditation, University of Scranton has baccalaureate program accreditation with AACSB, ABET, APTA, CSAB, NLN, ACOTE, CCNE, and CACREP. The 58-acre campus is in an urban area 125 miles north of Philadelphia. Including any residence halls, there are 67 buildings.

STUDENT LIFE: 60% of undergraduates are from out of state, mostly the Middle Atlantic. Students are from 24 states, and 12 foreign countries. 81% are White; 7% Hispanic; 6% race unknown; 3% Asian American; 2% African American; 2% two or more races. 75% are Catholic. **Female To Male Ratio:** 1.3:1. The average age of freshmen is 19; all undergraduates, 21. 12% do not continue beyond their first year; 83% remain to graduate. **Housing:** 2647 students can be accommodated in college housing, which includes dorms, on-campus apartments, off-campus apartments, and special-interest houses. On-campus housing is guaranteed for all 4 years. 64% of students live on campus. Upperclassmen may keep cars.

FACULTY/CLASSROOMS: 59% of faculty are male; 41% are female. No introductory courses are taught by graduate students. The average class size in a regular course is 20.

PROGRAMS OF STUDY: University of Scranton confers B.A. and B.S. degrees. Associate, master's, and doctoral degrees are also awarded. Bachelor's degrees are awarded in BIOLOGICAL SCIENCE (biochemistry, biology/biological science, biomathematics, biophysics, and neurosciences), BUSINESS (accounting, banking and finance, business administration and management, business economics, electronic business, human resources, information & communication technology, international business management, marketing/retailing/merchandising, and operations management), COMMUNICATIONS AND THE ARTS (communications, English, French, German, Greek, Latin, Spanish, and theatre arts), COMPUTER AND PHYSICAL SCIENCE (chemistry, computer science, information sciences and systems, mathematics, and physics), EDUCATION (early childhood education, elementary education, and secondary education), ENGINEERING AND ENVIRONMENTAL DESIGN (computer engineering, electrical/electronics engineering, and environmental science), HEALTH PROFESSIONS (community health work, exercise science, health care administration, medical laboratory technology, nursing, and occupational therapy), SOCIAL SCIENCE (criminal justice, economics, forensic studies, history, human services, international studies, philosophy, political science/government, psychology, sociology, theological studies, and women's studies). Chemistry, biology, and nursing are the strongest academically. Biology, communication, and nursing have the largest enrollments.

ACTIVITIES: There are no fraternities or sororities. There are 80 groups on campus, including art, band, cheerleading, chess, choir, chorale, chorus, communications, computers, dance, debate, drama, environmental, ethnic, film, forensics, honors, international, jazz band, literary magazine, musical theater, newspaper, orchestra, photography, political, professional, radio and TV, religious, social, social service, student government, symphony, and yearbook. Popular campus events include Spring Fest, Senior Formal, Royal Ball, Shamrockin' Eve, IGNITE Leadershop Conference, and Relay for Life. **Sports:** There are 9 intercollegiate sports for men and 9 for women, and 20 intramural sports for men and 19 for women. Facilities include a gym, basketball courts, wrestling and weight rooms, handball/racquetball and tennis courts, sand volleyball court, soccer/lacrosse field, softball field, a swimming pool, a physical therapy room, a 3-court multipurpose gym, fitness center, and a dance aerobics room. **Graduates:** From July 1, 2016 to June 30, 2017, 902 bachelor's degrees were awarded. The most popular majors were business/marketing (21%), health professions/related sciences (15%), and biological/life sciences (11%). In an average class, 73% graduate in 4 years or less, 79% graduate in 5 years or less, and 80% graduate in 6 years or less. Of the 2016 graduating class, 55% were enrolled in graduate school within 6 months of graduation, and 40% were employed.

SERVICES: Counseling and information services are available, as is tutoring in most subjects. There is a reader service for the blind. There is also time management, organizational skills, learning strategies, writing labs, math labs, and study skills. **Library/Resources:** The library contains 486,650 volumes, 26,241 microform items, and 21,285 audio/video tapes/CDs/DVDs, and subscribes to 75,198 periodicals including electronic. Computerized library services include interlibrary loans, database searching, Internet access, and Wi-Fi capability. Special learning facilities include a radio station, Hope Horn Gallery in Hyland Hall for paintings and sculpture, the Royal Theater and Studio Theater in the McDade Center for Literary and Performing Arts for University Players productions, television studio and broadcast FM-radio station, 700-seat performance hall in the Houlihan-McLean Center, and the Institute of Molecular Biology and Medicine offering proteomics, and genomics and PCR equipment. **Physically Challenged Students:** All of the campus is accessible. Facilities include wheelchair ramps, elevators, special parking, specially equipped restrooms, special class scheduling, lowered drinking fountains, lowered telephones, and special housing. **Special:** University of Scranton offers Honors, Business Leadership Honors & Special Jesuit Liberal Arts Honors Programs, First-year experience courses, service learning, faculty/student research, independent study, internships, study abroad in over 60 countries, cross registration, IB/AP/College Credit and Washington Center. The university also offers dual, student-designed, and interdisciplinary majors, including chemistry-business, chemistry-computers, electronics-business, and international language-business, credit by exam and for life/military/work experience, work-study, nondegree study, and pass/fail options. There are 32 national honor societies. **Visiting:** There are regularly scheduled orientations for prospective students, group information sessions, and tours are available most weekdays and Saturdays throughout the year. There are also personal meetings available with admissions counselors by appointment. To schedule a visit, contact the Office of Admissions. **Campus Safety and Security:** Measures include 24-hour foot and vehicle patrol, emergency notification system, self-defense education, and security escort services. There are emergency telephones, lighted pathways/sidewalks, and controlled access to dorms/residences.

REQUIREMENTS: The SAT or ACT is required. Applicants should be graduates of an accredited secondary school, though in some cases a GED may be accepted. They should complete 18 academic or Carnegie units, including 4 years of high school English, 3 each of math, science, history, and social studies, and 2 of foreign language. 2 letters of reference/recommendation are required. Essays are required. AP and CLEP credits are accepted. Important factors in the admissions decision are advanced placement or honors courses, leadership record, and extracurricular activities record. Students take general education requirements according to their area of study. All are required to take philosophy/theology, phys ed, English composition, speech, and computer literacy. The minimum GPA is 2.0, although some majors require a higher GPA. **Procedure:** Freshmen are admitted fall and spring. Entrance exams should be taken by fall of the senior year. There are deferred admissions and rolling admissions plans. Applications should be filed by March 1 for fall entry; December 15 for spring entry; and May 1 for summer entry. Notifications are sent December 15. 1087 applicants were on the 2017 waiting list; 57 were admitted. Applications are accepted on-line. **Transfer Students:** 89 transfer students enrolled in 2016-2017. Applicants should have earned a GPA of at least 2.5. 60 of 130 credits required for the bachelor's degree must be completed at University of Scranton. **International Students:** There are 40 international students enrolled. They must take the TOEFL with a minimum score of 500 on the paper-based TOEFL (PBT) or 61 on the Internet-based version (iBT).

ADMISSIONS: 69% of the 2017-2018 applicants were accepted. The SAT scores for the 2017-2018 freshman class were: Critical Reading-- 15% below 500, 56% between 500 and 599, 25% between 600 and 699, and 4% between 700 and 800. Math-- 12% below 500, 51% between 500 and 599, 31% between 600 and 699, and 5% between 700 and 800. 11 freshmen graduated first in their class. **Admissions Contact:** Joseph M. Roback, Associate Vice President for Admissions. Email: *admissions@scranton.edu* Web: *www.scranton.edu*

FINANCIAL AID: In 2017-2018, 90% of all full-time freshmen received some form of financial aid. 69% of all full-time freshmen received need-based aid. The average freshman award was $25,338. University of Scranton is a member of CSS. The FAFSA code is 003384. The priority date for freshman financial aid applications for fall entry is February 15.

UNIVERSITY OF THE ARTS *(The complete profile is made available exclusively on our website, www.barronspac.com)*

UNIVERSITY OF THE SCIENCES F-3

www.usciences.edu

Philadelphia, PA 19104 — **(215) 596-8815**, **(888) 996-8747**

Fax: (215) 596-8821	**Email: admit@usciences.edu**
Full-time: 729 men, 1214 women	**Faculty:** n/av
Part-time: 12 men, 28 women	**Ph.D.s:** n/av
Graduate: 153 men, 241 women	**Student/Faculty:** 10 to 1
Year: semesters, summer session	**Tuition:** see profile
Room & Board: see profile	**Freshman Class:** 3602 applied, 2188 accepted, 353 enrolled
SAT CR/M: 595/610 **ACT:** 26	**CEEB CODE:** 2663
Application Deadline: n/av	**VERY COMPETITIVE**

University of the Sciences has prepared students to be leaders and practitioners in the healthcare and science fields for nearly 200 years. Key to its distinctive education is a tradition of hands-on research and experiential learning that is evident in every graduate who has walked its campus. Since its founding in 1821 as Philadelphia College of Pharmacy, the first college of pharmacy in North America, USciences has grown to more than 30 degree-granting programs from bachelor's through doctoral degrees in the health sciences, bench sciences, and healthcare business and policy fields. The annual tuition and general fee for the current 2017-2018 school year is $38,850. However, in Fall 2018, tuition and general fee for incoming undergraduate students will be reduced to $25,000 per year. This pricing does not include room and board, health insurance, or any professional, clinical, or transportation fees. There are 4 undergraduate schools and 4 graduate schools. In addition to regional accreditation, USciences has baccalaureate program accreditation with ACBSP, ACPE, APTA, ACOTE, ACS, CAPTE, and NAACLS. The 35-acre campus is in an urban area in the heart of University City, Philadelphia, PA. Including any residence halls, there are 23 buildings.

STUDENT LIFE: 52% of undergraduates are from out of state, mostly the Middle Atlantic. Students are from 24 states, 28 foreign countries, and Canada. 8% are race unknown; 6% African American; 5% Hispanic; 44% White; 33% Asian American; 3% two or more races; 1% Foreign. **Female To Male Ratio:** 1.7:1. The average age of freshmen is 18; all undergraduates, 21. 12% do not continue beyond their first year; 80% remain to graduate. **Housing:** 768 students can be accommodated in college housing, which includes dorms, on-campus apartments, and honors houses. On-campus housing is available on a first-come, first-served basis, and on a lottery system for upperclassmen. 71% of students commute. Alcohol is not permitted. Upperclassmen may keep cars.

FACULTY/CLASSROOMS: 46% of faculty are male; 54% are female. No introductory courses are taught by graduate students. The average class size in an introductory lecture is 100; in a laboratory is 28; and in a regular course is 25.

PROGRAMS OF STUDY: University of the Sciences confers B.S. and B.S.H.S. degrees. Master's and doctoral degrees are also awarded. Bachelor's degrees are awarded in BIOLOGICAL SCIENCE (biochemistry, bioinformatics, biology/biological science, microbiology, and toxicology), BUSINESS (marketing management and recreational facilities management), COMPUTER AND PHYSICAL SCIENCE (chemistry, computer science, and physics), ENGINEERING AND ENVIRONMENTAL DESIGN (environmental science), HEALTH PROFESSIONS (health science, medical technology, mental health/human services, occupational therapy, pharmaceutical chemistry, pharmaceutical science, pharmacology, pharmacy, physical therapy, and physician's assistant), SOCIAL SCIENCE (humanities and social science, interdisciplinary studies, and psychology). Pharmacy, physical therapy, occupational therapy and pre-physician assistant studies are the strongest academically. Pharmacy, physical therapy, and biology have the largest enrollments.

ACTIVITIES: 7% of men belong to 3 local and 7 national fraternities; 7% of women belong to 3 local and 5 national sororities. There are 69 groups on campus, including art, band, cheerleading, chess, choir, chorale, chorus, computers, dance, drama, environmental, ethnic, honors, international, LGBT, literary magazine, martial arts, musical theater, newspaper, orchestra, political, professional, religious, social, social service, and student government. Popular campus events include Student Appreciation Weekend, Founder's Day, Usciences Scholarly Day, and Convocation. **Sports:** There are 6 intercollegiate sports for men and 6 for women, and 4 intramural sports for men and 4 for women. Facilities include an indoor track, a gym, baseball, basketball, cross country, golf, volleyball, field hockey, tennis courts, softball field, and a jogging path. **Graduates:** From July 1, 2016 to June 30, 2017, 453 bachelor's degrees were awarded. The most popular majors were pharmacy (41%), physical therapy/occupational therapy, health science (32%), and biology (5%). In an average class, 65% graduate in 4 years or less, 79% graduate in 5 years or less, and 80% graduate in 6 years or less. Of the 2016 graduating class, 14% were enrolled in graduate school within 6 months of graduation, and 74% were employed.

SERVICES: Counseling and information services are available, as is tutoring in every subject. There is remedial math and writing. **Library/Resources:** The library contains 497,246 volumes, and subscribes to 38,447 periodicals including electronic. Computerized library services include interlibrary loans, database searching, Internet access, and Wi-Fi capability. **Physically Challenged Students:** 90% of the campus is accessible. Facilities include wheelchair ramps, elevators, special parking, specially equipped restrooms, and special class scheduling. **Special:** USciences offers 5- and 6-year integrated professional programs in pharmacy, occupational therapy, physical therapy, and physician's assistant studies. Internships are required in all health science disciplines. Study abroad is available in Asia, Africa, and Europe through the NYU Study Abroad program. A 2-year undeclared major program is offered, as is a program of curriculum and advisement to prepare students to enter medical school. Students may elect dual majors or a minor in communications, economics, psychology, sociology, math, physics, computer science, biochemistry, biology, chemistry, humanities, math, microbiology, neurosciences, social sciences, and writing. There are 7 national honor societies and a freshman honors program. **Visiting:** There are regularly scheduled orientations for prospective students, as well as student visits, that consist of summer open houses for rising seniors, campus day visits, campus tours, and meetings with faculty members. There are guides for informal visits and visitors may sit in on classes. To schedule a visit, contact the Admission Office. **Campus Safety and Security:** Measures include 24-hour foot and vehicle patrol, self-defense education, and security escort services. There are shuttle buses, emergency telephones, lighted pathways/sidewalks, controlled access to dorms/residences, and required key and student identification for dorm entry.

REQUIREMENTS: The SAT or ACT is required. Applicants must be high school graduates or hold the GED. Minimum academic requirements include 4 credits in English, 1 credit each in American history and social science, and 4 credits in academic electives. Math requirements include 2 years of algebra and 1 year of geometry. The university strongly recommends an additional year of higher-level math, such as precalculus or calculus. In addition, 3 science credits are required, and the university strongly recommends that students have 1 credit each in biology, chemistry, and physics. A strong background in English, science, and math is recommended. A GPA of 3.0 is required. AP and CLEP credits are accepted. Important factors in the admissions decision are advanced placement or honors courses, leadership record, and extracurricular activities record. Total credits required for graduation range from 120 to 210 depending on the major, with a 2.0 GPA for BS majors, and higher minimum gpa's for professional programs and other specific programs. The core curriculum consists of 38 credits including 16 credits of natural science, 6 each of math, social sciences, communication, and an intellectual heritage sequence, 3 of literature, world culture, history, and advanced social sciences, and 1 of phys ed, along with 3 of electives. Students must pass a writing proficiency exam and demonstrate proficiency in computer applications. **Procedure:** Freshmen are admitted in the fall. Entrance exams should be taken by the end of the junior year or the fall of the senior year. There are early admissions, deferred admissions, and rolling admissions plans. Application deadlines are open. Notification is sent on a rolling basis. Applications are accepted on-line. **Transfer Students:** 117 transfer students enrolled in 2016-2017. To be considered, pharmacy and physical therapy applicants must present a minimum GPA of 3.0. All other majors must have at least a 2.7 GPA. All applicants must meet high school requirements as well. 51 of 120 credits required for the bachelor's degree must be completed at USciences. **International Students:** There are 38 international students enrolled. They must take the TOEFL with a minimum score of 550 on the paper-based TOEFL (PBT) or 80 on the Internet-based version (iBT). Students must take the college's own test. They must also take the SAT or ACT.

ADMISSIONS: 61% of the 2017-2018 applicants were accepted. The SAT scores for the 2017-2018 freshman class were: Math-- 1% below 500, 44% between 500 and 599, 45% between 600 and 699, and 10% between 700 and 800. Evidence-Based Reading/Writing-- 3% below 500, 46% between 500 and 599, 44% between 600 and 699, and 7% between 700 and 800. The ACT scores were 23% between 18 and 23, 58% between 24 and 29, and 19% above 30. **Admissions Contact:** Carolyn Giorando, Associate Provost. Email: *admit@usciences.edu* Web: *www.usciences.edu*

FINANCIAL AID: The FAFSA code is 003353. The priority date for freshman financial aid applications for fall entry is March 15.

URSINUS COLLEGE E-3
www.ursinus.edu

Collegeville, PA 19426 **(610) 409-3200**

Fax: (610) 409-3197
Email: admission@ursinus.edu
Full-time: 721 men, 821 women
Faculty: 121; IIB, av$
Part-time: 7 men, 7 women
Ph.D.s: 93%
Graduate: n/av
Student/Faculty: 11 to 1
Year: semesters
Tuition: $49,370
Room & Board: $12,320
Freshman Class: 2491 applied, 2053 accepted, 382 enrolled
SAT or ACT: required
CEEB CODE: 2931
Application Deadline: February 1
VERY COMPETITIVE

The mission of Ursinus College is to enable students to become independent, responsible, and thoughtful individuals through a program of liberal education, preparing them to live creatively and usefully, and provide leadership for their society in an interdependent world. There is 1 undergraduate school. In addition to regional accreditation, UC has baccalaureate program accreditation with ACS. The 170-acre campus is in a suburban area 25 miles west of Philadelphia. Including any residence halls, there are 65 buildings.

STUDENT LIFE: 56% of undergraduates are from Pennsylvania. Others are from 33 states, and 9 foreign countries. 67% are from public schools. 74% are White; 6% African American; 6% Hispanic; 4% Asian American; 3% Foreign; 3% two or more races; 3% race unknown; 1% American Indian/Alaska Native. **Female To Male Ratio:** 1.1:1. The average age of freshmen is 18; all undergraduates, 20. 12% do not continue beyond their first year; 79% remain to graduate. **Housing:** 1576 students can be accommodated in college housing, which includes single-sex, coed dorms, on-campus apartments, and off-campus apartments, and special-interest houses. On-campus housing is guaranteed for all 4 years. 95% of students live on campus; of those, 90% remain on campus on weekends. Upperclassmen may keep cars.

FACULTY/CLASSROOMS: 41% of faculty are male; 59% are female. All teach undergraduates and do research. No introductory courses are taught by graduate students.

PROGRAMS OF STUDY: UC confers B.A., and B.S., degrees. Bachelor's degrees are awarded in BIOLOGICAL SCIENCE (biochemistry, biology/biological science, and neurosciences), BUSINESS (business economics), COMMUNICATIONS AND THE ARTS (art history, art, communications, dance, dramatic arts, English, French, German, music, and Spanish), COMPUTER AND PHYSICAL SCIENCE (chemistry, computer science, mathematics, and physics), ENGINEERING AND ENVIRONMENTAL DESIGN (environmental science), HEALTH PROFESSIONS (exercise science), SOCIAL SCIENCE (American studies, anthropology, East Asian studies, economics, history, international relations, philosophy, political science/government, psychology, religious studies, and sociology). Biology, chemistry, and history are the strongest academically. Biology, applied economics, and health & exercise physiology have the largest enrollments.

ACTIVITIES: 19% of men belong to 5 local and 4 national fraternities; 25% of women belong to 4 local and 1 national sororities. There are 100 groups on campus, including art, band, cheerleading, chess, choir, chorale, chorus, computers, dance, debate, drama, environmental, ethnic, film, forensics, honors, international, jazz band, LGBT, literary magazine, newspaper, pep band, photography, political, professional, radio and TV, religious, social, social service, student government, and yearbook. Popular campus events include Air Band Competition, Relay for Life, and Family Day. **Sports:** There are 12 intercollegiate sports for men and 13 for women. Facilities include a fitness center and weight room, indoor track, indoor tennis courts, a dance studio, basketball courts, wrestling room, swimming pool, squash, racquetball courts, and a gymnastics space. Outdoor athletic and recreational facilities include turf fields for football, soccer, lacrosse, track & field, field hockey, baseball, softball, cross-country, and tennis courts. **Graduates:** From July 1, 2015 to June 30, 2016, 367 bachelor's degrees were awarded. The most popular majors were biology/life sciences (31%), social sciences (20%), and psychology (10%). In an average class, 73% graduate in 4 years or less, 78% graduate in 5 years or less, and 78% graduate in 6 years or less.

SERVICES: Counseling and information services are available, as is tutoring in every subject. There is a reader service for the blind. The college also provides appropriate services as-needed, including group tutoring. **Library/Resources:** The library contains 387,800 volumes, 300 microform items, and 24,800 audio/video tapes/CDs/DVDs, and subscribes to 21,500 periodicals including electronic. Computerized library services include interlibrary loans, database searching, Internet access, and Wi-Fi capability. Special learning facilities include an art gallery, planetarium, radio station, TV station, and an observatory. **Physically Challenged Students:** 95% of the campus is accessible. Facilities include wheelchair ramps, elevators, special parking, specially equipped restrooms, special class scheduling, lowered drinking fountains, lowered telephones, and special housing. **Special:** The college offers study abroad, student-designed majors, internships, a Washington semester, dual majors, and a 3-2 engineering degree with Columbia University. There are 16 national honor societies, Phi Beta Kappa, and 29 departmental honors programs. **Visiting:** There are regularly scheduled orientations for prospective students, including a campus interview and a tour. There are guides for informal visits, visitors may sit in on classes, and stay overnight. To schedule a visit, contact Office of Admission. **Campus Safety and Security:** Measures include 24-hour foot and vehicle patrol, emergency notification system, self-defense education, and security escort services. There are also emergency telephones and lighted pathways/sidewalks.

REQUIREMENTS: The SAT or ACT, the ACT Writing Test, and SAT Subject Tests are recommended. Applicants should prepare with 16 academic credits, including 4 years of English, 3 of math, 2 of foreign language, and 1 each of science and social studies. An interview is recommended. Following are the exceptions for which applicants must submit testing results: students applying for our Early Assurance program to medical school in cooperation with the Drexel University School of Medicine are required to submit SAT Reasoning Test (preferred) or ACT score results. To be considered for the Early Assurance program, applicants must meet the November 15 submission deadline and achieve at least: a) a minimal SAT Critical Reading and Mathematics combined score of 1300 with no subset less than 560 (the Writing section of the SAT test is not included); or b) an ACT composite score of 31. Homeschooled students and students who attend schools that provide narrative comments in lieu of grades are required to submit results from one or more standardized tests (SAT Reasoning Test, SAT Subject Tests, or ACT). AP credits are accepted. Important factors in the admissions decision are advanced placement or honors courses, recommendations by school officials, and leadership record. All students must fulfill requirements in the common intellectual experience, math or logic, foreign language, humanities, social science, natural science plus a lab, and an independent learning experience. A total of 128 semester hours, with 32 to 40 in the major, is required, as is a GPA of at least 2.0. **Procedure:** Freshmen are admitted in the fall and spring. Entrance exams should be taken in the junior or senior year. There are early decision, deferred admissions, and rolling admissions plans. Early decision applications should be filed by December 1; regular applications, by February 1 for fall entry; and December 1 for spring entry. Applications are accepted online. **Transfer Students:** Transfer applicants must submit transcripts from all institutions attended. 64 of 128 credits required for the bachelor's degree must be completed at UC. **International Students:** There are 40 international students enrolled. The school actively recruits these students. They must take the TOEFL with a minimum score of 80 on the Internet-based version (iBT). They must also take the SAT.

ADMISSIONS: 82% of the 2016-2017 applicants were accepted. 42% of the current freshmen were in the top fifth of their class; 79% were in the top two fifths. **Admissions Contact:** Scott Myers, Director of Admission. Email: *smyer@ursinus.edu* Web: *www.ursinus.edu*

FINANCIAL AID: In 2016-2017, 99% of all full-time freshmen received some form of financial aid. UC is a member of CSS. The CSS/Profile is required. The FAFSA code is 003385. The deadline for filing freshman financial aid applications for fall entry is February 15.

VILLANOVA UNIVERSITY E-3
www.villanova.edu

Villanova, PA 19085 **(610) 519-4000**

Fax: (610) 519-6450
Email: gotovu@villanova.edu
Full-time: 3073 men, 3452 women
Faculty: 618; IIA, +$
Part-time: 211 men, 230 women
Ph.D.s: 84%
Graduate: 1983 men, 2034 women
Student/Faculty: 11 to 1
Year: semesters, summer session
Tuition: $51,374
Room & Board: $13,548
Freshman Class: n/av
SAT CR/M/W: 650/670/650 **ACT:** 31
CEEB CODE: 2959
Application Deadline: January 15
MOST COMPETITIVE

Villanova University was founded in 1842 by the Order of Saint Augustine. To this day, Villanova's Augustinian Catholic intellectual tradition is the cornerstone of an academic community in which students learn to think critically, act compassionately and succeed while serving others. Villanova prepares students to become ethical leaders who create positive change everywhere life takes them. The University has six colleges: the College of Liberal Arts and Sciences, the Villanova School of Business, the College of Engineering, the College of Nursing, the College of Professional Studies and the Villanova University Charles Widger School of Law. In addition to regional accreditation, VU has baccalaureate program accreditation with AACSB, ABET, NLN, and ABA. The 260-acre campus is in a suburban area 12 miles west of Philadelphia. Including any residence halls, there are 69 buildings.

STUDENT LIFE: 79% of undergraduates are from out of state, mostly the Middle Atlantic. Students are from 48 states, 44 foreign countries, and Canada. 52% are from public schools. 8% are Hispanic; 74% White; 6% Asian American; 5% African American; 3% two or more races; 2% Foreign; 2% race unknown. 70% are Catholic; 12% Protestant. **Female To Male Ratio:** 1.1:1. The average age of freshmen is 18; all undergraduates, 20. 5% do not continue beyond their first year; 90% remain to graduate. **Housing:** 4500 students can be accommodated in college housing, which includes dorms and on-campus apartments. In addition, there are honors houses, learning communities for freshmen and 1 special sophomore residence hall, a living learning community, and a quiet study hall. On-campus housing is available on a lottery system for upperclassmen. 66% of students live on campus. Upperclassmen may keep cars.

FACULTY/CLASSROOMS: 58% of faculty are male; 42% are female. 90% teach undergraduates, 74% do research, and 74% do both. Graduate students teach 1% of introductory courses. The average class size in a regular course is 22.

PROGRAMS OF STUDY: VU confers B.A., B.S., B.B.A., B.S.N. and B.I.S. degrees. Associate, master's, and doctoral degrees are also awarded. Bachelor's degrees are awarded in AGRICULTURE (environmental studies), BIOLOGICAL SCIENCE (biochemistry and biology/biological science), BUSINESS (accounting, banking and finance, business administration and management, business economics, finance, international business management, management information systems, management, marketing/retailing/merchandising, and real estate), COMMUNICATIONS AND THE ARTS (art history and appreciation, classics, communications, English, French, Italian, and Spanish), COMPUTER AND PHYSICAL SCIENCE (astronomy, astrophysics, chemistry, computer science, information sciences and systems, mathematics, physics, science, and statistics), EDUCATION (secondary education), ENGINEERING AND ENVIRONMENTAL DESIGN (chemical engineering, civil engineering, computer engineering, electrical/electronics engineering, environmental science, and mechanical engineering), HEALTH PROFESSIONS (nursing), SOCIAL SCIENCE (behavioral science, cognitive science, criminal justice, crosscultural studies, economics, gender studies, geography, history, humanities, interdisciplinary studies, Latin American studies, liberal arts/general studies, philosophy, political science/government, psychology, religion, sociology, and theological studies). Nursing, engineering, and business have the largest enrollments.

ACTIVITIES: 17% of men belong to 13 national fraternities; 32% of women belong to 14 national sororities. There are 265 groups on campus, including service and advocacy, multicultural, art, band, Blue Key Ambassadors, cheerleading, choir, chorale, chorus, communications, computers, dance, debate, drama, drill team, environmental, ethnic, film, forensics, honors, international, jazz band, LGBT, literary magazine, marching band, musical theater, newspaper, pep band, photography, political, professional, radio and TV, religious, social, social service, student government, and yearbook. Popular campus events include Special Olympics, Hoops Mania, and Diwahni, Diwali, and Holi. **Sports:** There are 11 intercollegiate sports for men and 13 for women, and 11 intramural sports for men and 11 for women. Facilities include a 400-meter outdoor track, a swimming pool, weight rooms, field house, basketball and volleyball courts, softball field, soccer fields and tennis courts. **Graduates:** From July 1, 2016 to June 30, 2017, 1770 bachelor's degrees were awarded. The most popular majors were business/marketing (31%), social sciences (12%), and engineering (11%). In an average class, 87% graduate in 4 years or less, 90% graduate in 5 years or less, and 90% graduate in 6 years or less. Of the 2016 graduating class, 17% were enrolled in graduate school within 6 months of graduation, and 73% were employed.

SERVICES: Counseling and information services are available, as is tutoring in some subjects. There is a reader service for the blind. Tutoring is open to all students and some tutoring is offered through individual departments and colleges for first and second year courses. There is also a writing center, math center study skills and academic coaching available. **Library/Resources:** The library contains 1.2 million volumes, 10,000 microform items, and 6,376 audio/video tapes/CDs/DVDs, and subscribes to 85,876 periodicals including electronic. Computerized library services include interlibrary loans, database searching, Internet access, and Wi-Fi capability. Special learning facilities include an art gallery, radio station, TV station, an observatory. **Physically Challenged Students:** 90% of the campus is accessible. Facilities include wheelchair ramps, elevators, special parking, specially equipped restrooms, special class scheduling, lowered drinking fountains, and lowered telephones. There is also a specially equipped van for campus transportation and proximity card readers for several buildings with automatic doors. **Special:** Internships are available for each college in the Philadelphia area as well as in New York City and Washington D.C. Students may study abroad worldwide. Villanova offers a Washington semester, an accelerated degree program in biology for allied health program, dual majors, a general studies degree, and credit by exam. There are 36 national honor societies, Phi Beta Kappa, and a freshman honors program. **Visiting:** There are regularly scheduled orientations for prospective students, consisting of group admission presentations, and campus tours that are conducted throughout the year. There are guides for informal visits and visitors may sit in on classes. To schedule a visit, contact the Office of University Admission. **Campus Safety and Security:** Measures include 24-hour foot and vehicle patrol, emergency notification system, self-defense education, and security escort services. There are shuttle buses, emergency telephones, lighted pathways/sidewalks, and controlled access to dorms/residences.

REQUIREMENTS: The SAT or ACT and the ACT Optional Writing test are required. Applicants must be graduates of an accredited secondary school and should have completed 16 academic units. The specific courses required vary according to college. A GED is accepted. An essay is required. AP and CLEP credits are accepted. Important factors in the admissions decision are leadership record, advanced placement or honors courses, and evidence of special talent. All students are required to take core courses in humanities, Augustine and Culture, social science, religious studies, natural sciences, philosophy, and math. Students must complete a minimum of 122 credit hours and achieve at least a 2.0 overall GPA. **Procedure:** Freshmen are admitted in the fall. Entrance exams should be taken by December of the senior year. There is a deferred admissions plan. Early decision applications should be filed by November 1; regular applications, by January 15 for fall entry. The fall 2017 application fee was $80. Notification of early decision is sent December 20; regular decision, April 1. 2677 applicants were on the 2017 waiting list; 26 were admitted. Applications are accepted on-line. **Transfer Students:** 60 of 122 credits required for the bachelor's degree must be completed at Villanova. **International Students:** There are 111 international students enrolled. They must take the TOEFL with a minimum score of 550 on the paper-based TOEFL (PBT) or 85 on the Internet-based version (iBT). They must also take the SAT or ACT.

ADMISSIONS: The SAT scores for the 2017-2018 freshman class were: Critical Reading-- 3% below 500, 19% between 500 and 599, 52% between 600 and 699, and 25% between 700 and 800. Math-- 2% below 500, 15% between 500 and 599, 47% between 600 and 699, and 36% between 700 and 800. Writing-- 4% below 500, 20% between 500 and 599, 50% between 600 and 699, and 25% between 700 and 800. The ACT scores were 2% between 18 and 23, 23% between 24 and 29, and 75% above 30. **Admissions Contact:** Michael Gaynor, Director of Admission. Email: *gotovu@villanova.edu* Web: *www.villanova.edu*

FINANCIAL AID: In 2017-2018, 48% of all full-time freshmen received some form of financial aid. 44% of all full-time freshmen received need-based aid. The average freshman award was $35,801. Need-based scholarships or need-based grants averaged $31,433; need-based self-help aid (loans and jobs) averaged $5,922; non-need-based athletic scholarships averaged $44,836; and other non-need-based awards and non-need-based scholarships averaged $14,527. Villanova is a member of CSS. The CSS/Profile, the state aid form, the college's own financial statement, parent and student federal income tax return, and W2s are required. The FAFSA code is 003388. The priority date for freshman financial aid applications for fall entry is January 15. The deadline for filing freshman financial aid applications for fall entry is February 7.

WASHINGTON & JEFFERSON COLLEGE A-3

www.washjeff.edu

Washington, PA 15301 **(724) 223-6025** **(888) 926-3529**
Fax: (724) 223-6534 **Email: admission@washjeff.edu**

Full-time: 730 men, 668 women
Part-time: 4 men, 3 women
Graduate: 3 men, 4 women
Year: 4-1-4, summer session
Room & Board: $12,066
Faculty: 111; IIB, +$
Ph.D.s: 93%
Student/Faculty: 11 to 1
Tuition: $46,628
Freshman Class: 5358 applied, 2564 accepted, 339 enrolled
SAT EBR-W/M: 610/600 **ACT:** 26
CEEB CODE: 2967
Application Deadline: March 1
VERY COMPETITIVE

Washington & Jefferson College, founded in 1781, is a selective, residential, private liberal arts and sciences college. There is 1 undergraduate school and 1 graduate school. In addition to regional accreditation, W&J has baccalaureate program accreditation with ACS. The 60-acre campus is in a small town 27 miles southwest of Pittsburgh, PA. Including any residence halls, there are 53 buildings.

STUDENT LIFE: 72% of undergraduates are from Pennsylvania. Others are from 32 states, 28 foreign countries, and Canada. 82% are from public schools. 74% are White; 5% African American; 5% Hispanic; 5% Foreign; 5% race unknown; 4% two or more races; 2% Asian American. **Male To Female Ratio:** 1.1:1. The average age of freshmen is 18; all undergraduates, 20. 13% do not continue beyond their first year; 70% remain to graduate. **Housing:** 1422 students can be accommodated in college housing, which includes single-sex, coed dorms, and on-campus apartments. In addition, there are language/international houses, special-interest houses, fraternity houses, sorority houses, on-campus suites, wellness housing, pet house, STEM house, substance-free house, cultural connection's community, social justice community, and engagement community. On-campus housing is guaranteed for all 4 years. 94% of students live on campus. All students may keep cars.

FACULTY/CLASSROOMS: 51% of faculty are male; 49% are female. All teach undergraduates and do research. No introductory courses are taught by graduate students. The average class size in an introductory lecture is 16; in a laboratory is 14; and in a regular course is 16.

PROGRAMS OF STUDY: W&J confers B.A. degrees. Master's degrees are also awarded. Bachelor's degrees are awarded in AGRICULTURE (environmental studies), BIOLOGICAL SCIENCE (biochemistry, biology/biological science, biophysics, cell biology, and neurosciences), BUSINESS (accounting, business administration and management, and international business management), COMMUNICATIONS AND THE ARTS (communication rhetoric/communication, English, French, German, music, Spanish, and studio art), COMPUTER AND PHYSICAL SCIENCE (chemistry, computer information technology, mathematics, and physics), EDUCATION (art education and education), ENGINEERING AND ENVIRONMENTAL DESIGN (environmental science), SOCIAL SCIENCE (economics, history, interdisciplinary studies, international studies, philosophy, political science/government, psychology, public affairs, and sociology). Biology, chemistry, and political science are the strongest academically. Business/accounting, psychology, and English have the largest enrollments.

ACTIVITIES: 33% of men belong to 6 national fraternities; 30% of women belong to 4 national sororities. There are 93 groups on campus, including yoga and zumba., young entrepreneurs society, art, band, cheerleading, choir, chorale, chorus, computers, dance, debate, drama, environmental, equestrian, ethnic, film, honors, international, jazz band, LGBT, literary magazine, musical theater, newspaper, pep band, photography, political, professional, radio and TV, religious, social, social service, student government, and yearbook. Popular campus events include Welcome Week/Involvement Expo, Street Fair, Holiday Kick-Off Week, Spring Concert, International Week, and Late Night Breakfast. **Sports:** There are 12 intercollegiate sports for men and 12 for women, and 15 intramural sports for men and 15 for women. Facilities include a recreation center featuring indoor track lanes, indoor multi-sport courts, yoga and exercise rooms, batting cages, a pole-vault pen, swimming and diving pools, an all-weather track, weight room, football, baseball, softball, soccer/lacrosse fields, basketball, volleyball, squash, racquetball, tennis courts, and fitness center. **Graduates:** From July 1, 2016 to June 30, 2017, 253 bachelor's degrees were awarded. The most popular majors were business administration/accounting (16%), psychology (12%), and English (5%). In an average class, 1% graduate in 3 years or less, 68% graduate in 4 years or less, 72% graduate in 5 years or less, and 70% graduate in 6 years or less. Of the 2016 graduating class, 37% were enrolled in graduate school within 6 months of graduation, and 92% were employed.

SERVICES: Counseling and information services are available, as is tutoring in most subjects, accounting, such as biology, chemistry, computing and information studies, economics, math (general and probability & statistics), modern languages (Chinese, French, German, Russian, Spanish), physics, psychology and writing. **Library/Resources:** The library contains 128,645 volumes, 15,684 microform items, 3,818 audio/video tapes/CDs/DVDs, and subscribes to 47,836 periodicals including electronic. Computerized library services include interlibrary loans, database searching, Internet access, and Wi-Fi capability. Special learning facilities include an art gallery, radio station, biological field station, microplate reader, cell culture labs, isolator lab, X-ray diffraction unit, neuropsychology lab, atomic absorption unit, nuclear magnetic resonance lab, refrigerated centrifuge, global learning unit, language lab, spectrometers, and laser scanning confocal microscope facility. **Physically Challenged Students:** 90% of the campus is accessible. Facilities include wheelchair ramps, elevators, special parking, specially equipped restrooms, special class scheduling, lowered drinking fountains, and special housing. **Special:** The college offers semester-long off-campus study in Australia, Austria, Canada, Costa Rica, Ecuador and the Galapagos Islands, France, Germany, Greece, Hong Kong, Ireland, Italy, Japan, Netherlands, Russia, South Africa, South Korea, Spain, United Kingdom and the United States. There are also internships in all majors, dual and student-designed majors, credit by exam, and pass/fail options available. Concentrations are offered in American studies, computational science, conflict and resolution studies, entrepreneurship, graphic design, interfaith leadership studies, professional writing and Russian area studies. Special programs are offered in education, engineering, pre-law, ROTC and pre-health professions. The college also offers emphases in economic development, entrepreneurship, film studies, finance, financial economics, human resource management, marketing, operations analytics, public relations, theatre and thematic emphasis, computer science, digital media, interaction design, web and mobile technologies and an emphasis in Big Data available to CIS majors. Students can take electives in Arabic, Chinese, earth and space science, physical activity and wellness, Russian, and interdisciplinary courses. There is a 3-3 law program with Duquesne University and the University of Pittsburgh, medicine program with Temple University School of Medicine, optometry program with Pennsylvania College of Optometry at Salus University, physician assistant program, physical therapy program and an occupational therapy program at Chatham University. In addition, there is 3-2 engineering program with Case Western Reserve University, Washington University and Columbia University and a 3-4 program known as the Integrated Program in Human Health with the Sidney Kimmel Medical College at The Jefferson. A Washington semester is available with American University. W&J's proprietary Magellan Project provides financial support for students who wish to pursue summer internships or independent study abroad, making these opportunities available to every W&J student. There are 22 national honor societies, Phi Beta Kappa, a freshman honors program, and 18 departmental honors programs. **Visiting:** There are regularly scheduled orientations for prospective students, student visits include a general session, departmental meetings, preprofessional meetings, a financial aid meeting, and class scheduling. There are guides for informal visits, visitors may sit in on classes, and stay overnight. To schedule a visit, contact Anna Koffler at (724) 223-6025. **Campus Safety and Security:** Measures include 24-hour foot and vehicle patrol, emergency notification system, self-defense education, and security escort services. There are emergency telephones, lighted pathways/sidewalks, controlled access to dorms/residences, blue light emergency phones, and security cameras monitored 24/7.

REQUIREMENTS: The SAT or ACT is recommended. Applicants must complete 15 academic credits or Carnegie units, including 3 credits of English and math, 2 of foreign language, 1 of history, social science, or nautural science and 6 or more academic courses from the aforementioned areas. An essay is required and interviews are recommended. A GED is accepted. AP credits are accepted. Important factors in the admissions decision are advanced placement or honors courses, evidence of special talent, and personality/intangible qualities. Students must complete the general education requirement of at least 8 courses in 4 divisions. Other requirements include phys ed, first-year seminar, freshman composition, foreign language, cultural diversity, oral communication, quantitative reasoning, academic skills, and 8 to 10 elective courses. A total of 34 courses, with 8 to 10 courses in the major, is required for graduation, as is a 2.0 GPA. **Procedure:** Freshmen are admitted in the fall, winter, and spring. Entrance exams should be taken junior or senior year. There are early decision, early admissions, deferred admissions, and rolling admissions plans. Early decision applications should be filed by December 1; regular applications, by March 1 for fall entry; December 15 for winter entry; and January 15 for spring entry. The fall 2017 application fee was $25. Notification of early decision is sent December 15; regular decision, April 1. 11 early decision candidates were accepted for the 2017-2018 class. 12 applicants were on the 2017 waiting list; 7 were admitted. Applications are accepted on-line. **Transfer Students:** 18 transfer students enrolled in 2016-2017. Transfer students are required to submit an official high school transcript with standardized test results from the SAT or ACT unless they are applying score optional. 64 of 136 credits required for the bachelor's degree must be completed at W&J. **International Students:** There are 75 international students enrolled. They must take the TOEFL with a minimum score of 563 on the paper-based TOEFL (PBT) or 85 on the Internet-based version (iBT).

ADMISSIONS: 48% of the 2017-2018 applicants were accepted. The SAT scores for the 2017-2018 freshman class were: Math-- 5% below 500, 49% between 500 and 599, 34% between 600 and 699, and 12% between 700 and 800. Evidence-Based Reading/Writing-- 4% below 500, 34% between 500 and 599, 56% between 600 and 699, and 6% between 700 and 800. The ACT scores were 27% between 18 and 23, 58% between 24 and 29, and 15% above 30. 53% of the current freshmen were in the top fifth of their class; 80% were in the top two fifths. 9 freshmen graduated first in their class. **Admissions Contact:** Robert J. Gould, Vice President for Enrollment. Email: *admission@washjeff.edu* Web: *www.washjeff.edu*

FINANCIAL AID: In 2017-2018, 100% of all full-time freshmen received some form of financial aid. 80% of all full-time freshmen received need-based aid. The average freshman award was $38,035. Need-based scholarships or need-based grants averaged $10,960; need-based self-help aid (loans and jobs) averaged $4,810; and other non-need-based awards and non-need-based scholarships averaged $22,265. 46% of undergraduate students work part-time. The average financial indebtedness of the 2017 graduate was $27,019. The FAFSA code is 003389. The priority date for freshman financial aid applications for fall entry is February 15.

WAYNESBURG UNIVERSITY — B-4

www.waynesburg.edu

Waynesburg, PA 15370 — (724) 852-3216, (800) 225-7393

Fax: (724) 627-8124 — **Email:** admissions@waynesburg.edu

Full-time: 550 men, 780 women	**Faculty:** 72; IIB, -$
Part-time: 12 men, 34 women	**Ph.D.s:** 65%
Graduate: 85 men, 275 women	**Student/Faculty:** 18 to 1
Year: semesters, summer session	**Tuition:** $23,710
Room & Board: $9820	**Freshman Class:** 1608 applied, 1533 accepted, 400 enrolled
SAT CR/M/W: 540/520/520 **ACT:** 22	**CEEB CODE:** 2969
Application Deadline: open	**COMPETITIVE**

Waynesburg University, founded in 1849 by the Cumberland Presbyterian Church, is a private, comprehensive Christian university offering doctoral, graduate and undergraduate programs in more than 70 academic concentrations. The University has three adult centers located in the Pittsburgh region. The University is 1 of only 21 schools in the country to offer the Bonner Scholarship that affords local, regional and international opportunities to touch the lives of others through service. There is 1 undergraduate school and 1 graduate school. In addition to regional accreditation, Waynesburg University has baccalaureate program accreditation with CCNE, CAATE, and IACBE. The 30-acre campus is in a small town in Waynesburg, 50 miles south of Pittsburgh. Including any residence halls, there are 40 buildings.

STUDENT LIFE: 79% of undergraduates are from Pennsylvania. Others are from 33 states, and 4 foreign countries. 80% are from public schools. 86% are White; 4% African American; 4% race unknown; 3% two or more races; 2% Hispanic; 1% Asian American. 58% are Protestant; 23% Catholic; 17% Unknown, Agnostic, and Jehovah Witness. **Female To Male Ratio:** 1.7:1. The average age of freshmen is 18; all undergraduates, 20. 25% do not continue beyond their first year; 65% remain to graduate. **Housing:** 1045 students can be accommodated in college housing, which includes dorms. On-campus housing is guaranteed for all 4 years. 79% of students live on campus. Alcohol is not permitted. Upperclassmen may keep cars.

FACULTY/CLASSROOMS: 46% of faculty are male; 54% are female. No introductory courses are taught by graduate students.

PROGRAMS OF STUDY: Waynesburg confers B.A., B.S., B.S.B.A., B.S.M.B., and B.S.N. degrees. Master's and doctoral degrees are also awarded. Bachelor's degrees are awarded in BIOLOGICAL SCIENCE (biology/biological science, forensic science, and marine biology), BUSINESS (accounting, entrepreneurial studies, finance, international business management, management science, and marketing/retailing/merchandising), COMMUNICATIONS AND THE ARTS (advertising, art, arts administration/management, broadcasting, communication rhetoric/communication, creative writing, English, graphic design, literature, multimedia, and public relations), COMPUTER AND PHYSICAL SCIENCE (chemistry, computer science, information sciences and systems, and mathematics), EDUCATION (athletic training, early childhood education, elementary education, middle school education, and special education), ENGINEERING AND ENVIRONMENTAL DESIGN (engineering and environmental science), HEALTH PROFESSIONS (exercise science, nursing, predentistry, premedicine, prephysical therapy, and preveterinary science), SOCIAL SCIENCE (biblical studies, criminal justice, history, human services, international studies, ministries, prelaw, psychology, social science, and sociology). Nursing, business, and communication are the strongest academically. Nursing, business, and criminal justice have the largest enrollments.

ACTIVITIES: There are no fraternities or sororities. There are 51 groups on campus, including band, cheerleading, choir, chorale, chorus, drama, environmental, ethnic, film, honors, jazz band, literary magazine, marching band, musical theater, newspaper, orchestra, pep band, photography, professional, radio and TV, religious, social, social service, student government, and yearbook. Popular campus events include Spring Weekend Formal, VIP Forum, and Fine Arts Series. **Sports:** There are 9 intercollegiate sports for men and 9 for women, and 7 intramural sports for men and 7 for women. Facilities include a stadium, a gym, an arena, fitness center, basketball and racquetball courts, wrestling and weight rooms, golf driving net, all-weather tennis courts, table tennis and billiards tables. **Graduates:** From July 1, 2016 to June 30, 2017, 375 bachelor's degrees were awarded. The most popular majors were registered nurse (29%), business administration (14%), and criminal justice administration (10%). In an average class, 58% graduate in 4 years or less, 66% graduate in 5 years or less, and 67% graduate in 6 years or less.

SERVICES: Counseling and information services are available, as is tutoring in every subject. There is remedial writing. **Library/Resources:** The library contains 221,872 volumes, and 7,083 audio/video tapes/CDs/DVDs, and subscribes to 101,662 periodicals including electronic. Computerized library services include interlibrary loans, database searching, Internet access, and Wi-Fi capability. Special learning facilities include an art gallery, natural history museum, radio station, and TV station. **Physically Challenged Students:** 99% of the campus is accessible. Facilities include wheelchair ramps, elevators, special parking, specially equipped restrooms, special class scheduling, lowered drinking fountains, and special housing. **Special:** The college offers internships, an accelerated degree program in marketing and business management, dual majors, a student-designed interdisciplinary major, credit for experience, non-degree study, and pass/fail options. There is a 3-2 engineering degree program with Penn State University and a 3-1 in marine biology with Florida Institute of Technology or University of North Carolina Wilmington. A variety of study abroad experiences are available in countries around the world. There are 17 national honor societies and a freshman honors program. **Visiting:** There are regularly scheduled orientations for prospective students, including visits with faculty, students, administrators, and financial aid officers, and a tour of the campus. There are guides for informal visits, visitors may sit in on classes, and stay overnight. To schedule a visit, contact the Admissions Office at (724) 852-3248. **Campus Safety and Security:** Measures include 24-hour foot and vehicle patrol, emergency notification system, and security escort services. There are emergency telephones, lighted pathways/sidewalks, and 24-hour security access.

REQUIREMENTS: The SAT or ACT is required. Applicants must be graduates of an accredited secondary school or have a GED certificate and have completed 16 academic credits, including 4 in English, 3 in math, and 2 in sciences, history, or social studies. AP and CLEP credits are accepted. Important factors in the admissions decision are advanced placement or honors courses, recommendations by school officials, and extracurricular activities record. To graduate, students must complete a minimum of 124 semester hours, including at least 30 in the major, with a minimum 2.0 GPA. Requirements include 15 credits of humanities and social and behavioral sciences, 8 of natural and physical sciences, 6 each of English and literature/arts, 3 credits each in math and computer science and 1 each of life skills, service learning, and Fiat Lux. Students must also pass an English usage and written competency test and a math test. **Procedure:** Freshmen are admitted in the fall, spring, and summer. Entrance exams should be taken in April of the junior year or December of the senior year. There is a rolling admissions plan. Application deadlines are open. The fall 2017 application fee was $20. Applications are accepted on-line. **Transfer Students:** 34 transfer students enrolled in 2016-2017. Students must submit a high school transcript and complete transcripts from all colleges previously attended. 45 of 124 credits required for the bachelor's degree must be completed at Waynesburg. **International Students:** There are 3 international students enrolled. They must take the TOEFL with a minimum score of 80 on the Internet-based version (iBT).

Admissions Contact: Jacquelin Palko, Director of Admissions. Email: *admissions@waynesburg.edu* Web: *www.waynesburg.edu*

FINANCIAL AID: In 2017-2018, 100% of all full-time freshmen received some form of financial aid. 81% of all full-time freshmen received need-based aid. The average freshman award was $23,000. Need-based scholarships or need-based grants averaged $1,600 ($10,000 maximum); need-based self-help aid (loans and jobs) averaged $7,000 ($11,000 maximum); and other non-need-based awards and non-need-based scholarships averaged $9,000 ($33,830 maximum). 24% of undergraduate students work part-time. The average financial indebtedness of the 2017 graduate was $31,000. The FAFSA code is 003391. The deadline for filing freshman financial aid applications for fall entry is rolling.

WEST CHESTER UNIVERSITY OF PENNSYLVANIA — E-3

www.wcupa.edu

West Chester, PA 19383	**(610) 436-3411** **(877) 315-2165**
Fax: (610) 436-2907	**Email: ugadmiss@wcupa.edu**
Full-time: 5278 men, 7742 women	**Faculty:** n/av
Part-time: 658 men, 773 women	**Ph.D.s:** n/av
Graduate: 929 men, 1926 women	**Student/Faculty:** n/av
Year: semesters, summer session	**Tuition:** $10,111 ($21,591)
Room & Board: $9060	**Freshman Class:** 12667 applied, 8677 accepted, 2624 enrolled
SAT EBR-W/M: 585/573 **ACT:** 24	**CEEB CODE:** 2959
Application Deadline: open	**VERY COMPETITIVE**

West Chester University, founded in 1871, is a leading comprehensive university that excels in teacher education, business, health, natural and social sciences, music and the arts. WCU is committed to high quality education at every level and offers more than 180 undergraduate and graduate programs, through in-class instruction, hybrid models, and online options. There are 7 undergraduate schools and 6 graduate schools. In addition to regional accreditation, WCU has baccalaureate program accreditation with AACSB, ABET, CSWE, NASAD, NASM, ACCME, ACEND, ACS, AOSA, ASHA, CAAHEP, CAATE, CACREP, CCNE, CEPH, CoARC, FEPAC, EHAC, MSCHE, NASPAA, NAST, OAKE, and PDE. The 409-acre campus is in a suburban area 25 miles west of Philadelphia. Including any residence halls, there are 116 buildings.

STUDENT LIFE: 89% of undergraduates are from Pennsylvania. Others are from 32 states, 81 foreign countries, and Canada. 87% are from public schools. 76% are White; 6% Hispanic; 3% two or more races; 2% Asian American; 11% African American; 1% race unknown. **Female To Male Ratio:** 1.5:1. The average age of freshmen is 18; all undergraduates, 21. 15% do not continue beyond their first year; 73% remain to graduate. **Housing:** 5146 students can be accommodated in college housing, which includes gender neutral, coed dorms and on-campus apartments. In addition, there are special-interest houses, international student sections. On-campus housing is available on a first-come, first-served basis, and is available on a lottery system for upperclassmen. 64% of students commute. Alcohol is not permitted. Upperclassmen may keep cars.

FACULTY/CLASSROOMS: No introductory courses are taught by graduate students.

PROGRAMS OF STUDY: WCU confers B.A., B.S., B.F.A., B.Mus., B.S.Ed., B.S.N. and B.S.W. degrees. Master's and doctoral degrees are also awarded. Bachelor's degrees are awarded in BIOLOGICAL SCIENCE (biology ecology and field biology, biochemistry, biology/biological science, biology/general science secondary education, cell biology, cell & molecular biology, environmental biology, marine science, microbiology, molecular biology, and nutrition), BUSINESS (accounting, banking and finance, business administration and management, business administration - international, business administration marketing, business economics, international business, business management, and marketing management), COMMUNICATIONS AND THE ARTS (applied music, art, communication studies, communications, dance, dramatic arts, English, English literature, English Writing, French, German, German studies, Germanic languages and literature, jazz, keyboard - piano concentration, literature, music, music history and appreciation, music performance, music theory and composition, musical theater, performing arts, piano performance, Russian, Russian languages and literature, Spanish, studio art, theatre arts, theater design, theatre production, theatre studies, theater management, visual and performing arts, vocal performance, voice, and vocal music education), COMPUTER AND PHYSICAL SCIENCE (actuarial mathematics, chemistry, chemistry / chemical biology, chemistry education, chemistry/forensic chemistry, chemistry/general science second education, chemistry secondary education, computer science, earth science, earth & space science, geoenvironmental studies, geology, geoscience, mathematics, mathematics-actuarial concentration, mathematics/computational, physics, and statistics), EDUCATION (athletic training, childhood education, early childhood education, elementary education, English secondary education, English education, health education, health and physical education, mathematics education, middle school education, music education, physical education, science education, secondary education, social studies education, special education, and special education/early child dual program), ENGINEERING AND ENVIRONMENTAL DESIGN (engineering physics and urban planning technology), HEALTH PROFESSIONS (environmental health science, exercise science, health, health science, medical technology, nursing, pharmaceutical science, predentistry, premedicine, prephysical therapy, public health, respiratory therapy, speech pathology/audiology, and sports medicine), SOCIAL SCIENCE (American studies, anthropology, communication sciences & disorders, criminal justice, dietetics, early childhood studies, economics, government, forensic studies, French studies, geography, history, international relations, liberal arts/general studies, liberal arts, sciences, general studies, humanities, philosophy, philosophy and religion, political science/government, prelaw, psychology, Russian and Slavic studies, social work, sociology, Spanish studies, women & gender studies, and women's studies). Premedical is the strongest academically. Undeclared general, psychology, and early grades PK-4 have the largest enrollments.

ACTIVITIES: 12% of men belong to 14 national fraternities; 18% of women belong to 18 national sororities. There are 286 groups on campus, including art, band, cheerleading, chess, choir, chorale, chorus, communications, computers, dance, debate, drama, drill team, drum and bugle corps, environmental, ethnic, film, forensics, honors, international, jazz band, LGBT, literary magazine, marching band, musical theater, newspaper, opera, orchestra, pep band, photography, political, professional, radio and TV, religious, social, social service, student government, symphony, and yearbook. Popular campus events include Martin Luther King Day, University Festival, Student Involvement Fair, Homecoming, Greek Week, and Spring Weekend. **Sports:** There are 10 intercollegiate sports for men and 14 for women, and 7 intramural sports for men and 7 for women. Facilities include a field house, gyms, swimming pools and diving well, several practice and game fields, softball complex, tennis courts, basketball facility, a baseball stadium, field hockey/lacrosse complex two fitness centers, fi mile track, climbing wall, and a recreational outdoor pursuits education (ROPE) course. **Graduates:** From July 1, 2016 to June 30, 2017, 3707 bachelor's degrees were awarded. The most popular majors were psychology (6%), finance (6%), and business management (6%). In an average class, 54% graduate in 4 years or less, 71% graduate in 5 years or less, and 73% graduate in 6 years or less.

SERVICES: Counseling and information services are available, as is tutoring in some subjects, such as seventy 100, and 200 level general education courses. There is a reader service for the blind, and remedial math, reading, and writing. **Library/Resources:** The library contains 1.5 million volumes, 768,443 microform items, 58,312 audio/video tapes/CDs/DVDs, and subscribes to 101,028 periodicals including electronic. Computerized library services include interlibrary loans, database searching, Internet access, and Wi-Fi capability. Special learning facilities include an art gallery, planetarium, radio station, TV station, observatory, an herbarium, a speech and hearing clinic, an autism clinic and retail training program, a center for government and community affairs, a 151-acre natural area for environmental studies, mineral museum, music library, fully-equipped food preparation laboratory for nutrition and dietetics program, nursing skills laboratory, athletic training rooms, HEAT (Heat Illness Evaluation Avoidance and Treatment) Institute, dance studio, poetry center, Outdoor Classroom & Native Plant & Ornithology, Microsoft Demonstration and Application Center. The entire campus forest is designated an Arboretum Level II by ArbNet. **Physically Challenged Students:** 95% of the campus is accessible. Facilities include wheelchair ramps, elevators, special parking, specially equipped restrooms, special class scheduling, lowered drinking fountains, and lowered telephones. **Special:** There is cross-registration with Cheyney University and a 3-2 engineering program with Pennsylvania State University and Philadelphia University. The university offers some accelerated degree programs, a Washington semester, some student-designed majors, credit by examination for life, military, and work experience, and pass/fail options. Students arrange study-abroad programs through a third party. There are also several faculty-led study programs. There are 33 national honor societies and a freshman honors program. **Visiting:** There are regularly scheduled orientations for prospective students, campus tours are offered daily, some include an information session. WCU also host preview days for prospective students. They include faculty presentations, sessions on financial aid, tours of campus and interactions with administrative staff. There are guides for informal visits and visitors may sit in on classes. To schedule a visit, contact the Office of Admissions. **Campus Safety and Security:** Measures include 24-hour foot and vehicle patrol, emergency notification system, self-defense education, and security escort services. There are shuttle buses, emergency telephones, lighted pathways/sidewalks, controlled access to dorms/residences, bike patrol, card access/CCTV/security alarms on doors in all resident halls, security officers are posted in residence halls overnight, crime prevention programming with alcohol-free alternative events and personal self-defense courses.

REQUIREMENTS: A college preparatory curriculum in high school, standardized test scores from the SAT or ACT, and a personal statement are required. An interview is required for premedical, pharmaceutical product development and respiratory care programs. An audition is required for music applicants and a portfolio for art applicants. Specific course prerequisites depend on major selection. Additional documentation is required of candidates for the summer academic development program. The GED is acceptable. WCU requires applicants to be in the upper 40% of their class. AP and CLEP credits are accepted. All students must satisfy requirements in English composition, mathematics, public speaking, diverse communities study, interdisciplinary study, and writing emphasis. General Education distribution requirements include 6 credit hours each of science, behavioral and social science, and humanities, and 3 credit hours in the arts. A total of 120 (126 or 124 for some degrees) credit hours and a 2.0 GPA are required. **Procedure:** Freshmen are admitted fall and spring. Entrance exams should be taken in spring of the junior year or fall of the senior year. There is a rolling admissions plan. Application deadlines are open. The fall 2017 application fee was $45. Notification is sent on a rolling basis. 104 applicants were on the 2017 waiting list; 74 were admitted. Applications are accepted on-line. **Transfer Students:** 1328 transfer students enrolled in 2016-2017. Applicants must submit official copies of college transcripts for every institution attended. In some cases students will be required to submit a midterm progress report. If a transfer applicant has completed less than 24 credits they must submit a high school transcript and standardized test scores if they have been out of high school for less than 3 years. Audition is required for music applicants, portfolio for art applicants, and interview for Pre-Med, Pharmaceutical Product Development, and Respiratory Care. 30 of 120 credits required for the bachelor's degree must be completed at WCU. **International Students:** There are 59 international students enrolled. They must take the TOEFL with a minimum score of 550 on the paper-based TOEFL (PBT) or 80 on the Internet-based version (iBT) and the college's own test, Passing ELS Language School's Level 112 or the IELTS (overall band 6.0 or above). The SAT is recommended.

ADMISSIONS: 69% of the 2017-2018 applicants were accepted. The SAT scores for the 2017-2018 freshman class were: Math-- 6% below 500, 62% between 500 and 599, 30% between 600 and 699, and 3% between 700 and 800. Evidence-Based Reading/Writing-- 3% below 500, 58% between 500 and 599, 36% between 600 and 699, and 3% between 700 and 800. The ACT scores were 43% between 18 and 23, 50% between 24 and 29, and 7% above 30. 2 freshmen graduated first in their class. **Admissions Contact:** Sarah Freed, Interim Executive Director of Admissions. Email: *ugadmiss@wcupa.edu* Web: *www.wcupa.edu*

FINANCIAL AID: In 2017-2018, 82% of all full-time freshmen received some form of financial aid. 61% of all full-time freshmen received need-based aid. The average freshman award was $7,999. Need-based scholarships or need-based grants averaged $6,673 ($29,589 maximum); need-based self-help aid (loans and jobs) averaged $3,184 ($11,300 maximum); non-need-based athletic scholarships averaged $2,528 ($8,500 maximum); and other non-need-based awards and non-need-based scholarships averaged $4,882. 8% of undergraduate students work part-time. The average financial indebtedness of the 2017 graduate was $34,160. WCU is a member of CSS. The FAFSA code is 003328. The priority date for freshman financial aid applications for fall entry is February 15.

WESTMINSTER COLLEGE — B-2

www.westminster.edu

New Wilmington, PA 16172	**(800) 748-4753** **(800) 942-8033**
Fax: (801) 832-2200	**Email: admissions@westminstercollege.edu**
Full-time: 872 men, 1141 women	**Faculty:** 154; IIB, -$
Part-time: 58 men, 56 women	**Ph.D.s:** 83%
Graduate: 247 men, 317 women	**Student/Faculty:** 9 to 1
Year: semesters, summer session	**Tuition:** $32,104
Room & Board: $9618	**Freshman Class:** 1938 applied, 1820 accepted, 434 enrolled
SAT CR/M: 555/550 **ACT:** 25	**CEEB CODE:** 2975
Application Deadline: open	**COMPETITIVE**

Westminster College, founded in 1852, is a private liberal arts institution related to the Presbyterian Church. There is 1 undergraduate school. In addition to regional accreditation, Westminster College has baccalaureate program accreditation with NASM. The 350-acre campus is in a rural area 60 miles north of Pittsburgh. Including any residence halls, there are 25 buildings.

STUDENT LIFE: 53% of undergraduates are from Pennsylvania. Others are from 23 states, and 1 foreign country. 90% are from public schools. 71% are White; 4% race unknown; 3% Asian American; 2% African American; 2% two or more races; 10% Hispanic. 56% are Protestant; 34% Catholic. **Female To Male Ratio:** 1.3:1. The average age of freshmen is 18; all undergraduates, 22. 11% do not continue beyond their first year; 76% remain to graduate. **Housing:** 1098 students can be accommodated in college housing, which includes dorms and on-campus apartments. In addition, there are fraternity houses, apartments for single students. On-campus housing is guaranteed for all 4 years. 71% of students live on campus. Alcohol is not permitted. All students may keep cars.

FACULTY/CLASSROOMS: 53% of faculty are male; 47% are female. All teach undergraduates. No introductory courses are taught by graduate students. The average class size in an introductory lecture is 20; in a laboratory is 20; and in a regular course is 22.

PROGRAMS OF STUDY: Westminster confers B.A., B.S., and B.M. degrees. Master's degrees are also awarded. Bachelor's degrees are awarded in BIOLOGICAL SCIENCE (biology/biological science and molecular biology), BUSINESS (accounting, banking and finance, business administration and management, international business management, and marketing/retailing/merchandising), COMMUNICATIONS AND THE ARTS (art, broadcasting, communications, dramatic arts, English, fine arts, French, German, Latin, music, music performance, music theory and composition, public relations, and Spanish), COMPUTER AND PHYSICAL SCIENCE (chemistry, computer science, mathematics, and physics), EDUCATION (Christian education, elementary education, guidance education, music education, and secondary education), HEALTH PROFESSIONS (predentistry and premedicine), SOCIAL SCIENCE (criminal justice, economics, history, international relations, philosophy, political science/government, prelaw, psychology, religion, religious music, social science, and sociology). Sciences, business, and education are the strongest academically and have the largest enrollments.

ACTIVITIES: 33% of men belong to 5 national fraternities; 34% of women belong to 5 national sororities. There are 60 groups on campus, including cheerleading, choir, chorale, chorus, communications, dance, debate, drama, drill team, ethnic, forensics, honors, jazz band, LGBT, literary magazine, musical theater, newspaper, opera, orchestra, pep band, political, radio and TV, religious, social, social service, student government, and symphony. Popular campus events include Mock Conventions, Mardi Gras, and Volleyrock. **Sports:** There are 9 intercollegiate sports for men and 9 for women, and 7 intramural sports for men and 6 for women. Facilities include a natatorium, racquetball, tennis, and basketball courts, an all-weather track, and weight and aerobics rooms. **Graduates:** From July 1, 2016 to June 30, 2017, 402 bachelor's degrees were awarded. The most popular majors were health professions (29%), business marketing (28%), and history (19%). Of the 2016 graduating class, 90% were employed within 6 months of graduation.

SERVICES: Counseling and information services are available, as is tutoring in most subjects. There is a reader service for the blind, and remedial math, reading, and writing. **Library/Resources:** The library contains 283,070 volumes, 9,737 microform items, 14,251 audio/video tapes/CDs/DVDs, and subscribes to 848 periodicals including electronic. Computerized library services include interlibrary loans, database searching, Internet access, and Wi-Fi capability. Special learning facilities include an art gallery, planetarium, radio station, TV station, electron microscope labs in the science center, and a graphics computer center. **Physically Challenged Students:** 50% of the campus is accessible. Facilities include wheelchair ramps, elevators, special parking, specially equipped restrooms, and special class scheduling. **Special:** The college offers internships, study abroad in many countries, a Washington semester, various dual and student-designed majors, a 3-2 engineering degree with Case Western Reserve, Pennsylvania State, and Washington Universities, London study at Regent's College, a 3-3 J.D. program with Duquesne, and nondegree study. There are 12 national honor societies and a freshman honors program. **Visiting:** There are regularly scheduled orientations for prospective students, consisting of an introduction, a student panel, a financial aid workshop, a campus tour, and a faculty fair. There are 2 visitation days in the fall and 2 in the spring. There are guides for informal visits, visitors may sit in on classes, and stay overnight. To schedule a visit, contact the Office of Admissions. **Campus Safety and Security:** Measures include 24-hour foot and vehicle patrol, self-defense education, and security escort services. There are shuttle buses, emergency telephones, and lighted pathways/sidewalks.

REQUIREMENTS: The SAT or ACT is required, with a minimum recommended composite score of 900 on the SAT or 20 on the ACT. Applicants must be graduates of an accredited secondary school and have a minimum of 16 academic credits, including 4 units in English, 3 in math, and 2 each in foreign language, science, and social studies, 1 in history, and 2 in academic electives. The GED will be considered with a minimum composite score of 270. A portfolio, audition, and interview are recommended. An essay is required. Applications are accepted on-line. Westminster requires applicants to be in the upper 50% of their class. A GPA of 2.5 is required. AP and CLEP credits are accepted. Important factors in the admissions decision are advanced placement or honors courses, leadership record, evidence of special talent, personality/intangible qualities, and recommendations by school officials. First-year students are required to take Inquiry I and II, as well as writing and a speech course. Students must fulfill a distribution requirement by taking a course in one of each of the Intellectual Perspectives: Visual and Performing Arts, Quantitative Reasoning, Social Thought and Tradition, Humanity and Culture, Scientific Discovery, Foreign Language, and Religious and Philosophical Thought. A capstone experience in their major and community service are also required. Students must complete 132 semester hours with a minimum of 84 outside their majors, and have a minimum of 2.0 GPA in all courses. Majors require between 32 and 60 hours of coursework. **Procedure:** Freshmen are admitted fall, winter, and spring. Entrance exams should be taken during the junior year. There are deferred admissions and rolling admissions plans. Early decision applications should be filed by November 15. The fall 2017 application fee was $35. Notification of early decision is sent December 1; regular decision, December 1. Applications are accepted on-line. **Transfer Students:** 161 transfer students enrolled in 2016-2017. Applicants must have a college GPA of 2.0 or better. 60 of 132 credits required for the bachelor's degree must be completed at Westminster. **International Students:** There are 2 international students enrolled. They must take the TOEFL or MELAB. Students who come from a country where English is the spoken language they also must take the SAT.

ADMISSIONS: 94% of the 2017-2018 applicants were accepted. The SAT scores for the 2017-2018 freshman class were: Critical Reading-- 23% below 500, 45% between 500 and 599, 28% between 600 and 699, and 4% between 700 and 800. Math-- 24% below 500, 48% between 500 and 599, 24% between 600 and 699, and 4% between 700 and 800. The ACT scores were 2% between 12 and 17, 42% between 18 and 23, 44% between 24 and 29, and 12% above 30. 48% of the current freshmen were in the top fifth of their class; 80% were in the top two fifths. 8 freshmen graduated first in their class. **Admissions Contact:** Dawn Chapman, Director of Admissions. Email: *admissions@westminstercollege.edu* Web: *www.westminster.edu*

FINANCIAL AID: In 2017-2018, 98% of all full-time freshmen received some form of financial aid. 81% of all full-time freshmen received need-based aid. The average freshman award was $27,834. Need-based scholarships or need-based grants averaged $22,738; need-based self-help aid (loans and jobs) averaged $5,679; non-need-based athletic scholarships averaged $6,133; and other non-need-based awards and non-need-based scholarships averaged $14,729. The average financial indebtedness of the 2017 graduate was $30,442. Westminster is a member of CSS. The college's own financial statement is required. The FAFSA code is 003392. The priority date for freshman financial aid applications for fall entry is March 1.

WIDENER UNIVERSITY F-4
www.widener.edu

Chester, PA 19013 **(610) 499-4126**

Fax: (610) 499-4676 **Email:** admissions.office@widener.edu
Full-time: 1324 men, 1595 women **Faculty:** 203
Part-time: 164 men, 344 women **Ph.D.s:** 90%
Graduate: 852 men, 2239 women **Student/Faculty:** 13 to 1
Year: semesters, summer session **Tuition:** $44,166
Room & Board: $14,024 **Freshman Class:** 6028 applied, 3948 accepted, 770 enrolled
SAT CR/M: 551/551 **CEEB CODE:** 2642
Application Deadline: February 15 **COMPETITIVE**

Widener University, founded in 1821, is a private liberal arts institution offering undergraduate programs in the arts and sciences, business administration, engineering, nursing, and hospitality management. Other campuses are in Harrisburg and Wilmington, Delaware. There are 6 undergraduate schools and 7 graduate schools. In addition to regional accreditation, WU has baccalaureate program accreditation with AACSB, ABET, APTA, CSWE, ABA, and CCNE. The 105-acre campus is in a suburban area 12 miles south of Philadelphia. Including any residence halls, there are 90 buildings.

STUDENT LIFE: 57% of undergraduates are from Pennsylvania. Others are from 34 states, and 15 foreign countries. 65% are White; 6% Hispanic; 4% race unknown; 3% Asian American; 3% Foreign; 3% two or more races; 17% African American. **Female To Male Ratio:** 1.8:1. The average age of freshmen is 18; all undergraduates, 22. 20% do not continue beyond their first year; 57% remain to graduate. **Housing:** 1700 students can be accommodated in college housing, which includes dorms. In addition, there are honors houses, special-interest houses, sorority houses, substance-free housing, affinity housing, wellness housing, and quiet/study wings. On-campus housing is guaranteed for all 4 years and is available on a lottery system for upperclassmen. 55% of students commute. All students may keep cars.

FACULTY/CLASSROOMS: 44% of faculty are male; 56% are female. No introductory courses are taught by graduate students. The average class size in an introductory lecture is 30; in a laboratory is 14; and in a regular course is 24.

PROGRAMS OF STUDY: WU confers B.A., B.S., B.S.B., B.S.C.E., B.S.Ch.E., B.S.E.E., B.S. in H.M., B.S.M.E., B.S.N. and B.S.W. degrees.

Associate, master's, and doctoral degrees are also awarded. Bachelor's degrees are awarded in BIOLOGICAL SCIENCE (biochemistry and biology/biological science), BUSINESS (accounting, business administration and management, business economics, finance, hospitality management services, international business management, and management information systems), COMMUNICATIONS AND THE ARTS (art, communications, creative writing, English, fine arts, French, media arts, modern language, and Spanish), COMPUTER AND PHYSICAL SCIENCE (chemistry, computer science, information sciences and systems, informatics and computer science, mathematics, physics, and science), EDUCATION (early childhood education, elementary education, mathematics education, science education, and special education), ENGINEERING AND ENVIRONMENTAL DESIGN (biomedical engineering, chemical engineering, civil engineering, electrical/electronics engineering, engineering, environmental science, mechanical engineering, and preengineering), HEALTH PROFESSIONS (nursing and prephysical therapy), SOCIAL SCIENCE (anthropology, behavioral science, criminal justice, economics, gender studies, history, humanities, international relations, political science/government, psychology, social work, sociology, and women's studies). Computer science, engineering, and psychology are the strongest academically. Nursing, psychology, and engineering have the largest enrollments.

ACTIVITIES: 10% of men belong to 5 national fraternities; 9% of women belong to 3 national sororities. There are 106 groups on campus, including model UN, art, cheerleading, chess, choir, chorale, chorus, computers, dance, drama, environmental, environmental, ethnic, film, honors, international, jazz band, LGBT, literary magazine, musical theater, pep band, photography, political, professional, radio and TV, religious, social, social service, student government, and yearbook. Popular campus events include Greek Week, Hundredth Night, and Honors Week. **Sports:** There are 11 intercollegiate sports for men and 12 for women, and 7 intramural sports for men and 7 for women. Facilities include a stadium, a basketball gym, a field house, a championship pool, a weight training room, an exercise room, tennis courts, outdoor game and practice fields, and an 8-lane all weather championship track. **Graduates:** From July 1, 2016 to June 30, 2017, 746 bachelor's degrees were awarded. The most popular majors were nursing/health professions (30%), business (19%), and engineering (16%). In an average class, 45% graduate in 4 years or less, 55% graduate in 5 years or less, and 57% graduate in 6 years or less. Of the 2016 graduating class, 13% were enrolled in graduate school within 6 months of graduation, and 76% were employed.

SERVICES: Counseling and information services are available, as is tutoring in every subject. There is a reader service for the blind. Academic support is offered as needed for all students. **Library/Resources:** Computerized library services include interlibrary loans, database searching, Internet access, and Wi-Fi capability. Special learning facilities include an art gallery, radio station, TV station, a child development center, and a charter school. **Physically Challenged Students:** All of the campus is accessible. Facilities include wheelchair ramps, elevators, special parking, specially equipped restrooms, special class scheduling, lowered drinking fountains, and lowered telephones. **Special:** Widener offers internships, study abroad in 12 countries, a Washington semester, accelerated degree programs, dual, student-designed, and interdisciplinary majors, including chemistry management, nondegree study, and pass/fail options. Co-op programs are available in business administration, computer science, and engineering and are required in hospitality management. There are 31 national honor societies, a freshman honors program, and 8 departmental honors programs. **Visiting:** There are regularly scheduled orientations for prospective students. There are guides for informal visits, visitors may sit in on classes, and stay overnight. To schedule a visit, contact the Office of Admissions. **Campus Safety and Security:** Measures include 24-hour foot and vehicle patrol, emergency notification system, self-defense education, and security escort services. There are shuttle buses, emergency telephones, lighted pathways/sidewalks, controlled access to dorms/residences, residence hall briefings on personal safety, housing security, enforcement procedures, and bike patrols.

REQUIREMENTS: The SAT is required. Applicants must be graduates of an accredited secondary school and have completed 4 units each of English and social studies, 3 units each of math and science, and 1 unit each of art, history, and music. The GED is accepted under limited circumstances. An interview is recommended. AP credits are accepted. Important factors in the admissions decision are advanced placement or honors courses, recommendations by school officials, and extracurricular activities record. All students must complete 12 credits each in humanities, social sciences, and science/math, and 1 credit in phys ed. For graduation, students must have 121 credit hours and a GPA of 2.0. Hours in the major vary by program. There is a university-wide writing requirement for all students. **Procedure:** Freshmen are admitted in the fall and spring. Entrance exams should be taken in the junior year and November or December of the senior year. There are early admissions, deferred admissions, and rolling admissions plans. Applications should be filed by February 15 for fall entry; January 3 for spring entry. Notification of early decision is sent December 15; regular decision, February 15. 20 applicants were on the 2017 waiting list. Applications are accepted online. **Transfer Students:** 112 transfer students enrolled in 2016-2017. Applicants must have at least 12 college credits with a minimum GPA of 2.0 (2.5 for nursing students). An associate's degree and an interview are recommended. 45 of 121 credits required for the bachelor's degree must be completed at WU. **International Students:** There are 148 international students enrolled. They must take the TOEFL.

ADMISSIONS: 65% of the 2017-2018 applicants were accepted. The SAT scores for the 2017-2018 freshman class were: Critical Reading-- 20% below 500, 58% between 500 and 599, 19% between 600 and 699, and 3% between 700 and 800. Math-- 20% below 500, 57% between 500 and 599, 20% between 600 and 699, and 3% between 700 and 800. The ACT scores were 7% between 12 and 17, 53% between 18 and 23, 35% between 24 and 29, and 5% above 30. **Admissions Contact:** Courtney Kelly, Executive Director of Admissions. Email: *admissions.office@widener.edu* Web: *www.widener.edu*

FINANCIAL AID: In 2017-2018, 99% of all full-time freshmen received some form of financial aid. 74% of all full-time freshmen received need-based aid. Widener is a member of CSS. The FAFSA code is 003313. The priority date for freshman financial aid applications for fall entry is December 15. The deadline for filing freshman financial aid applications for fall entry is February 15.

WILKES UNIVERSITY — E-2

www.wilkes.edu

Wilkes Barre, PA 18766	**(570) 408-4400** **(800) WILKESU**
Fax: (570) 408-4904	**Email: admissions@wilkes.edu**
Full-time: 1219 men, 1014 women	**Faculty:** IIA, av$
Part-time: 112 men, 146 women	**Ph.D.s:** 91%
Graduate: 714 men, 2340 women	**Student/Faculty:** 14 to 1
Year: semesters, summer session	**Tuition:** $34,896
Room & Board: $14,270	**Freshman Class:** 4067 applied, 3063 accepted, 580 enrolled
SAT CR/M: 564/564 **ACT:** 24	**CEEB CODE:** 2977
Application Deadline: open	**COMPETITIVE**

Wilkes University, founded in 1933, is an independent comprehensive university offering undergraduate programs in 45 fields, including the arts and sciences, business, and engineering. There are 7 undergraduate schools and 1 graduate school. In addition to regional accreditation, Wilkes has baccalaureate program accreditation with ABET, ACBSP, ACPE, and CCNE. The 27-acre campus is in an urban area 120 miles west of New York City. Including any residence halls, there are 54 buildings.

STUDENT LIFE: 81% of undergraduates are from Pennsylvania. Others are from 23 states, and 12 foreign countries. 80% are from public schools. 70% are White; 9% Foreign; 6% Hispanic; 4% African American; 4% race unknown; 3% two or more races; 2% Asian American; 1% American Indian/Alaska Native. **Female To Male Ratio:** 1.7:1. The average age of freshmen is 18; all undergraduates, 21. 24% do not continue beyond their first year; 60% remain to graduate. **Housing:** 1099 students can be accommodated in college housing, which includes dorms and on-campus apartments. On-campus housing is guaranteed for all 4 years and is available on a lottery system for upperclassmen. 57% of students commute. Alcohol is not permitted. All students may keep cars.

FACULTY/CLASSROOMS: 54% of faculty are male; 46% are female. No introductory courses are taught by graduate students. The average class size in an introductory lecture is 22; in a laboratory is 15; and in a regular course is 18.

PROGRAMS OF STUDY: Wilkes confers B.A., B.S., B.F.A. and B.B.A.

degrees. Master's and doctoral degrees are also awarded. Bachelor's degrees are awarded in BIOLOGICAL SCIENCE (biochemistry, biology/biological science, and neurosciences), BUSINESS (accounting, business administration and management, entrepreneurial studies, finance, hospitality management services, marketing and distribution, and sports management), COMMUNICATIONS AND THE ARTS (communications, dramatic arts, English, media arts, musical theater, and Spanish), COMPUTER AND PHYSICAL SCIENCE (chemistry, computer science, earth science, geology, information sciences and systems, mathematics, and physics), EDUCATION (elementary education and middle school education), ENGINEERING AND ENVIRONMENTAL DESIGN (electrical/electronics engineering, engineering and applied science, engineering management, environmental engineering, and mechanical engineering), HEALTH PROFESSIONS (medical technology, nursing, and prepharmacy), SOCIAL SCIENCE (criminology, history, international studies, liberal arts/general studies, philosophy, political science/government, psychology, public administration, and sociology). Prepharmacy, biology, and engineering are the strongest academically. Nursing, biology, and mechanical engineering have the largest enrollments.

ACTIVITIES: There are no fraternities or sororities. There are 80 groups on campus, including art, band, cheerleading, choir, chorus, computers, dance, debate, drama, environmental, ethnic, honors, international, jazz band, LGBT, literary magazine, marching band, musical theater, newspaper, orchestra, pep band, political, professional, radio and TV, religious, social, social service, and student government. Popular campus events include Casino Night, Junior-Senior Dinner Dance, and Winter Weekend. **Sports:** There are 11 intercollegiate sports for men and 11 for women. Facilities include tennis courts, a stadium, a gym, a game room, weight and exercise rooms, and an indoor recreation and athletic center. **Graduates:** From July 1, 2016 to June 30, 2017, 576 bachelor's degrees were awarded. The most popular majors were business (20%), nursing (16%), and engineering (14%). In an average class, 47% graduate in 4 years or less, 58% graduate in 5 years or less, and 60% graduate in 6 years or less. Of the 2016 graduating class, 20% were enrolled in graduate school within 6 months of graduation, and 73% were employed.

SERVICES: Counseling and information services are available, as is tutoring in every subject. There is remedial math, reading, and writing. The Learning Center also provides individual tutoring, group study sessions, and small-group supplemental instruction seminars. **Library/Resources:** The library contains 185,000 volumes, and 1,359 audio/video tapes/CDs/DVDs. Computerized library services include interlibrary loans, database searching, Internet access, and Wi-Fi capability. Special learning facilities include an art gallery, radio station, and TV station. **Physically Challenged Students:** All of the campus is accessible. Facilities include wheelchair ramps, elevators, special parking, specially equipped restrooms, special class scheduling, lowered drinking fountains, and lowered telephones. **Special:** Wilkes offers cooperative education, cross-registration with King's College and Misericordia University, internships, and study abroad. Dual majors in all disciplines, credit for military experience, and nondegree study are also offered. There are 19 national honor societies and a freshman honors program. **Visiting:** There are regularly scheduled orientations for prospective students, including a general orientation session, a tour of the campus, and a meeting with faculty from the department of the student's intended major. There are guides for informal visits, visitors may sit in on classes, and stay overnight. To schedule a visit, contact the Admissions Office. **Campus Safety and Security:** Measures include 24-hour foot and vehicle patrol, emergency notification system, and security escort services. There are shuttle buses, emergency telephones, lighted pathways/sidewalks, controlled access to dorms/residences, personal alarm devices for students who wish to carry one, and engraving of personal belongings. Students and others may contact security anonymously.

REQUIREMENTS: The SAT or ACT is required. Applicants must be graduates of an accredited secondary school or have the GED. Secondary-school preparation should include 4 years of English, 3 years each of math and social studies, and 2 years of science. Theater majors must audition. Wilkes requires applicants to be in the upper 50% of their class. A GPA of 2.5 is required. AP and CLEP credits are accepted. Important factors in the admissions decision are recommendations by school officials, advanced placement or honors courses, and leadership record. To graduate, all students must complete at least 120 credit hours, with a minimum of 30 in the major, and a cumulative GPA of at least 2.0 overall and in the major. Students must demonstrate competency in written communication, computer literacy, oral communication, and qualitative reasoning. General education requirements consist of 12 to 15 credits in humanities, 9 to 12 in sciences, 6 to 9 in social sciences, and 3 in fine arts. **Procedure:** Freshmen are admitted in the fall, spring, and summer. Entrance exams should be taken before the second semester of the senior year in high school. There are early admissions, deferred admissions, and rolling admissions plans. Application deadlines are open. The fall 2017 application fee was $40. Notification is sent on a rolling basis. Applications are accepted on-line. **Transfer Students:** Applicants must have a minimum college GPA of 2.0 and at least 30 earned credits. A GPA of 2.5 is required for engineering majors. Students with fewer than 30 credits must submit official high school transcripts and SAT or ACT scores. An interview is recommended. 60 of 120 credits required for the bachelor's degree must be completed at Wilkes. **International Students:** There are 213 international students enrolled. They must take the TOEFL with a minimum score of 500 on the paper-based TOEFL (PBT) or 60 on the Internet-based version (iBT). They must also take the SAT or ACT.

ADMISSIONS: 75% of the 2017-2018 applicants were accepted. The SAT scores for the 2017-2018 freshman class were: Math-- 15% below 500, 53% between 500 and 599, 27% between 600 and 699, and 4% between 700 and 800. Evidence-Based Reading/Writing-- 14% below 500, 53% between 500 and 599, 31% between 600 and 699, and 2% between 700 and 800. The ACT scores were 9% between 12 and 17, 38% between 18 and 23, 46% between 24 and 29, and 7% above 30. **Admissions Contact:** Terese Wignot, Associate Provost Enrollment Services. Email: *admissions@wilkes.edu* Web: *www.wilkes.edu*

FINANCIAL AID: In 2017-2018, 94% of all full-time freshmen received some form of financial aid. 30% of undergraduate students work part-time. The average financial indebtedness of the 2017 graduate was $43,956. The FAFSA code is 003394. The deadline for filing freshman financial aid applications for fall entry is March 1.

WILSON COLLEGE *(The complete profile is made available exclusively on our website, www.barronspac.com)*

YORK COLLEGE OF PENNSYLVANIA — D-4

www.ycp.edu

York, PA 17403	**(717) 849-1600** **(800) 455-8018**
Fax: (717) 849-1607	**Email: admissions@ycp.edu**
Full-time: 1743 men, 2068 women	**Faculty:** 173; IIA, av$
Part-time: 134 men, 134 women	**Ph.D.s:** 87%
Graduate: 78 men, 166 women	**Student/Faculty:** 16 to 1
Year: semesters, summer session	**Tuition:** $18,780
Room & Board: $10,460	**Freshman Class:** 5217 applied, 3637 accepted, 990 enrolled
SAT CR/M/W: 520/535/500 **ACT:** 23	**CEEB CODE:** 2991
Application Deadline: September 15	**COMPETITIVE**

York College of Pennsylvania, founded in 1787, is a private institution offering undergraduate programs in the liberal arts and sciences, and professional programs. There is 1 undergraduate school. In addition to regional accreditation, York College has baccalaureate program accreditation with ABET, ACBSP, NASM, NLN, NRPA, CoARC, CCNE, CANRPE, and CANAEP. The 190-acre campus is in a suburban area 45 miles north of Baltimore. Including any residence halls, there are 46 buildings.

STUDENT LIFE: 58% of undergraduates are from Pennsylvania. Others are from 32 states, and 7 foreign countries. 85% are from public schools. 80% are White; 5% African American; 6% Hispanic; 3% two or more races; 3% race unknown; 2% Asian American. 36% claim no religious affiliation; 25% Protestant; 24% Catholic; 13% Muslim, and Unknown denominations. **Female To Male Ratio:** 1.2:1. The average age of freshmen is 18; all undergraduates, 21. 25% do not continue beyond their first year; 58% remain to graduate. **Housing:** 2575 students can be accommodated in college housing, which includes dorms and on-campus apartments. In addition, there are special-interest houses, fraternity houses, and sorority houses. On-campus housing is guaranteed for the freshman year only, and is available on a first-come, first-served basis. 57% of students live on campus. Alcohol is not permitted. All students may keep cars.

FACULTY/CLASSROOMS: 57% of faculty are male; 43% are female. All

teach undergraduates. No introductory courses are taught by graduate students. The average class size in an introductory lecture is 22; in a laboratory is 17; and in a regular course is 19.

PROGRAMS OF STUDY: York College confers B.A. and B.S. degrees. Associate, master's, and doctoral degrees are also awarded. Bachelor's degrees are awarded in BIOLOGICAL SCIENCE (biology/biological science), BUSINESS (accounting, banking and finance, business administration and management, entrepreneurial studies, management information systems, marketing/retailing/merchandising, recreation and leisure services, and sports management), COMMUNICATIONS AND THE ARTS (broadcasting, communications, creative writing, dramatic arts, English, English literature, fine arts, graphic design, music, music technology, public relations, and Spanish), COMPUTER AND PHYSICAL SCIENCE (chemistry, computer science, and mathematics), EDUCATION (education, elementary education, English education, mathematics education, music education, science education, secondary education, social studies education, and special education), ENGINEERING AND ENVIRONMENTAL DESIGN (computer engineering, electrical/electronics engineering, engineering, engineering management, and mechanical engineering), HEALTH PROFESSIONS (medical laboratory science, nuclear medical technology, nursing, and respiratory therapy), SOCIAL SCIENCE (behavioral science, criminal justice, economics, history, humanities, parks and recreation management, philosophy, political science/government, psychology, and sociology). Electrical, computer, and mechanical engineering are the strongest academically. Nursing, education, and criminal justice have the largest enrollments.

ACTIVITIES: 4% of men belong to 8 national fraternities; 6% of women belong to 6 national sororities. There are 80 groups on campus, including band, cheerleading, chess, choir, chorale, chorus, computers, debate, drama, environmental, ethnic, forensics, honors, international, jazz band, LGBT, literary magazine, musical theater, newspaper, orchestra, photography, political, professional, radio and TV, religious, social, social service, student government, and symphony. Popular campus events include Fall Weekend, Spring Weekend, and Spartalooza. **Sports:** There are 10 intercollegiate sports for men and 10 for women, and 10 intramural sports for men and 10 for women. Facilities include gyms, a track, swimming pool, game room, fitness center, weight training rooms, tennis courts, soccer, hockey, baseball, softball, and athletic/intramural fields. **Graduates:** From July 1, 2016 to June 30, 2017, 936 bachelor's degrees were awarded. The most popular majors were business administration (18%), nursing (14%), and criminal justice (13%). In an average class, 37% graduate in 4 years or less, 55% graduate in 5 years or less, and 61% graduate in 6 years or less.

SERVICES: Counseling and information services are available, as is tutoring in most subjects. There is remedial math and writing. There is also an education learning resource center. **Library/Resources:** The library contains 300,000 volumes, 500,000 microform items, and 11,000 audio/video tapes/CDs/DVDs, and subscribes to 1,500 periodicals including electronic. Computerized library services include interlibrary loans, database searching, and Internet access. Special learning facilities include an art gallery, radio station, TV station, a telecommunications center, Abraham Lincoln artifacts collection, rare books collection, oral history room, and a nursing education center. **Physically Challenged Students:** 90% of the campus is accessible. Facilities include wheelchair ramps, elevators, special parking, specially equipped restrooms, special class scheduling, lowered drinking fountains, and lowered telephones. **Special:** YCP offers internships for upper-division students and a co-op program in mechanical engineering. Study abroad is offered in England, Mexico, Japan, Puerto Rico, Korea, and other countries. Dual majors in any combination, nondegree study, and pass/fail options are available. There are 6 national honor societies. **Visiting:** There are regularly scheduled orientations for prospective students, including 2 open houses in October/November; 1 junior open house in April; and 2 spring orientation programs in April/May, featuring a general orientation, academic and support services sessions, and campus tours. There are guides for informal visits and visitors may sit in on classes. To schedule a visit, contact the Admissions Office. **Campus Safety and Security:** Measures include 24-hour foot and vehicle patrol, emergency notification system, and security escort services. There are shuttle buses, emergency telephones, lighted pathways/sidewalks, Safety seminars, crime prevention speakers, a desk monitor in residence halls, and a personal property engraving program.

REQUIREMENTS: The SAT or ACT, and the ACT Optional Writing test are required. Applicants must be graduates of an accredited secondary school or have a GED certificate. 15 academic credits are required, including 4 units in English, 3 or 4 in math, 3 each in science and social studies, and 2 in foreign language. Music students must audition. A GPA of 2.5 is required. AP and CLEP credits are accepted. Important factors in the admissions decision are advanced placement or honors courses, leadership record, personality/intangible qualities, and extracurricular activities record. To graduate, all students must complete at least 124 credit hours, with 60 to 80 in the major. The required core curriculum consists of English Composition, Writing about Literature, Human Communications, Critical Thinking and Problem Solving in Mathematics, Information Literacy, and physical education. Distribution requirements include 6 credits in fine arts and humanities, 6 in social and behavioral sciences, 6 to 8 in laboratory sciences, 6 in American civilization/government and Western civilization, and 6 in international studies/foreign language. A minimum GPA of 2.0 is required. **Procedure:** Freshmen are admitted in the fall and spring. Entrance exams should be taken in the spring of the junior year or the fall of the senior year. There are deferred admissions and rolling admissions plans. Application deadlines are open. Notification is sent on a rolling basis. Applications are accepted on-line. **Transfer Students:** 176 transfer students enrolled in 2016-2017. Applicants must have a minimum GPA of 2.0 from a regionally accredited institution. Students with fewer than 30 credit hours must submit a high school transcript. An interview is recommended. 30 of 124 credits required for the bachelor's degree must be completed at York College. **International Students:** There are 14 international students enrolled. They must take the TOEFL with a minimum score of 530 on the paper-based TOEFL (PBT) or 72 on the Internet-based version (iBT). They must also take the SAT or ACT or take the IELTS with a score of 6.

ADMISSIONS: 43% of the 2017-2018 applicants were accepted. The SAT scores for the 2017-2018 freshman class were: Critical Reading-- 37% below 500, 48% between 500 and 599, 13% between 600 and 699, and 1% between 700 and 800. Math-- 30% below 500, 49% between 500 and 599, 19% between 600 and 699, and 1% between 700 and 800. Writing-- 50% below 500, 39% between 500 and 599, and 11% between 600 and 699. The ACT scores were 5% between 12 and 17, 57% between 18 and 23, 36% between 24 and 29, and 3% above 30. 4 freshmen graduated first in their class. **Admissions Contact:** Ines Ramirez, Director of Admissions. Email: *admissions@ycp.edu* Web: *www.ycp.edu*

FINANCIAL AID: In 2017-2018, 90% of all full-time freshmen received some form of financial aid. 74% of all full-time freshmen received need-based aid. The average freshman award was $14,604. Need-based scholarships or need-based grants averaged $5,219 ($15,100 maximum); need-based self-help aid (loans and jobs) averaged $6,231 ($5,700 maximum); other non-need-based awards and non-need-based scholarships averaged $6,350 ($27,340 maximum); and $5,681 from other forms of aid. 20% of undergraduate students work part-time. The average financial indebtedness of the 2017 graduate was $39,334. York is a member of CSS. The FAFSA code is 003399. The priority date for freshman financial aid applications for fall entry is March 1.

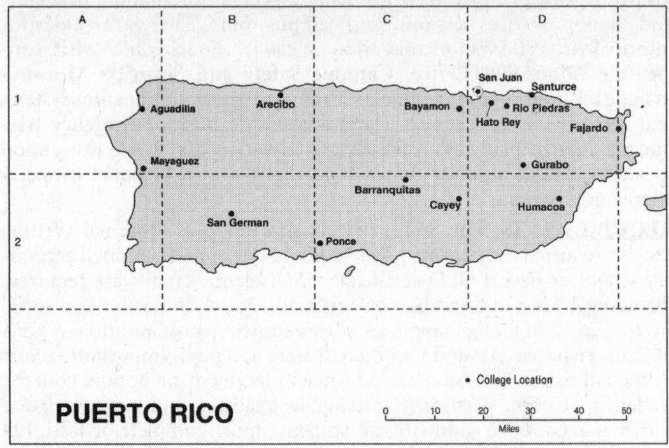

BAYAMON CENTRAL UNIVERSITY *(The complete profile is made available exclusively on our website, www.barronspac.com)*

CARIBBEAN UNIVERSITY *(The complete profile is made available exclusively on our website, www.barronspac.com)*

CONSERVATORY OF MUSIC OF PUERTO RICO *(The complete profile is made available exclusively on our website, www.barronspac.com)*

ESCUELA DE ARTES PLASTICAS DE PUERTO RICO *(The complete profile is made available exclusively on our website, www.barronspac.com)*

INTER-AMERICAN UNIVERSITY OF PUERTO RICO PONCE *(The complete profile is made available exclusively on our website, www.barronspac.com)*

INTER-AMERICAN UNIVERSITY OF PUERTO RICO-AGUADILLA CAMPUS *(The complete profile is made available exclusively on our website, www.barronspac.com)*

INTER-AMERICAN UNIVERSITY OF PUERTO RICO-ARECIBO CAMPUS *(The complete profile is made available exclusively on our website, www.barronspac.com)*

INTER-AMERICAN UNIVERSITY OF PUERTO RICO-BARRANQUITAS *(The complete profile is made available exclusively on our website, www.barronspac.com)*

INTER-AMERICAN UNIVERSITY OF PUERTO RICO-BAYAMON *(The complete profile is made available exclusively on our website, www.barronspac.com)*

INTER-AMERICAN UNIVERSITY OF PUERTO RICO-FAJARDO CAMPUS *(The complete profile is made available exclusively on our website, www.barronspac.com)*

INTER-AMERICAN UNIVERSITY OF PUERTO RICO-METROPOLITAN CAMPUS *(The complete profile is made available exclusively on our website, www.barronspac.com)*

INTER-AMERICAN UNIVERSITY OF PUERTO RICO-SAN GERMÁN *(The complete profile is made available exclusively on our website, www.barronspac.com)*

PONTIFICAL CATHOLIC UNIVERSITY OF PUERTO RICO *(The complete profile is made available exclusively on our website, www.barronspac.com)*

UNIVERSIDAD ADVENTISTA DE LAS ANTILLAS *(The complete profile is made available exclusively on our website, www.barronspac.com)*

UNIVERSIDAD DEL TURABO *(The complete profile is made available exclusively on our website, www.barronspac.com)*

UNIVERSIDAD METROPOLITANA *(The complete profile is made available exclusively on our website, www.barronspac.com)*

UNIVERSIDAD POLITECNICA DE PUERTO RICO, HATO REY CAMPUS *(The complete profile is made available exclusively on our website, www.barronspac.com)*

UNIVERSITY OF PUERTO RICO, AT ARECIBO *(The complete profile is made available exclusively on our website, www.barronspac.com)*

UNIVERSITY OF PUERTO RICO, AT BAYAMON *(The complete profile is made available exclusively on our website, www.barronspac.com)*

UNIVERSITY OF PUERTO RICO, AT CAYEY *(The complete profile is made available exclusively on our website, www.barronspac.com)*

UNIVERSITY OF PUERTO RICO, AT HUMACAO *(The complete profile is made available exclusively on our website, www.barronspac.com)*

UNIVERSITY OF PUERTO RICO, AT MAYAGUEZ *(The complete profile is made available exclusively on our website, www.barronspac.com)*

UNIVERSITY OF PUERTO RICO-RIO PIEDRAS CAMPUS *(The complete profile is made available exclusively on our website, www.barronspac.com)*

UNIVERSITY OF THE SACRED HEART *(The complete profile is made available exclusively on our website, www.barronspac.com)*

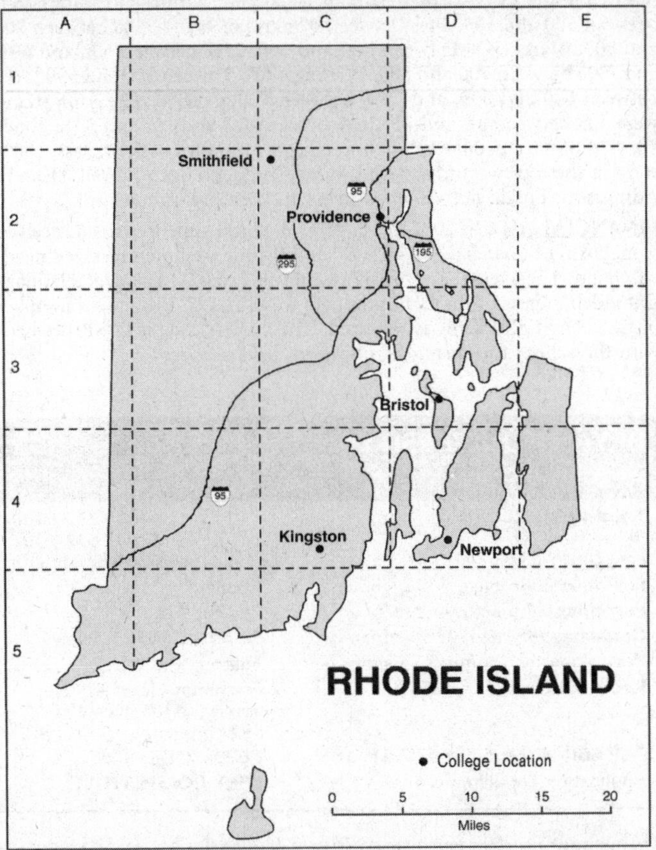

BROWN UNIVERSITY C-2

www.brown.edu

Providence, RI 02912 **(401) 863-2378**

Fax: (401) 863-9300
Full-time: 3133 men, 3423 women
Part-time: 10 men, 14 women
Graduate: 1206 men, 1049 women
Year: semesters, summer session
Room & Board: $1320

Email: admission@brown.edu
Faculty: 770; I, +$
Ph.D.s: 100%
Student/Faculty: 9 to 1
Tuition: $51,366
Freshman Class: 32390 applied, 3015 accepted, 1684 enrolled

SAT CR/M/W: 740/750/740 **ACT:** 33
Application Deadline: January 1

CEEB CODE: 3094
MOST COMPETITIVE

Brown University is the seventh-oldest college in the United States founded in 1764. Brown is an independent Ivy League institution comprised of undergraduate and graduate programs, plus the Alpert Medical School, School of Public Health, School of Engineering, and School of Professional Studies. There is 1 undergraduate school and 2 graduate schools. In addition to regional accreditation, Brown University has baccalaureate program accreditation with ABET. The 154-acre campus is in an urban area 45 miles south of Boston, MA. Including any residence halls, there are 240 buildings.

STUDENT LIFE: 95% of undergraduates are from out of state, mostly the Northeast. Students are from 50 states, 81 foreign countries, and Canada. 70% are from public schools. 43% are White; 14% Asian American; 12% Hispanic; 11% Foreign; 7% African American; 6% two or more races; 6% race unknown; 1% American Indian/Alaska Native. **Female To Male Ratio:** 1.0:1. The average age of freshmen is 18; all undergraduates, 20. 2% do not continue beyond their first year; 96% remain to graduate. **Housing:** 4858 students can be accommodated in college housing, which includes married student dorms, on-campus apartments, and off-campus apartments. In addition, there are language/international houses, special-interest houses, fraternity houses, sorority houses, international house, technology house, environmental studies house, and cooperatives housing. On-campus housing is guaranteed for all 4 years and is available on a lottery system for upperclassmen. 76% of students live on campus. Upperclassmen may keep cars.

FACULTY/CLASSROOMS: 66% of faculty are male; 34% are female. All teach undergraduates and all do research. Graduate students teach 5% of introductory courses.

PROGRAMS OF STUDY: Brown confers A.B., and Sc.B. degrees. Master's and doctoral degrees are also awarded. Bachelor's degrees are awarded in AGRICULTURE (environmental studies), BIOLOGICAL SCIENCE (biology ecology and field biology, biochemistry, biology/biological science, biology and society, biological sciences, biomathematics, biophysics, ecology, coastal environmental studies, environmental biology, human biology, health, and society, marine biology, molecular biology, and neurosciences), BUSINESS (business economics, economics – statistics, entrepreneurial studies, and organizational leadership and management), COMMUNICATIONS AND THE ARTS (Africana studies, American literature, art history, art, art history and appreciation, classics, comparative literature, creative writing, English, English literature, French language and literature, French and Francophone studies, German studies, Germanic languages and literature, Italian, linguistics, media arts, music, music composition, musicology/ethnomusicology, performing arts, Portuguese, Russian languages and literature, theatre arts, and visual and performing arts), COMPUTER AND PHYSICAL SCIENCE (applied mathematics, astronomy, astronomy and physics, astrophysics, chemical physics, chemistry, computer mathematics, computer science, earth & space science, environmental geology, geochemistry, geology, geoscience, mathematics, mathematics/computational, mathematics – economics, mathematics/theoretical, physics and mathematics, physics, physics with astrophysics option, planetary and space science, and statistics), EDUCATION (education), ENGINEERING AND ENVIRONMENTAL DESIGN (architectural history, architecture, bioengineering, biomedical engineering, chemical engineering, computational sciences, computer engineering, computer graphics, engineering, engineering physics, environmental engineering, environmental science, history of architecture / urban development, materials engineering, materials science, materials science and engineering, and mechanical engineering), HEALTH PROFESSIONS (biology, biomedical science, community health work, electrical engineering, human biology, and public health), SOCIAL SCIENCE (African studies, African American studies, American Indian studies, American studies, anthropology, archeology, architectural studies, Asian/American studies, classical/ancient civilization, classical and near eastern civilization, cognitive science, developmental psychology, East Asian studies, economics, ethnic studies, French studies, gender studies, German area studies, Hispanic American studies, history, human development, international relations, international studies, Italian studies, Judaic studies, Latin American studies, Luso-Brazilian studies, medieval studies, Middle Eastern studies, Native American studies, philosophy, political science/government, psychology, public administration, religion, religious studies, Russian and Slavic studies, Sanskrit and Indian studies, science and society, sociology, South Asian studies, Third World studies, urban studies, women & gender studies, and women's studies). Applied mathematics, computer science, and creative writing are the strongest academically. Economics, biology, and computer science have the largest enrollments.

ACTIVITIES: 12% of men belong to 11 national fraternities; 9% of women belong to 4 national sororities. There are 400 groups on campus, including ethnic groups, volunteer, art, band, cheerleading, chess, choir, chorale, chorus, computers, dance, debate, drama, environmental, ethnic, film, honors, international, jazz band, LGBT, literary magazine, marching band, musical theater, newspaper, opera, orchestra, pep band, photography, political, professional, public service, radio and TV, religious, social, social service, student government, symphony, and yearbook. Popular campus events include Commencement, Spring Weekend, Family Weekend, and Student of Color Heritage Series. **Sports:** There are 17 intercollegiate sports for men and 21 for women, and 19 intramural sports for men and 19 for women. Facilities include a stadium, Olympic-size pool, 6-lane track, hockey rink, playing fields, weight-training rooms, facilities for wrestling, and courts for squash, handball, racquetball, tennis, basketball, and volleyball. **Graduates:** From July 1, 2016 to June 30, 2017, 1591 bachelor's degrees were awarded. The most popular majors were economics (8%), computer science (6%), and biology (6%). In an average class, 83% graduate in 4 years or less, 94% graduate in 5 years or less, and 96% graduate in 6 years or less. Of the 2016 graduating class, 20% were enrolled in graduate school within 6 months of graduation, and 69% were employed.

SERVICES: Counseling and information services are available, as is tutoring in most subjects. There is a reader service for the blind, class note taking, books on tape, diagnostic testing services, oral tests, tutors, and untimed tests. **Library/Resources:** The library contains 4.4 million volumes, 2.0 million microform items, and 100,000 audio/video tapes/CDs/DVDs, and subscribes to 106,301 periodicals including electronic. Computerized library services include interlibrary loans, database searching, Internet access, and Wi-Fi capability. Special learning facilities include an art gallery, radio station, TV station, art center, museum of anthropology, language resource center, child language lab, infant research lab, educational technology center, a center for information technology, Forbes center for culture and media studies, institute for archaeology & the ancient world, center for creative arts, Brown design workshop, digital scholarship lab, microelectronics processing facility, electron microscope central facility, Nanotools facilities, two virtual reality spaces: The YURT, and The Cave. **Physically Challenged Students:** Facilities include wheelchair ramps, elevators, special parking, specially equipped restrooms, special class scheduling, lowered drinking fountains, lowered telephones, and special housing. **Special:** Students may cross-register with Rhode Island School of Design (RISD) or study abroad in any of 120 programs in 11 countries. A combined A.B.-S.C.B. degree is possible in any major field with five years of study. Dual and student-designed majors and community internships are available. Students may pursue five year programs in the arts or sciences, or the eight year Program in the Liberal Medical Education continuum, or the five year Brown/RISD dual degree program. Undergraduates study abroad in regions across the world. There are 3 national honor societies and a chapter of Phi Beta Kappa. **Visiting:** There are regularly scheduled orientations for prospective students. Group Information Sessions are usually conducted Monday through Friday at 10:15 a.m. and 2:15 p.m. from mid-February through November and on Saturday mornings from mid-September to mid-November. There are guides for informal visits and visitors may sit in on classes. To schedule a visit, contact the Admissions Office. **Campus Safety and Security:** Measures include 24-hour foot and vehicle patrol, emergency notification system, self-defense education, and security escort services. There are shuttle buses, emergency telephones, lighted pathways/sidewalks, controlled access to dorms/residences, SafeWALK, and SafeRIDE programs.

REQUIREMENTS: Applicants must be graduates of accredited high schools or have completed an appropriate home school curriculum. Preparation is expected to include courses in English, foreign language, math, lab science, the arts (music or art), and history. A personal essay is required, and two teacher recommendations. They may submit the SAT with or without essay, or they may submit the ACT with Writing recommended. (Applicants should check the Admission Office website for the current policy regarding SAT Subject Tests.) The high school transcript is the central criterion for admission. AP credits are accepted. Important factors in the admissions decision are advanced placement or honors courses, evidence of special talent, and personality/intangible qualities. Undergraduates at Brown design individualized programs of study across multiple departments. A strong advising network helps students engage fully with the Brown curriculum. To graduate, students must pass 30 courses in eight semesters, including 8 to 21 courses in the major. Students must also demonstrate writing proficiency throughout their time at Brown. With the exception of required courses specific to each major, there are no separate distribution requirements nor is there a core curriculum shared by all Brown undergraduates. Most students will complete a Capstone Project or Thesis by the time they graduate. **Procedure:** Freshmen are admitted in the fall. Entrance exams should be taken in the junior or early in the senior year. There are early decision and deferred admissions plans. Early decision applications should be filed by November 1; regular applications, by January 1 for fall entry. The fall 2017 application fee was $75. Notification of early decision is sent December 15; regular decision, March 31. 669 early decision candidates were accepted for the 2017-2018 class. Applications are accepted on-line. **Transfer Students:** 51 transfer students enrolled in 2016-2017. Transfer applicants must submit high school and college transcripts, two recommendations from college professors, scores on the ACT or on the SAT and any two SAT Subject tests, a letter of good standing from their original institution, and a personal essay. 15 of 30 credits required for the bachelor's degree must be completed at Brown. **International Students:** There are 744 international students enrolled. They must take the TOEFL with a minimum score of 100 on the Internet-based version (iBT). If a student receives at least a 600 on their SAT Critical Reading, they need not take the TOEFL. They must also take the SAT or ACT.

ADMISSIONS: 9% of the 2017-2018 applicants were accepted. The SAT scores for the 2017-2018 freshman class were: Critical Reading-- 5% between 500 and 599, 24% between 600 and 699, and 71% between 700 and 800. Math-- 4% between 500 and 599, 23% between 600 and 699, and 73% between 700 and 800. Writing-- 6% between 500 and 599, 21% between 600 and 699, and 73% between 700 and 800. The ACT scores were 1% between 18 and 23, 16% between 24 and 29, and 83% above 30. 97% of the current freshmen were in the top fifth of their class; 100% were in the top two fifths. **Admissions Contact:** Logan Powell, Dean of Admission. Email: *admission@brown.edu* Web: *www.brown.edu*

FINANCIAL AID: In 2017-2018, 45% of all full-time freshmen received some form of financial aid. 43% of all full-time freshmen received need-based aid. The average freshman award was $45,071. The average financial indebtedness of the 2017 graduate was $22,197. Brown is a member of CSS. The CSS/Profile is required. The FAFSA code is 003401. Check with the school for current application deadlines.

BRYANT UNIVERSITY — C-2
www.bryant.edu

Smithfield, RI 02917	**(401) 232-6100** **(800) 622-7001**
Fax: (401) 232-6741	**Email: admission@bryant.edu**
Full-time: 2086 men, 1332 women	**Faculty:** 162; IIA, ++$
Part-time: 29 men, 30 women	**Ph.D.s:** 79%
Graduate: 138 men, 136 women	**Student/Faculty:** 21 to 1
Year: semesters, summer session	**Tuition:** $42,109
Room & Board: $15,095	**Freshman Class:** 7242 applied, 5385 accepted, 892 enrolled
SAT EBR-W/M: 600/607 **ACT:** 26	**CEEB CODE:** 3095
Application Deadline: n/av	**VERY COMPETITIVE**

Throughout its 150-year history, Bryant University has earned a distinguished reputation for innovative academic programs and technology that are marketplace driven and highly attuned to the emerging needs of industry and society. Bryant's close-knit, student-centered community of scholars delivers challenging academic programs that integrate business and the arts and sciences, with an emphasis on real-world application and a global perspective. Abundant co-curricular opportunities, service learning programs, internships, and practicums allow students to put theory into practice while building character and leadership skills. There are 2 undergraduate schools and 3 graduate schools. In addition to regional accreditation, Bryant has baccalaureate program accreditation with AACSB and AAC+U. The 435-acre campus is in a suburban area 10 miles northwest of Providence, 45 miles southwest of Boston, 190 miles from New York City. Including any residence halls, there are 55 buildings.

STUDENT LIFE: 86% of undergraduates are from out of state, mostly the Northeast. Students are from 38 states, 53 foreign countries, and Canada. 71% are from public schools. 73% are White; 8% Foreign; 7% Hispanic; 4% African American; 4% Asian American; 2% race unknown; 1% American Indian/Alaska Native; 1% two or more races. **Male To Female Ratio:** 1.5:1. The average age of freshmen is 18; all undergraduates, 20. 10% do not continue beyond their first year; 79% remain to graduate. **Housing:** 2952 students can be accommodated in college housing, which includes gender neutral dorms and on-campus apartments. In addition, there are honors houses and special-interest houses. On-campus housing is guaranteed for all 4 years and is available on a lottery system for upperclassmen. 80% of students live on campus. All students may keep cars.

FACULTY/CLASSROOMS: 57% of faculty are male; 43% are female. 94% teach undergraduates, 39% do research, and 39% do both. No introductory courses are taught by graduate students. The average class size in an introductory lecture is 27; in a laboratory is 13; and in a regular course is 24.

PROGRAMS OF STUDY: Bryant confers B.A, B.S., B.S.B.A., B.S.I.B., and B.Sc.I.T. degrees. Master's degrees are also awarded. Bachelor's degrees are awarded in AGRICULTURE (conservation and regulation, environmental studies, natural resource/environmental economics, natural resources, and natural resource management), BIOLOGICAL SCIENCE (biology ecology and field biology, biochemistry, biology/biological science, biological sciences, cell biology, cell & molecular biology, ecology, environmental biology, environmental earth resources, forensic science, microbiology, molecular biology, and wildlife conservation biology), BUSINESS (accounting, banking and finance, business administration with legal studies, business administration and management, business administration international, business administration marketing, business communications, business data processing, business economics, business information systems, business intelligence and analytics, business law, business leadership, business statistics, business systems analysis, economics-statistics, entrepreneurial studies, environment & national resource economics, finance, financial institutions management, financial services, finance (financial planning), global/general management, human resources, industrial and labor relations, human resources/organizational management, institutional management, information & communication technology, insurance, international accounting, international business, insurance and risk management, international business information systems, international business management, international economics, investments and securities, international entrepreneurial management, international finance, international marketing, international supply and value chain management, labor studies, leadership, logistics, business management, management information systems, management, management science, marketing, management & strategic leadership, marketing and distribution, marketing management, marketing/retailing/merchandising, nonprofit/public organization management, operations research, organizational behavior, organizational leadership and management, personal financial planning, retailing, sports management, sports marketing, supply chain management, sustainable management, and professional program in accounting), COMMUNICATIONS AND THE ARTS (American literature, art and design, Chinese, communication design, communication studies, communications, communication rhetoric/communication, communication science, comparative literature, design and environmental analysis, English, English literature, foreign language, French, French and Francophone studies, information technology, intermedia/multimedia, languages, literature, modern language, public relations, romance languages and literature, Spanish, Spanish and Hispanic studies, speech/debate/rhetoric, communication arts-speech, sports administration, sport & lifestyle studies, sports communication, sports media, strategic communication, visual communication, and visual design), COMPUTER AND PHYSICAL SCIENCE (actuarial science, actuarial mathematics, applied mathematics, applied science, chemistry/chemical biology, clinical laboratory science, computer management, computer information technology, computer information systems, computer science, computer science & informatics, earth science, geoenvironmental studies, inform, science, systms & technology, information sciences and systems, information science, informatics and computer science, mathematics, mathematics - actuarial concentration, mathematics/computational, mathematics – economics, quantitative methods, science of earth systems, science of natural and environmental systems, statistics, sustainable energy, and sustainable energy science), EDUCATION (general studies, global studies, sports and wellness studies, and sports studies), ENGINEERING AND ENVIRONMENTAL DESIGN (computational sciences, computer technology, environmental design, and environmental science), HEALTH PROFESSIONS (biology, medical science, prehealth studies, prehealth biological studies, premedicine, and prephysician assistant), SOCIAL SCIENCE (American studies, applied psychology, applied social science, Chinese Studies, community services, cultural studies/critical theory & analysis, economics, government, forensic studies, French studies, gender studies, history, history and political science, humanities, humanities and social science, Iberian studies, international political science, international relations, international studies, law, legal studies, liberal arts/general studies, liberal arts, sciences, general studies, humanities, philosophy (history/contemporary thought), philosophy (political thought), political science/government, prelaw, psychology, public administration, public affairs, social science, sociology, Spanish studies, water resources, women & gender studies, and women's studies). Accounting, applied mathematics, and entrepreneurship are the strongest academically. Finance, marketing, and accounting have the largest enrollments.

ACTIVITIES: 5% of men belong to 4 national fraternities; 11% of women belong to 4 national sororities. There are 111 groups on campus, including art, band, cheerleading, chess, choir, chorale, chorus, communications, computers, dance, debate, drama, drill team, environmental, ethnic, film, forensics, honors, international, jazz band, LGBT, literary magazine, musical theater, newspaper, orchestra, pep band, photography, political, professional, radio and TV, religious, social, social service, student government, and yearbook. Popular campus events include Student Arts & Speaker Series, Black History Month, Women's Summit, Research & Engagement Day, World Trade Day, Reunion @ Homecoming, Family & Friends Weekend, and Festival of Lights. **Sports:** There are 18 intercollegiate sports for men and 19 for women, and 20 intramural sports for men and 20 for women. Facilities include a wellness fitness center, a stadium, a gym, track & turf complex, softball, tennis complex, multipurpose athletic center, and weight room. **Graduates:** From July 1, 2016 to June 30, 2017, 754 bachelor's degrees were awarded. The most popular majors were business/marketing (19%), mathematics and statistics (17%), and communications/journalism (15%). In an average class, 1% graduate in 3 years or less, 73% graduate in 4 years or less, 76% graduate in 5 years or less, and 77% graduate in 6 years or less. Of the 2016 graduating class, 18% were enrolled in graduate school within 6 months of graduation, and 81% were employed.

SERVICES: Counseling and information services are available, as is tutoring in most subjects. The Academic Center for Excellence offers tutoring for all students and is certified by the College Reading and Learning Association. **Library/Resources:** The library contains 242,563 volumes, 14,451 microform items, and 3,642 audio/video tapes/CDs/DVDs, and subscribes to 51,042 periodicals including electronic. Computerized library services include interlibrary loans, database searching, Internet access, and Wi-Fi capability. Special learning facilities include a radio station, TV station, a center for information and technology, financial markets center, a media wall, technology center and communications complex, a multimedia student exhibition, a center for international business, center for global and regional economic studies, intercultural center, a women's center, an interfaith center, and a center for student involvement. **Physically Challenged Students:** 90% of the campus is accessible. Facilities include wheelchair ramps, elevators, special parking, specially equipped restrooms, special class scheduling, lowered drinking fountains, lowered telephones, and special housing. **Special:** First-Year Gateway: 10 credits includes Global Foundations of Character & Leadership, Global Foundations of Organizations and Business, a writing course, and during winter session a 72 hour intensive course, IDEA (Innovation and Design Experience for All) experiential learning generating creative solutions to a real-world situation, plus co-curricular programs with Student Life. Honors Program culminating in a Senior Capstone Project, an interdisciplinary topic of personal interest and aligned to future career or study. Sophomore International Experience (3 credit pre-travel class work plus travel abroad during winter and summer sessions). Study Abroad (semester length via nine providers in over 54 countries). Exchange Programs for semester or year in Japan, Great Britain, and Spain. Service Learning through student organizations and/or coursework in Sociology, Management, Literary & Cultural Studies, and/or History, volunteering in community service, learning, reflecting, and devising solutions in classroom and in service. Academic Internships, 3 credits for professional work experience with faculty advisor. Practicum, 6 to 9 credits for professional work experience culminating in a major research project. The Washington Center, a full-time internship and seminar program offered during the fall, spring and summer semesters in DC. Eligible students can earn 9 to 15 credits for one semester by living, learning and working in DC. The internship placement, seminar program, one evening course and housing is provided. Work Study: Bryant provides part-time employment opportunities for work-study eligible students to assist them in meeting the cost of education. Army ROTC. There are 10 national honor societies, a freshman honors program, and 13 departmental honors programs. **Visiting:** There are regularly scheduled orientations for prospective students, Student-guided tours, admissions staff information sessions, day with class, interviews offered. To schedule a visit, contact the Office of Admission. **Campus Safety and Security:** Measures include 24-hour foot and vehicle patrol, emergency notification system, self-defense education, and security escort services. There are shuttle buses, emergency telephones, lighted pathways/sidewalks, controlled access to dorms/residences. The campus has only one vehicular entrance monitored by an Entry Control Station.

REQUIREMENTS: Accredited high school diploma or GED. High school general college prepatory program. Academic units: 4 English, 4 math, 2 each in lab science, foreign language, and history. Very important: rigor of high school record, GPA. Important: class rank, standardized test scores, application essay, recommendations. AP and CLEP credits are accepted. Important factors in the admissions decision are extracurricular activities record, advanced placement or honors courses, and recommendations by school officials. Students must complete 122-125 credits. First-Year Gateway: 10 credits includes Global Foundations of Character & Leadership, Global Foundations of Organizations and

Business, Writing Workshop, and during winter session a 72 hour intensive course, IDEA (Innovation and Design Experience for All) experiential learning generating creative solutions to a real-world situation. Upper Level Gateway: a culminating course across all disciplines. Liberal Arts Core: includes Literary Studies, Micro and Macro-Economics, Mathematics, and Statistics courses. Liberal Arts Distribution: includes two social science, two laboratory science, history, and literature courses. Business Core: includes accounting, finance, information technology, management, and marketing courses. Cross college minors: College of Arts & Sciences majors must minor in a College of Business field, and College of Business majors must minor in a College of Arts & Sciences field. All majors include a senior capstone course, a senior research seminar, and/or a senior practicum combining classroom and work experience related to the major. **Procedure:** Freshmen are admitted fall and spring. Entrance exams should be taken prior to enrollment. There are early decision, early admissions, and deferred admissions plans. Early decision applications should be filed by November 1; regular applications, by February 1 for spring entry. The fall 2017 application fee was $50. Notification of early decision is sent December 15; regular decision, March 15. 122 early decision candidates were accepted for the 2017-2018 class. 158 applicants were on the 2017 waiting list; 40 were admitted. Applications are accepted on-line. **Transfer Students:** 116 transfer students enrolled in 2016-2017. List of courses and course numbers not included on the transcript that the applicant expects to complete before enrollment. Transfers with fewer than 30 college credits required to submit SAT or ACT scores, or, if electing test optional must submit several short essay questions. 30 of 123 credits required for the bachelor's degree must be completed at Bryant. **International Students:** There are 251 international students enrolled. They must take the TOEFL with a minimum score of 550 on the paper-based TOEFL (PBT) or 80 on the Internet-based version (iBT).

ADMISSIONS: 67% of the 2017-2018 applicants were accepted. The SAT scores for the 2017-2018 freshman class were: Math-- 3% below 500, 46% between 500 and 599, 45% between 600 and 699, and 8% between 700 and 800. Evidence-based Reading/Writing-- 3% below 500, 44% between 500 and 599, 49% between 600 and 699, and 4% between 700 and 800. The ACT scores were 17% between 18 and 23, 60% between 24 and 29, and 23% above 30. 39% of the current freshmen were in the top fifth of their class; 79% were in the top two fifths. **Admissions Contact:** Michelle Cloutier, Vice President Enrollment Management. Email: *admission@bryant.edu* Web: *www.bryant.edu*

FINANCIAL AID: Bryant is a member of CSS. The FAFSA code is 003402. Check with the school for current application deadlines.

JOHNSON & WALES UNIVERSITY/ PROVIDENCE CAMPUS C-2

www.jwu.edu/providence

Providence, RI 02903 (401) 598-1000

Email: admissions.pvd@jwu.edu

Full-time: 4123 men, 3475 women	**Faculty:** 294
Part-time: 219 men, 299 women	**Ph.D.s:** 25%
Graduate: 353 men, 512 women	**Student/Faculty:** 20 to 1
Year: trimesters, summer session	**Tuition:** $31,508
Room & Board: $13,260	**Freshman Class:** 11971 applied, 9807 accepted, 2006 enrolled
	CEEB CODE: 3465
Application Deadline: n/av	**COMPETITIVE**

Johnson & Wales University/Providence Campus, was founded in 1914. Providence Campus is the largest of all JWU campuses and offers more than 50 majors in business, hospitality, culinary arts, technology, and graduate programs. There are 4 undergraduate schools and 2 graduate schools. The 166-acre campus is in a small town in Providence, 45 minutes from Boston, Cape Cod, and Newport and 3 hours from New York. Including any residence halls, there are 38 buildings.

STUDENT LIFE: 84% of undergraduates are from out of state, mostly the Northeast. Students are from 50 states, 91 foreign countries, and Canada. 8% are Foreign; 7% two or more races; 55% White; 4% race unknown; 13% African American; 12% Hispanic; 1% Asian American. **Male To Female Ratio:** 1.1:1. The average age of freshmen is 18; all undergraduates, 21. **Housing:** 3748 students can be accommodated in college housing, which includes dorms and on-campus apartments, coed dorms, apartments for single students, theme housing, and cooperative housing. On-campus housing is available on a lottery system for upperclassmen. 56% of students commute. Alcohol is not permitted. All students may keep cars.

FACULTY/CLASSROOMS: 56% of faculty are male; 44% are female. 95% teach undergraduates. No introductory courses are taught by graduate students.

PROGRAMS OF STUDY: Providence Campus confers B.S. degrees. Associate, master's, and doctoral degrees are also awarded. Bachelor's degrees are awarded in AGRICULTURE (equine science), BUSINESS (accounting, business administration and management, entrepreneurial studies, fashion merchandising, hospitality management services, hotel/motel and restaurant management, international business management, management information systems, marketing and distribution, marketing management, marketing/retailing/merchandising, office supervision and management, recreation and leisure services, recreational facilities management, retailing, secretarial studies/office management, small business management, sports management, tourism, and transportation and travel marketing), COMMUNICATIONS AND THE ARTS (advertising), COMPUTER AND PHYSICAL SCIENCE (computer management, computer science, information sciences and systems, systems analysis, and web services), EDUCATION (marketing and distribution education), ENGINEERING AND ENVIRONMENTAL DESIGN (electrical/electronics engineering, food services technology, and technological management), SOCIAL SCIENCE (clothing and textiles management/production/services, criminal justice, food production/management/services, paralegal studies, parks and recreation management, and systems science). Culinary arts, hotel/restaurant management, and marketing are the strongest academically. Culinary arts, hotel/restaurant management, and sports entertainment event management have the largest enrollments.

ACTIVITIES: 2% of men belong to 9 national fraternities; 2% of women belong to 7 national sororities. There are 100 groups on campus, including cheerleading, computers, dance, debate, drama, environmental, ethnic, honors, international, LGBT, multicultural clubs, musical theater, newspaper, pep band, political, professional, religious, social, social service, and student government. **Sports:** There are 8 intercollegiate sports for men and 6 for women, and 7 intramural sports for men and 4 for women. Facilities include exercise machines, weight management, personal exercise, wellness programs, body composition analysis, strength training, physical fitness testing, nutritional analysis, and physical fitness assessments. **Graduates:** From July 1, 2016 to June 30, 2017, 1853 bachelor's degrees were awarded. The most popular majors were business/marketing (38%), family and consumer sciences (24%), parks and recreation, and personal and culinary services (10%).

SERVICES: Counseling and information services are available, as is tutoring in every subject. Workshops in stress and time management and wellness and learning centers are available. **Library/Resources:** The library contains 108,706 volumes, 439,822 microform items, and 3,832 audio/video tapes/CDs/DVDs, and subscribes to 26,160 periodicals including electronic. Computerized library services include interlibrary loans, database searching, Internet access, and Wi-Fi capability. **Physically Challenged Students:** All of the campus is accessible. Facilities include wheelchair ramps, elevators, special parking, specially equipped restrooms, special class scheduling, lowered drinking fountains, lowered telephones, and special housing. **Special:** The university offers 11-week internships in most majors, study abroad in 19 countries, work-study programs, accelerated degree programs, and dual majors. Students have the opportunity to receive hands-on experience through 2 JWU programs: Summer Work Experience (SWEP) and Cooperative Education. There is 1 national honor society, a freshman honors program, and 5 departmental honors programs. **Visiting:** There are regularly scheduled orientations for prospective students, including tours conducted by JWU students. These tours include an introduction to the academic and social aspects of the campus experience through interactive sessions. There are guides for informal visits, visitors may sit in on classes, and stay overnight. To schedule a visit, contact the Admissions Office. **Campus Safety and Security:** Measures include 24-hour foot and vehicle patrol, emergency notification system, and security escort services. There are shuttle buses, emergency telephones, lighted pathways/sidewalks, controlled access to dorms/residences, 24-hour dorm coverage, a phone hot line for campus emergencies, and crime alerts in the student weekly newspaper.

REQUIREMENTS: Although SAT and ACT scores are required only for students applying for honors admissions, students who have taken these tests are encouraged to submit their scores. GED is accepted. Applicants must complete 4 years of English, 3 years each of mathematics and science, and 2 years of social studies. AP and CLEP credits are accepted. Important factors in the admissions decision are advanced placement or honors courses, extracurricular activities record, evidence of special talent, personality/intangible qualities, recommendations by alumni, and recommendations by school officials. To graduate, students must complete 180 quarter credit hours, including at least 36 in the major, with a minimum GPA of 2.0. Required classes include English, math, history, economics, science, psychology, sociology, and professional development. **Procedure:** There are deferred admissions and rolling admissions plans. Application deadlines are open. **Transfer Students:** 408 transfer students enrolled in 2016-2017. Applicants are required to submit official high school and college transcripts and must have earned a minimum college GPA of 2.0. Students may enroll in the fall, winter, spring and summer. 45 of 180 credits required for the bachelor's degree must be completed at JWU. **International Students:** There are 949 international students enrolled.

ADMISSIONS: 82% of the 2017-2018 applicants were accepted. **Admissions Contact:** Kim Medina, Director of Admissions. Email: *admissions.pvd@jwu.edu* Web: *www.jwu.edu/providence*

FINANCIAL AID: The average freshman award was $23,037. Need-based scholarships or need-based grants averaged $6,048; need-based self-help aid (loans and jobs) averaged $4,303; other non-need-based awards and non-need-based scholarships averaged $3,395; and $9,619 from other forms of aid. The FAFSA code is 003404. Check with the school for current application deadlines.

PROVIDENCE COLLEGE C-2

www.providence.edu

Providence, RI 02918	**(401) 865-2535** **(800) 721-6444**
Fax: (401) 865-2826	**Email: pcadmiss@providence.edu**
Full-time: 1810 men, 2239 women	**Faculty:** 297; IIA, +$
Part-time: 111 men, 146 women	**Ph.D.s:** 93%
Graduate: 239 men, 329 women	**Student/Faculty:** 7 to 1
Year: semesters, summer session	**Tuition:** $48,630
Room & Board: $14,240	**Freshman Class:** 11251 applied, 5797 accepted, 1062 enrolled
SAT CR/M/W: 620/620/610 **ACT:** 28	**CEEB CODE:** 3693
Application Deadline: January 15	**HIGHLY COMPETITIVE**

Providence College is a primarily undergraduate, liberal arts, independent, not-for-profit, Catholic institution of higher education. Committed to fostering academic excellence rooted in the arts and sciences, the college provides a variety of opportunities for intellectual, social, and spiritual growth in a supportive environment. There are 4 undergraduate schools and 3 graduate schools. In addition to regional accreditation, Providence has baccalaureate program accreditation with AACSB, CSWE, NASM, and ACS. The 105-acre campus is in a suburban area 50 miles south of Boston. Including any residence halls, there are 44 buildings.

STUDENT LIFE: 91% of undergraduates are from out of state, mostly the Northeast. Students are from 39 states, 28 foreign countries, and Canada. 9% are Hispanic; 78% White; 4% African American; 4% race unknown; 2% Foreign; 2% two or more races; 1% Asian American. 71% are Catholic; 11% claim no religious affiliation. **Female To Male Ratio:** 1.3:1. The average age of freshmen is 18; all undergraduates, 20. **Housing:** 2994 students can be accommodated in college housing, which includes single-sex dorms, coed dorms, and on-campus apartments. On-campus housing is available on a first-come, first-served basis, and is available on a lottery system for upperclassmen. 80% of students live on campus. Upperclassmen may keep cars.

FACULTY/CLASSROOMS: 56% of faculty are male; 44% are female. 93% teach undergraduates. No introductory courses are taught by graduate students. The average class size in an introductory lecture is 19; in a laboratory is 18; and in a regular course is 20.

PROGRAMS OF STUDY: Providence confers B.A. and B.S. degrees. Associate and master's degrees are also awarded. Bachelor's degrees are awarded in BIOLOGICAL SCIENCE (biochemistry), BUSINESS (accounting, business administration and management, business economics, finance, management, marketing, and professional studies), COMMUNICATIONS AND THE ARTS (art history, classics, creative writing, English, foreign language, French, German, Italian, music, musical theater, Spanish, studio art, and theatre arts), COMPUTER AND PHYSICAL SCIENCE (applied physics, chemistry, chemistry secondary education, computer science, mathematics, and physics secondary education), EDUCATION (elementary education, English secondary education, foreign languages education, global studies, mathematics education, music education, secondary education, and special education), ENGINEERING AND ENVIRONMENTAL DESIGN (engineering and preengineering), HEALTH PROFESSIONS (biology, health administration and policy, and premedicine), SOCIAL SCIENCE (American studies, community services, economics, history, humanities, liberal arts/general studies, philosophy, political science/government, psychology, social science, social work, sociology, theological studies, and women's studies). Business, and biology are the strongest academically. Finance, marketing, and biology have the largest enrollments.

ACTIVITIES: There are no fraternities or sororities. There are 125 groups on campus, including art, band, cheerleading, choir, chorale, chorus, computers, dance, debate, drama, environmental, ethnic, honors, international, intramural sports and social justice, jazz band, LGBT, literary magazine, musical theater, newspaper, orchestra, pep band, photography, political, professional, radio and TV, religious, social, social service, student government, and yearbook. Popular campus events include Late Night Madness, Clam Jam, Provapalooza, Cheesefest, Spring Concert, and Cultural Jamboree. **Sports:** There are 16 intercollegiate sports for men and 14 for women, and 22 intramural sports for men and 22 for women. Facilities include an ice arena, indoor track, tennis courts, basketball courts, volleyball court, a pool, intercollegiate strength and conditioning facilities, softball field, an outdoor track, and outdoor artificial fields. **Graduates:** From July 1, 2016 to June 30, 2017, 944 bachelor's degrees were awarded. The most popular majors were finance (13%), marketing (12%), and biology (8%). In an average class, 80% graduate in 4 years or less, 84% graduate in 5 years or less, and 84% graduate in 6 years or less. Of the 2016 graduating class, 26% were enrolled in graduate school within 6 months of graduation, and 70% were employed.

SERVICES: Counseling and information services are available, as is tutoring in most subjects. There is assistance with time management and study skills. **Library/Resources:** The library contains 1.4 million volumes, 11,110 microform items, and 3,199 audio/video tapes/CDs/DVDs, and subscribes to 61,021 periodicals including electronic. Computerized library services include interlibrary loans, database searching, Internet access, and Wi-Fi capability. Special learning facilities include an art gallery, radio station, TV station, Blackfriars Theater, Smith Center for the Arts, a science complex, Ruane Center for the Humanities, Smith Hill Annex- a community learning space, computer and language labs. **Physically Challenged Students:** 90% of the campus is accessible. Facilities include wheelchair ramps, elevators, special parking, specially equipped restrooms, lowered drinking fountains, and special housing. **Special:** Providence College offers internships in a variety of fields, including politics, broadcasting, journalism and business. Study abroad is available to students in every major. PC approves over 350 study abroad program options in more than 50 different countries. Also available are student-designed majors, a 3-2 engineering program with Columbia University or Washington University in St. Louis, non-degree study, a Washington semester, work-study, B.A.-B.S. degrees and pass/fail options. There are 22 national honor societies, a freshman honors program, and 16 departmental honors programs. **Visiting:** There are regularly scheduled orientations for prospective students, including campus tours and information sessions. Visitors may sit in on classes. To schedule a visit, contact the Office of Admissions. **Campus Safety and Security:** Measures include 24-hour foot and vehicle patrol, emergency notification system, self-defense education, and security escort services. There are shuttle buses, emergency telephones, lighted pathways/sidewalks, and controlled access to dorms/residences.

REQUIREMENTS: Applicants must be graduates of an accredited secondary school. An unweighted GPA of 3.25 in a rigorous curriculum is recommended. High school preparation should include 4 years each of English, and math, 3 years each of one foreign language, and science with at least 2 years of lab science, 2 years each of history/social studies, and other academic subjects. An essay and 2 academic letters of recommendation are required. Submission of standardized tests is optional. AP and CLEP credits are accepted. Important factors in the admissions decision are advanced placement or honors courses, extracurricular activities record, and personality/intangible qualities. To graduate, all students must complete at least 120 credit hours including all requirements for the student's major, and maintain an overall and major GPA of at least 2.0. Students must also meet all core requirements, including 16 credits in Development of Western Civilization, 6 credits in theology, 6 credits in philosophy (3 in ethics and 3 in a non-ethics philosophy course), 3 credits each in natural science, social science, fine arts and quantitative reasoning. Courses in the major or elective courses must include two intensive writing courses, as well as courses which address oral communication skills, diversity and civic engagement, and a set of two linked courses outside the major. **Procedure:** Freshmen are admitted fall and spring. Entrance exams should be taken by February 15. There are early decision, early admissions, and deferred admissions plans. Early decision applications should be filed by November 15; regular applications, by January 15 for fall entry; and December 1 for spring entry. The fall 2017 application fee was $65. Notification of early decision is sent January 1; regular decision, April 1. 198 early decision candidates were accepted for the 2017-2018 class. 3010 applicants were on the 2017 waiting list; 319 were admitted. Applications are accepted on-line. **Transfer Students:** 49 transfer students enrolled in 2016-2017. Students must complete the Common Application and forms for Transfer students, and submit a final official high school transcript, college transcript (s), essay, statement of good standing from prior institution (s) and a minimum college grade point average of 3.0 on a 4.0 scale. Submission of standardized tests is optional. Class syllabi should be sent to syllabi@providence.edu for transfer credit evaluation. Transfer student policies listed here apply to our traditional undergraduate day school only. However, we also have a School of Continuing Education that enrolls transfer students and they are included in our above transfer student totals. The School of Continuing Education has a variety of different transfer credit policies and requirements. If applying to our School of Continuing Education program, please contact them directly for guidelines. 60 of 120 credits required for the bachelor's degree must be completed at Providence. **International Students:** There are 96 international students enrolled. They must take the TOEFL with a minimum score of 577 on the paper-based TOEFL (PBT) or 90 on the Internet-based version (iBT). Student must take the IELTS.

ADMISSIONS: 52% of the 2017-2018 applicants were accepted. The SAT scores for the 2017-2018 freshman class were: Math-- 2% below 500, 34% between 500 and 599, 53% between 600 and 699, and 11% between 700 and 800. Evidence-Based Reading/Writing-- 2% below 500, 29% between 500 and 599, 59% between 600 and 699, and 11% between 700 and 800. The ACT scores were 8% between 18 and 23, 62% between 24 and 29, and 29% above 30. 59% of the current freshmen were in the top fifth of their class; 84% were in the top two fifths. 7 freshmen graduated first in their class. **Admissions Contact:** Raul A. Fonts, Dean of Admission. Email: *pcadmiss@providence.edu* Web: *www.providence.edu*

FINANCIAL AID: In 2017-2018, 80% of all full-time freshmen received some form of financial aid. 54% of all full-time freshmen received need-based aid. The average freshman award was $30,789. Need-based scholarships or need-based grants averaged $25,034 ($58,380 maximum); need-based self-help aid (loans and jobs) averaged $5,966 ($7,300 maximum); non-need-based athletic scholarships averaged $31,384 ($73,266 maximum); and other non-need-based awards and non-need-based scholarships averaged $18,200 ($47,870 maximum). 28% of undergraduate students work part-time. The average financial indebtedness of the 2017 graduate was $41,383. Providence College is a member of CSS. The CSS/Profile is required. The FAFSA code is 003406. The deadline for filing freshman financial aid applications for fall entry is February 1.

RHODE ISLAND COLLEGE *(The complete profile is made available exclusively on our website, www.barronspac.com)*

RHODE ISLAND SCHOOL OF DESIGN *(The complete profile is made available exclusively on our website, www.barronspac.com)*

ROGER WILLIAMS UNIVERSITY — D-3

www.rwu.edu

Bristol, RI 02809	**(401) 254-3500** **(800) 458-7144**
Fax: (401) 254-3557	**Email: admit@rwu.edu**
Full-time: 1905 men, 2137 women	**Faculty:** 214; IIA, ++$
Part-time: 311 men, 350 women	**Ph.D.s:** 93%
Graduate: 129 men, 192 women	**Student/Faculty:** 14 to 1
Year: semesters, summer session	**Tuition:** $32,510
Room & Board: $15,564	**Freshman Class:** 9515 applied, 7830 accepted, 1135 enrolled
SAT or ACT: required	**CEEB CODE:** 3729
Application Deadline: February 1	**VERY COMPETITIVE**

Roger Williams University, founded in 1956, is a leading independent, coeducational university with over 45 majors in arts and sciences, professional studies, architecture, and law. Across two campuses, one on the water in Bristol, and one in the heart of Providence, Rhode Island, students become community and globally-minded citizens through project-based, experiential learning. Since 2012, RWU has provided each incoming undergraduate class with a tuition guarantee for the duration of their four-year full-time studies, providing added peace of mind for financial planning. There are 8 undergraduate schools and 6 graduate schools. In addition to regional accreditation, RWU has baccalaureate program accreditation with AACSB, ABET, ACCE, NAAB, NASDTEC, ABA, ACS, and RIDE. The 140-acre campus is in a suburban area 18 miles southeast of Providence. Including any residence halls, there are 42 buildings.

STUDENT LIFE: 79% of undergraduates are from out of state, mostly the Northeast. Students are from 41 states, 62 foreign countries, and Canada. 85% are from public schools. 73% are White; 6% Hispanic; 2% African American; 2% Asian American; 2% Foreign; 2% two or more races; 12% race unknown. **Female To Male Ratio:** 1.1:1. The average age of freshmen is 18; all undergraduates, 21. 21% do not continue beyond their first year; 65% remain to graduate. **Housing:** 2996 students can be accommodated in college housing, which includes dorms and on-campus apartments. In addition, there are honors houses, special-interest houses, Academic major Living Learning Communities, and theme and wellness housing. On-campus housing is guaranteed for all 4 years and is available on a lottery system for upperclassmen. 76% of students live on campus. Upperclassmen may keep cars.

FACULTY/CLASSROOMS: 55% of faculty are male; 45% are female. All teach undergraduates. No introductory courses are taught by graduate students. The average class size in a laboratory is 15 and in a regular course is 19.

PROGRAMS OF STUDY: RWU confers B.A., B.S., B.Arch., B.F.A., and B.G.S degrees. Associate and master's degrees are also awarded. Bachelor's degrees are awarded in BIOLOGICAL SCIENCE (biochemistry, biology/biological science, and marine biology), BUSINESS (accounting, banking and finance, business administration and management, business law, international business management, management science, and marketing/retailing/merchandising), COMMUNICATIONS AND THE ARTS (art history and appreciation, communications, creative writing, dance, dramatic arts, English, graphic design, historic preservation, journalism, languages, media arts, music, theatre arts, and visual and performing arts), COMPUTER AND PHYSICAL SCIENCE (chemistry, computer science, computer security and information assurance, mathematics, web services, and web technology), EDUCATION (education, elementary education, and secondary education), ENGINEERING AND ENVIRONMENTAL DESIGN (architecture, construction management, engineering, environmental science, industrial engineering technology, and technological management), HEALTH PROFESSIONS (health care administration), SOCIAL SCIENCE (American studies, anthropology, community services, criminal justice, economics, history, humanities, international relations, legal studies, paralegal studies, philosophy, political science/government, psychology, public administration, social science, and sociology). Architecture, business and engineering are the strongest academically. Architecture, business and criminal justice have the largest enrollments.

ACTIVITIES: There are no fraternities or sororities. There are 75 groups on campus, including a radio station, art, cheerleading, chess, choir, chorale, chorus, communications, computers, dance, debate, drama, environmental, ethnic, honors, international, LGBT, literary magazine, newspaper, orchestra, photography, political, professional, religious, social service, student government, and yearbook. Popular campus events include Late Night Breakfast, Spring Concert (Spring Week), and Spring Comedian. **Sports:** There are 13 intercollegiate sports for men and 13 for women, and 13 intramural sports for men and 13 for women. Facilities include athletic facilities with a fitness center, an aquatic center, dance studios and exercise classes, racquetball/squash courts and a regulation squash court. The athletic facilities extend outdoors, sailing and kayaking, soccer and lacrosse, softball and baseball, outdoor tennis, volleyball, and basketball courts.**Graduates:** From July 1, 2016 to June 30, 2017, 884 bachelor's degrees were awarded. The most popular majors were business/marketing (28%), homeland security, law enforcement, and firefighting (10%), and architecture (9%). In an average class, 55% graduate in 4 years or less, 63% graduate in 5 years or less, and 65% graduate in 6 years or less. Of the 2016 graduating class, 18% were enrolled in graduate school within 6 months of graduation.

SERVICES: Counseling and information services are available, as is tutoring in most subjects, such as writing, math, science, and foreign language. There is a reader service for the blind. **Library/Resources:** The library contains 219,429 volumes, 136,194 microform items, and 15,907 audio/video tapes/CDs/DVDs, and subscribes to 53,078 periodicals including electronic. Computerized library services include interlibrary loans, database searching, Internet access, and Wi-Fi capability. Special learning facilities include an art gallery, RWU Marine and Natural Sciences building is home to a marine biology wet-lab and shellfish hatchery. The University also accesses an 80 acre field site on nearby Prudence Island, which includes Jenny's Creek Salt Marsh and the Oyster Nursey Pond. **Physically Challenged Students:** Facilities include wheelchair ramps, elevators, special parking, specially equipped restrooms, special class scheduling, lowered drinking fountains, and lowered telephones. **Special:** RWU offers co-op programs, internships, accelerated degree programs, study abroad in 30 countries, work-study, individualized majors, and dual majors. There are 17 national honor societies, a freshman honors program, and 15 departmental honors programs. **Visiting:** There are regularly scheduled orientations for prospective students. There are guides for informal visits and visitors may sit in on classes. To schedule a visit, contact the Office of Admission. **Campus Safety and Security:** Measures include 24-hour foot and vehicle patrol, emergency notification system, and security escort services. There are shuttle buses, emergency telephones, lighted pathways/sidewalks, and controlled access to dorms/residences.

REQUIREMENTS: Applicants should be graduates of an accredited secondary school with a minimum GPA of 2.0. The GED is accepted. Students should have 4 years of English, 3-4 years of math, natural sciences (of which 2 must be lab units), 3 of social studies, 2-3 years of history, and 2-3 electives, and 3-1 of other for a total of 16-26 Carnegie units. Art and architecture students must submit portfolios. An essay is required, and an interview is recommended. See admission requirements for individual colleges. AP and CLEP credits are accepted. Important factors in the admissions decision are leadership record, advanced placement or honors courses, personality/intangible qualities, recommendations by school officials, and extracurricular activities record. All students must: Earn a minimum cumulative grade point average (GPA) of 2.0 in order to graduate. Each college or school may also require a minimum GPA in the major. Successfully complete a minimum of 30 credits of course work in a major, all University Core Curriculum requirements and the Service Learning Requirement. Complete 45 of the last 60 credits at RWU or at an RWU Semester Abroad program. All financial obligations must be satisfied. **Procedure:** Freshmen are admitted fall and spring. Entrance exams should be taken September or October of the senior year. There are early admissions, deferred admissions, and rolling admissions plans. Applications should be filed by February 1 for fall entry. The fall 2017 application fee was $50. Notification of early decision is sent December 15; regular decision, March 15. 542 applicants were on the 2017 waiting list; 60 were admitted. Applications are accepted on-line. **Transfer Students:** 66 transfer students enrolled in 2016-2017. 45 of 120 credits required for the bachelor's degree must be completed at RWU. **International Students:** There are 116 international students enrolled. They must take the TOEFL and the college's own test. SAT scores are required for all education majors.

ADMISSIONS: 82% of the 2017-2018 applicants were accepted. **Admissions Contact:** Amy Tibero, AVP for Enrollment Mgmt and Marketing. Email: *admit@rwu.edu* Web: *www.rwu.edu*

FINANCIAL AID: In 2017-2018, 72% of all full-time freshmen received some form of financial aid. 33% of all full-time freshmen received need-based aid. The average freshman award was $19,985. Need-based scholarships or need-based grants averaged $14,297; need-based self-help aid (loans and jobs) averaged $5,688; and other non-need-based awards and non-need-based scholarships averaged $13,516. 35% of undergraduate students work part-time. The average financial indebtedness of the 2017 graduate was $44,225. RWU is a member of CSS. The CSS/Profile is required. The FAFSA code is 003410. The priority date for freshman financial aid applications for fall entry is January 1.

SALVE REGINA UNIVERSITY — D-4
www.salve.edu

Newport, RI 02840	**(401) 341-2908** **(888) GO-SALVE**
Fax: (401) 848-2823	**Email: sruadmis@salve.edu**
Full-time: 704 men, 1383 women	**Faculty:** 127; IIA, av$
Part-time: 20 men, 73 women	**Ph.D.s:** 84%
Graduate: 230 men, 413 women	**Student/Faculty:** 16 to 1
Year: semesters, summer session	**Tuition:** $38,986
Room & Board: $14,060	**Freshman Class:** 4991 applied, 3588 accepted, 598 enrolled
SAT EBR-W/M: 588/576 **ACT:** 25	**CEEB CODE:** 3759
Application Deadline: February 1	**VERY COMPETITIVE**

Salve Regina University, founded in 1934 and sponsored by the Sisters of Mercy, is an independent institution affiliated with the Roman Catholic Church. The university offers programs in liberal arts, business, health science, and professional training. There is 1 undergraduate school and 1 graduate school. In addition to regional accreditation, SRU has baccalaureate program accreditation with CSWE, NASAD, IACBE, CORE, and AACN. The 80-acre campus is in a suburban area 35 miles south of Providence and 60 miles south of Boston with an off-site location in Warwick, Rhode Island. Including any residence halls, there are 51 buildings.

STUDENT LIFE: 80% of undergraduates are from out of state, mostly the Northeast. Students are from 33 states, 21 foreign countries, and Canada. 72% are from public schools. 80% are White; 7% Hispanic; 5% race unknown; 3% two or more races; 2% African American; 2% Foreign; 1% Asian American. **Female To Male Ratio:** 2.0:1. The average age of freshmen is 18; all undergraduates, 21. 16% do not continue beyond their first year; 70% remain to graduate. **Housing:** 1289 students can be accommodated in college housing, which includes single sex dorms, coed dorms, on-campus apartments, and off-campus apartments. In addition, there are language/international houses, special-interest houses, living learning dorms. On-campus housing is available on a first-come, first-served basis, and is available on a lottery system for upperclassmen. 60% of students live on campus. Upperclassmen may keep cars.

FACULTY/CLASSROOMS: 43% of faculty are male; 57% are female. All teach undergraduates, 50% do research, and 50% do both. No introductory courses are taught by graduate students. The average class size in an introductory lecture is 22; in a laboratory is 17; and in a regular course is 18.

PROGRAMS OF STUDY: SRU confers B.A., B.S. and B.A.S. degrees. Associate, master's, and doctoral degrees are also awarded. Bachelor's degrees are awarded in BIOLOGICAL SCIENCE (biology/biological science and environmental biology), BUSINESS (accounting, business administration and management, finance, international business management, management science, and marketing and distribution), COMMUNICATIONS AND THE ARTS (art history and appreciation, communications, communications technology, dramatic arts, English, French, historic preservation, media arts, music, Spanish, and studio art), COMPUTER AND PHYSICAL SCIENCE (chemistry and mathematics), EDUCATION (early childhood education, elementary education, secondary education, and special education), HEALTH PROFESSIONS (health administration and policy and nursing), SOCIAL SCIENCE (American studies, criminal justice, economics, history, international studies, liberal arts/general studies, philosophy, political science/government, psychology, religion, social work, and sociology). Social work, nursing, and administration of justice are the strongest academically. Business, administration of justice, nursing and teacher education have the largest enrollments.

ACTIVITIES: There are no fraternities or sororities. There are 42 groups

on campus, including art, band, cheerleading, choir, chorus, computers, dance, drama, environmental, ethnic, film, honors, international, jazz band, LGBT, literary magazine, musical theater, newspaper, outdoor clubs, pep band, photography, political, professional, radio and TV, religious, social, social service, student government, and yearbook. Popular campus events include September Welcome-Back Weekend, Octoberfest Weekend, and New Year's Eve Ball. **Sports:** There are 8 intercollegiate sports for men and 10 for women, and 8 intramural sports for men and 9 for women. Facilities include a recreation center, tennis courts, indoor and outdoor basketball courts, a weight room, fitness center, soccer, baseball, and softball fields. **Graduates:** From July 1, 2016 to June 30, 2017, 424 bachelor's degrees were awarded. The most popular majors were nursing (21%), administration of justice (10%), and business administration (9%). In an average class, 1% graduate in 3 years or less, 63% graduate in 4 years or less, 6% graduate in 5 years or less, and 1% graduate in 6 years or less. Of the 2016 graduating class, 20% were enrolled in graduate school within 6 months of graduation, and 85% were employed.

SERVICES: Counseling and information services are available, as is tutoring in most subjects. There is remedial math, reading, and writing. There also is a writing center and a computer-based tutorial program. **Library/Resources:** The library contains 158,092 volumes, 46,067 microform items, and 64,829 audio/video tapes/CDs/DVDs, and subscribes to 1,041 periodicals including electronic. Computerized library services include interlibrary loans, database searching, Internet access, and Wi-Fi capability. Special learning facilities include an art gallery, radio station, biology, chemistry and nursing labs, graphic design and studio art facilities, information systems and computer labs. **Physically Challenged Students:** 80% of the campus is accessible. Facilities include wheelchair ramps, elevators, special parking, specially equipped restrooms, special class scheduling, lowered drinking fountains, and lowered telephones. **Special:** Salve offers internships in most academic disciplines as well as work-study programs on campus. Study abroad in 18 countries, a Washington semester, B.A.-B.S. degrees in biology, business, and economics, dual majors in many programs, and accelerated degree programs in administration of justice, business, international relations, holistic counseling leadership, and rehabilitation counseling are available. A liberal studies degree, credit for life, military, and work experience, non degree study, and pass/fail options are also offered. There are 15 national honor societies, a freshman honors program, and 10 departmental honors programs. **Visiting:** There are regularly scheduled orientations for prospective students, including information sessions led by an admissions professional with question/answer sessions and a student-led campus tour. There are guides for informal visits, visitors may sit in on classes, and stay overnight. To schedule a visit, contact the Admissions Office. **Campus Safety and Security:** Measures include 24-hour foot and vehicle patrol, emergency notification system, self-defense education, and security escort services. There are shuttle buses, emergency telephones, lighted pathways/sidewalks, and controlled access to dorms/residences.

REQUIREMENTS: Applicants must be high school graduates or hold a GED. Students should have 16 Carnegie units, consisting of 4 in English and electives, 3 in math including algebra and geometry, 2 each in science and foreign language, and 1 in history. An essay is required. The submission of standardized test scores is optional at Salve Regina unless you are considering a major in education or nursing. Students who decide not to submit scores will not be at any disadvantage during the admission process. AP and CLEP credits are accepted. Important factors in the admissions decision are advanced placement or honors courses, recommendations by school officials, and leadership record. To graduate, students must have 120 credit hours including approximately 36 in the major and must maintain a minimum GPA of 2.0. Distribution requirements include 9 credit hours in social science, 6 each in religious studies, science, English, and foreign language, and 3 each in visual and performing arts, philosophy, and math. **Procedure:** Freshmen are admitted fall and spring. Entrance exams should be taken as early as possible. There are early admissions and deferred admissions plans. Applications should be filed by February 1 for fall entry; December 1 for spring entry. The fall 2017 application fee was $50. Notifications are sent December 25. 40 applicants were on the 2017 waiting list. Applications are accepted on-line. **Transfer Students:** 31 transfer students enrolled in 2016-2017. Applicants must have a college GPA of 2.7 or better and follow the regular admissions process. 36 of 120 credits required for the bachelor's degree must be completed at Salve. **International Students:** There are 43 international students enrolled. They must take the TOEFL with a minimum score of 550 on the paper-based TOEFL (PBT) or 80 on the Internet-based version (iBT). The submission of standardized test scores is optional unless you are considering a major in education or nursing.

ADMISSIONS: 72% of the 2017-2018 applicants were accepted. The SAT scores for the 2017-2018 freshman class were: Math-- 7% below 500, 57% between 500 and 599, 34% between 600 and 699, and 2% between 700 and 800. Evidence-Based Reading/Writing-- 4% below 500, 54% between 500 and 599, 40% between 600 and 699, and 2% between 700 and 800. The ACT scores were 40% between 18 and 23, 51% between 24 and 29, and 5% above 30. 29% of the current freshmen were in the top fifth of their class; 65% were in the top two fifths. 2 freshmen graduated first in their class. **Admissions Contact:** Colleen Emerson, MBA, Dean of Admissions. Email: *sruadmis@salve.edu* Web: *www.salve.edu*

FINANCIAL AID: Salve Regina University is a member of CSS. The FAFSA code is 003411. The priority date for freshman financial aid applications for fall entry is March 1.

UNIVERSITY OF RHODE ISLAND — C-4
www.uri.edu

Kingston, RI 02881 — **(401) 874-1000**

Fax: (401) 874-5523	**Email: admission@uri.edu**
Full-time: 5604 men, 7011 women	**Faculty:** I, -$
Part-time: 975 men, 1502 women	**Ph.D.s:** 87%
Graduate: 1201 men, 1805 women	**Student/Faculty:** 17 to 1
Year: semesters, summer session	**Tuition:** $13,792 ($30,042)
Room & Board: $12,274	**Freshman Class:** 22667 applied, 15618 accepted, 3398 enrolled
SAT CR/M: 588/579 **ACT:** 26	**CEEB CODE:** 3919
Application Deadline: February 1	**VERY COMPETITIVE**

University of Rhode Island, founded in 1892, is a land-grant, sea-grant, and urban-grant institution offering programs in liberal arts, business, engineering, human services, nursing, and pharmacy. The university has strong marine and environmental programs. There are satellite campuses in Providence, West Greenwich, and Narragansett. URI is small enough to be friendly, intimate, safe, and student-centered, with more than 100 undergraduate and 80 graduate degree programs. There are 9 undergraduate schools and 3 graduate schools. In addition to regional accreditation, University of Rhode Island has baccalaureate program accreditation with AACSB, ABET, ACPE, ADA, ASLA, NASM, NCATE, and NLN. The 1245-acre campus is in a small town, within driving distances of Providence, Boston, and New York. Including any residence halls, there are 327 buildings.

STUDENT LIFE: 54% of undergraduates are from Rhode Island. Others are from 44 states, 62 foreign countries, and Canada. 71% are White; 6% race unknown; 5% African American; 3% Asian American; 3% two or more races; 2% Foreign; 10% Hispanic. **Female To Male Ratio:** 1.3:1. The average age of freshmen is 178; all undergraduates, 20. 15% do not continue beyond their first year; 66% remain to graduate. **Housing:** 6946 students can be accommodated in college housing, which includes language/international houses, special-interest houses, first year focused residence halls, living learning communities by academic college and program. On-campus housing is guaranteed for the freshman year only and is available on a lottery system for upperclassmen. 58% of students commute. All students may keep cars.

FACULTY/CLASSROOMS: No introductory courses are taught by graduate students.

PROGRAMS OF STUDY: University of Rhode Island confers B.F.A., B.I.S., B.L.A., B.O.A., B.O.M., and B.O.S. degrees. Master's and doctoral degrees are also awarded. Bachelor's degrees are awarded in AGRICULTURE (animal science, aquaculture & fishery technology, environmental studies, and plant science), BIOLOGICAL SCIENCE (biological sciences, cell & molecular biology, marine affairs, marine biology, microbiology, and wildlife conservation biology), BUSINESS (accounting, business administration and management, business administration - international, business institutions, environment & natural resource economics, finance, management information systems, management, marketing, supply chain management, and sustainable management), COMMUNICATIONS AND THE ARTS (Africana studies, art history, art, Chinese, communication studies, communication rhetoric/communication, English, film, television and digital media, French, German, Italian, journalism, music, public relations, Spanish, theatre arts, and writing & rhetoric), COMPUTER AND PHYSICAL SCIENCE (chemistry, chemistry/

forensic chemistry, computer science, data science, geology & geology oceanography, mathematics, physics & physical oceanography, and physics), EDUCATION (classical studies, elementary education, health education, and secondary education), ENGINEERING AND ENVIRONMENTAL DESIGN (biomedical engineering, chemical engineering, civil engineering, computer engineering, electrical and computer engineering, environmental science, industry & systems engineering, landscape architecture, mechanical engineering, ocean engineering, textile marketing, textile, and fashion merchandising & design), HEALTH PROFESSIONS (biology, communicative disorders, health promotion, health services administration, human studies, kinesiology, medical laboratory science, nursing, nutrition and dietetics, and pharmaceutical science), SOCIAL SCIENCE (anthropology, criminal justice, criminology, economics, gender studies, history, human development & family studies, Latin American studies, philosophy, political science/government, psychology, and sociology). Pharmacy, engineering, and biology are the strongest academically. Nursing, psychology, and communication studies have the largest enrollments.

ACTIVITIES: 15% of men belong to 15 national fraternities; 22% of women belong to 9 national sororities. There are 100 groups on campus, including band, cheerleading, chess, choir, chorale, chorus, computers, dance, drama, ethnic, honors, international, jazz band, LGBT, literary magazine, marching band, musical theater, newspaper, orchestra, pep band, photography, political, professional, radio and TV, religious, social, social service, student government, and yearbook. Popular campus events include First Night, Welcome Week, and Winterfest. **Sports:** Facilities include an area, a stadium, swimming pools, a multipurpose field house with an indoor track, a fitness center, fitness rooms, and courts for basketball, tennis, and volleyball. There are also outdoor tennis courts, an all-weather track, and varsity and practice fields. **Graduates:** From July 1, 2016 to June 30, 2017, 3233 bachelor's degrees were awarded. The most popular majors were nursing (7%), communication studies (6%), and psychology (6%). In an average class, 42% graduate in 4 years or less, 17% graduate in 5 years or less, and 63% graduate in 6 years or less.

SERVICES: Counseling and information services are available, as is tutoring in some subjects, such as ELS, freshman courses, math, physics, chemistry, and biology. There is a reader service for the blind, and remedial math, reading, and writing. **Library/Resources:** The library contains 1.8 million volumes, 1.7 million microform items, and 1,200 audio/video tapes/CDs/DVDs, and subscribes to 248,194 periodicals including electronic. Computerized library services include interlibrary loans, database searching, Internet access, and Wi-Fi capability. Special learning facilities include an art gallery, planetarium, radio station, TV station, a historic textile collection, and early childhood education center. **Physically Challenged Students:** Facilities include wheelchair ramps, elevators, special parking, specially equipped restrooms, special class scheduling, lowered drinking fountains, lowered telephones, and special housing. **Special:** Cross-registration is available with Rhode Island College and Community College of Rhode Island. URI also offers a Washington semester as well as semester-long internships with businesses and state agencies, study abroad in 40 countries, a B.A.-B.S. degree in German and engineering and in languages and business, a general studies degree, dual majors, pass/fail options, and credit for life, military, and work experience. The College of Engineering offers co-op programs and an international internship. There are 30 national honor societies, Phi Beta Kappa, and a freshman honors program. **Visiting:** There are regularly scheduled orientations for prospective students, including campus tours and information sessions. Visitors may sit in on classes. To schedule a visit, contact the Admission Office. **Campus Safety and Security:** Measures include 24-hour foot and vehicle patrol, emergency notification system, self-defense education, and security escort services. There are shuttle buses, emergency telephones, lighted pathways/sidewalks, and controlled access to dorms/residences.

REQUIREMENTS: The SAT or ACT is required. Applicants should be high school graduates, having completed 18 courses, including 4 of English, 3 to 4 of math, and 2 each of science (chemistry and physics for engineering majors), foreign language, and history or social studies. Remaining units should be college preparatory. Music majors must audition. AP and CLEP credits are accepted. Important factors in the admissions decision are evidence of special talent, personality/intangible qualities, extracurricular activities record, recommendations by alumni, geographical diversity, and recommendations by school officials. To graduate, the student must earn 120 to 150 credit hours, at least 30 in the major, with a GPA of 2.0. Distribution requirements include 6 credits each in English communication, fine arts and literature, foreign language or culture, letters, natural science, and social sciences, as well as 3 credits in math and quantitative reasoning. **Procedure:** Freshmen are admitted fall and spring. Entrance exams should be taken during the spring of the junior year or fall of the senior year. There are early admissions, deferred admissions, and rolling admissions plans. Applications should be filed by February 1 for fall entry; December 1 for spring entry. The fall 2017 application fee was $65. Notification is sent on a rolling basis. 1020 applicants were on the 2017 waiting list; 2 were admitted. Applications are accepted on-line. **Transfer Students:** 531 transfer students enrolled in 2016-2017. Applicants must submit transcripts from high school and all colleges or universities attended. A minimum GPA of 2.5 is required; many programs require higher. An essay or personal statement is required and a statement of good standing from prior institutions. 24 of 120 credits required for the bachelor's degree must be completed at URI. **International Students:** There are 197 international students enrolled. They must take the TOEFL with a minimum score of 550 on the paper-based TOEFL (PBT) or 79 on the Internet-based version (iBT), or the English proficiency test administered by the American Consulate. They must also take the SAT or ACT.

ADMISSIONS: 69% of the 2017-2018 applicants were accepted. The SAT scores for the 2017-2018 freshman class were: Math-- 9% below 500, 53% between 500 and 599, 34% between 600 and 699, and 4% between 700 and 800. Evidence-Based Reading/Writing-- 5% below 500, 50% between 500 and 599, 41% between 600 and 699, and 4% between 700 and 800. The ACT scores were % below 12, 1% between 12 and 17, 30% between 18 and 23, 59% between 24 and 29, and 10% above 30. 48% of the current freshmen were in the top fifth of their class; 85% were in the top two fifths. **Admissions Contact:** Cynthia Bonn, Dean of Admissions. Email: *admission@uri.edu* Web: *www.uri.edu*

FINANCIAL AID: In 2017-2018, 73% of all full-time freshmen received some form of financial aid. 70% of all full-time freshmen received need-based aid. The average freshman award was $16,577. Need-based scholarships or need-based grants averaged $10,594 ($19,515 maximum); need-based self-help aid (loans and jobs) averaged $6,147 ($6,700 maximum); and non-need-based athletic scholarships averaged $944 ($46,997 maximum). 23% of undergraduate students work part-time. The average financial indebtedness of the 2017 graduate was $23,554. The FAFSA code is 003414. The priority date for freshman financial aid applications for fall entry is March 1.

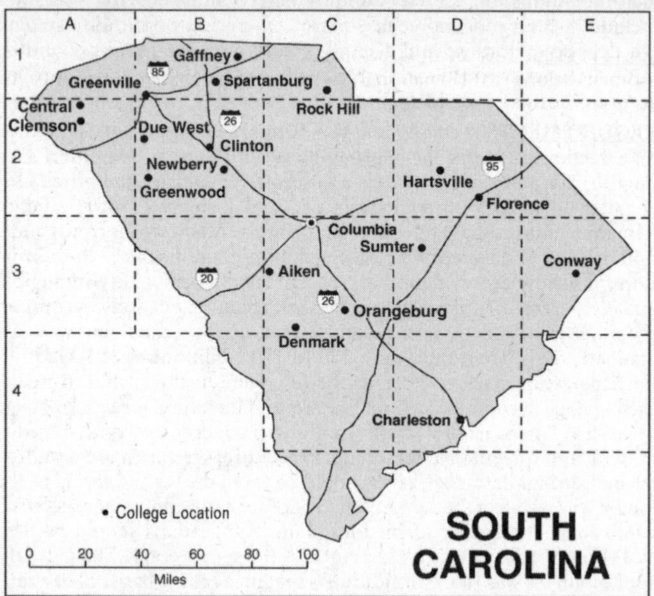

ALLEN UNIVERSITY *(The complete profile is made available exclusively on our website, www.barronspac.com)*

BENEDICT COLLEGE *(The complete profile is made available exclusively on our website, www.barronspac.com)*

CHARLESTON SOUTHERN UNIVERSITY D-4
www.csuniv.edu

Charleston, SC 29423 **(843) 863-7050**
(800) 947-7474
Fax: (843) 863-7070 **Email: enroll@csuniv.edu**

Full-time: 805 men, 1205 women	**Faculty:** 93
Part-time: 160 men, 320 women	**Ph.D.s:** 71%
Graduate: 100 men, 140 women	**Student/Faculty:** 16 to 1
Year: semesters, summer session	**Tuition:** $24,800
Room & Board: $9900	**Freshman Class:** n/av
SAT or ACT: recommended	**CEEB CODE:** 5079
Application Deadline: August 15	**COMPETITIVE**

Charleston Southern University, founded in 1964, is a private liberal arts institution affiliated with the South Carolina Baptist Convention. The figures given in the above capsule and in this profile are approximate. There are 5 undergraduate schools and 3 graduate schools. In addition to regional accreditation, CSU has baccalaureate program accreditation with NASDTEC, NASM, CAEP, AMTA, and NLNAC. The 300-acre campus is in a suburban area in Charleston, SC. Including any residence halls, there are 16 buildings.

STUDENT LIFE: 81% of undergraduates are from South Carolina. Others are from 26 states, 21 foreign countries, and Canada. 85% are from public schools. 60% are White; 5% Hispanic; 3% Foreign; 27% African American; 1% Asian American. 50% claim no religious affiliation; 42% Protestant. **Female To Male Ratio:** 1.6:1. The average age of freshmen is 18; all undergraduates, 25. 28% do not continue beyond their first year; 31% remain to graduate. **Housing:** 1250 students can be accommodated in college housing, which includes married student dorms. On-campus housing is guaranteed for the freshman year only, is available on a first-come, and first-served basis. 56% of students commute. Alcohol is not permitted. All students may keep cars.

FACULTY/CLASSROOMS: 55% of faculty are male; 45% are female. All teach undergraduates. No introductory courses are taught by graduate students. The average class size in an introductory lecture is 40; in a laboratory is 15; and in a regular course is 25.

PROGRAMS OF STUDY: CSU confers B.A., B.S., and B.Tech. degrees. Associate and master's degrees are also awarded. Bachelor's degrees are awarded in BIOLOGICAL SCIENCE (biochemistry and biology/biological science), BUSINESS (business administration and management), COMMUNICATIONS AND THE ARTS (dramatic arts, English, fine arts, music, Spanish, and speech/debate/rhetoric), COMPUTER AND PHYSICAL SCIENCE (chemistry, computer science, geology, mathematics, and natural sciences), EDUCATION (early childhood education, elementary education, music education, physical education, and science education), ENGINEERING AND ENVIRONMENTAL DESIGN (environmental science), HEALTH PROFESSIONS (music therapy and nursing), SOCIAL SCIENCE (criminal justice, economics, geography, history, humanities, political science/government, psychology, religion, religious music, social science, sociology, and youth ministry).

ACTIVITIES: There are no fraternities or sororities. There are 20 groups on campus, including art, band, cheerleading, choir, chorus, clubs for health promotions, drama, honors, international, jazz band, literary magazine, marching band, newspaper, radio and TV, religious, social service, student government, and yearbook. **Sports:** There are 9 intercollegiate sports for men and 9 for women, and 4 intramural sports for men and 4 for women. Facilities include a gym, tennis courts, softball, track and field, football and soccer fields, a baseball diamond, training and weight rooms, a 3-hole golf course with driving range, and a wellness center. **Graduates:** From July 1, 2016 to June 30, 2017, 275 bachelor's degrees were awarded. The most popular majors were business administration (21%), education (14%), and psychology/social science (9%). In an average class, 31% graduate in 4 years or less. Of the 2016 graduating class, 27% were enrolled in graduate school within 6 months of graduation, and 63% were employed.

SERVICES: Counseling and information services are available, as is tutoring in most subjects. There is remedial math, reading, and writing. **Library/Resources:** The library contains 212,666 volumes, 212,539 microform items, and 7,527 audio/video tapes/CDs/DVDs, and subscribes to 9,788 periodicals including electronic. Computerized library services include database searching. Special learning facilities include a radio station, an earthquake education center and a field physics laboratory. **Physically Challenged Students:** All of the campus is accessible. Facilities include wheelchair ramps, elevators, special parking, specially equipped restrooms, and lowered drinking fountains. **Special:** CSU offers internships, cross-registration through the Trident Area Consortium, work-study programs, dual majors, and nondegree study. Nonmajor preprofessional programs are available in dentistry, engineering, law, medicine, and ministry. There are 5 national honor societies, a freshman honors program, and 100 departmental honors programs. **Visiting:** There are regularly scheduled orientations for prospective students and parents, placement testing, and a tour. There are guides for informal visits and visitors may sit in on classes. To schedule a visit, contact the Office of Enrollment Services. **Campus Safety and Security:** Measures include 24-hour foot and vehicle patrol and security escort services. There are emergency telephones and lighted pathways/sidewalks.

REQUIREMENTS: The SAT or ACT is recommended. Applicants must be graduates of an accredited secondary school. The GED is accepted. Character references are preferred. An English proficiency exam is required for all entering students. AP and CLEP credits are accepted. Important factors in the admissions decision are evidence of special talent, leadership record, and advanced placement or honors courses. To graduate, students must complete 125 credit hours, including all core curriculum, major, and minor requirements, with a GPA of 2.0. At least 45 hours must be in the major. Core courses include 24 hours of communications and fine arts, 11 of natural science/math, and 9 of social studies. **Procedure:** Freshmen are admitted to all sessions. Entrance exams should be taken any time before filing for admission. There is a rolling admissions plan. Applications should be filed by August 15 for fall entry. The fall 2017 application fee was $25. Applications are accepted on-line. **Transfer Students:** 278 transfer students enrolled in 2016-2017. Applicants must submit official transcripts from all previous colleges attended. Accepted transfers must take an English proficiency exam. 30 of 125 credits required for the bachelor's degree must be completed at CSU. **International Students:** There are 69 international students enrolled. They must take the TOEFL, and either the SAT or ACT.

ADMISSIONS: 1 freshman graduated first in the class. **Admissions Contact:** Kimberly Ford, Director of Admission. Email: *enroll@csuniv.edu* Web: *www.csuniv.edu*

FINANCIAL AID: In 2017-2018, 95% of all full-time freshmen received

some form of financial aid and need-based aid. 26% of undergraduate students work part-time. CSU is a member of CSS. The CSS/Profile is required. The FAFSA code is 003419. The deadline for filing freshman financial aid applications for fall entry is May 1.

CLAFLIN UNIVERSITY *(The complete profile is made available exclusively on our website, www.barronspac.com)*

CLEMSON UNIVERSITY — A-2

www.clemson.edu

Clemson, SC 29634 — (864) 656-2287

Fax: (864) 656-0622 — Email: cuadmissions@clemson.edu

Full-time: 9311 men, 8572 women	**Faculty:** I, -$
Part-time: 414 men, 302 women	**Ph.D.s:** 88%
Graduate: 2481 men, 2326 women	**Student/Faculty:** 18 to 1
Year: semesters, summer session	**Tuition:** $14,708 ($34,590)
Room & Board: $9144	**Freshman Class:** 23506 applied, 11891 accepted, 3685 enrolled
SAT CR/M: 611/641 **ACT:** 28	**CEEB CODE:** 5111
Application Deadline: December 1	**HIGHLY COMPETITIVE**

Clemson University, founded in 1889, is a public institution with programs in agriculture, architecture, commerce and industry, education, engineering, forest and recreation resources, liberal arts, nursing, and sciences. There are 5 undergraduate schools and 1 graduate school. In addition to regional accreditation, CU has baccalaureate program accreditation with AACSB, ABET, CSAB, NAAB, CAEP, NLN, and NRPA. The 1400-acre campus is in a small town 32 miles west of Greenville. Including any residence halls, there are 587 buildings.

STUDENT LIFE: 69% of undergraduates are from South Carolina. Others are from 50 states, 96 foreign countries, and Canada. 81% are from public schools. 78% are White; 6% African American; 4% Foreign; 2% Asian American; 2% Hispanic. **Male To Female Ratio:** 1.1:1. The average age of freshmen is 18; all undergraduates, 21. 10% do not continue beyond their first year; 80% remain to graduate. **Housing:** 6448 students can be accommodated in college housing, which includes dorms and on-campus apartments. In addition, there are honors houses, special-interest houses, fraternity houses, sorority houses, and living learning communities. On-campus housing is guaranteed for the freshman year only and is available on a lottery system for upperclassmen. All students may keep cars.

FACULTY/CLASSROOMS: 66% of faculty are male; 34% are female. 99% teach undergraduates, 73% do research, and 72% do both. Graduate students teach 18% of introductory courses. The average class size in an introductory lecture is 45; in a laboratory is 19; and in a regular course is 29.

PROGRAMS OF STUDY: CU confers B.A., B.S., B.F.A., and B.L.A. degrees. Master's and doctoral degrees are also awarded. Bachelor's degrees are awarded in AGRICULTURE (agriculture, animal science, forestry production and processing, forestry and related sciences, horticulture, and soil science), BIOLOGICAL SCIENCE (biochemistry, biology/biological science, and microbiology), BUSINESS (accounting, banking and finance, business administration and management, management science, and marketing/retailing/merchandising), COMMUNICATIONS AND THE ARTS (communications, design, English, fine arts, French, German, modern language, and Spanish), COMPUTER AND PHYSICAL SCIENCE (chemistry, computer science, geology, information sciences and systems, mathematics, and physics), EDUCATION (agricultural education, early childhood education, elementary education, industrial arts education, secondary education, and special education), ENGINEERING AND ENVIRONMENTAL DESIGN (agricultural engineering, ceramic engineering, chemical engineering, civil engineering, computer engineering, construction management, electrical/electronics engineering, graphic arts technology, industrial administration/management, industrial engineering, landscape architecture/design, mechanical engineering, and textile technology), HEALTH PROFESSIONS (medical laboratory technology, nursing, predentistry, premedicine, prepharmacy, preveterinary science, and speech pathology/audiology), SOCIAL SCIENCE (economics, food science, history, parks and recreation management, philosophy, political science/government, prelaw, psychology, and sociology). Engineering, architecture, and biological sciences are the strongest academically. Marketing has the largest enrollment.

ACTIVITIES: 18% of men belong to 18 national fraternities; 24% of women belong to 17 national sororities. There are 350 groups on campus, including art, bagpipe, band, cheerleading, choir, chorus, computers, dance, debate, drama, drill team, ethnic, honors, international, jazz band, LGBT, literary magazine, marching band, musical theater, newspaper, orchestra, pep band, photography, political, professional, radio and TV, religious, social, social service, student government, symphony, and yearbook. Popular campus events include First Friday Parade, Tigerama, Welcome Back Festival, and Annual Shakespeare. **Sports:** There are 10 intercollegiate sports for men and 9 for women, and 45 intramural sports for men and 45 for women. Facilities include an indoor tennis facility, a recreation center, a stadium, and coliseum. **Graduates:** From July 1, 2016 to June 30, 2017, 3075 bachelor's degrees were awarded. The most popular majors were biological sciences (7%), management (6%), and psychology (5%). In an average class, 61% graduate in 4 years or less, 80% graduate in 5 years or less, and 82% graduate in 6 years or less.

SERVICES: Counseling and information services are available, as is tutoring in most subjects. There is a reader service for the blind, testing modifications, library assistance, interpreters, and note takers. **Library/Resources:** The library contains 1.2 million volumes, 1.2 million microform items, 140,000 audio/video tapes/CDs/DVDs, and subscribes to 11,400 periodicals, including electronic. Computerized library services include interlibrary loans, database searching, Internet access, and Wi-Fi capability. Special learning facilities include an art gallery, natural history museum, planetarium, radio station, TV station, a geology museum, experimental forest, research park, and state botanical gardens. **Physically Challenged Students:** 75% of the campus is accessible. Facilities include wheelchair ramps, elevators, special parking, specially equipped restrooms, special class scheduling, lowered drinking fountains, lowered telephones, and special housing. **Special:** Co-op programs are available in all majors except nursing. Work-study programs and study abroad in 39 countries are offered. There are 24 national honor societies, Phi Beta Kappa, a freshman honors program, and 40 departmental honors programs. **Visiting:** There are regularly scheduled orientations for prospective students, including a series of 2-day summer programs of advisement, student services presentations, and registration for the fall semester. There are guides for informal visits and visitors may sit in on classes. To schedule a visit, contact the Visitors Center at (864) 656-4789. **Campus Safety and Security:** Measures include 24-hour foot and vehicle patrol, emergency notification system, self-defense education, and security escort services. There are shuttle buses, emergency telephones, lighted pathways/sidewalks, electronic card access to residence halls, and limited outdoor surveillance cameras.

REQUIREMENTS: The SAT or ACT is required, as is the ACT Optional Writing test. Applicants should be graduates of an accredited secondary school. The GED is accepted. AP and CLEP credits are accepted. Important factors in the admissions decision are advanced placement or honors courses, parents or siblings attended your school, and evidence of special talent. To graduate, students must complete 120 to 157 credit hours, including 89 to 108 hours in the major, with a GPA of 2.0. Courses are required in English, humanities, math, science, and social science. **Procedure:** Freshmen are admitted fall, spring, and summer. Entrance exams should be taken during spring of the junior year or fall of the senior year. Applications should be filed by December 1 for fall entry. The fall 2017 application fee was $70. Notifications are sent February 15. Applications are accepted on-line. **Transfer Students:** 1096 transfer students enrolled in 2016-2017. Transfer applicants must have completed at least 30 semester hours with approximately a 2.5 GPA. 37 of 120 credits required for the bachelor's degree must be completed at Clemson. **International Students:** There are 160 international students enrolled. They must take the TOEFL with a minimum score of 550 on the paper-based TOEFL (PBT), and either take the SAT or ACT.

ADMISSIONS: 51% of the 2017-2018 applicants were accepted. The SAT scores for the 2017-2018 freshman class were: Critical Reading-- 6% below 500, 34% between 500 and 599, 47% between 600 and 699, and 12% between 700 and 800. Math-- 3% below 500, 22% between 500 and 599, 51% between 600 and 699, and 24% between 700 and 800. The ACT scores were 9% between 18 and 23, 50% between 24 and 29, and 41% above 30. 179 freshmen graduated first in their class. **Admissions Contact:** Robert S. Barkley, Director of Admissions. Email: *cuadmissions@clemson.edu* Web: *www.clemson.edu*

FINANCIAL AID: In 2017-2018, 95% of all full-time freshmen received

some form of financial aid. 54% of all full-time freshmen received need-based aid. The average freshman award was $16,281. Need-based scholarships or need-based grants averaged $5,054 ($9,315 maximum); need-based self-help aid (loans and jobs) averaged $4,696 ($11,000 maximum); non-need-based athletic scholarships averaged $28,056 ($55,598 maximum); and other non-need-based awards and non-need-based scholarships averaged $8,578 ($48,616 maximum). 57% of undergraduate students work part-time. The average financial indebtedness of the 2017 graduate was $30,270. The FAFSA code is 003425. The priority date for freshman financial aid applications for fall entry is March 1.

COASTAL CAROLINA UNIVERSITY E-3

www.coastal.edu

Conway, SC 29528 (843) 349-2170 (800) 277-7000

Fax: (843) 349-6436 Email: admissions@coastal.edu

Full-time: 4190 men, 4831 women	**Faculty:** 419; IIA, -$
Part-time: 394 men, 483 women	**Ph.D.s:** 80%
Graduate: 224 men, 541 women	**Student/Faculty:** 21 to 1
Year: semesters, summer session	**Tuition:** $11,200 ($25,872)
Room & Board: $9140	**Freshman Class:** 18563 applied, 11359 accepted, 2390 enrolled
SAT CR/M: 554/544 **ACT:** 22	**CEEB CODE:** 5837
Application Deadline: August 1	**COMPETITIVE**

Coastal Carolina University, established in 1954, is a public liberal arts institution offering undergraduate programs through the colleges of business, science, education, humanities, fine arts and university college. Graduate programs are offered through the colleges of business, education, humanities and fine arts, and science. There are 5 undergraduate schools and 4 graduate schools. In addition to regional accreditation, CCU has baccalaureate program accreditation with AACSB, ABET, NASAD, NASM, NAST, AAHE, and ACEN. The 633-acre campus is in a suburban area 9 miles west of Myrtle Beach. Including any residence halls, there are 115 buildings.

STUDENT LIFE: 51% of undergraduates are from out of state, mostly the Northeast. Students are from 48 states, 70 foreign countries, and Canada. 86% are from public schools. 68% are White; 5% two or more races; 4% Hispanic; 2% Foreign; 19% African American; 1% Asian American; 1% race unknown. **Female To Male Ratio:** 1.2:1. The average age of freshmen is 18; all undergraduates, 21. 33% do not continue beyond their first year; 42% remain to graduate. **Housing:** 4685 students can be accommodated in college housing, which includes dorms, off-campus apartments, and honors houses and special-interest houses. On-campus housing is available on a first-come, first-served basis, and is available on a lottery system for upperclassmen. 56% of students commute. Alcohol is not permitted. All students may keep cars.

FACULTY/CLASSROOMS: 49% of faculty are male; 51% are female. 93% teach undergraduates, 50% do research, and 50% do both. No introductory courses are taught by graduate students. The average class size in an introductory lecture is 23; in a laboratory is 20; and in a regular course is 22.

PROGRAMS OF STUDY: CCU confers B.A., B.F.A., B.S., B.S.N., B.A.Ed., B.A.I.S., B.S.B.A., B.S.Ed., B.S.I.S., and B.S.P.E. degrees. Master's and doctoral degrees are also awarded. Bachelor's degrees are awarded in BIOLOGICAL SCIENCE (biochemistry, biology/biological science, and marine science), BUSINESS (accounting, banking and finance, business administration and management, information & communication technology, marketing/retailing/merchandising, sports management, and tourism), COMMUNICATIONS AND THE ARTS (communications, dramatic arts, English, fine arts, graphic design, music, musical theater, Spanish, and studio art), COMPUTER AND PHYSICAL SCIENCE (chemistry, computer science, information sciences and systems, mathematics, and physics), EDUCATION (early childhood education, elementary education, middle school education, physical education, and special education), HEALTH PROFESSIONS (exercise science, health, health care administration, and nursing), SOCIAL SCIENCE (economics, history, interdisciplinary studies, philosophy, political science/government, psychology, and sociology). Accounting, marine science, and political science are the strongest academically. Marine science, management, and exercise & sport science have the largest enrollments.

ACTIVITIES: 3% of men belong to 10 national fraternities; 7% of women belong to 9 national sororities. There are 164 groups on campus, including art, band, cheerleading, choir, chorale, chorus, computers, dance, drama, environmental, ethnic, honors, international, jazz band, LGBT, literary magazine, marching band, musical theater, newspaper, pep band, political, professional, radio and TV, religious, social, social service, and student government. Popular campus events include CINO Day, Cultural Celebration, Club Recruitment Day, and Homecoming. **Sports:** There are 8 intercollegiate sports for men and 10 for women, and 13 intramural sports for men and 13 for women. Facilities include the Student Recreation and Convocation Center, a gym, a football stadium, baseball, soccer, softball fields, tennis, basketball, volleyball, racquetball courts, indoor Olympic-size swimming pool, an aerobic dance room, weight rooms, and a track. **Graduates:** From July 1, 2016 to June 30, 2017, 1821 bachelor's degrees were awarded. The most popular majors were management (10%), communication (9%), and exercise and sport science (8%). In an average class, 26% graduate in 4 years or less, 40% graduate in 5 years or less, and 42% graduate in 6 years or less.

SERVICES: Counseling and information services are available, as is tutoring in some subjects, such as English, foreign languages, math and statistics. There is also a reader service for the blind. **Library/Resources:** The library contains 116,498 volumes, 1,108 microform items, and 5,998 audio/video tapes/CDs/DVDs, and subscribes to 11,366 periodicals including electronic. Computerized library services include interlibrary loans, database searching, Internet access, and Wi-Fi capability. Special learning facilities include an art gallery, radio station, and a marine science research center. **Physically Challenged Students:** 95% of the campus is accessible. Facilities include wheelchair ramps, elevators, special parking, specially equipped restrooms, special class scheduling, lowered drinking fountains, and special housing. **Special:** Internships are offered in most majors, as well as study abroad in 15 countries. Interdisciplinary studies and a 3-2 engineering degree with Clemson University are available. There are 17 national honor societies and a freshman honors program. **Visiting:** There are regularly scheduled orientations for prospective students, including sessions for academic requirements, housing, financial aid, and student life, parents' orientation, tours, cook-outs, and entertainment. Visitors may sit in on classes. To schedule a visit, contact Holley Aufdemorte in Admissions. **Campus Safety and Security:** Measures include 24-hour foot and vehicle patrol, emergency notification system, self-defense education, and security escort services. There are shuttle buses, emergency telephones, and lighted pathways/sidewalks.

REQUIREMENTS: The SAT or ACT is required, as is graduation from an accredited secondary or homeschool program. A GED will be accepted with appropriate scores. Applicants are required to submit complete specific high school credits, including 4 years of college prep English, 4 units of mathematics (algebra ll required), 3 units of lab science, 3 units of social sciences (U.S. history required), 2 units of the same foreign language, 1 advanced electives (from computer science, math, additional science, foreign language, social science, humanities, and arts), 1 unit of visual/performing arts, and 1 unit of physical education or ROTC. An interview is recommended. AP and CLEP credits are accepted. Important factors in the admissions decision are advanced placement or honors courses, recommendations by school officials, and evidence of special talent. Students must successfully complete a minimum of 120 credits, varying with major department requirements, and must maintain a minimum GPA of 2.0. A 4-year core curriculum of 34 to 41 hours is required for proficiency in the broad areas of writing, library research, a foreign language, and computer usage. **Procedure:** Freshmen are admitted to all sessions. Entrance exams should be taken in spring of the junior year or fall of the senior year. There are deferred admissions and rolling admissions plans. Applications should be filed by August 1 for fall entry; December 1 for spring entry. The fall 2017 application fee was $45. Notification is sent on a rolling basis. Applications are accepted on-line. **Transfer Students:** 787 transfer students enrolled in 2016-2017. A minimum GPA of 2.0 is required. Transfers with fewer than 30 hours earned must also meet freshman admission requirements. Students must submit college transcripts and be eligible to return to the last institution attended. 30 of 120 credits required for the bachelor's degree must be completed at CCU. **International Students:** There are 200 international students enrolled. They must take the TOEFL with a minimum score of 550 on the paper-based TOEFL (PBT) or 79 on the Internet-based version (iBT). Students must also take the SAT or ACT.

ADMISSIONS: 61% of the 2017-2018 applicants were accepted. The SAT scores for the 2017-2018 freshman class were: Math-- 17% below

500, 64% between 500 and 599, 18% between 600 and 699, and 1% between 700 and 800. Evidence-Based Reading/Writing-- 14% below 500, 63% between 500 and 599, 22% between 600 and 699, and 1% between 700 and 800. The ACT scores were 5% between 12 and 17, 64% between 18 and 23, 29% between 24 and 29, and 2% above 30. 36% of the current freshmen were in the top fifth of their class; 71% were in the top two fifths. **Admissions Contact:** Amanda Craddock, Assistant Provost for Admissions. Email: *admissions@coastal.edu* Web: *www.coastal.edu*

FINANCIAL AID: In 2017-2018, 99% of all full-time freshmen received some form of financial aid. 63% of all full-time freshmen received need-based aid. The average freshman award was $19,547. Need-based scholarships or need-based grants averaged $3,592; need-based self-help aid (loans and jobs) averaged $3,394; non-need-based athletic scholarships averaged $8,329; other non-need-based awards and non-need-based scholarships averaged $2,263; and $8,283 from other forms of aid. 19% of undergraduate students work part-time. The average financial indebtedness of the 2017 graduate was $37,037. The FAFSA code is 003451. The priority date for freshman financial aid applications for fall entry is March 1.

COKER COLLEGE D-2
www.coker.edu

Hartsville, SC 29550	(843) 383-8050 (800) 950-1908
Fax: (843) 383-8056	Email: admissions@coker.edu
Full-time: 381 men, 528 women	**Faculty:** 70
Part-time: 28 men, 71 women	**Ph.D.s:** 70%
Graduate: 35 men, 51 women	**Student/Faculty:** 14 to 1
Year: semesters, summer session	**Tuition:** $28,684
Room & Board: $9512	**Freshman Class:** 1389 applied, 857 accepted, 210 enrolled
SAT CR/M: 520/500 **ACT:** 19	**CEEB CODE:** 5112
Application Deadline: August 1	**COMPETITIVE**

Coker College, founded in 1908, is a private institution offering undergraduate programs. There is 1 undergraduate school and 1 graduate school. In addition to regional accreditation, CC has baccalaureate program accreditation with CSWE, NASAD, NASM, and NCATE. The 37-acre campus is in a small town 25 miles west of Florence, 71 miles northeast of Columbia and 82 miles southeast of Charlotte. Including any residence halls, there are 28 buildings.

STUDENT LIFE: 76% of undergraduates are from South Carolina. Others are from 29 states, 15 foreign countries, and Canada. 6% are two or more races; 52% White; 33% African American; 3% Hispanic; 3% Foreign; 1% American Indian/Alaska Native; 1% race unknown. **Female To Male Ratio:** 1.5:1. The average age of freshmen is 19; all undergraduates, 25. 40% do not continue beyond their first year; 48% remain to graduate. **Housing:** 565 students can be accommodated in college housing, which includes coed dorms, off-campus apartments, honors houses, and sophomore scholars housing. On-campus housing is guaranteed for the freshman year only, and is available on a first-come, first-served basis, and is available on a lottery system for upperclassmen. 55% of students live on campus. All students may keep cars.

FACULTY/CLASSROOMS: 49% of faculty are male; 51% are female. 98% teach undergraduates. No introductory courses are taught by graduate students. The average class size in an introductory lecture is 15 and in a laboratory is 14.

PROGRAMS OF STUDY: CC confers B.A., B.F.A., B.S., B.M.E., and B.S.W. degrees. Master's degrees are also awarded. Bachelor's degrees are awarded in BIOLOGICAL SCIENCE (biology/biological science, biology/ gen science secondary education, and molecular biology), BUSINESS (business administration and management), COMMUNICATIONS AND THE ARTS (art, communications, dance, dramatic arts, English, graphic design, music, musical theater, photography, and Spanish), COMPUTER AND PHYSICAL SCIENCE (chemistry, chemistry/general science second education, computer science, and mathematics), EDUCATION (art education, early childhood education, education, elementary education, English education, mathematics education, music education, physical education, and social science education), HEALTH PROFESSIONS (medical laboratory technology and premedicine), SOCIAL SCIENCE (criminology, history, political science/government, psychology, social work, and sociology). Business, physical education, and criminology have the largest enrollments.

ACTIVITIES: There are no fraternities or sororities. There are 34 groups on campus, including art, band, cheerleading, choir, chorus, communications, dance, drama, ethnic, honors, literary magazine, musical theater, photography, political, religious, social service, and student government. Popular campus events include Coker Olympics of Winter (COW Days), Crew Race, and Bandfest. **Sports:** There are 9 intercollegiate sports for men and 8 for women, and 5 intramural sports for men and 5 for women. Facilities include a gym, weight room, soccer, baseball and softball fields, tennis courts, a boathouse with canoes and access to a golf course. **Graduates:** From July 1, 2016 to June 30, 2017, 221 bachelor's degrees were awarded. The most popular majors were business (25%), physical education (14%), and sociology (9%). In an average class, 43% graduate in 4 years or less, 49% graduate in 5 years or less, and 55% graduate in 6 years or less.

SERVICES: Counseling and information services are available, as is tutoring in most subjects, such as English, math, anatomy, biology, chinese, and spanish chemistry. There is also a writing lab. **Library/Resources:** The library contains 81,626 volumes, 15,760 microform items, and 3,737 audio/video tapes/CDs/DVDs, and subscribes to 112 periodicals including electronic. Computerized library services include interlibrary loans, database searching, Internet access, and Wi-Fi capability. Special learning facilities include an art gallery, a botanical garden and a nature preserve. **Physically Challenged Students:** 60% of the campus is accessible. Facilities include wheelchair ramps, elevators, special parking, specially equipped restrooms, special class scheduling, lowered drinking fountains, and special housing. **Special:** Internships, study abroad in many countries, on-campus and community service work-study programs, cross-registration with Central College and dual and student-designed majors are offered. A 3-1 in medical technology with McLeod Regional Medical Center is possible. Also available are credit for military experience, non-degree study and pass/fail options. The college's round-table approach allows students and professors to discuss topics and research in small settings. There are 4 national honor societies, a freshman honors program, and 6 departmental honors programs. **Visiting:** There are regularly scheduled orientations for prospective students, consisting of orientation, a meal, campus tours and discussions with faculty and a student panel. There are guides for informal visits, visitors may sit in on classes, and stay overnight. To schedule a visit, contact Sarah Peterka at (800) 950-1908. **Campus Safety and Security:** Measures include 24-hour foot and vehicle patrol, emergency notification system, and security escort services. There are lighted pathways/sidewalks and controlled access to dorms/residences.

REQUIREMENTS: Coker has a selective admissions process that does require a specific median high school GPA and either SAT/ACT test scores. AP and CLEP credits are accepted. Important factors in the admissions decision are advanced placement or honors courses, personality/intangible qualities, leadership record, parents or siblings attended your school, evidence of special talent, extracurricular activities record, recommendations by alumni, geographical diversity, and recommendations by school officials. For the undergraduate program: distribution requirements include 53-55 hours in general education including; 19-22 hours of core skills (English, Math, Communication, Language), and 24 hours of liberal arts. A minimum of 120 semester hours including 30 hours in courses number 300 or above is required as well a minimum 2.0 GPA in order to graduate. The final 30 semester hours must be taken in residence at Coker. **Procedure:** Freshmen are admitted in the fall, spring, and summer. Entrance exams should be taken during the junior year or the first part of the senior year. There are deferred admissions and rolling admissions plans. Application deadlines are open. Notifications are sent June 1. Applications are accepted on-line. **Transfer Students:** 105 transfer students enrolled in 2016-2017. Applicants with fewer than 24 semester hours must submit high school transcripts and SAT scores. A minimum 2.0 GPA is required. 30 of 120 credits required for the bachelor's degree must be completed at Coker. **International Students:** There are 40 international students enrolled. They must take the TOEFL with a minimum score of 66 on the Internet-based version (iBT). The SAT with a score of 450 or ACT English score of 18 is required.

ADMISSIONS: 62% of the 2017-2018 applicants were accepted. The SAT scores for the 2017-2018 freshman class were: Math-- 47% below 500, 42% between 500 and 599, 10% between 600 and 699, and 1% between 700 and 800. Evidence-Based Reading/Writing-- 35% below 500, 52% between 500 and 599, and 13% between 600 and 699. The ACT scores were 31% between 12 and 17, 55% between 18 and 23, 12% between 24 and 29, and 2% above 30. 18% of the current freshmen were in the top fifth of their class; 45% were in the top two fifths. **Admissions Contact:** Adam Connolly, Vice President of Enrollment Management. Email: *admissions@coker.edu* Web: *www.coker.edu*

FINANCIAL AID: In 2017-2018, 100% of all full-time freshmen received some form of financial aid. 82% of all full-time freshmen received need-based aid. The average freshman award was $15,951. Need-based scholarships or need-based grants averaged $4,224 ($9,810 maximum); need-based self-help aid (loans and jobs) averaged $1,732 ($3,750 maximum); non-need-based athletic scholarships averaged $3,984 ($11,144 maximum); other non-need-based awards and non-need-based scholarships averaged $5,914 ($18,654 maximum); and $1,493 from other forms of aid. 7% of undergraduate students work part-time. The average financial indebtedness of the 2017 graduate was $22,734. The FAFSA code is 003427. The deadline for filing freshman financial aid applications for fall entry is June 30.

COLLEGE OF CHARLESTON D-4

www.cofc.edu

Charleston, SC 29424	(843) 953-5670
Fax: (843) 953-6322	**Email:** admissions@cofc.edu
Full-time: 3249 men, 5834 women	**Faculty:** 522; IIA, av$
Part-time: 380 men, 432 women	**Ph.D.s:** 92%
Graduate: 249 men, 719 women	**Student/Faculty:** 17 to 1
Year: semesters, summer session	**Tuition:** $11,998 ($30,386)
Room & Board: $12,048	**Freshman Class:** 11900 applied, 9574 accepted, 1840 enrolled
SAT EBR-W/M: 595/566 **ACT:** 25	**CEEB CODE:** 5113
Application Deadline: February 15	**VERY COMPETITIVE**

College of Charleston, founded in 1770 is a nationally recognized public liberal arts and sciences university. The College is among the nation's top universities for quality education, student life and affordability. There are 7 undergraduate schools and 1 graduate school. In addition to regional accreditation, CC has baccalaureate program accreditation with AACSB, ABET, NASM, NCATE, NAST, CAATE, and NASPAA. The 66-acre campus is in an urban area in the heart of historic Charleston, S.C. Including any residence halls, there are 127 buildings.

STUDENT LIFE: 67% of undergraduates are from South Carolina. Others are from 51 states, 62 foreign countries, and Canada. 74% are from public schools. 77% are White; 8% African American; 5% Hispanic; 4% two or more races; 2% Asian American; 2% race unknown; 1% American Indian/Alaska Native; 1% Foreign. **Female To Male Ratio:** 1.8:1. The average age of freshmen is 18; all undergraduates, 21. 22% do not continue beyond their first year; 78% remain to graduate. **Housing:** 3409 students can be accommodated in college housing, which includes single sex dorms, coed dorms, and on-campus apartments. In addition, there are honors houses, language/international houses, special-interest houses, fraternity houses, and sorority houses. There are also restored Historic Charleston houses used as residence halls, some with kitchen facilities in suites. On-campus housing is available on a first-come, first-served basis. 69% of students commute. Some may keep cars.

FACULTY/CLASSROOMS: 51% of faculty are male; 49% are female. 98% teach undergraduates. No introductory courses are taught by graduate students. The average class size in an introductory lecture is 29; in a laboratory is 19; and in a regular course is 21.

PROGRAMS OF STUDY: CC confers B.A., B.S., A.B., and B.P.S degrees. Master's degrees are also awarded. Bachelor's degrees are awarded in BIOLOGICAL SCIENCE (biochemistry, biology/biological science, and marine biology), BUSINESS (accounting, business administration and management, finance, hospitality management services, international business management, marketing, supply chain management, and professional studies), COMMUNICATIONS AND THE ARTS (art history, arts administration/management, classics, communications, dance, English, German, historic preservation, music, Spanish, studio art, and theatre arts), COMPUTER AND PHYSICAL SCIENCE (astronomy, astrophysics, chemistry, computer information systems, computer science, data processing, geology, mathematics, and physics), EDUCATION (athletic training, early childhood education, elementary education, foreign languages education, middle school education, physical education, secondary education, and special education), HEALTH PROFESSIONS (exercise science and public health), SOCIAL SCIENCE (African American studies, anthropology, archeology, economics, French studies, history, international studies, Judaic studies, Latin American studies, philosophy, political science/government, psychology, religious studies, sociology, urban studies, and women's studies). Business, biology, and psychology have the largest enrollments.

ACTIVITIES: 18% of men belong to 10 national fraternities; 35% of women belong to 14 national sororities. There are 200 groups on campus, including art, band, cheerleading, chess, choir, chorale, chorus, communications, computers, dance, debate, drama, environmental, ethnic, film, forensics, honors, international, jazz band, LGBT, literary magazine, musical theater, newspaper, opera, orchestra, pep band, photography, political, professional, radio and TV, religious, social, social service, student government, and symphony. Popular campus events include Pep Supper, Homecoming Spirit Cup Competition, Georgestock, Weeks of Welcome, Cougarpalooza, and Midnight Breakfasts. **Sports:** There are 7 intercollegiate sports for men and 12 for women, and 25 intramural sports for men and 25 for women. Facilities include basketball and volleyball, Hall of Fame areas, strength and conditioning areas, practice area, an academic support area and a spacious sports medicine facility, coed tennis, women's offshore sailing, coed golf and Storybook Farms equestrian, courts for basketball, volleyball, and squash, an indoor running track, strength and conditioning facility with cardio machines and other resistance training equipment, a dance room, and an outdoor recreation field. **Graduates:** From July 1, 2016 to June 30, 2017, 2304 bachelor's degrees were awarded. The most popular majors were business administration (10%), biology (8%), and psychology (7%). In an average class, 56% graduate in 4 years or less, 67% graduate in 5 years or less, and 69% graduate in 6 years or less. Of the 2016 graduating class, 21% were enrolled in graduate school within 6 months of graduation, and 65% were employed.

SERVICES: Counseling and information services are available, as is tutoring in most subjects. There is Walk-in tutoring labs for Spanish, math, accounting, writing, natural/decision sciences, and computer science. By appointment tutoring for foreign languages, psychology, music theory, finance, economics, and additional courses with demonstrated needs. There is also a reader service for the blind, and remedial math, reading, and writing. Study strategies appointments, Supplemental Instruction (SI), peer academic coaching, study skills workshops are also available. **Library/Resources:** The library contains 1.3 million volumes, 3,300 microform items, 10,127 audio/video tapes/CDs/DVDs, and subscribes to 84,016 periodicals, including electronic. Computerized library services include interlibrary loans, database searching, Internet access, and Wi-Fi capability. Special learning facilities include an art gallery, a natural history museum, a radio station, iCat program (accelerator), a center for supply chain management, an observatory, marine science laboratory, early childhood development center, bronze sculpture foundry, a sailing center, an Avery Research Center for African American History and Culture, a center for entrepreneurship, a real estate center, English Language Institute, Halsey Institute of Contemporary Art, Riley Center for Livable Communities, a S.C. Space Grant Consortium, the Center for Social Research, and Carolina Lowcountry and Atlantic World. **Physically Challenged Students:** 70% of the campus is accessible. Facilities include wheelchair ramps, elevators, special parking, specially equipped restrooms, special class scheduling, lowered drinking fountains, and lowered telephones. **Special:** Cross-registration is possible with the Medical University of South Carolina. Co-op programs and internships in all majors, a Washington semester, study abroad in 36 countries, work-study programs, B.A.-B.S. degrees, and dual majors are offered. A 2-2 program in allied health, biometry or nursing is offered with the Medical University of South Carolina. The college's 3-week Maymester session offers unconventional courses and programs using alternative methods of instruction. There is an interdisciplinary honors program available to qualified students. There is a freshman honors program. **Visiting:** There are regularly scheduled orientations for prospective students; visits typically consist of a campus tour and an information session. These visits are available most weekdays, and some Saturdays throughout the academic year and in the summer. We also host several "open house" programs, and visitors may sit in on classes. To schedule a visit, contact the Admissions Office. **Campus Safety and Security:** Measures include 24-hour foot and vehicle patrol, an emergency notification system, self-defense education, and security escort services. There are shuttle buses, emergency telephones, lighted pathways/sidewalks, and controlled access to dorms/residences.

REQUIREMENTS: The admissions committee carefully weighs the student's academic preparation (which includes grades, rank in class, and rigor of courses taken), SAT/ACT results, personal statements and essays, leadership qualification, and special talents. Applicants should have completed the following high school units: 4 units each of English and math, 3 units each of lab science, foreign language and academic electives, 2 units of social studies, 1 unit each of history (2 recommended), computer science (advanced math, computer science or any combination of the two will fulfill this), and fine arts are recommended. The GED is accepted. AP and CLEP credits are accepted. In order to graduate with a BA or a BS degree, a student must satisfy the liberal arts and sciences general education requirement, select and complete the requirements for at least one academic major program with a minimum grade point average of 2.0 in all major courses, and complete elective coursework such that the total credit hours reach a minimum of 122 with a minimum cumulative grade point average of 2.0 based on all courses taken at the College. All students, regardless of major, must satisfy General Education requirements by completing approved courses distributed across seven areas: Writing, Foreign Languages, History, Humanities, Natural Science, Mathematics or Logic, and Social Science. All students entering the College of Charleston with less than one year of college experience are also required to complete a First Year Experience by selecting a First Year Seminar course or two courses organized into a Learning Community. As required by South Carolina statute, all degree-seeking students must complete instruction in the essentials of the Declaration of Independence, Federalist Papers, and the Constitution and achieve satisfactory performance on an accompanying examination. **Procedure:** Freshmen are admitted in the fall and spring. Entrance exams should be taken by March 1; by June 1 for state scholarship consideration. There are early decision, early admissions, and deferred admissions plans. Early decision applications should be filed by November 1; regular applications, by February 15 for fall entry; and November 1 for spring entry. The fall 2017 application fee was $50. Notification of early decision is sent December 1; regular decision, April 1. Applications are accepted on-line. **Transfer Students:** 633 transfer students enrolled in 2016-2017. Applicants must have 24 hours and must have a 2.6 GPA for in-state residents and 3.0 for out-of-state residents. 30 of 122 credits required for the bachelor's degree must be completed at CC. **International Students:** There are 121 international students enrolled. They must take the TOEFL with a minimum score of 80 on the Internet-based version (iBT). Students must also take either the IELTS, or the ITEP. The SAT or ACT are required for some applicants.

ADMISSIONS: 80% of the 2017-2018 applicants were accepted. The SAT scores for the 2017-2018 freshman class were: Math-- 11% below 500, 60% between 500 and 599, 25% between 600 and 699, and 4% between 700 and 800. Evidence-Based Reading/Writing-- 4% below 500, 48% between 500 and 599, 42% between 600 and 699, and 6% between 700 and 800. The ACT scores were 1% between 12 and 17, 38% between 18 and 23, 50% between 24 and 29, and 11% above 30. 43% of the current freshmen were in the top fifth of their class; 78% were in the top two fifths. 12 freshmen graduated first in their class. **Admissions Contact:** Mackenzie Chasteen, Director, Recruitment and Enrollment. Email: *admissions@cofc.edu* Web: *www.cofc.edu*

FINANCIAL AID: In 2017-2018, 53% of all full-time freshmen received some form of financial aid. 39% of all full-time freshmen received need-based aid. The average freshman award was $13,421. Need-based scholarships or need-based grants averaged $2,775; need-based self-help aid (loans and jobs) averaged $2,994; non-need-based athletic scholarships averaged $25,635; and other non-need-based awards and non-need-based scholarships averaged $10,982. The average financial indebtedness of the 2017 graduate was $26,203. The FAFSA code is 003428. The priority date for freshman financial aid applications for fall entry is March 1.

COLUMBIA COLLEGE C-3

www.columbia.edu

Columbia, SC 29203	**(803) 786-3871** **(800) 277-1301**
Fax: (803) 786-3674	**Email: admissions-ugrad@sc.edu**
Full-time: 6 men, 978 women	**Faculty:** n/av
Part-time: 24 men, 231 women	**Ph.D.s:** 80%
Graduate: 17 men, 255 women	**Student/Faculty:** 11 to 1
Year: semesters, summer session	**Tuition:** $28,900
Room & Board: $7650	**Freshman Class:** 1097 applied, 833 accepted, 271 enrolled
SAT CR/M: 500/500 **ACT:** recommended	**CEEB CODE:** 5117
Application Deadline: August 1	**COMPETITIVE**

Columbia College, founded in 1854, is a private primarily women's liberal arts college affiliated with the United Methodist Church. The figures in the above capsule and in this profile are approximate. There is 1 undergraduate school and 1 graduate school. In addition to regional accreditation, CC has baccalaureate program accreditation with CSWE, NASAD, NASDTEC, NASM, CAEP, and CASE. The 53-acre campus is in an urban area in the northern section of Columbia. Including any residence halls, there are 26 buildings.

STUDENT LIFE: 90% of undergraduates are from South Carolina. Others are from 23 states, and 10 foreign countries. 52% are White; 39% African American; 2% Hispanic; 1% Asian American; 1% Foreign. 84% are Protestant; 17% claim no religious affiliation. **Female To Male Ratio:** 31.1:1. The average age of freshmen is 18; all undergraduates, 23. 30% do not continue beyond their first year; 70% remain to graduate. **Housing:** 650 students can be accommodated in college dorms, and honors houses. On-campus housing is guaranteed for all 4 years. 63% of students live on campus. Alcohol is not permitted. All students may keep cars.

FACULTY/CLASSROOMS: 36% of faculty are male; 64% are female. 95% teach undergraduates. No introductory courses are taught by graduate students. The average class size in an introductory lecture is 20 and in a laboratory is 20.

PROGRAMS OF STUDY: CC confers B.A., B.F.A., and B.Mus. degrees. Master's degrees are also awarded. Bachelor's degrees are awarded in BIOLOGICAL SCIENCE (biology/biological science), BUSINESS (accounting and business administration and management), COMMUNICATIONS AND THE ARTS (communications, dance, English, French, languages, music, music performance, performing arts, piano/organ, Spanish, and studio art), COMPUTER AND PHYSICAL SCIENCE (chemistry, information sciences and systems, and mathematics), EDUCATION (Christian education, dance education, early childhood education, elementary education, music education, special education, and speech correction), HEALTH PROFESSIONS (medical laboratory technology), SOCIAL SCIENCE (history, political science/government, psychology, public affairs, religion, religious music, social work, and sociology). Education, sciences, and performing arts have the largest enrollments.

ACTIVITIES: There are no fraternities or sororities. There are 57 groups on campus, including women interested in sustainability and the environment (WISE), art, band, choir, chorus, computers, dance, drama, equestrian club, ethnic, honors, international, literary magazine, musical theater, newspaper, opera, photography, political, professional, radio and TV, religious, social, social service, and student government. Popular campus events include Fine Arts Series, Follies, Christmas Tree Lighting, Commencement Bibles, Dad's Night, Mom's Day, Surcies, and Ludy Bowl. **Sports:** There are 4 intercollegiate sports and 4 intramural sports for women. Facilities include an athletic field, basketball, golf, soccer, softball, volleyball, lacrosse, tennis courts, a gym, an Olympic-size pool, a fitness lab, cross country, track and field, and a dance studio.

SERVICES: Counseling and information services are available. Peer tutoring and remedial instruction are offered in some subjects. **Library/Resources:** The library contains 170,000 volumes, 8,353 microform items, 29,834 audio/video tapes/CDs/DVDs, and subscribes to 633 periodicals, including electronic. Computerized library services include interlibrary loans, database searching, Internet access, and Wi-Fi capability. Special learning facilities include an art gallery, radio station, women's leadership center, and a science and technology center. **Physically Challenged Students:** 90% of the campus is accessible. Facilities include wheelchair ramps, elevators, special parking, specially equipped restrooms, and special class scheduling. **Special:** The Center for Contractual Studies allows qualified students to pursue individualized programs through independent study, practicums, and a senior project. The college also offers internships, study abroad, a Washington semester, dual majors, and credit for life, military, and work experience. Nondegree study and pass/fail options are available. There is a freshman honors program. **Visiting:** There are regularly scheduled orientations for prospective students, consisting of meetings with faculty advisers, classroom visits, campus tours, lunch, and student life and financial aid presentations. There are guides for informal visits and visitors may sit in on classes. To schedule a visit, contact the Admissions Office. **Campus Safety and Security:** Measures include 24-hour foot and vehicle patrol, emergency notification system, self-defense education, and security escort services. There are emergency telephones and lighted pathways/sidewalks.

REQUIREMENTS: The SAT is required. The ACT is recommended.

Applicants must be graduates of an accredited secondary school or have earned a GED. They should complete 16 Carnegie units, including 4 years of English, 3 of math, and 2 each of foreign language and lab science, as well as courses in history and social studies. An essay and an interview are recommended, as is a portfolio or an audition for fine or performing arts students. AP and CLEP credits are accepted. Important factors in the admissions decision are recommendations by school officials, advanced placement or honors courses, and leadership record. To graduate, students must complete 127 semester hours, with a minimum GPA of 2.5 in the major and 2.0 overall. General education requirements for the B.A. degree include 15 hours of communication skills, 12 of social science, 9 of aesthetics, 8 of natural science, 6 of religion, and 3 each of math and phys ed. Students also must satisfy proficiency requirements in English and math. **Procedure:** Freshmen are admitted to all sessions. Entrance exams should be taken near the end of the junior year or by December of the senior year. There is a rolling admissions plan. Applications should be filed by August 1 for fall entry. The fall 2017 application fee was $25. Applications are accepted on-line. **Transfer Students:** 118 transfer students enrolled in 2016-2017. An interview is recommended for transfer students. Applicants with fewer than 24 semester hours must present ACT or SAT scores and high school transcripts. Grades of C or better transfer for credit. 30 of 127 credits required for the bachelor's degree must be completed at CC. **International Students:** There are 13 international students enrolled. They must take the TOEFL.

ADMISSIONS: 76% of the 2017-2018 applicants were accepted. The SAT scores for the 2017-2018 freshman class were: Critical Reading-- 49% below 500, 32% between 500 and 599, 16% between 600 and 699, and 3% between 700 and 800. Math-- 50% below 500, 36% between 500 and 599, 13% between 600 and 699, and 1% between 700 and 800. **Admissions Contact:** Julie A. King, Director of Admissions. Email: *admissions-ugrad@sc.edu* Web: *www.columbia.edu*

FINANCIAL AID: The FAFSA code is 003430. Check with the school for current application deadlines.

CONVERSE COLLEGE — B-1

www.converse.edu

Spartanburg, SC 29302 — **(864) 596-9040**, **(800) 766-1125**

Fax: (864) 596-9225 — **Email: admissions@converse.edu**

Full-time: 608 women	**Faculty:** 76; IIB, --$
Part-time: 82 women	**Ph.D.s:** 89%
Graduate: 120 men, 411 women	**Student/Faculty:** 11 to 1
Year: 4-1-4, summer session	**Tuition:** $17,680
Room & Board: $10,610	**Freshman Class:** 1383 applied, 710 accepted, 183 enrolled
SAT CR/M: 530/520 **ACT:** 23	**CEEB CODE:** 5121
Application Deadline: September 1	**COMPETITIVE**

Converse College, founded in 1889, is a private women's liberal arts college. Men are admitted to the graduate programs. The figures in the above capsule and in this profile are approximate. There are 3 undergraduate schools and 2 graduate schools. In addition to regional accreditation, CC has baccalaureate program accreditation with NASAD, NASM, and CAEP. The 72-acre campus is in an urban area 80 miles southwest of Charlotte. Including any residence halls, there are 27 buildings.

STUDENT LIFE: 65% of undergraduates are from South Carolina. Others are from 27 states, 11 foreign countries, and Canada. 70% are from public schools. 8% are African American; 45% White; 3% Hispanic; 1% Asian American; 1% Foreign. **Female To Male Ratio:** 9.2:1. The average age of freshmen is 18; all undergraduates, 20. 26% do not continue beyond their first year; 54% remain to graduate. **Housing:** 700 students can be accommodated in college housing, which includes dorms, on-campus apartments, a wellness dorm, and a special residence hall for students enrolled in the South Carolina Institute of Leadership for Women. On-campus housing is guaranteed for all 4 years. 85% of students live on campus. Alcohol is not permitted. All students may keep cars.

FACULTY/CLASSROOMS: 46% of faculty are male; 54% are female. All teach undergraduates, 50% do research, and 50% do both. No introductory courses are taught by graduate students. The average class size in an introductory lecture is 20; in a laboratory is 15; and in a regular course is 11.

PROGRAMS OF STUDY: CC confers B.A., B.S., B.F.A., and B.Mus. degrees. Master's degrees are also awarded. Bachelor's degrees are awarded in BIOLOGICAL SCIENCE (biology/biological science), BUSINESS (accounting and business administration and management), COMMUNICATIONS AND THE ARTS (English, fine arts, French, languages, modern language, music, and Spanish), COMPUTER AND PHYSICAL SCIENCE (chemistry, computer science, and mathematics), EDUCATION (art education, early childhood education, elementary education, foreign languages education, music education, science education, and secondary education), ENGINEERING AND ENVIRONMENTAL DESIGN (interior design), HEALTH PROFESSIONS (art therapy, predentistry, and premedicine), SOCIAL SCIENCE (economics, history, political science/government, prelaw, psychology, and religion). English, politics, and biology are the strongest academically. Music, education, and business have the largest enrollments.

ACTIVITIES: There are no fraternities or sororities. There are 50 groups on campus, including art, cheerleading, choir, chorale, chorus, computers, dance, debate, drama, ethnic, honors, international, LGBT, literary magazine, musical theater, newspaper, opera, orchestra, photography, political, professional, religious, social service, student government, symphony, and yearbook. Popular campus events include Founders Day, May Day, and Family Weekend. **Sports:** There are 9 intercollegiate sports for women, and 6 intramural sports for women. Facilities include an athletic field, a field house with training, weight rooms, a gym, pool, dance studio, weight room, tennis courts, and bowling lanes. **Graduates:** From July 1, 2016 to June 30, 2017, 153 bachelor's degrees were awarded. The most popular majors were psychology (10%), biology (8%), and music (5%). In an average class, 1% graduate in 3 years or less, 48% graduate in 4 years or less, 53% graduate in 5 years or less, and 54% graduate in 6 years or less. Of the 2016 graduating class, 31% were enrolled in graduate school within 6 months of graduation, and 63% were employed.

SERVICES: Counseling and information services are available, as is tutoring in most subjects. There is a reader service for the blind. **Library/Resources:** The library contains 150,000 volumes, 310 microform items, 12,000 audio/video tapes/CDs/DVDs, and subscribes to 700 periodicals, including electronic. Computerized library services include interlibrary loans and database searching. Special learning facilities include an art gallery and a natural history museum. **Physically Challenged Students:** 75% of the campus is accessible. Facilities include wheelchair ramps, elevators, special parking, and specially equipped restrooms. **Special:** There are co-op programs and cross-registration with Wofford College. Internships, study abroad, a work-study program, accelerated degree programs, B.A.-B.S. degrees in business, economics, sociology, biology, and chemistry, and dual and student-designed majors are offered. There are 10 national honor societies, a freshman honors program, and 100 departmental honors programs. **Visiting:** There are regularly scheduled orientations for prospective students, consisting of faculty meetings, panel discussions, campus tours, tours of Spartanburg, and private interview sessions. There are guides for informal visits, visitors may sit in on classes, and stay overnight. To schedule a visit, contact the Admissions Office. **Campus Safety and Security:** Measures include 24-hour foot and vehicle patrol, self-defense education, and security escort services. There are emergency telephones and lighted pathways/sidewalks.

REQUIREMENTS: The SAT or ACT is recommended. Applicants should be graduates of an accredited secondary school, having completed 20 Carnegie units, including 4 years of English, 3 of math, 2 each of foreign language, science, and social studies, and 1 of history. The GED is accepted. An interview is recommended for all students and an audition is recommended for music students. A GPA of 2.0 is required. AP and CLEP credits are accepted. Important factors in the admissions decision are advanced placement or honors courses, recommendations by school officials, and leadership record. To graduate, students must complete 120 semester hours, including 52 hours across the liberal arts discipline, with a minimum GPA of 2.0. Courses in ideas and culture, computer literacy, public speaking, and phys ed are required. **Procedure:** Freshmen are admitted to all sessions. Entrance exams should be taken by the senior year of high school. There are deferred admissions and rolling admissions plans. Applications should be filed by September 1 for fall entry. **Transfer Students:** 16 transfer students enrolled in 2016-2017. Transfer applicants should have a minimum GPA of 2.0. 42 of 120 credits required for the bachelor's degree must be completed at Converse. **International Students:** There are 14 international students enrolled. They must take the TOEFL.

ADMISSIONS: 51% of the 2017-2018 applicants were accepted. The

SAT scores for the 2017-2018 freshman class were: Critical Reading-- 29% below 500, 43% between 500 and 599, 25% between 600 and 699, and 3% between 700 and 800. Math-- 35% below 500, 50% between 500 and 599, 14% between 600 and 699, and 1% between 700 and 800. The ACT scores were 32% below 12, 25% between 12 and 17, 25% between 18 and 23, 13% between 24 and 29, and 6% above 30. 5 freshmen graduated first in their class. **Admissions Contact:** April Lewis, Director of Admissions. Email: *admissions@converse.edu* Web: *www.converse.edu*

FINANCIAL AID: The FAFSA code is 003431. The priority date for freshman financial aid applications for fall entry is October 1.

ERSKINE COLLEGE — B-2

www.erskine.edu

Due West, SC 29639	(864) 379-8830 (800) 241-8721
Fax: (864) 379-2167	**Email:** admissions@erskine.edu
Full-time: 250 men, 291 women	**Faculty:** 41
Part-time: 9 men, 3 women	**Ph.D.s:** 85%
Graduate: n/av	**Student/Faculty:** 11 to 1
Year: 4-1-4, summer session	**Tuition:** $34,560
Room & Board: $10,900	**Freshman Class:** 500 applied, 373 accepted, 144 enrolled
SAT CR/M: 531/543 **ACT:** required	**CEEB CODE:** 5188
Application Deadline: open	**COMPETITIVE**

Erskine College, founded in 1839, is a private liberal arts college affiliated with the Associate Reformed Presbyterian Church. The figures in the above capsule and in this profile are approximate. There is 1 undergraduate school and 1 graduate school. In addition to regional accreditation, EC has baccalaureate program accreditation with CAEP, CAEP, and ATS. The 85-acre campus is in a rural area in Abbeville County, 90 miles west of Columbia. Including any residence halls, there are 30 buildings.

STUDENT LIFE: 76% of undergraduates are from South Carolina. Others are from 19 states, 8 foreign countries, and Canada. 85% are from public schools. 8% are African American; 72% White; 4% Foreign; 2% Hispanic; 1% Asian American. **Female To Male Ratio:** 1.1:1. The average age of freshmen is 18; all undergraduates, 20. 23% do not continue beyond their first year; 69% remain to graduate. **Housing:** 654 students can be accommodated in college housing, and dorms. On-campus housing is guaranteed for all 4 years. 89% of students live on campus. Alcohol is not permitted. All students may keep cars.

FACULTY/CLASSROOMS: 61% of faculty are male; 39% are female. All teach undergraduates. No introductory courses are taught by graduate students. The average class size in an introductory lecture is 22; in a laboratory is 25; and in a regular course is 14.

PROGRAMS OF STUDY: EC confers A.B. and B.S. degrees. Master's and doctoral degrees are also awarded. Bachelor's degrees are awarded in BIOLOGICAL SCIENCE (biology/biological science), BUSINESS (business administration and management and sports management), COMMUNICATIONS AND THE ARTS (art, English, music, and visual and performing arts), COMPUTER AND PHYSICAL SCIENCE (chemistry, mathematics, natural sciences, and physics), EDUCATION (athletic training, Christian education, early childhood education, elementary education, foreign languages education, physical education, and special education), SOCIAL SCIENCE (American studies, behavioral science, history, philosophy, psychology, religion, and social studies). Mathematics, chemistry, philosophy, and Spanish are the strongest academically. Business administration, and biology have the largest enrollments.

ACTIVITIES: There are no fraternities or sororities. There are 51 groups on campus, including art, cheerleading, choir, chorale, chorus, computers, dance, drama, ethnic, honors, jazz band, literary magazine, newspaper, pep band, political, professional, radio and TV, religious, social, social service, student government, and yearbook. Popular campus events include Spring Fling, Back to School Bash, and Freshman Follies. **Sports:** There are 6 intercollegiate sports for men and 8 for women. Facilities include a physical activities center, gyms, racquetball courts, soccer and baseball fields, tennis and basketball courts, an outdoor pavilion, an outdoor pool, sand volleyball courts, a weight room, a dance/aerobics studio, and a climbing wall. **Graduates:** From July 1, 2016 to June 30, 2017, 141 bachelor's degrees were awarded. The most popular majors were biology (21%), business (20%), and education (13%). In an average class, 63% graduate in 5 years or less and 69% graduate in 6 years or less.

SERVICES: Counseling and information services are available, as is tutoring in every subject. There is a reader service for the blind. **Library/Resources:** The library contains 217,947 volumes, 63,064 microform items, and 2,979 audio/video tapes/CDs/DVDs, and subscribes to 1,125 periodicals including electronic. Computerized library services include interlibrary loans, database searching, Internet access, and Wi-Fi capability. Special learning facilities include an art gallery and radio station. **Physically Challenged Students:** 75% of the campus is accessible. Facilities include wheelchair ramps, elevators, special parking, specially equipped restrooms, and special class scheduling. **Special:** Externships are available during the January term. Study abroad in 5 countries, 3-2 engineering degrees with Clemson University, the University of Tennessee at Knoxville, and Medical University of South Carolina, and pass/fail options are offered. There are 7 national honor societies and 10 departmental honors programs. **Visiting:** There are guides for informal visits, visitors may sit in on classes, and stay overnight. To schedule a visit, contact the Admissions Office. **Campus Safety and Security:** Measures include emergency notification system and security escort services. There are lighted pathways/sidewalks.

REQUIREMENTS: Grades from college preparatory courses are weighed twice as heavily as the SAT or ACT scores. Applicants must be graduates of an accredited secondary school. The GED is accepted. Applicants should have a minimum of 14 high school academic credits, including 4 credits of English and 2 credits each of math, science, and history. AP and CLEP credits are accepted. Important factors in the admissions decision are advanced placement or honors courses, recommendations by school officials, and extracurricular activities record. Students must complete 124 semester hours with an average of 27 credits in a major and a minimum GPA of 2.0. A basic curriculum of arts and letters, humanities, natural science and math, social sciences, and phys ed is required. Attendance at 17 convocations per semester is also required. **Procedure:** Freshmen are admitted to all sessions. Entrance exams should be taken in the spring of the junior year or the fall of the senior year. There are deferred admissions and rolling admissions plans. Application deadlines are open. The fall 2017 application fee was $25. Notification is sent on a rolling basis. Applications are accepted on-line. **Transfer Students:** 17 transfer students enrolled in 2016-2017. Transfer applicants should have a minimum GPA of 2.0. An interview is recommended. 60 of 124 credits required for the bachelor's degree must be completed at Erskine. **International Students:** There are 20 international students enrolled. They must take the TOEFL. They must also take the SAT.

ADMISSIONS: 75% of the 2017-2018 applicants were accepted. The SAT scores for the 2017-2018 freshman class were: Critical Reading-- 40% below 500, 36% between 500 and 599, 19% between 600 and 699, and 5% between 700 and 800. Math-- 37% below 500, 35% between 500 and 599, 23% between 600 and 699, and 5% between 700 and 800. 65% of the current freshmen were in the top fifth of their class; 87% were in the top two fifths. **Admissions Contact:** Buck Brown, Director of Admissions. Email: *admissions@erskine.edu* Web: *www.erskine.edu*

FINANCIAL AID: The college's own financial statement is required. The FAFSA code is 003432. The deadline for filing freshman financial aid applications for fall entry is April 1.

FRANCIS MARION UNIVERSITY *(The complete profile is made available exclusively on our website, www.barronspac.com)*

FURMAN UNIVERSITY — B-1

www.furman.edu

Greenville, SC 29613	(864) 294-2034
Fax: (864) 294-2018	**Email:** admissions@furman.edu
Full-time: 1085 men, 1573 women	**Faculty:** 235; IIB, ++$
Part-time: 36 men, 52 women	**Ph.D.s:** 100%
Graduate: 29 men, 174 women	**Student/Faculty:** 10 to 1
Year: semesters, summer session	**Tuition:** $48,348
Room & Board: $12,750	**Freshman Class:** 5143 applied, 3268 accepted, 671 enrolled
SAT or ACT: required	**CEEB CODE:** 5222
Application Deadline: January 15	**VERY COMPETITIVE+**

Furman University, founded in 1826, is an independent liberal arts institution offering undergraduate and graduate programs. There is 1 undergraduate school. In addition to regional accreditation, Furman has baccalaureate program accreditation with NASM, and CAEP. The 750-acre campus is in a suburban area 5 miles north of Greenville. Including any residence halls, there are 69 buildings.

STUDENT LIFE: 72% of undergraduates are from out of state, mostly the South. Students are from 42 states, 27 foreign countries, and Canada. 60% are from public schools. 76% are White; 6% African American; 5% Hispanic; 5% Foreign; 3% race unknown; 23% two or more races; 2% Asian American. 51% are Protestant; 31% claim no religious affiliation; 15% Catholic. **Female To Male Ratio:** 1.6:1. The average age of freshmen is 18; all undergraduates, 20. 7% do not continue beyond their first year; 93% remain to graduate. **Housing:** 2394 students can be accommodated in college housing, which includes single sex dorms, coed dorms, and on-campus apartments. In addition, there are language/international houses, special-interest houses, and an environmental community. On-campus housing is guaranteed for all 4 years. 96% of students live on campus. All students may keep cars.

FACULTY/CLASSROOMS: 59% of faculty are male; 41% are female. 99% teach undergraduates, 80% do research, and 80% do both. No introductory courses are taught by graduate students. The average class size in an introductory lecture is 19; in a laboratory is 10; and in a regular course is 16.

PROGRAMS OF STUDY: Furman confers B.A., B.S., B.L.A., and B.M. degrees. Master's degrees are also awarded. Bachelor's degrees are awarded in BIOLOGICAL SCIENCE (biology/biological science and neurosciences), BUSINESS (accounting, business administration and management, mathematical business economics, and urban administration), COMMUNICATIONS AND THE ARTS (art history, art, church music, classics, communications, dramatic arts, English, French, German, Greek, Japanese, Latin, music, music composition, music performance, music theory and composition, Spanish, studio art, and theatre acting), COMPUTER AND PHYSICAL SCIENCE (chemistry, computer science, information sciences and systems, mathematics, physics, and sustainable energy science), EDUCATION (education, elementary education, and music education), ENGINEERING AND ENVIRONMENTAL DESIGN (environmental science, military science, and preengineering), HEALTH PROFESSIONS (health science and public health), SOCIAL SCIENCE (anthropology, Asian/Oriental studies, economics, history, philosophy, political science/government, psychology, religion, religious music, sociology, and urban studies). Chemistry, health sciences, and biology are the strongest academically. Political science, health sciences, and business administration have the largest enrollments.

ACTIVITIES: 30% of men belong to 6 national fraternities; 58% of women belong to 8 national sororities. There are 150 groups on campus, including art, band, cheerleading, choir, chorale, chorus, dance, debate, drama, environmental, ethnic, honors, international, jazz band, LGBT, literary magazine, marching band, musical theater, newspaper, orchestra, pep band, political, professional, radio and TV, religious, social, social service, student government, symphony, and yearbook. Popular campus events include Beach Weekend and Mountain Weekend. **Sports:** There are 9 intercollegiate sports for men and 9 for women, and 20 intramural sports for men and 20 for women. Facilities include Homecoming, Fall Fest, Family Weekend, Winter Wonderland, Last Day of Class (LDOC) Celebration. MLK Day of Service, various heritage month events throughout the year. **Graduates:** From July 1, 2016 to June 30, 2017, 684 bachelor's degrees were awarded. The most popular majors were business administration (12%), political science (2%), and health sciences (2%). In an average class, 1% graduate in 3 years or less, 80% graduate in 4 years or less, 83% graduate in 5 years or less, and 84% graduate in 6 years or less. Of the 2016 graduating class, 32% were enrolled in graduate school within 6 months of graduation, and 62% were employed.

SERVICES: Counseling and information services are available, as is tutoring in every subject. There is also a reader service for the blind. **Library/Resources:** The library contains 621,903 volumes, 862,324 microform items, and 9,550 audio/video tapes/CDs/DVDs, and subscribes to 179,800 periodicals including electronic. Computerized library services include interlibrary loans, database searching, Internet access, and Wi-Fi capability. Special learning facilities include an art gallery, planetarium, radio station, an observatory, biometrics lab, finance and business analytics lab, and a science center. **Physically Challenged Students:** 99% of the campus is accessible. Facilities include wheelchair ramps, elevators, special parking, specially equipped restrooms, special class scheduling, lowered drinking fountains, lowered telephones, and special housing. **Special:** A 3-2 engineering degree is offered with the Georgia Institute of Technology, Clemson, North Carolina State, and Auburn and Washington Universities. Internships, study abroad in at least 17 countries, a Washington semester with an internship in a government agency or political organization, and work-study programs are offered. B.A.-B.S. degrees, dual majors, interdisciplinary majors such as computer science-math, math-economics, and computing-business, and student-designed majors are available. A bachelor of general studies degree is granted in the evening division. Nondegree study and pass/fail options are possible. Furman features student/faculty research programs. There are 24 national honor societies and a chapter of Phi Beta Kappa. **Visiting:** There are regularly scheduled orientations for prospective students, Consisting of an individual or group session with an admissions counselor and a campus tour. There are guides for informal visits; visitors may sit in on classes and stay overnight. To schedule a visit, contact the Admissions Office. **Campus Safety and Security:** Measures include 24-hour foot and vehicle patrol, an emergency notification system, self-defense education, and security escort services. There are shuttle buses, emergency telephones, lighted pathways/sidewalks, and controlled access to dorms/residences.

REQUIREMENTS: Applicants must be high school graduates or hold a GED. Students should have earned at least 20 units in high school, including 4 of English, 3 each of history, math, and science, and 2 each of social studies and foreign language. A portfolio or an audition, where appropriate, is required. AP credits are accepted. Important factors in the admissions decision are advanced placement or honors courses, evidence of special talent, personality/intangible qualities, extracurricular activities record, leadership record, and parents or siblings attended your school. Students must complete at least 1 to 3 courses in foreign languages, 2 empirical studies focused on natural world courses, 2 empirical studies on human and social behavior, 3 courses in humanities, 2 courses in global awareness, 1 course in math and formal reasoning, 1 course in ultimate questions, and 1 course considering the mind and body. To graduate students muct complete 128 credits, typically including 24 to 44 in the major, with a GPA of at least 2.0. **Procedure:** Freshmen are admitted in the fall. Entrance exams should be taken junior or senior year. There are early decision and early admissions plans. Early decision applications should be filed by November 1; regular applications, by January 15 for fall entry. The fall 2017 application fee was $50. Notification of early decision is sent November 15; regular decision, March 1. 104 early decision candidates were accepted for the 2017-2018 class. 1412 applicants were on the 2017 waiting list; 59 were admitted. Applications are accepted online. **Transfer Students:** 18 transfer students enrolled in 2016-2017. Applicants should complete at least 1 year elsewhere before seeking admission. 64 of 128 credits required for the bachelor's degree must be completed at Furman. **International Students:** There are 130 international students enrolled. They must take the TOEFL with a minimum score of 85 on the Internet-based version (iBT).

ADMISSIONS: 64% of the 2017-2018 applicants were accepted. The SAT scores for the 2017-2018 freshman class were: Math-- 3% below 500, 29% between 500 and 599, 47% between 600 and 699, and 21% between 700 and 800. Evidence-Based Reading/Writing-- 2% below 500, 22% between 500 and 599, 53% between 600 and 699, and 23% between 700 and 800. The ACT scores were 1% between 12 and 17, 9% between 18 and 23, 51% between 24 and 29, and 39% above 30. 64% of the current freshmen were in the top fifth of their class; 89% were in the top two fifths. **Admissions Contact:** Brad Pochard, Dean of Admission. Email: *admissions@furman.edu* Web: *www.furman.edu*

FINANCIAL AID: In 2017-2018, 97% of all full-time freshmen received some form of financial aid. 47% of all full-time freshmen received need-based aid. The average freshman award was $33,273. Need-based scholarships or need-based grants averaged $36,996 ($52,514 maximum); need-based self-help aid (loans and jobs) averaged $3,776 ($7,000 maximum); non-need-based athletic scholarships averaged $35,867 ($62,498 maximum); and other non-need-based awards and non-need-based scholarships averaged $16,603 ($48,968 maximum). 49% of undergraduate students work part-time. The average financial indebtedness of the 2017 graduate was $32,919. Furman is a member of CSS. The CSS/Profile is required. The FAFSA code is 003434. The priority date for freshman financial aid applications for fall entry is March 1. The deadline for filing freshman financial aid applications for fall entry is January 15.

LANDER UNIVERSITY B-2
www.lander.edu

Greenwood, SC 29649 **(864) 388-8307**

Fax: (864) 388-8125 **Email: admissions@lander.edu**

Full-time: 735 men, 1361 women
Part-time: 75 men, 192 women
Graduate: 6 men, 42 women
Year: semesters, summer session
Room & Board: $25,300

SAT CR/M: 470/500 **ACT:** 21
Application Deadline: open

Faculty: 130
Ph.D.s: 63%
Student/Faculty: 14 to 1
Tuition: $11,700 ($21,300)
Freshman Class: 2230 applied, 946 accepted, 433 enrolled
CEEB CODE: 5363
COMPETITIVE

Lander University, founded in 1872, is a state-supported institution offering undergraduate programs in liberal arts, science and math, business, education, nursing, and phys ed and exercise studies. The figures given in the above capsule and in this profile are approximate. There are 10 undergraduate schools and 1 graduate school. In addition to regional accreditation, Lander has baccalaureate program accreditation with AACSB, NASAD, NASM, and CCSACS. The 100-acre campus is in a small town in the city of Greenwood, 75 miles west of Columbia. Including any residence halls, there are 6 buildings.

STUDENT LIFE: 92% of undergraduates are from South Carolina. Others are from 23 states, 21 foreign countries, and Canada. 67% are White; 3% Foreign; 24% African American; 1% Asian American; 1% American Indian/Alaska Native; 1% Hispanic. **Female To Male Ratio:** 2.0:1. The average age of freshmen is 19; all undergraduates, 26. 38% do not continue beyond their first year; 62% remain to graduate. **Housing:** 1082 students can be accommodated in college housing, which includes dorms, on-campus apartments, and off-campus apartments. On-campus housing is available on a first-come, first-served basis. 68% of students commute. Alcohol is not permitted. All students may keep cars.

FACULTY/CLASSROOMS: 47% of faculty are male; 53% are female. All teach undergraduates. No introductory courses are taught by graduate students. The average class size in a regular course is 22.

PROGRAMS OF STUDY: Lander confers B.A., B.S., and B.M.Ed. degrees. Master's degrees are also awarded. Bachelor's degrees are awarded in BIOLOGICAL SCIENCE (biology/biological science), BUSINESS (business administration and management), COMMUNICATIONS AND THE ARTS (communications, dramatic arts, English, music, Spanish, speech/debate/rhetoric, and visual and performing arts), COMPUTER AND PHYSICAL SCIENCE (chemistry, computer science, and mathematics), EDUCATION (early childhood education, elementary education, music education, physical education, and special education), ENGINEERING AND ENVIRONMENTAL DESIGN (environmental science), HEALTH PROFESSIONS (exercise science, nursing, and sports medicine), SOCIAL SCIENCE (history, interdisciplinary studies, political science/government, psychology, and sociology). Premedical, and dual engineering are the strongest academically. Business administration, education, and behavioral science have the largest enrollments.

ACTIVITIES: 11% of men belong to 5 national fraternities; 12% of women belong to 5 national sororities. There are 65 groups on campus, including art, band, cheerleading, choir, chorale, chorus, computers, dance, drama, ethnic, honors, international, jazz band, literary magazine, musical theater, newspaper, orchestra, pep band, political, professional, religious, social, social service, and student government. Popular campus events include The Greenwood Performing Arts Series. **Sports:** There are 5 intercollegiate sports for men and 6 for women, and 11 intramural sports for men and 11 for women. Facilities include a gym, basketball courts, a weight room, softball field, soccer and tennis courts, golf, volleyball, equestrian, ultimate disc, rugby, indoor pool, and an indoor suspended track. **Graduates:** From July 1, 2016 to June 30, 2017, 485 bachelor's degrees were awarded. The most popular majors were business (23%), education (14%), and social and political sciences (13%). In an average class, 2% graduate in 3 years or less, 28% graduate in 4 years or less, 39% graduate in 5 years or less, and 40% graduate in 6 years or less.

SERVICES: Counseling and information services are available, as is tutoring in most subjects. There is also a reader service for the blind, and remedial math, reading, and writing. **Library/Resources:** The library contains 174,624 volumes, 157,707 microform items, and 2,592 audio/video tapes/CDs/DVDs, and subscribes to 656 periodicals including electronic. Computerized library services include interlibrary loans, database searching, and Internet access. Special learning facilities include an art gallery, and a media center. **Physically Challenged Students:** All of the campus is accessible. Facilities include wheelchair ramps, elevators, special parking, specially equipped restrooms, special class scheduling, lowered drinking fountains, and lowered telephones. **Special:** Lander offers internships, co-op and work-study programs, accelerated degrees, B.A.-B.S. degrees, dual engineering degree's with Clemson University, student-designed majors in interdisciplinary studies, credit for military experience, and nondegree study. Students in the Honors International Program study abroad in England for 1 semester during their sophomore year. There are 7 national honor societies and a freshman honors program. **Visiting:** There are regularly scheduled orientations for prospective students, consisting of open houses. There are guides for informal visits and visitors may sit in on classes. To schedule a visit, contact the Admissions Office. **Campus Safety and Security:** Measures include 24-hour foot and vehicle patrol, emergency notification system, self-defense education, and security escort services. There are emergency telephones, lighted pathways/sidewalks, and controlled access to dorms/residences.

REQUIREMENTS: The SAT or ACT is required. Applicants must be high school graduates with 20 credits, including 4 each of English and academic electives, and 3 each of math and lab science, 2 each of foreign language and social studies, and 1 each of American history and phys ed or ROTC. An interview and a portfolio or an audition, if appropriate, are recommended. AP and CLEP credits are accepted. To graduate, students must complete 125 semester hours, including 36 in the major, with a GPA of 2.0. **Procedure:** Freshmen are admitted to all sessions. Entrance exams should be taken in the junior year. There are early admissions, deferred admissions, and rolling admissions plans. Application deadlines are open. The fall 2017 application fee was $35. Notification is sent on a rolling basis. Applications are accepted on-line. **Transfer Students:** 203 transfer students enrolled in 2016-2017. Applicants must have a minimum college GPA of 2.0, otherwise they may be considered on the strength of military or work experience. Transcripts from every school attended should be submitted. Students under 21 with fewer than 30 semester credits must submit high school transcripts and SAT or ACT results as well. An interview is recommended. 30 of 125 credits required for the bachelor's degree must be completed at Lander. **International Students:** Students must take the TOEFL with a minimum score of 550 on the paper-based TOEFL (PBT), and either the SAT or ACT.

ADMISSIONS: 42% of the 2017-2018 applicants were accepted. The SAT scores for the 2017-2018 freshman class were: Critical Reading-- 59% below 500, 32% between 500 and 599, and 8% between 600 and 699. Math-- 47% below 500, 38% between 500 and 599, 14% between 600 and 699, and 1% between 700 and 800. The ACT scores were 47% below 12, 32% between 12 and 17, 15% between 18 and 23, 4% between 24 and 29, and 2% above 30. 33% of the current freshmen were in the top fifth of their class; 69% were in the top two fifths. 5 freshmen graduated first in their class. **Admissions Contact:** Brooks Schadell, Director of Admissions. Email: *admissions@lander.edu* Web: *www.lander.edu*

FINANCIAL AID: The FAFSA code is 003435. Check with the school for current application deadlines.

LIMESTONE COLLEGE B-1
www.limestone.edu

Gaffney, SC 29340 **(864) 489-7151**
(800) 795-7151

Fax: (864) 487-8706 **Email: admissions@limestone.edu**

Full-time: 771 men, 456 women
Part-time: 14 men, 5 women
Graduate: 32 men, 42 women
Year: semesters, summer session
Room & Board: $8200

SAT CR/M: 500/510 **ACT:** 21
Application Deadline: August 23

Faculty: 81
Ph.D.s: 79%
Student/Faculty: 14 to 1
Tuition: $23,900
Freshman Class: 3196 applied, 1653 accepted, 526 enrolled
CEEB CODE: 5366
COMPETITIVE

Limestone College, founded in 1845, is an independent, accredited, coeducational, Christian non-denominational, four-year liberal arts college, offering programs in the arts, sciences, business, and teacher preparation. Its programs lead to the Bachelor of Arts, Bachelor of Fine Arts, Bachelor of Science, Bachelor of Social Work, Associate of Arts, and Associate of Science degrees. At the graduate level, a Master of Business Administration is offered. There is 1 undergraduate school and 1 graduate school. In addition to regional accreditation, Limestone has baccalaureate program accreditation with CSWE, NASM, CAEP, and CAATE. The 125-acre campus is in a suburban area 50 miles south of Charlotte, NC and 25 miles north of Spartanburg, SC. Including any residence halls, there are 33 buildings.

STUDENT LIFE: 58% of undergraduates are from South Carolina. Others are from 36 states, 31 foreign countries, and Canada. 9% are Foreign; 48% White; 4% Hispanic; 34% African American; 3% two or more races; 1% race unknown. **Male To Female Ratio:** 1.6:1. The average age of freshmen is 18; all undergraduates, 19. 45% do not continue beyond their first year; 66% remain to graduate. **Housing:** 823 students can be accommodated in college housing, which includes dorms, on-campus apartments, and off-campus apartments. On-campus housing is guaranteed for the freshman year only, is available on a first-come, and first-served basis. 58% of students live on campus. Alcohol is not permitted. All students may keep cars.

FACULTY/CLASSROOMS: 51% of faculty are male; 49% are female. All teach undergraduates, 20% do research, and 20% do both. No introductory courses are taught by graduate students. The average class size in an introductory lecture is 22; in a laboratory is 16; and in a regular course is 14.

PROGRAMS OF STUDY: Limestone confers B.A., B.S., B.F.A., and B.S.W. degrees. Associate and master's degrees are also awarded. Bachelor's degrees are awarded in BIOLOGICAL SCIENCE (biology/biological science), BUSINESS (accounting, business administration and management, business economics, electronic business, finance, human resources, management science, marketing, marketing and distribution, personnel management, and sports management), COMMUNICATIONS AND THE ARTS (communications, English, English Writing, graphic design, jazz, music, musical theater, studio art, and theatre arts), COMPUTER AND PHYSICAL SCIENCE (chemistry, computer programming, computer information technology, computer science, computer security and information assurance, information sciences and systems, mathematics, web services, and web technology), EDUCATION (athletic training, early childhood education, elementary education, English education, mathematics education, music education, and physical education), ENGINEERING AND ENVIRONMENTAL DESIGN (computer technology), HEALTH PROFESSIONS (health care administration), SOCIAL SCIENCE (child care/child and family studies, criminal justice, economics, history, liberal arts/general studies, physical fitness/movement, prelaw, psychology, and social work). Business administration, sport management, and criminal justice have the largest enrollments.

ACTIVITIES: 2% of men belong to 1 local fraternity; 3% of women belong to 1 local sorority. There are 32 groups on campus, including art, band, cheerleading, choir, chorus, computers, dance, drama, environmental, honors, international, jazz band, LGBT, literary magazine, marching band, musical theater, pep band, professional, religious, social, social service, student government, and symphony. Popular campus events include Christmas on Campus and Homecoming. **Sports:** There are 13 intercollegiate sports for men and 12 for women, and 28 intramural sports for men and 28 for women. Facilities include a basketball gym, Olympic size indoor swimming pool, equipment room, athletic support, lighted tennis courts, lacrosse, soccer and field hockey, football practice field with additional practice fields, the physical education center is the main athletic weight room, and the student recreation center features the basketball court, fitness center and intramural offices. **Graduates:** From July 1, 2016 to June 30, 2017, 142 bachelor's degrees were awarded. The most popular majors were business administration (16%), PE-strength and conditioning (11%), and sport management (10%). In an average class, 20% graduate in 4 years or less and 42% graduate in 6 years or less. Of the 2016 graduating class, 19% were enrolled in graduate school within 6 months of graduation.

SERVICES: Counseling and information services are available, as is tutoring in every subject. There is remedial math, reading, and writing. Special assistance is also available to students with documented learning disabilities through the Program for Alternative Learning Styles (PALS). **Library/Resources:** The library contains 77,342 volumes, 2,924 microform items, and 4,032 audio/video tapes/CDs/DVDs, and subscribes to 277,823 periodicals including electronic. Computerized library services include interlibrary loans, database searching, Internet access, and Wi-Fi capability. **Physically Challenged Students:** 75% of the campus is accessible. Facilities include wheelchair ramps, elevators, special parking, specially equipped restrooms, special class scheduling, lowered drinking fountains, and special housing. individual accommodations are made on an as-needed basis. **Special:** The College offers senior internships in public and private organizations for 3 to 6 semester credit hours, as well as a work-study program, on- and off-campus evening courses, and courses on the Internet. The College confers a liberal studies degree and may grant credit for military experience. Double majors are possible; however, granting of 2 baccalaureate degrees requires an additional 31 semester hours. There are 5 national honor societies and a freshman honors program. **Visiting:** There are regularly scheduled orientations for prospective students, tour of campus, faculty presentations, an Academic Fair, and a Question & Answer session. There are guides for informal visits, visitors may sit in on classes, and stay overnight. To schedule a visit, contact Jennifer Ledbetter at (864) 488-4552. **Campus Safety and Security:** Measures include 24-hour foot and vehicle patrol, emergency notification system, and security escort services. There are emergency telephones, lighted pathways/sidewalks, and controlled access to dorms/residences.

REQUIREMENTS: The SAT or ACT is required. SAT combined score (critical reading and math) of 910 or ACT combined score (English and math) of 19. The College recommends that students present 4 units of English, 3 each of math and social science, and 2 of lab science. The GED is accepted. An interview is recommended. A GPA of 2.0 is required. AP and CLEP credits are accepted. Important factors in the admissions decision are advanced placement or honors courses, leadership record, and evidence of special talent. To graduate a student must complete a minimum of 123 credit hours for a baccalaureate degree or 62 credit hours for an associate degree with a minimum overall GPA of 2.0, including within their major. **Procedure:** Freshmen are admitted fall and spring. Entrance exams should be taken during fall of the senior year of high school. There are deferred admissions and rolling admissions plans. Application deadlines are open. The fall 2017 application fee was $25. Notification is sent on a rolling basis. Applications are accepted online. **Transfer Students:** 95 transfer students enrolled in 2016-2017. Applicants must have a minimum GPA of 2.0 and be in good standing at their previous school. 31 of 123 credits required for the bachelor's degree must be completed at Limestone. **International Students:** There are 112 international students enrolled. They must take the TOEFL with a minimum score of 500 on the paper-based TOEFL (PBT) or 75 on the Internet-based version (iBT). They must also take the SAT or ACT, scoring 910.

ADMISSIONS: 52% of the 2017-2018 applicants were accepted. The SAT scores for the 2017-2018 freshman class were: Critical Reading-- 60% below 500, 31% between 500 and 599, and 8% between 600 and 699. Math-- 39% below 500, 51% between 500 and 599, and 9% between 600 and 699. The ACT scores were 75% between 18 and 23, 19% between 24 and 29, and 4% above 30. 18% of the current freshmen were in the top fifth of their class; 38% were in the top two fifths. 1 freshman graduated first in the class. **Admissions Contact:** Travis McDowell, Director of Admissions. Email: *admissions@limestone.edu* Web: *www.limestone.edu*

FINANCIAL AID: In 2017-2018, 92% of all full-time freshmen received some form of financial aid and need-based aid. The average freshman award was $16,675. Need-based scholarships or need-based grants averaged $5,660 ($9,825 maximum); need-based self-help aid (loans and jobs) averaged $6,575 ($12,500 maximum); non-need-based athletic scholarships averaged $6,985 ($25,600 maximum); other non-need-based awards and non-need-based scholarships averaged $4,875 ($28,800 maximum); and $1,650 from other forms of aid. 31% of undergraduate students work part-time. The average financial indebtedness of the 2017 graduate was $30,950. Limestone is a member of CSS. The FAFSA code is 003436. The priority date for freshman financial aid applications for fall entry is February 1. The deadline for filing freshman financial aid applications for fall entry is June 30.

MORRIS COLLEGE *(The complete profile is made available exclusively on our website, www.barronspac.com)*

NEWBERRY COLLEGE B-2
www.newberry.edu

Newberry, SC 29108	(803) 321-5127 (800) 845-4955
Fax: (803) 321-5138	Email: admissions@newberry.edu
Full-time: 435 men, 325 women	**Faculty:** 46; IIB, ++$
Part-time: 10 men, 25 women	**Ph.D.s:** 70%
Graduate: n/av	**Student/Faculty:** 16 to 1
Year: semesters, summer session	**Tuition:** $27,000
Room & Board: $9550	**Freshman Class:** n/av
SAT or ACT: required	**CEEB CODE:** 5493
Application Deadline: open	**COMPETITIVE**

Newberry College, founded in 1856, is a private liberal arts institution affiliated with the Evangelical Lutheran Church in America. The figures given in the above capsule and in this profile are approximate. There is 1 undergraduate school. In addition to regional accreditation, NC has baccalaureate program accreditation with NASM, CAEP, and AVMA. The 90-acre campus is in a small town 40 miles northwest of Columbia. Including any residence halls, there are 22 buildings.

STUDENT LIFE: 84% of undergraduates are from South Carolina. Others are from 13 states, 8 foreign countries, and Canada. 90% are from public schools. 71% are White; 26% African American; 1% Hispanic; 1% Foreign. 80% are Protestant; 12% claim no religious affiliation. **Male To Female Ratio:** 1.3:1. The average age of freshmen is 18; all undergraduates, 20. 49% do not continue beyond their first year; 47% remain to graduate. **Housing:** 622 students can be accommodated in college housing, which includes dorms, and honors houses. On-campus housing is guaranteed for all 4 years. 77% of students live on campus. All students may keep cars.

FACULTY/CLASSROOMS: 58% of faculty are male; 41% are female. All teach undergraduates. No introductory courses are taught by graduate students. The average class size in an introductory lecture is 30; in a laboratory is 30; and in a regular course is 25.

PROGRAMS OF STUDY: NC confers B.A., B.S., B.M., and B.M.E. degrees. Bachelor's degrees are awarded in BIOLOGICAL SCIENCE (biology/biological science), BUSINESS (business administration and management), COMMUNICATIONS AND THE ARTS (applied music, art, communications, dramatic arts, English, French, German, languages, music, music performance, music theory and composition, and Spanish), COMPUTER AND PHYSICAL SCIENCE (chemistry, computer science, and mathematics), EDUCATION (early childhood education, elementary education, music education, and physical education), HEALTH PROFESSIONS (veterinary science), SOCIAL SCIENCE (history, philosophy, political science/government, psychology, religion, and sociology). Education, and natural sciences are the strongest academically. Business administration, education, and physical education have the largest enrollments.

ACTIVITIES: 11% of men belong to 6 national fraternities; 13% of women belong to 3 national sororities. There are 50 groups on campus, including band, cheerleading, choir, chorale, chorus, computers, dance, drama, ethnic, honors, international, jazz band, literary magazine, marching band, musical theater, newspaper, orchestra, pep band, political, professional, radio and TV, religious, social, social service, student government, and yearbook. Popular campus events include Fall Fling and Spring Fling. **Sports:** There are 8 intercollegiate sports for men and 9 for women, and 6 intramural sports for men and 5 for women. Facilities include a stadium, a phys ed complex with racquetball courts a basketball arena, an outdoor pool, tennis courts, baseball, softball, cross country, lacrosse, golf, field hockey, volleyball, wrestling, and soccer fields. **Graduates:** The most popular majors were business and management (16%), education (13%), and social sciences and history (9%). Of the 2016 graduating class, 20% were enrolled in graduate school within 6 months of graduation, and 60% were employed.

SERVICES: Counseling and information services are available, as is tutoring in most subjects. There is remedial math, reading, and writing. **Library/Resources:** The library contains 79,464 volumes, 7,153 microform items, and 1,217 audio/video tapes/CDs/DVDs, and subscribes to 258 periodicals including electronic. Computerized library services include interlibrary loans, database searching, and Internet access. Special learning facilities include a radio station, TV station, and herbarium. **Physically Challenged Students:** 90% of the campus is accessible. Facilities include wheelchair ramps, elevators, special parking, specially equipped restrooms, and special class scheduling. **Special:** Internships, dual and student-designed majors, study abroad, a Washington semester, work-study programs, independent study, and cooperative education are offered. A 3-2 engineering degree program with Clemson University, a 3-2 forestry program with Duke University, a 3-3 cytotechnology program, and a 3-1 medical technology program are available. Nondegree study is possible. There are 3 national honor societies, a freshman honors program, and 3 departmental honors programs. **Visiting:** There are regularly scheduled orientations for prospective students, including a campus tour, informational sessions, and meetings with faculty, staff, and students. There are guides for informal visits; visitors may sit in on classes and stay overnight. To schedule a visit, contact the Admissions Office. **Campus Safety and Security:** Measures include 24-hour foot and vehicle patrol, emergency notification system, and security escort services. There are emergency telephones, lighted pathways/sidewalks, and controlled access to dorms/residences.

REQUIREMENTS: The SAT or ACT is required. Applicants should have completed 18 high school academic units, including 4 of English, 3 each of math and social science (1 of U.S. history), 2 each of lab science and foreign language, and 1 in elective. The GED is accepted. An essay is recommended. AP and CLEP credits are accepted. Important factors in the admissions decision are leadership record, evidence of special talent, and recommendations by school officials. To graduate, students must complete 126 semester hours, with a minimum GPA of 2.0. Core curriculum requirements include 10 to 11 hours of math and natural science, 9 each of communication skills, humanities or fine arts, and history or social sciences, up to 6 of foreign language, 3 of religion, and 2 of phys ed. There is also a 24-event fine arts and lectures requirement. All students must fulfill Communications Across the Curriculum writing projects. **Procedure:** Freshmen are admitted to all sessions. Entrance exams should be taken in the spring of the junior year or the fall of the senior year. There are deferred admissions and rolling admissions plans. Application deadlines are open. The fall 2017 application fee was $30. **Transfer Students:** 57 transfer students enrolled in 2016-2017. Applicants must be eligible to return to their previous school. A 2.0 minimum GPA is recommended. 32 of 126 credits required for the bachelor's degree must be completed at NC. **International Students:** There are 8 international students enrolled. They must take the TOEFL and the college's own test. They must also take the SAT or ACT.

Admissions Contact: Joel Vander Horst, Director of Admissions. Email: *admissions@newberry.edu* Web: *www.newberry.edu*

FINANCIAL AID: In 2017-2018, 91% of all full-time freshmen received some form of financial aid. 63% of all full-time freshmen received need-based aid. The average freshman award was $12,450. 12% of undergraduate students work part-time. The average financial indebtedness of the 2017 graduate was $3,135. NC is a member of CSS. The FAFSA code is 003440. The priority date for freshman financial aid applications for fall entry is March 30.

NORTH GREENVILLE UNIVERSITY
www.ngu.edu

Tigerville, SC 29688	(864) 977-7001 (800) 468-6642
	Email: admissions@ngu.edu
Full-time: 1163 men, 1046 women	**Faculty:** 137
Part-time: 75 men, 197 women	**Ph.D.s:** 50%
Graduate: 115 men, 95 women	**Student/Faculty:** 14 to 1
Year: semesters, summer session	**Tuition:** $16,290
Room & Board: $9640	**Freshman Class:** 1593 applied, 919 accepted, 531 enrolled
SAT CR/M/W: 562/552/528 **ACT:** 24	**CEEB CODE:** 005498
Application Deadline: open	**COMPETITIVE**

North Greenville University, founded in 1892, is a public university offering the Master of Christian Ministry, the Master of Business Administration, the Master of Education, the Master of Arts in Teaching, and the Doctor of Ministry. NGU also has undergraduate online degree programs in business administration, elementary studies, Christian Ministries, criminal justice and legal studies, general studies, and psychology. NGU mission is to offer a quality education in a biblically sound, Christ-centered environment. There are 7 undergraduate schools and 2 graduate schools. In addition to regional accreditation, NGU has baccalaureate program accreditation with NASM, CAEP, and NLN. The 315-acre campus is in a rural area in Tigerville in the foothills of the Blue Ridge Mountains, 18 miles north of Greenville, SC. Including any residence halls, there are 100 buildings.

STUDENT LIFE: 66% of undergraduates are from South Carolina. Others are from 35 states, and Canada. 79% are White; 7% African American; 7% race unknown; 3% Hispanic; 3% two or more races. 87% are Protestant; 12% claim no religious affiliation. **Male To Female Ratio:** 1.0:1. The average age of freshmen is 18; all undergraduates, 20. **Housing:** 1550 students can be accommodated in college housing, which includes dorms. On-campus housing is guaranteed for all 4 years, is available on a first-come, and first-served basis. 65% of students live on campus. All students may keep cars.

FACULTY/CLASSROOMS: 57% of faculty are male; 43% are female. All teach undergraduates. No introductory courses are taught by graduate students. The average class size in an introductory lecture is 30; in a laboratory is 20; and in a regular course is 20.

PROGRAMS OF STUDY: NGU confers B.A. and B.S. degrees. Master's and doctoral degrees are also awarded. Bachelor's degrees are awarded in BIOLOGICAL SCIENCE (biological sciences), BUSINESS (accounting, international business information systems, marketing, and sports management), COMMUNICATIONS AND THE ARTS (broadcasting, music performance, Spanish, studio art, and theatre arts), COMPUTER AND PHYSICAL SCIENCE (mathematics), EDUCATION (education, English secondary education, mathematics education, music education, outdoor leadership/education, and social studies education), HEALTH PROFESSIONS (health promotion), SOCIAL SCIENCE (Christian studies, history and political science, psychology, and youth ministry). Business, sport management, and biology are the strongest academically. Business, education, and biology have the largest enrollments.

ACTIVITIES: There are no fraternities or sororities. There are 16 groups on campus, including art, band, cheerleading, choir, chorale, chorus, computers, debate, drama, honors, jazz band, literary magazine, marching band, musical theater, newspaper, orchestra, political, professional, social, social service, student government, and yearbook. Popular campus events include Homecoming and the Miss NGU pagent. **Sports:** There are 10 intercollegiate sports for men and 10 for women, and Facilities include a gym, baseball and softball fields, football and soccer/lacrosse stadiums, practice fields, an athletic weight training facility, tennis courts, and an all-weather track. **Graduates:** From July 1, 2016 to June 30, 2017, 378 bachelor's degrees were awarded. The most popular majors were education (12%), health promotion & wellness (8%), and business administration (7%). In an average class, 42% graduate in 4 years or less, 55% graduate in 5 years or less, and 56% graduate in 6 years or less. Of the 2016 graduating class, 27% were enrolled in graduate school within 6 months of graduation, and 66% were employed.

SERVICES: Counseling and information services are available, as is tutoring in most subjects. There is remedial math, reading, and writing. **Library/Resources:** The library contains 67,637 volumes, and 4,548 audio/video tapes/CDs/DVDs. Computerized library services include interlibrary loans, database searching, Internet access, and Wi-Fi capability. **Physically Challenged Students:** 90% of the campus is accessible. Facilities include wheelchair ramps, elevators, special parking, specially equipped restrooms, and lowered drinking fountains. **Special:** There are a freshman honors program. **Visiting:** There are guides for informal visits, visitors may sit in on classes, and stay overnight. **Campus Safety and Security:** Measures include 24-hour foot and vehicle patrol, self-defense education, and security escort services. There are lighted pathways/sidewalks and controlled access to dorms/residences.

REQUIREMENTS: The SAT or ACT is required. AP and CLEP credits are accepted. Important factors in the admissions decision are advanced placement or honors courses, leadership record, and personality/intangible qualities. A GPA of 2.5 is required. Students at NGU will experience a general education curriculum that seeks to develop students who can apply Biblical truths and principles to learning and life, and students who will be good stewards of a Christian mind and body given to us by God. Students are exposed to courses in the liberal arts, fine arts, the social and behavioral sciences, and the natural and logical sciences. Such a curriculum will enable students to develop a broad knowledge of civilization, literature, religious traditions, and the human condition needed for successful interaction with individuals and institutions. Specific general education requirements may be found listed within each major, requiring a minimum of thirty-eight general education hours. **Procedure:** Freshmen are admitted to all sessions. There are early admissions, deferred admissions, and rolling admissions plans. Application deadlines are open. The fall 2017 application fee was $30. Applications are accepted on-line. **Transfer Students:** 179 transfer students enrolled in 2016-2017. 30 of 120 credits required for the bachelor's degree must be completed at NGU. **International Students:** There are 12 international students enrolled. They must take the TOEFL with a minimum score of 550 on the paper-based TOEFL (PBT) or 80 on the Internet-based version (iBT), and either the SAT or ACT.

ADMISSIONS: 58% of the 2017-2018 applicants were accepted. The SAT scores for the 2017-2018 freshman class were: Critical Reading-- 15% below 500, 60% between 500 and 599, 21% between 600 and 699, and 4% between 700 and 800. Math-- 21% below 500, 54% between 500 and 599, 22% between 600 and 699, and 3% between 700 and 800. Writing-- 20% below 500, 53% between 500 and 599, 21% between 600 and 699, and 6% between 700 and 800. The ACT scores were 4% between 12 and 17, 42% between 18 and 23, 45% between 24 and 29, and 9% above 30. 24% of the current freshmen were in the top fifth of their class; 75% were in the top two fifths. **Admissions Contact:** Keli Sewell, Vice President for Enrollment Services. Email: *admissions@ngu.edu* Web: *www.ngu.edu*

FINANCIAL AID: In 2017-2018, 75% of all full-time freshmen received some form of financial aid. 73% of all full-time freshmen received need-based aid. The average freshman award was $5,074. Need-based scholarships or need-based grants averaged $5,074; need-based self-help aid (loans and jobs) averaged $5,074; non-need-based athletic scholarships averaged $8,654; and other non-need-based awards and non-need-based scholarships averaged $7,576. The average financial indebtedness of the 2017 graduate was $2,000. NGU is a member of CSS. The state aid form is required. The FAFSA code is 003441. The priority date for freshman financial aid applications for fall entry is March 1.

PRESBYTERIAN COLLEGE — B-2

www.presby.edu

Clinton, SC 29325 — **(864) 833-8194**, **(800) 960-7583**

Fax: (864) 833-8195 — **Email: admissions@presby.edu**

Full-time: 476 men, 520 women	**Faculty:** 77
Part-time: 17 men, 50 women	**Ph.D.s:** 97%
Graduate: 96 men, 194 women	**Student/Faculty:** 13 to 1
Year: semesters, summer session	**Tuition:** $37,142
Room & Board: $10,044	**Freshman Class:** 2636 applied, 1577 accepted, 287 enrolled
SAT CR/M: 550/540 **ACT:** required	**CEEB CODE:** 5540
Application Deadline: February 1	**COMPETITIVE**

Presbyterian College, founded in 1880, is a private liberal arts institution affiliated with the Presbyterian Church. PC also has a graduate school of pharmacy that offers a doctorate in pharmacy (PharmD). There is 1 undergraduate school and 1 graduate school. In addition to regional accreditation, PC has baccalaureate program accreditation with ACPE, NASM, SACSCOC, ASBMB, and CAEP. The 240-acre campus is in a small town 40 miles south of Greenville. Including any residence halls, there are 71 buildings.

STUDENT LIFE: 66% of undergraduates are from South Carolina. Others are from 28 states, 20 foreign countries, and Canada. 8% are Foreign; 72% White; 3% Hispanic; 2% two or more races; 13% African American; 1% Asian American; 1% race unknown. 73% are Protestant; 16% claim no religious affiliation. **Female To Male Ratio:** 1.3:1. The average age of freshmen is 18; all undergraduates, 20. 18% do not continue beyond their first year; 70% remain to graduate. **Housing:** 1151 students can be accommodated in college housing, which includes dorms, on-campus apartments, and off-campus apartments. In addition, there are special-interest houses, fraternity houses, housing for international students and students with an interest in studying abroad or experiencing international cultures. On-campus housing is guaranteed for all 4 years. 99% of students live on campus. All students may keep cars.

FACULTY/CLASSROOMS: 59% of faculty are male; 41% are female. All teach undergraduates and all do research. No introductory courses are taught by graduate students. The average class size in an introductory lecture is 20; in a laboratory is 15; and in a regular course is 15.

PROGRAMS OF STUDY: PC confers B.A. and B.S. degrees. Doctoral degrees are also awarded. Bachelor's degrees are awarded in BIOLOGICAL SCIENCE (biochemistry and biology/biological science), BUSINESS (business administration and management and business economics), COMMUNICATIONS AND THE ARTS (art, art history and appreciation, creative writing, dramatic arts, English, French, modern language, music, and Spanish), COMPUTER AND PHYSICAL SCIENCE (chemistry, mathematics, medical physics, and physics), EDUCATION (early childhood education, elementary education, and middle school education), HEALTH PROFESSIONS (pharmacy), SOCIAL SCIENCE (history, international studies, philosophy and religion, political science/government, psychology, religion, religious education, and sociology). Arts and humanities, social sciences, and natural sciences are the strongest academically. Business administration, biology, and psychology have the largest enrollments.

ACTIVITIES: 38% of men belong to 6 national fraternities; 50% of women belong to 3 national sororities. There are 80 groups on campus, including art, bagpipe, band, cheerleading, choir, chorale, chorus, computers, dance, drama, environmental, ethnic, film, honors, international, jazz band, LGBT, literary magazine, newspaper, orchestra, pep band, photography, political, professional, religious, social, social service, student government, symphony, and yearbook. Popular campus events include Week of Welcome, First Weekend Stadium Dance, Scotoberfest, College-wide Thanksgiving Lunch, Annual Christmas Concert, MLK Day of Service, Greek Week, and Spring Fling. **Sports:** There are 7 intercollegiate sports for men and 8 for women, and 10 intramural sports for men and 10 for women. Facilities include a football stadium, basketball, tennis and volleyball, weight rooms, a stadium, baseball complex and softball complex, lacrosse field, and a golf course. The outdoor recreation program and intramurals includes basketball, billiards, dodgeball, flag, football, giant kickball, sand volleyball, soccer, co-ed softball, table tennis and ultimate frisbee. **Graduates:** From July 1, 2016 to June 30, 2017, 226 bachelor's degrees were awarded. The most popular majors were business administration (23%), psychology (14%), and biology (11%). In an average class, 62% graduate in 4 years or less, 68% graduate in 5 years or less, and 70% graduate in 6 years or less. Of the 2016 graduating class, 30% were enrolled in graduate school within 6 months of graduation, and 65% were employed.

SERVICES: Counseling and information services are available, as is tutoring in every subject. There is a reader service for the blind. **Library/Resources:** The library contains 122,528 volumes, 1,146 microform items, and 10,832 audio/video tapes/CDs/DVDs, and subscribes to 16,642 periodicals including electronic. Computerized library services include interlibrary loans, database searching, Internet access, and Wi-Fi capability. Special learning facilities include an art gallery. **Physically Challenged Students:** 95% of the campus is accessible. Facilities include wheelchair ramps, elevators, special parking, specially equipped restrooms, lowered drinking fountains, and special housing. **Special:** Educational internships, study abroad and a Washington semester are available. Dual majors, work-study programs, B.A.-B.S. degrees, and a 3-2 engineering degree with Auburn University, Clemson University, Georgia Institute of Technology, University of South Carolina and Vanderbilt University are offered. There is a forestry environmental studies program with Duke University. Credit for military experience, auditing courses, and pass/fail options are also possible. There are 12 national honor societies, a freshman honors program, and 16 departmental honors programs. **Visiting:** There are regularly scheduled orientations for prospective students, which include academics, student activity, financial aid information, a tour, and lunch. There are guides for informal visits, visitors may sit in on classes, and stay overnight. To schedule a visit, contact Brian J. Fortman at (800) 960-7583. **Campus Safety and Security:** Measures include 24-hour foot and vehicle patrol, emergency notification system, and security escort services. There are shuttle buses, emergency telephones, lighted pathways/sidewalks, controlled access to dorms/residences, and 24-hour key card dorm locks.

REQUIREMENTS: Applicants must be graduates of an accredited secondary school with 18 academic credits, including 4 years of English, 3 of math, and 2 or more each of foreign language, history, science, and social studies. The GED is accepted. For music scholarships, an audition is required. Depending on high school GPA, some students will be required to submit either SAT or ACT scores. The SAT and ACT scores above do not reflect the entire incoming freshman class, rather they include scores from all freshmen with a GPA below 3.25, and scores from freshmen with a GPA at or above 3.25 that did not apply as a test-optional student. AP and CLEP credits are accepted. Important factors in the admissions decision are advanced placement or honors courses, evidence of special talent, and leadership record. To graduate, students must complete a minimum of 122 semester hours with a minimum GPA of 2.0. Distribution requirements include 8 hours of natural science, 6 hours each of English, history, social science, and religion, 4 to 6 hours of intercultural/internship experience, 3 hours each of mathematics and fine arts, 2 to 3 hours, 1 hour of freshman experience and 1 to 3 hours of senior capstone courses (specific to the major), and a minimum of 3 hours (intermediate level) of foreign language. **Procedure:** Freshmen are admitted to all sessions. Entrance exams should be taken in the spring of the junior year or fall of the senior year. There are early decision, early admissions, and deferred admissions plans. Early decision applications should be filed by November 1; regular applications, by February 1 for fall entry; and December 1 for spring entry. Notification of early decision is sent December 1; regular decision, March 15. 46 early decision candidates were accepted for the 2017-2018 class. Applications are accepted on-line. **Transfer Students:** 30 transfer students enrolled in 2016-2017. Transfer students are admitted based on the academic record of all colleges or universities a student has attended, their high school record, and scores from the SAT or ACT. For additional information, see pages 11 & 12 of the 2016-17 Presbyterian College Catalog. 48 of 122 credits required for the bachelor's degree must be completed at PC. **International Students:** There are 88 international students enrolled. They must take the TOEFL with a minimum score of 550 on the paper-based TOEFL (PBT) or 80 on the Internet-based version (iBT). They must also take the SAT or ACT.

ADMISSIONS: 60% of the 2017-2018 applicants were accepted. The SAT scores for the 2017-2018 freshman class were: Critical Reading-- 21% below 500, 52% between 500 and 599, 21% between 600 and 699, and 6% between 700 and 800. Math-- 20% below 500, 48% between 500 and 599, 26% between 600 and 699, and 6% between 700 and 800. The ACT scores were 3% between 12 and 17, 33% between 18 and 23, 46% between 24 and 29, and 18% above 30. 53% of the current freshmen were in the top fifth of their class; 81% were in the top two fifths. 8 freshmen graduated first in their class. **Admissions Contact:** Suzanne M. Petrusch, VP for Enrollment Management & Marketing. Email: *admissions@presby.edu* Web: *www.presby.edu*

FINANCIAL AID: In 2017-2018, 100% of all full-time freshmen received some form of financial aid. 76% of all full-time freshmen received need-based aid. The average freshman award was $33,838. Need-based scholarships or need-based grants averaged $5,219 ($12,908 maximum); need-based self-help aid (loans and jobs) averaged $2,321 ($5,057 maximum); non-need-based athletic scholarships averaged $16,530 ($27,886 maximum); other non-need-based awards and non-need-based scholarships averaged $11,929 ($29,318 maximum); and $940 from other forms of aid. 34% of undergraduate students work part-time. The average financial indebtedness of the 2017 graduate was $42,809. The FAFSA code is 003445. The priority date for freshman financial aid applications for fall entry is February 15. The deadline for filing freshman financial aid applications for fall entry is May 15.

SOUTH CAROLINA STATE UNIVERSITY *(The complete profile is made available exclusively on our website, www.barronspac.com)*

SOUTHERN WESLEYAN UNIVERSITY *(The complete profile is made available exclusively on our website, www.barronspac.com)*

THE CITADEL, THE MILITARY COLLEGE OF SOUTH CAROLINA — D-4

www.citadel.edu

Charleston, SC 29409 — (843) 953-5230, (800) 868-1842

Fax: (843) 953-7036 — **Email:** admissions@citadel.edu

Full-time: 2308 men, 195 women
Part-time: 150 men, 40 women
Graduate: 323 men, 484 women
Year: semesters, summer session
Room & Board: $7924

Faculty: 193
Ph.D.s: 94%
Student/Faculty: 12 to 1
Tuition: $12,755 ($34,518)
Freshman Class: 2620 applied, 2156 accepted, 734 enrolled

SAT CR/M: 525/530 **ACT:** 23
Application Deadline: July 15

CEEB CODE: 5108
COMPETITIVE

The Citadel, The Military College of South Carolina, established in 1842 by the South Carolina legislature, is a liberal arts military college supported by the state and offers degrees in the humanities, business, math, science, engineering, and education. Tuition figures for students in the Corps of Cadets include charges for lab fees, athletic fees, most books, school supplies, uniforms, alterations, and laundry and dry cleaning. There are 5 undergraduate schools and 1 graduate school. In addition to regional accreditation, The Citadel, has baccalaureate program accreditation with AACSB, ABET, and ACS. The 300-acre campus is in a suburban area in Charleston, SC. Including any residence halls, there are 69 buildings.

STUDENT LIFE: 60% of undergraduates are from South Carolina. Others are from 43 states, and 12 foreign countries. 9% are African American; 76% White; 7% Hispanic; 4% two or more races; 2% Asian American; 1% American Indian/Alaska Native; 1% Foreign. **Male To Female Ratio:** 3.9:1. The average age of freshmen is 18; all undergraduates, 20. 15% do not continue beyond their first year; 85% remain to graduate. **Housing:** 2135 students can be accommodated in college dorms. All cadets live in barracks. On-campus housing is guaranteed for all 4 years. Alcohol is not permitted. Upperclassmen may keep cars.

FACULTY/CLASSROOMS: All teach undergraduates and do research. No introductory courses are taught by graduate students. The average class size in an introductory lecture is 25 and in a regular course is 20.

PROGRAMS OF STUDY: The Citadel, confers B.A., B.S., B.S.B.A., B.S.C.E., and B.S.E.E. degrees. Master's degrees are also awarded. Bachelor's degrees are awarded in BIOLOGICAL SCIENCE (biology/biological science), BUSINESS (business administration and management), COMMUNICATIONS AND THE ARTS (English, French, German, and Spanish), COMPUTER AND PHYSICAL SCIENCE (chemistry, computer science, mathematics, and physics), EDUCATION (health education, physical education, and secondary education), ENGINEERING AND ENVIRONMENTAL DESIGN (civil engineering and electrical/electronics engineering), SOCIAL SCIENCE (criminal justice, history, political science/government, and psychology). Engineering is the strongest academically. Business administration has the largest enrollment.

ACTIVITIES: There are no fraternities or sororities. There are 100 groups on campus, including bagpipe, band, cheerleading, choir, chorale, debate, drill team, ethnic, honors, literary magazine, marching band, newspaper, pep band, political, professional, religious, student government, and yearbook. Popular campus events include Parents Weekend, Corps Day, and Parades most friday afternoons during fall and spring semesters. **Sports:** There are 8 intercollegiate sports for men and 6 for women, and 24 intramural sports for men and 24 for women. Facilities include a stadium, field house, golf driving range, wrestling room, baseball batting tunnel, weight and wrestling rooms, tennis courts, an all-weather track, and playing fields. The boating center is on campus and the Citadel Beach House is within a half-hour drive of the college. **Graduates:** From July 1, 2016 to June 30, 2017, 651 bachelor's degrees were awarded. The most popular majors were business/marketing (29%), engineering (19%), and homeland security (17%). In an average class, 60% graduate in 4 years or less, 68% graduate in 5 years or less, and 66% graduate in 6 years or less. Of the 2016 graduating class, 90% were employed within 6 months of graduation.

SERVICES: Counseling and information services are available, as is tutoring in every subject. **Library/Resources:** The library contains 193,992 volumes, 1.2 million microform items, and 5,538 audio/video tapes/CDs/DVDs, and subscribes to 1,260 periodicals including electronic. Computerized library services include interlibrary loans, database searching, Internet access, and Wi-Fi capability. **Physically Challenged Students:** 80% of the campus is accessible. Facilities include wheelchair ramps, elevators, special parking, and specially equipped restrooms. **Special:** Work-study programs, internships, dual majors, independent study, and study abroad are available. Qualified students may enroll in a separate honors program. There is a teacher certification program. There are 8 national honor societies, Phi Beta Kappa, a freshman honors program, and 1 departmental honors program. **Visiting:** There are regularly scheduled orientations for prospective students, including an interview with an admissions counselor and a campus tour guided by a cadet. There are guides for informal visits, visitors may sit in on classes, and stay overnight. To schedule a visit, contact the Admissions Office. **Campus Safety and Security:** Measures include 24-hour foot and vehicle patrol, emergency notification system, and security escort services. There are emergency telephones, lighted pathways/sidewalks, and controlled access to dorms/residences.

REQUIREMENTS: The SAT or ACT is required. High school diploma is required and GED is accepted. Applicants must be between 17 and 22, unmarried, and must meet certain physical requirements. 19 high school preparation should include 4 units in English and math, 3 in lab science: biology, chemistry, or physics, 2 each in foreign language and social science, 1 each in academic elective, visual/perfoming arts, phys ed or ROTC, and 1 in American history. AP and CLEP credits are accepted. Important factors in the admissions decision are advanced placement or honors courses, extracurricular activities record, and leadership record. To graduate, students must complete 121 to 139 credit hours, depending on the major, with an overall GPA of 2.0 (2.5 for education and health, exercise, and sport science majors). The required core curriculum for all majors includes study in 5 areas: English, history, math, science, social sciences, computer literacy, and foreign languages. Specific course requirements include 8 semesters of ROTC, 4 of English and science, 2 of math and history, and 1 of social science. In addition, cadets must satisfy disciplinary requirements and observe the honor system. **Procedure:** Freshmen are admitted in the fall. Entrance exams should be taken by February of the senior year. There is a rolling admissions plan. Application deadlines are open. The fall 2017 application fee was $40. Notification is sent on a rolling basis. Applications are accepted on-line. **Transfer Students:** 98 transfer students enrolled in 2016-2017. Applicants must meet freshmen entrance requirements and submit official transcripts from high school and all previous colleges attended. Transfer students must have completed a minimum of 2 semesters as full-time students (minimum 12 hours each semester) and maintained a GPA of 2.0. A full year of coursework, including half the required hours in the major, must be completed at The Citadel. A statement of good standing from prior institutions and an interview are required. **International Students:** There are 26 international students enrolled. They must take the TOEFL with a minimum score of 550 on the paper-based TOEFL (PBT) or 80 on the Internet-based version (iBT).

ADMISSIONS: 82% of the 2017-2018 applicants were accepted. The SAT scores for the 2017-2018 freshman class were: Critical Reading-- 39% below 500, 40% between 500 and 599, 18% between 600 and 699, and 3% between 700 and 800. Math-- 31% below 500, 49% between 500 and 599, 19% between 600 and 699, and 1% between 700 and 800. The ACT scores were 5% between 12 and 17, 56% between 18 and 23, 34% between 24 and 29, and 5% above 30. 30% of the current freshmen were in the top fifth of their class; 59% were in the top two fifths. **Admissions Contact:** Lt. Col. John Powell, Director of Admissions. Email: *admissions@citadel.edu* Web: *www.citadel.edu*

FINANCIAL AID: In 2017-2018, 84% of all full-time freshmen received some form of financial aid. 61% of all full-time freshmen received need-based aid. The average freshman award was $14,144. Need-based scholarships or need-based grants averaged $13,821; need-based self-help aid (loans and jobs) averaged $3,447; non-need-based athletic scholarships averaged $26,632; other non-need-based awards and non-need-based scholarships averaged $3,447; and $7,300 from other forms of aid. The average financial indebtedness of the 2017 graduate was $34,955. The FAFSA code is 003423. The priority date for freshman financial aid applications for fall entry is March 1.

UNIVERSITY OF SOUTH CAROLINA AIKEN C-3

www.usca.edu

Aiken, SC 29801 (803) 641-3366

Fax: (803) 641-3727 Email: admit@usca.edu

Full-time: 963 men, 1755 women
Part-time: 229 men, 407 women
Graduate: 36 men, 116 women
Year: semesters, summer session
Room & Board: $7592

SAT EBR-W/M: 522/505 **ACT:** 20
Application Deadline: August 1

Faculty: 154
Ph.D.s: 73%
Student/Faculty: 18 to 1
Tuition: $10,502 ($20,702)
Freshman Class: 3075 applied, 1628 accepted, 573 enrolled
CEEB CODE: 5840
COMPETITIVE

University of South Carolina Aiken, founded in 1961 is a comprehensive liberal arts institution committed to active learning through teaching, faculty and student scholarship, research, creative activities and service. The university offers degrees in the arts and sciences and in the professional disciplines of business, education, and nursing. There are 5 undergraduate schools and 3 graduate schools. In addition to regional accreditation, USCA has baccalaureate program accreditation with AACSB, ABET, NASM, and CCNE. The 453-acre campus is in a suburban area 55 miles from Columbia, South Carolina, 15 miles from Augusta, Georgia. Including any residence halls, there are 25 buildings.

STUDENT LIFE: 88% of undergraduates are from South Carolina. Others are from 31 states, 21 foreign countries, and Canada. 59% are White; 4% Hispanic; 4% two or more races; 3% Foreign; 26% African American; 2% race unknown; 1% Asian American. **Female To Male Ratio:** 1.9:1. The average age of freshmen is 18; all undergraduates, 22. 32% do not continue beyond their first year; 41% remain to graduate. **Housing:** 974 students can be accommodated in college housing, which includes dorms and on-campus apartments. On-campus housing is available on a first-come, first-served basis, and is available on a lottery system for upperclassmen. 75% of students commute. All students may keep cars.

FACULTY/CLASSROOMS: 50% of faculty are male; 50% are female. All teach undergraduates. No introductory courses are taught by graduate students. The average class size in an introductory lecture is 16 and in a laboratory is 14.

PROGRAMS OF STUDY: USCA confers B.A., B.S., B.S.Business Administration, B.A.Ed, B.S.Ed, B.A.Spec.Ed, B.A.I.S, and B.S.N. degrees. Master's degrees are also awarded. Bachelor's degrees are awarded in BIOLOGICAL SCIENCE (biology/biological science), BUSINESS (business administration and management), COMMUNICATIONS AND THE ARTS (communications, English, and fine arts), COMPUTER AND PHYSICAL SCIENCE (applied mathematics, chemistry, clinical laboratory science, and computer mathematics), EDUCATION (early childhood education, elementary education, middle school education, music education, secondary education, and special education), ENGINEERING AND ENVIRONMENTAL DESIGN (engineering/mechanical emp/energy sys focus), HEALTH PROFESSIONS (exercise science and nursing), SOCIAL SCIENCE (history, interdisciplinary studies, political science/government, psychology, and sociology). Business, nursing, exercise and sports science have the largest enrollments.

ACTIVITIES: 7% of men belong to 7 national fraternities; 6% of women belong to 7 national sororities. There are 84 groups on campus, including band, cheerleading, choir, chorus, dance, drama, ethnic, honors, international, jazz band, LGBT, literary magazine, musical theater, newspaper, pep band, political, professional, religious, social, social service, and student government. Popular campus events include Homecoming, Midnight Madness, and Fall Fest. **Sports:** There are 5 intercollegiate sports for men and 6 for women, and 10 intramural sports for men and 10 for women. Facilities include an activities center, baseball, basketball, a soccer/intramural/softball field, cross-country, equestrian, football (non-tackle) tennis, golf, volleyball, ultimate Frisbee, and a wellness/exercise center. **Graduates:** From July 1, 2016 to June 30, 2017, 496 bachelor's degrees were awarded. The most popular majors were business administration (25%), nursing (18%), and exercise and sports science (10%). In an average class, 1% graduate in 3 years or less, 21% graduate in 4 years or less, 35% graduate in 5 years or less, and 41% graduate in 6 years or less.

SERVICES: Counseling and information services are available, as is tutoring in most subjects, such as math and writing. There is a reader service for the blind, and individual subject tutoring available upon request. **Library/Resources:** The library contains 138,795 volumes, 1,478 microform items, and 4,695 audio/video tapes/CDs/DVDs, and subscribes to 106,345 periodicals including electronic. Computerized library services include interlibrary loans, database searching, Internet access, and Wi-Fi capability. Special learning facilities include an art gallery, planetarium, a science education center, a language lab, adult (reentering) programs, career counseling, employment services for undergraduates, minority student services, on-campus day care, and veteran & military student center. **Physically Challenged Students:** All of the campus is accessible. Facilities include wheelchair ramps, elevators, special parking, specially equipped restrooms, lowered drinking fountains, lowered telephones, and special housing. **Special:** Cross-registration is permitted with other schools in the University of South Carolina system. Co-op programs, internships, study abroad, student-designed majors, and work-study programs are offered. B.A.-B.S. degrees in Interdisciplinary Studies, nondegree study, and pass/fail options are possible. There are 14 national honor societies, a freshman honors program, and 11 departmental honors programs. **Visiting:** There are regularly scheduled 2-day orientations for prospective students. There are guides for informal visits and visitors may sit in on classes. To schedule a visit, contact the Admissions Office. **Campus Safety and Security:** Measures include 24-hour foot and vehicle patrol, emergency notification system, self-defense education, and security escort services. There are emergency telephones, lighted pathways/sidewalks, and controlled access to dorms/residences.

REQUIREMENTS: The SAT or ACT is required. Admission is based on a combination of an applicant's scores on college entrance exams and high school GPA. Applicants are required to submit 21 academic credits, including 4 units each of English and math, 3 units of science (with lab), 2 units each of foreign language and social studies, 1 of US history, and phys ed or ROTC, and 4 electives from 3 different areas such as computer science, English, fine arts, foreign language, humanities, certain lab sciences, a math above algebra II, and social science. It is strongly suggested that 1 unit be in computer science programming. AP and CLEP credits are accepted. Important factors in the admissions decision are advanced placement or honors courses, recommendations by school officials, and leadership record. Students must complete a minimum of 120 credit hours, with at least a 2.0 GPA. USC Aiken has a strong liberal arts emphasis. General education requirements include courses in English, math, applied speech, natural science, social and behavioral sciences, humanities, non-western studies, and history. In addition, students must complete a critical inquiry course, a prescribed number of writing intensive courses and inter-curricular enrichment events. **Procedure:** Freshmen are admitted to all sessions. Entrance exams should be taken by the fall of the senior year. There are early admissions, deferred admissions, and rolling admissions plans. Applications should be filed by August 1 for fall entry; December 1 for spring entry. The fall 2017 application fee was $45. Notification is sent on a rolling basis. Applications are accepted on-line. **Transfer Students:** 397 transfer students enrolled in 2016-2017. The college GPA is considered. A high school transcript is required of applicants with fewer than 30 semester hours. 30 of 120 credits required for the bachelor's degree must be completed at USCA. **International Students:** There are 102 international students enrolled. They must take the TOEFL with a minimum score of 551 on the paper-based TOEFL (PBT) or 80 on the Internet-based version (iBT). They must also take the SAT or ACT.

ADMISSIONS: 53% of the 2017-2018 applicants were accepted. The SAT scores for the 2017-2018 freshman class were: Math-- 45% below 500, 45% between 500 and 599, and 10% between 600 and 699. Evidence-Based Reading/Writing-- 38% below 500, 46% between 500 and 599, 14% between 600 and 699, and 2% between 700 and 800. The ACT scores were 21% between 12 and 17, 59% between 18 and 23, 18% between 24 and 29, and 1% above 30. 33% of the current freshmen were in the top fifth of their class; 65% were in the top two fifths. 8 freshmen graduated first in their class. **Admissions Contact:** Andrew Hendrix, Director of Admissions. Email: *admit@usca.edu* Web: *www.usca.edu*

FINANCIAL AID: The average freshman award was $11,028. Need-based scholarships or need-based grants averaged $7,179; need-based self-help aid (loans and jobs) averaged $3,177; non-need-based athletic scholarships averaged $4,597; and other non-need-based awards and non-need-based scholarships averaged $4,087. The average financial indebtedness of the 2017 graduate was $27,739. The FAFSA code is 003449. The priority date for freshman financial aid applications for fall entry is February 15. The deadline for filing freshman financial aid applications for fall entry is March 15.

UNIVERSITY OF SOUTH CAROLINA AT COLUMBIA — C-3

www.sc.edu

Columbia, SC 29208 — **(803) 777-7700**, **(800) 868-5872**

Fax: (803) 777-0101 — **Email: admissions-ugrad@sc.edu**

Full-time: 10,835 men, 12,790 women	**Faculty:** 854
Part-time: 820 men, 663 women	**Ph.D.s:** 84%
Graduate: 3374 men, 4918 women	**Student/Faculty:** 25 to 1
Year: semesters, summer session	**Tuition:** $11,854 ($28,528)
Room & Board: $9872	**Freshman Class:** 25057 applied, 17073 accepted, 5110 enrolled
SAT CR/M: 605/605 **ACT:** required	**CEEB CODE:** 5818
Application Deadline: December 1	**VERY COMPETITIVE**

University of South Carolina at Columbia, founded in 1801, is a publicly assisted institution serving the entire state of South Carolina. In addition to the main campus at Columbia, there are 3 senior campuses at Aiken, Beaufort, and Upstate, and 4 regional campuses at Lancaster, Salkehatchie, Sumter, and Union. There are 11 undergraduate schools and 12 graduate schools. In addition to regional accreditation, USCC has baccalaureate program accreditation with AACSB, ABET, ACEJMC, ACPE, CSAB, NASM, and NLN. The 444-acre campus is in an urban area in the downtown area of Columbia. Including any residence halls, there are 181 buildings.

STUDENT LIFE: 65% of undergraduates are from South Carolina. Others are from 50 states, 115 foreign countries, and Canada. 9% are African American; 77% White; 4% Hispanic; 4% two or more races; 3% Asian American; 2% Foreign; 1% race unknown. **Female To Male Ratio:** 1.2:1. The average age of freshmen is 18; all undergraduates, 21. 13% do not continue beyond their first year; 72% remain to graduate. **Housing:** 6838 students can be accommodated in college housing, which includes married student dorms and on-campus apartments. In addition, there are honors houses, language/international houses, special-interest houses, fraternity houses, sorority houses, wellness, residential college, and environmentally housing. On-campus housing is guaranteed for the freshman year only and is available on a lottery system for upperclassmen. 64% of students commute. All students may keep cars.

FACULTY/CLASSROOMS: 59% of faculty are male; 41% are female. All teach undergraduates all do research, and 61% do both. No introductory courses are taught by graduate students. The average class size in an introductory lecture is 30; in a laboratory is 23; and in a regular course is 29.

PROGRAMS OF STUDY: USCC confers B.A., B.A.I.S., B.A.I.S., B.A.J.M.C., B.F.A., B.M., B.S., B.S.B.A., B.S.C., B.S.C.S., B.S.E., B.S.I.S., B.S.N., B.S.P.E., B.S.W., and BarSc. degrees. Associate, master's, and doctoral degrees are also awarded. Bachelor's degrees are awarded in BIOLOGICAL SCIENCE (biology/biological science and marine science), BUSINESS (accounting, banking and finance, business administration and management, business economics, hotel/motel and restaurant management, insurance, management science, marketing/retailing/merchandising, office supervision and management, real estate, retailing, and sports management), COMMUNICATIONS AND THE ARTS (advertising, art history and appreciation, broadcasting, classics, communications, comparative literature, dance, dramatic arts, English, fine arts, French, German, journalism, media arts, music, public relations, Russian, Spanish, speech/debate/rhetoric, and studio art), COMPUTER AND PHYSICAL SCIENCE (chemistry, computer science, geology, geophysics and seismology, mathematics, physics, and statistics), EDUCATION (art education, early childhood education, elementary education, middle school education, music education, and physical education), ENGINEERING AND ENVIRONMENTAL DESIGN (biomedical engineering, chemical engineering, civil engineering, computer engineering, electrical/electronics engineering, environmental science, and mechanical engineering), HEALTH PROFESSIONS (exercise science, nursing, and public health), SOCIAL SCIENCE (African American studies, anthropology, criminal justice, economics, European studies, experimental psychology, geography, history, interdisciplinary studies, Latin American studies, philosophy, political science/government, psychology, religion, social work, sociology, and women's studies). Engineering, business, and nursing are the strongest academically. Biology, nursing, and experimental psychology have the largest enrollments.

ACTIVITIES: 13% of men belong to 22 national fraternities; 28% of women belong to 16 national sororities. There are 387 groups on campus, including art, band, cheerleading, chess, choir, chorale, chorus, computers, dance, debate, drama, drill team, ethnic, film, forensics, honors, international, jazz band, LGBT, literary magazine, marching band, musical theater, newspaper, opera, orchestra, pep band, photography, political, professional, radio and TV, religious, social, social service, student government, symphony, and yearbook. Popular campus events include First-Year Reading Experience, Civil Rights Tour, Parents Weekend, Alternative Spring and Fall Break Trips, Homecoming Week, and Carolina Cares. **Sports:** There are 9 intercollegiate sports for men and 11 for women, and 29 intramural sports for men and 29 for women. Facilities include football and soccer stadiums, a basketball coliseum, a field house, volleyball and basketball practice facility, baseball, softball, and practice fields, and an all-weather track. There is also a recreation center with badminton, basketball, handball/racquetball, an aquatics center, climbing wall, and weight room. **Graduates:** From July 1, 2016 to June 30, 2017, 7162 bachelor's degrees were awarded. The most popular majors were buisness/marketing (28%), biological life sciences (11%), education, and and health professions and related programs (9%). In an average class, 56% graduate in 4 years or less, 70% graduate in 5 years or less, and 72% graduate in 6 years or less. Of the 2016 graduating class, 23% were enrolled in graduate school within 6 months of graduation.

SERVICES: Counseling and information services are available, as is tutoring in every subject. There is a reader service for LD students, as well as listening devices, and sign language interpreting. There is also a reader service for the blind. **Library/Resources:** The library contains 4.5 million volumes, 5.5 million microform items. Computerized library services include interlibrary loans, database searching, Internet access, and Wi-Fi capability. Special learning facilities include an art gallery, natural history museum, planetarium, radio station, and TV station. **Physically Challenged Students:** 85% of the campus is accessible. Facilities include wheelchair ramps, elevators, special parking, specially equipped restrooms, special class scheduling, lowered drinking fountains, transportation, and special housing. **Special:** USC transmits live interactive televised instruction to more than 20 locations in the state. Cross-registration is offered with the National Technological University in Engineering and through the National Student Exchange. Internships in many fields, study abroad in many countries through the Byrnes International Center, co-op programs, and work-study programs are available. Double majors through the colleges of humanities and social sciences and science and math, student-designed majors, an interdisciplinary studies degree, and a 3-2 engineering degree with the College of Charleston are offered. Credit for military experience, nondegree study, and pass/fail options also are possible. There are 28 national honor societies, Phi Beta Kappa, and a freshman honors program. **Visiting:** There are regularly scheduled orientations for prospective students, placement tests, and advisement on registrations for classes. Day and a half. There are guides for informal visits. To schedule a visit, contact the USC Visitor's Center. **Campus Safety and Security:** Measures include 24-hour foot and vehicle patrol, emergency notification system, self-defense education, and security escort services. There are shuttle buses, emergency telephones, lighted pathways/sidewalks, and controlled access to dorms/residences. All police officers have state wide authority.

REQUIREMENTS: Admission as a freshman is primarily based upon a combination of grades earned in specific high-school courses and official SAT or ACT scores. Additional factors may be taken into consideration, such as extraordinary personal circumstances, special talents, outstanding extracurricular activities, and evidence of leadership. AP and CLEP credits are accepted. Important factors in the admissions decision are leadership record and advanced placement or honors courses. All students must maintain a GPA of 2.0 in 120 semester hours including 24 in their major. Distribution requirements include 6 hours in English, 6 in Numerical/Analytical Reasoning, 12 in Liberal Arts, 7 in Natural Sciences, and Foreign Language demonstrated proficiency. **Procedure:** Freshmen are admitted to all sessions. Entrance exams should be taken during spring of the junior year and fall of the senior year, if necessary. There is a rolling admissions plan. Applications should be filed by December 1 for fall entry; November 1 for spring entry; and May 1 for summer entry. The fall 2017 application fee was $50. Applications are accepted on-line. **Transfer Students:** 1965 transfer students enrolled in 2016-2017. They must have a cumulative GPA of 2.25 from all regionally accredited colleges (remedial courses are not included in the GPA computation). Freshman requirements must be met if the student has attempted fewer than 30 semester hours. Transfer requirements are higher for certain majors. Please refer to http:/www.sc.edu/admissions/transrequire.php for current information. 30 of 120 credits required for the bachelor's degree must be completed at USCC. **International Students:** There are 390 international students enrolled. They must take the TOEFL with a minimum score of 550 on the paper-based TOEFL (PBT) or 77 on the Internet-based version (iBT). The SAT and ACT are recommended.

ADMISSIONS: 68% of the 2017-2018 applicants were accepted. The SAT scores for the 2017-2018 freshman class were: Critical Reading-- 4% below 500, 42% between 500 and 599, 44% between 600 and 699, and 10% between 700 and 800. Math-- 4% below 500, 37% between 500 and 599, 48% between 600 and 699, and 10% between 700 and 800. The ACT scores were 12% between 18 and 23, 62% between 24 and 29, and 26% above 30. 57% of the current freshmen were in the top fifth of their class; 88% were in the top two fifths. 66 freshmen graduated first in their class. **Admissions Contact:** R. Scott Verzyl, Associate Vice President for Enrollment. Email: *admissions-ugrad@sc.edu* Web: *www.sc.edu*

FINANCIAL AID: In 2017-2018, 96% of all full-time freshmen received

some form of financial aid. The average freshman award was $8,614. Need-based scholarships or need-based grants averaged $5,433; need-based self-help aid (loans and jobs) averaged $3,375; non-need-based athletic scholarships averaged $13,670; other non-need-based awards and non-need-based scholarships averaged $5,886; and $3,335 from other forms of aid. The average financial indebtedness of the 2017 graduate was $31,073. USCC is a member of CSS. The deadline for filing freshman financial aid applications for fall entry is April 15.

UNIVERSITY OF SOUTH CAROLINA UPSTATE *(The complete profile is made available exclusively on our website, www.barronspac.com)*

VOORHEES COLLEGE — C-3

www.voorhees.edu

Denmark, SC 29042 — **(803) 780-1023**

Fax: (803) 780-1430 — **Email: admissions@voorhees.edu**

Full-time: 185 men, 222 women	**Faculty:** 30
Part-time: 4 men, 4 women	**Ph.D.s:** 43%
Graduate: n/av	**Student/Faculty:** 7 to 1
Year: semesters, summer session	**Tuition:** $12,630
Room & Board: $7346	**Freshman Class:** n/av
SAT or ACT: recommended	**CEEB CODE:** 5863
Application Deadline: n/av	**COMPETITIVE**

Voorhees College, founded in 1897, is a historically black liberal arts college affiliated with the Protestant Episcopal Church. There is 1 undergraduate school. In addition to regional accreditation, Voorhees has baccalaureate program accreditation with ACBSP. The 342-acre campus is in a small town 50 miles south of Columbia. Including any residence halls, there are 26 buildings.

STUDENT LIFE: 70% of undergraduates are from South Carolina. Others are from 17 states, and 1 foreign country. 80% are from public schools. 93% are African American; 2% White; 2% race unknown; 1% Hispanic; 1% Foreign. 90% are Protestant. **Female To Male Ratio:** 1.2:1. The average age of freshmen is 18; all undergraduates, 22. 40% remain to graduate. **Housing:** 537 students can be accommodated in college dorms. On-campus housing is guaranteed for all 4 years. 72% of students live on campus. Alcohol is not permitted. All students may keep cars.

FACULTY/CLASSROOMS: 58% of faculty are male; 42% are female. All teach undergraduates. No introductory courses are taught by graduate students. The average class size in an introductory lecture is 30; in a laboratory is 20; and in a regular course is 25.

PROGRAMS OF STUDY: Voorhees confers B.A. and B.S. degrees. Bachelor's degrees are awarded in BIOLOGICAL SCIENCE (biology/biological science), BUSINESS (accounting, business administration and management, organizational leadership and management, and recreation and leisure services), COMMUNICATIONS AND THE ARTS (communications and English), COMPUTER AND PHYSICAL SCIENCE (computer science and mathematics), HEALTH PROFESSIONS (health), SOCIAL SCIENCE (criminal justice and sociology). Biology, and business administration are the strongest academically. Biology, business administration, and sports management have the largest enrollments.

ACTIVITIES: 20% of men belong to 4 national fraternities; 20% of women belong to 4 national sororities. There are 20 groups on campus, including cheerleading, choir, chorus, computers, honors, newspaper, pep band, political, professional, radio and TV, religious, social, student government, and yearbook. Popular campus events include Career Awareness Week, Black History Month, Religious Emphasis Week, National Women's History Month, Business Week, National Library Week, and Founders Day Week. **Sports:** There are 4 intercollegiate sports for men and 4 for women, and 4 intramural sports for men and 4 for women. Facilities include a gym, swimming pool, tennis and basketball courts, baseball and softball fields, track field, a weight room, a dance studio, and a student center. **Graduates:** From July 1, 2016 to June 30, 2017, 70 bachelor's degrees were awarded. The most popular majors were criminal justice (19%), sports management (14%), biology, and child development and health and recreation (10%). In an average class, 44% graduate in 4 years or less, 46% graduate in 5 years or less, and 10% graduate in 6 years or less.

SERVICES: Counseling and information services are available, as is tutoring in most subjects. There is remedial math, reading, and writing. **Library/Resources:** The library contains 309,479 volumes, 26,110 microform items, and 298 audio/video tapes/CDs/DVDs, and subscribes to 14,522 periodicals including electronic. Computerized library services include interlibrary loans, database searching, Internet access, and Wi-Fi capability. Special learning facilities include a radio station, an academic success center and a writing center. **Physically Challenged Students:** 90% of the campus is accessible. Facilities include wheelchair ramps, elevators, special parking, specially equipped restrooms, and lowered drinking fountains. **Special:** Voorhees offers cooperative education, internships in some programs, work-study, an evening/Saturday program, off-campus summer study, dual majors, credit by exam, and a degree completion program. Cross-registration with Denmark Technical College and interdisciplinary majors, such as health and recreation, are possible. There are 3 national honor societies and 1 departmental honors program. **Visiting:** There are regularly scheduled orientations for prospective students, consisting of senior visitation days held January through April. There are guides for informal visits, visitors may sit in on classes, and stay overnight. To schedule a visit, contact Adrian West. **Campus Safety and Security:** Measures include 24-hour foot and vehicle patrol and emergency notification system. There are lighted pathways/sidewalks.

REQUIREMENTS: The SAT or ACT is recommended, with a satisfactory minimum score of 600 on the SAT or 16 on the ACT. Applicants must be high school graduates or hold a GED. Students should have earned 24 academic credits in high school, including 4 units each of English and math, 3 units of science, 1 unit each of foreign language (optional), history, social studies, economics/government, physical education, and computer science/keyboarding, and 7 electives. A campus visit is advised. AP and CLEP credits are accepted. Important factors in the admissions decision are advanced placement or honors courses, recommendations by school officials, and alumni. To graduate, students must earn at least 122 credit hours, with at least 30 in the major, and have a minimum GPA of 2.0. The 50-hour general education requirement includes 12 hours of English/speech, 5 hours of humanities, 3 hours of foreign language, 1 hour of freshmen orientation, 2 hours of physical fitness, 12 hours of economics and history and 15 hours of mathematics, science and technology. A number of free electives and a senior seminar are also required. An English proficiency exam and an exit exam must be passed. **Procedure:** Freshmen are admitted to all sessions. Entrance exams should be taken in the senior year. There are deferred admissions and rolling admissions plans. Applications should be filed by December 16 for spring entry. The fall 2017 application fee was $25. Notification of early decision is sent August 16; regular decision, December 16. **Transfer Students:** 20 transfer students enrolled in 2016-2017. Transfer students must submit complete records, including a confidential report from each college attended. The confidential report form is provided by the Office of Admission and Recruitment. Students with fewer than 30 semester hours must submit their high school record with rank in class and GPA. The SAT is recommended; a satisfactory composite score is expected. An interview is advised. **International Students:** There are 3 international students enrolled. They must take the TOEFL. They must also take the SAT or ACT.

Admissions Contact: Diondra Smalls, Director of Admissions and Recruitment. Email: *admissions@voorhees.edu* Web: *www.voorhees.edu*

FINANCIAL AID: The average freshman award was $14,315. Need-based self-help aid (loans and jobs) averaged $5,500. Voorhees is a member of CSS. The college's own financial statement, and or SAR is required. The FAFSA code is 003455. The priority date for freshman financial aid applications for fall entry is April 16.

WINTHROP UNIVERSITY — C-1

www.winthrop.edu

Rock Hill, SC 29733 — **(803) 323-2191**, **(800) 946-8476**

Fax: (803) 323-2137 — **Email: admissions@winthrop.edu**

Full-time: 1350 men, 3138 women	**Faculty:** 280; IIA, -$
Part-time: 172 men, 354 women	**Ph.D.s:** 76%
Graduate: 244 men, 815 women	**Student/Faculty:** 14 to 1
Year: semesters, summer session	**Tuition:** $15,220 ($29,136)
Room & Board: $8740	**Freshman Class:** 4562 applied, 3350 accepted, 1050 enrolled
SAT CR/M: 556/531 **ACT:** 22	**CEEB CODE:** 5910
Application Deadline: May 1	**COMPETITIVE**

Winthrop University, is a public, comprehensive institution, nationally recognized for quality and value blending liberal arts, professional programs, global awareness, and civic engagement. No matter what students study at Winthrop, they are prepared for successful careers, engaged in our democratic society, responsive to local and global concerns, and grounded in values that give meaning to their lives. Winthrop embodies the characteristics essential to being one of the best – a high-achieving, diverse student body, a national caliber curriculum, an undergraduate residential experience emphasizing community, and institutional values centered around global learning, undergraduate research, and engaged public service. There are 4 undergraduate schools and 4 graduate schools. In addition to regional accreditation, WU has baccalaureate program accreditation with AACSB, ABET, ACEJMC, CSAB, CSWE, NASAD, NASM, and CIDA. The 445-acre campus is in a small town 23 miles south of Charlotte, North Carolina. Including any residence halls, there are 75 buildings.

STUDENT LIFE: 91% of undergraduates are from South Carolina. Others are from 42 states, 45 foreign countries, and Canada. 60% are White; 5% Hispanic; 3% two or more races; 28% African American; 2% Foreign; 1% Asian American. **Female To Male Ratio:** 2.4:1. The average age of freshmen is 18; all undergraduates, 21. 27% do not continue beyond their first year; 74% remain to graduate. **Housing:** 2519 students can be accommodated in college housing, which includes dorms and on-campus apartments. In addition, there are honors houses, special-interest houses, fraternity houses, sorority houses, and independent housing. On-campus housing is guaranteed for the freshman year only, is available on a first-come, and first-served basis. 53% of students live on campus. All students may keep cars.

FACULTY/CLASSROOMS: 38% of faculty are male; 62% are female. All teach undergraduates. No introductory courses are taught by graduate students. The average class size in an introductory lecture is 30 and in a laboratory is 15.

PROGRAMS OF STUDY: WU confers B.A., B.S., B.F.A., B.M., B.M.E., and B.S.W. degrees. Master's degrees are also awarded. Bachelor's degrees are awarded in AGRICULTURE (environmental studies), BIOLOGICAL SCIENCE (biology/biological science and nutrition), BUSINESS (business administration and management, electronic business, and sports management), COMMUNICATIONS AND THE ARTS (art, art history and appreciation, communications, dance, English, English literature, fine arts, French, German, modern language, music, music performance, public relations, Spanish, technical and business writing, and theatre arts), COMPUTER AND PHYSICAL SCIENCE (chemistry, computer science, and mathematics), EDUCATION (athletic training, early childhood education, elementary education, middle school education, music education, physical education, secondary education, special education, and sports and wellness studies), ENGINEERING AND ENVIRONMENTAL DESIGN (environmental science and interior design), HEALTH PROFESSIONS (exercise science and medical laboratory technology), SOCIAL SCIENCE (economics, history, philosophy, philosophy and religion, political science/government, psychology, religion, social work, sociology, and Spanish studies). Business administration, biology, psychology, and fine arts have the largest enrollments.

ACTIVITIES: 3% of men belong to 7 national fraternities; 9% of women belong to 9 national sororities. There are 160 groups on campus, including art, band, cheerleading, chess, choir, chorale, chorus, computers, dance, drama, environmental, ethnic, honors, international, jazz band, LGBT, literary magazine, musical theater, newspaper, opera, pep band, political, professional, radio and TV, religious, social, social service, and student government. Popular campus events include Welcome Week, Convocation and Picnic, Basketball Game Tailgaiting, Homecoming Talent Show, and Movies at DiGiorgio Campus Center. **Sports:** There are 7 intercollegiate sports for men and 9 for women, and 16 intramural sports for men and 16 for women. Facilities include a coliseum, athletics and recreational fields, ropes course, an 18-hole disc golf course, tennis complex, a track & field stadium and a soccer field. The Physical Ed and Wellness center includes a climbing wall, raquetball courts, 25 yd pool, basketball courts, weight room, cardio room space, and aerobic/activity rooms. **Graduates:** From July 1, 2016 to June 30, 2017, 1006 bachelor's degrees were awarded. The most popular majors were business administration (19%), education (16%), and psychology (6%). In an average class, 39% graduate in 4 years or less, 55% graduate in 5 years or less, and 58% graduate in 6 years or less. Of the 2016 graduating class, 25% were enrolled in graduate school within 6 months of graduation, and 46% were employed.

SERVICES: Counseling and information services are available, as is tutoring in some subjects, such as math, a writing center, and subjects tutoring program within residence halls. There is a reader service for the blind. The Academic Success Center focuses on helping students achieve academic excellence and earn their college degree. **Library/Resources:** The library contains 454,562 volumes, 1.2 million microform items, and 15,277 audio/video tapes/CDs/DVDs, and subscribes to 40,755 periodicals including electronic. Computerized library services include interlibrary loans, database searching, Internet access, and Wi-Fi capability. Special learning facilities include an art gallery, radio station, TV station, an audio recording studio, an early childhood lab school, the MIDI lab, the instructional technology center, a theatre, mathematics tutorial center, and the conservatory of music. **Physically Challenged Students:** 95% of the campus is accessible. Facilities include wheelchair ramps, elevators, special parking, specially equipped restrooms, special class scheduling, lowered drinking fountains, lowered telephones, and special housing. **Special:** Cross-registration is permitted with the Charlotte Area Educational Consortium. Internships in Business, Education, Visual and Performing Arts and Arts and Sciences. Study abroad in 20 countries and on-campus work-study programs are offered. Interdisciplinary majors such as science communication, nondegree study, and pass/fail options are possible. There are 15 national honor societies, Phi Beta Kappa, a freshman honors program, and 24 departmental honors programs. **Visiting:** There are regularly scheduled orientations for prospective students. There are guides for informal visits, visitors may sit in on classes, and stay overnight. To schedule a visit, contact the Admissions Office. **Campus Safety and Security:** Measures include 24-hour foot and vehicle patrol, emergency notification system, self-defense education, and security escort services. There are emergency telephones, lighted pathways/sidewalks, and controlled access to dorms/residences.

REQUIREMENTS: The SAT or ACT is required, as is graduation from an accredited secondary school. The GED will be accepted. Applicants must have successfully completed 4 credits in high school English, 3 each in math, and lab science, 2 each in social studies and foreign language, 1 in United States history, and 4 in electives that must be taken from at least three different fields selected from among computer science, English, fine arts, foreign languages, humanities, laboratory science (excluding earth science, general physical science, general environmental science, or other introductory science courses for which biology and/or chemistry is not a prerequisite), mathematics above the level of Algebra II, and social sciences. It is suggested that 1 unit be in computer science which includes programming (not just keyboarding) and 1 unit in fine arts (i.e. appreciation of, history, or performance). A GPA of 3.0 is required. AP and CLEP credits are accepted. Important factors in the admissions decision are advanced placement or honors courses, evidence of special talent, and geographical diversity. Students must complete a minimum of 120 semester hours, including a 38 to 53 hour general education distribution requirement, and maintain a minimum GPA of 2.0. Specific courses in writing, oral communication, computer information systems, critical issues, and the American Constitution are required. **Procedure:** Freshmen are admitted to all sessions. Entrance exams should be taken December of senior year. There are deferred admissions and rolling admissions plans. Applications should be filed by May 1 for fall entry; January 2 for spring entry. The fall 2017 application fee was $40. Notification is sent on a rolling basis. Applications are accepted on-line. **Transfer Students:** 357 transfer students enrolled in 2016-2017. Applicants must be eligible to return to the previous institution and submit college transcripts. 30 of 120 credits required for the bachelor's degree must be completed at Winthrop. **International Students:** There are 69 international students enrolled. They must take the TOEFL with a minimum score of 520 on the paper-based TOEFL (PBT) or 68 on the Internet-based version (iBT). They must also take the SAT or ACT.

ADMISSIONS: 73% of the 2017-2018 applicants were accepted. The SAT scores for the 2017-2018 freshman class were: Critical Reading--22% below 500, 46% between 500 and 599, 27% between 600 and 699, and 5% between 700 and 800. Math-- 28% below 500, 51% between 500 and 599, 16% between 600 and 699, and 2% between 700 and 800. The ACT scores were 13% between 12 and 17, 51% between 18 and 23, 32% between 24 and 29, and 5% above 30. **Admissions Contact:** Eduardo Prieto, Vice President for Access and Enrollment. Email: *admissions@winthrop.edu* Web: *www.winthrop.edu*

FINANCIAL AID: 18% of undergraduate students work part-time. Winthrop is a member of CSS. The FAFSA code is 003456. The priority date for freshman financial aid applications for fall entry is March 1.

WOFFORD COLLEGE B-1
www.wofford.edu

Spartanburg, SC 29303 (864) 597-4130

Fax: (864) 597-4147
Email: admission@wofford.edu
Full-time: 800 men, 749 women
Faculty: 130; IIB, av$
Part-time: 17 men, 18 women
Ph.D.s: 90%
Graduate: n/av
Student/Faculty: 11 to 1
Year: 4-1-4, summer session
Tuition: $38,705
Room & Board: $11,180
Freshman Class: 2718 applied, 1870 accepted, 415 enrolled
SAT CR/M: 585/597 **ACT:** 26
CEEB CODE: 5912
Application Deadline: February 1
VERY COMPETITIVE

Wofford College, founded in 1854, is a private four-year institution affiliated with the United Methodist Church, offering programs in liberal arts and preprofessional studies. It is especially known for leadership in studies abroad, service learning, and its innovative apartment-style housing, known as "The Wofford Village." There is 1 undergraduate school. In addition to regional accreditation, Wofford has baccalaureate program accreditation with NASDTEC. The 170-acre campus is in an urban area 70 miles southwest of Charlotte. Including any residence halls, there are 72 buildings.

STUDENT LIFE: 56% of undergraduates are from South Carolina. Others are from 37 states, and 12 foreign countries. 67% are from public schools. 80% are White; 8% African American; 3% Asian American; 3% Hispanic; 3% two or more races; 2% Foreign; 1% race unknown. 67% are Protestant; 18% Unknown Religious affiliation; 12% Catholic. **Male To Female Ratio:** 1.1:1. The average age of freshmen is 18; all undergraduates, 20. 10% do not continue beyond their first year; 82% remain to graduate. **Housing:** 1479 students can be accommodated in college housing, which includes dorms and on-campus apartments. On-campus housing is guaranteed for all 4 years. 94% of students live on campus. All students may keep cars.

FACULTY/CLASSROOMS: 60% of faculty are male; 40% are female. All teach undergraduates, 30% do research, and 30% do both. No introductory courses are taught by graduate students. The average class size in an introductory lecture is 21; in a laboratory is 21; and in a regular course is 17.

PROGRAMS OF STUDY: Wofford confers B.A. and B.S. degrees. Bachelor's degrees are awarded in AGRICULTURE (environmental studies), BIOLOGICAL SCIENCE (biology/biological science), BUSINESS (accounting, banking and finance, business economics, and finance), COMMUNICATIONS AND THE ARTS (art history, Chinese, creative writing, dramatic arts, English, French, German, Spanish, studio art, and theatre arts), COMPUTER AND PHYSICAL SCIENCE (applied mathematics, chemistry, computer science, mathematics, and physics), SOCIAL SCIENCE (African American studies, crosscultural studies, economics, gender studies, history, humanities, Latin American studies, philosophy, political science/government, psychology, religion, and sociology). Biology, foreign languages, and finance/accounting are the strongest academically. Biology, business economics, and Spanish have the largest enrollments.

ACTIVITIES: 43% of men belong to 8 national fraternities; 55% of women belong to 4 national sororities. There are 98 groups on campus, including interfaith youth core, band, cheerleading, choir, chorale, chorus, college bowl team, computers, dance, drama, environmental, ethnic, international, jazz band, LGBT, literary magazine, newspaper, orchestra, pep band, photography, political, professional, religious, social, social service, student government, and yearbook. Popular campus events Phi Beta Kappa Day, Honors Day, Novel Experience, and Winter Lighting. **Sports:** There are 9 intercollegiate sports for men and 8 for women, and 10 intramural sports for men and 10 for women. Facilities include a stadium, arena, tennis complex, soccer and baseball fields, a wellness and athletic center, sand volleyball court and basketball court. **Graduates:** From July 1, 2016 to June 30, 2017, 374 bachelor's degrees were awarded. The most popular majors were business/marketing (26%), biological/life sciences (18%), and foreign languages (12%). In an average class, 78% graduate in 4 years or less, 81% graduate in 5 years or less, and 82% graduate in 6 years or less.

SERVICES: Counseling and information services are available, as is tutoring in every subject. There is a reader service for the blind. **Library/Resources:** The library contains 184,715 volumes, 21,150 microform items, and 3,866 audio/video tapes/CDs/DVDs, and subscribes to 47,528 periodicals including electronic. Computerized library services include interlibrary loans, database searching, Internet access, and Wi-Fi capability. Special learning facilities include an art gallery, international studies center with simultaneous translation capabilities, arboretum, greenhouse, the Goodall environmental studies center at Glendale Shoals, Montgomery Music Building, and The Space in The Mungo Center that houses several programs: The Space to: Prepare (houses the Career Services office, the Sophomore Experience and the Institute); The Space to: Impact (a competitive four-year program teaching design thinking, entrepreneurship, project management & the consultative approach to problem solving; The Space to: Launch (supports students in the concept, development & launch of a business idea); The Space to: Consult (student consulting group providing business & organizations strategies to improve performance); The Space to: Explore (helps make the Wofford liberal arts degree global-ready by providing internship & travel opportunities). **Physically Challenged Students:** 95% of the campus is accessible. Facilities include wheelchair ramps, elevators, special parking, specially equipped restrooms, special class scheduling, lowered drinking fountains, and lowered telephones. **Special:** Special academic programs include study abroad in 70 countries, a Washington semester, and a concentration in Latin American and Caribbean studies. In addition, students can major or minor in multiple fields or complete interdisciplinary, humanities, or intercultural studies majors. The January interim allows students to concentrate on a single study project, internship, or travel experience. There are 9 national honor societies and a chapter of Phi Beta Kappa. **Visiting:** There are regularly scheduled orientations for prospective students, information sessions are offered Mon-Fri at 10:00am and 2:00pm. A visit consists of an information session with an admission counselor and campus tour. There are guides for informal visits, visitors may sit in on classes, and stay overnight. To schedule a visit, contact the Director of Admission. **Campus Safety and Security:** Measures include 24-hour foot and vehicle patrol, emergency notification system, self-defense education, and security escort services. There are emergency telephones, lighted pathways/sidewalks, and controlled access to dorms/residences.

REQUIREMENTS: The SAT or ACT is required, as is the ACT Optional Writing test. Applicants must be graduates of an accredited secondary school. The GED is accepted. Students should have completed 4 years each of high school English and math, 3 units of lab science, foreign language, and social studies. An essay is required and an interview is strongly recommended. AP and CLEP credits are accepted. Important factors in the admissions decision are advanced placement or honors courses, leadership record, and personality/intangible qualities. To graduate, students must complete 124 credits, with 24 to 40 credits in the major and a minimum GPA of 2.0. General education requirements include 3 credits each of history, philosophy, religion, mathematics and cultures & peoples, 3-4 credits of fine arts, 4-10 credits of foreign languages, 4-16 credits of natural sciences, 6 credits of English, and 2 credits of phys ed. Students must complete 4 interim projects, and a freshman humanities seminar. **Procedure:** Freshmen are admitted to all sessions. Entrance exams should be taken in the spring of the junior year or fall of the senior year. There are early decision, early admissions, and deferred admissions plans. Early decision applications should be filed by November 1; regular applications, by February 1 for fall entry. The fall 2017 application fee was $35. Notification of early decision is sent December 1; regular decision, March 15. 1155 early decision candidates were accepted for the 2017-2018 class. 52 applicants were on the 2017 waiting list; 52 were admitted. Applications are accepted on-line. **Transfer Students:** 19 transfer students enrolled in 2016-2017. Transfers should have a minimum GPA of 2.5 from a 4-year college or 3.0 from a 2-year college, or they may submit ACT or SAT scores. An interview is recommended. 30 of 124 credits required for the bachelor's degree must be completed at Wofford. **International Students:** There are 28 international students enrolled. They must take the TOEFL with a minimum score of 550 on the paper-based TOEFL (PBT) or 80 on the Internet-based version (iBT). They must also take the SAT or ACT.

ADMISSIONS: 69% of the 2017-2018 applicants were accepted. The SAT scores for the 2017-2018 freshman class were: Critical Reading-- 12% below 500, 40% between 500 and 599, 42% between 600 and 699, and 6% between 700 and 800. Math-- 11% below 500, 35% between 500 and 599, 42% between 600 and 699, and 11% between 700 and 800. Writing-- 21% below 500, 38% between 500 and 599, 37% between 600 and 699, and 4% between 700 and 800. The ACT scores were 3% below 12, 15% between 12 and 17, 27% between 18 and 23, 23% between 24 and 29, and 32% above 30. 69% of the current freshmen were in the top fifth of their class; 96% were in the top two fifths. 7 freshmen graduated first in their class. **Admissions Contact:** John W. Birney, Director of Admission. Email: *admission@wofford.edu* Web: *www.wofford.edu*

FINANCIAL AID: In 2017-2018, 93% of all full-time freshmen received some form of financial aid. 65% of all full-time freshmen received need-based aid. The average freshman award was $27,649. Need-based scholarships or need-based grants averaged $28,257; need-based self-help aid (loans and jobs) averaged $3,312; non-need-based athletic scholarships averaged $21,855; and other non-need-based awards and non-need-based scholarships averaged $14,262. 19% of undergraduate students work part-time. The average financial indebtedness of the 2017 graduate was $24,721. Wofford is a member of CSS. The FAFSA code is 003457. The deadline for filing freshman financial aid applications for fall entry is March 15.

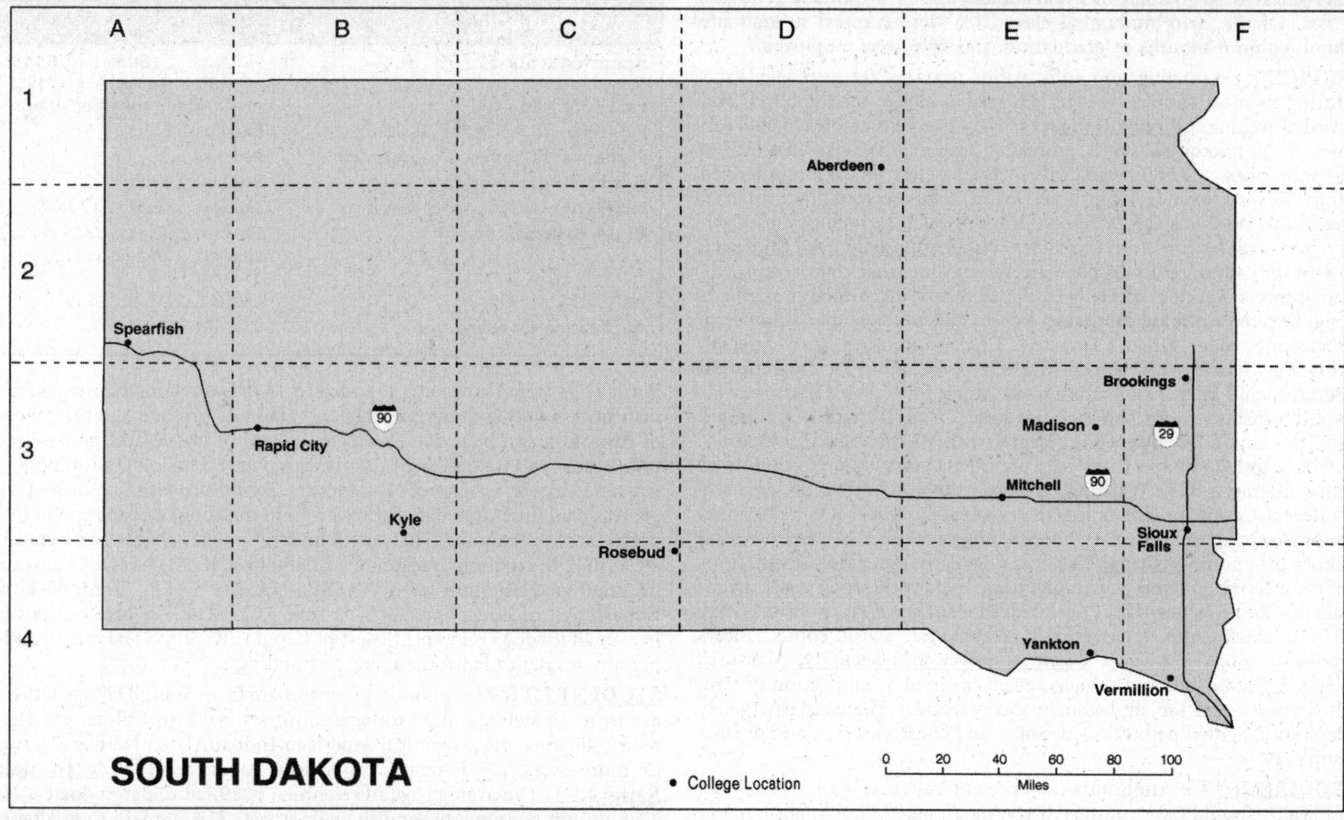

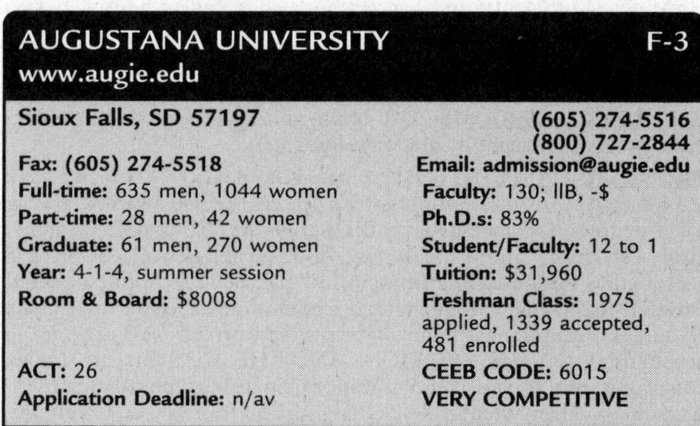

AUGUSTANA UNIVERSITY F-3

www.augie.edu

Sioux Falls, SD 57197	(605) 274-5516 (800) 727-2844
Fax: (605) 274-5518	Email: admission@augie.edu
Full-time: 635 men, 1044 women	Faculty: 130; IIB, -$
Part-time: 28 men, 42 women	Ph.D.s: 83%
Graduate: 61 men, 270 women	Student/Faculty: 12 to 1
Year: 4-1-4, summer session	Tuition: $31,960
Room & Board: $8008	Freshman Class: 1975 applied, 1339 accepted, 481 enrolled
ACT: 26	CEEB CODE: 6015
Application Deadline: n/av	VERY COMPETITIVE

Augustana University, founded in 1860, is a comprehensive liberal arts and professional university of the Lutheran church. There is 1 undergraduate school and 1 graduate school. In addition to regional accreditation, Augustana has baccalaureate program accreditation with NASM, ACGC, CED, CCNE, CAATE, ACS, SDBN, and NAACLS. The 100-acre campus is in an urban area of Sioux Falls, SD. Including any residence halls, there are 47 buildings.

STUDENT LIFE: 53% of undergraduates are from out of state, mostly the Midwest. Students are from 33 states, and 31 foreign countries. 89% are from public schools. 84% are White; 8% Foreign; 3% Hispanic; 2% African American; 1% Asian American; 1% American Indian/Alaska Native; 1% two or more races. 57% are Protestant; 21% Catholic. **Female To Male Ratio:** 1.9:1. The average age of freshmen is 18; all undergraduates, 20. 14% do not continue beyond their first year; 71% remain to graduate. **Housing:** 1277 students can be accommodated in college housing, which includes married student dorms, on-campus apartments, and off-campus apartments. In addition, there are special-interest houses, and theme houses. On-campus housing is guaranteed for all 4 years, is guaranteed for the freshman year only, is available on a first-come, and first-served basis. 67% of students live on campus. Alcohol is not permitted. All students may keep cars.

FACULTY/CLASSROOMS: 49% of faculty are male; 51% are female. 91% teach undergraduates and all do research. No introductory courses are taught by graduate students. The average class size in an introductory lecture is 32; in a laboratory is 18; and in a regular course is 20.

PROGRAMS OF STUDY: Augustana confers B.A. and B.S. degrees. Master's degrees are also awarded. Bachelor's degrees are awarded in BIOLOGICAL SCIENCE (biochemistry and biology/biological science), BUSINESS (accounting, business administration and management, business communications, and sports management), COMMUNICATIONS AND THE ARTS (American Sign Language, art, classics, communications, dramatic arts, English, French, German, journalism, modern language, music, Spanish, and theatre arts), COMPUTER AND PHYSICAL SCIENCE (chemical physics, chemistry, computer science, information sciences and systems, mathematics, and physics), EDUCATION (athletic training, drama education, elementary education, health education, middle school education, music education, physical education, social studies education, and special education), ENGINEERING AND ENVIRONMENTAL DESIGN (engineering physics), HEALTH PROFESSIONS (exercise science, medical laboratory science, and nursing), SOCIAL SCIENCE (American studies, anthropology, economics, history, interdisciplinary studies, international studies, philosophy, philosophy and religion, physical fitness/movement, political science/government, psychology, religion, and sociology). Nursing, biology, and business are the strongest academically. Nursing, biology, and education have the largest enrollments.

ACTIVITIES: There are no fraternities or sororities. There are 80 groups on campus, including art, band, cheerleading, chess, choir, chorale, chorus, computers, dance, drama, drill team, environmental, ethnic, honors, international, jazz band, LGBT, literary magazine, musical theater, newspaper, opera, orchestra, pep band, photography, political, professional, religious, social, social service, student government, symphony, and yearbook. Popular campus events include Christmas at Augustana, Viking Days, Boe Forum on Public Affairs, and Semester Shutdown. **Sports:** There are 9 intercollegiate sports for men and 10 for women, and 55 intramural sports for men and 55 for women. Facilities include an athletic facility, practice gyms, football complex with stadium, soccer, baseball and softball fields, a pool, weight/cardio work-out room, and a health, phys ed, and recreation center. **Graduates:** From July 1, 2016 to June 30, 2017, 359 bachelor's degrees were awarded. The most popular majors were business/marketing (17%), nursing/health professions

(17%), and education (16%). In an average class, 56% graduate in 4 years or less, 69% graduate in 5 years or less, and 71% graduate in 6 years or less. Of the 2016 graduating class, 21% were enrolled in graduate school within 6 months of graduation, and 99% were employed.

SERVICES: Counseling and information services are available, as is tutoring in most subjects. There is a reader service for the blind, and remedial writing. **Library/Resources:** The library contains 245,600 volumes, 8,450 microform items, and 8,200 audio/video tapes/CDs/DVDs, and subscribes to 7,500 periodicals including electronic. Computerized library services include interlibrary loans, database searching, Internet access, and Wi-Fi capability. Special learning facilities include an art gallery, and a center for Western studies. **Physically Challenged Students:** 75% of the campus is accessible. Facilities include wheelchair ramps, elevators, special parking, specially equipped restrooms, special class scheduling, lowered drinking fountains, lowered telephones, special housing, Arkenstone reader, Dragon Dictate, TTYs, and doorbell lights. **Special:** Cross-registration with Upper Midwest Association for Intercultural Education and Higher Education Consortium for Urban Affairs is available. Internships (both national and local), study abroad in unlimited countries, and a 3-2 engineering degree with Washington University in St. Louis and Columbia University are offered. A Washington semester with Lutheran College Washington Consortium or American University is offered. Credit for life experience is possible. There are 12 national honor societies, a freshman honors program, and 21 departmental honors programs. **Visiting:** There are regularly scheduled orientations for prospective students, a campus tour, visits with professors, current students, and coaches. There are guides for informal visits, visitors may sit in on classes, and stay overnight. To schedule a visit, contact Alexis Fredin at (605) 274-5516. **Campus Safety and Security:** Measures include 24-hour foot and vehicle patrol, emergency notification system, self-defense education, and security escort services. There are emergency telephones, lighted pathways/sidewalks, and controlled access to dorms/residences.

REQUIREMENTS: Applicants may present either ACT or SAT scores. Applicants should have completed 4 years of high school English, math, and science, 2 years of a foreign language and 3 years of history. A transcript is required. Recommendation and essay are not required, but considered if submitted. A GPA of 2.7 is required. AP and CLEP credits are accepted. Important factors in the admissions decision are advanced placement or honors courses, extracurricular activities record, leadership record, and personality/intangible qualities. Students must complete 124 semester hours, with a minimum GPA of 2.0. General education requirements total 59 semester hours, including component courses in writing for graduation. **Procedure:** Freshmen are admitted to all sessions. Entrance exams should be taken in the spring of the junior year or early fall of the senior. There are deferred admissions and rolling admissions plans. Application deadlines are open. Notification is sent on a rolling basis. Applications are accepted on-line. **Transfer Students:** 53 transfer students enrolled in 2016-2017. Applicants must have a 2.25 GPA in previous college work. 30 of 124 credits required for the bachelor's degree must be completed at Augustana. **International Students:** There are 153 international students enrolled. They must take the TOEFL with a minimum score of 550 on the paper-based TOEFL (PBT) or 79 on the Internet-based version (iBT). They must also take the SAT or ACT, scoring 20.

ADMISSIONS: 68% of the 2017-2018 applicants were accepted. The SAT scores for the 2017-2018 freshman class were: Math-- 10% below 500, 42% between 500 and 599, 38% between 600 and 699, and 10% between 700 and 800. Evidence-Based Reading/Writing-- 16% below 500, 42% between 500 and 599, 36% between 600 and 699, and 6% between 700 and 800. The ACT scores were 1% between 12 and 17, 32% between 18 and 23, 47% between 24 and 29, and 20% above 30. 60% of the current freshmen were in the top fifth of their class; 80% were in the top two fifths. **Admissions Contact:** Nancy L. Davidson, Vice President of Enrollment. Email: *admission@augie.edu* Web: *www.augie.edu*

FINANCIAL AID: In 2017-2018, 100% of all full-time freshmen received some form of financial aid. 72% of all full-time freshmen received need-based aid. The average freshman award was $27,792. Need-based scholarships or need-based grants averaged $24,784; need-based self-help aid (loans and jobs) averaged $4,342; non-need-based athletic scholarships averaged $12,639; and other non-need-based awards and non-need-based scholarships averaged $18,116. 37% of undergraduate students work part-time. The average financial indebtedness of the 2017 graduate was $24,405. The FAFSA code is 003458. The priority date for freshman financial aid applications for fall entry is March 1.

BLACK HILLS STATE UNIVERSITY — A-2

www.bhsu.edu

Spearfish, SD 57799	**(605) 642-6343** **(800) ALL-BHSU**
Fax: (605) 642-6022	**Email: admissions@bhsu.edu**
Full-time: 859 men, 1420 women	**Faculty:** 231
Part-time: 601 men, 1140 women	**Ph.D.s:** n/av
Graduate: 113 men, 356 women	**Student/Faculty:** 20 to 1
Year: semesters, summer session	**Tuition:** $8602 ($12,802)
Room & Board: $6820	**Freshman Class:** 1355 applied, 1267 accepted, 507 enrolled
ACT: 21	**CEEB CODE:** 003459
Application Deadline: n/av	**COMPETITIVE**

Black Hills State University, founded in 1883 is a comprehensive public institution offering undergraduate and graduate programs in the college of education and behavioral sciences, college of liberal arts, and college of business and natural sciences offering over 80 majors and minors, 5 master's degree programs, 4 associate degree programs and 20 pre-professional programs. The figures given in the above capsule and in this profile are approximate. There are 3 undergraduate schools and 1 graduate school. In addition to regional accreditation, BHSU has baccalaureate program accreditation with AACSB, NASM, CAEP, South Dakota Department of Education, AASCU, and ACU. The 123-acre campus is in a small town 45 miles northwest of Rapid City, South Dakota. Including any residence halls, there are 20 buildings.

STUDENT LIFE: 74% of undergraduates are from South Dakota. Others are from 44 states, and 29 foreign countries. 82% are White; 4% Hispanic; 4% race unknown; 3% American Indian/Alaska Native; 3% two or more races; 2% Foreign; 1% African American. **Female To Male Ratio:** 1.9:1. The average age of freshmen is 19; all undergraduates, 24. 37% do not continue beyond their first year; 31% remain to graduate. **Housing:** 840 students can be accommodated in college housing, which includes married student dorms and on-campus apartments. On-campus housing is guaranteed for the freshman year only. 79% of students commute. Alcohol is not permitted. All students may keep cars.

FACULTY/CLASSROOMS: 95% teach undergraduates. No introductory courses are taught by graduate students.

PROGRAMS OF STUDY: BHSU confers B.A., B.G.S., B.A.T.S., B.S., and B.S.Ed degrees. Associate and master's degrees are also awarded. Bachelor's degrees are awarded in BIOLOGICAL SCIENCE (biology/adolescence education and biology/biological science), BUSINESS (accounting, business administration and management, business administration marketing, entrepreneurial studies, human resources, human resources/organizational mgmt, tourism, and professional program in accounting), COMMUNICATIONS AND THE ARTS (art, art studies, communication studies, communications, English, graphic communications management, graphic design, English and Professional Communication, music, Spanish, speech/debate/rhetoric, and communication arts - speech), COMPUTER AND PHYSICAL SCIENCE (applied science, chemistry, chemistry/adolescence education, industrial technology, mathematics, physical sciences, and science), EDUCATION (business education, early childhood education, elementary education, English education, general studies, mathematics education, outdoor leadership/education, physical education, reading education, science education, social science education, Spanish education K-12, and special education), ENGINEERING AND ENVIRONMENTAL DESIGN (construction technology and manufacturing technology), HEALTH PROFESSIONS (biology and exercise science), SOCIAL SCIENCE (American Indian studies, economics, history, history and political science, human services, Native American studies, political science/government, psychology, social science, and sociology). Elementary education, biology, and business administration are the strongest academically and have the largest enrollments.

ACTIVITIES: Groups on campus include art, band, cheerleading, choir, chorale, chorus, computers, dance, debate, drama, drill team, environmental, ethnic, forensics, honors, international, jazz band, LGBT, musical theater, newspaper, pep band, photography, political, professional, radio and TV, religious, social, social service, student government, and yearbook. Popular campus events include Swarm Week. **Sports:** There are 5 intercollegiate sports for men and 7 for women. Facilities include a stadium, gymnasium with basketball and volleyball courts, tennis courts, swimming pools, indoor and outdoor tracks, golf course, baseball and softball complex. **Graduates:** In an average class, 27% graduate in 4 years or less and 50% graduate in 6 years or less.

SERVICES: Counseling and information services are available, as is tutoring in most subjects. There is remedial math, reading, and writing. **Library/Resources:** Computerized library services include interlibrary loans, database searching, Internet access, and Wi-Fi capability. Special learning facilities include an art gallery, radio station, TV station, a gymnasium, and theater. **Physically Challenged Students:** Facilities include wheelchair ramps, elevators, special parking, specially equipped restrooms, lowered drinking fountains, and special housing. **Special:** There is a chapter of Phi Beta Kappa and a freshman honors program. **Visiting:** There are regularly scheduled orientations for prospective students, consisting of open houses, receptions, green and gold days. There are guides for informal visits, visitors may sit in on classes, and stay overnight. To schedule a visit, contact Beth Oaks at Beth.Oaks@BHSU.edu. **Campus Safety and Security:** Measures include 24-hour foot and vehicle patrol, emergency notification system, and security escort services. There are lighted pathways/sidewalks and controlled access to dorms/residences.

REQUIREMENTS: ACT Composite Score of 18 or above, or rank in the top 60 percent of your graduating class, or high school GPA of 2.6 on a 4.0 scale. All baccalaureate or general studies students under 24 years of age, including students transferring with fewer than 24 credit hours, must meet the following minimum high school course requirements with an overall grade point average of "C" or higher: 4 years of English, or an ACT English subtest score of 18 or above, or an advanced placement language and composition or literature and composition score of 3 or above, 3 years of advanced math (algebra and above) or an ACT mathematics subtest score of 20 or above, or an advanced placement calculus AB or calculus BC score of 3 or above, 3 years of laboratory science (biology, chemistry, or physics, or approved physical science or earth science), or an ACT science reasoning subtest score of 17 or above, or an advanced placement biology, chemistry, or physics B score of 3 or above, 3 years of social sciences, or an ACT social studies subtest score of 17 or above, or an advanced placement microeconomics, macroeconomics, comparative or US government and policies, European or US history, or psychology score of 3 or above, and 1 year of fine arts. Applications received from students with deficiencies will be reviewed on an individual basis. A GPA of 2.0 is required. AP and CLEP credits are accepted. **Procedure:** Freshmen are admitted to all sessions. Entrance exams should be taken during the senior year of high school. There are early admissions and rolling admissions plans. Application deadlines are open. The fall 2017 application fee was $20. Applications are accepted on-line. **Transfer Students:** 313 transfer students enrolled in 2016-2017. Transfer to Baccalaureate Program - Students who are under the age of 24 at the start of the term, and who are transferring into baccalaureate degree programs with fewer than 24 transfer credit hours may be required to fulfill the baccalaureate degree admission requirements. Students with 24 or more transfer credit hours with a cumulative GPA of at least 2.0 may transfer into baccalaureate degree programs. Specific degree programs may include additional admissions requirements. If students are applying for federal financial aid, they must meet federal guidelines for transfer students. Transfer to Associate Degree Program - Students who are under the age of 24 at the start of the term and who are transferring into associate degree programs with fewer than 12 transfer credit hours must meet the associate degree admission requirements. Students with 12 or more transfer credit hours with a cumulative GPA of at least 2.0 may transfer into associate degree programs. Specific degree programs may include additional admissions requirements. Non-Regental Accredited Colleges or Universities – Transfer students may be accepted from other non-Regental universities outside of the SD system; preferential consideration will be given to applicants from institutions which are accredited by their respective regional accrediting association. Non-Accredited Colleges – BHSU is not required to accept credits from a non-accredited college or university. The university may admit the applicant on a provisional basis and provide a means for the evaluation of some or all of the credits. If the last institution attended was outside the Regental system, and the transfer applicant left under academic suspension, the applicant will not be considered for admission during the period of suspension or, if suspended for an indefinite period, until one semester has passed since the last date of attendance at the previous school. Application Procedure: Transfer applicants should submit a completed admission application, a $20 non-refundable application fee, a current complete official transcript sent directly from each college, school or institution attended since high school, and an official high school transcript. The application fee is not charged to students who transfer from other South Dakota Regental schools. Applicant who are 21 years of age or younger must submit Enhanced ACT (or SAT-I) results. Applicants who are over 21 need to submit their scores if they have taken the test within the last five years. Note: Transfer students applying for federal financial aid must meet federal guidelines for transfer students. **International Students:** They must take the TOEFL. They must also take the ACT, scoring 18.

ADMISSIONS: 94% of the 2017-2018 applicants were accepted. **Admissions Contact:** Beth Oaks, Director of Admissions. Email: *admissions@bhsu.edu* Web: *www.bhsu.edu*

FINANCIAL AID: The FAFSA code is 003459. Check with the school for current application deadlines.

DAKOTA STATE UNIVERSITY E-3

www.dsu.edu

Madison, SD 57042	**(605) 256-5139** **(888) DSU-9988**
Fax: (605) 256-5020	**Email: admissions@dsu.edu**
Full-time: n/av	**Faculty:** IIB, av$
Part-time: n/av	**Ph.D.s:** n/av
Graduate: n/av	**Student/Faculty:** n/av
Year: semesters, summer session	**Tuition:** $8927 ($11,843)
Room & Board: $3359	**Freshman Class:** 600 accepted, 360 enrolled
SAT or ACT: required	**CEEB CODE:** 6247
Application Deadline: open	**COMPETITIVE**

Dakota State University, founded in 1881, is a public institution offering undergraduate programs through the Colleges of Business and Information Systems, Education, and Arts and Sciences. The figures given in the above capsule and in this profile are approximate. There are 3 undergraduate schools and 1 graduate school. In addition to regional accreditation, DSU has baccalaureate program accreditation with ACBSP, AHEA, AHIMA, and CoARC. The 56-acre campus is in a rural area 45 miles northwest of Sioux Falls. Including any residence halls, there are 22 buildings.

STUDENT LIFE: Housing: 659 students can be accommodated in college housing, which includes dorms and on-campus apartments. On-campus housing is guaranteed for the freshman year only, is available on a first-come, first-served basis, and is available on a lottery system for upperclassmen. Alcohol is not permitted. All students may keep cars.

FACULTY/CLASSROOMS: No introductory courses are taught by graduate students.

PROGRAMS OF STUDY: DSU confers B.S., B.B.A., B.G.S., and B.S.Ed. degrees. Associate, master's, and doctoral degrees are also awarded. Bachelor's degrees are awarded in BIOLOGICAL SCIENCE (biology/biological science), BUSINESS (business administration and management), COMMUNICATIONS AND THE ARTS (communications technology, English, and information technology), COMPUTER AND PHYSICAL SCIENCE (computer programming, computer game design/development, computer science, computer security and information assurance, digital arts/technology, information sciences and systems, mathematics, and physical sciences), EDUCATION (business education, computer education, elementary education, English education, health education, health information management, marketing and distribution education, mathematics education, and secondary education), ENGINEERING AND ENVIRONMENTAL DESIGN (computer graphics), HEALTH PROFESSIONS (medical records administration/services, premedicine, and respiratory therapy).

ACTIVITIES: There are no fraternities or sororities. There are 36 groups on campus, including art, band, cheerleading, choir, chorale, chorus, computers, dance, drama, ethnic, honors, international, literary magazine, musical theater, newspaper, pep band, political, professional, radio and TV, religious, social, and student government. Popular campus events include Homecoming, Convocation, and Frost Bites Week. **Sports:** There are 6 intercollegiate sports for men and 6 for women, and 3 intramural sports for men and 3 for women. Facilities include courts for basketball and racquetball, a football field, a weight room, and a swimming pool. **Graduates:** From July 1, 2016 to June 30, 2017, 145 bachelor's degrees were awarded. In an average class, 24% graduate in 4 years or less, 42% graduate in 5 years or less, and 15% graduate in 6 years or less. Of the 2016 graduating class, 1% were enrolled in graduate school within 6 months of graduation, and 96% were employed.

SERVICES: Counseling and information services are available, as is tutoring in every subject. There is a reader service for the blind, and remedial math, reading, and writing. **Library/Resources:** The library contains 177,454 volumes, 3,669 microform items, and 3,426 audio/video tapes/CDs/DVDs, and subscribes to 350 periodicals including electronic. Computerized library services include interlibrary loans, database searching, Internet access, and Wi-Fi capability. Special learning facilities include an art gallery, natural history museum, and radio station. **Physically Challenged Students:** 80% of the campus is accessible. Facilities include wheelchair ramps, elevators, special parking, specially equipped restrooms, special class scheduling, and lowered drinking fountains. **Special:** The university offers co-op programs with South Dakota State University, internships, study abroad in London, and on-campus work-study programs. Also available are the general studies degree, a 3-2 engineering degree with the University of Minnesota/Twin Cities, credit for life, military, and work experience, nondegree study, and pass/fail options. There are 2 national honor societies and a freshman honors program. **Visiting:** There are regularly scheduled orientations for prospective students, including general information and academic sessions, a campus tour, and financial aid information. There are guides for informal visits, visitors may sit in on classes, and stay overnight. To schedule a visit, contact the Admissions Office. **Campus Safety and Security:** Measures include self-defense education and security escort services. There are emergency telephones, lighted pathways/sidewalks, controlled access to dorms/residences, and foot patrol.

REQUIREMENTS: The SAT or ACT is required, with a minimum composite score of 18 on the ACT. Applicants must be graduates of an accredited secondary school or have a GED certificate, and have completed 4 years of English, 3 years each of math, science, and social studies, and 1/2 year of computer science and the fine arts. A GPA of 2.6 is required. AP and CLEP credits are accepted. All students seeking a bachelor's degree are required to complete 30 credit hours of general education coursework (math, English, science, humanities) as well as 11 credit hours of institutional specific coursework (information technology and personal health). Associate's degree seeking students are required to complete 18 credit hours of general education coursework as well as 6 credit hours of institutional specific coursework. Graduates must have a 2.0 GPA. A general education assessment exam and exit assessment are required of all students. **Procedure:** Freshmen are admitted to all sessions. Entrance exams should be taken before students register for classes. There is a rolling admissions plan. Application deadlines are open. The fall 2017 application fee was $15. Notification is sent on a rolling basis. Applications are accepted on-line. **Transfer Students:** 67 transfer students enrolled in 2016-2017. Transfer applicants must have a minimum 2.0 GPA. 32 of 128 credits required for the bachelor's degree must be completed at DSU. **International Students:** There are 120 international students enrolled. They must take the TOEFL.

ADMISSIONS: 9 freshmen graduated first in their class. **Admissions Contact:** Amy Crissinger, Director of Admission. Email: *admissions@dsu.edu* Web: *www.dsu.edu*

FINANCIAL AID: The average freshman award was $5,836. The average financial indebtedness of the 2017 graduate was $16,588. The FAFSA code is 003463. The deadline for filing freshman financial aid applications for fall entry is March 1.

DAKOTA WESLEYAN UNIVERSITY *(The complete profile is made available exclusively on our website, www.barronspac.com)*

MOUNT MARTY COLLEGE — E-4

www.mtmc.edu

Yankton, SD 57078	**(605) 668-1545** **(800) 658-4552**
Fax: (605) 668-1607	**Email: mmcadmit@mtmc.edu**
Full-time: 215 men, 500 women	**Faculty:** 35; IIB, -$
Part-time: 76 men, 301 women	**Ph.D.s:** 64%
Graduate: 50 men, 50 women	**Student/Faculty:** 10 to 1
Year: semesters, summer session	**Tuition:** $29,170
Room & Board: $7692	**Freshman Class:** 397 accepted, 190 enrolled
ACT: required	**CEEB CODE:** 6416
Application Deadline: open	**COMPETITIVE**

Mount Marty College is a private, Catholic Benedictine, liberal and coeducational arts college, open to students of all faiths and backgrounds. Mount Marty prepares students for a contemporary world of work, service to the human community, and personal growth. The figures given in the above capsule and in this profile are approximate. There are 2 undergraduate schools and 3 graduate schools. In addition to regional accreditation, MMC has baccalaureate program accreditation with ADA and NLN. The 80-acre campus is in a small town in Yankton, 60 miles northwest of Sioux City, Iowa, and 80 miles southwest of Sioux Falls. Including any residence halls, there are 11 buildings.

STUDENT LIFE: 60% of undergraduates are from South Dakota. Others are from 25 states, and 5 foreign countries. 79% are from public schools. 94% are White; 3% Hispanic; 1% African American; 1% Asian American; 1% American Indian/Alaska Native. 42% are Catholic; 36% claim no religious affiliation. **Female To Male Ratio:** 2.5:1. The average age of freshmen is 19; all undergraduates, 26. 22% do not continue beyond their first year; 61% remain to graduate. **Housing:** College-sponsored housing includes dorms. On-campus housing is guaranteed for all 4 years. 75% of students live on campus. Alcohol is not permitted. All students may keep cars.

FACULTY/CLASSROOMS: 54% of faculty are male; 46% are female. All teach undergraduates. No introductory courses are taught by graduate students. The average class size in an introductory lecture is 30; in a laboratory is 15; and in a regular course is 20.

PROGRAMS OF STUDY: MMC confers B.A., B.S. and B.S.N. degrees. Associate and master's degrees are also awarded. Bachelor's degrees are awarded in BIOLOGICAL SCIENCE (biology/biological science), BUSINESS (accounting and business administration and management), COMMUNICATIONS AND THE ARTS (English, journalism, and music), COMPUTER AND PHYSICAL SCIENCE (chemistry, computer science, mathematics, and radiological technology), EDUCATION (athletic training, elementary education, physical education, secondary education, and special education), ENGINEERING AND ENVIRONMENTAL DESIGN (environmental science), HEALTH PROFESSIONS (health care administration, medical technology, and nursing), SOCIAL SCIENCE (behavioral science, criminal justice, food production/management/services, history, religion, and social science). Nursing, business, and teacher education are the strongest academically.

ACTIVITIES: There are no fraternities or sororities. There are 50 groups on campus, including business, dentistry, nursing, psychology, art, band, choir, chorus, clubs in theatre, computers, drama, ethnic, forensics, honors, jazz band, literary magazine, musical theater, newspaper, pep band, photography, political, professional, religious, social, social service, and student government. Popular campus events include Blue & Gold Days, Formal Dances, Benedictine Lecture Series, Bowling, Carmike Movie Night, Ice Skating, Yoga, Zumba, Family Weekend, and Homecoming. **Sports:** There are 6 intercollegiate sports for men and 6 for women, and 4 intramural sports for men and 4 for women. Facilities include volleyball and basketball courts, a jogging track, racquetball courts, weight and training rooms, a stadium, an indoor gym, and an auditorium. **Graduates:** The most popular majors were health professions (28%), business (23%), and education (15%). In an average class, 30% graduate in 4 years or less and 41% graduate in 5 years or less. Of the 2016 graduating class, 5% were enrolled in graduate school within 6 months of graduation, and 96% were employed.

SERVICES: Counseling and information services are available, as is tutoring in most subjects. There is remedial math, reading, and writing. **Library/Resources:** The library contains 79,228 volumes, 11,624 microform items, and 8,465 audio/video tapes/CDs/DVDs, and subscribes to 439 periodicals including electronic. Computerized library services include interlibrary loans, database searching, Internet access, and Wi-Fi capability. Special learning facilities include an art gallery. **Physically Challenged Students:** All of the campus is accessible. Facilities include wheelchair ramps, elevators, special parking, specially equipped restrooms, special class scheduling, lowered drinking fountains, and lowered telephones. **Special:** Mount Marty offers co-op programs, internships, student-designed majors in selected studies, an accelerated degree program in business administration, credit for work, life, and military experience, and pass/fail options. There are 8 national honor societies, a freshman honors program, and 7 departmental honors programs. **Visiting:** There are regularly scheduled orientations for prospective students, including campus tours, faculty appointments, and admission and financial aid information. There are guides for informal visits, visitors may sit in on classes, and stay overnight. To schedule a visit, contact the Director of Admissions. **Campus Safety and Security:** Measures include

24-hour foot and vehicle patrol and security escort services. There are emergency telephones and lighted pathways/sidewalks.

REQUIREMENTS: The ACT is required. Applicants must be graduates of an accredited secondary school or have a GED certificate. An audition and an interview are recommended. A GPA of 2.0 is required. AP and CLEP credits are accepted. To graduate, all students must complete at least 128 credit hours, with a minimum GPA of 2.0. General education requirements include 10 credit hours in religious studies/philosophy, 9 in humanities, 6 in English, 4 each in math, natural science, and lab science, and 3 in speech. **Procedure:** Freshmen are admitted fall, spring, and summer. Entrance exams should be taken by October of the senior year. There are deferred admissions and rolling admissions plans. Application deadlines are open. The fall 2017 application fee was $25. Notification is sent on a rolling basis. Applications are accepted on-line. **Transfer Students:** 60 transfer students enrolled in 2016-2017. Transfer students with fewer than 28 semester hours must submit high school and college transcripts. A minimum GPA of 2.0 and at least 64 credit hours are required. An interview is recommended. 32 of 128 credits required for the bachelor's degree must be completed at Mount Marty. **International Students:** There are 5 international students enrolled. They must take the TOEFL.

ADMISSIONS: The ACT scores were 10% below 12, 50% between 12 and 17, 30% between 18 and 23, 5% between 24 and 29, and 5% above 30. 10% of the current freshmen were in the top fifth of their class; 56% were in the top two fifths. 5 freshmen graduated first in their class. **Admissions Contact:** Jill Paulson, Director of Admissions. Email: *mmcadmit@mtmc.edu* Web: *www.mtmc.edu*

FINANCIAL AID: In 2017-2018, 99% of all full-time freshmen received some form of financial aid. 84% of all full-time freshmen received need-based aid. The average freshman award was $12,343. The average financial indebtedness of the 2017 graduate was $17,407. The FAFSA code is 003465. The deadline for filing freshman financial aid applications for fall entry is March 1.

NORTHERN STATE UNIVERSITY — D-1

www.northern.edu

Aberdeen, SD 57401	**(605) 626-2544** **(800) 678-5330**
Fax: (605) 626-2587	**Email: admissions@northern.edu**
Full-time: 666 men, 811 women	**Faculty:** 90
Part-time: 597 men, 927 women	**Ph.D.s:** 86%
Graduate: 121 men, 409 women	**Student/Faculty:** 21 to 1
Year: semesters, summer session	**Tuition:** $8280 ($11,210)
Room & Board: $7290	**Freshman Class:** 1379 applied, 1143 accepted, 363 enrolled
ACT: 22	**CEEB CODE:** 6487
Application Deadline: September 1	**COMPETITIVE**

Northern State University, established in 1901, is a state-supported institution offering undergraduate and graduate programs in the liberal arts and sciences, business, and education. Distance delivery technology is a core mission in all programs, especially all levels of teacher preparation. The figures in the above capsule and in this profile are approximate. There are 4 undergraduate schools and 1 graduate school. In addition to regional accreditation, NSU has baccalaureate program accreditation with NASM and CAEP. The 72-acre campus is in an urban area 1.5 miles south of Aberdeen's city center. Including any residence halls, there are 21 buildings.

STUDENT LIFE: 77% of undergraduates are from South Dakota. Others are from 41 states, 36 foreign countries, and Canada. 87% are White; 3% Hispanic; 2% African American; 2% American Indian/Alaska Native; 2% race unknown. **Female To Male Ratio:** 1.6:1. The average age of freshmen is 18; all undergraduates, 22. 30% do not continue beyond their first year; 70% remain to graduate. **Housing:** 850 students can be accommodated in college housing, which includes married student dorms and on-campus apartments, and living learning communities. On-campus housing is guaranteed for all 4 years. 59% of students commute. Alcohol is not permitted. All students may keep cars.

FACULTY/CLASSROOMS: 50% of faculty are male; 50% are female. All teach undergraduates and all do research. No introductory courses are taught by graduate students. The average class size in an introductory lecture is 25 and in a laboratory is 18.

PROGRAMS OF STUDY: NSU confers B.A., B.S., B.M.E., B.G.S., and B.S.Ed. degrees. Associate and master's degrees are also awarded. Bachelor's degrees are awarded in BIOLOGICAL SCIENCE (biology/biological science), BUSINESS (accounting, banking and finance, business administration and management, business economics, international business management, marketing/retailing/merchandising, and personnel management), COMMUNICATIONS AND THE ARTS (English, fine arts, French, German, music, and Spanish), COMPUTER AND PHYSICAL SCIENCE (chemistry and mathematics), EDUCATION (art education, business education, early childhood education, elementary education, foreign languages education, health education, middle school education, music education, physical education, science education, secondary education, and special education), ENGINEERING AND ENVIRONMENTAL DESIGN (environmental science), HEALTH PROFESSIONS (medical laboratory technology, predentistry, premedicine, and speech pathology/audiology), SOCIAL SCIENCE (community services, criminal justice, economics, history, human services, physical fitness/movement, political science/government, prelaw, psychology, social science, and sociology). Business and education are the strongest academically.

ACTIVITIES: There are no fraternities or sororities. There are 100 groups on campus, including art, band, cheerleading, chess, choir, chorale, chorus, computers, dance, debate, drama, drill team, drum and bugle corps, environmental, ethnic, forensics, honors, international, jazz band, LGBT, literary magazine, marching band, musical theater, newspaper, orchestra, pep band, photography, political, professional, radio and TV, religious, social, social service, student government, and symphony. Popular campus events include Gypsy Day, Gypsy Week, and I Hate Winter Weekend. **Sports:** There are 6 intercollegiate sports for men and 7 for women, and 11 intramural sports for men and 11 for women. Facilities include a sports complex, football stadium, all-weather track, a 160-meter track, an Olympic-size pool, weight room, racquetball courts, human performance lab, basketball courts, and arena. **Graduates:** From July 1, 2016 to June 30, 2017, 300 bachelor's degrees were awarded. The most popular majors were business (33%), education (20%), and social sciences (10%). Of the 2016 graduating class, 33% were enrolled in graduate school within 6 months of graduation, and 99% were employed.

SERVICES: Counseling and information services are available, as is tutoring in most subjects. There is remedial math, reading, and writing. There is an educational media center, a math lab, reading and writing centers, an ASL interpreter for the deaf, and a speech, language, and hearing clinic. **Library/Resources:** The library contains 179,721 volumes, 381,874 microform items, and 10,092 audio/video tapes/CDs/DVDs, and subscribes to 45,379 periodicals including electronic. Computerized library services include interlibrary loans, database searching, Internet access, and Wi-Fi capability. Special learning facilities include an art gallery, radio station, TV station, a fine arts center. **Physically Challenged Students:** 90% of the campus is accessible. Facilities include wheelchair ramps, elevators, special parking, specially equipped restrooms, lowered drinking fountains. **Special:** Opportunities are provided for internships, a Washington semester, work-study programs, a B.A.-B.S. degree, dual majors, a general studies degree, credit by exam, and nondegree study. Study abroad and a co-op program in international business are available. Technology proficiency certification is available with a diverse selection of certifications. There are 4 national honor societies, Phi Beta Kappa, a freshman honors program, and 4 departmental honors programs. **Visiting:** There are regularly scheduled orientations for prospective students, consisting of a welcome presentation, registration, refreshments, an academic visit, a campus tour, lunch, a financial aid presentation, a student panel, and cost and scholarship presentation. There are guides for informal visits, visitors may sit in on classes, and stay overnight. To schedule a visit, contact the Admissions Office. **Campus Safety and Security:** Measures include emergency notification system, self-defense education, and security escort services. There are emergency telephones, lighted pathways/sidewalks, and controlled access to dorms/residences.

REQUIREMENTS: Minimum ACT composite score of 18, or students must earn a high school GPA of at least 2.6 on a 4.0 scale, or rank in the top 60% of their graduating class. Graduation from an accredited secondary school is required; a GED will be accepted. Applicants should submit a minimum academic record distributed as follows: 4 years of English, 3 each of math, science, and social studies, and 1 year of fine arts. AP and CLEP credits are accepted. Important factors in the admissions decision are evidence of special talent, advanced placement or honors courses, and extracurricular activities record. Students must complete a minimum of 120 semester hours, with 27 to 36 in the major, and must maintain a 2.0 minimum GPA. The core curriculum consists of courses in English, history, fine arts, science, math, and psychology. In addition, there are specific course requirements. All students must pass a comprehensive exam. **Procedure:** Freshmen are admitted fall, spring, and summer. Entrance exams should be taken during the summer before the senior year. There are early admissions, deferred admissions, and rolling admissions plans. Applications should be filed by September 1 for fall entry. The fall 2017 application fee was $20. Notification is sent on a rolling basis. **Transfer Students:** 119 transfer students enrolled in 2016-2017. Applicants must submit official transcripts from all previous colleges attended. D grades do not transfer. If the applicant has not maintained a C average, an ACT score that places the applicant in the upper 50% of college-bound freshmen may be submitted for consideration. 24 of 120 credits required for the bachelor's degree must be completed at NSU. **International Students:** There are 107 international students enrolled. They must take the TOEFL with a minimum score of 525 on the paper-based TOEFL (PBT) or 61 on the Internet-based version (iBT).

ADMISSIONS: 83% of the 2017-2018 applicants were accepted. The SAT scores for the 2017-2018 freshman class were: Critical Reading-- 58% below 500, 30% between 500 and 599, 8% between 600 and 699, and 4% between 700 and 800. Math-- 47% below 500, 38% between 500 and 599, 12% between 600 and 699, and 3% between 700 and 800. The ACT scores were 42% below 12, 26% between 12 and 17, 15% between 18 and 23, 14% between 24 and 29, and 3% above 30. **Admissions Contact:** JoEllen Lindner, VP Student Affairs & Enrollment Management. Email: *admissions@northern.edu* Web: *www.northern.edu*

FINANCIAL AID: In 2017-2018, 90% of all full-time freshmen received some form of financial aid and need-based aid. NSU is a member of CSS. The CCS/Profile, FAFSA, and either the FFS, or SFS is required. The FAFSA code is 003466. The priority date for freshman financial aid applications for fall entry is March 1.

OGLALA LAKOTA COLLEGE *(The complete profile is made available exclusively on our website, www.barronspac.com)*

PRESENTATION COLLEGE *(The complete profile is made available exclusively on our website, www.barronspac.com)*

SINTE GLESKA UNIVERSITY *(The complete profile is made available exclusively on our website, www.barronspac.com)*

SOUTH DAKOTA SCHOOL OF MINES AND TECHNOLOGY B-3

www.sdsmt.edu

Rapid City, SD 57701 (605) 394-2414 (877) 877-6044
Fax: (605) 394-1979 **Email:** admissions@sdsmt.edu

Full-time: 1350 men, 370 women	**Faculty:** 143
Part-time: 223 men, 158 women	**Ph.D.s:** 88%
Graduate: 243 men, 80 women	**Student/Faculty:** 13 to 1
Year: semesters, summer session	**Tuition:** $10,400 ($14,580)
Room & Board: $8170	**Freshman Class:** 1127 applied, 991 accepted, 454 enrolled
SAT CR/M/W: 560/600/500 **ACT:** 26	**CEEB CODE:** 6652
Application Deadline: August 15	**COMPETITIVE+**

South Dakota School of Mines and Technology, founded in 1885, is a public university offering undergraduate and graduate programs in engineering, science, and mathematics. The figures given in the above capsule and in this profile are approximate. There is 1 undergraduate school and 1 graduate school. In addition to regional accreditation, SDSMT has baccalaureate program accreditation with ABET, CSAB, and ACS. The 120-acre campus is in a suburban area 350 miles northeast of Denver. Including any residence halls, there are 21 buildings.

STUDENT LIFE: 55% of undergraduates are from South Dakota. Others are from 45 states, 39 foreign countries, and Canada. 82% are White; 6% Foreign; 3% Hispanic; 3% two or more races; 2% American Indian/Alaska Native; 1% African American; 1% Asian American; 1% race unknown. **Male To Female Ratio:** 3.0:1. The average age of freshmen is 19; all undergraduates, 22. 20% do not continue beyond their first year; 55% remain to graduate. **Housing:** 671 students can be accommodated in college housing, which includes dorms and off-campus apartments. In addition, there are fraternity houses and sorority houses. On-campus housing is available on a first-come and first-served basis. 67% of students commute. Alcohol is not permitted. All students may keep cars.

FACULTY/CLASSROOMS: 76% of faculty are male; 24% are female. All teach undergraduates and 31% do research. Graduate students teach 4% of introductory courses. The average class size in an introductory lecture is 38; in a laboratory is 17; and in a regular course is 21.

PROGRAMS OF STUDY: SDSMT confers B.S. degrees. Associate, master's, and doctoral degrees are also awarded. Bachelor's degrees are awarded in COMPUTER AND PHYSICAL SCIENCE (chemistry, computer science, geology, mathematics, and physics), ENGINEERING AND ENVIRONMENTAL DESIGN (chemical engineering, civil engineering, computer engineering, electrical/electronics engineering, environmental engineering, geological engineering, industrial engineering, mechanical engineering, metallurgical engineering, and mining and mineral engineering), SOCIAL SCIENCE (interdisciplinary studies). Engineering is the strongest academically. Mechanical engineering, civil engineering, and electrical engineering have the largest enrollments.

ACTIVITIES: 8% of men belong to 4 national fraternities; 9% of women belong to 2 national sororities. There are 135 groups on campus, including ski club, biking, art, band, cheerleading, choir, chorale, chorus, circle k, computers, dance, drama, drill team, environmental, ethnic, film, honors, international, jazz band, LGBT, newspaper, orchestra, pep band, political, professional, radio and TV, religious, social, social service, and student government. Popular campus events include M-Week, Christmas Chorale Concert, International Cultural Exposition, and Engineers Week. **Sports:** There are 7 intercollegiate sports for men and 6 for women, and 10 intramural sports for men and 10 for women. Facilities include a football field, a track, gym, sand volleyball court, swimming pool, squash/racquetball courts, weight room, and wellness center. **Graduates:** The most popular majors were mechanical engineering (15%), civil engineering (7%), and electrical engineering (6%). Of the 2016 graduating class, 26% were enrolled in graduate school within 6 months of graduation, and 83% were employed.

SERVICES: Counseling and information services are available, as is tutoring in most subjects. There is a reader service for the blind, and remedial math. **Library/Resources:** The library contains 172,180 volumes, 18,958 microform items, and 10,357 audio/video tapes/CDs/DVDs, and subscribes to 7,364 periodicals including electronic. Computerized library services include interlibrary loans, database searching, Internet access, and Wi-Fi capability. Special learning facilities include an art gallery, natural history museum, planetarium, radio station, a Geology and Paleontology Museum, and an Apex Gallery. **Physically Challenged Students:** 81% of the campus is accessible. Facilities include wheelchair ramps, elevators, special parking, specially equipped restrooms, special class scheduling, lowered drinking fountains, and special housing. ADA lab with specialized workstations, software, and hardware to aid students with visual, auditory, and mobility impairments and dyslexia. **Special:** Opportunities are provided for study abroad, co-op programs, internships, dual degrees, undergraduate research experiences, interdisciplinary design teams, credit by exam, and nondegree study. There are 5 national honor societies and a chapter of Phi Beta Kappa. **Visiting:** There are regularly scheduled orientations for prospective students, including a campus tour, discussions, training, and a meal. There are guides for informal visits, visitors may sit in on classes, and stay overnight. To schedule a visit, contact the Admissions Office. **Campus Safety and Security:** Measures include 24-hour foot and vehicle patrol, emergency notification system, self-defense education, and security escort services. There are emergency telephones, lighted pathways/sidewalks, and controlled access to dorms/residences.

REQUIREMENTS: A minimum composite score of 920 (420 critical reading/writing and 500 math) on the SAT, or a minimum composite score of 18 on the ACT. Graduation from an accredited secondary school is required. A GED is accepted. Applicants must submit high school credits, distributed as follows: 4 years of English, 3 each of math, lab science, and social studies, and 1/2 year each of fine arts and computer science. A GPA of 2.8 is required. AP and CLEP credits are accepted. Students must complete 120 credits for the science major or 130 credits for the engineering major, and maintain a minimum GPA of 2.0. Included in these requirements are 16 credit hours each of math at a level of calculus and above, basic science, and humanities/social science (for engineering, 3 credits must be at the 300 or above level). State regents mandated distribution requirements include 6 credits each of written communications, social sciences, arts/humanities, science, and cultural diversity, 3 credits each of speech communications and math, and 2 credits of information technology literacy, plus completion of an exam. **Procedure:** Freshmen are admitted fall, spring, and summer. Entrance exams should be taken preferably in October and December. There is a rolling admissions plan. Application deadlines are open. The fall 2017 application fee was $20. Notification is sent on a rolling basis. Applications are accepted on-line. **Transfer Students:** 103 transfer students enrolled in 2016-2017. Transfer students must submit an official transcript from their high school or GED and their previous college (s) and must have maintained a minimum GPA 2.75 or higher. 30 of 130 credits required for the bachelor's degree must be completed at SDSMT. **International Students:** There are 35 international students enrolled. They must take the TOEFL with a minimum score of 520 on the paper-based TOEFL (PBT) or 68 on the Internet-based version (iBT). Students must take the IELTS. They must also take the ACT.

ADMISSIONS: 88% of the 2017-2018 applicants were accepted. The SAT scores for the 2017-2018 freshman class were: Critical Reading-- 31% below 500, 40% between 500 and 599, 22% between 600 and 699, and 7% between 700 and 800. Math-- 12% below 500, 40% between 500 and 599, 29% between 600 and 699, and 19% between 700 and 800. Writing-- 42% below 500, 40% between 500 and 599, 16% between 600 and 699, and 2% between 700 and 800. The ACT scores were 4% below 12, 17% between 12 and 17, 35% between 18 and 23, 20% between 24 and 29, and 24% above 30. 39% of the current freshmen were in the top fifth of their class; 65% were in the top two fifths. 24 freshmen graduated first in their class. **Admissions Contact:** Office of Admissions Email: *admissions@sdsmt.edu* Web: *www.sdsmt.edu*

FINANCIAL AID: The average freshman award was $13,258. Need-based scholarships or need-based grants averaged $4,115; need-based self-help aid (loans and jobs) averaged $3,646; non-need-based athletic scholarships averaged $3,868; and other non-need-based awards and non-need-based scholarships averaged $2,799. The FAFSA code is 003470. The deadline for filing freshman financial aid applications for fall entry is March 15.

SOUTH DAKOTA STATE UNIVERSITY F-3

www.sdstate.edu

Brookings, SD 57007 — **(605) 688-4121**, **(800) 952-3541**

Fax: (605) 688-6891 — **Email: sdsu.admissions@sdstate.edu**

Full-time: 4227 men, 4198 women	**Faculty:** n/av
Part-time: 920 men, 1551 women	**Ph.D.s:** 89%
Graduate: 715 men, 916 women	**Student/Faculty:** 16 to 1
Year: semesters, summer session	**Tuition:** $8441 ($11,688)
Room & Board: $7433	**Freshman Class:** 5551 applied, 5072 accepted, 2273 enrolled
ACT: required	**CEEB CODE:** 6653
Application Deadline: open	**COMPETITIVE**

South Dakota State University, founded in 1881, as South Dakota's Morrill Act land-grant university. There are 8 undergraduate schools and 1 graduate school. In addition to regional accreditation, SDSU has baccalaureate program accreditation with ABET, ACEJMC, ACPE, NAAB, NASM, ACEND, ASABE, ASBMB, AABI, CAATE, CoAES, CCNE, CIDA, CAEP, NAACLS, SRM, ACPHA, AAM, AAVLD, ASHP, CORE, HLC, and NAEYC. The 363-acre campus is in a small town 50 miles north of Sioux Falls, 200 miles west of Minneapolis. Including any residence halls, there are 175 buildings.

STUDENT LIFE: Students are from 50 states, 81 foreign countries, and Canada. 88% are White; 4% Foreign; 2% African American; 2% Hispanic; 2% two or more races; 1% Asian American; 1% American Indian/Alaska Native. **Female To Male Ratio:** 1.1:1. **Housing:** 4359 students can be accommodated in college housing, which includes married student dorms and on-campus apartments. In addition, there are honors houses, special-interest houses, fraternity houses, sorority houses, and living learning communities. On-campus housing is available on a first-come and first-served basis. All students may keep cars.

FACULTY/CLASSROOMS: 50% of faculty are male; 50% are female. No introductory courses are taught by graduate students.

PROGRAMS OF STUDY: SDSU confers B.A., B.G.S., B.S., B.S.Ed., B.F.A., B.M.E., and B.L.A degrees. Associate, master's, and doctoral degrees are also awarded. Bachelor's degrees are awarded in AGRICULTURE (agricultural business management, agricultural communications, agricultural economics, agriculture, agronomy, animal science, dairy science, fish and game management, forestry and related sciences, horticulture, natural resource management, plant science, and range/farm management), BIOLOGICAL SCIENCE (biochemistry, biology/biological science, biotechnology, ecology, environmental biology, microbiology, nutrition, and wildlife biology), BUSINESS (apparel and accessories marketing, entrepreneurial studies, and hotel/motel and restaurant management), COMMUNICATIONS AND THE ARTS (art, communications, dramatic arts, English, German, graphic design, journalism, music, and Spanish), COMPUTER AND PHYSICAL SCIENCE (chemistry, computer science, geoscience, mathematics, physics, and software engineering), EDUCATION (agricultural education, art education, athletic training, early childhood education, education, health education, home economics education, music education, physical education, secondary education, technical education, and vocational education), ENGINEERING AND ENVIRONMENTAL DESIGN (agricultural engineering, agricultural engineering technology, architecture, aviation administration/management, aviation maintenance management, civil engineering, construction management, electrical/electronics engineering, electrical/electronics engineering technology, engineering, engineering physics, engineering technology, environmental engineering, industrial administration/management, interior design, landscape architecture/design, manufacturing technology, and mechanical engineering), HEALTH PROFESSIONS (clinical science, exercise science, medical laboratory science, nursing, pharmaceutical science, and pharmacy), SOCIAL SCIENCE (consumer services, early childhood studies, economics, family/consumer resource management, family/consumer studies, food production/management/services, food science, French studies, geography, history, human development, liberal arts/general studies, parks and recreation management, philosophy and religion, political science/government, psychology, rural sociology, safety management, and sociology).

ACTIVITIES: 4% of men belong to 8 national fraternities; 3% of women belong to 4 national sororities. There are 200 groups on campus, including human powered vehicle team, art, badminton, band, bowling, cheerleading, chess, choir, chorale, chorus, computers, dance, debate, drama, drill team, environmental, ethnic, film, forensics, honors, international, jazz band, LGBT, literary magazine, marching band, musical theater, newspaper, opera, orchestra, pep band, photography, political, professional, radio and TV, religious, rodeo, social, social service, student government, and symphony. Popular campus events include Little International, Engineering Exploration Days, Capers, Cavorts, and Hobo Days. **Sports:** There are 9 intercollegiate sports for men and 10 for women, and 16 intramural sports for men and 17 for women. Facilities include a physical education complex, outdoor track, lighted tennis courts, a wellness center, football and softball fields, rugby, soccer fields, wrestling, hockey, rock climbing, karate, cricket, Frisbee, and water polo. **Graduates:** From July 1, 2016 to June 30, 2017, 1979 bachelor's degrees were awarded. The most popular majors were health professions and related programs (24%), agriculture (17%), and social sciences (7%).

SERVICES: Counseling and information services are available, as is tutoring in most subjects, such as accounting, biology, chemistry, economics, physics, and history. There is a reader service for the blind, and remedial math, reading, and writing. **Library/Resources:** The library contains 965,651 volumes, 160,489 microform items, and 4,462 audio/video tapes/CDs/DVDs, and subscribes to 37,318 periodicals including electronic. Computerized library services include interlibrary loans, database searching, Internet access, and Wi-Fi capability. Special learning facilities include an art gallery, radio station, McCrory Gardens Education and Visitor Center which includes an Arboretum, Agricultural Heritage Museum, Northern Plains Biostress Laboratory, and Animal Disease Research and Diagnostic Laboratory. **Physically Challenged Students:** 99% of the campus is accessible. Facilities include wheelchair ramps, elevators, special parking, specially equipped restrooms, special class scheduling, lowered drinking fountains, lowered telephones, and special housing. All academic programs can be made accessible. **Special:** Co-op programs in elementary education and social work, internships, work-study programs, B.A.-B.S. degrees, and interdisciplinary majors including agricultural journalism, environmental management, and wildlife and fisheries science, are available. SDSU offers cross-registration with Dakota State University, Black Hills State University, and the University of South Dakota, Northern State University and South Dakota School of Mines and Technology. Opportunities are provided for dual majors, study abroad in more than 50 countries, credit by examination, student-designed majors, credit for military experience, nondegree study, a general studies degree, and pass/fail options. There are 32 national honor societies and a freshman honors program. **Visiting:** There are regularly scheduled orientations for prospective students, student orientation sessions which are offered each June. Students become acquainted with the university and student resources. They also meet with an academic adviser and register for fall semester classes. Information is sent to all admitted students. There are guides for informal visits, visitors may sit in on classes, and stay overnight. To schedule a visit, contact the Admissions Office. **Campus Safety and Security:** Measures include 24-hour foot and vehicle patrol, emergency notification system, self-defense education, and security escort services. There are emergency telephones, lighted pathways/sidewalks, and controlled access to dorms/residences.

REQUIREMENTS: The ACT is required. Students must have an 18 ACT composite score, or be in the top 60% of their class, or have a 2.6 GPA in required classes. Graduation from an accredited secondary school is required. A GED will be accepted. Applicants must submit 4 years of English, 3 years each of advanced math-algebra 1 and higher, laboratory science, and social science, and 1 year of fine arts. Basic computer skills (students should have basic keyboarding, word processing, spreadsheet and internet skills). AP and CLEP credits are accepted. Important factors in the admissions decision are advanced placement or honors courses, evidence of special talent, and extracurricular activities record. Students must complete at least 120 semester credit hours for the baccalaureate degree (see individual professional college requirements) and 60 semester credit hours for the associate degree. Remedial course credits are not counted as meeting degree requirements. A Cumulative Grade Point Average of 2.0. **Procedure:** Freshmen are admitted to all sessions. Entrance exams should be taken by spring of the junior year. There is a rolling admissions plan. Application deadlines are open. The fall 2017 application fee was $20. Notification is sent on a rolling basis. Applications are accepted on-line. **Transfer Students:** To be eligible for transfer, students must have been in good standing at the previous college and must have maintained a minimum GPA of 2.0 to 2.5, depending on the student's major. 30 of 120 credits required for the bachelor's degree must be completed at SDSU. **International Students:** They must take the TOEFL with a minimum score of 500 on the paper-based TOEFL (PBT) or 61 on the Internet-based version (iBT).

ADMISSIONS: 91% of the 2017-2018 applicants were accepted. The ACT scores were 7% between 12 and 17, 49% between 18 and 23, 37% between 24 and 29, and 7% above 30. 50% of the current freshmen were in the top fifth of their class; 68% were in the top two fifths. **Admissions Contact:** Shawn Helmbolt, Interim Director. Email: *sdsu.admissions@sdstate.edu* Web: *www.sdstate.edu*

FINANCIAL AID: SDSU is a member of CSS. The FAFSA code is 003471. The priority date for freshman financial aid applications for fall entry is March 15.

UNIVERSITY OF SIOUX FALLS — F-3

www.usiouxfalls.edu

Sioux Falls, SD 57105 — **(605) 331-6600**, **(800) 888-1047**

Fax: (605) 331-6615 — **Email: admissions@usiouxfalls.edu**

Full-time: 375 men, 658 women	**Faculty:** 60; IIB, av$
Part-time: 57 men, 84 women	**Ph.D.s:** 70%
Graduate: 113 men, 125 women	**Student/Faculty:** 12 to 1
Year: 4-1-4, summer session	**Tuition:** $18,280
Room & Board: $7350	**Freshman Class:** 1602 applied, 1474 accepted, 280 enrolled
SAT EBR-W/M: 555/550 **ACT:** 23	**CEEB CODE:** 6651
Application Deadline: rolling	**COMPETITIVE**

University of Sioux Falls, founded in 1883, is a private liberal arts institution affiliated with the American Baptist Churches. USF offers more than 40 undergraduate majors, on-line and on-campus adult, and graduate programs. In addition to regional accreditation, USF has baccalaureate program accreditation with CSWE, CAEP, CCNE, and IACBE. The 140-acre campus is in a suburban area in Sioux Falls, 240 miles from Minneapolis/St. Paul, and 560 miles from Chicago, IL. Including any residence halls, there are 18 buildings.

STUDENT LIFE: 57% of undergraduates are from out of state, mostly the Midwest. Students are from 28 states, 5 foreign countries, and Canada. 95% are from public schools. 85% are White; 5% African American; 4% two or more races; 1% Asian American; 1% American Indian/Alaska Native; 1% Hispanic; 1% Foreign. 42% are Luthern, Baptist, Methodist, Presbyterian, Evangelical, and reformed; 11% Catholic. **Female To Male Ratio:** 1.6:1. The average age of freshmen is 19; all undergraduates, 21. 32% do not continue beyond their first year; 68% remain to graduate. **Housing:** 350 students can be accommodated in college housing, which includes single sex dorms, coed dorms, and on-campus apartments. On-campus housing is guaranteed for the freshman year only, is available on a first-come, first-served basis, and is available on a lottery system for upperclassmen. 55% of students live on campus. Alcohol is not permitted. All students may keep cars.

FACULTY/CLASSROOMS: 55% of faculty are male; 45% are female. All teach undergraduates and 60% do research. No introductory courses are taught by graduate students. The average class size in an introductory lecture is 40; in a laboratory is 15; and in a regular course is 20.

PROGRAMS OF STUDY: USF confers B.A. and B.S. degrees. Associate and master's degrees are also awarded. Bachelor's degrees are awarded in BIOLOGICAL SCIENCE (biology/biological science), BUSINESS (accounting, business administration and management, business economics, and marketing/retailing/merchandising), COMMUNICATIONS AND THE ARTS (communications, English, fine arts, music, and speech/debate/rhetoric), COMPUTER AND PHYSICAL SCIENCE (chemistry, computer science, mathematics, and natural sciences), EDUCATION (art education, early childhood education, elementary education, middle school education, music education, science education, and secondary education), HEALTH PROFESSIONS (medical laboratory technology, nursing, and premedicine), SOCIAL SCIENCE (history, humanities, philosophy, political science/government, prelaw, psychology, religion, social science, social work, and sociology). Business, and elementary education are the strongest academically, and have the largest enrollments.

ACTIVITIES: There are no fraternities or sororities. There are 35 groups on campus, including art, band, cheerleading, choir, chorale, chorus, computers, dance, drama, ethnic, honors, international, jazz band, musical theater, newspaper, opera, orchestra, pep band, photography, political, professional, radio and TV, religious, social, social service, and student government. Popular campus events include USF Olympics, and Madrigals. **Sports:** There are 9 intercollegiate sports for men and 9 for women. Facilities include a student lounge, 160-meter running track, volleyball, tennis, badminton, racquetball, and basketball courts, aerobics facilities, exercise machines, and a gym. **Graduates:** From July 1, 2016 to June 30, 2017, 385 bachelor's degrees were awarded. The most popular majors were business/marketing (28%), health professions and related programs (16%), and psychology (9%).

SERVICES: Counseling and information services are available, as is tutoring in most subjects. There is remedial math, reading, and writing. **Library/Resources:** The library contains 81,545 volumes, and 4,600 audio/video tapes/CDs/DVDs, and subscribes to 450 periodicals including electronic. Computerized library services include interlibrary loans, database searching, Internet access, and Wi-Fi capability. Special learning facilities include an art gallery, radio station, and TV station. **Physically Challenged Students:** 54% of the campus is accessible. Facilities include wheelchair ramps, elevators, special parking, specially equipped restrooms, special class scheduling, lowered drinking fountains, and lowered telephones. **Special:** There are co-op programs with Augustana College, the Center for Public Higher Education, Dakota State University, and the North American Baptist Seminary. USF offers internships, study abroad in Japan, Central America, and China, an American Studies Program in Washington, D.C., and a January interim. Also available are on-campus work-study programs, B.A.-B.S. degrees, dual and student-designed interdisciplinary majors, a general studies degree, a 3-2 engineering degree, credit for life and work experience, and pass/fail options. There are 3 national honor societies, a freshman honors program, and 2 departmental honors programs. **Visiting:** There are regularly scheduled orientations for prospective students, including meetings with faculty and staff, attendance at class, a campus tour, and a financial aid session. There are guides for informal visits, visitors may sit in on classes, and stay overnight. To schedule a visit, contact the Admissions Office. **Campus Safety and Security:** Measures include self-defense education and security escort services. There are emergency telephones and lighted pathways/sidewalks.

REQUIREMENTS: A minimum score for the critical reading and math section of the SAT is 1050 or the ACT is 22. Applicants must be graduates of an accredited secondary school or have a GED certificate. Students should have completed 4 years of English, 3 years each of math and science with lab, 2 years of social studies, and 2 years recommended of foreign language, and 3 years of academic electives. USF requires applicants to be in the upper 50% of their class. A GPA of 2.5 is required. AP and CLEP credits are accepted. Important factors in the admissions decision are advanced placement or honors courses, evidence of special talent, and leadership record. To graduate, all students must complete a minimum of 128 credit hours, with 64 hours in the major. Required courses include phys ed, computer science, religion, history, English, science, economics, political science, psychology, math, social science, cross-cultural experience, speech, and fine arts. A writing proficiency test and a minimum 2.0 GPA are also required. **Procedure:** Freshmen are admitted to all sessions. Entrance exams should be taken during the junior or senior year of high school. There are early admissions and rolling admissions plans. Application deadlines are open. The fall 2017 application fee was $25. Notifications are sent June 1. Applications are accepted on-line. **Transfer Students:** 72 transfer students enrolled in 2016-2017. Transfer students must meet freshman admission requirements and have completed at least 24 hours of college courses with a minimum 2.0 GPA. College transcript (s) are required. The SAT or the ACT and an interview are recommended. Transfers may enroll in the fall, spring, and summer. 30 of 128 credits required for the bachelor's degree must be completed at USF. **International Students:** They must take the TOEFL. They must also take the ACT.

ADMISSIONS: 92% of the 2017-2018 applicants were accepted. The SAT scores for the 2017-2018 freshman class were: Evidence-Based Reading/Writing-- 25% below 500, 33% between 500 and 599, and 42% between 600 and 699. The ACT scores were 6% between 12 and 17, 54% between 18 and 23, 36% between 24 and 29, and 4% above 30. **Admissions Contact:** Ben Weins, Associate Director of Admissions. Email: *admissions@usiouxfalls.edu* Web: *www.usiouxfalls.edu*

FINANCIAL AID: In 2017-2018, 100% of all full-time freshmen received some form of financial aid and need-based aid. The average freshman award was $22,378. Need-based scholarships or need-based grants averaged $18,249; need-based self-help aid (loans and jobs) averaged $4,216; non-need-based athletic scholarships averaged $11,219; other non-need-based awards and non-need-based scholarships averaged $13,675; and $3,828 from other forms of aid. The average financial indebtedness of the 2017 graduate was $26,933. USF is a member of CSS. The CCS/Profile, FAFSA, and either the FFS or SFS are required. The FAFSA code is 003469. The priority date for freshman financial aid applications for fall entry is January 1.

UNIVERSITY OF SOUTH DAKOTA F-4
www.usd.edu

Vermillion, SD 57069	**(605) 677-5434** **(877) COYOTES**
Fax: (605) 677-6323	**Email: admission@usd.edu**
Full-time: 1927 men, 2805 women	**Faculty:** 383
Part-time: 895 men, 2006 women	**Ph.D.s:** 85%
Graduate: 1125 men, 1477 women	**Student/Faculty:** 17 to 1
Year: semesters, summer session	**Tuition:** $8938 ($11,336)
Room & Board: $7171	**Freshman Class:** 3606 applied, 3469 accepted, 1342 enrolled
SAT CR/M: 509/527 **ACT:** 23	**CEEB CODE:** 6681
Application Deadline: open	**COMPETITIVE**

University of South Dakota, founded in 1862, is a public institution with undergraduate programs in arts and sciences, education, fine arts, business, health sciences, and professional schools of law, medicine, audiology, and physcial therapy. The figures given in the above capsule and in this profile are approximate. South Dakota National Guard members may be eligible for a reduction equal to 50% of the resident state-support tuition rate, limited to 128 credit hours. There are 6 undergraduate schools and 7 graduate schools. In addition to regional accreditation, USD has baccalaureate program accreditation with AACSB, APTA, CSWE, NASAD, NASM, and NLN. The 284-acre campus is in a small town between Sioux City, Iowa and Sioux Falls, South Dakota. Including any residence halls, there are 69 buildings.

STUDENT LIFE: 69% of undergraduates are from South Dakota. Others are from 48 states, 27 foreign countries, and Canada. 86% are White; 3% Hispanic; 3% two or more races; 2% African American; 2% American Indian/Alaska Native; 1% Asian American; 1% Foreign; 1% race unknown. **Female To Male Ratio:** 1.6:1. The average age of freshmen is 18; all undergraduates, 22. 25% do not continue beyond their first year; 56% remain to graduate. **Housing:** 2218 students can be accommodated in college housing, which includes married student dorms and on-campus apartments. In addition, there are fraternity houses and sorority houses. On-campus housing is guaranteed for the freshman year only, is available on a first-come, and first-served basis. 72% of students commute. Alcohol is not permitted. All students may keep cars.

FACULTY/CLASSROOMS: 50% of faculty are male; 50% are female. 95% teach undergraduates and do research. Graduate students teach 8% of introductory courses. The average class size in an introductory lecture is 29; in a laboratory is 19; and in a regular course is 23.

PROGRAMS OF STUDY: USD confers B.A., B.S., B.B.A., B.F.A., B.G.S., B.M., B.S.Ed, B.S.N., and B.S.R. degrees. Associate, master's, and doctoral degrees are also awarded. Bachelor's degrees are awarded in BIOLOGICAL SCIENCE (biology/biological science), BUSINESS (accounting, banking and finance, finance, human resources, management science, recreation and leisure services, and sports management), COMMUNICATIONS AND THE ARTS (art, communication studies, communications technology, dramatic arts, English, German, journalism, media management, music, music performance, Spanish, and theatre studies), COMPUTER AND PHYSICAL SCIENCE (chemistry, computer science, earth science, mathematics, and physics), EDUCATION (art education, education, elementary education, journalism education, music education, physical education, secondary education, and special education), HEALTH PROFESSIONS (dental hygiene, exercise science, health care administration, health science, medical technology, nursing, and speech pathology/audiology), SOCIAL SCIENCE (addiction studies, American Indian studies, anthropology, criminal justice, economics, French studies, history, international studies, liberal arts/ general studies, philosophy, political science/government, psychology, social work, sociology, and women & gender studies). Business, biology, and chemistry are the strongest academically. Business, psychology, and biology have the largest enrollments.

ACTIVITIES: 18% of men belong to 7 national fraternities; 11% of women belong to 8 national sororities. There are 140 groups on campus, including art, band, cheerleading, chess, choir, chorale, chorus, computers, dance, debate, drama, drill team, ethnic, forensics, honors, international, jazz band, LGBT, literary magazine, marching band, musical theater, newspaper, opera, orchestra, pep band, photography, political, professional, radio and TV, religious, social, social service, student government, and symphony. Popular campus events include Dakota Days, Strollers (a variety production), and Rockfest. **Sports:** There are 7 intercollegiate sports for men and 10 for women, and 12 intramural sports for men and 12 for women. Facilities include a wellness center, football field, basketball courts, a swimming pool, an 8-lane, 200-meter track, a fitness center, batting cages, racquetball, volleyball, and tennis courts. Outdoor areas include a softball complex, soccer fields, flag football fields, and tennis courts. **Graduates:** The most popular majors were health professions (21%), business/marketing (15%), and education (11%). Of the 2016 graduating class, 30% were enrolled in graduate school within 6 months of graduation, and 60% were employed.

SERVICES: Counseling and information services are available, as is tutoring in most subjects. There is a reader service for the blind, and remedial math, reading, and writing. There is an academic advising and testing center. **Library/Resources:** The library contains 863,292 volumes, 740,454 microform items, and 15,185 audio/video tapes/CDs/DVDs, and subscribes to 64,575 periodicals including electronic. Computerized library services include interlibrary loans, database searching, Internet access, and Wi-Fi capability. Special learning facilities include an art gallery, natural history museum, radio station, TV station, music museum, historical study center, institutes of American Indian studies, social science research, child welfare training, business and governmental research bureaus, centers for speech and hearing, international studies, fine arts, and telecommunications, natural sciences field station, and archeology and human factors labs. **Physically Challenged Students:** 95% of the campus is accessible. Facilities include wheelchair ramps, elevators, special parking, specially equipped restrooms, special class scheduling, lowered drinking fountains, and lowered telephones. **Special:** USD offers internships, study abroad in 7 countries, and work-study programs. B.A.-B.S. degrees in 34 majors, a student-designed liberal studies major, dual majors, nondegree study, and pass/fail options are available.

The Arts Outreach program provides arts activities and noncredit classes. There are 16 national honor societies, Phi Beta Kappa, a freshman honors program, and 19 departmental honors programs. **Visiting:** There are regularly scheduled orientations for prospective students, student visits include an introductory session with an admission counselor, academic department visits, a campus tour with a student guide, and any other requested units. To schedule a visit, contact the Admissions Office. **Campus Safety and Security:** Measures include 24-hour foot and vehicle patrol, emergency notification system, self-defense education, and security escort services. There are shuttle buses, emergency telephones, and lighted pathways/sidewalks.

REQUIREMENTS: Applicants must have earned a 2.0 GPA in 4 years of English, 3 years each of lab science, math, and social studies, and 2 semesters of fine arts. They must also rank in the top 60% of their graduation class, have an ACT score of 18, or have a high school GPA of 2.6. AP and CLEP credits are accepted. Students must complete 132 hours with a minimum GPA of 2.0. At least 32 hours must be at the 300/400 level. All students should complete 9 hours of interdisciplinary course work, 6 hours each in composition, humanities, social science, natural science, and multicultural diversity, 1 hour each in fine arts, and a computer literacy course. **Procedure:** Freshmen are admitted fall, spring, and summer. There are deferred admissions and rolling admissions plans. Application deadlines are open. The fall 2017 application fee was $20. Applications are accepted on-line. **Transfer Students:** 635 transfer students enrolled in 2016-2017. Applicants should have a minimum college GPA of 2.0 and be in good standing at their previous school. 32 of 130 credits required for the bachelor's degree must be completed at USD. **International Students:** There are 91 international students enrolled. They must take the TOEFL with a minimum score of 550 on the paper-based TOEFL (PBT).

ADMISSIONS: 96% of the 2017-2018 applicants were accepted. The SAT scores for the 2017-2018 freshman class were: Critical Reading-- 46% below 500, 34% between 500 and 599, 18% between 600 and 699, and 2% between 700 and 800. Math-- 39% below 500, 32% between 500 and 599, 25% between 600 and 699, and 4% between 700 and 800. The ACT scores were 24% below 12, 31% between 12 and 17, 26% between 18 and 23, 11% between 24 and 29, and 8% above 30. 31% of the current freshmen were in the top fifth of their class; 60% were in the top two fifths. 66 freshmen graduated first in their class. **Admissions Contact:** Travis Vlasman, Dean of Enrollment. Email: *admission@usd.edu* Web: *www.usd.edu*

FINANCIAL AID: In 2017-2018, 95% of all full-time freshmen received some form of financial aid. The average freshman award was $10,479. Need-based scholarships or need-based grants averaged $1,389 ($14,150 maximum); need-based self-help aid (loans and jobs) averaged $2,148 ($10,150 maximum); non-need-based athletic scholarships averaged $609 ($18,818 maximum); and other non-need-based awards and non-need-based scholarships averaged $2,992 ($19,856 maximum). 15% of undergraduate students work part-time. The average financial indebtedness of the 2017 graduate was $26,629. The FAFSA code is 003474. The priority date for freshman financial aid applications for fall entry is March 15.

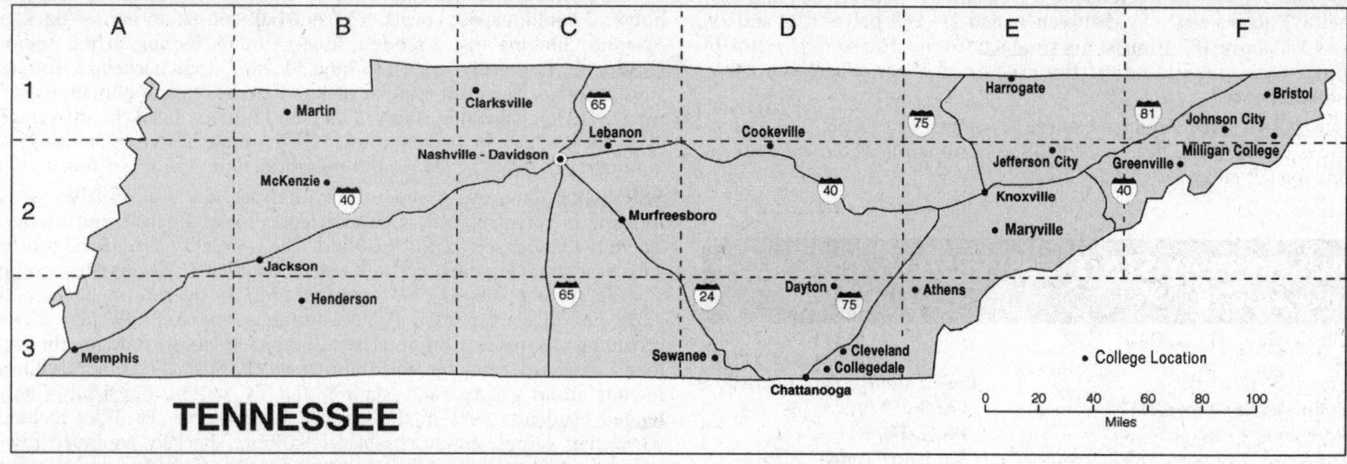

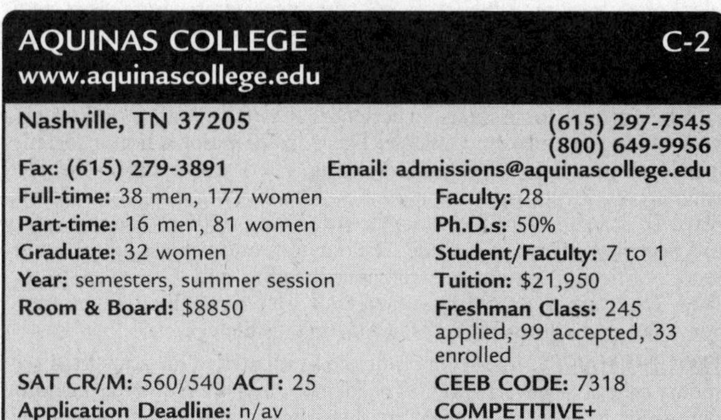

AQUINAS COLLEGE C-2

www.aquinascollege.edu

Nashville, TN 37205 (615) 297-7545
(800) 649-9956
Fax: (615) 279-3891 Email: admissions@aquinascollege.edu

Full-time: 38 men, 177 women
Part-time: 16 men, 81 women
Graduate: 32 women
Year: semesters, summer session
Room & Board: $8850

SAT CR/M: 560/540 **ACT:** 25
Application Deadline: n/av

Faculty: 28
Ph.D.s: 50%
Student/Faculty: 7 to 1
Tuition: $21,950
Freshman Class: 245 applied, 99 accepted, 33 enrolled
CEEB CODE: 7318
COMPETITIVE+

Aquinas College is a Catholic community of learning in the Dominican Tradition with Christ at its center. The College directs all its efforts to the intellectual, moral, spiritual, and professional formation of the human person in wisdom. Students are formed individually in a Christian community so that the harmonious integration between faith and reason can permeate every dimension of their lives. Immersed in exploring the relationship between human civilization and the message of salvation, the college community embraces the Dominican imperative to preach the Gospel, serve others, and engage culture in truth and charity. There are 4 undergraduate schools. In addition to regional accreditation, AC has baccalaureate program accreditation with ACEN. The 83-acre campus is in an urban area in the western section of metropolitan Nashville, four miles from downtown. Including any residence halls, there are 8 buildings.

STUDENT LIFE: 67% of undergraduates are from Tennessee. Others are from 29 states, 6 foreign countries, and Canada. 76% are White; 6% African American; 4% Hispanic; 4% Foreign; 4% two or more races; 4% race unknown; 2% Asian American; 1% American Indian/Alaska Native. 60% are Catholic. **Female To Male Ratio:** 5.4:1. The average age of freshmen is 18; all undergraduates, 25. 17% do not continue beyond their first year; 83% remain to graduate. **Housing:** 190 students can be accommodated in college housing, which includes dorms. On-campus housing is guaranteed for the freshman year only, and is available on a first-come, first-served basis. 78% of students commute. All students may keep cars. Alcohol is not permitted.

FACULTY/CLASSROOMS: 31% of faculty are male; 69% are female. All teach undergraduates. No introductory courses are taught by graduate students. The average class size in an introductory lecture is 12; in a laboratory is 8; and in a regular course is 12.

PROGRAMS OF STUDY: AC confers B.A., B.B.A., B.S., and B.S.N. degrees. Associate and master's degrees are also awarded. Bachelor's degrees are awarded in BUSINESS (business administration and management, finance, and marketing management), COMMUNICATIONS AND THE ARTS (English), COMPUTER AND PHYSICAL SCIENCE (mathematics), EDUCATION (elementary education and secondary education), HEALTH PROFESSIONS (nursing), SOCIAL SCIENCE (history, interdisciplinary studies, liberal arts/general studies, philosophy, psychology, and theological studies). Nursing, education, and management have the largest enrollments.

ACTIVITIES: There are no fraternities or sororities. There are 11 groups on campus, including house life, literary magazine, professional, religious, social, and social service. Popular campus events include House competitions and lectures, Fall Fest, Spring Fling, and St. Thomas Aquinas Day. **Sports:** There is no sports program at AC. Facilities include softball, basketball, tennis and volleyball. Students frequently initiate house competitions, including Capture the Flag and other less-formalized sporting activities. **Graduates:** From July 1, 2016 to June 30, 2017, 25 bachelor's degrees were awarded. The most popular majors were nursing (48%), education (20%), and English (12%).

SERVICES: Counseling and information services are available, as is tutoring in some subjects, such as nursing, theology, philosophy, math, writing, and biology. There is remedial math and writing. The Write Reason Writing Center, is available to all students for assistance with writing assignments for any course. **Library/Resources:** The library contains 129,919 volumes, 140,602 microform items, and 2,251 audio/video tapes/CDs/DVDs, and subscribes to 18,724 periodicals including electronic. Computerized library services include interlibrary loans, database searching, Internet access, and Wi-Fi capability. **Physically Challenged Students:** 75% of the campus is accessible. Facilities include wheelchair ramps, special parking, specially equipped restrooms, special class scheduling, and lowered drinking fountains. **Special:** The RN-BSN program is offered in an accelerated format. Students of the School of Business must complete an internship as a component of their program of study. A study abroad program (in Bracciano, Italy) is also available. There are 3 national honor societies. **Visiting:** There are regularly scheduled orientations for prospective students, including campus tours and information on admissions, financial aid, student life, and degree programs. There are guides for informal visits and visitors may sit in on classes. To schedule a visit, contact Connie Hansom in Admissions. **Campus Safety and Security:** Measures include 24-hour foot and vehicle patrol, emergency notification system, self-defense education, and security escort services. There are lighted pathways/sidewalks and controlled access to dorms/residences.

REQUIREMENTS: The SAT or ACT is required. The GED is accepted. AP and CLEP credits are accepted. Courses in theology and philosophy are required in every undergraduate curriculum. **Procedure:** Freshmen are admitted to all sessions. There is a rolling admissions plan. Application deadlines are open. Applications are accepted on-line. **Transfer Students:** 84 transfer students enrolled in 2016-2017. Transfer applicants must have a 2.4 GPA in previous college work. Transfer students with less than 30 semester hours of college-level coursework must also submit their high school transcripts and SAT/ACT scores. 30 of 120 credits required for the bachelor's degree must be completed at Aquinas. **International Students:** There are 11 international students enrolled. They must take the TOEFL with a minimum score of 80 on the Internet-based version (iBT). Students must take the IELTS, and either the SAT or ACT, scoring 21.

ADMISSIONS: 40% of the 2017-2018 applicants were accepted. The SAT scores for the 2017-2018 freshman class were: Critical Reading--21% below 500, 42% between 500 and 599, 16% between 600 and 699, and 21% between 700 and 800. Math-- 26% below 500, 37% between 500 and 599, 32% between 600 and 699, and 5% between 700 and 800. The ACT scores were 48% between 18 and 23, 39% between 24 and 29, and 13% above 30. **Admissions Contact:** Connie Hansom, Director of Admissions. Email: *admissions@aquinascollege.edu* Web: *www.aquinascollege.edu*

FINANCIAL AID: Aquinas College is a member of CSS. The FAFSA code is 003477. The deadline for filing freshman financial aid applications for fall entry is February 15.

AUSTIN PEAY STATE UNIVERSITY C-1

www.apsu.edu

Clarksville, TN 37044	**(931) 221-7661** **(800) 844-2778**
Fax: (931) 221-6168	**Email: admissions@apsu.edu**
Full-time: 2834 men, 4122 women	**Faculty:** 370; IIA, --$
Part-time: 1166 men, 1391 women	**Ph.D.s:** n/av
Graduate: 242 men, 589 women	**Student/Faculty:** 18 to 1
Year: semesters, summer session	**Tuition:** $7689 ($22,929)
Room & Board: $8708	**Freshman Class:** 6272 applied, 5570 accepted, 1963 enrolled
ACT: 22	**CEEB CODE:** 1028
Application Deadline: August 8	**COMPETITIVE**

Austin Peay State University, established in 1927, is a public institution offering undergraduate degrees in the liberal arts and sciences and professional preparation. There are 6 undergraduate schools and 1 graduate school. In addition to regional accreditation, APSU has baccalaureate program accreditation with ABET, CSWE, NASAD, NASM, NLN, ACS, NAACLS, and JRCERT. The 182-acre campus is in an urban area 47 miles from Nashville. Including any residence halls, there are 82 buildings.

STUDENT LIFE: 89% of undergraduates are from Tennessee. Others are from 43 states, 17 foreign countries, and Canada. 62% are White; 6% Hispanic; 6% two or more races; 3% race unknown; 21% African American; 2% Asian American. **Female To Male Ratio:** 1.4:1. The average age of freshmen is 19; all undergraduates, 24. 29% do not continue beyond their first year; 39% remain to graduate. **Housing:** 1817 students can be accommodated in college housing, which includes married student dorms, on-campus apartments, and honors houses. On-campus housing is available on a first-come, first-served basis. 83% of students commute. All students may keep cars. Alcohol is not permitted.

FACULTY/CLASSROOMS: 45% of faculty are male; 55% are female. All teach undergraduates. No introductory courses are taught by graduate students. The average class size in an introductory lecture is 24; in a laboratory is 20; and in a regular course is 19.

PROGRAMS OF STUDY: APSU confers B.A., B.S., B.B.A., B.F.A., B.P.S., and B.S.N. degrees. Associate and master's degrees are also awarded. Bachelor's degrees are awarded in AGRICULTURE (agriculture), BIOLOGICAL SCIENCE (biology/biological science), BUSINESS (accounting, business administration and management, finance, marketing, and professional studies), COMMUNICATIONS AND THE ARTS (art, communications, English, foreign language, languages, music, and theatre/dance), COMPUTER AND PHYSICAL SCIENCE (chemistry, computer science, geoscience, mathematics, physics, and radiological technology), EDUCATION (general studies, health education, and special education), ENGINEERING AND ENVIRONMENTAL DESIGN (engineering technology), HEALTH PROFESSIONS (medical laboratory science, nursing, and radiological science), SOCIAL SCIENCE (criminal justice, history, interdisciplinary studies, liberal arts/general studies, philosophy and religion, political science/government, psychology, public administration, social work, and sociology). Biology, nursing, and physics are the strongest academically. Business, health and human performance, and nursing have the largest enrollments.

ACTIVITIES: 8% of men belong to 11 national fraternities; 9% of women belong to 9 national sororities. There are 182 groups on campus, including art, band, cheerleading, choir, chorus, debate, drama, ethnic, honors, international, jazz band, LGBT, literary magazine, marching band, newspaper, orchestra, pep band, political, professional, radio and TV, religious, social, social service, student government, and yearbook. Popular campus events include Graduation, Parents Day and Mud Bowl.

Sports: There are 6 intercollegiate sports for men and 9 for women, and 14 intramural sports for men and 14 for women. The recreation complex houses 3 multipurpose courts, 4 racquetball courts, an indoor track, a dynamic climbing area, 2 modern fitness studios, indoor cycling studio. **Graduates:** From July 1, 2016 to June 30, 2017, 1558 bachelor's degrees were awarded. The most popular majors were health and human performance (13%), general business (11%), and nursing (8%). In an average class, 3% graduate in 3 years or less, 19% graduate in 4 years or less, 35% graduate in 5 years or less, and 39% graduate in 6 years or less.

SERVICES: Counseling and information services are available, as is tutoring in some subjects, such as science, math, English, and history. There is a reader service for the blind. The university also provides help with academic, learning, and test-taking problems. **Library/Resources:** The library contains 219,393 volumes, 668,958 microform items, and 7,378 audio/video tapes/CDs/DVDs, and subscribes to 54,392 periodicals including electronic. Computerized library services include interlibrary loans, database searching, and Internet access. Special learning facilities include an art gallery, radio station, and TV station. **Physically Challenged Students:** 90% of the campus is accessible. Facilities include wheelchair ramps, elevators, special parking, specially equipped restrooms, special class scheduling, lowered drinking fountains, and lowered telephones. **Special:** APSU offers cooperative programs in nuclear medicine with Vanderbilt University and a pre-engineering (2-year transfer) program in which a student will earn a degree in physics and an engineering degree from one of Tennessee's colleges of engineering. Credit may be granted for military experience. Pass/fail grading options and work-study programs are available. There are 20 national honor societies and a freshman honors program. **Visiting:** There are regularly scheduled orientations for prospective students. There are guides for informal visits. To schedule a visit, contact the Admissions Office. **Campus Safety and Security:** Measures include 24-hour foot and vehicle patrol, emergency notification system, self-defense education, and security escort services. There are shuttle buses, emergency telephones, lighted pathways/sidewalks, and controlled access to dorms/residences.

REQUIREMENTS: Applicants must be graduates of an accredited secondary school or have a GED. 14 academic units are required, including 4 units of English, 3 units of mathematics, 2 units each of natural/physical science, and foreign language, and 1 unit each of visual and/or performing arts, social studies, and U.S. history. Applicants who do not meet these requirements may be considered for admission. A GPA of 2.8 is required. AP and CLEP credits are accepted. To graduate, students must earn a minimum of 120 semester hours, of which 39 hours are in upper division courses, earn a cumulative GPA of 2.0, complete a Common General Education Core, and complete the First Year Experience Course. **Procedure:** Freshmen are admitted in the fall, spring, and summer. There is a rolling admissions plan. Applications should be filed by August 8 for fall entry, December 14 for spring entry, and May 21 for summer entry. The fall 2017 application fee was $25. Applications are accepted on-line. **Transfer Students:** 913 transfer students enrolled in 2016-2017. Applicants must have a 2.0 GPA and be in good standing with the last institution attended. Grades of D or better will be considered for credit. Application deadlines are the same as those for freshmen. Transfer students having attended only non-regionally accredited institutions are considered new students. 30 of 120 credits required for the bachelor's degree must be completed at APSU. **International Students:** There are 40 international students enrolled. They must take the TOEFL with a minimum score of 500 on the paper-based TOEFL (PBT) or 61 on the Internet-based version (iBT).

ADMISSIONS: 89% of the 2017-2018 applicants were accepted. The ACT scores were 12% between 12 and 17, 61% between 18 and 23, 24% between 24 and 29, and 3% above 30. 29% of the current freshmen were in the top fifth of their class; 57% were in the top two fifths. **Admissions Contact:** Amy Corlew, Director of Admissions. Email: *admissions@apsu.edu* Web: *www.apsu.edu*

FINANCIAL AID: In 2017-2018, 99% of all full-time freshmen received some form of financial aid. 65% of all full-time freshmen received need-based aid. The FAFSA code is 003478. The priority date for freshman financial aid applications for fall entry is October 1.

BELMONT UNIVERSITY C-2

www.belmont.edu

Nashville, TN 37212 **(615) 460-6785**

Fax: (615) 460-5434 **Email:** buadmission@belmont.edu
Full-time: 2152 men, 4009 women
Part-time: 139 men, 197 women
Graduate: 545 men, 970 women
Year: semesters, summer session
Room & Board: $11,680
Faculty: IIA, +$
Ph.D.s: n/av
Student/Faculty: 14 to 1
Tuition: $32,820
Freshman Class: 7737 applied, 4483 accepted, 1565 enrolled
SAT CR/M: 630/595 **ACT:** 27
CEEB CODE: 1058
Application Deadline: August 1
VERY COMPETITIVE+

Belmont University, founded in 1890, is a private, Christian liberal arts university. There are 8 undergraduate schools and 8 graduate schools. In addition to regional accreditation, BU has baccalaureate program accreditation with AACSB, ABET, CSWE, NASAD, NASM, NLN, and NASAD. The 75-acre campus is in an urban area in Nashville, TN. Including any residence halls, there are 41 buildings.

STUDENT LIFE: 70% of undergraduates are from out of state, mostly the South. Students are from 50 states, 28 foreign countries, and Canada. 5% are Hispanic; 1% Foreign. **Female To Male Ratio:** 1.8:1. The average age of freshmen is 18; all undergraduates, 21. 15% do not continue beyond their first year; 70% remain to graduate. **Housing:** College-sponsored housing includes dorms and on-campus apartments. On-campus housing is guaranteed for the freshman year only, and is available on a first-come, first-served basis. 52% of students live on campus. All students may keep cars. Alcohol is not permitted.

FACULTY/CLASSROOMS: No introductory courses are taught by graduate students. The average class size in a regular course is 20.

PROGRAMS OF STUDY: BU confers B.A., B.S., B.B.A., B.F.A., B.M., B.S.W., and B.S.N. degrees. Master's and doctoral degrees are also awarded. Bachelor's degrees are awarded in BIOLOGICAL SCIENCE (biochemistry, biology/biological science, environmental biology, and neurosciences), BUSINESS (accounting, business administration and management, entrepreneurial studies, finance, international business management, international economics, management science, and marketing/retailing/merchandising), COMMUNICATIONS AND THE ARTS (art history, art studies, audio technology, church music, communications, design, English, French, German, journalism, multimedia, music, music business management, music performance, music theory and composition, musical theater, public relations, Spanish, studio art, theatre arts, theater design, and visual and performing arts), COMPUTER AND PHYSICAL SCIENCE (applied mathematics, chemistry, computer science, mathematics, medical physics, physics, and web technology), EDUCATION (art education, early childhood education, elementary education, middle school education, and physical education), ENGINEERING AND ENVIRONMENTAL DESIGN (engineering physics), HEALTH PROFESSIONS (exercise science, medical technology, nursing, and pharmaceutical science), SOCIAL SCIENCE (Asian/Oriental studies, biblical languages, biblical studies, Christian studies, economics, food production/management/services, history, liberal arts/general studies, ministries, philosophy, political science/government, psychology, religion, social work, and sociology). Entertainment and music business, visual and performing arts, liberal arts and social sciences have the largest enrollments.

ACTIVITIES: There are 73 groups on campus, including art, band, cheerleading, choir, chorale, chorus, computers, dance, debate, drama, environmental, ethnic, film, forensics, honors, international, jazz band, LGBT, literary magazine, marching band, musical theater, newspaper, orchestra, pep band, photography, political, professional, radio and TV, religious, social, social service, student government, and symphony. **Sports:** There are 7 intercollegiate sports for men and 8 for women, and 10 intramural sports for men and 10 for women. The Fitness and Recreation Center has 2 regulation-size racquetball courts, a rock climbing wall, a group exercise room, a gymnasium and weight room featuring free weights, weight machines, treadmills, ellipticals and stationary bikes, intramural sports, ultimate Frisbee, flag football, soccer, basketball, walleyball, and dodgeball. **Graduates:** From July 1, 2016 to June 30, 2017, 1374 bachelor's degrees were awarded. The most popular majors were music business, nursing, and audio engineering technology. In an average class, 62% graduate in 4 years or less, 68% graduate in 5 years or less, and 70% graduate in 6 years or less.

SERVICES: Counseling and information services are available, as is tutoring in some subjects. There are also writing and computer labs. **Library/Resources:** The library contains 232,140 volumes, 29,999 microform items, 34,506 audio/video tapes/CDs/DVDs, and subscribes to 788 periodicals, including electronic. Computerized library services include interlibrary loans, database searching, and Internet access. Special learning facilities include an art gallery, radio station, TV station, including a 19th century Antebellum mansion. **Physically Challenged Students:** 98% of the campus is accessible. Facilities include wheelchair ramps, elevators, special parking, specially equipped restrooms, special class scheduling, and lowered drinking fountains. **Special:** BU offers study abroad, student-designed majors, dual majors in math, physics, and chemistry. Dual degree programs are available. Programs require 3 years of study at BU followed by 2 years at the other institution. There are 11 national honor societies, a freshman honors program, and 1 departmental honors program. **Visiting:** There are regularly scheduled orientations for prospective students, consisting of a 2-day program in summer and 4-day program right before classes begin. There are guides for informal visits; visitors may sit in on classes and stay overnight. To schedule a visit, contact the Admissions Office. **Campus Safety and Security:** Measures include 24-hour foot and vehicle patrol, an emergency notification system, self-defense education, and security escort services. There are shuttle buses, emergency telephones, lighted pathways/sidewalks, and controlled access to dorms/residences.

REQUIREMENTS: The ACT is required. The SAT is recommended. The university expects a composite score of at least 21 on the ACT and 1000 on the SAT. Applicants should be high school graduates or hold the GED. Secondary preparation should include 4 units of English, 3 of math, and 2 each of foreign language, history, science, and social studies. Potential music majors must audition. AP and CLEP credits are accepted. All students must complete at least 128 hours with a C average, including 22 to 24 hours in the major field. B.A. candidates are required to pursue a minor field. All programs except the B.B.A. require a core curriculum, which includes courses in language and literature, humanities (including religion), social sciences, science, math, and physical education. **Procedure:** Freshmen are admitted in the fall, spring, and summer. Entrance exams should be taken during the junior or senior year. There are early admissions and rolling admissions plans. Applications should be filed by August 1 for fall entry; December 1 for spring entry. The fall 2017 application fee was $50. Notification is sent on a rolling basis. Applications are accepted online. **Transfer Students:** 466 transfer students enrolled in 2016-2017. Applicants should present an above average GPA in previous college work and be able to meet freshman entrance requirements. Those with fewer than 64 credit hours must also submit SAT or ACT scores. 32 of 128 credits required for the bachelor's degree must be completed at BU. **International Students:** There are 85 international students enrolled. They must take the TOEFL with a minimum score of 550 on the paper-based TOEFL (PBT) or 80 on the Internet-based version (iBT).

ADMISSIONS: 58% of the 2017-2018 applicants were accepted. The SAT scores for the 2017-2018 freshman class were: Critical Reading-- 2% below 500, 28% between 500 and 599, 58% between 600 and 699, and 12% between 700 and 800. Math-- 6% below 500, 47% between 500 and 599, 37% between 600 and 699, and 10% between 700 and 800. The ACT scores were 23% between 18 and 23, 56% between 24 and 29, and 21% above 30. 56% of the current freshmen were in the top fifth of their class; 87% were in the top two fifths. **Admissions Contact:** Mary Lucus, Director, Institutional Research. Email: *buadmission@belmont.edu* Web: *www.belmont.edu*

FINANCIAL AID: 54% of all full-time freshmen received need-based aid. The average freshman award was $20,078. Need-based scholarships or need-based grants averaged $16,960; need-based self-help aid (loans and jobs) averaged $4,505; non-need-based athletic scholarships averaged $29,293; and other non-need-based awards and non-need-based scholarships averaged $8,348. The average financial indebtedness of the 2017 graduate was $29,207. The FAFSA code is 003479. The deadline for filing freshman financial aid applications for fall entry is March 1.

BETHEL UNIVERSITY B-2
www.bethelu.edu

McKenzie, TN 38201 (731) 352-4030

Fax: (731) 352-4069 Email: undergrad-admission@bethel.edu

Full-time: 738 men, 996 women	**Faculty:** 80
Part-time: 147 men, 351 women	**Ph.D.s:** 35%
Graduate: 190 men, 309 women	**Student/Faculty:** 16 to 1
Year: semesters, summer session	**Tuition:** $16,552
Room & Board: $10,590	**Freshman Class:** 598 applied, 317 accepted, 198 enrolled
	CEEB CODE: 1063
Application Deadline: August 30	**COMPETITIVE**

Bethel University, established in 1842, is a private institution affiliated with the Cumberland Presbyterian Church. The 3 colleges of BU offer undergraduate degrees through a variety of traditional and nontraditional programs. The figures given in the above capsule and in this profile are approximate. The 100-acre campus is in a small town in McKenzie, Tenn, and 120 miles northeast of Memphis. Including any residence halls, there are 18 buildings.

STUDENT LIFE: 89% of undergraduates are from Tennessee. Others are from 26 states, 25 foreign countries, and Canada. 99% are from public schools. 49% are White; 33% African American; 2% Foreign; 1% Hispanic. 72% are Protestant. **Female To Male Ratio:** 1.5:1. The average age of freshmen is 26; all undergraduates, 31. 38% do not continue beyond their first year; 37% remain to graduate. **Housing:** 530 students can be accommodated in college housing, which includes dorms, on-campus apartments. On-campus housing is available on a first-come, first-served basis. 75% of students commute. All students may keep cars. Alcohol is not permitted.

FACULTY/CLASSROOMS: 54% of faculty are male; 46% are female. All teach undergraduates. No introductory courses are taught by graduate students. The average class size in an introductory lecture is 25; in a laboratory is 15; and in a regular course is 12.

PROGRAMS OF STUDY: BU confers B.A., B.S., and B.S.N. degrees. Master's degrees are also awarded. Bachelor's degrees are awarded in BIOLOGICAL SCIENCE (biology/biological science), BUSINESS (business administration and management and management science), COMMUNICATIONS AND THE ARTS (English, music, music business management, and theater management), COMPUTER AND PHYSICAL SCIENCE (chemistry and mathematics), EDUCATION (education of the exceptional child, music education, and physical education), HEALTH PROFESSIONS (nursing and premedicine), SOCIAL SCIENCE (child psychology/development, history, human services, psychology, and sociology). Education, physicians assistant studies, and nursing are the strongest academically. Education, and organizational management have the largest enrollments.

ACTIVITIES: 25% of men belong to 5 local fraternities; 25% of women belong to 5 local sororities. There are 25 groups on campus, including art, band, cheerleading, choir, chorale, chorus, drama, honors, marching band, musical theater, pep band, political, professional, religious, social, social service, student government, and yearbook. **Sports:** There are 12 intercollegiate sports for men and 12 for women, and 9 intramural sports for men and 8 for women. Facilities include a gym with a pool, weight room, field house, health and fitness complex, football, soccer, tennis courts, track, and baseball fields. **Graduates:** From July 1, 2016 to June 30, 2017, 388 bachelor's degrees were awarded. The most popular majors were management and organizational development (66%), business management (14%), and nursing (9%). In an average class, 16% graduate in 3 years or less, 35% graduate in 4 years or less, 37% graduate in 5 years or less, and 37% graduate in 6 years or less.

SERVICES: Counseling and information services are available, as is tutoring in every subject, which is free to students. There is also remedial math, reading, and writing. **Library/Resources:** The library contains 79,164 volumes, 185 microform items, and 2,166 audio/video tapes/CDs/DVDs, and subscribes to 1,208 periodicals including electronic. Computerized library services include interlibrary loans, database searching, Internet access, and Wi-Fi capability. **Physically Challenged Students:** 75% of the campus is accessible. Facilities include wheelchair ramps, elevators, special parking, specially equipped restrooms, special class scheduling, and lowered drinking fountains. **Special:** BU offers evening classes for adults, in-service training for teachers, off-site classes, an accelerated degree program in organizational management, student-designed majors, internships, work-study, non-degree study, a pass/fail option, and portfolio credit for prior learning and work experience. There is 1 national honor society, a freshman honors program, and 11 departmental honors programs. **Visiting:** There are regularly scheduled orientations for prospective students. Students may tour the campus, dorms, review the lap-top program, and meet with advisers, financial aid and business staff, and register for classes. There are guides for informal visits; visitors may sit in on classes and stay overnight. To schedule a visit, contact the Admissions Office. **Campus Safety and Security:** Measures include 24-hour foot and vehicle patrol, self-defense education, and security escort services. There are lighted pathways/sidewalks, controlled access to dorms/residences, and security cameras in some buildings.

REQUIREMENTS: Applicants must graduate from an accredited secondary school. Students ranking in the upper half of their class or scoring a satisfactory score on the SAT or ACT are granted regular acceptance. Other applicants may be admitted conditionally. Other factors in the admission procedure are standardized test scores, an interview, evidence of special talent, and personality. Open admission is available for the nontraditional bachelor of science in the Management and Organizational Development program. Admission for all other programs is competitive. BU requires applicants to be in the upper 50% of their class. AP and CLEP credits are accepted. Important factors in the admissions decision are advanced placement or honors courses, leadership record, and evidence of special talent. Requirements for graduation include courses in English, history, lab science, math, physical education, and religion. Students must complete 128 to 132 hours with a minimum GPA of 2.0. A thesis is required in some majors. **Procedure:** Freshmen are admitted to all sessions. Entrance exams should be taken prior to enrollment, preferably by fall of the senior year. There is a rolling admissions plan. Applications should be filed by August 30 for fall entry; January 10 for spring entry; and June 5 for summer entry. The fall 2017 application fee was $30. Notification is sent on a rolling basis. Applications are accepted on-line. **Transfer Students:** 56 transfer students enrolled in 2016-2017. Applicants must meet the GPA requirements for the number of hours they previously earned. Up to 68 hours may be transferred from community or junior colleges. Students with fewer than 12 semester hours must submit high school transcripts and ACT or SAT scores. 32 of 128 credits required for the bachelor's degree must be completed at Bethel. **International Students:** There are 55 international students enrolled. They must also take the SAT or ACT, scoring 860.

ADMISSIONS: 53% of the 2017-2018 applicants were accepted. **Admissions Contact:** Bret Hyder, Director of Admissions. Email: *undergrad-admission@bethel.edu* Web: *www.bethelu.edu*

FINANCIAL AID: In 2017-2018, 95% of all full-time freshmen received some form of financial aid. 67% of all full-time freshmen received need-based aid. The college's own financial statement is required. The FAFSA code is 003480. The deadline for filing freshman financial aid applications for fall entry is March 15.

BRYAN COLLEGE D-3
www.bryan.edu

Dayton, TN 37321 (423) 775-2041 (800) 277-9522

Fax: (423) 775-7199 Email: admiss@bryan.edu

Full-time: 453 men, 521 women	**Faculty:** 40
Part-time: 17 men, 20 women	**Ph.D.s:** 85%
Graduate: 48 men, 24 women	**Student/Faculty:** 14 to 1
Year: semesters, summer session	**Tuition:** $25,600
Room & Board: $7300	**Freshman Class:** 680 applied, 369 accepted, 175 enrolled
SAT: required **ACT:** 23	**CEEB CODE:** 1908
Application Deadline: open	**COMPETITIVE**

Bryan College, founded in 1930, is a private, Christian institution that is evangelical and nondenominational. BC offers undergraduate degrees in the liberal arts, business, health science, fine arts, Bible and religious studies, music, and teacher preparation. There is 1 undergraduate school and 1 graduate school. The 128-acre campus is in a small town in Dayton, TN, 35 minutes north of Chattanooga. Including any residence halls, there are 28 buildings.

STUDENT LIFE: 55% of undergraduates are from out of state, mostly the South. Students are from 41 states, 9 foreign countries, and Canada. 83% are White; 5% African American; 3% Hispanic; 3% race unknown; 2% Foreign; 2% two or more races; 1% Asian American. 99% are Protestant. **Female To Male Ratio:** 1.1:1. The average age of freshmen is 18; all undergraduates, 20. 24% do not continue beyond their first year; 56% remain to graduate. **Housing:** 615 students can be accommodated in college housing, which includes married student dorms. On-campus housing is guaranteed for all 4 years. 58% of students live on campus. All students may keep cars. Alcohol is not permitted.

FACULTY/CLASSROOMS: 63% of faculty are male; 36% are female. All teach undergraduates. No introductory courses are taught by graduate students. The average class size in an introductory lecture is 27; in a laboratory is 13; and in a regular course is 16.

PROGRAMS OF STUDY: BC confers B.A. and B.S. degrees. Associate and master's degrees are also awarded. Bachelor's degrees are awarded in BIOLOGICAL SCIENCE (biology/biological science), BUSINESS (business administration and management and marketing), COMMUNICATIONS AND THE ARTS (communications, creative writing, English, music, musical theater, and theatre arts), COMPUTER AND PHYSICAL SCIENCE (mathematics), EDUCATION (elementary education, physical education, and science education), HEALTH PROFESSIONS (exercise science), SOCIAL SCIENCE (Christian studies, criminal justice, history, liberal arts/general studies, ministries, missions, philosophy and religion, political science/government, psychology, and religion). Business, and education are the strongest academically. Business, education, and psychology have the largest enrollments.

ACTIVITIES: There are no fraternities or sororities. There are 17 groups on campus, including art, cheerleading, choir, chorale, computers, debate, drama, film, honors, international, literary magazine, musical theater, newspaper, orchestra, photography, professional, religious, social, social service, student government, and yearbook. Popular campus events include Fine Arts Series. **Sports:** There are 6 intercollegiate sports for men and women, and 6 intramural sports for men and women. Facilities include a gym, soccer fields, baseball field, softball field, fitness center, outdoor swimming pool, and 4 tennis courts. **Graduates:** From July 1, 2016 to June 30, 2017, 230 bachelor's degrees were awarded. The most popular majors were business/marketing (51%), education/psychology/exercise and health science (8%), and theology and religious vocations (4%). In an average class, 47% graduate in 6 years or less.

SERVICES: Counseling and information services are available, as is tutoring in some subjects, such as math and English. There is also remedial math, reading, and writing. **Library/Resources:** The library contains 383,829 volumes, and 124,880 audio/video tapes/CDs/DVDs, and subscribes to 37,213 periodicals including electronic. Computerized library services include interlibrary loans, database searching, Internet access, and Wi-Fi capability. **Physically Challenged Students:** All of the campus is accessible. Facilities include wheelchair ramps, elevators, special parking, specially equipped restrooms, and lowered drinking fountains. **Special:** Special academic programs include practicums in business and psychology, and psychology internships. An American Studies Program in Washington and a study-abroad Latin American Studies Program are offered through the Christian College Coalition. There is 1 national honor society, a freshman honors program, and 7 departmental honors programs. **Visiting:** There are regularly scheduled orientations for prospective students, consisting of college visitation weekends, which include a tour of the campus, sitting in on classes and chapel, meeting with professors in the area of academic interest, and staying with current students in residence halls. There are guides for informal visits, visitors may sit in on classes, and stay overnight. To schedule a visit, contact Kerrie Murphy at visit@bryan.edu. **Campus Safety and Security:** Measures include an emergency notification system, self-defense education, and security escort services. There are lighted pathways/sidewalks and controlled access to dorms/residences.

REQUIREMENTS: Admission is granted to applicants who have graduated from an approved high school and who have a minimum GPA of 2.5 with a minimum composite score of 18 on the ACT or 940 RSAT (860 on the old SAT); admission is also granted to applicants with a minimum GPA of 2.0 and a composite score of 20 on the ACT or RSAT 1000 (920 on the old SAT). The high school record should include a minimum of 18 academic credits with a recommended distribution of 4 units of English, 3 units each of math, science, and social science/humanities, and 2 of foreign language. The GED is also accepted. An interview (preferred) or essay is required. AP and CLEP credits are accepted. To graduate, students must complete 124 semester hours, with a minimum of 30 in the major, and maintain a GPA of at least 2.0. Distributions requirements include 16 semester hours in Bible, 9 in communications, 7 each in personal development and natural science, and 6 each in the humanities and social science. Specific courses that must be taken include 7 semester hours in science, 6 hours each in freshman English, foreign language, and history of Western civilization, and 3 each in speech, general psychology, introduction to literature, fine arts, and phys ed. In addition, math and English proficiency must be met, and a comprehensive exam in the major is also required. **Procedure:** Freshmen are admitted in the fall and spring. Entrance exams should be taken before the fall of the senior year in high school. There are deferred admissions and rolling admissions plans. Application deadlines are open. The fall 2017 application fee was $35. Applications are accepted on-line. **Transfer Students:** 59 transfer students enrolled in 2016-2017. Applicants need a minimum GPA of 2.0 with 24 credits. Students with fewer than 24 credits must also submit their high school transcript and test scores. All students must complete an interview or essay. 30 of 124 credits required for the bachelor's degree must be completed at BC. **International Students:** There are 33 international students enrolled. They must take the TOEFL with a minimum score of 75 on the Internet-based version (iBT). They must also take the SAT or ACT, scoring 18ACT/940SAT.

ADMISSIONS: 54% of the 2017-2018 applicants were accepted. The ACT scores were 5% between 12 and 17, 52% between 18 and 23, 36% between 24 and 29, and 7% above 30. 44% of the current freshmen were in the top fifth of their class; 89% were in the top two fifths. **Admissions Contact:** Joshua Hood, Director of Admissions. Email: *admiss@bryan.edu* Web: *www.bryan.edu*

FINANCIAL AID: In 2017-2018, 92% of all full-time freshmen received some form of financial aid and need-based aid. The average financial indebtedness of the 2017 graduate was $16,077. The college's own financial statement is required. The FAFSA code is 003536. The priority date for freshman financial aid applications for fall entry is January 31.

CARSON-NEWMAN UNIVERSITY E-2

www.cn.edu

Jefferson City, TN 37760	(865) 471-3223 (800) 678-9061
Fax: (865) 471-4817	**Email:** admitme@cn.edu
Full-time: 675 men, 934 women	**Faculty:** n/av
Part-time: n/av	**Ph.D.s:** 77%
Graduate: n/av	**Student/Faculty:** 12 to 1
Year: semesters, summer session	**Tuition:** $27,900
Room & Board: $8000	**Freshman Class:** 2515 applied, 2260 accepted, 395 enrolled
SAT: required **ACT:** 23	**CEEB CODE:** 1102
Application Deadline: August 1	**COMPETITIVE**

Carson-Newman University, founded in 1851, is a private liberal arts college affiliated with the Tennessee Baptist Convention. In addition to regional accreditation, CNU has baccalaureate program accreditation with ADA, AHEA, NASAD, NASM, CAEP, and NLN. The 100-acre campus is in a small town 27 miles northeast of Knoxville, TN. Including any residence halls, there are 27 buildings.

STUDENT LIFE: 86% of undergraduates are from Tennessee. Others are from 29 states, 17 foreign countries, and Canada. 92% are from public schools. 81% are White; 3% Foreign; 2% Hispanic; 2% two or more races; 2% race unknown; 10% African American. 84% are Protestant. **Female To Male Ratio:** 1.4:1. The average age of freshmen is 18; all undergraduates, 22. 25% do not continue beyond their first year; 60% remain to graduate. **Housing:** 1430 students can be accommodated in college housing, which includes married student dorms, on-campus apartments, honors houses and special-interest houses. On-campus housing is guaranteed for all 4 years. 50% of students commute. Alcohol is not permitted. All students may keep cars.

FACULTY/CLASSROOMS: 53% of faculty are male; 47% are female. All teach undergraduates and 40% do research. No introductory courses are taught by graduate students. The average class size in an introductory lecture is 25; in a laboratory is 16; and in a regular course is 17.

PROGRAMS OF STUDY: CNU confers B.A., B.S., B.M., B.S.M., and B.S.N. degrees. Associate and master's degrees are also awarded. Bachelor's degrees are awarded in BIOLOGICAL SCIENCE (biology/biological science), BUSINESS (accounting, business administration and management, and business economics), COMMUNICATIONS AND THE ARTS (communications, English, fine arts, French, languages, music, and Spanish), EDUCATION (art education, early childhood education, elementary education, foreign languages education, health education, home economics education, middle school education, music education, science education, and secondary education), HEALTH PROFESSIONS (nursing and physical therapy), SOCIAL SCIENCE (economics, history, philosophy, psychology, religion, social science, and sociology). Nursing, music, and biology are the strongest academically. Nursing, business, and education have the largest enrollments.

ACTIVITIES: 20% of men belong to 2 local and 1 national fraternities; 20% of women belong to 2 local and 1 national sororities. There are 50 groups on campus, including art, band, cheerleading, chess, choir, chorale, chorus, computers, dance, debate, drama, drill team, ethnic, film, forensics, honors, international, jazz band, literary magazine, marching band, musical theater, orchestra, pep band, photography, political, professional, religious, social, social service, and student government. Popular campus events include Formal, International Festival/Fair, and Honors Convocation. **Sports:** There are 9 intercollegiate sports for men and 8 for women, and 40 intramural sports for men and women. Facilities include a football stadium, soccer, baseball, softball, and intramural fields, and a student center with 3 racquetball courts, 3 gyms, a weight room, an Olympic-size pool, and ropes course. **Graduates:** From July 1, 2016 to June 30, 2017, 340 bachelor's degrees were awarded. The most popular majors were education (22%), health professions and related programs (18%), and business/marketing (18%). In an average class, 41% graduate in 4 years or less, 54% graduate in 5 years or less, and 55% graduate in 6 years or less.

SERVICES: Counseling and information services are available, as is tutoring in most subjects. There is remedial math, reading, and writing. **Library/Resources:** The library contains 300,000 volumes, 221,960 microform items, 15,000 audio/video tapes/CDs/DVDs, and subscribes to 2,000 periodicals, including electronic. Computerized library services include interlibrary loans, database searching, and Internet access. Special learning facilities include an art gallery, natural history museum, and TV station. **Physically Challenged Students:** 50% of the campus is accessible. Facilities include wheelchair ramps, elevators, special parking, specially equipped restrooms, and special class scheduling. **Special:** The college offers internships, study in England, France, Japan, Hong Kong, and Spain, a Washington semester, on-campus work-study programs, B.A.-B.S. degrees, dual majors, a general studies degree, student-designed majors, and pass/fail options. Students may receive credit for life, military, or work experience. There is 1 national honor society, a freshman honors program, and 16 departmental honors programs. **Visiting:** There are regularly scheduled orientations for prospective students, including information sessions, meetings with advisers, and preregistration. There are guides for informal visits and visitors may sit in on classes. To schedule a visit, contact Jann Walker at visit@cn.edu. **Campus Safety and Security:** Measures include 24-hour foot and vehicle patrol, emergency notification system, self-defense education, and security escort services. There are lighted pathways/sidewalks and controlled access to dorms/residences.

REQUIREMENTS: Students must have a minimum composite score of 19 on the ACT or a satisfactory score on the SAT. Applicants should be graduates of an accredited secondary school. The GED is accepted. 20 academic credits are required, including 4 units of English and 2 units each of history, math, science, and social studies. An essay, a portfolio, an audition, or an interview are accepted if students wish to submit them for admission or for campus programs. A GPA of 2.3 is required. AP and CLEP credits are accepted. All students must complete 120-128 credit hours, including Composition I and II, Survey of Old Testament, Survey of New Testament, 15 hours in English and communications, 9 in social sciences, 6 each in religion, humanities, and science, and 3 each in history, literature, and math. The major requires 40 to 48 hours. Students must achieve a minimum GPA of 2.0. **Procedure:** Freshmen are admitted to all sessions. Entrance exams should be taken in the spring of junior year or early fall of the senior year. There are deferred admissions and rolling admissions plans. Applications should be filed by August 1 for fall entry; December 15 for spring entry; and April 15 for summer entry. Applications are accepted on-line. **Transfer Students:** 86 transfer students enrolled in 2016-2017. Transfer students should have a minimum GPA of 2.0 and must submit a transfer judicial check form. 32 of 120 credits required for the bachelor's degree must be completed at CNU. **International Students:** There are 55 international students enrolled. They must take the TOEFL, or score 4 on the APIEL, and take the English proficiency and math placement exams.

ADMISSIONS: 90% of the 2017-2018 applicants were accepted. The ACT scores were 9% below 12, 7% between 12 and 17, 49% between 18 and 23, 35% between 24 and 29, and 6% above 30. 10 freshmen graduated first in their class. **Admissions Contact:** Kate Amburn, Associate Director of Admissions. Email: *admitme@cn.edu* Web: *www.cn.edu*

FINANCIAL AID: CNU is a member of CSS. The college's own financial statement is required. The FAFSA code is 003481. The priority date for freshman financial aid applications for fall entry is November 17.

CHRISTIAN BROTHERS UNIVERSITY A-3

www.cbu.edu

Memphis, TN 38104	**(901) 321-4208** **(800) 288-7576**
Fax: (901) 321-3202	**Email: admissions@cbu.edu**
Full-time: 564 men, 631 women	**Faculty:** 94; IIA
Part-time: 52 men, 104 women	**Ph.D.s:** 87%
Graduate: 222 men, 255 women	**Student/Faculty:** 13 to 1
Year: semesters, summer session	**Tuition:** $28,600
Room & Board: $3070	**Freshman Class:** 1853 applied, 889 accepted, 290 enrolled
ACT: 25	**CEEB CODE:** 1121
Application Deadline: August 1	**VERY COMPETITIVE**

Christian Brothers University, founded in 1871, is a private Catholic university providing undergraduate educational opportunities in the arts, business, engineering, the sciences, and teacher education, and specialized graduate programs. There are 4 undergraduate schools and 4 graduate schools. In addition to regional accreditation, CBU has baccalaureate program accreditation with ABET, and CCNE. The 75-acre campus is in an urban area in Memphis, about 4 miles east of downtown. Including any residence halls, there are 23 buildings.

STUDENT LIFE: 79% of undergraduates are from Tennessee. Others are from 23 states, 26 foreign countries, and Canada. 70% are from public schools. 5% are Asian American; 48% White; 30% African American; 2% Hispanic; 2% Foreign. 50% are Protestant; 41% Buddhist, Muslim and unknown; 29% claim no religious affiliation; 21% Catholic. **Female To Male Ratio:** 1.2:1. The average age of freshmen is 18; all undergraduates, 23. 26% do not continue beyond their first year; 56% remain to graduate. **Housing:** 576 students can be accommodated in college housing, which includes dorms and on-campus apartments, quiet floors in residence halls, and a living learning community. On-campus housing is available on a first-come, first-served basis, and is available on a lottery system for upperclassmen. 67% of students live on campus. All students may keep cars.

FACULTY/CLASSROOMS: 56% of faculty are male; 44% are female. 83% teach undergraduates. No introductory courses are taught by graduate students. The average class size in an introductory lecture is 17; in a laboratory is 12; and in a regular course is 17.

PROGRAMS OF STUDY: CBU confers B.A., B.F.A., and B.S. degrees. Master's degrees are also awarded. Bachelor's degrees are awarded in BIOLOGICAL SCIENCE (biochemistry and biology/biological science), BUSINESS (accounting and business administration and management), COMMUNICATIONS AND THE ARTS (English and studio art), COMPUTER AND PHYSICAL SCIENCE (chemistry, computer science, mathematics, natural sciences, and physics), EDUCATION (early childhood education and special education), ENGINEERING AND ENVIRONMENTAL DESIGN (chemical engineering, civil engineering, electrical/electronics engineering, engineering management, engineering physics, and mechanical engineering), HEALTH PROFESSIONS (biomedical science), SOCIAL SCIENCE (applied psychology, history, liberal arts/general studies, philosophy and religion, and psychology). Engineering and biology are the strongest academically. Psychology, business, and electrical have the largest enrollments.

ACTIVITIES: 25% of men belong to 5 national fraternities; 19% of women belong to 6 national sororities. There are 37 groups on campus, including art, chess, chorale, chorus, computers, drama, ethnic, honors, international, LGBT, literary magazine, musical theater, political, professional, religious, social, social service, student government, and yearbook. Popular campus events include Bacchus, Sofapalooza, and Up Til Dawn. **Sports:** There are 5 intercollegiate sports for men and 6 for women, and 10 intramural sports for men and women. Facilities include a swimming pool, a gym, multimedia auditorium, a batting cage, a jogging track, basketball/volleyball and handball/racquetball courts, baseball and soccer fields, tennis courts, cross-country, and weight-training facilities. **Graduates:** From July 1, 2016 to June 30, 2017, 257 bachelor's degrees were awarded. The most popular majors were business (41%), psychology (15%), and engineering (15%). In an average class, 39% graduate in 4 years or less, 54% graduate in 5 years or less, and 55% graduate in 6 years or less.

SERVICES: Counseling and information services are available, as is tutoring in most subjects. CBU also has centers for math and writing. **Library/Resources:** The library contains 165,796 volumes, 61,523 microform items, and 2,004 audio/video tapes/CDs/DVDs. Computerized library services include interlibrary loans, database searching, Internet access, and Wi-Fi capability. Special learning facilities include an art gallery. **Physically Challenged Students:** 90% of the campus is accessible. Facilities include wheelchair ramps, elevators, special parking, specially equipped restrooms, lowered drinking fountains, and lowered telephones. **Special:** Special academic programs include on-campus work-study, study abroad in 4 countries, and internships for all juniors and seniors. There is cross-registration with the Greater Memphis Consortium, Rhodes College, and the University of Memphis. An accelerated degree program is available to all business and psychology majors through the professional studies program, and a general studies degree is offered. Up to 36 hours of nondegree study is possible, as are dual majors, an honors program, and pass/fail options. Numerous teacher licensure programs are also offered. There are 9 national honor societies and a freshman honors program. **Visiting:** There are regularly scheduled orientations for prospective students, including attendance at classes, meetings with professors and students, a campus tour, and meetings with admissions and financial aid representatives. There are guides for informal visits; visitors may sit in on classes and stay overnight. To schedule a visit, contact the Dean of Admissions. **Campus Safety and Security:** Measures include 24-hour foot and vehicle patrol, an emergency notification system, and security escort services. There are emergency telephones, lighted pathways/sidewalks, and controlled access to dorms/residences.

REQUIREMENTS: The ACT is required, with a score of 21, and a high school GPA of at least 2.5. Other admissions requirements include graduation from an accredited secondary school, with a college-preparatory curriculum recommended. The GED is also accepted. An interview is advised. ACT scores between 18 and 20 with a high school GPA of 3.0 or better are considered. AP and CLEP credits are accepted. Important factors in the admissions decision are advanced placement or honors courses, leadership record, and recommendations by school officials. In addition to meeting degree requirements for a particular major, a student at CBU is required to have a broad understanding of self, others, and the contemporary world. The graduate of CBU shall have cultivated, through the arts and sciences, the necessary skills of inquiry, reasoning, and communication, and shall have developed an awareness of the religious dimension of human existence. All students take a broad range of courses; common requirements are 9 hours of English, 3 hours of math, 4 hours of natural and physical sciences, 6 hours of religious studies, 3 hours of moral values, and 6 hours of social science/history for a total of 31 general education hours. Students must take a minimum of 30 hours of general education courses. **Procedure:** Freshmen are admitted to all sessions. Entrance exams should be taken by the end of the junior year. There are deferred admissions and rolling admissions plans. Applications should be filed by August 1 for fall entry; December 1 for spring entry; and May 1 for summer entry. The fall 2017 application fee was $25. Notifications are sent December 1. Applications are accepted online. **Transfer Students:** 41 transfer students enrolled in 2016-2017. Transfer students should have a minimum GPA of 2.5 and be in good academic and disciplinary standing. 35 of 122 credits required for the bachelor's degree must be completed at CBU. **International Students:** There are 35 international students enrolled. They must take the TOEFL with a minimum score of 500 on the paper-based TOEFL (PBT).

ADMISSIONS: 48% of the 2017-2018 applicants were accepted. The ACT scores were 4% below 12, 42% between 12 and 17, 28% between 18 and 23, 11% between 24 and 29, and 15% above 30. 68% of the current freshmen were in the top fifth of their class; 84% were in the top two fifths. 4 freshmen graduated first in their class. **Admissions Contact:** Kristi Forman, Director of Admissions. Email: *admissions@cbu.edu* Web: *www.cbu.edu*

FINANCIAL AID: In 2017-2018, 95% of all full-time freshmen received some form of financial aid. The average freshman award was $21,283. Need-based scholarships or need-based grants averaged $24,188; and non-need-based athletic scholarships averaged $8,937. 91% of undergraduate students work part-time. The average financial indebtedness of the 2017 graduate was $29,207. The FAFSA code is 003482. Check with the school for current application deadlines.

CUMBERLAND UNIVERSITY — C-2

www.cumberland.edu

Lebanon, TN 37087 — (615) 547-1246, (800) 467-0562

Fax: (615) 444-2569 — **Email:** admissions@cumberland.edu

Full-time: 461 women	**Faculty:** n/av
Part-time: 69 men, 93 women	**Ph.D.s:** 49%
Graduate: 82 men, 185 women	**Student/Faculty:** n/av
Year: semesters, summer session	**Tuition:** $20,160
Room & Board: $7550	**Freshman Class:** 602 applied, 367 accepted, 212 enrolled
SAT: recommended **ACT:** 21	**CEEB CODE:** 1146
Application Deadline: open	**COMPETITIVE**

Cumberland University, founded in 1842, is a private institution offering undergraduate and graduate degrees in business, education, and social sciences. The figures given in the above capsule and in this profile are approximate. There is 1 undergraduate school and 4 graduate schools. In addition to regional accreditation, CU has baccalaureate program accreditation with AACSB and NLN. The 44-acre campus is in a small town 28 miles east of Nashville. Including any residence halls, there are 17 buildings.

STUDENT LIFE: 87% of undergraduates are from Tennessee. Others are from 29 states, 29 foreign countries, and Canada. 89% are from public schools. 72% are White; 3% Foreign; 2% Hispanic; 14% African American; 1% Asian American; 1% American Indian/Alaska Native. **Female To Male Ratio:** 4.9:1. The average age of freshmen is 18; all undergraduates, 22. 44% do not continue beyond their first year; 35% remain to graduate. **Housing:** 400 students can be accommodated in college housing, which includes dorms. On-campus housing is available on a first-come, first-served basis. 62% of students commute. Alcohol is not permitted. All students may keep cars.

FACULTY/CLASSROOMS: 52% of faculty are male; 48% are female. 82% teach undergraduates. No introductory courses are taught by graduate students. The average class size in an introductory lecture is 20; in a laboratory is 20; and in a regular course is 20.

PROGRAMS OF STUDY: CU confers B.A., B.S., B.B.A., and B.S.N. degrees. Associate and master's degrees are also awarded. Bachelor's degrees are awarded in BIOLOGICAL SCIENCE (biology/biological science), BUSINESS (accounting, business administration and management, management science, marketing management, and recreation and leisure services), COMMUNICATIONS AND THE ARTS (English, fine arts, and music), COMPUTER AND PHYSICAL SCIENCE (mathematics), EDUCATION (elementary education, middle school education, music education, physical education, secondary education, and special education), HEALTH PROFESSIONS (nursing), SOCIAL SCIENCE (American studies, criminal justice, history, political science/government, psychology, social science, and sociology). Business, education, and nursing have the largest enrollments.

ACTIVITIES: 17% of men belong to 3 national fraternities; 7% of women belong to 2 national sororities. There are 15 groups on campus, including art, band, cheerleading, chorale, chorus, computers, dance, drama, honors, international, jazz band, marching band, musical theater, newspaper, pep band, political, professional, religious, social, social service, and student government. Popular campus events include Fall Frolic, Halloween at CU, and Fall and Spring Preview Days. **Sports:** There are 9 intercollegiate sports for men and 8 for women, and 4 intramural sports for men and 5 for women. Facilities include a gym, a field house, a weight room, baseball and soccer fields, tennis courts, outdoor volleyball courts, football field, and a softball field. **Graduates:** From July 1, 2016 to June 30, 2017, 154 bachelor's degrees were awarded. The most popular majors were nursing (45%), education (27%), and business administration (17%). In an average class, 10% graduate in 4 years or less, 20% graduate in 5 years or less, and 5% graduate in 6 years or less.

SERVICES: Counseling and information services are available, as is tutoring in most subjects. There is remedial math, reading, and writing. **Library/Resources:** The library contains 37,056 volumes, 590 microform items, 1,260 audio/video tapes/CDs/DVDs, and subscribes to 357 periodicals, including electronic. Computerized library services include interlibrary loans, database searching, and Internet access. Special learning facilities include an art gallery and a natural history museum. **Physically Challenged Students:** All of the campus is accessible. Facilities include wheelchair ramps, special parking, and lowered telephones. **Special:** Internships with local businesses and with the state legislature are available. Nondegree study, pass/fail options, and an accelerated degree program in general business are offered. There are 13 national honor societies, a freshman honors program, and 5 departmental honors programs. **Visiting:** There are regularly scheduled orientations for prospective students, consisting of campus tours, testing, information sessions pertaining to college life, and academic advising. A parent orientation is provided in conjunction with student orientation programs. There are guides for informal visits and visitors may sit in on classes. To schedule a visit, contact the Admissions Office. **Campus Safety and Security:** Measures include 24-hour foot and vehicle patrol and emergency notification system. There are emergency telephones, lighted pathways/sidewalks, and controlled access to dorms/residences.

REQUIREMENTS: The SAT and ACT Writing Test are recommended. A minimum composite ACT score of 19 and a GPA of 2.5 are expected. Applicants must be high school graduates or have earned the GED with a composite 50 score. AP and CLEP credits are accepted. To graduate, students must complete 120 to 132 (depending on major) semester hours, including a 41-hour core curriculum, and maintain a GPA of 2.0. **Procedure:** Freshmen are admitted in the fall, spring, and summer. Entrance exams should be taken during spring of the junior year or fall of the senior year. There is a rolling admissions plan. Application deadlines are open. The fall 2017 application fee was $25. Applications are accepted on-line. **Transfer Students:** 131 transfer students enrolled in 2016-2017. Transfer applicants should have a GPA of at least 2.0. 33 of 120 credits required for the bachelor's degree must be completed at Cumberland. **International Students:** There are 40 international students enrolled. They must take the TOEFL with a minimum score of 500 on the paper-based TOEFL (PBT). They must also take the SAT or ACT.

ADMISSIONS: 61% of the 2017-2018 applicants were accepted. The SAT scores for the 2017-2018 freshman class were: Critical Reading-- 65% below 500, 30% between 500 and 599, and 5% between 700 and 800. Math-- 50% below 500 and 50% between 500 and 599. Writing-- 88% between 500 and 599 and 12% between 600 and 699. The ACT scores were 44% below 12, 33% between 12 and 17, 10% between 18 and 23, 11% between 24 and 29, and 2% above 30. 38% of the current freshmen were in the top fifth of their class; 73% were in the top two fifths. **Admissions Contact:** Larry Vaughan, Director of Institutional Research. Email: *admissions@cumberland.edu* Web: *www.cumberland.edu*

FINANCIAL AID: In 2017-2018, 95% of all full-time freshmen received some form of financial aid. 33% of all full-time freshmen received need-based aid. The average freshman award was $6,133. Need-based scholarships or need-based grants averaged $5,191 ($9,972 maximum); need-based self-help aid (loans and jobs) averaged $2,800 ($11,500 maximum); non-need-based athletic scholarships averaged $7,899 ($20,020 maximum); and other non-need-based awards and non-need-based scholarships averaged $3,212 ($14,710 maximum). The college's own financial statement is required. The FAFSA code is 003485. The priority date for freshman financial aid applications for fall entry is February 1.

EAST TENNESSEE STATE UNIVERSITY F-1

www.etsu.edu

Johnson City, TN 37614	(423) 439-4213 (800) 462-3878
Fax: (423) 439-4630	Email: gozetsu@etsu.edu
Full-time: 3400 men, 4550 women	**Faculty:** 350; I, --$
Part-time: 650 men, 980 women	**Ph.D.s:** 75%
Graduate: 620 men, 1225 women	**Student/Faculty:** 23 to 1
Year: semesters, summer session	**Tuition:** $10,105 ($28,783)
Room & Board: $8036	**Freshman Class:** n/av
SAT or ACT: required	**CEEB CODE:** 1198
Application Deadline: open	**COMPETITIVE**

East Tennessee State University, founded in 1911, is a public institution, and part of the State University and Community College System of Tennessee. ETSU's undergraduate and graduate programs stress the liberal arts, business, art, fine arts, professional training, music, teacher preparation, technical studies, and health science. The figures given in the above capsule and in this profile are approximate. There are 6 undergraduate schools and 2 graduate schools. In addition to regional accreditation, ETSU has baccalaureate program accreditation with AACSB, ABET, ACEJMC, ADA, CSAB, CSWE, NASAD, NASM, NLN, ACS, CAAHEP, and NEHSPAC. The 366-acre campus is in a small town 90 miles northeast of Knoxville, TN. Including any residence halls, there are 68 buildings.

STUDENT LIFE: 89% of undergraduates are from Tennessee. Others are from 38 states, 46 foreign countries, and Canada. 97% are from public schools. 91% are White; 4% African American; 1% Asian American; 1% American Indian/Alaska Native; 1% Hispanic; 1% Foreign. **Female To Male Ratio:** 1.4:1. The average age of freshmen is 19; all undergraduates, 23. 33% do not continue beyond their first year; 38% remain to graduate. **Housing:** 2478 students can be accommodated in college housing, which includes married student dorms and on-campus apartments. On-campus housing is available on a first-come, first-served basis. 79% of students commute. All students may keep cars. Alcohol is not permitted.

FACULTY/CLASSROOMS: 55% of faculty are male; 45% are female. 85% teach undergraduates. No introductory courses are taught by graduate students. The average class size in an introductory lecture is 30; in a laboratory is 15; and in a regular course is 25.

PROGRAMS OF STUDY: ETSU confers B.A., B.S., B.A.S., B.B.A., B.F.A., B.G.S., B.M., B.S.D.H., B.S.Ed., B.S.E.H., B.S.M.T., B.S.N., and B.S.W. degrees. Associate, master's, and doctoral degrees are also awarded. Bachelor's degrees are awarded in BIOLOGICAL SCIENCE (biology/biological science), BUSINESS (accounting, management science, and marketing/retailing/merchandising), COMMUNICATIONS AND THE ARTS (art, communications, English, fine arts, music, and speech/debate/rhetoric), COMPUTER AND PHYSICAL SCIENCE (chemistry, computer science, information sciences and systems, mathematics, and physics), EDUCATION (foreign languages education, physical education, and special education), ENGINEERING AND ENVIRONMENTAL DESIGN (engineering technology and survey and mapping technology), HEALTH PROFESSIONS (allied health, dental hygiene, environmental health science, health science, nursing, and public health), SOCIAL SCIENCE (child psychology/development, criminal justice, economics, geography, history, human development, interdisciplinary studies, liberal arts/general studies, philosophy, political science/government, psychology, social work, and sociology). Engineering technology, computer science, and nursing have the largest enrollments.

ACTIVITIES: 4% of men belong to 8 national fraternities; 4% of women belong to 1 local and 6 national sororities. There are 200 groups on campus, including art, band, cheerleading, choir, chorale, chorus, computers, dance, drama, drill team, ethnic, forensics, honors, international, jazz band, LGBT, literary magazine, newspaper, pep band, photography, political, professional, radio and TV, religious, social, social service, and student government. Popular campus events include Leadership Retreat, National Clean Up for Hunger, and Winter Cruise. **Sports:** There are 6 intercollegiate sports for men and 8 for women, and 8 intramural sports for men and women. Facilities include a gym, a domed stadium which includes a basketball arena, tennis and handball/racquetball courts, a track, and weight and training rooms. **Graduates:** From July 1, 2016 to June 30, 2017, 1499 bachelor's degrees were awarded. The most popular majors were nursing (8%), psychology (6%), and finance and elementary education (5%). In an average class, 12% graduate in 4 years or less, 29% graduate in 5 years or less, and 38% graduate in 6 years or less.

SERVICES: Counseling and information services are available, as is tutoring in most subjects. There is a reader service for the blind, and remedial math, reading, and writing. **Library/Resources:** The library contains 1.1 million volumes, 1.7 million microform items, 23,658 audio/video tapes/CDs/DVDs, and subscribes to 3,714 periodicals, including electronic. Computerized library services include interlibrary loans, database searching, and Internet access. Special learning facilities include an art gallery, planetarium, radio station, TV station, and a regional art and history museum. **Physically Challenged Students:** 75% of the campus is accessible. Facilities include wheelchair ramps, elevators, special parking, specially equipped restrooms, special class scheduling, lowered drinking fountains, lowered telephones, special housing, and adaptive computer equipment. **Special:** Special academic programs include cooperative education programs, cross-registration with Milligan College, internships in political science, applied human sciences, and management,and dual majors study abroad in Scotland, England, France, and Spain, and B.A.-B.S. degrees and dual majors in most arts and sciences undergraduate majors. A general studies degree is offered. Credit for military experience may be granted, and nondegree study and pass/fail options are possible. There are 19 national honor societies, a freshman honors program, and 12 departmental honors programs. **Visiting:** There are regularly scheduled orientations for prospective students, including 5; 2-day orientation programs held during spring and summer for new students admitted to the fall term. There are guides for informal visits; visitors may sit in on classes and stay overnight. To schedule a visit, contact the Admissions Office. **Campus Safety and Security:** Measures include 24-hour foot and vehicle patrol, self-defense education, and security escort services. There are shuttle buses, emergency telephones, lighted pathways/sidewalks, and engravers available to identify personal property.

REQUIREMENTS: Students must have a minimum composite score of 890 on the SAT I or a minimum score of 19 on the ACT. Other admissions requirements include graduation from an accredited secondary school, with 20 Carnegie units and 14 academic credits, including 4 of English, 3 of math, 2 each of foreign language and science, and 1 each of history, social studies, and art. In-state students who pass the Tennessee State Proficiency Test are eligible to apply for admission. Applicants whose ACT/SAT I is below a certain score must complete the Academic Assessment Placement Program (AAPP) test battery before registration for classes. The GED is also accepted. A GPA of 2.3 is required. AP and CLEP credits are accepted. All students must complete 120 semester hours, with 30 to 60 in the major, and maintain a minimum GPA of 2.0. Distribution requirements, which total 46 semester hours, include English, American history, physical education, natural science, social and behavioral science, the humanities, analysis, and a 3-hour computer literacy course. An exit exam is also required. **Procedure:** Freshmen are admitted to all sessions. Entrance exams should be taken during the junior and/or senior year. There is a rolling admissions plan. Application deadlines are open. The fall 2017 application fee was $15. Notification is sent on a rolling basis. Applications are accepted on-line. **Transfer Students:** 857 transfer students enrolled in 2016-2017. Transfer students must have a minimum GPA of 2.0 in 12 or more semester credit hours of course work from a regionally accredited institution. Transfer students must also satisfy high school unit requirements if deficiencies exist. 34 of 120 credits required for the bachelor's degree must be completed at ETSU. **International Students:** There are 99 international students enrolled. They must take the TOEFL with a minimum score of 500 on the paper-based TOEFL (PBT) or 61 on the Internet-based version (iBT). They must also take the SAT or ACT.

Admissions Contact: Dr. Jeff S. Howard, Dean of Students. Email: *gozetsu@etsu.edu* Web: *www.etsu.edu*

FINANCIAL AID: In 2017-2018, 74% of all full-time freshmen received some form of financial aid. 55% of all full-time freshmen received need-based aid. The average freshman award was $7,407. Need-based scholarships or need-based grants averaged $5,002; need-based self-help aid (loans and jobs) averaged $2,992; and other non-need-based awards and non-need-based scholarships averaged $1,760. The average financial indebtedness of the 2017 graduate was $17,668. The FAFSA code is 003487. The priority date for freshman financial aid applications for fall entry is April 15.

FISK UNIVERSITY *(The complete profile is made available exclusively on our website, www.barronspac.com)*

FREED-HARDEMAN UNIVERSITY — B-3

www.fhu.edu

Henderson, TN 38340	**(731) 989-6651** **(800) 630-3480**
Fax: (731) 989-6047	**Email: admissions@fhu.edu**
Full-time: 541 men, 678 women	**Faculty:** 90; IIA, --$
Part-time: 51 men, 62 women	**Ph.D.s:** 69%
Graduate: 197 men, 335 women	**Student/Faculty:** 15 to 1
Year: semesters, summer session	**Tuition:** $21,950
Room & Board: $7950	**Freshman Class:** n/av
ACT: 23	**CEEB CODE:** 1230
Application Deadline: open	**COMPETITIVE**

Freed-Hardeman University, founded in 1869, is a private, liberal arts institution associated with the Church of Christ. The figures given in the above capsule and in this profile are approximate. There are 6 undergraduate schools and 4 graduate schools. In addition to regional accreditation, FHU has baccalaureate program accreditation with ACBSP and CSWE. The 120-acre campus is in a small town in Henderson, TN, 85 miles east of Memphis. Including any residence halls, there are 39 buildings.

STUDENT LIFE: 52% of undergraduates are from out of state, mostly the South. Students are from 33 states, 20 foreign countries, and Canada. 75% are from public schools. 91% are White; 4% African American; 3% Foreign; 1% Asian American; 1% Hispanic. 99% are Protestant. **Female To Male Ratio:** 1.4:1. The average age of freshmen is 19; all undergraduates, 21. 26% do not continue beyond their first year; 57% remain to graduate. **Housing:** College-sponsored housing includes dorms, on-campus apartments, and student teacher houses. On-campus housing is guaranteed for all 4 years. 75% of students live on campus. All students may keep cars. Alcohol is not permitted.

FACULTY/CLASSROOMS: 68% of faculty are male; 32% are female. 91% teach undergraduates. No introductory courses are taught by graduate students. The average class size in a laboratory is 22 and in a regular course is 20.

PROGRAMS OF STUDY: FHU confers B.A., B.S., B.B.A., and B.S.W. degrees. Associate and master's degrees are also awarded. Bachelor's degrees are awarded in BIOLOGICAL SCIENCE (biochemistry and biology/biological science), BUSINESS (accounting, banking and finance, and business administration and management), COMMUNICATIONS AND THE ARTS (art, broadcasting, communications, dramatic arts, English, fine arts, journalism, public relations, and speech/debate/rhetoric), COMPUTER AND PHYSICAL SCIENCE (chemistry, computer programming, computer science, information sciences and systems, mathematics, and physical sciences), EDUCATION (art education, early childhood education, elementary education, health education, middle school education, music education, physical education, science education, secondary education, and special education), ENGINEERING AND ENVIRONMENTAL DESIGN (preengineering), HEALTH PROFESSIONS (predentistry, premedicine, preoptometry, prepharmacy, and preveterinary science), SOCIAL SCIENCE (biblical studies, child care/child and family studies, criminal justice, family/consumer studies, history, ministries, psychology, and social work). Premedicine, preengineering, and business are the strongest academically. Business, Bible, and elementary education have the largest enrollments.

ACTIVITIES: There are no fraternities or sororities. There are 52 groups on campus, including art, band, cheerleading, choir, chorus, communications, computers, drama, drum and bugle corps, ethnic, honors, international, jazz band, musical theater, newspaper, orchestra, pep band, photography, political, professional, radio and TV, religious, social, social service, student government, and yearbook. Popular campus events include Makin' Music and Annual Bible Lectureship. **Sports:** There are 3 intercollegiate sports for men and 4 for women, and 7 intramural sports for men and 7 for women. Facilities include 2 gyms, playing fields, tennis courts, a walking track, 2 weight rooms, and racquetball courts.

SERVICES: Counseling and information services are available, as is tutoring in most subjects. There is remedial math, reading, and writing. **Library/Resources:** The library contains 175,748 volumes, 240,000 microform items, 43,000 audio/video tapes/CDs/DVDs, and subscribes to 1,650 periodicals, including electronic. Computerized library services include interlibrary loans, database searching, and Internet access. Special learning facilities include an art gallery, radio station, TV station, and an undergraduate research center. **Physically Challenged Students:** 70% of the campus is accessible. Facilities include wheelchair ramps, elevators, special parking, specially equipped restrooms, special class scheduling, lowered drinking fountains, and lowered telephones. **Special:** FHU offers study abroad in Belgium and Italy, a B.A.-B.S. degree in Bible, biology, communication, and arts and humanities, co-op programs, a dual major, field practicum opportunities in several majors, student-designed majors, 3-2 engineering degrees with 6 universities, and nondegree study. There are 4 national honor societies, a freshman honors program, and 13 departmental honors programs. **Visiting:** There are regularly scheduled orientations for prospective students, including an orientation during the 5 days prior to classes beginning in the fall. There are guides for informal visits; visitors may sit in on classes and stay overnight. **Campus Safety and Security:** Measures include 24-hour foot and vehicle patrol, an emergency notification system, security escort services, and lighted pathways/sidewalks.

REQUIREMENTS: The ACT is required. Students must have a minimum composite score of 19. Candidates for admission should be graduates of an accredited secondary school. An interview is recommended. A GPA of 2.3 is required. AP and CLEP credits are accepted. Important factors in the admissions decision are personality/intangible qualities, recommendations by school officials, and leadership record. To graduate, students must complete 132 semester hours, including 44 in upper-division courses in Bible, skills, humanities, and science, plus 3 hours of speech communication and 2 hours of physical education. The major requires a minimum of 30 semester hours, including 15 upper-division hours. Students must maintain a GPA of 2.0. All students must demonstrate, by approved tests or criteria, basic competence in reading, writing, oral communication, math, and computers. **Procedure:** Freshmen are admitted in the fall, spring, and summer. Entrance exams should be taken in early fall or summer before senior year. There are early admissions and rolling admissions plans. Application deadlines are open. Applications are accepted on-line. **Transfer Students:** Applicants should have a minimum college GPA of 2.0. Those with fewer than 30 college credits must also submit a high school transcript and ACT or SAT scores. 33 of 132 credits required for the bachelor's degree must be completed at FHU. **International Students:** They must take the TOEFL with a minimum score of 500 on the paper-based TOEFL (PBT) or 61 on the Internet-based version (iBT). They must also take the ACT, scoring 19.

ADMISSIONS: The ACT scores were 30% below 12, 27% between 12 and 17, 21% between 18 and 23, 10% between 24 and 29, and 12% above 30. **Admissions Contact:** Joe Askew, Director of Admissions. Email: *admissions@fhu.edu* Web: *www.fhu.edu*

FINANCIAL AID: In 2017-2018, 98% of all full-time freshmen received some form of financial aid and need-based aid. The FAFSA code is 003492. The priority date for freshman financial aid applications for fall entry is October.

KING UNIVERSITY F-1

www.king.edu

Bristol, TN 37620	(423) 652-4861 (800) 362-0014
Fax: (423) 652-4727	Email: admissions@king.edu
Full-time: 624 men, 984 women	Faculty: 98
Part-time: 75 men, 116 women	Ph.D.s: 47%
Graduate: 83 men, 280 women	Student/Faculty: 13 to 1
Year: semesters, summer session	Tuition: $28,572
Room & Board: $8424	Freshman Class: n/av
SAT or ACT: required	CEEB CODE: 1371
Application Deadline: open	COMPETITIVE

King University, founded in 1867, is a Presbyterian-affiliated Christian academic community dedicated to the integration of rigorous academic programming and the exploration of faith. The University establishes students in a robust liberal arts foundation and offers specialization in a contemporary range of undergraduate degrees. These include nursing, security and intelligence studies, exercise studies, and digital media and design, as well as more traditional majors such as mathematics, history and political science, English, biology, and more. Undergraduates have the opportunity to engage in a variety of real-world economic and scientific research opportunities, and to interact with prominent voices examining the intersection of faith and culture. On-campus and online learning programs are available, plus a dual degree program in Engineering. Graduate and Professional offerings include master's degrees in nursing, business and education, and a doctoral degree in nursing practice. There are 7 undergraduate schools and 3 graduate schools. In addition to regional accreditation, KU has baccalaureate program accreditation with CCNE and CAATE. The 135-acre campus is in a small town 2 miles east of Bristol, Tennessee. Including any residence halls, there are 20 buildings.

STUDENT LIFE: 59% of undergraduates are from Tennessee. Others are from 34 states, 26 foreign countries, and Canada. 94% are from public schools. 79% are White; 7% African American; 4% Hispanic; 3% Foreign; 3% race unknown; 2% two or more races; 1% Asian American. 57% are 57% unknown; 38% Protestant. **Female To Male Ratio:** 1.8:1. The average age of freshmen is 18; all undergraduates, 28. 31% do not continue beyond their first year; 46% remain to graduate. **Housing:** 443 students can be accommodated in college housing, which includes dorms, and honors houses. On-campus housing is guaranteed for all 4 years, and is available on a first-come, first-served basis. 81% of students commute. All students may keep cars. Alcohol is not permitted.

FACULTY/CLASSROOMS: 42% of faculty are male; 58% are female. No introductory courses are taught by graduate students. The average class size in an introductory lecture is 17; in a laboratory is 12; and in a regular course is 12.

PROGRAMS OF STUDY: KU confers B.A., B.B.A., B.S., B.S.N., B.S.W. degrees. Associate, master's, and doctoral degrees are also awarded. Bachelor's degrees are awarded in BIOLOGICAL SCIENCE (biochemistry, bioinformatics, biology/biological science, biology/ gen science secondary education, cell and molecular biology, forensic science, and neurosciences), BUSINESS (business administration, business administration marketing, and business economics), COMMUNICATIONS AND THE ARTS (communications, digital media, English, English literature, English Writing, French, information technology, instrumental music education, music, Spanish, technical communication, theatre arts, and vocal music education), COMPUTER AND PHYSICAL SCIENCE (applied science, chemistry, chemistry secondary education, digital arts/ technology, mathematics, and physics), EDUCATION (athletic training, elementary education, English secondary education, general studies, health information management, history education, learner designed area of study, mathematics education, music education, physical education, social studies education, and Spanish education K-12), HEALTH PROFESSIONS (exercise science, health care administration, human biology, and nursing), SOCIAL SCIENCE (biblical studies, criminal justice, history, interdisciplinary studies, international relations, philosophy, psychology, religious studies, social work, and youth ministry). Nursing and natural sciences is the strongest academically. Nursing, business, and information technology have the largest enrollments.

ACTIVITIES: There are no fraternities or sororities. There are 15 groups on campus, including band, cheerleading, choir, chorale, chorus, dance, drama, environmental, honors, international, jazz band, literary magazine, musical theater, newspaper, pep band, political, professional, religious, social, social service, and student government. Popular campus events include Dogwood Homecoming Weekend, Late Night Breakfast, and Rhythm and Roots Reunion. **Sports:** There are 11 intercollegiate sports for men and 14 for women, and 6 intramural sports for men and 6 for women. Facilities include basketball and volleyball, acrobatics and tumbling, wrestling, a weight room and cardiovascular space, a racquetball court, practice facility, soccer field, outdoor baseball field, softball field and tennis courts. **Graduates:** From July 1, 2016 to June 30, 2017, 951 bachelor's degrees were awarded. The most popular majors were business (37%), nursing (26%), and information technology (7%). In an average class, 1% graduate in 3 years or less, 24% graduate in 4 years or less, 19% graduate in 5 years or less, and 1% graduate in 6 years or less. Of the 2016 graduating class, 18% were enrolled in graduate school within 6 months of graduation, and 73% were employed.

SERVICES: Counseling and information services are available, as is tutoring in every subject. There is a reader service for the blind. The Academic Center for Excellence, offers a writing center, math center, and a speaking center. 24-hour online tutoring in all subjects and an online writing center are also available. **Library/Resources:** The library contains 78,462 volumes, 12,465 microform items, 6,142 audio/video tapes/CDs/ DVDs, and subscribes to 156 periodicals, including electronic. Computerized library services include interlibrary loans, database searching, Internet access, and Wi-Fi capability. Special learning facilities include an art gallery, an observatory, a printing press, and a nuclear physics laboratory. **Physically Challenged Students:** 60% of the campus is accessible. Facilities include wheelchair ramps, elevators, special parking, specially equipped restrooms, special class scheduling, lowered drinking fountains, lowered telephones, and special housing. **Special:** King also offers cooperative education, internships, and dual majors in all programs, as well as a pharmacy dual degree program, interdisciplinary and student-designed majors. King offers a first-year experience program with an Experience Washington DC component, a transfer experience, a Washington semester, and work-study programs. Non-degree study and pass/fail options for special students are available. King cooperates with the American Institute for Foreign Study (AIFS) to offer study abroad and internship experiences at universities throughout the world. AIFS currently offers multi-country programs in Argentina, Australia, Austria, Brazil, Chile, China, Costa Rica, Czech Republic, England, France, Germany, Greece, India, Ireland, Italy, New Zealand, Russia, South Africa, Spain, and Turkey. King and Arcadia University jointly offer study-abroad experiences at universities and colleges in Australia,

Chile, Cuba, England, France, Germany, Greece, Ireland, Italy, New Zealand, Scotland, South Africa, Spain, Turkey and Wales. These programs are available for a semester, year, or summer term. International Studies Abroad: King students have access to study abroad an internship opportunities at colleges and universities in Argentina, Australia, Belgium, Brazil, Chile, China, Colombia, Costa Rica, Czech Republic, Dominican Republic, England, Fiji, France, Germany, Greece, India, Ireland, Italy, Japan, Jordan, Morocco, Peru, Scotland, South Africa, South Korea, Spain, Thailand, and Turkey. There is 1 national honor society, a freshman honors program, and 1 departmental honors program. **Visiting:** There are regularly scheduled orientations for prospective students, including a campus tour; sessions on admission, athletics, financial aid, and academics/meeting with faculty. There are guides for informal visits; visitors may sit in on classes and stay overnight. To schedule a visit, contact Tom VerDow at admissions@king.edu. **Campus Safety and Security:** Measures include 24-hour foot and vehicle patrol, emergency notification system, self-defense education, and security escort services. There are emergency telephones, lighted pathways/sidewalks, and controlled access to dorms/residences.

REQUIREMENTS: Admission as a new freshman is complete when the following materials have been submitted: a completed application form (along with essay, if required), and official transcripts of all high school courses and grades (must include a minimum of 6 completed semesters). OPTIONAL: Scores from either the Scholastic Aptitude Test (SAT I) of the College. Entrance Examination Board or the American College Testing Program (ACT). General requirements for admission as a new freshman include graduation, with a standard or higher diploma, from an accredited or recognized high school or secondary institution, with a minimum of 17 academic units, distributed as follows: 4 units of English, 2 units each of algebra (algebra I and II), 1 unit of geometry, 4 units each of foreign language, history and the social studies, natural science, and any other academic electives. AP and CLEP credits are accepted. Undergraduate students must complete a minimum of 124 semester credit hours with 32 to 76 in the major. The minimum 48 semester hours of core curriculum include courses in English, history, math, Bible, humanities, science, social science, and physical education. Students must have a minimum GPA of 2.0 in most majors (may vary according to field of study). A comprehensive exam in the student's major area of concentration is required. **Procedure:** Freshmen are admitted in the fall, spring, and summer. Entrance exams should be taken by May 1. There are deferred admissions and rolling admissions plans. Application deadlines are open. Applications are accepted on-line. **Transfer Students:** 718 transfer students enrolled in 2016-2017. Transfer candidates for admission to undergraduate degree programs must submit these documents: a completed application form, official transcripts from all institutions of higher education previously attended, and an official high school transcript (only for any student who has not completed an associate or bachelor degree). King University will recognize transfer candidates who have earned a degree prior to matriculation at a regionally accredited college or university. The following degrees are accepted as meeting the general education requirements of King University: Associate of Arts, Associate of Science, Associate of Arts and Science, and Bachelor's Degree. 48 of 124 credits required for the bachelor's degree must be completed at King. **International Students:** There are 63 international students enrolled. They must take the TOEFL with a minimum score of 600 on the paper-based TOEFL (PBT) or 84 on the Internet-based version (iBT).

ADMISSIONS: 23% of the current freshmen were in the top fifth of their class; 39% were in the top two fifths. 5 freshmen graduated first in their class. **Admissions Contact:** Tom VerDow, Director of Undergraduate Enrollment. Email: *admissions@king.edu* Web: *www.king.edu*

FINANCIAL AID: In 2017-2018, 100% of all full-time freshmen received some form of financial aid. 87% of all full-time freshmen received need-based aid. The average freshman award was $30,462. Need-based scholarships or need-based grants averaged $18,004 ($38,002 maximum); need-based self-help aid (loans and jobs) averaged $4,210 ($7,500 maximum); non-need-based athletic scholarships averaged $929 ($18,921 maximum); and other non-need-based awards and non-need-based scholarships averaged $7,319 ($18,500 maximum). 36% of undergraduate students work part-time. The average financial indebtedness of the 2017 graduate was $23,950. The college's own financial statement is required. The FAFSA code is 003496. The priority date for freshman financial aid applications for fall entry is March 1.

LANE COLLEGE *(The complete profile is made available exclusively on our website, www.barronspac.com)*

LEE UNIVERSITY — D-3

www.leeuniversity.edu

Cleveland, TN 37320 — (423) 614-8500, (800) 533-9930

Fax: (423) 614-8533 **Email:** admissions@leeuniversity.edu

Full-time: 1544 men, 2222 women	**Faculty:** 158; IIA, --$
Part-time: 195 men, 155 women	**Ph.D.s:** 73%
Graduate: 251 men, 231 women	**Student/Faculty:** 17 to 1
Year: semesters, summer session	**Tuition:** $15,000
Room & Board: $7045	**Freshman Class:** 1745 applied, 1554 accepted, 756 enrolled
SAT CR/M: 520/480 **ACT:** 24	**CEEB CODE:** 1401
Application Deadline: September 1	**COMPETITIVE**

Lee University, founded in 1918, is a private liberal arts institution affiliated with the Church of God. There are 5 undergraduate schools and 5 graduate schools. In addition to regional accreditation, Lee has baccalaureate program accreditation with ACBSP, AND NASM. The 120-acre campus is in a suburban area 20 miles north of Chattanooga. Including any residence halls, there are 50 buildings.

STUDENT LIFE: 55% of undergraduates are from out of state, mostly the South. Students are from 49 states, 54 foreign countries, and Canada. 83% are White; 6% Foreign; 5% African American; 4% Hispanic; 2% Asian American. **Female To Male Ratio:** 1.3:1. The average age of freshmen is 18; all undergraduates, 23. **Housing:** 1870 students can be accommodated in college housing, which includes married student dorms, on-campus apartments, off-campus apartments, and apartments for single students. On-campus housing is guaranteed for the freshman year only, and is available on a first-come, first-served basis. 56% of students commute. All students may keep cars. Alcohol is not permitted.

FACULTY/CLASSROOMS: 63% of faculty are male; 37% are female. All teach undergraduates, 20% do research, and 20% do both. No introductory courses are taught by graduate students. The average class size in an introductory lecture is 25; in a laboratory is 15; and in a regular course is 28.

PROGRAMS OF STUDY: Lee confers B.A., B.S., B.C.M., B.M., and B.M.E. degrees. Master's degrees are also awarded. Bachelor's degrees are awarded in BIOLOGICAL SCIENCE (biochemistry and biology/biological science), BUSINESS (accounting and business administration and management), COMMUNICATIONS AND THE ARTS (communications, dramatic arts, English, French, music, music business management, music performance, public relations, Spanish, and telecommunications), COMPUTER AND PHYSICAL SCIENCE (chemistry, information sciences and systems, mathematics, and science), EDUCATION (athletic training, business education, elementary education, health education, mathematics education, middle school education, music education, physical education, and special education), HEALTH PROFESSIONS (health care administration, health science, and medical laboratory technology), SOCIAL SCIENCE (anthropology, biblical studies, crosscultural studies, history, human development, humanities, interdisciplinary studies, ministries, political science/government, psychology, religious music, sociology, and youth ministry). Business administration, communication, and human development are the strongest academically. Education, business, and psychology have the largest enrollments.

ACTIVITIES: 10% of men belong to 5 local fraternities; 10% of women belong to 5 local sororities. There are 95 groups on campus, including art, band, cheerleading, choir, chorale, chorus, computers, debate, drama, ethnic, honors, international, jazz band, literary magazine, musical theater, newspaper, opera, orchestra, pep band, photography, political, professional, religious, social, social service, student government, symphony, and yearbook. Popular campus events include Lee Day, Parade of Favorites, and Dorm Wars. **Sports:** There are 6 intercollegiate sports for men and women, and 11 intramural sports for men and women. Facilities include an arena, recreation complex, softball field, tennis center, soccer field, baseball field, and a playing field. **Graduates:** From July 1, 2016 to June 30, 2017, 781 bachelor's degrees were awarded. The most popular majors were education, and theology and religious studies (18%), psychology, and business/marketing (9%), and health professions and related programs (7%). In an average class, 1% graduate in 3 years or less, 29% graduate in 4 years or less, 44% graduate in 5 years or less, and 49% graduate in 6 years or less.

SERVICES: Counseling and information services are available, as is

tutoring in every subject. There is a reader service for the blind, and remedial math, reading, and writing. **Library/Resources:** The library contains 271,897 volumes, 51,385 microform items, 1,671 audio/video tapes/CDs/DVDs, and subscribes to 34,881 periodicals, including electronic. Computerized library services include interlibrary loans, database searching, Internet access, and Wi-Fi capability. **Physically Challenged Students:** 73% of the campus is accessible. Facilities include wheelchair ramps, elevators, special parking, specially equipped restrooms, special class scheduling, lowered drinking fountains, and lowered telephones. **Special:** Lee offers internships, cross-registration with the Coalition for Christian Colleges and Universities, study abroad in 25 countries, a Washington semester, numerous work-study programs, an accelerated degree program in Christian leadership, dual and student-designed majors, nondegree study, and limited pass/fail options. Every student completes a minor in religion. There are 16 national honor societies, a freshman honors program, and 6 departmental honors programs. **Visiting:** There are regularly scheduled orientations for prospective students, with a complete campus tour upon request. There are guides for informal visits and visitors may sit in on classes. To schedule a visit, contact the Admissions Office. **Campus Safety and Security:** Measures include 24-hour foot and vehicle patrol, emergency notification system, and security escort services. There are shuttle buses, emergency telephones, and lighted pathways/sidewalks.

REQUIREMENTS: The SAT or ACT is recommended. Students must be graduates of accredited secondary schools. The GED is accepted. A portfolio is recommended. 13 high school units are required, (14 recommended) includes 4 units in English, 3 units in math, and 2 units each in science, and social studies, and 1 unit each in foreign language and history, and 1 in computer science (recommended). Students with 16 college semester hours, 24 for TN residents, are not required to provide test scores. AP and CLEP credits are accepted. Important factors in the admissions decision are advanced placement or honors courses, leadership record, personality/intangible qualities, parents or siblings attended your school, evidence of special talent, extracurricular activities record, geographical diversity, and recommendations by school officials. All students must complete a minimum of 130 credit hours, including a core curriculum and 36 hours in the major, with a 2.0 GPA (2.5 for education majors). A Global Perspectives seminar and cross-cultural experience are required, in addition to a major field test the last semester before graduation in all fields except preprofessional science and teacher licensure. **Procedure:** Freshmen are admitted in the fall and spring. Entrance exams should be taken prior to registration. There are early admissions, deferred admissions, and rolling admissions plans. Early decision applications should be filed by January 1; regular applications, by September 1 for fall entry. The fall 2017 application fee was $25. Notifications are sent September 1. Applications are accepted on-line. **Transfer Students:** 232 transfer students enrolled in 2016-2017. Transfer students must take the SAT or the ACT unless they have 16 credit hours with a GPA of 2.0 or better. Students must have official transcripts from all prior colleges. 30 of 130 credits required for the bachelor's degree must be completed at Lee. **International Students:** There are 208 international students enrolled. They must take the TOEFL and either the SAT or ACT.

ADMISSIONS: 89% of the 2017-2018 applicants were accepted. The SAT scores for the 2017-2018 freshman class were: Critical Reading-- 39% below 500, 38% between 500 and 599, 21% between 600 and 699, and 2% between 700 and 800. Math-- 46% below 500, 40% between 500 and 599, 11% between 600 and 699, and 2% between 700 and 800. 43% of the current freshmen were in the top fifth of their class; 68% were in the top two fifths. **Admissions Contact:** Phil Cook, Vice President for Enrollment. Email: *admissions@leeuniversity.edu* Web: *www.leeuniversity.edu*

FINANCIAL AID: In 2017-2018, 89% of all full-time freshmen received some form of financial aid, and need-based aid. The average freshman award was $12,763. Need-based scholarships or need-based grants averaged $10,615; need-based self-help aid (loans and jobs) averaged $3,565; non-need-based athletic scholarships averaged $9,134; other non-need-based awards and non-need-based scholarships averaged $8,465; and $3,528 from other forms of aid. The average financial indebtedness of the 2017 graduate was $32,162. The college's own financial statement is required. The FAFSA code is 003500. The priority date for freshman financial aid applications for fall entry is March 15.

LEMOYNE-OWEN COLLEGE — A-3

www.loc.edu

Memphis, TN 38126	**(901) 435-1528** **(800) 737-7778**
Fax: (901) 942-6233	**Email: admissions@loc.edu**
Full-time: 300 men, 340 women	**Faculty:** 45
Part-time: 65 men, 80 women	**Ph.D.s:** 80%
Graduate: n/av	**Student/Faculty:** 14 to 1
Year: semesters, summer session	**Tuition:** $10,880
Room & Board: $6100	**Freshman Class:** n/av
SAT or ACT: required	**CEEB CODE:** 1403
Application Deadline: n/av	**COMPETITIVE**

LeMoyne-Owen College, founded in 1862, is a private, liberal arts college affiliated with the United Church of Christ and the Tennessee Baptist, Missionary and Educational Convention, offering degrees in the liberal arts and sciences and business administration. There is 1 undergraduate school. The 15-acre campus is in an urban area in Memphis, TN. Including any residence halls, there are 18 buildings.

STUDENT LIFE: 87% of undergraduates are from Tennessee. Others are from 17 states, and 10 foreign countries. 95% are from public schools. 97% are African American; 1% White; 1% Hispanic; 1% Foreign. 87% are Protestant. **Female To Male Ratio:** 1.2:1. The average age of freshmen is 18; all undergraduates, 26. **Housing:** 336 students can be accommodated in college housing, which includes dorms. On-campus housing is available on a first-come, first-served basis. 80% of students commute. All students may keep cars. Alcohol is not permitted.

FACULTY/CLASSROOMS: All teach undergraduates and 40% do research. No introductory courses are taught by graduate students. The average class size in an introductory lecture is 15; in a laboratory is 15; and in a regular course is 12.

PROGRAMS OF STUDY: LeMoyne-Owen confers B.A., B.S., and B.B.A. degrees. Associate degrees are also awarded. Bachelor's degrees are awarded in BIOLOGICAL SCIENCE (biology/biological science), BUSINESS (accounting and business administration and management), COMMUNICATIONS AND THE ARTS (art, English, information technology, language arts, and music), COMPUTER AND PHYSICAL SCIENCE (chemistry, computer science, mathematics, natural sciences, and science), EDUCATION (early childhood education, education, and special education), SOCIAL SCIENCE (criminal justice, history, humanities, interdisciplinary studies, political science/government, social science, social work, sociology, and urban studies). Business, biology, and education are the strongest academically. Business, and biology have the largest enrollments.

ACTIVITIES: 8% of men belong to 4 national fraternities; 5% of women belong to 4 national sororities. There are 15 groups on campus, including cheerleading, choir, chorus, community outreach, drama, ethnic, newspaper, professional, religious, social service, and student government. Popular campus events include Homecoming and Black History Month. **Sports:** There are 4 intercollegiate sports for men and 5 for women. Facilities include a gym, a pool, and other physical education installations. **Graduates:** From July 1, 2016 to June 30, 2017, 118 bachelor's degrees were awarded. The most popular majors were business management (37%), liberal studies (12%), and education (12%).

SERVICES: Counseling and information services are available, as is tutoring in every subject. There is also remedial math, reading, and writing. **Library/Resources:** The library contains 90,000 volumes, 1,000 audio/video tapes/CDs/DVDs, and subscribes to 300 periodicals, including electronic. Computerized library services include interlibrary loans, database searching, Internet access, and Wi-Fi capability. Special learning facilities include an art gallery. **Physically Challenged Students:** All of the campus is accessible. Facilities include wheelchair ramps, elevators, special parking, and special class scheduling. **Special:** Students may cross-register with other institutions of the Greater Memphis Consortium. The college offers a work-study program, dual and student-designed majors, internships, nondegree study, and a pass/fail grading option. There is 1 national honor society, a freshman honors program, and 1 departmental honors program. **Visiting:** There are regularly scheduled orientations for prospective students. There are guides for informal visits and visitors may sit in on classes. **Campus Safety and Security:** Measures include 24-hour foot and vehicle patrol and security escort services. There are emergency telephones and lighted pathways/sidewalks.

REQUIREMENTS: The SAT or ACT is required. Applicants must graduate from an accredited secondary school, having completed 20 high school units. The college recommends 4 years of English, 2 each of math, science, and social studies, and 1 of a foreign language. Applicants must submit 2 letters of recommendation. Students 23 or older may be admitted to the division of lifelong learning, which accepts the GED. AP and CLEP credits are accepted. Important factors in the admissions decision are advanced placement or honors courses, evidence of special talent, and parents or siblings attended your school. Successfully, completed at least 120 semester hours of course work with a minimum cumulative GPA of 2.0. The last 30 of these credit hours must have been earned at LeMoyne-Owen College, and must include at least three credit hours in Core II courses. Only courses completed with a grade of A, B, C, D or P can be credited toward the degree. Earned at least 45 credit hours in 300 and 400 numbered courses at the junior/senior level. Completed the General and Liberal Arts Education Core Requirements with a minimum grade of C in all Core I and six of the Core II courses. Met the specific course requirements for a major concentration area with a minimum grade of C in all courses required for the major including cognate courses. Submitted a formal application for the degree and completed the College exit interview. All recent high school graduates must participate in the Freshman Year Experience Program. **Procedure:** Freshmen are admitted to all sessions. Entrance exams should be taken in the spring of the junior year. There are early admissions, deferred admissions, and rolling admissions plans. Applications should be filed by November 1 for spring entry; March 1 for summer entry. The fall 2017 application fee was $25. Notifications are sent July 1. **Transfer Students:** 122 transfer students enrolled in 2016-2017. Applicants should have a GPA of 2.0 and must submit 2 copies of official transcripts plus a statement of good standing from the previous college attended. Students with fewer than 28 college credit hours must also submit a high school transcript and, if below age 21, ACT or SAT I scores. 30 of 120 credits required for the bachelor's degree must be completed at Lemoyne-Owen. **International Students:** They must take the TOEFL and take the ACT.

Admissions Contact: Delphia Harris, Director of Admissions. Email: *admissions@loc.edu* Web: *www.loc.edu*

FINANCIAL AID: In 2017-2018, 90% of all full-time freshmen received some form of financial aid. 80% of all full-time freshmen received need-based aid. 90% of undergraduate students work part-time. LeMoyne-Owen is a member of CSS. The college's own financial statement is required. The FAFSA code is 003501. The priority date for freshman financial aid applications for fall entry is May 1.

LINCOLN MEMORIAL UNIVERSITY — E-1

www.lmunet.edu

Harrogate, TN 37752 — **(423) 869-6280**, **(800) 325-0900**

Fax: (423) 869-6370 — **Email: admissions@lmunet.edu**

Full-time: 350 men, 1000 women	**Faculty:** n/av
Part-time: 84 men, 220 women	**Ph.D.s:** n/av
Graduate: 408 men, 1078 women	**Student/Faculty:** 12 to 1
Year: semesters, summer session	**Tuition:** $20,880
Room & Board: $7550	**Freshman Class:** 1350 applied, 494 accepted, 184 enrolled
SAT or ACT: required	**CEEB CODE:** 1408
Application Deadline: open	**COMPETITIVE**

Lincoln Memorial University, founded in 1897, is an independent institution offering degree programs in the arts and sciences, business, education, and preprofessional training. The figures given in the above capsule and in this profile are approximate. There are 4 undergraduate schools and 2 graduate schools. In addition to regional accreditation, LMU has baccalaureate program accreditation with CAHEA and NLN. The 1000-acre campus is in a rural area 55 miles north of Knoxville. Including any residence halls, there are 32 buildings.

STUDENT LIFE: 67% of undergraduates are from Tennessee. Others are from 25 states, 22 foreign countries, and Canada. 89% are from public schools. 94% are White; 4% Foreign; 2% African American. **Female To Male Ratio:** 2.7:1. The average age of freshmen is 19; all undergraduates, 23. 20% do not continue beyond their first year; 50% remain to graduate. **Housing:** 500 students can be accommodated in college housing, which includes married student dorms and on-campus apartments. On-campus housing is guaranteed for the freshman year only, and is available on a first-come, first-served basis. 70% of students commute. All students may keep cars. Alcohol is not permitted.

FACULTY/CLASSROOMS: 49% of faculty are male; 51% are female. 80% teach undergraduates. No introductory courses are taught by graduate students. The average class size in an introductory lecture is 20; in a laboratory is 25; and in a regular course is 20.

PROGRAMS OF STUDY: LMU confers B.A., B.S., B.B.A., B.S.N., and B.S.W. degrees. Associate and master's degrees are also awarded. Bachelor's degrees are awarded in AGRICULTURE (wildlife management), BIOLOGICAL SCIENCE (biology/biological science), BUSINESS (accounting and business administration and management), COMMUNICATIONS AND THE ARTS (broadcasting, communications, English, and fine arts), COMPUTER AND PHYSICAL SCIENCE (chemistry, information sciences and systems, and mathematics), EDUCATION (athletic training, business education, early childhood education, elementary education, health education, middle school education, science education, and secondary education), ENGINEERING AND ENVIRONMENTAL DESIGN (environmental science), HEALTH PROFESSIONS (medical laboratory technology, nursing, predentistry, premedicine, and veterinary science), SOCIAL SCIENCE (history, prelaw, psychology, social science, and social work). Nursing, business, and education have the largest enrollments.

ACTIVITIES: There are 26 groups on campus, including art, cheerleading, choir, chorus, computers, drama, drill team, honors, international, literary magazine, newspaper, photography, radio and TV, religious, social service, student government, and yearbook. Popular campus events include Lincoln Day. **Sports:** There are 6 intercollegiate sports for men and women, and 4 intramural sports for men and women. Facilities include an arena, a gym, golf complex, soccer complex, tennis complex, and sports fields. **Graduates:** From July 1, 2016 to June 30, 2017, 145 bachelor's degrees were awarded. The most popular majors were nursing (30%), elementary education (27%), and business (26%). In an average class, 42% graduate in 4 years or less.

SERVICES: Counseling and information services are available, as is tutoring in most subjects. There is remedial math, reading, and writing. **Library/Resources:** The library contains 200,000 volumes, 160,506 microform items, and 254 audio/video tapes/CDs/DVDs, and subscribes to 893 periodicals, including electronic. Computerized library services include interlibrary loans, database searching, and Internet access. Special learning facilities include a radio station, TV station, and the Lincoln Museum. **Physically Challenged Students:** 60% of the campus is accessible. Facilities include wheelchair ramps, elevators, special parking, and special class scheduling. **Special:** LMU offers pass/fail options and credit for life, military, and work experience. Some internships are available. **Visiting:** There are regularly scheduled orientations for prospective students, including introductory sessions for both students and their parents and opportunities for advising, and registration sessions. There are guides for informal visits, visitors may sit in on classes, and stay overnight. To schedule a visit, contact the Office of Admissions and Recruitment. **Campus Safety and Security:** Measures include 24-hour foot and vehicle patrol, and lighted pathways/sidewalks.

REQUIREMENTS: Applicants must score 19 on the ACT or satisfactorily on the SAT, or graduate with a GPA of at least 2.3. Candidates for admission should be graduates of accredited secondary schools or have the GED. Students should have completed 4 years of English, 2 each of math and science, and 1 each of history and social studies. LMU requires applicants to be in the upper 50% of their class. AP and CLEP credits are accepted. Important factors in the admissions decision are recommendations by school officials, personality/intangible qualities, and leadership record. To graduate, all students must complete at least 128 semester credit hours, including the general studies requirements of the declared major and a minimum of 30 hours of in the major. Students must achieve a minimum GPA of 2.0. **Procedure:** Freshmen are admitted in the fall, spring, and summer. Entrance exams should be taken in the spring of the junior year. There are early admissions, deferred admissions, and rolling admissions plans. Application deadlines are open. The fall 2017 application fee was $25. **Transfer Students:** Transfer students who have completed 12 or more semester credit hours of potentially transferable coursework at a regionally accredited college or university will be considered for transfer admissions. Students with fewer that 12 semester credit hours are subject to freshman admission procedures. Official transcripts from all colleges and universities must be submitted. 32 of 128 credits required for the bachelor's degree must be completed at LMU. **International Students:** There are 48 international students enrolled. They must take the TOEFL.

ADMISSIONS: 37% of the 2017-2018 applicants were accepted. **Admissions Contact:** Carla Brandon, Assistant Director of Admissions. Email: *admissions@lmunet.edu* Web: *www.lmunet.edu*

FINANCIAL AID: LMU is a member of CSS. The CCS/Profile, FAFSA, and the FFS or SFS are required. The FAFSA code is 003502. Check with the school for current application deadlines.

LIPSCOMB UNIVERSITY — C-2
www.lipscomb.edu

Nashville, TN 37204	(615) 966-6150 (877) 582-4766
Fax: (615) 966-1804	Email: admissions@lipscomb.edu
Full-time: 1074 men, 1649 women	Faculty: 175
Part-time: 96 men, 168 women	Ph.D.s: 83%
Graduate: 574 men, 1081 women	Student/Faculty: 16 to 1
Year: semesters, summer session	Tuition: $30,932
Room & Board: $12,052	Freshman Class: 3581 applied, 2164 accepted, 641 enrolled
SAT CR/M: 600/580 ACT: 26	CEEB CODE: 1161
Application Deadline: open	VERY COMPETITIVE

Lipscomb University is a private coeducational institution whose principal focus is undergraduate education in the liberal arts and sciences, combined with a number of undergraduate professional and preprofessional fields, master's and doctoral degree programs. Its primary mission is to integrate Christian faith and practice with academic excellence. This mission is carried out not only in the classroom but also by involvement in numerous services to the church and the larger community. There are 10 undergraduate schools and 16 graduate schools. In addition to regional accreditation, LU has baccalaureate program accreditation with ABET, ACBSP, ACPE, ADA, CSWE, NASM, CAEP, CAAHEP, ACS, and ATS. The 89-acre campus is in a suburban area 2 miles south of downtown Nashville. Including any residence halls, there are 48 buildings.

STUDENT LIFE: 61% of undergraduates are from Tennessee. Others are from 47 states, 50 foreign countries, and Canada. 56% are from public schools. 77% are White; 7% Hispanic; 6% African American; 3% Asian American; 3% Foreign; 3% two or more races; 1% race unknown. 79% are Protestant. **Female To Male Ratio:** 1.7:1. The average age of freshmen is 18; all undergraduates, 21. **Housing:** 1620 students can be accommodated in college housing, which includes dorms and on-campus apartments. On-campus housing is guaranteed for the freshman year only, and is available on a first-come, first-served basis. 53% of students live on campus. All students may keep cars. Alcohol is not permitted.

FACULTY/CLASSROOMS: 56% of faculty are male; 44% are female. 64% teach undergraduates and 2% do research. No introductory courses are taught by graduate students.

PROGRAMS OF STUDY: LU confers B.A., B.S., B.B.A., B.F.A., B.M., B.S.N., B.S.W., and B.P.S. degrees. Associate, master's, and doctoral degrees are also awarded. Bachelor's degrees are awarded in AGRICULTURE (conservation and regulation), BIOLOGICAL SCIENCE (biochemistry, biology/adolescence education, biology/biological science, biophysics, and molecular biology), BUSINESS (accounting, business administration and management, entrepreneurial studies, fashion merchandising, finance, human resources/organizational management, international business management, management information systems, marketing management, marketing/retailing/merchandising, sports management, supply chain management, and sustainable management), COMMUNICATIONS AND THE ARTS (acting, art, communications, English, French, German, graphic design, journalism, music, music composition, music ministry, music performance, musical theater, Spanish, studio art, theatre arts, and visual and performing arts), COMPUTER AND PHYSICAL SCIENCE (applied mathematics, chemistry, chemistry/adolescence education, computer science, mathematics, physics, software engineering, and web services), EDUCATION (art education, drama education, early childhood education, education, elementary education, English education, foreign languages education, health education, mathematics education, middle school education, music education, and physical education), ENGINEERING AND ENVIRONMENTAL DESIGN (civil engineering, computer engineering, electrical/electronics engineering, environmental science, mechanical engineering, and preengineering), HEALTH PROFESSIONS (art therapy, exercise science, medical technology, nursing, predentistry, premedicine, preoptometry, prepharmacy, prephysical therapy, and preveterinary science), SOCIAL SCIENCE (American studies, biblical languages, biblical studies, dietetics, economics, European studies, family/consumer studies, food production/management/services, history, interdisciplinary studies, international studies, legal studies, liberal arts/general studies, missions, philosophy, political science/government, prelaw, psychology, social work, textiles and clothing, urban studies, and youth ministry). Biology, education, and engineering are the strongest academically. Business, biology, and nursing have the largest enrollments.

ACTIVITIES: 16% of men belong to 6 local fraternities; 17% of women belong to 7 local sororities. There are 55 groups on campus, including art, band, cheerleading, choir, chorale, chorus, computers, drama, environmental, ethnic, honors, international, jazz band, musical theater, newspaper, orchestra, pep band, photography, political, professional, radio and TV, religious, social, social service, student government, and yearbook. Popular campus events include Singarama, Annual Service Day, International Square Fair, StompFest, Anteater's Ball, Paint the Herd, and Battle of the Boulevard. **Sports:** There are 7 intercollegiate sports for men and 8 for women, and 13 intramural sports for men and 13 for women. Facilities include a basketball/multi-purpose court, student activity center with 2 full-size basketball courts, 4 racquetball courts, a jogging course, and weight, aerobics, spinning, and recreation rooms for both men and women. **Graduates:** From July 1, 2016 to June 30, 2017, 687 bachelor's degrees were awarded. The most popular majors were business administration and marketing (22%), health professions and related programs (15%), and education (8%). In an average class, 48% graduate in 4 years or less, 56% graduate in 5 years or less, and 58% graduate in 6 years or less. Of the 2016 graduating class, 30% were enrolled in graduate school within 6 months of graduation, and 60% were employed.

SERVICES: Counseling and information services are available, as is tutoring in some subjects, such as math, English, biology, and chemistry. There is also a reader service for the blind, and remedial math, reading, and writing. **Library/Resources:** The library contains 158,948 volumes, 402,464 microform items, 5,726 audio/video tapes/CDs/DVDs, and subscribes to 653 periodicals, including electronic. Computerized library services include interlibrary loans, database searching, Internet access, and Wi-Fi capability. Special learning facilities include an art gallery, radio station, and a multimedia production studio. **Physically Challenged Students:** All of the campus is accessible. Facilities include wheelchair ramps, elevators, special parking, specially equipped restrooms, special class scheduling, and lowered drinking fountains. **Special:** Some majors require an internship. There are study-abroad options through Lipscomb programs in Austria, Chile, and England, as well as a cooperative program with the Council for Christian Colleges and Universities (CCCU) that allows students to choose from multiple countries. Several degree programs can be completed in an accelerated three-year format. A B.A.-B.S. option is available in music, and a B.F.A. option is available in art and theatre. Students can pursue an integrated studies major that allows them to custom design a course of study to match their personal and professional interests and goals. There are dual bachelor's/master's degree options available in accounting, biology, and information technology. There are 5 national honor societies and a freshman honors program. **Visiting:** There are regularly scheduled orientations for prospective students. There are guides for informal visits; visitors may sit in on classes and stay overnight. To schedule a visit, contact Dana Anderson at (615) 966-1776. **Campus Safety and Security:** Measures include 24-hour foot and vehicle patrol, an emergency notification system, self-defense education, and security escort services. There are shuttle buses, emergency telephones, lighted pathways/sidewalks, controlled access to dorms/residences, and residence hall security systems.

REQUIREMENTS: The SAT or ACT is required. Candidates for admission should be graduates of accredited secondary schools. The GED is accepted. 14 academic units are required. Students should have completed 4 units of English and 2 units each of history, math, and science, 2 units of foreign language are highly recommended, 2 additional units each of English, foreign language, history, math, science, and social studies are also required. AP and CLEP credits are accepted. All students must take 18 hours of Bible/theology courses. Other general education requirements include Lipscomb Seminar (freshman seminar class), 6 semester hours each in communications, humanities, science, history, and social science, 3 in math, 2 physical education, and 2 service learning experiences. Students must complete a total of 126 semester hours and have a minimum GPA of 2.0. At least 25% of credit hours must be earned at LU. Students are required to take and pass a proficiency test of basic computer concepts. **Procedure:** Freshmen are admitted to all sessions. There is a rolling admissions plan. Application deadlines are open. The fall 2017 application fee was $50. Applications are accepted on-line. **Transfer Students:** 161 transfer students enrolled in 2016-2017. College transcripts, an interview, and a statement of good standing from prior institutions are required. 32 of 126 credits required for the bachelor's degree must be completed at LU. **International Students:** There are 85 international students enrolled. They must take the TOEFL with a minimum score of 550 on the paper-based TOEFL (PBT) or 80 on the Internet-based version (iBT) or take the MELAB. They must also take the SAT or ACT.

ADMISSIONS: 60% of the 2017-2018 applicants were accepted. The SAT scores for the 2017-2018 freshman class were: Critical Reading-- 11% below 500, 36% between 500 and 599, 36% between 600 and 699, and 17% between 700 and 800. Math-- 15% below 500, 42% between 500 and 599, 33% between 600 and 699, and 10% between 700 and 800. The ACT scores were 31% between 18 and 23, 46% between 24 and 29, and 23% above 30. 13 freshmen graduated first in their class. **Admissions Contact:** Johnathan Akin, Senior Director of Admissions. Email: *admissions@lipscomb.edu* Web: *www.lipscomb.edu*

FINANCIAL AID: In 2017-2018, 99% of all full-time freshmen received some form of financial aid. 108% of undergraduate students work part-time. The FAFSA code is 003486. The priority date for freshman financial aid applications for fall entry is January 31.

MARYVILLE COLLEGE E-2

www.maryvillecollege.edu

Maryville, TN 37804	**(865) 981-8206** **(800) 597-2687**
Fax: (865) 981-8005	**Email: admissions@maryvillecollege.edu**
Full-time: 518 men, 644 women	**Faculty:** 78; IIB, --$
Part-time: 8 men, 6 women	**Ph.D.s:** 91%
Graduate: n/av	**Student/Faculty:** 15 to 1
Year: 4-1-4, summer session	**Tuition:** $33,542
Room & Board: $10,868	**Freshman Class:** 1584 applied, 1203 accepted, 317 enrolled
SAT CR/M/W: 537/535/528 **ACT:** 24	**CEEB CODE:** 1454
Application Deadline: March 1	**COMPETITIVE**

Maryville College, founded in 1819, is a private liberal arts college affiliated with the Presbyterian Church. The figures given in the above capsule and in this profile are approximate. There is 1 undergraduate school. In addition to regional accreditation, MC has baccalaureate program accreditation with NASM. The 350-acre campus is in a suburban area 15 miles south of Knoxville. Including any residence halls, there are 22 buildings.

STUDENT LIFE: 76% of undergraduates are from Tennessee. Others are from 32 states, 20 foreign countries, and Canada. 87% are from public schools. 85% are White; 6% African American; 4% Foreign; 2% Hispanic; 1% Asian American; 1% American Indian/Alaska Native. 64% are Protestant. **Female To Male Ratio:** 1.2:1. The average age of freshmen is 18; all undergraduates, 21. 28% do not continue beyond their first year; 52% remain to graduate. **Housing:** 802 students can be accommodated in college housing, which includes dorms, on-campus apartments, and off-campus apartments. In addition, there are language/international houses and special-interest houses. On-campus housing is guaranteed for all 4 years. 69% of students live on campus. All students may keep cars.

FACULTY/CLASSROOMS: 45% of faculty are male; 55% are female. All teach undergraduates and do research. No introductory courses are taught by graduate students. The average class size in an introductory lecture is 28; in a laboratory is 15; and in a regular course is 16.

PROGRAMS OF STUDY: MC confers B.A. and B.Mus. degrees. Bachelor's degrees are awarded in AGRICULTURE (environmental studies), BIOLOGICAL SCIENCE (biochemistry and biology/biological science), BUSINESS (business administration and management and recreation and leisure services), COMMUNICATIONS AND THE ARTS (American Sign Language, art, art history and appreciation, creative writing, dramatic arts, English, English as a second/foreign language, music, music performance, and Spanish), COMPUTER AND PHYSICAL SCIENCE (chemical physics, chemistry, computer science, and mathematics), EDUCATION (elementary education, music education, physical education, science education, and secondary education), ENGINEERING AND ENVIRONMENTAL DESIGN (engineering and preengineering), HEALTH PROFESSIONS (nursing, predentistry, and premedicine), SOCIAL SCIENCE (economics, history, international relations, interpreter for the deaf, political science/government, prelaw, psychology, religion, social science, and sociology). Biology, chemistry, and English are the strongest academically. Business, biology, and psychology have the largest enrollments.

ACTIVITIES: There are no fraternities or sororities. There are 53 groups on campus, including gospel music club, art, band, cheerleading, choir, chorus, computers, dance, drama, equestrianclub, ethnic, honors, international, jazz band, LGBT, literary magazine, musical theater, newspaper, orchestra, pep band, photography, political, professional, radio and TV, religious, social service, student government, and symphony. Popular campus events include Dogwood Arts Festival, Blister-in-the-Sun, and Spring Fling. **Sports:** There are 7 intercollegiate sports for men and 7 for women, and 12 intramural sports for men and 11 for women. Facilities include a physical education building with an indoor pool, tennis and racquetball courts, a weight room, and football, soccer, baseball, and softball fields, and off-campus equestrian arena. **Graduates:** From July 1, 2016 to June 30, 2017, 201 bachelor's degrees were awarded. The most popular majors were business/commerce (16%), child development (11%), and psychology (6%). In an average class, 45% graduate in 4 years or less, 50% graduate in 5 years or less, and 52% graduate in 6 years or less. Of the 2016 graduating class, 28% were enrolled in graduate school within 6 months of graduation, and 67% were employed.

SERVICES: Counseling and information services are available, as is tutoring in every subject. There is a reader service for the blind, and remedial math. There are sign language interpreters for deaf students. **Library/Resources:** The library contains 133,686 volumes, 8,263 microform items, and subscribes to 16,525 periodicals, including electronic. Computerized library services include interlibrary loans, database searching, Internet access, and Wi-Fi capability. Special learning facilities include an art gallery, a radio station, and a greenhouse. **Physically Challenged Students:** 75% of the campus is accessible. Facilities include wheelchair ramps, elevators, special parking, specially equipped restrooms, special class scheduling, lowered drinking fountains, lowered telephones, and special housing. **Special:** MC offers cross-registration with the University of Tennessee and Vanderbilt University, internships, study abroad in 9 countries, a Washington semester, accelerated degree programs, a B.A.-B.S. degree in engineering, and dual and student-designed majors. There are 3-2 engineering degrees offered with regional universities. Nondegree study and pass/fail options are possible. There are 6 national honor societies, a freshman honors program, and 100 departmental honors programs. **Visiting:** There are regularly scheduled orientations for prospective students, including an overnight in a residence hall, class attendance, meeting with students and faculty, a campus tour, and an interview. There are guides for informal visits; visitors may sit in on classes and stay overnight. To schedule a visit, contact the Admissions Office. **Campus Safety and Security:** Measures include 24-hour foot and vehicle patrol, security escort services, and lighted pathways/sidewalks.

REQUIREMENTS: The SAT or ACT is required. Candidates should be graduates of accredited secondary schools or have the GED. They should also have 15 academic credits with 4 years of English, 3 of math and science, 2 years of foreign language, history or social studies. An essay, portfolio, audition, and interview are all recommended. AP and CLEP credits are accepted. Important factors in the admissions decision are advanced placement or honors courses, extracurricular activities record, and leadership record. Each degree has its own general education requirements, which include humanities and a foreign language. Students must complete at least 128 total credit hours, including 48 in the major, and must maintain a minimum 2.0 GPA. A year-long freshman seminar and orientation are required in addition to a senior thesis in all majors and senior comprehensive exams. **Procedure:** Freshmen are admitted in the fall, spring, and summer. Entrance exams should be taken by October of the senior year. There are early decision, early admissions, and deferred admissions plans. Early decision applications should be filed by November 15; regular applications, by March 1 for fall entry; November 1 for spring entry; and May 1 for summer entry. Notification of early decision is sent December 1; regular decision, April 1. 84 early decision candidates were accepted for the 2017-2018 class. Applications are accepted on-line.

Transfer Students: 53 transfer students enrolled in 2016-2017. Transfer applicants must have a minimum GPA of 2.0 and a recommended 15 credit hours earned. An interview is also recommended. 45 of 128 credits required for the bachelor's degree must be completed at Maryville. **International Students:** There are 44 international students enrolled. They must take the TOEFL with a minimum score of 525 on the paper-based TOEFL (PBT) or 74 on the Internet-based version (iBT). Students must take the IELTS or the STEP test grade pre-One.

ADMISSIONS: 76% of the 2017-2018 applicants were accepted. The SAT scores for the 2017-2018 freshman class were: Critical Reading-- 35% below 500, 34% between 500 and 599, 27% between 600 and 699, and 4% between 700 and 800. Math-- 34% below 500, 42% between 500 and 599, 23% between 600 and 699, and 1% between 700 and 800. Writing-- 35% below 500, 37% between 500 and 599, 25% between 600 and 699, and 3% between 700 and 800. The ACT scores were 20% below 12, 26% between 12 and 17, 23% between 18 and 23, 16% between 24 and 29, and 15% above 30. 52% of the current freshmen were in the top fifth of their class; 80% were in the top two fifths. 5 freshmen graduated first in their class. **Admissions Contact:** Doug Carter, Assistant Director of Admissions. Email: *admissions@maryvillecollege.edu* Web: *www.maryvillecollege.edu*

FINANCIAL AID: In 2017-2018, 100% of all full-time freshmen received some form of financial aid. 97% of all full-time freshmen received need-based aid. The average freshman award was $26,518. Need-based scholarships or need-based grants averaged $17,728 ($36,610 maximum); need-based self-help aid (loans and jobs) averaged $2,859 ($7,500 maximum); and other non-need-based awards and non-need-based scholarships averaged $1,947 ($23,000 maximum). The average financial indebtedness of the 2017 graduate was $14,344. MC is a member of CSS. The FAFSA code is 003505. The priority date for freshman financial aid applications for fall entry is March 1.

MEMPHIS COLLEGE OF ART *(The complete profile is made available exclusively on our website, www.barronspac.com)*

MIDDLE TENNESSEE STATE UNIVERSITY C-2

www.mtsu.edu

Murfreesboro, TN 37132 **(615) 898-2111**

Fax: (615) 898-5478
Full-time: 9204 men, 9708 women
Part-time: 1577 men, 1810 women
Graduate: 963 men, 1926 women
Year: semesters, summer session
Room & Board: $4650
SAT: required **ACT:** 22
Application Deadline: July 1

Email: admissions@mtsu.edu
Faculty: n/av
Ph.D.s: 68%
Student/Faculty: n/av
Tuition: $4000 ($11,900)
Freshman Class: 9431 applied, 6616 accepted, 1758 enrolled
CEEB CODE: 1466
COMPETITIVE

Middle Tennessee State University, founded in 1911, is a comprehensive public university that offers undergraduate and graduate programs reflecting an emphasis on research, creative arts, and public and professional service activities. The figures given in the above capsule and in this profile are approximate. There are 7 undergraduate schools and 1 graduate school. In addition to regional accreditation, MTSU has baccalaureate program accreditation with AACSB, ABET, ACEJMC, ADA, CSAB, CSWE, FIDER, NASAD, NASM, NLN, NRPA, ACS, NAIT, AAFCS, CAA, NASP, and CACREP. The 500-acre campus is in an urban area 32 miles southeast of Nashville, TN. Including any residence halls, there are 159 buildings.

STUDENT LIFE: 93% of undergraduates are from Tennessee. Others are from 47 states, 70 foreign countries, and Canada. 80% are White; 3% Asian American; 2% Hispanic; 14% African American. 45% are Protestant; 43% claim no religious affiliation. **Female To Male Ratio:** 1.1:1. The average age of freshmen is 18; all undergraduates, 19. **Housing:** 3294 students can be accommodated in college housing, which includes married student dorms and on-campus apartments. In addition, there are honors houses, fraternity houses, sorority houses, first year experience program, and various learning community programs. On-campus housing is available on a first-come, first-served basis. 85% of students commute. All students may keep cars. Alcohol is not permitted.

FACULTY/CLASSROOMS: 53% of faculty are male; 47% are female. No introductory courses are taught by graduate students. The average class size in an introductory lecture is 24; in a laboratory is 18; and in a regular course is 23.

PROGRAMS OF STUDY: MTSU confers B.A., B.S., B.B.A., B.F.A., B.Mus., B.S.N., B.S.W., and B.U.S. degrees. Master's and doctoral degrees are also awarded. Bachelor's degrees are awarded in AGRICULTURE (agricultural business management, animal science, and plant science), BIOLOGICAL SCIENCE (biology/biological science and nutrition), BUSINESS (accounting, banking and finance, business administration and management, entrepreneurial studies, marketing/retailing/merchandising, office supervision and management, and recreation and leisure services), COMMUNICATIONS AND THE ARTS (communications, English, French, German, graphic design, music, music business management, public relations, Spanish, and studio art), COMPUTER AND PHYSICAL SCIENCE (chemistry, computer science, information sciences and systems, mathematics, physics, and science), EDUCATION (art education, athletic training, business education, early childhood education, health education, physical education, and special education), ENGINEERING AND ENVIRONMENTAL DESIGN (engineering technology, environmental science, industrial engineering technology, and interior design), HEALTH PROFESSIONS (health science and nursing), SOCIAL SCIENCE (anthropology, criminal justice, economics, family/consumer studies, geography, history, interdisciplinary studies, international relations, philosophy, political science/government, prelaw, psychology, public administration, social work, sociology, and textiles and clothing). Nursing, and science are the strongest academically. Recording industry has the largest enrollment.

ACTIVITIES: 9% of men belong to 16 national fraternities; 11% of women belong to 1 local and 11 national sororities. There are 153 groups on campus, including art, band, cheerleading, chess, choir, chorale, chorus, computers, dance, debate, drama, drill team, ethnic, film, honors, international, jazz band, LGBT, literary magazine, marching band, musical theater, newspaper, pep band, photography, political, professional, radio and TV, religious, social, social service, student government, and symphony. Popular campus events include Founders Day, Family Day, and African American History Month. **Sports:** There are 8 intercollegiate sports for men and 9 for women, and 13 intramural sports for men and 13 for women. Facilities include an athletic center with a stadium, a gym, a soccer/track complex, tennis courts, and baseball and softball fields, and a recreation center with 12 courts, an indoor track, indoor and outdoor pools, a rock-climbing wall, and a sand volleyball court. **Graduates:** From July 1, 2016 to June 30, 2017, 3629 bachelor's degrees were awarded. The most popular majors were business/marketing (20%), visual and performing arts (11%), and interdisciplinary studies (10%).

SERVICES: Counseling and information services are available, as is tutoring in most subjects. There is a reader service for the blind, and remedial math, reading, and writing. **Library/Resources:** The library contains 702,764 volumes, 1.3 million microform items, and subscribes to 3,798 periodicals, including electronic. Computerized library services include interlibrary loans, database searching, and Internet access. Special learning facilities include an art gallery, planetarium, radio station, TV station, and numerous research centers. **Physically Challenged Students:** All of the campus is accessible. Facilities include wheelchair ramps, elevators, special parking, specially equipped restrooms, special class scheduling, lowered drinking fountains, and lowered telephones. **Special:** MTSU offers co-op programs in aerospace, computer science, math, engineering technology, and industrial studies, cross-registration with Tennessee State University, internships, study abroad, work-study, double majors, a general studies degree, student-designed majors, non-degree study, and pass/fail options. Credit for life, military, and work experience may be granted. There are 2 national honor societies, a freshman honors program, and 25 departmental honors programs. **Visiting:** There are regularly scheduled orientations for prospective students, including campus tours and a meeting with a departmental adviser. There are guides for informal visits and visitors may sit in on classes. To schedule a visit, contact the Office of Admissions. **Campus Safety and Security:** Measures include 24-hour foot and vehicle patrol, self-defense education, and security escort services. There are shuttle buses, emergency telephones, and lighted pathways/sidewalks.

REQUIREMENTS: The SAT or ACT is required. Applicants must have a minimum composite score of 22 on the ACT if the GPA is less than 3.0. A high school diploma is required, the GED is accepted. The number of academic credits required is 14, including 4 years of English, 3 of math, 2 each of a foreign language and science, and 1 each of social studies, U.S. history, and visual and/or performance arts, with an additional unit of math, language, or art (recommended). AP and CLEP credits are accepted. To graduate, a total of at least 132 hours, including at least 48 of upper-level courses, is needed with a minimum overall GPA of 2.0. All students must complete the general studies requirements, including 9 hours each of natural science/math and humanities, 6 each of English composition, and history, 2 each of phys ed., arts/fine arts, social science, demonstrate computer literacy. A major field test and general studies exam are required. **Procedure:** Freshmen are admitted to all sessions. Entrance exams should be taken in the first half of the senior year. There are deferred admissions and rolling admissions plans. Applications should be filed by July 1 for fall entry. The fall 2017 application fee was $25. Notification is sent on a rolling basis. Applications are accepted on-line. **Transfer Students:** Applicants must have a minimum 2.0 GPA and submit official transcripts from all previous colleges attended. If transferring fewer than 9 semester hours, they must also meet freshman admission requirements. 24 of 120 credits required for the bachelor's degree must be completed at MTSU. **International Students:** There are 124 international students enrolled. They must take the TOEFL or MELAB. They must also take the SAT or ACT, scoring 20.

ADMISSIONS: 70% of the 2017-2018 applicants were accepted. The ACT scores were 32% below 12, 35% between 12 and 17, 20% between 18 and 23, 7% between 24 and 29, and 5% above 30. 31 freshmen graduated first in their class. **Admissions Contact:** Linda Elaine Olsen, Director of Admissions. Email: *admissions@mtsu.edu* Web: *www.mtsu.edu*

FINANCIAL AID: In 2017-2018, 35% of all full-time freshmen received some form of financial aid. 19% of all full-time freshmen received need-based aid. The average freshman award was $6,265. Need-based scholarships or need-based grants averaged $2,295 ($6,150 maximum); need-based self-help aid (loans and jobs) averaged $1,589 ($10,500 maximum); non-need-based athletic scholarships averaged $11,180 ($9,500 maximum); and other non-need-based awards and non-need-based scholarships averaged $4,057 ($5,000 maximum). 84% of undergraduate students work part-time. The average financial indebtedness of the 2017 graduate was $19,800. The FAFSA code is 003510. Check with the school for current application deadlines.

MILLIGAN COLLEGE F-1
www.milligan.edu

Milligan College, TN 37682	(423) 461-8757 (800) 262-8337
Fax: (423) 461-8982	Email: operations@milligan.edu
Full-time: 330 men, 443 women	Faculty: 68; IIB, --$
Part-time: 38 men, 57 women	Ph.D.s: 75%
Graduate: 124 men, 188 women	Student/Faculty: 13 to 1
Year: semesters, summer session	Tuition: $32,500
Room & Board: $6950	Freshman Class: 621 applied, 417 accepted, 204 enrolled
SAT CR/M/W: 568/555 ACT: 25	CEEB CODE: 1469
Application Deadline: August 1	COMPETITIVE

Milligan College, founded in 1866, is a private institution affiliated with the Christian Church that offers degree programs in liberal arts and professional studies. There are 5 undergraduate schools and 5 graduate schools. In addition to regional accreditation, MC has baccalaureate program accreditation with CAEP, ACOTE, CCNE, and ATS. The 235-acre campus is in a suburban area 4 miles south of Johnson City, TN. Including any residence halls, there are 50 buildings.

STUDENT LIFE: 62% of undergraduates are from Tennessee. Others are from 32 states, 14 foreign countries, and Canada. 80% are from public schools. 83% are White; 4% African American; 4% Hispanic; 4% Foreign; 2% Asian American; 2% two or more races. 83% are Protestant. **Female To Male Ratio:** 1.4:1. The average age of freshmen is 18; all undergraduates, 24. 24% do not continue beyond their first year; 64% remain to graduate. **Housing:** 628 students can be accommodated in college housing, which includes married student dorms and on-campus apartments. On-campus housing is guaranteed for all 4 years. 70% of students live on campus. All students may keep cars. Alcohol is not permitted.

FACULTY/CLASSROOMS: 50% of faculty are male; 50% are female. 96% teach undergraduates. No introductory courses are taught by graduate students. The average class size in an introductory lecture is 50; in a laboratory is 15; and in a regular course is 15.

PROGRAMS OF STUDY: MC confers B.A., B.S., B.S.W., and B.S.N. degrees. Master's and doctoral degrees are also awarded. Bachelor's degrees are awarded in BIOLOGICAL SCIENCE (biology/biological science), BUSINESS (accounting, business administration w/legal studies, and business administration and management), COMMUNICATIONS AND THE ARTS (art, communications, English, fine arts, music, photography, and piano performance), COMPUTER AND PHYSICAL SCIENCE (chemistry, computer information systems, computer science, information sciences and systems, and mathematics), EDUCATION (early childhood education, mathematics education, music education, and special education), ENGINEERING AND ENVIRONMENTAL DESIGN (engineering), HEALTH PROFESSIONS (allied health, exercise science, nursing, pre-health studies, premedicine, and prepharmacy), SOCIAL SCIENCE (biblical studies, history, humanities, liberal arts, sciences, general studies, humanities, psychology, religious music, social work, sociology, and youth ministry). Engineering, and nursing are the strongest academically. Business, psychology, and nursing have the largest enrollments.

ACTIVITIES: There are no fraternities or sororities. There are 44 groups on campus, including art, band, cheerleading, choir, chorale, chorus, computers, dance, drama, ethnic, film, honors, international, literary magazine, musical theater, newspaper, orchestra, photography, political, professional, radio and TV, religious, social, social service, student government, and yearbook. Popular campus events include Wonderful Wednesday, Campus Theater Productions, and Faculty Auction. **Sports:** There are 9 intercollegiate sports for men and 11 for women, and 7 intramural sports for men and 7 for women. Facilities include a 25-meter swimming pool, basketball court, a stadium, gym, tennis courts, baseball, softball, and soccer fields, a wellness center complete with workout rooms and exercise equipment. **Graduates:** From July 1, 2016 to June 30, 2017, 210 bachelor's degrees were awarded. The most popular majors were business administration (22%), health professions and related programs (18%), and psychology (10%). In an average class, 60% graduate in 4 years or less, 63% graduate in 5 years or less, and 64% graduate in 6 years or less.

SERVICES: Counseling and information services are available, as is tutoring in most subjects. There is remedial math, reading, and writing. **Library/Resources:** The library contains 434,436 volumes, 3,497 microform items, 3,894 audio/video tapes/CDs/DVDs, and subscribes to 22,100 periodicals, including electronic. Computerized library services include interlibrary loans, database searching, Internet access, and Wi-Fi capability. Special learning facilities include an art gallery, radio station, TV station, editing rooms, theater, prop shop, and darkroom. **Physically Challenged Students:** 80% of the campus is accessible. Facilities include wheelchair ramps, elevators, special parking, specially equipped restrooms, and lowered drinking fountains. **Special:** MC offers a Washington semester, study abroad in England, Australia, China, Costa Rica, Egypt, Russia, and Uganda, co-op programs and internships in several majors, work-study, nondegree study, and dual majors. 3 credits are offered for students participating in the annual summer tour of Europe. There are 5 national honor societies and a freshman honors program. **Visiting:** There are regularly scheduled orientations for prospective students, consisting of 1-day open houses that include a campus tour, a financial aid workshop, and the opportunity to meet faculty and to learn about student life. There are new student orientation weekends in April, June, and August. There are guides for informal visits; visitors may sit in on classes and stay overnight. To schedule a visit, contact the Campus Visits Coordinator at REBooher@milligan.edu. **Campus Safety and Security:** Measures include 24-hour foot and vehicle patrol and emergency notification system. There are emergency telephones, lighted pathways/sidewalks, controlled access to dorms/residences, and evening vehicle patrol.

REQUIREMENTS: The SAT or ACT is required. Students must be graduates of an accredited secondary school, with 18 Carnegie units and 18 academic credits, including 4 each in English, math, science, history and social studies, and speech, music or art, along with 2 years of a foreign language. Music students must audition. The GED is accepted. Other factors in the admission decision include character, recommendations by school officials, advanced placement, dual enrollment, or honor courses, ability, preparation, and Christian commitment. AP and CLEP credits are accepted. Important factors in the admissions decision are leadership record, recommendations by school officials, and personality/intangible qualities. Students must complete at least 128 semester hours, including 24 to 62 in the major, and 59 to 71 in the general education core, with a minimum GPA of 2.0. Required disciplines include 24 credit hours of humanities, 9 of Bible studies, 8 of lab science, 6 of social science, 3 each of math, speech, and ethnic studies, 2 of physical education, and 1 of introduction to college; B.A. candidates must also complete 6 to 12 in foreign language. All students must demonstrate computer literacy and attend all required chapel/convocation sessions. Measures of Academic Proficiency and Progress and an exam in the major are also required. **Procedure:** Freshmen are admitted in the fall, spring, and summer. Entrance exams should be taken beginning in the spring of the junior year. There are deferred admissions and rolling admissions plans. Applications should be filed by August 1 for fall entry; December 15 for spring entry. The fall 2017 application fee was $30. Notification is sent on a rolling basis. Applications are accepted online. **Transfer Students:** 66 transfer students enrolled in 2016-2017. A minimum GPA of 2.5 is preferred. Applicants must submit transcripts of all previous college work, as well as church or character reference, and a academic reference. 45 of 128 credits required for the bachelor's degree must be completed at MC. **International Students:** There are 39 international students enrolled. They must take the TOEFL with a minimum score of 550 on the paper-based TOEFL (PBT) or 79 on the Internet-based version (iBT). Student must take the MELAB. They must also take the SAT or ACT.

ADMISSIONS: 67% of the 2017-2018 applicants were accepted. The SAT scores for the 2017-2018 freshman class were: Math-- 24% below 500, 53% between 500 and 599, 16% between 600 and 699, and 7% between 700 and 800. Evidence-Based Reading/Writing-- 19% below 500, 45% between 500 and 599, 27% between 600 and 699, and 9% between 700 and 800. The ACT scores were 2% between 12 and 17, 32% between 18 and 23, 52% between 24 and 29, and 26% above 30. **Admissions Contact:** Allison Zetterburg, Operations Manager. Email: *operations@milligan.edu* Web: *www.milligan.edu*

FINANCIAL AID: In 2017-2018, 99% of all full-time freshmen received some form of financial aid. 58% of all full-time freshmen received need-based aid. The average freshman award was $31,170. 36% of undergraduate students work part-time. The average financial indebtedness of the 2017 graduate was $29,277. The FAFSA code is 003511. The priority date for freshman financial aid applications for fall entry is December 1.

RHODES COLLEGE — A-3

www.rhodes.edu

Memphis, TN 38112	**(901) 843-3700** **(800) 844-5969**
Fax: (901) 843-3631	**Email: adminfo@rhodes.edu**
Full-time: 846 men, 1170 women	**Faculty:** 174; IIB, +$
Part-time: 6 men, 9 women	**Ph.D.s:** 92%
Graduate: 13 men, 10 women	**Student/Faculty:** 11 to 1
Year: semesters, summer session	**Tuition:** $41,572
Room & Board: $10,328	**Freshman Class:** 3382 applied, 2029 accepted, 507 enrolled
SAT CR/M/W: 630/630/620 **ACT:** 28	**CEEB CODE:** 1730
Application Deadline: January 15	**HIGHLY COMPETITIVE**

Rhodes College, founded in 1848, is a private, church-affiliated institution of the arts and sciences. The campus is in a Gothic architectural style, and 13 of its buildings are listed on the National Register of Historic Places. There is 1 undergraduate school and 1 graduate school. The 100-acre campus is in an urban area in Memphis, TN. Including any residence halls, there are 45 buildings.

STUDENT LIFE: 74% of undergraduates are from out of state, mostly the South. Students are from 47 states, and 15 foreign countries. 53% are from public schools. 75% are White; 6% African American; 6% Asian American; 4% Hispanic; 3% Foreign; 3% two or more races; 2% race unknown; 1% American Indian/Alaska Native. **Female To Male Ratio:** 1.4:1. The average age of freshmen is 18; all undergraduates, 20. 11% do not continue beyond their first year; 80% remain to graduate. **Housing:** 1488 students can be accommodated in college housing, dorms, on-campus apartments, and living learning communities. On-campus housing is guaranteed for the freshman year only, and is available on a lottery system for upperclassmen. 71% of students live on campus. All students may keep cars.

FACULTY/CLASSROOMS: 52% of faculty are male; 48% are female. All teach undergraduates and all do research. No introductory courses are taught by graduate students. The average class size in an introductory lecture is 14; in a laboratory is 14; and in a regular course is 14.

PROGRAMS OF STUDY: RC confers B.A. and B.S. degrees. Master's degrees are also awarded. Bachelor's degrees are awarded in AGRICULTURE (environmental studies), BIOLOGICAL SCIENCE (biochemistry, biology/biological science, molecular biology, and neurosciences), BUSINESS (business administration and management), COMMUNICATIONS AND THE ARTS (art, English, French, German, music, Spanish, and theatre arts), COMPUTER AND PHYSICAL SCIENCE (chemistry, computer science, mathematics, and physics), ENGINEERING AND ENVIRONMENTAL DESIGN (environmental science), SOCIAL SCIENCE (anthropology, classical/ancient civilization, economics, history, interdisciplinary studies, international studies, Latin American studies, philosophy, political science/government, psychology, religion, Russian and Slavic studies, sociology, and urban studies). Business administration, biology, psychology and English are the strongest academically and have the largest enrollments.

ACTIVITIES: 35% of men belong to 8 national fraternities; 65% of women belong to 7 national sororities. There are 103 groups on campus, including Black Student Association, club sports, contents under pressure (comedy improv troupe), art, cheerleading, chess, choir, chorale, chorus, computers, dance, debate, drama, environmental, ethnic, Honor Council, honors, international, LGBT, literary magazine, musical theater, newspaper, orchestra, pep band, photography, political, professional, religious, social, social service, student government, symphony, and yearbook. Popular campus events include Rites of Spring, All-Sing, and Hunger for Homelessness. **Sports:** There are 11 intercollegiate sports for men and 12 for women, and 16 intramural sports for men and 16 for women. Facilities include the campus life center, which includes a performance gym, a multi-use gym, racquetball, and squash courts, a fitness center, and an indoor jogging track. Outdoor facilities include a pool, tennis courts, soccer fields, a football field, a track, and baseball, softball and intramural fields. **Graduates:** From July 1, 2016 to June 30, 2017, 433 bachelor's degrees were awarded. The most popular majors were business (15%), english, and psychology (9%), biology, and and history (8%). In an average class, 76% graduate in 4 years or less, 80% graduate in 5 years or less, and 80% graduate in 6 years or less.

SERVICES: Counseling and information services are available, as is tutoring in some subjects, such as math, writing, modern languages, biology, chemistry, economics, business, computer science, and physics. There is a reader service for the blind. **Library/Resources:** The library contains 304,512 volumes, 110,513 microform items, 14,017 audio/video tapes/CDs/DVDs, and subscribes to 7,355 periodicals, including electronic. Computerized library services include interlibrary loans, database searching, Internet access, and Wi-Fi capability. Special learning facilities include an art gallery, electron microscopes, astronomical observatory, GIS and archeology labs, and modern language labs. **Physically Challenged Students:** 90% of the campus is accessible. Facilities include wheelchair ramps, elevators, special parking, specially equipped restrooms, special class scheduling, lowered drinking fountains, lowered telephones, and an infrared hearing system in one of the auditoriums. **Special:** More than half of RC students have an internship experience, in which off-campus work and significant academic work are combined for credit. Study abroad in 11 countries, a Washington semester, cross-registration with Memphis College of Art and Christian Brothers University, and a science semester at Oak Ridge National Laboratory are also offered. A 3-2 engineering degree with Washington University is available. The B.A.-B.S. degree and dual majors are offered in any combination, and student-designed majors can be arranged. Nondegree study and pass/fail options are possible. There are 20 national honor societies and a chapter of Phi Beta Kappa. **Visiting:** There are regularly scheduled orientations for prospective students, including class visits, meetings with students and faculty, tours, and an overnight stay with students if desired. Interviews also are available. To schedule a visit, contact the Admissions Office. **Campus Safety and Security:** Measures include 24-hour foot and vehicle patrol, an emergency notification system, self-defense education, and security escort services. There are emergency telephones, lighted pathways/sidewalks, controlled access to dorms/residences24/7 staffed guard house, electronic readers on all gate entrances and residential dorms, security cameras monitored 24 hours a day, and a fenced campus.

REQUIREMENTS: The SAT or ACT is required. Graduation from an accredited secondary school is required, with 16 or more academic credits, including 4 years of English, 3 of math, and 2 each of a foreign language, science, and social studies/history. The GED is accepted. An essay is required; an interview is recommended. AP credits are accepted. Important factors in the admissions decision are advanced placement or honors courses, recommendations by school officials, and extracurricular activities record. To graduate, students must complete 128 credit hours with a variable number of hours in the major, and maintain a minimum GPA of 2.0. There is a basic degree requirement in 12 foundation areas. Students must complete 3 courses examining questions of meaning and value, 2 courses in writing, 1 course in each of literature, art, math, natural science, human interaction and contemporary institutions, and cultural perspective. Students must further demonstrate intermediate proficiency with a second language, engage in 1 for-credit activity broadening connections between the classroom and the world, participate in three half-semesters of physical education, and complete a senior seminar in the major. **Procedure:** Freshmen are admitted in the fall and spring. Entrance exams should be taken prior to December of the senior year. There are early decision, early admissions, and deferred admissions plans. Early decision applications should be filed by November 1; regular applications, by January 15 for fall entry; and December 1 for spring entry. Notification of early decision is sent December 1; regular decision, April 1. 75 early decision candidates were accepted for the 2017-2018 class. 738 applicants were on the 2017 waiting list; 52 were admitted. Applications are accepted on-line. **Transfer Students:** 15 transfer students enrolled in 2016-2017. Applicants must submit all high school and college transcripts, as well as SAT or ACT scores, and must be in good standing at the last institution they attended. 64 of 128 credits required for the bachelor's degree must be completed at Rhodes. **International Students:** There are 47 international students enrolled. They must take the TOEFL with a minimum score of 550 on the paper-based TOEFL (PBT) or 80 on the Internet-based version (iBT). They must also take the SAT or ACT.

ADMISSIONS: 60% of the 2017-2018 applicants were accepted. The SAT scores for the 2017-2018 freshman class were: Critical Reading-- 3% below 500, 20% between 500 and 599, 53% between 600 and 699, and 24% between 700 and 800. Math-- 2% below 500, 22% between 500 and 599, 56% between 600 and 699, and 20% between 700 and 800. The ACT scores were 4% between 12 and 17, 22% between 18 and 23, 24% between 24 and 29, and 46% above 30. **Admissions Contact:** Carey Thompson, Vice President of Enrollment and Communications. Email: *adminfo@rhodes.edu* Web: *www.rhodes.edu*

FINANCIAL AID: In 2017-2018, 95% of all full-time freshmen received some form of financial aid. 52% of all full-time freshmen received need-based aid. The average freshman award was $34,061. 26% of undergraduate students work part-time. The average financial indebtedness of the 2017 graduate was $27,077. RC is a member of CSS. The CSS/Profile is required. The FAFSA code is 003519. The deadline for filing freshman financial aid applications for fall entry is March 1.

SEWANEE: THE UNIVERSITY OF THE SOUTH — D-3

www.sewanee.edu

Sewanee, TN 37383	**(931) 598-1238** **(800) 522-2234**
Fax: (931) 538-3248	**Email: admiss@sewanee.edu**
Full-time: 798 men, 889 women	**Faculty:** 15
Part-time: 5 men, 10 women	**Ph.D.s:** n/av
Graduate: 46 men, 30 women	**Student/Faculty:** 10 to 1
Year: semesters, summer session	**Tuition:** $45,120
Room & Board: $12,880	**Freshman Class:** 4218 applied, 1971 accepted, 448 enrolled
SAT EBR-W/M: 658/632 **ACT:** 28	**CEEB CODE:** 1842
Application Deadline: February 1	**HIGHLY COMPETITIVE+**

Sewanee: The University of the South, founded in 1857, is an independent liberal arts institution affiliated with the Episcopal Church. There is 1 undergraduate school and 2 graduate schools. In addition to regional accreditation, Sewanee has baccalaureate program accreditation with SACSCOC. The 13000-acre campus is in a small town 93 miles southeast of Nashville and 52 miles northwest of Chattanooga. Including any residence halls, there are 102 buildings.

STUDENT LIFE: 78% of undergraduates are from out of state, mostly the South. Students are from 44 states, and 27 foreign countries. 48% are from public schools. 82% are White; 6% Hispanic; 5% African American; 3% Foreign; 3% two or more races; 1% Asian American. **Female To Male Ratio:** 1.1:1. The average age of freshmen is 18; all undergraduates, 20. 12% do not continue beyond their first year; 77% remain to graduate. **Housing:** 1800 students can be accommodated in college housing, which includes single sex dorms, coed dorms, married student dorms and on-campus apartments. In addition, there are language/international houses, special-interest houses, fraternity houses, and sorority houses. On-campus housing is guaranteed for all 4 years. 99% of students live on campus. All students may keep cars.

FACULTY/CLASSROOMS: All teach undergraduates. No introductory courses are taught by graduate students.

PROGRAMS OF STUDY: Sewanee confers B.A. and B.S. degrees. Master's and doctoral degrees are also awarded. Bachelor's degrees are awarded in AGRICULTURE (environmental studies, forestry and related sciences, and natural resources), BIOLOGICAL SCIENCE (biochemistry and biology/biological science), COMMUNICATIONS AND THE ARTS (art history, classical languages, English, fine arts, French, German, Greek, Latin, music, Russian, Spanish, and theatre arts), COMPUTER AND PHYSICAL SCIENCE (chemistry, computer science, geology, mathematics, and physics), SOCIAL SCIENCE (American studies, anthropology, Asian/Oriental studies, economics, history, international studies, medieval studies, philosophy, political science/government, psychology, religion, and women's studies). English, economics/pre-business, and natural resources and the environment are the strongest academically. Economics, English, and psychology have the largest enrollments.

ACTIVITIES: 70% of men belong to 2 local and 9 national fraternities; 80% of women belong to 8 local and 1 national sororities. There are 100 groups on campus, including backpacking, bouldering, canoeing, caving, cycling, hiking, kayaking, art, cheerleading, chess, choir, chorale, chorus, communications, computers, dance, drama, environmental, ethnic, film, honors, international, jazz band, LGBT, literary magazine, musical theater, newspaper, orchestra, pep band, photography, political, professional, radio and TV, religious, social, social service, student government, symphony, The Sewanee Outing Program - offers sport climbing, and yearbook. Popular campus events include Tennessee Williams Theatre Festival, Perpetual Motion student dance performances, Sewaneroo Music Festival, and Sewanee Monologues. **Sports:** There are 11 intercollegiate sports for men and 13 for women, and 4 intramural sports for men and 4 for women. Facilities include a sport and fitness center with multipurpose volleyball and basketball courts, an indoor pool with diving well, an indoor track, a batting cage, racquetball, squash courts, indoor and outdoor tennis courts, dance and fitness studios, a climbing wall, a golf course, a multiweather track, an equestrian center and stables, 15 playing fields, and areas for rappelling, mountain biking, caving, hiking, and rock climbing. **Graduates:** From July 1, 2016 to June 30, 2017, 400 bachelor's degrees were awarded. The most popular majors were economics (15%), psychology (12%), and English (9%). In an average class, 73% graduate in 4 years or less, 77% graduate in 5 years or less, and 77% graduate in 6 years or less.

SERVICES: Counseling and information services are available, as is tutoring in most subjects. There is a reader service for the blind. Study skills training is also offered. **Library/Resources:** The library contains 506,847 volumes, 112,666 microform items, 142,757 audio/video tapes/CDs/DVDs, and subscribes to 18,974 periodicals, including electronic. Computerized library services include interlibrary loans, database searching, Internet access, and Wi-Fi capability. Special learning facilities include an art gallery, radio station, an observatory, materials analysis lab with an electron scanning microscope, rare books collection, archives, and a music room. **Physically Challenged Students:** 90% of the campus is accessible. Facilities include wheelchair ramps, elevators, special parking, specially equipped restrooms, special class scheduling, lowered drinking fountains, and special housing. Special administrative services, and a telecommunications device for the deaf are available. **Special:** Sewanee offers internships in economics and public affairs, study abroad through almost 400 programs, a Washington semester, and student-designed majors. Peace Corps, medical, law, and veterinary preparation are available. A 3-2 engineering degree is offered with Columbia University, Rensselaer Polytechnic Institute, Vanderbilt University, and Washington University in St. Louis. There are 10 national honor societies and a chapter of Phi Beta Kappa. **Visiting:** There are regularly scheduled orientations for prospective students, include a tour, an interview, class visits, and a meeting with an admission counselor. There are guides for informal visits; visitors may sit in on classes and stay overnight. To schedule a visit, contact the Office of Admission. **Campus Safety and Security:** Measures include 24-hour foot and vehicle patrol, emergency notification system, self-defense education, and security escort services. There are shuttle buses, emergency telephones, lighted pathways/sidewalks, and controlled access to dorms/residences.

REQUIREMENTS: The SAT or ACT is recommended. Candidates for admission should have 15 secondary school academic credits, including 4 years of English, 3 of math, and 2 each of lab science, foreign language, and history or social science. An essay and 2 letters of recommendation are required and an interview is recommended. AP credits are accepted. Important factors in the admissions decision are advanced placement or honors courses, leadership record, and evidence of special talent. To graduate, students must complete at least 32 full courses (128 semester hours) with a minimum GPA of 2.0. Comprehensive exams in the major field of study are required. Students must complete a general education curriculum that encourages intellectual curiosity and exposure to significant traditions and ways of seeing the world that our disciplines and interdisciplinary programs present. **Procedure:** Freshmen are admitted in the fall. Entrance exams should be taken by December of the senior year. There are early decision, early admissions, and deferred admissions plans. Early decision applications should be filed by November 15; regular applications, by February 1 for fall entry. Notification of early decision is sent December 15; regular decision, in March. 116 early decision candidates were accepted for the 2017-2018 class. 107 applicants were on the 2017 waiting list; 15 were admitted. Applications are accepted online. **Transfer Students:** 19 transfer students enrolled in 2016-2017. Applicants should have a cumulative college GPA of 3.0 or above on a 4.0 scale. They must submit official transcripts from high school and all previous colleges attended, a letter of recommendation from a college instructor, and a statement of good standing from their current college. An interview is recommended. 64 of 128 credits required for the bachelor's degree must be completed at Sewanee. **International Students:** There are 57 international students enrolled. They must take the TOEFL with a minimum score of 577 on the paper-based TOEFL (PBT) or 90 on the Internet-based version (iBT).

ADMISSIONS: 47% of the 2017-2018 applicants were accepted. The SAT scores for the 2017-2018 freshman class were: Math-- 32% between 500 and 599, 48% between 600 and 699, and 20% between 700 and 800. Evidence-Based Reading/Writing-- 14% between 500 and 599, 61% between 600 and 699, and 25% between 700 and 800. The ACT scores were 5% between 18 and 23, 60% between 24 and 29, and 35% above 30. **Admissions Contact:** Lee Ann Backlund, Dean of Admission and Financial Aid. Email: *admiss@sewanee.edu* Web: *www.sewanee.edu*

FINANCIAL AID: In 2017-2018, 92% of all full-time freshmen received some form of financial aid. 55% of all full-time freshmen received need-based aid. The average freshman award was $31,982. Need-based scholarships or need-based grants averaged $19,229 ($61,250 maximum); need-based self-help aid (loans and jobs) averaged $2,140 ($11,150 maximum); other non-need-based awards and non-need-based scholarships averaged $8,489 ($61,650 maximum); and $2,124 from other forms of aid. 34% of undergraduate students work part-time. The average financial indebtedness of the 2017 graduate was $26,772. Sewanee is a member of CSS. The CSS/Profile is required. The FAFSA code is 003534. The priority date for freshman financial aid applications for fall entry is December 1.

SOUTHERN ADVENTIST UNIVERSITY D-3

www.southern.edu

Collegedale, TN 37315	(423) 236-2835 (800) 768-8437
Fax: (423) 236-1835	Email: admissions@southern.edu
Full-time: 985 men, 1172 women	**Faculty:** 132
Part-time: 130 men, 190 women	**Ph.D.s:** 64%
Graduate: 56 men, 107 women	**Student/Faculty:** 16 to 1
Year: semesters, summer session	**Tuition:** $21,550
Room & Board: $6700	**Freshman Class:** 1513 applied, 1074 accepted, 603 enrolled
SAT: recommended **ACT:** 22	**CEEB CODE:** 1727
Application Deadline: open	**COMPETITIVE**

Southern Adventist University, founded in 1892, is a private liberal arts institution affiliated with the Seventh-day Adventist Church. The figures given in the above capsule and in this profile are approximate. There are 9 undergraduate schools. In addition to regional accreditation, SAU has baccalaureate program accreditation with CSWE, NASM, and NLN. The 1000-acre campus is in a small town 18 miles southeast of Chattanooga. Including any residence halls, there are 17 buildings.

STUDENT LIFE: 78% of undergraduates are from out of state, mostly the South. Students are from 46 states, 42 foreign countries, and Canada. 16% are from public schools. 63% are White; 6% Foreign; 5% Asian American; 15% Hispanic; 11% African American. 97% are Protestant. **Female To Male Ratio:** 1.3:1. The average age of freshmen is 19; all undergraduates, 21. 31% do not continue beyond their first year; 45% remain to graduate. **Housing:** 1837 students can be accommodated in college housing, which includes married student dorms and on-campus apartments. On-campus housing is guaranteed for all 4 years. 65% of students live on campus. All students may keep cars. Alcohol is not permitted.

FACULTY/CLASSROOMS: 60% of faculty are male; 40% are female. 98% teach undergraduates. No introductory courses are taught by graduate students. The average class size in an introductory lecture is 40; in a laboratory is 25; and in a regular course is 13.

PROGRAMS OF STUDY: SAU confers B.A., B.S., B.B.A., B.F.A., B.Mus., and B.S.W. degrees. Associate and master's degrees are also awarded. Bachelor's degrees are awarded in BIOLOGICAL SCIENCE (biology/biological science), BUSINESS (accounting, banking and finance, business administration and management, entrepreneurial studies, international business management, marketing/retailing/merchandising, and nonprofit/public organization management), COMMUNICATIONS AND THE ARTS (animation, art, broadcasting, communications, English, film arts, fine arts, graphic design, journalism, music, and public relations), COMPUTER AND PHYSICAL SCIENCE (chemistry, computer management, computer science, information sciences and systems, mathematics, physics, and web services), EDUCATION (elementary education, music education, physical education, and recreation education), HEALTH PROFESSIONS (health care administration, health science, medical technology, and nursing), SOCIAL SCIENCE (behavioral science, history, international studies, psychology, public administration, religious education, social work, and theological studies). Business, nursing, and education are the strongest academically, and have the largest enrollments.

ACTIVITIES: There are no fraternities or sororities. There are 30 groups on campus, including band, choir, chorus, drama, ethnic, honors, international, jazz band, newspaper, orchestra, professional, radio and TV, religious, social, student government, symphony, and yearbook. Popular campus events include Alumni Weekend, Strawberry Festival, and Week of Spiritual Emphasis. **Sports:** There are 10 intramural sports for men and 10 for women. Facilities include a field house, 8 tennis courts, 3 athletic fields, a pool, 4 racquetball courts, a track, soccer fields, a gym, 3 weight rooms, and a 3-hole golf course. **Graduates:** From July 1, 2016 to June 30, 2017, 371 bachelor's degrees were awarded. The most popular majors were nursing (21%), business (15%), and education (8%). In an average class, 22% graduate in 4 years or less, 36% graduate in 5 years or less, and 48% graduate in 6 years or less. Of the 2016 graduating class, 15% were enrolled in graduate school within 6 months of graduation, and 41% were employed.

SERVICES: Counseling and information services are available, as is tutoring in most subjects. There is remedial math, reading, and writing. **Library/Resources:** The library contains 166,905 volumes, 410,551 microform items, 6,666 audio/video tapes/CDs/DVDs, and subscribes to 2,123 periodicals, including electronic. Computerized library services include interlibrary loans, database searching, Internet access, and Wi-Fi capability. Special learning facilities include an art gallery and a radio station. **Physically Challenged Students:** 70% of the campus is accessible. Facilities include wheelchair ramps, elevators, special parking, specially equipped restrooms, and special class scheduling. **Special:** Internships are available in long-term care, nursing, and journalism. A social work practicum, an accelerated degree program in nursing, and study abroad in Austria, Spain, Argentina, Italy, Germany, Mexico, and France are offered. The B.A.-B.S. degree and dual majors in any combination including business administration and automotive service and business administration and public relations, and interdisciplinary student-designed majors are available. Credit may be granted for 4 years of military experience. Pass/fail options are possible only for physical education activity classes. There are paraprofessional and pre-professional programs in dentistry and medicine, and various other health-related fields, as well as in law. There are 9 national honor societies. **Visiting:** There are regularly scheduled orientations for prospective students, including taking a tour of the campus and dorms, appointments with academic departments, and interview with an admissions officer. There are guides for informal visits, visitors may sit in on classes, and stay overnight. To schedule a visit, contact the Admissions Office. **Campus Safety and Security:** Measures include 24-hour foot and vehicle patrol, an emergency notification system, security escort services, emergency telephones and lighted pathways/sidewalks.

REQUIREMENTS: The ACT is required, with a minimum composite score of 22. The SAT is recommended. Students must graduate from an accredited secondary school with 14 academic credits, including 4 units of English and 2 each of a foreign language, math, science, social studies, and history. The GED is accepted. An essay must be submitted if home schooled. AP and CLEP credits are accepted. Important factors in the admissions decision are advanced placement or honors courses, recommendations by school officials, and leadership record. Students must complete 124 semester hours with at least 30 in the major, and maintain a minimum GPA of 2.0. General education requirements include 12 semester hours of religion, 6 of history, language, literature, and fine arts, 6 to 9 of English and natural science, 5 of behavioral, family, and health science, 3 each of activity skills, computer competencies, oral communication, and of political and economic systems, and up to 3 of math, depending on the ACT scores. **Procedure:** Freshmen are admitted in the fall, spring, and summer. Entrance exams should be taken prior to admission. There is a rolling admissions plan. Application deadlines are open. The fall 2017 application fee was $25. Notification is sent on a rolling basis. Applications are accepted on-line. **Transfer Students:** 165 transfer students enrolled in 2016-2017. Transfer applicants must have a cumulative GPA of at least 2.0 and a minimum ACT composite score of 18. 2 letters of recommendation are also required. 30 of 124 credits required for the bachelor's degree must be completed at SAU. **International Students:** There are 110 international students enrolled. They must take the TOEFL with a minimum score of 550 on the paper-based TOEFL (PBT) or 79 on the Internet-based version (iBT) or take the MELAB. They must also take the ACT, scoring 18.

ADMISSIONS: 71% of the 2017-2018 applicants were accepted. The ACT scores were 34% below 12, 27% between 12 and 17, 21% between 18 and 23, 10% between 24 and 29, and 8% above 30. **Admissions Contact:** Ryan Herman, Director of Admissions. Email: *admissions@southern.edu* Web: *www.southern.edu*

FINANCIAL AID: In 2017-2018, 93% of all full-time freshmen received some form of financial aid. 77% of all full-time freshmen received need-based aid. The average freshman award was $20,130. Need-based scholarships or need-based grants averaged $4,697 ($10,000 maximum); need-based self-help aid (loans and jobs) averaged $3,740 ($5,800 maximum); and other non-need-based awards and non-need-based scholarships averaged $2,290 ($16,205 maximum). The average financial indebtedness of the 2017 graduate was $17,524. The FAFSA code is 003518. The priority date for freshman financial aid applications for fall entry is March 1.

TENNESSEE STATE UNIVERSITY *(The complete profile is made available exclusively on our website, www.barronspac.com)*

TENNESSEE TECHNOLOGICAL UNIVERSITY D-2

www.tntech.edu

Cookeville, TN 38505 **(931) 372-3888** **(800) 255-8881**

Fax: (931) 372-6250 **Email: admissions@tntech.edu**

Full-time: 4599 men, 3786 women
Part-time: 433 men, 365 women
Graduate: 496 men, 557 women
Year: semesters, summer session
Room & Board: $9416

Faculty: 381
Ph.D.s: 83%
Student/Faculty: 18 to 1
Tuition: $8513 ($15,870)
Freshman Class: 5940 applied, 3992 accepted, 1608 enrolled

SAT CR/M: 525/550 **ACT:** 24
Application Deadline: August 1
CEEB CODE: 1804
COMPETITIVE

Tennessee Technological University, founded in 1915 and a member of the state university and community college system of Tennessee, is a public institution offering undergraduate and graduate programs in the liberal arts, business, engineering, agriculture studies, art and fine arts, music, professional training, teacher preparation, nursing, home economics, and crafts. There are 8 undergraduate schools and 5 graduate schools. In addition to regional accreditation, TTU has baccalaureate program accreditation with AACSB, ABET, NASAD, NASM, NLN, and AAFCS. The 235-acre campus is in a small town 78 miles east of Nashville. Including any residence halls, there are 97 buildings.

STUDENT LIFE: 96% of undergraduates are from Tennessee. Others are from 33 states, 55 foreign countries, and Canada. 82% are White; 5% Foreign; 4% African American; 3% Hispanic; 3% two or more races; 2% Asian American. 55% claim no religious affiliation. **Male To Female Ratio:** 1.2:1. The average age of freshmen is 18; all undergraduates, 22. 27% do not continue beyond their first year; 44% remain to graduate. **Housing:** College-sponsored housing includes married student dorms and on-campus apartments. In addition, there are honors houses, special-interest houses, and private room dorms for upper class students. On-campus housing is guaranteed for all 4 years. 75% of students commute. All students may keep cars. Alcohol is not permitted.

FACULTY/CLASSROOMS: 64% of faculty are male; 36% are female. 99% teach undergraduates, 73% do research, and 70% do both. Graduate students teach 5% of introductory courses. The average class size in an introductory lecture is 27; in a laboratory is 30; and in a regular course is 26.

PROGRAMS OF STUDY: TTU confers B.A., B.S., B.F.A., B.M., B.S.Agr., B.S.B.A., B.S.C.E., B.S.Ch.E., B.S.Ed., B.S.E.E., B.S.H.E., B.S.I.E., B.S.Ind.Tech., B.S.M.E., and B.S.N. degrees. Master's and doctoral degrees are also awarded. Bachelor's degrees are awarded in AGRICULTURE (agricultural economics, agriculture, animal science, fish and game management, plant science, soil science, and wildlife management), BIOLOGICAL SCIENCE (biochemistry and biology/biological science), BUSINESS (accounting, banking and finance, business administration and management, management science, and marketing/retailing/merchandising), COMMUNICATIONS AND THE ARTS (English, fine arts, French, German, journalism, Spanish, and technical and business writing), COMPUTER AND PHYSICAL SCIENCE (chemistry, computer science, geology, mathematics, physics, and web technology), EDUCATION (agricultural education, art education, home economics education, music education, physical education, secondary education, and special education), ENGINEERING AND ENVIRONMENTAL DESIGN (chemical engineering, civil engineering, electrical/electronics engineering, engineering, environmental engineering, industrial engineering, industrial engineering technology, manufacturing engineering, and mechanical engineering), HEALTH PROFESSIONS (nursing), SOCIAL SCIENCE (child care/child and family studies, economics, history, human ecology, political science/government, psychology, and sociology). Engineering, business, and education are the strongest academically. Mechanical engineering, multidisciplinary studies, and exercise science have the largest enrollments.

ACTIVITIES: 19% of men belong to 13 national fraternities; 24% of women belong to 9 national sororities. There are 178 groups on campus, including art, band, cheerleading, chess, choir, chorale, chorus, communications, computers, dance, debate, drama, drill team, ethnic, forensics, honors, international, jazz band, LGBT, literary magazine, marching band, musical theater, newspaper, opera, orchestra, pep band, photography, political, professional, radio and TV, religious, social, social service, student government, symphony, and yearbook. Popular campus events include Intramural Events, Greek Week, and Parents Day. **Sports:** There are 7 intercollegiate sports for men and 9 for women, and 10 intramural sports for men and 8 for women. Facilities include volleyball, basketball, 2 indoor tennis courts, a fitness center with a pool, handball courts, weight and meeting rooms. The Athletic Performance Center includes a turf practice field and strength center, baseball, football, cross country, soccer, and golf. **Graduates:** From July 1, 2016 to June 30, 2017, 1354 bachelor's degrees were awarded. The most popular majors were business (22%), education (20%), and engineering (13%). In an average class, 1% graduate in 3 years or less, 17% graduate in 4 years or less, 36% graduate in 5 years or less, and 51% graduate in 6 years or less. Of the 2016 graduating class, 10% were enrolled in graduate school within 6 months of graduation, and 80% were employed.

SERVICES: Counseling and information services are available, as is tutoring in some subjects, such as English and lower levels of mathematics. There is a reader service for the blind, and remedial math, reading, and writing. **Library/Resources:** The library contains 353,000 volumes, 100,005 microform items, 38,000 audio/video tapes/CDs/DVDs, and subscribes to 30,050 periodicals, including electronic. Computerized library services include interlibrary loans, database searching, and Internet access. Special learning facilities include an art gallery, radio station, and TV station. **Physically Challenged Students:** 95% of the campus is accessible. Facilities include wheelchair ramps, elevators, special parking, specially equipped restrooms, special class scheduling, lowered drinking fountains, lowered telephones, and special housing. **Special:** Co-op programs in most academic areas, internships in community-based programs, study abroad, a Washington semester, multidisciplinary majors and work-study programs are available. Accelerated degree programs are offered in all specified majors with 3 calendar years of continuous studies. A B.A.-B.S. degree is available, as are dual majors in all areas. Credit may be granted for military experience, and nondegree study and pass/fail options are offered. There are 29 national honor societies and a freshman honors program. **Visiting:** There are regularly scheduled orientations for prospective students, including visits either morning or afternoon each weekday, and meetings with an admission officer, faculty member in student's major, and a campus tour. There are guides for informal visits and visitors may sit in on classes. To schedule a visit, contact the Admissions Office. **Campus Safety and Security:** Measures include 24-hour foot and vehicle patrol, self-defense education, and security escort services. There are emergency telephones, lighted pathways/sidewalks, and student safety organization.

REQUIREMENTS: The ACT is required, with a minimum composite score of 19. Other admissions requirements include graduation from an accredited secondary school with 14 academic credits, including 4 of English, 3 of math, 2 each in science and a single foreign language, 1 in American history, 1 in world history, ancient history, modern history, world geography or European history, and 1 in music/art. The GED is also accepted. AP and CLEP credits are accepted. Students must complete 120 semester hours, with a variable number of hours in the major, and maintain a minimum GPA of 2.0. 9 semester hours of English, 8 of a lab science, 6 of American history, 6 each of social sciences and humanities, and 3 hours each of math and speech. **Procedure:** Freshmen are admitted to all sessions. Entrance exams should be taken during the senior year. There are deferred admissions and rolling admissions plans. Applications should be filed by August 1 for fall entry; December 1 for spring entry; and May 1 for summer entry. The fall 2017 application fee was $15. Applications are accepted on-line. **Transfer Students:** 716 transfer students enrolled in 2016-2017. Transfer students should have a minimum of 12 credit hours earned; the minimum GPA depends on the number of credit hours accumulated. Official transcripts must be submitted, and the ACT is required, depending on age (for applicants 21 or older it is not required). If an applicant has fewer than 12 credit hours, admissions requirements are the same as for freshmen. 30 of 120 credits required for the bachelor's degree must be completed at TTU. **International Students:** There are 209 international students enrolled. They must take the TOEFL with a minimum score of 500 on the paper-based TOEFL (PBT) or 61 on the Internet-based version (iBT). Students must also take the college's own test, and the SAT or ACT, scoring 17.

ADMISSIONS: 67% of the 2017-2018 applicants were accepted. The SAT scores for the 2017-2018 freshman class were: Critical Reading-- 36% below 500, 40% between 500 and 599, 20% between 600 and 699, and 4% between 700 and 800. Math-- 24% below 500, 47% between 500 and 599, 26% between 600 and 699, and 3% between 700 and 800. The ACT scores were 3% between 12 and 17, 41% between 18 and 23, 43% between 24 and 29, and 13% above 30. 48% of the current freshmen were in the top fifth of their class; 80% were in the top two fifths. **Admissions Contact:** Alexis Pope, Associate Director of Admissions. Email: *admissions@tntech.edu* Web: *www.tntech.edu*

FINANCIAL AID: In 2017-2018, 91% of all full-time freshmen received some form of financial aid. The average freshman award was $8,120. Need-based scholarships or need-based grants averaged $3,922; need-based self-help aid (loans and jobs) averaged $2,405; non-need-based athletic scholarships averaged $13,681; and other non-need-based awards and non-need-based scholarships averaged $5,271. The average financial indebtedness of the 2017 graduate was $14,478. The deadline for filing freshman financial aid applications for fall entry is December 15.

TENNESSEE WESLEYAN UNIVERSITY *(The complete profile is made available exclusively on our website, www.barronspac.com)*

THE UNIVERSITY OF MEMPHIS A-3

www.memphis.edu

Memphis, TN 38152 **(800) 669-2678**

Email: admissions@memphis.edu

Full-time: 5277 men, 7093 women	**Faculty:** 861; I, --$
Part-time: 1371 men, 2214 women	**Ph.D.s:** 79%
Graduate: 1610 men, 2331 women	**Student/Faculty:** 16 to 1
Year: semesters, summer session	**Tuition:** $9125 ($23,684)
Room & Board: $9153	**Freshman Class:** 13216 applied, 12388 accepted, 2743 enrolled
SAT CR/M/W: 523/500/500 **ACT:** 22	**CEEB CODE:** 1459
Application Deadline: July 1	**COMPETITIVE**

The University of Memphis, founded in 1912, is a public metropolitan research university and is part of the Tennessee Board of Regents. In addition to regional accreditation, UM has baccalaureate program accreditation with AACSB, ABET, ACEJMC, ADA, ASLA, CAHEA, CSWE, FIDER, NASAD, NASM, NLN, AAFCS, ACS, APA, CACREP, CCNE, NASPAA, NASPE, and NAST. The 1607-acre campus is in an urban area in Memphis, TN. Including any residence halls, there are 239 buildings.

STUDENT LIFE: 91% of undergraduates are from Tennessee. Others are from 44 states, 54 foreign countries, and Canada. 5% are Hispanic; 49% White; 4% two or more races; 38% African American; 3% Asian American; 1% Foreign. **Female To Male Ratio:** 1.4:1. The average age of freshmen is 18; all undergraduates, 24. **Housing:** 2557 students can be accommodated in college housing, which includes married student dorms and on-campus apartments. In addition, there are special-interest houses, fraternity houses, sorority houses, and cooperative housing. On-campus housing is guaranteed for all 4 years. 51% of students commute. All students may keep cars. Alcohol is not permitted.

FACULTY/CLASSROOMS: 53% of faculty are male; 47% are female. No introductory courses are taught by graduate students.

PROGRAMS OF STUDY: UM confers B.A., B.S., B.B.A., B.F.A., B.L.S., B.M., B.P.S., B.S.B.E., B.S.C.E., B.S.Ch., B.S.C.P., B.S.Ed., B.S.E.E., B.S.E.T., B.S.M.E., and B.S.N. degrees. Master's and doctoral degrees are also awarded. Bachelor's degrees are awarded in BIOLOGICAL SCIENCE (biology/biological science and microbiology), BUSINESS (accounting, banking and finance, business economics, hospitality management services, international business management, logistics, management information systems, management science, marketing management, and recreation and leisure services), COMMUNICATIONS AND THE ARTS (art, art history and appreciation, communications, dramatic arts, English, journalism, languages, music, and music business management), COMPUTER AND PHYSICAL SCIENCE (chemistry, computer science, earth science, mathematics, and physics), EDUCATION (physical education and special education), ENGINEERING AND ENVIRONMENTAL DESIGN (architecture, biomedical engineering, civil engineering, computer engineering, computer technology, electrical/electronics engineering, electrical/electronics engineering technology, engineering technology, manufacturing engineering, and mechanical engineering), HEALTH PROFESSIONS (health science and nursing), SOCIAL SCIENCE (African American studies, anthropology, criminal justice, criminology, economics, geography, history, human development, interdisciplinary studies, international studies, liberal arts/general studies, philosophy, political science/government, psychology, social work, and sociology). Nursing, professional studies, and psychology have the largest enrollments.

ACTIVITIES: 11% of men belong to 14 national fraternities; 13% of women belong to 11 national sororities. There are 140 groups on campus, including art, band, cheerleading, chess, choir, chorale, chorus, computers, dance, drama, drill team, environmental, ethnic, honors, international, jazz band, LGBT, literary magazine, marching band, musical theater, newspaper, opera, orchestra, pep band, photography, political, professional, religious, social, social service, student government, and symphony. Popular campus events include Black History Month, Step Shows by Greek organizations, and International Night. **Sports:** There are 9 intercollegiate sports for men and 9 for women, and 10 intramural sports for men and 10 for women. Facilities include a gym, football stadium, baseball field, swimming pools, track, weight room, tennis, handball, and racquetball courts. **Graduates:** From July 1, 2016 to June

30, 2017, 2991 bachelor's degrees were awarded. The most popular majors were business/marketing (20%), interdisciplinary studies (11%), and health professional and related programs (9%). In an average class, 13% graduate in 4 years or less, 34% graduate in 5 years or less, and 40% graduate in 6 years or less.

SERVICES: Counseling and information services are available, as is tutoring in most subjects. There is a reader service for the blind, and remedial math, reading, and writing. **Library/Resources:** Computerized library services include interlibrary loans, database searching, Internet access, and Wi-Fi capability. Special learning facilities include an art gallery, an earthquake research center, a center for electron microscopy, Chucalissa Indian Village and Museum, a speech and hearing center, center for the humanities, institute for intelligent systems, Institute of Egyptian Art and Archaeology, Ecological Research Center, and Biological Station. **Physically Challenged Students:** 95% of the campus is accessible. Facilities include wheelchair ramps, elevators, special parking, specially equipped restrooms, special class scheduling, lowered drinking fountains, lowered telephones, and special housing, including transportation service when needed. **Special:** The university offers co-op programs, dual enrollment, internships, study abroad and domestic student exchange, accelerated degree programs, double and student-designed majors, independent study, distance learning, an external degree program, preprofessional and professional studies programs, teacher certification, ESL, nondegree study, and pass/fail options. Students may receive credit for life, military, and work experience. There are 20 national honor societies, a freshman honors program, and 17 departmental honors programs. **Visiting:** There are regularly scheduled orientations for prospective students, including daily campus tour programs Monday-Friday and the first Saturday of the month. There are guides for informal visits, visitors may sit in on classes, and stay overnight. To schedule a visit, contact Recruitment and Orientation Services at (800) 669-2678. **Campus Safety and Security:** Measures include 24-hour foot and vehicle patrol, emergency notification system, and security escort services. There are shuttle buses, emergency telephones, lighted pathways/sidewalks, controlled access to dorms/residences, digital video cameras, a computerized entry system, a gated parking lot, parking lot fences, parking lot security towers, campus safety forums, and a personal safety program.

REQUIREMENTS: The SAT or ACT is required. Candidates for admission should be graduates of an accredited secondary school and have 15 academic credits. The GED is accepted. Academic preparation should include 4 units in English, 3 in math, 2 each in science (1 must be lab), and foreign language, 1 each in history, social studies, and visual and performing arts. An interview is required for University College applicants, a portfolio is required for art program applicants, and an audition is required for music applicants. AP and CLEP credits are accepted. Important factors in the admissions decision are advanced placement or honors courses, parents or siblings attended your school, personality/intangible qualities, and recommendations by school officials. To graduate, students must complete a minimum of 120 credit hours with a GPA of 2.0 and demonstrate proficiency in computer skills. Requirements include 9 hours of humanities and fine arts with at least 1 literature course, 8 hours of natural science, 6 of English composition, 6 of social and behavioral science, 6 of U.S. history, 3 each of math, and oral communication. **Procedure:** Freshmen are admitted in the fall, spring, and summer. Entrance exams should be taken in the spring of the junior year or October of the senior year. There are deferred admissions and rolling admissions plans. Applications should be filed by July 1 for fall entry; December 1 for spring entry; and May 1 for summer entry. The fall 2017 application fee was $25. Notification is sent on a rolling basis. Applications are accepted on-line. **Transfer Students:** 1395 transfer students enrolled in 2016-2017. Applicants must have honorable dismissal from the last institution attended and have a cumulative GPA that meets the required minimum established by the Tennessee State Board of Regents. 30 of 120 credits required for the bachelor's degree must be completed at UM. **International Students:** There are 133 international students enrolled. They must take the TOEFL with a minimum score of 500 on the paper-based TOEFL (PBT) or 61 on the Internet-based version (iBT). They must also take the SAT or ACT.

ADMISSIONS: 94% of the 2017-2018 applicants were accepted. The SAT scores for the 2017-2018 freshman class were: Critical Reading-- 42% below 500, 32% between 500 and 599, 19% between 600 and 699, and 6% between 700 and 800. Math-- 10% below 500, 38% between 500 and 599, 15% between 600 and 699, and 4% between 700 and 800. Writing-- 46% below 500, 36% between 500 and 599, 15% between 600 and 699, and 3% between 700 and 800. The ACT scores were 12% between 12 and 17, 50% between 18 and 23, 31% between 24 and 29, and 7% above 30. **Admissions Contact:** Dr. Justin Lawhead, Interim Associate, Vice President Dean of Students. Email: *admissions@memphis.edu* Web: *www.memphis.edu*

FINANCIAL AID: In 2017-2018, 72% of all full-time freshmen received some form of financial aid and need-based aid. The average freshman award was $10,415. Need-based scholarships or need-based grants averaged $6,519; need-based self-help aid (loans and jobs) averaged $3,367; non-need-based athletic scholarships averaged $14,687; other non-need-based awards and non-need-based scholarships averaged $7,855; and $3,342 from other forms of aid. The FAFSA code is 003509. The priority date for freshman financial aid applications for fall entry is March 1.

THE UNIVERSITY OF TENNESSEE AT CHATTANOOGA D-3

www.utc.edu

Chattanooga, TN 37403 **(423) 425-4662**

Fax: (423) 425-4157 **Email: info@utc.edu**
Full-time: 3884 men, 5078 women
Part-time: 610 men, 604 women
Graduate: 591 men, 820 women
Year: semesters, summer session
Room & Board: $8676
SAT CR/M: 577/558 **ACT:** 23
Application Deadline: May 1
Faculty: IIA, -$
Ph.D.s: 80%
Student/Faculty: 19 to 1
Tuition: $8664 ($24,782)
Freshman Class: n/av
CEEB CODE: 1831
COMPETITIVE+

The University of Tennessee at Chattanooga, founded in 1886, is a public institution and part of the state's university system, offering programs in liberal and fine arts, business, engineering, health science, and teacher preparation. There are 5 undergraduate schools and 1 graduate school. In addition to regional accreditation, Chattanooga has baccalaureate program accreditation with AACSB, ABET, ACEJMC, AHEA, APTA, CSWE, NASAD, NASM, NLN, CCNE, CAPTE, and CACREP. The 425-acre campus is in an urban area 120 miles north of Atlanta. Including any residence halls, there are 90 buildings.

STUDENT LIFE: 93% of undergraduates are from Tennessee. Others are from 40 states, 35 foreign countries, and Canada. 75% are from public schools. 76% are White; 4% Hispanic; 4% two or more races; 2% Asian American; 2% Foreign; 2% race unknown; 10% African American. **Female To Male Ratio:** 1.3:1. The average age of freshmen is 18; all undergraduates, 21. 27% do not continue beyond their first year; 44% remain to graduate. **Housing:** 3146 students can be accommodated in college housing, which includes on-campus apartments. In addition, there are language/international houses, special-interest houses, and theme housing. On-campus housing is guaranteed for the freshman year only, and is available on a first-come, first-served basis. 69% of students commute. All students may keep cars. Alcohol is not permitted.

FACULTY/CLASSROOMS: 49% of faculty are male; 51% are female. No introductory courses are taught by graduate students.

PROGRAMS OF STUDY: UTC confers B.A., B.S., B.F.A., B.M., B.S.E., B.S.E.E., B.S.M.E., B.S.N., B.S.W., B.S.ChE., and B.S.C.E. degrees. Master's and doctoral degrees are also awarded. Bachelor's degrees are awarded in BIOLOGICAL SCIENCE (biology/biological science), BUSINESS (business administration and management and recreation and leisure services), COMMUNICATIONS AND THE ARTS (art, communications, dramatic arts, English, fine arts, French, Greek, Latin, music, and Spanish), COMPUTER AND PHYSICAL SCIENCE (applied mathematics, chemistry, computer science, geology, mathematics, and physics), EDUCATION (art education, early childhood education, education, education of the exceptional child, English education, music education, secondary education, and special education), ENGINEERING AND ENVIRONMENTAL DESIGN (chemical engineering, civil engineering, construction management, electrical/electronics engineering, engineering, engineering management, environmental engineering, environmental science, industrial engineering, interior design, mechanical engineering, and nuclear engineering), HEALTH PROFESSIONS (nursing), SOCIAL SCIENCE (criminal justice, economics, history, humanities, legal studies, philosophy, political science/government, psychology, social work, and sociology). Education, physical therapy, and engineering are the strongest academically. Business, nursing, and health and human performance have the largest enrollments.

ACTIVITIES: 10% of men belong to 14 national fraternities; 19% of

women belong to 11 national sororities. There are 130 groups on campus, including band, cheerleading, chess, choir, chorale, chorus, communications, computers, dance, debate, drama, drill team, environmental, ethnic, film, honors, international, jazz band, LGBT, literary magazine, marching band, musical theater, newspaper, opera, orchestra, pep band, photography, political, professional, radio and TV, religious, social, social service, student government, and symphony. Popular campus events include Homecoming and Welcome Week. **Sports:** There are 6 intercollegiate sports for men and 7 for women, and 6 intramural sports for men and 6 for women. Facilities include an aquatic and recreation center, an arena, tennis and racquet center, swimming pool, 2 fields, and soccer field. **Graduates:** From July 1, 2016 to June 30, 2017, 2093 bachelor's degrees were awarded. The most popular majors were psychology (7%), nursing (7%), and health and human performance (6%). In an average class, 22% graduate in 4 years or less, 41% graduate in 5 years or less, and 45% graduate in 6 years or less.

SERVICES: Counseling and information services are available, as is tutoring in most subjects. There is a reader service for the blind, and remedial math, reading, and writing. **Library/Resources:** The library contains 799,387 volumes, 130,284 audio/video tapes/CDs/DVDs, and subscribes to 55,954 periodicals, including electronic. Computerized library services include interlibrary loans, database searching, Internet access, and Wi-Fi capability. Special learning facilities include an art gallery, a radio station, an observatory, and the Challenger Center. **Physically Challenged Students:** 95% of the campus is accessible. Facilities include wheelchair ramps, elevators, special parking, specially equipped restrooms, special class scheduling, lowered drinking fountains, and lowered telephones. **Special:** Cooperative programs are offered in accounting, business systems, chemistry, communications, engineering, environmental studies, nursing, and psychology. UTC offers internships, study abroad in England, work-study and accelerated degree programs, B.A.-B.S. degrees, dual majors, interdisciplinary majors, including theater and speech, 3-2 engineering degrees, and nondegree study. Credit is given for life, military, or work experience. There are 33 national honor societies, a freshman honors program, and 29 departmental honors programs. **Visiting:** There are regularly scheduled orientations for prospective students. There are guides for informal visits; visitors may sit in on classes and stay overnight. To schedule a visit, contact the Admissions Office. **Campus Safety and Security:** Measures include 24-hour foot and vehicle patrol, emergency notification system, self-defense education, and security escort services. There are shuttle buses, emergency telephones, lighted pathways/sidewalks, and controlled access to dorms/residences.

REQUIREMENTS: The SAT or ACT is required. Secondary school credits should include 4 each in English and math, 3 in science with labs, 2 each in foreign language and history, 1 in visual performing arts. The GED is accepted. AP and CLEP credits are accepted. Important factors in the admissions decision are advanced placement or honors courses, personality/intangible qualities, evidence of special talent, and extracurricular activities record. All students must complete at least 120 semester hours and maintain a minimum GPA of 2.0. General education requirements include 9 hours in humanities and fine arts, 6 hours in English and math, 8 hours in natural sciences, 9 hours in cultures and civilizations, and 6 hours in behavioral and social sciences. Students must complete at least 25% of the minimum credit hours under the direction of UTC faculty, complete 60 credit hours at an accredited senior institution, complete the last 24 credit hours at UTC, and complete at least 39 credit hours at the senior (300-400) level. They must also complete a minimum 12 hours at the senior level in the UTC major department or program offering the degree and also complete the senior exit exam. Other requirements vary by major. **Procedure:** Freshmen are admitted in the fall and spring. Entrance exams should be taken in spring of the junior year. There are deferred admissions and rolling admissions plans. Applications should be filed by May 1 for fall entry; November 1 for spring entry; and April 15 for summer entry. The fall 2017 application fee was $30. Applications are accepted on-line. **Transfer Students:** 816 transfer students enrolled in 2016-2017. Transfer students must have pursued courses appropriate to the curriculum at UTC, be eligible to return to their previous institution, and meet UTC's continuation standards. 24 of 120 credits required for the bachelor's degree must be completed at UTC. **International Students:** There are 146 international students enrolled. They must take the TOEFL with a minimum score of 500 on the paper-based TOEFL (PBT) or 61 on the Internet-based version (iBT). They must also take the SAT or ACT if it is available in the student's country.

ADMISSIONS: The SAT scores for the 2017-2018 freshman class were: Critical Reading-- 15% below 500, 43% between 500 and 599, 37% between 600 and 699, and 5% between 700 and 800. Math-- 15% below 500, 59% between 500 and 599, 22% between 600 and 699, and 4% between 700 and 800. The ACT scores were 2% between 12 and 17, 52% between 18 and 23, 38% between 24 and 29, and 8% above 30. **Admissions Contact:** Lee Pierce, Director of Admissions. Email: *info@utc.edu* Web: *www.utc.edu*

FINANCIAL AID: In 2017-2018, 61% of all full-time freshmen received some form of financial aid. 59% of all full-time freshmen received need-based aid. The average freshman award was $10,601. Need-based scholarships or need-based grants averaged $8,382; need-based self-help aid (loans and jobs) averaged $3,288; non-need-based athletic scholarships averaged $14,473; and other non-need-based awards and non-need-based scholarships averaged $3,245. The average financial indebtedness of the 2017 graduate was $22,917. The FAFSA code is 003529. The priority date for freshman financial aid applications for fall entry is April 1.

THE UNIVERSITY OF TENNESSEE AT KNOXVILLE E-2

www.utk.edu

Knoxville, TN 37996 **(865) 974-2184**

Email: admissions@utk.edu

Full-time: 10,136 men, 10,042 women	**Faculty:** 1324; I, av$
Part-time: 668 men, 550 women	**Ph.D.s:** 85%
Graduate: 3983 men, 4582 women	**Student/Faculty:** 17 to 1
Year: semesters, summer session	**Tuition:** $12,186 ($30,636)
Room & Board: $9926	**Freshman Class:** 15442 applied, 11555 accepted, 4701 enrolled
SAT CR/M: 575/585 **ACT:** 27	**CEEB CODE:** 1843
Application Deadline: December 1	**VERY COMPETITIVE**

The University of Tennessee at Knoxville was founded in 1794. There are 9 undergraduate schools and 11 graduate schools. In addition to regional accreditation, Knoxville has baccalaureate program accreditation with AACSB, ABET, ACEJMC, ACPE, ADA, ASLA, CAHEA, CSWE, FIDER, NAAB, NASAD, NASM, NLN, NRPA, SAF, AAFCS, ABA, ACS, AVMA, and CCNE. The 560-acre campus is in an urban area in Knoxville, TN. Including any residence halls, there are 236 buildings.

STUDENT LIFE: 90% of undergraduates are from Tennessee. Others are from 50 states, 113 foreign countries, and Canada. 81% are White; 7% African American; 4% Asian American; 3% Hispanic; 3% two or more races; 2% race unknown. **Female To Male Ratio:** 1.0:1. The average age of freshmen is 18; all undergraduates, 21. 15% do not continue beyond their first year; 85% remain to graduate. **Housing:** 7312 students can be accommodated in college housing, which includes dorms and on-campus apartments. In addition, there are honors houses, special-interest houses, fraternity houses, sorority houses, and theme housing. On-campus housing is guaranteed for the freshman year only, and is available on a first-come, first-served basis. 63% of students commute. All students may keep cars. Alcohol is not permitted.

FACULTY/CLASSROOMS: 58% of faculty are male; 42% are female. 76% teach undergraduates. No introductory courses are taught by graduate students.

PROGRAMS OF STUDY: UTK confers B.A., B.S., B.Arch., B.F.A., B.M., B.S.ArtEd., B.S.Ag.E., BSAN, BSFS, B.S.F., B.S.P.S., BSID, B.S.C., B.S.B.A., B.A.C., B.S.H.S., B.S.Ed., B.S.Ch.E., B.S.C.E., BSCOME, B.S.C.S., B.S.E.E., B.S.I.E., B.S.A.E., B.S.M.E., B.S.N., and B.S.S.W. degrees. Master's and doctoral degrees are also awarded. Bachelor's degrees are awarded in AGRICULTURE (agricultural economics, agriculture, animal science, forestry and related sciences, natural resources, plant science, and soil science), BIOLOGICAL SCIENCE (biology/biological science, nutrition, and wildlife biology), BUSINESS (accounting, business systems analysis, finance, hotel/motel and restaurant management, human resources, logistics, management science, retailing, and sports management), COMMUNICATIONS AND THE ARTS (advertising, art history, art, classics, communications, English, French, German, graphic design, Italian, journalism, music, public relations, Russian, studio art, and theatre arts), COMPUTER AND PHYSICAL SCIENCE (chemistry, computer science, geology, mathematics, physics, and statistics), EDUCATION (education, health information management, marketing and distribution education, recreation education, and special education), ENGINEERING AND ENVIRONMENTAL DESIGN (aerospace studies, architecture, biomedical engineering, chemical engineering, civil engineering, computer engineering, electrical/electronics engineering, environmental science, industrial engineering, interior design, materials engineering, mechanical engineering, and nuclear engineering), HEALTH PROFESSIONS (clinical science, dental hygiene, medical technology, nursing, predentistry, premedicine, prepharmacy, and preveterinary science), SOCIAL SCIENCE (anthropology, child care/child and family studies, economics, food science, geography, Hispanic American studies, history, interdisciplinary studies, philosophy, political science/government, psychology, public administration, religion, social work, and sociology). Engineering, business, and nursing are the strongest academically. Logistics, accounting, and psychology have the largest enrollments.

ACTIVITIES: 16% of men belong to 24 national fraternities; 25% of women belong to 18 national sororities. There are 296 groups on campus, including art, band, cheerleading, chess, choir, chorale, chorus, computers, dance, debate, drama, environmental, ethnic, film, honors, international, jazz band, LGBT, literary magazine, marching band, musical theater, newspaper, opera, orchestra, pep band, photography, political, professional, radio and TV, religious, social, social service, student government, symphony, and yearbook. Popular campus events include All-Sing, Torch Night, International Festival, Volapalooza, Vol Night Long, Dance Marathon, Carnius, football and basketball games. **Sports:** There are 9 intercollegiate sports for men and 11 for women, and 50 intramural sports for men and 50 for women. Facilities include a basketball arena, basketball practice facility, an Olympic track, Olympic indoor and outdoor pools, a baseball stadium, and softball and soccer fields. The Recreation Center has 4 multi-purpose gym courts, a raised running/jogging/walking track, a stretching area, fitness areas (with cardio equipment, selectorized equipment and free weight areas), cycling studio, 3 group exercise studios, 3 racquetball courts, indoor soccer, floor hockey, roller blading, volleyball and basketball, a fencing club for practice, 2 multi-purpose court areas, a small weight room, racquetball courts, 3 squash courts, a multi-purpose gym area with a climbing wall and bouldering, 8 rectangular multi-use fields (4 astroturf and 4 natural turf), 2 softball fields, 3 sand volleyball courts, athletic trainers room, and 8 tennis courts. **Graduates:** From July 1, 2016 to June 30, 2017, 4771 bachelor's degrees were awarded. The most popular majors were business/marketing (19%), engineering (10%), and social sciences (9%). In an average class, 36% graduate in 4 years or less, 62% graduate in 5 years or less, and 66% graduate in 6 years or less. Of the 2016 graduating class, 12% were enrolled in graduate school within 6 months of graduation, and 86% were employed.

SERVICES: Counseling and information services are available, as is tutoring in some subjects. There is a reader service for the blind. There is supplemental instruction in math and chemistry, as well as tutoring in English, math, chemistry and most lower division courses. **Library/Resources:** The library contains 3.1 million volumes, 4.7 million microform items, 80,122 audio/video tapes/CDs/DVDs, and subscribes to 58,765 periodicals, including electronic. Computerized library services include interlibrary loans, database searching, Internet access, and Wi-Fi capability. Special learning facilities include an art gallery, radio station, the Scripps Laboratory, an emergent communications technology facility with workstations and facilities to conduct focus-group research, hands-on media experience at WUTK is a student-run radio station and UTTV, a television production, the Masters Investment Learning Center, a finance laboratory with real-time stock quotes from the world's financial markets, and the Anderson Center for Entrepreneurship and Innovation, a learning environment for those interested in starting and growing new businesses. The Clarence Brown Theatre produces plays and musicals featuring nationally renowned guest artists. UTK is also home to the Clarence Brown Theatre Professional Company, the University Company, and the undergraduate performance group. The theatre also provides students with space to rehearse and perform experimental stage plays. UT is one of only 27 universities nationwide that is affiliated with the League of Resident Theatres (LORT). This professional theatre affiliation allows students regular opportunities to work alongside professional actors, directors, designers, and production artists. There is also the McClung Museum of Natural History and Culture, and that The Ewing Gallery of Art and Architecture, emphasizes historic and current trends in art and architecture and supports creative works by students. The Commons in Hodges Library is a learning environment designed to meet the changing needs of students with the latest technological advances in a private yet collaborative workspace. In addition UTK has The Humanities and Social Sciences Building. **Physically Challenged Students:** 95% of the campus is accessible. Facilities include wheelchair ramps, elevators, special parking, specially equipped restrooms, special class scheduling, lowered drinking fountains, lowered telephones, special housing. **Special:** Students can design a wide variety of interdisciplinary majors through the College of Arts and Sciences. Honors programs exist within several colleges. University-wide honors programs include the Baker Scholars, Haslam Scholars and Chancellor's Honors Programs. The university offers many dual graduate and professional degrees that include law and business, public administration and law, business and engineering, and recreation and sport management and business. New graduate programs include a master's in landscape architecture, a master's in public health, a master's in business analytics, a doctorate in energy science and engineering, a doctorate of nursing practice, and a doctorate in social work. Study-abroad programs are offered in more than fifty-nine countries. There are 27 national honor societies, Phi Beta Kappa, and a freshman honors program. **Visiting:** There are regularly scheduled orientations for prospective students, including 2 open houses yearly where prospective students can meet with faculty, administrators, and students to discuss admissions, housing, financial aid, and student activities. There are guides for informal visits and visitors may sit in on classes. **Campus Safety and Security:** Measures include 24-hour foot and vehicle patrol, emergency notification system, self-defense education, and security escort services. There are shuttle buses, emergency telephones, lighted pathways/sidewalks, and campus safety educational programs.

REQUIREMENTS: The ACT or SAT is accepted. Applicants should be high school graduates or have the GED. Required secondary school courses include 4 credits in English and math, 3 in science with lab, and 2 foreign language, 1 each in history, social studies, and visual/performing arts. AP and CLEP credits are accepted. Important factors in the admissions decision are advanced placement or honors courses, evidence of special talent, leadership record, parents or siblings attended your school, extracurricular activities record, and geographical diversity. All students must complete at least 120 credits with a minimum 2.0 GPA. Students must take 3 courses in communicating through writing: 2 courses in oral communication, quantitative reasoning, natural sciences, arts and humanities, social sciences, and cultures and civilizations, including 8 courses to develop broadening perspectives. **Procedure:** Freshmen are admitted to all sessions. Entrance exams should be taken in spring of the junior yearor fall of the senior year. Applications should be filed by December 1 for fall entry; November 1 for spring entry; and December 1 for summer entry. The fall 2017 application fee was $40. Notifications are sent March 31. 2051 applicants were on the 2017 waiting list; 19 were admitted. Applications are accepted on-line. **Transfer Students:** 1265 transfer students enrolled in 2016-2017. Transfer applicants should present a minimum 2.0 GPA in previous college work, although many specific programs have higher requirements. Transfer applicants must have completed a minimum of 15 transferable college credits by the date they apply. 30 of 120 credits required for the bachelor's degree must be completed at Knoxville. **International Students:** There are 385 international students enrolled. They must take the TOEFL with a minimum score of 523 on the paper-based TOEFL (PBT) or 70 on the Internet-based version (iBT). Student must take the Comprehensive English Language Test and the college's own test. Student must also take either the ILETS, the SAT or ACT.

ADMISSIONS: 75% of the 2017-2018 applicants were accepted. Critical Reading-- 15% below 500, 47% between 500 and 599, 29% between 600 and 699, and 10% between 700 and 800. Math-- 14% below 500, 44% between 500 and 599, 32% between 600 and 699, and 10% between 700 and 800. **Admissions Contact:** Tom Broadhead, Director of Admissions. Email: *admissions@utk.edu* Web: *www.utk.edu*

FINANCIAL AID: In 2017-2018, 51% of all full-time freshmen received some form of financial aid and need-based aid. The average freshman award was $13,793. Need-based scholarships or need-based grants averaged $11,207; need-based self-help aid (loans and jobs) averaged $5,219; non-need-based athletic scholarships averaged $15,303; other non-need-based awards and non-need-based scholarships averaged $5,093; and $5,042 from other forms of aid. The average financial indebtedness of the 2017 graduate was $23,870. The FAFSA code is 003530. The priority date for freshman financial aid applications for fall entry is March 1.

THE UNIVERSITY OF TENNESSEE AT MARTIN B-1

www.utm.edu

Martin, TN 38238	(731) 587-7020 (800) 829-8861
Fax: (731) 587-7029	Email: admitme@utm.edu
Full-time: 2112 men, 2838 women	**Faculty:** 286; IIA, --$
Part-time: 495 men, 913 women	**Ph.D.s:** 71%
Graduate: 137 men, 305 women	**Student/Faculty:** 15 to 1
Year: semesters, summer session	**Tuition:** $9236 ($14,996)
Room & Board: $5976	**Freshman Class:** 4884 applied, 3004 accepted, 1052 enrolled
ACT: 23	**CEEB CODE:** 1844
Application Deadline: August 1	**COMPETITIVE**

The University of Tennessee at Martin, founded in 1900, is the primary campus in the University of Tennessee System and is known for providing high-quality undergraduate and graduate academic programs. As a comprehensive public university, Martin remains committed to preparing students for success in the global economy by offering more than 100 different areas of study at the undergraduate and graduate levels. There are 5 undergraduate schools and 4 graduate schools. In addition to regional accreditation, Martin has baccalaureate program accreditation with AACSB, ABET, ACEJMC, CSWE, NASM, ACS, CAEP, ACEN, ACEND, AAFCS, AVMA, and and CVTEA. The 250-acre campus is in a rural area 125 miles northeast of Memphis and 150 miles northwest of Nashville. Including any residence halls, there are 48 buildings.

STUDENT LIFE: 92% of undergraduates are from Tennessee. Others are from 43 states, 17 foreign countries, and Canada. 92% are from public schools. 79% are White; 13% African American; 3% Hispanic; 2% Foreign; 2% two or more races; 1% Asian American. 61% are Protestant; 34% claim no religious affiliation. **Female To Male Ratio:** 1.5:1. The average age of freshmen is 19; all undergraduates, 23. 24% do not continue beyond their first year; 50% remain to graduate. **Housing:** 2217 students can be accommodated in college housing, which includes married student dorms and on-campus apartments. In addition, there are honors houses, special-interest houses, and living learning communities. On-campus housing is guaranteed for the freshman year only, and is available on a first-come, first-served basis. 71% of students commute. All students may keep cars. Alcohol is not permitted.

FACULTY/CLASSROOMS: 51% of faculty are male; 49% are female. All teach undergraduates, 76% do research, and 76% do both. No introductory courses are taught by graduate students. The average class size in an introductory lecture is 20; in a laboratory is 16; and in a regular course is 19.

PROGRAMS OF STUDY: UTM confers B.A., B.S., B.A.Mus., B.F.A., B.Mus., B.S.Agri., B.S.Bus.Admn., B.S.Chem., B.S.Crim.Just., B.S.Ed., B.S.Eng., B.S.Fam.C.S., B.S.Health/HP., B.S.N.R.M., B.S.N., B.S.S.W. and B.I.S. degrees. Master's degrees are also awarded. Bachelor's degrees are awarded in AGRICULTURE (agricultural business management, agriculture, animal science, natural resource management, and plant science), BIOLOGICAL SCIENCE (biology/biological science and nutrition), BUSINESS (accounting, business administration and management, business economics, management science, and marketing/retailing/merchandising), COMMUNICATIONS AND THE ARTS (communications, English, fine arts, French, music, performing arts, and Spanish), COMPUTER AND PHYSICAL SCIENCE (chemistry, computer science, geology, information sciences and systems, and mathematics), EDUCATION (education administration, elementary education, secondary education, and special education), ENGINEERING AND ENVIRONMENTAL DESIGN (engineering), HEALTH PROFESSIONS (health science and nursing), SOCIAL SCIENCE (child care/child and family studies, criminal justice, economics, geography, history, international studies, philosophy, political science/government, psychology, public administration, social work, and sociology). Agriculture, health and human performance, nursing, and management are the strongest academically. Agriculture, health and human performance, and nursing have the largest enrollments.

ACTIVITIES: 12% of men belong to 11 national fraternities; 15% of women belong to 9 national sororities. There are 160 groups on campus, including art, band, cheerleading, choir, chorale, chorus, computers, dance, drama, drill team, environmental, ethnic, film, honors, international, jazz band, LGBT, literary magazine, marching band, musical theater, newspaper, opera, pep band, photography, political, professional, radio and TV, religious, social, social service, student government, and yearbook. Popular campus events include Greekfest, Homecoming, and Pyramid. **Sports:** There are 7 intercollegiate sports for men and 9 for women, and 10 intramural sports for men and 10 for women. Facilities include an Olympic-size swimming pool, racquetball courts, a running/walking track, weight room, basketball, volleyball, badminton and tennis court combinations, a 1.5 mile fitness track, tennis courts, a soccer field, and lighted intramural playing fields. **Graduates:** From July 1, 2016 to June 30, 2017, 1231 bachelor's degrees were awarded. The most popular majors were business/marketing (17%), agriculture (14%), and interdisciplinary studies (11%). In an average class, 23% graduate in 4 years or less, 44% graduate in 5 years or less, and 50% graduate in 6 years or less. Of the 2016 graduating class, 19% were enrolled in graduate school within 6 months of graduation, and 73% were employed.

SERVICES: Counseling and information services are available, as is tutoring in some subjects, such as astronomy, biology, chemistry, computer science, English, French, geography, geology, German, history, Japanese, math, psychology, and Spanish. **Library/Resources:** The library contains 349,683 volumes, 3,734 microform items, 19,181 audio/video tapes/CDs/DVDs, and subscribes to 346 periodicals, including electronic. Computerized library services include interlibrary loans, database searching, Internet access, and Wi-Fi capability. Special learning facilities include a natural history museum, radio station, TV station, a teacher resource center, 680-acre agriculture and natural resources teaching and demonstration complex, a teaching/research facility, and a Center for Global Studies and International education. **Physically Challenged Students:** All of the campus is accessible. Facilities include wheelchair ramps, elevators, special parking, specially equipped restrooms, special class scheduling, lowered drinking fountains, lowered telephones, and special housing. **Special:** UTM offers co-op programs in engineering, agriculture, computer science, business, and chemistry, for-credit internships, study abroad, B.A.-B.S. degrees, dual and student-designed majors, National Forensic Academy Collegiate Program and pass/fail options. There are 15 national honor societies, a freshman honors program, and 10 departmental honors programs. **Visiting:** There are regularly scheduled orientations for prospective students, campus visits include Summer Orientation and Registration (SOAR); 4 sessions conducted for students and parents that include information sessions and class registration. There are guides for informal visits; visitors may sit in on classes and stay overnight. To schedule a visit, contact the Admissions Office. **Campus Safety and Security:** Measures include 24-hour foot and vehicle patrol, an emergency notification system, and self-defense education. There are emergency telephones, lighted pathways/sidewalks, controlled access to dorms/residences, bicycle patrol, security cameras in residence halls, auto dialer alert system, text messaging alert system, and severe weather siren alert system.

REQUIREMENTS: Students should have a minimum composite score of 21 on the ACT with a 2.70 minimum GPA, or 19 on the ACT with a GPA minimum of 3.0. Candidates for admission should be graduates of an accredited secondary school with 14 academic credits. The GED is accepted with a score of 500. Secondary school units should include 4 of English, 3 of math, 2 of a foreign language, and 1 each of science, history, social studies, and fine and performing arts. A GPA of 2.7 is required. AP and CLEP credits are accepted. The number of credit hours required for graduation ranges from 120 to 134 (based on degree). All students must have at least a 2.0 GPA. Specific courses and major requirements vary by the program selected. There is a 1 year or 30 hour UTM residency requirement. The general education core curriculum is 38 hours; English and communications courses are required. Major field and general education tests are required. **Procedure:** Freshmen are admitted in the fall, spring, and summer. Entrance exams should be taken by the spring of the junior year. There are deferred admissions and rolling admissions plans. Applications should be filed by August 1 for fall entry. The fall 2017 application fee was $30. Notification is sent on a rolling basis. Applications are accepted on-line. **Transfer Students:** 557 transfer students enrolled in 2016-2017. Transfer students should have a minimum GPA of 2.0. 30 of 120 credits required for the bachelor's degree must be completed at UTM. **International Students:** There are 150 international students enrolled. They must take the TOEFL with a minimum score of 500 on the paper-based TOEFL (PBT) or 61 on the Internet-based version (iBT). Students must take the writing proficiency exam.

ADMISSIONS: 62% of the 2017-2018 applicants were accepted. The

ACT scores were 1% between 12 and 17, 59% between 18 and 23, 35% between 24 and 29, and 5% above 30. 36% of the current freshmen were in the top fifth of their class; 67% were in the top two fifths. 17 freshmen graduated first in their class. **Admissions Contact:** Destin Tucker, Director of Admissions. Email: *admitme@utm.edu* Web: *www.utm.edu*

FINANCIAL AID: In 2017-2018, 77% of all full-time freshmen received some form of financial aid. 54% of all full-time freshmen received need-based aid. The average freshman award was $12,512. Need-based scholarships or need-based grants averaged $6,711 ($13,920 maximum); need-based self-help aid (loans and jobs) averaged $3,521 ($10,000 maximum); non-need-based athletic scholarships averaged $11,106 ($33,110 maximum); and other non-need-based awards and non-need-based scholarships averaged $2,426 ($5,500 maximum). 22% of undergraduate students work part-time. The average financial indebtedness of the 2017 graduate was $27,335. The FAFSA code is 003531. The priority date for freshman financial aid applications for fall entry is March 1.

TREVECCA NAZARENE UNIVERSITY C-2

www.trevecca.edu

Nashville, TN 37210 **(615) 248-1320**

Fax: (615) 248-7406 **Email: admissions@trevecca.edu**

Full-time: 505 men, 671 women
Part-time: 237 men, 264 women
Graduate: 295 men, 634 women
Year: semesters, summer session
Room & Board: $8060
SAT CR/M: 530/520 **ACT:** 23
Application Deadline: August 1

Faculty: IIA, --$
Ph.D.s: 90%
Student/Faculty: 18 to 1
Tuition: $23,126
Freshman Class: 1029 applied, 752 accepted, 320 enrolled
CEEB CODE: 1809
COMPETITIVE

Trevecca Nazarene University, founded in 1901, is a private institution affiliated with the Church of the Nazarene offering degrees in liberal arts and sciences and a number of professional content areas. TNU provides a variety of nontraditional continuing education professional specializations at the undergraduate and graduate levels. The figures given in the above capsule and in this profile are approximate. There are 4 undergraduate schools and 4 graduate schools. In addition to regional accreditation, TNU has baccalaureate program accreditation with NASM, CCNE, and ARC-PA. The 80-acre campus is in an urban area. Including any residence halls, there are 26 buildings.

STUDENT LIFE: 62% of undergraduates are from Tennessee. Others are from 42 states, 15 foreign countries, and Canada. 71% are White; 11% race unknown; 9% African American; 4% Hispanic; 3% two or more races; 1% Asian American; 1% American Indian/Alaska Native; 1% Foreign. 51% are Protestant; 15% claim no religious affiliation. **Female To Male Ratio:** 1.5:1. The average age of freshmen is 19; all undergraduates, 26. 21% do not continue beyond their first year; 51% remain to graduate. **Housing:** 759 students can be accommodated in college housing, which includes married student dorms, on-campus apartments, and off-campus apartments. On-campus housing is guaranteed for all 4 years. 53% of students commute. All students may keep cars. Alcohol is not permitted.

FACULTY/CLASSROOMS: 63% of faculty are male; 37% are female. No introductory courses are taught by graduate students.

PROGRAMS OF STUDY: TNU confers B.A., B.S., B.B.A., B.S.N., and B.S.S.W. degrees. Associate, master's, and doctoral degrees are also awarded. Bachelor's degrees are awarded in BIOLOGICAL SCIENCE (biology/biological science), BUSINESS (accounting, business administration and management, business administration - international, electronic business, management science, marketing, marketing/retailing/merchandising, and sports management), COMMUNICATIONS AND THE ARTS (communication studies, digital communications, dramatic arts, English, journalism, music, and music business management), COMPUTER AND PHYSICAL SCIENCE (chemistry, chemistry/adolescence education, computer information technology, information sciences and systems, mathematics, physics, and science), EDUCATION (business education, drama education, early childhood education, education, English education, mathematics education, music education, physical education, science education, secondary education, and special education), HEALTH PROFESSIONS (biology, exercise science, and nursing), SOCIAL SCIENCE (behavioral science, criminal justice, history, pastoral studies, political science/government, psychology, religion, social work, and sociology). Management and human relations, religion, and biology have the largest enrollments.

ACTIVITIES: There are no fraternities or sororities. There are 23 groups on campus, including art, band, cheerleading, choir, chorale, chorus, drama, environmental, forensics, honors, international, jazz band, literary magazine, marching band, musical theater, newspaper, orchestra, pep band, professional, religious, social service, student government, symphony, and yearbook. Popular campus events include drama productions and athletic events. **Sports:** There are 6 intercollegiate sports for men and 7 for women, and 10 intramural sports for men and 10 for women. Facilities include a gym, a jogging track, handball, racquetball, and tennis courts, exercise and weight rooms, and playing fields. **Graduates:** From July 1, 2016 to June 30, 2017, 353 bachelor's degrees were awarded. The most popular majors were business/management (42%), religion/christian ministry (6%), and psychology (5%). In an average class, 39% graduate in 4 years or less, 49% graduate in 5 years or less, and 51% graduate in 6 years or less.

SERVICES: Counseling and information services are available, as is tutoring in every subject. There is a reader service for the blind, and remedial math, reading, and writing. An academic enrichment program for students scoring below 19 on the ACT provides tutoring in math, reading, writing, and study skills. **Library/Resources:** The library contains 183,605 volumes. Computerized library services include interlibrary loans, database searching, Internet access, and Wi-Fi capability. **Physically Challenged Students:** Facilities include wheelchair ramps, elevators, special parking, specially equipped restrooms, special class scheduling, and lowered drinking fountains. **Special:** TNU offers cross registration with other Nazarene colleges and universities in the United States, as well as internships, practicums, and a Washington semester and study abroad through the Council of Christian Colleges and Universities. TNU also offers 3 adult degree-completion programs leading to bachelor degrees, as well as a 3-2 nursing program offered with Belmont University. There is 1 national honor society. **Visiting:** There are regularly scheduled orientations for prospective students, including a tour and meetings with admissions and financial aid personnel and faculty. There are guides for informal visits; visitors may sit in on classes and stay overnight. To schedule a visit, contact the Admissions Office. **Campus Safety and Security:** Measures include 24-hour foot and vehicle patrol and an emergency notification system, and lighted pathways/sidewalks.

REQUIREMENTS: The ACT is preferred, with a composite score of at least 18. Candidates should have completed at least 15 academic secondary credits, including 4 units in English, 2 each in math, foreign language, and social science, and 1 in natural science. A GED of at least 45 is also accepted. The teacher education program has special admission requirements. A GPA of 2.5 is required. AP and CLEP credits are accepted. To graduate, students must complete at least 120 semester hours with a minimum 2.0 GPA. The required 54-hour general education curriculum includes courses in English, communications, religion and philosophy, fine arts, history and social science (including foreign language), science, math, financial stewardship and health and wellness. **Procedure:** Freshmen are admitted in the fall, spring, and summer. Entrance exams should be taken in the junior or senior year. There are deferred admissions and rolling admissions plans. Applications should be filed by August 1 for fall entry. The fall 2017 application fee was $25. Applications are accepted on-line. **Transfer Students:** 87 transfer students enrolled in 2016-2017. Transfer applicants must present official transcripts and recommendations from a regionally accredited institution. 30 of 120 credits required for the bachelor's degree must be completed at TNU. **International Students:** There are 18 international students enrolled. They must take the TOEFL with a minimum score of 500 on the paper-based TOEFL (PBT) or 61 on the Internet-based version (iBT). They must also take the SAT or ACT.

ADMISSIONS: 73% of the 2017-2018 applicants were accepted. The SAT scores for the 2017-2018 freshman class were: Critical Reading-- 31% below 500, 44% between 500 and 599, 15% between 600 and 699, and 10% between 700 and 800. Math-- 37% below 500, 41% between 500 and 599, 18% between 600 and 699, and 4% between 700 and 800. The ACT scores were 28% below 12, 29% between 12 and 17, 22% between 18 and 23, 8% between 24 and 29, and 13% above 30. **Admissions Contact:** Melinda Miller, Director Undergraduate Admissions. Email: *admissions@trevecca.edu* Web: *www.trevecca.edu*

FINANCIAL AID: In 2017-2018, 94% of all full-time freshmen received some form of financial aid. The FAFSA code is 003526. The priority date for freshman financial aid applications for fall entry is February 1.

TUSCULUM COLLEGE *(The complete profile is made available exclusively on our website, www.barronspac.com)*

UNION UNIVERSITY B-2
www.uu.edu

Jackson, TN 38305	(731) 661-5009
Fax: (731) 338-6466	Email: admissions@uu.edu
Full-time: 803 men, 1369 women	Faculty: 239
Part-time: 303 men, 354 women	Ph.D.s: 80%
Graduate: 428 men, 739 women	Student/Faculty: 11 to 1
Year: 4-1-4, summer session	Tuition: $31,660
Room & Board: $9500	Freshman Class: 1930 applied, 1432 accepted, 452 enrolled
SAT CR/M: 590/590 ACT: 25	CEEB CODE: 1826
Application Deadline: August 15	VERY COMPETITIVE

Union University, founded in 1823, is a private, institution affiliated with the Southern Baptist Convention. The university offers programs in arts and sciences, education, business, and nursing. The figures given in the above capsule and in this profile are approximate. There are 5 undergraduate schools and 3 graduate schools. In addition to regional accreditation, Union has baccalaureate program accreditation with AACSB, ABET, CSWE, NASAD, NASM, NLN, ACS, CCNE, and CAAHEP. The 360-acre campus is in a suburban area 80 miles east of Memphis. Including any residence halls, there are 40 buildings.

STUDENT LIFE: 69% of undergraduates are from Tennessee. Others are from 44 states, 35 foreign countries, and Canada. 75% are from public schools. 75% are White; 5% race unknown; 2% Hispanic; 14% African American; 1% Asian American. 94% are Protestant. **Female To Male Ratio:** 1.6:1. The average age of freshmen is 18; all undergraduates, 20. 7% do not continue beyond their first year; 64% remain to graduate. **Housing:** 1180 students can be accommodated in college housing, which includes married student dorms and on-campus apartments. On-campus housing is guaranteed for all 4 years. 65% of students live on campus. All students may keep cars. Alcohol is not permitted.

FACULTY/CLASSROOMS: 53% of faculty are male; 47% are female. All teach undergraduates, and 25% do research. No introductory courses are taught by graduate students. The average class size in an introductory lecture is 25; in a laboratory is 18; and in a regular course is 15.

PROGRAMS OF STUDY: Union confers B.A., B.S., B.M., B.S.B.A., B.S.M.T., and B.S.N. degrees. Associate, master's, and doctoral degrees are also awarded. Bachelor's degrees are awarded in BIOLOGICAL SCIENCE (biology/biological science), BUSINESS (accounting, banking and finance, business administration and management, management science, marketing management, marketing/retailing/merchandising, and sports management), COMMUNICATIONS AND THE ARTS (advertising, art, broadcasting, communications, dramatic arts, English, English as a second/foreign language, English literature, French, graphic design, Greek, journalism, music, music performance, music theory and composition, piano/organ, public relations, Spanish, and voice), COMPUTER AND PHYSICAL SCIENCE (chemistry, computer science, mathematics, physical chemistry, physical sciences, and physics), EDUCATION (education, elementary education, middle school education, music education, physical education, secondary education, special education, and teaching English as a second/foreign language (TESOL/TEFOL), ENGINEERING AND ENVIRONMENTAL DESIGN (preengineering), HEALTH PROFESSIONS (medical laboratory technology, nursing, predentistry, premedicine, prepharmacy, and sports medicine), SOCIAL SCIENCE (biblical languages, biblical studies, Christian studies, economics, family and community services, history, ministries, missions, pastoral studies, philosophy, political science/government, prelaw, psychology, religion, religious music, social work, sociology, and youth ministry). Business, nursing, and education have the largest enrollments.

ACTIVITIES: 27% of men belong to 3 national fraternities; 23% of women belong to 3 national sororities. There are 73 groups on campus, including art, band, cheerleading, choir, chorus, computers, debate, drama, ethnic, film, honors, international, jazz band, literary magazine, musical theater, newspaper, opera, orchestra, photography, political, professional, religious, social, social service, student government, and symphony. Popular campus events include Campus Day, Parents Weekend, and Variety Show. **Sports:** There are 5 intercollegiate sports for men and 5 for women, and 12 intramural sports for men and 12 for women. Facilities include racquetball courts, a student recreation center, an indoor swimming pool, a wellness center, 2 gyms, 2 soccer fields, and baseball and softball complexes. **Graduates:** From July 1, 2016 to June 30, 2017, 640 bachelor's degrees were awarded. The most popular majors were business/marketing (26%), health professions and related science (20%), and education (15%). In an average class, 4% graduate in 3 years or less, 47% graduate in 4 years or less, 59% graduate in 5 years or less, and 60% graduate in 6 years or less. Of the 2016 graduating class, 40% were enrolled in graduate school within 6 months of graduation, and 78% were employed.

SERVICES: Counseling and information services are available, as is tutoring in most subjects. There is also assistance with study skills, time management, note taking, reading comprehension, and writing. **Library/Resources:** The library contains 146,055 volumes, 479,357 microform items, 11,088 audio/video tapes/CDs/DVDs, and subscribes to 705 periodicals, including electronic. Computerized library services include interlibrary loans, database searching, and Internet access. Special learning facilities include an art gallery, a radio and TV lab facilities. **Physically Challenged Students:** 98% of the campus is accessible. Facilities include wheelchair ramps, elevators, special parking, specially equipped restrooms, special class scheduling, lowered drinking fountains, lowered telephones, and special housing. **Special:** Cooperative and accelerated degree programs are available in business department majors. Cross-registration with Freed-Hardeman Universities, internships, study abroad in 7 countries, a Washington semester, work-study programs, composite majors in religion and church ministry, religion and Greek, and religion and philosophy, dual and student-designed majors, 3-2 engineering degrees, and nondegree study are also offered. There are 15 national honor societies, a freshman honors program, and 14 departmental honors programs. **Visiting:** There are regularly scheduled orientations for prospective students, including campus tours, class visits, and appointments with counselors. There are guides for informal visits, visitors may sit in on classes, and stay overnight. To schedule a visit, contact Robbie Graves at (731) 661-5590. **Campus Safety and Security:** Measures include 24-hour foot and vehicle patrol, emergency notification system, self-defense education, and security escort services. There are emergency telephones and lighted pathways/sidewalks.

REQUIREMENTS: The SAT is required. The ACT is preferred. A minimum composite score of 20 on the ACT or 820 on the SAT I is recommended. Candidates must be graduates of an accredited secondary school or have the GED. A minimum of 20 academic credits is required, including at least 14 in English, math, foreign language, and social and natural sciences. An interview is also recommended. Union requires applicants to be in the upper 50% of their class. AP and CLEP credits are accepted. Important factors in the admissions decision are leadership record, advanced placement or honors courses, and recommendations by school officials. All students must complete 128 credit hours, with at least 30 in the major, and maintain a minimum overall GPA of 2.0. The general core requirements are 8 credit hours of lab sciences, 6 each of history, composition, literature, and religion, 3 each of math, oral communication, social sciences/humanities, and fine arts, and 2 of physical education. Students must pass comprehensive exams in each course and at completion of the major. **Procedure:** Freshmen are admitted to all sessions. Entrance exams should be taken in the spring of the junior year. There are early decision, early admissions, deferred admissions, and rolling admissions plans. Applications should be filed by August 15 for fall entry. The fall 2017 application fee was $35. 14 early decision candidates were accepted for the 2017-2018 class. Applications are accepted on-line. **Transfer Students:** 145 transfer students enrolled in 2016-2017. Candidates must have a minimum GPA of 2.0 in more than 12 semester hours and submit a student transfer form from the last institution attended. 32 of 128 credits required for the bachelor's degree must be completed at Union. **International Students:** There are 40 international students enrolled. They must take the TOEFL. If the TOEFL has not been taken, the ACT or the SAT is required.

ADMISSIONS: 74% of the 2017-2018 applicants were accepted. The SAT scores for the 2017-2018 freshman class were: Critical Reading-- 13% below 500, 23% between 500 and 599, 30% between 600 and 699, and 23% between 700 and 800. Math-- 13% below 500, 35% between 500 and 599, 36% between 600 and 699, and 10% between 700 and 800. The ACT scores were 16% below 12, 21% between 12 and 17, 22% between 18 and 23, 12% between 24 and 29, and 29% above 30. 66% of the current freshmen were in the top fifth of their class; 89% were in the top two fifths. 44 freshmen graduated first in their class. **Admissions Contact:** Ted Wingo, Assistant Director of UGA. Email: *admissions@uu.edu* Web: *www.uu.edu*

FINANCIAL AID: The college's own financial statement is required. The FAFSA code is 003528. Check with the school for current application deadlines.

VANDERBILT UNIVERSITY C-2

www.vanderbilt.edu

Nashville, TN 37203	**(615) 343-3282** **(800) 288-0432**
Fax: (615) 343-7765	**Email: admissions@vanderbilt.edu**
Full-time: 3322 men, 3483 women	**Faculty:** 975; I, +$
Part-time: 41 men, 39 women	**Ph.D.s:** 94%
Graduate: 2337 men, 3370 women	**Student/Faculty:** 7 to 1
Year: semesters, summer session	**Tuition:** $47,664
Room & Board: $15,584	**Freshman Class:** 31462 applied, 3415 accepted, 1607 enrolled
SAT or ACT: required	**CEEB CODE:** 1871
Application Deadline: January 1	**MOST COMPETITIVE**

Vanderbilt University offers excellent academic rigor, a vibrant campus life, and an urban location which attract exceptionally talented students from around the world. Undergraduate students are immersed in multidisciplinary research and creative engagement across four schools: the College of Arts and Science, School of Engineering, Peabody College of Education and Human Development, and School of Engineering. Over 50 percent of undergraduate students participate in research. In addition to regional accreditation, VU has baccalaureate program accreditation with AACSB, ABET, and CAHEA. The 330-acre campus is in an urban area in Nashville, TN. Including any residence halls, there are 227 buildings.

STUDENT LIFE: 90% of undergraduates are from out of state, mostly the South. Students are from 51 states, 48 foreign countries, and Canada. 65% are from public schools. 8% are Foreign; 5% two or more races; 5% race unknown; 48% White; 13% Asian American; 10% African American; 10% Hispanic. **Female To Male Ratio:** 1.2:1. The average age of freshmen is 18; all undergraduates, 19. 3% do not continue beyond their first year; 93% remain to graduate. **Housing:** 6039 students can be accommodated in college housing, which includes married student dorms and on-campus apartments. In addition, there are language/international houses, special-interest houses, fraternity houses, and sorority houses. On-campus housing is guaranteed for the freshman year only, and is available on a first-come, first-served basis, and is available on a lottery system for upperclassmen. 90% of students live on campus. Upperclassmen may keep cars.

FACULTY/CLASSROOMS: 59% of faculty are male; 41% are female. No introductory courses are taught by graduate students. The average class size in an introductory lecture is 20; in a laboratory is 31; and in a regular course is 19.

PROGRAMS OF STUDY: VU confers B.A., B.S., B.E., and B.Mu. degrees. Master's and doctoral degrees are also awarded. Bachelor's degrees are awarded in AGRICULTURE (environmental studies), BIOLOGICAL SCIENCE (biochemistry, biology/biological science, ecology, molecular biology, and neurosciences), COMMUNICATIONS AND THE ARTS (art history, art, classical languages, classics, communications, composition, English, French, German, media arts, music performance, music theory and composition, Russian, Spanish, and theatre arts), COMPUTER AND PHYSICAL SCIENCE (chemistry, computer science, earth science, mathematics, and physics), EDUCATION (Asian studies, early childhood education, education, elementary education, music education, secondary education, and special education), ENGINEERING AND ENVIRONMENTAL DESIGN (bioengineering, biomedical engineering, chemical engineering, civil engineering, computer engineering, electrical/electronics engineering, engineering and applied science, and mechanical engineering), HEALTH PROFESSIONS (medicine and health and society), SOCIAL SCIENCE (African American studies, American studies, anthropology, child psychology/development, cognitive science, East Asian studies, economics, European studies, history, human development, interdisciplinary studies, Italian studies, Judaic studies, Latin American studies, philosophy, political science/government, psychology, public affairs, religious studies, sociology, and women and gender studies). Social science, engineering, and education have the largest enrollments.

ACTIVITIES: 34% of men belong to 17 national fraternities; 50% of women belong to 15 national sororities. There are 500 groups on campus, including art, band, cheerleading, chess, choir, chorale, chorus, computers, dance, debate, drama, drill team, environmental, ethnic, film, honors, international, jazz band, LGBT, literary magazine, marching band, musical theater, newspaper, opera, orchestra, pep band, photography, political, professional, radio and TV, religious, social, social service, student government, symphony, and yearbook. Popular campus events include Rites of Spring, International Lens Film Series, Diwali Festival, and IMPACT Speakers Series. **Sports:** There are 6 intercollegiate sports for men and 9 for women, and 32 intramural sports for men and 31 for women. Facilities include a gym, pool, football and intramural fields, indoor football field, student recreation and tennis centers, basketball and racquetball courts, a suspended indoor track, and a climbing wall. **Graduates:** From July 1, 2016 to June 30, 2017, 1716 bachelor's degrees were awarded. The most popular majors were social sciences (30%), engineering (14%), and interdisciplinary studies (11%). In an average class, 86% graduate in 4 years or less, 91% graduate in 5 years or less, and 92% graduate in 6 years or less. Of the 2016 graduating class, 33% were enrolled in graduate school within 6 months of graduation, and 76% were employed.

SERVICES: Counseling and information services are available, as is tutoring in most subjects. There is a reader service for the blind. **Library/Resources:** The library contains 4.6 million volumes, 3.1 million microform items, and 64,912 audio/video tapes/CDs/DVDs, and subscribes to 95,722 periodicals including electronic. Computerized library services include interlibrary loans, database searching, Internet access, and Wi-Fi capability. Special learning facilities include an art gallery, radio station, 2 observatories, and a TV news archive. **Physically Challenged Students:** 90% of the campus is accessible. Facilities include wheelchair ramps, elevators, special parking, specially equipped restrooms, special class scheduling, lowered drinking fountains, and lowered telephones. **Special:** Vanderbilt offers honors programs, teacher licensure, accelerated degree programs, and the opportunity to double major and/or add one or more minors. Forty percent of students study abroad at one of 120+ programs offered in more than 35 countries. In each of the four undergraduate schools, students can apply to programs that allow them to earn both a bachelor's and a master's degree in five years. The School of Engineering offers a three-two program with certain liberal arts colleges as well as a dual degree program with Fisk University. Immersion Vanderbilt calls for every student to participate in an intensive learning experience that takes place in and beyond the classroom. There are 6 national honor societies, Phi Beta Kappa, a freshman honors program, and 21 departmental honors programs. **Visiting:** There are regularly scheduled orientations for prospective students, including group information sessions and campus tours available Monday through Saturday during the academic year and Monday through Friday during the summer. Schedules vary, so visitors must call in advance. There are guides for informal visits, visitors may sit in on classes, and stay overnight. To schedule a visit, contact the Office of Undergraduate Admissions. **Campus Safety and Security:** Measures include 24-hour foot and vehicle patrol, an emergency notification system, self-defense education, and security escort services. There are shuttle buses, emergency telephones, lighted pathways/sidewalks, a bicycle patrol, and student dorm monitors.

REQUIREMENTS: Requirements for first-year applicants: All required parts of either the Common Application or the Universal College Application, $50 nonrefundable application fee, or fee waiver for qualified students, official high school transcript, counselor letter of recommendation, 2 academic teacher letters of recommendation, and official SAT or ACT scores (SAT code: 1871 / ACT code: 4036), and if applicable, TOEFL, IELTS, or Pearson applicants to the Blair School of Music must complete an additional application, which includes a prescreening audition video. Please visit the Blair website for details. AP credits are accepted. Important factors in the admissions decision are advanced placement or honors courses, extracurricular activities record, and evidence of special talent. Graduation requirements vary with the student's program of study but include a minimum of 120 hours (at least 60 of which must have been earned at Vanderbilt) and a minimum cumulative GPA of 2.0. A degree candidate must also have a 2.0 cumulative GPA in his or her major. **Procedure:** Freshmen are admitted in the fall. Entrance exams should be taken in spring of the junior year or the fall of the senior year. There are early decision and deferred admissions plans. Early decision applications should be filed by November 1; regular applications, by January 1 for fall entry. The fall 2017 application fee was $50. Notification of early decision is sent December 15; regular decision, April 1. 863 early decision candidates were accepted for the 2017-2018 class. Applications are accepted on-line. **Transfer Students:** 218 transfer students enrolled in 2016-2017. To be a transfer student, a minimum of 12 hours of college credit must have been earned. Requirements for transfer applicants: All required parts of either the Common Application Transfer Application or the Universal College Application Transfer Application, $50 nonrefundable application fee, or fee waiver for qualified students, official high school transcript, official college transcript(s) (from each institution attended), Transfer College Report (from the institution you are transferring from), 2 academic teacher letters of recommendation (we prefer that at least one letter is from a college professor/instructor), official SAT or ACT scores (SAT code: 1871 / ACT code: 4036), and if applicable, TOEFL, IELTS, or Pearson. 60 of 120 credits required for the bachelor's degree must be completed at Vanderbilt. **International Students:** There are 530 international students enrolled. They must take the TOEFL, and either the SAT or ACT.

ADMISSIONS: 11% of the 2017-2018 applicants were accepted. The SAT scores for the 2017-2018 freshman class were: Math-- 1% below 500, 5% between 500 and 599, 19% between 600 and 699, and 76% between 700 and 800. Evidence-Based Reading/Writing-- 5% between 500 and 599, 15% between 600 and 699, and 80% between 700 and 800. The ACT scores were 1% between 18 and 23, 8% between 24 and 29, and 91% above 30. 94% of the current freshmen were in the top fifth of their class; 98% were in the top two fifths. 74 freshmen graduated first in their class. **Admissions Contact:** Linda Forceno, Associate Institutional Research Analyst. Email: *admissions@vanderbilt.edu* Web: *www.vanderbilt.edu*

FINANCIAL AID: In 2017-2018, 54% of all full-time freshmen received some form of financial aid. 53% of all full-time freshmen received need-based aid. The average freshman award was $50,356. Need-based scholarships or need-based grants averaged $48,559; need-based self-help aid (loans and jobs) averaged $2,595; non-need-based athletic scholarships averaged $51,245; and other non-need-based awards and non-need-based scholarships averaged $23,629. The average financial indebtedness of the 2017 graduate was $24,122. The CSS/Profile, and tax return information are required. The FAFSA code is 003535. The priority date for freshman financial aid applications for fall entry is February 2.

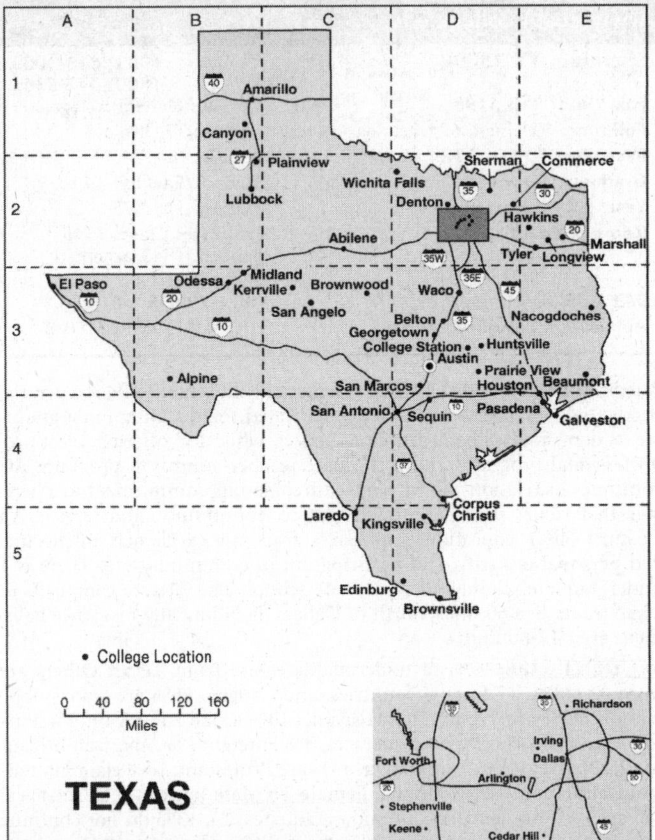

ABILENE CHRISTIAN UNIVERSITY C-2
www.acu.edu

Abilene, TX 79699 **(325) 674-2650** **(800) 460-6228**
Email: info@admissions.acu.edu

Full-time: 1457 men, 2055 women
Part-time: 68 men, 90 women
Graduate: 513 men, 966 women
Year: semesters, summer session
Room & Board: $10,378
SAT EBR-W/M: 568/558 **ACT:** 24
Application Deadline: February 15

Faculty: 266; IIA, -$
Ph.D.s: 79%
Student/Faculty: 16 to 1
Tuition: $33,330
Freshman Class: 9827 applied, 5952 accepted, 972 enrolled
CEEB CODE: 6001
COMPETITIVE+

Abilene Christian University, provides exceptional academics in a Christ-centered community, with colleges of Arts and Sciences, Biblical Studies, Business Administration, and Education and Human Services. Graduate and Professional Studies, and Honors include the Graduate School of Theology, and the schools of Information Technology and Computing, Nursing, and Social Work. ACU is affiliated with the Churches of Christ and is one of the largest private universities in the Southwest. There are 8 undergraduate schools and 10 graduate schools. In addition to regional accreditation, Abilene Christian University has baccalaureate program accreditation with AACSB, ABET, ACEJMC, CSWE, FIDER, NASM, ACEND, and CCNE. The 250-acre campus is in a small town 180 miles west of the Dallas-Fort Worth metroplex. Including any residence halls, there are 52 buildings.

STUDENT LIFE: 85% of undergraduates are from Texas. Others are from 41 states, 33 foreign countries, and Canada. 64% are from public schools. 9% are African American; 64% White; 5% two or more races; 4% Foreign; 17% Hispanic; 1% Asian American. 63% are Protestant. **Female To Male Ratio:** 1.5:1. The average age of freshmen is 18; all undergraduates, 20. 23% do not continue beyond their first year; 61% remain to graduate. **Housing:** 2013 students can be accommodated in college housing, which includes single-sex dorms and on-campus apartments. On-campus housing is available on a first-come, first-served basis, and is available on a lottery system for upperclassmen. 53% of students commute. All students may keep cars. Alcohol is not permitted.

FACULTY/CLASSROOMS: 59% of faculty are male; 41% are female. 84% teach undergraduates, 14% do research, and 6% do both. Graduate students teach 1% of introductory courses. The average class size in an introductory lecture is 34; in a laboratory is 16; and in a regular course is 23.

PROGRAMS OF STUDY: Abilene Christian University confers B.A., B.S., B.B.A., B.F.A., B.M., B.S.E., and B.S.N. degrees. Associate, master's, and doctoral degrees are also awarded. Bachelor's degrees are awarded in AGRICULTURE (agricultural business management and animal science), BIOLOGICAL SCIENCE (biochemistry, biology/biological science, biology/general science secondary education, and nutrition), BUSINESS (accounting, finance, information and communication technology, management science, and marketing/retailing/merchandising), COMMUNICATIONS AND THE ARTS (advertising, art, communications, dramatic arts, English, fine arts, graphic design, journalism, multimedia, music, piano performance, public relations, Spanish, and vocal performance), COMPUTER AND PHYSICAL SCIENCE (chemistry, computer game design/development, computer science, information sciences and systems, mathematics, mathematics/computational, and physics), EDUCATION (computer education, English secondary education, English education, foreign languages education, global studies, journalism education, mathematics education, middle school education, music education, secondary education, and special education), ENGINEERING AND ENVIRONMENTAL DESIGN (engineering, environmental science, and interior design), HEALTH PROFESSIONS (kinesiology and nursing), SOCIAL SCIENCE (biblical studies, child care/child and family studies, communication sciences and disorders, criminal justice, history, liberal arts/general studies, ministries, political science/government, psychology, social work, and sociology). Accounting, biology, and engineering are the strongest academically. Management, nursing, and kinesiology have the largest enrollments.

ACTIVITIES: 28% of men belong to 7 local fraternities; 35% of women belong to 7 local sororities. There are 110 groups on campus, including art, band, cheerleading, chess, choir, chorale, chorus, computers, dance, debate, drama, environmental, ethnic, film, forensics, honors, international, jazz band, LGBT, literary magazine, marching band, musical theater, newspaper, opera, orchestra, photography, political, professional, radio and TV, religious, social, social service, student government, and symphony. Popular campus events include Freshman Follies, Homecoming Carnival and Parade, Sing Song Festival, and Summit Bible Lectures. **Sports:** There are 7 intercollegiate sports for men and 7 for women, and 7 intramural sports for men and 7 for women. Facilities include the student recreation and wellness center with an aquatic center, a fitness center, group exercise studios, bouldering wall, gyms, racquetball courts, a coliseum, track/soccer, baseball, softball, and football stadiums, a tennis center, and a disc golf course. **Graduates:** From July 1, 2016 to June 30, 2017, 746 bachelor's degrees were awarded. The most popular majors were psychology (7%), management (7%), and nursing (6%). In an average class, 4% graduate in 3 years or less, 48% graduate in 4 years or less, 61% graduate in 5 years or less, and 61% graduate in 6 years or less. Of the 2016 graduating class, 35% were enrolled in graduate school within 6 months of graduation, and 51% were employed.

SERVICES: There is a reader service for the blind, and remedial math and writing. There is also a sign language interpreter. **Library/Resources:** The library contains 545,467 volumes, 1.2 million microform items, 66,790 audio/video tapes/CDs/DVDs, and subscribes to 104 periodicals, including electronic. Computerized library services include interlibrary loans, database searching, Internet access, and Wi-Fi capability. Special learning facilities include an art gallery, a planetarium, radio and TV stations, a writing center, a speaking center, AT&T Learning Studio, a maker lab, a Center for Christian Service and Leadership, a converged media newsroom, a Center for Speech and Language Disorders, the Rhoden Farm, and a center for restoration studies. **Physically Challenged Students:** 95% of the campus is accessible. Facilities include wheelchair ramps, elevators, special parking, specially equipped restrooms, special class scheduling, and lowered drinking fountains. **Special:** ACU offers health professions cooperative degrees in Animal Science, Biochemistry and Biology. ACU offers cross-registration with Hardin-Simmons, and McMurry Universities, internships are possible in most majors. Study abroad in 3 countries; England, Uruguay, and Germany. B.A.-B.S. degrees in biology, bio-chemistry, communication, convergence journalism, criminal justice, and mathematics. Double majors are available. AN individualized composite Interdisciplinary major may be approved for a student whose life & career goals will be served by such a major. There are 18 national honor societies and a freshman honors program. **Visiting:** There are regularly scheduled orientations for prospective students, consisting of academic department, attend chapel, financial aid and admission information, and special interest sessions. There are guides for informal visits and visitors may sit in on classes. To schedule a visit, contact the Director of Campus Visits at (800) 460-6228. **Campus Safety and Security:** Measures include 24-hour foot and vehicle patrol, an emergency notification system, self-defense education, and security escort services. There are shuttle buses, emergency telephones, lighted pathways/sidewalks, controlled access to dorms/residences, and fire safety discussions.

REQUIREMENTS: Satisfactory SAT or ACT score, with at least one Berklee College of Musicwriting score. Applicants must be graduates of an accredited secondary school or have the GED and have completed 12 academic credits, including 4 in English, 3 each in math and science, and 2 years of the same foreign language. Art majors need to submit a portfolio, and music and theater majors must audition. ACU requires applicants to be in the upper 50% of their class. AP and CLEP credits are accepted. Important factors in the admissions decision are leadership record, recommendations by alumni, and advanced placement or honors courses. To graduate, students must complete courses in Bible (9 hours), English, communication, science, mathematics, social science, kinesiology (2 hours), including historical literacy and cultural awareness. 33 semester hours of advanced work must be taken and a minimum 2.0 GPA maintained. A minimum of 128 credit hours is needed (more in some programs) and 30 to 64 hours of that is in the major, 18 of which must be upper division. **Procedure:** Freshmen are admitted to all sessions. Entrance exams should be taken by February of the senior year. There is an early admissions plan. Applications should be filed by February 15 for fall entry. The fall 2017 application fee was $50. Notification of early decision is sent November 1. Applications are accepted on-line. **Transfer Students:** 106 transfer students enrolled in 2016-2017. Transfer students are evaluated for admission on the basis of their college GPA. Entrance exam scores and high school transcripts will be reviewed for students with GPA's below 2.5. 40 of 128 credits required for the bachelor's degree must be completed at ACU. **International Students:** There are 165 international students enrolled. They must take the TOEFL with a minimum score of 400 on the paper-based TOEFL (PBT) or 80 on the Internet-based version (iBT). They must also take the SAT or ACT.

ADMISSIONS: 61% of the 2017-2018 applicants were accepted. The SAT scores for the 2017-2018 freshman class were: Math-- 19% below 500, 53% between 500 and 599, 25% between 600 and 699, and 3% between 700 and 800. Evidence-Based Reading/Writing-- 19% below 500, 44% between 500 and 599, 33% between 600 and 699, and 4% between 700 and 800. The ACT scores were 4% between 12 and 17, 46% between 18 and 23, 42% between 24 and 29, and 8% above 30. 46% of the current freshmen were in the top fifth of their class; 75% were in the top two fifths. 1 freshman graduated first in the class. **Admissions Contact:** Tamara Long, Dean of Admissions. Email: *info@admissions.acu.edu* Web: *www.acu.edu*

FINANCIAL AID: In 2017-2018, 100% of all full-time freshmen received some form of financial aid. 76% of all full-time freshmen received need-based aid. The average freshman award was $25,064. Need-based scholarships or need-based grants averaged $22,817; need-based self-help aid (loans and jobs) averaged $3,511; non-need-based athletic scholarships averaged $26,744; and other non-need-based awards and non-need-based scholarships averaged $15,291. 28% of undergraduate students work part-time. The FAFSA code is 003537. The deadline for filing freshman financial aid applications for fall entry is March 1.

ANGELO STATE UNIVERSITY *(The complete profile is made available exclusively on our website, www.barronspac.com)*

AUSTIN COLLEGE — D-2

www.austincollege.edu

Sherman, TX 75090 (903) 813-3000
(800) 442-5363
Fax: (903) 813-3198 **Email:** admission@austincollege.edu

Full-time: 591 men, 624 women	**Faculty:** 77; IIB, av$
Part-time: 5 men, 3 women	**Ph.D.s:** 98%
Graduate: 9 men, 5 women	**Student/Faculty:** 14 to 1
Year: 4-1-4, summer session	**Tuition:** $38,825
Room & Board: $12,234	**Freshman Class:** 3545 applied, 1849 accepted, 332 enrolled
SAT EBR-W/M: 634/625 **ACT:** 26	**CEEB CODE:** 6016
Application Deadline: March 1	**HIGHLY COMPETITIVE**

Austin College, founded by the Presbyterian Church in 1849, is a private, residential, co-educational college, dedicated to educating undergraduate students in the liberal arts and sciences, while also offering select pre-professional programs and a graduate teacher education program. AC continues its relationship with the church and its commitment to a heritage that values personal growth, justice, community, and service. An Austin College education emphasizes academic excellence, intellectual and personal integrity, and participation in community life. There is 1 undergraduate school and 1 graduate school. The 70-acre campus is in a suburban area 60 miles north of Dallas. Including any residence halls, there are 34 buildings.

STUDENT LIFE: 92% of undergraduates are from Texas. Others are from 32 states, 17 foreign countries, and Canada. 85% are from public schools. 49% are White; 21% Hispanic; 13% Asian American; 9% African American; 4% two or more races; 3% Foreign; 1% American Indian/Alaska Native; 1% race unknown. 44% are Protestant; 18% claim no religious affiliation; 17% Catholic. **Female To Male Ratio:** 1.0:1. The average age of freshmen is 18; all undergraduates, 23. 13% do not continue beyond their first year; 68% remain to graduate. **Housing:** 1072 students can be accommodated in college housing, which includes coed dorms, on-campus apartments, and language/international houses. On-campus housing is available on a lottery system for upperclassmen. 81% of students live on campus. All students may keep cars.

FACULTY/CLASSROOMS: 63% of faculty are male; 37% are female. All teach undergraduates, and all do research. No introductory courses are taught by graduate students. The average class size in an introductory lecture is 19; in a laboratory is 16; and in a regular course is 20.

PROGRAMS OF STUDY: AC confers B.A. degrees. Master's degrees are also awarded. Bachelor's degrees are awarded in AGRICULTURE (natural resources), BIOLOGICAL SCIENCE (biochemistry and biology/biological science), BUSINESS (business administration and management and international economics), COMMUNICATIONS AND THE ARTS (art history, art, classical languages, classics, communications, East Asian languages and literature, English, French, German, Latin, music, Spanish, and visual and performing arts), COMPUTER AND PHYSICAL SCIENCE (chemistry, computer science, mathematics, natural sciences, physical sciences, and physics), HEALTH PROFESSIONS (health administration and policy), SOCIAL SCIENCE (American studies, economics, history, interdisciplinary studies, international studies, Latin American studies, philosophy, political science/government, psychology, religion, social science, sociology, and women and gender studies). Biology, psychology, and political science are the strongest academically. Business administration has the largest enrollment.

ACTIVITIES: 26% of men belong to 10 local fraternities; 17% of women belong to 5 local sororities. There are 55 groups on campus, including art, cheerleading, choir, chorale, chorus, communications, dance, drama, environmental, ethnic, film, honors, international, jazz band, LGBT, literary magazine, Model UN and International Student organizations, musical theater, newspaper, orchestra, pep band, photography, political, professional, religious, social, social service, student government, symphony, and yearbook. Popular campus events include Christmas Pops, Kangapalooza (spring concert), Great Day of Service, Film Series, and Diwali Dinner. **Sports:** There are 7 intercollegiate sports for men and 7 for women, and 8 intramural sports for men and 8 for women. Facilities include an athletic/recreation complex that includes gyms, a natatorium, a fitness pavilion, a tennis stadium, and soccer and baseball fields. **Graduates:** From July 1, 2016 to June 30, 2017, 292 bachelor's degrees were awarded. The most popular majors were business/marketing (20%), biological/life sciences (16%), and psycholgy (12%). In an average class, 96% graduate in 4 years or less. Of the 2016 graduating class, 44% were enrolled in graduate school within 6 months of graduation, and 47% were employed.

SERVICES: Counseling and information services are available, as is tutoring in some subjects, such as introductory-level courses. There is also individual and group assistance to strengthen reading, writing, and study skills. **Library/Resources:** The library contains 272,776 volumes, 29,526 microform items, 15,575 audio/video tapes/CDs/DVDs, and subscribes to 33,936 periodicals, including electronic. Computerized library services include interlibrary loans, database searching, Internet access, and Wi-Fi capability. Special learning facilities include an art gallery, a social science lab, television studios for media instruction, environmental research areas near Lake Texoma, a facility for advanced computing and 3-D graphics, a mock courtroom, and a domed observatory housing a 24-inch telescope with an astronomical high-resolution image camera. **Physically Challenged Students:** All of the campus is accessible. Facilities include wheelchair ramps, elevators, special parking, specially equipped restrooms, special class scheduling, and lowered drinking fountains. **Special:** AC offers study abroad in 58 countries, internships during the January and summer terms, and in the fall, spring, and summer, there are internships in Washington, D.C. There are also work-study programs, accelerated degree programs in all majors, and dual and student-designed majors. There is a 3-2 engineering degree program in conjunction with the University of Texas at Dallas and Washington University in St. Louis, as well as cooperative agreements with Columbia University and Texas A&M University. There are 14 national honor societies and a chapter of Phi Beta Kappa. **Visiting:** There are regularly scheduled orientations for prospective students, 1-day and 2-day preview programs held for high school juniors, seniors and parents. Individual appointments may be made as well. There are guides for informal visits; visitors may sit in on classes and stay overnight. To schedule a visit, contact the Admissions Office at admissions@austincollege.edu. **Campus Safety and Security:** Measures include 24-hour foot and vehicle patrol, emergency notification system, self-defense education, and security escort services. There are emergency telephones and lighted pathways/sidewalks.

REQUIREMENTS: The SAT or ACT is required. The ACT writing test is recommended. Applicants must be graduates of an accredited secondary school, home school, or have a GED. The required academic requirements are 4 credits in English, 3-4 each in math and science with 1 lab (2 recommended), 2-4 each in social studies and foreign language, and 1 in visual performing arts. An essay and recommendation are also required. AC is test optional for admission. If a student elects to be test optional, and they do not submit test scores, they may submit an expository writing paper. AP and CLEP credits are accepted. Important factors in the admissions decision are advanced placement or honors courses, recommendations by school officials, leadership record, parents or siblings attended your school, evidence of special talent, personality/intangible qualities, extracurricular activities record, recommendations by alumni, and geographical diversity. Core requirements for graduation include completion of the Foundation Dimension, the Breadth Dimension, and 1 course in Lifetime Sports. To graduate, students must have a minimum 2.0 GPA and a total of 34 course credits (136 semester hours). Students must demonstrate an ability in a modern or classical language other than their own, quantitative competency with an approved course or test, and the required skills in written communication with approved coursework. A minor or a 2nd major is required. **Procedure:** Freshmen are admitted in the fall. Entrance exams should be taken by the junior year or the fall of the senior year. There are early decision, deferred admissions, and rolling admissions plans. Early decision applications should be filed by November 1; regular applications, by March 1 for fall entry. Notification of early decision is sent December 4; regular decision, April 1. 4 early decision candidates were accepted for the 2017-2018 class. Applications are accepted online. **Transfer Students:** 31 transfer students enrolled in 2016-2017. Applicants must have a minimum 3.0 GPA, submit official college transcripts and 2 recommendations, and be in good standing at most recently attended schools. Students with fewer than 30 credit hours must submit SAT or ACT scores and their high school transcript or GED. 17 credits required for the bachelor's degree must be completed at AC. **International Students:** There are 31 international students enrolled. They must take the TOEFL with a minimum score of 550 on the paper-based TOEFL (PBT) or 80 on the Internet-based version (iBT). They must also take the SAT or ACT.

ADMISSIONS: 52% of the 2017-2018 applicants were accepted. The SAT scores for the 2017-2018 freshman class were: Math-- 4% below 500, 34% between 500 and 599, 44% between 600 and 699, and 18% between 700 and 800. Evidence-Based Reading/Writing-- 2% below 500, 25% between 500 and 599, 55% between 600 and 699, and 18% between 700 and 800. The ACT scores were 25% between 18 and 23, 52% between 24 and 29, and 23% above 30. 76% of the current freshmen were in the top fifth of their class; 96% were in the top two fifths. **Admissions Contact:** Alan Ramirez, Director of Admission. Email: *admission@austincollege.edu* Web: *www.austincollege.edu*

FINANCIAL AID: In 2017-2018, 87% of all full-time freshmen received some form of financial aid. 66% of all full-time freshmen received need-based aid. The average freshman award was $35,402. Need-based scholarships or need-based grants averaged $32,493; need-based self-help aid (loans and jobs) averaged $4,123; other non-need-based awards and non-need-based scholarships averaged $3,344; and $24,114 from other forms of aid. AC is a member of CSS. The FAFSA code is 003543. The priority date for freshman financial aid applications for fall entry is March 1.

BAYLOR UNIVERSITY — D-3
www.baylor.edu

Waco, TX 76798 — **(254) 710-3435**

Email: admissions@baylor.edu

Full-time: 5804 men, 8296 women	**Faculty:** I, -$
Part-time: 107 men, 109 women	**Ph.D.s:** 83%
Graduate: 1438 men, 1305 women	**Student/Faculty:** 14 to 1
Year: semesters, summer session	**Tuition:** $43,790
Room & Board: $13,013	**Freshman Class:** n/av
SAT or ACT: required	**CEEB CODE:** 6032
Application Deadline: February 1	**HIGHLY COMPETITIVE**

Baylor University Chartered in 1845 by the Republic of Texas is a private Christian university and research institution, offering undergraduate programs in liberal arts and sciences, business, computer science, education, engineering, health and human services, music, nursing, social work, and an honors college. There are 9 undergraduate schools and 10 graduate schools. In addition to regional accreditation, BU has baccalaureate program accreditation with AACSB, ABET, ACEJMC, APTA, CSWE, FIDER, NASM, NAST, and ACS. The 1000-acre campus is in a small town 100 miles south of Dallas/Fort Worth. Including any residence halls, there are 127 buildings.

STUDENT LIFE: 70% of undergraduates are from Texas. Others are from 50 states, 73 foreign countries, and Canada. 63% are White; 6% African American; 6% Asian American; 5% two or more races; 3% Foreign; 15% Hispanic; 1% American Indian/Alaska Native. 17% are Catholic. **Female To Male Ratio:** 1.3:1. The average age of freshmen is 19; all undergraduates, 20. 11% do not continue beyond their first year; 74% remain to graduate. **Housing:** 5395 students can be accommodated in college housing, which includes married student dorms, on-campus apartments, and off-campus apartments. In addition, there are honors houses, language/international houses, special-interest houses, and living learning communities. On-campus housing is guaranteed for the freshman year only, and is available on a first-come, first-served basis. 65% of students commute. All students may keep cars. Alcohol is not permitted.

FACULTY/CLASSROOMS: 59% of faculty are male; 41% are female. No introductory courses are taught by graduate students. The average class size in a regular course is 26.

PROGRAMS OF STUDY: BU confers B.A., B.B.A., B.F.A., B.M., B.M.E., B.S., B.S.Av.Sc., B.S.C., B.S.C.S., B.S.E., B.S.E.C.E., B.S.Ed., B.S.F.C.S., B.S.I., B.S.M.E., B.S.N., B.S.P.H., and B.S.W. degrees. Master's and doctoral degrees are also awarded. Bachelor's degrees are awarded in BIOLOGICAL SCIENCE (biochemistry, bioinformatics, biology/biological science, life science, neurosciences, and nutrition), BUSINESS (accounting, apparel and accessories marketing, banking and finance, business administration and management, business economics, business statistics, business systems analysis, entrepreneurial studies, fashion merchandising, human resources, insurance, international business management, management information systems, marketing/retailing/merchandising, personnel management, real estate, and sports marketing), COMMUNICATIONS AND THE ARTS (acting, apparel design, applied music, art history, art, art history and appreciation, broadcasting, choral music, classics, communications, creative writing, dramatic arts, English, French, German, Greek (classical), journalism, languages, Latin, literature, music, music history and appreciation, music performance, music theory and composition, performing arts, Russian, Spanish, speech/debate/rhetoric, studio art, telecommunications, theater design, and theatre studies), COMPUTER AND PHYSICAL SCIENCE (applied mathematics, chemistry, computer science, earth science, geology, geophysics and seismology, information sciences and systems, mathematics, and physics), EDUCATION (art education, business education, computer education, drama education, elementary education, English education, foreign languages education, health education, home economics education, journalism education, mathematics education, museum studies, music education, physical education, reading education, recreation education, science education, secondary education, social science education, social studies education, and special education), ENGINEERING AND ENVIRONMENTAL DESIGN (airline piloting and navigation, aviation administration/management, computer engineering, electrical/electronics engineering, engineering, environmental science, interior design, and mechanical engineering), HEALTH PROFESSIONS (health science, medical laboratory technology, nursing, optometry, predentistry, premedicine, public health, speech pathology/audiology, and speech therapy), SOCIAL SCIENCE (American studies, anthropology, area studies, Asian/Oriental studies, child care/child and family studies, dietetics, economics, family/consumer studies, fashion design and technology, forensic studies, history, interdisciplinary studies, international public service, Latin American studies, Middle Eastern studies, philosophy, physical fitness/movement, political science/government, psychology, public administration, religion, religious education, religious music, Russian and Slavic studies, social work, sociology, and urban studies). Business/prebusiness, biology/prebiology, and health science studies have the largest enrollments.

ACTIVITIES: 16% of men belong to 2 local and 19 national fraternities; 31% of women belong to 1 local and 17 national sororities. There are 316 groups on campus, including academic (language, discipline specific), art, band, cheerleading, chess, choir, chorale, chorus, computers, dance, debate, drama, environmental, ethnic, film, forensics, honors, international, jazz band, literary magazine, marching band, musical theater, newspaper, opera, orchestra, pep band, photography, political, professional, radio and TV, religious, social, social service, sport clubs (non-NCAA athletics), student government, symphony, and yearbook. Popular campus events include Dia del Oso (Day of the Bear), Campus Sing, and Pigskin Review. **Sports:** There are 20 intercollegiate sports for men and 19 for women, and 23 intramural sports for men and 23 for women. Facilities include a football stadium, athletic facilities, softball stadium, baseball stadium, soccer complex, outdoor and indoor tennis facilities, a basketball facility, and volleyball. **Graduates:** From July 1, 2016 to June 30, 2017, 3127 bachelor's degrees were awarded. The most popular majors were biology (7%), nursing (7%), and accounting (5%). In an average class, 2% graduate in 3 years or less, 60% graduate in 4 years or less, 73% graduate in 5 years or less, and 74% graduate in 6 years or less.

SERVICES: Counseling and information services are available, as is tutoring in some subjects. There is a reader service for the blind. **Library/Resources:** The library contains 2.6 million volumes, 2.3 million microform items, 197,369 audio/video tapes/CDs/DVDs, and subscribes to 185,062 periodicals, including electronic. Computerized library services include interlibrary loans, database searching, Internet access, and Wi-Fi capability. Special learning facilities include an art gallery, natural history museum, radio station, TV station, and a speech/hearing clinic. **Physically Challenged Students:** 95% of the campus is accessible. Facilities include wheelchair ramps, elevators, special parking, specially equipped restrooms, and lowered drinking fountains. **Special:** BU offers internships in each school, study abroad and student exchange in more than 30 countries, and pass/fail options. There are also honors and university scholars programs and faculty exchange with 4 schools in China and 1 each in Japan, Thailand, and Russia. There are 36 national honor societies, Phi Beta Kappa, and a freshman honors program. **Visiting:** There are regularly scheduled orientations for prospective students, including day-and-a-half sessions in June and a Welcome Week in August. There are guides for informal visits; visitors may sit in on classes and stay overnight. To schedule a visit, contact Campus Visitation Program at (254) 710-2407. **Campus Safety and Security:** Measures include 24-hour foot and vehicle patrol, emergency notification system, and security escort services. There are shuttle buses, emergency telephones, lighted pathways/sidewalks, and controlled access to dorms/residences.

REQUIREMENTS: The SAT or ACT is required. Applicants must be graduates of an accredited secondary school. An interview is recommended. AP and CLEP credits are accepted. All degree programs require a minimum of 124 hours and a 2.0 GPA to graduate. Basic requirements for the B.A. degree include 18 semester hours of social science, 12 hours each of English and science, 6 to 9 hours of fine arts, 6 hours of religion, 4 hours of physical education, 3 to 16 hours of foreign language, 3 hours of math, and 2 semesters of chapel forum. Requirements for other degrees vary. **Procedure:** Freshmen are admitted in the fall, spring, and summer. Entrance exams should be taken in spring of the junior year or fall of the senior year. There are early admissions and deferred admissions plans. Early decision applications should be filed by November 1; regular applications, by February 1 for fall entry. Notification of early decision is sent January 15; regular decision, April 10. Applications are accepted online. **Transfer Students:** 430 transfer students enrolled in 2016-2017. Transfer students should begin studies no later than the end of the sophomore year because of the 60-semester-hour residence requirement for a bachelor's degree. Students with fewer than 30 credit hours earned must meet the entrance requirements for freshmen. 60 of 124 credits required for the bachelor's degree must be completed at BU. **International Students:** There are 630 international students enrolled. They must take the TOEFL with a minimum score of 540 on the paper-based TOEFL (PBT) or 76 on the Internet-based version (iBT). Student must have a satisfactory score on the SAT or ACT.

ADMISSIONS: 39% of the 2017-2018 applicants were accepted. 69% of the current freshmen were in the top fifth of their class; 91% were in the top two fifths. **Admissions Contact:** Jessica King Gereghty, Assistant Vice President of Undergraduate Admissions. Email: *admissions@baylor.edu* Web: *www.baylor.edu*

FINANCIAL AID: The FAFSA code is 003545. The priority date for freshman financial aid applications for fall entry is February 15.

CONCORDIA UNIVERSITY TEXAS — D-3

www.concordia.edu

Austin, TX 78705	**(512) 486-2000** **(800) 865-4282**
Fax: (512) 486-1350	**Email: admissions@concordia.edu**
Full-time: 350 men, 410 women	**Faculty:** n/av
Part-time: 85 men, 185 women	**Ph.D.s:** 74%
Graduate: 20 men, 70 women	**Student/Faculty:** 18 to 1
Year: semesters, summer session	**Tuition:** $30,600
Room & Board: $11,320	**Freshman Class:** 728 applied, 532 accepted, 194 enrolled
SAT or ACT: required	**CEEB CODE:** 6127
Application Deadline: August 15	**COMPETITIVE**

Concordia University Texas, founded in 1926, is a private college affiliated with the Lutheran Church-Missouri Synod. It offers undergraduate programs in liberal arts, behavioral science, business, communication, education, environmental science, and church music. The figures given in the above capsule and in this profile are approximate. There are 4 undergraduate schools. In addition to regional accreditation, CUT has baccalaureate program accreditation with SACSCOC. The 389-acre campus is in an urban area in Northwest Austin,TX. Including any residence halls, there are 20 buildings.

STUDENT LIFE: 93% of undergraduates are from Texas. Others are from 21 states and 13 foreign countries. 89% are from public schools. 9% are African American; 63% White; 16% Hispanic; 1% Asian American. 78% are Protestant; 16% Catholic. **Female To Male Ratio:** 1.5:1. The average age of freshmen is 19; all undergraduates, 25. 40% do not continue beyond their first year; 35% remain to graduate. **Housing:** 245 students can be accommodated in college housing, which includes dorms, and residence halls. On-campus housing is guaranteed for the freshman year only, and is available on a first-come, first-served basis. 68% of students commute. All students may keep cars.

FACULTY/CLASSROOMS: 69% of faculty are male; 31% are female. All teach undergraduates. No introductory courses are taught by graduate students. The average class size in a laboratory is 16 and in a regular course is 21.

PROGRAMS OF STUDY: CUT confers B.A. degrees. Associate and master's degrees are also awarded. Bachelor's degrees are awarded in BUSINESS (accounting and business administration and management),

COMMUNICATIONS AND THE ARTS (communications, English, music, and Spanish), COMPUTER AND PHYSICAL SCIENCE (computer science), EDUCATION (elementary education and secondary education), ENGINEERING AND ENVIRONMENTAL DESIGN (environmental science), SOCIAL SCIENCE (behavioral science, history, liberal arts/general studies, Mexican-American/Chicano studies, and religious music). Education is the strongest academically. Business management, education, and communication have the largest enrollments.

ACTIVITIES: There are no fraternities or sororities. There are 9 groups on campus, including band, choir, chorus, dance, drama, ethnic, religious, social, and student government. Popular campus events include Fall Festival Weekend, Parents Day, and Founders Day. **Sports:** There are 6 intercollegiate sports for men and 5 for women, and 10 intramural sports for men and 9 for women. Facilities include an activities center, a gym, auditorium, baseball field, beach volleyball court, and tennis courts. **Graduates:** From July 1, 2016 to June 30, 2017, 151 bachelor's degrees were awarded. The most popular majors were business/marketing (44%), education (12%), and social sciences (9%). In an average class, 20% graduate in 4 years or less and 30% graduate in 5 years or less.

SERVICES: Counseling and information services are available, as is tutoring in most subjects. **Library/Resources:** The library contains 56,146 volumes, 8,504 microform items, 3,213 audio/video tapes/CDs/DVDs, and subscribes to 514 periodicals, including electronic. Computerized library services include interlibrary loans and database searching. Special learning facilities include a TV station. **Physically Challenged Students:** 75% of the campus is accessible. Facilities include wheelchair ramps, elevators, special parking, specially equipped restrooms, and lowered drinking fountains. **Special:** CUT offers internships in communications, behavioral science, business, environmental science, and Mexican-American studies, study abroad in Mexico, an accelerated degree program in business management, dual majors, credit for prior experiential learning, nondegree study, pass/fail options, and a preseminary program. There is 1 national honor society. **Visiting:** There are regularly scheduled orientations for prospective students, consisting of placement exams, scheduling and registration of classes, and information sessions for parents with faculty and administrators. There are guides for informal visits; visitors may sit in on classes and stay overnight. To schedule a visit, contact the Admissions Office. **Campus Safety and Security:** Measures include 24-hour foot and vehicle patrol and security escort services, and lighted pathways/sidewalks.

REQUIREMENTS: The recommended minimum composite score is 860 on the SAT I or 17 on the ACT. Applicants must be graduates of an accredited secondary school or have the GED. A GPA of 2.5 is required. AP and CLEP credits are accepted. To graduate, all students must complete 12 hours each of English, social/behavioral science, and religion, 6 to 8 hours of natural science, and 3 hours each of fine arts, math, physical education, and speech. Students must earn 128 semester hours, including 39 upper-level hours and 33 to 48 hours in the major. A minimum 2.0 GPA is required, plus a 2.25 GPA in the major. **Procedure:** Freshmen are admitted in the fall, spring, and summer. There are early admissions, deferred admissions, and rolling admissions plans. Applications should be filed by August 15 for fall entry. The fall 2017 application fee was $25. **Transfer Students:** 71 transfer students enrolled in 2016-2017. Transfer students with fewer than 18 hours earned must meet freshman admissions requirements and submit high school and college transcripts; those with 18 or more hours earned must be in good standing at the previously attended college with a minimum 2.5 GPA. 45 of 128 credits required for the bachelor's degree must be completed at CUT. **International Students:** They must take the TOEFL.

ADMISSIONS: 73% of the 2017-2018 applicants were accepted. **Admissions Contact:** Dr. Michael Mogavero, Vice President of Enrollment Services. Email: *admissions@concordia.edu* Web: *www.concordia.edu*

FINANCIAL AID: In 2017-2018, 80% of all full-time freshmen received some form of financial aid and need-based aid. The average freshman award was $16,678. Need-based scholarships or need-based grants averaged $10,250; need-based self-help aid (loans and jobs) averaged $3,034; and other non-need-based awards and non-need-based scholarships averaged $6,896. The average financial indebtedness of the 2017 graduate was $15,084. The college's own financial statement is required. The FAFSA code is 003557. The priority date for freshman financial aid applications for fall entry is May 1.

DALLAS BAPTIST UNIVERSITY D-2

www.dbu.edu

Dallas, TX 75211 (214) 333-5360 (800) 460-1328

Fax: (214) 333-5447 **Email:** admiss@dbu.edu

Full-time: 1021 men, 1402 women
Part-time: 288 men, 450 women
Graduate: 764 men, 1142 women
Year: 4-1-4, summer session
Room & Board: $7740

Faculty: 107
Ph.D.s: 81%
Student/Faculty: 13 to 1
Tuition: $27,480
Freshman Class: 3770 applied, 1486 accepted, 542 enrolled

SAT EBR-W/M: 599/577 **ACT:** required
CEEB CODE: 6159
Application Deadline: n/av
VERY COMPETITIVE

Dallas Baptist University is a Christ-centered comprehensive, liberal arts university offering 7 Associate, 73 Bachelor, 63 Accelerated Bachelor/Master, 31 Master, 74 Dual Master, and 2 Doctoral degree programs. DBU integrates faith and academic learning, giving students freedom to explore their faith in the classroom and the encouragement to live out their faith as servant leaders in the world. DBU offers working adults the convenience and flexibility they need to complete their degree with online, weekend and evening classes. There are 7 undergraduate schools and 31 graduate schools. In addition to regional accreditation, DBU has baccalaureate program accreditation with ACBSP, NASM, TEA, and CEA. The 293-acre campus is in a suburban area 13 miles from downtown Dallas and 29 miles from downtown Fort Worth. Including any residence halls, there are 49 buildings.

STUDENT LIFE: 83% of undergraduates are from Texas. Others are from 40 states, 43 foreign countries, and Canada. 9% are Foreign; 59% White; 2% Asian American; 16% Hispanic; 12% African American; 1% American Indian/Alaska Native. 92% are Protestant. **Female To Male Ratio:** 1.4:1. The average age of freshmen is 18; all undergraduates, 24. 23% do not continue beyond their first year; 59% remain to graduate. **Housing:** 2105 students can be accommodated in college housing, which includes single-sex dorms, on-campus apartments, and off-campus apartments. In addition, there are language/international houses. On-campus housing is available on a first-come, first-served basis. 62% of students live on campus. Alcohol is not permitted. All students may keep cars.

FACULTY/CLASSROOMS: 57% of faculty are male; 43% are female. 71% teach undergraduates. No introductory courses are taught by graduate students. The average class size in a regular course is 12.

PROGRAMS OF STUDY: DBU confers B.A., B.S., B.A.S., B.B.A., B.B.S., B.M., B.M.E., and B.M.A. degrees. Associate, master's, and doctoral degrees are also awarded. Bachelor's degrees are awarded in BIOLOGICAL SCIENCE (biology/biological science and cell biology), BUSINESS (accounting, business administration and management, business administration - international, entrepreneurial studies, finance, hospitality management services, human resources/organizational management, international business, management information systems, marketing, and sports management), COMMUNICATIONS AND THE ARTS (applied music, art, broadcasting, choral music, church music, communication design, communications, English, film, television and digital media, fine arts, graphic design, keyboard - piano concentration, music, music business management, music performance, music theory and composition, piano performance, public relations, and vocal performance), COMPUTER AND PHYSICAL SCIENCE (computer science, mathematics, natural sciences, and science), EDUCATION (Christian education, early childhood education, education, elementary education, English education, middle school education, physical education, reading education, science education, and secondary education), ENGINEERING AND ENVIRONMENTAL DESIGN (environmental science), HEALTH PROFESSIONS (biology and health care administration), SOCIAL SCIENCE (biblical studies, Christian studies, counseling/psychology, criminal justice, cultural studies/critical theory and analysis, economics, history, interdisciplinary studies, liberal arts/general studies, ministries, philosophy, physical fitness/movement, political science/government, psychology, religion, religious education, religious studies, religious music, sociology, and youth ministry). Biology, premed, prenursing, business, educator preparation, music, and Biblical studies are the strongest academically. Business administration/management, psychology, and education have the largest enrollments.

ACTIVITIES: 14% of men belong to 4 local fraternities; 20% of women belong to 6 local sororities. There are 48 groups on campus, including community outreach, art, cheerleading, choir, chorale, chorus, communications, dance, drama, drill team, ethnic, honors, international, leadership/mission work, musical theater, opera, pep band, political, professional, religious, social, social service, student government, and yearbook. Popular campus events include All Night Party, Battle at the Burg, Mr. Big Chief, Christmas Tree Lighting, Family Weekend, Great Pumpkin Chase, Homecoming, Red Rally, Sadie Hawkins, Singled Out, Welcome Week, Winter Ball, and SWAT. **Sports:** There are 11 intercollegiate sports for men and 9 for women, and 7 intramural sports for men and 7 for women. Facilities include a fitness center, tennis courts, a baseball field and clubhouse, batting cages, soccer field, a golf facility, 3 pools, sand volleyball courts, indoor/outdoor basketball courts, ping pong, billiards, and Foosball tables, intramural fields, and athletic training center. **Graduates:** From July 1, 2016 to June 30, 2017, 670 bachelor's degrees were awarded. The most popular majors were multi/interdisciplinary studies (15%), business administration and management (14%), and psychology (9%). In an average class, 43% graduate in 4 years or less, 58% graduate in 5 years or less, and 59% graduate in 6 years or less. Of the 2016 graduating class, 16% were enrolled in graduate school within 6 months of graduation, and 62% were employed.

SERVICES: Counseling and information services are available, as is tutoring in most subjects, such as math, biology, chemistry, physics, physical science, writing, English, computer science, Spanish, music, accounting. There is a reader service for the blind, and remedial math. **Library/Resources:** The library contains 305,355 volumes, 511,000 microform items, and 7,986 audio/video tapes/CDs/DVDs, and subscribes to 64,497 periodicals, including electronic. Computerized library services include interlibrary loans, database searching, Internet access, and Wi-Fi capability. **Physically Challenged Students:** 90% of the campus is accessible. Facilities include wheelchair ramps, elevators, special parking, specially equipped restrooms, special class scheduling, lowered drinking fountains, lowered telephones, and special housing. **Special:** Study abroad programs are available in Brisbane, Australia; San Jose, Costa Rica; Oxford, England; Amman, Jordan; Belfast, Ireland, and Mukono, Uganda. National Culture-Shaping Programs include American Studies Program in Washington, D.C.; Contemporary Music Center in Nashville, Tennessee; and the L.A. Film Studies Center in Los Angeles, California. There are 9 national honor societies and a freshman honors program. **Visiting:** There are regularly scheduled orientations for prospective students. There are also Patriot Preview days in the fall, spring, and summer providing parents and students information about life at DBU, such as admissions, financial aid, campus life, and meeting with the faculty and administration staff, and a tour of the campus. There are guides for informal visits and visitors may sit in on classes. To schedule a visit, contact the Undergraduate Admissions Office. **Campus Safety and Security:** Measures include 24-hour foot and vehicle patrol, an emergency notification system, self-defense education, and security escort services. There are shuttle buses, emergency telephones, lighted pathways/sidewalks, and controlled access to dorms/residences.

REQUIREMENTS: The ACT Optional Writing test is required. Applicants must be graduates, or expect to graduate, from an accredited secondary school, home school, or have a GED. A composite SAT score of at least 1020 (Critical Reading and Math sections) or a composite ACT score of at least 21 is required, along with a minimum high school GPA of 2.5. An essay is required, and an interview is encouraged. Recommended high school courses should include 4 years each of English and history/social studies, 3 years of math, 2 years of science (including 1 year Lab Science), and 2 to 3 years of a foreign language. DBU requires applicants to be in the upper 50% of their class. A GPA of 2.5 is required. AP and CLEP credits are accepted. Important factors in the admissions decision are leadership record, personality/intangible qualities, and extracurricular activities record. To graduate with a bachelor degree, students must have a minimum GPA of 2.0 and complete a minimum of 120 credit hours, including 24 hours in the major and 42 upper-level hours. At least 12 credit hours in the major program must be completed at DBU, including 9 upper-level credits. Students must complete a minimum of 25% of credit hours in residence at DBU; complete 30 of the last 36 credit hours with courses offered by DBU; and complete the General Studies requirements including English, history, religion, fine arts, computer science, math, kinesiology, natural science, and social science. Chapel attendance is required. **Procedure:** Freshmen are admitted to all sessions. Entrance exams should be taken during the spring of the junior year or the fall of the senior year. There are deferred admissions and rolling admissions plans. Application deadlines are open. The fall 2017 application fee was $25. Applications are accepted on-line. **Transfer Students:** 480 transfer students enrolled in 2016-2017. Applicants must submit an essay along with their application and fee and transcripts of all previous college work. Applicants should have a cumulative GPA of 2.5 or higher on all previous college work. Students with fewer than 30 credit hours must furnish high school transcripts and ACT or SAT scores. 30 of 120 credits required for the bachelor's degree must be completed at DBU. **International Students:** There are 193 international students enrolled. They must take the TOEFL with a minimum score of 525 on the paper-based TOEFL (PBT) or 71 on the Internet-based version (iBT). Students must take the MELAB, the Comprehensive English Language Test, and the college's own test. They must also take the IELTS, PTE, CAE, ITEP, SAT, IB, or complete the DBU intensive English program.

ADMISSIONS: 39% of the 2017-2018 applicants were accepted. The SAT scores for the 2017-2018 freshman class were: Math-- 9% below 500, 55% between 500 and 599, 33% between 600 and 699, and 3% between 700 and 800. Evidence-Based Reading/Writing-- 9% below 500, 38% between 500 and 599, 44% between 600 and 699, and 9% between 700 and 800. The ACT scores were 11% between 12 and 17, 63% between 18 and 23, 23% between 24 and 29, and 4% above 30. 5 freshmen graduated first in their class. **Admissions Contact:** Bobby Soto, Director of Admissions. Email: *admiss@dbu.edu* Web: *www.dbu.edu*

FINANCIAL AID: In 2017-2018, 98% of all full-time freshmen received some form of financial aid. 54% of all full-time freshmen received need-based aid. The average freshman award was $20,350. Need-based scholarships or need-based grants averaged $6,504 ($12,966 maximum); need-based self-help aid (loans and jobs) averaged $2,921 ($8,500 maximum); non-need-based athletic scholarships averaged $19,197 ($38,130 maximum); other non-need-based awards and non-need-based scholarships averaged $9,475 ($34,554 maximum); and $8,984 from other forms of aid. 24% of undergraduate students work part-time. The average financial indebtedness of the 2017 graduate was $32,146. The college's own financial statement is required. The FAFSA code is 003560. The priority date for freshman financial aid applications for fall entry is March 1.

EAST TEXAS BAPTIST UNIVERSITY E-2

www.etbu.edu

Marshall, TX 75670	**(903) 923-2000** **(800) 804-ETBU**
Fax: (903) 923-2001	**Email: admissions@etbu.edu**
Full-time: 512 men, 584 women	**Faculty:** 73
Part-time: 54 men, 83 women	**Ph.D.s:** 84%
Graduate: 34 men, 41 women	**Student/Faculty:** 15 to 1
Year: semesters, summer session	**Tuition:** $24,420
Room & Board: $10,024	**Freshman Class:** 843 applied, 807 accepted, 342 enrolled
SAT CR/M: 490/510 **ACT:** 21	**CEEB CODE:** 6187
Application Deadline: August 17	**COMPETITIVE**

East Texas Baptist University, established in 1912, provides a Christ-centered education that emphasizes the integration of faith and learning. The ETBU experience is known for Embracing Faith, Engaging Minds, and Empowering Leaders. There are 7 undergraduate schools and 4 graduate schools. In addition to regional accreditation, ETBU has baccalaureate program accreditation with NASM, CCNE, and CAATE. The 250-acre campus is in a small town 40 miles west of Shreveport, Louisiana, 23 miles east of Longview, Texas, and 61 miles east of Tyler, Texas. Including any residence halls, there are 27 buildings.

STUDENT LIFE: 91% of undergraduates are from Texas. Others are from 17 states, 12 foreign countries, and Canada. 73% are from public schools. 63% are White; 21% African American; 2% Foreign; 2% two or more races; 10% Hispanic; 1% race unknown. 73% are Protestant; 21% claim no religious affiliation. **Female To Male Ratio:** 1.2:1. The average age of freshmen is 18; all undergraduates, 20. 48% do not continue beyond their first year; 46% remain to graduate. **Housing:** 1079 students can be accommodated in college housing, which includes married student dorms and on-campus apartments. On-campus housing is guaranteed for the freshman year only, and is available on a first-come, first-served basis, and is available on a lottery system for upperclassmen. 85% of students live on campus. All students may keep cars. Alcohol is not permitted.

FACULTY/CLASSROOMS: 56% of faculty are male; 44% are female. 97% teach undergraduates, 25% do research, and 25% do both. No introductory courses are taught by graduate students. The average class size in an introductory lecture is 21; in a laboratory is 12; and in a regular course is 18.

PROGRAMS OF STUDY: ETBU confers B.A., B.S., B.A.S., B.M., B.S.E., and B.S.N. degrees. Master's degrees are also awarded. Bachelor's degrees are awarded in BIOLOGICAL SCIENCE (biology/biological science), BUSINESS (business administration and management and business administration marketing), COMMUNICATIONS AND THE ARTS (communications, English, English literature, English Writing, music, music performance, piano/organ, piano performance, Spanish, speech/debate/rhetoric, theatre arts, visual and performing arts, vocal performance, and voice), COMPUTER AND PHYSICAL SCIENCE (chemistry and mathematics), EDUCATION (athletic training, drama education, early childhood education, education, elementary education, English education, foreign languages education, general studies, history education, mathematics education, music education, physical education, science education, secondary education, social studies education, social studies secondary school education, speech correction, and university studies), HEALTH PROFESSIONS (biology, exercise science, health science, kinesiology, and nursing), SOCIAL SCIENCE (biblical studies, child psychology/development, counseling/psychology, criminal justice, history, interdisciplinary studies, international studies, ministries, missions, pastoral studies, physical fitness/movement, political science/government, psychology, religion, religious education, religious music, sociology, and youth ministry). Nursing, athletic training, and business are the strongest academically. Nursing, business administration, and teacher education have the largest enrollments.

ACTIVITIES: 1% of men belong to 2 local and 1 national fraternities; 1% of women belong to 1 local and 1 national sororities. There are 29 groups on campus, including band, cheerleading, choir, chorale, chorus, communications, dance, debate, drama, drill team, ethnic, honors, international, jazz band, literary magazine, marching band, musical theater, newspaper, opera, orchestra, pep band, photography, political, professional, religious, social, social service, student government, symphony, and yearbook. Popular campus events include Tiger Camp, Family Weekend, Connexus, Christmas on the Hill, Homecoming, Miss ETBU, Tiger Football Tailgates, Chill on the Hill, Fall Formal, 2k in Color, ETBU Cares, Bonfire, Tigers Serve Days, and athletic games. **Sports:** There are 7 intercollegiate sports for men and 7 for women, and 8 intramural sports for men and 6 for women. Facilities include a baseball field, tennis courts, a weight room, a gym, soccer field, softball field, intramural field, a practice gym, football practice fields, and a stadium. **Graduates:** From July 1, 2016 to June 30, 2017, 174 bachelor's degrees were awarded. The most popular majors were interdisciplinary studies (19%), education (18%), and business (15%). In an average class, 5% graduate in 3 years or less, 19% graduate in 4 years or less, 37% graduate in 5 years or less, and 46% graduate in 6 years or less. Of the 2016 graduating class, 36% were enrolled in graduate school within 6 months of graduation, and 87% were employed.

SERVICES: Counseling and information services are available, as is tutoring in most subjects. There is remedial math, reading, and writing. **Library/Resources:** The library contains 5.6 million volumes, 10,000 microform items, 307,542 audio/video tapes/CDs/DVDs, and subscribes to 42,777 periodicals, including electronic. Computerized library services include interlibrary loans, database searching, Internet access, and Wi-Fi capability. Special learning facilities include a **Physically Challenged Students:** 95% of the campus is accessible. Facilities include wheelchair ramps, elevators, special parking, specially equipped restrooms, special class scheduling, lowered drinking fountains, lowered telephones, and special housing. **Special:** ETBU students have the opportunity to study in many different national and international arenas through service-learning courses in a variety of disciplines. In addition, through the Council for Christian College and Universities, ETBU provides semester abroad programs in Washington D. C., Oxford, Australia, and Uganda as well as other US and international locations. ETBU also has exchange partnerships with Hong Kong Baptist University, Jana Dlugosza University, and Lanzhou University of Technology. Internships are offered in business, religion, education, biology, communication, psychology, and sociology. Students also may take advantage of undergraduate majors like Religion and Business that provide for the completion of both undergraduate and graduate degrees in 5 years. ETBU is a member of the Council for Christian Colleges and Universities. There are 8 national honor societies, a freshman honors program, and 13 departmental honors programs. **Visiting:** There are regularly scheduled orientations for prospective students, including campus tours, scholarship interviews/testing, faculty visits, class visits, sports/entertainment, and financial aid seminars. Visitors may sit in on classes, and stay overnight. To schedule a visit, contact Alicia Earle at (903) 923-2000. **Campus Safety and Security:** Measures include 24-hour foot and vehicle patrol, an emergency notification system, self-defense education, and security escort services. There are emergency telephones, lighted pathways/sidewalks, controlled access to dorms/residences. ETBU partnered with the local police department for campus security.

REQUIREMENTS: The SAT or ACT is required. Applicants must be graduates of an accredited secondary school or have the GED, and must have composite scores of at least 18 on the ACT or 860 on the SAT (critical reading and math), or rank in the top 30% of their graduating class. Students not meeting these requirements may be admitted conditionally for 1 term or semester. AP and CLEP credits are accepted. To graduate, students must complete general education requirements and maintain a minimum GPA of 2.0. A total of 120 to 130 semester hours, with at least 30 in the major, is required. **Procedure:** Freshmen are admitted fall, spring, and summer. Entrance exams should be taken in the first semester of the senior year. There are deferred admissions and rolling admissions plans. Applications should be filed by August 17 for fall entry; January 15 for spring entry. The fall 2017 application fee was $25. Applications are accepted on-line. **Transfer Students:** 135 transfer students enrolled in 2016-2017. Transfer students must have a minimum GPA of 2.0 and be eligible to return to the last college attended. 33 of 120 credits required for the bachelor's degree must be completed at ETBU. **International Students:** There are 14 international students enrolled. They must take the TOEFL with a minimum score of 500 on the paper-based TOEFL (PBT) or 61 on the Internet-based version (iBT). They must also take the SAT or ACT.

ADMISSIONS: 96% of the 2017-2018 applicants were accepted. The SAT scores for the 2017-2018 freshman class were: Critical Reading-- 61% below 500, 27% between 500 and 599, 11% between 600 and 699, and 1% between 700 and 800. Math-- 41% below 500, 45% between 500 and 599, 13% between 600 and 699, and 1% between 700 and 800. The ACT scores were 15% between 12 and 17, 66% between 18 and 23, and 19% between 24 and 29. 36% of the current freshmen were in the top fifth of their class; 63% were in the top two fifths. 5 freshmen graduated first in their class. **Admissions Contact:** Vince Blankenship, Vice President for Enrollment Management and Marketing. Email: *admissions@etbu.edu* Web: *www.etbu.edu*

FINANCIAL AID: In 2017-2018, 99% of all full-time freshmen received some form of financial aid. 75% of all full-time freshmen received need-based aid. The average freshman award was $26,076. Need-based scholarships or need-based grants averaged $6,070 ($14,775 maximum); need-based self-help aid (loans and jobs) averaged $3,561 ($5,820 maximum); and other non-need-based awards and non-need-based scholarships averaged $19,549 ($35,910 maximum). 22% of undergraduate students work part-time. The average financial indebtedness of the 2017 graduate was $35,716. The college's own financial statement is required. The FAFSA code is 003564. The priority date for freshman financial aid applications for fall entry is June 1.

HARDIN-SIMMONS UNIVERSITY C-2

www.hsutx.edu

Abilene, TX 79698	**(325) 670-1206** **(877) 464-7889**
Fax: (325) 670-1527	**Email: enroll@hsutx.edu**
Full-time: 776 men, 992 women	**Faculty:** 120; IIA, --$
Part-time: 91 men, 171 women	**Ph.D.s:** 77%
Graduate: 184 men, 221 women	**Student/Faculty:** 12 to 1
Year: semesters, summer session	**Tuition:** $26,240
Room & Board: $9785	**Freshman Class:** 1757 applied, 635 accepted, 465 enrolled
SAT CR/M/W: 510/520/510 **ACT:** 22	**CEEB CODE:** 6268
Application Deadline: open	**COMPETITIVE**

Hardin-Simmons University, founded in 1891, is a private liberal arts institution affiliated with the Baptist General Convention of Texas. HSU offers The HSU Commitment that means your tuition rate will not increase while you are enrolled as a full-time undergraduate student during consecutive fall/spring semesters and making satisfactory progress toward a degree. There are 7 undergraduate schools and 1 graduate school. In addition to regional accreditation, HSU has baccalaureate program accreditation with ACBSP, CSWE, NASM, CCNE, CAPTE, CCSACS, and SACS. The 220-acre campus is in an urban area 150 miles west of Fort Worth. Including any residence halls, there are 41 buildings.

STUDENT LIFE: 96% of undergraduates are from Texas. Others are from 23 states, 19 foreign countries, and Canada. 88% are from public schools. 74% are White; 5% African American; 2% Foreign; 10% Hispanic; 1% Asian American; 1% American Indian/Alaska Native. 66% are Protestant; 13% claim no religious affiliation. **Female To Male Ratio:** 1.3:1. The average age of freshmen is 18; all undergraduates, 21. 34% do not continue beyond their first year; 49% remain to graduate. **Housing:** 1111 students can be accommodated in college housing, which includes married student dorms and off-campus apartments. On-campus housing is available on a first-come, first-served basis. 56% of students commute. All students may keep cars. Alcohol is not permitted.

FACULTY/CLASSROOMS: 64% of faculty are male; 39% are female. 87% teach undergraduates. No introductory courses are taught by graduate students. The average class size in an introductory lecture is 23; in a laboratory is 15; and in a regular course is 17.

PROGRAMS OF STUDY: HSU confers B.A., B.S., B.B.A., B.B.S., B.F.A., B.Mus., and B.S.N. degrees. Master's and doctoral degrees are also awarded. Bachelor's degrees are awarded in AGRICULTURE (agricultural business management, agriculture, and animal science), BIOLOGICAL SCIENCE (biochemistry, biology/biological science, and molecular biology), BUSINESS (accounting, banking and finance, business administration and management, finance, management science, and marketing management), COMMUNICATIONS AND THE ARTS (art, broadcasting, communications, dramatic arts, English, graphic design, music, music business management, music history and appreciation, music performance, music theory and composition, piano/organ, public relations, radio/television technology, Spanish, speech/debate/rhetoric, strings, theatre studies, and voice), COMPUTER AND PHYSICAL SCIENCE (chemistry, computer science, geology, mathematics, and physics), EDUCATION (art education, athletic training, business education, computer education, drama education, early childhood education, education, elementary education, English education, foreign languages education, mathematics education, middle school education, music education, physical education, reading education, science education, secondary education, and social studies education), ENGINEERING AND ENVIRONMENTAL DESIGN (environmental science), HEALTH PROFESSIONS (exercise science, health science, nursing, predentistry, premedicine, and speech pathology/audiology), SOCIAL SCIENCE (biblical studies, corrections, criminal justice, economics, history, legal studies, ministries, missions, philosophy, political science/government, prelaw, psychology, religious studies, religious music, social work, sociology, theological studies, and youth ministry). English, speech pathology, and music are the strongest academically. Education, biology, and nursing have the largest enrollments.

ACTIVITIES: 5% of men belong to 4 local fraternities; 16% of women belong to 4 local sororities. There are 57 groups on campus, including art, band, cheerleading, choir, chorale, computers, debate, drama, drill team, ethnic, honors, international, literary magazine, marching band, musical theater, newspaper, opera, orchestra, pep band, photography, political, professional, radio and TV, religious, social, social service, student government, and symphony. Popular campus events include Western Heritage Day, All-School SING, Cowboy Fridays, and Founders Day. **Sports:** There are 6 intercollegiate sports for men and 6 for women, and 17 intramural sports for men and 17 for women. Facilities include a rodeo arena, 2 running ovals, a practice field, football stadium, soccer field, softball and baseball fields, outdoor and indoor swimming pools, bowling alleys, a fitness course, basketball, racquetball, tennis, and badminton/paddleball courts, and a Nautilus weight-lifting room. **Graduates:** From July 1, 2016 to June 30, 2017, 383 bachelor's degrees were awarded. The most popular majors were education (18%), business/marketing (13%), and communication/journalism (9%). In an average class, 2% graduate in 3 years or less, 27% graduate in 4 years or less, 45% graduate in 5 years or less, and 49% graduate in 6 years or less.

SERVICES: Counseling and information services are available, as is tutoring in most subjects. There is remedial math, reading, and writing. **Library/Resources:** The library contains 443,979 volumes, 23,734 microform items, 12,013 audio/video tapes/CDs/DVDs, and subscribes to 33,942 periodicals, including electronic. Computerized library services include interlibrary loans, database searching, Internet access, and Wi-Fi capability. Special learning facilities include an art gallery, a radio station, and observatory. **Physically Challenged Students:** All of the campus is accessible. Facilities include wheelchair ramps, elevators, special parking, specially equipped restrooms, special class scheduling, lowered drinking fountains, lowered telephones, and special housing. **Special:** Cross-registration may be arranged with Abilene Christian and McMurry Universities. HSU offers cooperative programs, internships, dual majors, credit by exam, nondegree study, and pass/fail options. Students may study abroad in England, Austria, China, Spain, Italy and Israel, where HSU is involved in an ongoing archeological excavation of early Christian sites. There are 9 national honor societies and a freshman honors program. **Visiting:** There are regularly scheduled orientations for prospective students, including Cowboy Fridays, plus Fall and Winter preview and Spring Round-Up. There are guides for informal visits and visitors may sit in on classes. To schedule a visit, contact the Visitor Coordinator at (325) 670-5890. **Campus Safety and Security:** Measures include 24-hour foot and vehicle patrol. There are emergency telephones and lighted pathways/sidewalks.

REQUIREMENTS: The SAT or ACT and the ACT Optional Writing test are required, with a minimum SAT score of 1390 and a minimum ACT score of 20. Graduation from an accredited secondary school is required; a GED will be accepted. Applicants should submit an academic record of at least 16 units, distributed as follows: 3 units of English, 2 units each of math, science, and social studies, and 7 units of electives, with a GPA of 2.0 or above. 3 letters of recommendation are also required. HSU requires applicants to be in the upper 75% of their class. AP and CLEP credits are accepted. To graduate, students must complete a minimum of 124 semester hours with a minimum 2.0 GPA. A minimum of 18 to 30 hours are required in the major (18 must be advanced and 12 of the advanced must be from HSU). 42 hours in upper-division courses are required. Core courses that must be taken include 12 to 18 hours of social science, 9 of English, 7 of natural science (from 2 separate fields and 1 requiring a lab), 6 each of Bible and humanities (3 of fine arts and 3 of non-fine arts), 3 to 6 each of math, 3 to 4 of phys ed, 3 of oral communication, and computer science. All students must satisfy chapel attendance requirements and must demonstrate proficiency in written English. **Procedure:** Freshmen are admitted to all sessions. There are deferred admissions and rolling admissions plans. Application deadlines are open. The fall 2017 application fee was $50. Notification is sent on a rolling basis. Applications are accepted online. **Transfer Students:** 155 transfer students enrolled in 2016-2017. Applicants must submit official transcripts from all previous colleges. Students may petition to transfer up to 2 D grades if the overall GPA is 2.0 or higher. Students transferring from a 2-year college may receive credit for up to 66 semester hours of transferable courses. Applicants with fewer than 24 semester hours must submit a high school transcript and official report of ACT or SAT scores. Students ineligible to continue at another institution are not eligible for regular admission to HSU. 31 of 124 credits required for the bachelor's degree must be completed at HSU. **International Students:** There are 16 international students enrolled. They must take the TOEFL with a minimum score of 550 on the paper-based TOEFL (PBT). They must also take the SAT or ACT.

ADMISSIONS: 36% of the 2017-2018 applicants were accepted. The SAT scores for the 2017-2018 freshman class were: Critical Reading-- 43% below 500, 35% between 500 and 599, 20% between 600 and 699, and 2% between 700 and 800. Math-- 38% below 500, 44% between 500 and 599, 17% between 600 and 699, and 1% between 700 and 800. Writing-- 43% below 500, 45% between 500 and 599, 11% between 600 and 699, and 1% between 700 and 800. The ACT scores were 39% below 12, 25% between 12 and 17, 24% between 18 and 23, 6% between 24 and 29, and 6% above 30. 44% of the current freshmen were in the top fifth of their class; 71% were in the top two fifths. 10 freshmen graduated first in their class. **Admissions Contact:** Vicki House, Director of Admissions and Recruiting. Email: *enroll@hsutx.edu* Web: *www.hsutx.edu*

FINANCIAL AID: In 2017-2018, 72% of all full-time freshmen received some form of financial aid. 56% of all full-time freshmen received need-based aid. The average freshman award was $17,609. Need-based scholarships or need-based grants averaged $5,439 ($7,808 maximum); need-based self-help aid (loans and jobs) averaged $3,550 ($5,900 maximum); and other non-need-based awards and non-need-based scholarships averaged $10,062 ($25,272 maximum). 21% of undergraduate students work part-time. The average financial indebtedness of the 2017 graduate was $31,934. The priority date for freshman financial aid applications for fall entry is March 15.

HOUSTON BAPTIST UNIVERSITY E-3

www.hbu.edu

Houston, TX 77074	(281) 649-3211 (800) 969-3210
Fax: (281) 649-3217	Email: admissions@hbu.edu
Full-time: 839 men, 1298 women	**Faculty:** 118
Part-time: 111 men, 199 women	**Ph.D.s:** 69%
Graduate: 238 men, 602 women	**Student/Faculty:** 15 to 1
Year: semesters, summer session	**Tuition:** $28,800
Room & Board: $7650	**Freshman Class:** n/av
SAT CR/M/W: 530/540/520 **ACT:** 22	**CEEB CODE:** 6282
Application Deadline: open	**COMPETITIVE**

Houston Baptist University, founded in 1960, is a private institution affiliated with the Baptist General Convention of Texas and offering undergraduate programs in nursing, arts and science, music, and business administration. There are 8 undergraduate schools and 5 graduate schools. In addition to regional accreditation, HBU has baccalaureate program accreditation with ACBSP and NLN. The 100-acre campus is in an urban area in Southwest Houston. Including any residence halls, there are 29 buildings.

STUDENT LIFE: 95% of undergraduates are from Texas. Others are from 32 states, 27 foreign countries, and Canada. 6% are race unknown; 4% Foreign; 4% two or more races; 28% White; 24% African American; 23% Hispanic; 11% Asian American. 49% are Protestant; 31% claim no religious affiliation; 11% Catholic. **Female To Male Ratio:** 1.8:1. The average age of freshmen is 19; all undergraduates, 21. 30% do not continue beyond their first year; 70% remain to graduate. **Housing:** 568 students can be accommodated in college housing, which includes dorms and on-campus apartments. On-campus housing is available on a first-come, first-served basis, and is available on a lottery system for upperclassmen. 61% of students commute. All students may keep cars. Alcohol is not permitted.

FACULTY/CLASSROOMS: 45% of faculty are male; 55% are female. 94% teach undergraduates. No introductory courses are taught by graduate students. The average class size in a laboratory is 14 and in a regular course is 10.

PROGRAMS OF STUDY: HBU confers B.A., B.S., B.B.A., B.M., and B.S.N. degrees. Master's degrees are also awarded. Bachelor's degrees are awarded in BIOLOGICAL SCIENCE (biology/biological science and molecular biology), BUSINESS (accounting, banking and finance, business administration and management, and entrepreneurial studies), COMMUNICATIONS AND THE ARTS (art, communications, English, French, music, music performance, music theory and composition, and Spanish), COMPUTER AND PHYSICAL SCIENCE (chemistry, information sciences and systems, mathematics, and physics), EDUCATION (art education, early childhood education, elementary education, mathematics education, music education, physical education, reading education, secondary education, special education, and teaching English as a second/foreign language (TESOL/TEFOL), HEALTH PROFESSIONS (nursing), SOCIAL SCIENCE (biblical languages, Christian studies, economics, history, liberal arts/general studies, physical fitness/movement, political science/government, psychology, religious music, and sociology). Premedical studies, health professions, nursing are the strongest academically. Biology, nursing, and business administration have the largest enrollments.

ACTIVITIES: 3% of men belong to 1 local and 1 national fraternities; 5% of women belong to 3 national sororities. There are 51 groups on campus, including art, band, cheerleading, choir, chorale, chorus, computers, debate, drama, ethnic, forensics, honors, international, jazz band, newspaper, opera, pep band, photography, political, professional, radio and TV, religious, social service, student government, and symphony. Popular campus events include Welcome Days for New Students, Husky Fest Fall Festival, and Winter Formal. **Sports:** There are 6 intercollegiate sports for men and 7 for women, and 12 intramural sports for men and 12 for women. Facilities include volleyball, basketball, and tennis courts, an indoor track, softball, baseball, and soccer fields, and areas for track. **Graduates:** From July 1, 2016 to June 30, 2017, 365 bachelor's degrees were awarded. The most popular majors were nursing (21%), biology (10%), and psychology (8%). In an average class, 24% graduate in 4 years or less, 40% graduate in 5 years or less, and 44% graduate in 6 years or less.

SERVICES: Counseling and information services are available, as is tutoring in most subjects. There is remedial math and writing. **Library/Resources:** The library contains 235,026 volumes, 98,065 microform items, 9,591 audio/video tapes/CDs/DVDs, and subscribes to 29,992 periodicals, including electronic. Computerized library services include interlibrary loans, database searching, Internet access, and Wi-Fi capability. Special learning facilities include an art gallery, a radio station, a TV station, a Museum of American Architecture and Decorative Arts, the Dunham Family Bible in America Museum, a Museum of Southern History, and the Morris Cultural Arts Center. **Physically Challenged Students:** 90% of the campus is accessible. Facilities include wheelchair ramps, elevators, special parking, specially equipped restrooms, lowered drinking fountains, lowered telephones, and special housing. **Special:** HBU offers internships through its academic colleges, B.A.-B.S. degrees, and dual majors in most areas, work-study programs, credit for military experience, and pass/fail options. There is a freshman honors program. **Visiting:** There are guides for informal visits; visitors may sit in on classes and stay overnight. To schedule a visit, contact the Office of Admissions. **Campus Safety and Security:** Measures include 24-hour foot and vehicle patrol, an emergency notification system, and security escort services. There are emergency telephones and lighted pathways/sidewalks.

REQUIREMENTS: The SAT or ACT and the ACT Optional Writing test are required, with a recommended satisfactory score on the SAT or ACT composite score of 20. One counselor or teacher written recommendation, and an official high school transcript or GED scores are also required. AP and CLEP credits are accepted. Important factors in the admissions decision are recommendations by school officials, personality/intangible qualities, and advanced placement or honors courses. To graduate, students must complete a minimum of 130 semester hours, including at least 48 semester hours of upper-level courses and 24 to 36 hours in the major. They must complete courses in Christianity, written and oral communications, math, lab science, computer, kinetics, social and behavioral sciences, humanities, and fine arts. No grade below "C" within majors and program requirements and a cumulative GPA of 2.0 is required. Proficiency is required in reading, computer, communication, and math. Spiritual Life Program participation is also a graduation requirement. **Procedure:** Freshmen are admitted to all sessions. Entrance exams should be taken in the fall of the senior year. There are early decision and rolling admissions plans. Application deadlines are open. The fall 2017 application fee was $25. Applications are accepted online. **Transfer Students:** 334 transfer students enrolled in 2016-2017. Applicants with fewer than 30 semester hours earned must submit high school and college transcripts and SAT or ACT scores. All students must have a minimum 2.0 GPA and submit all previous college transcripts. 32 of 130 credits required for the bachelor's degree must be completed at HBU. **International Students:** There are 110 international students enrolled. They must take the TOEFL with a minimum score of 550 on the paper-based TOEFL (PBT) or 80 on the Internet-based version (iBT). Students must the IELTS.

ADMISSIONS: The SAT scores for the 2017-2018 freshman class were: Critical Reading-- 37% below 500, 38% between 500 and 599, 22% between 600 and 699, and 3% between 700 and 800. Math-- 35% below 500, 41% between 500 and 599, 22% between 600 and 699, and 2% between 700 and 800. Writing-- 39% below 500, 40% between 500 and 599, 17% between 600 and 699, and 4% between 700 and 800. The ACT scores were 40% below 12, 30% between 12 and 17, 16% between 18 and 23, 8% between 24 and 29, and 6% above 30. 38% of the current freshmen were in the top fifth of their class; 67% were in the top two fifths. **Admissions Contact:** Eduardo Borges, Director of Admissions. Email: *admissions@hbu.edu* Web: *www.hbu.edu*

FINANCIAL AID: In 2017-2018, 90% of all full-time freshmen received some form of financial aid. 27% of all full-time freshmen received need-based aid. The average freshman award was $14,957. Need-based scholarships or need-based grants averaged $9,941 ($22,941 maximum); need-based self-help aid (loans and jobs) averaged $5,352 ($9,000 maximum); non-need-based athletic scholarships averaged $13,994 ($25,671 maximum); and other non-need-based awards and non-need-based scholarships averaged $7,613 ($23,203 maximum). 100% of undergraduate students work part-time. The average financial indebtedness of the 2017 graduate was $23,000. The college's own financial statement is required. The FAFSA code is 003576. The priority date for freshman financial aid applications for fall entry is March 1.

HOWARD PAYNE UNIVERSITY C-3
www.hputx.edu

Brownwood, TX 76801
(325) 649-8020
(800) 880-4478
Fax: (325) 649-8901
Email: enroll@hputx.edu

Full-time: 516 men, 435 women	**Faculty:** 80
Part-time: 53 men, 59 women	**Ph.D.s:** 72%
Graduate: 58 men, 26 women	**Student/Faculty:** 10 to 1
Year: semesters, summer session	**Tuition:** $27,690
Room & Board: $8304	**Freshman Class:** 953 applied, 836 accepted, 330 enrolled
SAT: required **ACT:** 21	**CEEB CODE:** 6278
Application Deadline: March 15	**COMPETITIVE**

Howard Payne University, founded in 1889, is a liberal arts college affiliated with the Baptist General Convention of Texas. HPU is a liberal arts college. Chapel is an important part of student life at HPU, and is a required element for graduation. There are 6 undergraduate schools. In addition to regional accreditation, Howard Payne University has baccalaureate program accreditation with CSWE, NASM, IACBE, SACSCC, and NCAA. The 29-acre campus is in a rural area 150 miles from Dallas, 77 miles from Abilene. Including any residence halls, there are 31 buildings.

STUDENT LIFE: 98% of undergraduates are from Texas. Others are from 18 states and 2 foreign countries. 93% are from public schools. 74% are White; 6% African American; 14% Hispanic; 1% Asian American; 1% American Indian/Alaska Native; 1% Foreign. 85% are Protestant. **Male To Female Ratio:** 1.2:1. The average age of freshmen is 19; all undergraduates, 22. 40% do not continue beyond their first year; 33% remain to graduate. **Housing:** 764 students can be accommodated in college housing, which includes married student dorms, on-campus apartments, and apartments for single students. On-campus housing is available on a lottery system for upperclassmen. 86% of students live on campus. All students may keep cars. Alcohol is not permitted.

FACULTY/CLASSROOMS: All teach undergraduates. No introductory courses are taught by graduate students. The average class size in an introductory lecture is 22; in a laboratory is 20; and in a regular course is 18.

PROGRAMS OF STUDY: HPU confers B.A., B.S., B.A.A.S., B.B.A., and B.M. degrees. Associate degrees are also awarded. Bachelor's degrees are awarded in BIOLOGICAL SCIENCE (biology/biological science), BUSINESS (accounting and business administration and management), COMMUNICATIONS AND THE ARTS (art, communications, dramatic arts, English, multimedia, music, and Spanish), COMPUTER AND PHYSICAL SCIENCE (chemistry, computer science, and mathematics), EDUCATION (athletic training, elementary education, secondary education, and teaching English as a second/foreign language (TESOL/TEFOL)), ENGINEERING AND ENVIRONMENTAL DESIGN (occupational safety and health), HEALTH PROFESSIONS (exercise science), SOCIAL SCIENCE (Christian studies, history, liberal arts/general studies, political science/government, psychology, social work, and sociology). Biology, chemistry, and political science are the strongest academically. Business management, elementary education, and exercise and sports science have the largest enrollments.

ACTIVITIES: 14% of men belong to 5 local fraternities; 17% of women belong to 6 local sororities. There are 33 groups on campus, including art, band, cheerleading, choir, chorus, drama, drill team, ethnic, honors, jazz band, literary magazine, marching band, model UN, musical theater, newspaper, photography, professional, radio and TV, religious, social, social service, student government, and yearbook. Popular campus events include S.W.A.R.M. Day, Spring Street Party, Spring Sing, Paynt Rave, Impact Day, Meet the Greeks, Family Weekend, Christian Concerts, HPU Feast, and College Preview Weekends. **Sports:** There are 5 intercollegiate sports for men and 5 for women, and 5 intramural sports for men and 5 for women. Facilities include a stadium, an auditorium, basketball and volleyball courts, an indoor walking track, free weights and exercise equipment, tennis, football and non-tackle football, golf, soccer, tennis and table tennis, ultimate Frisbee, a student union, baseball, and softball. **Graduates:** From July 1, 2016 to June 30, 2017, 240 bachelor's degrees were awarded. The most popular majors were business/marketing (20%), education (19%), and Theology and religious vocations (9%). In an average class, 2% graduate in 3 years or less, 23% graduate in 4 years or less, 34% graduate in 5 years or less, and 46% graduate in 6 years or less. Of the 2016 graduating class, 20% were enrolled in graduate school within 6 months of graduation.

SERVICES: Counseling and information services are available, as is tutoring in some subjects. There is remedial math, reading, and writing. There is also a writing lab and computer lab for English, math, and computer science. **Library/Resources:** The library contains 118,825 volumes, 271,542 microform items, and subscribes to 30,598 periodicals, including electronic. Computerized library services include interlibrary loans, database searching, Internet access, and Wi-Fi capability. Special learning facilities include a radio station, a children's literature center, audio production facility, TV production studio, video editing facility, Faith and Life Leadership center, an art center, and a center for social justice. **Physically Challenged Students:** 90% of the campus is accessible. Facilities include wheelchair ramps, elevators, special parking, specially equipped restrooms, special class scheduling, and lowered drinking fountains. **Special:** Cross-registration is offered with several hospitals, and internships are available in many fields. HPU offers credit for experience for B.A.A.S. candidates only, study abroad in Israel and England, pass/fail options, and work-study programs. Special programs include the Douglas MacArthur Academy of Freedom, an interdisciplinary honors program in the social sciences, a chemistry honors program, and a provisional program for underprepared students. There are 4 national honor societies, a freshman honors program, and 1 departmental honors program. **Visiting:** There are regularly scheduled orientations for prospective students, Orientation/Welcome week (Jacket Journey) is held 5 days before the fall semester classes begin. There is also an afternoon program held in January prior to the beginning of the spring semester. There are guides for informal visits; visitors may sit in on classes and stay overnight. To schedule a visit, contact the Enrollment Services Office. **Campus Safety and Security:** Measures include 24-hour foot and vehicle patrol. There are emergency telephones, lighted pathways/sidewalks, monthly dorm meetings, 2 security seminars, and 24-hour telephone availability with on-duty officers.

REQUIREMENTS: The SAT or ACT is required. Applicants must be graduates of an accredited secondary school or have a GED. It is recommended that they have completed 4 units each in English, math, science (with 3 units of lab), 3 units of social studies, and 2 units of foreign language and history, .5 in computer science, 1 unit in visual/performing arts, and 4.5 in any academic electives. Graduates of high schools or home study programs that are not accredited by a regional or state accrediting agency will have their work reviewed by the admissions committee on an individual basis. An interview may be required by the admissions committee for select applicants. Students must audition for the music program. A GPA of 3.0 is required. AP and CLEP credits are accepted. Important factors in the admissions decision are leadership record, recommendations by school officials, and personality/intangible qualities. To graduate, students must complete a minimum of 128 credit hours, 49 in general education courses, 30 to 36 in the major, and 18 to 24 in a minor, plus electives. A minimum 2.0 GPA is required. The general education core includes Bible, English, social science, computer science, fine arts, phys ed, lab science, speech, and math courses. Requirements for students not obtaining the B.A. or B.S. vary. All students must complete 6 semester credits of chapel/convocation attendance. **Procedure:** Freshmen are admitted to all sessions. Entrance exams should be taken during the senior year. There are early admissions and rolling admissions plans. Applications should be filed by March 15 for fall entry. The fall 2017 application fee was $25. Notifications are sent October 15. **Transfer Students:** 67 transfer students enrolled in 2016-2017. Transfer students must be able to return to the university they are leaving and submit official transcripts from all previously attended colleges/universities. Students younger than 21 with fewer than 12 semester hours must submit the SAT or ACT scores. The same GPA per number of hours attempted is required of transfers as for continuing HPU students. 32 of 128 credits required for the bachelor's degree must be completed at HPU. **International Students:** There are 11 international students enrolled. They must take the TOEFL with a minimum score of 79 on the Internet-based version (iBT). A TOEFL score is not required for International students entering English as a Second Language (ESL). Students must score 19 on the ACT or 830 on the SAT for unconditional admission; otherwise, a provisional program may be available.

ADMISSIONS: 88% of the 2017-2018 applicants were accepted. The SAT scores for the 2017-2018 freshman class were: Critical Reading--62% below 500, 28% between 500 and 599, 8% between 600 and 699, and 2% between 700 and 800. Math-- 58% below 500, 34% between 500 and 599, and 8% between 600 and 699. The ACT scores were 20% between 12 and 17, 56% between 18 and 23, 20% between 24 and 29, and 4% above 30. 32% of the current freshmen were in the top fifth of their class; 60% were in the top two fifths. 4 freshmen graduated first in their class. **Admissions Contact:** PJ Grambling, Director of Admission. Email: *enroll@hputx.edu* Web: *www.hputx.edu*

FINANCIAL AID: The average freshman award was $19,567. Need-based scholarships or need-based grants averaged $16,945; need-based self-help aid (loans and jobs) averaged $5,687; other non-need-based awards and non-need-based scholarships averaged $3,412; and $11,998 from other forms of aid. 65% of undergraduate students work part-time. The average financial indebtedness of the 2017 graduate was $34,875. The FAFSA code is 003575. The deadline for filing freshman financial aid applications for fall entry is March 1.

HUSTON-TILLOTSON UNIVERSITY *(The complete profile is made available exclusively on our website, www.barronspac.com)*

JARVIS CHRISTIAN COLLEGE *(The complete profile is made available exclusively on our website, www.barronspac.com)*

LAMAR UNIVERSITY *(The complete profile is made available exclusively on our website, www.barronspac.com)*

LETOURNEAU UNIVERSITY E-2

www.letu.edu

Longview, TX 75607	**(903) 233-3000** **(800) 759-8811**
Fax: (903) 233-3411	**Email: admissions@letu.edu**
Full-time: 853 men, 449 women	**Faculty:** 87
Part-time: 189 men, 344 women	**Ph.D.s:** 76%
Graduate: 91 men, 301 women	**Student/Faculty:** 14 to 1
Year: semesters, summer session	**Tuition:** $29,320
Room & Board: $9870	**Freshman Class:** 1780 applied, 838 accepted, 321 enrolled
SAT or ACT: required	**CEEB CODE:** 6365
Application Deadline: n/av	**VERY COMPETITIVE**

LeTourneau University is the premier Christian polytechnic university in the nation where educators engage students to nurture Christian virtue, develop competency and ingenuity in their professional fields, integrate faith and work, and serve the local and global community. LETU offers undergraduate and graduate degree programs across a range of disciplines and delivery models at LETU's residential campus in Longview, Texas, and online at centers in Dallas and Houston. There are 8 undergraduate schools and 1 graduate school. In addition to regional accreditation, LTU has baccalaureate program accreditation with ABET, CCNE, and Texas State Board for Educator Certification. The 162-acre campus is in a small town 60 miles west of Shreveport, Louisiana, and 120 miles east of the Dallas/Fort Worth metroplex. Including any residence halls, there are 58 buildings.

STUDENT LIFE: 65% of undergraduates are from Texas. Others are from 46 states, 29 foreign countries, and Canada. 68% are White; 8% African American; 8% race unknown; 5% Hispanic; 5% two or more races; 3% Foreign; 2% Asian American; 1% American Indian/Alaska Native. **Male To Female Ratio:** 1.0:1. The average age of freshmen is 19; all undergraduates, 25. **Housing:** College-sponsored housing includes married student dorms and on-campus apartments. In addition, there are honors houses and special-interest houses. On-campus housing is guaranteed for all 4 years. 70% of students live on campus. Alcohol is not permitted. All students may keep cars.

FACULTY/CLASSROOMS: 63% of faculty are male; 37% are female. No introductory courses are taught by graduate students.

PROGRAMS OF STUDY: LTU confers B.A., B.S., and B.B.A. degrees. Associate and master's degrees are also awarded. Bachelor's degrees are awarded in BIOLOGICAL SCIENCE (biology/biological science), BUSINESS (accounting, business administration and management, management information systems, marketing management, and marketing/retailing/merchandising), COMMUNICATIONS AND THE ARTS (English), COMPUTER AND PHYSICAL SCIENCE (chemistry, computer mathematics, computer science, and mathematics), EDUCATION (business education, elementary education, physical education, science education, and secondary education), ENGINEERING AND ENVIRONMENTAL DESIGN (aeronautical science, aeronautical technology, computer engineering, computer technology, electrical/electronics engineering, engineering, engineering technology, industrial administration/management, mechanical engineering, and welding engineering), HEALTH PROFESSIONS (health, nursing, premedicine, and preveterinary science), SOCIAL SCIENCE (biblical studies, history, interdisciplinary studies, prelaw, psychology, and public administration).

ACTIVITIES: There are no fraternities or sororities. Groups on campus include chorale, drama, honors, international, jazz band, religious, student government, and yearbook. **Sports:** There are 7 intercollegiate sports for men and 8 for women. **Graduates:** From July 1, 2016 to June 30, 2017, 432 bachelor's degrees were awarded. The most popular majors were business (24%), engineering (23%), and education (11%). In an average class, 37% graduate in 4 years or less, 49% graduate in 5 years or less, and 53% graduate in 6 years or less.

SERVICES: Counseling and information services are available, as is tutoring in every subject. There is remedial math and writing. **Library/Resources:** Computerized library services include interlibrary loans, database searching, Internet access, and Wi-Fi capability. **Physically Challenged Students:** Facilities include wheelchair ramps, elevators, special parking, specially equipped restrooms, special class scheduling, lowered drinking fountains, lowered telephones, special housing, and automated doors. **Special:** There is a freshman honors program. **Visiting:** There are regularly scheduled orientations for prospective students, visits are individualized and may include touring the school, attending classes, special events, or chapel, meeting with faculty and financial aid personnel, and stay overnight. **Campus Safety and Security:** Measures include 24-hour foot and vehicle patrol, an emergency notification system, self-defense education, and security escort services. There are lighted pathways/sidewalks and controlled access to dorms/residences.

REQUIREMENTS: AP and CLEP credits are accepted. **Procedure:** Freshmen are admitted in the fall, spring, and summer. There are deferred admissions and rolling admissions plans. Application deadlines are open. Applications are accepted online. **Transfer Students:** 172 transfer students enrolled in 2016-2017. **International Students:** They must take the TOEFL with a minimum score of 525 on the paper-based TOEFL (PBT) or 80 on the Internet-based version (iBT).

ADMISSIONS: 47% of the 2017-2018 applicants were accepted. The SAT scores for the 2017-2018 freshman class were: Math-- 9% below 500, 38% between 500 and 599, 38% between 600 and 699, and 15% between 700 and 800. Evidence-Based Reading/Writing-- 8% below 500, 44% between 500 and 599, 36% between 600 and 699, and 12% between 700 and 800. The ACT scores were 2% between 12 and 17, 41% between 18 and 23, 38% between 24 and 29, and 20% above 30. **Admissions Contact:** Mike VanBrocklin, Director of Admissions. Email: *admissions@letu.edu* Web: *www.letu.edu*

FINANCIAL AID: LTU is a member of CSS. The FAFSA code is 003584. Check with the school for current application deadlines.

LUBBOCK CHRISTIAN UNIVERSITY B-2

www.lcu.edu

Lubbock, TX 79407	**(806) 720-7155** **(800) 933-7601**
Fax: 806-720-7162	**Email: admissions@lcu.edu**
Full-time: 543 men, 733 women	**Faculty:** 84
Part-time: 74 men, 134 women	**Ph.D.s:** 66%
Graduate: 81 men, 318 women	**Student/Faculty:** 13 to 1
Year: semesters, summer session	**Tuition:** $21,794
Room & Board: $7478	**Freshman Class:** 810 applied, 762 accepted, 310 enrolled
SAT EBR-W/M: 542/527 **ACT:** 22	**CEEB CODE:** 6378
Application Deadline: August 15	**COMPETITIVE**

Lubbock Christian University, founded in 1957, is affiliated with the Churches of Christ offering undergraduate degrees in liberal arts and professional studies, and graduate degrees in Biblical studies and education, behavioral sciences and nursing. There are 4 undergraduate schools and 2 graduate schools. In addition to regional accreditation, LCU has baccalaureate program accreditation with CSWE, ACEN, and Texas Education Agency Educator Cert. and Standard. The 65-acre campus is in a suburban area 350 miles from Dallas and 325 miles from Albuquerque. Including any residence halls, there are 37 buildings.

STUDENT LIFE: 91% of undergraduates are from Texas. Others are from 32 states, 17 foreign countries, and Canada. 81% are from public schools. 67% are White; 5% African American; 24% Hispanic; 1% Asian American; 1% American Indian/Alaska Native; 1% Foreign; 1% race unknown. 54% are Protestant; 11% Catholic. **Female To Male Ratio:** 1.7:1. The average age of freshmen is 18; all undergraduates, 23. 31% do not continue beyond their first year; 69% remain to graduate. **Housing:** 589 students can be accommodated in college housing, which includes married student dorms and on-campus apartments. On-campus housing is guaranteed for the freshman year only, and is available on a first-come, first-served basis. 64% of students commute. All students may keep cars. Alcohol is not permitted.

FACULTY/CLASSROOMS: 53% of faculty are male; 47% are female. All teach undergraduates. No introductory courses are taught by graduate students. The average class size in an introductory lecture is 25; in a laboratory is 15; and in a regular course is 14.

PROGRAMS OF STUDY: LCU confers B.A., B.S., B.B.A., B.F.A., B.M., B.S.I.S., B.S.N., and B.S.W. degrees. Associate and master's degrees are also awarded. Bachelor's degrees are awarded in AGRICULTURE (animal science and natural resource management), BIOLOGICAL SCIENCE (biochemistry and biology/biological science), BUSINESS (accounting, banking and finance, business administration and management, finance, management information systems, management, marketing, organizational leadership and management, and sports management), COMMUNICATIONS AND THE ARTS (communications, communications technology, creative writing, drawing, graphic design, journalism, literature, music, music business management, and theatre arts), COMPUTER AND PHYSICAL SCIENCE (chemistry, digital arts/technology, information sciences and systems, and mathematics), EDUCATION (art education, athletic training, early childhood education, middle school education, music education, physical education, secondary education, and Spanish education K-12), ENGINEERING AND ENVIRONMENTAL DESIGN (engineering and preengineering), HEALTH PROFESSIONS (health promotion, medical technology, music therapy, nursing, predentistry, premedicine, prepharmacy, prephysician assistant, prephysical therapy, preveterinary science, and sports psychology), SOCIAL SCIENCE (biblical studies, criminal justice, economics, family/consumer studies, history, humanities, ministries, missions, physical fitness/movement, prelaw, psychology, social work, and youth ministry). Education, nursing, and business are the strongest academically. Early childhood education, nursing, and prenursing have the largest enrollments.

ACTIVITIES: 18% of men belong to 3 local fraternities; 31% of women belong to 4 local sororities. There are 32 groups on campus, including art, band, cheerleading, choir, chorus, drama, ethnic, honors, international, jazz band, musical theater, newspaper, pep band, political, professional, radio and TV, religious, social, social service, student government, symphony, and yearbook. Popular campus events include Master Follies, Family Weekend, and Spiritual Renewal Week. **Sports:** There are 5 intercollegiate sports for men and 5 for women, and 7 intramural sports for men and 8 for women. Facilities include the Rip Griffin center, and the Rhodes Perrin Recreation center for intramural and physical education activities with an indoor track, a rock wall, basketball courts, volleyball, futsball, ping pong, and a fitness center. **Graduates:** From July 1, 2016 to June 30, 2017, 342 bachelor's degrees were awarded. The most popular majors were nursing (25%), early childhood education (8%), and psychology (5%). In an average class, 2% graduate in 3 years or less, 30% graduate in 4 years or less, 43% graduate in 5 years or less, and 47% graduate in 6 years or less. Of the 2016 graduating class, 28% were enrolled in graduate school within 6 months of graduation, and 16% were employed.

SERVICES: Counseling and information services are available, as is tutoring in every subject. There is a reader service for the blind, and remedial math, reading, and writing. **Library/Resources:** The library contains 125,248 volumes, 55 audio/video tapes/CDs/DVDs, and subscribes to 3,981 periodicals, including electronic. Computerized library services include interlibrary loans, database searching, Internet access, and Wi-Fi capability. Special learning facilities include an art gallery and a radio station. **Physically Challenged Students:** Facilities include wheelchair ramps, elevators, special parking, specially equipped restrooms, special class scheduling, and lowered drinking fountains. **Special:** LCU offers co-op programs in engineering, medical technology, and criminal justice, internships in several fields, and cross-registration with Texas Tech University and other regional schools. A general studies degree, nondegree study, and pass/fail options are also available. A 3-2 engineering degree with Texas Tech University is offered. There are 3 national honor societies, a freshman honors program, and 1 departmental honors programs. **Visiting:** There are regularly scheduled orientations for prospective students. There are guides for informal visits, visitors may sit in on classes, and stay overnight. To schedule a visit, contact the Admissions Office. **Campus Safety and Security:** Measures include 24-hour foot and vehicle patrol, an emergency notification system, and security escort services. There are lighted pathways/sidewalks and controlled access to dorms/residences.

REQUIREMENTS: The SAT or ACT is required. In addition, Applicants must be graduates of an accredited secondary school or have a GED certificate. Unconditional admission is granted to freshmen who score 18 or higher on the ACT or 860 or higher on the SAT and who meet all other admission requirements. AP and CLEP credits are accepted. Important factors in the admissions decision are personality/intangible qualities, parents or siblings attended your school, and geographical diversity. To graduate, students must complete 120 credit hours, including at least 39 in upper-division courses, 18 in the major, and 15 in residence after achieving senior status, with a minimum GPA of 2.25 overall and 2.5 in the major. All students must fulfill general education and biblical studies course requirements, including courses in English, math, history, science, communication, computer science, and exercise science. The core curriculum totals 45 hours. **Procedure:** Freshmen are admitted in the fall, spring, and summer. Entrance exams should be taken before registration. There are early decision, early admissions, and rolling admissions plans. Early decision applications should be filed by October 31; regular applications, by August 15 for fall entry. The fall 2017 application fee was $25. Notification of early decision is sent December 15; regular decision, December 15. Applications are accepted on-line. **Transfer Students:** 197 transfer students enrolled in 2016-2017. Transfer students with fewer than 16 hours of college credit must meet freshman admission requirements. All transfers must submit an official transcript from previously attended colleges or universities and be in good academic standing. Only courses with a grade of C or above are transferred from another institution. 30 of 126 credits required for the bachelor's degree must be completed at LCU. **International Students:** There are 20 international students enrolled. They must take the TOEFL with a minimum score of 525 on the paper-based TOEFL (PBT) or 71 on the Internet-based version (iBT) or take the MELAB. They must also take the SAT or ACT, scoring 18.

ADMISSIONS: 94% of the 2017-2018 applicants were accepted. The SAT scores for the 2017-2018 freshman class were: Math-- 36% below 500, 42% between 500 and 599, 19% between 600 and 699, and 3% between 700 and 800. Evidence-Based Reading/Writing-- 31% below 500, 44% between 500 and 599, 22% between 600 and 699, and 3% between 700 and 800. The ACT scores were 10% between 12 and 17, 50% between 18 and 23, 32% between 24 and 29, and 8% above 30. 29% of the current freshmen were in the top fifth of their class; 55% were in the top two fifths. 6 freshmen graduated first in their class. **Admissions Contact:** Chris Hayes, Director of Recruiting. Email: *admissions@lcu.edu* Web: *www.lcu.edu*

FINANCIAL AID: In 2017-2018, 69% of all full-time freshmen received some form of financial aid. 69% of all full-time freshmen received need-based aid. The average freshman award was $15,604. Need-based scholarships or need-based grants averaged $11,234; need-based self-help aid (loans and jobs) averaged $5,031; non-need-based athletic scholarships averaged $11,164; and other non-need-based awards and non-need-based scholarships averaged $5,486. 16% of undergraduate students work part-time. The average financial indebtedness of the 2017 graduate was $25,835. The college's own financial statement is required. The FAFSA code is 003586. The priority date for freshman financial aid applications for fall entry is June 1.

MCMURRY UNIVERSITY *(The complete profile is made available exclusively on our website, www.barronspac.com)*

MIDWESTERN STATE UNIVERSITY *(The complete profile is made available exclusively on our website, www.barronspac.com)*

OUR LADY OF THE LAKE UNIVERSITY *(The complete profile is made available exclusively on our website, www.barronspac.com)*

PAUL QUINN COLLEGE *(The complete profile is made available exclusively on our website, www.barronspac.com)*

PRAIRIE VIEW A&M UNIVERSITY *(The complete profile is made available exclusively on our website, www.barronspac.com)*

RICE UNIVERSITY E-3

www.rice.edu

Houston, TX 77251	(713) 348-7423
Fax: (713) 348-5952	Email: admission@rice.edu
Full-time: 1999 men, 1825 women	**Faculty:** 671; I, +$
Part-time: 37 men, 18 women	**Ph.D.s:** 99%
Graduate: 1850 men, 1011 women	**Student/Faculty:** 6 to 1
Year: semesters, summer session	**Tuition:** $45,608
Room & Board: $13,850	**Freshman Class:** 18236 applied, 2785 accepted, 981 enrolled
SAT CR/M/W: 730/760/725 **ACT:** 34	**CEEB CODE:** 6609
Application Deadline: January 1	**MOST COMPETITIVE**

Rice University, founded in 1912, is a comprehensive research university offering more than 50 undergraduate and graduate programs through its schools of engineering, natural sciences, humanities, social sciences, music, and architecture. The school of business offers graduate degrees and an undergraduate minor. There are 6 undergraduate schools and 7 graduate schools. In addition to regional accreditation, RU has baccalaureate program accreditation with AACSB, ABET, and NAAB. The 295-acre campus is in an urban area 3 miles southwest of downtown Houston. Including any residence halls, there are 75 buildings.

STUDENT LIFE: 45% of undergraduates are from out of state, mostly the South. Students are from 50 states, 44 foreign countries, and Canada. 7% are African American; 4% two or more races; 37% White; 24% Asian American; 14% Hispanic; 12% Foreign; 1% American Indian/Alaska Native. 33% are Protestant; 32% claim no religious affiliation; 18% Catholic; 13% Hindu, Muslim, and Unknown denomination. **Male To Female Ratio:** 1.4:1. The average age of freshmen is 18; all undergraduates, 20. 3% do not continue beyond their first year; 93% remain to graduate. **Housing:** 2080 students can be accommodated in college housing, which includes dorms. On-campus housing is available on a lottery system for upperclassmen. 72% of students live on campus. All students may keep cars.

FACULTY/CLASSROOMS: All teach undergraduates and do research. No introductory courses are taught by graduate students. The average class size in a regular course is 14.

PROGRAMS OF STUDY: RU confers B.A., B.S., B.Arch., B.F.A., B.Mus., and B.S.E degrees. Master's and doctoral degrees are also awarded. Bachelor's degrees are awarded in BIOLOGICAL SCIENCE (biology/biological science), BUSINESS (management science), COMMUNICATIONS AND THE ARTS (art history and appreciation, classics, English, linguistics, music, music history and appreciation, music performance, music theory and composition, and visual and performing arts), COMPUTER AND PHYSICAL SCIENCE (applied mathematics, chemistry, computer science, earth science, geology, geophysics and seismology, mathematics, physics, and statistics), ENGINEERING AND ENVIRONMENTAL DESIGN (architectural engineering, architecture, bioengineering, chemical engineering, civil engineering, electrical/electronics engineering, environmental engineering, and mechanical engineering), HEALTH PROFESSIONS (exercise science), SOCIAL SCIENCE (anthropology, Asian/Oriental studies, classical/ancient civilization, cognitive science, economics, French studies, German area studies, Hispanic American studies, history, medieval studies, philosophy, political science/government, psychology, public affairs, religion, sociology, and women's studies). Biochemistry and cell biology, mechanical engineering, and political science have the largest enrollments.

ACTIVITIES: There are no fraternities or sororities. There are 225 groups on campus, including art, band, cheerleading, chess, choir, chorale, chorus, computers, dance, debate, drama, environmental, ethnic, film, forensics, honors, international, jazz band, LGBT, literary magazine, marching band, musical theater, newspaper, opera, orchestra, pep band, photography, political, professional, radio and TV stations, religious, social, social service, student government, symphony, and yearbook. Popular campus events include Baker Shakespeare Festival, Annual Biking Relay Race, Archi Arts, and a Costume Ball. **Sports:** There are 19 intercollegiate sports for men and 18 for women, and 14 intramural sports for men and 13 for women. Facilities include a recreation center with a pool, a 50-meter competition pool, indoor and outdoor basketball courts, an indoor soccer and hockey arena, racquetball courts, squash courts, a weight and cardio workout room, and multipurpose rooms for group fitness and dance classes, a gym, a track, fields for soccer, lacrosse, and rugby, courts for tennis, squash, racquetball, volleyball, and basketball, and a stadium. **Graduates:** From July 1, 2016 to June 30, 2017, 1002 bachelor's degrees were awarded. The most popular majors were engineering (19%), social sciences (15%), and biological/life sciences (9%). In an average class, 82% graduate in 4 years or less, 92% graduate in 5 years or less, and 93% graduate in 6 years or less. Of the 2016 graduating class, 43% were enrolled in graduate school within 6 months of graduation, and 49% were employed.

SERVICES: Counseling and information services are available, as is tutoring in every subject. **Library/Resources:** The library contains 2.6 million volumes, 3.3 million microform items, 62,279 audio/video tapes/CDs/DVDs, and subscribes to 72,352 periodicals, including electronic. Computerized library services include interlibrary loans, database searching, Internet access, and Wi-Fi capability. Special learning facilities include an art gallery, a media center, and observatory. **Physically Challenged Students:** 90% of the campus is accessible. Facilities include wheelchair ramps, elevators, special parking, specially equipped restrooms, special class scheduling, lowered drinking fountains, lowered telephones, special housing, and a stair lift. **Special:** An 8-year guaranteed medical school program with the Baylor College of Medicine; a 5-year joint degree program for the B.S.E./M.S.E. in engineering; a 5-year joint degree for the B.S.E./M.B.A. in engineering and business; and a 3-2 engineering degree are possible, as are cross-registration, internships, study abroad, work-study, dual majors, and student-designed majors. There are 10 national honor societies, Phi Beta Kappa, and 9 departmental honors programs. **Visiting:** There are regularly scheduled orientations for prospective students, consisting of information sessions and tours available year-round. There are guides for informal visits, visitors may sit in on classes, and stay overnight. To schedule a visit, contact the Office of Admissions. **Campus Safety and Security:** Measures include 24-hour foot and vehicle patrol, emergency notification system, self-defense education, and security escort services. There are shuttle buses, emergency telephones, lighted pathways/sidewalks, controlled access to dorms/residences, and campus police department with a variety of outreach programs.

REQUIREMENTS: Official high school transcript (s), 1 counselor recommendation, and 1 teacher recommendation are required. To satisfy the testing requirement, students must submit either the SAT plus 2 SAT Subject Tests or the ACT with the Writing Test. Music students must arrange an audition. Architecture students must submit a portfolio. An interview is recommended but not required. Candidates should have completed 16 college preparatory units, including 4 years of English, 3 of math, or academic electives, and 2 each of social studies, foreign language, and lab science. AP credits are accepted. Important factors in the admissions decision are leadership record, advanced placement or honors courses, evidence of special talent, personality/intangible qualities, and extracurricular activities record. All students must complete at least 120 credits, with a 1.67 overall GPA and a 2.0 GPA in the major field. Distribution requirements include 12 credit/semester hours in natural sciences, social sciences, or humanities, depending on the major, and additional courses in these fields to meet distribution requirements. All students take 2 semesters of phys ed. At least 48 semester hours in upper-level courses are required. **Procedure:** Freshmen are admitted in the fall. Entrance exams should be taken no later than December of the senior year. There is a early decision plan. Early decision applications should be filed by November 1; regular applications, by January 1 for fall entry. The fall 2017 application fee was $75. Notification of early decision is sent December 15; regular decision, April 1. 220 early decision candidates were accepted for the 2017-2018 class. Applications are accepted online. **Transfer Students:** 36 transfer students enrolled in 2016-2017. Transfer applicants should present at least a 3.2 GPA in previous college work, SAT scores, 2 college teacher recommendations, high school and college transcripts, and a letter from the dean of their current college. 60 of 120 credits required for the bachelor's degree must be completed at RU. **International Students:** There are 220 international students enrolled. They must take the TOEFL with a minimum score of 600 on the paper-based TOEFL (PBT) or 90 on the Internet-based version (iBT). They must also take the SAT or ACT.

ADMISSIONS: 15% of the 2017-2018 applicants were accepted. The SAT scores for the 2017-2018 freshman class were: Critical Reading-- 1%

below 500, 4% between 500 and 599, 23% between 600 and 699, and 72% between 700 and 800. Math-- 1% below 500, 3% between 500 and 599, 14% between 600 and 699, and 82% between 700 and 800. Writing-- 2% below 500, 4% between 500 and 599, 27% between 600 and 699, and 68% between 700 and 800. The ACT scores were 3% between 18 and 23, 8% between 24 and 29, and 89% above 30. **Admissions Contact:** Julie M. Browning, Dean for Undergraduate Enrollment. Email: *admission@rice.edu* Web: *www.rice.edu*

FINANCIAL AID: In 2017-2018, 100% of all full-time freshmen received some form of financial aid. The average freshman award was $42,573. Need-based scholarships or need-based grants averaged $37,258; need-based self-help aid (loans and jobs) averaged $3,540; non-need-based athletic scholarships averaged $39,971; other non-need-based awards and non-need-based scholarships averaged $23,037; and $2,892 from other forms of aid. The average financial indebtedness of the 2017 graduate was $40,858. Rice is a member of CSS. The CSS/Profile, and parents' and student's tax returns are required. The FAFSA code is 003604. The priority date for freshman financial aid applications for fall entry is March 1.

SAM HOUSTON STATE UNIVERSITY D-3

www.shsu.edu

Huntsville, TX 77341	**(936) 294-1845** **(866) 232-7528**
Fax: (936) 294-3758	**Email: admissions@shsu.edu**
Full-time: 5429 men, 7010 women	**Faculty:** 582; I, --$
Part-time: 1041 men, 1515 women	**Ph.D.s:** 95%
Graduate: 911 men, 1711 women	**Student/Faculty:** 20 to 1
Year: semesters, summer session	**Tuition:** $10,112 ($18,583)
Room & Board: $8680	**Freshman Class:** 7070 applied, 5473 accepted, 2069 enrolled
SAT or ACT: required	**CEEB CODE:** 6643
Application Deadline: August 1	**COMPETITIVE**

Sam Houston University, founded in 1879, is a public institution offering programs in fine arts and mass communication, applied sciences, business administration, criminal justice, education, and humanities and social sciences. There are 6 undergraduate schools and 6 graduate schools. In addition to regional accreditation, SHSU has baccalaureate program accreditation with AACSB, ABET, ADA, and NASM. The 1256-acre campus is in a small town 70 miles north of Houston. Including any residence halls, there are 228 buildings.

STUDENT LIFE: 98% of undergraduates are from Texas. Others are from 48 states, 59 foreign countries, and Canada. 71% are White; 14% African American; 12% Hispanic; 1% Asian American; 1% American Indian/Alaska Native; 1% Foreign. **Female To Male Ratio:** 1.4:1. The average age of freshmen is 18; all undergraduates, 22. 31% do not continue beyond their first year; 40% remain to graduate. **Housing:** 3293 students can be accommodated in college housing, which includes dorms, on-campus apartments, and off-campus apartments. In addition, there are honors houses, special-interest houses, fraternity houses, and sorority houses. On-campus housing is guaranteed for all 4 years. 73% of students commute. All students may keep cars.

FACULTY/CLASSROOMS: 53% of faculty are male; 47% are female. All teach undergraduates, and all do research. Graduate students teach 5% of introductory courses.

PROGRAMS OF STUDY: SHSU confers B.A., B.S., B.A.A.S., B.B.A., B.F.A., and B.M. degrees. Master's and doctoral degrees are also awarded. Bachelor's degrees are awarded in AGRICULTURE (agriculture, animal science, and horticulture), BIOLOGICAL SCIENCE (biology/biological science), BUSINESS (accounting, banking and finance, business administration and management, and marketing/retailing/merchandising), COMMUNICATIONS AND THE ARTS (art, dance, dramatic arts, English, French, German, graphic design, journalism, music, music performance, music theory and composition, musical theater, photography, Spanish, and speech/debate/rhetoric), COMPUTER AND PHYSICAL SCIENCE (chemistry, computer science, geology, mathematics, and physics), EDUCATION (physical education), ENGINEERING AND ENVIRONMENTAL DESIGN (environmental science), HEALTH PROFESSIONS (health, medical technology, and music therapy), SOCIAL SCIENCE (criminal justice, economics, geography, history, law enforcement and corrections, philosophy, physical fitness/movement, political science/government, psychology, and sociology). Criminal justice, general business, and psychology have the largest enrollments.

ACTIVITIES: 9% of men belong to 15 local fraternities; 5% of women belong to 13 local sororities. There are 235 groups on campus, including art, band, cheerleading, choir, chorale, chorus, computers, dance, drama, drill team, environmental, ethnic, film, forensics, honors, international, jazz band, LGBT, marching band, musical theater, newspaper, orchestra, pep band, photography, political, professional, radio and TV stations, religious, social, social service, student government, and symphony. Popular campus events include Organization Fair, Greek Week, and Welcome Week. **Sports:** There are 7 intercollegiate sports for men and 7 for women, and 13 intramural sports for men and 13 for women. Facilities include a stadium, a gym, 4 basketball courts, 10 racquetball courts, 3 swimming pools, and 2 weight rooms. **Graduates:** From July 1, 2016 to June 30, 2017, 3188 bachelor's degrees were awarded. The most popular majors were business/marketing (25%), homeland security (16%), and interdisciplinary studies (13%). In an average class, 17% graduate in 4 years or less and 41% graduate in 6 years or less.

SERVICES: Counseling and information services are available, as is tutoring in every subject. There is a reader service for the blind, and remedial math, reading, and writing. **Library/Resources:** The library contains 1.3 million volumes, 3,744 audio/video tapes/CDs/DVDs, and subscribes to 7,175 periodicals, including electronic. Computerized library services include interlibrary loans, database searching, Internet access, and Wi-Fi capability. Special learning facilities include a planetarium, radio station, TV station, and the Sam Houston Museum. **Physically Challenged Students:** 90% of the campus is accessible. Facilities include wheelchair ramps, elevators, special parking, specially equipped restrooms, lowered drinking fountains, closed-circuit television, computer workstations with large print and speech output capabilities, and telecommunication devices for the disabled. **Special:** Work-study programs with the university, study abroad in 6 countries, duel degrees, and B.A.-B.S. degrees are available. There are 10 national honor societies and a freshman honors program. **Visiting:** There are regularly scheduled orientations for prospective students, including a tour of the campus, dorms, and departments. There are guides for informal visits. To schedule a visit, contact the Visitor Center at visitsam@shsu.edu. **Campus Safety and Security:** Measures include 24-hour foot and vehicle patrol, an emergency notification system, and security escort services. There are emergency telephones and lighted pathways/sidewalks.

REQUIREMENTS: The SAT or ACT is required. Applicants must have secondary school credits as follows: 4 of English, 2 each of math, history, and science, 1 1/2 of phys ed, and a half credit each of social studies and health education. The GED is accepted. AP and CLEP credits are accepted. All students must maintain a GPA of 2.0 while taking 128 semester hours, including 30 in the major. The core curriculum includes 15 hours of social and behavioral sciences, 9 hours of humanities and visual and performing arts, 8 hours of natural sciences, 6 hours of communication, 4 hours of an institutionally designated option, and 3 hours of math. **Procedure:** Freshmen are admitted in the fall, spring, and summer. There are early admissions and rolling admissions plans. Applications should be filed by August 1 for fall entry. The fall 2017 application fee was $40. Notification is sent on a rolling basis. **Transfer Students:** 2153 transfer students enrolled in 2016-2017. Transfer applicants must present a 2.0 GPA on all previous college work. 42 of 128 credits required for the bachelor's degree must be completed at SHSU. **International Students:** There are 105 international students enrolled. They must take the TOEFL with a minimum score of 550 on the paper-based TOEFL (PBT). They must also take the SAT or ACT.

ADMISSIONS: 77% of the 2017-2018 applicants were accepted. 32% of the current freshmen were in the top fifth of their class; 67% were in the top two fifths. 10 freshmen graduated first in their class. **Admissions Contact:** Donna Artho, Assistant Vice President Effectiveness. Email: *admissions@shsu.edu* Web: *www.shsu.edu*

FINANCIAL AID: 5% of undergraduate students work part-time. The average financial indebtedness of the 2017 graduate was $19,188. The FAFSA code is 003606. The priority date for freshman financial aid applications for fall entry is March 31.

SCHREINER UNIVERSITY *(The complete profile is made available exclusively on our website, www.barronspac.com)*

SOUTHERN METHODIST UNIVERSITY D-2

www.smu.edu

Dallas, TX 75275 (214) 768-2058
(800) 323-0672
Fax: (214) 768-0103 **Email:** ugadmission@smu.edu

Full-time: 3150 men, 3090 women
Part-time: 107 men, 105 women
Graduate: 2828 men, 2509 women
Year: semesters, summer session
Room & Board: $16,510
SAT or ACT: required
Application Deadline: January 15

Faculty: 676; I, av$
Ph.D.s: 82%
Student/Faculty: 11 to 1
Tuition: $52,498
Freshman Class: 13128 applied, 6402 accepted, 1423 enrolled
CEEB CODE: 6660
MOST COMPETITIVE

Southern Methodist University, founded in 1911, is a private nonsectarian institution affiliated with the United Methodist Church, offering undergraduate and graduate programs in humanities and sciences, business, arts, education, engineering, and applied sciences. There are 5 undergraduate schools and 7 graduate schools. In addition to regional accreditation, SMU has baccalaureate program accreditation with AACSB, ABET, NASAD, NASM, ACS, NASD, and NAST. The 235-acre campus is in an urban area 5 miles north of downtown Dallas. Including any residence halls, there are 132 buildings.

STUDENT LIFE: 55% of undergraduates are from out of state, mostly the Southwest. Students are from 47 states, 62 foreign countries, and Canada. 44% are from public schools. 6% are African American; 6% Asian American; 58% White; 3% two or more races; 15% Foreign; 11% Hispanic; 1% race unknown. 27% are Protestant; 15% Catholic. **Male To Female Ratio:** 1.1:1. The average age of freshmen is 18; all undergraduates, 20. 9% do not continue beyond their first year; 81% remain to graduate. **Housing:** 3803 students can be accommodated in college housing, which includes married student dorms and on-campus apartments. In addition, there are honors houses, special-interest houses, fraternity houses, sorority houses, and living learning community. On-campus housing is available on a first-come and first-served basis. 54% of students live on campus. All students may keep cars. Alcohol is not permitted.

FACULTY/CLASSROOMS: 59% of faculty are male; 41% are female. No introductory courses are taught by graduate students.

PROGRAMS OF STUDY: SMU confers B.A., B.S., B.B.A., B.F.A., B.M., B.S.C.P.E., B.S.C.E., B.S.E.E., B.S.Env.E., and B.S.M.E. degrees. Master's and doctoral degrees are also awarded. Bachelor's degrees are awarded in AGRICULTURE (environmental studies), BIOLOGICAL SCIENCE (biochemistry and biology/biological science), BUSINESS (accounting, business administration and management, economics – statistics, finance, finance (financial planning), insurance and risk management, management science, marketing/retailing/merchandising, real estate, and real estate finance), COMMUNICATIONS AND THE ARTS (advertising, art history and appreciation, broadcasting, communications, creative writing, dance, dramatic arts, English, film arts, fine/studio arts, general, French, German, journalism, languages, media arts, music performance, music theory and composition, performing arts, piano/organ, public relations, Spanish, sports administration, and studio art), COMPUTER AND PHYSICAL SCIENCE (chemistry, computer science, environmental geology, geology, geophysics and seismology, mathematics, physics, and statistics), EDUCATION (health education and music education), ENGINEERING AND ENVIRONMENTAL DESIGN (civil engineering, computer engineering, electrical/electronics engineering, environmental engineering, environmental science, and mechanical engineering), HEALTH PROFESSIONS (music therapy), SOCIAL SCIENCE (African American studies, anthropology, economics, history, humanities, Iberian studies, international relations, international studies, Italian studies, Latin American studies, liberal arts/general studies, medieval studies, Mexican-American/Chicano studies, philosophy, physical fitness/movement, political science/government, psychology, public affairs, religion, and sociology). Finance, mechanical engineering, and economics with finance applications have the largest enrollments.

ACTIVITIES: 28% of men belong to 15 national fraternities; 36% of women belong to 14 national sororities. There are 180 groups on campus, including art, band, cheerleading, choir, chorale, chorus, computers, dance, debate, drama, drill team, ethnic, forensics, honors, international, jazz band, LGBT, literary magazine, marching band, musical theater, opera, orchestra, pep band, photography, political, professional, religious, social, social service, student government, and symphony. Popular campus events include Celebration of Lights and Community Service Day. **Sports:** There are 6 intercollegiate sports for men and 11 for women, and 20 intramural sports for men and 20 for women. Facilities include a gym and weight rooms, a dance studio, indoor and outdoor jogging tracks, indoor and outdoor pools, outdoor and indoor stadium, courts for basketball, volleyball, tennis, badminton, and racquetball. **Graduates:** From July 1, 2016 to June 30, 2017, 1778 bachelor's degrees were awarded. The most popular majors were economics (10%), finance (10%), and accounting (6%). In an average class, 2% graduate in 3 years or less, 71% graduate in 4 years or less, 80% graduate in 5 years or less, and 81% graduate in 6 years or less.

SERVICES: Counseling and information services are available, as is tutoring in most subjects. There is a reader service for the blind, and remedial reading and writing. The Learning Enhancement Center provides study skills workshops, note-taking techniques, and time management skills seminars. **Library/Resources:** The library contains 3.1 million volumes, 2.0 million microform items, 58,145 audio/video tapes/ CDs/DVDs, and subscribes to 29,852 periodicals, including electronic. Computerized library services include interlibrary loans, database searching, Internet access, and Wi-Fi capability. Special learning facilities include an art gallery, a natural history museum, and a TV station. The Meadows Museum which houses one of the finest Spanish art collections outside Spain; SMU's engineering school, the nation's first to host a Lockheed Martin Skunk Works Lab modeled after the California research facility; and performance facilities that include theatres with classical thrust stage, proscenium stage and black box area; and a journalism complex that includes a digital newsroom and TV studio. **Physically Challenged Students:** 95% of the campus is accessible. Facilities include wheelchair ramps, elevators, special parking, specially equipped restrooms, special class scheduling, lowered drinking fountains, lowered telephones, and automatic doors. **Special:** SMU offers a co-op program in engineering, work-study programs, B.A.-B.S. degrees, study abroad in 50 countries with 150 programs, dual majors in any combination, student-designed majors, numerous internships, and interdisciplinary majors, including economics with finance applications and economics with systems analysis. A 3-2 advanced degree in business is available, as are evening degree programs in humanities and social sciences, and teacher certification programs. There are 30 national honor societies, Phi Beta Kappa, and a freshman honors program. **Visiting:** There are regularly scheduled orientations for prospective students, including information about academic studies, financial aid sessions, discussions with current students, lunch with faculty and students, and a tour of the campus. There is also a Spring Fest visitation in March for high school sophomores and juniors. There are guides for informal visits; visitors may sit in on classes and stay overnight. To schedule a visit, contact the Undergraduate Admissions Office. **Campus Safety and Security:** Measures include 24-hour foot and vehicle patrol, an emergency notification system, self-defense education, and security escort services. There are shuttle buses, emergency telephones, lighted pathways/sidewalks, controlled card key access to dorms/residences.

REQUIREMENTS: The SAT or ACT is recommended. Applicants should graduate from an accredited high school with a minimum of 15 academic credits: 4 in English, 3 in higher math, including algebra I, II, and plane geometry, 3 each in natural science and social science, and 2 in a foreign language. Home School Certificate applicants may qualify with the SAT or ACT and 3 SAT Subject Tests in math, literature, and science. Performing arts majors must audition. AP and CLEP credits are accepted. Important factors in the admissions decision are advanced placement or honors courses, leadership record, and recommendations by school officials. Basic requirements consist of 122 semester hours, including the major requirements for one of SMU's over 100 majors, as well as the University Curriculum (UC), which consists of three, main course-based components: Foundations, Pillars and Capstone. The Foundations emphasize reading and writing, quantitative reasoning, applied critical thinking, and wellness. The five UC Pillars cover the natural sciences, the arts and humanities, and the social and behavioral sciences. The Capstone completes each student's general education. In addition to the three core components, there are eight proficiencies and experiences that can be satisfied through coursework or out-of-class activities. **Procedure:** Freshmen are admitted to all sessions. Entrance exams should be taken by December of the senior year. There are early decision, deferred admissions, and rolling admissions plans. Early decision applications should be filed by November 1; regular applications, by January 15 for fall entry. The fall 2017 application fee was $60. Notification of early decision is sent April 1; regular decision, on a rolling basis. 266 early decision candidates were accepted for the 2017-2018 class. 582 applicants were on the 2017 waiting list; 69 were admitted. Applications are accepted on-line. **Transfer Students:** 279 transfer students enrolled in 2016-2017. A minimum 2.5 GPA is generally required for transfer, but specific requirements vary according to the program of study. Candidates must demonstrate math proficiency. A foreign language requirement may be met through high school or college work. 60 of 122 credits required for the bachelor's degree must be completed at SMU. **International Students:** There are 555 international students enrolled. They must take the TOEFL with a minimum score of 550 on the paper-based TOEFL (PBT) or 80 on the Internet-based version (iBT), and the IELTS, with a minimum score of 6.5.

ADMISSIONS: 49% of the 2017-2018 applicants were accepted. 79% of the current freshmen were in the top fifth of their class; 95% were in the top two fifths. **Admissions Contact:** Elena D. Hicks, Dean of Undergraduate Admission. Email: *ugadmission@smu.edu* Web: *www.smu.edu*

FINANCIAL AID: In 2017-2018, 76% of all full-time freshmen received some form of financial aid. 23% of all full-time freshmen received need-based aid. The average freshman award was $38,446. Need-based scholarships or need-based grants averaged $18,843; need-based self-help aid (loans and jobs) averaged $6,138; non-need-based athletic scholarships averaged $60,964; and other non-need-based awards and non-need-based scholarships averaged $27,732. The average financial indebtedness of the 2017 graduate was $32,468. SMU is a member of CSS. The CSS/Profile is required. The FAFSA code is 003613. The priority date for freshman financial aid applications for fall entry is February 15.

SOUTHWESTERN ADVENTIST UNIVERSITY *(The complete profile is made available exclusively on our website, www.barronspac.com)*

SOUTHWESTERN UNIVERSITY D-3

www.southwestern.edu

Georgetown, TX 78626 **(512) 863-1200** **(800) 252-3166**

Fax: (512) 863-9601 **Email: admission@southwestern.edu**

Full-time: 581 men, 786 women
Part-time: 16 men, 13 women
Graduate: n/av
Year: semesters, summer session
Room & Board: $11,810
SAT EBR-W/M: 610/600 **ACT:** 26
Application Deadline: February 1
Faculty: 113; IIB, av$
Ph.D.s: 100%
Student/Faculty: 11 to 1
Tuition: $40,560
Freshman Class: 4134 applied, 1783 accepted, 362 enrolled
CEEB CODE: 6674
VERY COMPETITIVE

Southwestern University, founded in 1840, is a private, national liberal arts institution affiliated with the United Methodist Church. There are 2 undergraduate schools. In addition to regional accreditation, SWU has baccalaureate program accreditation with NASM, SACS, University Senate of United Methodist Church, and TEA. The 700-acre campus is in a suburban area 28 miles north of Austin. Including any residence halls, there are 36 buildings.

STUDENT LIFE: 90% of undergraduates are from Texas. Others are from 34 states, 12 foreign countries, and Canada. 79% are from public schools. 60% are White; 24% Hispanic; 5% African American; 5% two or more races; 3% Asian American; 1% American Indian/Alaska Native; 1% Foreign; 1% race unknown. 59% are Protestant; 26% Catholic. **Female To Male Ratio:** 1.3:1. The average age of freshmen is 18; all undergraduates, 20. 14% do not continue beyond their first year; 74% remain to graduate. **Housing:** 1090 students can be accommodated in college housing, which includes gender neutral, single-sex dorms, coed dorms, on-campus apartments, and special-interest houses and fraternity houses. On-campus housing is available on a first-come, first-served basis, and is available on a lottery system for upperclassmen. 76% of students live on campus. All students may keep cars.

FACULTY/CLASSROOMS: 49% of faculty are male; 51% are female. All teach undergraduates and do research. No introductory courses are taught by graduate students. The average class size in an introductory lecture is 19; and in a laboratory is 17.

PROGRAMS OF STUDY: SWU confers B.A., B.S., B.F.A., B.S.Ed., and B.M. degrees. Bachelor's degrees are awarded in AGRICULTURE (environmental studies), BIOLOGICAL SCIENCE (biochemistry and biology/biological science), BUSINESS (business administration and management), COMMUNICATIONS AND THE ARTS (art history, art, classics, communications, English, French, German, Greek, Latin, music composition, music history and appreciation, music performance, Spanish, and theatre studies), COMPUTER AND PHYSICAL SCIENCE (applied science, chemistry, computer mathematics, computer science, mathematics, mathematics/computational, and physics), EDUCATION (education), SOCIAL SCIENCE (anthropology, economics, history, international studies, Latin American studies, philosophy, political science/government, psychology, religion, sociology, and women's studies). Psychology, business, and communication have the largest enrollments.

ACTIVITIES: 28% of men belong to 4 national fraternities; 23% of women belong to 4 national sororities. There are 105 groups on campus, including art, band, cheerleading, choir, chorus, communications, computers, dance, debate, drama, environmental, ethnic, film, honors, international, jazz band, LGBT, literary magazine, musical theater, newspaper, opera, orchestra, political, professional, radio and TV station, religious, social, social service, student government, and symphony. Popular campus events include Homecoming, Sing, Pirate Parties, Candlelight Chapel Service, and Shilling Lecture. **Sports:** There are 10 intercollegiate sports for men and 10 for women, and 20 intramural sports for men and 20 for women. Facilities include a recreation center, a performance gym, indoor jogging track, racquetball and handball courts, an indoor swimming pool, weight room and fitness area. Outdoor facilities has baseball, softball, soccer and lacrosse fields, tennis courts, recreational fields, an athletic field house with weight room, athletic training center, football practice fields, outdoor track and field complex, and sand volleyball. **Graduates:** From July 1, 2016 to June 30, 2017, 427 bachelor's degrees were awarded. The most popular majors were business (12%), psychology (9%), and communication studies (8%). In an average class, 2% graduate in 3 years or less, 66% graduate in 4 years or less, 73% graduate in 5 years or less, and 73% graduate in 6 years or less. Of the 2016 graduating class, 23% were enrolled in graduate school within 6 months of graduation, and 68% were employed.

SERVICES: Counseling and information services are available, as is tutoring in every subject. There is a reader service for the blind and remedial writing. **Library/Resources:** The library contains 293,784 volumes, 57,660 microform items, 14,800 audio/video tapes/CDs/DVDs, and subscribes to 5,119 periodicals, including electronic. Computerized library services include interlibrary loans, database searching, Internet access, and Wi-Fi capability. Special learning facilities include an art gallery, radio station, an observatory. **Physically Challenged Students:** 90% of the campus is accessible. Facilities include wheelchair ramps, elevators, special parking, specially equipped restrooms, special class scheduling, lowered drinking fountains, lowered telephones, and special housing. **Special:** Students may study abroad in a multitude of countries. The university offers a fall London semester, a Washington semester, dual, student-designed, and independent majors, and internships in government, fine arts, psychology, sociology, science, and other fields, including those in the New York Arts Program. An Applied Physics major allows students to spend several years at Southwestern, then finish their Southwestern degree with a year's qualifying engineering coursework at another university. There are 7 national honor societies, Phi Beta Kappa, and 21 departmental honors programs. **Visiting:** There are regularly scheduled orientations for prospective students, as well as individually arranged visits throughout the year. All visits typically include tours, faculty appointments and interviews, and class visits. There are guides for informal visits; visitors may sit in on classes and stay overnight. To schedule a visit, contact the Admission's Office. **Campus Safety and Security:** Measures include 24-hour foot and vehicle patrol, an emergency notification system, self-defense education, and security escort services. There are emergency telephones, lighted pathways/sidewalks, and controlled access to dorms/residences.

REQUIREMENTS: Applicants should be graduates of an accredited high school or have the GED. Secondary preparation should include: 4 years each of English and math, 3 years each of science, social science, and history, 2 years of foreign language, and year of an academic elective. The SAT or ACT score, an essay, a counselor recommendation are required; and an interview is recommended. AP and CLEP credits are accepted. Important factors in the admissions decision are leadership record and advanced placement or honors courses. All degrees require a 2.0 or higher GPA in 127 or more credits. Each requires a first year seminar, two fitness and recreational activity credits, at least one course tagged for social justice, and a third semester proficiency in a foreign language. Exploration and breadth requirements stipulate completion of six courses from six unique disciplines outside of the core major. These six must include one to two courses from each of the following areas: humanities; natural sciences; social sciences, and fine arts. Major requirements vary but require a minimum of 30 credits, including a capstone. **Procedure:** Freshmen are admitted in the fall. Entrance exams should be taken in the fall or early spring of the senior year. There are early decision, early admissions, and deferred admissions plans. Early decision applications should be filed by November 1; regular applications, by February 1 for fall entry. Notification of early decision is sent December 1; regular decision, April 1. 20 early decision candidates were accepted for the 2017-2018 class. 117 applicants were on the 2017 waiting list; 9 were admitted. Applications are accepted online. **Transfer Students:** 53 transfer students enrolled in 2016-2017. Preference is given to students having a 3.0 in all college work. 64 of 127 credits required for the bachelor's degree must be completed at SWU. **International Students:** There are 16 international students enrolled. They must take the TOEFL with a minimum score of 570 on the paper-based TOEFL (PBT) or 88 on the Internet-based version (iBT). Students must take the IELTS, and either the SAT or ACT.

ADMISSIONS: 43% of the 2017-2018 applicants were accepted. The SAT scores for the 2017-2018 freshman class were: Math-- 4% below 500, 44% between 500 and 599, 43% between 600 and 699, and 9% between 700 and 800. Evidence-Based Reading/Writing-- 3% below 500, 38% between 500 and 599, 44% between 600 and 699, and 15% between 700 and 800. The ACT scores were 1% between 12 and 17, 27% between 18 and 23, 51% between 24 and 29, and 21% above 30. 65% of the current freshmen were in the top fifth of their class; 89% were in the top two fifths. 3 freshmen graduated first in their class. **Admissions Contact:** Bob Baldwin, Director of Admission. Email: *admission@southwestern.edu* Web: *www.southwestern.edu/admission*

FINANCIAL AID: In 2017-2018, 98% of all full-time freshmen received some form of financial aid. 69% of all full-time freshmen received need-based aid. The average freshman award was $35,991. Need-based scholarships or need-based grants averaged $31,462; need-based self-help aid (loans and jobs) averaged $4,733; and other non-need-based awards and non-need-based scholarships averaged $22,395. 42% of undergraduate students work part-time. The average financial indebtedness of the 2017 graduate was $34,788. SWU is a member of CSS. The FAFSA code is 003620. The priority date for freshman financial aid applications for fall entry is March 1.

ST. EDWARD'S UNIVERSITY D-3

www.stedwards.edu

Austin, TX 78704	**(512) 448-8500** **(800) 555-0164**
Fax: (512) 464-8877	**Email: seu.admit@stedwards.edu**
Full-time: 1426 men, 2184 women	**Faculty:** n/av
Part-time: 166 men, 280 women	**Ph.D.s:** 82%
Graduate: 178 men, 367 women	**Student/Faculty:** n/av
Year: semesters, summer session	**Tuition:** $40,928
Room & Board: $12,172	**Freshman Class:** 6046 applied, 4468 accepted, 864 enrolled
SAT EBR-W/M: 590/570 **ACT:** 25	**CEEB CODE:** 6619
Application Deadline: May 1	**VERY COMPETITIVE**

St. Edward's University, founded in 1885 by the Congregation of the Holy Cross, and is an independent, Roman Catholic, liberal arts university. St. Edward is part of a small, yet diverse community that provides global learning and encourages students to think critically and creatively, make ethical decisions, solve problems rationally, and lead effectively. Through hands-on service projects and internships, students develop a deeper understanding of their role in the world and gain the confidence to excel and make a difference in the community. There are 6 undergraduate schools and 4 graduate schools. In addition to regional accreditation, SEU has baccalaureate program accreditation with CSWE. The 160-acre campus is in an urban area in Austin. Including any residence halls, there are 57 buildings.

STUDENT LIFE: 13% of undergraduates are from out of state, mostly the West. Students are from 49 states, 54 foreign countries, and Canada. 74% are from public schools. 8% are Foreign; 41% Hispanic; 4% African American; 37% White; 3% Asian American; 3% two or more races; 2% race unknown. 43% are Muslim, Buddhist, Christian, Hindu, Mormon, and unknown; 27% Catholic; 15% Protestant. **Female To Male Ratio:** 1.6:1. The average age of freshmen is 18; all undergraduates, 22. 19% do not continue beyond their first year; 64% remain to graduate. **Housing:** 1448 students can be accommodated in college housing, which includes dorms, on-campus apartments, and off-campus apartments, and living learning communities. On-campus housing is guaranteed for the freshman year only, and is available on a first-come, first-served basis, and is available on a lottery system for upperclassmen. 63% of students commute. All students may keep cars.

FACULTY/CLASSROOMS: 47% of faculty are male; 53% are female. No introductory courses are taught by graduate students.

PROGRAMS OF STUDY: St. Edward's confers B.A., B.S., B.B.A., B.F.A., and B.L.S. degrees. Master's degrees are also awarded. Bachelor's degrees are awarded in BIOLOGICAL SCIENCE (biochemistry, bioinformatics, biology/biological science, and biology/general science secondary education), BUSINESS (accounting, banking and finance, business administration and management, entrepreneurial studies, international business management, and marketing management), COMMUNICATIONS AND THE ARTS (acting, art, communications, digital communications, English literature, English Writing, French, game design and development, graphic design, photography, Spanish, and theatre arts), COMPUTER AND PHYSICAL SCIENCE (chemistry, chemistry/gen science second education, computer information technology, computer science, environmental chemistry, information sciences and systems, and mathematics), EDUCATION (art education, athletic training, drama education, English education, foreign languages education, global studies, mathematics education, physical education, physical science secondary school education, science education, social studies education, and special education), ENGINEERING AND ENVIRONMENTAL DESIGN (environmental science and preengineering), HEALTH PROFESSIONS (human studies, medical laboratory science, predentistry, premedicine, and prephysical therapy), SOCIAL SCIENCE (criminal justice, criminology, economics, forensic studies, history, interdisciplinary studies, international relations, liberal arts/general studies, philosophy, physical fitness/movement, political science/government, prelaw, psychology, religion, social work, and sociology). Psychology, biology, and communication have the largest enrollments.

ACTIVITIES: There are no fraternities or sororities. There are 136 groups on campus, including art, cheerleading, choir, chorale, chorus, computers, dance, debate, drama, drill team, environmental, ethnic, film, forensics, honors, international, jazz band, LGBT, literary magazine, musical theater, newspaper, orchestra, pep band, photography, political, professional, radio and TV, religious, social, social service, and student government. Popular campus events include Welcome Barbecue, Halloween Block Party, Homecoming, Involvement Fair, Hillfest, Casino Night, Leadershape, Festival of Lights, The Change Institute, End of Year Party, Anchors, Legacy Walk, Medallion Ceremony, and The Big Event. **Sports:** There are 6 intercollegiate sports for men and 7 for women, and 10 intramural sports for men and 10 for women. Facilities include gyms, baseball and softball fields, a soccer field, tennis, basketball, racquetball/handball, and volleyball courts, indoor pool, fitness center, sand volleyball courts, recreation multipurpose field and a fitness studio. **Graduates:** From July 1, 2016 to June 30, 2017, 847 bachelor's degrees were awarded. The most popular majors were communication (9%), psychology (9%), and global studies (6%). In an average class, 3% graduate in 3 years or less, 50% graduate in 4 years or less, 61% graduate in 5 years or less, and 64% graduate in 6 years or less.

SERVICES: Counseling and information services are available, as is tutoring in some subjects, such as accounting, biology, business, computer, chemistry, economics, French, math, physics, psychology, and Spanish. There is a reader service for the blind, and remedial math, reading, and writing. **Library/Resources:** The library contains 672,393 volumes, 4,144 audio/video tapes/CDs/DVDs, and subscribes to 2,601 periodicals, including electronic. Computerized library services include interlibrary loans, database searching, Internet access, and Wi-Fi capability. Special learning facilities include an art gallery, radio station, fine arts facility with a photography laboratory, 60 Global Digital classrooms in the Munday Library and throughout the campus, Mary Moody Northen Theatre, Our Lady Queen of Peace Chapel, Interdisciplinary research laboratory at Wild Basin Wilderness Preserve. In addition, there is a partner campus in Angers, France at Universite Catholique de l'Ouest, and 21 international partner universities. **Physically Challenged Stu-**

dents: 93% of the campus is accessible. Facilities include wheelchair ramps, elevators, special parking, specially equipped restrooms, special class scheduling, lowered drinking fountains, lowered telephones, and special housing. **Special:** Internships and study abroad in a variety of countries through the ISEP, SEU, and other university programs are available. Student-designed majors, nondegree study, and pass/fail options also are possible. A flexible program for working adults is offered through New College. There are 13 national honor societies and a freshman honors program. **Visiting:** There are regularly scheduled orientations for prospective students, including a tour, financial aid session, academic session, class visits, and entertainment. There are guides for informal visits; visitors may sit in on classes and stay overnight. To schedule a visit, contact Lisa Furler at (512) 448-8500. **Campus Safety and Security:** Measures include 24-hour foot and vehicle patrol, an emergency notification system, self-defense education, and security escort services. There are emergency telephones, lighted pathways/sidewalks, and controlled access to dorms/residences.

REQUIREMENTS: The SAT or ACT is required. Successful applicants should be in the top half of their graduating class with testing at or above a combined Evidenced Based Reading and Writing and Math score of 1080 on the SAT, or a composite score, not including writing, of 21 on the ACT. The GED is accepted. An interview is recommended. An essay is required. SEU requires applicants to be in the upper 50% of their class. AP and CLEP credits are accepted. Important factors in the admissions decision are advanced placement or honors courses, extracurricular activities record, and leadership record. All students must maintain a minimum GPA of 2.0 while taking 120 semester hours, including 36 to 81 in the major. The core curriculum includes courses from Foundational Skills, Cultural Foundations, and Foundations for Values and Decisions. In the required capstone class, seniors identify a problem in society, research it, present their solutions orally and in writing, and perform a civic engagement activity that supports their position. **Procedure:** Freshmen are admitted in the fall and spring. Entrance exams should be taken in spring of the junior year or in summer or fall of the senior year. There are deferred admissions and rolling admissions plans. Early decision applications should be filed by February 1; regular applications, by May 1 for fall entry; November 15 for spring entry; and May 1 for summer entry. The fall 2017 application fee was $50. Notification is sent on a rolling basis. 985 applicants were on the 2017 waiting list; 137 were admitted. Applications are accepted on-line. **Transfer Students:** 270 transfer students enrolled in 2016-2017. Transfer applicants must have a minimum GPA of 2.5. 30 of 120 credits required for the bachelor's degree must be completed at SEU. **International Students:** There are 312 international students enrolled. They must take the TOEFL with a minimum score of 500 on the paper-based TOEFL (PBT) or 61 on the Internet-based version (iBT), or IELTS; IB (English Higher Level) and AP (English or English Literature) may be submitted. Students may take the SAT or ACT in place of TOEFL or IELTS.

ADMISSIONS: 74% of the 2017-2018 applicants were accepted. The SAT scores for the 2017-2018 freshman class were: Math-- 9% below 500, 58% between 500 and 599, 30% between 600 and 699, and 3% between 700 and 800. Evidence-Based Reading/Writing-- 5% below 500, 47% between 500 and 599, 40% between 600 and 699, and 9% between 700 and 800. The ACT scores were 1% between 12 and 17, 36% between 18 and 23, 52% between 24 and 29, and 11% above 30. 52% of the current freshmen were in the top fifth of their class; 79% were in the top two fifths. 3 freshmen graduated first in their class. **Admissions Contact:** Tracy Manier, Associate Vice President and Dean of Admission. Email: *seu.admit@stedwards.edu* Web: *www.stedwards.edu*

FINANCIAL AID: In 2017-2018, 86% of all full-time freshmen received some form of financial aid. 72% of all full-time freshmen received need-based aid. The average freshman award was $35,885. Need-based scholarships or need-based grants averaged $23,009; need-based self-help aid (loans and jobs) averaged $3,973; non-need-based athletic scholarships averaged $21,661; and other non-need-based awards and non-need-based scholarships averaged $17,959. 28% of undergraduate students work part-time. The average financial indebtedness of the 2017 graduate was $37,337. SEU is a member of CSS. The FAFSA code is 003621. The priority date for freshman financial aid applications for fall entry is February 1.

ST. MARY'S UNIVERSITY — D-4

www.stmarytx.edu

San Antonio, TX 78228 — (210) 436-3126, (800) 367-7868, Email: uadm@stmarytx.edu

Full-time: 1008 men, 1220 women	**Faculty:** 152; IIA, +$
Part-time: 51 men, 48 women	**Ph.D.s:** 93%
Graduate: 641 men, 681 women	**Student/Faculty:** 11 to 1
Year: semesters, summer session	**Tuition:** $29,300
Room & Board: $9820	**Freshman Class:** 4346 applied, 3375 accepted, 587 enrolled
SAT M/W: 560/510 **ACT:** 22	**CEEB CODE:** 6637
Application Deadline: open	**COMPETITIVE**

St. Mary's University, founded in 1852 by Marianist brothers and priests, is the first institution of higher learning in San Antonio and the oldest Catholic university in Texas and the Southwest. The university provides a Catholic education experience that evokes academic excellence while integrating liberal studies, professional preparation and ethical commitment. Personal attention and powerful academic programs have made St. Mary's a nationally recognized liberal arts institution. There are 3 undergraduate schools and 2 graduate schools. In addition to regional accreditation, SMU has baccalaureate program accreditation with AACSB and ABET. The 135-acre campus is in a suburban area 5 miles northwest of downtown San Antonio. Including any residence halls, there are 45 buildings.

STUDENT LIFE: 87% of undergraduates are from Texas. Others are from 27 states, 33 foreign countries, and Canada. 68% are from public schools. 9% are Foreign; 67% Hispanic; 3% African American; 2% race unknown; 2% Asian American; 15% White. 42% are Catholic; 15% Baptist, Buddhist, Eastern Orthodox, Episcopal, and Hindu. **Female To Male Ratio:** 1.1:1. The average age of freshmen is 18; all undergraduates, 26. 27% do not continue beyond their first year; 64% remain to graduate. **Housing:** 1454 students can be accommodated in college housing, which includes dorms, and theme housing. On-campus housing is guaranteed for the freshman year only, and is available on a first-come, first-served basis. 56% of students live on campus. All students may keep cars.

FACULTY/CLASSROOMS: 64% of faculty are male; 36% are female. 75% teach undergraduates. No introductory courses are taught by graduate students. The average class size in an introductory lecture is 30; in a laboratory is 60; and in a regular course is 25.

PROGRAMS OF STUDY: SMU confers B.A., B.S., and B.B.A. degrees. Master's and doctoral degrees are also awarded. Bachelor's degrees are awarded in BIOLOGICAL SCIENCE (biochemistry and biology/biological science), BUSINESS (accounting, banking and finance, business administration and management, human resources, international business management, and marketing/retailing/merchandising), COMMUNICATIONS AND THE ARTS (communications, English, French, German, music, Spanish, and speech/debate/rhetoric), COMPUTER AND PHYSICAL SCIENCE (chemistry, computer science, earth science, mathematics, and physics), EDUCATION (business education, elementary education, science education, and secondary education), ENGINEERING AND ENVIRONMENTAL DESIGN (computer engineering, electrical/electronics engineering, engineering, environmental science, industrial engineering, and mechanical engineering), HEALTH PROFESSIONS (predentistry and premedicine), SOCIAL SCIENCE (criminal justice, economics, history, international relations, international studies, Latin American studies, philosophy, political science/government, prelaw, psychology, sociology, and theological studies). Biology, psychology, and exercise and sport science are the strongest academically and have the largest enrollments.

ACTIVITIES: 15% of men belong to 1 local and 4 national fraternities; 13% of women belong to 1 local and 3 national sororities. There are 55 groups on campus, including art, band, cheerleading, choir, chorale, dance, drama, ethnic, honors, international, jazz band, musical theater, newspaper, opera, pep band, photography, political, professional, religious, social, social service, and student government. Popular campus events include Campus Ministry Retreat, Hunger Awareness Week, Fiesta Oyster Bake, President's Peace Commision, and Lin Great Speaker. **Sports:** There are 5 intercollegiate sports for men and 5 for women, and 28 intramural sports for men and 28 for women. Facilities include a gym, a weight room, tennis, handball, basketball courts, a pool, a dance studio, baseball and softball stadium, batting cages, a soccer field, and sports arena. **Graduates:** From July 1, 2016 to June 30, 2017, 504 bachelor's degrees were awarded. The most popular majors were business marketing (20%), biological/life sciences15 (16%), and social science (15%). In an average class, 55% graduate in 6 years or less.

SERVICES: Counseling and information services are available, as is tutoring in most subjects, such as biology, chemistry, physics, psychology, languages, math, writing, accounting, statistics, English, and engineering. There is also remedial math, reading, and writing, biochemistry, organic chemistry, programming, macro/micro economics, philosphy, and electronics. The Learning Assistance Center provides academic support and instructional resources to students. **Library/Resources:** The library contains 222,220 volumes, 367,294 microform items, 5,741 audio/video tapes/CDs/DVDs, and subscribes to 36,954 periodicals, including electronic. Computerized library services include interlibrary loans, database searching, Internet access, and Wi-Fi capability. Special learning facilities include an art gallery, and a natural history museum. the learning assistance center is a learner-oriented service that provides academic support and instructional resources. **Physically Challenged Students:** 80% of the campus is accessible. Facilities include wheelchair ramps, elevators, special parking, specially equipped restrooms, special class scheduling, lowered drinking fountains, and special housing. **Special:** St. Mary's offers cooperative programs and internships in all majors, depending on the student's needs. Students may cross-register at any of the United Colleges of San Antonio, spend a semester in Washington, D.C., or study in England, Austria, or Mexico. Dual majors are possible in computer science and engineering and public justice and sociology, political science, or psychology. Accelerated degree programs are offered in law, (J.D./M.B.A.). Required theology courses may be taken on a pass/fail basis. There are 10 national honor societies, a freshman honors program, and 3 departmental honors programs. **Visiting:** There are regularly scheduled orientations for prospective students, a campus tour, admissions/financial aid session, student only activities, parent only activities, and placement testing. There are guides for informal visits, visitors may sit in on classes, and stay overnight. To schedule a visit, contact the Undergraduate Admissions Office. **Campus Safety and Security:** Measures include 24-hour foot and vehicle patrol, emergency notification system, self-defense education, and security escort services. There are emergency telephones, lighted pathways/sidewalks, controlled access to dorms/residences, and a crime prevention awareness program each semester.

REQUIREMENTS: All applicants must be high school graduates or have the GED, rank in the upper half of their graduating classes, and score in the 50th percentile on SAT I or ACT. Secondary school preparation should include 4 units of English, 3-4 units each of math and social studies, 2-3 units of foreign language, and 1 in academic electives. Potential science and engineering majors should have 4 units of math and 3 of lab science, including chemistry or physics. AP and CLEP credits are accepted. Important factors in the admissions decision are leadership record and advanced placement or honors courses. All students must complete at least 128 semester hours, 24 to 30 in the major, with a minimum 2.0 GPA. Core curriculum requirements include courses in fine arts, English, foreign language, speech, natural science, math, social science, philosophy, and theology. Students must also take computer science, demonstrate computer literacy, and take interdisciplinary electives. 128 hours includes CORE, Major and Minor (if applicable), and elective requirements. 6 advanced writing, intensive courses in major. **Procedure:** Freshmen are admitted in the fall and spring. Entrance exams should be taken by the fall of the senior year. There are early admissions, deferred admissions, and rolling admissions plans. Application deadlines are open. Notification is sent on a rolling basis. Applications are accepted on-line. **Transfer Students:** 116 transfer students enrolled in 2016-2017. Prospective transfer students possessing the aptitude and motivation to succeed at St. Mary's are encouraged to apply for admission. To be considered for admission, a minimum cumulative GPA of 2.5 (on a 4.0 scale) in all academic work attempted and good standing at the college or university last attended are required. Applicants in good standing with the last institution attended and who present a GPA between 2.0 and 2.49 (on a 4.0 scale) may be considered for probationary admission. (Developmental or technical coursework is not considered in the evaluation of the academic GPA.) Possession of the minimum GPA for consideration does not imply admissibility to St. Mary's University. The merits of each application are considered on a case-by-case basis. Academic credits ordinarily will be accepted in transfer from another college if the grade (s) earned is/are at least C (2.0 on a 4.0 scale). The school (s) must be accredited by one of the six regional accrediting associations. 45 of 126 credits required for the bachelor's degree must be completed at St. Mary's. **International Students:** There are 117 international students enrolled. They must take the TOEFL with a minimum score of 550 on the paper-based TOEFL (PBT) or 80 on the Internet-based version (iBT). Students must take the IELTS. They must also take the SAT or ACT.

ADMISSIONS: 80% of the 2017-2018 applicants were accepted. The SAT scores for the 2017-2018 freshman class were: Math-- 13% below 500, 54% between 500 and 599, 29% between 600 and 699, and 4% between 700 and 800. Writing-- 48% below 500, 39% between 500 and 599, 12% between 600 and 699, and 1% between 700 and 800. The ACT scores were 3% between 12 and 17, 56% between 18 and 23, 35% between 24 and 29, and 6% above 30. 7 freshmen graduated first in their class. **Admissions Contact:** Ryan Konkright, Director of Undergraduate Admission. Email: *rkonkright@stmarytx.edu* Web: *www.stmarytx.edu*

FINANCIAL AID: The average freshman award was $25,269. Need-based scholarships or need-based grants averaged $20,303; need-based self-help aid (loans and jobs) averaged $6,829; non-need-based athletic scholarships averaged $14,521; other non-need-based awards and non-need-based scholarships averaged $19,334; and $3,500 from other forms of aid. SMU is a member of CSS. The CSS/Profile is required. The FAFSA code is 003623. The priority date for freshman financial aid applications for fall entry is March 1.

STEPHEN F. AUSTIN STATE UNIVERSITY *(The complete profile is made available exclusively on our website, www.barronspac.com)*

SUL ROSS STATE UNIVERSITY *(The complete profile is made available exclusively on our website, www.barronspac.com)*

TARLETON STATE UNIVERSITY *(The complete profile is made available exclusively on our website, www.barronspac.com)*

TEXAS A&M UNIVERSITY AT COLLEGE STATION D-3

www.tamu.edu

College Station, TX 77843 **(979) 845-3741**

Fax: (979) 847-8737	**Email:** admissions@tamu.edu
Full-time: 23,853 men, 22,433 women	**Faculty:** 3193
Part-time: 3842 men, 2937 women	**Ph.D.s:** 88%
Graduate: 8095 men, 6673 women	**Student/Faculty:** 24 to 1
Year: semesters, summer session	**Tuition:** $10,403 ($37,154)
Room & Board: $10,368	**Freshman Class:** 35854 applied, 24988 accepted, 11063 enrolled
SAT CR/M/W: 617/629/617 **ACT:** 27	**CEEB CODE:** 6003
Application Deadline: December 1	**VERY COMPETITIVE+**

Texas A&M University at College Station, founded in 1876, is part of the Texas A&M University system. Undergraduate degrees are offered in agriculture and life sciences, architecture, business administration, education, engineering, geosciences, liberal arts, science, and biomedical science. There are 15 undergraduate schools and 17 graduate schools. In addition to regional accreditation, TAMU has baccalaureate program accreditation with AACSB, ABET, ACCE, ACEJMC, ADA, ASLA, CSAB, NAAB, CAEP, and SAF. The 11492-acre campus is in an urban area 90 miles northwest of Houston. Including any residence halls, there are 796 buildings.

STUDENT LIFE: 94% of undergraduates are from Texas. Others are from 50 states, 126 foreign countries, and Canada. 8% are Foreign; 7% Asian American; 58% White; 4% African American; 21% Hispanic; 2% two or more races; 1% race unknown. **Male To Female Ratio:** 1.1:1. The average age of freshmen is 18; all undergraduates, 20. 4% do not continue beyond their first year; 46% remain to graduate. **Housing:** 11079 students can be accommodated in college housing, which includes married student dorms, on-campus apartments, and off-campus apartments. In addition, there are honors houses, fraternity houses, and sorority houses. On-campus housing is available on a first-come and first-served basis. 76% of students commute. All students may keep cars.

FACULTY/CLASSROOMS: 63% of faculty are male; 37% are female.

57% teach undergraduates, 55% do research, and 30% do both. Graduate students teach 8% of introductory courses. The average class size in an introductory lecture is 57; in a laboratory is 33; and in a regular course is 40.

PROGRAMS OF STUDY: TAMU confers B.A., B.S., B.B.A., B.Ed., B.L.A., and B.S.N. degrees. Master's and doctoral degrees are also awarded. Bachelor's degrees are awarded in AGRICULTURE (agricultural business management, agricultural communications, agricultural economics, agricultural sciences, agronomy, animal science, food technology for companion animals, horticulture, plant science, poultry science, range/farm management, and wildlife science), BIOLOGICAL SCIENCE (biochemistry, biology/biological science, ecology, entomology, genetics, marine biology, marine science, microbiology, molecular biology, nutrition, and zoology), BUSINESS (accounting, business administration and management, business systems analysis, finance, human resources, management information systems, management science, marketing and distribution, recreational facilities management, and supply chain management), COMMUNICATIONS AND THE ARTS (communications, English, French, German, modern language, music, performing arts, Russian, Spanish, speech/debate/rhetoric, telecommunications, and theatre acting), COMPUTER AND PHYSICAL SCIENCE (applied mathematics, chemistry, computer science, geology, geophysics and seismology, mathematics, and physics), EDUCATION (agricultural education, elementary education, physical education, and secondary education), ENGINEERING AND ENVIRONMENTAL DESIGN (aerospace engineering, bioengineering, biomedical engineering, chemical engineering, civil engineering, computer engineering, electrical/electronics engineering, engineering technology, environmental design, environmental science, geological engineering, industrial engineering technology, landscape architecture, landscape architecture/design, manufacturing technology, marine engineering, marine engineering systems, marine transportation, maritime science, mechanical engineering, nuclear engineering, ocean engineering, petroleum/natural gas engineering, and technological management), HEALTH PROFESSIONS (biomedical science, community health work, dental hygiene, health, nursing, public health, and radiological science), SOCIAL SCIENCE (anthropology, economics, forensic studies, geography, history, international studies, philosophy, political science/government, psychology, sociology, Spanish studies, and urban and regional studies). Biomedical science, business administration, and engineering are the strongest academically, and have the largest enrollments.

ACTIVITIES: 8% of men belong to 2 local and 28 national fraternities. There are 1111 groups on campus, including campus services, community/volunteer service, enthusiasts/special interest, healthy living, military, recreation, spirit and tradition, academic, art, band, cheerleading, chess, choir, chorale, chorus, computers, dance, debate, drill team, drum and bugle corps, environmental, ethnic, film, honors, international, literary magazine, marching band, newspaper, orchestra, photography, political, professional, radio and TV, religious, social, social service, student government, and symphony. Popular campus events include Midnight Yell Practice, Silver Taps, and Muster. **Sports:** There are 8 intercollegiate sports for men and 10 for women, and 11 intramural sports for men and 11 for women. Facilities include a natatorium, handball/racquetball courts, badminton, weight and activity rooms, jogging trails, tennis courts, a squash court, an 18-hole golf course, auditorium/arena, driving range, flag football fields, soccer fields, outdoor basketball courts, and walking trails. Intercollegiate athletic facilities include a football stadium, indoor basketball and volleyball coliseum, a baseball stadium, softball complex, soccer complex, a natatorium, track-and-field complex, tennis center, and physical strength and conditioning lab. **Graduates:** From July 1, 2016 to June 30, 2017, 11169 bachelor's degrees were awarded. The most popular majors were engineering (19%), business/marketing (16%), and agriculture (8%). In an average class, 54% graduate in 4 years or less, 79% graduate in 5 years or less, and 82% graduate in 6 years or less.

SERVICES: Counseling and information services are available, as is tutoring in most subjects. There is a reader service for the blind, and remedial math, reading, and writing. Workshops in time management, basic study techniques, and test-taking skills are also available. **Library/Resources:** The library contains 5.6 million volumes, 6.5 million microform items, 956,695 audio/video tapes/CDs/DVDs, and subscribes to 134,626 periodicals, including electronic. Computerized library services include interlibrary loans, database searching, Internet access, and Wi-Fi capability. Special learning facilities include an art gallery, radio and TV stations, a weather station, an observatory, cyclotron, wind tunnel, visualization lab, nuclear reactor, ocean wave pool, and the Bush Museum and Library. **Physically Challenged Students:** 85% of the campus is accessible. Facilities include wheelchair ramps, elevators, special parking, specially equipped restrooms, special class scheduling, lowered drinking fountains, and lowered telephones. **Special:** The university offers extensive opportunities through the Career Center and Study Abroad Office. B.A.- B.S. degrees, study abroad in 12 countries, internships, a Washington semester, credit for military experience, nondegree study, co-op programs, dual majors, and pass/fail options are available. A 5-year graduate business/liberal arts program is offered, as well as a 3-2 engineering degree with Sam Houston State University. There are 25 national honor societies, including Phi Beta Kappa, and a freshman honors program. **Visiting:** There are regularly scheduled orientations for prospective students. New-student conferences are held for students to meet with academic advisers to select courses, become acquainted with student life activities, and tour the campus. There are guides for informal visits and visitors may sit in on classes. To schedule a visit, contact the Aggieland Visitor Center at (979) 845-5851. **Campus Safety and Security:** Measures include 24-hour foot and vehicle patrol, an emergency notification system, self-defense education, and security escort services. There are shuttle buses, emergency telephones, lighted pathways/sidewalks, a security awareness committee, and crime-watch and safety tip lines.

REQUIREMENTS: The SAT or ACT and the ACT Optional Writing test are required. Secondary school graduation is a condition of freshman admission. Required high school courses include 4 credits in English, 3 1/2 credits in math, 3 credits in science (2 from biology, chemistry, or physics), 2 credits of social studies and the same foreign language, and 1 of history. AP and CLEP credits are accepted. Important factors in the admissions decision are leadership record, evidence of special talent, and extracurricular activities record. To graduate, students must complete at least 128 credit hours, including 30 to 33 in the major. A minimum 2.0 GPA is required. Students must complete a core curriculum of 48 hours in 8 subject areas, including courses in American history and government, phys ed, computers, foreign language, speech and writing skills, math/logical reasoning, science, humanities, and social science. Requirements in the major vary. **Procedure:** Freshmen are admitted in the fall and spring. Entrance exams should be taken during the spring of the junior year or by December of the senior year. There is a rolling admissions plan. Applications should be filed by December 1 for fall entry; October 15 for spring entry. The fall 2017 application fee was $75. Notifications are sent March 31. Applications are accepted online. **Transfer Students:** 12146 transfer students enrolled in 2016-2017. Applicants must submit transcripts from previously attended colleges. Requirements vary, depending on how many semester hours were attempted and the grades for those hours. Transfer applicants must submit high school transcripts and, if they have fewer than 12 graded semester hours, SAT or ACT scores. 30 of 128 credits required for the bachelor's degree must be completed at TAMU. **International Students:** There are 680 international students enrolled. They must take the TOEFL with a minimum score of 600 on the paper-based TOEFL (PBT) or 100 on the Internet-based version (iBT). The SAT or ACT is required for graduates of U.S. high schools only.

ADMISSIONS: 70% of the 2017-2018 applicants were accepted. The SAT scores for the 2017-2018 freshman class were: Critical Reading-- 5% below 500, 32% between 500 and 599, 50% between 600 and 699, and 14% between 700 and 800. Math-- 4% below 500, 30% between 500 and 599, 45% between 600 and 699, and 21% between 700 and 800. Writing-- 26% below 500, 43% between 500 and 599, 26% between 600 and 699, and 5% between 700 and 800. The ACT scores were 1% between 12 and 17, 18% between 18 and 23, 55% between 24 and 29, and 26% above 30. 79% of the current freshmen were in the top fifth of their class; 97% were in the top two fifths. 364 freshmen graduated first in their class. **Admissions Contact:** Admissions Counseling Email: *admissions@tamu.edu* Web: *www.tamu.edu*

FINANCIAL AID: In 2017-2018, 73% of all full-time freshmen received some form of financial aid. 50% of all full-time freshmen received need-based aid. The average freshman award was $7,893. Need-based scholarships or need-based grants averaged $4,707 ($17,000 maximum); need-based self-help aid (loans and jobs) averaged $2,939 ($25,000 maximum); non-need-based athletic scholarships averaged $5,563 ($24,400 maximum); and other non-need-based awards and non-need-based scholarships averaged $5,144 ($41,000 maximum). 21% of undergraduate students work part-time. The average financial indebtedness of the 2017 graduate was $23,063. The FAFSA code is 003632. The priority date for freshman financial aid applications for fall entry is March 15.

TEXAS A&M UNIVERSITY AT COMMERCE D-2

www.tamu.edu

Commerce, TX 75429	(903) 886-5072
Fax: (903) 468-8685	**Email:** admissions@tamuc.edu
Full-time: 1547 men, 2470 women	**Faculty:** 206
Part-time: 438 men, 730 women	**Ph.D.s:** 65%
Graduate: 1416 men, 2420 women	**Student/Faculty:** 19 to 1
Year: semesters, summer session	**Tuition:** $5126 ($13,466)
Room & Board: $5370	**Freshman Class:** n/av
SAT or ACT: required	**CEEB CODE:** 6205
Application Deadline: August 15	**COMPETITIVE**

Texas A&M University at Commerce, founded in 1889, offers undergraduate and graduate programs in business and technology, arts and sciences, and education. There are 3 undergraduate schools and 1 graduate school. In addition to regional accreditation, TAMC has baccalaureate program accreditation with AACSB, CSWE, NASM, and CAEP. The 1883-acre campus is in a small town 65 miles northeast of Dallas. Including any residence halls, there are 121 buildings.

STUDENT LIFE: 97% of undergraduates are from Texas. Others are from 30 states, 21 foreign countries, and Canada. 98% are from public schools. 9% are Hispanic; 65% White; 6% Foreign; 2% Asian American; 17% African American; 1% American Indian/Alaska Native. **Female To Male Ratio:** 1.7:1. The average age of freshmen is 19; all undergraduates, 25. 42% do not continue beyond their first year; 57% remain to graduate. **Housing:** 1910 students can be accommodated in college housing, which includes married student dorms, women's dorms, on-campus apartments, and off-campus apartments. In addition, there are honors houses, special-interest houses, fraternity houses, sorority houses, and theme housing. On-campus housing is guaranteed for the freshman year only, is available on a first-come, and first-served basis. 71% of students commute. All students may keep cars. Alcohol is not permitted.

FACULTY/CLASSROOMS: 53% of faculty are male; 47% are female. 77% teach undergraduates, 46% do research, and 37% do both. Graduate students teach 21% of introductory courses. The average class size in an introductory lecture is 30; in a laboratory is 20; and in a regular course is 25.

PROGRAMS OF STUDY: TAMC confers B.A., B.S., B.A.C.J., B.B.A., B.F.A., B.G.S., B.M., B.M.Ed., B.S.C.J., B.S.Lib.Sci., and B.S.W. degrees. Master's and doctoral degrees are also awarded. Bachelor's degrees are awarded in AGRICULTURE (agricultural economics, agriculture, animal science, and wildlife management), BIOLOGICAL SCIENCE (biology/biological science and botany), BUSINESS (accounting, banking and finance, business administration and management, and marketing/retailing/merchandising), COMMUNICATIONS AND THE ARTS (advertising, broadcasting, dramatic arts, English, fine arts, French, German, journalism, languages, music, photography, printmaking, and Spanish), COMPUTER AND PHYSICAL SCIENCE (chemistry, computer science, earth science, geology, mathematics, and physics), EDUCATION (agricultural education, business education, early childhood education, elementary education, guidance education, health education, industrial arts education, music education, science education, and secondary education), ENGINEERING AND ENVIRONMENTAL DESIGN (engineering technology and preengineering), HEALTH PROFESSIONS (predentistry, premedicine, and prepharmacy), SOCIAL SCIENCE (anthropology, criminal justice, economics, geography, history, political science/government, prelaw, psychology, religion, social work, and sociology). Education, computer science, and business administration are the strongest academically and have the largest enrollments.

ACTIVITIES: 15% of men belong to 9 national fraternities; 12% of women belong to 7 national sororities. There are 96 groups on campus, including art, band, cheerleading, chess, choir, chorale, chorus, dance, drama, ethnic, film, honors, international, jazz band, LGBT, literary magazine, marching band, musical theater, newspaper, orchestra, pep band, photography, political, professional, radio and TV, religious, social, social service, and student government. Popular campus events include Sam Rayburn Symposium, Christmas Feast of Carols, and Spring Fest. **Sports:** There are 5 intercollegiate sports for men and 5 for women, and 7 intramural sports for men. Facilities include an auditorium, a stadium, a gym, handball and racquetball courts, a bowling alley, swimming pool, weight room, tennis courts, a field house, and intramural fields. **Graduates:** From July 1, 2016 to June 30, 2017, 1476 bachelor's degrees were awarded. The most popular majors were interdisciplinary studies (32%), business/marketing (16%), and psychology (5%).

SERVICES: Counseling and information services are available, as is tutoring in some subjects, such as math and writing. There is also remedial math, reading, and writing. **Library/Resources:** The library contains 1.2 million volumes, 1.2 million microform items, and subscribes to 16,222 periodicals including electronic. Computerized library services include interlibrary loans, database searching, Internet access, and Wi-Fi capability. Special learning facilities include a planetarium, radio station, TV station, performing arts center, and a teaching farm. **Physically Challenged Students:** All of the campus is accessible. Facilities include wheelchair ramps, elevators, special parking, and specially equipped restrooms. **Special:** TAMUC offers co-op programs with E-Systems Inc. and numerous other firms, cross-registration by independent arrangement, study abroad in England, and work-study programs. B.A.-B.S. degrees, second degrees, dual majors, a general studies degree, credit for life experience, internships, nondegree study, and pass/fail options are also available. There are 18 national honor societies, a freshman honors program, and 26 departmental honors programs. **Visiting:** There are regularly scheduled orientations for prospective students. There are guides for informal visits and visitors may sit in on classes. To schedule a visit, contact the Admissions Office. **Campus Safety and Security:** Measures include 24-hour foot and vehicle patrol, self-defense education, and security escort services. There are emergency telephones, lighted pathways/sidewalks, a victim assistance officer, a police service for special and social events, crime and date-rape prevention presentations, and motorist assistance.

REQUIREMENTS: The SAT or ACT is required, with a minimum recommended composite score of 800 or 20, respectively. Applicants need not be graduates of an accredited secondary school, although high school graduation is required. The GED is also accepted. AP and CLEP credits are accepted. To graduate, all students must earn a GPA of 2.0 while taking at least 126 semester hours, including 24 hours in the major. Distribution requirements include 24 in culture courses such as American history and foreign languages, 12 each in English composition, math, and speech skills, 8 in sciences, 6 in upper-division courses, and 4 in physical education. **Procedure:** Freshmen are admitted to all sessions. Entrance exams should be taken prior to enrollment. There are deferred admissions and rolling admissions plans. Applications should be filed by August 15 for fall entry. The fall 2017 application fee was $25. Notification is sent on a rolling basis. **Transfer Students:** 1175 transfer students enrolled in 2016-2017. Applicants must have a college GPA of 2.0 with a minimum of 21 credit hours. The SAT or ACT is not required. College transcripts and a statement of good standing from the prior institution are required. 30 of 126 credits required for the bachelor's degree must be completed at TAMUC. **International Students:** There are 61 international students enrolled. They must take the TOEFL, and either the SAT or ACT.

ADMISSIONS: 47% of the 2017-2018 applicants were accepted. The SAT scores for the 2017-2018 freshman class were: 42% of the current freshmen were in the top fifth of their class; 72% were in the top two fifths. **Admissions Contact:** Jody Tod Hunter, Interim Director of Admissions. Email: *admissions@tamuc.edu* Web: *www.tamu.edu*

FINANCIAL AID: The average freshman award was $12,250. Need-based scholarships or need-based grants averaged $10,903; need-based self-help aid (loans and jobs) averaged $3,520; non-need-based athletic scholarships averaged $4,393; other non-need-based awards and non-need-based scholarships averaged $3,459; and $2,145 from other forms of aid. The college's own financial statement is required. The FAFSA code is 003565. The deadline for filing freshman financial aid applications for fall entry is October 1.

TEXAS A&M UNIVERSITY AT CORPUS CHRISTI *(The complete profile is made available exclusively on our website, www.barronspac.com)*

TEXAS A&M UNIVERSITY AT KINGSVILLE *(The complete profile is made available exclusively on our website, www.barronspac.com)*

TEXAS CHRISTIAN UNIVERSITY D-2

www.tcu.edu

Fort Worth, TX 76129	**(817) 257-7490** **(800) TCU-FROG**
Fax: (817) 257-7268	**Email: frogmail@tcu.edu**
Full-time: 3531 men, 5207 women	**Faculty:** I, av$
Part-time: 137 men, 136 women	**Ph.D.s:** 85%
Graduate: 656 men, 822 women	**Student/Faculty:** 14 to 1
Year: semesters, summer session	**Tuition:** $44,760
Room & Board: $12,360	**Freshman Class:** 19740 applied, 8110 accepted, 1955 enrolled
SAT or ACT: required	**CEEB CODE:** 6820
Application Deadline: February 15	**HIGHLY COMPETITIVE**

Texas Christian University, founded in 1873, is a private institution affiliated with the Christian Church (Disciples of Christ), offering undergraduate programs in arts, sciences, business, education, fine arts, communications, nursing, and engineering. There are 8 undergraduate schools and 8 graduate schools. In addition to regional accreditation, TCU has baccalaureate program accreditation with AACSB, ABET, ACEJMC, CSWE, NASAD, NASM, ACS, ASHA, CAATE, CIDA, COA, AACN, ACEND, CCNE, BON, TEA, NAEYC, SACS CASI, UCIEP, NASD, SAIS, TANS, and AAIEP. The 290-acre campus is in a suburban area 5 miles southwest of downtown Fort Worth. Including any residence halls, there are 128 buildings.

STUDENT LIFE: 51% of undergraduates are from Texas. Others are from 49 states, 80 foreign countries, and Canada. 58% are from public schools. 71% are White; 5% African American; 5% Foreign; 3% Asian American; 14% Hispanic; 1% American Indian/Alaska Native; 1% race unknown. 48% are Protestant; 25% Catholic; 20% claim no religious affiliation. **Female To Male Ratio:** 1.4:1. The average age of freshmen is 18; all undergraduates, 20. 9% do not continue beyond their first year; 83% remain to graduate. **Housing:** 4257 students can be accommodated in college housing, which includes single sex dorms, coed dorms, and on-campus apartments. In addition, there are honors houses, language/international houses, fraternity houses, and sorority houses. On-campus housing is available on a lottery system for upperclassmen. 52% of students commute. All students may keep cars.

FACULTY/CLASSROOMS: No introductory courses are taught by graduate students. The average class size in an introductory lecture is 31 and in a laboratory is 20.

PROGRAMS OF STUDY: TCU confers B.A., B.B.A., B.F.A., B.G.S., B.Mus., B.S., B.S.Ed., B.S.N., B.S.W., B.C.J., B.Mus.Ed., B.S.athletic training, and B.C.S. degrees. Master's and doctoral degrees are also awarded. Bachelor's degrees are awarded in BIOLOGICAL SCIENCE (biochemistry, neurosciences, and nutrition), BUSINESS (accounting, business information systems, entrepreneurial studies, finance, international economics, marketing, real estate finance, and supply chain management), COMMUNICATIONS AND THE ARTS (acting, art history, ballet, church music, communication studies, design, English, film, television and digital media, fine/studio arts, general, French language and literature, Germanic languages and literature, graphic design, journalism, modern dance, music, music composition, music theory and composition, musical theater, organ performance, percussion, piano pedagogy, piano performance, printmaking, sculpture, Spanish, strategic communication, strings, studio art ceramics, studio art painting, theatre arts, theater design, theatre production, theatre studies, vocal performance, winds, and writing), COMPUTER AND PHYSICAL SCIENCE (applied climate science, astronomy and physics, chemistry, combined science, computer information technology, computer science, geology, mathematics, mathematics - actuarial concentration, and physics), EDUCATION (art education, athletic training, early childhood education, educational studies, English secondary education, general studies, mathematics education, middle school education, music education, physical education, physical ed teacher education, science education, social science education, social studies education, and social studies secondary school education), ENGINEERING AND ENVIRONMENTAL DESIGN (engineering/mechanical emp/energy system focus, environmental science, interior design, mechanical engineering, textile, and fashion merchandising and design), HEALTH PROFESSIONS (biology, electrical engineering, habilitation of the deaf, health and physical activity, movement science, nursing, speech pathology/audiology, and sports psychology), SOCIAL SCIENCE (anthropology, child psychology/development, criminal justice, dietetics, economics, ethnic studies, food production/management/services, geography, history, interdisciplinary studies, Latin American studies, philosophy, political science/government, psychology, religion, social work, and sociology). General business, nursing, and biology have the largest enrollments.

ACTIVITIES: 41% of men belong to 19 national fraternities; 58% of women belong to 1 local and 21 national sororities. There are 256 groups on campus, including art, band, cheerleading, choir, chorale, chorus, communications, computers, dance, debate, drama, drill team, environmental, ethnic, film, forensics, honors, international, jazz band, LGBT, literary magazine, marching band, musical theater, newspaper, opera, orchestra, pep band, photography, political, professional, radio and TV, religious, social, social service, student government, symphony, and yearbook. Popular campus events include Frog Camp, Frogs First Weekend, Family Weekend, Second Year Pinning, Homecoming, Christmas Tree Lighting, and Carols by Candlelight. **Sports:** There are 8 intercollegiate sports for men and 11 for women, and 19 intramural sports for men and 19 for women. Facilities include a recreation facility that includes a natatorium, outdoor swimming pool, racquetball courts, squash court, track, 2 multi-use gymnasiums sports, weight training, a cardiovascular fitness area, multi-purpose exercise studios, and a climbing wall. **Graduates:** From July 1, 2016 to June 30, 2017, 2099 bachelor's degrees were awarded. The most popular majors were nursing (9%), communication studies (6%), and strategic communication (5%). In an average class, 1% graduate in 3 years or less, 69% graduate in 4 years or less, 82% graduate in 5 years or less, and 83% graduate in 6 years or less. Of the 2016 graduating class, 31% were enrolled in graduate school within 6 months of graduation, and 71% were employed.

SERVICES: **Library/Resources:** The library contains 1.4 million volumes, 511,613 microform items, 70,092 audio/video tapes/CDs/DVDs, and subscribes to 815,971 periodicals, including electronic. Computerized library services include interlibrary loans, database searching, Internet access, and Wi-Fi capability. Special learning facilities include an art gallery, a natural history museum, a radio and TV stations, an observatory, a speech and hearing clinic, energy institute, behavioral research institute, laboratory schools, and various other centers within each college. **Physically Challenged Students:** All of the campus is accessible. Facilities include wheelchair ramps, elevators, special parking, specially equipped restrooms, lowered drinking fountains, and lowered telephones. **Special:** A general studies degree and a combined B.A.-B.S. degree in numerous majors are offered. TCU also accepts credit by exam and credit for life, military, and work experience. Accelerated programs are available in education and nursing. Internships are available in almost all major areas. The university also offers a Washington semester and study abroad in approximately 25 countries. TCU has a student-designed major, Interdisciplinary Inquiry, available on the BA, or BS degree. There are 36 national honor societies, Phi Beta Kappa, and a freshman honors program. **Visiting:** There are regularly scheduled orientations for prospective students, student-led tours, group info sessions, optional personal interviews, and departmental visits. There are guides for informal visits; visitors may sit in on classes and stay overnight. To schedule a visit, contact TCU Admissions Office. **Campus Safety and Security:** Measures include 24-hour foot and vehicle patrol, an emergency notification system, self-defense education, and security escort services. There are shuttle buses, emergency telephones, lighted pathways/sidewalks, controlled access to dorms/residences, bike patrol, and video monitoring of most parking lots.

REQUIREMENTS: The SAT or the ACT is required for admission. Candidates should be graduates of an accredited secondary school and have completed at least 17 Carnegie units, including 4 years of English, 3 years each of math, science, and social studies, and 2 years each of the same foreign language and of academic electives. TCU also requires an essay, a counselor's recommendation and a teacher's recommendation. A personal interview is optional. AP and CLEP credits are accepted. Important factors in the admissions decision are advanced placement or honors courses, leadership record, and extracurricular activities record. TCU requires completion of the TCU Core Curriculum Requirements, which are divided into the Essential Competencies Curriculum (12 hours plus 6 hours Writing Emphasis); Human Experiences and Endeavors Curriculum (27 hours; the Heritage, Mission, Vision and Values Curriculum (18 hours). Courses in the TCU Core Curriculum may overlay with other requirements of the student's degree program. The overlay feature provides the flexibility for core requirement to be satisfied in a range between 39 and 63 hours. At least 124 semester hours of credit (58 of which must be in residence) with a 2.0 GPA, 42 hours of upper division work, at least 30 hours in residence, and a major or concentration. **Procedure:** Freshmen are admitted in the fall, spring, and summer. Entrance exams should be taken during or before the fall semester of the senior year. There are early decision, early admissions, and deferred admissions plans. Early decision applications should be filed by November 1; regular applications, by February 15 for fall entry. The fall 2017 application fee was $50. Notification of early decision is sent December 5; regular decision, April 1. 362 early decision candidates were accepted for the 2017-2018 class. 763 applicants were on the 2017 waiting list; 473 were admitted. Applications are accepted online. **Transfer Students:** 506 transfer students enrolled in 2016-2017. The recommended GPA is 2.7 and a minimum GPA of 2.0 is required. Applicants must complete an application form and submit official transcripts from each college attended. If fewer than 24 semester hours of transferable work have been completed at the time of application, SAT or ACT scores and secondary school transcripts are required. 58 of 124 credits required for the bachelor's degree must be completed at TCU. **International Students:** There are 418 international students enrolled. They must take the TOEFL with a minimum score of 550 on the paper-based TOEFL (PBT) or 80 on the Internet-based version (iBT), or IELTS. The SAT or ACT is required for freshmen whose high school was taught in English or who want to be considered for scholarships.

ADMISSIONS: 41% of the 2017-2018 applicants were accepted. **Admissions Contact:** Heath Einstein, Dean of Admissions. Email: *frogmail@tcu.edu* Web: *www.tcu.edu*

FINANCIAL AID: In 2017-2018, 79% of all full-time freshmen received some form of financial aid. 41% of all full-time freshmen received need-based aid. The average freshman award was $30,725. Need-based scholarships or need-based grants averaged $20,285 ($60,310 maximum); need-based self-help aid (loans and jobs) averaged $2,872 ($9,000 maximum); non-need-based athletic scholarships averaged $42,118 ($78,464 maximum); and other non-need-based awards and non-need-based scholarships averaged $15,965 ($63,066 maximum). 23% of undergraduate students work part-time. The average financial indebtedness of the 2017 graduate was $42,212. TCU is a member of CSS. The CSS/Profile is required. The FAFSA code is 003636. The priority date for freshman financial aid applications for fall entry is February 15.

TEXAS LUTHERAN UNIVERSITY — D-4

www.tlu.edu

Seguin, TX 78155	**(830) 372-8050** **(800) 771-8521**
Fax: (830) 372-8096	**Email: admissions@tlu.edu**
Full-time: 636 men, 662 women	**Faculty:** 83; IIB, -$
Part-time: 23 men, 38 women	**Ph.D.s:** 86%
Graduate: 19 men, 16 women	**Student/Faculty:** 14 to 1
Year: semesters, summer session	**Tuition:** $30,050
Room & Board: $9720	**Freshman Class:** 2250 applied, 1092 accepted, 417 enrolled
SAT EBR-W/M: 530/530 **ACT:** 21	**CEEB CODE:** 6823
Application Deadline: August 1	**COMPETITIVE**

Texas Lutheran University, founded in 1891, is an exclusively undergraduate university of the liberal arts, sciences, and professional studies. The university's mission is to prepare students academically, spiritually, and socially for lives of leadership and service. There is 1 undergraduate school and 1 graduate school. In addition to regional accreditation, TLU has baccalaureate program accreditation with ACBSP, NASM, and CAATE. The 184-acre campus is in a small town 37 miles east of San Antonio and 50 miles south of Austin. Including any residence halls, there are 37 buildings.

STUDENT LIFE: 98% of undergraduates are from Texas. Others are from 13 states, 6 foreign countries, and Canada. 51% are White; 36% Hispanic; 3% race unknown; 10% African American; 1% Asian American. 39% claim no religious affiliation; 30% Protestant; 14% Catholic. **Female To Male Ratio:** 1.1:1. The average age of freshmen is 18; all undergraduates, 21. 28% do not continue beyond their first year; 52% remain to graduate. **Housing:** 896 students can be accommodated in college housing, which includes married student dorms and on-campus apartments. On-campus housing is guaranteed for the freshman year only, and is available on a first-come, first-served basis. 60% of students live on campus. All students may keep cars.

FACULTY/CLASSROOMS: 49% of faculty are male; 51% are female. All teach undergraduates. No introductory courses are taught by graduate students. The average class size in an introductory lecture is 20; in a laboratory is 20; and in a regular course is 12.

PROGRAMS OF STUDY: TLU confers B.A., B.S., B.B.A., B.S.N., and B.M.MAacy, M.S.Business Data Analytics, M.S.Athletic training degrees. Master's degrees are also awarded. Bachelor's degrees are awarded in BIOLOGICAL SCIENCE (biochemistry and biology/biological science), BUSINESS (accounting and business administration and management), COMMUNICATIONS AND THE ARTS (art, communications, dramatic arts, English, music, and Spanish), COMPUTER AND PHYSICAL SCIENCE (applied science, chemistry, computer science, information sciences and systems, mathematics, and physics), EDUCATION (athletic training, education, and physical education), HEALTH PROFESSIONS (nursing), SOCIAL SCIENCE (economics, history, international studies, philosophy, political science/government, psychology, sociology, and theological studies). Business, biology, and psychology are the strongest academically. Business, education, and kinesiology have the largest enrollments.

ACTIVITIES: 7% of men belong to 3 local fraternities; 11% of women belong to 5 local sororities. There are 47 groups on campus, including art, band, cheerleading, choir, chorus, computers, dance, drama, environmental, ethnic, forensics, honors, international, jazz band, LGBT, literary magazine, musical theater, newspaper, orchestra, pep band, political, professional, religious, science club, social, social service, student government, and symphony. Popular campus events include Christmas Vespers, Spring Fling, and Student Academic Symposium. **Sports:** There are 8 intercollegiate sports for men and 8 for women, and 14 intramural sports for men and 14 for women. Facilities include a football and track stadium, a gym, a fitness center, an 8-lane swimming pool, softball, baseball, and soccer fields, intramural/recreation fields, golf practice greens, a lighted walking track, a practice gym, lighted sand volleyball courts, tennis courts, and racquetball courts. **Graduates:** From July 1, 2016 to June 30, 2017, 323 bachelor's degrees were awarded. The most popular majors were business administration (16%), kinesiology (11%), and education (9%). In an average class, 30% graduate in 4 years or less, 49% graduate in 5 years or less, and 52% graduate in 6 years or less.

SERVICES: Counseling and information services are available, as is tutoring in most subjects. There is a reader service for the blind, and assistance with writing assignments. **Library/Resources:** The library contains 385,764 volumes, 117,357 microform items, 5,599 audio/video tapes/CDs/DVDs, and subscribes to 51,974 periodicals, including electronic. Computerized library services include interlibrary loans, database searching, Internet access, and Wi-Fi capability. **Physically Challenged Students:** 90% of the campus is accessible. Facilities include wheelchair ramps, elevators, special parking, specially equipped restrooms, special class scheduling, lowered drinking fountains, and special housing. **Special:** Internships are available in most majors. Study abroad in all countries affiliated with ISEP, Augsburg College, Central College, Equador Exchange, and Kansai Gaidai, a Washington semester with American University, and work-study programs are available. The college offers student-designed majors and dual majors. There is a 3-2 engineering program with Texas A&M, Baylor University, and Southern Methodist University. There are 11 national honor societies, a freshman honors program, and 20 departmental honors programs. **Visiting:** There are regularly scheduled orientations for prospective students, including a campus tour, classroom visits, a financial aid presentation, a study abroad session, an athlete session, and a student panel. There are guides for informal visits, visitors may sit in on classes, and stay overnight. To schedule a visit, contact the Admissions Office. **Campus Safety and Security:** Measures include 24-hour foot and vehicle patrol, self-defense education, and security escort services. There are lighted pathways/sidewalks, and coded locks in residence halls.

REQUIREMENTS: The SAT or ACT is required. Applicants must have 16 Carnegie units, including 4 years in English, 3 each of social studies, math, and science, and 2 in foreign language. The GED is accepted. AP and CLEP credits are accepted. Important factors in the admissions decision are advanced placement or honors courses, recommendations by school officials, and extracurricular activities record. All students must complete 124 semester hours, including 24 to 54 in their major, with a 2.0 GPA. Between 45 and 49 hours of distribution courses are required. A senior seminar, project, or concert is required in all majors. **Proce-**

dure: Freshmen are admitted in the fall, spring, and summer. Entrance exams should be taken in the spring of the junior year or the summer before the senior year. There are early decision and early admissions plans. Early decision applications should be filed by December 15; regular applications, by August 1 for fall entry. Applications are accepted online. **Transfer Students:** 48 transfer students enrolled in 2016-2017. Applicants for transfer must have a GPA of at least 2.25 and be in good academic standing. 33 of 124 credits required for the bachelor's degree must be completed at TLU. **International Students:** There are 7 international students enrolled. They must take the TOEFL with a minimum score of 550 on the paper-based TOEFL (PBT) or 79 on the Internet-based version (iBT). They must also take the SAT or ACT, scoring 960.

ADMISSIONS: 49% of the 2017-2018 applicants were accepted. The SAT scores for the 2017-2018 freshman class were: Math-- 31% below 500, 52% between 500 and 599, 14% between 600 and 699, and 3% between 700 and 800. Evidence-Based Reading/Writing-- 33% below 500, 47% between 500 and 599, 18% between 600 and 699, and 2% between 700 and 800. The ACT scores were 15% between 12 and 17, 58% between 18 and 23, 23% between 24 and 29, and 4% above 30. 34% of the current freshmen were in the top fifth of their class; 66% were in the top two fifths. **Admissions Contact:** Adam Navarro-Jusino, Director of Admissions. Email: *admissions@tlu.edu* Web: *www.tlu.edu*

FINANCIAL AID: In 2017-2018, 99% of all full-time freshmen received some form of financial aid. 57% of all full-time freshmen received need-based aid. The average freshman award was $26,587. Need-based scholarships or need-based grants averaged $22,639; and need-based self-help aid (loans and jobs) averaged $5,286. The average financial indebtedness of the 2017 graduate was $32,437. The state aid form, and the TASFA is required. The FAFSA code is 003641. The priority date for freshman financial aid applications for fall entry is March 1.

TEXAS SOUTHERN UNIVERSITY *(The complete profile is made available exclusively on our website, www.barronspac.com)*

TEXAS STATE UNIVERSITY D-3
www.txstate.edu

San Marcos, TX 78666 **(512) 245-2364**

Fax: (512) 245-8044
Email: admissions@txstate.edu
Full-time: 11,701 men, 16,318 women
Faculty: 1419; IIA, -$
Part-time: 2839 men, 3322 women
Ph.D.s: 78%
Graduate: 1570 men, 2916 women
Student/Faculty: 21 to 1
Year: semesters, summer session
Tuition: $10,621 ($23,071)
Room & Board: $8100
Freshman Class: 24277 applied, 17717 accepted, 5874 enrolled
SAT EBR-W/M: 566/554 **ACT:** 23
CEEB CODE: 6667
Application Deadline: March 1
COMPETITIVE

Texas State University, founded in 1899, is part of the Texas State University System, offering programs in general studies, applied arts, business, education, fine arts, health professions, liberal arts, science, engineering, and technology. TSU offers 98 Bachelor degrees, 91 Master degrees, 12 Doctoral degrees and 1 Special Professional degree. There are 9 undergraduate schools and one graduate school. In addition to regional accreditation, TSU has baccalaureate program accreditation with AACSB, ABET, ACCE, ACEJMC, ADA, AHEA, CSAB, CSWE, FIDER, NASM, NRPA, NAACLS, CAAHEP, and and TEA. The 495-acre campus is in a suburban area 30 miles south of Austin and 45 miles northeast of San Antonio. Including any residence halls, there are 313 buildings.

STUDENT LIFE: 98% of undergraduates are from Texas. Others are from 49 states, 52 foreign countries, and Canada. 98% are from public schools. 46% are White; 4% two or more races; 37% Hispanic; 2% Asian American; 10% African American; 1% Foreign. **Female To Male Ratio:** 1.4:1. The average age of freshmen is 18; all undergraduates, 21. 22% do not continue beyond their first year; 54% remain to graduate. **Housing:** 6940 students can be accommodated in college housing, which includes single-sex dorms, coed dorms, and on-campus apartments. In addition, there are honors houses, special-interest houses, fraternity houses, sorority houses, international housing, upper-division housing, and first-time freshmen experience housing. On-campus housing is guaranteed for the freshman year only, and is available on a first-come, first-served basis. 80% of students commute. All students may keep cars.

FACULTY/CLASSROOMS: 48% of faculty are male; 52% are female. 86% teach undergraduates, 41% do research, and 39% do both. Graduate students teach 8% of introductory courses. The average class size in an introductory lecture is 44; in a laboratory is 20; and in a regular course is 36.

PROGRAMS OF STUDY: TSU confers B.A., B.A.A.S., B.A.I.S., B.B.A., B.E.S.S., B.F.A., B.G.S., B.H.A., B.H.W.P., B.M., B.P.A., B.S., B.S.A.G., B.S.C.D., B.S.C.L.S., B.S.C.J., B.S.F.C.S., B.S.H.I.M., B.S.N, B.S.R.A., B.S.R.C., B.S.R.T., B.S.T., and B.S.W. degrees. Master's and doctoral degrees are also awarded. Bachelor's degrees are awarded in AGRICULTURE (agricultural business management, agriculture, animal science, and aquaculture & fishery technology), BIOLOGICAL SCIENCE (biochemistry, biology/biological science, marine biology, microbiology, nutrition, physiology, wildlife biology, and zoology), BUSINESS (accounting, banking and finance, business administration and management, business economics, fashion merchandising, finance, management, marketing/retailing/merchandising, and recreational facilities management), COMMUNICATIONS AND THE ARTS (advertising, applied art, art, art history and appreciation, audio technology, broadcasting, communication design , communication studies, communications, dance, digital media, dramatic arts, English, French, general art studio, German, jazz, journalism, music, music performance, musical theater, photography, public relations, Spanish, studio art, and theatre arts), COMPUTER AND PHYSICAL SCIENCE (applied mathematics, chemistry, computer information systems, computer science, mathematics, and physics), EDUCATION (athletic training, education, general studies, health education, health information management, physical education, special education, and technical education), ENGINEERING AND ENVIRONMENTAL DESIGN (cartography, city/community/regional planning, construction management, construction technology, electrical/electronics engineering, engineering technology, environmental science, industrial engineering, industrial engineering technology, interior design, land use management and reclamation, manufacturing engineering, manufacturing technology, technological management, urban planning technology, and water and wastewater technology), HEALTH PROFESSIONS (clinical science, exercise science, health and physical activity, health care administration, health promotion, medical records administration/services, nursing, radiation therapy, respiratory therapy, and speech pathology/audiology), SOCIAL SCIENCE (American studies, anthropology, Asian/Oriental studies, child care/child and family studies, communication sciences & disorders, corrections, criminal justice, economics, ethnic studies, European studies, family/consumer studies, geography, geography information science, history, interdisciplinary studies, international relations, international studies, law enforcement and corrections, liberal arts/general studies, Middle Eastern studies, philosophy, political science/government, psychology, public administration, social work, and sociology). Geography, anthropology, education, engineering, and physics are the strongest academically. Education, business, and psychology have the largest enrollments.

ACTIVITIES: 5% of men belong to 6 local and 15 national fraternities; 5% of women belong to 12 national sororities. There are 388 groups on campus, including art, band, cheerleading, chess, choir, chorale, chorus, communications, computers, dance, debate, drama, drill team, ethnic, film, honors, international, jazz band, LGBT, literary magazine, marching band, musical theater, newspaper, opera, orchestra, pep band, photography, political, professional, radio and TV stations, religious, social, social service, student government, symphony, and yearbook. Popular campus events include Unversity Common Experience, Welcome Week, Trade Up Days, Moonlight Breakfast, Philosophy Dialogues Series, Encore Series of Music and Theatrical Performances. **Sports:** There are 5 intercollegiate sports for men and 7 for women, and 10 intramural sports for men and 10 for women. The sport facilities include a gym, baseball, and a softball stadium, tennis courts, a spring-fed pool, and an aquatic sports center. The student recreation center has basketball and volleyball courts, racquetball courts, an indoor jogging/walking track, weight-lifting equipment, exercise machines, and rooms for fitness, dance, and aerobics. Intramural fields include softball, soccer, lacross, and a separate walking/running track. **Graduates:** From July 1, 2016 to June 30, 2017, 7067 bachelor's degrees were awarded. The most popular majors were business/marketing (17%), communication/journalism (9%), and interdisciplinary studies in education (8%). In an average class, 2% graduate in 3 years or less, 27% graduate in 4 years or less, 48% graduate in 5 years or less, and 54% graduate in 6 years or less. Of the

2016 graduating class, 10% were enrolled in graduate school within 6 months of graduation, and 77% were employed.

SERVICES: Counseling and information services are available, as is tutoring in most subjects, such as any core curriculum subjects, and advanced science and mathematics courses. There is a reader service for the blind, and remedial math, reading, and writing. Tutoring is available for all core curriculum classes. **Library/Resources:** The library contains 4.5 million volumes, 1.6 million microform items, and 1.4 million audio/video tapes/CDs/DVDs, and subscribes to 175,660 periodicals including electronic. Computerized library services include interlibrary loans, database searching, Internet access, and Wi-Fi capability. Special learning facilities include an art gallery, a planetarium, a radio station, a recording studio, 17 inch telescope, a clean room for manufacturing micro chips, anthropology forensics laboratory, and special collections library in southwest writing and photography. **Physically Challenged Students:** 90% of the campus is accessible. Facilities include wheelchair ramps, elevators, special parking, specially equipped restrooms, special class scheduling, lowered drinking fountains, lowered telephones, special housing, curb cuts, pay TTY text telephones, adaptive computer technology, sign language interpreter, and reading recorder services for the visually impaired. **Special:** Co-op programs in medicine, dentistry, engineering, architecture, law, pharmacy, nursing, occupational therapy, and veterinary medicine, internships in many departments not exclusive of education and business, study abroad in 26 countries, and Washington semesters are available. Dual majors, credit for life experience, and non-degree study also are possible. Two summer sessions are offered in most programs. A 3-2 engineering degree is possible with the University of Texas, Texas A&M, Texas Tech University, and University of Texas at San Antonio. Texas State also offers 3 engineering majors and a Master's level engineering program. There are 24 national honor societies, a freshman honors program, and 1 departmental honors program. **Visiting:** There are regularly scheduled orientations for prospective students, consisting of a 2-day event; parents may attend with registration, it includes registration instructions, policies and procedures, and student services. There are guides for informal visits and visitors may sit in on classes. To schedule a visit, contact the Admissions Office. **Campus Safety and Security:** Measures include 24-hour foot and vehicle patrol, an emergency notification system, self-defense education, and security escort services. There are shuttle buses, emergency telephones, lighted pathways/sidewalks, and controlled access to dorms/residences.

REQUIREMENTS: The SAT or ACT is required. Minimum test scores are determined by high school class rank. Applicants need 26 academic credits, including 4 units each in English, math, and science (2 with labs), 3 in social studies, 2 in foreign language, 1 in fine arts, and 8 in academic electives. The GED is accepted; applicants with a GED are treated as though they were in the 4th quarter of their graduating class which requires an SAT (math and verbal) of 1270 or and ACT of 29. AP and CLEP credits are accepted. Important factors in the admissions decision are advanced placement or honors courses, leadership record, and extracurricular activities record. All students must earn a minimum GPA of 2.0 while taking at least 120 semester hours, including 30 SCH in their major. The core curriculum includes basic skills, language and communication, mathematics, history and political science, natural science, social science, philosophy, international perspectives, literature, fine arts, and physical fitness. **Procedure:** Freshmen are admitted in the fall, spring, and summer. Entrance exams should be taken at the end of the junior year. There is a rolling admissions plan. Applications should be filed by March 1 for fall entry; November 15 for spring entry; and March 1 for summer entry. The fall 2017 application fee was $75. Notifications are sent September 1. Applications are accepted online. **Transfer Students:** 5215 transfer students enrolled in 2016-2017. Transfer students with 29 or fewer credits must meet freshman requirements; those with 30 or more credits must submit official transcripts to verify a minimum 2.25 GPA and good standing at their previous institution. 30 of 120 credits required for the bachelor's degree must be completed at TSU. **International Students:** There are 160 international students enrolled. They must take the TOEFL with a minimum score of 550 on the paper-based TOEFL (PBT) or 78 on the Internet-based version (iBT). They must also take the SAT or ACT.

ADMISSIONS: 73% of the 2017-2018 applicants were accepted. The SAT scores for the 2017-2018 freshman class were: Math-- 13% below 500, 64% between 500 and 599, 21% between 600 and 699, and 2% between 700 and 800. Writing-- 56% below 500, 36% between 500 and 599, 7% between 600 and 699, and 1% between 700 and 800. Evidence-Based Reading/Writing-- 13% below 500, 56% between 500 and 599, 28% between 600 and 699, and 3% between 700 and 800. The ACT scores were 9% between 12 and 17, 57% between 18 and 23, 31% between 24 and 29, and 3% above 30. 38% of the current freshmen were in the top fifth of their class; 77% were in the top two fifths. 32 freshmen graduated first in their class. **Admissions Contact:** Stephanie Anderson, Assistant Vice President for Enrollment Management. Email: *admissions@txstate.edu* Web: *www.txstate.edu*

FINANCIAL AID: In 2017-2018, 83% of all full-time freshmen received some form of financial aid. 61% of all full-time freshmen received need-based aid. The average freshman award was $8,470. Need-based scholarships or need-based grants averaged $4,567 ($11,260 maximum); need-based self-help aid (loans and jobs) averaged $1,996 ($5,263 maximum); non-need-based athletic scholarships averaged $5,475 ($11,690 maximum); and other non-need-based awards and non-need-based scholarships averaged $2,142 ($15,000 maximum). 56% of undergraduate students work part-time. The average financial indebtedness of the 2017 graduate was $26,568. The FAFSA code is 003615. The priority date for freshman financial aid applications for fall entry is January 15.

TEXAS TECH UNIVERSITY — B-2

www.ttu.edu

Lubbock, TX 79409 — **(806) 742-1480**

Fax: (806) 742-0062	**Email: admissions@ttu.edu**
Full-time: 14,548 men, 12,770 women	**Faculty:** I, --$
Part-time: 1965 men, 1454 women	**Ph.D.s:** n/av
Graduate: 2977 men, 3282 women	**Student/Faculty:** 20 to 1
Year: semesters, summer session	**Tuition:** $10,772 ($23,012)
Room & Board: $9384	**Freshman Class:** 25207 applied, 17438 accepted, 5883 enrolled
SAT EBR-W/M: 580/570 **ACT:** 24	**CEEB CODE:** 6827
Application Deadline: August 1	**COMPETITIVE+**

Texas Tech University, founded in 1923, is a large, comprehensive public university offering undergraduate and graduate programs in a variety of professional fields. There are 11 undergraduate schools and 1 graduate school. In addition to regional accreditation, TTU has baccalaureate program accreditation with AACSB, ABET, CSAB, CSWE, NAAB, NASAD, and NASM. The 1839-acre campus is in an urban area in Lubbock, TX. Including any residence halls, there are 164 buildings.

STUDENT LIFE: 91% of undergraduates are from Texas. 88% are from public schools. 8% are Foreign; 7% African American; 55% White; 25% Hispanic; 2% Asian American; 2% two or more races; 1% race unknown. **Male To Female Ratio:** 1.1:1. The average age of freshmen is 18; all undergraduates, 21. 16% do not continue beyond their first year; 59% remain to graduate. **Housing:** 8186 students can be accommodated in college housing, which includes single-sex dorms, coed dorms and on-campus apartments. In addition, there are honors houses, language/international houses, special-interest houses, living learning communities. On-campus housing is guaranteed for the freshman year only, and is available on a first-come, first-served basis. 74% of students commute. All students may keep cars. Alcohol is not permitted.

FACULTY/CLASSROOMS: 58% of faculty are male; 42% are female. All teach undergraduates. No introductory courses are taught by graduate students. The average class size in an introductory lecture is 48 and in a laboratory is 22.

PROGRAMS OF STUDY: TTU confers B.A., B.A.AS., B.B.A., B.F.A., B.G.S., B.I.D., B.L.A., B.M., B.S., B.S.ARCH., B.S.CE., B.S.CHE., B.S.EE., B.S.ENEGR., B.S.FCS., B.S.IE., B.S.INECO., B.S.ME., B.S.PE., and B.S.RHIM degrees. Master's and doctoral degrees are also awarded. Bachelor's degrees are awarded in AGRICULTURE (agricultural business management, agricultural communications, agricultural economics, agriculture, animal science, conservation and regulation, natural resource management, and plant science), BIOLOGICAL SCIENCE (biochemistry, cell & molecular biology, microbiology, nutrition, and zoology), BUSINESS (accounting, finance, hotel/motel and restaurant management, international business, international economics, management information systems, management, marketing, personal financial planning, resource economy and commerce, retailing, sports management, and supply chain management), COMMUNICATIONS AND THE ARTS (advertising, apparel design, applied art, art, classics, communication studies, dance, digital media, English, French, German, information technology, journalism, journalism - newswriting /edit, languages, literature, media management, music, public relations, Spanish, technical communication, television and digital media production, theatre arts, and winds), COMPUTER AND PHYSICAL SCIENCE (chemistry, computer science, geoscience, mathematics, and physics), EDUCATION (early childhood education, general studies, global studies, and university studies), ENGINEERING AND ENVIRONMENTAL DESIGN (architecture, chemical engineering, civil engineering, computer engineering, construction engineering, environmental engineering, industrial engineering, interior design, landscape architecture, mechanical engineering, and petroleum/natural gas engineering), HEALTH PROFESSIONS (biology, electrical engineering, human studies, kinesiology, multidisciplinary studies, and nutrition and dietetics), SOCIAL SCIENCE (addiction studies, anthropology, child care/ child and family studies, economics, family/consumer studies, food science, geography, history, human development & family studies, liberal arts/general studies, philosophy, political science/government, psychology, Russian and Slavic studies, social work, and sociology). Business, agriculture, wind energy, personal financial planning are the strongest academically. Kinesiology, biology, and psychology have the largest enrollments.

ACTIVITIES: 5% of men belong to 34 national fraternities; 8% of women belong to 23 national sororities. There are 579 groups on campus, including art, band, cheerleading, chess, choir, chorale, chorus, communications, computers, dance, debate, drama, drill team, environmental, ethnic, film, forensics, honors, international, jazz band, LGBT, literary magazine, marching band, musical theater, newspaper, opera, orchestra, pep band, photography, political, professional, radio and TV, religious, social, social service, student government, symphony, and yearbook. Popular campus events include Carol of Lights, Homecoming Week, Arbor Day, RaiderGate, Diversity Week, and Tech to Town. **Sports:** There are 8 intercollegiate sports for men and 9 for women, and 12 intramural sports for men and 11 for women. The student recreation center is equipped for basketball courts, a rock wall, a free-weight room, workout space, tennis courts, a turf field complex, a bike shop/rental program, indoor aquatic center, and outdoor leisure pool, lap pool, diving well, water basketball, volleyball courts, and an athletic training center. **Graduates:** From July 1, 2016 to June 30, 2017, 5574 bachelor's degrees were awarded. The most popular majors were kinesiology (5%), multidisciplinary studies (5%), and marketing (4%). In an average class, 3% graduate in 3 years or less, 36% graduate in 4 years or less, 55% graduate in 5 years or less, and 59% graduate in 6 years or less.

SERVICES: Counseling and information services are available, as is tutoring in some subjects, such as accounting, biology, chemistry, computer science, economics, engineering, English, foreign language, history, math, physics, political science, and statistics. There is a reader service for the blind, and remedial math, reading, and writing. The Learning Center offers academic coaching on topics such as time management, note taking, stress management, computer lab, and study area and class presentations. The Student Disability Services office provides in-class accommodations based on the documented needs of each student. **Library/Resources:** The library contains 2.9 million volumes, 2.5 million microform items, 92,298 audio/video tapes/CDs/DVDs, and subscribes to 155,098 periodicals, including electronic. Computerized library services include interlibrary loans, database searching, Internet access, and Wi-Fi capability. Special learning facilities include an art gallery, a natural history museum, a planetarium, radio and TV stations, a museum, an observatory, a national ranching heritage center, special collections library, archaeological dig/state park, international cultural center, fiber and biopolymer research institute, arid and semi-arid land studies center, child development research center, institutes for environmental and human health, the Vietnam center, planetarium, National Wind Institute, Burkhart Center for Autism Education and Research, and an innovation hub. **Physically Challenged Students:** All of the campus is accessible. Facilities include wheelchair ramps, elevators, special parking, specially equipped restrooms, special class scheduling, lowered drinking fountains, lowered telephones, and special housing. **Special:** TTU offers many bachelor-to-masters accelerated degree programs, internships, study abroad in over 70 countries, dual degrees, dual majors, extended studies, and pass/fail options. We also offer in accelerated program, cooperative education, independent study, and student design program. There are 31 national honor societies, Phi Beta Kappa, and a freshman honors program. **Visiting:** There are regularly scheduled orientations for prospective students, including summer orientation conferences offering new students an opportunity to meet with advisers, register early for the fall semester, and get acquainted with the campus. There are guides for informal visits and visitors may sit in on classes. To schedule a visit, contact Visitor Center at (806) 742-1299. **Campus Safety and Security:** Measures include 24-hour foot and vehicle patrol and an emergency notification system. There are shuttle buses, emergency telephones, lighted pathways/sidewalks, controlled access to dorms/residences, crime prevention programs, Operation ID, and bike registration.

REQUIREMENTS: The SAT or ACT is required. Applicants should be graduates of an accredited high school or have the GED. The university requires 4 credits in English, 3-4 in math, science with laboratory sciences, and 2 in foreign language, 3-3.5 in social studies and history, 5-6 in academic electives, 1 each in visual performing art, and physical education, recommended .5 in speech and economics. AP and CLEP credits are accepted. Important factors in the admissions decision are advanced placement or honors courses, recommendations by school officials, and extracurricular activities record. All students seeking a bachelor's degree must meet the requirements of the core curriculum. A minimum of 120 credits hours is required, depending on the degree program. A minimum GPA of 2.0 is required. The last 30 hours and 25% of all credit hours must be from TTU. **Procedure:** Freshmen are admitted in the fall, spring, and summer. Entrance exams should be taken before registering for classes. Applications should be filed by August 1 for fall entry; November 1 for spring entry; and May 1 for summer entry. The fall 2017 application fee was $75. Notification is sent on a rolling basis. Applications are accepted online. **Transfer Students:** 2623 transfer students enrolled in 2016-2017. If a student has any transferable credits earned after high school graduation, then they must apply as a transfer student. Twelve credit hours are required to be considered a full transfer, and if a student has fewer than twelve transferable credit hours, then they are evaluated by both high school and college coursework for admission. A transfer student is considered assured admit if they have a 2.5 GPA with 12-23 hours, or if they have a 2.25 GPA with 24+ hours. 30 of 120 credits required for the bachelor's degree must be completed at TTU. **International Students:** There are 836 international students enrolled. They must take the TOEFL with a minimum score of 550 on the paper-based TOEFL (PBT) or 79 on the Internet-based version (iBT), and any one of these tests: the IELTS, Cambridge Exam, PTE Academic, and ELS Intensive Program. They must also take the SAT or ACT, scoring 1270.

ADMISSIONS: 69% of the 2017-2018 applicants were accepted. The SAT scores for the 2017-2018 freshman class were: Math-- 7% below 500, 56% between 500 and 599, 32% between 600 and 699, and 5% between 700 and 800. Evidence-Based Reading/Writing-- 7% below 500, 55% between 500 and 599, 34% between 600 and 699, and 4% between 700 and 800. The ACT scores were 1% between 12 and 17, 44% between 18 and 23, 46% between 24 and 29, and 9% above 30. 39% of the current freshmen were in the top fifth of their class; 77% were in the top two fifths. 134 freshmen graduated first in their class. **Admissions Contact:** Jamie Hansard, Executive Director/Undergraduate Admissions. Email: *admissions@ttu.edu* Web: *www.ttu.edu*

FINANCIAL AID: The FAFSA code is 003644. The priority date for freshman financial aid applications for fall entry is March 15.

TEXAS WESLEYAN UNIVERSITY D-2

www.txwes.edu

Fort Worth, TX 76105	**(817) 531-4422** **(800) 580-8980**
Fax: (817) 531-7515	**Email: admissions@txwes.edu**
Full-time: 725 men, 772 women	**Faculty:** 123; IIA, av$
Part-time: 75 men, 102 women	**Ph.D.s:** 89%
Graduate: 264 men, 495 women	**Student/Faculty:** 13 to 1
Year: semesters, summer session	**Tuition:** $27,800
Room & Board: $9538	**Freshman Class:** 4097 applied, 1404 accepted, 306 enrolled
SAT CR/M/W: 510/527/533 **ACT:** 23	**CEEB CODE:** 6828
Application Deadline: open	**COMPETITIVE**

Texas Wesleyan University, founded in 1890, is a liberal arts institution affiliated with the United Methodist Church. There are 4 undergraduate schools and 3 graduate schools. In addition to regional accreditation, TWU has baccalaureate program accreditation with AACSB, ACBSP,

NASM, and CAATE. The 79-acre campus is in an urban area 2 miles east of downtown Fort Worth. Including any residence halls, there are 38 buildings.

STUDENT LIFE: 82% of undergraduates are from Texas. Others are from 25 states, 45 foreign countries, and Canada. 88% are from public schools. 39% are White; 26% Hispanic; 17% African American; 10% Foreign; 8% Asian American; 3% two or more races; 3% race unknown; 1% American Indian/Alaska Native. 44% claim no religious affiliation; 41% Protestant; 12% Catholic. **Female To Male Ratio:** 1.3:1. The average age of freshmen is 19; all undergraduates, 26. 43% do not continue beyond their first year; 36% remain to graduate. **Housing:** 541 students can be accommodated in college housing, which includes dorms and on-campus apartments. On-campus housing is available on a first-come, first-served basis. 68% of students commute. Alcohol is not permitted. All students may keep cars.

FACULTY/CLASSROOMS: 43% of faculty are male; 57% are female. 86% teach undergraduates. No introductory courses are taught by graduate students. The average class size in an introductory lecture is 16 and in a laboratory is 12.

PROGRAMS OF STUDY: TWU confers B.A., B.A.A.S., B.B.A., B.M., B.S., B.S.A.T., and B.S.H.S. degrees. Master's and doctoral degrees are also awarded. Bachelor's degrees are awarded in BIOLOGICAL SCIENCE (biochemistry, biology/adolescence education, and biology/biological science), BUSINESS (accounting, business administration and management, business economics, marketing management, and marketing/retailing/merchandising), COMMUNICATIONS AND THE ARTS (dramatic arts, English, journalism, music, Spanish, and theater design), COMPUTER AND PHYSICAL SCIENCE (chemistry and computer science), EDUCATION (athletic training, education, elementary education, foreign languages education, mathematics education, physical education, social science education, social studies education, and teaching English as a second/foreign language (TESOL/TEFOL)), HEALTH PROFESSIONS (biology, biomedical science, and exercise science), SOCIAL SCIENCE (criminal justice, history, industrial and organizational psychology, interdisciplinary studies, paralegal studies, political science/government, prelaw, psychology, religion, religious education, and sociology). General business, criminal justice, and liberal studies have the largest enrollments.

ACTIVITIES: 5% of men belong to 1 local and 3 national fraternities; 4% of women belong to 1 local and 2 national sororities. There are 34 groups on campus, including art, band, cheerleading, choir, chorale, computers, dance, drama, ethnic, forensics, honors, international, jazz band, LGBT, literary magazine, musical theater, newspaper, opera, political, professional, radio and TV, religious, social, social service, and student government. Popular campus events include We Are Wesleyan Concert, RAM JAM, and University College Day. **Sports:** There are 9 intercollegiate sports for men and 10 for women, and 7 intramural sports for men and 7 for women. Facilities include on-campus am athletic center, and tennis courts. Off-campus is baseball park, softball and soccer fields. **Graduates:** From July 1, 2016 to June 30, 2017, 307 bachelor's degrees were awarded. The most popular majors were general business (11%), management (9%), and finance (8%). In an average class, 1% graduate in 3 years or less, 19% graduate in 4 years or less, 32% graduate in 5 years or less, and 35% graduate in 6 years or less. Of the 2016 graduating class, 5% were enrolled in graduate school within 6 months of graduation, and 87% were employed.

SERVICES: Counseling and information services are available, as is tutoring in most subjects. There is remedial math, reading, and writing. **Library/Resources:** The library contains 175,506 volumes, 170 microform items, 6,720 audio/video tapes/CDs/DVDs, and subscribes to 1,499 periodicals, including electronic. Computerized library services include interlibrary loans, database searching, Internet access, and Wi-Fi capability. Special learning facilities include an art gallery, a radio station, and a theater. **Physically Challenged Students:** Facilities include wheelchair ramps, elevators, special parking, specially equipped restrooms, special class scheduling, and lowered telephones. **Special:** Study abroad is offered in more than 25 countries. A 3-2 engineering degree is offered in conjunction with a number of universities. Pass/fail options are available, as are B.A.-B.S. degrees and internships in sports management, business, psychology, mass communication, and sociology. A predentistry program is available. There are 15 national honor societies and 10 departmental honors programs. **Visiting:** There are regularly scheduled orientations for prospective students. There are guides for informal visits; visitors may sit in on classes and stay overnight. To schedule a visit, contact the Office of Admissions. **Campus Safety and Security:** Measures include 24-hour foot and vehicle patrol, an emergency notification system, self-defense education, and security escort services. There are emergency telephones, lighted pathways/sidewalks, controlled access to dorms/residences, and residence hall programs.

REQUIREMENTS: Applicants must be graduates of an accredited secondary school or have a GED equivalent, with satisfactory scores of 19 ACT composite score or 920 SAT combined score in critical reading and math only. AP and CLEP credits are accepted. Important factors in the admissions decision are leadership record, extracurricular activities record, and recommendations by alumni. A minimum GPA of 2.0 and a minimum of 124 credit hours are required to graduate. All students must complete a general education requirement of 51 credits, including courses in writing, literature, religion, lab science, history, math, political or economic systems, fine arts, humanities, physical education, and social science, philosophy, or psychology. The total number of hours in the major varies. **Procedure:** Freshmen are admitted to all sessions. Entrance exams should be taken as early as possible. There is a rolling admissions plan. Application deadlines are open. Applications are accepted online. **Transfer Students:** 299 transfer students enrolled in 2016-2017. Applicants with fewer than 30 credit hours must submit a high school transcript and the results of either the SAT or the ACT. A minimum GPA of 2.0 is required. 45 of 124 credits required for the bachelor's degree must be completed at Texas Wesleyan. **International Students:** There are 195 international students enrolled. They must take the TOEFL with a minimum score of 520 on the paper-based TOEFL (PBT) or 68 on the Internet-based version (iBT). Students must take the IELTS and score at least 6.0. The score must be less than 2 years old.

ADMISSIONS: 34% of the 2017-2018 applicants were accepted. The SAT scores for the 2017-2018 freshman class were: Critical Reading-- 37% below 500, 55% between 500 and 599, 7% between 600 and 699, and 1% between 700 and 800. Math-- 43% below 500, 50% between 500 and 599, and 7% between 600 and 699. Writing-- 66% below 500, 25% between 500 and 599, 6% between 600 and 699, and 3% between 700 and 800. The ACT scores were 3% between 12 and 17, 61% between 18 and 23, 30% between 24 and 29, and 6% above 30. 26% of the current freshmen were in the top fifth of their class; 58% were in the top two fifths. **Admissions Contact:** Djuana Young, Associate Vice President for Enrollment. Email: *admissions@txwes.edu* Web: *www.txwes.edu*

FINANCIAL AID: In 2017-2018, 80% of all full-time freshmen received some form of financial aid. 74% of all full-time freshmen received need-based aid. The average freshman award was $21,000. Need-based scholarships or need-based grants averaged $20,526; need-based self-help aid (loans and jobs) averaged $3,931; non-need-based athletic scholarships averaged $10,561; and other non-need-based awards and non-need-based scholarships averaged $11,954. 12% of undergraduate students work part-time. The average financial indebtedness of the 2017 graduate was $33,233. The college's own financial statement is required. The FAFSA code is 003645. The deadline for filing freshman financial aid applications for fall entry is March 1.

TEXAS WOMAN'S UNIVERSITY *(The complete profile is made available exclusively on our website, www.barronspac.com)*

THE UNIVERSITY OF TEXAS AT AUSTIN D-3

www.utexas.edu

Austin, TX 78712 **(512) 471-3833**

Fax: (512) 471-8950 **Email: admissions@austin.texas.edu**

Full-time: 17,325 men, 19,701 women	**Faculty:** 2599
Part-time: 1488 men, 1162 women	**Ph.D.s:** 75%
Graduate: 5835 men, 5327 women	**Student/Faculty:** 18 to 1
Year: semesters, summer session	**Tuition:** $10,136 ($35,766)
Room & Board: $10,070	**Freshman Class:** 47511 applied, 19182 accepted, 8719 enrolled
SAT: required **ACT:** 29	**CEEB CODE:** 6882
Application Deadline: December 1	**MOST COMPETITIVE**

The University of Texas at Austin, founded in 1883, is a major research institution within the University of Texas System that provides a broad range of degree programs. There are 18 undergraduate schools and 15 graduate schools. In addition to regional accreditation, UTA has baccalaureate program accreditation with AACSB, ABET, ACEJMC, ACPE, ADA, CSWE, FIDER, NAAB, NASAD, and NASM. The 431-acre campus is in an urban area near downtown Austin, just off the interstate. Including any residence halls, there are 120 buildings.

STUDENT LIFE: 92% of undergraduates are from Texas. Others are from 50 states, 127 foreign countries, and Canada. 5% are Foreign; 43% White; 4% African American; 4% two or more races; 23% Hispanic; 21% Asian American. 11% are Unknown denomination. **Female To Male Ratio:** 1.1:1. The average age of freshmen is 18; all undergraduates, 20. 7% do not continue beyond their first year; 93% remain to graduate. **Housing:** 6815 students can be accommodated in college housing, which includes married student dorms and off-campus apartments. In addition, there are honors houses, language/international houses, and the living learning centers are for first-time freshmen students. On-campus housing is available on a first-come and first-served basis. 61% of students live on campus. All students may keep cars.

FACULTY/CLASSROOMS: 51% of faculty are male; 40% are female. All teach undergraduates, and all do research. No introductory courses are taught by graduate students.

PROGRAMS OF STUDY: UTA confers B.A., B.S., B.Arch., B.B.A., B.F.A., B.M., B.J., and B.S.W. degrees. Master's and doctoral degrees are also awarded. Bachelor's degrees are awarded in BIOLOGICAL SCIENCE (biochemistry, biology/biological science, microbiology, molecular biology, and nutrition), BUSINESS (accounting, banking and finance, business administration and management, management information systems, management science, and marketing management), COMMUNICATIONS AND THE ARTS (advertising, applied music, Arabic, art history and appreciation, classics, creative writing, dance, design, dramatic arts, English, film arts, French, German, Greek, Hebrew, Italian, journalism, Latin, linguistics, music, music theory and composition, Portuguese, public relations, Russian, Scandinavian languages, Slavic languages, Spanish, speech/debate/rhetoric, studio art, and visual and performing arts), COMPUTER AND PHYSICAL SCIENCE (astronomy, chemistry, computer science, geology, geophysics and seismology, mathematics, and physics), ENGINEERING AND ENVIRONMENTAL DESIGN (aerospace studies, architectural engineering, architecture, biomedical engineering, chemical engineering, civil engineering, electrical/electronics engineering, geophysical engineering, interior design, landscape architecture/design, mechanical engineering, and petroleum/natural gas engineering), HEALTH PROFESSIONS (medical technology, nursing, pharmacy, and speech pathology/audiology), SOCIAL SCIENCE (American studies, anthropology, archeology, Asian/Oriental studies, child care/child and family studies, classical/ancient civilization, dietetics, Eastern European studies, economics, ethnic studies, geography, history, human ecology, humanities, Islamic studies, Judaic studies, Latin American studies, liberal arts/general studies, Middle Eastern studies, philosophy, physical fitness/movement, political science/government, psychology, religion, Russian and Slavic studies, social work, sociology, textiles and clothing, and urban studies). Biological sciences, electrical and computer engineering, and government have the largest enrollments.

ACTIVITIES: 13% of men belong to 27 national fraternities; 16% of women belong to 23 national sororities. There are 100 groups on campus, including art, band, cheerleading, chess, choir, chorale, chorus, computers, dance, drama, ethnic, film, forensics, honors, international, LGBT, literary magazine, marching band, musical theater, newspaper, orchestra, photography, political, professional, radio and TV, religious, social, social service, student government, symphony, and yearbook. Popular campus events include Gone to Texas (welcome for new students), Cinco de Mayo, and Texas Revue (talent show). **Sports:** There are 8 intercollegiate sports for men and 10 for women, and 45 intramural sports for men and 45 for women. Facilities include a football stadium, basketball, volleyball, baseball, Olympic swimming pool, multipurpose indoor recreational/athletic, racquetball, weight training, outdoor facilities tennis, racquetball, softball stadium, a track, and soccer stadium. **Graduates:** From July 1, 2016 to June 30, 2017, 10165 bachelor's degrees were awarded. The most popular majors were social sciences (12%), business/marketing (12%), and education (12%). In an average class, 55% graduate in 4 years or less, 76% graduate in 5 years or less, and 81% graduate in 6 years or less.

SERVICES: Counseling and information services are available, as is tutoring in most subjects. There is a reader service for the blind, and remedial math, reading, and writing. **Library/Resources:** The library contains 10.2 million volumes, 6.7 million microform items, 14.1 million audio/video tapes/CDs/DVDs, and subscribes to 103,589 periodicals, including electronic. Computerized library services include interlibrary loans, database searching, Internet access, and Wi-Fi capability. Special learning facilities include an art gallery, a natural history museum, radio and TV stations, an observatory, marine science institute, fusion reactor, the Lyndon Baines Johnson Library and Museum, and the Texas Memorial Museum collection. **Physically Challenged Students:** 98% of the campus is accessible. Facilities include wheelchair ramps, elevators, special parking, specially equipped restrooms, lowered drinking fountains, lowered telephones, special housing, specially equipped reading rooms, a speech and hearing center, academic accommodations specific to the student's disability, and interpreters for the hearing impaired. **Special:** Cooperative programs are available in most engineering courses, microbiology, chemistry, computer science, geology, and actuarial studies. Cross-registration is provided in pharmacy with the University of Texas at San Antonio. Internships, study abroad, B.A.-B.S. degrees, dual majors, student-designed majors for humanities students, and pass/fail options are offered. There are approximate 450 study abroad programs, and 78 countries where study abroad is offered. There are 45 national honor societies, Phi Beta Kappa, a freshman honors program, and 50 departmental honors programs. **Visiting:** There are regularly scheduled orientations for prospective students. There are guides for informal visits and visitors may sit in on classes. To schedule a visit, contact the Office of Admissions. **Campus Safety and Security:** Measures include 24-hour foot and vehicle patrol, self-defense education, and security escort services. There are shuttle buses, emergency telephones, lighted pathways/sidewalks, There is also a crime prevention unit and closed-circuit TV covering some parking areas and offices.

REQUIREMENTS: All students graduating in the top 10% of their class from an accredited Texas high school are eligible for admission. Applicants not meeting that requirement are reviewed based on SAT or ACT scores, class rank, writing samples, and related factors; consideration may be given to socioeconomic and geographic information. In addition, applicants need 26 academic credits, 4 each in English, math, science and social studies, 2 in foreign language, and 6 in electives. An audition is required for applied music majors. The GED is accepted, with supportive information. Home-schooled students are required to submit the results of either the SAT: Subject tests or AP exams in English, math, and a third subject of the student's choosing. AP and CLEP credits are accepted. Important factors in the admissions decision are leadership record, evidence of special talent, extracurricular activities record, and geographical diversity. All students must maintain a GPA of 2.0 while satisfactorily completing 120 to 167 semester hours. Distribution requirements include 6 hours each in American government, American history, natural science, and courses containing a substantial writing component (with at least 3 hours being upper-division), 3 hours each in math, social science, English composition, literature, and humanities/fine arts, plus 3 additional hours in either math, natural science, computer science, or social science, and a fourth semester proficiency in a single foreign language. **Procedure:** Freshmen are admitted in the fall, spring, and summer. Entrance exams should be taken in the junior year or early in the senior year. There are deferred admissions and rolling admissions plans. Applications should be filed by December 1 for fall entry; October 1 for spring entry; and February 1 for summer entry. The fall 2017 application fee was $75. 1007 applicants were on the 2017 waiting list; 374 were admitted. Applications are accepted on-line. **Transfer Students:** 2511 transfer students enrolled in 2016-2017. Applicants must have at least 24 transferable hours (30 for business). Students may apply in the fall (March 1), spring (October 1), and summer (March 1) which are closing dates. 60 of 120 credits required for the bachelor's degree must be completed at UTA. **International Students:** There are 1189 international students enrolled. They must take the TOEFL with a minimum score of 550 on the paper-based TOEFL (PBT) or 79 on the Internet-based version (iBT). They must also take the SAT or ACT.

ADMISSIONS: 40% of the 2017-2018 applicants were accepted. The ACT scores were 1% between 12 and 17, 11% between 18 and 23, 37% between 24 and 29, and 51% above 30. 88% of the current freshmen were in the top fifth of their class; 98% were in the top two fifths. **Admissions Contact:** Susan L. Kearns, Director of Undergraduate Admission. Email: *admissions@austin.texas.edu* Web: *www.utexas.edu*

FINANCIAL AID: In 2017-2018, 68% of all full-time freshmen received

some form of financial aid. 70% of all full-time freshmen received need-based aid. The average freshman award was $11,349. Need-based scholarships or need-based grants averaged $9,642; need-based self-help aid (loans and jobs) averaged $3,593; non-need-based athletic scholarships averaged $6,836; other non-need-based awards and non-need-based scholarships averaged $3,406; and $2,208 from other forms of aid. The average financial indebtedness of the 2017 graduate was $19,848. UTA is a member of CSS. The college's own financial statement is required. The FAFSA code is 003658. The priority date for freshman financial aid applications for fall entry is March 31.

THE UNIVERSITY OF TEXAS AT SAN ANTONIO D-4

www.utsa.edu

San Antonio, TX 78249	(210) 458-4536 (800) 669-0919
Fax: (210) 458-7857	**Email:** onestop@utsa.edu
Full-time: 9781 men, 10,214 women	**Faculty:** 784; I, --$
Part-time: 2213 men, 1828 women	**Ph.D.s:** 74%
Graduate: 1837 men, 2296 women	**Student/Faculty:** 23 to 1
Year: semesters, summer session	**Tuition:** $9380 ($20,634)
Room & Board: $11,680	**Freshman Class:** 15500 applied, 11843 accepted, 4378 enrolled
SAT CR/M/W: 505/520/480 **ACT:** 23	**CEEB CODE:** 6919
Application Deadline: June 1	**COMPETITIVE**

The University of Texas at San Antonio, founded in 1969, is dedicated to the advancement of knowledge through research and discovery, teaching and learning, community engagement, and public service. As an institution of access and excellence, UTSA embraces multicultural traditions, and serves as a center for intellectual and creative resources as well as a catalyst for socioeconomic development and the commercialization of intellectual property for Texas, the nation, and the world. There are 9 undergraduate schools and 7 graduate schools. In addition to regional accreditation, UTSA has baccalaureate program accreditation with AACSB, ABET, NASAD, NASM, NASPAA, CIDA, and ACS. The 725-acre campus is in a suburban area approximately 18 miles northwest of downtown San Antonio. Including any residence halls, there are 121 buildings.

STUDENT LIFE: 98% of undergraduates are from Texas. Others are from 50 states, 96 foreign countries, and Canada. 9% are African American; 54% Hispanic; 5% Asian American; 3% two or more races; 24% White; 2% Foreign. **Female To Male Ratio:** 1.0:1. The average age of freshmen is 18; all undergraduates, 22. 37% do not continue beyond their first year; 34% remain to graduate. **Housing:** 4298 students can be accommodated in college housing, which includes dorms, on-campus apartments, and theme housing. On-campus housing is available on a first-come, first-served basis. 59% of students commute. All students may keep cars.

FACULTY/CLASSROOMS: 58% of faculty are male; 42% are female. 81% teach undergraduates. Graduate students teach 13% of introductory courses. The average class size in an introductory lecture is 55 and in a laboratory is 21.

PROGRAMS OF STUDY: UTSA confers B.A., B.S., B.A.A.S., B.B.A., B.F.A., B.M., B.S.C.E., B.S.E.E., B.P.A., and B.S.M.E. degrees. Master's and doctoral degrees are also awarded. Bachelor's degrees are awarded in BIOLOGICAL SCIENCE (biochemistry and biology/biological science), BUSINESS (accounting, business administration and management, business statistics, finance, human resources, management science, and marketing management), COMMUNICATIONS AND THE ARTS (art, art history and appreciation, classics, communications, English, modern language, music, and Spanish), COMPUTER AND PHYSICAL SCIENCE (actuarial science, actuarial mathematics, chemistry, computer science, computer security and information assurance, geology, information sciences and systems, mathematics, physics, and statistics), EDUCATION (childhood education, early childhood education, and education), ENGINEERING AND ENVIRONMENTAL DESIGN (architecture, biomedical engineering, civil engineering, computer engineering, construction management, electrical/electronics engineering, engineering, environmental science, interior design, and mechanical engineering), HEALTH PROFESSIONS (health), SOCIAL SCIENCE (American studies, anthropology, child care/child and family studies, criminal justice, economics, geography, history, humanities, interdisciplinary studies, Mexican-American/Chicano studies, philosophy, philosophy and religion, political science/government, public administration, sociology, and women's studies). Honors college, business, and engineering are the strongest academically. Business, biology, and psychology have the largest enrollments.

ACTIVITIES: 4% of men belong to 12 national fraternities; 6% of women belong to 10 national sororities. There are 217 groups on campus, including art, band, cheerleading, chess, choir, chorale, chorus, computers, dance, debate, drama, environmental, ethnic, film, forensics, honors, international, jazz band, LGBT, marching band, newspaper, orchestra, pep band, political, professional, religious, social, social service, student government, and symphony. Popular campus events include Fiesta UTSA, Best Fest, and the Rowdy Rampage Fireworks Spectacular. **Sports:** There are 7 intercollegiate sports for men and 8 for women, and 26 intramural sports for men and 26 for women. Facilities include numerous gyms, basketball, volleyball, badminton, indoor soccer, inline hockey, weight rooms, a 400-meter track, a tennis center, a cardio room, dance studios, racquetball courts, wallyball courts, a rock wall, an indoor 1/6-mile track, a climbing wall, a swimming pool, sand volleyball courts, an outdoor basketball court, outdoor multipurpose fields, and a Frisbee golf course. **Graduates:** From July 1, 2016 to June 30, 2017, 4703 bachelor's degrees were awarded. The most popular majors were business/marketing (23%), engineering (8%), and psycholgy (8%). In an average class, 65% graduate in 6 years or less.

SERVICES: Counseling and information services are available, as is tutoring in some subjects. There is a reader service for the blind, and remedial math, reading, and writing. **Library/Resources:** The library contains 1.9 million volumes, 2.9 million microform items, and 3.6 million audio/video tapes/CDs/DVDs, and subscribes to 70,467 periodicals including electronic. Computerized library services include interlibrary loans, database searching, Internet access, and Wi-Fi capability. Special learning facilities include an art gallery, and the institute of Texan cultures. **Physically Challenged Students:** All of the campus is accessible. Facilities include wheelchair ramps, elevators, special parking, specially equipped restrooms, special class scheduling, lowered drinking fountains, lowered telephones, and special housing. **Special:** UTSA offers a wide variety of programs to enrich educational opportunities for students. Programs such as University College, ROTC and the Honors College are designed to provide opportunities for research, service and leadership. There are also programs for Pre-Professional Studies (Pre-Med and Pre-Law), internships and a degree in Multidisciplinary Studies where students have an opportunity to choose three focus areas. There are 40 national honor societies, a freshman honors program, and 17 departmental honors programs. **Visiting:** There are regularly scheduled orientations for prospective students. There are guides for informal visits. To schedule a visit, contact the Visitor Center at (210) 458-5143. **Campus Safety and Security:** Measures include 24-hour foot and vehicle patrol, an emergency notification system, self-defense education, and security escort services. There are shuttle buses, emergency telephones, lighted pathways/sidewalks, and controlled access to dorms/residences.

REQUIREMENTS: Admission is based on a formula derived from high school class rank and SAT or ACT scores. Applicants must be graduates of accredited high schools or have earned the GED. Students should have completed 23 academic units 4 in English, 3 units each in social studies, math and science, 2 units in foreign language, and 1 unit each in history, visual performing arts, including 5 academic electives. If a student submits the Texas Success Initiative Exam it is considered for placement. AP and CLEP credits are accepted. Important factors in the admissions decision are leadership record, advanced placement or honors courses, evidence of special talent, and personality/intangible qualities. In order to receive a bachelor's degree from UTSA, a student must meet these minimum requirements: complete a minimum of 120 semester credit hours, at least 39 of which must be upper-division level. Complete the University Core Curriculum requirements outlined in this profile. Complete at least one course in the University Core Curriculum designated as a Q-course to satisfy the Quantitative Scholarship requirement. Complete the major and support work requirements and the free elective requirements for the desired degree. Free electives refer to any semester credit hours accepted by UTSA in transfer or awarded by UTSA that, for degree purposes, are not applied to Core Curriculum, major, minor, or support work requirements. Meet all requirements for a degree as put forth by the Texas State Education Code, including the following: meet the minimum UTSA residence requirements. Achieve an overall 2.0 GPA in all work attempted at UTSA and a 2.0 GPA in all work included in the major. Be in good academic standing at UTSA. Apply formally for the degree before the deadline in the Office of the Registrar. **Procedure:** Freshmen are admitted to all sessions. Entrance exams should be taken in the spring of the junior year. There is a rolling admissions plan. Applications should be filed by June 1 for fall entry; October 15 for spring entry; and March 1 for summer entry. The fall 2017 application fee was $60. Notifications are sent March 1. Applications are accepted online. **Transfer Students:** 2463 transfer students enrolled in 2016-2017. Admissions requirements for transfer students with 30+ hours completed at time of application (work in progress is not considered) must: Have at least a cumulative 2.25 GPA on a 4.0 scale in all transferable college coursework from a regionally accredited institutions. Submit your official transcripts from each college or university attended, including Dual Credit work, be eligible to return to most recent institution (includes academic and disciplinary actions) Note: When calculating the cumulative grade point average for admission, all attempted work is considered. Repeated courses are not excluded. 30 of 120 credits required for the bachelor's degree must be completed at UTSA. **International Students:** There are 1104 international students enrolled. They must take the TOEFL with a minimum score of 500 on the paper-based TOEFL (PBT) or 61 on the Internet-based version (iBT). Students must take the IELTS, with a minimum score of 5. They must also take the SAT or ACT.

ADMISSIONS: 76% of the 2017-2018 applicants were accepted. The SAT scores for the 2017-2018 freshman class were: Critical Reading-- 45% below 500, 40% between 500 and 599, 14% between 600 and 699, and 2% between 700 and 800. Math-- 37% below 500, 46% between 500 and 599, 15% between 600 and 699, and 2% between 700 and 800. Writing-- 56% below 500, 35% between 500 and 599, and 7% between 600 and 699. The ACT scores were 11% between 12 and 17, 55% between 18 and 23, 32% between 24 and 29, and 4% above 30. 23 freshmen graduated first in their class. **Admissions Contact:** George Norton, Director of Admissions. Email: *onestop@utsa.edu* Web: *www.utsa.edu*

FINANCIAL AID: In 2017-2018, 56% of all full-time freshmen received some form of financial aid. 52% of all full-time freshmen received need-based aid. The average freshman award was $10,174. Need-based scholarships or need-based grants averaged $8,345; need-based self-help aid (loans and jobs) averaged $3,524; non-need-based athletic scholarships averaged $13,999; other non-need-based awards and non-need-based scholarships averaged $3,346; and $2,801 from other forms of aid. The average financial indebtedness of the 2017 graduate was $15,634. The college's own financial statement is required. The FAFSA code is 010115. The priority date for freshman financial aid applications for fall entry is March 15.

TRINITY UNIVERSITY — D-4

www.trinity.edu

San Antonio, TX 78212 — (210) 999-7207

Email: admissions@trinity.edu

Full-time: 1092 men, 1251 women	**Faculty:** 260
Part-time: 26 men, 16 women	**Ph.D.s:** n/av
Graduate: 82 men, 94 women	**Student/Faculty:** 9 to 1
Year: semesters, summer session	**Tuition:** $41,344
Room & Board: $13,136	**Freshman Class:** 4792 applied, 2946 accepted, 642 enrolled
SAT EBR-W/M: 665/659 **ACT:** 30	**CEEB CODE:** 6831
Application Deadline: February 1	**MOST COMPETITIVE**

Trinity University is known for its challenging and supportive academic environment, personalized attention from outstanding faculty, large school resources, post-graduate preparation, and vibrant campus life. Trinity encourages students to discover, grow, and become global citizens engaged with the community and the world. There is 1 undergraduate school and 1 graduate school. In addition to regional accreditation, Trinity has baccalaureate program accreditation with AACSB, ABET, and CAHME. The 117-acre campus is in an urban area 3 miles north of downtown San Antonio. Including any residence halls, there are 45 buildings.

STUDENT LIFE: 73% of undergraduates are from Texas. Others are from 48 states, 42 foreign countries, and Canada. 64% are from public schools. 7% are Asian American; 6% Foreign; 56% White; 5% two or more races; 4% African American; 21% Hispanic; 2% race unknown. 24% are Protestant; 21% Catholic; 19% Buddhist, Eastern Orthodox, Hindu, Muslim, and Other Denominations; 13% claim no religious affiliation. **Female To Male Ratio:** 1.1:1. The average age of freshmen is 18; all undergraduates, 20. 11% do not continue beyond their first year; 80% remain to graduate. **Housing:** 4032 students can be accommodated in college housing, which includes dorms and off-campus apartments. In addition, there are language/international houses and special-interest houses. On-campus housing is guaranteed for all 4 years. 80% of students live on campus. All students may keep cars.

FACULTY/CLASSROOMS: 57% of faculty are male; 43% are female. All teach and do research. No introductory courses are taught by graduate students. The average class size in an introductory lecture is 20; in a laboratory is 32; and in a regular course is 19.

PROGRAMS OF STUDY: Trinity confers B.A., B.S., and B.M. degrees. Master's degrees are also awarded. Bachelor's degrees are awarded in AGRICULTURE (environmental studies), BIOLOGICAL SCIENCE (biochemistry, biology/biological science, ecology, and neurosciences), BUSINESS (accounting, business administration and management, business intelligence and analytics, business and technology, finance, and international business), COMMUNICATIONS AND THE ARTS (art history, art, China Asia-Pacific studies, Chinese, choral music, classics, communications, dramatic arts, English, French, German, German studies, Greek, Latin, music, music performance, Russian, Spanish, and theatre studies), COMPUTER AND PHYSICAL SCIENCE (chemistry, computer science, earth science, geoscience, mathematics, and physics), EDUCATION (education and music education), ENGINEERING AND ENVIRONMENTAL DESIGN (engineering and applied science), SOCIAL SCIENCE (anthropology, Chinese Studies, economics, history, international relations, philosophy, political science/government, psychology, religion, sociology, and urban studies). Business administration, accounting, and communication have the largest enrollments.

ACTIVITIES: 17% of men belong to 6 local fraternities; 32% of women belong to 7 local sororities. There are 79 groups on campus, including art, band, cheerleading, chess, choir, chorale, chorus, communications, computers, dance, debate, drama, drill team, environmental, ethnic, film, forensics, honors, international, jazz band, LGBT, literary magazine, musical theater, newspaper, opera, orchestra, pep band, photography, political, professional, radio and TV, religious, social, social service, student government, symphony, wind ensemble and gaming, and yearbook. Popular campus events include TigerFest Gala, Chocolate Festival, and Trinity Spotlight. **Sports:** There are 9 intercollegiate sports for men and 9 for women, and 9 intramural sports for men and 9 for women. Facilities include Athletic facilities for football, soccer and basketball to water polo and sand volleyball. Our facilities offer football, soccer, basketball, volleyball, tennis, weight rooms, a cardio center, racquetball courts, tennis courts, and indoor and outdoor pools. **Graduates:** From July 1, 2016 to June 30, 2017, 479 bachelor's degrees were awarded. The most popular majors were business administration (7%), communication (7%), and accounting concentration (6%). In an average class, 66% graduate in 4 years or less, 75% graduate in 5 years or less, and 80% graduate in 6 years or less. Of the 2016 graduating class, 23% were enrolled in graduate school within 6 months of graduation, and 55% were employed.

SERVICES: Counseling and information services are available, as is tutoring in most subjects. **Library/Resources:** The library contains 716,500 volumes, 37,000 microform items, and 37,624 audio/video tapes/CDs/DVDs, and subscribes to 1,907 periodicals including electronic. Computerized library services include interlibrary loans, database searching, Internet access, and Wi-Fi capability. Special learning facilities include an art gallery, radio station, and TV station. **Physically Challenged Students:** Facilities include wheelchair ramps, elevators, special parking, specially equipped restrooms, special class scheduling, lowered drinking fountains, lowered telephones, and special housing. Accommodations for students with disabilities are determined through the office of Disability Services for Students. **Special:** The university offers student-designed interdisciplinary majors, double majors, significant opportunities for undergraduate research in the humanities and sciences, an entrepreneurship minor and program, a robust business curriculum, study abroad in 35 countries, and internship experiences outside the normal classroom for credit, as well as teacher certification. There are 21 national honor societies, Phi Beta Kappa, and 14 departmental honors programs. **Visiting:** There are regularly scheduled orientations for prospective students, campus tour, information session, and meetings with current students, faculty, or staff. There are guides for informal visits, visitors may sit in on classes, and stay overnight. To schedule a visit, contact the Admissions Office. **Campus Safety and Security:** Measures include 24-hour foot and vehicle patrol, emergency notification system, self-defense education, and security escort services. There are emergency telephones, lighted pathways/sidewalks, controlled access to dorms/residences, and shuttle carts.

REQUIREMENTS: The SAT or ACT is required. In addition, Applicants are expected to have completed 4 years of English, 3 of math, 3 each of lab science and social studies, and 2 foreign language. A personal essay, standardized test scores, an official high school transcript, high school counselor recommendation, and teacher evaluation are required. A campus visit is also recommended. AP credits are accepted. Important factors in the admissions decision are advanced placement or honors courses, recommendations by school officials, and extracurricular activities record. To graduate, students must satisfy the Pathways curriculum, complete at least one major, the residency requirements, and complete a minimum of 124 credit hours (129 for B.S. in engineering science and 141 for a B.M. in performance and composition). Students must complete at least six of the Curricular Requirements and 30 hours in upper-division courses. A minimum 2.0 GPA is required. **Procedure:** Freshmen are admitted fall, spring, and summer. Entrance exams should be taken late in the junior year or early in the senior year. There are early decision, early admissions, and deferred admissions plans. Early decision applications should be filed by November 1; regular applications, by February 1 for fall entry; and November 15 for spring entry. Notification of early decision is sent December 15; regular decision, April 1. 64 early decision candidates were accepted for the 2017-2018 class. Applications are accepted on-line. **Transfer Students:** 25 transfer students enrolled in 2016-2017. Transcripts for all colleges attended or attending, high school transcripts, an essay, standardized test scores, and a statement of good standing from the prior institution are required. An interview and visit to campus is recommended. 62 of 124 credits required for the bachelor's degree must be completed at Trinity. **International Students:** There are 137 international students enrolled. They must take the TOEFL. They must also take the SAT or ACT.

ADMISSIONS: 61% of the 2017-2018 applicants were accepted. The SAT scores for the 2017-2018 freshman class were: Math-- 16% between 500 and 599, 53% between 600 and 699, and 31% between 700 and 800. Evidence-Based Reading/Writing-- 12% between 500 and 599, 55% between 600 and 699, and 33% between 700 and 800. The ACT scores were 1% between 18 and 23, 44% between 24 and 29, and 55% above 30. 66% of the current freshmen were in the top fifth of their class; 88% were in the top two fifths. 11 freshmen graduated first in their class. **Admissions Contact:** Office of Admissions Email: *admissions@trinity.edu* Web: *www.trinity.edu*

FINANCIAL AID: In 2017-2018, 99% of all full-time freshmen received some form of financial aid. 52% of all full-time freshmen received need-based aid. The average freshman award was $33,567. Need-based scholarships or need-based grants averaged $33,960; need-based self-help aid (loans and jobs) averaged $6,618; other non-need-based awards and non-need-based scholarships averaged $20,558; and $7,944 from other forms of aid. The average financial indebtedness of the 2017 graduate was $40,800. Trinity is a member of CSS. The CSS/Profile is required. The priority date for freshman financial aid applications for fall entry is February 15.

UNIVERSITY OF DALLAS D-2

www.udallas.edu

Irving, TX 75062	**(972) 721-5266** **(800) 628-6999**
Fax: (972) 721-5017	**Email: crusader@udallas.edu**
Full-time: 622 men, 749 women	**Faculty:** 152; IIA, -$
Part-time: 11 men, 11 women	**Ph.D.s:** 88%
Graduate: 553 men, 389 women	**Student/Faculty:** 7 to 1
Year: semesters, summer session	**Tuition:** $33,800
Room & Board: $13,200	**Freshman Class:** 2135 applied, 1718 accepted, 371 enrolled
SAT CR/M/W: 590/575/570 **ACT:** 27	**CEEB CODE:** 6868
Application Deadline: August 1	**VERY COMPETITIVE**

University of Dallas, founded in 1955, is a private Catholic liberal arts institution. The university has 4 schools: Constantin College of Liberal Arts (undergraduates), Braniff Graduate School of Liberal Arts, Satish and Yasmin Gupta College of Business and School of Ministry. There are 3 graduate schools. In addition to regional accreditation, UD has baccalaureate program accreditation with AACSB and IACBE. The 750-acre campus is in an urban area in Irving, Texas, 10 miles west of Dallas, 30 miles east of Fort Worth. Including any residence halls, there are 33 buildings.

STUDENT LIFE: 50% of undergraduates are from out of state, mostly the Midwest. Students are from 50 states, 15 foreign countries, and Canada. 45% are from public schools. 63% are White; 6% Asian American; 3% Foreign; 3% two or more races; 22% Hispanic; 2% African American; 1% race unknown. 84% are Catholic. **Male To Female Ratio:** 1.0:1. The average age of freshmen is 18; all undergraduates, 20. 20% do not continue beyond their first year; 73% remain to graduate. **Housing:** 838 students can be accommodated in college housing, which includes dorms and on-campus apartments. On-campus housing is guaranteed for the freshman year only, and is available on a first-come, first-served basis. 87% of students live on campus. All students may keep cars.

FACULTY/CLASSROOMS: 60% of faculty are male; 39% are female. 90% teach undergraduates. No introductory courses are taught by graduate students. The average class size in an introductory lecture is 22; in a laboratory is 16; and in a regular course is 19.

PROGRAMS OF STUDY: UD confers B.A. and B.S. degrees. Master's and doctoral degrees are also awarded. Bachelor's degrees are awarded in BIOLOGICAL SCIENCE (biochemistry and biology/biological science), BUSINESS (business administration and management), COMMUNICATIONS AND THE ARTS (art history and appreciation, ceramic art and design, classics, dramatic arts, English, French, German, painting, printmaking, sculpture, and Spanish), COMPUTER AND PHYSICAL SCIENCE (chemistry, computer science, mathematics, and physics), EDUCATION (art education, education, and elementary education), ENGINEERING AND ENVIRONMENTAL DESIGN (electrical/electronics engineering technology), HEALTH PROFESSIONS (nursing), SOCIAL SCIENCE (economics, history, pastoral studies, philosophy, political science/government, psychology, and theological studies). Biology, classics, and English are the strongest academically. Business, biology, and English have the largest enrollments.

ACTIVITIES: There are no fraternities or sororities. There are 50 groups on campus, including art, chess, choir, chorale, chorus, computers, dance, debate, drama, ethnic, film, honors, international, literary magazine, musical theater, newspaper, opera, photography, political, professional, religious, social, social service, student government, and yearbook. Popular campus events include Charity Week, Groundhog Celebration, Lazy Faire, Mallapalooza, Winter Cotillion, Battle of the Bands, Alumni and Family Weekend, TGIT, and Spring Formal. **Sports:** There are 7 intercollegiate sports for men and 8 for women, and 6 intramural sports for men and 3 for women. Facilities include an athletic center with a gym, a weight room, aerobics, an outdoor pool, and outdoor tennis courts. A collegiate soccer field, baseball field, multipurpose field, and jogging trails. **Graduates:** From July 1, 2016 to June 30, 2017, 275 bachelor's degrees were awarded. The most popular majors were business/marketing (15%), Theology and religious vocations, and English (11%), biological/life sciences, and and social sciences (10%). In an average class, 66% graduate in 4 years or less and 70% graduate in 6 years or less. Of the 2016 graduating class, 21% were enrolled in graduate school within 6 months of graduation.

SERVICES: Counseling and information services are available, as is tutoring in most subjects. There is remedial math and writing. There are also writing and math labs, and an academic success office. **Library/Resources:** The library contains 364,691 volumes, 4,526 microform items, 432 audio/video tapes/CDs/DVDs, and subscribes to 64,000 periodicals, including electronic. Computerized library services include interlibrary loans, database searching, Internet access, and Wi-Fi capability. Special learning facilities include an art gallery, an 80-seat theater, a performance lab and an observatory. **Physically Challenged Students:** 70% of the campus is accessible. Facilities include wheelchair ramps, elevators, special parking, specially equipped restrooms, special class scheduling, and lowered drinking fountains. **Special:** UD offers internships in field experience or an off-campus research semester. The majority of students participate in the Rome Program, a semester-long experience on the UD Rome campus, and summer programs are available in Rome, as well. 3-2 electrical engineering degree (UT-Arlington) and 3-2 nursing degree (Texas Woman's University) are available. There are myriad opportunities for on-campus work-study programs. B.A.-B.S. degrees and double majors are available, as well as 33 concentrations to combine with any major. There are 5 national honor societies, Phi Beta Kappa, and 4 departmental honors programs. **Visiting:** There are regularly scheduled orientations for prospective students, including a campus tour, meeting with a admission counselor, scholarship competition, tour of residence halls, sitting in on classes, lunch with students in the cafeteria, mass and one-on-one meetings with professors. There are guides for informal visits; visitors may sit in on classes and stay overnight. To schedule a visit, contact the Office of Admission. **Campus Safety and Security:** Measures include 24-hour foot and vehicle patrol, an emergency notification system, self-defense education, and security escort services. There are emergency telephones, lighted pathways/sidewalks, and controlled access to dorms/residences.

REQUIREMENTS: The university seeks high school students who have pursued a curriculum of college preparatory courses including 4 units in English, 3 units each in math, science, social studies, history, and academic electives, and 1 unit in visual/performing arts. Although the university is flexible in its admission requests, applicants should be in the upper third of their graduating class and should present satisfactory SAT or ACT scores. AP and CLEP credits are accepted. Important factors in the admissions decision are personality/intangible qualities, recommendations by school officials, leadership record, advanced placement or honors courses, evidence of special talent, and extracurricular activities record. To graduate with a B.A., students must complete at least 120 credits, including 38 in advanced credits, which included 12 in the major, with a 2.0 GPA. Completion of the 60-credit-hour Core curriculum as well as major requirements is required. To graduate with a B.S degree, students must complete the above requirements for a B.A. plus 12 additional hours in the major. Seniors must pass a comprehensive exam, write a thesis or complete a research or capstone project in their major. **Procedure:** Freshmen are admitted in the fall and spring. Entrance exams should be taken during the junior year or by the fall of the senior year. There are early admissions, deferred admissions, and rolling admissions plans. Early decision applications should be filed by November 1; regular applications, by August 1 for fall entry. The fall 2017 application fee was $50. Notification is sent on a rolling basis. Applications are accepted on-line. **Transfer Students:** 48 transfer students enrolled in 2016-2017. Applicants must have a minimum 2.5 GPA from an accredited college or university. Official transcripts from all previous colleges attended, a writing sample, a personal statement, and an academic letter of recommendation are required. Students with fewer than 30 transferable credits must also submit SAT or ACT scores and an official high school transcript. 60 of 120 credits required for the bachelor's degree must be completed at UD. **International Students:** There are 34 international students enrolled. They must take the TOEFL with a minimum score of 79 on the Internet-based version (iBT). The SAT or ACT scores may be submitted in place of the TOEFL.

ADMISSIONS: 80% of the 2017-2018 applicants were accepted. The SAT scores for the 2017-2018 freshman class were: Critical Reading-- 12% below 500, 40% between 500 and 599, 30% between 600 and 699, and 17% between 700 and 800. Math-- 18% below 500, 44% between 500 and 599, 31% between 600 and 699, and 7% between 700 and 800. Writing-- 20% below 500, 42% between 500 and 599, 27% between 600 and 699, and 10% between 700 and 800. The ACT scores were 25% between 18 and 23, 47% between 24 and 29, and 27% above 30. 68% of the current freshmen were in the top fifth of their class; 80% were in the top two fifths. **Admissions Contact:** Elizabeth Griffin Smith, Director of Admission. Email: *crusader@udallas.edu* Web: *www.udallas.edu*

FINANCIAL AID: In 2017-2018, 96% of all full-time freshmen received some form of financial aid. 82% of all full-time freshmen received need-based aid. The average freshman award was $31,642. Need-based scholarships or need-based grants averaged $34,091; need-based self-help aid (loans and jobs) averaged $4,580; other non-need-based awards and non-need-based scholarships averaged $23,470; and $16,109 average dollar amount of institutional non-need and grant award. 15% of undergraduate students work part-time. The average financial indebtedness of the 2017 graduate was $31,161. The priority date for freshman financial aid applications for fall entry is March 1.

UNIVERSITY OF HOUSTON — E-3

www.uh.edu

Houston, TX 77004 (713) 743-1010

Email: admissions@uh.edu

Full-time: 13,538 men, 13,621 women
Part-time: 5217 men, 4839 women
Graduate: 4001 men, 4148 women
Year: semesters, summer session
Room & Board: $9984

Faculty: 959; I, ++$
Ph.D.s: 86%
Student/Faculty: 28 to 1
Tuition: $11,887 ($27,337)
Freshman Class: 20768 applied, 12691 accepted, 4962 enrolled

SAT EBR-W/M: 602/606 **ACT:** 25
Application Deadline: June 30

CEEB CODE: 6870
VERY COMPETITIVE

University of Houston is a Carnegie-designated Tier One public research university that serves the globally competitive Houston and Gulf Coast Region by providing world-class faculty, experiential learning, and strategic industry partnerships. There are 10 undergraduate schools and 4 graduate schools. In addition to regional accreditation, UH has baccalaureate program accreditation with AACSB, ABET, ACCE, ACPE, NAAB, NASM, CAEP, ACS, CSAC, and ACCE. The 594-acre campus is in an urban area 3 miles from downtown Houston, Texas. Including any residence halls, there are 161 buildings.

STUDENT LIFE: 94% of undergraduates are from Texas. Others are from 48 states, 107 foreign countries, and Canada. 93% are from public schools. 9% are Foreign; 30% Hispanic; 3% two or more races; 26% White; 21% Asian American; 10% African American; 1% race unknown. **Male To Female Ratio:** 1.0:1. The average age of freshmen is 18; all undergraduates, 22. 15% do not continue beyond their first year; 54% remain to graduate. **Housing:** 8008 students can be accommodated in college housing, which includes coed, married student dorms, on-campus apartments, and off-campus apartments. In addition, there are honors houses, special-interest houses, fraternity houses, and sorority houses. On-campus housing is available on a first-come and first-served basis. 83% of students commute. All students may keep cars.

FACULTY/CLASSROOMS: 61% of faculty are male; 39% are female. 53% teach undergraduates. Graduate students teach 17% of introductory courses. The average class size in an introductory lecture is 77; in a laboratory is 26; and in a regular course is 4.

PROGRAMS OF STUDY: UH confers B.A., B.S., B.A.C.Y., B.Arch., B.B.A., B.F.A., B.M., B.S.C.E., B.S.Ch.E., B.S.C.P.E., B.S.E.E., B.S.I.E., B.S.M.E., B.S.B.E., B.S.N., and B.S.P.E.T.E. degrees. Master's and doctoral degrees are also awarded. Bachelor's degrees are awarded in BIOLOGICAL SCIENCE (biology/biological science), BUSINESS (accounting, hotel/motel and restaurant management, management information systems, marketing and distribution, and supply chain management), COMMUNICATIONS AND THE ARTS (American Sign Language, applied music, art, Chinese, communications, dance, English, French, industrial design, Spanish, and studio art), COMPUTER AND PHYSICAL SCIENCE (chemistry, geology, mathematics, and physics), ENGINEERING AND ENVIRONMENTAL DESIGN (architecture, biomedical engineering, chemical engineering, civil engineering, computer engineering, construction management, electrical/electronics engineering, environmental design, environmental science, industrial engineering, mechanical engineering, mechanical engineering technology, and petroleum/natural gas engineering), HEALTH PROFESSIONS (health and pharmaceutical science), SOCIAL SCIENCE (anthropology, interdisciplinary studies, Italian studies, liberal arts/general studies, and philosophy). Business, and engineering are the strongest academically. Business, biology, and psychology have the largest enrollments.

ACTIVITIES: 3% of men belong to 25 national fraternities; 4% of women belong to 23 national sororities. There are 448 groups on campus, including art, band, cheerleading, chess, choir, chorale, chorus, computers, dance, debate, drama, drill team, environmental, ethnic, film, forensics, honors, international, jazz band, LGBT, literary magazine, marching band, musical theater, newspaper, opera, orchestra, pep band, photography, political, professional, radio and TV, religious, social, social service, student government, symphony, and yearbook. Popular campus events include Frontier Fiesta, Homecoming, and Cat's Back. **Sports:** There are 7 intercollegiate sports for men and 10 for women, and 31 intramural sports for men and 31 for women. The athletics facilities has football, baseball, basketball, volleyball, an indoor track, soccer, an outdoor track, tennis, swimming and diving, and softball. **Graduates:** From July 1, 2016 to June 30, 2017, 6726 bachelor's degrees were awarded. The most popular majors were business/marketing (29%), engineering (8%), and psychology (6%). In an average class, 25% graduate in 4 years or less, 45% graduate in 5 years or less, and 54% graduate in 6 years or less.

SERVICES: Counseling and information services are available, as is tutoring in most subjects. There is a reader service for the blind, and remedial math, reading, and writing. Assistance is also available for students taking exams, or who need help with coursework. **Library/Resources:** The library contains 3.5 million volumes, 155,656 microform items, 30,928 audio/video tapes/CDs/DVDs, and subscribes to 167,961 periodicals, including electronic. Computerized library services include interlibrary loans, database searching, Internet access, and Wi-Fi capability. Special learning facilities include an art gallery, radio and TV stations, and an observatory. **Physically Challenged Students:** 98% of the campus is accessible. Facilities include wheelchair ramps, elevators, special parking, specially equipped restrooms, special class scheduling, lowered drinking fountains, lowered telephones, and special housing. **Special:** Many colleges at the University of Houston offer internships and cooperative education opportunities in such areas as business, engineering, government/policy, education, hospitality, research, healthcare/health education, communications/media, sports, science, math, and technology. UH also offers a 3-2 program with the School of Nursing at the University of Texas Health Science Center, and a 3-3 program with the University of Houston Law Center. Dual degree and accelerated degrees are offered in the disciplines of business, computer science, global retailing, human resource development, health, hospitality, and political science. Learning Abroad programs include Faculty-Led programs, such as those offered through the Department of Modern and Classical Languages to China and France, and through the African American Studies Program to Africa, Bauer Study Abroad Programs to Chile and India, Affiliated Programs through organizations such as International Studies Abroad (ISA), and the University Study Abroad Consortium (USAC), Reciprocal Exchange Studies, and Service Learning or Internships abroad. There are 18 national honor societies, Phi Beta Kappa, a freshman honors program, and 12 departmental honors programs. **Visiting:** There are regularly scheduled orientations for prospective students, consisting of a tour, information sessions that help with the transition from high school to college and have scheduled time with an academic advisor. There are guides for informal visits and visitors may stay overnight. To schedule a visit, contact the Office of Admission. **Campus Safety and Security:** Measures include 24-hour foot and vehicle patrol, an emergency notification system, self-defense education, and security escort services. There are shuttle buses, emergency telephones, lighted pathways/sidewalks, controlled access to dorms/residences, community dialogues, and assistance with disabled vehicles.

REQUIREMENTS: The SAT or ACT is required. Automatic enrollment is granted to applicants who rank in top-tenth of secondary school class and submit a completed application by August 1st. All other students are reviewed using a holistic review process. A GPA of 2.0 is required. AP and CLEP credits are accepted. Important factors in the admissions decision are evidence of special talent, recommendations by school officials, and advanced placement or honors courses. To graduate, student must complete 120 semester credit hours, including at least 36 in advance-level courses, with a minimum GPA of 2.0. Core Curriculum requires each student complete 42 hours of coursework from select courses under 10 different component areas such as math, history, creative arts and the sciences. **Procedure:** Freshmen are admitted to all sessions. Entrance exams should be taken by November 15. There is a rolling admissions plan. Applications should be filed by June 30 for fall entry; December 1 for spring entry; and April 1 for summer entry. The fall 2017 application fee was $75. Applications are accepted on-line. **Transfer Students:** 5200 transfer students enrolled in 2016-2017. Applicants must be eligible to return to their last college. A 2.0 GPA is required for students with 30 or more semester hours of college credit, a 2.5 GPA for those with 15 to 29. 30 of 120 credits required for the bachelor's degree must be completed at UH. **International Students:** There are 1333 international students enrolled. They must take the TOEFL with a minimum score of 550 on the paper-based TOEFL (PBT) or 79 on the Internet-based version (iBT). They must also take the SAT or ACT.

ADMISSIONS: 61% of the 2017-2018 applicants were accepted. The SAT scores for the 2017-2018 freshman class were: Critical Reading-- 20% below 500, 48% between 500 and 599, 26% between 600 and 699, and 6% between 700 and 800. Math-- 4% below 500, 46% between 500 and 599, 45% between 600 and 699, and 5% between 700 and 800. Evidence-Based Reading/Writing-- 6% below 500, 43% between 500 and 599, 48% between 600 and 699, and 3% between 700 and 800. The ACT scores were 2% between 12 and 17, 34% between 18 and 23, 51% between 24 and 29, and 13% above 30. 57% of the current freshmen were in the top fifth of their class. 39 freshmen graduated first in their class. **Admissions Contact:** Mara Affre, Associate Vice President for Enrollment Service. Email: *admissions@uh.edu* Web: *www.uh.edu*

FINANCIAL AID: In 2017-2018, 85% of all full-time freshmen received some form of financial aid. 60% of all full-time freshmen received need-based aid. The average freshman award was $11,286. Need-based scholarships or need-based grants averaged $9,008 ($21,920 maximum); need-based self-help aid (loans and jobs) averaged $3,626 ($9,500 maximum); non-need-based athletic scholarships averaged $15,798 ($34,811 maximum); and other non-need-based awards and non-need-based scholarships averaged $5,206 ($38,790 maximum). 7% of undergraduate students work part-time. The average financial indebtedness of the 2017 graduate was $23,746. The priority date for freshman financial aid applications for fall entry is March 15.

UNIVERSITY OF HOUSTON-DOWNTOWN *(The complete profile is made available exclusively on our website, www.barronspac.com)*

UNIVERSITY OF MARY HARDIN-BAYLOR D-3

www.umhb.edu

Belton, TX 76513 — (254) 295-4513, (800) 727-8642

Fax: (254) 295-5049 — **Email:** admission@umhb.edu

Full-time: 1104 men, 1941 women
Part-time: 94 men, 194 women
Graduate: 247 men, 334 women
Year: semesters, summer session
Room & Board: $7592
SAT or ACT: required
Application Deadline: rolling

Faculty: 143
Ph.D.s: 78%
Student/Faculty: 18 to 1
Tuition: $27,700
Freshman Class: 8289 applied, 6535 accepted, 754 enrolled
CEEB CODE: 6396
COMPETITIVE+

University of Mary Hardin-Baylor, founded in 1845, is a private facility affiliated with the Baptist General Convention of Texas. It offers undergraduate degrees in liberal arts, fine arts, music, business, education, nursing, and social work, as well as masters degrees in business, information systems, education, psychology/counseling, and nursing, and doctorates in educational administration, physical therapy and nurse practitioner. There are 7 undergraduate schools and 7 graduate schools. In addition to regional accreditation, UMHB has baccalaureate program accreditation with CSWE, BCAT, CAATE, CCNE, and TEA. The 340-acre campus is in a small town in central Texas halfway between San Antonio and Dallas/Fort Worth. Including any residence halls, there are 80 buildings.

STUDENT LIFE: 96% of undergraduates are from Texas. Others are from 29 states, 29 foreign countries, and Canada. 56% are White; 21% Hispanic; 15% African American; 3% two or more races; 2% Asian American; 2% race unknown; 1% American Indian/Alaska Native; 1% Foreign. 15% are Catholic; 15% claim no religious affiliation. **Female To Male Ratio:** 1.7:1. The average age of freshmen is 18; all undergraduates, 22. 27% do not continue beyond their first year; 48% remain to graduate. **Housing:** 1929 students can be accommodated in college housing, which includes dorms and on-campus apartments. On-campus housing is guaranteed for the freshman year only, and is available on a first-come, first-served basis. 57% of students live on campus. All students may keep cars. Alcohol is not permitted.

FACULTY/CLASSROOMS: 44% of faculty are male; 56% are female. No introductory courses are taught by graduate students. The average class size in an introductory lecture is 25; in a laboratory is 20; and in a regular course is 17.

PROGRAMS OF STUDY: UMHB confers B.A., B.B.A., B.C.M., B.F.A., B.G.S., B.M., B.S., B.S.N., and B.S.W. degrees. Master's and doctoral degrees are also awarded. Bachelor's degrees are awarded in BIOLOGICAL SCIENCE (biology/adolescence education and biology/biological science), BUSINESS (accounting, business administration and management, business information systems, finance, international business, marketing/retailing/merchandising, organizational leadership and management, and sports management), COMMUNICATIONS AND THE ARTS (art, church music, communications, English, film, television and digital media, journalism, multimedia, music, music performance, performing arts, Spanish, speech/debate/rhetoric, and visual design), COMPUTER AND PHYSICAL SCIENCE (chemistry, chemistry/adolescence education, computer science, information sciences and systems, and mathematics), EDUCATION (art education, early childhood education, elementary education, English education, foreign languages education, mathematics education, middle school education, music education, physical education, physical education/exercise science, science education, secondary education, social studies education, and sports and wellness studies), ENGINEERING AND ENVIRONMENTAL DESIGN (computer graphics and engineering science), HEALTH PROFESSIONS (exercise science, nursing, and prephysical therapy), SOCIAL SCIENCE (biblical studies, Christian studies, criminal justice, economics, history, interdisciplinary studies, ministries, political science/government, psychology, social work, and sociology). Nursing, business, and education are the strongest academically and have the largest enrollments are the strongest academically.

ACTIVITIES: There are no fraternities or sororities. There are 59 groups on campus, including art, band, cheerleading, chess, choir, chorale, chorus, computers, debate, drama, drill team, ethnic, film, honors, international, jazz band, literary magazine, musical theater, newspaper, opera, orchestra, pep band, photography, political, professional, religious, social service, student government, and yearbook. Popular campus events include Miss UMHB Pageant, Mr. Crusader Knights, Play Day, Stunt Night, and Easter Pageant. **Sports:** There are 6 intercollegiate sports for men and 6 for women, and 21 intramural sports for men and 21 for women. Facilities include a football stadium and training facility, a tennis center, soccer fields, and a campus recreation center housing a pool, basketball courts, and cardio and weight equipment. **Graduates:** From July 1, 2016 to June 30, 2017, 640 bachelor's degrees were awarded. The most popular majors were health professions and related programs (26%), business/marketing (16%), and education (12%). In an average class, 31% graduate in 4 years or less, 44% graduate in 5 years or less, and 48% graduate in 6 years or less.

SERVICES: Counseling and information services are available, as is tutoring in most subjects. There is a reader service for the blind, and remedial math, reading, and writing. Academic counselors and software for the blind are also available. **Library/Resources:** The library contains 211,271 volumes, 2,761 microform items, 8,830 audio/video tapes/CDs/DVDs, and subscribes to 145,598 periodicals, including electronic. Computerized library services include interlibrary loans, database searching, Internet access, and Wi-Fi capability. Special learning facilities include an art gallery, and a nature walk. **Physically Challenged Students:** 85% of the campus is accessible. Facilities include wheelchair ramps, elevators, special parking, specially equipped restrooms, special class scheduling, lowered drinking fountains, lowered telephones, and special housing. **Special:** Study abroad in 5 countries, internships, a work-study program, dual majors, a professional studies degree, an applied science bachelor's degree, post-baccalaureate certification in education, and a 5-year B.B.A./M.B.A. accounting specialization are offered. There are 7 national honor societies and a freshman honors program. **Visiting:** There are regularly scheduled orientations for prospective students, consisting of campus tours and visits with counselors to discuss admissions, financial aid, housing, and degree plans. There are guides for informal visits; visitors may sit in on classes and stay overnight. To schedule a visit, contact the Admissions Office. **Campus Safety and Security:** Measures include 24-hour foot and vehicle patrol, an emergency notification system, self-defense education, and security escort services. There are emergency telephones, lighted pathways/sidewalks, controlled access to dorms/residences, and a campus police force.

REQUIREMENTS: Students who rank in the top half of their high school graduating class must score a minimum of 950 on the SAT or 20 on the ACT. Those who graduate in the lower half of their class must score a minimum of 990 on the SAT or 21 on the ACT. There is no minimum test score for students who rank in the top 10% of their high school graduating class. All students should be graduates of an accredited high school and have 24 units of credit, including 4 in English, 3 each in math and social science, 2 in foreign language, and 3 1/2 in social studies. AP and CLEP credits are accepted. Important factors in the admissions decision are leadership record, advanced placement or honors courses, parents or siblings attended your school, evidence of special talent, personality/intangible qualities, extracurricular activities record, recommendations by alumni, geographical diversity, and recommendations by school officials. To graduate all students must complete at least 124 credits, including at least 24 in the major field and at least 36 upper-level credits, with a 2.0 GPA. Requirements include 6 credits each in English, social sciences, religion, and electives, 3 each in math and communication, an additional 3 to 4 in math, lab science, or foreign language, and a 1-credit Success in Academics course. There is a chapel attendance requirement for full-time students and a residency requirement of 31 hours. **Procedure:** Freshmen are admitted fall, spring, and summer. Entrance exams should be taken by the fall of the senior year. There is a rolling admissions plan. Application deadlines are open. The fall 2017 application fee was $35. Notification is sent on a rolling basis. Applications are accepted online. **Transfer Students:** 250 transfer students enrolled in 2016-2017. Applicants must present at least a 2.0 GPA, be in good standing at their previous institutions, and submit all college transcripts. Those with fewer than 12 transferable credits must also meet freshman requirements. 31 of 124 credits required for the bachelor's degree must be completed at UMHB. **International Students:** There are 23 international students enrolled. They must take the TOEFL with a minimum score of 40 on the Internet-based version (iBT).

ADMISSIONS: 79% of the 2017-2018 applicants were accepted. The SAT scores for the 2017-2018 freshman class were: Critical Reading-- 17% below 500, 51% between 500 and 599, 29% between 600 and 699, and 3% between 700 and 800. Math-- 19% below 500, 60% between 500 and 599, 20% between 600 and 699, and 1% between 700 and 800. The ACT scores were 12% between 12 and 17, 51% between 18 and 23, 32% between 24 and 29, and 5% above 30. **Admissions Contact:** Dr. Brent Burks, Director of Admissions and Recruiting. Email: *admission@umhb.edu* Web: *www.umhb.edu*

FINANCIAL AID: In 2017-2018, 97% of all full-time freshmen received some form of financial aid. 91% of all full-time freshmen received need-based aid. The average freshman award was $25,712. Need-based scholarships or need-based grants averaged $13,139 ($37,987 maximum); need-based self-help aid (loans and jobs) averaged $2,883 ($7,300 maximum); and other non-need-based awards and non-need-based scholarships averaged $9,690. 15% of undergraduate students work part-time. The average financial indebtedness of the 2017 graduate was $24,400. The priority date for freshman financial aid applications for fall entry is March 1.

UNIVERSITY OF NORTH TEXAS D-2

www.unt.edu

Denton, TX 76203 **(940) 565-2681**
(800) UNT-8211

Fax: (940) 565-2408 **Email: unt.freshman@unt.edu**

Full-time: 12,048 men, 13,542 women	**Faculty:** 1034; I, -$
Part-time: 3030 men, 2821 women	**Ph.D.s:** 80%
Graduate: 2726 men, 3954 women	**Student/Faculty:** 25 to 1
Year: semesters, summer session	**Tuition:** $23,780
Room & Board: see profile	**Freshman Class:** 18508 applied, 13385 accepted, 4900 enrolled
SAT: required **ACT:** 24	**CEEB CODE:** 6481
Application Deadline: August 1	**COMPETITIVE**

University of North Texas is a student-focused public research university, offering 97 bachelor's, 88 master's and 40 doctoral degree programs. UNT's mission is to develop new knowledge and solutions, while giving rise to the next generation of engineers, scientists, artists, educators and business leaders. UNT also is a top draw for transfer students, leading the state and ranking fourth nationally among public universities for its transfer student enrollment. The average cost in the capsule is for the 2016-2017 attendance and it covers tuition, fee, room and board, and other expenses. There are 12 undergraduate schools and 1 graduate school. In addition to regional accreditation, UNT has baccalaureate program accreditation with AACSB, ABET, ACCE, ACEJMC, CSAB, CSWE, FIDER, NASM, and NRPA. The 875-acre campus is in a suburban area 35 miles north of Dallas/Fort Worth. Including any residence halls, there are 166 buildings.

STUDENT LIFE: 82% of undergraduates are from Texas. Others are from 50 states, 131 foreign countries, and Canada. 47% are White; 23% Hispanic; 14% African American; 7% Asian American; 6% Foreign; 4%

two or more races; 2% American Indian/Alaska Native; 1% race unknown. **Female To Male Ratio:** 1.1:1. The average age of freshmen is 18; all undergraduates, 23. 20% do not continue beyond their first year; 53% remain to graduate. **Housing:** 6200 students can be accommodated in college housing, which includes married student dorms, on-campus apartments, and off-campus apartments. In addition, there are honors houses, special-interest houses, fraternity houses, sorority houses, theme, and wellness housing. On-campus housing is available on a first-come, first-served basis. 84% of students commute. All students may keep cars.

FACULTY/CLASSROOMS: 55% of faculty are male; 45% are female. 80% teach undergraduates. Graduate students teach 34% of introductory courses. The average class size in an introductory lecture is 52 and in a laboratory is 51.

PROGRAMS OF STUDY: University of North Texas confers B.A., B.A.A.S., B.B.A., B.F.A., B.M., B.S., B.S.B.C., B.S.Bio, B.S.Chem., B.S.Eco., B.S.E.P., B.S.E.T., B.S.Math., B.S.M.T., B.S.Phy., and B.S.W. degrees. Master's and doctoral degrees are also awarded. Bachelor's degrees are awarded in BIOLOGICAL SCIENCE (biochemistry and biology/biological science), BUSINESS (accounting, banking and finance, business administration and management, electronic business, entrepreneurial studies, hospitality management services, human resources, insurance, investments and securities, logistics, management information systems, management science, marketing/retailing/ merchandising, operations management, organizational behavior, organizational leadership and management, purchasing/inventory management, real estate, and recreation and leisure services), COMMUNICATIONS AND THE ARTS (applied art, art, art history and appreciation, broadcasting, choral music, communications, dance, design, dramatic arts, English, French, German, jazz, journalism, music, music history and appreciation, music performance, music theory and composition, musical theater, performing arts, radio/television technology, Spanish, studio art, telecommunications, theater design, theater management, and visual and performing arts), COMPUTER AND PHYSICAL SCIENCE (chemistry, computer science, information sciences and systems, mathematics, and physics), ENGINEERING AND ENVIRONMENTAL DESIGN (aviation administration/management, commercial art, computer engineering, construction engineering, electrical/electronics engineering, electrical/electronics engineering technology, emergency/disaster science, engineering physics, engineering technology, interior design, manufacturing engineering, mechanical engineering, mechanical engineering technology, and nuclear engineering technology), HEALTH PROFESSIONS (cytotechnology, health, medical laboratory technology, rehabilitation therapy, and speech pathology/audiology), SOCIAL SCIENCE (anthropology, applied psychology, child care/child and family studies, criminal justice, economics, fashion design and technology, geography, history, home furnishings and equipment management/production/services, human services, interdisciplinary studies, international studies, liberal arts/general studies, philosophy, physical fitness/movement, political science/ government, psychology, social science, social work, and sociology). Jazz studies, public administration, and accounting are the strongest academically. Biology, psychology, and interdisciplinary studies have the largest enrollments.

ACTIVITIES: 5% of men belong to 25 national fraternities; 6% of women belong to 16 national sororities. There are 440 groups on campus, including band, cheerleading, chess, choir, chorale, chorus, computers, dance, debate, drama, ethnic, film, honors, international, jazz band, LGBT, literary magazine, marching band, musical theater, newspaper, opera, orchestra, pep band, photography, political, professional, radio and TV, religious, social, social service, student government, and symphony. Popular campus events include First Flight, Homecoming, Union Day, and Earth Day. **Sports:** There are 6 intercollegiate sports for men and 10 for women, and 23 intramural sports for men and 20 for women. Facilities include a football stadium, a weight-training building, tennis courts, indoor swimming pools, gyms, handball and racquetball courts, gymnastics equipment, intramural fields, and a recreational sports complex. **Graduates:** From July 1, 2016 to June 30, 2017, 6519 bachelor's degrees were awarded. The most popular majors were integrative studies (9%), applied arts and sciences (5%), and psychology (4%). In an average class, 31% graduate in 4 years or less, 49% graduate in 5 years or less, and 53% graduate in 6 years or less.

SERVICES: Counseling and information services are available, as is tutoring in most subjects. There is a reader service for the blind, and remedial math, reading, and writing. **Library/Resources:** The library contains 3.9 million volumes, 3.4 million microform items, 230,810 audio/video tapes/CDs/DVDs, and subscribes to 133,889 periodicals, including electronic. Computerized library services include interlibrary loans, database searching, Internet access, and Wi-Fi capability. Special learning facilities include an art gallery, a planetarium, radio and TV stations, an observatory, and a TV and film production unit. **Physically Challenged Students:** 90% of the campus is accessible. Facilities include wheelchair ramps, elevators, special parking, specially equipped restrooms, special class scheduling, lowered drinking fountains, lowered telephones, and dorm rooms adapted for disabled students. **Special:** UNT offers co-op programs, internships, and work-study programs with the university. Students may study abroad in several locations. An accelerated degree program in math and science allows Texas high school students to obtain 2 years of college credit during their last 2 years in high school. Dual degrees, a general studies degree, and pass/fail options are also offered. There are 42 national honor societies and a freshman honors program. **Visiting:** There are regularly scheduled orientations for prospective students, including 3-day, 2-night sessions throughout the summer. There are guides for informal visits; visitors may sit in on classes and stay overnight. **Campus Safety and Security:** Measures include 24-hour foot and vehicle patrol, emergency notification system, self-defense education, and security escort services. There are shuttle buses, emergency telephones, lighted pathways/sidewalks, controlled access to dorms/residences, there is a crime prevention program, sexual assault information services, and a full-time crime prevention officer on duty.

REQUIREMENTS: The SAT or ACT is required. Applicants must be graduates of an accredited high school and submit a high school transcript. The required minimum score for entrance exams is determined by high school class rank. 26 high school academic units are required such as 4 each in English, math, science with labs, 2 units each in social studies, foreign language, and history, and 1 unit each in computer science, and visual/ performing arts, and 3.5 unites in academic electives. Others could be .5 in health, 1.5 in P.E. and .5 speech. AP and CLEP credits are accepted. All students must complete at least 120 semester hours, including a minimum of 42 hours in the major, with a 2.0 GPA. The core requirements include English, natural science, U.S. history, political science, visual/performing arts, and humanities. Proficiency in English composition must be demonstrated. **Procedure:** Freshmen are admitted fall, spring, and summer. Entrance exams should be taken at least 2 months before admissions deadlines. There are early admissions, deferred admissions, and rolling admissions plans. Applications should be filed by August 1 for fall entry; December 3 for spring entry; and May 12 for summer entry. The fall 2017 application fee was $75. Notification is sent on a rolling basis. Applications are accepted on-line. **Transfer Students:** 3934 transfer students enrolled in 2016-2017. Applicants with fewer than 30 hours from an accredited college must have a 2.5 GPA and meet freshman entrance requirements. Applicants with at least 30 but no more than 44 transferable hours must have a 2.3 GPA; those with more than 44 hours must have a 2.0 GPA. Students may enroll in the fall, spring, and summer. 30 of 120 credits required for the bachelor's degree must be completed at UNT. **International Students:** There are 1895 international students enrolled. They must take the TOEFL with a minimum score of 550 on the paper-based TOEFL (PBT) or 79 on the Internet-based version (iBT), or take the MELAB, and any one of these tests: the ECPE, FCE, CAE, CPE, IELTS, or ELPT. U.S. high school graduates who are not U.S. citizens may take either the SAT I or ACT instead of the TOEFL.

ADMISSIONS: 72% of the 2017-2018 applicants were accepted. The SAT scores for the 2017-2018 freshman class were: Math-- 11% below 500, 55% between 500 and 599, 2% between 600 and 699, and 7% between 700 and 800. Evidence-Based Reading/Writing-- 9% below 500, 46% between 500 and 599, 38% between 600 and 699, and 7% between 700 and 800. The ACT scores were 6% between 12 and 17, 46% between 18 and 23, 40% between 24 and 29, and 8% above 30. 53% of the current freshmen were in the top fifth of their class; 90% were in the top two fifths. **Admissions Contact:** Dr. Rebecca Lothringer, Director of Undergraduate Admissions. Email: *unt.freshman@unt.edu* Web: *www.unt.edu*

FINANCIAL AID: The priority date for freshman financial aid applications for fall entry is March 15.

UNIVERSITY OF ST. THOMAS - HOUSTON E-3

www.stthom.edu

Houston, TX 77006	(713) 525-3500
Fax: (713) 525-3558	**Email:** admissions@stthom.edu
Full-time: 475 men, 961 women	**Faculty:** 119; IIA
Part-time: 239 men, 189 women	**Ph.D.s:** 93%
Graduate: 433 men, 940 women	**Student/Faculty:** 12 to 1
Year: semesters, summer session	**Tuition:** $32,660
Room & Board: $8850	**Freshman Class:** 1060 applied, 858 accepted, 295 enrolled
SAT EBR-W/M: 582/575 **ACT:** 24	**CEEB CODE:** 6880
Application Deadline: May 1	**VERY COMPETITIVE**

University of St. Thomas in Houston offers a Catholic liberal arts education for a lifetime of opportunities. Liberal arts degrees provide invaluable training to a range of careers including business, teaching and health. UST offers 33 undergraduate and 15 graduate degree programs. There are 4 undergraduate schools and 6 graduate schools. In addition to regional accreditation, UST-Houston has baccalaureate program accreditation with AACSB, CAEP, ATS, and CCNE. The 23-acre campus is in an urban area 3 miles from Downtown Houston. Including any residence halls, there are 65 buildings.

STUDENT LIFE: 97% of undergraduates are from Texas. Others are from 24 states, 38 foreign countries, and Canada. 76% are from public schools. 8% are Foreign; 6% African American; 44% Hispanic; 3% two or more races; 3% race unknown; 24% White; 11% Asian American. 53% are Catholic; 26% claim no religious affiliation; 12% Protestant. **Female To Male Ratio:** 1.8:1. The average age of freshmen is 18; all undergraduates, 26. 15% do not continue beyond their first year; 85% remain to graduate. **Housing:** 397 students can be accommodated in college housing, which includes dorms and on-campus apartments. In addition, there are special-interest houses, first-year and upperclassmen faith-based living learning communities, residents are grouped by classification and gender. On-campus housing is available on a first-come, first-served basis. 79% of students commute. All students may keep cars.

FACULTY/CLASSROOMS: 54% of faculty are male; 46% are female. 69% teach undergraduates. Graduate students teach 1% of introductory courses. The average class size in an introductory lecture is 19 and in a laboratory is 18.

PROGRAMS OF STUDY: UST-Houston confers B.A., B.F.A., B.S., B.S.N., B.B.A., and B.I.B. degrees. Master's and doctoral degrees are also awarded. Bachelor's degrees are awarded in AGRICULTURE (environmental studies), BIOLOGICAL SCIENCE (biochemistry, bioinformatics, and biology/biological science), BUSINESS (accounting, business administration and management, finance, international business, and marketing), COMMUNICATIONS AND THE ARTS (communications, dramatic arts, English, French, music, Spanish, and studio art), COMPUTER AND PHYSICAL SCIENCE (applied mathematics, chemistry, computer science, and mathematics), EDUCATION (education and music education), ENGINEERING AND ENVIRONMENTAL DESIGN (environmental science), HEALTH PROFESSIONS (nursing), SOCIAL SCIENCE (criminology, economics, history, international studies, liberal arts/general studies, liberal arts, sciences, general studies, humanities, philosophy, political science/government, psychology, and theological studies). Biology is the strongest academically. Biology, psychology, and nursing have the largest enrollments.

ACTIVITIES: There are no fraternities or sororities. There are 103 groups on campus, including art, cheerleading, choir, communications, dance, drama, environmental, ethnic, film, forensics, honors, international, jazz band, LGBT, literary magazine, musical theater, newspaper, orchestra, political, professional, religious, social, social service, and student government. Popular campus events include Research Symposium, Mass of Holy Spirit, Mass of St. Thomas Aquinas, Family and Alumni Weekend, Celts Day of Service, Deck the Mall, Neewollah, Late Night Breakfast, SAB's Formal, and I-Fest (international festival). **Sports:** There are 4 intercollegiate sports for men and 5 for women, and 10 intramural sports for men and 10 for women. Facilities include a gym, racquetball courts, a weight room, a fitness room, a dance room, swimming pool, and sand volleyball court. Outdoor facilities include a 120' x 120' turf field. **Graduates:** From July 1, 2016 to June 30, 2017, 327 bachelor's degrees were awarded. The most popular majors were nursing (10%), biology (9%), and finance (9%). In an average class, 31% graduate in 4 years or less, 51% graduate in 5 years or less, and 57% graduate in 6 years or less.

SERVICES: Counseling and information services are available, as is tutoring in most subjects. There is remedial math, reading, and writing, as well as Kurzweil Educational software and Jaws for the visually impaired, IBM SPSS Statistics for Psychology, QuickBooks File Manager for Accounting, Matlab for Math. **Library/Resources:** The library contains 262,245 volumes, 2,133 microform items, and 2,133 audio/video tapes/CDs/DVDs, and subscribes to 74,347 periodicals, including electronic. Computerized library services include interlibrary loans, database searching, Internet access, and Wi-Fi capability. Special learning facilities include an art gallery and a meditation garden. **Physically Challenged Students:** 90% of the campus is accessible. Facilities include wheelchair ramps, elevators, special parking, specially equipped restrooms, lowered drinking fountains, lowered telephones, and special housing. **Special:** UST has a cooperative 3-2 engineering program with the University of Houston, Texas A&M University, University of Notre Dame, and Catholic University of America. Internships in the major field of study and study abroad in 11 countries are also available. Dual and joint majors and 5 year joint bachelor's and master's degree programs, combining BBA/MBA are available. There are 22 national honor societies, a freshman honors program, and 1 departmental honors programs. **Visiting:** There are regularly scheduled orientations for prospective students, including campus tours, class visitations, introductions to faculty, administrative members, and currently enrolled students, financial aid, and social activities. There are guides for informal visits; visitors may sit in on classes and stay overnight. To schedule a visit, contact Karen Bautista at (713) 525-3500. **Campus Safety and Security:** Measures include 24-hour foot and vehicle patrol, an emergency notification system, self-defense education, and security escort services. There are shuttle buses, emergency telephones, lighted pathways/sidewalks, controlled access to dorms/residences, fire suppression system, fire extinguishers, smoke detectors, and annual fire drills; and IP security cameras.

REQUIREMENTS: The SAT or ACT and the ACT Optional Writing test are required. Applicants must graduate from an accredited secondary school, home school program or successfully complete the GED. Additionally, applicants should have competitive grades (mimimum high school GPA of 2.80 on a 4.0 scale) in a minimum of 18 college preparatory high school units: including 4 units of English, 3 units each of social science, mathematics, and science, 2 units of the same classical or modern language other than English, and 3 units of electives in college preparatory classes. Applicants should also have competitive official SAT or ACT scores and competitive class rank if high school ranks graduates. If appropriate, applicants should submit official transcripts of home school coursework. Home schooled students may also need to submit course descriptions, reading lists, or other information if requested. UST requires applicants to be in the upper 50% of their class. A GPA of 2.5 is required. AP and CLEP credits are accepted. Important factors in the admissions decision are advanced placement or honors courses, recommendations by school officials, and extracurricular activities record. To graduate, students must complete the core curriculum and 30 to 48 hours in their selected majors. In some cases, students need to complete special projects according to the requirements of specific majors. Students must have a minimum 2.0 GPA in a total of 126 credit hours, including 36 hours of upper-division credits and the final 36 hours competed in residence at the University. **Procedure:** Freshmen are admitted in the fall, spring, and summer. Entrance exams should be taken as early as possible. There are early admissions and deferred admissions plans. Early decision applications should be filed by December 1; regular applications, by May 1 for fall entry; December 1 for spring entry; and May 1 for summer entry. Notification of early decision is sent December 15; regular decision, on a rolling basis. Applications are accepted online. **Transfer Students:** 202 transfer students enrolled in 2016-2017. Transfer students must have a minimum 2.50 cumulative GPA from all colleges/universities attended and have a high school diploma or GED. 36 of 126 credits required for the bachelor's degree must be completed at UST. **International Students:** There are 138 international students enrolled. They must take the TOEFL with a minimum score of 550 on the paper-based TOEFL (PBT) or 79 on the Internet-based version (iBT), and the English Proficiency Level 112 for English language test. They must also take the SAT or ACT, scoring 23.

ADMISSIONS: 81% of the 2017-2018 applicants were accepted. The SAT scores for the 2017-2018 freshman class were: Math-- 6% below 500, 58% between 500 and 599, 29% between 600 and 699, and 6%

between 700 and 800. Evidence-Based Reading/Writing-- 8% below 500, 48% between 500 and 599, 41% between 600 and 699, and 3% between 700 and 800. The ACT scores were 51% between 18 and 23, 37% between 24 and 29, and 11% above 30. 47% of the current freshmen were in the top fifth of their class; 75% were in the top two fifths. 5 freshmen graduated first in their class. **Admissions Contact:** Arthur Ortiz, Vice President of Enrollment Management. Email: *admissions@stthom.edu* Web: *www.stthom.edu*

FINANCIAL AID: In 2017-2018, 94% of all full-time freshmen received some form of financial aid. 80% of all full-time freshmen received need-based aid. The average freshman award was $28,016. Need-based scholarships or need-based grants averaged $25,352; need-based self-help aid (loans and jobs) averaged $3,775; non-need-based athletic scholarships averaged $5,823; and other non-need-based awards and non-need-based scholarships averaged $12,504. 16% of undergraduate students work part-time. The average financial indebtedness of the 2017 graduate was $29,857. The priority date for freshman financial aid applications for fall entry is April 15.

UNIVERSITY OF TEXAS AT ARLINGTON D-2

www.uta.edu

Arlington, TX 76019 **(817) 272-6287**

Fax: (817) 272-3435
Email: admissions@uta.edu
Full-time: 8043 men, 8620 women
Faculty: n/av
Part-time: 4457 men, 11425 women
Ph.D.s: 81%
Graduate: 4916 men, 7591 women
Student/Faculty: 25 to 1
Year: semesters, summer session
Tuition: $9952 ($25,152)
Room & Board: $8924
Freshman Class: 12558 applied, 8768 accepted, 3054 enrolled
SAT CR/M/W: 520/550/500 **ACT:** 23
CEEB CODE: 6013
Application Deadline: June 1
COMPETITIVE

University of Texas at Arlington, founded in 1895, is part of the University of Texas System and is organized into colleges and schools, including business administration, engineering, liberal arts, science, architecture, nursing, social work, graduate studies, urban and public affairs, and education. There are 9 undergraduate schools and 10 graduate schools. In addition to regional accreditation, UTA has baccalaureate program accreditation with AACSB, ABET, ASLA, CSWE, FIDER, NAAB, NASM, NLN, ACS, and NASPAA. The 420-acre campus is in an urban area in the center of the Dallas/Fort Worth metroplex. Including any residence halls, there are 100 buildings.

STUDENT LIFE: 97% of undergraduates are from Texas. Others are from 45 states, 88 foreign countries, and Canada. 38% are White; 3% Foreign; 3% two or more races; 26% Hispanic; 15% African American; 11% Asian American; 1% American Indian/Alaska Native. **Female To Male Ratio:** 1.6:1. The average age of freshmen is 19; all undergraduates, 28. 31% do not continue beyond their first year; 31% remain to graduate. **Housing:** 3303 students can be accommodated in college housing, which includes married student dorms, on-campus apartments, and off-campus apartments. In addition, there are honors houses, fraternity houses, sorority houses, family housing (priority given to students with dependent children), and theme housing. On-campus housing is available on a first-come, first-served basis. 58% of students commute. All students may keep cars. Alcohol is not permitted.

FACULTY/CLASSROOMS: 60% of faculty are male; 40% are female. Graduate students teach 17% of introductory courses. The average class size in an introductory lecture is 47 and in a laboratory is 25.

PROGRAMS OF STUDY: UTA confers B.A., B.S., B.A.I.S., B.B.A., B.F.A., B.M., B.S.A.S.E., B.S.C.E., B.S.C.S., B.S.C.S.E., B.S.E.E., B.S.I.E., B.S.I.S., B.S.M.E., B.S.N., and B.S.W. degrees. Master's and doctoral degrees are also awarded. Bachelor's degrees are awarded in BIOLOGICAL SCIENCE (biochemistry, biology/biological science, and microbiology), BUSINESS (accounting, banking and finance, business administration and management, business economics, financial services, international business information systems, management science, marketing/retailing/merchandising, and real estate), COMMUNICATIONS AND THE ARTS (art history and appreciation, broadcasting, communications, dramatic arts, English, French, German, journalism, linguistics, music, Russian, Spanish, speech/debate/rhetoric, and studio art), COMPUTER AND PHYSICAL SCIENCE (chemistry, computer science, geology, information sciences and systems, mathematics, and physics), EDUCATION (physical education), ENGINEERING AND ENVIRONMENTAL DESIGN (architecture, civil engineering, computer engineering, electrical/electronics engineering, industrial engineering technology, interior design, landscape architecture/design, and mechanical engineering), HEALTH PROFESSIONS (medical technology and nursing), SOCIAL SCIENCE (anthropology, classical/ancient civilization, criminal justice, economics, history, interdisciplinary studies, philosophy, political science/government, psychology, social work, and sociology). Liberal arts, business, and engineering have the largest enrollments.

ACTIVITIES: 8% of men belong to 12 national fraternities; 6% of women belong to 10 national sororities. There are 225 groups on campus, including art, band, cheerleading, chess, choir, chorale, chorus, communications, computers, dance, drama, drill team, drum and bugle corps, ethnic, forensics, honors, international, jazz band, LGBT, marching band, opera, orchestra, photography, political, professional, religious, social, social service, student government, symphony, and yearbook. Popular campus events include Charity Week, The Big Event and Last Day Blast, Oozeball, Bed Races, and Maverick Stampede. **Sports:** There are 6 intercollegiate sports for men and 6 for women, and 10 intramural sports for men and 10 for women. Facilities include racquetball courts, basketball and volleyball courts, lighted tennis courts, an indoor track, outdoor track, cross country, softball, golf, wheelchair basketball, an Olympic-size pool, weight rooms, a stadium, and a gym. **Graduates:** From July 1, 2016 to June 30, 2017, 7481 bachelor's degrees were awarded. The most popular majors were health professions and related programs (43%), business marketing (11%), engineering, and and liberal arts (5%). In an average class, 1% graduate in 3 years or less, 9% graduate in 4 years or less, 23% graduate in 5 years or less, and 31% graduate in 6 years or less.

SERVICES: Counseling and information services are available, as is tutoring in most subjects, such as English, math, computer science, and foreign languages. There is a reader service for the blind, and remedial math, reading, and writing, a math tutorial clinic, a nursing learning resource center, a reading lab, a science learning center, and a writing lab. **Library/Resources:** The library contains 1.1 million volumes, 1.5 million microform items, and 3,468 audio/video tapes/CDs/DVDs, and subscribes to 5,073 periodicals, including electronic. Computerized library services include interlibrary loans and database searching. Special learning facilities include an art gallery, a planetarium, cartographic history library, and nano lab. **Physically Challenged Students:** All of the campus is accessible. Facilities include wheelchair ramps, elevators, special parking, specially equipped restrooms, special class scheduling, lowered drinking fountains, lowered telephones, and special housing. **Special:** Cooperative education programs provide opportunities to gain experience in local business through the colleges of engineering and business. Cross-registration with the Summer Institute of Linguistics and the University of Texas Health Science Center, as well as with other members of the University of Texas System, is available. Study abroad in 10 countries, work-study at the university, B.A.-B.S. degrees, dual majors, student-designed interdisciplinary majors, credit for military experience, and pass/fail options are also offered. There are 2 national honor societies, a freshman honors program, and 10 departmental honors programs. **Visiting:** There are regularly scheduled orientations for prospective students, and 1-day orientations for transfers and returning adult students. There are guides for informal visits and visitors may sit in on classes. To schedule a visit, contact the Admissions Office. **Campus Safety and Security:** Measures include 24-hour foot and vehicle patrol, self-defense education, and security escort services. There are shuttle buses, emergency telephones, lighted pathways/sidewalks, and crime prevention programs.

REQUIREMENTS: Students ranked in the top 10% of their high school class are admitted regardless of SAT I/ACT. Those in the second quarter of their class must submit a minimum of 950 on the SAT I or 20 on the ACT. Those in the third quarter must score 1000 on the SAT I or 21 on ACT. The bottom quarter must score 1150 on the SAT I or 25 on ACT. The GED is accepted under certain circumstances. Applicants must have 26 academic credits, including 4 units each of English, math, social studies, and science, and 2 units of foreign language, 5.5 units of academic electives, and recommended 1 unit each of computer science, visual/performing arts, or from education, fine arts, and .5 of speech or 1.5 physical education. Currently, the application form can be downloaded from the UTA web site. The Texas Common Application is also accepted. AP and CLEP credits are accepted. All students must earn a GPA of 2.0 while taking at least 124 semester hours, including 30 in their major. The core curriculum requires 8 hours of science, 6 each of English composition, math, U.S. history, and U.S. political science, and 3 each of literature, liberal arts, social/cultural studies, and fine arts/philosophy. Students must demonstrate proficiency in oral presentations and computer use. Proficiency exams, or completion of a department-designated course, may be required by the major department. These are also required of members of the Honors College. **Procedure:** Freshmen are admitted to all sessions. Entrance exams should be taken during the fall of the senior year. There are early admissions, deferred admissions, and rolling admissions plans. Applications should be filed by June 1 for fall entry; December 1 for spring entry; and April 1 for summer entry. The fall 2017 application fee was $35. Notification is sent on a rolling basis. Applications are accepted online. **Transfer Students:** 6398 transfer students enrolled in 2016-2017. Transfer students with 30 or more transferable semester hours need a 2.0 GPA or evidence of high school or GED completion and SAT I or ACT scores comparable to the high school associated rank (varies by student). Transfer students with fewer than 30 transferable semester hours must have a 2.0 GPA and also meet admission requirements for entering freshmen. 25 credits required for the bachelor's degree must be completed at UTA. **International Students:** There are 682 international students enrolled. They must take the TOEFL with a minimum score of 550 on the paper-based TOEFL (PBT). They must also take the SAT, scoring 900.

ADMISSIONS: 70% of the 2017-2018 applicants were accepted. The SAT scores for the 2017-2018 freshman class were: Critical Reading-- 32% below 500, 41% between 500 and 599, 22% between 600 and 699, and 4% between 700 and 800. Math-- 21% below 500, 43% between 500 and 599, 29% between 600 and 699, and 7% between 700 and 800. Writing-- 42% below 500, 40% between 500 and 599, 16% between 600 and 699, and 2% between 700 and 800. The ACT scores were 7% between 12 and 17, 42% between 18 and 23, 42% between 24 and 29, and 9% above 30. **Admissions Contact:** Hahns Gatterdam, Director of Undergraduate Admissions. Email: *admissions@uta.edu* Web: *www.uta.edu*

FINANCIAL AID: In 2017-2018, 65% of all full-time freshmen received some form of financial aid. The average freshman award was $10,555. Need-based scholarships or need-based grants averaged $7,427; need-based self-help aid (loans and jobs) averaged $3,608; non-need-based athletic scholarships averaged $3,787; other non-need-based awards and non-need-based scholarships averaged $5,465; and $3,587 from other forms of aid. The average financial indebtedness of the 2017 graduate was $13,332. The priority date for freshman financial aid applications for fall entry is April 17.

UNIVERSITY OF TEXAS AT DALLAS — D-2

www.utdallas.edu

Richardson, TX 75080 — **(972) 883-2270**

Fax: (972) 883-2599	**Email:** interest@utdallas.edu
Full-time: 8693 men, 6600 women	**Faculty:** 672; I, --$
Part-time: 1779 men, 1316 women	**Ph.D.s:** 92%
Graduate: 5299 men, 3954 women	**Student/Faculty:** 21 to 1
Year: semesters, summer session	**Tuition:** $12,528 ($34,644)
Room & Board: $11,112	**Freshman Class:** 13703 applied, 7747 accepted, 3182 enrolled
SAT CR/M: 650/670 **ACT:** 29	**CEEB CODE:** 6897
Application Deadline: July 1	**HIGHLY COMPETITIVE**

University of Texas at Dallas, founded in 1969 as part of the University of Texas system, offers undergraduate and graduate programs in the liberal arts and sciences, business, engineering, computer science, cognitive science, and neuroscience. There are 8 undergraduate schools and 8 graduate schools. In addition to regional accreditation, UTD has baccalaureate program accreditation with AACSB, ABET, ACS, and NASPAA. The 550-acre campus is in a suburban area 18 miles north of downtown Dallas. Including any residence halls, there are 158 buildings.

STUDENT LIFE: 93% of undergraduates are from Texas. Others are from 49 states, 78 foreign countries, and Canada. 94% are from public schools. 5% are African American; 30% White; 3% two or more races; 23% Asian American; 22% Foreign; 2% race unknown; 14% Hispanic. **Male To Female Ratio:** 1.3:1. The average age of freshmen is 18; all undergraduates, 22. 13% do not continue beyond their first year; 70% remain to graduate. **Housing:** 6954 students can be accommodated in college housing, which includes married student dorms, on-campus apartments, and living learning communities. On-campus housing is available on a first-come, first-served basis. 75% of students commute. All students may keep cars.

FACULTY/CLASSROOMS: 68% of faculty are male; 32% are female. 55% teach undergraduates, 3% do research, and 42% do both. Graduate students teach 7% of introductory courses. The average class size in an introductory lecture is 45; in a laboratory is 33; and in a regular course is 41.

PROGRAMS OF STUDY: UTD confers B.A., B.S., B.S.EE., and B.S.TE. degrees. Master's and doctoral degrees are also awarded. Bachelor's degrees are awarded in BIOLOGICAL SCIENCE (biochemistry, biology/biological science, molecular biology, and neurosciences), BUSINESS (accounting, banking and finance, business administration and management, international business management, marketing management, and supply chain management), COMMUNICATIONS AND THE ARTS (game design and development, literature, media arts, and visual and performing arts), COMPUTER AND PHYSICAL SCIENCE (actuarial science, chemistry, computer science, geoscience, information sciences and systems, mathematics, physics, and software engineering), ENGINEERING AND ENVIRONMENTAL DESIGN (biomedical engineering, computer engineering, electrical/electronics engineering, and mechanical engineering), HEALTH PROFESSIONS (health care leadership, health science biology interdisciplinary, and speech pathology/audiology), SOCIAL SCIENCE (American studies, child psychology/development, cognitive science, criminology, economics, geography information science, history, interdisciplinary studies, international public service, political science/government, psychology, public administration, public policy, and sociology). Electrical engineering, biological sciences, and business administration are the strongest academically. Biology, business administration, and computer science have the largest enrollments.

ACTIVITIES: 2% of men belong to 12 national fraternities; 3% of women belong to 11 national sororities. There are 438 groups on campus, including art, band, cheerleading, chess, choir, chorale, chorus, computers, dance, debate, drama, drill team, environmental, ethnic, film, forensics, honors, international, jazz band, LGBT, literary magazine, musical theater, newspaper, opera, orchestra, pep band, photography, political, professional, radio and TV, religious, social, social service, and student government. Popular campus events include Welcome Week, Homecoming, Holiday Sing, Oozeball, and Green Lecture Series. **Sports:** There are 6 intercollegiate sports for men and 7 for women, and 27 intramural sports for men and 27 for women. Facilities include racquetball courts, squash courts, tennis courts, indoor and outdoor basketball courts, a sand volleyball court, a 1-mile gravel track, soccer fields, softball fields, a junior Olympic pool/natatorium, a gym, and a weight room. **Graduates:** From July 1, 2016 to June 30, 2017, 3434 bachelor's degrees were awarded. The most popular majors were biology (8%), accounting (7%), and computer science (6%). In an average class, 6% graduate in 3 years or less, 52% graduate in 4 years or less, 66% graduate in 5 years or less, and 70% graduate in 6 years or less. Of the 2016 graduating class, 36% were enrolled in graduate school within 6 months of graduation, and 68% were employed.

SERVICES: Counseling and information services are available, as is tutoring in most subjects. There is a reader service for the blind, and remedial math, reading, and writing. **Library/Resources:** The library contains 3.2 million volumes, 727,521 microform items, 15,407 audio/video tapes/CDs/DVDs, and subscribes to 284,693 periodicals, including electronic. Computerized library services include interlibrary loans, database searching, and Internet access. Special learning facilities include an art gallery, radio and TV stations, a center for communications disorders, a rare books library, and special library collections on aviation history, geophysics, philatelic research, and botanicals. **Physically Challenged Students:** All of the campus is accessible. Facilities include wheelchair ramps, elevators, special parking, specially equipped restrooms, lowered drinking fountains, and lowered telephones. **Special:** Cross-registration is available with other University of Texas campuses. Accelerated degree programs and B.A.-B.S. degrees are offered in several majors, as is a 3-2 engineering degree. Co-op programs, internships, work-study programs with several major corporations, dual majors, student-designed majors and Washington semester are also possible. In addition, students may study abroad in Europe, Asia, Mexico and New

Zealand. There are 5 national honor societies, a freshman honors program, and 16 departmental honors programs. **Visiting:** There are regularly scheduled orientations for prospective students, including meetings with faculty and an admissions counselor, and a campus tour. There are guides for informal visits and visitors may sit in on classes. To schedule a visit, contact the Office of Enrollment Services at (972) 883-2270. **Campus Safety and Security:** Measures include 24-hour foot and vehicle patrol, emergency notification system, self-defense education, and security escort services. There are emergency telephones, lighted pathways/sidewalks, controlled access to dorms/residences, campus crime watch bulletins, bicycle patrols, crime prevention programs, ID engraving, and police liaison who works with students on security issues.

REQUIREMENTS: The SAT or ACT and the ACT Optional Writing test are required. Applicants should be graduates of an accredited secondary school. In-state students who rank in the top 10% of their class gain automatic admission to UTD. Credentials for other students must include completion of 4 units of English, 3 units each of social science and lab science, 3.5 of math, 2 units of foreign language, and coursework in fine arts and electives, with health and physical education courses recommended. AP and CLEP credits are accepted. Important factors in the admissions decision are advanced placement or honors courses, leadership record, and evidence of special talent. To graduate, students must complete at least 120 credit hours, including 30 in the major and 51 in upper-division courses, with a minimum GPA of 2.0. Core courses include 15 credits in social science (with 6 each in U.S./Texas government and U.S./Texas history), 9 in natural science, and 6 each in communications, math, and humanities/fine arts. Magna and summa cum laude graduates must complete a thesis. **Procedure:** Freshmen are admitted to all sessions. Entrance exams should be taken at the end of the junior year or beginning of the senior year. There are deferred admissions and rolling admissions plans. Applications should be filed by July 1 for fall entry; November 1 for spring entry; and April 1 for summer entry. The fall 2017 application fee was $50. Applications are accepted online. **Transfer Students:** 1979 transfer students enrolled in 2016-2017. Sophomore applicants must present a GPA of 3.0 and 12 credits in the general education core. Upper-division applicants should have a GPA of 2.5 and be in good standing at the last school attended. 30 of 120 credits required for the bachelor's degree must be completed at UTD. **International Students:** There are 611 international students enrolled. They must take the TOEFL with a minimum score of 550 on the paper-based TOEFL (PBT) or 80 on the Internet-based version (iBT). They must also take the SAT or ACT.

ADMISSIONS: 57% of the 2017-2018 applicants were accepted. The SAT scores for the 2017-2018 freshman class were: Critical Reading-- 2% below 500, 22% between 500 and 599, 51% between 600 and 699, and 25% between 700 and 800. Math-- 1% below 500, 16% between 500 and 599, 46% between 600 and 699, and 37% between 700 and 800. The ACT scores were 5% between 18 and 23, 47% between 24 and 29, and 48% above 30. 56% of the current freshmen were in the top fifth of their class; 82% were in the top two fifths. 95 freshmen graduated first in their class. **Admissions Contact:** Wray Weldon, Assistant Provost, Enrollment Management. Email: *interest@utdallas.edu* Web: *www.utdallas.edu*

FINANCIAL AID: In 2017-2018, 49% of all full-time freshmen received some form of financial aid. 44% of all full-time freshmen received need-based aid. The average freshman award was $13,429. Need-based scholarships or need-based grants averaged $10,535; need-based self-help aid (loans and jobs) averaged $3,568; and other non-need-based awards and non-need-based scholarships averaged $12,775. 6% of undergraduate students work part-time. The average financial indebtedness of the 2017 graduate was $20,432. The FAFSA code is 009741. The priority date for freshman financial aid applications for fall entry is March 31.

UNIVERSITY OF TEXAS AT EL PASO *(The complete profile is made available exclusively on our website, www.barronspac.com)*

UNIVERSITY OF TEXAS RIO GRANDE VALLEY *(The complete profile is made available exclusively on our website, www.barronspac.com)*

UNIVERSITY OF THE INCARNATE WORD *(The complete profile is made available exclusively on our website, www.barronspac.com)*

WAYLAND BAPTIST UNIVERSITY *(The complete profile is made available exclusively on our website, www.barronspac.com)*

WEST TEXAS A&M UNIVERSITY — B-1

www.wtamu.edu

Canyon, TX 79016 — (806) 651-2020, (800) 999-8268

Fax: (806) 651-5285 — **Email:** admissions@wtamu.edu

Full-time: 2487 men, 3036 women	**Faculty:** 210; IIA, --$
Part-time: 637 men, 748 women	**Ph.D.s:** 70%
Graduate: 509 men, 964 women	**Student/Faculty:** 21 to 1
Year: semesters, summer session	**Tuition:** $6970 ($7870)
Room & Board: $6508	**Freshman Class:** 1665 applied, 1204 accepted, 801 enrolled
SAT: required **ACT:** 21	**CEEB CODE:** 6938
Application Deadline: August 15	**COMPETITIVE**

West Texas A&M University, founded in 1910, is a public institution, and a member of the Texas A&M University System, offering programs in the liberal arts and sciences, fine arts, agriculture, nursing, and education. There are 4 undergraduate schools and 1 graduate school. In addition to regional accreditation, WTAMU has baccalaureate program accreditation with ACBSP, CSWE, NASM, and CCNE. The 135-acre campus is in a small town 17 miles south of Amarillo. Including any residence halls, there are 82 buildings.

STUDENT LIFE: 89% of undergraduates are from Texas. Others are from 39 states, 26 foreign countries, and Canada. 93% are from public schools. 76% are White; 4% African American; 4% Foreign; 14% Hispanic; 1% Asian American; 1% American Indian/Alaska Native. **Female To Male Ratio:** 1.3:1. The average age of freshmen is 18; all undergraduates, 24. 36% do not continue beyond their first year; 66% remain to graduate. **Housing:** 1520 students can be accommodated in college housing, which includes dorms. In addition, there are special-interest houses, sorority units within the residence halls, 24-hour quiet areas, and an honors hall. On-campus housing is guaranteed for all 4 years. 82% of students commute. All students may keep cars. Alcohol is not permitted.

FACULTY/CLASSROOMS: 56% of faculty are male; 44% are female. 95% teach undergraduates, 47% do research, and 47% do both. Graduate students teach 16% of introductory courses. The average class size in an introductory lecture is 28; in a laboratory is 23; and in a regular course is 26.

PROGRAMS OF STUDY: WTAMU confers B.A., B.S., B.A.A.S., B.B.A., B.F.A., B.G.S., B.M., B.S.M.T., and B.S.N. degrees. Master's and doctoral degrees are also awarded. Bachelor's degrees are awarded in AGRICULTURE (agricultural business management, agricultural economics, agriculture, animal science, plant protection (pest management), plant science, and soil science), BIOLOGICAL SCIENCE (biology/biological science, biotechnology, and wildlife biology), BUSINESS (accounting, banking and finance, business administration and management, business economics, management science, and marketing/retailing/merchandising), COMMUNICATIONS AND THE ARTS (applied art, art, broadcasting, dance, dramatic arts, English, graphic design, music, music theory and composition, musical theater, performing arts, public relations, publishing, Spanish, speech/debate/rhetoric, and studio art), COMPUTER AND PHYSICAL SCIENCE (chemistry, computer science, geology, information sciences and systems, mathematics, and physics), EDUCATION (art education, athletic training, business education, drama education, English education, foreign languages education, mathematics education, music education, physical education, reading education, science education, social studies education, and special education), ENGINEERING AND ENVIRONMENTAL DESIGN (emergency/disaster science, engineering technology, environmental science, mechanical engineering, and preengineering), HEALTH PROFESSIONS (allied health, exercise science, medical technology, music therapy, nursing, predentistry, premedicine, prepharmacy, preveterinary science, and speech pathology/audiology), SOCIAL SCIENCE (criminal justice, economics, geography, history, interdisciplinary studies, liberal arts/general studies, political science/government, prelaw, psychology, public administration, social science, social work, and sociology). Education and music are the strongest academically. Education has the largest enrollment.

ACTIVITIES: 4% of men belong to 1 local and 4 national fraternities; 4% of women belong to 2 local and 3 national sororities. There are 97 groups on campus, including academic club, art, band, cheerleading, choir, chorale, chorus, computers, dance, debate, drama, ethnic, film, forensics, honors, international, jazz band, literary magazine, marching band, musical theater, newspaper, opera, orchestra, photography, political, professional, radio and TV, religious, social, social service, student government, and symphony. Popular campus events include Workathon, RHA Mud Pull, and Buffalo Branding. **Sports:** There are 6 intercollegiate sports for men and 6 for women, and 39 intramural sports for men and 39 for women. Facilities include a swimming pool, an 8-lane bowling alley, weight-training rooms, a stadium, handball, racquetball, tennis, badminton, basketball, and volleyball courts, a flag football field, and softball fields. **Graduates:** From July 1, 2016 to June 30, 2017, 980 bachelor's degrees were awarded. The most popular majors were general studies (23%), business (19%), and nursing/interdisciplinary studies (10%). In an average class, 1% graduate in 3 years or less, 14% graduate in 4 years or less, 28% graduate in 5 years or less, and 32% graduate in 6 years or less. Of the 2016 graduating class, 40% were enrolled in graduate school within 6 months of graduation.

SERVICES: Counseling and information services are available, as is tutoring in most subjects, such as in the core curriculum courses. There is a reader service for the blind, and remedial math, reading, and writing. **Library/Resources:** The library contains 1.1 million volumes, 1.3 million microform items, 1,555 audio/video tapes/CDs/DVDs, and subscribes to 16,973 periodicals, including electronic. Computerized library services include interlibrary loans, database searching, Internet access, and Wi-Fi capability. Special learning facilities include an art gallery, a natural history museum, a radio station, an alternative energy institute, an electronic learning center, a communications disorders center, and a nursing learning center. **Physically Challenged Students:** All of the campus is accessible. Facilities include wheelchair ramps, elevators, special parking, specially equipped restrooms, special class scheduling, lowered drinking fountains, lowered telephones, and special housing. **Special:** WTAMU offers work-study programs, a Washington semester, internships, co-op programs, credit by exam, B.A.-B.S. degrees, a general studies degree, interdisciplinary studies in elementary/secondary education fields, nondegree study, and pass/fail options. There are 12 national honor societies, a freshman honors program, and 14 departmental honors programs. **Visiting:** There are regularly scheduled orientations for prospective students, including a tour of campus, admissions and financial services sessions, selection of a major, and a visit with faculty. There are guides for informal visits; visitors may sit in on classes and stay overnight. To schedule a visit, contact the Admissions Office. **Campus Safety and Security:** Measures include 24-hour foot and vehicle patrol, self-defense education, and security escort services. There are shuttle buses, emergency telephones, lighted pathways/sidewalks.

REQUIREMENTS: Applicants should have graduated from an accredited secondary school or have a GED. Admission requires graduation in the top 50% of the student's high school class or a minimum composite score of 20 on the ACT or 950 on the SAT I. Students should have completed 4 units each in English, math and science, 3.5 units in social science, 2 units in foreign language, 1 unit each in fine arts and physical education, 6 units in electives and .5 in speech. AP and CLEP credits are accepted. A general education requirement of 46 hours includes courses in analytic reasoning and communication skills, cultural heritage, English, computer literacy, math, science, history, political science, humanities, and sports and exercise sciences. Additional core requirements vary according to major. A minimum 2.0 GPA and 127 credit hours, including at least 36 of advanced work, up to a maximum of 60, 30 of which must be at WTAMU, are required to graduate. At least 33 hours must be earned in residence at WTAMU, including at least 24 of the last 30 hours counted toward a degree. **Procedure:** Freshmen are admitted to all sessions. Entrance exams should be taken in the fall of the senior year. There are deferred admissions and rolling admissions plans. Application deadlines are open. The fall 2017 application fee was $40. Applications are accepted on-line. **Transfer Students:** 799 transfer students enrolled in 2016-2017. A 2.0 GPA is generally required for transfer students. 30 of 127 credits required for the bachelor's degree must be completed at WTAMU. **International Students:** They must take the TOEFL, and either the SAT or ACT.

ADMISSIONS: 72% of the 2017-2018 applicants were accepted. The ACT scores were 49% below 12, 28% between 12 and 17, 15% between 18 and 23, 5% between 24 and 29, and 2% above 30. 44% of the current freshmen were in the top fifth of their class; 82% were in the top two fifths. 27 freshmen graduated first in their class. **Admissions Contact:** Jose Topete, Assistant Director of Admissions. Email: *admissions@wtamu.edu* Web: *www.wtamu.edu*

FINANCIAL AID: In 2017-2018, 51% of all full-time freshmen received some form of financial aid. 39% of all full-time freshmen received need-based aid. The average freshman award was $5,958. Need-based scholarships or need-based grants averaged $3,282 ($4,562 maximum); need-based self-help aid (loans and jobs) averaged $1,376 ($2,160 maximum); and $260 from other forms of aid. 4% of undergraduate students work part-time. The FAFSA code is 003665. The priority date for freshman financial aid applications for fall entry is April 15.

WILEY COLLEGE — E-2

www.wileyc.edu

Marshall, TX 75670 — (903) 927-3311

Fax: (903) 938-8100	**Email:** admissions@wileyc.edu
Full-time: 350 men, 391 women	**Faculty:** 35
Part-time: n/av	**Ph.D.s:** 63%
Graduate: n/av	**Student/Faculty:** 21 to 1
Year: semesters, summer session	**Tuition:** $12,306
Room & Board: $6946	**Freshman Class:** n/av
SAT or ACT: required	**CEEB CODE:** 3940
Application Deadline: September 3	**COMPETITIVE**

Wiley College, founded in 1873 as an institution for black students, is affiliated with the United Methodist Church. The college offers programs in the liberal arts, sciences, and teacher training. The figures given in the above capsule and in this profile are approximate. There are 3 undergraduate schools. The 70-acre campus is in a small town on the west side of Marshall, Texas. Including any residence halls, there are 17 buildings.

STUDENT LIFE: **Female To Male Ratio:** 1.1:1. **Housing:** College-sponsored housing includes a living learning community.

FACULTY/CLASSROOMS: All teach undergraduates. No introductory courses are taught by graduate students.

PROGRAMS OF STUDY: WC confers B.A., B.S., and B.B.A. degrees. Bachelor's degrees are awarded in BIOLOGICAL SCIENCE (biology/biological science), BUSINESS (business administration and management, hotel/motel and restaurant management, and office supervision and management), COMMUNICATIONS AND THE ARTS (communications, English, music, music performance, and Spanish), COMPUTER AND PHYSICAL SCIENCE (chemistry, computer science, mathematics, and physics), EDUCATION (business education, elementary education, English education, mathematics education, music education, physical education, secondary education, social science education, and special education), SOCIAL SCIENCE (history, liberal arts/general studies, philosophy, religion, social science, and sociology).

ACTIVITIES: There are no fraternities or sororities. Groups on campus include cheerleading, choir, and religious. **Sports:** There is no sports program at WC. Facilities include a basketball arena, a wellness center, baseball, soccer, track and field, cross-country, and volleyball.

SERVICES: **Library/Resources:** The library contains 80,000 volumes, and subscribes to 298 periodicals, including electronic.

REQUIREMENTS: The SAT or ACT is required. Applicants must be graduates of an accredited secondary school or have scored at least 40 on the GED. A letter of recommendation from a high school counselor or teacher is required. Core requirements include courses in education, English, humanities, history, religion, science, and math. 2 credits in physical education and 3 in computer science are required. A 2.0 GPA and 124 semester hours are needed to graduate. **Procedure:** There are early decision and early admissions plans. Applications should be filed by September 3 for fall entry. The fall 2017 application fee was $50. **Transfer Students:** Transfer applicants must be in good standing at their last college, and official transcripts. 30 of 124 credits required for the bachelor's degree must be completed at Wiley. **International Students:** They must take the TOEFL.

Admissions Contact: Bishop B. Curry, Director of Admissions. Email: *admissions@wileyc.edu* Web: *www.wileyc.edu*

FINANCIAL AID: The FAFSA code is 003669. Check with the school for current application deadlines.

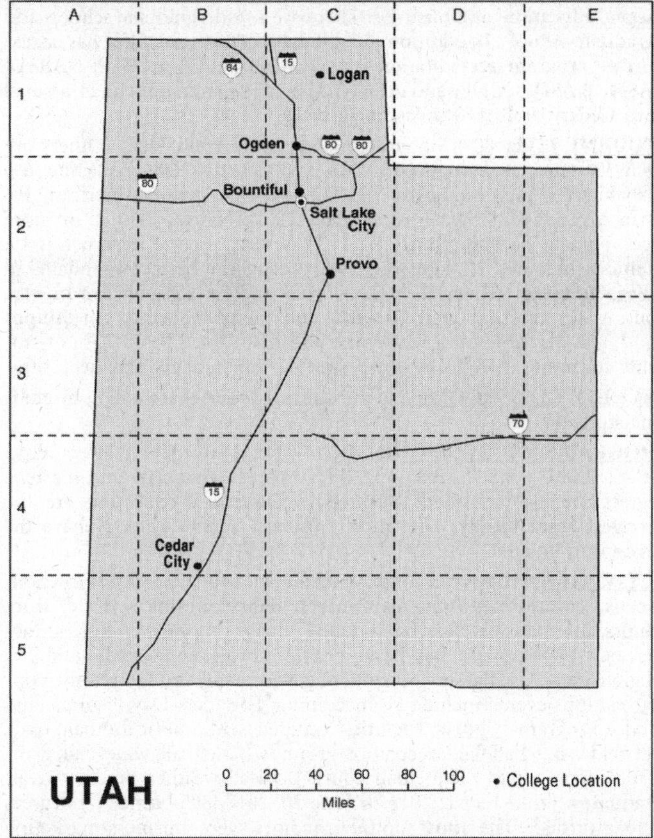

BRIGHAM YOUNG UNIVERSITY C-2

www.byu.edu

Provo, UT 84602 **(801) 422-2500**

Fax: (801) 422-0005 **Email: ugrad@byu.edu**

Full-time: 14,388 men, 13,768 women
Part-time: 1632 men, 1445 women
Graduate: 1908 men, 1193 women
Year: semesters, summer session
Room & Board: $7628

SAT EBR-W/M: 660/650 **ACT:** 30
Application Deadline: December 15

Faculty: 1256
Ph.D.s: 93%
Student/Faculty: 20 to 1
Tuition: $5620 ($11,240)
Freshman Class: 12858 applied, 3738 accepted, 5440 enrolled
CEEB CODE: 4019
MOST COMPETITIVE

Brigham Young University, founded in 1875, is a private university affiliated with the Church of Jesus Christ of Latter-day Saints. The university follows a semester calendar with spring and summer terms. There are 10 undergraduate schools and 1 graduate school. In addition to regional accreditation, BYU has baccalaureate program accreditation with AACSB, ABET, ACCE, ACEJMC, ADA, ASLA, CSAB, CSWE, NASAD, NASDTEC, NASM, NLN, NRPA, AAMFT, CAEP, APA, ASHA, CAAMEP, CAAHEP, CCNE, NASD, NAACLS, and NASO. The 557-acre campus is in a suburban area 45 miles south of Salt Lake City. Including any residence halls, there are 330 buildings.

STUDENT LIFE: 66% of undergraduates are from out of state, mostly the West. Students are from 50 states, 121 foreign countries, and Canada. 82% are White; 6% Hispanic; 4% two or more races; 3% Foreign; 2% Asian American; 1% African American. **Male To Female Ratio:** 1.1:1. The average age of freshmen is 19; all undergraduates, 22. 11% do not continue beyond their first year; 77% remain to graduate. **Housing:** 6302 students can be accommodated in college housing, which includes single-sex dorms, married student dorms, and on-campus apartments. In addition, there are honors houses, language/international houses, special-interest houses, and student family residences. On-campus housing is available on a first-come and first-served basis. 80% of students commute. Alcohol is not permitted. All students may keep cars.

FACULTY/CLASSROOMS: 79% of faculty are male; 21% are female. No introductory courses are taught by graduate students.

PROGRAMS OF STUDY: BYU confers B.A., B.S., B.F.A., B.G.S., B.M., and B.Mus. degrees. Master's and doctoral degrees are also awarded. Bachelor's degrees are awarded in AGRICULTURE (agricultural business management, environmental studies, plant science, and wildlife management), BIOLOGICAL SCIENCE (biochemistry, bioinformatics, biology/biological science, biophysics, biotechnology, botany, microbiology, molecular biology, neurosciences, nutrition, physiology, plant genetics, and plant physiology), BUSINESS (accounting, business administration and management, management information systems, management science, marketing management, recreation and leisure services, and tourism), COMMUNICATIONS AND THE ARTS (advertising, animation, art, art history and appreciation, audio technology, Chinese, classical languages, classics, communications, comparative literature, dance, dramatic arts, English, fine arts, French, German, graphic design, Greek, illustration, industrial design, Italian, Japanese, jazz, Korean, Latin, linguistics, literature, media arts, music, music performance, music technology, music theory and composition, musical theater, performing arts, photography, Portuguese, public relations, Russian, Spanish, studio art, and visual and performing arts), COMPUTER AND PHYSICAL SCIENCE (actuarial science, astronomy, chemistry, computer science, geology, information sciences and systems, mathematics, physics, and statistics), EDUCATION (art education, dance education, drama education, early childhood education, elementary education, English education, home economics education, mathematics education, music education, science education, social science education, special education, and technical education), ENGINEERING AND ENVIRONMENTAL DESIGN (chemical engineering, city/community/regional planning, civil engineering, computer engineering, construction management, electrical/electronics engineering, electrical/electronics engineering technology, environmental design, food services technology, landscape architecture/design, manufacturing engineering, manufacturing technology, and mechanical engineering), HEALTH PROFESSIONS (clinical science, exercise science, health science, nursing, and speech pathology/audiology), SOCIAL SCIENCE (American studies, anthropology, archeology, Asian/American studies, Asian/Oriental studies, classical/ancient civilization, dietetics, economics, family/consumer studies, food science, geography, history, human development, humanities, international relations, Latin American studies, Middle Eastern studies, Near Eastern studies, philosophy, political science/government, psychology, social work, and sociology). Engineering, accounting and business are the strongest academically. Business, communications, and exercise science have the largest enrollments.

ACTIVITIES: There are no fraternities or sororities. There are 390 groups on campus, including art, band, cheerleading, chess, choir, chorale, chorus, computers, dance, debate, drama, drill team, environmental, ethnic, film, honors, international, jazz band, literary magazine, marching band, musical theater, newspaper, opera, orchestra, pep band, photography, political, professional, radio and TV, religious, social, social service, student government, and symphony. Popular campus events include Fall and Spring Fling, and Preference Dances. **Sports:** There are 10 intercollegiate sports for men and 11 for women, and 34 intramural sports for men and 32 for women. Facilities include tennis and racquetball courts, pools, gyms, tracks, fields, and a strength and conditioning complex. **Graduates:** From July 1, 2016 to June 30, 2017, 6457 bachelor's degrees were awarded. The most popular majors were business marketing (17%), biological/life sciences (10%), and education (8%). In an average class, 31% graduate in 4 years or less and 77% graduate in 6 years or less.

SERVICES: Counseling and information services are available, as is tutoring in most subjects. There is a reader service for the blind, and remedial math, reading, and writing. **Library/Resources:** The library contains 4.0 million volumes, 3.5 million microform items, and 304,688 audio/video tapes/CDs/DVDs, and subscribes to 198,871 periodicals including electronic. Computerized library services include interlibrary loans, database searching, Internet access, and Wi-Fi capability. Special learning facilities include an art gallery, natural history museum, planetarium, radio station, TV station, an archeological museum, an earth science museum, reading and writing labs, and math, language, and computer labs. **Physically Challenged Students:** 97% of the campus is accessible. Facilities include wheelchair ramps, elevators, special parking, specially equipped restrooms, special class scheduling, lowered drinking fountains, lowered telephones, and special housing. **Special:** Brigham Young offers cooperative programs, national and international internships, study abroad in 55 countries, a Washington semester, dual majors, nondegree study, and credit for life and work experience. There are 22 national honor societies, Phi Beta Kappa, a freshman honors program, and 100 departmental honors programs. **Visiting:** There are regularly scheduled orientations for prospective students, including a campus tour, visits with the prospective major's department and advisement center, and an interview with a school relations counselor. There are guides for informal visits and visitors may sit in on classes. To schedule a visit, contact the Admissions Office. **Campus Safety and Security:** Measures include 24-hour foot and vehicle patrol, emergency notification system, self-defense education, and security escort services. There are emergency telephones, lighted pathways/sidewalks, bicycle patrol, academic building security officers from 7 p.m. to 2 a.m., and night time limited access to dorms.

REQUIREMENTS: The SAT or ACT is required. Applicants must be graduates of an accredited secondary school. The GED is accepted. The school recommends that applicants complete 4 years of English and math, 3 years of science, 2 years each of foreign language and academic electives. Essays and letters of recommendation are required with the application. AP and CLEP credits are accepted. Important factors in the admissions decision are advanced placement or honors courses, recommendations by school officials, and evidence of special talent. To graduate, students must complete 120 semester hours with a minimum GPA of 2.0. All students must take a total of 14 semester hours of religion and 2 hours of phys ed. There are general education requirements in English, advanced writing, foreign language or math, arts and letters, natural sciences, social sciences, and American heritage. **Procedure:** Freshmen are admitted to all sessions. Entrance exams should be taken by December of the senior year. There are early admissions, deferred admissions, and rolling admissions plans. Applications should be filed by December 15 for fall entry. The fall 2017 application fee was $35. Notifications are sent March 1. Applications are accepted on-line. **Transfer Students:** 643 transfer students enrolled in 2016-2017. For applicants, primary consideration will be given to basic general education subjects (English, math, history, and foreign languages) and major subjects. The GPA from those subjects must be near 3.5 to be competitive for admission. 30 credits required for the bachelor's degree must be completed at BYU. **International Students:** There are 943 international students enrolled. They must take the TOEFL with a minimum score of 550 on the paper-based TOEFL (PBT) or 80 on the Internet-based version (iBT). They must also take the SAT or ACT.

ADMISSIONS: 29% of the 2017-2018 applicants were accepted. The SAT scores for the 2017-2018 freshman class were: Math-- 2% below 500, 20% between 500 and 599, 52% between 600 and 699, and 25% between 700 and 800. Evidence-Based Reading/Writing-- 2% below 500, 16% between 500 and 599, 51% between 600 and 699, and 31% between 700 and 800. The ACT scores were 6% between 18 and 23, 46% between 24 and 29, and 48% above 30. 80% of the current freshmen were in the top fifth of their class. **Admissions Contact:** Tom Gourley, Director of Admissions Office. Email: *ugrad@byu.edu* Web: *www.byu.edu*

FINANCIAL AID: In 2017-2018, 63% of all full-time freshmen received some form of financial aid. 19% of all full-time freshmen received need-based aid. The average freshman award was $6,921. Need-based scholarships or need-based grants averaged $4,721; need-based self-help aid (loans and jobs) averaged $3,136; non-need-based athletic scholarships averaged $8,563; other non-need-based awards and non-need-based scholarships averaged $3,136; and $4,216 from other forms of aid. 54% of undergraduate students work part-time. The FAFSA code is 003670. The priority date for freshman financial aid applications for fall entry is April 15. The deadline for filing freshman financial aid applications for fall entry is June 30.

SOUTHERN UTAH UNIVERSITY — B-4

www.suu.edu

Cedar City, UT 84720 — **(435) 586-7740**

Fax: (435) 865-8223	**Email:** adminfo@suu.edu
Full-time: 2545 men, 3056 women	**Faculty:** 282; IIA, --$
Part-time: 381 men, 371 women	**Ph.D.s:** 66%
Graduate: 373 men, 489 women	**Student/Faculty:** 19 to 1
Year: semesters, summer session	**Tuition:** $6676 ($20,288)
Room & Board: $7067	**Freshman Class:** 10573 applied, 7642 accepted, 1523 enrolled
SAT CR/M/W: 515/505/495 **ACT:** 23	**CEEB CODE:** 4092
Application Deadline: May 1	**COMPETITIVE**

Southern Utah University, founded in 1897, is part of the Utah System of Higher Education and offers undergraduate degrees in arts and letters, science, education, and business. There are 7 undergraduate schools and 4 graduate schools. In addition to regional accreditation, SUU has baccalaureate program accreditation with AACSB, ABET, ACBSP, NASAD, NASM, NASD, CCNE, and AACN. The 133-acre campus is in a small town Cedar, Utah, 170 miles north of Las Vegas.

STUDENT LIFE: 80% of undergraduates are from Utah. Others are from 50 states, 28 foreign countries, and Canada. 76% are White; 6% Hispanic; 6% race unknown; 4% Foreign; 2% African American; 1% Asian American; 1% American Indian/Alaska Native; 1% two or more races. **Female To Male Ratio:** 1.2:1. The average age of freshmen is 19; all undergraduates, 22. **Housing:** 599 students can be accommodated in college housing, which includes dorms and on-campus apartments, housing for international students, and theme housing. On-campus housing is available on a first-come and first-served basis. 72% of students commute. Alcohol is not permitted. All students may keep cars.

FACULTY/CLASSROOMS: No introductory courses are taught by graduate students.

PROGRAMS OF STUDY: Southern Utah University confers B.A., B.F.A., B.M.U., B.S.N., B.S., and B.I.S. degrees. Associate and master's degrees are also awarded. Business, science, and education are the strongest academically. Education, business, and psychology have the largest enrollments.

ACTIVITIES: Groups on campus include art, band, cheerleading, choir, chorus, communications, computers, dance, drama, ethnic, film, honors, international, jazz band, LGBT, literary magazine, musical theater, newspaper, opera, pep band, political, professional, radio and TV, religious, social, social service, student government, and symphony. Popular campus events include Homecoming, Founders Day, Dances, and Service Programs. **Sports:** Facilities include a stadium for football, track and field, a baseball field, recreation grounds, basketball, volleyball, gymnastics, tennis, and racquetball courts, and all-weather practice areas. **Graduates:** From July 1, 2016 to June 30, 2017, 895 bachelor's degrees were awarded. The most popular majors were business/marketing (13%), education (12%), and family and consumer sciences (8%).

SERVICES: Counseling and information services are available, as is tutoring in most subjects. There is a reader service for the blind, and remedial math, reading, and writing. **Library/Resources:** The library contains 289,486 volumes, 28,525 microform items, and 10,821 audio/video tapes/CDs/DVDs, and subscribes to 749 periodicals including electronic. Computerized library services include interlibrary loans, database searching, and Internet access. Special learning facilities include an art gallery, natural history museum, planetarium, radio station, and TV station. **Physically Challenged Students:** Facilities include wheelchair ramps, elevators, special parking, specially equipped restrooms, special class scheduling, lowered drinking fountains, lowered telephones, and special housing. **Special:** SUU offers co-op programs with Weber State University, work-study programs, study abroad, dual majors, student-designed majors leading to a B.I.S. degree, and internships with government officials in Washington, D.C. Other programs offered include distance learning, ESL, independent study, liberal arts/career combinations, a teacher certification program, and weekend college. **Visiting:** There are regularly scheduled orientations for prospective students, including campus tours, which can be arranged by appointment. There are guides for informal visits, visitors may sit in on classes, and stay overnight. To schedule a visit, contact the Admissions Welcome Center at (435) 586-7741. **Campus Safety and Security:** Measures include self-defense education and security escort services. There are emergency telephones and lighted pathways/sidewalks.

REQUIREMENTS: The SAT or ACT is required. Applicants should be graduates of an accredited secondary school or have a GED, and should have completed 4 years of English, (composition and literature emphasis), 3 of math, at least 2 of which are elementary algebra or beyond, 3 each of biological/physical sciences (1 with a lab) and social studies including U.S. history/government, and 2 years of a foreign language. A GPA of 2.0 is required. AP and CLEP credits are accepted. To graduate, all students must complete at least 122 credit hours with a minimum 2.0 GPA. Students must satisfy general education, major, minor, and basic skills requirements, including 4 courses each in social and physical sciences, 2 each in English, fine arts, and humanities, 1 each in math, phys ed, and communications, and a course in either history, political science, or economics to fulfill the U.S. government requirement. Other courses required for graduation include computer literacy and philosophy. **Procedure:** Freshmen are admitted fall, spring, and summer. There are deferred admissions and rolling admissions plans. Applications should be filed by May 1 for fall entry; December 1 for spring entry. The fall 2017 application fee was $50. Applications are accepted on-line. **Transfer Students:** 398 transfer students enrolled in 2016-2017. Applicants must submit transcripts from previously attended colleges and have a minimum 2.0 GPA in college courses and a 2.0 high school GPA. ACT scores as well as high school transcripts are required from students who have not completed English or math courses at another institution or who have not completed a minimum of 24 credit hours at an institution of higher education. 30 of 120 credits required for the bachelor's degree must be completed at SUU. **International Students:** There are 287 international students enrolled. They must take the TOEFL with a minimum score of 525 on the paper-based TOEFL (PBT) or 71 on the Internet-based version (iBT). Students must take the IELTS.

ADMISSIONS: 72% of the 2017-2018 applicants were accepted. The SAT scores for the 2017-2018 freshman class were: Critical Reading-- 41% below 500, 39% between 500 and 599, 16% between 600 and 699, and 3% between 700 and 800. Math-- 49% below 500, 34% between 500 and 599, 15% between 600 and 699, and 3% between 700 and 800. Writing-- 53% below 500, 36% between 500 and 599, and 10% between 600 and 699. The ACT scores were 7% between 12 and 17, 46% between 18 and 23, 41% between 24 and 29, and 6% above 30. **Admissions Contact:** Christine Proctor, Associate Director of Admissions. Email: *adminfo@suu.edu* Web: *www.suu.edu*

FINANCIAL AID: The average freshman award was $9,641. Need-based scholarships or need-based grants averaged $4,218; need-based self-help aid (loans and jobs) averaged $2,869; other non-need-based awards and non-need-based scholarships averaged $6,308; and $6,503 from other forms of aid. The average financial indebtedness of the 2017 graduate was $10,152. The college's own financial statement is required. The FAFSA code is 003678. The priority date for freshman financial aid applications for fall entry is December 1. The deadline for filing freshman financial aid applications for fall entry is March 1.

THE UNIVERSITY OF UTAH C-2

admissions.utah.edu

Salt Lake City, UT 84112	(801) 581-8761
Fax: (801) 585-7864	**Email:** admissions@utah.edu
Full-time: 9599 men, 8467 women	**Faculty:** 1282
Part-time: 3509 men, 3060 women	**Ph.D.s:** 83%
Graduate: 4366 men, 3759 women	**Student/Faculty:** 16 to 1
Year: semesters, summer session	**Tuition:** $8884 ($28,127)
Room & Board: $9867	**Freshman Class:** 22400 applied, 14818 accepted, 4119 enrolled
SAT EBR-W/M: 610/610 **ACT:** 25	**CEEB CODE:** 4853
Application Deadline: April 1	**VERY COMPETITIVE**

The University of Utah, founded in 1850, is part of the Utah System of Higher Education and offers graduate and undergraduate programs. Step one: Imagine. Step two: Do. Imagine what you want to accomplish, then really make it happen. Imagine designing and publishing a video game before earning your diploma, starting a business while studying business, and doing all this in a setting that begs you to get out and do something. Imagine, then Do. Opportunity awaits and all things are possible at a place we call Imagine U The University of Utah. There are 13 undergraduate schools and 16 graduate schools. In addition to regional accreditation, The University of Utah has baccalaureate program accreditation with AACSB, ABET, ACEJMC, ACPE, ADA, APTA, CAHEA, CSWE, NAAB, NRPA, CCNE, and PAB. The 1534-acre campus is in an urban area in Salt Lake City. Including any residence halls, there are 370 buildings.

STUDENT LIFE: 69% of undergraduates are from Utah. Others are from 50 states, 105 foreign countries, and Canada. 95% are from public schools. 68% are White; 6% Asian American; 5% Foreign; 5% two or more races; 2% race unknown; 13% Hispanic; 1% African American. **Male To Female Ratio:** 1.1:1. The average age of freshmen is 18; all undergraduates, 23. 10% do not continue beyond their first year; 67% remain to graduate. **Housing:** 5412 students can be accommodated in college housing, which includes gender neutral, single-sex, coed, and married student dorms, on-campus apartments, and off-campus apartments. In addition, there are honors houses, language/international houses, special-interest houses, theme houses, and 24-hour quiet housing. On-campus housing is available on a first-come and first-served basis. 86% of students commute. Alcohol is not permitted. All students may keep cars.

FACULTY/CLASSROOMS: 60% of faculty are male; 40% are female. 86% teach undergraduates, 74% do research, and 64% do both. Graduate students teach 21% of introductory courses. The average class size in an introductory lecture is 57 and in a laboratory is 21.

PROGRAMS OF STUDY: University of Utah confers B.A., B.F.A., B.Mus., B.S., B.S.W., and B.U.S. degrees. Master's and doctoral degrees are also awarded. Bachelor's degrees are awarded in AGRICULTURE (environmental studies), BIOLOGICAL SCIENCE (biology/biological science and biology/general science secondary education), BUSINESS (accounting, business administration and management, entrepreneurial studies, finance, management information systems, management science, marketing management, marketing/retailing/merchandising, operations management, and recreation and leisure services), COMMUNICATIONS AND THE ARTS (art history, art, ballet, Chinese, classics, communications, comparative literature, design, English, film arts, film, television and digital media, French, German, Hebrew, Japanese, linguistics, modern dance, music, Russian, Spanish, theatre arts, and writing), COMPUTER AND PHYSICAL SCIENCE (applied mathematics, atmospheric sciences and meteorology, chemistry, computer science, earth science, environmental geology, geology, geophysics and seismology, geoscience, information sciences and systems, mathematics, physics secondary education, and physics), EDUCATION (art education, athletic training, elementary education, English education, French studies K-12 education, health education, history education, mathematics education, social science education, special education, and teaching English as a second/foreign language (TESOL/TEFOL), ENGINEERING AND ENVIRONMENTAL DESIGN (biomedical engineering, chemical engineering, civil engineering, computer engineering, electrical/electronics engineering, engineering, geological engineering, materials engineering, materials science, mechanical engineering, metallurgical engineering, mining and mineral engineering, and urban planning technology), HEALTH PROFESSIONS (exercise science, health administration and policy, medical laboratory science, medical laboratory technology, medical science, nursing, and speech pathology/audiology), SOCIAL SCIENCE (anthropology, architectural studies, Asian/Oriental studies, behavioral science, consumer services, economics, ethnic studies, family/consumer studies, gender studies, geography, history, international studies, Latin American studies, Middle Eastern studies, parks and recreation management, peace studies, philosophy, political science/government, psychology, religious studies, social science, social work, sociology, and urban studies). Business, computer science, and biology have the largest enrollments.

ACTIVITIES: 6% of men belong to 10 national fraternities; 7% of women belong to 7 national sororities. There are 605 groups on campus, including art, band, cheerleading, chess, choir, chorale, chorus, computers, dance, debate, drama, drill team, drum and bugle corps, environmental, ethnic, film, forensics, honors, international, jazz band, LGBT, marching band, musical theater, newspaper, opera, orchestra, pep band, photography, political, professional, radio and TV, religious, social, social service, student government, and symphony. Popular campus events include Redfest, Plazafest, and Welcome Week. **Sports:** There are 15 intercollegiate sports for men and 16 for women, and 11 intramural sports for men and 11 for women. Facilities include a stadium, a basketball arena, indoor gyms, indoor tennis courts, sand volleyball court, indoor swimming pools, gymnastics room, weight rooms, handball/racquetball/squash courts, indoor track, outdoor track, disc golf course, outdoor playing fields, bowling, basketball and football. **Graduates:** From July 1, 2016 to June 30, 2017, 5214 bachelor's degrees were awarded. The most popular majors were communication (7%), psychology (5%), and economics (5%). In an average class, 31% graduate in 4 years or less, 55% graduate in 5 years or less, and 65% graduate in 6 years or less. Of the 2016 graduating class, 14% were enrolled in graduate school within 6 months of graduation, and 69% were employed.

SERVICES: Counseling and information services are available, as is tutoring in most subjects. There is a reader service for the blind, and remedial math. There are also support services for the deaf, including readers, scribes, tutors, and interpreters. The on-campus Center for Disability Services directs students to on-campus services for people with disabilities and provides a supportive environment so they can achieve their academic goals. **Library/Resources:** The library contains 3.7 million volumes, 3.0 million microform items, and 94,200 audio/video tapes/CDs/DVDs, and subscribes to 11,400 periodicals including electronic. Computerized library services include interlibrary loans, database searching, Internet access, and Wi-Fi capability. Special learning facilities include an art gallery, natural history museum, radio station, TV station, and arboretum. **Physically Challenged Students:** 90% of the campus is accessible. Facilities include wheelchair ramps, elevators, special parking, specially equipped restrooms, special class scheduling, lowered drinking fountains, lowered telephones, and special housing. **Special:** The university offers numerous opportunities for cross-registration through the Western Undergraduate Exchange (WUE) as part of the Western Interstate Commission for Higher Education (WICHE), study abroad in more than 60 countries, internships, work-study, accelerated degree programs, and BS/MS combined degrees in Information Systems, Chemistry, Math, Nursing, Mining Engineering, and Geological Engineering. Also available are the Washington semester, student-designed and dual majors, credit for military experience, nondegree study, and pass/fail options. There are 44 national honor societies, Phi Beta Kappa, a freshman honors program, and 52 departmental honors programs. **Visiting:** There are regularly scheduled orientations for prospective students, including an information session with an admissions counselor to discuss academic and student involvement opportunities, scholarships, financial aid, admissions requirements, and deadlines, along with a campus tour and tour of residence halls. If time permits, prospective students are encouraged to meet with academic advisers on various majors, visit classrooms, and stay overnight in a residence hall. There are guides for informal visits, visitors may sit in on classes, and stay overnight. To schedule a visit, contact the Office of Admissions. **Campus Safety and Security:** Measures include 24-hour foot and vehicle patrol, emergency notification system, self-defense education, and security escort services. There are shuttle buses, emergency telephones, lighted pathways/sidewalks, and controlled access to dorms/residences.

REQUIREMENTS: Most applicants submit the ACT but the SAT is accepted. Applicants must be graduates of an accredited secondary school or have the GED. Academic credits required include 4 years each of English and electives, 2 years each of foreign language and math, 3 years of biological and/or physical science, and 1 year of history. A GPA of 2.6 is required. AP and CLEP credits are accepted. To graduate, all students must satisfy requirements in the general education and intellectual exploration programs. General education requirements include 1 course each in American institutions and lower-division writing; 2 in quantitative reasoning; and 2 each in fine arts, humanities, physical/life science, applied science, social/behavioral science, excluding the major area. Additionally, students must take 2 quantitative intensive courses and 1 course each in diversity, international, and upper-division communication/writing. Students must complete at least 122 credit hours. A minimum 2.0 GPA is required. **Procedure:** Freshmen are admitted fall, spring, and summer. Entrance exams should be taken in the junior year of high school. There are deferred admissions and rolling admissions plans. Applications should be filed by April 1 for fall entry; November 1 for spring entry; and March 15 for summer entry. The fall 2017 application fee was $55. Notification is sent on a rolling basis. Applications are accepted on-line. **Transfer Students:** 2689 transfer students enrolled in 2016-2017. Transfer students must have completed at least 45 quarter (30 semester) hours with a minimum 2.6 GPA. 30 of 122 credits required for the bachelor's degree must be completed at the University of Utah. **International Students:** There are 985 international students enrolled. They must take the TOEFL with a minimum score of 550 on the paper-based TOEFL (PBT) or 80 on the Internet-based version (iBT). They must also take the SAT or ACT.

ADMISSIONS: 66% of the 2017-2018 applicants were accepted. The ACT scores were 4% between 12 and 17, 34% between 18 and 23, 42% between 24 and 29, and 20% above 30. **Admissions Contact:** Matthew Lopez, Admissions Director. Email: *admissions@utah.edu* Web: *admissions.utah.edu*

FINANCIAL AID: In 2017-2018, 79% of all full-time freshmen received some form of financial aid. 46% of all full-time freshmen received need-based aid. The average freshman award was $22,575. Need-based scholarships or need-based grants averaged $7,754 ($15,532 maximum); need-based self-help aid (loans and jobs) averaged $10,085 ($40,512 maximum); non-need-based athletic scholarships averaged $26,745 ($41,688 maximum); and other non-need-based awards and non-need-based scholarships averaged $7,276 ($46,000 maximum). 21% of undergraduate students work part-time. The average financial indebtedness of the 2017 graduate was $34,066. The FAFSA code is 003675. The priority date for freshman financial aid applications for fall entry is March 15.

UTAH STATE UNIVERSITY — C-1

www.usu.edu

Logan, UT 84322 — (435) 797-1079, (800) 488-8108

Fax: (435) 797-3708 — **Email:** admit@usu.edu

Full-time: 8351 men, 8837 women	**Faculty:** 927; I, --$
Part-time: 3149 men, 4281 women	**Ph.D.s:** 81%
Graduate: 1388 men, 1673 women	**Student/Faculty:** 21 to 1
Year: semesters, summer session	**Tuition:** $7175 ($20,727)
Room & Board: $6060	**Freshman Class:** 15401 applied, 13899 accepted, 4466 enrolled
SAT CR/M: 559/569 **ACT:** 24	**CEEB CODE:** 4857
Application Deadline: n/av	**COMPETITIVE**

Utah State University, founded in 1888, is a public institution that offers degree programs in the liberal arts and sciences, agriculture and natural resources, engineering, business, education, fine arts, music, family life, and the sciences. There are 8 undergraduate schools and 1 graduate school. In addition to regional accreditation, USU has baccalaureate program accreditation with AACSB, ABET, ADA, AHEA, ASLA, CSWE, FIDER, NASM, NRPA, and SAF. The 332-acre campus is in a small town 86 miles north of Salt Lake City. Including any residence halls, there are 104 buildings.

STUDENT LIFE: 73% of undergraduates are from Utah. Others are from 50 states, 78 foreign countries, and Canada. 82% are White; 6% Hispanic; 4% race unknown; 2% American Indian/Alaska Native; 2% Foreign; 2% two or more races; 1% African American; 1% Asian American. **Female To Male Ratio:** 1.1:1. The average age of freshmen is 19; all undergraduates, 23. 27% do not continue beyond their first year. **Housing:** 3615 students can be accommodated in college housing, which includes married student dorms and on-campus apartments. In addition, there are honors houses, special-interest houses, fraternity houses, and sorority houses. On-campus housing is available on a first-come and first-served basis. Alcohol is not permitted. All students may keep cars.

FACULTY/CLASSROOMS: 60% of faculty are male; 40% are female. Graduate students teach 5% of introductory courses. The average class size in an introductory lecture is 35; in a laboratory is 20; and in a regular course is 25.

PROGRAMS OF STUDY: USU confers B.A., B.S., B.F.A., B.I.D., B.L.A., B.M., and B.S.N. degrees. Associate, master's, and doctoral degrees are also awarded. Bachelor's degrees are awarded in AGRICULTURE (agricultural business management, agricultural economics, agriculture international, animal science, dairy science, forestry and related sciences, natural resource management, plant science, range/farm management, soil science, and wildlife management), BIOLOGICAL SCIENCE (biochemistry, biology/biological science, and microbiology), BUSINESS (accounting, banking and finance, business administration and management, business economics, fashion merchandising, international business management, management information systems, marketing/retailing/merchandising, and personnel management), COMMUNICATIONS AND THE ARTS (dance, dramatic arts, English, fine arts, French, German, journalism, music, and Spanish), COMPUTER AND PHYSICAL SCIENCE (chemistry, computer science, earth science, geology, information sciences and systems, mathematics, physics, and statistics), EDUCATION (agricultural education, art education, business education, early childhood education, elementary education, foreign languages education, health education, home economics education, industrial arts education, mathematics education, music education, physical education, science education, secondary education, and special education), ENGINEERING AND ENVIRONMENTAL DESIGN (agricultural engineering, civil engineering, electrical/electronics engineering, engineering, environmental science, industrial engineering, industrial engineering technology, interior design, landscape architecture/design, and mechanical engineering), HEALTH PROFESSIONS (medical laboratory technology, music therapy, predentistry, premedicine, public health, speech pathology/audiology, and veterinary science), SOCIAL SCIENCE (American studies, child care/child and family studies, economics, food science, geography, history, home economics, human development, international relations, liberal arts/general studies, parks and recreation management, philosophy, political science/government, prelaw, psychology, social work, and sociology). Natural resources, engineering, and special education are the strongest academically. Humanities, business, and education have the largest enrollments.

ACTIVITIES: 4% of men belong to 8 national fraternities; 4% of women belong to 3 national sororities. There are 230 groups on campus, including art, bagpipe, band, cheerleading, choir, chorale, chorus, computers, dance, drama, drill team, environmental, ethnic, film, honors, international, jazz band, LGBT, literary magazine, marching band, musical theater, newspaper, opera, orchestra, pep band, photography, political, professional, radio and TV, religious, social, social service, student government, and symphony. Popular campus events include Festival of the American West, Halloween Howl, Homecoming, and A-Day. **Sports:** There are 7 intercollegiate sports for men and 9 for women, and 18 intramural sports for men and 18 for women. Facilities include various gyms, indoor and outdoor tennis courts, swimming pools, a recreation center with climbing walls, a field house, golf, and skiing areas. **Graduates:** From July 1, 2016 to June 30, 2017, 3846 bachelor's degrees were awarded. The most popular majors were economics (10%), communicative disorders and deaf education (7%), and business administration (5%). In an average class, 46% graduate in 6 years or less.

SERVICES: Counseling and information services are available, as is tutoring in most subjects. There is a reader service for the blind, and remedial math, reading, and writing. There is also a writing lab and a tutor room. **Library/Resources:** The library contains 1.9 million volumes, 23,840 microform items, and 23,209 audio/video tapes/CDs/DVDs, and subscribes to 118,174 periodicals including electronic. Computerized library services include interlibrary loans, database searching, Internet access, and Wi-Fi capability. Special learning facilities include an art gallery, natural history museum, radio station, a laboratory school, a historical farm, a fine arts center, and a developmental center for people who are disabled. **Physically Challenged Students:** 99% of the campus is accessible. Facilities include wheelchair ramps, elevators, special parking, specially equipped restrooms, special class scheduling, lowered drinking fountains, lowered telephones and special phones to receive calls from the deaf, and a disability resource center. **Special:** Internships are available in most departments through the Cooperative Education Program. The National Student Exchange Program allows students to cross-register in designated institutions and programs, and the International Student Exchange Program enables students to study abroad. There is also cross-registration with the University of the Americas of Mexico. A general studies degree and student-designed majors are available. Nondegree study, work-study programs, co-op programs, B.A.-B.S. degrees, pass/fail options, and credit for military experience are offered. There are 12 national honor societies, a freshman honors program, and 36 departmental honors programs. **Visiting:** There are regularly scheduled orientations for prospective students, consisting of a campus tour, including a meeting with an academic adviser, lunch, and a housing tour, available at 10:30 a.m. and 1:30 p.m., September to May, and 1:30 p.m., June to August. To schedule a visit, contact the Admissions Office. **Campus Safety and Security:** Measures include 24-hour foot and vehicle patrol, emergency notification system, self-defense education, and security escort services. There are shuttle buses, emergency telephones, lighted pathways/sidewalks, and campus police.

REQUIREMENTS: USU requires that either the SAT or ACT be provided. The ACT has been the preferred choice, but either is accepted. In addition, students should graduate from an accredited secondary school with 16.5 academic units, including 4 in English and Math, 3 in science, and 3.5 in social sciences. GED equivalency is accepted, provided ACT scores are 19 or higher. Students not meeting entrance requirements may be considered for admission on a provisional basis. A GPA of 2.7 is required. AP and CLEP credits are accepted. The core curriculum of 30 semester credits includes at least 6 of writing; the total number of credits required for graduation is 120. Students must maintain a minimum GPA of 2.5. The number of credits required in the major varies, but there is a minimum of 40 in major classes. **Procedure:** Freshmen are admitted to all sessions. Entrance exams should be taken in the spring of the junior year. There are deferred admissions and rolling admissions plans. Application deadlines are open. The fall 2017 application fee was $50. Applications are accepted on-line. **Transfer Students:** 2615 transfer students enrolled in 2016-2017. A minimum 2.2 GPA, higher for some majors, is required for transfer students. Those applicants with fewer than 45 credits must also submit ACT scores. 30 of 120 credits required for the bachelor's degree must be completed at USU. **International Students:** There are 234 international students enrolled. They must take the TOEFL with a minimum score of 525 on the paper-based TOEFL (PBT) or 71 on the Internet-based version (iBT) or the MELAB.

ADMISSIONS: 90% of the 2017-2018 applicants were accepted. The SAT scores for the 2017-2018 freshman class were: Critical Reading-- 26% below 500, 46% between 500 and 599, 15% between 600 and 699, and 13% between 700 and 800. Math-- 18% below 500, 42% between 500 and 599, 33% between 600 and 699, and 7% between 700 and 800. The ACT scores were 9% between 12 and 17, 39% between 18 and 23, 38% between 24 and 29, and 14% above 30. **Admissions Contact:** Katie Nielsen, Director of Admissions Office. Email: *admit@usu.edu* Web: *www.usu.edu*

FINANCIAL AID: The FAFSA code is 003677. The priority date for freshman financial aid applications for fall entry is March 1.

WEBER STATE UNIVERSITY — C-1

www.weber.edu

Ogden, UT 84408 — **(801) 626-7670**

Fax: (801) 626-6747	**Email:** admissions@weber.edu
Full-time: 5294 men, 6017 women	**Faculty:** 551; IIA, -$
Part-time: 7054 men, 8746 women	**Ph.D.s:** 79%
Graduate: 389 men, 449 women	**Student/Faculty:** 21 to 1
Year: semesters, summer session	**Tuition:** $5712 ($15,260)
Room & Board: $8400	**Freshman Class:** 6245 applied, 6245 accepted, 2524 enrolled
ACT: 21	**CEEB CODE:** 4941
Application Deadline: August 28	**COMPETITIVE**

Weber State University provides associate, baccalaureate and master degree programs in liberal arts, sciences, and technical and professional fields. Encouraging freedom of expression and valuing diversity, the university provides excellent educational experiences for students through extensive personal contact among faculty, staff and students in and out of the classroom. Through academic programs, research, artistic expression, public service and community-based learning, the university serves as an educational, cultural and economic leader for the region. There are 8 undergraduate schools and 13 graduate schools. In addition to regional accreditation, WSU has baccalaureate program accreditation with AACSB, ABET, ACCE, ADA, CSWE, NASAD, NASM, NCATE, NLN, ACEN, ACS, AUPHA, CAAHEP, CAATE, CAHIM, CARC, CEA, CIDA, CODA, NAACLS, NAEYC, NCFR, and NKBA. The 509-acre campus is in an urban area on the foothills of the Wasatch Mountains, 33 miles north of Salt Lake City. Including any residence halls, there are 114 buildings.

STUDENT LIFE: 92% of undergraduates are from Utah. Others are from 50 states, 61 foreign countries, and Canada. 99% are from public schools. 75% are White; 11% Hispanic; 6% race unknown; 3% two or more races; 2% Asian American; 1% African American; 1% American Indian/Alaska Native; 1% Foreign. **Female To Male Ratio:** 1.2:1. The average age of freshmen is 20; all undergraduates, 26. 38% do not continue beyond their first year; 35% remain to graduate. **Housing:** 1001 students can be accommodated in college housing, which includes married student dorms and on-campus apartments. On-campus housing is available on a first-come and first-served basis. 96% of students commute. Alcohol is not permitted. All students may keep cars.

FACULTY/CLASSROOMS: 52% of faculty are male; 48% are female. All teach undergraduates. No introductory courses are taught by graduate students. The average class size in an introductory lecture is 30; in a laboratory is 17; and in a regular course is 18.

PROGRAMS OF STUDY: WSU confers B.A., B.S., B.F.A., B.I.S., B.M., and B.M.E. degrees. Associate and master's degrees are also awarded. Bachelor's degrees are awarded in BIOLOGICAL SCIENCE (biology/biological science, botany, microbiology, and zoology), BUSINESS (accounting, banking and finance, business administration and management, business economics, finance, human resources, international economics, management information systems, marketing management, personnel management, purchasing/inventory management, and supply chain management), COMMUNICATIONS AND THE ARTS (advertising, art, communications, creative writing, dance, dramatic arts, English, fine arts, French, German, graphic design, instrumental performance, instrumental music education, journalism, media arts, music, music performance, musical theater, photography, piano/organ, public relations, Spanish, strings, technical and business writing, theatre arts, visual and performing arts, visual design, and voice), COMPUTER AND PHYSICAL SCIENCE (applied mathematics, chemistry, chemistry education, computer networks & systems, computer programming, computer science, computer security and information assurance, earth science, earth science/adolescence education, geology, information sciences and systems, mathematics, and physics), EDUCATION (art education, athletic training, business education, early childhood education, education, elementary education, English education, foreign languages education, health education, health information management, history education, mathematics education, music education, physical education, physical science secondary school education, psychology education, science education, secondary education, social science education, special education, and teaching English as a second/foreign language (TESOL/TEFOL), ENGINEERING AND ENVIRONMENTAL DESIGN (automotive technology, computer engineering, construction management, electrical/electronics engineering, electrical/electronics engineering technology, environmental science, interior design, manufacturing engineering, manufacturing technology, mechanical engineering technology, plastics engineering, plastics technology, and welding engineering), HEALTH PROFESSIONS (cardiac sonography, clinical science, dental hygiene, health care administration, health promotion, health services administration, health services technology, medical laboratory science, nuclear medicine, nursing, radiation therapy, radiograph medical technology, radiological science, radiologic imaging modalities, respiratory therapy, and vascular sonography), SOCIAL SCIENCE (anthropology, child care/child and family studies, criminal justice, early childhood studies, economics, family/consumer studies, geography, gerontology, history, interdisciplinary studies, law enforcement and corrections, liberal arts/general studies, philosophy, political science/government, psychology, public history/archives, social work, and sociology). Nursing, business administration, and computer science are the strongest academically. Nursing, computer science, and business administration have the largest enrollments.

ACTIVITIES: 1% of men belong to 2 local fraternities; 1% of women belong to 2 local sororities. There are 222 groups on campus, including art, band, cheerleading, chess, choir, chorale, chorus, communications, computers, dance, debate, drama, drill team, drum and bugle corps, environmental, ethnic, film, forensics, honors, international, jazz band, LGBT, literary magazine, marching band, musical theater, newspaper, opera, orchestra, pep band, photography, political, professional, radio and TV, religious, social, social service, student government, symphony, and The Latter-day Saint Student Association is established by the Ogden Institute of Religion to help students attending a Weber State University have a balanced secular and spiritual educational experience during their years of formal education. Popular campus events include Homecoming, Graduation, and Back to School Block Party. **Sports:** There are 6 intercollegiate sports for men and 8 for women, and 9 intramural sports for men and 9 for women. Facilities include an indoor track, a strength-training center, indoor basketball and volleyball courts, group fitness areas, a pool, racquetball and tennis courts, a stadium, an ice skating rink, outdoor playing fields, and a rock climbing wall. **Graduates:** From July 1, 2016 to June 30, 2017, 2458 bachelor's degrees were awarded. The most popular majors were nursing (10%), technical sales (6%), and criminal justice (4%). In an average class, 14% graduate in 4 years or less, 26% graduate in 5 years or less, and 35% graduate in 6 years or less.

SERVICES: Counseling and information services are available, as is tutoring in every subject. There is a reader service for the blind, and remedial math, reading, and writing. There are also translators for the hearing impaired. **Library/Resources:** The library contains 498,531 volumes, 16,834 microform items, and 21,365 audio/video tapes/CDs/DVDs, and subscribes to 425 periodicals including electronic. Computerized library services include interlibrary loans, database searching, Internet access, and Wi-Fi capability. Special learning facilities include an art gallery, natural history museum, planetarium, radio station, and TV station. Weber State University is also home to a working crime lab. **Physically Challenged Students:** 99% of the campus is accessible. Facilities include wheelchair ramps, elevators, special parking, specially equipped restrooms, special class scheduling, lowered drinking fountains, lowered telephones, and special housing. **Special:** Weber State University offers co-op programs and internships in many majors, a Washington semester, study abroad in Mexico and England, work-study programs with community businesses, B.A.-B.S. degrees, dual majors in many combinations, student-designed majors resulting in a B.I.S. degree, a general studies degree, credit for military experience, non-degree study, and pass/fail options. There are 20 national honor societies, a freshman honors program, and 17 departmental honors programs. **Visiting:** There are regularly scheduled orientations for prospective students. There are guides for informal visits, visitors may sit in on classes, and stay overnight. **Campus Safety and Security:** Measures include 24-hour foot and vehicle patrol, emergency notification system, self-defense education, and security escort services. There are shuttle buses, emergency telephones, lighted pathways/sidewalks, and controlled access to dorms/residences.

REQUIREMENTS: The ACT is recommended. Applicants must be graduates of an accredited secondary school or have a GED. Other requirements vary by department. Out-of-state residents must have a minimum high school GPA of 2.0. AP and CLEP credits are accepted. To graduate, students must demonstrate math competency and complete courses in government/history, English, humanities, math, biological/physical sciences, and social sciences. For a bachelor's degree, a student must complete at least 120 semester credit hours, with 45 at the upper-division level, and a minimum GPA of 2.0 are required. Hours in the major and distribution requirements vary with the degree. **Procedure:** Freshmen are admitted to all sessions. Entrance exams should be taken junior or senior year of high school. There are early admissions, deferred admissions, and rolling admissions plans. Applications should be filed by August 28 for fall entry. The fall 2017 application fee was $30. Applications are accepted on-line. **Transfer Students:** 1284 transfer students enrolled in 2016-2017. Transfer students must submit official transcripts from previously attended colleges or universities and have a minimum GPA of 2.0. 30 of 120 credits required for the bachelor's degree must be completed at WSU. **International Students:** There are 326 international students enrolled.

ADMISSIONS: 100% of the 2017-2018 applicants were accepted. The ACT scores were 23% between 12 and 17, 49% between 18 and 23, 23% between 24 and 29, and 4% above 30. **Admissions Contact:** Scott Teichert, Director of Admissions. Email: *admissions@weber.edu* Web: *www.weber.edu*

FINANCIAL AID: In 2017-2018, 78% of all full-time freshmen received some form of financial aid. 47% of all full-time freshmen received need-based aid. The average freshman award was $2,747. Need-based scholarships or need-based grants averaged $2,061; need-based self-help aid (loans and jobs) averaged $3,271; non-need-based athletic scholarships averaged $3,293; and other non-need-based awards and non-need-based scholarships averaged $1,830. 41% of undergraduate students work part-time. The average financial indebtedness of the 2017 graduate was $22,556. The college's own financial statement is required. The FAFSA code is 003680. The priority date for freshman financial aid applications for fall entry is April 1.

WESTMINSTER COLLEGE C-2

www.westminstercollege.edu

Salt Lake City, UT 84105	**(801) 832-2200** **(800) 748-4753**
Fax: (801) 832-3101	**Email: admission@westminstercollege.edu**
Full-time: 872 men, 1141 women	**Faculty:** 154
Part-time: 58 men, 56 women	**Ph.D.s:** 93%
Graduate: 247 men, 318 women	**Student/Faculty:** 13 to 1
Year: 4-1-4, summer session	**Tuition:** $32,104
Room & Board: $8974	**Freshman Class:** 1938 applied, 1820 accepted, 434 enrolled
SAT CR/M: 540/540 **ACT:** 24	**CEEB CODE:** 4948
Application Deadline: August 15	**COMPETITIVE**

Westminster College is a private, independent, and comprehensive college where students experience the liberal arts blended with professional programs in an atmosphere dedicated to civic engagement. With the goal of enabling its graduates to live vibrant, just, and successful lives, Westminster provides transformational learning experiences for both undergraduate and graduate students in a truly student-centered environment. Faculty focus on teaching, learning, and developing distinctive, innovative programs. There are 4 undergraduate schools and 4 graduate schools. In addition to regional accreditation, WC has baccalaureate program accreditation with ACBSP, AABI, CEPH, CCNE, and COA. The 27-acre campus is in an urban area 6 miles southeast of downtown Salt Lake City. Including any residence halls, there are 31 buildings.

STUDENT LIFE: 77% of undergraduates are from Utah. Others are from 42 states, 15 foreign countries, and Canada. 73% are from public schools. 71% are White; 5% Foreign; 4% two or more races; 4% race unknown; 3% Asian American; 2% African American; 10% Hispanic. **Female To Male Ratio:** 1.3:1. The average age of freshmen is 18; all undergraduates, 22. 79% remain to graduate. **Housing:** 809 students can be accommodated in college housing, which includes dorms and on-campus apartments. There are also themed living floors. On-campus housing is available on a first-come, first-served basis, and is available on a lottery system for upperclassmen. 68% of students commute. All students may keep cars.

FACULTY/CLASSROOMS: 49% of faculty are male; 51% are female. All teach undergraduates. No introductory courses are taught by graduate students.

PROGRAMS OF STUDY: Westminster confers B.A., B.S. and B.F.A. degrees. Master's degrees are also awarded. Bachelor's degrees are awarded in AGRICULTURE (environmental studies), BIOLOGICAL SCIENCE (biology/biological science and neurosciences), BUSINESS (accounting, banking and finance, business administration and management, international business management, investments and securities, and marketing/retailing/merchandising), COMMUNICATIONS AND THE ARTS (art, arts administration/management, communications, dramatic arts, English, fine arts, and music), COMPUTER AND PHYSICAL SCIENCE (chemistry, computer science, information sciences and systems, mathematics, and physics), EDUCATION (early childhood education, elementary education, and special education), ENGINEERING AND ENVIRONMENTAL DESIGN (aviation administration/management and aviation computer technology), HEALTH PROFESSIONS (nursing), SOCIAL SCIENCE (criminal justice, economics, gender studies, history, homeland security, philosophy, political science/government, prelaw, psychology, social science, sociology, and Spanish studies). Nursing, business, and biologica/life science, are the strongest academically and have the largest enrollments.

ACTIVITIES: There are no fraternities or sororities. There are 40 groups on campus, including art, choir, chorale, chorus, dance, debate, drama, environmental, ethnic, film, honors, jazz band, LGBT, literary magazine, musical theater, newspaper, orchestra, photography, political, professional, religious, social service, student government, and symphony. Popular campus events include Westminster Welcome Week, Griffin Swoop Ins, Pizza Tasting, Halloween Dance, Documentary Film and Lecture Series, Homecoming Week, and Late Night Breakfast. **Sports:** There are 8 intercollegiate sports for men and 9 for women, and 9 intramural sports for men and 9 for women. Facilities include elevated soccer/lacrosse field, a health and wellness recreation center, basketball/volleyball and multipurpose courts, weight room, lap pool, racquetball courts, dance studio, cardio equipment, a climbing wall, and training rooms. **Graduates:** From July 1, 2016 to June 30, 2017, 509 bachelor's degrees were awarded. The most popular majors were business (25%), health professions (24%), and biological/life sciences (8%). In an average class, 45% graduate in 4 years or less, 60% graduate in 5 years or less, and 62% graduate in 6 years or less.

SERVICES: Counseling and information services are available, as is tutoring in most subjects. There is a reader service for the blind, and remedial math, reading, and writing. **Library/Resources:** The library contains 462,759 volumes, 128,054 microform items, and 159,539 audio/video tapes/CDs/DVDs, and subscribes to 323,137 periodicals including electronic. Computerized library services include interlibrary loans, database searching, Internet access, and Wi-Fi capability. **Physically Challenged Students:** 90% of the campus is accessible. Facilities include wheelchair ramps, elevators, special parking, specially equipped restrooms, lowered drinking fountains, and special housing. **Special:** The college offers internships in every major, study abroad, dual and student-designed majors, an accelerated degree, work-study, independent study, weekend college, and freshman seminar courses. A 3-2 engineering degree with USC in Los Angeles or Washington University in St. Louis, Missouri, is also possible. There is 1 national honor society, a freshman honors program, and 1 departmental honors program. **Visiting:** There are regularly scheduled orientations for prospective students, including a welcome program, lunch, various workshops, a campus tour, and meetings with faculty. There are guides for informal visits, visitors may sit in on classes, and stay overnight. To schedule a visit, contact Darlene Dilley at admission@westminstercollege.edu. **Campus Safety and Security:** Measures include 24-hour foot and vehicle patrol, emergency notification system, and security escort services. There are emergency telephones, lighted pathways/sidewalks, and controlled access to dorms/residences.

REQUIREMENTS: The SAT or ACT is required. Applicants must be graduates of an accredited secondary school or have a GED certificate. College preparatory work should include 4 units of English, 3 of science, 2 each of math, foreign language, social studies, and electives, and 1 of history. An interview is recommended. AP and CLEP credits are accepted. Important factors in the admissions decision are evidence of special talent, extracurricular activities record, and advanced placement or honors courses. To be eligible for a bachelor's degree, students must satisfy the following requirements: complete a minimum of 124 semester credit hours, 30 of which must be upper division courses numbered 300 or above from a four-year institution, fulfill all WCore (liberal education) requirements, maintain an overall grade point average of 2.0 or above, meet all course requirements and grade point average requirements in the major, complete the last 36 credit hours in residency, and maintain good academic standing **Procedure:** Freshmen are admitted to all sessions. Entrance exams should be taken in the junior or senior year of high school. There are deferred admissions and rolling admissions plans. Applications should be filed by August 15 for fall entry. The fall 2017 application fee was $50. Notifications are sent September 1. Applications are accepted on-line. **Transfer Students:** 161 transfer students enrolled in 2016-2017. Transfer students are recommended to have a minimum 2.5 GPA and be in good standing at all previously attended institutions. They must provide college transcripts and submit an essay. An interview is recommended. Some students may need to present standardized test scores and high school transcripts. 36 of 124 credits required for the bachelor's degree must be completed at Westminster. **International Students:** There are 94 international students enrolled. They must take the TOEFL with a minimum score of 550 on the paper-based TOEFL (PBT) or 79 on the Internet-based version (iBT). They must also take the SAT or ACT.

ADMISSIONS: 94% of the 2017-2018 applicants were accepted. The SAT scores for the 2017-2018 freshman class were: Critical Reading-- 22% below 500, 45% between 500 and 599, 28% between 600 and 699, and 4% between 700 and 800. Math-- 21% below 500, 48% between 500 and 599, 24% between 600 and 699, and 4% between 700 and 800. The ACT scores were 1% between 12 and 17, 42% between 18 and 23, 44% between 24 and 29, and 12% above 30. 40% of the current freshmen were in the top fifth of their class; 72% were in the top two fifths. 10 freshmen graduated first in their class. **Admissions Contact:** Darlene Dilley, Interim Chief Enrollment Officer. Email: *admission@westminstercollege.edu* Web: *www.westminstercollege.edu*

FINANCIAL AID: In 2017-2018, 99% of all full-time freshmen received some form of financial aid. 68% of all full-time freshmen received need-based aid. The average freshman award was $28,357. Need-based scholarships or need-based grants averaged $19,781 ($40,243 maximum); need-based self-help aid (loans and jobs) averaged $5,680 ($12,000 maximum); non-need-based athletic scholarships averaged $6,493 ($32,104 maximum); and other non-need-based awards and non-need-based scholarships averaged $15,636 ($32,404 maximum). 28% of undergraduate students work part-time. The average financial indebtedness of the 2017 graduate was $30,442. Westminster is a member of CSS. The FAFSA code is 003681. The priority date for freshman financial aid applications for fall entry is March 1.

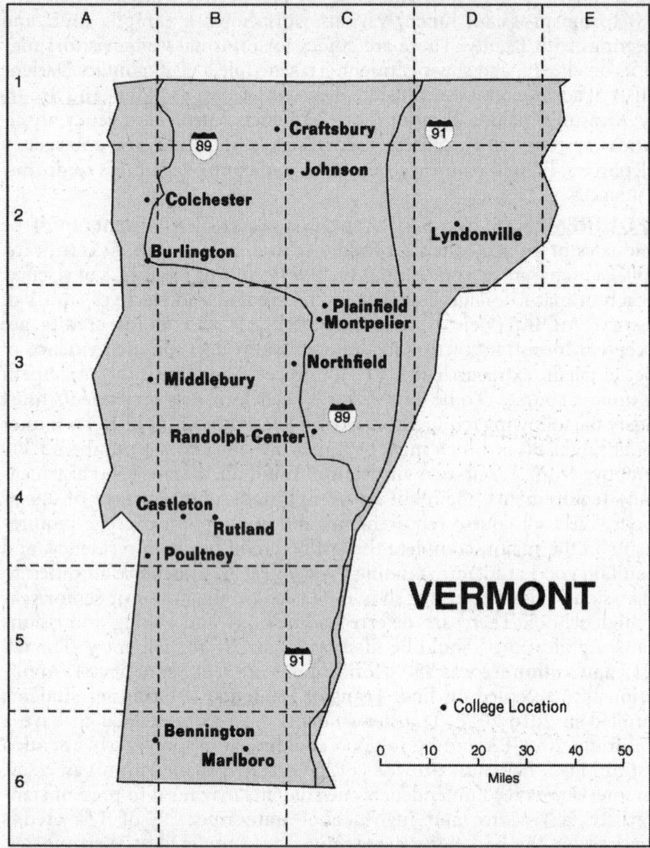

BENNINGTON COLLEGE A-6

www.bennington.edu

Bennington, VT 05201 (802) 440-4312
(800) 833-6845
Fax: (802) 440-4320 **Email:** hnbui@bennington.edu

Full-time: 244 men, 440 women
Part-time: 1 men, 3 women
Graduate: 27 men, 111 women
Year: other
Room & Board: $15,040
SAT CR/M/W: 690/610/660 **ACT:** 29
Application Deadline: January 3

Faculty: 64
Ph.D.s: 70%
Student/Faculty: 11 to 1
Tuition: $51,920
Freshman Class: 1236 applied, 779 accepted, 197 enrolled
CEEB CODE: 3080
MOST COMPETITIVE

Bennington College, founded in 1932, is a private liberal arts institution characterized by cross-disciplinary learning, a close working relationship between student and teacher, a self-directed academic planning process, and a connection to the world through its winter internship term. The figures given in the above capsule and in this profile are approximate. There are 4 undergraduate schools and 4 graduate schools. The 440-acre campus is in a small town in the southwestern corner of Vermont, 160 miles north of New York City and 150 miles west of Boston. Including any residence halls, there are 70 buildings.

STUDENT LIFE: 96% of undergraduates are from out of state, mostly the Middle Atlantic. Students are from 46 states, 35 foreign countries, and Canada. 57% are from public schools. 77% are White; 7% Foreign; 5% Hispanic; 4% race unknown; 3% two or more races; 2% African American; 2% Asian American. **Female To Male Ratio:** 2.0:1. The average age of freshmen is 18; all undergraduates, 20. 17% do not continue beyond their first year; 64% remain to graduate. **Housing:** 661 students can be accommodated in college housing, which includes dorms, on-campus apartments, and off-campus apartments. In addition, there are special-interest houses. On-campus housing is guaranteed for all 4 years. 95% of students live on campus. All students may keep cars.

FACULTY/CLASSROOMS: 51% of faculty are male; 49% are female. All teach undergraduates and all do research. No introductory courses are taught by graduate students. The average class size in an introductory lecture is 16; in a laboratory is 15; and in a regular course is 10.

PROGRAMS OF STUDY: Bennington College confers B.A. degrees. Master's degrees are also awarded. Bachelor's degrees are awarded in AGRICULTURE (environmental studies), BIOLOGICAL SCIENCE (biology/biological science, botany, ecology, environmental biology, evolutionary biology, and zoology), COMMUNICATIONS AND THE ARTS (American literature, animation, art, ceramic art and design, Chinese, comparative literature, creative writing, dance, design, digital communications, dramatic arts, drawing, English, English literature, film arts, fine arts, French, Germanic languages and literature, illustration, Italian, Japanese, jazz, journalism, languages, literature, multimedia, music, music performance, music theory and composition, painting, performing arts, photography, piano/organ, playwriting/screenwriting, printmaking, sculpture, Spanish, strings, studio art, theater design, video, visual and performing arts, and voice), COMPUTER AND PHYSICAL SCIENCE (astronomy, chemistry, computer science, digital arts/technology, mathematics, physical sciences, physics, and science), EDUCATION (drama education, early childhood education, education, elementary education, foreign languages education, mathematics education, middle school education, and secondary education), ENGINEERING AND ENVIRONMENTAL DESIGN (architecture and environmental science), HEALTH PROFESSIONS (premedicine), SOCIAL SCIENCE (American studies, anthropology, child psychology/development, European studies, fashion design and technology, history, humanities, humanities and social science, interdisciplinary studies, international relations, international studies, Judaic studies, Latin American studies, liberal arts/general studies, philosophy, political science/government, prelaw, psychology, social psychology, social science, sociology, and women's studies). Literature, languages, and visual & performing arts are the strongest academically. Literature, and interdisciplinary studies have the largest enrollments.

ACTIVITIES: There are no fraternities or sororities. There are 37 groups on campus, including student educational policies committee, campus activities board, student endowment for the arts, sustainability committee, art, chess, choir, chorale, chorus, computers, dance, debate, drama, environmental, ethnic, film, international, jazz band, LGBT, literary magazine, musical theater, newspaper, opera, outing club, photography, political, radio and TV, religious, social, social service, student government, and symphony. Popular campus events include Sunfest, Faculty Concerts, and Student-Work Performances. **Sports:** There are 2 intercollegiate sports for men and 2 for women, and 15 intramural sports for men and 15 for women. Facilities include a recreation barn equipped with an aerobic room, free weights, weight training, yoga and martial arts, cardiovascular machines, a rock climbing wall, dance studio, tennis courts, soccer field, and basketball court. **Graduates:** From July 1, 2016 to June 30, 2017, 151 bachelor's degrees were awarded. The most popular majors were visual and performing arts (46%), social sciences (10%), and english language and literature (10%). In an average class, 59% graduate in 4 years or less, 63% graduate in 5 years or less, and 64% graduate in 6 years or less.

SERVICES: Counseling and information services are available, as is tutoring in some subjects. There is remedial writing. Tutoring for learning disabilities is available in the town of Bennington at a cost to the student. **Library/Resources:** The library contains 125,000 volumes, and 6,000 audio/video tapes/CDs/DVDs, and subscribes to 14,500 periodicals including electronic. Computerized library services include interlibrary loans, database searching, Internet access, and Wi-Fi capability. Special learning facilities include an art gallery, radio station, a center for the Advancement of Public Action with unique tiered symposium space for U.N.-style dialogue and web-casting, observatory, greenhouse, digital arts lab, art gallery, architecture, drawing, painting, printmaking, and sculpture studios, ceramics studio and kilns, photography darkrooms, film and video editing studio, several fully equipped theaters, dance studios, scripts library, costume shop, electronic music and sound recording studios, music practice rooms and music library, student-run cafe and bar, and 440 acres of forest, ponds, wetlands and fields for recreation and scientific study. **Physically Challenged Students:** 80% of the campus is accessible. Facilities include wheelchair ramps, elevators, special parking, specially equipped restrooms, lowered drinking fountains, and special housing. **Special:** 7-week work/internships (during January and February) are required each year in residence. Cross-registration with Williams

College, Southern Vermont College, and Massachusetts College of Liberal Arts is possible. In addition, study abroad, dual, and student-designed majors are offered. Students receive narrative evaluations with the option of letter grades. **Visiting:** There are regularly scheduled orientations for prospective students, including a tour of campus, classes, lunch in the dining hall, and meeting with an admissions counselor. Overnight visits are also possible during the term. There are guides for informal visits, visitors may sit in on classes, and stay overnight. To schedule a visit, contact the Admissions Office. **Campus Safety and Security:** Measures include 24-hour foot and vehicle patrol, emergency notification system, and security escort services. There are shuttle buses, emergency telephones, and lighted pathways/sidewalks.

REQUIREMENTS: In addition, Bennington admits students who have demonstrated a passion for learning and academic excellence. The Common Application as well as the Bennington Supplement are required. Submission of standardized test scores is optional. A majority of applicants are interviewed in person or by phone. A minimum of 128 credit hours is required to graduate. Students must also complete a Field Work Term (job/internship) for each year in residence. Student's programs must reflect breadth and depth in curricular choices, and their academic plan process must be approved by a faculty committee. **Procedure:** Freshmen are admitted fall and spring. Entrance exams should be taken during the spring of the junior year or the fall of the senior year. There are early decision, early admissions, and deferred admissions plans. Early decision applications should be filed by November 15; regular applications, by January 3 for fall entry; and November 15 for spring entry. The fall 2017 application fee was $60. Notification of early decision is sent December 20; regular decision, April 1. 21 early decision candidates were accepted for the 2017-2018 class. 152 applicants were on the 2017 waiting list; 27 were admitted. Applications are accepted on-line. **Transfer Students:** 15 transfer students enrolled in 2016-2017. Applicants must submit the common application for transfer students, including essays, secondary school reports, college transcripts, and recommendations from 2 faculty members at the college from which they are transferring. They must also interview with a member of the admissions staff. Submission of SAT or ACT scores is optional. 64 of 128 credits required for the bachelor's degree must be completed at Bennington. **International Students:** There are 48 international students enrolled. They must take the TOEFL with a minimum score of 577 on the paper-based TOEFL (PBT) or 90 on the Internet-based version (iBT). A band score of 7 or more on the Academic Module of the IELTS exam is also acceptable.

ADMISSIONS: 63% of the 2017-2018 applicants were accepted. The SAT scores for the 2017-2018 freshman class were: Critical Reading-- 13% between 500 and 599, 46% between 600 and 699, and 41% between 700 and 800. Math-- 2% below 500, 38% between 500 and 599, 48% between 600 and 699, and 13% between 700 and 800. Writing-- 2% below 500, 21% between 500 and 599, 51% between 600 and 699, and 27% between 700 and 800. The ACT scores were 5% below 12, 23% between 18 and 23, 23% between 24 and 29, and 50% above 30. 56% of the current freshmen were in the top fifth of their class; 84% were in the top two fifths. **Admissions Contact:** Bui Hung, Vice President Dean. Email: *hnbui@bennington.edu* Web: *www.bennington.edu*

FINANCIAL AID: In 2017-2018, 95% of all full-time freshmen received some form of financial aid. 58% of all full-time freshmen received need-based aid. The average freshman award was $33,336. Need-based scholarships or need-based grants averaged $23,448; need-based self-help aid (loans and jobs) averaged $4,696; and other non-need-based awards and non-need-based scholarships averaged $13,019. 20% of undergraduate students work part-time. The average financial indebtedness of the 2017 graduate was $25,716. Bennington is a member of CSS. The CSS/Profile and the college's own financial statement, student and parent tax returns and W-2s are required. The FAFSA code is 003682. The priority date for freshman financial aid applications for fall entry is February 1.

CASTLETON UNIVERSITY — B-4

www.castleton.edu

Castleton, VT 05735	(802) 468-1352 (800) 639-8521
Fax: (802) 468-5237	Email: info@castleton.edu
Full-time: 859 men, 861 women	**Faculty:** 102
Part-time: 97 men, 168 women	**Ph.D.s:** 99%
Graduate: 49 men, 150 women	**Student/Faculty:** 14 to 1
Year: semesters, summer session	**Tuition:** $10,772 ($25,436)
Room & Board: $9414	**Freshman Class:** 2397 applied, 1868 accepted, 382 enrolled
SAT or ACT: required	**CEEB CODE:** 3765
Application Deadline: open	**COMPETITIVE**

Castleton University, founded in 1787, is the oldest institution of higher learning in Vermont. As part of the Vermont State Colleges system, it offers a state-supported undergraduate and graduate program in liberal arts, teacher preparation, and professional studies. There is 1 undergraduate school and 1 graduate school. In addition to regional accreditation, CU has baccalaureate program accreditation with CSWE and NLN. The 165-acre campus is in a rural area 12 miles west of Rutland. Including any residence halls, there are 24 buildings.

STUDENT LIFE: 85% are White; 6% race unknown; 2% African American; 2% Hispanic; 2% Foreign; 2% two or more races; 1% Asian American; 1% American Indian/Alaska Native. **Female To Male Ratio:** 1.2:1. The average age of freshmen is 18; all undergraduates, 21. **Housing:** 1100 students can be accommodated in college housing, which includes dorms, and wellness housing. On-campus housing is guaranteed for the freshman year only and is available on a lottery system for upperclassmen. 54% of students live on campus. All students may keep cars.

FACULTY/CLASSROOMS: 50% of faculty are male; 50% are female. All teach undergraduates, 50% do research, and 50% do both. No introductory courses are taught by graduate students. The average class size in an introductory lecture is 25; in a laboratory is 14; and in a regular course is 18.

PROGRAMS OF STUDY: Castleton confers B.A., B.S., B.M., and B.S.W. degrees. Associate and master's degrees are also awarded. Bachelor's degrees are awarded in BIOLOGICAL SCIENCE (biology/biological science and ecology), BUSINESS (business administration and management and sports management), COMMUNICATIONS AND THE ARTS (art, communications, English, literature, music, Spanish, and theatre arts), COMPUTER AND PHYSICAL SCIENCE (chemistry, computer science, geology, mathematics, and natural sciences), EDUCATION (athletic training, education, global studies, health education, music education, and physical education), ENGINEERING AND ENVIRONMENTAL DESIGN (environmental science), HEALTH PROFESSIONS (exercise science, health science, and nursing), SOCIAL SCIENCE (criminal justice, economics, history, liberal arts/general studies, philosophy, political science/government, psychology, social science, social work, sociology, and women & gender studies). Business, nursing, and teacher preparation have the largest enrollments.

ACTIVITIES: There are no fraternities or sororities. There are 40 groups on campus, including art, band, cheerleading, choir, chorale, chorus, computers, dance, drama, drill team, environmental, ethnic, film, honors, international, jazz band, LGBT, literary magazine, marching band, musical theater, newspaper, pep band, photography, political, professional, radio and TV, religious, social, social service, and student government. Popular campus events include Spring, Winter, and Alumni Weekends. **Sports:** There are 10 intercollegiate sports for men and 10 for women, and 10 intramural sports for men and 10 for women. Facilities include gymnasiums, a swimming pool, racquetball courts, fitness centers, a recreation gym, an ice hockey rink, an outdoor skating facility, multi-purpose turf field, baseball and softball fields, grass fields, athletic training rooms, a rock climbing wall, and an extensive trail system for hiking, running, and X-C skiing. **Graduates:** From July 1, 2016 to June 30, 2017, 372 bachelor's degrees were awarded. The most popular majors were health professions and related programs (20%), business/marketing (13%), and communication/journalism (10%). In an average class, 34% graduate in 4 years or less, 47% graduate in 5 years or less, and 51% graduate in 6 years or less.

SERVICES: Counseling and information services are available, as is tutoring in every subject. There is a reader service for the blind, and remedial math, reading, and writing. **Library/Resources:** The library contains 272,223 volumes, 626,965 microform items, and 22,349 audio/video tapes/CDs/DVDs, and subscribes to 67,896 periodicals including electronic. Computerized library services include interlibrary loans, database searching, Internet access, and Wi-Fi capability. Special learning facilities include an art gallery, radio station, TV studio, observatory, and theater. **Physically Challenged Students:** 95% of the campus is accessible. Facilities include wheelchair ramps, elevators, special parking, specially equipped restrooms, special class scheduling, lowered drinking fountains, and lowered telephones. **Special:** Cross-registration with other Vermont State Colleges, co-op programs, internships, study abroad, and work-study programs are available. In addition, B.A.-B.S. degrees, dual majors, student-designed majors in history, math, and social sciences, credit for life experience, nondegree study, and pass/fail options are offered. There are 8 national honor societies, a freshman honors program, and 4 departmental honors programs. **Visiting:** There are regularly scheduled orientations for prospective students, including meetings with admissions counselors, faculty, and coaches as well as a campus tour. There are guides for informal visits and visitors may sit in on classes. To schedule a visit, contact the Admissions Office. **Campus Safety and Security:** Measures include 24-hour foot and vehicle patrol, emergency notification system, self-defense education, and security escort services. There are emergency telephones, lighted pathways/sidewalks, and controlled access to dorms/residences.

REQUIREMENTS: The SAT or ACT is required. The college requires that candidates have 4 years of English, 3 years each of math, social studies or history, and sciences (two of which must be a lab). The college recommends 2 years of a foreign language. The GED is accepted. An interview is recommended. A GPA of 2.9 is required. AP and CLEP credits are accepted. Important factors in the admissions decision are advanced placement or honors courses, leadership record, and recommendations by school officials. All students must maintain a GPA of 2.0 while taking 122 semester hours, including 30 or more in their major. Distribution requirements include 3 courses each in literature and the arts, 2 each in math and natural sciences, and 1 each in foreign cultures, history, philosophy and psychology, and social analysis. Specific courses include computers, communication, and an introduction to liberal arts. **Procedure:** Freshmen are admitted fall and spring. Entrance exams should be taken during the spring of the junior year or fall of the senior year. There are early admissions, deferred admissions, and rolling admissions plans. Application deadlines are open. The fall 2017 application fee was $40. Applications are accepted on-line. **Transfer Students:** 183 transfer students enrolled in 2016-2017. All transfer applicants must have a 2.0 GPA and submit both previous college transcripts and an essay/personal statement. Some transfer applicants will be asked to submit high school transripts, standardized test scores, and a statement of good standing from the prior institution. An interview may also be required of some transfer students. 30 of 122 credits required for the bachelor's degree must be completed at Castleton. **International Students:** There are 27 international students enrolled. They must take the TOEFL with a minimum score of 550 on the paper-based TOEFL (PBT) or 80 on the Internet-based version (iBT). They must also take the SAT or ACT.

ADMISSIONS: 78% of the 2017-2018 applicants were accepted. 3 freshmen graduated first in their class. **Admissions Contact:** Maurice Ouimet, Dean of Enrollment. Email: *info@castleton.edu* Web: *www.castleton.edu*

FINANCIAL AID: Castleton is a member of CSS. The FAFSA code is 003683. The deadline for filing freshman financial aid applications for fall entry is April 1.

CHAMPLAIN COLLEGE — A-2
www.champlain.edu

Burlington, VT 05402	**(802) 865-5740** **(800) 570-5858**
Fax: (802) 860-2767	**Email: admission@champlain.edu**
Full-time: 1354 men, 810 women	**Faculty:** 114
Part-time: 32 men, 20 women	**Ph.D.s:** 71%
Graduate: 351 men, 464 women	**Student/Faculty:** 14 to 1
Year: semesters, summer session	**Tuition:** $39,818
Room & Board: $14,906	**Freshman Class:** 5197 applied, 3900 accepted, 587 enrolled
SAT EBR-W/M: 608/581 **ACT:** 26	**CEEB CODE:** 3291
Application Deadline: January 15	**VERY COMPETITIVE**

Champlain College, founded in 1878, has been preparing passionate students for rewarding careers. Today, our innovative Upside-Down Curriculum puts you in major-specific classes on day one, giving you the education you want. Each Champlain degree shares one goal: to prepare you to be a leader in your chosen field. In a highly competitive world, nothing less will do. Our multidimensional approach to education will equip you with the professional and life-management skills to reach your full potential. There is 1 undergraduate school. In addition to regional accreditation, Champlain College has baccalaureate program accreditation with CSWE, ASCLD, and JRCERT. The 22-acre campus is in an urban area just up the hill from the city's downtown area and Lake Champlain, and at the edge of Vermont's Green Mountains and within sight of New York's Adirondack Mountains. Including any residence halls, there are 51 buildings.

STUDENT LIFE: 79% of undergraduates are from out of state, mostly the Northeast. Students are from 42 states, 22 foreign countries, and Canada. 74% are White; 10% race unknown; 6% Hispanic; 3% Asian American; 3% two or more races; 2% African American; 1% Foreign. **Male To Female Ratio:** 1.3:1. The average age of freshmen is 18; all undergraduates, 20. 21% do not continue beyond their first year. **Housing:** 1472 students can be accommodated in college housing, which includes dorms and off-campus apartments. In addition, there are special-interest houses, international student housing, and sophomore housing. On-campus housing is guaranteed for the freshman year only, is available on a first-come, first-served basis, and is available on a lottery system for upperclassmen. 64% of students live on campus. Alcohol is not permitted. No one may keep cars.

FACULTY/CLASSROOMS: 59% of faculty are male; 41% are female. All teach undergraduates. No introductory courses are taught by graduate students. The average class size in a laboratory is 8 and in a regular course is 16.

PROGRAMS OF STUDY: Champlain College confers B.S., B.F.A., B.S.W., and B.S.B.A. degrees. Associate and master's degrees are also awarded. Bachelor's degrees are awarded in AGRICULTURE (environmental studies), BUSINESS (accounting, business administration and management, finance, international business management, management science, marketing, and marketing management), COMMUNICATIONS AND THE ARTS (advertising, broadcasting, communications, communications technology, film arts, fine arts, game design and development, game art, game programming, graphic design, graphic design & media, information technology, media arts, multimedia, public relations, and writing), COMPUTER AND PHYSICAL SCIENCE (computer game design/development, computer information technology, computer science, computer security and information assurance, cyber intelligence/security studies, information sciences and systems, radiological technology, and web services), EDUCATION (early childhood education, elementary education, health information management, middle school education, and secondary education), ENGINEERING AND ENVIRONMENTAL DESIGN (computational sciences), SOCIAL SCIENCE (criminal justice, forensic studies, legal studies, liberal arts/general studies, psychology, and social work). Game design & programming, graphic design, and digital forensics are the strongest academically. Computer networking & cybersecurity, game design, and computer science & innovation have the largest enrollments.

ACTIVITIES: There are no fraternities or sororities. There are 50 groups on campus, including sailing club, Parkour, Quidditch, art, chess, chorale, computers, dance, debate, drama, environmental, ethnic, forensics, honors, international, LGBT, literary magazine, newspaper, photography, professional, radio and TV, religious, ski and ride, social, social service, and student government. Popular campus events include Skiing, Snowboarding Trips, and Spring Meltdown. **Sports:** There are 16 intramural sports for men and 16 for women. Facilities include a wellness and fitness center, a gym, women and gender center, and game centers. **Graduates:** From July 1, 2016 to June 30, 2017, 496 bachelor's degrees were awarded. The most popular majors were business administration (7%), communication (6%), and game programming (6%). In an average class, 50% graduate in 4 years or less, 59% graduate in 5 years or less, and 60% graduate in 6 years or less. Of the 2016 graduating class, 4% were enrolled in graduate school within 6 months of graduation, and 90% were employed.

SERVICES: Counseling and information services are available, as is tutoring in some subjects, math, accounting, and writing. Peer tutoring is available. **Library/Resources:** The library contains 364,689 volumes, and 983 audio/video tapes/CDs/DVDs, and subscribes to 50,457 periodicals including electronic. Computerized library services include interlibrary loans, database searching, Internet access, and Wi-Fi capability. Special learning facilities include an art gallery, and radio station. Champlain College offers on-campus learning centers in studio-like environments in which students across majors work on professional projects that put Champlain students' classroom knowledge to the test through practical application on real projects. These Centers include; CCM (Center for Communications and Creative Media), EMC (Emergent Media Center), BYOBiz (Build Your Own Business), LCDI (Leahy Center for Digital Investigation) and the Publishing Initiative. A video production studio, broadcasting studio, several multimedia and graphic design studios and game design and production studio.**Physically Challenged Students:** 79% of the campus is accessible. Facilities include wheelchair ramps, elevators, special parking, specially equipped restrooms, special class scheduling, lowered drinking fountains, and lowered telephones. **Special:** Champlain College offers Bachelor of Science (BS) degrees in various fields of study in the areas of business, communication and creative media, education, human studies, and computer and information technology. We also offer the Bachelor of Social Work degree (BSW), the Bachelor of Fine Arts (BFA) degrees in creative media, filmmaking and graphic design; and the Bachelor of Business Administration (BSBA). The College also offers study abroad opportunities with campuses in Dublin, Ireland and Montreal, Canada, in addition to global partnerships with institutions around the world. The courses offered at the Champlain Abroad campuses fit across majors with a variety of professional, liberal arts, and interdisciplinary options that provide students with an understanding of culture and global perspective. Located in Burlington, Vermont, the college is accredited by the New England Association of Schools and Colleges (NEASC), which allows the credit transfer process to be seamless. We also prioritize creating internship opportunities. As a professionally focused institution, Champlain emphasizes the value of getting as much time in the field as possible. We go to great lengths to create the best options for our students to do so. If you have the drive, we will work with you extensively to help you find or create an internship that will give you a chance to really dig into the work of your profession, build up your professional portfolio and capture impressive credentials for your resume. Champlain has established close ties with the local business community, and Champlain students are the interns of choice at numerous businesses in and around Vermont. The college has developed a relationship with other area schools that allows students to take classes at their campuses as part of their regular class load. Champlain students can register for select classroom courses offered during the academic year at St. Michael's College or Burlington College. The agreement does not apply to summer session or online courses. The college maintains guaranteed admissions arrangements with NYU's School of Continuing and Professional Studies and the Vermont Law School. Students who meet the G.P.A. and other admission requirements of the programs are guaranteed admission into one of 14 Masters programs offered through NYU including an M.S. in Management and Systems and an M.S. in Global Affairs or into the J.D. program at Vermont Law School. An additional agreement with Clarkson University for a 4+1 graduate program allows students to complete the M.B.A. or M.S. in Management in one additional year. Through a special agreement with the prestigious Thunderbird School of Global Management, Champlain students may be able to pursue a Certificate of Advanced Global Studies during the fall of the fourth year, and upon successful completion, have those credits apply towards one of Thunderbird's masters programs. Students are also eligible for a 15% reduction in price per credit hour for certain Thunderbird Master's programs. **Visiting:** There are regularly scheduled orientations for prospective students, including a group information session followed by a tour. Personal interviews are also available with an admissions counselor. There are guides for informal visits and visitors may sit in on classes. To schedule a visit, contact the Admissions Office at admission@champlain.edu. **Campus Safety and Security:** Measures include 24-hour foot and vehicle patrol, emergency notification system, self-defense education, and security escort services. There are shuttle buses, emergency telephones, lighted pathways/sidewalks, and controlled access to dorms/residences.

REQUIREMENTS: The SAT or ACT is required. Applicants must be graduates of an accredited high school or the equivalent. AP and CLEP credits are accepted. Important factors in the admissions decision are extracurricular activities record, recommendations by school officials, and advanced placement or honors courses. Traditional Student: a GPA of 2.0 and 120 credits are required for baccalaureate degrees. Students must take between 40 and 60 hours in the major. Every undergraduate takes Champlain's Core Curriculum, a four-year course of interdisciplinary study that cultivates the intellectual leadership prized by a complex economy and a rapidly changing world. All undergraduate students also participate in the Career Flagship Program, a four-year program designed to help develop competencies in career positioning and personal finance. CPS Student: adult undergraduate students complete a professionally focused general education curriculum intentionally designed to support courses in the major. **Procedure:** Freshmen are admitted fall and spring. Entrance exams should be taken prior to applying. There are early decision and deferred admissions plans. Early decision applications should be filed by November 15; regular applications, by January 15 for fall entry. 314 early decision candidates were accepted for the 2017-2018 class. 85 applicants were on the 2017 waiting list; 20 were admitted. Applications are accepted on-line. **Transfer Students:** 68 transfer students enrolled in 2016-2017. High school and college transcripts are required. 45 of 120 credits required for the bachelor's degree must be completed at Champlain. **International Students:** There are 21 international students enrolled. They must take the TOEFL with a minimum score of 550 on the paper-based TOEFL (PBT) or 79 on the Internet-based version (iBT). Students whose high school was conducted in English must take the SAT or ACT.

ADMISSIONS: 75% of the 2017-2018 applicants were accepted. The SAT scores for the 2017-2018 freshman class were: Math-- 12% below 500, 46% between 500 and 599, 35% between 600 and 699, and 7% between 700 and 800. Evidence-Based Reading/Writing-- 8% below 500, 36% between 500 and 599, 45% between 600 and 699, and 11% between 700 and 800. The ACT scores were 10% between 12 and 17, 28% between 18 and 23, 41% between 24 and 29, and 21% above 30. 2 freshmen graduated first in their class. **Admissions Contact:** Chris Perlongo, Director of Admissions. Email: *admission@champlain.edu* Web: *www.champlain.edu*

FINANCIAL AID: The FAFSA code is 003684. The priority date for freshman financial aid applications for fall entry is January 15.

COLLEGE OF ST JOSEPH *(The complete profile is made available exclusively on our website, www.barronspac.com)*

GODDARD COLLEGE — C-3
www.goddard.edu

Plainfield, VT 05667	**(802) 454-8311** **(800) 906-8312**
Fax: (802) 454-1029	**Email: admissions@goddard.edu**
Full-time: 73 men, 136 women	**Faculty:** 16
Part-time: n/av	**Ph.D.s:** 87%
Graduate: 108 men, 274 women	**Student/Faculty:** n/av
Year: semesters	**Tuition:** $15,476
Room & Board: $1564	**Freshman Class:** n/av **CEEB CODE:** 3416
Application Deadline: open	**VERY COMPETITIVE**

Goddard College, founded in 1863, is a private college that stresses progressive, individualized education for personal and community transformation, based on John Dewey's learning-by-engagement philosophy. There is 1 undergraduate school and 1 graduate school. The 200-acre campus is in a rural area 10 miles from Montpelier, and 45 miles from Burlington, Vermont. Including any residence halls, there are 28 buildings.

STUDENT LIFE: 85% of undergraduates are from out of state, mostly the Northeast. 73% are White; 6% Hispanic; 4% two or more races; 2% African American; 13% race unknown; 1% Asian American; 1% American Indian/Alaska Native. **Female To Male Ratio:** 2.3:1. The average age of freshmen is 32; all undergraduates, 34. **Housing:** 175 students can be accommodated in college housing, which includes dorms. In addition, there are special-interest houses, family-friendly dorm, and substance-free (i.e. no perfumes, etc.) dorm. All students may keep cars.

FACULTY/CLASSROOMS: 23% of faculty are male; 77% are female. No introductory courses are taught by graduate students.

PROGRAMS OF STUDY: Goddard confers B.A. and B.F.A. degrees. Master's degrees are also awarded. Bachelor's degrees are awarded in AGRICULTURE (environmental studies), BIOLOGICAL SCIENCE (nutrition), BUSINESS (sustainable management), COMMUNICATIONS AND THE ARTS (applied art, art, comparative literature, creative writing, dramatic arts, English, English Writing, fine arts, folklore and mythology, intermedia/multimedia, literature, media arts, photography, playwriting/screenwriting, and visual and performing arts), EDUCATION (art education, collaborative education, early childhood education, education, elementary education, English education, health education, learner designed area of study, middle school education, and secondary education), HEALTH PROFESSIONS (health, health promotion, and health science), SOCIAL SCIENCE (addiction studies, clinical psychology, counseling/psychology, crosscultural studies, cultural studies/critical theory & analysis, ethics, politics and social policy, history, human development, human ecology, humanities and social science, industrial and organizational psychology, interdisciplinary studies, justice and society, liberal arts/general studies, psychology, social psychology, social science, and women & gender studies). Creative writing, individualized studies, and BA-to-MA Fast Track in psychology are the strongest academically. Psychology, and creative writing have the largest enrollments.

ACTIVITIES: There are no fraternities or sororities. There are 9 groups on campus, including art, drama, environmental, literary magazine, radio and TV, and student government. **Sports:** There is no sports program at Goddard. Facilities include workout room and hiking trails. **Graduates:** From July 1, 2016 to June 30, 2017, 92 bachelor's degrees were awarded.

SERVICES: There is remedial writing. **Library/Resources:** The library contains 173,000 volumes, and 400 audio/video tapes/CDs/DVDs, and subscribes to 10,000 periodicals including electronic. Computerized library services include interlibrary loans, database searching, Internet access, and Wi-Fi capability. Special learning facilities include a radio station. **Physically Challenged Students:** 60% of the campus is accessible. Facilities include wheelchair ramps, elevators, special parking, and specially equipped restrooms. **Special:** The BA/MA Fast Track in Psychology saves students a semester toward earning an MA while completing their bachelor's degree. All programs entail students designing their own studies. The B.A. in Sustainability, B.A. in Education, B.A. in Health Arts & Sciences, and B.F.A. in Creative Writing are upper-division programs, requiring 60 prior credits. The main undergraduate program encompasses both lower and upper divisions. **Visiting:** There are regularly scheduled orientations for prospective students, One Discover Goddard Day held each fall and spring, one visiting day during every residency, and individual meetings by appointment. There are guides for informal visits and visitors may sit in on classes. To schedule a visit, contact respective admissions counselor for the program. **Campus Safety and Security:** Measures include 24-hour foot and vehicle patrol. There are lighted pathways/sidewalks and controlled access to dorms/residences.

REQUIREMENTS: Goddard admits students who can contribute to its learning community and who will thrive in a self-directed degree program. The admission decision is based on the application, including essays, letters of recommendation, transcripts, samples of the student's creative or academic work, and an interview. Standardized test scores are unhelpful and not required. Homeschooled students are welcome to apply. AP and CLEP credits are accepted. Important factors in the admissions decision are personality/intangible qualities, recommendations by alumni, and evidence of special talent. Students come to campus for eight days at the beginning of each semester, then study independently the rest of the term, at home or elsewhere. Collaborating with a faculty advisor, students design and carry out programs of study specifically tailored to their own personal and professional interests and goals. Assessment takes the form of narrative evaluations rather than letter grades; students must pass comprehensive reviews of performance and progress. There are no declared majors, but in the last semester of enrollment, all students must complete a culminating senior study or project that may be multidisciplinary and requires extensive foundational work comparable to a major. A total of 120 credits is required to graduate. Students must conduct, or transfer in, substantive studies in the arts, humanities, social sciences, natural sciences, and quantitative reasoning. **Procedure:** Freshmen are admitted to all sessions. There are deferred admissions and rolling admissions plans. Check with the school for current application deadlines. The fall 2017 application fee was $65. Notification is sent on a rolling basis. Applications are accepted on-line. **Transfer Students:** Official transcripts from previous institutions, writing samples, an essay, letters of recommendation, and an interview are required. 45 of 120 credits required for the bachelor's degree must be completed at Goddard. **International Students:** There are 2 international students enrolled.

Admissions Contact: Admissions Office Email: *admissions@goddard.edu* Web: *www.goddard.edu*

FINANCIAL AID: The average freshman award was $9,515. Need-based scholarships or need-based grants averaged $5,662; and need-based self-help aid (loans and jobs) averaged $3,853. The average financial indebtedness of the 2017 graduate was $25,856. The FAFSA code is 003686. Check with the school for current application deadlines.

GREEN MOUNTAIN COLLEGE *(The complete profile is made available exclusively on our website, www.barronspac.com)*

JOHNSON STATE COLLEGE B-2

www.jsc.edu

Johnson, VT 05656 (802) 635-1219 (800) 635-2356

Fax: (802) 635-1230 **Email:** Patrick.Rogers@jsc.edu

Full-time: 505 men, 610 women
Part-time: 105 men, 320 women
Graduate: 60 men, 170 women
Year: semesters, summer session
Room & Board: $10,598

SAT CR/M: 500/500 **ACT:** required
Application Deadline: n/av

Faculty: 62
Ph.D.s: 90%
Student/Faculty: 19 to 1
Tuition: $12,074 ($25,394)
Freshman Class: 1333 applied, 1093 accepted, 410 enrolled
CEEB CODE: 3766
COMPETITIVE

Johnson State College, founded in 1828, is a public liberal arts and science college, offering more than 30 academic and professional degree programs. The figures given in the above capsule and in this profile are approximate. There is 1 undergraduate school and 1 graduate school. In addition to regional accreditation, JSC has baccalaureate program accreditation with NEASC. The 350-acre campus is in a small town in the heart of the Green Mountains, 1 hour from Burlington, and 3.5 hours from Boston. Including any residence halls, there are 14 buildings.

STUDENT LIFE: 63% of undergraduates are from Vermont. Others are from 23 states, 6 foreign countries, and Canada. 90% are White; 5% African American; 2% American Indian/Alaska Native; 2% Hispanic; 1% Foreign. **Female To Male Ratio:** 1.6:1. The average age of freshmen is 19; all undergraduates, 21. 30% do not continue beyond their first year; 45% remain to graduate. **Housing:** 549 students can be accommodated in college housing, which includes married student dorms and on-campus apartments. In addition, there are special-interest houses, an alcohol-free residence hall. On-campus housing is guaranteed for all 4 years. 57% of students live on campus. Alcohol is not permitted. All students may keep cars.

FACULTY/CLASSROOMS: 58% of faculty are male; 42% are female. All teach undergraduates. No introductory courses are taught by graduate students.

PROGRAMS OF STUDY: JSC confers B.A., B.S. and B.F.A. A.A., A.S., M.A., and M.F.A. degrees. Associate and master's degrees are also awarded. Bachelor's degrees are awarded in AGRICULTURE (natural resource management), BIOLOGICAL SCIENCE (biology/biological science and cell biology), BUSINESS (business administration and management, business systems analysis, hospitality management services, recreational facilities management, small business management, and tourism), COMMUNICATIONS AND THE ARTS (art, creative writing, English, fine arts, jazz, journalism, music, music business management, music history and appreciation, music performance, performing arts, studio art, theater design, theater management, visual and performing arts, and writing), COMPUTER AND PHYSICAL SCIENCE (mathematics), EDUCATION (art education, athletic training, education, elementary education, English education, environmental education, mathematics education, middle school education, music education, physical education, recreation education, science education, and secondary education), ENGINEERING AND ENVIRONMENTAL DESIGN (environmental science), HEALTH PROFESSIONS (allied health, health science, and premedicine), SOCIAL SCIENCE (anthropology, behavioral science, history, humanities, liberal arts/general studies, physical fitness/movement, political science/government, prelaw, psychology, and sociology). Environmental science, elementary/secondary/middle school education, and wellness & alternative medicine have the largest enrollments.

ACTIVITIES: There are no fraternities or sororities. There are 35 groups on campus, including ski & snowboard club, finance & investment club, hospitality, humans vs zombies, leadership, magic the gathering club, art, band, choir, chorale, chorus, dance, debate, drama, environmental, jazz band, LGBT, literary magazine, musical theater, newspaper, outdoor, photography, political, professional, radio and TV, religious, social, social service, and student government. Popular campus events include Winter Carnival and Coffee House (weekly live entertainment). **Sports:** There are 6 intercollegiate sports for men and 6 for women, and 20 intramural sports for men and 20 for women. Facilities include a multiuse facility with health monitoring and exercise equipment, gyms, weight room, indoor pool, basketball court, racquetball courts, indoor climbing and bouldering wall, and squash court. **Graduates:** The most popular majors were business, education, and behavioral sciences.

SERVICES: Counseling and information services are available, as is tutoring in most subjects. There is a reader service for the blind, and remedial math, reading, and writing. The Academic Support Services Department provides accommodations for students with a documented learning disability. **Library/Resources:** The library contains 111,000 volumes, 180,158 microform items, and 7,200 audio/video tapes/CDs/ DVDs, and subscribes to 42,884 periodicals including electronic. Computerized library services include interlibrary loans, database searching, Internet access, and Wi-Fi capability. Special learning facilities include an art gallery and radio station. **Physically Challenged Students:** 60% of the campus is accessible. Facilities include wheelchair ramps, elevators, special parking, specially equipped restrooms, special class scheduling, and lowered drinking fountains. **Special:** All students are encouraged to complete an internship. Through the National Student Exchange Program, students may study at another institution or abroad for a semester or a year. Co-op programs are offered in business, tourism, hospitality management, and education, and cross-registration is available with other Vermont state colleges. There is 1 national honor society. **Visiting:** There are regularly scheduled orientations for prospective students, including a campus tour and an admission interview. Students may request to meet with a faculty member. There are guides for informal visits and visitors may sit in on classes. To schedule a visit, contact the Admissions Office. **Campus Safety and Security:** Measures include 24-hour foot and vehicle patrol, self-defense education, and security escort services. There are shuttle buses, emergency telephones, and lighted pathways/sidewalks.

REQUIREMENTS: The SAT or ACT is required. Successful candidates for admission have generally completed a college preparatory curriculum consisting of 4 years of English, 3 of math (2 of algebra, 1 of geometry), 3 of social sciences, and 2 of science (including 1 lab science). An official high school transcript or GED test score must be submitted with the application. In addition, 1 letter of recommendation, preferably from a guidance counselor, and SAT or ACT scores should be sent with the application or under separate cover. A GPA of 2.3 is required. AP and CLEP credits are accepted. Important factors in the admissions decision are advanced placement or honors courses, recommendations by school officials, and extracurricular activities record. The bachelor's degree requires completion of at least 120 credit hours of course work (not including basic skills credits), with a minimum cumulative GPA of 2.0. In addition, students must complete the general education core curriculum and an approved major as well as take a writing proficiency exam. **Procedure:** Freshmen are admitted fall and spring. There are deferred admissions and rolling admissions plans. Applications should be filed by December 1 for spring entry. The fall 2017 application fee was $37. Applications are accepted on-line. **Transfer Students:** A GPA of at least 2.0 is required. 30 of 120 credits required for the bachelor's degree must be completed at Johnson State. **International Students:** They must take the TOEFL with a minimum score of 500 on the paper-based TOEFL (PBT) or 80 on the Internet-based version (iBT). They must also take the SAT or ACT, scoring 1400.

ADMISSIONS: 82% of the 2017-2018 applicants were accepted. **Admissions Contact:** Patrick Rogers, Director of Admissions. Email: *Patrick.Rogers@jsc.edu* Web: *www.jsc.edu*

FINANCIAL AID: JSC is a member of CSS. The FAFSA code is 003688. The priority date for freshman financial aid applications for fall entry is November 1.

LYNDON STATE COLLEGE — D-2

www.lyndonstate.edu

Lyndonville, VT 05851 — **(802) 626-6413** **(800) 225-1998**

Fax: (802) 626-6335 — **Email: nolan.atkins@lyndonstate.edu**

Full-time: 560 men, 570 women	**Faculty:** 56
Part-time: 70 men, 230 women	**Ph.D.s:** 60%
Graduate: 1 men, 5 women	**Student/Faculty:** 20 to 1
Year: semesters, summer session	**Tuition:** $11,018 ($22,418)
Room & Board: $9696	**Freshman Class:** n/av
SAT or ACT: required	**CEEB CODE:** 3767
Application Deadline: open	**COMPETITIVE**

Lyndon State College, founded in 1911 as a teachers' college, became a liberal arts school in 1962, offering undergraduate and graduate courses. The figures given in the above capsule and in this profile are approximate. There is 1 undergraduate school and 1 graduate school. In addition to regional accreditation, LSC has baccalaureate program accreditation with NRPA. The 175-acre campus is in a small town in northeastern Vermont, 184 miles north of Boston. Including any residence halls, there are 17 buildings.

STUDENT LIFE: 60% of undergraduates are from Vermont. Others are from 24 states, 12 foreign countries, and Canada. 99% are White. **Female To Male Ratio:** 1.3:1. The average age of freshmen is 18; all undergraduates, 24. 33% do not continue beyond their first year; 41% remain to graduate. **Housing:** 600 students can be accommodated in college housing, which includes dorms. In addition, there are special-interest houses. On-campus housing is available on a first-come and first-served basis. 56% of students commute. All students may keep cars.

FACULTY/CLASSROOMS: 66% of faculty are male; 34% are female. All teach undergraduates. No introductory courses are taught by graduate students. The average class size in an introductory lecture is 20; in a laboratory is 16; and in a regular course is 16.

PROGRAMS OF STUDY: LSC confers B.A. and B.S. degrees. Associate and master's degrees are also awarded. Bachelor's degrees are awarded in BUSINESS (accounting, business administration and management, recreation and leisure services, and sports management), COMMUNICATIONS AND THE ARTS (communications, English, graphic design, journalism, multimedia, and radio/television technology), COMPUTER AND PHYSICAL SCIENCE (atmospheric sciences and meteorology, mathematics, natural sciences, and science), EDUCATION (early childhood education, elementary education, English education, physical education, recreation education, and science education), SOCIAL SCIENCE (human services, interdisciplinary studies, psychology, and social science). Meteorology, natural science, and math are the strongest academically. Education, communications, and business have the largest enrollments.

ACTIVITIES: There are no fraternities or sororities. There are 22 groups on campus, including snowmobile club, anime, flight club, LAN party club and Lyndon sports broadcasting club, capella club, cheerleading, choir, chorale, chorus, communications, dance, drama, film, honors, international, jazz band, LGBT, literary magazine, newspaper, photography, political, professional, radio and TV, religious, social, social service, student government, and yearbook. Popular campus events include Family Weekend, Alumni Weekend, and a Concert Series. **Sports:** There are 5 intercollegiate sports for men and 5 for women, and 12 intramural sports for men and 12 for women. Facilities include a fitness center, features cardiovascular, selectorized and free weight equipment, racquetball courts, auxiliary gym, and Olympic-size pool, outdoor tennis courts, ice hockey, cross-country ski trails and running trails, softball, soccer, basketball and rugby fields. **Graduates:** The most popular majors were psychology/human services (19%), business (10%), and education (10%). In an average class, 21% graduate in 4 years or less, 35% graduate in 5 years or less, and 41% graduate in 6 years or less.

SERVICES: Counseling and information services are available, as is tutoring in every subject. There is remedial math, reading, and writing. A math lab and a writing center are available for student use. **Library/ Resources:** The library contains 100,000 volumes, and 3,600 audio/video tapes/CDs/DVDs, and subscribes to 48,000 periodicals including electronic. Computerized library services include interlibrary loans, database searching, and Internet access. Special learning facilities include an art gallery, radio station, TV station, a founder's museum, and meteorology lab. **Physically Challenged Students:** 70% of the campus is accessible. Facilities include wheelchair ramps, elevators, special parking, specially equipped restrooms, and lowered drinking fountains. **Special:** Cooperative programs in a variety of businesses, including local ski areas, social agencies, and radio and TV stations, internships in recreation programs and communications, and study abroad in Nova Scotia and England are available. B.A.-B.S. degrees, work-study, a general studies degree, dual and student-designed majors, a 3-2 engineering degree with Norwich University in Vermont, credit for life experience, nondegree study, cross-registration, work study, accelerated degree programs and pass/fail options also are offered. There is 1 national honor society, a freshman honors program, and 1 departmental honors program. **Visiting:** There are regularly scheduled orientations for prospective students, including a tour, an information session, and faculty presentations. There are guides for informal visits, visitors may sit in on classes, and stay overnight. To schedule a visit, contact the Admissions Office. **Campus Safety**

and Security: Measures include 24-hour foot and vehicle patrol, self-defense education, and security escort services. There are emergency telephones, lighted pathways/sidewalks, a security and safety service on campus as well as a 24-hour emergency rescue squad.

REQUIREMENTS: The SAT or ACT is required. LSC recommends that applicants have 4 years of English and 2 each of math, foreign language, history, and science. An essay is required, as is a recommendation from the high school principal or guidance counselor. An interview is recommended. The GED is accepted. AP and CLEP credits are accepted. Important factors in the admissions decision are advanced placement or honors courses, recommendations by school officials, and leadership record. All students must maintain a minimum GPA of 2.0 while taking 122 semester hours, including 42 hours in liberal arts. Distribution requirements include 28 credits in arts, humanities, math and science, and social and behavioral sciences. Required courses include freshman English and college algebra. **Procedure:** Freshmen are admitted fall and spring. There are early decision, early admissions, deferred admissions, and rolling admissions plans. Application deadlines are open. The fall 2017 application fee was $32. Notification of early decision is sent December 1; regular decision, on a rolling basis. Applications are accepted on-line. **Transfer Students:** 115 transfer students enrolled in 2016-2017. Interviews are recommended for transfer students. An official transcript from each college attended is required. 30 of 122 credits required for the bachelor's degree must be completed at LSC. **International Students:** There are 10 international students enrolled. They must take the TOEFL.

ADMISSIONS: 4 freshmen graduated first in their class. **Admissions Contact:** Nolan Atkins, Interim Dean. Email: *nolan.atkins@lyndonstate.edu* Web: *www.lyndonstate.edu*

FINANCIAL AID: In 2017-2018, 89% of all full-time freshmen received some form of financial aid. 89% of all full-time freshmen received need-based aid. The average freshman award was $8,079. Need-based scholarships or need-based grants averaged $3,879 ($5,000 maximum); need-based self-help aid (loans and jobs) averaged $3,817 ($4,625 maximum); and other non-need-based awards and non-need-based scholarships averaged $3,860 ($5,646 maximum). The average financial indebtedness of the 2017 graduate was $18,084. LSC is a member of CSS. The FAFSA code is 003689. The priority date for freshman financial aid applications for fall entry is January 1.

MARLBORO COLLEGE — B-6

www.marlboro.edu

Marlboro, VT 05344	**(802) 258-9261** **(800) 343-0049**
Fax: (802) 258-9300	**Email: blawler@marlboro.edu**
Full-time: 88 men, 102 women	**Faculty:** 38
Part-time: 1 men, 1 women	**Ph.D.s:** 77%
Graduate: 31 men, 39 women	**Student/Faculty:** 5 to 1
Year: semesters	**Tuition:** $40,030
Room & Board: $10,802	**Freshman Class:** 144 applied, 136 accepted, 35 enrolled
SAT CR/M/W: 670/555/620 **ACT:** 25	**CEEB CODE:** 3509
Application Deadline: January 15	**VERY COMPETITIVE+**

Marlboro College, established in 1946, is a small, private institution offering degrees in the liberal and fine arts and humanities, and employing self-designed programs of study. The figures given in the above capsule and in this profile are approximate. There is 1 undergraduate school and 1 graduate school. The 300-acre campus is in a rural area in the southern Vermont town of Marlboro, approximately 9 miles west of Brattleboro, and just 1.5 hours from Albany and Hartford. Including any residence halls, there are 36 buildings.

STUDENT LIFE: 88% of undergraduates are from out of state, mostly the Northeast. Students are from 37 states, 4 foreign countries, and Canada. 70% are from public schools. 78% are White; 8% race unknown; 4% two or more races; 3% African American; 3% Hispanic; 2% Asian American; 1% American Indian/Alaska Native; 1% Foreign. **Female To Male Ratio:** 1.2:1. The average age of freshmen is 19; all undergraduates, 21. 28% do not continue beyond their first year; 48% remain to graduate. **Housing:** 266 students can be accommodated in college housing, which includes married student dorms and on-campus apartments, residence halls, alcohol-free & smoke-free dorms, theme housing, wellness housing, and cottages. On-campus housing is guaranteed for all 4 years, is available on a first-come, and first-served basis. 78% of students live on campus. All students may keep cars.

FACULTY/CLASSROOMS: 62% of faculty are male; 38% are female. All teach undergraduates. No introductory courses are taught by graduate students. The average class size in a laboratory is 8 and in a regular course is 8.

PROGRAMS OF STUDY: Marlboro confers B.A. and B.S. degrees. Master's degrees are also awarded. Bachelor's degrees are awarded in AGRICULTURE (environmental studies), BIOLOGICAL SCIENCE (biochemistry, biology/biological science, botany, and microbiology), COMMUNICATIONS AND THE ARTS (art history and appreciation, creative writing, dance, dramatic arts, English, fine arts, French, German, Greek, Italian, languages, Latin, linguistics, music, photography, Russian, Spanish, and theatre studies), COMPUTER AND PHYSICAL SCIENCE (chemistry, computer science, mathematics, and physics), HEALTH PROFESSIONS (premedicine), SOCIAL SCIENCE (anthropology, economics, history, interdisciplinary studies, international studies, liberal arts, sciences, general studies, humanities, philosophy, political science/government, prelaw, psychology, religion, social science, and sociology). Sciences, humanities, and world studies are the strongest academically. Literature, biology, and sociology have the largest enrollments.

ACTIVITIES: There are no fraternities or sororities. There are 25 groups on campus, including art, chess, chorus, communications, computers, dance, drama, environmental, ethnic, film, international, jazz band, LGBT, literary magazine, musical theater, newspaper, photography, political, professional, religious, social, social service, and student government. Popular campus events include Green-up Day, Creativity Lecture Series, and Visiting Writers Series. **Sports:** There is 1 intercollegiate sport for men and 1 for women, and 1 intramural sport for men and 1 for women. Facilities include a soccer field, volleyball court, cross-country trails, basketball court, weight room, climbing wall, field trips for canoeing, white-water rafting, hiking, and skiing. **Graduates:** From July 1, 2016 to June 30, 2017, 44 bachelor's degrees were awarded. The most popular majors were film/vido studies, literature, and psychology. In an average class, 66% graduate in 6 years or less. Of the 2016 graduating class, 76% were employed within 6 months of graduation.

SERVICES: Counseling and information services are available, as is tutoring in some subjects, such as writing and languages, math, and organic chemistry. **Library/Resources:** The library contains 75,000 volumes, 5,799 microform items, and 2,990 audio/video tapes/CDs/DVDs, and subscribes to 188 periodicals including electronic. Computerized library services include interlibrary loans, database searching, Internet access, and Wi-Fi capability. Special learning facilities include an art gallery, an observatory. **Physically Challenged Students:** 90% of the campus is accessible. Facilities include wheelchair ramps, elevators, special parking, specially equipped restrooms, and special class scheduling. **Special:** Marlboro offers a variety of internships, cross-registration with Huron University in London, and study abroad in many countries, including China, Cambodia, Thailand, New Zealand, Hungary and Mexico. The World Studies Program combines liberal arts with international studies, including 5 to 8 months of internship work in another culture. Accelerated and B.A.-B.S. degree programs are available. Students may pursue dual majors. Majors reflect an integrated course of study designed by students and their faculty advisers during the junior year. **Visiting:** There are regularly scheduled orientations for prospective students, Campus tour, visit with admissions staff, optional class visit, optional interview. There are guides for informal visits, visitors may sit in on classes, and stay overnight. To schedule a visit, contact the Office of Admissions. **Campus Safety and Security:** Measures include self-defense education.

REQUIREMENTS: Applicants typically graduate from an accredited secondary school or have a GED. They are encouraged to earn 14 Carnegie units and complete 4 years of English and 3 years each of math, science, and 2 years each of history, social studies, and foreign language. Supplementary essays and analytical writing samples are required. Interviews are required. Standardized test scores (SAT, ACT, etc.) are not required, but may be submitted. It is encouraged to submit scores if a student feels it will strengthen their application. Any additional materials a student wishes to submit, such as an art portfolio or writing project, are encouraged and will be accepted and reviewed. AP and CLEP credits are accepted. Important factors in the admissions decision are personality/intangible qualities, leadership record, and extracurricular activities record. To graduate, students must complete a Plan of Concentration, a writing requirement, and a freshman seminar. A minimum GPA of 2.0 is required. Students must earn 120 credits, with 50 credits in the major, and complete a thesis and an oral exam. **Procedure:** Freshmen are admitted fall and spring. Entrance exams should be taken by October before entry. There are early decision, early admissions, deferred admissions, and rolling admissions plans. Early decision applications should be filed by November 15; regular applications, by January 15 for fall entry; and December 15 for spring entry. The fall 2017 application fee was $50. Notification of early decision is sent December 1; regular decision, May 1. Applications are accepted on-line. **Transfer Students:** 15 transfer students enrolled in 2016-2017. Transfers must have a minimum GPA of 2.0. All high school and college transcripts. An essay and interview are also required. Students may apply for admissions fall and spring. 42 of 120 credits required for the bachelor's degree must be completed at Marlboro. **International Students:** There are 6 international students enrolled. They must take the TOEFL.

ADMISSIONS: 94% of the 2017-2018 applicants were accepted. The SAT scores for the 2017-2018 freshman class were: Critical Reading-- 8% below 500, 25% between 500 and 599, 17% between 600 and 699, and 50% between 700 and 800. Math-- 17% below 500, 58% between 500 and 599, 17% between 600 and 699, and 8% between 700 and 800. Writing-- 8% below 500, 17% between 500 and 599, 67% between 600 and 699, and 8% between 700 and 800. The ACT scores were 35% between 12 and 17, 29% between 18 and 23, 29% between 24 and 29, and 7% above 30. 46% of the current freshmen were in the top fifth of their class; 82% were in the top two fifths. 2 freshmen graduated first in their class. **Admissions Contact:** Brigid Lawler, Director of Admissions. Email: *blawler@marlboro.edu* Web: *www.marlboro.edu*

FINANCIAL AID: In 2017-2018, 85% of all full-time freshmen received some form of financial aid. 68% of all full-time freshmen received need-based aid. The average freshman award was $33,928. Need-based scholarships or need-based grants averaged $15,969; need-based self-help aid (loans and jobs) averaged $29,231; other non-need-based awards and non-need-based scholarships averaged $13,000; and $34,912 from other forms of aid. 68% of undergraduate students work part-time. Marlboro is a member of CSS. The CSS/Profile is required. The FAFSA code is 003690. The priority date for freshman financial aid applications for fall entry is March 1.

MIDDLEBURY COLLEGE — A-3

www.middlebury.edu

Middlebury, VT 05753	(802) 443-3000
Fax: (802) 443-2065	**Email:** admissions@middlebury.edu
Full-time: 1222 men, 1309 women	**Faculty:** 293; IIB, ++$
Part-time: 13 men, 17 women	**Ph.D.s:** 96%
Graduate: 7 men, 35 women	**Student/Faculty:** 8 to 1
Year: 4-1-4	**Tuition:** $52,496
Room & Board: $14,968	**Freshman Class:** 8819 applied, 1423 accepted, 606 enrolled
SAT EBR-W/M: 700/704 **ACT:** 32	**CEEB CODE:** 3526
Application Deadline: January 1	**MOST COMPETITIVE**

Middlebury College, founded in 1800, is a small, private, liberal arts institution offering degree programs in languages, humanities, and social and natural sciences. There is 1 undergraduate school and 3 graduate schools. The 355-acre campus is in a small town 35 miles south of Burlington. Including any residence halls, there are 115 buildings.

STUDENT LIFE: 94% of undergraduates are from out of state, mostly the Northeast. Students are from 52 states, 68 foreign countries, and Canada. 63% are White; 11% Foreign; 10% Hispanic; 6% Asian American; 4% African American; 4% two or more races; 2% race unknown. **Female To Male Ratio:** 1.1:1. The average age of freshmen is 18; all undergraduates, 20. 4% do not continue beyond their first year; 96% remain to graduate. **Housing:** 2560 students can be accommodated in college housing, which includes married student dorms and on-campus apartments. In addition, there are language/international houses, special-interest houses, coed social, multicultural, and environmental houses. On-campus housing is guaranteed for all 4 years and is available on a lottery system for upperclassmen. 96% of students live on campus. All students may keep cars.

FACULTY/CLASSROOMS: 54% of faculty are male; 46% are female. All teach undergraduates. No introductory courses are taught by graduate students. The average class size in an introductory lecture is 18 and in a regular course is 18.

PROGRAMS OF STUDY: Middlebury confers A.B. degrees. Master's and doctoral degrees are also awarded. Bachelor's degrees are awarded in AGRICULTURE (environmental studies), BIOLOGICAL SCIENCE (biochemistry, biology/biological science, molecular biology, and neurosciences), BUSINESS (international economics), COMMUNICATIONS AND THE ARTS (Arabic, Chinese, classics, comparative literature, dance, dramatic arts, English, film arts, French, German, Italian, Japanese, music, Russian, Spanish, and studio art), COMPUTER AND PHYSICAL SCIENCE (chemistry, computer science, geology, mathematics, and physics), EDUCATION (museum studies), ENGINEERING AND ENVIRONMENTAL DESIGN (architectural history), SOCIAL SCIENCE (African American studies, American studies, anthropology, East Asian studies, economics, European studies, geography, history, Latin American studies, liberal arts/general studies, Middle Eastern studies, philosophy, political science/government, psychology, religion, Russian and Slavic studies, sociology, South Asian studies, and women's studies). Foreign languages, international studies, and sciences are the strongest academically. Economics, environmental studies, and computer science have the largest enrollments.

ACTIVITIES: There are no fraternities or sororities. There are 178 groups on campus, including art, band, cheerleading, chess, choir, chorus, communications, computers, dance, debate, drama, environmental, ethnic, film, honors, international, jazz band, LGBT, literary magazine, Middlebury Mountain Club, musical theater, newspaper, orchestra, pep band, photography, political, professional, radio and TV, religious, social, social service, student government, and yearbook. Popular campus events include Winter Carnival, Student Concert Series, and Clifford Symposium. **Sports:** There are 12 intercollegiate sports for men and 11 for women, and 16 intramural sports for men and 16 for women. Facilities include playing fields and athletic facilities, football and lacrosse complex, baseball and softball fields, golf course, cross country trail, hockey arena, Olympic-size natatorium, squash courts, tennis courts, climbing wall, gymnasium, astro-turf fields, and all-weather outdoor track.**Graduates:** From July 1, 2016 to June 30, 2017, 677 bachelor's degrees were awarded. The most popular majors were economics (16%), political science (7%), and environmental studies (6%). In an average class, 86% graduate in 4 years or less, 93% graduate in 5 years or less, and 95% graduate in 6 years or less. Of the 2016 graduating class, 9% were enrolled in graduate school within 6 months of graduation, and 70% were employed.

SERVICES: Counseling and information services are available, as is tutoring in every subject. There is a reader service for the blind. **Library/ Resources:** The library contains 970,734 volumes, 620 microform items, and 74,487 audio/video tapes/CDs/DVDs, and subscribes to 181,350 periodicals including electronic. Computerized library services include interlibrary loans, database searching, Internet access, and Wi-Fi capability. Special learning facilities include an art gallery, planetarium, and radio station. **Physically Challenged Students:** 65% of the campus is accessible. Facilities include wheelchair ramps, elevators, special parking, specially equipped restrooms, special class scheduling, lowered drinking fountains, lowered telephones, and special housing. **Special:** In addition to extensive study abroad opportunities, Middlebury College offers preprofessional combined programs as well as Washington semester, maritime studies, and exchange programs with Spelman and Swarthmore Colleges and the Association of Vermont Independent Colleges. Other opportunities include a semester at Woods Hole Marine Biological Laboratory and dual-degree engineering programs with Dartmouth and Columbia. There is a chapter of Phi Beta Kappa and 38 departmental honors programs. **Visiting:** There are regularly scheduled orientations for prospective students, including campus tours and a group or individual interview. There are guides for informal visits and visitors may sit in on classes. To schedule a visit, contact the Admissions Office. **Campus Safety and Security:** Measures include 24-hour foot and vehicle patrol, emergency notification system, self-defense education, and security escort services. There are shuttle buses, emergency telephones, lighted pathways/sidewalks, and controlled access to dorms/residences.

REQUIREMENTS: The SAT or ACT is required. AP credits are accepted. Important factors in the admissions decision are leadership record, advanced placement or honors courses, evidence of special talent, personality/intangible qualities, extracurricular activities record, geographical diversity, recommendations by school officials, and parents or siblings attended your school. Candidates for the Bachelor of Arts degree must complete 36 courses. At least 18 of these courses must be Middlebury courses. Courses taken at Middlebury summer Language Schools or at the Middlebury Schools Abroad will count in the 18-course total and the grades will count in the undergraduate grade point average. **Procedure:** Freshmen are admitted fall and spring. Entrance exams should be taken by December of the senior year. There are early decision, early admissions, and deferred admissions plans. Early decision applications should be filed by November 1; regular applications, by January 1 for fall entry. The fall 2017 application fee was $65. Notification of early decision is sent January 1; regular decision, March 30. 398 early decision candidates were accepted for the 2017-2018 class. 565 applicants were on the 2017 waiting list; 7 were admitted. Applications are accepted on-line. **Transfer Students:** 11 transfer students enrolled in 2016-2017. Transfer students must have the strongest academic record possible through high school and a minimum 3.0 average in college. 18 of 36 credits required for the bachelor's degree must be completed at Middlebury. **International Students:** There are 269 international students enrolled. They must take the TOEFL. They must also take the SAT or ACT and fulfill the same requirements as first-year applicants.

ADMISSIONS: 16% of the 2017-2018 applicants were accepted. The SAT scores for the 2017-2018 freshman class were: Math-- 6% between 500 and 599, 37% between 600 and 699, and 57% between 700 and 800. Evidence-Based Reading/Writing-- 5% between 500 and 599, 38% between 600 and 699, and 57% between 700 and 800. The ACT scores were 2% between 18 and 23, 18% between 24 and 29, and 81% above 30. **Admissions Contact:** Greg Buckles, Dean of Admissions. Email: *admissions@middlebury.edu* Web: *www.middlebury.edu*

FINANCIAL AID: In 2017-2018, 46% of all full-time freshmen received some form of financial aid and need-based aid. The average freshman award was $50,113. Need-based scholarships or need-based grants averaged $47,092; need-based self-help aid (loans and jobs) averaged $3,908; and other non-need-based awards and non-need-based scholarships averaged $5,000. Middlebury is a member of CSS. The CSS/Profile, and federal tax forms, non-custodial profile are required. The FAFSA code is 003691. The priority date for freshman financial aid applications for fall entry is November 15.

NORWICH UNIVERSITY C-3

www.norwich.edu

Northfield, VT 05663	**(802) 485-2001** **(800) 468-6679**
Fax: (802) 485-2032	**Email: nuadm@norwich.edu**
Full-time: 1360 men, 502 women	**Faculty:** 117; IIA, -$
Part-time: 34 men, 7 women	**Ph.D.s:** 85%
Graduate: 537 men, 211 women	**Student/Faculty:** 16 to 1
Year: semesters, summer session	**Tuition:** $42,862
Room & Board: $13,372	**Freshman Class:** 1899 applied, 1470 accepted, 578 enrolled
SAT: required **ACT:** 22	**CEEB CODE:** 3669
Application Deadline: n/av	**COMPETITIVE**

Norwich University, founded in 1819, is the oldest private military college in the country and the birthplace of the Reserve Officers' Training Corps (ROTC). Norwich is a coeducational four-year university where students choose either a military or civilian lifestyle. Norwich offers both undergraduate and graduate programs. There are 6 undergraduate schools and 2 graduate schools. In addition to regional accreditation, NU has baccalaureate program accreditation with ABET, ACBSP, NLN, and CAAHEP. The 1125-acre campus is in a rural area 11 miles south of Montpelier. Including any residence halls, there are 36 buildings.

STUDENT LIFE: 80% of undergraduates are from out of state, mostly the Northeast. Students are from 39 states, 13 foreign countries, and Canada. 82% are White; 3% African American; 3% Hispanic; 2% Asian American; 2% Foreign. **Male To Female Ratio:** 2.7:1. The average age of freshmen is 18; all undergraduates, 21. 25% do not continue beyond their first year; 52% remain to graduate. **Housing:** 1598 students can be accommodated in college housing, which includes dorms. On-campus housing is guaranteed for the freshman year only and is available on a lottery system for upperclassmen. 83% of students live on campus. Alcohol is not permitted. Upperclassmen may keep cars.

FACULTY/CLASSROOMS: 74% of faculty are male; 26% are female. 82% teach undergraduates and do research. No introductory courses are taught by graduate students. The average class size in an introductory lecture is 20; in a laboratory is 13; and in a regular course is 18.

PROGRAMS OF STUDY: Norwich confers B.A., B.S., and B.Arch. degrees. Associate degrees are also awarded. Bachelor's degrees are awarded in BIOLOGICAL SCIENCE (biochemistry and biology/biological science), BUSINESS (accounting, business administration and management, and business economics), COMMUNICATIONS AND THE ARTS (communications and English), COMPUTER AND PHYSICAL SCIENCE (chemistry, computer science, computer security and information assurance, geology, information sciences and systems, mathematics, and physics), EDUCATION (physical education), ENGINEERING AND ENVIRONMENTAL DESIGN (architecture, civil engineering, computer engineering, electrical/electronics engineering, environmental science, mechanical engineering, and military science), HEALTH PROFESSIONS (medical laboratory technology, nursing, and sports medicine), SOCIAL SCIENCE (criminal justice, history, international studies, liberal arts/general studies, peace studies, political science/government, and psychology). Engineering, and architecture are the strongest academically. Criminal justice, and nursing have the largest enrollments.

ACTIVITIES: There are no fraternities or sororities. There are 75 groups on campus, including band, cheerleading, chess, choir, chorus, communications, computers, drama, drill team, ethnic, honors, international, jazz band, literary magazine, marching band, musical theater, newspaper, orchestra, pep band, photography, political, professional, radio and TV, religious, social service, and student government. Popular campus events include Regimental Ball, Winter Carnival, and Junior Weekend. **Sports:** There are 12 intercollegiate sports for men and 7 for women, and 8 intramural sports for men and 8 for women. Facilities include an ice hockey arena, field house with track, swimming pool, aerobics room, weight and wrestling rooms, playing fields, basketball arena, and a hockey arena. **Graduates:** From July 1, 2016 to June 30, 2017, 269 bachelor's degrees were awarded. The most popular majors were criminal justice (18%), management (12%), and nursing/civil engineering (7%). In an average class, 37% graduate in 4 years or less, 49% graduate in 5 years or less, and 52% graduate in 6 years or less.

SERVICES: Counseling and information services are available, as is tutoring in most subjects. There is remedial math, reading, and writing. **Library/Resources:** The library contains 245,931 volumes, 90,435 microform items, and 2,872 audio/video tapes/CDs/DVDs, and subscribes to 815 periodicals including electronic. Computerized library services include interlibrary loans, database searching, Internet access, and Wi-Fi capability. Special learning facilities include an art gallery, natural history museum, radio station, a greenhouse, and 5 computer labs. **Physically Challenged Students:** Facilities include wheelchair ramps, elevators, special parking, specially equipped restrooms, and lowered drinking fountains. **Special:** Norwich offers internships, a Washington semester, work-study on-and-off-campus for service organizations and criminal justice programs, a B.A.-B.S. degree in communications, and study abroad in 15 countries through other schools and organizations and through the Vermont Overseas Studies Program. International studies majors must study abroad in a country whose language they are studying. There are 5 national honor societies, Phi Beta Kappa, and 5 departmental honors programs. **Visiting:** There are regularly scheduled orientations for prospective students, including meetings with representatives in admissions, financial aid, academic offices, Dean of Students or Commandant's Office, athletics (if desired), and a campus tour. To schedule a visit, contact the Admissions Office. **Campus Safety and Security:** Measures include 24-hour foot and vehicle patrol. There are lighted pathways/sidewalks.

REQUIREMENTS: The SAT or ACT is required. Applicants should graduate from an accredited secondary school with 18 academic credits or achieve the GED equivalent. AP and CLEP credits are accepted. Important factors in the admissions decision are leadership record, extracurricular activities record, and evidence of special talent. The total number of required credits and courses vary by program. All students are required to complete 3 credit hours in history and English 101-102, and 2 semesters in phys ed. A 2.0 GPA is required to graduate. **Procedure:** Freshmen are admitted fall and spring. Entrance exams should be taken starting with spring of the junior year. There is a rolling admissions plan. Application deadlines are open. The fall 2017 application fee was $35. 60 early decision candidates were accepted for the 2017-2018 class. Applications are accepted on-line. **Transfer Students:** 91 transfer students enrolled in 2016-2017. Transfer students should present a 2.0 GPA and meet all standards for entering freshmen. 60 of 116 credits required for the bachelor's degree must be completed at Norwich. **International Students:** There are 39 international students enrolled. They must take the TOEFL.

ADMISSIONS: 77% of the 2017-2018 applicants were accepted. The ACT scores were 40% below 12, 28% between 12 and 17, 20% between 18 and 23, 7% between 24 and 29, and 5% above 30. 30% of the current freshmen were in the top fifth of their class; 58% were in the top two fifths. 3 freshmen graduated first in their class. **Admissions Contact:** Karen McGarth, Dean of Enrollment Management. Email: *nuadm@norwich.edu* Web: *www.norwich.edu*

FINANCIAL AID: In 2017-2018, 97% of all full-time freshmen received some form of financial aid. 90% of all full-time freshmen received need-based aid. 50% of undergraduate students work part-time. The average financial indebtedness of the 2017 graduate was $26,072. Norwich is a member of CSS. The CSS/Profile is required. The FAFSA code is 003692. The priority date for freshman financial aid applications for fall entry is March 1.

SAINT MICHAEL'S COLLEGE A-2

www.smcvt.edu

Colchester, VT 05439	**(802) 654-3000** **(800) 762-8000**
Fax: (802) 654-2906	**Email: admission@smcvt.edu**
Full-time: 810 men, 1029 women	**Faculty:** 147; IIB, +$
Part-time: 16 men, 8 women	**Ph.D.s:** 91%
Graduate: 63 men, 259 women	**Student/Faculty:** 11 to 1
Year: semesters, summer session	**Tuition:** $41,975
Room & Board: $11,300	**Freshman Class:** 5013 applied, 3860 accepted, 461 enrolled
SAT CR/M/W: 600/585/580 **ACT:** 27	**CEEB CODE:** 3757
Application Deadline: February 1	**VERY COMPETITIVE+**

Saint Michael's College, founded in 1904 by the Society of Saint Edmund, is a selective Catholic liberal arts college. There is 1 undergraduate school and 1 graduate school. In addition to regional accreditation, SMC has baccalaureate program accreditation with ACS, ROPA, and CELPA. The 440-acre campus is in a suburban area 2 miles east of Burlington, Vermont. Including any residence halls, there are 52 buildings.

STUDENT LIFE: 83% of undergraduates are from out of state, mostly the Northeast. Students are from 33 states, 46 foreign countries, and Canada. 69% are from public schools. 85% are White; 4% Hispanic; 4% Foreign; 2% African American; 2% Asian American; 2% two or more races; 2% race unknown. 46% are Catholic; 34% claim no religious affiliation. **Female To Male Ratio:** 1.5:1. The average age of freshmen is 18; all undergraduates, 20. 13% do not continue beyond their first year; 76% remain to graduate. **Housing:** 2077 students can be accommodated in college housing, which includes dorms and on-campus apartments. In addition, there are honors houses, special-interest houses, theme housing, substance-free housing, and international housing. On-campus housing is guaranteed for all 4 years. 98% of students live on campus. All students may keep cars.

FACULTY/CLASSROOMS: 57% of faculty are male; 43% are female. All teach undergraduates and all do research. No introductory courses are taught by graduate students. The average class size in an introductory lecture is 24; in a laboratory is 18; and in a regular course is 19.

PROGRAMS OF STUDY: SMC confers B.A. and B.S. degrees. Master's degrees are also awarded. Bachelor's degrees are awarded in AGRICULTURE (environmental studies), BIOLOGICAL SCIENCE (biochemistry, biology/biological science, and neurosciences), BUSINESS (accounting and business administration and management), COMMUNICATIONS AND THE ARTS (dramatic arts, English, fine arts, French, journalism, music, and Spanish), COMPUTER AND PHYSICAL SCIENCE (chemistry, computer science, information sciences and systems, mathematics, physical sciences, and physics), EDUCATION (art education, elementary education, foreign languages education, science education, and secondary education), ENGINEERING AND ENVIRONMENTAL DESIGN (preengineering), HEALTH PROFESSIONS (preallied health and prepharmacy), SOCIAL SCIENCE (American studies, anthropology, economics, gender studies, history, international relations, philosophy, political science/government, prelaw, psychology, religion, and sociology). Biology, mathematics, and history are the strongest academically. Business administration, biology, and psychology have the largest enrollments.

ACTIVITIES: There are no fraternities or sororities. There are 50 groups on campus, including mobilization of volunteer efforts club, cycling, skiing, wilderness program, art, band, choir, chorale, chorus, communications, dance, drama, environmental, ethnic, film, fire and rescue, honors, international, jazz band, LGBT, literary magazine, musical theater, newspaper, photography, political, professional, radio and TV, religious, social, social service, student government, and yearbook. Popular campus events include Family Weekend, Homecoming, Martin Luther King, Jr. Convocation, Research Symposium, and Jib Fest. **Sports:** There are 10 intercollegiate sports for men and 11 for women, and 15 intramural sports for men and 15 for women. Facilities include a gym and field house with basketball, volleyball, tennis, and badminton courts, multipurpose courts, a 6-lane swimming pool, fitness center, training room, weight room, climbing wall, table tennis, suspended track, soccer, racquetball and squash courts, field hockey, lacrosse, baseball, and softball fields. **Graduates:** From July 1, 2016 to June 30, 2017, 478 bachelor's degrees were awarded. The most popular majors were business administration and accounting (19%), social sciences (14%), and biological/life sciences (12%). In an average class, 73% graduate in 4 years or less, 74% graduate in 5 years or less, and 76% graduate in 6 years or less. Of the 2016 graduating class, 13% were enrolled in graduate school within 6 months of graduation, and 70% were employed.

SERVICES: Counseling and information services are available, as is tutoring in every subject. Tutoring can be arranged on an individual basis. The following are available: peer tutoring, writing center, quantitative skills, study skills, and research help. **Library/Resources:** The library contains 469,578 volumes, 137,000 microform items, and 12,984 audio/video tapes/CDs/DVDs, and subscribes to 13,000 periodicals including electronic. Computerized library services include interlibrary loans, database searching, Internet access, and Wi-Fi capability. Special learning facilities include an art gallery, radio station, an observatory, the Maker Space, and McCarthy Arts Center. **Physically Challenged Students:** 75% of the campus is accessible. Facilities include wheelchair ramps, elevators, special parking, specially equipped restrooms, special class scheduling, lowered drinking fountains, lowered telephones, and special housing. Other accommodations are provided on an individual basis. **Special:** A variety of special academic programs and enriching academic experiences are available at Saint Michael's College. During the most recent academic year over 40% of our graduates participated in a "for credit" internship, most of which were associated with the student's major. On-campus work-study opportunities are available in departments and offices throughout the college. Students can choose from more than 100 study abroad programs in countries spanning the globe. There are also opportunities for semester long domestic "study away" programs including a Washington semester with American University. Student-designed majors may be pursued and nearly 20% of our most recent graduating class completed a double major. During the last four years an average of nearly 40% of the graduating classes participated in "for credit" study abroad experiences including summer and winter sessions as well as short term faculty led programs. The college offers a 3-2 engineering degree program in cooperation with Clarkson University and the University of Vermont and a 4+1 graduate business program is available with Clarkson University. A B.S./Pharm.D. degree is also available with the Albany College of Pharmacy and Health Services. Nondegree study and pass/fail grading options are offered on a limited basis. Independent research and undergraduate research opportunities with faculty are available through most departments. There are 11 national honor societies, Phi Beta Kappa, a freshman honors program, and 1 departmental honors program. **Visiting:** There are regularly scheduled orientations for prospective students. A campus visit begins with a group information session led by an admission counselor, which includes information about admission criteria and financial aid. It is followed by a student-led tour. Informational interviews are available after. To schedule a visit, contact the Admissions Office. **Campus Safety and Security:** Measures include 24-hour foot and vehicle patrol, emergency notification system, self-defense education, and security escort services. There are shuttle buses, emergency telephones, lighted pathways/sidewalks, controlled access to dorms/residences, and a campus fire and rescue squad.

REQUIREMENTS: The SAT or ACT and ACT Writing Test are recommended. Applicants must graduate from an accredited secondary school or have a GED. They must complete 16 Carnegie units. The college requires 4 credits in English and math, 3-4 in science (with lab 2-3), 2 -4 in foreign language, 3-4 in social studies. An essay is required and an interview is recommended. Stanardized tests are optional. There are three application deadlines: early action 1- November 1, early action 2- December 1, regular decision- February 1. AP and CLEP credits are accepted. Important factors in the admissions decision are advanced placement or honors courses, evidence of special talent, and recommendations by school officials. To earn the degree of Bachelor of Arts or the degree of Bachelor of Science a student must: Complete a minimum of 128 credit hours (equivalent to 32 full-courses). Complete the degree requirements of one of the established majors or a self-designated major approved by the Curriculum and Education Policy Committee. Complete the Liberal Studies Curriculum requirements (see below). Achieve a minimum cumulative quality point average of 2.0 and a minimum of a 2.0 average in courses taken in the major. Complete a minimum of twenty-four of the last thirty-two credits at Saint Michael's. The Liberal Studies Curriculum (LSC) is fulfilled through specific course requirement options and courses within the student's major field. Areas of study within the LSC include: Fundamental Philosophical Questions, Study of Christian Traditions and Thought, Ethical Decision Making, Global Issues that Impact the Common Good, Historical Studies, Literary Studies, Processes of Scientific Reasoning, Quantitative Reasoning, Second Language (depending on placement), Social and Institutional Dimensions of Human Behavior, Artistic Experience, Experiential Learning, and Oral and Written Communication. **Procedure:** Freshmen are admitted fall and spring. Entrance exams should be taken in the fall of the senior year. There are early admissions and deferred admissions plans. Applications should be filed by February 1 for fall entry; December 1 for winter entry; and November 1 for spring entry. The fall 2017 application fee was $50. Notifications are sent April 1. 53 applicants were on the 2017 waiting list; 14 were admitted. Applications are accepted online. **Transfer Students:** 34 transfer students enrolled in 2016-2017. Transfer applicants must have a minimum GPA of 3.0. The SAT is optional. An interview is recommended. 64 of 128 credits required for the bachelor's degree must be completed at Saint Michael's. **International Students:** There are 63 international students enrolled. They must take the TOEFL with a minimum score of 550 on the paper-based TOEFL (PBT) or 79 on the Internet-based version (iBT) and the college's own test. The SAT or ACT is optional for international students but recommended. The TOEFL may be used in place of the SAT.

ADMISSIONS: 77% of the 2017-2018 applicants were accepted. The SAT scores for the 2017-2018 freshman class were: Critical Reading-- 5% below 500, 45% between 500 and 599, 42% between 600 and 699, and 9% between 700 and 800. Math-- 6% below 500, 53% between 500 and 599, 37% between 600 and 699, and 4% between 700 and 800. Writing-- 6% below 500, 51% between 500 and 599, 39% between 600 and 699, and 4% between 700 and 800. 50% of the current freshmen were in the top fifth of their class; 74% were in the top two fifths. 5 freshmen graduated first in their class. **Admissions Contact:** Jacqueline Murphy, Director of Office of Admission. Email: *admission@smcvt.edu* Web: *www.smcvt.edu*

FINANCIAL AID: In 2017-2018, 99% of all full-time freshmen received some form of financial aid. 83% of all full-time freshmen received need-based aid. The average freshman award was $32,135. Need-based scholarships or need-based grants averaged $24,168 ($40,425 maximum); need-based self-help aid (loans and jobs) averaged $6,125 ($13,250 maximum); non-need-based athletic scholarships averaged $53,312 ($51,725 maximum); other non-need-based awards and non-need-based scholarships averaged $17,100 ($40,425 maximum); and $4,965 from other forms of aid. 39% of undergraduate students work part-time. The average financial indebtedness of the 2017 graduate was $40,275. SMC is a member of CSS. The FAFSA code is 003694. The priority date for freshman financial aid applications for fall entry is December 15.

SOUTHERN VERMONT COLLEGE *(The complete profile is made available exclusively on our website, www.barronspac.com)*

STERLING COLLEGE — B-1

www.sterlingcollege.edu

Craftsbury Common, VT 05827 — (802) 586-7711, (800) 648-3591

Fax: (802) 586-2596 — **Email:** admission@sterlingcollege.edu

Full-time: 57 men, 46 women	**Faculty:** 14
Part-time: 1 men, 1 women	**Ph.D.s:** 29%
Graduate: n/av	**Student/Faculty:** 7 to 1
Year: semesters, summer session	**Tuition:** $32,790
Room & Board: $9104	**Freshman Class:** 97 applied, 74 accepted, 30 enrolled
SAT or ACT: required	**CEEB CODE:** 3752
Application Deadline: February 15	**VERY COMPETITIVE**

Sterling College is a small and progressive liberal arts college in northern Vermont. Our small size, our environmental focus, and our commitment to grassroots sustainability all make us unique. We offer a liberal arts education through the lens of ecology. The figures given in the above capsule and in this profile are approximate. There is 1 undergraduate school. The 430-acre campus is in a rural area 40 miles north of Montpelier and 60 miles from Burlington. Including any residence halls, there are 16 buildings.

STUDENT LIFE: 82% of undergraduates are from out of state, mostly the Northeast. Students are from 22 states. 70% are White; 2% Hispanic. **Male To Female Ratio:** 1.2:1. The average age of freshmen is 19; all undergraduates, 21. 33% do not continue beyond their first year; 60% remain to graduate. **Housing:** 90 students can be accommodated in college housing, which includes dorms. On-campus housing is guaranteed for all 4 years. 77% of students live on campus. All students may keep cars.

FACULTY/CLASSROOMS: 50% of faculty are male; 50% are female. All teach undergraduates, 25% do research, and 25% do both. No introductory courses are taught by graduate students. The average class size in an introductory lecture is 12; in a laboratory is 12; and in a regular course is 12.

PROGRAMS OF STUDY: Sterling confers B.A. degrees. Bachelor's degrees are awarded in AGRICULTURE (agriculture), BIOLOGICAL SCIENCE (ecology), SOCIAL SCIENCE (humanities and social science). Ecology, sustainable agriculture, and sustainable food systems are the strongest academically. Sustainable agriculture, sustainable food systems, and ecology have the largest enrollments.

ACTIVITIES: There are no fraternities or sororities. Groups on campus include folk music, social and environmental justice, art, environmental, LGBT, photography, social, student government, and yearbook. Popular campus events include All-College Work Days, Earth Day, and Annual Wood Projects Show. **Sports:** There are 2 intercollegiate sports for men and 2 for women, and 1 intramural sport for men and 1 for women. Facilities include a climbing tower, nature trails on campus, ski trails managed by a nearby sports center. There is a soccer field and access to a gym at a local high school. **Graduates:** From July 1, 2016 to June 30, 2017, 27 bachelor's degrees were awarded. In an average class, 40% graduate in 4 years or less, 52% graduate in 5 years or less, and 56% graduate in 6 years or less. Of the 2016 graduating class, 30% were employed within 6 months of graduation.

SERVICES: Counseling and information services are available, as is tutoring in every subject. There is remedial math. In addition, there is a learning support coordinator as well as a writing center. **Library/Resources:** The library contains 13,630 volumes, and 600 audio/video tapes/CDs/DVDs, and subscribes to 127 periodicals including electronic. Computerized library services include interlibrary loans, database searching, Internet access, and Wi-Fi capability. Special learning facilities include an art gallery, a woodshop, darkroom, managed woodlot, organic garden, working livestock farm, 30-foot-tall climbing wall, challenge course, greenhouse, blacksmith shop, sugar house, sugar bush, and a 300-acre boreal forest/wetland research area. **Physically Challenged Students:** Facilities include wheelchair ramps and specially equipped restrooms. **Special:** Internships are required. Study abroad, work study, and student-designed majors are available. We are the only federally recognized Work College in the Northeast; all students, regardless of financial aid, must work on campus. **Visiting:** There are regularly scheduled orientations for prospective students, including a student-led campus tour, an interview with admissions, and a meal in the dining hall. Weekend Open Houses offer a more comprehensive view of the college. There are 2 open houses per year. Monday Visit Days are similar to open houses, but students may sit in on classes. To schedule a visit, contact Tim Patterson at tpatterson@sterlingcollege.edu. **Campus Safety and Security:** Measures include emergency notification system.

REQUIREMENTS: Well-written essays, quality of the interview, and the comments provided by references are equal to the value of high school and college transcripts. Home-schooled students are strongly encouraged to contact the admissions office to discuss their particular needs and interests. AP credits are accepted. Important factors in the admissions decision are advanced placement or honors courses, recommendations by school officials, and leadership record. Candidates for the Bachelor of Arts degree must earn a minimum of 120 credits with a minimum cumulative G.P.A. of 2.0 and pass the Mathematics Competency requirement. Candidates must also complete all required Core Courses, complete six credits each of Natural Science, Social Science, and Humanities electives, including a minimum of four credits emphasizing textual analysis and written critical response, and complete an approved major. All resident students must receive a satisfactory grade in the College's Work Program during their final semester of academic enrollment. Non-resident students must receive a satisfactory grade in their final semester of record in the College's Work Program. **Procedure:** Freshmen are admitted fall and spring. There are early decision, early admissions, and deferred admissions plans. Early decision applications should be filed by November 15; regular applications, by February 15 for fall entry. The fall 2017 application fee was $35. Notification of early decision is sent December 15; regular decision, April 1. One early decision candidate was accepted for the 2017-2018 class. Applications are accepted on-line. **Transfer Students:** 15 transfer students enrolled in 2016-2017. In addition to the standard application, transfer students must provide copies of college transcripts. They may begin in the spring semester. 30 of 120 credits required for the bachelor's degree must be completed at Sterling. **International Students:** There are 4 international students enrolled. They must take the TOEFL with a minimum score of 500 on the paper-based TOEFL (PBT).

ADMISSIONS: 76% of the 2017-2018 applicants were accepted. 20% of the current freshmen were in the top fifth of their class; 40% were in the top two fifths. **Admissions Contact:** Tim Patterson, Director of Admission. Email: *admission@sterlingcollege.edu* Web: *www.sterlingcollege.edu*

FINANCIAL AID: In 2017-2018, 100% of all full-time freshmen received some form of financial aid. 90% of all full-time freshmen received need-based aid. The average freshman award was $22,000. Need-based scholarships or need-based grants averaged $15,000 ($35,000 maximum); need-based self-help aid (loans and jobs) averaged $10,000 ($30,000 maximum); and other non-need-based awards and non-need-based scholarships averaged $10,000 ($20,000 maximum). 100% of undergraduate students work part-time. The FAFSA code is 014991. The priority date for freshman financial aid applications for fall entry is March 1.

UNIVERSITY OF VERMONT A-2

www.uvm.edu

Burlington, VT 05401	**(802) 656-4672**
Fax: (802) 656-8611	**Email: admissions@uvm.edu**
Full-time: 4357 men, 6038 women	**Faculty:** 629
Part-time: 404 men, 540 women	**Ph.D.s:** 84%
Graduate: 808 men, 1193 women	**Student/Faculty:** 17 to 1
Year: semesters, summer session	**Tuition:** $17,740 ($41,356)
Room & Board: $12,052	**Freshman Class:** 21991 applied, 14777 accepted, 2642 enrolled
SAT EBR-W/M: 637/623 **ACT:** 28	**CEEB CODE:** 3920
Application Deadline: January 15	**HIGHLY COMPETITIVE**

Since 1791, the University of Vermont has worked to move humankind forward. Our research labs are engineering new ways of fighting cancer, looking deep into geologic time to advance our understanding of climate change, and discovering the biochemistry of what makes cheese so delicious. Professors here are world-class researchers, scholars, and artists bringing their discoveries into the classroom and their students into the field. There are 7 undergraduate schools and 2 graduate schools. In addition to regional accreditation, UV has baccalaureate program accreditation with AACSB, ABET, APTA, ASLA, CAHEA, CSWE, and CCNE. The 460-acre campus is in a suburban area 90 miles south of Montreal, and 200 miles north of Boston. Including any residence halls, there are 115 buildings.

STUDENT LIFE: 71% of undergraduates are from out of state, mostly the Northeast. Students are from 48 states, 72 foreign countries, and Canada. 81% are White; 6% Foreign; 4% Hispanic; 3% Asian American; 3% two or more races; 2% race unknown; 1% African American. **Female To Male Ratio:** 1.4:1. The average age of freshmen is 18; all undergraduates, 20. 14% do not continue beyond their first year; 75% remain to graduate. **Housing:** 5717 students can be accommodated in college housing, which includes married student dorms, on-campus apartments, and off-campus apartments. In addition, there are honors houses, language/international houses, special-interest houses, fraternity houses, sorority houses, and living learning center provides an integrated, theme-based academic and residential option. On-campus housing is guaranteed for all 4 years and is available on a lottery system for upperclassmen. 51% of students live on campus. Upperclassmen may keep cars.

FACULTY/CLASSROOMS: 49% of faculty are male; 51% are female. No introductory courses are taught by graduate students. The average class size in a regular course is 33.

PROGRAMS OF STUDY: UV confers B.A., B.S., B.Mus., B.S.A.E., B.S.B.A., B.S.Ed., B.S.C.E., B.S.C.S., B.S.E.E., B.S.E.M., B.S.M., B.S.M.E., B.S.M.S., B.A.E., B.S.E., B.S.E.V., B.S.M.S.C. and B.S.B.M.E. degrees. Master's and doctoral degrees are also awarded. Bachelor's degrees are awarded in AGRICULTURE (animal science, environmental studies, fishing and fisheries, forestry and related sciences, natural resources, and plant science), BIOLOGICAL SCIENCE (biochemistry, biology/biological science, botany, genetics, microbiology, molecular biology, neurosciences, nutrition, wildlife biology, and zoology), BUSINESS (business administration and management and international economics), COMMUNICATIONS AND THE ARTS (art, art history and appreciation, Chinese, classics, communications, dramatic arts, English, film arts, French, German, Greek, Japanese, Latin, linguistics, music, Russian, and Spanish), COMPUTER AND PHYSICAL SCIENCE (chemistry, computer science, geology, information sciences and systems, mathematics, physics, and statistics), EDUCATION (art education, athletic training, early childhood education, education, elementary education, English education, foreign languages education, global studies, mathematics education, middle school education, music education, physical education, science education, secondary education, social studies education, and special education), ENGINEERING AND ENVIRONMENTAL DESIGN (civil engineering, electrical/electronics engineering, engineering, engineering management, environmental engineering, environmental science, and mechanical engineering), HEALTH PROFESSIONS (biomedical science, exercise science, health science, medical laboratory science, nuclear medical technology, nursing, radiation therapy, and speech pathology/audiology), SOCIAL SCIENCE (anthropology, area studies, Asian/Oriental studies, child care/child and family studies, communication sciences & disorders, dietetics, economics, ethnic studies, European studies, food science, gender studies, geography, history, human development, human development & family studies, Italian studies, Latin American studies, parks and recreation management, philosophy, political science/government, psychology, religion, Russian and Slavic studies, social work, and sociology). Business Administration, Engineering, Environmental Studies have the largest enrollments.

ACTIVITIES: 8% of men belong to 9 national fraternities; 7% of women belong to 6 national sororities. There are 168 groups on campus, including environmental clubs, outing club, art, band, cheerleading, chess, choir, chorale, chorus, communications, community service, computers, dance, debate, drama, environmental, ethnic, film, forensics, honors, international, jazz band, LGBT, literary magazine, musical theater, newspaper, orchestra, pep band, photography, political, professional, radio and TV, religious, social, social service, and student government. Popular campus events include Winterfest, Community Serve-a-thon, and Sugar on Snow day. **Sports:** There are 7 intercollegiate sports for men and 10 for women, and 24 intramural sports for men and 24 for women. Facilities include an ice hockey stadium, turffield, a field house, soccer and baseball fields, fitness center, indoor and outdoor tracks, a natatorium, indoor tennis courts, racquetball court, climbing facility, dance studio, and a gymnastics facility. **Graduates:** From July 1, 2016 to June 30, 2017, 2390 bachelor's degrees were awarded. The most popular majors were Business (10%), Environmental studies (5%), and Psychology (4%). In an average class, 62% graduate in 4 years or less, 73% graduate in 5 years or less, and 75% graduate in 6 years or less. Of the 2016 graduating class, 18% were enrolled in graduate school within 6 months of graduation, and 75% were employed.

SERVICES: Counseling and information services are available, as is tutoring in most subjects. There is a reader service for the blind. There is also supplemental instruction, note-taking and test-taking seminars, time management instruction, outreach programs, exam proctoring, writing tutors, and support for ESL students. **Library/Resources:** The library contains 3.3 million volumes, 626,225 microform items, and 27,798 audio/video tapes/CDs/DVDs, and subscribes to 90,542 periodicals including electronic. Computerized library services include interlibrary loans, database searching, Internet access, and Wi-Fi capability. Special learning facilities include an art gallery, natural history museum, radio station, TV station, health care center (the University of Vermont Medical Center), 4 research farms, the Fleming Museum, geology museum, 9 natural areas, lakeshore science center, and aquatic research vessel. **Physically Challenged Students:** Facilities include wheelchair ramps, elevators, special parking, specially equipped restrooms, special class scheduling, lowered drinking fountains, and lowered telephones. First-priority routes in poor weather, a TTY phone system for hearing-impaired students, and closed-caption video decoders. **Special:** Special academic programs include co-op programs, internships, study abroad in 70 countries, accelerated degree programs, and student-designed majors. In addition, a 3-4 veterinary medicine degree is offered with Tufts University and a 3-2 Juris Doctor degree with Vermont Law School. UVM also offers service learning courses, an undergraduate research office, and a Wellness Environment. There are 28 national honor societies, Phi Beta Kappa, a freshman honors program, and 14 departmental honors programs. **Visiting:** There are regularly scheduled orientations for prospective students, group information sessions and tours most weekdays and many Saturdays year round. Visitors may sit in on classes. To schedule a visit, contact the Admissions Office. **Campus Safety and Security:** Measures include 24-hour foot and vehicle patrol, emergency notification system, self-defense education, and security escort services. There are shuttle buses, emergency telephones, lighted pathways/sidewalks, controlled access to dorms/residences, bike registration, identification of property, and certified police officers.

REQUIREMENTS: The SAT or ACT is required. Requirements include graduation from an accredited secondary school with 16 Carnegie units. Required high school course work includes 4 years of English, 3 years each of social science and math, including algebra I and II and geometry, and 2 years each of the same foreign language and science (one of which must be a lab science). Some academic units require additional course work. An essay must be submitted. The GED is also accepted. AP and CLEP credits are accepted. Important factors in the admissions decision are advanced placement or honors courses, extracurricular activities record, and recommendations by school officials. Degree requirements vary among the individual colleges, but all require at least a 2.0 GPA and 122 credit hours to graduate. Most students must enroll in at least 30 distribution credits (approximately 10 courses) in the arts, humanities, social sciences, languages, literature, math, and the sciences. All academic units require 2 courses in Race and Culture. **Procedure:** Freshmen are admitted fall and spring. Entrance exams should be taken by November of the senior year. There are early admissions and deferred admissions plans. Early decision applications should be filed by November 1; regular applications, by January 15 for fall entry; and November 1 for spring entry. The fall 2017 application fee was $55. Notification of early decision is sent December 15; regular decision, March 15. 3988 applicants were on the 2017 waiting list. Applications are accepted on-line. **Transfer Students:** 600 transfer students enrolled in 2016-2017. Successful transfer students have a cumulative grade point average of at least 2.8 in credited courses and meet the same entrance requirements as first-year applicants. Considerations include the college and high school records, the major indicated, and availability of space at UVM. 30 of 122 credits required for the bachelor's degree must be completed at UV. **International Students:** There are 568 international students enrolled. They must take the TOEFL with a minimum score of 90 on the Internet-based version (iBT). Students must take the IELTS. They must also take the SAT or ACT.

ADMISSIONS: 67% of the 2017-2018 applicants were accepted. The SAT scores for the 2017-2018 freshman class were: Math-- 2% below 500, 32% between 500 and 599, 53% between 600 and 699, and 13% between 700 and 800. Evidence-Based Reading/Writing-- 2% below 500, 23% between 500 and 599, 58% between 600 and 699, and 17% between 700 and 800. The ACT scores were 11% between 18 and 23, 55% between 24 and 29, and 34% above 30. 66% of the current freshmen were in the top fifth of their class; 92% were in the top two fifths. **Admissions Contact:** Mr. Ryan Hargraves, Director of Admission. Email: *admissions@uvm.edu* Web: *www.uvm.edu*

FINANCIAL AID: In 2017-2018, 98% of all full-time freshmen received some form of financial aid. 63% of all full-time freshmen received need-based aid. The average freshman award was $23,420. Need-based scholarships or need-based grants averaged $10,351 ($49,620 maximum); need-based self-help aid (loans and jobs) averaged $4,238 ($10,700 maximum); non-need-based athletic scholarships averaged $27,947 ($59,036 maximum); and other non-need-based awards and non-need-based scholarships averaged $13,340 ($56,920 maximum). The average financial indebtedness of the 2017 graduate was $32,238. The FAFSA code is 003696. The priority date for freshman financial aid applications for fall entry is February 1.

VERMONT TECHNICAL COLLEGE — C-4

www.vtc.edu

Randolph Center, VT 05061 — **(802) 728-1000**

Email: admissions@vtc.edu

Full-time: 655 men, 378 women	**Faculty:** 71
Part-time: 165 men, 158 women	**Ph.D.s:** 54%
Graduate: n/av	**Student/Faculty:** 15 to 1
Year: semesters	**Tuition:** $15,080 ($27,392)
Room & Board: $10,290	**Freshman Class:** 757 applied, 528 accepted, 314 enrolled
SAT or ACT: required	**CEEB CODE:** 3941
Application Deadline: n/av	**COMPETITIVE**

Vermont Tech College is the only public institution of higher learning in Vermont whose mission is applied education. Vermont Tech takes an optimistic, rooted and personal approach to education to support students in gaining the confidence and practical skills necessary to not only see their potential, but to experience it. Our academic programs encompass a wide range of engineering technology, agricultural, health, and business fields that are vital to producing the knowledgeable workers needed most by employers in the state and in the region. The figures given in the above capsule and in this profile are approximate. There are 5 undergraduate schools. In addition to regional accreditation, VTC has baccalaureate program accreditation with ABET, NLNAC, AVMA, and CODA. The 544-acre campus is in a rural area in Randolph Center, VT. Including any residence halls, there are 19 buildings.

STUDENT LIFE: 60% of undergraduates are from Vermont. Others are from 12 states, and 2 foreign countries. 90% are from public schools. 94% are White; 2% Asian American; 2% Hispanic; 1% African American; 1% American Indian/Alaska Native. **Male To Female Ratio:** 1.5:1. The average age of freshmen is 25; all undergraduates, 26. 25% do not continue beyond their first year; 55% remain to graduate. **Housing:** 550 students can be accommodated in college housing, which includes dorms. On-campus housing is guaranteed for all 4 years. 60% of students commute. All students may keep cars.

FACULTY/CLASSROOMS: 58% of faculty are male; 42% are female. All teach undergraduates. No introductory courses are taught by graduate students. The average class size in an introductory lecture is 28; in a laboratory is 16; and in a regular course is 32.

PROGRAMS OF STUDY: VTC confers B.S. degrees. Associate degrees are also awarded. Bachelor's degrees are awarded in COMPUTER AND PHYSICAL SCIENCE (information sciences and systems and software engineering), EDUCATION (business education), ENGINEERING AND ENVIRONMENTAL DESIGN (architectural engineering, computer engineering, and electromechanical technology). Electromechanical engineering technology is the strongest academically. Architectural engineering technology, and business have the largest enrollments.

ACTIVITIES: There are no fraternities or sororities. Groups on campus include chess, computers, drama, ethnic, international, LGBT, photography, professional, radio and TV, religious, social, social service, and student government. Popular campus events include Harvest Days, Winter Carnival, and Spring Fling. **Sports:** There are 6 intercollegiate sports for men and 5 for women, and 21 intramural sports for men and 21 for women. Facilities include a double-court gym, racquetball courts, swimming pool, fitness center, outdoor soccer, baseball, and softball fields, trails for cross-country skiing, and downhill ski run. **Graduates:** From July 1, 2016 to June 30, 2017, 64 bachelor's degrees were awarded. The most popular majors were business (37%) and electromechanical engineering (25%). In an average class, 50% graduate in 4 years or less, 55% graduate in 5 years or less, and 59% graduate in 6 years or less. Of the 2016 graduating class, 97% were employed within 6 months of graduation.

SERVICES: Counseling and information services are available, as is tutoring in every subject. **Library/Resources:** The library contains 59,480 volumes, 5,920 microform items, and 4,122 audio/video tapes/CDs/DVDs, and subscribes to 348 periodicals including electronic. Computerized library services include interlibrary loans, database searching, and Internet access. Special learning facilities include a radio station, Vermont Interactive Technologies and Anaerobic Digester. **Physically Challenged Students:** All of the campus is accessible. Facilities include wheelchair ramps, elevators, special parking, specially equipped restrooms, special class scheduling, lowered drinking fountains, and lowered telephones. **Special:** Cross-registration, internships, work-study programs, and dual majors are offered. There are 2 national honor societies, a freshman honors program, and 2 departmental honors programs. **Visiting:** There are regularly scheduled orientations for prospective students. There are guides for informal visits, visitors may sit in on classes, and stay overnight. To schedule a visit, contact the Admissions Office. **Campus Safety and Security:** Measures include 24-hour foot and vehicle patrol, self-defense education, and security escort services. There are emergency telephones and lighted pathways/sidewalks.

REQUIREMENTS: The SAT or ACT is required. AP and CLEP credits are accepted. To graduate, students must complete 120 to 130 credit hours with a minimum GPA of 2.0. Required courses include those in English, technical communications, math, and computer. **Procedure:** Freshmen are admitted fall and spring. There is a rolling admissions plan. Application deadlines are open. The fall 2017 application fee was $30. Applications are accepted on-line. **Transfer Students:** 251 transfer students enrolled in 2016-2017. Transcripts are required from all colleges attended. 50 of 120 credits required for the bachelor's degree must be completed at VTC. **International Students:** There are 2 international students enrolled. They must take the TOEFL. They must also take the SAT or ACT, and the college's own entrance exam.

ADMISSIONS: 70% of the 2017-2018 applicants were accepted. 23% of the current freshmen were in the top fifth of their class; 70% were in the top two fifths. **Admissions Contact:** Dwight Cross, Assistant Dean of Enrollment. Email: *admissions@vtc.edu* Web: *www.vtc.edu*

FINANCIAL AID: In 2017-2018, 77% of all full-time freshmen received some form of financial aid. 63% of all full-time freshmen received need-based aid. The average freshman award was $12,400. Need-based scholarships or need-based grants averaged $4,000 ($13,200 maximum); need-based self-help aid (loans and jobs) averaged $2,750 ($5,025 maximum); and other non-need-based awards and non-need-based scholarships averaged $5,650 ($37,800 maximum). 26% of undergraduate students work part-time. The average financial indebtedness of the 2017 graduate was $12,000. The FAFSA code is 003698. The deadline for filing freshman financial aid applications for fall entry is March 1.

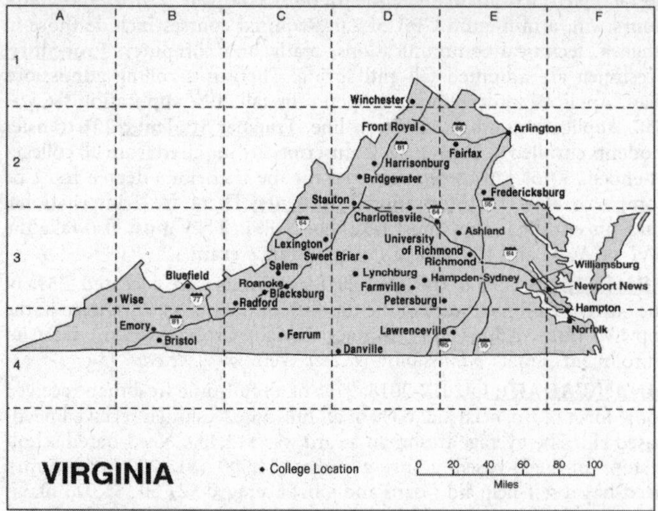

AVERETT UNIVERSITY *(The complete profile is made available exclusively on our website, www.barronspac.com)*

BLUEFIELD COLLEGE — B-3
www.bluefield.edu

Bluefield, VA 24605	**(276) 326-4339** **(800) 872-0175**
Fax: (276) 326-4288	**Email: admissions@bluefield.edu**
Full-time: 287 men, 405 women	**Faculty:** 33; IIA
Part-time: 27 men, 57 women	**Ph.D.s:** 61%
Graduate: n/av	**Student/Faculty:** 21 to 1
Year: semesters, summer session	**Tuition:** $25,010
Room & Board: $9701	**Freshman Class:** 731 applied, 358 accepted, 110 enrolled
SAT or ACT: required	**CEEB CODE:** 1523
Application Deadline: August 31	**COMPETITIVE**

Bluefield College is a Christ-centered liberal arts college in covenant with the Baptist General Association of Virginia. We offer a challenging academic experience within a diverse Christian environment. Our academic and co-curricular programs transform students' lives by integrating liberal arts with career-oriented studies and service to God and the global community. We are committed to graduating students who think critically, communicate effectively, and adapt readily to a changing world. The figures in the above capsule and in this profile are approximate. There is 1 undergraduate school. In addition to regional accreditation, BC has baccalaureate program accreditation with CAEP and SCHEV. The 82-acre campus is in a small town 100 miles west of Roanoke on the Virginia-West Virginia state line. Including any residence halls, there are 26 buildings.

STUDENT LIFE: 80% of undergraduates are from Virginia. Others are from 19 states, and 2 foreign countries. 79% are White; 18% African American; 1% Asian American; 1% American Indian/Alaska Native; 1% Foreign. **Female To Male Ratio:** 1.5:1. **Housing:** 330 students can be accommodated in college housing, which includes married student dorms and on-campus apartments. On-campus housing is available on a lottery system for upperclassmen. 65% of students live on campus. Alcohol is not permitted. All students may keep cars.

FACULTY/CLASSROOMS: 70% of faculty are male; 30% are female. All teach undergraduates, 30% do research, and 30% do both. No introductory courses are taught by graduate students. The average class size in an introductory lecture is 17; in a laboratory is 12; and in a regular course is 10.

PROGRAMS OF STUDY: BC confers B.A., B.S., and M.A. degrees. Bachelor's degrees are awarded in BIOLOGICAL SCIENCE (biology/biological science), BUSINESS (business administration and management), COMMUNICATIONS AND THE ARTS (communications, English, fine arts, and music), COMPUTER AND PHYSICAL SCIENCE (chemistry and mathematics), EDUCATION (middle school education and secondary education), HEALTH PROFESSIONS (exercise science), SOCIAL SCIENCE (Christian studies, criminal justice, history, interdisciplinary studies, psychology, religion, and social studies). Business, teacher education, and biology are the strongest academically. Business, organizational management and development, and criminal justice have the largest enrollments.

ACTIVITIES: 5% of men belong to 2 local fraternities; 10% of women belong to 2 local sororities. There are 15 groups on campus, including art, cheerleading, choir, chorale, chorus, communications, dance, drama, honors, literary magazine, musical theater, newspaper, orchestra, professional, religious, social, and student government. Popular campus events include Homecoming, and Mud Pig Day. **Sports:** There are 6 intramural sports for men and 6 for women. Facilities include a gym with game courts, excercise facility, student activities center, a game room, tennis courts, and sand volleyball court. **Graduates:** From July 1, 2016 to June 30, 2017, 246 bachelor's degrees were awarded. In an average class, 1% graduate in 3 years or less, 47% graduate in 4 years or less, 50% graduate in 5 years or less, and 55% graduate in 6 years or less. Of the 2016 graduating class, 16% were enrolled in graduate school within 6 months of graduation.

SERVICES: Counseling and information services are available, as is tutoring in most subjects. There is remedial math and writing. **Library/Resources:** The library contains 47,000 volumes, and 3,477 audio/video tapes/CDs/DVDs, and subscribes to 70,000 periodicals including electronic. Computerized library services include interlibrary loans, database searching, and Internet access. **Physically Challenged Students:** 95% of the campus is accessible. Facilities include wheelchair ramps, elevators, special parking, specially equipped restrooms, and lowered drinking fountains. **Special:** The college offers credit for life/military/work experience, nondegree study through the Fine Arts Community School, study abroad in England, an accelerated degree program in organizational management and development and in criminal justice, and internships in criminal justice, psychology, and recreation. There are 4 national honor societies, a freshman honors program, and 7 departmental honors programs. **Visiting:** There are regularly scheduled orientations for prospective students, including campus tours, opportunities to develop class schedules, and financial aid workshops. Visitors may sit in on classes and stay overnight. To schedule a visit, contact the Admissions Office. **Campus Safety and Security:** Measures include 24-hour foot and vehicle patrol, emergency notification system, and security escort services. There are lighted pathways/sidewalks and controlled access to dorms/residences.

REQUIREMENTS: The SAT or ACT is required. Applicants must be graduates of an accredited secondary school or have a GED certificate, and have completed 4 years of English, 2 of social sciences, 1 of science, and 5 of electives. AP and CLEP credits are accepted. Important factors in the admissions decision are leadership record, advanced placement or honors courses, and recommendations by school officials. To graduate, students must have completed a minimum of 126 semester hours, including a liberal arts requirement of 51 to 53 hours, with 30 to 45 hours in the major, and a minimum 2.0 GPA. Other requirements vary by program. All graduates must demonstrate computer proficiency by testing, passing computer courses, or having components in required courses. **Procedure:** Freshmen are admitted to all sessions. Entrance exams should be taken early in the senior year. There are deferred admissions and rolling admissions plans. Applications should be filed by August 31 for fall entry. The fall 2017 application fee was $30. Notification is sent on a rolling basis. Applications are accepted on-line. **Transfer Students:** 337 transfer students enrolled in 2016-2017. Prospective students must submit transcripts of all academic work, a financial aid transcript, and SAT or ACT scores if they have fewer than 30 hours of college level work. 32 of 126 credits required for the bachelor's degree must be completed at BC. **International Students:** There are 2 international students enrolled. They must take the TOEFL.

ADMISSIONS: 49% of the 2017-2018 applicants were accepted. 38% of the current freshmen were in the top fifth of their class; 64% were in the top two fifths. **Admissions Contact:** Evan Sherman, Director of Admissions. Email: *admissions@bluefield.edu* Web: *www.bluefield.edu*

FINANCIAL AID: In 2017-2018, 99% of all full-time freshmen received some form of financial aid and need-based aid. The college's own financial statement is required. The FAFSA code is 003703. The deadline for filing freshman financial aid applications for fall entry is March 10.

BRIDGEWATER COLLEGE D-2
www.bridgewater.edu

Bridgewater, VA 22812	**(540) 828-5469** **(800) 759-8328**
Fax: (540) 828-5481	**Email: admissions@bridgewater.edu**
Full-time: 853 men, 1023 women	**Faculty:** 120
Part-time: 5 men, 1 women	**Ph.D.s:** 82%
Graduate: 1 men, 6 women	**Student/Faculty:** 16 to 1
Year: semesters, summer session	**Tuition:** $33,820
Room & Board: $12,440	**Freshman Class:** 7241 applied, 3764 accepted, 534 enrolled
SAT EBR-W/M: 551/524 **ACT:** 22	**CEEB CODE:** 5069
Application Deadline: May 1	**COMPETITIVE**

Bridgewater College, founded in 1880, is a private liberal arts institution affiliated with the Church of the Brethren. There is 1 undergraduate school and 1 graduate school. In addition to regional accreditation, Bridgewater has baccalaureate program accreditation with CAATE. The 300-acre campus is in a small town 2 hours southwest of Washington, D.C., and 8 miles south of Harrisonburg, Virginia. Including any residence halls, there are 44 buildings.

STUDENT LIFE: 74% of undergraduates are from Virginia. Others are from 29 states, and 20 foreign countries. 92% are from public schools. 66% are White; 6% Hispanic; 5% two or more races; 4% race unknown; 2% Foreign; 16% African American; 1% Asian American. 52% are Protestant; 29% claim no religious affiliation. **Female To Male Ratio:** 1.2:1. The average age of freshmen is 18; all undergraduates, 20. 25% do not continue beyond their first year; 61% remain to graduate. **Housing:** 1542 students can be accommodated in college housing, which includes single sex and coed dorms and on-campus apartments, and honors houses. On-campus housing is available on a first-come, first-served basis, and is available on a lottery system for upperclassmen. 81% of students live on campus. Alcohol is not permitted. All students may keep cars.

FACULTY/CLASSROOMS: 50% of faculty are male; 50% are female. All teach undergraduates and 50% do research. No introductory courses are taught by graduate students. The average class size in an introductory lecture is 23; in a laboratory is 15; and in a regular course is 19.

PROGRAMS OF STUDY: Bridgewater confers B.A., B.S., and B.G.S. degrees. Master's degrees are also awarded. Bachelor's degrees are awarded in BIOLOGICAL SCIENCE (biochemistry, biology/biological science, and nutritional sciences), BUSINESS (business administration and management and management information systems), COMMUNICATIONS AND THE ARTS (art, communications, English, French, music, and Spanish), COMPUTER AND PHYSICAL SCIENCE (applied physics, chemistry, computer science, mathematics, physics and mathematics, and physics), EDUCATION (athletic training, global studies, and health and physical education), ENGINEERING AND ENVIRONMENTAL DESIGN (environmental science), HEALTH PROFESSIONS (exercise science), SOCIAL SCIENCE (economics, family/consumer studies, history, history and political science, liberal arts/general studies, philosophy and religion, political science/government, psychology, and sociology). Biology, chemistry, and English are the strongest academically. Business administration, biology, and health/exercise science have the largest enrollments.

ACTIVITIES: There are no fraternities or sororities. There are 88 groups on campus, including band, cheerleading, choir, chorale, chorus, communications, computers, dance, drama, environmental, ethnic, honors, international, jazz band, LGBT, literary magazine, newspaper, pep band, political, professional, radio and TV, religious, social, social service, student government, and yearbook. Popular campus events include Homecoming, Welcome Week Activities, and Spring Fest. **Sports:** There are 10 intercollegiate sports for men and 11 for women, and 26 intramural sports for men and 26 for women. Facilities include a gym, a football stadium, swimming pool, tennis courts, an all-weather track, playing fields for baseball, lacrosse, softball, football, field hockey, and soccer, basketball, volleyball, racquetball courts, indoor track, an fitness center, a cardiac and weight-training center, aerobics/dance rooms, an equestrian center with barns and stalls, and indoor and outdoor arenas. **Graduates:** From July 1, 2016 to June 30, 2017, 371 bachelor's degrees were awarded. The most popular majors were business administration (17%), biology (10%), and health & exercise science (9%). In an average class, 53% graduate in 4 years or less, 61% graduate in 5 years or less, and 61% graduate in 6 years or less.

SERVICES: Counseling and information services are available, as is tutoring in every subject. There is a reader service for the blind. The Academic Support Center provides services that assist students in their development of skills necessary for effective performance in a learning environment. **Library/Resources:** The library contains 116,121 volumes, 5,892 audio/video tapes/CDs/DVDs, and subscribes to 15,720 periodicals, including electronic. Computerized library services include interlibrary loans, database searching, Internet access, and Wi-Fi capability. Special learning facilities include an art gallery and a radio station. **Physically Challenged Students:** 95% of the campus is accessible. Facilities include wheelchair ramps, elevators, special parking, specially equipped restrooms, special class scheduling, lowered drinking fountains, lowered telephones, and special housing. **Special:** Bridgewater offers internships to junior and seniors; study abroad in over 50 countries; participation in the Smithsonian-Mason Semester for Conservation Studies; and a teacher certification program in elementary and secondary education. Interdisciplinary majors include environmental science, history and political science, global studies, liberal studies, nutrition and wellness, philosophy and religion, and physics and math. Dual-degree programs are offered in engineering with Virginia Tech (3-2) and in Veterinary Medicine (3-4) with Virginia Tech. There are 9 national honor societies, a freshman honors program, and 16 departmental honors programs. **Visiting:** There are regularly scheduled orientations for prospective students, including information on academic programs, student services, housing options, student organizations, intercollegiate athletics, financial aid, and campus events. Also included are placement tests and assistance with pre-registration from faculty advisors. There are guides for informal visits and visitors may sit in on classes. To schedule a visit, contact the Admissions Office. **Campus Safety and Security:** Measures include 24-hour foot and vehicle patrol, an emergency notification system, self-defense education, and security escort services. There are emergency telephones, lighted pathways/sidewalks, and controlled access to dorms/residences.

REQUIREMENTS: The SAT or ACT is required, with the SAT preferred; an interview is recommended. Applicants must be graduates of an accredited secondary school or have a GED certificate, and have completed 17 units, including 4 in English, 3 in math, 3 in science, 3 in history and social studies, and 4 electives. AP and CLEP credits are accepted. Important factors in the admissions decision are advanced placement or honors courses, recommendations by school officials, and leadership record. To graduate, all students must 1.Complete a minimum of 120 credit hours with a minimum of 45 credit hours chosen from junior and senior level courses; 2. Complete FILA general education requirements; 3. Complete course requirements for the major; 4. Earn a minimum cumulative GPA of 2.0 and a minimum GPA of 2.0 in courses required for the major; and 5. Complete a minimum of 33 credit hours with 30 of the last 33 credit hours of academic work in residence at Bridgewater College or at a College approved study abroad program. In addition, students must complete at least 9 credit hours of the major at Bridgewater College. **Procedure:** Freshmen are admitted in the fall and spring. Entrance exams should be taken in spring of the junior year or fall of the senior year. There are deferred admissions and rolling admissions plans. Applications should be filed by May 1 for fall entry; January 1 for spring entry. 60 applicants were on the 2017 waiting list; 18 were admitted. Applications are accepted on-line. **Transfer Students:** 56 transfer students enrolled in 2016-2017. A degree from an accredited high school and a 2.2 GPA in all undergraduate work are required. 33 of 123 credits required for the bachelor's degree must be completed at Bridgewater. **International Students:** There are 29 international students enrolled. They must take the TOEFL with a minimum score of 550 on the paper-based TOEFL (PBT) or 79 on the Internet-based version (iBT), The SAT may replace the TOEFL. Most international students take the SAT rather than TOEFL. They must also take the SAT or ACT.

ADMISSIONS: 52% of the 2017-2018 applicants were accepted. The SAT scores for the 2017-2018 freshman class were: Math-- 34% below 500, 50% between 500 and 599, 14% between 600 and 699, and 2% between 700 and 800. Evidence-Based Reading/Writing-- 23% below 500, 50% between 500 and 599, 24% between 600 and 699, and 3% between 700 and 800. The ACT scores were 20% between 12 and 17, 504% between 18 and 23, 29% between 24 and 29, and 5% above 30. 27% of the current freshmen were in the top fifth of their class; 59% were in the top two fifths. 2 freshmen graduated first in their class. **Admissions Contact:** Jarret L. Smith, Director of Admissions. Email: *admissions@bridgewater.edu* Web: *www.bridgewater.edu*

FINANCIAL AID: In 2017-2018, 100% of all full-time freshmen

received some form of financial aid. 85% of all full-time freshmen received need-based aid. The average freshman award was $32,931. Need-based scholarships or need-based grants averaged $29,262 ($39,770 maximum); need-based self-help aid (loans and jobs) averaged $4,916 ($7,500 maximum); and other non-need-based awards and non-need-based scholarships averaged $22,511 ($36,300 maximum). 23% of undergraduate students work part-time. The average financial indebtedness of the 2017 graduate was $33,567. Bridgewater is a member of CSS. The state aid form is required. The FAFSA code is 003704. The priority date for freshman financial aid applications for fall entry is March 1.

CHRISTENDOM COLLEGE D-2

www.christendom.edu

Front Royal, VA 22630
(540) 636-2900
(800) 877-5456
Fax: (540) 636-1655
Email: admissions@christendom.edu

Full-time: 177 men, 255 women	**Faculty:** 32
Part-time: 1 men	**Ph.D.s:** 65%
Graduate: n/av	**Student/Faculty:** 15 to 1
Year: semesters	**Tuition:** $23,900
Room & Board: $8700	**Freshman Class:** 228 applied, 211 accepted, 104 enrolled
SAT CR/M/W: 632/570/616 **ACT:** 25	**CEEB CODE:** 5691
Application Deadline: March 1	**VERY COMPETITIVE**

Christendom College, founded in 1977, is a private liberal arts institution affiliated with the Roman Catholic Church. There is 1 undergraduate school and 1 graduate school. In addition to regional accreditation, Christendom has baccalaureate program accreditation with SACS. The 120-acre campus is in a rural area 65 miles west of Washington, D.C. Including any residence halls, there are 21 buildings.

STUDENT LIFE: 74% of undergraduates are from out of state, mostly the Middle Atlantic. Students are from 43 states, 2 foreign countries, and Canada. 91% are White; 4% Hispanic; 2% Asian American; 2% Foreign; 1% African American. 100% are Catholic. **Female To Male Ratio:** 1.4:1. The average age of freshmen is 18; all undergraduates, 20. 7% do not continue beyond their first year; 70% remain to graduate. **Housing:** College-sponsored housing includes dorms and on-campus apartments. On-campus housing is guaranteed for all 4 years. 95% of students live on campus. Alcohol is not permitted. All students may keep cars.

FACULTY/CLASSROOMS: 79% of faculty are male; 21% are female. All teach undergraduates. No introductory courses are taught by graduate students. The average class size in an introductory lecture is 22 and in a regular course is 20.

PROGRAMS OF STUDY: Christendom confers B.A. degrees. Associate and master's degrees are also awarded. Bachelor's degrees are awarded in COMMUNICATIONS AND THE ARTS (English), SOCIAL SCIENCE (classical/ancient civilization, history, philosophy, political science/government, and theological studies). Philosophy is the strongest academically, and has the largest enrollment.

ACTIVITIES: There are no fraternities or sororities. There are 15 groups on campus, including chess, choir, chorale, computers, debate, drama, film, literary magazine, musical theater, newspaper, photography, political, professional, radio and TV, religious, social, social service, student government, and yearbook. Popular campus events include Christmas Dinner Dance, Coffee House, and St. Patrick's Day. **Sports:** There are 4 intercollegiate sports for men and 3 for women, and 7 intramural sports for men and 7 for women. Facilities include indoor basketball and volleyball courts, racquetball courts, playing fields, table games, a recreation center, and outdoor swimming pool. **Graduates:** From July 1, 2016 to June 30, 2017, 69 bachelor's degrees were awarded. In an average class, 70% graduate in 4 years or less and 70% graduate in 6 years or less. Of the 2016 graduating class, 12% were enrolled in graduate school within 6 months of graduation, and 80% were employed.

SERVICES: **Library/Resources:** The library contains 90,000 volumes, 860 microform items, and 1,345 audio/video tapes/CDs/DVDs, and subscribes to 279 periodicals including electronic. Computerized library services include interlibrary loans and database searching. Special learning facilities include a radio station, and a writing center. **Physically Challenged Students:** 60% of the campus is accessible. Facilities include wheelchair ramps, elevators, special parking, and specially equipped restrooms. **Special:** Christendom offers summer internships in Washington, D.C. for political science students and also sponsors a semester in Rome during the junior year. Students may pursue dual majors. There is a work-study program with the college. There are 5 departmental honors programs. **Visiting:** There are guides for informal visits, visitors may sit in on classes, and stay overnight. To schedule a visit, contact the Admissions Counselor at admission@christendom.edu. **Campus Safety and Security:** Measures include 24-hour foot and vehicle patrol and security escort services. There are emergency telephones and lighted pathways/sidewalks.

REQUIREMENTS: The SAT or ACT is required, with the SAT preferred. A minimum composite score of 1500 on the newest SAT or 21 on the ACT is required. Applicants need not be graduates of an accredited secondary school. GED certificates are accepted. Essays and letters of recommendation are required. A campus visit and a meeting with the Admissions Director are highly recommended. Christendom requires applicants to be in the upper 50% of their class. A GPA of 3.0 is required. AP credits are accepted. To graduate, all students must complete a total of 126 credit hours, including a 30-hour major and an 86-credit core curriculum, which includes 18 hours each in theology and philosophy. A minimum 2.0 GPA is required. All students must demonstrate proficiency in a foreign language and complete a thesis. **Procedure:** Freshmen are admitted fall and spring. Entrance exams should be taken in the spring of the junior year or fall of the senior year. There is an early admissions plan. Early decision applications should be filed by December 1; regular applications, by March 1 for fall entry; and January 2 for spring entry. The fall 2017 application fee was $25. Notification of early decision is sent December 15; regular decision, April 1. Applications are accepted on-line. **Transfer Students:** 9 transfer students enrolled in 2016-2017. Students must have a minimum 2.0 GPA and meet all other applicable standard admissions requirements. The SAT or ACT is recommended. 36 of 126 credits required for the bachelor's degree must be completed at Christendom. **International Students:** There are 7 international students enrolled. They must take the TOEFL.

ADMISSIONS: 93% of the 2017-2018 applicants were accepted. The SAT scores for the 2017-2018 freshman class were: Critical Reading-- 5% below 500, 33% between 500 and 599, 33% between 600 and 699, and 29% between 700 and 800. Math-- 20% below 500, 46% between 500 and 599, 24% between 600 and 699, and 10% between 700 and 800. Writing-- 11% below 500, 24% between 500 and 599, 43% between 600 and 699, and 22% between 700 and 800. The ACT scores were 3% below 12, 28% between 12 and 17, 50% between 18 and 23, 12% between 24 and 29, and 7% above 30. 40% of the current freshmen were in the top fifth of their class; 85% were in the top two fifths. **Admissions Contact:** Samuel J. Phillips, Director of Admissions. Email: *admissions@christendom.edu* Web: *www.christendom.edu*

FINANCIAL AID: In 2017-2018, 69% of all full-time freshmen received some form of financial aid. 56% of all full-time freshmen received need-based aid. The average freshman award was $17,236. Need-based scholarships or need-based grants averaged $6,270; need-based self-help aid (loans and jobs) averaged $7,530; and other non-need-based awards and non-need-based scholarships averaged $8,183. 40% of undergraduate students work part-time. The average financial indebtedness of the 2017 graduate was $28,084. The college's own financial statement is required. Check with the school for current application deadlines.

CHRISTOPHER NEWPORT UNIVERSITY F-3

www.cnu.edu

Newport News, VA 23606
(757) 594-7015
(800) 333-4268
Fax: (757) 594-7333
Email: admit@cnu.edu

Full-time: 2115 men, 2752 women	**Faculty:** 279; IIB, +$
Part-time: 51 men, 36 women	**Ph.D.s:** 91%
Graduate: 46 men, 81 women	**Student/Faculty:** 17 to 1
Year: semesters, summer session	**Tuition:** $13,654 ($25,850)
Room & Board: $11,224	**Freshman Class:** 6948 applied, 5030 accepted, 1293 enrolled
SAT EBR-W/M: 620/590 **ACT:** 26	**CEEB CODE:** 5128
Application Deadline: February 1	**VERY COMPETITIVE+**

Christopher Newport University is a public school offering a private school experience in the liberal arts and sciences. All freshmen students are assigned a core faculty advisor who mentors them for two years, provides academic support, helps with course selection, and introduces campus resources and engagement opportunities. There are 4 undergraduate schools and 1 graduate school. In addition to regional accreditation, CNU has baccalaureate program accreditation with AACSB, ABET, CSWE, NASM, NAST, and ACS. The 260-acre campus is in a suburban area in the heart of Newport News, Virginia, and 3 hours south of Washington, D.C. Including any residence halls, there are 49 buildings.

STUDENT LIFE: 92% of undergraduates are from Virginia. Others are from 32 states, 34 foreign countries, and Canada. 76% are White; 7% African American; 5% Hispanic; 5% two or more races; 4% race unknown; 3% Asian American. **Female To Male Ratio:** 1.3:1. The average age of freshmen is 18; all undergraduates, 20. 12% do not continue beyond their first year; 75% remain to graduate. **Housing:** 3805 students can be accommodated in college housing, which includes dorms and on-campus apartments. In addition, there are special-interest houses, fraternity houses, sorority houses, and living learning communities. On-campus housing is available on a lottery system for upperclassmen. 78% of students live on campus. Alcohol is not permitted. All students may keep cars.

FACULTY/CLASSROOMS: 53% of faculty are male; 47% are female. All teach undergraduates. No introductory courses are taught by graduate students.

PROGRAMS OF STUDY: CNU confers B.A., B.S., B.M., B.S.B.A., and B.S.I.S. degrees. Master's degrees are also awarded. Bachelor's degrees are awarded in AGRICULTURE (environmental studies), BIOLOGICAL SCIENCE (biochemistry, biology/biological science, cellular and molecular biology, environmental biology, and neurosciences), BUSINESS (accounting, business administration and management, finance, integrative studies, management, and marketing), COMMUNICATIONS AND THE ARTS (communications, English, fine arts, French, German, information technology, music, Spanish, and theatre arts), COMPUTER AND PHYSICAL SCIENCE (applied mathematics, applied physics, chemistry, computer science, information science, mathematics, and mathematics/computational), ENGINEERING AND ENVIRONMENTAL DESIGN (computer engineering and electrical and computer engineering), HEALTH PROFESSIONS (predentistry, premedicine, prepharmacy, prephysical therapy, and preveterinary science), SOCIAL SCIENCE (American studies, classical/ancient civilization, economics, history, interdisciplinary studies, philosophy, political science/government, prelaw, psychology, social work, and sociology). Psychology, communication studies and cellular and molecular physiological biology have the largest enrollments.

ACTIVITIES: 24% of men belong to 10 national fraternities; 34% of women belong to 10 national sororities. There are 200 groups on campus, including art, band, cheerleading, chess, choir, chorale, chorus, communications, computers, dance, debate, drama, environmental, ethnic, film, honors, international, jazz band, LGBT, literary magazine, marching band, musical theater, newspaper, opera, orchestra, pep band, photography, political, professional, radio and TV, religious, social, social service, student government, and symphony. Popular campus events include Glow in the Dar-Capella, Campus Tie Dye, Candlelight Ceremony, Captain's Ball, Club Fair, Day of Service, FallFest, Family Weekend, Ferguson Center for the Arts, Food 4 Thought, Lighting of the Lawn, Midnight Madness, and Spectrum Drag Ball. **Sports:** There are 12 intercollegiate sports for men and 12 for women, and 9 intramural sports for men and 9 for women. Facilities include volleyball, indoor track and field programs, basketball courts (2 housed in a separate Auxiliary gymnasium) a fitness pavilion, a football stadium which includes a 400-meter track, outdoor tennis courts, fields for soccer and field hockey/lacrosse, and fields for baseball and softball. **Graduates:** From July 1, 2016 to June 30, 2017, 1168 bachelor's degrees were awarded. The most popular majors were psychology (12%), communications (9%), cellular, molecular, and physiological biology (9%). In an average class, 2% graduate in 3 years or less, 68% graduate in 4 years or less, 71% graduate in 5 years or less, and 75% graduate in 6 years or less.

SERVICES: Counseling and information services are available, as is tutoring in most subjects. **Library/Resources:** The library contains 607,363 volumes, 199,503 microform items, and 15,815 audio/video tapes/CDs/DVDs, and subscribes to 65,919 periodicals, including electronic. Computerized library services include interlibrary loans, database searching, Internet access, and Wi-Fi capability. Special learning facilities include an art gallery, a radio station, a TV station, and the Ferguson Center for the Arts. **Physically Challenged Students:** 96% of the campus is accessible. Facilities include wheelchair ramps, elevators, special parking, specially equipped restrooms, special class scheduling, lowered drinking fountains, and special housing. **Special:** CNU offers cross-registration, dual majors, a student-designed interdisciplinary studies major, internships, and study abroad. Special course offerings: Honors Program, the President's Leadership Program and Freshman Learning Communities. There are 31 national honor societies, a freshman honors program, and 29 departmental honors programs. **Visiting:** There are regularly scheduled orientations for prospective students, Information sessions and walking campus tours are available Monday through Friday; and there is a information session and tour on Saturday. There are also special events on-and-off campus, and receptions as scheduled annually. Visitors may sit in on classes and stay overnight. To schedule a visit, contact Kimberly McDaniel at (757) 594-7334. **Campus Safety and Security:** Measures include 24-hour foot and vehicle patrol, an emergency notification system, self-defense education, and security escort services. There are emergency telephones, lighted pathways/sidewalks, controlled access to dorms/residences, campus police, and a full time communication center for emergency radio and telephone communications.

REQUIREMENTS: CNU requires Virginia's Advanced Studies Diploma (ASD) or similar college preparatory diploma from an accredited high school with a satisfactory score on the SAT verbal and math or ACT composite. The GED is not accepted in lieu of a final high school transcript for freshman admission, as GED recipients do not meet ASD requirements. A total of 24 academic credits are recommended, including 4 units each of English, social science, math, and science and either 3 units of 1 foreign language (preferred) or 2 years of 2 foreign languages. An essay and a personal statement are required. SAT or ACT scores are not required for students with a 3.5 or higher high school GPA in a rigorous curriculum that includes college level work. Letters of recommendation and interviews are strongly recommended but not required. AP and CLEP credits are accepted. Important factors in the admissions decision are recommendations by school officials, extracurricular activities record, and evidence of special talent. To graduate, all students must fulfill the liberal learning core, including mathematics, second language literacy, written communication (with minimum grades of C- or better), logical reasoning, economic modeling and analysis, civic and democratic engagement, global and multicultural perspectives, creative expressions, science lecture with laboratory, Western traditions, and two writing intensive designated courses, with a minimum of 120 semester hours and with 45 credits in residence, and 30 of the last 36 credit hours, including the last 12 credit hours within the major in residence. In addition, students must complete all requirements specific to the major, present an overall and an in-major GPA of at least 2.0, and enroll in at least one CNU course during the semester of the degree conferral. **Procedure:** Freshmen are admitted fall and spring. Entrance exams should be taken before the senior year. There are early decision, early admissions, and deferred admissions plans. Early decision applications should be filed by November 15; regular applications, by February 1 for fall entry; and November 1 for spring entry. The fall 2017 application fee was $65. Notification of early decision is sent December 15; regular decision, March 15. 324 early decision candidates were accepted for the 2017-2018 class. 921 applicants were on the 2017 waiting list; 107 were admitted. Applications are accepted on-line. **Transfer Students:** 143 transfer students enrolled in 2016-2017. Applicants must present a minimum 3.0 GPA, and be academically eligible to return to the most recently attended college or university. All transfer applicants must submit official college and high school transcripts. SAT or ACT scores are recommended if high school graduation is within the last five years. In addition, transfer applicants must submit the Transfer College Report certified from each college or university attended. 45 of 120 credits required for the bachelor degree must be completed at CNU. **International Students:** There are 17 international students enrolled. They must take the TOEFL with a minimum score of 530 on the paper-based TOEFL (PBT) or 71 on the Internet-based version (iBT). Students must take any one of the following tests: the IELTS, iTep, SAT, or ACT.

ADMISSIONS: 72% of the 2017-2018 applicants were accepted. The SAT scores for the 2017-2018 freshman class were: Math-- 4% below 500, 47% between 500 and 599, 44% between 600 and 699, and 5% between 700 and 800. Evidence-Based Reading/Writing-- 1% below 500, 32% between 500 and 599, 56% between 600 and 699, and 11% between 700 and 800. The ACT scores were 1% between 12 and 17, 24% between 18 and 23, 60% between 24 and 29, and 15% above 30. 40% of the current freshmen were in the top fifth of their class; 73% were in the top two fifths. **Admissions Contact:** Robert J. Lange III, Dean of Admission. Email: *admit@cnu.edu* Web: *www.cnu.edu*

FINANCIAL AID: In 2017-2018, 73% of all full-time freshmen received some form of financial aid. 40% of all full-time freshmen received need-based aid. The average freshman award was $13,260. Need-based scholarships or need-based grants averaged $6,902 ($8,300 maximum); need-based self-help aid (loans and jobs) averaged $3,465 ($4,500 maximum); and other non-need-based awards and non-need-based scholarships averaged $9,249 ($37,426 maximum). 32% of undergraduate students work part-time. The average financial indebtedness of the 2017 graduate was $32,994. The FAFSA code is 003706. The priority date for freshman financial aid applications for fall entry is March 1.

COLLEGE OF WILLIAM & MARY — E-3

www.wm.edu

Williamsburg, VA 23187 — **(757) 221-4223**

Fax: (757) 221-1242	**Email:** admission@wm.edu
Full-time: 2618 men, 3581 women	**Faculty:** I, av$
Part-time: 46 men, 40 women	**Ph.D.s:** n/av
Graduate: 1210 men, 1245 women	**Student/Faculty:** n/av
Year: semesters, summer session	**Tuition:** $23,108 ($43,670)
Room & Board: $11,799	**Freshman Class:** n/av
SAT or ACT: required	**CEEB CODE:** 5115
Application Deadline: January 1	**MOST COMPETITIVE**

College of William & Mary, founded by Royal Charter in 1693, is the second-oldest institution of higher education in the country. It has a long history of liberal arts education and a growing research and science curriculum that demonstrates a strong commitment to undergraduate research. There are 2 undergraduate schools and 5 graduate schools. In addition to regional accreditation, CWM has baccalaureate program accreditation with AACSB and CAEP. The 1200-acre campus is in a small town 50 miles southeast of Richmond. Including any residence halls, there are 173 buildings.

STUDENT LIFE: 66% of undergraduates are from Virginia. Others are from 50 states, 91 foreign countries, and Canada. 9% are Hispanic; 8% Asian American; 7% African American; 6% Foreign; 59% White; 5% two or more races; 5% race unknown. **Female To Male Ratio:** 1.3:1. The average age of freshmen is 18; all undergraduates, 20. 5% do not continue beyond their first year. **Housing:** 5000 students can be accommodated in college housing, which includes dorms and on-campus apartments. In addition, there are honors houses, language/international houses, special-interest houses, fraternity houses, sorority houses, smoke-free, substance free, multicultural housing, and Africana house. On-campus housing is guaranteed for the freshman year only and is available on a lottery system for upperclassmen. 72% of students live on campus. Upperclassmen may keep cars.

FACULTY/CLASSROOMS: No introductory courses are taught by graduate students.

PROGRAMS OF STUDY: CWM confers B.A., B.S., and B.B.A. degrees. Master's and doctoral degrees are also awarded. Bachelor's degrees are awarded in BIOLOGICAL SCIENCE (neurosciences), BUSINESS (accounting, banking and finance, business administration and management, business intelligence and analytics, entrepreneurial studies, and marketing management), COMMUNICATIONS AND THE ARTS (Africana studies, art history, art, Chinese, English, French, German, linguistics, music, and theatre arts), COMPUTER AND PHYSICAL SCIENCE (chemistry, computer science, geology, mathematics, and physics), HEALTH PROFESSIONS (biology, health science, and kinesiology), SOCIAL SCIENCE (American studies, anthropology, classical/ancient civilization, economics, gender studies, history, interdisciplinary studies, international relations, Latin American studies, medieval studies, philosophy, political science/government, psychology, public affairs, religion, sociology, Spanish studies, and women's studies). Biology, government, and economics have the largest enrollments.

ACTIVITIES: 27% of men belong to 15 national fraternities; 31% of women belong to 12 national sororities. There are 475 groups on campus, including art, band, cheerleading, chess, choir, chorale, chorus, computers, dance, debate, drama, drill team, environmental, ethnic, film, honors, international, jazz band, LGBT, literary magazine, musical theater, newspaper, opera, orchestra, pep band, photography, political, professional, radio and TV, religious, social, social service, student government, symphony, and yearbook. Popular campus events include Yule Log Ceremony, Raft Debate, and Senior Walk Across Campus (Commencement). **Sports:** There are 11 intercollegiate sports for men and 12 for women, and 28 intramural sports for men and 26 for women. Facilities include a football stadium, basketball, baseball, field for lacrosse and soccer, outdoor tennis courts, indoor tennis courts, field hockey field, a gymnasium with pool, volleyball courts, strength training center, a fitness room, weight rooms, racquetball courts, and squash courts. **Graduates:** From July 1, 2016 to June 30, 2017, 1591 bachelor's degrees were awarded. The most popular majors were business administration (13%), government (8%), and kinesiology & health sciences (8%). Of the 2016 graduating class, 22% were enrolled in graduate school within 6 months of graduation.

SERVICES: Counseling and information services are available, as is tutoring in most subjects. There is a reader service for the blind. **Library/Resources:** The library contains 1.5 million volumes, 179,143 microform items, 46,186 audio/video tapes/CDs/DVDs, and subscribes to 152,990 periodicals including electronic. Computerized library services include interlibrary loans, database searching, Internet access, and Wi-Fi capability. Special learning facilities include an art gallery, radio station, an anthropology museum, an art studio, a greenhouse, the Center for Archaeological Research, and the Omohundro Institute of Early American History and Culture. **Physically Challenged Students:** 95% of the campus is accessible. Facilities include wheelchair ramps, elevators, special parking, specially equipped restrooms, special class scheduling, lowered drinking fountains. There are also modified recreational facilities, braille signage, Kurzweil reader, and a special learning lab for the visually impaired. Individual accommodations are made on a case-by-case basis. **Special:** CWM has various special academic programs available to students: including study abroad in 23 countries around the world, and work-study programs with various employers including campus departments and off-campus community agencies. A Washington Program is open to students in all majors and disciplines. Also available are an accelerated degree program in Computer Science and Public Policy with an option whereby a small number of current CWM undergraduates will be able to earn both a Bachelor's degree and a Master degree in a total of five years of coursework; student self-designed majors are also available in interdisciplinary studies, as is a Combined Degree Program in engineering with Columbia University; a Joint Degree programme with the University of St Andrews in Scotland; The Department Honors programs administered by the Roy R. Charles Center; Internships for credit; and the opportunity to double major across the curriculum. There are 16 national honor societies, Phi Beta Kappa, a freshman honors program, and 27 departmental honors programs. **Visiting:** There are regularly scheduled orientations for prospective students, group information session followed by a student-led tour. Visitors may sit in on classes. To schedule a visit, contact the Office of Admissions. **Campus Safety and Security:** Measures include 24-hour foot and vehicle patrol, emergency notification system, self-defense education, and security escort services. There are shuttle buses, emergency telephones, lighted pathways/sidewalks, controlled access to dorms/residences, and crime prevention programs.

REQUIREMENTS: CWM Supplement to the Common Application, Secondary School Report form, complete with a high school transcript and counselor letter of recommendation, Midyear School Report form, and official report of standardized test scores (SAT and/or ACT), application fee, or a fee waiver request. AP and CLEP credits are accepted. Important factors in the admissions decision are advanced placement or honors courses, extracurricular activities record, leadership record, evidence of special talent, personality/intangible qualities, and geographical diversity. The College Curriculum (COLL), requires a "big ideas" course, a writing-intensive seminar, three integrative sophomore/junior-level courses, an experience beyond the college, and a capstone course. To graduate, students must complete the COLL courses and demonstrate proficiencies in foreign language, creative/performing arts, and mathematics; other proficiencies, such as digital information literacy, writing, and other forms of communication, are built into COLL courses. Distribution requirements include courses in Arts, Letters, and Values, Cultures, Societies, and the Individual and Natural World and Quantitative Reasoning. Students must complete 120 credit hours, with 33 to 48 in the major, a minimum 2.0 GPA cumulatively and in the major, and a minimum of 60 credit hours in residence at the College. **Procedure:** Freshmen are admitted in the fall. Entrance exams should be taken in spring of the junior year or fall of the senior year. There are early decision and deferred admissions plans. Early decision applications should be filed by November 1; regular applications, by January 1 for fall entry; and November 1 for spring entry. The fall 2017 application fee was $70. Notification of early decision is sent December 1; regular decision, April 1. 519 early decision candidates were accepted for the 2017-2018 class. 4392 applicants were on the 2017 waiting list; 69 were admitted. Applications are accepted on-line. **Transfer Students:** 170 transfer students enrolled in 2016-2017. William & Mary recommends that students interested in transferring to the College take challenging courses in the liberal arts and sciences. Typically, competitive transfer applicants have a GPA of 3.5 or higher at their current institution. Additional application requirements include: official transcripts from all colleges and universities attended, official high school transcript or copy of GED certificate. If you have completed less than a full year of college coursework when you apply, you must submit SAT or ACT scores. If you have been out of high school for more than five years, SAT or ACT scores are not required. Test scores listed on the high school transcript will be accepted. Midterm grades are due November 22 for students applying for spring and March 28 for students applying for fall. Student must use the Midterm Report form to submit current grades. 60 of 120 credits required for the bachelor's degree must be completed at William & Mary. **International Students:** There are 392 international students enrolled. They must take the TOEFL with a minimum score of 600 on the paper-based TOEFL (PBT) or 100 on the Internet-based version (iBT). Students must take the IELTS. They must also take the SAT or ACT. SAT II: Subject tests are considered if they are submitted.

ADMISSIONS: 95% of the current freshmen were in the top fifth of their class; 99% were in the top two fifths. **Admissions Contact:** David Trott, Associate Dean. Email: *admission@wm.edu* Web: *www.wm.edu*

FINANCIAL AID: The college's own financial statement, and the CSS Profile are required for early decision enrollees. The FAFSA code is 003705. The deadline for filing freshman financial aid applications for fall entry is March 1.

EASTERN MENNONITE UNIVERSITY D-2
www.emu.edu

Harrisonburg, VA 22802	**(540) 432-4118** **(800) 368-2665**
Fax: (540) 432-4444	**Email: admiss@emu.edu**
Full-time: 388 men, 699 women	**Faculty:** 89; IIA
Part-time: 44 men, 90 women	**Ph.D.s:** 79%
Graduate: 177 men, 375 women	**Student/Faculty:** 10 to 1
Year: semesters, summer session	**Tuition:** $32,300
Room & Board: $10,250	**Freshman Class:** 1762 applied, 1098 accepted, 257 enrolled
SAT CR/M: 505/503 **ACT:** 22	**CEEB CODE:** 5181
Application Deadline: n/av	**COMPETITIVE**

Eastern Mennonite University, founded in 1917, is a private Christian liberal arts university affiliated with the Mennonite Church. The university offers programs in the arts and sciences, education, biology, and nursing. EMU also offers some master's degrees at both Harrisonburg and Lancaster, PA. There is 1 undergraduate school and 6 graduate schools. In addition to regional accreditation, EMU has baccalaureate program accreditation with ACPE, CSWE, CAEP, and NLN. The 97-acre campus is in a small town Harrisonburg, VA., 110 miles southwest of Washington, D.C. Including any residence halls, there are 46 buildings.

STUDENT LIFE: 56% of undergraduates are from Virginia. Others are from 33 states, 38 foreign countries, and Canada. 58% are from public schools. 8% are Hispanic; 71% White; 3% Asian American; 3% Foreign; 10% African American. 91% are Protestant; 13% claim no religious affiliation. **Female To Male Ratio:** 1.9:1. The average age of freshmen is 18; all undergraduates, 25. 27% do not continue beyond their first year; 61% remain to graduate. **Housing:** 667 students can be accommodated in college housing, which includes married student dorms, on-campus apartments, off-campus apartments, and an international community. On-campus housing is guaranteed for all 4 years. 63% of students live on campus. Alcohol is not permitted. All students may keep cars.

FACULTY/CLASSROOMS: 58% of faculty are male; 42% are female. 75% teach undergraduates, 38% do research, and 35% do both. No introductory courses are taught by graduate students. The average class size in an introductory lecture is 40; in a laboratory is 17; and in a regular course is 18.

PROGRAMS OF STUDY: EMU confers B.A., and B.S. degrees. Associate and master's degrees are also awarded. Bachelor's degrees are awarded in BIOLOGICAL SCIENCE (biochemistry and biology/biological science), BUSINESS (accounting, business administration and management, international business management, and recreational facilities management), COMMUNICATIONS AND THE ARTS (art, communications, congregational and youth ministries, digital media, English, music, outdoor ministry & adventure leadership, photography, Spanish, theatre arts, and writing), COMPUTER AND PHYSICAL SCIENCE (chemistry, clinical laboratory science, computer science, and mathematics), EDUCATION (early childhood education, elementary education, health and physical education, physical education, secondary education, and special education), ENGINEERING AND ENVIRONMENTAL DESIGN (environmental science and preengineering), HEALTH PROFESSIONS (medical laboratory technology, nursing, predentistry, premedicine, pre-occupational therapy, preosteopathy, prepharmacy, pre-physician assistant, and prephysical therapy), SOCIAL SCIENCE (biblical studies, economics, history, liberal arts/general studies, ministries, peace studies, philosophy, psychology, religion, social science, social work, sociology, and theological studies). Biology/pre-med, education, and nursing are the strongest academically. Business, education, and nursing have the largest enrollments.

ACTIVITIES: There are no fraternities or sororities. There are 37 groups on campus, including art, chess, choir, chorale, chorus, computers, dance, drama, environmental, ethnic, film, honors, international, jazz band, literary magazine, musical theater, newspaper, orchestra, pep band, photography, political, professional, radio and TV, religious, social, social service, student government, student women's association and peace fellowship, and yearbook. Popular campus events include Spring Fling, Fall Festival, and Multicultural Week. **Sports:** There are 7 intercollegiate sports for men and 8 for women, and 15 intramural sports for men and 15 for women. Facilities include a fitness center, an aerobics room, indoor track, a climbing wall, and a gym. Outside facilities include a lighted artificial turf playing field, tennis courts, baseball, softball, and soccer fields, a rubberized outdoor track, basketball, and sand volleyball courts. **Graduates:** From July 1, 2016 to June 30, 2017, 360 bachelor's degrees were awarded. The most popular majors were nursing (36%), business (14%), and education (6%). In an average class, 50% graduate in 4 years or less, 58% graduate in 5 years or less, and 61% graduate in 6 years or less.

SERVICES: Counseling and information services are available, as is tutoring in most subjects, such as core curriculum courses. There is a reader service for the blind, and remedial reading and writing. EMU's technology has the ability to burn textbooks onto CD's, for visually impaired and special learning need students. **Library/Resources:** The library contains 340,838 volumes, 63,490 microform items, 32,240 audio/video tapes/CDs/DVDs, and subscribes to 86,373 periodicals including electronic. Computerized library services include interlibrary loans, database searching, Internet access, and Wi-Fi capability. Special learning facilities include an art gallery, natural history museum, planetarium, radio station, an arboretum and greenhouse, nursing laboratory, and a cadaver laboratory. **Physically Challenged Students:** 75% of the campus is accessible. Facilities include wheelchair ramps, elevators, special parking, specially equipped restrooms, special class scheduling, lowered drinking fountains, special housing, and some buildings on campus have accessible telephones. **Special:** EMU offers study-abroad programs each semester and during the summer at a variety of locations around the world. Students may also choose to study 1 or 2 semesters in Washington, D.C. There are internships in a variety of majors, dual majors, a student-designed major, and a 2 year general studies degree. There is 1 national honor society and a freshman honors program. **Visiting:** There are regularly scheduled orientations for prospective students, an address by the president, a financial aid seminar, a review of general education, the opportunity to sit in on classes, meet with professors and admissions representatives, sleep in residence halls, and eat in the cafeteria. To schedule a visit, contact Admissions Office. **Campus Safety and Security:** Measures include emergency notification system, self-defense education, and security escort services. There are emergency telephones, lighted pathways/sidewalks, and controlled access to dorms/residences. There is a 12-hour foot, and vehicle watchman.

REQUIREMENTS: SAT or ACT scores are required with a minimum SAT score of 900 (reading and math), and a minimum ACT composite score of 19. A minimum 2.6 GPA is required for admission. Applicants must be graduates of an accredited secondary school or have a GED certificate. The university recommends that students have completed 4 credits of English, 3 each of math, science, and social studies, 2 or more of foreign language and chemistry for nursing majors. AP and CLEP credits are accepted. Important factors in the admissions decision are leadership record, extracurricular activities record, and recommendations by school officials. To graduate, students must complete interdisciplinary core courses, courses in Bible and religion, cross-cultural study, writing, speech, and math, a major (minors are optional), and a variety of electives for a minimum of 128 semester hours. A minimum cumulative GPA of 2.0 is required while some majors require a higher GPA in the major or overall. **Procedure:** Freshmen are admitted in the fall and spring. Entrance exams should be taken in the spring of the junior year or the fall of the senior year. There are deferred admissions and rolling admissions plans. Application deadlines are open. The fall 2017 application fee was $25. Applications are accepted on-line. **Transfer Students:** 77 transfer students enrolled in 2016-2017. Transfer students must have a minimum college GPA of 2.0. 63 of 128 credits required for the bachelor's degree must be completed at EMU. **International Students:** There are 60 international students enrolled. They must take the TOEFL with a minimum score of 500 on the paper-based TOEFL (PBT) or 61 on the Internet-based version (iBT). They must also take the SAT or ACT, scoring 900 SAT, 19 ACT.

ADMISSIONS: 62% of the 2017-2018 applicants were accepted. The SAT scores for the 2017-2018 freshman class were: Critical Reading-- 41% below 500, 26% between 500 and 599, 13% between 600 and 699, and 1% between 700 and 800. Math-- 43% below 500, 25% between 500 and 599, 11% between 600 and 699, and 2% between 700 and 800. The ACT scores were 6% between 12 and 17, 16% between 18 and 23, 9% between 24 and 29, and 4% above 30. 36% of the current freshmen were in the top fifth of their class; 65% were in the top two fifths. **Admissions Contact:** Ms. Chris Hoover Seidel, Director of Admissions. Email: *admiss@emu.edu* Web: *www.emu.edu*

FINANCIAL AID: EMU is a member of CSS. The state aid form is required. The FAFSA code is 003708. The deadline for filing freshman financial aid applications for fall entry is April 15.

EMORY AND HENRY COLLEGE B-4

www.ehc.edu

Emory, VA 24327	(276) 944-6133 (800) 848-5493
Fax: (276) 944-6935	Email: admission@ehc.edu
Full-time: 464 men, 410 women	**Faculty:** 72; IIB, av$
Part-time: 12 men, 11 women	**Ph.D.s:** n/av
Graduate: 14 men, 34 women	**Student/Faculty:** 10 to 1
Year: semesters, summer session	**Tuition:** $34,500
Room & Board: $11,820	**Freshman Class:** 1217 applied, 878 accepted, 244 enrolled
SAT or ACT: required	**CEEB CODE:** 5185
Application Deadline: April 15	**COMPETITIVE**

Emory and Henry College, founded in 1836, is a private liberal arts institution affiliated with the United Methodist Church. The figures given in the above capsule and in this profile are approximate. There is 1 undergraduate school. In addition to regional accreditation, Emory and Henry has baccalaureate program accreditation with CAAHEP. The 331-acre campus is in a rural area in Emory, Southwest Virginia.

STUDENT LIFE: 64% of undergraduates are from Virginia. Others are from 26 states, 5 foreign countries, and Canada. 99% are from public schools. 80% are White; 10% African American; 1% Asian American; 1% Hispanic; 1% Foreign. **Male To Female Ratio:** 1.1:1. The average age of freshmen is 18; all undergraduates, 20. **Housing:** College-sponsored housing includes dorms, on-campus apartments, and off-campus apartments. In addition, there are honors houses and special-interest houses. On-campus housing is guaranteed for all 4 years. 77% of students live on campus. Alcohol is not permitted. All students may keep cars.

FACULTY/CLASSROOMS: 59% of faculty are male; 41% are female. All teach undergraduates. No introductory courses are taught by graduate students. The average class size in an introductory lecture is 25; in a laboratory is 13; and in a regular course is 22.

PROGRAMS OF STUDY: Emory and Henry confers B.A. and B.S. degrees. Master's degrees are also awarded. Bachelor's degrees are awarded in BIOLOGICAL SCIENCE (biology/biological science), BUSINESS (business administration and management), COMMUNICATIONS AND THE ARTS (art, communications, creative writing, dramatic arts, English literature, journalism, literature, modern language, music performance, and music theory and composition), COMPUTER AND PHYSICAL SCIENCE (chemistry, computer management, computer science, mathematics, and physics), EDUCATION (English education, mathematics education, and physical education), ENGINEERING AND ENVIRONMENTAL DESIGN (environmental science), SOCIAL SCIENCE (community services, East Asian studies, economics, European studies, geography, history, interdisciplinary studies, international studies, Middle Eastern studies, philosophy, political science/government, psychology, public affairs, religion, and sociology).

ACTIVITIES: 15% of men belong to 9 local fraternities; 30% of women belong to 6 local sororities. There are 50 groups on campus, including art, band, cheerleading, choir, chorus, dance, debate, drama, ethnic, international, LGBT, literary magazine, musical theater, newspaper, opera, pep band, photography, political, professional, radio and TV, religious, social, social service, student government, and yearbook. Popular campus events include Homecoming, Founder's Day, Martin Luther King Junior Day, Fall Formals, Parents Day, Greek Air Band, and the Literary Festival. **Sports:** Facilities include a gym, pool, a racquetball court, outdoor volleyball courts, tennis courts, a weight room, dance room, golf course, baseball and football fields, and a horseshoe area.

SERVICES: Counseling and information services are available, as is tutoring in most subjects. There is a reader service for the blind, and remedial math and writing. **Library/Resources:** The library contains 271,209 volumes, 207,000 microform items, and 7,950 audio/video tapes/CDs/DVDs, and subscribes to 352 periodicals including electronic. Computerized library services include interlibrary loans, database searching, and Internet access. Special learning facilities include an art gallery, radio station, and TV station. **Physically Challenged Students:** 50% of the campus is accessible. Facilities include wheelchair ramps, elevators, special parking, specially equipped restrooms, special class scheduling, lowered drinking fountains, and special housing. **Special:** A cooperative program in medical technology and 2-2, 4-1, and 3-2 engineering degrees are available. Dual and student-designed majors, an interdisciplinary English major, combined B.A.-B.S. degrees, internships, a Washington Semester, work-study, nondegree study, and pass/fail options are also available. There are 10 national honor societies and 8 departmental honors programs. **Visiting:** There are regularly scheduled orientations for prospective students, including a program for students to meet faculty and staff and to attend education sessions on college life. There are guides for informal visits, visitors may sit in on classes, and stay overnight. To schedule a visit, contact the Admissions Office. **Campus Safety and Security:** Measures include 24-hour foot and vehicle patrol, self-defense education, and security escort services. There are lighted pathways/sidewalks.

REQUIREMENTS: The SAT or ACT is required. Applicants should be high school graduates. High school courses required include 4 years of English, 3 or more units of math including algebra I, algebra II, and geometry, 2 or more units of lab science, 2 units of same foreign language, and 2 or more units of social studies and history. One additional unit in fine arts is strongly recommended. A personal essay is required. AP credits are accepted. Important factors in the admissions decision are advanced placement or honors courses, recommendations by school officials, and evidence of special talent. All students must complete a general studies curriculum covering Western traditions, great books, religion, ethical values inquiry, and global studies and must demonstrate proficiency in oral skills. Specific courses include a first-year writing course, 1 each from 3 disciplines, including social sciences, humanities and arts, and natural sciences, and according to major, either a foreign language or quantitative methods. A total of 120 semester hours for a B.A. or 124 for a B.S., with a GPA of 2.0, is required for graduation. The total number of hours in the major varies. **Procedure:** Freshmen are admitted fall, spring, and summer. Entrance exams should be taken in November of the senior year. There are early decision, deferred admissions, and rolling admissions plans. Early decision applications should be filed by November 1; regular applications, by April 15 for fall entry. The fall 2017 application fee was $30. Applications are accepted on-line. **Transfer Students:** 64 transfer students enrolled in 2016-2017. Transfers must have at least a 2.5 GPA in previous college work. Those with at least 24 credits may be admitted without high school data; those with fewer than 24 credits must meet freshman admission standards. 33 of 120 credits required for the bachelor's degree must be completed at Emory and Henry. **International Students:** There are 5 international students enrolled. They must take the TOEFL.

Admissions Contact: Dave Voskuil, Vice President of Enrollment Management. Email: *admission@ehc.edu* Web: *www.ehc.edu*

FINANCIAL AID: The state aid form and the college's own financial statement are required. The FAFSA code is 003709. The priority date for freshman financial aid applications for fall entry is April 1.

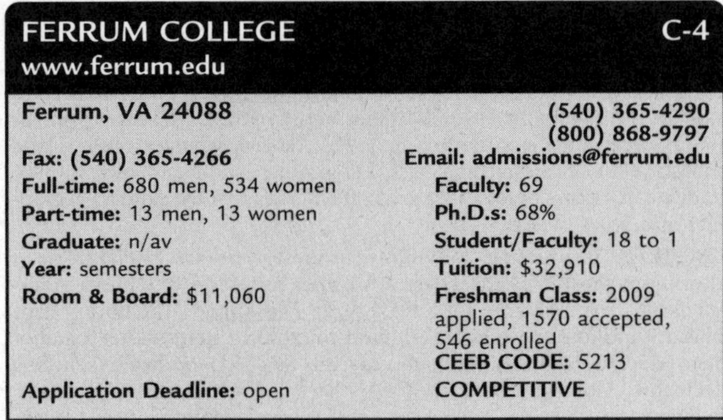

FERRUM COLLEGE C-4
www.ferrum.edu

Ferrum, VA 24088	**(540) 365-4290** **(800) 868-9797**
Fax: (540) 365-4266	**Email: admissions@ferrum.edu**
Full-time: 680 men, 534 women	**Faculty:** 69
Part-time: 13 men, 13 women	**Ph.D.s:** 68%
Graduate: n/av	**Student/Faculty:** 18 to 1
Year: semesters	**Tuition:** $32,910
Room & Board: $11,060	**Freshman Class:** 2009 applied, 1570 accepted, 546 enrolled
	CEEB CODE: 5213
Application Deadline: open	**COMPETITIVE**

Ferrum College, founded in 1913, is a private, primarily residential, 4-year institution offering both professional and liberal arts majors. The figures given in the above capsule and in this profile are approximate. There is 1 undergraduate school. In addition to regional accreditation, Ferrum has baccalaureate program accreditation with CSWE and SACS. The 700-acre campus is in a rural area in the Blue Ridge Mountains of southwestern Virginia. Including any residence halls, there are 54 buildings.

STUDENT LIFE: 86% of undergraduates are from Virginia. Others are from 24 states, and 5 foreign countries. 59% are White; 25% African American; 2% Hispanic; 1% Asian American; 1% American Indian/ Alaska Native; 1% Foreign. 29% claim no religious affiliation. **Male To Female Ratio:** 1.3:1. The average age of freshmen is 18; all undergraduates, 21. 40% do not continue beyond their first year; 35% remain to graduate. **Housing:** 1300 students can be accommodated in college housing, which includes married student dorms, on-campus apartments, off-campus apartments, and theme floors. On-campus housing is guaranteed for all 4 years. 86% of students live on campus. All students may keep cars.

FACULTY/CLASSROOMS: 57% of faculty are male; 43% are female. All teach undergraduates and do research. No introductory courses are taught by graduate students. The average class size in an introductory lecture is 20; in a laboratory is 15; and in a regular course is 13.

PROGRAMS OF STUDY: Ferrum confers B.A., B.S., B.F.A., and B.S.W. degrees. Bachelor's degrees are awarded in AGRICULTURE (agriculture and horticulture), BIOLOGICAL SCIENCE (biology/biological science), BUSINESS (accounting, business administration and management, recreation and leisure services, and sports management), COMMUNICATIONS AND THE ARTS (art, dramatic arts, English, performing arts, Russian, and Spanish), COMPUTER AND PHYSICAL SCIENCE (chemistry, information sciences and systems, and mathematics), EDUCATION (physical education), ENGINEERING AND ENVIRONMENTAL DESIGN (environmental science), HEALTH PROFESSIONS (health science), SOCIAL SCIENCE (criminal justice, history, international studies, liberal arts/general studies, philosophy, political science/ government, psychology, religion, social studies, and social work). Chemistry, biology, and environmental science are the strongest academically. Business administration, criminal justice, and liberal arts/ teacher education have the largest enrollments.

ACTIVITIES: 6% of men belong to 2 local fraternities; 9% of women belong to 3 local sororities. There are 63 groups on campus, including art, cheerleading, choir, chorale, chorus, communications, computers, dance, drama, environmental, ethnic, film, honors, international, jazz band, LGBT, literary magazine, musical theater, newspaper, photography, political, professional, radio and TV, religious, social, social service, and student government. Popular campus events include Spring Fling, Blue Ridge Folklife Festival, Relay for Life, and Snow Ball. **Sports:** There are 7 intercollegiate sports for men and 7 for women, and 13 intramural sports for men and 13 for women. Facilities include a gym, field house, tennis courts, weight room, an indoor pool, outdoor volleyball court, football stadium, soccer field, baseball field, women's softball field, recreation center (with indoor basketball courts, racquetball courts, and universal weights), and hiking/mountain biking trails. **Graduates:** From July 1, 2016 to June 30, 2017, 157 bachelor's degrees were awarded. The most popular majors were business administration (22%), criminal justice (11%), and parks and recreation (10%). In an average class, 17% graduate in 4 years or less, 27% graduate in 5 years or less, and 29% graduate in 6 years or less. Of the 2016 graduating class, 13% were enrolled in graduate school within 6 months of graduation, and 100% were employed.

SERVICES: Counseling and information services are available, as is tutoring in most subjects. There is remedial math, reading, and writing. College skills classes, individual assistance for study strategies, and subject-specific tutoring by professors and students are available. **Library/ Resources:** The library contains 219,774 volumes, 7,578 microform items, and 2,285 audio/video tapes/CDs/DVDs, and subscribes to 21,014 periodicals including electronic. Computerized library services include interlibrary loans, database searching, Internet access, and Wi-Fi capability. Special learning facilities include an art gallery, radio station, a folklife museum, and a living history museum. **Physically Challenged Students:** 75% of the campus is accessible. Facilities include wheelchair ramps, elevators, special parking, specially equipped restrooms, special class scheduling, and lowered drinking fountains. **Special:** The college encourages internships, and some majors require internships. Study abroad, work-study programs, dual majors, an accelerated degree program in social work, and B.A.-B.S. degrees are offered. A liberal studies degree and nondegree study are available. There are 6 national honor societies, a freshman honors program, and 33 departmental honors programs. **Visiting:** There are regularly scheduled orientations for prospective students, including faculty information sessions, parent-to-parent and student-to-student sessions, and tours of the campus and residence halls. There are guides for informal visits, visitors may sit in on classes, and stay overnight. To schedule a visit, contact the Director of Admissions. **Campus Safety and Security:** Measures include 24-hour foot and vehicle patrol, self-defense education, and security escort services. There are emergency telephones, lighted pathways/sidewalks, and controlled access to dorms/residences.

REQUIREMENTS: Applicants must be graduates of an accredited secondary school or receive a GED certificate. Applicants should complete 18 high school academic credits. The Admissions Committee considers courses taken, grades, extracurricular activities, SAT or ACT scores, and recommendations. Personal interviews may be required for students lacking appropriate GPA or standardized test scores. AP and CLEP credits are accepted. Important factors in the admissions decision are advanced placement or honors courses, leadership record, and evidence of special talent. To graduate, students must complete at least 121 semester hours with a minimum GPA of 2.0. There are 37 hours of distribution requirements, including social sciences, natural sciences, English, religion/philosophy, math, literature, fine arts, and phys ed. A major may require up to 57 semester hours, and 30 hours of the total must be in upper-level courses. **Procedure:** Freshmen are admitted to all sessions. There are deferred admissions and rolling admissions plans. Application deadlines are open. The fall 2017 application fee was $25. Notification is sent on a rolling basis. Applications are accepted on-line. **Transfer Students:** 73 transfer students enrolled in 2016-2017. Applicants for transfer must be in good academic standing at their current schools. 32 of 127 credits required for the bachelor's degree must be completed at Ferrum. **International Students:** There are 9 international students enrolled. They must take the TOEFL. They must also take the SAT or ACT.

ADMISSIONS: 78% of the 2017-2018 applicants were accepted. 13% of the current freshmen were in the top fifth of their class; 33% were in the top two fifths. **Admissions Contact:** Jason Byrd, Dean of Admissions. Email: *admissions@ferrum.edu* Web: *www.ferrum.edu*

FINANCIAL AID: In 2017-2018, 99% of all full-time freshmen received some form of financial aid and need-based aid. The state aid form is required. The FAFSA code is 003711. The deadline for filing freshman financial aid applications for fall entry is April 1.

GEORGE MASON UNIVERSITY E-2

www.gmu.edu

Fairfax, VA 22030 **(703) 993-2400**

Fax: (703) 993-4622
Full-time: 7147 men, 8042 women
Part-time: 2203 men, 2310 women
Graduate: 5117 men, 7248 women
Year: semesters, summer session
Room & Board: $7700

SAT CR/M: 560/570 **ACT:** required
Application Deadline: January 15

Email: admissions@gmu.edu
Faculty: 1041; I, -$
Ph.D.s: 90%
Student/Faculty: 15 to 1
Tuition: $12,184 ($34,630)
Freshman Class: 13732 applied, 8691 accepted, 2656 enrolled
CEEB CODE: 5827
COMPETITIVE

George Mason University, founded in 1972, is an entrepreneurial public institution with national distinction in a range of academic fields. The university has undergraduate and graduate degree programs in engineering, information technology, biotechnology, and health care. The figures given in the above capsule and in this profile are approximate. There are 8 undergraduate schools and 11 graduate schools. In addition to regional accreditation, George Mason University has baccalaureate program accreditation with AACSB, ABET, CSAB, CSWE, NASM, NCATE, ACS, CAAHEP, and CCNE. The 806-acre campus is in a suburban area in the Greater Washington Metropolitan area, 21 miles southwest of Washington, D.C. Including any residence halls, there are 115 buildings.

STUDENT LIFE: 88% of undergraduates are from Virginia. Others are from 50 states, 131 foreign countries, and Canada. 86% are from public schools. 9% are African American; 9% Hispanic; 7% Foreign; 59% White; 16% Asian American. **Female To Male Ratio:** 1.2:1. The average age of freshmen is 18; all undergraduates, 23. 15% do not continue beyond their first year; 69% remain to graduate. **Housing:** 5057 students can be accommodated in college housing, which includes dorms, on-campus apartments, and off-campus apartments. In addition, there are honors houses and special-interest houses. On-campus housing is guaranteed for all 4 years, and is available on a first-come, first-served basis. 74% of students commute. All students may keep cars.

FACULTY/CLASSROOMS: 55% of faculty are male; 45% are female. 84% teach undergraduates. Graduate students teach 12% of introductory courses. The average class size in an introductory lecture is 43; in a laboratory is 23; and in a regular course is 25.

PROGRAMS OF STUDY: GMU confers B.A., B.S., B.F.A., B.I.S., B.S.E.D., and B.S.N. degrees. Master's and doctoral degrees are also awarded. Bachelor's degrees are awarded in AGRICULTURE (environmental studies), BIOLOGICAL SCIENCE (biology/biological science and neurosciences), BUSINESS (accounting, banking and finance, business administration and management, marketing/retailing/merchandising, operations management, and tourism), COMMUNICATIONS AND THE ARTS (art history and appreciation, communications, communications technology, dance, dramatic arts, English, film arts, French, music, Spanish, video, and visual and performing arts), COMPUTER AND PHYSICAL SCIENCE (astronomy, chemistry, computer science, earth science, geology, information sciences and systems, mathematics, physics, science and management, and software engineering), EDUCATION (athletic training and physical education), ENGINEERING AND ENVIRONMENTAL DESIGN (civil engineering, computational sciences, computer engineering, electrical/electronics engineering, industrial engineering, and systems engineering), HEALTH PROFESSIONS (community health work, health science, medical technology, and nursing), SOCIAL SCIENCE (anthropology, criminal justice, economics, geography, history, interdisciplinary studies, international relations, Latin American studies, parks and recreation management, philosophy, political science/government, psychology, public administration, religion, Russian and Slavic studies, social work, and sociology). Accounting, biology, and psychology have the largest enrollments.

ACTIVITIES: 7% of men belong to 23 national fraternities; 6% of women belong to 15 national sororities. There are 255 groups on campus, including art, band, cheerleading, chess, choir, chorale, chorus, computers, dance, drama, environmental, ethnic, film, forensics, honors, international, jazz band, LGBT, literary magazine, musical theater, newspaper, opera, orchestra, pep band, photography, political, professional, radio and TV, religious, social, social service, student government, symphony, and yearbook. Popular campus events include Welcome Week, Mason Day, and Patriot Day. **Sports:** There are 11 intercollegiate sports for men and 11 for women, and 11 intramural sports for men and 11 for women. Facilities include an arena for basketball, indoor soccer, a sports and recreation complex that includes a 200-meter track, basketball, handball/racquetball, tennis, volleyball courts, baseball and softball diamonds, batting cages, weight room, a golf and archery net, 400-meter outdoor track, and playing fields. The aquatic and fitness center with cardio and weight training equipment, a recreational pool, and Olympic-size competition pool and diving well. **Graduates:** From July 1, 2016 to June 30, 2017, 4009 bachelor's degrees were awarded. The most popular majors were business/marketing (22%), social sciences (14%), and English (9%). In an average class, 2% graduate in 3 years or less, 39% graduate in 4 years or less, 58% graduate in 5 years or less, and 63% graduate in 6 years or less.

SERVICES: Counseling and information services are available, as is tutoring in most subjects. There is a reader service for the blind. Additional tutoring is offered for a fee. **Library/Resources:** The library contains 1.9 million volumes, 3.2 million microform items, 43,289 audio/video tapes/CDs/DVDs, and subscribes to 56,433 periodicals including electronic. Computerized library services include interlibrary loans, database searching, Internet access, and Wi-Fi capability. Special learning facilities include an art gallery, radio station, TV station, an astronomy observatory, and the Smithsonian Conservation and Research Center. **Physically Challenged Students:** 95% of the campus is accessible. Facilities include wheelchair ramps, elevators, special parking, specially equipped restrooms, special class scheduling, lowered drinking fountains, lowered telephones, and special housing. Special arrangements can be made for testing, readers, note takers, and interpreters. **Special:** Mason offers internships through academic departments and on-campus work-study programs. Also available are dual and student-designed majors, accelerated degrees, non-degree study, and pass/fail options. New Century College is an integrated program of study that emphasizes collaboration, experimental learning, and self-reflection. Mason also offers the Smithsonian Semester, a 16-credit resident program in conservation studies at the Smithsonian Conservation and Research Center in Front Royal, Virginia. There are 4 national honor societies, a freshman honors program, and 1 departmental honors program. **Visiting:** There are regularly scheduled orientations for prospective students, including campus tours and an information session. There are guides for informal visits and visitors may sit in on classes. To schedule a visit, contact the Admissions Office. **Campus Safety and Security:** Measures include 24-hour foot and vehicle patrol, emergency notification system, self-defense education, and security escort services. There are shuttle buses, lighted pathways/sidewalks, controlled access to dorms/residences. There are security call boxes located throughout the campus.

REQUIREMENTS: The ACT is recommended. A score-optional review of applications allows applicants to be considered for admission without submitting test scores. Applicants must be graduates of an accredited secondary school or have a GED certificate. A minimum high school GPA of 3.5 is recommended. A minimum of 18 academic credits is required, including 4 years of English, 3 each of math, science, lab science, social studies, and academic electives, and 2 of foreign language. A written personal statement, and a GPA of 2.0 are required. AP and CLEP credits are accepted. Important factors in the admissions decision are advanced placement or honors courses, evidence of special talent, and recommendations by school officials. To graduate, all students must complete a core of study that includes 6 credits written communication, 3 to 4 credits information technology, 4 credits lab science, 3 credits each oral communication, quantitative reasoning, literature, arts, Western civilization/world history, social and behavioral science, natural science, and global understanding, and 1 to 6 credits synthesis as well as at least 45 hours of upper-division work. Hours in the major vary. A minimum 2.0 GPA is required and a total of 120 to 133 credit hours must be completed. **Procedure:** Freshmen are admitted fall, spring, and summer. Entrance exams should be taken during the spring of the junior year. There is a deferred admissions plan. Applications should be filed by January 15 for fall entry; October 15 for spring entry. The fall 2017 application fee was $75. Notifications are sent April 1. Applications are accepted on-line. **Transfer Students:** 2600 transfer students enrolled in 2016-2017. Applicants must have a minimum 2.0 GPA and generally have completed 30 or more transferable credits from an accredited college or university. Official transcripts (including high school if 30 credits or less have been completed) are required. SAT or ACT scores must be submitted if 30 credits or less have been completed unless applicant graduated from high school more than 5 years before application. 30 of 120 credits required for the bachelor's degree must be completed at Mason. **International Students:** There are 488 international students enrolled. They must take the TOEFL with a minimum score of 570 on the paper-based TOEFL (PBT) or 88 on the Internet-based version (iBT). They must also take the SAT or ACT.

ADMISSIONS: 63% of the 2017-2018 applicants were accepted. The SAT scores for the 2017-2018 freshman class were: Critical Reading-- 15% below 500, 52% between 500 and 599, 28% between 600 and 699, and 6% between 700 and 800. Math-- 12% below 500, 49% between 500 and 599, 34% between 600 and 699, and 5% between 700 and 800. The ACT scores were 4% below 12, 30% between 12 and 17, 37% between 18 and 23, 15% between 24 and 29, and 14% above 30. 44% of the current freshmen were in the top fifth of their class; 83% were in the top two fifths. **Admissions Contact:** Andrew Flagel, Dean of Undergraduate Admissions. Email: *admissions@gmu.edu* Web: *www.gmu.edu*

FINANCIAL AID: In 2017-2018, 67% of all full-time freshmen received some form of financial aid. 43% of all full-time freshmen received need-based aid. The average freshman award was $12,012. Need-based scholarships or need-based grants averaged $7,182 ($24,800 maximum); need-based self-help aid (loans and jobs) averaged $3,660 ($8,500 maximum); non-need-based athletic scholarships averaged $16,156 ($36,533 maximum); and other non-need-based awards and non-need-based scholarships averaged $5,940 ($33,540 maximum). The average financial indebtedness of the 2017 graduate was $19,582. The FAFSA code is 003749. The priority date for freshman financial aid applications for fall entry is March 1.

HAMPDEN-SYDNEY COLLEGE D-3

www.hsc.edu

Hampden-Sydney, VA 23943	**(434) 223-6120** **(800) 755-0733**
Fax: (434) 223-6346	**Email: hsapp@hsc.edu**
Full-time: 1045 men, 1 women	**Faculty:** 95; IIB, av$
Part-time: n/av	**Ph.D.s:** 89%
Graduate: n/av	**Student/Faculty:** 10 to 1
Year: semesters, summer session	**Tuition:** $44,386
Room & Board: $13,420	**Freshman Class:** 3573 applied, 1967 accepted, 312 enrolled
SAT CR/M: 587/571 **ACT:** 25	**CEEB CODE:** 5291
Application Deadline: March 1	**VERY COMPETITIVE**

Hampden-Sydney College, founded in 1775, is a private men's liberal arts institution affiliated with the Presbyterian Church. There is 1 undergraduate school. The 1343-acre campus is in a rural area 60 miles southwest of Richmond. Including any residence halls, there are 121 buildings.

STUDENT LIFE: 69% of undergraduates are from Virginia. Others are from 26 states, and 9 foreign countries. 65% are from public schools. 86% are White; 4% African American; 4% Hispanic; 3% two or more races; 1% American Indian/Alaska Native; 1% race unknown. 64% are Protestant; 19% claim no religious affiliation; 15% Catholic. **Male To Female Ratio:** 1045.0:1. The average age of freshmen is 18; all undergraduates, 20. 16% do not continue beyond their first year; 70% remain to graduate. **Housing:** 1122 students can be accommodated in college housing, which includes single-sex and married student dorms, on-campus apartments, and off-campus apartments. In addition, there are honors houses, language/international houses, special-interest houses, fraternity houses, minority student house, men's dorm, theme housing, substance-free house, and foreign & LGBT inclusion house. On-campus housing is guaranteed for all 4 years. 95% of students live on campus. All students may keep cars.

FACULTY/CLASSROOMS: 74% of faculty are male; 26% are female. All teach undergraduates and do research. No introductory courses are taught by graduate students. The average class size in an introductory lecture is 14; in a laboratory is 14; and in a regular course is 14.

PROGRAMS OF STUDY: Hampden-Sydney confers B.A. and B.S. degrees. Bachelor's degrees are awarded in BIOLOGICAL SCIENCE (biology/biological science and molecular biology), BUSINESS (business economics), COMMUNICATIONS AND THE ARTS (classics, English, French, German, Greek, Latin, Spanish, studio art, theatre arts, theatre studies, and visual and performing arts), COMPUTER AND PHYSICAL SCIENCE (applied mathematics, chemistry, computer science, mathematics, and physics), ENGINEERING AND ENVIRONMENTAL DESIGN (engineering physics), SOCIAL SCIENCE (economics, history, humanities, international relations, philosophy, political science/government, psychology, and religion). Sciences, economics, and rhetoric are the strongest academically. Economics & business, economics, and biology have the largest enrollments.

ACTIVITIES: 34% of men belong to 11 national fraternities. There are no sororities. There are 83 groups on campus, including and mountain climbing, art, band, chess, choir, chorale, chorus, communications, computers, debate, drama, environmental, ethnic, film, honors, international, LGBT, literary magazine, newspaper, photography, political, professional, radio and TV, religious, social, social service, student government, and yearbook. Other groups are Union Philanthropic Literary Society, that facilitates lively discussion and debate about current events; and Outsiders, that hosts trips such as white-water kayaking. Popular campus events include Greek Week, Macon Week, and Midwinters CAC events. **Sports:** There are 11 intercollegiate sports for men, and 12 intramural sports for men. Facilities include a field house with indoor basketball courts, outdoor basektball courts, racquetball/handball courts, an outdoor track, a pool, squash courts, a weight room, gym, tennis courts, a beach volleyball court, and many playing fields. **Graduates:** From July 1, 2016 to June 30, 2017, 216 bachelor's degrees were awarded. The most popular majors were economics and business (30%), economics (14%), and biology (13%). In an average class, 61% graduate in 4 years or less, 63% graduate in 5 years or less, and 64% graduate in 6 years or less. Of the 2016 graduating class, 10% were enrolled in graduate school within 6 months of graduation, and 35% were employed.

SERVICES: Counseling and information services are available, as is tutoring in every subject. **Library/Resources:** The library contains 232,898 volumes, 6,841 microform items, and 10,631 audio/video tapes/CDs/DVDs, and subscribes to 53 periodicals including electronic. Computerized library services include interlibrary loans, database searching, Internet access, and Wi-Fi capability. Special learning facilities include an art gallery, planetarium, radio station, an international communications center, college history museum, an observatory, men's studies, Wilson Center for Leadership, and an energy research laboratory. **Physically Challenged Students:** 80% of the campus is accessible. Facilities include wheelchair ramps, elevators, special parking, specially equipped restrooms, special class scheduling, lowered drinking fountains, and lowered telephones. **Special:** The college offers co-op programs with Longwood, Randolph-Macon, Randolph College, Hollins, Mary Baldwin University and Washington and Lee University. Cross-registration with Longwood College, internships, study abroad, a 3-2 engineering program with the University of Virginia, dual-degree program in Physics and Engineering from Hampden-Sydney College and Old Dominion University, Eastern Virginia Medical School Joint program, The George Washington University School of Medicine Early Selection program, the VCU-MCV early selection program, Duke University Fuqua School of Business Early Admission program; Master of Management Studies, The UVA Darden School of Business preferred consideration program; Master of Business Administration, Washington semester, work-study programs, B.A.-B.S. degree, and dual majors are available. There is a public service concentration in all majors. There are 15 national honor societies, Phi Beta Kappa, a freshman honors program, and 11 departmental honors programs. **Visiting:** There are regularly scheduled orientations for prospective students, consisting of lectures, information sessions, tours, and an athletic event. There are guides for informal visits, visitors may sit in on classes, and stay overnight. To schedule a visit, contact Rachel N. Atkinson at (434) 223-6123. **Campus Safety and Security:** Measures include 24-hour foot and vehicle patrol, emergency notification system, and self-defense education. There are emergency telephones, lighted pathways/sidewalks, controlled access to dorms/residences, There is also a fire department on campus and a first responder unit for emergency medical assistance. The dorm phone lines are connected to 911.

REQUIREMENTS: The SAT or ACT is required. Applicants must be graduates of an accredited secondary school and have completed 16 high school academic credits, including 4 of English, 3-4 of math, 2 of foreign language, and 2-3 of science; of those 1 must be lab, and 1 each of social studies, and history, and 3 academic electives. An essay is required and an interview is recommended. The GED is accepted. AP credits are accepted. Important factors in the admissions decision are advanced placement or honors courses and personality/intangible qualities. To graduate, students must complete 120 credit hours with a minimum GPA of 2.0. Distribution requirements include 7 courses in humanities,

4 in math and natural sciences, and 3 in social sciences. All students must also take rhetoric and foreign language and pass a rhetoric exam. **Procedure:** Freshmen are admitted in the fall and spring. Entrance exams should be taken during the junior or senior year of high school. There are early decision and early admissions plans. Early decision applications should be filed by November 1; regular applications, by March 1 for fall entry; and December 1 for spring entry. The fall 2017 application fee was $30. Notification of early decision is sent December 1; regular decision, April 15. 74 early decision candidates were accepted for the 2017-2018 class. Applications are accepted on-line. **Transfer Students:** 114 transfer students enrolled in 2016-2017. Applicants must have high school transcript, college transcript(s), an essay or personal statement, standardized test scores, and statement of good standing from prior institutions, a minimum GPA of 2.5, and must take either the SAT or the ACT. An interview is recommended. Student may transfer in the spring and fall 60 of 120 credits required for the bachelor's degree must be completed at Hampden-Sydney. **International Students:** There are 11 international students enrolled. They must take the TOEFL with a minimum score of 114 on the Internet-based version (iBT). They must also take the SAT or ACT.

ADMISSIONS: 55% of the 2017-2018 applicants were accepted. The SAT scores for the 2017-2018 freshman class were: Critical Reading-- 14% below 500, 42% between 500 and 599, 36% between 600 and 699, and 9% between 700 and 800. Math-- 16% below 500, 47% between 500 and 599, 32% between 600 and 699, and 5% between 700 and 800. 14% of the current freshmen were in the top fifth of their class; 33% were in the top two fifths. **Admissions Contact:** Anita H. Garland, Dean of Admissions. Email: *hsapp@hsc.edu* Web: *www.hsc.edu*

FINANCIAL AID: In 2017-2018, 100% of all full-time freshmen received some form of financial aid. 73% of all full-time freshmen received need-based aid. The average freshman award was $35,420. Need-based scholarships or need-based grants averaged $29,908 ($40,000 maximum); need-based self-help aid (loans and jobs) averaged $5,183 ($11,000 maximum); and other non-need-based awards and non-need-based scholarships averaged $17,872 ($35,000 maximum). 22% of undergraduate students work part-time. The average financial indebtedness of the 2017 graduate was $35,921. The FAFSA code is 223713. The priority date for freshman financial aid applications for fall entry is March 1.

HAMPTON UNIVERSITY — F-3

www.hamptonu.edu

Hampton, VA 23668	(757) 727-5328 (800) 624-3328
Fax: (757) 727-5095	**Email:** helpdesk@hamptonu.edu
Full-time: 1189 men, 2462 women	**Faculty:** 288
Part-time: 58 men, 90 women	**Ph.D.s:** 84%
Graduate: 247 men, 573 women	**Student/Faculty:** 8 to 1
Year: semesters, summer session	**Tuition:** $25,192
Room & Board: $11,218	**Freshman Class:** n/av
SAT CR/M: 535/518 **ACT:** 22	**CEEB CODE:** 5292
Application Deadline: March 1	**COMPETITIVE**

Hampton University, founded in 1868, is a historically-black, private, university. Programs are offered through the following schools: Business, Engineering and Technology, Liberal Arts and Education, Scripps Howard School of Journalism and Communications, Nursing, Pharmacy, Science, University College, College of Virginia Beach, and the Graduate College. There are 9 undergraduate schools and 1 graduate school. In addition to regional accreditation, HU has baccalaureate program accreditation with ABET, ACEJMC, ACPE, NAAB, NASM, CAEP, ACS, IACBE, and CCNE. The 314-acre campus is in a suburban area 6 miles from Norfolk. Including any residence halls, there are 84 buildings.

STUDENT LIFE: 73% of undergraduates are from out of state, mostly the Northeast. Students are from 44 states, 22 foreign countries, and Canada. 90% are from public schools. 92% are African American; 4% White; 1% Asian American; 1% Hispanic; 1% Foreign; 1% race unknown. **Female To Male Ratio:** 2.1:1. The average age of freshmen is 18; all undergraduates, 20. **Housing:** 3066 students can be accommodated in college housing, which includes coed dorms and off-campus apartments. In addition, there are honors houses, and student cottages. On-campus housing is guaranteed for the freshman year only, is available on a first-come, first-served basis, and is available on a lottery system for upperclassmen. 64% of students live on campus. Alcohol is not permitted. Upperclassmen may keep cars.

FACULTY/CLASSROOMS: 50% of faculty are male; 50% are female. All teach undergraduates, and 10% do research. No introductory courses are taught by graduate students. The average class size in an introductory lecture is 50; in a laboratory is 20; and in a regular course is 25.

PROGRAMS OF STUDY: HU confers B.A., B.S., and B.S.Nurs. degrees. Associate, master's, and doctoral degrees are also awarded. Bachelor's degrees are awarded in BIOLOGICAL SCIENCE (biology/biological science), BUSINESS (accounting, banking and finance, business administration and management, marketing/retailing/merchandising, and sports management), COMMUNICATIONS AND THE ARTS (art, communications, dramatic arts, English, and music), COMPUTER AND PHYSICAL SCIENCE (chemistry, computer science, information sciences and systems, mathematics, and physics), EDUCATION (physical education), ENGINEERING AND ENVIRONMENTAL DESIGN (architecture, chemical engineering, and electrical/electronics engineering), HEALTH PROFESSIONS (nursing, recreation therapy, and speech pathology/audiology), SOCIAL SCIENCE (economics, history, political science/government, psychology, and sociology). Architecture, biology, and physics are the strongest academically. Biological sciences, psychology, and business administration have the largest enrollments.

ACTIVITIES: 5% of men belong to 5 national fraternities; 4% of women belong to 4 national sororities. There are 114 groups on campus, including art, band, cheerleading, choir, chorale, chorus, communications, computers, dance, debate, drama, drill team, environmental, ethnic, honors, international, jazz band, literary magazine, marching band, musical theater, newspaper, opera, orchestra, pep band, photography, political, professional, radio and TV, religious, social, social service, student government, symphony, and yearbook. Popular campus events include Career Day, High School Day, Parents' Weekend, Homecoming, Founder's Day, and Convocation. **Sports:** There are 8 intercollegiate sports for men and 9 for women, and 10 intramural sports for men and 10 for women. Facilities include a football stadium, Convocation Center, outdoor tennis courts, open fields for intramural sports, basketball courts, swimming pools, volleyball court, exercise and training room. A student center with health center, bowling, and indoor track. **Graduates:** From July 1, 2016 to June 30, 2017, 856 bachelor's degrees were awarded. The most popular majors were business/marketing (24%), communication/journalism (16%), and biologicial lige/psychology (9%). In an average class, 65% graduate in 6 years or less. Of the 2016 graduating class, 25% were enrolled in graduate school within 6 months of graduation, and 40% were employed.

SERVICES: Counseling and information services are available, as is tutoring in most subjects. There is remedial math, reading, and writing. **Library/Resources:** The library contains 411,671 volumes, 640,000 microform items, and 8,381 audio/video tapes/CDs/DVDs, and subscribes to 76,000 periodicals including electronic. Computerized library services include interlibrary loans, database searching, Internet access, and Wi-Fi capability. Special learning facilities include an art gallery, natural history museum, radio station, and TV station. **Physically Challenged Students:** 90% of the campus is accessible. Facilities include wheelchair ramps, elevators, special parking, specially equipped restrooms, lowered drinking fountains, lowered telephones, and special housing. **Special:** The college offers co-op programs in most majors, cross-registration with 6 schools, internships, and student-designed majors. Work study, study abroad, and dual majors are also available. Students may receive credit for life, military, and work experience. There are pass/fail options. There are 15 national honor societies and a freshman honors program. **Visiting:** There are regularly scheduled orientations for prospective students. We invite you to visit the campus and experience our diverse culture, beautiful scenery, and meet future classmates through group, personal, online, or virtual tour options. There are guides for informal visits and visitors may sit in on classes. To schedule a visit, contact the Office of Admission. **Campus Safety and Security:** Measures include 24-hour foot and vehicle patrol, emergency notification system, and self-defense education. There are shuttle buses, emergency telephones, lighted pathways/sidewalks, bike patrols, on-campus police officers, video cameras, gated campus, identification of valuables, limited access to campus, smoke detectors in residence halls, motorist assistance, and civilian support team.

REQUIREMENTS: Applicants must be graduates of an accredited secondary school, or the GED is accepted. Students should complete 17 Carnegie units, including 4 units of English, 3 units of math, (algebra

I and II and geometry), 2 years of science (chemistry and biology), 2 years of social studies, and 6 academic electives. An interview is recommended. Additional important factors that may be considered into the admissions decision are demonstrated leadership qualities, essays, and extracurricular activities. A GPA of 2.5 is required. AP and CLEP credits are accepted. Important factors in the admissions decision are advanced placement or honors courses, personality/intangible qualities, leadership record, extracurricular activities record, recommendations by school officials, and recommendations by alumni. Student must meet the minimum of 120 semester hours. A minimum cumulative GPA of 2.0. A grade of at least "C" (2.0) in all courses in the major area of study. Courses in General Education Sequence totaling 44-58 semester hours. Courses in major field, related subjects, and free electives totaling a minimum of 74 semester hours. The minimum number of credits needed to graduate is 120. Student must be in resident the final 30 semester hours prior to the completion of the degree requirements. Passing of English 101-102, Communication 103 and Computer Science 120 with grade of "C" (2.0) or better. **Procedure:** Freshmen are admitted in the fall and spring. Entrance exams should be taken during the junior year or fall of the senior year. There are early admissions, deferred admissions, and rolling admissions plans. Early decision applications should be filed by November 1; regular applications, by March 1 for fall entry; and November 1 for spring entry. The fall 2017 application fee was $35. Notification of early decision is sent December 31; regular decision, on a rolling basis. Applications are accepted on-line. **Transfer Students:** 68 transfer students enrolled in 2016-2017. Applicants for transfer must have a minimum GPA of 2.5 and 15 transferable hours. Students must have at least 60 semester or 90 quarter hours. 30 of 120 credits required for the bachelor's degree must be completed at HU. **International Students:** There are 26 international students enrolled. They must take the TOEFL with a minimum score of 550 on the paper-based TOEFL (PBT).

ADMISSIONS: 36% of the 2017-2018 applicants were accepted. The SAT scores for the 2017-2018 freshman class were: Critical Reading-- 31% below 500, 54% between 500 and 599, 14% between 600 and 699, and 1% between 700 and 800. Math-- 33% below 500, 57% between 500 and 599, 9% between 600 and 699, and 1% between 700 and 800. The ACT scores were 68% between 18 and 23, 28% between 24 and 29, and 4% above 30. 17% of the current freshmen were in the top fifth of their class; 35% were in the top two fifths. 2 freshmen graduated first in their class. **Admissions Contact:** Angela Boyd, Dean of Admission. Email: *helpdesk@hamptonu.edu* Web: *www.hamptonu.edu*

FINANCIAL AID: In 2017-2018, 66% of all full-time freshmen received some form of financial aid and need-based aid. The average freshman award was $5,975. Need-based scholarships or need-based grants averaged $5,355 ($24,370 maximum); need-based self-help aid (loans and jobs) averaged $7,854 ($36,298 maximum); non-need-based athletic scholarships averaged $26,510 ($34,926 maximum); and other non-need-based awards and non-need-based scholarships averaged $2,582 ($5,000 maximum). 7% of undergraduate students work part-time. The average financial indebtedness of the 2017 graduate was $36,260. The FAFSA code is 003714. The priority date for freshman financial aid applications for fall entry is February 15.

HOLLINS UNIVERSITY — C-3
www.hollins.edu

Roanoke, VA 24020	**(540) 362-6401** **(800) 456-9595**
Fax: (540) 362-6218	**Email: huadm@hollins.edu**
Full-time: 3 men, 638 women	**Faculty:** 70; IIB, av$
Part-time: 13 women	**Ph.D.s:** 97%
Graduate: 23 men, 122 women	**Student/Faculty:** 9 to 1
Year: 4-1-4	**Tuition:** $38,285
Room & Board: $13,120	**Freshman Class:** 2842 applied, 1375 accepted, 155 enrolled
SAT CR/M: 630/560 **ACT:** 26	**CEEB CODE:** 5294
Application Deadline: February 1	**VERY COMPETITIVE**

Hollins University, founded in 1842, is Virginia's first chartered women's college offering a broad liberal arts curriculum. The figures given in the above capsule and in this profile are approximate. There is 1 undergraduate school and 1 graduate school. The 475-acre campus is in a suburban area in Roanoke County. Including any residence halls, there are 73 buildings.

STUDENT LIFE: 53% of undergraduates are from out of state, mostly the South. Students are from 43 states, and 19 foreign countries. 84% are from public schools. 65% are White; 11% African American; 6% two or more races; 5% Hispanic; 5% Foreign; 4% race unknown; 2% Asian American; 1% American Indian/Alaska Native. 45% claim no religious affiliation; 29% Protestant; 20% Agnostic, Buddhist, Hindu, Muslim, Orthodox, Wicca, and Unitarian. **Female To Male Ratio:** 29.7:1. The average age of freshmen is 19; all undergraduates, 21. 23% do not continue beyond their first year; 53% remain to graduate. **Housing:** 688 students can be accommodated in college housing, which includes on-campus apartments. In addition, there are language/international houses, special-interest houses, a women's dorm, theme, and wellness housing. On-campus housing is guaranteed for all 4 years. 87% of students live on campus. All students may keep cars.

FACULTY/CLASSROOMS: 43% of faculty are male; 57% are female. All teach undergraduates. Graduate students teach 1% of introductory courses. The average class size in an introductory lecture is 11; in a laboratory is 11; and in a regular course is 14.

PROGRAMS OF STUDY: Hollins confers B.A., B.S., and B.A./B.F.A. degrees. Master's degrees are also awarded. Bachelor's degrees are awarded in AGRICULTURE (environmental studies), BIOLOGICAL SCIENCE (biology/biological science), BUSINESS (business administration and management), COMMUNICATIONS AND THE ARTS (art history and appreciation, classical languages, communications, dance, English, film arts, French, music, Spanish, studio art, and theatre arts), COMPUTER AND PHYSICAL SCIENCE (chemistry and mathematics), EDUCATION (classical studies), ENGINEERING AND ENVIRONMENTAL DESIGN (environmental science), SOCIAL SCIENCE (economics, gender studies, history, interdisciplinary studies, international studies, philosophy, political science/government, psychology, religion, and sociology). Art history, classical studies, and biology are the strongest academically. English/creative writing, biology, and psychology have the largest enrollments.

ACTIVITIES: There are no fraternities or sororities. There are 20 groups on campus, including art, choir, chorale, dance, drama, environmental, ethnic, film, honors, international, LGBT, literary magazine, musical theater, political, religious, social, social service, and student government. Popular campus events include Day of Service, Tinker Day, Ring Night, Founder's Day, Holiday Tea, Dance & Theatre Productions, and Women's History Month. **Sports:** There are 9 intercollegiate sports for women. Facilities include a swimming center, fitness center, weight rooms, a gym, an auxilary gym, an equestrian center, a 1.5-mile jogging loop, outdoor tennis courts, playing fields, a putting green, an exercise studio, training rooms, and a climbing wall. **Graduates:** From July 1, 2016 to June 30, 2017, 132 bachelor's degrees were awarded. The most popular majors were English/creative writing (21%), biology (12%), and business (12%). In an average class, 58% graduate in 4 years or less, 63% graduate in 5 years or less, and 63% graduate in 6 years or less. Of the 2016 graduating class, 29% were enrolled in graduate school within 6 months of graduation, and 68% were employed.

SERVICES: Counseling and information services are available, as is tutoring in most subjects. There is a reader service for the blind, and remedial writing. There is also a writing center and a quantitative reasoning center. **Library/Resources:** The library contains 243,837 volumes, 3,168 microform items, and 16,160 audio/video tapes/CDs/DVDs, and subscribes to 30,050 periodicals including electronic. Computerized library services include interlibrary loans, database searching, Internet access, and Wi-Fi capability. Special learning facilities include an art gallery. **Physically Challenged Students:** 42% of the campus is accessible. Facilities include wheelchair ramps, elevators, special parking, specially equipped restrooms, special class scheduling, lowered drinking fountains, and special housing. **Special:** Hollins offers internships during the January term, dual majors, student-designed majors, accelerated degrees, and study abroad in 16 countries. There is cross-registration with the Virginia Seven College Exchange and Roanoke College. A Washington Semester is available through The American University. There is also a domestic student exchange program. There are 17 national honor societies, Phi Beta Kappa, a freshman honors program, and 20 departmental honors programs. **Visiting:** There are regularly scheduled orientations for prospective students, including 2 open houses for seniors, in October and November. Sophomores and Juniors are invited to Spring Visit Day in March and May. Admitted students are invited to campus in April. There are guides for informal visits, visitors may sit in on classes, and stay overnight. To schedule a visit, contact Rena Musyt at (540) 362-6401. **Campus Safety and Security:** Measures include 24-hour foot and vehicle patrol, emergency notification system, self-defense education, and security escort services. There are emergency telephones, lighted pathways/sidewalks, and emergency buttons located along walkways and in labs.

REQUIREMENTS: The SAT or ACT is required. Applicants must be graduates of an accredited secondary school. With proper documentation, the GED and home-schooled students are accepted. Applicants should complete 16 high school academic credits, 4 credits of English and 3 credits each of math, science, and social studies, and 2 of foreign language. Official high school transcripts and letters of recommendation are required. An essay is also required, and an interview is recommended. AP credits are accepted. Important factors in the admissions decision are advanced placement or honors courses, personality/intangible qualities, and leadership record. To graduate, students must complete 128 credits for the B.A., 140 credits for the B.S., and 150 credits for the B.A./B.F.A., plus 4 short terms. At least 32 hours in the major and a 2.0 GPA are required. All students must fulfill Hollins' general education program (Education Through Skills and Perspectives). Students are also required to take 2 semesters of phys ed or participate in a varsity sport. A thesis is required for some majors. **Procedure:** Freshmen are admitted in the fall and spring. Entrance exams should be taken by January of the senior year. There are early decision, deferred admissions, and rolling admissions plans. Early decision applications should be filed by November 1; regular applications, by February 1 for fall entry; and December 1 for spring entry. Notification of early decision is sent November 15; regular decision, November 1. 5 early decision candidates were accepted for the 2017-2018 class. Applications are accepted on-line. **Transfer Students:** 12 transfer students enrolled in 2016-2017. Applicants for transfer should have a minimum college GPA of 2.5. Other criteria are the same as for entering freshmen, such as high school transcript, all college transcripts, an essay or personal statement, and a statement of good standing from prior institution (s). Students may enroll in the fall, and spring. 64 of 128 credits required for the bachelor's degree must be completed at Hollins. **International Students:** There are 34 international students enrolled. They must take the TOEFL with a minimum score of 550 on the paper-based TOEFL (PBT) or 79 on the Internet-based version (iBT). The SAT scores may be submitted in lieu of the TOEFL; however, if SAT scores are low the TOEFL may also be required.

ADMISSIONS: 48% of the 2017-2018 applicants were accepted. The SAT scores for the 2017-2018 freshman class were: Math-- 8% below 500, 61% between 500 and 599, 27% between 600 and 699, and 4% between 700 and 800. Evidence-Based Reading/Writing-- 29% below 500, 28% between 500 and 599, 54% between 600 and 699, and 17% between 700 and 800. The ACT scores were 3% between 12 and 17, 31% between 18 and 23, 50% between 24 and 29, and 16% above 30. 52% of the current freshmen were in the top fifth of their class; 84% were in the top two fifths. **Admissions Contact:** Ashley Browning, VP for Enrollment Management. Email: *huadm@hollins.edu* Web: *www.hollins.edu*

FINANCIAL AID: In 2017-2018, 100% of all full-time freshmen received some form of financial aid. 61% of all full-time freshmen received need-based aid. The average freshman award was $43,400. Need-based scholarships or need-based grants averaged $5,298 ($9,920 maximum); need-based self-help aid (loans and jobs) averaged $4,152 ($7,500 maximum); and other non-need-based awards and non-need-based scholarships averaged $39,117 ($58,652 maximum). 47% of undergraduate students work part-time. The average financial indebtedness of the 2017 graduate was $31,211. The state aid form, and FAFSA is recommended but not required. The FAFSA code is 003715. The priority date for freshman financial aid applications for fall entry is February 1.

JAMES MADISON UNIVERSITY — D-2

www.jmu.edu

Harrisonburg, VA 22807 — **(540) 568-5681**

Fax: (540) 568-3332
Email: admissions@jmu.edu
Full-time: 6999 men, 10330 women
Faculty: 840; IIA, av$
Part-time: 400 men, 378 women
Ph.D.s: 78%
Graduate: 559 men, 1261 women
Student/Faculty: 20 to 1
Year: semesters, summer session
Tuition: $10,066 ($25,200)
Room & Board: $9018
Freshman Class: 22648 applied, 14392 accepted, 4325 enrolled
SAT CR/M/W: 570/580/565 **ACT:** required
CEEB CODE: 5392
Application Deadline: January 15
VERY COMPETITIVE

James Madison University, founded in 1908, is a public institution with programs in science and math, business, education, arts and letters, visual and performing arts, and integrated science and technology. The figures given in the above capsule and in this profile are approximate. There are 7 undergraduate schools and 1 graduate school. In addition to regional accreditation, JMU has baccalaureate program accreditation with AACSB, ABET, ADA, AHEA, CSWE, FIDER, NASAD, NASM, CAEP, ACS, AOTA, APA, CACREP, and NAST. The 712-acre campus is in a small town 123 miles southwest of Washington, D.C. Including any residence halls, there are 111 buildings.

STUDENT LIFE: 71% of undergraduates are from Virginia. Others are from 45 states, 55 foreign countries, and Canada. 81% are White; 6% Asian American; 4% African American; 3% Hispanic; 1% Foreign; 1% two or more races. 32% are Catholic; 26% Protestant; 23% claim no religious affiliation. **Female To Male Ratio:** 1.5:1. The average age of freshmen is 18; all undergraduates, 21. 8% do not continue beyond their first year; 81% remain to graduate. **Housing:** 6100 students can be accommodated in college housing, which includes dorms and off-campus apartments. In addition, there are honors houses, special-interest houses, fraternity houses, sorority houses, substance-free and international communities, and living learning communities for education, health, psychology, community service, biology, ecology, wellness housing, and theme housing. On-campus housing is guaranteed for the freshman year only. 64% of students commute. Upperclassmen may keep cars.

FACULTY/CLASSROOMS: 52% of faculty are male; 48% are female. 92% teach undergraduates. Graduate students teach 1% of introductory courses. The average class size in an introductory lecture is 39; in a laboratory is 22; and in a regular course is 31.

PROGRAMS OF STUDY: JMU confers B.A., B.S., B.B.A., B.F.A., B.I.S., B.M., B.S.N., and B.S.W. degrees. Master's and doctoral degrees are also awarded. Bachelor's degrees are awarded in BIOLOGICAL SCIENCE (biology/biological science and biotechnology), BUSINESS (accounting, banking and finance, business administration and management, business economics, hospitality management services, international business management, marketing/retailing/merchandising, recreation and leisure services, and tourism), COMMUNICATIONS AND THE ARTS (art, art history and appreciation, communications, communications technology, dance, dramatic arts, English, fine arts, media arts, modern language, music, and speech/debate/rhetoric), COMPUTER AND PHYSICAL SCIENCE (chemistry, computer science, geology, information sciences and systems, mathematics, physics, quantitative methods, science technology, and statistics), EDUCATION (athletic training), ENGINEERING AND ENVIRONMENTAL DESIGN (engineering), HEALTH PROFESSIONS (health care administration, health science, nursing, and speech pathology/audiology), SOCIAL SCIENCE (anthropology, criminal justice, dietetics, economics, geography, history, international studies, liberal arts/general studies, philosophy, physical fitness/movement, political science/government, psychology, public administration, religion, social science, social work, and sociology). Interdisciplinary liberal studies, health science, and kinesiology have the largest enrollments.

ACTIVITIES: 12% of men belong to 15 national fraternities; 12% of women belong to 9 national sororities. There are 298 groups on campus, including art, band, cheerleading, chess, choir, chorale, chorus, computers, dance, drama, environmental, ethnic, honors, international, jazz band, LGBT, literary magazine, marching band, musical theater, newspaper, opera, orchestra, pep band, photography, political, professional, radio and TV, religious, social, social service, student government, symphony, and yearbook. Popular campus events include Madison Symposium, James Madison Week, and International Week. **Sports:** There are 6 intercollegiate sports for men and 12 for women, and 10 intramural sports for men and 10 for women. Facilities include a stadium, convocation center, an all-weather track, a gym, natatorium, tennis courts, lighted Astroturf field, and baseball, soccer, and softball fields. A recreation center houses a fitness center, racquetball courts, basketball gyms, an indoor track, a pool, and a climbing wall. **Graduates:** From July 1, 2016 to June 30, 2017, 4096 bachelor's degrees were awarded. The most popular majors were health professions and related programs (15%), business/marketing (14%), and communication/journalism (9%). In an average class, 64% graduate in 4 years or less, 80% graduate in 5 years or less, and 81% graduate in 6 years or less. Of the 2016 graduating class, 27% were enrolled in graduate school within 6 months of graduation, and 46% were employed.

SERVICES: Counseling and information services are available, as is tutoring in every subject. There is a reader service for the blind. Support is also available in time management, organization, test preparation, and test taking. **Library/Resources:** The library contains 645,740 volumes, 1.1 million microform items, and 42,676 audio/video tapes/CDs/DVDs, and subscribes to 12,662 periodicals including electronic. Computerized library services include interlibrary loans, database searching, and Internet access. Special learning facilities include an art gallery, planetarium, radio station, an arboretum, a music library, CISAT library services, a mineral museum, and science on a sphere. **Physically Challenged Students:** 90% of the campus is accessible. Facilities include wheelchair ramps, elevators, special parking, specially equipped restrooms, special class scheduling, lowered drinking fountains, lowered telephones, and special housing. **Special:** JMU offers internships, work-study programs, a Washington semester, and study abroad in London, Antwerp, Florence, and Salamanca. There is a combined program in forestry with Virginia Tech. An individualized study degree, nondegree study, pass/fail options, and credit for life, military, and work experience are available. There are 28 national honor societies, Phi Beta Kappa, a freshman honors program, and 82 departmental honors programs. **Visiting:** There are regularly scheduled orientations for prospective students, including daily campus tours during the week and on Saturdays, and tours following group conferences with admissions counselors. There are guides for informal visits. To schedule a visit, contact the Admissions Office. **Campus Safety and Security:** Measures include 24-hour foot and vehicle patrol, emergency notification system, self-defense education, and security escort services. There are emergency telephones, lighted pathways/sidewalks, and controlled access to dorms/residences. There are public bus transportation routes through the campus.

REQUIREMENTS: The SAT or ACT is required. Applicants must be graduates of an accredited secondary school. They must show solid achievement in 4 or more academic courses each year of high school including some honors or advanced coursework. A personal statement is optional. Art students must present a portfolio. Theater, dance, and music students must audition. Nursing students must apply to the nursing department in addition to applying for undergraduate admission. AP credits are accepted. Important factors in the admissions decision are advanced placement or honors courses, recommendations by school officials, and extracurricular activities record. To graduate, students must complete a minimum of 120 credit hours, with a GPA of at least 2.0, meet the general education requirements and the requirements of their major, have been enrolled at JMU a minimum of two regular semesters, and have earned a minimum of 30 credit hours at JMU during that period of enrollment. **Procedure:** Freshmen are admitted in the fall. Entrance exams should be taken in the spring of the junior year or the fall of the senior year. There are early admissions and deferred admissions plans. Early decision applications should be filed by November 1; regular applications, by January 15 for fall entry. The fall 2017 application fee was $50. Notification of early decision is sent January 15; regular decision, April 1. 1431 applicants were on the 2017 waiting list; 7 were admitted. Applications are accepted on-line. **Transfer Students:** 621 transfer students enrolled in 2016-2017. Applicants must have a minimum GPA of 2.0 and must submit a complete application, official college transcripts, and secondary school records or a copy of their GED. A one-page personal statement is optional. If applicants have fewer than 30 credit hours completed at the time of application, they must submit SAT scores unless they are 25 years old or older. 30 of 120 credits required for the bachelor's degree must be completed at JMU. **International Students:** There are 272 international students enrolled. They must take the TOEFL with a minimum score of 550 on the paper-based TOEFL (PBT) or 81 on the Internet-based version (iBT).

ADMISSIONS: 64% of the 2017-2018 applicants were accepted. The SAT scores for the 2017-2018 freshman class were: Critical Reading-- 13% below 500, 52% between 500 and 599, 31% between 600 and 699, and 4% between 700 and 800. Math-- 10% below 500, 47% between 500 and 599, 39% between 600 and 699, and 4% between 700 and 800. Writing-- 14% below 500, 51% between 500 and 599, 31% between 600 and 699, and 4% between 700 and 800. 21 freshmen graduated first in their class. **Admissions Contact:** Adam Anderson, Associate Dean of Admissions. Email: *admissions@jmu.edu* Web: *www.jmu.edu*

FINANCIAL AID: In 2017-2018, 32% of all full-time freshmen received some form of financial aid. 35% of all full-time freshmen received need-based aid. The average freshman award was $9,509. Need-based scholarships or need-based grants averaged $7,560; need-based self-help aid (loans and jobs) averaged $4,736; non-need-based athletic scholarships averaged $18,500; other non-need-based awards and non-need-based scholarships averaged $4,695; and $3,384 from other forms of aid. 20% of undergraduate students work part-time. The average financial indebtedness of the 2017 graduate was $23,562. The FAFSA code is 003721. The deadline for filing freshman financial aid applications for fall entry is March 1.

LIBERTY UNIVERSITY — D-3

www.liberty.edu

Lynchburg, VA 24502	**(434) 582-7307** **(800) 543-5317**
Fax: (434) 582-2421	**Email: admissions@liberty.edu**
Full-time: 2800 men, 3300 women	**Faculty:** 200
Part-time: 110 men, 120 women	**Ph.D.s:** 67%
Graduate: n/av	**Student/Faculty:** 31 to 1
Year: semesters, summer session	**Tuition:** $23,165
Room & Board: $8250	**Freshman Class:** n/av
SAT or ACT: required	**CEEB CODE:** 5385
Application Deadline: October 4	**COMPETITIVE**

Liberty University, founded in 1971, is a private liberal arts institution affiliated with the Baptist Church. The figures given in the above capsule and in this profile are approximate. There are 6 undergraduate schools and 5 graduate schools. In addition to regional accreditation, LU has baccalaureate program accreditation with NASM and NLN. The 160-acre campus is in a suburban area 45 miles east of Roanoke. Including any residence halls, there are 73 buildings.

STUDENT LIFE: 60% of undergraduates are from out of state, mostly the Middle Atlantic. Students are from 48 states, 76 foreign countries, and Canada. 78% are White; 4% Asian American; 3% Hispanic; 11% African American; 1% American Indian/Alaska Native. 89% are Protestant. **Female To Male Ratio:** 1.2:1. The average age of freshmen is 19; all undergraduates, 21. **Housing:** 4303 students can be accommodated in college housing, which includes dorms and on-campus apartments. On-campus housing is guaranteed for all 4 years. 64% of students live on campus. Alcohol is not permitted. All students may keep cars.

FACULTY/CLASSROOMS: 67% of faculty are male; 33% are female. 90% teach undergraduates. No introductory courses are taught by graduate students. The average class size in an introductory lecture is 43; in a laboratory is 22; and in a regular course is 23.

PROGRAMS OF STUDY: LU confers B.A., B.S., B.M., and B.S.N. degrees. Associate, master's, and doctoral degrees are also awarded. Bachelor's degrees are awarded in BIOLOGICAL SCIENCE (biology/biological science), BUSINESS (accounting, business administration and management, management information systems, and sports management), COMMUNICATIONS AND THE ARTS (communications, English, English as a second/foreign language, music, and Spanish), COMPUTER AND PHYSICAL SCIENCE (computer science and mathematics), EDUCATION (athletic training, elementary education, and physical education), HEALTH PROFESSIONS (community health work, exercise science, and nursing), SOCIAL SCIENCE (family/consumer studies, history, interdisciplinary studies, international studies, liberal arts/general studies, political science/government, psychology, religion, and social science). Education, psychology, and business are the strongest academically. Business, psychology, and education have the largest enrollments.

ACTIVITIES: There are no fraternities or sororities. There are 40 groups on campus, including band, cheerleading, choir, chorale, chorus, communications, computers, debate, drama, drill team, ethnic, honors, international, marching band, musical theater, newspaper, opera, orchestra, pep band, political, professional, radio and TV, religious, social service, student government, and yearbook. Popular campus events include Super Conference, and Missions Emphasis Week. **Sports:** There are 9 intercollegiate sports for men and 8 for women, and 16 intramural sports for men and 16 for women. Facilities include football stadium, basketball arena/convention center, baseball and soccer fields, a track complex, and a tennis center. **Graduates:** From July 1, 2016 to June 30, 2017, 945 bachelor's degrees were awarded. The most popular majors were psychology (17%), business (16%), and religion (14%).

SERVICES: Counseling and information services are available, as is tutoring in every subject. There is remedial math, reading, and writing. **Library/Resources:** The library contains 211,092 volumes, 95,329 microform items, 7,149 audio/video tapes/CDs/DVDs, and subscribes to 10,806 periodicals including electronic. Computerized library services include interlibrary loans, database searching, and Internet access. Special learning facilities include a radio station and TV station. **Physically Challenged Students:** 90% of the campus is accessible. Facilities include wheelchair ramps, elevators, special parking, specially equipped restrooms, special class scheduling, lowered drinking fountains, lowered telephones, and special housing. **Special:** Liberty offers internships, B.A.-B.S. degrees, and student-designed majors in interdisciplinary and general studies. There are 8 national honor societies, Phi Beta Kappa, and a freshman honors program. **Visiting:** There are regularly scheduled orientations for prospective students, a 2-day program where applicants can attend classes and special meetings. There are guides for informal visits, visitors may sit in on classes, and stay overnight. To schedule a visit, contact the Visitor's Center at visitorscenter@liberty.edu. **Campus Safety and Security:** Measures include 24-hour foot and vehicle patrol, self-defense education, and security escort services. There are shuttle buses and lighted pathways/sidewalks.

REQUIREMENTS: The SAT or ACT is required. Applicants must have completed 16 high school academic credits. The GED is accepted. An essay is required. AP and CLEP credits are accepted. Important factors in the admissions decision are recommendations by school officials and advanced placement or honors courses. Students must complete 120 to 123 credit hours to graduate, with a minimum GPA of 2.0. with few exceptions, by major, all must complete 18 hours of foundational studies in English, math, speech communications, and general education. An additional 42 credits of investigative studies are required; these vary according to the degree sought, either B.A. or B.S., but include English, natural sciences, history, arts, music, languages, government, social sciences, philosophy, theology, Bible studies, and integrated studies. **Procedure:** Freshmen are admitted to all sessions. Entrance exams should be taken during the junior year. There are early decision, early admissions, deferred admissions, and rolling admissions plans. Application deadlines are open. The fall 2017 application fee was $35. Notification is sent on a rolling basis. Applications are accepted on-line. **Transfer Students:** 743 transfer students enrolled in 2016-2017. Applicants for transfer must have a GPA of 2.0. If transferring fewer than 60 hours, a high school transcript and test scores are required. 30 of 120 credits required for the bachelor's degree must be completed at LU. **International Students:** There are 238 international students enrolled. They must take the TOEFL or MELAB. They must also take the SAT or ACT.

Admissions Contact: David Hart, Associate Director of Admissions. Email: *admissions@liberty.edu* Web: *www.liberty.edu*

FINANCIAL AID: In 2017-2018, 98% of all full-time freshmen received some form of financial aid. 64% of all full-time freshmen received need-based aid. The average freshman award was $8,506. Need-based scholarships or need-based grants averaged $1,800 ($4,000 maximum); need-based self-help aid (loans and jobs) averaged $3,725 ($3,940 maximum); non-need-based athletic scholarships averaged $8,172 ($18,850 maximum); and other non-need-based awards and non-need-based scholarships averaged $4,667 ($15,220 maximum). 15% of undergraduate students work part-time. The average financial indebtedness of the 2017 graduate was $15,619. The FAFSA code is 010392. The priority date for freshman financial aid applications for fall entry is September 18.

LONGWOOD UNIVERSITY — D-3

www.longwood.edu

Farmville, VA 23909	**(434) 395-2060** **(800) 281-4677**
Fax: (434) 395-2332	**Email: admissions@longwood.edu**
Full-time: 1283 men, 2635 women	**Faculty:** 238; IIA, av$
Part-time: 166 men, 291 women	**Ph.D.s:** 77%
Graduate: 77 men, 430 women	**Student/Faculty:** 18 to 1
Year: semesters, summer session	**Tuition:** $22,184 ($36,614)
Room & Board: see profile	**Freshman Class:** 4055 applied, 3299 accepted, 1111 enrolled
SAT CR/M: 500/500 **ACT:** 21	**CEEB CODE:** 5368
Application Deadline: March 1	**COMPETITIVE**

Longwood University, founded in 1839, is a state-supported institution with programs in liberal arts, business, and teacher preparation. The figures given in the above capsule includes tuition, and fees for 15 credit hours, including room and board on a 14 meal/week plan. There are 3 undergraduate schools and 1 graduate school. In addition to regional accreditation, LU has baccalaureate program accreditation with AACSB, CSWE, NASM, NCATE, and NRPA. The 160-acre campus is in a small town 60 miles west of Richmond and 60 miles south of Charlottesville. Including any residence halls, there are 44 buildings.

STUDENT LIFE: 94% of undergraduates are from Virginia. Others are from 39 states, 23 foreign countries, and Canada. 93% are from public schools. 9% are African American; 76% White; 4% Hispanic; 4% race unknown; 3% two or more races; 1% Asian American; 1% Foreign. **Female To Male Ratio:** 2.2:1. The average age of freshmen is 18; all undergraduates, 20. 20% do not continue beyond their first year; 66% remain to graduate. **Housing:** College-sponsored housing includes dorms and off-campus apartments. In addition, there are honors houses, a substance-free dorm, international studies, fraternity/sorority, and ecology floors. On-campus housing is guaranteed for the freshman year only, is available on a first-come, first-served basis, and is available on a lottery system for upperclassmen. 74% of students live on campus. Upperclassmen may keep cars.

FACULTY/CLASSROOMS: 45% of faculty are male; 55% are female. All teach undergraduates, 50% do research, and 50% do both. No introductory courses are taught by graduate students. The average class size in an introductory lecture is 21 and in a regular course is 21.

PROGRAMS OF STUDY: LU confers B.A., B.S., B.F.A., B.M., and B.S.B.A. degrees. Master's degrees are also awarded. Bachelor's degrees are awarded in BIOLOGICAL SCIENCE (biology/biological science), BUSINESS (business administration and management), COMMUNICATIONS AND THE ARTS (art, communications, English, modern language, music, and visual and performing arts), COMPUTER AND PHYSICAL SCIENCE (chemistry, computer science, mathematics, and physics), EDUCATION (art education, athletic training, elementary education, music education, physical education, and special education), HEALTH PROFESSIONS (community health work, nursing, and recreation therapy), SOCIAL SCIENCE (anthropology, criminal justice, criminology, economics, history, liberal arts/general studies, political science/government, psychology, social work, and sociology). Natural sciences, and secondary education are the strongest academically. Business, biology, and elementary education have the largest enrollments.

ACTIVITIES: 22% of men belong to 12 national fraternities; 22% of women belong to 10 national sororities. There are 176 groups on campus, including art, band, cheerleading, chess, choir, chorus, computers, dance, drama, ethnic, honors, international, jazz band, LGBT, musical theater, newspaper, pep band, photography, political, professional, radio and TV, religious, social, social service, and student government. Popular campus events include Spring Weekend, and Oktoberfest. **Sports:** There are 6 intercollegiate sports for men and 8 for women, and 14 intramural sports for men and 16 for women. Facilities include a 9-hole golf course, a weight training area, a gym, racquetball courts, lighted tennis courts, pools, a bowling alley, sand volleyball courts, a fitness trail, a frisbee golf course, outdoor basketball courts, soccer, baseball, and softball fields. **Graduates:** In an average class, 1% graduate in 3 years or less, 40% graduate in 4 years or less, 56% graduate in 5 years or less, and 59% graduate in 6 years or less.

SERVICES: Counseling and information services are available, as is tutoring in some subjects, such as learning strategies, study skills, organizational skills and time management. There is a reader service for the blind, and remedial writing. There is also assistance in study skills, learning strategies, advocacy training, and compensatory strategy instruction. **Library/Resources:** The library contains 362,151 volumes, 667,409 microform items, and 23,331 audio/video tapes/CDs/DVDs. Computerized library services include interlibrary loans, database searching, Internet access, and Wi-Fi capability. Special learning facilities include an art gallery, radio station, a greenhouse, a language lab, 6 computer labs, and psychology lab. **Physically Challenged Students:** Facilities include wheelchair ramps, elevators, special parking, special class scheduling, lowered drinking fountains, lowered telephones, and special housing. **Special:** Longwood offers internships or directed research projects in all majors, study abroad in 15 countries, and B.A.-B.S. degrees in many majors. Cross-registration is possible with Hampden-Sydney College, as are 3-2 engineering degrees with several regional universities. Also, there is a 3-3 preprofessional program in physical therapy with University of Virginia, Old Dominion, and Virginia Commonwealth Universities. There are 10 national honor societies and a freshman honors program. **Visiting:** There are regularly scheduled orientations for prospective students, including informational and tour programs, and open houses September to December and March to May. Visitors may sit in on classes and stay overnight. To schedule a visit, contact the Admissions Office. **Campus Safety and Security:** Measures include 24-hour foot and vehicle patrol, emergency notification system, self-defense education, and security escort services. There are shuttle buses, emergency telephones, lighted pathways/sidewalks, controlled access to dorms/residences, electronic card key entry into dorms, and video cameras.

REQUIREMENTS: The SAT or ACT is required. Applicants must be graduates of an accredited secondary school; the GED is accepted. Students should complete 4 years of high school English, 2 years of foreign language and 3 years of science (including 2 lab courses), 2 years each of history, algebra I, II, and geometry. A personal statement is required. An audition is required for music students. AP and CLEP credits are accepted. Important factors in the admissions decision are advanced placement or honors courses, leadership record, and evidence of special talent. To graduate, students must complete 120 to 145 credits, including 36 to 77 in the major, with a minimum GPA of 2.0 overall. A 41-hour general education core curriculum, 4 intensive writing courses, a phys ed course, and 30 upper-level credit hours are also required. **Procedure:** Freshmen are admitted to all sessions. Entrance exams should be taken in the fall of the senior year. There are early admissions and rolling admissions plans. Early decision applications should be filed by December 1; regular applications, by March 1 for fall entry; October 15 for winter entry; October 15 for spring entry; and March 1 for summer entry. The fall 2017 application fee was $50. Notification is sent on a rolling basis. Applications are accepted on-line. **Transfer Students:** 214 transfer students enrolled in 2016-2017. Applicants for transfer must have a GPA of at least 2.5 in all college coursework attempted. Other criteria are the same as for entering freshmen. 30 of 120 credits required for the bachelor's degree must be completed at LU. **International Students:** They must take the TOEFL with a minimum score of 550 on the paper-based TOEFL (PBT) or 79 on the Internet-based version (iBT). They must also take the SAT or ACT.

ADMISSIONS: 81% of the 2017-2018 applicants were accepted. The SAT scores for the 2017-2018 freshman class were: Critical Reading-- 43% below 500, 44% between 500 and 599, 10% between 600 and 699, and 1% between 700 and 800. Math-- 44% below 500, 45% between 500 and 599, and 9% between 600 and 699. **Admissions Contact:** Johnice Brown, Associate Director/Undergraduate Admission. Email: *admissions@longwood.edu* Web: *www.longwood.edu*

FINANCIAL AID: The FAFSA code is 003719. The priority date for freshman financial aid applications for fall entry is March 1.

MARY BALDWIN UNIVERSITY D-2

www.marybaldwin.edu

Staunton, VA 24401	**(540) 887-7019** **(800) 468-2262**
Fax: (540) 887-7292	**Email: admit@marybaldwin.edu**
Full-time: 41 men, 695 women	**Faculty:** 57; IIB, -$
Part-time: 44 men, 355 women	**Ph.D.s:** 81%
Graduate: 84 men, 435 women	**Student/Faculty:** 11 to 1
Year: 4-1-4, summer session	**Tuition:** $31,085
Room & Board: $9410	**Freshman Class:** 1370 applied, 1321 accepted, 107 enrolled
SAT EBR-W/M: 560/522 **ACT:** 23	**CEEB CODE:** 5397
Application Deadline: n/av	**COMPETITIVE**

Mary Baldwin University, founded as Augusta Female Seminary in 1842, has a proud legacy of innovating to best serve our students as the world changes. Mary Baldwin students experience the proven advantages of a close-knit women's college combined with the opportunities and access of a multifaceted, coed university, preparing them to lead both on the job and around the world. MBU offers a range of degree programs through the University's four academic colleges: the College of Arts and Sciences, the College of Business and Professional Studies, the College of Education, and the Murphy Deming College of Health Sciences. Master's degrees in education and undergraduate degrees through Baldwin Online and Adult Programs are available on campus, online, and at locations throughout the state, including Master's and doctoral programs in the health sciences at a branch campus in nearby Fishersville, Virginia. There are 4 undergraduate schools and 4 graduate schools. In addition to regional accreditation, MBU has baccalaureate program accreditation with CSWE, CAEP, SACS-COC, and CCNE. The 58-acre campus is in a small town in downtown Staunton, Virginia. Including any residence halls, there are 40 buildings.

STUDENT LIFE: 77% of undergraduates are from Virginia. Others are from 39 states, 13 foreign countries, and Canada. 89% are from public schools. 58% are White; 22% African American; 7% Hispanic; 5% race unknown; 4% two or more races; 2% Asian American; 1% American Indian/Alaska Native; 1% Foreign. 92% includes: Agnostic, Atheist, Christian Scientist, Mormon, Other, Unitarian Universalist, and Unknown. **Female To Male Ratio:** 8.8:1. The average age of freshmen is 18; all undergraduates, 24. 35% do not continue beyond their first year; 45% remain to graduate. **Housing:** 775 students can be accommodated in college housing, which includes dorms and on-campus apartments. In addition, there are honors houses, special-interest houses, and lofts and suites. On-campus housing is guaranteed for all 4 years and is available on a lottery system for upperclassmen. 85% of students live on campus. All students may keep cars.

FACULTY/CLASSROOMS: 28% of faculty are male; 72% are female. 82% teach undergraduates. No introductory courses are taught by graduate students. The average class size in an introductory lecture is 16; in a laboratory is 13; and in a regular course is 15.

PROGRAMS OF STUDY: MBU confers B.A., B.S., B.S.N., and B.S.W. degrees. Master's and doctoral degrees are also awarded. Bachelor's degrees are awarded in BIOLOGICAL SCIENCE (biology/biological science), BUSINESS (business administration and management, business economics, and marketing), COMMUNICATIONS AND THE ARTS (arts administration/management, communication studies, English, film arts, music, performing arts, studio art, and theatre arts), COMPUTER AND PHYSICAL SCIENCE (applied mathematics, chemistry, mathematics, and physics), HEALTH PROFESSIONS (clinical science, health care administration, health science, and nursing), SOCIAL SCIENCE (criminal justice, economics, history, international relations, liberal arts/general studies, political science/government, psychology, social work, and sociology). Nursing, healthcare administration, and biology are the strongest academically. Liberal arts & interdisciplinary studies, business, and social work have the largest enrollments.

ACTIVITIES: There are no fraternities or sororities. There are 49 groups on campus, including civic engagement, and event planning, leadership, wellness, art, choir, chorale, chorus, communications, dance, drama, drill team, drum and bugle corps, environmental, ethnic, film, hiking, honors, international, LGBT, literary magazine, marching band, musical theater, orchestra, photography, political, professional, religious, social, social service, student government, and yearbook. Popular campus events include Apple Day, Junior Dads & Family Weekend, Signature Ball, Halloween pumpkin carving, Las Posadas, Kwanzaa, International Festival, and Capstone Festival. **Sports:** There are 7 intercollegiate sports for women, and 6 intramural sports for women. Facilities include Physical Activities Center which has a main gym for basketball, volleyball, a dance studio, fencing, aerobics and group fitness classes, a cardio and weight room, a climbing wall, racquetball courts, a track, tennis courts, and softball. **Graduates:** From July 1, 2016 to June 30, 2017, 222 bachelor's degrees were awarded. The most popular majors were business (14%), psychology (11%), and liberal arts & interdisciplinary studies (9%). In an average class, 3% graduate in 3 years or less, 42% graduate in 4 years or less, 46% graduate in 5 years or less, and 46% graduate in 6 years or less. Of the 2016 graduating class, 20% were enrolled in graduate school within 6 months of graduation, and 84% were employed.

SERVICES: Counseling and information services are available, as is tutoring in most subjects. There is a reader service for the blind, and remedial math and writing. **Library/Resources:** The library contains 471,905 volumes, 31,392 audio/video tapes/CDs/DVDs, and subscribes to 36,745 periodicals including electronic. Computerized library services include interlibrary loans, database searching, Internet access, and Wi-Fi capability. Special learning facilities include an art gallery, the Staunton Military Academy/Virginia Women's Institute for Leadership Museum, dedicated to preserving local military history while inspiring future service members. In addition, the Spencer Center for Civic and Global Engagement at the heart of campus provides connections to local and regional service organizations, coordinates study abroad and international visitors, and offers meeting and event space. **Physically Challenged Students:** 30% of the campus is accessible. Facilities include wheelchair ramps, elevators, special parking, and specially equipped restrooms. **Special:** Special Programs: Self-designed majors, double majors, independent study, accelerated study, pass/fail grading option, internships, distance learning, external degree program, certificate programs,

Virginia State Teacher Licensure via the College of Education in undergraduate, master of arts in teaching, and post-baccalaureate teacher Licensure programs. Cooperative Education Programs: Dual-degree programs in education (BA/MAT and BA/MEd) and Shakespeare studies (BA/MLitt) through Mary Baldwin; 3-2 program in engineering (BS/MS) in partnership with the University of Virginia; 3-2 program in nursing (BS/MSN) with Vanderbilt University. Pre-Professional Programs: Pre-Chiropractic Medicine, Pre-Dentistry, Pre-Law, Pre-Medicine, Pre-Occupational Therapy, Pre-Optometry, Pre-Pharmacy, Pre-Physical Therapy, Pre-Physician Assistant, Pre-Podiatry, Pre-Speech Pathology, Pre-Veterinary Medicine. Study Abroad: Study abroad locations vary from year to year, and can include Costa Rica, Mexico, Japan, China, England, South Korea, Italy, Bermuda, Wales, The Netherlands, France, and Peru. Cadets in the Virginia Women's Institute for Leadership are eligible for special study opportunities in India and at Norwich University in Connecticut. Exchange programs with: Doshisha Women's College, Kansai Gaidai University, Lady Doak College, National Chengchi University, Oxford U, Soka University, and Sunshin Women's University. MBU and six other private colleges in Virginia (Hampden-Sydney College, Hollins University, Randolph-Macon College, Randolph College, Sweet Briar College, and Washington and Lee University) form a consortium through which students may attend another of the participating colleges for a semester or a year. An articulation agreement with the Virginia Community College System provides that a student with a transfer-oriented degree may qualify for guaranteed admission. There are 18 national honor societies, Phi Beta Kappa, a freshman honors program, and 29 departmental honors programs. **Visiting:** There are regularly scheduled orientations for prospective students, a tour, an interview, meet faculty, attend class, eat in dining hall, student events, athletic tours and other activities as requested or available. There are guides for informal visits, visitors may sit in on classes, and stay overnight. To schedule a visit, contact the Admissions Office. **Campus Safety and Security:** Measures include 24-hour foot and vehicle patrol, emergency notification system, self-defense education, and security escort services. There are emergency telephones, lighted pathways/sidewalks, controlled access to dorms/residences, 24-hour locked residence halls; video surveillance in all-night computer labs and access areas, and in the Exceptionally Gifted Center.

REQUIREMENTS: The SAT or ACT is required. Applicants must graduate from an accredited secondary school, have a GED, or meet state equivalency requirements for homeschooling. Admission to Mary Baldwin's programs is based on a student's academic potential; achievement in secondary school, when applicable; strength and maturity of character; and any special talents and abilities. In judging academic ability, the secondary school record, when applicable, is the primary factor considered. Candidates for admission should have completed at least 16 college preparatory courses. The university recommends that candidates include four or five academic subjects in their course loads each year in meeting the following recommended school program: 4 units of English, 3 units each of mathematics, history, and social studies, 2 units each of lab science and foreign language. AP and CLEP credits are accepted. Important factors in the admissions decision are extracurricular activities record, leadership record, and advanced placement or honors courses. Students seeking a bachelor's degree must complete a minimum of 126 semester hours. A maximum of 7 semester hours in physical/health education and a maximum of 15 semester hours in internships can be applied to the total hours to graduation. A maximum of 6 semester hours of graduate-level course-work (unless admitted into a joint bachelor's-master's program) can be applied to total hours to graduation. A cumulative, unrounded GPA of at least a 2.0 overall and a cumulative, un-rounded GPA of at least 2.0 in the major are also required. A minimum of 18 semester hours in the major, including the senior project, must be completed at Mary Baldwin University. A minimum of 36 total semester hours must be completed at Mary Baldwin. The Common Curriculum, which is organized by three learning outcomes (understanding of the liberal arts and sciences, understanding of the self in relationship to the broader community, and the capacity to make a positive difference in the world), includes 6 hours or more each in natural sciences, social sciences, arts, and humanities and history, 6 hours each in courses focused on writing, quantitative reasoning, and diverse cultures in a global context (foreign language, cross-cultural studies, and/or study abroad), 3 hours each in courses emphasizing oral communication, role of race and ethnicity, role of gender, and research and information literacy, 2 hours of health and physical education, and 1 hour of community involvement credit. Additional requirements for the Bachelor of Science (offered in biology, business, chemistry, economics, mathematics, physics, policy analysis, psychology) are 6 semester hours in mathematics at the 200-level or above, 3 hours emphasizing quantitative reasoning/data analysis, and at least two 200-level lab science courses. All graduates must complete a senior requirement for a minimum of 3 and a maximum of 6 semester hours of credit. The purpose of the senior requirement is to serve as a context within which students may establish themselves as capable of independent scholarship on a significant level. **Procedure:** Freshmen are admitted in the fall and spring. Entrance exams should be taken in the junior or senior year. There are early admissions, deferred admissions, and rolling admissions plans. Application deadlines are open. Applications are accepted online. **Transfer Students:** 184 transfer students enrolled in 2016-2017. Transfer applicants must have at least a 2.0 GPA at the institution where they are currently enrolled. 36 of 126 credits required for the bachelor's degree must be completed at MBU. **International Students:** There are 31 international students enrolled. They must take the TOEFL with a minimum score of 500 on the paper-based TOEFL (PBT) or 61 on the Internet-based version (iBT).

ADMISSIONS: The SAT scores for the 2017-2018 freshman class were: Math-- 41% below 500, 41% between 500 and 599, 13% between 600 and 699, and 5% between 700 and 800. Evidence-Based Reading/Writing-- 26% below 500, 38% between 500 and 599, 28% between 600 and 699, and 8% between 700 and 800. The ACT scores were 12% between 12 and 17, 49% between 18 and 23, 29% between 24 and 29, and 10% above 30. 34% of the current freshmen were in the top fifth of their class; 71% were in the top two fifths. **Admissions Contact:** Matt Munsey, Director of Admissions. Email: *admit@marybaldwin.edu* Web: *www.marybaldwin.edu*

FINANCIAL AID: In 2017-2018, 99% of all full-time freshmen received some form of financial aid. 95% of all full-time freshmen received need-based aid. The average freshman award was $36,257. Need-based scholarships or need-based grants averaged $6,425 ($36,680 maximum); need-based self-help aid (loans and jobs) averaged $3,095 ($14,724 maximum); and other non-need-based awards and non-need-based scholarships averaged $9,429 ($22,805 maximum). 20% of undergraduate students work part-time. The average financial indebtedness of the 2017 graduate was $31,274. The state aid form is required. The FAFSA code is 003723. The priority date for freshman financial aid applications for fall entry is March 1.

MARYMOUNT UNIVERSITY E-2

www.marymount.edu

Arlington, VA 22207	**(703) 284-1500** **(800) 548-7638**
Fax: (703) 522-0349	**Email: admissions@marymount.edu**
Full-time: 728 men, 1341 women	**Faculty:** 122; IIA, -$
Part-time: 76 men, 160 women	**Ph.D.s:** 88%
Graduate: 266 men, 804 women	**Student/Faculty:** 16 to 1
Year: semesters, summer session	**Tuition:** $30,426
Room & Board: $12,805	**Freshman Class:** 2416 applied, 2229 accepted, 405 enrolled
SAT EBR-W/M: 537/512 **ACT:** 22	**CEEB CODE:** 5405
Application Deadline: rolling	**COMPETITIVE**

Marymount University, founded in 1950, is a Catholic-affiliated, comprehensive university. Undergraduate and graduate programs are offered through the Schools of Arts and Sciences, Business Administration, Education & Human Services, and Malek School of Health Professions. There are 4 undergraduate schools and 4 graduate schools. In addition to regional accreditation, MU has baccalaureate program accreditation with ACBSP, CAEP, CAEP, CCNE, and CIDA. The 21-acre campus is in a suburban area 6 miles southwest of Washington, D.C. Including any residence halls, there are 15 buildings.

STUDENT LIFE: 60% of undergraduates are from Virginia. Others are from 42 states, 66 foreign countries, and Canada. 85% are from public schools. 35% are White; 17% Hispanic; 17% Foreign; 14% African American; 7% Asian American; 5% race unknown; 4% two or more races; 1% American Indian/Alaska Native. 33% are Catholic; 30% claim no religious affiliation; 19% Protestant; 17% Muslim, Orthodox, Hindu, and Buddhist. **Female To Male Ratio:** 2.2:1. The average age of freshmen is 18; all undergraduates, 22. 22% do not continue beyond their first year; 52% remain to graduate. **Housing:** 920 students can be accommodated in college housing, which includes single sex dorms, coed dorms off-campus apartments, and theme housing. On-campus housing is available on a lottery system for upperclassmen. 69% of students commute. Upperclassmen may keep cars.

FACULTY/CLASSROOMS: 34% of faculty are male; 66% are female. 78% teach undergraduates. No introductory courses are taught by graduate students.

PROGRAMS OF STUDY: MU confers B.A., B.S., B.B.A., and B.S.N. degrees. Master's and doctoral degrees are also awarded. Bachelor's degrees are awarded in BIOLOGICAL SCIENCE (biochemistry and biology/biological science), BUSINESS (business administration and management and fashion merchandising), COMMUNICATIONS AND THE ARTS (art, communications, English, graphic design & media, and information technology), COMPUTER AND PHYSICAL SCIENCE (computer security and information assurance and mathematics), EDUCATION (art education, English education, health information management, mathematics education, and special education), ENGINEERING AND ENVIRONMENTAL DESIGN (interior design), HEALTH PROFESSIONS (health science, nursing, premedicine, and prephysical therapy), SOCIAL SCIENCE (criminal justice, economics, fashion design and technology, history, liberal arts/general studies, philosophy, political science/government, psychology, sociology, and theological studies). Business administration, nursing, and information technology have the largest enrollments.

ACTIVITIES: There are no fraternities or sororities. There are 42 groups on campus, including art, cheerleading, choir, chorus, communications, dance, drama, environmental, ethnic, film, honors, international, literary magazine, newspaper, political, professional, religious, social, social service, student government, and yearbook. Popular campus events include Portfolio in Motion (Fashion Show), Snowball (Winter Formal Dance), International Week and Banquet, Saintsfest, Midnight Madness, Engagement Fair, Dancing with the MU Stars, Family Weekend, Homecoming, Halloweenfest. **Sports:** There are 9 intercollegiate sports for men and 8 for women, and 6 intramural sports for men and 4 for women. Facilities include basketball arena, practice field, recreational gymnasium, swimming pool, aerobics and weight rooms, and off-campus baseball field. **Graduates:** From July 1, 2016 to June 30, 2017, 605 bachelor's degrees were awarded. The most popular majors were nursing (24%), business administration (16%), and information technology (8%). In an average class, 36% graduate in 4 years or less, 49% graduate in 5 years or less, and 52% graduate in 6 years or less. Of the 2016 graduating class, 65% were employed within 6 months of graduation.

SERVICES: Counseling and information services are available, as is tutoring in most subjects. There is a reader service for the blind, and remedial math, reading, and writing. **Library/Resources:** Computerized library services include interlibrary loans, database searching, Internet access, and Wi-Fi capability. Special learning facilities include an art gallery, and a center for teaching and learning. **Physically Challenged Students:** Facilities include wheelchair ramps, elevators, special parking, specially equipped restrooms, special class scheduling, lowered drinking fountains, lowered telephones, and special housing. **Special:** Students can cross-register with the Consortium of Universities of the Washington Metropolitan Area and participate in short-term and semester-long study abroad in various countries. Marymount offers student-designed majors, an accelerated degree program in nursing, and dual-degree programs in business administration, information technology, and health sciences. An internship, research, or student teaching experience is required in all majors except nursing. There are 12 national honor societies and a freshman honors program. **Visiting:** There are regularly scheduled orientations for prospective students, campus visit days, information nights, and summer orientation. There are guides for informal visits, visitors may sit in on classes, and stay overnight. To schedule a visit, contact the Admissions Office. **Campus Safety and Security:** Measures include 24-hour foot and vehicle patrol, emergency notification system, and security escort services. There are shuttle buses, emergency telephones, lighted pathways/sidewalks, controlled access to dorms/residences, and student patrols.

REQUIREMENTS: Applicants must graduate from an accredited secondary school or have a GED. Marymount requires 15 academic credits in preparatory courses and strongly recommends biology and chemistry for Nursing candidates. First-time freshmen with a high school GPA of 3.0 or higher have the option of submitting SAT/ACT scores. If both SAT and ACT scores are submitted, the highest equivalent test score will be used. A GPA of 2.6 is required. AP and CLEP credits are accepted. Important factors in the admissions decision are advanced placement or honors courses, extracurricular activities record, and evidence of special talent. To graduate, students must complete all course requirements with a minimum cumulative grade point average of 2.0. Students must earn 120 credits by completing all liberal arts core requirements, all general education university requirements, and all major requirements. Core curriculum includes courses in humanities, mathematics and sciences, philosophy and theology, written communication, and freshman seminar. **Procedure:** Freshmen are admitted in the fall, spring, and summer. Entrance exams scores must be received by August 15 for fall-term admission. There are deferred admissions and rolling admissions plans. Application deadlines are open. The fall 2017 application fee was $40. Notification is sent on a rolling basis. Applications are accepted on-line. **Transfer Students:** 267 transfer students enrolled in 2016-2017. One letter of recommendation is required. Transfer applicants with fewer than 30 credits must meet freshman admission requirements. There are additional requirements for nursing and international applicants. 36 of 120 credits required for the bachelor's degree must be completed at Marymount. **International Students:** There are 383 international students enrolled. They must take the TOEFL with a minimum score of 550 on the paper-based TOEFL (PBT) or 79 on the Internet-based version (iBT). Students must take the IELTS. They must also take the SAT or ACT, scoring 950.

ADMISSIONS: 92% of the 2017-2018 applicants were accepted. The SAT scores for the 2017-2018 freshman class were: Math-- 45% below 500, 41% between 500 and 599, 13% between 600 and 699, and 1% between 700 and 800. Evidence-Based Reading/Writing-- 30% below 500, 49% between 500 and 599, 19% between 600 and 699, and 2% between 700 and 800. The ACT scores were 13% between 12 and 17, 52% between 18 and 23, 25% between 24 and 29, and 10% above 30. **Admissions Contact:** Dana Matassino, Director of Undergraduate Admissions. Email: *admissions@marymount.edu* Web: *www.marymount.edu*

FINANCIAL AID: In 2017-2018, 94% of all full-time freshmen received some form of financial aid. The average freshman award was $28,770. 20% of undergraduate students work part-time. The average financial indebtedness of the 2017 graduate was $34,023. The FAFSA code is 003724. The priority date for freshman financial aid applications for fall entry is March 1.

NORFOLK STATE UNIVERSITY *(The complete profile is made available exclusively on our website, www.barronspac.com)*

OLD DOMINION UNIVERSITY F-4
www.odu.edu

Norfolk, VA 23529	**(757) 683-3648** **(800) 348-7926**
Fax: (757) 683-3255	**Email: admissions@odu.edu**
Full-time: 6814 men, 8222 women	**Faculty:** 840; I, --$
Part-time: 1931 men, 2573 women	**Ph.D.s:** 81%
Graduate: 1979 men, 2856 women	**Student/Faculty:** 24 to 1
Year: semesters, summer session	**Tuition:** $10,350 ($28,200)
Room & Board: $11,268	**Freshman Class:** 11159 applied, 9566 accepted, 2938 enrolled
SAT EBR-W/M: 560/530 **ACT:** 21	**CEEB CODE:** 5126
Application Deadline: February 1	**COMPETITIVE**

Old Dominion University is Virginia's forward-focused public doctoral research university, established in 1930 as the Norfolk Division of the College of William & Mary. Today, the school is one of the largest universities in Virginia, offering 91 bachelors, 41 masters, 22 doctoral degrees and 2 education specialist programs through its colleges of Arts and Letters, Business, Continuing Education and Professional Studies, Education, Engineering and Technology, Health Sciences, Sciences and Honors College. There are 6 undergraduate schools and 6 graduate schools. In addition to regional accreditation, ODU has baccalaureate program accreditation with AACSB, ABET, ADA, NASAD, NASM, CAEP, NRPA, CCNE, COAES, EHAC, NAACLS, and NAST. The 251-acre campus is in an urban area in Norfolk, VA, and 3 hours from Washington, DC. Including any residence halls, there are 145 buildings.

STUDENT LIFE: 92% of undergraduates are from Virginia. Others are from 47 states, 85 foreign countries, and Canada. 93% are from public schools. 9% are Hispanic; 7% two or more races; 5% Asian American;

42% White; 32% African American; 2% Foreign; 2% race unknown. **Female To Male Ratio:** 1.3:1. The average age of freshmen is 19; all undergraduates, 22. 20% do not continue beyond their first year; 54% remain to graduate. **Housing:** 4830 students can be accommodated in college housing, which includes gender neutral, single-sex and coed dorms, and on-campus apartments. In addition, there are honors houses, language/international houses, special-interest houses, and living learning communities. On-campus housing is guaranteed for the freshman year only, and is available on a first-come, first-served basis, and is available on a lottery system for upperclassmen. 76% of students commute. Upperclassmen may keep cars.

FACULTY/CLASSROOMS: 55% of faculty are male; 45% are female. 75% teach undergraduates, and 3% do research. No introductory courses are taught by graduate students. The average class size in an introductory lecture is 32; in a laboratory is 22; and in a regular course is 30.

PROGRAMS OF STUDY: ODU confers B.A., B.S., B.F.A., B.M., B.S.B.A., B.S.C.E., B.S.C.O.M.E., B.S.C.S., B.S.D.H., B.S.E.E., B.S.E.H., B.S.E.T., B.S.H.S., B.S.M.&S.E., B.S.M.E., B.S.M.T., B.S.N. and B.S.N.M.T. degrees. Master's and doctoral degrees are also awarded. Bachelor's degrees are awarded in BIOLOGICAL SCIENCE (biochemistry, biology/adolescence education, biology/biological science, and marine biology), BUSINESS (accounting, business administration and management, business intelligence and analytics, electronic business, fashion merchandising, finance, financial services, insurance, international business management, leadership, management information systems, marketing management, personal financial planning, real estate, sports management, supply chain management, tourism, and professional studies), COMMUNICATIONS AND THE ARTS (art history and appreciation, communications, creative writing, dance, drawing, English, fiber/textiles/weaving, film arts, fine arts, fine arts education, French, German, graphic design, journalism, linguistics, literature, music, music production/recording technology, music performance, music theory and composition, painting, performing arts, printmaking, Spanish, studio art, theatre arts, theatre education, and writing), COMPUTER AND PHYSICAL SCIENCE (chemistry, chemistry/adolescence education, computer science, cyber intelligence/security studies, earth science, earth science/adolescence education, geology, industrial technology, information sciences and systems, mathematics, oceanography, physics secondary education, physics & physical oceanography, and physics), EDUCATION (art education, dance education, elementary education, English education, foreign languages education, French studies K-12 education, history education, mathematics education, music education, physical education, physical ed teacher education, secondary education, Spanish adolescense education, special education, and technology & science education), ENGINEERING AND ENVIRONMENTAL DESIGN (civil engineering, civil engineering technology, computer engineering, electrical/electronics engineering, electrical/ electronics engineering technology, engineering technology, mechanical engineering, and mechanical engineering technology), HEALTH PROFESSIONS (cytotechnology, dental hygiene, environmental health science, exercise science, health administration and policy, health science, medical technology, nuclear medical technology, nursing, public health, and speech pathology/audiology), SOCIAL SCIENCE (African studies, African American studies, Asian/Oriental studies, criminal justice, economics, geography, geography information science, history, human services, interdisciplinary studies, international studies, parks and recreation management, philosophy, political science/government, psychology, religious studies, sociology, and women's studies). Criminal justice, accounting, and speech pathology are the strongest academically. Psychology, nursing and criminal justice have the largest enrollments.

ACTIVITIES: 9% of men belong to 20 national fraternities; 6% of women belong to 11 national sororities. There are 290 groups on campus, including art, band, cheerleading, chess, choir, chorale, chorus, communications, computers, dance, debate, drama, drill team, environmental, ethnic, film, forensics, honors, international, jazz band, LGBT, marching band, musical theater, newspaper, pep band, photography, political, professional, radio and TV, religious, social, and student government. Popular campus events include Unity Fest, Exam Jam, Homecoming, Greek Week, and Relay for Life. **Sports:** There are 8 intercollegiate sports for men and 8 for women, and 16 intramural sports for men and 16 for women. Facilities include indoor tennis center, and outdoor courts, baseball stadium, basketball arena, field for soccer, a gym, wrestling, turf field stadium for field hockey and lacrosse, practice football fields, 9-hole golf course with driving range, sailing centers, varsity rowing, and swimming pool. **Graduates:** From July 1, 2016 to June 30, 2017, 4015 bachelor's degrees were awarded. The most popular majors were psychology (7%), nursing (7%), and criminology (7%). In an average class, 1% graduate in 3 years or less, 29% graduate in 4 years or less, 51% graduate in 5 years or less, and 55% graduate in 6 years or less.

SERVICES: Counseling and information services are available, as is tutoring in some subjects, such as English, sciences, math, and remedial writing. **Library/Resources:** The library contains 2.7 million volumes, 168,900 microform items, 153,385 audio/video tapes/CDs/DVDs, and subscribes to 12,400 periodicals including electronic. Computerized library services include interlibrary loans, database searching, Internet access, and Wi-Fi capability. Special learning facilities include an art gallery, planetarium, radio station, a music library and composers collections, university special collections and archives, an art library, and a digital library. **Physically Challenged Students:** All of the campus is accessible. Facilities include wheelchair ramps, elevators, special parking, specially equipped restrooms, special class scheduling, lowered drinking fountains, and special housing. **Special:** Old Dominion offers cross-registration with schools in the Tidewater Consortium program. There are co-op programs, guaranteed internships, study abroad in 56 countries, and a work-study program. Students may take a BA-BS degree in engineering and liberal arts. An interdisciplinary program, dual majors, 3-2 engineering degrees in business and engineering, non-degree study, pass/fail options, and credit for military and life experience are available. There are 29 national honor societies and a freshman honors program. **Visiting:** There are regularly scheduled orientations for prospective students. Orientation is a 1 day where students will meet with advisors in the academic area, and select their class schedule. There are guides for informal visits and visitors may sit in on classes. To schedule a visit, contact the Admissions Office. **Campus Safety and Security:** Measures include 24-hour foot and vehicle patrol, emergency notification system, self-defense education, and security escort services. There are shuttle buses, emergency telephones, lighted pathways/sidewalks, controlled access to dorms/residences, and bicycle patrol.

REQUIREMENTS: The SAT or ACT is required. Applicants must be graduates of an accredited secondary school. The GED is accepted. Applicants should have completed 4 years of math and 3 years each of English, foreign languages, science, and social science. An essay and recommendation are required. A list of extracurricular activities is required. Applications are accepted on-line. AP and CLEP credits are accepted. Important factors in the admissions decision are advanced placement or honors courses, recommendations by school officials, and leadership record. At least 120 credits, with a minimum GPA of 2.0, are required to graduate. Students must complete the university's general education program, consisting of specific skills and perspectives courses outside the student's major. English composition is a required course, and students must pass a writing proficiency exam. **Procedure:** Freshmen are admitted in the fall, spring, and summer. Entrance exams should be taken in May of the junior year or November/December of the senior. There are early admissions, deferred admissions, and rolling admissions plans. Applications should be filed by February 1 for fall entry; October 1 for spring entry; and March 15 for summer entry. The fall 2017 application fee was $50. Notification is sent on a rolling basis. 1042 applicants were on the 2017 waiting list; 9 were admitted. Applications are accepted on-line. **Transfer Students:** 2145 transfer students enrolled in 2016-2017. Applicants must have a minimum GPA of 2.5 and at least 24 semester hour credits. Applicants with fewer semester hours must meet the same requirements as freshmen. 30 of 120 credits required for the bachelor's degree must be completed at ODU. **International Students:** There are 258 international students enrolled. They must take the TOEFL with a minimum score of 550 on the paper-based TOEFL (PBT) or 79 on the Internet-based version (iBT). Students must take the college's own test, and the IELTS with a score of 6.5 overall.

ADMISSIONS: 86% of the 2017-2018 applicants were accepted. The SAT scores for the 2017-2018 freshman class were: Math-- 30% below 500, 49% between 500 and 599, 19% between 600 and 699, and 1% between 700 and 800. Evidence-Based Reading/Writing-- 21% below 500, 48% between 500 and 599, 29% between 600 and 699, and 2% between 700 and 800. The ACT scores were 17% between 12 and 17, 49% between 18 and 23, 30% between 24 and 29, and 4% above 30. 23% of the current freshmen were in the top fifth of their class; 55% were in the top two fifths. 4 freshmen graduated first in their class. **Admissions Contact:** Shereen Williams, Customer Service Manager, Admissions. Email: *admissions@odu.edu* Web: *www.odu.edu*

FINANCIAL AID: In 2017-2018, 72% of all full-time freshmen received

some form of financial aid. 62% of all full-time freshmen received need-based aid. The average freshman award was $19,640. Need-based scholarships or need-based grants averaged $7,999 ($26,074 maximum); need-based self-help aid (loans and jobs) averaged $4,103 ($26,074 maximum); non-need-based athletic scholarships averaged $20,472 ($26,074 maximum); and other non-need-based awards and non-need-based scholarships averaged $4,080 ($26,074 maximum). 10% of undergraduate students work part-time. The average financial indebtedness of the 2017 graduate was $30,410. The FAFSA code is 003728. The priority date for freshman financial aid applications for fall entry is February 15.

RADFORD UNIVERSITY C-3
www.radford.edu

Radford, VA 24142 **(540) 831-5371**

Fax: (540) 831-5038 **Email: admissions@radford.edu**

Full-time: 3423 men, 4626 women
Part-time: 168 men, 201 women
Graduate: 230 men, 770 women
Year: semesters, summer session
Room & Board: $9131

Faculty: 460; IIA, -$
Ph.D.s: 83%
Student/Faculty: 16 to 1
Tuition: $10,627 ($22,262)
Freshman Class: 14620 applied, 10866 accepted, 1848 enrolled

SAT EBR-W/M: 530/510 **ACT:** required
CEEB CODE: 5565

Application Deadline: February 1
COMPETITIVE

Radford University, founded in 1910, is a comprehensive, coeducational student-focused public institution with diverse curricula in science and technology, business and economics, nursing, allied health and human services, education and human development, visual and performing arts, and graduate and professional studies. There are 6 undergraduate schools and 1 graduate school. In addition to regional accreditation, Radford University has baccalaureate program accreditation with AACSB, ABET, CSWE, FIDER, NASM, NRPA, CAEP, APA, and CCNE. The 204-acre campus is in a small town 36 miles southwest of Roanoke, directly down Interstate 81. Including any residence halls, there are 59 buildings.

STUDENT LIFE: 94% of undergraduates are from Virginia. Others are from 41 states, 64 foreign countries, and Canada. 93% are from public schools. 67% are White; 17% African American; 7% Hispanic; 5% two or more races; 2% race unknown; 1% Asian American; 1% American Indian/Alaska Native; 1% Foreign. **Female To Male Ratio:** 1.5:1. The average age of freshmen is 18; all undergraduates, 21. 24% do not continue beyond their first year; 55% remain to graduate. **Housing:** 3156 students can be accommodated in college housing, which includes gender neutral, single-sex dorm, and coed dorms, on-campus apartments, and off-campus apartments. In addition, there are honors houses and special-interest houses. On-campus housing is guaranteed for the freshman year only, is available on a first-come, and first-served basis. 59% of students commute. Alcohol is not permitted. All students may keep cars.

FACULTY/CLASSROOMS: 47% of faculty are male; 53% are female. 86% teach undergraduates. Graduate students teach 7% of introductory courses. The average class size in an introductory lecture is 33; in a laboratory is 21; and in a regular course is 31.

PROGRAMS OF STUDY: Radford confers B.A., B.S., B.B.A., B.F.A., B.M., B.S.N., and B.S.W. degrees. Master's and doctoral degrees are also awarded. Bachelor's degrees are awarded in BIOLOGICAL SCIENCE (biology/biological science), BUSINESS (accounting, banking and finance, business administration and management, marketing/retailing/merchandising, and recreation and leisure services), COMMUNICATIONS AND THE ARTS (art, communications, dance, design, English, fine arts, media arts, music, speech/debate/rhetoric, and theatre arts), COMPUTER AND PHYSICAL SCIENCE (chemistry, computer science, geology, geoscience, information sciences and systems, mathematics, and physics), EDUCATION (athletic training, education, education administration, foreign languages education, mathematics education, physical education, and special education), HEALTH PROFESSIONS (exercise science, nursing, nutrition and dietetics, and speech pathology/audiology), SOCIAL SCIENCE (anthropology, criminal justice, economics, history, human development, interdisciplinary studies, liberal arts/general studies, philosophy and religion, political science/government, psychology, social science, social work, and sociology). Nursing and education is the strongest academically. Interdisciplinary studies, criminal justice, and exercise have the largest enrollments.

ACTIVITIES: 11% of men belong to 13 national fraternities; 10% of women belong to 11 national sororities. There are 275 groups on campus, including art, band, cheerleading, choir, chorale, communications, computers, dance, drama, environmental, ethnic, film, honors, international, jazz band, LGBT, literary magazine, Model UN, musical theater, newspaper, pep band, photography, political, professional, radio and TV, religious, social, social service, student government, and yearbook. Popular campus events include Highlander Festival. **Sports:** There are 6 intercollegiate sports for men and 9 for women. Facilities include a student fitness and wellness center, a facility, with indoor sloped running track, a gymnasium, multi-purpose activity courts, basketball courts, weight and cardio rooms, and fitness and nutritional instruction classrooms. The intramural complex provides additional fields for intramural soccer, lacrosse, flag football and rugby, a 1/6-mile jogging track, basketball and volleyball courts, a pole vault practice runway, an indoor golf room, and student-athlete support facilities such as a weight room, a rehabilitaion and training room, and an academic center. Outdoor facilities include a jogging trail, tennis courts, baseball, a track, soccer, field hockey, and softball. **Graduates:** From July 1, 2016 to June 30, 2017, 1911 bachelor's degrees were awarded. The most popular majors were exercise, sport, and health education (8%), psychology (8%), and criminal justice (7%). In an average class, 38% graduate in 4 years or less, 53% graduate in 5 years or less, and 55% graduate in 6 years or less. Of the 2016 graduating class, 12% were enrolled in graduate school within 6 months of graduation.

SERVICES: Counseling and information services are available, as is tutoring in most subjects. **Library/Resources:** The library contains 271,383 volumes, and 13,933 audio/video tapes/CDs/DVDs. Computerized library services include interlibrary loans, database searching, Internet access, and Wi-Fi capability. Special learning facilities include an art gallery, natural history museum, planetarium, radio station, real-time trading room, visual and performing arts with performance hall, museum of the earth sciences, nursing simulation labs, speech and hearing clinic, conservatory with observatory, athletic trainer lab, forensics institute, advanced GIS and GPS capabilities, digitally advanced classrooms, animation, modeling and simulation (GAMeS) lab, TV studio with LTN uplink, podcast studio, video editing labs, audio editing studios, and mobile journalism lab.**Physically Challenged Students:** 94% of the campus is accessible. Facilities include wheelchair ramps, elevators, special parking, specially equipped restrooms, special class scheduling, lowered drinking fountains, lowered telephones, and special housing. **Special:** RU offers internships, study abroad in 16 countries, and on-campus work-study. There are accelerated degree programs in criminal justice, nursing, and communication, and dual and student-designed majors are possible. There are 3-2 engineering, chemistry, physics, and math degree programs with Virginia Tech. There are 24 national honor societies and a freshman honors program. **Visiting:** There are regularly scheduled orientations for prospective students, consisting of open houses in the fall, information sessions and tours Monday through Friday, and Admitted Student Days in the spring. There are guides for informal visits and visitors may sit in on classes. To schedule a visit, contact the Office of Admissions. **Campus Safety and Security:** Measures include 24-hour foot and vehicle patrol, emergency notification system, self-defense education, and security escort services. There are shuttle buses, emergency telephones, lighted pathways/sidewalks, and controlled access to dorms/residences.

REQUIREMENTS: The SAT or ACT is recommended. Most successful applicants have taken 4 units each of English, math, and social sciences, including American history, and 3 or 4 units each of laboratory sciences and foreign language. The GED is accepted. AP and CLEP credits are accepted. To graduate, students must complete at least 120 credit hours, including 30 to 90 in the major, with a 2.0 GPA. There are core curriculum requirements in English, communication, math, natural sciences, humanities, visual and performing arts, social and behavioral sciences, U.S. and global perspectives, and health and wellness. **Procedure:** Freshmen are admitted in the fall, spring, and summer. There are early admissions and deferred admissions plans. Early decision applications should be filed by December 1; regular applications, by February 1 for fall entry. Notifications are sent April 1. 860 applicants were on the 2017 waiting list; 481 were admitted. Applications are accepted on-line. **Transfer Students:** 662 transfer students enrolled in 2016-2017. Applicants must have a minimum GPA of 2.0 for consideration. Those with fewer than 24 semester hours of college work must submit their high school record. 45 of 120 credits required for the bachelor's degree must be completed at Radford. **International Students:** There are 91 international students enrolled. They must take the TOEFL with a minimum score of 520 on the paper-based TOEFL (PBT) or 68 on the Internet-based version (iBT).

ADMISSIONS: 74% of the 2017-2018 applicants were accepted. The SAT scores for the 2017-2018 freshman class were: Math-- 43% below 500, 49% between 500 and 599, and 8% between 600 and 699. Evidence-Based Reading/Writing-- 32% below 500, 51% between 500 and 599, 16% between 600 and 699, and 1% between 700 and 800. The ACT scores were 25% between 12 and 17, 54% between 18 and 23, 19% between 24 and 29, and 2% above 30. 10% of the current freshmen were in the top fifth of their class; 18% were in the top two fifths. 8 freshmen graduated first in their class. **Admissions Contact:** Mildred Johnson, Dean of Admissions. Email: *admissions@radford.edu* Web: *www.radford.edu*

FINANCIAL AID: In 2017-2018, 86% of all full-time freshmen received some form of financial aid. 63% of all full-time freshmen received need-based aid. The average freshman award was $15,900. Need-based scholarships or need-based grants averaged $7,794 ($22,720 maximum); need-based self-help aid (loans and jobs) averaged $3,483 ($6,110 maximum); non-need-based athletic scholarships averaged $15,291 ($35,518 maximum); and other non-need-based awards and non-need-based scholarships averaged $5,775 ($12,000 maximum). 13% of undergraduate students work part-time. The average financial indebtedness of the 2017 graduate was $31,463. The FAFSA code is 003732. The priority date for freshman financial aid applications for fall entry is February 15.

RANDOLPH COLLEGE — D-3

www.randolphcollege.edu

Lynchburg, VA 24503 — **(434) 947-8000**, **(800) 745-7692**

Fax: (434) 947-8996 — **Email: admissions@randolphcollege.edu**

Full-time: 234 men, 409 women	**Faculty:** 70
Part-time: 4 men, 4 women	**Ph.D.s:** 89%
Graduate: 8 men, 13 women	**Student/Faculty:** 9 to 1
Year: semesters	**Tuition:** $39,695
Room & Board: $13,580	**Freshman Class:** 1696 applied, 1466 accepted, 202 enrolled
SAT EBR-W/M: 550/520 **ACT:** 22	**CEEB CODE:** 5557
Application Deadline: November 15	**COMPETITIVE**

Randolph College, founded in 1891, is an independent, coeducational, liberal arts institution. The college's curriculum offers the best feature of an honors education with a global outlook. Students are encouraged to travel, to take on real problems, to pursue and achieve a goal with personal meaning. Embedded within a student's education are opportunities to study abroad, both national and international internships, career guidance, leadership development, and one-on-one faculty advising. There is 1 undergraduate school and 1 graduate school. In addition to regional accreditation, Randolph has baccalaureate program accreditation with NASDTEC and CAEP. The 100-acre campus is in a suburban area within minutes of the Blue Ridge Mountains, 1 hour southwest of Charlottesville. Including any residence halls, there are 18 buildings.

STUDENT LIFE: 76% of undergraduates are from Virginia. Others are from 36 states, 32 foreign countries, and Canada. 72% are from public schools. 69% are White; 6% Hispanic; 6% Foreign; 4% two or more races; 2% Asian American; 13% African American. 55% are Protestant; 15% Catholic; 15% claim no religious affiliation; 12% Muslim, Hindu, Buddhist, and Orthodox. **Female To Male Ratio:** 1.7:1. The average age of freshmen is 19; all undergraduates, 20. 20% do not continue beyond their first year; 64% remain to graduate. **Housing:** 675 students can be accommodated in college housing, which includes coed dorms. In addition, there are special-interest houses, apartments for single students, wellness and theme housing, and gender-neutral housing. On-campus housing is guaranteed for all 4 years. 79% of students live on campus. All students may keep cars.

FACULTY/CLASSROOMS: All teach undergraduates, 58% do research, and 58% do both. No introductory courses are taught by graduate students. The average class size in an introductory lecture is 16; in a laboratory is 11; and in a regular course is 12.

PROGRAMS OF STUDY: Randolph confers B.A., B.S., and B.F.A. degrees. Master's degrees are also awarded. Bachelor's degrees are awarded in AGRICULTURE (environmental studies), BIOLOGICAL SCIENCE (biology/biological science), BUSINESS (business administration and management), COMMUNICATIONS AND THE ARTS (art, classics, communications, dance, dramatic arts, English, French, music, and Spanish), COMPUTER AND PHYSICAL SCIENCE (chemistry, mathematics, and physics), EDUCATION (education and physical education), ENGINEERING AND ENVIRONMENTAL DESIGN (engineering physics and environmental science), HEALTH PROFESSIONS (health science), SOCIAL SCIENCE (economics, history, international studies, philosophy, political science/government, psychology, religion, and sociology). Biology, psychology, and political science have the largest enrollments.

ACTIVITIES: There are no fraternities or sororities. There are 35 groups on campus, including campus ministries, environmental, Model UN, outdoor adventures, art, chorale, chorus, dance, debate, drama, environmental, equestrian, ethnic, honors, international, LGBT, literary magazine, newspaper, pep band, photography, political, professional, radio and TV, social, social service, student government, and yearbook. Popular campus events include Tacky Party, Never-ending Weekend, Senior Dinner Dance, and Dell Parties. **Sports:** There are 6 intercollegiate sports for men and 8 for women, and 6 intramural sports for men and 6 for women. Facilities include a multi-purpose playing field and track, gym, indoor swimming pool, dance studios, aerobic and weight rooms, tennis courts, athletic fields, frisbee golf course, a riding center with teaching, show rings, and indoor and outdoor arenas. **Graduates:** From July 1, 2016 to June 30, 2017, 160 bachelor's degrees were awarded. The most popular majors were biological/life sciences (15%), social sciences (13%), and visual and performing arts (12%). In an average class, 2% graduate in 3 years or less, 63% graduate in 4 years or less, 64% graduate in 5 years or less, and 69% graduate in 6 years or less. Of the 2016 graduating class, 35% were enrolled in graduate school within 6 months of graduation, and 60% were employed.

SERVICES: Counseling and information services are available, as is tutoring in every subject. There is a computing and study skills resource room, a writing lab, science and math center available for students. **Library/Resources:** The library contains 197,332 volumes, 187,000 microform items, and 3,600 audio/video tapes/CDs/DVDs, and subscribes to 618 periodicals including electronic. Computerized library services include interlibrary loans, database searching, and Internet access. Special learning facilities include an art gallery, radio station, an observatory, collection of American art in the Maier Museum, 2 theaters, recital hall, organic garden, a 100-acre equestrian center, and 3 nature preserves. **Physically Challenged Students:** 50% of the campus is accessible. Facilities include wheelchair ramps, elevators, special parking, specially equipped restrooms, special class scheduling, special housing. **Special:** Randolph offers a spring semester American Culture Program, as well as study abroad in 11 countries, including its own program in England, and both domestic and international internships. A Washington semester at American University is available, as is the Tri-College Consortium with Sweet Briar and Lynchburg Colleges, and the Seven-College Exchange Program with Hampden-Sydney, Hollins, Mary Baldwin, Randolph-Macon, and Sweet Briar Colleges, and Washington and Lee University. There is a 3-2 nursing program with Johns Hopkins University and Vanderbilt University and a 3-2 engineering degree with several institutions. There are 17 national honor societies, Phi Beta Kappa, and 16 departmental honors programs. **Visiting:** There are regularly scheduled orientations for prospective students, including a campus tour, student panels, faculty panels, class visits, and individual sessions with admissions and financial planning counselor. There are guides for informal visits, visitors may sit in on classes, and stay overnight. To schedule a visit, contact the Admissions Office. **Campus Safety and Security:** Measures include 24-hour foot and vehicle patrol, emergency notification system, self-defense education, and security escort services. There are emergency telephones, lighted pathways/sidewalks, and controlled access to dorms/residences.

REQUIREMENTS: Applicants must be graduates of an accredited secondary school with at least 16 academic credits, including 4 units in English, 3 units in math (4 recommended), 3-4 units recommended in foreign language, 3 units in science with 2 units in lab, 2 units in history, and 1 unit in academic electives (3 recommended). An interview is strongly encouraged. A GED is accepted. High school diploma is required. Either SAT and SAT Subject tests or ACT if submitted will be considered. AP and CLEP credits are accepted. Important factors in the admissions decision are advanced placement or honors courses, recommendations by school officials, extracurricular activities record, recommendations by alumni, leadership record, parents or siblings attended your school, evidence of special talent, and personality/intangible qualities. To graduate, all students must complete at least 124 credit hours with a minimum GPA of 2.0. Students must satisfy the requirements for the general education and major programs and must have a minimum GPA of 2.0 in the major. **Procedure:** Freshmen are admitted in the fall and spring. Entrance exams should be taken in the junior or senior year. There are early admissions and deferred admissions plans. Applications should be filed by November 15 for fall entry. The fall 2017 application fee was $35. Notification is sent on a rolling basis. Applications are accepted on-line. **Transfer Students:** 35 transfer students enrolled in 2016-2017. Transfer students must submit college transcripts and for high school transcripts, required by some students, a letters of recommendation from a college official. An interview is recommended. 62 of 124 credits required for the bachelor's degree must be completed at Randolph. **International Students:** There are 66 international students enrolled. They must take the TOEFL with a minimum score of 550 on the paper-based TOEFL (PBT) or 79 on the Internet-based version (iBT).

ADMISSIONS: 86% of the 2017-2018 applicants were accepted. The SAT scores for the 2017-2018 freshman class were: Math-- 38% below 500, 44% between 500 and 599, 16% between 600 and 699, and 2% between 700 and 800. Evidence-Based Reading/Writing-- 28% below 500, 37% between 500 and 599, 34% between 600 and 699, and 2% between 700 and 800. The ACT scores were 14% between 12 and 17, 55% between 18 and 23, 23% between 24 and 29, and 7% above 30. 71% of the current freshmen were in the top fifth of their class; 91% were in the top two fifths. **Admissions Contact:** Margaret Blount, Director of Recruitment. Email: *admissions@randolphcollege.edu* Web: *www.randolphcollege.edu*

FINANCIAL AID: In 2017-2018, 99% of all full-time freshmen received some form of financial aid. 76% of all full-time freshmen received need-based aid. The average freshman award was $34,868. Need-based scholarships or need-based grants averaged $30,826; need-based self-help aid (loans and jobs) averaged $4,599; other non-need-based awards and non-need-based scholarships averaged $23,718; and $3,909 from other forms of aid. 66% of undergraduate students work part-time. The average financial indebtedness of the 2017 graduate was $35,199. The state aid form is required. The priority date for freshman financial aid applications for fall entry is March 1.

RANDOLPH-MACON COLLEGE E-3

www.rmc.edu

Ashland, VA 23005	**(804) 752-7305** **(800) 888-1762**
Fax: (804) 752-4707	**Email: admissions@rmc.edu**
Full-time: 649 men, 773 women	**Faculty:** 110; IIB, av$
Part-time: 10 men, 6 women	**Ph.D.s:** 95%
Graduate: n/av	**Student/Faculty:** 8 to 1
Year: 4-1-4, summer session	**Tuition:** $40,000
Room & Board: $11,480	**Freshman Class:** 2820 applied, 1755 accepted, 374 enrolled
SAT EBR-W/M: 580/550 **ACT:** 24	**CEEB CODE:** 5566
Application Deadline: March 1	**VERY COMPETITIVE**

Randolph-Macon College is a private, coeducational liberal arts and sciences college. The college mission is to develop the mind and the character of its students which underlies the college's ultimate purpose: to prepare undergraduates for successful lives. R-MC enrolls undergraduate students who pursue their academic paths in 54 areas of study (including majors, minors, pre-professional programs, and other areas). There is 1 undergraduate school. In addition to regional accreditation, R-MC has baccalaureate program accreditation with ACS, and CAEP. The 116-acre campus is in a suburban area 15 miles north of Richmond and 90 miles south of Washington, D.C. Including any residence halls, there are 142 buildings.

STUDENT LIFE: 75% of undergraduates are from Virginia. Others are from 24 states, and 19 foreign countries. 75% are from public schools. 77% are White; 9% African American; 4% Hispanic; 4% two or more races; 2% Asian American; 1% American Indian/Alaska Native; 1% Foreign; 1% race unknown. 45% are Protestant; 14% Catholic. **Female To Male Ratio:** 1.2:1. The average age of freshmen is 18; all undergraduates, 20. 16% do not continue beyond their first year; 63% remain to graduate. **Housing:** 1290 students can be accommodated in college housing, which includes dorms and on-campus apartments. In addition, there are honors houses, language/international houses, special-interest houses, fraternity houses, sorority houses, senior apartments, Greek housing, and several college-owned houses. On-campus housing is guaranteed for all 4 years and is available on a lottery system for upperclassmen. 80% of students live on campus. All students may keep cars.

FACULTY/CLASSROOMS: 50% of faculty are male; 50% are female. All teach undergraduates and do research. No introductory courses are taught by graduate students. The average class size in an introductory lecture is 19; in a laboratory is 18; and in a regular course is 17.

PROGRAMS OF STUDY: R-MC confers B.A. and B.S. degrees. Bachelor's degrees are awarded in AGRICULTURE (environmental studies), BIOLOGICAL SCIENCE (biology/biological science and neurosciences), BUSINESS (accounting and business administration and management), COMMUNICATIONS AND THE ARTS (art history and appreciation, arts administration/management, classics, communications, dramatic arts, English, French, German, Greek, Latin, music, Spanish, and studio art), COMPUTER AND PHYSICAL SCIENCE (chemistry, computer science, mathematics, and physics), ENGINEERING AND ENVIRONMENTAL DESIGN (engineering physics), SOCIAL SCIENCE (archeology, Asian/Oriental studies, economics, history, international studies, philosophy, political science/government, psychology, religion, sociology, and women's studies). Biology, communications, and business have the largest enrollments.

ACTIVITIES: 28% of men belong to 8 national fraternities; 25% of women belong to 4 national sororities. There are 80 groups on campus, including diversity council, leadership fellows, art, cheerleading, choir, chorale, chorus, communications, computers, dance, debate, drama, environmental, equestrian club, ethnic, film, forensics, honors, international, jazz band, LGBT, literary magazine, musical theater, newspaper, opera, pep band, photography, political, professional, radio and TV, religious, social, social service, and student government. Popular campus events include the Cultural Arts Series, Monster Bash, and Beat Hampden-Sydney Week. **Sports:** There are 9 intercollegiate sports for men and 9 for women, and 15 intramural sports for men and 15 for women. Facilities include tennis courts, several playing fields, gyms, indoor pool, all-weather turf football/lacrosse field, weight room and training room. The sports and recreation center includes racquetball and squash courts, aerobics room, a track, multipurpose gym, and a climbing wall. **Graduates:** From July 1, 2016 to June 30, 2017, 310 bachelor's degrees were awarded. The most popular majors were communication (14%), business (12%), and biology (12%). In an average class, 4% graduate in 3 years or less, 88% graduate in 4 years or less, 6% graduate in 5 years or less, and 2% graduate in 6 years or less. Of the 2016 graduating class, 20% were enrolled in graduate school within 6 months of graduation, and 78% were employed.

SERVICES: Counseling and information services are available, as is tutoring in every subject. There is a reader service for the blind. There are also advisors for learning-disabled students. **Library/Resources:** The library contains 138,901 volumes, and 2,229 audio/video tapes/CDs/DVDs, and subscribes to 102,127 periodicals including electronic. Computerized library services include interlibrary loans, database searching, Internet access, and Wi-Fi capability. Special learning facilities include an art gallery, radio station, an academic center, observatory with radio telescope, scanning and transmission electron microscopy, human behavior lab, rodent lab, dark room, herbarium room, a greenhouse, a chamber music studio and music technology lab, and an auditorium with adjoining blackbox theater. **Physically Challenged Students:** 90% of the campus is accessible. Facilities include wheelchair ramps, elevators, special parking, specially equipped restrooms, special class scheduling, and special housing. **Special:** The College offers special programs in engineering with Columbia University and the University of Virginia, in forestry with Duke University, and in accounting with Virginia Commonwealth University. The College has a Guaranteed Admission Agreement with the George Washington University School of Nursing. An Early Assurance Program (EAP) exists with the Eastern Virginia Medical School (EVMS). The College also offers a preferred applicant track agreements into medical schools with VCU. Study-abroad programs are offered in 45 countries. Internships, dual majors, and a Washington semester are also available. B.A.-B.S. degrees are possible in all majors.

Travel classes are available during January term. There are 18 national honor societies, Phi Beta Kappa, and a freshman honors program. **Visiting:** There are regularly scheduled orientations for prospective students, including interviews, information sessions, tours, open houses, and visitation days. There are guides for informal visits, visitors may sit in on classes, and stay overnight. To schedule a visit, contact the Office of Admissions. **Campus Safety and Security:** Measures include 24-hour foot and vehicle patrol, emergency notification system, self-defense education, and security escort services. There are emergency telephones, lighted pathways/sidewalks, and controlled access to dorms/residences.

REQUIREMENTS: The SAT is required. Applicants must be graduates of an accredited secondary school or have completed their GED. Applicants should complete a minimum of 16 high school academic credits, including 4 years of English, 3 to 4 years each of math and science, and 2 to 3 years of foreign language, history, and social studies. An essay is required, and an interview is recommended. A GPA of 2.0 is required. AP and CLEP credits are accepted. Important factors in the admissions decision are advanced placement or honors courses, recommendations by school officials, and extracurricular activities record. To graduate, students must complete 110 credit hours, with 30 to 42 hours in the major and a minimum GPA of 2.0. All students must complete a Capstone course culminating the academic experience. All students must satisfy requirements in math, social science, lab science, literature, philosophy/theology, phys ed, fine arts, foreign language, history, and writing. There are also requirements for Western, non-Western, computing, multidisciplinary, and experiential courses. **Procedure:** Freshmen are admitted in the fall and spring. Entrance exams should be taken by January of the senior year. There are early admissions and deferred admissions plans. Early decision applications should be filed by November 15; regular applications, by March 1 for fall entry; and December 1 for spring entry. The fall 2017 application fee was $30. Notification of early decision is sent January 1; regular decision, April 1. Applications are accepted on-line. **Transfer Students:** 44 transfer students enrolled in 2016-2017. Applicants must have a minimum GPA of 2.0 and must be eligible to return to their previous institution. They must submit high school and college transcripts and SAT scores (the SAT requirement is waived for students who have earned an associate degree). 37 of 110 credits required for the bachelor's degree must be completed at R-MC. **International Students:** There are 26 international students enrolled. They must take the TOEFL with a minimum score of 550 on the paper-based TOEFL (PBT) or 80 on the Internet-based version (iBT). Students must take the IELTS, and the SAT or ACT if they are non-native English speakers.

ADMISSIONS: 62% of the 2017-2018 applicants were accepted. The SAT scores for the 2017-2018 freshman class were: Math-- 16% below 500, 55% between 500 and 599, 25% between 600 and 699, and 4% between 700 and 800. Evidence-Based Reading/Writing-- 5% below 500, 45% between 500 and 599, 45% between 600 and 699, and 8% between 700 and 800. The ACT scores were 2% between 12 and 17, 39% between 18 and 23, 45% between 24 and 29, and 13% above 30. 48% of the current freshmen were in the top fifth of their class; 78% were in the top two fifths. **Admissions Contact:** David Lesesne, Director. Email: *admissions@rmc.edu* Web: *www.rmc.edu*

FINANCIAL AID: In 2017-2018, 100% of all full-time freshmen received some form of financial aid. 75% of all full-time freshmen received need-based aid. The average freshman award was $29,326. Need-based scholarships or need-based grants averaged $26,710; need-based self-help aid (loans and jobs) averaged $3,875; and other non-need-based awards and non-need-based scholarships averaged $20,925. 46% of undergraduate students work part-time. The average financial indebtedness of the 2017 graduate was $34,426. R-MC is a member of CSS. The state aid form and the college's own financial statement are required. The FAFSA code is 003733. The priority date for freshman financial aid applications for fall entry is February 15.

ROANOKE COLLEGE C-3

www.roanoke.edu

Salem, VA 24153	**(540) 375-2270** **(800) 388-2276**
Fax: (540) 375-2267	**Email: admissions@roanoke.edu**
Full-time: 833 men, 1140 women	**Faculty:** 165; IIB, av$
Part-time: 28 men, 36 women	**Ph.D.s:** 88%
Graduate: n/av	**Student/Faculty:** 12 to 1
Year: semesters, summer session	**Tuition:** $42,694
Room & Board: $13,258	**Freshman Class:** 5117 applied, 3438 accepted, 557 enrolled
SAT EBR-W/M: 584/558 **ACT:** 24	**CEEB CODE:** 5571
Application Deadline: March 15	**VERY COMPETITIVE**

Roanoke College helps its students find their true passions, and enables them to pursue those passions with a broad education along with specific skills and in-depth knowledge of a chosen discipline. Students receive a strong liberal arts foundation through a unique Intellectual Inquiry core curriculum, emphasizing learning firsthand in topic based courses where fundamental concepts and skills are taught and then applied to real problems and issues. Experiential learning is emphasized throughout the curriculum. The college offers undergraduate programs in the arts and sciences, and in business administration. There is 1 undergraduate school. In addition to regional accreditation, Roanoke College has baccalaureate program accreditation with ACBSP, VDE, ACS, CAATE, and ASBMB. The 80-acre campus is in a suburban area 7 miles west of Roanoke, VA, in the Blue Ridge Mountains. Including any residence halls, there are 70 buildings.

STUDENT LIFE: 52% of undergraduates are from Virginia. Others are from 40 states, 32 foreign countries, and Canada. 82% are from public schools. 80% are White; 6% African American; 5% Hispanic; 5% two or more races; 4% Foreign; 1% Asian American. 35% are Protestant; 27% claim no religious affiliation; 20% Other 20% mix of various religious faiths, both western and non-western; 17% Catholic. **Female To Male Ratio:** 1.4:1. The average age of freshmen is 18; all undergraduates, 20. 16% do not continue beyond their first year; 67% remain to graduate. **Housing:** 1523 students can be accommodated in college housing, which includes single-sex dorms and on-campus apartments. In addition, there are honors houses, special-interest houses, fraternity houses, sorority houses, and living learning communities. On-campus housing is guaranteed for the freshman year only, is available on a first-come, first-served basis, and is available on a lottery system for upperclassmen. 78% of students live on campus. All students may keep cars.

FACULTY/CLASSROOMS: 48% of faculty are male; 52% are female. All teach undergraduates, 75% do research, and 75% do both. No introductory courses are taught by graduate students. The average class size in an introductory lecture is 19; in a laboratory is 17; and in a regular course is 18.

PROGRAMS OF STUDY: RC confers B.A., B.S. and B.B.A. degrees. Bachelor's degrees are awarded in AGRICULTURE (environmental studies), BIOLOGICAL SCIENCE (biochemistry and biology/biological science), BUSINESS (business administration and management and sports management), COMMUNICATIONS AND THE ARTS (art, art history and appreciation, communications, creative writing, French, literature, music, Spanish, and theatre arts), COMPUTER AND PHYSICAL SCIENCE (actuarial science, chemistry, computer science, mathematics, and physics), EDUCATION (physical education), HEALTH PROFESSIONS (exercise science and public health), SOCIAL SCIENCE (Christian studies, criminal justice, economics, history, interdisciplinary studies, international relations, philosophy, political science/government, psychology, religion, and sociology). Biology, chemistry, and philosophy are the strongest academically. Business administration, psychology, and biology have the largest enrollments.

ACTIVITIES: 22% of men belong to 5 national fraternities; 22% of women belong to 3 national sororities. There are 100 groups on campus, including art, band, cheerleading, choir, chorale, chorus, computers, dance, debate, drama, environmental, ethnic, honors, international, jazz band, LGBT, literary magazine, newspaper, orchestra, pep band, photography, political, professional, radio and TV, religious, social, social service, and student government. Popular campus events include Family weekend, President's Ball, Fridays on the Quad (FOTQ), Winterfest, and Alumni Weekend. **Sports:** There are 9 intercollegiate sports for men and 10 for women, and 11 intramural sports for men and 11 for women. Facilities include a field turf stadium, an athletic facility with 200 meter indoor track, a performance gym, and athletic training facilities, an all-weather track, practice and playing fields, tennis and racquetball courts, a swimming pool, and a fitness center. **Graduates:** From July 1, 2016 to June 30, 2017, 441 bachelor's degrees were awarded. The most popular majors were business administration (21%), psychology (11%), and biology (8%). In an average class, 1% graduate in 3 years or less, 62% graduate in 4 years or less, 66% graduate in 5 years or less, and 67% graduate in 6 years or less. Of the 2016 graduating class, 21% were enrolled in graduate school within 6 months of graduation, and 76% were employed.

SERVICES: Counseling and information services are available, as is tutoring in every subject. A supervised peer tutoring program is available at no charge to students, as well as the writing center and the center for learning and teaching. **Library/Resources:** The library contains 224,560 volumes, 141,461 microform items, and 8,233 audio/video tapes/CDs/

DVDs, and subscribes to 75,297 periodicals including electronic. Computerized library services include interlibrary loans, database searching, Internet access, and Wi-Fi capability. Special learning facilities include an art gallery, radio station, media classrooms, a video production facility, and multimedia computer labs. **Physically Challenged Students:** 85% of the campus is accessible. Facilities include wheelchair ramps, elevators, special parking, specially equipped restrooms, special class scheduling, and special housing. **Special:** We offer cross-registration with Hollins University and study abroad in many countries. Roanoke also offers internships, research with faculty, a Washington semester, the Virginia at Oxford Program, a semester of study in the Yucatan, a dual degree engineering degree with Virginia Polytechnic Institute and State University, credit by exam, and pass/fail options. A special May Term offers unique intensive travel and local experiences. Nondegree study is available to those students admitted with special status. There are 27 national honor societies, Phi Beta Kappa, a freshman honors program, and 15 departmental honors programs. **Visiting:** There are regularly scheduled orientations for prospective students, open houses that provide a sampling of college life at Roanoke, as well as discussing financial aid and admissions. Student/faculty panels answer questions, and campus tours are given. There are guides for informal visits, visitors may sit in on classes, and stay overnight. To schedule a visit, contact the Admissions Office. **Campus Safety and Security:** Measures include 24-hour foot and vehicle patrol, emergency notification system, self-defense education, and security escort services. There are shuttle buses, emergency telephones, lighted pathways/sidewalks, and controlled access to dorms/residences.

REQUIREMENTS: The SAT or ACT is required. An essay, and an interview are recommended. Applicants must be graduates of accredited secondary schools or have earned a GED. The college requires 18 (20 recommended) academic units, including 4 years of English, 3 courses in math, 4 courses (2 required) in foreign language (recommended), and 2 courses each in lab science and social studies. An audition is also recommended for performing arts majors. Students who have at least a 3.0 academic GPA may submit two graded writing samples in lieu of SAT or ACT test scores. AP and CLEP credits are accepted. Important factors in the admissions decision are advanced placement or honors courses, leadership record, and personality/intangible qualities. Requirements for graduation include completion of 33.5 courses, including about 9 to 12 in the major and about 11 to 14 in the Intellectual Inquiry core curriculum. The core consists of 2 first-year seminars; 5 to 7 topical courses drawn from the mathematical and natural sciences, the social sciences, and the humanities; a capstone that addresses a contemporary issue; and an intensive learning course. Students must also demonstrate competency in a foreign language at an intermediate level and complete 2 physical education courses. A 2.0 GPA is required. **Procedure:** Freshmen are admitted in the fall, spring, and summer. Entrance exams should be taken by January of the senior year. There are early decision, deferred admissions, and rolling admissions plans. Early decision applications should be filed by November 15; regular applications, by March 15 for fall entry; and December 15 for spring entry. The fall 2017 application fee was $30. Notification of early decision is sent December 15; regular decision, on a rolling basis. 70 early decision candidates were accepted for the 2017-2018 class. 174 applicants were on the 2017 waiting list; 16 were admitted. Applications are accepted on-line. **Transfer Students:** 88 transfer students enrolled in 2016-2017. Transfers must have a minimum GPA of 2.2. SAT or ACT scores and an interview are recommended. Transfers must be in good academic standing with their previous institution. 17 of 34 credits required for the bachelor's degree must be completed at RC. **International Students:** There are 82 international students enrolled. They must take the TOEFL with a minimum score of 80 on the Internet-based version (iBT). They must also take the SAT or ACT.

ADMISSIONS: 67% of the 2017-2018 applicants were accepted. The SAT scores for the 2017-2018 freshman class were: Math-- 16% below 500, 55% between 500 and 599, 25% between 600 and 699, and 4% between 700 and 800. Evidence-Based Reading/Writing-- 10% below 500, 47% between 500 and 599, 38% between 600 and 699, and 5% between 700 and 800. The ACT scores were 4% between 12 and 17, 37% between 18 and 23, 49% between 24 and 29, and 9% above 30. 30% of the current freshmen were in the top fifth of their class; 64% were in the top two fifths. 5 freshmen graduated first in their class. **Admissions Contact:** Dr. Brenda Poggendorf, Vice President of Enrollment. Email: *admissions@roanoke.edu* Web: *www.roanoke.edu*

FINANCIAL AID: In 2017-2018, 99% of all full-time freshmen received some form of financial aid. 80% of all full-time freshmen received need-based aid. The average freshman award was $36,817. Need-based scholarships or need-based grants averaged $7,966 ($23,498 maximum); need-based self-help aid (loans and jobs) averaged $4,866 ($12,500 maximum); and other non-need-based awards and non-need-based scholarships averaged $22,607 ($54,366 maximum). 46% of undergraduate students work part-time. The average financial indebtedness of the 2017 graduate was $41,187. The state aid form is required. The FAFSA code is 003736. The priority date for freshman financial aid applications for fall entry is March 1.

SHENANDOAH UNIVERSITY — D-1

www.su.edu

Winchester, VA 22601	**(540) 665-4581** **(800) 432-2266**
Fax: (540) 665-4627	**Email: admit@su.edu**
Full-time: 797 men, 1194 women	**Faculty:** 189; I, --$
Part-time: 25 men, 47 women	**Ph.D.s:** 79%
Graduate: 475 men, 1306 women	**Student/Faculty:** 11 to 1
Year: semesters, summer session	**Tuition:** $31,920
Room & Board: $10,180	**Freshman Class:** 2294 applied, 1947 accepted, 438 enrolled
SAT CR/M: 560/542 **ACT:** 23	**CEEB CODE:** 5613
Application Deadline: rolling	**COMPETITIVE**

Shenandoah University, founded in 1875, is a private, nationally recognized university that blends the best of professional studies and the liberal arts. SU is affiliated with the United Methodist Church and offers undergraduate programs in arts and sciences, nursing, respiratory care, business, music, theater, and dance. Graduate programs include: business, music, performance, pedagogy, music education, education, organizational leadership, nursing, pharmacy, athletic training, occupational therapy, physical therapy and physician assistant studies. SU empowers its students to help the human condition and to be professionals and leaders wherever they go. There are 4 undergraduate schools and 7 graduate schools. In addition to regional accreditation, SU has baccalaureate program accreditation with AACSB, ACPE, NASM, CAEP, CCNE, AMTA, and CoARC. The 315-acre campus is in a small town 72 miles west of Washington, D.C. Including any residence halls, there are 49 buildings.

STUDENT LIFE: 59% of undergraduates are from Virginia. Others are from 48 states and 22 foreign countries. 57% are White; 16% race unknown; 11% African American; 7% Hispanic; 4% Foreign; 3% Asian American; 3% American Indian/Alaska Native; 2% two or more races. 62% claim no religious affiliation; 20% Protestant. **Female To Male Ratio:** 2.0:1. The average age of freshmen is 18; all undergraduates, 21. 33% do not continue beyond their first year; 67% remain to graduate. **Housing:** 1029 students can be accommodated in college housing, which includes dorms, on-campus apartments, and off-campus apartments. In addition, there are special-interest houses, and community service housing. On-campus housing is guaranteed for the freshman year only, is available on a first-come, first-served basis, and is available on a lottery system for upperclassmen. 52% of students commute. All students may keep cars.

FACULTY/CLASSROOMS: 43% of faculty are male; 57% are female. 70% teach undergraduates. No introductory courses are taught by graduate students. The average class size in an introductory lecture is 18; in a laboratory is 11; and in a regular course is 13.

PROGRAMS OF STUDY: SU confers B.A., B.S., B.B.A., B.F.A., B.M., and B.M.T. degrees. Master's and doctoral degrees are also awarded. Bachelor's degrees are awarded in BIOLOGICAL SCIENCE (biology/biological science), BUSINESS (business administration and management, economics and finance, entrepreneurial studies, and sports management), COMMUNICATIONS AND THE ARTS (acting, church music, collaborative piano, composition, dance, dramatic arts, English, jazz, mass communications, music production/recording technology, music technology, music theatre accompanying, musical theater, performing arts, Spanish, theater design, and theatre production), COMPUTER AND PHYSICAL SCIENCE (chemistry and mathematics), EDUCATION (core studies, global studies, music education, and university studies), ENGINEERING AND ENVIRONMENTAL DESIGN (environmental science), HEALTH PROFESSIONS (exercise science, health care administration, kinesiology, music therapy, nursing, public health, and respiratory therapy), SOCIAL SCIENCE (criminal justice, economics, history, political science/government, psychology, religion, and sociology). Nursing, business administration, and music are the strongest academically. Nursing, business administration, and exercise science have the largest enrollments.

ACTIVITIES: There are no fraternities or sororities. There are 90 groups on campus, including art, band, cheerleading, choir, chorale, chorus, dance, debate, drama, environmental, ethnic, film, honors, international, jazz band, LGBT, literary magazine, musical theater, newspaper, online radio station, orchestra, pep band, political, professional, religious, social, social service, student government, and symphony. Popular campus events include Rock the Bloom, Movie Nights, Wine Tasting, Jazz Trio Social, Relay for Life, Welcome Back, Sun Block Party, International Days, Homecoming and Family Weekend, WATTS Night Out, Bingo and Bowling, and MLK Day Services. **Sports:** There are 10 intercollegiate sports for men and 11 for women, and 8 intramural sports for men and 8 for women. Facilities include volleyball and basketball courts, a regulation track, a turf field for football, soccer, field hockey, and lacrosse, a four-lane 400-meter track and throwing area, a multi-use grass field for practices and intramurals, indoor batting cages, a weight room with cardio equipment, selectorized weights, power racks, free weights, and plate loaded equipment and dumbells, and 2 athletic training facilities. **Graduates:** From July 1, 2016 to June 30, 2017, 539 bachelor's degrees were awarded. The most popular majors were nursing (25%), business administration (12%), and exercise science (9%). In an average class, 40% graduate in 4 years or less, 55% graduate in 5 years or less, and 56% graduate in 6 years or less. Of the 2016 graduating class, 14% were enrolled in graduate school within 6 months of graduation, and 67% were employed.

SERVICES: Counseling and information services are available, as is tutoring in every subject. **Library/Resources:** The library contains 126,142 volumes, 55,410 microform items, and 13,770 audio/video tapes/CDs/DVDs, and subscribes to 86,560 periodicals, including electronic. Computerized library services include interlibrary loans, database searching, Internet access, and Wi-Fi capability. Special learning facilities include an art gallery, the Pharmacy Apothecary Museum, environmental studies, a green rooftop garden, a cadaver lab, a nursing simulation station, a center for literacy, an academic enrichment center, a children's literature center, a media center, 2 book scan stations, and an online research room. There is also a Discovery Center: it is designed to provide a single, unified search interface for nearly all of the university's digital, and a print library content, including a wireless everywhere, print anywhere printing system. The Shenandoah Conservatory is an all-Steinway school and has 3 academic observation rooms: a recording studio, a music therapy clinic, and the Collins Music Learning Suite. There is also a Mac Lab, which has classrooms for music, piano, film and acting, voice, and a voice science lab. **Physically Challenged Students:** 91% of the campus is accessible. Facilities include wheelchair ramps, elevators, special parking, specially equipped restrooms, special class scheduling, lowered drinking fountains, special housing, electric doors, and 22 defibrillators. **Special:** SU offers internships; dual majors (Pharm-MBA, DPT/MSAT, PA-MPH); accelerated degree programs: ASD NUR.BS, 3+2 model with AT, 3+4 model with PharmD; public health fast-track to MPH program (3+2); cross-registration collaborative agreements with James Madison University (Nursing), Johns Hopkins School of Nursing, Marshall University School of Nursing, Old Dominion University School of Nursing, West Virginia Wesleyan Department of Nursing, George Washington University (Pharmacy), and B.A. Interdisciplinary Studies. Study abroad: Choice of 166 Global Partner institutions among 55 nations. No work-study programs are available; non-degree study is possible. During breaks (winter, spring and summer) with adviser approval, students may participate in service learning, volunteer, and third-party programs abroad. Study abroad opportunities with Global Experiential Learning (GEL): short-term, credit-bearing, faculty-led programs are offered during winter, spring and summer breaks. SU also has the Global Citizenship Project (GCP). Selected students, faculty, and staff travel with their group during spring break to one of five destinations around the world. GCP is an exclusive offering created and funded by Shenandoah University. Applicants are selected according to their application and one-page essay submission. We also participate in the VFIC Foreign Language project. There is also a 4+1 option for Conservatory undergraduates to earn their PLM.MS in one year by taking credits during undergraduate study plus a summer course prior to a start of a master's degree. There are 3 national honor societies. **Visiting:** There are regularly scheduled orientations for prospective students, including information sessions with faculty and staff, student-guided campus tours, and lunch in the dining hall. There are guides for informal visits; visitors may sit in on classes and stay overnight. To schedule a visit, contact Andrew Woodall at (800) 432-2266. **Campus Safety and Security:** Measures include 24-hour foot and vehicle patrol, emergency notification system, self-defense education, and security escort services. There are shuttle buses, emergency telephones, lighted pathways/sidewalks, controlled access to dorms/residences. There is also a lock-out car and dead-car battery jump assistance, LIVESAFE app (Safer in 60 Seconds), an emergency operation plan program for each building, self-defense classes, a responsible alcohol use and peer intervention training class, and a Safe Walk Safe Ride around the campus.

REQUIREMENTS: The SAT is required. The high school transcript should indicate courses pursued; 4 units of English, 3 units of mathematics (Algebra I, Algebra II and Geometry), 2 units each of social studies, and science (including one laboratory science), and foreign language are strongly recommended. Other classes may be appropriate for some curricula and will be evaluated on an individual basis by the Office of Admissions. Applicants are strongly advised to indicate community and extra-curricular involvement. Shenandoah Conservatory applicants are also required to successfully complete an audition or portfolio review. The most heavily weighted factor in an applicant's total profile is actual academic performance, as indicated by the high school transcript. The SAT or the ACT is required there is no preference as to which one a student submits. Applicants to music, theatre and dance programs must complete an audition or portfolio review. A GPA of 2.5 is required. AP and CLEP credits are accepted. Important factors in the admissions decision are advanced placement or honors courses, extracurricular activities record, and evidence of special talent. To graduate with a bachelor's degree, all undergraduate students must have taken the required core curriculum with a cumulative GPA of 2.0. Some programs require a higher grade-point average in the major. The minimum number of credit hours required for a baccalaureate degree is 120. Other requirements vary depending on the program of study. Candidates for baccalaureate degrees must earn a minimum of 30 credit hours of the 120 credit-hour requirement at Shenandoah University. At least 30 credit hours must be at or above the 300 level. **Procedure:** Freshmen are admitted in the fall and spring. Entrance exams should be taken by the junior year or early in the senior year. There are deferred admissions and rolling admissions plans. Application deadlines are open. The fall 2017 application fee was $30. Notification is sent on a rolling basis. Applications are accepted online. **Transfer Students:** 161 transfer students enrolled in 2016-2017. Transfer applicants must submit evidence of good standing at the college last attended and an official transcript(s) of credits earned at all institutions previously attended. A minimum cumulative 2.0 GPA and 24 college credits are required. Students who have earned fewer than 24 college credits need to submit their high school transcript and SAT or ACT scores for admission review. 30 of 120 credits required for the bachelors degree must be completed at SU. **International Students:** There are 57 international students enrolled. They must take the TOEFL with a minimum score of 550 on the paper-based TOEFL (PBT) or 79 on the Internet-based version (iBT). Students must take the IELTS. They must also take the SAT or ACT.

ADMISSIONS: 85% of the 2017-2018 applicants were accepted. The SAT scores for the 2017-2018 freshman class were: Critical Reading-- 19% below 500, 48% between 500 and 599, 29% between 600 and 699, and 4% between 700 and 800. Math-- 24% below 500, 54% between 500 and 599, 20% between 600 and 699, and 2% between 700 and 800. The ACT scores were 6% between 12 and 17, 50% between 18 and 23, 34% between 24 and 29, and 10% above 30. **Admissions Contact:** Andrew Woodall, Executive Director of Recruitment and Admissions. Email: *admit@su.edu* Web: *www.su.edu*

FINANCIAL AID: In 2017-2018, 100% of all full-time freshmen received some form of financial aid. 70% of all full-time freshmen received need-based aid. The average freshman award was $28,835. Need-based scholarships or need-based grants averaged $4,055 ($16,017 maximum); need-based self-help aid (loans and jobs) averaged $2,648 ($4,454 maximum); and other non-need-based awards and non-need-based scholarships averaged $11,255 ($30,500 maximum). 49% of undergraduate students work part-time. The average financial indebtedness of the 2017 graduate was $28,941. The state aid form and Virginia United Methodist Scholarship application are required. The FAFSA code is 003737. Check with the school for current application deadlines.

UNIVERSITY OF LYNCHBURG D-3
www.lynchburg.edu

Lynchburg, VA 24501 **(800) 426-8101**

Fax: (434) 544-8653 **Email:** admissions@lynchburg.edu

Full-time: 767 men, 1161 women	**Faculty:** 157; IIA, --$
Part-time: 40 men, 82 women	**Ph.D.s:** 89%
Graduate: 243 men, 517 women	**Student/Faculty:** 13 to 1
Year: semesters, summer session	**Tuition:** $37,690
Room & Board: $10,680	**Freshman Class:** 4880 applied, 3638 accepted, 543 enrolled
SAT EBR-W/M: 555/534 **ACT:** 22	**CEEB CODE:** 5372
Application Deadline: open	**COMPETITIVE**

University of Lynchburg, formerly Lynchburg College, established in 1903, is a private institution affiliated with the Christian Church (Disciples of Christ). UL offers bachelor's degrees in 40 majors, master's degrees in 16 programs, and 4 doctoral degrees (physical therapy, medical science, physician assistant & leadership studies). The mission of University of Lynchburg is to develop students with strong character and balanced perspectives and prepare them for engagement in a global society and effective leadership in the civic, professional, and spiritual dimensions of life. There are 6 undergraduate schools and 1 graduate school. In addition to regional accreditation, UL has baccalaureate program accreditation with ACBSP, NASM, CCNE, CAAHEP, and CACREP. The 264-acre campus is in a suburban area 180 miles southwest of Washington, D.C., and 120 west of Richmond. Including any residence halls, there are 40 buildings.

STUDENT LIFE: 69% of undergraduates are from Virginia. Others are from 42 states, 13 foreign countries, and Canada. 8% are race unknown; 70% White; 4% Hispanic; 3% two or more races; 2% Foreign; 10% African American; 1% Asian American. **Female To Male Ratio:** 1.7:1. The average age of freshmen is 18; all undergraduates, 25. 13% do not continue beyond their first year; 75% remain to graduate. **Housing:** 1800 students can be accommodated in college housing, which includes coed dorms and on-campus apartments, honors houses, language/international houses, special-interest houses, fraternity houses, and sorority houses. On-campus housing is guaranteed for all 4 years. 72% of students live on campus. Upperclassmen may keep cars.

FACULTY/CLASSROOMS: 47% of faculty are male; 53% are female. 93% teach undergraduates. No introductory courses are taught by graduate students. The average class size in a regular course is 17.

PROGRAMS OF STUDY: UL confers B.A. and B.S. degrees. Master's and doctoral degrees are also awarded. Bachelor's degrees are awarded in AGRICULTURE (environmental studies), BIOLOGICAL SCIENCE (biology/biological science), BUSINESS (accounting, business administration and management, human resources, management science, marketing/retailing/merchandising, and sports management), COMMUNICATIONS AND THE ARTS (art, communications, English, French, music, Spanish, and theatre arts), COMPUTER AND PHYSICAL SCIENCE (chemistry, computer science, mathematics, and physics), EDUCATION (athletic training, education, elementary education, and music education), ENGINEERING AND ENVIRONMENTAL DESIGN (environmental science), HEALTH PROFESSIONS (biomedical science, exercise science, health promotion, and nursing), SOCIAL SCIENCE (criminology, economics, history, international relations, liberal arts/general studies, philosophy, physical fitness/movement, political science/government, psychology, religion, and sociology). Nursing, exercise physiology and criminology have the largest enrollments.

ACTIVITIES: 10% of men belong to 5 national fraternities; 14% of women belong to 5 national sororities. There are 80 groups on campus, including art, cheerleading, choir, chorus, communications, computers, dance, drama, environmental, ethnic, honors, international, jazz band, LGBT, literary magazine, musical theater, newspaper, orchestra, political, professional, religious, social, social service, and student government. Popular campus events include Homecoming, Turkey Bowl, and Campus Days. **Sports:** There are 10 intercollegiate sports for men and 11 for women, and 12 intramural sports for men and 12 for women. Facilities include fields for soccer, field hockey & lacrosse, weight room, exercise physiology lab, field house, athletic fields, ropes course, climbing wall, and hiking/mountain biking trails. **Graduates:** From July 1, 2016 to June 30, 2017, 488 bachelor's degrees were awarded. The most popular majors were nursing (10%), communication studies (9%), and elementary education (8%). In an average class, 3% graduate in 3 years or less, 51% graduate in 4 years or less, 60% graduate in 5 years or less, and 59% graduate in 6 years or less.

SERVICES: Counseling and information services are available, as is tutoring in most subjects. Tutoring is available in most freshman and sophomore subjects, some upperclass subjects, and in math and writing. **Library/Resources:** The library contains 465,878 volumes, 466,605 microform items, and 6,629 audio/video tapes/CDs/DVDs, and subscribes to 139 periodicals including electronic. Computerized library services include interlibrary loans, database searching, Internet access, and Wi-Fi capability. Special learning facilities include an art gallery, astronomical observatory, nature center (470 acre farm used for science classes), a theatre, and 2 cadaver labs. **Physically Challenged Students:** 95% of the campus is accessible. Facilities include wheelchair ramps, elevators, special parking, specially equipped restrooms, special class scheduling, lowered drinking fountains, lowered telephones, and special housing. **Special:** Students may cross-register with Sweet Briar and Randolph Colleges as part of the Tri-College Consortium, and they may also study abroad in 20 countries. More than half of our graduates complete an external internship. A 3-2 engineering degree is available in cooperation with Old Dominion University and the University of Virginia. There are 14 national honor societies and a freshman honors program. **Visiting:** There are regularly scheduled orientations for prospective students, including individual appointments. There are guides for informal visits, visitors may sit in on classes, and stay overnight. To schedule a visit, contact the Admissions Office. **Campus Safety and Security:** Measures include 24-hour foot and vehicle patrol, emergency notification system, and security escort services. There are emergency telephones, lighted pathways/sidewalks, controlled access to dorms/residences. All residence halls are locked 24 hours a day. Admission is only by scanning an ID card.

REQUIREMENTS: The SAT or ACT is required. SAT: Subject Tests are recommended. GED's are reviewed on a case-by-case basis. Applicants should have earned between 16 to 20 academic high school credits in English, math and social science, lab science, and foreign language. AP and CLEP credits are accepted. Important factors in the admissions decision are advanced placement or honors courses, leadership record, and recommendations by school officials. The 51 hour core includes foreign language, fine arts, written composition, history, lab science, literature, math, oral communications, philosophy, religious studies, social science, and wellness. A senior symposium is also required, as is a senior project/thesis in some programs. Students must complete 124 credit hours to graduate, with a minimum 2.0 GPA, and 30 to 69 hours in their major. **Procedure:** Freshmen are admitted in the fall, spring, and summer. Entrance exams should be taken in the junior year and in the first semester of the senior year. There are early decision, deferred admissions, and rolling admissions plans. Early decision applications should be filed by November 15. The fall 2017 application fee was $30. Notification of early decision is sent December 15; regular decision, Applications are accepted on-line. **Transfer Students:** 88 transfer students enrolled in 2016-2017. Transfer students must have a minimum GPA of 2.0 to be considered, and must be in good academic and social standing. The SAT or ACT is not required for transfer students. An interview is recommended. 48 of 124 credits required for the bachelor's degree must be completed at UL. **International Students:** There are 69 international students enrolled. They must take the TOEFL with a minimum score of 550 on the paper-based TOEFL (PBT) or 78 on the Internet-based version (iBT). They must also take the SAT or ACT.

ADMISSIONS: 75% of the 2017-2018 applicants were accepted. The SAT scores for the 2017-2018 freshman class were: Math-- 30% below 500, 51% between 500 and 599, 18% between 600 and 699, and 2% between 700 and 800. Evidence-Based Reading/Writing-- 21% below 500, 51% between 500 and 599, 24% between 600 and 699, and 4% between 700 and 800. The ACT scores were 13% between 12 and 17, 59% between 18 and 23, 25% between 24 and 29, and 3% above 30. **Admissions Contact:** Sharon Walters-Bower, Director of Admissions. Email: *admissions@lynchburg.edu* Web: *www.lynchburg.edu*

FINANCIAL AID: In 2017-2018, 80% of all full-time freshmen received some form of financial aid and need-based aid. The average freshman award was $29,360. Need-based scholarships or need-based grants averaged $26,691; need-based self-help aid (loans and jobs) averaged $3,465; and other non-need-based awards and non-need-based scholarships averaged $20,157. 35% of undergraduate students work part-time. The average financial indebtedness of the 2017 graduate was $35,000. UL is a member of CSS. The state aid form is required. The FAFSA code is 003720. The deadline for filing freshman financial aid applications for fall entry is March 1.

THE UNIVERSITY OF VIRGINIA'S COLLEGE AT WISE *(The complete profile is made available exclusively on our website, www.barronspac.com)*

UNIVERSITY OF MARY WASHINGTON E-2

www.umw.edu

Fredericksburg, VA 22401	**(540) 654-2000** **(800) 468-5614**
Fax: (540) 654-1857	**Email: admit@umw.edu**
Full-time: 1357 men, 2524 women	**Faculty:** 244; IIB, av$
Part-time: 244 men, 390 women	**Ph.D.s:** 89%
Graduate: 176 men, 402 women	**Student/Faculty:** 14 to 1
Year: semesters, summer session	**Tuition:** $12,128 ($27,374)
Room & Board: $10,911	**Freshman Class:** 4847 applied, 3724 accepted, 955 enrolled
SAT CR/M/W: 570/560/560 **ACT:** 25	**CEEB CODE:** 5398
Application Deadline: February 1	**COMPETITIVE+**

University of Mary Washington is a premier, selective public liberal arts and sciences university that is highly respected for its commitment to academic excellence, and strong undergraduate programs. The university, features colleges of business, education, arts, and sciences. There are 3 campuses; a residential campus in Fredericksburg, VA, a second in nearby Stafford, and a third in Dahlgren, VA, which serves as a center of development of educational and research partnerships between the Navy, higher education institutions, and the region's employers. The figures given in the above capsule and in this profile are approximate. In addition to regional accreditation, UMW has baccalaureate program accreditation with NASM. The 176-acre campus is in a suburban area 50 miles south of Washington, D.C., and 50 miles north of Richmond. Including any residence halls, there are 48 buildings.

STUDENT LIFE: 87% of undergraduates are from Virginia. Others are from 38 states, 23 foreign countries, and Canada. 87% are from public schools. 64% are White; 6% African American; 6% Hispanic; 5% Asian American; 4% two or more races; 14% race unknown; 1% Foreign. **Female To Male Ratio:** 1.9:1. The average age of freshmen is 18; all undergraduates, 22. 17% do not continue beyond their first year; 76% remain to graduate. **Housing:** 2820 students can be accommodated in college housing, which includes dorms, and on-campus apartments. In addition, there are language/international houses, special-interest houses, living and learning communities, and gender neutral. On-campus housing is available on a lottery system for upperclassmen. 61% of students live on campus. Upperclassmen may keep cars.

FACULTY/CLASSROOMS: 51% of faculty are male; 49% are female. All teach undergraduates. No introductory courses are taught by graduate students. The average class size in an introductory lecture is 27; in a laboratory is 22; and in a regular course is 20.

PROGRAMS OF STUDY: UMW confers B.A., B.S., and B.L.S. degrees. Master's degrees are also awarded. Bachelor's degrees are awarded in BIOLOGICAL SCIENCE (biology/biological science), BUSINESS (business administration and management), COMMUNICATIONS AND THE ARTS (art history and appreciation, classics, dramatic arts, English, French, German, historic preservation, music, Spanish, and studio art), COMPUTER AND PHYSICAL SCIENCE (chemistry, computer science, mathematics, and physics), ENGINEERING AND ENVIRONMENTAL DESIGN (environmental science), SOCIAL SCIENCE (American studies, anthropology, economics, geography, history, international relations, liberal arts/general studies, philosophy, political science/government, psychology, religion, and sociology). Historic preservation, history, and political science are the strongest academically. Business administration, psychology, and biology have the largest enrollments.

ACTIVITIES: There are no fraternities or sororities. There are 140 groups on campus, including students helping Honduras, art, bagpipe, cheerleading, choir, chorale, chorus, class council, computers, dance, debate, drama, environmental, ethnic, film, honors, international, jazz band, LGBT, literary magazine, musical theater, newspaper, opera, orchestra, pep band, photography, political, professional, radio and TV, religious, social, social service, student government, symphony, and yearbook. Popular campus events include Rocktoberfest, Junior Ring Dance and Multicultural Fair. **Sports:** There are 10 intercollegiate sports for men and 12 for women, and 16 intramural sports for men and 20 for women. Facilities include all-weather-turf recreational sports field, 6-lane, 25-yard indoor pool, basketball and volleyball courts, a weight room, batting cages, training rooms, playing fields for all outdoor sports, a running course, handball/racquetball courts, an 8-lane, 400-meter track, a fitness and recreation facility, and an indoor tennis center. **Graduates:** From July 1, 2016 to June 30, 2017, 868 bachelor's degrees were awarded. The most popular majors were English (11%), business administration (11%), and psychology (9%). In an average class, 69% graduate in 4 years or less, 75% graduate in 5 years or less, and 76% graduate in 6 years or less. Of the 2016 graduating class, 24% were enrolled in graduate school within 6 months of graduation, and 95% were employed.

SERVICES: Counseling and information services are available, as is tutoring in most subjects. There is a reader service for the blind. There is also a writing center, and a speaking center. **Library/Resources:** The library contains 424,417 volumes, 610,498 microform items, and 2,206 audio/video tapes/CDs/DVDs, and subscribes to 62,985 periodicals including electronic. Computerized library services include interlibrary loans, database searching, Internet access, and Wi-Fi capability. Special learning facilities include an art gallery, radio station, the center for historic preservation, a center for Asian Studies, and a multicultural center. **Physically Challenged Students:** 75% of the campus is accessible. Facilities include wheelchair ramps, elevators, special parking, specially equipped restrooms, lowered drinking fountains, lowered telephones, and special housing. **Special:** Study abroad anywhere in the world, a Washington semester, and credit for off-campus work experience are available. The university also offers dual majors, work-study programs, student-designed majors, pass/fail options, more than 500 internships for credit. Teacher licensure preparation is offered for elementary and secondary education. Elementary education is a 5-year bachelor's-master's degree program. There are 23 national honor societies, Phi Beta Kappa, and a freshman honors program. **Visiting:** There are regularly scheduled orientations for prospective students, including information sessions, available Monday through Friday followed by a student-guided tour, and 2 Saturday open houses each semester. Visitors may sit in on classes and stay overnight. To schedule a visit, contact the Office of Admissions. **Campus Safety and Security:** Measures include 24-hour foot and vehicle patrol, emergency notification system, self-defense education, and security escort services. There are emergency telephones, lighted pathways/sidewalks, and controlled access to dorms/residences.

REQUIREMENTS: The SAT or ACT and ACT Writing Test are recommended. Applicants must be graduates of an accredited secondary school or hold the GED. The Admissions Committee recommends that applicants complete 4 years of each of math, English, foreign language, science, and social studies. A SAT: Subject test is strongly recommended. Application essays are required. A counselor or teacher recommendation is also required. AP and CLEP credits are accepted. Important factors in the admissions decision are advanced placement or honors courses, evidence of special talent, and recommendations by school officials. To graduate, students must complete 120 credit hours and a minimum GPA of 2.0. Hours required in the major vary. The B.A. and B.S. general education curriculum includes a first-year seminar, courses in quantitative reasoning, natural science, human experience and society, global inquiry, language, arts, literature and performance, and experiential learning. The experiential learning requirement may be fulfilled through study abroad, service learning, undergraduate research, or career internships. Students complete 4 writing-intensive courses and 2 speaking-intensive courses from across the curriculum. A thesis is required in some majors and programs of study. The B.L.S. degreee program is a flexible, adult-oriented alternative that features slightly different requirements. **Procedure:** Freshmen are admitted in the fall and spring. Entrance exams should be taken by January of the senior year. There are early admissions and deferred admissions plans. Applications should be filed by February 1 for fall entry; November 1 for spring entry. The fall 2017 application fee was $50. Notifications are sent April 1. 352 applicants were on the 2017 waiting list; 73 were admitted. Applications are accepted on-line. **Transfer Students:** 309 transfer students enrolled in 2016-2017. The university recommends that applicants for transfer have a minimum GPA of 3.0 and 30 college credits. The SAT and high school transcripts are required. Graduates from Virginia community colleges are given preference for admission. 30 of 120 credits required for the bachelor's degree must be completed at UMW. **International Students:** There are 38 international students enrolled. They must take the TOEFL with a minimum score of

88 on the Internet-based version (iBT). They must also take the SAT or ACT.

ADMISSIONS: 77% of the 2017-2018 applicants were accepted. The SAT scores for the 2017-2018 freshman class were: Critical Reading-- 10% below 500, 42% between 500 and 599, 37% between 600 and 699, and 10% between 700 and 800. Math-- 14% below 500, 47% between 500 and 599, 34% between 600 and 699, and 4% between 700 and 800. Writing-- 12% below 500, 45% between 500 and 599, 37% between 600 and 699, and 6% between 700 and 800. The ACT scores were 7% below 12, 24% between 12 and 17, 34% between 18 and 23, 18% between 24 and 29, and 17% above 30. 5 freshmen graduated first in their class. **Admissions Contact:** Candace Fox, Assistant Director of Admissions. Email: *admit@umw.edu* Web: *www.umw.edu*

FINANCIAL AID: In 2017-2018, 66% of all full-time freshmen received some form of financial aid. 34% of all full-time freshmen received need-based aid. The average freshman award was $4,800. Need-based scholarships or need-based grants averaged $6,493 ($2,455 maximum); need-based self-help aid (loans and jobs) averaged $3,324 ($7,500 maximum); and other non-need-based awards and non-need-based scholarships averaged $15,423 ($30,371 maximum). 28% of undergraduate students work part-time. The average financial indebtedness of the 2017 graduate was $23,300. The college's own financial statement is required. The FAFSA code is 003746. The deadline for filing freshman financial aid applications for fall entry is March 1.

UNIVERSITY OF RICHMOND E-3
www.richmond.edu

University of Richmond, VA 23173 (804) 289-8640 (800) 700-1662
Fax: (804) 287-6003 **Email:** admission@richmond.edu

Full-time: 1404 men, 1555 women	**Faculty:** 337; IIB, ++$
Part-time: 25 men, 15 women	**Ph.D.s:** 94%
Graduate: 247 men, 257 women	**Student/Faculty:** 9 to 1
Year: semesters, summer session	**Tuition:** $50,910
Room & Board: $11,820	**Freshman Class:** 10013 applied, 3301 accepted, 801 enrolled
SAT EBR-W/M: 680/680 **ACT:** 31	**CEEB CODE:** 5569
Application Deadline: January 15	**MOST COMPETITIVE**

University of Richmond provides an academically challenging, intellectually vibrant, and collaborative community dedicated to the holistic development of students. A Richmond education prepares students for lives of purpose, thoughtful inquiry, and responsible leadership in a diverse world. Through close mentoring and small classes taught by dedicated teacher-scholars and the opportunities and environment made possible by talented and engaged staff, the university challenges students to recognize their full potential, supports the development of their resilience, and encourages their growth as socially responsible community members. There are 3 undergraduate schools and 2 graduate schools. In addition to regional accreditation, UR has baccalaureate program accreditation with AACSB, CAEP, ACS, ASBMB, and ABA. The 350-acre campus is in a suburban area 6 miles west of Richmond. Including any residence halls, there are 81 buildings.

STUDENT LIFE: 80% of undergraduates are from out of state, mostly the Northeast. Students are from 48 states, 71 foreign countries, and Canada. 61% are from public schools. 9% are Hispanic; 8% Asian American; 7% African American; 55% White; 4% two or more races; 4% race unknown; 12% Foreign. **Female To Male Ratio:** 1.1:1. The average age of freshmen is 18; all undergraduates, 20. 7% do not continue beyond their first year; 93% remain to graduate. **Housing:** 2677 students can be accommodated in college housing, which includes gender neutral, single sex dorms, coed dorms, on-campus apartments, and special-interest houses. On-campus housing is available on a first-come, first-served basis, and is available on a lottery system for upperclassmen. 92% of students live on campus. All students may keep cars.

FACULTY/CLASSROOMS: 56% of faculty are male; 44% are female. All teach undergraduates. No introductory courses are taught by graduate students. The average class size in an introductory lecture is 18; in a laboratory is 13; and in a regular course is 17.

PROGRAMS OF STUDY: UR confers B.A., B.S., and B.S.B.A. degrees. Master's and doctoral degrees are also awarded. Bachelor's degrees are awarded in AGRICULTURE (environmental studies), BIOLOGICAL SCIENCE (biochemistry, biology/biological science, and molecular biology), BUSINESS (accounting and business administration and management), COMMUNICATIONS AND THE ARTS (Arabic, art history, communication rhetoric/communication, dance, English, film arts, French, German studies, Greek, journalism, Latin, music, Spanish, studio art, and theatre arts), COMPUTER AND PHYSICAL SCIENCE (chemistry, computer science, mathematics, and physics), HEALTH PROFESSIONS (health science), SOCIAL SCIENCE (American studies, anthropology, Chinese Studies, classical/ancient civilization, cognitive science, economics, geography, history, interdisciplinary studies, international studies, Italian studies, philosophy, political science/government, psychology, religion, Russian and Slavic studies, sociology, and women's studies). Business adminstration, leadership studies, and biology have the largest enrollments.

ACTIVITIES: 21% of men belong to 8 national fraternities; 28% of women belong to 8 national sororities. There are 171 groups on campus, including art, band, cheerleading, choir, chorale, chorus, communications, computers, dance, debate, drama, drill team, environmental, ethnic, film, honors, international, jazz band, LGBT, literary magazine, musical theater, newspaper, orchestra, pep band, photography, political, professional, radio and TV, religious, social, social service, and student government. Popular campus events include Homecoming, Pig Roast, and SpiderFest. **Sports:** There are 7 intercollegiate sports for men and 10 for women, and 15 intramural sports for men and 15 for women. Facilities include a gym, football stadium, soccer/track complex, lighted intramural fields, an intramural gym, aerobics and weight rooms, swimming pool, tennis, racquetball, disc golf, high ropes and squash courts. **Graduates:** From July 1, 2016 to June 30, 2017, 800 bachelor's degrees were awarded. The most popular majors were business/marketing (41%), social sciences (12%), and biological/life sciences (9%). In an average class, 83% graduate in 4 years or less, 87% graduate in 5 years or less, and 88% graduate in 6 years or less. Of the 2016 graduating class, 17% were enrolled in graduate school within 6 months of graduation, and 96% were employed.

SERVICES: Counseling and information services are available, as is tutoring in most subjects. There are support centers for help with academic skills, writing, and speech. **Library/Resources:** The library contains 937,386 volumes, 141,297 microform items, and 32,996 audio/video tapes/CDs/DVDs, and subscribes to 149,575 periodicals including electronic. Computerized library services include interlibrary loans, database searching, Internet access, and Wi-Fi capability. Special learning facilities include an art gallery, natural history museum, radio station, Joel and Lila Harnett Print Study Center, the Museum of Art, and the Lora Robins Gallery of Design from Nature. **Physically Challenged Students:** 95% of the campus is accessible. Facilities include wheelchair ramps, elevators, special parking, specially equipped restrooms, special class scheduling, lowered drinking fountains, and special housing. **Special:** Study abroad in Argentina, Australia, Austria, Barbados, Belgium, Bhutan, Bolivia, Bonaire, Botswana, Brazil, Cambodia, Cameroon, Chile, China, Costa Rica, Cuba, the Czech Republic, Denmark, the Dominican Republic, Ecuador, France, Germany, Ghana, Hungary, India, Indonesia, Ireland, Israel, Italy, Jamaica, Japan, Jordan, Kenya Coast Republic, Madagascar, Mexico, Mongolia, Morocco, Nepal, the Netherlands, New Zealand, Nicaragua, Panama, Peru, Poland, Portugal, Russia, Rwanda, Samoa, Senegal, Singapore, South Africa, South Korea, Spain, Sweden, Switzerland, Taiwan, Tanzania, Thailand, Trinidad and Tobago, Tunisia, Turks and Caicos, Uganda, the United Arab Emirates, the United Kingdom, and Vietnam. Dual degree engineering programs with the Columbia University School of Engineering and Applied Science and the University of Virginia. Students can earn a Masters of Environmental Management (MEM) or a Masters of Forestry (MF) through Duke University's Nicholas School of the Environment or a Masters of Environment Studies from Virginia Commonwealth University. Students may apply for visiting away status for approved programs. The following list includes approved visiting away programs: American University-Washington Semester (students should check with the appropriate department to see how different programs will transfer). Duke University Marine Sciences Laboratory (Undergraduate Catalog-Biology), Marine Biological Laboratory Semester in Environmental Science-Woods Hole (Undergraduate Catalog-Biology), and Boston University Washington DC Internship Program. There are 6 national honor societies, Phi Beta Kappa, and 22 departmental honors programs. **Visiting:** There are regularly scheduled orientations for prospective students, all first-time visitors are encouraged to schedule a regular campus visit, which typically includes an information session (a 45-minute presentation by an admission representative) and a campus tour (90-minute walking tour of campus led by a student). There are guides for informal visits and visitors may sit in on classes. To schedule a visit, contact the Admissions Office. **Campus Safety and Security:** Measures include 24-hour foot and vehicle patrol, emergency notification system, self-defense education, and security escort services. There are shuttle buses, emergency telephones, lighted pathways/sidewalks. There is also a card-access system in all residence halls, vehicle assistance, emergency first aid service, fingerprinting, firearms storage, and personal property engraving and identification.

REQUIREMENTS: Candidates for admission must have a high school diploma (or recognized equivalent), and completed a minimum of 16 units of secondary school coursework. Minimum requirements include four units in English, 3 in college preparatory mathematics (including Algebra I, II, and Geometry), and at least 2 each in history, laboratory science, and foreign language (or 2 units of the same foreign language, not including American Sign Language, which will not satisfy the requirement for foreign language). Competitive candidates for admission typically exceed the minimum requirements and have taken 4 units in all 5 core areas at the highest levels available in their school setting. Applicants should submit the Common Application, and may submit SAT or ACT test scores. The University of Richmond's application review is need-blind, and the University guarantees to meet 100% of each family's demonstrated need. AP and CLEP credits are accepted. A candidate for the Bachelor of Arts, Bachelor of Science, or Bachelor of Science in Business Administration degree must satisfactorily complete all degree requirements and 35 units. Undergraduate degree candidates must earn a grade point average of not less than 2.0 on all coursework attempted. All undergraduate degrees at the University of Richmond require satisfactory completion of one major. Multiple majors and/or minors may also be pursued and upon completion will be recorded on the permanent academic record. In the Robins School of Business and Jepson School of Leadership Studies a student must complete the requirements for the degree, as stated in the catalog at the time of entrance, within five years from the date of original entry. Reinstatement to a program after five years requires permission of the academic council of the student's school. If an extension of time is granted, the student may be required to satisfy the degree requirements in effect at the time of re-entrance. Additional Degree Requirements: 17.5 unit on-campus residency requirement (transfer students should see section on Transfer Credit), 28 unit residency requirement, to include work taken on approved exchange and study abroad programs and visiting away and off-campus programs as well as courses taken through dual degree and cross-registration programs (this requirement is pro-rated for transfer students), application for degree and attendance at Commencement, completion of financial and administrative obligations. **Procedure:** Freshmen are admitted in the fall. Entrance exams should be taken in the fall of the senior year. There are early decision and deferred admissions plans. Early decision applications should be filed by November 1; regular applications, by January 15 for fall entry. The fall 2017 application fee was $50. Notification of early decision is sent December 15; regular decision, April 1. 319 early decision candidates were accepted for the 2017-2018 class. 3383 applicants were on the 2017 waiting list; 56 were admitted. Applications are accepted on-line. **Transfer Students:** 54 transfer students enrolled in 2016-2017. Applicants must have earned a minimum of 24 credit hours in transferable courses. A minimum GPA of 2.0 is required. 60 credits required for the bachelor's degree must be completed at UR. **International Students:** There are 342 international students enrolled. They must take the TOEFL with a minimum score of 550 on the paper-based TOEFL (PBT) or 80 on the Internet-based version (iBT). They must also take the SAT or ACT.

ADMISSIONS: 33% of the 2017-2018 applicants were accepted. The SAT scores for the 2017-2018 freshman class were: Math-- 15% between 500 and 599, 46% between 600 and 699, and 39% between 700 and 800. Evidence-Based Reading/Writing-- 9% between 500 and 599, 50% between 600 and 699, and 41% between 700 and 800. The ACT scores were 2% between 18 and 23, 28% between 24 and 29, and 70% above 30. 90% of the current freshmen were in the top fifth of their class; 98% were in the top two fifths. 16 freshmen graduated first in their class. **Admissions Contact:** Gil Villanueva, Dean of Admissions. Email: *admission@richmond.edu* Web: *www.richmond.edu*

FINANCIAL AID: In 2017-2018, 62% of all full-time freshmen received some form of financial aid. 42% of all full-time freshmen received need-based aid. The average freshman award was $48,645. Need-based scholarships or need-based grants averaged $42,220; need-based self-help aid (loans and jobs) averaged $3,730; non-need-based athletic scholarships averaged $37,500; and other non-need-based awards and non-need-based scholarships averaged $33,995. 48% of undergraduate students work part-time. The average financial indebtedness of the 2017 graduate was $27,125. UR is a member of CSS. The CSS/Profile, parent and student federal tax return, and noncustodial parent profile are required. The FAFSA code is 003744. The deadline for filing freshman financial aid applications for fall entry is February 1.

UNIVERSITY OF VIRGINIA — D-3

www.virginia.edu

Charlottesville, VA 22904 — **(434) 982-3200**

Fax: (434) 924-3587 — **Email:** undergradadmission@virginia.edu

Full-time: 7253 men, 8521 women	**Faculty:** 1313; I, +$
Part-time: 288 men, 593 women	**Ph.D.s:** 91%
Graduate: 3690 men, 4015 women	**Student/Faculty:** 15 to 1
Year: semesters, summer session	**Tuition:** $16,147 ($47,662)
Room & Board: $11,220	**Freshman Class:** 36779 applied, 10058 accepted, 3788 enrolled
SAT EBR-W/M: 690/690 **ACT:** 32	**CEEB CODE:** 5820
Application Deadline: January 1	**MOST COMPETITIVE**

The University of Virginia, founded in 1819, is a public institution with undergraduate programs in architecture, arts and sciences, commerce, education, engineering and applied science, and nursing. There are 7 undergraduate schools and 10 graduate schools. In addition to regional accreditation, UV has baccalaureate program accreditation with AACSB, ABET, ASLA, NAAB, CAEP, ACS, APA, ASHA, and CCNE. The 1167-acre campus is in a suburban area 70 miles northwest of Richmond, VA. Including any residence halls, there are 537 buildings.

STUDENT LIFE: 70% of undergraduates are from Virginia. Others are from 49 states, 125 foreign countries, and Canada. 72% are from public schools. 7% are African American; 7% Hispanic; 6% race unknown; 58% White; 5% Foreign; 4% two or more races; 14% Asian American. **Female To Male Ratio:** 1.2:1. The average age of freshmen is 18; all undergraduates, 20. 4% do not continue beyond their first year; 94% remain to graduate. **Housing:** 6500 students can be accommodated in college housing, which includes married student dorms and on-campus apartments. In addition, there are honors houses, language/international houses, special-interest houses, and residential housing. On-campus housing is guaranteed for the freshman year only, is available on a first-come, first-served basis, and is available on a lottery system for upperclassmen. 61% of students commute. Upperclassmen may keep cars.

FACULTY/CLASSROOMS: 61% of faculty are male; 39% are female. 89% teach undergraduates. Graduate students teach 13% of introductory courses. The average class size in an introductory lecture is 47 and in a laboratory is 30.

PROGRAMS OF STUDY: UV confers B.A., B.S., B.Ar.H., B.I.S., B.P.S., B.S.C., B.S.Ed., B.S.N., and B.U.E.P. degrees. Master's and doctoral degrees are also awarded. Bachelor's degrees are awarded in BIOLOGICAL SCIENCE (biology/biological science), BUSINESS (business administration and management), COMMUNICATIONS AND THE ARTS (art, classics, comparative literature, dramatic arts, English, French, German, Italian, music, Slavic languages, and Spanish), COMPUTER AND PHYSICAL SCIENCE (astronomy, chemistry, computer science, mathematics, and physics), EDUCATION (physical education / exercise science), ENGINEERING AND ENVIRONMENTAL DESIGN (aerospace studies, architectural history, architecture, biomedical engineering, chemical engineering, city/community/regional planning, civil engineering, computer engineering, electrical/electronics engineering, engineering and applied science, environmental science, mechanical engineering, systems engineering, and urban design), HEALTH PROFESSIONS (health care administration, nursing, and speech pathology/audiology), SOCIAL SCIENCE (African American studies, anthropology, area studies, child psychology/development, economics, history, interdisciplinary studies, international relations, philosophy, political science/government, psychology, public administration, religion, and sociology). English, history, and biology are the strongest academically. Commerce, biology, and economics have the largest enrollments.

ACTIVITIES: 24% of men belong to 31 national fraternities; 28% of

women belong to 16 national sororities. Groups on campus include art, band, cheerleading, chess, choir, chorale, chorus, computers, dance, debate, drama, environmental, ethnic, film, forensics, honors, international, jazz band, judiciary and tour guides, LGBT, literary magazine, marching band, musical theater, newspaper, opera, orchestra, pep band, photography, political, professional, radio and TV, religious, social, social service, student government, symphony, and yearbook. Popular campus events include Culturefest, and Family Weekend. **Sports:** There are 12 intercollegiate sports for men and 13 for women, and 18 intramural sports for men and 18 for women. Facilities include a stadium, an arena, recreation centers, and an aquatics and fitness center. **Graduates:** From July 1, 2016 to June 30, 2017, 4015 bachelor's degrees were awarded. The most popular majors were economics (11%), commerce (8%), and biology (7%). In an average class, 3% graduate in 3 years or less, 88% graduate in 4 years or less, 94% graduate in 5 years or less, and 95% graduate in 6 years or less.

SERVICES: Counseling and information services are available, as is tutoring in every subject. There is a reader service for the blind. There are transcribers, note takers, and taped readings for disabled students. **Library/Resources:** The library contains 5.8 million volumes, 1.5 million microform items, and 140,466 audio/video tapes/CDs/DVDs, and subscribes to 189,860 periodicals including electronic. Computerized library services include interlibrary loans, database searching, Internet access, and Wi-Fi capability. Special learning facilities include an art gallery, radio station, TV station, an art museum and observatory. **Physically Challenged Students:** All of the campus is accessible. Facilities include wheelchair ramps, elevators, special parking, specially equipped restrooms, special class scheduling, lowered drinking fountains, lowered telephones, curb cuts, voice synthesizers, braille printers, and large-screen monitors. **Special:** The college offers internships, study abroad, accelerated degree programs, B.A.-B.S. degrees in biology, environmental sciences, chemistry and physics, co-op programs in engineering, and nondegree study. Dual majors in most arts and sciences programs, student-designed majors, an interdisciplinary major and Echols, and Rodman Scholars program (invited students design their own curricula with many requirements waived), and pass/fail options are available. There is a chapter of Phi Beta Kappa, a freshman honors program, and 35 departmental honors programs. **Visiting:** There are regularly scheduled orientations for prospective students, with visits consisting of comprehensive information sessions and campus tours. There are guides for informal visits, visitors may sit in on classes, and stay overnight. To schedule a visit, contact the Monroe Society at (434) 924-3321. **Campus Safety and Security:** Measures include 24-hour foot and vehicle patrol, emergency notification system, self-defense education, and security escort services. There are shuttle buses, emergency telephones, lighted pathways/sidewalks, controlled access to dorms/residences, and bicycle registration.

REQUIREMENTS: Applicants can substitute the ACT for the SAT. Two SAT subject tests of the student's choosing are strongly recommended. With few exceptions, candidates graduate from accredited secondary schools. While the GED is accepted, it is rare for candidates for first-year admission who have this credential to be competitive in the admissions process. Applicants should complete 16 high school academic courses, including 4 courses each of English, and math, 2 courses each of physics, biology, foreign language, and chemistry (3 if applying to engineering), and 1 course of social science. A letter of recommendation (preferably from the secondary school) is required; also, a teacher's recommendation is recommended. AP credits are accepted. To graduate, students must complete 120 credit hours, with 18 to 42 hours in the major and a minimum GPA of 2.0. Distribution requirements include 12 hours of math and science, 6 hours each of humanities, composition, and social sciences, 4 semesters of foreign languages, 3 hours of historical studies, and 3 hours of non-Western perspectives. **Procedure:** Freshmen are admitted in the fall. Entrance exams should be taken by December of the senior year. There are early admissions and deferred admissions plans. Applications should be filed by January 1 for fall entry. The fall 2017 application fee was $60. Notifications are sent April 1. 3615 applicants were on the 2017 waiting list; 117 were admitted. Applications are accepted on-line. **Transfer Students:** 648 transfer students enrolled in 2016-2017. For the largest school (Arts and Sciences) an applicant for transfer admission must be in good academic, and social standing at any college that he or she is currently attending or has previously attended and must be eligible to return there. To be competitive for admission, we recommend that a transfer student have a cumulative grade point average of B+ or better in all college work attempted. 60 of 120 credits required for the bachelor's degree must be completed at UV. **International Students:** There are 734 international students enrolled. They must take the TOEFL, and the IELTS. They must also take the SAT or ACT.

ADMISSIONS: 27% of the 2017-2018 applicants were accepted. The SAT scores for the 2017-2018 freshman class were: Math-- 1% below 500, 9% between 500 and 599, 38% between 600 and 699, and 52% between 700 and 800. Evidence-Based Reading/Writing-- 1% below 500, 5% between 500 and 599, 40% between 600 and 699, and 54% between 700 and 800. The ACT scores were 4% between 18 and 23, 21% between 24 and 29, and 75% above 30. 97% of the current freshmen were in the top fifth of their class; 99% were in the top two fifths. **Admissions Contact:** Gregory W. Roberts, Dean of Admissions. Email: *undergradadmission@virginia.edu* Web: *www.virginia.edu*

FINANCIAL AID: In 2017-2018, 58% of all full-time freshmen received some form of financial aid. 39% of all full-time freshmen received need-based aid. The average freshman award was $22,822. Need-based scholarships or need-based grants averaged $22,597; need-based self-help aid (loans and jobs) averaged $5,692; non-need-based athletic scholarships averaged $32,504; and other non-need-based awards and non-need-based scholarships averaged $10,110. The average financial indebtedness of the 2017 graduate was $24,501. The CSS/Profile is required. The deadline for filing freshman financial aid applications for fall entry is March 1.

VIRGINIA COMMONWEALTH UNIVERSITY E-3

www.vcu.edu

Richmond, VA 23284	**(804) 828-8476** **(800) 841-3638**
Fax: (804) 828-1899	**Email: ugrad@vcu.edu**
Full-time: 8197 men, 12,141 women	**Faculty:** 1242
Part-time: 1554 men, 2118 women	**Ph.D.s:** n/av
Graduate: 2667 men, 4359 women	**Student/Faculty:** 18 to 1
Year: semesters, summer session	**Tuition:** $13,624 ($33,656)
Room & Board: $10,187	**Freshman Class:** 16847 applied, 12901 accepted, 4201 enrolled
SAT CR/M/W: 590/560/530 **ACT:** 24	**CEEB CODE:** 5570
Application Deadline: January 15	**VERY COMPETITIVE**

Virginia Commonwealth University is 1 of 28 public institutions with academic medical centers to be designated by the Carnegie Foundation as "Community Engaged" with "Very High Research Activity" and among the nation's premier urban, public research universities. VCU has more than 200 degree and certificate programs and encompasses one of the largest academic health centers in the nation. VCU graduate programs and first-professional programs are consistently ranked among the top 50 nationally, including number one sculpture and nurse anesthesia programs. And, through the guidance of its strategic plan, Quest for Distinction, VCU is working to meet the demands of diverse populations through impactful research and creativity, rigorous study, and extensive community engagement. This mission traces its roots to two institutions that merged in 1968 to create VCU: the Medical College of Virginia, established in 1838 as the medical department of Hampden-Sydney College, and Richmond Professional Institute, founded in 1917. VCU and VCU Health have been honored with prestigious national and international recognition for top-quality graduate, professional, and medical care programs, reflecting a commitment to be among America's top research universities, supporting students, faculty and the VCU community. There are 14 undergraduate schools and 1 graduate school. In addition to regional accreditation, VCU has baccalaureate program accreditation with AACSB, ABET, ACEJMC, ACPE, ADA, APTA, CSAB, CSWE, FIDER, NASAD, NASDTEC, NASM, CAEP, NLN, NRPA, CAATE, and CACREP. The 173-acre campus is in an urban area 2 miles west of downtown Richmond and 90 miles from Washington, D.C. Including any residence halls, there are 249 buildings.

STUDENT LIFE: 90% of undergraduates are from Virginia. Others are from 50 states, 101 foreign countries, and Canada. 7% are Hispanic; 6% Foreign; 50% White; 5% two or more races; 4% race unknown; 16% African American; 12% Asian American. **Female To Male Ratio:** 1.5:1. The average age of freshmen is 18; all undergraduates, 21. **Housing:** 5158 students can be accommodated in college housing, which includes dorms and on-campus apartments. In addition, there are honors houses, and ASPIRE which is an innovative and comprehensive community engagement-focused living-learning program for sophmores. On-campus housing is guaranteed for the freshman year only, and is available on a first-come, first-served basis. All students may keep cars.

FACULTY/CLASSROOMS: 55% of faculty are male; 45% are female. No introductory courses are taught by graduate students.

PROGRAMS OF STUDY: VCU confers B.A., B.S., B.I.S., B.M., B.S.W., and B.F.A. degrees. Master's and doctoral degrees are also awarded. Bachelor's degrees are awarded in AGRICULTURE (environmental studies), BIOLOGICAL SCIENCE (bioinformatics and biology/biological science), BUSINESS (accounting, business administration and management, marketing/retailing/merchandising, and sports management), COMMUNICATIONS AND THE ARTS (art history and appreciation, communications, crafts, dance, dramatic arts, English, film arts, graphic design, languages, media arts, music, painting, photography, and sculpture), COMPUTER AND PHYSICAL SCIENCE (chemistry, computer science, information sciences and systems, mathematics, physics, and science), EDUCATION (art education, foreign languages education, and health education), ENGINEERING AND ENVIRONMENTAL DESIGN (bioengineering, biomedical engineering, chemical engineering, computer engineering, electrical/electronics engineering, electrical/electronics engineering technology, interior design, and mechanical engineering), HEALTH PROFESSIONS (clinical science, dental hygiene, and nursing), SOCIAL SCIENCE (African American studies, anthropology, criminal justice, economics, fashion design and technology, forensic studies, history, homeland security, interdisciplinary studies, international studies, philosophy, philosophy and religion, political science/government, psychology, religion, safety science, social work, sociology, and urban studies). Biology, psychology, and health physical education and exercise science have the largest enrollments.

ACTIVITIES: There are 468 groups on campus, including art, band, cheerleading, chess, choir, chorale, chorus, computers, dance, debate, drama, ethnic, film, forensics, honors, international, jazz band, LGBT, literary magazine, musical theater, newspaper, opera, pep band, photography, political, professional, radio and TV, religious, social, social service, student government, symphony, and yearbook. Popular campus events include Annual Fall Step Show, Greek Week, Homecoming International Festival, Spring Fest, and Welcome Week. **Sports:** There are 8 intercollegiate sports for men and 9 for women, and 16 intramural sports for men and 16 for women. Facilities include a multipurpose indoor facility for intercollegiate athletics and recreational space with a fitness center, an activity center, a wellness resource center, a stadium for soccer, track and field, tennis courts, a gym, a weight room, cardiovascular fitness space, a jogging track. There is also a baseball field, an aquatic and recreational facility with a 6-lane pool, and handball/racquetball and squash courts. Students also have full access to the Cary Street Gym on the Monroe Park Campus, and the MCV Campus Recreation & Aquatic Center. **Graduates:** From July 1, 2016 to June 30, 2017, 5207 bachelors degrees were awarded. The most popular majors were psychology, business, and biology. In an average class, 62% graduate in 6 years or less.

SERVICES: Counseling and information services are available, as is tutoring in most subjects. There is a reader service for the blind, and remedial math, reading, and writing. **Library/Resources:** The library contains 3.0 million volumes. Computerized library services include interlibrary loans, database searching, Internet access, and Wi-Fi capability. Special learning facilities include an art gallery, radio station, and TV station. **Physically Challenged Students:** 90% of the campus is accessible. Facilities include wheelchair ramps, elevators, special parking, specially equipped restrooms, special class scheduling, and lowered drinking fountains. **Special:** Special study options include accelerated programs, cooperative education program, distance learning, double majors, dual enrollment, English as a second language (ESL), honors program, independent study, internships, student-designed majors, study abroad, and teacher certification program. There are 13 national honor societies and a freshman honors program. **Visiting:** There are regularly scheduled orientations for prospective students and daily tours every Monday-Saturday except holidays and holiday weekends. The information session is followed by an hour-long guided walk tour of Monroe Park. Registration is required for attendance at these daily sessions. To schedule a visit, contact the Office of Admissions. **Campus Safety and Security:** Measures include 24-hour foot and vehicle patrol, an emergency notification system, self-defense education, and security escort services. There are shuttle buses, emergency telephones, lighted pathways/sidewalks, controlled access to dorms/residences, formal presentations, online crime prevention program, annual security report, crime prevention through environmental design, community police officers/certified prevention specialists, security inspections of facilities, operation ID bike and computer registration, and a victim/witness assistance program.

REQUIREMENTS: Candidates for admission to VCU are reviewed based on their academic performance in an accredited high school or on GED scores and either the SAT Reasoning Test or ACT scores. The college preparatory curriculum is highly preferred, and a minimum of 20 units is required for admissions. Applicants should present a minimum of 4 units of English, 3 units each of mathematics (algebra I and either geometry or algebra II), history, social studies (or government), science (with at least one laboratory), and foreign language (or 2 units of 2 foreign languages are strongly recommended). A GPA of 2.0 is required for graduation. The AP and CLEP credits are accepted. The total number of semester credits required for graduation depends upon the degree program. A student must have completed 25 percent of the semester-hour credits required for the bachelor's degree including at least 30 of the last 45 credits. **Procedure:** Freshmen are admitted in the fall and spring. Entrance exams should be taken and SAT or ACT scores must be received for fall term admission by March 1. There are early admissions, deferred admissions, and rolling admissions plans. Applications should be filed by January 15 for fall entry. The fall 2017 application fee was $65. Notifications are sent April 1. Applications are accepted on-line. **Transfer Students:** 1911 transfer students enrolled in 2016-2017. All credits taken at regionally accredited institutions that meet the VCU transfer requirements may be posted to the VCU transcript. However, there may be a difference between the credits VCU will post and the credits each VCU department/school will apply to the desired degree program. Students should meet with their program advisers, who will assist them in determining their VCU degree their VCU degree requirements and will advise them on what transfer courses the program specifically will apply toward their degree requirements. Regardless of how many transfer credits are accepted, students must satisfy all VCU graduation requirements noted in the graduation checklist, including the following: completion of at least 25 percent of the semester – hour credits required for their bachelor's degree program at VCU and completion of at least 30 of the last 45 semester hour credits. **International Students:** There are 747 international students enrolled. They must take the TOEFL, the college's own test, and the IELTS.

ADMISSIONS: 77% of the 2017-2018 applicants were accepted. The SAT scores for the 2017-2018 freshman class were: Critical Reading-- 44% between 500 and 599 and 9% between 700 and 800. Math-- 53% between 500 and 599, 27% between 600 and 699, and 5% between 700 and 800. Writing-- 37% below 500, 41% between 500 and 599, 18% between 600 and 699, and 3% between 700 and 800. The ACT scores were 4% between 12 and 17, 42% between 18 and 23, 39% between 24 and 29, and 15% above 30. 21 freshmen graduated first in their class. **Admissions Contact:** Admissions Department. Email: *ugrad@vcu.edu* Web: *www.vcu.edu*

FINANCIAL AID: The FAFSA code is 003735. The priority date for freshman financial aid applications for fall entry is March 1.

VIRGINIA MILITARY INSTITUTE C-3

www.vmi.edu

Lexington, VA 24450	**(540) 464-7211** **(800) 767-4207**
Fax: (540) 464-7746	**Email: admissions@vmi.edu**
Full-time: 1518 men, 195 women	**Faculty:** 133; IIB, av$
Part-time: n/av	**Ph.D.s:** 97%
Graduate: n/av	**Student/Faculty:** 11 to 1
Year: semesters, summer session	**Tuition:** $17,492 ($41,801)
Room & Board: $8968	**Freshman Class:** 1779 applied, 940 accepted, 405 enrolled
SAT CR/M/W: 580/580/550 **ACT:** 26	**CEEB CODE:** 5858
Application Deadline: February 1	**VERY COMPETITIVE**

Virginia Military Institute, established in 1839, is the nation's first state-supported military college, offering academic programs in engineering, sciences, and liberal arts. All students are members of the Corps of Cadets, live in barracks, eat together in the mess hall, wear uniforms, and adhere to the Honor System. There is 1 undergraduate school. In addition to regional accreditation, VMI has baccalaureate program accreditation with AACSB, ABET, and ACS. The 134-acre campus is in a small town 50 miles north of Roanoke, Va. Including any residence halls, there are 68 buildings.

STUDENT LIFE: 60% of undergraduates are from Virginia. Others are from 45 states, and 6 foreign countries. 78% are from public schools. 85% are White; 6% African American; 4% Asian American; 3% Hispanic; 2% Foreign. 64% are Protestant; 28% Catholic. **Male To Female Ratio:** 7.8:1. The average age of freshmen is 18; all undergraduates, 20. 26% do not continue beyond their first year; 74% remain to graduate. **Housing:** College-sponsored housing includes barracks, with 3-5 students in a room. On-campus housing is guaranteed for all 4 years. Alcohol is not permitted. Upperclassmen may keep cars.

FACULTY/CLASSROOMS: 70% of faculty are male; 30% are female. All teach undergraduates. No introductory courses are taught by graduate students. The average class size in an introductory lecture is 17; in a laboratory is 13; and in a regular course is 12.

PROGRAMS OF STUDY: VMI confers B.A. and B.S. degrees. Bachelor's degrees are awarded in BIOLOGICAL SCIENCE (biology/biological science), BUSINESS (business economics), COMMUNICATIONS AND THE ARTS (English), COMPUTER AND PHYSICAL SCIENCE (chemistry, computer science, mathematics, and physics), ENGINEERING AND ENVIRONMENTAL DESIGN (civil engineering, electrical/electronics engineering, and mechanical engineering), SOCIAL SCIENCE (history, international studies, and psychology). Engineering (civil, electrical, and mechanical), and sciences are the strongest academically. International studies, business/economics, and civil engineering have the largest enrollments.

ACTIVITIES: There are no fraternities or sororities. There are 50 groups on campus, including bagpipe, band, cheerleading, choir, chorus, communications, drama, drill team, ethnic, honors, international, investment, jazz band, LGBT, literary magazine, marching band, newspaper, orchestra, pep band, political, professional, religious, social, social service, student government, and yearbook. Popular campus events include Ring Figure, Virginia Transportation Conference, and Dance and Concert Weekends. **Sports:** There are 11 intercollegiate sports for men and 6 for women, and 4 intramural sports for men and 4 for women. Facilities include courts for basketball, racquetball, and tennis, fields for lacrosse, football, baseball, and soccer, a swimming pool, rifle range, indoor and outdoor running tracks, wrestling facility, access to a golf course, weight training and aerobic facility, and auxiliary indoor and outdoor basketball courts. **Graduates:** From July 1, 2016 to June 30, 2017, 372 bachelor's degrees were awarded. The most popular majors were social sciences (32%), engineering (25%), and history (12%). In an average class, 58% graduate in 4 years or less, 71% graduate in 5 years or less, and 73% graduate in 6 years or less. Of the 2016 graduating class, 89% were enrolled in graduate school within 6 months of graduation, and 99% were employed.

SERVICES: Counseling and information services are available, as is tutoring in some subjects. **Library/Resources:** The library contains 240,000 volumes, 12,963 microform items, 5,747 audio/video tapes/CDs/DVDs, and subscribes to 26,789 periodicals including electronic. Computerized library services include interlibrary loans, database searching, Internet access, and Wi-Fi capability. **Physically Challenged Students:** 75% of the campus is accessible. Facilities include wheelchair ramps, elevators, special parking, and specially equipped restrooms. **Special:** Study abroad in 14 countries and work-study programs are available, as are for-credit internships in English and international studies and summer internships in foreign countries. VMI offers dual majors in any combination and B.A.-B.S. degrees in liberal arts, physical sciences, and engineering. Minors are offered in each field of study. There are 11 national honor societies, a freshman honors program, and 3 departmental honors programs. **Visiting:** There are regularly scheduled orientations for prospective students, consisting of tours, conferences with academic and ROTC instructors, interaction with current freshmen, and overnight stays. There are guides for informal visits, visitors may sit in on classes, and stay overnight. To schedule a visit, contact the Admissions Office. **Campus Safety and Security:** Measures include 24-hour foot and vehicle patrol and self-defense education. There are emergency telephones and lighted pathways/sidewalks.

REQUIREMENTS: The SAT or ACT is required. Applicants must be graduates of an accredited secondary school. Applicants should complete 16 to 19 high school academic units, including 4 years of English, 3 to 4 each of math, science with lab, and foreign language, 2 of social studies, and 1 of history. An essay is encouraged and an interview is recommended. A GPA of 2.0 is required. AP credits are accepted. Important factors in the admissions decision are advanced placement or honors courses, personality/intangible qualities, extracurricular activities record, and leadership record. To graduate, students must complete 136 to 144 semester hours, with a GPA of 2.0. All students must pass chemistry, English, history, math, phys ed, ROTC, and public speaking. In addition, all cadets must pass swimming, boxing, and wrestling. **Procedure:** Freshmen are admitted in the fall. Entrance exams should be taken spring of the junior year or fall of the senior year. There are early decision, early admissions, and rolling admissions plans. Early decision applications should be filed by November 15; regular applications, by February 1 for fall entry. The fall 2017 application fee was $40. Notification of early decision is sent December 15; regular decision, 166 early decision candidates were accepted for the 2017-2018 class. 150 applicants were on the 2017 waiting list; 15 were admitted. **Transfer Students:** 27 transfer students enrolled in 2016-2017. Applicants for transfer must have a minimum GPA of 2.0, and 24 transferable credit hours, and a satisfactory high school record. The SAT or the ACT is required. 135 credits required for the bachelor's degree must be completed at VMI. **International Students:** There are 25 international students enrolled. They must take the TOEFL. International students who play intercollegiate athletics sports must take the SAT or ACT.

ADMISSIONS: 53% of the 2017-2018 applicants were accepted. The SAT scores for the 2017-2018 freshman class were: Critical Reading-- 11% below 500, 47% between 500 and 599, 35% between 600 and 699, and 7% between 700 and 800. Math-- 10% below 500, 48% between 500 and 599, 39% between 600 and 699, and 5% between 700 and 800. Writing-- 24% below 500, 48% between 500 and 599, 26% between 600 and 699, and 1% between 700 and 800. 21% of the current freshmen were in the top fifth of their class; 43% were in the top two fifths. **Admissions Contact:** Col. Vernon L. Beitzel, Director of Admissions. Email: *admissions@vmi.edu* Web: *www.vmi.edu*

FINANCIAL AID: In 2017-2018, 89% of all full-time freshmen received some form of financial aid and need-based aid. The average freshman award was $17,430. Need-based scholarships or need-based grants averaged $16,738; need-based self-help aid (loans and jobs) averaged $3,920; non-need-based athletic scholarships averaged $19,303; other non-need-based awards and non-need-based scholarships averaged $6,606; and $3,920 from other forms of aid. The average financial indebtedness of the 2017 graduate was $26,720. VMI is a member of CSS. The college's own financial statement is required. The priority date for freshman financial aid applications for fall entry is March 1.

VIRGINIA POLYTECHNIC INSTITUTE AND STATE UNIVERSITY C-3

www.vt.edu

Blacksburg, VA 24061 **(540) 231-6267**

Fax: (540) 231-3242 **Email: admissions@vt.edu**

Full-time: 14,352 men, 10,823 women	**Faculty:** 1744; I, av$
Part-time: 377 men, 173 women	**Ph.D.s:** 90%
Graduate: 4191 men, 3188 women	**Student/Faculty:** 14 to 1
Year: semesters, summer session	**Tuition:** $13,230 ($31,014)
Room & Board: $8690	**Freshman Class:** 25000 applied, 17718 accepted, 5929 enrolled
SAT CR/M/W: 590/620/580 **ACT:** required	**CEEB CODE:** 5859
Application Deadline: January 15	**VERY COMPETITIVE**

Virginia Polytechnic Institute and State University, founded in 1872, is a public land-grant institution, offering a cadet program within the larger, nonmilitary student body. There are 7 undergraduate schools and 2 graduate schools. In addition to regional accreditation, Virginia Tech has baccalaureate program accreditation with AACSB, ABET, ACCE, ADA, AHEA, ASLA, FIDER, NAAB, NCATE, and SAF. The 2600-acre campus is in a rural area 40 miles southwest of Roanoke. Including any residence halls, there are 110 buildings.

STUDENT LIFE: 77% of undergraduates are from Virginia. Others are from 49 states, 77 foreign countries, and Canada. 67% are White; 6% Hispanic; 6% Foreign; 4% African American; 4% two or more races; 3% race unknown; 10% Asian American. **Male To Female Ratio:** 1.3:1. The average age of freshmen is 18; all undergraduates, 20. 12% do not continue beyond their first year; 78% remain to graduate. **Housing:** 9125 students can be accommodated in college housing, which includes dorms. In addition, there are honors houses, special-interest houses, fraternity houses, sorority houses, theme housing, wellness housing, and international housing. The Cadets live in the Cadet Residence Halls. On-campus housing is guaranteed for the freshman year only and is available on a lottery system for upperclassmen. 99% of students live on campus. Upperclassmen may keep cars.

FACULTY/CLASSROOMS: 74% teach undergraduates and do research. Graduate students teach 12% of introductory courses. The average class size in an introductory lecture is 46 and in a laboratory is 30.

PROGRAMS OF STUDY: Virginia Tech confers B.A., B.S., B.Arch., B.F.A., B.Land.Arch., B.S.Bus., B.S.E., and B.S.Ed. degrees. Master's and doctoral degrees are also awarded. Bachelor's degrees are awarded in AGRICULTURE (agricultural economics, animal science, dairy science, forestry and related sciences, horticulture, poultry science, and soil science), BIOLOGICAL SCIENCE (biochemistry, biology/biological science, and nutrition), BUSINESS (accounting, apparel and accessories marketing, banking and finance, business economics, entrepreneurial studies, hotel/motel and restaurant management, management science, marketing management, and tourism), COMMUNICATIONS AND THE ARTS (art, communications, dramatic arts, English, French, German, industrial design, music, and Spanish), COMPUTER AND PHYSICAL SCIENCE (chemistry, computer science, geology, mathematics, physics, planetary and space science, and statistics), EDUCATION (agricultural education, business education, environmental education, foreign languages education, science education, and secondary education), ENGINEERING AND ENVIRONMENTAL DESIGN (aerospace studies, agricultural engineering, architecture, chemical engineering, civil engineering, computer engineering, construction engineering, construction management, electrical/electronics engineering, engineering mechanics, environmental science, industrial engineering, interior design, landscape architecture/design, materials engineering, mechanical engineering, mining and mineral engineering, and ocean engineering), HEALTH PROFESSIONS (physical therapy, predentistry, and premedicine), SOCIAL SCIENCE (dietetics, economics, food science, geography, history, human development, interdisciplinary studies, international studies, interpreter for the deaf, parks and recreation management, philosophy, physical fitness/movement, political science/government, prelaw, psychology, public affairs, sociology, and urban studies). Engineering, architecture, and business are the strongest academically. Engineering, computer science, and biology have the largest enrollments.

ACTIVITIES: 14% of men belong to 43 national fraternities; 18% of women belong to 21 national sororities. There are 600 groups on campus, including art, band, cheerleading, chess, choir, chorale, chorus, computers, dance, drama, drill team, drum and bugle corps, ethnic, film, honors, international, jazz band, LGBT, literary magazine, marching band, musical theater, newspaper, orchestra, pep band, photography, political, professional, radio and TV, religious, social, social service, student government, and yearbook. Popular campus events include Quad Jams, Ring Dance, and German's Mid-Winter Dance. **Sports:** There are 11 intercollegiate sports for men and 10 for women, and 24 intramural sports for men and 24 for women. Facilities include a football stadium, basketball coliseum, a field house, indoor tennis pavilion, 9-hole golf course, soccer and baseball fields, a swimming pool and diving well, basketball, volleyball, racquetball, handball, squash, multipurpose recreation fields, a weight-room and exercise facilities with gyms. **Graduates:** From July 1, 2016 to June 30, 2017, 5940 bachelor's degrees were awarded. The most popular majors were engineering (24%), business marketing (19%), and family and consumer sciences (9%). Of the 2016 graduating class, 19% were enrolled in graduate school within 6 months of graduation, and 57% were employed.

SERVICES: Counseling and information services are available, as is tutoring in most subjects. There is a reader service for the blind, and remedial reading. **Library/Resources:** The library contains 2.3 million volumes, 6.3 million microform items, 27,574 audio/video tapes/CDs/DVDs, and subscribes to 35,596 periodicals including electronic. Computerized library services include interlibrary loans, database searching, and Internet access. Special learning facilities include an art gallery, natural history museum, radio station, an airport, wind tunnels, agricultural stations, radio/visual observatories, satellite up-link station, multimedia, digital music, writing, CAD/CAM labs, math emporium, and CAVE (cave automatic virtual environment). **Physically Challenged Students:** 60% of the campus is accessible. Facilities include wheelchair ramps, elevators, special parking, specially equipped restrooms, special class scheduling, lowered drinking fountains, lowered telephones, and special housing. There is also a special services library room for the visually impaired. **Special:** Students may cross-register with Miami University in Ohio, Oxford Polytechnic Institute, California Polytechnic Institute, and Florida A & M. Study abroad in 36 countries, internships in nearly every major, a Washington semester, and a wide range of work-study programs are available, as well as co-ops in 48 majors. There are honors options for most majors, B.A.-B.S. degrees, dual and student-designed majors, credit for independent study or research, nondegree study, and pass/fail options. The Corps of Cadets, a militarily structured organization, is open to men and women. Undergraduate advising programs are available to students wishing to prepare for professional school in law, dentistry, medicine, pharmacy, physical therapy, and veterinary medicine. There are 13 national honor societies, Phi Beta Kappa, and a freshman honors program. **Visiting:** There are regularly scheduled orientations for prospective students, consisting of a fall Open House Series: half-day on-campus programs that include presentations, tours, and question-and-answer sessions. There are guides for informal visits and visitors may sit in on classes. To schedule a visit, contact the Office of Undergraduate Admissions. **Campus Safety and Security:** Measures include 24-hour foot and vehicle patrol, emergency notification system, self-defense education, and security escort services. There are shuttle buses, emergency telephones, and lighted pathways/sidewalks.

REQUIREMENTS: The SAT or ACT is required. Applicants must be graduates of an accredited secondary school, or have a GED. Applicants should complete 18 high school academic credits, including 4 years of English, 3-4 of math, including algebra II and geometry, 2 of lab science, to be chosen from biology, chemistry, or physics, and 1 each of history and social studies. An additional 3 years from college preparatory courses, and 4 from any credit course offerings are required. AP and CLEP credits are accepted. Important factors in the admissions decision are advanced placement or honors courses. To graduate, students must complete between 120 and 156 credit hours (depending on the major), with a minimum GPA of 2.0. There is a required core curriculum that includes 8 hours of science and 6 hours each of humanities, social science, math, and writing and discourse. Students must also meet a foreign language requirement. **Procedure:** Freshmen are admitted to all sessions. Entrance exams should be taken by January 1 of the senior year. There are early decision and deferred admissions plans. Early decision applications should be filed by November 1; regular applications, by January 15 for fall entry; October 1 for spring entry; and April 22 for summer entry. The fall 2017 application fee was $60. Notification of early decision is sent December 15; regular decision, 1137 early decision candidates were accepted for the 2017-2018 class. 1544 applicants were on the 2017 waiting list. Applications are accepted on-line. **Transfer Students:** 1012 transfer students enrolled in 2016-2017. Applicants must have a minimum GPA of 2.0 and must specify a major, (a competitive GPA is 3.0). Student may enroll in the fall and summer. 30 of 120 credits required for the bachelor's degree must be completed at Virginia Tech. **International Students:** They must take the TOEFL. They must also take the SAT or ACT.

ADMISSIONS: 71% of the 2017-2018 applicants were accepted. The SAT scores for the 2017-2018 freshman class were: Critical Reading-- 10% below 500, 42% between 500 and 599, 40% between 600 and 699, and 9% between 700 and 800. Math-- 5% below 500, 32% between 500 and 599, 44% between 600 and 699, and 18% between 700 and 800. Writing-- 12% below 500, 44% between 500 and 599, 37% between 600 and 699, and 6% between 700 and 800. 82% of the current freshmen were in the top fifth of their class; 97% were in the top two fifths. **Admissions Contact:** Mildred R. Johnson, Director of Undergraduate Admissions. Email: *admissions@vt.edu* Web: *www.vt.edu*

FINANCIAL AID: In 2017-2018, 92% of all full-time freshmen received some form of financial aid, and need-based aid. The average freshman award was $17,742. Need-based scholarships or need-based grants averaged $7,550; need-based self-help aid (loans and jobs) averaged $4,032; non-need-based athletic scholarships averaged $21,395; other non-need-based awards and non-need-based scholarships averaged $3,945; and $3,765 from other forms of aid. The average financial indebtedness of the 2017 graduate was $31,590. The priority date for freshman financial aid applications for fall entry is January 1.

VIRGINIA STATE UNIVERSITY E-3
www.vsu.edu

Petersburg, VA 23806	**(804) 524-5902** **(800) 871-7611**
Fax: (804) 524-5055	**Email: admiss@vsu.edu**
Full-time: 1400 men, 1800 women	**Faculty:** 168
Part-time: 200 men, 200 women	**Ph.D.s:** 74%
Graduate: 220 men, 580 women	**Student/Faculty:** 19 to 1
Year: semesters, summer session	**Tuition:** $9240 ($22,542)
Room & Board: $10,562	**Freshman Class:** 4138 applied, 2028 accepted, 1011 enrolled
SAT or ACT: required	**CEEB CODE:** 5860
Application Deadline: n/av	**COMPETITIVE+**

Virginia State University is a historically black public land-grant institution of higher education providing academic programs that integrate instruction, research, and extension/public service. The figures given in the above capsule and in this profile are approximate. Tuition cost is based on undergraduate programs; 9-15 credit hours. There are 4 undergraduate schools and 1 graduate school. In addition to regional accreditation, VSU has baccalaureate program accreditation with ABET, ADA, CSWE, NASM, and CAEP. The 652-acre campus is in a suburban area 25 miles south of Richmond. Including any residence halls, there are 52 buildings.

STUDENT LIFE: 65% of undergraduates are from Virginia. Others are from 35 states, and 1 foreign country. 96% are from public schools. 90% are African American; 8% White; 1% Hispanic. **Female To Male Ratio:** 1.4:1. The average age of freshmen is 18; all undergraduates, 21. 40% do not continue beyond their first year; 18% remain to graduate. **Housing:** 2050 students can be accommodated in college housing, which includes dorms, and honors houses. On-campus housing is guaranteed for the freshman year only, is available on a first-come, and first-served basis. 52% of students live on campus. Alcohol is not permitted. Upperclassmen may keep cars.

FACULTY/CLASSROOMS: 67% of faculty are male; 33% are female. Graduate students teach 2% of introductory courses.

PROGRAMS OF STUDY: VSU confers B.A., B.S., B.F.A., B.I.S. and B.Mus. degrees. Master's degrees are also awarded. Bachelor's degrees are awarded in AGRICULTURE (agriculture), BIOLOGICAL SCIENCE (biology/biological science), BUSINESS (accounting, business administration and management, hotel/motel and restaurant management, management information systems, and marketing management), COMMUNICATIONS AND THE ARTS (English literature, music performance, and visual and performing arts), COMPUTER AND PHYSICAL SCIENCE (chemistry, mathematics, and physics), EDUCATION (athletic training, business education, physical education, and trade and industrial education), ENGINEERING AND ENVIRONMENTAL DESIGN (engineering technology), SOCIAL SCIENCE (economics, history, home economics, interdisciplinary studies, political science/government, psychology, public administration, social work, and sociology). Business administration, accounting, and business information systems have the largest enrollments.

ACTIVITIES: 10% of men belong to 4 national fraternities; 10% of women belong to 4 national sororities. There are 44 groups on campus, including band, cheerleading, chess, choir, chorus, computers, dance, drama, drill team, ethnic, honors, international, jazz band, marching band, musical theater, newspaper, orchestra, pep band, photography, political, professional, radio and TV, religious, social, student government, symphony, and yearbook. Popular campus events include High School Day, VSU Day, and Commencement. **Sports:** There are 7 intercollegiate sports for men and 6 for women, and 5 intramural sports for men and 6 for women. Facilities include a gym, an Olympic-size pool, dance studio, tennis courts, track field, football field, baseball field, and indoor and outdoor basketball courts. **Graduates:** In an average class, 10% graduate in 4 years or less, 26% graduate in 5 years or less, and 33% graduate in 6 years or less.

SERVICES: Counseling and information services are available, as is tutoring in most subjects. There is a reader service for the blind. **Library/Resources:** The library contains 280,599 volumes, 662,075 microform items, and 3,939 audio/video tapes/CDs/DVDs, and subscribes to 1,198 periodicals including electronic. Computerized library services include interlibrary loans and database searching. Special learning facilities include an art gallery, radio station, and TV station. **Physically Challenged Students:** 75% of the campus is accessible. Facilities include wheelchair ramps, elevators, special parking, and specially equipped restrooms. **Special:** VSU offers dual majors, a general studies degree, a 3-2 engineering degree program, nondegree study, and a pass/fail grading option. There are 10 national honor societies, Phi Beta Kappa, a freshman honors program, and 7 departmental honors programs. **Visiting:** There are regularly scheduled orientations for prospective students. There are guides for informal visits and visitors may sit in on classes. To schedule a visit, contact the Admissions Office. **Campus Safety and Security:** Measures include 24-hour foot and vehicle patrol. There are emergency telephones and lighted pathways/sidewalks.

REQUIREMENTS: The SAT or ACT is required. Applicants must graduate from an accredited secondary school with 16 academic credits and 12 Carnegie units, or have a GED. Students must take 4 years of English, 2 each of a foreign language, math, and science, and 1 each of history and social studies. Essays, 2 letters of recommendation, evidence of physical condition, interviews, and, if appropriate, auditions are required. AP and CLEP credits are accepted. Important factors in the admissions decision are advanced placement or honors courses, recommendations by school officials, and leadership record. To graduate, students must have a minimum GPA of 2.0. They must earn at least 120 credits, with the last 27 semester hours in residence. Requirements include those in phys ed, freshman writing, math, biology, social or physical science, history, and psychology. Freshman orientation must also be completed. **Procedure:** Freshmen are admitted fall and spring. There are deferred admissions and rolling admissions plans. Early decision applications should be filed by May 1. Applications are accepted on-line. **Transfer Students:** Applicants must have a minimum GPA of 2.0. Those transferring fewer than 25 semester hours must meet freshman standards. 30 of 120 credits required for the bachelor's degree must be completed at VSU. **International Students:** They must take the TOEFL. They must also take the SAT or ACT.

ADMISSIONS: 49% of the 2017-2018 applicants were accepted. **Admissions Contact:** Irene Logan, Director of Admissions. Email: *admiss@vsu.edu* Web: *www.vsu.edu*

FINANCIAL AID: In 2017-2018, 95% of all full-time freshmen received some form of financial aid. VSU is a member of CSS. The CSS/Profile and the college's own financial statement are required. Check with the school for current application deadlines.

VIRGINIA UNION UNIVERSITY E-3
www.vuu.edu

Richmond, VA 23220	**(804) 342-3570** **(800) 368-3227**
Fax: (804) 342-3511	**Email: visitus@vuu.edu**
Full-time: 400 men, 800 women	**Faculty:** 82
Part-time: 30 men, 30 women	**Ph.D.s:** 55%
Graduate: 209 men, 114 women	**Student/Faculty:** 16 to 1
Year: semesters, summer session	**Tuition:** $16,948
Room & Board: $8110	**Freshman Class:** n/av
SAT: required	**CEEB CODE:** 5862
Application Deadline: n/av	**COMPETITIVE**

Virginia Union University, established in 1865 and affiliated with the Baptist Church, is a private institution offering undergraduate programs in education and psychology, business, humanities, natural science and math, and social sciences. There are 2 undergraduate schools and 1 graduate school. In addition to regional accreditation, VUU has baccalaureate program accreditation with ACBSP and CSWE. The 72-acre campus is in an urban area in the city of Richmond. Including any residence halls, there are 18 buildings.

STUDENT LIFE: 52% of undergraduates are from Virginia. Others are from 27 states, and 4 foreign countries. 85% are from public schools. 98% are African American. **Female To Male Ratio:** 1.5:1. The average age of freshmen is 18. 31% do not continue beyond their first year; 55% remain to graduate. **Housing:** 700 students can be accommodated in college housing, which includes dorms, and honors houses. On-campus housing is available on a first-come and first-served basis. Alcohol is not permitted. All students may keep cars.

FACULTY/CLASSROOMS: 55% of faculty are male; 45% are female. 86% teach undergraduates. No introductory courses are taught by grad-

uate students. The average class size in an introductory lecture is 28; in a laboratory is 20; and in a regular course is 22.

PROGRAMS OF STUDY: VUU confers B.A., B.S. and B.S.W. degrees. Master's and doctoral degrees are also awarded. Bachelor's degrees are awarded in BIOLOGICAL SCIENCE (biology/biological science), BUSINESS (accounting, banking and finance, and business administration and management), COMMUNICATIONS AND THE ARTS (English, journalism, and music), COMPUTER AND PHYSICAL SCIENCE (chemistry and mathematics), EDUCATION (art education, business education, early childhood education, elementary education, music education, secondary education, and special education), SOCIAL SCIENCE (criminology, history, political science/government, psychology, religion, social work, and sociology). Teacher education, accounting, and history/political science are the strongest academically. Teacher education, criminology, and business administration have the largest enrollments.

ACTIVITIES: There are 32 groups on campus, including cheerleading, drama, international, newspaper, religious, student government, and yearbook. Popular campus events include Films, Lectures, and Concerts. **Sports:** There are 6 intercollegiate sports for men and 6 for women, and 3 intramural sports for men and 2 for women. Facilities include a gym-auditorium, and a stadium. **Graduates:** The most popular majors were business administration, history/political science, and psychology.

SERVICES: Counseling and information services are available, as is tutoring in every subject. There is remedial math, reading, and writing. **Library/Resources:** The library contains 145,305 volumes, 62,079 microform items, and 1,523 audio/video tapes/CDs/DVDs, and subscribes to 308 periodicals including electronic. Computerized library services include database searching. Special learning facilities include an art gallery. **Physically Challenged Students:** 90% of the campus is accessible. Facilities include wheelchair ramps, elevators, and special parking. **Special:** The university offers cross-registration with Virginia Commonwealth and Virginia State Universities, and the University of Richmond. Internships, co-op programs, federal work-study programs, a general studies degree, a joint law degree with St. John's University School of Law in New York, a 3-2 degree in engineering with the Universities of Michigan and Iowa and Howard University, and exchange programs are also offered. There are 2 national honor societies and a freshman honors program. **Visiting:** There are guides for informal visits and visitors may sit in on classes. To schedule a visit, contact the Admissions Office. **Campus Safety and Security:** Measures include 24-hour foot and vehicle patrol and security escort services. There are emergency telephones and lighted pathways/sidewalks.

REQUIREMENTS: The SAT is required. Graduation from an accredited secondary school is required; the GED is accepted. 16 academic units are required, including 4 of English, 3 each of math and academic electives, and 2 each of foreign language, social science, and natural science. Special consideration is given to disadvantaged students. Children of alumni are given some preference. AP and CLEP credits are accepted. Important factors in the admissions decision are extracurricular activities record, advanced placement or honors courses, and leadership record. To graduate, all students must complete at least 124 credit hours with a GPA of at least 2.0. Courses in religion, English, math, science, social science, a foreign language, and phys ed are required. There are also chapel and VUU events attendance requirements. All students must successfully complete a computer science course and must take an English essay exam, usually by the end of the junior year, as well as a comprehensive exam in their major. **Procedure:** Freshmen are admitted fall and spring. Entrance exams should be taken between March of the junior year and March of the senior year. There are early admissions, deferred admissions, and rolling admissions plans. Check with the school for current application deadlines. Notification is sent on a rolling basis. **Transfer Students:** 51 transfer students enrolled in 2016-2017. Transfer students must be in good standing at their previous institutions and must submit all college transcripts. 30 of 124 credits required for the bachelor's degree must be completed at VUU. **International Students:** They must take the TOEFL. They must also take the SAT or ACT.

Admissions Contact: Gil Powell, Director of Admissions. Email: *visitus@vuu.edu* Web: *www.vuu.edu*

FINANCIAL AID: VUU is a member of CSS. The CSS/Profile is required. The FAFSA code is 003766. Check with the school for current application deadlines.

VIRGINIA WESLEYAN UNIVERSITY *(The complete profile is made available exclusively on our website, www.barronspac.com)*

WASHINGTON AND LEE UNIVERSITY C-3

www.wlu.edu

Lexington, VA 24450 **(540) 458-8710**

Fax: (540) 458-8062	**Email: admissions@wlu.edu**
Full-time: 941 men, 883 women	**Faculty:** 204; IIB, ++$
Part-time: 4 men, 2 women	**Ph.D.s:** 96%
Graduate: 182 men, 148 women	**Student/Faculty:** 8 to 1
Year: other	**Tuition:** $48,267
Room & Board: $11,380	**Freshman Class:** 5101 applied, 1203 accepted, 466 enrolled
SAT CR/M/W: 690/690/683 **ACT:** 32	**CEEB CODE:** 5887
Application Deadline: January 1	**MOST COMPETITIVE**

Washington and Lee University, founded in 1749, is a private, highly selective liberal arts university. There are 2 undergraduate schools and 1 graduate school. In addition to regional accreditation, Washington & Lee has baccalaureate program accreditation with AACSB, ACEJMC, and ACS. The 415-acre campus is in a small town 50 miles northeast of Roanoke, VA, and 190 miles southwest of Washington, DC. Including any residence halls, there are 128 buildings.

STUDENT LIFE: 85% of undergraduates are from out of state, mostly the South. Students are from 50 states, 31 foreign countries, and Canada. 51% are from public schools. 83% are White; 4% Hispanic; 4% Foreign; 3% Asian American; 3% two or more races; 2% African American; 1% race unknown. 39% claim no religious affiliation; 38% Protestant; 17% Catholic. **Male To Female Ratio:** 1.1:1. The average age of freshmen is 18; all undergraduates, 20. 4% do not continue beyond their first year; 92% remain to graduate. **Housing:** 1485 students can be accommodated in college housing, which includes dorms and on-campus apartments. In addition, there are language/international houses, special-interest houses, fraternity houses, and sorority houses. On-campus housing is available on a lottery system for upperclassmen. 74% of students live on campus. All students may keep cars.

FACULTY/CLASSROOMS: 60% of faculty are male; 40% are female. All teach undergraduates. No introductory courses are taught by graduate students. The average class size in an introductory lecture is 16; in a laboratory is 13; and in a regular course is 15.

PROGRAMS OF STUDY: Washington & Lee confers B.A. and B.S. degrees. Master's and doctoral degrees are also awarded. Bachelor's degrees are awarded in BIOLOGICAL SCIENCE (biochemistry, biology/biological science, and neurosciences), BUSINESS (accounting and business administration and management), COMMUNICATIONS AND THE ARTS (art history and appreciation, classics, dramatic arts, English, French, German, Germanic languages and literature, journalism, music, romance languages and literature, Russian languages and literature, Spanish, and studio art), COMPUTER AND PHYSICAL SCIENCE (chemistry, computer science, geology, mathematics, natural sciences, and physics), ENGINEERING AND ENVIRONMENTAL DESIGN (chemical engineering, engineering physics, and environmental science), SOCIAL SCIENCE (anthropology, archeology, East Asian studies, economics, history, interdisciplinary studies, medieval studies, philosophy, political science/government, psychology, public affairs, religion, and sociology). Neuroscience, economics, and psychology are the strongest academically. Business administration, economics, and accounting have the largest enrollments.

ACTIVITIES: 73% of men belong to 11 national fraternities; 75% of women belong to 6 national sororities. There are 100 groups on campus, including leadership, Spanish, volunteer, cheerleading, choir, chorale, chorus, communications, dance, debate, drama, environmental, ethnic, film, forensics, honors, international, jazz band, LGBT, literary magazine, musical theater, newspaper, orchestra, outdoor club, pep band, photography, political, professional, radio and TV, religious, social, social service, student government, symphony, and yearbook. Popular campus events include Presidential Mock Convention, Fancy Dress Ball, and NABORS Service Day. **Sports:** There are 12 intercollegiate sports for men and 12 for women, and 10 intramural sports for men and 10 for women. Facilities include a gym, an arena, a stadium, swimming pool, fitness center, weight training and exercise rooms, handball, racquetball, squash, and tennis courts, outdoor track, baseball and practice fields, indoor tennis facility, soccer/lacrosse stadium, and a turf field for hockey and lacrosse. **Graduates:** From July 1, 2016 to June 30, 2017, 470 bachelor's degrees were awarded. The most popular majors were business administration (10%), accounting (9%), and economics (9%). In an average class, 88% graduate in 4 years or less, 91% graduate in 5 years or less, and 92% graduate in 6 years or less. Of the 2016 graduating class, 23% were enrolled in graduate school within 6 months of graduation, and 73% were employed.

SERVICES: Counseling and information services are available, as is tutoring in every subject. There is a reader service for the blind. **Library/ Resources:** The library contains 1.3 million volumes, 1.4 million microform items, 15,078 audio/video tapes/CDs/DVDs, and subscribes to 66,967 periodicals including electronic. Computerized library services include interlibrary loans, database searching, Internet access, and Wi-Fi capability. Special learning facilities include an art gallery, radio station, TV station, special collections, history, fine arts, archeological museums, the Lee Chapel and museum, a gallery, a center for the performing arts, the Reeves center with a Japanese tea room, a multimedia center for foreign language, instrumental laboratory, and a seismograph/scanning electron microscope, light microscopy with digital imaging/ electrophysiological recording facilities. **Physically Challenged Students:** 55% of the campus is accessible. Facilities include wheelchair ramps, elevators, special parking, specially equipped restrooms, special class scheduling, lowered drinking fountains, and special housing. **Special:** Special academic programs are available throughout the college and the Williams School of Commerce. Internship opportunities include the Washington Term, and study abroad opportunities in over 50 countries. Students may earn dual degrees and double majors, over 30 departments offer honors programs, and a teacher certification is offered in consortium with Southern Virginia University. There are 17 national honor societies, Phi Beta Kappa, and 31 departmental honors programs. **Visiting:** There are regularly scheduled orientations for prospective students, hourly interviews and campus tours, 2 group information sessions daily, seasonal Saturday tours and interviews. There are guides for informal visits and visitors may sit in on classes. To schedule a visit, contact the Admissions Office. **Campus Safety and Security:** Measures include 24-hour foot and vehicle patrol, emergency notification system, self-defense education, and security escort services. There are shuttle buses, emergency telephones, lighted pathways/sidewalks, controlled access to dorms/residences, and required safety programs for first-year students.

REQUIREMENTS: The SAT or ACT is required. A high school diploma is not required. Applicants must earn 17 units (24 recommended), including 4 units in English, 3 units each in math (4 recommended), foreign language (4 recommended), and 1 each in history (2 recommended) and natural science (4 recommended with 1 lab science). Coursework in social sciences (1) is also required (2 recommended). Essays, test scores, a transcript, and recommendation letters are needed to apply. An interview is recommended. AP credits are accepted. Important factors in the admissions decision are advanced placement or honors courses, leadership record, extracurricular activities record, and recommendations by school officials. To graduate, students must achieve proficiency in a foreign language and English composition and complete at least 1 course in fine arts and humanities, lab science and math, and literature and 2 courses in social sciences. A total of 113 credits, with a minimum GPA of 2.0, is required. All students must take 4 skills courses in physical education and pass a swimming test. **Procedure:** Freshmen are admitted in the fall. Entrance exams should be taken prior to January of the senior year. There are early decision and deferred admissions plans. Early decision applications should be filed by November 1; regular applications, by January 1 for fall entry. The fall 2017 application fee was $50. Notification of early decision is sent December 22; regular decision, April 1. 268 early decision candidates were accepted for the 2017-2018 class. 1529 applicants were on the 2017 waiting list; 652 were admitted. Applications are accepted on-line. **Transfer Students:** 9 transfer students enrolled in 2016-2017. Transfer applicants must have a GPA of at least 2.0 (at least 3.5 to be competitive); no more than 56 credits will transfer. There is a 2-year residency requirement. 57 of 113 credits required for the bachelor's degree must be completed at Washington & Lee. **International Students:** There are 71 international students enrolled. They must take the TOEFL with a minimum score of 600 on the paper-based TOEFL (PBT) or 100 on the Internet-based version (iBT). Students must take the APIEL or ELPT. They must also take the SAT or ACT.

ADMISSIONS: 24% of the 2017-2018 applicants were accepted. The SAT scores for the 2017-2018 freshman class were: Critical Reading-- 5% between 500 and 599, 47% between 600 and 699, and 47% between 700 and 800. Math-- 2% between 500 and 599, 49% between 600 and 699, and 48% between 700 and 800. Writing-- 5% between 500 and 599, 55% between 600 and 699, and 40% between 700 and 800. The ACT scores were 12% between 24 and 29, and 88% above 30. 97% of the current freshmen were in the top fifth of their class; 100% were in the top two fifths. 22 freshmen graduated first in their class. **Admissions Contact:** Sally S. Richmond, V.P. for Admissions and Financial Aid. Email: *admissions@wlu.edu* Web: *www.wlu.edu*

FINANCIAL AID: In 2017-2018, 52% of all full-time freshmen received some form of financial aid. 45% of all full-time freshmen received need-based aid. The average freshman award was $46,056. Need-based scholarships or need-based grants averaged $40,072; need-based self-help aid (loans and jobs) averaged $1,089; and other non-need-based awards and non-need-based scholarships averaged $44,684. The average financial indebtedness of the 2017 graduate was $26,397. Washington & Lee is a member of CSS. The CSS/Profile, and federal tax returns for parents and students and business tax returns are required. The FAFSA code is 003768. The deadline for filing freshman financial aid applications for fall entry is February 1.

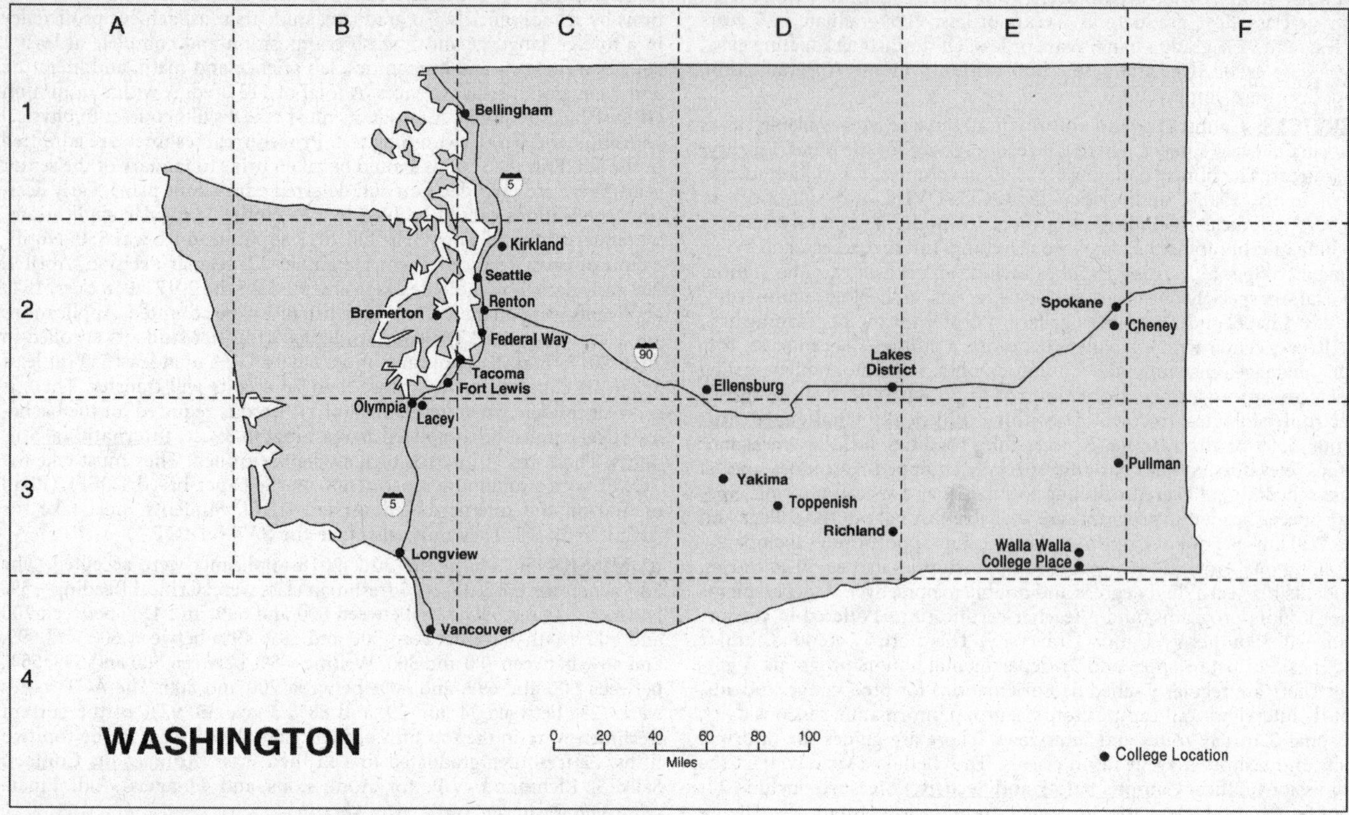

CENTRAL WASHINGTON UNIVERSITY D-2

www.cwu.edu

Ellensburg, WA 98926	**(509) 963-1211** **(866) 298-4968**
Fax: (509) 963-3022	**Email: admissions@cwu.edu**
Full-time: 4646 men, 4827 women	**Faculty:** 451; IIA, -$
Part-time: 750 men, 824 women	**Ph.D.s:** 82%
Graduate: 351 men, 573 women	**Student/Faculty:** 19 to 1
Year: trimesters, summer session	**Tuition:** $7023 ($20,826)
Room & Board: $9780	**Freshman Class:** 7295 applied, 5800 accepted, 1885 enrolled
SAT CR/M/W: 530/523/466 **ACT:** 21	**CEEB CODE:** 4044
Application Deadline: April 1	**COMPETITIVE**

Central Washington University is a public university offering undergraduate and graduate programs in the arts and sciences, business administration, and education and professional studies. There are 4 undergraduate schools and 1 graduate school. In addition to regional accreditation, CWU has baccalaureate program accreditation with AACSB, ABET, ACCE, ADA, NASM, CAPE, and NRPA. The 380-acre campus is in a small town 100 miles east of Seattle. Including any residence halls, there are 107 buildings.

STUDENT LIFE: 95% of undergraduates are from Washington. Others are from 39 states, 14 foreign countries, and Canada. 57% are White; 14% Hispanic; 11% race unknown; 6% two or more races; 4% African American; 4% Asian American; 3% Foreign; 1% American Indian/Alaska Native. **Female To Male Ratio:** 1.1:1. The average age of freshmen is 19; all undergraduates, 24. **Housing:** 3700 students can be accommodated in college housing, which includes married student dorms, on-campus apartments, and off-campus apartments. In addition, there are honors houses, language/international houses, special-interest houses, a freshman-only enrichment hall, a residence hall for transfers and upperclassmen only, and theme and wellness housing. On-campus housing is guaranteed for the freshman year only, is available on a first-come, and first-served basis. 68% of students commute. All students may keep cars.

FACULTY/CLASSROOMS: 58% of faculty are male; 42% are female. All teach undergraduates and all do research. No introductory courses are taught by graduate students. The average class size in an introductory lecture is 45; in a laboratory is 20; and in a regular course is 40.

PROGRAMS OF STUDY: CWU confers B.A., B.S., B.A.Ed. and B.F.A. degrees. Master's degrees are also awarded. Bachelor's degrees are awarded in BIOLOGICAL SCIENCE (biology/biological science), BUSINESS (accounting, banking and finance, business administration and management, business economics, fashion merchandising, international business management, marketing/retailing/merchandising, recreation and leisure services, and tourism), COMMUNICATIONS AND THE ARTS (art, broadcasting, Chinese, communications, dramatic arts, English, fine arts, French, German, guitar, Japanese, journalism, language arts, music, music business management, music theory and composition, percussion, piano/organ, public relations, Russian, Spanish, speech/debate/rhetoric, strings, studio art, visual and performing arts, and voice), COMPUTER AND PHYSICAL SCIENCE (actuarial science, chemistry, computer programming, computer science, earth science, geology, information sciences and systems, mathematics, physics, and software engineering), EDUCATION (art education, business education, early childhood education, elementary education, English education, foreign languages education, health education, home economics education, industrial arts education, marketing and distribution education, mathematics education, middle school education, music education, physical education, science education, secondary education, social studies education, and special education), ENGINEERING AND ENVIRONMENTAL DESIGN (aeronautical technology, aviation administration/management, aviation maintenance management, construction management, electrical/electronics engineering, engineering technology, industrial engineering technology, and mechanical engineering), HEALTH PROFESSIONS (community health work, emergency medical technologies, exercise science, and public health), SOCIAL SCIENCE (anthropology, Asian/Oriental studies, criminal justice, economics, family and community services, family/consumer studies, food science, geography, gerontology, history, liberal arts/general studies, paralegal studies, parks and recreation management, philosophy, political science/government, prelaw, psychology, public administration, safety science, social science, social work, and sociology). Accounting, music, and geology are the strongest academically. Business and education have the largest enrollments.

ACTIVITIES: There are no fraternities or sororities. There are 125

groups on campus, including art, band, cheerleading, chess, choir, chorale, chorus, computers, dance, drama, environmental, ethnic, film, honors, international, jazz band, LGBT, literary magazine, marching band, musical theater, newspaper, opera, orchestra, pep band, photography, political, professional, radio and TV, religious, social, social service, student government, and symphony. Popular campus events include Homecoming, Holiday Ware Fair, PolyFest, Day of the Dead, Showtime at Central, MLK Celebration, Jazz Night, Yakima River Clean-Up, Science in a Pint, and Nature of Night. **Sports:** There are 6 intercollegiate sports for men and 6 for women, and 21 intramural sports for men and 21 for women. Facilities include a student union and recreation center that features an indoor rock climbing wall, a gymnasium, fitness studios, strength training and cardio fitness areas, indoor elevated track, athletics complex for basketball, volleyball, weight-training and physical therapy facilities, fields for baseball, rugby, softball, and soccer. The Aquatic Center features a 25-yard by 25-meter pool with springboards, and water polo capabilities. **Graduates:** From July 1, 2016 to June 30, 2017, 2432 bachelor's degrees were awarded. The most popular majors were business/marketing (27%), education (14%), and social sciences (10%). In an average class, 1% graduate in 3 years or less, 24% graduate in 4 years or less, 45% graduate in 5 years or less, and 52% graduate in 6 years or less.

SERVICES: Counseling and information services are available, as is tutoring in most subjects. There is a reader service for the blind, and remedial math, reading, and writing. **Library/Resources:** The library contains 980,976 volumes, 47,567 microform items, and 22,565 audio/video tapes/CDs/DVDs, and subscribes to 72,352 periodicals including electronic. Computerized library services include interlibrary loans, database searching, Internet access, and Wi-Fi capability. Special learning facilities include an art gallery, natural history museum, planetarium, radio station, an anthropology museum, a botanical greenhouse, and a primate research lab. **Physically Challenged Students:** All of the campus is accessible. Facilities include wheelchair ramps, elevators, special parking, specially equipped restrooms, special class scheduling, lowered drinking fountains, lowered telephones, and special housing. **Special:** Students may study abroad; there are formal exchange programs with universities in Australia, England, France, Japan, Scotland, and South Korea. There are 3-2 physics/engineering degree programs in conjunction with the University of Puget Sound, the University of Washington, and Washington State University. CWU also offers co-op programs, internships, work-study programs, a competency based program, credit/no credit options, dual and student-designed majors, dual admission, Running Start, college in the high school, dual enrollment, undergraduate research, William O. Douglas Honors College, Bachelor of Applied Science programs, and alternative pathway to teacher certification. Students may earn additional credit by prior learning, credit by exam, and credit for military experience. Non-degree study is offered through adult/continuing education or international programs. This includes the Asia University America Program (AUAP) and University English as a Second Language (UESL). There are 11 national honor societies, a freshman honors program, and 12 departmental honors programs. **Visiting:** There are regularly scheduled orientations for prospective students, consisting of an information session, a tour of residence halls, a tour of the campus, prearranged appointments with faculty, and a financial aid presentation. There are guides for informal visits, visitors may sit in on classes, and stay overnight. To schedule a visit, contact the Admissions Office. **Campus Safety and Security:** Measures include 24-hour foot and vehicle patrol, emergency notification system, self-defense education, and security escort services. There are shuttle buses, emergency telephones, lighted pathways/sidewalks, controlled access to dorms/residences, and controlled-entry residence halls.

REQUIREMENTS: The SAT or ACT is required. Test scores and GPA are considered in combination according to a sliding scale. Applicants must be graduates of accredited secondary schools or have earned a GED. The university requires 15 academic credits or Carnegie units: 4 years of English, 3 units each of math and social studies, 2 units each of the same foreign language, and science (with 1 unit a lab), and 1 unit of performing arts or an academic elective, U.S. history and U.S. government are recommended and will count towards social studies requirements. A GPA of 2.0 is required. AP and CLEP credits are accepted. Important factors in the admissions decision are leadership record, evidence of special talent, personality/intangible qualities, and extracurricular activities record. Students must complete a minimum of 180 quarter credits, including 60 credits in upper-division courses and a minimum of 45 credits in the major plus a minor or 60 credits in the major. Core curriculum requirements include 15-18 of Basic and Breadth courses, including 3 courses each in arts and humanities, social and behavioral sciences, and natural science. An academic advising seminar, 2 courses of English composition, one course in math, one reasoning course, and a computer fundamentals course are also required. Students are required to have either one year of college level foreign language or two years of high school foreign language. (Exemptions may apply). Students must maintain a 2.25 GPA in the major (higher for some programs) and 2.0 GPA overall. Some academic programs have thesis or senior project options. **Procedure:** Freshmen are admitted to all sessions. Entrance exams should be taken before the fall of the senior year. There is a rolling admissions plan. Applications should be filed by April 1 for fall entry; November 1 for winter entry; February 1 for spring entry; and June 1 for summer entry. The fall 2017 application fee was $50. Notification is sent on a rolling basis. Applications are accepted on-line. **Transfer Students:** Students presenting an associate degree need a minimum GPA of 2.5 for automatic offer of admission; students with a GPA between 2.0 and 2.5 will be asked to provide additional information for review. 40 of 180 credits required for the bachelor's degree must be completed at CWU. **International Students:** There are 296 international students enrolled. They must take the TOEFL. They must also take the SAT or ACT.

ADMISSIONS: 80% of the 2017-2018 applicants were accepted. The SAT scores for the 2017-2018 freshman class were: Critical Reading-- 33% below 500, 47% between 500 and 599, 18% between 600 and 699, and 2% between 700 and 800. Math-- 34% below 500, 52% between 500 and 599, 12% between 600 and 699, and 2% between 700 and 800. Writing-- 66% below 500, 28% between 500 and 599, 5% between 600 and 699, and 1% between 700 and 800. The ACT scores were 1% below 12, 20% between 12 and 17, 52% between 18 and 23, 24% between 24 and 29, and 3% above 30. **Admissions Contact:** Kathy Gaer-Carlton, Director of Admissions. Email: *admissions@cwu.edu* Web: *www.cwu.edu*

FINANCIAL AID: In 2017-2018, 90% of all full-time freshmen received some form of financial aid. 88% of all full-time freshmen received need-based aid. The average financial indebtedness of the 2017 graduate was $26,360. The FAFSA code is 003771. The priority date for freshman financial aid applications for fall entry is March 1. The deadline for filing freshman financial aid applications for fall entry is May 1.

CITY UNIVERSITY OF SEATTLE *(The complete profile is made available exclusively on our website, www.barronspac.com)*

CORNISH COLLEGE OF THE ARTS *(The complete profile is made available exclusively on our website, www.barronspac.com)*

EASTERN WASHINGTON UNIVERSITY *(The complete profile is made available exclusively on our website, www.barronspac.com)*

GONZAGA UNIVERSITY — E-2

www.gonzaga.edu

Spokane, WA 99258	**(509) 313-6572** **(800) 322-2584**
Fax: (509) 313-5780	**Email: admissions@gonzaga.edu**
Full-time: 2444 men, 2666 women	**Faculty:** 370
Part-time: 51 men, 48 women	**Ph.D.s:** 84%
Graduate: 810 men, 1487 women	**Student/Faculty:** 12 to 1
Year: semesters, summer session	**Tuition:** $41,330
Room & Board: $11,550	**Freshman Class:** 7613 applied, 4937 accepted, 1257 enrolled
SAT EBR-W/M: 629/628 **ACT:** 28	**CEEB CODE:** 4330
Application Deadline: February 1	**HIGHLY COMPETITIVE**

Gonzaga University, founded in 1887, is a private, liberal arts institution affiliated with the Roman Catholic Church and the Society of Jesus (Jesuits). The university offers undergraduate and graduate degrees in arts and sciences, business, education, engineering, law, leadership, nursing and human physiology. There are 5 undergraduate schools and 7 graduate schools. In addition to regional accreditation, GU has baccalaureate program accreditation with AACSB, ABET, CAEP, CACREP, CCNE, and CSLE/ABA. The 152-acre campus is in an urban residential area along the Spokane River in the University District, just one-half mile from downtown core business district. Including any residence halls, there are 104 buildings.

STUDENT LIFE: 51% of undergraduates are from out of state, mostly the West. Students are from 43 states, 28 foreign countries, and Canada. 68% are from public schools. 72% are White; 11% Hispanic; 6% two or more races; 5% Asian American; 3% race unknown; 1% African American; 1% American Indian/Alaska Native; 1% Foreign. 47% are Catholic; 25% claim no religious affiliation; 24% Protestant. **Female To Male Ratio:** 1.3:1. The average age of freshmen is 18; all undergraduates, 20. 6% do not continue beyond their first year; 94% remain to graduate. **Housing:** 3028 students can be accommodated in college housing, which includes single sex dorms, coed dorms, married student dorms, on-campus apartments, and off-campus apartments. In addition, there are special-interest houses, living and learning communities within residence halls. On-campus housing is guaranteed for the freshman year only, is available on a first-come, first-served basis, and is available on a lottery system for upperclassmen. 55% of students live on campus. All students may keep cars.

FACULTY/CLASSROOMS: 52% of faculty are male; 48% are female. 75% do both. No introductory courses are taught by graduate students. The average class size in an introductory lecture is 24; in a laboratory is 13; and in a regular course is 24.

PROGRAMS OF STUDY: GU confers B.A., B.S., B.B.A., B.Ed., and B.S.N. degrees. Master's and doctoral degrees are also awarded. Bachelor's degrees are awarded in AGRICULTURE (environmental studies), BIOLOGICAL SCIENCE (biochemistry and biology/biological science), BUSINESS (accounting, business administration and management, business economics, and sports management), COMMUNICATIONS AND THE ARTS (art, broadcasting, classics, communications, dramatic arts, English, French, journalism, literature, music, public relations, Spanish, speech/debate/rhetoric, and theatre acting), COMPUTER AND PHYSICAL SCIENCE (chemistry, computer science, mathematics, and physics), EDUCATION (music education, physical education, and special education), ENGINEERING AND ENVIRONMENTAL DESIGN (civil engineering, computer engineering, electrical/electronics engineering, engineering management, and mechanical engineering), HEALTH PROFESSIONS (exercise science, kinesiology, and nursing), SOCIAL SCIENCE (classical/ancient civilization, criminology, economics, history, interdisciplinary studies, international studies, Italian studies, philosophy, political science/government, psychology, religious studies, and sociology). Engineering, biology, and nursing are the strongest academically. Business, engineering, and social sciences have the largest enrollments.

ACTIVITIES: There are no fraternities or sororities. There are 140 groups on campus, including art, band, cheerleading, chess, choir, chorale, chorus, communications, computers, dance, debate, drama, drill team, environmental, ethnic, honors, international, jazz band, LGBT, literary magazine, mock trial club, musical theater, newspaper, orchestra, pep band, photography, political, professional, radio and TV, religious, social, social service, student government, symphony, and yearbook. Popular campus events include Search and other Spiritual Retreats, GEL Weekend, Charity Ball, Diversity Monologues, and Fall Family Weekend. **Sports:** There are 9 intercollegiate sports for men and 9 for women, and 30 intramural sports for men and 30 for women. Facilities include a nutrition center, a basketball arena, 2 basketball/volleyball courts, indoor golf, tennis with 6 courts, soccer, baseball stadium and field, indoor rowing room, student fitness center with cardiovascular and weight areas, multipurpose synthetic turf field, 3 multipurpose courts, 4 racquetball courts, 2 aerobics rooms, indoor running track, and a 6-lane 25-yard swimming pool. **Graduates:** From July 1, 2016 to June 30, 2017, 1285 bachelor's degrees were awarded. The most popular majors were business/accounting (24%), engineering majors (15%), and various social science majors (12%). In an average class, 1% graduate in 3 years or less, 78% graduate in 4 years or less, 86% graduate in 5 years or less, and 87% graduate in 6 years or less. Of the 2016 graduating class, 19% were enrolled in graduate school within 6 months of graduation, and 65% were employed.

SERVICES: Counseling and information services are available, as is tutoring in most subjects. There is a reader service for the blind. Informal peer tutoring in English and math is available. **Library/Resources:** The library contains 398,985 volumes, 16,939 microform items, and 4,917 audio/video tapes/CDs/DVDs, and subscribes to 60,559 periodicals including electronic. Computerized library services include interlibrary loans, database searching, Internet access, and Wi-Fi capability. Special learning facilities include an art gallery, radio station, and TV station. **Physically Challenged Students:** 90% of the campus is accessible. Facilities include wheelchair ramps, elevators, special parking, specially equipped restrooms, special class scheduling, lowered drinking fountains, lowered telephones, and special housing. Academic adjustments are provided for students with disabilities who provide appropriate documentation and request services from Disability Access Office. Accessible rooms exist in some residence halls and apartments. **Special:** Honors program, cross-registration with Whitworth University, internships available for credit or no credit in every academic program, capstone experiences, study abroad in 45 countries (including a Gonzaga-in-Florence campus), a Washington semester, summer faculty-led programs and on- and off-campus work-study programs are offered. There is a limited pass/fail option for some coursework and double and triple majors and degrees are possible in all academic programs (though seeking multiple majors/degrees may increase time to degree). High school juniors and seniors may take 6 credits per semester in certain areas. Also offered are several 3-2 or 4-1 degrees that allow an undergraduate to also earn a graduate degree in a fifth year. During the fourth year of coursework, undergraduates majoring in Communication Arts or International Studies, or minoring in Leadership Studies may enroll in master's level courses in two M.A. graduate programs, completing both an undergraduate and master's degree in as little as five years. Engineering undergraduates may enroll in the MBA program earning both degrees in as little as five years. Accounting undergraduates may enroll in the Accountancy or Taxation graduate program earning both degrees in as little as five years. There are 19 national honor societies and a freshman honors program. **Visiting:** There are regularly scheduled orientations for prospective students, day visits are permitted Monday through Friday with campus tours offered multiple times per day; overnight visits, Sunday through Thursday (except for holiday periods). To schedule a visit, contact the Gonzaga Visit Office at (509) 13-6531. **Campus Safety and Security:** Measures include 24-hour foot and vehicle patrol, emergency notification system, self-defense education, and security escort services. There are emergency telephones, lighted pathways/sidewalks, and controlled access to dorms/residences.

REQUIREMENTS: The SAT or ACT is required. Applicants should be graduates of an accredited secondary school with a high school diploma; GED is not accepted. They must have completed 17 academic credits consisting of 4 years of English, 3-4 years of math, 2-3 years of the same foreign language (world language preferred, ASL accepted), 2-3 years of history, 2-3 years of social studies, and 3-4 years of natural or physical laboratory science. The Common Application for undergraduate admission, and a personal essay and activities list are required. A letter of recommendation from a teacher/professor in an academic area is required. An interview is optional but recommended for students with a GPA lower than 3.2 or SAT score less than 1070 for Verbal/Critical plus Math, or 23 ACT Composite. NURSING: Gonzaga University's Undergraduate Nursing Program accepts first-year applications only. Applicants interested in the Nursing Program must choose "Nursing" on their application to be considered. Students not admitted into the Nursing Program through the application process will not be permitted to change their major to nursing. ENGINEERING: The School of Engineering and Applied Science has competitive, direct admission for engineering programs. This includes civil, computer, electrical, mechanical, engineering management as well as students who are undecided but desire a major in an engineering discipline. Please note that direct admission does not apply to the computer science program. Applicants interested in pursuing any of the majors in the School of Engineering and Applied Science as a first-year student should be ready for college calculus and (with the exception of computer science applicants) should have completed physics in high school. Students not meeting these criteria are encouraged to consider majors outside the school. AP credits are accepted. Important factors in the admissions decision are advanced placement or honors courses, leadership record, parents or siblings attended your school, evidence of special talent, extracurricular activities record, recommendations by alumni, recommendations by school officials, and geographical diversity. All students must complete at least 128 credit hours with a minimum 2.0 GPA. The major requirements are 18 hours in upper-division courses and supporting courses required by the major department. Students must complete courses that support University Core. The University Core requires students to complete specific courses including a first year seminar, Writing, Reasoning, Math, Communication, Scientific Inquiry, Philosophy, Christianity & Catholic Traditions, Ethics, World or Comparative Religion, and a senior year integration seminar. Additional requirements let students choose classes that fulfill the following requirements: 3 credits each of History, Literature, Fine Arts & Design, and Social & Behavioral Science, 3 credits with a Global Studies designation, 3 credits with a Social Justice designation, and 6 credits with a Writing-Enriched designation. **Procedure:** Freshmen are admitted fall and spring. Entrance exams should be taken by February 15. There are early admissions and deferred admissions plans. Early decision applications should be filed by November 15; regular applications, by February 1 for fall entry; and November 15 for spring entry. The fall 2017 application fee was $50. Notification of early decision is sent January 15; regular decision, March 15. 602 applicants were on the 2017 waiting list; 17 were admitted. Applications are accepted on-line. **Transfer Students:** 120 transfer students enrolled in 2016-2017. A minimum college GPA of 2.7 and high school GPA of 3.1 is required. All applicants must provide college transcripts, an essay or personal statement, and a statement of good standing from prior institution(s). An interview is recommended. Some applicants may be required to submit their high school transcript and standardized test scores. 30 of 128 credits required for the bachelor's degree must be completed at Gonzaga. **International Students:** There are 71 international students enrolled. They must take the TOEFL with a minimum score of 550 on the paper-based TOEFL (PBT) or 80 on the Internet-based version (iBT). Student must also take any one of these tests: the IELTS, APIEL, SAT, ACT, or the Gonzaga ESL Program Exit Exam, which includes a writing test.

ADMISSIONS: 65% of the 2017-2018 applicants were accepted. The SAT scores for the 2017-2018 freshman class were: Math-- 1% below 500, 29% between 500 and 599, 55% between 600 and 699, and 15% between 700 and 800. Evidence-Based Reading/Writing-- 1% below 500, 25% between 500 and 599, 62% between 600 and 699, and 12% between 700 and 800. The ACT scores were 7% between 18 and 23, 59% between 24 and 29, and 34% above 30. 75% of the current freshmen were in the top fifth of their class; 96% were in the top two fifths. **Admissions Contact:** Julie McCulloh, Dean of Admission. Email: *admissions@gonzaga.edu* Web: *www.gonzaga.edu*

FINANCIAL AID: In 2017-2018, 98% of all full-time freshmen received some form of financial aid. 80% of all full-time freshmen received need-based aid. The average freshman award was $27,736. Need-based scholarships or need-based grants averaged $21,414; need-based self-help aid (loans and jobs) averaged $6,222; non-need-based athletic scholarships averaged $24,528; and other non-need-based awards and non-need-based scholarships averaged $15,510. 33% of undergraduate students work part-time. The average financial indebtedness of the 2017 graduate was $29,692. Gonzaga is a member of CSS. The FAFSA code is 003778. The priority date for freshman financial aid applications for fall entry is February 1.

HERITAGE UNIVERSITY *(The complete profile is made available exclusively on our website, www.barronspac.com)*

NORTHWEST UNIVERSITY — C-2

www.northwestu.edu

Kirkland, WA 98033 — (425) 889-7821, (800) 669-3781

Fax: (425) 889-5224	**Email:** admissions@northwestu.edu
Full-time: 322 men, 572 women	**Faculty:** 49; IIB, --$
Part-time: 5 men, 12 women	**Ph.D.s:** 41%
Graduate: 99 men, 200 women	**Student/Faculty:** 20 to 1
Year: semesters, summer session	**Tuition:** $30,320
Room & Board: $8400	**Freshman Class:** n/av
SAT or ACT: required	**CEEB CODE:** 4541
Application Deadline: August 15	**VERY COMPETITIVE**

Northwest University has continually built a learning community wholly dedicated to spiritual vitality, academic excellence, and empowered engagement with human need, and offers over 70 majors and programs. Providing unparalleled opportunity for career development, over 70% of students fulfill internships in local businesses and organizations. There are 4 undergraduate schools and 4 graduate schools. In addition to regional accreditation, NU has baccalaureate program accreditation with AACTE. The 56-acre campus is in a suburban area in Kirkland, 10 miles east of Seattle. Including any residence halls, there are 27 buildings.

STUDENT LIFE: 75% of undergraduates are from Washington. Others are from 27 states, 23 foreign countries, and Canada. 67% are White; 9% Hispanic; 5% Asian American; 5% Foreign; 5% two or more races; 4% African American; 2% American Indian/Alaska Native; 1% race unknown. 97% are Protestant. **Female To Male Ratio:** 1.8:1. The average age of freshmen is 19; all undergraduates, 22. 20% do not continue beyond their first year; 59% remain to graduate. **Housing:** 544 students can be accommodated in college housing, which includes single-sex and married student dorms and on-campus apartments. On-campus housing is guaranteed for all 4 years. 65% of students live on campus. Alcohol is not permitted. All students may keep cars.

FACULTY/CLASSROOMS: 65% of faculty are male; 35% are female. All teach undergraduates. No introductory courses are taught by graduate students. The average class size in an introductory lecture is 30; in a laboratory is 20; and in a regular course is 24.

PROGRAMS OF STUDY: NU confers B.A., and B.S. degrees. Associate, master's, and doctoral degrees are also awarded. Bachelor's degrees are awarded in BUSINESS (accounting, business administration and management, international business management, management, and marketing), COMMUNICATIONS AND THE ARTS (communication studies, English, English literature, English Writing, music, and music business management), COMPUTER AND PHYSICAL SCIENCE (information technology management and mathematics), EDUCATION (education, elementary education, middle school education, physical education, secondary education, and special education), ENGINEERING AND ENVIRONMENTAL DESIGN (environmental science), HEALTH PROFESSIONS (biology, exercise science, and nursing), SOCIAL SCIENCE (behavioral science, biblical studies, counseling/psychology, history, interdisciplinary studies, liberal arts/general studies, ministries, missions, pastoral studies, political science/government, psychology, religion, religious education, religious music, theological studies, and youth ministry). Nursing, biology, English, and church ministries are the strongest academically. Nursing, psychology, and business administration have the largest enrollments.

ACTIVITIES: There are no fraternities or sororities. There are 20 groups on campus, including band, chess, choir, chorale, chorus, communications, debate, drama, ethnic, forensics, international, jazz band, literary magazine, musical theater, newspaper, orchestra, photography, professional, religious, social, social service, and student government. Popular campus events include Christmas Holiday Social, Screaming Eagles Week, and Roomies Night-out. **Sports:** There are 4 intercollegiate sports for men and 5 for women, and 2 intramural sports for men and 2 for women. Facilities include a gym pavilion, outdoor tennis courts, a practice field for soccer and intramural football, access to the Seattle Seahawks' former practice fields, outdoor basketball, and sand volleyball. **Graduates:** From July 1, 2016 to June 30, 2017, 252 bachelor's degrees were awarded.

SERVICES: There is a reader service for the blind, and remedial math and writing. The Academic Success and Advising Office provides assistance in most areas, including study skills. **Library/Resources:** The library contains 311,925 volumes, and 887 audio/video tapes/CDs/DVDs, and subscribes to 30,000 periodicals including electronic. Computerized library services include interlibrary loans, database searching, and Internet access. **Physically Challenged Students:** 75% of the campus is accessible. Facilities include wheelchair ramps, elevators, and special parking. **Special:** NU offers study abroad in several locations in the U.S. and foreign countries through the Council for Christian Colleges and Universities, such as Korea, Russia, Australia, Sri Lanka, and Vietnam. Dual majors are also available. There are 2 national honor societies, a freshman honors program, and 1 departmental honors program. **Visiting:** There are regularly scheduled orientations for prospective students. There are guides for informal visits, visitors may sit in on classes, and stay overnight. **Campus Safety and Security:** Measures include 24-hour foot and vehicle patrol, self-defense education, and security escort services. There are shuttle buses, emergency telephones, lighted pathways/sidewalks, and controlled access to dorms/residences.

REQUIREMENTS: The SAT or ACT is required. A GPA of 2.3 is required. AP and CLEP credits are accepted. Important factors in the admissions decision are personality/intangible qualities, recommendations by alumni, and leadership record. The core curriculum for all students includes the following: Bible and Theology (12 credits), Written and Verbal Communication (9 credits), Humanities (9 credits), Social Sciences (9 credits), Science and Mathematics (7 credits), and Formation and Calling (5 credits). Bachelor's degrees are a total of 125 semester credits. A minimum GPA of 2.0 is required for graduation. **Procedure:** Freshmen are admitted to all sessions. Entrance exams should be taken in the spring of the junior year. There are early decision, deferred admissions, and rolling admissions plans. Applications should be filed by August 15 for fall entry; December 15 for spring entry; and April 15 for summer entry. The fall 2017 application fee was $30. Notification of early decision is sent December 1; regular decision, on a rolling basis. 56 early decision candidates were accepted for the 2017-2018 class. **Transfer Students:** 205 transfer students enrolled in 2016-2017. Transfers must have a minimum 2.3 GPA from high school and college and must submit SAT I or ACT scores, an essay, and 2 letters of reference. 30 of 125 credits required for the bachelor's degree must be completed at NU. **International Students:** There are 19 international students enrolled. They must take the TOEFL.

Admissions Contact: Andy Hall, Director of Traditional Admissions. Email: *admissions@northwestu.edu* Web: *www.northwestu.edu*

FINANCIAL AID: In 2017-2018, 94% of all full-time freshmen received some form of financial aid and need-based aid. 67% of undergraduate students work part-time. The college's own financial statement is required. The FAFSA code is 003783. The deadline for filing freshman financial aid applications for fall entry is March 1.

PACIFIC LUTHERAN UNIVERSITY C-2

www.plu.edu

Tacoma, WA 98447 **(253) 535-8145**

Fax: (253) 536-8760	**Email:** admissions@plu.edu
Full-time: 991 men, 1711 women	**Faculty:** 205; IIA, -$
Part-time: 44 men, 36 women	**Ph.D.s:** 94%
Graduate: 95 men, 199 women	**Student/Faculty:** 13 to 1
Year: 4-1-4, summer session	**Tuition:** $39,450
Room & Board: $10,510	**Freshman Class:** 3769 applied, 2896 accepted, 678 enrolled
SAT CR/M/W: required **ACT:** 25	**CEEB CODE:** 4597
Application Deadline: October 1	**COMPETITIVE**

Pacific Lutheran University, founded in 1890 by Norwegian immigrants. PLU offers programs in the liberal arts and professional. PLU is a private university affiliated with the Evangelical Lutheran Church in America. The university offers three pathways to academic distinction: global education and service to the world, robust student-faculty collaborative research and creative projects, and helping students discern meaning and purpose in their lives. There are 7 undergraduate schools and 5 graduate schools. In addition to regional accreditation, PLU has baccalaureate program accreditation with AACSB, ABET, CSWE, NASM, CCNE, and WSNCQA. The 156-acre campus is in a suburban area 7 miles south of Tacoma, WA. Including any residence halls, there are 42 buildings.

STUDENT LIFE: 76% of undergraduates are from Washington. Others are from 29 states, 26 foreign countries, and Canada. 66% are White; 9% Asian American; 9% Hispanic; 8% two or more races; 3% African American; 3% Foreign; 1% American Indian/Alaska Native; 1% race unknown. 33% are Protestant; 17% claim no religious affiliation; 12% Catholic. **Female To Male Ratio:** 1.7:1. The average age of freshmen is 18; all undergraduates, 21. 21% do not continue beyond their first year; 71% remain to graduate. **Housing:** 1582 students can be accommodated in college housing, which includes married student dorms and on-campus apartments. In addition, there are honors houses, language/international houses, special-interest houses, living learning communities, themed communities, gender neutral housing, international hall, and a social action and leadership wing. On-campus housing is guaranteed for the freshman year only. 52% of students commute. All students may keep cars.

FACULTY/CLASSROOMS: 42% of faculty are male; 58% are female. 92% teach undergraduates, and 90% do research. No introductory courses are taught by graduate students. The average class size in an introductory lecture is 23; in a laboratory is 14; and in a regular course is 17.

PROGRAMS OF STUDY: PLU confers B.A., B.A.C., B.A.E., B.A.K., B.B.A., B.F.A., B.M., B.M.A., B.M.E., B.S., B.S.K. and B.S.N. degrees. Master's and doctoral degrees are also awarded. Bachelor's degrees are awarded in BIOLOGICAL SCIENCE (biology/biological science), BUSINESS (business administration and management), COMMUNICATIONS AND THE ARTS (art history, classical languages, classics, communications, English, French, German, music, music performance, music theory and composition, Norwegian, piano/organ, Spanish, studio art, theatre arts, and voice), COMPUTER AND PHYSICAL SCIENCE (applied physics, chemistry, computer science, geoscience, mathematics, mathematics - actuarial concentration, and physics), EDUCATION (elementary education, global studies, mathematics education, music education, physical education, and secondary education), ENGINEERING AND ENVIRONMENTAL DESIGN (engineering and applied science and environmental science), HEALTH PROFESSIONS (kinesiology and nursing), SOCIAL SCIENCE (anthropology, Chinese Studies, economics, Hispanic American studies, history, philosophy, political science/government, psychology, religion, Scandinavian studies, social work, sociology, and women & gender studies). Business administration, nursing, and biology have the largest enrollments.

ACTIVITIES: There are no fraternities or sororities. There are 70 groups on campus, including art, band, cheerleading, choir, chorale, chorus, computers, dance, debate, drama, environmental, ethnic, film, forensics, honors, international, jazz band, LGBT, literary magazine, musical theater, newspaper, opera, orchestra, pep band, photography, political, professional, radio and TV, religious, social, social service, student government, student leadership institute, and symphony. Popular campus events include Wang Symposium, EXPLORE! Retreat, Holocaust Education Conference, Relay for Life, unPLUg, Songfest, Family Weekend, Homecoming, PLUtonic concerts, Berry Festival, Clay Crows - improv, and dance ensemble. **Sports:** There are 9 intercollegiate sports for men and 10 for women, and 18 intramural sports for men and 17 for women. Facilities include a gym/auditorium, fitness center, pool, racquetball, and tennis courts, volleyball, basketball, soccer field, softball, baseball fields, track and other fields for practice. Access to the Sparks Stadium for football and indoor tennis center. **Graduates:** From July 1, 2016 to June 30, 2017, 736 bachelor's degrees were awarded. The most popular majors were business administration (14%), nursing (10%), and biology (7%). In an average class, 5% graduate in 3 years or less, 58% graduate in 4 years or less, 69% graduate in 5 years or less, and 71% graduate in 6 years or less.

SERVICES: Counseling and information services are available, as is tutoring in most subjects, such as anthropology, biology, business, chemistry, geosciences, global studies, history, languages, math, music, nursing, philosophy, and religion. There is also a reader service for the blind, study groups, and free flashcards, pretest and posttest reviews. **Library/Resources:** The library contains 323,926 volumes, 228,386 microform items, and 11,858 audio/video tapes/CDs/DVDs, and subscribes to 4,474 periodicals including electronic. Computerized library services include interlibrary loans, database searching, Internet access, and Wi-Fi capability. Special learning facilities include an art gallery, radio station, TV station, observatory, marriage and family therapy center, nuclear magnetic resonance spectrometer, an herbarium, greenhouse and native plant garden, invertebrate and vertebrate museums, a biology field station, Northwest history collections, a Scandinavian history collection, and a language resource center. **Physically Challenged Students:** 90% of the campus is accessible. Facilities include wheelchair ramps, elevators, special parking, specially equipped restrooms, special class scheduling, lowered drinking fountains, lowered telephones, and special housing. **Special:** PLU offers 2 different bachelor's degrees simultaneously, 3-2 engineering degrees with Washington University in St. Louis and Columbia University, and accelerated degree programs in most majors. Dual majors and student-designed majors can be arranged. Extensive internships with local businesses and nonprofit organizations, work-study programs, non-degree study, and pass/fail options are also available. The Wang Center for International Programs supports the university's internationally focused academic programs. There are 17 national honor societies and a freshman honors program. **Visiting:** There are regularly scheduled orientations for prospective students, consisting of activities based on the students' individual interests-tour, class visits, and meeting with coaches and/or faculty. There are guides for informal visits, visitors may sit in on classes, and stay overnight. To schedule a visit, contact the Office of Admission. **Campus Safety and Security:** Measures include 24-hour foot and vehicle patrol, emergency notification system, self-defense education, and security escort services. There are emergency telephones, lighted pathways/sidewalks, controlled access to dorms/residences, and automated emergency notification system.

REQUIREMENTS: The SAT or ACT is required. Applicants should be graduates of accredited secondary schools, although GED certificates are accepted. PLU requires 2 years each of college preparatory math, and foreign language, and recommends 4 years of English, 2 each of social studies and lab science, 1 of fine or performing arts, and 3 of electives. Essay and recommendation are required. AP and CLEP credits are accepted. Important factors in the admissions decision are advanced placement or honors courses, leadership record, and evidence of special talent. All students must complete a minimum of 128 semester hours with a grade point average (GPA) of 2.00. A 2.50 is required in the Schools of Business and Education and Kinesiology, plus the Departments of Economics, History, Languages and Literatures (Hispanic Studies), Sociology, and Social Work. Of the 128 semester hours, a minimum of 40 semester hours must be completed from courses numbered 300 or above. The required General Education Program is a minimum of 48 semester hours plus a culminating seminar. The program is rooted in the classical liberal arts and sciences as understood within the Lutheran educational tradition, and is grounded in an understanding of scientific perspectives, mathematics, languages, and the long-standing traditions of critical discourse about nature, humanity and the world. **Procedure:** Freshmen are admitted fall and spring. Entrance exams should be taken by January of the senior year. There are deferred admissions and rolling admissions plans. Application deadlines are open. The fall 2017 application fee was $40. Notification is sent on a rolling basis. Applications are accepted on-line. **Transfer Students:** 268 transfer students enrolled in 2016-2017. Candidates must be in good academic and personal standing at the institutions last attended full time. Although it does not guarantee admission, a 2.5 GPA in all college work is usually required. For applicants with fewer than 30 semester hours or 45 quarter hours, secondary school records and standardized test scores must be submitted. All students must meet the foreign language and math entrance requirements. 32 of 128 credits required for the bachelor's degree must be completed at PLU. **International Students:** There are 80 international students enrolled. They must take the TOEFL with a minimum score of 550 on the paper-based TOEFL (PBT) or 79 on the Internet-based version (iBT).

ADMISSIONS: 77% of the 2017-2018 applicants were accepted. The SAT scores for the 2017-2018 freshman class were: Critical Reading-- 27% below 500, 41% between 500 and 599, 26% between 600 and 699, and 6% between 700 and 800. Math-- 25% below 500, 42% between 500 and 599, 28% between 600 and 699, and 5% between 700 and 800. Writing-- 34% below 500, 46% between 500 and 599, 18% between 600 and 699, and 2% between 700 and 800. The ACT scores were 6% between 12 and 17, 30% between 18 and 23, 48% between 24 and 29, and 16% above 30. **Admissions Contact:** Melody Ferguson, Director of Admission. Email: *admissions@plu.edu* Web: *www.plu.edu*

FINANCIAL AID: In 2017-2018, 99% of all full-time freshmen received some form of financial aid. 63% of all full-time freshmen received need-based aid. The average freshman award was $34,402. Need-based scholarships or need-based grants averaged $28,524; and need-based self-help aid (loans and jobs) averaged $9,284. The average financial indebtedness of the 2017 graduate was $28,214. The FAFSA code is 003785. The priority date for freshman financial aid applications for fall entry is January 31.

SAINT MARTIN'S UNIVERSITY B-3

www.stmartin.edu

Lacey, WA 98503	(360) 438-4592 (800) 368-8803
Fax: (360) 412-6189	Email: admissions@stmartin.edu
Full-time: 568 men, 551 women	**Faculty:** 84
Part-time: 110 men, 81 women	**Ph.D.s:** 90%
Graduate: 93 men, 162 women	**Student/Faculty:** 11 to 1
Year: semesters, summer session	**Tuition:** $34,356
Room & Board: $10,700	**Freshman Class:** 1367 applied, 1333 accepted, 279 enrolled
SAT EBR-W/M: 545/535 **ACT:** 21	**CEEB CODE:** 4674
Application Deadline: July 31	**COMPETITIVE**

Saint Martin's University, founded in 1895, is a private, non-profit Roman Catholic institution conducted by the Benedictine order, offering undergraduate and graduate programs in liberal arts and sciences, business, education, and engineering. There are 4 undergraduate schools and 3 graduate schools. In addition to regional accreditation, SMU has baccalaureate program accreditation with ABET, ACBSP, CSWE, CCNE, and MPCAC. The 300-acre campus is in a suburban area 3 miles from Olympia and 60 miles south of Seattle. Including any residence halls, there are 17 buildings.

STUDENT LIFE: 78% of undergraduates are from Washington. Others are from 28 states, 9 foreign countries, and Canada. 80% are from public schools. 48% are White; 13% Hispanic; 9% Asian American; 6% African American; 6% Foreign; 6% two or more races; 6% race unknown; 1% American Indian/Alaska Native. 39% claim no religious affiliation; 36% 16% Christian; 25% Catholic. **Female To Male Ratio:** 1.0:1. The average age of freshmen is 18; all undergraduates, 24. 19% do not continue beyond their first year; 55% remain to graduate. **Housing:** 630 students can be accommodated in college housing, which includes dorms, and living learning communities. On-campus housing is guaranteed for the freshman year only, is available on a first-come, and first-served basis. 63% of students commute. Alcohol is not permitted. All students may keep cars.

FACULTY/CLASSROOMS: 57% of faculty are male; 43% are female. 91% teach undergraduates. No introductory courses are taught by graduate students. The average class size in an introductory lecture is 11; in a laboratory is 11; and in a regular course is 11.

PROGRAMS OF STUDY: SMU confers B.A., B.S., B.S.W., B.S.N., B.S.C.E. and B.S.M.E. degrees. Master's degrees are also awarded. Bachelor's degrees are awarded in AGRICULTURE (environmental studies), BIOLOGICAL SCIENCE (biology/biological science), BUSINESS (accounting and business administration and management), COMMUNICATIONS AND THE ARTS (communications, English, music, and theatre arts), COMPUTER AND PHYSICAL SCIENCE (chemistry, computer science, and mathematics), EDUCATION (educational studies, elementary education, and special education), ENGINEERING AND ENVIRONMENTAL DESIGN (civil engineering and mechanical engineering), HEALTH PROFESSIONS (nursing), SOCIAL SCIENCE (criminology, history, interdisciplinary studies, political science/government, psychology, religious studies, social work, and sociology). Engineering is the strongest academically. Business administration, mechanical engineering, and biology have the largest enrollments.

ACTIVITIES: There are no fraternities or sororities. There are 30 groups on campus, including band, choir, chorale, computers, drama, environmental, ethnic, honors, international, jazz band, LGBT, musical theater, newspaper, pep band, political, professional, religious, social, social service, and student government. Popular campus events include Career Fair, International Day, and Capital Food and Wine Festival. **Sports:** There are 6 intercollegiate sports for men and 7 for women, and 9 intramural sports for men and 9 for women. Facilities include a multipurpose pavilion, recreation center, and athletic fields. **Graduates:** From July 1, 2016 to June 30, 2017, 319 bachelor's degrees were awarded. The most popular majors were business administration (18%), psychology (9%), and mechanical engineering (8%). In an average class, 4% graduate in 3 years or less, 47% graduate in 4 years or less, 57% graduate in 5 years or less, and 59% graduate in 6 years or less.

SERVICES: Counseling and information services are available, as is tutoring in some subjects, such as accounting, biology, business, chemistry, computer science, economics, physics, math, and world languages. There is a reader service for the blind, and remedial math, reading, and writing. **Library/Resources:** The library contains 281,777 volumes, 166,184 microform items, and 2,415 audio/video tapes/CDs/DVDs, and subscribes to 74,406 periodicals including electronic. Computerized library services include interlibrary loans, database searching, Internet access, and Wi-Fi capability. Special learning facilities include an art gallery. **Physically Challenged Students:** 90% of the campus is accessible. Facilities include wheelchair ramps, elevators, special parking, specially equipped restrooms, lowered drinking fountains, and lowered telephones. **Special:** Double majors, work-study with the state of Washington, nonprofit organizations, internships in all disciplines, a Washington semester with American University, and pass/fail options are offered. The FOCUS program offers credit for job experience. Nondegree study and study abroad is possible. There are 3 national honor societies and 3 departmental honors programs. **Visiting:** There are regularly scheduled orientations for prospective students, including a campus tour and faculty, student service, and financial aid presentations. There are guides for informal visits, visitors may sit in on classes, and stay overnight. **Campus Safety and Security:** Measures include 24-hour foot and vehicle patrol, emergency notification system, and security escort services. There are emergency telephones, lighted pathways/sidewalks, and controlled access to dorms/residences.

REQUIREMENTS: The SAT or ACT is required. Applicants must be graduates of an accredited secondary school or have a GED, with a minimum of 16 academic units, including 4 units in English, 2 or 3 units in math, 2 units in history/social science, 1 or 2 units each in foreign language and lab science, and 7 units in electives. Class standing is also considered. An essay and recommendation from a teacher or counselor are required. Students should have a score of 800 on the SAT I and a 2.5 GPA. AP and CLEP credits are accepted. Important factors in the admissions decision are advanced placement or honors courses, recommendations by school officials, and personality/intangible qualities. All students must complete freshman composition and general education requirements, including 2 courses in social sciences and world languages, 1 course each in literature, philosophy, the arts, religious studies, natural science with lab, math (precalculus), U.S. history, and non-U.S. history. A total of 120 semester credits with a 2.0 GPA is required. **Procedure:** Freshmen are admitted fall, spring, and summer. There is a rolling admissions plan. Applications should be filed by July 31 for fall entry; December 15 for spring entry. Notification is sent on a rolling basis. Applications are accepted on-line. **Transfer Students:** 252 transfer students enrolled in 2016-2017. Transfer applicants must submit transcripts from all colleges previously attended and have a 2.0 GPA. 30 of 120 credits required for the bachelor's degree must be completed at SMU. **International Students:** There are 62 international students enrolled. They must take the TOEFL with a minimum score of 525 on the paper-based TOEFL (PBT) or 71 on the Internet-based version (iBT). They must also take the SAT or ACT.

ADMISSIONS: 98% of the 2017-2018 applicants were accepted. The SAT scores for the 2017-2018 freshman class were: Math-- 32% below 500, 46% between 500 and 599, 20% between 600 and 699, and 2% between 700 and 800. Evidence-Based Reading/Writing-- 29% below 500, 45% between 500 and 599, 23% between 600 and 699, and 3% between 700 and 800. The ACT scores were 20% between 12 and 17, 53% between 18 and 23, 21% between 24 and 29, and 6% above 30. 42% of the current freshmen were in the top fifth of their class; 69% were in the top two fifths. 6 freshmen graduated first in their class. **Admissions Contact:** Emilie Schnabel, Assistant Director, Admissions. Email: *admissions@stmartin.edu* Web: *www.stmartin.edu*

FINANCIAL AID: In 2017-2018, 83% of all full-time freshmen received some form of financial aid and need-based aid. The average freshman award was $28,575. Need-based scholarships or need-based grants averaged $26,248; need-based self-help aid (loans and jobs) averaged $3,330; non-need-based athletic scholarships averaged $7,302; and other non-need-based awards and non-need-based scholarships averaged $15,645. SMU is a member of CSS. The FAFSA code is 003794. The priority date for freshman financial aid applications for fall entry is January 1. The deadline for filing freshman financial aid applications for fall entry is March 1.

SEATTLE PACIFIC UNIVERSITY — C-2

www.spu.edu

Seattle, WA 98119	(206) 281-2561 (800) 366-3344
Fax: (206) 281-2669	**Email:** admissions@spu.edu
Full-time: 995 men, 2089 women	**Faculty:** n/av
Part-time: 42 men, 76 women	**Ph.D.s:** 88%
Graduate: 265 men, 708 women	**Student/Faculty:** 15 to 1
Year: quarters, summer session	**Tuition:** $37,086
Room & Board: $10,353	**Freshman Class:** 5227 applied, 4266 accepted, 688 enrolled
SAT CR/M: 560/560 **ACT:** 25	**CEEB CODE:** 4694
Application Deadline: March 1	**COMPETITIVE+**

Seattle Pacific University, founded in 1891, is a private institution affiliated with the Free Methodist Church. It offers programs in business and economics, education, fine and performing arts, health science, humanities, natural and mathematical sciences, phys ed and athletics, religion, and social and behavioral sciences. The figures given in the above capsule and in this profile are approximate. There are 6 undergraduate schools and 6 graduate schools. In addition to regional accreditation, SPU has baccalaureate program accreditation with AACSB, ABET, NASM, CAEP, NLN, CADE, and CCNE. The 41-acre campus is in an urban area 7 minutes from downtown Seattle. Including any residence halls, there are 94 buildings.

STUDENT LIFE: 64% of undergraduates are from Washington. Others are from 41 states, 55 foreign countries, and Canada. 58% are White; 10% Asian American; 8% Hispanic; 8% race unknown; 7% two or more races; 4% African American; 4% Foreign; 1% American Indian/Alaska Native. **Female To Male Ratio:** 2.2:1. The average age of freshmen is 18; all undergraduates, 21. 75% remain to graduate. **Housing:** 1761 students can be accommodated in college housing, which includes married student dorms, on-campus apartments, off-campus apartments, and theme houses. 52% of students live on campus. Alcohol is not permitted. All students may keep cars.

FACULTY/CLASSROOMS: 54% of faculty are male; 46% are female. No introductory courses are taught by graduate students. The average class size in a regular course is 18.

PROGRAMS OF STUDY: SPU confers B.A. and B.S. degrees. Master's and doctoral degrees are also awarded. Bachelor's degrees are awarded in BIOLOGICAL SCIENCE (biochemistry and biology/biological science), BUSINESS (accounting and business administration and management), COMMUNICATIONS AND THE ARTS (art, classics, communications, creative writing, English, fine arts, French, German, language arts, Latin, linguistics, literature, music, Russian, and Spanish), COMPUTER AND PHYSICAL SCIENCE (chemistry, computer science, information sciences and systems, mathematics, and physics), EDUCATION (education, elementary education, home economics education, mathematics education, music education, nursing education, physical education, science education, secondary education, social science education, special education, and teaching English as a second/foreign language (TESOL/TEFOL)), ENGINEERING AND ENVIRONMENTAL DESIGN (electrical/electronics engineering, engineering, engineering and applied science, and interior design), HEALTH PROFESSIONS (exercise science and nursing), SOCIAL SCIENCE (Christian studies, clinical psychology, economics, European studies, family/consumer resource management, family/consumer studies, food science, history, Latin American studies, liberal arts/general studies, philosophy, physical fitness/movement, political science/government, prelaw, psychology, social science, sociology, and theological studies). Education, nursing, and business administration have the largest enrollments.

ACTIVITIES: There are no fraternities or sororities. There are 51 groups on campus, including art, chess, choir, chorale, drama, ethnic, honors, international, jazz band, literary magazine, newspaper, orchestra, pep band, political, professional, radio, religious, social, social service, student government, and symphony. Popular campus events include Family Weekend, Talent Show, and Ivy Cutting at Graduation. **Sports:** Facilities include a soccer field, an oval track, tennis and basketball courts, crew house and crew dock, indoor gym with auditorium. There is also free access to a community swimming pool. **Graduates:** From July 1, 2016 to June 30, 2017, 759 bachelor's degrees were awarded. The most popular majors were nursing (10%), psychology (8%), and business administration (8%). In an average class, 71% graduate in 6 years or less.

SERVICES: Counseling and information services are available, as is tutoring in most subjects. There is a reader service for the blind, and remedial math and writing. **Library/Resources:** The library contains 227,332 volumes, 497,248 microform items, and 8,915 audio/video tapes/CDs/DVDs, and subscribes to 2,841 periodicals including electronic. Computerized library services include interlibrary loans, database searching, Internet access, and Wi-Fi capability. Special learning facilities include an art gallery, a science center, performing arts theater, a writing lab, and a media center. **Physically Challenged Students:** Facilities include wheelchair ramps, elevators, special parking, specially equipped restrooms, and special class scheduling. **Special:** There is a cooperative program with Fashion Institute of Technology in New York City, Fashion Institute of Design and Merchandising in Los Angeles, and Han Nam University in Korea, cross-registration with the Christian College Consortium and Christian College Coalition, and a Washington semester in American studies through the Christian College Coalition. SPU offers internships, study abroad in more than 5 countries, work-study programs, dual and student-designed majors, interdisciplinary majors such as language arts, and a liberal studies major for associate degree graduates. A general studies degree, pass/no credit options, and nondegree study are available. There are 5 national honor societies, a freshman honors program, and 10 departmental honors programs. **Visiting:** There are regularly scheduled orientations for prospective students. There are guides for informal visits, visitors may sit in on classes, and stay overnight. To schedule a visit, contact the Admissions Office. **Campus Safety and Security:** Measures include 24-hour foot and vehicle patrol, emergency notification system, and security escort services. There are emergency telephones, lighted pathways/sidewalks, controlled access to dorms/residences, and closed-circuit TV monitors.

REQUIREMENTS: The SAT or ACT is required. The SAT I is preferred, with a minimum required composite score of 950. Candidates should be graduates of an accredited secondary school with a minimum high school GPA of 2.5 or hold a GED certificate. A strong college preparatory program in high school is recommended, including 4 years of English, 3 each of math, science, and foreign language, 2 of history, and 1 of social studies. An essay and 2 letters of recommendation are required, and an interview is recommended. AP and CLEP credits are accepted. Important factors in the admissions decision are advanced placement or honors courses, leadership record, and extracurricular activities record. All students must demonstrate competency in math and English. Students must complete 15 quarter credits in Christian heritage and values, 56 in general education, plus up to 15 credits of foreign language competency, and at least 45 to 60 in the major, depending on the program. A minimum of 180 credits is needed for the bachelor's degree, with a 2.0 GPA overall. At least 60 credits must be earned in 3000-level courses or higher. **Procedure:** Freshmen are admitted to all sessions. Entrance exams should be taken by January of the senior year. There are early decision and rolling admissions plans. Early decision applications should be filed by November 15; regular applications, by March 1 for fall entry. The fall 2017 application fee was $45. Notification of early decision is sent February 15; regular decision, on a rolling basis. Applications are accepted on-line. **Transfer Students:** 245 transfer students enrolled in 2016-2017. A minimum 2.5 GPA is required, and an interview is recommended. Transcripts from all previous colleges attended and from high school are required, along with 2 letters of recommendation and an essay or personal statement. Evidence of honorable dismissal from the previous school is also required. Students with at least 30 credits earned are not required to take the SAT or ACT. 45 of 180 credits required for the bachelor's degree must be completed at SPU. **International Students:** There are 127 international students enrolled. They must take the TOEFL, and the Michigan Test must be administered through SPU.

ADMISSIONS: 82% of the 2017-2018 applicants were accepted. The SAT scores for the 2017-2018 freshman class were: Critical Reading-- 18% below 500, 44% between 500 and 599, 32% between 600 and 699, and 6% between 700 and 800. Math-- 21% below 500, 44% between 500 and 599, 29% between 600 and 699, and 6% between 700 and 800. Writing-- 23% below 500. The ACT scores were 2% between 12 and 17, 29% between 18 and 23, 54% between 24 and 29, and 15% above 30. **Admissions Contact:** Ineliz Soto-Fuller, Director of Undergraduate Admissions. Email: *admissions@spu.edu* Web: *www.spu.edu*

FINANCIAL AID: The FAFSA code is 003788. The deadline for filing freshman financial aid applications for fall entry is June 30.

SEATTLE UNIVERSITY C-2

www.seattleu.edu

Seattle, WA 98122	**(206) 296-2000** **(800) 426-7123**
Fax: (206) 296-5656	**Email: admissions@seattleu.edu**
Full-time: 1665 men, 2718 women	**Faculty:** 424; IIA, av$
Part-time: 110 men, 154 women	**Ph.D.s:** 78%
Graduate: 1015 men, 1616 women	**Student/Faculty:** 11 to 1
Year: quarters, summer session	**Tuition:** $42,885
Room & Board: $12,072	**Freshman Class:** 8576 applied, 6329 accepted, 957 enrolled
SAT CR/M/W: 590/590/580 **ACT:** 27	**CEEB CODE:** 4695
Application Deadline: January 15	**VERY COMPETITIVE**

Seattle University is Seattle's university. That means a centralized urban location in one of the world's most innovative, vibrant and culturally rich metropolitan cities. Graduates recognize how SU enhances and strengthens abilities that businesses and organizations prize critical thinking, effective communication, global perspectives and solving complex problems across disciplines. Undergraduate, graduate and certificate programs include science and engineering, business, liberal arts, humanities, nursing, education, theology and law. Service is an element of learning that enriches spirituality at SU. It's a free-thinking approach that underscores this independent university's commitment to empower leaders for a just and humane world. There are 7 undergraduate schools and 7 graduate schools. In addition to regional accreditation, SU has baccalaureate program accreditation with AACSB, ABET, CAHEA, CAEP, CSWE, and NLN. The 46-acre campus is in an urban area east of downtown Seattle in the Capitol Hill neighborhood. Including any residence halls, there are 34 buildings.

STUDENT LIFE: 59% of undergraduates are from out of state, mostly the West. Students are from 47 states, 50 foreign countries, and Canada. 62% are from public schools. 8% are two or more races; 5% race unknown; 44% White; 3% African American; 16% Asian American; 12% Hispanic; 10% Foreign. 25% are Catholic. **Female To Male Ratio:** 1.6:1. The average age of freshmen is 18; all undergraduates, 21. 16% do not continue beyond their first year; 74% remain to graduate. **Housing:** 2085 students can be accommodated in college housing, which includes single-sex dorms and on-campus apartments. In addition, there are language/international houses, and 24-hour quiet floors. On-campus housing is available on a lottery system for upperclassmen. 55% of students commute. Some may keep cars.

FACULTY/CLASSROOMS: 43% of faculty are male; 57% are female. No introductory courses are taught by graduate students. The average class size in a regular course is 18.

PROGRAMS OF STUDY: SU confers B.A., B.S., B.A.B.A., B.A.E., B.A.H., B.C.J., B.M., B.F.A., B.S.B., B.S.B.C., B.S.P., B.S.C.E., B.S.C.S., B.S.D.U., B.S.E.E., B.S.E.S., B.S.G.S., B.S.M., B.S.M.E., B.S.N. and B.S.W. degrees. Master's and doctoral degrees are also awarded. Bachelor's degrees are awarded in AGRICULTURE (environmental studies), BIOLOGICAL SCIENCE (biochemistry, biology/adolescence education, biology/biological science, cell biology, and marine biology), BUSINESS (accounting, business administration and management, business economics, finance, international business management, international economics, marketing management, and organizational leadership and management), COMMUNICATIONS AND THE ARTS (art history, communications, creative writing, English, film arts, fine arts, French, journalism, music, photography, Spanish, strings, theatre arts, and visual and performing arts), COMPUTER AND PHYSICAL SCIENCE (applied mathematics, chemistry, chemistry/adolescence education, computer science, digital arts/technology, mathematics, mathematics - actuarial concentration, mathematics/theoretical, physics, science, and web technology), EDUCATION (Asian studies, environmental education, and mathematics education), ENGINEERING AND ENVIRONMENTAL DESIGN (civil engineering, computer engineering, electrical/electronics engineering, environmental engineering, environmental science, and mechanical engineering), HEALTH PROFESSIONS (exercise science, medical technology, nursing, and ultrasound technology), SOCIAL SCIENCE (anthropology, criminal justice, economics, forensic studies, history, humanities, international studies, liberal arts/general studies, philosophy, political science/government, psychology, public administration, religion, social work, sociology, theological studies, urban ecology, and women & gender studies). Nursing, criminal justice, and business are the strongest academically. Nursing, engineering, and business have the largest enrollments.

ACTIVITIES: There are no fraternities or sororities. There are 61 groups on campus, including art, cheerleading, choir, chorale, communications, dance, debate, drama, environmental, ethnic, film, forensics, honors, international, jazz band, LGBT, literary magazine, musical theater, newspaper, photography, political, professional, radio and TV, religious, social, social service, and student government. Popular campus events include Hawaiian Luau, Quad Stock, and International Student Dinner. **Sports:** There are 8 intercollegiate sports for men and 10 for women, and 14 intramural sports for men and 14 for women. Facilities include a recreational, fitness and athletic space center with swimming pools, cardio, weight rooms, group exercise, yoga, martial arts classrooms, racquetball, squash courts, basketball courts, outdoor track, soccer and softball fields, tennis courts, and astroturf gym for indoor soccer/tennis with batting cages. **Graduates:** From July 1, 2016 to June 30, 2017, 1298 bachelor's degrees were awarded. The most popular majors were registered nursing (12%), finance (7%), and psychology (6%). In an average class, 64% graduate in 4 years or less, 73% graduate in 5 years or less, and 75% graduate in 6 years or less. Of the 2016 graduating class, 92% were employed within 6 months of graduation.

SERVICES: Counseling and information services are available, as is tutoring in most subjects, such as math, English, accounting, language and science. There is a reader service for the blind and a writing center. **Library/Resources:** The library contains 582,577 volumes, 1.8 million microform items, and 9,402 audio/video tapes/CDs/DVDs, and subscribes to 69,109 periodicals including electronic. Computerized library services include interlibrary loans, database searching, Internet access, and Wi-Fi capability. Special learning facilities include an art gallery, planetarium, radio station, an electron microscope, a recording studio, and MRI. **Physically Challenged Students:** 95% of the campus is accessible. Facilities include wheelchair ramps, elevators, special parking, specially equipped restrooms, special class scheduling, lowered drinking fountains, lowered telephones, and special housing. **Special:** SU provides many opportunities for dual majors, local, national and international internships, and on and off-campus work study positions. In addition, distinctive programs include: International Development Internship Program (IDIP), with a goal of instilling in students a lifelong commitment to the Jesuit mission of service and promotion of social justice, IDIP is a 20-credit, three-phase academic program designed for undergraduates. In our study abroad program about 500 students now participate in educational and service programs in more than 40 countries. Short-term programs at SU are slightly more popular than long-term ones. Developing a long-term relationship with a sister Jesuit school, the University of Central America (UCA) in Nicaragua, also has increased opportunities abroad for SU students. SU runs one of the oldest and strongest Project Centers in the country. It's a great experiential learning opportunity for students in engineering, computer science and business. Sponsoring companies come back year after year; it's a great way for them to connect with SU and engage with great students. In fact, many students do go on to work for the sponsors of their projects. Albers Mentor Program is a unique opportunity for graduate-level and senior undergraduate business students to interact with upper level executives from leading Puget Sound companies and organizations. It offers opportunities to develop business contacts, access industry information, and gain valuable insights from experienced and successful professionals. There is a freshman honors program and 23 departmental honors programs. **Visiting:** There are regularly scheduled orientations for prospective students. Consisting of an hour of sharing what it's like to live and learn in our distinct urban setting, get a chance to see classroom spaces, a residence hall room, our Chapel of St. Ignatius, and the Lemieux Library among many others. To schedule a visit, contact the Undergraduate Admissions Office. **Campus Safety and Security:** Measures include 24-hour foot and vehicle patrol, emergency notification system, self-defense education, and security escort services. There are shuttle buses, emergency telephones, lighted pathways/sidewalks, and controlled access to dorms/residences.

REQUIREMENTS: The SAT or ACT is required. Admissions requirements include graduation from an accredited secondary school, with 16 academic credits, including 4 years of English, 3 each of math and social studies, 2 each of foreign language, lab science, and academic electives, 4 years of math and lab physics and chemistry are required of science and engineering students, lab biology and chemistry are needed by nursing students. The GED is also accepted. A GPA of 2.7 is required. AP and CLEP credits are accepted. Students must complete 180 to 192 quarter hours, depending on the degree, with 70 to 90 in the major, and maintain a minimum GPA of 2.25 to 2.5. Core curriculum requirements include 12 courses (60 credits) and a major-specific capstone course divided into four modules: Enagaging Academic Inquiry, Exploring the Self and Others, Engaging the World, and Reflection. **Procedure:** Freshmen are admitted to all sessions. Entrance exams should be taken during the fall of the senior year. There are early admissions and deferred admissions plans. Applications should be filed by January 15 for fall entry; November 1 for winter entry; February 15 for spring entry; and May 1 for summer entry. The fall 2017 application fee was $55. Notifications are sent March 15. 31 early decision candidates were accepted for the 2017-2018 class. 539 applicants were on the 2017 waiting list; 59 were admitted. Applications are accepted on-line. **Transfer Students:** 422 transfer students enrolled in 2016-2017. Generally, transfer students should have a college GPA of at least 2.25. An associate degree is recommended; a 2.75 GPA is required for nursing and business administration students. 45 of 180 credits required for the bachelor's degree must be completed at SU. **International Students:** There are 500 international students enrolled. They must take the TOEFL with a minimum score of 520 on the paper-based TOEFL (PBT) or 68 on the Internet-based version (iBT).

ADMISSIONS: 74% of the 2017-2018 applicants were accepted. The SAT scores for the 2017-2018 freshman class were: Critical Reading-- 11% below 500, 43% between 500 and 599, 36% between 600 and 699, and 9% between 700 and 800. Math-- 11% below 500, 42% between 500 and 599, 39% between 600 and 699, and 8% between 700 and 800. Writing-- 14% below 500, 45% between 500 and 599, 32% between 600 and 699, and 10% between 700 and 800. The ACT scores were 15% between 18 and 23, 58% between 24 and 29, and 27% above 30. **Admissions Contact:** Melore Nielsen, Dean of Admissions. Email: *admissions@seattleu.edu* Web: *www.seattleu.edu*

FINANCIAL AID: In 2017-2018, 97% of all full-time freshmen received some form of financial aid. 94% of all full-time freshmen received need-based aid. The average freshman award was $31,667. Need-based scholarships or need-based grants averaged $17,026 ($50,103 maximum); need-based self-help aid (loans and jobs) averaged $5,940 ($9,500 maximum); non-need-based athletic scholarships averaged $16,244 ($53,267 maximum); and other non-need-based awards and non-need-based scholarships averaged $22,598 ($62,007 maximum). The average financial indebtedness of the 2017 graduate was $22,628. The FAFSA code is 003790. The priority date for freshman financial aid applications for fall entry is February 1.

THE EVERGREEN STATE COLLEGE B-3

www.evergreen.edu

Olympia, WA 98505 **(360) 867-6170**

Fax: (360) 867-5114 **Email: admissions@evergreen.edu**

Full-time: 1498 men, 1960 women	**Faculty:** 137
Part-time: 151 men, 178 women	**Ph.D.s:** 87%
Graduate: 98 men, 204 women	**Student/Faculty:** 22 to 1
Year: quarters, summer session	**Tuition:** $7239 ($23,712)
Room & Board: $9360	**Freshman Class:** 1901 applied, 1853 accepted, 572 enrolled
SAT CR/M/W: 545/495/509 **ACT:** 23	**CEEB CODE:** 4292
Application Deadline: February 1	**COMPETITIVE**

The Evergreen State College, founded in 1967, is a public liberal arts and sciences college distinguished by interdisciplinary, collaborative, and team-taught academic programs, narrative evaluations of student work, and student-designed academic pathways. The 1000-acre campus is in a small town 5 miles northwest of downtown Olympia. Including any residence halls, there are 57 buildings.

STUDENT LIFE: 75% of undergraduates are from Washington. Others are from 46 states, 19 foreign countries, and Canada. 66% are White; 11% Hispanic; 8% two or more races; 5% African American; 4% race unknown; 3% Asian American; 2% American Indian/Alaska Native; 1% Foreign. **Female To Male Ratio:** 1.3:1. The average age of freshmen is 19; all undergraduates, 25. 25% do not continue beyond their first year. **Housing:** 991 students can be accommodated in college housing, which includes married student dorms and on-campus apartments. In addition, there are special-interest houses, theme housing includes: substance-free, first-year experience, quiet, LGBTQ+, the outdoor program, community action, sustainability, and over 30. Freshman students are in residence halls. On-campus housing is guaranteed for the freshman year only, is available on a first-come, and first-served basis. 77% of students commute. Alcohol is not permitted. All students may keep cars.

FACULTY/CLASSROOMS: 45% of faculty are male; 55% are female. 91% teach undergraduates. No introductory courses are taught by graduate students.

PROGRAMS OF STUDY: Evergreen confers B.A., B.S. and B.A.S degrees. Master's degrees are also awarded. Bachelor's degrees are awarded in BIOLOGICAL SCIENCE (biology/biological science, physiology, and zoology), COMMUNICATIONS AND THE ARTS (languages and visual and performing arts), COMPUTER AND PHYSICAL SCIENCE (mathematics and natural sciences), HEALTH PROFESSIONS (health), SOCIAL SCIENCE (anthropology, geography, history, liberal arts/general studies, political science/government, and sociology).

ACTIVITIES: There are no fraternities or sororities. There are 66 groups on campus, including art, choir, chorale, communications, dance, drama, environmental, ethnic, film, international, LGBT, literary magazine, newspaper, photography, political, professional, radio and TV, religious, social, social service, and student government. Popular campus events include Campus clam bake, Return to Evergreen reunion events, Winter Tree Lighting, Longhouse Native Arts Fair, and Day of Absence/Day of Presence. **Sports:** There are 3 intercollegiate sports for men and 4 for women, and 4 intramural sports for men and 4 for women. The Costantino Recreation Center features an Olympic-size 11-lane swimming pool, a diving well, a gymnasium, exercise and weight training rooms, racquetball courts, dance/movement rooms, and indoor and outdoor climbing walls. The campus also offers a covered pavilion with artificial turf, tennis courts, playing fields, and a challenge course. There are also bike paths, jogging paths and hiking trails. **Graduates:** From July

1, 2016 to June 30, 2017, 1019 bachelor's degrees were awarded. The most popular majors were liberal arts and sciences (83%) and interdisciplinary natural sciences (17%). In an average class, 9% graduate in 3 years or less, 43% graduate in 4 years or less, 53% graduate in 5 years or less, and 56% graduate in 6 years or less. Of the 2016 graduating class, 87% were enrolled in graduate school within 6 months of graduation, and 80% were employed.

SERVICES: The Writing Center offers assistance in writing; the Quantitive and Symbolic Reasoning Center offers assistance with all levels of math, economics, statistics, chemistry, biology, physics, and computer science. There is a reader service for the blind. **Library/Resources:** The library contains 322,238 volumes, 60,542 microform items, and 16,987 audio/video tapes/CDs/DVDs, and subscribes to 54,696 periodicals including electronic. Computerized library services include interlibrary loans, database searching, Internet access, and Wi-Fi capability. Special learning facilities include a radio station, organic farm, the sustainable agriculture laboratory and community gardens, Longhouse Education and Cultural Center, a Native American carving studio, art galleries, animation and design studio, ceramics studio, metal shop, wood shop, Center for Creative and Applied Media (video production and studios), photography studios and darkrooms, science laboratories, media equipment loan program, computer labs, and access to scientific equipment. **Physically Challenged Students:** 85% of the campus is accessible. Facilities include wheelchair ramps, elevators, special parking, specially equipped restrooms, lowered drinking fountains, and lowered telephones. **Special:** All work at the college is interdisciplinary, and the programs of study change annually. The college's credit-generating options include the comprehensive Coordinated Study Program model, which allows students and faculty to work together intensively over multiple quarters. Credits may be earned through cooperative programs, work-study programs, internships, independent contracts, or from prior learning and military experience. All students develop personalized academic pathways based on their goals and areas of interest (equivalent to student-designed majors). The Center for Community-Based Learning and Action facilitates service learning opportunities in non-profit agencies. There are parallel opportunities in government agencies and private businesses, including off-campus work-study opportunities. Evergreen offers a wide range of study abroad opportunities through academic programs, consortium partnerships, individual learning contracts, and domestic and international exchange programs. **Visiting:** There are regularly scheduled orientations for prospective students, includes admissions session, a class visit, and a campus tour. There are guides for informal visits, visitors may sit in on classes, and stay overnight. To schedule a visit, contact Student Visitor Program. **Campus Safety and Security:** Measures include 24-hour foot and vehicle patrol, emergency notification system, self-defense education, and security escort services. There are emergency telephones and lighted pathways/sidewalks.

REQUIREMENTS: The SAT or ACT is required. Candidates should be graduates of an accredited secondary school and have completed 15 academic credits, consisting of 4 in English, 3 each in math and social studies, 2 each in foreign language and science (one of which must be a lab science in biology, chemistry, or physics), and 1 in fine, visual, or performing arts or other college preparatory elective from another area mentioned in list. A GED certificate is acceptable. A GPA of 2.0 is required. AP and CLEP credits are accepted. Important factors in the admissions decision are advanced placement or honors courses and evidence of special talent. Students must earn a minimum of 180 quarter hours of credit to receive a B.A. or B.S. degree. For a B.S. students must have completed 72 credits of science, math, or computer science, 48 of which must be upper division. For a B.A.S. dual degree, 225 credits are required and students must meet the requirements of a B.A. and B.S. All students must also complete a summative academic statement at the conclusion of their studies. **Procedure:** Freshmen are admitted fall, winter, and spring. Entrance exams should be taken during spring of the junior year or fall of the senior year. Applications should be filed by February 1 for fall entry; October 1 for winter entry; and December 1 for spring entry. The fall 2017 application fee was $50. Applications are accepted on-line. **Transfer Students:** 712 transfer students enrolled in 2016-2017. A 2.0 minimum GPA is required. An associate degree is recommended. All applicants must submit all college transcripts. Applicants with fewer than 40 credits must submit SAT or ACT scores and a high school transcript. 45 of 180 credits required for the bachelor's degree must be completed at Evergreen. **International Students:** There are 26 international students enrolled. They must take the TOEFL with a minimum score of 550 on the paper-based TOEFL (PBT) or 79 on the Internet-based version (iBT). They must also take the SAT or ACT.

ADMISSIONS: 97% of the 2017-2018 applicants were accepted. The SAT scores for the 2017-2018 freshman class were: Critical Reading-- 32% below 500, 35% between 500 and 599, 27% between 600 and 699, and 6% between 700 and 800. Math-- 49% below 500, 37% between 500 and 599, 13% between 600 and 699, and 1% between 700 and 800. Writing-- 41% below 500, 43% between 500 and 599, 14% between 600 and 699, and 2% between 700 and 800. The ACT scores were 1% below 12, 12% between 12 and 17, 37% between 18 and 23, 40% between 24 and 29, and 10% above 30. **Admissions Contact:** Eric Pedersen, Director of Admissions. Email: *admissions@evergreen.edu* Web: *www.evergreen.edu*

FINANCIAL AID: Evergreen is a member of CSS. The college's own financial statement is required. The FAFSA code is 008155. The priority date for freshman financial aid applications for fall entry is February 2.

UNIVERSITY OF PUGET SOUND — C-2

www.pugetsound.edu

Tacoma, WA 98416 — **(253) 879-3211**

Fax: (253) 879-3993
Email: jdmiller@pugetsound.edu

Full-time: 951 men, 1439 women
Part-time: 11 men, 12 women
Graduate: 68 men, 220 women
Year: semesters, summer session
Room & Board: $12,120
SAT EBR-W/M: 635/625 **ACT:** 28
Application Deadline: January 15

Faculty: 233
Ph.D.s: 93%
Student/Faculty: 11 to 1
Tuition: $48,090
Freshman Class: 5827 applied, 4616 accepted, 652 enrolled
CEEB CODE: 4067
HIGHLY COMPETITIVE

University of Puget Sound is a residential national liberal arts college, drawing students and faculty from around the country and throughout the world. Named one of the "Colleges That Change Lives," Puget Sound graduates include Rhodes and Fulbright scholars, notables in the arts and culture, entrepreneurs and elected officials, and leaders in business and finance in the U.S. and abroad. A low student-faculty ratio provides Puget Sound students with personal attention from faculty members who have a strong commitment to teaching and offer 1,200 courses each year in more than 50 areas of study. Puget Sound is the only national, independent undergraduate liberal arts college in Western Washington, and one of just five independent colleges in the Pacific Northwest granted a charter by Phi Beta Kappa, the nation's most prestigious academic honor society. The college also offers sought-after graduate programs in education, physical therapy, and occupational therapy. There is 1 undergraduate school and 3 graduate schools. In addition to regional accreditation, Puget Sound has baccalaureate program accreditation with NASM, ACS, ACOTE, and CAPTE. The 97-acre campus is in an urban area near Commencement Bay in the historic North End neighborhood of Tacoma, Washington. Including any residence halls, there are 135 buildings.

STUDENT LIFE: 79% of undergraduates are from out of state, mostly the West. Students are from 47 states, 12 foreign countries, and Canada. 68% are from public schools. 8% are Hispanic; 8% two or more races; 71% White; 6% Asian American; 4% race unknown; 1% African American. 57% claim no religious affiliation; 24% Protestant. **Female To Male Ratio:** 1.6:1. The average age of freshmen is 18; all undergraduates, 20. 13% do not continue beyond their first year; 77% remain to graduate. **Housing:** 1751 students can be accommodated in college housing, which includes dorms and on-campus apartments. In addition, there are honors houses, language/international houses, special-interest houses, fraternity houses, sorority houses, theme and wellness housing, and suite style housing. On-campus housing is available on a first-come, first-served basis, and is available on a lottery system for upperclassmen. 65% of students live on campus. All students may keep cars.

FACULTY/CLASSROOMS: 50% of faculty are male; 50% are female. 85% teach undergraduates. No introductory courses are taught by graduate students. The average class size in an introductory lecture is 18; in a laboratory is 12; and in a regular course is 15.

PROGRAMS OF STUDY: Puget Sound confers B.A., B.M. and B.S. degrees. Master's and doctoral degrees are also awarded. Bachelor's degrees are awarded in BIOLOGICAL SCIENCE (biochemistry, biology/biological science, cell biology, and molecular biology), BUSINESS (business administration and management and international economics), COMMUNICATIONS AND THE ARTS (art, Chinese, classics, communications, dramatic arts, East Asian languages and literature, English, French, German, Japanese, music, music performance, and Spanish), COMPUTER AND PHYSICAL SCIENCE (chemistry, computer science, geology, mathematics, natural sciences, and physics), EDUCATION (music education), HEALTH PROFESSIONS (exercise science), SOCIAL SCIENCE (Asian/Oriental studies, economics, history, philosophy, political science/government, psychology, religion, science and society, and sociology). Psychology, exercise science, and business have the largest enrollments.

ACTIVITIES: 29% of men belong to 4 national fraternities; 26% of women belong to 4 national sororities. There are 125 groups on campus, including diversity awareness, art, band, cheerleading, choir, chorale, chorus, computers, dance, debate, drama, environmental, ethnic, forensics, honors, international, jazz band, LGBT, literary magazine, musical theater, newspaper, opera, orchestra, pep band, photography, political, professional, religious, social, social service, student government, symphony, and yearbook. Popular campus events include Foolish Pleasures (student film festival), Mistletoast Holiday, Hawaiian Luau, and Drag Show. **Sports:** There are 11 intercollegiate sports for men and 12 for women, and 8 intramural sports for men and 8 for women. Facilities include a basketball and volleyball gym, a 6-lane pool, football, soccer, lacrosse, and track stadium, indoor tennis courts, fitness center with free weights and aerobics equipment, dance studio, track, baseball, softball, and intramural fields (one of which is synthetic), an indoor climbing wall, auxiliary gym for intramurals and recreation. **Graduates:** From July 1, 2016 to June 30, 2017, 568 bachelor's degrees were awarded. The most popular majors were social science (17%), business and marketing (12%), and biological/life sciences (11%).

SERVICES: Counseling and information services are available, as is tutoring in most subjects. There is a reader service for the blind. **Library/Resources:** The library contains 520,919 volumes, 19,806 microform items, and 28,528 audio/video tapes/CDs/DVDs, and subscribes to 68,497 periodicals including electronic. Computerized library services include interlibrary loans, database searching, Internet access, and Wi-Fi capability. Special learning facilities include an art gallery, natural history museum, sculpture building, theatres, greenhouse, transmission and scanning electron microscopes, confocal microscope, DNA sequencer, X-ray diffractometer, microcomputer labs, sedimentology lab, stereoscopic and petrographic microscopes, computerized plotting/digitizing board and image analysis system, portable seismograph, gravimeter, proton precession magnetometer, ICP, GPS GIS lab, electronic music composition lab, electronic music keyboard lab with MIDI workstations, three electronic music classrooms, and one music V-room. **Physically Challenged Students:** 80% of the campus is accessible. Facilities include wheelchair ramps, elevators, special parking, specially equipped restrooms, special class scheduling, lowered drinking fountains, lowered telephones, and special housing. **Special:** International programs: Include 130 study abroad programs in 45 countries, as well as local, national, and international internships in conjunction with an internship seminar. A curricular strength in Asian studies includes the full academic year Pacific Rim/Asian Study-Travel Program. Interdisciplinary programs: A highly interdisciplinary curriculum includes undergraduate studies in Asian languages and cultures; biochemistry, bioethics, and biophysics; a liberal arts-focused business leadership program; environmental policy and decision making; gender and queer studies; global development studies; international political economy; science, technology, and society; a student-designed interdisciplinary major; and more, including a conservatory quality School of Music and an Honors Program. Many students choose to double major. Internships: Internship programs are available through the Alumni Sharing Knowledge network and Career and Employment Services, with companies such as Amazon, Boeing, Google, and Microsoft. Engineering: A 3-2 engineering degree offered with Washington University in St. Louis, Columbia University, Duke University, and the University of Southern California. Fellowships: Puget Sound is a top producer of Fulbright Scholars; Peace Corps volunteers; graduates who earn doctorates, with high acceptance rates to graduate programs in law and medicine; and prestigious fellowships including the Watson, Boren, and National Science Foundation. There are 15 national honor societies, Phi Beta Kappa, a freshman honors program, and 13 departmental honors programs. **Visiting:** There are regularly scheduled orientations for prospective students, tour of campus, meetings with counselors, faculty, and coaches, and classroom visits. There are guides for informal visits, visitors may sit in on classes, and stay overnight. To schedule a visit, contact Carolyn Johnson at crjohnson@pugetsound.edu. **Campus Safety and Security:** Measures include 24-hour foot and vehicle patrol, emergency notification system, and security escort services. There are emergency telephones, lighted pathways/sidewalks, controlled access to dorms/residences, and 24-hour live dispatch center.

REQUIREMENTS: Puget Sound only accepts the Common Application for undergraduate admission. Admission requirements include graduation from an accredited secondary school with a recommended 4 years of English, 3 to 4 of mathematics, 3 to 4 years of natural, and/or physical, laboratory science, 3 of social studies or history, 2 to 3 of foreign language, and 1 year of fine, visual, or performing arts. Also required are letters of personal recommendation from a teacher and counselor. An essay must be submitted, and an interview is recommended. The GED is also accepted. AP credits are accepted. Important factors in the admissions decision are advanced placement or honors courses, evidence of special talent, and personality/intangible qualities. In order to receive the baccalaureate degree from the University of Puget Sound, a student must: Earn a minimum of 32 units. The 32 units may include up to 4 academic courses graded pass/fail, up to 2 units in activity courses, and up to 4 units of independent study. Earn a minimum of 16 units, including the last 8, in residence at Puget Sound. Residence requirements also exist in core, majors, minors, and graduation honors. (See also the section on study abroad). Maintain a minimum GPA of 2.0 in all graded courses, including transfer courses, in the major (s) and the minor (s). Successfully complete Puget Sound's core requirements. The faculty of Puget Sound has designed the core curriculum to give undergraduates an integrated and demanding introduction to the life of the mind and to established methods of intellectual inquiry. The Puget Sound undergraduate's core experience begins with two first-year seminars that guide the student through an in-depth exploration of a focused area of interest and that sharpen the student's skills in constructing persuasive arguments. In the first three years of their Puget Sound college career, students also study five "Approaches to Knowing" (fine arts, humanities, mathematics, natural science, and social science). These core areas develop the student's understanding of different disciplinary perspectives on society, culture, and the physical world, and explore both the strengths of those disciplinary approaches and their limitations. Connections, an upper-level integrative course, challenges the traditional boundaries of disciplines and examines the benefits and limits of interdisciplinary approaches to knowledge. Further, in accordance with the stated educational goals of Puget Sound, core curriculum requirements have been established: (a) to improve each student's grasp of the intellectual tools necessary for the understanding and communication of ideas; (b) to enable each student to understand herself or himself as a thinking person capable of making ethical and aesthetic choices, (c) to help each student comprehend the diversity of intellectual approaches to understanding human society and the physical world, and (d) to increase each student's awareness of his or her place in those broader contexts. Students choose from a set of courses in eight Core areas, developing over four years an understanding of the liberal arts as the foundation for a lifetime of learning. Satisfy the foreign language graduation requirement in one of the following ways:(a) Successfully complete 2 semesters of a foreign language at the 101-102 college level, or 1 semester of a foreign language at the 200 level or above (courses taken pass/fail will not fulfill the foreign language graduation requirement); (b) Pass a Puget Sound-approved foreign language proficiency exam at the third-year high school or first-year college level, (c) Receive a score of 4 or 5 on an Advanced Placement foreign language exam or a score of 5, 6, or 7 on an International Baccalaureate Higher Level foreign language exam. **Procedure:** Freshmen are admitted fall and spring. Entrance exams should be taken during the fall of the senior year. There are early decision and deferred admissions plans. Early decision applications should be filed by November 15; regular applications, by January 15 for fall entry; November 1 for spring entry; and March 1 for summer entry. The fall 2017 application fee was $60. Notification of early decision is sent December 15; regular decision, April 1. 114 early decision candidates were accepted for the 2017-2018 class. 480 applicants were on the 2017 waiting list; 21 were admitted. Applications are accepted on-line. **Transfer Students:** 54 transfer students enrolled in 2016-2017. Applicants must have had an honorable dismissal from the institution(s) previously attended and be in good academic standing with a minimum GPA of 2.0. All college transcripts and the rigor of prior coursework and resulting grades are evaluated. High school transcripts and SAT or ACT scores are required if less than 1 year of college has been completed. An interview is recommended. An essay is required. Puget Sound only accepts the Common Application for undergraduate transfer admission. Students may apply in the fall, spring and summer. 64 of 128 credits required for the bachelor's degree must be completed at Puget Sound. **International Students:**

There are 10 international students enrolled. They must take the TOEFL with a minimum score of 550 on the paper-based TOEFL (PBT) or 80 on the Internet-based version (iBT). All freshman applicants and transfers with less than 1 full year of college work must take the SAT or ACT.

ADMISSIONS: 79% of the 2017-2018 applicants were accepted. The SAT scores for the 2017-2018 freshman class were: Math-- 5% below 500, 36% between 500 and 599, 42% between 600 and 699, and 17% between 700 and 800. Evidence-Based Reading/Writing-- 4% below 500, 24% between 500 and 599, 50% between 600 and 699, and 23% between 700 and 800. The ACT scores were 1% between 12 and 17, 13% between 18 and 23, 53% between 24 and 29, and 33% above 30. 58% of the current freshmen were in the top fifth of their class; 86% were in the top two fifths. **Admissions Contact:** James Miller, Director of Admission. Email: *jdmiller@pugetsound.edu* Web: *www.pugetsound.edu*

FINANCIAL AID: In 2017-2018, 99% of all full-time freshmen received some form of financial aid. 53% of all full-time freshmen received need-based aid. The average freshman award was $30,650. Need-based scholarships or need-based grants averaged $29,392; need-based self-help aid (loans and jobs) averaged $6,998; non-need-based athletic scholarships averaged $17,530; and other non-need-based awards and non-need-based scholarships averaged $5,584. 44% of undergraduate students work part-time. The average financial indebtedness of the 2017 graduate was $34,791. Puget Sound is a member of CSS. The CSS/Profile is required of early decision candidates. The FAFSA code is 003797. The priority date for freshman financial aid applications for fall entry is March 15.

UNIVERSITY OF WASHINGTON C-2

www.washington.edu

Seattle, WA 98195 **(206) 543-9686**

Fax: (206) 685-3655

Full-time: 13,493 men, 15,224 women	**Faculty:** 2128
Part-time: 895 men, 863 women	**Ph.D.s:** 91%
Graduate: 6781 men, 7843 women	**Student/Faculty:** 17 to 1
Year: trimesters, summer session	**Tuition:** $10,974 ($34,473)
Room & Board: $12,117	**Freshman Class:** 44877 applied, 20833 accepted, 6793 enrolled
SAT EBR-W/M: 640/665 **ACT:** 30	**CEEB CODE:** 4854
Application Deadline: November 15	**MOST COMPETITIVE**

University of Washington, founded in 1861, is a public research university offering a broad range of degree programs. The Husky Promise guarantees that qualified Washington State students' full tuition and standard fees will be covered by means of financial grants or scholarship support. There are 16 undergraduate schools and 1 graduate school. In addition to regional accreditation, UW has baccalaureate program accreditation with AACSB, ABET, CAEP, and NLN. The 643-acre campus is in an urban area 5 miles from downtown Seattle. Including any residence halls, there are 279 buildings.

STUDENT LIFE: 79% of undergraduates are from Washington. Others are from 44 states, 107 foreign countries, and Canada. 8% are Hispanic; 7% two or more races; 40% White; 3% African American; 24% Asian American; 15% Foreign; 1% race unknown. **Female To Male Ratio:** 1.1:1. The average age of freshmen is 18; all undergraduates, 20. 8% do not continue beyond their first year; 75% remain to graduate. **Housing:** 5200 students can be accommodated in college housing, which includes married student dorms and on-campus apartments. In addition, there are honors houses, language/international houses, special-interest houses, fraternity houses, sorority houses, freshman house, theme housing, apartments for singles, and substance and alcohol free environment. On-campus housing is guaranteed for all 4 years. 70% of students live on campus. Alcohol is not permitted. All students may keep cars.

FACULTY/CLASSROOMS: 85% teach undergraduates, and 85% do research. No introductory courses are taught by graduate students.

PROGRAMS OF STUDY: UW confers B.A., B.S., B.A.B.A., B.C.H.S., B.L.Arch., B.Mus., B.S.A.&A., B.S.B.C., B.S.Cer.E., B.S.Comp.E., B.S.F., B.S.Fish., B.S.I.E., B.S.M.E., B.S.Med.Tech., B.S.Met.E., and B.S.Nur. degrees. Master's and doctoral degrees are also awarded. Bachelor's degrees are awarded in AGRICULTURE (fishing and fisheries, forest engineering, and forestry production and processing), BIOLOGICAL SCIENCE (biochemistry, biology/biological science, botany, microbiology, neurosciences, and zoology), BUSINESS (accounting, banking and finance, business administration and management, business economics, international business management, marketing/retailing/merchandising, and personnel management), COMMUNICATIONS AND THE ARTS (art history and appreciation, classics, communications, comparative literature, dance, dramatic arts, English, French, Germanic languages and literature, graphic design, Italian, Japanese, jazz, music history and appreciation, music performance, painting, photography, Scandinavian languages, sculpture, Slavic languages, Spanish, speech/debate/rhetoric, studio art, and technical and business writing), COMPUTER AND PHYSICAL SCIENCE (astronomy, atmospheric sciences and meteorology, computer science, geology, information sciences and systems, mathematics, oceanography, physics, quantitative methods, and statistics), EDUCATION (music education), ENGINEERING AND ENVIRONMENTAL DESIGN (aeronautical engineering, ceramic engineering, chemical engineering, civil engineering, computer engineering, construction engineering, electrical/electronics engineering, engineering, landscape architecture/design, materials science, ocean engineering, and paper and pulp science), HEALTH PROFESSIONS (dental hygiene, environmental health science, health care administration, medical laboratory technology, nursing, and speech pathology/audiology), SOCIAL SCIENCE (African American studies, anthropology, Asian/American studies, Asian/Oriental studies, Canadian studies, economics, ethnic studies, food science, geography, history, international relations, Judaic studies, liberal arts/general studies, Near Eastern studies, philosophy, political science/government, psychology, religion, Russian and Slavic studies, social work, sociology, South Asian studies, and women's studies). Business, political science, and art have the largest enrollments.

ACTIVITIES: Groups on campus include band, cheerleading, chess, choir, chorale, chorus, communications, computers, dance, debate, drama, ethnic, film, honors, international, jazz band, LGBT, literary magazine, marching band, musical theater, newspaper, opera, orchestra, pep band, political, professional, radio and TV, religious, social, social service, student government, and symphony. Popular campus events include Convocation, Dawg Daze, and Washington Weekend. **Sports:** There are 11 intercollegiate sports for men and 12 for women, and 13 intramural sports for men and 12 for women. Facilities include a football stadium, a baseball field, track and field complex, tennis courts, intramurals building, golf driving range, and swimming pool. **Graduates:** From July 1, 2016 to June 30, 2017, 7772 bachelor's degrees were awarded. The most popular majors were social sciences (14%), biological/life sciences (13%), and business/marketing (11%).

SERVICES: Counseling and information services are available, as is tutoring in every subject. There is a reader service for the blind, and remedial math, reading, and writing. **Library/Resources:** The library contains 7.0 million volumes. Computerized library services include interlibrary loans, database searching, Internet access, and Wi-Fi capability. Special learning facilities include an art gallery, natural history museum, planetarium, radio station, TV station, a state museum, a full teaching hospital, a marine science lab, 200-acre arboretum, and field research forest. **Physically Challenged Students:** 95% of the campus is accessible. Facilities include wheelchair ramps, elevators, special parking, specially equipped restrooms, special class scheduling, lowered drinking fountains, lowered telephones, and special housing. **Special:** A wide variety of internships, including those for minority students in engineering, concurrent dual majors, study abroad in 60 countries, a Washington semester, a general studies degree, and co-op programs are available. Work-study programs, cross-registration with the National Student Exchange, credit/no credit options, student-designed majors, accelerated degree programs, nondegree study, and a 5-year B.A.-B.S. degree also are offered. There are 20 national honor societies, Phi Beta Kappa, a freshman honors program, and 36 departmental honors programs. **Visiting:** There are regularly scheduled orientations for prospective students, including attending a class, a meeting with an admissions counselor and/or academic advisor, going on a campus tour, and attending information sessions. There are guides for informal visits and visitors may sit in on classes. To schedule a visit, contact the Student Visitation Program at (206) 543-5429. **Campus Safety and Security:** Measures include 24-hour foot and vehicle patrol, emergency notification system, self-defense education, and security escort services. There are shuttle buses, emergency telephones, and lighted pathways/sidewalks.

REQUIREMENTS: The SAT or ACT is required. The ACT Optional Writing test is also required. Applicants must have completed 15 academic units, including 4 years of English, 3 each of math and social studies, 2 each of foreign language and science (with lab), and 1/2 year each in fine/visual performing arts and electives from required subject list. Admission is based on a comprehensive review. AP credits are accepted. Important factors in the admissions decision are leadership record, parents or siblings attended your school, evidence of special talent, personality/intangible qualities, and extracurricular activities record. All students must maintain a GPA of 2.0 while taking 180 quarter credits, with 50 in the major. Distribution requirements include 40 credits from the humanities, social sciences, and math/natural sciences, with 12 credits in English composition/writing and a course in quantitative/symbolic reasoning. **Procedure:** Freshmen are admitted to all sessions. Entrance exams should be taken by December of the senior year. Applications should be filed by November 15 for fall entry; September 1 for winter entry; December 15 for spring entry; and February 15 for summer entry. The fall 2017 application fee was $70. Notifications are sent March 15. 773 applicants were on the 2017 waiting list; 332 were admitted. Applications are accepted on-line. **Transfer Students:** 1508 transfer students enrolled in 2016-2017. The school gives priority to Washington community colleges students. Admission is based on a comprehensive review, high school transcript, college transcript (s) and an essay. Transfer student may apply for admissions fall, winter, spring, and summer. 45 of 180 credits required for the bachelor's degree must be completed at UW. **International Students:** There are 1095 international students enrolled. They must take the TOEFL with a minimum score of 540 on the paper-based TOEFL (PBT) or 57 on the Internet-based version (iBT).

ADMISSIONS: 46% of the 2017-2018 applicants were accepted. The SAT scores for the 2017-2018 freshman class were: Math-- 3% below 500, 19% between 500 and 599, 40% between 600 and 699, and 38% between 700 and 800. Evidence-Based Reading/Writing-- 5% below 500, 22% between 500 and 599, 50% between 600 and 699, and 23% between 700 and 800. The ACT scores were 2% between 12 and 17, 9% between 18 and 23, 41% between 24 and 29, and 49% above 30. 97% of the current freshmen were in the top fifth of their class; 99% were in the top two fifths. **Admissions Contact:** Paul C Seegert, Office of Admissions. Web: *www.washington.edu*

FINANCIAL AID: In 2017-2018, 82% of all full-time freshmen received some form of financial aid. The average freshman award was $17,800. Need-based scholarships or need-based grants averaged $14,000; need-based self-help aid (loans and jobs) averaged $7,200; non-need-based athletic scholarships averaged $10,500; other non-need-based awards and non-need-based scholarships averaged $5,500; and $6,000 from other forms of aid. The average financial indebtedness of the 2017 graduate was $31,300. The FAFSA code is 003798. The priority date for freshman financial aid applications for fall entry is January 15.

WALLA WALLA UNIVERSITY — E-3
www.wallawalla.edu

College Place, WA 99324	**(509) 527-2608** **(800) 541-8900**
Fax: (509) 527-2397	**Email: info@wallawalla.edu**
Full-time: 795 men, 790 women	**Faculty:** 100; I
Part-time: 53 men, 41 women	**Ph.D.s:** 38%
Graduate: 48 men, 145 women	**Student/Faculty:** 15 to 1
Year: quarters, summer session	**Tuition:** $27,495
Room & Board: $7350	**Freshman Class:** 1963 applied, 1219 accepted, 387 enrolled
SAT CR/M/W: 530/535/510 **ACT:** 24	**CEEB CODE:** 4940
Application Deadline: open	**COMPETITIVE**

Walla Walla University, founded in 1892, is a private comprehensive institution, affiliated with the Seventh-day Adventist Church, and offers liberal arts, professional, and technical programs. There are 6 undergraduate schools and 4 graduate schools. In addition to regional accreditation, Walla Walla has baccalaureate program accreditation with ABET, ACBSP, CSWE, NASM, and NLN. The 55-acre campus is in a small town in College Place, Washington, 120 miles southwest of Spokane. Including any residence halls, there are 34 buildings.

STUDENT LIFE: 69% of undergraduates are from out of state, mostly the West. 6% are Asian American; 5% two or more races; 45% White; 3% African American; 3% Foreign; 15% Hispanic. **Female To Male Ratio:** 1.1:1. The average age of freshmen is 18; all undergraduates, 21. **Housing:** 1500 students can be accommodated in college housing, which includes married student dorms, on-campus apartments, and off-campus apartments. On-campus housing is guaranteed for all 4 years. 93% of students live on campus. Alcohol is not permitted. All students may keep cars.

FACULTY/CLASSROOMS: All teach undergraduates. No introductory courses are taught by graduate students. The average class size in an introductory lecture is 24 and in a regular course is 13.

PROGRAMS OF STUDY: Walla Walla confers B.A., B.S., B.B.A., B.Mus., B.S.E., and B.S.W. degrees. Associate and master's degrees are also awarded. Bachelor's degrees are awarded in BIOLOGICAL SCIENCE (biochemistry, biology/biological science, and biophysics), BUSINESS (business administration and management and finance), COMMUNICATIONS AND THE ARTS (art, communications, English, French, German, graphic communications, graphic design, music, music performance, Spanish, and speech/debate/rhetoric), COMPUTER AND PHYSICAL SCIENCE (chemistry, computer science, digital arts/technology, information sciences and systems, mathematics, physics, and radiological technology), EDUCATION (business education, elementary education, music education, nursing education, physical education, physical education/exercise science, and special education), ENGINEERING AND ENVIRONMENTAL DESIGN (automotive technology, aviation computer technology, bioengineering, engineering, and environmental science), HEALTH PROFESSIONS (chiropractic, dental hygiene, health, nursing, occupational therapy, optometry, pharmacy, physical therapy, physical therapy assistant, physician's assistant, public health, and veterinary science), SOCIAL SCIENCE (biblical languages, history, humanities, psychology, religion, social work, sociology, and theological studies). Social work, business, and engineering are the strongest academically. Nursing, engineering, and business have the largest enrollments.

ACTIVITIES: There are no fraternities or sororities. Groups on campus include atlas, aviation, robotics, auto, art, band, choir, chorale, chorus, drama, ethnic, honors, international, jazz band, literary magazine, newspaper, orchestra, photography, professional, radio and TV, religious, social service, student government, symphony, and yearbook. Popular campus events include Mud Bowl Football Game, Sonneberg Series Basketball Tournament, and Welcome Back Bash. **Sports:** There are 6 intercollegiate sports for men and 3 for women, and 9 intramural sports for men and 8 for women. Facilities include a track, tennis and racquetball courts, basketball, softball, golf, soccer, volleyball, a gym, swimming pool, climbing wall, several weight rooms, floor hockey, flag football, badminton, and table tennis. **Graduates:** From July 1, 2016 to June 30, 2017, 325 bachelor's degrees were awarded. The most popular majors were health professions and related sciences (24%), business/marketing and engineering (13%), and visual and performing and related programs (7%).

SERVICES: Counseling and information services are available, as is tutoring in most subjects, such as math, languages, sciences, business, and engineering. There is remedial math, reading, and writing. Student can access the Teaching Learning Center for support. **Library/Resources:** The library contains 184,493 volumes, 151,946 microform items, and 3,451 audio/video tapes/CDs/DVDs, and subscribes to 3,727 periodicals including electronic. Computerized library services include interlibrary loans and database searching. Special learning facilities include an art gallery, radio station, TV station, audio listening/music library, and observatory. **Physically Challenged Students:** 90% of the campus is accessible. Facilities include wheelchair ramps, elevators, special parking, specially equipped restrooms, special class scheduling, and special housing. **Special:** Opportunities are provided for internships, co-op programs, cross-registration with Whitman College, study abroad programs offered in Argentina, Austria, Brazil, China, England, France, Germany, Israel, Italy, Lebanon, Spain, and Ukraine, work-study programs, a B.A.-B.S. degree, dual majors, credit by exam, and nondegree study. There is a freshman honors program and 6 departmental honors programs. **Visiting:** There are guides for informal visits, visitors may sit in on classes, and stay overnight. To schedule a visit, contact Guest Relations at (509) 527-2327. **Campus Safety and Security:** Measures include 24-hour foot and vehicle patrol, emergency notification system, self-defense education, and security escort services. There are emergency telephones, lighted pathways/sidewalks, programs on sexual assault, bomb threats, earthquake, crime & violence, and drug & alcohol, dangerous weather, first aid and medical instructions.

REQUIREMENTS: The SAT or ACT is required. These scores are used for placement and academic advisement. Graduation from an accredited secondary school is required; a GED will be accepted. Applicants should submit an academic record containing at a minimum 4 years of English, 3-4 of math, including algebra and geometry, 2 of history, and 1 of science with lab, along with a letter of recommendation from a teacher or school official. AP and CLEP credits are accepted. Important factors in the admissions decision are advanced placement or honors courses, recommendations by school officials, leadership record, and personality/intangible qualities. To graduate, students must successfully complete 192 quarter hours, including at least 45 in the major and at least 60 in upper-level work, with a minimum GPA of 2.0. Grades below C- will not apply toward the major. Students must also meet a general studies requirement that includes 16 to 20 quarter hours in religion and theology, 13 to 21 in language arts, 12 to 20 in history and social science, 12 to 16 in humanities and math/natural science, and 2 to 6 in health and phys ed. A comprehensive exam is required, as is attendance at chapel and assemblies. **Procedure:** Freshmen are admitted to all sessions. Entrance exams should be taken during the junior or senior year. There are early decision, early admissions, deferred admissions, and rolling admissions plans. Application deadlines are open. The fall 2017 application fee was $40. Applications are accepted on-line. **Transfer Students:** 111 transfer students enrolled in 2016-2017. Applicants should have a 2.0 minimum GPA and must submit all college transcripts and a letter of recommendation (3 for nursing majors) from a former teacher or school official. 36 of 192 credits required for the bachelor's degree must be completed at Walla Walla. **International Students:** They must take the TOEFL with a minimum score of 550 on the paper-based TOEFL (PBT) or 79 on the Internet-based version (iBT). They must also take the SAT or ACT.

ADMISSIONS: 62% of the 2017-2018 applicants were accepted. The SAT scores for the 2017-2018 freshman class were: Critical Reading-- 33% below 500, 40% between 500 and 599, 20% between 600 and 699, and 6% between 700 and 800. Math-- 37% below 500, 37% between 500 and 599, 23% between 600 and 699, and 3% between 700 and 800. Writing-- 42% below 500, 40% between 500 and 599, 17% between 600 and 699, and 1% between 700 and 800. The ACT scores were 8% below 12, 25% between 12 and 17, 40% between 18 and 23, 20% between 24 and 29, and 6% above 30. **Admissions Contact:** Dallas Weis, Director of Admissions. Email: *info@wallawalla.edu* Web: *www.wallawalla.edu*

FINANCIAL AID: The average freshman award was $21,879. Need-based scholarships or need-based grants averaged $5,605; need-based self-help aid (loans and jobs) averaged $8,843; other non-need-based awards and non-need-based scholarships averaged $10,457; and $3,421 from other forms of aid. The average financial indebtedness of the 2017 graduate was $33,018. The college's own financial statement is required. The FAFSA code is 003799. The priority date for freshman financial aid applications for fall entry is February 15.

WASHINGTON STATE UNIVERSITY — E-3

www.wsu.edu

Pullman, WA 99164	**(509) 335-5586** **(888) 468-6978**
Fax: (509) 335-4902	**Email: admissions@wsu.edu**
Full-time: 10,656 men, 11,510 women	**Faculty:** I, -$
Part-time: 1367 men, 1744 women	**Ph.D.s:** 88%
Graduate: 2609 men, 2728 women	**Student/Faculty:** 16 to 1
Year: semesters, summer session	**Tuition:** $11,391 ($25,817)
Room & Board: $11,356	**Freshman Class:** n/av
SAT or ACT: required	**CEEB CODE:** 4705
Application Deadline: January 31	**COMPETITIVE**

Washington State University, founded in 1890 as a land-grant institution, is now a major public research university. It has locations statewide (Pullman, Spokane, Tri-Cities, Vancouver, and Everett) and an online Global Campus that reaches students around the world. WSU's undergraduate and graduate offerings span the liberal arts and sciences, business, communication, education, engineering and architecture, agricultural, human and natural resource sciences, and the health sciences, including nursing, pharmacy, and veterinary medicine. There are 11 undergraduate schools and 1 graduate school. In addition to regional accreditation, WSU has baccalaureate program accreditation with AACSB, ABET, ACCE, ACPE, ADA, NAAB, NASM, ACS, NASM, NASPAA, CAA, LAAB, AAHA, ASHA, AACP, APA, AVMA, PESB, AACN, AAALAC, NPSMA, APACA, CADE, CCNE, CIDA, ACEND, CAHME, AAVLD, NWCCU, and ASLA. The 620-acre campus is in a small town 75 miles south of Spokane, and 286 miles east of Seattle. Including any residence halls, there are 545 buildings.

STUDENT LIFE: 87% of undergraduates are from Washington. Others are from 49 states, 72 foreign countries, and Canada. 61% are White; 15% Hispanic; 7% two or more races; 6% Asian American; 5% Foreign; 3% African American; 3% race unknown; 1% American Indian/Alaska Native. **Female To Male Ratio:** 1.1:1. The average age of freshmen is 19; all undergraduates, 22. 19% do not continue beyond their first year; 62% remain to graduate. **Housing:** 7324 students can be accommodated in college housing, which includes married student dorms and on-campus apartments. In addition, there are honors houses, language/international houses, special-interest houses, fraternity houses, sorority houses, living learning communities, and first-year focus (freshmen students only). On-campus housing is guaranteed for the freshman year only. 76% of students commute. All students may keep cars.

FACULTY/CLASSROOMS: 54% of faculty are male; 46% are female. Graduate students teach 17% of introductory courses.

PROGRAMS OF STUDY: WSU confers B.A., B.S., B.F.A., B. Mus., and B.L.A. degrees. Master's and doctoral degrees are also awarded. Bachelor's degrees are awarded in AGRICULTURE (agricultural business management, agricultural communications, agricultural economics, agricultural mechanics, agricultural sciences, agriculture, agronomy, animal science, forestry production and processing, forestry and related sciences, horticulture, natural resource management, plant protection (pest management), plant science, range/farm management, soil science, viticulture and enology, turfgrass and landscape management, and wildlife management), BIOLOGICAL SCIENCE (biochemistry, biology/biological science, biotechnology, botany, cell biology, entomology, genetics, microbiology, neurosciences, plant genetics, plant pathology, wildlife biology, and zoology), BUSINESS (accounting, business administration and management, business economics, business law, business statistics, electronic business, entrepreneurial studies, finance, hospitality management services, hotel/motel and restaurant management, human resources, insurance, international business, international business management, management information systems, management, marketing, marketing management, office supervision and management, operations management, real estate, and sports management), COMMUNICATIONS AND THE ARTS (advertising, art, broadcasting, Chinese, communications, digital communications, English, fine arts, fine/studio arts, general, foreign language, French, German, Japanese, journalism - magazine journalism, journalism - news & information, journalism - newswriting /edit, linguistics, multimedia, music, music composition, music performance, music theory and composition, public relations, Russian, Spanish, communication arts - speech, strategic communication, and theatre arts), COMPUTER AND PHYSICAL SCIENCE (applied mathematics, chemistry, computer science, data analytics, digital arts/technology, earth science, geology, mathematics, physical sciences, physics, science, and software engineering), EDUCATION (agricultural education, Asian studies, athletic training, bilingual/bicultural education, early childhood education, education, elementary education, English education, foreign languages education, global studies, music education, physical education, science education, secondary education, social studies education, and special education), ENGINEERING AND ENVIRONMENTAL DESIGN (agricultural engineering, agricultural engineering technology, architectural engineering, architecture, bioengineering, biomedical engineering, chemical engineering, civil engineering, computer engineering, construction management, electrical/electronics engineering, environmental science, industrial administration/management, industrial engineering technology, interior design, landscape architecture/design, manufacturing engineering, manufacturing technology, materials engineering, materials science, materials science and engineering, and mechanical engineering), HEALTH PROFESSIONS (biology, biomedical science, electrical engineering, exercise science, health and physical activity, nursing, predentistry, premedicine, preoptometry, prepharmacy, prephysical therapy, preveterinary science, and speech pathology/audiology), SOCIAL SCIENCE (American studies, anthropology, architectural studies, Chinese Studies, clothing and textiles management/production/services, criminal justice, criminology, crosscultural studies, economics, ethnic studies, family/consumer studies, food science, history, human development, human development & family studies, humanities, humanities and social science, interdisciplinary studies, liberal arts/general studies, liberal arts, sciences, general studies, humanities, philosophy, political science/government, prelaw, psychology, public affairs, religion, religious studies, social science, social studies, social work, sociology, and women's studies). Veterinary medicine, nursing, communications, engineering, and crop & soil sciences are the strongest academically. Arts and sciences, business, and engineering have the largest enrollments.

ACTIVITIES: 15% of men belong to 29 national fraternities; 18% of women belong to 14 national sororities. There are 350 groups on campus, including art, band, cheerleading, choir, chorale, chorus, computers, dance, debate, drama, environmental, ethnic, film, honors, international, jazz band, LGBT, literary magazine, marching band, musical theater, newspaper, opera, orchestra, pep band, photography, political, professional, radio and TV, religious, social, social service, student government, symphony, and yearbook. Popular campus events include Convocation, Showcase, All-Campus Picnic, Cougfest, Week of Welcome, Mom's Weekend, Dad's Weekend, Springfest, Homecoming, and Civic Engagement Week. **Sports:** There are 6 intercollegiate sports for men and 9 for women, and 53 intramural sports for men and 53 for women. Facilities include a stadium, a coliseum, indoor and outdoor tracks, tennis courts, a student recreation center, an 18-hole championship golf course, an indoor practice facility with roll-out turf system, baseball and soccer fields, indoor swimming pools, racquetball and squash courts, a climbing wall, gyms, an indoor rowing facility, an outdoor recreation center, basketball courts, sand volleyball courts, and intramural playing fields. **Graduates:** From July 1, 2016 to June 30, 2017, 5597 bachelor's degrees were awarded. The most popular majors were business/marketing (21%), engineering (11%), and social sciences (10%). In an average class, 37% graduate in 4 years or less, 55% graduate in 5 years or less, and 62% graduate in 6 years or less.

SERVICES: Counseling and information services are available, as is tutoring in most subjects, such as accounting, anatomy and physiology, biology, chemistry, computer science, engineering, finance, math (through calculus), Microsoft Office, physics, Spanish, statistics, writing, sciences, and social sciences. There is a reader service for the blind, and remedial math. The Academic Success and Career Center offers learning assistance through tutoring and workshops that address study skills, note taking, test preparation, time management, reading strategies, career/major choice, stress management, life skills, peer tutoring, and career services. WSU is also a member of the Northwest eTutoring Consortium which offers unlimited FREE online tutoring to all WSU students. **Library/Resources:** The library contains 2.4 million volumes, 4.0 million microform items, 41,674 audio/video tapes/CDs/DVDs, and subscribes to 133,691 periodicals including electronic. Computerized library services include interlibrary loans, database searching, Internet access, and Wi-Fi capability. Special learning facilities include an art gallery, a planetarium, a radio station, a natural history museum, museum of art, museum of anthropology, an entomological collection, a veterinary anatomy teaching museum, geology museums, radio and TV stations, digital recording studio, a music listening library, fine arts studio facilities with specialized equipment, a cultural center, an international center for exchanging cultural, a child development lab, financial markets lab (trading room), food sensory evaluation lab, culinary lab with a teaching kitchen and creamery, social and economic sciences research center, and astronomical observatory. There are specialized teaching and research labs for science and engineering, including a bio-molecular x-ray crystallography center, a genomics and gene sequencing lab, a virtual reality computer-integrated manufacturing lab, a hydraulics lab, and a laboratory for atmospheric research. Wildlife center, an ecological reserves, greenhouses, vivaria, and herbaria, agronomic research farms, a horticultural orchard, an organic teaching farm, an teaching apiary, a livestock center, labs, barns, beef and dairy centers, a cattle-feeding lab, and a feed plant. On-campus market for locally grown, alumni-grown, and organic produce. There is also a veterinary teaching hospital, human anatomy lab, water research center, nuclear radiation center, and a digital classroom. **Physically Challenged Students:** Facilities include wheelchair ramps, elevators, special parking, specially equipped restrooms, special class scheduling, lowered drinking fountains, lowered telephones, and special housing. **Special:** Undergraduates can become involved in faculty research, internships, over 1,500 study-abroad programs in more than 80 countries, an Honors College, academic club projects and competitions, civic engagement projects, work-study programs, and co-op programs in numerous majors. Dual majors are available, as are B.A.-B.S. degrees in computer science and psychology and student-designed majors in general studies. Interior design and veterinary medicine programs offer accelerated pathways to advanced degrees. Credit may be granted for military service, and non-degree and pass/fail options are offered. Some academic programs are offered in partnership with the Universities of Idaho and Washington, Eastern Washington University, and Wenatchee Valley College. Students can register for jointly offered courses either at WSU or at one of the other participating universities. There are 22 national honor societies, Phi Beta Kappa, and a freshman honors program. **Visiting:** There are regularly scheduled orientations for prospective students, consisting of a campus tour and a presentation about admissions, financial aid, and scholarship opportunities. There are guides for informal visits and visitors may sit in on classes. **Campus Safety and Security:** Measures include 24-hour foot and vehicle patrol, emergency notification system, self-defense education, and security escort services. There are shuttle buses, emergency telephones, lighted pathways/sidewalks, controlled access to dorms/residences. The Campus Safety Plan contains a list of university policies, procedures, statistics, and information related to campus safety, campus outdoor warning system (COWS), alert crisis communication system (WSU Alert). The Alert email list serves the college website, crime prevention and personal safety education, monitored lighting levels on campus, a women's transit service, residence hall security hours, an intern program with the campus police department, and housing patrols.

REQUIREMENTS: The SAT or ACT is required. Students should be high school graduates, and completed high school courses: 4 credits of English; 3 credits each of math (1 credit each of algebra, geometry, and algebra II) and social science; 2 credits each of the same world language (includes Native American languages and American Sign Language), and lab science including 1 algebra-based; and 1 year of fine, visual or performing arts, or elective from any of the other required subjects. A combination of the high school GPA and test scores is considered. The GED is also accepted. (1 credit equals 1 year) A GPA of 2.0 is required. AP and CLEP credits are accepted. Important factors in the admissions decision are advanced placement or honors courses. Students must complete 120 semester credits, with fulfillment of a major, 40 credits of upper-division work, 30 credits in residence, and maintain a minimum GPA of 2.0. General university requirements include 7 credits of science, 9 of arts and humanities and social sciences, 6 of writing and communication, 3 each of global issues, math, diversity, and an integrative capstone. Students must complete a writing portfolio and pass a writing qualifying exam prior to graduation. **Procedure:** Freshmen are admitted fall, spring, and summer. Entrance exams should be taken during spring of the junior year or fall of the senior year. Applications should be filed by January 31 for fall entry; November 15 for spring entry. The fall 2017 application fee was $50. Notifications are sent November 1. Applications are accepted on-line. **Transfer Students:** 2697 transfer students enrolled in 2016-2017. Admission to WSU is offered to qualified students on a first-come, first-served basis. Applications completed by the priority application date of January 31 will receive first consideration. Applicants who have less than a full year of college credit to transfer may be asked to submit a high school transcript (or G.E.D.) and test scores (SAT or ACT). Transcripts and test scores must be sent directly from the school or testing agency to WSU via secure electronic document transfer, fax, or mail. Email is not accepted. 30 of 120 credits required for the bachelor's degree must be completed at WSU. **International Students:** There are 1164 international students enrolled. They must take the TOEFL with a minimum score of 550 on the paper-based TOEFL (PBT) or 79 on the Internet-based version (iBT) or MELAB, and any one of these tests: the IELTS, IB with a passing score in English, or SAT with a 500 critical reading sub score.

Admissions Contact: Wendy Peterson, Director of Admissions. Email: *admissions@wsu.edu* Web: *www.wsu.edu*

FINANCIAL AID: In 2017-2018, 87% of all full-time freshmen received some form of financial aid. 46% of all full-time freshmen received need-based aid. The average freshman award was $12,199. Need-based scholarships or need-based grants averaged $11,534 ($48,202 maximum); need-based self-help aid (loans and jobs) averaged $3,437 ($15,814 maximum); non-need-based athletic scholarships averaged $25,860 ($48,209 maximum); and other non-need-based awards and non-need-based scholarships averaged $4,233 ($26,504 maximum). 17% of undergraduate students work part-time. The average financial indebtedness of the 2017 graduate was $25,951. The state aid form, the college's own financial statement, and WSU General Scholarship Application are required. The FAFSA code is 003800. The priority date for freshman financial aid applications for fall entry is January 31.

WESTERN WASHINGTON UNIVERSITY C-1
www.wwu.edu

Bellingham, WA 98225 **(360) 650-3966**

Email: admit@wwu.edu

Full-time: 5889 men, 7839 women
Part-time: 625 men, 615 women
Graduate: 339 men, 608 women
Year: quarters, summer session
Room & Board: $10,971

SAT EBR-W/M: 600/580 **ACT:** 25
Application Deadline: January 31

Faculty: 637
Ph.D.s: 89%
Student/Faculty: 22 to 1
Tuition: $7933 ($22,445)
Freshman Class: 11244 applied, 9534 accepted, 3114 enrolled
CEEB CODE: 4947
VERY COMPETITIVE

Western Washington University, founded in 1893, is a nonprofit, public institution whose emphasis is on the liberal arts and sciences, business and business administration, economics, art, fine arts, performing arts, music, teacher preparation, interdisciplinary learning, and environmental studies. There are 7 undergraduate schools and 1 graduate school. In addition to regional accreditation, WWU has baccalaureate program accreditation with AACSB, ABET, ASLA, NASM, CAEP, and NRPA. The 195-acre campus is in a small town 60 miles south of Vancouver, British Columbia, and 90 miles north of Seattle. Including any residence halls, there are 80 buildings.

STUDENT LIFE: 88% of undergraduates are from Washington. Others are from 47 states, 43 foreign countries, and Canada. 91% are from public schools. 9% are Hispanic; 8% two or more races; 71% White; 6% Asian American; 2% African American; 1% Foreign; 1% race unknown. **Female To Male Ratio:** 1.3:1. The average age of freshmen is 18; all undergraduates, 21. 19% do not continue beyond their first year; 73% remain to graduate. **Housing:** 4145 students can be accommodated in college housing, which includes gender neutral, coed, and married student dorms, on-campus apartments, and off-campus apartments. In addition, there are honors houses, special-interest houses, substance-free living, and quiet hall. On-campus housing is guaranteed for the freshman year only, is available on a first-come, and first-served basis. 73% of students commute. All students may keep cars.

FACULTY/CLASSROOMS: 50% of faculty are male; 50% are female. All teach undergraduates. Graduate students teach 1% of introductory courses. The average class size in an introductory lecture is 49; in a laboratory is 24; and in a regular course is 29.

PROGRAMS OF STUDY: WWU confers B.A., B.S., B.A.E., B.F.A. B.S.N. and B.Mus. degrees. Master's degrees are also awarded. Bachelor's degrees are awarded in AGRICULTURE (environmental studies), BIOLOGICAL SCIENCE (biochemistry, biology/biological science, cell biology, ecology, life science, marine biology, marine science, and molecular biology), BUSINESS (accounting, business administration and management, fashion merchandising, human resources, international business management, international economics, management information systems, management science, marketing/retailing/merchandising, and operations management), COMMUNICATIONS AND THE ARTS (apparel design, Arabic, art, ceramic art and design, classics, communications, creative writing, dance, design, dramatic arts, English, fine arts, French, German, Japanese, journalism, linguistics, multimedia, music, music history and appreciation, painting, photography, Russian, sculpture, Spanish, theatre arts, theater design, and visual and performing arts), COMPUTER AND PHYSICAL SCIENCE (applied mathematics, applied physics, chemistry, computer science, earth science, geology, mathematics, physics, and polymer science), EDUCATION (art education, early childhood education, education administration, elementary education, foreign languages education, health education, music education, nursing education, physical education, reading education, recreation education, science education, secondary education, special education, and technical education), ENGINEERING AND ENVIRONMENTAL DESIGN (electrical/electronics engineering, electrical/ electronics engineering technology, engineering technology, environmental science, industrial engineering technology, manufacturing technology, mechanical design technology, mechanical engineering technology, plastics engineering, and technology and public affairs), HEALTH PROFESSIONS (nursing, rehabilitation therapy, and speech pathology/audiology), SOCIAL SCIENCE (American studies, anthropology, behavioral science, Canadian studies, child psychology/ development, East Asian studies, economics, geography, history, human services, interdisciplinary studies, international studies, liberal arts/ general studies, parks and recreation management, philosophy, political science/government, psychology, public affairs, social studies, sociology, women & gender studies, and women's studies). Manufacturing and supply chain management, industrial design, and vehicle design are the strongest academically. Health & human development, English, and psychology have the largest enrollments.

ACTIVITIES: There are no fraternities or sororities. There are 230 groups on campus, including art, band, cheerleading, chess, choir, chorale, chorus, computers, dance, debate, drama, environmental, ethnic, film, forensics, honors, international, jazz band, LGBT, literary magazine, musical theater, newspaper, opera, orchestra, pep band, photography, political, professional, religious, social, social service, student government, and symphony. Popular campus events include Fall Info Fair, AS Outdoor Movie, Viking Union Late Night, Queer Resource Center (QRC) Ice Cream Social, Rec Center Late Night, Ethnic Student Center (ESC) Culture Shock, Low Rider Show, and Lawnstock (spring outdoor concert). **Sports:** There are 18 intercollegiate sports for men and 18 for women, and 14 intramural sports for men and 14 for women. Facilities include a center with pool, rock wall, weight and fitness equipment, basketball courts, multi-activity court, artificial-surfaced soccer practice field, a track, and a softball complex. **Graduates:** From July 1, 2016 to June 30, 2017, 3607 bachelor's degrees were awarded. The most popular majors were business and marketing (13%), social sciences (13%), and interdisciplinary studies (7%). In an average class, 37% graduate in 4 years or less, 64% graduate in 5 years or less, and 69% graduate in 6 years or less. Of the 2016 graduating class, 13% were enrolled in graduate school within 6 months of graduation, and 83% were employed.

SERVICES: Counseling and information services are available, as is tutoring in some subjects, such as English, math and natural sciences. There is a reader service for the blind. **Library/Resources:** The library contains 1.2 million volumes, 106,265 microform items, and 56,557 audio/video tapes/CDs/DVDs, and subscribes to 78,351 periodicals including electronic. Computerized library services include interlibrary loans, database searching, Internet access, and Wi-Fi capability. **Physically Challenged Students:** All of the campus is accessible. Facilities include wheelchair ramps, elevators, special parking, specially equipped restrooms, special class scheduling, lowered drinking fountains, and lowered telephones. WWU complies with federal and state law to ensure equal access to university sponsored programs and services. **Special:** Special academic programs include internships through various academic departments and study abroad in over 75 countries. Dual majors are available through various departments. We offer a Multidisciplinary Studies degree, multiple student-faculty designed majors and accelerated master's degree options in Business, Mathematics and Computer Science. There are 12 national honor societies and a freshman honors program. **Visiting:** There are regularly scheduled orientations for prospective students, student visits include tours, class visits, and advisement. There are guides for informal visits and visitors may sit in on classes. To schedule a visit, contact Brent Bode at (360) 650-3861. **Campus Safety and Security:** Measures include 24-hour foot and vehicle patrol, emergency notification system, self-defense education, and security escort services. There are shuttle buses, emergency telephones, and lighted pathways/sidewalks.

REQUIREMENTS: The SAT or ACT is required. Other admissions requirements include completion of 16 academic units, comprised of 4 years of college preparatory English composition and literature courses, 3 units each of college preparatory math (with 2 years each of algebra), social studies/history, science (with 1 lab and 1 algebra-based science), and foreign language, 1 unit each of fine and performing arts, and another in any academic field. The GED is accepted for admission. Other factors taken into consideration include curricular rigor (level of difficulty of courses), grade trends, leadership, community involvement, special talent, multicultural experience, and personal hardship or circumstances. A GPA of 2.5 is required. AP credits are accepted. Important factors in the admissions decision are advanced placement or honors courses, leadership record, and extracurricular activities record. Students must complete at least 180 quarter hours, with fulfillment of a major and at least 60 credits in upper-division study, and maintain at least a 2.0 GPA. General university requirements include 70 to 75 credits, and students must satisfy writing proficiency requirements as well. Fairhaven College has a separate interdisciplinary core program. **Procedure:** Freshmen are admitted fall, winter, and spring. Entrance exams should be taken by fall of the senior year. There are early admissions, deferred admissions, and rolling admissions plans. Applications should be filed by January 31 for fall entry; September 15 for winter entry; and January 1 for spring entry. The fall 2017 application fee was $60. Notifications are sent March 15. 226 applicants were on the 2017 waiting list; 55 were admitted. Applications are accepted on-line. **Transfer Students:** 1744 transfer students enrolled in 2016-2017. Minimum requirements for transfer admission include a 2.0 cumulative transferable GPA and a 2.0 in the quarters prior to application review and enrollment. Applicants with fewer than 45 completed transferable quarter credits also must meet freshman admission standards. Meeting minimum requirements is not a guarantee for admission, as the number of qualified applicants exceeds the number of available enrollment spaces. 45 of 180 credits required for the bachelor's degree must be completed at WWU. **International Students:** There are 172 international students enrolled. They must take the TOEFL with a minimum score of 550 on the paper-based TOEFL (PBT) or 80 on the Internet-based version (iBT). Students must take the IELTS.

ADMISSIONS: 85% of the 2017-2018 applicants were accepted. The SAT scores for the 2017-2018 freshman class were: Math-- 11% below 500, 51% between 500 and 599, 33% between 600 and 699, and 5% between 700 and 800. Evidence-Based Reading/Writing-- 8% below 500, 41% between 500 and 599, 43% between 600 and 699, and 8% between 700 and 800. The ACT scores were 3% between 12 and 17, 34% between 18 and 23, 49% between 24 and 29, and 14% above 30. 44% of the current freshmen were in the top fifth of their class; 77% were in the top two fifths. 62 freshmen graduated first in their class. **Admissions Contact:** Jeanne Gaffney, Associate Director of Admissions. Email: *admit@wwu.edu* Web: *www.wwu.edu*

FINANCIAL AID: In 2017-2018, 61% of all full-time freshmen received some form of financial aid. 55% of all full-time freshmen received need-based aid. The average freshman award was $16,627. Need-based scholarships or need-based grants averaged $8,947; need-based self-help aid (loans and jobs) averaged $4,188; non-need-based athletic scholarships averaged $5,905; and other non-need-based awards and non-need-based scholarships averaged $2,099. The average financial indebtedness of the 2017 graduate was $15,663. The priority date for freshman financial aid applications for fall entry is February 15.

WHITMAN COLLEGE — E-3

www.whitman.edu

Walla Walla, WA 99362	**(509) 527-5176** **(877) 462-9448**
Fax: (509) 527-4967	**Email: admission@whitman.edu**
Full-time: 636 men, 857 women	**Faculty:** 165; IIB, +$
Part-time: 14 men, 26 women	**Ph.D.s:** 95%
Graduate: n/av	**Student/Faculty:** 8 to 1
Year: semesters	**Tuition:** $47,862
Room & Board: $11,910	**Freshman Class:** 3931 applied, 1979 accepted, 425 enrolled
SAT CR/M/W: 650/650/650 **ACT:** 30	**CEEB CODE:** 4951
Application Deadline: January 15	**MOST COMPETITIVE**

Whitman College, founded in 1883, is a nonprofit, private, independent residential liberal arts and sciences college. There is 1 undergraduate school. In addition to regional accreditation, WC has baccalaureate program accreditation with ACS. The 117-acre campus is in a small town 150 miles south of Spokane, 260 miles southeast of Seattle, and 235 miles east of Portland. Including any residence halls, there are 41 buildings.

STUDENT LIFE: 65% of undergraduates are from out of state, mostly the Northwest. Students are from 47 states, 26 foreign countries, and Canada. 71% are White; 7% Hispanic; 7% two or more races; 6% Foreign; 5% Asian American; 3% race unknown; 1% African American. **Female To Male Ratio:** 1.4:1. The average age of freshmen is 18; all undergraduates, 20. 6% do not continue beyond their first year; 87% remain to graduate. **Housing:** 857 students can be accommodated in college housing, which includes dorms and off-campus apartments. In addition, there are language/international houses, special-interest houses, and fraternity houses. On-campus housing is guaranteed for the freshman year only and is available on a lottery system for upperclassmen. All students may keep cars.

FACULTY/CLASSROOMS: 51% of faculty are male; 49% are female. All teach undergraduates and all do research. No introductory courses are taught by graduate students. The average class size in an introductory lecture is 22; in a laboratory is 19; and in a regular course is 17.

PROGRAMS OF STUDY: WC confers B.A. degrees. Bachelor's degrees are awarded in AGRICULTURE (environmental studies and forestry and related sciences), BIOLOGICAL SCIENCE (biochemistry, biophysics, and molecular biology), COMMUNICATIONS AND THE ARTS (art history, art, classics, communication rhetoric/communication, English, French, Greek (classical), jazz, Latin, film and media studies, music, music composition, music history and appreciation, music performance, music theory and composition, Spanish, speech/debate/rhetoric, and theatre arts), COMPUTER AND PHYSICAL SCIENCE (astronomy, astrophysics, chemistry, computer mathematics, geology, mathematics, mathematics – economics, oceanography, physics and mathematics, and physics), ENGINEERING AND ENVIRONMENTAL DESIGN (environmental science and preengineering), HEALTH PROFESSIONS (biology), SOCIAL SCIENCE (anthropology, Asian/Oriental studies, economics, ethnic studies, gender studies, German area studies, history, international studies, philosophy, political science/government, prelaw, psychology, religion, and sociology). Biology, psychology, and economics have the largest enrollments.

ACTIVITIES: 39% of men belong to 4 national fraternities; 43% of women belong to 4 national sororities. There are 55 groups on campus, including art, chess, choir, chorale, chorus, dance, drama, environmental, ethnic, film, forensics, honors, international, jazz band, LGBT, literary magazine, musical theater, newspaper, opera, orchestra, photography, political, professional, radio and TV, religious, social, social service, student government, symphony, and yearbook. Popular campus events include Renaissance Fair, Choral Contest, Mr. Whitman, Arts & Crafts Fair, and Interest House Block Party. **Sports:** There are 7 intercollegiate sports for men and 8 for women, and 14 intramural sports for men and 13 for women. Facilities include a stadium, gyms, squash and handball courts, saunas, climbing walls, aerobic/dance room, athletics center with weights/cardiovascular area, 8-lane swimming pool, outdoor and indoor tennis courts, soccer field, dance studio, soccer, baseball, and track facilities. **Graduates:** From July 1, 2016 to June 30, 2017, 367 bachelor's degrees were awarded. The most popular majors were psychology (11%), biology (10%), biochemistry, biophysics, and molecular biology (9%). In an average class, 80% graduate in 4 years or less and 87% graduate in 5 years or less. Of the 2016 graduating class, 60% were enrolled in graduate school within 6 months of graduation.

SERVICES: Counseling and information services are available, as is tutoring in most subjects. There is a reader service for the blind. The Academic Resource Center and Learning Commons provides tutoring, academic assistance and workshops in study skills and writing. Department tutors are also available for students. **Library/Resources:** The library contains 627,812 volumes, and 32,433 audio/video tapes/CDs/DVDs, and subscribes to 98,012 periodicals including electronic. Computerized library services include interlibrary loans, database searching, Internet access, and Wi-Fi capability. Special learning facilities include an art gallery, natural history museum, planetarium, radio station, an electron microscope lab, a multimedia development lab, an observatory, astronomical telescopes, an Asian Art collection, a video-conferencing center, organic garden, and Penrose Library and Welty Student Health Center are open 24/7. **Physically Challenged Students:** 96% of the campus is accessible. Facilities include wheelchair ramps, elevators, special parking, specially equipped restrooms, lowered drinking fountains, lowered telephones, any other modifications necessary for a specific cases will be made. **Special:** Special academic programs include more than 500 internships, over 80 semester or year-long study abroad programs in 40 countries, a Washington semester, and study programs in Chicago and Philadelphia. Dual majors are available in any area, and student-designed majors are offered. There is a 3-2 environmental management and forestry program with Duke University and a 3-2 engineering program with Washington University in St. Louis, California Institute of Technology and Applied Science, Columbia and Duke Universities, and University of Washington. A 3-3 law program is offered through Columbia University. A 4-1 education program is available through Bank Street College of Education and University of Puget Sound Cooperative. Certification is offered for elementary and secondary education. A pass-D-fail option is available. A 3-2 program in international studies is available with the Monterey Institute of International Studies. A 3-2 program in oceanography is available with University of Washington. There are 3 national honor societies, Phi Beta Kappa, and a freshman honors program. **Visiting:** There are regularly scheduled orientations for prospective students, The agenda for visits are catered to each individual student and their interests. There are guides for informal visits, visitors may sit in on classes, and stay overnight. To schedule a visit, contact Mary Beth Ehrhardt at (509) 527-5176. **Campus Safety and Security:** Measures include 24-hour foot and vehicle patrol, emergency notification system, self-defense education, and security escort services. There are emergency telephones, lighted pathways/sidewalks, and controlled access to dorms/ residences.

REQUIREMENTS: Whitman is test-optional, we encourage applicants to decide for themselves whether they wish to submit ACT or SAT results as an additional measure of their academic preparedness. The GED is accepted. 3 essays must be submitted, and an interview is recommended. Credit by challenge examination is accepted. AP credits are accepted. Important factors in the admissions decision are advanced placement or honors courses, personality/intangible qualities, evidence of special talent, recommendations by alumni, recommendations by school officials, and extracurricular activities record. Students must complete 124 credits, with 32 to 36 in the major, and maintain a minimum GPA of 2.0. Distribution requirements include a minimum of 6 credits in social sciences, humanities, fine arts, and science (including 1 course with a lab), 1 course of 3 or more credits in quantitative analysis, and 2 courses that fulfill the alternative voices requirement. Freshman must take the year-long Encounters (great works) course. All majors require an oral exam as well as a thesis project or comprehensive written exam. **Procedure:** Freshmen are admitted in the fall. Entrance exams should be taken by fall of the senior year. There are early decision and deferred admissions plans. Early decision applications should be filed by November 15; regular applications, by January 15 for fall entry. The fall 2017 application fee was $50. Notification of early decision is sent December 20; regular decision, April 1. 123 early decision candidates were accepted for the 2017-2018 class. 872 applicants were on the 2017 waiting list; 67 were admitted. Applications are accepted on-line. **Transfer Students:** 20 transfer students enrolled in 2016-2017. Transfer applicants must submit the common application, a transfer supplement, a school report completed by the applicant's secondary school counselor, an academic recommendation from a high school teacher or college instructor, a statement of good standing from prior institutions, their official high school and college transcripts, and the application fee. SAT or ACT scores are optional. 54 of 124 credits required for the bachelor's degree must be completed at Whitman. **International Students:** There are 86 international students enrolled. They must take the TOEFL with a minimum score of 560 on the paper-based TOEFL (PBT) or 85 on the Internet-based version (iBT).

ADMISSIONS: 50% of the 2017-2018 applicants were accepted. The SAT scores for the 2017-2018 freshman class were: Critical Reading-- 4% below 500, 19% between 500 and 599, 44% between 600 and 699, and 34% between 700 and 800. Math-- 2% below 500, 19% between 500 and 599, 53% between 600 and 699, and 25% between 700 and 800. Writing-- 1% below 500, 23% between 500 and 599, 48% between 600 and 699, and 28% between 700 and 800. The ACT scores were 3% between 18 and 23, 40% between 24 and 29, and 57% above 30. 80% of the current freshmen were in the top fifth of their class; 96% were in the top two fifths. 25 freshmen graduated first in their class. **Admissions Contact:** Tony Cabasco, Dean of Admission and Financial Aid. Email: *admission@whitman.edu* Web: *www.whitman.edu*

FINANCIAL AID: In 2017-2018, 74% of all full-time freshmen received some form of financial aid. 42% of all full-time freshmen received need-based aid. The average freshman award was $32,500. Need-based scholarships or need-based grants averaged $29,148 ($59,050 maximum); need-based self-help aid (loans and jobs) averaged $7,819 ($9,000 maximum); and other non-need-based awards and non-need-based scholarships averaged $13,960 ($19,000 maximum). The average financial indebtedness of the 2017 graduate was $18,444. Whitman is a member of CSS. The CSS/Profile is required. The FAFSA code is 003803. The priority date for freshman financial aid applications for fall entry is November 15.

WHITWORTH UNIVERSITY E-2

www.whitworth.edu

Spokane, WA 99251 (509) 777-4348 (800) 533-4668

Fax: (509) 777-3758 **Email:** admission@whitworth.edu

Full-time: 878 men, 1314 women	**Faculty:** 144; IIB, -$
Part-time: 17 men, 18 women	**Ph.D.s:** 87%
Graduate: 140 men, 236 women	**Student/Faculty:** 11 to 1
Year: 4-1-4, summer session	**Tuition:** $42,186
Room & Board: $11,496	**Freshman Class:** 3166 applied, 2818 accepted, 505 enrolled
SAT or ACT: recommended	**CEEB CODE:** 4953
Application Deadline: March 1	**VERY COMPETITIVE**

Whitworth University, founded in 1890, is an independent, comprehensive institution affiliated with the Presbyterian Church. The emphasis of its undergraduate and graduate programs is on the liberal arts, business, art and fine arts, music, religious studies, and teacher preparation. There are 4 undergraduate schools and 3 graduate schools. In addition to regional accreditation, WU has baccalaureate program accreditation with NASM, NLN, Washington State Board of Nursing, CCNE, and CAATE. The 200-acre campus is in a suburban area in a residential area 7 miles north of downtown Spokane. Including any residence halls, there are 40 buildings.

STUDENT LIFE: 67% of undergraduates are from Washington. Others are from 26 states, 42 foreign countries, and Canada. 88% are from public schools. 70% are White; 9% Hispanic; 7% two or more races; 5% Asian American; 4% Foreign; 2% African American; 1% American Indian/Alaska Native; 1% race unknown. 64% are Protestant; 20% claim no religious affiliation. **Female To Male Ratio:** 1.5:1. The average age of freshmen is 18; all undergraduates, 20. 15% do not continue beyond their first year; 75% remain to graduate. **Housing:** 1356 students can be accommodated in college housing, which includes dorms. In addition, there are special-interest houses, and theme houses. On-campus housing is guaranteed for all 4 years. 50% of students commute. Alcohol is not permitted. All students may keep cars.

FACULTY/CLASSROOMS: 57% of faculty are male; 43% are female. All teach undergraduates. No introductory courses are taught by graduate students. The average class size in an introductory lecture is 30; in a laboratory is 15; and in a regular course is 19.

PROGRAMS OF STUDY: WU confers B.A., B.B.A., and B.S. degrees. Master's degrees are also awarded. Bachelor's degrees are awarded in BIOLOGICAL SCIENCE (bioinformatics, biology/biological science, and biophysics), BUSINESS (accounting, business administration and management, international business management, and marketing management), COMMUNICATIONS AND THE ARTS (art, communications, dramatic arts, English, French, journalism, music, Spanish, speech/ debate/rhetoric, theatre arts, and visual design), COMPUTER AND PHYSICAL SCIENCE (applied physics, chemistry, computer science, mathematics, mathematics – economics, physics, and quantitative methods), EDUCATION (athletic training, elementary education, English education, foreign languages education, mathematics education, music education, science education, secondary education, and social studies education), ENGINEERING AND ENVIRONMENTAL DESIGN (engineering and engineering physics), HEALTH PROFESSIONS (community health work, health science, nursing, predentistry, and premedicine), SOCIAL SCIENCE (American studies, crosscultural studies, economics, history, international studies, peace studies, philosophy, political science/government, prelaw, psychology, sociology, theological studies, and women's studies). Sciences, education, and music are the strongest academically. Health sciences, business, and math & computer science have the largest enrollments.

ACTIVITIES: There are no fraternities or sororities. There are 45 groups on campus, including art, band, cheerleading, choir, chorale, chorus, communications, computers, dance, debate, drama, environmental, ethnic, forensics, honors, international, jazz band, literary magazine, musical theater, newspaper, orchestra, photography, political, professional, radio and TV, religious, social, social service, student government, symphony, and yearbook. Popular campus events include Guest Speakers, Student Research Conference, and Community Building Day. **Sports:** There are 10 intercollegiate sports for men and 11 for women, and 10 intramural sports for men and 8 for women. Facilities include a recreation center complete with climbing walls, a stadium, gym, field house, an aquatic center, and playing fields. **Graduates:** From July 1, 2016 to June 30, 2017, 526 bachelor's degrees were awarded. The most popular majors were business/marketing (13%), interdisciplinary studies (10%), and education (10%). In an average class, 4% graduate in 3 years or less, 63% graduate in 4 years or less, 76% graduate in 5 years or less, and 75% graduate in 6 years or less. Of the 2016 graduating class, 30% were enrolled in graduate school within 6 months of graduation, and 86% were employed.

SERVICES: Counseling and information services are available, as is tutoring in most subjects. **Library/Resources:** The library contains 292,113 volumes, 1,112 microform items, and 9,412 audio/video tapes/CDs/DVDs, and subscribes to 36,517 periodicals including electronic. Computerized library services include interlibrary loans, database searching, Internet access, and Wi-Fi capability. Special learning facilities include an art gallery, radio station, a writing center. **Physically Challenged Students:** 80% of the campus is accessible. Facilities include wheelchair ramps, elevators, special parking, specially equipped restrooms, special class scheduling, lowered drinking fountains, and lowered telephones. **Special:** Special academic programs include many work-study opportunities, 1 to 3 internship course credits. Study abroad is available in many countries. Accelerated degree programs are possible, as is a 3-2 engineering degree, and students may choose to specialize in an area of concentration in lieu of a major. Credit may be granted for life, military, or work experience. Nondegree study is possible for those auditing or in seminars, and there is 1 pass/fail option allowed per year. A special feature of the school is the 4-1-1 semester calendar, which affords unusual opportunities for internships, study tours, and other activities during January term. There is a freshman honors program. **Visiting:** There are regularly scheduled orientations for prospective students. A visit includes an admissions/financial aid presentation, campus tour, class visit, student panel, lunch in the dining hall and overnight stay (if desired). To schedule a visit, contact Lara Ramsay at visitus@whitworth.edu. **Campus Safety and Security:** Measures include 24-hour foot and vehicle patrol, emergency notification system, and security escort services. There are emergency telephones, lighted pathways/sidewalks, and controlled access to dorms/residences.

REQUIREMENTS: Whitworth recommends a rigorous college-preparatory high school curriculum and also considers, in the admissions review process, participation in extra-curricular, service and leadership activities, a writing sample included in the application and counselor/teacher recommendations. Students have the option of submitting either SAT or ACT scores (no preference) or, if they have a weighted GPA of 3.0 or higher, can choose to do an admissions interview instead of submitting test scores. AP and CLEP credits are accepted. Important factors in the admissions decision are advanced placement or honors courses, recommendations by alumni, and extracurricular activities record. Students must complete 126 credit hours, with about 45 in the major, and maintain a GPA of at least 2.0. The curriculum includes 3 core courses on religious, rationalist, and scientific traditions. Distribution requirements are comprised of 3 phys ed activity courses, 2 each in a foreign language and science/math, and 1 course each in biblical literature, oral communication, fine arts, social science, and humanities. Additionally, global perspectives and an American diversity course must be fulfilled. **Procedure:** Freshmen are admitted fall, winter, and spring. Entrance exams should be taken by fall of senior year, but scores are accepted later. There are early admissions, deferred admissions, and rolling admissions plans. Early decision applications should be filed by November 15; regular applications, by March 1 for fall entry. Notification of early decision is sent December 15; regular decision, March 15. Applications are accepted on-line. **Transfer Students:** 93 transfer students enrolled in 2016-2017. Transfer students must have a GPA of at least 2.75. 32 of 126 credits required for the bachelor's degree must be completed at WU. **International Students:** There are 99 international students enrolled. They must take the TOEFL with a minimum score of 79 on the Internet-based version (iBT).

ADMISSIONS: 89% of the 2017-2018 applicants were accepted. The SAT scores for the 2017-2018 freshman class were: Math-- 12% below 500, 41% between 500 and 599, 39% between 600 and 699, and 8% between 700 and 800. Evidence-Based Reading/Writing-- 9% below 500, 34% between 500 and 599, 45% between 600 and 699, and 13% between 700 and 800. The ACT scores were 6% between 12 and 17, 26% between 18 and 23, 44% between 24 and 29, and 23% above 30. 61% of the current freshmen were in the top fifth of their class; 88% were in the top two fifths. **Admissions Contact:** Greg Orwig, Vice President, Admissions and Financial Aid. Email: *admission@whitworth.edu* Web: *www.whitworth.edu*

FINANCIAL AID: In 2017-2018, 99% of all full-time freshmen received some form of financial aid. 78% of all full-time freshmen received need-based aid. The average freshman award was $38,694. Need-based scholarships or need-based grants averaged $15,131 ($55,244 maximum); need-based self-help aid (loans and jobs) averaged $6,162 ($12,000 maximum); and other non-need-based awards and non-need-based scholarships averaged $20,099 ($50,300 maximum). 53% of undergraduate students work part-time. The average financial indebtedness of the 2017 graduate was $26,882. WU is a member of CSS. The FAFSA code is 003804. The priority date for freshman financial aid applications for fall entry is December 1.

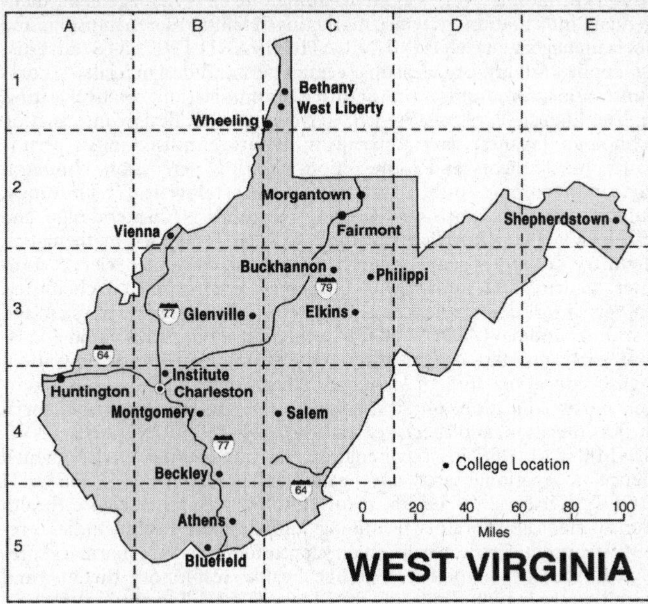

ALDERSON BROADDUS UNIVERSITY *(The complete profile is made available exclusively on our website, www.barronspac.com)*

BETHANY COLLEGE *(The complete profile is made available exclusively on our website, www.barronspac.com)*

BLUEFIELD STATE COLLEGE *(The complete profile is made available exclusively on our website, www.barronspac.com)*

CONCORD UNIVERSITY *(The complete profile is made available exclusively on our website, www.barronspac.com)*

DAVIS & ELKINS COLLEGE *(The complete profile is made available exclusively on our website, www.barronspac.com)*

FAIRMONT STATE UNIVERSITY C-2

www.fairmontstate.edu

Fairmont, WV 26554 **(304) 367-4892**
(800) 641-5678
Fax: (304) 367-4789 **Email: admit@fairmontstate.edu**

Full-time: 1489 men, 1744 women	**Faculty:** n/av
Part-time: 156 men, 309 women	**Ph.D.s:** 65%
Graduate: 73 men, 161 women	**Student/Faculty:** 15 to 1
Year: semesters, summer session	**Tuition:** $6950 ($14,666)
Room & Board: $8776	**Freshman Class:** 2943 applied, 1930 accepted, 826 enrolled
SAT: required **ACT:** 21	**CEEB CODE:** 5211
Application Deadline: August 15	**COMPETITIVE**

Fairmont State University, founded in 1865, is a student centered institution of first choice among students who desire a flexible and relevant learning experience. There are 6 undergraduate schools and 4 graduate schools. In addition to regional accreditation, Fairmont has baccalaureate program accreditation with ABET, ACBSP, CAEP, NLN, IACBE, and ACEN. The 120-acre campus is in a small town 75 miles south of Pittsburgh, 135 miles north of Charleston WV, and 218 miles west of Washington DC. Including any residence halls, there are 20 buildings.

STUDENT LIFE: 91% of undergraduates are from West Virginia. Others are from 24 states, and 19 foreign countries. 98% are from public schools. 90% are White; 4% African American; 2% Foreign; 1% Asian American; 1% Hispanic. **Female To Male Ratio:** 1.3:1. The average age of freshmen is 19; all undergraduates, 23. 34% do not continue beyond their first year; 67% remain to graduate. **Housing:** 1189 students can be accommodated in college housing, which includes dorms and on-campus apartments. On-campus housing is guaranteed for the freshman year only, and is available on a first-come, first-served basis. 76% of students commute. Alcohol is not permitted. All students may keep cars.

FACULTY/CLASSROOMS: 49% of faculty are male; 51% are female. All teach undergraduates. No introductory courses are taught by graduate students. The average class size in an introductory lecture is 35; in a laboratory is 20; and in a regular course is 30.

PROGRAMS OF STUDY: Fairmont confers B.A., B.S., B.S.E.T. and B.S.N. degrees. Associate and master's degrees are also awarded. Bachelor's degrees are awarded in BIOLOGICAL SCIENCE (biology/biological science), BUSINESS (accounting, business administration and management, and marketing/retailing/merchandising), COMMUNICATIONS AND THE ARTS (communications, English, graphic design, Spanish, speech/debate/rhetoric, and theatre acting), COMPUTER AND PHYSICAL SCIENCE (chemistry, computer science, and mathematics), EDUCATION (art education, early childhood education, elementary education, foreign languages education, health education, middle school education, music education, science education, and secondary education), ENGINEERING AND ENVIRONMENTAL DESIGN (architectural technology, architecture, civil engineering technology, electrical/electronics engineering technology, engineering technology, mechanical engineering technology, and occupational safety and health), HEALTH PROFESSIONS (nursing and predentistry), SOCIAL SCIENCE (criminal justice, forensic studies, history, political science/government, psychology, and sociology). Nursing, and education are the strongest academically. Business, health careers, and criminal justice have the largest enrollments.

ACTIVITIES: 4% of women belong to 1 local and 2 national sororities. There are 80 groups on campus, including art, band, cheerleading, chess, choir, chorus, computers, debate, drama, honors, international, jazz band, LGBT, literary magazine, marching band, musical theater, newspaper, photography, political, professional, religious, social, student government, symphony, and yearbook. Popular campus events include Multicultural Events. **Sports:** There are 7 intercollegiate sports for men and 9 for women, and 24 intramural sports for men and 24 for women. Facilities include a phys ed center, a stadium, a basketball arena, and playing fields. **Graduates:** From July 1, 2016 to June 30, 2017, 602 bachelor's degrees were awarded. The most popular majors were engineering technologies (12%), homeland security (11%), education, and and health professions and related programs (10%). In an average class, 29% graduate in 6 years or less. Of the 2016 graduating class, 18% were enrolled in graduate school within 6 months of graduation, and 80% were employed.

SERVICES: Counseling and information services are available, as is tutoring in most subjects. There is a reader service for the blind, and remedial math, reading, and writing. **Library/Resources:** The library contains 275,000 volumes, 54,241 microform items, 12,000 audio/video tapes/CDs/DVDs, and subscribes to 1,175 periodicals including electronic. Computerized library services include interlibrary loans, database searching, Internet access, and Wi-Fi capability. Special learning facilities include an art gallery. **Physically Challenged Students:** All of the campus is accessible. Facilities include wheelchair ramps, elevators, special parking, specially equipped restrooms, special class scheduling, lowered drinking fountains, lowered telephones, and special housing. **Special:** The college offers internships in teacher education, retailing, and psychology, and awards a B.S. degree in chemistry/math. There are 4 national honor societies, a freshman honors program, and 4 departmental honors programs. **Visiting:** There are regularly scheduled orientations for prospective students. There are guides for informal visits and visitors may sit in on classes. To schedule a visit, contact the Office of Admissions. **Campus Safety and Security:** Measures include 24-hour foot and vehicle patrol and emergency notification system. There are emergency telephones, lighted pathways/sidewalks, and controlled access to dorms/residences.

REQUIREMENTS: Students must be high school graduates or completed GED requirements fewer than 5 years prior to seeking admission. A satisfactory score is required on the SAT or 17 on the ACT. The college requires 4 credits each in English and math (algebra I and at least 1 higher), 3 in science of those 2 lab science, 2 in foreign language, and social studies (1 in U.S. history), and 8 academic electives. AP and CLEP credits are accepted. To graduate, students must complete 128 hours with a GPA of 2.0. (2.5 in education specializations). They must also complete 50 core curriculum hours for the B.S. or B.A. degree. All students must take 2 hours of phys ed. A course and distribution requirements vary according to the program. **Procedure:** Freshmen are admitted in the fall, spring, and summer. Entrance exams should be taken during the fall of the senior year. There is a rolling admissions plan. Applications should be filed by August 15 for fall entry. Applications are accepted on-line. **Transfer Students:** 359 transfer students enrolled in 2016-2017. Applicants must have a GPA of 2.0. The ACT is required for applicants with fewer than 30 college credits. Students may enroll in the fall, spring, and summer. 60 of 128 credits required for the bachelor's degree must be completed at Fairmont. **International Students:** There are 69 international students enrolled. They must take the TOEFL. If ACT or SAT scores are not supplied, the ACT must be taken upon arrival on campus.

ADMISSIONS: 66% of the 2017-2018 applicants were accepted. The ACT scores were 18% between 12 and 17, 60% between 18 and 23, 21% between 24 and 29, and 1% above 30. **Admissions Contact:** Amie Fazalare, Admissions Director. Email: *admit@fairmontstate.edu* Web: *www.fairmontstate.edu*

FINANCIAL AID: The average freshman award was $8,985. Need-based scholarships or need-based grants averaged $6,596; need-based self-help aid (loans and jobs) averaged $3,049; non-need-based athletic scholarships averaged $5,315; other non-need-based awards and non-need-based scholarships averaged $3,015; and $6,272 from other forms of aid. The average financial indebtedness of the 2017 graduate was $10,840. Fairmont is a member of CSS. The FAFSA code is 003812. The priority date for freshman financial aid applications for fall entry is March 1.

GLENVILLE STATE COLLEGE *(The complete profile is made available exclusively on our website, www.barronspac.com)*

MARSHALL UNIVERSITY — A-4

www.marshall.edu

Huntington, WV 25755 — (304) 696-3170, (800) 642-3499

Fax: (304) 696-3135	**Email:** admissions@marshall.edu
Full-time: 3413 men, 4454 women	**Faculty:** IIA, --$
Part-time: 595 men, 1030 women	**Ph.D.s:** 83%
Graduate: 1014 men, 1781 women	**Student/Faculty:** 21 to 1
Year: semesters, summer session	**Tuition:** $7918 ($17,976)
Room & Board: $10,126	**Freshman Class:** n/av
SAT or ACT: required	**CEEB CODE:** 5396
Application Deadline: n/av	**COMPETITIVE**

Marshall University, founded in 1837, is a comprehensive institution that provides a diverse in-depth real-world learning environment. There are 9 undergraduate schools and 3 graduate schools. In addition to regional accreditation, Marshall has baccalaureate program accreditation with AACSB, ABET, ACEJMC, CSWE, NASM, NRPA, JRCERT, ACEND, and NAACLS. The 100-acre campus is in an urban area in Huntington, West Virginia, which is 126 miles east of Lexington, Kentucky, and 50 miles west of Charleston, West Virginia. Including any residence halls, there are 53 buildings.

STUDENT LIFE: 81% of undergraduates are from West Virginia. Others are from 49 states, 56 foreign countries, and Canada. 78% are White; 6% race unknown; 5% African American; 4% Foreign; 2% Hispanic; 2% two or more races; 1% Asian American. **Female To Male Ratio:** 1.4:1. The average age of freshmen is 19; all undergraduates, 21.7. **Housing:** 2499 students can be accommodated in college housing, which includes single sex dorms, coed dorms, living learning communities, honors floors, and freshman interest groups. On-campus housing is available on a first-come, first-served basis. Alcohol is not permitted. All students may keep cars.

FACULTY/CLASSROOMS: 56% of faculty are male; 44% are female. No introductory courses are taught by graduate students. The average class size in a regular course is 22.

PROGRAMS OF STUDY: Marshall confers B.A., B.B.A., B.F.A., B.S., B.S.E., B.S.E.E., B.S.M.E., B.S.W., and R.B.A. degrees. Associate, master's, and doctoral degrees are also awarded. Bachelor's degrees are awarded in AGRICULTURE (natural resource management), BIOLOGICAL SCIENCE (anatomy, biochemistry, biology/biological science, biotechnology, cell biology, ecology, evolutionary biology, molecular biology, and nutrition), BUSINESS (accounting, banking and finance, business economics, finance, international business management, management information systems, marketing/retailing/merchandising, and sports management), COMMUNICATIONS AND THE ARTS (advertising, applied art, art, broadcasting, ceramic art and design, classics, communications, communication rhetoric/communication, creative writing, English, English literature, French, German, graphic design, information technology, Japanese, jazz, journalism, literature, music, music performance, music theory and composition, painting, percussion, photography, piano/organ, public relations, radio/television technology, sculpture, Spanish, sports media, strings, theatre arts, theater design, and voice), COMPUTER AND PHYSICAL SCIENCE (applied mathematics, chemistry, computer game design/development, computer science, computer security and information assurance, environmental chemistry, geology, information sciences and systems, mathematics, physics, and science technology), EDUCATION (athletic training, childhood education, early childhood education, education, elementary education, English education, foreign languages education, middle school education, music education, physical education, secondary education, social studies education, and special education), ENGINEERING AND ENVIRONMENTAL DESIGN (civil engineering, engineering, environmental science, occupational safety and health, and preengineering), HEALTH PROFESSIONS (allied health, cytotechnology, exercise science, health science, medical laboratory technology, nursing, pre-health studies, predentistry, premedicine, preoptometry, preosteopathy, prepharmacy, prephysical therapy, prepodiatry, public health, respiratory therapy, and speech pathology/audiology), SOCIAL SCIENCE (criminal justice, dietetics, economics, forensic studies, geography, history, humanities, international relations, parks and recreation management, philosophy, physical fitness/movement, political science/government, prelaw, psychology, safety and security technology, safety management, social work, sociology, and women's studies). Nursing, biological science, education elemantary & secondary have the largest enrollments.

ACTIVITIES: There are 200 groups on campus, including art, band, cheerleading, choir, chorale, chorus, communications, computers, dance, debate, drama, environmental, ethnic, forensics, honors, international, jazz band, LGBT, literary magazine, marching band, musical theater, newspaper, opera, orchestra, pep band, photography, political, professional, radio and TV, religious, social, social service, student government, symphony, and yearbook. Popular campus events include Week of Welcome, Parents Weekend, Homecoming, Springfest, and International Festival. **Sports:** There are 6 intercollegiate sports for men and 10 for women, and 9 intramural sports for men and 9 for women. Facilities include a basketball arena, a football stadium, tennis courts, a softball field, an Olympic-size pool, auxiliary gym, health and fitness center, racquetball courts, basketball courts, and human performance enhancement lab. **Graduates:** From July 1, 2016 to June 30, 2017, 1457 bachelor's degrees were awarded. The most popular majors were regents (12%), nursing (8%), and management (6%). In an average class, 45% graduate in 6 years or less.

SERVICES: Counseling and information services are available, as is tutoring in most subjects. There is a reader service for the blind, and remedial math, reading, and writing. There are also study skills courses and other services for students with disabilities. **Library/Resources:** The library contains 2.2 million volumes, 1.0 million microform items, 43,449 audio/video tapes/CDs/DVDs, and subscribes to 45,508 periodicals including electronic. Computerized library services include interlibrary loans, database searching, Internet access, and Wi-Fi capability. Special learning facilities include an art gallery, natural history museum, radio station, TV station, and a greenhouse. **Physically Challenged Students:** All of the campus is accessible. Facilities include wheelchair ramps, elevators, special parking, specially equipped restrooms, special class scheduling, lowered drinking fountains, lowered telephones, special housing, and attendant care program. **Special:** Many programs require or offer internships. Work-study opportunities are available on campus. Students participate in student exchange and study abroad programs. B.A.-B.S. degrees, dual majors and minors, nondegree study, credit for life experience, and credit/no-credit options are available. There are 20 national honor societies and a freshman honors program. **Visiting:** There are regularly scheduled orientations for prospective students. There are guides for informal visits, visitors may sit in on classes, and stay overnight. To schedule a visit, contact the Office of Admissions. **Campus Safety and Security:** Measures include 24-hour foot and vehicle patrol, emergency notification system, self-defense education, and security escort services. There are emergency telephones, lighted pathways/sidewalks, and controlled access to dorms/residences.

REQUIREMENTS: General freshman admission is open to all applicants with a high school diploma, with an overall GPA of 2.0 on a 4.0 scale, an ACT Composite score of 19 or SAT total score of 980 or an overall GPA of 3.0 on a 4.0 scale. An ACT Composite of 16 or SAT Total Score of 860 is required for regular freshman admission. High school equivalency diploma exams (GED, HiSET, TASC) are also considered with scores acceptable for admission. Majors within the College of Information Technology and Engineering have additional requirements for admission. Please consult the current undergraduate academic catalog for specific information regarding requirements. The following high school units are recommended for admission: 4 units each of English (including English 12CR and courses in grammar, composition, and literature) and mathematics (three units must be Algebra I and higher or Math I or higher; Transitional Math for Seniors will also be accepted). Courses designed as "support courses" such as Math I Lab or Math I Support, that provide extra instructional time but no additional content, shall not be acceptable as meeting the required 4 mathematics course core requirements, 3 units each of social studies (including U.S. studies/ history), and science (all units must be college-preparatory laboratory science, preferably including units from biology, chemistry, and physics), and 2 units of world language (two units of the same world language; sign language is also acceptable), and 1 unit of arts. A GPA of 2.0 is required. AP and CLEP credits are accepted. Marshall utilizes a core curriculum that applies through all colleges and majors and incorporates critical thinking, multicultural, writing intensive, and international components. Most degrees require 120 for graduation. Overall and major-specific GPAs vary with degrees. **Procedure:** Freshmen are admitted to all sessions. Entrance exams should be taken during the junior year or early in the senior year. There is a rolling admissions plan. Check with the school for current application deadlines. The fall 2017 application fee was $40. Notification is sent on a rolling basis. Applications are accepted on-line. **Transfer Students:** 835 transfer students enrolled in 2016-2017. All transfer students must be eligible to return to the institution they most recently attended. Students who have fewer than 30 earned semester hours must meet the current freshman admission standards, or have earned 12 graded college-level semester hours while maintaining a 2.00 cumulative college GPA. 24 of 120 credits required for the bachelor's degree must be completed at Marshall. **International Students:** There are 167 international students enrolled. They must take the TOEFL with a minimum score of 547 on the paper-based TOEFL (PBT) or 78 on the Internet-based version (iBT) or take either the MELAB or IELTS.

ADMISSIONS: The ACT scores were 10% between 12 and 17, 55% between 18 and 23, 30% between 24 and 29, and 5% above 30. **Admissions Contact:** Dr. Tammy R. Johnson, Admissions. Email: *admissions@marshall.edu* Web: *www.marshall.edu*

FINANCIAL AID: In 2017-2018, 96% of all full-time freshmen received some form of financial aid. 80% of all full-time freshmen received need-based aid. The average freshman award was $14,404. Need-based scholarships or need-based grants averaged $6,928 ($19,229 maximum); need-based self-help aid (loans and jobs) averaged $5,542 ($14,500 maximum); non-need-based athletic scholarships averaged $13,330 ($29,402 maximum); and other non-need-based awards and non-need-based scholarships averaged $7,271 ($30,340 maximum). 3% of undergraduate students work part-time. The average financial indebtedness of the 2017 graduate was $28,095. Marshall is a member of CSS. The FAFSA code is 003815. The deadline for filing freshman financial aid applications for fall entry is March 1.

OHIO VALLEY UNIVERSITY B-2

www.ovu.edu

Vienna, WV 26105	(304) 865-6202
Fax: (304) 865-6175	**Email:** admissions@ovu.edu
Full-time: 250 men, 275 women	**Faculty:** 21; IIB
Part-time: 12 men, 22 women	**Ph.D.s:** 75%
Graduate: n/av	**Student/Faculty:** 18 to 1
Year: semesters, summer session	**Tuition:** $21,100
Room & Board: $7700	**Freshman Class:** 304 applied, 170 accepted, 85 enrolled
ACT: 23	**CEEB CODE:** 5519
Application Deadline: August 15	**COMPETITIVE**

Ohio Valley University, founded in 1960, is a liberal arts institution affiliated with the Church of Christ, offering 36 degrees along with myraid minors. The figures given in the above capsule and in this profile are approximate. There are 4 undergraduate schools and 1 graduate school. In addition to regional accreditation, OVU has baccalaureate program accreditation with IACBE, AACRAO, ACA, ASCD, and NCAA. The 266-acre campus is in a suburban area in Vienna, West Virginia. Including any residence halls, there are 9 buildings.

STUDENT LIFE: 65% of undergraduates are from out of state, mostly the Midwest. Students are from 28 states, 13 foreign countries, and Canada. 97% are from public schools. 88% are White; 6% Foreign; 4% African American; 1% Asian American; 1% Hispanic. 97% are Protestant. **Female To Male Ratio:** 1.1:1. The average age of freshmen is 18; all undergraduates, 22. 26% do not continue beyond their first year; 35% remain to graduate. **Housing:** 500 students can be accommodated in college housing, which includes married student dorms and on-campus apartments. On-campus housing is guaranteed for all 4 years. 55% of students live on campus. Alcohol is not permitted. All students may keep cars.

FACULTY/CLASSROOMS: 68% of faculty are male; 32% are female. All teach undergraduates. No introductory courses are taught by graduate students. The average class size in an introductory lecture is 30; in a laboratory is 20; and in a regular course is 15.

PROGRAMS OF STUDY: OVU confers B.A. and B.S. degrees. Associate degrees are also awarded. Bachelor's degrees are awarded in BIOLOGICAL SCIENCE (biochemistry), BUSINESS (accounting, business administration and management, organizational leadership and management, and sports management), COMMUNICATIONS AND THE ARTS (English), COMPUTER AND PHYSICAL SCIENCE (computer information technology and mathematics), EDUCATION (elementary education, English education, health education, mathematics education, and science education), HEALTH PROFESSIONS (biology and health), SOCIAL SCIENCE (biblical studies, criminal justice, history, humanities, interdisciplinary studies, psychology, and sociology). Business is the strongest academically. Elementary education, psychology, and business administration have the largest enrollments.

ACTIVITIES: There are no fraternities or sororities. There are 16 groups on campus, including Women for Christ, band, cheerleading, choir, chorale, chorus, communications, diversity club, drama, jazz band, newspaper, pep band, religious, social, and student government. Popular campus events include Expressions, and a Schoolwide Musical Review. **Sports:** There are 5 intercollegiate sports for men and 4 for women, and 11 intramural sports for men and 10 for women. Facilities include a weight room, a recreation facility and activity center, 2 gyms, baseball, basketball, cross country, golf, soccer, lacrosse, softball, and wrestling. **Graduates:** From July 1, 2016 to June 30, 2017, 101 bachelor's degrees were awarded. The most popular majors were business (46%), education (25%), and psychology (16%). In an average class, 18% graduate in 4 years or less, 35% graduate in 5 years or less, and 27% graduate in 6 years or less.

SERVICES: Counseling and information services are available, as is tutoring in most subjects. There is remedial math, reading, and writing. **Library/Resources:** The library contains 31,750 volumes, 51,530 microform items, 2,946 audio/video tapes/CDs/DVDs, and subscribes to 165 periodicals including electronic. Computerized library services include interlibrary loans, database searching, Internet access, and Wi-Fi capability. **Physically Challenged Students:** 30% of the campus is accessible. Facilities include wheelchair ramps, elevators, special parking, specially equipped restrooms, special class scheduling, and lowered telephones. **Special:** Ohio Valley offers internships with churches for student ministers. Study abroad programs are frequently offered in England, France and Italy. OVU is also affiliated with the Washington Center for Internships and Academic Seminars. There is 1 national honor society and 1 departmental honors program. **Visiting:** There are guides for informal visits, visitors may sit in on classes, and stay overnight. To schedule a visit, contact the Office of Admissions. **Campus Safety and Security:** Measures include 24-hour foot and vehicle patrol.

REQUIREMENTS: The ACT is required. Applicants should be graduates of an accredited secondary school or have earned a GED. Ohio Valley requires applicants to be in the upper 50% of their class. AP and CLEP credits are accepted. Important factors in the admissions decision are recommendations by school officials, personality/intangible qualities, and leadership record. To graduate, students must complete 128 credit hours, including 53 to 60 in the major, with a minimum GPA of 2.0. General requirements include 4 courses of Bible studies, 2 of English composition, 1 to 2 of history, and 1 each of speech, computer literacy, math, and social science. There is also a phys ed requirement. Students must attend chapel daily and take 1 Bible class each semester. **Procedure:** Freshmen are admitted in the fall and spring. Entrance exams should be taken during the senior year. There are early admissions and rolling admissions plans. Applications should be filed by August 15 for fall entry. Notification is sent on a rolling basis. **Transfer Students:** Transfer applicants must provide high school, college, and financial aid transcripts, and test scores. 32 of 128 credits required for the bachelor's degree must be completed at OVU. **International Students:** There are 33 international students enrolled. They must take the TOEFL with a minimum score of 500 on the paper-based TOEFL (PBT) or 61 on the Internet-based version (iBT). They must also take the SAT or ACT, scoring 18.

ADMISSIONS: 56% of the 2017-2018 applicants were accepted. The ACT scores were 75% below 12, 25% between 12 and 17, 9% between 18 and 23, 3% between 24 and 29, and 2% above 30. 10% of the current freshmen were in the top fifth of their class; 32% were in the top two fifths. 10 freshmen graduated first in their class. **Admissions Contact:** Rob E. Dudley, Director of Admissions. Email: *admissions@ovu.edu* Web: *www.ovu.edu*

FINANCIAL AID: In 2017-2018, 95% of all full-time freshmen received some form of financial aid. 70% of all full-time freshmen received need-based aid. The average freshman award was $9,768. Need-based scholarships or need-based grants averaged $7,219; need-based self-help aid (loans and jobs) averaged $3,248 ($5,500 maximum); non-need-based athletic scholarships averaged $5,442 ($16,796 maximum); and other non-need-based awards and non-need-based scholarships averaged $7,732 ($15,000 maximum). 44% of undergraduate students work part-time. The average financial indebtedness of the 2017 graduate was $9,035. OVU is a member of CSS. The FAFSA code is 003819. The priority date for freshman financial aid applications for fall entry is February 14.

SALEM INTERNATIONAL UNIVERSITY C-4

www.salemu.edu

Salem, WV 26426	**(304) 782-5336** **(800) 283-4562**
Fax: (304) 782-5592	**Email: admissions@salemu.edu**
Full-time: 284 men, 284 women	**Faculty:** 26
Part-time: n/av	**Ph.D.s:** 88%
Graduate: 121 men, 122 women	**Student/Faculty:** 13 to 1
Year: other, summer session	**Tuition:** $14,690
Room & Board: $6520	**Freshman Class:** n/av
SAT: required **ACT:** 21	**CEEB CODE:** 5608
Application Deadline: open	**COMPETITIVE**

Salem International University, founded in 1888, is a private institution offering oriented degree programs, including international business, education, criminal justice, nursing, and computer science/information technology. There are 3 undergraduate schools and 2 graduate schools. In addition to regional accreditation, SIU has baccalaureate program accreditation with ACBSP and CAEP. The 300-acre campus is in a rural area 120 miles south of Pittsburgh, Pennsylvania. Including any residence halls, there are 19 buildings.

STUDENT LIFE: 69% of undergraduates are from out of state, mostly the Middle Atlantic. Students are from 34 states, 26 foreign countries, and Canada. 9% are African American; 53% White; 22% Foreign; 2% Hispanic; 1% Asian American; 1% American Indian/Alaska Native. **Female To Male Ratio:** 1.0:1. The average age of freshmen is 19; all undergraduates, 21. 37% do not continue beyond their first year; 51% remain to graduate. **Housing:** 454 students can be accommodated in college housing, which includes dorms. In addition, there are honors houses and special-interest houses. On-campus housing is guaranteed for all 4 years. 90% of students live on campus. All students may keep cars.

FACULTY/CLASSROOMS: 54% of faculty are male; 46% are female. All teach undergraduates and do research. No introductory courses are taught by graduate students. The average class size in an introductory lecture is 25; in a laboratory is 10; and in a regular course is 14.

PROGRAMS OF STUDY: SIU confers B.A. and B.S. degrees. Associate and master's degrees are also awarded. Bachelor's degrees are awarded in AGRICULTURE (equine science), BIOLOGICAL SCIENCE (biology/biological science and molecular biology), BUSINESS (business administration and management and sports management), COMMUNICATIONS AND THE ARTS (communications and English as a second/foreign language), COMPUTER AND PHYSICAL SCIENCE (computer mathematics and information sciences and systems), EDUCATION (athletic training, elementary education, and secondary education), ENGINEERING AND ENVIRONMENTAL DESIGN (aviation administration/management and environmental science), SOCIAL SCIENCE (criminal justice, human services, Japanese studies, and liberal arts/general studies). Molecular biology, and Japanese studies are the strongest academically. Management studies, equine, and criminal justice have the largest enrollments.

ACTIVITIES: 10% of men belong to 2 local fraternities; 12% of women belong to 3 local sororities. There are 25 groups on campus, including cheerleading, ethnic, honors, international, LGBT, newspaper, professional, radio and TV, religious, social, social service, student government, and yearbook. Popular campus events include Winterfest, Spring Arts Series, and Spring Fling. **Sports:** There are 6 intercollegiate sports for men and 6 for women, and 12 intramural sports for men and 12 for women. Facilities include a gym, swimming pool, weight room, tennis courts, a soccer stadium, fitness trail, racquetball courts, track and field, bowling, softball, basketball, baseball and horseback-riding trails. **Graduates:** From July 1, 2016 to June 30, 2017, 93 bachelor's degrees were awarded. The most popular majors were criminal justice (14%), equine (9%), and molecular bio/biotechnology (6%). In an average class, 32% graduate in 4 years or less and 47% graduate in 6 years or less.

SERVICES: Counseling and information services are available, with most classes have a tutoring option. There is a reader service for the blind, and remedial math, reading, and writing. **Library/Resources:** The library contains 66,000 volumes, 284,302 microform items, 974 audio/video tapes/CDs/DVDs, and subscribes to 94 periodicals including electronic. Computerized library services include interlibrary loans, database searching, Internet access, and Wi-Fi capability. Special learning facilities include a radio station. **Physically Challenged Students:** 90% of the campus is accessible. Facilities include wheelchair ramps, elevators, special parking, specially equipped restrooms, special class scheduling. **Special:** A student may cross-register with another college within the Mountain State Association of Colleges. Many internships are available. Study abroad is offered. Dual majors, credit by exam, and credit for life experience may be arranged. There are 2 national honor societies. **Visiting:** There are regularly scheduled orientations for prospective students, consisting of meetings with academic and administrative department heads, tours, question-and-answer sessions, and a reception. Visitors may sit in on classes, and stay overnight. To schedule a visit, contact the Admissions Office. **Campus Safety and Security:** Measures include 24-hour foot and vehicle patrol and security escort services. There are emergency telephones, lighted pathways/sidewalks, and dial-a-ride on weekends.

REQUIREMENTS: The SAT or ACT is required. Applicants should be graduates of an accredited secondary school with 15 academic courses, including 4 in English, 3 each in math, science, and social studies, and 2 in a foreign language. AP and CLEP credits are accepted. Important factors in the admissions decision are advanced placement or honors courses, evidence of special talent, and extracurricular activities record. All students must take 24 credits of international business in the core curriculum, including communication skills, humanities, science/math, social studies, psychology, and health and phys ed. A minimum 2.0 GPA overall, with a minimum 2.25 GPA in the major, and 128 credit hours are required to graduate. **Procedure:** Freshmen are admitted to all sessions. Entrance exams should be taken in the junior year or fall of the senior year. There are deferred admissions and rolling admissions plans. Application deadlines are open. The fall 2017 application fee was $25. Notification is sent on a rolling basis. Applications are accepted on-line. **Transfer Students:** 43 transfer students enrolled in 2016-2017. A minimum GPA of 2.0 is required for acceptance as a transfer student. 32 of 128 credits required for the bachelor's degree must be completed at SIU. **International Students:** There are 77 international students enrolled. They must take the TOEFL.

ADMISSIONS: The ACT scores were 51% below 12, 29% between 12 and 17, 18% between 18 and 23, and 2% between 24 and 29. 11% of the current freshmen were in the top fifth of their class; 18% were in the top two fifths. **Admissions Contact:** Todd Breland, Director of Admissions. Email: *admissions@salemu.edu* Web: *www.salemu.edu*

FINANCIAL AID: In 2017-2018, 99% of all full-time freshmen received some form of financial aid and need-based aid. The average freshman award was $17,579. Need-based scholarships or need-based grants averaged $6,912 ($12,662 maximum); need-based self-help aid (loans and jobs) averaged $5,430 ($11,290 maximum); non-need-based athletic scholarships averaged $5,213 ($10,085 maximum); and other non-need-based awards and non-need-based scholarships averaged $8,815 ($19,219 maximum). 34% of undergraduate students work part-time. The average financial indebtedness of the 2017 graduate was $18,228. SIU is a member of CSS. The FAFSA code is 003820. The deadline for filing freshman financial aid applications for fall entry is July 15.

SHEPHERD UNIVERSITY, WEST VIRGINIA E-2
www.shepherd.edu

Shepherdstown, WV 25443 (304) 876-5212 (800) 344-5231
Fax: (304) 876-5165 **Email: admission@shepherd.edu**

Full-time: 1089 men, 1525 women	**Faculty:** 130; IIA, --$
Part-time: 399 men, 408 women	**Ph.D.s:** 91%
Graduate: 88 men, 227 women	**Student/Faculty:** 20 to 1
Year: semesters, summer session	**Tuition:** $7328 ($17,873)
Room & Board: $10,054	**Freshman Class:** 1573 applied, 1402 accepted, 598 enrolled
SAT EBR-W/M: 540/520 **ACT:** 21	**CEEB CODE:** 5615
Application Deadline: n/av	**COMPETITIVE**

Shepherd University, West Virginia, founded in 1871, is a state-supported institution offering programs in the liberal and creative arts, business administration, teacher education, social and natural sciences, health fields, and other career-oriented areas. There are 4 undergraduate schools and 1 graduate school. In addition to regional accreditation, SUWV has baccalaureate program accreditation with CSWE, NASAD, NASM, CAEP, CCNE, WVBOERN, IACBE, and COAPRT. The 323-acre campus is in a small town 70 miles northwest of Washington, D.C. and Baltimore. Including any residence halls, there are 52 buildings.

STUDENT LIFE: 60% of undergraduates are from West Virginia. Others are from 50 states, and 14 foreign countries. 94% are from public schools. 80% are White; 7% African American; 4% Hispanic; 3% two or more races; 2% Asian American; 2% race unknown; 1% American Indian/Alaska Native; 1% Foreign. **Female To Male Ratio:** 1.4:1. The average age of freshmen is 18; all undergraduates, 23. 35% do not continue beyond their first year; 42% remain to graduate. **Housing:** 1225 students can be accommodated in college housing, which includes gender neutral, single sex, coed dorms, and on-campus apartments. In addition, there are honors houses, special-interest houses, and Trio housing. On-campus housing is guaranteed for all 4 years. 67% of students commute. All students may keep cars.

FACULTY/CLASSROOMS: 48% of faculty are male; 52% are female. 94% teach undergraduates. No introductory courses are taught by graduate students. The average class size in an introductory lecture is 21; in a laboratory is 18; and in a regular course is 13.

PROGRAMS OF STUDY: SUWV confers B.A., B.S., B.F.A., B.M.E., B.S.N., B.S.W., B.M.P., and R.B.A. degrees. Master's and doctoral degrees are also awarded. Bachelor's degrees are awarded in AGRICULTURE (environmental studies), BIOLOGICAL SCIENCE (biology/biological science), BUSINESS (accounting, business administration and management, and recreation and leisure services), COMMUNICATIONS AND THE ARTS (art, communications, English, music, Spanish, and theatre studies), COMPUTER AND PHYSICAL SCIENCE (chemistry, computer science, information sciences and systems, mathematics, and mathematics/computational), EDUCATION (art education, elementary education, English education, global studies, health education, home economics education, mathematics education, music education, physical education, science education, secondary education, and social studies education), ENGINEERING AND ENVIRONMENTAL DESIGN (computer engineering, computer technology, and engineering science), HEALTH PROFESSIONS (nursing), SOCIAL SCIENCE (economics, family/consumer studies, history, political science/government, psychology, social work, and sociology). Biology, business, education, nursing, and political science are the strongest academically. Nursing, business, and recreation and sport studies have the largest enrollments.

ACTIVITIES: 3% of men belong to 5 national fraternities; 4% of women belong to 3 national sororities. There are 87 groups on campus, including art, band, cheerleading, choir, chorale, chorus, computers, dance, debate, drama, environmental, ethnic, honors, international, jazz band, LGBT, literary magazine, marching band, musical theater, newspaper, opera, orchestra, political, professional, radio and TV, religious, social, social service, student government, and symphony. Popular campus events include Family Day, Midnight Breakfast, Appalachian Heritage Festival, Appalachian Writer in Residence, Glow Rage, Homecoming Spirit Week, and Relay for Life. **Sports:** There are 6 intercollegiate sports for men and 6 for women, and 6 intramural sports for men and 6 for women. Facilities include a football and lacrosse field, soccer fields, softball and baseball fields, a gym, outdoor and indoor tennis courts, outdoor sand volleyball courts, a fitness/wellness center with a basketball court, racquetball courts, 1/10 of a mile indoor track, cardio area, free weight area, exercise studio, and an 8-lane/25-yard indoor swimming pool. **Graduates:** From July 1, 2016 to June 30, 2017, 762 bachelor's degrees were awarded. The most popular majors were regents bachelor of arts (17%), nursing (10%), and business administration (9%). In an average class, 25% graduate in 4 years or less, 39% graduate in 5 years or less, and 42% graduate in 6 years or less. Of the 2016 graduating class, 86% were enrolled in graduate school within 6 months of graduation, and 32% were employed.

SERVICES: Counseling and information services are available, as is tutoring in most subjects. There is remedial math, reading, and writing. **Library/Resources:** The library contains 192,615 volumes, 26,941 microform items, 5,072 audio/video tapes/CDs/DVDs, and subscribes to 242 periodicals including electronic. Computerized library services include interlibrary loans, database searching, Internet access, and Wi-Fi capability. Special learning facilities include an art gallery, radio station, 3 theaters, a Center for the Study of the Civil War, and the Robert C. Byrd Center for Congressional History and Education. **Physically Challenged Students:** 90% of the campus is accessible. Facilities include wheelchair ramps, elevators, special parking, specially equipped restrooms, special class scheduling, lowered drinking fountains, lowered telephones, and automatic door openers. **Special:** Shepherd offers study abroad, a B.A.-B.S. degree in communication and new media, and internships and co-op programs that are available in most majors. There is a Washington semester, and dual majors are possible in any 2 majors. Credit by exam, life experience credentialing through the Regents degree, nondegree study, and pass/fail options for electives are offered. 4+1 M.B.A. Program. Intensive English Language Program. There are 11 national honor societies, a freshman honors program, and 20 departmental honors programs. **Visiting:** There are regularly scheduled orientations for prospective students, two fall open houses and one spring open house, weekday campus tours, and ccepted Student Day. There are guides for informal visits and visitors may sit in on classes. To schedule a visit, contact the Admissions Office. **Campus Safety and Security:** Measures include 24-hour foot and vehicle patrol, emergency notification system, and security escort services. There are shuttle buses, emergency telephones, lighted pathways/sidewalks, and controlled access to dorms/residences.

REQUIREMENTS: The SAT or ACT is required, with a minimum composite score of 900 on the SAT (critical reading and math) or 19 on the ACT. Applicants should be graduates of an accredited secondary school and have earned academic credits including 4 each in English and math, 3 each in history or social science, with 1 in American history and lab science, 1 in art, and the rest in computer, foreign language, and other academic electives. Applicants must have a minimum 2.0 academic core GPA. The GED is accepted. AP and CLEP credits are accepted. Important factors in the admissions decision are advanced placement or honors courses, leadership record, and extracurricular activities record. To graduate, students must complete a minimum of 120 semester hours with a 2.0 GPA overall and 42 upper division credits in the major and minor fields. The core curriculum totals 42: 6 in written English, 3 each in mathematics, history, arts, and wellness, 8 in sciences, 1 in first-year experience, 6 in humanities, and 9 in social sciences. Students pursuing the Bachelor of Arts degree (not including education) are required to complete 12 semester hours in the same foreign language, except music students whose requirements must be approved by the chairs of the Music and English and Modern Languages departments. Two years of German or French or both are recommended for students who anticipate going to graduate or professional school. The foreign language requirement for the B.A. degree can be satisfied through advanced placement or CLEP tests. **Procedure:** Freshmen are admitted in the fall, spring, and summer. Entrance exams should be taken during the junior year. There are early decision, early admissions, deferred admissions, and rolling admissions plans. Application deadlines are open. The fall 2017 application fee was $45. Notification is sent on a rolling basis. 567 early decision candidates were accepted for the 2017-2018 class. Applications are accepted on-line. **Transfer Students:** 360 transfer students enrolled in 2016-2017. Applicants must have a 2.0 cumulative GPA in a minimum of 24 semester hours of college-level work completed and must submit a transcript from each college attended. 30 of 120 credits required for the bachelor's degree must be completed at Shepherd. **International Students:** There are 14 international students enrolled. They must take the TOEFL with a minimum score of 550 on the paper-based TOEFL (PBT) or 79 on the Internet-based version (iBT) or take the MELAB, and any one of these tests the IELTS or EIKEN. They must also take the SAT or ACT, scoring 820.

ADMISSIONS: 89% of the 2017-2018 applicants were accepted. The SAT scores for the 2017-2018 freshman class were: Math-- 34% below 500, 51% between 500 and 599, and 15% between 600 and 699. Evidence-Based Reading/Writing-- 29% below 500, 51% between 500 and 599, 19% between 600 and 699, and 1% between 700 and 800. The ACT scores were 14% between 12 and 17, 59% between 18 and 23, 25% between 24 and 29, and 2% above 30. **Admissions Contact:** Kristen Lorenz, Director of Admissions. Email: *admission@shepherd.edu* Web: *www.shepherd.edu*

FINANCIAL AID: In 2017-2018, 91% of all full-time freshmen received some form of financial aid. 41% of all full-time freshmen received need-based aid. The average freshman award was $11,803. Need-based scholarships or need-based grants averaged $5,559; need-based self-help aid (loans and jobs) averaged $3,366; and non-need-based athletic scholarships averaged $6,074. 15% of undergraduate students work part-time. The average financial indebtedness of the 2017 graduate was $28,230. The state aid form is required. The FAFSA code is 003822. The priority date for freshman financial aid applications for fall entry is March 1.

UNIVERSITY OF CHARLESTON *(The complete profile is made available exclusively on our website, www.barronspac.com)*

WEST LIBERTY UNIVERSITY — C-1

www.westliberty.edu

West Liberty, WV 26074	**(304) 336-8076** **(800) 732-6204**
Fax: (304) 336-8403	**Email: admissions@westliberty.edu**
Full-time: 693 men, 1127 women	**Faculty:** 119
Part-time: 94 men, 195 women	**Ph.D.s:** 60%
Graduate: 787 men, 1322 women	**Student/Faculty:** 13 to 1
Year: semesters, summer session	**Tuition:** $7038 ($14,394)
Room & Board: $9120	**Freshman Class:** 1781 applied, 1277 accepted, 434 enrolled
SAT: required **ACT:** 21	**CEEB CODE:** 5901
Application Deadline: August 1	**COMPETITIVE**

West Liberty University, founded in 1837, is a state-assisted college offering programs in teacher education, liberal and fine arts, sciences, business, and preprofessional and technical fields. There are 4 undergraduate schools. In addition to regional accreditation, WLU has baccalaureate program accreditation with ADA, CAHEA, NASM, CAEP, NLN, CIHE, and NCACS. The 263-acre campus is in a rural area in West Liberty, WV, 10 miles north of Wheeling and 56 miles southwest of Pittsburgh. Including any residence halls, there are 50 buildings.

STUDENT LIFE: 67% of undergraduates are from West Virginia. Others are from 46 states, 26 foreign countries, and Canada. 90% are from public schools. 63% are White; 32% race unknown; 2% African American; 1% Asian American; 1% Hispanic; 1% Foreign; 1% two or more races. **Female To Male Ratio:** 1.7:1. The average age of freshmen is 18; all undergraduates, 21. 30% do not continue beyond their first year; 43% remain to graduate. **Housing:** College-sponsored housing includes on-campus apartments for married students, coed dorms and single sex dorms. In addition, there are honors houses, fraternity houses, and sorority houses. On-campus housing is available on a first-come and first-served basis. 81% of students live on campus. Alcohol is not permitted. All students may keep cars.

FACULTY/CLASSROOMS: 59% of faculty are male; 41% are female. All teach undergraduates. No introductory courses are taught by graduate students. The average class size in an introductory lecture is 25; in a laboratory is 20; and in a regular course is 20.

PROGRAMS OF STUDY: WLU confers B.A., B.S., and B.S.N. degrees. Associate degrees are also awarded. Bachelor's degrees are awarded in BIOLOGICAL SCIENCE (biology/biological science, ecology, and microbiology), BUSINESS (accounting, banking and finance, business administration and management, business economics, management science, marketing/retailing/merchandising, organizational leadership and management, and tourism), COMMUNICATIONS AND THE ARTS (advertising, broadcasting, communications, English, fine arts, graphic design, music, and public relations), COMPUTER AND PHYSICAL SCIENCE (chemistry, information sciences and systems, and mathematics), EDUCATION (art education, early childhood education, elementary education, health education, middle school education, music education, outdoor leadership/education, physical education, science education, secondary education, social science education, and special education), ENGINEERING AND ENVIRONMENTAL DESIGN (pre-engineering), HEALTH PROFESSIONS (clinical science, dental hygiene, disabilities studies, nursing, predentistry, premedicine, prepharmacy, and speech pathology/audiology), SOCIAL SCIENCE (criminal justice, economics, history, interdisciplinary studies, physical fitness/movement, political science/government, prelaw, psychology, social science, social studies, and sociology). Business, natural sciences, and health sciences are the strongest academically. Business, elementary education, and criminal justice have the largest enrollments.

ACTIVITIES: 2% of men belong to 4 local fraternities; 3% of women belong to 1 local and 3 national sororities. There are 48 groups on campus, including tourism, hospitality, art, cheerleading, choir, chorus, communications, dance, drama, ethnic, honors, international, jazz band, literary magazine, marching band, musical theater, newspaper, pep band, photography, professional, radio and TV, religious, social, social service, steel drum band, and student government. Popular campus events include Multi-Cultural Day, Greek Week, and Spring Fling. **Sports:** There are 8 intercollegiate sports for men and 7 for women, and 8 intramural sports for men and 7 for women. Facilities include handball and racquetball courts, training rooms, gyms, an indoor track, a wellness center, an indoor swimming pool, a game area with pool tables and table tennis, all-weather-surface tennis courts, and football and softball/baseball fields. **Graduates:** From July 1, 2016 to June 30, 2017, 503 bachelor's degrees were awarded. The most popular majors were education (33%), business administration (21%), and criminal justice (11%). In an average class, 19% graduate in 4 years or less, 37% graduate in 5 years or less, and 42% graduate in 6 years or less. Of the 2016 graduating class, 10% were enrolled in graduate school within 6 months of graduation, and 85% were employed.

SERVICES: Counseling and information services are available, as is tutoring in every subject. There is a reader service for the blind, and remedial math and writing. **Library/Resources:** The library contains 196,338 volumes, 131,000 microform items, and subscribes to 485 periodicals including electronic. Computerized library services include interlibrary loans and database searching. Special learning facilities include an art gallery, radio station, TV station, and a publication area. **Physically Challenged Students:** 90% of the campus is accessible. Facilities include wheelchair ramps, elevators, special parking, specially equipped restrooms, lowered drinking fountains, and lowered telephones. **Special:** Communications, exercise physiology, criminal justice, hospitality, tourism management, sports management, and golf management require an on-campus internship. The Washington Center Program, an internship, is also offered. However, students may also choose to complete an internship in the areas of business, clinical lab science, phys ed, or nursing. Interdisciplinary studies is a student-designed degree taken as either a B.A. or B.S. Biology, chemistry, and math are offered as a B.S. degree but may also be taken as a B.A. degree in education. Work and life experience credit is accepted in the Regents B.A. degree program. There are 10 national honor societies, a freshman honors program, and 6 departmental honors programs. **Visiting:** There are guides for informal visits, visitors may sit in on classes, and stay overnight. To schedule a visit, contact the Office of Admissions. **Campus Safety and Security:** Measures include 24-hour foot and vehicle patrol, self-defense education, and security escort services. There are emergency telephones, lighted pathways/sidewalks, and late night transport.

REQUIREMENTS: The SAT or ACT is required. Applicants must graduate from an accredited secondary school with a minimum GPA of 2.0, or have a composite minimum score of 18 on the ACT, or a minimum combined verbal, critical reading, and math score of 870. Students must have completed 4 years each of English and math, 3 of science, 2 each of foreign language and social studies, 1 unit each of U.S. history and academic electives. The GED is accepted. AP and CLEP credits are accepted. The required core curriculum varies for B.A. and B.S. candidates, but both include courses in communications, fine arts and humanities, natural science and math, social science and history, and phys ed and health. A minimum GPA of 2.0 and 128 credit hours are required to graduate. **Procedure:** Freshmen are admitted to all sessions. Entrance exams should be taken in time so that all admissions credentials, including test scores, are received 2 weeks prior to the beginning of the term. There are deferred admissions and rolling admissions plans. Applications should be filed by August 1 for fall entry. Applications are accepted on-line. **Transfer Students:** 175 transfer students enrolled in 2016-2017. Students must be eligible to return to the institution from which they wish to transfer. An official college transcript and a minimum GPA of 2.0 overall are required. Admissions criteria are the same as for freshmen if the student has completed fewer than 28 hours of college-level course work. 36 of 128 credits required for the bachelor's degree must be completed at WLU. **International Students:** There are 13 international students enrolled. They must take the TOEFL. They must also take the SAT or ACT, scoring 17.

ADMISSIONS: 72% of the 2017-2018 applicants were accepted. The ACT scores were 19% between 12 and 17, 59% between 18 and 23, 20% between 24 and 29, and 2% above 30. **Admissions Contact:** Brenda King, Director of Admissions. Email: *admissions@westliberty.edu* Web: *www.westliberty.edu*

FINANCIAL AID: In 2017-2018, 91% of all full-time freshmen received some form of financial aid and need-based aid. The average freshman award was $5,023. 99% of undergraduate students work part-time. The average financial indebtedness of the 2017 graduate was $12,568. The FAFSA code is 003823. The deadline for filing freshman financial aid applications for fall entry is March 1.

WEST VIRGINIA STATE UNIVERSITY *(The complete profile is made available exclusively on our website, www.barronspac.com)*

WEST VIRGINIA UNIVERSITY C-2

www.wvu.edu

Morgantown, WV 26506 **(304) 293-2121**
(800) 344-9881

Fax: (304) 293-3080 **Email: wvuadmissions@mail.wvu.edu**

Full-time: 11,064 men, 9649 women	**Faculty:** I, -$
Part-time: 815 men, 976 women	**Ph.D.s:** 67%
Graduate: 2613 men, 3292 women	**Student/Faculty:** 21 to 1
Year: semesters, summer session	**Tuition:** $8376 ($23,616)
Room & Board: $10,576	**Freshman Class:** 5225 enrolled
SAT: required **ACT:** 24	**CEEB CODE:** 5904
Application Deadline: August 1	**VERY COMPETITIVE**

West Virginia University, founded in 1867, is a comprehensive, public land-grant research university offering more than 100 undergraduate degrees in liberal arts and sciences, health science, and professional training. There are 15 undergraduate schools and 13 graduate schools. In addition to regional accreditation, WVU has baccalaureate program accreditation with AACSB, ABET, ACEJMC, ACPE, ADA, APTA, ASLA, CAHEA, CSWE, FIDER, NASAD, NASM, CAEP, NLN, NRPA, and SAF. The 1887-acre campus is in a small town 75 miles south of Pittsburgh, and 200 miles west of Baltimore. Including any residence halls, there are 275 buildings.

STUDENT LIFE: 50% of undergraduates are from out of state, mostly the Middle Atlantic. Students are from 50 states, 107 foreign countries, and Canada. 79% are White; 7% Foreign; 4% African American; 4% Hispanic; 4% two or more races; 2% Asian American. **Male To Female Ratio:** 1.0:1. The average age of freshmen is 19; all undergraduates, 21. **Housing:** 6500 students can be accommodated in college housing, which includes married student dorms, on-campus apartments, and off-campus apartments. In addition, there are honors houses, language/international houses, special-interest houses, fraternity houses, sorority houses, and designated halls for special programming. On-campus housing is available on a first-come, first-served basis, and is available on a lottery system for upperclassmen. 76% of students commute. Alcohol is not permitted. All students may keep cars.

FACULTY/CLASSROOMS: 55% of faculty are male; 45% are female. No introductory courses are taught by graduate students.

PROGRAMS OF STUDY: WVU confers B.A., B.S., B.F.A., B.M., B.Md.S., B.S.A.E., B.S.Agr., B.S.B.Ad., B.S.B.S., B.S.C.E., B.S.Ch.E., B.S.Cp.E., B.S.E.E., B.S.F., B.S.C.S., B.S.I.E., B.S.J., B.S.L.A., B.S.M.E., B.S.Min.E., B.S.N., B.S.Pnge., B.S.R., R.B.A., B.S.Bm.E., and B.S.W. degrees. Master's and doctoral degrees are also awarded. Bachelor's degrees are awarded in AGRICULTURE (agricultural economics, agricultural sciences, agriculture, agronomy, animal science, fish and game management, fishing and fisheries, forestry and related sciences, horticulture, natural resource management, plant science, wildlife management, and wood science), BIOLOGICAL SCIENCE (biology/biological science, forensic science, genetics, and nutrition), BUSINESS (accounting, banking and finance, business administration and management, business administration marketing, business law, entrepreneurial studies, fashion merchandising, finance, management information systems, marketing, marketing and distribution, recreation and leisure services, sports management, and tourism), COMMUNICATIONS AND THE ARTS (advertising, art, broadcasting, communications, creative writing, dance, dramatic arts, English, foreign language, journalism, music, public relations, speech/debate/rhetoric, and visual and performing arts), COMPUTER AND PHYSICAL SCIENCE (applied mathematics, chemistry, computer science, geology, geoscience, mathematics, physics, and science), EDUCATION (agricultural education, art education, athletic training, education administration, environmental education, general studies, library science, physical education, and reading education), ENGINEERING AND ENVIRONMENTAL DESIGN (aeronautical engineering, aerospace studies, chemical engineering, civil engineering, computer engineering, electrical/electronics engineering, engineering, environmental science, interior design, landscape architecture/design, mechanical engineering, military science, mining and mineral engineering, petroleum/natural gas engineering, and systems engineering), HEALTH PROFESSIONS (biology, dental hygiene, kinesiology, nursing, occupational therapy, pharmacy, physical therapy, speech pathology/audiology, and veterinary science), SOCIAL SCIENCE (American Indian studies, anthropology, child care/child and family studies, criminology, economics, family/consumer resource management, forensic studies, gender studies, geography, history, interdisciplinary studies, international studies, law, liberal arts/general studies, parks and recreation management, philosophy, political science/government, psychology, social work, and sociology). Engineering & mineral resources, psychology, and political science are the strongest academically. Business & economics, engineering & mineral resources, and health sciences have the largest enrollments.

ACTIVITIES: 7% of men belong to 16 national fraternities; 7% of women belong to 1 local and 8 national sororities. There are 469 groups on campus, including art, band, cheerleading, chess, choir, chorale, chorus, computers, dance, debate, drama, environmental, ethnic, film, forensics, honors, international, jazz band, LGBT, marching band, newspaper, opera, orchestra, pep band, photography, political, professional, radio and TV, religious, social, social service, student government, and symphony. Popular campus events include Mountaineer Week, Greek Week, and Fall Fest. **Sports:** There are 7 intercollegiate sports for men and 9 for women, and 17 intramural sports for men and 17 for women. Facilities include tennis courts, weight and exercise space, turf field, lacrosse, frisbee, basketball courts, a 50 foot high climbing wall, a natatorium with swimming and diving pools, rifle facilities, indoor/outdoor tracks, bowling alley, a gym, lacrosse, baseball, football, and soccer fields, a stadium, basketball, wrestling, volleyball, gymnastics, and a soccer stadium. **Graduates:** From July 1, 2016 to June 30, 2017, 4524 bachelor's degrees were awarded. The most popular majors were engineering (15%), business (13%), and health field (9%).

SERVICES: Counseling and information services are available, as is tutoring in most subjects. There is a reader service for the blind, and remedial math, reading, and writing. **Library/Resources:** The library contains 2.4 million volumes, 263,203 microform items, 15,663 audio/video tapes/CDs/DVDs, and subscribes to 89,824 periodicals including electronic. Computerized library services include interlibrary loans, database searching, Internet access, and Wi-Fi capability. Special learning facilities include an art gallery, planetarium, radio station, a discovery lab for inventors, coal, mining, and minerals history museum, a pharmacy museum, art museum, and an arboretum. **Physically Challenged Students:** 90% of the campus is accessible. Facilities include wheelchair ramps, elevators, special parking, specially equipped restrooms, special class scheduling, lowered drinking fountains, lowered telephones, and special housing. Academic programs are made accessible by transferring class to an architecturally accessible facility. Other facilities include tactile signage, specially designed lab facilities, portable lab stations, a Kurzweil reading machine, and a specially equipped van for inner-city transportation. **Special:** A co-op program in engineering and cross-registration with schools in the Southern Regional Education Board through the Academic Common Market are possible. Internships, study abroad in 25 countries, a Washington semester, student-designed majors, dual majors in business and foreign languages, and B.A.-B.S. degrees in economics, chemistry, physics, biology, math, psychology, and geology are available. A liberal studies degree, credit by exam, credit for life experience, nondegree study, and pass/fail options are also offered. There are 261 national honor societies, Phi Beta Kappa, and a freshman honors program. **Visiting:** There are regularly scheduled orientations for prospective students, including 2-day sessions with campus tours, placement testing, academic and advisement meetings, parent/student orientation discussions, and transitional meetings. There are guides for informal visits and visitors may sit in on classes. To schedule a visit, contact the Visitors Resource Center at (304) 293-3489. **Campus Safety and Security:** Measures include 24-hour foot and vehicle patrol, emergency notification system, self-defense education, and security escort services. There are shuttle buses, emergency telephones, lighted pathways/sidewalks, neighborhood watch programs, and sexual assault prevention booths staffed by city and university police.

REQUIREMENTS: The ACT Optional Writing test is required. West Virginia residents must have a minimim GPA of 2.0 and either a composite ACT score of 19 or a combined SAT score of 910 (critical reading and math). Nonresidents must have a minimum GPA of 2.5 and either 21 on the ACT or 990 on the SAT. AP and CLEP credits are accepted. Important factors in the admissions decision are leadership record, evidence of special talent, and advanced placement or honors courses. All students are required to take 12 credit hours in each of 3 areas: humanities and fine arts, social and behavioral sciences, and natural sciences and math. The 36 credit hours must include international/minority/gender studies, math, composition, and an advanced course emphasizing writing skills. A minimum 2.0 GPA and at least 128 credit hours are required to graduate. **Procedure:** Freshmen are admitted in the fall, spring, and summer. Entrance exams should be taken by spring of the junior year. There are deferred admissions and rolling admissions plans. Applications should be filed by August 1 for fall entry. The fall 2017 application fee was $60. Applications are accepted on-line. **Transfer Students:** 844 transfer students enrolled in 2016-2017. Students must have a minimum 2.0 GPA in all college work attempted. Those with fewer than 12 transferable credit hours must also meet freshman admission standards. Some programs have different course and higher GPA requirements. 30 of 128 credits required for the bachelor's degree must be completed at WVU. **International Students:** There are 1528 international students enrolled. They must take the TOEFL with a minimum score of 500 on the paper-based TOEFL (PBT) or 61 on the Internet-based version (iBT), international students serving as graduate teaching assistants must also demonstrate mastery of spoken English. They must also take the SAT or ACT, scoring 950.

ADMISSIONS: The SAT scores for the 2017-2018 freshman class were: Math-- 23% below 500, 53% between 500 and 599, 21% between 600 and 699, and 2% between 700 and 800. Evidence-Based Reading/Writing-- 23% below 500, 53% between 500 and 599, 22% between 600 and 699, and 2% between 700 and 800. The ACT scores were 8% between 12 and 17, 48% between 18 and 23, 37% between 24 and 29, and 7% above 30. **Admissions Contact:** Stephen Lee, Ex Director of Admissions and Records. Email: *wvuadmissions@mail.wvu.edu* Web: *www.wvu.edu*

FINANCIAL AID: In 2017-2018, 56% of all full-time freshmen received some form of financial aid. 44% of all full-time freshmen received need-based aid. The average freshman award was $6,752. Need-based scholarships or need-based grants averaged $5,357; need-based self-help aid (loans and jobs) averaged $3,268; non-need-based athletic scholarships averaged $18,928; and other non-need-based awards and non-need-based scholarships averaged $3,590. The state aid form is required. The FAFSA code is 003827. The deadline for filing freshman financial aid applications for fall entry is March 1.

WEST VIRGINIA UNIVERSITY INSTITUTE OF TECHNOLOGY B-4

www.wvutech.edu

Montgomery, WV 25136
(304) 442-3164
(888) 554-TECH
Email: tech-admissions@mail.wvu.edu

Full-time: 636 men, 343 women	**Faculty:** 83
Part-time: 91 men, 46 women	**Ph.D.s:** 52%
Graduate: n/av	**Student/Faculty:** 11 to 1
Year: semesters, summer session	**Tuition:** $6960 ($17,544)
Room & Board: $11,304	**Freshman Class:** 929 applied, 571 accepted, 268 enrolled
SAT: required **ACT:** 21	**CEEB CODE:** 5902
Application Deadline: n/av	**COMPETITIVE**

West Virginia University Institute of Technology, part of the Western Virginia University system and founded in 1895, is a public institution offering programs in business and accounting, psychology and sciences, nursing, and engineering & engineering technology. The figures given in the above capsule and in this profile are approximate. There are 3 undergraduate schools. In addition to regional accreditation, WVUIT has baccalaureate program accreditation with ABET, ADA, and NLN. The 112-acre campus is in a small town 28 miles southeast of Charleston. Including any residence halls, there are 15 buildings.

STUDENT LIFE: 75% of undergraduates are from West Virginia. Others are from 25 states, 24 foreign countries, and Canada. 95% are from public schools. 87% are White; 6% African American; 4% Foreign; 1% Asian American; 1% American Indian/Alaska Native; 1% Hispanic. **Male To Female Ratio:** 1.9:1. The average age of freshmen is 19; all undergraduates, 22. 35% do not continue beyond their first year; 40% remain to graduate. **Housing:** 500 students can be accommodated in college dorms. On-campus housing is guaranteed for all 4 years, is available on a first-come, and first-served basis. 69% of students commute. Alcohol is not permitted. All students may keep cars.

FACULTY/CLASSROOMS: 70% of faculty are male; 30% are female. All teach undergraduates and 10% do research. No introductory courses are taught by graduate students. The average class size in an introductory lecture is 30; in a laboratory is 15; and in a regular course is 20.

PROGRAMS OF STUDY: WVUIT confers B.A., B.S., B.E.T., B.M.E.T., B.S.C.E., B.S.E. and B.S.E.E. degrees. Bachelor's degrees are awarded in BIOLOGICAL SCIENCE (biology/biological science), BUSINESS (accounting and business administration and management), COMPUTER AND PHYSICAL SCIENCE (chemistry, computer programming, computer science, and physics), ENGINEERING AND ENVIRONMENTAL DESIGN (chemical engineering, civil engineering, electrical/electronics engineering, electrical/electronics engineering technology, engineering technology, industrial administration/management, industrial engineering technology, and mechanical engineering), HEALTH PROFESSIONS (health care administration and nursing), SOCIAL SCIENCE (history and public administration). Engineering is the strongest academically. Nursing has the largest enrollment.

ACTIVITIES: 10% of men belong to 5 national fraternities; 8% of women belong to 2 national sororities. There are 42 groups on campus, including art, cheerleading, computers, drama, ethnic, international, musical theater, newspaper, photography, political, professional, religious, social, social service, and student government. Popular campus events include Comedy and Film Series, Black History Month, and Greek Week. **Sports:** There are 5 intercollegiate sports for men and 4 for women, and 8 intramural sports for men and 8 for women. Facilities include a gym, weight room, tennis courts, student union, football field a stadium, an Olympic-size swimming pool, game rooms, and a fitness center. **Graduates:** From July 1, 2016 to June 30, 2017, 152 bachelor's degrees were awarded. The most popular majors were engineering (29%), business (11%), and homeland security (10%). In an average class, 19% graduate in 6 years or less.

SERVICES: Counseling and information services are available, as is tutoring in most subjects. There is remedial math, reading, and writing. There is also a math center, and student success center. **Library/Resources:** The library contains 166,967 volumes, 438,232 microform items, and subscribes to 510 periodicals including electronic. Computerized library services include interlibrary loans and database searching. Special learning facilities include an art gallery. **Physically Challenged**

Students: 60% of the campus is accessible. Facilities include wheelchair ramps, elevators, special parking, specially equipped restrooms, special class scheduling, and lowered drinking fountains. **Special:** An extensive co-op program is offered in all areas as well as a number of internships in public service and industrial relations. Credit for armed service experience and credit by departmental exam are available. **Visiting:** There are regularly scheduled orientations for prospective students. There are guides for informal visits, visitors may sit in on classes, and stay overnight. To schedule a visit, contact the Admissions Office. **Campus Safety and Security:** Measures include 24-hour foot and vehicle patrol, self-defense education, security escort services, and lighted pathways/sidewalks.

REQUIREMENTS: The SAT or ACT is required, with a minimum composite score of 870 on the SAT or 18 on the ACT (higher for engineering and health majors). Students should have completed 17 academic units such as 4 in English and math, 3 in science, of those including lab, and social studies, 2 in foreign language, and 1 in visual/performing arts. Applicants should be graduates from an accredited secondary school or have qualifying scores on the GED. AP and CLEP credits are accepted. Core curriculum requirements include 8 hours of lab science, 6 to 12 each of humanities and social science, 6 each of English and math/computer science, and 2 of phys ed and health. Other requirements vary according to the degree sought. To graduate, students must complete 128 semester hours with a minimum 2.0 GPA overall and in the major. **Procedure:** Freshmen are admitted to all sessions. Entrance exams should be taken in sufficient time for the scores to reach the institute by the application deadline. There are early admissions and rolling admissions plans. Applications should be filed by December 15 for spring entry; May 1 for summer entry. Notifications are sent August 1. **Transfer Students:** 109 transfer students enrolled in 2016-2017. Minimum of 30 credit hours with a GPA of 2.0. Students may enroll in the fall, spring and winter. 30 of 128 credits required for the bachelor's degree must be completed at WVUIT. **International Students:** There are 74 international students enrolled. They must take the TOEFL with a minimum score of 62 on the Internet-based version (iBT). They must also take the SAT or ACT.

ADMISSIONS: 61% of the 2017-2018 applicants were accepted. The ACT scores were 27% between 12 and 17, 51% between 18 and 23, and 21% between 24 and 29. 11 freshmen graduated first in their class. **Admissions Contact:** Jeretta Ford, Admissions Director. Email: *tech-admissions@mail.wvu.edu* Web: *www.wvutech.edu*

FINANCIAL AID: In 2017-2018, 86% of all full-time freshmen received some form of financial aid. 49% of all full-time freshmen received need-based aid. The average freshman award was $2,480. Need-based scholarships or need-based grants averaged $6,822; need-based self-help aid (loans and jobs) averaged $54; non-need-based athletic scholarships averaged $1,350; other non-need-based awards and non-need-based scholarships averaged $1,992; and $2,532 from other forms of aid. 15% of undergraduate students work part-time. The average financial indebtedness of the 2017 graduate was $11,064. WVUIT is a member of CSS. The FAFSA code is 003825. The priority date for freshman financial aid applications for fall entry is March 15.

WEST VIRGINIA WESLEYAN COLLEGE C-3

www.wvwc.edu

Buckhannon, WV 26201	**(304) 473-8510** **(800) 722-9933**
Fax: (304) 473-8108	**Email: admissions@wvwc.edu**
Full-time: 600 men, 700 women	**Faculty:** 78; IIB, --$
Part-time: 13 men, 14 women	**Ph.D.s:** 77%
Graduate: 16 men, 26 women	**Student/Faculty:** 17 to 1
Year: semesters, summer session	**Tuition:** $30,752
Room & Board: $8436	**Freshman Class:** 1272 applied, 984 accepted, 369 enrolled
SAT: required **ACT:** 23	**CEEB CODE:** 5905
Application Deadline: August 1	**COMPETITIVE**

West Virginia Wesleyan College, founded in 1890, is an independent liberal and applied arts institution affiliated with the United Methodist Church. The figures given in the above capsule and in this profile are approximate. There are 7 undergraduate schools. In addition to regional accreditation, WVWC has baccalaureate program accreditation with CAEP, NLN, IACBE, and CAAHEP. The 80-acre campus is in a small town in the Appalachian foothills, 135 miles south of Pittsburgh, Pennsylvania. Including any residence halls, there are 23 buildings.

STUDENT LIFE: 53% of undergraduates are from West Virginia. Others are from 37 states, 12 foreign countries, and Canada. 85% are from public schools. 88% are White; 5% African American; 4% Foreign; 1% Asian American; 1% American Indian/Alaska Native; 1% Hispanic. 53% are Protestant; 20% Catholic. **Female To Male Ratio:** 1.2:1. The average age of freshmen is 18; all undergraduates, 21. **Housing:** 1275 students can be accommodated in college housing, which includes dorms and on-campus apartments. In addition, there are honors houses, quiet study living areas, and substance-free small group living units. On-campus housing is guaranteed for all 4 years. 83% of students live on campus. Alcohol is not permitted. All students may keep cars.

FACULTY/CLASSROOMS: 79% of faculty are male; 21% are female. All teach undergraduates. No introductory courses are taught by graduate students. The average class size in an introductory lecture is 24; in a laboratory is 12; and in a regular course is 21.

PROGRAMS OF STUDY: WVWC confers B.A., B.S., B.M.E., and B.S.N. degrees. Master's degrees are also awarded. Bachelor's degrees are awarded in AGRICULTURE (environmental studies), BIOLOGICAL SCIENCE (biochemistry, biology/biological science, biological sciences, and nutrition), BUSINESS (accounting, business administration and management, international business, and marketing/retailing/merchandising), COMMUNICATIONS AND THE ARTS (communication studies, dramatic arts, English, music, public relations, speech/debate/rhetoric, and theatre arts), COMPUTER AND PHYSICAL SCIENCE (chemistry, computer science, mathematics, and physics), EDUCATION (art education, Christian education, elementary education, music education, physical education, and secondary education), ENGINEERING AND ENVIRONMENTAL DESIGN (engineering, engineering physics, environmental science, and petroleum/natural gas engineering), HEALTH PROFESSIONS (exercise science and nursing), SOCIAL SCIENCE (criminal justice, economics, gender studies, history, international studies, philosophy, political science/government, psychology, religion, religious education, social science, and sociology). Physical & natural sciences, and accounting are the strongest academically. Business, biology, and education have the largest enrollments.

ACTIVITIES: 25% of men belong to 5 national fraternities; 25% of women belong to 5 national sororities. There are 75 groups on campus, including art, band, cheerleading, choir, chorale, chorus, communications, computers, dance, drama, ethnic, forensics, honors, international, jazz band, literary magazine, musical theater, newspaper, political, professional, radio and TV, religious, social, social service, student government, and yearbook. Popular campus events include Founders Day, Festivals of Lessons and Carols, and Spring Sing. **Sports:** There are 9 intercollegiate sports for men and 8 for women, and 9 intramural sports for men and 8 for women. Facilities include baseball and football fields, a phys ed center with a basketball court, handball courts, an auxiliary gym, indoor tennis, volleyball, golf and wrestling practice areas, a dance studio, gymnastics and weight rooms, cross country, soccer, swimming, softball, and track and field. **Graduates:** From July 1, 2016 to June 30, 2017, 303 bachelor's degrees were awarded. The most popular majors were business (14%), elementary education (12%), and biology (8%). In an average class, 1% graduate in 3 years or less, 44% graduate in 4 years or less, 52% graduate in 5 years or less, and 55% graduate in 6 years or less.

SERVICES: Counseling and information services are available, as is tutoring in every subject. There is a reader service for the blind, and remedial math, reading, and writing. **Library/Resources:** The library contains 116,240 volumes, 39,119 microform items, 6,322 audio/video tapes/CDs/DVDs, and subscribes to 14,126 periodicals including electronic. Computerized library services include interlibrary loans, database searching, Internet access, and Wi-Fi capability. Special learning facilities include an art gallery, planetarium, and radio station. **Physically Challenged Students:** 75% of the campus is accessible. Facilities include wheelchair ramps, elevators, special parking, specially equipped restrooms, special class scheduling, and lowered drinking fountains. **Special:** WVWC offers cross-registration with the Mountain State Association of Colleges. Students may participate in a wide variety of internships, including a Washington center internship and work-study and study-abroad programs; there are exchange agreements in Korea, the People's Republic of China, Norway, and Bulgaria. Nondegree and pass/fail study, dual, student-designed, and contract majors, and credit for life, military, and work experience are available. A 3-2 engineering degree offered with WVWC. There is 1 national honor society and a freshman honors program. **Visiting:** There are regularly scheduled orientations for prospective students. There are guides for informal visits, visitors may sit in on classes, and stay overnight. To schedule a visit, contact the Admission Office. **Campus Safety and Security:** Measures include 24-hour foot and vehicle patrol, self-defense education, and security escort services. There are emergency telephones, lighted pathways/sidewalks, rape awareness educational programs, and appropriate training for residence hall staff.

REQUIREMENTS: The SAT or ACT is required. The minimum composite score needed is 800 on SAT, 420 verbal and 380 math, or 18 on the ACT. In addition, applicants must be high school graduates, or hold a GED. Students should have earned 26 academic credits, consisting of 4 in English, 3 each in math, science, and academic electives, and 2 each in foreign language, lab science, and social studies, as well as a total of 7 academic credits in fine arts, technology education, health, and phys ed. An essay and an interview are recommended. A GPA of 2.2 is required. AP and CLEP credits are accepted. Important factors in the admissions decision are extracurricular activities record, recommendations by school officials, and leadership record. To graduate, students must earn 120 semester hours with a minimum GPA of 2.0; 24 to 51 hours must be in the major, 48 to 53 in general studies. Required disciplines are cultural studies, natural science and math, social sciences, health and phys ed, religion, philosophy, humanities and fine arts, and communications. **Procedure:** Freshmen are admitted in the fall and spring. Entrance exams should be taken in fall of the senior year or spring/summer of the junior year. There are early decision, deferred admissions, and rolling admissions plans. Early decision applications should be filed by December 1; regular applications, by August 1 for fall entry; and January 10 for spring entry. The fall 2017 application fee was $25. Notifications are sent November 1. Applications are accepted online. **Transfer Students:** 34 transfer students enrolled in 2016-2017. Transfer applicants must supply a high school transcript if their GPA for college work is less than 2.5. An associate degree and an interview are recommended. 30 of 120 credits required for the bachelor's degree must be completed at WVWC. **International Students:** They must take the TOEFL. They must also take the SAT or ACT if they are seeking scholarships.

ADMISSIONS: 77% of the 2017-2018 applicants were accepted. The ACT scores were 18% below 12, 19% between 12 and 17, 16% between 18 and 23, 6% between 24 and 29, and 4% above 30. 10 freshmen graduated first in their class. **Admissions Contact:** John Waltz, VP for Enrollment Management. Email: *admissions@wvwc.edu* Web: *www.wvwc.edu*

FINANCIAL AID: In 2017-2018, 98% of all full-time freshmen received some form of financial aid. 77% of all full-time freshmen received need-based aid. The average freshman award was $21,700. 41% of undergraduate students work part-time. The average financial indebtedness of the 2017 graduate was $18,000. The FAFSA code is 003830. The deadline for filing freshman financial aid applications for fall entry is March 1.

WHEELING JESUIT UNIVERSITY *(The complete profile is made available exclusively on our website, www.barronspac.com)*

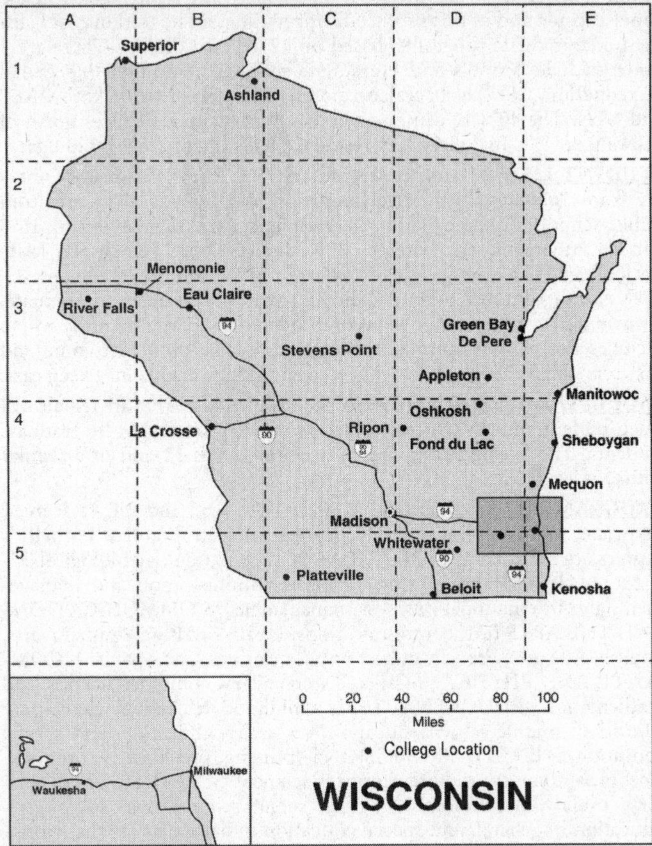

ALVERNO COLLEGE *(The complete profile is made available exclusively on our website, www.barronspac.com)*

BELOIT COLLEGE — D-5
www.beloit.edu

Beloit, WI 53511	**(608) 363-2500**
Fax: (608) 363-2075	**Email: admiss@beloit.edu**
Full-time: 620 men, 717 women	**Faculty:** 107; IIB, av$
Part-time: 19 men, 38 women	**Ph.D.s:** 98%
Graduate: n/av	**Student/Faculty:** 12 to 1
Year: semesters, summer session	**Tuition:** $47,060
Room & Board: $8146	**Freshman Class:** 3855 applied, 2693 accepted, 382 enrolled
SAT CR/M: 630/620 **ACT:** 27	**CEEB CODE:** 1059
Application Deadline: January 15	**HIGHLY COMPETITIVE**

Beloit College, founded in 1846, is a private liberal arts institution. There is 1 undergraduate school. The 44-acre campus is in a small town 50 miles south of Madison, 80 miles southwest of Milwaukee, 90 miles northwest of Chicago, IL. Including any residence halls, there are 70 buildings.

STUDENT LIFE: 85% of undergraduates are from out of state, mostly the Midwest. Students are from 49 states, 28 foreign countries, and Canada. 64% are from public schools. 9% are Hispanic; 61% White; 5% African American; 4% race unknown; 3% Asian American; 3% two or more races; 14% Foreign. **Female To Male Ratio:** 1.2:1. The average age of freshmen is 18; all undergraduates, 20. 12% do not continue beyond their first year; 81% remain to graduate. **Housing:** 1206 students can be accommodated in college housing, which includes dorms and on-campus apartments. In addition, there are language/international houses, special-interest houses, fraternity houses, and sorority houses. On-campus housing is guaranteed for the freshman year only. 87% of students live on campus. All students may keep cars.

FACULTY/CLASSROOMS: 44% of faculty are male; 56% are female. All teach undergraduates. No introductory courses are taught by graduate students. The average class size in an introductory lecture is 15; in a laboratory is 15; and in a regular course is 15.

PROGRAMS OF STUDY: Beloit confers B.A. and B.S. degrees. Bachelor's degrees are awarded in AGRICULTURE (environmental studies and forestry and related sciences), BIOLOGICAL SCIENCE (biology ecology and field biology, biochemistry, biology/biological science, cell biology, ecology, and environmental biology), BUSINESS (business administration and management, business economics, and international economics), COMMUNICATIONS AND THE ARTS (art history, art, Chinese, classical languages, classics, comparative literature, creative writing, dance, dramatic arts, East Asian languages and literature, English, English literature, French, German, intermedia/multimedia, literature, modern language, music, Russian, Spanish, and studio art), COMPUTER AND PHYSICAL SCIENCE (applied physics, chemistry, computer science, environmental geology, geology, mathematics, and physics), EDUCATION (art education and education), ENGINEERING AND ENVIRONMENTAL DESIGN (preengineering), HEALTH PROFESSIONS (premedicine), SOCIAL SCIENCE (anthropology, Chinese Studies, classical/ancient civilization, cognitive science, economics, gender studies, history, interdisciplinary studies, international relations, philosophy, philosophy and religion, political science/government, prelaw, psychology, religion, religious studies, sociology, and women's studies). Anthropology, creative writing, and biology are the strongest academically. Psychology, international relations, and biology have the largest enrollments.

ACTIVITIES: 19% of men belong to 3 national fraternities; 20% of women belong to 1 local and 3 national sororities. There are 117 groups on campus, including small instrument ensembles and string, entrepreneurial, science fiction and fantasy, wind, art, band, choir, chorus, computers, dance, drama, environmental, ethnic, film, honors, international, jazz band, LGBT, literary magazine, musical theater, newspaper, photography, political, professional, radio and TV, religious, social, social service, student government, and yoga. Popular campus events include Great Lecture Series, Advising Day, Folk and Blues Weekend, and Spring Day. **Sports:** There are 9 intercollegiate sports for men and 9 for women, and 8 intramural sports for men and 7 for women. Facilities include an arena for basketball and volleyball, racquetball/handball courts, fitness center, a natatorium, a field house with a running track, an indoor soccer area, batting/pitching cage, indoor tennis, a stadium hosting football, soccer, lacrosse, and track and field, outdoor playing fields, dance studio, tennis court complex. **Graduates:** From July 1, 2016 to June 30, 2017, 282 bachelor's degrees were awarded. The most popular majors were education (6%), anthropology/sociology (6%), and psychology (6%). In an average class, 69% graduate in 4 years or less, 80% graduate in 5 years or less, and 81% graduate in 6 years or less. Of the 2016 graduating class, 15% were enrolled in graduate school within 6 months of graduation, and 89% were employed.

SERVICES: Counseling and information services are available, as is tutoring in most subjects, such as advanced courses, if available, and requested by student. There is also a reader service for the blind. **Library/ Resources:** The library contains 505,586 volumes, 7,314 microform items, and 9,301 audio/video tapes/CDs/DVDs, and subscribes to 1,052 periodicals including electronic. Computerized library services include interlibrary loans, database searching, and Internet access. Special learning facilities include an art gallery, natural history museum, planetarium, radio station, TV station, a teaching anthropology museum, a teaching art museum, a comprehensive language lab, an observatory, a center for entrepreneurship, dance facilities, science laboratories, and a theater complex. **Physically Challenged Students:** 50% of the campus is accessible. Facilities include wheelchair ramps, elevators, special parking, specially equipped restrooms, special class scheduling, lowered drinking fountains, and lowered telephones. **Special:** Beloit offers cross-registration with the University of Wisconsin/Madison, internships, study abroad in more than 38 countries, and a Washington semester. Dual majors, student-designed and interdisciplinary majors, and non-degree study are available. A 3-2 engineering degree is offered with 9 institutions, and co-op programs are available in social services, forestry and environmental management, engineering, and business administration. An intensive summer language program is offered in Russian, Arabic, Japanese, and Chinese. There are 6 national honor societies and including Phi Beta Kappa. **Visiting:** There are regularly scheduled orientations for prospective students, A visit may include an interview, a tour, class visits, and meetings with professors. Enrolled students serve as tour guides and hosts for overnight stays. There are guides for informal visits, visitors may sit in on classes, and stay overnight. To schedule a visit, contact The Office of Admissions. **Campus Safety and Security:** Measures include 24-hour foot and vehicle patrol, emergency notification system, and security escort services. There are emergency telephones, lighted pathways/sidewalks, and controlled access to dorms/residences.

REQUIREMENTS: Submission of test scores is optional for most applicants. Home-schooled applicants and candidates applying from schools that do not provide grades are asked to submit results from one or more standardized tests, such as SAT or ACT. Applicants must be graduates of an accredited secondary school or home-school program, with 4 years of English, 3 each of math, science, and history/social sciences, and 2 of foreign language. The GED is accepted. An essay and a letter of recommendation are required, and an interview is strongly recommended. A GPA of 2.5 is required. AP and CLEP credits are accepted. Important factors in the admissions decision are advanced placement or honors courses, recommendations by school officials, and leadership record. To graduate, students must complete 31 units, including 8 to 15 in the major, with a minimum GPA of 2.0. Students must complete 3 writing designated courses, 1 quantitative reasoning designated course, and 1 intercultural literacy designated course. Breadth requirements include 1 courses in each of the following domains: Conceptual and Foundational Systems, Artistic and Creative Practices, Social Analysis of Human Behavior, Scientific Inquiry into the Physical and Biological Universe, and Textual Cultures and Analysis. Students are also expected to complete a liberal arts in practice experience that integrates learning from inside and outside the classroom, typically in the junior year, and a capstone experience, in the senior year. **Procedure:** Freshmen are admitted in the fall and spring. There are early decision, early admissions, deferred admissions, and rolling admissions plans. Early decision applications should be filed by November 1; regular applications, by January 15 for fall entry; and November 1 for spring entry. Notification of early decision is sent November 30; regular decision, March 15. 32 applicants were on the 2017 waiting list; 3 were admitted. Applications are accepted online. **Transfer Students:** 27 transfer students enrolled in 2016-2017. Applicants must have a minimum GPA of 2.5 and submit official transcripts of all college work completed. The SAT and the ACT are both optional. An interview is recommended. A letter of recommendation from a professor at a current/previous institution is also required. 16 of 31 credits required for the bachelor's degree must be completed at Beloit. **International Students:** There are 196 international students enrolled. Requirements vary by student background. Applicants from some countries must supply a school-leaving exam/certificate.

ADMISSIONS: 70% of the 2017-2018 applicants were accepted. The SAT scores for the 2017-2018 freshman class were: Critical Reading-- 11% below 500, 34% between 500 and 599, 30% between 600 and 699, and 25% between 700 and 800. Math-- 13% below 500, 31% between 500 and 599, 43% between 600 and 699, and 13% between 700 and 800. The ACT scores were 2% between 12 and 17, 18% between 18 and 23, 52% between 24 and 29, and 28% above 30. 60% of the current freshmen were in the top fifth of their class. **Admissions Contact:** Emily McEntee, Assistant Director of Admission. Email: *admiss@beloit.edu* Web: *www.beloit.edu*

FINANCIAL AID: In 2017-2018, 63% of all full-time freshmen received some form of financial aid. 70% of all full-time freshmen received need-based aid. 79% of undergraduate students work part-time. Beloit is a member of CSS. The FAFSA code is 003835. The deadline for filing freshman financial aid applications for fall entry is March 1.

CARDINAL STRITCH UNIVERSITY — E-4

www.stritch.edu

Milwaukee, WI 53217 — (414) 410-4040, (800) 347-8822

Fax: (414) 410-4049
Email: admityou@stritch.edu
Full-time: 910 men, 2000 women
Faculty: 98
Part-time: 50 men, 170 women
Ph.D.s: 54%
Graduate: 820 men, 1900 women
Student/Faculty: 30 to 1
Year: semesters, summer session
Tuition: $28,844
Room & Board: $8292
Freshman Class: n/av
SAT or ACT: required
CEEB CODE: 1100
Application Deadline: August 1
COMPETITIVE

Cardinal Stritch University, founded in 1937, is a private, Catholic institution sponsored by the Sisters of St. Francis. The figures given in the above capsule and in this profile are approximate. The tuition cost is for the undergraduate programs, based on 12-18 credit hours. There are 4 undergraduate schools and 1 graduate school. In addition to regional accreditation, CSU has baccalaureate program accreditation with CAEP and NLN. The 40-acre campus is in a suburban area 10 miles north of Milwaukee, WI. Including any residence halls, there are 9 buildings.

STUDENT LIFE: 89% of undergraduates are from Wisconsin. Others are from 16 states, 27 foreign countries, and Canada. 60% are from public schools. 72% are White; 3% Hispanic; 2% Asian American; 16% African American; 1% Foreign. 27% are Catholic. **Female To Male Ratio:** 2.3:1. The average age of freshmen is 19; all undergraduates, 32. 27% do not continue beyond their first year; 43% remain to graduate. **Housing:** 278 students can be accommodated in college housing, which includes dorms. On-campus housing is available on a first-come and first-served basis. 95% of students commute. All students may keep cars.

FACULTY/CLASSROOMS: 49% of faculty are male; 51% are female. All teach undergraduates. No introductory courses are taught by graduate students. The average class size in a laboratory is 12 and in a regular course is 11.

PROGRAMS OF STUDY: CSU confers B.A., B.S., and B.F.A. degrees. Associate, master's, and doctoral degrees are also awarded. Bachelor's degrees are awarded in BIOLOGICAL SCIENCE (biology/biological science), BUSINESS (accounting, business administration and management, and international business management), COMMUNICATIONS AND THE ARTS (art, communications, creative writing, dramatic arts, English, fine arts, French, music, public relations, and Spanish), COMPUTER AND PHYSICAL SCIENCE (chemistry, computer science, and mathematics), EDUCATION (early childhood education, elementary education, middle school education, secondary education, and special education), HEALTH PROFESSIONS (nursing, predentistry, premedicine, preoptometry, and preveterinary science), SOCIAL SCIENCE (history, prelaw, psychology, religion, social science, and sociology). Education in general, and special education in particular are the strongest academically. Business, education, and nursing have the largest enrollments.

ACTIVITIES: There are no fraternities or sororities. There are 50 groups on campus, including art, band, cheerleading, choir, chorus, computers, dance, drama, ethnic, film, honors, international, jazz band, musical theater, newspaper, orchestra, photography, political, professional, radio and TV, religious, social, social service, student government, and yearbook. Popular campus events include Thursday night events, and weekly activities. **Sports:** There are 5 intercollegiate sports for men and 5 for women, and 2 intramural sports for men and 2 for women. Facilities include basketball and volleyball courts, an indoor track, a weight and exercise room, an area for table tennis and billiards, and a soccer field. **Graduates:** From July 1, 2016 to June 30, 2017, 285 bachelor's degrees were awarded. The most popular majors were management (35%), business administration (25%), and management information systems (9%). In an average class, 4% graduate in 3 years or less, 19% graduate in 4 years or less, 39% graduate in 5 years or less, and 43% graduate in 6 years or less.

SERVICES: Counseling and information services are available, as is tutoring in every subject. There is remedial math, reading, and writing. **Library/Resources:** The library contains 132,293 volumes, 173,216 microform items, and 6,310 audio/video tapes/CDs/DVDs, and subscribes to 1,309 periodicals including electronic. Computerized library services include interlibrary loans and database searching. Special learning facilities include an art gallery and radio station. **Physically Challenged Students:** 80% of the campus is accessible. Facilities include wheelchair ramps, special parking, specially equipped restrooms, special class scheduling, and lowered telephones. **Special:** Students may participate in a variety of internships with Milwaukee businesses and organizations. Stritch offers an accelerated degree program and a B.A.-B.S. degree in business, dual majors, a general studies degree, and nondegree study. There is study abroad, work-study programs, pass/fail options, and credit for life, military, and work experience. An accelerated evening program and a management program are offered for working adults. There are 9 national honor societies and a freshman honors program. **Visiting:** There are regularly scheduled orientations for prospective students, including a campus tour, meetings with admissions and financial aid counselors, and possible meetings with department chairs. There are guides for informal visits, visitors may sit in on classes, and stay overnight. To schedule a visit, contact the Admissions Office. **Campus Safety**

and Security: Measures include 24-hour foot and vehicle patrol. There are lighted pathways/sidewalks.

REQUIREMENTS: The SAT or ACT is required, with a recommended minimum composite score of 20 on the ACT or 950 on the SAT I. Applicants must be graduates of an accredited secondary school, with 16 academic credits, including 4 years of English and 2 years each of math (algebra required), science, and social studies. The GED is accepted. Stritch requires an essay and recommends an interview. Applications are accepted on-line. AP and CLEP credits are accepted. Important factors in the admissions decision are leadership record, evidence of special talent, and advanced placement or honors courses. To graduate, students must complete 128 credits, 34 to 72 in the major, with a GPA of at least 2.0. Required disciplines include history, foreign language, literature, written communication, and communication arts. 5 courses are required in humanities, 3 in social/behavioral sciences, 2 each in communication arts and written communication, and 1 each in math and natural science. An English proficiency exam must be taken. **Procedure:** Freshmen are admitted to all sessions. Entrance exams should be taken as early as possible. There are deferred admissions and rolling admissions plans. Applications should be filed by August 1 for fall entry. The fall 2017 application fee was $25. Notification is sent on a rolling basis. Applications are accepted on-line. **Transfer Students:** 164 transfer students enrolled in 2016-2017. Applicants for transfer should have a minimum GPA of 2.0, and be eligible for return to the previous institution. 32 of 128 credits required for the bachelor's degree must be completed at Stritch. **International Students:** There are 35 international students enrolled. They must take the TOEFL, and the college's own entrance exam. They must also take the SAT or ACT.

Admissions Contact: David Wegener, Director of Admissions. Email: *admityou@stritch.edu* Web: *www.stritch.edu*

FINANCIAL AID: The college's own financial statement is required. The FAFSA code is 003837. Check with the school for current application deadlines.

CARROLL UNIVERSITY D-5

www.carrollu.edu

Waukesha, WI 53186	**(262) 524-7220** **(262) 547-1211**
Fax: (262) 524-7139	**Email: info@carrollu.edu**
Full-time: 953 men, 1753 women	**Faculty:** 101; IIA, --$
Part-time: 102 men, 207 women	**Ph.D.s:** 71%
Graduate: 134 men, 297 women	**Student/Faculty:** 23 to 1
Year: semesters, summer session	**Tuition:** $29,535
Room & Board: $8550	**Freshman Class:** 2969 applied, 2400 accepted, 762 enrolled
SAT: required **ACT:** 24	**CEEB CODE:** 1101
Application Deadline: open	**COMPETITIVE+**

Carroll University, founded in 1846, is an independent, co-educational comprehensive college grounded in the liberal arts tradition. There are 2 undergraduate schools and 2 graduate schools. In addition to regional accreditation, CU has baccalaureate program accreditation with APTA and NLN. The 133-acre campus is in a suburban area 15 miles west of Milwaukee. Including any residence halls, there are 56 buildings.

STUDENT LIFE: 71% of undergraduates are from Wisconsin. Others are from 28 states, 29 foreign countries, and Canada. 85% are White; 6% Hispanic; 4% Asian American; 2% two or more races; 1% African American; 1% Foreign; 1% race unknown. **Female To Male Ratio:** 1.9:1. The average age of freshmen is 18; all undergraduates, 21. 21% do not continue beyond their first year; 58% remain to graduate. **Housing:** 1785 students can be accommodated in college housing, which includes dorms, on-campus apartments, and special interest floors. On-campus housing is guaranteed for all 4 years. 58% of students live on campus. All students may keep cars.

FACULTY/CLASSROOMS: 45% of faculty are male; 55% are female. All teach undergraduates. No introductory courses are taught by graduate students.

PROGRAMS OF STUDY: CU confers B.A., B.S., and B.S.N. degrees. Master's and doctoral degrees are also awarded. Bachelor's degrees are awarded in BIOLOGICAL SCIENCE (biochemistry, biology/biological science, and marine biology), BUSINESS (accounting, business administration and management, business economics, finance, management & strategic leadership, organizational leadership and management, small business management, and professional tennis management), COMMUNICATIONS AND THE ARTS (art, communications, dramatic arts, English, graphic communications management, information technology, languages, music, photography, Spanish, theatre arts, and writing), COMPUTER AND PHYSICAL SCIENCE (actuarial science, applied physics, chemistry, computer science, mathematics, and radiological technology), EDUCATION (art education, athletic training, early childhood education, education, elementary education, music education, physical education, and science education), ENGINEERING AND ENVIRONMENTAL DESIGN (computational sciences, environmental science, and graphic arts technology), HEALTH PROFESSIONS (diagnostic medical sonography, exercise science, health care administration, music therapy, nursing, occupational therapy, physical therapy, physician's assistant, prepharmacy, and public health), SOCIAL SCIENCE (criminal justice, economics, history, political science/government, prelaw, psychology, religion, and sociology). Nursing, communication, and criminal justice have the largest enrollments.

ACTIVITIES: There are 54 groups on campus, including activities board, art, band, cheerleading, choir, chorale, chorus, computers, dance, drama, environmental, ethnic, honors, international, jazz band, LGBT, literary magazine, musical theater, newspaper, orchestra, photography, political, professional, radio and TV, religious, social, social service, student government, and symphony. Popular campus events include Celebrate Carroll, Madrigal Dinner, Spring Fling, Involvement Fair, Freshman Day of Service, Carroll's Got Talent, Alcohol Awareness Week, Learn 2 Lead Month, Byron's Run/Walk/Roll to Cure Paralysis, and Pioneer Games. **Sports:** There are 11 intercollegiate sports for men and 11 for women, and 6 intramural sports for men and 6 for women. Facilities include an all-purpose field house/gym which includes multi-purpose courts for volleyball, basketball, batting cages, an indoor track, athletic training rooms, a weight room, an exercise/physiology laboratory and a 6-lane pool. An additional gym provides a multi-purpose court, dance studio and fitness center. Outdoor facilities include tennis courts, sand volleyball court, a football/soccer/lacrosse field, a practice field, softball diamond, and track and field complex. The Carroll YMCA, is a 24/7 exercise facility with weights, cardio, resistance training equipment and dance studio. The campus center houses ping pong tables, pool tables, dart machine and video games. **Graduates:** From July 1, 2016 to June 30, 2017, 646 bachelor's degrees were awarded. The most popular majors were exercise science (16%), business administration (11%), and nursing (9%). In an average class, 42% graduate in 4 years or less, 55% graduate in 5 years or less, and 56% graduate in 6 years or less. Of the 2016 graduating class, 33% were enrolled in graduate school within 6 months of graduation.

SERVICES: Counseling and information services are available, as is tutoring in most subjects. There is a reader service for the blind. Academic coaching is also available. **Library/Resources:** The library contains 92,593 volumes, 17 microform items, and 3,643 audio/video tapes/CDs/DVDs, and subscribes to 144,006 periodicals including electronic. Computerized library services include interlibrary loans, database searching, Internet access, and Wi-Fi capability. Special learning facilities include an art gallery, radio station, a studio theater, and recital hall. **Physically Challenged Students:** Facilities include wheelchair ramps, elevators, special parking, specially equipped restrooms, special class scheduling, and lowered drinking fountains. **Special:** The Cross-Cultural Experience is a signature component of Carroll's Pioneer Core curriculum, which is characterized by an integrating theme of culture and a requirement for domestic or international cross-cultural immersion. This experience challenges students to apply classroom-based examinations of culture and to interact with cultures other than their own in an off-campus setting. Carroll University, the University of Wisconsin Platteville and the University of Wisconsin Milwaukee offer an inter-university program that allows students to earn two degrees: a B.S. in Applied Physics from Carroll University, and a B.S. in Engineering from the UW-Platteville or UW-Milwaukee. There is also an option to earn a B.S. in Applied Physics from Carroll University and an M.S. in Engineering from UW- Milwaukee. There are 2 national honor societies and a freshman honors program. **Visiting:** There are regularly scheduled orientations for prospective students, consisting of a campus tour, financial aid/admissions counseling, academic department meetings, and extracurricular activities meetings. There are guides for informal visits, visitors may sit in on classes, and stay overnight. To schedule a visit, contact the Office of Admissions. **Campus Safety and Security:** Measures include 24-hour foot and vehicle patrol, emergency notification system, self-defense education, and security escort services. There are shuttle buses, emergency telephones, lighted pathways/sidewalks, and controlled access to dorms/residences.

REQUIREMENTS: The SAT or ACT is required. Applicants must be graduates of an accredited secondary school. The GED is accepted. An essay and interview are recommended for all students, and a portfolio or audition is advised for art and music students, respectively. AP and CLEP credits are accepted. Important factors in the admissions decision are advanced placement or honors courses, recommendations by school officials, and evidence of special talent. To graduate, students must complete 128 credit hours, 32 to 88 in the major, with a minimum GPA of 2.0. Carroll's Pioneer Core curriculum requires students to complete 5 General Education courses outside their major area of study as well as a Cross-Cultural Component. 2 computer science courses and a math course are needed for the B.S.; 8 credits of modern language or the humanities and math competency is needed for the B.A. **Procedure:** Freshmen are admitted in the fall and spring. Entrance exams should be taken during the junior year of high school. There are deferred admissions and rolling admissions plans. Application deadlines are open. Applications are accepted on-line. **Transfer Students:** 197 transfer students enrolled in 2016-2017. Applicants for transfer must have a minimum GPA of 2.0. An interview is required. 32 of 128 credits required for the bachelor's degree must be completed at Carroll. **International Students:** There are 36 international students enrolled. They must take the TOEFL.

ADMISSIONS: 81% of the 2017-2018 applicants were accepted. The ACT scores were 17% below 12, 31% between 12 and 17, 29% between 18 and 23, 13% between 24 and 29, and 10% above 30. **Admissions Contact:** James V. Wiseman, Vice President of Enrollment. Email: *info@carrollu.edu* Web: *www.carrollu.edu*

FINANCIAL AID: In 2017-2018, 98% of all full-time freshmen received some form of financial aid. 85% of all full-time freshmen received need-based aid. The average freshman award was $22,239. Need-based scholarships or need-based grants averaged $17,807; need-based self-help aid (loans and jobs) averaged $4,470; and other non-need-based awards and non-need-based scholarships averaged $14,566. 59% of undergraduate students work part-time. The average financial indebtedness of the 2017 graduate was $25,875. CU is a member of CSS. The FAFSA code is 003838. Check with the school for current application deadlines.

CARTHAGE COLLEGE — E-5

www.carthage.edu

Kenosha, WI 53140 — (262) 551-6000, (800) 351-4058

Fax: (262) 551-5762 — **Email:** admissions@carthage.edu

Full-time: 1265 men, 1370 women	**Faculty:** 102
Part-time: 160 men, 380 women	**Ph.D.s:** 90%
Graduate: 20 men	**Student/Faculty:** 17 to 1
Year: 4-1-4, summer session	**Tuition:** $38,375
Room & Board: $10,460	**Freshman Class:** n/av
SAT or ACT: required	**CEEB CODE:** 1103
Application Deadline: open	**COMPETITIVE**

Carthage College, founded in 1847, is an independent liberal arts institution affiliated with the Evangelical Lutheran Church. There is 1 undergraduate school and one graduate school. In addition to regional accreditation, CC has baccalaureate program accreditation with CSWE and NASM. The 75-acre campus is in a suburban area 30 miles south of Milwaukee and 60 miles north of Chicago, on the shore of Lake Michigan. Including any residence halls, there are 16 buildings.

STUDENT LIFE: 52% of undergraduates are from out of state, mostly the Midwest. Students are from 23 states, 14 foreign countries, and Canada. 88% are from public schools. 76% are White; 6% African American; 6% race unknown; 5% Hispanic; 4% two or more races; 3% Asian American; 1% American Indian/Alaska Native. 31% are Catholic; 26% claim no religious affiliation; 13% Protestant. **Female To Male Ratio:** 1.2:1. The average age of freshmen is 18; all undergraduates, 20. 22% do not continue beyond their first year; 65% remain to graduate. **Housing:** 1800 students can be accommodated in college housing, which includes dorms, on-campus apartments, study-intensive floors, and a health and wellness floor. On-campus housing is guaranteed for all 4 years. 70% of students live on campus. All students may keep cars. Alcohol is not permitted.

FACULTY/CLASSROOMS: 68% of faculty are male; 33% are female. All teach undergraduates. No introductory courses are taught by graduate students. The average class size in an introductory lecture is 19; in a laboratory is 19; and in a regular course is 17.

PROGRAMS OF STUDY: CC confers B.A. and B.S.N. degrees. Master's degrees are also awarded. Bachelor's degrees are awarded in BIOLOGICAL SCIENCE (biology/biological science), BUSINESS (accounting, business administration and management, international economics, and marketing management), COMMUNICATIONS AND THE ARTS (art, English, fine arts, French, German, graphic design, languages, music, performing arts, Spanish, studio art, theatre arts, and theatre production), COMPUTER AND PHYSICAL SCIENCE (chemistry, mathematics, natural sciences, and physics), EDUCATION (elementary education, English education, foreign languages education, mathematics education, middle school education, music education, physical education, and secondary education), HEALTH PROFESSIONS (nursing), SOCIAL SCIENCE (criminal justice, economics, geography, history, philosophy, political science/government, psychology, religion, social science, social work, and sociology). Education, business, and sciences are the strongest academically. Business, biology, and education have the largest enrollments.

ACTIVITIES: 28% of men belong to 5 local and 3 national fraternities; 22% of women belong to 4 local and 2 national sororities. There are 125 groups on campus, including habitat for humanity, art, band, choir, chorus, computers, dance, debate, drama, environmental, ethnic, film, forensics, honors, international, jazz band, LGBT, literary magazine, musical theater, newspaper, orchestra, pep band, photography, political, professional, radio and TV, religious, social, social service, student government, and yearbook. Popular campus events include May Madness, Little Sibling Weekend, and Casino Night. **Sports:** There are 12 intercollegiate sports for men and 12 for women, and 10 intramural sports for men and 5 for women. Facilities include a physical education center, a stadium, a gym, tennis courts, baseball, soccer, softball fields, and natatorium. **Graduates:** The most popular majors were business, education, and biology. Of the 2016 graduating class, 95% were employed within 6 months of graduation.

SERVICES: Counseling and information services are available, as is tutoring in most subjects. **Library/Resources:** The library contains 130,000 volumes, 9,000 microform items, 1,300 audio/video tapes/CDs/DVDs, and subscribes to 450 periodicals including electronic. Computerized library services include interlibrary loans and database searching. Special learning facilities include an art gallery, planetarium, and radio station. **Physically Challenged Students:** 90% of the campus is accessible. Facilities include wheelchair ramps, elevators, special parking, specially equipped restrooms, special class scheduling, lowered drinking fountains, and lowered telephones. **Special:** Internships are available during the January term or, in some cases, for a semester. Carthage offers study abroad in many countries, cross-registration with the University of Wisconsin, work-study programs, and dual and student-designed majors. Students may take a 3-2 engineering degree with Case Western, and the University of Minnesota-Twin Cities or the University of Wisconsin/Madison, or a 3-2 occupational therapy degree with Washington University. There are 3 national honor societies and a freshman honors program. **Visiting:** There are regularly scheduled orientations for prospective students, including small group meetings with first year adviser and faculty members, class selection, and curriculum overview. Informational sessions for parents are offered. There are guides for informal visits, visitors may sit in on classes, and stay overnight. To schedule a visit, contact the Office of Admissions. **Campus Safety and Security:** Measures include 24-hour foot and vehicle patrol, emergency notification system, self-defense education, and security escort services. There are shuttle buses, emergency telephones, lighted pathways/sidewalks, controlled access to dorms/residences, and electronic exit locks on residence halls.

REQUIREMENTS: The SAT or ACT is required. Applicants should be graduates of an accredited secondary school, having earned 16 academic credits, including English, foreign language, math, science, and social studies. The GED is accepted. An interview is recommended. AP and CLEP credits are accepted. Important factors in the admissions decision are advanced placement or honors courses, leadership record, and extracurricular activities record. To graduate, students must complete 138 credits, with up to 56 in the major, and a minimum GPA of 2.0 (education requires 2.75). Students must complete 50 credits in liberal arts studies, including the Heritage Seminar Series, which includes 3 courses that help develop competencies in cultural studies, writing, thinking, reading, speaking, and listening. 2 courses each are required in religion and foreign language, and 1 in math. There is also a phys ed requirement. Each student must complete one of the junior symposia, a series of 3 interdependent courses, and a senior project in the major. **Procedure:** Freshmen are admitted to all sessions. Entrance exams should be taken in spring of the junior year or fall of the senior year. There are deferred admissions and rolling admissions plans. Application deadlines are open. The fall 2017 application fee was $25. Notification is sent on a rolling basis. Applications are accepted on-line. **Transfer Students:** 76 transfer students enrolled in 2016-2017. Transfer students are accepted based on academic performance at their previous school; they should have a GPA greater than 2.0. If they have fewer than 12 credits, the high school record is considered. Either the SAT I or ACT and an interview are recommended. **International Students:** They must take the TOEFL.

Admissions Contact: Thomas J. Augustine, Director of Admissions and Financial Aid. Email: *admissions@carthage.edu* Web: *www.carthage.edu*

FINANCIAL AID: In 2017-2018, 95% of all full-time freshmen received some form of financial aid. 35% of undergraduate students work part-time. The FAFSA code is 003839. The deadline for filing freshman financial aid applications for fall entry is February 15.

CONCORDIA UNIVERSITY WISCONSIN E-4

www.cuw.edu

Mequon, WI 53097	**(414) 243-4500**
Fax: (414) 243-4545	**Email: admission@cuw.edu**
Full-time: 1502 men, 1502 women	**Faculty:** 195
Part-time: 667 men, 667 women	**Ph.D.s:** 75%
Graduate: 1964 men, 1965 women	**Student/Faculty:** 13 to 1
Year: 4-1-4, summer session	**Tuition:** $26,130
Room & Board: $9780	**Freshman Class:** 1947 accepted, 639 enrolled
ACT: 22	**CEEB CODE:** 1139
Application Deadline: August 15	**COMPETITIVE**

Concordia University Wisconsin, established in 1881, is a private institution affiliated with the Lutheran Church-Missouri Synod. There are 5 undergraduate schools and 1 graduate school. In addition to regional accreditation, CUW has baccalaureate program accreditation with NLN, ACOTE, CAAHEP, CAPTE, CCNE, IACBE, and ACPE. The 155-acre campus is in a suburban area 15 miles north of Milwaukee. Including any residence halls, there are 20 buildings.

STUDENT LIFE: 60% of undergraduates are from Wisconsin. Others are from 47 states, and 25 foreign countries. 75% are White; 3% Hispanic; 2% Foreign; 17% African American; 1% Asian American; 1% American Indian/Alaska Native. 79% are Protestant; 21% Catholic. **Female To Male Ratio:** 1.0:1. The average age of freshmen is 18; all undergraduates, 20. 20% do not continue beyond their first year; 60% remain to graduate. **Housing:** 1500 students can be accommodated in college housing, which includes dorms. On-campus housing is guaranteed for all 4 years, and is available on a first-come, first-served basis. 69% of students live on campus. Alcohol is not permitted. All students may keep cars.

FACULTY/CLASSROOMS: 43% of faculty are male; 57% are female. All teach undergraduates. No introductory courses are taught by graduate students. The average class size in a regular course is 17.

PROGRAMS OF STUDY: CUW confers B.A., B.S., and B.S.N. degrees. Associate, master's, and doctoral degrees are also awarded. Bachelor's degrees are awarded in BIOLOGICAL SCIENCE (biology/biological science), BUSINESS (accounting, banking and finance, business administration and management, management science, and marketing/retailing/merchandising), COMMUNICATIONS AND THE ARTS (art, communications, English, graphic design, music, Spanish, speech/debate/rhetoric, and telecommunications), COMPUTER AND PHYSICAL SCIENCE (mathematics and radiological technology), EDUCATION (athletic training, early childhood education, elementary education, physical education, and secondary education), ENGINEERING AND ENVIRONMENTAL DESIGN (interior design), HEALTH PROFESSIONS (nursing, occupational therapy, and sports medicine), SOCIAL SCIENCE (biblical languages, criminal justice, history, humanities, ministries, paralegal studies, pastoral studies, psychology, religion, religious music, social science, social work, and theological studies). Education, business, and health sciences are the strongest academically.

ACTIVITIES: There are no fraternities or sororities. There are 20 groups on campus, including art, band, cheerleading, choir, chorale, drama, drill team, ethnic, honors, international, jazz band, literary magazine, musical theater, newspaper, orchestra, pep band, political, professional, radio and TV, religious, and student government. Popular campus events include Winterfest and Springfest. **Sports:** There are 11 intercollegiate sports for men and 10 for women, and 10 intramural sports for men and 9 for women. Facilities include a field house, a stadium, fitness center, athletic fields, and a baseball stadium. **Graduates:** From July 1, 2016 to June 30, 2017, 664 bachelor's degrees were awarded. The most popular majors were health professions, business, and education. In an average class, 60% graduate in 6 years or less. Of the 2016 graduating class, 52% were employed within 6 months of graduation.

SERVICES: Counseling and information services are available, as is tutoring in every subject. There is a reader service for the blind, and remedial math, reading, and writing. **Library/Resources:** The library contains 120,000 volumes, 270,602 microform items, and 4,152 audio/video tapes/CDs/DVDs, and subscribes to 37,000 periodicals including electronic. Computerized library services include interlibrary loans, database searching, and Internet access. Special learning facilities include an art gallery, radio station, a curriculum library for education students, and sustainable environmental center. **Physically Challenged Students:** All of the campus is accessible. Facilities include wheelchair ramps, elevators, special parking, and specially equipped restrooms. **Special:** Internships, study abroad, pass/fail options, and credit for life, military, and work experience are available. Concordia offers a general studies degree, dual, student-designed, and interdisciplinary majors, including justice and public policy, and nondegree study. Accelerated degree programs are available in several fields. There is 1 national honor society. **Visiting:** There are regularly scheduled orientations for prospective students, including a tour and financial aid and academic information sessions. There are guides for informal visits, visitors may sit in on classes, and stay overnight. To schedule a visit, contact Michelle Hoffman in the Admissions Office. **Campus Safety and Security:** Measures include 24-hour foot and vehicle patrol and emergency notification system. There are lighted pathways/sidewalks, controlled access to dorms/residences, and security guards.

REQUIREMENTS: A satisfactory score on the SAT or on the ACT is required. Applicants must be graduates of an accredited secondary school, having completed 16 academic credits, including 3 of English and 2 each of math, science, and social studies. The GED is accepted. AP and CLEP credits are accepted. Important factors in the admissions decision are leadership record, recommendations by school officials, and personality/intangible qualities. To graduate, students must complete 126 credits, including at least 30 in the major, with a minimum GPA of 2.0. The 47 1/2 credit core curriculum includes theology/philosophy, humanities, cross culture, social science, natural science, communication, math, and phys ed. **Procedure:** Freshmen are admitted to all sessions. Entrance exams should be taken in the junior year. There is a rolling admissions plan. Applications should be filed by August 15 for fall entry. The fall 2017 application fee was $35. **Transfer Students:** 128 transfer students enrolled in 2016-2017. Applicants for transfer must have a minimum GPA of 2.0 and meet the same entrance exam criteria as entering freshmen. 36 of 126 credits required for the bachelor's degree must be completed at CUW. **International Students:** There are 86 international students enrolled. They must take the TOEFL and the college's own test. If the student's TOEFL score is below 500, they must take an English proficiency exam for placement.

Admissions Contact: Michelle Hoffman, Director of Admissions. Email: *admission@cuw.edu* Web: *www.cuw.edu*

FINANCIAL AID: In 2017-2018, 82% of all full-time freshmen received some form of financial aid. The average freshman award was $23,007. The CSS/Profile and the college's own financial statement, and income tax forms are required. The deadline for filing freshman financial aid applications for fall entry is April 30.

EDGEWOOD COLLEGE C-4
www.edgewood.edu

Madison, WI 53711	(608) 663-2294 (800) 444-4861
Fax: (608) 663-2214	Email: admissions@edgewood.edu
Full-time: 441 men, 1109 women	**Faculty:** n/av
Part-time: 96 men, 167 women	**Ph.D.s:** 72%
Graduate: 226 men, 639 women	**Student/Faculty:** 11 to 1
Year: semesters, summer session	**Tuition:** $26,550
Room & Board: $9400	**Freshman Class:** 1160 applied, 891 accepted, 298 enrolled
ACT: 23	**CEEB CODE:** 1202
Application Deadline: August 14	**COMPETITIVE**

Edgewood College, established in 1927, is a private Catholic institution sponsored by the Sinsinawa Dominican Sisters. The figures given in the above capsule and in this profile are approximate. There is 1 undergraduate school and 1 graduate school. In addition to regional accreditation, EC has baccalaureate program accreditation with ACBSP, CAEP, and CCNE. The 55-acre campus is in a suburban area 5 miles southwest of Madison. Including any residence halls, there are 15 buildings.

STUDENT LIFE: 89% of undergraduates are from Wisconsin. Others are from 20 states, 29 foreign countries, and Canada. 92% are from public schools. 79% are White; 6% Hispanic; 4% Foreign; 3% African American; 3% Asian American; 3% two or more races; 3% race unknown. 27% are Christian; 23% Catholic. **Female To Male Ratio:** 2.5:1. The average age of freshmen is 18; all undergraduates, 22. 19% do not continue beyond their first year; 60% remain to graduate. **Housing:** 536 students can be accommodated in college housing, which includes dorms and on-campus apartments. On-campus housing is guaranteed for the freshman year only and is available on a lottery system for upperclassmen. 70% of students commute. Upperclassmen may keep cars.

FACULTY/CLASSROOMS: 39% of faculty are male; 61% are female. All teach undergraduates. No introductory courses are taught by graduate students.

PROGRAMS OF STUDY: EC confers B.A. and B.S. degrees. Master's and doctoral degrees are also awarded. Bachelor's degrees are awarded in AGRICULTURE (environmental studies), BIOLOGICAL SCIENCE (biology/adolescence education), BUSINESS (accounting, business administration and management, and organizational leadership and management), COMMUNICATIONS AND THE ARTS (art, communication studies, English, French, graphic design, music, music industry, music production/recording technology, Spanish, and theatre arts), COMPUTER AND PHYSICAL SCIENCE (chemistry, chemistry education, information sciences and systems, mathematics, natural sciences, physics, and web technology), EDUCATION (art education, business education, computer education, early childhood education, education of the exceptional child, educational studies, elementary education, English education, French studies K-12 education, mathematics education, music education, Spanish education K-12, and special education), HEALTH PROFESSIONS (art therapy, biology, cytotechnology, medical science, and nursing), SOCIAL SCIENCE (child care/child and family studies, criminal justice, economics, ethnic studies, history, international relations, political science/government, psychology, religious education, religious studies, social studies, and sociology). Liberal arts is the strongest academically. Business, education, and nursing have the largest enrollments.

ACTIVITIES: There are no fraternities or sororities. There are 48 groups on campus, including art, band, choir, chorale, chorus, communications, dance, drama, environmental, ethnic, honors, international, jazz band, LGBT, literary magazine, musical theater, newspaper, orchestra, political, professional, religious, social, social service, student government, and symphony. Popular campus events include Winterfrost, Fall Fest, and Spring Fest. **Sports:** There are 8 intercollegiate sports for men and 9 for women, and 4 intramural sports for men and 4 for women. Facilities include a gym, soccer, baseball, and softball fields, a fitness center, and access to tennis courts off campus. **Graduates:** From July 1, 2016 to June 30, 2017, 459 bachelor's degrees were awarded. The most popular majors were nursing (16%), business (9%), and psychology (8%). In an average class, 38% graduate in 4 years or less, 60% graduate in 5 years or less, and 60% graduate in 6 years or less.

SERVICES: Counseling and information services are available, as is tutoring in some subjects, such as sciences, introductory math courses, and Spanish. There is a reader service for the blind, and remedial math, reading, and writing. **Library/Resources:** The library contains 205,058 volumes, 9,524 microform items, 6,226 audio/video tapes/CDs/DVDs, and subscribes to 31,200 periodicals, including electronic. Computerized library services include interlibrary loans, database searching, Internet access, and Wi-Fi capability. Special learning facilities include an art gallery. **Physically Challenged Students:** 90% of the campus is accessible. Facilities include wheelchair ramps, elevators, special parking, specially equipped restrooms, special class scheduling, lowered drinking fountains, lowered telephones, special housing, automated doors in the library, science center, activities center, and residence halls and a chairlift. **Special:** Students may cross-register with the University of Wisconsin/Madison. Internships, study abroad, dual and student-designed majors, nondegree study, pass/fail options, and credit for prior learning experience are available. There are accelerated undergraduate degree programs for working adults. There are 5 national honor societies and a freshman honors program. **Visiting:** There are regularly scheduled orientations for prospective students, including Experience Edgewood Days, a program where admitted freshmen spend a day on campus as if they were Edgewood college students. They choose their own schedule for the day, which may include sitting in on classes, attending athletics presentations, and learning about study abroad opportunities, residence life, and student activities. Students also have the opportunity to take campus tours and exclusive tours of the residence halls. Complimentary lunch is included. There are guides for informal visits, visitors may sit in on classes, and stay overnight. To schedule a visit, contact the Admissions Office. **Campus Safety and Security:** Measures include 24-hour foot and vehicle patrol, emergency notification system, self-defense education, and security escort services. There are shuttle buses, emergency telephones, lighted pathways/sidewalks, controlled access to dorms/residences, residence halls have alarms, a security card system, and campus security guards. RAs are on duty 24 hours a day and weekends.

REQUIREMENTS: Students must meet two of the following three requirement: must present a cumulative high school GPA of 2.5 on a 4.0 scale, a rank in the top 50% of their high school graduating class and/or a composite score of 18 on the ACT or an equivalent SAT score. Edgewood requires applicants to be in the upper 50% of their class. AP and CLEP credits are accepted. To graduate, students must complete a minimum of 120 credit hours with a minimum cumulative GPA of 2.0. There are general education requirements, and each student must complete a major field of study and required core courses. **Procedure:** Freshmen are admitted in the fall and spring. Entrance exams should be taken by the senior year. There are deferred admissions and rolling admissions plans. Applications should be filed by August 14 for fall entry; January 12 for spring entry. The fall 2017 application fee was $30. Applications are accepted on-line. **Transfer Students:** 161 transfer students enrolled in 2016-2017. Transfer students must complete an Application for Undergraduate Admission and have official transcripts from each high school, and college or university attended, sent directly to the Office of Admissions. High school transcripts should include class rank and cumulative GPA. GEDs are accepted. Students are expected to present a minimum of 12 academic-level credits and a cumulative college grade point average of 2.0 (on a 4.0 scale) from an accredited institution. Students dismissed from a previous college must wait one full year prior to applying to Edgewood and supply additional information. 32 of 120 credits required for the bachelor's degree must be completed at EC. **International Students:** There are 62 international students enrolled. They must take the TOEFL with a minimum score of 525 on the paper-based TOEFL (PBT) or 71 on the Internet-based version (iBT).

ADMISSIONS: 77% of the 2017-2018 applicants were accepted. The ACT scores were 9% between 12 and 17, 51% between 18 and 23, 36% between 24 and 29, and 4% above 30. 25% of the current freshmen were in the top fifth of their class; 59% were in the top two fifths. **Admissions Contact:** Christine Benedict, VP for Enrollment Management. Email: *admissions@edgewood.edu* Web: *www.edgewood.edu*

FINANCIAL AID: In 2017-2018, 79% of all full-time freshmen received some form of financial aid and need-based aid. The average freshman award was $22,004. Need-based scholarships or need-based grants averaged $16,868; and need-based self-help aid (loans and jobs) averaged $5,732. 82% of undergraduate students work part-time. The average financial indebtedness of the 2017 graduate was $30,574. Edgewood is a member of CSS. The college's own financial statement and a tax return are required. The FAFSA code is 003848. Check with the school for current application deadlines.

LAKELAND UNIVERSITY E-4
www.lakeland.edu

Plymouth, WI 53073	(920) 565-1217 (800) 242-3347
Fax: (920) 565-1206	Email: admissions@lakeland.edu
Full-time: 390 men, 400 women	**Faculty:** 41; IIB, --$
Part-time: 20 men, 30 women	**Ph.D.s:** 59%
Graduate: 50 men, 130 women	**Student/Faculty:** 19 to 1
Year: semesters, summer session	**Tuition:** $26,880
Room & Board: $8250	**Freshman Class:** n/av
SAT or ACT: required	**CEEB CODE:** 1393
Application Deadline: September 1	**COMPETITIVE**

Lakeland University, established in 1862, is a private institution affiliated with the United Church of Christ. The 4-4-1 academic calendar consists of 4-month fall and spring terms, and an optional 3-week May term. There are 3 undergraduate schools and 1 graduate school. The 240-acre campus is in a rural area 10 miles northwest of Sheboygan. Including any residence halls, there are 24 buildings.

STUDENT LIFE: 79% of undergraduates are from Wisconsin. Others are from 16 states, 31 foreign countries, and Canada. 90% are from public schools. 8% are Foreign; 76% White; 5% African American; 4% Asian American; 1% Hispanic. 32% are Protestant; 29% Catholic; 25% claim no religious affiliation. **Female To Male Ratio:** 1.2:1. The average age of all undergraduates is 22. 32% do not continue beyond their first year; 43% remain to graduate. **Housing:** 488 students can be accommodated in college housing, which includes on-campus apartments. In addition, there are honors houses, male-only and female-only dorms, and housing for students with senior standing. On-campus housing is guaranteed for all 4 years. 57% of students live on campus. All students may keep cars.

FACULTY/CLASSROOMS: 51% of faculty are male; 49% are female. All teach undergraduates and do research. No introductory courses are taught by graduate students. The average class size in an introductory lecture is 20; in a laboratory is 15; and in a regular course is 16.

PROGRAMS OF STUDY: LU confers B.A. degrees. Master's degrees are also awarded. Bachelor's degrees are awarded in BIOLOGICAL SCIENCE (biology/biological science), BUSINESS (accounting, business administration and management, business economics, hospitality management services, international business management, and marketing management), COMMUNICATIONS AND THE ARTS (art, creative writing, dramatic arts, English, German, music, and Spanish), COMPUTER AND PHYSICAL SCIENCE (chemistry, computer science, and mathematics), EDUCATION (business education, early childhood education, elementary education, music education, and secondary education), SOCIAL SCIENCE (behavioral science, criminal justice, economics, history, philosophy, physical fitness/movement, psychology, public administration, religion, and sociology). Business, education, and accounting are the strongest academically. Education, business, and computer science have the largest enrollments.

ACTIVITIES: 17% of men belong to 3 local fraternities; 11% of women belong to 3 local sororities. There are 27 groups on campus, including band, choir, chorus, dance, drama, ethnic, honors, international, literary magazine, newspaper, pep band, professional, radio and TV, religious, social, student government, and yearbook. Popular campus events include Winter Carnival and Spring Celebration. **Sports:** There are 8 intercollegiate sports for men and 7 for women, and 2 intramural sports for men and 2 for women. Facilities include a sports complex, a fitness lab, 3 full-size basketball courts, a weight room, indoor and outdoor tennis courts, indoor pitching and batting facilities, softball, baseball, football, soccer, and practice fields. **Graduates:** From July 1, 2016 to June 30, 2017, 145 bachelor's degrees were awarded. The most popular majors were education (28%), business administration (17%), and computer science (10%). In an average class, 13% graduate in 3 years or less, 30% graduate in 4 years or less, 43% graduate in 5 years or less, and 46% graduate in 6 years or less. Of the 2016 graduating class, 10% were enrolled in graduate school within 6 months of graduation, and 95% were employed.

SERVICES: Counseling and information services are available, as is tutoring in every subject. There is a reader service for the blind, and remedial math, reading, and writing. **Library/Resources:** The library contains 57,447 volumes, 33,169 microform items, 2,099 audio/video tapes/CDs/DVDs, and subscribes to 322 periodicals, including electronic. Computerized library services include interlibrary loans and database searching. Special learning facilities include an art gallery, radio station, and a college history museum. **Physically Challenged Students:** 83% of the campus is accessible. Facilities include wheelchair ramps, elevators, special parking, specially equipped restrooms, and lowered drinking fountains. **Special:** Internships in all majors, study abroad in Germany and Japan, a Washington semester, and work-study programs are available. There are some dual majors, a general studies degree, a 3-2 engineering degree with the University of Wisconsin-Madison, a 2-2 1/2 nursing program with Bellin College of Nursing, and nondegree study. There is a freshman honors program and 10 departmental honors programs. **Visiting:** There are regularly scheduled orientations for prospective students, consisting of meetings with faculty and financial aid personnel, activities meetings, and a campus tour. There are guides for informal visits, visitors may sit in on classes, and stay overnight. To schedule a visit, contact the Admissions Office. **Campus Safety and Security:** Measures include security escort services. There are emergency telephones, lighted pathways/sidewalks, and foot patrol on weekends and evenings.

REQUIREMENTS: The SAT or ACT is required, with a minimum composite score of 950 on the SAT I or 19 on the ACT. Applicants must be graduates of an accredited secondary school or have the GED. An interview is recommended. Applications are accepted on-line via the college's website. AP and CLEP credits are accepted. Important factors in the admissions decision are advanced placement or honors courses, leadership record, and evidence of special talent. To graduate, students must complete 128 semester hours, with at least 32 in the major and a minimum 2.0 GPA. There are requirements in history, humanities, natural sciences, social sciences, and religion. **Procedure:** Freshmen are admitted in the fall, spring, and summer. Entrance exams should be taken after the enrollment commitment is made. There is a rolling admissions plan. Applications should be filed by September 1 for fall entry; December 15 for spring entry. The fall 2017 application fee was $20. Notification is sent on a rolling basis. Applications are accepted on-line. **Transfer Students:** 115 transfer students enrolled in 2016-2017. Applicants should have a GPA of at least 2.0. Lakeland recommends an interview. 36 of 128 credits required for the bachelor's degree must be completed at LU. **International Students:** There are 100 international students enrolled. They must take the TOEFL.

Admissions Contact: Kristin Henning, Senior Director of Admissions/Recruitment. Email: *admissions@lakeland.edu* Web: *www.lakeland.edu*

FINANCIAL AID: In 2017-2018, 100% of all full-time freshmen received some form of financial aid. 86% of all full-time freshmen received need-based aid. The average freshman award was $11,895. 30% of undergraduate students work part-time. The average financial indebtedness of the 2017 graduate was $20,558. LU is a member of CSS. The college's own financial statement is required. The FAFSA code is 003854. The deadline for filing freshman financial aid applications for fall entry is July 1.

LAWRENCE UNIVERSITY D-3
www.lawrence.edu

Appleton, WI 54911	(920) 832-6500 (800) 227-0982
Fax: (920) 832-6782	Email: admissions@lawrence.edu
Full-time: 683 men, 809 women	**Faculty:** 165; IIB, av$
Part-time: 12 men, 3 women	**Ph.D.s:** 92%
Graduate: n/av	**Student/Faculty:** 8 to 1
Year: trimesters	**Tuition:** $46,101
Room & Board: $10,032	**Freshman Class:** 3579 applied, 2254 accepted, 374 enrolled
SAT CR/M/W: 624/646/630 **ACT:** 29	**CEEB CODE:** 1398
Application Deadline: January 15	**HIGHLY COMPETITIVE+**

Lawrence University, founded in 1847, is a private liberal arts institution with a conservatory of music. The figures given in the above capsule and in this profile are approximate. There is 1 undergraduate school. In addition to regional accreditation, LU has baccalaureate program accreditation with NASM. The 84-acre campus is in an urban area 100 miles north of Milwaukee, 30 miles south of Green Bay. Including any residence halls, there are 58 buildings.

STUDENT LIFE: 73% of undergraduates are from out of state, mostly

the Midwest. Students are from 45 states, 35 foreign countries, and Canada. 75% are from public schools. 8% are Foreign; 77% White; 5% American Indian/Alaska Native; 4% Hispanic; 3% African American; 3% Asian American. 69% claim no religious affiliation. **Female To Male Ratio:** 1.2:1. The average age of freshmen is 18; all undergraduates, 20. 12% do not continue beyond their first year; 76% remain to graduate. **Housing:** 1364 students can be accommodated in college housing, which includes married student dorms and on-campus apartments. In addition, there are language/international houses, special-interest houses, fraternity houses, sorority houses, single apartments and theme housing. On-campus housing is guaranteed for all 4 years. All students may keep cars.

FACULTY/CLASSROOMS: 62% of faculty are male; 38% are female. All teach undergraduates and all do research. No introductory courses are taught by graduate students. The average class size in an introductory lecture is 24; in a laboratory is 15; and in a regular course is 15.

PROGRAMS OF STUDY: LU confers B.A. and B.Mus. degrees. Bachelor's degrees are awarded in AGRICULTURE (environmental studies), BIOLOGICAL SCIENCE (biochemistry and biology/biological science), COMMUNICATIONS AND THE ARTS (art history and appreciation, Chinese, classics, dramatic arts, English, French, German, Japanese, linguistics, music performance, music theory and composition, Russian, Spanish, and studio art), COMPUTER AND PHYSICAL SCIENCE (chemistry, computer science, geology, mathematics, and physics), EDUCATION (music education), SOCIAL SCIENCE (anthropology, cognitive science, East Asian studies, economics, gender studies, history, international studies, philosophy, political science/government, and psychology). Biology, music, and physics are the strongest academically. Psychology, biology, and English have the largest enrollments.

ACTIVITIES: 22% of men belong to 5 national fraternities; 18% of women belong to 3 national sororities. There are 100 groups on campus, including art, band, chess, choir, chorale, chorus, computers, dance, drama, environmental, ethnic, film, honors, international, jazz band, LGBT, literary magazine, musical theater, newspaper, online radio station, opera, orchestra, pep band, photography, political, professional, religious, social, social service, student government, and symphony. Popular campus events include Midwest Trivia Contest, International Cabaret, Mardis Gras, and Shack-a-thon. **Sports:** There are 12 intercollegiate sports for men and 10 for women, and 23 intramural sports for men and 23 for women. Facilities include a football stadium, outdoor track, indoor track, baseball, soccer, practice fields, tennis, squash, and racquetball/handball courts, gyms for basketball, volleyball, and badminton, batting cages, an 8-lane swimming pool with diving well, weight rooms, cardio exercise rooms, and dance studio. **Graduates:** From July 1, 2016 to June 30, 2017, 356 bachelor's degrees were awarded. The most popular majors were visual and performing arts (20%), social science (16%), and biological/life sciences (13%). In an average class, 1% graduate in 3 years or less, 68% graduate in 4 years or less, 70% graduate in 5 years or less, and 76% graduate in 6 years or less. Of the 2016 graduating class, 30% were enrolled in graduate school within 6 months of graduation, and 50% were employed.

SERVICES: Counseling and information services are available, as is tutoring in every subject. There is a reader service for the blind. The writing lab focuses on enhancing writing skills, and remedial writing. **Library/Resources:** The library contains 420,502 volumes, 102,629 microform items, 25,897 audio/video tapes/CDs/DVDs, and subscribes to 2,505 periodicals, including electronic. Computerized library services include interlibrary loans, database searching, Internet access, and Wi-Fi capability. Special learning facilities include an art gallery and natural history museum. **Physically Challenged Students:** 95% of the campus is accessible. Facilities include wheelchair ramps, elevators, special parking, specially equipped restrooms, special class scheduling, lowered drinking fountains, and special housing. **Special:** Lawrence offers Chicago-based programs in urban studies, urban education, and the arts, a humanities program at the Newberry Library, and a science internship at Oak Ridge National Laboratory. There are study-abroad programs in 28 countries, a Washington semester, limited pass/fail options, student-designed majors, and nondegree study. Students may take a 3-2 engineering degree with Columbia or Washington Universities, or Rensselaer Polytechnic Institute. Also available are 3-2 programs in forestry and environmental studies with Duke University, in occupational therapy with Washington University in St. Louis. A 5-year B.A.-B.Mus. degree is offered. There are 5 national honor societies and a chapter of Phi Beta Kappa. **Visiting:** There are regularly scheduled orientations for prospective students, visiting students can participate in an extensive day-long program with many choices of classes and presentations. There are guides for informal visits; visitors may sit in on classes and stay overnight. To schedule a visit, contact the Visit Coordinator in the Office of Admissions. **Campus Safety and Security:** Measures include 24-hour foot and vehicle patrol, emergency notification system, self-defense education, and security escort services. There are emergency telephones, lighted pathways/sidewalks, controlled access to dorms/residences, and whistle stop program.

REQUIREMENTS: It is recommended that applicants should complete 16 high school academic credits 4 units in English, 3 units each in math and science, 2 units each in foreign language, social studies, and history. Lawrence requires an essay, reports from a teacher and counselor, and an audition for music majors. For art majors Lawrence recommends an interview, and a portfolio. AP credits are accepted. Important factors in the admissions decision are advanced placement or honors courses, evidence of special talent, personality/intangible qualities, and extracurricular activities record. Students must complete 216 units (270 units for a double-degree program), including 48 to 72 in the major, with a minimum GPA of 2.0. All students must take Freshmen Studies. Distribution requirements include 12 units each in humanities, social sciences, and natural sciences, including a lab course, and 6 units in fine arts. Competency requirements must also be met in writing, speaking, foreign language, and quantitative analysis. Some majors require a comprehensive exam or a thesis. **Procedure:** Freshmen are admitted in the fall. Entrance exams should be taken in the spring of the junior year or fall of the senior year. There are early decision, early admissions, and deferred admissions plans. Early decision applications should be filed by November 15; regular applications, by January 15 for fall entry. The fall 2017 application fee was $40. Notification of early decision is sent December 1; regular decision, 43 early decision candidates were accepted for the 2017-2018 class. 56 applicants were on the 2017 waiting list; 38 were admitted. Applications are accepted on-line. **Transfer Students:** 25 transfer students enrolled in 2016-2017. Applicants must present official transcripts of their college and secondary school work, and the recommendation of a college professor. Typically, candidates with a college GPA of 2.75 or higher will receive serious consideration. 108 of 216 credits required for the bachelor's degree must be completed at Lawrence. **International Students:** There are 104 international students enrolled. They must take the TOEFL with a minimum score of 577 on the paper-based TOEFL (PBT) or 90 on the Internet-based version (iBT). Students must take either the ACT, IELTS, or SAT.

ADMISSIONS: 63% of the 2017-2018 applicants were accepted. The SAT scores for the 2017-2018 freshman class were: Critical Reading-- 13% below 500, 21% between 500 and 599, 40% between 600 and 699, and 26% between 700 and 800. Math-- 5% below 500, 23% between 500 and 599, 37% between 600 and 699, and 35% between 700 and 800. Writing-- 10% below 500, 25% between 500 and 599, 42% between 600 and 699, and 23% between 700 and 800. The ACT scores were 13% between 18 and 23, 40% between 24 and 29, and 47% above 30. 74% of the current freshmen were in the top fifth of their class; 95% were in the top two fifths. 13 freshmen graduated first in their class. **Admissions Contact:** Marybeth Petrie, Director of Admission. Email: *admissions@lawrence.edu* Web: *www.lawrence.edu*

FINANCIAL AID: In 2017-2018, 95% of all full-time freshmen received some form of financial aid. 64% of all full-time freshmen received need-based aid. The average freshman award was $38,758. Need-based scholarships or need-based grants averaged $33,637 ($38,205 maximum); need-based self-help aid (loans and jobs) averaged $6,841 ($8,000 maximum); other non-need-based awards and non-need-based scholarships averaged $22,716 ($38,205 maximum); and $5,023 from other forms of aid. The average financial indebtedness of the 2017 graduate was $44,328. LU is a member of CSS. The college's own financial statement is required. The FAFSA code is 003856. The priority date for freshman financial aid applications for fall entry is February 1.

MARIAN UNIVERSITY D-4

Fond du Lac, WI 54935 (920) 923-7650 (800) 262-7426

Fax: (920) 923-8755 **Email: admission@marianuniversity.edu**

Full-time: 398 men, 805 women	**Faculty:** 72; I, +$
Part-time: 79 men, 189 women	**Ph.D.s:** 57%
Graduate: 122 men, 341 women	**Student/Faculty:** 18 to 1
Year: semesters, summer session	**Tuition:** $27,400
Room & Board: $7222	**Freshman Class:** 1684 applied, 1138 accepted, 352 enrolled
ACT: 21	**CEEB CODE:** 1443
Application Deadline: open	**COMPETITIVE**

Marian University, founded in 1936, is a private, Catholic, liberal arts institution offering degree programs in the arts and sciences, business, education, and health fields. There are 2 undergraduate schools and 1 graduate school. In addition to regional accreditation, MU has baccalaureate program accreditation with CSWE, CAEP, NLN, IACBE, and CCNE. The 78-acre campus is in a small town 60 miles north of Milwaukee. Including any residence halls, there are 30 buildings.

STUDENT LIFE: 82% of undergraduates are from Wisconsin. Others are from 40 states, 8 foreign countries, and Canada. 70% are from public schools. 82% are White; 5% race unknown; 4% African American; 4% Hispanic; 2% Foreign; 1% Asian American; 1% American Indian/Alaska Native; 1% two or more races. 32% are Catholic; 30% claim no religious affiliation; 28% Protestant. **Female To Male Ratio:** 2.2:1. The average age of freshmen is 19; all undergraduates, 24. 34% do not continue beyond their first year; 48% remain to graduate. **Housing:** 538 students can be accommodated in college housing, which includes single-sex dorms and on-campus apartments. In addition, there are special-interest houses. On-campus housing is available on a first-come, first-served basis, and is available on a lottery system for upperclassmen. 65% of students commute. All students may keep cars.

FACULTY/CLASSROOMS: 37% of faculty are male; 59% are female. 82% teach undergraduates. No introductory courses are taught by graduate students. The average class size in an introductory lecture is 17; in a laboratory is 16; and in a regular course is 14.

PROGRAMS OF STUDY: MU confers B.A., B.S., B.B.A., B.C.J., B.I.S, B.O.C., B.S.B.A., B.S.Ed., B.S.N., B.S.R.T., and B.S.W. degrees. Master's and doctoral degrees are also awarded. Bachelor's degrees are awarded in BIOLOGICAL SCIENCE (biology/biological science), BUSINESS (accounting, business administration and management, management science, marketing/retailing/merchandising, and sports management), COMMUNICATIONS AND THE ARTS (art, communications, English, and music), COMPUTER AND PHYSICAL SCIENCE (chemistry, information sciences and systems, mathematics, and radiological technology), EDUCATION (art education, early childhood education, elementary education, English education, mathematics education, middle school education, music education, science education, secondary education, and social science education), HEALTH PROFESSIONS (cytotechnology and nursing), SOCIAL SCIENCE (criminal justice, history, homeland security, interdisciplinary studies, psychology, and social work). Nursing, education, and business have the largest enrollments.

ACTIVITIES: There are no fraternities; 2% of women belong to 2 national sororities. There are 27 groups on campus, including art, band, choir, chorale, chorus, drama, environmental, ethnic, honors, international, jazz band, LGBT, multicultural and campus ministry, newspaper, orchestra, photography, professional, religious, social, social service, student government, and symphony. Popular campus events include Academic Symposium, and Big Band. **Sports:** There are 10 intercollegiate sports for men and 10 for women, and 6 intramural sports for men and 6 for women. Facilities include baseball field, soccer field, softball field, a gym, game room, outdoor volleyball, and a weight room. **Graduates:** From July 1, 2016 to June 30, 2017, 392 bachelor's degrees were awarded. The most popular majors were nursing (32%), criminal justice (12%), and radiologic technology (7%). In an average class, 28% graduate in 4 years or less, 39% graduate in 5 years or less, and 42% graduate in 6 years or less. Of the 2016 graduating class, 7% were enrolled in graduate school within 6 months of graduation, and 80% were employed.

SERVICES: Counseling and information services are available, as is tutoring in most subjects. There is a reader service for the blind, and remedial math, reading, and writing. **Library/Resources:** The library contains 200,158 volumes, 3,570 microform items, 3,544 audio/video tapes/CDs/DVDs, and subscribes to 1,503 periodicals including electronic. Computerized library services include interlibrary loans, database searching, Internet access, and Wi-Fi capability. **Physically Challenged Students:** All of the campus is accessible. Facilities include wheelchair ramps, elevators, special parking, specially equipped restrooms, and lowered telephones. **Special:** Internships are offered in most areas of study, cooperative education programs in all majors, and accelerated-degree programs in nursing, business administration, and operation management. Student-designed and dual majors, credit for prior learning, work-study, nondegree study, and cooperative education (paid work experience) are available. Study abroad is available through ISA (International Studies Abroad). There are evening degree completion programs for working adults. There are 7 national honor societies and a freshman honors program. **Visiting:** There are regularly scheduled orientations for prospective students, consisting of sessions in April, May, June, and July for course selection and meeting with advisors. There are guides for informal visits, visitors may sit in on classes, and stay overnight. To schedule a visit, contact the Admissions Office. **Campus Safety and Security:** Measures include 24-hour foot and vehicle patrol, emergency notification system, self-defense education, and security escort services. There are emergency telephones, lighted pathways/sidewalks, and controlled access to dorms/residences.

REQUIREMENTS: The required minimum ACT composite score is 18. Applicants must be graduates of an accredited secondary school or have earned a GED. An interview is recommended. AP and CLEP credits are accepted. To graduate, students must complete 120 credits with a minimum GPA of 2.0 (social work, 2.75 and education 3.0). Core requirements include 25 credits in arts and humanities, 12 to 13 in social and behavioral science, and 12 in math and natural science, as well as a freshman seminar. **Procedure:** Freshmen are admitted to all sessions. Entrance exams should be taken in the junior year. There are early admissions, deferred admissions, and rolling admissions plans. Application deadlines are open. Notification is sent on a rolling basis. Applications are accepted on-line. **Transfer Students:** 161 transfer students enrolled in 2016-2017. The school recommends a minimum GPA of 2.0, the SAT or ACT (if <30 credits), and an interview. 32 of 120 credits required for the bachelor's degree must be completed at Marian. **International Students:** There are 21 international students enrolled. They must take the TOEFL with a minimum score of 525 on the paper-based TOEFL (PBT) or 70 on the Internet-based version (iBT). TOEFL may be substituted for the ACT.

ADMISSIONS: 68% of the 2017-2018 applicants were accepted. The ACT scores were 24% between 12 and 17, 53% between 18 and 23, 21% between 24 and 29, and 2% above 30. 21% of the current freshmen were in the top fifth of their class; 47% were in the top two fifths. 2 freshmen graduated first in their class. **Admissions Contact:** Shannon Laluzerne, Director of Admissions. Email: *admission@marianuniversity.edu*

FINANCIAL AID: In 2017-2018, 93% of all full-time freshmen received some form of financial aid, and need-based aid. The average freshman award was $23,725. Need-based scholarships or need-based grants averaged $13,591 ($32,700 maximum); need-based self-help aid (loans and jobs) averaged $4,892 ($17,482 maximum); and other non-need-based awards and non-need-based scholarships averaged $4,471 ($16,500 maximum). 30% of undergraduate students work part-time. The average financial indebtedness of the 2017 graduate was $30,000. The college's own financial statement is required. The FAFSA code is 003861. The deadline for filing freshman financial aid applications for fall entry is March 15.

MARQUETTE UNIVERSITY — E-4

www.marquette.edu

Milwaukee, WI 53201	**(414) 288-7302** **(800) 222-6544**
Fax: (414) 288-3764	**Email: admissions@marquette.edu**
Full-time: 3734 men, 4268 women	**Faculty:** 646; I, -$
Part-time: 168 men, 164 women	**Ph.D.s:** 91%
Graduate: 1496 men, 1661 women	**Student/Faculty:** 14 to 1
Year: semesters, summer session	**Tuition:** $41,870
Room & Board: $11,220	**Freshman Class:** 12957 applied, 11574 accepted, 2023 enrolled
SAT EBR-W/M: 615/605 **ACT:** 27	**CEEB CODE:** 1448
Application Deadline: December 1	**VERY COMPETITIVE+**

Marquette University, established in 1881, is a private Roman Catholic Jesuit institution. There are 8 undergraduate schools and 4 graduate schools. In addition to regional accreditation, MU has baccalaureate program accreditation with AACSB, ABET, ACEJMC, ADA, APTA, CAEP, ARCPA, ACS, and ACNM. The 107-acre campus is in an urban area in the heart of Milwaukee. Including any residence halls, there are 69 buildings.

STUDENT LIFE: 71% of undergraduates are from out of state, mostly the Midwest. Students are from 47 states, 39 foreign countries, and Canada. 60% are from public schools. 72% are White; 5% Asian American; 4% African American; 4% Foreign; 4% two or more races; 10% Hispanic. 63% are Catholic; 14% Protestant. **Female To Male Ratio:** 1.1:1. The average age of freshmen is 18; all undergraduates, 20. 10% do not continue beyond their first year; 79% remain to graduate. **Housing:** 4800 students can be accommodated in college housing, which includes single sex, coed, married student dorms, and on-campus apartments. In addition, there are honors houses, language/international houses, special-interest houses, fraternity houses, sorority houses, theme and wellness housing, engineering, and nursing housing. On-campus housing is guaranteed for the freshman year only and is available on a lottery system for upperclassmen. 52% of students live on campus. All students may keep cars.

FACULTY/CLASSROOMS: 57% of faculty are male; 43% are female. 76% teach undergraduates. No introductory courses are taught by graduate students.

PROGRAMS OF STUDY: MU confers B.A., B.S., B.S.N., B.S.B.E., B.S.C.E., B.S.C.M., B.S.C.O., B.S.E.E., and B.S.M.E. degrees. Master's and doctoral degrees are also awarded. Bachelor's degrees are awarded in BIOLOGICAL SCIENCE (biochemistry, biology/biological science, molecular biology, and physiology), BUSINESS (accounting, business administration and management, business economics, entrepreneurial studies, finance, human resources, international business management, management information systems, marketing/retailing/merchandising, operations management, organizational leadership and management, real estate, and supply chain management), COMMUNICATIONS AND THE ARTS (advertising, broadcasting, classical languages, classics, communications, dramatic arts, English, French, German, information technology, journalism, media arts, public relations, Spanish, theatre arts, and writing), COMPUTER AND PHYSICAL SCIENCE (chemistry, computer science, mathematics, physics, and statistics), EDUCATION (athletic training, education, and secondary education), ENGINEERING AND ENVIRONMENTAL DESIGN (bioengineering, biomedical engineering, civil engineering, computational sciences, computer engineering, construction engineering, electrical/electronics engineering, engineering, environmental engineering, and mechanical engineering), HEALTH PROFESSIONS (biomedical science, clinical science, exercise science, medical laboratory science, nursing, premedicine, and speech pathology/audiology), SOCIAL SCIENCE (anthropology, criminology, economics, history, interdisciplinary studies, international relations, peace studies, philosophy, political science/government, psychology, social science, sociology, and theological studies). Biomedical engineering, nursing, and premedicine are the strongest academically. Biomedical sciences, nursing, and mechanical engineering have the largest enrollments.

ACTIVITIES: 4% of men belong to 11 national fraternities; 14% of women belong to 13 national sororities. There are 270 groups on campus, including art, band, cheerleading, chess, choir, chorale, chorus, community awareness and recreational, computers, dance, debate, drama, drill team, ethnic, film, honors, international, jazz band, LGBT, literary magazine, musical theater, newspaper, orchestra, pep band, photography, political, professional, radio and TV, religious, social, social service, student government, and symphony. Popular campus events include Student Organizational Fest, Winter Flurry, and Hunger Clean Up. **Sports:** There are 7 intercollegiate sports for men and 7 for women, and 40 intramural sports for men and 40 for women. Facilities include recreation centers and valley fields, outdoor soccer, track, and football facility. **Graduates:** The most popular majors were business/marketing (27%), biological/life science (12%), and engineering (10%).

SERVICES: Counseling and information services are available, as is tutoring in some subjects, such as many lower-division classes taken by freshmen and sophomores. There is a reader service for the blind. There is also book taping and note taking available for the physically challenged. **Library/Resources:** The library contains 1.8 million volumes, 1.7 million microform items, and 23,503 audio/video tapes/CDs/DVDs, and subscribes to 46,685 periodicals including electronic. Computerized library services include interlibrary loans, database searching, Internet access, and Wi-Fi capability. Special learning facilities include an art gallery, radio station, and TV station. **Physically Challenged Students:** 90% of the campus is accessible. Facilities include wheelchair ramps, elevators, special parking, specially equipped restrooms, special class scheduling, lowered drinking fountains, lowered telephones, and special housing. **Special:** Marquette offers co-op programs in engineering, internships, study abroad in 16 countries, a Washington summer term, and work-study programs. Dual and student-designed majors, nondegree study, an accelerated degree program for pre-dental and pre-law students, and pass/fail options are available. Cross-registration is possible with Milwaukee Institute of Art and Design, and there is a 2-2 engineering program with Waukesha County Technical College. The Freshman Frontier Program offers academic support for selected freshmen who do not meet regular admission requirements but show potential for success. The Educational Opportunity Program affords students from minority groups and low-income families the opportunity to attend the school. There are 22 national honor societies, a chapter of Phi Beta Kappa, a freshman honors program, and 42 departmental honors programs. **Visiting:** There are regularly scheduled orientations for prospective students, including an agenda for visits that varies according to the specific program; open houses are available on scheduled weekends throughout the academic year. There are guides for informal visits, visitors may sit in on classes, and stay overnight. To schedule a visit, contact the Office of Undergraduate Admissions. **Campus Safety and Security:** Measures include 24-hour foot and vehicle patrol, emergency notification system, self-defense education, and security escort services. There are shuttle buses, emergency telephones, lighted pathways/sidewalks, controlled access to dorms/residences, closed-circuit cameras in selected parking lots and buildings throughout the campus. Public Safety has bicycle patrols and the Milwaukee police conduct patrols on horseback, and secure storage for bicycles in parking ramps monitored by Public Safety using closed-circuit cameras.

REQUIREMENTS: The ACT or the SAT is required. Applicants must be graduates of an accredited secondary school with required 16 credits, including 4 years of English, 2-4 each of math and science (with 2 lab), 2-3 social studies, recommended 2 unites each of foreign language and history, and 2-5 of academic electives. Applicants must demonstrate ability, preparation, and motivation. An interview is recommended. AP and CLEP credits are accepted. Important factors in the admissions decision are advanced placement or honors courses, recommendations by school officials, and leadership record. To graduate, students must complete a total of 126 to 135 credit hours and maintain a minimum GPA depending on major. The 36-credit-hour core of common studies includes 6 credit hours each of rhetoric, human nature and ethics, and theology, and 3 each of mathematical reasoning, individual and social behavior, science and nature, histories of cultures and societies, literature and performing arts, and diverse cultures. The total number of hours in the major varies. **Procedure:** Freshmen are admitted to all sessions. Entrance exams should be taken in the junior year and repeated early in the senior year if necessary. There is a deferred admissions plan. Applications should be filed by December 1 for fall entry. Notifications are sent December 23. 438 applicants were on the 2017 waiting list; 198 were admitted. Applications are accepted on-line. **Transfer Students:** 177 transfer students enrolled in 2016-2017. Applicants for transfer must have a minimum GPA of 2.0; some programs require a higher average. The SAT or ACT is required if the applicant has completed fewer than 12 hours of college-level work. An essay of personal statement is also required. Applications are in the fall (June 1) and summer (December 1) 30 of 126 credits required for the bachelor's degree must be completed at MU. **International Students:** There are 311 international students enrolled. MU requires success in final external secondary exams according to the student's country of education.

ADMISSIONS: 89% of the 2017-2018 applicants were accepted. The SAT scores for the 2017-2018 freshman class were: Evidence-Based Reading/Writing-- 4% below 500, 34% between 500 and 599, 53% between 600 and 699, and 9% between 700 and 800. The ACT scores were 17% between 18 and 23, 58% between 24 and 29, and 25% above 30. 34% of the current freshmen were in the top fifth of their class; 59% were in the top two fifths. 17 freshmen graduated first in their class. **Admissions Contact:** Jean Burke, Interim Dean of Admissions. Email: *admissions@marquette.edu* Web: *www.marquette.edu*

FINANCIAL AID: In 2017-2018, 99% of all full-time freshmen received some form of financial aid. 53% of all full-time freshmen received need-based aid. The average freshman award was $29,812. Need-based scholarships or need-based grants averaged $24,753; need-based self-help aid (loans and jobs) averaged $4,307; non-need-based athletic scholarships averaged $24,237; other non-need-based awards and non-need-based scholarships averaged $15,206; and $3,603 from other forms of aid. 41% of undergraduate students work part-time. The average financial indebtedness of the 2017 graduate was $44,968. MU is a member of CSS. The FAFSA code is 003863. The priority date for freshman financial aid applications for fall entry is January 9.

MILWAUKEE INSTITUTE OF ART & DESIGN *(The complete profile is made available exclusively on our website, www.barronspac.com)*

MILWAUKEE SCHOOL OF ENGINEERING E-4
www.msoe.edu

Milwaukee, WI 53202 (414) 277-6762
(800) 332-6763

Fax: (414) 277-7475 **Email:** explore@msoe.edu
Full-time: 1829 men, 679 women **Faculty:** 131; IIA, +$
Part-time: 84 men, 13 women **Ph.D.s:** 83%
Graduate: 133 men, 80 women **Student/Faculty:** 16 to 1
Year: quarters, summer session **Tuition:** $39,039
Room & Board: $9102 **Freshman Class:** 2893 applied, 1818 accepted, 522 enrolled
CEEB CODE: 1476
Application Deadline: n/av **HIGHLY COMPETITIVE+**

Milwaukee School of Engineering, established in 1903, is a private university offering bachelor's and master's degrees in engineering, business, mathematics, and nursing. There are 3 undergraduate schools and 1 graduate school. In addition to regional accreditation, Milwaukee School of Engineering has baccalaureate program accreditation with ABET, ACCE, and CCNE. The 22-acre campus is in an urban area in Milwaukee, WI. Including any residence halls, there are 18 buildings.

STUDENT LIFE: 66% of undergraduates are from Wisconsin. Others are from 37 states, 26 foreign countries, and Canada. 8% are race unknown; 67% White; 6% Hispanic; 4% Asian American; 3% two or more races; 2% African American; 10% Foreign. **Male To Female Ratio:** 2.7:1. The average age of freshmen is 18; all undergraduates, 21. 15% do not continue beyond their first year; 67% remain to graduate. **Housing:** 1278 students can be accommodated in college housing, which includes single sex, coed dorms, and on-campus apartments. In addition, there are special-interest houses, suites for upperclassmen, and honors floors. On-campus housing is guaranteed for all 4 years. 58% of students commute. All students may keep cars. Alcohol is not permitted.

FACULTY/CLASSROOMS: 63% of faculty are male; 37% are female. No introductory courses are taught by graduate students. The average class size in a regular course is 21.

PROGRAMS OF STUDY: Milwaukee School of Engineering confers B.A. and B.S. degrees. Master's degrees are also awarded. Bachelor's degrees are awarded in BIOLOGICAL SCIENCE (molecular biology), BUSINESS (business administration and management), COMMUNICATIONS AND THE ARTS (digital communications), COMPUTER AND PHYSICAL SCIENCE (actuarial science and software engineering), ENGINEERING AND ENVIRONMENTAL DESIGN (architectural engineering, biomedical engineering, civil engineering, computer engineering, construction management, electrical/electronics engineering, engineering, industrial engineering, and mechanical engineering), HEALTH PROFESSIONS (nursing). Mechanical engineering, electrical engineering, and software engineering have the largest enrollments.

ACTIVITIES: 3% of men belong to 1 local and 3 national fraternities; 11% of women belong to 3 local and 1 national sororities. There are 89 groups on campus, including badminton, baseball, bowling, disk golf, fencing, rock climbing, rowing, rugby, soccer, spike ball, tae kwon do, ultimate frisbee, band, cheerleading, chess, choir, chorus, communications, computers, dance, drama, drum and bugle corps, environmental, ethnic, hockey, honors, international, jazz band, LGBT, literary magazine, musical theater, orchestra, pep band, photography, political, professional, radio and TV, religious, social, social service, student government, and symphony. Popular campus events include St. Patrick's Week, Greek Week, and Sub-Zero Days. **Sports:** There are 12 intercollegiate sports for men and 8 for women, and 8 intramural sports for men and 8 for women. Facilities include a recreation athletic center, health and wellness center, with ice arena, a fitness center, wrestling room, field house, basketball arena, and indoor track facility. **Graduates:** From July 1, 2016 to June 30, 2017, 573 bachelor's degrees were awarded. The most popular majors were engineering (74%), health professions an related programs (12%), and business/marketing (11%). In an average class, 42% graduate in 4 years or less, 63% graduate in 5 years or less, and 67% graduate in 6 years or less. Of the 2016 graduating class, 8% were enrolled in graduate school within 6 months of graduation, and 97% were employed.

SERVICES: Counseling and information services are available, as is tutoring in most subjects, All freshman and sophomore classes, most junior classes, and some senior level classes There is a reader service for the blind and an ESL Program. **Library/Resources:** The library contains 51,408 volumes, 80,654 microform items, 3,067 audio/video tapes/CDs/DVDs, and subscribes to 5,154 periodicals including electronic. Computerized library services include interlibrary loans, database searching, Internet access, and Wi-Fi capability. Special learning facilities include an art gallery, radio station, campus ministries and counseling center. **Physically Challenged Students:** 95% of the campus is accessible. Facilities include wheelchair ramps, elevators, special parking, specially equipped restrooms, special class scheduling, lowered drinking fountains, lowered telephones, and special housing. **Special:** MSOE offers internships in the student's discipline, study abroad in France, Germany, India, and Czech Republic, on-campus work study programs, and non-degree study. A number of dual degrees along with a 5-year freshman-to-master's degree in civil engineering, are also available. There are 4 national honor societies, a freshman honors program, and 5 departmental honors programs. **Visiting:** There are regularly scheduled orientations for prospective students, consisting of personal visits, Spring and Fall Open Houses, Accepted Student Days, and Senior Visit Days. There are guides for informal visits, visitors may sit in on classes, and stay overnight. To schedule a visit, contact the Admission Office at (800) 332-6763. **Campus Safety and Security:** Measures include 24-hour foot and vehicle patrol, emergency notification system, self-defense education, and security escort services. There are shuttle buses, emergency telephones, lighted pathways/sidewalks, controlled access to dorms/residences, 24-hour security in residence halls.

REQUIREMENTS: The ACT is required. The SAT is recommended. Applicants must be graduates of an accredited secondary school, having completed 15 academic credits, including 4 units of English, 2 units each of science and math, and 1 unit each of social studies and history. Additional units in math, science, and English are strongly advised; 1 unit in computer science is recommended. The GED is accepted. An essay is required, and an interview is recommended. A GPA of 2.5 is required. AP and CLEP credits are accepted. To graduate, students must complete approximately 197 quarter credits with a minimum GPA of 2.0 overall and in the major. A minimum total of 49 credits must be earned in the three topical areas of General Education (i.e. mathematics and science, professional preparedness, and society and culture). **Procedure:** Freshmen are admitted to all sessions. Entrance exams should be taken during the junior year. There are deferred admissions and rolling admissions plans. Application deadlines are open. Applications are accepted on-line. **Transfer Students:** 177 transfer students enrolled in 2016-2017. Applicants for transfer should have a minimum GPA of 2.75, and must have completed 24 semester or 36 quarter credits. 100 of 197 credits required for the bachelor's degree must be completed at MSOE. **International Students:** There are 263 international students enrolled. They must take the TOEFL with a minimum score of 82 on the Internet-based version (iBT), and the IELTS.

ADMISSIONS: 63% of the 2017-2018 applicants were accepted. The SAT scores for the 2017-2018 freshman class were: Math-- 24% between 500 and 599, 44% between 600 and 699, and 32% between 700 and 800. Evidence-Based Reading/Writing-- 12% below 500, 35% between 500 and 599, 38% between 600 and 699, and 15% between 700 and 800. The ACT scores were 12% between 18 and 23, 62% between 24 and 29, and 26% above 30. **Admissions Contact:** Seandra Mitchell, Dean of Admission. Email: *explore@msoe.edu* Web: *www.msoe.edu*

FINANCIAL AID: The FAFSA code is 003868. The priority date for freshman financial aid applications for fall entry is March 15.

MOUNT MARY UNIVERSITY *(The complete profile is made available exclusively on our website, www.barronspac.com)*

NORTHLAND COLLEGE B-1
www.northland.edu

Ashland, WI 54806 (715) 682-1224
(800) 753-1840

Fax: (715) 682-1258 **Email:** admit@northland.edu
Full-time: 285 men, 364 women **Faculty:** 41
Part-time: 27 men, 63 women **Ph.D.s:** 85%
Graduate: n/av **Student/Faculty:** 10 to 1
Year: 4-1-4, summer session **Tuition:** $32,754
Room & Board: $8349 **Freshman Class:** 804 applied, 605 accepted, 181 enrolled
SAT: required **ACT:** 24 **CEEB CODE:** 1561
Application Deadline: n/av **COMPETITIVE+**

Northland College is a private liberal arts college with a progressive focus on the environment and sustainability. Northland's innovative curriculum and distinguished faculty draw students from across the country, who come to be part of a powerful educational community. The 80-acre campus is in a small town in Ashland, WI and 65 miles east of Duluth, MN. Including any residence halls, there are 20 buildings.

STUDENT LIFE: 65% of undergraduates are from out of state, mostly the Midwest. Students are from 43 states, 7 foreign countries, and Canada. 85% are from public schools. 84% are White; 3% Foreign; 2% African American; 2% American Indian/Alaska Native; 2% Hispanic; 1% Asian American. **Female To Male Ratio:** 1.4:1. The average age of freshmen is 20; all undergraduates, 21. 20% do not continue beyond their first year; 44% remain to graduate. **Housing:** 530 students can be accommodated in college housing, which includes dorms, on-campus apartments, and special-interest houses. On-campus housing is guaranteed for all 4 years. 70% of students live on campus. Alcohol is not permitted. All students may keep cars.

FACULTY/CLASSROOMS: 81% of faculty are male; 19% are female. All teach undergraduates and 25% do research. No introductory courses are taught by graduate students. The average class size in an introductory lecture is 30; in a laboratory is 30; and in a regular course is 15.

PROGRAMS OF STUDY: NC confers B.A. and B.S. degrees. Bachelor's degrees are awarded in AGRICULTURE (environmental studies, fish and game management, forestry and related sciences, and natural resource management), BIOLOGICAL SCIENCE (biology ecology and field biology, biology/biological science, and environmental biology), BUSINESS (business administration and management, environment and national resource economics, and sustainable management), COMMUNICATIONS AND THE ARTS (ceramic art and design, comparative literature, creative writing, English, fine arts, graphic design, and writing), COMPUTER AND PHYSICAL SCIENCE (atmospheric sciences and meteorology, chemistry, earth science, environmental chemistry, environmental geology, geology, information sciences and systems, and mathematics), EDUCATION (education, elementary education, environmental education, middle school education, and secondary education), ENGINEERING AND ENVIRONMENTAL DESIGN (environmental science and water and wastewater technology), SOCIAL SCIENCE (American Indian studies, history, humanities, Native American studies, parks and recreation management, psychology, public administration, religion, rural sociology, sociology, and women and gender studies). Biology, natural resources, and education are the strongest academically. Biology, education, and business have the largest enrollments.

ACTIVITIES: There are no fraternities or sororities. There are 40 groups on campus, including art, band, cheerleading, choir, chorale, chorus, computers, drama, ethnic, honors, international, jazz band, LGBT, literary magazine, newspaper, orchestra, photography, political, professional, religious, social, social service, student government, symphony, and yearbook. Popular campus events include Snow Festival, Pow Wow, Folk Festival, and the Sigurd Olsen Nature Writing Award. **Sports:** There are 7 intercollegiate sports for men and 8 for women, and 10 intramural sports for men and 10 for women. **Graduates:** From July 1, 2016 to June 30, 2017, 109 bachelor's degrees were awarded. The most popular majors were natural resources (15%), outdoor education (15%), and biology (15%). In an average class, 2% graduate in 3 years or less and 80% graduate in 4 years or less. Of the 2016 graduating class, 15% were enrolled in graduate school within 6 months of graduation, and 95% were employed.

SERVICES: Counseling and information services are available, as is tutoring in every subject. There is a reader service for the blind, and remedial math, reading, and writing. **Library/Resources:** The library contains 77,700 volumes, 9,300 microform items, and subscribes to 350 periodicals including electronic. Computerized library services include interlibrary loans and database searching. Special learning facilities include an art gallery, natural history museum, environmental research acreage, community garden, solar and geothermal energy, unparalleled access to Lake Superior and National Forest lands. **Physically Challenged Students:** 90% of the campus is accessible. Facilities include wheelchair ramps, elevators, special parking, specially equipped restrooms, and special class scheduling. **Special:** Opportunities are provided for cooperative programs in many majors and with other schools, internships, work-study programs with state and federal agencies, student-designed majors, credit for life experience, pass/fail options, and study abroad in 7 countries. Cross-registration is offered within the Eco-League and Kansai Gaidai University in Japan. 3-2 engineering degrees are available in conjunction with Michigan Technological University and Washington University in St. Louis. There are 2 national honor societies. **Visiting:** There are regularly scheduled orientations for prospective students, an interview, a tour, and class visits. There are guides for informal visits, visitors may sit in on classes, and stay overnight. To schedule a visit, contact the Admissions Office. **Campus Safety and Security:** Measures include emergency notification system and security escort services. There are emergency telephones, lighted pathways/sidewalks, and controlled access to dorms/residences.

REQUIREMENTS: The SAT or ACT is required. Graduation from an accredited secondary school is required; the GED is accepted. An essay and interview are recommended. AP and CLEP credits are accepted. Important factors in the admissions decision are advanced placement or honors courses, extracurricular activities record, and recommendations by school officials. Students must complete 124 credits, including 35 to 60 in the major, with a minimum GPA of 2.0. All students must meet requirements that include courses in English composition, literature, history, philosophy, social and natural sciences, physical science, fine arts, phys ed, and studies of other cultures. **Procedure:** Freshmen are admitted in the fall, winter, and spring. Entrance exams should be taken fall of the senior year. There are early admissions, deferred admissions, and rolling admissions plans. Application deadlines are open. Applications are accepted on-line. **Transfer Students:** Applicants must have maintained a minimum GPA of 2.0 in previously attended colleges. 30 of 124 credits required for the bachelor's degree must be completed at Northland. **International Students:** They must take the TOEFL or MELAB.

ADMISSIONS: 75% of the 2017-2018 applicants were accepted. 75% of the current freshmen were in the top fifth of their class; 74% were in the top two fifths. **Admissions Contact:** Teege Mettille, Executive Director of Admissions. Email: *admit@northland.edu* Web: *www.northland.edu*

FINANCIAL AID: In 2017-2018, 89% of all full-time freshmen received some form of financial aid. 83% of all full-time freshmen received need-based aid. 90% of undergraduate students work part-time. NC is a member of CSS. The college's own financial statement is required. The FAFSA code is 003875. The deadline for filing freshman financial aid applications for fall entry is April 15.

RIPON COLLEGE — D-4

www.ripon.edu

Ripon, WI 54971	(920) 748-8185 (800) 947-4766
Fax: (920) 748-8335	**Email:** adminfo@ripon.edu
Full-time: 343 men, 399 women	**Faculty:** 62; IIB, -$
Part-time: 6 men, 10 women	**Ph.D.s:** 97%
Graduate: n/av	**Student/Faculty:** 14 to 1
Year: semesters	**Tuition:** $41,835
Room & Board: $8156	**Freshman Class:** n/av
SAT or ACT: required	**CEEB CODE:** 1664
Application Deadline: August 1	**VERY COMPETITIVE**

Ripon College, established in 1851, is a private, residential, and liberal arts institution. There is 1 undergraduate school. The 250-acre campus is in a small town 80 miles north of Milwaukee in the east-central part of the state. Including any residence halls, there are 26 buildings.

STUDENT LIFE: 73% of undergraduates are from Wisconsin. Others are from 26 states, 11 foreign countries, and Canada. 60% are from public schools. 9% are Hispanic; 80% White; 4% African American; 4% Foreign; 2% two or more races; 1% Asian American. **Female To Male Ratio:** 1.2:1. The average age of freshmen is 18; all undergraduates, 20. 20% do not continue beyond their first year; 69% remain to graduate. **Housing:** 952 students can be accommodated in college housing, which includes dorms and on-campus apartments. Theme and interest groups may form living areas in the residence halls. On-campus housing is guaranteed for all 4 years and is available on a lottery system for upperclassmen. 90% of students live on campus. All students may keep cars.

FACULTY/CLASSROOMS: 63% of faculty are male; 37% are female. All teach undergraduates and do research. No introductory courses are taught by graduate students. The average class size in an introductory lecture is 54; in a laboratory is 18; and in a regular course is 20.

PROGRAMS OF STUDY: RC confers A.B. degrees. Bachelor's degrees are awarded in BIOLOGICAL SCIENCE (biochemistry and biology/biological science), BUSINESS (business administration and management), COMMUNICATIONS AND THE ARTS (art, art history and appreciation, communications, dramatic arts, English, music, Spanish, and studio art), COMPUTER AND PHYSICAL SCIENCE (chemistry, mathematics, physical sciences, and physics), EDUCATION (early childhood education, elementary education, middle school education, and secondary education), ENGINEERING AND ENVIRONMENTAL DESIGN (environmental science), HEALTH PROFESSIONS (exercise science), SOCIAL SCIENCE (anthropology, economics, history, international studies, philosophy, political science/government, psychobiology, psychology, religion, and sociology). Communication, biology, and chemistry are the strongest academically. Business, exercise science, and education have the largest enrollments.

ACTIVITIES: 33% of men belong to 2 local and 3 national fraternities; 19% of women belong to 3 national sororities. There are 78 groups on campus, including art, band, cheerleading, chess, choir, chorale, chorus, computers, dance, drama, environmental, ethnic, film, forensics, honors, international, jazz band, LGBT, literary magazine, musical theater, newspaper, orchestra, pep band, photography, political, professional, radio and TV, religious, social, social service, student government, symphony, and yearbook. Popular campus events include Theater Events, Homecoming Week, SpringFest, Quad Bash, and awareness programming based monthly and weekly. **Sports:** There are 9 intercollegiate sports for men and 9 for women, and 8 intramural sports for men and 8 for women. Facilities include a cycling path, a athletic center which includes an indoor track, dance studios, and wellness center. **Graduates:** From July 1, 2016 to June 30, 2017, 181 bachelor's degrees were awarded. The most popular majors were business (12%), psychology (12%), and biology (10%). In an average class, 1% graduate in 3 years or less, 60% graduate in 4 years or less, 67% graduate in 5 years or less, and 69% graduate in 6 years or less. Of the 2016 graduating class, 23% were enrolled in graduate school within 6 months of graduation, and 68% were employed.

SERVICES: Counseling and information services are available, as is tutoring in most subjects. Tutoring services are also available for learning-disabled students. **Library/Resources:** The library contains 282,034 volumes, 8,276 microform items, 1,330 audio/video tapes/CDs/DVDs, and subscribes to 60,147 periodicals, including electronic. Computerized library services include interlibrary loans, database searching, Internet access, and Wi-Fi capability. Special learning facilities include an art gallery, radio station, a music library, an art slide library, and college archives. **Physically Challenged Students:** 50% of the campus is accessible. Facilities include wheelchair ramps, elevators, special parking, specially equipped restrooms, special class scheduling, and lowered drinking fountains. **Special:** In addition to the two standard semesters, the calendar includes two short, intensive terms of three weeks-one before fall semester starts and one at the end of spring semester. Taught in short, intensive block, these optional In Focus courses offer a beneficial alternative and valuable supplement to those offered during the regular semester. Courses are immersion experiences that can involve off-campus experiences which may be in other countries including service learning; internships; field work; community engagement; all with an emphasis on mentoring and making connections with experts outside the campus community. There are 16 national honor societies and a chapter of Phi Beta Kappa. **Visiting:** There are regularly scheduled orientations for prospective students, including a tour, an interview, and meetings with professors and coaches. There are guides for informal visits and visitors may sit in on classes. To schedule a visit, contact the Admission Office. **Campus Safety and Security:** Measures include 24-hour foot and vehicle patrol, emergency notification system, and security escort services. There are emergency telephones, lighted pathways/sidewalks, controlled access to dorms/residences, and a paging system.

REQUIREMENTS: Applicants must be graduates of an accredited secondary school. The GED is accepted. Applicants should complete at least 17 Carnegie units, including 4 of English, 2 to 4 each of math, social studies, and natural sciences, and up to 7 of other college-preparatory electives. An essay may be required, and an interview is recommended. Ripon requires applicants to be in the upper 50% of their class. AP and CLEP credits are accepted. Important factors in the admissions decision are leadership record, recommendations by school officials, and advanced placement or honors courses. To graduate, students must complete 124 credit hours, as well as complete the concentration in applied innovation, completion of a major, and have a cumulative GPA of 2.0 or better. **Procedure:** Freshmen are admitted in the fall and spring. Entrance exams should be taken in the junior year or the fall of the senior year. There are deferred admissions and rolling admissions plans. Applications should be filed by August 1 for fall entry; December 15 for spring entry. The fall 2017 application fee was $30. Notification is sent on a rolling basis. Applications are accepted online. **Transfer Students:** 13 transfer students enrolled in 2016-2017. Applicants must have a minimum 2.0 GPA and be in good standing at their previous college. The SAT or ACT, a personal statement, and an interview are recommended. 32 of 124 credits required for the bachelor's degree must be completed at RC. **International Students:** There are 20 international students enrolled. They must take the TOEFL with a minimum score of 550 on the paper-based TOEFL (PBT) or 79 on the Internet-based version (iBT). They must also take the SAT.

ADMISSIONS: 30% of the current freshmen were in the top fifth of their class; 68% were in the top two fifths. 3 freshmen graduated first in their class. **Admissions Contact:** Jennifer Machacek, Vice President for Enrollment. Email: *adminfo@ripon.edu* Web: *www.ripon.edu*

FINANCIAL AID: In 2017-2018, 100% of all full-time freshmen received some form of financial aid. 90% of all full-time freshmen received need-based aid. The average freshman award was $37,764. Need-based scholarships or need-based grants averaged $32,694 ($38,177 maximum); and need-based self-help aid (loans and jobs) averaged $6,010 ($9,000 maximum). 47% of undergraduate students work part-time. The average financial indebtedness of the 2017 graduate was $29,071. The FAFSA code is 003884. The deadline for filing freshman financial aid applications for fall entry is March 1.

SILVER LAKE COLLEGE OF THE HOLY FAMILY *(The complete profile is made available exclusively on our website, www.barronspac.com)*

ST. NORBERT COLLEGE — D-3

www.snc.edu

De Pere, WI 54115	(920) 403-3005 (800) 236-4878
Fax: (920) 403-4072	**Email:** admit@snc.edu
Full-time: 872 men, 1149 women	**Faculty:** 142; IIA, --$
Part-time: 18 men, 28 women	**Ph.D.s:** 92%
Graduate: 41 men, 57 women	**Student/Faculty:** 13 to 1
Year: semesters, summer session	**Tuition:** $36,593
Room & Board: $9467	**Freshman Class:** 3860 applied, 3058 accepted, 526 enrolled
ACT: 25	**CEEB CODE:** 1706
Application Deadline: open	**VERY COMPETITIVE**

St. Norbert College is a liberal arts college that teaches critical thinking, problem-solving and leadership skills. There is 1 undergraduate school and 4 graduate schools. The 112-acre campus is in a suburban area 5 miles south of Green Bay. Including any residence halls, there are 44 buildings.

STUDENT LIFE: 78% of undergraduates are from Wisconsin. Others are from 28 states, 26 foreign countries, and Canada. 72% are from public schools. 87% are White; 4% Hispanic; 3% Foreign; 2% Asian American; 1% African American; 1% American Indian/Alaska Native; 1% two or more races. 41% are Catholic; 36% claim no religious affiliation; 21% Protestant. **Female To Male Ratio:** 1.3:1. The average age of freshmen is 18; all undergraduates, 20. 17% do not continue beyond their first year; 73% remain to graduate. **Housing:** 1892 students can be accommodated in college housing, which includes single sex dorms, coed dorms, off-campus houses, and on-campus apartments. In addition, there are special-interest houses, a townhouse complex, and a living center. On-campus housing is guaranteed for all 4 years. 85% of students live on campus. All students may keep cars.

FACULTY/CLASSROOMS: 54% of faculty are male; 46% are female. All teach undergraduates. No introductory courses are taught by graduate students. The average class size in an introductory lecture is 21 and in a regular course is 19.

PROGRAMS OF STUDY: St. Norbert confers B.A., B.B.A., B.Mus., and B.S. degrees. Master's degrees are also awarded. Bachelor's degrees are awarded in BIOLOGICAL SCIENCE (biology/biological science), BUSINESS (accounting, business administration and management, and international business management), COMMUNICATIONS AND THE

ARTS (art, communications, English, French, German, graphic design, music, Spanish, and theatre arts), COMPUTER AND PHYSICAL SCIENCE (chemistry, computer science, geology, mathematics, natural sciences, and physics), EDUCATION (elementary education and music education), ENGINEERING AND ENVIRONMENTAL DESIGN (commercial art and environmental science), SOCIAL SCIENCE (economics, history, humanities, international relations, philosophy, political science/government, psychology, religion, and sociology). Business administration, communications, and elementary education have the largest enrollments.

ACTIVITIES: 10% of men belong to 4 national fraternities; 10% of women belong to 4 national sororities. There are 94 groups on campus, including art, band, cheerleading, chess, choir, chorale, chorus, communications, computers, dance, drama, E2K Entertainment Tonight, environmental, ethnic, film, honors, international, jazz band, LGBT, literary magazine, musical theater, newspaper, opera, pep band, photography, political, professional, radio and TV, religious, social, social service, and student government. Popular campus events include Opening Campus Picnic/convocation, E2K Homecoming, and SNC Day. **Sports:** There are 12 intercollegiate sports for men and 12 for women, and 7 intramural sports for men and 7 for women. Facilities include a stadium, baseball and softball sports complex, an activity center with gymnasium and fitness center, fitness and sports center with pool, indoor track, volleyball courts and intramural basketball courts. **Graduates:** From July 1, 2016 to June 30, 2017, 443 bachelor's degrees were awarded. The most popular majors were business administration (20%), elementary education (11%), and communication and media studies (10%). In an average class, 73% graduate in 6 years or less. Of the 2016 graduating class, 13% were enrolled in graduate school within 6 months of graduation.

SERVICES: Counseling and information services are available, as is tutoring in most subjects. There is a reader service for the blind, and remedial math, reading, and writing. **Library/Resources:** The library contains 249,694 volumes, 16,084 microform items, 2,411 audio/video tapes/CDs/DVDs, and subscribes to 100,960 periodicals, including electronic. Computerized library services include interlibrary loans, database searching, Internet access, and Wi-Fi capability. Special learning facilities include an art gallery, radio station, TV station, innovation studio, center for women's and gender studies, center for peace, justice and public understanding, marina, fine and performing arts centers, center for international education, center for leadership and service, children's center, center for Norbertine studies, language labs, media center with satellite hookup, and environmental sciences research craft. **Physically Challenged Students:** 82% of the campus is accessible. Facilities include wheelchair ramps, elevators, special parking, specially equipped restrooms, special class scheduling, lowered drinking fountains, lowered telephones, and special housing. **Special:** A partnership program with Bellin College Nursing, cross-registration in Arabic courses with the University of Wisconsin-Green Bay, internships, study abroad in 29 countries, a Washington semester, and work-study programs are available. The college offers dual and student-designed majors, B.A.-B.S. degrees, nondegree study, and limited credit for military experience and work training. The Leadership and Service Program and leadership minor help students improve their leadership abilities through courses and activities. A Masters of Science in Applied Economics (MSAE) degree preparation agreement with Marquette University. A partnership with the Medical College of Wisconsin provides an accelerated route for students to earn both a Bachelor of Science degree in natural sciences from St. Norbert and their Pharm.D. degree from the Medical College of Wisconsin. There are 11 national honor societies and a freshman honors program. **Visiting:** There are regularly scheduled orientations for prospective students, including preregistrations, meetings with advisers, and meetings regarding programming and activities, housing, and student life. There are guides for informal visits, visitors may sit in on classes, and stay overnight. To schedule a visit, contact the Office of Admissions at (920) 403-3005. **Campus Safety and Security:** Measures include 24-hour foot and vehicle patrol, emergency notification system, self-defense education, and security escort services. There are emergency telephones, lighted pathways/sidewalks, controlled access to dorms/residences, motorist assistance, and a crime prevention program.

REQUIREMENTS: Admissions requirements are either graduation from an accredited secondary school with 16 units recommended, including 4 English, 3 math, 3 lab sciences, 2 each of foreign language, social studies, and history; or a GED recommended score in the 55% range; and either an SAT or ACT entrance exam. AP and CLEP credits are accepted. Important factors in the admissions decision are advanced placement or honors courses, extracurricular activities record, and recommendations by school officials. To graduate, students must complete 128 credits with at least a 2.0 GPA and a minimum of 40 semester credits in a particular major and a major GPA of at least a 2.0. There are general education requirements in the areas of religious studies, human nature, human relationships, natural science, creative expression, U.S. heritage, foreign heritages, foreign language, quantitative skills, Western tradition, global society, a writing-intensive course, and Senior Colloquium. **Procedure:** Freshmen are admitted to all sessions. Entrance exams should be taken by the end of the junior year. There are deferred admissions and rolling admissions plans. Application deadlines are open. Notification of early decision is sent December 15; regular decision, on a rolling basis. Applications are accepted on-line. **Transfer Students:** 32 transfer students enrolled in 2016-2017. Applicants should have a minimum GPA of 2.5. At least their senior year and 25% of their major credits must be taken at St. Norbert. 32 of 128 credits required for the bachelor's degree must be completed at St. Norbert. **International Students:** There are 59 international students enrolled. They must take the TOEFL with a minimum score of 555 on the paper-based TOEFL (PBT) or 80 on the Internet-based version (iBT). They must also take the SAT or ACT.

ADMISSIONS: 79% of the 2017-2018 applicants were accepted. The ACT scores were 1% between 12 and 17, 43% between 18 and 23, 47% between 24 and 29, and 9% above 30. **Admissions Contact:** Edward Lamm, Vice President of Enrollment Management and Communication. Email: *admit@snc.edu* Web: *www.snc.edu*

FINANCIAL AID: In 2017-2018, 99% of all full-time freshmen received some form of financial aid. 77% of all full-time freshmen received need-based aid. The average freshman award was $25,972. The average financial indebtedness of the 2017 graduate was $33,794. The FAFSA code is 003892. The priority date for freshman financial aid applications for fall entry is January 1.

UNIVERSITY OF WISCONSIN-EAU CLAIRE B-3

www.uwec.edu

Eau Claire, WI 54701	(715) 836-5188
Fax: (715) 831-4799	**Email:** admissions@uwec.edu
Full-time: 3621 men, 5726 women	**Faculty:** 387; IIA, --$
Part-time: 258 men, 417 women	**Ph.D.s:** 83%
Graduate: 302 men, 413 women	**Student/Faculty:** 22 to 1
Year: semesters, summer session	**Tuition:** $8816 ($16,736)
Room & Board: $7538	**Freshman Class:** 5990 applied, 5133 accepted, 2337 enrolled
SAT: required **ACT:** 24	**CEEB CODE:** 1913
Application Deadline: n/av	**VERY COMPETITIVE**

University of Wisconsin-Eau Claire, founded in 1916, fosters its students in creativity, critical insight, empathy, and intellectual courage, the hallmarks of a transformative liberal education and the foundation for active citizenship and lifelong inquiry. There are 4 undergraduate schools. In addition to regional accreditation, UW-Eau Claire has baccalaureate program accreditation with AACSB, ACEJMC, CSWE, and NASM. The 337-acre campus is in an urban area 95 miles east of Minneapolis, MN. Including any residence halls, there are 28 buildings.

STUDENT LIFE: 70% of undergraduates are from Wisconsin. Others are from 39 states, 32 foreign countries, and Canada. 88% are White; 4% Asian American; 3% Hispanic; 2% Foreign; 2% two or more races; 1% African American. **Female To Male Ratio:** 1.6:1. The average age of freshmen is 18; all undergraduates, 20. 18% do not continue beyond their first year; 82% remain to graduate. **Housing:** 4500 students can be accommodated in college housing, which includes dorms, on-campus apartments, and off-campus apartments. In addition, there are honors houses, special-interest houses, theme housing, and wellness housing. On-campus housing is available on a first-come, first-served basis, and is available on a lottery system for upperclassmen. 62% of students commute. All students may keep cars.

FACULTY/CLASSROOMS: 50% of faculty are male; 50% are female. All teach undergraduates. No introductory courses are taught by graduate students. The average class size in an introductory lecture is 37 and in a laboratory is 21.

PROGRAMS OF STUDY: UW-Eau Claire confers B.A., B.S., B.B.A.,

B.F.A., B.L.S., B.M., B.M.E., B.S.E.Ph., B.S.N., and B.S.W. degrees. Associate, master's, and doctoral degrees are also awarded. Bachelor's degrees are awarded in BIOLOGICAL SCIENCE (biochemistry and biology/biological science), BUSINESS (accounting, banking and finance, business administration and management, international business, and marketing), COMMUNICATIONS AND THE ARTS (art, communications, English, French, German, journalism, music, Spanish, and theatre arts), COMPUTER AND PHYSICAL SCIENCE (chemistry, computer science, geology, geoscience, information sciences and systems, mathematics, physical sciences, and physics), EDUCATION (athletic training, elementary education, physical education, science education, and special education), ENGINEERING AND ENVIRONMENTAL DESIGN (materials science and materials science and engineering), HEALTH PROFESSIONS (health care administration, nursing, predentistry, premedicine, preoptometry, prepharmacy, prephysical therapy, preveterinary science, and public health), SOCIAL SCIENCE (American Indian studies, communication sciences & disorders, criminal justice, economics, geography, history, Latin American studies, liberal arts/general studies, philosophy, political science/government, prelaw, psychology, religious studies, social studies, social work, sociology, and women's studies). Nursing, biology, and psychology have the largest enrollments.

ACTIVITIES: 1% of men belong to 3 national fraternities; 1% of women belong to 3 national sororities. There are 250 groups on campus, including art, band, cheerleading, chess, choir, chorale, chorus, communications, computers, dance, debate, drama, environmental, ethnic, film, forensics, honors, international, jazz band, LGBT, literary magazine, marching band, musical theater, newspaper, opera, orchestra, pep band, photography, political, professional, radio and TV, religious, social, social service, student government, and symphony. Popular campus events include Homecoming, Caberet, Viennese Ball, and Winter Carnival. **Sports:** There are 9 intercollegiate sports for men and 11 for women. Facilities include a gym, pool, intramural and recreation fields, billiards, Nautilus fitness center, racquetball courts, weight room, ropes course, a stadium, tennis courts, and a climbing wall. **Graduates:** From July 1, 2016 to June 30, 2017, 2023 bachelor's degrees were awarded. The most popular majors were marketing (22%), health professionals (16%), and education (8%). In an average class, 34% graduate in 4 years or less, 63% graduate in 5 years or less, and 67% graduate in 6 years or less.

SERVICES: Counseling and information services are available, as is tutoring in most subjects, such as writing, math/problem solving, and reading/study skills. There is a reader service for the blind, and remedial math, reading, and writing. Entry-level courses in foreign languages, humanities, and social and physical sciences are also available. **Library/Resources:** The library contains 733,630 volumes, 20,145 microform items, 34,171 audio/video tapes/CDs/DVDs, and subscribes to 216,718 periodicals, including electronic. Computerized library services include interlibrary loans, database searching, Internet access, and Wi-Fi capability. Special learning facilities include a radio station, TV station, art gallery, greenhouses, bird museum, communication and journalism center, human development center, materials science center (wide array of instrumentation for materials imaging, elemental/chemical analysis, physical/mechanical properties analysis and sample preparation), natural preserve, and nursing clinical simulation/skills lab. **Physically Challenged Students:** 90% of the campus is accessible. Facilities include wheelchair ramps, elevators, special parking, specially equipped restrooms, special class scheduling, lowered drinking fountains, lowered telephones, and special housing. **Special:** Numerous internships, work-study programs, and study abroad in 26 countries are offered. Dual majors and interdisciplinary majors are possible. Credit by examination, non-degree study, and pass/fail options are offered. There are 29 national honor societies, a freshman honors program, and 21 departmental honors programs. **Visiting:** There are regularly scheduled orientations for prospective students. Freshmen students meet with an advisor and peer guide to learn the registration system and select courses. They can attend informational sessions on housing, dining, financial aid, and tour the campus. Family orientation is also available. To schedule a visit, contact the Admissions Office. **Campus Safety and Security:** Measures include 24-hour foot and vehicle patrol and emergency notification system. There are shuttle buses, an emergency telephones, lighted pathways/sidewalks, and controlled access to dorms/residences.

REQUIREMENTS: The ACT or SAT is required. Applicants should graduate from an accredited secondary school or present its equivalent, with 17 academic credits including 4 in English, 3 each in social studies, college prep math, and science and 4 years of elective. Each application is given a comprehensive review. In addition to a rigorous curriculum, academic factors include: class rank, GPA, trends in grades, and test scores. Secondary non-academic factors include: leadership, service, achievement in arts, athletics, etc, and diversity in personal background and experience. AP and CLEP credits are accepted. Important factors in the admissions decision are advanced placement or honors courses, extracurricular activities record, and evidence of special talent. All students must complete 36 hours in liberal education, natural sciences, social sciences, humanities, fine arts, written and oral communications, mathematics, creativity, equity, diversity and inclusivity, global perspectives, civic and environmental issues, and integration, and also complete 30 or more hours of service-learning. A minimum 2.0 GPA and 120 credits hours are required to graduate. **Procedure:** Freshmen are admitted in the fall and spring. Entrance exams should be taken by April of the senior year. There are early admissions and rolling admissions plans. Application deadlines are open. The fall 2017 application fee was $50. 450 applicants were on the 2017 waiting list; 100 were admitted. Applications are accepted on-line. **Transfer Students:** 528 transfer students enrolled in 2016-2017. Transfer applicants must carry a minimum 2.0 GPA. Preference is given to transfers who have completed the equivalent of freshman composition and college algebra. Students with less than 30 semester credits must meet the freshman admissions requirements. 30 of 120 credits required for the bachelor's degree must be completed at UW-Eau Claire. **International Students:** There are 216 international students enrolled. They must take the TOEFL with a minimum score of 550 on the paper-based TOEFL (PBT) or 79 on the Internet-based version (iBT). They must also take the SAT or ACT.

ADMISSIONS: 86% of the 2017-2018 applicants were accepted. The SAT scores for the 2017-2018 freshman class were: Critical Reading-- 33% between 500 and 599 and 67% between 700 and 800. Math-- 33% below 500, 33% between 500 and 599, and 33% between 600 and 699. The ACT scores were 2% between 12 and 17, 48% between 18 and 23, 44% between 24 and 29, and 6% above 30. 50 freshmen graduated first in their class. **Admissions Contact:** Heather Kretz, Director of Admissions. Email: *kretzhm@uwec.edu* Web: *www.uwec.edu*

FINANCIAL AID: In 2017-2018, 89% of all full-time freshmen received some form of financial aid. 55% of all full-time freshmen received need-based aid. The average freshman award was $13,079. Need-based scholarships or need-based grants averaged $6,335; need-based self-help aid (loans and jobs) averaged $8,363; and other non-need-based awards and non-need-based scholarships averaged $7,979. 32% of undergraduate students work part-time. The average financial indebtedness of the 2017 graduate was $26,244. The FAFSA code is 003917. The priority date for freshman financial aid applications for fall entry is April 15.

UNIVERSITY OF WISCONSIN-GREEN BAY D-3
www.uwgb.edu

Green Bay, WI 54311 (920) 465-2111

Fax: (920) 465-2765	**Email: admissions@uwgb.edu**
Full-time: 1446 men, 2574 women	**Faculty:** 182; IIA, --$
Part-time: 903 men, 1892 women	**Ph.D.s:** 87%
Graduate: 140 men, 223 women	**Student/Faculty:** 22 to 1
Year: semesters, summer session	**Tuition:** $7878 ($15,728)
Room & Board: $7306	**Freshman Class:** 2151 applied, 2036 accepted, 975 enrolled
ACT: 22	**CEEB CODE:** 1859
Application Deadline: n/av	**COMPETITIVE**

University of Wisconsin-Green Bay, founded in 1968, is a public institution offering bachelors and masters programs in humanities and fine arts, natural sciences, social sciences, business, education, health, and preprofessional areas. There are 4 undergraduate schools and 1 graduate school. In addition to regional accreditation, UW-Green Bay has baccalaureate program accreditation with ADA, CSWE, NASM, and NLN. The 700-acre campus is in a suburban area 111 miles north of Milwaukee, WI. Including any residence halls, there are 49 buildings.

STUDENT LIFE: 91% of undergraduates are from Wisconsin. Others are from 42 states, 33 foreign countries, and Canada. 95% are from public schools. 85% are White; 5% Hispanic; 3% Asian American; 3% two or more races; 2% African American; 1% American Indian/Alaska Native; 1% Foreign. 40% are Catholic; 40% Protestant; 15% claim no religious affiliation. **Female To Male Ratio:** 1.9:1. The average age of freshmen is 19; all undergraduates, 25. 27% do not continue beyond their first year; 51% remain to graduate. **Housing:** 2000 students can be accommodated in college housing, which includes dorms and on-campus apartments. In addition, there are special-interest houses, and 3- 4- and 5-person dorm suites with private bedrooms. On-campus housing is available on a first-come, first-served basis, and is available on a lottery system for upperclassmen. 64% of students commute. All students may keep cars.

FACULTY/CLASSROOMS: 49% of faculty are male; 51% are female. 95% teach undergraduates, 85% do research, and 85% do both. No introductory courses are taught by graduate students. The average class size in an introductory lecture is 40; in a laboratory is 20; and in a regular course is 25.

PROGRAMS OF STUDY: UW-Green Bay confers B.A., B.S., B.A.S., B.B.A., B.M., B.S.N., and B.S.W. degrees. Associate and master's degrees are also awarded. Bachelor's degrees are awarded in AGRICULTURE (environmental studies), BIOLOGICAL SCIENCE (biology/biological science), BUSINESS (accounting, business administration and management, finance, human resources, and sustainable management), COMMUNICATIONS AND THE ARTS (art, arts administration/management, communications, creative writing, design, dramatic arts, English, English as a second/foreign language, fine arts, French, German, Germanic languages and literature, music, Spanish, and theatre arts), COMPUTER AND PHYSICAL SCIENCE (chemistry, computer science, earth science, geoscience, information sciences and systems, and mathematics), EDUCATION (art education, education, elementary education, English education, foreign languages education, health information management, mathematics education, middle school education, music education, and secondary education), ENGINEERING AND ENVIRONMENTAL DESIGN (city/community/regional planning, electrical/electronics engineering technology, engineering technology, environmental engineering technology, environmental science, and mechanical engineering technology), HEALTH PROFESSIONS (exercise science and nursing), SOCIAL SCIENCE (American Indian studies, dietetics, economics, French studies, gender studies, history, human development, humanities, interdisciplinary studies, liberal arts/general studies, philosophy, political science/government, psychology, public administration, social work, urban studies, and women's studies). Psychology, human development, environmental science, and human biology are the strongest academically. Business, human biology, and integrative leadership studies have the largest enrollments.

ACTIVITIES: 1% of men belong to 1 national fraternity; 1% of women belong to 2 national sororities. There are 127 groups on campus, including art, band, cheerleading, choir, chorale, chorus, computers, dance, drama, drill team, environmental, ethnic, film, honors, international, jazz band, LGBT, literary magazine, musical theater, newspaper, orchestra, pep band, photography, political, professional, radio and TV, religious, social, social service, and student government. Popular campus events include Frost Fest, GB Week, and Pow Wow. **Sports:** There are 7 intercollegiate sports for men and 9 for women, and 7 intramural sports for men and 7 for women. Facilities include a sports center with arena, auxiliary courts (basketball practice, student recreation), elevated running track, 28-foot climbing tower, weight areas with Magnum machines and free weights, group aerobics/fitness studio (cardio deck with stationary bikes, stair-climbers, elliptical machines, treadmills, video monitors), indoor turf gym, and pool. **Graduates:** From July 1, 2016 to June 30, 2017, 1191 bachelor's degrees were awarded. The most popular majors were business administration (17%), integrative leadership studies (14%), and nursing (9%). In an average class, 1% graduate in 3 years or less, 30% graduate in 4 years or less, 49% graduate in 5 years or less, and 51% graduate in 6 years or less. Of the 2016 graduating class, 23% were enrolled in graduate school within 6 months of graduation, and 87% were employed.

SERVICES: Counseling and information services are available, as is tutoring in most subjects. There is a reader service for the blind, and remedial math, reading, and writing. There is an academic support office, language and writing centers, student health services, and individual counseling. Available equipment includes a visual enlarger, automatic page turner, accessible computer station with attached voice syntheizer, slow speed cassette recorders, and a TDD device. Note takers, typists, readers, and aids are also available for students. **Library/Resources:** The library contains 366,860 volumes, 1.4 million microform items, 47,943 audio/video tapes/CDs/DVDs, and subscribes to 3,234 periodicals, including electronic. Computerized library services include interlibrary loans, database searching, Internet access, and Wi-Fi capability. Special learning facilities include an art gallery, natural history museum, radio station, TV station, a 270-acre arboretum, and a regional performing arts center. **Physically Challenged Students:** All of the campus is accessible. Facilities include wheelchair ramps, elevators, special parking, specially equipped restrooms, lowered drinking fountains, lowered telephones, and automatic door openers. All academic buildings on campus are connected by an underground concourse system which is widely accessed by the entire campus community and which makes the campus particularly accessible to wheelchair transportation. **Special:** UW-Green Bay offers cross-registration with Bellin College of Nursing and the University of Wisconsin at Milwaukee or Oshkosh. There are study-abroad programs and travel courses in numerous countries. Students can receive credit by examination or for life, military, or work experience. There are internships in almost all fields; interdisciplinary majors; and dual and student-designed majors, work-study, B.A.-B.S. degrees in most areas, nondegree study, a general studies degree, and pass/fail options. There are 6 national honor societies and 34 departmental honors programs. **Visiting:** There are regularly scheduled orientations for prospective students, including campus preview days, which consist of information sessions, academic area workshops, and campus tours. There are guides for informal visits and visitors may sit in on classes. To schedule a visit, contact the Office of Admissions. **Campus Safety and Security:** Measures include 24-hour foot and vehicle patrol and security escort services. There are emergency telephones, lighted pathways/sidewalks, and controlled access to dorms/residences.

REQUIREMENTS: The ACT is required. Candidates must be graduates of an accredited secondary school, approved home school program, or hold a GED certificate. They must have completed 17 academic credits consisting of 4 in English, 3 each in social sciences, science, and math, 2 in any of the above areas or a foreign language, and 2 other electives. Home schooled applicants are encouraged to apply and should contact the admissions office for additional information. AP and CLEP credits are accepted. Important factors in the admissions decision are advanced placement or honors courses, extracurricular activities record, and leadership record. All students must complete at least 120 semester hours, including an average of 36 in the major, with a minimum GPA of 2.0, depending on the major. Students must declare an interdisciplinary minor or major. Required general education includes courses in fine arts, humanities, natural and social sciences, Other culture studies, ethnic studies, a freshman seminar, and competency and capstone courses. **Procedure:** Freshmen are admitted to all sessions. Entrance exams should be taken between the junior and senior years. There are deferred admissions and rolling admissions plans. Application deadlines are open. The fall 2017 application fee was $50. Notification is sent on a rolling basis. Applications are accepted on-line. **Transfer Students:** 1134 transfer students enrolled in 2016-2017. Transfer students must have a minimum GPA of 2.0 based on at least 15 transferable credits; priority for admission is given to students with 24 credits and a minimum GPA of 2.5. 31 of 120 credits required for the bachelor's degree must be completed at UW-Green Bay. **International Students:** There are 83 international students enrolled. They must take the TOEFL with a minimum score of 500 on the paper-based TOEFL (PBT) or 61 on the Internet-based version (iBT). They must also take the SAT or ACT.

ADMISSIONS: 95% of the 2017-2018 applicants were accepted. The ACT scores were 7% between 12 and 17, 57% between 18 and 23, 31% between 24 and 29, and 5% above 30. **Admissions Contact:** Jen Jones, Director of Admissions. Email: *admissions@uwgb.edu* Web: *www.uwgb.edu*

FINANCIAL AID: In 2017-2018, 89% of all full-time freshmen received some form of financial aid. 59% of all full-time freshmen received need-based aid. The average freshman award was $11,750. Need-based scholarships or need-based grants averaged $6,533 ($16,858 maximum); need-based self-help aid (loans and jobs) averaged $3,786 ($8,000 maximum); non-need-based athletic scholarships averaged $11,855 ($31,465 maximum); other non-need-based awards and non-need-based scholarships averaged $6,069 ($19,610 maximum); and $4,643 from other forms of aid. 80% of undergraduate students work part-time. The average financial indebtedness of the 2017 graduate was $22,664. The FAFSA code is 003899. The deadline for filing freshman financial aid applications for fall entry is April 15.

UNIVERSITY OF WISCONSIN-LA CROSSE B-4

www.uwlax.edu

La Crosse, WI 54601 **(608) 785-8000**

Fax: (608) 785-8940
Email: admissions@uwlax.edu
Full-time: 3920 men, 5144 women
Faculty: 447; IIA, --$
Part-time: 300 men, 291 women
Ph.D.s: 84%
Graduate: 297 men, 521 women
Student/Faculty: 19 to 1
Year: semesters, summer session
Tuition: $9219 ($17,889)
Room & Board: $6206
Freshman Class: 5880 applied, 4783 accepted, 2106 enrolled
SAT M: 615 **ACT:** 25
CEEB CODE: 1914
Application Deadline: n/av
VERY COMPETITIVE

University of Wisconsin-La Crosse is the top-ranked regional public university in Wisconsin. Guided by our motto Mens Corpusque "Mind and Body" offering 91 undergraduate programs guided by caring faculty and staff who will challenge you to grow in a supportive, diverse learning environment. Internships and undergraduate research provide opportunities for real-world applications of your lessons learned in the classroom and through cocurricular activities. There are 5 undergraduate schools and 1 graduate school. In addition to regional accreditation, UW-La Crosse has baccalaureate program accreditation with AACSB, NASM, CAEP, ACS, JRCERT, and JRCNMT. The 121-acre campus is in a small town 142 miles west of Madison, WI, and 150 miles southeast of Minneapolis/St. Paul, MN. Including any residence halls, there are 32 buildings.

STUDENT LIFE: 82% of undergraduates are from Wisconsin. Others are from 29 states, 20 foreign countries, and Canada. 90% are from public schools. 90% are White; 3% Hispanic; 3% two or more races; 2% Asian American; 1% African American; 1% Foreign. **Female To Male Ratio:** 1.3:1. The average age of freshmen is 18; all undergraduates, 20. 17% do not continue beyond their first year; 71% remain to graduate. **Housing:** 3492 students can be accommodated in college housing, which includes gender neutral, single sex coed, coed, and on-campus apartments. In addition, there are language/international houses, and special-interest houses. On-campus housing is guaranteed for the freshman year only, and is available on a first-come, first-served basis. 64% of students commute. All students may keep cars.

FACULTY/CLASSROOMS: 50% of faculty are male; 5% are female. 95% teach undergraduates. No introductory courses are taught by graduate students. The average class size in an introductory lecture is 30; in a laboratory is 23; and in a regular course is 28.

PROGRAMS OF STUDY: UW-La Crosse confers B.A. and B.S. degrees. Associate, master's, and doctoral degrees are also awarded. Bachelor's degrees are awarded in BIOLOGICAL SCIENCE (biochemistry, biology/biological science, and microbiology), BUSINESS (accounting, finance, international business management, management, and marketing), COMMUNICATIONS AND THE ARTS (art, communication studies, English, French, German studies, music, Spanish, and theatre arts), COMPUTER AND PHYSICAL SCIENCE (chemistry, clinical laboratory science, computer science, information sciences and systems, mathematics, physics, and statistics), EDUCATION (athletic training, elementary education, health education, health information management, physical education, science education, secondary education, and social studies education), HEALTH PROFESSIONS (community health work, exercise science, nuclear medical technology, public health, radiation therapy, and recreation therapy), SOCIAL SCIENCE (archeology, economics, geography, history, parks and recreation management, philosophy, political science/government, psychology, public administration, sociology, and women's studies). Microbiology, nuclear medicine technology, and physics are the strongest academically. Biology, exercise and sport science, and psychology have the largest enrollments.

ACTIVITIES: 1% of men belong to 3 national fraternities; 1% of women belong to 2 national sororities. There are 200 groups on campus, including art, band, campus activity board, cheerleading, choir, chorale, chorus, computers, dance, drama, environmental, ethnic, honors, international, jazz band, LGBT, literary magazine, marching band, musical theater, newspaper, orchestra, photography, political, professional, radio and TV, religious, social, social service, student government, and symphony. Popular campus events include Parents Weekend, Community-Sponsored Oktoberfest, and International Banquet. **Sports:** There are 9 intercollegiate sports for men and 10 for women, and 21 intramural sports for men and 20 for women. Facilities include a wrestling room, an indoor track, indoor and outdoor tennis courts, a swimming pool, strength-training centers, dance studio, a climbing wall, racquetball courts, a stadium, and a gym. **Graduates:** From July 1, 2016 to June 30, 2017, 1951 bachelor's degrees were awarded. The most popular majors were biology (12%), exercise and sport science (11%), and psychology (9%). In an average class, 42% graduate in 4 years or less, 67% graduate in 5 years or less, and 71% graduate in 6 years or less. Of the 2016 graduating class, 22% were enrolled in graduate school within 6 months of graduation, and 58% were employed.

SERVICES: Counseling and information services are available, as is tutoring in most subjects. There is a reader service for the blind, and remedial math and writing. There is also a public speaking center, and writing center. **Library/Resources:** The library contains 842,223 volumes, 30,684 microform items, and 44,726 audio/video tapes/CDs/DVDs, and subscribes to 565,461 periodicals including electronic. Computerized library services include interlibrary loans, database searching, Internet access, and Wi-Fi capability. Special learning facilities include an art gallery, planetarium, radio station, and TV station. **Physically Challenged Students:** 98% of the campus is accessible. Facilities include wheelchair ramps, elevators, special parking, specially equipped restrooms, special class scheduling, lowered drinking fountains, lowered telephones, and special housing. **Special:** International study abroad options are available in many countries as well as a national exchange program throughout the US. Internships are also available to all students. UWL offers 3-2 engineering dual degree programs with the University of Wisconsin - Madison, Milwaukee, Platteville, the University of Minnesota - Duluth, and Winona State University. There are 11 national honor societies and 12 departmental honors programs. **Visiting:** There are regularly scheduled orientations for prospective students, campus close-up, open houses, and group information sessions. There are guides for informal visits and visitors may sit in on classes. To schedule a visit, contact the Admissions Office. **Campus Safety and Security:** Measures include 24-hour foot and vehicle patrol, emergency notification system, self-defense education, and security escort services. There are emergency telephones, lighted pathways/sidewalks, and controlled access to dorms/residences.

REQUIREMENTS: The SAT or ACT is required. Applicants for freshman admission must graduate from a recognized high school or the equivalent. Completion of the following 17 high school credits is minimal preparation and is required for admission consideration. Applicants are strongly recommended to take advanced courses beyond the required 17 high school credits: 4 credits of English, 3 credits each of mathematics, specifically algebra, advanced algebra, and geometry, credits of natural science with 2 credits from biology, chemistry, physics, earth science, or advanced courses in these disciplines, and social science, and 4 academic credits from the above and/or in the fine arts, computer science, foreign language, or other academic areas. All applications receive a comprehensive review. Due to enrollment limitations and the competitive nature of admission to the university, admission consideration will be primarily based on rigor of courses, high school rank, grade point average, and ACT/SAT scores. While academic preparation is the primary criterion used in the admissions review process, other non-academic secondary factors may contribute to the strength of an application. These may include qualities such as demonstrated leadership, extracurricular involvement, special talent, personal statement, recommendations, and/or adding a diverse dimension to our campus community. AP and CLEP credits are accepted. To graduate, students must earn 120 semester credits, including 74 in subjects outside the major and at least 40 in 300- or 400-level courses. The minimum GPA is 2.0, though it is considerably higher for some programs. Distribution requirements include 30 to 40 credits in liberal studies and 13 to 19 credits in skill courses. **Procedure:** Freshmen are admitted to all sessions. Entrance exams should be taken before the start of senior year. There is a rolling admissions plan. Application deadlines are open. The fall 2017 application fee was $50. Notification is sent on a rolling basis. Applications are accepted online. **Transfer Students:** 627 transfer students enrolled in 2016-2017. All applications receive a comprehensive review. Students with at least a cumulative 2.50 GPA in all previous transferable college level work will be considered stronger candidates for admission. Students with a cumulative GPA between a 2.0 and a 2.49 will be considered for admission on available space. In addition to grade point guidelines, students must be in good standing at their previous institution (s) to be admitted to UWL. New first year students must earn at least 18 transferable semester credits to be considered for admission. Due to enrollment limitations and the competitive nature of admission, primarily consideration will be based on academic preparation, other non-academic secondary factors may also contribute to the strength of an application. These may include qualities such as demonstrated leadership, extracurricular involvement, special talent, personal statement, recommendations, and/or adding a diverse dimension to our campus community. 30 of 120 credits required for the bachelor's degree must be completed at UW-La Crosse. **International Students:** There are 116 international students enrolled. They must take the TOEFL with a minimum score of 73 on the Internet-based version (iBT).

ADMISSIONS: 81% of the 2017-2018 applicants were accepted. The SAT scores for the 2017-2018 freshman class were: Math-- 48% between 500 and 599, 43% between 600 and 699, and 9% between 700 and 800. Evidence-Based Reading/Writing-- 4% below 500, 39% between 500 and 599, 48% between 600 and 699, and 9% between 700 and 800. The ACT scores were 39% between 18 and 23, 54% between 24 and 29, and 7% above 30. 47% of the current freshmen were in the top fifth of their class; 85% were in the top two fifths. 65 freshmen graduated first in their class. **Admissions Contact:** Corey Sjoquist, Director of Admissions. Email: *admissions@uwlax.edu* Web: *www.uwlax.edu*

FINANCIAL AID: In 2017-2018, 45% of all full-time freshmen received some form of financial aid. 39% of all full-time freshmen received need-based aid. The average freshman award was $10,975. Need-based scholarships or need-based grants averaged $6,033; need-based self-help aid (loans and jobs) averaged $3,599; and other non-need-based awards and non-need-based scholarships averaged $5,773. The average financial indebtedness of the 2017 graduate was $26,768. The FAFSA code is 003919. The priority date for freshman financial aid applications for fall entry is March 15.

UNIVERSITY OF WISCONSIN-MADISON C-4

www.wisc.edu

Madison, WI 53706 **(608) 262-3961**

Fax: (608) 262-7706 **Email:** onwisconsin@admissions.wisc.edu

Full-time: 14,035 men, 14,981 women	**Faculty:** 1965; I, av$
Part-time: 1676 men, 1504 women	**Ph.D.s:** 85%
Graduate: 5740 men, 5884 women	**Student/Faculty:** 18 to 1
Year: semesters, summer session	**Tuition:** $10,533 ($34,783)
Room & Board: $11,114	**Freshman Class:** 35615 applied, 19150 accepted, 6610 enrolled
SAT EBR-W/M: 653/706 **ACT:** 29	**CEEB CODE:** 1846
Application Deadline: February 1	**MOST COMPETITIVE**

University of Wisconsin-Madison, founded in 1849, is a public, land-grant institution offering undergraduate and graduate study in almost every major field. There are 9 undergraduate schools and 13 graduate schools. In addition to regional accreditation, UW-Madison has baccalaureate program accreditation with AACSB, ABET, ADA, ASLA, CSWE, FIDER, NASAD, NASM, SAF, CCNE, CAAHP, NAST, AOTA, ACS, SoAF, NASAS, CAATE, CFRB, and CIDA. The 936-acre campus is in an urban area 75 miles west of Milwaukee and 150 miles northwest of Chicago, IL.

STUDENT LIFE: 66% of undergraduates are from Wisconsin. Others are from 50 states, 105 foreign countries, and Canada. 72% are White; 6% Asian American; 5% Hispanic; 3% two or more races; 2% African American; 10% Foreign; 1% race unknown. **Female To Male Ratio:** 1.0:1. The average age of freshmen is 18; all undergraduates, 20. 5% do not continue beyond their first year; 87% remain to graduate. **Housing:** 7476 students can be accommodated in college housing, which includes married student dorms and on-campus apartments. In addition, there are honors houses, language/international houses, special-interest houses, co-op housing, residential learning communities, and housing for student families. No one may keep cars.

FACULTY/CLASSROOMS: 58% of faculty are male; 42% are female. No introductory courses are taught by graduate students.

PROGRAMS OF STUDY: UW-Madison confers B.A., B.S., B.B.A., B.F.A., B.M., B.S.Ed., and B.N.S. degrees. Master's and doctoral degrees are also awarded. Bachelor's degrees are awarded in AGRICULTURE (agricultural business management, agricultural communications, agricultural economics, agronomy, animal science, dairy science, environmental studies, forestry and related sciences, horticulture, poultry science, and soil science), BIOLOGICAL SCIENCE (biochemistry, biology/biological science, botany, entomology, genetics, microbiology, molecular biology, nutrition, plant pathology, wildlife biology, and zoology), BUSINESS (accounting, banking and finance, human resources, insurance and risk management, international business management, marketing/retailing/merchandising, nonprofit/public organization management, operations management, personal financial planning, real estate, and retailing), COMMUNICATIONS AND THE ARTS (African languages, art, art history and appreciation, Chinese, classics, communications, communication science, comparative literature, dance, dramatic arts, English, French, German, Italian, Japanese, journalism, Latin, linguistics, music, music performance, Polish, Portuguese, Russian, Spanish, and theatre arts), COMPUTER AND PHYSICAL SCIENCE (actuarial science, applied mathematics, astronomy, atmospheric sciences and meteorology, chemistry, computer science, geology, geophysics and seismology, information sciences and systems, mathematics, physics, and statistics), EDUCATION (art education, athletic training, elementary education, music education, physical education, secondary education, and special education), ENGINEERING AND ENVIRONMENTAL DESIGN (bioengineering, biomedical engineering, cartography, chemical engineering, civil engineering, computer engineering, electrical/electronics engineering, engineering mechanics, engineering physics, environmental science, geological engineering, industrial engineering, interior design, landscape architecture/design, materials engineering, materials science, mechanical engineering, naval architecture and marine engineering, nuclear engineering, and textile technology), HEALTH PROFESSIONS (kinesiology, nursing, pharmacology, and speech pathology/audiology), SOCIAL SCIENCE (African American studies, anthropology, Asian/Oriental studies, economics, family/consumer studies, food science, gender studies, geography, history, history of science, human development, international relations, international studies, Judaic studies, Latin American studies, legal studies, philosophy, political science/government, psychology, religion, rural sociology, Scandinavian studies, social studies, social work, sociology, textiles and clothing, and women's studies). Biology, economics, and computer science have the largest enrollments.

ACTIVITIES: There are 995 groups on campus, including art, band, cheerleading, chess, choir, chorale, chorus, communications, computers, dance, debate, drama, environmental, ethnic, film, forensics, honors, international, jazz band, LGBT, literary magazine, marching band, musical theater, newspaper, opera, orchestra, pep band, photography, political, professional, radio and TV, religious, social, social service, student government, symphony, and yearbook. **Sports:** There are 12 intercollegiate sports for men and 12 for women, and 14 intramural sports for men and 14 for women. **Graduates:** From July 1, 2016 to June 30, 2017, 6812 bachelor's degrees were awarded. The most popular majors were biology (7%), economics (7%), and computer science (5%). In an average class, 62% graduate in 4 years or less, 85% graduate in 5 years or less, and 87% graduate in 6 years or less.

SERVICES: Counseling and information services are available, as is tutoring in most subjects. There is a reader service for the blind. **Library/Resources:** The library contains 10.1 million volumes. Computerized library services include interlibrary loans, database searching, Internet access, and Wi-Fi capability. Special learning facilities include an art gallery, a natural history museum, a planetarium, a radio station, and TV station. **Physically Challenged Students:** 90% of the campus is accessible. Facilities include wheelchair ramps, elevators, special parking, specially equipped restrooms, special class scheduling, lowered drinking fountains, and lowered telephones. **Special:** Co-op programs, internships, study abroad, work-study programs, and accelerated degrees in any major are available. B.A.-B.S. degrees and dual and student-designed majors also are available. There is a chapter of Phi Beta Kappa and a freshman honors program. **Visiting:** There are regularly scheduled orientations for prospective students, a tour, admission information session, and class visits. There are guides for informal visits; visitors may sit in on classes and stay overnight. To schedule a visit, contact Visitor and Information Programs at (608) 263-2400. **Campus Safety and Security:** Measures include 24-hour foot and vehicle patrol, emergency notification system, self-defense education, and security escort services. There are shuttle buses, emergency telephones, lighted pathways/sidewalks, and controlled access to dorms/residences.

REQUIREMENTS: The SAT or ACT is required. Applicants must have completed the following number of units in high school (these are minimums; the number of units recommended is higher): 17 total units including 4 each in English and math, 3 each in science, social studies, and foreign language, and 2 academics/fine arts electives. AP and CLEP credits are accepted. Required courses vary with individual programs. A total of 120 to 136 credit hours, with at least 30 in the major, and a cumulative GPA of 2.0 are minimum requirements for graduation. In addition to courses required for each major, all students must complete general education in communication, quantitative reasoning, breadth (science, math, humanities, and social science), and ethnic studies. **Procedure:** Freshmen are admitted in the fall, spring, and summer. Entrance exams should be taken in the junior year. There is a deferred admissions plan. Early decision applications should be filed by November 1; regular applications, by February 1 for fall entry; October 3 for spring entry; and February 1 for summer entry. The fall 2017 application fee was $60. Notification of early decision is sent December 31; regular decision, March 31. Applications are accepted online. **Transfer Students:** 11281 transfer students enrolled in 2016-2017. Admission is competitive and varies by program. Generally, applicants must have at least sophomore standing. 30 of 120 credits required for the bachelor's degree must be completed at Wisconsin. **International Students:** There are 2649 international students enrolled. They must take the TOEFL with a minimum score of 550 on the paper-based TOEFL (PBT) or 80 on the Internet-based version (iBT), and take the IELTS (paper). They must also take the SAT or ACT.

ADMISSIONS: 54% of the 2017-2018 applicants were accepted. The SAT scores for the 2017-2018 freshman class were: Math-- 8% between 500 and 599, 34% between 600 and 699, and 69% between 700 and 800. Evidence-Based Reading/Writing-- 1% below 500, 13% between 500 and 599, 62% between 600 and 699, and 24% between 700 and 800. The ACT scores were 5% between 18 and 23, 52% between 24 and 29, and 43% above 30. **Admissions Contact:** Office of Admissions and Recruitment. Email: *onwisconsin@admissions.wisc.edu* Web: *www.wisc.edu*

FINANCIAL AID: 35% of all full-time freshmen received need-based aid. The average freshman award was $14,789. Need-based scholarships or need-based grants averaged $12,746; need-based self-help aid (loans and jobs) averaged $6,933; non-need-based athletic scholarships averaged $24,310; and other non-need-based awards and non-need-based scholarships averaged $5,954. The average financial indebtedness of the 2017 graduate was $27,979. The FAFSA code is 003895. The priority date for freshman financial aid applications for fall entry is December 1.

UNIVERSITY OF WISCONSIN-MILWAUKEE E-4

www.uwm.edu

Milwaukee, WI 53211 | **(414) 229-2222**

Fax: 414-229-3788	**Email: uwmlook@uwm.edu**
Full-time: 8120 men, 8935 women	**Faculty:** n/av
Part-time: 1319 men, 1287 women	**Ph.D.s:** n/av
Graduate: 1856 men, 2775 women	**Student/Faculty:** n/av
Year: semesters, summer session	**Tuition:** $10,978 ($22,258)
Room & Board: $10,560	**Freshman Class:** 10000 applied, 7153 accepted, 3228 enrolled
ACT: 22	**CEEB CODE:** 1473
Application Deadline: July 1	**COMPETITIVE**

University of Wisconsin-Milwaukee, founded in 1956, is Wisconsin's premier public urban research university. There are 11 undergraduate schools and 3 graduate schools. In addition to regional accreditation, UW-Milwaukee has baccalaureate program accreditation with AACSB, ABET, APTA, CAHEA, CSWE, NAAB, NASM, NLN, APA, NCA, and CCNE. The 104-acre campus is in an urban area in Milwaukee, WI. Including any residence halls, there are 58 buildings.

STUDENT LIFE: 89% of undergraduates are from Wisconsin. Others are from 50 states, 92 foreign countries, and Canada. 74% are from public schools. 7% are African American; 66% White; 6% Asian American; 6% Foreign; 4% two or more races; 10% Hispanic. **Female To Male Ratio:** 1.2:1. The average age of freshmen is 18; all undergraduates, 24. **Housing:** 4288 students can be accommodated in college housing, which includes married student dorms and off-campus apartments. In addition, there are honors houses, language/international houses, and special-interest houses. On-campus housing is available on a first-come, first-served basis. 82% of students commute. All students may keep cars.

FACULTY/CLASSROOMS: No introductory courses are taught by graduate students.

PROGRAMS OF STUDY: UW-Milwaukee confers B.A., B.B.A., B.F.A., B.S., B.S.E., and B.S.N. degrees. Master's and doctoral degrees are also awarded. Bachelor's degrees are awarded in BIOLOGICAL SCIENCE (biochemistry, biology/biological science, microbiology, molecular biology, nutrition, and nutritional sciences), BUSINESS (accounting, business administration and management, entrepreneurial studies, finance, human resources, international business, management information systems, marketing management, operations management, and real estate), COMMUNICATIONS AND THE ARTS (art history, art, art history and appreciation, classics, communications, comparative literature, dance, dramatic arts, English, film arts, French, Germanic languages and literature, information technology, linguistics, music, Russian languages and literature, and theatre arts), COMPUTER AND PHYSICAL SCIENCE (actuarial science, applied mathematics, atmospheric sciences and meteorology, chemistry, computer science, geology, inform, science, systems and technology, information sciences and systems, mathematics, physics, and web services), EDUCATION (art education, athletic training, education, journalism education, music education, and special education), ENGINEERING AND ENVIRONMENTAL DESIGN (architecture, civil engineering, computer engineering, electrical/electronics engineering, engineering, environmental science, industrial engineering, materials engineering, mechanical engineering, occupational safety and health, and urban planning technology), HEALTH PROFESSIONS (biomedical science, exercise science, health care administration, hospital administration, medical science, nursing, occupational therapy, premedicine, recreation therapy, and speech pathology/audiology), SOCIAL SCIENCE (African American studies, anthropology, Asian/American studies, behavioral science, communication sciences & disorders, criminal justice, economics, ethnic studies, forensic studies, geography, history, interdisciplinary studies, international studies, Italian studies, Judaic studies, Latin American studies, liberal arts/general studies, Near Eastern studies, peace studies, philosophy, political science/government, psychology, religion, Scandinavian studies, social work, sociology, Spanish studies, urban studies, and women's studies). Nursing, psychology, and marketing have the largest enrollments.

ACTIVITIES: There are 314 groups on campus, including art, band, cheerleading, chess, choir, chorale, chorus, communications, computers, dance, debate, drama, environmental, ethnic, film, honors, international, jazz band, LGBT, literary magazine, musical theater, newspaper, orchestra, pep band, photography, political, professional, religious, social, social service, student government, and symphony. Popular campus events include Fall Welcome, PantherFest, Concerts, Art Exhibitions, and Dance Performances. **Sports:** There are 6 intercollegiate sports for men and 7 for women. Facilities include a basketball court, volleyball court, baseball field, soccer field, natatorium, indoor track, exercise facilities, and racquetball courts. **Graduates:** From July 1, 2016 to June 30, 2017, 3829 bachelor's degrees were awarded. The most popular majors were business (22%), health professions and related programs (13%), and engineering (7%). In an average class, 15% graduate in 4 years or less, 34% graduate in 5 years or less, and 41% graduate in 6 years or less.

SERVICES: Counseling and information services are available, as is tutoring in some subjects. There is a reader service for the blind, and remedial math, reading, and writing. **Library/Resources:** The library contains 2.6 million volumes, 1.8 million microform items, 988,474 audio/video tapes/CDs/DVDs, and subscribes to 109,250 periodicals including electronic. Computerized library services include interlibrary loans, database searching, Internet access, and Wi-Fi capability. Special learning facilities include an art gallery, planetarium, The American Geographical Society Library, and Institute of Visual Arts. **Physically Challenged Students:** 95% of the campus is accessible. Facilities include wheelchair ramps, elevators, special parking, specially equipped restrooms, special class scheduling, lowered drinking fountains, and lowered telephones. **Special:** UWM offers cooperative education programs in computer science and engineering, accelerated degree programs, dual majors, student-designed majors, and study abroad opportunities in Africa, Asia, Europe, and South America. UWM also has a consortial nursing program with UW-Parkside, a graduate exchange program for graduate students with Marquette University, and a collaborative doctoral program in biomedical and health informatics with the Medical College of Wisconsin. There are 4 national honor societies, including Phi Beta Kappa, and a freshman honors program. **Visiting:** New Student Orientation is a one and a half day (overnight) program packed with information about UWM. At orientation new students will meet other students, learn about campus resources and student life, meet with advisors and register for classes. To schedule a visit, contact Department of Admissions and Recruitment. **Campus Safety and Security:** Measures include 24-hour foot and vehicle patrol, emergency notification system, self-defense education, and security escort services. There are shuttle buses, emergency telephones, lighted pathways/sidewalks, and controlled access to dorms/residences.

REQUIREMENTS: All freshmen applicants under the age of 21 must submit ACT or SAT scores; scores submitted via high school transcripts are acceptable. A GED certificate is accepted. Music, dance, and theatre majors must audition and art majors must submit a portfolio. For the School of Architecture and Urban Planning, higher rank and ACT requirements apply. Each application receives a comprehensive review, taking all factors into consideration. In addition to academic preparation, other factors considered include demonstrated leadership skills, motivation, and maturity, as addressed in a student's personal statement and/or recommendations. UWM provides broad access to individuals from many walks of life and encourages all interested students to apply. Certain programs, including Architecture, Engineering, and Nursing are more selective and higher standardized test scores may be required. A GPA of 2.0 is required. AP and CLEP credits are accepted. Generally, to be a candidate for the Bachelor's Degree, students must satisfactorily complete the following: English composition and math proficiency exams must be passed with satisfactory scores. A minimum of 120 undergraduate credits in courses numbered 100 through 500. The General Education requirements, university requirements and all major and/or minor requirements. Distribution requirements include 6 credits each in humanities, natural sciences, and socials sciences, and 3 credits each in the arts and cultural diversity. A minimum GPA of 2.0 or better both overall and in the major and minor fields; Business Administration and Accounting majors must have a cumulative GPA of 2.5 overall. A minimum of 30 credits overall and half of upper-level credits in majors and minors must be earned in residence at UW-Milwaukee. Other specific graduation criteria are set by individual colleges and schools. **Procedure:** Freshmen are admitted to all sessions. Entrance exams should be taken in the spring of the junior year. There are deferred admissions and rolling admissions plans. Applications should be filed by July 1 for fall entry; December 1 for spring entry. The fall 2017 application fee was $50. Notification is sent on a rolling basis. Applications are accepted on-line. **Transfer Students:** 1506 transfer students enrolled in 2016-2017. Students applying with less than 12 transferable credits must meet freshman admission requirements 30 of 120 credits required for the bachelor's degree must be completed at UWM. **International Students:** There are 760 international students enrolled. They must take the TOEFL with a minimum score of 75 on the Internet-based version (iBT). Students must also take the IELTS. All applicants to the College of Engineering and Applied Science must also submit official ACT or SAT scores.

ADMISSIONS: 72% of the 2017-2018 applicants were accepted. The ACT scores were 8% between 12 and 17, 56% between 18 and 23, 32% between 24 and 29, and 4% above 30. 30% of the current freshmen were in the top fifth of their class; 54% were in the top two fifths. 9 freshmen graduated first in their class. **Admissions Contact:** Department of Admissions and Recruitment Email: *uwmlook@uwm.edu* Web: *www.uwm.edu*

FINANCIAL AID: The FAFSA code is 003896. The priority date for freshman financial aid applications for fall entry is March 1. The deadline for filing freshman financial aid applications for fall entry is December 1.

UNIVERSITY OF WISCONSIN-OSHKOSH D-4

www.uwosh.edu

Oshkosh, WI 54901	**(920) 424-3164** **(920) 424-1234**
Fax: (920) 424-1207	**Email: admissions@uwosh.edu**
Full-time: 3466 men, 4785 women	**Faculty:** 407; IIA, --$
Part-time: 544 men, 707 women	**Ph.D.s:** 81%
Graduate: 365 men, 772 women	**Student/Faculty:** 20 to 1
Year: semesters, summer session	**Tuition:** $7600 ($15,174)
Room & Board: $7792	**Freshman Class:** 5635 applied, 3688 accepted, 1501 enrolled
ACT: 22	**CEEB CODE:** 1916
Application Deadline: n/av	**COMPETITIVE**

University of Wisconsin-Oshkosh, founded in 1871, is a public institution offering undergraduate and graduate programs in education, business, the arts and sciences, and health fields. There are 4 undergraduate schools and 1 graduate school. In addition to regional accreditation, UW-Oshkosh has baccalaureate program accreditation with AACSB, ACEJMC, CSWE, NASM, NCATE, and NLN. The 192-acre campus is in an urban area 90 miles north of Milwaukee, WI. Including any residence halls, there are 36 buildings.

STUDENT LIFE: 89% of undergraduates are from Wisconsin. Others are from 30 states, 32 foreign countries, and Canada. 85% are White; 4% Asian American; 4% Hispanic; 3% African American; 2% two or more races. **Female To Male Ratio:** 1.4:1. The average age of freshmen is 18; all undergraduates, 23. 29% do not continue beyond their first year; 55% remain to graduate. **Housing:** College-sponsored housing includes dorms, fraternity houses, sorority houses, designated quiet floors, smoke-free floors, theme housing, and university learning community floor. On-campus housing is guaranteed for all 4 years. 86% of students live on campus. All students may keep cars.

FACULTY/CLASSROOMS: 56% of faculty are male; 44% are female. No introductory courses are taught by graduate students. The average class size in an introductory lecture is 31 and in a laboratory is 21.

PROGRAMS OF STUDY: UW-Oshkosh confers B.A., B.S., B.Art Ed., B.B.A., B.F.A., B.L.S., B.M., B.M.E., B.S.N., and B.S.W. degrees. Associate and master's degrees are also awarded. Bachelor's degrees are awarded in BIOLOGICAL SCIENCE (biology/biological science and microbiology), BUSINESS (accounting, banking and finance, business administration and management, human resources, management information systems, and marketing/retailing/merchandising), COMMUNICATIONS AND THE ARTS (art, English, fine arts, French, German, journalism, music, Spanish, and speech/debate/rhetoric), COMPUTER AND PHYSICAL SCIENCE (chemistry, computer science, geology, mathematics, and physics), EDUCATION (art education, elementary education, music education, physical education, science education, secondary education, social science education, and special education), HEALTH PROFESSIONS (medical laboratory technology, music therapy, nursing, and speech pathology/audiology), SOCIAL SCIENCE (anthropology, criminal justice, economics, geography, history, human services, international studies, liberal arts/general studies, philosophy, political science/government, psychology, religion, social work, sociology, and urban studies). Business, education, and nursing have the largest enrollments.

ACTIVITIES: 4% of men belong to 8 national fraternities; 3% of women belong to 5 national sororities. There are 175 groups on campus, including art, band, cheerleading, chess, choir, computers, dance, debate, drama, ethnic, film, forensics, honors, international, LGBT, newspaper, pep band, political, professional, radio and TV, religious, social, social service, and student government. Popular campus events include Winter Carnival, Taste of UW Oshkosh, and Celebration of Racial Inclusiveness. **Sports:** There are 10 intercollegiate sports for men and 11 for women, and 15 intramural sports for men and 15 for women. Facilities include a hall for basketball and volleyball, a sports center for basketball, tennis, and indoor track, a pool, a stadium for football and outdoor track, indoor gym, and an arena. **Graduates:** From July 1, 2016 to June 30, 2017, 2045 bachelor's degrees were awarded. The most popular majors were business/marketing (19%), health professions and related programs, and education (13%), public administration and social sciences, social sciences, and and communication/journalism (7%). In an average class, 7% graduate in 4 years or less, 33% graduate in 5 years or less, and 42% graduate in 6 years or less. Of the 2016 graduating class, 97% were employed within 6 months of graduation.

SERVICES: Counseling and information services are available, as is tutoring in most subjects. There is a reader service for the blind, and remedial math, reading, and writing. **Library/Resources:** The library contains 487,000 volumes, 1.3 million microform items, 7,000 audio/video tapes/CDs/DVDs, and subscribes to 1,850 periodicals, including electronic. Computerized library services include interlibrary loans and database searching. Special learning facilities include an art gallery, planetarium, radio station, TV station, and a speech and hearing clinic. **Physically Challenged Students:** Facilities include wheelchair ramps, elevators, special parking, specially equipped restrooms, special class scheduling, lowered drinking fountains, and lowered telephones. **Special:** UW-Oshkosh offers internships and study abroad. There are 15 national honor societies and a freshman honors program. **Visiting:** There are regularly scheduled orientations for prospective students, including preview days, campus tours, and an individual appointment with an admissions counselor. There are guides for informal visits, visitors may sit in on classes, and stay overnight. To schedule a visit, contact the Admissions Office. **Campus Safety and Security:** Measures include 24-hour foot and vehicle patrol, self-defense education, and security escort services. There are emergency telephones and lighted pathways/sidewalks.

REQUIREMENTS: Students must graduate in the upper 50% of their class from an accredited secondary school or score a 22 on the enhanced ACT if ranked in the third quartile. They should have completed 17 academic credits, including 4 in English, 3 (4 recommended) each in math, social studies, natural sciences with lab, and 4 in academic electives. AP and CLEP credits are accepted. All students must complete a minimum of 120 credit hours with at least a 2.0 GPA. A minimum of 42 credits in general education requirements includes 9 credits each in humanities and social science, 8 in natural science, 6 in English composition, 3 in math or logic, 3 in non-Western culture, 3 in speech, and 2 in phys ed. **Procedure:** Freshmen are admitted to all sessions. Entrance exams should be taken in spring of the junior year or early fall of the senior year. There are deferred admissions and rolling admissions plans. Applications should be filed by January 1 for spring entry. The fall 2017 application fee was $50. Notification of early decision is sent September 15; regular decision, on a rolling basis. **Transfer Students:** 943 transfer students enrolled in 2016-2017. Candidates should have completed 30 or more semester credits; if not, high school transcripts are reviewed. Students must have at least a 2.0 cumulative GPA. Student may enroll in the fall, spring and summer. 30 of 120 credits required for the bachelor's degree must be completed at UW-Oshkosh. **International Students:** There are 75 international students enrolled. They must take the TOEFL.

ADMISSIONS: 65% of the 2017-2018 applicants were accepted. The ACT scores were 4% between 12 and 17, 63% between 18 and 23, 31% between 24 and 29, and 2% above 30. 19 freshmen graduated first in their class. **Admissions Contact:** Jill Endries, Director of Undergraduate Admissions. Email: *admissions@uwosh.edu* Web: *www.uwosh.edu*

FINANCIAL AID: In 2017-2018, 78% of all full-time freshmen received some form of financial aid and need-based aid. The average freshman award was $7,895. Need-based scholarships or need-based grants averaged $6,129; need-based self-help aid (loans and jobs) averaged $2,234; other non-need-based awards and non-need-based scholarships averaged $3,166; and $1,496 from other forms of aid. 60% of undergraduate students work part-time. UW-Oshkosh is a member of CSS. The FAFSA code is 003920. The priority date for freshman financial aid applications for fall entry is March 15.

UNIVERSITY OF WISCONSIN-PARKSIDE E-5
www.uwp.edu

Kenosha, WI 53141 **(262) 595-2355**

Fax: (262) 595-2008	**Email: admissions@uwp.edu**
Full-time: 1578 men, 1697 women	**Faculty:** 162; IIA, --$
Part-time: 401 men, 492 women	**Ph.D.s:** 76%
Graduate: 73 men, 67 women	**Student/Faculty:** 20 to 1
Year: semesters, summer session	**Tuition:** $7389 (15,378)
Room & Board: $7924	**Freshman Class:** 1743 applied, 1399 accepted, 712 enrolled
ACT: 21	**CEEB CODE:** 1860
Application Deadline: August 1	**COMPETITIVE**

University of Wisconsin-Parkside, founded in 1968, offers undergraduate programs in liberal arts, business, education, and science and technology. There are 4 undergraduate schools and 3 graduate schools. In addition to regional accreditation, UW-Parkside has baccalaureate program accreditation with AACSB. The 700-acre campus is in a suburban area approximately 30 miles south of Milwaukee and 60 miles north of Chicago, between the cities of Racine and Kenosha. Including any residence halls, there are 15 buildings.

STUDENT LIFE: 82% of undergraduates are from Wisconsin. Others are from 32 states, and 24 foreign countries. 65% are White; 16% Hispanic; 9% African American; 4% Asian American; 4% two or more races; 2% Foreign. **Female To Male Ratio:** 1.1:1. The average age of freshmen is 19; all undergraduates, 24. 26% do not continue beyond their first year; 33% remain to graduate. **Housing:** 1000 students can be accommodated in college housing, which includes dorms and on-campus apartments. On-campus housing is available on a first-come, first-served basis. 81% of students commute. All students may keep cars.

FACULTY/CLASSROOMS: 51% of faculty are male; 49% are female. All teach undergraduates. No introductory courses are taught by graduate students. The average class size in an introductory lecture is 33; in a laboratory is 18; and in a regular course is 25.

PROGRAMS OF STUDY: UW-Parkside confers B.A. and B.S. degrees. Associate and master's degrees are also awarded. Bachelor's degrees are awarded in AGRICULTURE (environmental studies), BIOLOGICAL SCIENCE (biology/biological science and molecular biology), BUSINESS (accounting, business administration and management, management information systems, marketing, and sports management), COMMUNICATIONS AND THE ARTS (art, communications, English, fine arts, graphic design, music, Spanish, and theatre arts), COMPUTER AND PHYSICAL SCIENCE (chemistry, computer science, geology, mathematics, and physics), EDUCATION (early childhood education, elementary education, health information management, secondary education, and special education), HEALTH PROFESSIONS (exercise and movement science and health science), SOCIAL SCIENCE (criminal justice, economics, geography, history, international studies, liberal arts, sciences, general studies, humanities, philosophy, political science/government, psychology, and sociology). Computer science, criminal justice, applied health sciences, and theatre arts are the strongest academically. Biology, business, computer science, criminal justice, and psychology have the largest enrollments.

ACTIVITIES: 1% of men belong to 3 national fraternities; 1% of women belong to 4 national sororities. There are 75 groups on campus, including art, band, cheerleading, choir, chorale, chorus, communications, computers, dance, debate, drama, environmental, ethnic, honors, international, jazz band, LGBT, literary magazine, musical theater, newspaper, orchestra, political, professional, radio and TV, religious, social, social service, and student government. Popular campus events include World Fest, Heritage Month Celebrations, Weeks of Welcome. **Sports:** There are 7 intercollegiate sports for men and 6 for women, and 10 intramural sports for men and 10 for women. Facilities include a national/cross-country course, playing fields, tennis courts, an all-purpose gym with a auditorium for athletic events and concerts, indoor track facility, swimming pool, weight room, and disc golf course. **Graduates:** From July 1, 2016 to June 30, 2017, 741 bachelor's degrees were awarded. The most popular majors were business management (16%), sociology (12%), and psychology (7%). In an average class, 11% graduate in 4 years or less, 19% graduate in 5 years or less, and 33% graduate in 6 years or less. Of the 2016 graduating class, 23% were enrolled in graduate school within 6 months of graduation, and 85% were employed.

SERVICES: Counseling and information services are available, as is tutoring in every subject. A reader service for the blind, remedial math, and online tutoring are also available. **Library/Resources:** The library contains 460,000 volumes, 972,991 microform items, 19,000 audio/video tapes/CDs/DVDs, and subscribes to 1,200 periodicals including electronic. Computerized library services include interlibrary loans, database searching, Internet access, and Wi-Fi capability. Special learning facilities include an art gallery and radio station. **Physically Challenged Students:** All of the campus is accessible. Facilities include wheelchair ramps, elevators, special parking, specially equipped restrooms, lowered drinking fountains, and lowered telephones. **Special:** UW-Parkside offers on-campus work-study programs, internships, study abroad, student-designed majors, and an accelerated premedicine program. Nondegree study and credit by exam are possible. Study abroad includes: Mexico, China, India, Cuba, Australia, Italy, Germany, Poland, Caribbean, Japan, Finland, and Russia. There is a freshman honors program. **Visiting:** There are regularly scheduled orientations for prospective students, including open houses and campus tours. There are guides for informal visits; visitors may sit in on classes and stay overnight. To schedule a visit, contact Cortney Payne at paynec@uwp.edu. **Campus Safety and Security:** Measures include 24-hour foot and vehicle patrol, an emergency notification system, self-defense education, and security escort services. There are shuttle buses, emergency telephones, lighted pathways/sidewalks, and controlled access to dorms/residences.

REQUIREMENTS: The ACT is required for in-state students; either the ACT or the SAT I for out-of-state students. A minimum score of 21 is required on the ACT. Students may use a lower ACT score in combination with class rank to gain admission. Candidates must be graduates of an accredited secondary school or hold a GED diploma. At least 16 academic credits are required, including 4 in English, 3 in social sciences, 2 in natural sciences, and 1 each in algebra and plane geometry. AP and CLEP credits are accepted. A total of 120 credits with at least 30 in the major and 30 at UW-Parkside with a GPA of 2.0 or higher are required for graduation. Students must complete a minimum of 12 credits in humanities and the arts, 12 in social and behavioral sciences, and 12 in natural sciences. Students in most majors with fewer than 2 units of foreign language in high school must also fulfill a foreign language requirement. **Procedure:** Freshmen are admitted to all sessions. Entrance exams should be taken by the fall of the senior year. There is a rolling admissions plan. Applications should be filed by August 1 for fall entry. The fall 2017 application fee was $44. Applications are accepted on-line. **Transfer Students:** 578 transfer students enrolled in 2016-2017. Students must have a GPA of 2.0 and be in good standing with the previous institution attended. 30 of 120 credits required for the bachelor's degree must be completed at UW-Parkside. **International Students:** There are 65 international students enrolled. They must take the TOEFL with a minimum score of 521 on the paper-based TOEFL (PBT) or 71 on the Internet-based version (iBT).

ADMISSIONS: 80% of the 2017-2018 applicants were accepted. The ACT scores were 17% between 12 and 17, 60% between 18 and 23, 20% between 24 and 29, and 3% above 30. 30% of the current freshmen were in the top fifth of their class; 61% were in the top two fifths. 7 freshmen graduated first in their class. **Admissions Contact:** Troy Moldenhauer, Director of Admissions and Recruitment. Email: *Moldenht@uwp.edu* Web: *www.uwp.edu*

FINANCIAL AID: The average financial indebtedness of the 2017 graduate was $26,000. UW-Parkside is a member of CSS. The CSS/Profile, FFS, and the college's own financial statement are required. The FAFSA code is 005015. The priority date for freshman financial aid applications for fall entry is March 15.

UNIVERSITY OF WISCONSIN-PLATTEVILLE — C-5

www.uwplatt.edu

Platteville, WI 53818 — (608) 342-1125, (800) 362-5515

Fax: (608) 342-1122 — **Email:** admit@uwplatt.edu

Full-time: 4442 men, 2309 women	**Faculty:** 316; IIA, --$
Part-time: 542 men, 227 women	**Ph.D.s:** 75%
Graduate: 491 men, 418 women	**Student/Faculty:** 21 to 1
Year: semesters, summer session	**Tuition:** $7543 ($15,393)
Room & Board: $7160	**Freshman Class:** 3711 applied, 2937 accepted, 1407 enrolled
SAT or ACT: required	**CEEB CODE:** 1917
Application Deadline: open	**COMPETITIVE**

University of Wisconsin-Platteville, takes its roots from the Platteville Normal School State Teachers College (1866) and the Wisconsin Mining Trade School (1908). Since then, the university's teaching mission has remained the same, develop strong graduates who can take their experience as a student directly to the workforce in an impactful way. UW-Platteville consists of 3 colleges: the college of business, industry, life science and agriculture; the college of engineering, mathematics and science; and the college of liberal arts and education. We have particular strengths in agriculture, biology, business, criminal justice, education, engineering, and industrial technology. In addition to regional accreditation, UW-Platteville has baccalaureate program accreditation with ABET, NASM, CAEP, ACS, ATMAE, and Wisconsin DPI. The 821-acre campus is in a small town 20 miles northeast of Dubuque, IA, and 75 miles southwest of Madison, WI. Including any residence halls, there are 39 buildings.

STUDENT LIFE: 76% of undergraduates are from Wisconsin. Others are from 42 states, and 29 foreign countries. 90% are from public schools. 89% are White; 3% Hispanic; 3% two or more races; 1% African American; 1% Asian American; 1% Foreign; 1% race unknown. **Male To Female Ratio:** 1.9:1. The average age of freshmen is 19; all undergraduates, 21. 23% do not continue beyond their first year; 52% remain to graduate. **Housing:** 3433 students can be accommodated in college housing, which includes dorms and on-campus apartments. In addition, there are special-interest houses, and Cooper living and learning center. 14% of students commute. All students may keep cars.

FACULTY/CLASSROOMS: 58% of faculty are male; 41% are female. No introductory courses are taught by graduate students.

PROGRAMS OF STUDY: UW-Platteville confers B.A. and B.S. degrees. Associate and master's degrees are also awarded. Bachelor's degrees are awarded in AGRICULTURE (agricultural business management, animal science, dairy science, horticulture, and soil science), BIOLOGICAL SCIENCE (biology/biological science), BUSINESS (accounting and business administration and management), COMMUNICATIONS AND THE ARTS (art, English, German, media arts, music, Spanish, communication arts - speech, and visual and performing arts), COMPUTER AND PHYSICAL SCIENCE (chemistry, computer science, mathematics, physical sciences, physics, and software engineering), EDUCATION (agricultural education, art education, education, elementary education, middle school education, music education, physical education, secondary education, and technical education), ENGINEERING AND ENVIRONMENTAL DESIGN (civil engineering, electrical/electronics engineering, engineering physics, environmental engineering, industrial engineering, industrial engineering technology, land use management and reclamation, mechanical engineering, and nanotechnology), SOCIAL SCIENCE (criminal justice, economics, forensic studies, geography, history, international studies, liberal arts/general studies, philosophy, political science/government, psychology, and social science). Engineering, agriculture, and business administration/marketing are the strongest academically. Engineering, agriculture, and homeland security have the largest enrollments.

ACTIVITIES: 4% of men belong to 1 local and 8 national fraternities; 4% of women belong to 1 local and 5 national sororities. There are 178 groups on campus, including art, band, cheerleading, choir, chorale, chorus, computers, dance, debate, drama, ethnic, film, forensics, honors, international, jazz band, LGBT, literary magazine, marching band, musical theater, newspaper, orchestra, pep band, photography, political, professional, radio and TV, religious, social, social service, student government, and symphony. Popular campus events include Homecoming, Pioneer Distinguished Lecturer Presentation, Mudfest Rugby Tournament, and Lighting and Whitewash of the M. **Sports:** There are 7 intercollegiate sports for men and 7 for women, and 13 intramural sports for men and 12 for women. Facilities include a gym, stadium, indoor track, outdoor track, basketball and volleyball courts, tennis, racquetball courts, a weight room, swimming pool, baseball diamonds, and soccer fields. **Graduates:** From July 1, 2016 to June 30, 2017, 1495 bachelor's degrees were awarded. The most popular majors were engineering (28%), agriculture (12%), and homeland security (12%). In an average class, 19% graduate in 4 years or less, 26% graduate in 5 years or less, and 53% graduate in 6 years or less.

SERVICES: Counseling and information services are available, as is tutoring in most subjects. There is a reader service for the blind, and remedial math, reading, and writing. In addition, there is pioneer academic and transitional help, services for students with disabilities, a student support services, and a testing center. **Library/Resources:** The library contains 234,055 volumes, 16,889 microform items, 8,357 audio/video tapes/CDs/DVDs, and subscribes to 266 periodicals, including electronic. Computerized library services include interlibrary loans, database searching, Internet access, and Wi-Fi capability. Special learning facilities include an art gallery, a radio station, TV station, Southwest Wisconsin room/archives, North American Manx Museum, forensic investigation crime scene house, a animal house, and a Pioneer Farm (400A education/research farm). **Physically Challenged Students:** 95% of the campus is accessible. Facilities include wheelchair ramps, elevators, special parking, specially equipped restrooms, special class scheduling, lowered drinking fountains, lowered telephones, and special housing. **Special:** UWP offers internships in business, industry, and communication, a co-op program in engineering, and study abroad in 16 countries. Credit by exam, credit for life, military, and work experience, work-study programs, dual majors, student-designed majors, nondegree study, and pass/fail options are also available. There are 13 national honor societies. **Visiting:** There are regularly scheduled orientations for prospective students. The Pioneer Previews, held on 6 dates each year, include group tours, an admissions briefing, and visits to specific colleges and departments. Daily visits (Monday through Friday) are also available. There are guides for informal visits, visitors may sit in on classes, and stay overnight. To schedule a visit, contact Amanda Witzig at (877) UWPLATT. **Campus Safety and Security:** Measures include 24-hour foot and vehicle patrol, an emergency notification system, and security escort services. There are shuttle buses, emergency telephones, lighted pathways/sidewalks, and controlled access to dorms/residences.

REQUIREMENTS: ACT and SAT scores are permissible for applicants. Applicants must have successfully completed 17 college preparatory units, including 4 units of English, 3 each of math (algebra, geometry and higher), social science, natural science (2 must include lab experiences), 4 from the above academic areas, foreign language, fine arts, computer science, or courses in vocational areas. Standard admission will be given to those students who are in the top 50% of their graduating class or have an ACT composite of 22 (SAT equivalency). UW-Platteville requires applicants to be in the upper 50% of their class. AP and CLEP credits are accepted. In order to graduate with Bachelor of Arts or Bachelor of Science degrees, students must earn a minimum of 120 college or university credits (some programs require more than 120 credits), and they must: satisfy all the requirements for the particular university degree and for the college in which they are enrolled; satisfy all requirements for a major; earn a minimum of 42 credits in upper division courses (courses numbered 3000 or above); earn a minimum of 32 credits in residence at UW-Platteville with at least 23 of the last 32 credits in residence; be in good academic standing; and earn cumulative grade point averages of at least 2.0 in all subjects and within a major field. Note that minimum academic standards set for particular majors, minors or colleges may be higher. **Procedure:** Freshmen are admitted to all sessions. Entrance exams should be taken in April or June of the junior year. There are deferred admissions and rolling admissions plans. Application deadlines are open. The fall 2017 application fee was $50. Applications are accepted on-line. **Transfer Students:** 470 transfer students enrolled in 2016-2017. Applicants must have a cumulative GPA of at least 2.0 in college transfer courses and be in good standing at the institution they are currently attending or have attended. Applicants must have 12 or more transferable credits from an accredited institution to be considered for admission as a transfer. 32 of 120 credits required for the bachelor's degree must be completed at UW-Platteville. **International Students:** There are 87 international students enrolled. They must take the TOEFL with a minimum score of 550 on the paper-based TOEFL (PBT) or 79 on the Internet-based version (iBT). In addition applicants must take the Wisconsin English and Math placement exam.

ADMISSIONS: 79% of the 2017-2018 applicants were accepted. **Admissions Contact:** Heidi Tuescher-Gille, Director of Admission and Enrollment Service. Email: *admit@uwplatt.edu* Web: *www.uwplatt.edu*

FINANCIAL AID: The FAFSA code is 003921. The priority date for freshman financial aid applications for fall entry is March 15.

UNIVERSITY OF WISCONSIN-RIVER FALLS A-3

www.uwrf.edu

River Falls, WI 54022	(715) 425-3500
Fax: (715) 425-0676	Email: admit@uwrf.edu
Full-time: 2500 men, 3500 women	**Faculty:** 221; IIA, --$
Part-time: 160 men, 230 women	**Ph.D.s:** 85%
Graduate: 160 men, 330 women	**Student/Faculty:** 23 to 1
Year: semesters, summer session	**Tuition:** $8015 ($15,589)
Room & Board: $6526	**Freshman Class:** n/av
ACT: required	**CEEB CODE:** 1918
Application Deadline: open	**COMPETITIVE**

University of Wisconsin-River Falls, founded in 1874, is a public institution offering undergraduate programs in arts and sciences, education, agriculture, and food and environmental sciences. The figures given in the above capsule and in this profile are approximate. There are 4 undergraduate schools and 1 graduate school. In addition to regional accreditation, UW-River Falls has baccalaureate program accreditation with ACEJMC, ASLA, CSWE, and NASM. The 225-acre campus is in a suburban area 29 miles east of Minneapolis-St. Paul, Minnesota. Including any residence halls, there are 28 buildings.

STUDENT LIFE: 52% of undergraduates are from Wisconsin. Others are from 25 states, 13 foreign countries, and Canada. 95% are from public schools. 95% are White; 2% Asian American; 1% African American; 1% Hispanic. **Female To Male Ratio:** 1.4:1. The average age of freshmen is 18; all undergraduates, 21. 25% do not continue beyond their first year; 54% remain to graduate. **Housing:** 2172 students can be accommodated in college housing, which includes dorms. On-campus housing is guaranteed for all 4 years. 59% of students commute. All students may keep cars.

FACULTY/CLASSROOMS: 70% of faculty are male; 30% are female. All teach undergraduates. No introductory courses are taught by graduate students. The average class size in an introductory lecture is 30; in a laboratory is 24; and in a regular course is 20.

PROGRAMS OF STUDY: UW-River Falls confers B.A., B.S., B.F.A, B.M.E., and B.S.W. degrees. Master's degrees are also awarded. Bachelor's degrees are awarded in AGRICULTURE (agricultural business management, agronomy, animal science, conservation and regulation, horticulture, and soil science), BIOLOGICAL SCIENCE (biology/biological science and biotechnology), BUSINESS (accounting and business administration and management), COMMUNICATIONS AND THE ARTS (art, communications, English, fine arts, journalism, modern language, music, and speech/debate/rhetoric), COMPUTER AND PHYSICAL SCIENCE (chemistry, computer programming, geology, mathematics, physics, and science), EDUCATION (agricultural education, art education, elementary education, foreign languages education, music education, physical education, and secondary education), ENGINEERING AND ENVIRONMENTAL DESIGN (agricultural engineering and land use management and reclamation), HEALTH PROFESSIONS (premedicine, prepharmacy, and speech pathology/audiology), SOCIAL SCIENCE (economics, food science, geography, history, political science/government, prelaw, psychology, social studies, social work, and sociology). Physics, chemistry, and elementary education are the strongest academically. Business, elementary education, and animal science have the largest enrollments.

ACTIVITIES: 5% of men belong to 5 national fraternities; 5% of women belong to 4 national sororities. There are 120 groups on campus, including agriculture, and academic, drug awareness, art, band, cheerleading, choir, chorus, clubs for rodeo, communications, computers, dance, debate, drama, ethnic, forensics, honors, international, jazz band, LGBT, literary magazine, musical theater, newspaper, orchestra, pep band, political, professional, radio and TV, religious, social, student government, and symphony. Popular campus events include Winter Carnival, Annual Rodeo, and Unity in the Community. **Sports:** There are 7 intercollegiate sports for men and 11 for women, and 11 intramural sports for men and 12 for women. Facilities include an ice arena, a stadium, multipurpose phys ed centers, swimming pool, multi gyms, handball courts, field house, an indoor track, an indoor rock-climbing wall, basketball, tennis, and volleyball courts. **Graduates:** From July 1, 2016 to June 30, 2017, 1045 bachelor's degrees were awarded. The most popular majors were education (18%), agriculture (15%), and business (15%). In an average class, 25% graduate in 4 years or less, 35% graduate in 5 years or less, and 54% graduate in 6 years or less.

SERVICES: Counseling and information services are available, as is tutoring in every subject. There is a reader service for the blind, and remedial math, reading, and writing. **Library/Resources:** The library contains 221,453 volumes, 726,035 microform items, 8,455 audio/video tapes/CDs/DVDs, and subscribes to 1,322 periodicals, including electronic. Computerized library services include interlibrary loans, database searching, and Internet access. Special learning facilities include an art gallery, planetarium, radio station, TV station, a greenhouse, climbing wall, communicative disorders lab, educational technology center, food science and meat facilities, 2 campus lab farms, and sundial. **Physically Challenged Students:** 95% of the campus is accessible. Facilities include wheelchair ramps, elevators, special parking, specially equipped restrooms, special class scheduling, lowered drinking fountains, and lowered telephones. **Special:** Co-op programs in food science and environmental science, on-campus work-study, and accelerated degree programs in several preprofessional areas are available. UW/River Falls also offers internships, student-designed majors, credit by examination, nondegree study, and pass/fail options. Study abroad is available through the National Student Exchange and the International Student Exchange Program in some 15 countries. There are 11 national honor societies and a freshman honors program. **Visiting:** There are regularly scheduled orientations for prospective students, including College Visit Days and tours. There are guides for informal visits and visitors may sit in on classes. To schedule a visit, contact the Admissions Office. **Campus Safety and Security:** Measures include 24-hour foot and vehicle patrol, self-defense education, and security escort services. There are emergency telephones and lighted pathways/sidewalks.

REQUIREMENTS: The ACT is required, with a minimum composite score of 22, or 18 if in upper 40% of high school class. Candidates must be graduates of an accredited secondary school and have completed at least 17 academic credits, including 4 in English, 3 in social sciences, and 3 each in math and science, with 4 college prep courses. A GED certificate is accepted. AP and CLEP credits are accepted. To graduate, students must complete at least 120 semester hours, with a GPA of 2.0 overall and 2.25 in the major field. General education requirements include 39 semester hours in English composition, speech and humanities, natural and social sciences, math, and phys ed. **Procedure:** Freshmen are admitted to all sessions. Entrance exams should be taken in the spring of the junior year. There are early admissions, deferred admissions, and rolling admissions plans. Application deadlines are open. The fall 2017 application fee was $35. Applications are accepted on-line. **Transfer Students:** Priority admission is given to students with a college GPA of 2.6 or higher. Students with a GPA of 2.0 to 2.6 are placed on a waiting list. Transfers in elementary education must have a GPA of 3.0. 30 of 120 credits required for the bachelor's degree must be completed at UW-River Falls. **International Students:** There are 47 international students enrolled. They must take the TOEFL, and the ACT.

Admissions Contact: Alan J. Tuchtenhagen, Admissions Director. Email: *admit@uwrf.edu* Web: *www.uwrf.edu*

FINANCIAL AID: 20% of undergraduate students work part-time. UW-River Falls is a member of CSS. The FAFSA code is 003923. The deadline for filing freshman financial aid applications for fall entry is March 15.

UNIVERSITY OF WISCONSIN-STEVENS POINT C-3

www.uwsp.edu

Stevens Point, WI 54481 **(715) 346-2441**

Fax: (715) 346-2441	**Email: admiss@uwsp.edu**
Full-time: 4159 men, 4476 women	**Faculty:** 413; IIA, --$
Part-time: 219 men, 264 women	**Ph.D.s:** 67%
Graduate: 93 men, 288 women	**Student/Faculty:** 20 to 1
Year: semesters, summer session	**Tuition:** $7505 ($15,078)
Room & Board: $6538	**Freshman Class:** 4915 applied, 3672 accepted, 1637 enrolled
SAT CR/M/W: 546/536/528 **ACT:** 23	**CEEB CODE:** 1919
Application Deadline: open	**COMPETITIVE**

University of Wisconsin-Stevens Point, founded in 1894, offers undergraduate programs in natural resources, education, business, arts and sciences, and professional studies. The figures given in the above capsule and in this profile are approximate. There are 4 undergraduate schools and 1 graduate school. In addition to regional accreditation, UW-Stevens Point has baccalaureate program accreditation with ABET, ASLA, NASAD, ACS, CADE, and NNACL. The 400-acre campus is in a small town 110 miles north of Madison. Including any residence halls, there are 35 buildings.

STUDENT LIFE: 89% of undergraduates are from Wisconsin. Others are from 30 states, 29 foreign countries, and Canada. 98% are from public schools. 89% are White; 2% Asian American; 2% Hispanic; 2% two or more races; 1% African American. **Female To Male Ratio:** 1.1:1. The average age of freshmen is 19; all undergraduates, 22. 20% do not continue beyond their first year; 61% remain to graduate. **Housing:** 3414 students can be accommodated in college housing, which includes dorms, and special-interest houses. 62% of students commute. All students may keep cars.

FACULTY/CLASSROOMS: 64% of faculty are male; 46% are female. All teach undergraduates, 98% do research, and 98% do both. No introductory courses are taught by graduate students.

PROGRAMS OF STUDY: UW-Stevens Point confers B.A., B.S., B.F.A., and B.M. degrees. Associate, master's, and doctoral degrees are also awarded. Bachelor's degrees are awarded in AGRICULTURE (fishing and fisheries, forestry and related sciences, natural resource management, and soil science), BIOLOGICAL SCIENCE (biochemistry, biology/biological science, nutrition, and wildlife biology), BUSINESS (accounting and business administration and management), COMMUNICATIONS AND THE ARTS (art, arts administration/management, communications, dance, dramatic arts, English, fine arts, French, German, music, and Spanish), COMPUTER AND PHYSICAL SCIENCE (chemistry, geoscience, information sciences and systems, mathematics, natural sciences, physics, and web services), EDUCATION (athletic training, early childhood education, education, education of the exceptional child, elementary education, health education, music education, and physical education), ENGINEERING AND ENVIRONMENTAL DESIGN (computer technology, interior design, and paper and pulp science), HEALTH PROFESSIONS (clinical science, health science, and speech pathology/audiology), SOCIAL SCIENCE (American studies, dietetics, economics, family/consumer studies, geography, history, international studies, liberal arts/general studies, philosophy, political science/government, psychology, public administration, social science, social work, and sociology). Natural resources, education, and social sciences have the largest enrollments.

ACTIVITIES: 1% of men belong to 1 local and 4 national fraternities; 1% of women belong to 2 local and 1 national sororities. There are 201 groups on campus, including art, band, cheerleading, choir, chorale, chorus, computers, dance, drama, environmental, ethnic, film, honors, international, jazz band, LGBT, literary magazine, musical theater, newspaper, orchestra, pep band, photography, political, professional, radio and TV, religious, social, social service, student government, and symphony. Popular campus events include Trivia Contest, International Club Dinner, and Spud Bowl. **Sports:** There are 8 intercollegiate sports for men and 10 for women, and 16 intramural sports for men and 16 for women. Facilities include gyms, a health enhancement center, cardio center, aquatic center, the University Center, a stadium, an indoor gym, and numerous outdoor fields. **Graduates:** From July 1, 2016 to June 30, 2017, 1717 bachelor's degrees were awarded. The most popular majors were natural resources and conservation (13%), education (10%), and social sciences (10%). In an average class, 22% graduate in 4 years or less and 59% graduate in 6 years or less. Of the 2016 graduating class, 17% were enrolled in graduate school within 6 months of graduation, and 55% were employed.

SERVICES: Counseling and information services are available, as is tutoring in most subjects. There is a reader service for the blind, and remedial math, reading, and writing. **Library/Resources:** The library contains 813,123 volumes, 50,349 microform items, 25,357 audio/video tapes/CDs/DVDs, and subscribes to 44,876 periodicals, including electronic. Computerized library services include interlibrary loans, database searching, Internet access, and Wi-Fi capability. Special learning facilities include an art gallery, a natural history museum, a planetarium, radio station, TV station, an observatory, a map center, 275-acre nature preserve, a groundwater center, and a wellness institute. **Physically Challenged Students:** All of the campus is accessible. Facilities include wheelchair ramps, elevators, special parking, specially equipped restrooms, special class scheduling, lowered drinking fountains, and lowered telephones. **Special:** A co-op program in nursing is offered with UW/Eau Claire and St. Joseph's Hospital. Internships, study abroad in 9 countries, work-study programs, dual and student-designed majors, independent study, and pass/fail options are also available. Credit is given for military, life, and work experience. There are 13 national honor societies and 3 departmental honors programs. **Visiting:** There are regularly scheduled orientations for prospective students. Students and parents can visit the campus on a scheduled day or participate in a one-day specialized program called ViewPoint, which is offered several times each fall and spring. UWSP also offers Info Nights in communities throughout WI and in IL to introduce students and parents to the university and answer detailed questions. There are guides for informal visits. To schedule a visit, contact the Office of Admissions. **Campus Safety and Security:** Measures include 24-hour foot and vehicle patrol, emergency notification system, and security escort services. There are emergency telephones, lighted pathways/sidewalks, and controlled access to dorms/residences.

REQUIREMENTS: The ACT is preferred. Applicants should have a high school rank of top 35% or above, or a cumulative high school GPA of 3.20 or higher, with an ACT composite score of 21 (SAT equivalent) or above; or rank in the top 50% of high school class. The GED is accepted. Required academic preparation includes 4 years of English, 3 years each of social studies, math, and lab science, along with 4 electives; 2 years of foreign language. The following non-academic factors are considered: involvement through work experience, extracurricular activities, and volunteerism; personal characteristics and accomplishments including special talents and abilities, honors, awards and personal qualities; diversity in background and experience; and life circumstances. While non-academic factors are considered, they will not necessarily make an applicant with a weak academic background a strong candidate for admission. AP and CLEP credits are accepted. To graduate, students must complete 120 credit hours (30 from UWSP and 40 at 300/400 level), with a minimum GPA of 2.0. Core curriculum requirements must also be fulfilled, along with courses in writing, natural science, non-Western culture, minorities studies, social science, humanities, and wellness, and 3 credits in phys ed. Some majors require additional credits and higher minimum GPAs. **Procedure:** Freshmen are admitted in the fall and spring. Entrance exams should be taken previous fall or spring. There are deferred admissions and rolling admissions plans. Application deadlines are open. The fall 2017 application fee was $44. 119 applicants were on the 2017 waiting list; 98 were admitted. Applications are accepted online. **Transfer Students:** 786 transfer students enrolled in 2016-2017. Applicants must submit high school and college transcripts, as well as a statement of good standing from prior institutions. A high school minimum GPA of 2.25 is required. If fewer than 12 credits have been completed, the student must enroll as a freshman. 30 of 120 credits required for the bachelor's degree must be completed at UWSP. **International Students:** There are 206 international students enrolled. They must take the TOEFL with a minimum score of 70 on the Internet-based version (iBT).

ADMISSIONS: 75% of the 2017-2018 applicants were accepted. The SAT scores for the 2017-2018 freshman class were: Critical Reading-- 23% below 500, 55% between 500 and 599, 14% between 600 and 699, and 9% between 700 and 800. Math-- 32% below 500, 41% between 500 and 599, 23% between 600 and 699, and 5% between 700 and 800. Writing-- 46% below 500, 32% between 500 and 599, and 23% between 600 and 699. The ACT scores were 27% below 12, 37% between 12 and 17, 23% between 18 and 23, 8% between 24 and 29, and 5% above 30. 27% of the current freshmen were in the top fifth of their class; 61% were in the top two fifths. 28 freshmen graduated first in their class. **Admissions Contact:** Bill Jordan, Dean of Students. Email: *admiss@uwsp.edu* Web: *www.uwsp.edu*

FINANCIAL AID: In 2017-2018, 58% of all full-time freshmen received some form of financial aid. 31% of all full-time freshmen received need-based aid. The average freshman award was $6,571. Need-based scholarships or need-based grants averaged $5,406; need-based self-help aid (loans and jobs) averaged $4,107; other non-need-based awards and non-need-based scholarships averaged $2,237; and $3,960 from other forms of aid. 38% of undergraduate students work part-time. The average financial indebtedness of the 2017 graduate was $22,788. The FAFSA code is 003924. The priority date for freshman financial aid applications for fall entry is March 15.

UNIVERSITY OF WISCONSIN-STOUT B-3

www.uwstout.edu

Menomonie, WI 54751 **(715) 232-1411**

Fax: (715) 232-1667	**Email: admissions@uwstout.edu**
Full-time: 3656 men, 3122 women	**Faculty:** 406; IIA, --$
Part-time: 817 men, 599 women	**Ph.D.s:** 78%
Graduate: 347 men, 465 women	**Student/Faculty:** 18 to 1
Year: 4-1-4, summer session	**Tuition:** $9203 ($16,949)
Room & Board: $10,464	**Freshman Class:** 3535 applied, 2964 accepted, 1534 enrolled
SAT: required **ACT:** 22	**CEEB CODE:** 1740
Application Deadline: open	**COMPETITIVE**

University of Wisconsin-Stout, founded in 1891, offers undergraduate programs in liberal studies, human environmental sciences, industry and technology, education, and human services. The figures given in the above capsule and in this profile are approximate. There are 4 undergraduate schools and 1 graduate school. In addition to regional accreditation, UW-Stout has baccalaureate program accreditation with ABET, ACCE, ADA, FIDER, NASAD, IACBE, and AAMFT. The 110-acre campus is in a rural area 60 miles east of Minneapolis/St. Paul. Including any residence halls, there are 33 buildings.

STUDENT LIFE: 69% of undergraduates are from Wisconsin. Others are from 26 states, 28 foreign countries, and Canada. 93% are White; 2% Asian American; 1% African American; 1% American Indian/Alaska Native; 1% Hispanic; 1% Foreign. **Male To Female Ratio:** 1.2:1. The average age of freshmen is 18; all undergraduates, 21. 27% do not continue beyond their first year. **Housing:** College-sponsored housing includes dorms, smoke-free, alcohol-free, quiet study, upper class/graduate housing, freshman housing, wellness housing, and living learning communities. On-campus housing is guaranteed for all 4 years. 60% of students commute. All students may keep cars.

FACULTY/CLASSROOMS: 58% of faculty are male; 42% are female. All teach undergraduates and do research. No introductory courses are taught by graduate students. The average class size in an introductory lecture is 31 and in a laboratory is 21.

PROGRAMS OF STUDY: UW-Stout confers B.A., B.S., and B.F.A. degrees. Master's and doctoral degrees are also awarded. Bachelor's degrees are awarded in BUSINESS (business administration and management, hospitality management services, hotel/motel and restaurant management, information and communication technology, management science, marketing/retailing/merchandising, property management, retailing, supply chain management, and sustainable management), COMMUNICATIONS AND THE ARTS (apparel design, art, communications, fine arts, game design and development, graphic communications management, studio art, and telecommunications), COMPUTER AND PHYSICAL SCIENCE (applied mathematics, applied science, and science), EDUCATION (art education, career, technical education and training, early childhood education, golf enterprise management, home economics education, marketing and distribution education, science education, special education, technical education, technology and science education, and vocational education), ENGINEERING AND ENVIRONMENTAL DESIGN (computer engineering, construction technology, engineering technology, food services technology, graphic arts technology, graphic and printing production, industrial administration/management, industrial engineering technology, manufacturing engineering, packaging science, and plastics engineering), HEALTH PROFESSIONS (health and rehabilitation therapy), SOCIAL SCIENCE (applied social science, child care/child and family studies, cognitive science, dietetics, family/consumer studies, food production/management/services, human development, and psychology). General business administration, art, and hotel restaurant have the largest enrollments.

ACTIVITIES: 2% of men belong to 3 local and 2 national fraternities; 3% of women belong to 3 national sororities. There are 117 groups on campus, including art, band, cheerleading, choir, chorale, chorus, computers, dance, debate, drama, ethnic, film, forensics, honors, international, jazz band, LGBT, literary magazine, marching band, model UN, musical theater, newspaper, pep band, photography, political, professional, religious, social, social service, and student government. Popular campus events include Family Weekend, Cheese Week, and Biggest House Party. **Sports:** There are 6 intercollegiate sports for men and 8 for women, and 20 intramural sports for men and 19 for women. Facilities include baseball, soccer, and football fields, indoor and outdoor tracks, a field house with basketball, racquetball, and volleyball courts, a pool, weight and gymnastics rooms, and indoor and outdoor tennis courts. **Graduates:** From July 1, 2016 to June 30, 2017, 1697 bachelor's degrees were awarded. The most popular majors were business marketing (34%), education (9%), engineering, family and consumer sciences, and and visual and performing arts (8%). In an average class, 14% graduate in 4 years or less and 41% graduate in 5 years or less.

SERVICES: Counseling and information services are available, as is tutoring in most subjects. There is a reader service for the blind, and remedial math, reading, and writing. **Library/Resources:** The library contains 225,672 volumes, 1.2 million microform items, and 14,254 audio/video tapes/CDs/DVDs, and subscribes to 1,012 periodicals including electronic. Computerized library services include interlibrary loans, database searching, Internet access, and Wi-Fi capability. Special learning facilities include an art gallery and a TV station. **Physically Challenged Students:** All of the campus is accessible. Facilities include wheelchair ramps, elevators, special parking, specially equipped restrooms, special class scheduling, lowered drinking fountains, lowered telephones, and special housing. **Special:** UW-Stout offers business and industry internships, cooperative programs, work-study programs, and study abroad in London. Dual majors, credit by examination, credit for life, military, and work experience, nondegree study, and pass/fail options are also available. There is 1 national honor society, a freshman honors program, and 3 departmental honors programs. **Visiting:** There are regularly scheduled orientations for prospective students, including an interview with an admissions counselor and a campus tour. There are also campus preview days throughout the academic year. There are guides for informal visits, visitors may sit in on classes, and stay overnight. **Campus Safety and Security:** Measures include 24-hour foot and vehicle patrol. There are lighted pathways/sidewalks, and safety training sessions.

REQUIREMENTS: The SAT or ACT is required, with a minimum composite score of 1030 on the SAT I. Minimum test scores are waived if students rank in the upper 50% of their class. Applicants should graduate from an accredited secondary school. The GED is accepted if applicants are over 21, or if their graduating class has been out for at least 2 years. Secondary school preparation should include 4 academic credits in

English, 3 each in social studies, math, and science, and 4 in electives, 2 units recommended in foreign language. UW-Stout requires applicants to be in the upper 50% of their class. A GPA of 2.8 is required. AP and CLEP credits are accepted. Important factors in the admissions decision are leadership record, advanced placement or honors courses, parents or siblings attended your school, evidence of special talent, personality/intangible qualities, extracurricular activities record, recommendations by alumni, recommendations by school officials, and geographical diversity. Students must complete a minimum of 124 credits, including a general education component. Some degree programs have specific general education courses that must be taken in order to satisfy certification, accreditation, or prerequisite standards. Students must also fulfill an ethnic studies requirement. **Procedure:** Freshmen are admitted in the fall, spring, and summer. Entrance exams should be taken in June of the junior year. There is a rolling admissions plan. Application deadlines are open. The fall 2017 application fee was $44. Notification is sent on a rolling basis. Applications are accepted on-line. **Transfer Students:** 734 transfer students enrolled in 2016-2017. A minimum college GPA of 2.50 preferred (2.75 required for education majors). ACT/SAT 1 recommended for applied science, plastics engineering, computer engineering, applied mathematics and computer science, and manufacturing engineering applicants. A high school transcript and a statement of good standing from prior institutions are required. 32 of 124 credits required for the bachelor's degree must be completed at UW-Stout. **International Students:** There are 39 international students enrolled. They must take the TOEFL.

ADMISSIONS: 84% of the 2017-2018 applicants were accepted. The ACT scores were 9% between 12 and 17, 59% between 18 and 23, 29% between 24 and 29, and 3% above 30. 18% of the current freshmen were in the top fifth of their class; 50% were in the top two fifths. 10 freshmen graduated first in their class. **Admissions Contact:** Joel Helms, Associate Director of Admissions. Email: *admissions@uwstout.edu* Web: *www.uwstout.edu*

FINANCIAL AID: In 2017-2018, 83% of all full-time freshmen received some form of financial aid. The average freshman award was $30,410. Need-based scholarships or need-based grants averaged $5,829; need-based self-help aid (loans and jobs) averaged $5,010; other non-need-based awards and non-need-based scholarships averaged $4,475; and $2,219 from other forms of aid. The average financial indebtedness of the 2017 graduate was $25,746. UW-Stout is a member of CSS. The FAFSA code is 003915. The priority date for freshman financial aid applications for fall entry is March 15.

UNIVERSITY OF WISCONSIN-SUPERIOR A-1

www.uwsuper.edu

Superior, WI 54880	(715) 394-8230
Fax: (715) 394-8407	**Email:** admissions@uwsuper.edu
Full-time: 744 men, 1084 women	**Faculty:** 117; IIA, --$
Part-time: 162 men, 378 women	**Ph.D.s:** 50%
Graduate: 67 men, 155 women	**Student/Faculty:** 14 to 1
Year: semesters, summer session	**Tuition:** $8108 ($15,609)
Room & Board: $6730	**Freshman Class:** 1002 applied, 718 accepted, 345 enrolled
ACT: 21	**CEEB CODE:** 1920
Application Deadline: August 1	**COMPETITIVE**

University of Wisconsin-Superior, founded in 1893, offers undergraduate programs in the liberal arts and sciences, business, education, fine arts, applied arts, and social sciences. In addition to regional accreditation, UW-Superior has baccalaureate program accreditation with CSWE and NASM. The 230-acre campus is in an urban area in Superior, Wisconsin, at the western tip of Lake Superior. UWS is accessible by Interstate 35 in Minnesota and U.S. Highway 53 in Wisconsin. Including any residence halls, there are 17 buildings.

STUDENT LIFE: 57% of undergraduates are from out of state, mostly the Midwest. Students are from 35 states, 44 foreign countries, and Canada. 71% are White; 4% Hispanic; 3% two or more races; 2% African American; 17% Foreign; 1% Asian American; 1% American Indian/Alaska Native. **Female To Male Ratio:** 1.6:1. The average age of freshmen is 19; all undergraduates, 23. 33% do not continue beyond their first year; 40% remain to graduate. **Housing:** 820 students can be accommodated in college housing, which includes dorms. On-campus housing is guaranteed for the freshman year only. 72% of students commute. All students may keep cars.

FACULTY/CLASSROOMS: 46% of faculty are male; 54% are female. 95% teach undergraduates. No introductory courses are taught by graduate students. The average class size in an introductory lecture is 20.

PROGRAMS OF STUDY: UWS confers B.A., B.S., B.F.A., B.M., and B.M.E. degrees. Associate and master's degrees are also awarded. Bachelor's degrees are awarded in BIOLOGICAL SCIENCE (biology/biological science), BUSINESS (accounting, business administration and management, finance, international business management, sustainable management, and transportation management), COMMUNICATIONS AND THE ARTS (art history, art, communications, dramatic arts, English, fine arts, music, music performance, speech/debate/rhetoric, studio art, theatre arts, visual and performing arts, and writing), COMPUTER AND PHYSICAL SCIENCE (chemistry, computer science, and mathematics), EDUCATION (art education, elementary education, English education, health education, mathematics education, music education, physical education, science education, secondary education, social science education, and social studies secondary school education), ENGINEERING AND ENVIRONMENTAL DESIGN (computational sciences), HEALTH PROFESSIONS (art therapy, biology, community health work, exercise science, health, health and physical activity, and health promotion), SOCIAL SCIENCE (criminal justice, economics, history, interdisciplinary studies, international studies, law, political science/government, psychology, public administration, social studies, social work, and sociology). Business administration, elementary education, and communicating arts have the largest enrollments.

ACTIVITIES: There are no fraternities or sororities. There are 59 groups on campus, including art, band, cheerleading, choir, chorale, chorus, computers, dance, drama, ethnic, honors, international, jazz band, LGBT, newspaper, orchestra, pep band, photography, political, professional, radio and TV, religious, social, social service, student government, and symphony. Popular campus events include World Culture Night and Jacket Racket. **Sports:** There are 7 intercollegiate sports for men and 8 for women, and 19 intramural sports for men and 19 for women. Facilities include a gym, an ice arena, swimming pool, weight training room, dance studio, racquetball courts, an all-weather track, high ropes course, zip line, a climbing wall, and softball and baseball fields. **Graduates:** From July 1, 2016 to June 30, 2017, 469 bachelor's degrees were awarded. The most popular majors were interdisciplinary studies (13%), biological/life sciences (12%), and business/marketing (11%). In an average class, 1% graduate in 3 years or less, 24% graduate in 4 years or less, 37% graduate in 5 years or less, and 40% graduate in 6 years or less.

SERVICES: Counseling and information services are available, as is tutoring in every subject. There is remedial math and writing. **Library/Resources:** Computerized library services include interlibrary loans, database searching, Internet access, and Wi-Fi capability. Special learning facilities include an art gallery, radio station, TV station, an aquatic lab, and an observatory. **Physically Challenged Students:** 95% of the campus is accessible. Facilities include wheelchair ramps, elevators, special parking, specially equipped restrooms, special class scheduling, lowered drinking fountains, and lowered telephones. **Special:** UW/Superior offers work-study and co-op programs in business and internships in social work, business, mass communication, and criminal justice. There is a comprehensive program of student-designed majors, along with a cooperative program in marine studies with Texas A&M University, and 3-2 engineering and forestry programs with Michigan Technological University. Students may cross-register for 2 classes per semester at the University of Minnesota/Duluth or the College of St. Scholastica. An extended degree is offered. Credit for life experience and pass/fail options are available. There are 4 national honor societies and 4 departmental honors programs. **Visiting:** There are regularly scheduled orientations for prospective students, consisting of two days of social and educational programs. There are guides for informal visits, visitors may sit in on classes, and stay overnight. To schedule a visit, contact the Admissions Office. **Campus Safety and Security:** Measures include 24-hour foot and vehicle patrol, an emergency notification system, self-defense education, and security escort services. There are emergency telephones, lighted pathways/sidewalks, and controlled access to dorms/residences.

REQUIREMENTS: The ACT is required. Out-of-state residents may submit SAT scores instead. Applicants must graduate from an accredited secondary school or the equivalent. Applicant must rank in at least the upper 50% of their graduating class or achieve a minimum composite score of 21 on the ACT. AP and CLEP credits are accepted. To graduate, students must complete 120 credit hours, with a GPA of 2.0. A minimum of 54 hours must be credited toward completion of 1 comprehensive major, 2 majors, or 1 major and 1 minor. The required core curriculum includes 55 credits in Communications, English, Math, Phys Ed, World Culture, Contemporary Society, Aesthetic Experience, Natural Science, and Human Behavior. A comprehensive exam and a senior project are required. **Procedure:** Freshmen are admitted in the fall, spring, and summer. Entrance exams should be taken spring of junior year or early fall of senior year. There are deferred admissions and rolling admissions plans. Applications should be filed by August 1 for fall entry. The fall 2017 application fee was $44. Notification is sent on a rolling basis. Applications are accepted on-line. **Transfer Students:** 256 transfer students enrolled in 2016-2017. A college GPA of 2.0 is required. 30 of 120 credits required for the bachelor's degree must be completed at UWS. **International Students:** There are 189 international students enrolled. They must take the TOEFL with a minimum score of 500 on the paper-based TOEFL (PBT) or 61 on the Internet-based version (iBT), or take the MELAB, complete an on-campus ESL program (if necessary). The ACT or SAT are generally required for native English speaking international students.

ADMISSIONS: 72% of the 2017-2018 applicants were accepted. The ACT scores were 15% between 12 and 17, 64% between 18 and 23, 19% between 24 and 29, and 2% above 30. 19% of the current freshmen were in the top fifth of their class; 44% were in the top two fifths. 3 freshmen graduated first in their class. **Admissions Contact:** Robert Strand, Admissions Director. Email: *admissions@uwsuper.edu* Web: *www.uwsuper.edu*

FINANCIAL AID: In 2017-2018, 54% of all full-time freshmen received some form of financial aid. 33% of all full-time freshmen received need-based aid. The average freshman award was $10,621. Need-based scholarships or need-based grants averaged $5,225; and need-based self-help aid (loans and jobs) averaged $4,595. The average financial indebtedness of the 2017 graduate was $29,139. The FAFSA code is 003925. The priority date for freshman financial aid applications for fall entry is April 1.

UNIVERSITY OF WISCONSIN-WHITEWATER D-5

www.uww.edu

Whitewater, WI 53190	(262) 472-1440
Fax: (262) 472-1515	**Email:** uwwadmit@mail.uww.edu
Full-time: 4986 men, 4890 women	**Faculty:** 384; IIA, --$
Part-time: 368 men, 340 women	**Ph.D.s:** 73%
Graduate: 554 men, 655 women	**Student/Faculty:** 22 to 1
Year: semesters, summer session	**Tuition:** $7650 ($16,222)
Room & Board: $6326	**Freshman Class:** 7279 applied, 5048 accepted, 2178 enrolled
SAT: recommended **ACT:** 23	**CEEB CODE:** 1921
Application Deadline: May 1	**COMPETITIVE**

University of Wisconsin-Whitewater, founded in 1868, offers programs in teacher education, business, liberal arts, preprofessional studies, fine arts and music. There are 4 undergraduate schools and 1 graduate school. In addition to regional accreditation, UW-Whitewater has baccalaureate program accreditation with AACSB, ASLA, CSWE, NASAD, NASM, CAEP, and ACS. The 385-acre campus is in a small town 50 miles southwest of Milwaukee, 45 miles southeast of Madison, 100 miles northwest of Chicago, 50 miles north of Rockford, IL. Including any residence halls, there are 45 buildings.

STUDENT LIFE: 85% of undergraduates are from Wisconsin. Others are from 38 states, 42 foreign countries, and Canada. 70% are from public schools. 82% are White; 6% Hispanic; 5% two or more races; 4% African American; 1% Asian American; 1% Foreign. **Male To Female Ratio:** 1.0:1. The average age of freshmen is 19; all undergraduates, 22. 19% do not continue beyond their first year; 81% remain to graduate. **Housing:** 4300 students can be accommodated in college housing, which includes dorms and off-campus apartments. On-campus housing is available on a first-come and first-served basis. 8% of students commute. All students may keep cars.

FACULTY/CLASSROOMS: 57% of faculty are male; 43% are female. All teach undergraduates and 78% do research. No introductory courses are taught by graduate students. The average class size in a regular course is 26.

PROGRAMS OF STUDY: UW-Whitewater confers B.A., B.S., B.B.A., B.F.A., B.M., and B.S.Ed. degrees. Associate, master's, and doctoral degrees are also awarded. Bachelor's degrees are awarded in BIOLOGICAL SCIENCE (biology/biological science), BUSINESS (accounting, banking and finance, business administration and management, business economics, marketing/retailing/merchandising, office supervision and management, and personnel management), COMMUNICATIONS AND THE ARTS (art history and appreciation, communications, dramatic arts, English, French, German, journalism, music, public relations, Spanish, and speech/debate/rhetoric), COMPUTER AND PHYSICAL SCIENCE (chemistry, computer programming, mathematics, and physics), EDUCATION (art education, business education, early childhood education, elementary education, foreign languages education, middle school education, music education, physical education, science education, secondary education, social studies education, and special education), SOCIAL SCIENCE (economics, geography, history, international studies, political science/government, prelaw, psychology, public administration, safety and security technology, social work, sociology, and women's studies). Accounting, education, and marketing are the strongest academically. Business/accounting, education, and letters and sciences have the largest enrollments.

ACTIVITIES: There are 220 groups on campus, including art, band, cheerleading, chess, choir, chorus, communications, computers, dance, debate, drama, drill team, environmental, ethnic, film, forensics, honors, international, jazz band, LGBT, marching band, musical theater, newspaper, orchestra, pep band, photography, political, professional, radio and TV, religious, social, social service, student government, symphony, and yearbook. Popular campus events include Job Fair, Performing Arts Series, and Athletic Contests. **Sports:** There are 9 intercollegiate sports for men and 11 for women, and 12 intramural sports for men and 12 for women. Facilities include tennis courts, pools, playing fields, weight rooms, a stadium, and gym. **Graduates:** In an average class, 50% graduate in 6 years or less.

SERVICES: Counseling and information services are available, as is tutoring in most subjects. There is a reader service for the blind, and remedial math, reading, and writing. Study skills instruction is also available. **Library/Resources:** The library contains 356,000 volumes, 993,000 microform items, 7,300 audio/video tapes/CDs/DVDs, and subscribes to 5,000 periodicals including electronic. Computerized library services include interlibrary loans, database searching, Internet access, and Wi-Fi capability. Special learning facilities include an art gallery, radio station, TV station, an observatory and weather station. **Physically Challenged Students:** 85% of the campus is accessible. Facilities include wheelchair ramps, elevators, special parking, specially equipped restrooms, special class scheduling, lowered drinking fountains, lowered telephones, and special housing. **Special:** Internships, study abroad in 9 nations, accelerated degree programs in safety studies and speech communication, student-designed majors, and a general studies degree are available. Credit by examination, nondegree study, and pass/fail options are also offered. There are 12 national honor societies, a freshman honors program, and 7 departmental honors programs. **Visiting:** There are regularly scheduled orientations for prospective students. There are guides for informal visits and visitors may sit in on classes. To schedule a visit, contact James Lanouette at lanouetj@uww.edu. **Campus Safety and Security:** Measures include 24-hour foot and vehicle patrol, an emergency notification system, self-defense education, and security escort services. There are emergency telephones, lighted pathways/sidewalks, and controlled access to dorms/residences.

REQUIREMENTS: The SAT or ACT is recommended. Applicants should graduate from an accredited secondary school or with 17 academic units, including 4 in English and 3 each in social studies, math, and science. The GED may be accepted. Applicants should rank in the upper 40% of their graduating class or achieve a combined high school and ACT/SAT percentile rank of 100% or above. AP and CLEP credits are accepted. Important factors in the admissions decision are evidence of special talent, advanced placement or honors courses, and recommendations by school officials. Students must complete 50 credits of general studies, a writing competency requirement, and 3 credits in minority issues. A GPA of 2.0 and 120 hours are required to graduate. **Procedure:** Freshmen are admitted to all sessions. There is a rolling admissions plan. Applications should be filed by May 1 for fall entry. The fall 2017 application fee was $50. Notification is sent on a rolling basis. Applications are accepted on-line. **Transfer Students:** 811 transfer students enrolled in 2016-2017. Applicants should have a minimum college GPA of 2.0. 30 of 120 credits required for the bachelor's degree must be completed at UW-Whitewater. **International Students:** There are 164 international students enrolled. They must take the TOEFL.

ADMISSIONS: 69% of the 2017-2018 applicants were accepted. **Admissions Contact:** Dr. Jeremy Reed, Director of Admissions. Email: *uwwadmit@mail.uww.edu* Web: *www.uww.edu*

FINANCIAL AID: In 2017-2018, 73% of all full-time freshmen received some form of financial aid. 45% of all full-time freshmen received need-based aid. The average freshman award was $6,000. UW-Whitewater is a member of CSS. The FAFSA code is 003926. Check with the school for current application deadlines.

VITERBO UNIVERSITY — B-4

www.viterbo.edu

La Crosse, WI 54601	**(608) 796-3010** **(800) 848-3726**
Fax: (608) 796-3020	**Email: admission@viterbo.edu**
Full-time: 437 men, 1132 women	**Faculty:** 107; IIA, --$
Part-time: 125 men, 411 women	**Ph.D.s:** 60%
Graduate: 211 men, 514 women	**Student/Faculty:** 12 to 1
Year: semesters, summer session	**Tuition:** $26,150
Room & Board: $8510	**Freshman Class:** 1655 applied, 1145 accepted, 304 enrolled
ACT: 23	**CEEB CODE:** 1878
Application Deadline: August 15	**COMPETITIVE**

Viterbo University, a Catholic, Franciscan ecumenical university, prepares students for leadership and service by providing a student-centered, values-based, learning-focused liberal arts education rooted in the values of human dignity and respect for the world. The figures given in the above capsule and in this profile are approximate. There are 5 undergraduate schools and 5 graduate schools. In addition to regional accreditation, Viterbo University has baccalaureate program accreditation with CSWE, NASM, CAEP, NLN, ACS, CADE, CCNE, and IACBE. The 72-acre campus is in a suburban area 150 miles from Minneapolis-St. Paul, 105 miles from Madison, and 230 miles from Chicago. Including any residence halls, there are 18 buildings.

STUDENT LIFE: 76% of undergraduates are from Wisconsin. Others are from 34 states, and 11 foreign countries. 93% are from public schools. 92% are White; 2% African American; 2% Asian American; 2% Hispanic; 1% American Indian/Alaska Native; 1% Foreign; 1% race unknown. 43% are Catholic; 34% Protestant; 14% Unidentified religions. **Female To Male Ratio:** 2.7:1. The average age of freshmen is 18; all undergraduates, 25. 26% do not continue beyond their first year; 52% remain to graduate. **Housing:** 686 students can be accommodated in college housing, which includes dorms and on-campus apartments. In addition, there are special-interest houses, on-campus houses, and special-interest floors. On-campus housing is guaranteed for the freshman year only, and is available on a first-come, first-served basis. 10% of students commute. Upperclassmen may keep cars. Alcohol is not permitted.

FACULTY/CLASSROOMS: 48% of faculty are male; 63% are female. 90% teach undergraduates, 53% do research, and 53% do both. No introductory courses are taught by graduate students. The average class size in an introductory lecture is 17; in a laboratory is 16; and in a regular course is 15.

PROGRAMS OF STUDY: VU confers B.A., B.S., B.Art.Ed., B.B.A., B.F.A., B.I.L., B.L.S., B.M., B.S.T., B.S.VC., B.S.Community-Medical Dietetics, B.S.Ed., and B.S.N. degrees. Associate and master's degrees are also awarded. Bachelor's degrees are awarded in AGRICULTURE (environmental studies), BIOLOGICAL SCIENCE (biochemistry and biology/biological science), BUSINESS (accounting, management information systems, management science, marketing/retailing/merchandising, organizational leadership and management, sports management, and sustainable management), COMMUNICATIONS AND THE ARTS (art, arts administration/management, communications, dramatic arts, English, graphic design, music performance, Spanish, studio art, and theatre studies), COMPUTER AND PHYSICAL SCIENCE (chemistry, digital arts/technology, mathematics, and natural sciences), EDUCATION (art education, business education, elementary education, English education, mathematics education, music education, science education, social studies education, and technology and science education), HEALTH PROFESSIONS (health care administration and nursing), SOCIAL SCIENCE (addiction studies, biopsychology, criminal justice, dietetics, history, liberal arts/general studies, philosophy, psychology, religious education, religious studies, social studies, social work, and sociology). Life sciences, nutrition/dietetics, and natural sciences are the strongest academically. Health professions, business, and education have the largest enrollments.

ACTIVITIES: There are no fraternities or sororities. There are 32 groups on campus, including art, choir, chorale, chorus, dance, drama, drill team, environmental, ethnic, honors, international, LGBT, literary magazine, musical theater, newspaper, opera, pep band, political, professional, religious, social, social service, and student government. Popular campus events include Orientation Weekend, Welcome Back Bash, Viterbo Days (Family Day), St. Francis Day Celebration, and Courtyard Carni. **Sports:** There are 7 intercollegiate sports for men and 8 for women, and 14 intramural sports for men and 14 for women. Facilities include a student activity center with weight training and fitness rooms and courts for basketball, volleyball, basketball and racquetball. The outdoor athletic complex has facilities for soccer, baseball, and softball, located 2 1/2 miles from campus. **Graduates:** From July 1, 2016 to June 30, 2017, 453 bachelor's degrees were awarded. The most popular majors were health (44%), letters and science (26%), and business (15%). In an average class, 33% graduate in 4 years or less and 52% graduate in 6 years or less. Of the 2016 graduating class, 7% were enrolled in graduate school within 6 months of graduation, and 97% were employed.

SERVICES: Counseling and information services are available, as is tutoring in every subject. There is a reader service for the blind, and remedial math, reading, and writing. **Library/Resources:** The library contains 92,300 volumes, 307 microform items, 5,110 audio/video tapes/CDs/DVDs, and subscribes to 229 periodicals, including electronic. Computerized library services include interlibrary loans, database searching, Internet access, and Wi-Fi capability. Special learning facilities include an art gallery, and a music resource center. **Physically Challenged Students:** 90% of the campus is accessible. Facilities include wheelchair ramps, elevators, special parking, specially equipped restrooms, special class scheduling, lowered drinking fountains, and lowered telephones. **Special:** Students may cross-register at the University of Wisconsin/LaCrosse, enroll for independent study, or earn a dual degree. Co-op programs, study abroad in 7 countries, double majors, student-designed majors, accelerated degree programs, work-study, internships in many areas, credit by exam, and credit/no credit options are available. There are 2 national honor societies, Phi Beta Kappa, and a freshman honors program. **Visiting:** There are regularly scheduled orientations for prospective students, including a meeting with an admissions staff member, a tour of the campus, and optional meetings with a financial aid officer and faculty members. There are guides for informal visits and visitors may sit in on classes. To schedule a visit, contact the Admission Office. **Campus Safety and Security:** Measures include emergency notification system, self-defense education, and security escort services. There are shuttle buses, emergency telephones, lighted pathways/sidewalks, controlled access to dorms/residences, an emergency evacuation plan, 24 hours a day, 7 days a week, phone access to security personnel, security patrol from 5 p.m. to 7 a.m., ID check-in in dorms after 10 p.m., and card access to all campus buildings after regular hours, and 6 emergency blue lights.

REQUIREMENTS: The ACT is required. Graduation from an accredited secondary school is required; the GED is accepted. Secondary preparation should include 16 credits, with 3 or 4 in English and 2 each in math, natural science, and social science or history. Fine arts students may be required to audition or submit a portfolio. Nursing, dietetics, and premedical students must have high school chemistry. A GPA of 2.0 is required. AP and CLEP credits are accepted. Students must complete a minimum of 128 semester hours of credit. A minimum of 43 of these must be upper division level. All students must complete the General Education requirements (45 credit hours from various disciplines) and competencies, as well as all of the specified requirements for their major. Also, students must complete a service component designed by their major program. All students must have a GPA of at least 2.0; and must take as a minimum the last 30 consecutive semester hours at Viterbo University or complete 45 of the last 60 semester hours from VU. Students seeking a B.S. must complete 7 credits of natural science and/or math in addition to the 4 credits of natural science in the General Education requirements. Students seeking a B.A. must complete the equivalent of 14 semester hours of the same modern foreign language. **Procedure:** Freshmen are admitted to all sessions. Entrance exams should be taken at orientation, prior to registration. There is a rolling admissions plan. Applications should be filed by August 15 for fall entry. The fall 2017 application fee was $25. Notification is sent on a rolling basis. Applications are accepted on-line. **Transfer Students:** 274 transfer students enrolled in 2016-2017. Transfer students must have a cumulative GPA of at least 2.0, are free to return to their previous school, and are considered to be in good academic standing both at their previous school and at VU. They must submit an application, the official transcripts of coursework in high school, official transcripts from all post-secondary institutions, and ACT/SAT results, if already taken. 30 of 128 credits required for the bachelor's degree must be completed at Viterbo. **International Students:** There are 24 international students enrolled. They must take the TOEFL with a minimum score of 525 on the paper-based TOEFL (PBT) or 93 on the Internet-based version (iBT).

ADMISSIONS: 69% of the 2017-2018 applicants were accepted. The ACT scores were 24% below 12, 34% between 12 and 17, 29% between 18 and 23, 8% between 24 and 29, and 5% above 30. 37% of the current freshmen were in the top fifth of their class; 72% were in the top two fifths. 6 freshmen graduated first in their class. **Admissions Contact:** Eric Schmidt, Director of Admission. Email: *admission@viterbo.edu* Web: *www.viterbo.edu*

FINANCIAL AID: In 2017-2018, 98% of all full-time freshmen received some form of financial aid. 100% of undergraduate students work part-time. The college's own financial statement is required. The FAFSA code is 003911. The priority date for freshman financial aid applications for fall entry is March 15.

WISCONSIN LUTHERAN COLLEGE E-4

www.wlc.edu

Milwaukee, WI 53226	(414) 443-8811
	Email: admissions@wlc.edu
Full-time: 300 men, 400 women	Faculty: 47
Part-time: 20 men, 20 women	Ph.D.s: 65%
Graduate: n/av	Student/Faculty: 14 to 1
Year: semesters, summer session	Tuition: $27,040
Room & Board: $9250	Freshman Class: n/av
ACT: required	CEEB CODE: 1513
Application Deadline: n/av	COMPETITIVE

Wisconsin Lutheran College is an independent, residential, Christian college, that serves traditional undergraduate, adult, and graduate students through its on-campus, on-location, and online programs. WLC prepares students for lives of Christian leadership, and is recognized for its academic excellence and superior student experience. Caring, Christian faculty work directly with students, who benefit from numerous research, service, and co-curricular opportunities designed to enhance academic and spiritual growth. There are 2 undergraduate schools and 1 graduate school. In addition to regional accreditation, WLC has baccalaureate program accreditation with CCNE. The 21-acre campus is in a suburban area on the western edge of Milwaukee. Including any residence halls, there are 11 buildings.

STUDENT LIFE: 80% of undergraduates are from Wisconsin. Others are from 27 states, and 6 foreign countries. 41% are from public schools. 95% are White; 2% African American; 2% Foreign; 1% Asian American; 1% Hispanic. 88% are Protestant. **Female To Male Ratio:** 1.3:1. The average age of freshmen is 18; all undergraduates, 20. 20% do not continue beyond their first year; 74% remain to graduate. **Housing:** 600 students can be accommodated in college housing, which includes dorms and on-campus apartments. On-campus housing is guaranteed for all 4 years. 68% of students live on campus. Alcohol is not permitted. All students may keep cars.

FACULTY/CLASSROOMS: 70% of faculty are male; 30% are female. All teach undergraduates and do research. No introductory courses are taught by graduate students. The average class size in an introductory lecture is 20; in a laboratory is 10; and in a regular course is 16.

PROGRAMS OF STUDY: WLC confers B.A., B.S. and B.S.N. degrees. Master's degrees are also awarded. Bachelor's degrees are awarded in AGRICULTURE (environmental studies), BIOLOGICAL SCIENCE (biochemistry, biology/biological science, and marine biology), BUSINESS (accounting and business administration and management), COMMUNICATIONS AND THE ARTS (art, communications, English, German, media arts, music, Spanish, television & digital media production, and theatre arts), COMPUTER AND PHYSICAL SCIENCE (chemistry, computer science, mathematics, and physics), EDUCATION (elementary education and secondary education), ENGINEERING AND ENVIRONMENTAL DESIGN (environmental science), HEALTH PROFESSIONS (exercise science and nursing), SOCIAL SCIENCE (Chinese Studies, history, human services, interdisciplinary studies, philosophy, psychology, social science, and theological studies). Nursing, education, and biology are the strongest academically.

ACTIVITIES: There are no fraternities or sororities. There are 31 groups on campus, including art, band, cheerleading, choir, communications, dance, drama, honors, international, jazz band, musical theater, newspaper, political, professional, religious, social, social service, and student government. Popular campus events include Musical and Theater Events, and Winterfest. **Sports:** There are 9 intercollegiate sports for men and 9 for women. Facilities include an outdoor athletics complex with football stadium, track, soccer fields, baseball and softball fields, and training facilities, basketball courts, a gym, weight room, fitness center, dance/aerobics room, training and therapy rooms, and a walking/running track. **Graduates:** From July 1, 2016 to June 30, 2017, 121 bachelor's degrees were awarded. The most popular majors were communication (17%), psychology (11%), and biology (11%). In an average class, 47% graduate in 4 years or less, 62% graduate in 5 years or less, and 74% graduate in 6 years or less.

SERVICES: Counseling and information services are available, as is tutoring in most subjects. **Library/Resources:** The library contains 81,660 volumes and 4,673 audio/video tapes/CDs/DVDs. Computerized library services include interlibrary loans, database searching, Internet access, and Wi-Fi capability. Special learning facilities include an art gallery. **Physically Challenged Students:** 90% of the campus is accessible. Facilities include wheelchair ramps, elevators, special parking, specially equipped restrooms, and lowered drinking fountains. **Special:** There is a freshman honors program. **Visiting:** There are regularly scheduled orientations for prospective students, including a tour of the campus, a meal, meetings with admissions, financial aid, cocurriculars, and faculty in academic areas of interest. There are guides for informal visits, visitors may sit in on classes, and stay overnight. To schedule a visit, contact the Admissions Office. **Campus Safety and Security:** Measures include 24-hour foot and vehicle patrol, emergency notification system, and security escort services. There are lighted pathways/sidewalks and controlled access to dorms/residences.

REQUIREMENTS: The ACT is required. A GPA of 2.7 is required. AP and CLEP credits are accepted. **Procedure:** Freshmen are admitted in the fall and spring. Entrance exams should be taken in the spring of the junior year. There is a rolling admissions plan. Applications should be filed by January 15 for spring entry. The fall 2017 application fee was $20. Notification is sent on a rolling basis. Applications are accepted on-line. **Transfer Students:** 30 of 128 credits required for the bachelor's degree must be completed at Wisconsin Lutheran. **International Students:** There are 10 international students enrolled. They must take the TOEFL, and either the SAT and ACT, scoring 970.

Admissions Contact: Lucas Faust, Executive Director of Admissions. Email: *admissions@wlc.edu* Web: *www.wlc.edu*

FINANCIAL AID: In 2017-2018, 100% of all full-time freshmen received some form of financial aid. The average freshman award was $14,526. The average financial indebtedness of the 2017 graduate was $13,707. The college's own financial statement is required. The FAFSA code is 014658. The priority date for freshman financial aid applications for fall entry is March 1.

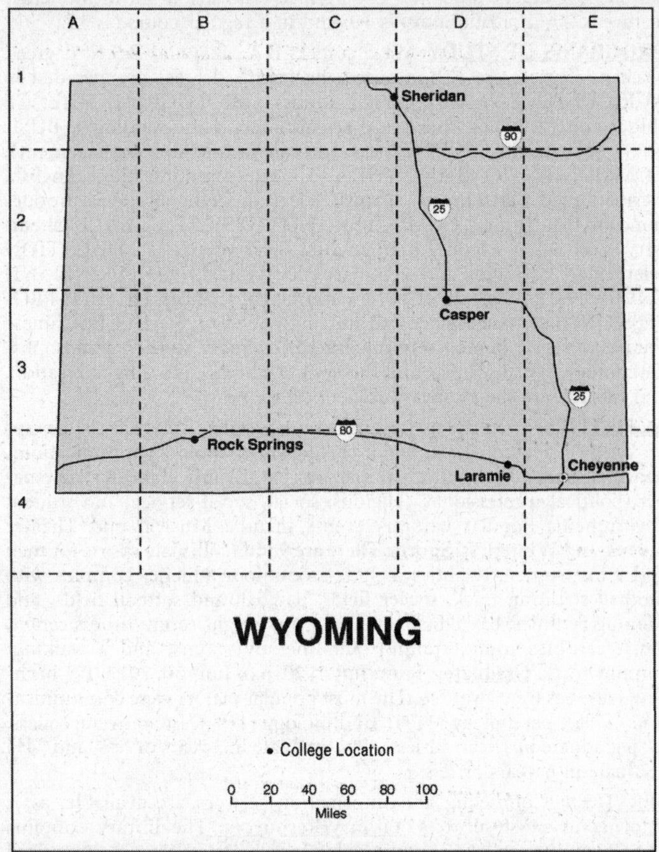

UNIVERSITY OF WYOMING D-4

www.uwyo.edu

Laramie, WY 82071 **(307) 766-5160**
(800) 342-5996

Fax: (307) 766-4042 **Email: admissions@uwyo.edu**

Full-time: 4127 men, 3975 women
Part-time: 698 men, 988 women
Graduate: 1224 men, 1354 women
Year: semesters, summer session
Room & Board: $10,320

SAT CR/M: 535/553 **ACT:** 24
Application Deadline: August 10

Faculty: 701; I, -$
Ph.D.s: 76%
Student/Faculty: 14 to 1
Tuition: $5217 ($16,827)
Freshman Class: 4883 applied, 4643 accepted, 1551 enrolled
CEEB CODE: 4855
COMPETITIVE

University of Wyoming, founded in 1886, is a public institution offering programs in agriculture and natural resources, arts and sciences, business, education, engineering and applied science, health sciences, and law. There are 9 undergraduate schools and 8 graduate schools. In addition to regional accreditation, UW has baccalaureate program accreditation with AACSB, ABET, ACPE, ADA, CSAB, CSWE, NASM, ABA, ACS, APA, PTSB, CACREP, CCNE, ACEND, CAA of ASHA, ACGME, AOBFP, AAVLD, Society for Range Management, and AAAHC. The 835-acre campus is in a small town 128 miles north of Denver and 50 miles west of Cheyenne. Including any residence halls, there are 189 buildings.

STUDENT LIFE: 62% of undergraduates are from Wyoming. Others are from 51 states, 68 foreign countries, and Canada. 73% are White; 9% race unknown; 7% Hispanic; 4% Foreign; 3% two or more races; 1% African American; 1% Asian American; 1% American Indian/Alaska Native. **Female To Male Ratio:** 1.0:1. The average age of freshmen is 18; all undergraduates, 23. 24% do not continue beyond their first year; 55% remain to graduate. **Housing:** 2789 students can be accommodated in college housing, which includes married student dorms, on-campus apartments, and off-campus apartments. In addition, there are honors houses, special-interest houses, fraternity houses, sorority houses, academic, upperclassmen, quiet-living, substance-free and freshman interest-group floors, 21 and over, and ROTC housing. On-campus housing is guaranteed for all 4 years. 77% of students commute. All students may keep cars.

FACULTY/CLASSROOMS: 60% of faculty are male; 40% are female. 97% teach undergraduates. Graduate students teach 16% of introductory courses. The average class size in a regular course is 39.

PROGRAMS OF STUDY: UW confers B.A., B.S., B.A.S., B.F.A., B.M., B.S.A.R., B.S.C.E., B.S.Ch., B.S.C.P., B.S.C.S., B.S.D.H., B.S.E.E., B.S.E.S.E., B.S.F.C., B.S.M.E., B.S.N., B.S.P.E., and B.S.W. degrees. Master's and doctoral degrees are also awarded. Bachelor's degrees are awarded in AGRICULTURE (agricultural business management, agricultural communications, animal science, environmental studies, fish and game management, and range/farm management), BIOLOGICAL SCIENCE (botany, ecology, microbiology, molecular biology, physiology, wildlife biology, and zoology), BUSINESS (accounting, business administration and management, business economics, finance, management science, marketing, and organizational leadership and management), COMMUNICATIONS AND THE ARTS (art, communications, dance, English, French, German, journalism, music, music performance, Russian, Spanish, and theatre acting), COMPUTER AND PHYSICAL SCIENCE (astronomy and physics, chemistry, computer science, earth science, environmental geology, geology, mathematics, physics, and statistics), EDUCATION (agricultural education, elementary education, music education, physical education, secondary education, special education, technical education, and trade and industrial education), ENGINEERING AND ENVIRONMENTAL DESIGN (architectural engineering, chemical engineering, civil engineering, computer engineering, electrical/electronics engineering, energy management technology, energy systems technology, mechanical engineering, and petroleum/natural gas engineering), HEALTH PROFESSIONS (biology, dental hygiene, kinesiology, medical laboratory technology, nursing, and speech pathology/audiology), SOCIAL SCIENCE (American Indian studies, American studies, anthropology, criminal justice, economics, family/consumer studies, geography, history, humanities, interdisciplinary studies, international studies, philosophy, political science/government, psychology, religious studies, social science, social work, sociology, and women & gender studies). Psychology, mechanical engineering, and nursing have the largest enrollments.

ACTIVITIES: 6% of men belong to 8 national fraternities; 6% of women belong to 5 national sororities. There are 152 groups on campus, including art, band, cheerleading, choir, chorale, chorus, communications, computers, dance, debate, drama, drill team, environmental, ethnic, film, forensics, honors, international, jazz band, LGBT, literary magazine, marching band, musical theater, newspaper, opera, orchestra, pep band, photography, political, professional, radio and TV, religious, social, social service, student government, and symphony. Popular campus events include President's Welcome, Family Weekend, and Homecoming. **Sports:** There are 8 intercollegiate sports for men and 9 for women, and 30 intramural sports for men and 30 for women. Facilities include a stadium, basketball arena, volleyball, badminton, racquetball courts, running track, swimming pools, weight rooms, indoor tennis complex, baseball, soccer and track stadiums, football training center, golf course, sports complex, climbing wall, and fitness rooms. **Graduates:** From July 1, 2016 to June 30, 2017, 2022 bachelor's degrees were awarded. The most popular majors were nursing (10%), elementary education (6%), and psychology (5%). In an average class, 26% graduate in 4 years or less, 49% graduate in 5 years or less, and 55% graduate in 6 years or less.

SERVICES: Counseling and information services are available, as is tutoring in most subjects. There is a reader service for the blind. Note-taking services, tape recorders, and interpreters for the hearing impaired. **Library/Resources:** The library contains 1.7 million volumes, 2.9 million microform items, and 22,535 audio/video tapes/CDs/DVDs, and subscribes to 163,861 periodicals including electronic. Computerized library services include interlibrary loans, database searching, Internet access, and Wi-Fi capability. Special learning facilities include an art gallery, natural history museum, planetarium, radio station, TV station, the American Heritage Center, specialized science and agriculture labs, Williams Botany Conservatory, Wyoming Infrared Observatory, Geology-Brinkerhoff Geology library, law library, library annex, a research library, and the Rocky Mountain Herbarium. **Physically Challenged Students:** 95% of the campus is accessible. Facilities include wheelchair ramps, elevators, special parking, specially equipped restrooms, special class scheduling, lowered drinking fountains, lowered telephones, and special housing. **Special:** UW offers internships, study abroad in many countries, national student exchange, Washington and U.N. semesters, work-study programs, dual and interdisciplinary majors, pass/fail options, credit by exam, accelerated degree programs, and credit for life, military, and work experience. There are 60 national honor societies, Phi Beta Kappa, a freshman honors program, and 27 departmental honors programs. **Visiting:** There are regularly scheduled orientations for prospective students, including campus tours and meetings with academic advisers. There are guides for informal visits. To schedule a visit, contact the Student Admissions Center at (307) 766-4075. **Campus Safety and Security:** Measures include 24-hour foot and vehicle patrol, emergency notification system, self-defense education, and security escort services. There are shuttle buses, emergency telephones, lighted pathways/sidewalks, and controlled access to dorms/residences.

REQUIREMENTS: The SAT or ACT is required for students under 21; the ACT is preferred. Applicants must be graduates of an accredited secondary school or hold a GED certificate. Secondary preparation should include at least 19 academic credits consisting of 4 years each of English, math, and science, 3 years of social science, 2 years of foreign language, and 2 years of any electives chosen from: fine and performing arts, social and behavioral studies, humanities, additional foreign language, or career-technical courses. A visit is suggested. A GPA of 3.0 is required. AP and CLEP credits are accepted. To graduate, students must complete 120 to 142 credit hours, depending on the major, with a minimum GPA of 2.0. The core curriculum includes required general education courses in the University Studies Program. Students must complete a minimum of 48 upper division or graduate-level semester credit hours, 30 of which must be earned from the University of Wyoming. **Procedure:** Freshmen are admitted fall, spring, and summer. Entrance exams should be taken in spring of the junior year or fall of the senior year. There are deferred admissions and rolling admissions plans. Applications should be filed by August 10 for fall entry; December 10 for spring entry. The fall 2017 application fee was $40. Applications are accepted on-line. **Transfer Students:** 967 transfer students enrolled in 2016-2017. Applicants with 30 or more transferable college-level credits must have a minimum GPA of 2.0. All applicants with fewer credits must apply as a new freshman. Those students under age 21 must also present SAT or ACT scores. 30 of 120 credits required for the bachelor's degree must be completed at UW. **International Students:** There are 366 international students enrolled. They must take the TOEFL with a minimum score of 525 on the paper-based TOEFL (PBT) or 71 on the Internet-based version (iBT). Students must take the Comprehensive English Language Test. They must also take the SAT or ACT scoring 21 or 980 math/critical reasoning combined.

ADMISSIONS: 95% of the 2017-2018 applicants were accepted. The SAT scores for the 2017-2018 freshman class were: Critical Reading-- 34% below 500, 41% between 500 and 599, 22% between 600 and 699, and 3% between 700 and 800. Math-- 27% below 500, 37% between 500 and 599, 31% between 600 and 699, and 5% between 700 and 800. The ACT scores were 4% between 12 and 17, 37% between 18 and 23, 47% between 24 and 29, and 11% above 30. 43% of the current freshmen were in the top fifth of their class; 72% were in the top two fifths. 65 freshmen graduated first in their class. **Admissions Contact:** Shelley Dodd, Director of Admissions. Email: *admissions@uwyo.edu* Web: *www.uwyo.edu*

FINANCIAL AID: In 2017-2018, 50% of all full-time freshmen received some form of financial aid. 30% of all full-time freshmen received need-based aid. The average freshman award was $10,788. Need-based scholarships or need-based grants averaged $5,261; need-based self-help aid (loans and jobs) averaged $3,508; non-need-based athletic scholarships averaged $2,267; and other non-need-based awards and non-need-based scholarships averaged $4,316. 28% of undergraduate students work part-time. The average financial indebtedness of the 2017 graduate was $25,378. The FAFSA code is 003932. The priority date for freshman financial aid applications for fall entry is March 1.

ARIZONA

ARIZONA CHRISTIAN UNIVERSITY C-4

Phoenix, AZ 85032 (602) 489-5300 (602) 404-2159

Full-time: 500 men, 237 women
Part-time: n/av
Graduate: n/av
Application Deadline: February 1
SAT or ACT: required
Faculty: 55
Tuition: $23,972
Room & Board: $9,308

Arizona Christian University, founded in 1960, is nondenominational. Its mission is transforming culture with the truth of Christ. The figures in the above capsule and in this profile are approximate. In addition to regional accreditation, the college is accredited by AABC and NCA. Arizona Christian University awards the B.A. and B.S. in elementary education, biblical studies, Christian ministries, secondary education, business administration, behavioral health, family studies and music education. The school also awards associate and bachelor's degrees. Web:*www.arizonachristian.edu*

ARKANSAS

CENTRAL BAPTIST COLLEGE C-3

Conway, AR 72034 (501) 329-6872 (501) 329-2941

Full-time: 347 men, 282 women
Part-time: 129 men, 134 women
Graduate: n/av
Application Deadline: August 15
SAT or ACT: required
Faculty: 75
Tuition: $13,500
Room & Board: $7500

Central Baptist College, founded in 1952, is affiliated with the Baptist Missionary Association of Arkansas. Its mission is to transform lives through education that integrates Christian faith and academic excellence in a Christ-centered environment. In addition to regional accreditation, the college is accredited by NCA. Central Baptist College awards the A.A., B.A., B.S., B.B.A., and B.S.E. in accounting, Bible, biology, business administration, church music, education (elementary education, health and physical education, middle level education, secondary level - English/language arts, secondary level - life sciences, secondary level - social sciences), English, general studies, health science, history, human resources, international business, journalism, kinesiology - exercise science, kinesiology - sports management, leadership, leadership and ministry, management, management information systems, marketing, missions, molecular bioscience, multimedia communication, music, organizational management, psychology, psychology & counseling, psychology & social services, worship arts. The school also awards associate and bachelor's degrees. Web:*www.cbc.edu*

CALIFORNIA

WILLIAM JESSUP UNIVERSITY B-3

Rocklin, CA 95678 (916) 577-2278 (916) 577-2220

Full-time: 260 men, 399 women
Part-time: 7 men, 6 women
Graduate: n/av
Application Deadline: June 1
ACT: required
Faculty: 74
Tuition: $29,950
Room & Board: $10,950

William Jessup University, founded in 1939, is affiliated with nondenominational. Its mission is to prepare Christians for leadership and service in church and society through Christian higher education, spiritual formation, and directed experiences. In addition to regional accreditation, the college is accredited by AABC. William Jessup University awards the B.A. and B.S. in Bible and theology, pastoral ministry, youth ministry, Christian education, Intercultural studies, counseling, music and worship, business management, liberal arts education and Christian leadership. The figures in the above capsule are approximate. The school also awards associate and bachelor's degrees. Web:*www.jessup.edu*

CONNECTICUT

HOLY APOSTLES COLLEGE & SEMINARY C-2

Cromwell, CT 06416 (860) 632-3033 (860) 632-3075

Full-time: 25 men, 7 women
Part-time: 7 men, 17 women
Graduate: 178 men, 82 women
Application Deadline: August 1
SAT: required
Faculty: 25
Tuition: $15,345
Room & Board: $12,200

Holy Apostles College & Seminary, founded in 1956, is affiliated with the Roman Catholic Church. Its mission is to cultivate lay, consecrated, and ordained Catholic leaders for the purpose of evangelization and to maintain excellence in teaching/learning, research/discovery, and service/engagement through the liberal arts, philosophy and theology. The figures in the above capsule are approximate. In addition to regional accreditation, the college is accredited by NEASC. Holy Apostles College & Seminary awards the B.A. in English in the humanities, history in the social sciences, philosophy and theology. The school also awards associate, bachelor's, and master's degrees. Web:*www.holyapostles.edu*

FLORIDA

JOHNSON UNIVERSITY FLORIDA D-3

Kissimmee, FL 34744 (407) 569-1172 (407) 847-3925

Full-time: 88 men, 92 women
Part-time: 3 men, 2 women
Graduate: n/av
Application Deadline: June 1
SAT or ACT: required
Faculty: 35
Tuition: $14,920
Room & Board: $3350

Johnson University Florida, founded in 1976, is affiliated with the Christian Churches/Churches of Christ/Independent. Its mission is to conduct a course of study educating men and women for Christian service, to provide a program of instruction on the college level, to grant appropriate degrees, and to serve as a resource to churches, especially in Florida. The figures in the above capsule are approximate. In addition to regional accreditation, the college is accredited by AABC and SACS. Johnson University Florida awards the B.A., B.S., and B.Th. in Bible, Christian education ministries, and Christian ministries. The school also awards associate and bachelor's degrees. Web:*www.johnsonu.edu/florida*

ST. JOHN VIANNEY COLLEGE SEMINARY E-5

Miami, FL 33165 (305) 223-4561 (305) 223-0650

Full-time: 74 men
Part-time: 1 men, 1 women
Graduate: n/av
Application Deadline: open
Faculty: 23
Tuition: $21,000
Room & Board: $11,000

St. John Vianney College Seminary, founded in 1959, is affiliated with the Roman Catholic Church. Its mission is to provide an undergraduate education for students whose stated objective is to serve the Catholic Church in the priesthood, and to provide spiritual and intellectual formation within an Anglo-Hispanic bilingual, bicultural setting. In addition to regional accreditation, the college is accredited by SACS. St. John Vianney College Seminary awards the B.A. and B.Phil. in philosophy. The figures in the above capsule are approximate. The school also awards bachelor's degrees. Web: *www.sjvcs.edu*

THE BAPTIST COLLEGE OF FLORIDA — B-1

Graceville, FL 32440 — (800) 328-2660, (850) 263-9026

Full-time: 237 men, 177 women — **Faculty:** 57
Part-time: 103 men, 29 women — **Tuition:** $11,880
Graduate: n/av — **Room & Board:** $4888
Application Deadline: August 1

The Baptist College of Florida, founded in 1943, is affiliated with the Florida Baptist Convention. Its mission is to promote, provide for, operate, and control a program of education and training for ministers and other religious workers. The figures in the above capsule are approximate. In addition to regional accreditation, the college is accredited by SACS. The Baptist College of Florida awards the B.A. in biblical studies, Christian counseling, Christian education, Christian studies, elementary education, English, English secondary education, history and social studies, history and social studies secondary education, leadership, ministry, missions, and music ministry. The school also awards associate and bachelor's degrees. Web: *www.baptistcollege.edu*

GEORGIA

POINT UNIVERSITY — B-2

West Point, GA 31833 — (706) 385-1000, (706) 645-9473

Full-time: 534 men, 639 women — **Faculty:** 120
Part-time: 142 men, 207 women — **Tuition:** $18,818 (30,392)
Graduate: n/av — **Room & Board:** $10,060
Application Deadline: August 1

Point University, founded in 1937, is affiliated with the Christian Churches and Churches of Christ. Its mission is to educate students for Christ-centered service and leadership throughout the world. The figures in the above capsule are approximate. In addition to regional accreditation, the college is accredited by SACSCOC. Point University awards the B.A., B.S., and B.B.A. in accounting, biblical studies, biblical studies and preaching ministry (dual major), biology, business administration, child and youth development, Christian ministry, counseling and human services, criminal justice, early childhood education, English, English and biblical studies (dual major), exercise science, history, human relations, humanities, humanities and biblical studies (dual major), management, marketing, middle grades education, music, organizational leadership, psychology, and sociology, with specialization in social work. The school also awards associate and bachelor's degrees. Web: *www.point.edu*

ILLINOIS

LINCOLN CHRISTIAN UNIVERSITY — D3

Lincoln, IL 62656-2111 — (217) 732-3168, (217) 732-4199

Full-time: 273 men, 265 women — **Faculty:** 99
Part-time: 52 men, 53 women — **Tuition:** $15,949
Graduate: 233 men, 117 women — **Room & Board:** $7564
Application Deadline: open
ACT: required

Lincoln Christian University, founded in 1944, is affiliated with the Christian Church/Church of Christ. Its mission is to nurture and equip Christians with a Biblical worldview to serve and lead in the church and the world. The figures in the above capsule are approximate. In addition to regional accreditation, the college is accredited by AABC and NCACS. Lincoln Christian University awards the B.A. and B.S. in Bible, business administration, Christian leadership and management, general ministry, intercultural studies, preaching ministry, youth ministry, Biblical exposition, children and family ministry, Christian spiritual formation, general studies, philosophy, psychology, and worship ministry. The school also awards associate, bachelor's, master's, and doctorate degrees. Web:*www.lincolnchristian.edu*

MOODY BIBLE INSTITUTE — E-2

Chicago, IL 60610 — (312) DL-MOODY, (312) 329-8955

Full-time: 848 men, 730 women — **Faculty:** 95
Part-time: 436 men, 389 women — **Tuition:** $19,280
Graduate: 261 men, 152 women — **Room & Board:** $5185
Application Deadline: December 1
ACT: required

Moody Bible Institute, founded in 1886, is Evangelical Protestant. Its mission is to educate and train individuals to proclaim the gospel of the Lord Jesus Christ, to promote evangelism, and to serve the Evangelical Christian Church vocationally and/or avocationally in its worldwide ministry. In addition to regional accreditation, the college is accredited by AABC and NCA. Moody Bible Institute awards the B.A., B.S., and B.Mus. in missionary aviation technology, biblical studies, evangelism/discipleship, communication, educational ministries, world missions, pastoral studies, religious education, church music, sacred music, Bible-theology, applied linguistics, youth ministry, urban ministry, Jewish and modern Israel studies, family ministries, women's ministries, and teaching English to speakers of other languages. The school also awards associate, bachelor's, and master's degrees. Web: *www.moody.edu*

IOWA

DIVINE WORD COLLEGE — E-2

Epworth, IA 52045-0380 — (563) 876-3353, (563) 876-5515

Full-time: 80 men, 34 women — **Faculty:** 29
Part-time: n/av — **Tuition:** $13,220
Graduate: n/av — **Room & Board:** $7200
Application Deadline: July 15

Divine Word College, founded in 1912, is affiliated with the Roman Catholic Church. Its mission is to combine a liberal arts education with a cross-cultural program of missionary formation for Divine Word Missionaries and other leaders in the Roman Catholic Church. The figures in the above capsule are approximate. In addition to regional accreditation, the college is accredited by NCA. Divine Word College awards the BA in philosophy, cross-cultural studies, and religious studies. The school also awards associate and bachelor's degrees. Web:*www.dwci.edu*

FAITH BAPTIST BIBLE COLLEGE AND THEOLOGICAL SEMINARY — C-3

Ankeny, IA 50023 — (515) 964-0601, (515) 964-1638

Full-time: 120 men, 186 women — **Faculty:** 36
Part-time: 22 men, 23 women — **Tuition:** $16,766
Graduate: 52 men, 14 women — **Room & Board:** $6800
Application Deadline: August 24
SAT or ACT: required

Faith Baptist Bible College and Theological Seminary, founded in 1921, is affiliated with the Baptist Church. Its mission is to provide an intensive biblical and vocational education on the college level with the goal of preparing students to minister effectively in Christian service through leadership positions in fundamental Baptist churches and other organizations of like convictions. The figures in the above capsule are approximate. In addition to regional accreditation, the college is accredited by AABC and NCA. Faith Baptist Bible College and Theological Seminary awards the B.A. and B.S. in Bible and theology, assistant pastor, Christian education, Christian school, missions, music ministries, and pastoral training. The school also awards associate, bachelor's, and master's degrees. Web:*www.faith.edu*

KENTUCKY

CLEAR CREEK BAPTIST BIBLE COLLEGE F-3

Pineville, KY 40977 **(606) 337-3196** **(606) 337-2372**

Full-time: 100 men, 24 women
Part-time: 50 men, 14 women
Graduate: n/av
Application Deadline: July 15
Faculty: 22
Tuition: $8100
Room & Board: $4034

Clear Creek Baptist Bible College, founded in 1926, is affiliated with the Southern Baptist Church. Its mission is to provide theological education for adults called to Christian service. The figures in the above capsule are approximate. In addition to regional accreditation, the college is accredited by AABC and SACS. Clear Creek Baptist Bible College awards the B.A. in Bible, and also awards associate and bachelor's degrees. *Web:www.ccbbc.edu*

LOUISIANA

SAINT JOSEPH ABBEY AND SEMINARY COLLEGE D-3

St. Benedict, LA 70457 **(985) 892-1800** **(985) 867-2270**

Full-time: 80 men
Part-time: 70 men
Graduate: n/av
Application Deadline: open
ACT: required
Faculty: 43
Tuition: $28,730
Room & Board: $14,120

Saint Joseph Abbey and Seminary College, founded in 1891, is affiliated with the Roman Catholic Church. Its mission is educate and train men for the priesthood in the Roman Catholic Church and to support preparation for lay ministry. The figures in the above capsule are approximate. In addition to regional accreditation, the college is accredited by SACS. Saint Joseph Abbey and Seminary College awards the B.A. in liberal arts, philosophy and theological studies. The figures in the above capsule are approximate. The school also awards bachelor's degrees. Web:*www.sjasc.edu*

MICHIGAN

SACRED HEART MAJOR SEMINARY E-5

Detroit, MI 48206 **(313) 883-8512** **(313) 883-8682**

Full-time: 46 men, 6 women
Part-time: 108 men, 102 women
Graduate: 124 men, 44 women
Application Deadline: August 15
Faculty: 78
Tuition: $15,770
Room & Board: $9484

Sacred Heart Major Seminary, founded in 1919, is affiliated with the Roman Catholic Church. Its mission is to prepares candidates for the Roman Catholic Priesthood and, further, prepares individuals for the diaconate, lay ministry and other leadership roles. Sacred Heart Major Seminary seeks to provide an excellent undergraduate formation based on an emphasis in Philosophy and ministry that will serve as a sound foundation to pursue theological studies. The graduate Theology programs seek to ensure a clearly Catholic professional and academic formation for ministerial service. The figures in the above capsule are approximate. In addition to regional accreditation, the college is accredited by NCA and ATS. Sacred Heart Major Seminary awards the A.B. and B.Phil. in Philosophy, and Pastoral Theology. The school also awards associate, bachelor's, and master's degrees. Web: *www.shms.edu*

MINNESOTA

CROWN COLLEGE C-4

Saint Bonifacius, MN 55375 **(952) 446-4100** **(952) 446-4149**

Full-time: 348 men, 465 women
Part-time: 96 men, 122 women
Graduate: 100 men, 67 women
Application Deadline: n/av
ACT: required
Faculty: n/av
Tuition: $25,430
Room & Board: $8410

Crown College, founded in 1916, is affiliated with the Christian and Missionary Alliance. Its mission is to provide a Biblically based education for Christian leadership in the Christian and Missionary Alliance, the church at large, and the world. The figures in the above capsule are approximate. In addition to regional accreditation, the college is accredited by NCA. Crown College awards the B.A., B.S., B.Mus.Ed., and B.S.N. in Biblical and Theological Studies, biology, business administration, child and family ministries, communication, criminal/social justice, discipleship ministries, elementary education, English, English education, ESL education, general studies, history, intercultural studies, liberal arts, linguistics, management, music, music education, new testament, nursing, pastoral leadership, physical education, psychology, science education, social entrepreneurship, social studies education, sports management, TESOL, urban studies, worship arts, youth and family, and youth/social ministry. The school also awards associate, bachelor's, and master's degrees. Web: *www.crown.edu*

MARTIN LUTHER COLLEGE C-4

New Ulm, MN 56073-3300 **(507) 354-8221** **(507) 354-8225**

Full-time: 515 men, 525 women
Part-time: 8 men, 9 women
Graduate: n/av
Application Deadline: April 15
ACT: required
Faculty: 98
Tuition: $14,680
Room & Board: $5790

Martin Luther College, founded in 1995, is affiliated with the Wisconsin Evangelical Lutheran Synod. Its mission is to provide training for elementary and secondary teaching, preseminary training for pastoral students, and training for other church vocations through the Staff Ministry Program. The figures in the above capsule are approximate. In addition to regional accreditation, the college is accredited by NCACS. Martin Luther College awards the B.A. and B.S.Ed. in education and preseminary studies, and also awards bachelor's degrees. Web: *www.mlc-wels.edu*

OAK HILLS CHRISTIAN COLLEGE B-2

Bemidji, MN 56601 **(218) 751-8670** **(218) 444-1311**

Full-time: 75 men, 75 women
Part-time: 15 men, 20 women
Graduate: n/av
Application Deadline: August 1
ACT: required
Faculty: 18
Tuition: $17,314
Room & Board: $6880

Oak Hills Christian College, founded in 1946, is interdenominational. Its mission is integrating faith and learning through biblical training. The figures in the above capsule are approximate. Oak Hills Christian College awards the B.A., B.S. in biblical studies, biblical studies and applied psychology, applied studies, campus ministry, contemporary worship, contemporary Christian ministry, intercultural studies, pastoral ministry, and youth ministry. The school also awards associate and bachelor's degrees. Web: *www.oakhills.edu*

MISSOURI

CONCEPTION SEMINARY COLLEGE A-1

Conception, MO 64433 **(660) 944-2886** **(660) 944-2829**

Full-time: 98 men
Part-time: 2 men
Graduate: n/av
Application Deadline: August 1
SAT or ACT: required
Faculty: 28
Tuition: $20,706
Room & Board: $12,316

Conception Seminary College, founded in 1886, is affiliated with Roman Catholic Church. Its mission is dedication to the formation and preparation of candidates for the ordained ministry in the Roman Catholic Church. It places emphasis on spiritual, character, academic and pastoral formation. The goal is for the student to integrate these aspects of formation into his life, whether as an ordained priest or as a Catholic layman. In addition to regional accreditation, the college is accredited by NCA. Conception Seminary College awards the Bachelor of Arts in Philosophy. The school also awards bachelor's degrees. Web: *www.conception.edu*

NORTH CAROLINA

MID-ATLANTIC CHRISTIAN UNIVERSITY F-2

Elizabeth City, NC 27909-4054 **(252) 334-2000** **(252) 334-2071**

Full-time: 87 men, 48 women
Part-time: 12 men, 22 women
Graduate: n/av
Application Deadline: n/av
SAT or ACT: required
Faculty: 23
Tuition: $13,440
Room & Board: $8200

Mid-Atlantic Christian University, founded in 1948, is affiliated with the Christian Church/Church of Christ. Its mission is to impact the world by transforming ordinary people into extraordinary Christian leaders. The figures in the above capsule are approximate. In addition to regional accreditation, the college is accredited by AABC and SACS. Mid-Atlantic Christian University awards the B.A., B.S., B.Th. in Biblical Exposition and cross-cultural ministry, Biblical exposition and general ministry, Biblical exposition and missions aviation, Biblical exposition and preaching, Biblical exposition with youth & family ministry, Biblical exposition & applied linguistics, Biblical studies with counseling & psychology, Biblical studies with leadership & administration, Biblical studies, and Biblical exposition. The school also awards associate and bachelor's degrees. Web: *www.macuniversity.edu*

NORTH DAKOTA

TRINITY BIBLE COLLEGE E-4

Ellendale, ND 58436 **(800) 523-1603** **(701) 349-5786**

Full-time: 131 men, 143 women
Part-time: 8 men, 25 women
Graduate: n/av
Application Deadline: August 15
Faculty: 30
Tuition: $16,040
Room & Board: $6060

Trinity Bible College, founded in 1948, is affiliated with the Assemblies of God. Its mission is to prepare pastors, church leaders, and Christian professionals in various fields in a Bible-based Pentecostal environment of academic excellence. In addition to regional accreditation, the college is accredited by AABC and NCACS. Trinity Bible College awards the B.A. in biblical studies, business administration, elementary education, ministerial studies, and missions. The figures in the above capsule are approximate. The school also awards associate and bachelor's degrees. Web: *www.trinitybiblecollege.edu*

OHIO

CINCINNATI CHRISTIAN UNIVERSITY A-5

Cincinnati, OH 45204-3200 **(800) 949-4CCU** **(513) 244-8111**

Full-time: 270 men, 236 women
Part-time: 85 men, 44 women
Graduate: 169 men, 86 women
Application Deadline: February 1
SAT or ACT: required
Faculty: 85
Tuition: $17,328
Room & Board: $8360

Cincinnati Christian University, founded in 1924, is affiliated with the Christian Churches/Churches of Christ. Its mission is to teach men and women to live by biblical principles and to equip and empower them with skills, insight, and vision to lead the church and impact society for Christ. The figures in the above capsule are approximate. In addition to regional accreditation, the college is accredited by AABC and NCA. Cincinnati Christian University awards the B.A., B.S., and B.Mus. in biblical studies (primary major), education, ministries, (second major), and signing interpreter's training program, psychology, preaching, youth ministry, worship, music, children's ministry, urban/intercultural ministry, music education and history. The school also awards associate, bachelor's, and master's degrees. Web: *www.CCUniversity.edu*

OHIO CHRISTIAN UNIVERSITY

Circleville, OH 43113 **(740) 474-8896**

Full-time: 372 men, 429 women
Part-time: 55 men, 75 women
Graduate: n/av
Application Deadline: May
SAT or ACT: required
Faculty: 135
Tuition: $20,240
Room & Board: $7996

Ohio Christian University, founded in 1948, is affiliated with the Churches of Christ in Christian Union (CCCU). Its mission is to provide a holistic Bible college education in the Wesleyan tradition that equips students to grow spiritually and intellectually and to serve effectively in society and the church. The figures in the above capsule are approximate. In addition to regional accreditation, the college is accredited by AABC and NCA. Ohio Christian University awards the B.A. in religion, business management, psychology, nursing, teacher education, international studies, ministries, music education, youth ministries, and christian ministries. The school also awards associate and bachelor's degrees. Web: *www.ohiochristian.edu*

PONTIFICAL COLLEGE JOSEPHINUM C-3

Columbus, OH 43235 **(614) 885-5585** **(614) 885-2307**

Full-time: 78 men
Part-time: n/av
Graduate: 51 men, 2 women
Application Deadline: July 31
SAT or ACT: required
Faculty: 41
Tuition: $22,650
Room & Board: $10,250

Pontifical College Josephinum, founded in 1888, is affiliated the with

Roman Catholic Church. Its mission is to prepare young men for the priesthood. In addition to regional accreditation, the college is accredited by NCACS and ATS. Pontifical College Josephinum awards the B.A. in philosophy and the humanities (English literature, Hispanic studies, history, and classical studies). The figures in the above capsule are approximate. The school also awards bachelor's and master's degrees. Web: *pcj .edu*

OKLAHOMA

MID-AMERICA CHRISTIAN UNIVERSITY D-3

Oklahoma City, OK 73170 (405) 692-3800
(405) 692-3165

Full-time: 338 men, 387 women **Faculty:** 45
Part-time: 87 men, 94 women **Tuition:** $17,132
Graduate: 116 men, 158 women **Room & Board:** $7956
Application Deadline: open
SAT or ACT: required

Mid-America Christian University, founded in 1953, is affiliated with Church of God in Anderson, Indiana. Its mission is to equip students to impact their world for Christ through achieving Bible-based academic excellence in a Christian environment so that students professionally serve in their chosen vocation/ministry. The figures in the above capsule are approximate. In addition to regional accreditation, the college is accredited by NCA. Mid-America Christian University awards the B.A. and B.S. in behavioral science, elementary education, English, music, performance, pastoral ministry, worship and music ministries, secondary education, specialized ministries, management and ethics, English/ business, and business administration. The school also awards associate, bachelor's, and master's degrees. Web: *www.macu.edu*

SOUTHWESTERN CHRISTIAN UNIVERSITY

Bethany, OK 73008 (405) 789-7661
(405) 495-0078

Full-time: 91 men, 92 women **Faculty:** 35
Part-time: 11 men, 15 women **Tuition:** $16,130
Graduate: 58 men, 20 women **Room & Board:** $7900
Application Deadline: open
ACT: required

Southwestern Christian University, founded in 1946, is affiliated with Pentecostal Holiness. Its mission is to educate and train for Christian service leading toward professional competence in the practice of various ministry forms. The figures in the above capsule are approximate. In addition to regional accreditation, the college is accredited by NCA. Southwestern Christian University awards the B.A. and B.S. and B.B.A. in Bibical studies, church growth, church music, music performace, missions, Christian education, Christian elementary education, pastoral ministry, youth ministry religion, Biblicial leadership, human and family services, business leadership, nonprofit organizational leadership, and business administration. The school also awards associate, bachelor's, and master's degrees. Web: *www.swcu.edu*

OREGON

MOUNT ANGEL ABBEY & SEMINARY B-2

St. Benedict, OR 97373 (503) 845-3030
(503) 845-3126

Full-time: 85 men **Faculty:** 40
Part-time: n/av **Tuition:** $19,589
Graduate: 87 men, 12 women **Room & Board:** $11,089
Application Deadline: July 15

Mount Angel Abbey & Seminary, founded in 1889, is affiliated with the Roman Catholic Church. Its mission is to prepare students of the Roman Catholic priesthood for religious orders and dioceses. The figures in the above capsule are approximate. In addition to regional accreditation, the college is accredited by NASC. Mount Angel Abbey & Seminary awards the B.A. in philosophy and literature, and also awards bachelor's and master's degrees. Web: *www.mountangelabbey.org*

PENNSYLVANIA

CLARKS SUMMIT UNIVERSITY E-2

South Abington Twp., PA 18411 (570) 586-2400
(570) 586-1753

Full-time: 192 men, 243 women **Faculty:** 30
Part-time: 68 men, 86 women **Tuition:** $23,170
Graduate: 213 men, 87 women **Room & Board:** $6150
Application Deadline: January 1
SAT or ACT: required

Clarks Summit University, founded in 1932, is affiliated with the Baptist Church. Its mission is to prepare men and women for service in a wide variety of ministries including teaching, counseling, pastors, missionaries, Christian education workers, church musicians, and secretaries. The figures in the above capsule are approximate. In addition to regional accreditation, the college is accredited by AABC and MSACS. Clarks Summit University awards the B.S. in Bible and B.S.M. in church music, communications, elementary and early childhood teacher education, pre-K teacher education, general missions, local church ministries, outreach and evangelism pastor, pastoral ministry, pastor of Christian education, preseminary, secondary social studies teacher education, secondary science teacher education, secondary math teacher education, secondary english teacher education, health and physical education teacher education, music teacher education, secretarial ministries, sports ministries, youth pastor, precounseling, general ministries, women's ministries, early childhood education, business, and office professionals. The school also awards associate, bachelor's, master's, and doctorate degrees. Web: *www.clarkssummitu.edu*

LANCASTER BIBLE COLLEGE E-3

Lancaster, PA 17601 (717) 569-7071
(717) 560-8213

Full-time: 302 men, 286 women **Faculty:** 86
Part-time: 110 men, 105 women **Tuition:** $23,400
Graduate: 90 men, 85 women **Room & Board:** $8750
Application Deadline: March 31
SAT or ACT: required

Lancaster Bible College, founded in 1933, is nondenominational. Its mission is to educate Christian men and women to live according to a biblical worldview and to serve through professional Christian ministries. The figures in the above capsule are approximate. In addition to regional accreditation, the college is accredited by AABC and MSA. Lancaster Bible College awards the B.S. in Bible and B.S.Ed. in Bible education, Bible ministry, children and family ministry, counseling (professional), cross-cultural ministry, elementary education/early level, elementary education/middle level, music education, music performance, pastoral ministry, pre-seminary, social work, spiritual formation and discipleship, student ministry, TESOL, women in Christian ministry, and worship arts. The school also awards associate, bachelor's, and master's degrees. Web: *www.lbc.edu*

SAINT CHARLES BORROMEO SEMINARY F-3

Wynnewood, PA 19096 (610) 785-6252
(610) 617-9267

Full-time: 90 men **Faculty:** 65
Part-time: 25 men, 35 women **Tuition:** $19,500
Graduate: 90 men, 30 women **Room & Board:** $12,300
Application Deadline: July 1

Saint Charles Borromeo Seminary, founded in 1832, is affiliated with the Roman Catholic Church. Its mission is to prepare and educate men for the Roman Catholic priesthood and to provide undergraduate and graduate programs for men and women pursuing theological studies. In addition to regional accreditation, the college is accredited by MSACS. Saint Charles Borromeo Seminary awards the B.A. in philosophy. The figures in the above capsule are approximate. The school also awards bachelor's and master's degrees. Web: *www.scs.edu*

SOUTH CAROLINA

COLUMBIA INTERNATIONAL UNIVERSITY C-3

Columbia, SC 29230 (803) 754-4100 (803) 786-4029

Full-time: 215 men, 259 women
Part-time: 33 men, 43 women
Graduate: 214 men, 186 women
Application Deadline: August 1
ACT: required
Faculty: 49
Tuition: $22,390
Room & Board: $7990

Columbia International University, founded in 1923, is multidenominational. Its mission is to prepare students to grow in spiritual maturity, Bible knowledge, and ministry skills in preparation for vocational or lay Christian ministry. The figures in the above capsule are approximate. In addition to regional accreditation, the college is accredited by AABC and SACS. Columbia International University awards the B.A. and B.S. in Bible, general studies, intercultural studies, psychology, biblical languages, music, Bible teaching, youth ministry, middle eastern studies, family and church education, teacher education, humanities, pastoral ministries, and communications. The school also awards associate, bachelor's, master's, and doctorate degrees. Web: *www.ciu.edu*

TENNESSEE

JOHNSON UNIVERSITY/TENNESSEE E-3

Knoxville, TN 37998 (865) 573-4517

Full-time: 408 men, 408 women
Part-time: 15 men, 16 women
Graduate: 47 men, 60 women
Application Deadline: June 1
SAT or ACT: required
Faculty: 62
Tuition: $15,115
Room & Board: $6160

Johnson University/Tennessee, founded in 1893, is affiliated with the Christian Churches and Churches of Christ. Its mission is to educate students for specialized Christian ministries. The figures in the above capsule are approximate. In addition to regional accreditation, the college is accredited by AABC and SACS. Johnson University/Tennessee awards the B.A. and B.S. in Bible. In addition, five professional programs require a second major, in counseling, preaching, as well as interdisciplinary major with focus on teacher education, music, and youth ministry/preaching. The school also awards associate, bachelor's, and master's degrees. Web: *www.johnsonu.edu*

WELCH COLLEGE C-2

Nashville, TN 37205 (615) 844-5000 (615) 269-6028

Full-time: 100 men, 92 women
Part-time: 54 men, 36 women
Graduate: n/av
Application Deadline: open
ACT: required
Faculty: 55
Tuition: $17,920
Room & Board: $7260

Welch College, founded in 1942, is affiliated with National Association of Free Will Baptists. Its mission is to educate leaders to serve Christ, His Church and His world through Biblical thought and life. The figures given in the above capsule are approximate. In addition to regional accreditation, the college is accredited by AABC, SACS, ABHE, and CHEA. Welch College awards the B.A. and B.S. in biblical studies, biblical and ministry studies, business administration, church music, church music and youth ministry, English, elementary education, music education, music performance, sports medicine, physical education, secondary English education, psychology, and learning. The school also awards associate and bachelor's degrees. Web: *www.welch.edu*

TEXAS

AUSTIN GRADUATE SCHOOL OF THEOLOGY D-3

Austin, TX 78752 (512) 476-2772 (512) 476-3919

Full-time: 4 men
Part-time: 15 men, 7 women
Graduate: 25 men, 5 women
Application Deadline: July 1
Faculty: 10
Tuition: $8750
Room & Board: n/app

Austin Graduate School of Theology, founded in 1917, is affiliated with the Church of Christ. Its mission is to equip ministers and other Christians for service in the kingdom of God. The figures in the above capsule are approximate. In addition to regional accreditation, the college is accredited by SACS. Austin Graduate School of Theology awards the B.A. in Christian studies, also awards bachelor's and master's degrees. Web: *www.austingrad.edu*

BAPTIST MISSIONARY ASSOCIATION THEOLOGICAL SEMINARY E-2

Jacksonville, TX 75766 (903) 586-2501 (903) 586-0378

Full-time: 23 men, 1 women
Part-time: 26 men, 22 women
Graduate: 49 men, 8 women
Application Deadline: July 31
Faculty: 13
Tuition: $8550
Room & Board: n/app

Baptist Missionary Association Theological Seminary, founded in 1955, is affiliated with the Baptist Missionary Association. Its mission is to train individuals for Christian ministry. The figures in the above capsule are approximate. In addition to regional accreditation, the college is accredited by SACS. Baptist Missionary Association Theological Seminary awards the B.A.R. in religion, and also awards associate, bachelor's, and master's degrees. Web:*www.bmats.edu*

CRISWELL COLLEGE D-2

Dallas, TX 75246 (214) 821-5433 (214) 370-0497

Full-time: 140 men, 30 women
Part-time: 160 men, 50 women
Graduate: 100 men, 20 women
Application Deadline: July 15
SAT or ACT: required
Faculty: 27
Tuition: $13,090
Room & Board: $11,000

Criswell College, founded in 1970, is affiliated with the Southern Baptist of Texas Convention. Its mission is to educate and train laymen and full-time Christian workers in biblical, theological, and professional studies so they can serve effectively in evangelistic, educational, pastoral, and missionary vocations of the Christian church. The figures in the above capsule are approximate. In addition to regional accreditation, the college is accredited by SACS. Criswell College awards the B.A. in biblical studies, counseling, missions, evangelism, pastoral, and urban ministries. The school also awards associate, bachelor's, and master's degrees. Web: *www.criswell.edu*

SOUTHWESTERN ASSEMBLIES OF GOD UNIVERSITY D-2

Waxahachie, TX 75165 (972) 825-4634
(972) 923-0006

Full-time: 587 men, 604 women
Part-time: 145 men, 122 women
Graduate: 168 men, 148 women
Application Deadline: open
SAT or ACT: required
Faculty: 129
Tuition: $9725
Room & Board: $6330

Southwestern Assemblies of God University, founded in 1927, is affiliated with the Assemblies of God. Its mission is to prepare undergraduate and graduate students spiritually, academically, professionally, and cross culturally, so as to successfully fill evangelistic, missionary and church ministry roles and to provide quality educational and professional Christian service wherever needed throughout the world. The figures in the above capsule are approximate. In addition to regional accreditation, the college is accredited by AABC and SACS. Southwestern Assemblies of God University awards the B.A. and B.S. in accounting, ancient studies, Biblical studies, business administration, children & family ministries, and church ministries, church planting & revitalization, communication, counseling, counseling ministries, criminal justice, digital media arts, drama, education, bilingual education, elementary education, middle & secondary, English language arts/reading, social studies/history, music education, instrumental, piano, vocal, physical education, English history, human services, management, management information systems, marketing, media ministries, music ministries, music performance, instrumental, piano, vocal, pastoral ministries, professional development, psychology, social work, sports management, theological studies, world ministries, youth & student ministries. The school also awards associate, bachelor's, and master's degrees. Web: *www.sagu.edu*

WISCONSIN

MARANATHA BAPTIST UNIVERSITY D-4

Watertown, WI 53094 (920) 261-9300
(920) 261-9109

Full-time: 350 men, 404 women
Part-time: 31 men, 45 women
Graduate: 27 men, 3 women
Application Deadline: n/av
ACT: required
Faculty: 57
Tuition: $14,260
Room & Board: $6720

Maranatha Baptist University, founded in 1968, is affiliated with the Baptist Church. Its mission is nurture students who are spiritually and academically prepared to serve the Lord. We want to develop servants of Christ who are disciplined, creative, and passionate about the field to which they have been called. The figure in the above capsule are approximate. In addition to regional accreditation, the college is accredited by NCA. Maranatha Baptist University awards the B.A. and B.S. in Bible, church ministries, education, general studies, fine arts, business, nursing, office administration, biology, and premed. The school also awards associate, bachelor's, and master's degrees. Web: *www.mbu.edu*

AIR FORCE

In the Air Force ROTC program, young men and women may earn commissions while attending college. The amount of academic credit given for Air Force ROTC varies from school to school.

Most new Air Force officers come through the Air Force ROTC program. It offers students the opportunity to attend a civilian college while studying officership as part of their undergraduate curriculum.

The AFROTC program begins with the General Military Course. Freshmen or sophomores attend one hour of ROTC classes and one to two hours of leadership laboratory weekly. During these first two years, study is focused on the history of the Air Force and the part it plays in the world today. During the summer between sophomore and junior years, students attend a four-week basic training course located at an Air Force base.

The Professional Officer Course is completed during the junior and senior years. Study includes management principles and defense policy and offers the opportunity for managing, organizing, directing, and evaluating the cadet corps activities. Cadets who are medically qualified will have the opportunity to compete for pilot or navigator positions. Upon graduation, students are commissioned as Second Lieutenants.

For academically qualified students in selected majors, the AFROTC offers scholarships, including tuition, fees and books, and a monthly nontaxable allowance during the school year.

The majority of scholarships are awarded in the technical degree areas of engineering and computer science, but there are opportunities in nontechnical areas as well. Scholarships are based on individual merit, not financial need. Those who receive a scholarship must still apply and be accepted by the school they wish to attend and notify the AFROTC headquarters of their selection.

The scholarship program is broken down into different types and durations. All scholarships include full or partial tuition, fees, textbook allowance, and $500 per month tax-free allowance during the academic year. Type 1 pays full tuition at any school offering AFROTC. Type 2 pays tuition and fees up to a maximum of $18,000 per year. There are two variations of the Type 7 scholarship. A Type 7 scholarship winner can attend any post-secondary institution (public or private) where tuition does not exceed $9,000 per year, or he/she can attend any public post-secondary institution where the student qualifies for in-state tuition rates.

The application deadline is December 1 of the senior year, but priority consideration is given to those who get the application in early. AFROTC only accepts on-line applications and they are available during the spring prior to the senior year of high school.

Further information can be obtained from the professor of aerospace studies at any of the host campuses where Air Force ROTC is offered. The listing that follows represents the host schools that offer these programs. Hundreds more schools have crosstown agreements with these institutions to make AFROTC more accessible to students. Please be sure to contact the school directly for more details. You may also find useful and current information at the Air Force Reserve Officer Training Corps web site, *www.afrotc.com*.

ALABAMA

- Alabama State University
- Auburn University at Auburn
- Samford University
- Troy University
- Tuskegee University
- University of Alabama
- University of South Alabama

ALASKA

- University of Alaska - Anchorage

ARIZONA

- Arizona State University
- Embry-Riddle Aeronautical University
- Northern Arizona University
- University of Arizona

ARKANSAS

- University of Arkansas

CALIFORNIA

- California State University, Fresno
- California State University, Sacramento
- California State University, San Bernadino
- Loyola Marymount University
- San Diego State University
- San Jose State University
- University of California at Berkeley
- University of California at Los Angeles
- University of Southern California

COLORADO

- Colorado State University
- University of Colorado at Boulder

CONNECTICUT

- University of Connecticut
- Yale University

DELAWARE

- University of Delaware

DISTRICT OF COLUMBIA

- Howard University

FLORIDA

- Embry-Riddle Aeronautical University
- Florida State University
- University of Central Florida
- University of Florida
- University of Miami
- University of South Florida

GEORGIA

- Georgia Institute of Technology
- University of Georgia
- Valdosta State University

HAWAII

- University of Hawaii at Manoa

ILLINOIS

- Illinois Institute of Technology
- Southern Illinois University
- University of Illinois at Champaign/Urbana

INDIANA

- Indiana State University
- Indiana University
- Purdue University
- University of Notre Dame

IOWA

- Iowa State University
- University of Iowa

KANSAS

- Kansas State University
- University of Kansas

KENTUCKY

- University of Kentucky
- University of Louisville

LOUISIANA

- Louisiana State University and Agricultural and Mechanical College
- Louisiana Tech University
- Tulane University

MARYLAND

- Howard University
- University of Maryland

MASSACHUSETTS

- Boston University
- Massachusetts Institute of Technology
- University of Massachusetts
- University of Massachusetts, Lowell
- Worcester Polytechnic Institute

MICHIGAN

- Michigan State University
- University of Michigan

MINNESOTA

- University of Minnesota/Duluth
- University of Minnesota
- University of St. Thomas

MISSISSIPPI

- Jackson State University
- Mississippi State University
- University of Mississippi
- University of Southern Mississippi

MISSOURI

- Missouri University of Science and Technology
- Saint Louis University
- University of Missouri/Columbia

MONTANA

- Montana State University

NEBRASKA

- University of Nebraska at Lincoln
- University of Nebraska at Omaha

NEVADA

- University of Nevada—Las Vegas

NEW HAMPSHIRE

- University of New Hampshire

NEW JERSEY

- New Jersey Institute of Technology
- Rutgers University

NEW MEXICO

- New Mexico State University
- University of New Mexico

NEW YORK

- Clarkson University
- Cornell University
- Manhattan College
- Rensselaer Polytechnic Institute
- Rochester Institute of Technology
- Syracuse University

NORTH CAROLINA

- Duke University
- East Carolina University
- Fayetteville State University
- North Carolina A&T State University
- North Carolina State University
- University of North Carolina at Chapel Hill
- University of North Carolina at Charlotte

NORTH DAKOTA

- North Dakota State University

OHIO

- Bowling Green University
- Kent State University
- Miami University
- Ohio State University, The
- Ohio University
- University of Cincinnati
- Wright State University

OKLAHOMA

- Oklahoma State University
- University of Oklahoma

OREGON

- Oregon State University
- University of Portland

PENNSYLVANIA

- Penn State University/Main Campus
- Saint Joseph's University
- University of Pittsburgh
- Wilkes University

PUERTO RICO

- University of Puerto Rico/Mayaguez
- University of Puerto Rico/Río Piedras

SOUTH CAROLINA

- Charleston Southern University
- The Citadel
- Clemson University
- University of South Carolina/Columbia

SOUTH DAKOTA

- South Dakota State University

TENNESSEE

- Tennessee State University
- University of Memphis
- University of Tennessee

TEXAS

- Angelo State University
- Baylor University
- Texas A&M University
- Texas Christian University
- Texas State University/San Marcos
- Texas Tech University
- University of Houston
- University of North Texas
- University of Texas at Austin
- University of Texas at San Antonio

UTAH

- Brigham Young University
- University of Utah
- Utah State University

VERMONT

- Norwich University

VIRGINIA

- University of Virginia
- Virginia Military Institute
- Virginia Polytechnic Institute

WASHINGTON

- Central Washington University
- University of Washington
- Washington State University

WEST VIRGINIA

- West Virginia University

WISCONSIN

- Marquette University
- University of Wisconsin/Madison

WYOMING

- University of Wyoming

ARMY

The Army Reserve Officers' Training Corps (ROTC) provides college students with the opportunity to combine leadership and management training with their other academic studies. The curriculum, which consists of a series of classroom and hands-on leadership training experiences, provides students with the necessary foundation to serve successfully in positions of responsibility in either the U.S. Army or the corporate world.

Those with a strong academic background, an active mindset, and the ability to rapidly assimilate information thrive in the program. These scholar-athlete-leaders note that the leadership skills developed through their participation in the program are further honed during their period of service as Army officers. After service as an Army lieutenant, many graduates elect to continue their service in uniform. Others elect to enter the corporate world where their leadership skills and experience as ROTC-trained Army officers allow them to advance rapidly.

Although the program is designed to be completed in four years, students may complete all requirements within a two-year period through participation in a summer training session called the Leaders' Training Course, normally held during the summer between the sophomore and junior years. A generous series of merit-based scholarships that cover tuition, fees, textbooks, and supplies exist to help students and their families defray the cost of college. For more information on the program, call (800) USA-ROTC (872–7682), or contact the professor of military science at a college that offers Army ROTC. Detailed information about the program is also available at *www.goarmy.com/rotc*.

ALABAMA

- Alabama A&M University
- Auburn University
- Auburn University at Montgomery
- Jacksonville State University
- Marion Military Institute
- The University of Alabama
- Tuskegee University
- University of Alabama at Birmingham
- University of North Alabama
- University of South Alabama

ALASKA

- University of Alaska/Anchorage
- University of Alaska/Fairbanks

ARIZONA

- Arizona State University
- Northern Arizona University
- University of Arizona

ARKANSAS

- Arkansas State University
- University of Arkansas
- University of Arkansas at Pine Bluff
- University of Central Arkansas

CALIFORNIA

- California Polytechnic State University at San Luis Obispo
- California State University at Fresno
- California State University at Fullerton
- Claremont McKenna College
- San Diego State University
- Santa Clara University
- University of California at Berkeley
- University of California at Davis
- University of California at Los Angeles
- University of California at Santa Barbara
- University of San Francisco
- University of Southern California

COLORADO

- Colorado State University
- University of Colorado at Boulder
- University of Colorado at Colorado Springs

CONNECTICUT

- University of Connecticut
- University of New Haven

DELAWARE

- University of Delaware

DISTRICT OF COLUMBIA

- Georgetown University
- Howard University

FLORIDA

- Embry-Riddle Aeronautical University
- Florida A&M University
- Florida Institute of Technology
- Florida International University
- Florida Southern College
- Florida State University
- University of Central Florida
- University of Florida
- University of South Florida
- University of Tampa
- University of West Florida

GEORGIA

- Columbus State University
- Fort Valley State University
- Georgia Institute of Technology
- Georgia Military College
- Georgia Regents University
- Georgia Southern University
- Georgia State University
- University of North Georgia
- University of Georgia

HAWAII

- University of Hawaii at Manoa

IDAHO

- Boise State University
- University of Idaho

ILLINOIS

- Eastern Illinois University
- Illinois State University
- Loyola University
- Northern Illinois University
- Southern Illinois University at Carbondale
- Southern Illinois University at Edwardsville
- University of Illinois at Chicago
- University of Illinois at Urbana-Champaign
- Western Illinois University
- Wheaton College

INDIANA

- Ball State University
- Indiana University-Purdue University at Indianapolis
- Indiana University at Bloomington
- Purdue University
- Rose-Hulman Institute of Technology
- University of Notre Dame

IOWA

- Iowa State University
- University of Iowa
- University of Northern Iowa

KANSAS

- Kansas State University
- Pittsburg State University
- University of Kansas

KENTUCKY

- Eastern Kentucky University
- Morehead State University
- University of Kentucky
- University of Louisville
- Western Kentucky University

LOUISIANA

- Grambling State University
- Louisiana State University
- Northwestern State University
- Southern University and A&M College
- Tulane University

MAINE

- University of Maine

MARYLAND

- Bowie State University
- Loyola University Maryland
- McDaniel College
- Morgan State University
- The Johns Hopkins University
- University of Maryland at College Park

MASSACHUSETTS

- Boston University
- Massachusetts Institute of Technology
- Northeastern University
- University of Massachusetts
- Worcester Polytechnic Institute

MICHIGAN

- Central Michigan University
- Eastern Michigan University
- Michigan State University
- Michigan Technological University
- Northern Michigan University
- University of Michigan
- Western Michigan University

MINNESOTA

- Minnesota State University, Mankato
- Saint John's University
- University of Minnesota/Twin Cities

MISSISSIPPI

- Alcorn State University
- Jackson State University
- Mississippi State University
- University of Mississippi
- University of Southern Mississippi

MISSOURI

- Lincoln University
- Missouri State University
- Missouri University of Science and Technology
- Missouri Western State University
- Truman State University
- University of Central Missouri
- University of Missouri/Columbia
- Washington University

MONTANA

- Montana State University
- University of Montana

NEBRASKA

- Chadron State College
- Creighton University
- University of Nebraska at Lincoln

NEVADA

- University of Nevada/Reno

NEW HAMPSHIRE

- University of New Hampshire

NEW JERSEY

- Princeton University
- Rutgers University
- Seton Hall University

NEW MEXICO

- New Mexico Military Institute
- New Mexico State University
- University of New Mexico

NEW YORK

- Canisius College
- City University of New York (CUNY)
- Clarkson University
- Cornell University
- Fordham University
- Hofstra University
- Niagara University
- Rochester Institute of Technology
- St. Bonaventure University
- St. John's University New York
- Siena College
- State University of New York (SUNY)/Brockport
- Syracuse University

NORTH CAROLINA

- Appalachian State University
- Campbell University
- Duke University
- East Carolina University
- Elizabeth City State University
- North Carolina Agricultural and Technical State University
- North Carolina State University
- Saint Augustine's College
- University of North Carolina at Chapel Hill
- University of North Carolina at Charlotte
- Wake Forest University

NORTH DAKOTA

- North Dakota State University
- University of North Dakota

OHIO

- Bowling Green State University
- Capital University
- Central State University
- John Carroll University
- Kent State University
- The Ohio State University
- Ohio University
- The University of Akron
- University of Cincinnati
- University of Dayton
- University of Toledo
- Wright State University
- Xavier University

OKLAHOMA

- Cameron University
- Oklahoma State University
- University of Central Oklahoma
- University of Oklahoma

OREGON

- Oregon State University
- University of Oregon
- University of Portland

PENNSYLVANIA

- Bucknell University
- Dickinson College
- Drexel University
- Edinboro University of Pennsylvania
- Gannon University
- Indiana University of Pennsylvania
- Lehigh University
- Lock Haven University of Pennsylvania
- Pennsylvania State University
- Shippensburg University
- Slippery Rock University
- Temple University
- University of Pittsburgh
- University of Scranton
- Valley Forge Military College
- Widener University

PUERTO RICO

- University of Puerto Rico/Mayaguez
- University of Puerto Rico/Río Piedras

RHODE ISLAND

- Providence College
- University of Rhode Island

SOUTH CAROLINA

- The Citadel
- Clemson University
- Furman University
- Presbyterian College
- South Carolina State University
- University of South Carolina
- Wofford College

SOUTH DAKOTA

- South Dakota School of Mines and Technology
- South Dakota State University
- University of South Dakota

TENNESSEE

- Austin Peay State University
- Carson-Newman College
- East Tennessee State University
- Middle Tennessee State University
- Tennessee Tech University
- University of Memphis
- University of Tennessee at Knoxville
- University of Tennessee at Martin
- Vanderbilt University

TEXAS

- Prairie View A&M University
- Saint Mary's University
- Sam Houston State University
- Stephen F. Austin State University
- Tarleton State University
- Texas A&M University-College Station
- Texas A&M-Corpus Christi
- Texas A&M University at Kingsville
- Texas Christian University
- Texas State University
- Texas Tech University
- University of Houston
- The University of Texas at Arlington
- The University of Texas at Austin
- University of Texas at El Paso
- University of Texas at Rio Grande Valley
- University of Texas at San Antonio

UTAH

- Brigham Young University
- University of Utah
- Weber State University

VERMONT

- Norwich University
- University of Vermont

VIRGINIA

- College of William and Mary
- George Mason University
- Hampton University
- James Madison University
- Norfolk State University
- Old Dominion University
- University of Richmond
- University of Virginia
- Virginia Military Institute
- Virginia State University
- Virginia Tech

WASHINGTON

- Central Washington University
- Eastern Washington University
- Gonzaga University
- Pacific Lutheran University
- Seattle University
- University of Washington
- Washington State University

WEST VIRGINIA

- Marshall University
- West Virginia State University
- West Virginia University

WISCONSIN

- Marquette University
- University of Wisconsin/La Crosse
- University of Wisconsin/Madison
- University of Wisconsin/Oshkosh
- University of Wisconsin/Stevens Point

WYOMING

- University of Wyoming

NAVY

The NROTC Program educates and trains qualified young men and women for service as commissioned officers in the unrestricted line Navy or Marine Corps. Two programs are available: the NROTC Scholarship Program and the NROTC College Program.

The NROTC Scholarship Program plays an important role in preparing young men and women for leadership and management positions in an increasingly technical Navy and Marine Corps. The four-year NROTC Scholarship Program is available to qualified students who graduate from high school before August 1 of the year they intend to start college. The two-year NROTC Scholarship Program is available to qualified college sophmores who have completed one year of differential and integral calculus with a grade of C or better and maintain a minimum GPA of 2.5.

Selected applicants for NROTC Scholarship Programs (four-year and two-year) are awarded scholarships through a highly competitive national selection process, and receive full tuition, fees, book stipend, and other financial benefits at many of the country's leading colleges and universities. Upon graduation, midshipmen are commissioned as officers in the unrestricted line Navy or Marine Corps.

Students selected for the NROTC Scholarship Program make their own arrangements for college enrollment and room and board, and take the normal course load required by the college or university for degree completion. Additionally, scholarship midshipmen are required to follow specific academic guidelines. Full information concerning the NROTC Scholarship Program is available from any of the colleges and universities with NROTC units or from Navy and Marine Corps recruiters.

For information on the NROTC scholarship programs, call 1-800-USA-NAVY or 1-800-NAV-ROTC, e-mail *PNSC_NROTC.scholarship@navy.mil*; or visit *www.nrotc.navy.mil.* Electronic application for the four-year scholarship program must be submitted by January 31.

The NROTC College Program may be either two or four years. Additional points include:

- Applicants are selected from students already attending or accepted by colleges with the NROTC program.
- Students selected for "advance standing" receive a stipend for a maximum of 20 months. Advance standing is only available starting in the junior year of college. Stipend per academic month is $350 junior year and $400 senior year.
- Students will complete naval science and other university courses, a few specific university courses, and attend one summer training session, normally at sea for Navy-option midshipmen and in Quantico, VA for Marine Corps-option midshipmen.

The following list shows the colleges and universities that have an NROTC unit on campus. Many more institutions offer the program through cross-town arrangements. We recommend that you visit *www.nrotc.navy.mil* for a listing of participating colleges and universities. Contact the schools directly for the most current and accurate information.

ALABAMA
- Auburn University
- Tuskegee University

ARIZONA
- Arizona State University
- University of Arizona

CALIFORNIA
- San Diego State University
- University of California/Berkeley
- University of California/Los Angeles
- University of San Diego
- University of Southern California

COLORADO
- University of Colorado

CONNECTICUT
- Yale University

DISTRICT OF COLUMBIA
- George Washington University

FLORIDA
- Embry Riddle Aeronautical University
- Florida A&M University
- Jacksonville University
- University of Florida
- University of South Florida

GEORGIA
- Georgia Institute of Technology
- Morehouse College
- Savannah State College

IDAHO
- University of Idaho

ILLINOIS
- Illinois Institute of Technology
- Northwestern University
- University of Illinois

INDIANA
- Purdue University
- University of Notre Dame

IOWA
- Iowa State University

KANSAS
- University of Kansas

LOUISIANA
- Southern University and A&M College
- Tulane University

MAINE
- Maine Maritime Academy

MARYLAND
- University of Maryland, College Park
- University of Maryland, Baltimore County

MASSACHUSETTS
- Boston University
- College of the Holy Cross
- Massachusetts Institute of Technology

MICHIGAN
- University of Michigan

MINNESOTA
- University of Minnesota

MISSISSIPPI
- University of Mississippi

MISSOURI
- University of Missouri

NEBRASKA
- University of Nebraska at Lincoln

NEW JERSEY
- Rutgers University, New Brunswick

NEW MEXICO
- University of New Mexico

NEW YORK
- Cornell University
- Rensselaer Polytechnic Institute
- State University of New York/Maritime College
- University of Rochester

NORTH CAROLINA
- Duke University
- North Carolina State University
- University of North Carolina

OHIO
- Miami University
- Ohio State University

OKLAHOMA

- University of Oklahoma

OREGON

- Oregon State University

PENNSYLVANIA

- Carnegie Mellon University
- Pennsylvania State University
- University of Pennsylvania
- Villanova University

SOUTH CAROLINA

- The Citadel
- University of South Carolina

TENNESSEE

- University of Memphis
- Vanderbilt University

TEXAS

- Prairie View A&M University
- Rice University
- Texas A&M University
- University of Texas

UTAH

- University of Utah

VERMONT

- Norwich University

VIRGINIA

- Hampton University
- Norfolk State University
- Old Dominion University
- University of Virginia
- Virginia Military Institute
- Virginia Polytechnic Institute and State University

WASHINGTON

- University of Washington

WISCONSIN

- Marquette University
- University of Wisconsin

ENROLLMENT IN CANADIAN SCHOOLS

Recently, Canadian universities hosted 1,016,000 full-time students and 290,000 part-time students. Universities are translating this priority into action at an increasing pace: 89% say that the pace of internationalization on their campuses has accelerated during the past three years. Eighty-one percent of Canadian universities offer collaborative academic programs with international partners, a major increase over the last eight years, when this number stood at 48%. Today, 63% of those that offer such academic programs offer dual or double degree programs and 45% offer joint degree programs.

Universities Canada, formerly known as the Association of Universities and Colleges of Canada (AUCC) represents 97 universities and university-level colleges. These institutions account for almost 99 percent of the total university enrollment in Canada. Almost all Canadian colleges are coeducational. This section contains individual profiles for those English-language universities that enroll more than 10,000 students.

Affiliated with each of these universities are a number of general, theological, or residential colleges, which also have been listed here. The names and addresses of the three French-speaking colleges with enrollments of more than 26,000 may be found at the end of this introduction.

Admissions Requirements

Each university has its own entrance requirements and will assess you on an individual basis. The university will determine the equivalency of your academic credentials. There is no nationwide set of entrance exams. For more details about this or any other part of the application process, contact the registrar at the university you wish to attend.

Admissions Procedure

Once you have determined which universities meet your needs, contact the registrar's office at each institution to obtain an application for a bachelor's program or a professional degree. If you anticipate pursuing postgraduate studies in Canada, you may obtain more information by contacting the dean of graduate studies at the universities that interest you. It is important to apply early. Remember that the Canadian academic year usually starts in September. Some programs, however, do admit students to courses that start in January and May.

Universities Canada's web site *www.univcan.ca* has links to the web pages of all Canadian universities, the majority of which accept applications via email.

To study at a Canadian university, you will need a study permit. You may also need a visitor's visa, which will be issued to you at the same time as your study permit. To apply for a study permit, please contact your nearest Canadian diplomatic post.

You will have to arrange for medical coverage before you arrive in Canada. Medical coverage varies from province to province and sometimes from university to university within each province. Please ask an official at the nearest Canadian diplomatic post for detailed information. Also, check whether the universities you are applying to have any medical insurance plans for international students.

Degrees Offered

Canadian universities, like those in the United States, grant three levels of degrees: bachelor's and first professional, master's, and doctoral as well as undergraduate certificates and diplomas and graduate diploma programs.

Earning the first degree can take three to five years. A general, or unspecialized, program leading to a Bachelor of Arts or Bachelor of Science usually can be completed in three years. An honors degree, earned in a specialized program, usually requires four years. Students must meet more rigorous requirements to enter an honors-degree program and must maintain high grades to remain in it. First professional degrees in some fields may take more than four years to earn, and students may be required to undertake two or three years of university study before enrolling in the professional program. Students who enter graduate programs with a general degree usually must study a year longer than those with honors degrees. Undergraduate diplomas and certificates may be from one to three years' duration and may (although not necessarily) be used as a basis for entry to a degree program. A graduate diploma may be considered as conferring a qualification that is intermediate between the bachelor's (or first professional degree) and master's degree. It may be completed in as little as two or as long as three academic years.

Organizations

Virtually all universities have organizations for international students, and sponsor international student centers and advisers. There also are national organizations that aid international students, including the World University Service of Canada and the Canadian Bureau for International Education, which arranges for representatives to meet international students arriving at Canadian airports.

Tuition, Fees, and Aid

Universities and colleges are heavily subsidized by provincial and federal governments, and tuition fees actually cover one third of university operating costs. Canadian institutions charge different fees for different programs, unlike American institutions, which charge the same tuition regardless of the program of study. Each profile in this book lists the range of tuitions, which may or may not include student fees. Some universities have higher fees for international students, and where that is the case, the profile includes just the international fees. All costs are given in Canadian (CDN) dollars. In all cases, you should check with the university in which you are interested to obtain the most up-to-date information about tuition and room-and-board charges.

Most awards available to international students through Canadian universities or from the Canadian government are restricted to graduate and post graduate studies. Some of the scholarship programs for international students to study in Canada include the Commonwealth Scholarship and Fellowship Plan, the Canadian International Development Agency awards, the Government of Canada awards program of cultural exchanges and the Programme canadien de bourses de la Francophonie. Students interested in applying for aid should contact a Canadian diplomatic mission in their home countries and, for information on cultural exchange programs, their own nation's education department or ministry.

Additional Information

Universities Canada
1710-350 Albert Street
Ottawa, Ontario, K1R 1B1 Canada
(613) 563-1236
Fax: (613) 563-9745
Email: info@univcan.ca
www.univcan.ca

Canadian Bureau for International Education
220 Laurier West, Suite 1550
Ottawa, ON Canada K1P 5Z9
(613) 237-4820
Fax: (613) 237-1073
Email: communication@cbie.ca
www.cbie.ca

Canada Immigration & Citizenship
www.cic.gc.ca
(publications include *Studying in Canada: Visas, Work and Immigration for International Students*, downloadable pdf publication)

Consulate General of Canada in New York
1251 Avenue of the Americas
Concourse Level (between 49th & 50th Streets, Midtown Manhattan)
New York, NY 10020-1175
(212) 596-1628
Fax: (212) 596-1790
Monday-Friday, 9am-5pm
Email: cngnyg@international.gc.ca
www.international.gc.ca

The Department of Foreign Affairs and International Trade
Enquiries Service (SXCI)
125 Sussex Drive
Ottawa, ON K1A 0G2 Canada
(613) 996-9709
1 (800) 267-8376
Fax: (613) 996-9709
Email: enqserv@international.gc.ca
www.international.gc.ca/international/index.aspx

Social Sciences and Humanities Research Council of Canada
350 Albert Street
P.O. Box 1610
Ottawa, ON K1P 6G4, Canada
(613) 992-0691
Email: research@sshrc-crsh.gc.ca
www.sshrc-crsh.gc.ca

Statistics Canada
150 Tunney's Pasture Driveway
Ottawa, Ontario K1A 0T6 Canada
Monday-Friday, 8:30am-4:30pm
1 (800) 263-1136
Or (514) 283-8300 (international)
Fax: (514) 283-9350
Email: infostats@statcan.gc.ca
www.statcan.gc.ca

World University Service of Canada
1404 Scott Street
Ottawa, ON K1Y 4M8 Canada
(613) 798-7477
(800) 267-8699
Fax: (613) 798-0990
Email: wusc@wusc.ca
www.wusc.ca

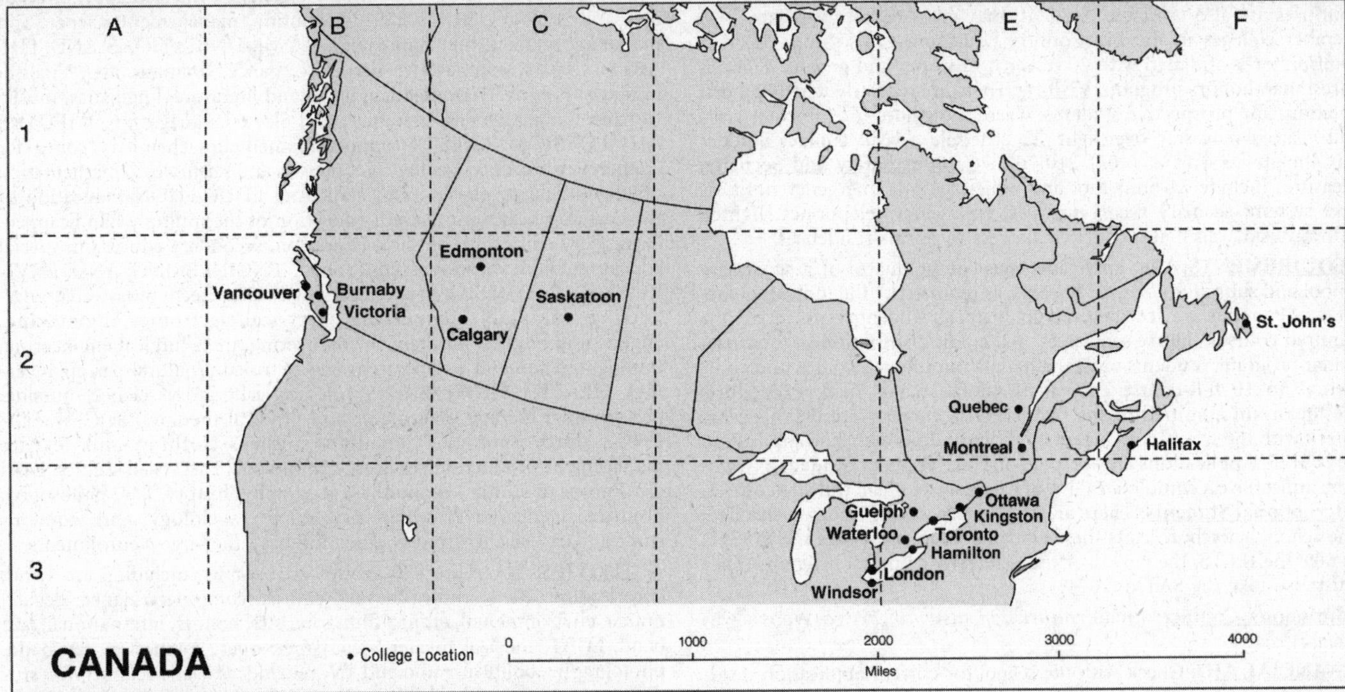

UNIVERSITY OF CALGARY C-2

www.ucalgary.ca

Calgary, AB T2N 1N4 **(403) 210-7625**

Fax: (403) 220-0762 **Email:** future.students@ucalgary.ca
Full-time: 10,667 men, 12,146 women
Part-time: 747 men, 1064 women
Graduate: 2795 men, 3099 women
Year: semesters, summer session
Room & Board: $9614
SAT or ACT: required
Application Deadline: n/av
Faculty: n/av
Ph.D.s: n/av
Student/Faculty: n/av
Tuition: $6590
Freshman Class: n/av
CEEB CODE: 0813

The University of Calgary is a leading Canadian university offering more than 200 undergraduate, graduate and professional degree programs. Ranked one of the top ten research universities, it houses over 70 Canada Research Chairs and over 80 research institutes and centers working to address society's most persistent and emerging challenges. There are 14 undergraduate schools and 2 graduate schools. The 526-acre campus is in an urban area in northwest Calgary, Alberta Canada. Including any residence halls, there are 48 buildings.

STUDENT LIFE: 82% of undergraduates are from Alberta. **Female To Male Ratio:** 1.1:1. The average age of all undergraduates is 22. **Housing:** 2812 students can be accommodated in college housing, which includes coed dorms, on-campus apartments, married student housing, honors houses, language houses, Upper, International & Transfer Students; business, engineering students, Scholar's Advantage (first year recipients of Prestige Scholarships and Awards). On-campus housing is guaranteed for all 4 years. Priority is given to out-of-town students. All students may keep cars.

FACULTY/CLASSROOMS: No introductory courses are taught by graduate students.

PROGRAMS OF STUDY: Master's and doctoral degrees are also awarded. Bachelor's degrees are awarded in BIOLOGICAL SCIENCE (biochemistry, bioinformatics, biology/biological science, botany, cell biology, ecology, and zoology), BUSINESS (accounting, business administration and management, hotel/motel and restaurant management, and marketing/retailing/merchandising), COMMUNICATIONS AND THE ARTS (communications, dance, dramatic arts, East Asian languages and literature, English, fine arts, French, German, Latin, linguistics, music, music history and appreciation, music performance, music theory and composition, Russian, and Spanish), COMPUTER AND PHYSICAL SCIENCE (actuarial science, applied mathematics, astrophysics, chemical physics, chemistry, computer science, earth science, geology, geophysics and seismology, mathematics, natural sciences, physics, and statistics), EDUCATION (education, elementary education, and secondary education), ENGINEERING AND ENVIRONMENTAL DESIGN (chemical engineering, civil engineering, computer engineering, electrical/electronics engineering, environmental science, mechanical engineering, petroleum/natural gas engineering, and surveying engineering), HEALTH PROFESSIONS (biomedical science, exercise science, nursing, public health, and sports medicine), SOCIAL SCIENCE (anthropology, archeology, Asian/Oriental studies, Canadian studies, Christian studies, classical/ancient civilization, East Asian studies, economics, geography, German area studies, history, international relations, Italian studies, Latin American studies, law, liberal arts/general studies, philosophy, physical fitness/movement, political science/government, psychology, religion, social work, sociology, urban studies, and women's studies). Engineering, and medicine are the strongest academically. Arts, science, and engineering have the largest enrollments.

ACTIVITIES: There are no fraternities or sororities. Groups on campus include art, band, chess, choir, chorus, computers, dance, debate, drama, environmental, ethnic, film, international, jazz band, LGBT, musical theater, newspaper, orchestra, political, professional, radio and TV, religious, social, social service, and student government. Popular campus events include Bermuda Shorts Day (last day of classes in April), Orientation Week and KickOff. **Sports:** There are 9 intercollegiate sports for men and 9 for women, and 20 intramural sports for men and 18 for women. Facilities include a swimming pool, gyms, a indoor track, climbing wall, indoor speed-skating arena, outdoor stadium, rooms for weight training room, aerobics, combatives, squash, tennis, and racquetball courts. There is also an outdoor recreation center. **Graduates:** The most popular majors were arts, science, and engineering.

SERVICES: Counseling and information services are available, as is tutoring in most subjects, a reader service for the blind, and remedial math and writing. **Library/Resources:** Computerized library services include interlibrary loans, database searching, Internet access, and Wi-Fi capability. Special learning facilities include an art gallery, radio station, TV station, an environmental research center, observatory, human performance and theater labs, arts museum, children's hospital, and Foothills medical center. **Physically Challenged Students:** All of the campus is accessible. Facilities include wheelchair ramps, elevators, special parking, specially equipped restrooms, special class scheduling, lowered drinking fountains, lowered telephones, and special housing. **Special:** The university offers co-op programs in arts, actuarial science, applied chemistry, business, arts, engineering, and computer science. Dual majors, combined degrees in many disciplines, and study abroad in 61 countries are also available. Students may cross-register with any of 8 member colleges in the Big Country Education Consortium. U of C sponsors or is affiliated with 20 research institutes and groups. There is a freshman honors program. **Visiting:** There are regularly scheduled orientations for prospective students. There are guides for informal visits and visitors may stay overnight. To schedule a visit, contact Student Enrollment Services at (403) 210-7625. **Campus Safety and Security:** Measures include 24-hour foot and vehicle patrol, emergency notification system, security escort services, emergency telephones, lighted pathways/sidewalks, and controlled access to dorms/residences.

REQUIREMENTS: U.S. applicants must be graduates of a secondary school and submit SAT or ACT scores, as required by the individual faculties. AP credits are accepted. To graduate, all students must satisfy the required courses, course sequences, and credit distribution in their particular program. Students must maintain a minimum 2.0 GPA and complete 7 to 10 full-course equivalents in the major field. **Procedure:** Freshmen are admitted in the fall. There is an early admissions plan. Check with the school for current application deadlines. The application fee is $125. Applications are accepted on-line. **Transfer Students:** Applicants must have a cumulative GPA of 2.0 or above on all transfer courses. **International Students:** There are 1637 international students enrolled. The school actively recruits these students. They must take the TOEFL, or take the IELTS, the CAEL, or the university's English program. They must also take the SAT or ACT.

Admissions Contact: Email: *future.students@ucalgary.ca* Web: *www.ucalgary.ca*

FINANCIAL AID: Check with the school for current application deadlines.

UNIVERSITY OF ALBERTA — C-2

www.ualberta.ca

Edmonton, AB T6G 2M7 — (780) 492-3113

Fax: (780) 492-7172
Email: admissions@ualberta.ca
Full-time: 12,346 men, 15,665 women
Faculty: 1659
Part-time: 691 men, 1147 women
Ph.D.s: 92%
Graduate: 3550 men, 3594 women
Student/Faculty: n/av
Year: semesters, summer session
Tuition: $5829 ($18,459)
Room & Board: $6502
Freshman Class: 10587 applied, 6131 accepted, 4812 enrolled
SAT: recommended
CEEB CODE: 0963
Application Deadline: November 1

University of Alberta, founded in 1908, is a publicly supported institution offering undergraduate and graduate programs in arts and science, agricultural sciences, business, education, engineering, nursing, phys ed, native studies, and professional studies. The figures in the above capsule and in this profile are approximate. The fall tuition cost is for Canadian citizens and permanent residents. Tuition cost varies by program chosen by student. There are 18 undergraduate schools and 1 graduate school. The 155-acre campus is in an urban area 2 miles southwest of downtown Edmonton, Canada. Including any residence halls, there are 90 buildings.

STUDENT LIFE: Students are from 130 foreign countries, and Canada. **Female To Male Ratio:** 1.2:1. The average age of freshmen is 19; all undergraduates, 22. **Housing:** 4900 students can be accommodated in college housing, which includes single-sex and coed dorms, on-campus apartments, off-campus apartments, and married student housing. In addition, there are honors houses, language houses, special-interest houses, fraternity houses, and sorority houses. 88% of students commute. All students may keep cars.

FACULTY/CLASSROOMS: All teach undergraduates, and all do research. No introductory courses are taught by graduate students. The average class size in an introductory lecture is 90; in a laboratory is 20; and in a regular course is 35.

PROGRAMS OF STUDY: U of A confers B.A., B.Comm., B.Ed., B.F.A., B.Mus., B.P.E., B.S.C., B.S.Cn. and B.des. degrees. Master's and doctoral degrees are also awarded. Bachelor's degrees are awarded in AGRICULTURE (agricultural economics, agriculture, animal science, and soil science), BIOLOGICAL SCIENCE (biochemistry, biology/biological science, botany, cell biology, entomology, genetics, microbiology, physiology, and zoology), BUSINESS (accounting, management science, and marketing/retailing/merchandising), COMMUNICATIONS AND THE ARTS (classics, comparative literature, dance, dramatic arts, English, film arts, French, Germanic languages and literature, linguistics, music, romance languages and literature, and Slavic languages), COMPUTER AND PHYSICAL SCIENCE (applied mathematics, chemistry, computer science, earth science, geology, geophysics and seismology, mathematics, physical sciences, physics, and statistics), EDUCATION (education of the deaf and hearing impaired, education of the multiply handicapped, elementary education, physical education, secondary education, special education, and vocational education), ENGINEERING AND ENVIRONMENTAL DESIGN (chemical engineering technology, civil engineering, computer engineering, electrical/electronics engineering, engineering physics, mechanical engineering, metallurgical engineering, mining and mineral engineering, and petroleum/natural gas engineering), HEALTH PROFESSIONS (medical laboratory science, nursing, occupational therapy, pharmacy, and physical therapy), SOCIAL SCIENCE (anthropology, Canadian studies, clothing and textiles management/production/services, criminology, East Asian studies, Eastern European studies, economics, geography, history, law, philosophy, political science/government, psychology, sociology, and women's studies). Arts, science, and engineering have the largest enrollments.

ACTIVITIES: There are 400 groups on campus, including art, band, cheerleading, chess, choir, chorale, chorus, computers, dance, debate, drama, environmental, ethnic, film, forensics, honors, international, jazz band, LGBT, musical theater, newspaper, opera, orchestra, pep band, photography, political, radio and TV, religious, social, social service, student government, and symphony. Popular campus events include WOW (week of welcome) and AntiFreeze (winter activity). **Sports:** There are 12 intercollegiate sports for men and 13 for women, and 60 intramural sports for men and 45 for women. Facilities include a stadium, swimming pools, gyms, combatives and weight rooms, ballet/fencing and aerobics studios, 400-meter outdoor track, an ice arena, racquetball and squash courts, wrestling, an indoor field house, sports medicine clinic, training center for disabled athletes, curling rinks, and tennis courts.

SERVICES: Counseling and information services are available, as is tutoring in most subjects. There is a reader service for the blind, and remedial math, reading, and writing. **Library/Resources:** The 13 libraries contain 5.4 million volumes and 3.7 million microform items. Computerized library services include interlibrary loans, database searching, Internet access, and Wi-Fi capability. Special learning facilities include an art gallery, radio station, an agricultural meteorological research station, ecological sanctuary, botanical garden, the Kurimoto Japanese Garden, and Timms Centre for the Arts. **Physically Challenged Students:** 98% of the campus is accessible. Facilities include wheelchair ramps, elevators, special parking, specially equipped restrooms, special class scheduling, lowered drinking fountains, lowered telephones, and automatic doors. **Special:** The university offers co-op programs in business and engineering. Opportunities for study abroad, internships, dual majors, bilingual classes in French and English, credit by exam (special assessment), and pass/fail options are also available. There is 1 national honor society and a freshman honors program. **Visiting:** There are regularly scheduled orientations for prospective students, including University Open House on the first weekend in October and Orientation for new students held on campus 2 days before classes begin in the fall term. There are guides for informal visits, visitors may sit in on classes, and stay overnight. To schedule a visit, contact the Office of the Registrar and Student Awards. **Campus Safety and Security:** Measures include 24-hour foot and vehicle patrol, emergency notification system, self-defense education, and security escort services. There are emergency telephones, lighted pathways/sidewalks, and controlled access to dorms/residences.

REQUIREMENTS: The SAT is recommended. Graduation from an accredited secondary school is required. A minimum GPA of 70 is required in all courses submitted for academic credit. Depending on the program selected by the student, an essay, portfolio, audition, or interview may be required. AP credits are accepted. The requirements for graduation vary according to the program. A minimum GPA of 2.0 and at least 120 credit hours are required for graduation. **Procedure:** Freshmen are admitted to all sessions. There is an early admissions plan. Applications should be filed by November 1 for fall entry; November 15 for winter entry; and March 1 for spring entry, along with a $115 fee. Notification of early decision is sent January 2; regular decision, August 1. Applications are accepted on-line. **Transfer Students:** 4609 transfer students enrolled in 2016-2017. Applicants must meet minimum matriculation requirements or complete 24 credits of transferable work with satisfactory standing. The deadlines to send in official documents for fall admission is June 15 for post-secondary transfer applicants. August 1 for high school applicants. 60 of 120 credits required for the bachelor's degree must be completed at U of A. **International Students:** There are 1885 international students enrolled. The school actively recruits these students. They must take the TOEFL with a minimum score of 580 on the paper-based TOEFL (PBT) or 86 on the Internet-based version (iBT) or take the MELAB, the IELTS, the CAEL, or the university's own test.

ADMISSIONS: 58% of the 2017-2019 applicants were accepted. **Admissions Contact:** Office of the Registrar and Student Awards Email: *admissions@ualberta.ca* Web: *www.ualberta.ca*

FINANCIAL AID: Check with the school for current application deadlines.

SIMON FRASER UNIVERSITY B-2

www.sfu.ca

Burnaby, BC V5A 1S6 **(778) 782-3995**

Fax: (778) 782-4969 **Email: reginfo@sfu.ca**

Full-time: 7000 men, 7094 women	**Faculty:** n/av
Part-time: 7094 men, 8293 women	**Ph.D.s:** 88%
Graduate: 2000 men, 3400 women	**Student/Faculty:** n/av
Year: varies, summer session	**Tuition:** $6724 ($17,984)
Room & Board: $7484	**Freshman Class:** n/av
SAT: required	**CEEB CODE:** 0999
Application Deadline: October 1	

Simon Fraser University, established in 1965, is a public institution offering undergraduate and graduate programs in the arts, sciences, business, education, and applied sciences. In addition to its main campus, the university maintains the Harbour Centre campus in downtown Vancouver to provide mid-career education to the urban population and the new SFU Surrey campus offering programs in information technology and interactive arts. The figures given in the above capsule and in this profile are approximate. There are 8 undergraduate schools and 35 graduate schools. The 400-acre campus is in a suburban area 9 miles east of Vancouver, Canada. Including any residence halls, there are 51 buildings.

STUDENT LIFE: 89% of undergraduates are from British Columbia. Others are from 107 foreign countries, and Canada. 92% are from public schools. **Female To Male Ratio:** 1.2:1. The average age of freshmen is 19; all undergraduates, 23. **Housing:** 1750 students can be accommodated in college housing, which includes single-sex and coed dorms, on-campus apartments, and married student housing. In addition, there are special-interest houses. On-campus housing is guaranteed for the freshman year only. Priority is given to out-of-town students. 92% of students commute. All students may keep cars.

FACULTY/CLASSROOMS: 71% of faculty are male; 29% are female. No introductory courses are taught by graduate students.

PROGRAMS OF STUDY: SFU confers B.A., B.A.Sc., B.B.A., B.E.D., B.F.A., B.G.S., and B.Sc. degrees. Master's and doctoral degrees are also awarded. Bachelor's degrees are awarded in BIOLOGICAL SCIENCE (biology/biological science, molecular biology, and physiology), BUSINESS (business administration and management and management science), COMMUNICATIONS AND THE ARTS (art, communications, dance, dramatic arts, English, film arts, French, linguistics, music, and visual and performing arts), COMPUTER AND PHYSICAL SCIENCE (actuarial science, applied mathematics, applied physics, chemistry, computer science, earth science, mathematics, physics, science, and statistics), EDUCATION (education), ENGINEERING AND ENVIRONMENTAL DESIGN (engineering and applied science and environmental science), SOCIAL SCIENCE (anthropology, archeology, Canadian studies, cognitive science, criminology, economics, geography, history, humanities, liberal arts/general studies, philosophy, physical fitness/movement, political science/government, psychology, sociology, and women's studies). Engineering science is the strongest academically. Business administration, psychology, and computing science have the largest enrollments.

ACTIVITIES: There are no fraternities or sororities. There are 35 groups on campus, including chess, choir, ethnic, international, LGBT, newspaper, political, professional, religious, social, social service, and student government. Popular campus events include Terry Fox Day, Gung Hagis Fat Choi, and Robbie Burns Day. **Sports:** There are 8 intercollegiate sports for men and 9 for women, and 8 intramural sports for men and 7 for women. Facilities include swimming and diving pools, multi gyms, a running track, weight rooms, playing fields, a combative room, tennis, squash, racquetball courts, and a fitness center. **Graduates:** The most popular majors were business, education, and economics.

SERVICES: There is a reader service for the blind. There are taped library books, and some lectures are taped. **Library/Resources:** The 3 libraries contain 2.6 million volumes, 936,808 microform items, and 22,649 audio/video tapes/CDs/DVDs, and subscribe to 67,000 periodicals including electronic. Computerized library services include interlibrary loans, database searching, Internet access, and Wi-Fi capability. Special learning facilities include an art gallery, an archeology museum, special literature and map collections, fine and performing arts theater, hypo/hyperbaric chamber, back test unit, rock climbing wall, apiary, underwater lab, television and photography studios, and dance floors. **Physically Challenged Students:** 95% of the campus is accessible. Facilities include wheelchair ramps, elevators, special parking, specially equipped restrooms, lowered drinking fountains, lowered telephones, and special housing. There is also a Braille printer, a visualtek machine, closed-circuit TV for text or graphic enlargement, note taking tutor support, adaptive technology, exam modifications, sign language interpreters, closed captioning in lectures, and alternate format texts. **Special:** Simon Fraser offers cooperative education in most areas of study, study abroad in 47 countries, many opportunities for joint majors, a general studies degree, work-study programs, dual-majors, student-designed majors, and a variety of certificate and diploma programs, as well as nondegree and evening study. Interdisciplinary majors are offered in such areas as chemical physics, management and systems science, mathematical physics, and physics and physiology. There is a freshman honors program and 48 departmental honors programs. **Visiting:** There are regularly scheduled orientations for prospective students, consisting of regularly scheduled 1-day campus orientations for prospective students. There are guides for informal visits and visitors may stay overnight. To schedule a visit, contact the Residence and Housing Office at (778) 782-4201. **Campus Safety and Security:** Measures include 24-hour foot and vehicle patrol and security escort services. There are emergency telephones, lighted pathways/sidewalks, controlled access to dorms/residences, safe-walk stations, and student patrols.

REQUIREMENTS: The ACT is recommended. The SAT is required for U.S. applicants. Applicants must be graduates of an accredited secondary school and have a minimum grade average of 70%. A GPA of 3.2 is required. AP credits are accepted. General bachelor's degrees require completion of 120 semester hours with a 2.0 cumulative GPA. For a honors degrees, students must complete 132 hours. Some programs require a thesis. **Procedure:** Freshmen are admitted to all sessions. There are early decision and early admissions plans. Early decision applications should be filed by July 10; regular applications, by October 1 for fall entry; and August 1 for spring entry. The fall 2017 application fee was $45. Applications are accepted online. **Transfer Students:** 2603 transfer students enrolled in 2016-2017. Applicants must have a minimum GPA of 2.0 and be in good standing at their previous school. 60 of 120 credits required for the bachelor's degree must be completed at SFU. **International Students:** There are 2889 international students enrolled. The school actively recruits these students. They must take the TOEFL, or take the IELTS (minimum score 6.5 on academic modules).

Admissions Contact: Dr. Gordon M. Myers, Associate VP of Academic. Email: *reginfo@sfu.ca* Web: *www.sfu.ca*

FINANCIAL AID: The FAFSA code is G08444. The priority date for freshman financial aid applications for fall entry is February 28.

THE UNIVERSITY OF BRITISH COLUMBIA B-2

www.ubc.ca

Vancouver, BC V6T 1Z1 **(604) 822-3014**
(877) 272-1422

Fax: (604) 822-3599 **Email: recruitment.ok@ubc.ca**

Full-time: 10,044 men, 11,332 women	**Faculty:** n/av
Part-time: 3357 men, 4090 women	**Ph.D.s:** 99%
Graduate: 6861 men, 8293 women	**Student/Faculty:** 15 to 1
Year: other, summer session	**Tuition:** $5175 ($21,150)
Room & Board: $6650	**Freshman Class:** 23102 applied, 12285 accepted, 6225 enrolled
SAT or ACT: required	**CEEB CODE:** 0965
Application Deadline: February 28	

University of British Columbia, established in 1908, is a publicly supported institution offering a wide range of undergraduate, graduate, and professional programs in the arts, sciences, and other fields of study. The figures in the above capsule and in this profile are approximate. There are 16 undergraduate schools and 1 graduate school. The 1000-acre campus is in an urban area 6 miles from the center of Vancouver, Canada. Including any residence halls, there are 500 buildings.

STUDENT LIFE: 87% of undergraduates are from British Columbia. Others are from 43 states, 139 foreign countries, and Canada. 98% are from public schools. 14% are Foreign. **Female To Male Ratio:** 1.2:1. The average age of freshmen is 20; all undergraduates, 21. 8% do not continue beyond their first year; 92% remain to graduate. **Housing:** 9500 students can be accommodated in college housing, which includes single-sex and coed dorms, on-campus apartments, and married student housing. In addition, there are special-interest houses, International houses: Japanese, Korean, Mexican and Hong Kong. On-campus housing is guaranteed for the freshman year only, and is available on a first-come, first-served basis, and is available on a lottery system for upperclassmen. Priority is given to out-of-town students. 80% of students commute. All students may keep cars.

FACULTY/CLASSROOMS: 62% of faculty are male; 38% are female. No introductory courses are taught by graduate students.

PROGRAMS OF STUDY: UBC confers B.A., B.A.H.S., B.A.Sc., B.B.R.E., B.Com.B.C.S., B.D.Sc., B.Ed., B.End., B.F.A., B.H.E., B.H.K., B.Mgt., B.M.LSc., B.Mus., B.Mw., B.Sc., B.Sc.Die., B.Sc.F., B.Sc.Pharm., B.S.F., B.S.N., B.S.W., and L.L.B. degrees. Master's and doctoral degrees are also awarded. Bachelor's degrees are awarded in AGRICULTURE (agricultural economics, animal science, forestry production and processing, forestry and related sciences, horticulture, natural resource management, and soil science), BIOLOGICAL SCIENCE (biochemistry, biology/biological science, biophysics, biotechnology, microbiology, nutrition, physiology, and zoology), BUSINESS (accounting, banking and finance, business administration and management, business economics, human resources, international business management, management information systems, marketing/retailing/merchandising, real estate, recreational facilities management, and transportation management), COMMUNICATIONS AND THE ARTS (art history and appreciation, Chinese, classics, creative writing, dramatic arts, English, film arts, fine arts, French, German, Italian, Japanese, linguistics, music, music history and appreciation, music performance, music theory and composition, romance languages and literature, and Spanish), COMPUTER AND PHYSICAL SCIENCE (astronomy, atmospheric sciences and meteorology, chemistry, computer science, earth science, geophysics and seismology, mathematics, oceanography, physics, science, and statistics), EDUCATION (elementary education, museum studies, and physical education), ENGINEERING AND ENVIRONMENTAL DESIGN (chemical engineering, civil engineering, computer engineering, electrical/electronics engineering, engineering, engineering physics, environmental design, environmental engineering, environmental science, geological engineering, mechanical engineering, metallurgical engineering, and mining and mineral engineering), HEALTH PROFESSIONS (exercise science, health, nursing, pharmacology, preveterinary science, and speech pathology/audiology), SOCIAL SCIENCE (anthropology, archeology, Asian/Oriental studies, Canadian studies, classical/ancient civilization, cognitive science, dietetics, economics, European studies, family/consumer studies, food production/management/services, food science, geography, Hispanic American studies, history, home economics, human ecology, international relations, Latin American studies, medieval studies, Native American studies, philosophy, political science/government, psychology, religion, sociology, South Asian studies, and women's studies). Applied sciences, and commerce are the strongest academically. Education, and arts have the largest enrollments.

ACTIVITIES: 6% of men belong to 7 national fraternities; 2% of women belong to 7 national sororities. There are 250 groups on campus, including varsity outdoors, art, band, cheerleading, chess, choir, chorale, chorus, computers, dance, debate, drama, environmental, ethnic, film, honors, international, jazz band, LGBT, literary magazine, musical theater, newspaper, opera, orchestra, photography, political, professional, radio and TV, religious, ski and snowboard, social, social service, student government, symphony, and yearbook. Popular campus events include Storm the Wall, Day of the Longboat, and Great Trek Run. **Sports:** There are 13 intercollegiate sports for men and 11 for women, and 18 intramural sports for men and 18 for women. Facilities include a winter sports center, a 3500-seat stadium, a gym, an aquatic center, playing fields, a recreation center, a tennis center, and a rowing centre. **Graduates:** The most popular majors were psychology, biology, and English.

SERVICES: Counseling and information services are available, as is tutoring in most subjects. There is a reader service for the blind, and remedial math, reading, and writing. **Library/Resources:** The 22 libraries contain 5.6 million volumes, 5.2 million microform items, and 840,000 audio/video tapes/CDs/DVDs, and subscribe to 63,000 periodicals including electronic. Computerized library services include interlibrary loans, database searching, Internet access, and Wi-Fi capability. Special learning facilities include an art gallery, natural history museum, radio station, a learning center, and anthropology museum. Canada's largest accelerator for subatomic physics, space observatory, center for integrated computer systems research, center for the study of global issues, and a center for the performing arts. **Physically Challenged Students:** 95% of the campus is accessible. Facilities include wheelchair ramps, elevators, special parking, specially equipped restrooms, special class scheduling, lowered drinking fountains, lowered telephones, and special housing. Accessible shower stalls in fitness facilities, tactile maps, TTY pay phones, an accessible security bus, and audible street crossing signals. **Special:** UBC offers co-op programs in science, applied science, commerce, arts, and forestry, and study abroad through 190 student exchange opportunities in 41 countries. Non-degree study is possible. A B.A.-B.A.Sc. degree, student-designed majors, dual majors in most faculties, and work-study programs are available. There are 1 national honor societies and 10 departmental honors programs. **Visiting:** There are regularly scheduled orientations for prospective students, Monday through Saturday. There are guides for informal visits, visitors may sit in on classes, and stay overnight. **Campus Safety and Security:** Measures include 24-hour foot and vehicle patrol and security escort services. There are shuttle buses, emergency telephones, lighted pathways/sidewalks, controlled access to dorms/residences, Royal Canadian mounted police detachment is on campus, awareness programs on theft, and personal safety lectures.

REQUIREMENTS: The SAT or ACT is required. The ACT Optional Writing test is also required. Graduation from an accredited secondary school is required. General admission for students following a U.S. system is based on 4 years of English and 3 years of math. There are also specific program requirements in math, chemistry, physics, and biology for students applying to science-based programs. U.S. curriculum students are required to submit SAT or ACT and writing scores. Exemptions may begin where these tests are not available. A GPA of 2.6 is required. AP credits are accepted. Important factors in the admissions decision are extracurricular activities record, leadership record, and recommendations by school officials. To graduate, students must complete 120 credits in arts or science, more for applied science. Total number of hours required in a major varies by faculty. English is required for all majors. **Procedure:** Freshmen are admitted fall and spring. There are early admissions, deferred admissions, and rolling admissions plans. Applications should be filed by February 28 for fall entry; February 28 for spring entry; and February 28 for summer entry, along with a $100 fee. Applications are accepted on-line. **Transfer Students:** 1829 transfer students enrolled in 2015-2016. Official transcripts, completion of the equivalent of 24 course credits, and no failures are required. A competitive GPA is required to get into the program at the second or third year. Applicants must have attended an accredited post-secondary institution. 60 of 120 credits required for the bachelor's degree must be completed at UBC. **International Students:** There are 4442 international students enrolled. The school actively recruits these students. They must also take the SAT or ACT.

ADMISSIONS: 53% of the 2017-2018 applicants were accepted. 96% of the current freshmen were in the top fifth of their class. **Admissions Contact:** Office of the Registrar Email: *recruitment.ok@ubc.ca* Web: *www.ubc.ca*

FINANCIAL AID: The college's own financial statement is required. The FAFSA code is G08369. Check with the school for current application deadlines.

UNIVERSITY OF VICTORIA — B-2

www.uvic.ca

Victoria, BC V8W 2YZ	(250) 721-7211
Fax: (250) 721-7212	**Email:** recruitment@uvic.ca
Full-time: 6000 men, 6046 women	**Faculty:** 721
Part-time: 2957 men, 2958 women	**Ph.D.s:** 96%
Graduate: 1180 men, 1384 women	**Student/Faculty:** 15 to 1
Year: semesters, summer session	**Tuition:** $6027
Room & Board: $8000	**Freshman Class:** 11576 applied, 8443 accepted, 4309 enrolled
	CEEB CODE: 0989
Application Deadline: February 28	

University of Victoria, founded in 1903, is a public institution operated by the province of British Columbia. It offers undergraduate and graduate programs in the arts and sciences, business, education, engineering, fine arts, human and social development, and law. There are 10 undergraduate schools and 2 graduate schools. The 400-acre campus is in an urban area in Victoria. Including any residence halls, there are 107 buildings.

STUDENT LIFE: 86% of undergraduates are from British Columbia. 92% are from public schools. **Female To Male Ratio:** 1.0:1. The average age of freshmen is 21. **Housing:** 2200 students can be accommodated in college housing, which includes single-sex and coed dorms, on-campus apartments, and married student housing. There is also an off-campus housing registry service. On-campus housing is guaranteed for the freshman year only, is available on a first-come, first-served basis, and is available on a lottery system for upperclassmen. Priority is given to out-of-town students. 89% of students commute. All students may keep cars.

FACULTY/CLASSROOMS: 61% of faculty are male; 39% are female. All teach undergraduates, and do research. No introductory courses are taught by graduate students. The average class size in an introductory lecture is 53 and in a regular course is 30.

PROGRAMS OF STUDY: UVic confers B.A., B.S., B.Com., B.Ed., B.Eng., B.F.A., B.Mus., B.Sc., B.S.N., B.S.W. and L.L.B. degrees. Master's and doctoral degrees are also awarded. Bachelor's degrees are awarded in AGRICULTURE (environmental studies), BIOLOGICAL SCIENCE (biochemistry, biology/biological science, and microbiology), BUSINESS (business administration and management, hospitality management services, international business management, and recreation and leisure services), COMMUNICATIONS AND THE ARTS (art history and appreciation, classics, creative writing, dramatic arts, English, French, Germanic languages and literature, linguistics, music, and visual and performing arts), COMPUTER AND PHYSICAL SCIENCE (astronomy, chemistry, computer science, earth science, mathematics, physics, software engineering, and statistics), EDUCATION (elementary education, physical education, and secondary education), ENGINEERING AND ENVIRONMENTAL DESIGN (computer engineering, electrical/electronics engineering, and mechanical engineering), HEALTH PROFESSIONS (health science and nursing), SOCIAL SCIENCE (anthropology, child care/child and family studies, economics, geography, Hispanic American studies, history, Italian studies, Latin American studies, medieval studies, Pacific area studies, philosophy, political science/government, psychology, Russian and Slavic studies, social work, sociology, and women's studies). Writing is the strongest academically.

ACTIVITIES: There are no fraternities or sororities. Groups on campus include art, chess, choir, chorus, computers, dance, debate, drama, environmental, ethnic, honors, international, jazz band, LGBT, musical theater, newspaper, orchestra, photography, political, radio and TV, religious, social, social service, student government, symphony, and yearbook. Popular campus events include Week of Welcome, the President's BBQ, and Experience Uvic (Spring open house). **Sports:** There are 7 intercollegiate sports for men and 7 for women, and 12 intramural sports for men and 12 for women. Facilities include 3 gyms, a dance studio, weight and fitness training rooms, racquetball and squash courts, playing fields, an outdoor stadium, tennis courts, swimming pools, a sailing compound, and jogging trails.

SERVICES: Counseling and information services are available, as is tutoring in most subjects. There is remedial reading and writing. **Library/Resources:** The 4 libraries contain 1.9 million volumes, 2.3 million microform items, and 110,600 audio/video tapes/CDs/DVDs, and subscribe to 40,000 periodicals including electronic. Computerized library services include interlibrary loans, database searching, Internet access, and Wi-Fi capability. Special learning facilities include an art gallery, radio station, and language labs. **Physically Challenged Students:** 95% of the campus is accessible. Facilities include wheelchair ramps, elevators, special parking, specially equipped restrooms, lowered drinking fountains, lowered telephones, and special housing. **Special:** A number of co-op and internship programs are available in specific disciplines as are many dual majors, including biochemistry/microbiology and Hispanic/Italian studies. Work-study is possible on a limited basis for Canadian students only. Study abroad is offered in 19 countries. There are 37 departmental honors programs. **Visiting:** There are regularly scheduled orientations for prospective students. There are guides for informal visits, visitors may sit in on classes, and stay overnight. To schedule a visit, contact the Campus Tours at (250) 472-4935. **Campus Safety and Security:** Measures include 24-hour foot and vehicle patrol, self-defense education, and security escort services. There are emergency telephones and lighted pathways/sidewalks.

REQUIREMENTS: Application requires high school graduation with a 2.5 GPA or higher, 4 semesters of English, 2 each of social science, math, science, and language, and 6 semesters of 2.5 work at grade 12 level. Applications are accepted online at the school's web site. A GPA of 67.0 is required. AP credits are accepted. To graduate, students must complete the university English requirement, a minimum of 60 units above the 100 level, at least 21 of which must be upper level, and have a 2.0 GPA. **Procedure:** Freshmen are admitted to all sessions. There are early admissions and deferred admissions plans. Early decision applications should be filed by November 30; regular applications, by February 28 for fall entry; and October 31 for winter entry. The fall 2017 application fee was $60. Applications are accepted on-line. **Transfer Students:** 2000 transfer students enrolled in 2016-2017. Requirements vary with the program and the individual. Check with the school's admissions requirements for transfer students. 30 of 60 credits required for the bachelor's degree must be completed at UVic. **International Students:** There are 2000 international students enrolled. The school actively recruits these students. They must take the TOEFL with a minimum score of 530 on the paper-based TOEFL (PBT) or 71 on the Internet-based version (iBT) or take the MELAB, or take the International English Language Testing System (IELTS).

ADMISSIONS: 73% of the 2017-2018 applicants were accepted. **Admissions Contact:** Wendy Joyce, Admissions Office. Email: *recruitment@uvic.ca* Web: *www.uvic.ca*

FINANCIAL AID: Check with the school for current application deadlines.

MEMORIAL UNIVERSITY OF NEWFOUNDLAND F-2

www.mun.ca

St. John's, NF A1C 5S7	(709) 864-4431 (866) 354-8896
Fax: (709) 864-4893	**Email:** admissions@mun.ca
Full-time: 5000 men, 7000 women	**Faculty:** 932
Part-time: 690 men, 1350 women	**Ph.D.s:** 50%
Graduate: 840 men, 760 women	**Student/Faculty:** 12 to 1
Year: varies, summer session	**Tuition:** $8800 ($11,440)
Room & Board: $10,307	**Freshman Class:** n/av **CEEB CODE:** 0885
Application Deadline: March 1	

Memorial University of Newfoundland, founded in 1925, is a public liberal arts institution. The figures in the above capsule and in this profile are approximate. There are 13 undergraduate schools and 12 graduate schools. The 220-acre campus is in an urban area in St. John's. Including any residence halls, there are 40 buildings.

STUDENT LIFE: 98% of undergraduates are from Newfoundland. Others are from 90 foreign countries. **Female To Male Ratio:** 1.4:1. **Housing:** 1750 students can be accommodated in college housing, which includes single-sex and coed dorms, on-campus apartments, off-campus apartments, and married student housing. On-campus housing is available on a first-come and first-served basis. Priority is given to out-of-town students. 89% of students commute. All students may keep cars.

FACULTY/CLASSROOMS: 80% of faculty are male; 20% are female. All teach undergraduates, and do research. Graduate students teach 71% of introductory courses. The average class size in an introductory lecture is 40.

PROGRAMS OF STUDY: MUN confers B.A., B.Sc., B.Comm.(Co-op.), B.Comm.(Gen.), B.Ed., B.Eng., B.F.A., B.Kin., B.M.S., B.Mus., B.Mus.Ed., B.Med.Sc., B.N., B.P.E., B.Rec., B.Sc.(Pharm.), B.Spec.Ed., B.S.W., B.Tech., and B.Voc.Ed. degrees. Master's and doctoral degrees are also awarded. Bachelor's degrees are awarded in AGRICULTURE (forestry and related sciences), BIOLOGICAL SCIENCE (biochemistry, biology/biological science, cell biology, ecology, entomology, environmental biology, evolutionary biology, marine biology, marine science, microbiology, and neurosciences), BUSINESS (entrepreneurial studies, human resources, labor studies, management science, marketing/retailing/merchandising, organizational behavior, and small business management), COMMUNICATIONS AND THE ARTS (dramatic arts, English, English literature, fine arts, folklore and mythology, French, German, linguistics, literature, music, music history and appreciation, music performance, music theory and composition, Russian, Spanish, and visual and performing arts), COMPUTER AND PHYSICAL SCIENCE (applied mathematics, applied physics, chemistry, computer science, earth science, information sciences and systems, mathematics, oceanography, and statistics), EDUCATION (athletic training, education, elementary education, guidance education, middle school education, music education, physical education, recreation education, secondary education, and special education), ENGINEERING AND ENVIRONMENTAL DESIGN (civil engineering, electrical/electronics engineering, engineering technology, maritime science, mechanical engineering, naval architecture and marine engineering, and ocean engineering), HEALTH PROFESSIONS (medical science, nursing, and pharmacy), SOCIAL SCIENCE (anthropology, archeology, Canadian studies, criminology, dietetics, economics, French studies, geography, German area studies, history, humanities, medieval studies, philosophy, physical fitness/movement, political science/government, psychology, religion, social studies, social work, sociology, Spanish studies, and women's studies). Marine biology, naval architecture, and business are the strongest academically. Arts, science, business, and engineering have the largest enrollments.

ACTIVITIES: There are no fraternities or sororities. There are 100 groups on campus, including an academic club, band, cheerleading, chess, choir, chorale, computers, dance, debate, drama, ethnic, international, jazz band, LGBT, literary magazine, musical theater, newspaper, orchestra, photography, political, professional, radio and TV, religious, single parent, social, social service, student government, symphony, and yearbook. Popular campus events include Winter Carnival and Orientation. **Sports:** There are 6 intercollegiate sports for men and 6 for women, and 6 intramural sports for men and 6 for women. Facilities include a gym, squash courts, a rifle range, a weight room, a soccer field, and swimming facilities. **Graduates:** The most popular majors were business, biology, and sociology.

SERVICES: There is a reader service for the blind, and remedial math, reading, and writing. Students staying in residence have access to tutoring in every subject. In addition, lectures are offered on topics such as public speaking, speed reading, and time management. **Library/Resources:** The 3 libraries contain 2.5 million volumes, and subscribe to 700 periodicals including electronic. Computerized library services include interlibrary loans and database searching. Special learning facilities include an art gallery, natural history museum, planetarium, radio station, TV station, and a language lab. **Physically Challenged Students:** 85% of the campus is accessible. Facilities include wheelchair ramps, elevators, special parking, specially equipped restrooms, special class scheduling, lowered drinking fountains, lowered telephones, classroom aids, note-taking volunteers, and other facilities based on individual needs. **Special:** The university offers co-op programs in commerce, phys ed, recreation, kinesiology, and engineering. Internships are available in education and nursing. Study abroad may be arranged in at least 20 countries. Work-study programs, dual majors, and B.A.-B.S. degrees are available. There are 3 departmental honors programs. **Visiting:** There are regularly scheduled orientations for prospective students, including various student activities, mock lectures, campus tours, and educational sessions. There are guides for informal visits and visitors may sit in on classes. To schedule a visit, contact the Student Development at (709) 737-2192. **Campus Safety and Security:** Measures include 24-hour foot and vehicle patrol, self-defense education, and security escort services. There are emergency telephones and lighted pathways/sidewalks.

REQUIREMENTS: Admission is based on a 70% high school average as computed from university preparatory courses required for admission. Applications are accepted online. A GPA of 70.0 is required. AP credits are accepted. Students must complete 40 to 50 credits to graduate. Each discipline has different requirements for graduation. **Procedure:** Freshmen are admitted to all sessions. There is a rolling admissions plan. Applications should be filed by March 1 for fall entry; October 1 for winter entry; February 1 for spring entry; and February 1 for summer entry. The fall 2016 application fee was $80. **Transfer Students:** 499 transfer students enrolled in 2015-2016. Applicants must be in good academic standing at the previous institution. 10 of 40 credits required for the bachelor's degree must be completed at MUN. **International Students:** The school actively recruits these students. They must take the TOEFL or MELAB.

Admissions Contact: Phyllis McCann, Manager of Admissions. Email: *admissions@mun.ca* Web: *www.mun.ca*

FINANCIAL AID: The FAFSA code is G09500. Check with the school for current application deadlines.

DALHOUSIE UNIVERSITY F-2

www.dal.ca

Halifax, NS B3H 4R2 **(902) 494-2450**

Fax: (902) 494-1630 **Email: admissions@dal.ca**

Full-time: 9000 men, 9500 women
Part-time: n/av
Graduate: n/av
Year: semesters, summer session
Room & Board: $9220

Application Deadline: March 1

Faculty: 999
Ph.D.s: 90%
Student/Faculty: 17 to 1
Tuition: $9234
Freshman Class: n/av
CEEB CODE: 0915

Dalhousie University, founded in 1818. Students study at the undergraduate, graduate and professional levels in more than 180 programs. The figures in the above capsule and in this profile are approximate. There are 12 undergraduate schools. The campus is in an urban area in Halifax and Truro, Nova Scotia.

STUDENT LIFE: 59% of undergraduates are from out of state. Students are from 110 foreign countries. **Female To Male Ratio:** 1.1:1. **Housing:** 2200 students can be accommodated in college housing, which includes single-sex and coed dorms, on-campus apartments, off-campus apartments, and married student housing. In addition, there are special-interest houses. On-campus housing is available on a first-come, first-served basis, and is available on a lottery system for upperclassmen. Some may keep cars.

FACULTY/CLASSROOMS: No introductory courses are taught by graduate students.

PROGRAMS OF STUDY: Master's and doctoral degrees are also awarded. Bachelor's degrees are awarded in AGRICULTURE (agricultural economics, agricultural sciences, and animal science), BIOLOGICAL SCIENCE (biochemistry, biology/biological science, marine biology, microbiology, and neurosciences), BUSINESS (accounting, banking and finance, business administration and management, business economics, and recreation and leisure services), COMMUNICATIONS AND THE ARTS (classics, dramatic arts, English, French, German, music, Russian, and Spanish), COMPUTER AND PHYSICAL SCIENCE (chemistry, computer science, earth science, mathematics, physics, and statistics), EDUCATION (health education), ENGINEERING AND ENVIRONMENTAL DESIGN (chemical engineering, city/community/regional planning, and engineering), HEALTH PROFESSIONS (dental hygiene, nursing, occupational therapy, pharmacy, physical therapy, predentistry, and premedicine), SOCIAL SCIENCE (Canadian studies, economics, history, international studies, law, philosophy, physical fitness/movement, political science/government, psychology, religion, social work, sociology, and women's studies).

ACTIVITIES: There are no fraternities or sororities. There are 280 groups on campus, including cheerleading, chess, chorale, communications, computers, dance, debate, drama, environmental, ethnic, honors, international, LGBT, musical theater, newspaper, photography, political, professional, radio and TV, religious, social, social service, and student government. **Sports:** Facilities include cardio and weight training equipment, soccer fields, outdoor tennis courts, a track, an Olympic-size swimming pool, squash and volleyball courts, a climbing wall, and dance studio.

SERVICES: Counseling and information services are available, as is tutoring in most subjects. There is a reader service for the blind, and remedial math and writing. **Library/Resources:** Computerized library services include interlibrary loans, database searching, and Internet access. Special learning facilities include an art gallery, natural history museum, planetarium, and radio station. **Physically Challenged Students:** The Advising and Access Services Centre is available to assist students who require support. **Special:** There is a freshman honors program. **Visiting:** There are regularly scheduled orientations for prospective students. There are guides for informal visits and visitors may sit in on classes. To schedule a visit, contact the Campus Tours at (902) 494-2587. **Campus Safety and Security:** Measures include 24-hour foot and vehicle patrol, emergency notification system, self-defense education, and security escort services. There are shuttle buses, emergency telephones, lighted pathways/sidewalks, and controlled access to dorms/residences.

REQUIREMENTS: Applicants from the US must have an SAT result of at least 1650 or an ACT composite score of 23 and no individual score less than 20. Grade 12 credit in English is required. An audition is necessary for music students. AP credits are accepted. **Procedure:** Freshmen are admitted to all sessions. There are early decision, early admissions, deferred admissions, and rolling admissions plans. Applications should be filed by March 1 for fall entry, along with a $65 fee. Applications are accepted online. **Transfer Students:** Applicants are assessed on an individual basis. **International Students:** The school actively recruits these students. US applicants may submit either the SAT or ACT.

Admissions Contact: Krista Cross, Director, Communication & Assessment. Email: *admissions@dal.ca* Web: *www.dal.ca*

FINANCIAL AID: The FAFSA code is G06838. Check with the school for current application deadlines.

UNIVERSITY OF GUELPH E-3

www.uoguelph.ca

Guelph, ON N1G 2W1 **(519) 821-2130**

Fax: (519) 766-9481
Full-time: n/av
Part-time: n/av
Graduate: n/av
Year: varies, summer session
Room & Board: $10,924

SAT or ACT: required
Application Deadline: March 1

Email: admission@uoguelph.ca
Faculty: 800
Ph.D.s: 98%
Student/Faculty: 19 to 1
Tuition: $7660 ($21,514)
Freshman Class: 18852 applied, 13765 accepted, 3479 enrolled
CEEB CODE: 0892

University of Guelph, founded in 1964, is a public institution offering programs in arts and sciences, agriculture, engineering, commerce, landscape architecture, veterinary medicine, applied science, and technology. The approximate figures in the above capsule are based upon Canada and International students and varies by programs chosen. There are 7 undergraduate schools and 56 graduate schools. The 1017-acre campus is in a suburban area 2 miles south of the center of Guelph, Canada. Including any residence halls, there are 80 buildings.

STUDENT LIFE: 93% of undergraduates are from Ontario. Others are from 100 foreign countries, and Canada. The average age of freshmen is 18; all undergraduates, 21. 9% do not continue beyond their first year; 89% remain to graduate. **Housing:** 5500 students can be accommodated in college housing, which includes single-sex and coed dorms, on-campus apartments, off-campus apartments, and married student housing. In addition, there are language houses, special-interest houses, an international house, La Maison Francaise, Eco house, an arts house, and study intensive and academic clusters. On-campus housing is guaranteed for the freshman year only, and on a first-come, first-served basis, and is available on a lottery system for upperclassmen. 67% of students commute. All students may keep cars.

FACULTY/CLASSROOMS: No introductory courses are taught by graduate students. The average class size in an introductory lecture is 300 and in a laboratory is 25.

PROGRAMS OF STUDY: U of G confers B.A., B.A.S., B.A.Sc, B.B.R.M., B.Comm, B.Comp, B.Eng, B.L.A., B.Sc-Agr, B.Sc-Eng, B.Sc-Env, and B.Sc degrees. Master's and doctoral degrees are also awarded. Bachelor's degrees are awarded in AGRICULTURE (agricultural economics, agriculture, agronomy, animal science, horticulture, and natural resource management), BIOLOGICAL SCIENCE (biochemistry, biology/biological science, biophysics, ecology, environmental biology, marine science, microbiology, molecular biology, nutrition, wildlife biology, and zoology), BUSINESS (hospitality management services, human resources, marketing management, and real estate), COMMUNICATIONS AND THE ARTS (art history and appreciation, classical languages, English, music, Spanish, and studio art), COMPUTER AND PHYSICAL SCIENCE (chemical physics, chemistry, computer science, earth science, information sciences and systems, physical sciences, physics, and statistics), ENGINEERING AND ENVIRONMENTAL DESIGN (biomedical engineering, engineering, environmental engineering, and landscape architecture/design), SOCIAL SCIENCE (anthropology, child care/child and family studies, classical/ancient civilization, criminal justice, economics, food science, French studies, geography, gerontology, history, interdisciplinary studies, philosophy, political science/government, psychology, public administration, rural sociology, sociology, water resources, and women's studies). Biological and physical sciences and veterinary medicine is the strongest academically. Biological and physical sciences, arts, and social sciences have the largest enrollments.

ACTIVITIES: There are no fraternities or sororities. There are 100 groups on campus, including art, cheerleading, chess, choir, chorale, computers, dance, debate, drama, environmental, ethnic, international, jazz band, LGBT, literary magazine, newspaper, photography, political, professional, radio and TV, religious, social, social service, student government, and yearbook. Popular campus events include College Royal open house weekend in March. **Sports:** There are 15 intercollegiate sports for men and 15 for women, and 17 intramural sports for men and 17 for women. Facilities include a twin-pad arena, ice surface, squash courts, a fitness gym, weight-training rooms, swimming pools, a fitness circuit, and gyms. Outdoor facilities include tennis courts, a running track, lighted football, field hockey, soccer, rugby and fastball fields, jogging trails, and multipurpose fields. There are also dance studios, a climbing wall, wrestling/combatives room, covered field with artificial turf, and a track.

SERVICES: Counseling and information services are available, as is tutoring in most subjects, and a reader service for the blind. ESL, learning, studying, and writing resources are available. **Library/Resources:** The library contains 2.0 million volumes, 1.5 million microform items, and 17,000 audio/video tapes/CDs/DVDs, and subscribes to 7,600 periodicals including electronic. Computerized library services include interlibrary loans, database searching, Internet access, and Wi-Fi capability. Special learning facilities include an art gallery, radio station, an observatory, a learning commons, a research park, and arboretum. **Physically Challenged Students:** 90% of the campus is accessible. Facilities include wheelchair ramps, elevators, special parking, specially equipped restrooms, special class scheduling, lowered drinking fountains, lowered telephones, special housing, special library services, equipment, and software. **Special:** U of G offers co-op programs in 30 majors, study abroad in 29 countries, and work-study programs. Accelerated degree programs, dual majors, a general studies degree, and non-degree study are available. There is a freshman honors program and 33 departmental honors programs. **Visiting:** Regularly scheduled orientations are available for prospective students, as are daily tours of the campus, Fall Preview Day, Campus Day and Spring Academic Open House. There are guides for informal visits and visitors may sit in on classes. To schedule a visit, contact The Assistant Manager at (519) 824-4120, ext. 58712. **Campus Safety and Security:** Measures include 24-hour foot and vehicle patrol, emergency notification system, self-defense education, and security escort services. There are also shuttle buses, emergency telephones, lighted pathways/sidewalks, controlled access to dorms/residences, a campus safe walk, and a campus police patrol.

REQUIREMENTS: The SAT or ACT, the ACT Optional Writing test are required. U.S. applicants must have a minimum cumulative unweighted grade point average of 3.0 from a regionally accredited high school, and a combined math and critical reading SAT score of 1100 or ACT score of 24. Where class rankings are reported on the transcript, a ranking in the top quarter is preferred. Students should include among their senior level courses, specific courses that are required for admission to the degree program of their choice. Particular attention is paid to performance in program prerequisites. Students should ensure that senior year final grades from first and second semester interim grades are submitted before the document deadline date. AP credits are accepted. Important factors in the admissions decision are advanced placement or honors courses, extracurricular activities record, and leadership record. To graduate, students must complete 30 credits (half courses) for a general degree and 40 credits (half courses) for an honors degree. U of G requires a minimum of 10 credits in the major. **Procedure:** Freshmen are admitted in the fall. There are early decision and deferred admissions plans. Early decision applications should be filed by January 1; regular applications, by March 1 for fall entry, along with a $165 fee. Notifications are sent in March. 5000 early decision candidates were accepted for the 2017-2018 class. Applications are accepted online. **Transfer Students:** Applicants must meet general admissions requirements and have a B average in all college-level courses. **International Students:** There are 700 international students enrolled. The school actively recruits these students. They must take the TOEFL with a minimum score of 600 on the paper-based TOEFL (PBT) or 89 on the Internet-based version (iBT) or take the MELAB and the college's own test, CAEL, IELTS, and PTE. U.S. students are required to submit SAT or ACT scores, with minimum acceptable scores.

ADMISSIONS: 73% of the 2017-2018 applicants were accepted. **Admis-**

sions Contact: Admission Services. Email: *admission@uoguelph.ca* Web: *www.uoguelph.ca*

FINANCIAL AID: 30% of undergraduate students work part-time. The college's own financial statement and the Federal and Provincial Government Canadian Form are required. The FAFSA code is G06683. Check with the school for current application deadlines.

MCMASTER UNIVERSITY E-3

www.future.mcmaster.ca

Hamilton, ON L8S 4L8 **(905) 525-9140**

Fax: (905) 527-1105
Email: macadmit@mcmaster.ca
Full-time: 5400 men, 7000 women
Part-time: 900 men, 1900 women
Graduate: 1190 men, 1030 women
Year: n/app
Room & Board: $8298
Faculty: 927
Ph.D.s: n/av
Student/Faculty: 13 to 1
Tuition: $7418 ($27,448)
Freshman Class: n/av
CEEB CODE: 0936
Application Deadline: January 17

McMaster University is a public nonsectarian institution, offering programs in the arts and sciences, business, engineering, health sciences, kinesiology, and social work. The figures given in the above capsule and in this profile are approximate. The 300-acre campus is in an urban area 60 miles southwest of Toronto. Including any residence halls, there are 44 buildings.

STUDENT LIFE: 95% of undergraduates are from Ontario. Others are from 12 states, and 79 foreign countries. **Female To Male Ratio:** 1.3:1. The average age of freshmen is 20; all undergraduates, 22. 1% do not continue beyond their first year. **Housing:** 2765 students can be accommodated in college housing, which includes single-sex and coed dorms and on-campus apartments. In addition, there are language houses, La Maison Francaise, an international house, and a quiet house. On-campus housing is guaranteed for the freshman year only and is available on a lottery system for upperclassmen. Priority is given to out-of-town students. 77% of students commute. All students may keep cars.

FACULTY/CLASSROOMS: 71% of faculty are male; 29% are female. All teach undergraduates, all do research, and all teach and do research. No introductory courses are taught by graduate students.

PROGRAMS OF STUDY: Mac confers B.A., B.S., B.A.S., B.A./B.S.W., B.C., B.Eng., B.Eng./Management, B.Eng./Society, B.H.S., B.Kinesiology, B.Mus., and B.S.N. degrees. Master's and doctoral degrees are also awarded. Bachelor's degrees are awarded in BIOLOGICAL SCIENCE (biochemistry, biology/biological science, and life science), BUSINESS (business administration and management and labor studies), COMMUNICATIONS AND THE ARTS (art, art history and appreciation, classics, comparative literature, dramatic arts, English, French, linguistics, modern language, music, and Russian), COMPUTER AND PHYSICAL SCIENCE (chemistry, computer science, earth science, geology, mathematics, physical sciences, physics, science, and statistics), ENGINEERING AND ENVIRONMENTAL DESIGN (chemical engineering, civil engineering, computer engineering, electrical/electronics engineering, engineering physics, environmental science, manufacturing engineering, materials engineering, materials science, and mechanical engineering), HEALTH PROFESSIONS (medical science, nursing, occupational therapy, and physical therapy), SOCIAL SCIENCE (anthropology, economics, geography, German area studies, gerontology, history, interdisciplinary studies, Japanese studies, Latin American studies, liberal arts/general studies, philosophy, physical fitness/movement, political science/government, psychology, religion, social work, sociology, and women's studies).

ACTIVITIES: There are no fraternities or sororities. There are 100 groups on campus, including academic club, art, band, cheerleading, chess, choir, chorale, chorus, computers, debate, drama, ethnic, international, jazz band, LGBT, musical theater, newspaper, orchestra, photography, political, radio and TV, religious, social, student government, and yearbook. Popular campus events include Marauder Weekend. **Sports:** There are 16 intercollegiate sports for men and 14 for women, and 16 intramural sports for men and 14 for women. Facilities include an outdoor track and field, a mini-weight room, a swimming pool, cross-country trails, rugby, soccer, football and flag football, tennis, squash, baseball, cricket, cycling, fencing, field hockey, golf, gymnastics, wrestling, water polo, tennis, lacrosse, ice hockey, rowing, ultimate Frisbee, badminton, and squash.

SERVICES: Counseling and information services are available, as is tutoring in some subjects. There is a reader service for the blind. **Library/Resources:** The 4 libraries contain 1.7 million volumes, 1.4 million microform items, and 19,500 audio/video tapes/CDs/DVDs, and subscribe to 11,976 periodicals including electronic. Computerized library services include interlibrary loans and database searching. Special learning facilities include an art gallery, planetarium, radio station, a nuclear reactor, tandem accelerator, a greenhouses, Chedoke-McMaster Hospital, a communication research lab, Bertrand Russell archives, Humanities Communication Centre, and computing labs. **Physically Challenged Students:** 60% of the campus is accessible. Facilities include wheelchair ramps, elevators, special parking, specially equipped restrooms, special class scheduling, lowered telephones, and basement-level and above-ground tunnels with connecting walkways. **Special:** All honors students have the option of taking a minor in a second subject area. Nondegree study is possible through the Center for Continuing Education. Internships and study abroad are offered. Students may repeat failed courses provided they are eligible to continue in the program. There are 37 departmental honors programs. **Visiting:** There are regularly scheduled orientations for prospective students, including campus tours, information sessions, and panel discussions. There are guides for informal visits and visitors may sit in on classes. To schedule a visit, contact the Tour Coordinator, Division of Student Liaison. **Campus Safety and Security:** Measures include 24-hour foot and vehicle patrol and security escort services. There are shuttle buses, emergency telephones, lighted pathways/sidewalks, additional services include the Emergency First-Response Team, Mac Alert bulletins, a campus watch program, a prevention programs officer, and video monitoring in some parking areas.

REQUIREMENTS: U.S. applicants must have a high school grade average of 80. Applicants must be graduates of an accredited secondary school. The required high school courses should include 5 years each of English and math. A portfolio is required for art students and an audition for music students. A supplementary application form is required for some programs. Offers of admission are made based on academic standing and audition/portfolio/supplementary application requirements where necessary. A GPA of 80.0 is required. Important factors in the admissions decision are evidence of special talent, extracurricular activities record, and leadership record. Requirements for graduation vary according to the program of study. A minimum 3.5 GPA in 90 to 150 units is required for most programs. **Procedure:** Freshmen are admitted to all sessions. There is an early decision plan. Applications should be filed by January 17 for fall entry. **Transfer Students:** Applicants are considered on an individual basis. Review of high school, college, and/or university work determines admission status. **International Students:** The school actively recruits these students. They must take the TOEFL or MELAB, or take the IELTS.

Admissions Contact: Sam Digiandomenico, Associate Registrar Admissions. Email: *macadmit@mcmaster.ca* Web: *www.future.mcmaster.ca*

FINANCIAL AID: The deadline for filing freshman financial aid applications for fall entry is July 15.

QUEEN'S UNIVERSITY E-3

www.queensu.ca

Kingston, ON K7L 3N6 **(613) 533-2218**

Fax: (613) 533-6810
Email: admission@queensu.ca
Full-time: 7000 men, 7000 women
Part-time: 1300 men, 1300 women
Graduate: 1400 men, 1400 women
Year: semesters, summer session
Room & Board: $13,242
SAT: required
Application Deadline: n/av
Faculty: 973
Ph.D.s: n/av
Student/Faculty: 13 to 1
Tuition: $17,824
Freshman Class: n/av
CEEB CODE: 0949

Queen's University, founded in 1841, is a public institution offering undergraduate and graduate programs in the arts and sciences, business, engineering, health sciences, and teacher education. The figures in the above capsule and in this profile are approximate. Cost is based upon domestic students, and varies by program chosen by student. There are 10 undergraduate schools and 5 graduate schools. The 160-acre campus is in an urban area 150 miles east of Toronto. Including any residence halls, there are 100 buildings.

STUDENT LIFE: Students are from 100 foreign countries, and Canada. 89% are from public schools. **Male To Female Ratio:** Is 1:1. 5% do not continue beyond their first year; 90% remain to graduate. **Housing:** 3071 students can be accommodated in college housing, which includes single-sex and coed dorms, on-campus apartments, off-campus apartments, and married student housing. In addition, there are language houses, study floors, nonsmoking floors, and special-interest houses. First year students live in the residence hall which is guaranteed for the first-year. 80% of students commute. All students may keep cars.

FACULTY/CLASSROOMS: 72% of faculty are male; 27% are female. All teach undergraduates. No introductory courses are taught by graduate students. The average class size in a laboratory is 40.

PROGRAMS OF STUDY: Queen's confers B.A., B.Sc., B.A./B.Ed., B.A./B.Phe., B.Comm., B.F.A., B.Mus., B.N.Sc., B.Sc./B.Ed., B.Sc./B.Phe., B.S.C.E., B.Sc.O.T., and B.Sc.P.T. degrees. Master's and doctoral degrees are also awarded. Bachelor's degrees are awarded in BIOLOGICAL SCIENCE (biochemistry, biology/biological science, and life science), COMMUNICATIONS AND THE ARTS (art history and appreciation, classics, dramatic arts, English, film arts, fine arts, French, German, Greek, Italian, Latin, music, and Spanish), COMPUTER AND PHYSICAL SCIENCE (chemistry, computer science, geology, mathematics, physics, and statistics), EDUCATION (elementary education, middle school education, and secondary education), ENGINEERING AND ENVIRONMENTAL DESIGN (chemical engineering, civil engineering, electrical/electronics engineering, engineering physics, geological engineering, and mechanical engineering), HEALTH PROFESSIONS (health, nursing, occupational therapy, and physical therapy), SOCIAL SCIENCE (economics, geography, history, Judaic studies, philosophy, political science/government, psychology, religion, sociology, and women's studies). Arts, science, and engineering have the largest enrollments.

ACTIVITIES: There are no fraternities or sororities. There are 220 groups on campus, including art, bagpipe, band, cheerleading, chess, choir, chorale, chorus, computers, dance, debate, drama, ethnic, film, international, jazz band, LGBT, literary magazine, marching band, musical theater, newspaper, orchestra, photography, political, professional, radio and TV, religious, social, social service, student government, symphony, and yearbook. Popular campus events include Orientation Week, Alumni Weekend, and Applied Science Formal. **Sports:** There are 19 intercollegiate sports for men and 21 for women, and 39 intramural sports for men and 39 for women. Facilities include a pool, an indoor track, a hockey arena, tennis, squash, racquetball courts, a weight room, dance studio, a projectile range, indoor gym and a football stadium.

SERVICES: Counseling and information services are available, as is tutoring in most subjects. There is a reader service for the blind, and remedial math, reading, and writing. **Library/Resources:** The 8 libraries contain 1.8 million volumes, 2.0 million microform items, and 7,000 audio/video tapes/CDs/DVDs, and subscribe to 15,000 periodicals including electronic. Computerized library services include interlibrary loans and database searching. Special learning facilities include a radio station, TV station, Queen's has 6 libraries, several art museums and arts facilities, including the Agnes Etherington Art Centre, and the Isabel Bader Centre for the Performing Arts, a geology museum, and an observatory. **Physically Challenged Students:** 80% of the campus is accessible. Facilities include wheelchair ramps, elevators, special parking, specially equipped restrooms, special class scheduling, lowered drinking fountains, and lowered telephones. **Special:** Internships are available in life science, commerce, and engineering. Students may study abroad in 25 countries. Dual majors are available. Cross-registration with St. Lawrence College for the B.S.N. is possible. There is a freshman honors program and 20 departmental honors programs. **Visiting:** There are regularly scheduled orientations for prospective students, consisting of a short briefing session and a walking tour. There are guides for informal visits, visitors may sit in on classes, and stay overnight. To schedule a visit, contact Student Recruitment at (613) 533-2217. **Campus Safety and Security:** Measures include 24-hour foot and vehicle patrol, self-defense education, and security escort services. There are shuttle buses, emergency telephones, and lighted pathways/sidewalks.

REQUIREMENTS: The SAT is required. Candidates for admission are required to submit a school profile. A GPA of 70.0 is required. Important factors in the admissions decision are evidence of special talent, leadership record, and extracurricular activities record. Each faculty and school establishes the academic requirements for the graduation of its students. **Procedure:** Freshmen are admitted in the fall. There are deferred admissions and rolling admissions plans. Check with the school for current application deadlines. The application fee is $125. Applications are accepted online. **Transfer Students:** 151 transfer students enrolled in 2016-2017. Admission requirements for transfer applicants vary by program. 10 of 19 credits required for the bachelor's degree must be completed at Queen's. **International Students:** There are 396 international students enrolled. The school actively recruits these students. They must take the TOEFL or MELAB. They must also take the SAT, scoring 1200.

Admissions Contact: Ann Tierney, Vice-Provost Dean. Email: *admission@queensu.ca* Web: *www.queensu.ca*

FINANCIAL AID: The FAFSA code is G06679. The deadline for filing freshman financial aid applications for fall entry is May 13.

UNIVERSITY OF WESTERN ONTARIO D-3

www.uwo.ca

London, ON N6A 3K7 **(519) 661-2100**

Fax: (519) 661-3710 **Email: liaison@uwo.ca**

Full-time: 11,675 men, 14,288 women
Part-time: 699 men, 973 women
Graduate: 2622 men, 2723 women
Year: varies, summer session
Room & Board: $8770
SAT: required
Application Deadline: May 15

Faculty: 1381
Ph.D.s: n/av
Student/Faculty: 20 to 1
Tuition: $6486 ($18,850)
Freshman Class: 32163 applied, 17817 accepted, 9644 enrolled
CEEB CODE: 0984

University of Western Ontario, founded in 1878 is one of Canada's oldest and largest universities. Today, we are a vibrant centre of learning - through our 12 faculties and professional schools, and three affiliated university colleges (Brescia, Huron and King's), we offer more than 400 different specializations, majors and minors at the undergraduate level. And, we are proud to provide the best student experience among Canada's leading research-intensive universities. There are 12 undergraduate schools and one graduate school. In addition to regional accreditation, uWO, has baccalaureate program accreditation with ASLA. The 1125-acre campus is in an urban area 120 miles from both Detroit, Michigan and Toronto, Ontario. Including any residence halls, there are 116 buildings.

STUDENT LIFE: 94% of undergraduates are from Ontario. Others are from 116 foreign countries, and Canada. **Female To Male Ratio:** 1.2:1. The average age of freshmen is 19; all undergraduates, 21. 7% do not continue beyond their first year. **Housing:** 5077 students can be accommodated in college housing, which includes single-sex and coed dorms, on-campus apartments, and married student housing. In addition, there are honors houses and special-interest houses. On-campus housing is guaranteed for the freshman year only and is available on a lottery system for upperclassmen. Priority is given to out-of-town students. 75% of students commute. All students may keep cars.

FACULTY/CLASSROOMS: 69% of faculty are male; 31% are female. No introductory courses are taught by graduate students.

PROGRAMS OF STUDY: uWO confers B.A., B.Sc., B.Ed., B.E.Sc., B.F.A., B.H.Sc., B.M.O.S., B.M.Sc., B.Mus., B.Mus.A., B.A.H.Ec., B.Sc.H.Ec., B.Sc.FN., B.Sc.N., B.S.W.Hons., J.D. and B.Th. degrees. Master's and doctoral degrees are also awarded. Bachelor's degrees are awarded in AGRICULTURE (environmental studies, natural resource management, and plant science), BIOLOGICAL SCIENCE (anatomy, biochemistry, bioinformatics, biology/biological science, biophysics, cell biology, ecology, genetics, microbiology, nutrition, physiology, and toxicology), BUSINESS (accounting, business administration and management, business communications, and human resources), COMMUNICATIONS AND THE ARTS (applied music, art, art history and appreciation, arts administration/management, Chinese, classical languages, classics, communications, communications technology, comparative literature, creative writing, digital communications, English, English literature, film arts, fine arts, French, German, Germanic languages and literature, Greek, Italian, Japanese, Latin, linguistics, media arts, modern language, music, music business management, music history and appreciation, music performance, music theory and composition, musicology/ethnomusicology, opera, piano/organ, public relations, radio/television technology, Russian, Spanish, strings, studio art, and visual and performing arts), COMPUTER AND PHYSICAL SCIENCE (actuarial science, applied mathematics, astronomy, astrophysics, chemistry, computer mathematics, computer programming, computer science, cybernetics, earth science, geology, geophysics and seismology, information sciences and systems, mathematics, medical physics, physics, planetary and space science, science, software engineering, and statistics), EDUCATION (education, elementary education, middle school education, museum studies, music education, physical education, and secondary education), ENGINEERING AND ENVIRONMENTAL DESIGN (aviation administration/management, biomedical engineering, chemical engineering, civil engineering, computer engineering, computer technology, electrical/electronics engineering, engineering, engineering management, environmental engineering, environmental science, materials engineering, materials science, and mechanical engineering), HEALTH PROFESSIONS (health science, medical science, nursing, and pharmacology), SOCIAL SCIENCE (American studies, anthropology, Asian/American studies, Asian/Oriental studies, biblical studies, Canadian studies, child psychology/development, classical/ancient civilization, clinical psychology, criminology, East Asian studies, economics, family/consumer studies, food science, French studies, gender studies, geography, gerontology, history, home economics, human ecology, humanities, humanities and social science, interdisciplinary studies, international relations, Italian studies, Japanese studies, Latin American studies, law, liberal arts/general studies, Native American studies, peace studies, philosophy, philosophy and religion, physical fitness/movement, political science/government, psychology, public administration, religion, social science, social work, sociology, Spanish studies, theological studies, urban studies, Western civilization/culture, and women's studies).

ACTIVITIES: There are no fraternities or sororities. There are 184 groups on campus, including art, band, cheerleading, chess, choir, chorale, chorus, computers, dance, debate, drama, environmental, ethnic, film, international, jazz band, LGBT, marching band, musical theater, newspaper, opera, orchestra, photography, political, professional, radio and TV, religious, social, social service, and student government. Popular campus events include Western Homecoming, Fall Preview Day, and Summer Academic Orientation. **Sports:** There are 20 intercollegiate sports for men and 21 for women, and 20 intramural sports for men and 19 for women. Facilities include Thompson recreation and athletic centre, and TD Waterhouse stadium.**Graduates:** From July 1, 2016 to June 30, 2017, 6791 bachelor's degrees were awarded. 393 companies recruited on campus in 2016-2017. Of the 2016 graduating class, 94% were employed within 6 months of graduation.

SERVICES: Counseling and information services are available, as is tutoring in most subjects. There is a reader service for the blind, and remedial math, reading, and writing. Details available through Learning Skills Services at the Student Development Centre. **Library/Resources:** The 7 libraries contain 3.7 million volumes, 4.1 million microform items, and 2.1 million audio/video tapes/CDs/DVDs, and subscribe to 86,179 periodicals including electronic. Computerized library services include interlibrary loans, database searching, Internet access, and Wi-Fi capability. Special learning facilities include an art gallery, radio station, TV station, International Centre for Olympic Studies, Fowler-Kennedy Sports Medicine Clinic, Cronyn Observatory, and Boundary Layer Wind Tunnel. **Physically Challenged Students:** 92% of the campus is accessible. Facilities include wheelchair ramps, elevators, special parking, specially equipped restrooms, special class scheduling, lowered drinking fountains, lowered telephones, and special housing. **Visiting:** There are regularly scheduled orientations for prospective students, academic counseling appointments and campus tours. There are guides for informal visits and visitors may sit in on classes. To schedule a visit, contact Liaison Officer & Events Planner at (519) 661-2100. **Campus Safety and Security:** Measures include 24-hour foot and vehicle patrol, emergency notification system, and security escort services. There are emergency telephones, lighted pathways/sidewalks, controlled access to dorms/residences, Campus community police, SERT: Student Emergency Response Team, western foot patrol.

REQUIREMENTS: The SAT is required. A GPA of 3.5 is required. AP credits are accepted. Important factors in the admissions decision are advanced placement or honors courses, recommendations by school officials, and leadership record. **Procedure:** Freshmen are admitted fall. There are deferred admissions and rolling admissions plans. Early decision applications should be filed by May 15; regular applications, by May 15 for fall entry. The fall 2017 application fee was $125. Notifications are sent February 1. Applications are accepted online. **Transfer Students:** 381 transfer students enrolled in 2016-2017. A minimum 3.0 GPA is required of transfer applicant; a maximum of 10.0 credits may be transferred. At least 5 credits in a 15-credit degree program or 10 credits in an honors program must be completed at The University of Western Ontario to earn a bachelor's degree. 5 of 15 credits required for the bachelor's degree must be completed at uWO. **International Students:** The school actively recruits these students. They must take the TOEFL with a minimum score of 550 on the paper-based TOEFL (PBT) or 83 on the Internet-based version (iBT) or take the MELAB, We accept MELAB, IELTS, CAEL, CanTEST, Fanshawe College and CultureWorks as alternatives to TOEFL.

ADMISSIONS: 55% of the 2017-2018 applicants were accepted. **Admissions Contact:** Lori Gribbon, Director, Recruitment and Admissions. Email: *liaison@uwo.ca* Web: *www.uwo.ca*

FINANCIAL AID: uWO is a member of CSS. The college's own financial statement is required. The FAFSA code is G08446. Check with the school for current application deadlines.

UNIVERSITY OF OTTAWA — E-3

www.uottawa.ca

Ottawa, ON K1N 6N5 — **(613) 562-5315** / **(877) 868-8292**

Fax: (613) 562-5790 — **Email: admissions@uottawa.ca**

Full-time: 11,124 men, 17,521 women	**Faculty:** n/av
Part-time: 2177 men, 3095 women	**Ph.D.s:** 96%
Graduate: 2430 men, 3252 women	**Student/Faculty:** 22 to 1
Year: semesters, summer session	**Tuition:** $7700 ($27,895)
Room & Board: $6159	**Freshman Class:** n/av
SAT: required	**CEEB CODE:** 0993
Application Deadline: n/av	

University of Ottawa, founded in 1848, is a bilingual (French/English) institution offering undergraduate and graduate degrees through the faculties of arts, law, health sciences, medicine, science, engineering, management, social sciences, and education. The figures in the above capsule and in this profile are approximate. There are 9 undergraduate schools and 9 graduate schools. In addition to regional accreditation, uOttawa has baccalaureate program accreditation with AACSB. The 43-acre campus is in an urban area in Ottawa, Ontario. Including any residence halls, there are 40 buildings.

STUDENT LIFE: 80% of undergraduates are from Ontario. **Female To Male Ratio:** 1.5:1. **Housing:** 2870 students can be accommodated in college housing, which includes single-sex and coed dorms, on-campus apartments, and married student housing. On-campus housing on a first-come, first-served basis, and is available on a lottery system for upperclassmen. All students may keep cars.

FACULTY/CLASSROOMS: 63% of faculty are male; 37% are female. All teach undergraduates, and do research. No introductory courses are taught by graduate students. The average class size in an introductory lecture is 60; in a laboratory is 30; and in a regular course is 30.

PROGRAMS OF STUDY: uOttawa confers B.A., B.Ad., B.A.Sc., B.Com., B.Ed., B.F.A., B.Mus., B.Sc., B.Sc.N., B.Soc.Sc., B.Jour., and B.H.Sc. degrees. Master's and doctoral degrees are also awarded. Bachelor's degrees are awarded in AGRICULTURE (environmental studies), BIOLOGICAL SCIENCE (biochemistry, biology/biological science, biotechnology, and life science), BUSINESS (accounting, banking and finance, electronic business, human resources, management information systems, management science, and marketing/retailing/merchandising), COMMUNICATIONS AND THE ARTS (Arabic, art history and appreciation, arts administration/management, classics, communications, English, English as a second/foreign language, French, German, Italian, journalism, Latin, linguistics, modern language, music, Spanish, and visual and performing arts), COMPUTER AND PHYSICAL SCIENCE (chemistry, computer science, earth science, geology, mathematics, physics, and software engineering), EDUCATION (education, elementary education, foreign languages education, and middle school education), ENGINEERING AND ENVIRONMENTAL DESIGN (biomedical engineering, chemical engineering, civil engineering, computer engineering, electrical/electronics engineering, environmental engineering, environmental science, and mechanical engineering), HEALTH PROFESSIONS (biomedical science, health science, nursing, and ophthalmic technology), SOCIAL SCIENCE (anthropology, Canadian studies, criminology, economics, ethics, politics, and social policy, ethnic studies, geography, gerontology, history, international studies, law, medieval studies, philosophy, political science/government, psychology, public administration, religion, Russian and Slavic studies, sociology, and women's studies). Law, medicine, and education are the strongest academically. Arts, social sciences, and science have the largest enrollments.

ACTIVITIES: There are no fraternities or sororities. There are 100 groups on campus, including art, band, cheerleading, chess, choir, chorale, computers, dance, debate, drama, environmental, ethnic, film, honors, international, jazz band, LGBT, newspaper, orchestra, photography, political, professional, radio and TV, religious, social, social service, student government, and symphony. Popular campus events include University of Ottawa Day, Gee-gees Football Games and International week. **Sports:** There are 5 intercollegiate sports for men and 7 for women, and 13 intramural sports for men and 11 for women. Facilities include sports complexes with weight-training and combat rooms, swimming pools, gyms, racquetball and squash courts, billiards and ping pong tables, indoor arena, and a multipurpose sports field. **Graduates:** From July 1, 2015 to June 30, 2016, 6836 bachelor's degrees were awarded.

SERVICES: Counseling and information services are available, as is tutoring in most subjects. There is a reader service for the blind, and remedial math, reading, and writing. **Library/Resources:** The 8 libraries contain 2.2 million volumes, 1.9 million microform items, and 777,349 audio/video tapes/CDs/DVDs, and subscribe to 60,522 periodicals including electronic. Computerized library services include interlibrary loans, database searching, Internet access, and Wi-Fi capability. Special learning facilities include an art gallery, radio station, TV station, a Museum of Classical Antiquities. **Physically Challenged Students:** 75% of the campus is accessible. Facilities include wheelchair ramps, elevators, special parking, specially equipped restrooms, special class scheduling, lowered drinking fountains, lowered telephones, special housing, automatic doors and specialized equipment. **Special:** Opportunities are provided for cooperative programs, study abroad in over 56 countries, a general studies degree in arts and in sciences, and combined programs in all fields in arts and in social sciences. There are 40 departmental honors programs. **Visiting:** There are regularly scheduled orientations for prospective students, open house and campus visits (ongoing, year round). There are guides for informal visits and visitors may sit in on classes. To schedule a visit, contact the Liaison Office at (613) 562-5800. **Campus Safety and Security:** Measures include 24-hour foot and vehicle patrol, emergency notification system, self-defense education, and security escort services. There are also shuttle buses, emergency telephones, lighted pathways/sidewalks, controlled access to dorms/residences, and a community crime-stoppers program.

REQUIREMENTS: The SAT is required. Graduation from an accredited secondary school is required. Those students planning to major in occupational or physical therapy must speak French. A portfolio is required for fine arts students, and an audition for music students. AP credits are accepted. Students must maintain a GPA of 3.5 out of 10 for all courses, including those in the major. Students must also complete a second language requirement: French for English students, and English for French students. **Procedure:** Freshmen are admitted in the fall and winter. There are early decision, early admissions, and rolling admissions plans. Check with the school for current application deadlines. The fall 2017 application fee was $105. **Transfer Students:** Admissions requirements vary according to program. 60 of 90 credits required for the bachelor's degree must be completed at uOttawa. **International Students:** There are 2234 international students enrolled. The school actively recruits these students. They must take the TOEFL with a minimum score of 580 on the paper-based TOEFL (PBT) or 92 on the Internet-based version (iBT) or take the MELAB and the college's own test, CanTest.

Admissions Contact: Andre-Pierre Lepage, International Admissions Administrator. Email: *admissions@uottawa.ca* Web: *www.uottowa.ca*

FINANCIAL AID: The FAFSA code is G06686. Check with the school for current application deadlines.

CARLETON UNIVERSITY — E-3

www.carleton.ca

Ottawa, ON K1S 5B6 — **(613) 520-3609**

Fax: (613) 520-4410 — **Email: admissions@carleton.ca**

Full-time: 9000 men, 9406 women
Part-time: 1502 men, 1216 women
Graduate: 1937 men, 1699 women
Year: semesters, summer session
Room & Board: $10,200

Faculty: n/av
Ph.D.s: 93%
Student/Faculty: n/av
Tuition: $8913 ($25,115)
Freshman Class: n/av
CEEB CODE: 0854

Application Deadline: June 1

Carleton University, founded in 1942, is a public institution operated by the province of Ontario. There are 14 undergraduate and 14 graduate degree programs offered. The figures in the above capsule and in this profile are approximate. Tuition varies according to program chosen by student. There are 5 undergraduate schools and 1 graduate school. The 152-acre campus is in a small town in Ottawa. Including any residence halls, there are 29 buildings.

STUDENT LIFE: 80% of undergraduates are from Ontario. **Male To Female Ratio:** 1.0:1. The average age of freshmen is 19; all undergraduates, 21. 13% do not continue beyond their first year; 72% remain to graduate. **Housing:** 2873 students can be accommodated in college housing, which includes single-sex and coed dorms. On-campus housing is available on a lottery system for upperclassmen. Priority is given to out-of-town students. All students may keep cars.

FACULTY/CLASSROOMS: 65% of faculty are male; 35% are female. No introductory courses are taught by graduate students. The average class size in an introductory lecture is 166 and in a regular course is 107.

PROGRAMS OF STUDY: Carleton confers B.A., B.Sc., B.Arch., B.Comm., B.C.S., B.Eng., B.Hum., B.I.B., B.I.D., B.I.T., B.J., B.Math., B.Mus., B.P.A.P.M. and B.S.W. degrees. Master's and doctoral degrees are also awarded. Bachelor's degrees are awarded in BIOLOGICAL SCIENCE (biochemistry, biology/biological science, biometrics and biostatistics, biotechnology, and neurosciences), BUSINESS (accounting, business systems analysis, human resources, international business management, marketing and distribution, marketing/retailing/merchandising, and operations research), COMMUNICATIONS AND THE ARTS (art history and appreciation, classics, communications, communications technology, English, English literature, film arts, French, German, industrial design, Italian, journalism, linguistics, music, Russian, and Spanish), COMPUTER AND PHYSICAL SCIENCE (chemistry, computer mathematics, computer programming, computer science, geology, information sciences and systems, mathematics, physical sciences, physics, and statistics), EDUCATION (teaching English as a second/foreign language (TESOL/TEFOL), ENGINEERING AND ENVIRONMENTAL DESIGN (aeronautical engineering, architecture, civil engineering, computer engineering, electrical/electronics engineering, engineering, engineering physics, environmental engineering, environmental science, mechanical engineering, and systems engineering), SOCIAL SCIENCE (anthropology, Canadian studies, child care/child and family studies, classical/ancient civilization, cognitive science, criminology, Eastern European studies, economics, European studies, geography, German area studies, history, human ecology, interdisciplinary studies, law, liberal arts/general studies, philosophy, political science/government, psychology, public administration, religion, social work, sociology, and women's studies). Arts, engineering, and commerce have the largest enrollments.

ACTIVITIES: There are no fraternities or sororities. There are 80 groups on campus, including cheerleading, chess, choir, computers, drama, environmental, ethnic, film, international, jazz band, LGBT, newspaper, pep band, photography, political, radio and TV, religious, social, social service, and student government. Popular campus events include Orientation. **Sports:** There are 16 intercollegiate sports for men and 18 for women, and 4 intramural sports for men and 3 for women. Facilities include a physical recreation center with an Olympic-size pool, squash courts, Nautilus and fitness centers, and a double gym, outdoor tennis courts and playing fields. **Graduates:** From July 1, 2016 to June 30, 2017, 3640 bachelor's degrees were awarded. The most popular majors were psychology (10%), economics (4%), and English (4%). In an average class, 3% graduate in 3 years or less, 38% graduate in 4 years or less, 62% graduate in 5 years or less, and 67% graduate in 6 years or less.

SERVICES: Counseling and information services are available, as is

tutoring in most subjects. There is a reader service for the blind. Study skills workshops are available in essay writing and preparation and writing of exams. There is special exam scheduling and a study center for disabled students and a PASS program (peer tutoring). **Library/Resources:** The library contains 1.8 million volumes, 1.4 million microform items, and 22,370 audio/video tapes/CDs/DVDs, and subscribes to 40,607 periodicals including electronic. Computerized library services include interlibrary loans, database searching, Internet access, and Wi-Fi capability. Special learning facilities include an art gallery, radio station, an environmental biology laboratories annex. **Physically Challenged Students:** All of the campus is accessible. Facilities include wheelchair ramps, elevators, special parking, specially equipped restrooms, lowered drinking fountains, lowered telephones. including automatic doors in some buildings, tactile control panels in elevators, tunnels connecting buildings, specially equipped residence rooms, and attendant services. **Special:** Carleton offers co-op programs in many majors and an exchange program with the University of Ottawa. Study abroad, internships in industrial design, dual and student-designed majors, accelerated degree programs, and interdisciplinary programs are available. The university also utilizes instructional television. **Visiting:** There are regularly scheduled orientations for prospective students, including a general information session and campus tour. There are guides for informal visits, visitors may sit in on classes, and stay overnight. To schedule a visit, contact the Undergraduate Recruitment Office at (613) 520-3663. **Campus Safety and Security:** Measures include 24-hour foot and vehicle patrol, emergency notification system, and security escort services. There are emergency telephones, lighted pathways/sidewalks, controlled access to dorms/residences, bike patrol, rape defence classes and student safety patrol.

REQUIREMENTS: Applicants must be graduates of an accredited secondary school. Architecture, humanities, and industrial design students must present a portfolio, social work students should submit a personal information form, and music students must audition. A GPA of 3.0 is required. AP and CLEP credits are accepted. Requirements for graduation vary according to programs. **Procedure:** Freshmen are admitted to all sessions. There are early admissions, deferred admissions, and rolling admissions plans. Applications should be filed by June 1 for fall entry, along with a $100 fee. Applications are accepted online. **Transfer Students:** Applicants are evaluated on individual merits. 30 of 120 credits required for the bachelor's degree must be completed at Carleton. **International Students:** There are 1565 international students enrolled. The school actively recruits these students. They must take the TOEFL with a minimum score of 580 on the paper-based TOEFL (PBT) or 86 on the Internet-based version (iBT) or take the MELAB and the college's own test, Canadian Academic English Language Assessment and the IETLS.

Admissions Contact: Janice O'Farrell, Director of Admissions. Email: *admissions@carleton.ca* Web: *www.carleton.ca*

FINANCIAL AID: The FAFSA code is G08368. The deadline for filing freshman financial aid applications for fall entry is February 1.

YORK UNIVERSITY — E-3

www.futurestudents.yorku.ca

Toronto , ON M3J 1P3 — **(416) 736-5825**

Fax: (416) 650-8195	**Email:** admissions@yorku.ca
Full-time: 13,500 men, 21,540 women	**Faculty:** 1357
Part-time: 2900 men, 4510 women	**Ph.D.s:** 98%
Graduate: 2500 men, 2700 women	**Student/Faculty:** n/av
Year: semesters, summer session	**Tuition:** $6376 ($17,512)
Room & Board: $5119	**Freshman Class:** n/av
SAT or ACT: required	**CEEB CODE:** 0894
Application Deadline: February 1	

York University, founded in 1959, is a public institution offering programs in computer science, design, education, environmental studies, fine arts, business, social science, law, engineering, health, humanities, human resources, pure and applied sciences, and social work. The figures in the above capsule and in this profile are approximate. There are 10 undergraduate schools and 43 graduate schools. The 635-acre campus is in an urban area in Northwest and midtown Toronto. Including any residence halls, there are 96 buildings.

STUDENT LIFE: 90% of undergraduates are from Ontario. Others are from 159 foreign countries. **Female To Male Ratio:** 1.5:1. The average age of freshmen is 18; all undergraduates, 22. 97% remain to graduate. **Housing:** 4000 students can be accommodated in college housing, which includes single-sex and coed dorms, on-campus apartments, and married student housing. In addition, there are language houses, special-interest houses, and Co-op housing. On-campus housing is available on a first-come, first-served basis, and is available on a lottery system for upperclassmen. Priority is given to out-of-town students. 93% of students commute. All students may keep cars.

FACULTY/CLASSROOMS: 59% of faculty are male; 41% are female. All teach undergraduates, and all do research. No introductory courses are taught by graduate students. The average class size in an introductory lecture is 72 and in a laboratory is 25.

PROGRAMS OF STUDY: York confers B.A., B.Sc., B.A.S., B.B.A., B.Des., B.Ed., B.E.S., B.F.A., B.H.R.M., B.H.S., B.Sc.N., B.S.W., I.B.B.A. and L.L.B. degrees. Master's and doctoral degrees are also awarded. Bachelor's degrees are awarded in AGRICULTURE (conservation and regulation and environmental studies), BIOLOGICAL SCIENCE (biochemistry, biology/biological science, biotechnology, and ecology), BUSINESS (accounting, banking and finance, business administration and management, business economics, business statistics, entrepreneurial studies, human resources, international business management, international economics, labor studies, management science, marketing and distribution, and organizational behavior), COMMUNICATIONS AND THE ARTS (art history and appreciation, classics, communications, creative writing, dance, design, dramatic arts, English, film arts, fine arts, French, German, Greek, Italian, linguistics, music, photography, Russian, Spanish, video, and visual and performing arts), COMPUTER AND PHYSICAL SCIENCE (applied mathematics, astronomy, atmospheric sciences and meteorology, chemistry, computer science, earth science, information sciences and systems, mathematics, physics, science, science technology, and statistics), EDUCATION (education, education of the deaf and hearing impaired, elementary education, middle school education, and secondary education), ENGINEERING AND ENVIRONMENTAL DESIGN (computer engineering, engineering, environmental science, and industrial administration/management), HEALTH PROFESSIONS (community health work, environmental health science, exercise science, health, health care administration, health science, nursing, and rehabilitation therapy), SOCIAL SCIENCE (African studies, anthropology, Canadian studies, Caribbean studies, cognitive science, criminal justice, criminology, East Asian studies, economics, European studies, French studies, geography, German area studies, gerontology, Hispanic American studies, history, humanities, international studies, Judaic studies, Latin American studies, law, liberal arts/general studies, peace studies, philosophy, physical fitness/movement, political science/government, psychology, public administration, religion, Russian and Slavic studies, science and society, social science, social work, sociology, South Asian studies, Third World studies, urban studies, and women's studies). Business, science, fine arts, and liberal arts are the strongest academically. Psychology, administrative studies, and sociology have the largest enrollments.

ACTIVITIES: There are no fraternities or sororities. There are 249 groups on campus, including art, band, cheerleading, chess, choir, communications, computers, dance, debate, drama, ethnic, film, international, jazz band, LGBT, literary magazine, musical theater, newspaper, orchestra, photography, political, professional, radio and TV, religious, social, social service, student government, and yearbook. Popular campus events include The Blue Bowl (football), Orientation Week, and Multicultural Week. **Sports:** There are 11 intercollegiate sports for men and 12 for women, and 17 intramural sports for men and 17 for women. Facilities include a stadium, a 6-rink ice arena, sport playing fields, softball diamonds, cricket pitch, indoor and outdoor track and field center, 26 indoor and outdoor tennis courts. There is a fitness center with cardio machines and free weights, a 25-meter swimming pool, gyms, squash courts, dance/aerobic studios, spinning studio, and a sports therapy clinic, a combative room, teaching labs, and an outdoor events facility.

SERVICES: Counseling and information services are available, as is tutoring in most subjects. There is a reader service for the blind. A writing support center, and a multimedia language center. The Counseling and Development Center offers a variety of services and workshops. **Library/Resources:** The 5 libraries contain 2.5 million volumes, 4.0 million microform items, and 54,184 audio/video tapes/CDs/DVDs, and subscribe to 24,576 periodicals including electronic. Computerized library services include interlibrary loans, database searching, Internet access, and Wi-Fi capability. Special learning facilities include an art gallery, radio station, TV station, an observatory, language labs, writing center, geographical information systems lab, computer science labs, science-related labs, and fine arts studios and labs (editing studios). **Physically Challenged Students:** 65% of the campus is accessible. Facilities include wheelchair ramps, elevators, special parking, specially equipped restrooms, special class scheduling, lowered drinking fountains, lowered telephones. The office for persons with disabilities offers a variety of additional services. **Special:** Co-op programs and cross-registration with Seneca, Centennial, Sheridan, and Humber Colleges, internships, study abroad in more than 100 countries, and work-study are available. York offers dual, student-designed, multi-, and interdisciplinary majors, including atmospheric chemistry, physics and astronomy, science, technology, culture, and society, social and political thought, space and communication sciences, and translation. Independent study and nondegree study are also possible. There are a freshman honors program. **Visiting:** There are regularly scheduled orientations for prospective students, consisting of a general information session and campus tour and 1 week of orientation prior to the start of classes. There are guides for informal visits, visitors may sit in on classes, and stay overnight. To schedule a visit, contact the International Admissions Office at (416) 736-5000. **Campus Safety and Security:** Measures include 24-hour foot and vehicle patrol, self-defense education, and security escort services. There are shuttle buses, emergency telephones, lighted pathways/sidewalks. There is also a bicycle patrol team monitoring the campuses.

REQUIREMENTS: U.S. applicants must present evidence of superior academic achievement. Secondary school record, SAT or ACT scores, and teacher or counselor recommendation will be taken into consideration. Applicants to a fine arts program are required to successfully pass an audition or evaluation, and business administration applicants are required to submit a supplementary application. Admission averages and course prerequisites vary by faculty. A GPA of 3.0 is required. AP credits are accepted. Students must maintain at least a C average in 90 credits to receive an ordinary degree and a C+ in 120 credits to receive an honors degree. Requirements for graduation vary according to the program. **Procedure:** Freshmen are admitted to all sessions. Entrance exams should be taken in the fall of the senior year. There are early admissions and rolling admissions plans. Applications should be filed by February 1 for fall entry; November 1 for winter entry; and March 1 for spring entry. The fall 2017 application fee was $60. Notification is sent on a rolling basis. Applications are accepted online. **Transfer Students:** 954 transfer students enrolled in 2016-2017. Requirements vary depending on the program. Postsecondary transcripts are required. **International Students:** There are 2708 international students enrolled. The school actively recruits these students. They must take the TOEFL, the Comprehensive English Language Test, and the college's own test, the York English Language Test (YELT), or take the IELTS. They must also take the SAT or ACT.

Admissions Contact: Office of International Admissions. Email: *admissions@yorku.ca* Web: *www.futurestudents.yorku.ca*

FINANCIAL AID: The FAFSA code is G07679. Check with the school for current application deadlines.

RYERSON UNIVERSITY — E-3

www.ryerson.ca

Toronto, ON M5B 2K3 — **(416) 979-5036**

Fax: (416) 979-5067	**Email:** studentinfo@ryerson.ca
Full-time: 12,000 men, 13,000 women	**Faculty:** n/av
Part-time: n/av	**Ph.D.s:** 63%
Graduate: 500 men, 1500 women	**Student/Faculty:** 23 to 1
Year: semesters, summer session	**Tuition:** $10,200 ($24,800)
Room & Board: $15,600	**Freshman Class:** 69000 applied, 24800 accepted, 8555 enrolled
SAT or ACT: recommended	**CEEB CODE:** 0886
Application Deadline: February 1	

Ryerson University, founded in 1948, is a public institution offering undergraduate programs in arts, applied arts, business, community services, and engineering and applied science. The figures in the above capsule and in this profile are approximate. Tuition varies by program chosen by student. There are 5 undergraduate schools and 3 graduate schools. In addition to regional accreditation, Ryerson has baccalaureate program accreditation with FIDER. The 20-acre campus is in an urban area in the heart of Toronto. Including any residence halls, there are 35 buildings.

STUDENT LIFE: 90% of undergraduates are from Ontario. Others are from 146 foreign countries. **Female To Male Ratio:** 1.2:1. **Housing:** 852 students can be accommodated in college housing, which includes coed dorms. On-campus housing is available on a first-come and first-served basis. Priority is given to out-of-town students. 96% of students commute. All students may keep cars.

FACULTY/CLASSROOMS: 32% are female. No introductory courses are taught by graduate students. The average class size in a regular course is 30.

PROGRAMS OF STUDY: Ryerson confers B.A., B.Arch.Sc., B.A.Sc., B.Comm., B.Des., B.Eng., B.H.Sc., B.Sc., B.S.W., B.Tech., and B.U.R.P.I. degrees. Master's and doctoral degrees are also awarded. Bachelor's degrees are awarded in BUSINESS (business administration and management, hospitality management services, and management information systems), COMMUNICATIONS AND THE ARTS (broadcasting, journalism, and photography), COMPUTER AND PHYSICAL SCIENCE (computer programming), EDUCATION (early childhood education), ENGINEERING AND ENVIRONMENTAL DESIGN (aeronautical engineering, architecture, chemical engineering, civil engineering, electrical/electronics engineering, graphic and printing production, industrial engineering, interior design, mechanical engineering, and urban planning technology), HEALTH PROFESSIONS (environmental health science and nursing), SOCIAL SCIENCE (child care/child and family studies, family/consumer studies, fashion design and technology, geography, public administration, and social work). Business management, nursing, and information technology management have the largest enrollments.

ACTIVITIES: There are no fraternities or sororities. There are 150 groups on campus, including choir, chorale, computers, drama, environmental, ethnic, film, international, LGBT, literary magazine, musical theater, newspaper, political, professional, radio and TV, religious, social, social service, student government, and yearbook. Popular campus events include orientation, a parade and picnic. **Sports:** There are 7 intercollegiate sports for men and 8 for women, and 20 intramural sports for men and 20 for women. Facilities include a recreation and athletic center, squash courts, a fitness training that has an indoor running track and weight-training equipment, a rehabilitation center, a 25-yard pool, and gyms.

SERVICES: Counseling and information services are available, as is tutoring in most subjects. There is a reader service for the blind, and remedial math, reading, and writing. Services are available in study skills development, critical reading seminars, time management skills, and exam workshops. **Library/Resources:** The library contains 477,739 volumes, 842,963 microform items, and 20,235 audio/video tapes/CDs/DVDs, and subscribes to 60,809 periodicals including electronic. Computerized library services include interlibrary loans, database searching, Internet access, and Wi-Fi capability. Special learning facilities include a radio station, the BlackStar Historical Black and White Photography Collection, Heidelberg Centre, George Vari Engineering and Computing Centre. The zone learning is a program designed with like-minded students from diverse disciplines and community groups. **Physically Challenged Students:** Facilities include wheelchair ramps, elevators, special parking, specially equipped restrooms, special class scheduling, lowered drinking fountains, lowered telephones, and special housing. There are also test and exam adaptations, computer-equipped exam and study rooms, assistive listening devices for personal use and for use in auditorium settings, advocacy services, individual needs assessment, and access to a wide range of technical devices. **Special:** The university offers co-op programs in applied chemistry and biology, chemical engineering, and midwifery. Accelerated degree programs are available in journalism, radio and television arts, nurse practitioner, and nursing. There is 1 national honor society and a freshman honors program. **Visiting:** There are regularly scheduled orientations for prospective students, student visits include a half-day tour and discussion session featuring campus tours and visits to specific schools and departments. There are guides for informal visits and visitors may sit in on classes. To schedule a visit, contact the Undergraduate Admissions and Recruitment at (416) 979-5036. **Campus Safety and Security:** Measures include 24-hour foot and vehicle patrol, emergency notification system, self-defense education, and security escort services. There are emergency telephones, lighted pathways/sidewalks, controlled access to dorms/residences, sexual assault training, harassment prevention and crime prevention programs, and community policing programs.

REQUIREMENTS: The SAT or ACT and ACT Writing Test are recommended. In addition, for U.S. students, there is a recommended minimum score of 550 on each section of the SAT I. Students should be high school graduates with a minimum B overall average. A GPA of 3.0 is required. AP credits are accepted. To graduate, students must have a 2.0 GPA and complete the requirements of their program of study. **Procedure:** Freshmen are admitted in the fall. Applications should be filed by February 1 for fall entry, along with a $130 fee. Notifications are sent in March. Applications are accepted online. **Transfer Students:** 700 transfer students enrolled in 2016-2017. Transfer applicants must have completed 1 year at the college level. Acceptance of transfer credits is at the discretion of the Office of Admissions/Liaison/Curriculum Advising. Half of the required credits for a particular degree program must be completed at Ryerson. **International Students:** There are 1000 international students enrolled. The school actively recruits these students. They must take the TOEFL with a minimum score of 560 on the paper-based TOEFL (PBT) or 83 on the Internet-based version (iBT) or take the MELAB and the college's own test, or take the IELTS.

ADMISSIONS: 36% of the 2017-2018 applicants were accepted. **Admissions Contact:** Barbara Cecchetto, Director of Admissions. Email: *studentinfo@ryerson.ca* Web: *www.ryerson.ca*

FINANCIAL AID: Ryerson is a member of CSS. The FAFSA code is G10720. Check with the school for current application deadlines.

UNIVERSITY OF TORONTO — E-3

www.utoronto.ca

Toronto, ON M5S 1A1 — **(416) 978-2190**

Fax: (416) 978-7022 — **Email:** admissions.help@utoronto.ca

Full-time: 25,000 men, 30,000 women	**Faculty:** n/av
Part-time: 4528 men, 3256 women	**Ph.D.s:** 91%
Graduate: 6843 men, 8339 women	**Student/Faculty:** n/av
Year: other, summer session	**Tuition:** $8095 ($41,920)
Room & Board: $10,000	**Freshman Class:** n/av
SAT: required	**CEEB CODE:** 0982
Application Deadline: January 17	

The University of Toronto, founded in 1827, is a public institution offering undergraduate programs in applied science and engineering, arts and science, education, dentistry, law, medicine, music, nursing, pharmacy, physical and health education, and radiation sciences. Degrees are also offered at the graduate level in a wide range of programs. The figures in the above capsule and in this profile are approximate. There are 2 undergraduate schools and 1 graduate school. The 1767-acre campus is in an urban area with 3 campuses in downtown and suburban Toronto. Including any residence halls, there are 242 buildings.

STUDENT LIFE: 88% of undergraduates are from Ontario. **Female To Male Ratio:** 1.1:1. The average age of freshmen is 18; all undergraduates, 21. 5% do not continue beyond their first year; 83% remain to graduate. **Housing:** 7903 students can be accommodated in college housing, which includes single-sex and coed dorms, on-campus apartments, off-campus apartments, and married student housing. On-campus housing is guaranteed for the freshman year only, and is available on a first-come, and first-served basis. Priority is given to out-of-town students. 80% of students commute. All students may keep cars.

FACULTY/CLASSROOMS: 55% of faculty are male; 45% are female. No introductory courses are taught by graduate students.

PROGRAMS OF STUDY: uToronto confers B.A., B.Sc., B.A.Sc., B.B.A., B.Com., B.Ed., B.Sc.Med.Rad.Sc., B.Sc.N., B.Sc.O.T., B.Sc.Phm., B.Sc.P.T., B.S.P.H.E., and Mus.Bac. degrees. Master's and doctoral degrees are also awarded. Bachelor's degrees are awarded in AGRICULTURE (environmental studies, forestry and related sciences, and natural resource management), BIOLOGICAL SCIENCE (biochemistry, biology/biological science, biophysics, biotechnology, botany, cell biology, ecology, evolutionary biology, life science, microbiology, molecular biology, neurosciences, nutrition, physiology, toxicology, and zoology), BUSINESS (banking and finance, business administration and management, business economics, electronic business, and human resources), COMMUNICATIONS AND THE ARTS (art history and appreciation, arts administration/management, classics, communications, communications technology, comparative literature, dramatic arts, English, film arts, French, German, Greek, Italian, journalism, Latin, linguistics, media arts, modern language, music, music history and appreciation, music theory and composition, musicology/ethnomusicology, Polish, Portuguese, Russian languages and literature, Slavic languages, Spanish, technical and business writing, and visual and performing arts), COMPUTER AND PHYSICAL SCIENCE (actuarial science, applied mathematics, applied physics, astronomy, astrophysics, chemical physics, chemistry, computer science, digital arts/technology, earth science, geology, mathematics, paleontology, physical sciences, physics, planetary and space science, statistics, and systems analysis), EDUCATION (education, education of the exceptional child, foreign languages education, music education, and physical education), ENGINEERING AND ENVIRONMENTAL DESIGN (architecture, chemical engineering, civil engineering, computer engineering, electrical/electronics engineering, engineering and applied science, environmental science, industrial engineering, materials engineering, materials science, mechanical engineering, mining and mineral engineering, and water and wastewater technology), HEALTH PROFESSIONS (environmental health science, health, nursing, occupational therapy, pharmacology, pharmacy, physical therapy, physician's assistant, and radiological science), SOCIAL SCIENCE (African studies, American studies, anthropology, applied psychology, archeology, behavioral science, Canadian studies, Caribbean studies, Celtic studies, Christian studies, classical/ancient civilization, cognitive science, criminology, East Asian studies, economics, ethics, politics, and social policy, European studies, forensic studies, geography, German area studies, Hispanic American studies, history, history of science, human ecology, humanities, international relations, international studies, Judaic studies, medieval studies, Middle Eastern studies, Native American studies, Pacific area studies, peace studies, philosophy, political science/government, psychology, public affairs, religion, Russian and Slavic studies, Scandinavian studies, sociology, South Asian studies, urban studies, and women's studies). Arts and science, applied science, and engineering have the largest enrollments.

ACTIVITIES: There are no fraternities or sororities. There are 200 groups on campus, including art, band, cheerleading, chess, choir, chorus, computers, dance, debate, drama, ethnic, film, international, jazz band, LGBT, literary magazine, musical theater, newspaper, opera, orchestra, photography, political, radio and TV, religious, social, student government, symphony, and yearbook. Popular campus events include uToronto Day, concerts, and theater productions. **Sports:** There are 27 intercollegiate sports for men and 26 for women, and 29 intramural sports for men and 29 for women. Facilities include swimming pools, an outdoor hockey rink, weight and exercise rooms, gyms, squash and multipurpose courts, a rifle range, dance studios, playing fields, a stadium, an arena, and indoor running track. **Graduates:** From July 1, 2016 to June 30, 2017, 9724 bachelor's degrees were awarded. In an average class, 83% graduate in 4 years or less.

SERVICES: Counseling and information services are available, as is tutoring in every subject. There is a reader service for the blind. **Library/Resources:** The 32 libraries contain 11.4 million volumes, 5.5 million microform items, 374,046 audio/video tapes/CDs/DVDs, and subscribe to 74,545 periodicals including electronic. Computerized library services include interlibrary loans, database searching, Internet access, and Wi-Fi capability. Special learning facilities include an art gallery, radio station, an observatory. **Physically Challenged Students:** Facilities include wheelchair ramps, elevators, special parking, specially equipped restrooms, lowered drinking fountains, and lowered telephones. **Special:** The university offers co-op programs in management, arts management, management and information technology, cell and molecular biology, computer science, mathematical and physical sciences, sociology, applied psychology, public policy, humanities, international development studies, psychology (including mental health studies), sciences, social sciences, and neuroscience. Study abroad, interdisciplinary programs, and various work-study programs are also available. **Visiting:** There are regularly scheduled orientations for prospective students. There are guides for informal visits. To schedule a visit, contact Student Recruitment at (416) 978-5000. **Campus Safety and Security:** Measures include 24-hour foot and vehicle patrol, self-defense education, and security escort services. There are also shuttle buses, emergency telephones, and lighted pathways/sidewalks.

REQUIREMENTS: The faculties of arts and science, of music, and physical education and health will consider Grade 12 applicants from an accredited U.S. high school with a high GPA and good scores on the SAT.

The ACT will also be considered. Engineering will consider excellent grade 12 students with high SAT scores who also are completing at least 2 advanced placement courses. The SAT Subject Tests and AP courses and exams must include math, physics, and chemistry. Other requirements may apply. Architecture students must submit a questionnaire and a portfolio. Music students must audition. A GPA of 3.0 is required. AP credits are accepted. Arts and science students must satisfy a breadth requirement, which includes 3 courses from outside the major. Students must complete 20 credits for a 4-year degree, plus prerequisite subjects. **Procedure:** Freshmen are admitted in the fall. There are early decision, early admissions, deferred admissions, and rolling admissions plans. Application deadlines are open. The fall 2016 application fee was $80. Notification is sent on a rolling basis. **Transfer Students:** 786 transfer students enrolled in 2016-2017. For the Arts and Science divisions, normally a B average is required. 5 of 20 credits required for the bachelor's degree must be completed at uToronto. **International Students:** There are 6884 international students enrolled. The school actively recruits these students. They must take the TOEFL with a minimum score of 600 on the paper-based TOEFL (PBT) or 100 on the Internet-based version (iBT) or take the MELAB, or the ELDA/COPE, the IELTS Academic Module, or the University of Toronto's Continuing Studies Academic English Course. They must also take the SAT or ACT, scoring 1800.

Admissions Contact: Admissions Counselor. Email: *admissions.help@utoronto.ca* Web: *www.utoronto.ca*

FINANCIAL AID: The FAFSA code is G06688. Check with the school for current application deadlines.

UNIVERSITY OF WATERLOO E-3

www.uwaterloo.ca

Waterloo, ON N2L 3G1 **(519) 888-4567**

Fax: (519) 746-8088
Email: myapplication@uwaterloo.ca
Full-time: 13,752 men, 9241 women
Faculty: n/av
Part-time: 400 men, 541 women
Ph.D.s: 93%
Graduate: 2921 men, 1599 women
Student/Faculty: 25 to 1
Year: varies, summer session
Tuition: $7058 ($19,524)
Room & Board: $8000
Freshman Class: 29859 applied, 20942 accepted, 6970 enrolled
CEEB CODE: 0996
Application Deadline: March 31

University of Waterloo, founded in 1957, is a public institution that offers undergraduate and graduate programs in applied health sciences, arts, engineering, environment, math, and science. Students have a home base in 1 of 6 faculties or 4 affiliated institutions. Most programs are offered in either the traditional or the cooperative system of study. The figures in the above capsule and in this profile are approximate. There are 10 undergraduate schools and 6 graduate schools. The 1000-acre campus is in a suburban area 60 miles southwest of Toronto. Including any residence halls, there are 65 buildings.

STUDENT LIFE: 95% of undergraduates are from Ontario. Others are from 13 states. **Male To Female Ratio:** 1.5:1. **Housing:** 6100 students can be accommodated in college housing, which includes single-sex and coed dorms, on-campus apartments, off-campus apartments, special-interest houses, language floors, and an off-campus housing service. On-campus housing is guaranteed for the freshman year only. Priority is given to out-of-town students. All students may keep cars.

FACULTY/CLASSROOMS: 75% of faculty are male; 25% are female. All teach undergraduates, all do research, and all teach and do research. No introductory courses are taught by graduate students.

PROGRAMS OF STUDY: Waterloo confers B.A., B.Sc., B.A.S., B.A.Sc., B.A.F.M., B. Arch., B.C.F.M., B.C.S., B.E.S., B.I.S., B.Math, BSc. Phm., B.S.E., B.S.W., and B.K.I. degrees. Master's and doctoral degrees are also awarded. Bachelor's degrees are awarded in AGRICULTURE (environmental studies), BIOLOGICAL SCIENCE (biochemistry, bioinformatics, biology/biological science, and biotechnology), BUSINESS (accounting, business administration and management, human resources, management engineering, management science, operations research, and recreation and leisure services), COMMUNICATIONS AND THE ARTS (art history and appreciation, arts administration/management, classics, dramatic arts, English, English literature, film arts, fine arts, French, German, music, Russian, Spanish, speech/debate/rhetoric, and studio art), COMPUTER AND PHYSICAL SCIENCE (actuarial science, applied mathematics, chemistry, computer mathematics, computer science, digital arts/technology, earth science, information sciences and systems, mathematics, physics, science, science and management, software engineering, and statistics), EDUCATION (foreign languages education, mathematics education, and science education), ENGINEERING AND ENVIRONMENTAL DESIGN (architecture, chemical engineering, city/community/regional planning, civil engineering, computational sciences, computer engineering, electrical/electronics engineering, engineering, environmental engineering, environmental science, geological engineering, mechanical engineering, and systems engineering), HEALTH PROFESSIONS (health, health science, optometry, preallied health, preoptometry, and respiratory therapy), SOCIAL SCIENCE (anthropology, economics, French studies, geography, history, international studies, medieval studies, philosophy, physical fitness/movement, political science/government, psychology, religion, Russian and Slavic studies, social work, sociology, and women's studies). Engineering, accounting, and math are the strongest academically. Arts has the largest enrollment.

ACTIVITIES: 1% of men belong to 1 national fraternity; 1% of women belong to 1 national sorority. There are 150 groups on campus, including social dance, juggling, martial arts, band, bridge, cheerleading, chess, choir, computers, dance, debate, drama, environmental, ethnic, film, honors, international, LGBT, literary magazine, marching band, musical theater, newspaper, photography, political, professional, radio and TV, religious, social, social service, student government, and yearbook. Popular campus events include Oktoberfest and Canada Day. **Sports:** There are 18 intercollegiate sports for men and 18 for women, and 16 intramural sports for men and 16 for women. Facilities include outdoor playing fields, an ice arena, swimming pool, diving tank, squash courts, weight rooms, gyms, a dance studio, tennis courts, and activity areas. **Graduates:** From July 1, 2015 to June 30, 2016, 4466 bachelor's degrees were awarded. The most popular majors were arts (32%), mathematics (21%), and engineering (18%).

SERVICES: Counseling and information services are available, as is tutoring in most subjects, and a reader service for the blind, and remedial math, reading, and writing. **Library/Resources:** The 8 libraries contain 2.0 million volumes, 1.7 million microform items, 1,179 audio/video tapes/CDs/DVDs, and subscribe to 24,074 periodicals including electronic. Computerized library services include interlibrary loans, database searching, Internet access, and Wi-Fi capability. Special learning facilities include an art gallery, radio station, 4 museums, 2 theaters, and an observatory. **Physically Challenged Students:** All of the campus is accessible. Facilities include wheelchair ramps, elevators, special parking, specially equipped restrooms, special class scheduling, lowered drinking fountains, and lowered telephones. Up-to-date technical equipment for the visually disabled and the hearing impaired. **Special:** Cross-registration with Wilfrid Laurier University, study abroad in 30 countries, dual, student-designed, and interdisciplinary majors, a combined bachelor's-master's degree in accounting and engineering, and noncredit courses are available. Students may study under the regular or cooperative system, which allows off-campus work terms in education, professional organizations and agencies, business, industry, or government. There are concurrent education programs in conjunction with the faculties of education at Brock and Queen's Universities. There are 55 departmental honors programs. **Visiting:** Regularly scheduled orientations are available for prospective students, student visits include tours and individual and group information sessions. There are guides for informal visits and visitors may sit in on classes. To schedule a visit, contact the Visitors Reception Center at (519) 888-4567, ext. 3614. **Campus Safety and Security:** Measures include 24-hour foot and vehicle patrol, emergency notification system, self-defense education, and security escort services. There are also shuttle buses, emergency telephones, and lighted pathways/sidewalks.

REQUIREMENTS: Candidates from the United States must have a high school diploma with exceptionally high standing and AP exams in prerequisite subjects or first-year university standing in acceptable subjects from an accredited university. An audition, portfolio, and/or interview may be required for certain programs. A GPA of 3.0 is required. AP credits are accepted. Important factors in the admissions decision are advanced placement or honors courses, extracurricular activities record, and leadership record. To graduate, all students must satisfy specific program requirements. These include a writing skills requirement. The total number of credits and minimum grade average vary. **Procedure:** Freshmen are admitted in the fall, winter, and spring. Entrance exams should be taken by the junior year. There are early admissions and deferred admissions plans. Applications should be filed by March 31 for fall entry; October 31 for winter entry; and March 1 for spring entry, along with a $130 fee. Notifications are sent May 25. Applications are accepted online. **Transfer Students:** Applicants are considered on an individual basis. 10 of 20 credits required for the bachelor's degree must be completed at Waterloo. **International Students:** There are 2398 international students enrolled. The school actively recruits these students. They must take the TOEFL, and also take the TWE and the TSE. The MELAB or the IELTS may also be submitted.

ADMISSIONS: 70% of the 2016-2017 applicants were accepted. **Admissions Contact:** Undergraduate Recruitment. Email: *myapplication@uwaterloo.ca* Web: *www.uwaterloo.ca*

FINANCIAL AID: Check with the school for current application deadlines.

UNIVERSITY OF WINDSOR — D-3

www.uwindsor.ca

Windsor, ON N9B 3P4 — **(519) 253-3000**

Fax: (519) 253-3653	**Email:** registrar@uwindsor.ca
Full-time: 6528 men, 6012 women	**Faculty:** 592
Part-time: 1170 men, 1325 women	**Ph.D.s:** 92%
Graduate: 1030 men, 228 women	**Student/Faculty:** 18 to 1
Year: trimesters, summer session	**Tuition:** $8700 ($21,045)
Room & Board: $9037	**Freshman Class:** n/av
SAT or ACT: required	**CEEB CODE:** 0904
Application Deadline: n/av	

University of Windsor, founded in 1857, is a public liberal arts institution offering undergraduate and graduate programs through 10 faculties and 6 schools. The figures in the above capsule and in this profile are approximate. There are 11 undergraduate schools and 1 graduate school. The 125-acre campus is in an urban area 2 kilometers from downtown Windsor, and 3 kilometers from downtown Detroit, Michigan. Including any residence halls, there are 58 buildings.

STUDENT LIFE: 90% of undergraduates are from Ontario. Others are from 90 foreign countries, and Canada. 95% are from public schools. **Male To Female Ratio:** 1.2:1. The average age of freshmen is 18; all undergraduates, 22. 10% do not continue beyond their first year. **Housing:** 1500 students can be accommodated in college housing, which includes coed dorms, on-campus apartments, and married student housing. On-campus housing is guaranteed for the freshman year only and is available on a lottery system for upperclassmen. 90% of students commute. All students may keep cars.

FACULTY/CLASSROOMS: 54% of faculty are male; 46% are female. All teach undergraduates, and all do research. No introductory courses are taught by graduate students. The average class size in an introductory lecture is 100; in a laboratory is 25; and in a regular course is 50.

PROGRAMS OF STUDY: uWindsor confers B.A., B.Sc., B.A.S., B.A.Sc., B.Comm., B.C.S., B.Ed., B.E.S., B.F.A., B.F.S., B.H.K., B. Math, B.Mus., B.Mus.Th., B.Sc.N., B.S.W. and L.L.B. degrees. Master's and doctoral degrees are also awarded. Bachelor's degrees are awarded in AGRICULTURE (environmental studies), BIOLOGICAL SCIENCE (biochemistry, biology/biological science, and biotechnology), BUSINESS (business administration and management and international business management), COMMUNICATIONS AND THE ARTS (art history and appreciation, classics, communications, comparative literature, creative writing, dramatic arts, English, French, languages, modern language, music, Spanish, and visual and performing arts), COMPUTER AND PHYSICAL SCIENCE (chemistry, computer science, geology, mathematics, physics, science, software engineering, and statistics), EDUCATION (drama education, education, and science education), ENGINEERING AND ENVIRONMENTAL DESIGN (automotive technology, civil engineering, electrical/electronics engineering, engineering, environmental engineering, environmental science, industrial engineering, and mechanical engineering), HEALTH PROFESSIONS (music therapy and nursing), SOCIAL SCIENCE (anthropology, Canadian studies, criminology, crosscultural studies, developmental psychology, economics, family/consumer studies, forensic studies, geography, history, international relations, law, philosophy, physical fitness/movement, political science/government, psychology, social work, sociology, urban studies, and women's studies). Science, engineering, and human kinetics are the strongest academically. Business, science, and education have the largest enrollments.

ACTIVITIES: 1% of men belong to 3 national fraternities; 1% of women belong to 3 national sororities. There are 135 groups on campus, including cheerleading, chess, choir, chorale, computers, dance, debate, drama, environmental, ethnic, film, forensics, honors, international, jazz band, LGBT, literary magazine, musical theater, newspaper, orchestra, political, professional, radio and TV, religious, social, and student government. Popular campus events include Head Start Orientation, Windsor Welcome Week and Homecoming. **Sports:** There are 7 intercollegiate sports for men and 6 for women, and 11 intramural sports for men and 9 for women. Facilities include a 6-lane 200-meter track, a multiuse gym, a field house, a stadium, an indoor pool, weight rooms, and a sports therapy clinic.

SERVICES: Counseling and information services are available, as is tutoring in most subjects, such as chemistry, biochemistry, physics, mathematics, statistics, and S.T.E.P.S. program. There is a reader service for the blind, and remedial math, reading, and writing. **Library/Resources:** The 2 libraries contain 1.7 million volumes, 1.5 million microform items, and 10,792 audio/video tapes/CDs/DVDs, and subscribe to 76,378 periodicals including electronic. Computerized library services include interlibrary loans, database searching, Internet access, and Wi-Fi capability. Special learning facilities include an art gallery, natural history museum, radio station, a video-conferencing center, a computing services theater, the Chrysler Canada/University of Windsor Research Center, and the Great Lakes Institute. **Physically Challenged Students:** 90% of the campus is accessible. Facilities include wheelchair ramps, elevators, special parking, specially equipped restrooms, special class scheduling, lowered drinking fountains, lowered telephones, and specially equipped residence rooms. **Special:** The university offers a variety of co-op programs and internships. Cross-registration may be arranged with the University of Detroit Mercy, Wayne State University, the University of Central Florida, and the University of Darby (England). There are 30 departmental honors programs. **Visiting:** There are regularly scheduled orientations for prospective students, student visits include a tour, counseling, and classes if requested. There are guides for informal visits and visitors may sit in on classes. To schedule a visit, contact the Office of Liason and Student Recruitment at 1-800-864-2860. **Campus Safety and Security:** Measures include 24-hour foot and vehicle patrol, emergency notification system, self-defense education, and security escort services. There are emergency telephones, lighted pathways/sidewalks, and controlled access to dorms/residences.

REQUIREMENTS: Each U.S. applicant must present scores from either the ACT or the SAT offered by the College Entrance Examination Board. Advanced Placement Examinations in certain prerequisite subjects may also be required. AP credits are accepted. To graduate, students must complete a total of 90 credit hours, including 30 in the major, with a C average. Honors students must complete 120 hours, including 60 in the major, with a B average. All students must fulfill the requirements of the core curriculum. **Procedure:** Freshmen are admitted to all sessions. Entrance exams should be taken as early as possible. There are early decision, early admissions, and rolling admissions plans. Check with the school for current application deadlines. Applications are accepted online. **Transfer Students:** Applicants must present an official transcript and be in good academic standing. **International Students:** There are 1209 international students enrolled. The school actively recruits these students. They must take the TOEFL or MELAB, or take the IELTS, CAEL, or MELAB.

Admissions Contact: Abby Nakhaie, Assistant to the Dean. Email: *registrar@uwindsor.ca* Web: *www.uwindsor.ca*

FINANCIAL AID: The FAFSA code is G06689. Check with the school for current application deadlines.

MCGILL UNIVERSITY E-2
www.mcgill.ca

Montreal, PQ H3A oG4 **(514) 398-7878**

Fax: (514) 398-5544 **Email: welcome@mcgill.ca**
Full-time: 6899 men, 10952 women
Part-time: 1200 men, 2056 women
Graduate: 3464 men, 3900 women
Year: semesters, summer session
Room & Board: $14,015

ACT: 29 **SAT:** required
Application Deadline: March 1

Faculty: n/av
Ph.D.s: 95%
Student/Faculty: n/av
Tuition: $3986 ($17,303)
Freshman Class: 18963 applied, 10689 accepted, 4834 enrolled
CEEB CODE: 0935

McGill University, founded in 1821, is a publicly funded private institution that grants undergraduate, graduate, and professional degrees. Tuition fees varies depending on program chosen by student. Higher rates are charged to international students. The figures in the above capsule and in this profile are approximate. There are 11 undergraduate schools and 79 graduate schools. In addition to regional accreditation, McGill has baccalaureate program accreditation with APTA. The 80-acre campus is in an urban area in downtown Montreal, with the MacDonald campus located on the far west end of the island. Including any residence halls, there are 150 buildings.

STUDENT LIFE: 53% of undergraduates are from Quebec. Others are from 140 foreign countries. 17% are Foreign. **Female To Male Ratio:** 1.5:1. The average age of freshmen is 19; all undergraduates, 21. **Housing:** 2080 students can be accommodated in college housing, which includes single-sex and coed dorms, off-campus apartments, and married student housing. On-campus housing is available on a lottery system for upperclassmen. Priority is given to out-of-town students. 83% of students commute.

FACULTY/CLASSROOMS: 67% of faculty are male; 33% are female. No introductory courses are taught by graduate students. The average class size in an introductory lecture is 30; in a laboratory is 25; and in a regular course is 45.

PROGRAMS OF STUDY: McGill confers B.A., B.C.L., B.Com., B.Ed., B.Eng., B.Mus., B.Sc., B.Sc.Agr., B.Sc.Agr.Eng., B.Sc.Arch., B.Sc.F.Sc., B.Sc.N., B.Sc.Nutr.Sc., B.Sc.Occ.Ther., B.Sc.Phys.Ther., B.S.W., B.Th., and LL.B. degrees. Master's and doctoral degrees are also awarded. Bachelor's degrees are awarded in AGRICULTURE (agricultural economics, agriculture, animal science, conservation and regulation, plant science, and soil science), BIOLOGICAL SCIENCE (anatomy, biochemistry, biology/biological science, botany, cell biology, environmental biology, microbiology, molecular biology, nutrition, physiology, wildlife biology, and zoology), BUSINESS (accounting, banking and finance, entrepreneurial studies, human resources, institutional management, insurance and risk management, international business management, labor studies, management information systems, management science, marketing management, and organizational behavior), COMMUNICATIONS AND THE ARTS (art history and appreciation, classics, English, French, jazz, linguistics, modern language, music history and appreciation, music performance, music technology, music theory and composition, Russian, and Spanish), COMPUTER AND PHYSICAL SCIENCE (applied mathematics, atmospheric sciences and meteorology, chemistry, computer science, earth science, geology, geophysics and seismology, information sciences and systems, mathematics, physics, planetary and space science, and software engineering), EDUCATION (elementary education, foreign languages education, music education, physical education, secondary education, special education, teaching English as a second/foreign language (TESOL/TEFOL), and vocational education), ENGINEERING AND ENVIRONMENTAL DESIGN (agricultural engineering, architecture, chemical engineering, civil engineering, computer engineering, electrical/electronics engineering, environmental science, mechanical engineering, metallurgical engineering, and mining and mineral engineering), HEALTH PROFESSIONS (clinical science, exercise science, nursing, occupational therapy, and physical therapy), SOCIAL SCIENCE (African studies, American studies, anthropology, Canadian studies, Caribbean studies, dietetics, East Asian studies, economics, food science, French studies, geography, German area studies, Hispanic American studies, history, humanities, international studies, Italian studies, Judaic studies, Latin American studies, law, Middle Eastern studies, philosophy, political science/government, psychology, religion, social work, sociology, Western civilization/culture, and women's studies).

ACTIVITIES: 4% of men belong to 1 local and 12 national fraternities; 2% of women belong to 4 national sororities. There are 180 groups on campus, including and drive-safe program, walk-safe, band, cheerleading, chess, choir, chorale, chorus, computers, dance, debate, drama, ethnic, film, honors, international, jazz band, LGBT, literary magazine, Model UN, musical theater, newspaper, opera, orchestra, photography, political, professional, radio and TV, religious, social, social service, student government, symphony, and yearbook. Popular campus events include Multicultural Festivals, 4-Floor Parties, Music, Film and Theatrical Productions. **Sports:** There are 23 intercollegiate sports for men and 24 for women, and 23 intramural sports for men and 15 for women. Facilities include a stadium, a competition hall, double gyms for basketball, volleyball, badminton, outdoor tennis courts, indoor tennis courts, a 400-meter outdoor track and a banked 6-lane 200-meter indoor track, weight-training rooms, dance, aerobics, and martial arts rooms, swimming pool, a gymnastics facility, sports fields, a fitness center, a sport medicine center, and hyperbaric chamber. **Graduates:** The most popular majors were social sciences (18%), health professions (11%), and biological/life sciences (10%).

SERVICES: Counseling and information services are available, as is tutoring in every subject. There is a reader service for the blind, and remedial math, reading, and writing. **Library/Resources:** The 14 libraries contain 3.3 million volumes, 1.6 million microform items, and 71,765 audio/video tapes/CDs/DVDs, and subscribe to 22,513 periodicals including electronic. Computerized library services include interlibrary loans and database searching. Special learning facilities include a natural history museum, radio station, McCord Museum of Canadian History, Mont St. Hilaire Nature Conservation Center, an herbarium, arboretum, a subarctic research station, the Institute of Air and Space Law, the Institute of Islamic Studies, the Redpath Museum of Natural History, the Lyman Entomological Museum, the Ecomuseum, the Osler Library of the History of Medicine, and the Lande Canadiana Collection. **Physically Challenged Students:** 80% of the campus is accessible. Facilities include wheelchair ramps, elevators, special parking, specially equipped restrooms, special class scheduling, lowered telephones, braille, variable-speed tape recorders, talking calculators, books on tape, exam accommodations, adapted computers (voice synthesis and voice recognition), sign language interpreters, computerized note taking, note takers, print enlargement, readers, and adapted transport. **Special:** There is cross-registration with area universities. Study abroad, work-study within the university, co-op programs in mining and metallurgical engineering, dual majors, internships, and student-designed majors are available. There are 6 departmental honors programs. **Visiting:** There are regularly scheduled orientations for prospective students, with a varying agenda (including campus tours and student for a day programs). There are guides for informal visits, visitors may sit in on classes, and stay overnight. To schedule a visit, contact the Welcome Center at (514) 398-6555 (tours). **Campus Safety and Security:** Measures include 24-hour foot and vehicle patrol and security escort services. There are emergency telephones and lighted pathways/sidewalks.

REQUIREMENTS: The SAT or ACT is required. McGill requires applicants to be in the upper 25% of their class. A GPA of 3.3 is required. AP credits are accepted. Important factors in the admissions decision are advanced placement or honors courses, recommendations by school officials, and evidence of special talent. To graduate, students must successfully complete a required number of approved credits, usually between 90 and 120. Students must also be in satisfactory standing, with a minimum cumulative GPA of 2.0. **Procedure:** Freshmen are admitted in the fall. Entrance exams should be taken during Spring of the junior year, fall of the senior year. There are deferred admissions and rolling admissions plans. Applications should be filed by March 1 for fall entry, along with a $60 fee. Applications are accepted online. **Transfer Students:** 528 transfer students enrolled in 2015-2016. Requirements varies by program. Standard admission requirements must also be met. Students must submit high school and college transcripts and have a 3.0 GPA in college coursework. 60 of 90 credits required for the bachelor's degree must be completed at McGill. **International Students:** The school actively recruits these students. They must take the TOEFL or MELAB, McGill Certificate of Proficiency in English must be earned. SAT and/or ACT tests are required for U.S. applicants and recommended for other international applicants.

ADMISSIONS: 56% of the 2017-2018 applicants were accepted. **Admis-**

sions Contact: Dr. Mara Ludwig, Vice-Dean of Academic Affairs. Email: *welcome@mcgill.ca* Web: *www.mcgill.ca*

FINANCIAL AID: The average freshman award was $5,855. Need-based scholarships or need-based grants averaged $3,022; and need-based self-help aid (loans and jobs) averaged $6,146. McGill is a member of CSS. The college's own financial statement is required. The FAFSA code is G06677. The deadline for filing freshman financial aid applications for fall entry is June 1.

UNIVERSITÉ DE MONTRÉAL E-2

www.umontreal.ca/English

Montreal, PQ H3C 3J7 (514) 343-7076

Fax: (514) 343-5788 Email: admissions@regis.umontreal.ca

Full-time: 13020 men, 17045 women
Part-time: 5410 men, 9025 women
Graduate: 6726 men, 8348 women
Year: trimesters, summer session
Room & Board: $3840
Faculty: n/av
Ph.D.s: 96%
Student/Faculty: n/av
Tuition: $3553 ($16,020)
Freshman Class: 31100 applied, 13923 accepted, 13174 enrolled
CEEB CODE: 0992
Application Deadline: March 1

Université de Montréal, founded in 1878, is the largest French-language university in North America, with 13 faculties, 2 affiliated schools, 62 teaching departments, and more than 170 research units. The figures in the above capsule and in this profile are approximate. The 145-acre campus is in an urban area in Montreal, Canada. Including any residence halls, there are 38 buildings.

STUDENT LIFE: Students are from 11 states and Canada. 88% are from public schools. **Female To Male Ratio:** 1.4:1. The average age of freshmen is 22; all undergraduates, 24. 20% do not continue beyond their first year; 80% remain to graduate. **Housing:** 1164 students can be accommodated in college housing, which includes coed off-campus apartments. On-campus housing is available on a first-come and first-served basis. 98% of students commute. All students may keep cars.

FACULTY/CLASSROOMS: 71% of faculty are male; 29% are female. All teach undergraduates. No introductory courses are taught by graduate students. The average class size in an introductory lecture is 48; in a laboratory is 19; and in a regular course is 40.

PROGRAMS OF STUDY: UdeM confers B.A., B.Sc., B.A.A., B.A.P., B.D.I., B.Gest., B.Ed., B.Ing., B.Int., B.Mus., and B.Th. degrees. Associate, master's, and doctoral degrees are also awarded. Bachelor's degrees are awarded in BIOLOGICAL SCIENCE (biochemistry, biology/biological science, biometrics and biostatistics, and nutrition), BUSINESS (business administration and management), COMMUNICATIONS AND THE ARTS (art history and appreciation, classics, English, film arts, French, German, industrial design, linguistics, and music), COMPUTER AND PHYSICAL SCIENCE (chemistry, computer science, mathematics, and physics), EDUCATION (education, physical education, and psychology education), ENGINEERING AND ENVIRONMENTAL DESIGN (architectural engineering, architecture, engineering, industrial administration/management, and landscape architecture/design), HEALTH PROFESSIONS (health science, nursing, occupational therapy, pharmacy, physical therapy, predentistry, premedicine, preveterinary science, speech pathology/audiology, and veterinary science), SOCIAL SCIENCE (anthropology, Asian/Oriental studies, criminology, economics, geography, history, law, philosophy, political science/government, psychology, social work, sociology, Spanish studies, theological studies, and urban studies). Law, medicine, and nursing have the largest enrollments.

ACTIVITIES: There are no fraternities or sororities. There are 100 groups on campus, including art, cheerleading, choir, chorale, computers, dance, debate, drama, environmental, ethnic, film, international, jazz band, literary magazine, newspaper, orchestra, photography, political, radio and TV, religious, social, social service, student government, and yearbook. Popular campus events include Multicultural Week, and Welcoming Week. **Sports:** There are 8 intercollegiate sports for men and 6 for women, and 12 intramural sports for men and 12 for women. Facilities include a skating rink, a football field, a gym, squash and racquetball courts, an Olympic-size pool, a diving pool, a running field with tennis courts, and aerobic and muscular exercise equipment. **Graduates:** The most popular majors were law (8%), medicine (5%), and nursing (5%).

SERVICES: Counseling and information services are available, as is tutoring in some subjects. There is a reader service for the blind, and remedial math, reading, and writing. **Library/Resources:** The 19 libraries contain 3.0 million volumes, 1.6 million microform items, and 2.0 million audio/video tapes/CDs/DVDs, and subscribe to 50,000 periodicals including electronic. Computerized library services include interlibrary loans, database searching, Internet access, and Wi-Fi capability. Special learning facilities include an art gallery, natural history museum, radio station, and a concert hall. **Physically Challenged Students:** 95% of the campus is accessible. Facilities include wheelchair ramps, elevators, special parking, specially equipped restrooms, lowered drinking fountains, lowered telephones, and special housing. There is also a specialized equipment center. **Special:** The university offers co-op programs in math, translation, mining, and civil, chemical, and software material engineering; and work-study programs in hospitals and businesses in Quebec. Dual majors in math and economics, math and physics, math and computer science, communication and politics, economics and politics, and 3-2 engineering degrees may also be arranged. Study abroad is available in 31 countries. There is a freshman honors program and 45 departmental honors programs. **Visiting:** There are regularly scheduled orientations for prospective students. Student visits include Orientation and Employment Week in November, guided tours February through May, and open house in January and August. There are guides for informal visits. To schedule a visit, contact the Director of Communications and Recruitment at (514) 343-6032. **Campus Safety and Security:** Measures include 24-hour foot and vehicle patrol, emergency notification system, and security escort services. There are emergency telephones, lighted pathways/sidewalks, controlled access to dorms/residences, and in-room safes.

REQUIREMENTS: Applicants in certain programs must take the university's admissions tests. An interview is also required in some programs. To graduate, students must have a GPA of 2.0 on a 4.3 scale. The total number of credits required in most programs is 90, although it can range up to 187. Professional programs, particularly those in health-related fields, require more hours. **Procedure:** Freshmen are admitted fall and winter. Applications should be filed by March 1 for fall entry, along with a $100 fee. Notifications are sent March 15. Applications are accepted online. **Transfer Students:** Transfers are considered if there are openings in the second or third year of the university's programs. 90 credits required for the bachelor's degree must be completed at UdeM. **International Students:** The school actively recruits these students.

ADMISSIONS: 45% of the 2017-2018 applicants were accepted. **Admissions Contact:** Jacinthe Gauthier, Responsible Admissions. Email: *admissions@regis.umontreal.ca* Web: *www.umontreal.ca/English*

FINANCIAL AID: The deadline for filing freshman financial aid applications for fall entry is March 31.

CONCORDIA UNIVERSITY MONTREAL E-2

www.concordia.ca

Montreal, PQ H3G IM8 (514) 848-4971

Fax: (514) 848-2621 Email: study@concordia.ca

Full-time: 9200 men, 9342 women
Part-time: 4270 men, 4271 women
Graduate: 2162 men, 2163 women
Year: semesters, summer session
Room & Board: $7900
SAT or ACT: recommended
Application Deadline: March 1
Faculty: 714
Ph.D.s: 84%
Student/Faculty: 17 to 1
Tuition: $3840 ($17,822)
Freshman Class: n/av
CEEB CODE: 0956

Concordia University Montreal, established in 1974, is a public institution operated by the province of Quebec. The figures in the above capsule and in this profile are approximate. Tuition varies according to program chosen by student. There are 5 undergraduate schools and 1 graduate school. In addition to regional accreditation, CUM has baccalaureate program accreditation with AACSB. The 1555-acre campus is in an urban area in downtown Montreal and in suburban Loyola. Including any residence halls, there are 80 buildings.

STUDENT LIFE: 90% of undergraduates are from Quebec. Others are from 29 states, 128 foreign countries, and Canada. **Female To Male**

Ratio: 1.0:1. The average age of freshmen is 21; all undergraduates, 25. 11% do not continue beyond their first year; 52% remain to graduate. **Housing:** 144 students can be accommodated in college housing, which includes single-sex and coed dorms and off-campus apartments. In addition, there are fraternity houses and sorority houses. On-campus housing is available on a first-come and first-served basis. Priority is given to out-of-town students. 75% of students commute. All students may keep cars.

FACULTY/CLASSROOMS: 65% of faculty are male; 35% are female. No introductory courses are taught by graduate students. The average class size in an introductory lecture is 50; in a laboratory is 50; and in a regular course is 50.

PROGRAMS OF STUDY: CUM confers B.A., B.Admin., B.Comm., B.Comp.Sci., B.Ed., B.Eng., B.F.A., and B.S.C. degrees. Master's and doctoral degrees are also awarded. Bachelor's degrees are awarded in BIOLOGICAL SCIENCE (biochemistry, biology/biological science, and microbiology), BUSINESS (accounting, banking and finance, business administration and management, business economics, international business management, marketing/retailing/merchandising, and personnel management), COMMUNICATIONS AND THE ARTS (communications, dance, design, dramatic arts, English, English as a second/foreign language, film arts, fine arts, journalism, languages, music, and photography), COMPUTER AND PHYSICAL SCIENCE (actuarial science, chemistry, computer programming, computer science, geology, information sciences and systems, mathematics, physics, and statistics), EDUCATION (art education, early childhood education, and elementary education), ENGINEERING AND ENVIRONMENTAL DESIGN (civil engineering, computer engineering, electrical/electronics engineering, industrial engineering, and mechanical engineering), SOCIAL SCIENCE (anthropology, East Asian studies, economics, geography, history, philosophy, political science/government, psychology, sociology, and urban studies). Computer engineering, accounting, and communication studies are the strongest academically. Accounting, and psychology have the largest enrollments.

ACTIVITIES: 1% of men belong to 3 national fraternities; 1% of women belong to 3 national sororities. There are 125 groups on campus, including art, choir, chorale, chorus, computers, dance, drama, ethnic, film, honors, international, jazz band, LGBT, literary magazine, musical theater, newspaper, orchestra, photography, political, professional, radio and TV, religious, social, social service, student government, symphony, and yearbook. **Sports:** There are 9 intercollegiate sports for men and 7 for women, and 16 intramural sports for men and 12 for women. Facilities include an arena, a gym, and a football stadium. **Graduates:** The most popular majors were arts and science (55%), commerce and administration (25%), and fine arts (10%).

SERVICES: Counseling and information services are available, as is tutoring in most subjects. There is a reader service for the blind, and remedial math, reading, and writing. **Library/Resources:** The 2 libraries contain 3.0 million volumes, 75,000 microform items, and 2,000 audio/video tapes/CDs/DVDs, and subscribe to 5,500 periodicals including electronic. Computerized library services include interlibrary loans and database searching. Special learning facilities include an art gallery, radio station, TV station, a greenhouse, audiovisual instruction service, and specialized research center. Career and Planning services (CAPS). **Physically Challenged Students:** 75% of the campus is accessible. Facilities include wheelchair ramps, elevators, special parking, specially equipped restrooms, special class scheduling, lowered drinking fountains, and lowered telephones. **Special:** The university offers programs in many majors with the Institute for Co-operative Education, internships, and study abroad in 12 countries. There are accelerated degree programs, B.A.-B.S. degrees, dual majors, a general studies degree, and student-designed majors. There is a Phi Beta Kappa Chapter and 21 departmental honors programs. **Visiting:** There are regularly scheduled orientations for prospective students. There are guides for informal visits and visitors may sit in on classes. To schedule a visit, contact the Office of Student Recruitment at (514) 848-4779. **Campus Safety and Security:** Measures include 24-hour foot and vehicle patrol, self-defense education, and security escort services. There are shuttle buses, emergency telephones, and lighted pathways/sidewalks.

REQUIREMENTS: The SAT or ACT is recommended. Applicants must be graduates of an accredited secondary school. The GED is accepted. An essay, an interview, a portfolio, or an audition may be required for some programs. A GPA of 2.5 is required. AP and CLEP credits are accepted. Important factors in the admissions decision are advanced placement or honors courses and recommendations by school officials. To graduate, students must complete 90 to 120 credits, depending on the degree, with a minimum GPA of 2.0. Between 42 and 54 credits are required in the major. All students must fulfill the requirements of the core curriculum and take the university writing test. **Procedure:** Freshmen are admitted to all sessions. There are early decision, early admissions, and rolling admissions plans. Early decision applications should be filed by February 1; regular applications, by March 1 for fall entry; November 1 for winter entry; and April 15 for summer entry, along with a $50 fee. **Transfer Students:** Applicants must have a minimum GPA of 2.2. 45 of 90 credits required for the bachelor's degree must be completed at CUM. **International Students:** The school actively recruits these students. They must take the TOEFL or MELAB and the college's own test. **Admissions Contact:** Jonathan Levinson, Executive Director of Institutional Plan. Email: *study@concordia.ca* Web: *www.concordia.ca*

FINANCIAL AID: The FAFSA code is G08365. Check with the school for current application deadlines.

UNIVERSITE LAVAL — E-2
www.ulaval.ca

Quebec, PQ G1K 7P4 — (418) 656-2764, (877) 785-2825

Fax: (418) 656-5216 — **Email: reg@reg.ulaval.ca**

Full-time: 9000 men, 13000 women
Part-time: 3345 men, 5487 women
Graduate: 4914 men, 5458 women
Year: semesters, summer session
Room & Board: $10,300
Faculty: n/av
Ph.D.s: 90%
Student/Faculty: n/av
Tuition: $3024 ($18,590)
Freshman Class: 28717 applied, 20234 accepted, 10726 enrolled
CEEB CODE: 0931
Application Deadline: March 1

Universite Lavel, founded in 1852, is the oldest French-language university in North America. It offers undergraduate and graduate programs through 17 faculties and 9 institutes. The figures in the above capsule and in this profile are approximate. There are 16 undergraduate schools and 17 graduate schools. In addition to regional accreditation, UL has baccalaureate program accreditation with AACSB, AUCC, and ACU. The 465-acre campus is in an urban area 2 miles west of old Quebec City. Including any residence halls, there are 35 buildings.

STUDENT LIFE: 94% of undergraduates are from Quebec. Others are from 105 foreign countries. **Female To Male Ratio:** 1.4:1. The average age of all undergraduates is 26. **Housing:** 2400 students can be accommodated in college housing, which includes single-sex and coed on-campus apartments. On-campus housing is available on a first-come and first-served basis. All students may keep cars.

FACULTY/CLASSROOMS: All teach undergraduates. No introductory courses are taught by graduate students.

PROGRAMS OF STUDY: UL confers B.A., B.Sc., B.A.A., B.A.V., B.Ed., B.Ens., B.Ing., B.Mus., B.Pharm., B.Sc.A., B.Sc.Arch., B.Serv.Soc., B.Th., and LL.B. degrees. Master's and doctoral degrees are also awarded. Bachelor's degrees are awarded in AGRICULTURE (agricultural business management, agricultural economics, agronomy, forest engineering, forestry and related sciences, and wood science), BIOLOGICAL SCIENCE (biochemistry, biology/biological science, microbiology, and nutrition), BUSINESS (business administration and management), COMMUNICATIONS AND THE ARTS (art, art history and appreciation, communications, dramatic arts, English, English as a second/foreign language, French, languages, linguistics, literature, music, and visual and performing arts), COMPUTER AND PHYSICAL SCIENCE (actuarial science, chemistry, computer science, geology, geoscience, mathematics, physics, software engineering, and statistics), EDUCATION (art education, athletic training, early childhood education, education, elementary education, music education, physical education, secondary education, and technical education), ENGINEERING AND ENVIRONMENTAL DESIGN (agricultural engineering, architecture, chemical engineering, civil engineering, computer engineering, electrical/electronics engineering, engineering and applied science, engineering physics, geological engineering, graphic arts technology, industrial administration/management, mechanical engineering, metallurgical engineering, and mining and mineral engineering), HEALTH PROFESSIONS (nursing, occupational therapy, pharmacy, physical therapy, predentistry, and premedicine), SOCIAL SCIENCE (anthropology, classical/ancient civilization, consumer services, counseling/psychology, economics, food science, French studies, geography, history, interdisciplinary studies, international studies, Judaic studies, law, philosophy, physical fitness/movement, political science/government, psychology, social work, sociology, Spanish studies, and theological studies). Business administration, sciences, and education have the largest enrollments.

ACTIVITIES: There are no fraternities or sororities. There are 150 groups on campus, including art, band, chess, choir, chorale, computers, dance, drama, ethnic, film, forensics, international, jazz band, LGBT, literary magazine, musical theater, newspaper, opera, orchestra, photography, political, radio and TV, religious, social, social service, student government, and symphony. Popular campus events include Thematic Weeks, Rendez-vous Laval, and student festivals. **Sports:** There are 13 intercollegiate sports for men and 10 for women, and 7 intramural sports for men and 7 for women. Facilities include track and tennis courts, a swimming pool with diving tower, a double ice arena, gyms, squash courts, handball and racquetball courts, judo, karate, and self-defense rooms, a dance studio, an open-air stadium with a running track, softball, football, soccer fields, outdoor tennis courts, physical training rooms, a golf driving range, an indoor golf practice room, outdoor basketball courts, and a jogging track. **Graduates:** The most popular majors were administration (18%), science and engineering (14%), and letters (13%).

SERVICES: There is a reader service for the blind, and remedial math and writing. Tutoring in French grammar is also available. **Library/Resources:** The 2 libraries contain 3.4 million volumes, 1.3 million microform items, and 37,832 audio/video tapes/CDs/DVDs, and subscribe to 17,625 periodicals including electronic. Computerized library services include interlibrary loans, database searching, and Internet access. Special learning facilities include an art gallery, natural history museum, radio station, a language lab, and business simulations. **Physically Challenged Students:** 95% of the campus is accessible. Facilities include wheelchair ramps, elevators, special parking, specially equipped restrooms, special class scheduling, lowered drinking fountains, lowered telephones, teletype machines for the deaf, computerized classrooms for the visually disabled, electric doors, sidewalks adjusted for physically disabled students, elevators equipped with speaking devices, and a campus plan in braille. **Special:** Laval offers co-op programs in forest operation, mining, metallurgical engineering, mineral engineering, and wood processing engineering, and study abroad in 65 countries. Dual majors are possible in anthropology and ethnology, economics and politics, international studies and modern languages, historical sciences and patrimonial studies, French language and professional writing, math and computer science. Intensive French courses are offered during the summer. **Visiting:** There are regularly scheduled orientations for prospective students. There are guides for informal visits and visitors may stay overnight. To schedule a visit, contact the Public Affairs Office at (877) 785-2825. **Campus Safety and Security:** Measures include 24-hour foot and vehicle patrol and security escort services. There are emergency telephones, lighted pathways/sidewalks, 24-hour camera surveillance in pedestrian tunnels and trained evacuating teams in all buildings. Security training for social events is offered to all student associations.

REQUIREMENTS: The only general requirement is the D.E.C. (Diploma of Collegial Studies 13 years of scholarity) or the equivalent. Some programs have specific requirements. All undergraduate students (except those who are nonfrancophones) must show a sufficient knowledge of the French language to obtain their bachelor's degree. Requirements for graduation vary according to the program. A minimum GPA of 2.0 out of 4.33 is required per 30 credits. **Procedure:** Freshmen are admitted to all sessions. Applications should be filed by March 1 for fall entry. Applications are accepted online. **Transfer Students:** 1662 transfer students enrolled in 2016-2017. Applicants must have the D.E.C. or the equivalent. **International Students:** The school actively recruits these students.

ADMISSIONS: 70% of the 2017-2018 applicants were accepted. **Admissions Contact:** Samuel Auger, Media Relations. Email: *reg@reg.ulaval.ca* Web: *www.ulaval.ca*

FINANCIAL AID: The FAFSA code is G06837. The deadline for filing freshman financial aid applications for fall entry is June 30.

UNIVERSITY OF SASKATCHEWAN — C-2
www.usask.ca

Saskatoon, SK S7N 5A2 — **(306) 966-5788**

Fax: (306) 966-2115
Email: admissions@usask.ca
Full-time: 10,000 men, 10,515 women
Faculty: n/av
Part-time: n/av
Ph.D.s: 87%
Graduate: n/av
Student/Faculty: n/av
Year: semesters, summer session
Tuition: $5043
Room & Board: $4275
Freshman Class: n/av
CEEB CODE: 0980
Application Deadline: April 1

University of Saskatchewan, founded in 1907, is a public institution offering programs in business, agriculture, arts and sciences, education, engineering, and health professions. The figures in the above capsule and in this profile are approximate. There are 13 undergraduate schools and 4 graduate schools. In addition to regional accreditation, uSaskatchewan has baccalaureate program accreditation with ACTEP, ITEP, NORTEP, and SUNTEP. The 1865-acre campus is in an urban area in Saskatoon.

STUDENT LIFE: 90% of undergraduates are from Saskatchewan. Others are from 100 foreign countries, and Canada. **Female To Male Ratio:** 1.1:1. 77% remain to graduate. **Housing:** 1600 students can be accommodated in college housing, which includes single-sex dorms, off-campus apartments, and married student housing. On-campus housing is available on a first-come and first-served basis. All students may keep cars.

FACULTY/CLASSROOMS: 65% of faculty are male; 35% are female. No introductory courses are taught by graduate students.

PROGRAMS OF STUDY: uSaskatchewan confers B.A., B.Sc., B.A.Sc., B.Comm., B.E., B.Ed., B.F.A., B.Mus., B.Mus/Mus.Ed., B.S.A., B.S.N., B.S.P., and B.Sc.Kin./Kin.Ed. degrees. Master's and doctoral degrees are also awarded. Bachelor's degrees are awarded in AGRICULTURE (agricultural business management, agricultural economics, agronomy, animal science, environmental studies, horticulture, plant science, range/farm management, and soil science), BIOLOGICAL SCIENCE (anatomy, biochemistry, bioinformatics, biology/biological science, biotechnology, cell biology, environmental biology, microbiology, nutrition, and physiology), BUSINESS (accounting, banking and finance, business administration and management, business economics, human resources, marketing/retailing/merchandising, and operations management), COMMUNICATIONS AND THE ARTS (art, art history and appreciation, dramatic arts, English, fine arts, French, German, Hebrew, Latin, linguistics, modern language, music, music performance, music theory and composition, musicology/ethnomusicology, Russian, Spanish, and studio art), COMPUTER AND PHYSICAL SCIENCE (applied mathematics, chemistry, computer science, environmental geology, geology, geophysics and seismology, mathematics, and physics), EDUCATION (education, elementary education, home economics education, physical education, secondary education, and teaching English as a second/foreign language (TESOL/TEFOL), ENGINEERING AND ENVIRONMENTAL DESIGN (agricultural engineering, bioengineering, bioresource engineering, chemical engineering, civil engineering, computer engineering, electrical/electronics engineering, electrical/electronics engineering technology, engineering physics, environmental engineering, environmental engineering technology, environmental science, geological engineering, land use management and reclamation, mechanical engineering, and urban planning technology), HEALTH PROFESSIONS (biomedical science, exercise science, health science, nursing, pharmacology, pharmacy, physical therapy, and veterinary science), SOCIAL SCIENCE (anthropology, archeology, dietetics, economics, food science, gender studies, geography, history, international studies, law, Native American studies, Near Eastern studies, philosophy, political science/government, psychology, public administration, religion, social work, sociology, and women's studies).

ACTIVITIES: There are no fraternities or sororities. Groups on campus include band, cheerleading, chess, choir, chorale, chorus, computers, drama, ethnic, international, jazz band, LGBT, literary magazine, newspaper, orchestra, photography, political, professional, religious, social, social service, and student government. Popular campus events include Powwow in the Bowl, Experience US!, and Greystone Scholar Spend-a-Day. **Sports:** There are 8 intercollegiate sports for men and 7 for women, and 17 intramural sports for men and 17 for women. Facilities include the Physical Activity Complex, which houses a climbing wall, a gym, fitness center and weight room, track, squash, racquetball courts, dance studio, swimming pool, football stadium, hockey rink, curling rink, track and field area, and outdoor soccer field.

SERVICES: Counseling and information services are available, as is tutoring in most subjects. There is also remedial math and writing. **Library/Resources:** The 8 libraries contain 2.5 million volumes, 3.1 million microform items, and subscribe to 47,055 periodicals including electronic. Computerized library services include interlibrary loans, database searching, Internet access, and Wi-Fi capability. Special learning facilities include an art gallery, natural history museum, and planetarium. **Physically Challenged Students:** All of the campus is accessible. Facilities include wheelchair ramps, elevators, special parking, specially equipped restrooms, special class scheduling, lowered drinking fountains, and lowered telephones. There is also a coordinator of services for students with disabilities, special funding application assistance, and special exam scheduling and accommodations. **Special:** The University of Saskatchewan offers interdisciplinary majors, including agricultural biology, agricultural chemistry, agricultural and bioresource engineering, agricultural extension, and anthropology and archaeology. Co-op programs are offered through the Program for Agricultural Cooperative Education. There are computer science internships, as well as internships offered through the Engineering Professional Internship program. The university has exchange agreements with 41 countries. **Visiting:** There are regularly scheduled orientations for prospective students. To schedule a visit, contact the Recruitment and Admissions at (306) 966-5788. **Campus Safety and Security:** Measures include 24-hour foot and vehicle patrol, emergency notification system, self-defense education, security escort services, emergency telephones, lighted pathways/sidewalks, and controlled access to dorms/residences.

REQUIREMENTS: Applicants must be graduates of an accredited secondary school. The decision is based solely on academic achievement in secondary school. In direct-entry programs, priority is given to Saskatchewan residents, with the exception being the College of Arts and Science. A GPA of 70.0 is required. AP credits are accepted. Requirements for graduation vary according to the program of study. **Procedure:** Freshmen are admitted to all sessions. There is an early decision plan. Applications should be filed by April 1 for fall entry; September 1 for winter entry; February 1 for spring entry; and March 1 for summer entry, along with a $90 fee. Applications are accepted online. **Transfer Students:** Applicants must meet promotion levels for the college to which transfer is sought. **International Students:** There are 1863 international students enrolled. The school actively recruits these students. They must take the TOEFL with a minimum score of 550 on the paper-based TOEFL (PBT) or 80 on the Internet-based version (iBT) or take the MELAB, or take the IELTS, CanTEST, CAEL, or iBT.

Admissions Contact: Recruitment and Admission, Email: *admissions@usask.ca* Web: *www.usask.ca*

FINANCIAL AID: The FAFSA code is G22192. Check with the school for current application deadlines.

Study abroad programs are now available in more than 60 countries in fields that range from Costa Rican tropical biology to Finnish architecture. Program directors have responded to the vocational interests of the student of the 21st century by organizing programs in international management, health care administration, and other career-oriented fields.

In fact, study in both traditional and nontraditional fields is enriched by overseas experience. An international perspective can benefit study of environmental sciences, anthropology, political science, urban planning, oceanography, hotel administration, psychology, social work, journalism, marketing and law, as well as film, art history, theater, music and dance.

The vast majority of U.S. students enter European schools through organized, ongoing programs sponsored and managed by the colleges and universities in which they are already enrolled. In this way, they automatically earn U.S. academic credit from their home institution for their overseas course work. Academic credit *directly* earned at a foreign institution is often not acceptable toward a U.S. degree. Applying directly to a foreign school is not difficult but unusual.

According to the Institute of International Education (IIE), in their *Open Doors 2017 Report on International Educational Exchange*, based on the recent academic year, 325,339 U.S. students received academic credit last year at the home campus for study abroad in 2015–2016, an increase of four percent from the previous year. The number of U.S. students studying abroad has more than tripled in the past two decades; however, the rate of growth had slowed following the financial crisis in 2008. The population of U.S. students studying abroad continues to diversify, with greater inclusion of students from underrepresented racial and ethnic backgrounds. The top host destinations for U.S. students studying abroad in 2015–2016 were the United Kingdom, Italy, Spain, France, and Germany. China dropped out of the top five host countries, as the number of U.S. students studying there decreased by 9 percent. Europe was the top host region, attracting more than 50 percent of Americans who studied abroad, followed by Latin America and the Caribbean, and Asia. Strong growth was noted in Australia (8.2%), Czech Republic (12.6%), Cuba (58.6%), Denmark (14.8%), Germany (8.1%), Ireland (8.2%), Japan (18%), Mexico (9.9%), the Netherlands (17.2%), New Zealand (14.5%), and South Africa (10.2%). The top fields for U.S. students studying abroad were: STEM fields (science, technology, engineering, and math), which had an increase of 9%. Other fields also saw an increase, including business and management (8.1%), social sciences (2.45%), and fine and applied arts (2.9%).

The report also indicated that during the 2016–2017 academic year, 1,078,822 international students were studying in the United States. This represented an increase of 3.4% from the previous year. The top fields of study for international students included: STEM fields (science, technology, engineering, and math) (48%), business and management (18.6%), social sciences (7.7%), fine and applied arts (5.7%), and intensive English (2.8%).

A Productive Experience

If you are interested in study abroad, plan ahead by taking the following steps to ensure that the experience is productive:

- **Assess the ways in which study abroad will benefit your educational and career plans.** Study abroad can be a casual choice or a pleasant way to spend a semester but you will derive the greatest benefit if you bring more thought to it: How will the overseas experience complement your other courses or your educational major? Can you maximize its value by seeking language as well as academic study or by combining independent study or an internship with traditional course work?
- **Consult your campus study-abroad adviser.** Most colleges and universities have a person or an office charged with the responsibility of counseling students on overseas study. The study-abroad adviser is best qualified to help you make the right choices.
- **Make sure your college will accept credit earned at the study-abroad program you have chosen.** Speak with both your academic adviser and your study-abroad adviser and resolve any issues before you leave. Many students have assumed incorrectly that credit is granted automatically for another institution's program. You cannot take this for granted.
- **Be realistic about your foreign language proficiency.** It is one thing to be able to order a meal or buy a train ticket in a foreign language. It is quite another to follow a professor lecturing on a complex subject. If you discover that your linguistic ability is inadequate, it is quite possible that you can find abroad the subject matter you want taught in English. You will get more out of the overseas experience however, if you make the effort to function in the language of the chosen country.
- **Look carefully at costs.** If you are dealing with a program sponsor that is not your home institution, it is wise to read program literature carefully. Ask questions before you go if you have any qualms! Are charges clearly specified? Does the literature specify what services *are* covered and more important, what services are *not* covered? What is the refund policy, if any? Is there a clearly identified organization with an official base in the United States which would be legally responsible in the event of disaster?

  While drawing up your budget, think about the extras. You will want to make the small side trips to new places that help to make overseas living rewarding. Try to give yourself some financial flexibility in working out your budget.
- **Think about what it means to live abroad.** Be sure to arrange for substitutes for the support systems you take for granted at home. Will your medical insurance cover you? Do you need vaccinations or a doctor who can manage your specific health problems while you are living abroad? What about visas?

  It is critically important to find out about housing before you leave. Student housing is difficult to find almost everywhere. Be sure to find out whether securing housing abroad is your responsibility and what the alternatives are in the country in which you plan to live.
- **Don't assume that you can work abroad.** Because of foreign labor laws, students should not plan to seek paid employment. The practice of working one's way through college is not common abroad, nor are the relatively high-paying part-time jobs that make it possible in the United States. However, increasing numbers of students are looking to combine practical work experience with study abroad. There are many work exchanges, volunteer opportunities, and internships available. Contact the Council on International Exchange, 300 Fore Street, Portland, ME 04101, (207) 553-4000, Fax: (207) 553-4299 or E-mail: contact@ciee.org for further information.
- **Find out what you can about the sponsoring agency, especially if it is not an accredited U.S. college or university.** Talk to your study-abroad adviser if you have any doubts. Most private agencies engaged in study abroad are legitimate organizations but their basic purposes may not match yours. Does the organization have experience in placing students in an academic environment, not just in arranging travel? Are descriptions of its study program specific or vague? Does it make unverifiable claims about the academic reputation of its programs, or their recognition by U.S. higher educational institutions?

For further information, consult:
Institute of International Education
809 United Nations Plaza
New York, NY 10017
(212) 883-8200 Fax: (212) 984-5452
For further information, consult the following publications:
IIE Passport: Study Abroad Directories, which are available at *www.iie.org/Research-and-Publications/Publications-and-Reports*

Council on International Educational Exchange (CIEE)
300 Fore Street
Portland, ME 04101
9am–5pm
(207) 553-4000 Fax: (207) 553-4299
E-mail: contact@ciee.org
Web site: *www.ciee.org*

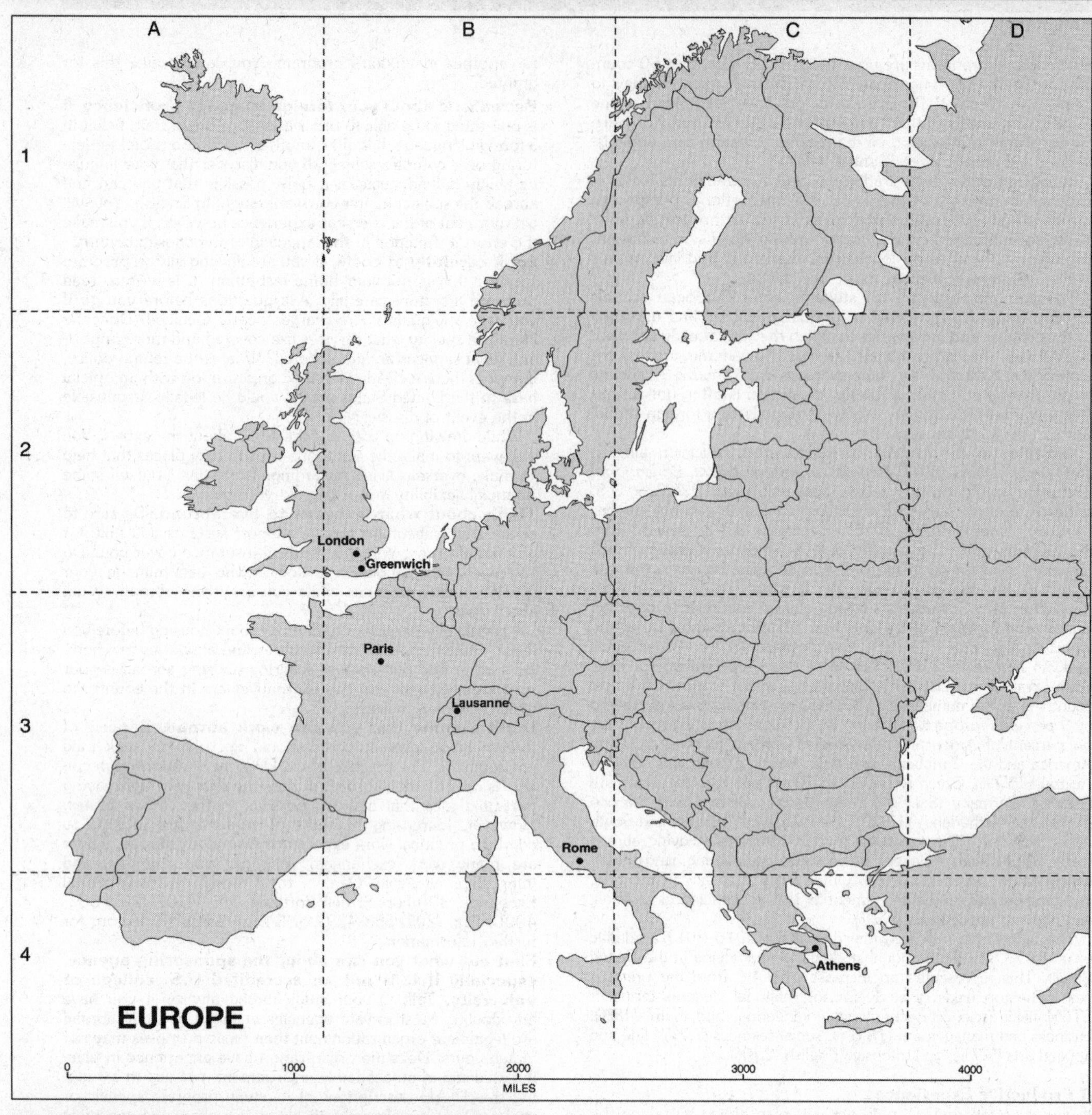

DEREE - THE AMERICAN COLLEGE OF GREECE C-4

www.acg.edu

Aghia Paraskevi Athens, 15342 **001 (857) 284 7908**

Email: mnisdeo@acg.edu

Full-time: 528 men, 611 women
Part-time: 905 men, 914 women
Graduate: 36 men, 146 women
Year: semesters, summer session
Room & Board: n/app

SAT or ACT: recommended
Application Deadline: June 15

Faculty: 86
Ph.D.s: 74%
Student/Faculty: 13 to 1
Tuition: $11,098
Freshman Class: 606 applied, 430 accepted, 407 enrolled
CEEB CODE: 0925

Deree is the undergraduate and graduate division of The American College of Greece (ACG), which was founded in 1875 as the American School for Girls. ACG has 1 campus in Athens. Deree offers bachelor's degrees in 27 areas of the liberal arts, fine and performing arts, and business. The graduate school offers masters in psychology and communications. The figures given in the above capsule and in this profile are approximate. There are 3 undergraduate schools and 2 graduate schools. In addition to regional accreditation, Deree has baccalaureate program accreditation with NEASC. The 64-acre campus is in a suburban area in Athens suburb of Aghia Paraskevi. Including any residence halls, there are 12 buildings.

STUDENT LIFE: 87% of undergraduates are from Greece. Others are from 69 foreign countries, and Canada. **Female To Male Ratio:** 1.1:1. The average age of freshmen is 19; all undergraduates, 23. 5% do not continue beyond their first year; 88% remain to graduate. **Housing:** 261 students can be accommodated in college housing, which includes off-campus apartments, studio apartments on availability only. Alcohol is not permitted. All students commute. No one may keep cars.

FACULTY/CLASSROOMS: 43% of faculty are male; 57% are female. No introductory courses are taught by graduate students. The average class size in an introductory lecture is 25; in a laboratory is 20; and in a regular course is 19.

PROGRAMS OF STUDY: Deree confers B.A. and B.S. degrees. Master's degrees are also awarded. Bachelor's degrees are awarded in AGRICULTURE (environmental studies), BUSINESS (accounting, entrepreneurial studies, finance, international business, logistics, management information systems, management, marketing/retailing/merchandising, sports management, and tourism), COMMUNICATIONS AND THE ARTS (art history, communications, dance, English, graphic design, music, music performance, theatre arts, theatre/dance, and visual and performing arts), COMPUTER AND PHYSICAL SCIENCE (information sciences and systems), HEALTH PROFESSIONS (health care administration), SOCIAL SCIENCE (economics, history, philosophy, psychology, and sociology). English, psychology, and marketing are the strongest academically. Psychology, management and communications have the largest enrollments.

ACTIVITIES: There are no fraternities or sororities. There are 54 groups on campus, including academic societies, innovation & entrepreneurship, art, choir, computers, dance, debate, drama, drill team, ethnic, film, health & social awareness, honors, international, LGBT, literary magazine, newspaper, orchestra, photography, professional, social, social service, and student government. Popular campus events include Fall Festival, Student Awards Night, and Business Week. **Sports:** Facilities include a gym, a fitness center, dance studios, aerobic rooms, outdoor tennis courts, a 50-meter swimming pool, a 400-meter track, tennis courts, basketball, and volleyball courts, and a soccer field. **Graduates:** From July 1, 2016 to June 30, 2017, 298 bachelor's degrees were awarded. The most popular majors were communications (20%), management (16%), and marketing (15%). In an average class, 1% graduate in 3 years or less, 35% graduate in 4 years or less, 47% graduate in 5 years or less, and 54% graduate in 6 years or less. Of the 2016 graduating class, 12% were enrolled in graduate school within 6 months of graduation, and 51% were employed.

SERVICES: Counseling and information services are available, as is tutoring in some subjects, math, such as accounting, finance and economics. There is also remedial writing, counseling and educational services, and career services are available. **Library/Resources:** The library contains 437,000 volumes, 6,450 microform items, and 1,700 audio/video tapes/CDs/DVDs, and subscribes to 13,000 periodicals including electronic. Computerized library services include interlibrary loans, database searching, Internet access, and Wi-Fi capability. Special learning facilities include an art gallery. **Physically Challenged Students:** 90% of the campus is accessible. Facilities include wheelchair ramps, elevators, special parking, specially equipped restrooms, special class scheduling, lowered drinking fountains, and special housing. **Special:** Study abroad, work-study programs, and dual majors in all disciplines are offered. Non-degree study and pass/fail options are available. **Visiting:** There are regularly scheduled orientations for prospective students, consisting of information sessions and campus tours. There are guides for informal visits and visitors may sit in on classes. To schedule a visit, contact the Office of Admissions at 0030-210 6009800 ext.1254. **Campus Safety and Security:** Measures include 24-hour foot and vehicle patrol and security escort services. There are shuttle buses, lighted pathways/sidewalks, and controlled access to dorms/residences.

REQUIREMENTS: The SAT or ACT and ACT Writing Test are recommended. In addition, applicants must be graduates of an accredited secondary school. The GED is accepted. English speakers are required to pass an English language proficiency test. AP and CLEP credits are accepted. Important factors in the admissions decision are recommendations by school officials, extracurricular activities record, and personality/intangible qualities. All students must maintain a minimum CI (cumulative index) of 2.0 and complete 121 semester hours, including 43 hours in general education, at least 30 in the concentration, and must meet the College's residency requirements by completing at least 30 credits (beyond the introductory level courses). Distribution requirements vary with the major but include composition, public speaking, humanities, ethics, computer, and social science. **Procedure:** Freshmen are admitted to all sessions. There are deferred admissions and rolling admissions plans. Applications should be filed by June 15 for fall entry; December 1 for spring entry; and April 1 for summer entry. Notification is sent on a rolling basis. Applications are accepted on-line. Application fees are waived if application is completed online. **Transfer Students:** 31 transfer students enrolled in 2016-2017. Applicants must be in Good Academic Standing. Students who wish to transfer from U.S institutions must have a minimum GPA of 2.75 and submit high school transcripts, an official catalog, and a diploma. English proficiency also must be demonstrated, if students are not native speakers of English. 36 of 121 credits required for the bachelor's degree must be completed at Deree. **International Students:** There are 388 international students enrolled. The school actively recruits these students. They must take the TOEFL with a minimum score of 567 on the paper-based TOEFL (PBT) or 87 on the Internet-based version (iBT) and the college's own test, or any one of these tests; GCE, IB, or IELTS.

ADMISSIONS: 71% of the 2017-2018 applicants were accepted. **Admissions Contact:** Mara Nisdeo, Dean of North American Enrollment. Email: *mnisdeo@acg.edu* Web: *www.acg.edu*

FINANCIAL AID: Deree is a member of CSS. The college's own financial statement, and Internal Revenue statement is required. The deadline for filing freshman financial aid applications for fall entry is September 1.

THE AMERICAN UNIVERSITY OF CAIRO

www.aucegypt.edu

New Cairo, 11835 **(212) 730-8800 (Egypt 20-2 615-2233)**

Fax: (212) 730-1600
Email: enrolauc@aucegypt.edu
Full-time: 2640 men, 2655 women
Faculty: 423
Part-time: n/av
Ph.D.s: 72%
Graduate: 633 men, 634 women
Student/Faculty: 14 to 1
Year: semesters, summer session
Tuition: $28,237
Room & Board: $5000
Freshman Class: 1543 applied, 1520 accepted, 1252 enrolled
SAT or ACT: required
Application Deadline: March 1

The American University in Cairo, founded in 1919, is a private liberal arts institution offering 36 undergraduate majors, and 50 graduate programs. The tuition is based on a flat rate of LE 9,800 for Egyptian students and $1,213 for international students per credit hour. Tuition and fees for international students must be paid in U.S. dollars, and subject to change at each semester. The figures given in the above capsule and in this profile are approximate. There are 5 undergraduate schools and 1 graduate school. In addition to regional accreditation, AUC has baccalaureate program accreditation with AACSB, ABET, and CSAB. The 260-acre campus is in an urban area in New Cairo, Egypt. Including any residence halls, there are 16 buildings.

STUDENT LIFE: 90% of undergraduates are from Egypt. Others are from 60 foreign countries, and Canada. **Female To Male Ratio:** 1.0:1. The average age of freshmen is 18; all undergraduates, 20. 6% do not continue beyond their first year; 82% remain to graduate. **Housing:** 830 students can be accommodated in college housing, which includes single-sex dorms and off-campus apartments. On-campus housing is guaranteed for all 4 years, is available on a first-come, and first-served basis. 91% of students commute. Alcohol is not permitted. All students may keep cars.

FACULTY/CLASSROOMS: 51% of faculty are male; 49% are female. No introductory courses are taught by graduate students. The average class size in an introductory lecture is 20; in a laboratory is 13; and in a regular course is 17.

PROGRAMS OF STUDY: AUC confers B.A. and B.S. degrees. Master's degrees are also awarded. Bachelor's degrees are awarded in BUSINESS (accounting, business administration and management, international business management, management information systems, and sports management), COMMUNICATIONS AND THE ARTS (Arabic, art, communications, English, fine/studio arts, general, French, German, Germanic languages and literature, graphic design, Greek, information technology, Italian, journalism, Spanish, theater design, and visual and performing arts), COMPUTER AND PHYSICAL SCIENCE (actuarial science, chemistry, computer science, mathematics, physical sciences, and physics), EDUCATION (general studies and journalism education), ENGINEERING AND ENVIRONMENTAL DESIGN (architectural engineering, computer engineering, construction engineering, engineering, and mechanical engineering), HEALTH PROFESSIONS (biology), SOCIAL SCIENCE (anthropology, archeology, economics, history, Middle Eastern studies, philosophy, political science/government, psychology, and sociology). Journalism, business administration, and political science have the largest enrollments.

ACTIVITIES: There are no fraternities or sororities. There are 62 groups on campus, including robotics club, anit-cancer, art, chess, choir, chorus, dance, debate, drama, ethnic, film, international, literary magazine, musical theater, newspaper, photography, political, professional, radio and TV, social, social service, student government, and yearbook. Popular campus events include International Day, National University Cultural Activities Competition and Model United Nations. **Sports:** There are 23 intercollegiate sports for men and 17 for women, and 10 intramural sports for men and 8 for women. Facilities include tennis courts, multipurpose courts for basketball, volleyball, and handball, Martial arts room, squash courts, an exercise gym, a weight training and aerobics room, tennis courts, a pool, and a stadium. **Graduates:** From July 1, 2016 to June 30, 2017, 778 bachelor's degrees were awarded. The most popular majors were business administration (24%), journalism and mass communication (18%), and political science (10%). 424 companies recruited on campus in 2016-2017. In an average class, 3% graduate in 3 years or less, 35% graduate in 4 years or less, 70% graduate in 5 years or less, and 82% graduate in 6 years or less.

SERVICES: There is remedial reading and writing. **Library/Resources:** The 2 libraries contain 673,103 volumes, 190,536 microform items, and 2,790 audio/video tapes/CDs/DVDs, and subscribe to 72,321 periodicals including electronic. Computerized library services include interlibrary loans, database searching, Internet access, and Wi-Fi capability. Special learning facilities include an art gallery, radio station, the largest English-language academic library collection in Egypt, with three theaters, and 15 cross-disciplinary research centers. The rare books and special collection, and the university archives. **Physically Challenged Students:** All of the campus is accessible. Facilities include wheelchair ramps, elevators, and specially equipped restrooms. **Special:** Study abroad through a consortium of U.S. schools, work-study programs with the university, and non-degree study are available. **Visiting:** There are regularly scheduled orientations for prospective students. There are guides for informal visits, visitors may sit in on classes, and stay overnight. To schedule a visit, contact the General Director of Admission in Egypt at 20-2 797-5551. **Campus Safety and Security:** Measures include 24-hour foot and vehicle patrol, emergency notification system, and security escort services. There are shuttle buses, lighted pathways/sidewalks, controlled access to dorms/residences, security personnel at all open entrances 24 hours a day.

REQUIREMENTS: The SAT or ACT is required. The ACT Optional Writing test is also required. In addition, U.S. applicants must also be graduates of an accredited secondary school and submit complete transcripts and a copy of their diploma. Others must submit the Egyptian Thanawiya Amma certificate or other national high school certificate recognized by the university as equivalent to it, or the GCE, GCSE, or IGCSE. A minimum high school GPA of 2.0 is required. Students should have taken courses in 3 of the following subjects: languages and humanities, math, social studies, and biological and physical sciences. AP credits are accepted. Important factors in the admissions decision are ability to finance college education, evidence of special talent, and extracurricular activities record. All students must maintain a C average and must complete from 120 to 162 semester credits, depending on the major. Core courses include a writing program, an interdisciplinary seminar in humanities, natural science, and social science, a scientific-thinking course, and Arab literature, history, and society. **Procedure:** Freshmen are admitted fall and spring. Entrance exams should be taken by July for fall admission. There is a rolling admissions plan. Early decision applications should be filed by April 1; regular applications, by March 1 for fall entry; November 1 for winter entry; October 15 for spring entry; and May 1 for summer entry. The fall 2017 application fee was $45. Applications are accepted on-line. **Transfer Students:** 20 transfer students enrolled in 2016-2017. Transfer students must have a C average on secondary school and college transcripts. 45 of 120 credits required for the bachelor's degree must be completed at AUC. **International Students:** There are 351 international students enrolled. The school actively recruits these students. Graduates of U.S. high schools must take the SAT or ACT.

ADMISSIONS: 99% of the 2017-2018 applicants were accepted. The SAT scores for the 2017-2018 freshman class were: Critical Reading-- 68% below 500, 27% between 500 and 599, 4% between 600 and 699, and 1% between 700 and 800. Math-- 15% below 500, 41% between 500 and 599, 38% between 600 and 699, and 6% between 700 and 800. Writing-- 22% below 500, 58% between 500 and 599, 19% between 600 and 699, and 1% between 700 and 800. **Admissions Contact:** American University in Cairo, New York Office. Email: *enrolauc@aucegypt.edu* Web: *www.aucegypt.edu*

FINANCIAL AID: In 2017-2018, 55% of all full-time freshmen received some form of financial aid. 43% of all full-time freshmen received need-based aid. The college's own financial statement is required. The FAFSA code is G05034. The priority date for freshman financial aid applications for fall entry is January 15. The deadline for filing freshman financial aid applications for fall entry is April 20.

THE AMERICAN UNIVERSITY OF PARIS B-3

www.aup.edu

Paris, 75007 **(33) 1 40 62 06 61**

Email: ssprenger@aup.edu

Full-time: 580 men, 596 women	**Faculty:** 62
Part-time: 80 men, 92 women	**Ph.D.s:** 69%
Graduate: n/av	**Student/Faculty:** 12 to 1
Year: semesters, summer session	**Tuition:** $28,795
Room & Board: $15,742	**Freshman Class:** n/av
SAT or ACT: recommended	**CEEB CODE:** 0866
Application Deadline: July 15	

The American University of Paris, founded in 1962, is a private institution that provides a liberal arts program in an international context. AUP offers 24 undergraduate programs, and 9 graduate programs in 12 academic departments. It has regional U.S. accreditation and is recognized by the French government as an institute of higher learning. Classes are in English except for foreign language and literature courses. The figures given in the above capsule and in this profile are approximate. There is 1 undergraduate school and 1 graduate school. In addition to regional accreditation, AUP has baccalaureate program accreditation with CHEMSA, ATHEA, and MSCHE. The campus is in an urban area in Paris, on the Left Bank, near the Eiffel Tower and the Seine. Including any residence halls, there are 9 buildings.

STUDENT LIFE: Students are from Paris and 142 foreign countries, and Canada. **Female To Male Ratio:** 1.0:1. The average age of freshmen is 19; all undergraduates, 21. **Housing:** 475 students can be accommodated in college housing, which includes coed off-campus apartments. First year students are to arrange housing with Comforts of Home, including Home Stays is an authentic Perisian life-style shared by 4 - 6 other students. On-campus housing is available on a first-come and first-served basis. No one may keep cars.

FACULTY/CLASSROOMS: No introductory courses are taught by graduate students. The average class size in an introductory lecture is 13; in a laboratory is 8; and in a regular course is 13.

PROGRAMS OF STUDY: AUP confers B.A. and B.S. degrees. Master's degrees are also awarded. Bachelor's degrees are awarded in BUSINESS (business administration and management, entrepreneurial studies, international business management, international economics, international finance, management information systems, management, and marketing), COMMUNICATIONS AND THE ARTS (art history, communications, comparative literature, creative writing, film arts, fine arts, French, and Latin), COMPUTER AND PHYSICAL SCIENCE (computer science), EDUCATION (journalism education), ENGINEERING AND ENVIRONMENTAL DESIGN (environmental science), SOCIAL SCIENCE (economics, European studies, gender studies, history, international political science, Middle Eastern studies, philosophy, psychology, and urban studies). Art history, international economics, and comparative literature are the strongest academically. International business administration, global communications, and international comparative politics have the largest enrollments.

ACTIVITIES: There are no fraternities or sororities. Groups on campus include wine society club, music & performing club, Paris fashion club, roots and shoots, theatre club, art, cheerleading, chess, computers, dance, debate, drama, environmental, ethnic, film, forensics, honors, international, LGBT, literary magazine, newspaper, photography, political, professional, radio and TV, religious, social, social service, starting a new club, and student government. Popular campus events include Student Clubs Night, Holiday Bash, Showcase, Spring Break, and Charity Week. **Sports:** There are 3 intercollegiate sports for men and 3 for women, and 6 intramural sports for men and 6 for women. Facilities include AUP Competitive Sports include equestrian, indoor soccer, basketball. Recreational sports are flag football, boxing, Zumba, Yoga, Brazilian Jiu Jitsu and running. **Graduates:** From July 1, 2016 to June 30, 2017, 131 bachelor's degrees were awarded. The most popular majors were global communications (17%), international and comparative politics (14%), and international business administration (14%). In an average class, 18% graduate in 3 years or less, 40% graduate in 4 years or less, 45% graduate in 5 years or less, and 46% graduate in 6 years or less.

SERVICES: Counseling and information services are available, as is tutoring in most subjects. There is remedial writing. Faculty project support, and pedagogical workshops, plagiarism-detection training and consultation, survey-building training, and disability support **Library/Resources:** The library contains 76,000 volumes, 1,000 microform items, and 500,000 audio/video tapes/CDs/DVDs, and subscribes to 40,000 periodicals including electronic. Computerized library services include interlibrary loans, database searching, Internet access, and Wi-Fi capability. Special learning facilities include an art gallery, radio station, The AUP Arts Gallery presents art by the community, students, alumni, faculty and by professional artist from different backgrounds and cultures. Health and Wellness, student support program, students accounting services, student immigration services, The iSPACE-Interactive teaching and learning, Links Peer tutoring program, instructional technology online teaching and learning. **Physically Challenged Students:** 50% of the campus is accessible. Facilities include wheelchair ramps, elevators, specially equipped restrooms, and special class scheduling. **Special:** There are co-operative partnership programs with, Eugene Lang College of the New School, The Fashion Institute of Technology, The George Washington University, The Goizueta Business School of Emory University, Loyola University in Maryland, Northeastern University, Salve Regina University, The University of Miami, The University of San Francisco, l' Université de Paris-Sorbonne, The American University of Cairo in Egypt, The University of Cape Town in South Africa, Lingnan University in Hong Kong, and The University of Oslo in Norway. Cross-registration is available in foreign language programs at 3 other French colleges. Juniors and seniors with good academic standing are encouraged to undertake internships. There are Study abroad institutions available for undergraduate students in USA, South Africa, Cairo, Egypt, Hong Kong, and Norway, second degrees, non-degree study, and pass/fail options also are offered. There is 1 national honor society and 10 departmental honors programs. **Visiting:** There are regularly scheduled orientations for prospective students, by appointment. There are guides for informal visits and visitors may sit in on classes. To schedule a visit, contact the Admissions Office at +331 40 62 0720.

REQUIREMENTS: The SAT or ACT is recommended. Candidates must be graduates of an accredited secondary school. An essay and 2 letters of recommendation are also needed. Knowledge of French is not required. Students may apply either through the AUP website, or through the Common Application. A GPA of 2.8 is required. AP credits are accepted. Important factors in the admissions decision are advanced placement or honors courses, recommendations by school officials, personality/intangible qualities, and extracurricular activities record. Undergraduate students must maintain a minimum GPA of 2.0 and earn at least 128 semester credits. The 128 credits required to graduate, include core major requirements, general education requirements and general electives. The general education requirement includes; mathematics, English, French, social sciences, science, and humanities courses. **Procedure:** Freshmen are admitted fall and spring. There are deferred admissions and rolling admissions plans. Application deadlines are open. Application fee is $70. Applications are accepted on-line. **Transfer Students:** 80 transfer students enrolled in 2016-2017. Transfer applicants must submit college and high school transcripts, and SAT I or ACT scores if they have fewer than 45 credits. Two letters of recommendation, and an essay are required. 64 of 128 credits required for the bachelor's degree must be completed at AUP. **International Students:** There are 697 international students enrolled. The school actively recruits these students. They must take the TOEFL and the college's own test. They must also take the TOEIC, or IELTS.

Admissions Contact: Scott Sprenger, Provost of Academic Affairs. Email: *ssprenger@aup.edu* Web: *www.aup.edu*

FINANCIAL AID: In 2017-2018, 43% of all full-time freshmen and 36% of continuing full-time students received some form of financial aid. 26% of all full-time freshmen and 28% of continuing full-time students received need-based aid. The average freshman award was $8,943. AUP is a member of CSS. The college's own financial statement is required. The priority date for freshman financial aid applications for fall entry is March 15.

THE AMERICAN UNIVERSITY OF ROME B-3

www.aur.edu

Rome, 00153 **+39 06 5833 0919 (228)**

Email: a.damico@aur.edu

Full-time: n/av	**Faculty:** 16
Part-time: n/av	**Ph.D.s:** 73%
Graduate: n/av	**Student/Faculty:** 16 to 1
Year: semesters, summer session	**Tuition:** $23,420
Room & Board: $9100	**Freshman Class:** n/av
SAT or ACT: required	**CEEB CODE:** 0262
Application Deadline: March 31	

The American University of Rome, founded in 1969, is a private institution offering programs in archeology, art history, business, communications, film and digital media, Italian studies, international relations, and liberal arts. The figures given in the above capsule and in this profile are approximate. There is 1 undergraduate school. In addition to regional accreditation, AUR has baccalaureate program accreditation with MSCHE. The campus is in a suburban area on the Janiculum Hill, 15 minutes walking distance from downtown Rome. Including any residence halls, there are 3 buildings.

STUDENT LIFE: Students are from Rome and 40 foreign countries, and Canada. 20% are from public schools. 83% are White; 7% Hispanic; 4% African American. The student base is all male. The average age of freshmen is 18; all undergraduates, 20. 30% remain to graduate. **Housing:** 350 students can be accommodated in college housing, which includes single-sex off-campus apartments. Freshman students are grouped together in housing the First Year Seminar which teaches you how to adjust to university life in Rome. On-campus housing is available on a first-come and first-served basis. 85% of students live on campus. Alcohol is not permitted. No one may keep cars.

FACULTY/CLASSROOMS: 40% of faculty are male; 60% are female. All teach undergraduates, and 70% do research. No introductory courses are taught by graduate students. The average class size in an introductory lecture is 18; in a laboratory is 12; and in a regular course is 18.

PROGRAMS OF STUDY: AUR confers B.A. and B.S. degrees. Associate degrees are also awarded. Bachelor's degrees are awarded in BUSINESS (business administration and management, marketing, and tourism), COMMUNICATIONS AND THE ARTS (art history and appreciation, communications, film arts, film, and television and digital media), SOCIAL SCIENCE (archeology, international relations, international studies, Italian studies, and religious studies). Business administration, international relations, and communications have the largest enrollments.

ACTIVITIES: There are no fraternities or sororities. Groups on campus include and cooking lessons with authentic Italian chefs, drama club, Italian language exchange, art, choir, dance, debate, drama, film, honors, international, LGBT, literary magazine, newspaper, photography, political, professional, religious, self-defense, social, social service, and student government. Popular campus events include Guest Lecture Series, Trips to Tuscany, Capri, Sorrento and Pompeii, Business Excursions, and International Relations Debates. **Sports:** There are 1 intercollegiate sports for men and 1 for women, and 3 intramural sports for men and 3 for women. Facilities include off-campus access to men's and women's soccer, tennis, swimming facilities, and performing arts. AUR fitness center offers cardio fitness, and muscle toning equipment/machines, yoga, Pilates, Boot camp, running track, martial arts, and rowing. **Graduates:** Of the 2016 graduating class, 32% were enrolled in graduate school within 6 months of graduation, and 48% were employed.

SERVICES: Counseling and information services are available, as is tutoring in some subjects, such as Italian language. There is remedial math and writing. **Library/Resources:** The library contains 15,000 volumes, 10,000 microform items, and 1,200 audio/video tapes/CDs/DVDs, and subscribes to 0 periodicals including electronic. Computerized library services include interlibrary loans, database searching, Internet access, and Wi-Fi capability. **Physically Challenged Students:** 30% of the campus is accessible. **Special:** Internships in business, international relations, communications, Italian studies, art history, film and digital media, and archeology are available. Study abroad programs are available in China, Denmark, Ecuador, England, Greece, and Spain. There are 99 departmental honors programs. **Visiting:** There are regularly scheduled orientations for prospective students, which AUR organizes directly and through its agents in many U.S. states and in other countries. Orientation is assisted by use of audiovisual materials. There are guides for informal visits and visitors may sit in on classes. To schedule a visit, contact the Enrollment Services at +39 06 5833 0919. **Campus Safety and Security:** Freshman students are grouped together in housing the First Year Seminar which teaches you how to adjust to university life in Rome.

REQUIREMENTS: The SAT or ACT is required. In addition, a high school diploma and transcript or the non-American equivalent is required, as are a letter of recommendation and 2 short answer essay questions, copy of valid photo ID or passport, an interview with the admissions office contact. The GED is accepted. A GPA of 2.5 is required. AP and CLEP credits are accepted. Important factors in the admissions decision are recommendations by school officials, advanced placement or honors courses, and personality/intangible qualities. To graduate, students must complete 120 credits, including 60 in the major, with a minimum GPA of 2.0. Distribution requirements include general education requirements, including Italian language, requirements in the major and free electives. A comprehensive exam in business and a thesis in other disciples is required. **Procedure:** Freshmen are admitted to all sessions. There are early decision, early admissions, deferred admissions, and rolling admissions plans. March 31 for fall entry; October 31 for spring entry, along with a $60 fee. Applications are accepted on-line. **Transfer Students:** Applicants must submit an application, a high school transcript, a diploma, all transcripts of universities attended, a letter of recommendation, and an essay. 45 of 120 credits required for the bachelor's degree must be completed at AUR. **International Students:** There are 240 international students enrolled. The school actively recruits these students. They must take the TOEFL with a minimum score of 79 on the Internet-based version (iBT) and the college's own test, the IELTS test score of 6.5.

Admissions Contact: Arianna D'Amico, Director of Admissions and F.A.. Email: *a.damico@aur.edu* Web: *www.aur.edu*

FINANCIAL AID: In 2017-2018, 38% of all full-time freshmen and 43% of continuing full-time students received some form of financial aid. 20% of all full-time freshmen and 17% of continuing full-time students received need-based aid. The FAFSA code is G31025. The deadline for filing freshman financial aid applications for fall entry is March 1.

FRANKLIN UNIVERSITY SWITZERLAND B-3

www.fus.edu

Sorengo, Lugano, 6924 (713) 623-1879 (011-41-91-986-3613)

Email: nmack@fus.edu

Full-time: 140 men, 276 women	**Faculty:** 25
Part-time: 3 women	**Ph.D.s:** 76%
Graduate: 4 men, 1 women	**Student/Faculty:** 16 to 1
Year: semesters, summer session	**Tuition:** $42,720
Room & Board: $13,290	**Freshman Class:** n/av
SAT: required	
Application Deadline: March 15	

Franklin University Switzerland, founded in 1969, is a dual-accredited American institution providing a liberal arts education through courses that are international in perspective and cross-cultural in content. The baccalaureate degree offers concentrations in international management, art history, modern languages (French, Italian, German), international relations, history/literature, visual and communication arts, and more. There is 1 undergraduate school and 1 graduate school. In addition to regional accreditation, Franklin has baccalaureate program accreditation with Swiss University Conference. The 4-acre campus is in a suburban area on a hillside above Lugano in the southern Italian-speaking region of Switzerland called Ticino. Including any residence halls, there are 13 buildings.

STUDENT LIFE: Students are from Southern Italy, 23 states, 55 foreign countries, and Canada. **Female To Male Ratio:** 1.9:1. The average age of freshmen is 18; all undergraduates, 20. 48% do not continue beyond their first year. **Housing:** College-sponsored housing includes single-sex dorms, on-campus apartments, and off-campus apartments. On-campus housing is guaranteed for all 4 years. 85% of students live on campus; of those, 60% remain on campus on weekends. All students may keep cars.

FACULTY/CLASSROOMS: 50% of faculty are male; 50% are female. All teach undergraduates. No introductory courses are taught by graduate students. The average class size in an introductory lecture is 15; in a laboratory is 10; and in a regular course is 15.

PROGRAMS OF STUDY: Franklin confers B.A., and M.S. degrees. Associate and master's degrees are also awarded. Bachelor's degrees are awarded in BUSINESS (international business management and international economics), COMMUNICATIONS AND THE ARTS (art history and appreciation, literature, media arts, and modern language), SOCIAL SCIENCE (European studies, history, and international relations). International management/international relations is the strongest academically.

ACTIVITIES: There are no fraternities or sororities. Groups on campus include art, drama, international, literary magazine, newspaper, photography, social, student government, and yearbook. Popular campus events include Academic Travel, International Food Night, and Tutte le Strade. **Sports:** There are 3 intramural sports for men and 2 for women. **Graduates:** From July 1, 2016 to June 30, 2017, 72 bachelor's degrees were awarded. The most popular majors were international management (35%), international relations (15%), and international economics (11%). In an average class, 20% graduate in 3 years or less and 80% graduate in 4 years or less.

SERVICES: Counseling and information services are available, as is tutoring in most subjects. **Library/Resources:** The library contains 33,500 volumes, 15 microform items, and 1,620 audio/video tapes/CDs/DVDs, and subscribes to 174 periodicals including electronic. Computerized library services include interlibrary loans and database searching. **Special:** Cross-registration with most U.S. colleges having an international management major, internships, study abroad as part of the academic travel requirement. We also offer accelerated degree programs in any major and dual majors and minors are offered. There are 4 departmental honors programs. **Visiting:** There are guides for informal visits and visitors may sit in on classes. **Campus Safety and Security:** There are emergency telephones and lighted pathways/sidewalks.

REQUIREMENTS: The SAT is required. The college recommends that applicants have completed 4 years of English grammar, composition, and literature, 3 years each of history, math and foreign language, and 2 years each of science. Electives in art, music, and computer science are recommended. An essay, a personal statement, and academic references are required. An interview is strongly encouraged. AP credits are accepted. Important factors in the admissions decision are leadership record, personality/intangible qualities, and extracurricular activities record. All students must complete 125 credit hours. A general core requirement includes foreign languages, global awareness, and writing. Academic travel is also required each year (each travel program is 3 academic credits). A minimum GPA of 2.0 overall and 42 credits or more in the major, with a C or better, are also required. Most majors require a thesis. **Procedure:** Freshmen are admitted to all sessions. Entrance exams should be taken in the fall prior to the desired entrance. There are early decision, early admissions, deferred admissions, and rolling admissions plans. Early decision applications should be filed by December 15; regular applications, by March 15 for fall entry; November 15 for spring entry; and May 1 for summer entry, along with a $50 fee. Notification of early decision is sent January 15; regular decision, on a rolling basis. **Transfer Students:** Applicants must have a C average and provide 1 recommendation. 60 of 120 credits required for the bachelor's degree must be completed at Franklin. **International Students:** The school actively recruits these students. They must take the TOEFL. They must also take the SAT or ACT.

Admissions Contact: Nathan Mack, Associate Director of Admissions. Email: *nmack@fus.edu* Web: *www.fus.edu*

FINANCIAL AID: In 2017-2018, 62% of all full-time freshmen received some form of financial aid. 62% of all full-time freshmen received need-based aid. The average freshman award was $19,594. 30% of undergraduate students work part-time. Average annual earnings from campus work are $1000. Franklin is a member of CSS. The college's own financial statement is required. The FAFSA code is G11683. The deadline for filing freshman financial aid applications for fall entry is May 1.

JOHN CABOT UNIVERSITY B-3
www.johncabot.edu

Rome, 00165 **+39 06 681 9121**

Email: jantonio@johncabot.edu

Full-time: 460 men, 467 women
Part-time: n/av
Graduate: n/av
Year: semesters, summer session
Room & Board: $10,790
SAT CR/M/W: 541/507/521
Application Deadline: July 15

Faculty: 20
Ph.D.s: 90%
Student/Faculty: 32 to 1
Tuition: $23,900
Freshman Class: n/av
CEEB CODE: 2795

John Cabot University, founded in 1972, is an independent, liberal arts college offering an American university education in the heart of Rome, Italy. John Cabot students enrich their international academic experience by pursuing international internships, taking part in student athletics and organizations, and traveling on educational exchange programs with John Cabot's partner universities abroad. There is 1 undergraduate school. In addition to regional accreditation, JCU has baccalaureate program accreditation with CHEMSA. The campus is in an urban area along the banks of the Tiber River in the historic center of Rome. Including any residence halls, there are 4 buildings.

STUDENT LIFE: 75% of undergraduates are from out of state, mostly the Mid-West. Students are from 30 states, 70 foreign countries, and Canada. **Female To Male Ratio:** 1.0:1. The average age of freshmen is 18; all undergraduates, 22. 13% do not continue beyond their first year; 87% remain to graduate. **Housing:** 500 students can be accommodated in college housing, which includes single-sex dorms, on-campus apartments, and off-campus apartments. In addition, there are special-interest houses. On-campus housing is guaranteed for all 4 years. Some may keep cars.

FACULTY/CLASSROOMS: 60% of faculty are male; 40% are female. All teach undergraduates, and 40% do research. No introductory courses are taught by graduate students. The average class size in an introductory lecture is 15 and in a regular course is 25.

PROGRAMS OF STUDY: JCU confers B.A., and B.B.A. degrees. Associate and master's degrees are also awarded. Bachelor's degrees are awarded in BUSINESS (business administration and management and marketing management), COMMUNICATIONS AND THE ARTS (art history and appreciation, classics, communications, and English literature), SOCIAL SCIENCE (economics, history, humanities, international studies, Italian studies, and political science/government). Business administration, and International affairs have the largest enrollments.

ACTIVITIES: There are no fraternities or sororities. There are 15 groups on campus, including art, cheerleading, chess, dance, debate, drama, environmental, ethnic, film, international, jazz band, LGBT, musical theater, newspaper, opera, photography, political, professional, social, social service, student government, and yearbook. Popular campus events include Trips to Florence, Capri, and Venice, Presidential Gala, 2 Musical Theater Productions per year, Presidental Lecture Series, and Inverse Poetry Festival. **Sports:** There are 4 intercollegiate sports for men and 4 for women, and 8 intramural sports for men and 10 for women. Facilities include a soccer field, volleyball court, and basketball. **Graduates:** From July 1, 2016 to June 30, 2017, 102 bachelor's degrees were awarded. The most popular majors were international business, international affairs, and art history. 32 companies recruited on campus in 2016-2017.

SERVICES: Counseling and information services are available, as is tutoring in some subjects, such as Italian, French, and Spanish. There is remedial math, reading, and writing. The career Service Center prepares students for internships, graduate programs, and careers **Library/Resources:** The library contains 32,000 volumes, and 1,300 audio/video tapes/CDs/DVDs, and subscribes to 72 periodicals including electronic. Computerized library services include interlibrary loans, database searching, Internet access, and Wi-Fi capability. **Physically Challenged Students:** Facilities include wheelchair ramps, elevators, specially equipped restrooms, special housing. **Special:** Qualifying students may intern through John Cabot Career Services with multinational and Italian businesses, governmental organizations, and embassies. Workstudy opportunities are also avaailable. Students may also study abroad at one of John Cabot's partner institutions in the United States, Europe, and Australia. There is a freshman honors program. **Visiting:** There are regularly scheduled orientations for prospective students, visits are conducted Monday-Friday at 10 a.m. and 2 p.m. Open Houses are scheduled monthly. Skype with an Admissions Counselor with concern questions. There are guides for informal visits and visitors may sit in on classes. To schedule a visit, contact the Admissions Office at +39-06-6819121. **Campus Safety and Security:** Measures include 24-hour foot and vehicle patrol, emergency notification system, self-defense education, and security escort services. There are emergency telephones, controlled access to dorms/residences, guards on duty 24/7 in dormitories and academic buildings.

REQUIREMENTS: SAT or ACT tests are required for U.S. high school graduates and are recommended for students graduating from other educational systems. Also required are a personal essay and 2 letters of academic recommendation. An interview is recommended; the GED diploma may be recognized for admission. A GPA of 2.8 is required. AP and CLEP credits are accepted. Important factors in the admissions decision are advanced placement or honors courses, leadership record, recommendations by school officials, and extracurricular activities record. To graduate, students must complete 120 semester hours with a GPA of 2.0, including required courses in writing, math, and foreign language. **Procedure:** Freshmen are admitted to all sessions. Entrance exams should be taken at the orientation session. There are early decision, early admissions, deferred admissions, and rolling admissions plans. Applications should be filed by July 15 for fall entry; November 15 for spring entry, along with a $50 fee. 20 early decision candidates were accepted for the 2017-2018 class. Applications are accepted on-line. **Transfer Students:** 80 transfer students enrolled in 2016-2017. Transfer applicants must be in good academic standing at the previous institution. 60 of 120 credits required for the bachelor's degree must be completed at JCU. **International Students:** There are 467 international students enrolled. The school actively recruits these students. They must take the TOEFL with a minimum score of 85 on the Internet-based version (iBT) and the college's own test, or take the IELTS. They must also take the SAT or ACT.

Admissions Contact: James Antonio, Associate Director of Admissions. Email: *jantonio@johncabot.edu* Web: *www.johncabot.edu*

FINANCIAL AID: 10% of undergraduate students work part-time. The college's own financial statement is required. The FAFSA code is G33293. Check with the school for current application deadlines.

RICHMOND, THE AMERICAN INTERNATIONAL UNIVERSITY IN LONDON B-2
www.richmond.ac.uk

Richmond, Surrey, TW10 6JP **1 (617) 958-9542**

Email: teressa.cleary@richmond.ac.uk

Full-time: 565 men, 570 women
Part-time: 6 men, 57 women
Graduate: 50 men, 50 women
Year: semesters, summer session
Room & Board: $12,100
SAT CR/M: 542/535 **ACT:** 24
Application Deadline: July 1

Faculty: 50
Ph.D.s: 90%
Student/Faculty: 19 to 1
Tuition: $38,000
Freshman Class: n/av

Richmond, The American International University in London, established in 1972, is an independent, international, liberal arts and professional studies university. The figures given are in US dollars in the above capsule and in this profile are approximate. There are 2 undergraduate schools and 2 graduate schools. In addition to regional accreditation, Richmond has baccalaureate program accreditation with MAS/CHE, NACAC, NASPA, and NESA. The 5-acre campus is in a suburban area JCU's two campus centers are located along the banks of the Tiber River in the historic center of Rome. Including any residence halls, there are 3 buildings.

STUDENT LIFE: Students are from London, 40 states, and 70 foreign countries. **Female To Male Ratio:** 1.1:1. **Housing:** College-sponsored housing includes dorms and on-campus apartments. Accommodations are predominantly for first and second year students, generally new students live at The Hill. On-campus housing is available on a first-come and first-served basis. No one may keep cars.

FACULTY/CLASSROOMS: 65% of faculty are male; 35% are female. 97% teach undergraduates. No introductory courses are taught by grad-

uate students. The average class size in an introductory lecture is 22; in a laboratory is 12; and in a regular course is 17.

PROGRAMS OF STUDY: Richmond confers B.A. and B.S. degrees. Associate and master's degrees are also awarded. Bachelor's degrees are awarded in BUSINESS (business administration and management, business administration - international, fashion merchandising, finance, international business management, and marketing), COMMUNICATIONS AND THE ARTS (art and design, art history and appreciation, communications, design, English as a second/foreign language, German, Latin, literature, film and media studies, music, performing arts, Russian, Spanish, studio art, theatre studies, and visual and performing arts), COMPUTER AND PHYSICAL SCIENCE (chemistry, computer programming, mathematics, and physics), ENGINEERING AND ENVIRONMENTAL DESIGN (environmental science and systems engineering), HEALTH PROFESSIONS (biology and pre-physician assistant), SOCIAL SCIENCE (American studies, anthropology, classical/ancient civilization, economics, French studies, gender studies, history, humanities and social science, international relations, political science/government, psychology, sociology, and world cultural studies). International relations & business, international affairs, art history, and English literature have the largest enrollments.

ACTIVITIES: There are no fraternities or sororities. Groups on campus include and investment club, self-defense club, yoga club, art, drama, ethnic, fashion club, film, honors, international, LGBT, newspaper, political, professional, religious, social, social service, and student government. Popular campus events include Movie Nights, Comedy Nights, and Theatre Trips, Wine Tasting, Day and Weekend Trips, Italian Cooking Classes, the Royal Albert Hall or Wembley Stadium for Concerts. **Sports:** Facilities include multi-purpose outdoor court for tennis, basketball, volleyball, and mini-soccer, football, soccer, games and basketball competitions, dodgeball matches, a 40 square meter fitness centre equipped with Cybex cardiovascular and weights machines. **Graduates:** From July 1, 2016 to June 30, 2017, 184 bachelor's degrees were awarded.

SERVICES: **Library/Resources:** The 2 libraries contain 60,000 volumes, and subscribe to 300 periodicals including electronic. Computerized library services include database searching. **Physically Challenged Students:** Facilities include special housing. At the time of Admissions provide the Office of Student Affairs with the appropriate medical documentation, so that we can make all reasonable accommodations to your needs. In addition, you must complete a Disability Form. **Special:** The International Internship Program utilizes London-based businesses and institutions. Study abroad is offered in London, Florence or Rome. A field study project in a developing country may be arranged during the summer. A limited number of students can be placed in family helper/au pair positions with British families. Joint degrees are offered in engineering with George Washington University. There is a freshman honors program. **Visiting:** There are regularly scheduled orientations for prospective students, open day registration, (Monday,Wednesday and Friday), postgraduation visit registration, and campus tour registration. There are guides for informal visits, visitors may sit in on classes, and stay overnight. To schedule a visit, contact the Admissions Counselor in the U.K. **Campus Safety and Security:** Measures include 24-hour foot and vehicle patrol.

REQUIREMENTS: The SAT or ACT is required. U.S. applicants should have completed secondary school with a 2.5 GPA. A GED equivalent is acceptable. An autobiographical essay is an important part of the application. A GPA of 2.5 is required. AP and CLEP credits are accepted. Important factors in the admissions decision are advanced placement or honors courses, geographical diversity, and recommendations by school officials. Students must complete 12 courses in 7 fields: English, humanities, social science, intercultural studies, math, science, and the creative arts. Proficiency in English composition, math, and computer skills is required. A 2.0 GPA and 120 credit hours are needed to graduate. **Procedure:** Freshmen are admitted to all sessions. There are deferred admissions and rolling admissions plans. Application deadlines are open. The fall 2017 application fee was $35. Notifications are sent August 1. **Transfer Students:** 48 transfer students enrolled in 2016-2017. A 2.0 GPA, official transcripts from all previous institutions, and 2 references are required for admission. All transfer students are required to complete a minimum of 54 upper division credits (18 courses) of which at least 45 credits must be taken at Richmond. 45 of 120 credits required for the bachelor's degree must be completed at Richmond. **International Students:** The school actively recruits these students. The school also requires placement exams in math and English.

Admissions Contact: Teressa Cleary, Director of Admissions/North America. Email: *teressa.cleary@richmond.ac.uk* Web: *www.richmond.ac.uk*

FINANCIAL AID: The college's own financial statement is required. The deadline for filing freshman financial aid applications for fall entry is April 15.

STUDY IN THE UNITED STATES

More and more American colleges and universities are welcoming students from foreign countries. Did you know that there are over 1,000,000 international students enrolled in U.S. institutions of higher learning, and that number continues to increase?

Why Colleges and Universities Seek International Students

There are several reasons why American colleges and universities seek international students. First, they recognize that international students help educate the American students on campus by introducing them to different ideas and cultures. Second, the number of college-age American students is declining, and international students can fill places that otherwise would go unfilled. Third, the money that international students spend on tuition and other expenses helps the U.S. economy; education is a valuable export for the United States. And fourth, education has long been an important part of America's foreign aid program, providing foreign nationals with skills that they can use to improve life in their homelands.

Why International Students Seek to Study in the United States

There are also a number of reasons why international students seek to study in the United States. For some students, colleges and universities in the United States offer opportunities to study major fields that are not available in their own countries. For other students, American colleges and universities offer an alternative to colleges and universities in their own countries where places may not be available for all of the qualified students who wish to attend. For still other students, study in the United States provides them not only with an education but also with experiences in living in another culture and in exchanging ideas with students from many nations.

Whatever *your* reason may be for studying in the United States, this book will help you make decisions and plans.

Investigating a College or University

Although most of the colleges and universities in the United States are very honest about their programs and services, a few have been known to misrepresent themselves. When choosing a college or university, as when making any other major purchase, you should investigate carefully. In addition to checking whether your exact major field is offered, you should compare the special services for international students offered by the schools that you are considering. You will want to know whether a representative of the school will pick you up at the airport when you arrive, whether dormitories or other housing is available, and whether there is a foreign student adviser to help you with decisions that you will have to make and problems that you may have to solve after you arrive.

The Difference Between a College and a University

Most international students want to know the difference between a college and a university. This is a difficult question because there is more than one correct answer. In fact, there are three definitions for the word *college* (as it refers to a college in the United States) listed in the *American Heritage Dictionary of the English Language*.

According to the dictionary, a *college* is (1) a school of higher learning that grants a bachelor's degree (undergraduate degree) in arts or sciences or both; (2) an undergraduate division of a university that offers courses and grants undergraduate degrees in a particular field of study; or (3) a technical or professional school, often affiliated with a university, that grants a bachelor's or master's degree in that field.

A *university* is a school of higher learning that grants a bachelor's degree (undergraduate degree), master's degree, and doctorate (Ph.D.) through various colleges within the university.

The Comparison of a College and a University

Many international students ask whether a university is better than a college. The answer is that a university has advantages and disadvantages for an international student, and a college has advantages and disadvantages.

The advantages of a university are that there are usually more research and recreational facilities, and more different kinds of courses offered. The disadvantages of a university are that courses taught to first-year students are often taught by teaching assistants who are graduate students themselves, and that the classes can be very large. The advantages of a college are that the courses are almost always taught by professors, and that the classes are usually small. The disadvantages of a college are that there are usually fewer research and recreational facilities.

Remember, as you decide what is best for you, that there are excellent colleges and there are excellent universities.

Accreditation

Unlike most countries, the United States does not have a national ministry of education that approves the programs at colleges and universities throughout the country. Instead, programs are approved by professional organizations and regional associations. This approval is called accreditation.

All of the schools listed in this book are accredited or are in the process of being accredited.

Requirements for Admission

Academic Preparation

To study in the United States, an international student should begin preparing in secondary school. A good secondary school report is one of the most important requirements for admission to a college or university. When applying to a college or university, you must submit an English translation of your grades with a seal and signature on it. This grade report is called a transcript. In addition, most colleges and universities require undergraduate students to submit standardized test scores. Some of the most common tests are the ACT (American College Test), the SAT (Scholastic Aptitude Test), and the SAT Subject Tests. Each test is described below.

ACT Achievement Test	A test of general academic preparation
SAT Reasoning Test	An aptitude test for college
SAT Subject Tests	Skill tests in academic subjects

The ACT is a national college admission examination that measures your general educational development in English, mathematics, reading, and science, as well as your writing ability in a thirty-minute optional essay. The SAT is a test that measures your general skills in critical reading, mathematics, and writing. The writing test is optional. In addition, the SAT Subject Tests measure your knowledge in key academic areas such as languages, social sciences, natural sciences, and mathematics. Some highly selective schools require applicants to take several SAT Subject Tests in addition to the SAT Reasoning Test. Both the SAT and the ACT are administered by Educational Testing Service for the College Board. For more information, visit *www.ets.org or www.collegeboard.com.*

The following books are available from Barron's Educational Series, Inc., 250 Wireless Boulevard, Hauppauge, New York 11788, USA, to help you prepare for the ACT and the SAT:

Barron's ACT
Pass Key to the ACT
Barron's SAT 1600
Barron's SAT
Pass Key to the SAT
Barron's 6 SAT Practice Tests
Picture These SAT Words

New SAT Flash Cards
SAT Word Master, Level I
SAT Word Master, Level II
ACT Flash Cards
Barron's ACT Math and Science Workbook
Barron's ACT English, Reading and Writing Workbook
Hot Words for the ACT
SAT and ACT Grammar Workbook
Barron's 6 ACT Practice Tests
Barron's ACT 36
SAT Vocabulary Flashcards
Barron's Math Workbook for the New SAT
Barron's Reading Workbook for the New SAT
Barron's Writing Workbook for the New SAT
Hot Words for the SAT

Barron's also has a series of study guides for the SAT Subject Tests in the following areas: Biology, Physics, Chemistry, Math, U.S. History, World History, Literature, French, and Spanish.

Barron's books are available worldwide at major bookstores or directly from the publisher at *www.barrons educ.com.* Click on Test Preparation for further information.

English Language Proficiency

In addition, if your native language is not English, you will probably have to take a test of your ability to use English. The most widely used of these tests is the TOEFL (Test of English as a Foreign Language), given at official test centers throughout the world. Two TOEFL formats are being used in different parts of the world: The Internet-Based TOEFL (iBT), and the Institutional Testing Program TOEFL (ITP). The Michigan English Language Assessment Battery (MELAB) and the IELTS (International English Language Testing System) are sometimes accepted as proof of English language proficiency also. These tests are described as follows:

TOEFL iBT	An Internet-based test. The newest TOEFL format being used throughout the world. A test of listening, speaking, reading, and writing.
TOEFL ITP	A pencil and paper alternative to the iBT available in remote locations or by special arrangement with the test administrator. A test of listening, structure, and reading, with a separate essay.
MELAB	The Michigan English Language Assessment Battery, which is sometimes accepted as evidence of English language proficiency instead of the TOEFL. A test of listening, writing, and multiple-choice items in grammar, vocabulary, and reading.
IELTS	The International English Language Testing System is available in academic or general formats. Listening, speaking, reading, and writing modules are included.

You can take the TOEFL at an official test center. To register, visit *www.ets.org* or register by mail or fax, using the form in the *TOEFL Bulletin of Information,* which can be downloaded from the web site or obtained in print at one of the regional registration sites or counseling centers around the world. For more information about the test, visit *www.ets.org/toefl*. For information about preparing for the test, visit *toeflprep.com*. To download a bulletin or to register for the MELAB, visit the official web site at *www.lsa.umich.edu/eli* or write to the MELAB Office at the following address: English Language Institute, 555 South Forest Avenue, Third Floor, Ann Arbor, MI 48104-2584. Phone: (734) 764-2413. E-mail: eli-information@umich.edu

To register for IELTS, visit the official web site at *www.ielts.org* or go to a local IELTS center.

Barron's TOEFL books are available worldwide at major bookstores or directly from the publisher at *www.barronseduc.com*. Click on Test Preparation, and then click on TOEFL/TOEIC/IELTS.

Barron's TOEFL iBT (available as book with MP3 CDs and book with MP3 CD and CD-ROM)
Barron's TOEFL Superpack
Barron's PASS KEY to the TOEFL iBT
Barron's Practice Exercises for the TOEFL
Barron's Writing for the TOEFL iBT
Barron's Essential Words for the TOEFL
TOEFL Strategies and Tips: Outsmart the TOEFL iBT
Barron's Michigan Test Battery
Barron's IELTS
Essential Words for the IELTS
IELTS Strategies and Tips
IELTS Practice Exams
Writing for the IELTS
IELTS Superpack

Financial Guarantees

All schools require that international students show proof of their ability to pay tuition, fees, and living expenses. Most schools require a statement from a bank that shows adequate finances for one year's study. If the name on the account is not the same as the name of the student, a signed letter from the person who has the account must accompany the bank statement. In the letter this person promises to support the international student while the student is in the United States. This person is called the student's sponsor.

Application Procedures

Select a few schools and write for information

When you are ready to apply—usually about a year before the date on which you hope to enter college—write to the schools that interest you for application materials. You should include the field you wish to study, a brief outline of your previous education, the number of years you have studied English, the amount of money you can spend, and the proposed date of enrollment. The college admissions officers will review this information and should let you know if the college cannot meet your needs. You should also ask the schools for information about special programs and organizations for international students.

Remember, this book provides general information about the requirements for admission to colleges and universities, but each school has the authority to set its own standards for admission. For the specific requirements for admission, you must write directly to the schools that most interest you. Some schools will be glad to send you a catalog free of charge; most schools will charge you a fee for the catalog.

Libraries of college catalogs also can be found at the offices of the Institute of International Education, a private, nonprofit, international educational exchange agency administered in 13 international locations. To find an office near you, visit *www.iie.org*. Counseling centers, generally located at U.S. embassies and the offices of binational and Fulbright commissions, also have collections of college catalogs. The Department of State supports a network of advising centers around the world. To find a center near you, visit *www.educationusa.state.gov*. Another web site that offers limited free access to college catalogs is *www.collegesource.org*. After a search for three catalogs and a time limit of ten days, a subscription is required to continue looking through their database. Online catalogs are available for many schools on their web sites.

Apply to more than one school

Remember, most American students apply to more than one college or university, and you should, too, especially if you are interested in competitive schools with very high admissions standards. By using this book and by reviewing catalogs from the schools that interest you, you can select several colleges and universities to which you can apply. Because the application fees are almost always nonrefundable, you should truly be serious about the schools where you make application.

Be sure that you have selected some schools where you are likely to be accepted. If you were an average student in high school and your standardized test scores are average, you have little chance of being accepted by a highly competitive school. Evaluate yourself realistically.

Remember, too, that the rating of colleges and universities in this book is based upon information about American students only. Although it is usually accurate for international students as well, some large state universities that are listed as noncompetitive have open admission for state residents. This means that anyone with a high school diploma who is a resident of that state may attend the state school. These schools, listed as noncompetitive, may actually be very competitive for students from other states and for international students. Nevertheless, the rating scale will be useful to you, especially for schools that are not large state universities.

Be sure that you submit all of the documents that the schools require along with application fees. The most common reason for delays in admission to American colleges and universities is because international students do not send everything that is required along with their application forms.

When you are ready to apply to the schools of your choice, consider the following points:

1. Be sure that the schools offer your major field of study.
2. Be sure that the schools are accredited.
3. Be sure that you apply to more than one school.
4. Be sure that you apply to schools where you meet the requirements for admission.
5. Be sure that you submit all of the documents and fees with your application to avoid delays.

Make a Decision

Some international students choose a school in the United States because their friends are going there. It is nice to have friends on campus, but the right school for your friend may not be the right school for you. There is no list of the best schools in the United States. A school may be the best in one major field and only average in another major field. It may have famous professors who only do research and do not teach. It may be well known but not academically excellent.

Consider the following points in making a decision where you will go to school.

1. Be sure that the school offers your major field of study or a premajor for your major field of study.
2. Be sure that the school is accredited.
3. Be sure that the school offers an English program if you need one.
4. Be sure that you understand how much credit you will receive if you are transferring from another school.
5. Be sure that the school has a foreign-student adviser or someone assigned to help international students.
6. Be sure that the expenses for the school are within your budget.

Going to the United States

You should start investigating requirements for visas from the United States and from your home country (if applicable) as soon as you decide to study overseas. You cannot apply for an American visa, however, until you have been accepted by a school in the United States. You must apply for the visa at a U.S. embassy or consulate. You probably will need the following items.

1. A passport (except for Canadians) from your own country.
2. A passport-sized photograph.
3. A Form I-20 (Certificate of Eligibility for Non-Immigrant Student Status) from the school that has accepted you.
4. A notarized bank statement or other proof that you have enough money available and/or financial aid promised to cover your expenses for the entire term of your program. (If you have been accepted to a bachelor's degree program, for instance, the term is four years.)
5. Evidence that you are in good health, including a recent chest X-ray and, in some countries, proof that you have been vaccinated against smallpox within the past three years.
6. A supplemental visa application, and a fee for the Student and Exchange Visitor Information Service, or other security information.

Most students are admitted to the United States under an F-1 (foreign student) visa. Those who come under certain grant or scholarship programs may qualify for a J-1 (exchange visitor) visa. After you have qualified for your visa, any spouse and children of yours may be admitted under F-2 or J-2 visas. You must provide evidence that there is enough money to support them while you are studying. For more information, visit *www.usimmigrationsupport.org*.

You may want to consider participating in predeparture orientation programs offered by education services abroad and by the U.S. Information Service. Information about these programs is available from the agency or from any U.S. embassy or consulate.

Many schools send representatives to meet students at local airports and bus and train stations, if they have correct arrival information. If your school offers this service, take advantage of it. Send your travel plans to the foreign-student adviser on your campus.

Arriving on Campus

As soon as you arrive on campus, you should visit the foreign-student adviser, an official who is responsible for the welfare of students from other countries. If your college has no such official, you should see the dean of students. Bring your passport and immigration documents.

Your university will also assign a faculty member to advise you on your academic program. Other services available through the school may include psychological counseling and health-care services. Although some schools provide limited health care to students at no charge, you should keep in mind that, in the United States, medical care is the responsibility of the individual, not the government. You would be wise to obtain health insurance. Many colleges offer such plans (some *require* foreign students to have health insurance) and your foreign-student adviser can provide information on them.

Most colleges and universities offer campus orientation programs for all new students; some also hold special orientations for foreign students. The latter are generally held during the summer and may continue on after the academic year has begun. On- and off-campus tours and placement exams may be included.

English Language and Cultural Orientation Programs

Many American colleges and universities provide English language instruction often in conjunction with courses and activities that orient foreign students to the various phases of life in the United States. Full-time English language programs generally involve at least 15 hours of intensive instruction per week and usually include orientation activities. Single courses involve fewer hours and are generally taken to help students engaged in academic courses.

You should know that your ability to speak and write English will affect your admission to most American colleges and universities. If your ability falls below that required for admission, you may be accepted conditionally, with the understanding that you will participate in an intensive English course or program. Some schools require that all foreign students enroll in such a course or program.

For more information, you should refer to the booklet *Intensive English Programs in the USA,* published by the Institute of International Education, 809 United Nations Plaza, New York, New York 10017 and available in their overseas offices and many U.S. embassy libraries as well as their web site, *www.iiebooks.org*. This publication gives detailed information on the intensive English-language courses and programs at many of the institutions in this book.

Expenses

Most colleges will expect you to pay all fixed costs—tuition, room-and-board, if you live and eat in college facilities and student fees—in U.S dollars at the beginning of each academic term. Some colleges provide installment plans, under which these costs may be paid monthly over the course of the term.

Keep in mind when determining your probable expenses that personal expenses, including travel, entertainment, and textbooks, may be considerable and generally are not listed as part of a college's tuition schedule. While some colleges will provide an estimate of a typical student's personal expenses, you should generally expect to spend considerably more.

International students generally are not permitted to hold jobs in the United States. Work permits are issued only when there is unexpected economic need. Part-time jobs on campus, however, are permitted and do not require government approval.

Financial aid may be available from your government, the U.S. government cultural exchange programs, corporations, the college you attend, or religious, fraternal, or special-interest groups. For information, contact a U.S. embassy or consulate and your government's ministry or department of education. If you are already in the United States, see your foreign-student adviser.

Pamela J. Sharpe, Ph.D.
Author, *Barron's TOEFL iBT, 15th Edition*

INDEX

Make Those College Essays Stand Out!

Essays That Will Get You Into College

4th Edition

Chris Dowhan, Roz Abero, Adrienne Dowhan, and Dan Kaufman

BARRON'S

ESSAYS That Will Get You Into COLLEGE

Fourth Edition

A STRONG ENTRANCE ESSAY INCREASES YOUR CHANCE OF ACCEPTANCE AT THE SCHOOL OF YOUR CHOICE

>> More Than 50 Model Essays . . . written by successful Ivy League school applicants, with critical comments pointing out essays' strong and weak points

>> Guidance . . . in planning and writing your own college application essay

>> Advice . . . from school admissions officers

ADRIENNE DOWHAN, ROZ ABERO, CHRIS DOWHAN, AND DAN KAUFMAN

Learn how to take your college admissions essay from "nothing special" to "nailed it!" This updated edition offers a wealth of strategies, tips, and guidance for the essay-writing portion of college applications. It includes:

- 50 model essays written by successful Ivy League college applicants
- Comments on each essay that explore strong and weak points in style and content
- Advice from students accepted into some of the nation's most competitive colleges
- Insights into choosing a theme, writing the first draft, editing until it's perfect, and more

Available at your local bookstore or visit **www.barronseduc.com**

You'll also find help with the Common Application and tips about preparing for important admissions interviews.

"Kaufman and his associates create an excellent resource for college-bound students . . . The book is extremely well organized and offers valuable advice on how to succeed in the admissions process." —*VOYA*

Paperback • ISBN 978-1-4380-0288-0 • $13.99, *Can$16.99*

Barron's Educational Series, Inc.
250 Wireless Blvd.
Hauppauge, N.Y. 11788
Order toll-free: 1-800-645-3476
Order by fax: 1-631-434-3217

In Canada:
Georgetown Book Warehouse
34 Armstrong Ave.
Georgetown, Ontario L7G 4R9
Canadian orders: 1-800-247-7160
Order by fax: 1-800-887-1594

(#280) R6/18

Prices subject to change without notice.